The Original

M000211588

THOROUGHBRED TIMES
RACING
ALMANAC™
2006

THOROUGHBRED TIMES BOOKS

The Original

THOROUGHBRED TIMES

RACING ALMANAC™

2006
A Thoroughbred Times Book™

Editor in Chief:	Mark Simon
Almanac Editor:	Don Clippinger
Director of Research:	John P. Sparkman
Editors:	Tom Law, Amy Owens
Information Technology:	Alan Johnson, Jonathan McKinney
Editorial Research:	Frank Angst, Jeff Apel, Steve Bailey, Liane Crossley, Mike Curry, Pete Denk, Ed DeRosa, Bill Heller, Myra Lewyn, Jeff Lowe, Tom Musgrave, Steve Schuelein
Statistical Research:	Gail Allensworth, Chris Bauer, Jessica Flounders, Melissa Humphrey, Colleen Jonsson, Aylett Melton
Editorial Assistants:	Deanna Lyons, Denise Steffanus
Art Director:	Jeanette Vance
Production Coordinator:	Erica Mitchell
Production Staff:	Gail Burge, Nicole Elliott, Betty Gee, Tami Helmreich-Zigo, David Kaplan, Laura Lacy, Amy McLean
Cover Photo:	Enzina Mastrippolito

Thoroughbred Times Co. Inc.

Publisher: Norman Ridker
Vice President Editorial: Mark Simon
Editorial Office: 2008 Mercer Rd., Lexington, KY 40511

THOROUGHBRED TIMES RACING ALMANAC welcomes comments and suggestions from readers. Every communication is read by the editors and receives consideration and attention. THOROUGHBRED TIMES RACING ALMANAC does not decide wagers.

THOROUGHBRED TIMES RACING ALMANAC™ and THOROUGHBRED TIMES ®
are registered trademarks of Thoroughbred Times Co. Inc.
International Standard Serial Number (ISSN) 1540-5486
ISBN Number 1-93-1993-65-3

THOROUGHBRED TIMES RACING ALMANAC ™
Thoroughbred Times Books™
An imprint of BowTie Press™
www.thoroughbredtimes.com
e-mail: letters@thoroughbredtimes.com

FOREWORD
My, how we have grown.

The premiere edition of the *Thoroughbred Times Racing Almanac* in 2003 came out at 656 pages, and it was an immediate hit with racing fans and racing journalists. One well-traveled journalist said it was an invaluable reference that he did not need a steamer trunk to carry around with him from city to city. Well, you still do not need a steamer trunk to transport the 2006 *Thoroughbred Times Racing Almanac*, but it is heftier. This year's issue has 976 pages, nearly 50% bigger than the premiere edition. We also have expanded the index over the four editions to make it more comprehensive and useful for our readers.

Why have we increased the size of the *Thoroughbred Times Racing Almanac* when everyone seemed to be pleased with the premiere edition? The reason is that we are not satisfied to stand still. In time, we knew *Thoroughbred Times Racing Almanac* users would want more information, and we have tried to anticipate our readers' wants and needs.

The growth of the *Thoroughbred Times Racing Almanac* has been a highly creative process that has challenged the entire THOROUGHBRED TIMES staff. Each staff member has made a contribution of expertise, brainstorms, and curiosity. More than a few new features have grown from such statements as, "Hey, don't you think you should have (fill in the blank) in the Almanac?"

Compiling so much data has led us to look beyond the raw numbers to the trends behind them. You will see some of these trends delineated in the State of the Industry chapter. One new feature in that chapter is a section on racinos, which essentially are racetracks with slot machines. In the last decade or so, racinos have become a significant source of purse revenue, and we felt it was important to chronicle that change in the Thoroughbred industry and to examine its implications.

Although the Almanac's page count has grown substantially, the size of the staff producing the words, statistics, and tables has not increased appreciably, although some notable additions have been made. The heart of the Almanac is the staff of the weekly THOROUGHBRED TIMES, recognized in 2004 by American Horse Publications as the best horse publication of any kind. Many of the features appearing in the Almanac first appeared in different forms in the weekly magazine. One example is the Industry Leaders features, which also are found in the People and Sires chapters. Two others are All About Purses and Auction Review. The History of Racing is condensed from Mary Simon's Eclipse Award-winning articles in THOROUGHBRED TIMES. Reports on the 2004 Breeders' Cup races and the '05 Triple Crown are drawn from staff reports.

Many other features are unique to the Almanac. One is the comprehensive annual listing of every stakes race in North America, and another is the graded stakes histories, which this year have been extended back to 1973, the first year that North American races were graded. Researcher Melissa Humphrey gathered and painstakingly verified that mountain of information. Under the guidance of John P. Sparkman, bloodstock/sales editor, the THOROUGHBRED TIMES Research Department gathered and verified data on a variety of topics. Colleen Jonsson tackled the colossal task of obtaining information on every race meet and racetrack in North America. Chris Bauer pulled together the sires data, Jessica Flounders compiled all the international information, Aylett Melton gathered the auctions entries, and Gail Allensworth lent an experienced eye to assure the accuracy of the information. Deanna Lyons, chief copy editor, assured the accuracy of the editorial matter.

Thoroughbred racing thrives on numbers, and making sense of all that data are knowledgeable information-technology practitioners Alan Johnson and Jonathan McKinney. They know the contents of the Jockey Club Information Systems database as well as the large THOROUGHBRED TIMES database, and, when confronted with a complex project for the Almanac, invariably will say, "We can do that." And, they deliver. This is the second issue of the Almanac for which Erica Mitchell has served as the production coordinator. She has contributed a consistent appearance to the book and has done a remarkable job of keeping the editor organized. In the end, the *Thoroughbred Times Racing Almanac* is the result of the vision of Publisher Norman Ridker and Editor in Chief Mark Simon, who perceived a need and a market for a comprehensive annual publication. With their support and their insights, the *Thoroughbred Times Racing Almanac* will be bigger and better, year by year. That's a promise.

Don Clippinger, Editor
Lexington, Kentucky
June 13, 2005

TABLE OF CONTENTS

GENERAL INDEX

STATE OF THE INDUSTRY
Thoroughbred Economy in 2004

In 2003, the Thoroughbred industry encountered a troubling and somewhat puzzling anomaly. While wagering in North America on Thoroughbred racing moved ahead, albeit by a relatively small amount, purses for those races declined. In 2004, the industry encountered another anomaly, and it was, at once, more troubling and more puzzling than the one of the previous year. While purses turned around and advanced in 2004 to $1.18-billion, total wagering on Thoroughbred races in the United States and Canada declined 0.7% to $15.6-billion. The wagering decline was the second in 11 years, following a dip in 1993, and the first since the National Thoroughbred Racing Association was created to rekindle the American public's passion for racing and racetrack gambling. The 2004 total for North America was the smallest since $15.14-billion was wagered in 2001.

Proportionally, the decline was significantly larger in Canada than in the United States. The U.S. wagering economy is so large that its dip determined the size of the overall decline. But the Canadian wagering decline was 6% after a 5.8% dip in 2003 and placed Canadian betting at its lowest point since '00.

The results of the previous two years ran counter to the longstanding tenet of the Thoroughbred economy that purses rise when wagering increases, and purses drop with wagering slips. In 1993, purses declined with the wagering total. Indeed, the recent consecutive years of diverging purses and wagering indicate that a fundamental change may now be under way in how purses are financed.

The wagering decline was all the more disturbing because it occurred in the midst of an expanding national economy. The 1993 decline in wagering occurred 21 months after the end

North American Purses

Year	Total Purses	Average Purse
2004	$1,177,769,765	$20,069
2003	1,154,238,845	19,626
2002	1,170,169,267	19,597
2001	1,146,337,367	18,936
2000	1,093,661,241	18,053
1999	1,008,162,608	6,770
1998	968,366,929	15,838
1997	888,667,752	13,997
1996	845,916,706	13,163
(Excluding Puerto Rico and Mexico)		

of a nine-month recession. The 2004 dip came 26 months after a milder recession that lasted for seven months, to November 2001. Other indicators of confidence and well-being in the economy moved upward. The Standard and Poor's Index of 500 large-capitalization stocks advanced 8.9% to 1,211.916, and the overall Thoroughbred auction economy surged forward by 23.7% and crossed the $1-billion sales mark for the first time since 2000.

The statistics also indicated that one trend, the erosion of on-track wagering to off-track facilities and locations, ground to a halt, at least temporarily. In 2004, 87.2% of all Thoroughbred wagers were placed at locales other than the track staging the live races. This figure was basically unchanged from 87% in 2003. In the span of two decades, racetrack wagering has moved from overwhelmingly on-track to largely off-track, the result of the explosion of full-card simulcasting in the middle and late 1990s.

Thus, the retreat from Thoroughbred race wagering was both widespread and consistent; fewer dollars were bet on-track on the live racing product, and an equal proportion of betting dollars

North American Pari-Mutuel Wagering
(Millions of Dollars)

Year	On-Track	United States Off-Track	Total	On-Track	Canada Off-Track	Total	Total Total	Total Change
2004	$1,860	$13,239	$15,099	$137	$364	$502	$15,601	−0.7%
2003	1,902	13,278	15,180	139	394	534	15,714	0.5%
2002	2,029	13,033	15,062	153	414	567	15,629	3.2%
2001	2,112	12,487	14,599	153	387	540	15,139	2.3%
2000	2,270	12,051	14,321	150	325	475	14,796	4.5%
1999	2,359	11,365	13,724	161	278	439	14,163	4.0%
1998	2,498	10,617	13,115	188	310	498	13,613	4.2%
1997	2,703	9,839	12,542	217	310	527	13,069	6.5%
1996	2,944	8,683	11,627	259	383	642	12,269	9.3%

were withheld by bettors away from the track staging the races. Wagering is a result of product and marketing, and the sport certainly had a marketing success in 2004 with Smarty Jones through his Triple Crown campaign, which crashed with a second-place finish in the Belmont Stakes (G1). But the big horse did not translate into big dollars—or even an equal number of dollars—through the betting windows. Indeed, much of the decline occurred in the second half of the year, after the dual classic winner had been retired to stud and at a time when heightened interest in the sport should have resulted in increased wagering.

The declining handle numbers confirm that the full-card simulcasting revolution has run its course and now is a mature product. The last decline in wagering occurred before the full-card revolution, and the sport enjoyed a steady advance in wagering—albeit most of it away from the host track—for almost a decade. Those days are over, but it was quite a ride. Full-card wagering pulled Thoroughbred racing out of a gradual decline that had spanned the 1980s and early '90s. With full-card simulcasting, racetracks became financially healthy, and the added revenues encouraged the consolidation of the sport under two conglomerates, Magna Entertainment Corp. and Churchill Downs Inc. It was during this time that a national office for racing was created, the National Thoroughbred Racing Association.

The industry staged fewer performances in 2004, and that 1.4% dip to 58,686 races may well be one factor in the wagering decline. The total number of starts, 486,106 in 2004, was off only 0.4% from 487,991 in the prior year.

The diverging numbers—purses down and wagering up in one year and purses up and wagering down in the next—very likely reflect the effects of two trends: increasing handle by rebating shops, which tends to increase wagering while contributing little or nothing to purses, and the increase in alternative forms of gaming at tracks, which pump money into purses without adding to wagering totals.

Both trends are relatively new, and the rapid growth of rebaters since 2000 has been discussed by racetrack executives with both alarm and a high level of frustration—because nothing can be done to stop the practice of giving rebates to big players and because racetracks are unwilling to give up the revenue that the rebate shops provide them.

The popularity of rebaters is, in many ways, a result of the high takeout rate on horse-racing wagers. In principle, the takeout pays for purses and racetrack operations; state taxes have generally become an increasingly smaller part of the takeout. Full-card simulcasting changed the traditional split of takeout, which had been 50-50 between the track and horsemen, to a four-way split among two racetracks and two sets of

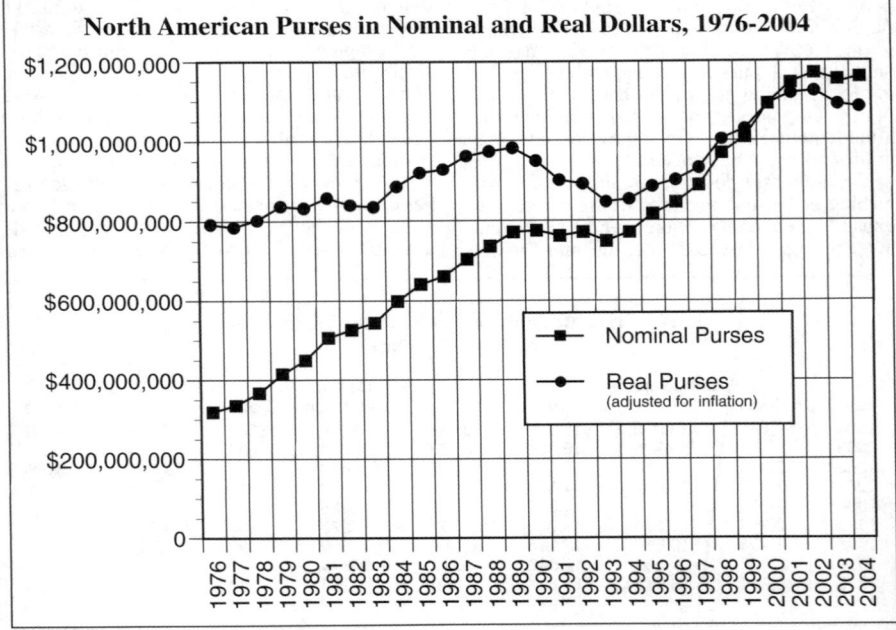

North American Purses in Nominal and Real Dollars, 1976-2004

Legend:
- ■ Nominal Purses
- ● Real Purses (adjusted for inflation)

horsemen if the wagers are placed at another track. The rebate shops have neither horsemen nor the expense of maintaining a racetrack, so they hold a substantial piece of the takeout with which to pay the rebates, which can run as high as 16% of total play.

The big players and their rebate shops also utilize sophisticated computer technology to search out and exploit mathematical inefficiencies in the wagering. Thus, they tend to win more often than the $2 bettor at the track. Racetrack operators also have found that the rebate-shop players put less of their winnings back into succeeding bets. Industry leaders expressed interest in doing something to limit the influence of rebate shops, but their discussions led to no across-the-board action in 2004.

The rise of racinos—casinos at racetracks—is discussed in detail later in this chapter. Slot machines and video lottery terminals can raise purses substantially. Across North America in 2004, purses were approximately 7.5% of total wagering. At Delaware Park in 2004, purses supplemented with slots revenue were 37.5% of total wagering on the track's races.

—Don Clippinger

Racing Dates, Races, Runners, Starts, Purses by State and Province in 2004

	Racing Dates	Races	Runners	Starts	Purses
NORTH AMERICA	6,950	58,798	74,193	487,095	$1,182,518,714
Arizona	260	2,002	3,178	15,991	13,889,990
Arkansas	55	558	1,784	4,858	13,139,300
California	755	5,128	8,064	38,797	157,388,294
Colorado	37	252	546	1,721	1,974,025
Delaware	134	1,202	3,327	8,891	33,948,230
Florida	363	3,766	8,225	32,455	81,121,618
Georgia	2	10	69	72	337,050
Idaho	47	275	473	1,795	902,849
Illinois	311	2,930	4,676	23,568	57,163,493
Indiana	107	1,076	2,788	9,217	12,298,600
Iowa	96	746	1,436	5,959	13,021,318
Kansas	57	279	951	2,320	1,493,816
Kentucky	268	2,649	7,125	23,150	85,611,318
Louisiana	375	3,833	7,437	33,486	70,123,684
Maryland	210	1,830	4,243	13,908	38,354,095
Massachusetts	128	1,180	1,591	9,356	13,349,816
Michigan	146	1,050	1,437	7,750	9,613,992
Minnesota	67	578	1,215	4,704	8,322,994
Montana	32	166	333	1,073	407,900
Nebraska	102	894	1,378	7,700	5,660,269
Nevada	6	36	129	213	104,003
New Hampshire	1	3	29	29	44,590
New Jersey	125	1,194	3,251	9,451	42,717,004
New Mexico	262	1,450	2,766	12,672	22,574,270
New York	412	3,745	6,920	30,946	136,489,493
North Carolina	4	18	83	106	245,800
North Dakota	20	103	272	682	308,577
Ohio	441	3,288	5,991	29,264	24,770,300
Oklahoma	142	857	2,197	7,957	7,577,310
Oregon	104	789	1,325	5,772	2,704,392
Pennsylvania	415	3,825	6,683	31,355	45,239,175
South Carolina	4	23	146	171	507,850
Tennessee	1	7	48	48	290,050
Texas	217	1,885	4,489	17,068	41,092,768
Virginia	44	397	1,851	3,420	7,803,191
Washington	107	879	1,533	6,293	8,625,475
West Virginia	450	4,638	10,265	42,609	89,532,035
Wyoming	18	36	120	259	67,325
UNITED STATES	**6,325**	**53,577**	**68,567**	**445,086**	**$1,048,816,259**
Alberta	192	1,364	1,789	10,355	16,079,534
British Columbia	82	731	1,062	5,576	12,775,415
Manitoba	71	583	900	4,634	5,476,982
Ontario	248	2,328	3,728	19,936	98,720,884
Saskatchewan	32	215	350	1,508	649,640
CANADA	**625**	**5,221**	**7,438**	**42,009**	**$133,702,455**

Revenues to Government From Horse Racing

Through much of the 20th century and into the 21st century, government has looked to gambling as a tax upon the willing, a way to ease the burden of most taxpayers by levying a heavy tax load on all gambling wagers. In the 1940s, the tax burden on racetracks exploded. In the 1970s and '80s, the states created lotteries, which had a heavy tax burden but nonetheless drew patrons through slick advertising and hefty jackpots. In the 1990s and beyond, the attention of state government shifted to slot machines and casino games. Some of the machine wagering was authorized for racetracks.

The following table, compiled by the Association of Racing Commissioners International, illustrates very clearly the rise of horse racing—principally Thoroughbred racing but also Quarter Horse and Standardbred racing—as a source of government income and its decline. In the depths of the Great Depression, the horse-racing industry was not taxed heavily, either in current dollars or inflation-adjusted dollars. That circumstance began to change in the late 1930s, as the nation began to emerge from the Depression and, with war on the horizon, to change to a military economy. For the first time in 1939, revenues to government passed the $10-

million level. By 1942, the tax had more than doubled, and it doubled again by '44.

After World War II, demands on states and local governments for schools and other services grew exponentially, and so did the taxes on horse racing. By 1951, horse racing contributed more than $100-million in taxes; by '56, the tax had doubled again. Also in 1956, the tax on racing surpassed $1-billion in inflation-adjusted dollars for the first time. It peaked at more than $2-billion in deflated dollars in 1975.

At approximately that time, Thoroughbred racing began a slow, steady slide. As racing lost patrons to other sports—all of which had, unlike racing, embraced television as a way to enlarge their fan bases—racetracks were transformed from monopolist profit centers to marginally profitable or even losing operations. The tracks made compelling arguments to state governments that unless pari-mutuel taxes were reduced drastically, the racetracks would be unable to remain in business, and the state would lose both jobs and revenue on wagers placed at the track. The argument that a small tax was better than nothing carried the day, and subsequently some states eliminated the pari-mutuel tax altogether.

Revenue to States from Horse Racing

Year	Current Dollars	Deflated Dollars	Year	Current Dollars	Deflated Dollars
2002	$346,799,090	$333,637,106	1967	$394,381,913	$1,650,616,971
2001	351,511,182	343,363,174	1966	388,452,125	1,676,096,501
2000	367,786,590	367,786,590	1965	369,892,036	1,641,411,298
1999	392,201,085	400,744,968	1964	350,095,928	1,581,925,480
1998	431,722,361	447,510,533	1963	316,570,791	1,452,292,830
1997	441,768,972	463,002,255	1962	287,930,030	1,334,925,263
1996	443,882,538	472,960,127	1961	264,853,077	1,244,727,310
1995	455,764,292	494,825,844	1960	258,030,385	1,226,364,645
1994	451,546,549	500,278,697	1959	243,388,655	1,172,900,848
1993	471,735,474	533,752,135	1958	222,049,651	1,083,274,715
1992	491,259,606	568,686,237	1957	216,747,621	1,081,682,907
1991	523,249,392	619,640,699	1956	207,456,272	1,069,748,218
1990	623,839,806	764,603,268	1955	186,989,588	997,650,259
1989	584,888,183	744,549,344	1954	178,015,828	966,584,286
1988	596,202,319	787,648,055	1953	167,426,465	917,757,304
1987	608,351,461	831,126,648	1952	142,489,696	790,643,081
1986	587,357,677	824,361,652	1951	117,250,564	661,759,589
1985	625,159,697	896,762,006	1950	98,366,167	601,591,138
1984	650,262,852	961,145,299	1949	95,327,053	582,968,768
1983	641,387,176	983,617,060	1948	95,803,364	584,808,717
1982	652,888,463	1,040,857,799	1947	97,926,984	631,542,525
1981	680,199,584	1,150,560,030	1946	94,035,859	672,357,064
1980	712,727,523	1,318,815,615	1945	65,265,405	522,541,273
1979	680,919,798	1,374,262,933	1944	55,971,233	460,062,740
1978	673,063,831	1,470,952,709	1943	38,194,727	321,342,142
1977	700,239,986	1,637,911,644	1942	22,005,278	195,099,548
1976	714,629,120	1,777,861,280	1941	21,128,173	201,893,674
1975	780,081,431	2,052,737,832	1940	16,145,182	164,612,378
1974	645,980,984	1,860,276,412	1939	10,369,807	106,960,361
1973	585,201,524	1,837,425,112	1938	9,576,335	97,817,518
1972	531,404,550	1,761,600,975	1937	8,434,792	83,653,595
1971	512,838,417	1,773,852,226	1936	8,611,538	89,100,238
1970	486,403,097	1,766,554,431	1935	8,386,255	87,740,688
1969	461,498,886	1,764,881,586	1934	6,024,193	64,292,348
1968	426,856,448	1,713,388,384			

Revenues to States From Thoroughbred Racing and All Forms of Racing in 2002

State	Thoroughbred	Mixed	Total
Alabama	$1,370,131		$1,370,131
Arizona*		$5,284,240	5,284,240
Arkansas	1,009,593	1,441,308	2,450,901
California	44,721,948	4,033,739	51,396,000
Colorado*		653,539	653,539
Connecticut		9,411,802	9,411,802
Delaware	34,899	192,085	239,031
Florida	11,891,408		13,594,436
Idaho*		631,126	631,126
Illinois	17,411,818	1,003,246	25,678,427
Indiana*		4,252,020	4,453,585
Iowa*		2,023,898	2,023,898
Kansas*		1,854,810	1,854,810
Kentucky	7,537,463		7,950,942
Louisiana*		5,961,806	5,961,806
Maine*		1,707,630	1,936,248
Maryland	2,036,337	1,509,940	4,310,451
Massachusetts	1,948,954	254,781	2,797,302
Michigan	8,462,515	13,840	13,557,902
Minnesota*	181,467	198,197	392,000
Montana*		94,040	94,040
Nebraska	886,974		886,974
Nevada*	4,437,661	2,636	4,877,565
New Hampshire	3,071,061		3,434,278
New Jersey	689,588	33,749	1,308,187
New Mexico*		1,183,736	1,183,736
New York	88,432,157	2,867,298	112,923,832
North Dakota		4,101,389	4,101,389
Ohio	1,229,885	8,644,705	11,477,407
Oklahoma	725,085	3,329,789	4,054,874
Oregon*		1,657,361	1,657,361
Pennsylvania	22,697,440		25,993,378
Rhode Island		3,406,415	3,406,415
South Dakota*		804,674	804,674
Texas*		7,415,054	7,415,054
Virginia	2,625,705	17,525	3,371,654
Washington	1,968,402	200	1,968,602
West Virginia	855,713	695,147	1,550,860
Wisconsin		88,196	88,196
Wyoming*		252,037	252,037
Totals	**$224,226,204**	**$75,021,958**	**$346,799,090**

* denotes tax revenue from mixed meets and in some cases full-card simulcasting Source: Association of Racing Commissioners International

Pari-Mutuel Wagering by State in 2002

State	On-Track	Intertrack	Off-Track	Total
Alabama		$45,671,018		$45,671,018
Arizona*	$22,010,352		$152,619,591	174,629,943
Arkansas	53,501,393	97,611,841		151,113,234
California	446,762,525		1,409,002,214	1,855,764,739
Colorado*	4,610,256		79,594,183	84,204,439
Connecticut			253,175,327	253,175,327
Delaware	22,228,588	122,347,033		144,575,621
Florida	195,062,616	661,534,545		856,597,161
Idaho*	2,523,370	23,462,407	54,667,023	80,652,800
Illinois	115,777,597	295,403,820	387,189,901	798,371,318
Indiana*	4,227,736		136,275,246	140,502,982
Iowa*	7,391,735	28,545,590		35,937,325
Kansas*	1,824,682	51,608,059		53,432,741
Kentucky	166,153,096	379,437,102	31,361,251	576,951,449
Louisiana*	57,907,203		330,542,616	388,449,819
Maryland	50,940,320	31,284,102	7,473,955	89,698,377
Massachusetts	25,463,954	174,328,128		199,792,082
Michigan	3,475,023	212,345,930		215,820,953
Minnesota*	15,255,902	59,355,633		74,611,535
Montana*	1,787,066		7,617,252	9,404,318
Nebraska	8,696,802	104,825,210		113,522,012
Nevada*	263,598		429,572,979	429,836,577
New Hampshire	12,872,792	150,874,202		163,746,994
New Jersey	87,980,115	550,030,349	93,305,156	731,315,620
New Mexico*	25,008,687	81,385,047		106,393,734
New York	381,179,369	290,873,404	1,626,324,620	2,298,377,393
North Dakota	76,030		172,081,155	172,157,185
Ohio	45,400,101	447,069,807	14,713,262	507,183,170
Oklahoma	5,758,954	13,569,718	11,610,275	30,938,947
Oregon*	3,031,717		226,966,098	229,997,815
Pennsylvania	43,865,074		879,141,292	923,006,366
Texas*	81,321,619	384,459,353		465,780,972
Virginia	3,641,863	1,842,046	91,571,592	97,055,501
Washington	27,417,047	104,473,069	11,690,456	143,580,572
West Virginia	48,064,660	69,580,860		117,645,520
Wyoming*	1,157,253		11,094,168	12,251,421
Totals	**$1,972,639,095**	**$4,381,918,273**	**$6,417,589,612**	**$12,772,146,980**

* handle includes mixed meets
Source: Association of Racing Commissioners International

Pari-Mutuel Takeout by State

Pari-mutuel takeout is the amount deducted from wagers before odds are calculated and payments are made to winning bettors. The money taken out from the wagers goes to state taxes, horsemen as purses, the racetrack operators, breed enhancement funds, and other funds.

Arizona—Up to 25% on win-place-show wagers; up to 30% on two-horse wagers; up to 35% on multiple-horse wagers.

Arkansas—17% on win-place-show wagers; 21% on multiple wagers.

California—15.63% on win-place-show wagers; 20.38% on exotic wagers.

Colorado—18.5% on win-place-show wagers; 25% on exotic wagers.

Delaware—17% on win-place-show wagers; 19% on daily doubles and exactas; 27% on all other exotic wagers.

Florida—Individual tracks determine takeout rate.

Idaho—23% on win-place-show wagers; 23.75% on exotic wagers.

Illinois—17% on total handle; 20.5% on two-horse wagers; 25% on wagers involving three or more horses.

Indiana—18% on win-place-show wagers; 21.5% on exotic wagers.

Iowa—Up to 18% on win-place-show wagers; up to 24% on two-horse wagers; up to 25% on all other wagers.

Kansas—18% on win-place-show wagers; up to 22% on multiple wagers.

Kentucky—At tracks above $1,200,000 daily average: 16% on win-place-show wagers; 19% on exotic wagers. At tracks below $1,200,000 daily average: 17.5% on win-place-show wagers; 19% on exotic wagers.

Louisiana—17% on win-place-show wagers; 20.5% on two-horse wagers; 25% on multiple-horse wagers.

Maryland—At mile tracks, 18% on win-place-show wagers; 21% on two-horse multiple wagers; 25.75% on three-horse multiple wagers.

Massachusetts—19% on win-place-show wagers; 26% on exotic wagers (24% at fairs).

Michigan—17% on win-place-show wagers; up to 28% on multiples; up to 35% on multiple wagers with permission of racing commissioner.

Minnesota—Up to 17% on win-place-show wagers; 23% on exotic wagers.

Missouri—18% on straight wagers, 20% on two-horse wagers, 25% on other wagers.

Montana—20% on win-place-show wagers; up to 25% on exotic wagers.

Nebraska—15% to 18% on win-place-show wagers; up to 24% on exotic wagers.

New Hampshire—19% on win-place-show wagers; 26% on multiple wagers.

New Jersey—17% on win-place-show wagers; 19% on two-horse wagers; 25% on all other wagers.

New Mexico—Class A tracks: 19% on win-place-show wagers; 21% to 25% on exotic wagers. Class B tracks: 18.75% to 25% on win-place-show wagers; 21% to 30% on exotic wagers.

New York—At NYRA racetracks, 15% on win-place-show wagers; 20% on multiple wagers; 25% on exotics and super exotics. At Finger Lakes, 18% on win-place-show wagers, 20% on multiple wagers, 25% on exotics and super exotics.

Ohio—18% on win-place-show wagers; 22.5% on exotic wagers.

Oklahoma—18% on win-place-show wagers; 20% on multiple-horse wagers; 20% on up to three-race wagers (such as Pick Three); 25% on multiple-race wagers (more than three races, such as Pick Six).

Oregon—19% on win-place-show wagers; 22% on multiple wagers. At fairs, up to 22% on all wagers.

Pennsylvania—17% on regular wagering pools; 19% if average daily handle is less than $300,000; 20% on exactas, daily doubles and quinellas; 26% to 35% on trifectas.

Texas—18% on win-place-show wagers; up to 21% on two-horse wagers; up to 25% on three-horse wagers.

Virginia—18% on win-place-show wagers; 22% on all other wagers.

Washington—16.1% on win-place-show wagers; 22.1% on all other wagers.

West Virginia—17.25% on win-place-show wagers; 19% on two-horse wagers; 25% on three horses or more.

Wyoming—20.9% on win-place-show wagers; 25.9% on exotic wagers.

Claiming Activity by Claiming Category by State and Province in 2004

NORTH AMERICA	No. Claims	Value	Average
Maiden Claiming	1,744	$32,825,175	$18,822
$0-$4,999	2,982	10,361,775	3,475
$5,000-$9,999	5,189	31,752,063	6,119
$10,000-$19,999	4,717	59,974,625	12,715
$20,000 and up	3,419	107,511,500	31,445
Total	16,307	$209,599,963	$12,853

UNITED STATES	No. Claims	Value	Average
Maiden Claiming	1,532	$28,369,550	$18,518
$0-$4,999	2,891	10,065,550	3,482
$5,000-$9,999	4,905	29,895,500	6,095
$10,000-$19,999	4,362	55,222,000	12,660
$20,000 and up	3,044	96,202,000	31,604
Total	15,202	$191,385,050	$12,589

Includes steeplechase races.

	No. Claims	Value	Average
Arizona			
Maiden Claiming	48	$285,000	$5,938
$0-$4,999	306	1,034,400	3,380
$5,000-$9,999	161	959,750	5,961
$10,000-$19,999	50	593,000	11,860
$20,000 and up	6	130,000	21,667
Total	**523**	**$2,717,150**	**$5,195**
Arkansas			
Maiden Claiming	40	757,500	18,938
$0-$4,999	0	0	0
$5,000-$9,999	71	440,000	6,197
$10,000-$19,999	92	1,175,000	12,772
$20,000 and up	78	2,145,000	27,500
Total	**241**	**$3,760,000**	**$15,602**
California			
Maiden Claiming	409	10,745,500	26,273
$0-$4,999	454	1,522,400	3,353
$5,000-$9,999	473	3,138,000	6,634
$10,000-$19,999	769	10,060,500	13,083
$20,000 and up	1,065	35,954,000	33,760
Total	**2,761**	**$50,674,900**	**$18,354**
Colorado			
Maiden Claiming	1	5,000	5,000
$0-$4,999	7	23,200	3,314
$5,000-$9,999	6	34,250	5,708
$10,000-$19,999	3	30,000	10,000
$20,000 and up	0	0	0
Total	**16**	**$87,450**	**$5,466**
Delaware			
Maiden Claiming	54	1,212,000	22,444
$0-$4,999	0	0	0
$5,000-$9,999	192	1,105,250	5,757
$10,000-$19,999	181	2,374,500	13,119
$20,000 and up	125	3,527,500	28,220
Total	**498**	**$7,007,250**	**$14,071**
Florida			
Maiden Claiming	190	3,874,500	20,392
$0-$4,999	0	0	0
$5,000-$9,999	243	1,668,250	6,865
$10,000-$19,999	486	6,620,500	13,622
$20,000 and up	271	8,674,500	32,009
Total	**1,000**	**$16,963,250**	**$16,963**
Idaho			
Maiden Claiming	3	9,000	3,000
$0-$4,999	17	50,800	2,988
$5,000-$9,999	1	5,000	5,000
$10,000-$19,999	0	0	0
$20,000 and up	0	0	0
Total	**18**	**$55,800**	**$3,100**
Illinois			
Maiden Claiming	68	1,053,600	15,494
$0-$4,999	101	385,600	3,818
$5,000-$9,999	210	1,251,250	5,958
$10,000-$19,999	416	5,401,500	12,984
$20,000 and up	159	4,817,500	30,299
Total	**886**	**$11,855,850**	**$13,381**
Indiana			
Maiden Claiming	4	19,000	4,750
$0-$4,999	53	212,000	4,000
$5,000-$9,999	52	306,250	5,889
$10,000-$19,999	5	62,500	12,500
$20,000 and up	0	0	0
Total	**110**	**$580,750**	**$5,280**

	No. Claims	Value	Average
Iowa			
Maiden Claiming	10	$120,000	$12,000
$0-$4,999	12	48,000	4,000
$5,000-$9,999	26	160,250	6,163
$10,000-$19,999	40	485,000	12,125
$20,000 and up	14	310,000	22,143
Total	**92**	**$1,003,250**	**$10,905**
Kansas			
Maiden Claiming	0	0	0
$0-$4,999	6	17,000	2,833
$5,000-$9,999	7	35,000	5,000
$10,000-$19,999	0	0	0
$20,000 and up	0	0	0
Total	**13**	**$52,000**	**$4,000**
Kentucky			
Maiden Claiming	145	2,737,000	18,876
$0-$4,999	17	68,000	4,000
$5,000-$9,999	263	1,665,250	6,332
$10,000-$19,999	320	4,028,000	12,588
$20,000 and up	253	7,936,000	31,368
Total	**853**	**$13,697,250**	**$16,058**
Louisiana			
Maiden Claiming	80	1,280,000	16,000
$0-$4,999	121	437,000	3,612
$5,000-$9,999	324	1,896,750	5,854
$10,000-$19,999	269	3,386,500	12,589
$20,000 and up	133	3,845,000	28,910
Total	**847**	**$9,565,250**	**$11,293**
Maryland			
Maiden Claiming	81	1,396,000	17,235
$0-$4,999	9	37,000	4,111
$5,000-$9,999	181	1,215,500	6,715
$10,000-$19,999	244	3,317,000	13,594
$20,000 and up	168	4,243,500	25,259
Total	**602**	**$8,813,000**	**$14,640**
Massachusetts			
Maiden Claiming	13	79,500	6,115
$0-$4,999	53	213,500	4,028
$5,000-$9,999	88	523,750	5,952
$10,000-$19,999	46	586,500	12,750
$20,000 and up	2	45,000	22,500
Total	**189**	**$1,368,750**	**$7,242**
Michigan			
Maiden Claiming	3	18,000	6,000
$0-$4,999	14	56,000	4,000
$5,000-$9,999	18	110,000	6,111
$10,000-$19,999	0	0	0
$20,000 and up	0	0	0
Total	**32**	**$166,000**	**$5,188**
Minnesota			
Maiden Claiming	1	15,000	15,000
$0-$4,999	12	48,000	4,000
$5,000-$9,999	46	305,000	6,630
$10,000-$19,999	18	228,000	12,667
$20,000 and up	2	50,000	25,000
Total	**78**	**$631,000**	**$8,090**
Montana			
Maiden Claiming	0	0	0
$0-$4,999	7	16,500	2,357
$5,000-$9,999	0	0	0
$10,000-$19,999	0	0	0
$20,000 and up	0	0	0
Total	**7**	**$16,500**	**$2,357**

	No. Claims	Value	Average
Nebraska			
Maiden Claiming	0	$0	$0
$0-$4,999	85	242,500	2,853
$5,000-$9,999	26	147,000	5,654
$10,000-$19,999	7	75,000	10,714
$20,000 and up	0	0	0
Total	118	$464,500	$3,936
New Jersey			
Maiden Claiming	22	421,500	19,159
$0-$4,999	0	0	0
$5,000-$9,999	119	769,250	6,464
$10,000-$19,999	126	1,623,500	12,885
$20,000 and up	134	3,670,000	27,388
Total	379	$6,062,750	$15,997
New Mexico			
Maiden Claiming	17	170,000	10,000
$0-$4,999	20	76,800	3,840
$5,000-$9,999	187	1,151,500	6,158
$10,000-$19,999	75	872,500	11,633
$20,000 and up	13	280,000	21,538
Total	295	$2,380,800	$8,071
New York			
Maiden Claiming	54	1,564,000	28,963
$0-$4,999	69	276,000	4,000
$5,000-$9,999	54	372,250	6,894
$10,000-$19,999	164	2,303,000	14,043
$20,000 and up	447	16,262,500	36,381
Total	734	$19,213,750	$26,177
Ohio			
Maiden Claiming	30	138,000	4,600
$0-$4,999	159	579,000	3,642
$5,000-$9,999	119	666,000	5,597
$10,000-$19,999	9	100,500	11,167
$20,000 and up	1	25,000	25,000
Total	288	$1,370,500	$4,759
Oklahoma			
Maiden Claiming	3	17,500	5,833
$0-$4,999	27	94,500	3,500
$5,000-$9,999	45	283,500	6,300
$10,000-$19,999	8	110,000	13,750
$20,000 and up	4	100,000	25,000
Total	84	$588,000	$7,000
Oregon			
Maiden Claiming	5	25,700	5,140
$0-$4,999	89	259,100	2,911
$5,000-$9,999	17	95,500	5,618
$10,000-$19,999	0	0	0
$20,000 and up	0	0	0
Total	106	$354,600	$3,345
Pennsylvania			
Maiden Claiming	57	638,000	11,193
$0-$4,999	193	732,500	3,795
$5,000-$9,999	339	2,120,500	6,255
$10,000-$19,999	236	2,896,500	12,273
$20,000 and up	64	1,616,500	25,258
Total	832	$7,366,000	$8,853
Texas			
Maiden Claiming	43	620,000	14,419
$0-$4,999	44	174,500	3,966
$5,000-$9,999	166	1,051,250	6,333
$10,000-$19,999	202	2,227,500	11,027
$20,000 and up	72	1,800,000	25,000
Total	484	$5,253,250	$10,854
Virginia			
Maiden Claiming	5	42,500	8,500
$0-$4,999	0	0	0
$5,000-$9,999	13	93,500	7,192

	No. Claims	Value	Average
$10,000-$19,999	5	$75,000	$15,000
$20,000 and up	6	150,000	25,000
Total	24	$318,500	$13,271
Washington			
Maiden Claiming	31	329,500	10,629
$0-$4,999	56	192,000	3,429
$5,000-$9,999	90	602,750	6,697
$10,000-$19,999	55	756,000	13,745
$20,000 and up	15	345,000	23,000
Total	216	$1,895,750	$8,777
West Virginia			
Maiden Claiming	115	796,250	6,924
$0-$4,999	959	3,265,750	3,405
$5,000-$9,999	1,368	7,723,000	5,645
$10,000-$19,999	536	5,834,000	10,884
$20,000 and up	12	275,000	22,917
Total	2,875	$17,097,750	$5,947
Wyoming			
Maiden Claiming	0	0	0
$0-$4,999	1	3,500	3,500
$5,000-$9,999	0	0	0
$10,000-$19,999	0	0	0
$20,000 and up	0	0	0
Total	1	$3,500	$3,500
CANADA			
Maiden Claiming	**212**	**$4,455,625**	**$21,017**
$0-$4,999	91	296,225	3,255
$5,000-$9,999	284	1,856,563	6,537
$10,000-$19,999	355	4,752,625	13,388
$20,000 and up	375	11,309,500	30,159
Total	1,105	$18,214,913	$16,484
Alberta			
Maiden Claiming	28	324,000	11,571
$0-$4,999	16	46,500	2,906
$5,000-$9,999	59	391,000	6,627
$10,000-$19,999	134	1,792,000	13,373
$20,000 and up	61	1,511,000	24,770
Total	270	$3,740,500	$13,854
British Columbia			
Maiden Claiming	45	532,000	11,822
$0-$4,999	7	30,000	4,286
$5,000-$9,999	93	588,000	6,323
$10,000-$19,999	53	705,000	13,302
$20,000 and up	34	823,000	24,206
Total	187	$2,146,000	$11,476
Manitoba			
Maiden Claiming	5	38,125	7,625
$0-$4,999	41	135,000	3,293
$5,000-$9,999	41	256,063	6,245
$10,000-$19,999	5	70,125	14,025
$20,000 and up	0	0	0
Total	87	$461,188	$5,301
Ontario			
Maiden Claiming	134	3,561,500	26,578
$0-$4,999	9	40,500	4,500
$5,000-$9,999	90	615,500	6,839
$10,000-$19,999	163	2,185,500	13,408
$20,000 and up	280	8,975,500	32,055
Total	542	$11,817,000	$21,803
Saskatchewan			
Maiden Claiming	0	0	0
$0-$4,999	18	44,225	2,457
$5,000-$9,999	1	6,000	6,000
$10,000-$19,999	0	0	0
$20,000 and up	0	0	0
Total	19	$50,225	$2,643

Auction Sales by State and Province in 2004

North America	Yearling	Two-Year-Old	Weanling	Broodmare	Others	Total
North America	$496,937,672	$171,333,601	$71,713,850	$298,241,142	$16,159,448	$1,054,385,713
Arizona	889,350	0	14,000	9,500	3,100	915,950
California	7,890,150	18,675,200	361,300	7,669,000	7,101,300	41,696,950
Florida	22,558,000	112,409,100	6,120,500	7,851,200	173,000	149,111,800
Idaho	0	0	0	0	0	0
Illinois	0	173,800	0	0	0	173,800
Indiana	25,500	0	1,000	11,950	8,550	47,000
Iowa	304,450	84,800	13,500	39,900	0	442,650
Kentucky	384,422,400	22,117,100	62,570,900	276,679,600	7,568,600	753,358,600
Louisiana	1,632,500	859,700	115,600	1,301,050	930,350	4,839,200
Maryland	11,191,600	13,356,300	1,907,600	2,471,100	258,000	29,184,600
Michigan	211,800	37,400	0	6,900	4,100	260,200
Minnesota	312,500	0	0	0	0	312,500
New Mexico	1,357,100	0	5,500	235,950	0	1,598,550
New York	51,477,800	0	328,100	708,500	11,300	52,525,700
Ohio	107,400	10,400	2,500	24,100	500	144,900
Oklahoma	111,300	25,100	0	357,150	58,050	551,600
Oregon	111,000	12,200	26,050	58,600	1,700	209,550
Texas	3,507,600	3,533,800	187,600	448,000	16,900	7,693,900
Washington	3,141,450	0	55,750	218,700	3,950	3,419,850
West Virginia	19,500	30,950	3,950	63,125	17,725	135,250
United States	$489,271,400	$171,325,850	$71,713,850	$298,154,325	$16,157,125	$1,046,622,550
Alberta	1,004,509	5,349	0	50,696	1,197	1,061,751
British Columbia	1,115,598	2,402	0	36,121	1,126	1,155,247
Manitoba	69,985	0	0	0	0	69,985
Ontario	5,476,180	0	0	0	0	5,476,180
Canada	$7,666,272	$7,751	$0	$86,817	$2,323	$7,763,163

Auction Sales in Current and Deflated Dollars, 1990-2004

	All Horses			Yearlings		
Year	No. Sold	Nominal Dollars	Deflated Dollars	No. Sold	Nominal Dollars	Deflated Dollars
2004	20,198	$1,054,385,713	$974,298,386	9,421	$496,937,672	$459,192,083
2003	18,916	855,123,171	806,735,194	8,839	425,079,960	401,026,397
2002	18,397	767,048,402	736,894,672	9,000	390,820,438	375,456,748
2001	19,191	846,478,571	826,857,248	9,084	473,517,056	462,540,959
2000	21,225	1,091,872,249	1,091,872,249	9,569	520,053,532	520,053,532
1999	20,117	1,001,718,775	1,023,540,662	8,757	440,149,579	449,737,993
1998	19,653	828,664,233	858,968,647	8,263	354,200,540	367,153,723
1997	18,698	700,362,250	734,024,619	8,067	307,711,712	322,501,637
1996	18,871	620,712,382	661,373,633	8,026	277,221,538	295,381,599
1995	18,518	526,647,938	571,784,616	7,881	243,391,708	264,251,740
1994	17,972	448,685,293	497,108,646	7,744	210,460,233	233,173,681
1993	16,605	364,519,425	412,440,938	7,459	187,228,694	211,842,697
1992	17,504	348,995,344	403,999,935	7,967	180,385,683	208,815,978
1991	18,977	401,102,091	474,991,818	8,179	213,940,466	253,351,885
1990	21,153	500,167,261	613,025,200	8,937	268,378,588	328,935,639

Average Auction Prices by State and Province in 2004

North America	Yearling	Two-Year-Old	Weanling	Broodmare	Others	Total
North America	$52,748	$58,918	$37,004	$55,694	$28,103	$52,205
Arizona	5,968	0	2,000	1,055	1,550	5,484
California	13,084	57,817	4,014	14,663	29,712	23,451
Florida	18,133	66,632	18,435	11,824	7,521	37,749
Idaho	0	0	0	0	0	0
Illinois	0	8,276	0	0	0	8,276
Indiana	1,961	0	1,000	919	1,221	1,382
Iowa	7,080	7,709	13,500	1,662	0	5,603
Kentucky	81,896	179,813	51,456	92,134	56,482	82,154
Louisiana	5,728	6,989	5,504	4,293	11,075	5,930
Maryland	19,668	36,195	12,976	10,605	10,750	21,747
Michigan	5,042	4,675	0	6,900	4,100	5,003
Minnesota	8,680	0	0	0	0	8,680
New Mexico	10,359	0	1,833	4,290	0	8,457
New York	166,594	0	10,936	6,500	2,260	115,950
Ohio	3,254	1,485	833	2,190	500	2,634
Oklahoma	2,928	1,930	0	3,132	2,902	2,981
Oregon	3,363	1,525	1,736	1,502	850	2,160
Texas	11,930	17,669	4,362	4,435	4,225	11,984
Washington	11,100	0	2,230	4,288	658	9,369
West Virginia	1,950	3,438	987	1,468	932	1,591
United States	$55,542	$59,037	$37,004	$56,298	$28,296	$53,628

	Yearling	Two-Year-Old	Weanling	Broodmare	Others	Total
Alberta	$5,580	$1,337	$0	$1,034	$399	$4,498
British Columbia	10,141	1,201	0	3,612	1,126	9,392
Manitoba	3,042	0	0	0	0	3,042
Ontario	18,314	0	0	0	0	18,314
Canada	**$12,526**	**$1,291**	**$0**	**$1,471**	**$580**	**$11,399**

Median Auction Prices by State and Province in 2004

	Yearling	Two-Year-Old	Weanling	Broodmare	Others	Total
North America	**$13,000**	**$20,000**	**$15,000**	**$9,000**	**$9,500**	**$13,000**
Arizona	3,500	0	1,200	1,000	1,550	3,000
California	6,000	20,000	2,500	3,000	15,000	6,000
Florida	8,500	25,000	11,000	6,000	4,000	14,000
Idaho	0	0	0	0	0	0
Illinois	0	6,500	0	0	0	6,500
Indiana	2,000	0	0	650	1,050	1,075
Iowa	4,250	6,000	0	1,025	0	3,250
Kentucky	30,000	100,000	25,000	25,000	14,000	27,000
Louisiana	3,200	5,000	1,700	2,100	6,500	3,450
Maryland	10,000	21,000	5,700	5,500	7,500	11,000
Michigan	3,200	5,150	0	0	0	3,350
Minnesota	4,350	0	0	0	0	4,350
New Mexico	5,500	0	1,500	1,500	0	3,500
New York	100,000	0	3,750	3,000	1,700	30,000
Ohio	2,000	1,000	900	700	0	1,500
Oklahoma	2,500	1,000	0	1,400	1,450	1,500
Oregon	3,000	1,500	1,500	1,200	850	1,600
Texas	6,350	8,000	2,500	2,500	4,250	6,000
Washington	7,500	0	1,100	2,900	650	5,200
West Virginia	1,475	3,200	950	650	775	950
United States	**$15,000**	**$20,000**	**$15,000**	**$9,500**	**$9,500**	**$14,000**
Alberta	3,366	878	0	878	399	2,027
British Columbia	6,759	1,201	0	3,755	0	6,008
Manitoba	2,628	0	0	0	0	2,628
Ontario	10,138	0	0	0	0	10,138
Canada	**$6,008**	**$1,201**	**$0**	**$1,038**	**$399**	**$5,257**

Yearling Auction Prices in Nominal and Deflated Dollars, 1990-2004

Year	Average	Change	Deflated Average	Median	Change	Deflated Median	S&P 500	Change S&P
2004	$52,748	9.7%	$48,741	$13,000	8.3%	$12,013	1,212	9.0%
2003	48,091	11%	45,370	12,000	14%	11,321	1,112	26%
2002	43,424	−17%	41,717	10,500	17%	10,087	880	−23%
2001	52,126	−4%	50,918	9,000	−22%	8,791	1,148	−13%
2000	54,347	8%	54,347	11,500	−4%	11,500	1,320	−10%
1999	50,262	17%	51,357	12,000	3%	12,261	1,469	20%
1998	42,865	12%	44,433	11,626	6%	12,051	1,229	27%
1997	38,144	10%	39,977	11,000	16%	11,529	971	31%
1996	34,540	12%	36,803	9,500	−5%	10,122	741	20%
1995	30,883	14%	33,530	10,000	11%	10,857	616	34%
1994	27,177	8%	30,110	9,000	13%	9,971	459	−2%
1993	25,101	11%	28,401	8,000	14%	9,052	466	7%
1992	22,641	−13%	26,209	7,000	17%	8,103	436	4%
1991	26,157	−13%	30,976	6,000	−14%	7,105	417	24%
1990	30,030	−6%	36,806	7,000	8%	8,579	336	−5%

North American Mares Bred, 2000-2004

	2004	2003	2002	2001	2000
NORTH AMERICA	62,574	62,755	63,725	63,778	64,289
Alabama	136	122	99	96	108
Alaska	3	2	1	1	0
Arizona	485	564	549	468	588
Arkansas	593	582	645	569	640
California	5,757	5,821	5,827	5,735	5,593
Colorado	431	496	473	447	455
Connecticut	1	0	0	7	5
Delaware	0	1	5	0	0
Florida	6,935	6,664	7,161	7,172	7,141
Georgia	116	120	135	103	103
Hawaii	0	0	0	1	1
Idaho	308	300	305	324	391
Illinois	1,067	1,155	1,237	1,283	1,315
Indiana	702	857	885	815	766
Iowa	505	633	669	743	784
Kansas	189	184	188	200	221

	2004	2003	2002	2001	2000
Kentucky	20,346	19,885	19,664	20,279	20,708
Louisiana	3,092	2,770	2,305	2,221	2,225
Maine	0	0	3	3	3
Maryland	1,603	1,651	1,845	1,863	1,853
Massachusetts	68	93	121	110	96
Michigan	544	527	522	567	413
Minnesota	341	341	313	259	204
Mississippi	72	73	75	74	50
Missouri	73	109	164	158	181
Montana	181	196	243	274	340
Nebraska	360	354	340	356	382
Nevada	15	19	12	30	13
New Hampshire	0	1	6	5	9
New Jersey	257	325	456	278	301
New Mexico	1,528	1,526	1,476	1,212	1,131
New York	2,654	2,745	2,534	2,274	2,135
North Carolina	61	73	72	73	85
North Dakota	110	75	106	123	105
Ohio	515	661	881	865	864
Oklahoma	1,488	1,594	1,768	1,955	1,964
Oregon	449	432	390	452	341
Pennsylvania	1,003	1,021	1,026	976	1,016
Rhode Island	1	2	0	0	0
South Carolina	140	154	176	232	190
South Dakota	111	127	154	167	149
Tennessee	56	90	113	94	100
Texas	2,882	3,218	3,623	3,643	3,663
Utah	216	123	151	212	296
Vermont	4	2	11	5	6
Virginia	387	456	548	590	642
Washington	1,160	1,154	1,159	1,361	1,664
West Virginia	1,048	1,023	917	665	535
Wisconsin	22	56	38	27	53
Wyoming	19	35	36	55	54
Puerto Rico	776	756	734	810	934
Virgin Islands	4	2	2	7	11
Unknown	69				
UNITED STATES	**58,883**	**59,170**	**60,163**	**60,239**	**60,827**
Alberta	922	882	902	855	832
British Columbia	786	765	733	829	895
Manitoba	184	211	239	229	211
New Brunswick	3	2	1	1	1
Nova Scotia	1	1	5	5	6
Ontario	1,619	1,591	1,493	1,448	1,320
Prince Edward Island	0	0	14	0	0
Quebec	13	9	16	16	15
Saskatchewan	163	124	159	156	182
CANADA	**3,691**	**3,585**	**3,562**	**3,539**	**3,462**

Source: Association of Racing Commissioners International

North American Stallions in Production, 2000-2004

	2004	2003	2002	2001	2000
NORTH AMERICA	**3,766**	**4,339**	**4,501**	**4,664**	**4,771**
Alabama	25	23	22	22	23
Alaska	1	1	1	1	0
Arizona	53	65	71	76	95
Arkansas	68	68	77	73	73
California	378	398	407	422	430
Colorado	62	86	84	82	75
Connecticut	1	0	0	3	1
Delaware	0	1	1	0	0
Florida	228	258	289	295	293
Georgia	20	21	33	24	24
Hawaii	0	0	0	1	1
Idaho	45	54	62	69	68
Illinois	111	117	122	136	156
Indiana	87	102	113	105	103
Iowa	45	50	61	68	71
Kansas	25	32	31	31	35
Kentucky	352	381	388	449	436
Louisiana	229	229	210	205	186
Maine	0	2	2	3	2
Maryland	67	92	105	110	116
Massachusetts	17	24	29	23	25
Michigan	57	73	72	76	62
Minnesota	32	37	39	33	29
Mississippi	14	17	16	15	13
Missouri	17	33	37	35	39
Montana	42	43	43	51	61
Nebraska	36	44	39	43	42
Nevada	6	9	6	7	7
New Hampshire	0	1	1	1	3
New Jersey	25	36	42	51	56
New Mexico	148	166	159	148	139
New York	144	159	156	136	134
North Carolina	17	19	24	25	27
North Dakota	19	17	12	20	16
Ohio	83	108	107	114	121
Oklahoma	171	214	226	240	273
Oregon	46	53	45	56	55
Pennsylvania	109	116	109	117	123
Rhode Island	1	2	0	0	0
South Carolina	24	26	33	25	27
South Dakota	9	15	17	18	16
Tennessee	13	24	31	30	29
Texas	319	398	434	438	465
Utah	27	34	35	48	51
Vermont	3	2	5	3	2
Virginia	53	72	81	92	92
Washington	94	101	107	133	144
West Virginia	77	82	66	58	54
Wisconsin	7	15	16	16	17
Wyoming	6	15	12	18	17
Puerto Rico	54	70	75	78	88
Virgin Islands	2	1	1	3	4
Unknown	16				
UNITED STATES	**3,485**	**4,006**	**4,154**	**4,326**	**4,419**
Alberta	73	93	92	86	93
British Columbia	58	65	78	83	83
Manitoba	21	22	28	24	26
New Brunswick	2	1	1	1	1
Nova Scotia	1	1	2	2	3
Ontario	102	129	112	111	112
Prince Edward Island	0	0	1	0	0
Quebec	4	2	8	5	4
Saskatchewan	20	20	25	26	30
CANADA	**281**	**333**	**347**	**338**	**352**

Mares Bred in North America, 1997-2004

Year	Mares Bred	Change
2004	62,574	−0.3%
2003	62,755	−1.5%
2002	63,725	−0.1%
2001	63,788	−0.8%
2000	64,289	5.9%
1999	60,732	2.1%
1998	59,458	1.5%
1997	58,596	0.6%

North American Live Foals, 1997-2004

Year	Live Foals	Change
2004	39,835	2.7%
2003	38,793	2.6%
2002	37,796	−6.2%
2001	40,309	10.2%
2000	36,567	5.7%
1999	34,594	1.7%
1998	34,030	1.8%
1997	33,443	

North American Live Foals, 2000-2004

	2004	2003	2002	2001	2000
NORTH AMERICA	39,835	38,793	37,796	40,309	36,567
Alabama	58	53	55	61	74
Alaska	1	1	0	0	1
Arizona	338	316	267	316	263
Arkansas	306	353	317	323	305
California	4,045	4,043	4,022	3,796	3,301
Colorado	264	225	217	205	203
Connecticut	0	0	4	5	3
Delaware	1	2	0	24	4
Florida	4,229	4,595	4,517	4,527	4,381
Georgia	55	68	58	51	71
Hawaii	0	0	1	0	0
Idaho	151	128	142	201	163
Illinois	600	593	658	630	444
Indiana	421	408	379	363	271
Iowa	342	314	403	384	348
Kansas	84	72	91	107	104
Kentucky	14,476	13,076	12,276	14,615	13,903
Louisiana	1,598	1,275	1,305	1,309	1,007
Maine	0	3	2	3	1
Maryland	1,081	1,231	1,189	1,213	1,229
Massachusetts	50	76	48	58	52
Michigan	318	284	317	236	176
Minnesota	194	168	138	90	90
Mississippi	33	33	37	26	10
Missouri	51	65	69	92	85
Montana	103	119	93	149	119
Nebraska	169	179	159	173	174
Nevada	11	9	18	5	5
New Hampshire	1	0	1	6	7
New Jersey	209	271	179	184	182
New Mexico	808	771	650	580	397
New York	1,703	1,587	1,423	1,411	1,176
North Carolina	33	37	35	54	50
North Dakota	42	43	56	46	37
Ohio	343	459	453	477	407
Oklahoma	814	897	1,016	1,069	893
Oregon	274	255	267	213	247
Pennsylvania	574	607	546	601	493
Puerto Rico	530	512	530	629	562
Rhode Island	1	0	0	0	0
South Carolina	51	76	117	89	106
South Dakota	40	46	63	64	45
Tennessee	44	54	31	38	31
Texas	1,835	1,881	1,979	2,009	1,623
Utah	58	55	121	124	132
Vermont	1	6	3	0	7
Virginia	285	311	323	373	461
Virgin Islands	2	0	0	0	0
Washington	603	706	823	987	874
West Virginia	548	468	350	295	189
Wisconsin	22	16	15	27	25
Wyoming	13	20	25	20	20
UNITED STATES	37,813	36,767	35,788	38,258	34,751
Alberta	449	456	446	485	418
British Columbia	452	441	473	511	547
Manitoba	82	91	95	106	104
New Brunswick	1	0	1	1	1
Nova Scotia	1	4	3	3	1
Ontario	958	941	896	832	659
Prince Edward Island	0	12	0	0	0
Quebec	0	8	4	5	1
Saskatchewan	60	73	90	108	85
CANADA	2,003	2,026	2,008	2,051	1,816

Aggregate Revenues From Stud Fees by Year

Year	Stud Fees	Change
2003	$495,882,125	−4.8%
2002	520,932,750	10.8%
2001	470,085,700	5.4%
2000	445,858,075	16.9%
1999	381,292,150	19.8%
1998	318,405,625	

Average North American Stud Fees by Year, 2000-2004

Year	Average	Change
2004	$4,023	−4.0%
2003	4,192	−18.1%
2002	5,117	0.6%
2001	5,084	8.8%
2000	4,673	

Aggregate Revenues From Stud Fees

Calculated by multiplying actual number of live foals by stallion times the stud fee.

	2003	2002	2001	2000	1999
NORTH AMERICA	$495,882,125	$520,932,750	$470,085,700	$445,858,075	$381,292,150
Alabama	27,500	34,200	20,250	18,800	25,750
Arizona	186,750	151,350	68,800	110,300	194,800
Arkansas	309,250	292,250	262,750	327,000	204,150
California	17,654,950	15,114,850	19,629,650	17,903,850	8,686,150
Colorado	187,000	181,300	85,600	70,000	80,000
Connecticut	0	0	2,250	3,750	2,250
Delaware	0	0	0	2,500	4,000
Florida	21,602,950	20,761,300	18,906,050	17,980,100	18,976,500
Georgia	28,450	27,400	31,050	7,950	17,900
Idaho	77,300	110,000	129,150	126,800	109,800
Illinois	698,950	668,950	722,200	673,150	387,250
Indiana	443,600	322,100	295,450	324,700	236,150

	2003	2002	2001	2000	1999
Iowa	$499,450	$349,300	$354,750	$328,750	$260,400
Kansas	16,450	27,750	50,800	62,250	52,500
Kentucky	420,514,550	448,111,500	399,539,750	379,143,300	327,608,300
Louisiana	1,933,700	1,348,350	1,348,050	1,276,250	985,500
Maine	0	1,000	0	0	0
Maryland	7,031,850	8,488,400	7,626,850	7,117,200	7,235,500
Massachusetts	31,000	41,500	38,500	50,450	17,000
Michigan	317,650	284,900	287,050	135,450	74,650
Minnesota	221,350	142,100	80,600	45,150	34,850
Mississippi	6,750	5,050	6,000	6,500	0
Missouri	9,500	13,700	34,100	23,500	30,200
Montana	32,600	45,700	48,450	45,300	40,750
Nebraska	112,000	132,500	88,450	174,750	103,350
Nevada	0	2,500	2,500	0	5,000
New Hampshire	0	0	0	750	3,000
New Jersey	505,250	658,500	167,750	194,000	134,500
New Mexico	917,000	645,350	434,650	402,100	309,350
New York	8,960,050	8,584,750	6,450,300	7,577,650	4,376,650
North Carolina	19,800	25,800	30,100	14,550	27,500
North Dakota	14,500	28,600	30,500	10,400	17,400
Ohio	210,450	360,100	415,200	419,200	265,950
Oklahoma	706,675	664,800	774,950	834,275	747,250
Oregon	294,800	264,000	378,350	335,900	154,900
Pennsylvania	998,750	960,250	793,550	942,050	780,050
Puerto Rico	311,000	117,500	204,000	208,500	272,500
South Carolina	17,850	22,500	113,000	116,000	120,250
South Dakota	27,900	20,100	20,200	5,700	5,300
Tennessee	9,800	13,000	2,800	2,000	5,200
Texas	3,916,550	4,238,000	3,136,000	2,443,150	2,279,600
Utah	8,800	10,100	74,500	129,000	127,350
Virginia	746,750	795,500	421,500	520,100	716,350
Washington	808,300	1,104,450	1,362,700	1,252,700	1,168,900
West Virginia	837,200	596,000	385,050	224,550	142,750
Wisconsin	2,800	0	1,200	4,000	2,950
Wyoming	2,950	0	1,000	400	1,500
UNITED STATES	**$491,260,725**	**$515,767,250**	**$464,856,350**	**$441,594,725**	**$377,031,900**
Alberta	637,000	701,250	603,200	596,750	565,750
British Columbia	1,032,000	940,350	1,026,100	612,550	1,271,800
Manitoba	45,800	55,800	78,350	66,250	69,600
Ontario	2,856,700	3,438,250	3,467,600	2,913,050	2,307,750
Quebec	0	0	400	0	600
Saskatchewan	49,900	29,850	53,700	74,750	44,750
CANADA	**$4,621,400**	**$5,165,500**	**$5,229,350**	**$4,263,350**	**$4,260,250**

Average North American Stud Fees, 2000-2004

	2004	2003	2002	2001	2000
NORTH AMERICA	**$4,023**	**$4,192**	**$5,117**	**$5,084**	**$4,673**
Alabama	930	930	1,040	800	783
Arizona	935	916	932	840	770
Arkansas	1,062	1,000	990	1,184	1,397
California	2,711	2,613	2,797	2,783	2,766
Colorado	958	866	935	823	885
Connecticut	687	687	612	566	612
Florida	3,712	3,638	3,648	3,422	3,256
Georgia	1,470	1,555	1,408	1,408	790
Idaho	1,002	845	980	1,176	1,054
Illinois	1,306	1,212	1,309	1,261	1,207
Indiana	1,168	1,035	976	1,043	1,168
Iowa	1,370	1,260	1,146	1,030	952
Kansas	687	583	625	583	583
Kentucky	20,404	19,795	21,797	19,809	16,498
Louisiana	1,256	1,145	1,106	1,070	973
Maine	1,000	750	500	750	650
Maryland	3,618	3,204	3,624	3,505	3,625
Massachusetts	2,666	2,222	2,200	2,712	2,587
Michigan	1,605	1,414	1,395	1,415	1,441
Minnesota	1,213	1,266	1,179	876	939
Mississippi	750	625	1,000	1,000	
Missouri	1,023	918	870	1,058	783
Montana	765	703	695	745	692
Nebraska	1,025	984	1,053	870	933
New Hampshire	400	400	300		
New Jersey	1,359	1,513	1,702	1,333	1,333

	2004	2003	2002	2001	2000
New Mexico	1,728	1,619	1,213	1,131	1,030
New York	3,108	3,228	3,287	2,627	2,970
North Carolina	991	922	937	818	762
North Dakota	780	780	825	760	633
Ohio	1,183	1,111	1,131	1,171	1,152
Oklahoma	976	979	1,018	1,073	1,053
Oregon	1,110	1,061	1,263	1,383	1,577
Pennsylvania	1,623	1,503	1,544	1,520	1,451
South Carolina	1,104	954	937	1,138	1,142
South Dakota	812	828	833	760	600
Tennessee	677	677	750	612	664
Texas	1,614	1,630	1,829	1,402	1,344
Utah	839	700	533	764	1,075
Virginia	1,357	1,376	1,450	1,298	1,138
Washington	1,315	1,262	1,405	1,292	1,344
West Virginia	1,165	1,102	976	887	825
Wisconsin	730	730	666	550	500
Wyoming	740	733	400		
UNITED STATES	**$4,176**	**$4,370**	**$5,322**	**$5,299**	**$4,831**
Alberta	1,598	1,570	1,560	1,339	1,410
British Columbia	1,972	1,977	2,063	2,133	1,784
Manitoba	875	812	800	907	1,000
Ontario	2,562	2,370	2,668	2,716	2,580
Saskatchewan	1,350	1,241	1,016	1,100	1,250
CANADA	**$2,040**	**$1,941**	**$2,118**	**$2,114**	**$2,058**

All About Purses 2004

by Mark Simon

Total purses in North America reached a record in 2004. That was the good news. The bad news was that total purses declined slightly when adjusted for inflation. Such was the state of racing in North America in 2004, when opportunity was rich for a select group of runners and the majority were average—or worse—when average is a poor economic proposition for an owner.

In 2004, as total purses in North America reached a record, incremental increases were attained in average earnings per runner and average purse per race because the number of races declined. But getting an average runner in 2004 was no picnic, because the average earnings per runner were $15,934. That amount would not cover all costs related to keeping a racehorse in training for a year on a major circuit.

A negative factor that affected averages was the continued increase in total number of runners. And, as the number of runners increased, a substantial number of horses failed to win a race or earn much money, a perilous proposition for any owner.

On the other hand, an owner who had a stakes horse or a horse in the top 1% of earners in 2004 fared quite well, as this annual review of purses indicates.

Highlights of the 2004 data in North America include:

• A record $1,177,769,765 in purses was distributed in 58,686 races, the fewest races held in North America since 1971.

• Average purse increased 2.3% to a record $20,069 after rising just 0.1% in 2003 over '02.

• Total number of runners, 73,915, increased for the sixth straight year.

• Average earnings per runner increased 1.6%, a rebound from the 2.8% decline in that measure in 2003.

• Nominal—in current dollars—median earnings per runner increased 2.9%, also rebounding after declining by a substantial 4.8% in 2003. Median earnings had peaked in 2001.

• Real average earnings per runner—when adjusted for inflation—declined 0.5%, marking the fourth straight year of decline.

• A total of 6,294 runners—8.5% of all starters—failed to earn any part of a purse.

• More than half of all starters—53.2%—failed to win a race in 2004.

• Horses that were able to win at least one race in 2004 earned an average of $30,193; horses that failed to win a race earned an average of $3,373.

• Horses that won a stakes race earned an average of $153,372.

• Winners collectively earned 88.7% of all purse money in 2004.

• 17.4% of all runners earned more than $25,000 and collectively won 68.3% of all purse money.

• Stakes races constituted 4.4% of all races and offered 23.8% of all purses.

• Claiming races—straight claiming and maiden claiming—accounted for 66.5% of all races and distributed just 37.9% of all purses.

• For runners three and up, almost half of all races—49.7%—were carded at six furlongs or shorter.

• The average number of starts per horse remained at 6.6 in 2004.

• Average field size remained steady at 8.3 starters per race.

"All About Purses" was first published in *The Thoroughbred Record* in 1973 and covered the '72 racing year. It has been published in THOROUGHBRED TIMES since 1990. The data reflect all Thoroughbred purses distributed to racehorses in North America in 2004, excluding Mexico and Puerto Rico, and were provided to THOROUGH-

---

Table 1

Selected Racing Statistics, North American Thoroughbred Racing, 1995-2004

Year	No. of Runners	No. of Races	Total Purses	Average Purse	Earnings per Runner Average	Median	Percentage of Runners Earning Purses
2004	73,915	58,686	$1,177,769,765	$20,069	$15,934	$5,877	91.5%
2003	73,614	58,813	1,154,238,845	19,626	15,680	5,714	90.3%
2002	72,504	59,712	1,170,169,267	19,597	16,139	6,003	89.6%
2001	70,942	60,538	1,146,337,367	18,936	16,159	6,010	90.6%
2000	69,230	60,579	1,093,661,241	18,053	15,798	5,796	90.2%
1999	68,435	60,118	1,008,162,608	16,770	14,732	5,310	89.1%
1998	68,419	61,141	968,366,929	15,838	14,153	4,939	88.8%
1997	69,067	63,491	888,667,752	13,997	12,867	4,425	88.9%
1996	70,371	64,263	845,916,706	13,163	12,021	3,937	88.1%
1995	72,316	68,197	815,987,125	11,965	11,283	3,702	88.9%
Change:							
2003-2004	0.4%	−0.2%	2.0%	2.3%	1.6%	2.9%	1.3%
1995-2004	22.1%	−13.9%	44.3%	67.7%	41.2%	58.8%	2.9%
Average change:							
1995-2004	2.2%	−1.4%	4.4%	6.8%	4.1%	5.9%	0.3%

Table 2
Distribution of Earnings of Runners for 2004

Earnings range	No. of Runners	Percent of Runners	Earnings	Percent of Earnings	Average Earnings
$300,000 or more	189	0.3%	$113,209,580	9.6%	$598,992
$200,000 - 299,999	184	0.2%	45,068,978	3.8%	244,940
$100,000 - 199,999	976	1.3%	128,284,850	10.9%	131,439
$75,000 - 99,999	1,013	1.4%	86,896,474	7.4%	85,781
$50,000 - 74,999	2,529	3.4%	153,048,666	13.0%	60,517
$25,000 - 49,999	8,006	10.8%	277,853,235	23.6%	34,706
$20,000 - 24,999	3,376	4.6%	75,436,243	6.4%	22,345
$15,000 - 19,999	4,780	6.5%	82,886,171	7.0%	17,340
$10,000 - 14,999	7,191	9.7%	88,503,119	7.5%	12,307
$9,000 - 9,999	1,835	2.5%	17,396,453	1.5%	9,480
$8,000 - 8,999	2,012	2.7%	17,078,590	1.5%	8,488
$7,000 - 7,999	2,194	3.0%	16,411,592	1.4%	7,480
$6,000 - 6,999	2,407	3.3%	15,604,005	1.3%	6,483
$5,000 - 5,999	2,577	3.5%	14,099,422	1.2%	5,471
$4,000 - 4,999	2,831	3.8%	12,728,752	1.1%	4,496
$3,000 - 3,999	3,093	4.2%	10,769,720	0.9%	3,482
$2,000 - 2,999	3,762	5.1%	9,320,077	0.8%	2,477
$1,000 - 1,999	5,388	7.3%	7,864,047	0.7%	1,460
$1 - 999	13,278	18.0%	5,309,791	0.5%	400
None	6,294	8.5%	0	0.0%	0
Totals	**73,915**	**100.0%**	**$1,177,769,765**	**100.0%**	**$ 15,934**

BRED TIMES based on data obtained from the Jockey Club Information Systems. Steeplechase races are excluded.

Purses Up in 2004

The best news for racehorse owners in 2004 came in the form of higher purses. Total purses in North America reached a record $1,177,769,765, a 2% increase over 2003 that eclipsed the previous mark set in '02. In 2003, total purses decreased in North America for the first time since 1993, a year that marked the end of a long recession in yearling prices and stud fees. The unexpected downturn in total purses in 2003 was accompanied by declines in average earnings per runner and median earnings per runner.

The big-picture statistics on racing in 2004, summarizing purses, runners, races, and earnings, are presented in Table 1. The table presents a ten-year snapshot of key statistics. As can be seen by the summary line that provides percent changes in the data in 2004 from '03, all key statistics improved. The only downward movement was number of races, and, for purses, that is a positive statistic. When races decline and purses increase, average purse per race increases.

Indeed, the combination of fewer races and higher purses pushed average purse over the $20,000 mark for the first time. Average purse increased 2.3% over 2003. Average purse has increased 67.7% in the decade to 2004. Average earnings per runner increased 1.6%, slightly less than purses because the number of runners increased 0.4%, thus suppressing the increase in average. Average earnings per runner were 1.4% below the all-time record average per runner of $16,159 set in 2001, when there were 4.2% fewer runners than in '04.

All major averages increased primarily because total purses increased 2% from 2003. After purses had generally stagnated from 1988 to '93, increasing just 1.6% in that time period, purses increased every year from '94 through 2002. The temporary dip in 2003 meant several key averages also declined that year, including average earnings per runner. Helping fuel increases in 2004 was a 0.2% decrease in the number of races, which continued a long, steady decline that began in 1990, after the number of races in North America peaked at 82,726 in '89. The number of races has declined every year but one since then, falling 29.1% since 1989.

For owners, the most disturbing key statistic listed in Table 1 is median earnings per runner. That measure was $5,877 in 2004, meaning that half of all runners earned more than that amount and half less. While median earnings increased 2.9% in 2004 and have risen 58.8% in the past ten years, horses that earn the median figure remain a financial drain on their owners. The good news about median is that at least it increased in 2004, after having declined in '02 and '03.

In 2004, the percentage of runners earning part of a purse increased once again, 1.3% to 91.5%, an all-time high. That number is not really significant because a small percentage of runners earn the lion's share of the spoils.

The relatively rosy picture of 2004 is tempered when the numbers are adjusted for inflation using the federal government's gross domestic product implicit price deflator, which is considered to be more conservative and more accurate than the widely quoted consumer price index. Total purses, though a record in nominal dollars, actually declined ever so slightly when adjusted for inflation. Average earnings per runner also declined, 0.5%,

Table 3
Earnings as a Function of Number of Wins for 2004

Races Won	No. of Runners	Percent of Runners	Total Earnings	Percent of Earnings	Average Earnings
More than 11	0	0.0%	$0	0.0%	$0
11	1	0.0%	27,016	0.0%	27,016
10	0	0.0%	0	0.0%	0
9	5	0.0%	547,247	0.0%	109,449
8	11	0.0%	882,668	0.1%	80,243
7	52	0.1%	5,822,222	0.5%	111,966
6	157	0.2%	24,125,425	2.0%	153,665
5	510	0.7%	47,702,514	4.1%	93,534
4	1,413	1.9%	98,933,950	8.4%	70,017
3	3,839	5.2%	203,022,596	17.2%	52,884
2	8,989	12.2%	309,111,407	26.2%	34,388
1	19,641	26.6%	355,039,383	30.1%	18,076
0	39,297	53.2%	132,555,337	11.3%	3,373
Totals	**73,915**	**100.0%**	**$1,177,769,765**	**100.0%**	**$15,934**

when adjusted for inflation. In real dollars, average earnings per runner fell to $14,724, down 6.8% from the record $15,798 achieved in 2000.

Deflated average earnings per runner have shown little improvement in the past 34 years. In 1971, deflated average earnings were $13,862, a figure not surpassed until '98. Since 1971, real average earnings per runner have increased just 6.2%.

Real median earnings per runner have fared a bit better, increasing 0.7% in 2004 and 35.1% over ten years. But, in looking over a longer time horizon, it is doing worse than real average earnings per runner. In 1971, real median earnings per runner were $5,569, higher than in 2004.

Total real purses in North America have been on a general increase during the duration of this study. In 1973, real total purses stood at $733.7-million (when nominal total purses were $233.7-million). Still, as other forms of gaming have increased their market share and revenues appreciably in that time period, Thoroughbred racing barely has been able to keep pace with inflation.

Table 2 breaks down distribution of earnings for all runners by earnings range. While the average earnings per runner in 2004 stood at $15,934, very few runners earned the average. In the category of runners that earned $15,000 to $19,999, just 4,780 horses, or 6.5% of all runners, fell into that bracket. That was because median earnings—the midpoint range—was just $5,877. This table indicates that 6,294 horses, or 8.5% of the total, earned nothing, and 18% earned some purse money but less than $1,000. In all, 19,572 runners earned less than $1,000 in 2004. Those 26.5% of all runners accounted for just 0.5% of all purse money. At the other end of the earnings spectrum, 1.8% of all runners, 1,349, earned $100,000 or more. Those runners took home 24.3% of all purse money, an average of $212,427 each. A total of 45,671 runners, 61.8% of all runners, earned less than $10,000 in 2004, with those runners collectively winning just 10.7% of all purse money.

Starting and Winning

A horse must start to earn money for its owner, and average earnings rise for every start made from one through ten. Horses that made five starts earned an average of $14,111; horses that made ten starts earned an average of $26,009. Horses that started fewer than six times earned less than the overall average earnings per starter for the year, $15,934.

Horses that started most frequently earned the most money; 19.9% of runners in 2004 made more than ten starts, and they earned 32.4% of all purse money. Average earnings per start in 2004 were $2,423. For horses starting more than ten times, mostly claiming horses, average earnings per start drop below the overall average.

The data reveal that the key to winning is starting. Winners start far more often and earn far more money than horses that earn some money but fail to win. And winners average more than four times as many starts as those horses that fail to earn any part of a purse. In 2004, winners started 8.9 times on average, nonwinning earners 5.0 times, and nonearners 2.0 times, for an overall average of 6.6 starts per runner.

By far the most important factor for earning money on the racetrack is winning. Table 3, which reports earnings as a function of number of wins, shows that winners take the spoils in racing. Horses that failed to win—39,297 runners, or 53.2% of the total in 2004—earned an average of $3,373. Horses that won once earned an average of $18,076, or more than five times as much as nonwinners. Horses that won twice earned $34,388, nearly twice as much as those that won just once. Horses that won three times earned an average of $52,884.

Earnings rise dramatically because once a horse is able to win a race, it has eliminated more than half of the competition for purses. The 34,618 winners effectively were splitting up the $1.045-billion in purses that the 39,297 winless horses could not share.

Horses that won six times earned an average

of $153,665, the most of any win category. Only 157 horses, or 0.2% of all runners, fall into that rich bracket. Only one horse was able to win more than nine races in 2004.

The 34,618 winners collectively won 58,778 races (there were 92 more wins than races due to dead heats). Winning one race is tough, two is even tougher, and so it is up the scale. Table 3 shows exactly how hard it is for one horse to win multiple times, as seen by the number of runners that are able to win at each successive level drops off substantially. Only 736 horses, 1% of all runners, were able to win five or more races in 2004.

Winners collectively earned 88.7% of all purse money, as shown in Figure 1. Based on best finish position, the 46.8% of runners that won a race earned 100% of first-place money, 75.1% of all second-place money, 71.2% of all third-place money, 68.8% of all fourth-place money, 66.4% of all fifth-place money, and 59.9% of all sixth-place money or lower, to earn an overall average per runner of $30,193. The 14.3% of runners that

could finish no better than second earned 7.9% of all purse money, an average of $8,818. Horses that finished first and second collectively earned 96.6% of all purse money.

The study of purses indicates that owners derive little benefit from minor placings. In 2004, horses that finished first earned 100% of first-place money, 75.1% of second-place money, 71.2% of third, 68.8% of fourth, 66.4% of fifth, and 59.9% of sixth or lower, for a total of 88.7% of all purse money. Horses that could finish no better than second, earned 7.9% of all purse money in 2004.

Distribution of purses by best finish position is presented as a pie chart in Figure 1. The distribution of money to horses based on best finish position has not changed much since this study started in 1973.

Runners by Age and Sex

Purse earnings potential differs by age and sex, and Table 4 details those differences. Three-year-olds have the most lucrative opportunities. While

Table 4
Distribution of Races and Purses by Age and Sex for 2004

Sex	No. of Races	Percent of Races	Purses	Percent of Purses	Average Purse per Race
			TWO-YEAR-OLDS		
Females	1,977	3.4%	$57,282,685	4.9%	$28,975
Males	59	0.1%	4,565,052	0.4%	77,374
Either Sex	2,277	3.9%	62,892,837	5.3%	27,621
Overall	4,313	7.3%	124,740,574	10.6%	28,922
			THREE-YEAR-OLDS		
Females	2,893	4.9%	83,720,872	7.1%	28,939
Males	52	0.1%	1,947,667	0.2%	37,455
Either Sex	3,220	5.5%	110,164,273	9.4%	34,213
Overall	6,165	10.5%	195,832,812	16.6%	31,765
			THREE-YEAR-OLDS AND UP		
Females	15,981	27.2%	287,737,185	24.4%	18,005
Males	65	0.1%	1,070,525	0.1%	16,470
Either Sex	23,807	40.6%	407,783,953	34.6%	17,129
Overall	39,853	67.9%	696,591,663	59.1%	17,479
			FOUR-YEAR-OLDS		
Females	78	0.1%	2,040,847	0.2%	26,165
Males	0	0.0%	0	0.0%	
Either Sex	99	0.2%	2,463,551	0.2%	24,884
Overall	177	0.3%	4,504,398	0.4%	25,449
			FOUR-YEAR-OLDS AND UP		
Females	3,112	5.3%	61,027,415	5.2%	19,610
Males	11	0.0%	440,762	0.0%	40,069
Either Sex	5,050	8.6%	94,613,859	8.0%	18,735
Overall	8,173	13.9%	156,082,036	13.3%	19,097
			FIVE-YEAR-OLDS AND UP		
Females	0	0.0%	0	0.0%	0
Males	0	0.0%	0	0.0%	0
Either Sex	5	0.0%	18,282	0.0%	3,656
Overall	5	0.0%	18,282	0.0%	3,656
			TOTALS		
Females	24,041	41.0%	$491,809,004	41.8%	$20,457
Males	187	0.3%	$8,024,006	0.7%	$42,909
Either Sex	34,458	58.7%	$677,936,755	57.6%	$19,674
Overall	58,686	100.0%	$1,177,769,765	100.0%	$20,069

Table 5
Distribution of Runners and Earnings by Age and Sex for 2004

Sex	No. of Runners	Percent of Runners	Earnings	Percent of Earnings	Average Earnings
			TWO-YEAR-OLDS		
Females	5,351	7.2%	$59,368,333	5.0%	$11,095
Males	5,490	7.4%	65,359,051	5.5%	11,905
Overall	10,843	14.7%	124,740,574	10.6%	11,504
			THREE-YEAR-OLDS		
Females	10,601	14.3%	$187,758,071	15.9%	$17,711
Males	11,107	15.0%	218,965,216	18.6%	19,714
Overall	21,709	29.4%	406,724,017	34.5%	18,735
			FOUR-YEAR-OLDS		
Females	8,043	10.9%	$141,775,840	12.0%	$17,627
Males	9,314	12.6%	171,688,368	14.6%	18,433
Overall	17,358	23.5%	313,467,015	26.6%	18,059
			FIVE-YEAR-OLDS		
Females	4,606	6.2%	$69,786,861	5.9%	$15,151
Males	6,295	8.5%	103,734,742	8.8%	16,479
Overall	10,901	14.7%	173,521,603	14.7%	15,918
			SIX-YEAR-OLDS AND UP		
Females	3,720	5.0%	$38,423,445	3.3%	$10,329
Males	9,384	12.7%	120,893,111	10.3%	12,883
Overall	13,104	17.7%	159,316,556	13.5%	12,158
			TOTALS		
Females	**32,321**	**43.7%**	**$497,112,550**	**42.2%**	**$15,380**
Males	**41,590**	**56.3%**	**$680,640,488**	**57.8%**	**$16,365**
Overall	**73,915**	**100.0%**	**$1,177,769,765**	**100.0%**	**$15,934**

10.5% of all races in 2004 were restricted to three-year-olds, those 6,165 races distributed 16.6% of all purses, an average purse of $31,765. Races restricted to sophomore males offered an average purse of $37,455, and those open to either sex an average of $34,213. Races restricted to three-year-old fillies offered an average purse of $28,939.

Two-year-old racing offered the second-most lucrative average purses, with the 4,313 races restricted to juveniles offering 10.6% of all purses for an average of $28,922. Races solely for juveniles accounted for 7.3% of all races in 2004.

The most common races were for horses three-year-olds and up, and the 39,853 races for horses in that category accounted for 67.9% of all races and 59.1% of all purses. The age bracket's average race purse of $17,479 was less than the overall average purse for the year, $20,069.

Differences in earnings potential between the sexes also are pronounced. Races open to either sex—which effectively means races for males—were far more abundant than races exclusively for females, with 58.7% of all races being open and 41% re-

stricted to females. Just 0.3% of races were restricted to males. The 24,041 races restricted to females had slightly higher purses on average than races open to either sex, by a margin of $20,457 to $19,674.

Table 5 examines in greater detail the differences in earnings potential by age and sex. Females earned an average of $15,380 and males $16,365. While females accounted for 43.7% of all runners, they collectively earned 42.2% of all purses. In every age bracket, males earned more than females. Among three-year-olds, the highest earnings bracket of all ages, males earned an average of $19,714, while females averaged $17,711.

Three-year-olds provided the largest group of runners, with 29.4% of the total, followed by four-year-olds, 23.5%. Three-year-olds earned the largest portion of purses, taking more than one-third of all purse money, 34.5%, with four-year-olds again coming next, at 26.6%. Three-year-olds are annually able to win the most money because average purses for three-year-olds are higher than those for any other age group (Table 4) and three-

Figure 1
Distribution of purses by best finish position

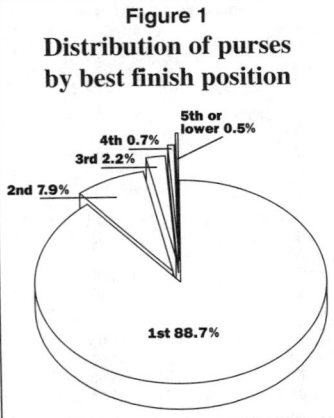

- 5th or lower 0.5%
- 4th 0.7%
- 3rd 2.2%
- 2nd 7.9%
- 1st 88.7%

Table 6
Distribution of Races by Class for 2004

	No. of Races	Percent of Races	No. of Starts	Average Starters	Purses	Percent of Purses	Avg. Purse per Race
MAIDEN CLAIMING	10,101	17.2%	89,592	8.9	$111,081,385	9.4%	$ 10,997
CLAIMING	28,909	49.3%	237,963	8.2	335,754,655	28.5%	11,614
$0 to 999	0	0.0%	0	0.0	0	0.0%	0
$1,000 to 1,999	142	0.2%	957	6.7	285,588	0.0%	2,011
$2,000 to 2,999	1,680	2.9%	13,537	8.1	8,465,184	0.7%	5,039
$3,000 to 3,999	3,294	5.6%	28,785	8.7	20,545,153	1.7%	6,237
$4,000 to 4,999	3,919	6.7%	33,565	8.6	27,374,017	2.3%	6,985
$5,000 to 5,999	5,389	9.2%	46,838	8.7	49,020,963	4.2%	9,096
$6,000 to 6,999	1,020	1.7%	8,129	8.0	9,209,773	0.8%	9,029
$7,000 to 7,999	2,201	3.8%	18,601	8.5	21,448,933	1.8%	9,745
$8,000 to 8,999	777	1.3%	6,057	7.8	8,066,806	0.7%	10,382
$9,000 to 9,999	30	0.1%	251	8.4	219,000	0.0%	7,300
$10,000 to 14,999	4,427	7.5%	35,389	8.0	58,507,042	5.0%	13,216
$15,000 to 19,999	2,119	3.6%	16,436	7.8	32,179,977	2.7%	15,186
$20,000 and up	3,911	6.7%	29,418	7.5	100,432,219	8.5%	25,679
TOTAL CLAIMING	**39,010**	**66.5%**	**327,555**	**8.4**	**$446,836,040**	**37.9%**	**$11,454**
Optional claiming	2,286	3.9%	16,372	7.2	73,467,786	6.2%	32,138
Starter allowance	1,212	2.1%	9,158	7.6	18,606,849	1.6%	15,352
Starter handicap	77	0.1%	614	8.0	1,535,389	0.1%	19,940
Maiden	6,527	11.1%	57,567	8.8	160,711,973	13.6%	24,623
Allowance	6,954	11.8%	54,540	7.8	194,521,810	16.5%	27,973
Handicap	49	0.1%	347	7.1	1,246,176	0.1%	25,432
Stakes	2,571	4.4%	19,953	7.8	280,843,742	23.8%	109,235
TOTAL NONCLAIMING	**19,676**	**33.5%**	**158,551**	**8.1**	**$730,933,725**	**62.1%**	**$ 37,148**
TOTAL ALL RACES	**58,686**	**100.0%**	**486,106**	**8.3**	**$1,177,769,765**	**100.0%**	**$ 20,069**

year-olds have a lot of opportunities outside their own age division in the fall. Two-year-olds earned an average of $11,504, less than any other age group, largely because two-year-olds start fewer times.

As any racegoer can tell you, claiming races dominate the average card. Table 6 shows how prevalent claiming races are in North America. In 2004, claiming races constituted almost exactly two out of every three races in North America. Of the 58,686 races, 39,010, or 66.5%, were for claimers, including maiden claiming, which accounted for 17.2% of all races. Straight claiming races accounted for almost half—49.3%—of all races. While claiming races are plentiful, they feature below-average purses; the $11,454 average claiming purse in 2004 was 42.9% below the overall average of $20,069. When this series began in the 1970s, claiming races made up approximately 73% of all races. After whole-card simulcasting began, and the number of runners and the number of races decreased, claiming races were less plentiful as allowance races and optional claiming races became more common. Percentage of claiming races dropped to an all-time low of 64.5% in 2000. As the number of runners has increased since 2000, the percentage of claiming races has increased.

The gap in the percentage of purses being dis-

Table 7
Distribution of all North American Races by Purse for 2004

Range of Purses	No. of Races	Total Purses
Less than $1,000	2	$600
$1,000-1,999	549	899,706
$2,000-2,999	1,208	2,966,845
$3,000-3,999	700	2,398,517
$4,000-4,999	3,833	16,719,972
$5,000-5,999	2,374	12,787,756
$6,000-6,999	4,009	25,685,812
$7,000-7,999	3,968	29,538,427
$8,000-8,999	3,472	29,108,472
$9,000-9,999	2,847	26,706,153
$10,000-12,499	7,184	79,362,613
$12,500-14,999	4,702	63,977,304
$15,000-19,999	6,011	101,895,035
$20,000-24,999	4,430	98,108,579
$25,000-29,999	3,898	104,385,110
$30,000-39,999	3,365	114,664,341
$40,000-49,999	3,085	135,449,685
$50,000-74,999	1,824	104,520,706
$75,000-99,999	318	25,768,479
$100,000-199,999	607	75,261,615
$200,000-299,999	155	35,662,338
$300,000-399,999	41	13,127,800
$400,000-499,999	18	7,666,200
$500,000-749,999	45	23,177,200
$750,000-999,999	19	14,700,670
$1,000,000 and up	22	33,229,830
Totals	**58,686**	**$1,177,769,765**

Table 8
Average Field Size and Number of Starts

Year	Avg Number of Starts	Avg Field Size	Year	Avg Number of Starts	Avg Field Size
2004	6.6	8.3	1994	7.8	8.3
2003	6.6	8.3	1993	7.9	8.6
2002	6.8	8.3	1992	7.9	8.6
2001	7.0	8.2	1991	7.9	8.7
2000	7.1	8.1	1990	7.9	8.9
1999	7.2	8.2	1989	8.0	8.8
1998	7.6	8.5	1988	8.0	9.1
1997	7.6	8.2	1987	8.1	9.0
1996	7.6	8.3	1986	8.2	9.1
1995	7.7	8.2			

tributed in claiming races versus nonclaiming races has been increasing over the years. In 1984, claiming races distributed 44.9% of all purses; in '94, claiming races distributed 39.1% of all purses; and in 2004, claiming races distributed 37.9% of all purses. That decline is partly attributable to the decline in percentage of claiming races during that time period; in '84, claiming races accounted for 72% of all races.

The $37,148 average nonclaiming purse in 2004 was 3.2 times larger than the $11,454 average claiming purse. Ten years earlier, the $21,903 average nonclaiming purse was 3.6 times larger than the $6,124 average claiming purse. Allowance races were the second-most common race type in 2004, accounting for two of every 17 races. Those 11.8% of all races offered an average purse of $27,973 and distributed 16.5% of all purses.

After a long, slow, steady decline for decades, the average number of starts per runner has leveled off, at least for now. In 2004, the average starter made 6.6 starts, the same as in '03. In 1972, the first year of this study, horses started an average of 10.1 times. The average number of starts per runner peaked in the mid-1950s.

Earnings are related to the number of starts, and, with the average number of starts declining, the opportunities to pick up purses also decline. The decline in starts comes at the same time as a decline in average field size. With fewer starters per race, it should be easier to get a horse into the starting gate, but average field size, like starts, has been in a slow decline. In 2004, average field size was 8.3, the same as the previous two years but well below the 9.1 average number of starters per race in 1986.

Table 7 presents the distribution of purses in North America in 2004 by value and helps to explain why so few horses earn six figures in any single year. In 2004, just 86 races, 0.15% of the total, offered a purse of $500,000 or more. Another 821 races, 1.4% of the total, offered purses of $100,000 to $499,999. Those 907 races, however, distributed $202,825,653, 17.2% of the total. At the other end of the purse spectrum, 2,459 races, 4.2% of the total, offered a purse of less than $4,000, and just 0.5% of all purses. In 2004, 39.1% of all races featured a purse of less than $10,000.

In summary, the overall health of Thoroughbred racing's purse structure improved in 2004 after a down year in '03, when total purses and average earnings per runner declined. That total purses reached a record in 2004 was welcome news to owners, trainers, breeders, and jockeys. The record purses also were a sign that growth in racing may have slowed a bit, but the industry is not stagnant. Purse money coming into racing from slots and other subsidies helped to support the entire infrastructure of racing.

Mark Simon is editor of THOROUGHBRED TIMES.

Table 9
Distribution of Races and Purses by Distance for 2004
(All two-year-old races omitted)

Distance	Number of Races	Percent of Races	Purses	Percent of Purses	Avg. Purse per Race
Less than 5 furlongs	2,531	4.7%	$26,926,647	2.6%	$10,639
5 furlongs	2,759	5.1%	38,900,414	3.7%	14,099
Between 5 and 6 furlongs	5,699	10.5%	61,358,236	5.8%	10,766
6 furlongs	16,048	29.5%	254,965,841	24.2%	15,888
Between 6 and 7 furlongs	4,108	7.6%	71,599,788	6.8%	17,429
7 furlongs	3,275	6.0%	75,897,995	7.2%	23,175
Between 7 and 8 furlongs	675	1.2%	10,352,037	1.0%	15,336
1 mile	7,288	13.4%	144,171,903	13.7%	19,782
1 mile 40 yds.	49	0.1%	658,100	0.1%	13,431
1 mile 70 yds.	3,538	6.5%	46,083,945	4.4%	13,025
1¹⁄₁₆ miles	6,488	11.9%	175,680,557	16.7%	27,078
1⅛ miles	1,468	2.7%	87,090,730	8.3%	59,326
1³⁄₁₆ miles	42	0.1%	5,494,129	0.5%	130,813
1¼ miles	177	0.3%	32,859,463	3.1%	185,647
1⁵⁄₁₆-1⅜ miles	99	0.2%	7,881,732	0.7%	79,613
1½ miles	90	0.2%	11,931,424	1.1%	132,571
More than 1½ miles	39	0.1%	1,176,149	0.1%	30,158
Totals	54,373	100.0%	$1,053,029,191	100.0%	$19,367

Purse Distribution by Track in 2004

Northeast

Track, State	Racing Days	Average Daily Purse Distribution (Change from Previous Year)		Average Purse	Average Stakes Purses (% Total Purse)	
Aqueduct, N.Y.	125	$368,055	(1%)	$41,004	$120,152	(20%)
Atlantic City Race Course, N.J.	4	151,950	(44%)	20,260	50,000	(8%)
Belmont Park, N.Y.	93	548,315	(–2%)	59,157	212,107	(40%)
Finger Lakes, N.Y.	157	105,755	(40%)	11,726	76,190	(8%)
Genesee Valley, N.Y.	1	27,300	(–2%)	13,650	0	(0%)
Meadowlands, N.J.	33	339,808	(54%)	36,057	87,501	(27%)
Monmouth Park, N.J.	87	349,443	(11%)	35,936	96,988	(26%)
Northampton Fair, Ma.	9	25,040	(–8%)	3,174	15,000	(7%)
Rockingham Park, N.H.	1	44,590		14,863	0	(0%)
Saratoga Race Course, N.Y.	36	634,957	(4%)	66,643	226,044	(44%)
Suffolk Downs, Ma.	119	110,290	(6%)	11,834	66,748	(12%)

Mid-Atlantic

Track, State	Racing Days	Average Daily Purse Distribution (Change from Previous Year)		Average Purse	Average Stakes Purses (% Total Purse)	
Charles Town Races, W.V.	231	$224,692	(52%)	$20,853	$67,094	(5%)
Colonial Downs, Va.	35	199,600	(3%)	20,191	99,233	(21%)
Delaware Park, De.	134	253,345	(8%)	28,243	115,628	(16%)
Laurel Park, Md.	62	165,499	(–11%)	18,389	78,856	(14%)
Mountaineer Race Track, W.V.	219	171,818	(–2%)	17,510	99,038	(7%)
Penn National Race Course, Pa.	196	74,142	(9%)	8,352	44,825	(2%)
Philadelphia Park, Pa.	216	140,737	(0%)	14,679	108,878	(8%)
Pimlico Race Course, Md.	135	197,722	(–14%)	22,640	113,523	(28%)
Timonium, Md.	8	131,228	(5%)	13,998	50,000	(10%)

Southeast

Track, State	Racing Days	Average Daily Purse Distribution (Change from Previous Year)		Average Purse	Average Stakes Purses (% Total Purse)	
Calder Race Course, Fl.	178	$229,102	(2%)	$21,726	$86,762	(27%)
Gulfstream Park, Fl.	91	301,358	(–10%)	30,505	171,339	(30%)
Ocala Training Center, Fl.	1	380,000	(3%)	63,333	63,333	(100%)
Tampa Bay Downs, Fl.	92	135,073	(3%)	12,693	82,373	(16%)

Midwest

Track, State	Racing Days	Average Daily Purse Distribution (Change from Previous Year)		Average Purse	Average Stakes Purses (% Total Purse)	
Anthony Downs, Ks.	6	$13,054	(8%)	$3,730	$8,013	(61%)
Arlington Park, Il.	96	274,276	(–2%)	29,387	135,722	(26%)
Beulah Park, Oh.	137	43,894	(0%)	5,678	37,083	(7%)
Canterbury Park, Mn.	67	124,224	(7%)	14,400	51,849	(22%)
Chippewa Downs, N.D.	6	8,596	(44%)	1,563	2,467	(14%)
Churchill Downs, Ky.	74	538,845	(24%)	52,884	312,442	(40%)
Columbus Races, Ne.	25	44,616	(20%)	5,140	12,422	(9%)
Ellis Park, Ky.	54	163,826	(–13%)	16,383	93,973	(12%)
Eureka Downs, Ks.	21	5,694	(–21%)	2,174	3,952	(3%)
Fairmount Park, Il.	101	64,186	(0%)	6,746	32,000	(8%)
Fonner Park, Ne.	37	59,837	(13%)	6,116	25,766	(19%)
Great Lakes Downs, Mi.	118	80,507	(6%)	9,424	67,982	(19%)
Hawthorne Race Course, Il.	114	213,598	(0%)	22,694	155,232	(16%)
Hoosier Park, In.	59	138,905	(23%)	12,765	92,982	(19%)
Horsemen's Atokad Downs, Ne.	3	71,392	(–12%)	11,899	0	(0%)
Horsemen's Park, Ne.	4	129,350	(2%)	32,338	43,400	(50%)
Indiana Downs, In.	48	85,483	(–25%)	9,454	41,775	(8%)
Keeneland Race Course, Ky.	32	614,178	(2%)	65,952	229,164	(44%)
Kentucky Downs, Ky.	6	227,833	(9%)	31,068	96,667	(42%)
Lincoln State Fair, Ne.	33	48,465	(9%)	5,692	13,027	(10%)
Mt. Pleasant Meadows, Mi.	28	4,076	(–34%)	2,718	0	(0%)
North Dakota Horse Fair, N.D.	14	18,357	(–11%)	3,671	12,884	(35%)
Prairie Meadows Racetrack, Ia.	96	135,639	(–4%)	17,455	76,305	(23%)
River Downs, Oh.	122	54,230	(–4%)	7,417	58,167	(13%)
Thistledown, Oh.	182	66,708	(12%)	9,081	63,043	(12%)
Turfway Park, Ky.	101	156,515	(1%)	15,667	96,491	(17%)
Woodlands, Ks.	30	43,197	(–18%)	6,384	21,783	(20%)

Southwest

Track, State	Racing Days	Average Daily Purse Distribution (Change from Previous Year)		Average Purse	Average Stakes Purses (% Total Purse)	
Blue Ribbon Downs, Ok.	49	$7,732	(0%)	$2,849	$9,179	(15%)
Delta Downs, La.	99	197,760	(0%)	19,213	89,273	(21%)
Downs at Albuquerque, N.M.	69	48,663	(–12%)	10,728	41,201	(33%)

Track, State	Racing Days	Average Daily Purse Distribution (Change from Previous Year)	Average Purse	Average Stakes Purses (% Total Purse)
Evangeline Downs, La.	92	$121,317 (67%)	12,158	$58,500 (5%)
Fair Grounds, La.	82	251,513 (–2%)	25,306	111,031 (27%)
Fair Meadows at Tulsa, Ok.	28	63,950 (162%)	13,264	46,315 (10%)
Gillespie County Fairgrounds, Tx.	8	14,000 (52%)	5,333	16,800 (15%)
Lone Star Park, Tx.	82	197,380 (–9%)	20,462	108,682 (26%)
Louisiana Downs, La.	102	183,924 (2%)	17,355	63,432 (19%)
Manor Downs, Tx.	16	16,144 (–58%)	5,381	12,667 (15%)
Oaklawn Park, Ar.	55	238,896 (2%)	23,547	153,673 (30%)
Remington Park, Ok.	65	83,198 (10%)	9,181	55,155 (20%)
Retama Park, Tx.	39	90,981 (–6%)	10,851	64,946 (26%)
Ruidoso Downs, N.M.	57	45,582 (–16%)	9,955	36,331 (35%)
Sam Houston Race Park, Tx.	72	104,930 (–5%)	10,949	56,971 (23%)
Sunland Park, N.M.	92	155,473 (–5%)	22,176	118,277 (22%)
SunRay Park, N.M.	44	52,611 (–28%)	10,021	54,707 (24%)

West Coast

Track, State	Racing Days	Average Daily Purse Distribution (Change from Previous Year)	Average Purse	Average Stakes Purses (% Total Purse)
Apache County Fair, Az.	4	$10,375 (15%)	$1,804	$0 (0%)
Arapahoe Park, Co.	37	53,352 (–3%)	7,833	29,646 (26%)
Bay Meadows Race Course, Ca.	104	161,482 (–4%)	19,128	77,012 (13%)
Bay Meadows Fair, Ca.	12	118,895 (–12%)	14,709	0 (0%)
Cochise County Fair, Az.	4	7,663 (3%)	1,613	0 (0%)
Cow Capital Turf Club, Mt.	3	6,400 (35%)	2,400	5,300 (28%)
Dayton, Wa.	2	4,190 (2,095)	0	(0%)
Del Mar, Ca.	43	488,820 (3%)	56,656	180,264 (35%)
Eastern Oregon Livestock Show, Or.	3	12,331 (27%)	2,312	0 (0%)
Elko County Fair, Nv.	6	17,334 (12%)	2,889	12,209 (35%)
Emerald Downs, Wa.	90	94,564 (8%)	10,468	56,099 (24%)
Fairplex Park, Ca.	17	251,201 (10%)	26,524	71,713 (29%)
Ferndale, Ca.	10	18,586 (32%)	5,467	8,809 (24%)
Flagstaff, Az.	4	27,575 (32%)	4,796	0 (0%)
Fresno, Ca.	10	57,179 (6%)	9,222	40,017 (7%)
Gila County Fair, Az.	4	9,661 (27%)	1,756	0 (0%)
Golden Gate Fields, Ca.	105	159,284 (–4%)	18,941	81,226 (11%)
Graham County Fair, Az.	4	9,504 (33%)	2,236	0 (0%)
Grants Pass, Or.	19	14,964 (5%)	2,138	3,704 (13%)
Great Falls, Mt.	9	13,450 (–5%)	2,328	5,900 (24%)
Greenlee County Fair, Az.	4	10,830 (6%)	1,805	5,696 (13%)
Kalispell, Mt.	3	9,100 (7%)	1,706	2,700 (10%)
Hollywood Park, Ca.	101	389,161 (–4%)	45,387	184,000 (34%)
Les Bois Park, Id.	46	19,614 (–7%)	3,293	13,259 (41%)
Los Alamitos, Ca.	188	13,149 (23%)	6,421	0 (0%)
Marias Fair, Mt.	2	7,562 (15%)	1,891	2,962 (39%)
Minidoka County Fair, Id.	1	600 (0%)	600	0 (0%)
Mohave County Fair, Az.	4	8,457 (–3%)	1,879	2,384 (14%)
Pleasanton, Ca.	11	143,953 (–9%)	17,401	50,587 (16%)
Portland Meadows, Or.	79	29,628 (–3%)	3,775	12,943 (17%)
Rillito Park, Az.	14	11,021 (4%)	1,882	3,726 (2%)
Sacramento, Ca.	11	97,314 (3%)	12,028	56,345 (11%)
Santa Anita Park, Ca.	110	437,710 (–2%)	50,897	181,183 (38%)
Santa Cruz County Fair, Az.	4	8,450 (12%)	1,988	4,953 (15%)
Santa Rosa, Ca.	12	138,131 (5%)	17,088	55,936 (20%)
Solano County Fair, Ca.	11	122,567 (3%)	14,343	49,158 (11%)
Stockton, Ca.	10	81,023 (–3%)	10,949	0 (0%)
Sun Downs, Wa.	10	8,296 (1%)	1,728	3,125 (8%)
Tillamook County Fair, Or.	3	14,142 (0%)	2,121	3,800 (9%)
Turf Paradise, Az.	158	73,857 (–2%)	8,318	36,522 (25%)
Waitsburg Race Track, Wa.	2	6,503 (1,858)	0	(0%)
Walla Walla, Wa.	3	3,467 (131%)	1,486	0 (0%)
Western Montana Fair, Mt.	6	19,238 (816%)	2,815	4,628 (32%)
Wyoming Downs, Wy.	18	3,740 (–4%)	1,870	4,432 (46%)
Yavapai Downs, Az.	56	30,289 (–4%)	4,791	14,219 (15%)
Yellowstone Downs, Mt.	9	12,200 (0%)	2,678	9,250 (17%)

Canada

Track, State	Racing Days	Average Daily Purse Distribution (Change from Previous Year)	Average Purse	Average Stakes Purses (% Total Purse)
Assiniboia Downs, Mb.	71	$77,141 (6%)	$9,394	$40,839 (23%)
Fort Erie, On.	81	191,755 (–4%)	19,439	98,261 (15%)
Grand Prairie, Ab.	21	11,614 (13%)	3,934	5,209 (36%)
Hastings Race Course, B.C.	71	178,441 (7%)	18,335	67,343 (24%)
Kamloops, B.C.	8	7,871 (–20%)	2,519	8,725 (28%)
Kin Park, B.C.	3	14,381 (32%)	2,876	7,415 (34%)
Lethbridge, Ab.	51	25,737 (5%)	4,898	11,996 (21%)
Marquis Downs, Sk.	29	21,960 (16%)	3,107	8,517 (24%)
Millarville, Ab.	2	10,900 (–7%)	4,360	5,500 (25%)
Northlands Park, Ab.	72	127,476 (8%)	14,662	57,322 (22%)
Stampede Park, Ab.	46	115,716 (3%)	13,208	45,833 (10%)
Woodbine, On.	167	498,136 (–13%)	54,407	198,956 (28%)
Yorkton Exh. Assoc., Sk.	3	4,267 (4%)	1,280	2,000 (16%)

Racing Enters the Racino Era

Racino is a highly descriptive new word, created by combining a racetrack with a casino. The concept also is relatively new, dating from the 1990s. Initially, the racino concept—which essentially puts video lottery terminals or slot machines into racetracks or free-standing facilities at racetracks—rescued three racing operations, Mountaineer Race Track in West Virginia, Prairie Meadows Racetrack in Iowa, and historic Delaware Park. Gaming machines have spread from those three locations to Louisiana, New Mexico, and New York. By the end of 2006, electronic gaming most likely will be in operation in Pennsylvania and Oklahoma, and possibly in Florida. In some cases, the gaming machines have saved racetracks from possible closure. In other jurisdictions, the machines have transformed marginal tracks into highly profitable businesses paying race purses near or above the North American average.

Governmental bodies such as state legislatures have passed electronic-gaming legislation over the opposition of antigambling organizations, and politicians have been willing to risk the wrath of these groups because slots and VLTs represent a tax upon the willing—that is, those individuals who go to the track or some other site to play the slots. Like the state's cut from lotteries, casino taxes tend to be high. Until the 1980s, horse racing represented a tax on the willing horseplayer who went to the track despite takeouts that included a hefty state tax. As horse racing began to be marginalized as a major sport and wagering handle stagnated or declined in the 1980s and '90s, states were forced to cut taxes on horse-racing wagers sharply.

Like most revolutions in the horse-racing industry, the era of racinos began with little notice and far from the recognized centers of the sport. The racino revolution began on June 8, 1990, at Mountaineer in Chester, West Virginia. Mountaineer, which was known as Waterford Park from its founding in 1951 until '87, certainly needed help. It paid very low purses, and its horses occupied racing's bottom rung. The West Virginia lottery, which began operation in 1986, put 160 voucher-spitting video lottery terminals at Mountaineer to help the track and to help itself. A dispute over the machines went to the state Supreme Court, which ruled that the video lottery terminals had to be authorized by the Legislature or shut down. With no interruption in play, the Legislature approved video lottery terminals in 1994, local voters endorsed the machines, and the newly legitimate VLTs began operating on May 10, 1994. Mountaineer changed its name to Mountaineer Race Track and Gaming Resort in 2001.

The state's other Thoroughbred track, Charles Town Races, was purchased in 1996 by Penn National Gaming Inc. after voters in the county in which the track is located approved machine gaming. While successful from the start, Mountaineer and Charles Town received a significant boost when the state Legislature authorized the tracks to install coin-drop video lottery terminals in fall 1999. Like tracks elsewhere, purses have increased tremendously in the years since the machines were installed, but both tracks have experienced declines in later years.

The second significant launch of video lottery terminals occurred on April 1, 1995, when the first slot machines began operation at Prairie Meadows Racetrack in Altoona, Iowa. Prairie Meadows had struggled from its first days in 1989. Even full-card simulcasting could not save the track from a bankruptcy filing in 1991, and the facility closed its doors on September 2, 1991. Because Polk County, which includes the track, had under written the $40-million in bonds to build the track, the county ended up owning the track in 1993, and racing resumed that May. Acting on a positive recommendation of a gambling task force, the Legislature and local voters authorized slot machines at the state's horse and dog tracks in 1994, and the machines began spewing revenues. The total play for 1995 totaled nearly $1-billion.

From the start, however, the county and horsemen were locked in a battle over who should get the lion's share of the slots revenue. The horsemen thought that they should; the county and several prominent citizens argued for minimal contribution to purses and maximum contribution to local government and civic projects. The issue has never been completely resolved, although the balance of power has tilted toward the property owner, Polk County. While Prairie Meadows's purses climbed toward the North American per-race average for several years, a new contract between the county and the track's operator in 2002 resulted in a purse cut beginning in '03. Purses fell further in 2004. This pattern—an initial sharp increase in purses followed by, for a number of reasons, stagnant or declining purses—has been repeated elsewhere.

Delaware Park followed a pattern similar to Prairie Meadows. Built in the later years of the Great Depression by William duPont Jr. and associates, the track near Wilmington opened in June 1937 and for many years was a magnet for racing fans in the Philadelphia area. In the 1970s and '80s, new competitors arose, and the Maryland tracks—which had used Delaware as a summer base—began racing year-round. In 1982, the track closed and was dormant until William Rickman Sr. bought it in late '83. The track reopened in 1984 and survived on creative management and fan loyalty for the next decade. Full-card simulcasting helped, but Delaware Park turned the corner with passage of the Horse Racing Redevelopment Act in June 1994. Delaware Park's slot machines began operation on December 29, 1995. To be sure, the racetrack and its purses received a generous portion of the slots revenue, but most money went to the state. In 2004, the state's share from Delaware Park and two Standardbred tracks was $222-million, or 8% of state revenue.

With the slots money, Delaware Park was able to rebuild its purse structure and its stakes program, and its purses are now well above the North American average. The track also has encountered changes in the purse payouts as events unrelated to the racetrack have affected slots play. For instance, after the state of Delaware banned smoking in public places in late 2002, slots play declined for a while, and as a result purses declined in '03, although they rose again in '04.

In the mid-1990s, New Mexico's racetracks were on the ropes. But the tracks and horsemen lobbied for slots, won approval for them, and entered the racino age in February 1999 at Sunland Park, which is just across the Texas border from El Paso. The state's other tracks followed suit, and all have experienced sizable increases in purses. By the end of 2004, Sunland was paying purses above the North American average. The casino boom proved so alluring that a new track, Zia Park, was built in Hobbs. Its casino began operation in November 2004, and racing at the $54-million facility was scheduled to begin in late '05.

Riverboat gambling began in Louisiana in 1993, video poker machines were added to the gambling mix in '98, and land-based casinos opened in '99. Slot machines arrived at the racetrack on February 13, 2002, in sleepy Vinton, not far from the Texas border at Delta Downs. By the time the first slot machines were played, gambling interests had readily identified the value of such a franchise. Las Vegas speculator Shawn Scott bought the track for $10-million in 1999; Boyd Gaming Corp. bought it for a reported $125-million two years later. Louisiana Gaming Control Board reports make clear why the price went through the roof. By the end of 2002, Delta's slots had generated $60-million in net win—after the 652,038 slots

players had gotten their share—with the state receiving $9.1-million in taxes. Purses and breeders' funds received $10.8-million.

Louisiana Downs, purchased by Harrah's Inc., opened its slots operation on May 21, 2003, and Evangeline Downs, relocated to St. Landry Parish after local voters rejected slots at its former site, began casino operations on December 19, 2003. Fair Grounds most likely will trade its video-poker machines for slots in 2006. Without question, Louisiana's purses have benefited greatly from slots. At Delta, purses increased from an average of $8,783 for its 2001-'02 meet to $19,675 per race for the 2003-'04 season. End-of-year figures indicate how profitable the machines are. In all, 3.2-million slots players went to Louisiana track facilities in 2004, and the net win was $142.9-million. After deductions for purses, breeders' funds, and community grants, the net taxable total was $117.1-million. Louisiana's tax was $21.7-million at 18.5%. The state's governor proposed in 2005 an increase in the tax to more than 30%.

Slot machines also were installed in Ontario's two Thoroughbred tracks, at Fort Erie in 1999 and Woodbine in 2000, with positive results initially. However, reduced play on the machines resulted in lower purses at both tracks in 2004. Canada was not the only location with a mixed picture from the slot machines. Although New York approved video lottery terminals at racetracks in the wake of the September 11, 2001, terrorist attack on the World Trade Center's twin towers, the first slots operation did not open until January 2003 at Saratoga Raceway, a Standardbred track, and Finger Lakes became the first Thoroughbred track in New York with VLTs on February 18, 2004. A proposed VLT operation at Aqueduct, which was expected to do a sizable volume, was repeatedly delayed but finally appeared to be moving forward in 2005.

Video lottery terminals were authorized in both Pennsylvania and Oklahoma in 2004, and those operations are likely to have machines operational no later than '06. In a 2005 referendum, voters in Broward County, Florida, authorized video lottery terminals at Gulfstream Park, but enabling legislation and tax issues were likely to delay the debut of machines at Gulfstream until 2006 at the earliest.—*Don Clippinger*

Racinos and Daily Purses, 1998-2004

Delaware
Delaware Park

Year	Types of Gaming	Racing Days	Avg. Daily Purse Distribution	Avg. Purse Change
2004	Pari-Mutuel, Slot Machines	134	$253,345	(8%)
2003	Pari-Mutuel, Slot Machines	141	233,813	(–20%)
2002	Pari-Mutuel, Slot Machines	141	291,204	(14%)
2001	Pari-Mutuel, Slot Machines	139	255,018	(4%)
2000	Pari-Mutuel, Slot Machines	149	245,466	(5%)
1999	Pari-Mutuel, Slot Machines	143	234,071	(19%)
1998	Pari-Mutuel, Slot Machines	140	195,935	(11%)

Iowa
Prairie Meadows Racetrack

Year	Types of Gaming	Racing Days	Avg. Daily Purse Distribution	Avg. Purse Change
2004	Pari-Mutuel, Slot Machines	96	$135,639	(–4%)
2003	Pari-Mutuel, Slot Machines	100	141,619	(–15%)
2002	Pari-Mutuel, Slot Machines	98	166,172	(4%)
2001	Pari-Mutuel, Slot Machines	97	160,447	(10%)
2000	Pari-Mutuel, Slot Machines	98	146,500	(17%)
1999	Pari-Mutuel, Slot Machines	98	125,414	(11%)
1998	Pari-Mutuel, Slot Machines	97	112,499	(19%)

Louisiana
Delta Downs

Year	Types of Gaming	Racing Days	Avg. Daily Purse Distribution	Avg. Purse Change
2004	Pari-Mutuel, Slot Machines	99	$197,760	(0%)
2003	Pari-Mutuel, Slot Machines	82	196,899	(85%)
2002	Pari-Mutuel, Slot Machines	88	106,421	(115%)
2001	Pari-Mutuel	85	49,404	(–4%)
2000	Pari-Mutuel	52	51,200	(32%)
1999	Pari-Mutuel	50	38,860	(16%)
1998	Pari-Mutuel	50	33,642	(–2%)

Evangeline Downs

Year	Types of Gaming	Racing Days	Avg. Daily Purse Distribution	Avg. Purse Change
2004	Pari-Mutuel, Slot Machines	92	$121,317	(67%)
2003	Pari-Mutuel	87	72,805	(–8%)
2002	Pari-Mutuel	82	79,104	(4%)
2001	Pari-Mutuel	82	75,848	(–4%)
2000	Pari-Mutuel	82	78,779	(–1%)
1999	Pari-Mutuel	82	79,840	(3%)
1998	Pari-Mutuel	82	77,489	(23%)

Fair Grounds

Year	Types of Gaming	Racing Days	Avg. Daily Purse Distribution	Avg. Purse Change
2004	Pari-Mutuel, Video Poker	82	$251,513	(–2%)
2003	Pari-Mutuel, Video Poker	83	256,249	(–4%)
2002	Pari-Mutuel, Video Poker	80	265,740	(–2%)
2001	Pari-Mutuel, Video Poker	89	271,595	(2%)
2000	Pari-Mutuel, Video Poker	90	266,958	(–2%)
1999	Pari-Mutuel, Video Poker	89	273,763	(15%)
1998	Pari-Mutuel, Video Poker	88	238,166	(14%)

Louisiana Downs

Year	Types of Gaming	Racing Days	Avg. Daily Purse Distribution	Avg. Purse Change
2004	Pari-Mutuel, Slot Machines	102	$183,924	(2%)
2003	Pari-Mutuel, Slot Machines	80	180,934	(14%)
2002	Pari-Mutuel	80	158,176	(27%)
2001	Pari-Mutuel	89	124,801	(–15%)
2000	Pari-Mutuel	83	146,226	(2%)
1999	Pari-Mutuel	82	143,137	(5%)
1998	Pari-Mutuel	86	136,463	(–3%)

New Mexico
Ruidoso Downs

Year	Types of Gaming	Racing Days	Avg. Daily Purse Distribution	Avg. Purse Change
2004	Pari-Mutuel, Slot Machines	57	$45,582	(–16%)
2003	Pari-Mutuel, Slot Machines	57	54,420	(25%)
2002	Pari-Mutuel, Slot Machines	57	43,458	(4%)
2001	Pari-Mutuel, Slot Machines	57	41,615	(7%)
2000	Pari-Mutuel, Slot Machines	57	38,890	(34%)
1999	Pari-Mutuel, Slot Machines	57	28,995	(27%)
1998	Pari-Mutuel	46	22,861	(41%)

Sunland Park

Year	Types of Gaming	Racing Days	Avg. Daily Purse Distribution	Avg. Purse Change
2004	Pari-Mutuel, Slot Machines	92	$155,473	(–5%)
2003	Pari-Mutuel, Slot Machines	75	162,876	(59%)
2002	Pari-Mutuel, Slot Machines	78	102,135	(31%)
2001	Pari-Mutuel, Slot Machines	79	78,144	(28%)
2000	Pari-Mutuel, Slot Machines	86	60,852	(116%)
1999	Pari-Mutuel, Slot Machines	87	28,211	(37%)
1998	Pari-Mutuel	59	20,556	(16%)

SunRay Park

Year	Types of Gaming	Racing Days	Avg. Daily Purse Distribution	Avg. Purse Change
2004	Pari-Mutuel, Slot Machines	44	$52,611	(–28%)
2003	Pari-Mutuel, Slot Machines	40	73,074	(–5%)
2002	Pari-Mutuel, Slot Machines	35	76,840	(65%)
2001	Pari-Mutuel, Slot Machines	46	46,621	(14%)
2000	Pari-Mutuel, Slot Machines	41	$41,063	(26%)
1999	Pari-Mutuel, Slot Machines	28	32,509	

The Downs at Albuquerque

Year	Types of Gaming	Racing Days	Avg. Daily Purse Distribution	Avg. Purse Change
2004	Pari-Mutuel, Slot Machines	69	$48,663	(–12%)
2003	Pari-Mutuel, Slot Machines	67	55,118	(–8%)
2002	Pari-Mutuel, Slot Machines	64	59,890	(13%)
2001	Pari-Mutuel, Slot Machines	63	52,892	(17%)
2000	Pari-Mutuel, Slot Machines	69	45,256	(30%)
1999	Pari-Mutuel	54	34,893	(–21%)
1998	Pari-Mutuel	52	44,115	(–9%)

New York
Finger Lakes

Year	Types of Gaming	Racing Days	Avg. Daily Purse Distribution	Avg. Purse Change
2004	Pari-Mutuel, Slot Machines	157	$105,755	(40%)
2003	Pari-Mutuel	154	75,282	(–4%)
2002	Pari-Mutuel	161	78,223	(0%)
2001	Pari-Mutuel	165	78,302	(–3%)
2000	Pari-Mutuel	167	80,655	(1%)
1999	Pari-Mutuel	176	80,048	(1%)
1998	Pari-Mutuel	170	79,128	(21%)

Ontario
Fort Erie

Year	Types of Gaming	Racing Days	Avg. Daily Purse Distribution	Avg. Purse Change
2004	Pari-Mutuel, Slot Machines	81	$191,755	(–4%)
2003	Pari-Mutuel, Slot Machines	114	200,504	(1%)
2002	Pari-Mutuel, Slot Machines	116	197,936	(16%)
2001	Pari-Mutuel, Slot Machines	116	170,310	(52%)
2000	Pari-Mutuel, Slot Machines	107	111,681	(32%)
1999	Pari-Mutuel, Slot Machines	107	84,554	(44%)
1998	Pari-Mutuel	75	58,823	(–8%)

Woodbine

Year	Types of Gaming	Racing Days	Avg. Daily Purse Distribution	Avg. Purse Change
2004	Pari-Mutuel, Slot Machines	167	$498,136	(–13%)
2003	Pari-Mutuel, Slot Machines	162	571,514	(2%)
2002	Pari-Mutuel, Slot Machines	166	558,598	(13%)
2001	Pari-Mutuel, Slot Machines	165	494,595	(2%)
2000	Pari-Mutuel, Slot Machines	160	483,979	(53%)
1999	Pari-Mutuel	165	316,586	(27%)
1998	Pari-Mutuel	171	249,594	(17%)

West Virginia
Charles Town Races

Year	Types of Gaming	Racing Days	Avg. Daily Purse Distribution	Avg. Purse Change
2004	Pari-Mutuel, Video Lottery	231	$224,692	(52%)
2003	Pari-Mutuel, Video Lottery	235	148,243	(13%)
2002	Pari-Mutuel, Video Lottery	254	131,273	(–8%)
2001	Pari-Mutuel, Video Lottery	233	142,154	(48%)
2000	Pari-Mutuel, Video Lottery	208	96,022	(25%)
1999	Pari-Mutuel, Video Lottery	213	76,933	(81%)
1998	Pari-Mutuel, Video Lottery	206	42,563	(23%)

Mountaineer Race Track

Year	Types of Gaming	Racing Days	Avg. Daily Purse Distribution	Avg. Purse Change
2004	Pari-Mutuel, Video Lottery	219	$171,818	(–2%)
2003	Pari-Mutuel, Video Lottery	222	175,244	(5%)
2002	Pari-Mutuel, Video Lottery	230	166,383	(14%)
2001	Pari-Mutuel, Video Lottery	228	145,463	(30%)
2000	Pari-Mutuel, Video Lottery	221	111,797	(32%)
1999	Pari-Mutuel, Video Lottery	211	84,760	(28%)
1998	Pari-Mutuel, Video Lottery	212	66,381	(43%)

YEAR IN REVIEW

2004 in Review: *Smarty's Smashing Party*

Triple Crown Bid by Rags-to-Riches
Colt Grabs Country's Attention and Affection

Bursting from the hills of Arkansas and the suburbs of Philadelphia, Smarty Jones stormed beyond the confines of Thoroughbred racing and into the hearts of people around the world. Upon his back he carried the dreams of everyday men and women who saw their own struggles in life mirrored in his 15.3-hand chestnut frame. Not only had he recovered from fractured bones in his skull after a starting gate mishap as a juvenile, but his modest pedigree and stature also clearly did not define the depth of his heart.

Racing for a trainer who five years earlier had sought divine guidance before continuing in an often-unrewarding profession, a jockey who had battled alcoholism, and owners who had nearly quit the game after the tragic murder of a previous trainer, Smarty Jones and his saga fired the public imagination in a way unseen for decades.

The Kentucky Derby (G1) and Preakness Stakes (G1) winner brought a record 120,139 fans to Belmont Park with him as he bid for Triple Crown glory in the Belmont Stakes (G1), and many of those in the crowd wept unabashedly when he lost by a length to Birdstone after running hard the entire 1½ miles.

And then—long before his fans were ready to surrender him from the racetrack, where trainer John Servis believed he could prove himself to be as indelible in racing lore as 1980 Horse of the Year Spectacular Bid—he was gone, retired to stud at Three Chimneys Farm in Midway, Kentucky, in a deal worth $39-million, the fifth largest in history.

More than a million Thoroughbred foals have been born in North America since Affirmed became the last horse to win the Triple Crown in 1978, but none grew larger in the public's consciousness than Smarty Jones, said Bill Nader, senior vice president of the New York Racing Association.

In the span of his five-week Triple Crown onslaught, Smarty Jones rose from being viewed as a somewhat fluky winner of the Derby on a sloppy track to an overpowering Preakness conquistador to a horse seemingly destined to do what none had been able to accomplish in 26 years. He was seen everywhere in that period of time, from the cover of *Sports Illustrated*—the first time a horse gained that prominent position in 21 years—to the cover of *ESPN The Magazine*, and he was a top name for invitations to settings as unlikely as the set of "The Tonight Show" in Burbank, California.

"It really was the *Rocky* story. It was really a story of overachievement," Nader said, referring to the 1976 Academy Award best picture about a fictional boxer from Philadelphia, the area where Smarty Jones was based. "I don't know that any horse since Spectacular Bid [in 1979] brought to Belmont the same hope. People felt as strongly about, or even more strongly about, the chances of Smarty Jones to win the Triple Crown. They came to see a coronation."

And they also watched on television. The Belmont generated ratings that topped all broadcasts during the week ended on June 6 and was among the highest for all sports events in 2004.

Some felt moved enough that they wanted to see him with their own eyes, up close, even when he was not racing. Thousands packed Philadelphia Park for some of his workouts, and a very tough sports town embraced him. Servis found himself answering a constantly ringing telephone, with calls of support and admiration. Box loads of fan mail barraged him daily from around the United States and as far away as Australia and Japan. But just at the dramatic peak of his box-office power, Smarty Jones's turn in racing's spotlight ended. Chronic bruising of the cannon bones in all four of his fetlock joints led owners and breeders Pat and Roy Chapman to announce in early August they were retiring him to Three Chimneys.

Although a backlash arose among some disappointed racing fans and journalists who had hoped he would race at four, as the Chapmans had indicated earlier, the popularity of Smarty Jones did not vanish when he left Philadelphia and arrived in the rolling Bluegrass of Kentucky. Three Chimneys President Dan Rosenberg said about 50 fans a day, not including professional horsemen, still come to see Smarty Jones. Smarty Jones, who stands for an advertised stud fee of $100,000, was to be bred to a book of 111 mares in 2005. Both fans and horsemen appreciated the quality in Smarty Jones that Servis describes as gritty determination, even though the trainer noted wryly that the same quality sometimes proved a difficult obstacle to overcome in training because "he was just so tough; when he would get his mind made up, it was tough to persuade him to go in another direction."

His stubborn determination also may have been his undoing in the Belmont when he refused to settle early for jockey Stewart Elliott. It was his only loss in nine career starts; with the $5-million bonus for winning the Arkansas Derby and Rebel Stakes at Oaklawn Park and the Kentucky Derby, Smarty Jones retired with career earnings of $7,613,155.

"For racing, I think he was the best thing that happened in a long time," said Servis. "I still have people come up to me every week that had never been to a horse race who fell in love with Smarty Jones and now go to the races and watch horse racing because of him."—*Michele MacDonald*

Each year, THOROUGHBRED TIMES editors and staff writers collectively determine the year's top news stories. The interest in racing generated by Smarty Jones was voted the year's leading story. Following are other top news events of 2004.

2. NTRA in transition. From its founding in the second half of the 1990s, the National Thoroughbred Racing Association has continued to make headlines, as it should in its role as a coalition of horse racing interests charged with increasing the popularity of racing and improving economic conditions for industry participants.

The NTRA maintained a relative status quo for the first half of 2004, embarking on the same advertising, television, group purchasing, and other programs it has pursued in previous years. In July, however, the NTRA faced a monumental change. Commissioner Tim Smith, the man who guided the NTRA since its debut in 1998, announced he would leave the organization on September 1 to pursue positions as president and chief executive officer with the New York Racing Association.

Smith's departure apparently had been in the works for several months, dating to earlier in the year, when tensions mounted between the NTRA and the Thoroughbred Owners and Breeders Association over the proposed Thoroughbred Championship Tour. A lightning rod for some within the industry, the Tour has failed to get off the ground despite strong support from several organizations. The NTRA board named the executive recruiting firm Russell Reynolds Associates, the same firm used when Smith was hired as commissioner, to find a new leader. Breeders' Cup Ltd. President D. G. Van Clief Jr., who had served as NTRA vice chairman since the two organizations merged in 2000, was given a vote of confidence by the board and named commissioner in April 2005.

3. Jockeys battle for more insurance, right to wear ads. Jockeys were involved in showdowns both on and off the racetrack, but the biggest battleground seemed to be at Churchill Downs. The first battle came in the form of a lawsuit against the Kentucky Horse Racing Authority by five jockeys who sought to overturn the authority's rule that prohibits jockeys wearing certain forms of advertising. The jockeys, describing themselves as independent contractors, received permission to wear the ads during the Kentucky Derby (G1) and supporting program when United States District Court Judge John Heyburn II granted a preliminary injunction on April 29 to Jerry Bailey, Shane Sellers, Jose Santos, John Velazquez, and Alex Solis. All riders on the Derby and Kentucky Oaks (G1) cards were allowed to wear ads that did not conflict with sponsors for the Churchill spring meeting.

At the start of Churchill's fall meeting, a group of riders refused to accept mounts for the November 10 program, citing concerns over what they characterized as inadequate insurance coverage, and track management banned them for the remainder of the meet. The actions and subsequent ban of the 14 riders, which included Robby Albarado and Rafael Bejarano, served as a catalyst for an industrywide assessment of the issue of jockey insurance and who should pay for it.

4. Continued controversy at NYRA. The focal point of an investigation by the state attorney general and federal prosecutors in 2003, the New York Racing Association took its share of lumps again in '04 while it gained a new leader. NYRA operated the year under the watchful eye of the federal-appointed monitor Getnick & Getnick, a Manhattan-based firm that focuses on antifraud litigation. NYRA had agreed to the monitor as part of its deferred prosecution settlement with federal prosecutors that included the promise to pay a $3-million fine and adopt anticorruption reforms.

The presence of Getnick & Getnick was felt primarily at Saratoga Race Course, where NYRA adhered to new security protocols, which prohibited many fans from some of the access they previously had received, including admission to the track's stable areas for morning workouts and for races in the afternoon. Signs posted around the track urged patrons to call a toll-free number to report all suspicions of fraud or misconduct.

Tim Smith, who was negotiating to accept the top NYRA executive positions, was a shadow to NYRA Chairman Barry Schwartz for most of the Saratoga meeting. By the time racing was in full swing at Belmont Park, Smith was no longer a candidate for the executive positions and Schwartz had announced his intentions to step down as NYRA's chairman and chief executive officer on December 31. Longtime publishing executive and former NYRA trustee Charles Hayward was named president and chief executive officer on November 4. NYRA's franchise to operate Aqueduct, Belmont, and Saratoga expires in 2007, and serious doubt remained over whether it will be renewed in its current form. Magna Entertainment Corp. has expressed an interest in operating the tracks, and Smith is leading an effort to possibly privatize NYRA.

5. Strength of bloodstock markets. The country's major bloodstock markets fared extremely well in 2003, but those results paled in comparison to the robust spending that set records in auction rings from New York to California in 2004. The spree started at the select two-year-olds in training sales in South Florida, with the Ocala Breeders' Sales Co. and Fasig-Tipton Co. setting records for its auctions at Calder Race Course. Serious fireworks went off at the Fasig-Tipton Calder sale, where a record $41.58-million changed hands for 142 juveniles. Fusao Sekiguchi spent a world record for a juvenile, $4.5-million for a colt by Fusaichi Pegasus.

The auction season continued with sharp increases at the Fasig-Tipton Kentucky July selected yearling sale and marginal declines at the Fasig-Tipton Saratoga selected yearling sale. They set the stage for the 14-day Keeneland September yearling sale, which posted total sales of $324,904,300, the most for any Thoroughbred sale on the planet. That figure was helped by the sale of a Storm Cat colt for a sale-record $8-million. Young and successful broodmares were in demand at Kentucky's fall mixed sales, and the dam of Smarty Jones sold for $5-million to highlight the Fasig-Tipton Kentucky selected November sale. Keeneland's November breeding stock sale posted near-record returns as 2,873 horses sold for $279,680,200 and a record average of $97,348.

6. Slaughter issue reaches new level of national interest. The battle to end the slaughter of horses in the United States for human consumption picked up steam in March 2004 when legislation to end the practice was introduced in Congress. Later in the year, it continued when high-profile trainer Nick Zito spoke out against slaughter on the "CBS Evening News with Dan Rather." In 2004, several people played a role in saving some Thoroughbreds that were bred or raced by some notable connections.

Zito, who serves as national spokesman for the National Horse Protection Coalition, explained the issue during a press conference that included several antislaughter groups the day before the Breeders' Cup World Thoroughbred Championships at Lone Star Park on October 30. "If I could take a message to America today, it would be to simply think about the word 'slaughter' for just a minute," Zito said. "How does that word make you feel? Have you ever heard the

word slaughter used in a positive way? Of course not. People need to take that to heart. Slaughter is wrong. Period."

7. Expanded gaming legislation passes in key states. Pennsylvania and Florida took important steps in 2004 toward placing slot machines at racetracks. Pennsylvania became the 18th state to legalize slot machine gambling on July 5, when Governor Ed Rendell signed a law at Philadelphia Park to allow 61,000 slot machines in the state at 14 sites, including seven racetracks.

The legalization in Pennsylvania put surrounding states immediately on alert. Philadelphia Park said its overnight purses could more than triple to an estimated $500,000 per day by 2006, on par with the nation's major racing centers in New York, California, and Kentucky.

In the November 2 election, Florida voters approved by nearly 100,000 votes a statewide amendment that authorized Broward and Miami-Dade counties to hold referendums as soon as spring 2005 to allow seven pari-mutuel facilities in the two counties to operate slots. In 2005 referenda, Broward approved the machines, Dade did not, and the Florida Legislature failed to act on enabling legislation.

8. Churchill Downs Inc. buys Fair Grounds. The on-again, off-again sale of Fair Grounds reached a conclusion that many within the industry thought would be realized years ago when Churchill Downs Inc. purchased the historic New Orleans racetrack in a deal worth $47-million. Churchill had long sought winter racing dates to fill out its Churchill Downs Simulcast Network and agreed to pay $25-million in cash to horsemen as part of a settlement between them and Fair Grounds over underpaid purses from video poker revenue. Fair Grounds, which was forced to file for Chapter 11 bankruptcy protection in August 2001, and Louisiana horsemen had settled a $90-million judgment against the track and averted the possible auction of the facility in bankruptcy court. The announcement of Churchill's purchase came less than two weeks after Fair Grounds had signed a deal with Thoroughbred owner and fast-food entrepreneur Mike Pegram to take control of the track under an amended reorganization plan. Pegram's deal was worth $25-million. A federal bankruptcy court approved the sale to Churchill in late September, and Fair Grounds opened its 2004-'05 meeting on Thanksgiving under the new owner's banner.

9. Training marks for Asmussen, Baird. The wins keep piling up for Steve Asmussen and Dale Baird. Asmussen toppled the 28-year-old record for victories in a single season when Coronado Rose won the Delta Belle Stakes on November 20 at Delta Downs. The victory was the

497th of the season for Asmussen, who broke Racing Hall of Fame trainer Jack Van Berg's mark of 496 set in 1976. Asmussen, 39, ended his history-making season with 555 victories. Although approximately half of his wins were in claiming races, Asmussen also notched victories at the highest level, including the Ballerina Handicap (G1) with Lady Tak, the Coolmore Lexington Stakes (G2) with Quintons Gold Rush, and the Amsterdam Stakes (G2) with Bwana Charlie.

Already Thoroughbred racing's all-time leading trainer by victories, Baird added to his résumé on November 5 when he saddled his 9,000th career winner. The victory came at Mountaineer Race Track, where the 69-year-old Baird has won every training title for 20 consecutive years.

10. Industry loses Young and Sangster. The Thoroughbred industry lost two significant members with the deaths of William T. Young and Robert Sangster. Young, master of Overbrook Farm in Lexington, left a huge legacy as horseman, entrepreneur, and philanthropist when he died of a heart attack at age 85 on January

12. Founder of Overbrook in 1972, Young was a gentleman to the core, and he was rarely seen at a private or public function without a jacket, necktie, and shined shoes. He celebrated victories in nearly every major race in the United States, including a cherished victory in the 1996 Kentucky Derby (G1) with Grindstone, and he enjoyed helping others equally if not more. Young was the benefactor to many causes, including his beloved University of Kentucky.

Sangster, who died at age 67 on April 7 after a lengthy battle with pancreatic cancer, was a revolutionary in racing and breeding. John Gaines, a visionary himself and one of Sangster's peers, said during a memorial service that "the record will forever show that Robert Edmund Sangster was the most influential horseman of his generation." Sangster, who personified the explosion of the breeding and sales market in the 1980s, campaigned more than 800 stakes winners, including more than 100 Group/Grade 1 winners. He was also a partner in the purchase of Seattle Dancer as a yearling in 1985 for a world-record $13.1-million.—*Tom Law*

Leaders of 2004

Category	Leader	Leading Statistic
Owner by Wins	Michael Gill	487
Owner by Earnings	Michael Gill	$10,835,561
Owner by Graded Stakes Winners	Edmund Gann	7
Owner by Grade 1 Wins	Gary Tanaka	6
Breeder by Wins	John Franks	529
Breeder by Earnings	Adena Springs	$14,122,256
Breeder by Graded Stakes Winners	Juddmonte Farms	7
Breeder by Grade 1 Wins	Juddmonte Farms	6
Trainer by Wins	Steve Asmussen	555
Trainer by Earnings	Todd Pletcher	$17,511,923
Trainer by Graded Stakes Wins	Bobby Frankel	44
Trainer by Grade 1 Wins	Bobby Frankel	13
Jockey by Wins	Rafael Bejarano	455
Jockey by Earnings	John Velazquez	$22,248,661
Jockey by Graded Stakes Wins	John Velazquez	40
Jockey by Grade 1 Wins	Edgar Prado	11
Horse by Wins	Tender Offer (Ire)	11
Horse by Earnings	Smarty Jones	$7,563,535
Horse by Graded Stakes Wins	Kitten's Joy	6
Horse by Grade 1 Wins	(tie) Ashado, Azeri, Pico Central (Brz), Sightseek	3
Oldest Graded Stakes Winner	Glick	8
Oldest Stakes Winner	Major Zee	11
Sire by Wins	Roar	237
Sire by Earnings	Elusive Quality	$10,865,792
Sire by Number of Winners	Royal Academy	148
Sire by Stakes Wins	(tie) A.P. Indy, Storm Cat, El Prado (Ire)	28
Sire by Graded Stakes Wins	Storm Cat	15
Broodmare by Earnings	I'll Get Along	$7,563,535
Top Yearling Price	c., Storm Cat—Welcome Surprise	$8,000,000
Top Two-Year-Old Price	Fusaichi Samurai	$4,500,000
Top Weanling Price	c., Dance in the Dark—Air Groove	$4,537,037
Top Broodmare Price	I'll Get Along	$5,000,000
Top Stallion Syndication	Smarty Jones	$39,000,000
Highest Stud Fee	Storm Cat	$500,000

Chronology of 2004 and 2005

January 2—Legendary veterinarian Alex Harthill announces his retirement from racetrack practice after 50 years of treating many of the world's top horses.

January 6—Kentucky Governor Ernie Fletcher abolishes the Kentucky Racing Commission and creates the 16-member Kentucky Horse Racing Authority to regulate the state's horse industry.

January 12—Eclipse Award-winning breeder W. T. Young, owner of Overbrook Farm and owner-breeder of leading sire Storm Cat and 1996 Kentucky Derby (G1) winner Grindstone, dies in Florida at age 85.

January 13—*Seabiscuit* becomes the best-selling drama on DVD, with retail sales of $125-million.

January 14—Bernie Hettel resigns as executive director of the newly disbanded Kentucky Racing Commission and as chief state steward.

January 15—Racing Hall of Fame jockey Russell Baze wins his ninth consecutive Isaac Murphy Award, given to the jockey with the year's highest winning percentage.

January 16—Keeneland's horses of all ages sale ends with hefty across-the-board increases over 2003, including a 49% rise in average.

January 19—A feature on the 2002 Ultra Pick Six scandal is televised nationally on the Court TV series "Masterminds."

January 22—Robby Albarado is announced as the 55th recipient of the George Woolf Memorial Jockey Award. Jockey C. C. Lopez scores his 3,000th victory, aboard Sunnyridge Sam at Aqueduct.

January 23—Keeneland announces that, for the second year, it will not conduct a 2004 July yearling sale. Jockey Josiah Hampshire Jr. scores his 3,000th victory, aboard Bluebird's Song at Laurel. Jockey Patrick Valenzuela is suspended indefinitely by Santa Anita stewards after failing to report for a mandatory drug test.

January 24—Florida-breds dominate Sunshine Millions program for the second straight year, winning six of the eight races against California-breds. Florida-bred Southern Image captures the $1-million Barretts/CTBA Sunshine Millions Classic Stakes.

January 26—Mineshaft is named 2003 Horse of the Year at the Eclipse Awards ceremony held in Florida. Experimental Free Handicap is released, with Action This Day, Cuvee, and Ruler's Court sharing top weight among males at 126 pounds; Halfbridled tops fillies at 124 pounds.

January 27—The movie *Seabiscuit* receives seven Academy Award nominations, including one for Best Picture, but wins none.

January 28—Saratoga Gaming and Raceway, a Standardbred track, opens as New York state's first racetrack VLT casino, handles $2.5-million on slots.

January 31—Magna Entertainment launches its new national pick five wager—the Magna 5—with guaranteed minimum pool of $500,000.

February 3—A son of Wild Rush brings $1.6-million at the Ocala Breeders' Sales Co. selected two-year-olds in training sale, setting a record for a juvenile sold by OBSC.

February 7—Jockey Corey Lanerie scores career victory 2,000 aboard Slow Walkin' John at Fair Grounds.

February 8—Jockey Perry Ouzts collects career victory 4,500 aboard Private Ambition at Turfway Park.

February 9—Jockey Michael Rowland dies from head injuries sustained in a February 4 racing accident

at Turfway Park, becoming the first North American jockey casualty in more than two years. Racing Hall of Fame rider Julie Krone is named by *USA Today* as one of America's ten toughest athletes.

February 18—Amazing Philly, who was born unexpectedly in a stall at Philadelphia Park in 2000 and whose sire is unknown, finishes third at the Philadelphia track in her career debut. Finger Lakes racetrack opens New York's first Thoroughbred racino.

February 22—Jockey Ronald Ardoin, one of 17 North American riders with 5,000 or more wins (5,226), retires from race riding.

February 24—A son of Fusaichi Pegasus sells for $4.5-million at Fasig-Tipton Calder, a world record for a two-year-old sold at public auction.

February 28—Racing Hall of Fame member Richard Mandella becomes the seventh trainer to saddle winners of more than $100-million, when Emeritus finishes fifth in a maiden race at Santa Anita Park.

March 2—A daughter of Awesome Again brings $2-million at Barretts Equine Ltd. March sale, setting a world auction record for a juvenile filly in training.

March 3—Santa Anita Park establishes a North American record for a pick six pool, at $7.3-million.

March 12—Jockey Rafael Bejarano sets a Turfway Park record by winning seven races on the 12-race card.

March 13—Jockey Edgar Prado becomes the 18th rider in North America to reach 5,000 wins, aboard Wynn Dot Comma in the Swale Stakes (G3).

March 17—Ocala Breeders' Sales Co.'s March select two-year-olds in training auction establishes sale records in gross, average, and median prices.

March 18—Jockey Zoe Cadman, Arlington Park's all-time leading female rider and the first of her sex to win a Chicago riding title, at Hawthorne Park in 2001, retires after winning 311 of 2,868 races.

March 27—Pleasantly Perfect and Medaglia d'Oro run first and second, respectively, in the $6-million Dubai World Cup (UAE-G1), duplicating their 2003 Breeders' Cup Classic (G1) finish.

March 28—Jockey Shane Sellers scores his 4,000th career victory, aboard Destiny Calls in the Red Camelia Handicap at Fair Grounds. A Louisiana district court judge rules that Fair Grounds owes horsemen $89.9-million from video poker proceeds earmarked for purses since 1994.

April 2—Santa Anita Park stewards extend jockey Pat Valenzuela's January 23 suspension through the end of 2004, but the California Horse Racing Board stays the suspension until the rider's appeal is heard, allowing him to resume riding on April 25.

April 3—In her seasonal debut, 2002 Horse of the Year Azeri wins her third straight Apple Blossom Handicap (G1) at Oaklawn Park.

April 7—Internationally renowned owner-breeder Robert Sangster dies in England at age 67.

April 15—Prospectors Delite, the dam of five stakes winners, including 2003 Horse of the Year Mineshaft, is named '03 Kentucky Broodmare of the Year. Trainer Jerry Hollendorfer becomes the sixth trainer to saddle 4,000 winners, with Gonetorule, at Bay Meadows Race Course.

April 16—Three jockeys file suit against the Kentucky Horse Racing Authority in U. S. District Court in Louisville, asking that Kentucky jockeys be allowed to wear the Jockeys' Guild patch during races.

April 17—Brazilian jockey Jorge Ricardo records his 8,700th career victory, at Gavea racecourse in Brazil.

April 19—Churchill Downs Inc. CEO Tom Meeker opens the NASDAQ stock market in New York to celebrate the 130th running of the Kentucky Derby.

April 21—Churchill Downs officials state that if jockeys wear advertising images that conflict with on-site sponsors during the Kentucky Derby (G1) program on May 1, they will be banned from riding on that day.

April 23—Jockey Ken Shino boots home his 2,000th career winner when he guides Els Editor to victory at Prairie Meadows Racetrack. Five high-profile jockeys file a lawsuit in United States District Court in Louisville, contending a state law banning jockeys from wearing certain forms of advertising violates their constitutional rights of free speech.

April 28—Churchill Downs oddsmaker Mike Battaglia makes The Cliff's Edge the 4-to-1 morning-line favorite for the Kentucky Derby.

April 29—A federal judge rules that five jockeys who sued the Kentucky Horse Racing Authority may wear advertising in the Kentucky Derby (G1). The authority suspends its rule barring commercial logos and allows all Kentucky jockeys to wear ads.

May 1—Favored Smarty Jones becomes the first undefeated Kentucky Derby (G1) winner since Seattle Slew in 1977. North American records are set for total betting on an individual event and for single-day handle, as $99.3-million is wagered on the Derby and $142.8-million on the 12-race Churchill Downs card. Derby television ratings jump 7.8% over 2003 and are the highest since 1992.

May 2—Green Mountain Park racetrack in Vermont is listed for sale for $2.5-million on eBay.

May 4—Jockey Jose Santos and Sackatoga Stable, connections of 2003 Kentucky Derby (G1) winner Funny Cide, file a $48-million libel suit against the Miami *Herald* and Knight-Ridder Inc.; the newspaper had published a controversial photo on May 10, 2003, and reported that Santos held a "cue ring" in his right hand near the finish of the Derby.

May 6—Jockey Kerwin Clark scores his 2,000th career victory, aboard Golden Rail at Evangeline Downs.

May 8—Approximately 5,000 fans turn out for the morning workouts at Philadelphia Park to see Smarty Jones in his first public appearance since winning the Kentucky Derby (G1).

May 10—Smarty Jones becomes the first Kentucky Derby (G1) winner in 21 years to be featured on the cover of *Sports Illustrated* magazine, and the first representative of horse racing since Julie Krone in 1989. Oaklawn Park President Charles Cella presents a $5-million bonus check to the owners of Smarty Jones, for sweeping the Rebel Stakes, Arkansas Derby (G2), and Kentucky Derby.

May 14—California Governor Arnold Schwarzenegger signs a bill increasing takeout on exotic wagers to help cover cost of workers' compensation policies held by state horse trainers.

May 15—Smarty Jones wins the Preakness Stakes (G1) by a record 11½ lengths to remain undefeated in eight starts. Pennsylvania Governor Edward Rendell proclaims "Smarty Jones Day" in the commonwealth that day. Pimlico Race Course reports all-time records for attendance and handle. Overnight Preakness television ratings are highest since 1990.

May 22—American-bred Bachelor Duke wins his maiden victory in the $494,120 Irish Two Thousand Guineas (Ire-G1) at the Curragh. Undefeated Attraction becomes the first winner of both the Irish (Ire-G1) and English (Eng-G1) One Thousand Guineas.

May 24—*Daily Racing Form* is sold to The Wicks Group of Companies for a reported $60-million.

May 26—Trainer Jerry Hollendorfer saddles five winners at Bay Meadows Race Course, equaling a Northern California single-card record for the third time in his career. Trainer Todd Pletcher sends out his 1,000th career winner with Kon Tiki, at Belmont Park.

May 28—Jockey Ricky Faul scores career victory 3,000 aboard Princeton Star at Evangeline Downs.

June 1—A Los Angeles judge denies jockey Pat Valenzuela's request that his suspension be delayed, so he can ride Rock Hard Ten in the Belmont.

June 4—Dual classic winner Smarty Jones becomes the first horse-racing subject to make the cover of *ESPN The Magazine* in the publication's six-year history.

June 5—Smarty Jones fails in his Triple Crown bid, finishing second by a length to Birdstone in the Belmont Stakes (G1). NYRA attendance and handle records are shattered. NBC's Belmont coverage produces highest overnight ratings for the race since 1981. Former United States President and lifetime racing enthusiast Ronald Reagan passes away at age 93.

June 11—Jockey David Clark scores his 2,500th career victory, on Devils Right Hand, at Woodbine.

June 13—Jockey Francine Villeneuve becomes the first female recipient of the Avelino Gomez Memorial Jockey Award, which honors top Canadian riders.

June 21—California Governor Arnold Schwarzenegger signs deals with five Native American tribes giving them the right to operate unlimited number of slot machines—while repeating his opposition to an initiative allowing state racetracks to operate slots.

June 24—Jockey Patricia Cooksey retires after a 25-year career, second behind Julie Krone on the all-time list for North American female jockeys, with 2,137 victories.

June 25—Dual 2004 classic winner Smarty Jones will stand at Three Chimneys Farm in Midway, Kentucky, at the conclusion of his racing career. Owner-breeder B. Wayne Hughes privately purchases historic Spendthrift Farm in Lexington.

June 30—The 60-share syndication of Smarty Jones for an approximate $39-million valuation is nearly completed. Owners-breeders Roy and Patricia Chapman retain half the shares.

July 2—Hollywood Park stewards suspend jockey Pat Valenzuela indefinitely for failing to provide hair samples for drug testing.

July 5—Pennsylvania Governor Ed Rendell signs laws allowing 61,000 slot machines in the state, at sites that include seven racetracks.

July 7—Well-known Southern California trainer Dan Hendricks is paralyzed in a motorcycle accident.

July 8—Top Argentine three-year-old Forty Mirage is kidnapped from his stall at Tandil Racecourse and held for $100,000 ransom. He is found unharmed the following day at a nearby shooting range.

July 13—Claiborne Farm announces that three-time leading North American sire Danzig has been pensioned from stud duty due to declining fertility.

July 15—Stewart Elliott, regular rider for dual classic winner Smarty Jones, is honored as the 2004 ESPY Award-winning jockey.

July 21—Jockey Ray Sibille announces his retirement from the saddle after 35 years and 4,264 victories.

July 27—Tim Smith resigns as commissioner and chief executive officer of the National Thoroughbred Racing Association, effective September 1. He subsequently breaks off negotiations to manage the New York Racing Association and forms Jockey Club-supported Friends of New York Racing for a possible bid for New York racing franchise in 2007. Citgo Petroleum Corp. signs a five-year agreement with the NTRA to be its official league sponsor. A record 4,891 yearlings are cataloged for Keeneland's September sale.

July 29—Jockey John Velazquez posts his 3,000th career victory, aboard Runingforpresident, at Saratoga.

August 2—Dual classic winner Smarty Jones is retired to Three Chimney Farms due to chronic bruising of the distal ends of his cannon bones.

August 6—Del Mar stewards uphold jockey Pat Valenzuela's suspension through 2004 on possible drug violations. Jockey Jerry Bailey becomes Saratoga's all-time leading rider, with 641 wins. Fair Grounds agrees to pay horsemen $25-million to settle a lawsuit over revenue-sharing of video poker proceeds for purses.

August 9—Jockeys Kent Desormeaux and Jimmy Winkfield, trainer Claude R. "Shug" McGaughey III, and Skip Away, Flawlessly, and Bowl of Flowers are inducted into the Racing Hall of Fame.

August 10—Miswaki, sire of 98 stakes winners, is pensioned from stud duty at Walmac International. Trainer Gary Danelson records his 1,000th career win, at Assiniboia Downs.

August 14—Ten-thousand Philadelphia Park fans say good-bye to Smarty Jones in his final public appearance. Kicken Kris wins the Arlington Million (G1) after the disqualification of Powerscourt (GB).

August 16—Fair Grounds agrees to partnership arrangement with Mike Pegram to forestall scheduled auction of the track.

August 17—Trainer Dick Clark saddles his 1,000th career winner, at Prairie Meadows Racetrack.

August 28—Birdstone wins the Travers Stakes (G1) in his first start since denying Smarty Jones's Triple Crown bid in the Belmont Stakes (G1).

August 29—Jockey Larry Reynolds records his 3,000th career victory, on Secret Missile, at Timonium racetrack. Owner-breeder Eugene Melnyk pledges $1-million toward construction of a child-care center for backstretch workers at Saratoga Race Course.

September 1—English champion jockey Kieren Fallon is one of 16 people arrested by British police as part of an investigation into race fixing. Fallon denies the charge. In a reversal of its previous deal with Mike Pegram, Fair Grounds agrees to be acquired by Churchill Downs Inc. for $47-million. A federal bankruptcy court subsequently approves the deal for the New Orleans track and its ten off-track betting sites.

September 2—Officials of the Oak Tree Racing Association say they plan to test for alkalizing agents, commonly known as bicarbonate milkshaking, at its upcoming meet. Magna's Santa Anita Park meet subsequently adopts similar standards, and the California Horse Racing Board publishes proposed rules barring the practice.

September 4—Zippy Chippy, America's most famous maiden, loses his 99th consecutive race, at Northampton Fair.

September 9—Smarty Jones's 2005 stud fee is announced at $100,000.

September 10—Two-time leading North American sire Deputy Minister dies at age 25. Zippy Chippy extends his winless streak to 100 with a last-place finish at Northampton Fair.

September 14—A son of Storm Cat and Welcome Surprise sets a Keeneland September sale record when he sells for $8-million.

September 21—After eight sessions, Keeneland's September yearling sale surpasses its previous record for total sales, with $297-million.

September 22—Breeders' Cup Ltd. announces that it has sold all 51,034 seats for the Breeders' Cup at Lone Star Park on October 30.

September 24—The NTRA board appoints D. G. Van Clief Jr. as commissioner, succeeding Tim Smith.

September 29—Jockey Jose Amy is cleared to ride in New York, 24 years after being stripped of his license for holding back horses in a high-profile bribery case.

October 1—Florida's Division of Administrative Hearings upholds Division of Pari-Mutuel Wagering's bid to revoke Hialeah racetrack's operating permit and to deny the track 2005 race dates.

October 4—NYRA and ABC sign a contract for the television network to begin broadcasting the Belmont Stakes (G1) in 2006, thus breaking up the unified television contract under Triple Crown Productions. NYRA broke away because of high ratings for the third Triple Crown race and Churchill Downs's refusal to cede a portion of its 50% share of revenues.

October 6—A five-track California coalition drops its political efforts to place slot machines in racetracks and card clubs.

October 8—New York Racing Association Chairman and Chief Executive Officer Barry Schwartz announces his resignation from those positions, effective December 31. Grandstand of defunct Ak-Sar-Ben racetrack in Nebraska is demolished, to make way for residential and retail development.

October 9—Racing Hall of Fame jockey Chris McCarron resigns as general manager of Santa Anita Park.

October 13—Jockey Carlos Marquez Jr. registers his 2,000th career victory, aboard Fiery Diablo, at Hawthorne Race Course.

October 15—Churchill Downs Inc. completes its $47-million purchase of Fair Grounds in New Orleans.

October 16—Brazilian-based Jorge Ricardo, the world's leading active jockey, scores career victory 8,834, passing Bill Shoemaker for second behind Laffit Pincay Jr. among all-time winning riders.

October 17—Jockey Jose Amy, 50, finishes eighth in a Belmont Park maiden race while competing for the first time since losing his license in 1980 for holding back horses.

October 19—Hall of Fame jockey Gary Stevens says he will not ride in the Breeders' Cup at Lone Star Park because Texas lacks adequate workers' compensation insurance for injured jockeys.

October 22—Breeders' Cup and NTRA announce an increase in medical insurance coverage for jockeys at Lone Star Park, from $100,000 to $500,000, for three racing dates ending October 30.

October 30—Lone Star Park hosts the 21st Breeders' Cup championship day. Ghostzapper wins the $4-million Classic in track- and race-record time. NBC Sports registers the lowest overnight ratings ever for its Breeders' Cup telecast.

November 1—Sunshine Forever, 1988 champion turf male, is pensioned at 19 at Hurstland Farm in Kentucky, as part of the Old Friends retirement program.

November 2—Oklahoma voters approve a bill that would allow electronic gaming machines at three state racetracks. California voters soundly defeat an initiative that could have led to installation of slot machines at five state racetracks.

November 4—NYRA announces that former *Daily Racing Form* chief executive Charles Hayward will be its new president and CEO.

November 5—All-time winningest trainer Dale Baird saddles his 9,000th career winner, at Mountaineer Racetrack in West Virginia.

November 7—Churchill Downs jockeys attempt to organize boycott due to lack of adequate medical insurance; eight riders, including Shane Sellers, are evicted from the grounds. Riders subsequently force cancellation of a racing program at Hoosier Park, co-owned by Churchill Downs Inc. I'll Get Along, dam of Smarty Jones, brings $5-million at Fasig-Tipton Kentucky's November mixed sale.

November 17—Breeders' Cup Filly and Mare Turf (G1) winner Ouija Board (GB), who scored an Epsom Oaks (Eng-G1) and Irish Oaks (Ire-G1) double in 2004, is named European Horse of the Year.

November 18—Racing Hall of Fame jockey Russell Baze scores victory number 8,772, moving into third on the all-time North American wins list, behind Laffit Pincay Jr. and Bill Shoemaker.

November 19—Keeneland's 12-day November breeding stock sale ends with a record average of $97,348 and near-record total receipts of $280-million.

November 20—Trainer Steve Asmussen saddles his 497th winner of 2004, breaking Jack Van Berg's 28-year record for single-season victories.

November 22—Newly formed Jockeys' Medical Insurance Working Panel, comprising 31 industry representatives, meets at Turfway Park and endorses concept to increase insurance for riders beyond current $100,000 per incident.

December 3—Jockey Dean Sarvis registers his 1,000th career victory, at Turfway Park.

December 6—Zippy Chippy, America's most celebrated maiden with 100 consecutive defeats, is retired from racing at age 13.

December 9—Jockey Robby Albarado scores career victory number 3,000, at Fair Grounds. Lonny Powell resigns as president of the Association of Racing Commissioners International to become vice president of public affairs for Youbet.com Inc.

December 11—World-record-priced $4.5-million two-year-old Fusaichi Samurai wins his career debut at Hollywood Park.

December 14—Jockey Shane Sellers, winner of 4,070 races, announces his retirement due to lack of adequate insurance coverage for injured riders.

December 15—Agents from the New York State Attorney General's Office and state police raid Aqueduct, Belmont Park, and Saratoga Race Course, with target reported to be weights carried by jockeys in races. Smarty Jones is named one of Beliefnet.com's ten nominees as most inspiring "person" of the year, along with Nancy Reagan and former NFL player Pat Tillman, who was killed in Afghanistan. (Tillman won.)

December 17—Soaring Free is honored as Canada's Horse of the Year and champion turf male at the Sovereign Awards banquet in Toronto. Jockeys' Guild extends by five years the management contract of Matrix Capital Associates, headed by L. Wayne Gertmenian, Ph.D., the Guild's controversial president.

December 23—Champion Azeri, North America's all-time leading money-winning female with $4,079,820, is retired.

December 29—A record 2,073 horses are catalogued for the Keeneland January horses of all ages sale.

December 31—Jockey John Velasquez finishes the year as North America's leading rider by earnings, with purses of $22.2-million, ending Jerry Bailey's three-year reign. Todd Pletcher tops all trainers with $17.5-million.

2005

January 2—Apprentice jockey Jordan Charkoudian scores her first career victory, aboard Sadies Lad, at Tampa Bay Downs.

January 3—Gulfstream Park announces that it will test horses for milkshaking. Mr. Light (Arg) establishes a world-record mile of 1:31.41 in a race on Gulfstream's rebuilt turf course.

January 4—Churchill Downs announces it has doubled the guaranteed purse for the 2005 Kentucky Derby (G1) to $2-million.

January 7—The California Horse Racing Board accepts a judge's recommendation that clears the way for jockey Pat Valenzuela to resume his riding career after a series of drug problems.

January 9—Santa Anita Park becomes the first Southern California track in a decade to cancel racing due to heavy rain.

January 12—Coolmore Stud's auction of stallion seasons raises $3.5-million for Red Cross tsunami relief in Southeast Asia.

January 13—Jockey Rene Douglas boots home his 3,000th career winner, aboard Grey Misty, at Santa Anita Park. New York trainer Greg Martin is indicted in federal court on charges of wire fraud, conspiracy, and horse doping to fix the outcome of a race on December 18 at Aqueduct.

January 15—Keeneland announces that for the third consecutive year it will not hold a July selected yearling sale.

January 17—Owner Ken Ramsey, a 2004 Eclipse Award finalist, receives a $25,000 fine and seven-day suspension from the Kentucky Horse Racing Authority for offering money to an owner to scratch a horse out of a December 31 race at Turfway Park.

January 19—Former jockey Chris McCarron announces that he will leave his executive position with Magna Entertainment Corp. to open a jockey school.

January 20— Seven United States racing commissions approve the Racing Medication and Testing Consortium's model rules on medications. Jockey Ramon Dominguez is honored with the 2004 Isaac Murphy Award for the jockey with the highest winning percentage, supplanting nine-time winner Russell Baze.

January 21—Jockey Jorge Chavez scores his 4,000th career victory, aboard A Rizzi Rueben at Gulfstream.

January 22—Racing Hall of Fame rider Russell Baze passes Bill Shoemaker and moves into second place on the North American all-time wins list with a victory aboard Hollow Memories at Golden Gate Fields.

January 23—Laurel Park reopens after a ten-month closing for rebuilding of its dirt and turf courses. The main track was widened from 75 to 95 feet.

January 24—Ghostzapper outpolls Smarty Jones to claim 2004 Horse of the Year honors at the Eclipse Awards ceremony in Los Angeles. Declan's Moon and Wilko top the 2004 Experimental Free Handicap at 126 pounds; Sweet Catomine tops all fillies at 124.

January 30—Jockey Gary Boulanger, winner of 3,104 races, is critically injured in a spill during the running of the Mac Diarmida Handicap (G3) at Gulfstream Park. Gulfstream subsequently increases its catastrophic coverage to $500,000 per incident from $100,000.

February 1—Jockeys' Guild conditionally agrees to allow the California Horse Racing Board to inspect how it has spent the about $1-million it receives annually for health insurance claims of jockeys in the state. Approximately 30 jockeys in Northern California form new group and seek to represent California jockeys.

February 2—Maryland racing leaders release a plan under which Laurel Park would become the state's preeminent track and Pimlico Race Course would operate a six-week meet that includes the Preakness Stakes (G1).

February 4—Racing Services Inc. founder Susan Bala is convicted of operating an illegal gambling operation in North Dakota. She appeals. Jockey Richard Migliore scores his 4,000th career win, aboard Benjamin Baby at Aqueduct.

February 10—Champions Declan's Moon and Sweet Catomine open as future-book favorites for the Kentucky Derby (G1) and Oaks (G1).

February 11—Industry innovator John R. Gaines, whose ideas included the Breeders' Cup and Kentucky Horse Park, dies at age 76.

February 16—NYRA begins pre- and post-race testing for "milkshakes," an alkalizing agent given to a horse by nasogastric tube before it competes. Jockey Calvin Borel records his 4,000th career victory, aboard Jet Angel at Oaklawn Park.

February 17—Irish trainer Dermot Weld scores his 3,000th career victory, with King Jock at Nad al Sheba racecourse in Dubai.

February 20—Retired jockey Ray Sibille is named 2005 recipient of the George Woolf Memorial Award.

February 21—Maryland-based trainer Howard Wolfendale saddles career win number 1,000, with Warison at Laurel Park. Jockey Jose Amy, who had been suspended in 1980 for holding back horses, rides his first winner in nearly 25 years, at Aqueduct.

February 25—Jockey Leslie Mawing scores his 1,000th career victory, aboard Wata Sunrise at Turf Paradise.

March 1—A colt by Tale of the Cat sets a world record for a juvenile sold at auction when he brings $5.2-million at the Fasig-Tipton Calder selected two-year-olds in training sale.

March 2—MI Developments Inc., parent company of Magna Entertainment Corp., reports an $8.5-million loss for 2004. Fasig-Tipton's Calder selected sale ends after breaking all-time records for a juvenile auction in both total sales and average price.

March 9—Two-time Horse of the Year John Henry celebrates his 30th birthday at the Kentucky Horse Park, with 200 fans, including retired jockey Chris McCarron, in attendance.

March 11—Undefeated juvenile champion and early Kentucky Derby favorite Declan's Moon is indefinitely sidelined with a knee injury. Jockey Tyler Baze posts his 1,000th career victory, aboard Mashiko at Santa Anita.

March 15—Churchill Downs quarantines two barns at its Trackside Louisville training center after a horse is diagnosed with the highly contagious bacterial respiratory disease known as strangles.

March 20—Jockey Joe Martinez scores his 2,000th career victory, aboard Roll On Retsina at Sunland Park.

March 24—Seven horses test positive for strangles at Palm Meadows Training Center in Florida.

March 26—American-based Roses in May captures the $6-million Dubai World Cup (UAE-G1).

March 29—Jockey Glen Murphy scores career win number 2,000, aboard Red Lifesaver, at Sunland Park.

April 3—Silent Witness notches his 16th consecutive victory, at Sha Tin in Hong Kong, equaling the 20th-century North American record of Citation and Cigar.

April 7—Jockey Jon Court wins his 3,000th lifetime victory, with Brite Lorelei, at Santa Anita Park.

April 9—Champion filly Sweet Catomine finishes a well-beaten fifth as the even-money favorite in the Santa Anita Derby (G1). Bellamy Road wins the Wood Memorial Stakes (G1) by 17½ lengths, equaling Aqueduct's record of 1:47 for 1⅛ miles. Procreate sets a five-furlong world record of :53.79 in winning the Yankee Affair Stakes at Gulfstream Park.

April 19—D. G. Van Clief Jr. is named NTRA commissioner and chief executive officer through 2007.

April 23—Hollywood Park stewards drop a complaint filed by the California Horse Racing Board against Sweet Catomine co-owner Martin Wygod following her poor Santa Anita Derby performance. Three days earlier, the 2004 champion juvenile filly had been retired without explanation and booked to A.P. Indy.

April 24—Hong Kong sensation Silent Witness scores his 17th consecutive victory, surpassing 20th-century North American and European marks of 16 straight set by Citation, *Ribot, and Cigar. Brazilian-based jockey Jorge Ricardo joins Laffit Pincay Jr. as the only riders to reach the 9,000-win milestone.

April 27—Dear Birdie, dam of champion Bird Town and classic winner Birdstone, is selected as 2004 Broodmare of the Year.

May 2—Visa International announces it will not renew its ten-year sponsorship of the Triple Crown series and will instead sponsor only the Kentucky Derby beginning in 2006.

May 5—Racing Hall of Fame rider Ted Atkinson dies at age 88. The United States House of Representatives passes a resolution to honor Jimmy Winkfield, one of the last great African-American jockeys. Jockey Martin Ramirez notches his 1,000th career win, at Woodbine.

May 6—Churchill Downs sets a Kentucky Oaks (G1) day attendance record of 111,243. Jockey Steve Bahen scores career victory 1,000, at Woodbine.

May 7—Maiden winner Giacomo scores a 50.30-to-1 Kentucky Derby upset. The Derby becomes North America's first race to surpass $100-million in wagers. Total on- and off-track wagering on the 12-race Derby day program establishes an American record of $155,133,631.

May 10—Florida-based Farnsworth Farms, Eclipse Award-winning breeder of 1996, announces it will cease operations in 2005.

May 14—Silent Witness's historic 17-race win streak ends in the Champions Mile at Sha Tin racecourse in Hong Kong.

May 18—Tests confirm that several horses stabled at Churchill Downs are suffering from equine herpesvirus; three barns are quarantined.

May 21—Favored Afleet Alex wins the Preakness Stakes (G1) after recovering from a dramatic near spill entering the stretch.

June 11—Afleet Alex wins the Belmont Stakes (G1) by seven lengths.

June 13—Reigning Horse of the Year Ghostzapper is retired due to a chipped sesamoid.

2004-2005 Obituaries

Billy Adams, 57, longtime Fairmount Park trainer who saddled more than 250 winners in a 35-year career, including 2004 Seattle Slew Handicap winner Living a Dream; of a heart attack, at Fairmount in Collinsville, Illinois.

Frank "Dooley" Adams, 77, Racing Hall of Fame steeplechase rider, winner of seven national steeplechase titles, rode champions Elkridge, Neji, Oedipus, and Ancestor; on November 12, 2004, in Southern Pines, North Carolina.

Mike Allen, 60, noted jazz musician who played at many major Central Kentucky horse parties and events; on January 10, 2005, in Lexington.

Dilip Amarsingh, 31, exercise rider and occasional jockey, rode 25 career winners from 388 starts; stabbed to death near the Belmont Park track kitchen, on September 14, 2004.

Leland Anderson, 78, former Nebraska-based trainer, father of trainer Doug Anderson; after a lengthy battle with emphysema, on January 23, 2004.

Sir Tristan Antico, 81, prominent Australian owner and breeder, former proprietor of Baramul Stud, bred Group-winning fillies Verdi and Shannara; on December 27, 2004, in Sydney, Australia.

Bernard T. Applegarth, 95, longtime Midwest-based owner-breeder, member of the Nebraska Thoroughbred Association; on April 29, 2005, in Alliance, Nebraska.

John Appleton, 55, son of Arthur I. Appleton, owner of Bridlewood Farm in Florida; in a skydiving accident, on May 1, 2005, in Texas.

V. "Nod" Argante, 91, Northern California-based owner, breeder, and trainer since 1941; on July 13, 2004, in California.

Ted Atkinson, 88, Racing Hall of Fame jockey and leading American rider of 1944 and '46, whose 3,795 career winners included champions Tom Fool, Nashua, Devil Diver, Gallorette, and Capot; at his home, on May 5, 2005, in Beaver Dam, Virginia.

Chuck Badone, 67, veteran handicapper, writer for *Daily Racing Form*, author, and Lone Star Park's first morning-line oddsmaker; of esophageal cancer, on April 29, 2004, in Phoenix.

Bud Baedeker, 90, longtime Southern California-based handicapper, father of Hollywood Park President Rick Baedeker; on February 28, 2004.

Ivor Balding, 96, long-time farm manager and trainer for leading breeder C.V. Whitney, who urged Whitney to import *Mahmoud, retired seven-goal professional polo player, uncle of top English trainers Ian and Toby Balding; on January 21, 2005, in Camden, South Carolina.

Thomasine Bandle, 73, a trainer for more than a half-century, who was denied a Kentucky trainer's license at age 20 but a year later became one of Ellis Park's first female trainers; in April 2004, from a blood clot in the lungs, in Shawneetown, Illinois.

Edward J. Barrier, 82, retired Illinois steward and racing secretary, owner, and trainer; of an apparent heart attack, on November 1, 2004, in Belleville, Illinois.

Tony Basile, 82, trainer, saddled major stakes winners Coraggioso, It's Freezing, and T. V. Commercial, who finished third in the 1968 Kentucky Derby; twice leading trainer at Keeneland; on January 22, 2004, in Hallandale, Florida.

Art Baumohl, 78, noted bloodstock agent and handicapper, co-breeder of 15 stakes winners, uncle of Hopewell Farm owner Rick Trontz, adviser to prominent breeder Nelson Bunker Hunt; of congestive heart failure, on January 12, 2005, in Lexington.

Ian Baxter, 58, Australian Thoroughbred industry executive, past chairman and director of the Brisbane Turf Club, and a founding director of the QBBS Thoroughbred sales company in Queensland; on February 5, 2005, in Australia.

William "Red" Beaton, 72, former New England-based trainer and paddock judge; of cancer, in October 2004 in Ocala.

Dick Becker, 82, former vice president of Thoroughbred Racing Associations, executive director and general manager of Ak-Sar-Ben Racetrack; on January 7, 2004, in Omaha.

Willie Belmonte, 38, trainer of nearly 700 winners, jockey who rode Zippy Chippy in his 100th consecutive defeat, son of former leading rider Eddie Belmonte; of cancer, on December 29, 2004, in Charles Town, West Virginia.

Piers Bengough, 75, Queen Elizabeth II's longtime representative at Ascot, former amateur rider, owner, Jockey Club steward, and racetrack executive; on April 18, 2005, in England.

George Berry, 73, longtime administrator for American Totalisator Co., predecessor to AmTote International Inc.; of heart failure related to cancer, on June 18, 2004, in Westminster, Maryland.

James H. Binger, 88, noted owner, breeder, and philanthropist; co-bred classic winners Unbridled and Codex and 1978 sprint champion Dr. Patches in the name of Tartan Farms; of colon cancer, on November 3, 2004, in Minneapolis.

Sylvia Bishop, 84, the first black female licensed as a Thoroughbred trainer in the United States; on December 27, 2004, in Ranson, West Virginia.

Tony Blickenstaff, 33, exercise rider and former jockey at Mid-Atlantic racetracks; on February 17, 2005, at his home in Funkstown, Maryland.

Hannah Blumenthal, 52, pony rider at Belmont Park; of injuries sustained in a riding accident, on January 7, 2004, in Mineola, New York.

James Bohanon, 59, longtime Thoroughbred owner and breeder, who was a partner for several years in Claim to Fame Stables; on May 11, 2005, in Louisville.

David Bourke, 74, well-known Australian racing executive for more than 50 years, former chairman of the Victoria Racing Club; in May 2005, in Melbourne, Australia.

Merle Hunter Boyce, 78, owner, breeder, and member of the California Thoroughbred Breeders Association whose stakes-winning Confederate Yankee competed in the 1974 Kentucky Derby (G1); in January 2005, in California.

Larry Boyle, 68, former Midwest-based trainer of multiple stakes winner Tondi, jockey's agent; on October 13, 2003, in Council Bluffs, Iowa.

Bill Braucher, 77, sports writer and columnist for the Miami *Herald* until his retirement in 1992, a strong proponent of Florida racing, of lung cancer, on March 26, 2004, in Florida.

Bruce Brinkley, 67, presiding steward at Sunland Park, former Thoroughbred and Quarter Horse jockey based in the Southwest; on April 4, 2005, in El Paso, Texas.

Dana Broccoli, 82, owner, author, film executive, widow of James Bond movie producer Albert Broccoli, with whom she campaigned 1993 Breeders' Cup Juvenile (G1) winner Brocco; on February 29, 2004.

Colin Browell, 33, among the leading jockeys in Victoria during the late 1980s and '90s; of leukemia, on February 22, 2005, in Bendigo, Australia.

John T. Bryans, Ph.D., 80, renowned equine researcher, who helped develop vaccines for equine viral abortion, equine viral arteritis, and strangles, member of the University of Kentucky's Equine Research Hall of Fame; of cancer, on October 2, 2004, in Lexington.

George Bucknam Jr., 82, owner, breeder, and chief sound engineer at Del Mar from 1968 to 1992; on May 25, 2004, in California.

Doug Cameron, 87, owner, who raced Canadian champions Rainbow Connection and New Connection during the 1980s; on February 1, 2004, in Toronto.

Al Carpenito, 60, owner, whose wife Noreen campaigned graded stakes winners Devil's Honor and In Contention; on February 11, 2004, in Holmdel, New Jersey.

Snowden Carter, 83, longtime Maryland horse owner, award-winning journalist, former editor of *The Maryland Horse*, general manager of the Maryland Horse Breeders Association; of heart failure, on February 3, 2005, in Owings Mills, Maryland.

Joe Catanese, 72, East Coast-based trainer for more than 40 years; after a long illness, on January 8, 2004.

Andrew Robert Buxton Cavendish, 84, the 11th Duke of Devonshire, who campaigned England's 1969 Horse of the Year Park Top and 1997 Group 1 winner Compton Place; on May 3, 2004, in Derbyshire, England.

Dan Chandler, 70, son of two-time Kentucky Governor A. B. "Happy" Chandler, newspaper executive for whom graded stakes winner Danthebluegrassman was named; of apparent heart failure, on April 27, 2004, in Versailles, Kentucky.

Richard "Tote" Cherry-Downes, 62, British bloodstock agent, a leading buyer at North American auctions during the 1980s who in 1987 purchased the Keeneland September sale's first $1-million yearling; after a long illness, on April 30, 2005.

Richard Chew, 72, former California trainer who saddled stakes winners Lulutorch and Westward Sal in a five-decade career, father of trainer Matt Chew; of cancer, on October 29, 2004, in Bonsall, California.

Gerald Chige, 87, owner-breeder who campaigned for 20 years on the East Coast under the name Chige Stable and raced stakes winner Wild Moment; of a brain tumor, on February 3, 2005, in Dunedin, Florida.

Peter Chiodo, 59, Canadian-based owner who campaigned 1996 Sovereign Award-winning three-year-old filly Silent Fleet; on May 8, 2005, in Toronto.

Al Christensen, 67, a Midwest-based trainer since 1978, whose top runner was multiple 2004 stakes winner Grayglen; of a heart attack, in his shedrow at Fonner Park in Grand Island, Nebraska.

Bennie Ciboron, 80, former Michigan-based trainer whose 313 career winners included Satan's Hills, winner of the $100,000 Hazel Park Handicap in 1977; of cancer, on December 7, 2004, in Maybee, Michigan.

Ruth Claflin, 65, longtime Texas-based horsewoman, who with her husband owned and operated Golden Owl Farm and Training Center, trainer of more than 200 winners, including multiple stakes winner Hattab Voladora; in a traffic accident, on June 17, 2004, in Texas.

Sir Rupert Clark, 85, chairman of Australia's Victoria Amateur Turf Club between 1972 and '88, chairman of the trustees of Caulfield Racecourse Reserve; after a long illness, on February 4, 2005, in Melbourne.

Sandra D. Clark, 64, owner of Glen Echo Farm near Cynthiana, Kentucky, former bloodstock agent, breeder of 11 stakes winners; of pancreatic and liver cancer, on April 20, 2004, in Kentucky.

Thomas Bartlett Clark, 61, author of a collection of inspirational racing stories entitled "Down on the Backside," volunteer with the Arizona chapter of the Race Track Chaplaincy of America; of cancer, on March 6, 2004.

William G. Clark Sr., 80, co-breeder of 1972 champion sprinter Chou Croute, former owner of Highlands Farm in Midway, Kentucky, member of the Keeneland Association and the Thoroughbred Club of America; after a lengthy illness, on August 30, 2004, in Lexington.

Sir Stanley Clarke, 71, racetrack executive in Great Britain, member of the English Jockey Club, and prominent owner of steeplechasers, who campaigned 1997 Grand National winner Lord Gyllene; after a long illness, on September 19, 2004, in Staffordshire, England.

Joss Collins, 56, internationally known bloodstock agent who in 1985 signed the world-record $13.1-million ticket for the yearling Seattle Dancer, and also involved in purchases of Nureyev and Caerleon; of liver cancer, on February 8, 2004, in England.

Daniel S. Combs II, 44, former manager of the Kentucky Training Center, son of former Spendthrift Farm President Brownell Combs II, grandson of the late Spendthrift owner Leslie Combs II; of an apparent heart ailment, on February 27, 2004, in Fort Myers, Florida.

Robert Congleton, 80, construction entrepreneur, co-owner of 1984 Broodmare of the Year Hasty Queen II, former owner of Oakland Farm in Versailles, Kentucky; of heart failure, on March 29, 2005, in Kentucky.

Juan Carlos Contreras, 79, trainer, former top Argentine jockey who guided two-time Horse of the Year *Yatasto to victory in that country's 1951 Quadruple Crown; on March 13, 2004.

John E. "Jack" Cooper, 93, racing secretary, handicapper, and longtime executive secretary of the National Steeplechase Association, winner of the 1974 F. Ambrose Clark Award for distinguished service to American steeplechasing; of pneumonia, on September 9, 2004, in Litchfield, Connecticut.

Paul Cooper, 92, former trainer who developed Canadian champion Almoner; of a stroke, on April 4, 2004, in Toronto.

William J. Cortesi, 85, a Thoroughbred owner since 1957, who bred and raced Illinois Horse of the Year Magic Doe; of cancer, on October 25, 2004, in Illinois.

Perry Cotton, 90, breeder, trainer, and longtime member of the California Thoroughbred Breeders Association who trained such homebred stakes winners as Cotton Bloomers and Liz Tasto; in June 2004, in California.

Nelson Crews, 46, a Mid-Atlantic-based trainer of 33 winners, including 1998 St. Brendan Stakes winner Kool Krafty; of injuries sustained in a propane explosion at his home, on January 6, 2005, in Elk Township, Pennsylvania.

Joey Cuffari, 71, former jockey, who rode on the East Coast during the 1950s and 1960s; of heart complications, on November 7, 2004, in California.

Ash Daley, a leading New Zealand-based owner, whose runners included 1996 AJC Oaks (NZ-G1) winner Savana City; after a lengthy illness, in November, 2004, Matamata, New Zealand.

Roger Danjean, 60, former jockey who rode more than 700 winners, including Timely Writer in his 1981 Hopeful Stakes (G1) win; in a car accident, on January 23, 2005, in Hollywood, Florida.

Michael Dargan, 86, past chairman of Goffs Bloodstock Sales and Aer Lingus airline and a former senior steward of the Irish Turf Club; on January 11, 2005, at his home in Dublin, Ireland.

Bruce Davis, 72, longtime jockey's agent whose clients had included Patricia Cooksey and Sam Siciliano; on April 2, 2004.

Austin Delahoussaye, 82, father of Racing Hall of Fame jockey Eddie Delahoussaye, longtime Louisiana-based owner, on September 6, 2004, in Louisiana.

Alphonse DeRossi, 84, lifelong Thoroughbred racing fan and owner of the popular Saratoga Springs restaurant DeRossi's; on February 2, 2005, in New York.

Ed Devine, 78, veterinarian whose patients included five-time Horse of the Year Kelso and 1980 Horse of the Year Spectacular Bid; on December 14, 2004, in New Jersey.

Celestino DiLibero, 76, former owner and breeder, who stood Lawmaker at his Florida farm; in 1986 the stallion broke a 70-year-old record by siring 30 two-year-old winners; in September 2004 in Ocala.

Bernard "Buddy D" Diliberto, 73, longtime New Orleans sports commentator and racing fan, father of Fair Grounds oddsmaker and director of broadcast media Mike Diliberto; of an apparent heart attack, on January 7, 2005, at his home in Metairie, Louisiana.

Peter DiPasquale, 83, longtime Canadian-based owner and trainer, among the leading trainers at Woodbine in the mid-1970s, father of trainer Sam DiPasquale; on May 31, 2004, in Canada.

Charles F. "Chuck" Di Rocco, 69, founder and publisher of *Gaming Today* magazine, credited with conceiving and promoting the idea of simulcasting horse race cards in Las Vegas during the early 1970s; on March 6, 2004, in Las Vegas.

Vonda Pate Dixon, 81, longtime member of the Oklahoma Thoroughbred Association; on December 16, 2004, in Guymon, Oklahoma.

Victor Doleski, 82, longtime Kentucky-based trainer, whose best runner was three-time Ben Ali H. (G3) winner Knight Counter; on January 19, 2005, in Louisville.

Charlie Dougherty, 85, former Northern California-based steward, owner, and breeder; of congestive heart failure, on March 25, 2005, in Burlingame, California.

Thomas "Wally" Dunn, 92, noted West Coast trainer and member of the British Columbia Hall of Fame, saddled 1954 and '64 Hollywood Gold Cup winners Correspondent and *Colorado King, and 1964 Kentucky Oaks winner Blue Norther; in April 2004 in Arcadia, California.

Joseph Durso, 80, longtime New York *Times* sports writer, whose beat included Thoroughbred racing and Major League Baseball; of cancer, on December 31, 2004, in Stony Brook, New York.

Dale Duspiva, 53, racetrack publicist at Bay Meadows Race Course and Golden Gate Fields, former longtime chart caller for *Daily Racing Form*; from a brain tumor, on June 16, 2004, in San Bruno, California.

Noel Eales, 73, a noted trainer in New Zealand for nearly 50 years, saddled 1,348 winners and ranks fifth on that country's all-time list, conditioned 1994 New Zealand Horse of the Year The Phantom; after a long illness, on June 8, 2004, in New Zealand.

Robert Edens, 81, former jockey and assistant trainer to his wife, Mary, helped in developing 1978 champion juvenile filly Candy Eclair; on January 3, 1004, in Aiken, South Carolina.

Meggs Elkington, 77, former jockey who later trained Australian classic winners Begonia Belle, Venus And Mars, and several other Group 1 winners, father of trainer Bruce Elkington; on February 2, 2005, in Australia.

Christopher Elser, 20, son of Kirkwood Stables owner Kip Elser, frequently attended Thoroughbred auctions around the country and worked on stable crew at Fasig-Tipton Saratoga yearling sales; of stab wounds sustained in a mugging, on April 18, 2004, in Baltimore.

Andy Engel, 79, longtime trainer based in the Midwest; after a lengthy illness, on March 8, 2004, in Silver Creek, Nebraska.

Fritz Engel, 71, well-known Nebraska auctioneer, involved in the state's Thoroughbred industry since 1969, a past director of the Nebraska HBPA; on March 22, 2004, in Clarks, Nebraska.

Morley Engelson, 69, co-owner of multiple Grade 1 winner Marquetry; in a double homicide, on June 13, 2004, in Los Angeles.

George Evans Jr., 86, former member of the Kentucky Racing Commission; after a long illness, on May 9, 2005, in Lexington.

Mike Ewing, 58, former Midwest-based jockey for more than 20 years, rode more than 1,000 winners, regular rider of 1983 Ohio Horse of the Year Rollin On Over; after a short illness, on January 18, 2004, in Daytona Beach, Florida.

Sally Fanning, California-based owner and breeder, wife of California trainer Jerry Fanning; on July 10, 2004, in California.

Daniel "Skeeter" Figgins, 58, former broodmare manager at Sagamore Farm for Alfred G. Vanderbilt, and later at Stoneworth Farm; on August 7, 2005, in Maryland.

Jimmy FitzGerald, 69, a steeplechase trainer in England for more than 30 years, who influenced the early career of six-time English champion flat jockey Kieren Fallon; following a long illness, on October 6, 2004, in England.

Robert Fitzgerald Jr., 78, a former jockey who trained on the East Coast for more than four decades; on July 12, 2004, in Lancaster, Pennsylvania.

James W. Fitzsimmons, 85, grandson of Racing Hall of Fame trainer James "Sunny Jim" Fitzsimmons, former assistant general manager of Saratoga Raceway harness track; in September, at his home near Lake Desolation, New York.

Thomas "Peaches" Fleming, 94, trainer for more than 60 years, former jockey and owner; on February 19, 2005, in Texas.

Peter Fortay, 56, well-known Mid-Atlantic owner and trainer, saddled 110 winners between 1993 and 2002, including 1997 Sorority Stakes (G3) winner Unky and Ally; of a kidney ailment; on June 4, 2004.

Ciro Frare, 67, a top breeder in Brazil, a former Jockey Club de Parana director, and past member of the Brazilian Breeders and Owners Association; shot to death by a former employee, on June 27, 2004, in Parana, Brazil.

Carol Pyle Jones Fry, 93, award-winning artist, mother of Russell and Richard Jones, operators of Walnut Green Bloodstock; from injuries suffered in a car accident, on July 25, 2004, near West Marlborough Township, Pennsylvania.

Frank Gabriel Sr., former owner, trainer, jockey's agent, and racing secretary, father of Arlington Park executive Frank Gabriel Jr.; following a long illness, on March 1, 2005, in Florida.

Robert Gaffglione, 68, former jockey who rode for more than 40 years, leading rider at Calder Race Course in 1971, rode Rexson's Hope to a tenth-place finish in the 1984 Kentucky Derby (G1); of complications from Parkinson's disease, on December 5, 2004, in Fort Lauderdale, Florida.

John R. Gaines, 76, a Thoroughbred industry pioneer who conceived the idea of the Breeders' Cup, established Gainesway farm, was a leading force in creating the Kentucky Horse Park and a supporter of the National Thoroughbred Association, winner of an Eclipse Award of Merit; of diabetes, on February 11, 2005, in Lexington.

Raymond Gambone, 56, co-founder of Our Farm Inc., a boarding, training, and stallion facility near Norristown, Pennsylvania, raced stakes winners Iknowasecret and Dear Jane; of cancer, on February 13, 2004, in Philadelphia.

Richard L. Gelb, 79, owner-breeder, member of the Jockey Club, trustee emeritus of the New York Racing Association, and longtime chief executive of Bristol-Myers Squibb; of cancer, on April 4, 2005, in New York City.

Pat Glennon, 76, retired jockey, who rode *Sea-Bird to victory in the 1965 Prix de l'Arc de Triomphe and Epsom Derby, and twice won the Melbourne Cup in Australia; on February 14, 2004, in Australia.

Kevin Goemmer, 48, former track announcer at River Downs, Arlington Park, Sportsman's Park, and Hawthorne Park; of an apparent heart attack, in Independence, Kentucky, on January 27, 2004.

Louis Goodwin, 85, successful owner-breeder in Maryland for more than 30 years who campaigned in the name of Mom's Delight Stable; on February 10, 2005, in Baltimore.

William Grace, 69, president of Woodlands racetrack in Kansas, lobbyist for legalizing slot machines at state tracks; of cancer, on April 25, 2004, in Houston.

Douglas Gray, 94, British owner-breeder and former director of England's National Stud, who played a pivotal role in bringing champion Mill Reef to that facility as a stallion, and helped establish the National Racing Museum in Newmarket; in October 2004 in England.

Graham Green, 73, bookmaker, member of the Tattersalls committee that heard betting disputes; after a long illness, on March 11, 2004, in Stratford-upon-Avon, England.

John "Jack" Green, 67, longtime farrier at Maryland racetracks and farms; on July 9, 2004, in Maryland.

Stanley Greene, 82, who trained horses for several prominent owners during the 1960s before establishing the Virginia Stallion Station in 1977, former state steward at Charles Town Races; on March 12, 2005, in Purcellville, Virginia.

Otto Grohs, 83, former jockey, trainer, owner, and breeder, who rode Free for All to victory in the 1944 Arlington Futurity; on June 18, 2004, in Arcadia, California.

Michael Halay, 81, owner and breeder, former owner of Oak Lane Farms in Florida and Oak Meadow Farms in Louisiana, bred multiple stakes winner Cool Comfort; on September 29, 2004, in Louisiana.

Frank Handfield, 76, pony rider for the New York Racing Association for 40 years, who handled Secretariat, Spectacular Bid, Hoist the Flag, and Buckpasser; after a long illness, on August 20, 2004.

John Hanley, 70, former jockey, racing official, and general manager of Tampa Bay Downs; on September 7, 2004, at his home in Clearwater, Florida.

Gene Hargrove, 78, former trainer based in the Northeast; on February 2, 2004, in Fayre, Oklahoma.

Richard Harris, 73, former jockey in the Northwest and Canada, trainer for Cliff Roberts Stable; on November 17, 2004, in Harrison, Montana.

Kim Hart, president and chief executive of Horsepower Broadcasting Network International Ltd., past director and vice president of the HBPA of British Columbia, a leading owner at Hastings Park; on February 10, 2005, in British Columbia.

Elwood D. Heironimus, 83, longtime racing secretary and later a steward at Charles Town Races, also worked in the racing office at Shenandoah Downs; on October 21, 2004, in Charles Town, West Virginia.

Mary Lou Heleringer, 76, longtime Kentucky owner-breeder, member of the Thoroughbred Owners and Breeders Association, campaigned stakes winner Put Me In; on January 13, 2004, in Louisville.

Tony Hemmerick, 75, longtime East Coast trainer, began career as groom for Racing Hall of Fame horseman Hirsch Jacobs and later worked for Hall of Fame trainer John Nerud; of a stomach aneurysm, on December 1, 2004, in Hollywood, Florida.

Gary Henson, 60, announcer at Longacres in Washington state from 1973 to 1992, son of long-time Hollywood Park racecaller Harry Henson; after a lengthy illness, on May 22, 2004, in Renton, Washington.

Tom Hesketh, 75, owner-trainer based in Ohio and Kentucky; on May 18, 2004, in Cincinnati.

Jay Morgan Hickey, 60, lifelong horseman, assistant to Racing Hall of Fame trainer Bill Mott in the 1970s and early '80s; on November 17, 2004, in Fort Worth, Texas.

John Hilburn, 40, Midwest-based jockey who rode nearly 250 winners at Remington Park, and won stakes aboard Only Cash and Accomplished Lover; on November 1, 2004, in Oklahoma City.

Nancy Hilts, 64, longtime owner and trainer, who in 1960 became the first woman to be licensed as a Thoroughbred trainer in Ontario; on July 28, 2004, in Toronto.

Clark Holden, 65, long-time racetrack farrier, who had worked for such trainers as D. Wayne Lukas and Carl Nafzger, and most recently in Dubai for Godolphin Racing; of cancer, on May 26, 2004, in Oldsmar, Florida.

Donald Holmes, 70, former jockey, who ranked among the leading riders at Hazel Park, Detroit Race Course, and Fair Grounds, and guided Ask the Fare to victory in the 1967 Louisiana Derby; of cancer, on September 10, 2004, in Oak Park, Michigan.

Carroll "Frank" Hopkins Sr., 79, former member of the Maryland Racing Commission, two-term vice-president of the Maryland Horse Breeders Association, owner-breeder of 1997 Maryland Million Sprint winner Aberfoyle; of heart failure, on May 19, 2004, at Elberton Hill Farm, near Darlington, Maryland.

Roger Howard, 45, a longtime jockey's agent, brother of trainer Tom Howard; of cancer, on March 17, 2005.

John Casper "J. C." Howe, 83, former trainer and jockey, who rode the winners of more than 500 races in the South and Midwest; on May 14, 2004, in Chicago.

Dr. John A. Hoy, 94, longtime Maryland-based owner, breeder, and farm owner; on October 30, 2004, in Maryland.

Norman Hughes, 71, former trainer, co-founder of Silver Fox Stables, which specialized in quarantine services and repair of leg injuries; on April 29, 2005, in Florida.

Susan Hundley, 62, co-owner of Saxony Farm near Versailles, Kentucky, where champions Arazi and Ajdal were raised; of cancer, on January 24, 2004, in Kentucky.

Danny Hutt, 51, owner and trainer, who developed 1997 Arlington-Washington Futurity (G2) winner Cowboy Dan; on May 14, 2004, in Louisville.

Don Encrico Incisa, 70, well-known trainer in the north of England, noted for rejuvenating injured horses; on April 30, 2005, in England.

Angel Irastorza, 26, Argentine jockey; of injuries suffered in a December 27, 2003, spill at Hipodromo Palermo, on January 1, 2004, in Buenos Aires.

Barry James, 68, an East Coast racing official for more than 30 years, most recently at Penn National Race Course; on July 10, 2004, in Harrisburg, Pennsylvania.

Robert W. Jeans, 82, who groomed Racing Hall of Fame champion Buckpasser and other notable runners for trainer Eddie Neloy; on April 15, 2005.

Nick Jemas, 86, former jockey and longtime Jockeys' Guild executive director, who successfully advocated higher jockey mount fees, father of New Jersey Sports and Exposition Authority executive James Jemas; on April 14, 2005, in New Jersey.

Kay Eric Jensen, 86, a former leading jockey in Sweden and Denmark, and retired New York-based trainer who saddled graded stakes winners Golden Don, Heron Cove, and He's Vivacious; on May 13, 2005, in Warrenton, Virginia.

Jimmy Jimenez, 80, former jockey and trainer, who conditioned 1974 Hollywood Derby (G1) winner Agitate and four other stakes winners; of complications from surgery, on March 26, 2004, in Phoenix.

Mary Kay Johnson, 79, wife of Racing Hall of Fame trainer Philip G. Johnson, a principal in her family's Amherst Stable which campaigned homebred Volponi to win the 2002 Breeders' Cup Classic; of an apparent heart attack, on May 25, 2004, in Roslyn, New York.

Norman "Bootie" Johnson, 64, veteran Maryland-based trainer whose runners included stakes-winning Ayeaspecialgirl; on January 11, 2005, in Maryland.

Philip G. Johnson, 78, Racing Hall of Fame trainer, saddled winners at Saratoga Race Course for 36 consecutive years, conditioned 2002 Breeders' Cup Classic (G1) winner Volponi and major stakes winners Quiet Little Table, Kiri's Clown, etc; of cancer, on August 6, 2004, in Rockville Center, New York.

Susan Cocks Small Jones, 62, former general manager of Fair Hill Training Center, daughter of the late Racing Hall of Fame trainer W. Burling "Burley" Cocks; of breast cancer on October 16, 2004, in Unionville, Pennsylvania.

Attie Saffie Joseph Sr., 92, prominent Caribbean owner whose runners since the 1940s included winners of the Trinidad and United Barbados Derbys; on January 23, 2003, in Barbados.

Alex Kahn, 94, a United Press International journalist for 40 years, who covered horse racing at Hollywood Park and Santa Anita Park; of natural causes, on January 11, 2004, in Los Angeles.

Deb Kay, 50, who rehabilitated and retrained retired racehorses as proprietor of the Oaks of Kendall Woods; stabbed to death on January 30, 2005, at her home in Houston.

Edward I. Kelly, 83, trainer of 1959 champion sprinter Intentionally and Grade 1 winner I Enclose, brother of Racing Hall of Fame trainer Tommy Kelly; of a heart attack, on September 2, 2004, at his home in Brooksville, Florida.

Marty Kelly, 63, a jockeys' agent for nearly 40 years, and trainer of multiple stakes winner Commander Bold in the 1980s; after a lengthy battle with cancer, on November 14, 2004, in British Columbia.

Kevin Kerr, European-based trainer whose runners included Irish classic winners *Sea Charger and *Green Banner; in spring of 2005, in Dublin.

Vikki Kitchingman, 34, owner, exercise rider, and wife of California-based trainer Adam Kitchingham; of cancer, on July 23, 2004, in California.

Leo Klinkhammer, 85, breeder of 1988 Washington champion three-year-old male Steel an Emperor; on October 3, 2004, in Washington.

Jack L. Knight, 79, former owner and trainer; on October 11, 2004, in Chattanooga, Tennessee.

Ferdinand "Fred Schnozz" Krieger, 94, longtime jockey's agent and racing official; on May 22, 2004, in Atco, New Jersey.

George Krikorian Sr., 89, former East Coast trainer, father of Southern California-based owner George Krikorian Jr.; of cancer, on August 29, 2004, in Vista, California.

Dean Kutz, 48, retired jockey, who rode more than 2,800 winners in a 30-year career, recipient of the 2001 George Woolf Memorial Jockey Award and 2002 Mike Venezia Award, member of the Canterbury Downs and North Dakota Sports Halls of Fame; of cancer, on September 26, 2004, in Lexington.

Ray Lagemann, 73, well-known jockey's agent, whose clients had included Larry Snyder, Patricia Cooksey, and Steve Neff; of diabetes, in late October, 2004, in Cincinnati.

Joe Lamonte, 73, a former jockey who rode for nearly 30 years and a trainer for a quarter-century; on October 22, 2004, in Elm Grove, Louisiana.

Eric Langjahr, 47, a pioneer in computer handicapping of Thoroughbred racing, president of International Thoroughbred Superhighway Inc.; of cancer, on January 2, 2004, in Las Vegas.

Russ Lawler, 84, longtime steward in Washington state, former trainer, jockey's agent, and clerk of scales, for whom Racing Hall of Fame jockey Russell Baze was named; of injuries sustained in a car accident, in late March 2005.

Adrian Ledger, 25, Australian jockey who had ridden approximately 150 winners; from head injuries sustained in a fall on March 13, 2005, at Corowa racecourse, in Canberra, Australia.

Adrian Gordon Lee, 74, owner and breeder, member of the Louisiana Thoroughbred Breeders Association and Florida Thoroughbred Breeders' and Owners' Association; on June 6, 2004, in Ocean Springs, Mississippi.

Don Lee, 82, Turf writer who covered racing for the Omaha *World Herald* and *Daily Racing Form*, member of the Nebraska Horse Racing Hall of Fame; on February 18, 2004, in Omaha.

Mike Lee, 55, noted handicapper and author; of a massive stroke, on September 8, 2004, in Las Vegas.

Frederick M. Lege III, 87, Virginia farm owner and breeder, who bred 1984 Sunny Slope Stakes (G3) winner Matthew T. Parker and other stakes winners; on March 23, 2005, in Virginia.

Jerome Leon, 54, Canadian-based trainer at Woodbine and Fort Erie for 25 years; of hypothermia in a skiing accident, in February 2004, in Missoula, Montana.

Mary R. Lester, 84, longtime Maryland-based owner and breeder, who with her late husband, William, raced under the name Will-Mar Stables; on July 19, in Annapolis, Maryland.

William Lester, 84, longtime Maryland-based owner and breeder, who with his wife, Mary, raced under the name Will-Mar Stables, author of the 1997 horse racing novel *The Gemini Fraud*, former sports writer for the Baltimore *Sun*; on May 7, 2004, in Annapolis, Maryland.

Robert Levine, 86, New York-based owner-trainer who saddled 187 winners, including 2005 Bonnie Miss Stakes (G2) winner Jill Robin L, and as an owner campaigned multiple Grade 2 winner Koluctoo's Jill; on March 17, 2005, in New York.

Donald S. Levinson, 91, owner whose best runner was millionaire Grade 1 winner Lost Code, member of the Maryland Racing Commission from 1973-'78; on January 9, 2004, in Palm Beach, Florida.

Alice Lewis, 83, Thoroughbred owner, who with her husband, James, campaigned multiple Grade 1 winner Mecke and 1992 Kentucky Derby (G1) entrant Sir Pinder; of heart failure, on May 2, 2005, in Florida.

James Lewis, 83, Thoroughbred owner, who with his wife, Alice, campaigned multiple Grade 1 winner Mecke and 1992 Kentucky Derby (G1) entrant Sir Pinder; of heart and kidney failure, on May 10, 2005, in Florida.

Melvin Lewis, 88, former jockey who rode for 51 years, first recipient of the Jack Robinson Memorial Award, representative for the Northern California Jockeys' Association; on January 21, 2004, in Escalon, California.

Brenda Linville, 41, stallion secretary at Lane's End; of pancreatic cancer, on January 5, 2005, in Lexington.

Gavin Lisk, 23, Australian apprentice jockey; from head and spinal injuries suffered in a fall at Moe racecourse, on March 15, 2005, in Melbourne, Australia.

Rick Littrell, 50, co-owner and founder of Viking Stud in Lexington nearly two decades ago, frequent consignor at major Kentucky sales; from a blood clot in his lung, on November 11, 2004, in Lexington.

Frank Lodato Jr., 52, former trainer, jockey's agent, and clocker at Fair Grounds; on April 8, 2005, at his home in New Orleans.

Mike Loomer, 62, California-based bloodstock agent, whose purchases for Team Valor included major stakes winner Demaloot Demashoot; on June 2, 2004, in California.

F. A. "Red" Lowry, 71, former Golden Gate Fields track superintendent and trainer for four decades; of a heart attack, in February 2004 in Phoenix.

Snowy Lupton, 84, longtime New Zealand-based trainer, who saddled Kiwi to victory in the 1983 Melbourne Cup (Aus-G1); on December 15, 2004, in Waverly, New Zealand.

Polly Lyman, 97, founder of Maui Meadow Farm in Pennsylvania in 1946 with her late husband, Gen. Charles Lyman, breeder of stakes winners Fleg and T. V. Alliance; on November 9, 2004 in West Chester, Pennsylvania.

Francisco Eduardo de Paula Machado, 90, former president of the Brazilian Jockey Club, prominent owner-breeder who campaigned North American Grade 1 winners Siphon (Brz) and Virginie (Brz); of a heart attack, on January 1, 2005, in Rio de Janeiro, Brazil.

Keith Mahoney, 42, Australian jockey, whose controversial 25-year career included nearly 100 suspensions and a victory in the 1991 Australia Cup (Aus-G2) aboard Heavenly Knight; found dead in his car on July 20, 2004, near Mingela, Australia.

Dominic Marotta, 74, longtime owner and trainer who, with his brother Frank Marotta built the track now known as Great Lake Downs; on October 24.

John Terry Marshall, 59, a trainer in Western Canada and Northern California, perennially among the leading conditioners at Hastings Park, saddled 33 stakes winners, including Canadian Grade 3 winner Grace For You; of heart failure, on April 17, 2004, in El Cerrito, California.

Robert "R. J." Martin, 77, former jockey who ranked among the leading New England-based riders for 40 years and won title at Narragansett Park in 1947; following a lengthy illness, on March 10, 2005, in Aventura, Florida.

Claude Mauberret Jr., 82, noted veterinarian, member of the Fair Grounds Racing Hall of Fame, former state steward and member of the Louisiana State Racing Commission; on February 23, 2004.

Joe Mazur, 66, veteran Ohio-based owner and trainer, who saddled more than 400 winners between 1976 and 2004, including two-time Ohio-bred champion Mimi's Missile; of cancer, on May 25, 2004, in Macedonia, Ohio.

James Michael McGrath, 76, retired jockey's agent, whose clients included Racing Hall of Fame riders Angel Cordero Jr. and Braulio Baeza; after a lengthy illness, on April 26, 2004, in New York.

Edward McKinsey, 74, former general manager of Atlantic City Race Course and Hialeah, Arlington, Monmouth, Delaware, and Gulfstream Parks; of complications from a surgical procedure, on January 29, 2005, in North Miami Beach, Florida.

Sam McRae, 16, New Zealand-based apprentice jockey; as the result of a freak riding accident at Riverton racecourse, on March 26, 2005, near Invergargill, New Zealand.

Michael Mehlhope, 49, former trainer, conditioned Grade 3 stakes winner Subtle 'n Sly and stakes-winning What Majesty; on January 20, 2004, in Lexington.

Louis Mondello, 81, former New York-based trainer, saddled several stakes winners, including Grade 2 winner Bar Dexter, Cavamore, and Mochila; on September 1, 2004, in Hicksville, New York.

Christine Moore, Thoroughbred owner and breeder in the Southwest for more than 30 years, mother of Texas Thoroughbred Association director Sherry Raska, owner of South 64 Ranch; on April 4, 2005, in Texas.

John Morish, 53, former leading Australian trainer, who saddled Group 1 winners March Hare, Arkday, and Rouslan; in a shooting accident, on September 4, 2004, near Wombungi Station, Australia.

George Morrison, 84, Mid-Atlantic-based trainer for more than 50 years, whose runners included stakes winners Dance for Jan, Jo Jo Dancer, and Adam Cat; on November 4, 2004.

Norm Morrison, 67, a Texas state steward for a decade; of cancer, on February 1, 2004, in Breckenridge, Texas.

William Murray, 78, well-known author of novels with horse racing settings, including *Tip on a Dead Crab* and *Dead Heat*; of a heart attack, on March 8, 2005, in New York City.

Patrick Myer, 61, former steeplechase jockey, trainer, and supervisor of dormitories for NYRA, saddled 89 winners and three stakes winners; after suffering two strokes, on July 5, 2004, in New York.

Peggy Neloy, 83, mother of trainer Del Carroll, widow of Racing Hall of Fame trainer Eddie Neloy; of a heart attack, on March 28, 2004, in Florida.

V. J. "Lefty" Nickerson, 75, retired trainer, conditioned champion John Henry in 1979 and Grade 1 winners Spout and Big Spruce, mentor to Racing Hall of Fame trainer Richard Mandella; on March 26, 2004, in Smithtown, New York.

Gerald Nielsen, 70, New York breeder, owner of Sunnyfield Farm, two-term president of the New York Thoroughbred Breeders Inc., bred millionaire Grade 1 winner Capades; January 2004.

J. Frank Northcutt, 61, leading apprentice rider of 1959 and third among all North American jockeys that year; of cancer, on February 21, 2004, in Ocala.

Norbert "Nub" Norton, 76, Northwest-based trainer for more than 50 years, six-time leading conditioner at Portland Meadows, trained Washington champion Travel Orb and Oregon champions Judy B. and Tempo's Tiger; after a long illness, on December 18, 2004, in Vancouver, Washington.

Charles O'Bannon, 85, former superintendent of Charles Town Races; on September 30, 2004, in Kearneysville, West Virginia.

Richard O'Connell, 54, trainer of more than 500 winners, including Grade 1 winners Thunder Rumble and Capades, three-time trainer of the year of New York breds; from pneumonia stemming from a blood disorder, on February 29, 2004.

Willard D. Omert, 86, noted West Coast veterinarian for more than 60 years, performed the first arthroscopic surgery, chief veterinarian for the 1984 Olympics in Los Angeles; on January 2, 2004, in California.

Pat O'Neill, 69, horse owner, avid horseplayer, and father of trainer Doug O'Neill; of a heart attack, on March 16, 2004, in California.

Deane Mitchell-Palm, 87, owner, breeder, and trainer; on August 22, 2004, in Pahrump, Nevada.

Richard Papa, 92, an owner and trainer during the past four decades, who in the mid-1980s owned and trained major stakes winner Banker's Jet; on July 20, 2004, in Ontario.

Sandra Helen Payson, 78, owner of Manhasset Stable, daughter of the late Greentree Stud owner Joan Whitney and Charles Shipman Payson, great-granddaughter of legendary owner-breeder William Collins Whitney; of cancer, on July 15, 2004, in New York City.

Nina Peace, 53, lawyer and judge, wife of former Rocketts Mill Farm owner and prominent Virginia breeder Ed Stevens; of an apparent heart attack, on February 29, 2004, in Ashland, Virginia.

Tony Pellegrino, 64, longtime New York Racing Association employee as an outrider, paddock judge, and clerk of scales; on November 22, 2004, in Lone Grove, Oklahoma.

David Penna, 46, jockey, winner of 1,772 races in a 19-year career, whose 178 stakes winners included Canadian champions Peteski, Regal Classic, Rainbows for Life, Sunny's Halo, and Ruling Angel; on January 13, 2004, in British Columbia.

Doug Peterson, 53, longtime trainer, best known for training Seattle Slew during his four-year-old championship campaign in 1978; of an apparent accidental drug overdose, on November 22, 2004, in Los Angeles.

Melvin Peterson, 83, retired jockey who rode *Olhaverry to victory in the 1947 Santa Anita Handicap, and who finished fourth aboard Billings in the 1948 Kentucky Derby; on January 3, 2005, in Phoenix.

Marion Plesa, the first bookkeeper at Calder Race Course, owner, mother and wife, respectively, of trainers Eddie Plesa Jr. and Eddie Plesa Sr.; after a long illness, on September 5, 2004, in Florida.

Harold Polk, 93, longtime Virginia-based owner-breeder, bred multiple stakes-winner Jim J., who finished second to Dr. Fager in the 1967 Vosburgh H; from spinal meningitis, on September 20, 2004, in Alexandria, Virginia.

Maj. Michael Pope, 87, noted English trainer for more than 25 years, saddled jockey Pat Eddery's first winner. Founding president of the National Trainers' Federation; on October 13, 2004, in England.

Taylor Powell, 72, former jockey, who rode 2,014 winners from 1950-1967, retired Idaho state steward and longtime regional manager of the Jockeys' Guild, father of industry executive Lonny Powell; on April 10, 2004, in Boise, Idaho.

John Boyce Pumphrey III, 80 equine consultant, farm manager, a leader in the fight to return pari-mutuel wagering to Texas, credited with helping Dorothy and Pamela Scharbauer purchase future 1988 Horse of the Year Alysheba; on February 13, 2004, in Fort Worth, Texas.

Bill Pyers, 71, former internationally renowned jockey, member of the Australian Racing Hall of Fame, rode classic winners in England, Ireland, and France and guided Dahlia to victories in Europe and North America; in October, 2004 in Adelaide, Australia.

Christopher Quinn, 42, a jockey based in the Midwest, who rode more than 150 winners of $853,325, including 1999 Woodlands Juvenile S. winner Wildwood Penny; from injuries related to a 2003 fall at Fairmount Park, on August 10, 2004, in Lincoln, Nebraska.

Jim Randle, 66, Arizona-based owner and breeder, founder and co-owner of Pinnacle Vista Ranch near Phoenix; on February 9, 2005, in Arizona.

Owen Range, 90, owner of Gleneagles Farm in Versailles, Kentucky, who declined to purchase eventual two-time Horse of the Year John Henry for $5,000; of congestive heart failure, on January 26, 2004, in Lexington.

Sheilah Moore Rathbun, 81, owner of a successful racing and breeding facility near Middleburg, Virginia, breeder of $548,432 stakes winner Shiny Sheet; of emphysema, on January 10, 2005, in Arlington, Virginia.

Ronald Reagan, 93, former owner, breeder, President of the United States, lifetime member of the California Thoroughbred Breeders Association, who as governor of California in the 1960s signed laws advantageous to horse racing; of Alzheimer's disease and pneumonia, on June 5, 2004, in Bel Air, California.

William O. Reed, 83, internationally noted veterinarian, whose patients included Racing Hall of Fame members Ruffian, Tim Tam, Stymie, Dr. Fager, Damascus, and Hoist the Flag, former owner of Mare Haven Farm in Kentucky; on October 23, 2004, in Mineola, New York.

Bruce Reid, 84, prominent Australian owner, co-owner of 2004 Cox Plate (Aus-G1) winner Savabeel and '04 Caulfield Guineas (Aus-G1) winner Econsul; of complications from heart surgery, on March 13, 2005, in Australia.

Russell Reineman, 86, prominent owner and breeder since 1941, campaigned champions War Emblem and Smart Deb, and Grade 1 winners Wise Times, Hurry Up Blue, and I'm Sweets; on March 23, 2004, near Chicago.

Arthur Renihan Jr., 77, former trainer and owner, past member of the Thoroughbred Club of America; on February 24, 2005, in Indiana.

Willys Rhodes Sr., 84, longtime Mississippi-based owner, breeder, and trainer, who saddled 71 winners, including stakes winner Burgled; on April 16, 2005, in Bay St. Louis, Mississippi.

Jerry Richards, 59, Nebraska-based jockey's agent; on July 24, 2004, in Des Moines, Iowa.

Vittorio Riva, 66, a leading Italian owner-breeder, who raced champion Red Arrow and bred Group 1 winner Mendez. Former vice president of the Italian Jockey Club; in April 2005, in Milan.

Thomas Roberts, 56, a trainer for two decades, who saddled 76 winners; as the result of an accident, on November 23, 2004, at his Kentucky farm.

Gil Robillard, 80, former trainer and jockey who rode Epigram to victory in the 1952 Queen's Plate; on January 13, 2004, in Barrie, Ontario.

Kevin Robinson, 75, noted Australian trainer who saddled Kenbelle for a victory in the 1996 Australian Jockey Club Oaks (Aus-G1); in May 2005, in Australia.

Einar Paul Robsham, 75, owner, campaigned Grade 1 winner Trust N Luck and 2003 graded stakes winner Feline Story, breeder of 1995 Alabama Stakes (G1) winner Pretty Discreet; of heart failure, on February 22, 2004, in Boston.

Ray Rogers, 87, former executive with Oak Tree Racing Association and the Los Angeles Turf Club at Santa Anita Park, who coordinated the 1993 Breeders' Cup program at Oak Tree; of a heart attack, on July 12, 2004, in California.

John Rooney, 78, longtime Delaware Park executive, over 44 years served as treasurer, finance controller, vice president of racing, and steward; on January 19, 2004, in New Jersey.

Edmund B. Ross, 85, longtime owner-breeder, raced stakes winner Royal Form, member of the Essex Hunt Club; following a brief illness, on January 17, 2005, in Morristown, New Jersey.

Michael Rowland, 41, jockey, rode 3,996 career winners and won 29 meet titles at Thistledown in Ohio; from head injuries sustained in a February 4 spill at Turfway Park, on February 9, 2004, in Cincinnati.

John Russell, 67, trainer who conditioned Racing Hall of Fame members Susan's Girl and Precisionist, and champion Track Robbery, chairman of the California Equine Retirement Foundation advisory board; of stomach cancer, on February 25, 2004, in Del Mar, California.

Edward St. George, 76, owner who raced English Group 1 winners Desert Prince (Ire), Continent, Bahamian Bounty, and Bahamian Pirate in the colors of Lucayan Stud; of a heart attack, on December 20, 2004, in Houston.

Leslie Salminen, owner, noted mathematician; of breast cancer, in May 2005, in Monongahela, Pennsylvania.

Abdussamed Samadi, 84, Maryland-based owner-breeder, who bred stakes winner Kayacan in the name of his Turkeli Farms; of complications from a stroke, on February 5, 2005, at his home near Hollywood, Maryland.

Robert Sangster, 67, owner-breeder who helped fuel the 1980s boom at Thoroughbred sales, with partners purchased a world record $13.1-million yearling in 1985, campaigned more than 800 stakes winners, including champions The Minstrel and Alleged, and homebred Sadler's Wells, five-time leading owner in England; of pancreatic cancer, on April 7, 2004, in London.

Francis Santangelo, 71, owner-breeder who raced several New York-bred stakes winners, including homebred Grade 3 winner Hilbys Brite Flite; on March 22, 2004, in Palm Beach, Florida.

Bertram D. Sarafan, 91, former chairman of the New York State Racing and Wagering Board; on December 5, 2004, in New York.

Dorothy Scharbauer, 73, who raced dual classic winner and 1988 Horse of the Year Alysheba with her daughter Pamela, co-owner of Valor Farm in Texas; of pancreatic cancer, on February 23, 2005, in Midland, Texas.

David Schmidt, 46, Canadian-based trainer who was among the 2003 leaders at Fort Erie Racetrack; after being kicked in the back by a horse, on January 5, 2004, in Ontario.

Harry L. Schmidt Jr., 81, who oversaw the early lives of Mr. Prospector and Majestic Prince as broodmare manager of Spendthrift Farm; on February 8, 2005, in Lexington.

Marge Schott, 75, former Thoroughbred owner-breeder, bred and raced Grade 1 winner Stub and Grade 2 winner Answer, owned the Cincinnati Reds baseball team; of lung-related problems, on March 2, 2004, in Cincinnati.

Bob Schwarzmann, 81, longtime Seattle *Times* Turf writer and handicapper, who covered racing at Longacres Racetrack for four decades until his retirement in 1987; on May 8, 2004, in Shoreline, Washington.

Tommy Scott, 83, longtime racing official at Fair Grounds and Sportsman's Park, member of the Fair Grounds Hall of Fame; on January 21, 2004.

Francis Sears Jr., 87, co-owner of 1983 Preakness Stakes (G1) winner Deputed Testamony; on February 4, 2004, in Hamilton, Massachusetts.

Woody Sedlacek, 85, a trainer for more than 50 years, who saddled multiple Grade 1 winner Bounding Basque and graded stakes winners Shy Dawn and Champagne Charlie; of cancer, on July 19, 2004, in Ocala.

Fred Selz, 81, racehorse owner for more than 40 years, whose top runners included 1979 Arlington-Washington Lassie (G2) winner Sissy's Time and 2000 Spring Fever Stakes winner Burn Brightly; of kidney problems, on July 12, 2004, in Little Rock, Arkansas.

Barbara Shinpoch, 73, chairwoman of the Washington Horse Racing Commission when the 1994 law was passed allowing Emerald Downs to be built; following a lengthy illness, on March 9, 2005, in Washington.

H. E. Sircy Jr., noted farrier, shod Affirmed and Alydar; on January 16, 2004, in Harrodsburg, Kentucky.

Kayla Skinner, 84, owner of Swiftsure Stables with her late husband, David, and raced stakes winners Dusky Damion and Hooplah; on July 10, 2004, in Washington.

Carol Sue Smalley, 59, member of the Thoroughbred Owners and Breeders Association and the Oklahoma Thoroughbred Association; on January 5, 2005, in Chelsea, Oklahoma.

R. Gene Smith, 70, Louisville-based owner, breeder, businessman, and philanthropist, campaigned graded stakes winner Inkatha; of a heart attack, on March 13, 2005, in Louisville.

Jere Smith Sr., 63, Midwest trainer, saddled graded stakes winners Recoup the Cash and Chicago Six, member of the Hawthorne Race Course Hall of Fame; of cancer, on January 14, 2004, in Chicago.

Gordon Smyth, 77, trainer of England's 1966 Horse of the Year Charlottown; after a long illness, on July 22, 2004, in Sussex, England.

Brad Smythe, 48, Sovereign Award winner as Canada's outstanding apprentice jockey of 1977; of cancer, on February 4, 2005, in Alberta.

Alfred Z. Solomon, 104, racing enthusiast and noted philanthropist, longtime fixture at Saratoga Race Course, benefactor of the National Museum of Racing, owner of Madcaps Farm near Saratoga Springs, New York; on September 4, 2004, in Saratoga Springs.

Alma Spence, 87, former jockey, trainer, blacksmith, and movie stunt-rider; on March 26, 2004, in Cottonwood, Arizona.

Hassel Spraberry, 74, owner-breeder of 2004 Win-Star Derby winner Hi Teck Man, campaigned 1997 New Mexico champion Missy Cherub, longtime member of the Texas Thoroughbred Association; on February 21, 2005, in Texas.

Ray Stark, 88, legendary Hollywood producer, owner of Rancho Corral de Quati in California, breeder of Grade 1 winner Cacoethes, producer of the movies *Funny Girl* and *The Sunshine Boys*; after a long illness, on January 17, 2004, in Los Angeles.

Alec Stewart, 49, Newmarket-based trainer, who conditioned English champion Mtoto and 2001 Canadian International Stakes (Can-G1) Mutamam (GB); of cancer, on August 4, 2004, in Newmarket.

George Stidham, 78, former jockey, trainer, and business manager-agent for Racing Hall of Fame rider Bill Hartack, father of trainer Mike Stidham; on April 1, 2005, in Glendora, California.

Everett L. Talbot, 82, Thoroughbred owner and breeder, real estate developer; on April 10, 2004, in Houma, Louisiana.

Jack Taylor, 70, noted New Zealand-based trainer, whose runners included 1984 New Zealand Two Thousand Guineas (NZ-G1) winner Kingdom Bay; in May 2005, in New Zealand.

William K. Taylor, 87, general manager of Claiborne Farm from 1957 to '75, former manager of Nelson Bunker Hunt's Bluegrass Farm, developer of Springland Farm in Paris, Kentucky; on February 8, 2005, in Lexington.

Chris Thomas, 55, award-winning sportscaster, owner, handicapper, earned a 1989 Eclipse Award for his report on the death of Secretariat; of cancer, on February 18, 2004, in Tampa, Florida.

Edwin W. Thomas, 85, retired veterinarian, farm owner, breeder of major stakes winner and sire Our Native; in his sleep, on March 19, 2004, in Lexington.

Dorothy "Dottie" Terrill, wife of trainer William "Red" Terrill, who conditioned multiple Grade 1 winner Turnback the Alarm; in late April 2004 at her home in Saratoga Springs, New York.

Alvin Toffel, 69, California-based owner and breeder, who co-bred and -raced stakes winners Riva Ranger, Only the Best, and Rexy Sexy; of a stroke, on March 5, 2005, in Las Vegas.

Gerald Turner, 58, five-time champion South African jockey who won numerous classic races in his native country, longtime chairman of the Transvaal Jockeys' Association; on February 9, 2005, in South Africa.

Don Valliere, 72, former general manager at Fort Erie Racetrack, founder of *Canadian Horse* magazine, and one-time publisher of *Turf & Sport Digest*; on October 15, 2004, in Fort Erie, Ontario.

John Valpredo, 96, a California owner-breeder for 50 years, father of Jockey Club member Don Valpredo, bred graded stakes winners Dimaggio and Fifty Six Ina Row, imported and raced major 1970s stakes winners *Lucie Manet and *Star Ball; on January 12, 2005, in Bakersfield, California.

Robert Vanaman, 57, employee of Gainsborough Farm, active member of the Thoroughbred Farm Managers' Club; on April 10, 2004, in Lexington.

Glen Richard Vandervort, 82, respected veterinarian for more than half a century, fondly known at Portland Meadows as "Doc Dickey;" in August 2004.

Marvin Waldman, 86, longtime Thoroughbred breeder, partner in Red Bull Stables, which bred dual classic winner and champion Bold Forbes and Group 1 or Grade 1 winners Green Desert, Dunbeath, and Group Plan, father of Overbrook Farm adviser Ric Waldman; on April 8, 2004, in Highland Beach, Florida.

Wilhelmine Waller, 90, New York owner-breeder, owner of Tanrackin Farm, a founder of the New York Breeding and Racing Program, president of the Eastern New York Thoroughbred Breeders Association, campaigned 14 homebred stakes winners; on April 7, 2004, in Bedford Hills, New York.

Martin Wansborough, 50, Canadian-based trainer who worked at the track for 35 years and saddled 146 winners, including multiple stakes winner Synchronized; after a long illness, on September 19, 2004, in Canada.

Paul Ward, 70, former jockey who consistently ranked among Ohio's leading riders during a 17-year riding career in the 1950s and '60s, outrider for more than 30 years at Beulah Park; on March 21, 2005, in Canal Winchester, Ohio.

C. L. "Bubba" Webb, 81, former chief steward for the Louisiana Racing Commission; after a long illness, on June 30, 2004, in Shreveport, Louisiana.

Jo Ann Weber, 70, executive director of the Texas Horse Racing Hall of Fame, former employee of the Texas Thoroughbred Association; of breast cancer, on November 22, 2004, in Texas.

Jay Weiss, 76, owner, breeder, and philanthropist, co-bred and -owned Grade 2 winner Queue; of lung cancer, on January 31, 2004, in Bal Harbour, Florida.

Lady Joan Westbrook, co-owner and -breeder of 2002 St. Leger S. (Eng-G1) winner Bollin Eric; on March 6, 2004.

Charles W. Whims Sr., 81, Maryland-based horseman for more than 50 years; on July 29, 2004, in Maryland.

Denis Whishaw, 50, co-owner of Armidale Stud in Australia, noted sales consignor, breeder of Group 2 winner Weasel Will; in a farm accident, in October 2004, at his farm in Northern Tasmania, Australia.

Herbert J. Whitmore, 86, state auditor for the Maine Thoroughbred Racing Commission for more than 25 years; on September 19, 2004, in Portland, Maine.

Karry Wilson, 44, former jockey, exercise rider, and racing official, graduate of the Race Track Industry Program at the University of Arizona; following a long illness, on August 12, 2004 in Poway, California.

Arthur Harrison Wilson Jr., 91, Virginia-based owner and breeder, former owner of Twin Orchards Farm, champion polo player; on November 17, 2004, in Fredericksburg, Virginia.

Fred Winter, 77, England's four-time champion steeplechase jockey and eight-time champion trainer, on April 5, 2004, in England.

Margaret "Sissy" Woolums, 68, an authority in pedigree research and cataloging, founder of Pedigree Associates, helped launch the Jockey Club Statistical Bureau, member of the International Cataloging Standards Committee; of pancreatic cancer, on February 28, 2004, in Lexington.

Peter Wragg, 76, bloodstock agent, whose purchases included Irish Derby winners *Talgo II and Fidalgo, and English champion Miralgo; after a long illness, in February 2004.

John C. Wyatt, 76, longtime Central Kentucky-based photographer who worked for Keeneland Race Course and for a local newspaper; on April 19, 2005, in Lexington.

Ron Yanke, 68, prominent Idaho horseman, businessman, and philanthropist, campaigned popular Idaho stakes winners Rosie Way and Head Table; of leukemia, on February 3, 2004, in Idaho.

Eleanor Anne Yearley, 56; **Henry Yearley**, 62; English owners, husband and wife, charged with having stolen nearly $2-million to support their racing stable; of apparent suicide, on June 25, 2004, in England.

William T. Young, 85, Eclipse Award-winning breeder, owner of Overbrook Farm, owned and bred leading sire Storm Cat, 1996 Kentucky Derby (G1) winner Grindstone, and Breeders' Cup winners Cat Thief, Boston Harbor, and Flanders, director emeritus of Churchill Downs; of an apparent heart attack, on January 12, 2004, in Florida.

Robert J. Zindorf Jr., 84, owner of Prospect Hill Farm in Maryland, longtime member of the Maryland Horse Breeders Association, noted sportsman, and former racing columnist; from injuries sustained in a fall, on October 1, 2004, in Baltimore.

2004-2005 Horse Deaths

ACATENANGO, 1982 ch. h., Surumu—Aggravate, by *Aggressor II. Two-time German Horse of the Year. Four-time leading sire in Germany. Sire of more than 60 stakes winners, including three champions; of injuries sustained in a paddock accident, on April 2, 2005, at Gestut Fahrhof in Germany.

AIR DE FRANCE, 1984 dk. b. or br. h., Seattle Slew—Allez France, by *Sea-Bird. 2-1-0-0, $11,032. Sire of ten stakes winners, including millionaire Group 1 winner Bomber Bill; after fracturing a leg in a breeding shed accident, in November 2004 at Tobermory Stud, Australia.

ALL ALONG (FR), 1979 b. m., Targowice—Agujita (Fr), by Vieux Manoir. 21-9-4-2, $2,125,828. U.S. Horse of the year, champion grass mare of 1983, champion in France. Won the 1983 Prix de l'Arc de Triomphe (Fr-G1), Turf Classic (G1), etc. Dam of French group winner Along All; of old age, on February 23, 2005, at Three Chimneys Farm in Midway, Kentucky.

ALLAMANDA, 2001 ch. f., A.P. Indy—Aldiza, by Storm Cat. By a leading sire, out of a Grade 1 winner. Unraced; after breaking down in a workout in early August 2004 at Saratoga Race Course.

AMERICAN CHANCE, 1989 dk. b. or br. h., Cure the Blues—American Dance, by Seattle Slew. 37-10-8-4, $847,977. Won the 1992 Jersey Derby (G2). Sire of more than 20 stakes winners, including Grade 1 winner America Alive; of colic, in late October 2004 at Haras La Providencia, Argentina.

AMONG MY SOUVENIRS, 2001 dk. b. or br. f., Souvenir Copy—Accountinquestion, by Classic Account. 4-3-0-0, $87,105. Won the 2004 Dearly Precious S. and Marshua S.; euthanized after breaking her right fore ankle in the Adena Stallions' Miss Preakness S. (G3), on May 14, 2004, at Pimlico Race Course.

Angel Fever, 1990 b. m., Danzig—Rowdy Angel, by Halo. 2-1-1-0, $25,665. Stakes-placed. Dam of 2000 Kentucky Derby (G1) winner Fusaichi Pegasus; after fracturing her pelvis in a paddock accident, on January 30, 2004, at Stone Farm in Paris, Kentucky.

ANNIE EDGE (IRE), 1980 ch. m., Nebbiolo—Friendly Court, by Be Friendly. 23-6-4-6, $277,526. Won the 1984 New York H. (G2), classic-placed in Ireland. Dam of six stakes winners, including European high-weight Selkirk; due to infirmities of old age, on October 13, 2004, at Derry Meeting Farm in Pennsylvania.

ARCHWAY, 1988 ch. h., Thatching—Rose of Jericho, by Alleged. 9-3-2-1, $93,482. Champion sprinter of 1991 in Ireland. Sire of more than 15 stakes winners, including champions Grand Archway and Sua; euthanized after breaking his neck in a paddock accident, on July 29, 2004, at Larneuk Stud in Victoria, Australia.

ARGOSY, 1981 b. h., Affirmed—My Charmer, by Poker. 3-2-0-0, $22,279. Former $1.5-million yearling purchase, half brother to Seattle Slew. Stakes winner in Ireland. Sire of at least nine stakes winners, including Group 1 winners Vistula and Lindberg; of laminitis in January 2005 at Southford Stud in South Africa.

AS DE PIK, 1999 dk. b. or br. h., Lode—Asqute, by Raise a Man. Won the 2003 Gran Premio 9 de Julio (Arg-G1). Considered one of Argentina's top handicap horses; of acute peritonitis, on March 5, 2004, in Argentina.

Atswhatimtalknbout, 2000 dk. b. or br. c., A. P. Indy—Lucinda K, by Red Ransom. 6-2-1-1, $209,120. Finished second by a nose in the 2003 San Felipe S. (G2), fourth in the Kentucky Derby (G1); of complications from intestinal surgery, on September 1, 2004, at San Luis Rey Equine Clinic in California.

AUENWEISE, 2002 dk. b. or br. f., Big Shuffle—Auenglocke, by Surumu. 2-1-1-0, $47,401. Stakes winner at two in Germany and a favorite for the 2005 Henkel-Rennen (Ger-G2) German One Thousand Guineas; after breaking down, in April 2005 in Germany.

AU PRINTEMPS, 1979 b. m., Dancing Champ—*Lorgnette II, by High Hat. 30-7-5-4, $124,383. Stakes winner. Dam of Canadian champion Charley Barley, 1987 Breeders' Cup Juvenile (G1) winner Success Express, and Grade 1 winner Greenwood Lake; two days after foaling, on May 10, 2005, at Pennbrook Farm in Lexington.

AVERTI, 1991 b. h., Warning (GB)—Imperial Jade, by Lochnager. 41-5-2-6, $218,993. Won the 1997 King George S. (Eng-G3). Sire of Group 2 winners Avonbridge and Wunders Dream; of a heart attack in December 2004 at Whitsbury Manor Stud in Salisbury, England.

AWAASIF, 1979 b. m., *Snow Knight—Royal Statute, by Northern Dancer. 14-4-0-1, $273,526. Champion three-year-old filly in 1982 in England. Won the Yorkshire Oaks (Eng-G1). Dam of 1989 Epsom Oaks (Eng-G1) winner Snow Bride and graded stakes winners Jarraar and Ibn Al Haitham (GB); on May 26, 2004, in Newmarket, England.

BATES MOTEL, 1979 b. h., Sir Ivor—Sunday Purchase, by T. V. Lark. 19-9-1-4, $851,050. Champion older male of 1983. Sire of more than 35 stakes winners, including four foreign champions and several U.S. Grade 2 winners; due to infirmities of old age, on October 12, 2004, at Gainesway in Lexington.

Battle Creek Girl, 1977 b. m., His Majesty—Far Beyond, by Nijinsky II. 20-3-3-1, $40,240. Stakes-placed. Dam of 1989 Canadian champion juvenile filly Wavering Girl and Grade 2 winners Tricky Creek, Parade Ground, Parade Leader, and Speed Dialer; from infirmities of old age, on August 25, 2004, at Lane's End in Versailles, Kentucky.

Beau Cougar, 1979 b. m., *Cougar II—Miss Beaustark, by Graustark. 31-5-3-12, $78,556. Multiple stakes-placed. Dam of Canadian champion Hasten To Add and Grade 1 winner See How She Runs; of old age, in 2004.

Beckys Shirt, 1991 b. m., Cure the Blues—Thundertee, by Ye. 17-5-4-3, $174,856. Grade 2-placed at three and four. Dam of 2003 Breeders' Cup Sprint (G1) winner Cajun Beat; of colic after foaling, on April 3, 2005, at Ashford Stud in Versailles, Kentucky.

Beekeeper, 1998 b. h., Rainbow Quest—Chief Bee, by Chief's Crown. 11-3-0-1, $264,140. Third in the 2002 Melbourne Cup (Aus-G1); euthanized after fracturing a leg during training, on May 9, 2004.

BE MY GUEST, 1974 ch. h., Northern Dancer—What a Treat, by *Tudor Minstrel. 7-4-1-0, $49,421. Group winner. Leading 1982 sire in England. Sired 80 stakes winners, including champions Assert (Ire) and Luth Enchantee (Fr); of old age, on February 19, 2004, at Coolmore, Ireland.

BEST WALKING, 1999 gr. or ro. m., Big Shuffle—Bergwelt, by Solarstern. 13-3-1-2, $83,886. Won the 2003 Prix de Saint-Georges (Fr-G3); of colic, in the spring of 2005, at Coolmore in Ireland.

BLACK BART, 1999 dk. b. or br. g., Stage Colony—Lyrical Pirate, by Pirate's Bounty. 34-9-4-3, $346,080. Won five stakes in 2004, including the TVG Khaled S. and Quicken Tree S.; after breaking down in the Native Diver H., on December 11, 2004, at Hollywood Park.

BLITEY, 1976 b. m., Riva Ridge—Lady Pitt, by Sword Dancer. 23-8-5-5, $297,746. Won the 1979 Maskette S. (G2). Dam of Grade 1 winners Dancing Spree, Fantastic Find, and Furlough, grandam of 1994 champion three-year-old filly Heavenly Prize; due to infirmities of old age, on November 26, 2004, at Claiborne Farm in Paris, Kentucky.

BOOKLET, 1999 b. h., Notebook—Crafty Bobbie, by Bob's Dusty. 14-7-2-1, $989,460. Won the 2002 Fountain of Youth S. (G1), Holy Bull S. (G3); of colic, on March 4, 2004, at Hagyard Equine Medical Institute in Lexington.

BOOMZEEBOOM, 2001 b. c., Explosive Red—Zee Lady, by Unreal Zeal. 10-3-3-1, $190,096. Won the 2004 Affirmed H. (G3); euthanized after injuring a cannon bone in a workout, on July 24, 2004, in California.

BORN WILD, 1992 dk. b. or br. h., Wild Again—Lady Winborne, by Secretariat. 31-8-2-5, $259,505. High-weighted at three on the Austrian Free Handicap. Won the 1996 Fair Grounds Breeders' Cup H. Sire of at least 14 winners; in 2004.

BOSSANOVA, 2000 dk. b. or br. c., Pine Bluff—Street Tappin, by Housebuster. 10-4-1-2, $234,426. Won the 2003 Fall Highweight H. (G3); euthanized after fracturing both sesamoid bones in his right foreleg during the Hollie Hughes H., on February 15, 2004, at Aqueduct.

Boston Brahmin, 2001 b. c., Boston Harbor—Shoreline, by Unbridled. 17-2-3-1, $82,365. Multiple stakes-placed, third in the 2003 Cowdin S.; after breaking down in a race, on August 29, 2004, at Saratoga Race Course.

BOSTON COMMON, 1999 b. g., Boston Harbor—Especially, by Mr. Prospector. 33-12-8-4, $609,317. Won the 2002 Jerome H. (G2). Euthanized after sustaining a condylar fracture to his right foreleg during a race on June 27, 2004, at Hollywood Park.

BRILLIANT MELODY, 1979 b. m., Cornish Prince—Pavlova, by Nijinsky II. Unraced. Dam of graded stakes winners Al's Helen and Straight Man; euthanized due to infirmities of age, on May 13, 2004, at Winding Oaks Farm in Ocala.

BUSHMANLAND, 1991 b. g., Centenary—Damaraland, by Quarrytown. Group 1 winner in South Africa. Sire of one stakes-placed runner. Gelded and returned to racing at 13; of a heart attack after flipping in the gate before a race at Kenilworth, in November 2004, in South Africa.

CAPITOL SOUTH, 1981 b. h., Roberto—Polylady, by Polynesian. 13-3-4-0, $116,550. Won the 1983 Hopeful S. (G1). Sire of four stakes winners; in October 2004, in Texas.

CAPO MAXIMO, 1985 ch. h., Farnesio (Arg)—Capa Chochi, by El Capo. 16-12-3-1, $236,468. Champion sprinter in Argentina in 1989. Sire of at least five known stakes winners, including 1997 champion Argentine sprinter Capo d' Oro and Group 1 winner Diegol; of natural causes, on June 17, 2004, at Haras Abolengo, Argentina.

CAPTAIN JAMES (IRE), 1974 b. h., Captain's Gig—Aliceva (Ire), by Alcide. 13-3-4-0, $60,833. Won the 1978 Waterford Crystal Mile (Eng-G2). Sire of six stakes winners, including Group 1 winners Creag-an-Sgor and Outof the Question; of old age, on September 10, 2004, at Getaway Thoroughbred Farm in Romoland, California.

CAROLS FOLLY, 1987 dk. b. or br. m., Taylor's Falls—No Tresspassing, by Bob's Dusty. 12-5-0-2, $32,756. Won the 1989 Airdrie S. Dam of millionaire Grade 1 winners Unbridled Elaine and Glitter Woman; after rupturing an intestine while foaling, on April 20, 2004, at Hagyard Equine Medical Institute in Lexington.

CARSON CITY, 1987 ch. h., Mr. Prospector—Blushing Promise, by Blushing Groom (Fr). 15-6-2-0, $306,240. Won the 1989 Sapling S. (G2). Sire of more than 70 stakes winners, including 2002 Canadian champion older mare Small Promises and Grade 1 winners City Zip, Carson Hollow, Cuvee, and City Band; of unknown causes, on December 24, 2004, at Overbrook Farm in Lexington.

CASAS CABALLO, 2000 b. c., Boston Harbor—One Beautiful Lady, by Broad Brush. 7-3-1-0, $93,800; euthanized after sustaining a condylar fracture to his left front cannon bone in the Potrero Grande Breeders' Cup H. (G2), on March 28, 2004, at Santa Anita Park.

CASTLE GANDOLFO, 1999 ch. h., Gone West—Golden Oriole, by Northern Dancer. 14-3-2-3, $214,408. Won the 2001 Juddmonte Beresford S. [Ire-G3]; of a broken neck in a farm accident, on September 5, 2004, at Haras Mocito Guapo, Chile.

CAT'S CAT, 2000 ch. m., Tabasco Cat—Catchofthecentury, by Carson City. 24-3-7-2, $168,513. Won the 2003 Hatoof S.; euthanized after breaking down in the San Felipe S., on January 8, 2005, at Sam Houston Race Park in Texas.

CENTAINE, 1980 br. h., Century—Rainbeam, by Vain. 6-2-2-2. Won the 1984 Autumn S. (Aus-G3). Sire of at least 56 stakes winners, including 1999 New Zealand champion juvenile Spring Rain; on April 19, 2004, at Waikato Stud in Matamata, New Zealand.

CENT HOME, 1995 br. g., Lord Ballina—Centuria, by Centaine. 37-11-4-3, $329,619. New Zealand highweighted older horse of 2001. Multiple Group 1 winner; euthanized after breaking down in the Zabeel Classic (NZ-G1), on January 3, 2005, in New Zealand.

CERTAIN HABIT, 1977 b. m., Ashabit—Charlotte Rhodes, by Lucifer. Unraced. Five-time New Zealand Broodmare of the Year. Dam of two-time New Zealand Horse of the Year Rough Habit and Group 3 winner Citi Habit; of a heart attack, in May 2004 in New Zealand.

CHARMING PRINCE, 2001 b. c., Barathea (Ire)—Most Charming, by Darshaan. 4-2-2-0, $145,277. Won the 2003 Prix des Jouvenceaux et des Jouvencelles, Group 3-placed; following a training accident, in February 2004 in Europe.

CHEROKEE COLONY, 1985 b. h., Pleasant Colony—Cherokee Phoenix, by Nijinsky II. 11-3-3-2, $474,380. Won the 1988 Flamingo S. (G1). Sire of ten stakes winners, including 2000 Dominican Horse of he Year Klindo and steeplechase winner Cherokeeinthehills; from an internal rupture, in December 2004 at the University of California at Davis Veterinary Hospital.

CHIC SHIRINE, 1984 b. m., Mr. Prospector—Too Chic, by Blushing Groom (Fr). 16-3-2-3, $237,944. Won the 1987 Ashland S. (G1). Dam of Grade 2 winners Waldoboro and Tara Roma; of complications from colic surgery, on May 3, 2004, in Kentucky.

CHIMES BAND, 1991 dk. b. or br. h., Dixieland Band—Chimes, by Mr. Prospector. 19-7-2-2, $416,961. Group/graded winner in France and the U.S. Three-time leading sire in New Mexico; euthanized in January 2005, due to complications following surgery for wobbler syndrome, in New Mexico.

CHRISTMAS BONUS, 1978 dk. b. or br. m., Key to the Mint—Sugar Plum Time, by Bold Ruler. 28-7-2-5, $140,557. Won a division of the 1982 Poquessing H. Dam of five stakes winners and grandam of Grade 1 winner Grand Slam; of old age, on August 18, 2004, at Spring Hill Farm in Casanova, Virginia.

Cisco Road, 1990 ch. h., Northern Baby—Mythographer, by Secretariat. 8-5-1-0, $97,034. Stakes-placed. Washington's leading freshman sire of 1998. Sire of more than 15 stakes winners; of cancer, in September 2004, in Washington.

CITI STATE, 2000 ch. m., Citidancer—Bal Du Bois, by Balzac. 32-3-3-5, $104,170; euthanized after falling over another horse on March 12, 2005, in the Conniver S. at Laurel Park in Maryland.

CLASSIFIED FACTS, 1993 b. h., Seattle Slew—Bald Facts, by In Reality. 15-2-3-0, $33,085. Sire of at least 27 winners from 31 starters; in 2005, in Illinois.

CLEVER TRICK, 1976 dk. b. or br. h., Icecapade—Kankakee Miss, by Better Bee. 29-18-2-1, $419,787. Multiple stakes winner. Sire of more than 65 stakes winners, including Phone Trick, Anet, and Weekend Delight; broodmare sire of more than 75 stakes winners; of kidney failure, on June 5, 2004, at Glencrest Farm in Midway, Kentucky.

COLONIAL SECRETARY, 1992 b. g., Pleasant Colony—Secretary's Story, by Secretariat. 78-22-14-11, $421,840. Won the 1996 Creme Fraiche S. at Meadowlands in track-record time; euthanized due to a leg injury, on March 16, 2004.

COME MY PRINCE, 1972 ro. m., Prince John—Come Hither Look, by *Turn-to. Unraced. Dam of Grade/Group 1 winner and 1995 leading American sire Palace Music; euthanized due to infirmities of old age, on March 7, 2004, at Warfield Stud, in Butler, Missouri.

COMMANCHE RUN, 1981 b. h., Run the Gantlet—Volley, by Ratification. 14-7-0-0, $607,912. Won the 1984 St. Leger Stakes (Eng-G1). Sire of 15 stakes winners, including Wavy Run (Ire) and Commanche Court; of heart failure, in March 2005, at Astley Grange Stud in England.

CONFLUENCE, 1995 b. m., Paris Opera—Tristrams Jewel, by *Sir Tristram. 13-6-3-2, $90,274. 2002 Singapore Horse of the Year; following surgery to fuse a fetlock joint, in November 2004 in Singapore.

CRIMINAL TYPE, 1985 ch. h., Alydar—Klepto, by No Robbery. 24-10-5-3, $2,351,274. Horse of the Year in 1990. Won the 1990 Hollywood Gold Cup H. (G1), Pimlico Special H. (G1). Sire of seven stakes winners. Broodmare sire of Ten Most Wanted; of a gastric rupture, on March 9, 2005, at Otsuka Bokujo in Japan.

CROCROCK, 1997 b. g., North Prospect—Spice Wreath, by Summing. 42-16-6-3, $359,977. Winner of nine stakes, including the 2000 Minnesota Derby; after breaking down in a race, on April 26, 2005, at Prairie Meadows Racetrack in Iowa.

CRYPTO'S REDJET, 1992 b. m., Cryptoclearance—Doc's Lear Jet, by Lear Fan. 39-17-3-7, $364,640. Two-time Ohio-bred horse of the year. Dam of stakes winner Crypto's Prospect; of complications after foaling, on April 14, 2005, at Willow Springs Farm near Columbus, Ohio.

CRYSTAL WATER, 1973 b. h., Windy Sands—Soft Snow, by T. V. Lark. 25-9-3-3, $845,072. California horse of the year in 1977. Won the 1977 Santa Anita H. (G1), Hollywood Gold Cup H. (G1). Sire of nine stakes winners, including Grade 2 winner Glacial Stream; in 2004, in California.

CUPECOY'S JOY, 1979 b. m., Northerly—Lady Abla (Arg), by Alsina. 22-6-7-4, $377,960. Won the 1982 Mother Goose S. (G1), Acorn S. (G1), and led for the opening mile of the Kentucky Derby (G1). Dam of three winners; in 2004, at Haras Lucy Grace in Otisville, New York.

DAHLIA'S DREAMER, 1989 ch. m., Theatrical (Ire)—Dahlia, by *Vaguely Noble. 22-5-7-3, $333,956. Won the 1994 Flower Bowl Invitational H. (G1). Half sister to three Grade 1 winners; of lymphangitis, on February 17, 2004, at Claiborne Farm in Paris, Kentucky.

DANCE OR PRANCE, 1975 dk. b. or br. m., Bold Reasoning—Make Or Break, by Cohoes. Unraced. Dam of three stakes winners, including Grade 3 winner Swingin Sway; euthanized on February 22, 2004, at Westview Farm in Paris, Kentucky.

DANCING KEY, 1983 b. m., Nijinsky II—Key Partner, by Key to the Mint. Unraced. Dam of four graded stakes winners, including champions Dance Partner (Jpn), Dance in the Dark and Dance in the Mood (Jpn); from complications of foaling, on March 30, 2004, at Shadai Farm, Japan.

DANESTORM, 1998 b. g., Danehill—Shalbourne, by Nureyev. 25-5-9-1, $337,573. Won the 2004 Brisbane Cup (Aus-G1); euthanized after fracturing a sesamoid in the Cranbourne Cup, on October 6, 2004, at Cranbourne Race Course, Australia.

DAVID, 1996 ch. h., Mt. Livermore—Fateful Beauty, by Turkoman. 14-5-3-2, $403,920. Won the 1999 New York Derby. Sire of winners; of complications following colic surgery, on December 30, 2004, at Stonewall Farm in Granite Springs, New York.

DEPUTY JANE WEST, 1990 dk. b. or br. m., Silver Deputy—Lady D' Arbanville, by Cornish Prince. 17-9-5-0, $593,410. Canadian champion filly at two and three. Dam of stakes winners Bag Lady Jane and Deputy Storm; of laminitis, in September 2004, at Clearbrook Farm in Paris, Kentucky.

DEPUTY MINISTER, 1979 dk. b. or br. h., Vice Regent—Mint Copy, by Bunty's Flight. 22-12-2-2, $696,964. Champion in the U.S. and Canadian Horse of the Year, 1981. Twice leading North American sire. Sire of more than 80 stakes winners and six champions, including Go for Wand, Open Mind, and Dehere; of cardiac failure, on September 10, 2004, at Ohio State University Veterinary Hospital in Columbus, Ohio.

DESERT DEER, 1998 ch. h., Cadeaux Genereux—Tuxford Hideaway, by Cawston's Clown. 14-7-3-1, $240,641. Won the 2003 Bet Attheraces Mile (Eng-G2); euthanized after fracturing a hind fetlock in the Juddmonte Lockinge S. (Eng-G1) on May 15, 2004, at Newbury Race Course, England.

DEVIL'S BAG, 1981 b. h., Halo—Ballade, by *Herbager. 9-8-0-0, $445,860. Undefeated champion at two in 1983. Sire of more than 40 stakes winners, including 1998 Japanese Horse of the Year and champion Taiki Shuttle and Grade 1 winners Devil His Due, Twilight Agenda, Buy the Sport, and Devil's Orchid; euthanized due to complications from a stall injury, on February 3, 2005, at Claiborne Farm in Paris, Kentucky.

DEVIOUS BOY (GB), 2000 dk. b. or br. g., Dr Devious (Ire)—Oh Hebe, by Night Shift. 17-5-6-3, $286,220. Won the 2003 Oak Tree Derby (G2); from complications of a virus, in May 2004 in California.

Devonwood, 1994 ch. h., Woodman—Golden Oriole, by Northern Dancer. 14-4-2-2, $248,345. Grade 1-placed. His first crop raced in 2004 and included stakes winner Speedy Gone Sally; on May 9, 2004, at Horizon Farm, Alberta.

DIAGHLYPHARD, 1982 b. h., Lyphard—Jump Seat, by Hasty Road. 13-4-4-0, $47,123. Twice leading sire in

Scandinavia. Sire of champions Songline and Kokomo; in early 2005, at Ravdansens Stuteri near Stockholm, Sweden.

DISTINCTIVE PRO, 1979 dk. b. or br. h., Mr. Prospector—Well Done, by Distinctive. 13-8-3-1, $179,187. Won the 1982 Hutcheson S. (G3). Sire of more than 40 stakes winners, including Grade 1 winner Quick Mischief; of laminitis, on February 22, 2005, at Sugar Maple Farm in Poughquag, New York.

DOLLAR BILL, 1998 b. h. 1998, Peaks and Valleys—Saratoga Dame, by Saratoga Six. 22-4-5-5, $1,225,546. Won the 2000 Kentucky Jockey Club S. (G2), Grade 1-placed; of laminitis, on August 3, 2004, at Houstondale Farm in Paris, Kentucky.

DR. BLUM, 1977 ch. h., Dr. Fager—Due Dilly, by Sir Gaylord. 23-9-5-2, $253,520. Multiple stakes winner. Sire of 19 stakes winners, including graded winners Richard R. and Medicine Woman, broodmare sire of champion Left Bank; euthanized due to a throat tumor, in October 2004 at Sugar Maple Farm in New York.

DR. DANZIG, b. h. 1982, Danzig—Dr. Feel Great, by Dr. Fager. 16-1-7-1, $50,604. Winner. Sire of at least four stakes winners, including Danzig Foxxy Woman and Medical History; in 2004 in Iowa.

EARTHMOVER, 1981 b. h., Chieftain—Runette, by Run Fool Run. 26-8-3-3, $145,408. Stakes winner, set a six-furlong track record of 1:08 at Hialeah Park in 1985; euthanized due to a leg injury, on April 3, 2004, at Seven Oaks Farm in Mt. Gilead, Ohio.

EASTERN ECHO, 1988 b. h., Damascus—Wild Applause, by Northern Dancer. 3-3-0-0, $93,960. Won the 1990 Futurity S. (G1). Sire of more than 20 stakes winners, including Grade 1 winners Buddy Gil and Swiss Yodeler; of a heart attack, on December 14, 2004, at Shamrock Farms in Woodbine, Maryland.

EASTOVER COURT, gr. h. 1991, Seattle Slew—Heavenly Cause, by *Grey Dawn II. Unraced. Sire of at least four stakes winners, including $527,897 earner Confucius Say; of pneumonia, in January 2004 at New Bolton Center in Pennsylvania.

EL ANGELO, 1992 dk. b. or br. h., El Gran Senor—Angela Serra (GB), by Arctic Tern. 47-8-6-10, $696,065. Won the 1997 American H. (G2). His first foals were two-year-olds of 2004; of colic, on January 31, 2004, in Indiana.

ELLE SEULE, 1983 ch. m., Exclusive Native—Fall Aspen, by Pretense. 16-3-4-2, $101,478. French Group 2 winner. Dam of four stakes winners, including 1994 Airlie Coolmore Irish One Thousand Guineas (Ire-G1) winner Mehthaaf and Group 1 winner Elnadim; of a ruptured aneurysm, on February 21, 2005, at Shadwell Farm in Lexington.

ELLIODOR, 1977 b. h., Lyphard—Ellida, by Crepello. 4-1-1-1, $15,969. Sire of at least 50 stakes winners, including South African champions Model Man, Special Parade, Dollar Fortune, and Warning Zone (SAf); euthanized due to infirmities of old age, in July 2004 at Daytona Stud, South Africa.

EMPRESS CLUB (ARG), 1988 dk. b. or br. m., Farnesio (Arg)—Elysee, by El Gran Capitan (Arg). 26-16-2-1, $1,155,235. South African Horse of the Year in 1992, champion at two, three, and four in South Africa. Dam of stakes winner Azouz Pasha; on December 19, 2004, at Gainesway Farm in Lexington.

EMPTY NEST, 1978 dk. b. or br. m., No Robbery—Everglow, by Jacinto. 22-1-4-3, $12,330. Dam of Grade 3 winners King's Nest and Mister S. M.; due to infirmities of age, on September 13, 2004, at Glade Valley Farms in Frederick, Maryland.

EPITOME, 1985 b. m., Summing—Honest and True, by Mr. Leader. 14-5-5-1, $631,755. Champion juvenile filly in 1987. Won Breeders' Cup Juvenile Fillies (G1). Dam of three stakes winners, including 1995 United Arab Emirates highweight Faltaat, Essence of Dubai, and Danjur; of a ruptured artery, on November 12, 2004, at Elmwood Farm in Versailles, Kentucky.

ESTRAPADE, 1980 ch. m., *Vaguely Noble—Klepto, by No Robbery. 30-12-5-5, $1,937,142. Champion grass female of 1986. Won five Grade 1 stakes, including the 1986 Arlington Million. Dam of stakes winner Rice; of a heart attack, on February 25, 2005, at Hill 'n' Dale Farm in Lexington.

EVENING KRIS, 1985 dk. b. or br. h., Kris S.—Evening Y'all, by Double Hitch. 42-5-9-2, $578,773. Won the 1988 Jerome H. (G1). Sire of at least three stakes winners, including New Jersey-bred champion Jersey Giant; on October 11, 2004, at Walnford Stud in Allentown, New Jersey.

EVIL ELAINE, 1984 b. m., Medieval Man—Distinctive Elaine, by Distinctive. 30-4-4-3, $119,729. Won the 1986 Coronado S. Dam of 1997 Horse of the Year Favorite Trick; of laminitis, on March 15, 2004, at Rood & Riddle Equine Hospital in Lexington.

EXCELLENT MEETING, 1996 b. m., General Meeting—Fitted Crown, by Chief's Crown. 20-8-5-3, $1,402,396. Winner of four Grade 1 stakes, including the 1999 Santa Anita Oaks (G1); during colic surgery, on March 23, 2004, at Rood & Riddle Hospital in Lexington.

EXCITING STORY, 1997 ch. h., Diablo—Appealing Story, by Valid Appeal. 25-7-6-1, $911,270. Canadian juvenile champion male in 1999. Won the 2001 Metropolitan H. (G1); euthanized due to a degenerative joint condition, in July 2004 at Lane's End Texas in Hempstead.

Exclusive Ribot, 1972 b. h., *Ribot—Exclusive, by Shut Out. 32-6-4-3, $43,974. Stakes-placed. Sire of six stakes winners, including millionaire Grade 2 winner Men's Exclusive; of heart failure, on August 8, 2004, at Dormello II Stud in Decatur, Texas.

FABULOUS DANCER, 1976 b. h., Northern Dancer—Last of the Line, by The Axe II. 8-4-1-1, $124,773. French Group 3 winner. France's leading sire of 1992. Sire of 53 stakes winners and five champions, including Fabulous La Fouine; on June 28, 2004, at Haras d'Etreham, France.

FAIR SALINIA (IRE), 1975 dk. b. or br. m., Petingo—Fair Arabella, by Chateaugay. 8-4-1-0, $268,971. Won the 1978 Epsom Oaks (Eng-G1), Yorkshire Oaks (Eng-G1). Dam of three stakes winners, including Group 3 winner Perfect Vintage; of old age, on March 31, 2004, at Haras de Vieux Pont, France.

FARMER JACK, 1996 b. g., Alflora—Cheryls Pet, by General Ironside. 27-10-3-1, $419,744. Multiple English stakes winner; of a probable heart attack after morning training on March 16, 2005, in England.

FEU D' ENFER, 1980 dk. b. or br. h., Tentam—La Bourrasque, by Victoria Park. 115-14-21-13, $271,245.

Won the 1983 Queenston S. Sire of 14 stakes winners, including Work Visa and Win a Feu; in 2004, in Canada.

FIELD NYMPH, 1977 b. m., Northfields—Conduct Unbecoming, by Silly Season. Unraced. Dam of Australasian Group 1 winners Field Dancer and Just a Dancer; euthanized due to infirmities of old age, on July 16, 2004, at Windsor Park Stud in Cambridge, New Zealand.

FLYING CONTINENTAL, 1986 ch. h., Flying Paster—Continental Girl, by Transworld. 51-12-15-10, $1,815,938. Won the 1990 Jockey Club Gold Cup (G1). Sire of more than 15 stakes winners, including millionaire Continental Red; died in his paddock, on November 8, 2004, at Harris Farms in Coalinga, California.

FOGOSO NOV, 2000 dk. b. or br. c., Romanov (Ire)—Foy, by Verbatim. 9-2-1-0, $28,234. Won the 2003 Polla de Potrillos (Arg-G1) (Argentine Two Thousand Guineas); euthanized after fracturing his right foreleg in a race, on March 2, 2004, at Hipodromo la Plata, Argentina.

FORMAL HUNCH, 2003 ch. f., Solid Hunch—Joyce's Last Love, by Formal Dinner. Of Eastern equine encephalitis, on September 24, 2004, in Wilmington, Massachusetts.

FOURSTARS ALLSTAR, b. h. 1988, Compliance—Broadway Joan, by Bold Arian. Won the 1991 Airlie Coolmore Irish Two Thousand Guineas (Ire-G1). Sire of three stakes winners; euthanized after breaking his neck in an accident, in February 2005, at Newmarket.

FREE HOUSE, 1994 gr. or ro. h., Smokester—Fountain Lake, by Vigors. 22-9-5-3, $3,178,971. Won the 1997 Santa Anita Derby (G1), '99 Santa Anita H. (G1). Sire of 2004 Fantasy S. (G2) winner House of Fortune; of injuries from a farm accident, on July 20, 2004, at Vessels Stallion Farm in Bonsal, California.

GA HAI, 1971 b.h., Determine—Goyala, by Goyamo. 43-13-2-5, $257,548. Won the 1975 and '76 Arcadia H. (G3). Sire of seven stakes winners; of old age, on March 17, 2004, at Reigle Heir Farms in Grantville, Pennsylvania.

Gallantsky, 1976 b. h., Nijinsky II—Queen Pot, by Buckpasser. 16-1-0-3, $30,701. Stakes-placed in France. Sire of at least 32 stakes winners, six champions, and United States Grade 1 winner Puerto Madero (Chi). Among the leading broodmare sires in Chile; of natural causes, in April 2004 at Haras Santa Olga, Chile.

GENERAL ASSEMBLY, 1976 ch. h., Secretariat—Exclusive Dancer, by Native Dancer. 17-7-6-1, $463,245. Won the 1979 Travers S. (G1). Sire of more than 30 stakes winners, including Hong Kong champion Steady Flame; euthanized due to heart and circulatory problems, in March 2005, at Gestut Olympia in Germany.

GENERAL MINOLTA, 1999 br. g., Nediym (Ire)—Minolta, by Luskin Star. 33-5-6-4, $223,518. Multiple stakes winner in Australia; after breaking down in the Grafton Cup (Aus-G3), on July 15, 2004, at Grafton racecourse in Australia.

GHADEER, 1978 b. h., Lyphard—Swanilda, by Habitat. 17-3-3-2, $68,935. Group 3 winner in Italy. Leading sire and broodmare sire in Brazil. Sire of more than 75 stakes winners. Broodmare sire of ten champions, including Riboletta (Brz); of heart failure, on February 10, 2005, at Haras Fazenda Mondesir in Brazil.

GILDED LILLY, 1979 ch. m., What a Pleasure—Luquillo, by *Princequillo. 25-4-3-4, $50,235. Dam of 14 winners from 16 starters, including 1992 champion juvenile male Gilded Time; from a ruptured aorta, on February 12, 2004, at Castleton Lyons Farm in Lexington.

GLOWING TRIBUTE, 1973 b. m., Graustark—Admiring, by Hail to Reason. 24-9-3-2, $230,819. Won the 1976 and '77 Sheepshead Bay H. (G2). Broodmare of the Year in 1993. Dam of seven stakes winners, including 1993 Kentucky Derby (G1) winner Sea Hero and Grade 1 winner Hero's Honor; of colic, on August 5, 2004, at Waggoner Farm in Lexington.

GOLDEN VOYAGER, 1987 b. h., Mr. Prospector—La Voyageuse, by Tentam. 14-3-3-3, $96,875. Sire of at least 16 stakes winners and seven champions, including 1999 Chilean Horse of the Year Crystal House (Chi); following colic surgery, on April 8, 2005, at Haras Old Friends in Brazil.

GO WEST, 1995 ch. c., Seeking the Gold—West Turn, by Cox's Ridge. 23-3-5-1, $109,578. Half brother to Grade 1 millionaire West by West. $450,000 1996 Keeneland July selected sale yearling purchase; in 2004, in South Carolina.

GRATIAEN, 1997 b. h., Cure the Blues—Adorable Minister, by Deputy Minister. 32-7-2-1, $288,164. Won the 2000 Albany H. at Saratoga Race Course; after breaking down in a race on February 5, 2005, at Aqueduct in New York.

GREEN TEAM, 1999 b. g., Huddle Up—Scare Tactics, by Moscow Ballet. 39-10-10-5, $620,827. Won the 2003 California Cup Sprint H; euthanized after fracturing a sesamoid in the Padua Stables Sprint S. on January 29, 2005, at Santa Anita Park in California.

GRENZEN, 1975 ch. m., Grenfall—My Poly, by Cyclotron. 24-8-7-3, $346,490. Won the 1978 Santa Susana S. (G2). Dam of Grade 1 winner Twilight Agenda; grandam of 2003 Irish highweight Refuse to Bend (Ire) and 1990 Belmont S. (G1) winner Go and Go (Ire); in July 2004 at Eaton Farms in Lexington.

GUINEVERE'S FOLLY, 1976 b. m., Round Table—Lodge, by Bold Lad. 14-4-1-3, $60,982. Stakes winner. Dam of stakes winner Lady Baiul, grandam of 1991 Prix de l'Arc de Triomphe (Fr-G1) winner Suave Dancer; of old age, on March 19, 2004, at Brickenhill Farm in Richmond, Kentucky.

HAIL THE RUCKUS, b. h. 1983, Bold Ruckus—Morning Miss, by Hail the Prince. 25-8-8-3, $274,691. Won the 1988 Suffolk Downs Sprint H. (G3). Sire of 1999 Canadian champion juvenile male Gomtuu; in 2004, in Canada.

Heaven's Wish, 1992 ch. h., Halo—Wishing Mood, by Coastal. 30-6-7-4, $193,674. Graded stakes-placed in Canada. Sire of at least eight winners; in January 2004 in Florida.

HEDONIST, 1995 dk. b. or br. m., Alydeed—Play all Day, by Steady Growth. 4-3-0-0, $200,400. Won the 1998 Santa Anita Oaks (G1); in 2004.

HERE WE COME, 1988 ch. h., Mr. Prospector—Minstress, by The Minstrel. Unraced. Among the leading Oklahoma sires. Sire of more than 15 stakes winners, including Toll Booth Willie and Mesquite Cowboy; on September 24, 2004, at B-T Ranch in Collinsville, Oklahoma.

HIGHEST, 1999 b. h., Selkirk—Pearl Kite, by Silver Hawk. 14-3-6-1, $434,706. Won the 2003 Dubai City of Gold S. (UAE-G3), second in the '02 St. Leger S. (Eng-G1); euthanized after rupturing a suspensory ligament in the Gold Cup (Eng-G1) on June 17, 2004, at Ascot, England.

Hook Call (Brz), 1995 b. g., Exile King—Yarrow, by Icecapade. 44-15-7-4, $309,727. Group 1-placed in Brazil, Grade 3-placed in the U.S.; after breaking down in a race at Philadelphia Park, on December 21, 2004, in Pennsylvania.

HOPELESSLY DEVOTED, 2001 b. f., Storm Creek—Silver Treego, by Silver Buck. 16-6-4-0, $499,385. Won the 2004 Calder Oaks; collapsed during the running of the Marshua's River S., on January 9, 2005, at Gulfstream Park in Florida.

HOPE OF GLORY, 1972 b. m., Mr. Leader—Daizel, by Manteau. 35-9-3-5, $168,421. Won the 1974 Alcibiades S. (G3) and '76 Falls City H. (G3). Dam of nine winners; of a stroke, on October 13, 2004, at Our Mims Retirement Haven in Paris, Kentucky.

HOT SHOT BROTHER, 1999 b. g., Key Business—Cold Fusion, by Protos. 16-6-5-1, $134,387. Won the 2003 A. J. Scahill S. (Aus-G3); after hemorrhaging during a workout on November 2, 2004, at Ascot Racecourse, Australia.

HOUSEBUSTER, 1987 dk. b. or br. h., Mt. Livermore—Big Dreams, by Great Above. 22-15-3-1, $1,229,696. Two-time champion sprinter. Leading sire in Virginia and West Virginia. Sire of more than 30 stakes winners, including champion Electronic Unicorn; of unknown causes, on May 15, 2005, in West Virginia.

Huckster, 1980 dk. b. or br. h., Mr. Prospector—Land Girl, by Sir Ivor. 60-8-6-14, $234,508. Stakes-placed. Sire of five stakes winners; euthanized due to infirmities of age, on April 17, 2005, at Sue Hubbard and Associates Farm in Paso Robles, California.

HUM ALONG, 1989 dk. b. or br. m., Fappiano—Minstress, by The Minstrel. 2-0-0-1, $4,680. Dam of champion Storm Song and $6.8-million record Keeneland September yearling Tasmanian Tiger; from complications of foaling, on February 23, 2005, at Ashford Stud in Versailles, Kentucky.

Hyde Park (Chi), 1997 b. h., Rich Man's Gold—Granita, by Roy. 10-2-3-0, $32,533. Group 1-placed in Chile; in a barn fire in March 2004 near Louisville.

IDABEL, 1986 b. m., Mr. Prospector—Impetuous Gal, by Briartic. 8-4-1-2, $145,835. Won the 1990 Ark-La-Tex H. (G3). Sire of seven stakes winners, including 1998 Hungarian champion juvenile Shine My Boots; of laminitis, on November 12, 2004, at Pegasus Farm in Bismarck, Arkansas.

IFINEEDYAILLCALLYA, 1996 ch. g., Al Sabin—Allegro Brillante, by Caro (Ire). 62-9-5-13, $261,884. Won the 2000 Best of Ohio Endurance S. and three other stakes; euthanized after breaking down in a race on August 30, 2004, at Mountaineer Race Track in West Virginia.

IMAGINARY LADY, 1986 b. m., Marfa—Dream Harder, by Hard Work. 12-7-3-0, $574,720. Won the 1989 Santa Anita Oaks (G1) and Black-Eyed Susan S. (G2); euthanized on July 16, 2004, after fracturing a leg in her paddock at Spendthrift Farm in Lexington.

I'ma Hell Raiser, 1977 ro. h., Raise a Native—I'm for Mama, by I'm For More. 10-5-2-2, $135,184. Grade 2-placed. Sire of 20 stakes winners, including Littlebitapleasure; euthanized in July 2004 at Traders Rest Farm in Carencro, Louisiana.

INCHMURRIN, 1985 b. m., Lomond—On Show, by Welsh Pageant. 12-6-1-0, $217,514. Italian highweight in 1988. Won the 1988 Child S. (Eng-G2). Dam of three stakes winners, including Group 3 winner and successful French sire Inchinor (GB); of cancer, on July 26, 2004, at Hascombe Stud, England.

INCITATUS (BAR), 1993 ch. h., Nosferatu—Balage, by Horage. 64-19-10-8, $698,505. Won the 2000 King Edward Breeders' Cup H. (Can-G2); of an apparent heart attack after a race on September 25, 2004, at Hastings Park, Canada.

INDIGENOUS, 1993 b. g., Marju—Sea Port, by Averof. 78-16-8-12, $5,124,919. Hong Kong Horse of the Year in 1999, all-time leading Hong Kong earner, twice won the Hong Kong Gold Cup (HK-G1) (1998-'99); of an unidentified illness, on August 8, 2004, at Tuen Mun Public Riding School, Hong Kong.

INDYGAL, 2001 ch. f., A.P. Indy—Garimpeiro, by Mr. Prospector. 3-1-0-0, $29,660. Half sister to Grade 1-winning millionaire Geri; euthanized after breaking down in a race, on May 29, 2004, at Churchill Downs.

IN HAND, 2000 dk. b. or br. g., Belong to Me—Summer Fantasy, by Summer Squall. 19-5-1-2, $222,199. Won the 2004 Greenwood Cup H. Euthanized on January 30, 2005, after breaking down in the Mac Diarmida H. (G3), at Gulfstream Park.

INTERSTELLAR, 1986 ch. h., Star Way—Gelu, by Agricola. Won the 1990 Canterbury Guineas (Aus-G1). Sire of millionaire and multiple Australian Group 1 winner Yippyio; in May 2005, at Copenhagen Stud in Victoria, Australia.

IN THE WINGS (GB), 1986 b. h., Sadler's Wells—High Hawk (Ire), by Shirley Heights. 11-7-1-0, $1,562,335. Won the 1990 Breeders' Cup Turf (G1), Group 1 winner in England, France. Sire of more than 50 stakes winners and four champions, including Singspiel (Ire); of laminitis, on April 3, 2004, at Kildangan Stud, Ireland.

IRISH RIVER (Fr), 1976 ch. h., Riverman—Irish Star, by *Klairon. 12-10-0-1, $622,739. Twice champion in France. Won the 1979 Poule d' Essai des Poulains (Fr-G1) (French Two Thousand Guineas). Among the leading sires in France and the United States. Sire of more than 85 stakes winners, including champions Hatoof and Paradise Creek. Broodmare sire of more than 110 stakes winners; on April 25, 2004, at Gainesway in Lexington.

I TWO STEP TOO, 1993 dk. b. or br. g., Spook Dance—Augustar, by Star Envoy. 53-7-13-13, $24,538. One of the horses who played Seabiscuit in the movie of that name; euthanized due to a rare nasal tumor, on March 7, 2005, at the Kentucky Horse Park.

IVORY POACHER, 1985 gr. g., Buckfinder—White Knuckles, by Cloudy Dawn. 9-3-1-1, $43,200. Won the 1993 Maryland Hunt Cup S.; euthanized due to complications from a kidney tumor, on August 4, 2004, in Maryland.

JADE ROBBERY, 1987 dk. b. or br. h., Mr. Prospector—Number, by Nijinsky II. 7-2-2-1, $246,845. Won the 1989 Grand Criterium (Fr-G1). Among the leading sires in Japan. Sire of 14 stakes winners, including champion Yamakatsu Suzuran; after abdominal surgery, in May 2004 at Shadai Farm, Japan.

JAIR DU COCHET, 1997 b. g., Rahotep—Dilaure, by Rose Laurel. 23-13-4-2, $428,043. Winner of eight jump stakes in England, including the 2004 Pillar Prop-

erty Stp.; after breaking his right hind leg in a workout in early March 2004, at Le Mathes, France.

JIVA COOLIT, 1972 b. g., Jussive—Hope Against Hope, by Mt. Hope. 113-36-32-26, $218,292. Won the 1977 Valley Sprint Championship H. Set four track records from four to six furlongs; in May 2005, in Virginia.

JOLYPHA, 1989 dk. b. or br. m., Lyphard—Navajo Princess, by Drone. 10-4-2-1, $988,691. European highweight at three. Won the 1992 Prix de Diane (Fr-G1) (French Oaks); of complications from foaling, on March 26, 2005, at Juddmonte Farms in Lexington.

J. R.'S HORIZON, 1987 dk. b. or br. g., Caveat—Metrica, by Holy War. 51-7-10-5, $282,570. Won the 1991 John B. Campbell H. (G3); after being hit by lightning, on May 14, 2005, at a farm near Middleburg, Virginia.

KALFAARI, 1997 dk. b. or br. g., Alfaari—Kellahan, by Sexist. 24-15-3-2, $232,964. Won eight Canadian stakes, including the 2003 Hastings Speed H.; of a heart attack, on May 11, 2004, at Assiniboia Downs, Manitoba.

KATIES (Ire), 1981 dk. b. or br. m., Nonoalco—Mortefontaine, by Polic. 10-4-2-1, $152,029. Champion three-year-old filly in England in 1984. Won the 1984 Goffs Irish One Thousand Guineas (Ire-G1). Dam of five stakes winners, including three-time Japanese champion and $7-million earner Hishi Amazon; euthanized on August 20, 2004, at Taylor Made Farm in Nicholasville, Kentucky.

KENVAIN, 1990 gr. h., Kenmare—Dancelot, by Vain. Highweighted older horse on the 1994 Australian Free Handicap for sprinters. Won the 1994 Oakleigh Plate (Aus-G1). Sire of at least nine stakes winners; of intestinal failure, in October 2004, at Mungrup Stud in Australia.

KHATANGO, 1979 b. h., Nijinsky II—Penny Flight, by Damascus. 24-6-4-2, $184,411. Won the 1983 Dixie H. (G2). Sire of at least nine stakes winners, including 2003 Brazilian Horse of the Year Gene de Campeao (Brz); of natural causes, in May 2004 at Haras Bandeirantes, Brazil.

Kipper Kelly, 1987 b. h., Valid Appeal—Plum Ten, by Tentam. 11-3-4-2, $94,619. Graded stakes-placed. Sire of 11 stakes winners, including millionaire Grade 1 winner Kelly Kip and Grade 3 winner Miss Inquisitive; of a heart attack, on September 11, 2004, at Indian Ridge Farm in Duson, Louisiana.

KRIS, 1976 ch. h., Sharpen Up (GB)—Doubly Sure (GB), by Reliance II. 16-14-0-0, $405,373. Twice champion miler in England (1979-'80). Sire of more than 80 stakes winners and five champions, including Oh So Sharp (Ire), All Gong (GB), and Unite (Ire). Broodmare sire of more than 80 stakes winners including Doyen, Epalo (Ger), Kiri's Clown; of heart failure, on November 18, 2004, at Plantation Stud in Newmarket, England.

LAKE WILLIAM, 1996 dk. b. or br. h., Salt Lake—Sol de Terre, by Mr. Prospector. 21-7-3-3, $320,091. Won the 2001 San Simeon H. (G3); of an ulcerated colon, in August 2004 at Chino Equine Medical Center, in Chino, California.

LANCE CORPORAL, 1996 b. g., Military Plume—Beading, by Lyphard. 39-8-5-4, $182,212. Won the 2003 Australian Grand National Steeplechase; euthanized after fracturing his pelvis in a race at Cheltenham, on March 5, 2005, in Australia.

LASER LIGHT, 1979 b. h., Majestic Light—Peaceful Union, by Royal Union. 13-2-3-2, $291,624. Won the 1981 Remsen S. (G1), second in the 1982 Kentucky Derby (G1). Sire of two winners from six foals; euthanized due to infirmities of age, on February 10, 2005, at Live Oak Stud in Ocala.

LILANDE, 1993 ch. m., Marscay—Ladyeri, by Salieri. 3-0-0-0, $0. Dam of multiple Australian Group 1 winner Defier; euthanized as a result of injuries sustained in a paddock accident, in February 2005, at Arrowfield Stud in Australia.

LION CAVERN, 1989 ch. h., Mr. Prospector—Secrettame, by Secretariat. Brother to Gone West. 16-5-4-3, $420,701. Won the 1993 True North H. (G2). Sire of more than 15 stakes winners, including European highweights Crimplene (Ire) and Silent Tribute; of colic, in July 2004 at Elia Stud Farms, Greece.

Lion Hunter, 1992 gr. h., Danehill—Pure of Heart, by Godswalk. 8-3-2-0, $90,428, Group 1-placed; Australia's leading first-season sire of 2001-'02; euthanized on February 4, 2004, at Oaklands Stud, Australia.

LORD BALLINA, b. h. 1979, Bletchingly—Sunset Girl, by Star Affair. Multiple Group 1 winner in Australia in 1985. Sire of more than 35 stakes winners, including three-time New Zealand champion Lord Tridan and four Australasian highweights; of a heart attack, on July 7, 2004, at Ardsley Stud, New Zealand.

LORD CARSON, 1992 b. h., Carson City—Bedgay's Lady, by Lord Gaylord. 27-12-5-0, $654,742. Won the 1996 Boojum H. (G2). Sire of seven stakes winners; of head injuries suffered in a breeding shed accident, on March 16, 2005, at Tommy Town Thoroughbreds in Santa Ynez, California.

LORD OF ALL, 1980 dk. b. or br. h., Seattle Slew—Twixt, by Restless Native. Unplaced. Sire of ten stakes winners, including McClure Mountain and Dancing Frona; in his sleep, on June 6, 2004, at St. Hilaire Thoroughbreds in Yakima, Washington.

Lost Opportunity, b. h. 1986, Mr. Prospector—Squander, by Buckpasser. 19-4-2-7, $145,910. Graded stakes-placed. Sire of Ecuadorian champion Espartaco and stakes winners Day Hunter and Fjr's Winner; in 2004, in Oklahoma.

MACHIAVELLIAN, 1987 dk. b. or br. h., Mr. Prospector—Coup de Folie, by Halo. 7-4-1-0, $355,790. European highweight in 1989. Won the 1989 Prix Morny (Fr-G1). Leading 2002 sire in United Arab Emirates. Sire of more than 50 stakes winners, including 2002 UAE Horse of the Year Street Cry (Ire); of laminitis, on June 25, 2004, at Dalham Hall Stud, England.

MAJOR FORCE, 1996 b. h., Woodman—Ready for Action, by Riverman. 11-5-0-1, $119,604. Group 3 winner in Ireland; in 2004.

MARKET GARDEN, 2000 b. m., Bold Badgett—Margaret's Native, by He's Our Native. 35-6-5-8, $363,958. Won the 2004 Pio Pico S.; collapsed and died after finishing unplaced in the B. Thoughtful S., on April 24, 2005, at Hollywood Park in California.

Matchlite, 1983 dk. b. or br. h., Clever Trick—Light Up My Life, by Sir Ivor. 11-3-0-1, $49,769. Stakes-placed. Leading Michigan sire. Sire of 14 stakes winners, including Pongo Boy and Match Trick; of an aneurysm, on October 31, 2004, in Michigan.

MAYBE JACK, 1993 b. g., Classic Account—Hester Lou, by Summing. 122-35-17-17, $534,715. Won the 1997 Bruce G. Smith Memorial S. at Suffolk Downs;

after finishing fourth in an $8,000 claiming race on January 22, 2005, at Gulfstream Park.

MILLEMIX, 2001 gr. c., Linamix—Milesime, by Riverman. 6-3-2-0, $175,195. Won the 2004 Prix Greffulhe (Fr-G2); euthanized after sustaining multiple leg fractures during a gallop, on May 25, 2004, at Chantilly.

MISS SNOWFLAKE, 1978 b. m., *Snow Sporting—Bold Jewel, by Any Time Now. 5-1-1-1, $2,308. Dam of 1986 champion three-year-old male Snow Chief and Group 2 winner Mujaazif; from complications of foaling, on April 2, 2004, at Knockgriffin Farm in Lexington.

MISTER MONET, 2001 b. c., Peintre Celebre—Breyani, by Commanche Run. 8-5-1-1, $213,357. Won the 2004 Prix Guillaume d' Ornano (Fr-G2), Rose of Lancaster S. (Eng-G3); after breaking down in the Champion S. (Eng-G1), on October 16, 2004, at Newmarket, England.

MISWAKI, 1978 ch. h., Mr. Prospector—Hopespringseternal, by Buckpasser. 13-6-4-1, $232,320. Won the 1980 Prix de la Salamandre (Fr-G1). Leading broodmare sire in England (2001) and France ('03). Sire of more than 95 stakes winners, including 2001 English and Irish Broodmare of the Year Urban Sea. Broodmare sire of more than 110 stakes winners and eight champions; on December 17, 2004, at Walmac Farm in Lexington.

MONEY BY CHOICE, 1987 dk. b. or br. m., Knights Choice—Pamlisa's Delight, by Drone. 40-11-9-6, $206,040. Washington champion older mare of 1991. Dam of stakes winner Kermit's Choice; in December 2004, in Washington.

Mr. Integrity, 1987 b. h., Mr. Prospector—Balletomane, by Nijinsky II. 10-4-1-0, $110,550. Stakes-placed. Sire of four stakes winners, including Wolfwithintegrity; in June 2004 at E.A. Ranches in Santa Ysabel, California.

MR. SHAWKLIT, ch. h. 1991, Afleet—Shawklit, by Groshawk. 25-8-5-0, $323,395. Won the 1995 Westchester H. (G3). Sire of stakes winner Courvoisier; in 2004, in Louisiana.

MULTIPLICATION, 2001 ch. c., Subordination—Tricky Move, by Tricky Creek. 4-2-1-0, $102,740. Won the 2004 Mike Lee S.; of an apparent heart attack after a workout, on July 10, 2004, at Belmont Park.

MY BEST VALENTINE, 1990 b. h., Try My Best—Pas de Calais, by Pas de Seul. 73-9-12-6, $295,310. Won the 1998 Prix de l'Abbaye de Longchamp (Fr-G1). Sire of three winners; of an apparent heart attack, on January 24, 2004, at Allevamento Fattoria Renaccino, Italy.

MY PRINCE CHARMING, 1983 ch. h., Sir Wimborne—Maid in Waiting, by Stage Door Johnny. 43-7-7-5, $363,583. Won the 1986 Fountain of Youth S. (G2). Leading New Jersey sire of 1999. Sire of stakes winner Mr. Denim; in February 2005, in New Jersey.

MYRENE, 2002 ch. f., Gold Fever—Mrs. Magnum, by Northjet (Ire). 3-1-0-0, $15,083. Maiden special winner by 16¾ lengths; after breaking down in the Silver Spur Breeders' Cup S., on October 1, 2004, at Lone Star Park, in Texas.

MY TURBULENT MISS, 1976 b. m., My Dad George—Turbulent Miss, by *Petare. Unraced. Dam of six stakes winners, including 1989 Breeders' Cup Turf (G1) winner Prized and Grade 2 winner Exploit; on May 13, 2005, at Our Mims Retirement Haven at Ahwenasa Farm in Paris, Kentucky.

NARAINGANG (BRZ), 1998 b. h., Gulf Star (Brz)—Grain Lady, by Greinton (GB). 22-8-1-1, $85,271. Group 1 winner in Brazil. Stakes winner in North America; euthanized due to complications from a fever, in August 2004 at Longfield Farm in Goshen, Kentucky.

NATIONAL CURRENCY, 1999 b. h., National Assembly—Enchanted Dollar, by Spend a Buck. 15-10-2-3, $490,210. Two-time South African champion; of toxemia and laminitis, on March 11, 2004, in Dubai.

NATIONAL TREASURE, 1993 dk. b. or br. m., Recusant—Ivory Treasure, by Sir Ivor. 36-9-3-3, $280,440. Won the 1998 Beaugay H. (G3); of foaling complications, on May 2, 2005, at Windfields Farm in Canada.

NAVEL ACADEMY, 1995 b. h., Slewpy—Summertime Silver, by True Colors. 20-7-3-4, $302,398. Won the 1998 Reb's Policy H., 2000 Aprisa H.; in 2004, in California.

NEW COLONY, 1983 dk. b. or br. h., French Colonial—Newfoundland, by Prince John. 63-9-11-14, $408,369. Won division 2 of the 1987 Canadian Turf H. (G2). Sire of more than 15 stakes winners, including Brazilian champions Gorylla (Brz) and Belo Colony; from a lung infection, on June 5, 2004, at Haras Valente, Brazil.

NIMBLE FEET, 1985 b. m., Danzig—Nimble Folly, by Cyane. 8-1-0-3, $11,106. Dam of four stakes winners, including graded/group winners Forest Gazelle and Eltish; of complications from foaling, on March 19, 2005, at Juddmonte Farms in Lexington.

NOPRO BLAMA, 1984 dk. b. or br. m., Dimaggio—In Prime Time, by Boldnesian. Unraced. Dam of 1994 California champion Soviet Problem; on April 12, 2004, at Heaven Trees Farm in Lexington.

NORTHERN TASTE, 1971 ch. h., Northern Dancer—Lady Victoria, by Victoria Park. 23-5-3-4, $154,177. Won the 1974 Prix de la Foret (Fr-G1). Nine-time leading sire in Japan, four-time leading broodmare sire. Sire of more than 45 stakes winners and six champions. Broodmare sire of more than 80 stakes winners and 11 champions; of old age, on December 11, 2004, at Shadai Stallion Station, Japan.

OLD COMRADE, 1997 br. g., Old Spice—Belgravia, by Ksar. 22-6-6-2, $935,276. Won the 2002 Australian Cup (Aus-G1) and three other Group 1 events; euthanized due to an infection from a cut on his hock, on May 3, 2004, in Australia.

OSCEOLA, 2001 ch. f., American Gipsy—Speed Daughter, by Rahy. 10-4-0-0, $35,013. Won the 2005 Diana S. (Brz-G1); of a heart attack, in March 2005, during a workout, in Rio de Janeiro, Brazil.

PARADE MARSHAL, 1983 dk. b. or br. h., Caro (Ire)—Stepping High, by No Robbery. 17-4-3-2, $184,644. Won the 1986 Governor's Cup H. Sire of more than 25 stakes winners, including two South American champions and United States Grade 1 winner Star Parade (Arg); of old age, in October 2004 at Haras La Esperanza, Argentina.

Paragon Queen, 2002 ch. f., Lord Carson—Storm Struck, by Storm Bird. 7-1-4-0, $85,540. Second in the Debutante S. (G3); after breaking down in the Sorority S., on September 4, 2004, at Monmouth Park.

Pato, 1982 b. m., High Top—Patosky, by Skymaster. 24-4-0-0, $22,373. Stakes-placed in England. Dam of European highweights Classic Cliche and My Emma; euthanized due to infirmities of age, in November 2004, in Newmarket, England.

Pennant Fever, 1989 dk. b. or br. m., Seattle Slew—Letty's Pennant, by Bold Forbes. 15-3-3-1, $87,222. Grade 3-placed. Dam of Grade 1 winner Raging Fever and Grade 3 winner Stormin Fever; of laminitis, on February 24, 2004, at Kentucky Equine Sports Medicine and Rehabilitation Center in Versailles, Kentucky.

PERSIAN PUNCH, 1993 ch. g., Persian Heights—Rum Cay, by Our Native. 63-20-8-11, $1,539,149. Two-time European champion stayer (2001, '03); of a heart attack 100 yards before the finish of the Sagaro S. (Eng-G3), on April 28, 2004, at Ascot, England.

PETTIBONE PRINCE, 1986 b. h., Brent's Prince—Pettibone Lass, by East Indian. 20-2-1-1, $32,503. Won the 1988 Ohio Graduate S. Sire of six winners from ten starters; in late December 2004 at Four Winds Farm in Lexington.

POHAVE, 1998 gr. or ro. g., Holy Bull—Trail Robbery, by Alydar. 27-5-9-4, $576,240. Won the 2004 Triple Bend Breeders' Cup Invitational H. (G1); euthanized after foundering while recovering from liver surgery, on April 28, 2005, in Dubai.

POINT PRINCE, 1999 dk. b. or br. g., Youmade-yourpoint—Princess of Note, by Notebook. 14-4-1-4, $156,080. Won the 2003 Appleton H. (G2); of a viral infection and pleurisy, in December 2004, in Florida.

POLE POSITION, 1976 ch. h., Draft Card—Miss Ooh La La, by Wallet Lifter. 35-16-7-4, $507,402. Won the 1979 San Felipe H. (G2). Leading sire in Saskatchewan, 1998-2001. Sire of more than 20 stakes winners, including Position Leader; euthanized on May 25, 2004, at Justanother Farm in Edmonton, Alberta.

PRECIOUS BEAUTY, 1981 wh. m., Jatullah—World O'Beauty, by Reverse. Unraced. A rare white Thoroughbred. Dam of the white winner Patchen Beauty; euthanized due to problems from an old injury, on May 21, 2004, at Patchen Wilkes Farm, in Lexington.

PRIMARILY, 1988 b. m., Lord At War (Arg)—Mostly, by *Grey Dawn II. 4-2-1-0, $63,036. Stakes winner. Canada's 2000 broodmare of the year. Dam of Canadian champions Primaly and Poetically, and sire Whiskey Wisdom; from injuries sustained in a fall, on March 30, 2005, at Adena Springs in Versailles, Kentucky.

PRIVATE ACCOUNT, 1976 b. h., Damascus—Numbered Account, by Buckpasser. 13-6-4-1, $339,396. Won the 1980 Widener H. (G1). Among America's leading sires. Sire of more than 60 stakes winners, including champions Personal Ensign and Inside Information. Broodmare sire of more than 80 stakes winners, including champion Aldebaran, My Flag; due to infirmities of old age, on November 25, 2004, at Claiborne Farm in Paris, Kentucky.

PRIVATE EMBLEM, 1999 dk. b. or br. h., Our Emblem—Merion Miss, by Halo. 24-7-3-5, $783,152. Won the 2002 Arkansas Derby (G2) and '04 Essex H. (G3); euthanized after fracturing both sesamoid bones in his left foreleg during the Kings Point H., on May 2, 2004, at Aqueduct.

PROSPECTOR'S MUSIC, 1989 dk. b. or br. h., Mr. Prospector—Minstrella, by The Minstrel. 3-0-0-0, $3,326. Sire of four stakes winners, including Grade 1 winner Gygistar; of a ruptured cecum, on December 10, 2004, in Washington, Oklahoma.

PUFFY SHIRT, 2000 ch. f., Gold Spring (Arg)—Norcliffe Dancer, by Ends Well. 5-3-0-1, $66,875; after breaking down in the Carousel S., on March 27, 2004, at Oaklawn Park.

PUZZLEMENT, 1999 b. h., Pine Bluff—Taine, by Sir Ivor. 22-6-3-5, $717,590. Won the 2003 Saratoga Breeders' Cup H. (G2) and '04 Hal's Hope H. (G3); euthanized due to a tendon infection, on June 16, 2004, at a Florida equine clinic.

QUICK NIP, 1999 ch. m., Whiskey Wisdom—Twist the Knife, by Crafty Prospector. 20-7-1-2, $115,400; of West Nile Virus, the first known racehorse to die from the disease at a California racetrack, on August 10, 2004, at Golden Gate Fields.

QUINTONS GOLD RUSH, 2001 ch. c., Wild Rush—Hollywood Gold, by Mr. Prospector. 10-3-1-0, $329,835. Won the 2004 Coolmore Lexington S. (G2); died while undergoing a biopsy, in mid-January 2005 at San Luis Rey Equine Hospital in Bonsall, California.

RAMBO DANCER, 1984 b. h., Northern Dancer—Fair Arabella, by Chateaugay. A former $2.6-million Keeneland July selected sale yearling purchase. 18-4-3-1, $160,556. Won the 1989 Red Smith H. (G2). Sire of 12 stakes winners, including European group winner Ramooz; after covering a mare, on September 20, 2004, at Summerhill Stud in KwaZulu-Natal, South Africa.

RAZYANA, 1981 b. m., His Majesty—Spring Adieu, by Buckpasser. 3-0-1-1, $2,412. Dam of four graded/group winners, including leading sire Danehill; after foaling, in February 2004 at Juddmonte Farm in Kentucky.

REAL SHADAI, 1979 dk. b. or br. h., Roberto—Desert Vixen, by In Reality. 8-2-2-2, $161,374. Won the 1982 Grand Prix de Deauville (Fr-G2). Leading 1993 sire in Japan. Sire of 18 stakes winners, including champion Shadai Kagura; of laminitis, on May 16, 2004, at Shadai Stallion Station, Japan.

REGAL REMARK, 1982 ch. h., Vice Regent—Male Strike, by Speak John. 19-7-5-2, $279,879. Won the 1985 Tampa Bay Derby (G3). Six-time leading sire in Alberta. Sire of more than 35 stakes winners; due to infirmities of age, on January 2, 2005, at Horizon Farm in Alberta.

REMEMBER SHEIKH, 1997 b. g., Sheikh Albadou (GB)—Remember the Day, by Settlement Day. 20-3-0-2, $227,495. Won the 2000 El Camino Real Derby (G3); of colic, in March 2004 in Ohio.

ROB 'N GIN, 1994 dk. b. or br. h., Farma Way—Windy Mindy, by Honey Jay. 30-9-7-5, $989,178. Won the 1997 Jersey Derby (G2). Sire of winners; of an unspecified injury, in August 2004, at Painted Desert Farm in Redmond, Oregon.

ROCK OPERA, 1999 ch. g., Royal Academy—Star de Rahy, by Rahy. 14-4-1-3, $248,800. Won a division of the 2002 Oceanside S.; after breaking down in a race, on June 5, 2004, at Hollywood Park.

ROO ART, 1982 b. h., Buckaroo—New Art, by *Ribot. 27-10-4-5, $1,011,723. Won the 1986 Suburban H. (G1), Philip H. Iselin H. (G1). Sire of eight stakes winners, including $723,895 earner Mary's Buckaroo; of kidney failure, on August 13, 2004, at Key Ranch in Salado, Texas.

ROOT BOY, 1988 b. h., Baederwood—Archdiocese, by King's Bishop. 32-12-5-8, $384,143. Won the 1993 Stephen Foster H. (G3). Sire of stakes winners Sneaks and Karen's Lullaby; euthanized after breaking an ankle in his paddock, on November 6, 2004, at Murmur Farm in Maryland.

ROSA MISS, 2001 dk. b. or br. f., Luhuk—Bebony, by Southern Halo. 2-2-0-0, $11,957. Won the 2004 Saturnino J. Unzue S. (Arg-G1); of laminitis, in May 2004, in Argentina.

ROSES FROM HEAVEN, 1991 ch. m., Mogambo—Roundup Rose, by Minnesota Mac. Unraced. Half sister to 1980 Preakness S. (G1) winner Codex. Dam of three winners; victim of a drive-by shooting, on September 29, 2004, at Shanbally Acres in Ocala.

ROSSARD (DEN), 1980 dk. b. or br. m., Glacial—Peas-Blossom, by Midsummer Night. Champion in Sweden and Denmark. Won the 1984 Flower Bowl H. (G1). Dam of stakes winner Unusual Heat; due to infirmities of age, on March 18, 2005, at Hunterton Farm in Paris, Kentucky.

ROUVRES (FR), 1999 dk. b. or br. h., Anabaa—Riziere, by Groom Dancer. 15-5-6-1, $427,826. Won the 2002 Prix Jean Prat (Fr-G1); from injuries sustained in a farm accident, in June 2004 at Greentree Stud, Ireland.

ROWDY ANGEL, 1979 b. m., Halo—Ramhyde, by Rambunctious. 13-0-2-3, $16,395. Dam of Grade 1 winners Pine Bluff and Demons Begone, grandam of 2000 Kentucky Derby (G1) winner Fusaichi Pegasus; of natural causes, on March 22, 2004, at Longfield Farm in Goshen, Kentucky.

Roy, 1983, b. h., Fappiano—Adlibber, by Never Bend. 17-3-2-3, $91,567. Grade 2-placed. Twice leading sire in Argentina (2001, '03). Leading 1994 sire in Chile. Sire of more than 110 stakes winners and 15 champions, including 1995-'96 Chilean Horse of the Year Gran Ducato; of a respiratory ailment, on January 7, 2004, at Haras La Esperanza, Argentina.

ROYAL CIRCLE, 1997 dk. b. or br. g., Palace Music—Dapple Up, by Black Zephyr. 47-5-8-6, $121,382. Won the 2002 Frank Underwood Quality Cup in Australia; in a racetrack paddock accident, in November 2004 in Australia.

ROYAL ROBERTO, 1979 dk. b. or br. h., Roberto—Princess Roycraft, by Royal Note. 27-9-2-2, $331,648. Sold in 1983 for a racing age auction record $2.2-million. Won a division of the 1982 Lexington S. (G2). Sire of 16 stakes winners, including 1997-'98 Argentine champion older mare Sea Girl; of a heart attack, in July 2004 at Hill 'N Dale Farm in Barrington, Illinois.

ROYAL SKI, 1974 ch. h., Raja Baba—Coz O'Nijinsky, by Involvement. 14-8-2-1, $324,895. Won the 1976 Laurel Futurity (G1). Sire of 20 stakes winners, including 1990 Japan champion three-year-old filly Agnes Flora and Grade 1 winners Snow Plow and Ski Goggle; on April 30, 2004, at the Japan Bloodhorse Breeders' Association's Nasu Stud Farm, Japan.

RULES OF WAR, 2001 b. g., Cromwell—Nannetta, by Falstaff. 9-3-1-1, $64,730. Won the 2004 Richmond Derby Trial H.; of a virus that caused him to founder, on May 5, 2005, in British Columbia.

SCENIC (IRE), 1986 dk. b. or br. h., Sadler's Wells—Idyllic, by Foolish Pleasure. 12-4-2-1, $245,011. Won the 1988 Three Chimneys Dewhurst S. (Eng-G1). Sire of more than 45 stakes winners, including Australian champion Universal Prince; of a heart attack, on March 6, 2005, at Durham Lodge Stud in Australia.

SCOOP THE GOLD, 1990 ch. m., Forty Niner—Leap Lively, by Nijinsky II. 21-4-2-2, $114,527. Won the

1995 Likely Exchange S. Dam of millionaire and Grade 1 winner High Yield; of a ruptured aorta, on April 17, 2005, at Fares Farm in Lexington.

SEATTLE MORN, 1990 ch. h., *Grey Dawn II— Tilting, by Seattle Slew. 39-8-10-3, $370,571. Won the 1994 Johnny Morris H., Grade 2-placed. Sire of two stakes winners; after colic surgery, in August 2004 in Colorado.

Shammy Davis, 1994 dk. b. or br. h., Temperence Hill—Sissy Sham, by Sham. 49-11-5-6, $308,790. Graded stakes-placed, 12th in the 1997 Kentucky Derby (G1); of colic, on January 29, 2004, at Buffalo Station Farm in Gladstone, Virginia.

SHARED INTEREST, 1988 b. m., Pleasant Colony—Surgery, by Dr. Fager. 23-10-5-3, $667,610. Won the 1993 Ruffian H. (G1). Dam of Grade 1 winners Cash Run and Forestry; of complications from foaling, on March 10, 2005, at Taylor Made Farm in Nicholasville, Kentucky.

SHE'S ZEALOUS, 2000 dk. b. or br. f., Cozzene—Zealous Connection, by Unreal Zeal. 9-4-2-0, $157,765. Won the 2004 Correction H.; after breaking down in a workout on March 7, 2004, at Aqueduct.

SHOT OF THUNDER, 1997 b. h., Thunder Gulch—My Brilliant Star, by Copper Kingdom. 35-7-5-4, $302,542. Won the 2002 Toorak H. (Aus-G1); euthanized after fracturing a femur in a breeding shed accident, in September 2004 at Glenlogan Park in Queensland, Australia.

SICYOS, 1981 ch. h., Lyphard—Sigy (Fr), by Habitat. 11-3-3-1, $83,948. Group 3 winner in France. Sire of 12 stakes winners, including Switzerland's 1991 Horse of the Year Three Well and '98 Del Mar Oaks (G1) winner Sicy d'Alsace (Fr); on January 26, 2004, at Haras du Petit Tellier, France.

SILVER WIZARD, 1990 b. h., Silver Hawk—Cherie's Hope, by Flying Paster. 33-8-3-7, $493,563. Stakes winner in England and the U.S. Grade 1-placed. Won the 1995 American H. (G2). Sire of winners; died early in 2005, in Italy.

SINTRA, 1981 ro. m., Drone—Misty Plum, by Misty Day. 19-9-3-1, $378,604. Won the 1984 Test S. (G2) and '85 Bewitch S. (G3). Dam of five winners; of melanoma, on October 13, 2004, at Indian Creek Farm in Georgetown, Kentucky.

SKATE AWAY, b. g. 1999, Belong to Me—Missouri Mist, by Little Missouri. 29-7-9-3, $479,730. Won the 2003 Edward J. DeBartolo Sr. Memorial Breeders' Cup H.; after collapsing from cardiac arrhythmia during the Woodford Reserve Turf Classic S. (G1) on May 1, 2004, at Churchill Downs.

SKY BEAUTY, 1990 b. m., Blushing Groom (Fr)—Maplejinsky, by Nijinsky II. 21-15-2-2, $1,336,000. Champion older female of 1994. Winner of the 1993 filly triple crown. Dam of three winners; euthanized after foundering, on July 2, 2004, at Creekview Farm in Paris, Kentucky.

Slewsbag, 2002 dk. b. or br. g., Devil's Bag—Slew's M. D., by Slew o' Gold. 14-1-2-2, $82,176. Graded stakes-placed at two; after breaking down in the Cal National Snow Chief S. on April 24, 2005, at Hollywood Park in California.

SLEW THE BRIDE, 1984 gr. h., Seattle Slew—Herecomesthebride, by Al Hattab. Unraced. Sire of Grade 3 winner Slew the Surgeon and $404,622 stakes winner Seattle Carla; in 2004 in California.

Smartest Thing, 2002 b. f., Smart Strike—Alycheer, by Alydeed. 3-1-2-0, $99,020. Stakes-placed; euthanized after breaking her right foreleg in a workout while prepping for the Ontario Lassie S., on November 30, 2004, at Woodbine.

SMOKESTER, 1988 dk. b. or br. h., Never Tabled—Small World, by Transworld. 4-2-0-3, $35,600. Among California's leading sires. Sire of nine stakes winners, including Grade 1 winner Free House; of an apparent heart attack, on February 21, 2005, at Cardiff Stud Farms in Creston, California.

SMOLDERIN HEART, 1995 gr. or ro. h., Two Punch—Sconneltown Road, by Ack Ack. 35-8-10-5, $467,686. Won the 1998 Lone Star Derby, 2000 King Cotton S. His first foals race in 2005; after fracturing a leg while recovering from colic surgery, in June 2004 in Arkansas.

SNACK, 2002 ch. c., Afternoon Deelites—Miss Riverton, by Fred Astaire. 9-4-2-2, $97,400. Won the 2005 Turfway Prevue S., WEBN S., 2004 Indiana Futurity; euthanized after breaking down in the Santa Catalina S. (G2) on March 5, 2005, at Santa Anita Park in California.

SNOW RIDGE, 2001 b. c., Indian Ridge—Snow Princess, by Ela-Mana-Mou. 5-2-1-0, $222,976. Won the 2003 Royal Lodge S. (Eng-G2); from laminitis, on September 9, 2004, in England.

SOBA, 1979 ch. m., Most Secret—Mild Wind, by *Porto Bello II. 33-13-1-0, $292,847. Won the 1983 King George S. (Eng-G3). Grandam of 1999 Italian highweight Dark Moondancer (GB); euthanized due to declining health, in September 2004 at Lane Side Farm, England.

SOMETHING SMITH, 2000 ch. g., Northern Idol—Summer Semester, by Better Arbitor. 17-7-5-1, $282,389. Won the 2004 Bernie Dowd H. and '03 Friendly Lover H.; euthanized following an infection, in August 2004 at Monmouth Park.

SORIANO CAT, 2001 ch. g., Bonus Time Cat—Bab's Beauty, by Glorious Flag. 15-3-3-3, $41,750. Won the 2003 Woodlands Juvenile S.; euthanized after breaking down in a race, on June 29, 2004, at Prairie Meadows Racetrack.

Soud, 1998 b. h., Mr. Prospector—Wasnah, by Nijinsky II. Half brother to Group 1 winner Bahri. 20-5-5-3, $260,580. Grade 3-placed, 1:33.60 miler; of an apparent heart attack, in June 2004 in Southern California.

SOUND OF GOLD, 1998 b. m., Mutakddim—Too Loud, by No Louder. 40-13-5-4, $268,243. 2003-'04 turf champion at Sam Houston Racing Park. Won the 2004 Jersey Lilly S.; after hemorrhaging after winning the Minnesota HBPA Mile S., on July 5, 2004, at Canterbury Downs.

SPANISH EMPIRE, 2000 dk. b. or br. c., Pleasant Colony—La Paz, by Hold Your Peace. $500,000 Keeneland mixed sale weanling purchase. 20-5-3-3, $276,714. Won the 2004 Fifth Season S. (G3); from an apparent heart attack in the Tenacious H., on December 4, 2004, at Fair Grounds.

Sparkling Ava, 1999 b. m., Royal Academy—Carolina Chant, by Linkage. 23-4-1-2, $158,429. Multiple stakes-placed; after breaking down in an allowance race on November 21, 2004, at Hollywood Park.

SPEED WEEK, 1995 ch. h., Rory's Jester—Vain

Princess, by Biscay. 19-6-3-0, $144,596. Won the 1998 Black Opal S. (Aus-G2); of colic, in November 2004, at Mungrup Stud in Australia.

SPORTSWORLD, 1988 b. h., Alleged—Gallanta (Fr), by Nureyev. 5-3-1-0, $104,736. Won the 1991 Windfields Farm Gallinule S. (Ire-G2). Sire of at least 13 stakes winners, including South African Group 1 winners Kournikova, Sport's Chestnut, and Jamaica; euthanized due to a hock injury, in January 2005 at Daytona Stud, South Africa.

STALWART, 1979 b. h., Hoist the Flag—Yes Dear Maggy, by Iron Ruler. 5-4-0-0, $528,595. Won the 1981 Norfolk S. (G1), Hollywood Futurity. Sire of 55 stakes winners, including 1998 Puerto Rican champion juvenile male Cedro Blanco and millionaire Stalwars; on April 2, 2004, at Nuckols Farm in Midway, Kentucky.

STAR OVER THE BAY, 1998 gr. or ro. g., Cozzene—Lituya Bay, by Empery. 43-10-4-3, $917,353. Won the 2004 Clement L. Hirsch Memorial Turf Championship S. (G1), Del Mar H. (G2); euthanized after breaking down in the International Cup (Sng-G1) on May 15, 2005, in Singapore.

STATELY SLEW, 1992 b. h., Seattle Slew—La Griffe, by Prince John. 17-2-5-0, $23,260. Half brother to 1989 champion older horse Blushing John. Sire of four winners; of colic, on February 23, 2004, at Circle L Farms in Breaux Bridge, Louisiana.

STORM BIRD, 1978 b. h., Northern Dancer—South Ocean, by New Providence. 6-5-0-0, $162,869. Champion at two in England and Ireland. Sire of at least 63 stakes winners, including leading sire Storm Cat. Broodmare sire of at least 107 stakes winners, including champion Thunder Gulch and 2004 Belmont S. (G1) winner Birdstone; of colic, on December 3, 2004, at Ashford Stud in Versailles, Kentucky.

Stormy Afternoon, 2002 ch. c., Afternoon Deelites—Temporada, by Summer Squall. 6-1-3-0, $49,965. Stakes-placed at two; of a massive heart attack, on April 15, 2005, while training at Churchill Downs in Louisville.

STRAWBERRY FAIR, 1984 b. m., Whiskey Road—Avellino, by Todman. Group 1 winner in Australia in 1988. Dam of South African group winner Taineberry and Australian stakes winner Galaxy Fair; after aborting a foal, on March 29, 2004.

STRIKE THE BRASS, 1997 b. g., Dixie Brass—Strike It Easy, by Easy Goer. 66-11-12-9, $314,719. Won the 2002 Wine Country H. and George W. Barker S.; after breaking down in a race on April 28, 2005, at Charles Town Races in West Virginia.

SUGAR AND SPICE, 1977 b. m., Key to the Mint—Sweet Tooth, by On-and-On. 18-5-3-3, $257,046. Half sister to champion Our Mims and to Alydar. Won the 1980 Mother Goose S. (G1). Dam of two stakes winners, including Grade 2 winner Cinnamon Sugar (Ire); of old age, on September 13, 2004, at Our Mims Retirement Haven in Paris, Kentucky.

Swift Attraction, 2001 dk. b. or br. c., Storm Cat—Golden Attraction, by Mr. Prospector. 6-1-0-1, $42,175. Third in the 2004 Kentucky Cup Sprint (G3); after breaking down in a race at Keeneland Race Course, on October 14, 2004, in Lexington.

TAATLETAIL, 2000 b. f., Faltaat—Defensive Lady, by Defensive Play. 6-5-1-0, $208,057. Won the 2003 New Zealand One Thousand Guineas (NZ-G1); euthanized following a stable accident, on February 7, 2004, in New Zealand.

TABA (ARG), 1973 b. m. Table Play—Filipina, by Fomento. Argentine champion and classic winner. Dam of 1986 Eclipse champion older male Turkoman; of natural causes, on February 11, 2005, at Our Mims Retirement Haven at Ahwenasa Farm in Paris, Kentucky.

TABASCO CAT, 1991 ch. h., Storm Cat—Barbicue Sauce, by Sauce Boat. 18-8-3-2, $2,347,671. Won the 1994 Preakness S. (G1), Belmont S. (G1). Sire of at least 23 stakes winners, including Grade 1 winners Snow Ridge, Habibti, and Island Sand of heart failure, on March 6, 2004, at Shizunai Stallion Station, Japan.

TARA ROMA, 1990 b. m., Lyphard—Chic Shirine, by Mr. Prospector. 16-5-2-1, $192,017. Won the 1994 Ladies H. (G2). Dam of Grade 1 winner Serra Lake and Grade 3 winner Cappuchino; of foaling complications, on March 31, 2004, at Middlebrook Farm in Lexington.

TASMANIAN TIGER, 1999 ch. g., Storm Cat—Hum Along, by Fappiano. 25-3-1-1, $154,543. Most expensive yearling of 2000, sold for $6.8-million at Keeneland September. Half brother to champion Storm Song; in June 2004, in Hong Kong.

TEMPERATURE, 2002 ch. g., Bering (GB)—Thermal Spring, by Zafonic. 3-2-0-0, $27,022. Won his first two starts impressively; after breaking down in the Prix Greffulhe (Fr-G2), on May 16, 2005, at St. Cloud racecourse in France.

TIMBERA, 1994 dk. b. or br. g., Commanche Run—Morry's Lady, by The Parson. 27-7-4-1, $211,526. Won the 2003 Irish Grand National Steeplechase; after breaking down in a race, on March 21, 2005, in Ireland.

TIMELY RUCKUS, 1993 dk. b. or br. g., Bold Executive—Shy Beauty, by Great Gladiator. 68-25-19-3, $618,004. Winner of 18 Canadian stakes; euthanized after contracting a virus, in December 2004, in Canada.

TIPICALLY IRISH, 1993 b. m., Metfield—Irish Izzy, by Full Out. 10-4-1-1, $231,895. Won the 1995 Oak Leaf S. (G1), Kentucky Cup Juvenile Fillies S. Dam of stakes winner Killenaule; in 2004.

Toby's Success, 2000 ch. g., Forty Won—Chad's Prospect, by Sutter's Prospect. 4-2-0-2, $49,830. Stakes-placed Fair Grounds record-setter; collapsed after finishing third in the Louisiana Premier Night Sprint S., on February 7, 2004, at Delta Downs.

TOUCHING WOOD, 1979 b. h., Roberto—Mandera, by *Vaguely Noble. 9-3-4-2, $388,989. Won the 1982 St. Leger (Eng-G1) and Irish St. Leger (Ire-G1). Sire of at least 23 stakes winners, including champions Golden Flare and Taldari; of old age, on March 31, 2004, at Fayette Park Stud, New Zealand.

TOUGH KNIGHT, 1984 dk. b. or br. h., Knights Choice—Countess Courage, by Captain Courageous. 6-3-0-1, $54,450. Multiple stakes winner. Among Washington's leading sires. Sire of 20 stakes winners, including Washington-bred champion Tough to Crack; of colic, on May 24, 2004, in Washington.

TRACK ROBBERY, 1976 ch. m., No Robbery—Left At Home, by Run For Nurse. 59-22-12-7, $1,098,537. Champion older female of 1982. Won the 1982 Spinster S. (G1), Apple Blossom H. (G1). Dam of Grade 3 winner Train Robbery; euthanized on October 24, 2004, at Fares Farm in Lexington.

TRUE PASSION, 1998 dk. b. or br. g., Petionville—Trumanita, by Capote. 47-13-6-3, $442,812. Won the 2002 Philadelphia Park Breeders' Cup H. (G3); after breaking down in a race at Belmont Park, on October 8, 2004, in New York.

Twilight Prince, 1996 b. g., Waquoit—Turn Capp, by Turn to Reason. 56-9-8-9, $244,371. Stakes-placed. Broke down in a race, on June 30, 2004, at Suffolk Downs.

TWO MILE HILL, 2000 b. m., A.P. Indy—Flat Fleet Feet, by Afleet. 12-4-2-1, $165,747. Won the 2004 Golden Sylvia H.; after breaking down in the Banshee Breeze S., on January 23, 2005, at Gulfstream Park in Florida.

Tycoon (GB), 2001 b. c., Sadler's Wells—Fleeting Glimpse, by Rainbow Quest. 13-1-2-5, $430,645. Classic-placed in England and Ireland; euthanized after breaking down in the Abu Dhabi Championship, on April 10, 2005, in the United Arab Emirates.

Unloosened, 1995 b. h., Unbridled—Flying Loose, by Giboulee. 28-6-3-7, $256,016. Grade 3-placed. First foals are two-year-olds of 2005; of septic shock, on September 4, 2004, at the University of Illinois Veterinary Clinic.

UNTOLD GOLD, 1994 b. h., Seeking the Gold—Torrie Ann, by Blushing Groom (Fr). 29-4-7-2, $65,677. Sire of at least two winners from three starters, including 2004 stakes winner Hush's Gold; in 2004, in New Mexico.

VALLEY CROSSING, 1988 dk. b. or br. h., Private Account—Chic and Sassy, by His Majesty. 48-8-13-8, $1,616,490. Won the 1993 Philip H. Iselin H. (G1). Leading 2002 Arkansas sire. Sire of 11 stakes winners, including Slew Valley; following colic surgery, in September 2004 at Rockin River Ranch in Winterset, Iowa.

WAVERING MONARCH, 1979 b. h., Majestic Light—Uncommitted, by Buckpasser. 13-6-1-3, $466,773. Won the 1982 Haskell Invitational H. (G1). Sire of 40 stakes winners, including champions Maria's Mon and Wavering Girl; broodmare sire of champion Prairie Bayou; due to infirmities of old age, on June 17, 2004, at Glencrest Farm in Midway, Kentucky.

WELL DECORATED, 1978 dk. b. or br. h., Raja Baba—Paris Breeze, by Majestic Prince. 16-6-4-2, $455,836. Won the 1980 Arlington-Washington Futurity (G1). Sire of 35 stakes winners. Broodmare sire of 45 stakes winners; of complications from arthritis, in December 2004, at Illinois Stud in Woodstock, Illinois.

WESTERN SYMPHONY, 1981 b. h., Nijinsky II—Millicent, by Cornish Prince. 8-3-2-2, $40,131. Won the 1983 Larkspur S. (Ire-G3). Sire of more than 25 stakes winners. Broodmare sire of three-time Australian Horse of the Year Sunline; in April 2005, at Emerald Park Stud in New Zealand.

WETHERLY, 2002 dk. b. or br. c., Expelled—Balla Balla, by Bolger. 3-1-0-0, $30,260; euthanized after breaking down in the Best Pal S. (G2), on August 15, 2004, at Del Mar.

WHARITE PRINCESS, 2000 ch. f., His Royal Highness—Regal Visit, by Vice Regal. Won the 2004 New Zealand Oaks (NZ-G1); collapsed and died from an apparent heart malfunction after a workout in early October 2004 at Awapuni Race Course, New Zealand.

WHAT A NUISANCE, 1978 b. g., St Puckle—Fashion Bell, by Belmura. Won ten races, including the 1985 Melbourne Cup (Aus-G1); of natural causes in his paddock at trainer Pat Hyland's farm, on April 20, 2005, in Australia.

WILDCAT QUEEN, 2000 b. f., Storm Cat—Jetapat, by Tri Jet. 5-1-1-0, $33,595. Former $1.5-million Keeneland September sale yearling purchase, euthanized after breaking down in an allowance race, on June 16, 2004, at Churchill Downs.

WITH ABILITY, 1998 b. m., A.P. Indy—Withallprobability, by Mr. Prospector. 19-7-4-2, $558,124. Won the 2002 Sixty Sails H. (G3); following surgery to repair a fractured pastern, on January 31, 2004, at Blue Ridge Equine Clinic in Free Union, Virginia.

WITHALLPROBABILITY, 1988 b. m., Mr. Prospector—Sulemeif, by Northern Dancer. 27-9-4-5, $643,438. Won the 1991 Bonnie Miss S. (G2). Dam of Grade 3 winner With Ability; of laminitis, on January 14, 2004, at Kentucky Equine Sports Medicine Rehabilitation Center in Versailles, Kentucky.

WIXOE EXPRESS (Ire), 1999 b. g., Anabaa—Esquiline, by Gone West. 20-6-2-3, $153,165. Won the 2004 Tanforan H.; euthanized after fracturing his left foreleg in an $80,000 claiming race on August 1, 2004, at Del Mar.

WOODLAND MELODY, 1995 b. m., Woodman—Eloquent Minister, by Deputy Minister. 4-3-0-0, $57,573. Group 3 winner in France in 1997; dam of stakes winner Shady Reflection; in 2004.

WOODMAN'S GIRL, 1990 b. m., Woodman—Becky Be Good, by Naskra. 28-3-3-5, $69,195. Dam of millionaire Grade 1 winner More Than Ready; of colic, following surgery to deliver her Mineshaft foal, on February 21, 2005, in Kentucky.

WORLD STAGE (Ire), 1993 b. h., Sadler's Wells—Rosa Mundi, by Secretariat. Brother to champion Correggio (Ire). Winner. Sire of stakes winners Final Prophecy and Worldly Victor; in 2004 in Florida.

World Trade, 1999 b. h., Storm Cat—Daring Bidder, by Bold Bidder. 19-4-1-3, $122,430. Stakes-placed half brother of champion Eliza and Grade 1 winner Dinard; after breaking down in an accident that claimed the life of jockey Michael Rowland, on February 4, 2004, at Turfway Park.

WYNN DOT COMMA, 2001 ch. c., Struggler (GB)—I Like Punch, by Two Punch. 8-6-1-0, $298,525. Won the 2004 Swale S. (G3), Spectacular Bid S. (G3); after fracturing both front ankles while galloping on March 23, 2004, at Calder Race Course.

XRAY, 1988 b. h., Allen's Prospect—Galafest, by Cornish Prince. 23-6-3-4, $206,462. Won the 1990 Maryland Nursery S. Sire of $206,994 stakes winner A Ray of Magic; in 2004, in California.

YARNY'S STAR, 1991 ch. g., Yarnallton Native—Wartime Lady, by Mighty Crafty. 131-27-23-13. Won the 1998 Brent's Prince H.; after breaking down in a race on July 15, 2004, at River Downs in Ohio.

YOUNG FLYER, 1984 dk. b. or br. m., Flying Paster—Youthful Lady, by Youth. 24-4-3-6, $215,000. Won the 1986 California Breeders' Champion S. Dam of Grade 1 winners River Flyer and Victory Ride; from complications of foaling, on March 25, 2004, at Ashford Stud in Versailles, Kentucky.

HISTORY OF RACING

by Mary Simon

Horse racing officially appeared in the annals of history in approximately 1000 B.C. when Greeks started racing horses with chariots drawn behind them, a dangerous game that subsequently was adopted by the Romans and Egyptians. For the 33rd Olympiad in 644 B.C., formal competition began with riders astride the horses. The Romans, who conquered England in 43 A.D. under Emperor Claudius and ruled it until 410 A.D., carried their horses and their sport to the island nation, where a millennium later it would blossom into the sport known as Thoroughbred racing.

By the late 1500s, racing had become a favorite pastime of English noblemen. King Henry VIII and his daughter Queen Elizabeth I both maintained racing stables, and Elizabeth's cousin King James I established Newmarket racecourse early in the 17th century. His son Charles I also was a racing enthusiast, but he was overthrown and beheaded in 1649, and Lord Protector Oliver Cromwell banned horse racing. After the restoration of the monarchy in 1660, racing flourished under its ardent devotee King Charles II.

Because of Charles II's love for the sport, racing became known as the sport of kings, and during his rule the first of three imported Arabian stallions began the genetic progression toward the Thoroughbred of today. In 1688, Capt. Robert Byerly purportedly returned from Hungary with a captured stallion who became known as the Byerly Turk. Sixteen years later, British consul Thomas Darley smuggled an Arabian stallion out of Syria and transplanted him to Yorkshire; he became known as the Darley Arabian. In approximately 1730, an Arabian stallion of unknown lineage appeared in the stable of the Earl of Godolphin and became known as the Godolphin Arabian. These three stallions would become the foundation sires of the Thoroughbred. The Darley Arabian sired Flying Childers, generally regarded as the first great Thoroughbred, in 1714. (For more on the development of the Thoroughbred, see Evolution of the Breed.)

In the late 18th century, racing began to assume a formal structure. Racecourses were established, and the first of the English classics, the St. Leger Stakes, was run in 1776. The Epsom Derby followed four years later, and the Two Thousand Guineas had its first running in 1809. As racing developed in England, it found its way to the American colonies. In 1665, New York Governor Richard Nicholls gave the name Newmarket to America's first racetrack. Although the first track was located in New York, horse racing tended to be frowned upon by religious leaders and communities in the North, but the sport flourished in the South. The first known Thoroughbred sire imported to North America from England was *Bulle Rock, an aged son of the Darley Arabian. Although *Bulle Rock had no lasting influence, pre-Revolution imports such as *Fearnought, pint-sized *Janus, and the *Cub mare influenced the breed's development.

19th Century

Early American presidents, particularly those from the South, were racing fans. Thomas Jefferson approved the Senate's practice of adjourning early to attend local meets. Senators of the day might have marveled at the fabled 28-foot stride of the great colt Florizel or witnessed the unbeatable brilliance of First Consul during his 21-race winning streak.

It was an era of often unrecorded and disputed genealogies, and races were crudely timed, if at all. The 1823 victory of American Eclipse over Henry in the North-South match at Long Island's Union Course proved a milestone in post-Colonial racing. The $20,000-a-side event drew a significant portion of the New York populace and helped American Eclipse stake his claim as the first American earnings champion, with $56,700. At the same time, *Leviathan was standing for America's highest known fee—$75—but he was not the most notable stallion of the period. That honor went to *Diomed, a British castoff after the Revolutionary War. The inaugural Epsom Derby winner in 1780, he arrived on American shores in Virginia in '98, acquired for a meager $250. *Diomed proceeded over 11 seasons to reshape the American Thoroughbred in his own remarkable image, getting runners that were uniformly taller, heavier of bone, stouter, stronger, and faster than their contemporaries.

Unlike England, where the Epsom Derby and St. Leger heralded a trend toward shorter races, America maintained its long heat races for the first half of the century. While the style of racing evolved over time, change of another kind arrived on March 17, 1850, when *Diomed's great-great grandson Lexington was born on a Central Kentucky farm. Brilliant on the racecourse and even more accomplished at stud, Lexington would reign 16 times—including 14 in succession—as the country's leading sire.

As the century progressed, races became shorter, purses rose, and racing began to become organized. Saratoga Race Course, Pimlico Race Course, Churchill Downs, and Fair Grounds opened for business. The Travers Stakes had its first running in 1864, and the Belmont Stakes was run for the first time in 1867. The Preakness Stakes followed in 1873, and the Kentucky Derby was staged for the first time in '75. Late in the century, the Jockey Club was established to oversee the growing sport, and it soon assumed control of the *American Stud Book.* In 1889, Miss Woodford became the first American Thoroughbred to top $100,000 in career earnings. Two-year-old racing gained popularity with the inaugural 1888 Futurity, worth $40,000 to the winner; five years later, a juvenile named Domino set a single-season earnings record of $170,790 that would stand for decades. Kingston—last of the great iron horses of a dying era—retired in 1894 with 89 victories, a record to this day. By the end of the 19th century, Kentucky had become the heart of America's Thoroughbred business, with more professional horsemen than any other region. America and its Thoroughbred industry were thus poised to enter a modern era of even greater change.

1901-'10

The American century's first decade was one of promise and turmoil for the Thoroughbred racing industry. Trouble brewed even as financier James R. Keene's great Commando blistered the track at the dawn of the century and as Commando's unbeatable son Colin carried the Keene colors to victory after brilliant victory a few years later. Even as Keene's stable racked up unprecedented earnings, as record purses were dispensed, and as Belmont Park opened its glorious gates, a dark cloud was settling ominously on racing's horizon.

Racing may have been the sport of kings, but it was also part of a larger gambling industry. Increasingly, the taint of corruption eroded public confidence in the sport as high-profile incidents were exposed. Keene's Sysonby, one of the sport's all-time greats, suffered his only loss in the 1904 Futurity after being drugged by a groom. Delhi, the 1904 Belmont Stakes winner, later ran sluggishly and was found to have sponges inserted far up into his nostrils. Electric prods, dopings, ringers, crooked jockeys, and diverse gambling scams involving track bookmakers were daily journalistic fodder.

By 1907, anti-racetrack wagering laws had been simmering for some time on legislative back burners across America. In June 1908, New York passed the Agnew-Hart bill with the ardent blessing of Governor Charles Evans Hughes, who used the legislation as a weapon against the Tammany Hall political machine, a major beneficiary of racing in the New York metropolitan area. Without revenues from legalized gambling, racing soon found it impossible to support itself. In 1910, historic Saratoga was among the racetracks that ceased operation, and E. J. "Lucky" Baldwin's original Santa Anita Park was forced to close.

A domino effect occurred as other states rushed to pass similar legislation. The national purse structure collapsed, declining from a 1907 average of $949 per race to $643 in '09. Top stables, including Keene's, shipped overseas in a European invasion so successful that it would pave the way for the next great blow to the American Thoroughbred industry—the English Jockey Club's 1913 passage of the "Jersey Act" banning most American-breds from their Stud Book. In 1908, Churchill Downs's energetic general manager, Col. Matt Winn, pulled some old pari-mutuel machines out of storage, dusted them off, and put them back into use. When racing resumed in the next decade, the pari-mutuel wagering system quickly would become dominant.

Despite all, several great competitors appeared on racing's stage to illuminate the era. Colin was one of nine future Racing Hall of Fame members who campaigned during the decade. Man o' War's fiery sire, Fair Play, was another, along with Commando, Sysonby, Artful, Beldame, Roseben, Broomstick, and Peter Pan.

1911-'20

As indignation among the American populace swelled over the puritan campaigners' assault on gambling and alcohol consumption, a group of wealthy horsemen began to stockpile a fund with which to hold future race meets. The future came quickly. Although the Agnew-Hart legislation moldered on the books until 1934, the penalties associated with it were stripped away by May 30, 1913, when Belmont Park opened for the first time since 1910. Between 1908 and '13, however, American breeders had sent overseas more than 1,500 horses, among them at least 24 champions. Some eventually came back, but many did not. Leading sires *Rock Sand and *Meddler, also part of the exodus, were lost forever to American breeding.

The British responded with the Jersey Act in 1913, which effectively barred many old American lines from England's *General Stud Book,* but the first shots of World War I one year later quickly changed the United States from an exporter of bloodstock into an aggressive importer. Between 1916-'20, numerous English-breds and French-breds became American champions, including *Short Grass, *Sun Briar, *Hourless, *Omar Khayyam, *Johren, *Sunbonnet, *Enfilade, and *Constancy.

Even in the shadow of war, the decade was memorable for its outstanding runners, including future Racing Hall of Fame geldings Roamer, Old Rosebud, and Exterminator. Together, they won 129 races and set or equaled 29 records from five furlongs to 2¼ miles at 14 different racetracks. Iron Mask set a North American record for 5½ furlongs that would stand for 30 years, and the mare Pan Zareta took a back seat to no male in the realm of blazing speed. H. P. Whitney's Regret routinely whipped the boys and in 1915 became the first filly to win the Kentucky Derby. The Triple Crown was won for the first time in 1919 by Sir Barton, although the sweep did not take on its popular name until the '30s.

Sir Barton won the Belmont on June 11, five days after the decade's finest specimen made his first career start at Belmont Park. Man o' War, considered the greatest American horse of all time, was ineligible for admission to the *General Stud Book*, but in 16 months of competition redefined greatness. He lost one race at two that he should have won, failing to overcome a bad start in the Sanford Stakes at Saratoga Race Course and losing to Upset, but he never lost again. In 1920, "Big Red" established five American and two track records in 11 starts and won his races by a combined 164 lengths. Man o' War capped his extraordinary career on October 12, 1920, by galloping away from Sir Barton in a winner-take-all race at Kenilworth Park in Canada. The $80,000 purse sent him to stud as the richest American Thoroughbred in history with $249,465.

1921-'30

On the surface at least, the Roaring Twenties were a time of outrageous fun—flappers and the fox trot are indelible images of the era—and horse racing rode the crest of this postwar celebration. Elaborate new racetracks were the overt symbol of this prosperity—at least 15 of note were constructed in the United States during the 1920s, including Arlington and Washington Parks in Chicago and Hialeah Park in Florida. Purses went through the roof. In 1923, Zev became the first American racehorse to bank $200,000 in a season and, by '30, Gallant Fox— the second Triple Crown winner and the first to be recognized for sweeping the three American classics—had raised that bar to $300,000. Jockey Earle Sande, trainer James Fitzsimmons, breeder Harry Payne Whitney, and owner Harry Sinclair each established earnings records that would stand for years. Bloodstock prices also went into orbit, with a yearling commanding a record $75,000 in 1928.

Because the Jersey Act remained in force, horses mostly migrated to the west. Future leading sires *St. Germans, *Sickle, and *Challenger II were among the importees, as was the great matron *La Troienne. In late 1925, *Sir Galla-

had III arrived at Claiborne Farm, where he would reign four times as America's premier sire and 12 times as its leading broodmare sire. *Sir Gallahad III's American-bred counterpart was Man o' War, a private stallion who had seven of his eight champions in his first four crops and in 1926—with only three crops racing—set a progeny earnings record of $409,927.

No single racehorse towered above all others in the 1920s as Man o' War and Colin had before, but the decade nonetheless yielded 15 Racing Hall of Fame members. Foremost among them was Exterminator, the wonderful gelding who scored a 20th-century record 34 stakes victories and retired as America's richest Thoroughbred. Grey Lag flirted with greatness, as did champions Sarazen, Blue Larkspur, Reigh Count, and Gallant Fox. Zev, Crusader, and Sun Beau were big money winners. Princess Doreen won 34 races and broke Miss Woodford's 40-year female earnings record with $174,745. Other notable fillies included 1924 Preakness winner Nellie Morse; multiple champions Black Maria and Bateau; and Rose of Sharon, considered best of either sex at three in 1929. For a time, it appeared the good times would go on forever, but the stock market crashed in October 1929, which led to events that caused the Great Depression.

1931-'40

As the Depression shrunk race purses 40%, the average yearling price slumped to $570 in 1932. But, as the Depression eased, the Thoroughbred industry entered one of its healthiest eras. Purses rose by decade's end to record heights, and yearling sales gained strength. Racing also had some wealthy, influential leaders. Joseph E. Widener, vice chairman of the New York Jockey Club, crusaded tirelessly to return the sport in the Empire State to its former glory. Jockey Club Chairman William Woodward campaigned 1935 Triple Crown winner Omaha, but more importantly that year he fired some of the angriest, most articulate words at England's discriminatory Jersey Act. During the decade, increasingly sophisticated stall starting gates were developed, photo-finish cameras were installed, and saliva testing for drugs gained widespread use. Keeneland Race Course, Del Mar Thoroughbred Club, Santa Anita Park, and Hollywood Park opened for business.

Although the 1930s featured many standout racehorses, including 17 future Racing Hall of Fame members and two Triple Crown winners, three in particular captured the hearts of America—C. V. Whitney's Equipoise, Australasian wonder *Phar Lap, and claimer-turned-champion Seabiscuit. Although bred in the purple and owned by one of America's wealthiest bluebloods, there was nothing pretentious about Equipoise, a son of Pennant who was a champion at two in 1930, a three-time handicap champion, and a world-record miler. Seabiscuit, an undersized Wheatley Stable reject, developed into a megastar, reigning as '38 Horse of the Year and twice as America's handicap champion. In one of the decade's greatest moments, Seabiscuit defeated 1937 Triple Crown winner War Admiral in the two-horse '38 Pimlico Special Stakes. *Phar Lap illuminated the Depression's darkest hour by winning the 1932 Agua Caliente Handicap in record time, but the huge New Zealander died just 17 days later under suspicious circumstances.

The 1930s launched a feminine revolution of sorts. Top Flight defeated males in the 1931 Futurity to become the first $200,000 juvenile earner and richest American female. Mrs. Payne Whitney's Twenty Grand won that year's Kentucky Derby, and Isabel Dodge Sloane became America's leading owner in 1934. As war in Europe approached, America imported several top stallions. In 1936, Hancock organized a syndicate to purchase *Blenheim II, for $250,000; four years later, C. V. Whitney acquired the stallion's classic-winning son, *Mahmoud.

1941-'50

Despite a world at war for half the decade, the 1940s very well may have been racing's finest hour, with four Triple Crown winners crowning the decade. The war years were grim for the sport, however. Southern California's tracks were shut down—Santa Anita was an internment camp for Japanese-Americans, Hollywood was an army storage unit, and Del Mar was used for assembling aircraft wings. Travel restrictions crippled the Saratoga yearling sale and led to the creation of the Breeders' Sales Co., precursor of Keeneland Sales. In late 1944, the government banned racing, and only victory in Europe saved the '45 Triple Crown.

Leavening the somber news from overseas were the exploits of Whirlaway, Calumet's "Mr. Longtail," winner of the 1941 Triple Crown. Then there was Alsab, a $700 yearling of peasant lineage who outgamed Whirlaway by a nose in a famous 1942 match race at Narragansett Park. Mrs. John D. Hertz's 1943 Triple Crown winner, Count Fleet, habitually crushed his opposition and romped to a 25-length Belmont Stakes victory, despite a career-ending injury. High-headed, flame-coated Stymie was not the best, but he was nevertheless beloved by fans who made him the people's horse. Claimed for $1,500 from King Ranch by trainer Hirsch Jacobs, Stymie became the first Thoroughbred to surpass $900,000 in career earnings. King Ranch had Assault, who overcame a deformed right fore foot to win the

1946 Triple Crown. The 1940s also produced several top fillies, including Racing Hall of Fame members Twilight Tear, Busher, Gallorette, Bewitch, Two Lea, and Bed o' Roses. Argentine-bred *Miss Grillo set a 2½-mile world record in the 1948 Pimlico Cup Handicap.

The decade virtually belonged to Warren Wright's magnificent Calumet Stable, whose champions were trained by Ben and Jimmy Jones and in many cases ridden by Eddie Arcaro—all Racing Hall of Fame members. Calumet reigned as America's top owner seven times during the decade, edged only by a trio of prominent women—Mrs. Payne Whitney (1942), Elizabeth Graham ('45), and Isabel Dodge Sloane ('50). Runners who carried the feared devil's red and blue silks during the 1940s included Racing Hall of Fame members Whirlaway, Twilight Tear, Armed, Citation, Bewitch, Coaltown, and Two Lea, and father-son Kentucky Derby winners Pensive and Ponder. Citation was not only Calumet's best but also one of the century's most talented runners. Champion at two and three, American Triple Crown hero, and winner of 16 consecutive races, Citation would become the sport's first millionaire in 1951.

Late in the decade, Claiborne Farm acquired *Nasrullah, a rogue stallion who would transform the American bloodstock industry. Also in 1949, England's Jockey Club backed down after 36 years and rescinded the despised Jersey Act, by now long outdated and hindering rather than helping the British breeding industry. America thus regained its former stature as a respected source of international bloodstock.

1951-'60

As it entered the second half of the 20th century, the U.S. confronted a rapidly changing world. It was at war in Korea, the threat of Nazism had been replaced by the peril of nuclear cataclysm, television was helping to create a truly national society, and polio had been conquered. America's appetite for racing seemed utterly insatiable; attendance and handle records were established almost annually. Perhaps it was too successful. In this decade, racing failed to build a lasting partnership with television—an arrogant decision that the industry would regret into the 21st century.

The 1950s were a time of rising incomes and rising expectations. In 1956, Nashua became the first million-dollar stallion syndication. Also that year, jockey Bill Hartack became the first to ride winners of $2-million in a single season; he topped $3-million the following year. The 1950s witnessed a growing interest in early competition—particularly after the spectacular 1953 debut of the world's richest race, the $270,000 Garden State Stakes for two-year-olds at Garden State Park in New Jersey. Soundness became an issue in the 1950s, with the high-profile breakdowns of such stars as Hail to Reason and Swaps. In the late 1950s, phenylbutazone—an anti-inflammatory drug popularly known as Bute—came into wide use to ease the aches and pains of thoroughbreds, though not legal for racing.

Racing in the 1950s had several stars but no Triple Crown winner. (Jockey Eddie Arcaro blamed himself for Nashua's loss to Swaps in the 1955 Derby. Nashua subsequently won the Preakness and Belmont.) The first equine superhero of the TV age was Native Dancer—the "Gray Ghost of Sagamore," whose only loss in 22 starts was by a head in the 1953 Kentucky Derby. Also racing at that time was Tom Fool, who carried heavy imposts to ten straight victories. As Native Dancer and Tom Fool exited the stage, the prodigiously talented pair of Nashua and Swaps took their place. They met twice, with Swaps winning the 1955 Derby and Nashua the '55 $100,000 Washington Park match race. The foal crop of 1954 contained Bold Ruler, Round Table, and *Gallant Man, all Racing Hall of Fame members. Round Table lasted the longest, 66 races, and was America's first great grass horse. Talent was so widespread that no one noticed an ordinary-looking bay gelding who won only a maiden race in 1959. But Kelso went on to become one of the major heroes of the 1960s.

1961-'70

The 1960s were a watershed for America and American racing. Inaugurated in January 1961 was John F. Kennedy, the first president born in the 20th century. Racial segregation was overthrown in the South, but lives were lost in the battle. Kennedy's assassination in 1963 shook America to its core, and soon the collective conformism of the '50s crumbled. As men walked on the moon, young soldiers were dying in an unpopular Vietnam war.

Racing increasingly became a game of haves and have-nots. In 1967, Damascus banked a single-season record $817,941. That same year, North America's earnings per runner averaged $3,359, or about half of training costs for a year. Medication also became an issue, especially when Dancer's Image was disqualified from his 1968 Kentucky Derby victory over a Bute positive.

State legislators looked to racing to plug budget gaps; at the end of the decade, proposed federal tax changes led to the creation of the American Horse Council to help lobby on behalf of horse racing and breeding interests. Simultaneously, racing was losing some of its audience as other professional sports and entertainment forms gained popularity. National attendance declined in 1967 for the first time since World War II, despite nearly 100 added racing days. During the 1960s, total racing days increased 35%, while average daily attendance declined 3%. At decade's end, off-track betting was approved in New York, which would lead to even larger attendance declines.

Against this chaotic and disquieting backdrop, Kelso—and others like him—redeemed this troubled era and made it one of the most remarkable in 200 years. Allaire duPont's Kelso tore through the handicap ranks, ruling as Horse of the Year from 1960 through '64. Carry Back emerged from Florida to win the 1961 Kentucky Derby and Preakness Stakes. Other outstanding performers of the era were Arts and Letters, Majestic Prince, Nodouble, Northern Dancer, and Fort Marcy, but the second half of the decade belonged to Buckpasser, Damascus, and Dr. Fager. Together, they started 85 times and compiled a 64-13-5 record.

Fillies of the 1960s deserve special mention. Cicada, Old Hat, Affectionately, Straight Deal, Tosmah, Politely, Gamely, and Shuvee averaged 56 career starts. Cicada set an earnings record; Moccasin became the first juvenile filly to take Horse of the Year honors in the 1965 Thoroughbred Racing Associations poll; Dark Mirage was first to sweep New York's filly triple crown in 1968; Dr. Fager's younger half sister, Ta Wee, toted an average of 136 pounds in 1970. Women gained the right to ride in races in 1969, and trailblazer Diane Crump rode in the '70 Derby. Bloodstock prices were heating up, and Nijinsky II was syndicated for a record $5.44-million in 1970.

1971-'80

In some respects, the decade between 1971 and '80 was one of the century's most satisfying periods for American Thoroughbred racing. Great runners and big money energized the era, but they also disguised some troubling problems, such as race fixing, increasingly lenient medication rules, and a declining audience. The 1970s were racing's best years since the '40s, with three Triple Crown winners within five years. The bloodstock markets were supercharged as well, with the beginning of the Northern Dancer era and the speculative buying that eventually damaged the markets in the 1980s.

Secretariat, Seattle Slew, and Affirmed, the three Triple Crown winners, attracted most of the attention, and they shared the limelight with Forego, Ruffian, and Spectacular Bid, among others. It has been said that Secretariat appeared at the precise moment when America and racing needed him most. A transcendent, larger-than-life figure bursting with almost supernatural vitality, he streaked across racing's stage in 1972 and '73, leaving behind an impression of pure greatness unrivaled since Man o' War. After he won the 1973 Kentucky Derby (G1) in record time (1:59⅖, a mark that still stands) and the Preakness Stakes (G1) with consummate ease (also probably a record even though the timing was botched), Secretariat quieted every skeptic with his 31-length triumph in the Belmont Stakes (G1) in 2:24, 2⅗ seconds—11 lengths—faster than the existing world record. Seattle Slew blazed through the Triple Crown, becoming the first to complete the sweep with an unbeaten record, and one year later Affirmed won the Triple Crown over his nemesis Alydar, who was second in all three races.

The Triple Crown winners did not stand alone in the spotlight. Twenty-two future Racing Hall of Fame members campaigned during this decade, including six from a remarkable 1970 foal crop. Among them were the first distaff millionaire, Dahlia, 12-for-12 juvenile La Prevoyante, and Forego, who was Horse of the Year three times. Ruffian cruised unbeaten through ten starts until the ill-fated 1975 match race with Kentucky Derby winner Foolish Pleasure that took her life. The era closed with yet another performer for the ages. The Triple Crown eluded Spectacular Bid, but not much else did between 1978 and '80. The compact gray colt set nine track, American, and world standards. In 1980, Genuine Risk became only the second filly in 106 years to win the Kentucky Derby.

The 1970s signaled the dramatic rise of top Hispanic jockeys, with none more prominent than Laffit Pincay Jr. Among trainers, the torch passed to Charlie Whittingham and Laz Barrera, whose West Coast-based stables also hailed the arrival of California as a centerpiece of American racing. The industry was changing in other ways, due in part to the 1971 introduction of off-track betting in New York. By 1977, OTB wagers finally exceeded money wagered on track in New York, and the gap would widen thereafter.

1981-'90

The breeding industry follows the fortunes of the racetrack, but for a few years in the 1980s that relationship became temporarily detached, or so it seemed, as rich foreign buyers pursued yearlings by Northern Dancer and his sons. In 1985, a Nijinsky II colt was sold for a record $13.1-million at the Keeneland July sale of selected yearlings, but by then the bloodstock markets had entered a slide that would last into the 1990s. Stud fees climbed to unsupportable levels on the fantasy, and everything came crashing down. On the track, attendance was falling while wagering and purses stagnated.

In 1982, at the peak of the bloodstock boom, horseman John Gaines worried over the industry's fundamentals and came up with an idea to market it. One year earlier, the Arlington Million had been inaugurated at Arlington Park as the world's first $1-million Thoroughbred race. Enthusiastically received, it had drawn a field of international grass stars and was won by John Henry. Gaines envisioned a single championship day of racing, offering millions of dollars in purse money, paid for by stallion and foal nomination fees. In November 1984 at Hollywood Park, his dream became reality at the first Breeders' Cup championship day, arguably the sport's greatest innovation since the Triple Crown.

Although he missed the first Breeders' Cup and never raced again, Dotsam Stable's John Henry proved once again that the American Dream was alive and well. He was a gelded son of an obscure sire, and he earned more than $6.5-million. In the 1980s, fillies shined brightest. Eight of the decade's 13 Racing Hall of Fame performers thus far have been members of the distaff set, including Horses of the Year All Along (Fr) and Lady's Secret, 1988 Kentucky Derby winner Winning Colors, undefeated champions Personal Ensign (13-for-13) and Landaluce (5-for-5 before her death), and two-time champion Go for Wand, who died on the track in the 1990 Breeders' Cup Distaff (G1). Also notable were two-time champions Bayakoa (Arg) and Miesque.

Although males of the 1980s lacked the brilliance of their female counterparts, they did provide memorable moments. Ferdinand gave Whittingham his first Kentucky Derby victory at age 73 in 1986, and in '87 he fought to the bitter end under Racing Hall of Fame member Bill Shoemaker to edge Derby winner Alysheba in the Breeders' Cup Classic (G1). The fierce 1989 rivalry between Sunday Silence and Easy Goer ranks among the sport's best, and also memorable was Conquistador Cielo's 14-length triumph in the 1982 Belmont Stakes, the first of trainer Woody Stephens's historic five straight wins in that classic. One of the decade's most poignant moments was trainer Carl Nafzger's spontaneous televised description of Unbridled's 1990 Kentucky Derby stretch run for 92-year-old owner Frances Genter. Trainer D. Wayne Lukas rewrote the record books repeatedly during these years, setting and breaking his own earnings standards.

1991-2000

The century's final decade was a breakthrough for America's racetracks, which built a solid foundation first on intrastate intertrack wagering and then on the true bonanza, interstate full-card wagering. The full-card explosion forever altered the sport. By mid-decade, off-site wagering accounted for 74% of racing's handle, a figure that jumped to 82% by 1999. Some tracks added slot machines to boost both purses and profits without putting any new patrons in the stands. The bloodstock markets recovered from a prolonged recession and rose to new heights as the decade ended.

Lexington ad executive Fred Pope, with counsel from John Gaines, in 1996 proposed an industry alliance to revitalize the sport and create a "major league of racing." Their National Thoroughbred Association, an owner-driven organization, soon was swallowed up by the National Thoroughbred Racing Association (NTRA), which was launched in April 1998 and reached into every corner of the sport. Racing series added hours of television coverage, and in 1999 Television Games Network (TVG) debuted on satellite and a few cable systems.

In the bloodstock market, stallion owners began breeding their stars to large books of mares and sent them to the Southern Hemisphere for double duty. A record for a stallion syndication was set in 2000 when Fusaichi Pegasus commanded a record $60-million to $70-million price tag.

A trio of sensational grays—Holy Bull, Silver Charm, and Skip Away—and Allen Paulson's marvelous bay Cigar captured the imagination of the racing public in the 1990s. Together they won classics, championships, and $30-million, but they were sired by stallions with average stud fees of just $7,800. Among females, Serena's Song and Dance Smartly were the decade's standouts.

It was an exciting classics decade, with the Triple Crown on the line each year between 1997 and '99, with Silver Charm, Real Quiet, and Charismatic winning the Derby and Preakness before coming up short in the Belmont. Silver Charm and Real Quiet were trained by Bob Baffert, but the classics of the 1990s virtually belonged to Lukas, who won six consecutive classic races with five different horses and also trained Charismatic for Robert and Beverly Lewis, Californians who owned Silver Charm and Serena's Song. Cigar, a two-time Horse of the Year, won 16 consecutive races but proved sterile.

Class I racing returned to Texas, but the first two tracks to open, Sam Houston Race Park and Retama Park, struggled initially. Lone Star Park in the populous Dallas-Fort Worth area was a success from its opening in April 1997. An important trend that began toward the end of the decade was the consolidation of racetrack ownership under Magna Entertainment Corp. and Churchill Downs Inc. That consolidation would continue into the 21st century.

2001-'05

The beginning of the new century was indelibly scarred by an act of unspeakable horror, a terrorist attack with commercial jetliners that killed approximately 3,000 innocent people in New York's World Trade Center towers, at the Pentagon, and in a rural Pennsylvania field, where passengers sacrificed their lives to protect American institutions from Islamist terrorists who had hijacked their plane. September 11, 2001, forever will be seared on the American psyche, along with December 7, 1941, and November 22, 1963. On each of those dates, America lost some of its innocence and confronted a changing and frightening world. In 2001, a racing event, the Breeders' Cup World Thoroughbred Championships, marked the first international sporting event in the New York region following the terrorist attacks.

In the first half of the 21st century's first decade, Thoroughbred racing experienced triumphs and it engaged in self-evaluation as the gambling element of the sport began to change. It also had to deal with an attempt to fix the outcome of a bet on the 2002 Breeders' Cup. Meanwhile, the consolidation of American racing into the hands of a few publicly traded companies continued. On the track, the dominant news events were three rags-to-riches horses who stepped out of obscurity and stood on the brink of the sport's ultimate prize, the Triple Crown. War Emblem was the first Derby-Preakness winner of the 21st century in 2002, and he was followed by Funny Cide, a crowd-pleasing gelding owned by a group of fun-loving friends. But without question the horse who captured America's heart was Smarty Jones, who won the 2004 Derby as the favorite and scored in the Preakness by a record margin. He finished second in the Belmont, however, and was whisked off to stud.

In the new century's first five years, the sport began to come to grips with a new phenomenon, offshore betting operations known as rebaters (because they rebated part of every bet to their high-dollar players). Some rebaters paid money to purses and others did not. As a result, total North American wagering rose in 2003 while purses declined. The following year, purses rose while wagering declined, a sign of the emergence of racinos—racetracks with slot-machine casinos attached to them.

The sport began an evaluation of its wagering systems in 2002 when three former fraternity brothers fixed the Breeders' Cup Ultra Pick Six wager. It was an inside job, by a programmer for tote provider Autotote, and the fix was quickly uncovered when 43.50-to-1 Volponi won the Breeders' Cup Classic (G1). Industry officials came together with the tote companies to strengthen safeguards and protect the integrity of horse-race wagering. In another stroke for the sport's integrity, the Racing Medication and Testing Consortium developed model rules on racing drugs and lobbied successfully for their adoption in most racing states. Also, the industry mobilized against alkalizing agents, known as milkshakes, which reputedly delayed the onset of muscle fatigue.

The Kentucky commercial breeding industry, plunged into recession after the 2001 terrorist attacks, sustained a significant blow in '01 and beyond from mare reproductive loss syndrome (MRLS), which caused the loss of more than 500 late-term fetuses and almost 3,000 early-term fetuses in Central Kentucky. Attributed to Eastern tent caterpillars, MRLS cost the Kentucky Thoroughbred industry an estimated $300-million and contributed to the demise of the Keeneland July sale of selected yearlings. The bloodstock markets recovered in 2003 and '04.

The consolidation of the American racetrack industry continued when Magna Entertainment Corp. bought Lone Star Park in Texas and controlling interest in Maryland's major tracks, Pimlico Race Course and Laurel Park, in 2002. In 2004, Churchill Downs Inc. bought Fair Grounds in New Orleans for $47-million.

Condensed from "Racing Through the Century," for which Mary Simon was awarded the 2000 Eclipse Award for outstanding features-enterprise writing and which was later published as a book with additional material.

History of Racing Silks

Worn by each jockey to represent a horse's owner, racing silks have been associated with horse racing for nearly two millennia. *Kennets Roman Antiquities* (1696) cites colors worn at chariot races: "At these races, the Romans rode in different colours, particularly the companies of Charioteers, to distinguish themselves." Nero was so fond of his green colors that he often wore a green toga when he attended the races during the first century.

The records of England's King Henry VIII mention jockeys' attire in the first half of the 16th century. His 1530 purse accounts show payments for "doublets [shirts] of Bruges Satin for the boys that runne the gueldings" and for "ryding cappes of Black Satin lyned with black vellute [velvet]." Silk, though expensive, was used for jockeys' jackets and caps because of its light weight and soft, smooth texture. Velvet also was used through the first half of the 19th century.

On October 4, 1762, 19 members of the English Jockey Club registered their colors at Newmarket "for the greater convenience of distinguishing the horses in running." Across the Atlantic Ocean just four years later, Philadelphia horsemen registered their silks with the Philadelphia Jockey Club. Registering yellow silks was Lewis Morris Jr., a signer of the Declaration of Independence.

One of the longest-used silks in America belonged to Howell E. Jackson, a relative of President Andrew Jackson who chose all-maroon colors first used in the early 1820s. The all-scarlet silks of Francis Morris (no relation to Lewis) were first worn in 1862 at the Union Course on Long Island. The Morris family used those colors for four generations through John A. Morris.

Rules published for the October 17-19, 1826, race meeting in Lexington required jockeys to wear a silk jacket and cap. The American Jockey Club, founded in 1894, registered silks for $1 annually or $25 lifetime. The most famous silks in American racing have been those of prominent, private stables—the devil's red and blue of Calumet Farm, the plain black jacket with cherry cap of the late Ogden Phipps, and the all-orange silks of Claiborne Farm.

Sporadically, racetracks have experimented with color-coded silks and jockeys' caps. In 1947, Portland Meadows assigned silks colors by post positions, an idea that was copied at Sportsman's Park and Prescott Downs. Narragansett Park matched the colors of jockeys' caps with post positions. Neither experiment caught on nationally.

In the evolution of Thoroughbred racing in the United States, silk has mostly yielded to nylon or Lycra as the preferred fabric of jockeys' colors. Aerodynamic silks have become commonplace in American racing. First unveiled in 1988 when trainer D. Wayne Lukas used them on all 12 of his horses in the Breeders' Cup, aerodynamic silks, though more costly, are widely available today.

Approximately 28,000 sets of silks are registered with the Jockey Club. Owners pay an annual fee of $15 or $60 every five years. The Jockey Club ceased registering lifetime silks in 1964 while perpetually reserving 3,500 designs.

The Jockey Club has registered silks with various punctuation marks, geometric figures, riding equipment, racetracks, vegetables, musical notes, instruments, birds, dogs, horses, foxes, and even an elephant. Though silks can vary from state to state, roughly 95% of all silks designs are registered with the Jockey Club.

—Bill Heller

Key Dates in American Racing History

1665 New York Governor Richard Nicolls establishes America's first formal racecourse on Long Island, names it "New Market."

1730 The Darley Arabian's son *Bulle Rock becomes the first recognized Thoroughbred imported to America, into the Virginia colony.

1752 The great racemare *Selima wins an intercolonial race in Virginia worth $10,000 **(December)**.

1764 Undefeated racehorse and foundation sire Eclipse is born in England during a solar eclipse. Future influential sire *Fearnought is imported to America.

1780 The inaugural Epsom Derby is won by Sir Charles Bunbury's *Diomed **(May 4)**.

1798 *Diomed is imported to Virginia at age 21 for the equivalent of $250; he becomes America's most important early sire. *Spread Eagle, 1795 Epsom Derby winner, is imported into Virginia.

1801 *Spread Eagle reportedly covers 234 mares. Leviathan, American racing's first great gelding, concludes a 23-race win streak, which remains an American record for more than two centuries.

1802 Leviathan wins a five-mile race carrying 180 pounds.

1804 *Sir Harry, 1798 Epsom Derby winner, is imported into Virginia.

1805 American foundation sire Sir Archy is foaled.

1806 Northern champion First Consul runs his undefeated streak to 21.

1808 *Diomed dies in Virginia at age 31 **(March 10)**.

1810 Maria runs five four-mile heats to win a $500 purse at Fairfield, Virginia **(October 3)**.

1820 American Eclipse covers 87 mares for a $12.50 fee.

1821 Union Course opens on Long Island, becomes America's first famous racetrack **(October 15)**.

1823 American Eclipse defeats Henry in North-South match over the Union Course; he becomes America's leading earner, with $56,700 **(May 27)**.

1833 Leading sires Sir Archy and his best son, Sir Charles, die on same day **(June 7)**.

1836 *Glencoe, winner of the 1834 Two Thousand Guineas, is imported into Alabama.

1842 Fashion defeats Boston in a Union Course match race before a crowd of more than 50,000 **(May 10)**.

1845 Peytona defeats Fashion in a $20,000 match race over two four-mile heats at the Union Course and surpasses American Eclipse as the leading American money winner, with $62,400 **(May 13)**. Fashion defeats Peytona in two four-mile heats at Camden, New Jersey **(May 28)**.

1850 Lexington is born **(March 17)**.

1852 Black Swan defeats Governor Pio Pico's non-Thoroughbred stallion Sarco in a nine-mile match race at Los Angeles for a $2,000 purse and 1,000 head of cattle **(March)**.

1855 Lexington sets a four-mile world record of 7:19¾ **(April 2)**. Lexington defeats Lecomte in a match race at New Orleans **(April 14)**.

1856 Lexington sells for an American record $15,000 to Robert A. Alexander.

1857 American-bred Prioress wins England's Cesarewitch Handicap at Newmarket **(October 13)**. Lexington retires to Woodburn Stud in Kentucky.

1860 Don Juan wins the first running of Canada's Queen's Plate **(June 27)**. Revenue becomes America's first leading sire based on progeny earnings instead of winners.

1861 Lexington leads the American sire list for the first of a record 16 times. Planet surpasses Peytona as America's leading money winner, with $69,700.

1864 Lexington's unbeaten son Norfolk wins America's first Derby—the $1,000 Jersey Derby at Paterson **(June 7)**. Saratoga Race Course opens; the inaugural Travers Stakes is won by Lexington's son Kentucky **(August 2)**. Asteroid, another undefeated son of Lexington, is stolen from Woodburn Stud by Confederate guerillas **(October 22)**, recovered a week later. Norfolk is sold for an American record $15,001.

1866 Jerome Park opens in New York **(September 25)**.

1867 The inaugural Belmont Stakes is won by the filly Ruthless at Jerome Park **(June 19)**. Robert A. Alexander dies at Woodburn at age 48 **(June 17)**.

1868 The Ladies Handicap is inaugurated at Jerome Park, becoming the first major American race to be carded annually for fillies and mares **(June 16)**.

1870 Monmouth Park opens in New Jersey **(July 30)**. Pimlico Race Course opens in Maryland **(October 25)**.

1872 Fair Grounds racetrack opens in New Orleans **(April 13)**.

1873 The inaugural Preakness Stakes at Pimlico is won by Survivor **(May 27)**. Volume I of the *American Stud Book* is published.

1874 Pari-mutuel wagering is introduced at Jerome Park.

1875 *Kentucky Livestock Record* begins publication **(February 5)**, with a subscription cost of $3 per year. Churchill Downs opens; the inaugural Kentucky Derby is won by Aristides **(May 17)**. Lexington dies **(July 1)**.

1877 Congress adjourns to watch Parole defeat Tom Ochiltree and Ten Broeck at Pimlico **(October 24)**.

1878 Ten Broeck defeats Mollie McCarthy in East-West match at Louisville **(July 4)**.

1880 America's first recorded post parade is held before the Belmont Stakes **(June 14)**. Sheepshead Bay racecourse opens in New York **(June 19)**. Blue Gown, the 1868 Epsom Derby winner, dies en route to America.

1881 Pierre Lorillard's Iroquois becomes the first American-owned and -bred Epsom Derby winner **(June 1)**. Hindoo wins his 18th consecutive race **(September 1)**. Parole retires as the leading American money winner, with $82,816.

1882 Fair Grounds racetrack installs electric lights in its grandstand.

1883	The Louisville Jockey Club racetrack is renamed Churchill Downs.
1884	Buchanan becomes the first maiden Kentucky Derby winner (**May 16**).
1886	Miss Woodford becomes the first American Thoroughbred to top $100,000 in earnings (**June 2**). Two-year-old Tremont wins each of his 13 career starts in a ten-week span that ends on **August 7**.
1887	Hanover wins 17 consecutive races.
1888	Trainer R. Wyndham Walden saddles a record seventh Preakness Stakes winner, Refund (**May 11**). King Thomas brings an American yearling auction record of $40,000 (**June 26**). The inaugural Futurity Stakes at Sheepshead Bay is worth $40,900 to winner Proctor Knott (**September 3**).
1889	Hanover ends Miss Woodford's reign as the leading American money winner (**August 29**), retiring with earnings of $118,887. U.S. purse distribution is $2.4-million; 4,820 races are run.
1890	The Preakness Stakes is run at Morris Park in New York (**June 10**). Salvator runs a world-record 1:35½ mile down the straightaway at Monmouth Park (**August 28**).
1891	Hawthorne Race Course opens near Chicago (**May 20**). *St. Blaise sells for a world auction record $100,000 at the August Belmont I estate dispersal (**October 16**).
1892	Kingston surpasses Hanover as America's top money winner, with $138,917.
1893	Boundless wins the American Derby at Washington Park, after an hour and 40-minute delay at the starting post (**June 24**). *Ormonde, regarded as Europe's best horse of the 19th century, arrives for stud duty in California (**September 8**). Two-year-old Domino sets a single-season earnings record of $170,890 and becomes America's leading money winner (**September 29**). Himyar sets a single-season progeny earnings record of $249,502.
1894	The Jockey Club is incorporated (**February 9**). Kingston scores a record 89th career victory (**August 21**). Aqueduct racetrack opens in New York (**September 27**). *Daily Racing Form* begins publication (**November 17**). *Sir Modred becomes the only California-based stallion to lead the American year-end sire list.
1895	*Livestock Record* changes its name to *The Thoroughbred Record* (**February 2**). August Belmont II heads the new Westchester Racing Association, the controlling body of New York racing (**August 14**). Domino retires with record American earnings of $193,550 (**September 17**).
1896	Domino arrives in Lexington and makes his last public appearance before entering stud (**February 3**).
1897	Jockey Club buys the *American Stud Book* from H. Sanders Bruce for $35,000 (**May 17**). Lucretia Borgia races against time at Oakland, California, setting a world four-mile record of 7:11 that remains on the books today. Domino dies of meningitis at age six (**July 29**).
1898	Fasig-Tipton auction company is incorporated. American-born jockey Tod Sloan introduces his high-stirrup, crouched ("monkey-on-a-stick") riding style to England.
1899	Fasig-Tipton Co. conducts its first Thoroughbred auction, under electric lights at Madison Square Garden, New York (**June 19**). Champion and four-time leading sire Hanover dies (**March 23**).
1900	Pari-mutuel wagering is introduced at Fair Grounds. The Jockey Club registers 3,476 foals. Johnny Reiff becomes the first American to top the English jockey standings, with 143 victories.
1901	William Collins Whitney becomes the second American owner to win the Epsom Derby, with Volodyovski (**June 5**). James R. Keene's American-bred Cap and Bells, by Domino, wins the Epsom Oaks (**June 7**). Racing Hall of Fame racehorse and leading sire Hindoo dies at age 23 (**July 4**). Champion Hamburg sells for $60,000 at the Marcus Daly estate dispersal (**October 1**). Future five-time leading sire *Star Shoot is imported.
1902	Savable earns the decade's largest winner's purse, $44,500, in the Futurity Stakes (**August 30**).
1903	Flocarline is the first filly to win the Preakness Stakes (**May 30**). Africander is the first three-year-old Suburban Handicap winner (**June 18**).
1904	Oaklawn Park opens in Arkansas (**February 24**). Leading owner W. C. Whitney dies (**March 7**). Elwood becomes the first Kentucky Derby winner owned and bred by women (**May 2**). Hamburg sells for $70,000 at the W. C. Whitney estate dispersal (**October 10**).
1905	Champion Commando dies of tetanus at age seven (**March 13**). Belmont Park opens (**May 4**). Tanya becomes the second filly to win the Belmont Stakes (**May 24**). Artful hands Sysonby his only defeat, in the Futurity Stakes (**August 27**). Roseben sets an American six-furlong record of 1:11⅗ under 147 pounds in the Manhattan Handicap (**October 6**).
1906	An earthquake destroys San Francisco's Ingleside racetrack (**April 18**). Sysonby dies of septic poisoning at age four (**June 17**). Roseben wins the Manhattan Handicap for a second time under 147 pounds (**October 12**). Kentucky appoints the first state racing commission.
1907	Colin launches his perfect 15-for-15 career with a maiden victory at Belmont Park (**May 29**). The original Santa Anita Park opens in California (**December 7**). Commando posthumously breaks his grandsire Himyar's single-season progeny earnings record, with $270,345.
1908	California-bred Rubio wins England's Grand National Steeplechase (**March 26**). Bookmakers are barred from Churchill Downs and 15 pari-mutuel machines are installed (**March**). Agnew-Hart legislation outlaws public betting in New York, though racing continues without wagering (**June 13**). Colin ends his career in the Tidal Stakes, a betless exhibition at Sheepshead Bay (**June 20**). The Locke Law ends racing in New Orleans.
1909	The Walker-Otis Anti-Racetrack Gambling Bill is passed in California, effectively blacking out racing there for a quarter-century (**February 19**). The Preakness winner's silks are painted on the Pimlico Clubhouse's weathervane for the first time (**May 12**).
1910	New York passes the Director's Criminal Liability Act, making racetrack operators and executives subject to imprisonment if gambling is found to occur on track premises. All New York tracks cease operation. A mass exodus of American breeding stock and racehorses to Europe begins.

1911 Laurel Race Course opens in Maryland **(October 2)**. Three-hundred ninety yearlings average $230 at U.S. auctions. The average U.S. purse reaches a 20th-century low $371.

1912 Wishing Ring wins at Latonia, paying a record $1,885.50 for a $2 wager **(June 17)**. James R. Keene sells Castleton Stud in Kentucky for $225 an acre. Star Charter is the season's leading money winner, with $14,655. Influential sire *Rock Sand and champion Tanya are included in the mass exportation of bloodstock to Europe.

1913 The English Jockey Club passes the Jersey Act, excluding most American pedigrees from admission to the *General Stud Book* **(April)**. Donerail wins the Kentucky Derby at record odds of 91.45-to-1 **(May 10)**. Belmont Park reopens without legal wagering **(May 30)**. Whisk Broom II becomes the first to sweep New York's handicap triple crown—the Metropolitan, Brooklyn, and Suburban Handicaps **(June 28)**. James R. Keene's estate dispersal is conducted at Madison Square Garden, and future Racing Hall of Fame member Peter Pan tops the sale at $38,000 **(September 2)**.

1914 Iron Mask carries 150 pounds to victory at Juarez, Mexico, setting a 5½-furlong world record of 1:03⅖ that stands for 30 years **(March 8)**. Old Rosebud sets a Kentucky Derby record of 2:03⅖ that stands for 17 years **(May 9)**.

1915 Pan Zareta gives ten pounds to Joe Blair and beats him in a match race at Juarez, setting a five-furlong world record of :57⅕ that stands for 36 years **(February 10)**. Pan Zareta carries 146 pounds to victory at Juarez, giving rivals from 31 to 54 pounds **(March 26)**. Regret becomes the first filly to win the Kentucky Derby **(May 8)**. The Preakness Stakes is run in two divisions for the only time **(May 15)**.

1916 *Star Shoot sires a record 27 juvenile winners.

1917 The New York State Racing Commission recommends to the Legislature that pari-mutuel wagering be legalized **(January)**. Man o' War is born **(March 29)**. *Omar Khayyam becomes the first foreign-bred Kentucky Derby winner **(May 12)**. Borrow wins the Brooklyn Handicap over Kentucky Derby winners Regret, Old Rosebud, and *Omar Khayyam **(June 25)**.

1918 Exterminator wins the Kentucky Derby at 29.60-to-1 odds **(May 11)**. Man o' War is sold to Samuel D. Riddle for $5,000 at the Saratoga yearling sale **(August 17)**. Roamer is the first to crack a 1:35 mile, running in 1:34⅘ at Saratoga **(August 21)**.

1919 Sir Barton, a maiden, wins the Kentucky Derby **(May 10)**; he becomes the first American Triple Crown winner in winning the Belmont Stakes **(June 18)**. Man o' War wins his first start, at Belmont Park **(June 6)**; he suffers his only career defeat, to Upset, in Saratoga's Sanford Memorial **(August 13)**. Purchase walks over in the inaugural Jockey Club Gold Cup **(September 13)**. The American Jockey Club registers a century-low 1,665 foals.

1920 Man o' War smashes the world record for 1⅜ miles in winning the Belmont Stakes by 20 lengths **(June 12)**; wins the Lawrence Realization Stakes by approximately 100 lengths **(September 4)**; carries 138 pounds to win the Potomac Handicap at Havre de Grace while setting a 1$\frac{1}{16}$-mile track record **(September 18)**; defeats Sir Barton in an $80,000 match race at Kenilworth Park in Canada **(October 12)**; retires as America's leading earner, with $249,465.

1921 Man o' War makes a farewell public gallop around the Kentucky Association racetrack in Lexington **(January 28)**. Counterclockwise racing begins at Belmont Park.

1922 Morvich scores his 11th victory in 11 starts in the Kentucky Derby **(May 13)**, joining Regret as the only undefeated Derby winners to that time. Kentucky Derby winner and future Racing Hall of Fame member Old Rosebud breaks down in a race at Jamaica racetrack and dies at age 11 **(May 23)**.

1923 Exterminator scores a record 34th stakes victory **(April 21)**. Kentucky Derby winner Zev defeats Epsom Derby winner *Papyrus in a Belmont Park match **(October 20)**. Zev becomes the first American racehorse to top $200,000 in single-season earnings ($272,008). Earl Sande rides the winners of $569,394, a record that stands for 20 years.

1924 Nellie Morse is the fourth and final filly Preakness winner **(May 12)**. Nine-year-old Exterminator finishes third in his 100th and final career start **(June 21)**. Three "international specials" are staged in the U.S. and are won by American-breds Wise Counsellor at Belmont Park **(September 1)**, Ladkin at Aqueduct **(September 27)**, and Sarazen at Latonia **(October 11)**. French star *Epinard finishes second in all three. Man o' War is represented by his first stakes winner when By Hisself wins the Autumn Days Stakes at Empire City **(October 20)**.

1925 Hialeah Park opens in Florida, ushering in an era of big-time winter racing **(January 15)**. Network radio's first broadcast of a Kentucky Derby is aired from Louisville's WHAS **(May 16)**. River Downs opens near Cincinnati **(July 6)**. War Feathers, a Man o' War–*Tuscan Red filly, sells at Saratoga for $50,500, an American yearling auction record **(August 10)**. *Sir Gallahad III arrives at Claiborne Farm from France, becoming the first major American stallion syndication **(December 15)**.

1926 Boot to Boot wins Washington Park's American Derby, the first U.S. race to offer a $100,000-added purse **(July 31)**. Man o' War sets a single-season progeny earnings record of $408,137 with just two crops racing. North American yearling sales average is $2,640.

1927 John Longden scores the first of his 6,032 career victories aboard Hugo K. Asher at Salt Lake City **(October 4)**. Arlington Park racetrack opens near Chicago **(October 13)**.

1928 New Broom, a yearling son of Whisk Broom II, sells for $75,000, an auction record that stands for 26 years **(August 7)**. Wirt G. Bowman becomes America's first flying Thoroughbred, traveling by airplane from San Diego to San Francisco **(October)**.

1929 The $100,000 Coffroth Handicap at Tijuana, Mexico, is won by Golden Prince **(March 17)**. Clyde Van Dusen becomes the eighth gelding to win the Kentucky Derby **(May 18)**. Whichone wins the Futurity Stakes, earning America's first six-figure winner's purse, $105,730 **(September 14)**.

1930 The Preakness Stakes is the first American classic to be started from a gate **(May 9)**. Gallant Fox sweeps the Triple Crown **(June 7)**. Jim Dandy defeats Gallant Fox at 100-to-1 odds in the Travers Stakes **(August 16)**. Gallant Fox becomes the first racehorse to surpass $300,000 in single-season earnings **(September 17)**.

1931 Hawthorne Park is the first track in the U.S. to use an electronic timer **(August 3)**. Top Flight becomes the leading distaff money winner and the first juvenile to top $200,000 in earnings **(November 7)**. Tropical Park racetrack opens in Florida **(December 26)**. Influential broodmare *La Troienne is imported.

1932 Eddie Arcaro rides his first winner, at Agua Caliente **(January 14)**. Australian wonder horse *Phar Lap wins the $50,000 Agua Caliente Handicap **(March 20)**; dies in California under mysterious circumstances **(April 5)**. Sportsman's Park opens near Chicago **(May 2)**. The North American yearling sales average declines to $570.

1933 The Woolwine-Maloney Bill legalizes pari-mutuel wagering in California **(February 19)**. Brokers Tip, a maiden, wins the Kentucky Derby in a "fighting finish" involving jockeys Don Meade and Herb Fisher, aboard Head Play **(May 6)**. Longacres racetrack opens in Washington state **(August 3)**. Saliva drug testing instituted at Hialeah Park. Legal bookmaking returns to New York. Walter Vosburgh compiles weights for the first Experimental Free Handicap.

1934 Bay Meadows Race Course opens in Northern California and is the first in America to use a photo-finish camera **(November 3)**. Santa Anita Park opens in Southern California **(December 25)**. The Kentucky Derby purse is reduced from $50,000 to $30,000. Hialeah Park builds the first modern American grass course.

1935 The inaugural $100,000 Santa Anita Handicap is won by *Azucar, with Twenty Grand and Equipoise in the beaten field **(February 23)**. Mary Hirsch is the first woman awarded a trainer's license from the Jockey Club **(April)**. Omaha becomes the third Triple Crown winner **(June 8)**. Suffolk Downs opens in Massachusetts **(July 10)**.

1936 Jockey Ralph Neves pronounced "dead" after a racing accident at Bay Meadows; he returns to the track that day **(May 12)**. Keeneland Race Course opens in Kentucky **(October 15)**. *Daily Racing Form* begins formal recognition of annual divisional champions, names Granville the first Horse of the Year. Black Toney stands for an American-high $2,000 fee.

1937 Stagehand receives 30 pounds from Seabiscuit and beats him by a nose in the Santa Anita Handicap **(March 5)**. War Admiral becomes the fourth Triple Crown winner **(June 5)**. Delaware Park opens **(June 26)**. Bing Crosby and Pat O'Brien open Del Mar racetrack in California **(July 3)**. Sir Barton, America's first Triple Crown winner, dies in Wyoming **(October 30)**.

1938 Hollywood Park opens in California **(June 10)**. Equipoise dies at age ten **(August 10)**. Seabiscuit defeats *Ligaroti in a Del Mar match race **(August 12)**; Seabiscuit defeats War Admiral in a two-horse Pimlico Special **(November 1)**.

1939 Gulfstream Park opens in Florida **(February 1)**. Ben A. Jones becomes Calumet Farm's trainer **(July)**. The Grayson Foundation is established to finance equine research **(August 12)**. Bay Meadows Race Course installs America's first electric, enclosed starting gate, developed by Clay Puett.

1940 In his third try, Seabiscuit wins the Santa Anita Handicap and retires as the world's leading money winner, with $437,730 **(March 2)**. Pari-mutuel wagering is legalized in New York **(April 1)**; Jamaica racetrack opens in New York with pari-mutuel wagering **(April 15)**.

1941 Golden Gate Fields opens in California **(February 1)**. Merrick dies at age 38, as the oldest known Thoroughbred **(March 13)**. Whirlaway becomes the fifth American Triple Crown winner **(June 7)**.

1942 Thoroughbred Racing Associations is formed **(March 19)**. Garden State Park opens in New Jersey **(July 18)**. Future leading American sire and broodmare sire *Princequillo is claimed for $2,500 **(August 20)**. Alsab defeats Whirlaway in a $25,000 match at Narragansett Park **(September 19)**. Jockey Eddie Arcaro is suspended by Jockey Club stewards for one year for dangerous riding in the Cowdin Stakes **(September 26)**. Whirlaway becomes the first $500,000 earner **(October 3)**. Santa Anita is used as an internment center for Japanese-Americans. Co. North American yearlings average $638, about half the 1941 average.

1943 Man o' War is pensioned from stud duty at age 26 **(March)**. Stymie is claimed by trainer Hirsch Jacobs for $1,500 **(June 2)**. Tanforan racetrack in California is utilized as a naval training base **(June 3)**. Count Fleet wins the Belmont Stakes by 25 lengths to become the sixth Triple Crown winner **(June 5)**. The Breeders' Sales Co. is organized in Kentucky **(September)**. A wartime ban on "pleasure driving" causes the cancellation or relocation of several race meetings.

1944 The only triple dead-heat in a North American stakes race occurs in Aqueduct's Carter Handicap, between Bossuet, Wait a Bit, and Brownie **(June 10)**. The Breeders' Sales Co. conducts its first yearling auction, at Keeneland **(July 31-August 3)**.

1945 Horse racing in the United States is called off by order of the War Mobilization Board **(January 3)**. American racing resumes four days after Nazi Germany surrenders **(May 12)**. Owner Fred Hooper wins the Kentucky Derby with his first horse, Hoop, Jr. **(June 9)**. North American yearling average soars to $5,146.

1946 Jockey George "The Iceman" Woolf dies following a spill at Santa Anita **(January 4)**. The first transcontinental flight with a Thoroughbred passenger is recorded when Historian flies from Chicago to Los Angeles **(May 29)**. Assault becomes the seventh Triple Crown winner **(June 1)**. Atlantic City Race Course opens **(July 22)**. *Fair Truckle is first to break 1:09 for six furlongs, running 1:08⅖ at Golden Gate Fields **(October 4)**. Assault becomes the first $400,000 single-season earner **(November 9)**. The first transatlantic flight with racehorses on board takes place, from Ireland to New Jersey **(November 26-27)**. Lip tattoos are adopted as a method of identifying racehorses.

1947 Stepfather brings a world auction record of $200,000 at the Louis B. Mayer dispersal **(February 27)**. Seabiscuit dies at age 14 **(May 17)**. Armed defeats Assault at Belmont Park in the first $100,000 winner-take-all match race **(September 27)**. Man o' War dies at age 30 **(November 1)**. Stymie retires with record earnings of $918,485. Calumet is the first stable to top $1-million in a season. Automatic hotwalking machines are introduced.

1948 *Alibhai is syndicated for a record $500,000. Citation becomes the eighth Triple Crown winner **(June 12)**. Gallorette is the first racemare to top $400,000 in career earnings **(July 17)**. Citation ends his campaign with a new single-season earnings record of $709,470 **(December 11)**. *Shannon II becomes the first to crack 2:00 for 1¼ miles, running the distance in 1:59⅘ at Golden Gate Fields **(October 23)**.

1949 Apprentice Bill Shoemaker rides his first winner, at Golden Gate Fields **(April 20)**. Hollywood Park's grandstand and clubhouse are destroyed by fire **(May 6)**. England's Jockey Club rescinds the Jersey Act after 36 years **(June)**. *Nasrullah is purchased by an American syndicate for $340,000. Keeneland installs America's first aluminum rail.

1950 Detroit Race Course opens **(May 25)**. Future five-time leading American sire *Nasrullah arrives at Claiborne Farm in Kentucky **(July)**. The National Museum of Racing is chartered at Saratoga Springs, New York **(October)**. Gordon Glisson wins the first George Woolf Memorial Jockey Award.

1951 The Santa Anita Maturity offers a record $205,700 purse, with a record winner's share of $144,325 going to Great Circle **(February 3)**. Citation becomes racing's first equine millionaire, winning the Hollywood Gold Cup in his final start **(July 14)**. Bewitch passes Gallorette as leading distaff earner with $462,605. **(July 14)**. The Pimlico Special, won by Bryan G., becomes the first nationally televised race **(November 16)**. Lloyd's of London pays off a $250,000 insurance claim on gravely injured Your Host, who survives to sire Kelso.

1952 The Kentucky Derby is broadcast for the first time on national television, by CBS, and is won by Hill Gail, Ben Jones's record sixth winner **(May 3)**. English representative *Wilwyn wins the inaugural Washington, D.C., International at Laurel Park **(October 18)**. Apprentice jockey Tony DeSpirito scores a single-season record 390 victories **(December 31)**.

1953 Dark Star, 24.90-to-1, hands Native Dancer his only defeat, in the Kentucky Derby **(May 2)**. Charlie Whittingham saddles his first career stakes winner, Porterhouse **(June 10)**. Tom Fool is the second New York handicap triple crown winner, taking the Brooklyn Handicap under 136 pounds **(July 11)**. The Garden State Stakes is inaugurated as the world's richest race, worth $239,000 **(October 31)**. R. H. "Red" McDaniel becomes the first trainer to saddle 200 winners in a season **(December 1)**. Santa Anita opens its Camino Real grass course **(December 26)**. Bill Shoemaker smashes the single-season win record, with 485 victories **(December)**. *Royal Charger is advertised at an American record $10,000 stud fee.

1954 The San Juan Capistrano Handicap is America's first $100,000 grass race **(March 6)**. Bold Ruler and Round Table are foaled at Claiborne Farm in Kentucky **(April 6)**. Determine becomes the first gray Kentucky Derby winner **(May 1)**. Never Say Die is the second American-bred Epsom Derby winner, 73 years after Iroquois **(June 2)**.

1955 The National Museum of Racing opens at Saratoga Springs; the Racing Hall of Fame is instituted **(August 6)**. Camarero's undefeated streak concludes after a world-record 56 consecutive victories, in Puerto Rico **(August)**. Nashua defeats Swaps in a $100,000 match race at Washington Park **(August 31)**. Nashua becomes the first $1-million stallion syndication, for $1,251,000. **(December 15)**. New York Racing Association Inc. is established. *Sir Gallahad III leads the American broodmare sire list for a record 12th time.

1956 Turf Paradise opens in Arizona **(January 7)**. Nashua becomes racing's second equine millionaire **(February 18)**. Woodbine opens in Canada **(June 12)**. John Longden becomes the world's winningest jockey, with 4,871 victories **(September 3)**. Bill Shoemaker and Bill Hartack become the first to ride winners of $2-million in a season. Swaps carries 130 pounds to a 1:39 clocking for 1⅟₁₆ miles, a mark that stands as a dirt record for 27 years **(June 23)**. The original Aqueduct racetrack is torn down.

1957 Florida Breeders' Sales Co. conducts the first two-year-olds in training sale, at Hialeah **(January 28)**. Bold Ruler defeats Round Table and *Gallant Man in the three-horse Trenton Handicap, described as the race of the year **(November 9)**. Bill Hartack is the first jockey to top $3-million in single-season earnings. The American foal crop tops 10,000 for the first time.

1958 Round Table becomes racing's third equine millionaire **(May 11)**. Future Hall of Fame jockey Jack Westrope is killed in a spill during the Hollywood Oaks **(June 19)**. Round Table supplants Nashua as the world's all-time leading money winner **(October 11)**.

1959 *Tomy Lee is the second foreign-bred winner of the Kentucky Derby **(May 2)**. Jamaica racetrack in New York is torn down to make way for a housing development **(August)**. Modern $32-million Aqueduct racetrack opens in New York **(September 14)**.

1960 Undefeated *Ribot arrives in the U.S. for stud duty **(June 23)**. Kelso wins the first of five Horse of the Year titles. The Animal Insurance Co. of America pays off a $1-million policy on Bally Ache, who died on October 28 **(December)**.

1961   Northern Dancer is born **(May 27)**. Ben A. Jones, Racing Hall of Fame trainer, dies **(June 13)**. A son of Swaps, Swapson, becomes the first six-figure American auction yearling, selling for $130,000 at Keeneland July **(July 24)**. National Association of State Racing Commissioners recommends a general ban on all drugs, narcotics, anesthetics, and analgesics. Kelso becomes the third winner of New York's handicap triple crown **(July 22)**. Racing Hall of Fame jockey Eddie Arcaro retires **(November 18)**.

1962   Champion Crimson Satan is the first high-profile positive finding for phenylbutazone after winning the Leonard Richards Handicap at Delaware Park **(July 23)**. Angel Cordero Jr. rides his first North American winner **(July 26)**. Crazy Kid is first to break 1:08 for six furlongs, clocking 1:07⅘ at Del Mar **(August 18)**. Never Say Die becomes the first American-bred to lead the English sire list.

1963   Bold Ruler leads the American sire list for the first of eight times.

1964   Northern Dancer wins the Kentucky Derby in track-record time of 2:00 **(May 2)**. Laffit Pincay Jr. scores his first career victory, in Panama **(May 19)**. Seven-year-old Kelso wins a fifth Jockey Club Gold Cup **(October 31)** and earns a record fifth Horse of the Year title. Wagering in the United States tops $3-billion.

1965   Affectionately wins the Vagrancy Handicap under 137 pounds, the most weight successfully carried by a filly in 49 years **(July 26)**. Buckpasser breaks the juvenile earnings record, with $568,096 **(October 16)**. Northern Dancer stands his first season for a $10,000 stud fee. Moccasin becomes the first juvenile filly to be named Horse of the Year, in the Thoroughbred Racing Associations poll.

1966   Graustark is syndicated for a record $2.4-million **(June)**. Kelso retires as the world's leading money winner, with $1,977,165 **(March 2)**. John Longden wins the San Juan Capistrano aboard George Royal in his final career ride and retires with a world record 6,032 victories **(March 12)**. Three-year-old Buckpasser becomes the youngest equine millionaire **(August 20)**. American foal registrations top 20,000 for the first time.

1967   Buckpasser concludes a 15-race win streak in the Metropolitan Handicap at Aqueduct **(May 30)**. Damascus defeats Buckpasser and Dr. Fager by ten lengths in the Woodward Stakes **(September 30)**; banks record single-season earnings of $817,941. Future double classic winner Majestic Prince brings a yearling auction record of $250,000 at Keeneland July **(July 24)**. National racetrack attendance declines for the first time since World War II. Buckpasser is syndicated for a record $4.8-million. Bold Ruler becomes the first to sire juvenile winners of more than $1-million in a season.

1968   Dancer's Image becomes the only disqualified Kentucky Derby winner, after the then-illegal phenylbutazone shows up in his post-race test **(May 4)**. American-bred Sir Ivor wins the Epsom Derby **(May 29)**. Dark Mirage is the first New York filly triple crown winner **(June 22)**. A *Sea-Bird filly sets a world auction record of $405,000 at Keeneland July **(July 23)**. Native Diver becomes the first California-bred millionaire **(July 15)**. Dr. Fager wins the Washington Park Handicap with 134 pounds, in a world-record 1:32⅕ mile **(August 24)**. Dr. Fager carries 139 pounds to victory in the Vosburgh Handicap, his final career start **(November 2)**. *Vaguely Noble is syndicated for $5-million.

1969   Male riders boycott a race at Tropical Park in which Barbara Jo Rubin was scheduled to ride **(January 15)**. Diane Crump becomes the first female to compete in an American Thoroughbred pari-mutuel race, finishing tenth at Hialeah **(February 7)**. Rubin becomes the first of her sex to a win a pari-mutuel Thoroughbred race in America, at Charles Town Races **(February 22)**; Diane Crump is the first female rider to win a stakes, on Easy Lime in Fair Grounds's Spring Fiesta Cup **(March 29)**. Richard Nixon is the first sitting 20th-century president to attend the Kentucky Derby **(May 3)**. Not-for-profit Oak Tree Racing Association launches its first meeting, at Santa Anita **(October 7)**.

1970   Secretariat is foaled in Virginia **(March 30)**. The New York Legislature votes to legalize city-operated off-track betting parlors **(April 8)**. New York Governor Nelson Rockefeller signs a bill legalizing OTB in the Empire State **(April 22)**. Diane Crump finishes 15th as the first female to ride in the Kentucky Derby **(May 2)**. Exacta wagering is introduced in New York and New Jersey **(June)**. Crowned Prince sets a $510,000 world yearling record at Keeneland July **(July 20)**. Citation dies at age 25 **(August 8)**. Bill Shoemaker passes John Longden as the all-time winning jockey, with victory number 6,033 **(September 7)**. Canadian-bred Nijinsky II sweeps undefeated through the English Triple Crown **(September 12)**. Nijinsky II is syndicated for a record $5.44-million.

1971   Eclipse Awards are instituted by Thoroughbred Racing Associations, *Daily Racing Form*, and National Turf Writers Association. Off-track betting begins in New York **(April 8)**. Canonero II, a $1,200 auction yearling, wins the Kentucky Derby **(May 1)** and Preakness Stakes **(May 15)**. Eight-time leading sire Bold Ruler dies at age 17 **(July 12)**. Former Illinois Governor Otto Kerner is indicted on federal charges that included bribery to influence racing matters **(December)**. National purse distribution tops $200-million.

1972   European racing authorities institute pattern system to rate best races. Jockey Bill Shoemaker sets an all-time stakes record with win number 555 **(March 2)**. What a Treat brings a $450,000 auction record for a female Thoroughbred **(March 6)**. *Morning Telegraph* daily racing newspaper suspends publication after 139 years **(April 10)**. Kentucky's Court of Appeals awards Forward Pass the winner's purse from the 1968 Kentucky Derby, making him Calumet Farm's eighth Derby winner **(April 28)**. American-owned and -bred Roberto wins the Epsom Derby (Eng-G1) **(June 7)**. Convenience defeats Typecast in a $250,000 Hollywood match race **(June 17)**. Secretariat finishes fourth in his debut **(July 4)** but goes on to win seven of nine starts and is voted Horse of the Year at the conclusion of his two-year-old season. Roberto ends Brigadier Gerard's 15-race win streak, in the Benson and Hedges Gold Cup (Eng-G1) **(August 15)**. Four-time leading breeder Arthur B. "Bull" Hancock Jr. dies **(September 14)**.

1973 At urging of European racing authorities, North American Graded Stakes Committee is formed and begins grading of North American races. Champion mare Typecast brings a world auction record of $725,000 **(January 28)**. Secretariat's record $6.08-million syndication is announced **(February 26)**. Sunday racing begins in California at Hollywood Park **(April 15)**. Secretariat sets a Kentucky Derby (G1) record of 1:59⅖ **(May 5)**. *Cougar II becomes the first foreign-bred millionaire **(May 5)**. Secretariat wins the Belmont Stakes (G1) by 31 lengths in a world record 2:24 for 1½ miles, becoming the ninth Triple Crown winner **(June 9)**. Secretariat is featured simultaneously on the covers of *Time, Newsweek*, and *Sports Illustrated* **(June 11)**. Wajima, from the last crop of Bold Ruler, brings a world record yearling price of $600,000 at Keeneland July **(July)**. Secretariat defeats stablemate Riva Ridge in the inaugural Marlboro Cup, setting a world record of 1:45⅖ for 1⅛ miles **(September 15)**. Secretariat ends his career triumphantly in the Canadian International Championship (G2) **(October 28)**. Count Fleet dies at age 33 **(December 3)**. Sandy Hawley is the first jockey to ride 500 winners in a season **(December 15)**.

1974 The centennial Kentucky Derby (G1) is won by Cannonade before a record crowd of 163,628 **(May 4)**. Chris Evert defeats Miss Musket by approximately 50 lengths in a $350,000 match race at Hollywood **(July 20)**. Dahlia is the first distaff millionaire **(August 20)**. D. Wayne Lukas saddles his first Thoroughbred stakes winner, Harbor Hauler, in a division of the Foothill Stakes at Pomona **(September 13)**. Dahlia becomes a stakes winner in five countries **(October 27)**. Louisiana Downs opens **(October 30)**. Apprentice jockey Chris McCarron sets a single-season win record of 546. Dan Lasater nearly doubles the previous single-season earnings record for an owner, with $3,020,521.

1975 Ruffian breaks down in Belmont Park's "battle of the sexes" match race against Foolish Pleasure **(July 6)**; dies following surgery and is buried in the Belmont infield **(July 7)**. Seattle Slew sells as a yearling for $17,500 at the Fasig-Tipton Kentucky July sale **(July 19)**. Two yearling colts are stolen from their stalls at the Keeneland fall sale **(September 7)** and are never recovered. On-track betting in the United States tops $5-billion for the first time. On-track attendance tops 50-million for the first time. Champion Wajima is syndicated for a world-record $7.2-million.

1976 Secretariat's son Canadian Bound is the world's first seven-figure auction yearling, bringing $1.5-million at Keeneland July **(July 20)**. Connecticut opens its Teletrack satellite wagering site. Forego wins his third straight Horse of the Year title. What a Pleasure is syndicated for a world-record $8-million.

1977 Washington Park is destroyed by fire **(February 5)**. Garden State Park's grandstand and clubhouse are destroyed by fire **(April 14)**. Seattle Slew becomes the first undefeated American Triple Crown winner **(June 11)**. Champion Fanfreluche is stolen from a pasture at Claiborne Farm **(June 24)**; recovered unharmed six months later. Seattle Slew suffers his first career loss in the Swaps Stakes at Hollywood Park **(July 3)**. Maryland Governor Marvin Mandel is convicted on racing-related racketeering and mail fraud charges **(August 23)**. The Meadowlands in New Jersey opens its first Thoroughbred meet **(September 6)**. American foal registrations top 30,000 for the first time. Lebon-*Cinzano ringer scandal breaks in New York **(September 23)**. Steve Cauthen becomes the first to ride winners of $6-million in a single season **(December 10)** and is later named *Sports Illustrated*'s Sportsman of the Year and Professional Athlete of the Year by the Associated Press. The Minstrel is syndicated for a world-record $9-million.

1978 John Henry wins a $25,000 claiming race **(May 21)**; switches to turf and wins for $35,000 claiming tag at Belmont Park **(June 1)**. Affirmed becomes the 11th Triple Crown winner **(June 10)**. Triple Crown winners meet for the first time, with Seattle Slew defeating Affirmed in the Marlboro Cup Handicap (G1) **(September 16)**. Affirmed is syndicated for a world-record $14.4-million.

1979 Affirmed becomes the first career $2-million earner **(June 24)**. Affirmed defeats Kentucky Derby (G1) and Preakness Stakes (G1) victor Spectacular Bid in the Jockey Club Gold Cup (G1); becomes the first to earn $1-million in a single season **(October 6)**. Hollywood Park introduces pick-six wagering **(April 23)**. Turf female division added to annual North American championships, won by Trillion.

1980 Genuine Risk becomes the second filly Kentucky Derby winner **(May 3)**. Ex-jockey Con Errico is convicted of race fixing in New York **(May 19)**, is later sentenced to ten years in prison. Spectacular Bid is unchallenged for Woodward Stakes (G1) and walks over **(September 20)**. Prerace drug testing of horses begins at Aqueduct **(October 14)**. Spectacular Bid is syndicated for a record $22-million.

1981 Julie Krone rides her first winner, at Tampa Bay Downs **(February 12)**. The Arlington Million is inaugurated at Arlington Park as the world's first $1-million Thoroughbred race, with John Henry defeating The Bart by a nose. **(August 30)**. Storm Bird is syndicated for a record $30-million.

1982 Mary Russ becomes the first female jockey to win a North American Grade 1 race, with Lord Darnley in the Widener Handicap **(February 27)**. Trainer Woody Stephens saddles the first of five consecutive Belmont Stakes (G1) winners, Conquistador Cielo **(June 5)**. A son of Nijinsky II—Spearfish brings a record $4.25-million at Keeneland July. Simulcasting begins at Woodbine and Fort Erie in Canada. John Gaines conceives the idea for the Breeders' Cup. Conquistador Cielo is syndicated for a record $36.4-million.

1983   European champion Shergar is stolen from Ballymany Stud in Ireland **(February 8)**; he was never recovered. Genuine Risk produces a stillborn colt by Secretariat, the first offspring of two Kentucky Derby (G1) winners **(April 4)**. Shareef Dancer is syndicated for a record $40-million. Jockey Angel Cordero Jr. rides to a record $10-million season. All Along (Fr) becomes America's first foreign-bred Horse of the Year. Simulcasting begins from the Meadowlands to Atlantic City Race Course **(September 28)**. John Henry becomes the first $4-million earner **(December 11)**. Fourteen Northern Dancer sales yearlings average $3,320,357. The Hollywood Futurity (G1) is carded as racing's first $1-million event for two-year-olds **(December 18)**. Horse racing loses its status as the nation's number one spectator sport, to baseball.

1984   A share in Seattle Slew sells for $3-million **(May)**. Swale collapses and dies eight days after winning the Belmont Stakes **(June 17)**. Equine viral arteritis (EVA) halts Kentucky breeding season two weeks early **(June)**. Fit to Fight becomes the fourth horse to sweep New York's handicap triple crown **(July 21)**. The inaugural Breeders' Cup is run at Hollywood Park before 64,625 on-track fans and 50-million television viewers; Wild Again wins the $3-million Breeders' Cup Classic (G1) **(November 10)**. Nine-year-old John Henry retires with record earnings of $6,597,947; he later earns a second Horse of the Year title.

1985   Bill Shoemaker is the first jockey to reach $100-million in purse winnings **(March 3)**. Garden State Park, rebuilt at a cost of approximately $200-million, reopens **(April 1)**. Spend a Buck earns $2.6-million in purse and bonus money following his Jersey Derby (G3) victory **(May 27)**. Steve Cauthen becomes the first American jockey to win both a Kentucky Derby (G1) and Epsom Derby (Eng-G1) **(June 5)**. Creme Fraiche becomes the first gelding to win the Belmont Stakes **(June 8)**. Seattle Dancer sells for a world auction record of $13.1-million at Keeneland July **(July 23)**. Arlington Park's grandstand is destroyed by fire **(July 31)**. Teleprompter (GB) wins the Arlington Million (G1) in front of a razed grandstand and an on-track crowd of 35,651 **(August 25)**. THOROUGHBRED TIMES weekly news magazine publishes its inaugural edition **(September 20)**. Miss Oceana brings a world-record broodmare price of $7-million at the Newstead Farm dispersal **(November 10)**. American foal registrations top 50,000 for the first time.

1986   A season to 25-year-old Northern Dancer sells at auction for $710,000 **(January)**. The Santa Anita Handicap (G1) becomes the first $1-million-guaranteed handicap, won by Greinton (GB) **(March 2)**. Jan Ciochetti is the first woman to call a race at a major track (Hialeah) **(March 21)**. Woody Stephens saddles his fifth straight Belmont Stakes (G1) winner, Danzig Connection **(June 7)**. Laurel Park inaugurates the Maryland Million **(October 18)**. Lawmaker breaks *Star Shoot's 70-year-old record by siring his 28th juvenile winner **(December 12)**; ends the year with 30 two-year-old winners. Jockey Club foal registrations reach an all-time annual high of 51,293. The Jockey Club launches a mandatory blood-typing program. Joint nomination to Triple Crown races begins.

1987   Jockey Chris Antley wins a record nine races in a single day, at Aqueduct and Meadowlands **(October 31)**. Tejano becomes the first juvenile millionaire **(December 12)**. Northern Dancer retires from breeding. Chrysler Corp. announced as the first sponsor of the $5-million Triple Crown Challenge.

1988   Winning Colors is the third filly Kentucky Derby (G1) winner **(May 7)**. Personal Ensign ends her 13-for-13 career with a thrilling victory over Winning Colors in the Breeders' Cup Distaff (G1) **(November 5)**. Alysheba wins the Breeders' Cup Classic (G1) and retires as the leading American money earner, with $6,679,242 **(November 5)**.

1989   E. P. Taylor, breeder of Northern Dancer and Nijinsky II, dies at age 88 **(May 14)**. Belmont Park is the first American racetrack to time races in hundredths of a second. Arlington International Racecourse opens **(June 28)**. Northern Park, the last Northern Dancer yearling sold at auction, brings $2.8-million at Keeneland **(July 18)**. Secretariat dies at age 19 **(October 4)**. Pari-mutuel wagering on horse racing returns to Texas for the first time since 1937 **(October 6)**. Jockey Kent Desormeaux establishes a single-season win record of 547 **(November 30)**; ends the year with 598 winners.

1990   Bill Shoemaker retires as the world's winningest jockey, with 8,833 victories **(February 3)**. D. Wayne Lukas becomes the first trainer to saddle career winners of $100-million **(May 12)**. Champion Go for Wand breaks down fatally in the Breeders' Cup Distaff (G1) **(October 27)**. Santa Anita hosts the inaugural California Cup Day **(November 3)**. Northern Dancer dies at age 29 **(November 16)**. Alydar dies at Calumet Farm under suspicious circumstances **(November 17)**.

1991   The American Championship Racing Series is launched as a designed-for-television event. Bill Shoemaker is paralyzed in a California car accident **(April 8)**. Equibase, a joint venture of the Jockey Club and Thoroughbred Racing Associations, is formed and begins gathering past-performance data in competition with *Daily Racing Form*.

1992   Video lottery terminals (VLTs) are installed at West Virginia and Louisiana racetracks. Henryk de Kwiatkowski buys Calumet Farm for $17-million at a bankruptcy auction **(March 26)**. Gilded Time runs the fastest six furlongs ever recorded by a two-year-old, 1:07.84, in the Sapling Stakes at Monmouth Park **(August 8)**.

1993   At age 16, Kentucky Derby (G1) winner Genuine Risk produces her first live foal, a colt by Rahy **(May 15)**. Julie Krone becomes the first female jockey to win an American classic, with Colonial Affair in the Belmont Stakes **(June 5)**. Claude R. "Shug" McGaughey III saddles five graded stakes winners at Belmont Park in single day **(October 16)**. Arcangues wins the Breeders' Cup Classic at record 133.60-to-1 odds **(November 6)**. Fair Grounds's historic grandstand is destroyed by fire **(December 17)**.

1994	Thoroughbred Racing Associations appoints Brian McGrath as its first and only commissioner **(January 17)**. The American Championship Racing Series is canceled. Class 1 racing begins in Texas at Sam Houston Race Park **(April 29)**. Hollywood Park's casino and card club opens **(July 1)**. Cigar begins his 16-race win streak **(October 28)**. Thoroughbred Owners of California is launched.
1995	New York becomes the last North American racing jurisdiction to legalize race-day use of the antibleeder medication furosemide **(September 1)**. Hoosier Park opens **(September 1)**. Visa International begins sponsorship of the American Triple Crown races. Jockey Jerry Bailey wins a single-season record $16-million in purse money. Delaware Park and Prairie Meadows Racetrack install slot machines.
1996	Cigar scores his 16th consecutive victory, tying Citation's modern record **(July 13)**. Cigar retires as the world's leading money winner, with $9,999,815 **(October 26)**. Serena's Song becomes the top North American distaff earner, with $3,283,388. The Breeders' Cup is held outside of the United States for the first time, at Woodbine in Canada **(October 26)**.
1997	Atticus is the first to crack a 1:32 mile, running the distance on grass in 1:31.89 **(March 3)**. A $25-million infertility insurance claim is paid off on Cigar **(March 24)**. Racing Hall of Fame member Exceller is killed in a Swedish slaughterhouse at age 24 **(April 7)**. Keeneland utilizes a public address system for the first time, at its spring meeting. Colonial Downs opens as Virginia's first pari-mutuel racetrack **(September 1)**. Arlington International announces that it will suspend racing because of financial losses, political climate in Illinois **(September 8)**. Chelsea Zupan sets an American record for a female jockey by winning seven consecutive races at Emerald Downs **(September 18-19)**. Racing Hall of Fame jockey Eddie Arcaro dies at age 81 **(November 14)**. Japanese-based Hokuto Vega retires as the world's richest Thoroughbred mare ($8,300,301).
1998	The National Thoroughbred Racing Association (NTRA) is launched **(April 1)**. Tim Smith is named NTRA commissioner **(April 21)**. Real Quiet fails by a nose in his quest for the Triple Crown **(June 6)**. Elusive Quality clocks a world-record 1:31.63 mile on Belmont Park's grass **(July 4)**. Company controlled by Frank Stronach buys Santa Anita Park. Equibase becomes the sport's sole provider of past-performance data and acquires *Daily Racing Form* database.
1999	Julie Krone retires as the all-time winningest female jockey, with 3,546 victories **(April 18)**. ESPN honors Secretariat as one of the top 50 athletes of the 20th century **(May 19)**. Mr. Prospector dies at age 29 **(June 1)**. Television Games Network (TVG) debuts **(July 14)**. Dale Baird becomes the first trainer to saddle 8,000 winners **(July 22)**. Churchill Downs Inc. purchases Hollywood Park for $140-million **(September 10)**. Laffit Pincay Jr. passes Bill Shoemaker as the world's winningest jockey **(December 10)**, with 8,834 victories. Frank Stronach-controlled Magna Entertainment Corp. buys Gulfstream Park, Golden Gate Fields, Thistledown, and Remington Park. Churchill Downs Inc. acquires Calder Race Course.
2000	Julie Krone becomes the first female elected to the Racing Hall of Fame **(May 2)**. Arlington Park reopens after a two-year hiatus **(May 14)**. NTRA and Breeders' Cup Ltd. consolidate **(May 18)**. Fusaichi Pegasus becomes the first favorite to win the Kentucky Derby in 21 years **(May 6)**; syndicated for a reported record $60-million to $70-million **(June 25)**. Leading breeder Allen Paulson dies at 78 **(July 19)**. Breeder Fred Hooper dies at 102 **(August 3)**. Churchill Downs Inc. buys Arlington Park **(September)**.
2001	Triple Crown winner Affirmed dies at 26 **(January 12)**. The Breeders' Cup becomes formally known as the Breeders' Cup World Thoroughbred Championships **(June 26)**. Jerry Bailey becomes the first jockey to ride winners of $20-million in a season **(October 7)**. Tiznow becomes the first two-time winner of the Breeders' Cup Classic **(October 27)**. The horse racing industry raises more than $5-million to benefit victims of the September 11 terrorist attacks. Laura Hillenbrand's *Seabiscuit: An American Legend* tops the New York *Times* bestseller list for nonfiction.
2002	Japan-based T.M.Opera O, the world's richest Thoroughbred, retires with earnings of $16,200,337 **(January 25)**. Seattle Slew, the last living American Triple Crown winner, dies at age 28 **(May 7)**. Racing Hall of Fame jockey Chris McCarron retires after career victory number 7,139 **(June 23)**. Volponi scores the second-biggest upset in Breeders' Cup Classic (G1) history, with an $89 payoff **(October 26)**. Ultra Pick Six wager on Breeders' Cup races is found to have been fixed, and three former Drexel University fraternity brothers plead guilty to $3-million scam. Julie Krone wins at Santa Anita in comeback after 3½ years in retirement **(November 7)**. Magna International buys Lone Star Park **(October 30)**, and the Maryland Racing Commission approves sale of controlling interest in Maryland tracks to Magna **(November 13)**.
2003	Johnny Longden dies on his 96th birthday **(February 14)**. Laffit Pincay Jr. retires as all-time leading jockey by wins, with 9,530 **(April 29)**. Funny Cide becomes first gelding to win Kentucky Derby since Clyde Van Dusen in 1929 **(May 3)**. *Seabiscuit*, the film, opens to good reviews **(July 25)**. Bill Shoemaker dies at age 72 **(October 12)**. Richard Mandella wins a record four Breeders' Cup races **(October 25)**. Trainer Bobby Frankel set records for single-season earnings and Grade 1 victories.
2004	Owner-breeder William T. Young dies at age 85 **(January 12)**. Smarty Jones wins the Kentucky Derby **(May 1)** and the Preakness by a record 11½ lengths **(May 15)**, but finishes second in the Belmont **(June 5)**. Churchill Downs buys Fair Grounds **(October 15)**. Ghostzapper wins the Breeders' Cup Classic in record time **(October 30)**.
2005	John R. Gaines, creator of the Breeders' Cup, dies at age 76 **(February 11)**. Giacomo wins Kentucky Derby at 50.30-to-1, second-longest odds ever **(May 7)**.

Notable Horses in Racing
Racing Hall of Fame members are listed in italics

The name of each horse is followed by year of birth and year of death, if known. Color and sex (colt, filly, or gelding) are followed by sire, dam, and broodmare sire. The horse's race record is detailed by number of starts, wins, seconds, thirds, and earnings, followed by championship honors and most important wins. Records from the 18th and 19th centuries may be incomplete, and earnings may be impossible to determine. If the horse sired or produced significant stakes winners, that information follows the race record. A sire's or dam's place in important male or female lines is also noted.

ACK ACK, 1966-1990. B. c., Battle Joined—Fast Turn, by *Turn-to. 27-19-6-0, $636,641, Horse of the Year in 1971, champion sprinter, champion older male, Santa Anita H., Hollywood Gold Cup H., etc. Sire of 54 stakes winners, including Youth, Broad Brush, Ack's Secret, Rascal Lass, Caline. Broodmare sire of Sharp Cat, Royal Anthem, Benny the Dip, North Sider, Lost Code.

AFFECTIONATELY, 1960-1979. Dk. b. or br. f., Swaps—Searching, by War Admiral. 52-28-8-6, $546,659, champion two-year-old filly, champion sprinter, champion older mare, Top Flight H., Spinaway S., etc. Dam of Personality.

AFFIRMED, 1975-2001. Ch. c., Exclusive Native—Won't Tell You, by Crafty Admiral. 29-22-5-1, $2,393,818, Horse of the Year in 1978-'79, champion two- and three-year-old male, champion older male, Triple Crown, Jockey Club Gold Cup (G1), etc. Sire of more than 80 stakes winners, including Flawlessly, Quiet Resolve, Affirmed Success, Peteski, Zoman, Charlie Barley, Bint Pasha. Broodmare sire of Chelsey Flower, Harlan's Holiday, Stinger, Balanchine.

AFRICANDER, 1900-unknown. B. c. *Star Ruby—Afric Queen, by *Darebin. 60-19-15-8, $102,325, champion three-year-old, Belmont S., Suburban H., etc.

ALARM, 1869-1895. B. c., *Eclipse—*Maud, by Stockwell. 9-6-2-1, $12,500, match race with Inverary. Sire of Himyar, Panique, Danger, Ann Fief, Fidele. First American male-line ancestor of Domino, Plaudit lines.

ALCIBIADES, 1927-1957. Ch. f., Supremus—*Regal Roman, by Roi Herode. 23-7-2-4, $47,860, champion two-year-old filly, Kentucky Oaks, etc. Dam of Menow, Lithe, Salaminia. Foundation mare of family that includes Sir Ivor, Firm Policy, Rash Statement, Twice the Vice, Shine Again, Halo America.

ALL ALONG (FR), 1979- . B. f., Targowice—Agujita (Fr), by Vieux Manoir. 21-9-4-2, $2,125,809, Horse of the Year in 1983, champion older female, champion older horse in France, Prix de l'Arc de Triomphe (Fr-G1), Turf Classic S. (G1), etc. Dam of Along All, Arnaqueur.

ALLEGED, 1974-2000. B. c., Hoist the Flag—Princess Pout, by Prince John. 10-9-1-0, $623,187, champion three-year-old in England and France, champion older horse in Europe, Prix de l'Arc de Triomphe (Fr-G1) twice, etc. One of only five horses to win consecutive runnings of the Prix de l'Arc de Triomphe. Sire of 100 stakes winners, including Miss Alleged, Law Society, Midway Lady, Shantou, Muhtarram, Romanette. Broodmare sire of Suave Dancer, Dr Devious (Ire), Dream Well (Fr), Go and Go (Ire), Sulamani (Ire).

ALLEZ FRANCE, 1970-1989. B. f., *Sea-Bird—Priceless Gem, by Hail to Reason. 21-13-3-1, $1,262,801, Horse of the Year in France in 1974, champion two- and three-year-old filly, champion older mare twice, Prix de l'Arc

de Triomphe (Fr-G1), etc. Dam of Action Francaise. Considered greatest filly ever trained in France.

ALMAHMOUD, 1947-1971. Ch. f., *Mahmoud—Arbitrator, by Peace Chance. 11-4-0-1, $32,760, Vineland H., etc. Dam of Cosmah, Natalma. Foundation mare of family that includes Northern Dancer, Halo, Danehill, Tosmah, Flawlessly, Arctic Tern, Machiavellian, Bago, L'Emigrant, Cannonade, La Prevoyante.

ALSAB, 1939-1963. B. c., Good Goods—Winds Chant, by Wildair. 51-25-11-5, $350,015, champion two- and three-year-old colt, Preakness S., American Derby, etc. Sire of 17 stakes winners, including Myrtle Charm, Armageddon, Sabette. Defeated Triple Crown winner Whirlaway in match race. Tail-male ancestor of line that leads to Broad Brush.

ALYDAR, 1975-1990. Ch. c., Raise a Native—Sweet Tooth, by On-and-On. 26-14-9-1, $957,195, Travers S. (G1), Florida Derby (G1), etc. Leading sire in 1990. Sire of 77 stakes winners, including Alysheba, Easy Goer, Criminal Type, Turkoman, Althea, Alydaress, Strike the Gold, Miss Oceana, Endear, Peinture Bleue, Winglet. Broodmare sire of Ajina, Amilynx, Anees, Cat Thief, General Meeting, Lakeway, Lure, Peintre Celebre.

ALYSHEBA, 1984- . B. c., Alydar—Bel Sheba, by Lt. Stevens. 26-11-8-2, $6,679,242, Horse of the Year in 1988, champion three-year-old male, champion older male, Kentucky Derby (G1), Preakness S. (G1), Breeders' Cup Classic (G1), etc. Sire of more than 15 stakes winners, including Alywow, Bright Moon, Moonlight Dance.

AMERICAN ECLIPSE, 1814-1847. Ch. c., Duroc—Millers Damsel, by *Messenger. 8-8-0-0, $56,700, North-South Match Race with (Sir) Henry. Sire of Black Maria, Ariel, Medoc, Fanny, Lance. First great American champion.

AMERICAN FLAG, 1922-1942. Ch. c., Man o' War—*Lady Comfey, by Roi Herode. 17-8-1-1, $82,725, champion three-year-old colt, Belmont S., Withers S., etc. Sire of 16 stakes winners including Nellie Flag, Gusto. Broodmare sire of Raise You, Mar-Kell.

ANCIENT TITLE, 1970-1981. Dk. b. or br. g., Gummo—Hi Little Gal, by Bar Le Duc. 57-24-11-9, $1,252,791, Hollywood Gold Cup Invitational H. (G1), Charles H. Strub S. (G1), etc. Won 20 stakes; leading California-bred money earner at the time of his death.

ANITA PEABODY, 1925-1934. B. or br. f., Luke McLuke—*La Dauphine, by The Tetrarch. 8-7-0-1, $113,105, champion two-year-old filly, Futurity S., Debutante S., etc. Dam of Our Count.

A.P. INDY, 1989- . Dk. b. or br. c., Seattle Slew—Weekend Surprise, by Secretariat. 11-8-0-1, $2,979,815, Horse of the Year in 1992, champion three-year-old male, Belmont S. (G1), Breeders' Cup Classic (G1), etc. Sire of more than 75 stakes winners, including Mineshaft, Tempera, Golden Missile, Aptitude, Lu Ravi, Secret Status, A P Valentine, Old Trieste.

ARAZI, 1989- . Ch. c., Blushing Groom (Fr)—Danseur Fabuleux, by Northern Dancer. 14-9-1-1, $1,212,351, champion two-year-old male, Horse of the Year in Europe, Breeders' Cup Juvenile (G1), Grand Criterium (Fr-G1), etc. Sire of 15 stakes winners, including Congaree, First Magnitude (Ire), America (Ire).

ARIEL, 1822-1843. Gr. f., American Eclipse—Young Empress, by Financier. 57-42-14-1, about $25,000. Ran four-mile heats 28 times, winning 18. Dam of three foals, no winners.

ARISTIDES, 1872-1893. Ch. c., *Leamington—Sarong, by Lexington. 21-9-5-1,$18,325, Kentucky Derby, Withers S., Jerome S., etc. First winner of Kentucky Derby in 1875.

ARMED, 1941-1964. Br. g., Bull Lea—Armful, by Chance Shot. 81-41-20-10, $817,475, Horse of the Year in 1947, champion handicap horse twice, Suburban H., Widener H. twice, Gulfstream Park H., etc.

ARTFUL, 1902-1927. B. f., Hamburg—Martha II, by Dandie Dinmont. 8-6-2-0, $81,125, Futurity S., etc. Only horse to defeat Sysonby. Tail-female ancestor of family that includes Runaway Groom.

ARTS AND LETTERS, 1966-1998. Ch. c., *Ribot—All Beautiful, by Battlefield. 23-11-6-1, $632,404, Horse of the Year in 1969, champion three-year-old colt, champion handicap horse, Belmont S., Jockey Club Gold Cup, etc. Sire of 30 stakes winners, including Codex, Winter's Tale, Illiterate.

ASSAULT, 1943-1971. Ch. c., Bold Venture—Igual, by Equipoise. 42-18-6-7, $675,470, Horse of the Year in 1946, champion three-year-old colt, Triple Crown, Suburban H., Brooklyn H. twice. Sterile at stud.

ASTEROID, 1861-1886. B. c., Lexington—Nebula, by *Glencoe. 12-12-0-0, $12,800, Woodlawn Vase, etc. One of three sons of Lexington, along with Kentucky and Norfolk, to be considered the best racehorses of the 1860s, called the "great triumvirate." Sire of Creedmoor, Ballankeel.

***AUSTRALIAN**, 1858-1879. Ch. c. West Australian—*Emilia, by Young Emilius. 10-3-3-3, $12,150, Doswell S., Galt House S. Sire of Spendthrift, Wildidle, Baden Baden, Fellowcraft, Joe Daniels, Springbok. American founder of male line that includes Man o' War, War Admiral, In Reality, Tiznow.

AZERI, 1998- . Ch. f., Jade Hunter—Zodiac Miss (Aus), by Ahonoora. 24-17-4-0, $4,079,820, Horse of the Year in 2002, champion older female 2002, '03, '04, Breeders' Cup Distaff (G1), Apple Blossom H. (G1) 2002-'04, etc. Leading North American distaff earner.

BALD EAGLE, 1955-1977. B. c., *Nasrullah—Siama, by Tiger. 29-12-5-4, $692,946, champion older horse, Metropolitan H., Suburban H., etc. Sire of 12 stakes winners, including Too Bald, San San. Broodmare sire of 33 stakes winners, including Exceller, Capote.

BALLOT, 1904-1937. Ch. c., *Voter—*Cerito, by Lowland Chief. 38-20-6-6, $154,545, Suburban H., etc. Sire of Midway, Chilhowee, Star Voter. Broodmare sire of Bull Lea.

BATTLEFIELD, 1948-1964. Ch. c., War Relic—Dark Display, by Display. 44-22-14-2, $474,727, champion two-year-old colt, Futurity S., Hopeful S., Travers S., etc. Sire of Yorktown. Broodmare sire of Arts and Letters, Steeple Jill.

BATTLESHIP, 1927-1958. Ch. c., Man o' War—*Quarantaine, by Sea Sick. 55-24-6-4, $71,641, Grand National Steeplechase in England and U.S., etc. Sire of Shipboard, War Battle.

BAYAKOA (Arg), 1984-1997. B. f., Consultant's Bid—Arlucea (Arg), by Good Manners. 39-21-9-0, $2,861,701, champion older female twice, Breeders' Cup Distaff (G1) twice, Spinster S. (G1) twice, etc.

BED O' ROSES, 1947-1953. B. f., Rosemont—Good Thing, by Discovery. 46-18-8-6, $383,925, champion two-year-old filly, champion handicap mare, Santa Margarita H., Matron S., etc.

BELDAME, 1901-1923. Ch. f., Octagon—*Bella Donna, by Hermit. 31-17-6-4, $102,135, Suburban H., Alabama S., Ladies H., etc. Dam of Belvale. Tail-female ancestor of family that includes Revoked, Lion Heart.

BEN ALI, 1883-unknown. Br. c., Virgil—Ulrica, by Lexington. 40-12-3-5, $25,090, Kentucky Derby, Hopeful S., etc.

BEN BRUSH, 1893-1918. B. c., Bramble—Roseville, by Reform. 40-25-5-5, $65,208, Kentucky Derby, Suburban H., etc. Leading sire in 1909. Sire of Broomstick, Sweep, Delhi, Meridian, Pebbles, Theo Cook, Von Tromp.

BEND OR, 1877-1903. Ch. c., Doncaster—Rouge Rose, by Thormanby. 14-10-2-0, $90,304, Epsom Derby, Champion S., etc. Sire of *Ormonde, Bona Vista, Kendal, Orvieto. Tail-male ancestor of Phalaris, *Teddy lines.

BEST PAL, 1988-1998. B. g., *Habitony—Ubetshedid, by King Pellinore. 47-18-11-4, $5,668,245, Santa Anita H. (G1), Hollywood Gold Cup H. (G1), etc. Leading California-bred money earner at retirement.

BEWITCH, 1945-1959. Br. f., Bull Lea—Potheen, by Wildair. 55-20-10-11, $462,605, champion two-year-old filly, champion handicap mare, Arlington Lassie S., Vanity H., etc. Defeated stablemate Citation in 1947 Washington Park Futurity.

BIMELECH, 1937-1966. B. c., Black Toney—*La Troienne, by *Teddy. 15-11-2-1, $248,745, champion two- and three-year-old colt, Preakness S., Belmont S., etc. Sire of 30 stakes winners, including Better Self, Be Faithful, Guillotine, Hilarious, Brookfield. Broodmare sire of Lalun, No Robbery. Full brother to Black Helen.

BIRDCATCHER, 1833-1860. Ch. c., Sir Hercules—Guiccioli, by Bob Booty. 18-6-4-4, $6,666 in Ireland, Madrid Plate, Peel Cup, etc. Sire of *Alfred, The Baron, Bird on the Wing, Chanticleer, Daniel O'Rourke, Kingfisher. Tail-male ancestor of Phalaris, *Teddy, Blandford male lines. Famous for passing on dark spots in his chestnut coat, known as "Birdcatcher spots."

BLACK GOLD, 1921-1928. Bl. c., Black Toney—Useeit, by Bonnie Joe. 35-18-5-4, $110,553, champion three-year-old colt, Kentucky Derby, Ohio Derby, etc. Broke down fatally at seven and buried in the infield at Fair Grounds.

BLACK HELEN, 1932-1957. B. f., Black Toney—*La Troienne, by *Teddy. 22-15-0-2, $61,800, champion three-year-old filly, Coaching Club American Oaks, Florida Derby, etc. Tail-female ancestor of family that includes Pleasant Tap, Go for Gin, But Why Not, Princess Rooney. Full sister to Bimelech.

BLACK MARIA, 1826-unknown. Bl. f., American Eclipse—Lady Lightfoot, by Sir Archy. 26-13-(placings unknown), $14,900, Jockey Club Purse, etc. Ran 17 times in four-mile heats. Won a five-heat, four-mile heat race that caused death of one opponent from exhaustion.

BLACK MARIA, 1923-1932. Bl. f., Black Toney—*Bird Loose, by Sardanapale. 52-18-14-6, $110,350, champion three-year-old filly, champion older mare twice, Kentucky Oaks, Metropolitan H., Ladies H. twice, etc. Tail-female ancestor of family that includes Polynesian, Air Forbes Won.

BLACK TIE AFFAIR (Ire), 1986- . Gr. or ro. c., Miswaki—Hat Tab Girl, by Al Hattab. 45-18-9-6, $3,370,694, Horse of the Year in 1991, champion older male, Breeders' Cup Classic (G1), Philip H. Iselin H. (G1), etc. Sire of more than 30 stakes winners, including Formal Gold, Evening Attire. Exported from the United States to Japan in 1997; returned in 2003.

BLACK TONEY, 1911-1938. Br. c., Peter Pan—Belgravia, by Ben Brush. 37-12-10-7, $12,815, Independence H., Valuation S., etc. Sire of more than 35 stakes winners, including Balladier, Big Hurry, Bimelech, Black Gold, Black Helen, Black Maria, Black Servant, Brokers Tip, Miss Jemima. Broodmare sire of more than 25 stakes winners, including Bridal Flower, Elkridge, Relic, Searching. Foundation sire of Col. E. R. Bradley's Idle Hour Farm.

BLANDFORD, 1919-1935. Br. c., Swynford—Blanche, by White Eagle. 4-3-1-0, $16,041, Princess of Wales's S., etc. Leading sire three times in England. Sire of *Blenheim II, *Bahram, Brantome, Windsor Lad, Campanula, Trigo, Dalmary, Mistress Ford, Pasch, Udaipur, Umidwar. Tail-male ancestor of line leading to The Axe II, Quadrangle, Crepello, Mtoto.

*BLENHEIM II, 1927-1958. Br. c., Blandford—Malva, by Charles O'Malley. 10-5-3-0, $73,060, Epsom Derby, etc. Leading sire in 1941. Sire of more than 45 stakes winners, including Whirlaway, *Mahmoud, Donatello II, Mar-Kell, Fervent, A Gleam, Jet Pilot. Broodmare sire of A Glitter, Coaltown, Hill Gail, Kauai King, Le Paillon, *Nasrullah, Wistful. Tail-male ancestor of line leading to The Axe II, Quadrangle, Crepello, Mtoto.

BLUE LARKSPUR, 1926-1947. B. c., Black Servant—Blossom Time, by *North Star III. 16-10-3-1, $272,070, regarded as Horse of the Year in 1929, champion three-year-old colt, champion handicap horse, Belmont S., Classic S., etc. Sire of 44 stakes winners, including But Why Not, Myrtlewood, Painted Veil, Blue Swords, Alablue, Revoked, Blue Delight, Bee Ann Mac. Broodmare sire of Alanesian, Be Faithful, Busanda, By Jimminy, Cohoes, Durazna, Real Delight, Twilight Tear.

BLUSHING GROOM (Fr), 1974-1992. Ch. c., Red God—Runaway Bride (GB), by Wild Risk. 10-7-1-2, $407,153, champion two-year-old in France, champion miler in France, Grand Criterium (Fr-G1), Poule d'Essai des Poulains (French Two Thousand Guineas) (Fr-G1), etc. Leading sire in England in 1989. Sire of 92 stakes winners, including Nashwan, Rainbow Quest, Arazi, Sky Beauty, Rahy, Blushing John, Runaway Groom, Al Bahathri, Blush With Pride, Mt. Livermore. Broodmare sire of Awesome Again, Flute, Kahyasi, Lammtarra, Macho Uno, Stravinsky, T.M. Opera O.

BOLD FORBES, 1973-2000. Dk. b. or br. c., Irish Castle—Comely Nell, by Commodore M. 18-13-1-4, $546,536, champion three-year-old male, champion two-year-old in Puerto Rico, Kentucky Derby (G1), Belmont S. (G1), etc. Sire of 29 stakes winners, including Tiffany Lass, Air Forbes Won.

BOLD LAD, 1962-1986. Ch. c., Bold Ruler—Misty Morn, by *Princequillo. 19-14-2-1, $516,465, champion two-year-old, Metropolitan H., Futurity S., Hopeful S., etc. Sire of 29 stakes winners, including Sirlad (Ire), Bold Fascinator, Gentle Thoughts, Rube the Great.

BOLD 'N DETERMINED, 1977-1997. B. f., Bold and Brave—Pidi, by Determine. 20-16-2-0, $949,599, Coaching Club American Oaks (G1), Kentucky Oaks (G1), etc. Winner of six Grade 1 races at three in 1980, she had the misfortune of being in the same crop as Kentucky Derby (G1) winner and champion three-year-old filly Genuine Risk. Defeated Genuine Risk in the 1980 Maskette Stakes (G2).

BOLD RULER, 1954-1971. Dk. b. c., *Nasrullah—Miss Disco, by Discovery. 33-23-4-2, $764,204, Horse of the Year in 1957, champion three-year-old colt, champion sprinter, Preakness S., Futurity S., Suburban H., etc. Leading sire eight times, seven in succession (1963-'69). Sire of 82 stakes winners, including Secretariat, Gamely, Lamb Chop, Bold Lad (out of Misty Morn), Bold Lad (out of *Barn Pride), Bold Bidder, Wajima, Queen Empress, Queen of the Stage, Boldnesian, Chieftain, Dewan, Reviewer. Broodmare sire of Autobiography, Christmas Past, Private Terms, Sensational. Tail-male ancestor of Seattle Slew line.

BOLD VENTURE, 1933-1958. Ch. c., *St. Germans—Possible, by Ultimus. 11-6-2-0, $68,300, champion three-year-old colt, Kentucky Derby, Preakness S.

Sire of 12 stakes winners, including Assault, Middleground. Broodmare sire of Miss Cavandish, Prove Out.

BON NOUVEL, 1960-unknown. B. g., Duc de Fer—Good News, by *Happy Argo. 51-16-11-7, $176,148, champion steeplechaser three times, Temple Gwathmey Stp. H., Brook Stp. H. twice, etc.

BORROW, 1908-unknown. Ch. g., Hamburg—Forget, by Exile. 91-24-20-12. $87,275, Middle Park Plate (in England), Brooklyn H., etc. Defeated three Kentucky Derby winners in 1917 Brooklyn H.

BOSTON, 1833-1850. Ch. c., Timoleon—Sister to Tuckahoe, by Ball's Florizel. 45-40-2-1, $51,700, champion of his era. Leading sire three times. Sire of Lexington, Lecomte, Commodore, Madeline, Nina, Ringgold, Red Eye. Won 70 of 81 heats, 47 at 4 miles. Lost famous match race with Fashion.

BOURTAI, 1942-1970. B. f., Stimulus—Escutcheon, by *Sir Gallahad III. 12-2-1-2, $3,850, 3rd Pimlico Nursery S. Dam of Bayou, Levee, Delta, Banta, Ambassador. Tail-female ancestor of Aptitude, Big Spruce, Coastal, Dike, Sacahuista, Shuvee, Sleepytime, Slew o' Gold, Talking Picture.

BOWL OF FLOWERS, 1958-unknown. Ch. f., Sailor—Flower Bowl, by *Alibhai. 16-10-3-3, $398,504, champion two- and three-year-old filly, Coaching Club American Oaks, Spinster S., etc. Dam of sires Whiskey Road, Big Burn.

BRIGADIER GERARD, 1968-'89. B. c., Queen's Hussar—La Paiva, by Prince Chevalier. 18-17-1-0, $631,199, Horse of the Year in England, champion miler twice, champion older horse, Two Thousand Guineas, King George VI and Queen Elizabeth II S., etc. Sire of 28 stakes winners, including Light Cavalry, Vayrann, Comrade in Arms, General (Fr). One of the greatest English horses of the 20th century and grandsire of Lord At War (Arg), one of the last representatives of the Fairway male line.

BROAD BRUSH, 1983-. B. c., Ack Ack—Hay Patcher, by Hoist the Flag. 27-14-5-5, $2,656,793, Santa Anita H. (G1), Suburban H. (G1), etc. Leading sire in 1994. Sire of more than 85 stakes winners, including Farda Amiga, Concern, Include, Broad Appeal, Pompeii.

BROOMSTICK, 1901-1931. B. c., Ben Brush—*Elf, by Galliard. 39-14-11-5, $74,730, Travers S., Brighton H., etc. Leading sire 1913-'15; leading broodmare sire 1932-'33. Sire of 69 stakes winners, including Regret, Whisk Broom II, Bostonian, Broomspun, Cudgel, Halcyon, Sweeper, Traffic, Transmute, Wildair, Escoba, Flying Witch, Remembrance. Broodmare sire of Equipoise, Mother Goose, Whichone.

BROWN BESS, 1982-. Dk. b. or br. f., *Petrone—Chickadee, by Windy Sands. 36-16-8-6, $1,300,920, champion grass female, Santa Barbara H. (G1), Ramona H. (G1), Yellow Ribbon Inv. S. (G1), etc.

BUCKPASSER, 1963-1978. B. c., Tom Fool—Busanda, by War Admiral. 31-25-4-1, $1,462,014, Horse of the Year in 1966, champion two- and three-year-old colt, champion handicap horse twice, Jockey Club Gold Cup, Metropolitan H., etc. Leading broodmare sire 1983-'84, '88-'89. Sire of 35 stakes winners, including Numbered Account, Relaxing, La Prevoyante, L'Enjoleur, Norcliffe, State Dinner, Silver Buck, Buckaroo, Quick as Lightning, Lassie Dear, Passing Mood. Broodmare sire of Slew o' Gold, Seeking the Gold, Coastal, Woodman, Private Account, Easy Goer, El Gran Senor, Miswaki, Touch Gold.

*BULL DOG, 1927-1954. Dk. b. or br. c., *Teddy—Plucky Liege, by Spearmint. 8-2-1-0, $7,802 Prix Daphnis, etc. Leading sire in 1943; leading broodmare sire in 1953, '54, '56. Sire of 52 stakes winners, including Bull Lea, Occupy, Our Boots, Occupation, Johns Joy, The Doge, Canina, Miss Dogwood, Miss Mommy, Tiger. Broodmare sire of Tom Fool, Decathlon, Dark Star, Rough'n Tumble. Full brother to *Sir Gallahad III; half brother to Bois Roussel, Admiral Drake.

*BULLE ROCK, 1709-unknown. B. c., Darley Arabian—Byerley Turk mare, by Byerley Turk. Earliest Thoroughbred recorded as imported (in 1730) to the United States in the *American Stud Book*. No horse matching his description and pedigree appears in the *General Stud Book*, but he is generally accepted as America's first Thoroughbred.

BULL LEA, 1935-1964. Br. c., *Bull Dog—Rose Leaves, by Ballot. 27-10-7-3, $94,825, Widener H., Blue Grass S., etc. Leading sire in 1947, '48, '49, '52, '53; leading broodmare sire 1958-'61. Sire of 57 stakes winners, ten champions, including Citation, Coaltown, Hill Gail, Two Lea, Twilight Tear, Bewitch, Real Delight, Iron Liege, Armed, Durazna, Next Move. Broodmare sire of Barbizon, Bramalea, Gate Dancer, Idun, Leallah, Pucker Up, Quadrangle, Tim Tam.

BUSHER, 1942-1955. Ch. f., War Admiral—Baby League, by Bubbling Over. 21-15-3-1, $334,035, Horse of the Year in 1945, champion two- and three-year-old filly, champion handicap mare, Hollywood Derby, Santa Margarita H., etc. Dam of Jet Action. Tail-female ancestor of family that includes Beau's Eagle, Play On.

BUSHRANGER, 1930-1937. Ch. g., *Stefan the Great—War Path, by Man o' War. 21-11-3-1, $20,635, champion steeplechaser, Grand National Stp. H., Broad Hollow Stp. H. twice, etc.

BYERLEY TURK, ca. 1680. Bl. c. of unknown parentage. Sire of Jigg, Basto, Black Hearty. One of three Thoroughbred male-line foundation sires. Tail-male ancestor of the Herod line leading to *Ambiorix, The Tetrarch, Dr Devious (Ire), Indian Ridge.

CAFE PRINCE, 1970-unknown. B. g., Creme dela Creme—Princess Blair, by Blue Prince. 52-18-5-4, $228,238, champion steeplechaser twice, Colonial Cup International Stp. twice, etc.

CANONERO II, 1968-1981. B. c., *Pretendre—Dixieland II, by Nantallah. 23-9-3-4, $360,933, champion three-year-old male, Kentucky Derby, Preakness S.-ntr, etc. Sire of five stakes winners, including Cannon Boy. First foreign-trained horse to win Kentucky Derby.

CAPOT, 1946-1974. Br. c., Menow—Piquet, by *St. Germans. 28-12-4-7, $347,260, Horse of the Year in 1949, champion three-year-old colt, Preakness S., Belmont S., etc. Sired 13 foals, no stakes winners.

CARBINE, 1885-1913. B. c., Musket—Mersey, by Knowsley. 43-33-6-3, $143,982, Melbourne Cup twice, Sydney Cup twice, etc.. Sire of Amberite, *Bomba, Fowling-Piece, Greatorex, Miss Gunning, Ramrod, Spearmint, Wallace. Won 1890 Melbourne Cup under 145 pounds. Still widely considered best New Zealand-bred of all time.

CARRY BACK, 1958-1983. Br. c., Saggy—Joppy, by Star Blen. 62-21-11-11, $1,241,165, champion three-year-old colt, Kentucky Derby, Preakness S., etc. Sire of ten stakes winners, including Taken Aback, Sharp Gary, Back in Paris.

CAVALCADE, 1931-1940. Br. c., *Lancegaye—*Hastily, by Hurry On. 22-8-5-3, $127,165, Horse of the Year in 1934, champion two- and three-year-old colt, Kentucky Derby, American Derby, etc. Sire of three stakes winners.

CHALLEDON, 1936-1958. B. c., *Challenger II—Laura Gal, by *Sir Gallahad III. 44-20-7-6, $334,660, Horse of the Year in 1939 and '40, champion three-year-

old colt, champion handicap horse, Preakness S., Whitney S., etc. Sire of 13 stakes winners, including Ancestor, Tenacious, Donor.

CHARISMATIC, 1996- . Ch. c., Summer Squall—Bali Babe, by Drone. 17-5-2-4, $2,038,064, Horse of the Year in 1999, champion three-year-old male, Kentucky Derby (G1), Preakness S. (G2), etc. Exported to Japan in 2002.

CHIEF'S CROWN, 1982-1997. B. c., Danzig—Six Crowns, by Secretariat. 21-12-3-3, $2,191,168, champion two-year-old male, Breeders' Cup Juvenile (G1), Travers S. (G1), etc. Sire of more than 50 stakes winners, including Erhaab, Grand Lodge, Chief Bearhart, Concerto, Chief Honcho.

CHRIS EVERT, 1971-2001. Ch. f., Swoon's Son—Miss Carmie, by T. V. Lark. 15-10-2-2, $679,475, champion three-year-old filly, filly triple crown, Coaching Club American Oaks (G1), Hollywood Special S. (match race with Miss Musket). Dam of Six Crowns, Wimbledon Star. Second dam of Chief's Crown.

CICADA, 1959-1981. B. f., Bryan G.—Satsuma, by Bossuet. 42-23-8-6, $783,674, champion two- and three-year-old filly, champion older mare, Kentucky Oaks, Beldame S., etc. Dam of Cicada's Pride. Retired as world's leading money-winning female.

CIGAR, 1990- . B. c., Palace Music—Solar Slew, by Seattle Slew. 33-19-4-5, $9,999,815, Horse of the Year in 1995 and '96, champion older male twice, Breeders' Cup Classic (G1), Dubai World Cup, etc. Leading earner of all-time in North America. Sterile at stud. Resides at Kentucky Horse Park.

CITATION, 1945-1970. B. c., Bull Lea—*Hydroplane II, by Hyperion. 45-32-10-2, $1,085,760, Horse of the Year in 1948, champion two- and three-year-old colt, champion handicap horse, Triple Crown, Jockey Club Gold Cup, Hollywood Gold Cup, etc. First $1-million earner. Sire of 12 stakes winners, including Silver Spoon, Fabius.

CLEOPATRA, 1917-unknown. Ch. f., Corcyra—*Gallice, by Gallinule. 26-8-10-4, $55,937, champion three-year-old filly, Coaching Club American Oaks, Alabama S., etc. Dam of Pompey, Laughing Queen; third dam of Tom Fool. Tail-female ancestor of family that includes Ambiopoise, Dust Commander.

CLIFFORD, 1890-1917. B. c., Bramble—Duchess, by Kingfisher. 63-42-14-5, $59,757 Second Special S., Flight S. twice, Phoenix S., etc. Defeated three Racing Hall of Fame members. Regarded as one of the worst gate horses ever, a trait that cost him several races he should have won.

COALTOWN, 1945-1965. B. c., Bull Lea—Easy Lass, by *Blenheim II. 39-23-6-3, $415,675, Horse of the Year in 1949, champion sprinter, champion handicap horse, Jerome H., Blue Grass S., etc. Never sired a stakes winner. Exported to France in 1955.

COLIN, 1905-1932. Br. c., Commando—*Pastorella, by Springfield. 15-15-0-0, $178,110, champion two- and three-year-old colt, Belmont S., Futurity S., etc. Sire of Jock, Neddie, On Watch. Shy breeder. Tail-male ancestor of line that leads to Broad Brush.

COMMANDO, 1898-1905. B. c., Domino—Emma C., by *Darebin. 9-7-2-0, $58,196, champion two- and three-year-old colt, Belmont S., Junior Champion S., etc. Leading sire in 1907. Sire of ten stakes winners from 27 foals, including Colin, Peter Pan, Celt, Hippodrome, Superman, Transvaal, and of Ultimus.

CONQUISTADOR CIELO, 1979-2002. B. c., Mr. Prospector—K D Princess, by Bold Commander. 13-9-0-2, $474,328, Horse of the Year in 1982, champion three-year-old male, Belmont S. (G1), Metropolitan H. (G1), etc. Sire of more than 65 stakes winners, including Marquetry, Forty Niner Days, Wagon Limit. Broodmare sire of more than 80 stakes winners, including Apelia, Dixie Dot Com, Thornfield.

CORRECTION, 1888–unknown. B. f., Himyar—Mannie Gray, by Enquirer. 122-38-35-22, $45,600, Toboggan Slide H., etc. Dam of Yankee, Miss Malaprop, Nature. Tail-female ancestor of family that includes Affirmed, Lil E. Tee, Ghostzapper. Full sister to Domino.

COSMAH, 1953–1979. B. f., Cosmic Bomb—Almahmoud, by *Mahmoud. 30-9-5-2, $86,525, Astarita S., etc. Broodmare of the Year in 1974. Dam of Tosmah, Halo, Fathers Image, Maribeau. Foundation mare of family that includes Flawlessly, L'Emigrant, Cannonade, Stephan's Odyssey.

***COUGAR II**, 1966–1989. Dk b. or br. c., Tale of Two Cities—*Cindy Lou II, by Madara. 50-20-7-17, $1,172,625, champion grass horse, Santa Anita H. (G1), Sunset H. (G1), etc. Sire of 24 stakes winners, including Gato Del Sol, Exploded.

COUNTERPOINT, 1948–1970. Ch. c., Count Fleet—Jabot, by *Sickle. 21-10-3-1, $284,575, Horse of the Year in 1951, champion three-year-old colt, Belmont S., Jockey Club Gold Cup, etc. Sire of 11 stakes winners, including Dotted Swiss, Harmonizing, Honey Dear, Snow White.

***COUNT FLEET**, 1940–1973. Br. c., Reigh Count—Quickly, by Haste. 21-16-4-1, $250,300, Horse of the Year in 1943, champion two- and three-year-old colt, Triple Crown, Champagne S., Withers S., etc. Leading sire in 1951; leading broodmare sire in 1963. Sire of 39 stakes winners, including Counterpoint, One Count, Kiss Me Kate, Count Turf, Straight Face, Count of Honor, Countess Fleet, County Delight, Juliets Nurse. Broodmare sire of Kelso, Prince John, Quill, Fleet Nasrullah, Gallant Romeo, Lamb Chop.

CREME FRAICHE, 1982–2003. B. g., Rich Cream—Likely Exchange, by Terrible Tiger. 64-17-12-13, $4,024,727, Belmont S. (G1), Jockey Club Gold Cup (G1) twice, Super Derby (G1), etc.

CRIMINAL TYPE, 1985–2005. Ch. c., Alydar—Klepto, by No Robbery. 24-10-5-3, $2,351,274, Horse of the Year in 1990, champion older male, Hollywood Gold Cup (G1), Pimlico Special H. (G1), Metropolitan H. (G1), etc. Sire of seven stakes winners, including Hoolie. Exported to Japan in 1992.

CRIMSON SATAN, 1959–1982. Ch. c., Spy Song—*Papila, by Requiebro. 58-18-9-9, $796,077, champion two-year-old colt, Garden State S., Charles H. Strub S., etc. Sire of 33 stakes winners, including Crimson Saint, Krislin, Whitesburg.

CRUSADER, 1923–1940. Ch. c., Man o' War—Star Fancy, by *Star Shoot. 42-18-8-4, $203,261, consensus Horse of the Year in 1926, champion three-year-old colt, Belmont S., Jockey Club Gold Cup, Suburban H. twice, etc. Sire of six stakes winners, including *Crossbow II.

DAHLIA, 1970–2001. Ch f., *Vaguely Noble—Charming Alibi, by Honeys Alibi. 48-15-3-7, $1,489,105, Horse of the Year in England in 1974 and '75, champion three-year-old in Ireland, champion three-year-old in England, champion grass horse in U.S., champion older mare twice in England, King George VI and Queen Elizabeth S. (Eng-G1) twice, Washington, D.C., International (G1), etc. Dam of Dahar, Rivlia, Delegant, Dahlia's Dreamer, Wajd, Llandaff. First distaff millionaire.

DALAKHANI, 2000– . Gr. c., Darshaan—Daltawa, by Miswaki. 9-8-1-0, $2,496,059, European Horse of the Year and champion three-year-old in 2003, Prix de l'Arc de Triomphe (Fr-G1), Prix du Jockey-Club (Fr-G1) (French Derby), etc.

DAMASCUS, 1964–1995. B. c., Sword Dancer—Kerala, by *My Babu. 32-21-7-3, $1,176,781, Horse of the Year in 1967, champion three-year-old colt, champion handicap horse, Preakness S., Belmont S., Jockey Club Gold Cup S., etc. Sire of 71 stakes winners, including Private Account, Desert Wine, Highland Blade, Ogygian, Honorable Miss, Time for a Change, Judger, Bailjumper, Timeless Moment, Cutlass. Broodmare sire of more than 155 stakes winners, including Boundary, Chilukki, Coronado's Quest, Shadeed.

DANCE SMARTLY, 1988– . Dk. b. or br. f., Danzig—Classy 'n Smart, by Smarten. 17-12-2-3, $3,263,835, champion three-year-old filly in U.S., Canadian Horse of the Year, champion two- and three-year-old filly in Canada, Canadian Triple Crown, Breeders' Cup Distaff (G1), Queen's Plate S., etc. Dam of Queen's Plate winners Scatter the Gold, Dancethruthedawn.

DANEHILL, 1986–2003. B. c., Danzig—Razyana, by His Majesty. 9-4-1-2, $321,064, Ladbroke Sprint S. (Eng-G1), etc. Brother to Eagle Eyed, Harpia, Shibboleth, half brother to Euphonic. Leading sire in Australia eight times, leading sire in France twice, leading sire in U.S. Sire of more than 280 stakes winners, including Rock of Gibraltar (Ire), Flying Spur, Danewin, Fairy King Prawn, Dane Ripper, Banks Hill (GB).

DANZIG, 1977– . B. c., Northern Dancer—Pas de Nom, by Admiral's Voyage. 3-3-0-0, $32,400. Leading sire 1991–'93. Sire of more than 185 stakes winners, including Chief's Crown, Polish Precedent, Dayjur, Danehill, Dance Smartly, Langfuhr, Anabaa, Green Desert, Pine Bluff. Broodmare sire of more than 125 stakes winners, including Caller One, Fusaichi Pegasus.

DARK MIRAGE, 1965–1969. Dk. b. or br. f., *Persian Road II—Home by Dark, by Hill Prince. 27-12-3-2, $362,788, champion three-year-old filly, first winner of the filly triple crown in New York, Kentucky Oaks, Delaware Oaks, etc. Won nine consecutive stakes and broke down trying for tenth. Died at four.

DARK STAR, 1950–1972. Br. c., *Royal Gem II—Isolde, by *Bull Dog. 13-6-2-2, $131,337, Kentucky Derby, Derby Trial, etc. Only horse to defeat Native Dancer. Sire of 26 stakes winners, including *Gazala II, My Dad George, Hidden Treasure. Broodmare sire of Youth, Mississipian, Too Bald.

DARLEY ARABIAN, 1700. B. c. of unknown parentage. Sire of Flying Childers, Aleppo, Almanzor, Bartlett's Childers. One of three male-line foundation sires of the Thoroughbred breed. Tail-male ancestor of the Eclipse male line leading to Phalaris, Blandford, Hyperion, *Teddy, Domino lines.

DARSHAAN, 1981–2001. Br. c., Shirley Heights—Delsy, by Abdos. 8-5-0-1, $226, 979, champion three-year-old in France, Prix du Jockey-Club (Fr-G1) (French Derby), etc. Leading sire in France in 2003, leading broodmare sire in England twice, leading broodmare sire in France. Sire of more than 90 stakes winners, including Dalakhani, Kotashaan (Fr), Aliysa (Ire), Mark of Esteem (Ire). Broodmare sire of High Chaparral (Ire), Ebadiyla, Islington (Ire), Yesterday (Ire).

DAVONA DALE, 1976– . B. f., Best Turn—Royal Entrance, by Tim Tam. 18-11-2-1, $641,612, champion three-year-old filly, filly triple crown, Kentucky Oaks (G1), etc.

DECATHLON, 1953–1972. B. c., Olympia—Dog Blessed, by *Bull Dog. 42-25-8-1, $269,530, champion sprinter twice, Oceanport H. twice, Hutcheson S., etc. Sire of 12 stakes winners, including Juanita.

***DELANCEY'S CUB MARE**, 1762. F., Cub—Second mare (dam of Amaranthus), by Second. One of the first great imported American foundation mares. Dam of (Maria) Slamerkin. Tail-female ancestor of family that includes Nearco, Neckar, Golden Trail, Parole, Imp, Black Gold, Mad Hatter, Sun Beau, Flirtilla, Sumpter, Artful, Delhi, Falsetto, Halma.

DEPUTY MINISTER, 1979-2004. Dk. b. or br. c., Vice Regent—Mint Copy, by Bunty's Flight. 22-12-2-2, $696,964, champion two-year-old male in U.S., Horse of the Year in Canada in 1981, champion two-year-old male in Canada, Laurel Futurity (G1), Donn H. (G2), etc. Leading sire in 1997 and '98. Sire of more than 80 stakes winners, including Go for Wand, Open Mind, Awesome Again, Dehere, Touch Gold. Broodmare sire of more than 105 stakes winners, including Halfbridled.

DESERT VIXEN, 1970-1982. Dk. b. or br. f., In Reality—Desert Trial, by Moslem Chief. 28-13-6-3, $421,538, champion three-year-old filly, champion older female, Alabama S. (G1), Beldame S. (G1) twice, etc. Dam of Real Shadai; full sister to Valid Appeal.

DETERMINE, 1951-1972. Gr. c., *Alibhai—Koubis, by *Mahmoud. 44-18-7-9, $573,360, Kentucky Derby, Santa Anita Derby, etc. First gray winner of the Kentucky Derby. Sire of 21 stakes winners, including Decidedly, Warfare, Donut King. Broodmare sire of Bold 'n Determined, Gummo, Princess Pout.

DEVIL DIVER, 1939-1961. B. c., *St. Germans—Dabchick, by *Royal Minstrel. 47-22-12-3, $261,064, champion handicap horse twice, Metropolitan H. twice, Suburban H., Whitney S., etc. Sire of 17 stakes winners, including Beau Diable, Call Over, Ruddy.

*DIOMED, 1777-1808. Ch. c., Florizel—Spectator mare (sister to Juno), by Spectator. 20-11-5-3, $38,200, champion three-year-old in England. First winner of the Epsom Derby. Sire of Sir Archy, Haynie's Maria, Ball's Florizel, Duroc, Fanny, Young Giantess, Potomac, Virginius. Imported to U.S. in 1798. Tail-male ancestor of Boston, Lexington.

DISCOVERY, 1931-1958. Ch. c., Display—Ariadne, by *Light Brigade. 63-27-10-10, $195,287, Horse of the Year in 1935, champion handicap horse twice, Whitney S. three times, Brooklyn H. three times, etc. Sire of 25 stakes winners, including Conniver, Miss Disco, Find, Loser Weeper, Traffic Court. Broodmare sire of Bold Ruler, Native Dancer, Intentionally, Hasty Road, Traffic Judge, Bed o' Roses. Famed as a weight carrier.

DISGUISE, 1897-1927. B. c., Domino—*Bonnie Gal, by Galopin. 8-3-0-4, $40,275, Jockey Club S., 3rd Epsom Derby, etc. Sire of Maskette, Court Dress, Harmonicon, Helmet, Miss Puzzle, Wonder, Comely.

DISPLAY, 1923-1944. B. c., Fair Play—*Cicuta, by *Nassovian. 103-23-25-27, $256,326, Preakness S., Hawthorne Gold Cup, etc. Sire of 11 stakes winners, including Discovery, Parade Girl.

DOMINO, 1891-1897. Br. c., Himyar—Mannie Gray, by Enquirer. 25-19-2-1, $193,550, Champion two-year-old, Futurity S., Withers S., etc. Sire of Commando, Cap and Bells, Disguise, Noonday, Running Stream, Pink Domino. Sired only 20 foals in two crops, eight stakes winners, two classic winners.

DR. FAGER, 1964-1976. B. c., Rough'n Tumble—Aspidistra, by Better Self. 22-18-2-1, $1,002,642, Horse of the Year in 1968, champion older horse, champion sprinter twice, champion grass horse, Whitney S., Vosburgh H. twice, etc. Leading sire in 1977. Sire of 35 stakes winners, including Dr. Patches, Dearly Precious, L'Alezane, Dr. Blum, Tree of Knowledge, Lie Low, Lady Love. Broodmare sire of Cure the Blues, Equalize, Fappiano, Quiet American, Sewickley. Won every championship for which he was eligible in 1968.

DUKE OF MAGENTA, 1875-1899. B. c., Lexington—Magenta, by *Yorkshire. 19-15-3-1, $45,913, Belmont S., Preakness S., Travers S., etc. Sire of Duke, Eric, Ballyhoo. Sent to England with Parole after three-year-old season, but became a roarer and never raced again.

*EASY GOER, 1986-1994. Ch. c., Alydar—Relaxing, by Buckpasser. 20-14-5-1, $4,873,770, champion two-year-old male, Belmont S. (G1), Jockey Club Gold Cup (G1), etc. Sire of nine stakes winners, including Will's Way, My Flag, Furlough. Broodmare sire of champion Storm Flag Flying.

ECLIPSE, 1764-1789. Ch. c., Marske—Spiletta, by Regulus. 18-18-0-0, undefeated champion in England, won 11 King's Plates. Never leading sire but runner-up 11 times. Sire of Pot8O's, King Fergus, Serjeant, Dungannon, Alexander, Joe Andrews, Mercury, Meteor, Saltram, Volunteer. Tail-male line ancestor of more than 95% of modern Thoroughbreds, including Phalaris, Hyperion, Blandford lines.

*ECLIPSE, 1855-1878. B. c., Orlando—Gaze, by Bay Middleton. 9-4-0-1, $9,015, Newmarket S., Clearwell S. Sire of Alarm, Ruthless. Tail-male line ancestor of Domino, Plaudit, Dr. Fager, Holy Bull, Broad Brush.

*EIGHT THIRTY, 1936-1965. B. c., Pilate—Dinner Time, by High Time. 27-16-3-5, $155,475, Travers S., Whitney S., Metropolitan H., etc. Sire of 45 stakes winners, including Sailor, Bolero, Royal Coinage, Rare Perfume, Sunday Evening, Make Tracks, Anyoldtime. Broodmare sire of Cornish Prince, Evening Out, Hold Your Peace, Jaipur, Rare Treat.

ELKRIDGE, 1938-1961. B. g., Mate—Best by Test, by Black Toney. 123-31-18-15, $230,680, champion steeplechaser twice, North American Stp. H. four times, Indian River Stp. H. four times, etc.

*EMPEROR OF NORFOLK, 1885-1907. B. c., Norfolk—Marian, by Malcolm. 29-21-2-4, $72,400, American Derby, Brooklyn Derby, etc. Sire of Americus (Rey del Carreras), Cruzados. Buried at Santa Anita Park.

ENDURANCE BY RIGHT, 1899-1908. B. f., Inspector B.—*Early Morn, by Silvester. 18-16-0-2, $27,645, champion two-year-old filly, Champagne S., Clipsetta S., etc. Dam of Stamina. Tail-female ancestor of family that includes Plucky Play, Windjammer, Racing Room.

ENQUIRER, 1867-1895. B. c., *Leamington—Lida, by Lexington. 11-7-0-0, $17,550, consensus champion three-year-old, Kenner S., Phoenix S., etc. Sire of Falsetto, Inspector B., Blue Eyes, Mannie Gray.

*EPINARD, 1920-unknown. Ch. c., Badajoz—Epine Blanche, by *Rock Sand. 20-12-6-0, $46,688, champion two-year-old in France, Grand Criterium, Prix d'Ispahan, etc. Great French champion who ran second in each of three international races in U.S. in 1925. Sire of Rodosto, Marica, Epithet.

EQUIPOISE, 1928-1938. Ch. c., Pennant—Swinging, by Broomstick. 51-29-10-4, $338,610, Horse of the Year in 1932 and '33, champion handicap horse three times, champion two-year-old colt, Metropolitan H. twice, Whitney S., etc. Leading sire in 1942. Sire of nine stakes winners, including Shut Out, Level Best, Bolingbroke, Attention, Swing and Sway. Broodmare sire of Assault, Myrtle Charm.

EXCELLER, 1973-1997. B. c., *Vaguely Noble—Too Bald, by Bald Eagle. 33-15-5-6, $1,674,587, Jockey Club Gold Cup (G1), Grand Prix de Paris (Fr-G1), etc. Sire of 19 stakes winners, including Slew's Exceller, Squan Song. Died in a slaughterhouse in Sweden.

*EXTERMINATOR, 1915-1945. Ch. g., *McGee—Fair Empress, by Jim Gore. 100-50-17-17, $252,996, Kentucky Derby, Saratoga Cup twice, etc. Won record 34 stakes races. Won 19 times carrying 130 pounds or more.

FAIRMOUNT, 1921-unknown. Ch. g., Fair Play—Sunflower, by *Rock Sand. 22-12-5-0, $74,075, Temple Gwathmey Memorial Steeplechase H. three times, Manley Memorial Steeplechase H., etc.

FAIR PLAY, 1905-1929. Ch. c., Hastings—*Fairy Gold, by Bend Or. 32-10-11-3, $86,950, Flash S., Coney Island Jockey Club S., etc. Leading sire in 1920, '24, '27; leading broodmare sire in 1931, '34, '38. Sire of Man o' War, Chance Play, Mad Hatter, Display, Chance Shot, Mad Play, Ladkin, Chatterton, Olambala, Stagecraft, Masda, Native Wit, Oval. Broodmare sire of High Quest, Jamestown, Stagehand, Sun Beau. Tail-male ancestor of line leading to In Reality, Valid Appeal, Tiznow.

FAIRWAY, 1925-1948. B. c., Phalaris—Scapa Flow, by Chaucer. 15-12-1-0, $194,685, champion three-year-old in England, St. Leger S., Champion S. twice, etc. Leading sire in England four times; leading broodmare sire in England in 1946 and '47. Sire of Blue Peter, Fair Copy, Fair Trial, Full Sail, Garden Path, Honeyway, Ribbon, Tide-Way, *Watling Street. Founder of sire line that leads to Shergar, Troy, Ela-Mana-Mou, Brigadier Gerard, Lord At War (Arg).

FALLASPEN, 1976-1998. Ch. f., Pretense—Change Water, by Swaps. 20-8-3-0, $198,037, Matron S. (G1), Prioress S., etc. Broodmare of the Year in 1994. Dam of nine stakes winners, including Timber Country, Northern Aspen, Hamas (Ire), Elle Seule, Colorado Dancer (Ire), Fort Wood. Tail-female ancestor of family that includes Dubai Millennium, Charnwood Forest (Ire), Elnadim, Mehthaaf, Occupandiste.

FASHION, 1837-1860. Ch. f., *Trustee—Bonnets o' Blue, by Sir Charles. 36-32-0-0, $41,500, won match race with Boston, etc. Dam of A la Mode. Greatest of four-mile heat fillies.

FAVORITE TRICK, 1995-. Dk. b. or br. c., Phone Trick—Evil Elaine, by Medieval Man. 16-12-0-1, $1,726,793, Horse of the Year in 1997, champion two-year-old male, Breeders' Cup Juvenile (G1), Hopeful S. (G1), etc. First two-year-old since Secretariat in 1972 to be voted Horse of the Year.

FEARNOUGHT, 1755-1776. B. c., Regulus—Silvertail, by Heneage's Whitenose. Five wins in England, won three King's Plates. Early American foundation sire. Sire of Symme's Wildair, Fitzhugh's Regulus, Spotswood's Apollo, Eden's Whynot, Gallant, Othello, Harris's Eclipse, Goldfinder.

FERDINAND, 1983-2002. Ch. c., Nijinsky II—Banja Luka, by Double Jay. 29-8-9-6, $3,777,978, Horse of the Year in 1987, champion older male, Kentucky Derby (G1), Breeders' Cup Classic (G1), etc. Sire of eight stakes winners, including Bull Inthe Heather. Exported to Japan in 1995 and slaughtered there.

FIRENZE (FIRENZI), 1884-1902. B. f., Glenelg—Florida, by Virgil. 82-47-21-9, $112,471, Gazelle S., Monmouth H., Jerome S. (beating Hanover), etc. Tail-female ancestor of family that includes Carry Back, Paul Jones.

FIRST FLIGHT, 1944-1975. B. f., *Mahmoud—Fly Swatter, by *Dis Donc. 24-11-3-3, $197,965, champion two-year-old filly, Matron S., Monmouth Oaks, etc. Defeated Jet Pilot in Futurity S.

FIRST LANDING, 1956-1987. B. c., *Turn-to—Hildene, by Bubbling Over. 37-19-9-2, $779,577, champion two-year-old colt, Champagne S., Hopeful S., etc. Sire of 27 stakes winners, including Riva Ridge, First Family, Gladwin.

FLATTERER, 1979-. Dk. b. or br. g., Mo Bay—Horizontal, by Nade. 51-24-7-5, $534,854, four-time champion steeplechaser 1983-'86, Marion duPont Scott Colonial Cup International Stp. three times, Temple Gwathmey Steeplechase H. twice, etc.

FLAWLESSLY, 1988-2002. B. f., Affirmed—La Confidence, by Nijinsky II. 28-16-4-3, $2,572,536, champion grass female twice, Beverly D. S. (G1), Matriarch S. (G1) three times, etc.

FLOWER BOWL, 1952-1968. B. f., *Alibhai—Flower Bed, by *Beau Pere. 32-7-4-3, $174,625, Ladies H., Delaware H., etc. Dam of Bowl of Flowers, Graustark, His Majesty.

FOOLISH PLEASURE, 1972-1994. B. c., What a Pleasure—Fool-Me-Not, by Tom Fool. 26-16-4-3, $1,216,705, champion two-year-old male, Kentucky Derby (G1), Suburban H. (G1), Great Match S. (with Ruffian), etc. Sire of 43 stakes winners, including Baiser Vole, Marfa, Kiri's Clown, Maudlin, Prayers'n Promises.

FOREGO, 1970-1997. B. g., *Forli—Lady Golconda, by Hasty Road. 57-34-9-7, $1,938,957, three-time Horse of the Year 1974-'76, champion older male 1974-'77, champion sprinter, Marlboro Cup H. (G1), Metropolitan H. (G1) twice, Woodward H. (G1) three times, etc. Last of the great weight carriers. Retired to Kentucky Horse Park.

FORLI, 1963-1988. Ch. c., Aristophanes—Trevisa, by Advocate. 10-9-1-0, $156,648, Horse of the Year in Argentina, Quadruple Crown, Gran Premio Carlos Pellegrini, Gran Premio Nacional (Argentine Derby), Coronado S.-ncr, etc. Brother to *Tirreno, Tibur. Sire of 60 stakes winners, including Forego, Thatch, Intrepid Hero, Sadeem, Formidable. Broodmare sire of Swale, Nureyev, Precisionist.

FORT MARCY, 1964-1991. B. g., *Amerigo—Key Bridge, by *Princequillo. 75-21-18-14, $1,109,791, Horse of the Year in 1970, champion grass horse twice, champion handicap horse, Washington, D.C., International S. twice, Man o' War S., etc. Half-brother to Key to the Mint.

FORWARD GAL, 1968-1984. Ch. f., Native Charger—Forward Thrust, by Jet Action. 26-12-4-6, $438,933, champion two-year-old filly, Frizette S., Monmouth Oaks, etc. Third dam of Freedom Cry (GB).

FOURSTARDAVE, 1985-2002. Ch. g., Compliance—Broadway Joan, by Bold Arian. 100-21-18-16, $1,636,737, St. Paul Derby (G2), Daryl's Joy S. (G3) twice, etc. Won a race at Saratoga Race Course for eight consecutive years. Full brother to Irish classic winner Fourstars All-star.

FREE FOR ALL, 1942-1964. Br. c., Questionnaire—Panay, by *Chicle. 7-6-0-0, $111,225, Arlington Futurity, Washington Park Futurity, etc. Sire of Rough'n Tumble. Tail-male ancestor of Dr. Fager, Holy Bull.

FRIAR ROCK, 1913-1928. Ch. c., *Rock Sand—*Fairy Gold, by Bend Or. 21-9-1-3, $20,365, champion three-year-old, Belmont S., Suburban H., Brooklyn H., etc. Sire of Pilate, Friar's Carse, Apprehension, Inchcape, Black Curl, Emotion, Heloise, Tenez.

FRIZETTE, 1905-unknown. B. f., Hamburg—*Ondulee, by St. Simon. 36-12-8-7, $16,135, Rosedale S., Laureate S., etc. Dam of Banshee, Durzetta, *Lespedeza II. Foundation mare of family that includes Myrtlewood, Seattle Slew, Mr. Prospector, Tourbillon, Sinndar, Cordova, Darshaan, Corejada, *Apollonia, Akiyda, Acamas, Akarad, *Priam II, *Djeddah, Sing Sing, Jet Pilot, Shecky Greene, Typecast, Bahri, Forestry, Chief Bearhart, Escena, Dahlia, Vitriolic, Vagrancy, Anees, Truly Bound, Baldric, Honorable Miss.

FUSAICHI PEGASUS, 1997-. B. c., Mr. Prospector—Angel Fever, by Danzig. 9-6-2-0, $1,994,400, Kentucky Derby (G1), Wood Memorial S. (G2), etc. Syndicated for a world-record $60-million to $70-million in 2000. Sire of Bandini.

GALLANT BLOOM, 1966-1991. B. f., *Gallant Man—Multiflora, by Beau Max. 22-16-1-1, $535,739, champion two- and three-year-old filly, champion handicap mare, Santa Margarita Invitational H., Spinster S., Monmouth Oaks, etc.

GALLANT FOX, 1927-1954. B. c., *Sir Gallahad III—Marguerite, by Celt. 17-11-3-2, $328,165, consensus Horse of the Year in 1930, champion three-year-old colt, Triple Crown, Jockey Club Gold Cup, etc. Sire of 18 stakes winners, including Omaha, Granville, Flares.

***GALLANT MAN**, 1954-1988. B. c., *Migoli—*Majideh, by *Mahmoud. 26-14-4-1, $510,355, Belmont S.-ntr, Jockey Club Gold Cup, etc. Sire of 51 stakes winners, including Gallant Bloom, Gallant Romeo, War Censor, Spicy Living, Ring Twice. Broodmare sire of Genuine Risk, Highbinder, Lord Avie.

GALLORETTE, 1942-1959. Ch. f., *Challenger II—Gallette, by *Sir Gallahad III. 72-21-20-13, $445,535, champion handicap mare, Metropolitan H., Whitney S., Beldame H., etc. World's leading money-earning female at retirement. Dam of Mlle. Lorette, Courbette. Foundation mare of family that includes Minstrella, Misty Gallore, Silver Ghost, White Gloves, Greenwood Lake, Dancing Moss.

GAMELY, 1964-1975. B. f., Bold Ruler—Gambetta, by *My Babu. 41-16-9-6, $574,961, champion three-year-old filly, champion older mare twice, Alabama S., Beldame S. twice, etc. Dam of Cellini.

GENUINE RISK, 1977- . Ch. f., Exclusive Native—Virtuous, by *Gallant Man. 15-10-3-2, $646,587, champion three-year-old filly, Kentucky Derby (G1), Ruffian H. (G1), etc. Second filly to win Kentucky Derby.

***GLENCOE**, 1831-1858. Ch. c., Sultan—Trampoline, by Tramp. 10-8-1-1, $33,459, Two Thousand Guineas, Ascot Gold Cup, etc. Sire of Pocahontas, Peytona, Reel, Pryor, Star Davis, Vandal. Male-line ancestor of Hanover, Hamburg.

GODOLPHIN ARABIAN, 1724-1753. Br. c. of unknown parentage. Leading sire in England three times. Sire of Cade, Lath, Dismal, Regulus, Babraham, Blank. One of three male-line foundation sires of the Thoroughbred breed. Tail-male ancestor of Matchem line leading to Man o' War, In Reality, Tiznow.

GO FOR WAND, 1987-1990. B. f., Deputy Minister—Obeah, by Cyane. 13-10-2-0, $1,373,338, champion two- and three-year-old filly, Alabama S. (G1), Breeders' Cup Juvenile Fillies (G1), etc. Died at three in Breeders' Cup Distaff (G1). Buried in infield at Saratoga Race Course.

GOOD AND PLENTY, 1900-1907. B. g., Rossington—Famine, by Jils Johnson. 21-14-4-1, $45,815, Grand National Steeplechase H., Westbury Steeplechase H., etc.

GRANVILLE, 1933-1951. B. c., Gallant Fox—Gravita, by *Sarmatian. 18-8-4-3, $111,820, Horse of the Year in 1936, champion three-year-old colt, Belmont S., Travers S., etc. Sired only two stakes winners.

GREY LAG, 1918-1942. Ch. c., *Star Shoot—Miss Minnie, by *Meddler. 47-25-9-3, $136,715, Horse of the Year in 1921, champion three-year-old colt, champion handicap horse twice, Belmont S., Metropolitan H., Suburban H., etc. Shy breeder, sired only one stakes winner from 17 foals.

GUN BOW, 1960-unknown. B. c., Gun Shot—Ribbons and Bows, by War Admiral. 42-17-8-4, $798,722, Metropolitan H., Whitney S., etc. Sire of six stakes winners, including Pistol Packer. Exported to Japan in 1973.

HAIL TO REASON, 1958-1976. Br. c., *Turn-to—Nothirdchance, by Blue Swords. 18-9-2-2, $328,434, champion two-year-old colt, Hopeful S., Sanford S., etc. Broke down and retired at end of two-year-old season. Leading sire in 1970. Sire of 43 stakes winners, including Roberto, Halo, Stop the Music, Mr. Leader, Bold Reason, Trillion, Priceless Gem, Straight Deal, Hail to All, Regal Gleam,

Personality, Proud Clarion, Admiring. Broodmare sire of Allez France, Escaline (Fr), Royal Glint, Silver Buck, Triptych. Tail-male ancestor of line that includes Saint Ballado, Sunday Silence, Red Ransom, Brian's Time.

HALO, 1969-2000. Dk. b. or br. c., Hail to Reason—Cosmah, by Cosmic Bomb. 31-9-8-5, $259,553, United Nations H. (G1), Tidal H. (G2), etc. Leading sire in 1983 and '89. Sire of 63 stakes winners, including Sunday Silence, Sunny's Halo, Glorious Song, Devil's Bag, Saint Ballado, Rainbow Connection, Goodbye Halo, Lively One, Jolie's Halo, Coup de Folie. Broodmare sire of Halo America, Machiavellian, Pine Bluff, Rahy, Singspiel (Ire).

HAMBURG, 1895-1915. B. c., Hanover—Lady Reel, by Fellowcraft. 21-16-3-2, $60,380, consensus champion three-year-old colt, Lawrence Realization, Brighton Cup, etc. Leading sire in 1905. Sire of Artful, Borrow, Burgomaster, Frizette, Prince Eugene, Lady Hamburg II, Biturica, Jersey Lightning, Rosie O'Grady.

HANOVER, 1884-1899. Ch. c., Hindoo—Bourbon Belle, by *Bonnie Scotland. 50-32-14-2, $118,887, consensus champion three-year-old colt, Belmont S., Lawrence Realization, etc. Won 17 consecutive races. Leading sire 1895-'98. Sire of Hamburg, Abe Frank, Blackstock, David Garrick, Halma, Handspun, Rhoda B., Tea's Over, The Commoner, Urania, Yankee.

HARRY BASSETT, 1868-1878. Ch. c., Lexington—Canary Bird, by *Albion. 36-23-6-3 $59,450, consensus champion three-year-old colt, Belmont S., Travers S., etc.

HASTINGS, 1893-1917. Br. c., Spendthrift—*Cinderella, by Tomahawk or Blue Ruin. 21-10-8-0, $16,340, Belmont S., Toboggan H., etc. Leading sire 1902, '08. Sire of Fair Play, Gunfire, Don Enrique, Flittergold, Masterman. Notorious for his savage temperament.

HAYNIE'S MARIA, 1808-unknown. Ch. f., *Diomed—Bellair mare, by Bellair. 9-8-1-0. Won at distances from four furlongs to four-mile heats. Famed as the nemesis of the stable of Andrew Jackson who said, "I could not beat her."

***HELIOPOLIS**, 1936-1959. B. c., Hyperion—Drift, by Swynford. 15-5-2-1, $71,216, Prince of Wales's S., Imperial Produce S., etc. Leading sire in 1950, '54. Sire of 53 stakes winners, including High Gun, Olympia, Helioscope, Grecian Queen, Parlo, Berlo, Aunt Jinny, Summer Tan, Princess Turia, Camargo. Broodmare sire of Riva Ridge, Summer Guest.

HENRY (SIR HENRY), 1819-1837. Ch. c., Sir Archy—Diomed mare, by *Diomed. Southern representative in first great North-South four-mile heat match race against American Eclipse at the Union Course, New York, in 1823. Won first heat, but beaten in second and third. Won four-mile and three-mile heat races, including 1823 Jockey Club Purse at Petersburg, Virginia. Sire of Post Boy, Decatur, Alice Grey.

HENRY OF NAVARRE, 1891-1917. Ch. c., Knight of Ellerslie—Moss Rose, by *The Ill-Used. 42-29-8-3, $68,985, champion three-year-old colt, Belmont S., Travers S., etc. Sire of Grave and Gay, Orienta.

HEROD, 1758-1780. B. c., Tartar—Cypron, by Blaze. 10-6-3-0, Match against Antinous, etc. Leading sire in England eight times. Sire of Highflyer, Florizel, Woodpecker, Bridget, Bagot, Maid Of The Oaks, Phenomenom. Tail-male ancestor of the Tetrarch, Tourbillon, *Ambiorix, Ahonoora, Dr Devious (Ire), Indian Ridge.

HIGHFLYER, 1774-1793. B. c., Herod—Rachel, by Blank. 12-12-0-0, Grosvenor S., Great Subscription Race, etc. Leading sire in England a record 13 times, record 12 in succession. Sire of Sir Peter Teazle, Delpini, Huncamunca, Noble, Rockingham, Skyscraper, Maid Of All Work, Prunella.

HIGH GUN, 1951-1962. Br. c., *Heliopolis—Rocket Gun, by Brazado. 24-11-5-4, $486,025, champion three-year-old colt, champion handicap horse, Belmont S., Jockey Club Gold Cup, etc. Virtually sterile; sired only four foals.

HILL PRINCE, 1947-1970. B. c., *Princequillo—Hildene, by Bubbling Over. 30-17-5-4, $422,140, Horse of the Year in 1950, champion two- and three-year-old colt, champion handicap horse, Preakness S., Jockey Club Gold Cup, etc. Sire of 23 stakes winners, including Bayou, Levee, Royal Living, Middle Brother. Broodmare sire of Dark Mirage, Shuvee.

HILLSDALE, 1955-1972. B. c., Take Away—Johann, by Johnstown. 41-23-6-4, $646,935, Hollywood Gold Cup H., Californian S., etc. Sire of nine stakes winners, including Bravery II and Hi Q.

HINDOO, 1878-1901. B. c., Virgil—Florence, by Lexington. 35-30-3-2, $71,875, champion two- and three-year-old colt, Kentucky Derby, Travers S., etc. Won 18 consecutive races at two and three. Sire of Hanover, Buddhist, Hindoo Rose, Jim Gore, Sallie McClelland.

HIS MAJESTY, 1968-'95. B. c., *Ribot—Flower Bowl, by *Alibhai. 22-5-6-3, $99,430, Everglades S., Leading sire in 1982. Sire of 59 stakes winners, including Pleasant Colony, Tight Spot, Majesty's Prince, Cetewayo, Mehmet. Broodmare sire of Danehill, Dynaformer, Midway Lady, Risen Star. Brother to Graustark, half brother to Bowl of Flowers.

HOLY BULL, 1991- . Gr. c., Great Above—Sharon Brown, by Al Hattab. 16-13-0-0, $2,481,760, Horse of the Year in 1994, champion three-year-old male, Travers S. (G1), Metropolitan H. (G1), etc. Sire of more than 20 stakes winners, including Macho Uno.

HONEYMOON, 1943-unknown. B. f., *Beau Pere—Panoramic, by Chance Shot. 78-20-14-9, $387,760, Top Flight H., Hollywood Oaks, etc. Dam of stakes winners Honeys Gem, Honeys Alibi from only three foals.

HYPERION, 1930-1960. Ch. c., Gainsborough—Selene, by Chaucer. 13-9-1-2, $124,386, champion three-year-old in England, Epsom Derby, St. Leger S., etc. Leading sire in England six times; leading broodmare sire in England four times. Sire of *Alibhai, Aristophanes, Aureole, Godiva, Gulf Stream, *Heliopolis, High Hat, *Khaled, Owen Tudor, Pensive, Sun Chariot. Broodmare sire of Alycidon, *Aunt Edith II, *Carrozza, Citation, Nearctic, Pretense. Foundation sire of line that leads to *Forli, Star Kingdom, *Vaguely Noble, Marscay, Nodouble, Efisio.

IMP, 1894-1909. Br. f., Wagner—Fondling, by Fonso. 171-62-35-29, $70,069, champion older mare twice, Suburban H., etc. Immortalized in verse as "My Coal Black Lady."

IRISH LAD, 1900-unknown. Dk. b or br. c., *Candlemas—Arrowgrass, by Enquirer. 23-12-5-2, $98,210, consensus champion older horse, Metropolitan H., Brooklyn H., etc. Sire in France of Banshee, Blarney.

IROQUOIS, 1878-1899. B. c., *Leamington—Maggie B.B., by *Australian. 26-12-4-3, $99,707, champion three-year-old in England, Epsom Derby, St. Leger S., etc. First American-bred winner of the Epsom Derby in 1881. Leading sire in 1892. Sire of Tammany, Huron.

JAIPUR, 1959-1987. Dk. b. c., *Nasrullah—Rare Perfume, by Eight Thirty. 19-10-6-0, $618,926, champion three-year-old colt, Belmont S., Travers S., etc. Sire of Amber Rama, Mansingh, Pontifex.

JANUS (LITTLE JANUS), 1746-1780. Ch. c., Janus—Fox mare, by Fox. Won twice in England and once in the U.S. at four-mile heats. Sire of Meade's Celer, Clodius, Goode's Old Twigg. Early Colonial Thor-

oughbred foundation sire and foundation sire of the original Virginia Quarter Horse.

JAY TRUMP, 1957-1988. Dk. b. or br. g., Tonga Prince—Be Trump, by *Bernborough. 29-13-5-2, Grand National Steeplechase H. in England, etc. Also won three Maryland Hunt Cups.

JIM DANDY, 1927-unknown. Ch. g., Jim Gaffney—Thunderbird, by *Star Shoot. 141-7-6-8, $49,570, Travers S., Grand Union Hotel S., etc. Upset Gallant Fox and Whichone in 1930 Travers S. at 100-to-1.

JOHN HENRY, 1975- . B. g., Ole Bob Bowers—Once Double, by Double Jay. 83-39-15-9, $6,591,860, Horse of the Year 1981, '84, champion grass male four times, Santa Anita H. (G1) twice, Jockey Club Gold Cup (G1), Oak Tree Invitational (G1) three times, Hollywood Invitational H. (G1) three times, etc.

JOHN P. GRIER, 1917-1943. Ch. c., Whisk Broom II—Wonder, by Disguise. 17-10-4-2, $37,006, Queens County H., Aqueduct H., etc. Sire of more than 25 stakes winners, including Boojum, El Chico, Jack High, White Lies. Pressed Man o' War to narrowest victory in 1920 Dwyer H.

JOHNSTOWN, 1936-1950. B. c., Jamestown—La France, by *Sir Gallahad III. 21-14-0-3, $169,315, Kentucky Derby, Belmont S., etc. Sire of Flood Town, Acoma. Broodmare sire of Nashua.

JOLLY ROGER, 1922-1948. Ch. g., Pennant—Lethe, by *All Gold. 49-18-9-9, $143,240, Grand National Steeplechase H. twice, Brook Stp. H., etc.

***KAYAK II**, 1935-1946. Dk. br. c., Congreve—Mosquita, by Your Majesty. 26-14-8-1, $213,205, champion handicap horse, Santa Anita H., Hollywood Gold Cup, etc. Shy breeder.

KELSO, 1957-1983. Dk. b. or br. g., Your Host—Maid of Flight, by Count Fleet. 63-39-12-2, $1,977,896, Horse of the Year 1960-'64, champion three-year-old male, champion older horse four times, handicap triple crown, Jockey Club Gold Cup five times, Woodward S. three times, etc. Only five-time Horse of the Year.

KENTUCKY, 1861-1875. B. c., Lexington—Magnolia, by *Glencoe. 23-21-0-0, $33,700, Travers S., Saratoga Cup twice, etc. Won 20 consecutive races; first winner of the Travers S. Sire of Nina, Woodbine. Along with Norfolk and Asteroid, one of three dominant sons of Lexington, called the "great triumvirate."

***KHALED**, 1943-1968. B. c., Hyperion—Eclair, by Ethnarch. 12-6-1-1, $38,860, Middle Park S., Coventry S., etc. Sire of 61 stakes winners, including Swaps, Terrang, Going Abroad, New Policy, Correspondent, A Glitter, Bushel-n-Peck. Broodmare sire of Candy Spots, Outing Class, Prove It.

KINCSEM, 1874-unknown. B. f., Cambuscan—Waternymph, by Cotswold. 54-54-0-0, Goodwood Cup, etc. All-time leader by number of wins among unbeaten horses. Greatest horse ever bred in Hungary. Raced all over Europe and in England.

KING'S BISHOP, 1969-1981. B. c., Round Table—Spearfish, by Fleet Nasrullah. 28-11-4-3, $308,079, Carter H. (G2), Fall Highweight H. (G3), etc. Sire of 30 stakes winners, including King's Swan, Possible Mate, Queen to Conquer, Queen Lib, Bishop's Ring.

KINGSTON, 1884-1912. Br. c., Spendthrift—*Kapanga, by Victorious. 138-89-33-12, $140,195, First Special S., etc. Leading sire in 1900, '10. Sire of Novelty, Wild Mint, Lida B. Holds American record for most races won at 89.

KINGSTON TOWN, 1976-'91. Dk. b. or br. g., Bletchingly—Ada Hunter (Ger), by Andrea Mantegna. 42-32-6-2, $1,565,015, Horse of the Year in Australia, champion miler, champion older horse, W. S. Cox Plate (Aus-G1) three times, AJC Derby (Aus-G1), Sydney Cup (Aus-G1), etc. Greatest Australian racehorse of second half of 20th century.

KOTASHAAN (FR), 1988- . Dk. b. or br. c., Darshaan—Haute Autorite, by Elocutionist. 22-10-5-2, Horse of the Year in 1993, champion grass male, Breeders' Cup Turf (G1), Eddie Read H. (G1), etc. Exported to Japan in 1994.

LADY LIGHTFOOT, 1812-1834. Br. f., Sir Archy—Black Maria, by *Shark. Won at least 23 races, 15 at four-mile heats. Dam of Black Maria, Terror.

LADY'S SECRET, 1982-2003. Gr. f., Secretariat—Great Lady M., by Icecapade. 45-25-9-3, $3,021,325, Horse of the Year in 1986, champion older female, Breeders' Cup Distaff (G1), Whitney H. (G1), etc. All-time distaff leading earner at time of retirement.

LANDALUCE, 1980-1982. Dk. b. or br. f., Seattle Slew—Strip Poker, by Bold Bidder. 5-5-0-0, $372,365, champion two-year-old filly, Oak Leaf S. (G1), Del Mar Debutante S. (G2), etc. Died at two.

LA PREVOYANTE, 1970-1974. B. f., Buckpasser—Arctic Dancer, by Nearctic. 39-25-5-3, $572,417, champion two-year-old filly in U.S., Horse of the Year in Canada in 1972, champion two-year-old filly in Canada, champion older female in Canada, Frizette S., Spinaway S., etc. Won all 12 of her starts at two. Died at four.

LA TROIENNE, 1926-1954. B. f., *Teddy—Helene de Troie, by Helicon. 7-0-1-1, $146. Greatest American foundation mare of the 20th century. Dam of Bimelech, Black Helen. Foundation mare of family that includes Buckpasser, Easy Goer, Allez France, Affectionately, Busher, Glamour, Numbered Account, Private Account, Woodman, Bee Ann Mac, Autobiography, Cohoes, The Axe II, Big Hurry, Searching, Relaxing, Bridal Flower, Caerleon, Straight Deal, Glowing Tribute, Sea Hero, Lite Light, Go for Gin, Pleasant Tap, Princess Rooney, Prairie Bayou.

LECOMTE, 1850-1856. Ch. c., Boston—Reel, by *Glencoe. 16-11-5-0, $12,630, Jockey Club Purse, etc. Only horse to defeat Lexington. Sire of Umpire, Sherrod.

L'ESCARGOT, 1963-1984. Ch. g., Escart III—What a Daisy, by Grand Inquisitor. 63-14-15-8, $237,572, champion steeplechaser, Cheltenham Gold Cup Steeplechase H. twice, Meadow Brook Steeplechase H., etc.

LEXINGTON, 1850-1875. B. c., Boston—Alice Carneal, by *Sarpedon. 7-6-1-0, $56,600, Great State Post S., etc. Leading sire 1861-'74, '76, '78. Sire of Asteroid, Norfolk, Kentucky, Tom Ochiltree, Duke of Magenta, Tom Bowling, Harry Bassett, Sultana, Maiden, Florence, General Duke, Hira, Idlewild, Lida, Preakness, Salina, Ulrica, War Dance. Leading sire record 16 times, 14 in succession.

LONESOME GLORY, 1988-2002. Ch. g., Transworld—Stronghold (Fr), by Green Dancer. 44-24-5-6, $1,325,868, champion steeplechaser five times, Carolina Cup Hurdle S. twice, Colonial Cup Steeplechase S. twice, etc. First steeplechase millionaire.

LONGFELLOW, 1867-1893. Br. c., *Leamington—Nantura, by Brawner's Eclipse. 16-13-2-0, $11,200, Monmouth Cup twice, Saratoga Cup, etc. Leading sire in 1891. Sire of Freeland, The Bard, Thora, Longstreet, Leonatus, Riley.

LUKE BLACKBURN, 1877-1904. B. c., *Bonnie Scotland—Nevada, by Lexington. 39-25-6-2, $49,460, Champion S., Kenner S., etc. Won 22 of 24 races at three. Sire of Proctor Knott.

LYPHARD, 1969-2005. B. c., Northern Dancer—Goofed, by *Court Martial. 12-6-1-0, $195,427, Prix Jacques

le Marois, Prix de la Foret, etc. Leading sire in U.S. in 1986, leading sire in France 1978 and '79; leading broodmare sire in France in 1985 and '86. Sire of 115 stakes winners, including Dancing Brave, Manila, Three Troikas (Fr), Reine de Saba (Fr), Jolypha, Dancing Maid (Fr), Pharly, Bellypha (Ire), Sangue (Ire), Sabin, Al Nasr (Fr), Elliodor, Featherhill (Fr), Lypheor (GB), Skimble. Broodmare sire of Bering (GB), Groom Dancer, Hatoof.

MAD HATTER, 1916-1935. B. or br. c., Fair Play—Madcap, by *Rock Sand. 98-32-22-15, $194,525, consensus champion handicap horse, Jockey Club Gold Cup twice, Toboggan H., etc. Sire of 22 stakes winners, including Snowflake, The Nut.

MAGGIE B.B., 1867-1889. B. f., *Australian—Madeline, by Boston. 7-3-4-0, $2,950, Sequel S. Greatest American broodmare of 19th century. Dam of Iroquois, Harold, Jaconet, Pera, Panique, Red and Blue. Tail-female ancestor of family that includes Alanesian, Boldnesian, Lawrin, Idun, Top Flight, Whisk Broom II, Life's Magic, Bald Eagle, Dubai Millennium.

MAHMOUD, 1933-1962. Gr. c., *Blenheim II—Mah Mahal, by Gainsborough. 11-4-2-3, $85,413, champion three-year-old in England, Epsom Derby, Champagne S., etc. Leading sire in 1946; leading broodmare sire in 1957. Sire of 66 stakes winners, including The Axe II, Oil Capitol, Cohoes, First Flight, Vulcan's Forge, Mount Marcy, Adile, Snow Goose, Almahmoud, Happy Mood, Mahmoudess. Broodmare sire of Cosmah, Determine, *Gallant Man, *Grey Dawn II, Misty Morn, Silver Spoon, Your Host. Made the gray coat color popular in America.

MAIDEN, 1862-1880. B. f., Lexington—Kitty Clark, by *Glencoe. 15-5-8-3, $5,500, Travers S., Produce S., etc. Second Travers S. winner. Dam of Parole, sixth dam of Nearco.

MAJESTIC PRINCE, 1966-1981. Ch. c., Raise a Native—Gay Hostess, by *Royal Charger. 10-9-1-0, $414,200, Kentucky Derby, Preakness S., etc. Sire of 33 stakes winners, including Majestic Light, Coastal, Sensitive Prince, Eternal Prince.

MAN O' WAR, 1917-1947. Ch. c., Fair Play—Mahubah, by *Rock Sand. 21-20-1-0, $249,465, consensus champion two- and three-year-old colt, Belmont S., Travers S., etc. Leading sire in 1926. Sire of 62 stakes winners, including War Admiral, Crusader, American Flag, War Relic, Bateau, Scapa Flow, Edith Cavell, Maid at Arms, Florence Nightingale, Battleship, Clyde Van Dusen, Hard Tack. Broodmare sire of Blue Swords, Helioscope, Mata Hari, Pavot, Vagrancy. Tail-male ancestor of line that leads to In Reality, Tiznow. Still considered by many to be the greatest racehorse of all time.

MASKETTE, 1906-c.1930. B. f., Disguise—Biturica, by Hamburg. 17-12-3-0, $77,090, consensus champion two- and three-year-old filly, Futurity S., Alabama S., Matron S., Spinaway S., etc.

MATA HARI, 1931-1957. Br. f., Peter Hastings—War Woman, by Man o' War. 16-7-0-2, $66,699, consensus champion two- and three-year-old filly, Breeders' Futurity, Kentucky Jockey Club S., Illinois Derby, etc. Dam of Spy Song, Mr. Music.

MATCHEM, 1748-1781. B. c., Cade—Partner mare, by Partner. 8 wins, The Whip, etc. Leading sire three times in England. Sire of Conductor, Pantaloon, Alfred, Hollandaise, Tetotum. Male-line ancestor of Man o' War, In Reality, Tiznow, Hurry On, Sassafras (Fr).

MATE, 1928-1953. Ch. c., Prince Pal—Killashandra, by *Ambassador IV. 75-20-14-19, $301,810, Preakness S., American Derby, etc. Great rival of Equipoise, Twenty Grand. Sire of five stakes winners, including two-time champion steeplechaser Elkridge.

*MEDLEY, 1776-1792. Gr. c., Gimcrack—Arminda, by Snap. 13 wins. Sire of Bellair, Calypso, Grey Diomed, Grey Medley, Lamplighter. Early American foundation sire.

*MESSENGER, 1780-1808. Gr. c., Mambrino—Turf mare, by Turf. 10 wins, $7,365. Sire of Miller's Damsel, Tippoo Saib, Potomac, Bright Phoebus, Mambrino. Early American foundation sire; also foundation sire of the American Standardbred breed.

MIDDLEGROUND, 1947-1972. Ch. c., Bold Venture—Verguenza, by Chicaro. 15-6-6-2, $237,725, Kentucky Derby, Belmont S., Hopeful S., etc. Sire of seven stakes winners, including Resaca. Shy breeder.

MIESQUE, 1984- . B. f., Nureyev—Pasadoble, by Prove Out. 16-12-3-1, $2,070,163, champion grass female twice in U.S., champion two-year-old in France, champion miler in England, champion older mare in France, Breeders' Cup Mile (G1) twice, One Thousand Guineas (Eng-G1), etc. Dam of Kingmambo, East of the Moon, Miesque's Son, Moon Is Up.

MILL REEF, 1968-1986. B. c., Never Bend—Milan Mill, by *Princequillo. 14-12-2-0, $450,533, Horse of the Year in Europe, champion three-year-old in England and France, champion older horse in France, Epsom Derby, Prix de l'Arc de Triomphe, etc. Leading sire in England twice. Sire of 62 stakes winners, including Reference Point, Shirley Heights, Acamas, Glint of Gold, Ibn Bey (GB). Broodmare sire of Last Tycoon (Ire), Pentire. Tail-male ancestor of line that includes Darshaan, Dalakhani, Daylami (Ire).

MINESHAFT, 1999-. Dk.b. or br. c., A. P. Indy—Propectors Delite, by Mr. Prospector. 18-10-3-1, $2,283,402. Horse of the Year in 2003, champion older male, Jockey Club Gold Cup (G1), etc.

MISS WOODFORD, 1880-1899. Br. f., *Billet—Fancy Jane, by Neil Robinson. 48-37-7-2, $118,270, Alabama S., Spinaway S., Pimlico S., etc. First American horse to earn $100,000.

MOCCASIN, 1963-1986. Ch. f., Nantallah—*Rough Shod II, by Gold Bridge. 21-11-2-4, $388,075, Horse of the Year in 1965 Thoroughbred Racing Associations poll, champion two-year-old filly, Gardenia S., Test S., etc. Dam of Apalachee, Scuff, Flippers.

MODESTY, 1881-unknown. Ch. f., War Dance—Ballet, by Planet. 82-35-8-11, $49,135, Kentucky Oaks, American Derby, etc. First filly winner of the American Derby. Tail-female ancestor of family that includes Regret, Thunderer, First Fiddle.

MOLLIE MCCARTHY, 1873-unknown. B. f., Monday—Hennie Farrow, by Shamrock. 17-15-0-0, $18,750, Winter S., Garden City Cup, etc. One of the last great four-mile heat fillies.

MONSIEUR TONSON, 1822-unknown. B. c., Pacolet—Madame Tonson, by Top Gallant. 12-11-0-0. Leading sire in 1834. Sire of Argyle. First horse bred west of the Appalachians to win in the East.

MORVICH, 1919-unknown. Bl. c., Runnymede—Hymir, by Dr. Leggo. 16-12-2-1, $172,909, Kentucky Derby, Hopeful S., etc. First California-bred winner of the Kentucky Derby in 1922, won first 12 starts. Sire of 12 stakes winners.

MOTHER GOOSE, 1922-unknown. Br. f., *Chicle—Flying Witch, by Broomstick. 10-3-1-3, $72,755, consensus champion two-year-old filly, Futurity S. (defeated 28 others in a record field), Fashion S., etc. Dam of Arbitrator. Full sister to Whichone. Tail-female ancestor of family that includes Northern Dancer, Halo, Arctic Tern, Machiavellian, La Prevoyante, Tosmah, Danehill.

MR. PROSPECTOR, 1970-1999. B. c., Raise a Native—Gold Digger, by Nashua. 14-7-4-2, $112,171, Gravesend H., Whirlaway S., etc. Leading sire in 1987-'88; leading broodmare sire in 1997-2004. Sire of 180 stakes winners, including Forty Niner, Fusaichi Pegasus, Seeking the Gold, It's in the Air, Fappiano, Woodman, Gulch, Carson City, Conquistador Cielo, Gone West, Gold Beauty, Kingmambo, Machiavellian, Miswaki. Broodmare sire of Dayjur, Fasliyev, Hollywood Wildcat, Pulpit, Mineshaft.

MUMTAZ MAHAL, 1921-1945. Gr. f., The Tetrarch—Lady Josephine, by Sundridge. 10-7-2-0, $67,421, champion two-year-old, champion sprinter, Champagne S., Nunthorpe S., etc. Dam of Mirza II, Badruddin. Tail-female ancestor of *Nasrullah, *Royal Charger, Abernant, Petite Etoile, Shergar, Octagonal, Oh So Sharp (GB), *Migoli, Aliya, Risen Star, Left Bank, Kalamoun. Known as "the Flying Filly." Still considered by many the fastest filly ever to race in England.

MY CHARMER, 1969-1993. B. f., Poker—Fair Charmer, by Jet Action. 32-6-4-2, $34,133, Fair Grounds Oaks. Dam of Seattle Slew, Lomond, Seattle Dancer (record $13.1-million yearling).

MYRTLEWOOD, 1932-1950. B. f., Blue Larkspur—*Frizeur, by *Sweeper. 22-15-4-2, $40,620, champion sprinter, champion handicap mare, Ashland S., Hawthorne Sprint H., etc. Set five track records and equaled three. Dam of Durazna, Miss Dogwood. Foundation mare of family that includes Seattle Slew, Mr. Prospector, Myrtle Charm, Lomond, Typecast, Siberian Express, Highest Trump, Bahri, Ajina, Escena, Sewickley, Forestry, Chief Bearhart.

NASHUA, 1952-1982. B. c., *Nasrullah—Segula, by Johnstown. 30-22-4-1, $1,288,565, Horse of the Year in 1955, champion two- and three-year-old colt, Preakness S., Belmont S., Jockey Club Gold Cup twice, etc. Sire of 77 stakes winners, including Shuvee, Noble Nashua, Diplomat Way, Producer, Marshua, Bramalea, Bombay Duck, Good Manners, Nalee. Broodmare sire of Mr. Prospector, Roberto. First $1-million syndicated stallion.

*NASRULLAH, 1940-1959. B. c., Nearco—Mumtaz Begum, by *Blenheim II. 10-5-1-2, $15,259, champion two-year-old colt in England, Champion S., Coventry S., etc. Leading sire in 1955-'56, '59-'60, '62 in U.S.; leading sire in England. Sire of 93 stakes winners, including Bold Ruler, Nashua, Never Bend, Nearula, *Musidora, Never Say Die, Jaipur, Bald Eagle, Red God, Delta, Grey Sovereign. Broodmare sire of Drumtop, Natashka, *Sovereign II, Talking Picture, Turkish Trousers. Tail-male ancestor of Bold Ruler, Never Bend, Blushing Groom (Fr), Caro (Ire) lines.

NATIVE DANCER, 1950-1967. Gr. c., Polynesian—Geisha, by Discovery. 22-21-1-0, $785,240, Horse of the Year in 1952, '54, champion two- and three-year-old colt, champion handicap horse, Belmont S., Preakness S., Travers S., Futurity S., etc. Sire of 43 stakes winners, including Raise a Native, Hula Dancer, Dan Cupid, Secret Step, Kauai King, Dancer's Image, Native Charger, Native Street, Exclusive Dancer. Broodmare sire of Northern Dancer, General Assembly, Icecapade, Ruffian. Founder of male line that includes Mr. Prospector, Alydar, *Sea-Bird, Forty Niner, Seeking the Gold, Woodman, Thunder Gulch.

NATIVE DIVER, 1959-1967. Br. g., Imbros—Fleet Diver, by Devil Diver. 81-37-7-12, $1,026,500, Hollywood Gold Cup three times, San Carlos H. twice, etc. Won 33 stakes. Became the first California-bred millionaire.

NEARCO, 1935-1957. B. c., Pharos—Nogara, by Havresac II. 14-14-0-0, $85,974, champion two- and three-year-old in Italy, Grand Prix de Paris, Derby Italiano, etc. Leading sire three times in England; leading broodmare sire three times in England. Sire of *Nasrullah, Dante, *Masaka, *Amerigo, Mossborough, Narrator, Nimbus, *Royal Charger, Sayajirao, Infatuation, *Malindi, Neasham Belle, Netherton Maid, *Rivaz. Broodmare sire of *Arctic Prince, Charlottesville, Saint Crespin III, Sheshoon, *Tulyar, *Vaguely Noble. Tail-male ancestor of Northern Dancer, Bold Ruler, Blushing Groom (Fr), Never Bend, Caro (Ire) male lines.

NEARCTIC, 1954-1973. Br. c., Nearco—*Lady Angela, by Hyperion. 47-21-5-3, $152,384, Horse of the Year in Canada in 1958, Michigan Mile, Saratoga Special S., Canadian Maturity, etc. Sire of 49 stakes winners, including Northern Dancer, Icecapade, Nonoalco, Briartic, Cool Reception, Cold Comfort, Cool Moon, Arctic Dancer, Christmas Wind. Broodmare sire of Kennedy Road, La Prevoyante.

NEEDLES, 1953-1984. B. c., Ponder—Noodle Soup, by Jack High. 21-11-3-3, $600,355, champion two- and three-year-old colt, Kentucky Derby, Belmont S., etc. Sire of 21 stakes winners, including Irish Rebellion. First Florida-bred winner of the Kentucky Derby.

NEJI, 1950-1982. Ch. g., *Hunters Moon IV—Accra, by Annapolis. 46-17-11-8, $270,694, champion steeplechaser three times, Temple Gwathmey Steeplechase H. twice, Grand National Steeplechase H. twice, etc.

NELLIE FLAG, 1932-1953. Ch. f., American Flag—Nellie Morse, by Luke McLuke. 22-6-5-1, $59,665, champion two-year-old filly, Kentucky Jockey Club S., Matron S., etc. Dam of Mar-Kell, Sunshine Nell, Nellie L. Foundation mare of family that includes Forego, Bold Forbes, Bet Twice, Lakeway, Mark-Ye-Well, Saratoga Six.

NELLIE MORSE, 1921-1941. B. f., Luke McLuke—La Venganza, by Abercorn. 34-7-9-3, $73,565, consensus champion three-year-old filly, Preakness S., Fashion S., etc. Dam of Nellie Flag, Count Morse.

NEVER SAY DIE, 1951-1975. Ch. c., *Nasrullah—Singing Grass, by War Admiral. 12-3-1-3, $89,200, champion three-year-old in England, Epsom Derby, St. Leger S., etc. Leading sire in England in 1962. Sire of 41 stakes winners, including Never Too Late, Saidam, Die Hard. Broodmare sire of 95 stakes winners. Second American-bred to win the Epsom Derby. First American-bred to lead English sire list.

NEXT MOVE, 1947-1968. Br. f., Bull Lea—Now What, by Chance Play. 46-17-11-3, $398,550, champion three-year-old filly, champion older mare, Coaching Club American Oaks, Beldame H. twice, etc. Dam of Good Move, Restless Native. Fourth dam of Peteski.

NIJINSKY II, 1967-1992. B. c., Northern Dancer—Flaming Page, by Bull Page. 13-11-2-0, $667,220, Horse of the Year in Europe in 1970, champion two- and three-year-old in England and Ireland, English Triple Crown, King George VI and Queen Elizabeth S., etc. Last winner of the English Triple Crown. Leading sire in England in 1986; leading broodmare sire in U.S. in 1993-'94. Sire of 155 stakes winners, including Caerleon, Lammtarra, Ferdinand, Ile de Bourbon, Sky Classic, Golden Fleece, Royal Academy, Green Dancer, Number, Javamine, Maplejinsky. Broodmare sire of more than 245 stakes winners, including Fantastic Light, Flawlessly, Forest Flower, Heavenly Prize, Java Gold, Rubiano, Sky Beauty.

NODOUBLE, 1965-1990. Ch. c., *Noholme II—Abla Jay, by Double Jay. 42-13-11-5, $846,749, champion handicap horse twice, Santa Anita H., Metropolitan H., etc. Leading sire in 1981. Sire of 91 stakes winners, including Overskate, Mairzy Doates, Coolawin, Chain Store. Broodmare sire of 89 stakes winners, including Sky Classic, Regal Classic.

*NOOR, 1945-1974. Br. c., *Nasrullah—Queen of Baghdad, by *Bahram. 31-12-5-3, $356,940, champion handicap horse, Santa Anita H., Hollywood Gold Cup H., etc. Sire of Yours, Flutterby, Noureddin. Broodmare sire of Dancer's Image, Delta Judge. Defeated Citation four times at five.

NORFOLK, 1861-1890. B. c., Lexington—Novice, by *Glencoe. 5-5-0-0, $10,550, Jersey Derby, etc. Sire of Emperor of Norfolk, El Rio Rey, Flood, Ralston. Member of sire Lexington's "great triumvirate" with Asteroid and Kentucky.

NORTHERN DANCER, 1961-1990. B. c. Nearctic—Natalma, by Native Dancer. 18-14-2-2, $580,647, champion three-year-old colt, Horse of the Year in 1964 in Canada, champion two-year-old colt in Canada, Kentucky Derby, Preakness S., etc. Leading sire in U.S. in 1971, leading broodmare sire in U.S. in 1991; leading sire in England four times. Sire of 146 stakes winners, including Nijinsky II, Sadler's Wells, Nureyev, The Minstrel, El Gran Senor, Storm Bird, Lyphard, Northern Taste, Northfields, Unfuwain, Northernette, Fanfreluche, Shareef Dancer, Try My Best, Be My Guest, Cool Mood, Dixieland Band. Broodmare sire of more than 240 stakes winners, including Arazi, Eillo, L'Alezane, L'Enjoleur, Narita Brian, Noverre, Rhythm, Ryafan, Southern Halo.

NUREYEV, 1977-2001. B. c., Northern Dancer—Special, by *Forli. 3-2-0-0, $42,522, champion miler in France, Prix Thomas Bryon (Fr-G3), Prix Djebel. Disqualified from victory in 1980 Two Thousand Guineas (Eng-G1). Leading sire twice in France. Sire of more than 135 stakes winners, including Miesque, Peintre Celebre, Theatrical (Ire), Soviet Star, Sonic Lady, Fasliyev, Polar Falcon, Reams of Verse, Stravinsky, Zilzal, Skimming. Broodmare sire of more than 135 stakes winners, including Desert King, East of the Moon, Kingmambo, Peteski, Zabeel.

OEDIPUS, 1946-1978. Br. g., Blue Larkspur—Be Like Mom, by *Sickle. 58-14-12-9, $132,405, champion steeplechaser three times, Grand National Steeplechase H., Brook Steeplechase H. twice, etc.

OLD ROSEBUD, 1911-1922. B. g., Uncle—Ivory Bells, by Himyar. 80-40-13-8, $74,729, Kentucky Derby, Carter H., Flash S., etc. Set Kentucky Derby record that stood for 17 years.

OMAHA, 1932-1959. Ch. c., Gallant Fox—Flambino, by *Wrack. 22-9-7-2, $154,705, champion three-year-old colt, Triple Crown, Dwyer S., Classic S., etc. Sire of seven stakes winners, including Prevaricator. Broodmare sire of Summer Tan.

ONE COUNT, 1949-1966. Dk. br. c., Count Fleet—Ace Card, by Case Ace. 23-9-3-3, $245,625, Horse of the Year in 1952, champion three-year-old colt, Belmont S., Travers S., etc. Sire of 12 stakes winners, including Airmans Guide. Broodmare sire of Fit to Fight, Obeah.

*ORMONDE, 1883-1904. B. c., Bend Or—Lily Agnes, by Macaroni. 16-16-0-0, $138,340, Champion at two, three, and four in England, English Triple Crown. Sire of Orme, Ormondale, *Gold Finch, Ossary. Progressively sterile. Tail-male ancestor of *Teddy line. Widely considered the greatest English racehorse of 19th century; he was a roarer.

PAN ZARETA, 1910-1918. Ch. f., Abe Frank—Caddie Griffith, by Rancocas. 151-76-31-21, $39,082, Juarez H., Rio Grande H., etc. Won carrying 140 pounds or more five times. Died at eight and is buried in infield at Fair Grounds. Holds record for most wins by American distaffer.

*PAPYRUS, 1920-1941. Br. c., Tracery—Miss Matty, by Marcovil. 18-9-5-1, $110,068, Epsom Derby, Chester

Vase, etc. First Epsom Derby winner to race in the U.S. in international match race against Zev in 1923. Sire of Barbara Burrini, *Cosquilla, *Osiris II, Honey Buzzard.

PARLO, 1951-1978. Ch. f., *Heliopolis—Fairy Palace, by Pilate. 34-8-6-3, $309,240, champion three-year-old filly, champion handicap mare twice, Alabama S., Beldame H., etc. Tail-female ancestor of Arts and Letters, Silverbulletday, Saudi Poetry, Zaccio, Waquoit.

PAROLE, 1873-1903. Br. g., *Leamington—Maiden, by Lexington. 127-59-22-16, $82,111, Saratoga Cup, Epsom Gold Cup (in England), etc. Leading American money winner 1881-1885.

PASEANA (Arg), 1987- . B. f., Ahmad—Pasiflin (Arg), by Flintham. 36-19-10-2, $3,317,427, champion older female twice, Breeders' Cup Distaff (G1), Milady H. (G1) twice, Apple Blossom H. (G1) twice, etc.

PAVOT, 1942-1975. Br. c., Case Ace—Coquelicot, by Man o' War. 32-14-6-2, $373,365, undefeated champion two-year-old colt, Belmont S., Futurity S., etc. Sire of 14 stakes winners, including Andre, Cigar Maid.

PERSONAL ENSIGN, 1984- . B. f., Private Account—Grecian Banner, by Hoist the Flag. 13-13-0-0, $1,679,880, champion older female, Breeders' Cup Distaff (G1), Beldame S. (G1) twice, etc. Broodmare of the Year in 1996. Dam of My Flag, Miner's Mark, Traditionally; grandam of Storm Flag Flying.

PETER PAN, 1904-1933. B. c., Commando—*Cinderella, by Hermit. 17-10-3-1, $115,450, Belmont S., Hopeful S., etc. Sire of Black Toney, Pennant, Peter Hastings, Tryster, Prudery, Vexatious, Panoply, Wendy.

PEYTONA, 1839-1858. Ch. f., *Glencoe—Giantess, by *Leviathan. 8-6-1-0, $62,400, Peyton S., North-South Match, etc. One-time leading American money earner; defeated Fashion in last great North-South match race.

PHALARIS, 1913-1931. B. c., Polymelus—Bromus, by Sainfoin. 24-16-2-1, $26,376, Challenge S. twice, Stud Produce S., etc. Leading sire twice in England. Sire of 65 stakes winners, including Pharos, Fairway, Colorado, Manna, Fair Isle, *Sickle, *Pharamond II, Chatelaine. Broodmare sire of *Easton, Godiva, Mid-day Sun, Picture Play. Tail-male ancestor of *Nasrullah, Northern Dancer, Native Dancer, Buckpasser sire lines.

PHARIS, 1936-1957. Br. c., Pharos—Carissima, by Clarissimus. 3-3-0 0, $47,531, champion three-year-old in France, Prix du Jockey-Club (French Derby), Grand Prix de Paris, etc. Leading sire in France four times. Sire of *Ardan, Auriban, Philius, Dynamiter, *Priam II, Asterblute. Greatest horse bred in France in first half of 20th century. Racing career cut short by World War II; confiscated by the Nazis during the war and spent five years in Germany.

PHAR LAP, 1926-1932. Ch. g., Night Raid—Entreaty, by Winkie. 51-37-3-2, $305,921, AJC Derby, Victoria Derby, W. S. Cox Plate twice; won Agua Caliente H. in only start in North America; died shortly after under mysterious circumstances. Considered Australia's greatest racehorse.

PLANET, 1855-1875. Ch. c., Revenue—Nina, by Boston. 31-27-4-0, $69,700, Great Post S. twice, etc. Sire of Katy Pease, Hubbard, Ballet. Replaced Peytona as America's leading money earner.

PLAUDIT, 1895-1919 B. c., Himyar—*Cinderella, by Tomahawk or Blue Ruin. 20-8-5-0, $32,715, Kentucky Derby, Champagne S., etc. Sire of King James, Casuarina, Rosa Mundi, Spoonful. Tail-male ancestor of Dr. Fager, Holy Bull, Giacomo.

POCAHONTAS, 1837-1870. B. f., *Glencoe—Marpessa, by Muley. 9-0-3-0, $0. Greatest English broodmare of 19th century, dam of Stockwell, King Tom,

Rataplan. Ancestress of modern families that include foundation mares Rosy Legend, Kizil-Kourgan, Traverse, Traffic Court, Segula as well as racehorses and sires Dante, Sayajirao, *Ksar, *Kantar, Traffic Judge, Hasty Road, Nashua, Louis Quatorze.

POINT GIVEN, 1998- . Ch. c., Thunder Gulch—Turko's Turn, by Turkoman. 13-9-3-0, $3,968,500, Horse of the Year in 2001, champion three-year-old male, Belmont S. (G1), Preakness S. (G1), etc.

POT8O'S, 1773-unknown. Ch. c., Eclipse—Sportsmistress, by Sportsman. 30 wins in England, Craven S., Jockey Club Plate three times, etc. Sire of Champion, Coriander, Mandane, Waxy. Tail-male line ancestor of Phalaris, Hyperion, Blandford, Domino lines.

PREAKNESS, 1867-1881. B. c., Lexington—Bayleaf, by *Yorkshire. 39-18-11-5, $43,679, Dinner Party S., Saratoga Cup, etc. Sire in England of Fiddler, Piccadilly.

PRECISIONIST, 1981- . Ch. c., Crozier—Excellently, by *Forli. 46-20-10-4, $3,485,398, champion sprinter, Breeders' Cup Sprint (G1), Woodward S. (G1), etc. Virtually sterile. Sired only four foals.

PRETTY POLLY, 1901-1931. Ch. f., Gallinule—Admiration, by Saraband. 24-22-2-0, $187,780, champion two- and three-year-old in England, Epsom Oaks, St. Leger S., Coronation Cup twice, etc. Dam of Molly Desmond, Polly Flinders. Tail-female ancestor of Abadan, Arabella, Brigadier Gerard, Carroll House, *Daumier, Donatello II, Flute Enchantee, Flying Water, Luthier, Marwell, Nearctic, Northern Taste, Premonition, Psidium, St. Paddy, Supreme Court, Swain (Ire). Widely regarded as the greatest English racemare of all time; known as "the peerless Pretty Polly."

PRIMONETTA, 1958-1993. Ch. f., Swaps—Banquet Bell, by Polynesian. 25-17-2-2, $306,690, champion older mare, Alabama S., Spinster S. twice, etc. Broodmare of the Year in 1978; dam of Prince Thou Art, Maud Muller, Cum Laude Laurie, Grenfall. Sister to Chateaugay.

***PRINCEQUILLO**, 1940-1964. B. c., Prince Rose—*Cosquilla, by *Papyrus. 33-12-5-7, $96,550, Jockey Club Gold Cup, Saratoga Cup, etc. Leading sire 1957-'58; leading broodmare sire 1966-'70, '72, '73, '76. Sire of 65 stakes winners, including Round Table, Dedicate, Prince John, How, Quill, Hill Prince, Misty Morn, Princessnesian, Discipline. Broodmare sire of Bold Lad, *Comtesse de Loir, Fort Marcy, Key to the Mint, Kris S., Mill Reef, Secretariat, Sham, Sir Gaylord.

PRINCESS DOREEN, 1921-1952. B. f., *Spanish Prince II—Lady Doreen, by Ogden. 94-34-15-17, $174,754, Coaching Club American Oaks, Saratoga H., etc. Dam of Miss Doreen. Tail-female ancestor of Brown Bess, Caller I. D.

PRINCESS ROONEY, 1980- . Gr. f., Verbatim—Parrish Princess, by Drone. 21-17-2-1, $1,343,339, champion older female, Breeders' Cup Distaff (G1), Spinster S. (G1), etc.

PRIORESS, 1853-1868. B. f., *Sovereign—Reel, by *Glencoe. 24-10-1-3, $22,637, Cesarewitch H., two Queen's Plates, etc. First American-bred to win in England, victorious in a runoff after a dead heat in the 1857 Cesarewitch H.

PROCTOR KNOTT, 1886-unknown. Ch. g., Luke Blackburn—Tallapoosa, by *Great Tom. 26-11-6-4, $80,040, Futurity S., Junior Champion S., 2nd Kentucky Derby, etc. First winner of the Futurity Stakes (now at Belmont Park) in 1888, the race that swung the pendulum of American racing toward two-year-old speed because of its large purse.

PRUDERY, 1918-1930. B. f., Peter Pan—Polly Flinders, by Burgomaster. 22-7-6-5, $47,625, consensus champion two-year-old filly, Alabama S., Spinaway S., etc. Dam of Whiskery, Victorian, Halcyon. Tail-female ancestor of Taylor's Special.

QUESTIONNAIRE, 1927-1950. B. c., Sting—Miss Puzzle, by Disguise. 45-19-8-4, $89,611, Metropolitan H., Brooklyn H., etc. Sire of 24 stakes winners, including Requested, Free For All, Carolyn A., Hash, Stefanita, Third Degree. Tail-male line ancestor of Dr. Fager, Holy Bull, Giacomo.

RAISE A NATIVE, 1961-1988. Ch. c., Native Dancer—Raise You, by Case Ace. 4-4-0-0, $45,955, champion two-year-old colt, Juvenile S., Great American S. Sire of 78 stakes winners, including Alydar, Mr. Prospector, Exclusive Native, Majestic Prince, Laomedonte, Crowned Prince, Native Royalty, Marshua's Dancer, Native Partner, Where You Lead. Broodmare sire of Ajdal, Meadowlake, Slightly Dangerous.

REAL DELIGHT, 1949-1969. B. f., Bull Lea—Blue Delight, by Blue Larkspur. 15-12-1-0, $261,822, champion three-year-old filly, champion handicap mare, Coaching Club American Oaks, Kentucky Oaks, etc. Dam of Plum Cake, No Fooling, Spring Sunshine. Foundation mare of family that includes Alydar, Our Mims, Codex, Rich Cream, Christmas Bonus, Grand Slam, Sugar and Spice, Christmas Past.

REAL QUIET, 1995- . B. c., Quiet American—Really Blue, by Believe It. 20-6-5-6, $3,271,802, champion three-year-old male, Kentucky Derby (G1), Preakness S. (G1), Hollywood Gold Cup S. (G1), etc. Came within a nose of winning Triple Crown in 1998 Belmont S. (G1). Sire of No Place Like It.

REEL, 1838-unknown. Gr. f., *Glencoe—*Gallopade, by Catton. 8-7-1-0. Dam of Lecomte, Prioress, Starke, War Dance. Tail-female ancestor of modern family that includes Two Lea, Tim Tam, Miz Clementine, Best Turn, Chris Evert, Chief's Crown, Winning Colors.

REGRET, 1912-1934. Ch. f., Broomstick—Jersey Lightning, by Hamburg. 11-9-1-0, $35,093, Kentucky Derby, Hopeful S., etc. First filly to win the Kentucky Derby. Tail-female ancestor of family that includes First Fiddle, Divine Comedy.

REIGH COUNT, 1925-1948. Ch. c., *Sunreigh—*Contessina, by Count Schomberg. 27-12-4-0, $178,170, champion two- and three-year-old colt, Kentucky Derby, Jockey Club Gold Cup S., Coronation Cup (in England), etc. Sire of 22 stakes winners, including Count Fleet, Triplicate, Count Arthur. Broodmare sire of Gallahadion.

REVENUE, 1843-unknown. B. c., *Trustee—Rosalie Somers, by Sir Charles. 21-16-5-0. Jockey Club Purse, Proprietor's Purse, etc. Leading sire in 1860. Sire of Planet, Fanny Washington, Revolver.

*RIBOT, 1952-1972. B. c., Tenerani—Romanella, by El Greco. 16-16-0-0, $288,648, champion at two, three, and four in Italy, champion at four in England and France, Prix de l'Arc de Triomphe twice, King George VI and Queen Elizabeth S., etc. Leading sire three times in England. Sire of 65 stakes winners, including Arts and Letters, Tom Rolfe, Graustark, His Majesty, Ragusa, Molvedo, *Prince Royal II. Broodmare sire of more than 100 stakes winners, including Cannonade, Cascapedia, Majestic Light, Grandsire of Pleasant Colony.

RIVA RIDGE, 1969-1985. B. c., First Landing—Iberia, by *Heliopolis. 30-17-3-1, $1,111,497, champion two-year-old male, champion handicap male, Kentucky Derby, Belmont S., etc. Sire of 29 stakes winners, including Tap Shoes, Rivalero, Blitey. Broodmare sire of more than 45 stakes winners, including Life At the Top.

RIVERMAN, 1969-1999. B. c., Never Bend—River Lady, by Prince John. 8-5-2-1, $223,960, Poule d'Essai des Poulains (French Two Thousand Guineas), etc. Leading sire in France in 1980-'81. Sire of 128 stakes winners, including Irish River (Fr), Triptych, Bahri, Gold River (Fr), Detroit (Fr), Imperfect Circle, Korveya. Broodmare sire of Bosra Sham, Carnegie (Ire), Erhaab, Hector Protector, Highest Honor (Fr), Saint Cyrien, Spinning World.

ROAMER, 1911-1919. B. g., *Knight Errant—*Rose Tree II, by Bona Vista. 98-39-26-9, $98,828, Travers S., Carter H., Saratoga H. three times, etc.

ROBERTO, 1969-1988. Ch. c., Hail to Reason—Bramalea, by Nashua. 14-7-4-0, $332,272, champion three-year-old in England in 1972, champion two-year-old in Ireland in 1971, Epsom Derby, etc. Sire of 85 stakes winners, including Sunshine Forever, Brian's Time, Plenty of Grace, Dynaformer, and Red Ransom. Broodmare sire of more than 145 stakes winners, including Blushing K. D., Commander in Chief, Warning (GB).

ROCK OF GIBRALTAR (Ire), 1999- . B. c., Danehill—Offshore Boom, by Be My Guest. 13-10-2-0, $1,888,048, Horse of the Year in Europe, champion three-year-old colt, highweighted colt at three on International Classification at 7-9½ furlongs, Two Thousand Guineas (Eng-G1), Sussex S. (Eng-G1), Prix du Moulin de Longchamp (Fr-G1), etc. Won record seven Group 1 races in succession in 2001-'02.

ROSEBEN, 1901-1918. B. g., *Ben Strome—Rose Leaf, by Duke of Montrose. 111-52-25-12, $75,110, Carter H., Manhattan H. twice, etc. Great sprinter who won 14 races under 140 pounds or more, known as "the big train."

ROUGH'N TUMBLE, 1948-1968. B. c., Free For All—Roused, by *Bull Dog. 16-4-5-4, $126,980, Santa Anita Derby, Primer S., etc. Sire of 24 stakes winners, including Dr. Fager, My Dear Girl, Flag Raiser, Ruffled Feathers, Minnesota Mac, Treasure Chest. Florida foundation sire.

*ROUGH SHOD II, 1944-1965. B. f., Gold Bridge—Dalmary, by Blandford. 7-1-1-1, $1,306. Dam of Moccasin, Ridan, Lt. Stevens, Gambetta, Thong. Foundation mare of family that includes Sadler's Wells, Nureyev, Thatch, Gamely, Drumtop, Fairy King, King Pellinore, El Condor Pasa, Number, Bienamado.

ROUND TABLE, 1954-1987. B. c., *Princequillo—*Knight's Daughter, by Sir Cosmo. 66-43-8-5, $1,749,869, Horse of the Year in 1958, champion grass horse three times, champion handicap horse twice, Santa Anita H., Hollywood Gold Cup H., etc. Leading sire in 1972. Sire of 83 stakes winners, including Baldric, Apalachee, Flirting Around, Targowice, Royal Glint, King Pellinore, Drumtop, Knightly Manner, Advocator, King's Bishop, Artaius, Dancealot, Foreseer, Poker, Tell. Broodmare sire of 125 stakes winners, including Bowl Game, Caerleon, Hidden Lake, Outstandingly, Topsider.

*ROYAL CHARGER, 1942-1961. Ch. c., Nearco—Sun Princess by Solario. 20-6-7-2, $20,291, Queen Anne S., Ayr Gold Cup, etc. Sire of 54 stakes winners, including *Turn-to, Mongo, *Royal Serenade, Royal Native, Idun, Royal Orbit, Gilles de Retz, Happy Laughter, Royal Palm, *Banri an Oir. Broodmare sire of Majestic Prince, Tudor Queen. Tail-male ancestor of Roberto, Halo lines.

ROYAL HEROINE (Ire), 1980- . Dk. b. or br. f., Lypheor (GB)—My Sierra Leone, by Relko. 21-10-4-2, $1,229,449, champion grass female, Breeders' Cup Mile (G1), Matriarch S. (G1), etc. Second dam of Carmine Lake (Ire).

RUFFIAN, 1972-1975. Dk. b. or br. f., Reviewer—Shenanigans, by Native Dancer. 11-10-0-0, $313,428, champion two- and three-year-old filly, filly triple crown, Spinaway S. (G1), etc. Broke down in match race with

Foolish Pleasure and euthanized when she reinjured leg after surgery. Buried in infield at Belmont Park.

RUTHLESS, 1864-1876. B. f., *Eclipse—Barbarity, by *Simoom. 11-7-4-0, $11,000, Belmont S., Travers S., etc. Won first Belmont S. Best of five high-class sisters out of Barbarity nicknamed "the barbarous battalion."

SABIN, 1980- . Ch. f., Lyphard—Beaconaire, by *Vaguely Noble. 25-18-0-2, $1,098,341, Yellow Ribbon Invitational S. (G1), etc. Dam of Sabina, Al Sabin.

SADLER'S WELLS, 1981-. B. c., Northern Dancer—Fairy Bridge, by Bold Reason. 11-6-3-0, $713,690, Irish Two Thousand Guineas (Ire-G1), Eclipse S. (Eng-G1), etc. Leading sire in England 14 times. Sire of more than 255 stakes winners, including Galileo (Ire), High Chaparral (Ire), In the Wings (GB), Salsabil (Ire), Old Vic, Northern Spur (Ire), El Prado (Ire), Montjeu (Ire), Carnegie (Ire), Barathea (Ire), Imagine, King of Kings (Ire), Fort Wood. Broodmare sire of more than 120 stakes winners.

SAFELY KEPT, 1986-. B. f., Horatius—Safely Home, by Winning Hit. 31-24-2-3, $2,194,206, champion sprinter, Breeders' Cup Sprint (G1), Test S. (G1), etc.

SALVATOR, 1886-1909. Ch. c., *Prince Charlie—Salina, by Lexington. 19-16-1-1, $113,240, consensus champion three-year-old, Suburban H., Lawrence Realization, etc. Sire of Salvation. Subject of the Ella Wheeler Wilcox poem "How Salvator Won."

SARAZEN, 1921-1940. Ch. g., High Time—Rush Box, by Box. 55-27-2-6, $225,000, Champagne S., Carter H., Dixie H. twice, etc. Defeated *Epinard in third race of the International Series of 1924.

SCEPTRE, 1899-1927. Br. f., Persimmon—Ornament, by Bend Or. 25-13-4-4, $192,544, champion three-year-old, champion older horse, Epsom Oaks, Two Thousand Guineas, One Thousand Guineas, St. Leger S., etc. Dam of Curia, Grosvenor. Tail-female ancestor of Buchan, Commanche Run, Craig an Eran, Relko, Reliance, *Match II, *Noor, *St. Germans, Sunny Jane, Torbido. One of two fillies to win four of the five English classics.

SEA-BIRD, 1962-1973. Ch. c., Dan Cupid—Sicalade, by Sicambre. 8-7-1-0, $645,283, Horse of the Year in France and England, Epsom Derby, Prix de l'Arc de Triomphe, etc. Sire of 33 stakes winners, including Allez France, Little Current, Gyr, Arctic Tern. Broodmare sire of Alydar's Best, Assert (Ire), Bikala, Miss Oceana. Considered France's greatest racehorse.

SEABISCUIT, 1933-1947. B. c., Hard Tack—Swing On, by Whisk Broom II. 89-33-15-13, $437,730, Horse of the Year in 1938, champion handicap male twice, Pimlico Special, Santa Anita H., etc. Sire of four stakes winners, including Sea Swallow.

SEARCHING, 1952-1973. B. f., War Admiral—Big Hurry, by Black Toney. 89-25-14-16, $327,381, Maskette H., Diana H. twice, etc. Dam of Affectionately, Priceless Gem, Admiring. Foundation mare of family that includes Allez France, Sea Hero, Lite Light, Personality, Al Mamoon.

SEATTLE SLEW, 1974-2002. Dk. b. or br. c., Bold Reasoning—My Charmer, by Poker. 17-14-2-0, $1,208,726, Horse of the Year in 1977, champion two- and three-year-old colt, champion older horse, Triple Crown, Woodward S. (G1), etc. Leading sire in 1984; leading broodmare sire 1995-'96. Sire of more than 110 stakes winners, including A.P. Indy, Swale, Slew o' Gold, Surfside, Capote, Landaluce, Vindication, Slew City Slew, Taiki Blizzard, Lakeway, Honest Lady, General Meeting, Avenue of Flags, Slewvescent, Slewacide. Broodmare sire of more than 135 stakes winners, including Cigar, Agnes World, Escena, Lemon Drop Kid, Golden Attraction, Seeking the Pearl. Only horse to win Triple Crown while undefeated.

SECRETARIAT, 1970-1989. Ch. c., Bold Ruler—Somethingroyal, by *Princequillo. 21-16-3-1, $1,316,808, Horse of the Year in 1972-'73, champion two- and three-year-old male, champion grass horse, Triple Crown, Marlboro Cup H., etc. Leading broodmare sire in 1992. Sire of 56 stakes winners, including Lady's Secret, Risen Star, Medaille d'Or, Terlingua, General Assembly, Tinners Way, Weekend Surprise, Secrettame, Six Crowns. Broodmare sire of more than 160 stakes winners, including A.P. Indy, Chief's Crown, Dehere, Gone West, Secreto, Storm Cat, Summer Squall.

SELIMA, 1745-1766. B. f., Godolphin Arabian—Shireborn mare, by Hobgoblin. 2-2-0-0, $10,200, Great Intercolonial Match Race with Tryal. Dam of Ariel, Selim, Ebony, Bellair, Lightfoot's Partner. Tail-female ancestor of family that includes Hanover, Inspector B., Peytona, Foxhall, The Vid, Pirate's Revenge, Cherokee Run.

SENSATION, 1877-1899. Br. c., *Leamington—Susan Beane, by Lexington. 8-8-0-0, $20,250, champion two-year-old colt, Flash S., Nursery S., etc. Sire of Democrat.

SERENA'S SONG, 1992- . B. f., Rahy—Imagining, by Northfields. 38-18-11-3, $3,283,388, champion three-year-old filly, Mother Goose S. (G1), Beldame S. (G1), etc. Leading North American money-earning female at time of retirement. Dam of Serena's Tune, Sophisticat, Grand Reward.

SHIRLEY JONES, 1956-1978. B. f., Double Jay—L'Omelette, by *Alibhai. 49-18-9-5, $282,313, Test S., Maskette H., etc.

SHUVEE, 1966-1986. Ch. f., Nashua—Levee, by Hill Prince. 44-16-10-6, $890,445, champion handicap mare, champion older female, filly triple crown, Jockey Club Gold Cup twice, etc. Dam of Tom Swift, Shukey, Benefice.

SICKLE, 1924-1943. Br. c., Phalaris—Selene, by Chaucer. 10-3-4-2, $23,629, Prince of Wales's S., etc. Leading sire in 1936, '38. Sire of 41 stakes winners, including Stagehand, Brevity, Unbreakable, Star Pilot, Cravat, Reaping Reward, Misty Isle, Jabot. Broodmare sire of Bornastar, Counterpoint, Dan Cupid, How, Social Outcast. Tail-male ancestor of Native Dancer sire line.

SILVER BULLETDAY, 1996-. B. f., Silver Deputy—Rokeby Rose, by Tom Rolfe. 23-15-3-1, $3,093,207, champion two- and three-year-old filly, Breeders' Cup Juvenile Fillies (G1), Kentucky Oaks (G1), etc.

SILVER CHARM, 1994-. Gr. or ro. c., Silver Buck—Bonnie's Poker, by Poker. 24-12-7-2, $6,944,369, champion three-year-old male, Kentucky Derby (G1), Preakness S. (G1), Dubai World Cup (UAE-G1), etc.

SILVER SPOON, 1956-1978. Ch. f., Citation—Silver Fog, by *Mahmoud. 27-13-3-4, $313,930, champion three-year-old filly, Santa Anita Derby, Milady H., etc. Dam of Inca Queen. Tail-female ancestor of family that includes Catinca, Metfield.

SIR ARCHY, 1805-1833. Ch. c., *Diomed—*Castianira, by Rockingham. 7-4-1-0, Post S. Leading Colonial sire. Sire of Sir Charles, Timoleon, Flirtilla, Bertrand, Henry, Kosciusko, Lady Lightfoot, Sumpter, Reality. Oldest member of the Racing Hall of Fame.

SIR BARTON, 1916-1937. Ch. c., *Star Shoot—Lady Sterling, by Hanover. 31-13-6-5, $116,857, consensus champion three-year-old colt, Triple Crown, Saratoga H., etc. First winner of the American Triple Crown. Sire of seven stakes winners, including Easter Stockings.

SIR GALLAHAD III, 1920-1949. B. c., *Teddy—Plucky Liege, by Spearmint. 24-11-3-3, $17,009, Poule d'Essai des Poulains (French Two Thousand Guineas), Prix Jacques le Marois, match race with *Epinard, etc. Leading sire 1930, '33-'34, '40; leading broodmare sire '39, '43-'52, '55. Sire of 56 stakes winners, including Gallant Fox, Gallahadion, High Quest, Vagrancy, Foxbrough, Fighting Fox, Hoop, Jr., Roman. Broodmare sire of 180 stakes winners, including Beaugay, Challedon, *Galatea II, Gallorette, Johnstown, Royal Native. Greatest American broodmare sire of the 20th century. First major American stallion syndication.

SKIP AWAY, 1993- . Gr. or ro. c., Skip Trial—Ingot Way, by Diplomat Way. 38-18-10-6, $9,616,360, Horse of the Year in 1998, champion three-year-old male, champion older male twice, Breeders' Cup Classic (G1), Jockey Club Gold Cup (G1) twice, etc. Sire of 11 stakes winners.

SKY BEAUTY, 1990- 2004. B. f., Blushing Groom (Fr)—Maplejinsky, by Nijinsky II. 21-15-2-2, $1,336,000, champion older female, filly triple crown, Alabama S. (G1), Ruffian H. (G1), etc.

SLEW O' GOLD, 1980- . B. c., Seattle Slew—Alluvial, by Buckpasser. 21-12-5-1, $3,533,534, champion three-year-old male, champion older male, Jockey Club Gold Cup (G1) twice, Woodward S. (G1) twice, etc. Sire of 29 stakes winners, including Golden Opinion, Gorgeous, Dramatic Gold, Thirty Six Red, Awe Inspiring. Broodmare sire of Kona Gold.

SOMETHINGROYAL, 1952-1983. B. f., *Princequillo—Imperatrice, by Caruso. 1-0-0-0, $0. Broodmare of the Year in 1973. Dam of Secretariat, Sir Gaylord, First Family, Syrian Sea, Somethingfabulous. Foundation mare of family that includes Saratoga Dew, Alada, John Cherry, Personal Business.

SPECTACULAR BID, 1976-2003. Gr. or ro. c., Bold Bidder—Spectacular, by Promised Land. 30-26-2-1, $2,781,608, Horse of the Year in 1980, champion two- and three-year-old male, champion older male, Kentucky Derby (G1), Preakness S. (G1), etc. Sire of more than 40 stakes winners, including Lotus Pool, Double Feint, Spectacular Love. Broodmare sire of more than 85 stakes winners.

SPEND A BUCK, 1982-2002. B. c., Buckaroo—Belle de Jour, by Speak John. 15-10-3-2, $4,220,689, Horse of the Year in 1985, champion three-year-old male, Kentucky Derby (G1), Monmouth H. (G1), etc. Sire of more than 30 stakes winners, including Antespend, Hard Buck (Brz). Exported to Brazil in 1997.

SPENDTHRIFT, 1876-1900. Ch. c., *Australian—Aerolite, by Lexington. 13-10-5-0, $27,250, Belmont S., Jersey Derby, etc. Sire of Kingston, Hastings, Lamplighter. Tail-male ancestor of line that leads to Fair Play, Man o' War, War Admiral, In Reality, Tiznow.

SPINAWAY, 1878-unknown. Ch. f., *Leamington—Megara, by *Eclipse. 9-7-2-0, $16,225, champion two-year-old filly, Hopeful S., Juvenile S., etc. Dam of Lazzarone. Tail-female ancestor of family that includes Giant's Causeway, Tanya, Floradora, Star Pilot, By Land By Sea, Gummo, Spearfish, Gaily, King's Bishop.

SPY SONG, 1943-1973. Br. c., Balladier—Mata Hari, by Peter Hastings. 36-15-9-4, $206,325, Arlington Futurity, Clang H., etc. Sire of 28 stakes winners, including Crimson Satan, Sly Pola, Sari's Song. Broodmare sire of 91 stakes winners, including Blue Tom, Faraway Son, Liloy (Fr), Singh.

*STAR SHOOT, 1898-1919. B. c., Isinglass—Astrology, by Hermit. 10-3-1-1, $34,747 in England, National Breeders' Produce S., etc. Leading sire 1911-'12, '16-'17, '19; leading broodmare sire 1924-'26, '28-'29. Sire of Sir Barton, Grey Lag, Uncle, Wistful, Daylight Saving, Mindful, Priscilla. Broodmare sire of Blazes, Crusader, Gusto, Jack High. Sired a record 27 juvenile winners in 1916 that stood for 70 years.

STOCKWELL, 1849-1870. Ch. c., The Baron—Pocahontas, by *Glencoe. 16-11-3-0, $48,457, champion

three-year-old in England, Two Thousand Guineas, St. Leger S., etc. Leading sire in England seven times. Sire of Doncaster, Achievement, Caller Ou, Cantiniere, Chevisaunce, Lord Lyon, Regalia, St. Albans, The Marquis. Known as the "Emperor of Stallions." Tail-male ancestor of Phalaris, *Teddy male lines.

STRAIGHT DEAL, 1962-1982. B. f., Hail to Reason—No Fiddling, by King Cole. 99-21-21-9, $733,020, champion handicap mare, Delaware H., Santa Margarita H., etc. Dam of Desiree, Reminiscing.

ST. SIMON, 1881-1908. Br. c., Galopin—St. Angela, by King Tom. 9-9-0-0, $23,121, Ascot Gold Cup, Epsom Gold Cup, Goodwood Cup, etc. Leading sire in England nine times. Sire of Persimmon, Diamond Jubilee, St. Frusquin, Rabelais, Chaucer, Memoir, La Fleche. Tail-male ancestor of *Ribot, *Princequillo male lines.

STYMIE, 1941-1962. Ch. c., Equestrian—Stop Watch, by On Watch. 131-35-33-28, $918,485, champion handicap horse, Metropolitan H. twice, Whitney S., etc. Sire of 12 stakes winners, including Rare Treat, Joe Jones, Paper Tiger. Broodmare sire of Regal Gleam, What a Treat. Retired as world's leading money earner in 1950.

SUN BEAU, 1925-1944. B. c., *Sun Briar—Beautiful Lady, by Fair Play. 74-33-12-10, $376,744, consensus champion handicap horse three times, Hawthorne Gold Cup three times, Aqueduct H., etc. Sire of six stakes winners, including Sun Lover. Leading money earner at his retirement in 1931.

*SUN BRIAR, 1915-1943. B. c., Sundridge—*Sweet Briar II, by St. Frusquin. 22-8-4-5, $74,355, consensus champion two-year-old colt, Travers S., Hopeful S., etc. Sire of more than 30 stakes winners, including Sun Beau, Pompey, Firethorn.

SUNDAY SILENCE, 1986-2002. Dk. b. or br. c., Halo—Wishing Well, by Understanding. 14-9-5-0, $4,968,554, Horse of the Year in 1989, champion three-year-old male, Kentucky Derby (G1), Preakness S. (G1), Breeders' Cup Classic (G1), etc. Leading sire in Japan 1995-2004. Sire of more than 135 stakes winners, including Air Shakur, Dance Partner, Marvelous Sunday, Dance in the Dark, Bubble Gum Fellow, Fuji Kiseki, Special Week, Stay Gold, Genuine, Tayasu Tsuyoshi. All-time leading sire by earnings, exceeding $530-million.

SUNLINE, 1995. B. f., Desert Sun (GB)—Songline, by Western Symphony. 48-32-9-3, $6,625,105, Horse of the Year three times in Australia, Cox Plate (Aus-G1) twice, Flight S. (Aus-G1), Doncaster H. (Aus-G1) twice, etc. All-time leading money winner in Australia and New Zealand.

SUSAN'S GIRL, 1969-1988. B. f., Quadrangle—Quaze, by *Quibu. 63-29-14-11, $1,251,668, champion three-year-old filly, champion older female twice, Spinster S. (G1) twice, Delaware H. (G1) twice, etc. Dam of Copelan, Paramount Jet.

SWALE, 1981-1984. Dk. b. or br. c., Seattle Slew—Tuerta, by *Forli. 14-9-2-2, $1,583,660, champion three-year-old male, Kentucky Derby (G1), Belmont S. (G1), etc. Died eight days after winning Belmont Stakes.

SWAPS, 1952-1972. Ch. c., *Khaled—Iron Reward, by *Beau Pere. 25-19-2-2, $848,900, Horse of the Year in 1956, champion handicap horse, Kentucky Derby, Hollywood Gold Cup H., etc. Sire of 35 stakes winners, including Affectionately, Chateaugay, Primonetta, No Robbery. Broodmare sire of Best Turn, Fall Aspen, Numbered Account, Personality.

SWOON'S SON, 1953-1977. B. c., The Doge—Swoon, by Sweep Like. 51-30-10-3, $970,605, American Derby, Arlington Classic, etc. Sire of 22 stakes winners, including Chris Evert, Loom, Mr. Washington. Won 22 stakes.

SWORD DANCER, 1956-1984. Ch. c., Sunglow—Highland Fling, by By Jimminy. 39-15-7-4, $829,610, Horse of the Year in 1959, champion three-year-old colt, champion handicap horse, Belmont S., Jockey Club Gold Cup, etc. Sire of 15 stakes winners, including Damascus, Lady Pitt.

SYSONBY, 1902-1906. B. c., *Melton—*Optime, by Orme. 15-14-0-1, $184,438, champion two- and three-year-old colt, Metropolitan H., Saratoga Special, etc. Died at four.

TANYA, 1902-1929. Ch. f., *Meddler—Handspun, by Hanover. 10-6-1-1, $73,127, Belmont S., Hopeful S., Spinaway S., etc. Second filly to win the Belmont S.

TA WEE, 1966-1980. Dk. b. or br. f., Intentionally—Aspidistra, by Better Self. 21-15-2-1, $284,941, champion sprinter twice, Vosburgh H., Fall Highweight H. twice, etc. Dam of Great Above, Tax Holiday, Entropy, Tweak.

***TEDDY**, 1913-1936. B. c., Ajax—Rondeau, by Bay Ronald. 8-5-1-2, Gran Premio de San Sebastian, Prix des Trois Ans, etc. Leading sire in France twice. Sire of *Sir Gallahad III, *Bull Dog, *La Troienne, *Ortello, Aethelstan, Asterus, Rose of England, Brumeux, Case Ace, Sun Teddy, Anne de Bretagne, Anna Bolena, Assignation, Boxeuse, Coeur a Coeur, La Moqueuse. Tail-male ancestor of line leading to Damascus, Private Account, Captain Steve.

TEMPTED, 1955-unknown. Ch. f., *Half Crown—Enchanted Eve, by Lovely Night. 45-18-4-9, $330,760, champion handicap mare, Alabama S., Ladies H., etc. Dam of Lead Me On.

TEN BROECK, 1872-1887. B. c., *Phaeton—Fanny Holton, by Lexington. 30-23-3-1, $27,550, Phoenix Hotel S., Louisville Cup, etc. Sire of Jim Gray. Once held every major American record from one to four miles.

TENNY, 1886-1909. B. c., *Rayon d'Or—Belle of Maywood, by Hunter's Lexington. 65-25-15-12, $88,442, Brooklyn H., First Special S., etc. Defeated Racing Hall of Fame members Firenze, Hanover, and Kingston, but consistently beaten by Racing Hall of Famer Salvator.

THAD STEVENS, 1865-unknown. Ch. g., Langford—Mary Chilton, by *Glencoe. Great California four-miler.

THE TETRARCH, 1911-1935. Gr. c., Roi Herode—Vahren, by Bona Vista. 7-7-0-0, $55,206, Champagne S., Coventry S., etc. Leading sire in England in 1924. Sire of Mumtaz Mahal, Tetratema, Salmon Trout, *Stefan the Great, Caligula, Polemarch, Paola, Snow Maiden, *The Satrap. Called "the Spotted Wonder"; revived the Herod male line in England and popularized the gray coat color.

THE VERY ONE, 1975-1992. B. f., One for All—*Veruschka, by Venture. 71-22-12-9, $1,104,623, Santa Barbara H. (G1), Black Helen H. (G2), etc.

THUNDER GULCH, 1992- . Ch. c., Gulch—Line of Thunder, by Storm Bird. 16-9-2-2, $2,915,086, champion three-year-old male, Kentucky Derby (G1), Belmont S. (G1), etc. Sire of more than 35 stakes winners, including Point Given, Spain, Tweedside.

TIMOLEON, 1813-1836. Ch. c., Sir Archy—Saltram mare, by *Saltram. 16-14-0-0. Sire of Boston, Hotspur, Sally Walker, Saluda, Omega, Washington.

TIM TAM, 1955-1982. Dk. b. c., Tom Fool—Two Lea, by Bull Lea. 14-10-1-2, $467,475, champion three-year-old colt, Kentucky Derby, Preakness S., etc. Sire of 14 stakes winners, including Tosmah, Timmy Lad, Nancy Jr. Broodmare sire of Before Dawn, Davona Dale, Known Fact, Mac Diarmida, Tentam.

TIPPITY WITCHET, 1915-unknown. B. g., Broomstick—*Lady Frivoles, by St. Simon. 266-78-52-42, $88,241. Raced to age 14, beginning his career in stakes but descending to the claiming ranks.

TIZNOW, 1997-. B. c., Cee's Tizzy—Cee's Song, by Seattle Song. 15-8-4-2, $6,427,830, Horse of the Year in 2000, champion three-year-old male, champion older male, Breeders' Cup Classic (G1) twice, Santa Anita H. (G1), etc. Only dual winner of the Breeders' Cup Classic.

T.M.OPERA O, 1996-. Ch. c., Opera House (GB)—Once Wed, by Blushing Groom (Fr). 26-14-6-3, $16,200,337, Horse of the Year in Japan, champion three-year-old in Japan, Japan Cup (Jpn-G1), etc. World's leading money-winning Thoroughbred.

TOM BOWLING, 1870-unknown. B. c., Lexington—Lucy Fowler, by *Albion. 17-14-3-0, $35,000, champion three-year-old colt, Travers S., Jersey Derby, Jerome S., Monmouth Cup, etc. Sire of General Monroe.

TOM FOOL, 1949-1976. B. c., Menow—Gaga, by *Bull Dog. 30-21-7-1, $570,165, Horse of the Year in 1953, champion two-year-old colt, champion handicap horse, champion sprinter, handicap triple crown, Futurity S., etc. Leading broodmare sire in England in 1965. Sire of 36 stakes winners, including Buckpasser, Tim Tam, Silly Season, Tompion, Dunce, Jester, Funloving, Sweet Folly, Dinner Partner, Dunce Cap II. Broodmare sire of 90 stakes winners, including Foolish Pleasure, Hatchet Man, Late Bloomer, *Meadow Court, Stop the Music, Majesty's Prince.

TOM ROLFE, 1962-1989. B. c., *Ribot—Pocahontas, by Roman. 32-16-5-5, $671,297, champion three-year-old colt, Preakness S., American Derby-ntr, etc. Sire of 49 stakes winners, including Hoist the Flag, Run the Gantlet, Droll Role, Bowl Game. Broodmare sire of more than 105 stakes winners, including Diminuendo, Environment Friend, Forty Niner, Life's Magic, Niniski, Notebook, Silverbulletday.

TOP FLIGHT, 1929-1949. Dk. br. f., *Dis Donc—Flyatit, by Peter Pan. 16-12-0-0, $275,900, champion two- and three-year-old filly, Coaching Club American Oaks, Futurity S., etc. Dam of Flight Command. Tail-female ancestor of family that includes Watch Fob, Sikeston. World's leading money-winning female at time of retirement.

TOSMAH, 1961-1992. B. f., Tim Tam—Cosmah, by Cosmic Bomb. 39-23-6-2, $612,588, champion two- and three-year-old filly, champion handicap mare, Frizette S., Beldame S., etc. Dam of La Guidecca.

TREMONT, 1884-1901. Bl. c., Virgil—Ann Fief, by Alarm. 13-13-0-0, $39,135, champion two-year-old colt, Great American S., etc.

TURNBACK THE ALARM, 1989- . Ro. f., Darn That Alarm—Boomie's Girl E., by *Figonero. 22-8-6-4, $960,504, Coaching Club American Oaks (G1), Mother Goose S. (G1), etc.

***TURN-TO**, 1951-1973. B. c., *Royal Charger—*Source Sucree, by Admiral Drake. 8-6-1-1, $280,032, Garden State S., Flamingo S., etc. Sire of 25 stakes winners, including First Landing, Hail to Reason, Sir Gaylord, Best Turn, Cyane. Broodmare sire of 63 stakes winners, including Ack Ack, Bessarabian, Chinook Pass. Male line ancestor of Halo, Roberto lines.

T. V. LARK, 1957-1975. B. c., *Indian Hemp—Miss Larksfly, by Heelfly. 72-19-13-6, $902,194, champion grass horse, Washington, D.C., International S., United Nations H., etc. Leading sire in 1974. Sire of 53 stakes winners, including Quack, T. V. Commercial, Pink Pigeon, Buffalo Lark, Golden Don, T. V. Vixen, Romeo. Broodmare sire of 85 stakes winners, including Bates Motel, Chris Evert.

TWENTY GRAND, 1928-1948. B. c., *St. Germans—Bonus, by *All Gold. 23-14-4-3, $261,790, Horse of the Year in 1931, champion three-year-old colt, Kentucky Derby, Belmont S., etc. Sterile at stud.

TWILIGHT TEAR, 1941-1954. B. f., Bull Lea—Lady Lark, by Blue Larkspur. 24-18-2-2, $202,165, Horse of the Year in 1944, champion two- and three-year-old filly, champion handicap mare, Coaching Club American Oaks, Pimlico Special, etc. Dam of A Gleam, Bardstown, Coiner. Tail-female ancestor of family that includes Before Dawn, Gleaming, A Glitter.

TWO LEA, 1946-1973. B. f., Bull Lea—Two Bob, by The Porter. 26-15-6-3, $309,250, champion three-year-old filly, champion handicap mare, Hollywood Gold Cup H., Santa Margarita H., etc. Dam of Tim Tam, On-and-On, Pied d'Or.

ULTIMUS, 1906-1921. Ch c., Commando—Running Stream, by Domino. Unraced. Sire of Luke McLuke, High Time, High Cloud, Infinite, Stimulus, Supremus. Broodmare sire of Bold Venture, Case Ace, Flying Heels. One of the very few unraced successful sires; inbred 2x2 to Domino.

UNBRIDLED, 1987-2001. B. c., Fappiano—Gana Facil, by *Le Fabuleux. 24-8-6-6, $4,489,475, champion three-year-old male, Kentucky Derby (G1), Breeders' Cup Classic (G1), etc. Sire of more than 40 stakes winners, including Banshee Breeze, Anees, Unbridled's Song, Halfbridled, Empire Maker, Red Bullet.

UPSET, 1917-1941. Ch. c., Whisk Broom II—Pankhurst, by *Voter. 17-5-7-1, $37,504, Sanford S., etc. Only horse to defeat Man o' War. Sire of 11 stakes winners, including Misstep.

VAGRANCY, 1939-1964. Dk. b. f., *Sir Gallahad III—Valkyr, by Man o' War. 42-15-8-8, $102,480, champion three-year-old filly, champion handicap mare, Coaching Club American Oaks, Alabama S., etc. Dam of Black Tarquin, Vulcania. Tail-female ancestor of family that includes Ferdinand, Fiddle Isle, Natashka, Tallahto, Hidden Light, Truly Bound, Anees.

VANDAL, 1850-unknown. B. c., *Glencoe—Tranby mare, by *Tranby. 6-4-1-1. Sire of Vandalite, Survivor, Virgil, Capitola, Vicksburg, Mollie Jackson, Ella D.

VERTEX, 1954-1981. Ch. c., The Rhymer—Kanace, by Case Ace. 25-17-3-1, $453,424, Pimlico Special, Gulfstream Park H., etc. Sire of 25 stakes winners, including Lucky Debonair, Top Knight, Vertee. Broodmare sire of 50 stakes winners.

VICTORIA PARK, 1957-1985. B. c., Chop Chop—Victoriana, by Windfields. 19-10-4-2, $250,076, Horse of the Year in Canada, Queen's Plate, Remsen S., etc. Sire of 25 stakes winners, including Kennedy Road, Solometeor, Victorian Era, Floral Victory. Broodmare sire of Northern Taste, The Minstrel.

VOLANTE, 1882-unknown. B. c., Grinstead—Sister Anne, by Glenelg. 84-35-28-12, $72,099, American Derby, Saratoga Cup, etc.

VOTER, 1894-unknown. Ch. c., Friar's Balsam—*Mavourneen, by Barcaldine. 49-26-6-7, $34,217, Metropolitan H., Toboggan H., etc. Sire of Ballot, Runnymede, Curiosity, Inaugural, Pankhurst.

WAGNER, 1834-1862. Ch. c., Sir Charles—Maria West, by Marion. 18-12-6-0, $34,150, Jockey Club Purse, etc. Sire of Starke, Lavender, Rhynodyne, Neil Robinson, Endorser.

WANDA, 1882-1905. Ch. f., *Mortemer—Minnie Minor, by Lexington. 24-12-8-0, $58,160, Monmouth Oaks, Champion Stallion S., etc. Tail-female ancestor of family that includes Swaps, Iron Liege, Flying Ebony,

Creme dela Creme, Cascapedia, Althea, Green Desert, *Durbar II, Kauai King.

WAR ADMIRAL, 1934-1959. Br. c., Man o' War—Brushup, by Sweep. 26-21-3-1, $273,240, Horse of the Year in 1937, champion three-year-old colt, Triple Crown, Jockey Club Gold Cup, Whitney S., etc. Leading sire in 1945; leading broodmare sire '62, '64. Sire of 40 stakes winners, including Busher, Blue Peter, Searching, Admiral Vee, Busanda, War Date, Blue Banner, Mr. Busher, Bee Mac, Striking. Broodmare sire of 112 stakes winners, including Affectionately, Better Self, Buckpasser, Crafty Admiral, Gun Bow, Hoist the Flag, Iron Liege, Never Say Die, Priceless Gem.

WAR RELIC, 1938-1963. Ch. c., Man o' War—Friar's Carse, by Friar Rock. 20-9-4-2, $89,495, Massachusetts H., Kenner S., etc. Sire of Battlefield, Intent, Relic, Missile. Broodmare sire of Hail to All, My Dear Girl. Tail-male ancestor of male line that includes Tiznow, In Reality, Relaunch.

WEEKEND SURPRISE, 1980-2001. B. f., Secretariat—Lassie Dear, by Buckpasser. 31-7-5-10, $402,892, Golden Rod S. (G3), Schuylerville S. (G3), etc. Broodmare of the Year in 1992. Dam of A.P. Indy, Summer Squall, Welcome Surprise, Honor Grades.

WHICHONE, 1927-1944. Br. c., *Chicle—Flying Witch, by Broomstick. 14-10-2-1, $192,705, consensus champion two-year-old colt, Futurity S., Champagne S., etc. Sire of ten stakes winners, including Handcuff, Today. Rival of Gallant Fox; first winner of $100,000 first-prize purse in 1929 Futurity. Broodmare sire of Lord Boswell, Vulcan's Forge. Full brother to Mother Goose.

WHIRLAWAY, 1938-1953. Ch. c., *Blenheim II—Dustwhirl, by Sweep. 60-32-15-9, $561,161, Horse of the Year in 1941-'42, champion two- and three-year-old colt, champion handicap horse, Triple Crown, Jockey Club Gold Cup, Travers S., etc. Sire of 18 stakes winners, including Scattered, Kurun, Whirl Some. Broodmare sire of Lady Pitt, Beau Prince. Exported to France in 1950.

WHISK BROOM II, 1907-1928. Ch. c., Broomstick—Audience, by Sir Dixon. 26-10-8-0, $38,776, first winner of America's handicap triple crown, Victoria Cup (in England), etc. Sire of Whiskery, Diavolo, Victorian, Whiskaway, John P. Grier, Broomshot, Swing On, Upset, Weno. Broodmare sire of Seabiscuit, Double Jay.

WINNING COLORS, 1985- . Ro. f., Caro (Ire)—All Rainbows, by Bold Hour. 19-8-3-1, $1,526,837, champion three-year-old filly, Kentucky Derby (G1), Santa Anita Derby (G1), etc. Third filly to win Kentucky Derby.

YO TAMBIEN, 1889-1896. Ch. f., Joe Hooker—Marian, by Malcolm. 73-44-11-9, $89,480, Garfield Park Derby, etc. Half sister to Emperor of Norfolk, El Rio Rey.

YOUR HOST, 1947-1961. Ch. c., *Alibhai—*Boudoir II, by *Mahmoud. 23-13-5-2, $384,795, Santa Anita Derby, Del Mar Futurity, etc. Sire of 16 stakes winners, including Kelso, Social Climber, Windy Sands. Broodmare sire of Tosho Boy, Terry's Secret, Ruken.

ZACCIO, 1976- . Ch. g., *Lorenzaccio—Delray Dancer, by Chateaugay. 42-22-7-3, $288,124, champion steeplechaser three times, Colonial Cup International Steeplechase twice, Temple Gwathmey Steeplechase H., etc.

ZEV, 1920-1943. Br. c., The Finn—Miss Kearney, by *Planudes. 43-23-8-5, $313,639, champion two- and three-year-old colt, Kentucky Derby, Belmont S., International Race S., etc. Sire of two stakes winners. Defeated *Papyrus in first international race in U.S. Retired as world's leading money earner.

Profiles of Oldest Notable Horses
Listed alphabetically by age

MERRICK (38), 1903-1941. Ch. g., *Golden Garter— Bianca, by Wildidle. 205-61-40-24, $26,785. Won Pontchartrain Selling S. Died on March 13, 1941, at Merrick Place in Lexington, where he was buried.

BARGAIN DAY (37), 1965-2002. B. h., Prove It— Special Price, by *Toulouse Lautrec. 43-13-3-7, $146,575. Won 1970 Bing Crosby H. at Del Mar in course record 1:27.60 for 7½ furlongs on grass. Sire of 24 stakes winners, including 1⅛-mile course-record-setter Hoedown's Day (1:38.40). Died of natural causes on June 24, 2002, at Van Mar Farm, in Galt, California.

LYPHARD (36), 1969-2005. See Notable Horses in Racing in this chapter.

PRIMONETTA (35), 1958-1993. See Notable Horses in Racing in this chapter.

STOP THE MUSIC (35), 1970- . B. h., Hail to Reason—Bebopper, by Tom Fool. 30-11-10-4, $448,922. Won 1972 Champagne S. (on disqualification of Secretariat), 1973 Dwyer S. (G2). Sire of 46 stakes winners, including champion and classic winner Temperence Hill and Grade 1 winners Music Merci, Dontstop Themusic, Cure the Blues, etc. Broodmare sire of at least 86 stakes winners including Giacomo. Pensioned at Gainesway, in Lexington.

*GALLANT MAN (34), 1954-1988. See Notable Horses in Racing in this chapter.

*GREEN VALLEY II (34), 1967-2001. Dk. b. or br. m., *Val de Loir—Sly Pola, by Spy Song. Unraced. Dam of six stakes winners, including French classic winner and leading sire Green Dancer and graded/group winners Val Danseur and Ercolano. Died on July 22, 2001, at Haras de Saint-Leonard, in France.

IMPERATRICE (34), 1938-1972. Dk. b. or br. m., Caruso—Cinquepace, by Brown Bud. 31-11-7-2, $37,255. Won the 1941 Test S., 1942 Fall Highweight H. Dam of six stakes winners, including Scattered, Squared Away, and Imperium. Grandam of Secretariat. Euthanized in October 1972 at The Meadow, in Doswell, Virginia, where she was buried.

*JANUS (34), 1746-1780. See Notable Horses in Racing in this chapter.

KENILWORTH (34), 1898-1932. Br. h., *Sir Modred—*Queen Bess, by Gilroy or St. Martin. 168-61-18-22, $31,270. Sire. Died of a ruptured artery, on December 16, 1932, at the ranch of owner L. M. Bugeia, in Marin County, California.

LUCKY SPELL (34), 1971- . B. m., Lucky Mel— Incantation, by Prince Blessed. 69-12-8-11, $253,655. Won 1974 Princess S. (G3) and Las Palmas H. (G3). Dam of three stakes winners, including English Group 3 winner Merlins Charm. Grandam of 1995 Breeders' Cup Juvenile (G1) winner Unbridled's Song. Pensioned in California.

MISS DEBBIE LEE (34), 1966-2000. B. m., Accomplish—Lucky Gay, by Blue Gay. 14-1-5-1, $6,152. Dam of four stakes winners, including Strate Sunshine and Strate Miss. Died in December 2000 at Dash Goff's ranch in Arkansas.

RAJA BABA (34), 1968-2002. B. h., Bold Ruler— Missy Baba, by *My Babu. 41-7-12-9, $123,287. Stakes winner. Leading American sire, juvenile sire of 1980. Leading 1976 freshman sire. Sire of 62 stakes winners, including champion Sacahuista and Grade 1 winners Is It True, Junius, Well Decorated, etc. Broodmare sire

of more than 75 stakes winners. Euthanized on October 9, 2002, at Hermitage Farm, in Goshen, Kentucky, where he stood his entire career. Buried on the farm.

VIEUX MANOIR (34), 1947-1981. B. h., Brantome— Vieille Canaille, by Finglas. Champion at three in France. Leading French sire of 1958. Among the leading French broodmare sires. Sire of 26 stakes winners, including French champion and leading sire *Val de Loir. Died November 19, 1981, at Haras de Meautry in Normandy, France.

AMERICAN ECLIPSE (33), 1814-1847. See Notable Horses in Racing in this chapter.

BALLOT (33), 1904-1937. See Notable Horses in Racing in this chapter.

BILLY BARTON (33), 1918-1951. Br. g., *Huon— Mary Le Bus, by *St. Savin. Great American steeplechaser. Second to Tipperary Tim in the 1928 Grand National at Aintree, England—the only two horses to finish that year. Died March 11, 1951, at Belmont Farm, in Elkridge, Maryland.

BROWN BERRY (33), 1960-1993. B. m., Mount Marcy—Brown Baby, by Phalanx. 29-6-3-3, $53,625. Won 1962 Del Mar Debutante. Dam of 1975 Belmont Stakes (G1) winner Avatar, 1988 French Derby (Fr-G1) winner Hours After, and 1972 Charles H. Strub S. winner Unconscious. Died May 18, 1993, at Brookdale Farm, in Versailles, Kentucky. Buried on the farm.

CHATEAUCREEK (33), 1970-2003. Ch. m., Chateaugay—Mooncreek, by Sailor. 29-6-1-2, $24,203. Stakes winner. Dam of 1980 champion and Epsom Derby (Eng-G1) winner Henbit. Grandam of Grade 1 winners Mr Purple and Queens Court Queen. Euthanized due to infirmities of age on August 7, 2003, at Mineola Farm, in Lexington. Buried on the farm.

COUNT FLEET (33), 1940-1973. See Notable Horses in Racing in this chapter.

GA HAI (33), 1971-2004. Gr. h., Determine—Goyala, by Goyamo. 43-13-2-5, $257,548. Won 1975 and 1976 Arcadia H. (G3). Sire of seven stakes winners. Pensioned in 1995. Died on March 17, 2004, at Reigle Heir Farms, in Grantville, Pennsylvania. Buried on the farm.

GREEN FINGER (33), 1958-1991. Dk. b. or br. m., Better Self—Flower Bed, by *Beau Pere. 18-1-3-1, $5,935. Dam of two stakes winners, including Grade 2 winner Free Hand. Died in 1991 and buried at Old Frankfort Stud (formerly King Ranch), near Lexington.

LUCKY MEL (33), 1954-1987. Ch. h., Olympia— *Royal Mink, by *Royal Charger. 12-7-0-1, $106,450. Stakes winner at two. Set five-furlong world record of :56.60, at Hollywood Park. Sire of 23 stakes winners, including graded winners Copper Mel and Lucky Spell. Broodmare sire of 44 stakes winners. Died at Old English Rancho, in Fresno, California.

MATCHEM (33), 1748-1781. See Notable Horses in Racing in this chapter.

MR. LEADER (33), 1966-1999. B. h., Hail to Reason—Jolie Deja, by *Djeddah. 25-10-3-3, $219,803. Won 1970 Tidal H., Stars and Stripes H. Sire of 83 stakes winners, including Grade 1 winners Ruhlmann, Hurry Up Blue, Wise Times, Quiet Little Table, Martial Law. Broodmare sire of more than 110 stakes winners, including champion Epitome. Euthanized on April 20, 1999, at Nuckols Farm in Midway, Kentucky, and buried at the farm.

Oldest Notable Horses of All Time

Age Died	Horse, YOB, Sex, Sire	Record (Starts-Wins-2nd-3rd)	Earnings
38	Merrick, 1903 g., by *Golden Garter	205-61-40-24	$26,785
37	Bargain Day, 1965 h., by Prove It	43-13-3-7	146,575
36	Lyphard, 1969 h., by Northern Dancer	12-6-1-0	195,427
35	Busted, 1963 h., by Crepello	11-5-0-0	140,308
	Primonetta, 1958 m., by Swaps	25-17-2-2	306,690
	Stop the Music, 1970 h., by Hail to Reason	*30-11-10-4*	*448,922*
	Young Langford, 1840 h., by *Langford	No record	
34	*Gallant Man, 1954 h., by *Migoli	26-14-4-1	510,355
	*Green Valley II, 1967 m., by *Val de Loir	Unraced	
	Imperatrice, 1938 m., by Caruso	31-11-7-2	37,255
	*Janus, 1746 h., by Janus	3 wins	
	Kenilworth, 1898 h., by *Sir Modred	163, 61 wins	31,270
	Raja Baba, 1968 h., by Bold Ruler	41-7-12-9	123,287
33	American Eclipse, 1814 h., by Duroc	8-8-0-0	56,700
	Ballot, 1904 h., by *Voter	38-20-6-6	154,545
	Billy Barton, 1918 g., by *Huon	No record	43,040
	Brown Berry, 1960 m., by Mount Marcy	29-6-3-3	53,625
	Chateaucreek, 1970 m., by Chateaugay	29-6-1-2	24,203
	Count Fleet, 1940 h., by Reigh Count	21-16-4-1	250,300
	Ga Hai, 1971 h., by Determine	43-13-2-5	257,548
	*Inspirado, 1964 h., by Souepi	37-4-10-5	9,932
	Lucky Mel, 1954 h., by Olympia	12-7-0-1	106,450
	Matchem, 1748 h., by Cade	8 wins	
	Miss Debbie Lee, 1966 m., by Accomplish	14-1-5-1	6,152
	Mr. Leader, 1966 h., by Hail to Reason	25-10-3-3	219,803
	Napalm, 1963 m., by *Nilo	17-2-2-5	9,575
	Northern Taste, 1971 h., by Northern Dancer	23-5-3-4	154,177
	Old Friendship, 1783 h., by Apollo	No record	
	Pocahontas, 1837 m., by *Glencoe	9-0-3-0	0
	Round Table, 1954 h., by *Princequillo	66-43-8-5	1,749,869
	Sweepida, 1937 g., by Sweepster	65-18-12-10	111,640
	Tamerett, 1962 m., by Tim Tam	35-4-6-10	25,415
	Tripping, 1908 m., by Delhi	No record	
32	Arts and Letters, 1966 h., by *Ribot	23-11-6-1	632,404
	Big Spruce, 1969 h., by *Herbager	40-9-9-7	673,117
	Come My Prince, 1972 m., by Prince John	Unraced	
	Crimson Saint, 1969 m., by Crimson Satan	11-7-0-2	91,770
	Exclusive Ribot, 1972 h., by *Ribot	32-6-4-3	43,974
	Fanfreluche, 1967 m., by Northern Dancer	21-11-6-2	238,688
	Honey Jay, 1968 h., by Double Jay	63-24-10-11	223,853
	Hope of Glory, 1972 m., by Mr. Leader	35-9-3-5	168,421
	Introductivo, 1969 h., by *Sensitivo	54-6-10-15	107,128
	Kittiwake, 1968 m., by *Sea-Bird	54-18-12-9	338,086
	Knightly Manner, 1961 h., by Round Table	67-16-13-10	436,676
	Legendra, 1944 m., by *Challenger II	32-6-2-5	23,220
	Little Current, 1971 h., by *Sea-Bird	16-4-3-1	354,704
	Little Hut, 1952 m., by Occupy	55-5-7-14	22,220
	Minnesota Mac, 1964 h., by Rough'n Tumble	11-4-2-2	63,275
	Miss Justice (GB), 1961 m., by King's Bench	2-1-0-0	970
	Oracle II, 1910 g., by Oxford	No record	
	*Philomela, 1954 m., by *Tudor Minstrel	23-1-2-2	560
	Queen Sucree, 1966 m., by *Ribot	4-1-0-0	3,925
	Sampson, 1745 h., by Blaze	No record	
	*Slady Castle, 1969 h., by *Tudor Melody	19-4-3-3	20,835
	S. S. Bellstar, 1966 h., by Eagle Admiral	36-10-10-5	40,637
	Taba (Arg), 1973 m., by Table Play	8-3-0-1	20,609
	*Tobin Bronze, 1962 h., by Arctic Explorer	60-28-10-5	391,447

Living as of June 15, 2005

NAPALM (33), 1963-1996. Ch. m., *Nilo—Fire Falls, by *Bull Dog. 17-2-2-5, $9,575. Dam of millionaire Grade 2 winner Fighting Fit and stakes winner Hot Words. Euthanized on February 9, 1996, at Nuckols Farm in Midway, Kentucky.

NORTHERN TASTE (33), 1971-2004. Ch. h., Northern Dancer—Lady Victoria, by Victoria Park. 23-5-3-4, $154,177. Won 1974 Prix de la Foret (Fr-G1). Nine-time leading sire in Japan, four-time leading Japanese broodmare sire. Sire of 48 stakes winners and six champions. Died in December 2004 at Shadai Stallion Station, on Hokkaido, Japan. Cremated and buried at the farm.

POCAHONTAS (33), 1837-1870. See Notable Horses in Racing in this chapter.

ROUND TABLE (33), 1954-1987. See Notable Horses in Racing in this chapter.

SWEEPIDA (33), 1937-1970. Br. g., Sweepster—Rapida, by *Hand Grenade. 65-18-12-10, $111,640. Won 1940 Santa Anita Derby, Bay Meadows H., etc. Died May 8, 1970, at the San Joaquin County Fair in Stockton, California, where he had lived as a pensioner. Buried in front of the racetrack grandstand.

TAMERETT (33), 1962-1995. Dk. b. or br. m., Tim Tam—*Mixed Marriage, by *Tudor Minstrel. 35-4-6-10, $25,415. Dam of five stakes winners, including English champion miler Known Fact and Grade 1 winner Tentam. Grandam of noted sire Gone West. Died September 15, 1995, at Mare Haven Farm, in Lexington and buried on the farm.

TRIPPING (33), 1908-1941. B. m., Delhi—*Fairy Slipper, by St. Serf. 20-2-0-4, $950. Dam of two stakes winners, including 1920 Futurity S. winner Step Lightly. Died September 21, 1941, at Haylands Farm, in Lexington.

TWOSY (33), 1942-1975. B. m., Bull Lea—Two Bob, by The Porter. 52-21-17-3, $101,375. Multiple stakes winner. Sister to Racing Hall of Fame member Two Lea and to major stakes winner Miz Clementine. Dam of four winners and one stakes-placed runner. Died and was buried at Calumet Farm in Lexington.

VICTORIAN HEIRESS (33), 1968-2001. B. m, Northern Dancer—Victoriana, by Windfields. 12-3-0-1, $20,590. Dam of Canadian champion Northern Blossom. Half sister to 1960 Canadian Horse of the Year Victoria Park. Died in fall 2001 at Tranquility Farm in Tehachapi, California.

ARTS AND LETTERS (32), 1966-1998. See Notable Horses in Racing in this chapter.

BIG SPRUCE (32), 1969-2001. Dk. b. or br. h., *Herbager—Silver Sari, by Prince John. 40-9-9-7, $673,117. Won 1974 Governors S. (G1). Sire of 43 stakes winners, including Grade 1 winners Super Moment, Acaroid, Catatonic, Splendid Spruce, Sweet Diane, Back Bay Barrister, and Spruce Needles. Euthanized due to infirmities of age on December 28, 2001, at Gainesway, in Lexington.

COME MY PRINCE (32), 1972-2004. Ro. m., Prince John—Come Hither Look, by *Turn-to. Unraced. Dam of Grade/Group 1 winner and 1995 leading North American sire Palace Music. Euthanized due to infirmities of age on March 7, 2004, at Warfield Stud, in Butler, Missouri.

CRIMSON SAINT (32), 1969-2001. Ch. m., Crimson Satan—Bolero Rose, by Bolero. 11-7-0-2, $91,770. Won 1973 Hollywood Express (G3). Equaled the four-furlong world record. Dam of four stakes winners, including Breeders' Cup Mile (G1) winner Royal Academy and Grade 2 winners Terlingua and Pancho Villa. Grandam of leading sire Storm Cat. Euthanized due to infirmities of age on May 12, 2001, at Offutt-Cole Farm, in Midway, Kentucky.

Exclusive Ribot (32), 1972-2004. B. h., *Ribot—Exclusive, by Shut Out. 32-6-4-3, $43,974. Stakes-placed. Half brother to two-time leading North American sire Exclusive Native. Sire of six stakes winners, including millionaire Grade 2 winner Men's Exclusive and Grade 2 winner Exclusive Partner. Died of heart failure on August 8, 2004, at Dormello II Stud in Decatur, Texas.

FANFRELUCHE (32), 1967-1999. B. m., Northern Dancer—Ciboulette, by Chop Chop. 21-11-6-2, $238,688. Canadian Horse of the Year in 1970. Canadian Broodmare of the Year in 1978. Dam of five stakes winners, including Canadian Horse of the Year L'Enjoleur and Canadian champions La Voyageuse and Medaille d' Or. Stolen from her Claiborne Farm paddock in 1977; later recovered. Euthanized in July 1999 at Big Sink Farm in Midway, Kentucky, and buried at the farm.

HONEY JAY (32), 1968-2000. B. h., Double Jay—Roman Honey, by Roman. 63-24-10-11, $223,853. Won 1972 and '73 Phoenix H. Sire of 44 stakes winners, including Grade 1 winner Sweet Missus. Broodmare sire of 40 stakes winners. Euthanized February 22, 2000, at Fair Winds Farm in Waynesville, Ohio, and buried on the farm.

HOPE OF GLORY (32), 1972-2004. B. m., Mr. Leader—Daizel, by Manteau. 35-9-3-5, $168,421. Mul-

tiple graded stakes winner. Dam of nine winners from nine starters, including stakes-placed Grab the Glory. Euthanized after suffering a stroke on October 13, 2004, at Our Mims Retirement Haven in Paris, Kentucky.

KITTIWAKE (32), 1968-2000. B. m., *Sea-Bird—Ole Liz, by Double Jay. 54-18-12-9, $338,086. Won 1973 Columbiana H. (G2). Dam of four stakes winners, including Grade 1 winners Miss Oceana and Kitwood, and Grade 2 winner Larida. Euthanized due to infirmities of age on May 19, 2000, at Lazy Lane Farms in Upperville, Virginia.

KNIGHTLY MANNER (32), 1961-1993. B. h., Round Table—Courtesy, by *Nasrullah. 67-16-13-10, $436,676. Won or placed in 27 stakes. Sire of 14 stakes winners, including Italian classic winner Azzurrina (GB), Ohio Derby (G2) winner Stonewalk, and Grade 2 winner Cycylya Zee. Died in August 1993 in Australia.

Legendra (32), 1944-1976. B. m., *Challenger II—Lady Legend, by Dark Legend. 32-6-2-5, $23,220. Stakes-placed. Dam of four stakes winners, including Sky Clipper and Rich Tradition. Great-grandam of champion Shareef Dancer. Died February 6, 1976, at Newstead Farm, in Upperville, Virginia.

LITTLE CURRENT (32), 1971-2003. Ch. h., *Sea-Bird—Luiana, by *My Babu. 16-4-3-1, $354,704. Champion at three. Won 1974 Preakness S. (G1) and Belmont S. (G1). Sire of 35 stakes winners, including Grade 1 winners Current Hope and Prize Spot. Broodmare sire of 46 stakes winners. Euthanized January 20, 2003, due to strangulation of the small intestine, at Pacific Equine Clinic in Monroe, Washington.

MINNESOTA MAC (32), 1964-1996. B. h., Rough 'n Tumble—*Cow Girl II, by Mustang. 11-4-2-2, $63,275. Stakes winner. Sire of 18 stakes winners, including 1978 grass champion Mac Diarmida. Paternal grandsire of Holy Bull. Pensioned in 1984 at Tartan Farms in Florida, where he died on April 25, 1996. Buried at the farm.

*MONADE (32), 1959-1991. Br. m., *Klairon—Mormyre, by Atys. 35-10-5-4, $252,016. Champion at three in England and France. Won 1962 Epsom Oaks. Dam of stakes winner Pressing Date.

*PHILOMELA (32), 1954-1986. Ch. m., Tudor Minstrel—Petrovna II, by Blue Peter. 23-1-2-2, $560. Dam of California champion and G2 winner Messenger of Song and stakes-winning Procne. Grandam of California champion and leading sire Flying Paster. Died September 14, 1986, at Murrieta Stud in Murrieta, California.

QUEEN SUCREE (32), 1966-1998. B. m., *Ribot—Cosmah, by Cosmic Bomb. 4-1-0-0, $3,925. Dam of four stakes winners, including 1974 Kentucky Derby (G1) winner Cannonade and graded stakes winner Circle Home. Grandam of Grade 1 winners Stephan's Odyssey and Lotka. Pensioned in 1994. Euthanized on June 27, 1998, at Windward Oaks Farm in Harrodsburg, Kentucky. Buried at the farm.

TABA (Arg) (32), 1973-2005. B. m., Table Play—Filipina, by Fomento. Champion at two in Argentina. Dam of champion Grade 1 winner Turkoman and stakes winner Slow Fuse.

*TOBIN BRONZE (32), 1962-1994. Ch. h., Arctic Explorer—Amarco, by Masthead. 60-28-10-5, $391,447. Champion older horse in Australia. Sire of 15 stakes winners, including Canadian champion Proud Tobin and Grade 1 winner Trojan Bronze. Euthanized due to infirmities of old age in 1994. Buried at Rancho de Esperanza, in Hemet, California.

ECLIPSE AWARDS
History of the Eclipse Awards

Thoroughbred racing's first official champions were recognized for the 1936 racing season by *Daily Racing Form*, which named Granville as Horse of the Year and selected champions in six divisions.

Beginning in the 1950 racing season, Thoroughbred Racing Associations, formed eight years earlier, announced its own set of champions. Usually the *Form*'s and TRA's separate lists of champions coincided, but sometimes they did not. For example, Horse of the Year titles went separately to One Count and Native Dancer in 1952, Bold Ruler and Dedicate in '57, Roman Brother and Moccasin in '65, and Fort Marcy and Personality in '70.

In 1971, J. B. Faulconer, then president of the Turf Publicists of America, an organization of marketing and public-relations representatives from racetrack and industry organizations, was asked by Monmouth Park executive Philip H. Iselin to head a special committee to consolidate the year-end championship honors. Faulconer helped to bring together the *Form*, TRA, and the National Turf Writers Association to select one set of champions.

Faulconer is credited with naming the Eclipse Award, which honors the great 18th-century English racehorse and sire from whom most modern-day Thoroughbreds descend in male line. He selected Lexington artist Adalin Wichman to design the award statuette of a lone Thoroughbred tacked in preparation for a race, and he served as master of ceremonies at the inaugural awards din-

ner on January 26, 1972, at New York's Waldorf Astoria. Faulconer was the host through 1976.

Today, the National Thoroughbred Racing Association has replaced the TRA in the three voting groups. Members of the three eligible organizations vote on winners of the ten divisional categories and then select the Horse of the Year. In addition, the groups vote on the outstanding breeder, owner, trainer, jockey, and apprentice jockey. The 2003 Eclipse Award winners were determined for the first time on a one-person, one-vote basis. Formerly, the Eclipse Award winners were determined by bloc voting, with each organization having equal weight.

Eclipse Awards generally are presented shortly after the conclusion of the previous year's racing season. Since the awards were founded, a few notable events have occurred. In 1978, a tie in the voting for outstanding two-year-old filly resulted in It's in the Air and Candy Eclair being named co-champions, while Dr. Patches and J. O. Tobin were voted co-champion sprinters. Voting procedures were changed to eliminate ties. In 1979, the champion turf horse division was divided into male and female categories. In Eclipse Award history, two-year-olds have been voted Horse of the Year just twice: Secretariat (1972) and Favorite Trick ('97).

While horses and horsemen are honored with Eclipse Awards, so too are members of the media. Selected committees vote on the outstanding submissions in several media categories.

Eclipse Award-Winning Horses

Horse of the Year

2004	Ghostzapper
2003	Mineshaft
2002	Azeri (female)
2001	Point Given
2000	Tiznow
1999	Charismatic
1998	Skip Away
1997	Favorite Trick
1996	Cigar
1995	Cigar
1994	Holy Bull
1993	Kotashaan (Fr)
1992	A.P. Indy
1991	Black Tie Affair (Ire)
1990	Criminal Type
1989	Sunday Silence
1988	Alysheba
1987	Ferdinand
1986	Lady's Secret (female)
1985	Spend a Buck
1984	John Henry
1983	All Along (Fr) (female)
1982	Conquistador Cielo
1981	John Henry
1980	Spectacular Bid
1979	Affirmed
1978	Affirmed
1977	Seattle Slew
1976	Forego
1975	Forego
1974	Forego
1973	Secretariat
1972	Secretariat
1971	Ack Ack

Two-Year-Old Male

2004	Declan's Moon
2003	Action This Day
2002	Vindication
2001	Johannesburg
2000	Macho Uno
1999	Anees
1998	Answer Lively
1997	Favorite Trick
1996	Boston Harbor
1995	Maria's Mon
1994	Timber Country
1993	Dehere
1992	Gilded Time
1991	Arazi
1990	Fly So Free
1989	Rhythm
1988	Easy Goer
1987	Forty Niner
1986	Capote
1985	Tasso
1984	Chief's Crown
1983	Devil's Bag
1982	Roving Boy
1981	Deputy Minister
1980	Lord Avie

Two-Year-Old Filly

2004	Sweet Catomine
2003	Halfbridled
2002	Storm Flag Flying
2001	Tempera
2000	Caressing
1999	Chilukki
1998	Silverbulletday
1997	Countess Diana
1996	Storm Song
1995	Golden Attraction
1994	Flanders
1993	Phone Chatter
1992	Eliza
1991	Pleasant Stage
1990	Meadow Star
1989	Go for Wand
1988	Open Mind
1987	Epitome
1986	Brave Raj
1985	Family Style
1984	Outstandingly

1979	Rockhill Native
1978	Spectacular Bid
1977	Affirmed
1976	Seattle Slew
1975	Honest Pleasure
1974	Foolish Pleasure
1973	Protagonist
1972	Secretariat
1971	Riva Ridge

1983	Althea
1982	Landaluce
1981	Before Dawn
1980	Heavenly Cause
1979	Smart Angle
1978	†It's in the Air
	†Candy Eclair
1977	Lakeville Miss
1976	Sensational
1975	Dearly Precious
1974	Ruffian
1973	Talking Picture
1972	La Prevoyante
1971	Numbered Account
	†Tied in voting, named co-champions

Three-Year-Old Male

2004	Smarty Jones
2003	Funny Cide
2002	War Emblem
2001	Point Given
2000	Tiznow
1999	Charismatic
1998	Real Quiet
1997	Silver Charm
1996	Skip Away
1995	Thunder Gulch
1994	Holy Bull
1993	Prairie Bayou
1992	A.P. Indy
1991	Hansel

1990 Unbridled	1995 Cigar	1999 Daylami (Ire)	1998 Reraise
1989 Sunday Silence	1994 The Wicked North	1998 Buck's Boy	1997 Smoke Glacken
1988 Risen Star	1993 Bertrando	1997 Chief Bearhart	1996 Lit de Justice
1987 Alysheba	1992 Pleasant Tap	1996 Singspiel (Ire)	1995 Not Surprising
1986 Snow Chief	1991 Black Tie Affair (Ire)	1995 Northern Spur (Ire)	1994 Cherokee Run
1985 Spend a Buck	1990 Criminal Type	1994 Paradise Creek	1993 Cardmania
1984 Swale	1989 Blushing John	1993 Kotashaan (Fr)	1992 Rubiano
1983 Slew o' Gold	1988 Alysheba	1992 Sky Classic	1991 Housebuster
1982 Conquistador Cielo	1987 Ferdinand	1991 Tight Spot	1990 Housebuster
1981 Pleasant Colony	1986 Turkoman	1990 Itsallgreektome	1989 Safely Kept (female)
1980 Temperence Hill	1985 Vanlandingham	1989 Steinlen (GB)	1988 Gulch
1979 Spectacular Bid	1984 Slew o' Gold	1988 Sunshine Forever	1987 Groovy
1978 Affirmed	1983 Bates Motel	1987 Theatrical (Ire)	1986 Smile
1977 Seattle Slew	1982 Lemhi Gold	1986 Manila	1985 Precisionist
1976 Bold Forbes	1981 John Henry	1985 Cozzene	1984 Eillo
1975 Wajima	1980 Spectacular Bid	1984 John Henry	1983 Chinook Pass
1974 Little Current	1979 Affirmed	1983 John Henry	1982 Gold Beauty (female)
1973 Secretariat	1978 Seattle Slew	1982 Perrault (GB)	1981 Guilty Conscience
1972 Key to the Mint	1977 Forego	1981 John Henry	1980 Plugged Nickle
1971 Canonero II	1976 Forego	1980 John Henry	1979 Star de Naskra
	1975 Forego	1979 Bowl Game	1978 †Dr. Patches
Three-Year-Old Filly	1974 Forego		†J. O. Tobin
2004 Ashado	1973 Riva Ridge	**Turf Female[1]**	1977 What a Summer
2003 Bird Town	1972 Autobiography	2004 Ouija Board (GB)	(female)
2002 Farda Amiga	1971 Ack Ack	2003 Islington (Ire)	1976 My Juliet (female)
2001 Xtra Heat		2002 Golden Apples (Ire)	1975 Gallant Bob
2000 Surfside	**Older Female**	2001 Banks Hill (GB)	1974 Forego
1999 Silverbulletday	2004 Azeri	2000 Perfect Sting	1973 Shecky Greene
1998 Banshee Breeze	2003 Azeri	1999 Soaring Softly	1972 Chou Croute
1997 Ajina	2002 Azeri	1998 Fiji (GB)	(female)
1996 Yanks Music	2001 Gourmet Girl	1997 Ryafan	1971 Ack Ack
1995 Serena's Song	2000 Riboletta (Brz)	1996 Wandesta (GB)	†Tied in voting, named
1994 Heavenly Prize	1999 Beautiful Pleasure	1995 Possibly Perfect	co-champions
1993 Hollywood Wildcat	1998 Escena	1994 Hatoof	
1992 Saratoga Dew	1997 Hidden Lake	1993 Flawlessly	**Steeplechaser**
1991 Dance Smartly	1996 Jewel Princess	1992 Flawlessly	2004 Hirapour (Ire)
1990 Go for Wand	1995 Inside Information	1991 Miss Alleged	2003 McDynamo
1989 Open Mind	1994 Sky Beauty	1990 Laugh and Be Merry	2002 Flat Top
1988 Winning Colors	1993 Paseana (Arg)	1989 Brown Bess	2001 Pompeyo (Chi)
1987 Sacahuista	1992 Paseana (Arg)	1988 Miesque	2000 All Gong (GB)
1986 Tiffany Lass	1991 Queena	1987 Miesque	1999 Lonesome Glory
1985 Mom's Command	1990 Bayakoa (Arg)	1986 Estrapade	1998 Flat Top
1984 Life's Magic	1989 Bayakoa (Arg)	1985 Pebbles (GB)	1997 Lonesome Glory
1983 Heartlight No. One	1988 Personal Ensign	1984 Royal Heroine (Ire)	1996 Correggio (Ire)
1982 Christmas Past	1987 North Sider	1983 All Along (Fr)	1995 Lonesome Glory
1981 Wayward Lass	1986 Lady's Secret	1982 April Run (Ire)	1994 Warm Spell
1980 Genuine Risk	1985 Life's Magic	1981 De La Rose	1993 Lonesome Glory
1979 Davona Dale	1984 Princess Rooney	1980 Just a Game (Ire)	1992 Lonesome Glory
1978 Tempest Queen	1983 Ambassador of Luck	1979 Trillion	1991 Morley Street (Ire)
1977 Our Mims	1982 Track Robbery		1990 Morley Street (Ire)
1976 Revidere	1981 Relaxing	**Turf Horse[1]**	1989 Highland Bud
1975 Ruffian	1980 Glorious Song	1978 Mac Diarmida	1988 Jimmy Lorenzo (GB)
1974 Chris Evert	1979 Waya (Fr)	1977 Johnny D.	1987 Inlander (GB)
1973 Desert Vixen	1978 Late Bloomer	1976 Youth	1986 Flatterer
1972 Susan's Girl	1977 Cascapedia	1975 *Snow Knight	1985 Flatterer
1971 Turkish Trousers	1976 Proud Delta	1974 Dahlia (female)	1984 Flatterer
	1975 Susan's Girl	1973 Secretariat	1983 Flatterer
Older Male	1974 Desert Vixen	1972 *Cougar II	1982 Zaccio
2004 Ghostzapper	1973 Susan's Girl	1971 Run the Gantlet	1981 Zaccio
2003 Mineshaft	1972 Typecast	[1]One turf category prior to 1979	1980 Zaccio
2002 Left Bank	1971 Shuvee		1979 Martie's Anger
2001 Tiznow		**Sprinter**	1978 Cafe Prince
2000 Lemon Drop Kid	**Turf Male[1]**	2004 Speightstown	1977 Cafe Prince
1999 Victory Gallop	2004 Kitten's Joy	2003 Aldebaran	1976 Straight and True
1998 Skip Away	2003 High Chaparral (Ire)	2002 Orientate	1975 Life's Illusion
1997 Skip Away	2002 High Chaparral (Ire)	2001 Squirtle Squirt	1974 *Gran Kan
1996 Cigar	2001 Fantastic Light	2000 Kona Gold	1973 Athenian Idol
	2000 Kalanisi (Ire)	1999 Artax	1972 Soothsayer
			1971 Shadow Brook

Eclipse Award-Winning Individuals

Owner

2004	Kenneth and Sarah Ramsey
2003	Juddmonte Farms
2002	Richard Englander
2001	Richard Englander
2000	Frank Stronach
1999	Frank Stronach
1998	Frank Stronach
1997	Carolyn Hine
1996	Allen E. Paulson
1995	Allen E. Paulson
1994	John Franks
1993	John Franks
1992	Juddmonte Farms
1991	Sam-Son Farm
1990	Mrs. Frances Genter
1989	Ogden Phipps
1988	Ogden Phipps
1987	Mr. and Mrs. Eugene Klein
1986	Mr. and Mrs. Eugene Klein
1985	Mr. and Mrs. Eugene Klein
1984	John Franks
1983	John Franks
1982	Viola Sommer
1981	Dotsam Stable
1980	Mr. and Mrs. Bertram Firestone
1979	Harbor View Farm
1978	Harbor View Farm
1977	Maxwell Gluck
1976	Dan Lasater
1975	Dan Lasater
1974	Dan Lasater
1973	Not awarded
1972	Not awarded
1971	Mr. and Mrs. E. E. Fogelson

Breeder

2004	Adena Springs (Frank Stronach)
2003	Juddmonte Farms
2002	Juddmonte Farms
2001	Juddmonte Farms
2000	Frank Stronach
1999	William S. Farish & Partners
1998	John and Betty Mabee
1997	John and Betty Mabee
1996	Farnsworth Farms
1995	Juddmonte Farms
1994	William T. Young
1993	Allen E. Paulson
1992	William S. Farish
1991	John and Betty Mabee
1990	Calumet Farm
1989	North Ridge Farm
1988	Ogden Phipps
1987	Nelson Bunker Hunt
1986	Paul Mellon
1985	Nelson Bunker Hunt
1984	Claiborne Farm
1983	E. P. Taylor
1982	Fred W. Hooper
1981	Golden Chance Farm
1980	Adele Paxson
1979	Claiborne Farm
1978	Harbor View Farm
1977	E. P. Taylor
1976	Nelson Bunker Hunt
1975	Fred W. Hooper
1974	John W. Galbreath
1973	Not awarded
1972	Not awarded
1971	Not awarded

Owner-Breeder

1973	Meadow Stable-Meadow Stud (C. T. Chenery)
1972	Meadow Stable-Meadow Stud (C. T. Chenery)
1971	Paul Mellon

Trainer

2004	Todd Pletcher
2003	Bobby Frankel
2002	Bobby Frankel
2001	Bobby Frankel
2000	Bobby Frankel
1999	Bob Baffert
1998	Bob Baffert
1997	Bob Baffert
1996	Bill Mott
1995	Bill Mott
1994	D. Wayne Lukas
1993	Bobby Frankel
1992	Ron McAnally
1991	Ron McAnally
1990	Carl Nafzger
1989	Charles Whittingham
1988	C. R. McGaughey
1987	D. Wayne Lukas
1986	D. Wayne Lukas
1985	D. Wayne Lukas
1984	Jack Van Berg
1983	Woody Stephens
1982	Charles Whittingham
1981	Ron McAnally
1980	Grover G. "Buddy" Delp
1979	Lazaro Barrera
1978	Lazaro Barrera
1977	Lazaro Barrera
1976	Lazaro Barrera
1975	Steve DiMauro
1974	Sherrill Ward
1973	H. Allen Jerkens
1972	Lucien Laurin
1971	Charles Whittingham

Jockey

2004	John Velazquez
2003	Jerry Bailey
2002	Jerry Bailey
2001	Jerry Bailey
2000	Jerry Bailey
1999	Jorge Chavez
1998	Gary Stevens
1997	Jerry Bailey
1996	Jerry Bailey
1995	Jerry Bailey
1994	Mike Smith
1993	Mike Smith
1992	Kent Desormeaux
1991	Pat Day
1990	Craig Perret
1989	Kent Desormeaux
1988	Jose Santos
1987	Pat Day
1986	Pat Day
1985	Laffit Pincay Jr.
1984	Pat Day
1983	Angel Cordero Jr.
1982	Angel Cordero Jr.
1981	William Shoemaker
1980	Chris McCarron
1979	Laffit Pincay Jr.
1978	Darrel McHargue

1977	Steve Cauthen
1976	Sandy Hawley
1975	Braulio Baeza
1974	Laffit Pincay Jr.
1973	Laffit Pincay Jr.
1972	Braulio Baeza
1971	Laffit Pincay Jr.

Apprentice Jockey

2004	Brian Hernandez Jr.
2003	Eddie Castro
2002	Ryan Fogelsonger
2001	Jeremy Rose
2000	Tyler Baze
1999	Ariel Smith
1998	Shaun Bridgmohan
1997	Roberto Rosado, Philip Teator (tie)
1996	Neil Poznansky
1995	Ramon Perez
1994	Dale Beckner
1993	Juan L. Umana
1992	†Rosemary Homeister Jr.
1991	Mickey Walls
1990	Mark Johnston
1989	Michael Luzzi
1988	Steve Capanas
1987	Kent Desormeaux
1986	Allen Stacy
1985	Art Madrid Jr.
1984	Wesley Ward
1983	Declan Murphy
1982	Alberto Delgado
1981	Richard Migliore
1980	Frank Lovato Jr.
1979	Cash Asmussen
1978	Ron Franklin
1977	Steve Cauthen
1976	George Martens
1975	Jimmy Edwards
1974	Chris McCarron
1973	Steve Valdez
1972	Thomas Wallis
1971	Gene St. Leon

†Jesus Bracho was originally awarded the title but relinquished it in 1994.

Eclipse Award of Merit

2004	Oaklawn Park and Cella Family
2003	Richard L. Duchossois
2002	Ogden Phipps
	Howard Battle
2001	Harry T. Mangurian Jr.
	Pete Pedersen
2000	Jim McKay
1999	Not awarded
1998	D. G. Van Clief Jr.
1997	Bob and Beverly Lewis
1996	Allen E. Paulson
1995	James E. "Ted" Bassett III
1994	Alfred G. Vanderbilt
1993	Paul Mellon
1992	Robert P. Strub, Joe Hirsch
1991	Fred W. Hooper
1990	Warner L. Jones
1989	Michael Sandler
1988	John Forsythe
1987	J. B. Faulconer
1986	Herman Cohen
1985	Keene Daingerfield

1984	John Gaines	1996	Not awarded	1976	William Shoemaker
1983	Not awarded	1995	Russell Baze	1975	Not awarded
1982	Not awarded	1994	Eddie Arcaro, John Longden	1974	Charles Hatton
1981	William Shoemaker	1993	Not awarded	1973	Not awarded
1980	John D. Schapiro	1992	Not awarded	1972	Not awarded
1979	Frank E. "Jimmy" Kilroe	1991	Not awarded	1971	Robert J. Kleberg
1978	Ogden Mills "Dinny" Phipps	1990	Not awarded		
1977	Steve Cauthen	1989	Richard L. Duchossois		**Man of the Year**
1976	Jack J. Dreyfus Jr.	1988	Edward J. DeBartolo Sr.	1975	John A. Morris
		1987	Anheuser-Busch	1974	William L. McKnight
	Special Award	1986	Not awarded	1973	Edward P. Taylor
2004	Dale Baird	1985	Arlington Park	1972	John W. Galbreath
2003	Not awarded	1984	C. V. Whitney		
2002	Keeneland Library	1983	Not awarded		**Outstanding Achievement**
2001	Sheikh Mohammed bin Rashid	1982	Not awarded	1972	Arthur B. Hancock Jr.
	al Maktoum	1981	Not awarded		(posthumously)
2000	John Hettinger	1980	John T. Landry, Pierre E. Bellocq	1971	Charles Engelhard
1999	Laffit Pincay Jr.	1979	Not awarded		(posthumously)
1998	Oak Tree Racing Association	1978	Not awarded		
1997	Not awarded	1977	Not awarded		

Eclipse Award Media Winners

Outstanding Newspaper Writing

1999 Maryjean Wall, Lexington *Herald-Leader*
1998 Tom Keyser, Baltimore *Sun*
1997 Maryjean Wall, Lexington *Herald-Leader*
1996 Tom Keyser, Baltimore *Sun*
1995 Stephanie Diaz, Riverside *Press-Enterprise*
1994 Mike Downey, Los Angeles *Times*
1993 Jennie Rees, Louisville *Courier-Journal*
1992 James Wallace, Seattle *Post Intelligencer*
1990 Paul Moran, *Newsday*
1989 Ronnie Virgets, *Gambit*
1988 Billy Reed, Lexington *Herald-Leader*
1987 Tim Layden, Capital Newspapers
1986 Edwin Pope, Miami *Herald*
1985 Paul Moran, *Newsday*
1984 Bill Christine, Los Angeles *Times*
      Eddie Donnally, Dallas *Morning News*
1983 Dave Koemer, Louisville *Times*
1982 Edwin Pope, Miami *Herald*
1981 Dave Kindred, Washington *Post*
1980 Maryjean Wall, Lexington *Herald*
1979 Billy Reed, Louisville *Courier-Journal*
1978 Joe Hirsch, *Daily Racing Form*
1977 Skip Bayless, Los Angeles *Times*
1976 Edwin Pope, Miami *Herald*
1975 Bob Harding, Newark *Star-Ledger*
1974 William H. Rudy, New York *Post*
1973 Red Smith, New York *Times*
1972 Phil Ranallo, Buffalo *Courier Express*
1971 Scott Young, Toronto *Telegram*

Outstanding Magazine Writing

1999 Tom Keyser, Baltimore *Sun*
1998 Laura Hillenbrand, *American Heritage*
1997 Bill Heller, *The Backstretch*
1996 Don Clippinger, *Mid-Atlantic Thoroughbred*
1995 Not awarded
1994 Jay Hovdey, *The Blood-Horse*
1993 Stephanie Diaz, *The Backstretch*
1992 Joseph P. Pons Jr., *The Blood-Horse*
1990 Bill Nack, *Sports Illustrated*
1989 Bill Nack, *Sports Illustrated*
1988 Jennie Rees, Lexington *Courier-Journal* (Sunday Magazine)
1987 Jack Mann, *Spur*
1986 Bill Nack, *Sports Illustrated*
1985 Bill Mooney, *The Thoroughbred Record*
1984 Frank Deford, *Sports Illustrated*

1983 Arnold Kirkpatrick, *Keeneland*
1982 Jay Hovdey, *Horsemen's Journal*
1981 Joseph P. Pons Jr., *The Blood-Horse*
1980 Clive Gammon, *Sports Illustrated*
1979 William Leggett, *Sports Illustrated*
1978 Bill Nack, *Sports Illustrated*
1977 Whitney Tower, *Classic*
1976 Whitney Tower, *Classic*
1975 Frank Deford, *Sports Illustrated*
1974 Chet Hagan, *Spur*
1973 Pete Axthelm, *Newsweek*
1972 Edward L. Bowen, *The Blood-Horse*
1971 Bill Surface, *Reader's Digest*

Outstanding Feature and Enterprise Writing

2004 Mike Jensen, Philadelphia *Inquirer*
2003 Bill Nack, *GQ*
2002 John Jeremiah Sullivan, *Harper's*
2001 Laura Hillenbrand, *EQUUS*
2000 Mary Simon, THOROUGHBRED TIMES

Outstanding Feature Writing

1991 Bill Nack, *Sports Illustrated*

Outstanding News Writing

1991 Bill Nack, *Sports Illustrated*

Outstanding News and Commentary Writing

2004 Bill Christine, Los Angeles *Times*
2003 Jay Hovdey, *Daily Racing Form*
2002 Joe Drape, New York *Times*
2001 Janet Patton, Lexington *Herald-Leader*
2000 Jay Hovdey, *Daily Racing Form*

Local Television Achievement

2004 WAVE-TV, Louisville
2003 WKYT, Lexington
2002 Fox Sports Net Southwest
2001 WTVI, Charlotte, NC
2000 WMAR-TV, Baltimore
1999 Amy Zimmerman and Michael Ewing, Fox-TV Sports West
1998 Jeff Lifson, WHAS-TV, Louisville
1997 Brian Blessing, Ontario Jockey Club
1996 Kenny Rice, WTVQ-TV, Lexington
1995 JCM Productions, New York
1994 Ronnie Virgets, WNXO, New Orleans
1993 Stephen Sadis, KBTC, Tacoma
1992 Rick Cushing, WKPC-TV, Louisville

1991 WABC-TV, New York
1990 Philip Von Borries, WKPC-TV, Louisville
1989 Chris Thomas, WFLA-TV, Tampa
1988 Joseph Kwong, KCET-TV, Los Angeles
1987 Arlington Park
1986 Louisiana Downs
1985 Oak Tree Racing Association
1984 NYRA/Cinema Mistral
1983 Cawood Ledford Productions
1982 ON-TV, Los Angeles
1981 WHAS, Louisville
1980 WCAU, Philadelphia
1979 Dave Johnson, ON-TV
1978 Cawood Ledford, WHAS, Louisville
1977 Jane Chastain, KABC, Los Angeles
1976 NYRA-OTB Race of the Week
1975 Cawood Ledford, WHAS, Louisville

National Television Achievement

1999 Mark Shapiro and William Rapaport, ESPN
1998 E. S. Lamoreaux III, *CBS News Sunday Morning*
1997 E. S. Lamoreaux III, *CBS News Sunday Morning*
1996 NBC Sports
1995 ABC's Wide World of Sports
1994 ABC's Wide World of Sports
1993 E. S. Lamoreaux III, CBS News, *Sunday Morning with Charles Kuralt*
1992 ABC Sports
1991 CBS News, *Sunday Morning with Charles Kuralt*
1990 ABC Sports
1989 ABC Sports
1988 Thoroughbred Sports, *Racing Across America*
1987 ABC
1986 ABC
1985 CBS
1984 NBC
1983 CBS
1982 ESPN
1981 Canadian Broadcasting Corp.
1980 ABC
1979 Don Ohlmeyer, NBC
1978 Roger Murphy, Public Broadcasting System
1977 Jack Whitaker, CBS
1976 CBS
1975 CBS
1974 Pen Densham, John Watson, Insight Productions
1973 Chuck Milton, Tony Verna, CBS
1972 Chuck Milton, Tony Verna, CBS
1971 Burt Bacharach, CBS

National Television—Live Racing Programming

2004 NBC Sports
2003 NBC Sports
2002 NBC Sports
2001 NBC
2000 ABC Sports
1999 Curt Gowdy Jr., Craig Janoff, Howard Katz, and John Filippelli, ABC Sports

National Television—Features

2004 ESPN
2003 MSNBC
      ESPN Classic
2002 NBC Sports
2001 ESPN Classic

Audio–Multimedia–Internet

2004 Premiere Radio Networks
2003 KSPN/ESPN Radio, Los Angeles
      WBAL, Baltimore
2002 Shelby Whitfield, Premiere Radio

Radio Achievement

2001 WBAL, Baltimore
2000 Shelby Whitfield, Premiere Radio
1999 Tom Leach, WVLK-AM, Lexington
1998 Not awarded
1997 John Patti, WBAL, Baltimore
1996 Robin Dawson, CJCL, Toronto
1995 Vic Stauffer, KKAR, Omaha
1994 John Asher, WHAS, Louisville
1993 Tom Leach, WVLK, Lexington
1992 John Asher, WHAS, Louisville
1991 Julia McEvoy, National Public Radio
1990 John Asher, WHAS, Louisville
1989 John Asher, WAVG, Louisville
1988 John Asher, WAVG, Louisville
1987 Bob Lauder, WHAS, Louisville
1986 ABC Radio Network
1985 Bob Lauder, WHAS, Louisville
1984 WBAL, Baltimore
1983 Tom Davis, WCBM, Baltimore
1982 ABC Radio Network
1981 WBAL, Baltimore
1980 Not awarded
1979 Dick Woolley, WITH, Baltimore
1978 Ted Patterson, WBAL, Baltimore
1977 Not awarded
1976 Win Elliot, CBS
1975 Not awarded
1974 Not awarded
1973 Not awarded
1972 Not awarded
1971 Win Elliot, CBS

Film Achievement

1972 Joseph Burnham

Photography Achievement

2004 Cindy Pierson Dulay, *Mid-Atlantic Thoroughbred*
2003 Frank Anderson, Thoroughbred Times
2002 Michael Clevenger, Louisville *Courier-Journal*
2001 Barbara Livingston, *The Thoroughbred Chronicle*
2000 Dave Landry, *Canadian Thoroughbred*
1999 Michael J. Marten, *Daily Racing Form*
1998 Ryan Haynes, Northlands Park
1997 Jean Raftery, Calder Race Course
1996 Skip Dickstein, *The Blood-Horse*
1995 Michael J. Marten, *Daily Racing Form*
1994 Tony Leonard, Thoroughbred Times
1993 Michael Burns, Ontario Jockey Club
1992 Barbara Livingston, *The Blood-Horse*
1991 Rayetta Burr, Benoit and Associates
1990 Michael Cartee, *Thoroughbred of California*
1989 Ron Cortes, Philadelphia *Inquirer*
1988 Ben Van Hook, Louisville *Courier-Journal*
1987 Dan Farrell, New York *Daily News*
1986 Janice Wilkman, Los Angeles *Times*
1985 Kim Pratt, Garden State Park
1984 Bill Straus, *The Thoroughbred Record*
1983 Rayetta Burr, *Paddock*
1982 Kay Coyte, *Horsemen's Journal*
1981 Tom Baker, River Downs
1980 Bob Coglianese, New York Racing Association
1979 Skip Ball, *Maryland Horse*
1978 Douglas Lees, Fauquier *Democrat*
1977 John Walther, Miami *Herald*
1976 John J. Vasile, Covina (California) *Sentinel*
1975 John Pineda, Miami *Herald*
1974 Michael Burns, Ontario Jockey Club
1973 Harry Leder, United Press International
1972 Bob Coglianese, New York Racing Association
1971 Art Rogers, Los Angeles *Times*

Owners of Eclipse Award Winners

Aga Khan—Kalanisi (Ire).

Alexander, Helen, David Aykroyd, and Helen Groves—Althea.

Allbritton, Joseph—Hansel.

Anderson, Frank, Verne H. Winchell, and Rick Carradini—Tight Spot.

Augustin Stables—Cafe Prince (1977, '78), Pompeyo (Chi).

Bacharach, Burt C.—Heartlight No. One.

Bailey, Richard E.—Dearly Precious.

Beal, Barry and L. R. French—Landaluce, Sacahuista.

Beal, Barry, L. R. French, and Eugene Klein—Capote.

Bell III, John A.—Epitome.

Blue Vista—Possibly Perfect.

Brant, Peter M.—Gulch, Just a Game (Ire), Waya (Fr).

Bray Jr., Dana S.—Johnny D.

Buckland Farm—Pleasant Colony, Pleasant Stage, Pleasant Tap.

Caibett, Edgar—Canonero II.

Calbourne Farm—Brown Bess.

Calumet Farm—Before Dawn, Davona Dale, Our Mims.

Calumet Farm and Jurgen Arnemann—Criminal Type.

Cee's Stable—Tiznow (2001).

Cella, Charles—Northern Spur (Ire).

Centennial Farms—Rubiano.

Christiana Stables—Go for Wand (1989, '90).

Claiborne Farm—Forty Niner, Swale.

Clark Jr., Mrs. F. Ambrose—*Gran Kan.

Clark Jr., Stephen C.—Shadow Brook.

Clay, Robert and Tracy Farmer—Hidden Lake.

Cooper, Audrey H. and Michael Fennessy—Yanks Music.

Couvercelle, Jean—Cardmania.

Cowan, Irving and Marjorie—Hollywood Wildcat.

Craig, Sidney and Jenny—Paseana (Arg) (1992, '93).

Croll Jr., Warren A.—Holy Bull.

Crown Stable—Eillo.

Darby Dan Farm—Little Current, Sunshine Forever, Tempest Queen.

Davison, Mrs. Richard—Guilty Conscience.

De Camargo, Jose, Winner Silk Inc., and Old Friends Inc.—Farda Amiga.

De Kwiatkowski, Henryk—Conquistador Cielo, De La Rose.

Lord Derby—Ouija Board (GB).

Dogwood Stable—Inlander (GB), Storm Song.

Dotsam Stable—John Henry (1980, '81, '83, '84).

Due Process Stables—Dehere.

East-West Stable—Wajima.

Eldon Farm—Hirapour (Ire).

Elmendorf Farm—Protagonist, Talking Picture.

Engel, Charles F.—Saratoga Dew.

Envoy Stable—Ambassador of Luck.

Equusequity Stable—Slew o' Gold (1983, '84).

Evergreen Farm—Lit de Justice.

Fares, Issam M.—Miss Alleged.

Farish, William S., James Elkins, and Temple Webber Jr.—Mineshaft.

Farish, Will, William Kilroy, Harold Goodman, and Tomonori Tsurumaki—A.P. Indy.

Fey, Barry, Moon Han, Class Racing Stable, Larry Opas, Frank Sinatra, and Craig Dollase—Reraise.

Firestone, Mr. and Mrs. Bertram R.—April Run (Ire), Genuine Risk, Honest Pleasure, Jimmy Lorenzo (GB), What a Summer.

505 Farms and Ed Nahem—Bertrando.

Flaxman Holdings—Aldebaran.

Flying Zee Stables—Wayward Lass.

Folsom Farm and J. Merrick Jones Jr.—Chou Croute.

Forked Lightning Ranch—Ack Ack.

Fradkoff, Serge and Baron Thierry Van Zuylen de Nyevelt—Perrault (GB).

Franks, John—Answer Lively.

Fuller, Peter—Mom's Command.

Genter, Frances A. Stable—Smile, Unbridled.

Gerry, Nancy—Flat Top (1998, 2002).

Godolphin Racing—Daylami (Ire), Fantastic Light, Tempera.

Green, Dolly—Brave Raj.

Grinstead, Carl and Ben Rochelle—Snow Chief.

Greentree Stable—Bowl Game, Late Bloomer.

Greer, John L.—Foolish Pleasure.

Griggs, John K.—Warm Spell.

Guest, Virginia—Life's Illusion.

Hamilton, Emory Alexander—Queena.

Hancock III, Arthur, Charlie Whittingham, and Dr. Ernest Gaillard—Sunday Silence.

Harbor View Farm—Affirmed (1977, '78, '79), Flawlessly (1992, '93), It's in the Air, Outstandingly.

Hatley, Melvin E. and Eugene V. Klein—Life's Magic.

Hawksworth Farm—Spectacular Bid (1978, '79, '80).

Henley Jr., Mrs. Jesse M.—Highland Bud.

Hersh, Trust of Philip and Sophie—The Wicked North.

Hibbert, Robert E.—Roving Boy.

Hickory Tree Stable—Devil's Bag.

Hine, Carolyn H.—Skip Away (1996, '97, '98).

Hi Yu Stable—Chinook Pass.

Hofmann, Mrs. Philip B.—Gold Beauty, Sky Beauty.

Hooper Sr., Fred W.—Precisionist, Susan's Girl (1972, '73, 1975).

Horton, Robert P.—Gallant Bob.

Houghland, Calvin—All Gong (GB).

Hughes, B. Wayne—Action This Day.

Hunt, Nelson Bunker—Dahlia, Youth.

Hunt, Nelson Bunker and Edward L. Stephenson—Trillion.

Hunter Farm—Spend a Buck.

Icahn, Carl—Meadow Star.

Jackson, Michael—Morley Street (Ire) (1990, '91).

Jay Em Ess Stable—Declan's Moon.

Jayeff B Stables and Barry Weisbord—Safely Kept.

Jeffords Jr., Mrs. Walter M.—Lonesome Glory (1992, '93, '95, '97, '99).

Jhayare Stables—Itsallgreektome.

Jones, Aaron U.—Lemhi Gold, Tiffany Lass.

Jones, Aaron and Marie—Riboletta (Brz).

Jones Jr., J. Merrick and Folsom Farm—Chou Croute.

Jones, Mrs. Mary F.—*Cougar II.

Juddmonte Farms—Banks Hill (GB), Ryafan, Wandesta (GB).

Kaster, Mr. and Mrs. Richard and Mr. and Mrs. Donald Propson—Countess Diana.

Keck, Mrs. Howard B.—Ferdinand, Turkish Trousers.

Kellman, Joseph—Shecky Greene.

Klein, Eugene V.—Family Style, Open Mind (1988, '89), Winning Colors.

Klein, Mr. and Mrs. Eugene V.—Lady's Secret.

Klein, Eugene, L. R. French, and Barry Beal—Capote.

Klein, Eugene V. and Melvin E. Hatley—Life's Magic.

LaCombe, Joseph—Favorite Trick.

Lamarque Racing Stable and Louis J. Roussel III—Risen Star.

Lancaster Jr., Carlyle, et al.—Star de Naskra.

Lanzman, David—Squirtle Squirt.

La Presle Farm—Kotashaan (Fr).

Lazy F Ranch—Forego (1974, '75, '76, '77).

Levesque, Jean-Louis—La Prevoyante.

Levy, Morton and Marjoh, and Donald and David Willmot—Deputy Minister.

Levy, Robert P.—Housebuster (1990, '91).

Levy, Robert, William Roberts, and Alex Karkenny—Smoke Glacken.

Lewis, Robert and Beverly—Charismatic, Orientate, Serena's Song, Silver Charm.

Lewis, Robert and Beverly, Gainesway Farm, and Overbrook Farm—Timber Country.

Lickle, William C.—Correggio (Ire).

Loblolly Stable—Prairie Bayou, Temperence Hill, Vanlandingham.

Locust Hill Farm—Ruffian (1974, '75).

Maktoum, Sheikh Maktoum bin Rashid al—Hatoof.

Maktoum, Sheikh Mohammed bin Rashid al—Pebbles (GB), Singspiel (Ire).

Maktoum, Sheikh Mohammed bin Rashid al and Allen E. Paulson—Arazi.

Mangurian Jr., Harry T.—Desert Vixen.

Meadow Stable—Riva Ridge, Secretariat (1972, '73).

Melnyk, Eugene and Laura—Speightstown.

Milch, David, Marc Silverman, and Jack Silverman—Gilded Time.

Mill House—Sensational.

Molasky, Irwin and Andrew, Bruce Headley, and High Tech Stable (Michael Singh)—Kona Gold.

Montpelier—Proud Delta, Sooth-

sayer.

Moran, Michael—McDynamo.

Murdock, Mrs. Lewis C.—Zaccio (1980, '81, '82).

Nerud, John A.—Cozzene.

Niarchos, Stavros—Miesque (1987, '88).

Nishiyama, Masayuki—Paradise Creek.

Oak, Harry A.—Rockhill Native.

Overbrook Farm—Boston Harbor, Flanders, Golden Attraction, Surfside.

Oxley, John C.—Beautiful Pleasure.

Padua Stables—Vindication.

Pape, William L.—Athenian Idol, Martie's Anger.

Pape, William L., George Harris, and Jonathan Sheppard—Flatterer (1983, '84, '85, '86).

Paraneck Stable—Artax.

Paternostro, Paul, and D. Wayne Lukas—North Sider.

Paulson, Allen E.—Ajina, Blushing John, Cigar (1995, '96), Eliza, Escena, Estrapade.

Paulson, Allen E. Living Trust—Azeri (2002, '03, '04).

Paulson, Allen E. and Bertram R. Firestone—Theatrical (Ire).

Paulson, Allen E. and Sheikh Mohammed bin Rashid al Maktoum—Arazi.

Paxson, Adele—Candy Eclair.

Pegram, Mike—Real Quiet, Silverbulletday (1998, '99).

Perry, William H.—Revidere.

Phillips Racing Partnership—Soaring Softly.

Phipps, Cynthia—Christmas Past.

Phipps, Mrs. Ogden—Straight and True.

Phipps, Ogden—Easy Goer, Heavenly Prize, Numbered Account, Personal Ensign, Relaxing.

Phipps, Ogden Mills—Inside Information, Rhythm, Storm Flag Flying.

Pin Oak Stable—Laugh and Be Merry.

Pollard, Carl F.—Caressing.

Pope Jr., George A.—J. O. Tobin.

Prestonwood Farm—Groovy, Victory Gallop.

Quarter B. Farm—Buck's Boy.

Ramsey, Kenneth and Sarah—Kitten's Joy.

Ridder, Bernard R.—Cascapedia.

Riordan, Michael D.—Bates Motel.

Robins, Gerald W. and Timothy Sams—Tasso.

Robinson, Jill E.—Cherokee Run.

Rokeby Stable—Key to the Mint, Run the Gantlet.

Rosen, Carl—Chris Evert.

Rosenthal, Mrs. Morton—Maria's Mon.

Ryehill Farm—Heavenly Cause, Smart Angle.

Salman, Prince Fahd bin—Fiji (GB).

Sams, Timothy and Gerald W. Robins—Tasso.

Sam-Son Farm—Chief Bearhart, Dance Smartly, Sky Classic.

Sangster, Robert E.—Royal Heroine (Ire).

Sackatoga Stable—Funny Cide.

Sarkowsky, Herman—Phone Chatter.

Saron Stable—Turkoman.

Scharbauer, Dorothy and Pamela—Alysheba (1987, '88).

Schiff, John M.—Plugged Nickle.

Shannon, Bradley M.—Manila.

SKS Stable—Lord Avie.

Sommer, Sigmund—Autobiography.

Star Crown Stable—Chief's Crown.

Starlight Stables, Paul Saylor, and Johns Martin—Ashado.

Stephen, Martha and Richard and The Thoroughbred Corp.—Jewel Princess.

Someday Farm—Smarty Jones.

Stone, Mrs. Whitney—Shuvee.

Stonerside Stable—Chilukki.

Straub-Rubens, Cecilia, and Michael Cooper—Tiznow (2000).

Stronach, Frank and Nelson Bunker Hunt—Glorious Song.

Stronach Stable—Ghostzapper, Macho Uno, Perfect Sting.

Sullivan, Jeffrey—Black Tie Affair (Ire).

Summa Stable—Track Robbery.

Tabor, Michael—Left Bank, Thunder Gulch.

Tabor, Michael and Susan Magnier—High Chaparral (Ire) (2002, '03), Johannesburg.

Tafel, James, Richard Santulli, and Jayeff B Stables—Banshee Breeze.

Tanaka, Gary—Golden Apples (Ire), Gourmet Girl.

Tartan Stable—Dr. Patches.

Tayhill Stable—Seattle Slew (1978).

Taylor, Mrs. Karen L.—Seattle Slew (1976, '77).

The Thoroughbred Corp.—Anees, Point Given.

The Thoroughbred Corp. and Russell Reineman—War Emblem.

Tizol, E. Rodriguez—Bold Forbes.

Torsney, Dr. Jerome M.—Mac Diarmida.

Tucker, Paula—Princess Rooney.

Valando, Thomas—Fly So Free.

Vance, Jeanne—Lemon Drop Kid.

Van Worp, Robert—Not Surprising.

Weasel Jr., George—My Juliet.

Weinsier, Randolph—Lakeville Miss.

Lord Weinstock, Executors of the late—Islington (Ire).

Wertheimer Farm—Halfbridled.

Westerly Stud—Typecast.

Whitham, Mr. and Mrs. Frank E.—Bayakoa (Arg) (1989, '90).

Whitney, Marylou—Bird Town.

Wildenstein, Daniel—All Along (Fr).

Wildenstein Stable—Steinlen (GB).

Windfields Farm and Neil Phillips—*Snow Knight.

Wygod, Martin and Pamela—Sweet Catomine.

Breeders of Eclipse Award Winners

Adams, Mrs. Vanderbilt—Desert Vixen.

Adena Springs—Ghostzapper, Macho Uno, Perfect Sting.

Aga Khan—Daylami (Ire), Hirapour (Ire), Kalanisi (Ire).

Alexander, Emory—Queena.

Allez France Stables—Steinlen (GB).

Augustus, Peggy—Johnny D.

Baker, Dr. Howard—Serena's Song.

Ballydoyle Stud—Correggio (Ire).

Ballymacoll Stud Farm—Islington (Ire).

Barnhart, Anna Marie—Skip Away (1996, '97, '98).

Bell, H. Bennett, and Jessica Bell Nicholson—Epitome.

Benjamin, Edward Bernard—Canonero II (Ire).

Benjamin, E. V. III, and William G. Clark—Chou Croute.

Bettersworth, J. R.—My Juliet.

Blue Bear Stud—Zaccio (1980, '81, '82).

Blue Diamond Ranch—Snow Chief.

Blue Seas Music Inc.—Heartlight No. One.

Brant, Peter M.—Gulch, Thunder Gulch.

Calbourne Farm—Brown Bess.

Calumet Farm—Before Dawn, Criminal Type, Davona Dale, Our Mims.

Cannata, Carl and Olivia—Gourmet Girl.

Carrion, Jaime S.—Action This Day, Meadow Star.

Castleman, Ben S.—Seattle Slew (1976, '77, '78).

Centurion Farms—Deputy Minister.

Chenery, Helen B.—Saratoga Dew.

Christiana Stables—Go for Wand (1989, '90).

Claiborne Farm—Forty Niner, Revidere, Slew o' Gold (1983, '84), Swale, Wajima.

Cleaboy Farms Co.—Inlander (GB).

Cohen, Ollie A.—Eillo.

Cojuangco, Edwardo M. Jr.—Manila.

Coughlan, Sean—High Chaparral (Ire) (2002, '03).

Cowan, Irving and Marjorie—Hollywood Wildcat.

Danada Farm—Proud Delta.

Darley Stud Management—Tempera.

Davison, Mrs. Richard—Guilty Conscience.

Dayton Ltd.—All Along (Fr), Waya (Fr).

Delta Thoroughbreds Inc.—Cardmania.

De Mestre, J. W.—Jimmy Lorenzo (GB).

Due Process Stables—Dehere, Open Mind (1988, '89).

Eaton Farms Inc. and Red Bull Stable—Bold Forbes.

Echo Valley Horse Farm Inc.—Chris Evert, Winning Colors.

Egan, James and David Hanley—Golden Apples (Ire).

Elmendorf Farm—Protagonist, Shadow Brook, Talking Picture.

Evans, Thomas Mellon—Pleasant Colony, Pleasant Tap.

Evans, Mrs. Thomas Mellon—Pleasant Stage.

Farfellow Farms Ltd.—Anees.

Farish, William S., James Elkins, and Temple Webber Jr.—Mineshaft.

Farish, William S., and W. S. Kilroy—A.P. Indy, Lemon Drop Kid.

Farish, William S., and Ogden Mills Phipps—Storm Song.

Farnsworth Farms—Beautiful Pleasure, Jewel Princess.

Feeney, F.—April Run (Ire).

Firestone, Mr. and Mrs. Bertram R.—Paradise Creek, Theatrical (Ire).

Flaxman Holdings Ltd.—Aldebaran, Miesque (1987, '88).

Floyd, William—Highland Bud.

Fox, Richard and Nathan, and Richard Kaster—McDynamo.

Franks, John—Answer Lively.

Freeman, Carl M.—Miss Alleged.

Fuller, C. T.—Ambassador of Luck.

Fuller, Peter—Mom's Command.

Gainesway Thoroughbreds Ltd.—Orientate.

Gainsborough Farm—Fantastic Light, Hatoof.

Galbreath, John W.—Little Current, Sunshine Forever.

Galbreath, Mrs. John W.—Tempest Queen.

Galbreath/Phillips Racing Partnership—Soaring Softly.

Genter Stable, Frances A.—Smile.

Golden Chance Farm Inc.—John Henry (1980, '81, '83, '84).

Greentree Stud—Bowl Game, Late Bloomer.

Groves, Helen, Helen Alexander, and David Aykroyd—Althea.

Guest, Raymond R.—Cascapedia.

Guest, Virginia D.—Life's Illusion.

Guggenheim, Harry F.—Ack Ack.

Hancock, Arthur B. III, and Leone J. Peters—Risen Star.

Happy Valley Farm—It's in the Air.

Haras El Huerton—*Gran Kan.

Haras General Cruz—*Cougar II.

Haras Principal—Bayakoa (Arg) (1989, '90).

Haras Santa Ana do Rio Grande—Riboletta (Brz).

Haras Santa Amelia—Pompeyo (Chi).

Haras Vacacion—Paseana (Arg) (1992, '93).

Harbor View Farm—Affirmed (1977-'79), Athenian Idol, Outstandingly, Flawlessly (1992, '93).

Hartigan, John H.—Mac Diarmida.

Hayden, Mr. and Mrs. David—Safely Kept.

Hibbert, Robert E.—Roving Boy.

Hickey, P. Noel—Buck's Boy.

Highclere Inc. and Clear Creek—Silverbulletday (1998, '99).

Hi Yu Stables—Chinook Pass.

Hofmann, Mr. and Mrs. Philip B.—Gold Beauty.

Homan, J. L.—Gallant Bob.

Hooper, Fred W.—Susan's Girl (1972, '73, '75).

Hooper, Fred W.—Precisionist.

Humphrey, G. Watts Jr., and William S. Farish III—Sacahuista.

Humphrey, Mrs. G. Watts Jr.—Genuine Risk.

Hundley, Bruce, and Wayne Garrison—Fly So Free.

Hunt, Nelson Bunker—Dahlia, Estrapade, Trillion, Youth.

Iandolo, Lewis E.—Conquistador Cielo.

Irish American Bloodstock Agency Ltd.—Yanks Music.

Irish Hill Farm and Rowe W. Harper—Spend a Buck.

Janney, Mr. and Mrs. Stuart S. Jr.—Ruffian (1974, '75).

Jason, Mrs. William M., and Mrs. William Gilmore—Spectacular Bid (1978, '79, '80).

Jeffords, Walter M. Jr.—Lonesome Glory (1992, '93, '95, '97, '99).

Jones, Aaron U.—Lemhi Gold, Tiffany Lass.

Jones, Aaron U. and Marie D.—Ashado, Speightstown.

Jones, Brereton C.—Caressing.

Juddmonte Farms—Banks Hill (GB), Ryafan, Wandesta (GB).

Karutz, Dr. Wallace—Brave Raj.

Kaster, Richard S.—Countess Diana.

Keck, Howard B.—Ferdinand, Turkish Trousers.

Kellman, Joseph—Shecky Greene.

Kitchen, Edgar—Track Robbery.

Kluener, Robert G.—Warm Spell.

Knight, Landon—Flat Top (1998, 2002).

Kris Syndicate, and Kirtlington Stud Ltd.—All Gong (GB).

Lancaster, Carlyle J.—Star de Naskra.

Lazy F Ranch—Forego (1974, '75, '76, '77).

Levesque, Jean-Louis—La Prevoyante.

Levy, Blanche P., and Murphy Stable—Housebuster (1990, '91).

Levy, Robert P., and Cisley Stable—North Sider.

Lilley, J. A. C.—*Snow Knight.

Little Hill Farm—Real Quiet.

Little, Marvin A. Jr.—Hansel.

Loblolly Stable—Prairie Bayou, Vanlandingham.

Lowquest Ltd.—Timber Country.

Luro, Horatio A.—Wayward Lass.

Lyster III, W. G. and Jayeff B Stables—Johannesburg.

Madden, Preston—Alysheba (1987, '88).

Maktoum, Sheikh Mohammed bin Rashid al—Singspiel (Ire).

Mangurian, Mr. and Mrs. Harry T. Jr.—Gilded Time.

Maynard, Richard D.—Chief Bearhart.

Meadow Stud—Riva Ridge, Secretariat (1972, '73).

Mellon, Paul—Key to the Mint, Run the Gantlet.

Mill House—Sensational.

Nahem, Ed—Bertrando.

Narducci, M.D., Audrey—Squirtle Squirt.

Nerud, John A.—Cozzene.

Newgate Stud Company—Fiji (GB).

North Ridge Farm—Blushing John, Capote.

Nuckols Brothers—Typecast.

Nuckols, Charles Jr. and Sons—Hidden Lake, War Emblem.

Oak Cliff Thoroughbreds Ltd.—Sunday Silence.

Onett, George C.—Cherokee Run.

Overbrook Farm—Boston Harbor, Flanders, Golden Attraction, Surfside.

Pancoast, Mrs. Jean R.—Dearly Precious.

Pape, William L., and Jonathan Sheppard—Flatterer (1983, '84, '85, '86), Martie's Anger.

Parkhill, Marshall—Morley Street (Ire) (1990, '91).

Parrish, Douglas, Estate of Emma Haggin Parrish, and Dr. David C.

Parrish III—Life's Magic.

Parrish Hill Farm and William S. Farish—Charismatic.

Paulson, Allen E.—Ajina, Azeri (2002, '03, '04), Cigar (1995, '96), Eliza, Escena.

Payson Stud—Farda Amiga, Vindication.

Paxson, Adele—Candy Eclair.

Ramsey, Kenneth and Sarah—Kitten's Joy

Pelican Stable—Holy Bull.

Perez, Carlos—Kona Gold.

Peskoff, Stephen D.—Black Tie Affair (Ire).

Phillips, Mrs. Jacqueline Getty—Bates Motel.

Phillips Racing Partnership/Galbreath—Soaring Softly.

Phipps, Cynthia—Christmas Past.

Phipps, Mrs. Ogden—Straight and True.

Phipps, Ogden—Easy Goer, Heavenly Prize, Numbered Account, Personal Ensign, Relaxing.

Phipps, Ogden Mills—Inside Information, Rhythm.

Phipps Stable—Storm Flag Flying.

Pin Oak Farm—Laugh and Be Merry.

Polinger, Milton—What a Summer.

Polk, Dr. Albert F. Jr.—Temperence Hill.

Pope, George A. Jr.—J. O. Tobin.

Ramsey, Kenneth and Sarah—Kitten's Joy.

Rathvale Stud—Just a Game (Ire).

Ravenbrook Farm Inc.—Not Surprising.

Ridgely, Brice—Declan's Moon.

Roach, Dr. Ben, and Tom Roach—Princess Rooney.

Robertson, Corbin—Turkoman.

Robins, Gerald W. and Timothy H. Sams—Tasso.

Robinson, Marshall T.—Groovy.

Rosebrock, Perry M.—Smoke Glacken.

Rosen, Carl—Chief's Crown.

Rosenthal, Morton—Maria's Mon.

Ryan, B. L.—Royal Heroine (Ire).

Ryehill Farm—Heavenly Cause, Smart Angle.

Sam-Son Farm—Dance Smartly, Sky Classic.

Sarkowsky, Herman—Phone Chatter.

Schiff, John M.—Plugged Nickle.

Scott, Mrs. Marion duPont—Soothsayer.

Selective Seasons—Family Style.

Sergent, Willard—Reraise.

Shead, A. D. and F. H. Sasse—Perrault (GB).

Someday Farm—Smarty Jones.

Spendthrift Farm and Francis Kernan—Landaluce.

Spreen, Robert H.—Lady's Secret.

Stanley Estate and Stud Co.—Ouija Board (GB).

Stone, Whitney—Shuvee.

Straub-Rubens, Cecilia—Tiznow (2000, '01).

Sugar Maple Farm—Itsallgreektome, Sky Beauty.

Swettenham Stud—Lit de Justice.

Swettenham Stud and Partners—Northern Spur (Ire).

Tafel, James B.—Banshee Breeze.

Tall Oaks Farm—Victory Gallop.

Tartan Farms Corp.—Dr. Patches, Unbridled.

Taylor, E. P.—Devil's Bag, Glorious Song.

The Thoroughbred Corp.—Point Given.

Third Kirsmith Racing Associates—Rubiano.

Thomas, Dr. E. W., and Carolaine Farm—Rockhill Native.

Viking Farms Ltd.—Lord Avie.

Vinery and Carondelet Farm—Artax.

Waldemar Farms Inc.—Foolish Pleasure, Honest Pleasure.

Warren Hill Stud and Mimika Financiera—Pebbles (GB).

Weinsier, Randolph—Lakeville Miss.

Wertheimer and Brother—Halfbridled, Kotashaan (Fr).

West, Dr. and Mrs. R. Smiser, and MacKenzie Miller—De La Rose.

West, Dr. and Mrs. R. Smiser, and Mr. and Mrs. MacKenzie Miller—Chilukki.

Wheatley Stable—Autobiography.

Whitney, Marylou—Bird Town.

WinStar Farm—Funny Cide.

Wilson, Ralph C. Jr.—Arazi.

Winchell, Verne H.—Cafe Prince (1977-'78), Tight Spot.

Witt, Mr. and Mrs. Robert—Possibly Perfect.

Wood, Mr. and Mrs. M. L.—Favorite Trick.

Wootton, Mary Lou—Silver Charm.

Wygod, Martin and Pamela—Sweet Catomine.

Youngblood, John, and Fletcher Gray—Left Bank.

Zurek, Edward N.—The Wicked North.

Trainers of Eclipse Award Winners

Albertrani, Louis—Artax.

Alexander, Frank—Cherokee Run.

Allard, Edward T.—Mom's Command.

Anderson, Laurie—Chinook Pass.

Arias, Juan—Canonero II.

Badgett Jr., William—Go for Wand (1989, '90).

Baffert, Robert—Chilukki, Point Given, Real Quiet, Silverbulletday (1998, '99), Silver Charm, Vindication, War Emblem.

Balding, Gerald B. "Toby"—Morley Street (Ire) (1990, '91).

Barnett, Robert—Answer Lively.

Barrera, Lazaro S.—Affirmed (1977, '78, '79), Bold Forbes, It's in the Air, J. O. Tobin, Lemhi Gold, Tiffany Lass.

Bary, Pascal—Miss Alleged (with Charles Whittingham).

Belanger Jr., Gerald W.—Glorious Song.

Bernstein, David—The Wicked North.

Biancone, Patrick L.—All Along (Fr).

Bin Suroor, Saeed—Daylami (Ire), Fantastic Light.

Bohannan, Thomas—Prairie Bayou.

Boutin, Francois—April Run (Ire), Arazi, Miesque (1987, '88).

Brittain, Clive E.—Pebbles (GB).

Brothers, Frank—Hansel.

Burch, J. Elliot—Key to the Mint, Run the Gantlet.

Byrne, Patrick—Countess Diana, Favorite Trick.

Campbell, Gordon C.—Cascapedia.

Campo, John P.—Pleasant Colony,

Protagonist, Talking Picture.
Canani, Julio—Sweet Catomine.
Cantey, Joseph B.—Temperence Hill.
Carroll, Henry—Smoke Glacken.
Cecil, Ben—Golden Apples (Ire).
Cocks, W. Burling—Zaccio (1980, '81, '82).
Croll Jr., Warren A.—Holy Bull, Housebuster (1990, '91).
Curtis Jr., William—Gold Beauty.
Day, Jim—Dance Smartly, Sky Classic.
Delp, Grover G.—Spectacular Bid (1978, '79, '80).
de Seroux, Laura—Azeri (2002, '03).
DiMauro, Steve—Dearly Precious, Wajima.
Dollase, Craig—Reraise.
Dollase, Wallace—Itsallgreektome, Jewel Princess.
Doyle, A. T.—Typecast.
Drysdale, Neil—A.P. Indy, Fiji (GB), Hollywood Wildcat, Princess Rooney, Tasso.
Dunham, Robert G.—Chou Croute.
Dunlop, Edward—Ouija Board (GB).
Elliot, Janet E.—Correggio (Ire), Flat Top (1998, 2002).
Ellis, Ron—Declan's Moon.
Euster, Eugene—My Juliet.
Fabre, Andre—Banks Hill (GB).
Fenstermaker, L. Ross—Precisionist, Susan's Girl (1975).
Fenwick, Charles—Inlander (GB).
Ferris, Richard D.—Star de Naskra.
Fout, Douglas—Hirapour (Ire).
Fout, Paul R.—Life's Illusion.
Frankel, Robert—Aldebaran, Bertrando, Ghostzapper, Possibly Perfect, Ryafan, Squirtle Squirt, Wandesta (GB).
Freeman, W. C.—Shuvee.
Furr, C.—*Gran Kan.
Frostad, Mark—Chief Bearhart.
Gambolati, Cam—Spend a Buck.
Gaver, John M.—Late Bloomer.
Gaver Jr., John M.—Bowl Game.
Goldberg, Alan E.—Safely Kept.
Goldfine, Lou M.—Shecky Greene.
Gosden, John H. M.—Bates Motel, Royal Heroine (Ire).
Griggs, John K.—Warm Spell.
Harty, Eoin—Tempera.
Hassinger Jr., Alex—Anees, Eliza.
Hauswald, Phil—Epitome.
Head, Christiane—Hatoof.
Headley, Bruce—Kona Gold.
Hendriks, Sanna Neilson—McDynamo, Pomeyo (Chi).
Hertler, John O.—Slew o' Gold (1983, '84).
Hickey, P. Noel—Buck's Boy.
Hine, Hubert—Guilty Conscience, Skip Away (1996, '97, '98).
Howard, Neil—Mineshaft.
Howe, Peter M.—Proud Delta, Soothsayer.
Inda, Eduardo—Riboletta (Brz).
Jenda, Charles J.—Brown Bess.

Jerkens, H. Allen—Sky Beauty.
Jolley, LeRoy—Foolish Pleasure, Genuine Risk, Honest Pleasure, Manila, Meadow Star, What a Summer.
Jones, Gary—Turkoman.
Kay, Michael—Johnny D.
Kelly, Thomas J.—Plugged Nickle.
Kimmel, John—Hidden Lake.
King Jr., S. Allen—Candy Eclair.
Laurin, Lucien—Riva Ridge, Secretariat (1972, '73).
Laurin, Roger—Chief's Crown, Numbered Account.
Lepman, Budd—Eillo.
Lobo, Paulo—Farda Amiga.
Lukas, D. Wayne—Althea, Azeri (2004), Boston Harbor, Capote, Charismatic, Criminal Type, Family Style, Flanders, Golden Attraction, Gulch, Lady's Secret, Landaluce, Life's Magic (1984, '85), North Sider, Open Mind (1988, '89), Orientate, Sacahuista, Serena's Song, Steinlen (GB), Surfside, Thunder Gulch, Timber Country, Winning Colors.
Lundy, Richard J.—Blushing John.
Mandella, Richard—Action This Day, Halfbridled, Kotashaan (Fr), Phone Chatter.
Manzi, Joseph—Roving Boy.
Marquette, Joseph D.—Gallant Bob.
Marti, Pedro—Heartlight No. One.
Martin, Frank—Autobiography, Outstandingly.
Martin, Jose—Groovy, Lakeville Miss, Wayward Lass.
McAnally, Ronald—Bayakoa (Arg) (1989, '90), John Henry (1980, '81, '83, '84), Northern Spur (Ire), Paseana (Arg) (1992, '93), Tight Spot.
McGaughey III, Claude R.—Easy Goer, Heavenly Prize, Inside Information, Personal Ensign, Queena, Rhythm, Storm Flag Flying, Vanlandingham.
Meredith, Derek—Cardmania.
Miller, F. Bruce—All Gong (GB), Lonesome Glory (1992, '93, '95, '97, '99).
Miller, MacKenzie—*Snow Knight.
Mott, Bill—Ajina, Cigar (1995, '96), Escena, Paradise Creek, Theatrical (Ire).
Nafzger, Carl A.—Banshee Breeze, Unbridled.
Nerud, Jan H.—Cozzene.
Nerud, John A.—Dr. Patches.
Nickerson, Victor J.—John Henry (1981).
Nobles, Reynaldo—Dehere.
O'Brien, Aidan—High Chaparral (Ire) (2002, '03), Johannesburg.
O'Brien, Leo—Yanks Music.
Orseno, Joseph F.—Macho Uno, Perfect Sting.
Penna, Angel—Relaxing.
Penna Jr., Angel—Christmas Past, Laugh and Be Merry.
Perlsweig, Daniel—Lord Avie.

Perdomo, Pico—Gourmet Girl.
Peterson, Douglas—Seattle Slew (1978).
Pletcher, Todd—Ashado, Left Bank, Speightstown.
Poulos, Ernie—Black Tie Affair (Ire).
Preger, Mitchell C.—Ambassador of Luck.
Robbins, Jay—Tiznow (2000, '01).
Romans Dale L.—Kitten's Joy.
Rondinello, Thomas L.—Little Current, Tempest Queen.
Root Sr., T. F.—Desert Vixen.
Roussel III, Louis J.—Risen Star.
Russell, John W.—Susan's Girl (1972, '73).
Sahadi, Jenine—Lit de Justice.
Schosberg, Richard—Maria's Mon.
Schulhofer, Flint S.—Fly So Free, Lemon Drop Kid, Mac Diarmida, Rubiano, Smile.
Sciacca, Gary—Saratoga Dew.
Servis, John—Smarty Jones.
Sheppard, Jonathan E.—Athenian Idol, Cafe Prince (1977, '78), Flatterer (1983, '84, '85, '86), Highland Bud, Jimmy Lorenzo (GB), Martie's Anger.
Smithwick, D. Michael—Straight and True.
Speckert, Chris—Pleasant Stage,

Pleasant Tap.
Starr, John—La Prevoyante.
Stephens, Woodford C.—Conquistador Cielo, De La Rose, Devil's Bag, Forty Niner, Heavenly Cause, Sensational, Smart Angle, Swale.
Stevens, Herbert—Rockhill Native.
Stoute, Sir Michael—Islington (Ire), Kalanisi (Ire), Singspiel (Ire).
Stute, Mel—Brave Raj, Snow Chief.
Tagg, Barclay—Funny Cide.
Tammaro, John—Deputy Minister.
Toner, James J.—Soaring Softly.
Trovato, Joseph A.—Chris Evert.

Turner Jr., William H.—Seattle Slew (1976-'77).
Van Berg, Jack—Alysheba (1987-'88).
Vance, David R.—Caressing.
Van Worp, Judson—Not Surprising.
Veitch, John M.—Before Dawn, Davona Dale, Our Mims, Sunshine Forever.
Vienna, Darrell—Gilded Time.
Walden, W. Elliott—Victory Gallop.
Ward, John T.—Beautiful Pleasure.
Ward, Sherrill W.—Forego (1974, '75).
Watters Jr., Sidney—Shadow Brook, Slew o' Gold (1983, '84).
Wheeler, Robert L. and John W. Russell—Track Robbery.

Whiteley, David A.—Just a Game (Ire), Revidere, Waya (Fr).
Whiteley Jr., Frank Y.—Forego (1976, '77), Ruffian (1974, '75).
Whittingham, Charles—Ack Ack, *Cougar II, Estrapade, Ferdinand, Flawlessly (1992, '93), Miss Alleged (with Pascal Bary), Perrault (GB), Sunday Silence, Turkish Trousers.
Zilber, Maurice—Youth, Dahlia, Trillion.
Zito, Nicholas P.—Bird Town, Storm Song.

Sires of Eclipse Award Winners

Ack Ack—Youth.
Affirmed—Flawlessly (1992, '93).
Ahmad—Paseana (Arg) (1992, '93).
Air Forbes Won—Yanks Music.
***Alcibiades II**—Athenian Idol.
Alleged—Flat Top (1998, 2002), Miss Alleged.
Alydar—Althea, Alysheba (1987, '88), Criminal Type, Easy Goer, Turkoman.
A.P. Indy—Mineshaft, Tempera.
Awesome Again—Ghostzapper.
Bagdad—Turkish Trousers.
Battle Joined—Ack Ack.
Best Turn—Davona Dale.
Blushing Groom (Fr)—Arazi, Blushing John, Sky Beauty.
Bold Bidder—Spectacular Bid (1978, '79, '80).
Bold Forbes—Tiffany Lass.
Bold Reasoning—Seattle Slew (1976, '77, '78).
Bold Ruler—Secretariat (1972, '73), Wajima.
Broad Brush—Farda Amiga.
Buckaroo—Spend a Buck.
Buckpasser—La Prevoyante, Numbered Account, Relaxing.
Bucksplasher—Buck's Boy.
Cape Cross (Ire)—Ouija Board (GB).
Cape Town—Bird Town.
Capote—Boston Harbor.
Caro (Ire)—Cozzene, Winning Colors.
Cee's Tizzy—Gourmet Girl, Tiznow (2000, '01).
Cherokee Run—Chilukki.
Chief's Crown—Chief Bearhart.
Chieftain—Cascapedia.
Cohoes—Shadow Brook.
Consultant's Bid—Bayakoa (Arg) (1989, '90).
Cormorant—Saratoga Dew.
Court Ruling—Guilty Conscience.
Cox's Ridge—Cardmania, Life's Magic 1984, '85), Vanlandingham.
Creme dela Creme—Cafe Prince (1977, '78).
Crozier—Precisionist.
Cryptoclearance—Victory Gallop.
Danehill—Banks Hill (GB).
Danzatore—Reraise.
Danzig—Chief's Crown, Dance Smartly.

Darshaan—Kotashaan (Fr).
Deep Run—Morley Street (Ire) (1990, '91).
Deerhound—Countess Diana.
Delta Judge—Proud Delta.
Deputy Minister—Dehere, Go for Wand (1989, '90), Open Mind (1988, '89).
Distorted Humor—Funny Cide.
Djakao—Perrault (GB).
Doyoun—Daylami (Ire), Kalanisi (Ire).
Dr. Fager—Dearly Precious, Dr. Patches.
Dynaformer—McDynamo.
El Gran Senor—Lit de Justice.
El Prado (Ire)—Kitten's Joy.
Elusive Quality—Smarty Jones.
Erins Isle (Ire)—Laugh and Be Merry.
Exclusive Native—Affirmed (1977, '78, '79), Genuine Risk, Outstandingly.
Fappiano—Tasso, Unbridled, Rubiano.
Faraway Son—Waya (Fr).
Far North—The Wicked North.
Firestreak—*Snow Knight.
First Landing—Riva Ridge.
***Forli**—Forego (1974, '75, '76, '77).
French Deputy—Left Bank.
Gallant Romeo—Gallant Bob, My Juliet.
Gone West—Speightstown.
Graustark—Key to the Mint, Tempest Queen.
Great Above—Holy Bull.
***Grey Dawn II**—Christmas Past, Heavenly Cause.
Gulch—Thunder Gulch.
Habitat—Steinlen (GB).
Hail the Pirates—Wayward Lass.
Hail to Reason—Trillion.
Halo—Devil's Bag, Glorious Song, Sunday Silence.
Hennessy—Johannesburg.
***Herbager**—Our Mims.
His Majesty—Pleasant Colony, Tight Spot.
Hoist the Flag—Sensational.
Holy Bull—Macho Uno.
Honour and Glory—Caressing.
Horatius—Safely Kept.
Ile de Bourbon—Inlander (GB).
In Reality—Desert Vixen, Smile.
In the Wings (GB)—Singspiel (Ire).

Leading Sires

By number of titles won, including Horse of the Year
11—Mr. Prospector
9—Seattle Slew
8—Alydar
7—Exclusive Native
7—*Forli
6—Bold Ruler
6—Ole Bob Bowers
5—Deputy Minister
5—Sadler's Wells
5—Transworld

By Individual Winners
10—Mr. Prospector
6—Seattle Slew
5—Alydar
4—Sadler's Wells

Irish Castle—Bold Forbes.
Irish River (Fr)—Hatoof, Paradise Creek.
Jade Hunter—Azeri (2002, '03, '04).
Java Gold—Kona Gold.
Kahyasi—Hirapour (Ire).
Key to the Mint—Jewel Princess, Plugged Nickle.
Kingmambo—Lemon Drop Kid.
Kris—All Gong (GB).
Kris S.—Action This Day, Hollywood Wildcat, Soaring Softly.
Lear Fan—Ryafan.
Licencioso—*Gran Kan.
Little Missouri—Prairie Bayou.
Lively One—Answer Lively.
Lord Gaylord—Lord Avie.
***Lorenzaccio**—Zaccio (1980, '81, '82).
Lt. Stevens—Chou Croute.
Lyphard—Manila.
Lypheor (GB)—Royal Heroine (Ire).
Malibu Moon—Declan's Moon.
Marquetry—Artax, Squirtle Squirt.
Maudlin—Beautiful Pleasure.
Meadowlake—Meadow Star.
Medieval Man—Not Surprising.
Minnesota Mac—Mac Diarmida.
Miswaki—Black Tie Affair (Ire).
Mo Bay—Flatterer (1983, '84, '85, '86).

Mr. Prospector—Aldebaran, Conquistador Cielo, Eillo, Forty Niner, Gold Beauty, Golden Attraction, Gulch, It's in the Air, Queena, Rhythm.
Mt. Livermore—Housebuster (1990, '91), Eliza, Orientate.
*Mystic II—Life's Illusion, Soothsayer.
Nashua—Shuvee.
Nashwan—Wandesta (GB).
Naskra—Star de Naskra.
Native Born—Chinook Pass.
Never Bend—J. O. Tobin, Straight and True.
Nijinsky II—De La Rose, Ferdinand, Sky Classic.
*Noholme II—Shecky Greene.
Norcliffe—Groovy.
No Robbery—Track Robbery.
Northern Baby—Highland Bud, Possibly Perfect, Warm Spell.
Northern Jove—Candy Eclair.
Nureyev—Miesque (1987, '88), Theatrical (Ire).
Nureyev Dancer—Pompeyo (Chi).
Olden Times—Roving Boy.
Ole Bob Bowers—John Henry (1980, '81, '83, '84).
Our Emblem—War Emblem.
Our Jimmy—Jimmy Lorenzo (GB).
Our Native—Rockhill Native.
Palace Music—Cigar (1995, '96).
*Petrone—Brown Bess.
Phone Trick—Favorite Trick, Phone Chatter.
Pivotal—Golden Apples (Ire).
Pleasant Colony—Pleasant Stage, Pleasant Tap.
*Pretendre—Canonero II.
Prince John—Protagonist, Typecast.
Private Account—Inside Information, Personal Ensign.
Quadrangle—Smart Angle, Susan's Girl (1972, '73, '75).
Quiet American—Hidden Lake, Real Quiet.
Rahy—Fantastic Light, Serena's Song.
Rainbow Quest—Fiji (GB).
Rainy Lake—Lakeville Miss.
Raise a Cup—Before Dawn.
Rajab—Brave Raj.
Raja Baba—Sacahuista.
Red Ransom—Perfect Sting.
Reflected Glory—Snow Chief.
Reviewer—Revidere, Ruffian (1974, '75).
Roberto—Sunshine Forever.
Rock Talk—Heartlight No. One.
Roi Normand—Riboletta (Brz).
Runaway Groom—Cherokee Run.
Run the Gantlet—April Run (Ire).
Sadler's Wells—Correggio (Ire), High Chaparral (Ire) (2002, '03), Islington (Ire), Northern Spur (Ire).
Saint Ballado—Ashado.
*Sea-Bird—Little Current.
Seattle Slew—A. P. Indy, Capote, Landaluce, Slew o' Gold (1983, '84), Surfside, Swale, Vindication.
Secretariat—Lady's Secret, Risen Star.
Seeking the Gold—Flanders, Heavenly Prize.
Sharpen Up (GB)—Pebbles (GB).
Silver Buck—Silver Charm.
Silver Deputy—Silverbulletday (1998, '99).
Sir Ivor—Bates Motel.
SkipTrial—Skip Away (1996, '97, '98).
*Sky High II—Autobiography.
Skywalker—Bertrando.
Sovereign Dancer—Itsallgreektome.
Speak John—Talking Picture.
Spring Double—Martie's Anger.
Stage Door Johnny—Johnny D., Late Bloomer.
State Dinner—Family Style.
Stop the Music—Temperence Hill.
Storm Cat—Storm Flag Flying, Sweet Catomine.
Strawberry Road (Aus)—Ajina, Escena.
Summer Squall—Charismatic, Storm Song.
Summing—Epitome.
Swoon's Son—Chris Evert.
Tale of Two Cities—*Cougar II.
Tarboosh—Just a Game (Ire).
Targowice—All Along (Fr).
Thunder Gulch—Point Given.
Time for a Change—Fly So Free.
Timeless Moment—Gilded Time.
Tom Rolfe—Bowl Game, Run the Gantlet.
Top Command—Mom's Command.
Topsider—North Sider.
Transworld—Lonesome Glory (1992, '93, '95, '97, '99).
Two Punch—Smoke Glacken.
Unbridled—Anees, Banshee Breeze, Halfbridled.
*Vaguely Noble—Dahlia, Estrapade, Lemhi Gold.
Verbatim—Princess Rooney.
Vice Regent—Deputy Minister.
Wavering Monarch—Maria's Mon.
What a Pleasure—Foolish Pleasure, Honest Pleasure.
What Luck—Ambassador of Luck, What a Summer.
Woodman—Hansel, Timber Country.

Daily Racing Form/NTRA
National Handicapping Championship

Consistency paid off handsomely for Jamie Michelson Jr., a West Bloomfield, Michigan, advertising executive who won the sixth annual *Daily Racing Form*/NTRA National Handicapping Championship on January 22, 2005, in Las Vegas. Although he placed no higher than fifth in the two days of competition, his $240.40 total gave him the title by $31.60 and the $200,000 first-place prize.

Michelson, who reached the finals through a You bet.com online contest, played with his father, James Michelson Sr., who had qualified by winning a contest at Thistledown. His father finished out of the money against 213 other players but counseled his son to stick with his picks. The younger Michelson said that advice probably gave him the victory.

Michelson is a lifelong friend of Steve Wolfson Jr.,

winner of the 2003 contest and a qualifier for the '05 tournament. They met as youngsters when their parents took them on trips to Saratoga Springs, New York, for the summer racing season.

The winner benefited from changes in the leader board for the two days of championship play. He finished fifth on the first day, and was 13th on the second day. But his two-day total was enough to give him the win over Michael Conway of Glencoe, Illinois, who had been third on the first day and briefly led on the second day. Michelson took home the first-place money with consistency in the eight required races and a $35.60 winner on one of his seven optional plays.

The winner of each year's championship is offered an opportunity to accept the Handicapper of the Year trophy at the Eclipse Awards ceremony.

Year	Winner	Residence	Winning Total
2005	Jamie Michelson Jr.	West Bloomfield, Mi.	$240.40
2004	Kent Meyer	Sioux City, Ia.	238.40
2003	Steve Wolfson Jr.	Port Orange, Fl.	279.60
2002	Herman Miller	Oakland, Ca.	205.30
2001	Judy Wagner	New Orleans, La.	237.70
2000	Steve Walker	Lincoln, Ne.	305.40

2004 Eclipse Award Winners

GHOSTZAPPER
Horse of the Year
Older Male
2000 b. h., Awesome Again—Baby Zip,
by Relaunch
Breeder: Adena Springs (Ky.)
Owner: Stronach Stables
Trainer: Bobby Frankel
2004 Record: 4-4-0-0, $2,590,000
Lifetime Record Through 2004: 10-8-0-1, $2,996,120
2004 Stakes Victories: Breeders' Cup Classic (G1),
Woodward S. (G1), Tom Fool H. (G2), Philip H. Iselin
Breeders' Cup H. (G3)

Ghostzapper claimed honors as champion older male and Horse of the Year off a perfect season, albeit the briefest Horse of the Year campaign ever. His four starts all were in stakes races, and he successfully progressed from seven furlongs in the Tom Fool Handicap (G2), his 2004 debut in July, through the 1¼ miles of the Breeders' Cup Classic (G1), in which he set a stakes and track record, 1:59.02. A son of 1998 Breeders' Cup Classic winner Awesome Again, Ghostzapper had established his credentials as a sprinter of the highest quality in 2003, when he won the Vosburgh Stakes (G1) in a fast time. After the Tom Fool, trainer Bobby Frankel next dispatched Ghostzapper to Monmouth Park, where he trounced his overmatched rivals in the Philip H. Breeders' Cup Handicap (G3). He encountered some traffic difficulties in the Woodward Stakes (G1) and won by only a neck over Saint Liam. Frank Stronach's homebred colt was at his best for the Breeders' Cup Classic, in which he went to the lead early and won by three lengths over Roses in May.

DECLAN'S MOON
Two-Year-Old Male
2002 dk. b. or br. g., Malibu Moon—Vee Vee Star, by
Norquestor
Breeder: Brice Ridgely (Md.)
Owner: Jay Em Ess Stable
Trainer: Ron Ellis
2004 Record: 4-4-0-0, $507,300
2004 Stakes Victories: Hollywood Futurity (G1), Del
Mar Futurity (G2), Hollywood Prevue S. (G3)

The juvenile season of Declan's Moon was perfection, four wins in four starts, but he had to wait until mid-December to lock up his title as champion two-year-old male. On December 18, the gelding scored a one-length victory over Giacomo in the Hollywood Futurity (G1), with upset Breeders' Cup Juvenile (G1) victor Wilko checking in third, a nose farther back. Declan's Moon won his maiden victory at Del Mar by five lengths and then upset 1-to-10 favorite Roman Ruler in the Del Mar Futurity (G2). Declan's Moon passed up the Juvenile and won the Hollywood Prevue Stakes (G3) before the Futurity. Declan's Moon and Wilko shared a 126-pound impost in the Experimental Free Handicap.

SWEET CATOMINE
Two-Year-Old Filly
2002 b. f., Storm Cat—Sweet Life, by Kris S.
Owners-Breeders: Martin and Pamela Wygod (Ky.)
Trainer: Julio Canani
2004 Record: 4-3-1-0, $799,800

2004 Stakes Victories: Breeders' Cup Juvenile Fillies
(G1), Del Mar Debutante S. (G1), Oak Leaf S. (G2)

After losing her debut in a race that probably was too short in distance for her, Sweet Catomine put together a perfect march to the two-year-old filly title with three wins that paralleled the course of 2003 champion juvenile filly Halfbridled. Sweet Catomine moved to the fore in the Del Mar Debutante Stakes (G1), scoring her maiden victory in the Grade 1 race, and then prepared for the Breeders' Cup Juvenile Fillies (G1) with a four-length victory in the Oak Leaf Stakes (G2) in 1:42.98 for 1¹⁄₁₆ miles. She was equally impressive in the Breeders' Cup race at Lone Star Park, overcoming traffic difficulties at the top of the stretch and winning by 3¾ lengths.

SMARTY JONES
Three-Year-Old Male
2001 ch. c., Elusive Quality—I'll Get Along, by Smile
Owner-Breeder: Someday Farm (Pa.)
Trainer: John C. Servis
2004 Record: 7-6-1-0, $7,563,535
Lifetime Record Through 2004: 9-8-1-0, $7,613,155
2004 Stakes Victories: Kentucky Derby (G1), Preakness S. (G1), Arkansas Derby (G2), Rebel S., Southwest S., Count Fleet S.

Few horses in recent decades have captured the affection of the American public—both racing fans and others—as completely and wholeheartedly as Smarty Jones, who missed winning the Triple Crown by a length in the Belmont Stakes (G1). His 1½-length victory in the Arkansas Derby (G2) was his first venture in a graded stakes; in his prior start, he had won the listed Rebel Stakes by 3¼ lengths to become eligible for Oaklawn Park's centennial $5-million bonus for sweeping the Arkansas track's major three-year-old races and the Kentucky Derby (G1). By the first Saturday in May, Smarty Jones was the horse to beat, and he triumphed easily in the Derby. Two weeks later, he soared away from his opponents and won the Preakness Stakes (G1) by a record 11½ lengths.

ASHADO
Three-Year-Old Filly
2001 dk. b. or br. f., Saint Ballado—Goulash,
by Mari's Book
Breeders: Aaron U. and Marie D. Jones (Ky.)
Owners: Starlight Stables, Paul Saylor, and Johns
Martin
Trainer: Todd A. Pletcher
2004 Record: 8-5-2-1, $2,259,640
Lifetime Record Through 2004: 14-9-3-2, $2,870,440
2004 Stakes Victories: Breeders' Cup Distaff (G1),
Kentucky Oaks (G1), Coaching Club American Oaks
(G1), Fair Grounds Oaks (G2), Cotillion H. (G2)

With three Grade 1 victories in 2004, including a decisive victory in the Breeders' Cup Distaff (G1), Ashado was the clear choice for champion three-year-old filly by season's end. Despite finishing on the board in all eight of her 2004 starts, her third-place finish behind Society Selection and Stellar Jayne in Saratoga Race Course's Alabama Stakes (G1) in August had raised some questions. Before that race, she had won the Fair Grounds Oaks (G2), Kentucky Oaks (G1), and Coaching Club American Oaks (G1), and had finished second in the Ashland Stakes (G1) and Mother Goose Stakes (G1). After the Alabama, trainer Todd Pletcher sent Ashado to Philadelphia Park for an easy Breeders' Cup warm-up in the Cotillion Handicap (G2).

AZERI
Older Female
1998 ch. m., Jade Hunter—Zodiac Miss (Aus), by Ahonoora
Breeder: Allen E. Paulson (Ky.)
Owner: Allen E. Paulson Living Trust
Trainer: D. Wayne Lukas
2004 Record: 8-3-2-0, $1,035,000
Lifetime Record Through 2004: 24-17-4-0, $4,079,820
2004 Stakes Victories: Apple Blossom H. (G1), Overbrook Spinster S. (G1), Go for Wand H. (G1)

Azeri concluded her amazing career in 2004 with her third consecutive title as champion older female. She also had been voted Horse of the Year in 2002. D. Wayne Lukas took over her training in 2004 from Laura de Seroux and the mare opened the season with her third straight victory in Oaklawn Park's Apple Blossom Handicap (G1). She was second in the Humana Distaff Handicap (G1), and then ran poorly in the Metropolitan Handicap (G1) against males. After a distant fourth in the Ogden Phipps Handicap (G1) at Belmont Park in June, she bounced back to win Saratoga Race Course's Go for Wand Handicap (G1). Azeri faded to finish second in the Personal Ensign Handicap (G1) at 1¼ miles, and then won Keeneland Race Course's Overbrook Spinster Stakes (G1). She passed up the Breeders' Cup Distaff (G1) and ran fifth in the Breeders' Cup Classic (G1). She was retired as the richest North American-raced female.

KITTEN'S JOY
Turf Male
2001 ch. c., El Prado (Ire)—Kitten's First, by Lear Fan
Owners-Breeders: Ken and Sarah Ramsey (Ky.)
Trainer: Dale L. Romans
2004 Record: 8-6-2-0, $1,625,796
Lifetime Record Through 2004: 12-8-3-0, $1,705,911
2004 Stakes Victories: Joe Hirsch Turf Classic Invitational S. (G1), Secretariat S. (G1), Virginia Derby (G3), American Turf S. (G3), Tropical Park Derby (G3), Palm Beach S. (G3)

With six stakes victories on six different turf courses, three-year-old Kitten's Joy became the first North American-based male turf champion since Buck's Boy in 1998. He ended the year with a troubled second-place finish in the Breeders' Cup Turf (G1), a race he very well might have won if he had not found himself in trouble repeatedly. After four Grade 3 wins, Kitten's Joy successfully made the jump to Grade 1 competition in the Secretariat Stakes at Arlington Park. He then showed himself to be the best North American grass competitor with a decisive win in the Joe Hirsch Turf Classic Invitational Stakes (G1) in October.

OUIJA BOARD (GB)
Turf Female
2001 b. f., Cape Cross (Ire)—Selection Board, by Welsh Pageant
Breeder: Stanley Estate and Stud Co. (GB)
Owner: Lord Derby

Trainer: Edward Dunlop
2004 Record: 5-4-0-1, $1,659,958
Lifetime Record Through 2004: 8-5-0-3, $1,671,768
2004 Stakes Victories: Breeders' Cup Filly and Mare Turf (G1), Epsom Oaks (Eng-G1), Darley Irish Oaks (Ire-G1), Pretty Polly S.

Bet down to 9-to-10 in the Breeders' Cup Filly and Mare Turf (G1), Lord Derby's Ouija Board (GB) won by 1½ lengths over Film Maker and solidified her dominance on both sides of the Atlantic Ocean. She won the Pretty Polly Stakes in her 2004 debut and then crushed her opponents in the Epsom Oaks (Eng-G1), drawing away to a seven-length victory. She then added a triumph in the Darley Irish Oaks (Ire-G1). She finished third against males in the Prix de l'Arc de Triomphe (Fr-G1) in early October before her trip to Lone Star Park.

SPEIGHTSTOWN
Sprinter
1998 ch. h., Gone West—Silken Cat, by Storm Cat
Breeders: Aaron U. and Marie D. Jones (Ky.)
Owners: Eugene and Laura Melnyk
Trainer: Todd A. Pletcher
2004 Record: 6-5-0-1, $1,045,556
Lifetime Record Through 2004: 16-10-2-2, $1,258,256
2004 Stakes Victories: Breeders' Cup Sprint (G1), Churchill Downs H. (G2), True North Breeders' Cup H. (G2), Alfred G. Vanderbilt H. (G2), Artax H.

A $2-million yearling purchase in 1999, Speightstown took several years to achieve the promise of his pedigree, and he did so with a rock-solid 2004 season that culminated with a decisive victory in the Breeders' Cup Sprint (G1). Trainer Todd Pletcher brought him along carefully, starting with a victory in the listed Artax Stakes at Gulfstream Park in late March and then sending him through a series of Grade 2 races, all victories. In his first Grade 1 attempt in the Vosburgh Stakes, however, he bobbled at the start and finished third behind Pico Central (Brz), the Metropolitan Handicap (G1) winner who passed up the Breeders' Cup.

HIRAPOUR (Ire)
Steeplechaser
1996 b. g., Kahyasi—Himara, by Mouktar
Breeder: H. H. the Aga Khan's Stud S. C. (Ire)
Owner: Eldon Farm
Trainer: P. Douglas Fout
2004 Record: 4-2-2-0, $199,625
Lifetime Record Through 2004: 32-13-5-2, $373,401
2004 Stakes Victories: Marion duPont Scott Colonial Cup Hurdle S., Royal Chase for the Sport of Kings Hurdle S.

Hirapour (Ire), a product of the Aga Khan's stud, had found his niche over hurdles in England in 2003, twice winning by 22 lengths, and he won his first two North American starts that fall in the silks of new owner Eldon Farm. The Kahyasi gelding came into his own in 2004, with major victories surrounding a second-place finish to '03 champion McDynamo in the Breeders' Cup Steeplechase. In mid-April, Hirapour won the Royal Chase for the Sport of Kings Hurdle Stakes at Keeneland Race Course. After missing the summer with minor foot problems, Hirapour was second in the Breeders' Cup Steeplechase before soaring to a 2¼-length triumph in the Marion duPont Scott Colonial Cup Hurdle Stakes in course-record time.

Champions Before Eclipse Awards

Daily Racing Form (DRF) began naming champions in 1936. Beginning in 1950, the Thoroughbred Racing Associations (TRA) began naming its own champions. The following tables reflect the horses named champions by those two organizations. Where neither the letter (D) nor (T) follows the name of the horse, both the DRF and the TRA named that horse champion. When there were different champions named in any category, the DRF champion is noted with the letter (D) and the TRA with the letter (T). *Daily Racing Form*, the TRA, and the National Turf Writers Association joined forces in 1971 to create the Eclipse Awards, which now recognize the champions of racing in North America.

†-filly, *-imported horse; (D) *Daily Racing Form*; (T) Thoroughbred Racing Associations

Horse of the Year

1970	Fort Marcy (D)
	Personality (T)
1969	Arts and Letters
1968	Dr. Fager
1967	Damascus
1966	Buckpasser
1965	Roman Brother (D)
	†Moccasin (T)
1964	Kelso
1963	Kelso
1962	Kelso
1961	Kelso
1960	Kelso
1959	Sword Dancer
1958	Round Table
1957	Bold Ruler (D)
	Dedicate (T)
1956	Swaps
1955	Nashua
1954	Native Dancer
1953	Tom Fool
1952	One Count (D)
	Native Dancer (T)
1951	Counterpoint
1950	Hill Prince
1949	Capot
1948	Citation
1947	Armed
1946	Assault
1945	†Busher
1944	†Twilight Tear
1943	Count Fleet
1942	Whirlaway
1941	Whirlaway
1940	Challedon
1939	Challedon
1938	Seabiscuit
1937	War Admiral
1936	Granville

Two-Year-Old Male

1970	Hoist the Flag
1969	Silent Screen
1968	Top Knight
1967	Vitriolic
1966	Successor
1965	Buckpasser
1964	Bold Lad
1963	Hurry to Market
1962	Never Bend
1961	Crimson Satan
1960	Hail to Reason
1959	Warfare
1958	First Landing
1957	Nadir (D)
	Jewel's Reward (T)

1956	Barbizon
1955	Needles
1954	Nashua
1953	Porterhouse
1952	Native Dancer
1951	Tom Fool
1950	Battlefield
1949	Hill Prince
1948	Blue Peter
1947	Citation
1946	Double Jay
1945	Star Pilot
1944	Pavot
1943	Platter
1942	Count Fleet
1941	Alsab
1940	Our Boots
1939	Bimelech
1938	El Chico
1937	Menow
1936	Pompoon

Two-Year-Old Filly

1970	Forward Gal
1969	Fast Attack (D)
	Tudor Queen (T)
1968	Gallant Bloom (D)
	Process Shot (T)
1967	Queen of the Stage
1966	Regal Gleam
1965	Moccasin
1964	Queen Empress
1963	Tosmah (D)
	Castle Forbes (T)
1962	Smart Deb
1961	Cicada
1960	Bowl of Flowers
1959	My Dear Girl
1958	Quill
1957	Idun
1956	Leallah (D)
	Romanita (T)
1955	Doubledogdare (D)
	Nasrina (T)
1954	High Voltage
1953	Evening Out
1952	Sweet Patootie
1951	Rose Jet
1950	Aunt Jinny
1949	Bed o' Roses
1948	Myrtle Charm
1947	Bewitch
1946	First Flight
1945	Beaugay
1944	Busher
1943	Durazna
1942	Askmenow

Three-Year-Old Male

1970	Personality
1969	Arts and Letters
1968	Stage Door Johnny
1967	Damascus
1966	Buckpasser
1965	Tom Rolfe
1964	Northern Dancer
1963	Chateaugay
1962	Jaipur
1961	Carry Back
1960	Kelso
1959	Sword Dancer
1958	Tim Tam
1957	Bold Ruler
1956	Needles
1955	Nashua
1954	High Gun
1953	Native Dancer
1952	One Count
1951	Counterpoint
1950	Hill Prince
1949	Capot
1948	Citation
1947	Phalanx
1946	Assault
1945	Fighting Step
1944	By Jimminy
1943	Count Fleet
1942	Alsab
1941	Whirlaway
1940	Bimelech
1939	Challedon
1938	Stagehand
1937	War Admiral
1936	Granville

Three-Year-Old Filly

1970	Office Queen (D)
	Fanfreluche (T)
1969	Gallant Bloom
1968	Dark Mirage
1967	Furl Sail (D)
	Gamely (T)
1966	Lady Pitt
1965	What a Treat
1964	Tosmah
1963	Lamb Chop
1962	Cicada
1961	Bowl of Flowers

1960	Berlo
1959	Royal Native (D)
	Silver Spoon (T)
1958	Idun
1957	Bayou
1956	Doubledogdare
1955	Misty Morn
1954	Parlo
1953	Grecian Queen
1952	Real Delight
1951	Kiss Me Kate
1950	Next Move
1949	‡Two Lea
	‡Wistful
1948	Miss Request
1947	But Why Not
1946	Bridal Flower
1945	Busher
1944	Twilight Tear
1943	Stefanita
1942	Vagrancy
1941	Painted Veil
1940	Not awarded
1939	Unerring
1938	Not awarded
1937	Not awarded
1936	Not awarded

‡ (D) co-champions

Handicap Male

1970	Fort Marcy (D)
	Nodouble (T)
1969	Arts and Letters (D)
	Nodouble (T)
1968	Dr. Fager
1967	Damascus (D)
	Buckpasser (T)
1966	Buckpasser (D)
	Bold Bidder (T)
1965	Roman Brother
1964	Kelso
1963	Kelso
1962	Kelso
1961	Kelso
1960	Bald Eagle
1959	Sword Dancer (D)
	Round Table (T)
1958	Round Table
1957	Dedicate
1956	Swaps
1955	High Gun
1954	Native Dancer
1953	Tom Fool
1952	Crafty Admiral
1951	Hill Prince
1950	*Noor
1949	Coaltown
1948	Citation
1947	Armed
1946	Armed
1945	Stymie
1944	Devil Diver
1943	Market Wise
	Devil Diver
1942	Whirlaway
1941	Mioland
1940	Challedon
1939	*Kayak II

1938	Seabiscuit
1937	Seabiscuit
1936	Discovery

Handicap Female

1970	Shuvee
1969	Gallant Bloom (D)
	Gamely (T)
1968	Gamely
1967	Straight Deal
1966	Open Fire (D)
	Summer Scandal (T)
1965	Old Hat
1964	Tosmah (D)
	Old Hat (T)
1963	Cicada
1962	Primonetta
1961	Airmans Guide
1960	Royal Native
1959	Tempted
1958	Bornastar
1957	Pucker Up
1956	Blue Sparkler
1955	Misty Morn (D)
	Parlo (T)
1954	Parlo (D)
	Lavender Hill (T)
1953	Sickle's Image
1952	Real Delight (D)
	Next Move (T)
1951	Bed o' Roses
1950	Two Lea
1949	Bewitch
1948	Conniver
1947	But Why Not
1946	Gallorette
1945	Busher
1944	Twilight Tear
1943	Mar-Kell
1942	Vagrancy
1941	Fairy Chant
1940	War Plumage
1939	Lady Maryland
1938	Marica
1937	Not awarded
1936	Myrtlewood

Sprinter

1970	†Ta Wee
1969	†Ta Wee
1968	Dr. Fager
1967	Dr. Fager
1966	Impressive
1965	†Affectionately
1964	Ahoy
1963	Not awarded
1962	Not awarded
1961	Not awarded
1960	Not awarded
1959	Intentionally
1958	Bold Ruler
1957	Decathlon
1956	Decathlon
1955	Berseem
1954	White Skies
1953	Tom Fool
1952	Tea-Maker
1951	Sheilas Reward
1950	Sheilas Reward

1949	Delegate
	Royal Governor
1948	Coaltown
1947	Polynesian

1947: first year category included

Turf Horse

1970	Fort Marcy
1969	*Hawaii
1968	Dr. Fager (D)
	Fort Marcy (T)
1967	Fort Marcy
1966	Assagai
1965	Parka
1964	*Turbo Jet II
1963	Mongo
1962	Not awarded
1961	T. V. Lark
1960	Not awarded
1959	Round Table
1958	Round Table
1957	Round Table
1956	Career Boy
1955	*St. Vincent
1954	*Stan
1953	*Iceberg II

1953: first year category included

Steeplechase

1970	Top Bid
1969	*L'Escargot
1968	Bon Nouvel
1967	Quick Pitch
1966	Mako (D)
	Tuscalee (T)
1965	Bon Nouvel
1964	Bon Nouvel
1963	Amber Diver
1962	Barnabys Bluff
1961	Peal
1960	Benguala
1959	Ancestor
1958	Neji
1957	Neji
1956	Shipboard
1955	Neji
1954	King Commander
1953	The Mast
1952	Jam (D)
	Oedipus (T)
1951	Oedipus
1950	Oedipus
1949	Trough Hill
1948	American Way
1947	War Battle
1946	Elkridge
1945	Mercator
1944	Rouge Dragon
1943	Brother Jones
1942	Elkridge
1941	Speculate
1940	Not awarded
1939	Not awarded
1938	Not awarded
1937	Jungle King
1936	Bushranger

RACING HALL OF FAME
History of Racing Hall of Fame

The Racing Hall of Fame was founded in 1955 to honor the all-time greats of the sport, though it is largely limited to horses, jockeys, and trainers. Housed in the National Museum of Racing in Saratoga Springs, New York, the Racing Hall of Fame contains plaques that summarize the accomplishments of each inductee.

Each spring, a panel votes on the horses and people nominated for induction into the Hall of Fame. The results are announced in May, and the induction ceremonies take place the second Monday of August in Saratoga Springs. Categories under consideration each year are Contemporary Male, Contemporary Female, Jockey, and Trainer.

Nominees for induction into the Hall of Fame are first obtained from the 125 members of the Hall of Fame voting panel. Unsuccessful candidates who appeared on the final ballot in the previous three years automatically are added to the initial list of candidates. The suggestions then go before a nomination committee, which narrows the names down to five for each category for that year's ballots.

Names of the five finalists in each division then go before the entire voting panel. Beginning in 2005, members of the voting panel cast ballots for three of the five candidates. A candidate must receive at least 75% of the votes cast to be eligible for induction. If more than one candidate receives more than 75% of the votes cast, the one with the most votes will be inducted. In case of ties for the top position, all candidates will be inducted. Before 2005, the top vote-getter in each category was selected as that year's inductee.

From time to time, the Historical Review Committee and the Steeplechase Committee make additional selections to the Hall of Fame.

Hall of Fame Eligibility Criteria:
1. Thoroughbreds become eligible when five calendar years have elapsed between their final racing year and their year of nomination.

2. Eligible Thoroughbreds are classified as Contemporary Male or Female if they have been retired between five and 25 years. Horses that have been retired for more than 25 years are classified as horses of yesteryear and are considered by the Historical Review Committee.

3. Beginning in 2006, active jockeys become eligible after riding Thoroughbreds for 20 years (any interruptions in their careers for injury are not counted against them). Before 2006, the requirement was 15 years.

4. Active trainers become eligible after 25 years as licensed Thoroughbred trainers.

5. The 20- and 25-year requirements may be waived for retired jockeys and trainers, but a five-year waiting period is then observed before they become eligible. In cases of fragile health, the Hall of Fame Committee may request that the five-year waiting period be waived at the discretion of the Executive Committee.

Members of the National Museum of Racing Hall of Fame
Exemplars of Racing (Year Inducted)

John W. Hanes (1982)
C. V. Whitney (1991)
Walter M. Jeffords (1973)
Paul Mellon (1989)
George D. Widener (1971)

Jockeys (Year Inducted)

Frank D. "Dooley" Adams (1970)
John Adams (1965)
Joe Aitcheson Jr. (1978)
Edward Arcaro (1958)
Ted Atkinson (1957)
Braulio Baeza (1976)
Jerry Bailey (1995)
George Barbee (1996)
Carroll K. Bassett (1972)
Russell Baze (1999)
Walter Blum (1987)
George "Pete" Bostwick (1968)
Sam Boulmetis Sr. (1973)
Steve Brooks (1963)
Don Brumfield (1996)
Thomas H. Burns (1983)
James H. Butwell (1984)
J. Dallett "Dolly" Byers (1967)
Steve Cauthen (1994)
Frank Coltiletti (1970)
Angel Cordero Jr. (1988)

Robert H. "Specs" Crawford (1973)
Pat Day (1991)
Eddie Delahoussaye (1993)
Kent Desormeaux (2004)
Lavelle "Buddy" Ensor (1962)
Laverne Fator (1955)
Earlie Fires (2001)
Jerry Fishback (1992)
Andrew "Mack" Garner (1969)
Edward "Snapper" Garrison (1955)
Avelino Gomez (1982)
Henry F. Griffin (1956)
Eric Guerin (1972)
William J. Hartack (1959)
Sandy Hawley (1992)
Albert Johnson (1971)
William J. Knapp (1969)
Julie Krone (2000)
Clarence Kummer (1972)
Charles Kurtsinger (1967)

John P. Loftus (1959)
John Longden (1958)
Daniel A. Maher (1955)
J. Linus McAtee (1956)
Chris McCarron (1989)
Conn McCreary (1975)
Rigan McKinney (1968)
James McLaughlin (1955)
Walter Miller (1955)
Isaac B. Murphy (1955)
Ralph Neves (1960)
Joe Notter (1963)
George M. Odom (1955)
Winfield "Winnie" O'Connor (1956)
Frank O'Neill (1956)
Ivan H. Parke (1978)
Gilbert W. Patrick (1970)
Laffit Pincay Jr. (1975)
Samuel Purdy (1970)
John Reiff (1956)
Alfred Robertson (1971)
John L. Rotz (1983)

Earl Sande (1955)
Carroll H. Schilling (1970)
William Shoemaker (1958)
Willie Simms (1977)
James "Tod" Sloan (1955)
Mike Smith (2003)
Alfred P. "Paddy" Smithwick (1973)
Gary Stevens (1997)
James Stout (1968)
Fred Taral (1955)
Bayard Tuckerman Jr. (1973)
Ron Turcotte (1979)
Nash Turner (1955)
Robert N. Ussery (1980)
Jacinto Vasquez (1998)
Jorge Velasquez (1990)
Thomas Walsh (2005)
Jack Westrope (2002)
George M. Woolf (1955)
Raymond Workman (1956)
Manuel Ycaza (1977)

Trainers (Year Inducted)

Lazaro S. Barrera (1979)
H. Guy Bedwell (1971)
Edward D. Brown (1984)
J. Elliott Burch (1980)
Preston M. Burch (1963)
William P. Burch (1955)
Fred Burlew (1973)
Frank E. Childs (1968)
Henry S. Clark (1982)
W. Burling Cocks (1985)
James P. Conway (1996)
Warren A. "Jimmy" Croll Jr. (1994)
Grover G. "Buddy" Delp (2002)
Neil Drysdale (2000)
William Duke (1956)
Louis Feustel (1964)
James Fitzsimmons (1958)
Robert Frankel (1995)
John M. Gaver Sr. (1966)
Thomas J. Healey (1955)

Sam C. Hildreth (1955)
Hubert "Sonny" Hine (2003)
Max Hirsch (1959)
William J. "Buddy" Hirsch (1982)
Thomas Hitchcock Sr. (1973)
Hollie Hughes (1973)
John J. Hyland (1956)
Hirsch Jacobs (1958)
H. Allen Jerkens (1975)
Philip G. Johnson (1997)
William R. Johnson (1986)
LeRoy Jolley (1987)
Ben A. Jones (1958)
Horace A. "Jimmy" Jones (1959)
Andrew Jackson Joyner (1955)
Thomas J. Kelly (1993)
Lucien Laurin (1977)
J. Howard Lewis (1969)
D. Wayne Lukas (1999)
Horatio Luro (1980)
John E. Madden (1983)

James W. Maloney (1989)
Richard Mandella (2001)
Frank "Pancho" Martin (1981)
Ron McAnally (1990)
Henry McDaniel (1956)
Claude R. "Shug" McGaughey III (2004)
MacKenzie "Mack" Miller (1987)
William Molter Jr. (1960)
William I. Mott (1998)
Winbert Mulholland (1967)
Edward A. Neloy (1983)
John A. Nerud (1972)
Burley Parke (1986)
Angel Penna Sr. (1988)
Jacob Pincus (1988)
John W. Rogers (1955)
James G. Rowe Sr. (1955)
Flint S. "Scotty" Schulhofer (1992)
Jonathan Sheppard (1990)

Robert A. Smith (1976)
Tom Smith (2001)
D. M. "Mike" Smithwick (1971)
Woodford C. "Woody" Stephens (1976)
Meshach "Mesh" Tenney (1991)
Henry J. Thompson (1969)
Harry Trotsek (1984)
Jack C. Van Berg (1985)
Marion H. Van Berg (1970)
Sylvester Veitch (1977)
Robert W. Walden (1970)
Michael Walsh (1997)
Sherrill Ward (1978)
Sidney Watters Jr. (2005)
Frank Whiteley Jr. (1978)
Charles Whittingham (1974)
Ansel Williamson (1998)
G. Carey Winfrey (1975)
William C. Winfrey (1971)
Nicholas P. Zito (2005)

Horses (Year Inducted, Year Foaled)

Ack Ack (1986, 1966)
Affectionately (1989, 1960)
Affirmed (1980, 1975)
All Along (Fr) (1990, 1979)
Alsab (1976, 1939)
Alydar (1989, 1975)
Alysheba (1993, 1984)
American Eclipse (1970, 1814)
A.P. Indy (2000, 1989)
Armed (1963, 1941)
Artful (1956, 1902)
Arts and Letters (1994, 1966)
Assault (1964, 1943)
Battleship (1969, 1927)
Bayakoa (Arg) (1998, 1984)
Bed o' Roses (1976, 1947)
Beldame (1956, 1901)
Ben Brush (1955, 1893)
Bewitch (1977, 1945)
Bimelech (1990, 1937)
Black Gold (1989, 1921)
Black Helen (1991, 1932)
Blue Larkspur (1957, 1926)
Bold 'n Determined (1997, 1977)
Bold Ruler (1973, 1954)
Bon Nouvel (1976, 1960)
Boston (1955, 1833)
Broomstick (1956, 1901)
Buckpasser (1970, 1963)
Busher (1964, 1942)
Bushranger (1967, 1930)
Cafe Prince (1985, 1970)
Carry Back (1975, 1958)
Cavalcade (1993, 1931)
Challedon (1977, 1936)
Chris Evert (1988, 1971)
Cicada (1967, 1959)
Cigar (2002, 1990)
Citation (1959, 1945)
Coaltown (1983, 1945)
Colin (1956, 1905)
Commando (1956, 1898)
Count Fleet (1961, 1940)

Crusader (1995, 1923)
Dahlia (1981, 1970)
Damascus (1974, 1964)
Dance Smartly (2003, 1988)
Dark Mirage (1974, 1965)
Davona Dale (1985, 1976)
Desert Vixen (1979, 1970)
Devil Diver (1980, 1939)
Discovery (1969, 1931)
Domino (1955, 1891)
Dr. Fager (1971, 1964)
Easy Goer (1997, 1986)
Eight Thirty (1994, 1936)
Elkridge (1966, 1938)
Emperor of Norfolk (1988, 1885)
Equipoise (1957, 1928)
Exceller (1999, 1973)
Exterminator (1957, 1915)
Fairmount (1985, 1921)
Fair Play (1956, 1905)
Fashion (1980, 1837)
Firenze (1981, 1884)
Flatterer (1994, 1979)
Flawlessly (2004, 1988)
Foolish Pleasure (1995, 1972)
Forego (1979, 1970)
Fort Marcy (1998, 1964)
Gallant Bloom (1977, 1966)
Gallant Fox (1957, 1927)
*Gallant Man (1987, 1954)
Gallorette (1962, 1942)
Gamely (1980, 1964)
Genuine Risk (1986, 1977)
Go for Wand (1996, 1987)
Good and Plenty (1956, 1900)
Granville (1997, 1933)
Grey Lag (1957, 1918)
Gun Bow (1999, 1960)
Hamburg (1986, 1895)
Hanover (1955, 1884)
Henry of Navarre (1985, 1891)

Hill Prince (1991, 1947)
Hindoo (1955, 1878)
Holy Bull (2001, 1991)
Imp (1965, 1894)
Jay Trump (1971, 1957)
John Henry (1990, 1975)
Johnstown (1992, 1936)
Jolly Roger (1965, 1922)
Kelso (1967, 1957)
Kentucky (1983, 1861)
Kingston (1955, 1884)
Lady's Secret (1992, 1982)
La Prevoyante (1995, 1970)
*L'Escargot (1977, 1963)
Lexington (1955, 1850)
Lonesome Glory (2005, 1988)
Longfellow (1971, 1867)
Luke Blackburn (1955, 1877)
Majestic Prince (1988, 1966)
Man o' War (1957, 1917)
Maskette (2001, 1906)
Miesque (1999, 1984)
Miss Woodford (1967, 1880)
Myrtlewood (1979, 1932)
Nashua (1965, 1952)
Native Dancer (1963, 1950)
Native Diver (1978, 1959)
Needles (2000, 1953)
Neji (1966, 1950)
*Noor (2002, 1945)
Northern Dancer (1976, 1961)
Oedipus (1978, 1946)
Old Rosebud (1968, 1911)
Omaha (1965, 1932)
Pan Zareta (1972, 1910)
Parole (1984, 1873)
Paseana (Arg) (2001, 1987)
Personal Ensign (1993, 1984)
Peter Pan (1956, 1904)
Precisionist (2003, 1981)
Princess Doreen (1982, 1921)
Princess Rooney (1991, 1980)

Real Delight (1987, 1949)
Regret (1957, 1912)
Reigh Count (1978, 1925)
Riva Ridge (1998, 1969)
Roamer (1981, 1911)
Roseben (1956, 1901)
Round Table (1972, 1954)
Ruffian (1976, 1972)
Ruthless (1975, 1864)
Salvator (1955, 1886)
Sarazen (1957, 1921)
Seabiscuit (1958, 1933)
Searching (1978, 1952)
Seattle Slew (1981, 1974)
Secretariat (1974, 1970)
Serena's Song (2002, 1992)
Shuvee (1975, 1966)
Silver Spoon (1978, 1956)
Sir Archy (1955, 1805)
Sir Barton (1957, 1916)
Skip Away (2004, 1993)
Slew o' Gold (1992, 1980)
Spectacular Bid (1982, 1976)
Stymie (1975, 1941)
Sun Beau (1996, 1925)
Sunday Silence (1996, 1986)
Susan's Girl (1976, 1969)
Swaps (1966, 1952)
Sword Dancer (1977, 1956)
Sysonby (1956, 1902)
Ta Wee (1994, 1966)
Ten Broeck (1982, 1872)
Tim Tam (1985, 1955)
Tom Fool (1960, 1949)
Top Flight (1966, 1929)
Tosmah (1984, 1961)
Twenty Grand (1957, 1928)
Twilight Tear (1963, 1941)
Two Lea (1982, 1946)
War Admiral (1958, 1934)
Whirlaway (1959, 1938)
Whisk Broom II (1979, 1907)
Winning Colors (2000, 1985)
Zaccio (1990, 1976)
Zev (1983, 1920)

Owners of Racing Hall of Fame Members

H. C. Applegate—Old Rosebud

Augustin Stables—Cafe Prince

E. J. "Lucky" Baldwin—Emperor of Norfolk

Edith W. Bancroft—Damascus

Belair Stud—Gallant Fox, Granville, Johnstown, Nashua, Omaha

August Belmont II—Beldame, Fair Play, Henry of Navarre

Col. E. R. Bradley—Bimelech, Black Helen, Blue Larkspur, Busher

William Brann—Challedon, Gallorette

Briardale Farm—Tosmah

Brookmeade Stable—Bowl of Flowers, Cavalcade, Sword Dancer

S. S. Brown—Broomstick

Calumet Farm—Alydar, Armed, Bewitch, Citation, Coaltown, Davona Dale, Real Delight, Tim Tam, Twilight Tear, Two Lea, Whirlaway

Christopher T. Chenery (Meadow Stable)—Hill Prince

Christiana Stable—Go for Wand

Claiborne Farm—Round Table

Gen. Nathaniel Coles—American Eclipse

E. T. Colton—Pan Zareta

Brownell Combs—Myrtlewood

Sidney H. Craig—Paseana (Arg)

Warren A. "Jimmy" Croll Jr.—Holy Bull

J. F. Cushman and E. V. Snedeker—Kingston

D & H Stable—Needles

Marcus Daly—Hamburg

Dotsam Stable—John Henry

Allaire duPont—Kelso

Mike Dwyer—Ben Brush

Phil and Mike Dwyer—Hanover, Hindoo, Kingston, Luke Blackburn, Miss Woodford

Rex Ellsworth—Swaps

Equusequity Stable—Slew o' Gold

Diana Firestone—Genuine Risk

Mr. and Mrs. E. E. Fogelson—Ack Ack

Dr. Ernest Gaillard, Arthur B. Hancock III, and Charles Whittingham—Sunday Silence

Gedney Farm—Gun Bow

Martha F. Gerry—Forego

William Gibbons—Fashion

Greentree Stable—Devil Diver, Tom Fool, Twenty Grand

John L. Greer—Foolish Pleasure

Harry Guggenheim—Ack Ack

James Ben Ali Haggin—Firenze, Salvator

Harbor View Farm—Affirmed, Flawlessly

Dan Harness—Imp

Frank Harper—Ten Broeck

John Harper—Longfellow

Hawksworth Farm—Spectacular Bid

Mrs. John D. Hertz—Count Fleet, Reigh Count

Carolyn Hine—Skip Away

Max Hirsch—Grey Lag

Thomas Hitchcock—Elkridge, Good and Plenty

Fred Hooper—Precisionist, Susan's Girl

Rosa M. Hoots—Black Gold

Charles S. Howard—*Noor, Seabiscuit

Nelson Bunker Hunt—Dahlia, Exceller

John Hunter, George Osgood, and William Travers—Kentucky

Ethel Jacobs—Affectionately, Searching, Stymie

Kay Jeffords—Lonesome Glory

Col. William R. Johnson—Boston, Sir Archy

Davy C. Johnson—Roseben

B. B. and Monfort Jones—Princess Doreen

James R. Keene—Colin, Commando, Maskette, Peter Pan, Sysonby

James R. and Foxhall Keene—Domino

Kerr Stable—Round Table

Willis Sharpe Kilmer—Exterminator, Sun Beau

King Ranch—Assault, Gallant Bloom

Eugene Klein—Winning Colors

Mr. and Mrs. Eugene Klein—Lady's Secret

Eugene Leigh and Ed Brown—Ben Brush

Jean-Louis Levesque—La Prevoyante

Robert and Beverly Lewis—Serena's Song

Locust Hill Farm—Ruffian

Pierre Lorillard—Parole

Ralph Lowe—*Gallant Man

John E. Madden—Hamburg

Harry Mangurian Jr.—Desert Vixen

Louis B. Mayer—Busher

Bryon McClelland—Henry of Navarre

Frank McMahon—Majestic Prince

Meadow Stable (Christopher T. Chenery)—Cicada, Riva Ridge, Secretariat

Paul Mellon (Rokeby Stable)—Arts and Letters

J. Cal Milam—Exterminator

Andrew Miller—Roamer

Kent Miller—Elkridge

Lloyd Miller—Dark Mirage

Francis Morris—Ruthless

Mrs. Lewis C. Murdock—Zaccio

J. F. Newman—Pan Zareta

Stavros Niarchos—Miesque

Jonathan Sheppard, William Pape, and George Harris—Flatterer

Allen E. Paulson—Cigar

William Haggin Perry—Gamely

Lillian Bostwick Phipps—Neji, Oedipus

Ogden Phipps—Buckpasser, Easy Goer, Personal Ensign

Powhatan—*L'Escargot

Jack Price—Carry Back

Rancocas Stable—Zev

Mrs. Theodore Randolph—Bon Nouvel

Glen Riddle Farm—Crusader, Man o' War, War Admiral

Nathaniel Rives—Boston

Rokeby Stable (Paul Mellon)—Fort Marcy

Carl Rosen—Chris Evert

Commander J. K. L. Ross—Sir Barton

Albert Sabath—Alsab

Walter J. Salmon Sr.—Battleship

Sam-Son Farm—Dance Smartly

Saron Stable—Bold 'n Determined

Dorothy and Pamela Scharbauer—Alysheba

Marion duPont Scott—Battleship

Mr. and Mrs. L. K. Shapiro—Native Diver

Harry Sinclair—Grey Lag

Mrs. Mary Stephenson—Jay Trump

Mrs. Whitney Stone—Shuvee

Tartan Farms—Dr. Fager, Ta Wee

Tayhill Stable—Seattle Slew

E. P. Taylor—Northern Dancer

Richard Ten Broeck—Lexington

Tomonori Tsurumaki and Farish-Goodman-Kilroy—A.P. Indy

Paula Tucker—Princess Rooney

Cornelius W. Van Ranst—American Eclipse

Alfred G. Vanderbilt—Bed o' Roses, Discovery, Native Dancer

Mrs. W. K. Vanderbilt III—Sarazen

Wheatley Stable—Bold Ruler

Frank and Janis Whitham—Bayakoa (Arg)

C. V. Whitney—Equipoise, Silver Spoon, Top Flight

Harry Payne Whitney—Artful, Regret, Whisk Broom II

Mrs. Payne Whitney—Jolly Roger

George D. Widener—Eight Thirty

Joseph E. Widener—Bushranger, Fairmount

Daniel Wildenstein—All Along (Fr)

Capt. Jim Williams—Luke Blackburn

Breeders of Racing Hall of Fame Members

Muriel Vanderbilt Adams—Desert Vixen

H. H. Aga Khan—*Noor

H. H. Aga Khan and Prince Aly Khan—*Gallant Man

Lucien O. Appleby—Henry of Navarre

F. Wallis Armstrong—Cavalcade

Dr. Howard Baker—Serena's Song

Mrs. Thomas Bancroft—Damascus

Anna Marie Barnhart—Skip Away

Belair Stud—Gallant Fox, Granville, Nashua, Omaha

August Belmont II—Beldame, Fair Play, Man o' War

Bieber-Jacobs Stables—Affectionately

Blue Bear Stud—Zaccio

Idle Hour Stock Farm—Bimelech, Black Helen, Blue Larkspur, Busher, Oedipus
William L. Brann—Challedon
Brookmeade Stable—Bowl of Flowers, Sword Dancer
S. S. Brown—Whisk Broom II
Preston Burch—Gallorette
Calumet Farm—Alydar, Armed, Bewitch, Citation, Coaltown, Davona Dale, Real Delight, Tim Tam, Twilight Tear, Two Lea, Whirlaway
Mrs. Thomas J. Carson—Roseben
Ben Castleman—Seattle Slew
Christopher T. Chenery—Hill Prince
Christiana Stables—Go for Wand
Claiborne Farm—Gamely, Round Table, Slew o' Gold
John Clay—Kentucky
Clay Brothers—Roamer
Gen. Nathaniel Coles—American Eclipse
Brownell Combs—Myrtlewood
Leslie Combs II—Majestic Prince
Dayton Ltd.—All Along (Fr)
Allaire duPont—Kelso
Echo Valley Farm—Chris Evert, Winning Colors
Rex Ellsworth—Swaps
Mrs. Charles W. Engelhard—Exceller
Con Enright—Hamburg
William S. Farish and W. S. Kilroy—A.P. Indy
Joseph F. Flanagan—Elkridge
Flaxman Holdings Ltd.—Miesque
Capt. James and A. C. Franklin—Luke Blackburn
William Gibbons—Fashion
Mrs. William Gilmore and Mrs. William Jason—Spectacular Bid
Golden Chance Farm—John Henry
Greentree Stable—Devil Diver, Jolly Roger, Twenty Grand
Harry Guggenheim—Ack Ack
Arthur B. Hancock Sr.—Johnstown
Haras Principal—Bayakoa (Arg)
Haras Vacacion—Paseana (Arg)
Harbor View Farm—Affirmed, Flawlessly
Dan Harness—Imp
Frank B. Harper—Good and Plenty
John Harper—Ten Broeck, Longfellow
Duval Headley—Dark Mirage, Tom Fool

Leading Breeders of Racing Hall of Fame Horses

11— Calumet Farm
6— James R. Keene
5— Idle Hour Stock Farm
    John Madden*
4— Belair Stud
    Ogden Phipps
3— August Belmont II
    Claiborne Farm
    Greentree Stable
    Meadow Stud
    Daniel Swigert
    Harry Payne Whitney
*Includes partnerships

Mrs. John D. Hertz—Count Fleet
Max Hirsch and King Ranch—Stymie
Fred Hooper—Precisionist, Susan's Girl
Rosa M. Hoots—Black Gold
Mrs. G. Watts Humphrey Jr.—Genuine Risk
Nelson Bunker Hunt—Dahlia
Mr. and Mrs. Stuart S. Janney Jr.—Ruffian
Mrs. William Jason and Mrs. William Gilmore—Spectacular Bid
Walter Jefford Jr.—Lonesome Glory
Marius E. Johnston—Sarazen
James R. Keene—Colin, Commando, Maskette, Peter Pan, Kingston, Sysonby
Willis Sharpe Kilmer—Reigh Count, Sun Beau
King Ranch—Assault, Gallant Bloom, Stymie
Dixie Knight—Exterminator
Gordon E. Layton—Bold 'n Determined
Lazy F Ranch—Forego
W. E. Leach—Needles
Jean-Louis Levesque—La Prevoyante
John E. Madden—Grey Lag, Old Rosebud, Princess Doreen, Zev
John E. Madden and Vivian A. Gooch—Sir Barton
Preston Madden—Alysheba
Maine Chance Farm—Gun Bow
Meadow Stud—Cicada, Riva Ridge, Secretariat
Paul Mellon—Arts and Letters, Fort Marcy
Mereworth Farm—Discovery
Eugene Mori—Tosmah

Francis Morris—Ruthless
J. F. Newman—Pan Zareta
Oak Cliff Thoroughbreds—Sunday Silence
Mrs. B. O'Neill—L'Escargot
William Pape and Jonathan Sheppard—Flatterer
Allen E. Paulson—Cigar
Pelican Stable—Holy Bull
Ogden Phipps—Buckpasser, Easy Goer, Personal Ensign, Searching
Thomas Piatt—Alsab
Jack Price—Carry Back
Dr. A. C. Randolph—Bon Nouvel
Capt. Archibald Randolph and Col. John Tayloe III—Sir Archy
Samuel D. Riddle—Crusader, War Admiral
Ben Roach and Tom Roach—Princess Rooney
Runnymede Farm—Ben Brush, Hanover
Walter J. Salmon—Discovery, Battleship
Sam-Son Farm—Dance Smartly
Marion duPont Scott—Neji
Jan Sensenich—Jay Trump
Mr. and Mrs. L. K. Shapiro—Native Diver
Robert H. Spreen—Lady's Secret
Whitney Stone—Shuvee
Daniel Swigert—Firenze, Hindoo, Salvator
Tartan Farms—Dr. Fager, Ta Wee
E. P. Taylor—Northern Dancer
Maj. Barak Thomas—Domino
Alfred G. Vanderbilt—Bed o' Roses, Native Dancer
Waldemar Farms—Foolish Pleasure
Elisha Warfield—Lexington
Aristides Welch—Parole
Wheatley Stable—Bold Ruler, Seabiscuit
C. V. Whitney—Silver Spoon
Harry Payne Whitney—Equipoise, Regret, Top Flight
William C. Whitney—Artful
John Wickham—Boston
George D. Widener—Eight Thirty
Joseph E. Widener—Bushranger, Fairmount
Verne H. Winchell—Cafe Prince
Theodore Winters—Emperor of Norfolk
Woodford and Clay—Miss Woodford
Col. Milton Young—Broomstick

Trainers of Racing Hall of Fame Members

Note: In instances when more than one trainer had a Hall of Fame horse during the horse's career, all are credited.

William Badgett—Go for Wand
Lazaro Barrera—Affirmed
Guy Bedwell—Sir Barton
John Belcher—Boston
Patrick Biancone—All Along (Fr)
Frank A. Bonsal—Ack Ack
George H. "Pete" Bostwick—Oedipus, Neji
Francois Boutin—Miesque
William Brennan—Twenty Grand
Charles Brossman—Imp
Ed Brown—Ben Brush
Henry Brown—Lexington
William Brown—Parole
J. Elliott Burch—Arts and Letters, Bowl

of Flowers, Fort Marcy, Sword Dancer
Fred Burlew—Beldame
Matt Byrnes—Firenze, Salvator
Don Cameron—Count Fleet
Hardy Campbell—Kingston
Edward A. Christmas—Gallorette
W. Burling Cocks—Zaccio
Harry Colston—Ten Broeck
E. T. Colton—Pan Zareta
George Conway—Crusader, War Admiral
Warren A. "Jimmy" Croll—Holy Bull
James E. Day—Dance Smartly
Grover G. "Bud" Delp—Spectacular Bid
Neil Drysdale—A.P. Indy, Bold 'n Determined, Princess Rooney
Richard Dutrow Sr.—Flawlessly
Ross Fenstermaker—Precisionist, Susan's Girl

Louis Feustel—Man o' War
James "Sunny Jim" Fitzsimmons—Bold Ruler, Gallant Fox, Granville, Johnstown, Nashua, Omaha
Hugh Fontaine—Needles
E. Foucon—Pan Zareta
Willard C. Freeman—Shuvee
John M. Gaver Sr.—Devil Diver, Tom Fool
Jack Goldsborough—Roamer
Carl Hanford—Kelso
John Harper—Longfellow
J.H. "Casey" Hayes—Cicada, Hill Prince
Thomas J. Healey—Equipoise, Top Flight
S. M. Henderson—Princess Doreen
John Hertler—Slew o' Gold
Sam Hildreth—Grey Lag, Zev
Hubert "Sonny" Hine—Skip Away
Max Hirsch—Assault, Gallant Bloom, Sarazen

William Hirsch—Gallant Bloom
Reg Hobbs—Battleship
Freddy Hopkins—Equipoise
Will Hurley—Bimelech, Black Helen
John Hyland—Beldame, Henry of Navarre
Hirsch Jacobs—Affectionately, Searching, Stymie
William R. Johnson—Boston, Sir Archy
LeRoy Jolley—Foolish Pleasure, Genuine Risk
Ben A. Jones—Armed, Bewitch, Citation, Coaltown, Real Delight, Twilight Tear, Two Lea, Whirlaway
Horace A. "Jimmy" Jones—Bewitch, Citation, Coaltown, Tim Tam, Two Lea
Andrew J. Joyner—Fair Play, Whisk Broom II
Charles Kiernan—Good and Plenty
Ray Kindred—Myrtlewood
Everett King—Dark Mirage
Billy Lakeland—Domino, Hamburg
Thomas Larkin—Sir Archy
Lucien Laurin—Riva Ridge, Secretariat
John Lee—Kelso
J. Howard Lewis—Bushranger, Fairmount
John Longden—Majestic Prince
D. Wayne Lukas—Lady's Secret, Serena's Song, Winning Colors
Horatio Luro—Northern Dancer
John E. Madden—Hamburg
James W. Maloney—Gamely
Francois Mathet—Exceller
Ron McAnally—Bayakoa (Arg), John Henry, Paseana (Arg)
Frank McCabe—Hanover
Byron McClelland—Henry of Navarre
John McClelland—Emperor of Norfolk
Henry McDaniel—Exterminator, Reigh Count
Claude R. "Shug" McGaughey III—Easy Goer, Personal Ensign
Joe Mergler—Tosmah
B. S. Michell—Reigh Count
Bruce Miller—Lonesome Glory
Kent Miller—Elkridge
Buster Millerick—Native Diver

Leading Trainers of Racing Hall of Fame Horses

10— James Rowe Sr.
8— Ben A. Jones
6— James "Sunny Jim" Fitzsimmons
5— Horace A. "Jimmy" Jones
   Charlie Whittingham
4— J. Elliott Burch
3— Neil Drysdale
   Max Hirsch
   Hirsch Jacobs
   D. Wayne Lukas
   Ron McAnally
   John Nerud
   Frank Whiteley Jr.
   William C. Winfrey

A. J. Minor—Ruthless
William Molter—Round Table
D. L. Moore—Neji, *L'Escargot
William I. Mott—Cigar
W. F. "Bert" Mulholland—Eight Thirty
Tom Murphy—Twenty Grand
Edward Neloy—Buckpasser, Gun Bow
John Nerud—Dr. Fager, *Gallant Man, Ta Wee
H. S. Newman—Pan Zareta
J. L. Newman—Susan's Girl
Victor J. "Lefty" Nickerson—John Henry
George Odom—Busher
Burley Parke—*Noor
Chuck Parke—Susan's Girl
Douglas R. Peterson—Seattle Slew
Vincent Powers—Jolly Roger
Jack Price—Carry Back
John B. Pryor—Lexington
John W. Rogers—Artful
Tommy Root Sr.—Desert Vixen
James Rowe Jr.—Twenty Grand
James Rowe Sr.—Colin, Commando, Hindoo, Luke Blackburn, Maskette, Miss Woodford, Peter Pan, Regret, Sysonby, Whisk Broom II

John Russell—Precisionist, Susan's Girl
Louis J. Schaefer—Challedon
Flint S. "Scotty" Schulhofer—Ta Wee
Jonathan Sheppard—Cafe Prince, Flatterer
A. Shuttinger—Sun Beau
Robert A. Smith—Cavalcade
Thomas Smith—Seabiscuit
Crompton "Tommy" Smith Jr.—Jay Trump
D. Michael Smithwick—Bon Nouvel, Neji
E. V. Snedeker—Kingston
John Starr—La Prevoyante
J. H. Stotler—Discovery
August "Sarge" Swenke—Alsab
Arthur Taylor—Boston, Sir Archy
M. A. "Mesh" Tenney—Swaps
Bob Thomas—Emperor of Norfolk
H. J. Thompson—Blue Larkspur
G. R. Tompkins—Crusader
Joseph Trovato—Chris Evert
Bob Tucker—Broomstick
William H. Turner Jr.—Seattle Slew
Jack Van Berg—Alysheba
John Veitch—Alydar, Davona Dale
Sherrill Ward—Forego
Sidney Watters Jr.—Slew o' Gold
Hanley Webb—Black Gold
Frank D. Weir—Old Rosebud, Roseben
R. L. Wheeler—Silver Spoon
Frank Whiteley Jr.—Damascus, Forego, Ruffian
Charles Whittingham—Ack Ack, Dahlia, Exceller, Flawlessly, Sunday Silence
J. Whyte—Sun Beau
Capt. Jim Williams—Luke Blackburn
Peter Wimmer—Broomstick, Imp
William C. Winfrey—Bed o' Roses, Buckpasser, Native Dancer
Maurice Zilber—Dahlia, Exceller
Unknown—American Eclipse, Fashion, Kentucky

Sires of Racing Hall of Fame Members

Abe Frank—Pan Zareta
Affirmed—Flawlessly
Ahmad—Paseana (Arg)
Alydar—Alysheba, Easy Goer
*Amerigo—Fort Marcy
Battle Joined—Ack Ack
Ben Brush—Broomstick
*Ben Strome—Roseben
Best Turn—Davona Dale
*Billet—Miss Woodford
Black Servant—Blue Larkspur
Black Toney—Bimelech, Black Gold, Black Helen
*Blenheim II—Whirlaway
Blue Larkspur—Myrtlewood, Oedipus
Bold and Brave—Bold 'n Determined
Bold Bidder—Spectacular Bid
Bold Reasoning—Seattle Slew
Bold Ruler—Gamely, Secretariat
Bold Venture—Assault
*Bonnie Scotland—Luke Blackburn

Boston—Lexington
Bramble—Ben Brush
Broomstick—Regret, Whisk Broom II
Bryan G.—Cicada
Buckpasser—La Prevoyante
Bull Lea—Armed, Bewitch, Citation, Coaltown, Real Delight, Twilight Tear, Two Lea
Caro (Ire)—Winning Colors
*Challenger II—Challedon, Gallorette
Citation—Silver Spoon
Commando—Colin, Peter Pan
Consultant's Bid—Bayakoa (Arg)
Creme dela Creme—Cafe Prince
Crozier—Precisionist
Danzig—Dance Smartly
Deputy Minister—Go for Wand
*Diomed—Sir Archy
*Dis Donc—Top Flight
Disguise—Maskette
Display—Discovery
Domino—Commando

Duc de Fer—Bon Nouvel
Duroc—American Eclipse
*Eclipse—Ruthless
Equestrian—Stymie
Escart III—*L'Escargot
Exclusive Native—Affirmed, Genuine Risk
Fair Play—Fairmount, Man o' War
First Landing—Riva Ridge
*Forli—Forego
Gallant Fox—Granville, Omaha
*Gallant Man—Gallant Bloom
Glenelg—Firenze
Good Goods—Alsab
Great Above—Holy Bull
Gun Shot—Gun Bow
Halo—Sunday Silence
Hamburg—Artful
Hanover—Hamburg
Hard Tack—Seabiscuit
Hastings—Fair Play
High Time—Sarazen

Himyar—Domino
Hindoo—Hanover
*Hunters Moon IV—Neji
Imbros—Native Diver
In Reality—Desert Vixen
Intentionally—Ta Wee
Jamestown—Johnstown
*Khaled—Swaps
*Knight Errant—Roamer
Knight of Ellerslie—Henry of Navarre
*Lancegaye—Cavalcade
*Leamington—Longfellow, Parole
Lexington—Kentucky
*Lorenzaccio—Zaccio
Man o' War—Battleship, Crusader, War Admiral
Mate—Elkridge
*McGee—Exterminator
*Melton—Sysonby
Menow—Tom Fool
*Migoli—*Gallant Man
Mo Bay—Flatterer
*Nasrullah—Bold Ruler, Nashua, *Noor
Nearctic—Northern Dancer
Norfolk—Emperor of Norfolk
Nureyev—Miesque
Octagon—Beldame
Ole Bob Bowers—John Henry
Palace Music—Cigar
Pennant—Equipoise, Jolly Roger
*Persian Road II—Dark Mirage
*Phaeton—Ten Broeck
Pilate—Eight Thirty
Polynesian—Native Dancer
Ponder—Needles
*Prince Charlie—Salvator

Leading Sires of Racing Hall of Fame Horses

7 — Bull Lea
3 — Black Toney
    Man o' War
    *Nasrullah
2 — Alydar
    Blue Larkspur
    Bold Ruler
    Broomstick
    *Challenger II
    Commando
    Exclusive Native
    Fair Play
    Gallant Fox
    *Leamington
    Pennant
    *Princequillo
    Raise a Native
    Seattle Slew
    *St. Germains
    *Star Shoot
    Tom Fool
    *Vaguely Noble
    War Admiral

*Princequillo—Hill Prince, Round Table
Private Account—Personal Ensign
Quadrangle—Susan's Girl
Rahy—Serena's Song
Raise a Native—Alydar, Majestic Prince
Reigh Count—Count Fleet
Reviewer—Ruffian
*Ribot—Arts and Letters

Rosemont—Bed o' Roses
Rossington—Good and Plenty
Rough'n Tumble—Dr. Fager
Saggy—Carry Back
Sailor—Bowl of Flowers
Seattle Slew—A.P. Indy, Slew o' Gold
Secretariat—Lady's Secret
*Sir Gallahad III—Gallant Fox
Skip Trial—Skip Away
*Spanish Prince II—Princess Doreen
Spendthrift—Kingston
*St. Germans—Devil Diver, Twenty Grand
*Star Shoot—Grey Lag, Sir Barton
*Stefan the Great—Bushranger
*Sun Briar—Sun Beau
Sunglow—Sword Dancer
*Sunreigh—Reigh Count
Swaps—Affectionately
Swoon's Son—Chris Evert
Sword Dancer—Damascus
Targowice—All Along (Fr)
The Finn—Zev
Tim Tam—Tosmah
Timoleon—Boston
Tom Fool—Buckpasser, Tim Tam
Tonga Prince—Jay Trump
Transworld—Lonesome Glory
*Trustee—Fashion
Uncle—Old Rosebud
*Vaguely Noble—Dahlia, Exceller
Verbatim—Princess Rooney
Virgil—Hindoo
Wagner—Imp
War Admiral—Busher, Searching
What a Pleasure—Foolish Pleasure
Your Host—Kelso

Regional Halls of Fame

Arlington Park

No new members have been inducted since 1989.

Horses
Armed
Buckpasser
Candy Spots
Citation
Coaltown
Dr. Fager
Equipoise
Nashua
Native Dancer
Round Table
Secretariat
Tom Rolfe
T. V. Lark
Twilight Tear
Jockeys
Eddie Arcaro

Braulio Baeza
Steve Brooks
Doug Dodson
Bill Hartack
Johnny Sellers
Bill Shoemaker
Trainers
William Hal Bishop
Ben Jones
H. A. "Jimmy" Jones
Harry Trotsek
Arnold Winick
Stables
Calumet Farm
Hasty House Farm
William Hal Bishop Stable

Calder Race Course

Calder Race Course created its Hall of Fame in 1995 and annually inducts at least one new member in each of four categories.

Horses (Year Inducted)
Brave Raj (1995)
Carterista (2004)
Chaposa Springs (2003)
Cherokee Run (1998)
Flying Pidgeon (2000)
Hollywood Wildcat (2002)
Judy's Red Shoes (1996)
Mecke (1999)
Princess Rooney (1995)
Smile (1995)
Spend a Buck (1995)
Spirit of Fighter (1997)

The Vid (2001)
Jockeys (Year Inducted)
Eibar Coa (2004)
Mike Gonzalez (2001)
Walter Guerra (1998)
Michael Lee (1996)
Gene St. Leon (1995)
Miguel Rivera (2000)
Mary Russ (2003)
Alex Solis (2002)
Jacinto Vasquez (1999)
Jose Velez Jr. (1997)

Owners-Breeders (Year Inducted)
Arthur Appleton (1999)
Gilbert Campbell (2004)
Cobble View Stable (2001)
Farnsworth Farms (1997)
John Franks (2003)
Frances Genter Stable (1998)
Fred Hooper (1995)
James Lewis Jr. (2000)
Harry T. Mangurian Jr. (1995)
Ocala Stud Farm (2002)
Tartan Farms (1996)

Trainers (Year Inducted)
James Bracken (2000)
Frank Gomez (1995)
Stanley Hough (1996)
Jose "Pepe" Mendez (2004)
Luis Olivares (2002)
Harold Rose (1997)
John Tammaro (1999)
Emanuel Tortora (1998)
Martin D. Wolfson (2003)
Ralph Ziade (2001)

Canterbury Park

Created to honor those who contributed to the track and Minnesota racing, the Canterbury Park Hall of Fame inducts from one to three new members each year.

Horses
Blair's Cove
Come Summer
Hoist Her Flag
Honor the Hero
John Bullit (NZ)
K Z Bay
Northbound Pride
Princess Elaine
Timeless Prince
Valid Leader
Who Doctor Who
Jockeys
Sandy Hawley
Dean Kutz
Luis Quinonez
Mike Smith
Scott Stevens
Trainers
Carl Nafzger

Doug Oliver
Bernell Rhone
Owners
Chuck Bellingham
Frances Genter
Bobbi Knapper
Paul Knapper
Dan Mjolsness
Breeders
Almar Farms
Art and Gretchen Eaton
Robert Morehouse
Others
Brooks Fields
Tom Ryther Sr.
Curtis, Randy, Russ, and Paul Sampson
Dark Star
Jim Wells

Fair Grounds

Fair Grounds established its Hall of Fame in 1971 to honor those who made lasting contributions to racing on both the local and national levels.

Horses
A Letter to Harry
Black Gold
Blushing K. D.
Cabildo
Chou Croute
Colonel Power
Concern
Davona Dale
Diplomat Way
Dixie Poker Ace
Furl Sail
Grindstone
Lecomte
Lexington
Marriage
Master Derby
Mike's Red
Mineshaft
Monarchist
Monique Rene
No Le Hace
Pan Zareta
*Princequillo
Quatrain
Reel
Risen Star
Scott's Scoundrel
Silverbulletday
Spanish Play
Taylor's Special
Tenacious
Tiffany Lass
Tippety Witchet
Whirlaway
Yorktown
Jockeys
Eddie Arcaro
Robby Albarado
Ron Ardoin
Robert L. Baird
Raymond Broussard
Pat Day
Eddie Delahoussaye
Andrew "Uncle Mack" Garner
Edward "Snapper" Garrison
Eric Guerin
Abe Hawkins
Johnny Heckmann
John Longden
J. D. Mooney
Jimmy Nichols
Winnie O'Connor
Craig Perret
Randy Romero
Earle Sande
Bill Shoemaker
James Forman "Tod" Sloan
Larry Snyder
David Whited
Owners-Breeders
Col. Edward R. Bradley

Dorothy Brown
Jack DeFee
Joseph P. Dorignac Jr.
John Franks
T. A. Grissom
William G. Helis Sr.
Samuel Clay Hildreth
Duncan Farrar Kenner
Lane's End
Harvey Peltier
J. R. Strauss Sr.
Thomas Jefferson Wells
Roger W. Wilson
Anthony Zuppardo
Trainers
Tom Amoss
Bobby Barnett
Angel Barrera
W. Hal Bishop
Frank Brothers
Joseph "Spanky" Broussard
Grover "Bud" Delp
Joey Dorignac III
Henry Forrest
Norman "Butsy" Hernandez
Neil Howard
Ben Jones
Jack Lohman
J. O. Meaux
Bill Mott
Homer Pardue
Anthony Pelleteri
Louie Roussel III
Clifford Scott
Dewey Smith
Harry Trotsek
Jack Van Berg
Marion H. Van Berg
C. W. "Cracker" Walker
Vester R. "Tennessee" Wright
Others
Frank "Buddy" Abadie
Eric Wolfson Blind
Richard Ten Broeck
John Blanks Campbell
John F. Clark Jr.
Capt. William Cottrill
Francis Dunne
Marie Krantz
Sylvester W. Labrot Jr.
Allen "Black Cat" LaCombe
John S. Letellier
John G. Masoni
Claude Mauberret Jr.
Mervin H. Muniz Jr.
Joseph A. Murphy
John Kenneth "Jack" O'Hara
Thomas P. Scott
Albert Stall Sr.

Gulfstream Park

Gulfstream Park's Garden of Champions inductees must be retired, have competed at Gulfstream at least once, and have been named divisional champions or have competed against the highest caliber of competition.

Horses
A.P. Indy
Ajina
Alydar
Armed
Artax
Arts and Letters
Bald Eagle

Banshee Breeze
Battlefield
Bayakoa (Arg)
Beautiful Pleasure
Black Tie Affair (Ire)
Blushing John
Bold Ruler
Bowl Game

Buck's Boy
Candy Eclair
Carry Back
Cherokee Run
Chief's Crown
Christmas Past
Cicada
Cigar
Coaltown
Counterpoint
Crafty Admiral
Cryptoclearance
Dark Star
Davona Dale
Daylami (Ire)
Decathlon
Dehere
De La Rose
Deputy Minister
Easy Goer
Eillo
Eliza
Escena
Favorite Trick
Fly So Free
Foolish Pleasure
Forego
Fort Marcy
Forty Niner
Forward Gal
Fraise
Funny Cide
Genuine Risk
Gilded Time
Go for Wand
Groovy
Hansel
Heavenly Prize
Hollywood Wildcat
Holy Bull
Honest Pleasure
Housebuster
Inside Information
Izvestia
Kelso
Lady's Secret
La Prevoyante
Late Bloomer
Left Bank
Lemon Drop Kid

Little Current
Lord Avie
Mac Diarmida
Nashua
Needles
Nodouble
Northern Dancer
Office Queen
Old Hat
Open Mind
Paradise Creek
Parka
Paseana (Arg)
Perfect Sting
Pleasant Colony
Pleasant Tap
Plugged Nickle
Princess Rooney
Roman Brother
Round Table
Rubiano
Sabin
Safely Kept
Sailor
Shecky Greene
Silverbulletday
Silver Charm
Skip Away
Sky Beauty
Sky Classic
Smile
Snow Chief
Soaring Softly
Spectacular Bid
Steinlen (GB)
Sunday Silence
Sunshine Forever
Swale
Swaps
Swoon's Son
Sword Dancer
Thunder Gulch
Tim Tam
Unbridled
Vanlandingham
Victory Gallop
Winning Colors
White Skies
With Approval

Hawthorne Race Course

Hawthorne Race Course launched its Hall of Fame on November 10, 1996, with a tribute to 21 jockey inductees. Trainers were honored for the first time in 1998.

Jockeys (Year Inducted)
Johnny Adams (1996)
Eddie Arcaro (1996)
Ted Atkinson (1996)
Braulio Baeza (1996)
Jerry Bailey (1996)
Robert L. Baird (1997)
Steve Brooks (1996)
Steve Cauthen (1996)
Angel Cordero Jr. (1996)
Pat Day (1996)
Eddie Delahoussaye (1996)
Juvenal Diaz (1998)
Earlie Fires (1997)
Gerland Gallitano (1997)
Chris McCarron (1996)

Randall Meier (1997)
Isaac Murphy (1996)
Laffit Pincay Jr. (1996)
Earle Sande (1996)
Shane Sellers (1997)
Bill Shoemaker (1996)
Ray Sibille (1998)
Carlos Silva (1998)
Ron Turcotte (1996)
Jorge Velasquez (1996)
George Woolf (1996)
Trainers (Year Inducted)
Ernie Poulos (1998)
Jere Smith Sr. (1998)
Other (Year Inducted)
Phil Georgeff (1996)

Monmouth Park

The Hall of Champions was established in 1986 to honor Monmouth-raced horses that achieved success on the national level.

Affectionately
Alydar

Alysheba
Bet Twice

Black Tie Affair (Ire)
Blue Sparkler
Bold Ruler
Buckpasser
Carry Back
Damascus
Dan Horn
Dearly Precious
Decathlon
Dehere
Desert Vixen
First Flight
Forego
Formal Gold
Forty Niner
Friendly Lover
Frisk Me Now
Hansel
Helioscope
Holy Bull
Inside Information
John Henry
Kelso
Lady's Secret
Lord Avie
Lost Code

Majestic Light
Misty Morn
Mongo
Nashua
Needles
Open Mind
Personal Ensign
Point Given
Politely
Polynesian
Riva Ridge
Ruffian
Safely Kept
Serena's Song
Silverbulletday
Skip Away
Smoke Glacken
Spectacular Bid
Spend a Buck
Stymie
Sword Dancer
Ta Wee
Teddy Drone
Touch Gold
With Anticipation

Nebraska Racing Hall of Fame

The Nebraska Racing Hall of Fame was established in 1966. No inductions have been made since 1993.

Horses (Year Inducted)
Gate Dancer (1991)
Omaha (1969)
Rose's Gem (1971)
Who Doctor Who (1993)
Jockeys (Year Inducted)
Irving Anderson (1976)
Steve Brooks (1971)
Earl Dew (1978)
Fred Ecoffey (1981)
Dave Erb (1972)
Ira Hanford (1968)
John Lively (1979)
Charley Thorpe (1978)
Trainers (Year Inducted)
Earl Beezley (1972)
Carl Hanford (1968)
Hoss Inman (1992)
C. B. Irwin (1979)
Robert Irwin (1973)
John Nerud (1970)
Lyman Rollins (1992)
Jack Van Berg (1976)
Marion H. Van Berg (1966)
Don Von Hemel (1991)
Robert L. Wheeler (1972)

Owners-Breeders (Year Inducted)
Mr. and Mrs. Al Cascio (1993)
Omer "Pete" Hall (1970)
Jack Fickler (1985)
Barton Ford (1978)
Mike Ford (1967)
William Fudge (1973)
Orville Kemling (1981)
Paul Kemling (1981)
Ken Opstein (1985)
Others (Year Inducted)
Warren Albert (1978)
Dale Becker (1985)
James E. "Tom" Bock (1973)
Ralph Boomer (1971)
Don Fair (1979)
Harry Farnham (1971)
J. J. "Jake" Isaacson (1969)
Don Lee (1992)
Earl Moyer (1967)
Murdock Platner (1979)
Grover Porter (1969)
Al Swihart (1992)
Howard Wolff (1969)

Prairie Meadows Racetrack

Iowa's first horse-racing facility established its Hall of Fame in 1998.

Horses (Year Inducted)
Dontforgethisname (1999)
Lady Tamworth (2003)
Nut N Better (2003)
Railroad Red (1998)
Prince Ariba (1999)
Sure Shot Biscuit (2004)
Vaguely Who (2001)
Owners-Breeders (Year Inducted)
Jim Bader (1998)

Jack Bishop (2002)
Bob and Marlene Bryant (2002)
Jim and Sandra Rasmussen (2000)
Others (Year Inducted)
Dick Clark (2004)
Keith Hopkins (2001)
Ed Skinner (1999)
Jim Woodward (1999)

Remington Park

The Remington Hall of Fame was established in 1999. No others have been inducted since the original group.

Jockey
Pat Steinberg
Trainer
Donnie K. Von Hemel

Owner-Breeder
Ran Ricks Jr.
Horse
Clever Trevor

Texas Horse Racing Hall of Fame

The Texas Horse Racing Hall of Fame was created in 1999 at Retama Park to pay tribute to the people and horses who have influenced the state's racing industry.

Horses (Year Inducted)
Assault (1999)
Groovy (2001)
Middleground (2000)
Pan Zareta (1999)
Staunch Avenger (2002)
Stymie (2000)
Two Altazano (2003)
Jockeys (Year Inducted)
Cash Asmussen (2003)
Jerry Bailey (2000)
Bill Shoemaker (1999)
Trainer (Year Inducted)
Max Hirsch (2000)
Willard Proctor (2003)

Owners-Breeders (Year Inducted)
Williams S. Farish (2004)
Nelson Bunker Hunt (2004)
Robert Kleberg Jr. (1999)
Walter Merrick (2000)
Clarence Scharbauer Jr. (2001)
Joe R. Straus Sr. (2001)
Emerson Woodward (2001)
Others (Year Inducted)
Allen Bogan (2003)
Charles "Doc" Graham (2002)
Patricia Link (2004)
B. F. Phillips (1999)
W. T. Waggoner (2001)

Virginia Thoroughbred Hall of Fame

The Virginia Thoroughbred Hall of Fame began inducting members in 1978.

Horses	People
Cicada	Ted Atkinson
Cyane	Christopher Chenery
First Landing	Melville Church II
Fort Marcy	Thomas Mellon Evans
Genuine Risk	Bertram and Diana Firestone
Hansel	J. Jorth Fletcher
Hildene	Kenneth Gilpin
Legendra	Tyson Gilpin
Lexington	Gordon Grayson
Majesty's Prince	Richard Hancock
Mill Reef	Taylor Hardin
Mongo	Abraham S. Hewitt
Norfolk	Dr. Fritz Howard
Paradise Creek	Howell E. Jackson
Pilate	Mrs. J. P. Jones
Pleasant Colony	Keswick Stables
Quadrangle	Dorothy N. Lee
Reigh Count	Paul Mellon
Saluter	James P. Mills
Sea Hero	Dr. Frank O'Keefe
Secretariat	George L. Ohrstrom Jr.
Seeking the Pearl	William Haggin Perry
Sir Archy	Mrs. A. C. Randolph
Somethingroyal	Marion duPont Scott
Sword Dancer	Isabell Dodge Sloan
Sun Beau	Whitney Stone
	Orme Wilson Jr.

Washington Thoroughbred Racing Hall of Fame

The first Washington Thoroughbred Racing Hall of Fame members were inducted in 2004.

Special Lifetime Achievement (Year Inducted)
Joe Gottstein (2003)
Breeders (Year Inducted)
Herb Armstrong (2003)
George Drumheller (2004)
Jerre Paxton (2003)
Jockeys (Year Inducted)
Gary Baze (2003)
Russell Baze (2004)
Ralph Neves (2003)
Gary Stevens (2003)

Trainers (Year Inducted)
Allen Drumheller Sr. (2003)
Jim Penney (2003)
Tom Smith (2003)
Charlie Whittingham (2004)
Horses (Year Inducted)
Captain Condo (2003)
Chinook Pass (2003)
Saratoga Passage (2004)
Trooper Seven (2003)
Turbulator (2004)

TRIPLE CROWN
History of the Triple Crown

As with other great sporting events such as the Olympics and the World Series, the Triple Crown has a rich tradition and history. While modern memory places the Triple Crown in a fixed format—the Kentucky Derby (G1) on the first Saturday in May, the Preakness Stakes (G1) two weeks later, and the Belmont Stakes (G1) three weeks after the Preakness—the series has undergone changes ranging from subtle to seismic in its history.

Origins

The Triple Crown did not start with the inauguration of the three races—the Belmont in 1867, the Preakness six years later, and the Derby in '75. Of the three races, only the Derby has been run continuously, with gaps in the history of the Preakness (1891-'93) and the Belmont (1911 and '12, when antigambling legislation shut down New York racing). In some years, the Derby and Preakness were run within days of each other, and in two years (1917 and '22) they were run on the same day. In some years, the Preakness was run before the Derby.

Far from its current summit as the most prestigious race for American three-year-olds, the Derby in the early 20th century was a struggling regional race. The marketing and showmanship genius of Churchill Downs track executive Col. Matt J. Winn elevated the race to national and international prominence during the first quarter of the century.

When Sir Barton became the first Triple Crown winner in 1919, he was not recognized as a Triple Crown winner, only as a fast-developing three-year-old who went from maiden to multiple major stakes winner within two months.

In fact, the origin of the term "Triple Crown" (which had been in use in England for decades) has been disputed for many years. For decades, credit for coining the expression generally was accorded to legendary *Daily Racing Form* columnist Charlie Hatton. While Hatton's stature

Triple Crown Television Ratings and Share					
	Kentucky Derby		Preakness Stakes		Belmont Stakes
Year	Rating	Share	Rating	Share	Rating	Share
2005	7.3	18	5.1	13	4.5	11
2004	7.4	18	6.1	15	11.3	26
2003	6.4	17	5.6	13	9.5	23
2002	7.1	18	5.7	14	7.6	21
2001	8.1	21	5.6	16	4.5	13
2000	5.8	17	3.6	10	2.8	9
1999	6.3	19	3.4	10	6.0	17
1998	6.1	18	3.6	11	5.9	18
1997	7.1	19	4.8	14	5.3	16
1996	7.4	21	3.7	11	2.9	9
1995	6.0	17	3.2	10	3.5	11
1994	7.5	21	4.4	14	3.9	12
1993	7.3	22	4.7	15	4.2	11

Each rating point represents 1,096,000 viewers as of September 20, 2004. Share is the percentage of televisions tuned to that program.

and repeated use of the term closely associated him with the Triple Crown, the phrase arguably was first put in print by New York *Times* writer Bryan Field, who used the expression in 1930 after Gallant Fox won the Belmont.

The Triple Crown has been characterized by clusters of winners, especially in the 1930s, '40s, and '70s, and long droughts in between. After Gallant Fox won the 1930 Triple Crown for owner-breeder Belair Stud, only five years passed before Gallant Fox's son Omaha won for Belair. Two years later in 1937, Man o' War's son War Admiral took the Triple Crown for Glen Riddle Farm.

The Triple Crown sweep was achieved four times in the 1940s. First, Calumet Farm and jockey Eddie Arcaro won in 1941 with Whirlaway, and Mrs. John D. Hertz's Count Fleet rolled to victory two years later with Johnny Longden in the saddle. In 1946, King Ranch's homebred Assault scored the triple, and two years later Arcaro and Calumet collected their second Triple Crown sweep with Citation.

In 1950, the Thoroughbred Racing Associations formally recognized the three-race series as the Triple Crown and commissioned Cartier to craft a three-sided trophy, one side for each race. The trophy was in storage many years before Secretariat breezed to a Triple Crown victory in 1973, the first sweep in a quarter-century. Four years later, the brilliant Seattle Slew became the first to win the series without a defeat on his record. In 1978, the first back-to-back Triple Crown sweep occurred when Affirmed defeated Alydar in three classic battles. Harbor View Farm's Affirmed would be the last Triple Crown winner of the 20th century as another long drought took hold.

Birthplaces of Triple Crown Race Winners			
Place of Birth	Winners	Place of Birth	Winners
Kentucky	272	New York	7
Virginia	21	Canada	4
Florida	19	Texas	4
New Jersey	13	Ireland	2
Maryland	11	Montana	2
Pennsylvania	11	Ohio	2
California	9	Illinois	1
United Kingdom	9	Kansas	1
Tennessee	8	Missouri	1

Modern Triple Crown

The perception that the Triple Crown's prestige made it an irresistible goal for the connections of leading three-year-olds was shaken twice in the 1980s. Gato Del Sol won the 1982 Derby, but trainer Eddie Gregson, speaking for owners-breeders Arthur Hancock III and Leone J. Peters, declined to run the colt in the Preakness. Well aware that Gato Del Sol was unsuited to a speed-favoring Pimlico Race Course for the Preakness, Gregson and his owners awaited the Belmont, in which Gato Del Sol finished a distant second to Conquistador Cielo.

Dennis Diaz's speedy Spend a Buck crushed his competition in the 1985 Derby, but Diaz turned his back on the Preakness and Belmont, opting for the $1-million Jersey Derby (G3) at the newly rebuilt Garden State Park and a $2-million bonus.

Through the remainder of the 20th century, five horses came within one race of winning the Triple Crown, but none collected the $5-million—first offered as a purse and bonus and exclusively as a bonus beginning in 1998. Alysheba won the first two races in 1987 but was a distant fourth to Bet Twice in the Belmont. Sunday Silence won two spirited battles with Easy Goer in 1989 and finished a well-beaten second to his nemesis in the Belmont. The Triple Crown bids of the 1990s occurred in three consecutive years, 1997-'99. In 1997, Derby and Preakness winner Silver Charm could not repel the late charge of Touch Gold in the Belmont. The following year, Real Quiet appeared to have the Belmont won but lost by a nose in the last stride to Victory Gallop. Charismatic, the 1999 Derby and Preakness winner, finished third by less than two lengths despite sustaining a leg fracture in the Belmont's late stages. At the start of the 21st century, War Emblem won the first two legs in 2002, only to finish eighth in the Belmont. In 2003, Funny Cide won the Derby and Preakness but finished third in the Belmont; in '04, Smarty Jones came within one length of becoming the 12th Triple Crown winner. Afleet Alex won the 2005 Preakness and Belmont after finishing third in the Derby—*John Harrell*

Triple Crown Productions

Charged with marketing the Kentucky Derby (G1), Preakness Stakes (G1), and Belmont Stakes (G1), Triple Crown Productions was created at a time of turmoil within the industry and especially at the three tracks that stage the races. Threatened with a hostile takeover, Churchill Downs Inc. reorganized in 1984 and hired Thomas Meeker, a lawyer, as its president. The following year, Garden State Park reopened and lured the Derby winner, Spend a Buck, off the Triple Crown trail to the Jersey Derby (G3) with a $2-million bonus. Robert E. Brennan, then Garden State's chairman, spoke of the Jersey Derby taking the place of the Preakness at Pimlico Race Course in the Triple Crown. The New York Racing Association also was mired in internal turmoil.

Incorporated in September 1985, Triple Crown Productions opened its office at Churchill Downs in January '86, with Audrey R. Korotkin as its first executive director. In addition to its marketing function, Triple Crown Productions inaugurated a common nomination form and fees for the races, with early nominations of $600 each closing in mid-January and late nominations, originally $3,000 and now $6,000, closing six weeks before the Derby. Previously, each track obtained nominations for its own races. Supplemental entries (initially $150,000 for the Derby and $100,000 each for the Preakness and Belmont) were permitted beginning in 1990. The Derby supplemary fee was increased to $200,000 in 2005, and Greeley's Galaxy became the first supplemental nominee.

In 1987, the company offered the first Triple Crown Challenge—$5-million in purse money and bonuses to a Triple Crown winner and a $1-million bonus to the horse with the best overall performances in all three races. Triple Crown Productions financed the first bonus year (Bet Twice collected $1-million after he finished second to Alysheba in the Derby and Preakness and won the Belmont). Chrysler Corp. became the sponsor of the bonus in '88.

Meeker, chairman of Triple Crown Productions, eliminated the executive director position in August 1989, but media attention the following

Nominations Since Unified Under Triple Crown Productions

Year	Early	Late	Total	Total Fees	Each Track's Share
2005	358	13	371	$292,800	$97,600
2004	434	14	448	344,400	114,800
2003	446	8	454	315,600	105,200
2002	405	12	417	315,000	105,000
2001	440	7	447	306,000	102,000
2000	387	13	400	310,200	103,400
1999	396	11	407	303,600	101,200
1998	384	6	390	266,800	88,933
1997	375	13	388	303,000	101,000
1996	354	7	361	254,800	84,800
1995	317	7	324	232,400	77,400
1994	354	9	363	266,400	88,800
1993	342	25	367	317,700	105,900
1992	389	18	407	314,400	104,800
1991	369	8	377	257,400	85,800
1990	315	33	348	282,000	94,000
1989	381	13	394	267,600	89,200
1988	381	20	401	288,600	96,200
1987	398	24	422	310,800	103,600
1986	422	30	452	343,200	144,400

Early nomination fee has been $600 since 1986; late nomination fee: 1986-'90, $3,000; 1991-'93, $4,500; 1994-present, $6,000.

winter led to hiring Edward Seigenfeld, a former NYRA marketing vice president, as the organization's executive director. In 1993, the $1-million bonus for the best overall finish was eliminated.

Chrysler bowed out as the Triple Crown Challenge sponsor after 1995 and was replaced by Visa USA, the credit-card marketing company. Beginning in 1998, a Triple Crown sweep would earn a $5-million bonus in addition to purse earnings from the three races. Visa ended its sponsorship in 2005. In 2004, NYRA abandoned the Triple Crown's joint television contract with NBC in a dispute over revenue splits. NYRA signed up with ABC beginning in 2006.

$5-Million Visa Triple Crown Bonus

Triple Crown Productions will pay a bonus of $5-million to the owner of any horse that is declared the official winner of the Kentucky Derby (G1), the Preakness Stakes (G1), and the Belmont Stakes (G1). The Visa Triple Crown Challenge Bonus for 2005 had the following rules:

1. In the event of a dead heat for first in any race, each horse involved in the dead heat shall be considered to have finished first for purposes of determining whether or not any horse has won all of the races.

In the event of a dead heat for first between the same horses in all three races, the bonus money shall be divided equally.

2. Triple Crown Productions will present the Triple Crown trophy to the owner of a horse winning all of the races.

3. The Visa Triple Crown Challenge Bonus of $5-million shall be paid by Triple Crown Productions within 30 days after the result of the final race is declared official, but only after any dispute arising with regard to the eligibility, disqualification, or finish of a horse or the official result of any race has been finally adjudicated. Pending final determination of any such dispute, the Triple Crown Challenge Bonus and the Triple Crown trophy shall be held by Triple Crown Productions until such dispute is finally adjudicated and, if the Triple Crown Challenge Bonus and/or the Triple Crown trophy have been awarded to an owner prior to such dispute, the owner agrees that such bonus and/or trophy shall be returned immediately to Triple Crown Productions to be held as provided herein.

The following horses received $1-million bonus payments, with the totals including the bonus and purse money won in Triple Crown races:

1987—Bet Twice, second in the Kentucky Derby and Preakness Stakes, first in the Belmont Stakes, with earnings of $1,499,160.

1988—Risen Star, third in the Kentucky Derby, first in the Preakness and Belmont, with earnings of $1,767,420.

1989—Sunday Silence, first in the Kentucky Derby and Preakness, second in the Belmont, with earnings of $2,164,053.

1990—Unbridled, first in the Kentucky Derby, second in the Preakness, and fourth in the Belmont, with earnings of $1,759,360.

1991—Hansel, tenth in the Kentucky Derby and first in the Preakness and Belmont, with earnings of $1,850,250.

1992—Pine Bluff, fifth in the Kentucky Derby, first in the Preakness, and third in the Belmont, with earnings of $1,575,896.

1993—Sea Hero, first in the Kentucky Derby, fifth in the Preakness, and seventh in the Belmont, with earnings of $1,735,900.

Triple Crown Race Conditions
(Note: All conditions below are based on 2005 conditions and are subject to change.)

First deadline: January 22, 2005—$600
Second deadline: March 26, 2005—$6,000

Nominations to each and all of the Triple Crown races, the Kentucky Derby, the Preakness Stakes, and the Belmont Stakes (the "races") may be made by payment of a single nomination fee to Triple Crown Productions LLC as agent for Churchill Downs Inc., the Maryland Jockey Club of Baltimore City Inc., and the New York Racing Association Inc. (the "Association" or "Associations" as the case may be). The nomination fee for nominations postmarked, by facsimile, or hand-delivered by January 22, 2005, is $600 and for nominations postmarked, by facsimile, or hand-delivered from January 23 through March 26, 2005, is $6,000. Horses nominated on or before March 26, 2005, shall be considered original nominees ("original nominees").

[At any time prior to the closing for the Kentucky Derby, as defined below, additional nominations to all three races may be made and the nominee will be eligible for the Visa Triple Crown Challenge Bonus upon payment of a supplementary fee of $200,000 to Churchill Downs Inc. Following the running of the Kentucky Derby, horses may be nominated at any time prior to closing for the Preakness Stakes or the Belmont Stakes (time of closing being defined below) but will not be eligible for the Visa Triple Crown Challenge Bonus. The supplementary fee payable for such nomination shall be $100,000 payable to the Maryland Jockey Club of Baltimore City for supplemental nomination to the Preakness Stakes and the Belmont Stakes or $100,000 payable to the New York Racing Association for supplemental nomination to the Belmont Stakes only. All supplemental fees will be included in the purse distribution for the race run by the association to which the supplemental nomination is paid, unless otherwise specified in the specific race rules below. The ability of horses nominated by payment of the foregoing supplementary fees ("supplemental nominees") to enter any race will be determined in accordance with the conditions of that race. All nominees, original, supplemental or otherwise, will be required to pay entry and starting fees for the race or races in which they participate before they may start. Triple Crown Productions will pay a bonus of $5-million to the owner of any horse that is declared the official winner of all the races in 2005 to be divided equally in the event of a dead heat between the same horses in all races. The bonus will be paid in accordance with the official rules of the Visa Triple Crown Challenge Bonus, which are incorporated herein by reference.

131st running of the Kentucky Derby (G1)
$2-million guaranteed minimum purse
To be run on Saturday, May 7, 2005
One mile and a quarter

For three-year olds, with an entry fee of $25,000 each and a starting fee of $25,000 each. Supplemental nominations may be made upon payment of $200,000 and in accordance with the rules set forth. All fees, including supplemental nominations, in excess of $500,000 in the aggregate shall be paid to the winner. Churchill Downs Inc. shall guarantee a minimum gross purse of $2-million (the "guaranteed purse"). The winner shall receive $1,240,000, second place shall receive $400,000, third place shall receive $200,000, fourth place shall receive $100,000, and fifth place shall receive $60,000 from the guaranteed purse (the guaranteed purse to each place to be divided equally in the event of a dead heat). Starters shall be named through the entry box on Wednesday, May 4, 2005, at 10 a.m. Eastern Daylight Time (the "closing"). The maximum number of starters shall be limited to 20. Colts and geldings shall each carry a weight of 126 pounds; fillies shall each carry 121 pounds. Supplemental nominees will be allowed to enter but will not have preference over any original nominee and will not be allowed to start the race if the maximum number of starters has otherwise been reached by original nominees prior to the closing. If the number of nominees exceeds the number of available starting positions at the closing, these conditions shall be applied to determine which nominees will be allowed to start. In the event that more than 20 entries pass through the entry box at the closing, the starters shall be determined at the closing from original nominees first, then supplemental nominees if starting positions are still available with preference given to those horses that have accumulated the highest earnings in the graded stakes races, including all monies actually paid for performance in such graded stakes races. For purposes of this preference, the graded status of each race shall be the graded status assigned to the race by the International Cataloguing Standards Committee in Part I of the International Cataloguing Standards as published by Jockey Club Information Systems each year. Should additional starters be needed to bring the field to 20, the remaining starters shall be determined at the closing with preference given to those horses that have accumulated the highest earnings in non-restricted sweepstakes. For purposes of this preference, a "non-restricted sweepstakes" shall mean those sweepstakes whose conditions contain no restrictions other that that of age or sex. In the case of ties resulting from preferences or otherwise, the additional starter(s) shall be determined by lot. Any horse excluded from running because of the aforementioned preference(s) shall be refunded the $25,000 entry fee and the $200,000 supplemental fee, if applicable. An "also-eligible" list will not be maintained and in no event will starters be added or allowed to run in the race which are not determined to be starters at the closing. Post position shall be determined as follows: A nontransferable lot number shall be drawn for each horse named as a starter at the closing. The lot number drawn for each starter shall determine the numerical order for selection of post position. Selection of post position shall be made by each owner of a horse (or, if more than one, the owners collectively) or the authorized agent of the horse's owner(s). Horses having common ties through ownership or training shall each be treated separately for purposes of selecting post position. Detailed rules governing the post position draw process are available from the racing secretary's office and will be distributed prior to the closing. These rules shall control. The owner of the winner of the race shall receive a gold trophy.

130th running of the Preakness Stakes (G1)
$1-million guaranteed purse
To be run on Saturday, May 21, 2005
One mile and three-sixteenths

For three-year-olds, $10,000 to pass the entry box, starters to pay $10,000 additional. Supplemental nominations may be made in accordance with the rules, upon payment of $100,000, 65% of the purse to the winner, 20% to second, 10% to third, and 5% to fourth. Weight: 126 pounds for colts and geldings, 121 pounds for fillies. Starters to be named through the entry box on Wednesday, May 18, 2005, three days before the race by the usual time of closing (the "closing"). The Preakness field will be limited to 14 entries and shall be determined on the Wednesday immediately preceding the day of the race. In the event that more than 14 horses are properly nominated and pass through the entry box by the usual time of closing, the starters will be determined at the closing with the first seven horses given preference by accumulating the highest earnings in graded stakes (lifetime), for purposes of this preference, the graded status of each race shall be the graded status assigned to the race by the International Cataloguing Standards Committee in Part 1 of the International Cataloguing Standards as published by Jockey Club Information Systems each year. The next four starters will be determined by accumulating the highest earnings (lifetime) in all non-restricted stakes. "Non-restricted sweepstakes" shall mean those sweepstakes whose conditions contain no restrictions other than that of age or sex. The remaining three starters shall be determined by accumulating the highest earnings (lifetime) in all races. Should this preference produce any ties, the additional starter(s) shall be determined by lot. In application of the above described rule, each horse will be separately considered without regard to identity of its owner. If the rules described in this paragraph result in the exclusion of any horse, the $10,000 entry fee previously paid will be refunded to the owner of said horse. The above conditions notwithstanding, no horse which earns purse money in the Kentucky Derby shall be denied the opportunity to enter and start in the Preakness Stakes. A replica of the Woodlawn Vase will be presented to the winning owner to remain his or her personal property.

137th running of the Belmont Stakes (G1)
$1-million purse
To be run on Saturday, June 11, 2005
One mile and a half

For three-year olds, by subscription of $600 each, to accompany the nomination, if made on or before January 22, 2005; or $6,000, if made on or before March 26, 2005; $10,000 to pass the entry box and $10,000 additional to start. At any time prior to the closing time of entries, horses may be nominated to the Belmont Stakes upon payment of a supplementary fee of $100,000 to the New York Racing Association. All entrants, supplemental or otherwise, will be required to pay entry and starting fees. The purse to be divided 60% to the winner, 20% to second, 11% to third, 6% to fourth, and 3% to fifth. Colts and geldings, 126 pounds; fillies, 121 pounds. Starters to be named at the closing time of entries. The Belmont field will be limited to 16 starters. In the event more than

16 entries pass through the entry box at the closing, the starters will be determined at the closing with the first eight starters given preference by accumulating the highest earnings in graded sweepstakes at a mile or over. For purposes of this preference, the graded status of each race shall be the grade assigned by the International Cataloguing Standards Committee in Part I of the International Cataloguing Standards as published annually by Jockey Club Information Systems. The next five starters will be determined by accumulating the highest earning in all non-restricted sweepstakes. "Non-restricted sweepstakes" shall mean those sweepstakes whose conditions contain no restrictions other than age or sex. The remaining three starters shall be determined by accumulating the highest earnings in all races. Should this preference produce any ties, the additional starter(s) shall be determined by lot. If the rules described result in the exclusion of any horse, the $10,000 entry fee will be refunded to the owner of said horse. The above conditions notwithstanding, any horse which earns purse money in either the Kentucky Derby or the Preakness Stakes shall be included in the initial eight (8) starters of the Belmont Stakes. The winning owner will be presented with the August Belmont Memorial Cup, to be retained for one year, as well as a trophy for permanent possession and trophies to the winning trainer and jockey.

Road to the Triple Crown

The following races are traditionally used as preps for the Triple Crown races. The table includes the dates and winners of the races in 2005.

Date	Race	Trk	Dist.	Time	First Three Finishers
1/1	Tropical Park Derby (G3)	Crc	1⅛mT	1:47.18	**LORD ROBYN**, Fire Path, **Crown Point**
1/8	Aventura S.	GP	1m	1:35.88	**HIGH FLY, Drum Major, Magna Graduate**
1/15	Count Fleet S.	Aqu	1m70yd	1:42.41	**SCRAPPY T, Naughty New Yorker**, Tani Maru
1/15	Golden Gate Derby	GG	1 1/16m	1:43.69	**BUZZARDS BAY, Sharp Writer, Dover Dere**
1/15	Lecomte S. (G3)	FG	1m	1:39.34	**STORM SURGE, Smooth Bid, Kansas City Boy**
1/15	San Rafael S. (G2)	SA	1m	1:36.69	**SPANISH CHESTNUT, Iced Out, Texcess**
1/17	San Miguel S.	SA	6f	1:09.62	**GOING WILD, So Long Birdie, General John B**
1/29	Black Gold H.	FG	1m	1:39.30	STRAW HAT, **Medigating (Fr)**, Krises Bells
1/29	Sunshine Millions Dash S.	GP	6f	1:09.96	LOST IN THE FOG, Santana Strings, Lucky Frolic
2/5	Holy Bull S. (G3)	GP	1⅛m	1:50.14	**CLOSING ARGUMENT, Kansas City Boy, High Fly**
2/5	Hutcheson S. (G2)	GP	7½f	1:29.90	**PROUD ACCOLADE, Park Avenue Ball, Vicarage**
2/5	Sham S.	SA	1⅛m	1:50.18	**GOING WILD, Papi Chullo, Giacomo**
2/12	Risen Star S. (G3)	FG	1 1/16m	1:44.54	**SCIPION, Real Dandy, Storm Surge**
2/12	San Mateo Mile S.	BM	1m	1:35.57	STELLAR MAGIC, **Texcess**, King Mobay
2/12	Turf Paradise Derby	TuP	1 1/16m	1:45.48	**GENERAL JOHN B**, Quiet Money, Lead for Speed
2/12	Whirlaway S.	Aqu	1 1/16m	1:43.32	**SORT IT OUT, Naughty New Yorker, Scrappy T**
2/13	San Vicente S. (G2)	SA	7f	1:22.59	**FUSAICHI ROCK STAR, Don't Get Mad, Kirkendahl**
2/19	Southwest S.	OP	1m	1:39.09	**GREATER GOOD**, Munificence, Humor At Last
2/26	Sam F. Davis S.	Tam	1 1/16m	1:46.63	**ANDROMEDA'S HERO**, Summer Legacy, Captain Lindsay
2/27	Borderland Derby	Sun	1 1/16m	1:43.18	**SOUTHERN AFRICA, Thor's Echo, Dover Dere**
3/5	Baldwin S.	SA	6½f	1:16.16	HIGH STANDARDS, Talking to John, Run Thruthe Sun
3/5	Fountain of Youth S. (G2)	GP	1⅛m	1:49.70	**HIGH FLY, Bandini, B. B. Best**
3/5	John Battaglia Memorial S.	TP	1 1/16m	1:43.94	**MAGNA GRADUATE, Pavo, Ultimate**
3/5	Santa Catalina S. (G2)	SA	1 1/16m	1:42.41	**DECLAN'S MOON, Going Wild, Spanish Chestnut**
3/5	Swale S. (G2)	GP	7f	1:22.21	LOST IN THE FOG, **Around the Cape**, More Smoke
3/12	El Camino Real Derby (G3)	BM	1 1/16m	1:42.22	UNCLE DENNY, **Wannawinemall, Buzzards Bay**
3/12	Louisiana Derby (G2)	FG	1 1/16m	1:42.74	**HIGH LIMIT, Vicarage, Storm Surge**
3/19	Gotham S. (G3)	Aqu	1m	1:35.61	**SURVIVALIST, Galloping Grocer, Naughty New Yorker**
3/19	Rebel S. (G3)	OP	1 1/16m	1:44.92	**GREATER GOOD, Rockport Harbor**, Batson Challenge
3/19	San Felipe S. (G2)	SA	1 1/16m	1:40.11	**CONSOLIDATOR, Giacomo, Don't Get Mad**
3/19	Tampa Bay Derby (G3)	Tam	1 1/16m	1:43.98	**SUN KING**, Forever Wild, Global Trader
3/26	Lane's End S. (G2)	TP	1⅛m	1:50.33	**FLOWER ALLEY, Wild Desert, Mr Sword**
3/26	Palm Beach S. (G3)	GP	1⅛mT	1:47.12	INTERPATATION, Tadreeb, Fishy Advice
3/26	Rushaway S.	TP	1 1/16m	1:44.49	**CAT SHAKER, Daddy Joe**, Catch Me
3/26	San Pedro S.	SA	6½f	1:16.58	HIGH STANDARDS, Ransom Demanded, Talking to John
3/26	UAE Derby (UAE-G2)	Nad	1800m	1:50.05	**BLUES AND ROYALS**, =Marenostrum (Brz), **Parole Board**
4/2	Florida Derby (G1)	GP	1⅛m	1:49.43	**HIGH FLY, Noble Causeway, B. B. Best**
4/2	WinStar Derby	Sun	1⅛m	1:49.59	**THOR'S ECHO, Southern Africa, Sort It Out**
4/8	Transylvania S. (G3)	Kee	1mT	1:35.28	**CHATTAHOOCHEE WAR, Guillaume Tell (Ire)**, Rey de Cafe
4/9	Bay Shore S. (G3)	Aqu	7f	1:21.33	LOST IN THE FOG, White Socks, **Big Top Cat**
4/9	Illinois Derby (G2)	Haw	1⅛m	1:49.62	**GREELEY'S GALAXY, Monarch Lane, Magna Graduate**
4/9	Santa Anita Derby (G1)	SA	1⅛m	1:49.18	**BUZZARDS BAY, General John B., Wilko**
4/9	Wood Memorial S. (G1)	Aqu	1⅛m	1:47.16	**BELLAMY ROAD, Survivalist, Scrappy T**
4/10	Lafayette S. (G3)	Kee	6f	1:09.88	MORE SMOKE, **Crimson Stag**, Razor
4/16	Arkansas Derby (G2)	OP	1⅛m	1:48.80	**AFLEET ALEX, Flower Alley, Andromeda's Hero**
4/16	Blue Grass S. (G1)	Kee	1⅛m	1:50.16	**BANDINI, High Limit, Closing Argument**
4/21	Forerunner S.	Kee	1⅛mT	1:48.51	GUN SALUTE, Mad Adam, Cosmic Kris
4/23	Coolmore Lexington S. (G2)	Kee	1 1/16m	1:45.76	**COIN SILVER, Sort It Out, Storm Surge**
4/30	Derby Trial S.	CD	1m	1:36.16	**DON'T GET MAD**, Gallardo, **Vicarage**
5/7	Kentucky Derby (G1)	CD	1¼m	2:02.75	**GIACOMO, Closing Argument, Afleet Alex**
5/21	Preakness S. (G1)	Pim	1 3/16m	1:55.04	**AFLEET ALEX, Scrappy T, Giacomo**
5/28	Peter Pan S. (G2)	Bel	1⅛m	1:46.35	ORATORY, **Reverberate**, Golden Man
6/11	Belmont S. (G1)	Bel	1½m	2:28.75	**AFLEET ALEX, Andromeda's Hero, Nolan's Cat**

Triple Crown nominees are listed in bold.

Triple Crown Winners

America's Triple Crown Winners

Year	Horse	Owner	Trainer	Jockey
1978	Affirmed	Harbor View Farm	Lazaro Barrera	Steve Cauthen
1977	Seattle Slew	Karen L. Taylor	William Turner Jr.	Jean Cruguet
1973	Secretariat	Meadow Stable	Lucien Laurin	Ron Turcotte
1948	Citation	Calumet Farm	H. A. "Jimmy" Jones	Eddie Arcaro
1946	Assault	King Ranch	Max Hirsch	Warren Mehrtens
1943	Count Fleet	Mrs. John D. Hertz	Don Cameron	John Longden
1941	Whirlaway	Calumet Farm	Ben A. Jones	Eddie Arcaro
1937	War Admiral	Samuel D. Riddle	George Conway	Charles Kurtsinger
1935	Omaha	Belair Stud	James Fitzsimmons	William Saunders
1930	Gallant Fox	Belair Stud	James Fitzsimmons	Earle Sande
1919	Sir Barton	J.K.L. Ross	H. Guy Bedwell	John Loftus

Triple Crown Trophy

The Triple Crown trophy was commissioned in 1950 by the Thoroughbred Racing Associations, which copyrighted the term Triple Crown, and has three sides to symbolize the three races in the series. The trophy was presented retroactively to the eight previous winners of the three races.

The first three-year-old with a chance to claim the silver Triple Crown trophy was Tim Tam, who won the 1958 Kentucky Derby and Preakness Stakes but finished second to *Cavan in the Belmont Stakes. Secretariat in 1973 was the first horse to be presented the trophy after sweeping the three races.

Sir Barton

At the start of 1919, Sir Barton was far down the pecking order in trainer H. Guy Bedwell's stable. Commander J.K.L. Ross had purchased the *Star Shoot colt at Saratoga for $10,000 in 1918, but Sir Barton was winless in his six starts as a two-year-old and made his three-year-old debut in the '19 Kentucky Derby. His role in the Derby on May 10, 1919, was to serve as a pacemaker for his highly fancied stablemate, Billy Kelly. They went off at 2.60-to-1, second choice behind the 2.10-to-1 entry of Sailor and Eternal. Ridden by Johnny Loftus, Sir Barton bucked the odds, leading all the way and winning the Derby by five lengths over his stablemate. He was immediately shipped to Baltimore and won the Preakness Stakes on May 14 (a Wednesday) by four lengths over Eternal as the 7-to-5 favorite. In the Belmont Stakes on June 11, Sir Barton was 2-to-5 against the entry of Sweep On, third in the Preakness, and Natural Bridge. Sir Barton allowed Natural Bridge to set the pace for three-quarters of a mile before taking the lead and winning by five lengths. Between his Preakness and Belmont victories, Sir Barton won the Withers Stakes.

Sir Barton's achievement was unprecedented, but he was overshadowed by the appearance of Man o' War, who sustained the only defeat of his career in that year's Sanford Memorial Stakes at Saratoga Race Course.

As a four-year-old in 1920, Sir Barton alternated

Ch. c., 1916, by *Star Shoot— Lady Sterling, by Hanover

Owner: Commander J. K. L. Ross
Breeders: Madden and Gooch (Ky.)
Trainer: H. Guy Bedwell
Jockey: Johnny Loftus

		Race Record			
Year	Starts	1st	2nd	3rd	Earnings
1918	6	0	1 (1)	0	$ 4,113
1919	13	8 (8)	3 (2)	2 (1)	88,250
1920	12	5 (5)	2 (2)	3 (3)	24,494
	31	13 (13)	6 (5)	5 (4)	$116,857

1919—1st Kentucky Derby, Preakness S., Belmont S., Withers S., Potomac H., Maryland H., Pimlico Fall Series No. 2, Pimlico Fall Series No. 3
1920—1st Saratoga H., Merchants' and Citizens' H., Dominion H., Climax H., Rennert H.

between brilliant and ordinary, winning five of 12 starts but finishing off the board twice. Because of his chronically sore feet and difficult temperament, he lost several races that he should have won against less talented opponents.

After losing a match race to Man o' War, Sir Barton faded from view. Retired to stud at the end of the 1920 season, he enjoyed only moderate success, was sold to the United States Cavalry Remount Station, and lived on a Wyoming ranch until his death in 1937.

Gallant Fox

Bred and owned by the Belair Stud of William Woodward, Gallant Fox marked a shift in the standards of American breeding. The introduction of *Sir Gallahad III to the United States from France in the late 1920s represented an important step forward for the American breeding industry. For the next several decades, American breeders went to Europe for proven stallions or prospects, particularly in England. The result was a significant increase in the quality of American racehorses. Woodward was one of the syndicate members involved in the purchase of *Sir Gallahad III, who stood at Claiborne Farm in Kentucky.

Gallant Fox was a good but not outstanding two-year-old, winning the Flash and Junior Champion Stakes and placing in three other stakes in his seven starts in 1929. In the care of trainer James "Sunny Jim" Fitzsimmons, Gallant Fox developed into an imposing physical specimen at three.

A four-length winner in Aqueduct's 1930 Wood Memorial Stakes, Gallant Fox hurtled through the Triple Crown, winning the Preakness on May 9 by three-quarters of a length, the Kentucky Derby eight days later by two lengths, and the Belmont on June 7 by three lengths over Whichone, his leading rival. Three weeks later,

B. c., 1927, by *Sir Gallahad III—Marguerite, by Celt				

Owner-Breeder: Belair Stud (Ky.)
Trainer: James Fitzsimmons
Jockey: Earl Sande

		Race Record			
Year	Starts	1st	2nd	3rd	Earnings
1929	7	2 (2)	2 (1)	2 (2)	$ 19,890
1930	10	9 (9)	1 (1)	0	308,275
	17	11 (11)	3 (2)	2 (2)	$328,165

1929—1st Flash S., Junior Champion S.
1930—1st Kentucky Derby, Preakness S., Belmont S., Wood Memorial S., Dwyer S., Classic S., Saratoga Cup, Lawrence Realization S., Jockey Cup Gold Cup

Gallant Fox added the Dwyer Stakes to his list of triumphs.

His only loss of the year occurred in the Travers Stakes at Saratoga Race Course, where he ran second to 100-to-1 longshot Jim Dandy.

At the end of the year, Gallant Fox was retired to stud at Claiborne, where he sired 1935 Triple Crown winner Omaha and '36 Belmont Stakes winner Granville. Gallant Fox died on November 13, 1954, and was buried at Claiborne alongside his sire and dam.

Omaha

Five years after his Gallant Fox became the second Triple Crown winner, William Woodward saw his decision to participate in the syndication of French runner *Sir Gallahad III for stud duty in the United States pay off with a second Triple Crown winner. Omaha, a son of Gallant Fox and grandson of *Sir Gallahad III, won nine of 22 starts, but his career did not measure up to that of his sire. At two, Omaha won only once in nine starts, although he finished second in the Sanford and Champagne Stakes.

Once again, trainer James "Sunny Jim" Fitzsimmons's patient hand allowed the chestnut colt to fill out nicely over the winter between his two- and three-year-old years. On May 4, 1935, Omaha stepped onto an off track at Churchill Downs as the 4-to-1 second choice for the Kentucky Derby (favored at 3.80-to-1 was the filly Nellie Flag). Omaha made his move for the lead on the far turn, led by two lengths at the top of the stretch, and won by a relatively easy 1½ lengths over Roman Soldier.

One week later, Omaha was a runaway, six-length winner of the Preakness Stakes over Firethorn, who had skipped the Derby. Despite losing two weeks later in the Withers Stakes, Omaha won the Belmont Stakes by 1½ lengths

Ch. c., 1932, by Gallant Fox—Flambino, by *Wrack				

Owner-Breeder: Belair Stud (Ky.)
Trainer: James Fitzsimmons
Jockey: Willie Saunders

		Race Record			
Year	Starts	1st	2nd	3rd	Earnings
1934 (U.S.)	9	1	4 (3)	0	$ 3,850
1935 (U.S.)	9	6 (5)	1 (1)	2 (2)	142,255
1936 (Eng.)	4	2 (2)	2 (2)	0	8,650
	22	9 (7)	7 (6)	2 (2)	$154,705

1935—1st Kentucky Derby, Preakness S., Belmont S., Dwyer S., Classic S.
1936—(In England) 1st Victor Wild S., Queen's Plate

on June 8. Omaha finished third in the Brooklyn Handicap in his next start but won his next two starts, the Dwyer Stakes and the Arlington Classic, before an injury ended his season.

As a four-year-old, Omaha was shipped to England and finished second in the Ascot Gold Cup. Omaha failed at stud, and Claiborne in 1943 sent him to a New York farm. Moved to a farm in Nebraska in 1950, Omaha died in '59 and was buried at Ak-Sar-Ben racetrack in Omaha.

War Admiral

Glen Riddle Farms owner Samuel Riddle owned War Admiral's famous sire, Man o' War, but chose to skip the Kentucky Derby with him in 1920. In Riddle's estimation, Churchill Downs was too far west, and the Derby was too early in the year for his comfort.

War Admiral, a striking brown colt out of the Sweep mare Brushup, had won three of six starts as a two-year-old, and his one stakes victory was in the minor Eastern Shore Handicap at Havre de Grace in Maryland. He returned to Havre de Grace for his first start of 1937 and won the Chesapeake Stakes. Riddle then decided to give War Admiral a shot at the Kentucky Derby.

Sent off as the 8-to-5 favorite in a Derby field of 20, War Admiral led at every point of call and easily held off champion two-year-old Pompoon in the final furlong to win by 1¾ lengths.

One week later, War Admiral was put to a much sterner test in the Preakness Stakes by Pompoon, who battled the Derby winner from the top of Pimlico Race Course's stretch. War Admiral won by a head. In the Belmont Stakes on June 5, War Admiral stumbled at the start, injuring his right foreleg, but the diminutive colt cruised to an easy, three-length victory over Sceneshifter.

Br. c., 1934, by Man o' War—Brushup, by Sweep					
Owner: Glen Riddle Farms					
Breeder: Samuel Riddle (Ky.)					
Trainer: George Conway					
Jockey: Charles Kurtsinger					
		Race Record			
Year	Starts	1st	2nd	3rd	Earnings
1936	6	3 (1)	2 (2)	1 (1)	$ 14,800
1937	8	8 (6)	0	0	166,500
1938	11	9 (8)	1 (1)	0	90,840
1939	1	1	0	0	1,100
	26	21 (15)	3 (3)	1 (1)	$273,240

1936—1st Eastern Shore H.
1937—1st Kentucky Derby, Preakness S., Belmont S., Chesapeake S., Pimlico Special, Washington H.
1938—1st Whitney S., Jockey Club Gold Cup, Saratoga Cup, Saratoga H., Wilson S., Queens County H., Rhode Island H., Widener H.

Voted Horse of the Year and champion three-year-old, War Admiral lost a 1938 match race to Seabiscuit in the Pimlico Special.

At stud, War Admiral sired 40 stakes winners and two champions from 320 starters, 12.5% of starters, in his 20-year stud career. He died in 1959.

Whirlaway

Prone to wild trips around the racetrack, Whirlaway could be a danger to himself and those around him, but he was worth the risk to train and run. In his three- and four-year-old seasons, he made 42 starts, won 25 times, finished second 13 times, and was third in his other four starts. Handled patiently by Racing Hall of Fame trainer Ben Jones, Whirlaway became the first of eight Kentucky Derby winners and two Triple Crown winners for Calumet Farm.

For the Derby on May 3, 1941, Jones fashioned new blinkers for Whirlaway, cutting away the left cup but leaving the right cup intact. He also made a rider change, with Eddie Arcaro replacing Wendall Eads. On Derby day, Whirlaway displayed his customary tendency to run near the back of the pack early. With a quarter-mile left, Whirlaway had moved up to fourth place and was flying. He exploded through a final quarter-mile, running it in :24, and won by eight lengths.

Despite walking out of the gate and trailing by more than nine lengths after a half-mile of the Preakness on May 10, Whirlaway again came on late and won by 5½ lengths. Nearly one month later in the Belmont Stakes, Whirlaway stunned his three rivals by taking off after a half-mile and opening up a seven-length lead after six furlongs. Despite entering the stretch a bit wide, he won

Ch. c., 1938, by *Blenheim II—Dustwhirl, by Sweep					
Owner-Breeder: Calumet Farm (Ky.)					
Trainer: Ben A. Jones					
Jockey: Eddie Arcaro					
		Race Record			
Year	Starts	1st	2nd	3rd	Earnings
1940	16	7 (4)	2 (2)	4 (3)	$77,275
1941	20	13 (8)	5 (5)	2	272,386
1942	22	12 (10)	8 (6)	2 (2)	211,250
1943	2	0	0	1	250
	60	32 (22)	15 (13)	9 (5)	$561,161

1940—1st Saratoga Special, Hopeful S., Breeders' Futurity, Walden S.
1941—1st Kentucky Derby, Preakness S., Belmont S., Travers S., Lawrence Realization S., Saranac H., Dwyer S., American Derby
1942—1st Brooklyn H., Jockey Club Gold Cup, Massachusetts H., Narragansett Special, Dixie H., Washington H., Louisiana H., Trenton H., Governor Bowie H., Clark H.

by 2½ lengths to become the fifth Triple Crown winner.

The colt maintained his brilliance through 1942, when he was named Horse of the Year a second time.

Sold to French interests, Whirlaway died in southern Normandy on April 6, 1953.

Count Fleet

In 1927, Yellow Cab founder John D. Hertz watched a two-year-old race in which one of the runners reached out and bit another horse dueling with him for the lead. It was a remarkable display of aggression and a single-minded will to win. Hertz was sufficiently impressed to buy the colt, Reigh Count, who won the 1928 Kentucky Derby. Hertz never had much faith in Reigh Count as a stallion and bred him to only a few mares each year, including Quickly, who on March 24, 1940, gave birth to a gangly brown package named Count Fleet. The youngster was so clumsy and awkward that Hertz considered selling him as a yearling and again early in his two-year-old campaign. At two, Count Fleet won ten of 15 starts, was voted champion two-year-old colt, and on the Experimental Free Handicap was accorded highweight of 132 pounds, still the highest weight ever assigned.

As a three-year-old, Count Fleet had no equal. He usually went to the lead early, discouraged his competition by the stretch, and won as he pleased.

In the Kentucky Derby on May 1, Count Fleet went off as the 2-to-5 favorite in the field of ten. He broke sharply under John Longden, went

Assault

As a foal, Assault stepped on a surveyor's stake at King Ranch, which left him with a malformed right front hoof. As a result, he was called the club-footed comet.

Trainer Max Hirsch initially was unsure that Assault could withstand training because of the injury, but the Bold Venture colt won two of nine starts at two in 1945. He went off at 8.20-to-1 in the Kentucky Derby on May 4, 1946. Assault, with jockey Warren Mehrtens up, blew past Spy Song and Knockdown early in the stretch and won by eight lengths.

One week later in the Preakness Stakes, Assault's Triple Crown dreams nearly ended. Mehrtens decided to go for the knockout punch and sent Assault after the leaders going into the far turn. Assault tired and staggered home, winning by a fast-diminishing neck over Lord Boswell.

When the Belmont Stakes came around on June 1, many racing fans believed the 1½ miles would expose Assault. Lord Boswell was sent off as the 1.35-to-1 favorite, with Assault the second choice at 7-to-5. Mehrtens allowed Assault to reach contention gradually. Trailing Natchez by two lengths in midstretch, Assault exploded past him in the final 200 yards and won by three lengths.

Horse of the Year in 1946, Assault won five of

Br. c., 1940, by Reigh Count— Quickly, by Haste

Owner-Breeder: Mrs. John D. Hertz (Ky.)
Trainer: Don Cameron
Jockey: John Longden

| Year | Starts | Race Record | | | Earnings |
		1st	2nd	3rd	
1942	15	10 (4)	4 (2)	1 (1)	$ 76,245
1943	6	6 (5)	0	0	174,055
	21	16 (9)	4 (2)	1 (1)	$250,300

1942—1st Champagne S., Pimlico Futurity, Walden S., Wakefield S.
1943—1st Kentucky Derby, Preakness S., Belmont S., Wood Memorial S., Withers S.

immediately to the lead, opened two lengths after six furlongs, and won by an easy three lengths over Blue Swords. One week later, Count Fleet won the Preakness by eight lengths. In the Belmont Stakes on June 5, Count Fleet, at odds of 1-to-20, won by 25 lengths in 2:28⅕.

A seemingly minor injury to Count Fleet's left front ankle did not respond to treatment and ended his career. At stud, he sired champions Counterpoint and Kiss Me Kate as well as Count Turf, upset winner of the 1951 Kentucky Derby. Count Fleet died on December 3, 1973.

Ch. c., 1943, by Bold Venture— Igual, by Equipoise

Owner-Breeder: King Ranch (Tx.)
Trainer: Max Hirsch
Jockey: Warren Mehrtens

| Year | Starts | Race Record | | | Earnings |
		1st	2nd	3rd	
1945	9	2 (1)	2	1 (1)	$ 17,250
1946	15	8 (8)	2 (2)	3 (3)	424,195
1947	7	5 (5)	1	1 (1)	181,925
1948	2	1	0	0	3,250
1949	6	1 (1)	1	1 (1)	45,900
1950	3	1	0	1	2,950
	42	18 (15)	6 (2)	7 (6)	$675,470

1945—1st Flash S.
1946—1st Kentucky Derby, Preakness S., Belmont S., Wood Memorial S., Dwyer S., Westchester H., Pimlico Special, Experimental Free H. No. 1
1947—1st Suburban H., Brooklyn H., Butler H., Grey Lag H., Dixie H.
1949—1st Brooklyn H.

seven starts in '47 and spent much of the year battling fellow handicappers Stymie and Armed for the all-time earnings crown.

Assault was retired to stud in early 1948 but proved to be sterile. Returned to the racetrack, he ran until he was seven. Pensioned at King Ranch, he was euthanized in 1971 after fracturing a leg.

Citation

Citation resulted from a mating of Calumet Farm's premier sire, Bull Lea, with *Hydroplane II, whom Warren Wright purchased from Lord Derby in the spring of 1941. Citation was foaled on April 11, 1945, and joined trainer H. A. "Jimmy" Jones's Maryland division in the spring of '47 to begin his racing career.

At two, his only loss was in the Washington Park Futurity to stablemate Bewitch.

Citation began his three-year-old season with two victories over older horses at Hialeah Park before winning the Everglades and Flamingo Stakes. His jockey, Al Snider, died in a boating accident after the Flamingo, and Jones induced Eddie Arcaro to take the mount.

In the Kentucky Derby against only five opponents on May 1, Citation spotted stablemate Coaltown six lengths in the opening half-mile and ran him down to win by 3½ lengths.

In the Preakness Stakes two weeks later, Citation set the pace and won by 5½ lengths as the 1-to-10 favorite. With four weeks between the Preakness and Belmont Stakes, Jones sent out Citation for an 11-length victory in the Jersey Stakes. On June 12 in the Belmont, Citation, at 1-to-5 odds, scored an eight-length triumph over Better Self.

Citation won 19 times in 1948, including a walkover in the Pimlico Special. At the end of his

B. c., 1945, by Bull Lea— *Hydroplane II, by Hyperion

Owner-Breeder: Calumet Farm (Ky.)
Trainers: Ben A. Jones and H. A. "Jimmy" Jones
Jockey: Eddie Arcaro

		Race Record			
Year	Starts	1st	2nd	3rd	Earnings
1947	9	8 (3)	1 (1)	0	$ 155,680
1948	20	19 (16)	1 (1)	0	709,470
1949	—	—	—	—	—
1950	9	2 (1)	7 (5)	0	73,480
1951	7	3 (2)	1 (1)	2	147,130
	45	32 (22)	10 (8)	2	$1,085,760

1947—1st Futurity S., Pimlico Futurity, Elementary S.
1948—1st Kentucky Derby, Preakness S., Belmont S., Jockey Club Gold Cup, Pimlico Special, Belmont Gold Cup, American Derby, Flamingo S., Jersey S., Stars and Stripes H., Tanforan H., Sysonby Mile, Chesapeake S., Seminole H., Derby Trial, Everglades H.
1950—1st Golden Gate Mile H.
1951—1st American H., Hollywood Gold Cup

three-year-old season, Citation had 27 victories and two seconds in 29 starts, with earnings of $865,150.

In 1951, Citation won the Hollywood Gold Cup, becoming racing's first $1-million earner. Immediately retired to Calumet, he was an undistinguished sire. He died on August 8, 1970.

Secretariat

Like Man o' War, Secretariat was known as Big Red, and both were big in accomplishments. Secretariat, by leading sire Bold Ruler out of the *Princequillo mare Somethingroyal, made his career debut on July 4, 1972, in a 5½-furlong maiden race at Aqueduct and finished fourth with a late surge. Secretariat subsequently won five stakes impressively and was voted Horse of the Year.

In February 1973, as Secretariat was being prepared for the Triple Crown campaign, he was syndicated by Claiborne Farm for a record $6.08-million. Secretariat easily won his first two starts of the year, the Bay Shore (G3) and the Gotham (G2) Stakes, but the colt ran third in the Wood Memorial Stakes (G1) on April 20, most likely due to a lip abscess. His Kentucky Derby (G1) was one that will forever be remembered. After breaking near the back of the pack, Secretariat began picking up horses on the first turn, collared Sham at the top of the lane, and drew away to a 2½-length victory in a Derby record 1:59⅖ for 1¼ miles.

In the Preakness Stakes (G1), jockey Ron Turcotte sensed a slow early pace and allowed Secretariat to surge to the lead as the six-horse field entered the backstretch. Secretariat dominated the rest of the race and again won by 2½ lengths over Sham. A timer malfunction effectively nullified what should have been a track record.

Ch. c., 1970, by Bold Ruler— Somethingroyal, by *Princequillo

Owner: Meadow Stable
Breeder: Meadow Stud (Va.)
Trainer: Lucien Laurin
Jockey: Ron Turcotte

		Race Record			
Year	Starts	1st	2nd	3rd	Earnings
1972	9	7 (5)	1 (1)	0	$ 456,404
1973	12	9 (9)	2 (2)	1 (1)	860,404
	21	16 (14)	3 (3)	1 (1)	$1,316,808

1972—1st Hopeful S., Futurity S., Garden State S., Laurel Futurity, Sanford S.
1973—1st Kentucky Derby (G1), Preakness S. (G1), Belmont S. (G1), Man o' War S. (G1), Canadian International Championship S. (G2), Marlboro Cup H., Arlington Invitational S., Gotham S. (G2), Bay Shore S. (G3)

Only Sham and three others showed up to oppose Secretariat in the Belmont Stakes (G1) on June 9. Secretariat and Sham dueled through the first six furlongs in 1:09⅘ before Sham surrendered. Secretariat steadily pulled away to win by 31 lengths while running 1½ miles in 2:24, an American record.

Retired to Claiborne, Secretariat was a good but not great sire. He died of complications from laminitis on October 4, 1989.

Seattle Slew

A son of Bold Reasoning out of My Charmer, by Poker, Seattle Slew was brought along patiently by his young trainer, Billy Turner Jr. He was voted champion two-year-old male after a stunning Champagne Stakes (G1) win in just his third start.

At three, Seattle Slew won Hialeah Park's Flamingo Stakes (G1) by four lengths on March 26 and took Aqueduct's Wood Memorial Stakes (G1) by 3¼ lengths on April 23.

For the Derby on May 7, Seattle Slew went off as the 1-to-2 favorite. Disaster nearly struck at the start when he swerved out and was sharply taken up by jockey Jean Cruguet. At the top of the stretch, Seattle Slew put away For The Moment and then cruised home by 1¾ lengths over Run Dusty Run.

Two weeks later in the Preakness Stakes (G1), 2-to-5 Seattle Slew took command leaving the backstretch and won by 1½ lengths over Iron Constitution. Seattle Slew then dominated the Belmont Stakes (G1), winning by four lengths over Run Dusty Run. Seattle Slew was the first to complete the series without a defeat. Turner suggested a rest, but owners Karen and Mickey Taylor and Sally and Jim Hill insisted on running in Hollywood Park's Swaps Stakes (G1). Slew finished fourth and did not race again in 1977.

Seattle Slew made seven starts as a four-year-old for trainer Doug Peterson, and his five victories

Dk. b. or br. c., 1974, by Bold Reasoning—My Charmer, by Poker					

Owners: Mickey and Karen L. Taylor, Dr. Jim and Sally Hill
Breeder: Ben S. Castleman (Ky.)
Trainers: William H. Turner Jr. (1976-'77); Doug Peterson (1978)
Jockey: Jean Cruguet

		Race Record			
Year	Starts	1st	2nd	3rd	Earnings
1976	3	3 (1)	0	0	$ 94,350
1977	7	6 (5)	0	0	641,370
1978	7	5 (3)	2 (2)	0	473,006
	17	14 (9)	2 (2)	0	$1,208,726

1976—1st Champagne S. (G1)
1977—1st Kentucky Derby (G1), Preakness S. (G1), Belmont S. (G1), Wood Memorial S. (G1), Flamingo S. (G1)
1978—1st Marlboro Cup Invitational H. (G1), Woodward S. (G1), Stuyvesant S. (G3)

included an epic win over Affirmed in the Marlboro Cup Invitational Handicap (G1), the first meeting of Triple Crown winners. Standing first at Spendthrift Farm and then at Three Chimneys Farm, he sired A.P. Indy, 1992 Horse of the Year, and more than 100 stakes winners. He died on May 7, 2002, at Hill 'n' Dale Farm, where he was moved shortly before his death.

Affirmed

The 1978 Triple Crown, the first won in back-to-back years, belonged to Affirmed, but his name will forever be linked with Alydar, the first horse to finish second in all three races to a Triple Crown winner.

Both colts dominated their arenas at three, and the Kentucky Derby (G1), in which Alydar went off as the 6-to-5 favorite with Affirmed at 9-to-5, was a clash of titans. Third early under jockey Steve Cauthen, Affirmed surged past Believe It early in the stretch and opened a two-length lead in midstretch. Alydar made a late charge but finished second, beaten 1½ lengths.

Two weeks later on May 20, the two would stage an epic duel in the Preakness Stakes (G1). Affirmed, 1-to-2, once again stalked the early pace and inherited the lead after a quarter-mile. Jorge Velasquez asked Alydar for speed on the backstretch, and the Raise a Native colt reached Affirmed's side leaving the turn. They fought to the wire, with Affirmed winning by a neck.

In the Belmont Stakes (G1) three weeks later, 3-to-5 Affirmed was the only speed in a field of five, and 11-to-10 Alydar shadowed him practically from the start. After a half-mile, Affirmed led by one length, and by the top of Belmont Park's stretch they were a head apart. Alydar appeared

Ch. c., 1975, by Exclusive Native— Won't Tell You, by Crafty Admiral					

Owner-Breeder: Harbor View Farm (Fl.)
Trainer: Lazaro Barrera
Jockey: Steve Cauthen

		Race Record			
Year	Starts	1st	2nd	3rd	Earnings
1977	9	7 (6)	2 (2)	0	$ 343,477
1978	11	8 (7)	2 (2)	0	901,541
1979	9	7 (6)	1 (1)	1 (1)	1,148,800
	29	22 (19)	5 (5)	1 (1)	$2,393,818

1977—1st Hopeful S. (G1), Futurity S. (G1), Laurel Futurity (G1), Sanford S. (G2), Hollywood Juvenile Championship S. (G2), Youthful S.
1978—1st Kentucky Derby (G1), Preakness S. (G1), Belmont S. (G1), Santa Anita Derby (G1), Hollywood Derby (G1), San Felipe H. (G2), Jim Dandy S. (G3)
1979—1st Jockey Club Gold Cup (G1), Hollywood Gold Cup (G1), Santa Anita H. (G1), Woodward S. (G1), Californian S. (G1), Charles H. Strub S. (G1)

to take a narrow lead inside the furlong pole, but Affirmed fought back and won by a head. He was voted Horse of the Year and repeated in 1979 with six consecutive Grade 1 victories. The sport's first $2-million earner, he sired more than 80 stakes winners. He died on January 12, 2001, at Jonabell Farm.

Near Triple Crown Winners

While the Triple Crown has been swept on 11 occasions, in 49 other years three-year-olds have won two legs of the Triple Crown. Among the 49 near successes were 20 horses who won the Kentucky Derby and Preakness Stakes but not the Belmont Stakes.

Of those 20, injury felled several in the Belmont (including Tim Tam and Charismatic), several have come agonizingly close (Silver Charm, Real Quiet, Smarty Jones), and two did not run in the Belmont (Burgoo King, Bold Venture) because of injuries before the race.

Following are the 49 horses who won two of the three races. Winner of the race the Triple Crown hopeful lost is in parentheses.

Year	Horse	Kentucky Derby	Preakness	Belmont
2005	Afleet Alex	3rd (Giacomo)	Won	Won
2004	Smarty Jones	Won	Won	2nd (Birdstone)
2003	Funny Cide	Won	Won	3rd (Empire Maker)
2002	War Emblem	Won	Won	8th (Sarava)
2001	Point Given	5th (Monarchos)	Won	Won
1999	Charismatic	Won	Won	3rd (Lemon Drop Kid)
1998	Real Quiet	Won	Won	2nd (Victory Gallop)
1997	Silver Charm	Won	Won	2nd (Touch Gold)
1995	Thunder Gulch	Won	3rd (Timber Country)	Won
1994	Tabasco Cat	6th (Go for Gin)	Won	Won
1991	Hansel	10th (Strike the Gold)	Won	Won
1989	Sunday Silence	Won	Won	2nd (Easy Goer)
1988	Risen Star	3rd (Winning Colors)	Won	Won
1987	Alysheba	Won	Won	4th (Bet Twice)
1984	Swale	Won	7th (Gate Dancer)	Won
1981	Pleasant Colony	Won	Won	3rd (Summing)
1979	Spectacular Bid	Won	Won	3rd (Coastal)
1976	Bold Forbes	Won	3rd (Elocutionist)	Won
1974	Little Current	5th (Cannonade)	Won	Won
1972	Riva Ridge	Won	4th (Bee Bee Bee)	Won
1971	Canonero II	Won	Won	4th (Pass Catcher)
1969	Majestic Prince	Won	Won	2nd (Arts and Letters)
1968	Forward Pass	Won†	Won	2nd (Stage Door Johnny)
1967	Damascus	3rd (Proud Clarion)	Won	Won
1966	Kauai King	Won	Won	4th (Amberoid)
1964	Northern Dancer	Won	Won	3rd (Quadrangle)
1963	Chateaugay	Won	2nd (Candy Spots)	Won
1961	Carry Back	Won	Won	7th (Sherluck)
1958	Tim Tam	Won	Won	2nd (*Cavan)
1956	Needles	Won	2nd (Fabius)	Won
1955	Nashua	2nd (Swaps)	Won	Won
1953	Native Dancer	2nd (Dark Star)	Won	Won
1950	Middleground	Won	2nd (Hill Prince)	Won
1949	Capot	2nd (Ponder)	Won	Won
1944	Pensive	Won	Won	2nd (Bounding Home)
1942	Shut Out	Won	5th (Alsab)	Won
1940	Bimelech	2nd (Gallahadion)	Won	Won
1939	Johnstown	Won	5th (Challedon)	Won
1936	Bold Venture	Won	Won	Did not start
1932	Burgoo King	Won	Won	Did not start
1931	Twenty Grand	Won	2nd (Mate)	Won
1923	Zev	Won	12th (Vigil)	Won
1922	Pillory	Did not start	Won	Won
1920	Man o' War	Did not start	Won	Won
1895	Belmar	Did not start	Won	Won
1881	Saunterer	Did not start	Won	Won
1880	Grenada	Did not start	Won	Won
1878	Duke of Magenta	Did not start	Won	Won
1877	Cloverbrook	Did not start	Won	Won

†Won on disqualification of Dancer's Image. Winner of race is in parentheses.

Leading Owners of Triple Crown Race Winners

17 Calumet Farm: Kentucky Derby: Whirlaway (1941), Pensive ('44), Citation ('48), Ponder ('49), Hill Gail ('52), Iron Liege ('57), Tim Tam ('58), Forward Pass ('68); Preakness: Whirlaway ('41), Pensive ('44), Faultless ('47), Citation ('48), Fabius ('56), Tim Tam ('58), Forward Pass ('68); Belmont: Whirlaway ('41), Citation ('48)

12 Belair Stud: Kentucky Derby: Gallant Fox (1930), Omaha ('35), Johnstown ('39); Preakness: Gallant Fox ('30), Omaha ('35), Nashua ('55); Belmont: Gallant Fox ('30), Omaha ('35), Nashua ('55), Granville ('36), Johnstown ('39), Nashua ('55)

10 Harry P. Whitney: Kentucky Derby: Regret (1915), Whiskery ('27); Preakness: Royal Tourist ('08), Broomspun ('21), Bostonian ('27), Victorian ('28); Belmont: Tanya ('05), Burgomaster ('06), Prince Eugene ('13), *Johren ('18)

9 E. R. Bradley (Idle Hour Stock Farm): Kentucky Derby: Behave Yourself (1921), Bubbling Over ('26), Burgoo King ('32), Brokers Tip ('33); Preakness: Kalitan ('17), Burgoo King ('32), Bimelech ('40); Belmont: Blue Larkspur ('29), Bimelech ('40)

8 Dwyer Brothers:
6—Dwyer Brothers (M. F. and Phil J.): Kentucky Derby: Hindoo (1881); Belmont: George Kinney ('83), Panique ('84), Inspector B. ('86), Hanover ('87), Sir Dixon ('88)
1—M. F. Dwyer: Kentucky Derby: Ben Brush (1896)
1—Phil J. Dwyer: Preakness: Half Time (1899)
George L. Lorillard: Preakness: Duke of Magenta (1878), Harold ('79), Grenada ('80), Saunterer ('81), Vanguard ('82); Belmont: Duke of Magenta ('78), Grenada ('80), Saunterer ('81)

7 August Belmont II: Preakness: Margrave (1896), Don Enrique (1907), Watervale ('11); Belmont: Hastings (1896), Masterman (1902), Friar Rock ('16), *Hourless ('17)
Glen Riddle Farms: Kentucky Derby: War Admiral (1937); Preakness: Man o'War ('20), War Admiral ('37); Belmont: Man o'War ('20), American Flag ('25), Crusader (1926), War Admiral ('37)
Greentree Stable: Kentucky Derby: Twenty Grand (1931), Shut Out ('42); Preakness: Capot ('49); Belmont: Twenty Grand ('31), Shut Out ('42), Capot ('49), Stage Door Johnny ('68)
James R. Keene:
6—James R. Keene: Belmont: Spendthrift (1879), Commando (1901), Delhi ('04), Peter Pan ('07), Colin ('08), Sweep ('10)
1—James R. Keene and Foxhall P. Keene: Preakness: Assignee (1894)

6 Robert and Beverly Lewis:
5—Robert and Beverly Lewis: Kentucky Derby: Silver Charm (1997), Charismatic ('99); Preakness: Silver Charm ('97), Charismatic ('99); Belmont: Commendable (2000)
1—Gainesway Farm, Robert and Beverly Lewis, and Overbrook Farm: Preakness: Timber Country (1995)
Meadow Stable (C. T. and Penny Chenery): Kentucky Derby: Riva Ridge (1972), Secretariat ('73); Preakness: Hill Prince ('50), Secretariat ('73); Belmont: Riva Ridge ('72), Secretariat ('73)

5 Overbrook Farm (W. T. Young):
2—Overbrook Farm: Kentucky Derby: Grindstone (1996); Belmont: Editor's Note ('96)
2—Overbrook Farm and David Reynolds: Preakness: Tabasco Cat (1994); Belmont: Tabasco Cat ('94)
1—Gainesway Farm, Robert and Beverly Lewis, and Overbrook Farm: Preakness: Timber Country (1995)
King Ranch: Kentucky Derby: Assault (1946), Middleground ('50); Preakness: Assault ('46); Belmont: Assault ('46), Middleground ('50), High Gun ('54)
Darby Dan Farm: Kentucky Derby: Chateaugay (1963), Proud Clarion ('67); Preakness: Little Current ('74); Belmont: Chateaugay ('63), Little Current ('74)

4 Brookmeade Stable: Kentucky Derby: Cavalcade (1934); Preakness: High Quest ('34), Bold ('51); Belmont: Sword Dancer ('59)
Mrs. John D. Hertz: Kentucky Derby: Reigh Count (1928), Count Fleet ('43); Preakness: Count Fleet ('43); Belmont: Count Fleet ('43)
J.K.L. Ross: Kentucky Derby: Sir Barton (1919); Preakness: Damrosch ('16), Sir Barton ('19); Belmont: Sir Barton ('19)

4 The Thoroughbred Corp: Kentucky Derby: War Emblem (2002); Preakness: Point Given ('01), War Emblem ('02); Belmont: Point Given ('01)

3 William Condren:
1—B. Giles Brophy, William Condren, and Joseph Cornacchia: Kentucky Derby: Strike the Gold (1991)
1—William Condren and Joseph Cornacchia: Kentucky Derby: Go for Gin (1994)
1—William Condren, Georgia Hofmann, and Joseph Cornacchia: Preakness: Louis Quatorze (1996)
Joseph Cornacchia:
1—B. Giles Brophy, William Condren, and Joseph Cornacchia: Kentucky Derby: Strike the Gold (1991)
1—William Condren and Joseph Cornacchia: Kentucky Derby: Go for Gin (1994)
1—William Condren, Georgia Hofmann, and Joseph Cornacchia: Preakness: Louis Quatorze (1996)
Arthur B. Hancock III:
1—Arthur B. Hancock III and Leone J. Peters: Kentucky Derby: Gato Del Sol (1982)
2—Arthur B. Hancock III, Ernest Gaillard, and Charlie Whittingham: Kentucky Derby: Sunday Silence (1989); Preakness: Sunday Silence ('89)
Harbor View Farm: Kentucky Derby: Affirmed (1978); Preakness: Affirmed ('78); Belmont: Affirmed ('78)
Loblolly Stable: Preakness: Pine Bluff (1992), Prairie Bayou ('93); Belmont: Temperence Hill ('80)
David McDaniel: Belmont: Harry Bassett (1871), Joe Daniels ('72), Springbok ('73)
Preakness Stable (James Galway): Preakness: Montague (1890), Belmar ('95); Belmont: Belmar ('95)

3   Rokeby Stable: Kentucky Derby: Sea Hero (1993); Belmont: Quadrangle ('64), Arts and Letters ('69)
Walter J. Salmon: Preakness: Vigil (1923), Display ('26), Dr. Freeland ('29)
H. F. Sinclair: Belmont: Grey Lag (1921), Zev ('23), Mad Play ('24)

3   Karen and Mickey Taylor and Sally and James Hill: Kentucky Derby: Seattle Slew (1977); Preakness: Seattle Slew ('77); Belmont: Seattle Slew ('77)
Joseph E. Widener: Belmont: Chance Shot (1927), Hurryoff ('33), Peace Chance ('34)
Richard T. Wilson Jr.: Preakness: The Parader (1901), Pillory ('22); Belmont: Pillory ('22)

Leading Breeders of Triple Crown Race Winners

18   Calumet Farm: Kentucky Derby: Whirlaway (1941), Pensive ('44), Citation ('48), Ponder ('49), Hill Gail ('52), Iron Liege ('57), Tim Tam ('58), Forward Pass ('68), Strike the Gold ('91); Preakness: Whirlaway ('41), Pensive ('44), Faultless ('47), Citation ('48), Fabius ('56), Tim Tam ('58), Forward Pass ('68); Belmont: Whirlaway ('41), Citation ('48)

15   A. J. Alexander: Kentucky Derby: Baden-Baden (1877), Fonso ('80), Joe Cotton ('85), Chant ('94); Preakness: Tom Ochiltree ('75), Shirley ('76), Grenada ('80), Duke of Magenta ('90); Belmont: Harry Bassett ('71), Joe Daniels ('72), Springbok ('73), Duke of Magenta ('78), Spendthrift ('79), Grenada ('80), Burlington ('90)

12   Harry P. Whitney: Kentucky Derby: Regret (1915), Whiskery ('27); Preakness: Royal Tourist ('08), Buskin ('13), Holiday ('14), Broomspun ('21), Bostonian ('27), Victorian ('28); Belmont: Tanya ('05), Burgomaster ('06), Prince Eugene ('13), *Johren ('18)

11   John E. Madden
       8—John E. Madden: Kentucky Derby: Old Rosebud (1914), Paul Jones ('20), Zev ('23), Flying Ebony ('25); Belmont: Joe Madden ('09), The Finn ('15), Grey Lag ('21), Zev ('23)
       3—John E. Madden and Vivian A. Gooch: Kentucky Derby: Sir Barton (1919); Preakness: Sir Barton ('19); Belmont: Sir Barton ('19)

10   Belair Stud: Kentucky Derby: Gallant Fox (1930), Omaha ('35); Preakness: Gallant Fox ('30), Omaha ('35), Nashua ('55); Belmont: Gallant Fox ('30), Faireno ('32), Omaha ('35), Granville ('36), Nashua ('55)
       August Belmont II: Preakness: Margrave (1896), Don Enrique (1907), Watervale ('11), Damrosch ('16), Man o' War ('20); Belmont: Masterman ('02), Friar Rock ('16), *Hourless ('17), Man o' War ('20), Chance Shot ('27)

8   E. R. Bradley (Idle Hour Stock Farm): Kentucky Derby: Behave Yourself (1921), Bubbling Over ('26), Burgoo King ('32), Brokers Tip ('33); Preakness: Burgoo King ('32), Bimelech ('40); Belmont: Blue Larkspur ('29), Bimelech ('40)

7   Greentree Stud: Kentucky Derby: Twenty Grand (1931), Shut Out ('42); Preakness: Capot ('49); Belmont: Twenty Grand ('31), Shut Out ('42), Capot ('49), Stage Door Johnny ('68)

6   William S. Farish
       3—William S. Farish and William S. Kilroy: Preakness: Summer Squall (1990); Belmont: A.P. Indy ('90), Lemon Drop Kid ('99)
       2—Parrish Hill Farm and William S. Farish: Kentucky Derby: Charismatic (1999); Preakness: Charismatic ('99)
       1—William S. Farish and E. J. Hudson: Belmont: Bet Twice (1987)

6   James Ben Ali Haggin: Kentucky Derby: Stone Street (1908); Preakness: Old England ('02), Cairngorm ('05), Rhine Maiden ('15); Belmont: Commanche (1893), Africander (1903)
Meadow Stud (C. T. Chenery): Kentucky Derby: Riva Ridge (1972), Secretariat ('73); Preakness: Hill Prince ('50), Secretariat ('73); Belmont: Riva Ridge ('72), Secretariat ('73)

5   Ezekiel F. Clay
       4—Clay and Woodford: Kentucky Derby: Ben Brush (1896); Preakness: Buddhist ('89); Belmont: Hanover ('87), Sir Dixon ('88)
       1—Ezekiel F. Clay: Kentucky Derby: Agile (1905)
       John W. Galbreath: Kentucky Derby: Chateaugay (1963), Proud Clarion ('67); Preakness: Little Current ('74); Belmont: Chateaugay ('63), Little Current ('74)
       James R. Keene: Belmont: Commando (1901), Delhi ('04), Peter Pan ('07), Colin ('08), Sweep ('10)
       King Ranch: Kentucky Derby: Assault (1946), Middleground ('50); Preakness: Assault ('46); Belmont: Assault ('46), Middleground ('50)
       Samuel D. Riddle: Kentucky Derby: War Admiral (1937); Preakness: War Admiral ('37); Belmont: American Flag ('25), Crusader ('26), War Admiral ('37)

4   Arthur B. Hancock III
       3—Arthur B. Hancock III and Leone J. Peters: Kentucky Derby: Gato Del Sol (1982); Preakness: Risen Star ('88); Belmont: Risen Star ('88)
       1—Arthur B. Hancock III and Stonerside Ltd.: Kentucky Derby: Fusaichi Pegasus (2000)
       Arthur B. Hancock Sr.
       3—Arthur B. Hancock: Kentucky Derby: Johnstown (1939); Preakness: Vigil ('23); Belmont: Johnstown ('39)
       1—Arthur B. Hancock and Mrs. R. A. Van Clief: Kentucky Derby: Jet Pilot (1947)
       Aristides Welch: Preakness: Harold (1879), Saunterer ('81); Belmont: Saunterer ('81), Panique ('84)

3   August Belmont I: Preakness: Jacobus (1883); Belmont: Fenian ('69), Forester ('82)
       A. J. Cassatt: Preakness: Montague (1890); Belmont: Foxford ('91), Patron ('92)
       Ben S. Castleman: Kentucky Derby: Seattle Slew (1977), Preakness: Seattle Slew ('77), Belmont: Seattle Slew ('77)
       Claiborne Farm: Kentucky Derby: Swale (1984); Belmont: Coastal ('79), Swale ('84)
       Harbor View Farm: Kentucky Derby: Affirmed (1978); Preakness: Affirmed ('78); Belmont: Affirmed ('78)

3   Mrs. John D. Hertz: Kentucky Derby: Count Fleet (1943); Preakness: Count Fleet ('43); Belmont: Count Fleet ('43)

George J. Long: Kentucky Derby: Azra (1892), Manuel (1899), Sir Huon (1906)

H. Price McGrath (McGrathiana Stud): Kentucky Derby: Aristides (1875); Preakness: Paul Kauvar ('97); Belmont: Calvin ('75)

Paul Mellon: Kentucky Derby: Sea Hero (1993); Belmont: Quadrangle ('64), Arts and Letters ('69)

3   Overbrook Farm
2—Overbrook Farm and David Reynolds: Preakness: Tabasco Cat (1994); Belmont: Tabasco Cat ('94)
1—Overbrook Farm: Kentucky Derby: Grindstone (1996)

Daniel Swigert: Kentucky Derby: Hindoo (1881), Apollo ('82), Ben Ali ('86)

Leading Trainers of Triple Crown Race Winners

13   James "Sunny Jim" Fitzsimmons: Kentucky Derby: Gallant Fox (1930), Omaha ('35), Johnstown ('39); Preakness: Gallant Fox ('30), Omaha ('35), Nashua ('55), Bold Ruler ('57); Belmont: Gallant Fox ('30), Faireno ('32), Omaha ('35), Granville ('36), Johnstown ('39), Nashua ('55)

D. Wayne Lukas: Kentucky Derby: Winning Colors (1988), Thunder Gulch ('95), Grindstone ('96), Charismatic ('99); Preakness: Codex ('80), Tank's Prospect ('85), Tabasco Cat ('94), Timber Country ('95), Charismatic ('99); Belmont: Tabasco Cat ('94), Thunder Gulch ('95), Editor's Note ('96), Commendable (2000)

11   James Rowe Sr.: Kentucky Derby: Hindoo (1881), Regret (1915); Preakness: Broomspun (1921); Belmont: George Kinney (1883), Panique (1884), Commando (1901), Delhi ('04), Peter Pan ('07), Colin ('08), Sweep ('10), Prince Eugene ('13)

R. Wyndham Walden: Preakness: Tom Ochiltree (1875), Duke of Magenta ('78), Harold ('79), Grenada ('80), Saunterer ('81), Vanguard ('82), Refund ('88); Belmont: Duke of Magenta ('78), Grenada ('80), Saunterer ('81), *Bowling Brook ('98)

9   Max Hirsch: Kentucky Derby: Bold Venture (1936), Assault ('46), Middleground ('50); Preakness: Bold Venture ('36), Assault ('46); Belmont: Vito ('28), Assault ('46), Middleground ('50), High Gun ('54)

B. A. "Ben" Jones: Kentucky Derby: Lawrin (1938), Whirlaway ('41), Pensive ('44), Citation ('48), Ponder ('49), Hill Gail ('52); Preakness: Whirlaway ('41), Pensive ('44); Belmont: Whirlaway ('41)

8   Bob Baffert: Kentucky Derby: Silver Charm (1997), Real Quiet ('98), War Emblem (2002); Preakness: Silver Charm ('97), Real Quiet ('98), Point Given (2001), War Emblem ('02); Belmont: Point Given ('01)

Woodford C. "Woody" Stephens: Kentucky Derby: Cannonade (1974), Swale ('84); Preakness: Blue Man ('52); Belmont: Conquistador Cielo ('82), Caveat ('83), Swale ('84), Creme Fraiche ('85), Danzig Connection ('86)

7   H. A. "Jimmy" Jones: Kentucky Derby: Iron Liege (1957), Tim Tam ('58); Preakness: Faultless ('47), Citation ('48), Fabius ('56), Tim Tam ('58); Belmont: Citation ('48)

Sam Hildreth: Belmont: Jean Bereaud (1899), Joe Madden (1909), Friar Rock ('16), *Hourless ('17), Grey Lag ('21), Zev ('23), Mad Play ('24)

6   Thomas J. Healy: Preakness: The Parader (1901), Pillory ('22), Vigil ('23), Display ('26), Dr. Freeland ('29); Belmont: Pillory ('22)

6   Lucien Laurin: Kentucky Derby: Riva Ridge (1972), Secretariat ('73); Preakness: Secretariat ('73); Belmont: Amberoid ('66), Riva Ridge ('73), Secretariat ('73)

5   John M. Gaver: Kentucky Derby: Shut Out (1942); Preakness: Capot ('49); Belmont: Shut Out ('42), Capot ('49), Stage Door Johnny ('68)

Lazaro Barrera: Kentucky Derby: Bold Forbes (1976), Affirmed ('78); Preakness: Affirmed ('78); Belmont: Bold Forbes ('76), Affirmed ('78)

H. J. "Dick" Thompson: Kentucky Derby: Behave Yourself (1921), Bubbling Over ('26), Burgoo King ('32), Brokers Tip ('33); Preakness: Burgoo King ('32)

4   Henry Forrest: Kentucky Derby: Kauai King (1966), Forward Pass ('68); Preakness: Kauai King ('66), Forward Pass ('68)

George Conway: Kentucky Derby: War Admiral (1937); Preakness: War Admiral ('37); Belmont: Crusader ('26), War Admiral ('37)

Frank McCabe: Preakness: Half Time (1899); Belmont: Inspector B. ('86), Hanover ('87), Sir Dixon ('88)

Nicholas P. Zito: Kentucky Derby: Strike the Gold (1991), Go for Gin ('94); Preakness: Louis Quatorze ('96); Belmont: Birdstone (2004)

3   H. Guy Bedwell: Kentucky Derby: Sir Barton (1919); Preakness: Sir Barton ('19); Belmont: Sir Barton ('19)

J. Elliott Burch: Belmont: Sword Dancer (1959), Quadrangle ('64), Arts and Letters ('69)

G. D. Cameron: Kentucky Derby: Count Fleet (1943); Preakness: Count Fleet ('43); Belmont: Count Fleet ('43)

Peter Coyne: Kentucky Derby: Sir Huon (1906); Belmont: Chance Shot ('27), Peace Chance ('34)

Edward Feakes: Preakness: Montague (1890), Belmar ('95); Belmont: Belmar ('95)

Thomas P. Hayes: Kentucky Derby: Donerail (1913); Preakness: Paul Kauvar (1897), Head Play (1933)

William Hurley: Preakness: Kalitan (1917), Bimelech ('40); Belmont: Bimelech ('40)

Horatio Luro: Kentucky Derby: Decidedly (1962), Northern Dancer ('64); Preakness: Northern Dancer ('64)

David McDaniel: Belmont: Harry Bassett (1871), Joe Daniels ('72), Springbok ('73)

James Rowe Jr.: Kentucky Derby: Twenty Grand (1931); Preakness: Victorian ('28), Belmont: Twenty Grand ('31)

William H. Turner Jr.: Kentucky Derby: Seattle Slew (1977); Preakness: Seattle Slew ('77); Belmont: ('77)

3   **James Whalen:** Preakness: Don Enrique (1907), Watervale ('11), Buskin ('13)
Frank Y. Whiteley Jr.: Preakness: Tom Rolfe (1965), Damascus ('67); Belmont: Damascus ('67)

3   **Charles Whittingham:** Kentucky Derby: Ferdinand (1986), Sunday Silence ('89); Preakness: Sunday Silence ('89)

Leading Jockeys of Triple Crown Race Winners

17   **Eddie Arcaro:** Kentucky Derby: Lawrin (1938), Whirlaway ('41), Hoop, Jr. ('45), Citation ('48), Hill Gail ('52); Preakness: Whirlaway ('41), Citation ('48), Hill Prince ('50), Bold ('51), Nashua ('55), Bold Ruler ('57); Belmont: Whirlaway ('41), Shut Out ('42), Pavot ('45), Citation ('48), One Count ('52), Nashua ('55)

11   **William Shoemaker:** Kentucky Derby: Swaps (1955), *Tomy Lee ('59), Lucky Debonair ('65), Ferdinand ('86); Preakness: Candy Spots ('63), Damascus ('67); Belmont: *Gallant Man ('57), Sword Dancer ('59), Jaipur ('62), Damascus ('67), Avatar ('75)

9   **Pat Day:** Kentucky Derby: Lil E. Tee (1992); Preakness: Tank's Prospect ('85), Summer Squall ('90), Tabasco Cat ('94), Timber Country ('95), Louis Quatorze ('96); Belmont: Easy Goer ('89), Tabasco Cat ('94), Commendable (2000)

9   **William J. Hartack:** Kentucky Derby: Iron Liege (1957), Venetian Way ('60), Decidedly ('62), Northern Dancer ('64), Majestic Prince ('69); Preakness: Fabius ('56), Northern Dancer ('64), Majestic Prince ('69); Belmont: *Celtic Ash ('60)

     Earl Sande: Kentucky Derby: Zev (1923), Flying Ebony ('25), Gallant Fox ('30); Preakness: Gallant Fox ('30); Belmont: Grey Lag ('21), Zev ('23), Mad Play ('24), Chance Shot ('27), Gallant Fox ('30)

8   **James McLaughlin:** Kentucky Derby: Hindoo (1881); Preakness: Tecumseh ('85); Belmont: Forester ('82), George Kinney ('83), Panique ('84), Inspector B. ('86), Hanover ('87), Sir Dixon ('88)

     Gary Stevens: Kentucky Derby: Winning Colors (1988), Thunder Gulch ('95), Silver Charm ('97); Preakness: Silver Charm ('97), Point Given (2001); Belmont: Thunder Gulch (1995), Victory Gallop ('98), Point Given (2001)

6   **Jerry Bailey:** Kentucky Derby: Sea Hero (1993), Grindstone ('96); Preakness: Hansel ('91), Red Bullet (2000); Belmont: Hansel (1991), Empire Maker (2003)

     Angel Cordero Jr.: Kentucky Derby: Cannonade (1974), Bold Forbes ('76), Spend a Buck ('85); Preakness: Codex ('80), Gate Dancer ('84); Belmont: Bold Forbes ('76)

     Charles Kurtsinger: Kentucky Derby: Twenty Grand (1931), War Admiral ('37); Preakness: Head Play ('33), War Admiral ('37); Belmont: Twenty Grand ('31), War Admiral ('37)

     Chris McCarron: Kentucky Derby: Alysheba (1987), Go for Gin ('94); Preakness: Alysheba ('87), Pine Bluff ('92); Belmont: Danzig Connection ('86), Touch Gold ('97)

     Ron Turcotte: Kentucky Derby: Riva Ridge (1972), Secretariat ('73); Preakness: Tom Rolfe ('65), Secretariat ('73); Belmont: Riva Ridge ('72), Secretariat ('73)

5   **Eddie Delahoussaye:** Kentucky Derby: Gato Del Sol (1982), Sunny's Halo ('83); Preakness: Risen Star ('88); Belmont: Risen Star ('88), A.P. Indy ('92)

5   **Lloyd Hughes:** Preakness: Tom Ochiltree (1875), Harold ('79), Grenada ('80); Belmont: Duke of Magenta ('78), Grenada ('80)

     John Loftus: Kentucky Derby: George Smith (1916), Sir Barton ('19); Preakness: *War Cloud ('18), Sir Barton ('19); Belmont: Sir Barton ('19)

     Willie Simms: Kentucky Derby: Ben Brush (1898), Plaudit ('98); Preakness: Sly Fox ('98); Belmont: Comanche ('93), Henry Of Navarre ('94)

4   **Braulio Baeza:** Kentucky Derby: Chateaugay (1963); Belmont: Sherluck ('61), Chateaugay ('63), Arts and Letters ('69)

     George Barbee: Preakness: Survivor (1873), Shirley ('76), Jacobus ('83); Belmont: Saxon ('74)

     William "Billy" Donohue: Kentucky Derby: Leonatus (1883); Preakness: Culpepper ('74), Dunboyne ('87); Belmont: Algerine ('76)

     Eric Guerin: Kentucky Derby: Jet Pilot (1947); Preakness: Native Dancer ('53); Belmont: Native Dancer ('53), High Gun ('54)

     Albert Johnson: Kentucky Derby: Morvich (1922), Bubbling Over ('26); Belmont: American Flag ('25), Crusader ('26)

     Clarence Kummer: Preakness: Man o' War (1920), Coventry ('25); Belmont: Man o' War ('20), Vito ('28)

     Conn McCreary: Kentucky Derby: Pensive (1944), Count Turf ('51); Preakness: Pensive ('44), Blue Man ('52)

     Laffit Pincay Jr.: Kentucky Derby: Swale (1984); Belmont: Conquistador Cielo ('82), Caveat ('83), Swale ('84)

     James Stout: Kentucky Derby: Johnstown (1939); Belmont: Granville ('36), Pasteurized ('38), Johnstown ('39)

     Fred Taral: Kentucky Derby: Manuel (1899); Preakness: Assignee ('94), Belmar ('95); Belmont: Belmar ('95)

     Ismael "Milo" Valenzuela: Kentucky Derby: Tim Tam (1958), Forward Pass ('68); Preakness: Tim Tam ('58), Forward Pass ('68)

3   **Chris Antley:** Kentucky Derby: Strike the Gold (1991), Charismatic ('99); Preakness: Charismatic ('99)

     William Boland: Kentucky Derby: Middleground (1950); Belmont: Middleground ('50), Amberoid ('66)

     James H. "Jimmy" Butwell: Preakness: Buskin (1913); Belmont: Sweep ('10), *Hourless ('17)

     Steve Cauthen: Kentucky Derby: Affirmed (1978); Preakness: Affirmed ('78); Belmont: Affirmed ('78)

     T. Costello: Preakness: Saunterer (1881), Vanguard ('82); Belmont: Saunterer ('81)

     Jean Cruguet: Kentucky Derby: Seattle Slew (1977), Preakness: Seattle Slew ('77); Belmont: Seattle Slew ('77)

     Kent Desormeaux: Kentucky Derby: Real Quiet (1998), Fusaichi Pegasus (2000); Preakness: Real Quiet (1998)

3   **Eddie Dugan**: Preakness: Royal Tourist (1908), Watervale ('11); Belmont: Joe Madden ('09)
    Mack Garner: Kentucky Derby: Cavalcade (1934); Belmont: Blue Larkspur ('29), Hurryoff ('33)
    C. Holloway: Preakness: Cloverbrook (1877), Duke of Magenta ('78); Belmont: Cloverbrook ('77)
    John Longden: Kentucky Derby: Count Fleet (1943); Preakness: Count Fleet ('43); Belmont: Count Fleet ('43)
    J. Linus "Pony" McAtee: Kentucky Derby: Whiskery (1927), Clyde Van Dusen ('29); Preakness: Damrosch ('16)
    Warren Mehrtens: Kentucky Derby: Assault (1946); Preakness: Assault ('46), Belmont: Assault ('46)

3   **Isaac Murphy**: Kentucky Derby: Buchanan (1884), Riley ('90), Kingman ('91)
    Jose Santos: Kentucky Derby: Funny Cide (2003); Preakness: Funny Cide (2003); Belmont: Lemon Drop Kid (1999)
    William "Smokey" Saunders: Kentucky Derby: Omaha (1935); Preakness: Omaha ('35); Belmont: Omaha ('35)
    John Sellers: Kentucky Derby: Carry Back (1961); Preakness: Carry Back ('61); Belmont: Hail to All ('65)
    Bobby Swim: Kentucky Derby: Vagrant (1876); Belmont: General Duke ('68), Calvin ('75)
    Wayne D. Wright: Kentucky Derby: Shut Out (1942); Preakness: Polynesian ('45); Belmont: Peace Chance ('34)

Leading Sires of Triple Crown Race Winners

7   **Lexington**: Preakness Stakes: Tom Ochiltree (1875), Shirley (1876), Duke of Magenta (1878); Belmont: General Duke (1868), Kingfisher (1870), Harry Bassett (1871), Duke of Magenta (1878)

6   **Bull Lea**: Kentucky Derby: Citation (1948), Hill Gail (1952), Iron Liege (1957); Preakness: Faultless (1947), Citation (1948); Belmont: Citation (1948)
    Man o' War: Kentucky Derby: Clyde Van Dusen (1929); War Admiral (1937); Preakness: War Admiral (1937); Belmont: American Flag (1925), Crusader (1926), War Admiral (1937)
    *Sir Gallahad III: Kentucky Derby: Gallant Fox (1930), Gallahadion (1940), Hoop, Jr. (1945); Preakness: Gallant Fox (1930), High Quest, (1934); Belmont: Gallant Fox (1930)

5   **Bold Venture**: Kentucky Derby: Assault (1946), Middleground (1950); Preakness: Assault (1946); Belmont: Assault (1946), Middleground (1950)
    Broomstick: Kentucky Derby: Meridian (1911), Regret (1915); Preakness: Holiday (1914), Broomspun (1921), Bostonian (1927)
    Fair Play: Preakness: Man o' War (1920), Display (1926); Belmont: Man o' War (1920), Mad Play (1924), Chance Shot (1927)

4   ***Australian**: Kentucky Derby: Baden-Baden (1877); Belmont: Joe Daniels (1872), Springbok (1873), Spendthrift (1879)
    Alydar: Kentucky Derby: Alysheba (1987), Strike the Gold (1991); Preakness: Alysheba (1987); Belmont: Easy Goer (1989)
    Black Toney: Kentucky Derby: Black Gold (1924), Brokers Tip (1933); Preakness: Bimelech (1940); Belmont: Bimelech (1940)
    *Blenheim II: Kentucky Derby: Whirlaway (1941), Jet Pilot (1947); Preakness: Whirlaway (1941); Belmont: Whirlaway (1941)
    Exclusive Native: Kentucky Derby: Affirmed (1978); Genuine Risk (1980); Preakness: Affirmed (1978); Belmont: Affirmed (1978)
    Falsetto: Kentucky Derby: Chant (1894), His Eminence (1901); Sir Huon (1906); Belmont: Patron (1892)
    Gallant Fox: Kentucky Derby: Omaha (1935); Preakness: Omaha (1935); Belmont: Omaha (1935), Granville (1936)

4   **King Alfonso**: Kentucky Derby: Fonso (1880); Joe Cotton (1885); Preakness: Grenada (1880); Belmont: Grenada (1880)
    *Leamington: Kentucky Derby: Aristides (1875); Preakness: Harold (1879), Saunterer (1881); Belmont: Saunterer (1881)
    *Nasrullah: Preakness: Nashua (1955), Bold Ruler (1957); Belmont: Nashua (1955), Jaipur (1962)
    *Star Shoot: Kentucky Derby: Sir Barton (1919); Preakness: Sir Barton (1919); Belmont: Sir Barton (1919), Grey Lag (1921)
    *St. Germans: Kentucky Derby: Twenty Grand (1931); Bold Venture (1936); Preakness: Bold Venture (1936); Belmont: Twenty Grand (1931)

3   **Bold Bidder**: Kentucky Derby: Cannonade (1974), Spectacular Bid (1979); Preakness: Spectacular Bid (1979)
    Bold Reasoning: Kentucky Derby: Seattle Slew (1977); Preakness: Seattle Slew (1977); Belmont: Seattle Slew (1977)
    Bold Ruler: Kentucky Derby: Secretariat (1973); Preakness: Secretariat (1973); Belmont: Secretariat (1973)
    Halo: Kentucky Derby: Sunny's Halo (1983); Sunday Silence (1989); Preakness: Sunday Silence (1989)
    Hamburg: Preakness: Buskin (1913); Belmont: Burgomeister (1906), Prince Eugene (1913)
    Longfellow: Kentucky Derby: Leonatus (1883); Riley (1890); Preakness: The Bard (1886)
    Mr. Prospector: Kentucky Derby: Fusaichi Pegasus (2000); Preakness: Tank's Prospect (1985); Belmont: Conquistador Cielo (1982)
    Reigh Count: Kentucky Derby: Count Fleet (1943); Preakness: Count Fleet (1943); Belmont: Count Fleet (1943)
    Seattle Slew: Kentucky Derby: Swale (1984); Belmont: Swale (1984), A.P. Indy (1992)
    The Finn: Kentucky Derby: Zev (1923), Flying Ebony (1925); Belmont: Zev (1923)
    Unbridled: Kentucky Derby: Grindstone (1996); Preakness: Red Bullet (2000); Belmont: Empire Maker (2003)
    Virgil: Kentucky Derby: Vagrant (1886), Hindoo (1881), Ben Ali (1886)
    Woodman: Preakness: Hansel (1991), Timber Country (1995); Belmont: Hansel (1991)

Kentucky Derby History

The Kentucky Derby was the dream of Col. Meriwether Lewis Clark Jr., grandson of William Clark of Lewis and Clark Expedition fame. Just 29 when the first Derby was run in 1875, Meriwether Clark had the family's sense of adventure and ambition but devoted his energies to equine pursuits.

Racing in Louisville was essentially dead in the early 1870s following the closure in '70 of Woodlawn Course, located east of the city. In 1872, Clark traveled to England to observe its racing scene.

He returned with grand ambitions of creating a racing palace in Louisville with races modeled on such leading events in England as the Epsom Derby, Epsom Oaks, and St. Leger Stakes. With $32,000 in investment capital, Clark set about building Louisville's new racetrack in 1874. The facility, built on 80 acres of land leased from Clark's uncles, John and Henry Churchill, was called the Louisville Jockey Club.

The Louisville Jockey Club opened on Monday, May 17, 1875, with four races. It was a sunny day with a crisp breeze, according to an account in the *Live Stock Record* (precursor of *The Thoroughbred Record* and THOROUGHBRED TIMES), and the "course was in splendid order, and all the appurtenances requisite for the comfort and convenience of racing was ready to hand."

All 42 nominees for the inaugural Derby were listed in the program and 15 started, with H. P. McGrath's nobly named Aristides becoming the first Derby winner.

One week after the first meet ended, the *Live Stock Record*'s editor, Benjamin G. Bruce, noted that, while he had attended the inaugural meet at Jerome Park and had visited Saratoga Race Course and Long Branch, "never have we seen such a grand success, taking it from its beginning to its close, as the late inaugural meeting of the Louisville Jockey Club."

While the first race meet was an artistic success, at least in Bruce's view, the financial situation of the Louisville Jockey Club was perilous almost from its start. For most of its first 40 years, the Derby would be regarded as a strong regional race at best and an embarrassing farce at worst. There were many reasons for the race's decline. Louisville was still considered western territory to many leading Eastern stables, and the situation grew worse when a track official insulted leading owner James Ben Ali Haggin in 1886. The race's initial 1½-mile distance was considered too taxing for three-year-olds in the spring.

The revival of the track and its signature race began in 1902. Col. Matt Winn, a Louisville tailor with no racetrack management experience but an undying love for the track—he attended every

Kentucky Derby Attendance

Year	Attendance	Year	Attendance
2005	156,435	1987	130,532
2004	140,054	1986	123,819
2003	148,530	1985	108,573
2002	145,033	1984	126,453
2001	154,210	1983	134,444
2000	153,204	1982	141,009
1999	151,051	1981	139,195
1998	143,215	1980	131,859
1997	141,981	1979	128,488
1996	142,668	1978	131,004
1995	144,110	1977	124,038
1994	130,594	1976	115,387
1993	136,817	1975	113,324
1992	132,543	1974	163,628
1991	135,554	1973	134,476
1990	128,257	1972	130,564
1989	122,653	1971	123,284
1988	137,694	1970	105,087

Kentucky Derby from 1875 to 1949—recruited a group of Louisvillians to purchase the track for $40,000. Winn spent a decade straightening out the financial mess at the track, which by then was known as Churchill Downs. Then, he set out to revive the Kentucky Derby.

The years 1913-'15 would establish the race's credentials from both a romantic and qualitative standpoint. The 1913 running was won by 91.45-to-1 longshot Donerail, who remains the race's longest-priced winner. The race also picked up an unofficial ambassador in winning rider Roscoe Goose, who lived for a half-century mere blocks from the track, dispensing wisdom and schooling such prospective jockeys as two-time Derby winner Charlie Kurtsinger.

The next year, the gallant gelding Old Rosebud won, enhancing the race's reputation. And, in 1915, New York owner Harry Payne Whitney shipped his marvelous, unbeaten filly Regret to Louisville, where she became the first filly to win the Derby. While some Eastern stables still shied away from shipping west for the Derby—most notably Samuel Riddle's decision not to run Man o' War in 1920—the Derby's reputation was set after 1915.

Winn was a showman who combined a promoter's instincts with a passion for the Derby. The Kentucky Derby benefited from Winn's skill until he died on October 6, 1949. By the time of his death, the Derby had become a national racing institution, traditionally run on the first Saturday in May and part of the Triple Crown, a three-race series for three-year-olds considered as the ultimate test for young horses. The track's twin spires, constructed in 1895 when the physical plant was rebuilt on what had been the backstretch side of the original track, were transformed from a unique architectural feature to an iconic symbol.

Before he died, however, Winn witnessed some amazing Derbys. Longshot Exterminator won the 1918 Derby in his three-year-old debut after he was purchased to help train another horse who did not make the race. There were two famous victories by maidens: Sir Barton's 1919 victory launched the first successful Triple Crown campaign, while Brokers Tip won in '33 after his jockey, Don Meade, fought with Head Play's rider, Herb Fisher, down the stretch.

Winn also had to adjust to the circumstances of World War II. Travel restrictions in 1943 gave that Derby a distinctly local flavor, and it became known as the "Street Car Derby." Further war restrictions shut down the sport in early 1945; when the restrictions were lifted after V-E Day, the Derby was scheduled for June 9, the only time the race has been run in June. Three years later, Citation won the Triple Crown—the eighth during Winn's tenure at Churchill.

History flows easily through the Kentucky Derby. Each year seems to bring an amazing, astounding, or simply amusing story. From the sublime (Bill Shoemaker standing up at the sixteenth pole and possibly costing *Gallant Man the 1957 Derby) to the ridiculous (the antics of unraced Nevada gelding One Eyed Tom, who failed to make it to the starting gate in 1972), the Derby has something to offer every racing fan.

Over the past 30 years, the Derby's story has been about the growth of the event as a local and international event. Attendance rose from the 120,000-to-130,000 level in the late 1980s to more than 150,000 starting in 1999. (Security restrictions following the September 11, 2001, terrorist attacks and Churchill's rebuilding program held attendance below 150,000 from 2002 through '04.) Unsuccessful Triple Crown bids by Silver Charm, Real Quiet, and Charismatic from 1997-'99 and by War Emblem, Funny Cide, and Smarty Jones from 2002-'04 created a heightened level of awareness in the Triple Crown races. The efforts of Godolphin Racing (Dubai), The Thoroughbred Corp. (Saudi Arabia and owner of War Emblem), and Michael Tabor and John Magnier (Monaco and Ireland, respectively) to win the race in the late 1990s and early 2000s have given the race an international flavor.—*John Harrell*

Presidents at the Derby

Since World War II, attending the Kentucky Derby has become a pastime of United States presidents. Getting them to attend while they are actually in office, however, has proved to be a challenge.

Eight U.S. presidents have been seen under the twin spires on the first Saturday in May, but Richard Nixon is the only one to attend the race while in office. He attended the event in 1968 while he was running for his first term and then fulfilled a promise when he returned the next year, his first in the Oval Office.

Also attending the Derby in 1969 were two future presidents, Gerald Ford and Ronald Reagan. Ford returned in 1983, along with Jimmy Carter, who defeated him in the 1976 presidential race, and future President George H. W. Bush. Bush returned in 2000, along with his son and future President George W. Bush.

Other presidents who attended the race—though they were not in the Oval Office at the time—were Harry Truman and Lyndon B. Johnson.

Kentucky Derby Trophy

The Kentucky Derby trophy, featuring a simple but classic design with a horse and garland of roses on top, was first presented in 1924, when Black Gold won the 50th running of the Derby.

The trophy had been commissioned for the golden anniversary Derby by Churchill Downs President Col. Matt Winn, who wanted a standard trophy for the connections of each Derby winner. The original design remains to this day, except for one change, when the horseshoe on the trophy was inverted upward starting with the 1999 Derby. The horseshoe had been pointed down for 75 years, according to ancient belief that an upside-down shoe afforded protection. But, since racing superstition maintains that luck runs out of horseshoes that are pointed down, the shoe was inverted.

The only other changes made to the Derby trophy were for the 75th (1949), 100th ('74), and 125th ('99) runnings, when additional jewels were added. Several Derby trophies are on display at the Kentucky Derby Museum; the oldest is Flying Ebony's trophy from the 1925 Derby.

Glasses and Mint Julep Cups

The popularity of the mint julep as the official Kentucky Derby drink grew in proportion with the introduction of Derby glasses and sterling silver julep cups as Derby souvenirs in the middle years of the 20th century.

The Derby glass made its introduction in 1938 after Churchill officials noted that patrons took water glasses from their tables on Derby day as souvenirs. In 1939, glass manufacturers were encouraged to add color to the glasses, making them as attractive as mint julep glasses. Sales of mint juleps increased threefold, according to track officials, and the glasses have gone on to become the most popular Derby souvenirs.

The sterling silver cups were introduced in 1951 as part of the legacy of Col. Matt Winn, who had died two years earlier. Winn wished to make the cups an official Derby souvenir, and they have been part of Derby lore now for more than a half-century. The cups, which hold 12 fluid ounces, were unchanged in design until 1984, when noted owner-breeder Leslie Combs II pointed out that the horseshoe on the glass pointed down, a superstitious sign of bad luck in racing, although an upside-down shoe was regarded in folklore as affording protection. The horseshoe was turned upright and remains so to this day.

Although some relatively minor errors have occurred in the printing on the glasses, two significant mistakes occurred on approximately 100,400 of the half-million Derby glasses manufactured for the 2002 Derby. The erroneous glasses had Burgoo King winning the Triple Crown in 1932 (he won the Derby and Preakness but did not compete in the Belmont Stakes) and War Admiral failing to win the 1937 Triple Crown (he did). These erroneous glasses immediately became collectors' items.

Enduring Twin Spires

The twin spires atop Churchill Downs's grandstand are arguably the best-known architectural feature of any racetrack in the world. They date from the reconstruction of the Louisville track in 1894-'95. Designed by 24-year-old Louisville architect Joseph D. Baldez, the twin spires were intended only as an ornamental feature of the new grandstand, which was constructed at a cost of $100,000. Col. Matt Winn, Churchill's longtime president, once told Baldez, "Joe, when you die there's one monument that will never be taken down, the twin spires."

The spires are checked periodically for structural soundness, and they underwent a renovation in 2002 as part of the $27-million first phase of Churchill's $121-million renewal project. Workmen inspecting the spires found a copy of the Louisville *Courier-Journal* from 1907 and a flag wrapped around a '08 copy of the *Courier-Journal*.

Kentucky Derby Wagering

Each year, the Kentucky Derby attracts the largest crowd in North American racing, usually in excess of 140,000. The Derby also is the sport's biggest day for wagering in North America. In 2005, the Derby set a North American record for most money bet on a single race. Wagering on the Derby totaled $103,325,510, which was 4% above the 2003 record total of $99,364,088 from all sources. On-track wagering on the Derby was $10,055,508, also a record, and all-sources wagering on the Derby day program was $155,133,631, a North American mark.

Kentucky Derby Festival

Conducted annually since 1956, the Kentucky Derby Festival has grown into a weeks-long celebration of Louisville's premier attraction. A not-for-profit community organization, the Kentucky Derby Festival recruits 4,000 volunteers for 70 special events that annually attract approximately 1.5-million people to venues in and around Louisville. Financed by 325 corporate sponsors and the sale of Pegasus Pins, the festival contributes an estimated $93-million to the local economy.

Three of the best-known events of the Kentucky Derby Festival are the Pegasus Parade, the Great Balloon Race, and the Great Steamboat Race. In 1990, the Kentucky Derby Festival added a new attraction, Thunder Over Louisville. Held three weeks before the Derby, it is billed as the nation's largest fireworks display and attracts thousands to the banks of the Ohio River each April.

The schedule of events for the 2005 Kentucky Derby Festival included:

Basketball Classic	April 16
They're Off! Luncheon	April 22
Fillies' Derby Ball	April 22
Thunder Over Louisville	April 23
Great Balloon Race	April 30
Great Bed Races	May 2
Knights of Columbus Charity Dinner	May 2
Run for the Rosé	May 3
Derby Trainers Dinner	May 3
Great Steamboat Race	May 4
Pegasus Parade	May 5

"My Old Kentucky Home"

As the Kentucky Derby field parades onto the racetrack from the paddock, the University of Louisville Marching Band plays "My Old Kentucky Home," a song whose meaning and involvement with the Derby are shrouded in some mystery. Stephen Collins Foster (1826-'64) wrote the song in 1853, while visiting cousins at Federal Hill in Bardstown, Kentucky, a short distance from Louisville.

According to contemporary accounts, the song was first played at the Derby in 1921, and Damon Runyon reported in '29 that the song was played several times on Derby day. The following year, according to the Philadelphia *Public Ledger*, the song was played as the field came onto the track for the Derby.

The sentimental melody and its lyrics may well have foreshadowed the sadness that would fall upon the nation in the Civil War. A Pittsburgh native who lived many years of his brief life there, Foster began writing minstrel songs and had a national hit with "Oh, Susanna" in 1848. His view of slaves and slavery apparently changed in the next few years. According to some accounts, Foster may have been inspired to write "My Old Kentucky Home" after reading Harriet Beecher

Stowe's *Uncle Tom's Cabin*, published in 1851. Foster's first draft in his song workbook was entitled "Poor Uncle Tome, Good Night."

"My Old Kentucky Home" came in the midst of Foster's most productive period. He wrote "Old Folks at Home" in 1851 and "Jeannie With the Light Brown Hair" in '54. Foster died in January 1864 after sustaining a cut, probably alcohol-related, at a New York boarding house. One of his best-known songs, "Beautiful Dreamer," was published posthumously.

"My Old Kentucky Home, Good-Night!" was adopted by Kentucky as its state song in 1928. The official lyrics were subsequently changed to remove references to "darkies" in the original version. The song had three verses, but only the first is now sung. Here are the modern lyrics:

The sun shines bright in the old Kentucky home
'Tis summer, the people are gay;
The corn top's ripe and the meadow's in the bloom,
While the birds make music all the day;
The young folks roll on the little cabin floor,
All merry, all happy, and bright,
By'n by hard times comes a-knocking at the door,
Then my old Kentucky home, good night!

Chorus

Weep no more, my lady,
Oh weep no more today!
We will sing one song for the old Kentucky home,
For the old Kentucky home far away.

Kentucky Derby Future Wager

For years, future-book wagers on the Kentucky Derby have enriched Las Vegas casinos, and Churchill Downs tapped into that bet in 1999 with the Kentucky Derby Future Wager. The bet is offered three times each year, with four days in each wagering period.

Bettors choose the horse they believe will win, with the final pool being offered approximately four weeks before the Derby. From modest beginnings, the wager gained popularity and achieved a record mark of $1,655,034 in 2005.

Here are the amounts wagered by year:

Year	Pool 1	Pool 2	Pool 3	Total
2005	$620,535	$511,655	$522,844	$1,655,034
2004	536,958	358,966	386,244	1,282,168
2003	516,906	391,002	222,261	1,130,169
2002	577,889	401,070	524,847	1,503,806
2001	510,815	372,961	425,871	1,309,647
2000	465,454	306,259	387,206	1,158,919
1999	267,748	178,811	229,674	676,233

Future Pool Payoffs

Year	Winner	Pool 1 Win Price	Pool 2 Win Price	Pool 3 Win Price	Derby Day Win Price
2005	Giacomo	$52.00	$54.20	$103.60	$102.60
2004	Smarty Jones	5.60†	10.80†	23.60	10.20
2003	Funny Cide	188.00	120.80	107.40	27.60
2002	War Emblem	7.60†	16.00†	24.00†	43.00
2001	Monarchos	36.60	13.00	15.80	23.00

Year	Winner	Pool 1 Win Price	Pool 2 Win Price	Pool 3 Win Price	Derby Day Win Price
2000	Fusaichi Pegasus	27.80	26.40	8.00	6.60
1999	Charismatic	10.20†	30.20†	26.60†	64.60

† Part of mutuel field

Derby Winner's Garland of Roses

Run for the roses, the popular nickname of the Kentucky Derby (G1), derives from the garland of roses that is laid over the winner's withers. By 1925, the rose garland was so much a part of the race's pageantry that New York sports columnist Bill Corum coined the "run for the roses" phrase. Corum would serve as Churchill Downs's president from 1950 to '58.

According to Derby lore, the rose was designated as the Derby's official flower in 1884 by Col. M. Lewis Clark, the race's founder. News articles reported that Ben Brush was presented with a collar of pink and white roses after his 1896 Derby win.

In 1931, Churchill commissioned Mrs. Kingsley Walker to create a rose garland for the Derby winner. Her design placed 500 dark-red roses and greenery on a cloth-backed blanket. Burgoo King wore the first Walker-designed garland in 1932, and she continued to craft the garlands until '74. Her daughter, Betty Korfhage, continued the tradition into the 1980s. Beginning in 1987, Kroger Co., a Cincinnati-based grocery chain, took over the task of creating the Derby winner's garland of roses.

Leading Derby Owners by Wins

8 **Calumet Farm:** Whirlaway, 1941; Pensive, 1944; Citation, 1948; Ponder, 1949; Hill Gail, 1952; Iron Liege, 1957; Tim Tam, 1958; Forward Pass, 1968.

4 **Col. E. R. Bradley:** Behave Yourself, 1921; Bubbling Over, 1926; Burgoo King, 1932; Brokers Tip, 1933.

3 **Belair Stud:** Gallant Fox, 1930; Omaha, 1935; Johnstown, 1939.

2 **Bashford Manor Stable:** Azra, 1892; Sir Huon, 1906.
Harry Payne Whitney: Regret, 1915; Whiskery, 1927.
Mrs. John D. Hertz: Reigh Count, 1928; Count Fleet, 1943.
Greentree Stable: Twenty Grand, 1931; Shut Out, 1942.
King Ranch: Assault, 1946; Middleground, 1950.
Darby Dan Farm: Chateaugay, 1963; Proud Clarion, 1967.
Meadow Stable: Riva Ridge, 1972; Secretariat, 1973.
William Condren and Joseph Cornacchia: Strike the Gold, 1991; Go for Gin, 1994.
Robert and Beverly Lewis: Silver Charm, 1997; Charismatic, 1999.

Owners With Most Derby Starters

Name	Strs.	Wins	2nd	3rd	Unplaced
Col. E. R. Bradley/ Idle Hour Stock Farm	28	4	4	1	19
Calumet Farm	20	8	4	1	7
Greentree Stable	19	2	2	1	14
Harry Payne Whitney	19	2	1	1	15
C. V. Whitney	15	0	1	1	13

Name	Strs.	Wins	2nd	3rd	Unplaced
Bashford Manor	11	2	2	1	6
† Overbrook Farm	11	1	0	2	8
† Michael Tabor	11	1	1	0	9
Milky Way Farm	10	1	0	2	7
Dixiana Farm	9	0	3	0	6
Belair Stud	8	3	1	0	4
Elmendorf Farm	8	0	0	0	8
Hal Price Headley	8	0	0	0	8
† Robert and Beverly Lewis	8	2	0	1	5
Three D's Stock Farm	8	0	0	1	7
† Includes partnerships					

Leading Breeders of Kentucky Derby Winners

9   Calumet Farm: Whirlaway, 1941; Pensive, 1944; Citation, 1948; Ponder, 1949; Hill Gail, 1952; Iron Liege, 1957; Tim Tam, 1958; Forward Pass, 1968; Strike the Gold, 1991.

5   John Madden: Old Rosebud, 1914; Sir Barton, 1919; Paul Jones, 1920; Zev, 1923; Flying Ebony, 1925.

4   A. J. Alexander: Baden-Baden, 1877; Fonso, 1880; Joe Cotton, 1885; Chant, 1894.

    E. R. Bradley (Idle Hour Stock Farm):
    1   E. R. Bradley: Behave Yourself, 1921.
    2   Idle Hour Stock Farm: Bubbling Over, 1926; Brokers Tip, 1933.
    1   H. N. Davis and Idle Hour Stock Farm: Burgoo King, 1932.

3   Bashford Manor Stable (George J. Long): Azra, 1892; Manuel, 1899; Sir Huon, 1906.

    Daniel Swigert: Hindoo, 1881; Apollo, 1882; Ben Ali, 1886.

2   Belair Stud: Gallant Fox, 1930; Omaha, 1935.

    Claiborne Farm: Johnstown, 1939; Swale, 1984.

    R. A. Fairbairn: Gallahadion, 1940; Hoop, Jr., 1945.

    John W. Galbreath: Chateaugay, 1963; Proud Clarion, 1967.

    Greentree Stable: Twenty Grand, 1931; Shut Out, 1942.

    Arthur B. Hancock III:
    1   A. B. Hancock III and Leone J. Peters: Gato Del Sol, 1982.
    1   A. B. Hancock III and Stonerside Ltd.: Fusaichi Pegasus, 2000.

    King Ranch: Assault, 1946; Middleground, 1950.

    Meadow Stud: Riva Ridge, 1972; Secretariat, 1973.

    Harry Payne Whitney: Regret, 1915; Whiskey, 1927.

    Milton Young: Montrose, 1887; Donau, 1910.

Leading Derby Trainers by Wins

6   Ben A. Jones: Lawrin, 1938; Whirlaway, 1941; Pensive, 1944; Citation, 1948; Ponder, 1949; Hill Gail, 1952.

4   H. J. "Dick" Thompson: Behave Yourself, 1921; Bubbling Over, 1926; Burgoo King, 1932; Brokers Tip, 1933.

    D. Wayne Lukas: Winning Colors, 1988; Thunder Gulch, 1995; Grindstone, 1996; Charismatic, 1999.

3   Bob Baffert: Silver Charm, 1997; Real Quiet, 1998; War Emblem, 2002.

    James "Sunny Jim" Fitzsimmons: Gallant Fox, 1930; Omaha, 1935; Johnstown, 1939.

    Max Hirsch: Bold Venture, 1936; Assault, 1946; Middleground, 1950.

2   John McGinty: Leonatus, 1883; Montrose, 1887.

    James Rowe Sr.: Hindoo, 1881; Regret, 1915.

    H. A. "Jimmy" Jones: Iron Liege, 1957; Tim Tam, 1958.

    Horatio Luro: Decidedly, 1962; Northern Dancer, 1964.

    Henry Forrest: Kauai King, 1966; Forward Pass, 1968.

    Lucien Laurin: Riva Ridge, 1972; Secretariat, 1973.

    W. C. "Woody" Stephens: Cannonade, 1974; Swale, 1984.

    LeRoy Jolley: Foolish Pleasure, 1975; Genuine Risk, 1980.

    Lazaro Barrera: Bold Forbes, 1976; Affirmed, 1978.

    Charlie Whittingham: Ferdinand, 1986; Sunday Silence, 1989.

    Nicholas P. Zito: Strike the Gold, 1991; Go for Gin, 1994.

Female Trainers in the Derby

A woman has yet to win the Kentucky Derby (G1) as either a jockey or a trainer, but several female trainers have come close to landing one of racing's biggest prizes.

Northern California-based trainer Shelley Riley came closest to notching a Kentucky Derby victory when her 29.90-to-1 longshot, Casual Lies, finished second to Lil E. Tee in 1992.

Mary Hirsch, daughter of Racing Hall of Fame trainer Max Hirsch, was the first female trainer to saddle a Derby starter. No Sir, also owned by Mary Hirsch, finished 13th in 1937.

The women who have trained Derby starters:

Trainer	Horse	Year	Finish
Kristin Mulhall	Imperialism	2004	3rd
Jennifer Pederson	Song of the Sword	2004	11th
Jenine Sahadi	The Deputy (Ire)	2000	14th
Akiko Gothard	K One King	1999	8th
Kathy Walsh	Hanuman Highway	1998	7th
Cynthia Reese	In Contention	1996	15th
Shelly Riley	Casual Lies	1992	2nd
Patti Johnson	Fast Account	1985	4th
Dianne Carpenter	Kingpost	1988	14th
	Biloxi Indian	1984	12th
Mary Keim	Mr. Pak	1965	6th
Mrs. Albert Roth	Senecas Coin	1949	DNF
Mary Hirsch	No Sir	1937	13th

Trainers With Most Derby Starters

Trainer	Strs.	Wins	2nd	3rd	Unplaced
D. Wayne Lukas	42	4	1	5	32
H. J. Thompson	24	4	2	1	17
James Rowe Sr.*	18	2	1	1	14
Max Hirsch	14	3	0	2	9
W. C. Stephens	14	2	3	3	6
Nicholas P. Zito	19	2	0	0	17
LeRoy Jolley	13	2	2	1	8
Bob Baffert	14	3	1	2	8
Todd Pletcher	12	0	1	1	10
James Fitzsimmons	11	3	1	0	7
Ben A. Jones	11	6	2	1	2

*Information on James Rowe Sr. is incomplete

Leading Derby Jockeys by Wins

5   Eddie Arcaro: Lawrin, 1938; Whirlaway, 1941; Hoop, Jr., 1945; Citation, 1948; Hill Gail, 1952.

   Bill Hartack: Iron Liege, 1957; Venetian Way, 1960; Decidedly, 1962; Northern Dancer, 1964; Majestic Prince, 1969.

4   Bill Shoemaker: Swaps, 1955; *Tomy Lee, 1959; Lucky Debonair, 1965; Ferdinand, 1986.

3   Isaac Murphy: Buchanan, 1884; Riley, 1890; Kingman, 1891.

   Earl Sande: Zev, 1923; Flying Ebony, 1925; Gallant Fox, 1930.

   Angel Cordero Jr.: Cannonade, 1974; Bold Forbes, 1976; Spend a Buck, 1985.

   Gary Stevens: Winning Colors, 1988; Thunder Gulch, 1995; Silver Charm, 1997.

Jockeys With Most Derby Mounts

Jockey	Strs.	Wins	2nd	3rd	Unplaced
Bill Shoemaker	26	4	3	4	15
Pat Day	22	1	4	2	15
Eddie Arcaro	21	5	3	2	11
Laffit Pincay Jr.	21	1	4	2	14
Angel Cordero Jr.	17	3	1	0	13
Chris McCarron	18	2	3	0	13
Gary Stevens	18	3	2	1	12
Jerry Bailey	17	2	2	1	12
Jorge Velasquez	14	1	1	2	10
Mack Garner	14	1	0	1	12
Don Brumfield	13	1	0	1	11
Johnny Adams	13	0	2	0	11

African-American Jockeys in the Derby

African-American jockeys dominated the Kentucky Derby during the race's first quarter-century. Between 1875 and 1902, 11 African-American riders won 15 runnings of the Derby. The most famous were Isaac Murphy, the first jockey to win the Derby three times, and Jimmy Winkfield, who won the Derby in 1901 and '02.

Marlon St. Julien became the first African-American rider in the Derby in 79 years when he finished seventh aboard Curule in the 2000 renewal.

African-American riders who have won the Derby:

Jockey	Year	Mount
Jimmy Winkfield	1902	Alan-a-Dale
	1901	His Eminence
Willie Simms	1898	Plaudit
	1896	Ben Brush
James "Soup" Perkins	1895	Halma
Alonzo "Lonnie" Clayton	1892	Azra
Isaac Murphy	1891	Kingman
	1890	Riley
	1884	Buchanan
Isaac Lewis	1887	Montrose
Erskine Henderson	1885	Joe Cotton
Babe Hurd	1882	Apollo
George Garret Lewis	1880	Fonso
William Walker	1877	Baden-Baden
Oliver Lewis	1875	Aristides

Female Jockeys in the Derby

Jockey	Mount	Year	Finish
Rosemary Homeister	Supah Blitz	2003	13th
Julie Krone	Suave Prospect	1995	11th
	Ecstatic Ride	1992	14th
Andrea Seefeldt	Forty Something	1991	16th
Patricia Cooksey	So Vague	1984	11th
Diane Crump	Fathom	1970	15th

Leading Sires of Derby Winners

3   Virgil: Vagrant, 1876; Hindoo, 1881; Ben Ali, 1886.

   Falsetto: Chant, 1894; His Eminence, 1901; Sir Huon, 1906.

   *Sir Gallahad III: Gallant Fox, 1930; Gallahadion, 1940; Hoop, Jr., 1945.

   Bull Lea: Citation, 1948; Hill Gail, 1952; Iron Liege, 1957.

2   King Alfonso: Fonso, 1880; Joe Cotton, 1885.

   Longfellow: Leonatus, 1883; Riley, 1890.

   Broomstick: Meridian, 1911; Regret, 1915.

   *McGee: Donerail, 1913; Exterminator, 1918.

   The Finn: Zev, 1923; Flying Ebony, 1925.

   Black Toney: Black Gold, 1924; Brokers Tip, 1933.

   Man o' War: Clyde Van Dusen, 1929; War Admiral, 1937.

   *St. Germans: Twenty Grand, 1931; Bold Venture, 1936.

   *Blenheim II: Whirlaway, 1941; Jet Pilot, 1947.

   Bold Venture: Assault, 1946; Middleground, 1950.

   Bold Bidder: Cannonade, 1974; Spectacular Bid, 1979.

   Exclusive Native: Affirmed, 1978; Genuine Risk, 1980.

   Halo: Sunny's Halo, 1983; Sunday Silence, 1989.

   Alydar: Alysheba, 1987; Strike the Gold, 1991.

Derby Winners Who Sired Winners

2   Bold Venture (1936): Assault, 1946; Middleground, 1950.

1   Halma (1895): Alan-a-Dale, 1902.

   Bubbling Over (1926): Burgoo King (1932)

   Reigh Count (1928): Count Fleet, 1943.

   Gallant Fox (1930): Omaha, 1935.

   Count Fleet (1943): Count Turf (1951)

   Pensive (1944): Ponder, 1949.

   Ponder (1949): Needles, 1956.

   Determine (1954): Decidedly, 1962.

   Swaps (1955): Chateaugay, 1963.

   Seattle Slew (1977): Swale, 1984.

   Unbridled (1990): Grindstone, 1996.

Fastest Derby Winning Times
1¼ miles

Year	Winner	Time	Cond.
1973	Secretariat	1:59⅖	Fast
2001	Monarchos	1:59.97	Fast
1964	Northern Dancer	2:00	Fast
1985	Spend a Buck	2:00⅕	Fast
1962	Decidedly	2:00⅖	Fast
1967	Proud Clarion	2:00⅗	Fast
1996	Grindstone	2:01.06	Fast
2000	Fusaichi Pegasus	2:01.12	Fast
2002	War Emblem	2:01.13	Fast

Year	Winner	Time	Cond.
1978	Affirmed	2:01⅕	Fast
1965	Lucky Debonair	2:01⅕	Fast
1995	Thunder Gulch	2:01.27	Fast

Time recorded in hundredths of a second beginning in 1991

1½ miles

Year	Winner	Time	Cond.
1889	Spokane	2:34½	Fast
1886	Ben Ali	2:36½	Fast
1879	Lord Murphy	2:37	Fast
1878	Day Star	2:37¼	Dusty
1885	Joe Cotton	2:37¼	Good

Fastest Derby Fractions

Quarter-mile: :21⅘, Top Avenger (1981)
Half-mile: :44.86, Songandaprayer (2001)
Six furlongs: 1:09.25, Songandaprayer (2001)
One mile: 1:34⅘, Spend a Buck (1985)

Slowest Derby Winning Times

1¼ miles

Year	Winner	Time	Cond.
1908	Stone Street	2:15⅕	Heavy
1907	Pink Star	2:12⅗	Heavy
1897	Typhoon II	2:12½	Heavy
1899	Manuel	2:12	Fast
1918	Exterminator	2:10⅘	Muddy
1929	Clyde Van Dusen	2:10⅘	Muddy
1905	Agile	2:10¾	Heavy
1928	Reigh Count	2:10⅖	Heavy
1919	Sir Barton	2:09⅘	Heavy
1912	Worth	2:09⅖	Muddy

1½ miles

Year	Winner	Time	Cond.
1891	Kingman	2:52¼	Slow
1890	Riley	2:45	Muddy
1883	Leonatus	2:43	Heavy
1892	Azra	2:41½	Heavy
1894	Chant	2:41	Fast

Evolution of Derby Stakes Record at 1¼ miles

Year	Winner	Time
1896	Ben Brush	2:07¾
1900	Lieut. Gibson	2:06¼
1911	Meridian	2:05
1913	Donerail	2:04⅘
1914	Old Rosebud	2:03⅖
1931	Twenty Grand	2:01⅘
1941	Whirlaway	2:01⅖
1962	Decidedly	2:00⅖
1964	Northern Dancer	2:00
1973	Secretariat	1:59⅖

Shortest-Priced Derby Beaten Favorites

Year	Horse	Odds	Finish
1976	Honest Pleasure	0.40-to-1	2nd
1940	Bimelech	0.40-to-1	2nd
1953	Native Dancer	0.70-to-1	2nd
1989	Easy Goer	0.80-to-1	2nd
1949	Olympia	0.80-to-1	6th
1936	Brevity	0.80-to-1	2nd
1992	Arazi	0.90-to-1	8th
1911	Governor Gray	1-to-1	2nd
1916	Thunderer	1.05-to-1	5th
1960	Tompion	1.10-to-1	4th
1962	Ridan	1.10-to-1	3rd
1946	Lord Boswell	1.10-to-1	4th
1921	Prudery	1.10-to-1	3rd

Shortest-Priced Winning Favorites

Year	Winner	Odds
1948	Citation	0.40-to-1
1943	Count Fleet	0.40-to-1
1977	Seattle Slew	0.50-to-1
1979	Spectacular Bid	0.60-to-1
1939	Johnstown	0.60-to-1
1912	Worth	0.80-to-1
1914	Old Rosebud	0.85-to-1
1931	Twenty Grand	0.88-to-1
1952	Hill Gail	1.10-to-1
1906	Sir Huon	1.10-to-1
1930	Gallant Fox	1.19-to-1

Longest Winning Odds

Year	Horse	Odds
1913	Donerail	91.45-to-1
2005	Giacomo	50.30-to-1
1940	Gallahadion	35.20-to-1
1999	Charismatic	31.30-to-1
1967	Proud Clarion	30.10-to-1
1918	Exterminator	29.60-to-1
1953	Dark Star	24.90-to-1
1995	Thunder Gulch	24.50-to-1
1908	Stone Street	23.72-to-1
1982	Gato Del Sol	21.20-to-1
2002	War Emblem	20.50-to-1
1936	Bold Venture	20.50-to-1
1923	Zev	19.20-to-1
1986	Ferdinand	17.70-to-1

Largest Winning Margins

Year	Winner	Lengths
1946	Assault	8
1941	Whirlaway	8
1939	Johnstown	8
1914	Old Rosebud	8
1880	Fonso	7
1945	Hoop, Jr.	6
1894	Chant	6
1985	Spend a Buck	5¼
1970	Dust Commander	5
1932	Burgoo King	5
1926	Bubbling Over	5
1919	Sir Barton	5
1895	Halma	5

Smallest Winning Margins

Year	Winner	Lengths
1996	Grindstone	nose
1959	*Tomy Lee	nose
1957	Iron Liege	nose
1933	Brokers Tip	nose
1902	Alan-a-Dale	nose
1898	Plaudit	nose
1896	Ben Brush	nose
1892	Azra	nose
1889	Spokane	nose
1997	Silver Charm	head

Year	Winner	Lengths
1953	Dark Star	head
1947	Jet Pilot	head
1936	Bold Venture	head
1927	Whiskery	head
1921	Behave Yourself	head
1920	Paul Jones	head

Birthplaces of Derby Winners

State	Winners
Kentucky	98
Florida	6
Virginia	4
California	3
Tennessee	3
New Jersey	2
Pennsylvania	2
Texas	2
Canada	2
Great Britain	2
Illinois	1
Kansas	1
Maryland	1
Missouri	1
Montana	1
New York	1
Ohio	1

Fillies in the Derby

In the long history of the Kentucky Derby, only three fillies have won the 1¼-mile classic: Regret in 1915, Genuine Risk in 1980, and Winning Colors in 1988.

Fillies to start in the Derby:

Year	Filly	Finish
1999	Excellent Meeting	5th
	Three Ring	19th
1995	Serena's Song	16th
1988	**Winning Colors**	1st
1984	Life's Magic	8th
	Althea	19th
1982	Cupecoy's Joy	10th
1980	**Genuine Risk**	1st
1959	Silver Spoon	5th
1945	Misweet	12th
1936	Gold Seeker	9th
1935	Nellie Flag	4th
1934	Mata Hari	4th
	Bazaar	9th
1932	Oscillation	13th
1930	Alcibiades	10th
1929	Ben Machree	18th
1922	Startle	8th
1921	Prudery	3rd
	Careful	5th
1920	Cleopatra	15th
1919	Regalo	9th
1918	Viva America	3rd
1915	**Regret**	1st
1914	Bronzewing	3rd
	Watermelon	7th
1913	Gowell	3rd
1912	Flamma	3rd
1911	Round the World	6th
1906	Lady Navarre	2nd
1883	Pike's Pride	6th
1879	Ada Glenn	7th
	Wissahickon	9th

Year	Filly	Finish
1877	Early Light	8th
1876	Lizzie Stone	6th
	Marie Michon	7th
1875	Ascension	10th
	Gold Mine	15th

Maiden Winners of the Derby

Year	Winner
Brokers Tip	1933
Sir Barton	1919
Buchanan	1884

Maiden Starters Since 1950

Maidens in the Derby were a common occurrence until the mid-1930s. Since 1950, only seven maidens have run in the Derby, and none came close to winning. The connections of several runners, most notably Great Redeemer in 1979, were harshly criticized for running.

Year	Horse	Finish
1998	Nationalore	9th
1990	Pendleton Ridge	13
1979	Great Redeemer	10th
1971	Fourulla	19th
1959	The Chosen One	14
1958	Flamingo	13th
1950	On the Mark	8th

Geldings in the Derby

In all, 106 geldings have started in the Derby since 1908. Before then, records of starters were incomplete. The geldings that have started in the Kentucky Derby since 1980:

Year	Gelding	Finish
2003	**Funny Cide**	1st
	Buddy Gil	6th
2002	Perfect Drift	3rd
	Easy Grades	13th
2001	Balto Star	14th
1999	General Challenge	11th
1998	Hanuman Highway (Ire)	7th
1997	Celtic Warrior	10th
1996	Cavonnier	2nd
	Alyrob	8th
	Zarb's Magic	13th
1993	Prairie Bayou	2nd
	Truth of It All	10th
1991	Best Pal	2nd
1989	Wind Splitter	11th
	Clever Trevor	13th
1988	Kingpost	14th
1986	Bachelor Beau	14th
1984	Raja's Shark	14th
1983	My Mac	14th
1982	Real Dare	19th
1981	Television Studio	5th
	Beau Rit	13th
1980	Rockhill Native	5th
	Execution's Reason	11th

Gelding Winners of the Derby

With Funny Cide's victory in the 2003 Derby, the losing streak for geldings ended after 74 years, dating to Clyde Van Dusen in 1929. In the 1990s, three geldings finished second: Best Pal (1991), Prairie Bayou ('93), and Cavonnier ('96). The winning geldings:

Year	Gelding
2003	Funny Cide
1929	Clyde Van Dusen
1920	Paul Jones
1918	Exterminator
1914	Old Rosebud
1888	Macbeth II
1882	Apollo
1876	Vagrant

Front-Running Derby Winners

The following Kentucky Derby winners were on the lead at all points of call.

Year	Winner	Winning Margin
2002	War Emblem	4
1988	Winning Colors	neck
1985	Spend a Buck	5¼
1976	Bold Forbes	1
1972	Riva Ridge	3¼
1966	Kauai King	½
1955	Swaps	1½
1953	Dark Star	head
1947	Jet Pilot	head
1945	Hoop, Jr.	6
1943	Count Fleet	3
1939	Johnstown	8
1937	War Admiral	1¾
1929	Clyde Van Dusen	2
1926	Bubbling Over	5
1923	Zev	1½
1922	Morvich	1½
1920	Paul Jones	head
1919	Sir Barton	5
1915	Regret	2
1914	Old Rosebud	8
1912	Worth	neck
1911	Meridian	¾
1910	Donau	½
1909	Wintergreen	4
1905	Agile	3
1902	Alan-a-Dale	nose
1901	His Eminence	1½
1900	Lieut. Gibson	3
1897	Typhoon II	neck
1895	Halma	5
1894	Chant	6
1893	Lookout	4
1887	Montrose	2
1883	Leonatus	3
1881	Hindoo	4
1880	Fonso	1
1878	Day Star	1
1875	Aristides	2

Winning Derby Post Positions

Winning Derby post positions since 1900:

Post	Winners	Post	Winners
1	12	11	3
2	9	12	3
3	8	13	4
4	10	14	2
5	12	15	3
6	6	16	3
7	7	17	0
8	8	18	1
9	4	19	0
10	10	20	1

Undefeated Starters

Smarty Jones, the 2004 Kentucky Derby winner, was only the fifth undefeated horse to win the Derby. The other four were Regret in 1915, Morvich in '22, Majestic Prince in '69, and Triple Crown winner Seattle Slew in '77.

The undefeated Derby starters since Regret in 1915:

Year	Horse	Pre-Derby Starts	Derby Finish
2004	**Smarty Jones**	6	**1st**
2000	China Visit	2	6th
	Trippi	4	11th
1998	Indian Charlie	4	3rd
1990	Mister Frisky	16	8th
1988	Private Terms	7	9th
1982	Air Forbes Won	4	7th
1978	Sensitive Prince	6	6th
1977	**Seattle Slew**	6	**1st**
1969	**Majestic Prince**	7	**1st**
1963	Candy Spots	6	3rd
	No Robbery	5	5th
1953	Native Dancer	11	2nd
1948	Coaltown	4	2nd
1940	Bimelech	8	2nd
1922	**Morvich**	11	**1st**
1916	Thunderer	3	5th
1915	**Regret**	3	**1st**

Derby Winners Sold at Public Auction and Privately

Derby	Winner	Year	Sale	Price
2003	Funny Cide	2001	FT Saratoga	$22,000
		2002	Private	75,000
2002	War Emblem	2000	Kee Sept	20,000
		2002	Private	900,000
2001	Monarchos	1999	FT Saratoga	90,000 (RNA)
		2000	FT Calder	170,000
2000	Fusaichi Pegasus	1998	Kee July	4,000,000
1999	Charismatic	1996	Private	200,000
1998	Real Quiet	1996	Kee Sept	17,000
1997	Silver Charm	1995	OBSC Aug	16,500
		1996	OBSC April	100,000
1995	Thunder Gulch	1993	Kee July	40,000
		1994	Kee April	120,000 (RNA)
1994	Go for Gin	1991	FT Ky	32,000
		1992	FT Saratoga	150,000
1992	Lil E. Tee	1991	OBSC April	25,000
1990	Unbridled	1987	Tartan dispersal	90,000
1989	Sunday Silence	1987	Kee July	17,000 (RNA)
		1988	CTS March	32,000
1988	Winning Colors	1986	Kee July	575,000
1987	Alysheba	1985	Kee July	500,000
1985	Spend a Buck	1983	Private	12,500
1980	Genuine Risk	1978	FT Ky	32,000
1979	Spectacular Bid	1977	Kee Sept.	37,000
1977	Seattle Slew	1975	FT Ky	17,500
1976	Bold Forbes	1975	FT Ky	15,200
1975	Foolish Pleasure	1973	FT Saratoga	20,000
1971	Canonero II	1969	Kee Sept	1,200
1970	Dust Commander	1968	Kee Sept	6,500
1969	Majestic Prince	1967	Kee July	250,000
1966	Kauai King	1968	FT Saratoga	42,000
1960	Venetian Way	1958	Kee July	10,500
1959	*Tomy Lee	1956	Tatt Dec	6,762
1954	Determine	1952	Kee July	12,500
1953	Dark Star	1951	Kee July	6,500
1951	Count Turf	1949	FT Saratoga	3,700
1947	Jet Pilot	1945	Kee July	41,000

Derby Winner	Year	Sale	Price
1945 Hoop, Jr.	1943	Kee July	10,200
1940 Gallahadion	1938	FT Saratoga	5,000
1934 Cavalcade	1932	FT Saratoga	1,200

FT Fasig-Tipton; CTS California Thoroughbred Sale; RNA Reserve Not Attained

Derby Winners Unraced at Two

A juvenile campaign of some sort is virtually a prerequisite for winning the Kentucky Derby. Only one horse, Apollo, has won the Derby without racing as a two-year-old, and he accomplished that feat in 1882, in the eighth running.

In recent years, only three horses have won the Derby after making only one start as a two-year-old. Tim Tam, trained by H. A. "Jimmy" Jones, won in 1958 after finishing unplaced in his only start at two. Also unplaced in his only juvenile start was Lucky Debonair, who won the 1965 Derby. Fusaichi Pegasus finished second in his only start as a two-year-old and won the Derby as the 2.30-to-1 favorite in 2000.

Derby Weather, Track Condition, and Temperature Since 1940

Year	Winner	Weather	Track Condition	Temp
2005	Giacomo	Clear	Fast	79
2004	Smarty Jones	Thunderstorm	Sloppy	68
2003	Funny Cide	Partly cloudy	Fast	67
2002	War Emblem	Clear	Fast	71
2001	Monarchos	Clear	Fast	83
2000	Fusaichi Pegasus	Clear	Fast	82
1999	Charismatic	Clear	Fast	72
1998	Real Quiet	Clear	Fast	70
1997	Silver Charm	Overcast	Fast	51
1996	Grindstone	Thunderstorm	Fast	75
1995	Thunder Gulch	Partly cloudy	Fast	72
1994	Go for Gin	Thunderstorm	Sloppy	57
1993	Sea Hero	Overcast	Fast	69
1992	Lil E. Tee	Overcast	Fast	78
1991	Strike the Gold	Overcast	Fast	80
1990	Unbridled	Mostly cloudy	Good	63
1989	Sunday Silence	Overcast	Muddy	51
1988	Winning Colors	Clear	Fast	72
1987	Alysheba	Mostly cloudy	Fast	79
1986	Ferdinand	Partly cloudy	Fast	63
1985	Spend a Buck	Partly cloudy	Fast	72
1984	Swale	Overcast	Fast	71
1983	Sunny's Halo	Thunderstorm	Fast	81
1982	Gato Del Sol	Partly cloudy	Fast	75
1981	Pleasant Colony	Clear	Fast	55
1980	Genuine Risk	Clear	Fast	72
1979	Spectacular Bid	Clear	Fast	55
1978	Affirmed	Clear	Fast	67
1977	Seattle Slew	Partly cloudy	Fast	69
1976	Bold Forbes	Overcast	Fast	62

Year	Winner	Weather	Track condition	Temp
1975	Foolish Pleasure	Overcast	Fast	63
1974	Cannonade	Partly cloudy	Fast	68
1973	Secretariat	Partly cloudy	Fast	69
1972	Riva Ridge	Partly cloudy	Fast	75
1971	Canonero II	Partly cloudy	Fast	73
1970	Dust Commander	Partly cloudy	Good	64
1969	Majestic Prince	Partly cloudy	Fast	87
1968	Forward Pass	Partly cloudy	Fast	71
1967	Proud Clarion	Overcast	Fast	61
1966	Kauai King	Partly cloudy	Fast	67
1965	Lucky Debonair	Clear	Fast	84
1964	Northern Dancer	Overcast	Fast	76
1963	Chateaugay	Partly cloudy	Fast	80
1962	Decidedly	Partly cloudy	Fast	81
1961	Carry Back	Overcast	Good	81
1960	Venetian Way	Partly cloudy	Good	64
1959	*Tomy Lee	Partly cloudy	Fast	94
1958	Tim Tam	Partly cloudy	Muddy	86
1957	Iron Liege	Overcast	Fast	47
1956	Needles	Clear	Fast	82
1955	Swaps	Overcast	Fast	85
1954	Determine	Overcast	Fast	84
1953	Dark Star	Clear	Fast	76
1952	Hill Gail	Clear	Fast	79
1951	Count Turf	Partly cloudy	Fast	67
1950	Middleground	Overcast	Fast	70
1949	Ponder	Partly cloudy	Fast	57
1948	Citation	Overcast	Sloppy	72
1947	Jet Pilot	Overcast	Fast	57
1946	Assault	Overcast	Slow	68
1945	Hoop, Jr.	Partly cloudy	Muddy	77
1944	Pensive	Partly cloudy	Good	54
1943	Count Fleet	Clear	Fast	54
1942	Shut Out	Partly cloudy	Fast	87
1941	Whirlaway	Partly cloudy	Fast	76
1940	Gallahadion	Clear	Fast	62

Derby Trivia

Largest field: 23 in 1974.

Smallest field: Three in 1892 and 1905.

Longest-priced runner since 1908: A Dragon Killer, seventh in 1958 at 294.40-to-1.

Most maidens in one race: Six in 1882 (Highflyer, seventh; Pat Malloy colt, ninth; Wallensee, tenth; Newsboy, 11th; Mistral, 12th; Robert Bruce, 14th).

Most lifetime starts going into Derby: 66, Florizar, 1900 (second).

Fewest lifetime starts going into Derby: Zero, 11 times, most recently by Col. Hogan, 1911 (seventh).

Mutuel field horses who won the Derby: Canonero II, 1971; Count Turf, 1951; Flying Ebony, 1925.

Derby winners who never started again: Grindstone, 1996; Bubbling Over, 1926.

Derby winner as both jockey and trainer: Johnny Longden, rider of Count Fleet in 1943 and trainer of Majestic Prince in '69.

Longest-priced Derby favorite: Harlan's Holiday, 6-to-1, in 2002.

Status of Kentucky Derby Winners Since 1970

Year	Winner	Birthdate	Status	Where Stands/Stood	Location	Death Date
2005	Giacomo	2/16/2002	In training			
2004	Smarty Jones	2/28/2001	Stallion	Three Chimneys Farm	Midway, Ky.	
2003	Funny Cide	4/20/2000	In training			
2002	War Emblem	2/20/1999	Stallion	Shadai Stallion Station	Hokkaido, Japan	
2001	Monarchos	2/9/1998	Stallion	Claiborne Farm	Paris, Ky.	
2000	Fusaichi Pegasus	4/12/1997	Stallion	Ashford Stud	Versailles, Ky.	
1999	Charismatic	3/13/1996	Stallion	JBBA Shizunai Stallion Station	Hokkaido, Japan	
1998	Real Quiet	3/7/1995	Stallion	Taylor Made Farm	Nicholasville, Ky.	
1997	Silver Charm	2/22/1994	Stallion	JBBA Shizunai Stallion Station	Hokkaido, Japan	

Year	Winner	Birthdate	Status	Where Stands/Stood	Location	Death Date
1996	Grindstone	1/23/1993	Stallion	Overbrook Farm	Lexington, Ky.	
1995	Thunder Gulch	5/23/1992	Stallion	Ashford Stud	Versailles, Ky.	
1994	Go for Gin	4/18/1991	Stallion	Bonita Farm	Darlington, Md.	
1993	Sea Hero	3/4/1990	Stallion	Izmit Pension Stud	Izmit, Turkey	
1992	Lil E. Tee	3/29/1989	Stallion	Old Frankfort Stud	Lexington, Ky.	
1991	Strike the Gold	3/21/1988	Stallion	Izmit Pension Stud	Izmit, Turkey	
1990	Unbridled	3/5/1987	Deceased	Claiborne Farm	Paris, Ky.	10/18/2001
1989	Sunday Silence	3/25/1986	Deceased	Shadai Stallion Station	Hokkaido, Japan	8/19/2002
1988	Winning Colors	3/14/1985	Broodmare	Gainesway	Lexington, Ky.	
1987	Alysheba	3/3/1984	Stallion	Janadriyah Stud Farm	Riyadh, Saudi Arabia	
1986	Ferdinand	3/12/1983	Deceased	Arrow Stud	Hokkaido, Japan	2002
1985	Spend a Buck	5/15/1982	Deceased	Haras Bage do Sul	Sao Paulo, Brazil	11/24/2002
1984	Swale	4/21/1981	Deceased			6/17/1984
1983	Sunny's Halo	2/11/1980	Deceased	Double S Thoroughbred Farm	Tyler, Tx.	6/3/2003
1982	Gato Del Sol	2/23/1979	Pensioned	Stone Farm	Paris, Ky.	
1981	Pleasant Colony	5/4/1978	Deceased	Lane's End	Versailles, Ky.	12/31/2002
1980	Genuine Risk	2/15/1977	Pensioned	Newstead Farm	Upperville, Va.	
1979	Spectacular Bid	2/17/1976	Deceased	Milfer Farm	Unadilla, N.Y.	6/9/2003
1978	Affirmed	2/21/1975	Deceased	Jonabell Farm	Lexington, Ky.	1/12/2001
1977	Seattle Slew	2/15/1974	Deceased	Three Chimneys Farm	Midway, Ky.	5/7/2002
1976	Bold Forbes	3/31/1973	Deceased	Stone Farm	Paris, Ky.	8/9/2000
1975	Foolish Pleasure	3/23/1972	Deceased	Horseshoe Ranch	Dayton, Wy.	11/17/1994
1974	Cannonade	5/12/1971	Deceased	Gainesway	Lexington, Ky.	8/3/1993
1973	Secretariat	3/30/1970	Deceased	Claiborne Farm	Paris, Ky.	10/4/1989
1972	Riva Ridge	4/13/1969	Deceased	Claiborne Farm	Paris, Ky.	4/21/1985
1971	Canonero II	4/24/1968	Deceased	Gainesway	Lexington, Ky.	11/11/1981
1970	Dust Commander	2/8/1967	Deceased	Springland Farm	Paris, Ky.	10/7/1991

Starts by Kentucky Derby Winners at Two and Three

Year	Winner	Starts at 2	Starts Before Derby at 3	Total Pre-Derby Starts	Total Starts at 3	Total Starts at 2-3	Derby Prep	Finish
2005	Giacomo	4	3	7	—	—	Santa Anita Derby (G1)	4
2004	Smarty Jones	2	4	6	7	9	Arkansas Derby (G2)	1
2003	Funny Cide	3	3	6	8	11	Wood Memorial S. (G1)	2
2002	War Emblem	3	4	7	10	13	Illinois Derby (G2)	1
2001	Monarchos	2	4	6	7	9	Wood Memorial S. (G2)	2
2000	Fusaichi Pegasus	1	4	5	8	9	Wood Memorial S. (G2)	1
1999	Charismatic	7	7	14	10	17	Lexington S. (G2)	1
1998	Real Quiet	9	3	12	6	15	Santa Anita Derby (G1)	2
1997	Silver Charm	3	3	6	7	10	Santa Anita Derby (G1)	2
1996	Grindstone	2	3	5	4	6	Arkansas Derby (G2)	2
1995	Thunder Gulch	6	3	9	10	16	Blue Grass S. (G2)	4
1994	Go for Gin	5	4	9	11	16	Wood Memorial S. (G1)	2
1993	Sea Hero	7	3	10	9	16	Blue Grass S. (G2)	4
1992	Lil E. Tee	4	4	8	6	10	Arkansas Derby (G2)	2
1991	Strike the Gold	3	4	7	12	15	Blue Grass S. (G2)	1
1990	Unbridled	6	4	10	11	17	Blue Grass S. (G2)	3
1989	Sunday Silence	3	3	6	9	12	Santa Anita Derby (G1)	1
1988	Winning Colors	2	4	6	10	12	Santa Anita Derby (G1)	1
1987	Alysheba	7	3	10	10	17	Blue Grass S. (G1)	1, pl 3
1986	Ferdinand	5	4	9	8	13	Santa Anita Derby (G1)	3
1985	Spend a Buck	8	3	3	7	15	Garden State S.	1
1984	Swale	7	4	11	7	14	Lexington S.	2
1983	Sunny's Halo	11	2	13	9	20	Arkansas Derby (G1)	1
1982	Gato Del Sol	8	4	12	9	17	Blue Grass S. (G1)	2
1981	Pleasant Colony	5	8	8	9	14	Wood Memorial S. (G1)	1
1980	Genuine Risk	4	3	7	8	12	Wood Memorial S. (G1)	3
1979	Spectacular Bid	9	5	14	12	21	Blue Grass S. (G1)	1
1978	Affirmed	9	4	13	11	20	Hollywood Derby (G1)	1
1977	Seattle Slew	3	3	6	7	10	Wood Memorial S. (G1)	1
1976	Bold Forbes	8	5	13	10	18	Wood Memorial S. (G1)	1
1975	Foolish Pleasure	7	4	11	11	18	Wood Memorial S. (G1)	1
1974	Cannonade	17	4	21	8	25	Churchill allowance	1
1973	Secretariat	9	3	12	12	21	Wood Memorial S. (G1)	3
1972	Riva Ridge	9	3	12	12	21	Blue Grass S.	1
1971	Canonero II	4	8	12	11	15	Series 4A-5A H.	3
1970	Dust Commander	14	8	22	23	37	Blue Grass S.	1
1969	Majestic Prince	2	5	7	8	10	Churchill allowance	1
1968	Forward Pass	10	7	17	13	23	Blue Grass S.	1
1967	Proud Clarion	3	5	8	13	16	Blue Grass S.	2
1966	Kauai King	4	8	12	12	16	Governor's Gold Cup	1
1965	Lucky Debonair	1	8	9	10	11	Blue Grass S.	1
1964	Northern Dancer	9	5	14	9	18	Blue Grass S.	1

Year	Winner	Starts at 2	Starts Before Derby at 3	Total Pre-Derby Starts	Total Starts at 3	Total Starts at 2-3	Derby Prep	Finish
1963	Chateaugay	5	3	8	12	17	Blue Grass S.	1
1962	Decidedly	8	4	12	12	20	Blue Grass S.	2
1961	Carry Back	21	7	28	16	37	Wood Memorial S.	2
1960	Venetian Way	9	5	14	11	20	Churchill allowance	2
1959	*Tomy Lee	8	4	12	7	15	Blue Grass S.	1
1958	Tim Tam	1	10	11	13	14	Derby Trial S.	1
1957	Iron Liege	8	9	17	17	25	Derby Trial S.	5
1956	Needles	10	3	13	8	18	Florida Derby	1
1955	Swaps	6	3	9	9	15	Churchill allowance	1
1954	Determine	14	8	22	15	29	Derby Trial S.	1
1953	Dark Star	6	5	11	7	13	Derby Trial S.	1
1952	Hill Gail	7	7	14	8	15	Derby Trial S.	1
1951	Count Turf	10	10	20	14	24	Wood Memorial S.	5
1950	Middleground	5	4	9	10	15	Derby Trial S.	2
1949	Ponder	4	8	12	21	25	Derby Trial S.	2
1948	Citation	9	7	16	20	29	Derby Trial S.	1
1947	Jet Pilot	12	2	14	5	17	Jamaica H.	1
1946	Assault	9	3	12	15	24	Derby Trial S.	4
1945	Hoop, Jr.	5	2	7	4	9	Cedar Manor Purse	2
1944	Pensive	5	7	12	17	22	Chesapeake S.	2
1943	Count Fleet	15	2	17	6	21	Wood Memorial S.	1
1942	Shut Out	9	2	11	12	21	Blue Grass S.	1
1941	Whirlaway	16	7	23	20	36	Derby Trial S.	2
1940	Gallahadion	5	9	14	17	22	Derby Trial S.	2
1939	Johnstown	12	3	15	9	21	Wood Memorial S.	1
1938	Lawrin	15	8	23	11	26	Derby Trial S.	2
1937	War Admiral	6	2	8	8	14	Chesapeake S.	1
1936	Bold Venture	8	1	9	3	11	South Shore Purse	1
1935	Omaha	9	2	11	9	18	Wood Memorial S.	3
1934	Cavalcade	11	2	13	7	18	Chesapeake S.	1
1933	Brokers Tip	4	1	5	5	9	Lexington allowance	2
1932	Burgoo King	12	1	13	4	16	Lexington allowance	2
1931	Twenty Grand	8	2	10	10	18	Preakness S.	2
1930	Gallant Fox	7	2	9	10	17	Preakness S.	1

Foreign-Based Runners in the Kentucky Derby

Following are horses that were trained primarily outside the U.S. prior to their start in the Kentucky Derby (G1). Horses that made more than one U.S. start at three prior to their start in the Derby are not included.

Derby	Starter	Derby Finish	Country Where Based or Last Started
2002	Johannesburg	8	Ireland
	Essence of Dubai	9	United Arab Emirates
	Castle Gandolfo	12	Ireland
2001	Express Tour	8	United Arab Emirates
2000	China Visit	6	United Arab Emirates
	Curule	7	United Arab Emirates
1999	Worldly Manner	7	United Arab Emirates
1995	Eltish	6	England
	Citadeed	9	England
	Ski Captain	14	Japan
1994	Ulises[1]	14	Panama
1993	El Bakan[2]	18	Panama
1992	Dr Devious (Ire)	7	England
	Arazi	8	France
	Thyer	13	England
1986	Bold Arrangement (GB)[3]	2	England
1974	*Sir Tristram[4]	11	France
	Set n' Go[5]	15	Venezuela
	Lexico	22	Venezuela
1972	Pacallo[6]	16	Puerto Rico
1971	**Canonero II**	**1**	Venezuela

[1] Ulises started in the Lexington Stakes (G2) at Keeneland 13 days prior to the Derby.
[2] El Bakan started in the Lexington Stakes (G2) at Keeneland 13 days prior to the Derby.
[3] Bold Arrangement started in the Blue Grass Stakes (G1) at Keeneland nine days prior to the Derby.
[4] *Sir Tristram started in the Stepping Stone Purse at Churchill seven days prior to the Derby.
[5] Set n' Go started in the Carl G. Rose Memorial Handicap at Hialeah 24 days prior to the Derby.
[6] Pacallo started in the Stepping Stone Purse at Churchill seven days prior to the Derby.

Winners' Total Starts Before Derby

Decade	Total Starts Before Derby	Average No. Starts
2000-'05	37	6.2
1990-'99	90	9
1980-'89	93	9.3
1970-'79	136	13.6
1960-'69	129	12.9
1950-'59	137	13.7
1940-'49	138	13.8

Derby Winners' Starts at Two

Decade	Total Starts at Two	Average No. Starts
2000-'05	15	2.5
1990-'99	52	5.2
1980-'89	60	6.0
1970-'79	89	8.9
1960-'69	72	7.2
1950-'59	75	7.5
1940-'49	89	8.9

Winners' Starts at Three Before Derby

Decade	Total Starts at Three Before Derby	Average No. Starts
2000-'05	22	3.7
1990-'99	38	3.8
1980-'89	33	3.3
1970-'79	47	4.7
1960-'69	57	5.7
1950-'59	62	6.2
1940-'49	49	4.9

Total Pre-Derby Starts

Decade	Starters	Starts	Avg. No. Starts
2000-'05	108	763	7.06
1990-'99	167	1,387	8.31
1980-'89	171	1,720	10.06
1970-'79	149	1,945	13.05
1960-'69	126	2,151	17.07
1950-'59	145	2,316	15.97
1940-'49	126	1,805	14.33

Derby Starters' Starts at Two

Decade	Starters	Starts at 2	Avg. No. Starts
2000-'05	108	397	3.67
1990-'99	167	749	4.49
1980-'89	171	954	5.58
1970-'79	149	1,016	6.82
1960-'69	126	1,272	10.1
1950-'59	145	1,405	9.69
1940-'49	126	1,241	9.85

Pre-Derby Starts at Three

Decade	Starters	Starts at 3 Before Derby	Average No. Starts
2000-'05	108	366	3.39
1990-'99	167	638	3.82
1980-'89	171	766	4.48
1970-'79	149	929	6.23
1960-'69	126	879	6.98
1950-'59	145	911	6.28
1940-'49	126	564	4.48

Most Total Starts by Winner Before Derby

Total Starts	Horse	Year	Starts at Two	At Three Before Derby
28	Carry Back	1961	21	7
23	Whirlaway	1941	16	7
22	Determine	1954	14	8
	Dust Commander	1970	14	8
21	Cannonade	1974	17	4
20	Count Turf	1951	10	10
17	Count Fleet	1943	15	2
	Iron Liege	1957	8	9
	Forward Pass	1968	10	7
16	Citation	1948	9	7
14	Gallahadion	1940	5	9
	Jet Pilot	1947	12	2
	Hill Gail	1952	7	7
	Venetian Way	1960	9	5
	Northern Dancer	1964	9	5
	Spectacular Bid	1979	9	5
	Charismatic	1999	7	7

Fewest Total Starts by Winner Before Derby

Total Starts	Horse	Year	Starts at Two	At Three Before Derby
5	Grindstone	1996	2	3
	Fusaichi Pegasus	2000	1	4
6	Seattle Slew	1977	3	3
	Winning Colors	1988	2	4
	Sunday Silence	1989	3	3
	Silver Charm	1997	3	3
	Monarchos	2001	2	4
	Funny Cide	2003	3	3
	Smarty Jones	2004	2	4
7	Hoop, Jr.	1945	5	2
	Majestic Prince	1969	2	5
	Genuine Risk	1980	4	3
	Strike the Gold	1991	3	4
	War Emblem	2002	3	4
	Giacomo	2005	4	3

Kentucky Derby Handle

Year	On-track	Off-track	Total
2005	$10,055,508	$93,270,002	$103,325,510
2004	9,488,539	89,875,549	99,364,088
2003	9,135,919	78,832,118	87,968,037
2002	8,630,408	70,464,398	79,094,806
2001	8,360,273	59,192,483	67,552,756
2000	8,737,659	53,059,793	61,797,452
1999	8,025,318	46,171,266	54,196,586
1998	7,890,907	44,586,385	52,477,292
1997	7,401,141	41,891,506	49,292,647
1996	7,488,725	37,734,438	45,223,163
1995	7,297,050	37,518,438	44,815,488
1994	7,449,744	37,289,274	44,739,018
1993	6,811,130	33,458,735	40,269,865
1992	6,690,746	28,250,209	34,940,955
1991	6,744,979	27,499,222	34,244,201
1990	6,948,762	27,452,177	34,400,939
1989	6,751,067	23,089,515	29,840,582
1988	7,346,411	25,525,312	32,871,723
1987	6,362,673	20,829,236	27,191,909
1986	6,165,119	19,932,231	26,097,350
1985	5,770,074	14,474,555	20,244,629
1984	5,420,787	13,521,146	18,941,933
1983	5,546,977	—	5,546,977
1982	5,011,575	—	5,011,575
1981	4,566,179	455,163	5,021,342

Kentucky Derby simulcast wagering began in 1981, when three tracks (Longacres, Yakima Meadows, and Centennial) wagered a total of $455,163. Simulcast wagering was shelved for two years and resumed in 1984. Off-track wagering includes interstate and intrastate wagering.

Kentucky Derby

Grade 1, Churchill Downs, three-year-olds, 1¼ miles, dirt. Held on May 7, 2005, with gross value of $2,399,600. First run in 1875. Weights: colts and geldings, 126 pounds; fillies, 121 pounds.

Year	Winner	Jockey	Second	Third	Strs	Time	Track	1st Purse
2005	**Giacomo**	M. Smith	Closing Argument	Afleet Alex	20	2:02.75	ft	$1,639,600
2004	**Smarty Jones**	S. Elliott	Lion Heart	Imperialism	18	2:04.06	sy	**6,184,800**
2003	**‡Funny Cide**	J. Santos	Empire Maker	Peace Rules	16	2:01.19	ft	800,200
2002	**War Emblem**	V. Espinoza	Proud Citizen	Perfect Drift	18	2:01.13	ft	1,875,000
2001	**Monarchos**	J. Chavez	Invisible Ink	Congaree	17	1:59.97	ft	812,000
2000	**Fusaichi Pegasus**	K. Desormeaux	Aptitude	Impeachment	19	2:01.12	ft	888,400
1999	**Charismatic**	C. Antley	Menifee	Cat Thief	19	2:03.29	ft	886,200
1998	**Real Quiet**	K. Desormeaux	Victory Gallop	Indian Charlie	15	2:02.38	ft	738,800
1997	**Silver Charm**	G. Stevens	Captain Bodgit	Free House	13	2:02.44	ft	700,000
1996	**Grindstone**	J. Bailey	‡Cavonnier	Prince of Thieves	19	2:01.06	ft	869,800
1995	**Thunder Gulch**	G. Stevens	Tejano Run	Timber Country	19	2:01.27	ft	707,400
1994	**Go for Gin**	C. McCarron	Strodes Creek	Blumin Affair	14	2:03.72	sy	628,800
1993	**Sea Hero**	J. Bailey	‡Prairie Bayou	Wild Gale	19	2:02.42	ft	735,900
1992	**Lil E. Tee**	P. Day	Casual Lies	Dance Floor	18	2:03.04	ft	724,800
1991	**Strike the Gold**	C. Antley	‡Best Pal	Mane Minister	16	2:03.08	ft	655,800
1990	**Unbridled**	C. Perret	Summer Squall	Pleasant Tap	15	2:02	gd	581,000
1989	**Sunday Silence**	P. Valenzuela	Easy Goer	Awe Inspiring	15	2:05	my	574,200
1988	**†Winning Colors**	G. Stevens	Forty Niner	Risen Star	17	2:02⅕	ft	611,200
1987	**Alysheba**	C. McCarron	Bet Twice	Avies Copy	17	2:03⅖	ft	618,600
1986	**Ferdinand**	W. Shoemaker	Bold Arrangement (GB)	Broad Brush	16	2:02⅘	ft	609,400
1985	**Spend a Buck**	A. Cordero Jr.	Stephan's Odyssey	Chief's Crown	13	2:00⅕	ft	406,800
1984	**Swale**	L. Pincay Jr.	Coax Me Chad	At the Threshold	20	2:02⅖	ft	537,400
1983	**Sunny's Halo**	E. Delahoussaye	Desert Wine	Caveat	20	2:02⅕	ft	426,000
1982	**Gato Del Sol**	E. Delahoussaye	Laser Light	Reinvested	19	2:02⅖	ft	428,850
1981	**Pleasant Colony**	J. Velasquez	Woodchopper	Partez	21	2:02	ft	317,200
1980	**†Genuine Risk**	J. Vasquez	Rumbo	Jaklin Klugman	13	2:02	ft	250,550
1979	**Spectacular Bid**	R. Franklin	General Assembly	Golden Act	10	2:02⅖	ft	228,650
1978	**AFFIRMED**	S. Cauthen	Alydar	Believe It	11	2:01⅕	ft	186,900
1977	**SEATTLE SLEW**	J. Cruguet	Run Dusty Run	Sanhedrin	15	2:02⅕	ft	214,700
1976	**Bold Forbes**	A. Cordero Jr.	Honest Pleasure	Elocutionist	9	2:01⅗	ft	165,200
1975	**Foolish Pleasure**	J. Vasquez	Avatar	Diabolo	15	2:02	ft	209,600
1974	**Cannonade**	A. Cordero Jr.	Hudson County	Agitate	**23**	2:04	ft	274,000
1973	**SECRETARIAT**	R. Turcotte	Sham	Our Native	13	**1:59⅖**	ft	155,050
1972	**Riva Ridge**	R. Turcotte	No Le Hace	Hold Your Peace	16	2:01⅘	ft	140,300
1971	**Canonero II**	G. Avila	Jim French	Bold Reason	20	2:03⅕	ft	145,500
1970	**Dust Commander**	M. Manganello	My Dad George	High Echelon	17	2:03⅖	gd	127,800
1969	**Majestic Prince**	W. Hartack	Arts and Letters	Dike	8	2:01⅘	ft	113,200
1968	**Forward Pass**	I. Valenzuela	Francie's Hat	T. V. Commercial	14	2:02⅕	ft	122,600
1967	**Proud Clarion**	R. Ussery	Barbs Delight	Damascus	14	2:00⅗	ft	119,700
1966	**Kauai King**	D. Brumfield	Advocator	Blue Skyer	15	2:02	ft	120,500
1965	**Lucky Debonair**	W. Shoemaker	Dapper Dan	Tom Rolfe	11	2:01⅕	ft	112,000
1964	**Northern Dancer**	W. Hartack	Hill Rise	The Scoundrel	12	2:00	ft	114,300
1963	**Chateaugay**	B. Baeza	Never Bend	Candy Spots	9	2:01⅘	ft	108,900
1962	**Decidedly**	W. Hartack	Roman Line	Ridan	15	2:00⅖	ft	119,650
1961	**Carry Back**	J. Sellers	Crozier	Bass Clef	15	2:04	gd	120,500
1960	**Venetian Way**	W. Hartack	Bally Ache	Victoria Park	13	2:02⅖	gd	114,850
1959	***Tomy Lee**	W. Shoemaker	Sword Dancer	First Landing	17	2:02⅕	ft	119,650
1958	**Tim Tam**	I. Valenzuela	Lincoln Road	Noureddin	14	2:05	my	116,400
1957	**Iron Liege**	W. Hartack	*Gallant Man	Round Table	9	2:02⅕	ft	107,950
1956	**Needles**	D. Erb	Fabius	Come On Red	17	2:03⅖	ft	123,450
1955	**Swaps**	W. Shoemaker	Nashua	Summer Tan	10	2:01⅘	ft	108,400
1954	**Determine**	R. York	Hasty Road	Hasseyampa	17	2:03	ft	102,050
1953	**Dark Star**	H. Moreno	Native Dancer	Invigorator	11	2:02	ft	90,050
1952	**Hill Gail**	E. Arcaro	Sub Fleet	Blue Man	16	2:01⅗	ft	96,300
1951	**Count Turf**	C. McCreary	Royal Mustang	‡Ruhe	20	2:02⅗	ft	98,050
1950	**Middleground**	W. Boland	Hill Prince	Mr. Trouble	14	2:01⅗	ft	92,650
1949	**Ponder**	S. Brooks	Capot	Palestinian	14	2:04⅕	ft	91,600
1948	**CITATION**	E. Arcaro	Coaltown	My Request	6	2:05⅖	sy	83,400
1947	**Jet Pilot**	E. Guerin	Phalanx	Faultless	13	2:06⅘	sl	92,160
1946	**ASSAULT**	W. Mehrtens	Spy Song	Hampden	17	2:06⅗	sl	96,400
1945	**Hoop, Jr.**	E. Arcaro	Pot o'Luck	‡Darby Dieppe	16	2:07	my	64,850
1944	**Pensive**	C. McCreary	Broadcloth	‡Stir Up	16	2:04⅕	gd	64,675
1943	**COUNT FLEET**	J. Longden	Blue Swords	Slide Rule	10	2:04	ft	60,725
1942	**Shut Out**	W. Wright	Alsab	Valdina Orphan	15	2:04⅖	ft	64,225
1941	**WHIRLAWAY**	E. Arcaro	Staretor	Market Wise	11	2:01⅖	ft	61,275
1940	**Gallahadion**	C. Bierman	Bimelech	‡Dit	8	2:05	ft	60,150
1939	**Johnstown**	J. Stout	Challedon	Heather Broom	8	2:03⅖	ft	46,350

Year	Winner	Jockey	Second	Third	Strs	Time	Track	1st Purse
1938	**Lawrin**	E. Arcaro	Dauber	Can't Wait	10	2:04⅘	ft	47,050
1937	**WAR ADMIRAL**	C. Kurtsinger	Pompoon	Reaping Reward	20	2:03⅕	ft	52,050
1936	**Bold Venture**	I. Hanford	Brevity	Indian Broom	14	2:03⅗	ft	37,725
1935	**OMAHA**	W. Saunders	Roman Soldier	Whiskolo	18	2:05	gd	39,525
1934	**Cavalcade**	M. Garner	Discovery	Agrarian	13	2:04	ft	28,175
1933	**Brokers Tip**	D. Meade	Head Play	Charley O.	13	2:06⅘	gd	48,925
1932	**Burgoo King**	E. James	Economic	Stepenfetchit	20	2:05⅕	ft	52,350
1931	**Twenty Grand**	C. Kurtsinger	Sweep All	Mate	12	2:01⅘	ft	48,725
1930	**GALLANT FOX**	E. Sande	Gallant Knight	Ned O.	15	2:07⅗	gd	50,725
1929	**‡Clyde Van Dusen**	L. McAtee	Naishapur	Panchio	21	2:10⅘	my	53,950
1928	**Reigh Count**	C. Lang	Misstep	Toro	22	2:10⅖	hy	55,375
1927	**Whiskery**	L. McAtee	‡Osmand	Jock	15	2:06	sl	51,000
1926	**Bubbling Over**	A. Johnson	Bagenbaggage	Rock Man	13	2:03⅘	ft	50,075
1925	**Flying Ebony**	E. Sande	Captain Hal	Son of John	20	2:07⅗	sy	52,950
1924	**Black Gold**	J. Mooney	Chilhowee	Beau Butler	19	2:05⅕	ft	52,775
1923	**Zev**	E. Sande	Martingale	Vigil	21	2:05⅖	ft	53,600
1922	**Morvich**	A. Johnson	Bet Mosie	John Finn	10	2:04⅗	ft	53,775
1921	**Behave Yourself**	C. Thompson	Black Servant	†Prudery	12	2:04⅕	ft	38,450
1920	**‡Paul Jones**	T. Rice	Upset	On Watch	17	2:09	sl	30,375
1919	**SIR BARTON**	J. Loftus	‡Billy Kelly	*Under Fire	12	2:09⅘	hy	20,825
1918	**‡Exterminator**	W. Knapp	Escoba	†Viva America	8	2:10⅘	my	14,700
1917	***Omar Khayyam**	C. Borel	Ticket	Midway	15	2:04⅗	ft	16,600
1916	**George Smith**	J. Loftus	Star Hawk	Franklin	9	2:04	ft	9,750
1915	**†Regret**	J. Notter	Pebbles	‡Sharpshooter	16	2:05⅖	ft	11,450
1914	**‡Old Rosebud**	J. McCabe	‡Hodge	†Bronzewing	7	2:03⅖	ft	9,125
1913	**Donerail**	R. Goose	Ten Point	†Gowell	8	2:04⅘	ft	5,475
1912	**Worth**	C. Schilling	Duval	†Flamma	7	2:09⅖	my	4,850
1911	**Meridian**	G. Archibald	‡Governor Gray	Colston	7	2:05	ft	4,850
1910	**Donau**	F. Herbert	Joe Morris	Fighting Bob	7	2:06⅖	ft	4,850
1909	**Wintergreen**	V. Powers	‡Miami	Dr. Barkley	10	2:08⅕	sl	4,850
1908	**Stone Street**	A. Pickens	‡Sir Cleges	Dunvegan	8	2:15⅕	hy	4,850
1907	**Pink Star**	A. Minder	Zal	Ovelando	6	2:12⅗	hy	4,850
1906	**Sir Huon**	R. Troxler	†Lady Navarre	James Reddick	6	2:08⅘	ft	4,850
1905	**Agile**	J. Martin	Ram's Horn	Layson	3	2:10¾	hy	4,850
1904	**Elwood**	F. Prior	Ed Tierney	Brancas	5	2:08½	ft	4,850
1903	**Judge Himes**	H. Booker	Early	Bourbon	6	2:09	ft	4,850
1902	**Alan-a-Dale**	J. Winkfield	Inventor	The Rival	4	2:08¾	ft	4,850
1901	**His Eminence**	J. Winkfield	Sannazarro	Driscoll	5	2:07¾	ft	4,850
1900	**Lieut. Gibson**	J. Boland	Florizar	Thrive	7	2:06¼	ft	4,850
1899	**Manuel**	F. Taral	‡Corsine	Mazo	5	2:12	ft	4,850
1898	**Plaudit**	W. Simms	Lieber Karl	Isabey	4	2:09	gd	4,850
1897	**Typhoon II**	F. Garner	Ornament	Dr. Catlett	6	2:12½	hy	4,850
1896	**Ben Brush**	W. Simms	Ben Eder	Semper Ego	8	2:07¾	dy	4,850
1895	**Halma**	J. Perkins	Basso	Laureate	4	2:37½	ft	2,970
1894	**Chant**	F. Goodale	Pearl Song	Sigurd	5	2:41	ft	4,020
1893	**Lookout**	E. Kunze	Plutus	Boundless	6	2:39¼	ft	3,840
1892	**Azra**	A. Clayton	Huron	Phil Dwyer	3	2:41½	hy	4,230
1891	**Kingman**	I. Murphy	Balgowan	High Tariff	4	2:52¼	sl	4,550
1890	**Riley**	I. Murphy	Bill Letcher	Robespierre	6	2:45	my	5,460
1889	**Spokane**	T. Kiley	‡Proctor Knott	Once Again	8	2:34½	ft	4,880
1888	**‡Macbeth II**	G. Covington	Gallifet	White	7	2:38¼	ft	4,740
1887	**Montrose**	I. Lewis	Jim Gore	‡Jacobin	7	2:39¼	ft	4,200
1886	**Ben Ali**	P. Duffy	Blue Wing	Free Knight	10	2:36½	ft	4,890
1885	**Joe Cotton**	E. Henderson	Bersan	‡Ten Booker	10	2:37¼	gd	4,630
1884	**Buchanan**	I. Murphy	Loftin	Audrain	9	2:40¼	gd	3,990
1883	**Leonatus**	W. Donohue	‡Drake Carter	Lord Raglan	7	2:43	hy	3,760
1882	**‡Apollo**	B. Hurd	Runnymede	Bengal	14	2:40¼	gd	4,560
1881	**Hindoo**	J. McLaughlin	‡Lelex	Alfambra	6	2:40	ft	4,410
1880	**Fonso**	G. Lewis	Kimball	‡Bancroft	5	2:37½	dy	3,800
1879	**Lord Murphy**	C. Shauer	Falsetto	Strathmore	9	2:37	ft	3,550
1878	**Day Star**	J. Carter	Himyar	Leveller	9	2:37¼	dy	4,050
1877	**Baden-Baden**	W. Walker	Leonard	King William	11	2:38	ft	3,300
1876	**‡Vagrant**	B. Swim	Creedmore	Harry Hill	11	2:38¼	ft	2,950
1875	**Aristides**	O. Lewis	Volcano	Verdigris	15	2:37¾	ft	2,850

†—filly, ‡—gelding, *—imported horse
1875-'95: 1½ miles; 1973-present: Grade 1; 1968: Dancer's Image finished first but was disqualified from purse money; bold indicates records set in number of starters, time, and winning purse; War Emblem's record winning purse includes a $1-million bonus awarded by Sportman's Park for winning the Illinois Derby (G2) and a Triple Crown race. Smarty Jones's 2004 purse includes $5-million bonus from Oaklawn Park. Triple Crown winners are in all capitalized letters.

History of the Preakness Stakes

Born out of a party boast and named for a horse who met an unfortunate end, the Preakness Stakes (G1) is the second jewel of the American Triple Crown and the second-oldest American classic.

Both the Preakness Stakes and Pimlico Race Course, the track where the classic race is staged annually on the third Saturday of May, trace their roots to a party hosted by Milton H. Sanford in Saratoga Springs, New York, in 1868. At the party, Maryland Governor Oden Bowie promised that a new racetrack would open in Baltimore to play host to the Dinner Party Stakes, to which he pledged a hefty purse.

A 70-acre track site, which had been known as Pimlico since the 1850s and had been used for racing since then, was purchased by the Maryland Agricultural Society from Robert Wylie in 1866. The organization held a fair meet at the site in 1869 but failed to raise enough money to complete the track.

Bowie, a horse owner and sportsman, helped another group, the Maryland Jockey Club, to negotiate a lease of the property—$1,000 annual rent for ten years. Gen. John Elliott designed the track, and Pimlico opened on October 25, 1870. Among the amenities was the Pimlico Clubhouse, a Baltimore landmark until it was destroyed by fire in 1966.

Sanford, a New York horseman who made a portion of his fortune by selling blankets to the army in the Civil War, sent his three-year-old colt Preakness to make his only start of that year in the new Dinner Party Stakes. Bred in Kentucky by A. J. Alexander, Sanford bought the colt by Lexington out of Bay Leaf, by *Yorkshire, as a yearling for $2,000. He named the colt after his farms in New Jersey and Kentucky, which also bore the name Preakness. The name is derived from the language of the Minisi Indians in northern New Jersey; in their language, "pra-qua-les" meant "quail woods."

Under English jockey Billy Hayward, Preakness won the first Dinner Party Stakes, which today is known as the Dixie Stakes (G2) and is run on grass. Three years later, in 1873, the Maryland Jockey Club staged its first spring meeting and honored the winner of the first Dinner Party Stakes by naming the 1½-mile race for three-year-olds the Preakness Stakes.

Second race on a three-race program on Tuesday, May 23, 1873, the first Preakness Stakes attracted a field of seven to compete for the $2,050 total purse. A crowd estimated at 12,000 made Bowie's Catesby the favorite, but John Chamberlin's Survivor won by ten lengths, which until 2004 was the race's largest winning

Preakness Attendance

Year	On-Track	Total	Year	On-Track	Total
2005	115,318	125,687	1987		87,945
2004	112,668	124,351	1986		87,652
2003	100,268	109,931	1985		81,235
2002	101,138	117,055	1984		80,566
2001	104,454	118,926	1983		71,768
2000	98,304	111,821	1982		80,724
1999	100,311	116,526	1981		84,133
1998	91,122	103,269	1980		83,455
1997	88,594	102,118	1979		72,607
1996	85,122	97,751	1978		81,261
1995	87,707	100,818	1977		77,346
1994	86,343	99,834	1976		62,256
1993	85,495	97,641	1975		75,216
1992	85,294	96,865	1974		54,911
1991	87,245	96,695	1973		61,657
1990	86,531	96,106	1972		48,721
1989	90,145	98,896	1971		47,221
1988	81,282	88,654	1970		42,474

Attendance figures from 1988 to 2003 include combined intertrack sites (Laurel, Rosecroft, Delmarva Downs) and exclude Maryland off-track betting sites. Pimlico and Laurel Park in, 2004-'05.

margin. In 2004, Roy and Patricia Chapman's Smarty Jones won by 11½ lengths.

Preakness, the horse for whom the race was named, continued to race until age eight, winning the 1875 Baltimore Cup and finishing in a dead heat with Springbok in that year's Saratoga Cup. Sold to England for stud, Preakness became difficult to handle in his later years and was shot to death by his owner, the Duke of Hamilton.

Pimlico staged the first 17 runnings of the Preakness, but the Maryland Jockey Club encountered financial difficulties in 1889, and the race was run the following year at Morris Park in New York. It was not run in 1891, '92, and '93—thus, though two years older than the Kentucky Derby, the Preakness has had one fewer running—and reappeared in 1894 at Gravesend Race Course in Brooklyn, where it would be renewed for 15 years.

Pimlico regained its financial health early in the new century, but the Preakness did not return to Baltimore until May 12, 1909, when Effendi set the pace and won by one length over Fashion Plate while running a mile in 1:39⅗. Unlike the Belmont Stakes, which was not run in 1911 and '12 because of New York antigambling legislation, the Preakness was run with betting through those years.

The race proved so popular that in 1918 the Preakness—then at 1⅛ miles—was run in two divisions, the only American classic race to be split. On May 14 of the following year, J.K.L. Ross's Sir Barton won the Preakness only four days after scoring his maiden victory in the Kentucky Derby. On June 11, 1919, the *Star Shoot colt defeated two opponents in the Belmont Stakes to become the first Triple Crown winner. The feat was noted after the fact when *Daily Racing Form* columnist Charles Hatton popularized the designation for the three races beginning in 1930.

The Preakness's reputation was sealed in 1920 when the great Man o' War opened his three-year-old season with a 1½-length victory over Upset, the only horse ever to defeat him. The Preakness remained at 1⅛ miles until 1925, when it was changed to its present 1³⁄₁₆ miles.

In 1930, the Preakness was the first race of Gallant Fox's Triple Crown, but after '31 the race took its place as second in the series. In 1945, after victory in Europe led to the lifting of a voluntary ban on racing, the Preakness was run one week after the Derby and one week before the Belmont.

Pimlico was the scene of three memorable Triple Crown efforts in the 1970s: Secretariat's sweeping move to the lead on the clubhouse turn in 1973, Seattle Slew's brilliance in '77, and the stretch-long battle of Affirmed and Alydar in '78.

The race has had its share of controversy as well. In 1962, Greek Money won by a nose over Ridan, whose rider, Manuel Ycaza, claimed foul. A head-on photo, however, disclosed that Ycaza was in fact using his hands and elbows to restrain Greek Money. In 1980, Kentucky Derby winner Genuine Risk was herded wide at the top of the stretch by winner Codex, ridden by Angel Cordero Jr. An objection by Genuine Risk's jockey, Jacinto Vasquez, was disallowed, and Bertram Firestone, the filly's co-owner, forced a long Maryland Racing Commission hearing into the result. The original order of finish was upheld.

The Preakness in the 1980s and '90s was notable for two close finishes: Sunday Silence's 1989 nose victory over Easy Goer and the '97 race, in which Silver Charm won by a head over Free House, with third-place finisher Captain Bodgit another head farther back.

In 2002, '03, and '04, the Derby winners scored victories in the Preakness. War Emblem won in 2002, and Funny Cide romped by 9¾ lengths, then the second-largest margin, in '03. Funny Cide was only the seventh gelding to win the Preakness. Smarty Jones won in 2004 by a record 11½ lengths. In 2005, Afleet Alex overcame a near fall and won by 4¾ lengths.—*Don Clippinger*

Woodlawn Vase

The Woodlawn Vase, said to be the most valuable trophy in sports, is presented annually to the owner of the Preakness Stakes winner. The trophy, 34 inches tall and weighing almost 30 pounds, was created in 1860 by Tiffany and Co. for the Woodlawn Racing Association in Louisville. After being buried during the Civil War to

prevent it from being melted down, the trophy was unearthed and remained in Louisville until 1878, when the Dwyer brothers won it. They presented it to the Coney Island Jockey Club, and it was subsequently presented at two other New York tracks, Jerome Park and Morris Park.

Thomas C. Clyde won the trophy in 1904 and gave it to the Maryland Jockey Club, of which he was a director, in '17. That year, E. R. Bradley's Kalitan was the first horse to win the Woodlawn Vase at Pimlico.

A Preakness Tradition

A Preakness Stakes tradition observed each year is the painting of the winner's silks on a weather vane atop the Preakness presentation stand. The practice dates to 1909, when lightning destroyed a weather vane atop the Members' Clubhouse, which dated to 1870. The track's directors commissioned a new weather vane depicting a horse and rider, and the weather vane was adorned with the colors of Effendi that year.

The clubhouse structure, an ornate Victorian building that contained dining rooms, sleeping rooms, and a library, burned to the ground in June 1966. Since then, winner's colors have been painted on a weather vane atop an infield replica of the old clubhouse's cupola.

Black-Eyed Susans in the Spring

The black-eyed Susan, Maryland's state flower since 1918, blooms each summer and fall in Maryland and other states, but not in the spring. Thus, the black-eyed Susans that adorn the Preakness Stakes (G1) winner's garland are not black-eyed Susans. Actually, they are Viking daisies in disguise.

The ersatz black-eyed Susans were first draped across Bimelech's withers after the 1940 Preakness. Today, the garland is 18" wide and 90" long, and assembling it requires two days. First, greenery is attached to a spongy rubber base, and then more than 80 bunches of daisies are secured to the base. Heavy felt is then attached to the back to protect the horse. After that, black lacquer is daubed on the center of the daisies to simulate black-eyed Susans.

Origins of the Alibi Breakfast

The Alibi Breakfast, a Preakness-week tradition, is a direct descendant of the informal gatherings on the porch of the historic Old Clubhouse in the 1930s, when trainers, journalists, racing officials, and others would gather during training hours to watch the horses and swap stories.

David Woods, Pimlico Race Course's publicity director in the 1940s, formalized the get-togethers as a Preakness event at which owners and trainers could explain why they believed their horses would win, or take the opportunity to propose an alibi or two in case they did not win.

The track's principal awards—the Old Hilltop Award, Special Award of Merit, and the David F. Woods Memorial Award—are presented during the breakfast.

"Maryland, My Maryland"

While the roots of "My Old Kentucky Home" most likely were opposition to slavery, "Maryland, My Maryland" was originally a nine-stanza poem written in support of the Confederacy.

The author was James Ryder Randall, who wrote it in April 1861 to protest Union troops marching through Baltimore. A Maryland native, Randall was then teaching in Louisiana.

His poem was set to the tune of "Lauriger Horatius" ("O, Tannenbaum"), and the song achieved wide popularity in Maryland and throughout the South before becoming the official state song in 1939.

The two stanzas that are sung:

The despot's heel is on thy shore,
Maryland!
His torch is at thy temple door,
Maryland!
Avenge the patriotic gore
That flecked the streets of Baltimore,
And be the battle queen of yore,
Maryland! My Maryland!

Thou wilt not cower in the dust,
Maryland!
Thy beaming sword shall never rust,
Maryland!
Remember Carroll's sacred trust,
Remember Howard's warlike thrust,
And all thy slumberers with the just,
Maryland! My Maryland!

Preakness Trivia

• Derby winners in recent years were not necessarily favored in the Preakness. Since 1986, the following Derby winners did not go off as the Preakness favorites: Ferdinand, 1986,

second; Sunday Silence, 1989, won; Lil E. Tee, 1992, fifth; Sea Hero, 1993, fifth; Silver Charm, 1997, won; Real Quiet, 1998, won; Charismatic, 1999, won; Giacomo, 2005, third.

• Two individuals have won the Preakness both as jockeys and trainers. Louis Schaefer rode Dr. Freeland to victory in 1929 and one decade later trained Challedon to a Preakness win. Johnny Longden rode Count Fleet in 1943 and trained Majestic Prince in '69.

• A starting gate was first used for the Preakness in 1930.

• The Preakness has been run at seven different distances since 1873. The race was as short as one mile in 1909 and '10, as long as 1¾ miles in 1889, and 1³⁄₁₆ miles since 1925.

• Two African-American jockeys have won the Preakness: George B. "Spider" Anderson aboard Buddhist in 1889 and Willie Simms on Sly Fox in '98. The only black jockey to ride in the Preakness in modern times was Wayne Barnett, who finished eighth aboard Sparrowvon in 1985.

• The Preakness preceded the Kentucky Derby on the racing calendar 11 times between 1888 and 1931.

• In 1890, the Preakness and the Belmont Stakes were run on the same card at Morris Park.

• From 1910 through '16, the Preakness was run as a handicap. From 1895 through 1907, the race was under allowance conditions, limiting it to horses that had not won a race worth a certain amount.

• The Preakness was run in divisions in 1918, when *War Cloud and Jack Hare Jr. won.

Leading Preakness Owners by Wins

7   **Calumet Farm:** Whirlaway, 1941; Pensive, 1944; Faultless, 1947; Citation, 1948; Fabius, 1956; Tim Tam, 1958; Forward Pass, 1968.

5   **George L. Lorillard:** Duke of Magenta, 1878; Harold, 1879; Grenada, 1880; Saunterer, 1881; Vanguard, 1882.

4   **Harry Payne Whitney:** Royal Tourist, 1908; Broomspun, 1921; Bostonian, 1927; Victorian, 1928.

Added Value of the Preakness

The purse value of the Preakness Stakes (G1) has increased from $1,000 in 1873 to $1-million guaranteed, with the winner currently collecting a check for $650,000. The increase is significant; $1,000 in 1873 would equal only $14,210 today, which is the purse level of a good-quality claiming race.

The Preakness purse has been decreased on occasion, including once during the Great Depression (1933) and in consecutive years, 1949 and 1950. Following is the progression of the Preakness purse:

Year	Added Value	Year	Added Value
1998	*$1,000,000	1918	**$15,000
1989	500,000	1917	5,000
1985	350,000	1912	1,500
1979	200,000	1909	2,000
1959	150,000	1907	2,500
1953	100,000	1904	2,000
1951	75,000	1902	1,500
1950	50,000	1899	1,000
1949	75,000	1895	2,000
1946	100,000	1983	250,000
1937	50,000	1894	1,000
1933	25,000	1890	1,500
1922	50,000	1873	1,000
1921	40,000	* guaranteed purse	
1919	25,000	** each division	

Supplemental Nominations to the Preakness

When Triple Crown Productions launched a common nomination in 1986, no supplemental entries were permitted. The rules were changed in 1991 to allow supplemental entries, although no horse owner has yet to put up $100,000 to gain a place in the Preakness Stakes (G1) starting gate.

Supplemental entries to the Preakness were first permitted in 1938, and the first supplemental entrant to win was Citation, who won the '48 Triple Crown. Calumet Farm owner Warren Wright supplemented both Citation and Coaltown for $3,000 each, but only Citation started. Hill Prince (1950) and Master Derby ('75) were supplemental winners.

Here are the supplemented Preakness starters since 1959:

Year	Horse	Supplement	Finish	Purse Winnings
1985	Tajawa	$20,000	6th	$ 0
	Sport Jet	20,000	10th	0
	Hajji's Treasure	20,000	11th	0
1984	Fight Over	15,000	3rd	30,000
1982	Reinvested	10,000	6th	0
1981	Paristo	10,000	3rd	20,000
1980	Lucky Pluck	10,000	8th	0
1975	**Master Derby**	10,000	1st	158,100
	Native Guest	10,000	7th	0
1974	Super Florin	10,000	10th	0
1970	Dust Commander	10,000	9th	0
1968	Nodouble	10,000	3rd*	15,000
1967	Barb's Delight	10,000	6th	0
1959	Manassah Mauler	10,000	8th	0

* moved up from fourth via disqualification

3 **Belair Stud:** Gallant Fox, 1930; Omaha, 1935; Nashua, 1955.

E. R. Bradley: Kalitan, 1917; Burgoo King, 1932; Bimelech, 1940.

Robert and Beverly Lewis: Timber Country (co-owners), 1995; Silver Charm, 1997; Charismatic, 1999.

Walter J. Salmon: Vigil, 1923; Display, 1926; Dr. Freeland, 1929.

2 **August Belmont II:** Don Enrique, 1907; Watervale, 1911.

Brookmeade Stable: High Quest, 1934; Bold, 1951.

J. F. Chamberlin: Survivor, 1873; Tom Ochiltree, 1875.

Glen Riddle Farm: Man o' War, 1920; War Admiral, 1937.

Loblolly Stable: Pine Bluff, 1992; Prairie Bayou, 1993.

Overbrook Farm: Tabasco Cat (co-owner), 1994; Timber Country (co-owner), 1995.

Preakness Stable: Montague, 1890; Belmar, 1895.

J. K. L. Ross: Damrosch, 1916; Sir Barton, 1919.

The Thoroughbred Corp.: Point Given, 2001; War Emblem 2002.

Owners with Most Starters

Owner	Starters	Wins
Greentree Stable	20	1
Harry Payne Whitney	15	4
Calumet Farm	14	7
August Belmont II	11	2
George L. Lorillard	11	5
Overbrook Farm	11	2
Brookmeade Stable	9	2
King Ranch	8	1
Robert and Beverly Lewis	8	3
Pierre Lorillard	8	1
Wheatley Stable	7	1
Rancocas Stable	6	0
Mrs. Ethel D. Jacobs	6	1

Leading Preakness Breeders by Wins

7 **Calumet Farm:** Whirlaway, 1941; Pensive, 1944; Faultless, 1947; Citation, 1948; Fabius, 1956; Tim Tam, 1958; Forward Pass, 1968.

6 **Harry Payne Whitney:** Royal Tourist, 1908; Buskin, 1913; Holiday, 1914; Broomspun, 1921; Bostonian, 1927; Victorian, 1928.

August Belmont II: Jacobus, 1883; Margrave, 1896; Don Enrique, 1907; Watervale, 1911; Damrosch, 1916; Man o' War, 1920.

4 **A. J. Alexander:** Tom Ochiltree, 1875; Shirley, 1876; Duke of Magenta, 1878; Grenada, 1880.

3 **Belair Stud:** Gallant Fox, 1930; Omaha, 1935; Nashua, 1955.

James Ben Ali Haggin: Old England, 1902; Cairngorm, 1905; Rhine Maiden, 1915.

2 **William S. Farish:** Summer Squall (co-breeder), 1990; Charismatic (co-breeder), 1999.

Idle Hour Stock Farm: Burgoo King (co-breeder), 1932; Bimelech, 1940.

Loblolly Stable: Pine Bluff, 1992; Prairie Bayou, 1993.

Raceland Stud: Whimsical, 1906; Colonel Holloway, 1912.

Walter J. Salmon: Display, 1926; Dr. Freeland, 1929.

R. W. Walden: Vanguard, 1882; Refund, 1882.

Aristides Welch: Harold, 1879; Saunterer, 1881.

Leading Preakness Trainers by Wins

7 **R. Wyndham Walden:** Tom Ochiltree, 1875; Duke of Magenta, 1878; Harold, 1879; Grenada, 1880; Saunterer, 1881; Vanguard, 1882; Refund, 1888.

5 **Thomas J. Healey:** The Parader, 1901; Pillory, 1922; Vigil, 1923; Display, 1926; Dr. Freeland, 1929.

D. Wayne Lukas: Codex, 1980; Tank's Prospect, 1985; Tabasco Cat, 1994; Timber Country, 1995; Charismatic, 1999.

4 **Bob Baffert:** Silver Charm, 1997; Real Quiet, 1998; Point Given, 2001; War Emblem, 2002.

4   James E. "Sunny Jim" Fitzsimmons: Gallant Fox, 1930; Omaha, 1935; Nashua, 1955; Bold Ruler, 1957.

H. A. "Jimmy" Jones: Faultless, 1947; Citation, 1948; Fabius, 1956; Tim Tam, 1958.

3   James Whalen: Don Enrique, 1907; Watervale, 1911; Buskin, 1913.

2   Thomas Bohannan: Pine Bluff, 1992; Prairie Bayou, 1993.

Edward Feakes: Montague, 1890; Belmar, 1895.

Henry Forrest: Kauai King, 1966; Forward Pass, 1968.

T. P. Hayes: Paul Kauvar, 1897; Head Play, 1933.

J. S. Healey: Layminster, 1910; Holiday, 1914.

Max Hirsch: Bold Venture, 1936; Assault, 1946.

William Hurley: Kalitan, 1917; Bimelech, 1940.

B. A. "Ben" Jones: Whirlaway, 1941; Pensive, 1944.

Andrew W. Joyner: Cairngorm, 1905; Royal Tourist, 1908.

2   Jack Van Berg: Gate Dancer, 1984; Alysheba, 1987.

Frank Y. Whiteley Jr.: Tom Rolfe, 1965; Damascus, 1967.

Trainers with Most Starters

Trainer	Starters	Wins
D. Wayne Lukas	31	5
Max Hirsch	19	2
James E. Fitzsimmons	18	4
James Rowe Sr.	14	1
Nicholas Zito	16	1
Bob Baffert	9	4
Woody Stephens	9	1
Preston Burch	8	1
John P. Campo	8	1

Female Trainers in the Preakness

Here are the female trainers with Preakness starters:

Year	Horse	Trainer	Finish
2004	Imperialism	Kristin Mulhall	5th
	Water Cannon	Linda Albert	10th
2003	New York Hero	Jennifer Pedersen	6th
	Kissin Saint	Lisa Lewis	10th
2002	Magic Weisner	Nancy H. Alberts	2nd
2001	Griffinite	Jennifer Leigh-Peterson	5th
1998	Silver's Prospect	Jean Rolfe	10th
1996	In Contention	Cynthia Reese	6th
1993	Hegar	Penny Lewis	9th
1992	Casual Lies	Shelley Riley	3rd
	Speakerphone	Dean Gaudet	14th
1990	Fighting Notion	Nancy Heil	5th
1980	Samoyed	Judith Zouck	6th
1968	Sir Beau	Judy Johnson	7th

Leading Preakness Jockeys by Wins

Eddie Arcaro, known as "The Master," held sway over the Preakness Stakes in his storied career, winning the race six times in 15 starts. His closest challenger is Pat Day, who has won the race three consecutive times, 1994-'96, and has five victories with 17 Preakness starters.

The leading Preakness jockeys with two or more victories:

6   Eddie Arcaro: Whirlaway, 1941; Citation, 1948; Hill Prince, 1950; Bold, 1951; Nashua, 1955; Bold Ruler, 1957.

5   Pat Day: Tank's Prospect, 1985; Summer Squall, 1990; Tabasco Cat, 1994; Timber Country, 1995; Louis Quatorze, 1996.

3   George Barbee: Survivor, 1873; Shirley, 1876; Jacobus, 1883.

William Hartack: Fabius, 1956; Northern Dancer, 1964; Majestic Prince, 1969.

L. Hughes: Tom Ochiltree, 1875; Harold, 1879; Grenada, 1880.

2   Jerry Bailey: Hansel, 1991; Red Bullet, 2000.

Angel Cordero Jr.: Codex, 1980; Gate Dancer, 1984.

Costello: Saunterer, 1881; Vanguard, 1882.

Fisher: Knight of Ellersie, 1884; The Bard, 1886.

C. Holloway: Cloverbrook, 1877; Duke of Magenta, 1878.

Clarence Kummer: Man o' War, 1920; Coventry, 1925.

Charles Kurtsinger: Head Play, 1933; War Admiral, 1937.

John Loftus: War Cloud, 1918; Sir Barton, 1919.

Chris McCarron: Alysheba, 1987; Pine Bluff, 1992.

Conn McCreary: Pensive, 1944; Blue Man, 1952.

Bill Shoemaker: Candy Spots, 1963; Damascus, 1967.

Gary Stevens: Silver Charm, 1997; Point Given, 2001.

Fred Taral: Assignee, 1894; Belmar, 1895.

Ismael Valenzuela: Tim Tam, 1958; Forward Pass, 1968.

Most Preakness Mounts

Jockey	Starts	Wins
Pat Day	17	5
Eddie Arcaro	15	6
Gary Stevens	16	2
Jerry Bailey	15	2
Angel Cordero Jr.	13	2
Chris McCarron	13	2
Bill Shoemaker	12	2
William Hartack	11	3
Jorge Velasquez	11	1
Braulio Baeza	10	0
Linus McAtee	10	1

Female Jockeys in the Preakness

Only two female jockeys have ridden in the Preakness, and the best finish was by Patricia Cooksey, who was sixth aboard Tajawa in 1985. Andrea Seefeldt, a Maryland-based rider, finished seventh in 1994 aboard Looming.

Jockey	Year	Horse	Finish
Andrea Seefeldt	1994	Looming	7th
Patricia Cooksey	1985	Tajawa	6th

Leading Preakness Sires by Wins

3   Lexington: Tom Ochiltree, 1875; Shirley, 1876; Duck of Magenta, 1878.

Preakness Wagering, 1980-2005

Year	Preakness Winner	Preakness In-State Handle	Preakness Simulcasting	Preakness Total Handle
2005	Afleet Alex	$4,079,858	$56,781,232	$60,861,090
2004	Smarty Jones	3,808,863	54,982,543	58,791,406
2003	Funny Cide	3,151,864	38,008,281	41,620,145
2002	War Emblem	3,440,321	44,254,871	47,695,192
2001	Point Given	3,342,237	37,352,557	40,694,884
2000	Red Bullet	2,482,262	26,550,064	29,032,326
1999	Charismatic	3,056,891	26,438,761	34,435,703
1998	Real Quiet	2,103,027	17,624,933	23,640,365
1997	Silver Charm	2,667,000	18,087,214	26,602,245
1996	Louis Quatorze	2,352,900	20,545,618	22,898,518
1995	Timber Country	2,519,388	20,869,915	23,389,303
1994	Tabasco Cat	2,548,282	21,461,540	24,009,822
1993	Prairie Bayou	2,269,946	19,293,287	21,563,233
1992	Pine Bluff	2,365,023	19,338,393	21,703,416
1991	Hansel	2,504,693	18,289,622	20,794,315
1990	Summer Squall	2,257,916	16,625,833	18,883,749
1989	Sunday Silence	2,519,893	17,306,821	19,826,714
1988	Risen Star	2,392,384	18,519,289	20,911,673
1987	Alysheba	1,846,768		
1986	Snow Chief	1,680,923		
1985	Tank's Prospect	1,461,997		
1884	Gate Dancer	1,358,444		
1983	Deputed Testamony	1,251,931		
1982	Aloma's Ruler	1,257,244		
1981	Pleasant Colony	1,387,797		
1980	Codex	1,215,664		

3 **Broomstick:** Holiday, 1914; Broomspun, 1921; Bostonian, 1927.

2 ***Leamington:** Harold, 1879; Saunterer, 1881.
***Watercress:** Watervale, 1911; Rhine Maiden, 1915.
Fair Play: Man o' War, 1920; Display, 1926.
***Sir Gallahad III:** Gallant Fox, 1930; High Quest, 1934.
Bull Lea: Faultless, 1947; Citation, 1948.
***Nasrullah:** Nashua, 1955; Bold Ruler, 1957.
Sovereign Dancer: Gate Dancer, 1984; Louis Quatorze, 1996.
Woodman: Hansel, 1991; Timber Country, 1995.

Preakness in the Pedigree

Preakness winners who have sired other Preakness winners:

Man o' War (1920): War Admiral (1937)
Gallant Fox (1930): Omaha (1935)
Bold Venture (1936): Assault (1946)
Polynesian (1945): Native Dancer (1953)
Citation (1948): Fabius (1956)
Native Dancer (1953): Kauai King (1966)
Bold Ruler (1957): Secretariat (1973)
Secretariat (1973): Risen Star (1988)
Summer Squall (1990): Charismatic (1999)

Fastest Runnings of the Preakness

Tank's Prospect and Louis Quatorze share the record for the fastest running of the Preakness Stakes, 1:53⅖. Louis Quatorze, the 1996 winner, was timed in 1:53.43, but Tank's Prospect in 1985 was timed in one-fifths of a second, the standard at that time.

Unofficially, Secretariat ran the Preakness's 1$\frac{3}{16}$ miles in the same time. He was caught in 1:53⅖ by *Daily Racing Form* clockers who were hand-timing the race. A malfunctioning official timer recorded a time of 1:55, but that was subsequently adjusted to 1:54⅖.

Year	Winner	Time	Cond.
1996	Louis Quatorze	1:53.43	Fast
1985	Tank's Prospect	1:53⅖	Fast
1984	Gate Dancer	1:53⅗	Fast
1990	Summer Squall	1:53⅘	Fast
1971	Canonero II	1:54	Fast
1979	Spectacular Bid	1:54⅕	Fast
1995	Timber Country	1:54.45	Fast
1980	Codex	1:54⅕	Fast
1973	Secretariat	1:54⅖*	Fast
1977	Seattle Slew	1:54⅖	Fast
1978	Affirmed	1:54⅖	Fast

* Hand-timed in 1:53⅖

Evolution of Preakness Stakes Record

Year	Winner	Time
1925	Coventry	1:59
1934	High Quest	1:58⅕
1942	Alsab	1:57
1949	Capot	1:56
1955	Nashua	1:54⅗
1971	Canonero II	1:54
1984	Gate Dancer	1:53⅗
1985	Tank's Prospect	1:53⅖
1996	Louis Quatorze	1:53⅖ (1:53.43)

Fastest Preakness Fractions

First quarter-mile: :22⅖ Flag Raiser (1965), Fight Over (1984), Eternal Prince (1985), Vicar (1999).
First half-mile: :45, Bold Forbes (1976).

First six furlongs: 1:09, Bold Forbes (1976).

Fastest first mile: 1:34⅕, Chief's Crown (1985), Sunday Silence (1989).

Fastest final three-sixteenths: :18, Summer Squall, 1990.

Slowest Preakness Times

Citation, a Triple Crown winner and regarded as one of the greatest Thoroughbreds of the 20th century, ran the slowest Preakness Stakes ever, 2:02⅖. But the *Daily Racing Form* chart characterized the track as heavy, which would have been considerably slower than today's speed-tuned racing surfaces.

Following are the slowest Preakness runnings since 1925, when the race's distance became 1³⁄₁₆ miles.

Year	Winner	Time	Cond.
1948	Citation	2:02⅖	Heavy
1933	Head Play	2:02	Slow
1927	Bostonian	2:01⅗	Good
1929	Dr. Freeland	2:01⅗	Fast
1946	Assault	2:01⅖	Fast
1930	Gallant Fox	2:00⅗	Fast
1928	Victorian	2:00⅕	Fast
1932	Burgoo King	1:59⅘	Fast
1938	Dauber	1:59⅘	Sloppy
1939	Challedon	1:59⅘	Muddy
1926	Display	1:59⅘	Fast
1950	Hill Prince	1:59⅕	Slow
1944	Pensive	1:59⅕	Fast

Largest Winning Margins

Year	Winner	Lengths
2004	Smarty Jones	11½
1873	Survivor	10
2003	Funny Cide	9¾
1943	Count Fleet	8
1889	Buddhist	8
1991	Hansel	7
1974	Little Current	7
1951	Bold	7
1938	Dauber	7
1968	Forward Pass	6
1935	Omaha	6
1878	Duke of Magenta	6
1979	Spectacular Bid	5½
1948	Citation	5½
1941	Whirlaway	5½
1950	Hill Prince	5
1912	Colonel Holloway	5

Smallest Winning Margins

Year	Winner	Margin
1989	Sunday Silence	nose
1962	Greek Money	nose
1936	Bold Venture	nose
1934	High Quest	nose
1928	Victorian	nose
1902	Old England	nose
1997	Silver Charm	head
1985	Tank's Prospect	head
1969	Majestic Prince	head
1949	Capot	head
1937	War Admiral	head
1932	Burgoo King	head
1926	Display	head
1922	Pillory	head
1905	Cairngorm	head
1900	Hindus	head

Preakness Odds-On Beaten Favorites

The shortest-priced beaten favorites in the Preakness Stakes were Riva Ridge in 1972 and Fusaichi Pegasus in 2000. Both entered the Preakness off Derby victories and both went off at 3-to-10. Riva Ridge fell to Bee Bee Bee on a sloppy track, and Fusaichi Pegasus finished second to Red Bullet.

Here are the odds-on beaten favorites in the Preakness:

Year	Horse	Odds	Finish
2000	Fusaichi Pegasus	0.30-to-1	2nd
1972	Riva Ridge	0.30-to-1	4th
1939	Gilded Knight-Johnstown entry	0.45-to-1	2nd 5th
1982	Linkage	0.50-to-1	2nd
1989	Easy Goer	0.60-to-1	2nd
1956	Needles	0.60-to-1	2nd
1984	Swale	0.80-to-1	7th
1964	Hill Rise	0.80-to-1	3rd
1976	Honest Pleasure	0.90-to-1	5th
1954	Correlation	0.90-to-1	2nd

Shortest-Priced Preakness Winners

Year	Winner	Odds
1979	Spectacular Bid	0.10-to-1
1948	Citation	0.10-to-1
1943	Count Fleet	0.15-to-1
1953	Native Dancer	0.20-to-1
1973	Secretariat	0.30-to-1
1955	Nashua	0.30-to-1
1937	War Admiral	0.35-to-1
1977	Seattle Slew	0.40-to-1
1934	High Quest	0.45-to-1
1978	Affirmed	0.50-to-1

Longest-Priced Preakness Winners

Year	Winner	Odds
1975	Master Derby	23.40-to-1
1925	Coventry	21.80-to-1
1926	Display	19.35-to-1
1972	Bee Bee Bee	18.70-to-1
1983	Deputed Testamony	14.50-to-1
1974	Little Current	13.10-to-1
1924	Nellie Morse	12.10-to-1
1945	Polynesian	12-to-1
1922	Pillory	11.15-to-1
1962	Greek Money	10.90-to-1
1976	Elocutionist	10.10-to-1

Winning Preakness Favorites Since 1979

Year	Winner	Odds
2005	Afleet Alex	3.30-to-1
2004	Smarty Jones	0.70-to-1

Year	Winner	Odds
2003	Funny Cide	1.90-to-1
2002	War Emblem	2.80-to-1
2001	Point Given	2.30-to-1
1995	Timber Country	1.90-to-1
1993	Prairie Bayou	2.20-to-1
1992	Pine Bluff	7-to-2
1987	Alysheba	2-to-1
1981	Pleasant Colony	3-to-2
1979	Spectacular Bid	1-to-10

Preakness Front-Running Winners

The following Preakness winners were on the lead at all points of call, beginning at a quarter-mile (approaching the clubhouse turn). Regarded as speed horses, neither Seattle Slew nor Affirmed led the opening quarter-mile in the Preakness.

Year	Winner	Winning margin
1996	Louis Quatorze	3¼
1982	Aloma's Ruler	½
1972	Bee Bee Bee	1½
1960	Bally Ache	4
1957	Bold Ruler	2
1954	Hasty Road	neck
1951	Bold	7
1948	Citation	5½
1945	Polynesian	2½
1943	Count Fleet	8
1940	Bimelech	3
1937	War Admiral	head
1934	High Quest	nose
1933	Head Play	4
1920	Man o' War	1½
1919	Sir Barton	4
1918	Jack Hare Jr.	2
1915	Rhine Maiden	1½
1914	Holiday	¾
1911	Watervale	1
1909	Effendi	1
1902	Old England	nose
1899	Half Time	1
1896	Margrave	1
1889	Buddhist	8
1882	Vanguard	neck

Winning Preakness Post Positions

Since 1909, Preakness Stakes winners have come out of the sixth post position 15 times. Only two Preakness winners, Display in 1926 and Point Given in 2001, have come out of the 11th starting position.

Twelve winners have come out of the fourth hole, and 11 each have broken from the second, third, and seventh slots.

Here are the winning post positions since 1909:

Post	Winners	Post	Winners
1	9	7	11
2	11	8	9
3	11	9	3
4	12	10	2
5	10	11	2
6	15	12	3

Preakness Wins by Geldings

Year	Winner
2003	Funny Cide
1993	Prairie Bayou
1914	Holiday
1913	Buskin
1910	Layminster
1907	Don Enrique
1876	Shirley

Geldings were barred from 1920-'34.

Fillies in the Preakness

Since Genuine Risk finished second behind Codex in the controversial 1980 Preakness Stakes (G1), only two other fillies have run in the race. Winning Colors finished a valiant third behind Risen Star after Forty Niner pressed her early, and Excellent Meeting did not finish in the 1999 Preakness.

Four fillies have won the Preakness: Flocarline in 1903, Whimsical in '06, Rhine Maiden in '15, and Nellie Morse in '24.

Here are the 52 fillies to compete in the Preakness:

Year	Horse	Owner	Finish
1999	Excellent Meeting	Golden Eagle Farm	DNF
1988	Winning Colors	Mr. & Mrs. Eugene V. Klein	3rd
1980	Genuine Risk	Diana Firestone	2nd
1939	Ciencia	King Ranch	6th
1937	Jewell Dorsett	J. W. Brown	8th
1935	Nellie Flag	Calumet Farm	7th
1930	Snowflake	W J. Salmon	3rd
1928	Bateau	W. M. Jeffords	8th
1927	Fair Star	Foxcatcher Farm	6th
1925	Maid At Arms	Glen Riddle Farm	11th
1924	**Nellie Morse**	H. C. Fisher	1st
1923	Sally's Alley	W. S. Kilmer	11th
1922	Miss Joy	Montford Jones	10th
1921	Polly Ann	S. L. Jenkins	2nd
	Careful	W. J. Salmon	12th
	Lough Storm	E. B. McLean	13th
1919	Milkmaid	J.K.L. Ross	8th
1918	Mary Maud	C. E. Clements	6th
	Quietude	A. H. Morris	9th
	Kate Bright	A. Neal	3rd
1917	Fruit Cake	E. T. Zollicoffer	4th
	Fox Trot	J. E. Griffith	14th
1915	**Rhine Maiden**	E. F. Whitney	1st
1913	Cadeau	J. G. Oxnard	5th
1912	Jeannette B.	C. C. Smithson	5th
1911	Heatherbroom	E. B. Cassatt	6th
1909	Hill Top	R. Angarola	3rd
	Arondack	Mrs. J. McLaughlin	6th
	Sans Souci II	G. J. Kraus	7th
	Grania	A. Garson	8th

Year	Horse	Owner	Finish
1906	Whimsical	T. J. Gaynor	1st
	Content	W. Clay	2nd
	Flip Flap	J. A. Bennet	7th
	Fatinitza	Palestine Stable	8th
1905	Kiamesha	Oneck Stable	2nd
	Coy Maid	Kenilworth Stable	3rd
	Bohemia	Albemarle Stable	5th
	Iota	H. B. Duryea	9th
1904	Possession	C. Oxx	7th
	Flammula	W. H. Kraft	8th
1903	Flocarline	M. H. Tichenor & Co.	1st
1902	Barouche	W. H. McCorkle	6th
	Sun Shower	Jere Dunn	7th
1901	Sadie S.	P. H. Sullivan	2nd
1896	Intermission	J. E. McDonald	3rd
	Cassette	A. Clason	4th
1895	Sue Kittie	O. A. Jones	3rd
	Bombazette	C. Littlefield Jr.	7th
1894	Flirt	Manhattan Stable	13th
1881	Aella	George L. Lorillard	6th

Year	Horse	Owner	Finish
1880	Emily F.	J. J. Bevins	3rd
1875	Australind	Harbeck & Johnson	7th

Where Preakness Winners Were Foaled

State	Winners
Kentucky	87
Maryland	8
Florida	7
Pennsylvania	6
Virginia	6
California	4
New Jersey	4
New York	3
Tennessee	2
Ohio	1
Texas	1
Canada	1
England	1

Status of Preakness Winners Since 1970

Year	Winner	Birthdate	Status	Where Stands or Stood	Location	Death Date
2005	Afleet Alex	5/9/2002	In training			
2004	Smarty Jones	2/28/2001	Stallion	Three Chimneys Farm	Midway, Ky.	
2003	Funny Cide	4/20/2000	In training			
2002	War Emblem	2/20/1999	Stallion	Shadai Stallion Station	Hokkaido, Japan	
2001	Point Given	3/27/1998	Stallion	Three Chimneys Farm	Midway, Ky.	
2000	Red Bullet	4/13/1997	Stallion	Adena Springs South	Ocala, Fl.	
1999	Charismatic	3/13/1996	Stallion	JBBA Shizunai Stallion Station	Hokkaido, Japan	
1998	Real Quiet	3/7/1995	Stallion	Taylor Made Farm	Nicholasville, Ky.	
1997	Silver Charm	2/22/1994	Stallion	JBBA Shizunai Stallion Station	Hokkaido, Japan	
1996	Louis Quatorze	3/13/1993	Stallion	Murmur Farm	Darlington, Md.	
1995	Timber Country	4/12/1992	Stallion	Shadai Stallion Station	Hokkaido, Japan	
1994	Tabasco Cat	4/15/1991	Deceased	JBBA Shizunai Stallion Station	Hokkaido, Japan	3/6/2004
1993	Prairie Bayou	3/14/1990	Deceased			6/5/1993
1992	Pine Bluff	5/10/1989	Stallion	Lane's End	Versailles, Ky.	
1991	Hansel	3/12/1988	Stallion	Hidaka Stallion Station	Hokkaido, Japan	
1990	Summer Squall	3/12/1987	Pensioned	Lane's End	Versailles, Kyy.	
1989	Sunday Silence	3/25/1986	Deceased	Shadai Stallion Station	Hokkaido, Japan	8/19/2002
1988	Risen Star	3/25/1985	Deceased	Walmac International	Lexington, Ky.	3/13/1998
1987	Alysheba	3/3/1984	Stallion	Janadriyah Stud Farm	Aljanadriya, Saudi Arabia	
1986	Snow Chief	3/17/1983	Stallion	Eagle Oak Ranch	Paso Robles, Ca.	
1985	Tank's Prospect	5/2/1982	Deceased	Venture Farms	Pilot Point, Tx.	3/2/1995
1884	Gate Dancer	3/31/1981	Deceased	Silverleaf Farm	Orange Lake, Fl.	3/6/1998
1983	Deputed Testamony	5/7/1980	Pensioned	Bonita Farm	Darlington, Md.	
1982	Aloma's Ruler	4/21/1979	Deceased	B & B Farm	Monee, Il.	6/21/2003
1981	Pleasant Colony	5/4/1978	Deceased	Lane's End	Versailles, Ky.	12/31/2002
1980	Codex	2/28/1977	Deceased	Tartan Farms	Ocala, Fl.	8/20/1984
1979	Spectacular Bid	2/17/1976	Deceased	Milfer Farm	Unadilla, Ny.	6/9/2003
1978	Affirmed	2/21/1975	Deceased	Jonabell Farm	Lexington, Ky.	1/12/2001
1977	Seattle Slew	2/15/1974	Deceased	Three Chimneys Farm	Midway, Ky.	5/7/2002
1976	Elocutionist	3/4/1973	Deceased	Airdrie Stud	Midway, Ky.	3/30/1995
1975	Master Derby	4/24/1972	Deceased	Not Just Another Horse Farm	Chino, Ca.	1/22/1999
1974	Little Current	4/5/1971	Deceased	Pacific Equine Clinic	Monroe, Wa.	1/19/2003
1973	Secretariat	3/30/1970	Deceased	Claiborne Farm	Paris, Ky.	10/4/1989
1972	Bee Bee Bee	4/3/1969	Deceased	JBBA Stallion Station	Hokkaido, Japan	
1971	Canonero II	4/24/1968	Deceased	Gainesway	Lexington, Ky.	11/11/1981
1970	Personality	5/27/1967	Deceased		Japan	1990

Preakness Stakes

Grade 1, Pimlico Race Course, three-year-olds, $1\frac{3}{16}$ miles, dirt. Held on May 15, 2004, with gross value of $1,000,000. First run in 1873. Weights: colts and geldings, 126 pounds; fillies, 121 pounds.

Year	Winner	Jockey	Second	Third	Strs	Time	Track	1st Purse
2005	Afleet Alex	J. Rose	Scrappy T	Giacomo	14	1:55.04	ft	$650,000
2004	Smarty Jones	S. Elliott	Rock Hard Ten	Eddington	10	1:55.59	ft	650,000
2003	‡Funny Cide	J. Santos	Midway Road	Scrimshaw	10	1:55.61	gd	650,000
2002	War Emblem	V. Espinoza	Magic Weisner	Proud Citizen	13	1:56.36	ft	650,000
2001	Point Given	G. Stevens	A P Valentine	Congaree	11	1:55.51	ft	650,000
2000	Red Bullet	J. Bailey	Fusaichi Pegasus	Impeachment	8	1:56.04	gd	650,000
1999	Charismatic	C. Antley	Menifee	Badge	13	1:55.32	ft	650,000
1998	Real Quiet	K. Desormeaux	Victory Gallop	Classic Cat	10	1:54.75	ft	**650,000**
1997	Silver Charm	G. Stevens	Free House	Captain Bodgit	10	1:54.84	ft	488,150
1996	Louis Quatorze	P. Day	Skip Away	Editor's Note	12	**1:53.43**	ft	458,120
1995	Timber Country	P. Day	Oliver's Twist	Thunder Gulch	11	1:54.45	ft	446,810
1994	Tabasco Cat	P. Day	Go for Gin	Concern	10	1:56.47	ft	447,720
1993	‡Prairie Bayou	M. Smith	Cherokee Run	‡El Bakan	12	1:56.61	ft	471,835
1992	Pine Bluff	C. McCarron	Alydeed	Casual Lies	14	1:55.60	gd	484,120
1991	Hansel	J. Bailey	Corporate Report	Mane Minister	8	1:54	ft	432,770
1990	Summer Squall	P. Day	Unbridled	Mister Frisky	9	1:53⅗	ft	445,900
1989	Sunday Silence	P. Valenzuela	Easy Goer	Rock Point	8	1:53⅘	ft	438,230
1988	Risen Star	E. Delahoussaye	Brian's Time	†Winning Colors	9	1:56⅕	gd	413,700
1987	Alysheba	C. McCarron	Bet Twice	Cryptoclearance	9	1:55⅘	ft	421,100
1986	Snow Chief	A. Solis	Ferdinand	Broad Brush	7	1:54⅘	ft	411,900
1985	Tank's Prospect	P. Day	Chief's Crown	Eternal Prince	11	**1:53⅖**	ft	423,200
1984	Gate Dancer	A. Cordero Jr.	Play On	Fight Over	10	1:53⅗	ft	243,600
1983	Deputed Testamony	D. A. Miller Jr.	Desert Wine	High Honors	12	1:55⅖	sy	251,200
1982	Aloma's Ruler	J. Kaenel	Linkage	Cut Away	7	1:55⅖	ft	209,900
1981	Pleasant Colony	J. Velasquez	Bold Ego	Paristo	13	1:54⅗	ft	200,800
1980	Codex	A. Cordero Jr.	†Genuine Risk	Colonel Moran	8	1:54⅕	ft	180,600
1979	Spectacular Bid	R. Franklin	Golden Act	Screen King	5	1:54⅕	gd	165,300
1978	AFFIRMED	S. Cauthen	Alydar	Believe It	7	1:54⅖	ft	136,200
1977	SEATTLE SLEW	J. Cruguet	Iron Constitution	Run Dusty Run	9	1:54⅖	ft	138,600
1976	Elocutionist	J. Lively	Play the Red	Bold Forbes	6	1:55	ft	129,700
1975	Master Derby	D. G. McHargue	Foolish Pleasure	Diabolo	10	1:56⅖	ft	158,100
1974	Little Current	M. A. Rivera	‡Neapolitan Way	Cannonade	13	1:54⅗	gd	156,500
1973	SECRETARIAT	R. Turcotte	Sham	Our Native	6	1:54⅖	ft	129,900
1972	Bee Bee Bee	E. Nelson	No Le Hace	Key to the Mint	7	1:55⅗	sy	135,300
1971	Canonero II	G. Avila	Eastern Fleet	Jim French	11	1:54	ft	137,400
1970	Personality	E. Belmonte	My Dad George	Silent Screen	14	1:56⅕	ft	151,300
1969	Majestic Prince	W. Hartack	Arts and Letters	Jay Ray	8	1:55⅗	ft	129,500
1968	Forward Pass	I. Valenzuela	Out of the Way	Nodouble	10	1:56⅘	ft	142,700
1967	Damascus	W. Shoemaker	In Reality	Proud Clarion	10	1:55⅕	ft	151,500
1966	Kauai King	D. Brumfield	Stupendous	Amberoid	9	1:55⅖	ft	129,000
1965	Tom Rolfe	R. Turcotte	Dapper Dan	Hail to All	9	1:56⅕	ft	128,100
1964	Northern Dancer	W. Hartack	The Scoundrel	Hill Rise	6	1:56⅘	ft	124,200
1963	Candy Spots	W. Shoemaker	Chateaugay	Never Bend	8	1:56⅕	ft	127,500
1962	Greek Money	J. L. Rotz	Ridan	Roman Line	11	1:56⅕	ft	135,800
1961	Carry Back	J. Sellers	Globemaster	Crozier	9	1:57⅗	ft	126,200
1960	Bally Ache	R. Ussery	Victoria Park	*Celtic Ash	6	1:57⅗	ft	121,000
1959	Royal Orbit	W. Harmatz	Sword Dancer	Dunce	11	1:57	ft	136,200
1958	Tim Tam	I. Valenzuela	Lincoln Road	Gone Fishin'	12	1:57⅕	ft	97,900
1957	Bold Ruler	E. Arcaro	Iron Liege	Inside Tract	7	1:56⅕	ft	66,300
1956	Fabius	W. Hartack	Needles	No Regrets	9	1:58⅖	ft	84,250
1955	Nashua	E. Arcaro	Saratoga	Traffic Judge	8	1:54⅗	ft	67,550
1954	Hasty Road	J. Adams	Correlation	Hasseyampa	11	1:57⅖	ft	91,600
1953	Native Dancer	E. Guerin	Jamie K.	Royal Bay Gem	7	1:57⅘	ft	65,200
1952	Blue Man	C. McCreary	‡Jampol	One Count	10	1:57⅖	ft	86,135
1951	Bold	E. Arcaro	Counterpoint	Alerted	8	1:56⅖	ft	83,110
1950	Hill Prince	E. Arcaro	Middleground	Dooly	6	1:59⅕	sl	56,115
1949	Capot	T. Atkinson	Palestinian	Noble Impulse	9	1:56	ft	79,985
1948	CITATION	E. Arcaro	Vulcan's Forge	Bovard	4	2:02⅖	hy	91,870
1947	Faultless	D. Dodson	On Trust	Phalanx	11	1:59	ft	98,005
1946	ASSAULT	W. Mehrtens	Lord Boswell	Hampden	10	2:01⅖	ft	96,620
1945	Polynesian	W. D. Wright	Hoop, Jr.	‡Darby Dieppe	9	1:58⅘	ft	66,170
1944	Pensive	C. McCreary	Platter	‡Stir Up	7	1:59⅕	ft	60,075
1943	COUNT FLEET	J. Longden	Blue Swords	Vincentive	4	1:57⅖	gd	43,190
1942	Alsab	B. James	dh-Requested	dh-Sun Again	10	1:57	ft	58,175
1941	WHIRLAWAY	E. Arcaro	King Cole	Our Boots	8	1:58⅘	gd	49,365
1940	Bimelech	F. A. Smith	Mioland	Gallahadion	9	1:58⅗	ft	53,230
1939	Challedon	G. Seabo	Gilded Knight	Volitant	6	1:59⅘	my	53,710

Year	Winner	Jockey	Second	Third	Strs	Time	Track	1st Purse
1938	**Dauber**	M. Peters	Cravat	Menow	9	1:59⅘	sy	51,875
1937	**WAR ADMIRAL**	C. Kurtsinger	Pompoon	Flying Scot	8	1:58⅖	gd	45,600
1936	**Bold Venture**	G. Woolf	Granville	Jean Bart	11	1:59	ft	27,325
1935	**OMAHA**	W. Saunders	Firethorn	Psychic Bid	8	1:58⅖	ft	25,325
1934	**High Quest**	R. Jones	Cavalcade	Discovery	7	1:58⅕	ft	25,175
1933	**Head Play**	C. Kurtsinger	Ladysman	Utopian	10	2:02	sl	26,850
1932	**Burgoo King**	E. James	Tick On	Boatswain	9	1:59⅘	ft	50,375
1931	**Mate**	G. Ellis	Twenty Grand	Ladder	7	1:59	ft	48,225
1930	**GALLANT FOX**	E. Sande	Crack Brigade	†Snowflake	11	2:00⅗	ft	51,925
1929	**Dr. Freeland**	L. Schaefer	Minotaur	African	11	2:01⅗	ft	52,325
1928	**Victorian**	R. Workman	Toro	Solace	**18**	2:00⅕	ft	60,000
1927	**Bostonian**	A. Abel	Sir Harry	Whiskery	12	2:01⅗	gd	53,100
1926	**Display**	J. Malben	Blondin	Mars	13	1:59⅘	ft	53,625
1925	**Coventry**	C. Kummer	‡Backbone	Almadel	12	1:59	ft	52,700
1924	**†Nellie Morse**	J. Merimee	Transmute	Mad Play	15	1:57⅕	sy	54,000
1923	**Vigil**	B. Marinelli	Gen. Thatcher	‡Rialto	13	1:53⅗	ft	52,000
1922	**Pillory**	L. Morris	Hea	June Grass	12	1:51⅗	ft	51,000
1921	**Broomspun**	F. Coltiletti	†Polly Ann	Jeg	14	1:54⅕	sl	43,000
1920	**Man o' War**	C. Kummer	Upset	Wildair	9	1:51⅗	ft	23,000
1919	**SIR BARTON**	J. Loftus	Eternal	Sweep On	12	1:53	ft	24,500
1918	***War Cloud**	J. Loftus	Sunny Slope	*Lanius	10	1:53⅗	gd	12,250
	Jack Hare, Jr.	C. Peak	The Porter	†Kate Bright	6	1:53⅖	gd	11,250
1917	**Kalitan**	E. Haynes	Al. M. Dick	‡Kentucky Boy	14	1:54⅖	ft	4,800
1916	**Damrosch**	L. McAtee	Greenwood	Achievement	9	1:54⅘	ft	1,380
1915	**†Rhine Maiden**	D. Hoffman	Half Rock	Runes	6	1:58	my	1,275
1914	**‡Holiday**	A. Schuttinger	Brave Cunarder	Defendum	6	1:53⅘	ft	1,355
1913	**‡Buskin**	J. Butwell	Kleburne	‡Barnegat	8	1:53⅖	ft	1,670
1912	**Col. Holloway**	C. Turner	Bwana Tumbo	Tipsand	7	1:56⅗	sl	1,450
1911	**Watervale**	E. Dugan	Zeus	‡The Nigger	7	1:51	ft	2,700
1910	**‡Layminster**	R. Estep	Dalhousie	Sager	12	1:40⅕	ft	2,800
1909	**Effendi**	W. Doyle	Fashion Plate	†Hill Top	10	1:39⅘	ft	2,725
1908	**Royal Tourist**	E. Dugan	Live Wire	‡Robert Cooper	4	1:46⅖	ft	2,455
1907	**‡Don Enrique**	G. Mountain	Ethon	Zambesi	7	1:45⅖	hy	2,260
1906	**†Whimsical**	W. Miller	†Content	Larabie	10	1:45	ft	2,355
1905	**Cairngorm**	W. Davis	†Kiamesha	†Coy Maid	10	1:45⅘	ft	2,145
1904	**Bryn Mawr**	E. Hildebrand	Wotan	‡Dolly Spanker	10	1:44⅕	ft	2,355
1903	**†Flocarline**	W. Gannon	Mackey Dwyer	Rightful	6	1:44⅘	ft	1,875
1902	**Old England**	L. Jackson	Major Daingerfield	Namtor	7	1:45⅘	hy	2,240
1901	**The Parader**	F. Landry	†Sadie S.	Dr. Barlow	5	1:47⅕	hy	1,605
1900	**Hindus**	H. Spencer	*Sarmatian	Ten Candles	10	1:48⅖	ft	1,900
1899	**Half Time**	R. Clawson	Filigrane	Lackland	3	1:47	ft	1,580
1898	**Sly Fox**	W. Simms	The Huguenot	Nuto	4	1:49¾	gd	1,450
1897	**Paul Kauvar**	C. Thorpe	Elkin	On Deck	7	1:51¼	sy	1,420
1896	**Margrave**	H. Griffin	Hamilton II	*Intermission	4	1:51	ft	1,350
1895	**Belmar**	F. Taral	‡April Fool	†Sue Kittie	7	1:50½	ft	1,350
1894	**Assignee**	F. Taral	Potentate	‡Ed Kearney	14	1:49¼	ft	1,830
1890	**Montague**	J. Martin	Philosophy	Barrister	4	2:36¾	ft	1,215
1889	**Buddhist**	G. Anderson	Japhet	———	2	2:17½	ft	1,130
1888	**Refund**	F. Littlefield	Judge Murray	Glendale	4	2:49	hy	1,185
1887	**Dunboyne**	W. Donohue	Mahony	Raymond	4	2:39½	ft	1,675
1886	**The Bard**	S. Fisher	Eurus	Elkwood	5	2:45	gd	2,050
1885	**Tecumseh**	J. McLaughlin	Wickham	‡John C.	4	2:49	hy	2,160
1884	**Knight of Ellerslie**	S. Fisher	Welcher	———	2	2:39½	ft	1,905
1883	**Jacobus**	G. Barbee	Parnell	———	2	2:42½	gd	1,635
1882	**Vanguard**	T. Costello	Heck	‡Col. Watson	3	2:44½	gd	1,250
1881	**Saunterer**	T. Costello	‡Compensation	Baltic	6	2:40½	gd	1,950
1880	**Grenada**	L. Hughes	Oden	†Emily F.	5	2:40½	ft	2,000
1879	**Harold**	L. Hughes	Jerico	‡Rochester	6	2:40½	ft	2,550
1878	**Duke of Magenta**	C. Holloway	Bayard	‡Albert	3	2:41¾	gd	2,100
1877	**Cloverbrook**	C. Holloway	Bombast	Lucifer	4	2:45½	sl	1,600
1876	**‡Shirley**	G. Barbee	Rappahannock	Compliments	8	2:44¾	gd	1,950
1875	**Tom Ochiltree**	L. Hughes	Viator	†Bay Final	9	2:43½	sl	1,900
1874	**Culpepper**	W. Donohue	*King Amadeus	Scratch	6	2:56½	my	1,900
1873	**Survivor**	G. Barbee	John Boulger	Artist	7	2:43	sl	1,800

†—filly; ‡—gelding; *—imported horse; dh-dead heat; bold indicates records set in starters, time, and 1st purse; Triple Crown winners are in all capitalized letters.

1894, 1½ miles; 1889, 1¼ miles; 1894-1900,1908, 1 1/16 miles; 1901-'07, 1 mile and 70 yards; 1909,1910, 1 mile; 1911-'24, 1⅛ miles. 1891-'93, not run. 1890 held at Morris Park, New York; 1894-1908 Gravesend, New York. Run in two divisions in 1918. 1973-present, Grade 1. Dancer's Image disqualified from third to eighth in 1968. Secretariat's time in 1973 originally reported as 1:55; hand-timed by *Daily Racing Form* clockers in 1:53⅖

Belmont Stakes History

Unforgettable horses, jockeys, and trainers punctuate the glorious history of the Belmont Stakes, a compelling race if only because two three-year-olds carrying equal weights of 126 pounds can battle its testing 1½-mile distance and be separated at the finish line by inches. It has happened more than once in the final race of the Triple Crown.

First run in 1867, the Belmont Stakes is named for August Belmont I, a prominent investment banker and Thoroughbred owner who was president of the American Jockey Club. The Belmont Stakes preceded the Preakness by six years and the Kentucky Derby by eight. Francis Morris's filly Ruthless won the first Belmont Stakes, which was contested at Jerome Park in the Bronx on a Thursday afternoon at 1⅝ miles, "cleverly by a head" over De Coursey. The purse was $2,500.

The first 23 runnings of the Belmont Stakes were held on a ribbon-like course at Jerome Park. In 1890, the Belmont Stakes moved to Morris Park, a 1⅜-mile track a few miles east of what is now Van Cortland Park in the Bronx. Fifteen years later, in 1905, the Belmont Stakes had a new home, Belmont Park, but the race was not run in 1911 and '12 because antigambling legislation shut down racing in New York in those years. Unlike the Belmont's current counterclockwise path, the race was run clockwise—like many English and European races—until 1921. By then, two great champions with a unique link had won the race known as the Test of Champions in strikingly different styles.

Colin is one of only two undefeated American champions with more than five starts in the past 96 years (the other is Personal Ensign). Colin nearly lost his unbeaten record because of a mistake by Joe Notter, his jockey in the 1908 Belmont Stakes. In a driving rainstorm so intense that no final time was taken, Notter misjudged the finish line on Colin, and his five-length lead was shaved to a head by a fast-closing Fair Play.

Colin continued to a perfect 15-for-15 record. Fair Play sired Man o' War, the once-beaten champion who won the Belmont by 20 lengths over his only challenger, Donnacona, at odds of 0.04-to-1.

Gallant Fox is one of only two Triple Crown winners who was not the favorite in the Belmont Stakes. The previous year, Whichone had beaten Gallant Fox in the 1929 Futurity and also had won the Champagne and Saratoga Special Stakes. Whichone missed the Kentucky Derby and Preakness Stakes the following spring because of knee problems, but he returned to win the

Belmont Attendance			
Year	Attendance	Year	Attendance
2005	62,274	1987	64,772
2004	120,139	1986	42,555
2003	101,864	1985	43,446
2002	103,222	1984	46,430
2001	73,857	1983	56,677
2000	67,810	1982	46,050
1999	85,818	1981	61,200
1998	80,162	1980	58,883
1997	70,682	1979	59,073
1996	40,797	1978	65,417
1995	37,171	1977	71,026
1994	42,695	1976	58,788
1993	45,037	1975	60,611
1992	50,204	1974	52,153
1991	51,766	1973	67,605
1990	50,123	1972	54,635
1989	64,959	1971	82,694
1988	56,223	1970	54,299

Withers Stakes and went off the 7-to-10 favorite in the 1930 Belmont Stakes.

Gallant Fox had won the Wood Memorial Stakes, Preakness, and Kentucky Derby (in that order), but he went off at odds of 8-to-5 in the field of just four in the Belmont. Gallant Fox uncharacteristically took the lead immediately and scampered to a surprisingly easy three-length victory in a stakes record of 2:31⅗ for 1½ miles.

Gallant Fox's winning Belmont Stakes margin paled next to the 25-length romp of Count Fleet, who completed his 1943 Triple Crown at odds of 1-to-20 "galloping," according to the Belmont chart. Three years later, Assault went off as the 7-to-5 second choice in the Belmont but, like Gallant Fox, he completed his Triple Crown with a three-length victory. Favored Lord Boswell finished fifth in the field of seven at 1.35-to-1.

In 1948, Citation cruised to an eight-length win in the Belmont to become the fourth Triple Crown winner in eight years. There would not be another for a quarter-century.

Plenty of upsets occurred in those 25 years from Citation to Secretariat, but none was more shocking than Sherluck's 1961 victory over 2-to-5 favorite Carry Back at odds of 65.05-to-1, which resulted in a then-record Belmont Stakes win payout of $132.10.

Carry Back, who finished seventh, joined Pensive (1944) and Tim Tam ('58) as Kentucky Derby and Preakness winners who lost in the Belmont Stakes. Five more followed Carry Back in the next ten years: Northern Dancer (1964), Kauai King ('66), Forward Pass ('68), Majestic Prince ('69), and Canonero II, who attracted 82,694, then the largest crowd in

Belmont Park history, on June 5, 1971, in his fourth-place finish to Pass Catcher, a 34.50-to-1 longshot.

Just when everybody thought there might not ever be another Triple Crown winner—the tremendous growth in the number of foals was frequently cited as a reason—along came Secretariat. To provide a perspective on his 31-length 1973 Belmont Stakes victory in a world record 2:24, consider that the next-fastest winners, Easy Goer in '89 and A.P. Indy in '92, went in 2:26, the equivalent of ten lengths slower.

Secretariat's 1973 Triple Crown was followed by two more in the ensuing five years: Seattle Slew, who in '77 became the first undefeated Triple Crown winner, and Affirmed one year later.

The Triple Crowns of 1977 and '78 were starkly different. Seattle Slew dominated his generation, while Affirmed was pushed to the limit by his nemesis, Alydar. The final sixteenth of a mile of the 1978 Belmont Stakes, with Affirmed on the inside under Steve Cauthen and Alydar at his throat under Jorge Velasquez, was a dramatic test of will in which Affirmed prevailed by a head. That was not the closest Belmont Stakes finish. Colin had won by the same margin, and Granville in 1936, Jaipur in '62, and Victory Gallop in '98 prevailed by a nose.

Spectacular Bid had a shot at becoming the third consecutive Triple Crown winner in 1979 but checked in third at 3-to-10 to Coastal in the Belmont after reportedly stepping on a safety pin that morning. Two years later, Derby and Preakness winner Pleasant Colony failed to sweep the series, finishing third to Summing.

Then, Woody Stephens took over. People questioned the Racing Hall of Fame trainer's judgment when he announced that Conquistador Cielo, who had just routed older horses by 7¼ lengths in the one-mile Metropolitan Handicap (G1) five days earlier, would start in the Belmont Stakes. Stephens knew his horse, and the colt won the Belmont by 14 lengths under Laffit Pincay Jr. Stephens-trained Caveat won the 1983 Belmont, and ill-fated Swale won in '84. Then Stephens ran first and second with Creme Fraiche and Stephan's Odyssey in 1985. In 1986, Stephens won his fifth consecutive Belmont Stakes with Danzig Connection, at odds of 8-to-1.

Three consecutive blowouts occurred in the late 1980s, with Bet Twice winning by 14 lengths over Derby and Preakness winner Alysheba (who finished fourth) in '87, Risen Star adding to his Preakness triumph with a 14¾-length Belmont romp, and Easy Goer avenging his Derby and Preakness losses to Sunday Silence

by winning the '89 Belmont Stakes by eight lengths.

The middle years of the 1990s were dominated by Racing Hall of Fame trainer D. Wayne Lukas, who secured consecutive victories with Tabasco Cat (1994), Thunder Gulch ('95), and Editor's Note ('96).

Julie Krone became the first female rider to win a Triple Crown race when she guided Colonial Affair to a 2¼-length win in the 1993 Belmont for trainer Flint S. "Scotty" Schulhofer. The Racing Hall of Fame trainer collected his second Belmont victory in 1999 when Lemon Drop Kid denied Lukas-trained Charismatic a Triple Crown before a then-record crowd of 85,818.

Charismatic's loss marked the third straight year that a Triple Crown was on the line. In 1997, Silver Charm, trained by Bob Baffert, led 100 yards before the finish but was passed by Touch Gold, who won by three-quarters of a length. One year later, Baffert-trained Real Quiet looked home free in the Belmont before weakening late and losing by a nose in the final stride to Victory Gallop. Two years later, Baffert recorded his first Belmont win with Point Given's 2001 victory before 73,857, the largest Belmont Stakes crowd without a Triple Crown on the line. A Triple Crown was at stake in each of the next three years, but War Emblem, Funny Cide, and Smarty Jones were defeated. A record crowd of 120,139 turned out in 2004 for Smarty Jones's bid.—*Bill Heller*

Belmont Trophy and Tray

The Belmont Stakes trophy is a solid silver bowl originally crafted by Tiffany's, and it was the trophy that August Belmont I's Fenian won in 1869 after taking the third running of the race. The Belmont family presented it as a perpetual trophy for the Belmont Stakes in 1926, and each winning owner is given the option of keeping the trophy for the year his horse wins. Atop the cover of the trophy is a silver figure of Fenian. The bowl is supported by three horses representing influential sires Eclipse, Herod, and Matchem. The winning owner also receives a permanent large silver tray with the names of previous Belmont Stakes winners engraved on it. Trays also are presented to the winning trainer, jockey, exercise rider, and groom.

Carnation Blanket

The Kentucky Derby (G1) has its roses, the Preakness Stakes (G1) has ersatz black-eyed Susans, and the carnation is the official flower of the Belmont Stakes (G1). Imported from either California or Colombia, between 300 and 400 carnations are glued onto a green velveteen backing to create the blanket that adorns the Belmont winner.

From "Sidewalks" to "New York, New York"

Until 1997, the song that escorted the Belmont Stakes field onto the track was "Sidewalks of New York," written in 1894 by Charles Lawlor, a vaudevillian, and James W. Blake, a hat salesman and lyricist. More than one version of the lyrics exist, but the best-known stanza is:

East Side, West Side, all around the town
The kids sang "ring around rosie," "London Bridge is falling down"

Boys and girls together, me and Mamie O'Rourke
We tripped the light fantastic on the sidewalks of New York.

"New York, New York" is of much more recent vintage, written by John Kander and Fred Ebb in 1977 for the movie of the same name. Composer Kander and and lyricist Ebb were one of Broadway's most successful teams; their credits included *Cabaret, Funny Lady, Woman of the Year,* and *Zorba. New York, New York,* not regarded as one of director Martin Scorsese's better films, starred Liza Minelli, who performed the song in the movie, and Robert de Niro. The song subsequently was recorded by Frank Sinatra and rose to number 32 on the hits chart in 1980.

Its lyrics:
Start spreading the news
I'm leaving today
I want to be a part of it, New York, New York
These vagabond shoes

Are longing to stray
And make a brand new start of it
New York, New York
I want to wake up in the city that never sleeps
To find I'm king of the hill, top of the heap
These little town blues
Are melting away
I'll make a brand new start of it
In old New York
If I can make it there
I'll make it anywhere
It's up to you, New York, New York.

Belmont Trivia

- The Belmont Stakes has not always been contested at 1½ miles. Prior to 1874, the race was run at 1⅝ miles. The Belmont was held at 1¼ miles from 1890 through '92, and in '95, 1904, and 1905. It was 1⅛ miles in 1893 and '94; at 1⅜ miles 1896 through 1903 and from 1906 through '25. The Belmont was run at 1½ miles from 1874 through '89 and from 1926 to the present.
- The Belmont Stakes was run at Aqueduct from 1963 through '67 while Belmont Park was being rebuilt.
- The smallest Belmont Stakes field was two. It happened in 1887, '88, '92, 1910, and '20. The largest Belmont Stakes field was 15 in 1983.
- Afleet Alex was the 54th bay to win the Belmont. Fifty winners have been chestnut, 28 dark bay or brown, three black, two gray, and one roan.

Belmont Wagering, 1980-2005

Year	Winner	On-Track Handle	OTB Handle	Simulcasting	Total Handle
2005	Afleet Alex	$2,736,948		$45,312,800	$48,049,748
2004	Birdstone	4,331,463		59,340,243	63,671,706
2003	Empire Maker	3,440,151		44,642,048	48,082,199
2002	Sarava	3,753,983		54,503,406	58,257,389
2001	Point Given	2,707,574		34,959,635	37,667,209
2000	Commendable	2,046,835		28,354,418	30,401,253
1999	Lemon Drop Kid	3,143,508		40,839,558	43,983,066
1998	Victory Gallop	2,521,457		25,864,228	28,385,685
1997	Touch Gold	2,229,860		22,546,860	24,776,720
1996	Editor's Note	1,639,134		18,714,712	20,353,846
1995	Thunder Gulch	1,571,891	3,672,079	15,310,597	20,554,567
1994	Tabasco Cat	1,717,684	3,299,616	13,848,321	18,865,621
1993	Colonial Affair	2,793,320	4,567,493	17,472,438	24,833,251
1992	A.P. Indy	2,058,039	4,365,205	12,581,848	19,005,092
1991	Hansel	2,222,049	5,206,757	12,877,258	20,306,064
1990	Go and Go (Ire)	1,588,767	3,832,777	8,985,594	14,407,138
1989	Easy Goer	2,565,156	4,062,020	12,269,211	18,896,387
1988	Risen Star	1,439,045	4,135,493	8,685,408	14,259,946
1987	Bet Twice	2,703,924	6,794,377	8,242,290	17,740,591
1986	Danzig Connection	2,038,445	4,469,831	5,869,281	12,377,557
1985	Creme Fraiche	1,840,198	4,982,800	4,518,679	11,341,677
1884	Swale	2,063,135	5,540,202	4,080,482	11,683,819
1983	Caveat	1,530,010	3,724,455	2,961,256	8,215,721
1982	Conquistador Cielo	1,201,491	2,248,366	2,488,107	5,937,964
1981	Smarten	1,420,517	3,204,415	465,950	5,090,882
1980	Temperence Hill	1,603,057	3,769,868		5,372,925

Beginning in 1996, figures for OTB and simulcasting handle were combined.

- Thirty-six of the 137 runnings of the Belmont have been run on off tracks, the most recent in 2003 when Empire Maker won.
- The 2001 Belmont drew a crowd of 73,857, the largest for the race without a horse going for the Triple Crown and seventh highest behind 120,139 in 2004, 103,222 in '02, 101,864 in 2003, 85,818 in 1999, 82,694 in '71, and 80,162 in '98.
- Sarava was the 17th Belmont winner whose name began with the letter 'S'. Twenty Belmont winners had names beginning with 'C'.

Leading Belmont Owners by Wins

6 James R. Keene: Spendthrift, 1879; Commando, 1901; Delhi, 1904; Peter Pan, 1907; Colin 1908; Sweep, 1910.

Belair Stud: Gallant Fox, 1930; Faireno, 1932; Omaha, 1935; Granville, 1936; Johnstown, 1939; Nashua, 1955.

5 Mike and Phil Dwyer: George Kinney, 1883; Panique, 1884; Inspector B., 1886; Hanover, 1887; Sir Dixon, 1888.

4 Glen Riddle Farms: Man o' War, 1920; American Flag, 1925; Crusader, 1926; War Admiral, 1937.

Greentree Stable: Twenty Grand, 1931; Shut Out, 1942; Capot, 1949; Stage Door Johnny, 1968.

3 August Belmont II: Masterman, 1902; Friar Rock, 1916; *Hourless, 1917.

King Ranch: Assault, 1946; Middleground, 1950; High Gun, 1954.

Owners with Most Belmont Starters

Name	Starts	Wins	2nd	3rd	Unplaced
C. V. Whitney	20	2	2	4	12
August Belmont I	19	2	4	4	9
Greentree Stable	15	4	1	2	8
Belair Stud	14	6	0	1	7
King Ranch	14	3	2	1	8
James R. Keene	12	6	2	1	3
Calumet Farm	11	2	5	2	2
Brookmeade Stable	11	2	1	1	7
Wheatley Stable	11	0	0	3	8
George D. Widener	10	1	3	2	4
George Lorillard	8	3	3	0	2
Marcus Daly	8	1	1	2	4
Pierre Lorillard	8	1	0	3	4
Ogden Phipps	8	1	0	1	6
Dwyer Brothers	7	5	1	0	1
August Belmont II	7	3	2	0	2
D. McDaniel	7	3	0	0	4
Darby Dan Farm	7	2	0	1	4
Meadow Stable	7	2	0	1	4
Walter M. Jeffords	7	1	1	0	5
Buckland Stable	7	0	0	1	6

Leading Belmont Breeders by Wins

7 A. J. Alexander: Harry Bassett, 1871; Joe Daniels, 1872; Springbok, 1873; Duke of Magenta, 1878; Spendthrift, 1879; Grenada, 1880; Burlington, 1890.

5 Belair Stud: Gallant Fox, 1930; Faireno, 1932; Omaha, 1935; Granville, 1936; Nashua, 1955.

J. R. Keene: Commando, 1901; Delhi, 1904; Peter Pan, 1907; Colin, 1908; Sweep, 1910.

John E. Madden: Joe Madden, 1909; The Finn, 1915; Sir Barton, 1919; Grey Lag, 1921; Zev, 1923.

4 August Belmont II: Masterman, 1902; Friar Rock, 1916; *Hourless, 1917; Man o' War, 1920.

Greentree: Twenty Grand, 1931; Shut Out, 1942; Capot, 1949; Stage Door Johnny, 1968.

H. P. Whitney: Tanya, 1905; Burgomaster, 1906; Prince Eugene, 1913; *Johren, 1918.

3 W. S. Farish: Bet Twice, 1987; A.P. Indy, 1991; Lemon Drop Kid, 1999.

Sam Riddle: American Flag, 1925; Crusader, 1926; War Admiral, 1937.

Leading Belmont Trainers by Wins

8 James Rowe: George Kinney, 1883; Panique, 1884; Commando, 1901; Delhi, 1904; Peter Pan, 1907; Colin, 1908; Sweep, 1910; Prince Eugene, 1913.

7 Sam Hildreth: Jean Bereaud, 1899; Joe Madden, 1909; Friar Rock, 1916; Hourless, 1917; Grey Lag, 1921; Zev, 1923; Mad Play, 1924.

6 James "Sunny Jim" Fitzsimmons: Gallant Fox, 1930; Faireno, 1932; Omaha, 1935; Granville, 1936; Johnstown, 1939; Nashua, 1955.

5 W. C. "Woody" Stephens: Conquistador Cielo, 1982; Caveat, 1983; Swale, 1984; Creme Fraiche, 1985; Danzig Connection, 1986.

4 Max Hirsch: Vito, 1928; Assault, 1946; Middleground, 1950; High Gun, 1954.

D. Wayne Lukas: Tabasco Cat, 1994; Thunder Gulch, 1995; Editor's Note, 1996; Commendable, 2000.

R. W. Walden: Duke of Magenta, 1878; Grenada, 1880; Saunterer, 1881; *Bowling Brook, 1898.

3 Elliott Burch: Sword Dancer, 1959; Quadrangle, 1964; Arts and Letters, 1969.

John M. Gaver: Shut Out, 1942; Capot, 1949; Stage Door Johnny, 1968.

Lucien Laurin: Amberoid, 1966; Riva Ridge, 1972; Secretariat, 1973.

Frank McCabe: Inspector B., 1886; Hanover, 1887; Sir Dixon, 1888.

David McDaniel: Harry Bassett, 1871; Joe Daniels, 1872; Springbok, 1873.

2 Tom Barry: *Cavan, 1958; *Celtic Ash, 1960.

Flint S. "Scotty" Schulhofer: Colonial Affair, 1993; Lemon Drop Kid, 1999.

Sylvester Veitch: Phalanx, 1947; Counterpoint, 1951.

Oscar White: Pavot, 1945; One Count, 1952.

Trainers with Most Belmont Starters Since 1972

Name	Starts	Wins	2nd	3rd	Unplaced
D. Wayne Lukas	19	4	0	1	14
Nicholas P. Zito	16	1	6	2	7
LeRoy Jolley	10	0	2	1	7
John P. Campo	10	0	0	1	9
Woodford C. Stephens	9	5	1	1	2
Flint S. Schulhofer	7	2	1	9	4
Bob Baffert	6	1	2	0	3
Lou Rondinello	6	1	0	2	3
C. R. McGaughey III	5	1	1	1	2
Alfredo Callejas	5	0	0	0	5

Female Trainers in the Belmont

Seven women have trained Belmont Stakes (G1) starters, and the best finish was that by Dianne Carpenter-trained Kingpost, who finished a distant second behind Risen Star in 1988. In 2002, owner-breeder-trainer Nancy Alberts saddled Magic Weisner for a fourth-place finish behind upset winner Sarava.

Women who have trained Belmont starters:

Year	Trainer	Horse	Finish
2003	Linda Rice	Supervisor	5th
2002	Nancy Alberts	Magic Weisner	4th
1996	Cynthia Reese	In Contention	9th
1992	Shelley Riley	Casual Lies	5th
1988	Dianne Carpenter	Kingpost	2nd
1985	Patricia Johnson	Fast Account	4th
1984	Sarah Lundy	Minstrel Star	11th

Leading Belmont Jockeys by Wins

6   **Eddie Arcaro:** Whirlaway, 1941; Shut Out, 1942; Pavot, 1945; Citation, 1948; One Count, 1952; Nashua, 1955.

     James McLaughlin: Forester, 1882; George Kinney, 1883; Panique, 1884; Inspector B., 1886; Hanover, 1887; Sir Dixon, 1888.

5   **Earle Sande:** Grey Lag, 1921; Zev, 1923; Mad Play, 1924; Chance Shot, 1927; Gallant Fox, 1930.

     Bill Shoemaker: Gallant Man, 1957; Sword Dancer, 1959; Jaipur, 1962; Damascus, 1967; Avatar, 1975.

3   **Braulio Baeza:** Sherluck, 1961; Chateaugay, 1963; Arts and Letters, 1969.

     Pat Day: Easy Goer, 1989; Tabasco Cat, 1994; Commendable, 2000.

     Laffit Pincay Jr.: Conquistador Cielo, 1982; Caveat, 1983; Swale, 1984.

     James Stout: Granville, 1936; Pasteurized, 1938; Johnstown, 1939.

Jockeys with Most Belmont Starters Since 1938

Name	Starts	Wins	2nd	3rd	Unplaced
Eddie Arcaro	22	6	3	2	11
Angel Cordero Jr.	21	1	2	4	14
Jerry Bailey	20	2	1	1	16
Pat Day	17	3	2	2	10
Braulio Baeza	14	3	2	0	9
Laffit Pincay Jr.	13	3	3	0	7
Jorge Velasquez	13	0	1	5	7
Bill Shoemaker	11	5	1	1	4
Eric Guerin	11	2	2	1	6
Chris McCarron	11	2	1	2	6
Edward Maple	11	2	0	1	8
Jose Santos	14	1	2	1	10
Jacinto Vasquez	10	0	3	1	6
Mike Smith	9	0	1	1	7
Gary Stevens	9	3	1	1	4
Ron Turcotte	9	2	1	9	6
Jorge Chavez	9	0	0	1	8
Ruben Hernandez	8	1	0	0	7
Bobby Ussery	8	0	1	0	7
John Sellers	7	1	1	1	4

Only One Female Jockey in Belmont

Julie Krone, the only female jockey in the Racing Hall of Fame, is the only female rider to have had a mount in the Belmont. Krone won the 1993 Belmont Stakes (G1) aboard Colonial Affair. She retired in 1999 but resumed her career in 2002 and retired in 2004.

Krone's Belmont Stakes mounts:

Year	Mount	Finish
1996	South Salem	DNF
1995	Star Standard	2nd
1993	**Colonial Affair**	1st
1992	Colony Light	6th
1991	Subordinated Debt	9th

Leading Sires of Belmont Winners

5   **Lexington:** General Duke, 1868; Kingfisher, 1870; Harry Bassett, 1871; Duke of Magenta, 1878; Saunterer, 1881.

3   ***Australian :** Joe Daniels, 1872; Springbok, 1873; Spendthrift, 1879.

     Fair Play: Man o' War, 1920; Mad Play, 1924; Chance Shot, 1927.

     Man o' War: American Flag, 1925; Crusader, 1926; War Admiral, 1937.

2   **Commando:** Peter Pan, 1907; Colin, 1908.

     Count Fleet: Counterpoint, 1951; One Count, 1952.

     Gallant Fox: Omaha, 1935; Granville, 1936.

     Hamburg: Burgomaster, 1906; Prince Eugene, 1913.

     *Nasrullah: Nashua, 1955; Jaipur, 1962.

     *Negofol: *Hourless, 1917; Vito, 1928.

     Seattle Slew: Swale, 1984; A.P. Indy, 1992.

     *Star Shoot: Sir Barton, 1919; Grey Lag, 1921.

Belmont Winners Who Sired Belmont Winners

3   **Man o' War (1920):** American Flag, 1925; Crusader, 1926; War Admiral, 1937.

2   **Commando (1901):** Peter Pan, 1907; Colin, 1908.

     Gallant Fox (1930): Omaha, 1935; Granville, 1936.

     Count Fleet (1943): Counterpoint, 1951; One Count, 1952.

     Seattle Slew (1977): Swale, 1984; A.P. Indy, 1992.

1   **Duke of Magenta (1878):** Eric, 1889.

     Spendthrift (1879): Hastings, 1896.

     Hastings (1896): Masterman, 1902.

     The Finn (1915): Zev, 1923.

     Sword Dancer (1959): Damascus, 1967.

     Secretariat (1973): Risen Star, 1988.

Derby-Preakness Winners Not Favored in the Belmont

Thirty-one three-year-olds swept the Kentucky Derby and Preakness to earn a chance at the Triple Crown. Ironically, the only two who were not the betting favorites in the Belmont Stakes became Triple Crown champions.

Gallant Fox in 1930 was the 8-to-5 second choice to 4-to-5 Whichone, who finished second. Assault in 1946 was the 7-to-5 second choice to 1.35-to-1 Lord Boswell, who finished fifth.

Fastest Belmont Times

Year	Winner	Time	Cond.
1973	Secretariat	2:24	Fast
1989	Easy Goer	2:26	Fast
1992	A.P. Indy	2:26	Good
1988	Risen Star	2:26⅖	Fast
2001	Point Given	2:26.56	Fast
1957	Gallant Man	2:26⅗	Fast
1978	Affirmed	2:26⅘	Fast
1994	Tabasco Cat	2:26.82	Fast

Fastest Fractions

Quarter-mile	:23	Another Review, 1991
Half-mile	:46⅕	Secretariat, 1973
Six furlongs	1:09⅘	Secretariat, 1973
One mile	1:34⅕	Secretariat, 1973
1¼ miles	1:59	Secretariat, 1973

Slowest Winning Times

Year	Winner	Time	Cond.
1970	High Echelon	2:34	Sloppy
1928	Vito	2:33⅕	Fast
1932	Faireno	2:32⅘	Fast
1929	Blue Larkspur	2:32⅘	Sloppy
1933	Hurryoff	2:32⅗	Fast
1927	Chance Shot	2:32⅖	Fast
1944	Bounding Home	2:32⅕	Fast
1926	Crusader	2:32⅕	Fast
1995	Thunder Gulch	2:32.02	Good
1930	Gallant Fox	2:31⅗	Fast
2000	Commendable	2:31.19	Fast
1941	Whirlaway	2:31	Fast

Evolution of Belmont Stakes Record at 1½ Miles

Year	Winner	Time	Cond.
1874	Saxon	2:39½	Fast
1926	Crusader	2:32⅕	Sloppy
1930	Gallant Fox	2:31⅗	Good
1931	Twenty Grand	2:29⅗	Fast
1934	Peace Chance	2:29⅕	Fast
1937	War Admiral	2:28⅗	Fast
1943	Count Fleet	2:28⅕	Fast
1957	Gallant Man	2:26⅗	Fast
1973	Secretariat	2:24	Fast

Shortest-Priced Winning Favorites

Winner	Year	Odds
Man o' War	1920	0.04-to-1
Count Fleet	1943	0.05-to-1
Hanover	1887	0.05-to-1
George Kinney	1883	0.08-to-1
Secretariat	1973	0.10-to-1
Johnstown	1939	0.12-to-1
Sweep	1910	0.12-to-1
Nashua	1955	0.15-to-1
Citation	1948	0.20-to-1
Forester	1882	0.20-to-1
Whirlaway	1941	0.25-to-1
Chance Shot	1927	0.25-to-1
*Hourless	1917	0.25-to-1
Sir Dixon	1888	0.36-to-1
Burgomaster	1906	0.40-to-1
Sir Barton	1919	0.40-to-1
Seattle Slew	1977	0.40-to-1
Native Dancer	1953	0.45-to-1
Colin	1908	0.50-to-1
Jean Bereaud	1899	0.50-to-1
Grenada	1880	0.50-to-1

Longest Winning Odds

Year	Horse	Odds
2002	Sarava	70.25-to-1
1961	Sherluck	65.05-to-1
1980	Temperence Hill	53.40-to-1
2004	Birdstone	36.00-to-1
1971	Pass Catcher	34.50-to-1
1999	Lemon Drop Kid	29.75-to-1
2000	Commendable	18.80-to-1
1944	Bounding Home	16.35-to-1

Odds-On Beaten Favorites

Year	Horse	Odds	Finish
1958	Tim Tam	0.15-to-1	2nd
1979	Spectacular Bid	0.30-to-1	3rd
1938	Dauber	0.33-to-1	2nd
1922	*Snob II	0.33-to-1	2nd
2004	Smarty Jones	0.35-to-1	2nd
1942	Alsab	0.40-to-1	2nd
1928	Victorian	0.40-to-1	5th
1961	Carry Back	0.45-to-1	7th
1963	Candy Spots	0.50-to-1	2nd
1952	Blue Man	0.50-to-1	2nd
1944	Pensive	0.50-to-1	2nd
1900	Missionary	0.50-to-1	3rd
1966	Kauai King	0.60-to-1	4th
1915	Pebbles	0.60-to-1	3rd
1971	Canonero II	0.70-to-1	4th
1913	Rock View	0.70-to-1	2nd
1947	Faultless	0.75-to-1	5th
1998	Real Quiet	0.80-to-1	2nd
1987	Alysheba	0.80-to-1	4th
1981	Pleasant Colony	0.80-to-1	3rd
1964	Northern Dancer	0.80-to-1	3rd
1949	Ponder	0.80-to-1	2nd
1930	Whichone	0.80-to-1	2nd
1895	Counter Tenor	0.80-to-1	2nd
1891	Montana	0.80-to-1	2nd
1889	Diablo	0.80-to-1	2nd
1960	Tompion	0.85-to-1	4th
1957	Bold Ruler	0.85-to-1	3rd
1950	Hill Prince	0.85-to-1	7th
1989	Sunday Silence	0.90-to-1	2nd

Belmont Front-Runners

Since Capot in 1949, only six horses have won the Belmont while leading at every point of call, and none since Swale in '84. The following Belmont Stakes winners were on the lead at all points of call.

Year	Winner	Winning Margin
1898	*Bowling Brook	8
1901	Commando	½
1902	Masterman	2
1904	Delhi	3½
1905	Tanya	½
1906	Burgomaster	4
1907	Peter Pan	1
1908	Colin	Head
1910	Sweep	6
1915	The Finn	4
1916	Friar Rock	3
1917	*Hourless	10
1920	Man o' War	20
1923	Zev	1½
1927	Chance Shot	1½
1930	Gallant Fox	3
1932	Faireno	1½
1937	War Admiral	3
1939	Johnstown	5
1943	Count Fleet	25
1948	Citation	8
1949	Capot	½
1972	Riva Ridge	7
1973	Secretariat	31
1976	Bold Forbes	Neck
1977	Seattle Slew	4
1978	Affirmed	Head
1984	Swale	4

Winning Belmont Post Positions

Post	Winners	Post	Winners
1	23	7	11
2	11	8	5
3	13	9	4
4	9	10	2
5	13	11	2
6	7		

Largest Winning Margins

Year	Horse	Margin in Lengths
1973	Secretariat	31
1943	Count Fleet	25
1920	Man o' War	20
1988	Risen Star	14¾
1987	Bet Twice	14
1982	Conquistador Cielo	14
2001	Point Given	12¼
1888	Sir Dixon	12
1931	Twenty Grand	10
1917	*Hourless	10

Smallest Winning Margins

Year	Horse	Margin
1998	Victory Gallop	nose
1962	Jaipur	nose
1936	Granville	nose
1999	Lemon Drop Kid	head
1991	Hansel	head

Year	Horse	Margin
1978	Affirmed	head
1908	Colin	head
1900	Ildrim	head
1899	Jean Bereaud	head
1895	Belmar	head
1893	Commanche	head
1889	Eric	head
1876	Algerine	head
1867	Ruthless	head
1981	Summing	neck
1976	Bold Forbes	neck
1975	Avatar	neck
1965	Hail to All	neck
1956	Needles	neck
1954	High Gun	neck
1953	Native Dancer	neck
1938	Pasteurized	neck
1936	Granville	neck
1896	Hastings	neck
1891	Foxford	neck
1881	Saunterer	neck
1874	Saxon	neck

Fillies in the Belmont

Ruthless left a tough act to follow when she won the inaugural Belmont Stakes in 1867. Only 20 other fillies have raced in the Belmont Stakes, and just one other, Tanya, in 1905, has won. Kentucky Derby winner and Preakness runner-up Genuine Risk was second to Temperence Hill in 1980, and six other fillies have finished third, most recently My Flag in '96.

Year	Filly	Finish
1999	Silverbulletday	7th
1996	My Flag	3rd
1988	Winning Colors	6th
1980	Genuine Risk	2nd
1954	Riverina	7th
1932	Laughing Queen	10th
1927	Flambino	3rd
1923	Miss Smith	8th
1913	Flying Fairy	3rd
1905	**Tanya**	1st
	Funders	7th
1885	Miss Palmer	9th
1871	Nellie Gray	4th
	Mary Clark	9th
1870	Midday	3rd
	Nellie James	4th
	Stamps	6th
1869	Invercauld	3rd
	Viola	7th
1868	Fanny Ludlow	3rd
1867	**Ruthless**	1st

Geldings in the Belmont

Creme Fraiche, owned by Elizabeth Moran's Brushwood Stable, remains the only gelding ever to have won the Belmont Stakes (G1). In its early years, the Belmont conditions allowed geldings to run in the classic race, but America subsequently bowed to European practice, which barred geldings from major races. Lanius, a gelding, ran in the 1918 Belmont, but it was not until '57 that geldings again were permitted in the race. Creme Fraiche was the first gelding to compete in the Belmont since 1979 champion juvenile male Rockhill Native finished third in '80.

Geldings who have started in the Belmont since 1985:

Year	Gelding	Finish
2004	Tap Dancer	6th
2003	Funny Cide	3rd
2002	Magic Weisner	4th
	Perfect Drift	10th
2001	Balto Star	8th
2000	Unshaded	3rd
1998	Thomas Jo	3rd
1997	Irish Silence	5th
1996	Jamies First Punch	8th

Year	Gelding	Finish
1996	Cavonnier	DNF
1993	Prairie Bayou	DNF
1991	Subordinated Debt	9th
1988	Kingpost	2nd
1985	**Creme Fraiche**	1st

Birthplaces of Belmont Winners

Place of Birth	Winners
Kentucky	88
Virginia	11
New Jersey	7
England	6
Florida	6
New York	3
Pennsylvania	3
Tennessee	3
California	2
Ireland	2
Maryland	2
Texas	2
Canada	1
Montana	1

Status of Belmont Stakes Winners Since 1970

Year	Winner	Birthdate	Status	Where Stands/Stood	Location	Death Date
2005	Afleet Alex	3/9/2002	In Training			
2004	Birdstone	5/16/2001	Stallion	Gainesway	Lexington, Ky.	
2003	Empire Maker	4/27/2000	Stallion	Juddmonte Farms	Lexington, Ky.	
2002	Sarava	3/2/1999	Stallion	CloverLeaf Farms II	Reddick, Fl.	
2001	Point Given	3/27/1998	Stallion	Three Chimneys Farm	Midway, Ky.	
2000	Commendable	4/13/1997	Stallion	South Korean Racing Association	South Korea	
1999	Lemon Drop Kid	5/26/1996	Stallion	Lane's End	Versailles, Ky.	
1998	Victory Gallop	5/30/1995	Stallion	WinStar Farm	Versailles, Ky.	
1997	Touch Gold	5/26/1994	Stallion	Adena Springs Kentucky	Versailles, Ky.	
1996	Editor's Note	4/26/1993	Stallion		Argentina	
1995	Thunder Gulch	5/23/1992	Stallion	Ashford Stud	Versailles, Ky.	
1994	Tabasco Cat	4/15/1991	Deceased	JBBA Shizunai Stallion Station	Hokkaido, Japan	3/6/2004
1993	Colonial Affair	4/19/1990	Stallion	Haras El Paraiso	Capitan Sarmiento, Argentina	
1992	A.P. Indy	3/31/1989	Stallion	Lane's End	Versailles, Ky.	
1991	Hansel	3/12/1988	Stallion	Hidaka Stallion Station	Hokkaido, Japan	
1990	Go and Go (Ire)	3/21/1987	Deceased	Waldorf Farm	North Chatham, N.Y.	3/2000
1989	Easy Goer	3/21/1986	Deceased	Claiborne Farm	Paris, Ky.	5/1/1994
1988	Risen Star	3/25/1985	Deceased	Walmac International	Lexington, Ky.	3/13/1998
1987	Bet Twice	4/20/1984	Deceased	Muirfield East	Chesapeake City, Md.	3/5/1999
1986	Danzig Connection	4/6/1983	Stallion	Allevamento Al-Ca Torre	Comiso, Italy	
1985	Creme Fraiche	4/7/1982	Deceased	Brushwood Farm	Malvern, Pa.	10/9/03
1984	Swale	4/21/1981	Deceased			6/17/1984
1983	Caveat	3/16/1980	Deceased	Northview Stallion Station	Chesapeake City, Md.	2/1/1995
1982	Conquistador Cielo	3/20/1979	Deceased	Claiborne Farm	Paris, Ky.	12/17/2002
1981	Summing	4/16/1978	Pensioned	Getaway Thoroughbred Farms	Romoland, Ca.	
1980	Temperence Hill	3/6/1977	Deceased	Swang Jei Farm	Nontaburi, Thailand	6/03/2003
1979	Coastal	4/6/1976	Pensioned	Summerhill Stud	Mooi River, South Africa	
1978	Affirmed	2/21/1975	Deceased	Jonabell Farm	Lexington, Ky.	1/12/2001
1977	Seattle Slew	2/15/1974	Deceased	Three Chimneys Farm	Midway, Ky.	5/7/2002
1976	Bold Forbes	3/31/1973	Deceased	Stone Farm	Paris, Ky.	8/9/2000
1975	Avatar	3/10/1972	Deceased	Frisch's Farm	Morrow, Oh.	12/3/1992
1974	Little Current	4/5/1971	Deceased	Pacific Equine Clinic	Monroe, Wa.	1/19/2003
1973	Secretariat	3/30/1970	Deceased	Claiborne Farm	Paris, Ky.	10/4/1989
1972	Riva Ridge	4/13/1969	Deceased	Claiborne Farm	Paris, Ky.	4/21/1985
1971	Pass Catcher	4/6/1968	Deceased	Ocala Stud Farm	Ocala, Fl.	1993
1970	High Echelon	3/22/1967	Deceased	Franks Farms	Ocala, Fl.	5/15/1991

Belmont Stakes

Grade 1, Belmont Park, three-year-olds, 1½ miles, dirt. Held on June 11, 2005, with gross value of $1,000,000. First run in 1867. Weights: colts and geldings, 126 pounds; fillies, 121 pounds.

Year	Winner	Jockey	Second	Third	Strs	Time	Track	1st Purse
2005	**Afleet Alex**	J. Rose	Andromeda's Hero	Nolan's Cat	11	2:28.75	ft	$600,000
2004	**Birdstone**	E. Prado	Smarty Jones	Royal Assault	9	2:27.50	ft	600,000
2003	**Empire Maker**	J. Bailey	Ten Most Wanted	Funny Cide	6	2:28.26	sy	600,000
2002	**Sarava**	E. Prado	Medaglia d'Oro	Sunday Break (Jpn)	11	2:29.71	ft	600,000
2001	**Point Given**	G. Stevens	A P Valentine	Monarchos	9	2:26.56	ft	600,000
2000	**Commendable**	P. Day	Aptitude	‡Unshaded	11	2:31.19	ft	600,000
1999	**Lemon Drop Kid**	J. Santos	Vision and Verse	Charismatic	12	2:27.88	ft	600,000
1998	**Victory Gallop**	G. Stevens	Real Quiet	‡Thomas Jo	11	2:29.16	ft	**600,000**
1997	**Touch Gold**	C. McCarron	Silver Charm	Free House	7	2:28.82	ft	432,600
1996	**Editor's Note**	R. Douglas	Skip Away	†My Flag	14	2:28.96	ft	437,880
1995	**Thunder Gulch**	G. Stevens	Star Standard	‡Citadeed	11	2:32.02	ft	415,440
1994	**Tabasco Cat**	P. Day	Go for Gin	Strodes Creek	6	2:26.82	ft	392,280
1993	**Colonial Affair**	J. Krone	Kissin Kris	Wild Gale	13	2:29.97	gd	444,540
1992	**A.P. Indy**	E. Delahoussaye	My Memoirs (GB)	Pine Bluff	11	2:26.13	gd	458,880
1991	**Hansel**	J. Bailey	Strike the Gold	Mane Minister	11	2:28.10	ft	417,480
1990	**Go and Go (Ire)**	M. Kinane	Thirty Six Red	Baron de Vaux	9	2:27⅕	gd	411,600
1989	**Easy Goer**	P. Day	Sunday Silence	Le Voyageur	10	2:26	ft	413,520
1988	**Risen Star**	E. Delahoussaye	‡Kingpost	Brian's Time	6	2:26⅖	ft	303,720
1987	**Bet Twice**	C. Perret	Cryptoclearance	Gulch	9	2:28⅕	ft	329,160
1986	**Danzig Connection**	C. McCarron	Johns Treasure	Ferdinand	10	2:29⅘	sy	338,640
1985	**‡Creme Fraiche**	E. Maple	Stephan's Odyssey	Chief's Crown	11	2:27	my	307,740
1984	**Swale**	L. Pincay Jr.	Pine Circle	Morning Bob	11	2:27⅕	ft	310,020
1983	**Caveat**	L. Pincay Jr.	Slew o' Gold	Barberstown	**15**	2:27⅘	ft	215,100
1982	**Conquistador Cielo**	L. Pincay Jr.	Gato Del Sol	Illuminate	11	2:28⅕	sy	159,720
1981	**Summing**	G. Martens	Highland Blade	Pleasant Colony	11	2:29	ft	170,580
1980	**Temperence Hill**	E. Maple	†Genuine Risk	Rockhill Native	10	2:29⅘	my	176,228
1979	**Coastal**	R. Hernandez	Golden Act	Spectacular Bid	8	2:29⅗	ft	161,400
1978	**AFFIRMED**	S. Cauthen	Alydar	Darby Creek Road	5	2:26⅘	ft	110,580
1977	**SEATTLE SLEW**	J. Cruguet	Run Dusty Run	Sanhedrin	8	2:29⅗	my	109,080
1976	**Bold Forbes**	A. Cordero Jr.	McKenzie Bridge	Great Contractor	10	2:29	ft	117,000
1975	**Avatar**	W. Shoemaker	Foolish Pleasure	Master Derby	9	2:28⅕	ft	116,160
1974	**Little Current**	M. Rivera	Jolly Johu	Cannonade	9	2:29⅕	ft	101,970
1973	**SECRETARIAT**	R. Turcotte	Twice a Prince	My Gallant	5	**2:24**	ft	90,120
1972	**Riva Ridge**	R. Turcotte	Ruritania	Cloudy Dawn	10	2:28	ft	83,540
1971	**Pass Catcher**	W. Blum	Jim French	Bold Reason	13	2:30⅗	ft	97,710
1970	**High Echelon**	J. Rotz	Needles n Pens	Naskra	10	2:34	sy	115,000
1969	**Arts and Letters**	B. Baeza	Majestic Prince	Dike	6	2:28⅘	ft	104,050
1968	**Stage Door Johnny**	H. Gustines	Forward Pass	Call Me Prince	9	2:27⅕	ft	117,700
1967	**Damascus**	W. Shoemaker	Cool Reception	Gentleman James	9	2:28⅘	ft	104,950
1966	**Amberoid**	W. Boland	Buffle	Advocator	11	2:29⅗	ft	117,700
1965	**Hail to All**	J. Sellers	Tom Rolfe	First Family	8	2:28⅖	ft	104,150
1964	**Quadrangle**	M. Ycaza	Roman Brother	Northern Dancer	8	2:28⅖	ft	110,850
1963	**Chateaugay**	B. Baeza	Candy Spots	Choker	7	2:30⅕	gd	101,700
1962	**Jaipur**	W. Shoemaker	Admiral's Voyage	Crimson Satan	8	2:28⅘	ft	109,550
1961	**Sherluck**	B. Baeza	Globemaster	Guadalcanal	9	2:29⅕	ft	104,900
1960	***Celtic Ash**	W. Hartack	Venetian Way	Disperse	7	2:29⅗	ft	96,785
1959	**Sword Dancer**	W. Shoemaker	Bagdad	Royal Orbit	9	2:28⅗	sy	93,525
1958	***Cavan**	P. Anderson	Tim Tam	‡Flamingo	8	2:30⅕	ft	73,440
1957	***Gallant Man**	W. Shoemaker	Inside Tract	Bold Ruler	6	2:26⅗	ft	78,350
1956	**Needles**	D. Erb	Career Boy	Fabius	8	2:29⅘	ft	83,600
1955	**Nashua**	E. Arcaro	Blazing Count	Portersville	8	2:29	ft	83,700
1954	**High Gun**	E. Guerin	Fisherman	*Limelight	13	2:30⅘	ft	89,000
1953	**Native Dancer**	E. Guerin	Jamie K.	Royal Bay Gem	6	2:28⅗	ft	82,500
1952	**One Count**	E. Arcaro	Blue Man	Armageddon	6	2:30⅕	ft	82,400
1951	**Counterpoint**	D. Gorman	Battlefield	Battle Morn	9	2:29	ft	82,000
1950	**Middleground**	W. Boland	Lights Up	Mr. Trouble	9	2:28⅗	ft	61,350
1949	**Capot**	T. Atkinson	Ponder	Palestinian	8	2:30⅕	ft	60,900
1948	**CITATION**	E. Arcaro	Better Self	Escadru	8	2:28⅕	ft	77,700
1947	**Phalanx**	R. Donoso	Tide Rips	Tailspin	9	2:29⅗	ft	78,900
1946	**ASSAULT**	W. Mehrtens	Natchez	Cable	7	2:30⅘	ft	75,400
1945	**Pavot**	E. Arcaro	Wildlife	Jeep	8	2:30⅕	ft	52,675
1944	**Bounding Home**	G. L. Smith	Pensive	Bull Dandy	7	2:32⅕	ft	55,000
1943	**COUNT FLEET**	J. Longden	Fairy Manhurst	‡Deseronto	3	2:28⅕	ft	35,340
1942	**Shut Out**	E. Arcaro	Alsab	Lochinvar	7	2:29⅕	ft	44,520
1941	**WHIRLAWAY**	E. Arcaro	Robert Morris	‡Yankee Chance	4	2:31	ft	39,770
1940	**Bimelech**	F. Smith	Your Chance	Andy K.	6	2:29⅗	ft	35,030
1939	**Johnstown**	J. Stout	Belay	Gilded Knight	6	2:29⅗	ft	37,020
1938	**Pasteurized**	J. Stout	Dauber	Cravat	6	2:29⅖	ft	34,530
1937	**WAR ADMIRAL**	C. Kurtsinger	Sceneshifter	Vamoose	7	2:28⅗	ft	38,020

Year	Winner	Jockey	Second	Third	Strs	Time	Track	1st Purse
1936	**Granville**	J. Stout	Mr. Bones	Hollyrood	10	2:30	ft	29,800
1935	**OMAHA**	W. Saunders	Firethorn	Rosemont	5	2:30$\frac{3}{5}$	sy	35,480
1934	**Peace Chance**	W. Wright	High Quest	Good Goods	8	2:29$\frac{1}{5}$	ft	43,410
1933	**Hurryoff**	M. Garner	Nimbus	Union	9	2:32$\frac{3}{5}$	ft	49,490
1932	**Faireno**	T. Malley	Osculator	Flag Pole	11	2:32$\frac{4}{5}$	ft	55,120
1931	**Twenty Grand**	C. Kurtsinger	Sun Meadow	Jamestown	3	2:29$\frac{3}{5}$	ft	58,770
1930	**GALLANT FOX**	E. Sande	Whichone	Questionnaire	4	2:31$\frac{3}{5}$	gd	66,040
1929	**Blue Larkspur**	M. Garner	African	Jack High	8	2:32$\frac{4}{5}$	sy	59,650
1928	**Vito**	C. Kummer	Genie	Diavolo	6	2:33$\frac{1}{5}$	ft	63,430
1927	**Chance Shot**	E. Sande	Bois de Rose	†Flambino	6	2:32$\frac{2}{5}$	ft	60,910
1926	**Crusader**	A. Johnson	Espino	Haste	9	2:32$\frac{1}{5}$	sy	48,550
1925	**American Flag**	A. Johnson	Dangerous	Swope	7	2:16$\frac{4}{5}$	ft	38,500
1924	**Mad Play**	E. Sande	Mr. Mutt	Modest	11	2:18$\frac{4}{5}$	gd	42,880
1923	**Zev**	E. Sande	Chickvale	‡Rialto	8	2:19	gd	38,000
1922	**Pillory**	C. H. Miller	*Snob II	Hea	4	2:18$\frac{4}{5}$	ft	39,200
1921	**Grey Lag**	E. Sande	Sporting Blood	Leonardo II	4	2:16$\frac{4}{5}$	ft	8,650
1920	**Man o' War**	C. Kummer	*Donnacona	————	2	2:14$\frac{1}{5}$	ft	7,950
1919	**SIR BARTON**	J. Loftus	Sweep On	Natural Bridge	3	2:17$\frac{2}{5}$	ft	11,950
1918	***Johren**	F. Robinson	*War Cloud	‡Cum Sah	4	2:20$\frac{2}{5}$	ft	8,950
1917	***Hourless**	J. Butwell	Skeptic	Wonderful	3	2:17$\frac{4}{5}$	gd	5,800
1916	**Friar Rock**	E. Haynes	Spur	Churchill	4	2:22	my	4,100
1915	**The Finn**	G. Byrne	Half Rock	Pebbles	3	2:18$\frac{2}{5}$	ft	1,825
1914	**Luke McLuke**	M. Buxton	‡Gainer	‡Charlestonian	3	2:20	ft	3,275
1913	**Prince Eugene**	R. Troxler	Rock View	†Flying Fairy	4	2:18	ft	3,075
1910	**Sweep**	J. Butwell	Duke of Ormonde	————	2	2:22	ft	9,700
1909	**Joe Madden**	E. Dugan	Wise Mason	‡Donald Macdonald	5	2:21$\frac{3}{5}$	ft	24,550
1908	**Colin**	J. Notter	Fair Play	King James	4	n/a	sy	22,765
1907	**Peter Pan**	G. Mountain	Superman	Frank Gill	5	n/a	ft	22,765
1906	**Burgomaster**	L. Lyne	The Quail	Accountant	6	2:20	gd	22,700
1905	**†Tanya**	E. Hildebrand	Blandy	Hot Shot	7	2:08	ft	17,240
1904	**Delhi**	G. Odom	Graziallo	Rapid Water	8	2:06$\frac{3}{5}$	ft	14,685
1903	**Africander**	J. Bullman	Whorler	Red Knight	4	2:21$\frac{3}{4}$	ft	12,285
1902	**Masterman**	J. Bullman	Ranald	King Hanover	6	2:22$\frac{3}{5}$	ft	12,020
1901	**Commando**	H. Spencer	The Parader	All Green	3	2:21	ft	11,595
1900	**Ildrim**	N. Turner	‡Petruchio	Missionary	7	2:21$\frac{1}{4}$	ft	14,790
1899	**Jean Bereaud**	R. Clawson	Half Time	Glengar	4	2:23	ft	10,680
1898	***Bowling Brook**	F. Littlefield	Previous	Hamburg	4	2:32	hy	7,810
1897	**Scottish Chieftain**	J. Scherrer	On Deck	Octagon	6	2:23$\frac{1}{4}$	ft	3,350
1896	**Hastings**	H. Griffin	Handspring	Hamilton II	4	2:24$\frac{1}{2}$	gd	3,025
1895	**Belmar**	F. Taral	Counter Tenor	Nanki Pooh	5	2:11$\frac{1}{2}$	hy	2,700
1894	**Henry of Navarre**	W. Simms	Prig	Assignee	3	1:56$\frac{1}{2}$	ft	6,680
1893	**Comanche**	W. Simms	Dr. Rice	Rainbow	5	1:53$\frac{1}{4}$	ft	5,310
1892	**Patron**	W. Hayward	Shellbark	————	2	2:12	my	6,610
1891	**Foxford**	E. Garrison	Montana	Laurestan	6	2:08$\frac{3}{4}$	gd	5,070
1890	**Burlington**	S. Barnes	Devotee	Padishah	9	2:07$\frac{3}{4}$	ft	8,560
1889	**Eric**	W. Hayward	Diablo	Zephyrus	3	2:47$\frac{1}{4}$	gd	4,960
1888	**Sir Dixon**	J. McLaughlin	Prince Royal	————	2	2:40$\frac{1}{4}$	ft	3,440
1887	**Hanover**	J. McLaughlin	Oneko	————	2	2:43$\frac{1}{2}$	hy	2,900
1886	**Inspector B.**	J. McLaughlin	The Bard	Linden	5	2:41	ft	2,720
1885	**Tyrant**	P. Duffy	‡St. Augustine	Tecumseh	6	2:43	gd	2,710
1884	**Panique**	J. McLaughlin	Knight of Ellerslie	Himalaya	4	2:42	gd	3,150
1883	**George Kinney**	J. McLaughlin	‡Trombone	Renegade	4	2:42$\frac{1}{2}$	ft	3,070
1882	**Forester**	J. McLaughlin	Babcock	‡Wyoming	3	2:43	ft	2,600
1881	**Saunterer**	T. Costello	Eole	Baltic	6	2:47	hy	3,000
1880	**Grenada**	W. Hughes	Ferncliffe	Turenne	4	2:47	gd	2,800
1879	**Spendthrift**	G. Evans	‡Monitor	Jericho	6	2:24$\frac{3}{4}$	sy	4,250
1878	**Duke of Magenta**	W. Hughes	Bramble	Sparta	6	2:43$\frac{1}{2}$	my	3,850
1877	**Cloverbrook**	C. Holloway	‡Loiterer	Baden-Baden	13	2:46	hy	5,200
1876	**Algerine**	W. Donohue	Fiddlesticks	Barricade	5	2:40$\frac{1}{2}$	ft	3,700
1875	**Calvin**	R. Swim	Aristides	Milner	14	2:42$\frac{1}{4}$	ft	4,450
1874	**Saxon**	G. Barbee	Grinstead	Aaron Pennington	9	2:39$\frac{1}{2}$	ft	4,200
1873	**Springbok**	J. Rowe	Count d'Orsay	Strachino	10	3:01$\frac{3}{4}$	fr	5,200
1872	**Joe Daniels**	J. Rowe	‡Meteor	Shylock	9	2:58$\frac{1}{4}$	fr	4,500
1871	**Harry Bassett**	W. Miller	Stockwood	By the Sea	11	2:56	ft	5,450
1870	**Kingfisher**	Dick	Foster	†Midday	7	2:59$\frac{1}{2}$	ft	3,750
1869	**Fenian**	C. Miller	Glenelg	†Invercauld	8	3:04$\frac{1}{4}$	hy	3,350
1868	**General Duke**	R. Swim	Northumberland	†Fanny Ludlow	6	3:02	ft	2,800
1867	**†Ruthless**	J. Gilpatrick	DeCourcey	Rivoli	4	3:05	hy	1,850

†—filly, ‡—gelding, *—imported horse

1867-'73, 1$\frac{5}{8}$ miles; 1890-'92, 1895, 1904-'05, 1$\frac{1}{4}$ miles; 1893-'94, 1$\frac{1}{8}$ miles; 1896-1903, 1906-'25, 1$\frac{3}{8}$ miles. 1867-'89, held at Jerome Park; 1890-1904, Morris Park; 1963-'67, Aqueduct. Not run 1911 and '12. 1973-present, Grade 1. Hansel (1991), Risen Star (1988), and Bet Twice (1987) earned $1-million bonus from Triple Crown Productions. 1907-'08 no official time recorded; bold-faced type shows records in starters, time, and purse earnings.

2005 Kentucky Derby: A 50.30-to-1 Surprise

The mantra of great expectations leading to great disappointments plays itself out time and time again in the weeks and days leading up to the Triple Crown. Once the 131st Kentucky Derby (G1) was complete on May 7 at Churchill Downs, owners-breeders Jerry and Ann Moss, trainer John Shirreffs, and jockey Mike Smith found out that the very dreams born from those expectations can be realized.

Smith was teased with the fulfillment of Derby dreams several times during his Racing Hall of Fame riding career, finishing second three times, third once, and off the board on two post-time favorites in 11 tries at America's most famous race. Shirreffs, a Vietnam veteran and patient trainer who got his start walking hots and breaking yearlings in California, never came close to the Derby and had saddled only three horses at Churchill during his career. The Mosses got a glimpse of the Derby experience in 1994 when their filly Sardula won the Kentucky Oaks (G1), but they too were untested in the Derby after more than three decades as owners and breeders.

They came to Louisville four days before the race and hitched their hopes to Giacomo, a son of Holy Bull still eligible for an entry-level allowance race who would be dismissed by the wagering public, the media, rival horsemen, and just about anyone else with an interest in the first American classic. Giacomo, one of four runners from the much-maligned Santa Anita Derby (G1) field to make the 20-member Kentucky Derby field, allowed his connections to live the dream when he ran down fellow longshot Closing Argument and 9-to-2 second choice Afleet Alex in the shadow of the wire to produce the second-biggest upset in Derby history. Giacomo, sent off at 50.30-to-1 in front of the second-largest announced Derby crowd in 156,435, won the $2,399,600 event by a half-length from Closing Argument, with Afleet Alex another half-length back in third.

Bellamy Road, the powerful winner of the Wood Memorial Stakes (G1) and one of five runners saddled by Nick Zito, contested the early pace and finished a disappointing seventh as the 2.60-to-1 favorite. Zito's other starters finished behind Bellamy Road. Giacomo's time for the 1¼ miles on a fast track in picture-perfect weather conditions was 2:02.75.

At the start, Spanish Chestnut took the field through a sharp opening quarter-mile in :22.28. Giacomo had only two horses beaten, Don't Get Mad and Greater Good, as the field flashed under the wire and in front of Churchill's $121-million newly renovated clubhouse the first time. Spanish Chestnut continued to show the way through the half in a blistering :45.38, the fourth fastest in the history of the race, with Going Wild, Flower Alley, High Fly, and Bellamy Road all within three lengths of the lead. As the field approached the half-mile pole and headed into the far turn, Smith and Giacomo were still languishing at the back of the pack as Spanish Chestnut clicked past the six-furlong split in 1:09.59. The time for that distance was second only to the 1:09.25 clocking through which Songandaprayer took the field in 2001.

Javier Castellano positioned Bellamy Road four paths off the rail heading into the far turn just outside Going Wild, High Fly, and Flower Alley, with a flight of four—Buzzards Bay, Closing Argument, Afleet Alex, and Sun King—tucked behind that group as High Limit started to retreat under Ramon Dominguez. High Fly under Jerry Bailey and Bellamy Road passed Spanish Chestnut almost simultaneously as the field approached the quarter pole and ran past the mile in 1:35.88.

High Fly stuck his nose in front briefly, but his burst was short-lived, and Bellamy Road stuck his head in front as Closing Argument, Afleet Alex, and Buzzards Bay took dead aim at the tiring leaders. Bellamy Road offered no response inside the three-sixteenths pole when confronted by Afleet Alex and Closing Argument.

Jockey Cornelio Velasquez angled Closing Argument out slightly and split Afleet Alex and Buzzards Bay before taking the lead and setting sights for the wire under a vigorous hand ride. While Closing Argument and Afleet Alex were taking aim at the early front-runners, Giacomo and Don't Get Mad, ridden by Tyler Baze, were weaving in and out of traffic while advancing steadily on the leaders. Smith angled Giacomo out slightly into the seventh path with a furlong to run, inching past Buzzards Bay, Bellamy Road, and High Fly.

Only Closing Argument and Afleet Alex were in front of Giacomo with a sixteenth to run and, after seven strong cracks of Smith's whip once he came alongside Closing Argument nearing the wire, Giacomo surged to victory.—*Tom Law*

Owners-Breeders

Jerry Moss, co-founder of A&M Records with trumpeter Herb Alpert, became a horse owner in 1970. He and his wife, **Ann**, had their greatest success before Giacomo with Ruhlmann, winner of the 1990 Santa Anita Handicap (G1), and Sardula, who took the '94 Kentucky Oaks (G1). Giacomo is their first major homebred winner.

Trainer

John Shirreffs, a Vietnam veteran, took out his trainer's license in 1978 and spent several years as a private trainer for 505 Farms and The Thoroughbred Corp., among others, before opening a public stable. Among the leading horses he has trained are Bertrando and Manistique. His wife, Dottie Ingordo-Shirreffs, is the longtime racing manager of Jerry and Ann Moss.

TENTH RACE 1¼ MILES (1:59⅖) on dirt. 131st running of the Kentucky Derby. Grade 1. 3-year-olds. Purse $2,000,000.

Churchill

May 7, 2005

Value of race $2,399,600; Winner $1,639,600; second $400,000; third $200,000; fourth $100,000, fifth $60,000. Mutuel WPS Pool $42,296,149. Exacta Pool $19,132,958. Trifecta Pool $22,189,155. Superfecta Pool $7,422,552.

Horse	M/Eqt.	Wt.	PP	¼	½	¾	1 mi.	Str.	Fin.	Jockey	Odds $1
Giacomo, 3, c	Ll	126	10	$18^{½}$	$18^{2½}$	$18^{1½}$	11^{hd}	$6^{½}$	$1^{½}$	M. Smith	50.30
Closing Argument, 3, c	Lc	126	18	5^{hd}	$6^{½}$	6^{hd}	4^{hd}	$1^{½}$	$2^{½}$	C. Velasquez	71.60
Afleet Alex, 3, c	Lf	126	12	11^{hd}	$11^{½}$	$9^{½}$	$6^{1½}$	2^{1}	$3^{2½}$	J. Rose	4.50
Don't Get Mad, 3, c		126	17	19^{6}	$19^{3½}$	$19^{3½}$	10^{hd}	$7^{½}$	$4^{2¾}$	T. Baze	29.20
Buzzards Bay, 3, c	Lf	126	20	$10^{½}$	10^{hd}	$7^{½}$	$5^{½}$	5^{hd}	$5^{½}$	M. Guidry	46.30
Wilko, 3, c	L	126	14	$13^{½}$	14^{hd}	$16^{2½}$	$13^{1½}$	$10^{½}$	6no	C. Nakatani	21.70
Bellamy Road, 3, c	Lc	126	16	$3^{½}$	5^{2}	5^{2}	2^{hd}	3^{hd}	$7^{¾}$	J. Castellano	2.60*
Andromeda's Hero, 3, c	Lc	126	2	16^{hd}	15^{2}	13^{hd}	16^{2}	$14^{1½}$	8no	R. Bejarano	57.30
Flower Alley, 3, c	Lb	126	7	4^{hd}	3^{hd}	2^{hd}	$7^{1½}$	8^{1}	9^{hd}	J. Chavez	41.30
High Fly, 3, c	Lc	126	11	6^{1}	4^{1}	3^{hd}	1^{hd}	4^{1}	10^{nk}	J. Bailey	7.10
Greeley's Galaxy, 3, c	L	126	9	17^{1}	$16^{½}$	14^{hd}	8^{hd}	$12^{2½}$	$11^{2¼}$	K. Desormeaux	21.00
Coin Silver, 3, c	L	126	5	$14^{½}$	12^{hd}	$12^{1½}$	9^{2}	11^{1}	$12^{1¼}$	P. Valenzuela	38.60
Greater Good, 3, r	L	126	8	20	20	20	$17^{½}$	$15^{½}$	$13^{¾}$	J. McKee	58.40
Noble Causeway, 3, c	Lc	126	4	12^{2}	$13^{2½}$	15^{hd}	12^{hd}	$13^{½}$	$14^{2½}$	G. Stevens	12.30
Sun King, 3, c	Lc	126	3	$9^{½}$	9^{hd}	8^{hd}	$15^{1½}$	16^{4}	15^{4}	E. Prado	15.70
Spanish Chestnut, 3, c		126	13	$1^{½}$	$1^{1½}$	$1^{1½}$	3^{hd}	9^{hd}	16^{7}	J. Bravo	71.00
Sort It Out, 3, c	L	126	1	$15^{½}$	17^{hd}	17^{hd}	18^{4}	$17^{2½}$	$17^{3¼}$	B. Blanc	61.90
Going Wild, 3, c	Lb	126	19	2^{1}	2^{1}	$4^{½}$	14^{hd}	$18^{5½}$	$18^{3½}$	J. Valdivia Jr.	59.50
Bandini, 3, c	L	126	15	7^{hd}	8^{2}	$11^{1½}$	20	19^{3}	19^{12}	J. Velazquez	6.80
High Limit, 3, c	L	126	6	8^{2}	7^{hd}	$10^{3½}$	19^{hd}	20	20	R. Dominguez	22.50

L=Salix b=blinkers c=mud calks f=front bandages

OFF AT 6:11. Times: :22.28, :45.38, 1:09.59, 1:35.88, 2:02.75.

Start: Good. Track: Fast. Weather: Cloudy. Winner: Eight wide, all out.

$2 Mutuel Prices:				
	10—GIACOMO	**102.60**	**45.80**	**19.80**
	18—CLOSING ARGUMENT		**70.00**	**24.80**
	12—AFLEET ALEX			**4.60**

$2 PICK THREE 8-9-10 PAID $21,335.20 $2 PICK FOUR 1-8-9-10 PAID $164,168.60
$2 PICK SIX 5-5/6-1-8-9-10 PAID $11,228.20
$2 DAILY DOUBLE 9-10 PAID $1,973.40 $2 DAILY DOUBLE OAKS/DERBY 5-10 PAID $595.20
$2 EXACTA 10-18 PAID $9,814.80 $2 TRIFECTA 10-18-12 PAID $133,134.80
$2 SUPERFECTA 10-18-12-17 PAID $1,728,507.00
$2 FUTURE WAGER POOL 1 (7) PAID $52.00 $2 FUTURE WAGER POOL 2 (8) PAID $54.20
$2 FUTURE WAGER POOL 3 (10) PAID $103.60

Gr/ro. c., by Holy Bull out of Set Them Free, by Stop the Music. Trainer: John Shirreffs. Breeder: Mr. and Mrs. Jerry S. Moss (Ky.)

GIACOMO, unhurried and four or five wide between rivals during the early stages, worked his way forward between horses six wide on the far turn, was alertly angled eight abreast to secure racing room at the furlong grounds, then closed determinedly under extreme left-handed urging to prevail. CLOSING ARGUMENT bobbled slightly at the break, gained a forward position while nine wide during the opening quarter, inched up between foes four or five wide entering the far turn, gained a narrow advantage leaving the three-sixteenths pole, and held on tenaciously to save the place. AFLEET ALEX, nicely placed under light rating, rallied near the inside around the far turn, came out and split rivals when straightened into the stretch, gained even terms for the lead in deep stretch and was not quite good enough. DON'T GET MAD was asked for his best nearing the three-eighths pole while circling foes eight wide, offered a serious bid entering the final furlong but could not sustain the momentum. BUZZARDS BAY commenced a sweeping bid seven wide approaching the final quarter, loomed menacingly but came up empty. WILKO, eased back early, began to advance on the far turn, came out between horses six or seven wide for the drive, and improved position while unable to threaten. BELLAMY ROAD, away in good order to track the leaders under light rating, gained a slight advantage when straightened into the stretch but weakened soon after. ANDROMEDA'S HERO, unhurried to the far turn and racing to the inside, came out six or seven wide entering the stretch and produced a mild gain. FLOWER ALLEY, a bit sluggish to begin, forced HIGH LIMIT into NOBLE CAUSEWAY, was steadied behind SPANISH CHESTNUT approaching the five-sixteenths pole, and weakened. HIGH FLY, nicely placed while working his way near the inside between foes, put a head in front near the final quarter but could not sustain the momentum. GREELEY'S GALAXY, tardy to start, reached contention when straightened for the drive and lacked a further account. COIN SILVER, eased back early, made a run around the far turn but was unable to continue. GREATER GOOD, void of early speed, failed to menace while improving position. NOBLE CAUSEWAY bumped with COIN SILVER at the start, was forced to check sharply when bumped by HIGH LIMIT nearing the wire the first time, and failed to reach serious contention. SUN KING, in contention near the inside for seven furlongs, gradually weakened thereafter. SPANISH CHESTNUT moved to the front early, held on for almost a mile, and tired. SORT IT OUT never reached contention. GOING WILD angled in early to press SPANISH CHESTNUT, was asked for more leaving the backstretch, failed to keep pace, and faded. BANDINI, in contention while racing in midpack between rivals, was finished entering the far turn. HIGH LIMIT, bumped passing the wire the first time and forced in on NOBLE CAUSEWAY, was finished after six furlongs.

2005 Preakness: Tragedy Averted

As the leaders wheeled out of Pimlico Race Course's final turn in the 130th Preakness Stakes (G1) on May 21, jockey Ramon Dominguez windmilled his left arm and whacked Scrappy T hard with his whip. Scrappy T literally leaped sideways away from the blow—right across the path of Afleet Alex, who was swinging wide while surging toward the lead. In one horrifying instant, Scrappy T went from one path inside Afleet Alex to one path outside and Afleet Alex clipped the heels of Scrappy T, who was on the lead.

His forelegs knocked sideways, Afleet Alex dove toward the ground while his jockey, Jeremy Rose, held onto his mane and started looking for a place to land. Then something very close to a miracle happened. As Afleet Alex's nose was about to scoop up dirt from the Pimlico surface, the agile little colt bounced off Scrappy T's hindquarters, managed to fling his front legs back out in front of him, and something seemed to nudge Rose back into the saddle.

Something or someone.

His legs back where they belonged, Afleet Alex quickly regained his momentum and spurted away from Scrappy T to win the Preakness by 4¾ lengths in 1:55.04 on a fast Pimlico track.

The back story resembles an episode of the popular, inspirational television show "Touched by an Angel." In the real-life story, a terminally ill little girl, Alex Scott, starts a lemonade stand to raise money for her hospital, touching the lives of millions, including a racehorse who shares her name. "Someone pulled me out of the fire on that one," Rose told NBC Sports as he rode back to the winner's circle on Afleet Alex. "Little Alex was watching me."

Scrappy T easily held on to second, five lengths in front of Kentucky Derby (G1) winner Giacomo, who did not work free from traffic in time to mount a serious challenge but finished strongly to claim

third, a length ahead of Sun King in fourth.

The story began on May 9, 2002, at Classic Oaks Farm in Ocala, where John M. Silvertand's young Hawkster mare Maggy Hawk foaled her third baby, a medium-sized bay from the third crop of then lightly regarded Florida stallion Northern Afleet. The mare had taken good care of her two previous foals, including Afleet Alex's two years older full brother, Unforgettable Max, who, at Afleet Alex's birth, was a year or so away from developing into a good stakes winner of $346,379. But, for whatever reason, Maggy Hawk's milk did not come in, which deprived the foal of her natural, protective colostrum and put the colt in mortal danger. The breeder's nine-year-old daughter, Lauren, took an interest in Maggy Hawk's foal, helping to feed him from a nipple attached to a Coors Lite bottle for the 12 days it took to find a nurse mare.

Six months later, John Silvertand was diagnosed with colon cancer. Doctors gave him only a few months to live, but the English-born horseman defied the odds, fighting through chemotherapy and several surgical procedures. Then, almost two years later, the little foal in whom Silvertand and his family had taken such an interest started winning races. It gave the breeder something to live for.

Silvertand had acquired Maggy Hawk and four other mares from John Devers and agreed to flip a coin with Devers for any foals. He lost the flip for Afleet Alex, and Devers consigned him to the 2004 Fasig-Tipton Midlantic sale of two-year-olds in training at Timonium, Maryland, just north of Baltimore.

Chuck Zacney of Philadelphia, who had raced a few horses in the early 1990s but had gotten out of the business, had the itch again. "Myself and four friends [Jennifer Reeves, Joe Judge, Joe Lerro, and Bob Brittingham], we were looking to put a group together," Zacney said. "It all came together when we chose Tim [Ritchey] as our trainer."

A lifelong horseman and former steeplechase rider based at nearby Delaware Park, Ritchey accompanied Zacney to the Timonium sale and selected the athletic-looking Northern Afleet colt. Zacney had to pay only $75,000 for him in the name of CJZ Racing Stable.

In the Preakness, Afleet Alex was favored at 3.30-to-1 off his third-place finish in the Kentucky Derby, in which he was beaten one length by winner Giacomo.

At the start, Rose maneuvered Afleet Alex to a position two paths off the rail heading into the first turn as High Limit, wearing blinkers for the first time, and Going Wild cleared the field through the first quarter-mile in :23.17. Giacomo, breaking from post 13 alongside Afleet Alex, also dropped

---

Owner

Cash is King stable is composed of Chuck Zacney of Philadelphia, the managing partner, and friends Jennifer Reeves, Joe Judge, Joe Lerro, and Bob Brittingham. All have connections to the Philadelphia area and some partners have business interests with Zacney-owned Sirrus Group, a regional medical billing company. Afleet Alex derived his name from Zacney's son Alex, Lerro's daughter Alexandra, and Brittingham's daughter, Alexandria.

Breeder

John Martin Silvertand, a resident of Palm Beach County, Florida, grew up in England, where his family built Southwell Racecourse. After serving in the Royal Air Force, he lived in Tanzania and the Bahamas before settling in the United States in 1990. He maintained a small broodmare band and was a half-owner of Florida sire Tour d'Or with Noel Hickey.

in toward the rail but was four wide around the first turn, while Withers Stakes (G3) winner Scrappy T tucked in behind the leaders, tugging at the bit. As High Limit led the field through honest fractions of :46.07 and 1:10.72 for the first six furlongs, Rose maneuvered Afleet Alex closer to the rail and, as the field banked into the final turn, he dove for a narrow hole on the fence and barely squeezed through. Mike Smith on Giacomo was alongside, two paths farther out, but could not find a way through.

Scrappy T attacked High Limit on the final turn, and the big, almost black Fit to Fight gelding forged to the front outside the quarter pole and began to pull away. Afleet Alex was flying at him, though, as Rose shifted him off the rail. As Dominguez smacked his horse on the left hip, Rose threw a cross on Afleet Alex, expecting the colt's momentum to take him right by the leader.

When Scrappy T jumped to his right, the pair clipped heels, Afleet Alex stumbled into Scrappy T's hindquarters, pushing the gelding farther to the right and probably helping himself find his feet. Quickly finding his best stride again, Afleet Alex forged to the lead and drew away to a heart-stopping victory.—*John P. Sparkman*

12th RACE
Pimlico
May 21, 2005

$1\frac{3}{16}$ MILES ($1{:}53\frac{2}{5}$) on dirt. 130th running of the Preakness Stakes. Grade 1. 3-year-olds. Purse $1,000,000.

Value of race $6,154,800; Winner $5,854,800; second $170,000; third $85,000; fourth $45,000. Mutuel WPS Pool $42,409,001. Exacta Pool $19,599,574. Trifecta Pool $20,500,979. Superfecta Pool $5,261,943.

Horse	M/Eqt.	Wt.	PP	¼	½	¾	1 mi.	Str.	Fin.	Jockey	Odds $1
Afleet Alex, 3, c	LAf	126	12	10	10^{2}	10^{1}	$7^{\frac{1}{2}}$	1^{hd}	$1^{4\frac{3}{4}}$	J. Rose	3.30*
Scrappy T, 3, g	LAbf	126	5	2	3^{2}	3^{hd}	2^{1}	2^{4}	2^{5}	R. Dominguez	13.30
Giacomo, 3, c	L	126	13	11	11^{hd}	$11^{3\frac{1}{2}}$	10^{hd}	5^{2}	3^{1}	M. Smith	6.00
Sun King, 3, c	LA	126	10	7	$8^{\frac{1}{2}}$	$9^{1\frac{1}{2}}$	9^{2}	4^{hd}	4^{1}	R. Bejarano	21.10
High Limit, 3, c	LAb	126	11	8	$1^{\frac{1}{2}}$	1^{hd}	$1^{\frac{1}{2}}$	3^{3}	$5^{6\frac{3}{4}}$	E. Prado	18.70
Noble Causeway, 3, c	LA	126	3	13	14	13^{1}	13^{3}	$7^{\frac{1}{2}}$	$6^{1\frac{1}{4}}$	G. Stevens	11.30
Greeley's Galaxy, 3, c	L	126	4	14	9^{1}	$8^{\frac{1}{2}}$	$5^{\frac{1}{2}}$	$6^{2\frac{1}{2}}$	7^{1}	D. Flores	9.40
Malibu Moonshine, 3, c	LAb	126	1	12	$13^{2\frac{1}{2}}$	$12^{\frac{1}{2}}$	12^{hd}	8^{3}	8^{6}	S. Hamilton	24.00
Closing Argument, 3, c	L	126	7	3	$5^{2\frac{1}{2}}$	$5^{\frac{1}{2}}$	6^{1}	9^{1}	$9^{2\frac{1}{4}}$	C. Velasquez	7.20
High Fly, 3, c	LA	126	2	1	6^{hd}	6^{1}	$8^{\frac{1}{2}}$	10^{3}	$10^{5\frac{1}{4}}$	J. Bailey	5.10
Hal's Image, 3, c	LA	126	6	4	12^{2}	14	14	13^{4}	$11^{\frac{3}{4}}$	J. Santos	23.50
Wilko, 3, c	LA	126	9	6	$7^{1\frac{1}{2}}$	7^{hd}	$11^{2\frac{1}{2}}$	$12^{1\frac{1}{2}}$	12^{1}	C. Nakatani	13.30
Galloping Grocer, 3, g	L	126	8	5	4^{hd}	4^{2}	$4^{\frac{1}{2}}$	11^{1}	13^{6}	J. Bravo	27.00
Going Wild, 3, c	Lb	126	14	9	2^{1}	$2^{1\frac{1}{2}}$	$3^{\frac{1}{2}}$	14	14	R. Albarado	26.50

OFF AT 6:21. Times: :23.17, :46.07, 1:10.72, 1:36.04, 1:55.04.
Start: Good. Track: Fast. Weather: Clear. Winner: Clipped heels, stumbled.

$2 Mutuel Prices:				
	12—AFLEET ALEX	8.60	5.00	3.20
	5—SCRAPPY T		11.20	5.80
	13—GIACOMO			4.80

$2 EXACTA 12-5 PAID $152.60 $2 TRIFECTA 12-5-13 PAID $872.00 $2 SUPERFECTA 12-5-13-10 PAID $20,724.60
$2 PICK THREE 7-7-12 PAID $222.40 $2 PICK FOUR 4-7-7-12 PAID $4,881.80
$2 DAILY DOUBLE PIMLICO SPECIAL/PREAKNESS 5-12 PAID $35.80 $2 DAILY DOUBLE 7-12 PAID $33.20

B. c., by Northern Afleet out of Maggy Hawk, by Hawkster. Trainer: Timothy F. Ritchey. Breeder: John Martin Silvertand (Fl.)

AFLEET ALEX saved ground early, angled out three to four wide leaving the five-sixteenths pole, stumbled badly when clipping the heels of SCRAPPY T entering the stretch, quickly recovered, angled inside that rival, surged to command a furlong out, and then drew clear under steady right-handed pressure. SCRAPPY T prompted the pace, lodged a two-wide bid around the far turn, moved to a clear advantage after 6½ furlongs, ducked out when roused left-handed entering the stretch, dueled briefly nearing the eighth pole, and was clearly second best. GIACOMO, sluggish early, was put to urging nearing the far turn, worked his way between foes leaving the eighth pole, and continued on with good energy. SUN KING, in midpack early, made a mild run to midstretch and then flattened out. HIGH LIMIT set a pressured pace into the far turn and gave way after the quarter pole. NOBLE CAUSEWAY, bumped at the break, ran six wide down the backstretch and failed to generate a solid response. GREELEY'S GALAXY broke inward into NOBLE CAUSEWAY, made a steady run along the rail into the far turn, angled out leaving the three-furlong marker, but had no further response. MALIBU MOONSHINE saved ground in an even effort. CLOSING ARGUMENT stalked the pace and tired after seven furlongs. HIGH FLY failed to make a serious impact and tired. HAL'S IMAGE lacked speed and failed to menace. WILKO chased the pace to the far turn and was eased in the final furlong. GALLOPING GROCER prompted the pace, faltered nearing the stretch, and was eased late. GOING WILD pressed the pace and stopped after six furlongs.

2005 Belmont: Alex Is Awesome

From the instant he sat down at the post-race press conference, the word to describe Afleet Alex's performance in the Belmont Stakes (G1) on June 11 was clear in jockey Jeremy Rose's mind. "Explosive," he said succinctly when prompted to describe the effort that brought a hearty roar from a slightly sweat-soaked crowd of 62,274 when Afleet Alex catapulted past the leaders at the top of Belmont Park's stretch en route to a seven-length victory in the Belmont. The statement was as emphatic as Afleet Alex, a son of Northern Afleet who has asserted himself as the best member of his generation with a pair of classic victories.

Afleet Alex was as dominant in the Belmont as he was courageous in the Preakness Stakes (G1) three weeks earlier at Pimlico Race Course, when he clipped the heels of Scrappy T at the top of the stretch, nearly fell, recovered, and went on to a 4¾-length win.

Afleet Alex encountered no traffic problems in the Belmont and blew the race wide open with a final quarter-mile clocking of :24.50 to win the 1½-mile Belmont by seven lengths from 11.90-to-1 fourth choice Andromeda's Hero. The maiden Nolan's Cat was another 6¾ lengths back in third and 2¼ lengths in front of Indy Storm in fourth. Giacomo, longshot winner of the Kentucky Derby (G1) who grabbed a brief lead at the top of the stretch, displaced his soft palate and struggled home in seventh place. Six days later, he was diagnosed with a chip in his left front ankle and would undergo surgery. Afleet Alex's time on a fast track that favored speed and yielded quick times all day was 2:28.75.

The final quarter-mile time by Afleet Alex was faster than any of the final quarters turned in by the six fastest Belmont winners in history, including 1973 Triple Crown winner Secretariat, who ran his final quarter-mile in :25. It was the fastest since Rokeby Stable's Arts and Letters zipped down the stretch in :24⅘ en route to a 5½-length win in '69.

Afleet Alex breezed once between the Preakness and the Belmont, going five furlongs with Rose aboard in 1:01.60 on June 1 at Pimlico Race Course. After a day of rest, trainer Tim Ritchey resumed his two-a-day training sessions with Afleet Alex, jogging the colt early and sending him out again after the maintenance break for jogs and gallops. On June 5, his first morning at Belmont, Afleet Alex jogged once and galloped once around the 1 ½-mile oval. Ritchey tightened the screws a bit on the second day, five days before the race, when Afleet Alex jogged two miles and then galloped not once, but twice around the expansive oval. Fans on and off track settled on Afleet Alex as the 1.15-to-1 favorite at post time in the race billed as a rubber match between the winners of the first two Triple Crown events. Giacomo was the only other member of the field at single-digit odds as the 5.10-to-1 second choice.

Sir Barton Stakes winner Pinpoint, one of three starters sent out by trainer Nick Zito, took the early initiative under John Velazquez and led through the opening quarter in :24.47 and half in :48.62 with token pressure from A. P. Arrow, Lone Star Derby (G3) winner Southern Africa, and Chekhov. They were followed by Giacomo, who was kept closer to the pace by jockey Mike Smith than he had in the Derby or Preakness, Watchmon, and Indy Storm.

Rose bided his time toward the back of the field as Pinpoint continued to lead past six furlongs in 1:12.92 and Giacomo started to inch up to be fourth. The front-runners began to tire around the final turn, and Giacomo took aim at the leaders while running four wide as Pinpoint held onto the lead through a mile in 1:38.05. Rose and Afleet Alex also were traveling well around the turn and were picking off rivals effortlessly as Giacomo stuck his head in front of A. P. Arrow and Southern Africa.

Afleet Alex was tipped out five wide approaching the quarter pole, drew on even terms briefly with Giacomo, who led through 1¼ miles in 2:04.25, and responded in an instant after some mild urging from Rose just before the field straightened for home. The race was over in the blink of an eye as Afleet Alex exploded past Giacomo and opened a clear lead after about five strides.

Meanwhile, Smith said, Giacomo was encountering difficulty with his breathing and backed up through the stretch.

Andromeda's Hero, who was 8¾ lengths behind Afleet Alex when third in the Arkansas Derby

Sire

NORTHERN AFLEET, 1993 b. h., Afleet–Nuryette, by Nureyev, 21-5-3-5, $626,671. Bred by Hermitage Farm and raced by Anderson and Waranach. Graded stakes winner at four, San Fernando Breeders' Cup S. (G2), San Carlos H. (G2), San Diego H. (G3). He stood his first season at stud in 1999 at Donald Dizney's Double Diamond Farm in Ocala. Acquired by Taylor Made Farm and WinStar Farm, he stood the 2005 breeding season for a $12,500 fee at Taylor Made in Nicholasville, Kentucky. He has sired at least eight stakes winners, including Afleet Alex's full brother, Unforgettable Max, and Grade 3 winner G P Fleet.

Dam

MAGGY HAWK, 1994 b. m., Hawkster–Qualique, by *Hawaii. 4-1-1-1, $15,080. Dam of five foals, two to race, both stakes winners. Afleet Alex won the Hopeful S. (G1) and Sanford S. (G2) at two, and the Preakness S. (G1), Belmont S. (G1), and Arkansas Derby (G2) at three. His full brother, Unforgettable Max, won the 2004 Shecky Greene S. and earned $374,579.

(G2), rallied from the back of the pack to become the sixth Belmont runner-up for Zito. The son of Fusaichi Pegasus, ridden by Rafael Bejarano, passed the tiring Southern Africa and Giacomo inside the eighth pole but was no match for the winner.

Nolan's Cat also earned a bit of redemption for trainer Dale Romans and owners Ken and Sarah Ramsey when he began a sustained run on the far turn under Norberto Arroyo Jr. The son of Catienus was coming off a close second behind A. P. Arrow in a 1¼-mile maiden race on May 14 at Churchill in his fifth career start.

Afleet Alex was the 18th runner since 1877 to complete the Preakness-Belmont double and the fifth—along with Risen Star, Hansel, Tabasco Cat, and Point Given—to pull off the double since Affirmed won the Triple Crown in 1978. Since Affirmed's memorable victories over Alydar in the 1978 classics, 17 three-year-olds have been dual classic winners, including Smarty Jones last year, Funny Cide in 2003, and War Emblem in '02.

The efforts by Afleet Alex were similar to those of Risen Star, who also finished third in the Derby before bouncing back to emphatic wins in the Preakness and Belmont. Damascus also finished third in the Derby before posting runaway wins in the Preakness and Belmont in 1967.—*Tom Law*

11TH RACE **Belmont** June 11, 2005	1½ MILES (2:24) on dirt. 137th running of the Belmont Stakes. Grade 1. 3-year-olds. Purse $1,000,000.											

Value of race $1,000,000; Winner $600,000; second $200,000; third $110,000; fourth $60,000, fifth $30,000. Total WPS Pool $15,878,182. Exacta Pool $9,583,612. Trifecta Pool $12,353,752. Superfecta Pool $4,834,612.

Horse	M/Eqt.	Wt.	PP	¼	½	1 mi.	1¼	Str.	Fin.	Jockey	Odds $1
Afleet Alex, 3, c	Lf	126	9	9^{hd}	8^{hd}	8^{hd}	$2½$	1^6	1^7	J. Rose	1.15*
Andromeda's Hero, 3, c	Lc	126	7	10^8	10^7	9^3	4^{hd}	$22½$	$26¾$	R. Bejarano	11.90
Nolan's Cat, 3, c	L	126	1	11	11	11	$7½$	5^2	$32¼$	N. Arroyo Jr.	20.50
Indy Storm, 3, c	Lc	126	10	$7½$	6^{hd}	$61½$	6^{hd}	$8½$	4^1	E. Prado	17.10
A. P. Arrow, 3, c	Lb	126	3	$2½$	2^{hd}	2^{hd}	$5½$	7^{hd}	5^{nk}	J. Bailey	16.40
Chekhov, 3, c		126	11	$4½$	$41½$	7^{hd}	9^6	6^{hd}	$6½$	G. Stevens	15.10
Giacomo, 3, c	L	126	5	$5½$	$5½$	$4½$	1^{hd}	$4½$	7^{hd}	M. Smith	5.10
Southern Africa, 3, c	Lb	126	4	$3½$	$3½$	$3½$	$32½$	$3½$	$84¼$	J. Court	15.40
Watchmon, 3, c	Lb	126	6	6^{hd}	$72½$	5^{hd}	$81½$	9^{12}	9^{12}	J. Castellano	20.60
Reverberate, 3, c	Lb	126	8	8^{hd}	$9½$	$102½$	$10½$	10^{hd}	$10¾$	J. Santos	11.80
Pinpoint, 3, c	Lbc	126	2	1^1	$1½$	1^{hd}	11	11	11	J. Velazquez	15.60

OFF AT 6:34. Times: :24.47, :48.62, 1:12.92, 1:38.05, 2:04.25, 2:28.75.
Start: Good for all but 8. Track: Fast. Weather: Cloudy. Winner: Quick move, drew away.

$2 Mutuel Prices:	9—AFLEET ALEX	4.30	3.60	3.00
	7—ANDROMEDA'S HERO		8.20	5.80
	1—NOLAN'S CAT			7.20

$2 EXACTA 9-7 PAID $44.00 $2 TRIFECTA 9-7-1 PAID $1,249.00 $2 SUPERFECTA 9-7-1-10 PAID $14,219.00
$2 PICK THREE 9-2-9 (3 CORRECT) PAID $314.50 $2 PICK FOUR 2-9-2-9 (4 CORRECT) PAID $490.00
$2 PICK SIX 7-6-2-9-2-9 (5 CORRECT) PAID $204.00 $2 PICK SIX 7-6-2-9-2-9 (6 CORRECT) PAID $19,758.00
$2 DAILY DOUBLE 2-9 PAID $88.00

B. c., by Northern Afleet out of Maggy Hawk, by Hawkster. Trainer: Timothy F. Ritchey. Breeder: John Martin Silvertand (Fl.).

AFLEET ALEX, angled to the inside in the early stages, was unhurried along the backstretch while slightly off the rail, launched a rally leaving the far turn, split rivals while rapidly gaining on the turn, swung five wide for clear sailing nearing the quarter pole, charged to the front at the top of the stretch, quickly opened a commanding lead under right-handed urging in upper stretch, and extended his lead to the finish. ANDROMEDA'S HERO, raced well back for six furlongs, moved up between horses on the far turn, made a move four wide outside the winner midway on the turn, swung wider in upper stretch, but was no match for AFLEET ALEX while holding willingly for the place. NOLAN'S CAT raced far back to the far turn, circled eight wide while closing the gap approaching the quarter pole, and then rallied belatedly in the middle of the track. INDY STORM raced in the middle of the pack along the backstretch, closed the gap a bit midway on the turn, and lacked a strong finishing bid. A. P. ARROW pressed the pace for six furlongs, remained a factor to the turn, and steadily tired thereafter. CHEKHOV stalked the pace while six wide along the backstretch and dropped back leaving the far turn. GIACOMO tucked in along the rail in the early stages, made a quick five-wide move to join the leaders midway on the final turn, surged to the front approaching the quarter pole, yielded to the winner at the top of the stretch, and steadily tired thereafter. SOUTHERN AFRICA stalked three wide for a mile, rallied between horses to challenge briefly midway on the turn, remained a factor into upper stretch, and then gave way. WATCHMON raced in midpack to the turn then lacked a further response. REVERBERATE stumbled at the start, steadied along the rail on the first turn, and was never close thereafter. PINPOINT set the pace under pressure for nearly a mile and a quarter, then faltered.

BREEDERS' CUP
Breeders' Cup History

John R. Gaines, one of the central figures in the North American commercial breeding industry in the last quarter of the 20th century, was renowned for his creativity and his powers of persuasion. In the early 1980s, Gaines needed all his considerable talents to get a fractious industry lined up behind his concept, which he believed would help to define the Thoroughbred industry and give it a centerpiece.

Gaines's creation was the Breeders' Cup. From the perspective of the 21st century, the Breeders' Cup stands as the most successful initiative of the Thoroughbred industry in the last half of the 20th century. Creation of the Breeders' Cup allowed the sport to hold a championship day of racing in late fall for the majority of age and sex divisions, an important element missing from a sport that had its major fall championship races scattered across the nation at several tracks.

Gaines conceived the idea in part out of anger and frustration. He was angered by a television program in the early 1980s that had depicted Thoroughbred racing as a haven of drug abuse. Indeed, permissive medication policies at racetracks had eroded confidence in the sport's integrity, and racing had continued its long, slow slide in popularity—a decline that began shortly after World War II. Even as the commercial bloodstock markets boomed in the early 1980s, race purses in real terms were shrinking.

The highly successful owner of Gainesway near Lexington and an innovator in the stallion-station concept, Gaines developed the idea for a championship day of racing with multimillion-dollar purses to attract the world's best runners, with the races being broadcast nationally on a major television network. The day of racing, as important as it was, would not be an end unto itself. The event would be used to build racing's popularity, with the organization in charge of the event becoming a leader in marketing the sport.

Given the sport's propensity for infighting, it is surprising the Breeders' Cup came into being in very much the form that Gaines first envisioned Thoroughbred racing's championship day. But it was not easy.

Gaines had to sell the concept to a skeptical industry in 1982, and he had to do it one person at a time. His first target was John W. Galbreath, owner of Darby Dan Farm and an influential sportsman in the United States and England. (At the time, Galbreath was the only person to have raced both a Kentucky Derby winner [Chateaugay] and an Epsom Derby victor [Roberto].)

Gaines went to Columbus, Ohio, to meet with Galbreath, who initially thought little of the idea. But, as Gaines sketched out his idea in detail, Galbreath came on board. Moving quickly, Gaines lined up other supporters, including Spendthrift Farm's Leslie Combs II, Nelson Bunker Hunt, Windfields Farms' Charles Taylor, Will Farish, Racing Hall of Fame trainer John Nerud, Brereton C. Jones, John T. L. Jones Jr., and Seth Hancock, who a decade earlier had taken over management of his family's Claiborne Farm.

All great ideas have their moments, and Gaines's idea came at just the right time for the Thoroughbred industry. Commercial breeders, who would pay a big part of the program's cost by nominating their stallions and foals, were enjoying unprecedented prosperity as bloodstock prices rose to record levels and stallion fees climbed.

Where Championship Days Were Held

Churchill Downs (5): 1988, 1991, 1994, 1998, 2000
Hollywood Park (3): 1984, 1987, 1997
Belmont Park (3): 1990, 1995, 2001
Gulfstream Park (3): 1989, 1992, 1999
Santa Anita Park (3): 1986, 1993, 2003
Arlington Park (1): 2002
Aqueduct (1): 1985
Lone Star Park (1): 2004
Woodbine (1) 1996

Breeders' Cup Attendance and Wagering by Year

Year	Site	On-Track Attendance	On-Track Wagering*	Total Wagering*
2004	Lone Star	53,717	$11,274,066	$109,838,668
2003	Santa Anita	51,486	**13,678,118**	107,535,731
2002	Arlington	46,118	12,143,114	108,885,673
2001	Belmont	52,987	12,067,995	98,008,747
2000	Churchill	76,043	13,579,798	101,283,427
1999	Gulfstream	45,124	11,065,973	96,485,255
1998	Churchill	**80,452**	13,544,859	91,338,477
1997	Hollywood	51,161	8,191,459	71,639,333
1996	Woodbine	42,243	5,925,469	67,738,890
1995	Belmont	37,246	7,590,332	64,075,207
1994	Churchill	71,671	10,146,524	78,224,530
1993	Santa Anita	55,130	12,142,750	79,744,742
1992	Gulfstream	45,415	9,915,542	76,876,726
1991	Churchill	66,204	11,945,562	67,588,113
1990	Belmont	51,236	9,107,270	55,328,195
1989	Gulfstream	51,342	10,216,258	55,345,677
1988	Churchill	71,237	9,219,083	42,932,379
1987	Hollywood	57,734	10,202,252	31,864,457
1986	Santa Anita	69,155	12,510,109	31,984,490
1985	Aqueduct	42,568	7,200,175	26,941,288
1984	Hollywood	64,254	8,443,070	16,452,179

*Breeders' Cup races only

At the same time, racing was perceived as a sport in trouble, and relatively low purse levels dissuaded some prospective owners from buying horses. Although overseas interests sent the bloodstock markets skyrocketing, many breeders realized the prices they received for their sale offerings and the stallion fees they charged were directly related to purses, which determined how much a sale purchase potentially could earn.

Gaines chose the sport's most prestigious event, the Kentucky Derby (G1), to announce his idea. He was honored at the Kentucky Derby Festival's "They're Off" luncheon on April 23, 1982, and there he outlined his idea, a $13-million afternoon featuring the world's best racehorses. Gaines named it the Breeders' Cup.

He moved quickly to name a board of directors and girded for the inevitable naysayers. New York racing interests were opposed because Gaines's proposal would diminish the importance of the New York Racing Association's fall races, which frequently decided year-end titles.

Smaller-scale breeders also voiced their opposition. Gaines said breeders could breed one more mare to a stallion to cover the cost of the stallion nomination fee each year. Such a strategy certainly would work for a breeder with barns filled with desirable stallions whose books were filled, and Gaines was one of those breeders. But, for a small-scale breeder trying to fill the book of a less-commercial stallion, the stallion nomination most likely would be paid out of the stallion owner's pocket.

Other breeders raised concerns that Gaines was putting all the money into one event, argu-

Television Ratings for Breeders' Cup

Date	Host Track	Rating/Share
2004	Lone Star Park	1.4/4
2003	Santa Anita Park	1.8/5
2002	Arlington Park	2.0/5
2001	Belmont Park	1.7/5
2000	Churchill Downs	1.8/5
1999	Gulfstream Park	1.9/5
1998	Churchill Downs	2.2/6
1997	Hollywood Park	2.2/6
1996	Woodbine	2.5/8
1995	Belmont Park	2.8/9
1994	Churchill Downs	2.7/8
1993	Santa Anita Park	3.4/9
1992	Gulfstream Park	3.0/8
1991	Churchill Downs	3.0/9
1990	Belmont Park	2.7/9
1989	Gulfstream Park	3.7/11
1988	Churchill Downs	4.0/11
1987	Hollywood Park	2.9/7
1986	Santa Anita Park	4.4/12
1985	Aqueduct	4.0/11
1984	Hollywood Park	5.1/13

ing that the money should be spread throughout the year to supplement purses of existing stakes races. On that point, a compromise was reached, with $10-million earmarked for the championship day and an equal portion going into Breeders' Cup-sponsored races around the country.

By the fall of 1982, the Breeders' Cup was beset with infighting, and Hancock delivered an unexpected blow when he did not nominate Claiborne's stallions on grounds that the organization had not developed a clear game plan. Gaines realized he had become a lightning rod for opponents and resigned the presidency on October 22, becoming chairman. C. Gibson Downing Jr., a Lexington lawyer with a modest-sized stud farm and a reputation for consensus building, became Breeders' Cup president. Hancock signed up after a rules book was written on how the money would be spent, and smaller breeders followed his lead. D. G. Van Clief Jr. came on board that fall as executive director.

For several months, Gaines and Nerud traveled around the country, selling breeders and racetrack operators on the concept. By April 15, 1983, 1,083 stallions had been nominated to the program, and the Breeders' Cup was up and running. Nerud said in 1985 that a decision was made early to hold the first Breeders' Cup in a warm climate so television viewers would see racing in a pleasant setting. Marjorie Everett, chief executive of Hollywood Park, lobbied heavily for the first event, and on February 24, 1983, the Inglewood, California, track was named as host of the first Breeders' Cup, to be held on November 10, 1984. In a bow to New York interests, Aqueduct was host of the second Breeders' Cup in 1985.

At Nerud's suggestion, marketers Mike Letis and Mike Trager of Sports Marketing and Television International were brought in to negotiate a television deal, and a contract with NBC was signed on September 13, 1983. The show would run for four hours on a Saturday afternoon and would include live coverage of all seven Breeders' Cup championship races. In January 1984, all seven races were granted Grade 1 status.

From the first race, won by Chief's Crown in the $1-million Breeders' Cup Juvenile (G1), the Breeders' Cup was an unprecedented success. That afternoon's races attracted a crowd of 64,254, and the day concluded with a breathtaking $3-million Breeders' Cup Classic (G1), in which supplemental entry Wild Again edged Gate Dancer and Slew o' Gold for the biggest race purse ever offered to that time.

An even larger crowd, 69,155, attended the third Breeders' Cup at Santa Anita Park in suburban Los Angeles, but that record lasted only two years until Churchill Downs hosted the fifth Breeders' Cup in 1988 before a crowd of 71,237. On a dreary, rainy, chilly day in Louisville, they were treated to one of the event's most exciting races when undefeated Personal Ensign closed relentlessly in the final yards and caught that year's Kentucky Derby winner, Winning Colors, at the finish line to win the Breeders' Cup Distaff (G1) by a nose. With that victory, Personal Ensign was retired unbeaten in 13 starts.

The Breeders' Cup traveled to Florida for the first time in 1989, and Gulfstream Park was the scene for another monumental struggle in which Sunday Silence fought off the challenge of Easy Goer to win the Breeders' Cup Classic. The event reached its nadir the following year at Belmont Park, when Go for Wand sustained a fatal breakdown near the finish line of the Breeders' Cup Distaff and was humanely destroyed. Earlier on the card, a spill in the Breeders' Cup Sprint (G1) led to the deaths of Mr. Nickerson and Shaker Knit. Subsequently, Breeders' Cup Ltd. instituted prerace examinations in an effort to limit breakdowns.

As rich races became more common, especially internationally, Breeders' Cup Ltd. increased its championship day purses, raising the Classic to $4-million in 1996 and the Distaff to $2-million in '98. In 1999, a new race, the $1-million Filly and Mare Turf (G1), was added, raising the afternoon's total purses to $13-million. In 2001, the championship day was renamed the Breeders' Cup World Thoroughbred Championships. By 2003, the Breeders' Cup Stakes program had grown to 104 stakes races, with purses exceeding $18.5-million.

In 2003, $500,000 each was added to the purses of the Breeders' Cup Mile (G1) and Juvenile, raising the afternoon's total purses to $14-million. At the same time, Breeders' Cup increased total entry fees 50% to 3% of the race purse.

—Don Clippinger

Breeders' Cup Trophy

The Breeders' Cup trophy is an authentic reproduction of the Torrie horse, created by Giovanni da Bologna in Florence, Italy, mostly likely in the late 1580s. The sculpture is known as an ecorche or flayed horse and shows the horse's muscles in great detail.

Although its original commission is not known, the sculpture may have been a study made for an equestrian statue of Duke Cosimo I, which was completed in 1591 and stands today in the Piazza della Signoria in Florence.

The sculptor's original ecorche in bronze was acquired by Sir James Erskine of Torrie in the early 1800s. It was bequeathed to the University of Edinburgh in 1836 and today is housed in the university's Museum of Fine Arts in Scotland.

The Breeders' Cup trophy was cast from the original under supervision of University of Edinburgh curators, and the replica is owned by Breeders' Cup Ltd. Smaller replicas are presented to winners of each Breeders' Cup race, and winning breeders, trainers, and jockeys also are presented with replicas.

Breeders' Cup Purses

When John Gaines first proposed the Breeders' Cup in 1982, he envisioned a purse structure of $13-million for the championship day. As the concept was put into final form for the first championship day in 1984, purses and nominator fees totaled $10-million. Five of seven races had $1-million purses (Juvenile, Juvenile Fillies, Sprint, Distaff, Mile); the Turf had a $2-million purse, and the Classic was $3-million.

In 1996, the Classic was increased to $4-million, and the Distaff was raised to $2-million two years later. The $1-million Filly and Mare Turf was added in 1999, and the Juvenile and Mile were increased to $1.5-million each in 2003, raising total purses to $14-million.

A 1997 change in the rules for supplemental nominations has resulted in higher purses. Beginning in 1998, supplemental-nomination money is added to the total purse. Thus, the 1998 Breeders' Cup Classic, which contained supplemental nominees Gentlemen (Arg), Silver Charm, and Skip Away, raised the total purse ($4,689,920) and nominator fees above $5-million, then the biggest race purse ever.

In addition to purse money paid to the horse's owner or owners, the Breeders' Cup purse structure contains 5% awards for both the stallion nominator and the foal nominator. Here is the 2004 distribution for a $1-million race:

Finish	Purse	Owner	Stallion Nominator	Foal Nominator
1st	57.2%	$520,000	$26,000	$26,000
2nd	22.0%	200,000	10,000	10,000
3rd	12.1%	110,000	5,500	5,500
4th	5.7%	57,000		
5th	3.0%	30,000		
Total	100.0%	$917,000	$41,500	$41,500

Largest Breeders' Cup Purses

(Not including stallion and foal nominator fees)

Year	Race	Purse	Winner	Value to Winner
1998	Classic	$4,689,920	Awesome Again	$2,662,400
2000	Classic	4,369,320	Tiznow	2,480,400
1997	Classic	4,030,400	Skip Away	2,288,000
2004	Classic	3,668,000	Ghostzapper	2,080,000
2003	Classic	3,668,000	Pleasantly Perfect	2,080,000
2002	Classic	3,664,000	Volponi	2,080,000
2001	Classic	3,664,000	Tiznow	2,080,000
1999	Classic	3,664,000	Cat Thief	2,080,000
1996	Classic	3,664,000	Alphabet Soup	2,080,000
1995	Classic	2,798,000	Cigar	1,560,000
1994	Classic	2,748,000	Concern	1,560,000
1993	Classic	2,748,000	Arcangues	1,560,000
1992	Classic	2,748,000	A.P. Indy	1,560,000
1991	Classic	2,748,000	Black Tie Affair (Ire)	1,560,000

From 1984 through '90, the Breeders' Cup Classic had a race purse of $2,739,000 and a winner's share of $1.35-million. The next highest purse was $2,271,680 in the 2000 Breeders' Cup Turf, won by Kalanisi (Ire).

Breeders' Cup Supplemental Entries

From its beginning, the Breeders' Cup program has allowed supplemental entries for its championship races, but the supplemental fee has been expensive to encourage stallion and foal owners to nominate their horses to the program. The supplemental fee was originally 12% for horses whose sires were nominated to the Breeders' Cup, the European Breeders' Fund, or a common fund of the two organizations. If a stallion was not nominated to the program at the time of the foal's conception, the supplementary fee was 20%.

For the foal to be nominated, the stallion must first be nominated to the program. Thus, when John Henry was pre-entered for the first $2-million Breeders' Cup Turf (G1) in 1984, owners Sam and Dorothy Rubin had to pay a $400,000 fee to start the gelding because his sire, Ole Bob Bowers, was not nominated to the program. The Rubins paid a $133,000 pre-entry fee, which was nonrefundable, and John Henry did not start because of a minor injury.

The hefty fees for horses whose sires were not nominated to the program worked against Southern Hemisphere horses in particular. Frank and Janis Whitham paid $200,000 to start Bayakoa (Arg) in the 1989 Breeders' Cup Distaff (G1) and again put up a $200,000 supplemental fee to start her the following year. Bayakoa won both times, earning a first-place purse of $450,000 each year. At that time, the supple-mental fees did not go into the race purses but were retained by Breeders' Cup Ltd.

The rules were changed for the 1998 Breeders' Cup championship. Beginning with foals of 1996, the supplemental fee for offspring of nominated stallions was reduced to 9%, while the fee remained at 12% for older horses and 20% for horses whose sires were not nominated to the program.

Another change allowed supplemented horses to receive a credit for the net supplementary fees, after pre-entry, entry, and starting fees were taken out. High Chaparral (Ire) started in the 2002 Breeders' Cup Turf with payment of a $180,000 supplemental fee. When he started the following year, he had a $120,000 credit for the supplemental fee—the original $180,000 payment less starting fees of 3% of the total purse, or $60,000. High Chaparral won in 2002 and finished in a dead heat for the win with Johar in '03.

A further change added the net supplemental fees to the race purse, also in 1998. As a result of this change, the Breeders' Cup Classic (G1) in 1998 had a record purse of $4,689,920 with the supplemental nominations of Gentlemen (Arg) and Silver Charm. Skip Away, who had won the race a year earlier, received a credit for his net supplementary fee in 1997. Silver Charm finished second to Awesome Again, while Skip Away and Gentlemen finished out of the money.

Breeders' Cup Leaders

Leading Owners by Wins

6 Allen E. Paulson (Escena, 1998 Distaff; Ajina, 1997 Distaff; Cigar, 1995 Classic; Eliza, 1992 Juvenile Fillies; Opening Verse, 1991 Mile; Theatrical [Ire], 1987 Turf)

5 Flaxman Holdings/Stavros Niarchos (Six Perfections [Fr], 2003 Mile; Domedriver [Ire], 2002 Mile; Spinning World, 1997 Mile; Miesque [twice], 1987, '88 Mile)

Eugene V. Klein (Is It True, 1988 Juvenile; Open Mind, 1988 Juvenile Fillies; Success Express, 1987 Juvenile; Twilight Ridge, 1985 Juvenile Fillies; Life's Magic, 1985 Distaff)

4 Stronach Stables (Ghostzapper, 2004 Classic; Macho Uno, 2000 Juvenile; Perfect Sting, 2000 Filly and Mare Turf; Awesome Again, 1998 Classic)

3 Godolphin Racing (Fantastic Light, 2001 Turf; Tempera, 2001 Juvenile Fillies; Daylami [Ire], 1999 Turf)

Overbrook Farm (Cat Thief, 1999 Classic; Boston Harbor, 1996 Juvenile; Flanders, 1994 Juvenile Fillies)

Ogden Phipps (My Flag, 1995 Juvenile Fillies; Dancing Spree, 1989 Sprint; Personal Ensign, 1988 Distaff)

Ogden Mills Phipps (Storm Flag Flying, 2002 Juvenile Fillies; Inside Information, 1995 Distaff; Rhythm, 1989 Juvenile)

The Thoroughbred Corp. (Johar, 2003 Turf; Spain, 2000 Distaff; Anees, 1999 Juvenile)

Leading Breeders by Wins

6 Allen E. Paulson (Azeri, 2002 Distaff; Escena, 1998 Distaff; Ajina, 1997 Distaff; Cigar, 1995 Classic; Fraise, 1992 Turf; Eliza, 1992 Juvenile Fillies)

5 Flaxman Holdings/Niarchos Family (Six Perfections [Fr], 2003 Mile; Domedriver [Ire], 2002 Mile; Spinning World, 1997 Mile; Miesque [twice], 1987, '88 Mile)

4 Ogden Phipps (Storm Flag Flying, 2002 Juvenile Fillies; My Flag, 1995 Juvenile Fillies; Dancing Spree, 1989 Sprint; Personal Ensign, 1988 Distaff)

Frank Stronach (Ghostzapper, 2004 Classic; Macho Uno, 2000 Juvenile; Perfect Sting, 2000 Filly and Mare Turf; Awesome Again, 1998 Classic)

3 Aga Khan (Kalanisi [Ire], 2000 Turf; Daylami [Ire], 1999 Turf; Lashkari [GB], 1984 Turf)

Sean Coughlan (High Chaparral [Ire] [twice], 2002, '03 Turf; Ridgewood Pearl [GB], 1995 Mile)

Overbrook Farm (Cat Thief, 1999 Classic; Boston Harbor, 1996 Juvenile; Flanders, 1994 Juvenile Fillies)

Leading Trainers by Wins

17 D. Wayne Lukas (Orientate, 2002 Sprint; Spain, 2000 Distaff; Cat Thief, 1999 Classic; Cash Run, 1999 Juvenile Fillies; Boston Harbor, 1996 Juvenile; Timber Country, 1994 Juvenile Fillies; Steinlen [GB], 1989 Mile; Is It True, 1988 Juvenile; Gulch, 1988 Sprint;

Open Mind, 1988 Juvenile Fillies; Success Express, 1987 Juvenile; Sacahuista, 1987 Distaff; Capote, 1986 Juvenile; Lady's Secret, 1986 Distaff; Life's Magic, 1985 Distaff; Twilight Ridge, 1985 Juvenile Fillies)

8   **Claude R. "Shug" McGaughey III** (Storm Flag Flying, 2002 Juvenile Fillies; Inside Information, 1995 Distaff; My Flag, 1995 Juvenile Fillies; Lure [twice], 1992, '93 Mile; Rhythm, 1989 Juvenile; Dancing Spree, 1989 Sprint; Personal Ensign, 1988 Distaff)

6   **Neil Drysdale** (War Chant, 2000 Mile; Hollywood Wildcat, 1993 Distaff; A.P. Indy, 1992 Classic; Prized, 1989 Turf; Tasso, 1985 Juvenile; Princess Rooney, 1984 Distaff)

    Richard Mandella (Pleasantly Perfect, 2003 Classic; Johar, 2003 Turf; Action This Day, 2003 Juvenile; Halfbridled, 2003 Juvenile Fillies; Kotashaan [Fr], 1993 Turf; Phone Chatter, 1993 Juvenile Fillies)

5   **William I. Mott** (Escena, 1998 Distaff; Ajina, 1997 Distaff; Cigar, 1995 Classic; Fraise, 1992 Turf; Theatrical [Ire], 1987 Turf)

4   **Ron McAnally** (Northern Spur [Ire], 1995 Turf; Paseana [Arg], 1992 Distaff; Bayakoa [Arg] [twice], 1989, '90 Distaff)

3   **Bob Baffert** (Vindication, 2002 Juvenile; Silverbulletday, 1998 Juvenile Fillies; Thirty Slews, 1992 Sprint)

    Pascal Bary (Six Perfections [Fr], 2003 Mile; Domedriver [Ire], 2002 Mile; Miss Alleged, 1991 Turf)

    Francois Boutin (Arazi, 1991 Juvenile; Miesque [twice], 1987, '88 Mile)

    Patrick Byrne (Awesome Again, 1998 Classic; Favorite Trick, 1997 Juvenile; Countess Diana, 1997 Juvenile Fillies)

    Julio Canani (Sweet Catomine, 2004 Juvenile Fillies; Val Royal (Fr), 2001 Mile; Silic (Fr), 1999 Mile)

    Andre Fabre (Banks Hill [GB], 2001 Filly and Mare Turf; In the Wings [GB], 1990 Turf; Arcangues, 1993 Classic)

    Robert Frankel (Ghostzapper, 2004 Classic; Starine [Fr], 2002 Filly and Mare Turf; Squirtle Squirt, 2001 Sprint)

    Aidan P. O'Brien (High Chaparral [Ire] [twice], 2002, '03 Turf; Johannesburg, 2001 Juvenile)

    Sir Michael Stoute (Islington [Ire], 2003 Filly and Mare Turf; Kalanisi [Ire], 2000 Turf; Pilsudski [Ire], 1996 Turf)

Leading Jockeys by Wins

14   **Jerry Bailey** (Six Perfections [Fr], 2003 Mile; Orientate, 2002 Sprint; Squirtle Squirt, 2001 Sprint; Macho Uno, 2000 Juvenile; Perfect Sting, 2000 Filly and Mare Turf; Soaring Softly, 1999 Filly and Mare Turf; Cash Run, 1999 Juvenile Fillies; Answer Lively, 1998 Juvenile; Cigar, 1995 Classic; My Flag, 1995 Juvenile Fillies; Concern, 1994 Classic; Arcangues, 1993 Classic; Black Tie Affair [Ire], 1991 Classic)

12   **Pat Day** (Unbridled Elaine, 2001 Distaff; Cat Thief, 1999 Classic; Awesome Again, 1998 Classic; Favorite Trick, 1997 Juvenile; Timber Country, 1994 Juvenile; Flanders, 1994 Juvenile Fillies; Dance Smartly, 1991 Distaff; Unbridled, 1990 Classic; Theatrical (Ire), 1987 Turf; Epitome,

1987 Juvenile Fillies; Lady's Secret, 1986 Distaff; Wild Again, 1984 Classic)

10   **Mike Smith** (Azeri, 2002 Distaff; Vindication, 2002 Juvenile; Skip Away, 1997 Classic; Ajina, 1997 Distaff; Unbridled's Song, 1995 Juvenile; Inside Information, 1995 Distaff; Tikkanen, 1994 Turf; Cherokee Run, 1994 Sprint; Lure [twice], 1992, '93 Mile)

9   **Chris McCarron** (Tiznow [twice], 2000, '01 Classic; Alphabet Soup, 1996 Classic; Northern Spur [Ire], 1995 Turf; Paseana [Arg], 1992 Distaff; Gilded Time, 1992 Juvenile; Sunday Silence, 1989 Classic; Alysheba, 1988 Classic; Precisionist, 1985 Sprint)

8   **Gary Stevens** (War Chant, 2000 Mile; Anees, 1999 Juvenile; Escena, 1998 Distaff; Silverbulletday, 1998 Juvenile Fillies; Da Hoss, 1996 Mile; One Dreamer, 1994 Distaff; Brocco, 1993 Juvenile; In the Wings [GB], 1990 Turf)

7   **Eddie Delahoussaye** (Hollywood Wildcat, 1993 Distaff; Cardmania, 1993 Sprint; A.P. Indy, 1992 Classic; Thirty Slews, 1992 Sprint; Pleasant Stage, 1991 Juvenile Fillies; Prized, 1989 Turf; Princess Rooney, 1984 Distaff)

    Laffit Pincay Jr. (Phone Chatter, 1993 Juvenile Fillies; Bayakoa [Arg], [twice], 1989, '90 Distaff; Is It True, 1988 Juvenile; Skywalker, 1986 Classic; Capote, 1986 Juvenile; Tasso, 1985 Juvenile)

    Jose Santos (Volponi, 2002 Classic; Chief Bearhart, 1997 Turf; Fly So Free, 1990 Juvenile; Meadow Star, 1990 Juvenile Fillies; Steinlen [GB], 1989 Mile; Success Express, 1987 Juvenile; Manila, 1986 Turf)

    Patrick Valenzuela (Adoration, 2003 Distaff; Fraise, 1992 Turf; Eliza, 1992 Juvenile Fillies; Arazi, 1991 Juvenile; Opening Verse, 1991 Mile; Very Subtle, 1987 Sprint; Brave Raj, 1986 Juvenile Fillies)

6   **Corey Nakatani** (Sweet Catomine, 2004 Juvenile Fillies; Silic [Fr], 1999 Mile; Reraise, 1998 Sprint; Elmhurst, 1997 Sprint; Jewel Princess, 1996 Distaff; Lit de Justice, 1996 Sprint)

    John Velazquez (Ashado, 2004 Distaff; Speightstown, 2004 Sprint; Storm Flag Flying, 2002 Juvenile Fillies; Starine (Fr), 2002 Filly and Mare Turf; Caressing, 2000 Juvenile Fillies; Da Hoss, 1998 Mile)

Leading Sires by Wins

6   **Sadler's Wells** (High Chaparral [Ire] [twice], 2002, '03 Turf; Islington [Ire], 2003 Filly and Mare Turf; Northern Spur [Ire], 1995 Turf; Barathea [Ire], 1994 Mile; In the Wings [GB], 1990 Turf)

5   **Danzig** (War Chant, 2000 Mile; Lure [twice], 1992, '93 Mile; Dance Smartly, 1991 Distaff; Chief's Crown, 1984 Juvenile)

    Kris S. (Action This Day, 2003 Juvenile; Soaring Softly, 1999 Filly and Mare Turf; Brocco, 1993 Juvenile; Hollywood Wildcat, 1993 Distaff; Prized, 1989 Turf)

4   **Gone West** (Da Hoss 1996 and '98 Mile; Johar, 2003 Turf; Speightstown, 2004 Sprint)

    Nureyev (Spinning World, 1997 Mile; Miesque [twice], 1987, '88 Mile; Theatrical [Ire], 1987 Turf)

    Storm Cat (Storm Flag Flying, 2002 Juvenile Fillies; Cat Thief, 1999 Classic; Desert Stormer, 1995 Sprint; Sweet Catomine, 2004 Juvenile Fillies)

3   **Cox's Ridge** (Cardmania, 1993 Sprint; Twilight Ridge, 1985 Juvenile Fillies; Life's Magic, 1985 Distaff)

3 Deputy Minister (Awesome Again, 1999 Classic; Go for Wand, 1989 Juvenile Fillies; Open Mind, 1988 Juvenile Fillies)
Mr. Prospector (Rhythm, 1989 Juvenile; Gulch, 1988 Sprint; Eillo, 1984 Sprint)
Nijinsky II (Royal Academy, 1990 Mile; Dancing Spree, 1989 Sprint; Ferdinand, 1987 Classic)
Seattle Slew (Vindication, 2002 Juvenile; A.P. Indy, 1992 Classic; Capote, 1986 Juvenile)
Strawberry Road (Aus) (Escena, 1998 Distaff; Ajina, 1997 Distaff; Fraise, 1992 Turf)
Unbridled (Halfbridled, 2003 Juvenile Fillies; Anees, 1999 Juvenile; Unbridled's Song, 1995 Juvenile)

Leading Owners by Purses Won

Owner	Starts	Wins	Earnings
Allen E. Paulson	32	6	$7,570,000
Frank Stronach/ Stronach Stables	22	4	7,538,000
Godolphin Racing	31	3	5,004,200
Susan Magnier and Michael Tabor	22	3	4,463,920
Overbrook Farm	28	3	4,387,000
The Thoroughbred Corp.	22	3	4,164,200
Wildenstein Stable	19	2	3,917,000
Ogden Phipps	19	3	3,611,000
Sheikh Mohammed bin Rashid al Maktoum	22	2	3,576,800
Juddmonte Farms	41	1	3,443,620
Sam-Son Farm	19	2	3,018,760
Frances A. Genter	8	2	2,835,000
Eugene V. Klein	18	4	2,701,000
Robert and Beverly Lewis	11	1	2,556,800

Owners With Most Starts

Owner	Starts	Wins	Earnings
Juddmonte Farms	41	1	$3,443,620
Allen E. Paulson	32	6	7,570,000
Godolphin Racing	31	3	5,004,200
Overbrook Farm	28	3	4,387,000
Flaxman Holdings/ S. Niarchos	25	5	3,762,000
The Thoroughbred Corp.	22	3	4,164,200
Susan Magnier and Michael Tabor	22	3	4,463,920
Sheikh Mohammed bin Rashid al Maktoum	22	2	3,576,800
Frank Stronach/ Stronach Stables	22	4	7,538,000
Ogden Phipps	19	3	3,611,000
Wildenstein Stable	19	2	3,917,000
Eugene V. Klein	18	4	2,701,000
Sam-Son Farm	19	2	3,018,760

Owners With Most Starters on a Program

Starters	Owner	Year
8	Godolphin Racing	2001
7	Eugene V. Klein	1987

Leading Breeders by Purses Won

Breeder	Starts	Wins	Earnings
Allen E. Paulson	28	6	$7,854,800
Frank Stronach/ Adena Springs	10	4	6,232,000

Cecilia Straub-Rubens	3	2	5,360,400
Overbrook Farm	26	3	4,618,000
Ogden Phipps	18	4	4,131,000
Flaxman Holdings/ S. Niarchos	25	5	3,762,000
Aga Khan	10	3	3,529,600
Sheikh Mohammed bin Rashid al Maktoum	12	2	3,461,000
Juddmonte Farms	37	1	3,207,200
Oak Cliff Thoroughbreds	3	2	2,700,000
Allez France Stables	9	2	2,332,800
Anna Marie Barnhart	2	1	2,288,000
The Thoroughbred Corp.	5	2	2,260,400
Bertram & Diana Firestone	13	1	2,240,000
Preston Madden	3	1	2,133,000

Breeders With Most Starts

Breeder	Starts	Wins	Earnings
Juddmonte Farms	41	1	$3,267,620
Allen E. Paulson	28	6	7,854,800
Overbrook Farm	25	3	4,618,000
John C. Mabee	20	0	1,555,800
Ogden Phipps	17	3	3,611,000
Sam-Son Farm	15	1	2,051,760
Bertram R. Firestone	13	1	2,240,000
Flaxman Holdings Ltd.	13	3	1,904,800
Ogden Mills Phipps	13	2	1,408,000
Mohammed bin Rashid al Maktoum	12	2	3,461,600
Harry T. Mangurian	11	1	720,000
John Franks	11	1	1,480,000
Kinghaven Farms	10	0	1,285,000
North Ridge Farm	10	1	1,109,000
Peter M. Brant	10	1	880,000
Thomas Mellon Evans	10	1	1,685,000
Joseph Allen	9	0	355,000
Moyglare Stud Farm	9	0	720,000
Wertheimer et Frere	9	2	1,560,000
Arthur I. Appleton	8	0	287,000
Edward P. Evans	8	0	0
Gainsborough Stud Mgmt.	8	0	638,000
George Strawbridge	8	1	1,634,000
H. H. Aga Khan	8	2	2,240,000
W. S. Farish and W. S. Kilroy	8	1	2,085,400

Leading Trainers by Purses Won

Trainer	Starts	Wins	Earnings
D. Wayne Lukas	143	17	$19,033,900
Bobby Frankel	63	3	9,679,820
William I. Mott	41	5	8,542,960
Claude R. McGaughey III	47	8	7,653,560
Richard Mandella	27	6	7,116,960
Andre Fabre	36	3	6,435,400
Neil Drysdale	31	6	6,095,840
Aidan O'Brien	30	3	5,551,020
Bob Baffert	41	3	5,349,800
Jay Robbins	6	2	4,938,400
Charles Whittingham	24	2	4,298,000
Saeed bin Suroor	22	2	4,099,800
David Hofmans	10	2	3,731,040
Sir Michael Stoute	24	3	3,724,600
Patrick Byrne	7	3	3,718,000
Jack Van Berg	15	2	3,611,784
Ron McAnally	27	4	3,518,000
Nick Zito	23	1	3,336,120

Trainers With Most Starts

Trainer	Starts	Wins	Earnings
D. Wayne Lukas	143	17	$19,033,900
Bobby Frankel	63	3	9,679,820
Claude R. McGaughey III	47	8	7,653,560
Bob Baffert	41	3	5,349,800
William I. Mott	41	5	8,542,960
Andre Fabre	36	3	6,435,400
Neil Drysdale	31	6	6,095,840
Aidan O'Brien	30	3	5,551,020
Richard Mandella	27	6	7,116,960
Ron McAnally	27	4	3,518,000
Flint S. Schulhofer	26	2	2,841,400

Trainers With Multiple Victories on Breeders' Cup Program

4 **Richard Mandella** (2003 Classic, Turf, Juvenile, Juvenile Fillies)

3 **D. Wayne Lukas** (1988 Juvenile, Juvenile Fillies, Sprint)

2 **Patrick Byrne** (1998 Juvenile, Juvenile Fillies); **D. Wayne Lukas** (five times) (1985 Distaff, Juvenile Fillies; 1986 Distaff, Juvenile; 1987 Distaff, Juvenile; 1994 Juvenile, Juvenile Fillies; 1999 Classic, Juvenile Fillies); **Richard Mandella** (1993 Turf, Juvenile Fillies); **C. R. "Shug" McGaughey III** (1989 Juvenile, Sprint); **Todd Pletcher** (2004 Distaff, Sprint)

Trainers With Most Starters on a Program

Starters	Trainer	Year
14	D. Wayne Lukas	1987
12	D. Wayne Lukas	1988
11	D. Wayne Lukas	1989
10	D. Wayne Lukas	1996
	D. Wayne Lukas	1985

Leading Jockeys by Purses Won

Jockey	Mounts	Wins	Earnings
Pat Day	117	12	$23,033,360
Jerry Bailey	96	14	19,589,340
Chris McCarron	101	9	17,669,600
Gary Stevens	93	8	13,441,160
Mike Smith	52	10	10,505,760
Jose Santos	59	7	8,008,800
Corey Nakatani	56	6	7,905,280
Eddie Delahoussaye	68	7	7,775,000
Alex Solis	47	3	6,827,660
Laffit Pincay Jr.	61	7	6,811,000
John Velazquez	47	6	6,361,800
Patrick Valenzuela	46	7	6,274,280
Lanfranco Dettori	34	4	6,159,160
Angel Cordero Jr.	48	4	6,020,000
Michael Kinane	25	3	4,590,920
Kent Desormeaux	50	2	4,773,200

Jockeys With Multiple Victories on Breeders' Cup Program

2 **Jerry Bailey** (four times) (1995 Classic, Juvenile Fillies; 1996 Juvenile, Mile; 1999 Filly and Mare Turf, Juvenile Fillies; 2000 Juvenile, Filly and Mare Turf); **Jorge Chavez** (1999 Distaff, Sprint); **Angel Cordero Jr.** (1988 Juvenile Fillies, Sprint); **Pat Day** (twice) (1987 Turf, Juvenile Fillies; 1994 Juvenile, Juvenile Fillies); **Eddie Delahoussaye** (twice) (1992 Classic, Sprint; 1993 Distaff, Sprint); **Chris McCarron** (1992 Distaff, Juvenile); **Corey Nakatani** (1996 Distaff, Sprint); **Laffit Pincay Jr.** (1986 Classic, Juvenile); **Jose Santos** (1990 Juvenile, Juvenile Fillies); **Mike Smith** (four times) (1994 Turf, Sprint; 1995 Distaff, Juvenile; 1997 Classic, Distaff; 2002 Distaff, Juvenile); **Alex Solis** (2003 Classic, Turf); **Gary Stevens** (1998 Distaff, Juvenile Fillies); **Patrick Valenzuela** (twice) (1991 Juvenile, Mile; 1992 Turf, Juvenile Fillies); **Jorge Velasquez** (1985 Classic, Juvenile Fillies); **John Velazquez** (twice) (2002 Filly and Mare Turf, Juvenile Fillies; 2004 Distaff, Sprint)

Jockeys With Most Mounts in Breeders' Cup

Jockey	Mounts	Wins	Earnings
Pat Day	117	12	$23,033,360
Chris McCarron	101	9	17,669,600
Jerry Bailey	96	14	19,589,340
Gary Stevens	93	8	13,441,160
Eddie Delahoussaye	68	7	7,775,000
Laffit Pincay Jr.	61	7	6,811,000
Jose Santos	59	7	8,008,800
Corey Nakatani	56	6	7,905,280
Mike Smith	52	10	10,505,760
Kent Desormeaux	50	2	4,773,200
Angel Cordero Jr.	48	4	6,020,000
Alex Solis	47	3	6,827,660
John Velazquez	47	6	6,361,800
Patrick Valenzuela	46	7	6,274,280

Jockeys with Most Mounts on a Program

Mounts	Jockey	Year
8	Corey Nakatani	2004
	Edgar Prado	2004
	John Velazquez	2004
	John Velazquez	2003
	John Velazquez	2002
	Jerry Bailey	2001
	Jerry Bailey	2000
	Jerry Bailey	1999

Leading Sires by Purses Won

Sire	Starts	Wins	Earnings
Storm Cat	37	4	$7,136,300
Sadler's Wells	38	6	6,982,900
Deputy Minister	25	3	5,370,560
Cee's Tizzy	3	2	5,360,400
Danzig	42	5	4,657,320
Seattle Slew	26	3	4,655,400
Pleasant Colony	20	2	4,541,320
Alydar	19	1	4,495,000
Kris S.	13	5	3,721,900
Cozzene	9	2	3,468,000
Mr. Prospector	42	3	3,421,680
Nureyev	23	4	3,408,400
Fappiano	15	2	3,386,000
Nijinsky II	12	3	3,283,000

Winners by Country and State Bred

Country	Starts	Wins
Ireland	130	13
Great Britain	109	8
France	44	5
Argentina	12	3
Canada	69	3

State	Starts	Wins
Kentucky	1,019	93
Florida	187	18
Maryland	24	3
Pennsylvania	19	3
California	57	2
Illinois	8	1
New Jersey	10	1
Oklahoma	3	1

Breeders' Cup Race Winners by Total Earnings

Horse	Breeders' Cup Victory	Total Earnings
Cigar	1995 Classic	$9,999,815
Skip Away	1997 Classic	9,616,360
Fantastic Light	2001 Turf	8,486,957
Pleasantly Perfect	2003 Classic	7,789,880
Alysheba	1988 Classic	6,679,242
Tiznow	2000, '01 Classic	6,427,830
High Chaparral (Ire)	2002, '03 Turf	5,331,231
Sunday Silence	1989 Classic	4,968,554
Daylami (Ire)	1999 Turf	4,614,762
Unbridled	1990 Classic	4,489,475
Awesome Again	1998 Classic	4,374,590
Pilsudski (Ire)	1996 Turf	4,080,297

Horses With Highest Earnings in Breeders' Cup Races

Horse	Year(s) Started	Earnings
Tiznow	2000, '01	$4,560,400
Awesome Again	1998	2,662,400
Pleasantly Perfect	2003, '04	2,520,000
Skip Away	1997, '98	2,288,000
Cat Thief	1998, '99, 2000	2,200,000
Alysheba	1986, '87, '88	2,080,000
Alphabet Soup	1996	2,080,000
Volponi	2002, '03	2,080,000
Cigar	1995, '96	2,080,000
High Chaparral (Ire)	2002, '03	2,021,600
Spain	1999, 2000, '01	1,755,200
Unbridled	1990, '91	1,710,000

Winning Favorites by Race

Race	Winning Favorites	Race	Winning Favorites
Distaff	47.6%	Filly and Mare Turf	50%
Juvenile Fillies	52.4%	Juvenile	38.1%
Mile	33.3%	Turf	38.1%
Sprint	23.8%	Classic	28.6%

Favored Winners and Average Odds by Year

Year	Site	Winning Favorites	Average Winning Odds
2004	Lone Star Park	50%	10.51-to-1
2003	Santa Anita Park	25%	14.90-to-1
2002	Arlington Park	50%	11.62-to-1
2001	Belmont Park	12.5%	8.63-to-1
2000	Churchill Downs	25%	16.65-to-1
1999	Gulfstream Park	25%	12.69-to-1
1998	Churchill Downs	28.6%	4.31-to-1
1997	Hollywood Park	71.4%	4.34-to-1
1996	Woodbine	28.6%	7.48-to-1
1995	Belmont Park	42.9%	4.46-to-1
1994	Churchill Downs	42.9%	12.06-to-1
1993	Santa Anita Park	42.9%	21.19-to-1
1992	Gulfstream Park	42.9%	6.59-to-1
1991	Churchill Downs	28.6%	15.36-to-1
1990	Belmont Park	57.1%	3.74-to-1
1989	Gulfstream Park	28.6%	5.00-to-1
1988	Churchill Downs	42.9%	4.59-to-1
1987	Hollywood Park	28.6%	12.74-to-1
1986	Santa Anita Park	28.6%	10.36-to-1
1985	Aqueduct	42.9%	3.31-to-1
1984	Hollywood Park	57.1%	15.98-to-1

Largest Winning Margins

Year	Winner	Race	Margin
1995	Inside Information	Distaff	13½
1997	Countess Diana	Juvenile Fillies	8½
1984	Princess Rooney	Distaff	7
1990	Bayakoa (Arg)	Distaff	6¾
2002	Volponi	Classic	6½
1985	Life's Magic	Distaff	6¼
1997	Skip Away	Classic	6

Smallest Winning Margins

Year	Winner	Race	Margin
2003	High Chaparral (Ire), Johar	Turf	DH
2001	Tiznow	Classic	nose
2000	Macho Uno	Juvenile	nose
1998	Escena	Distaff	nose
1996	Alphabet Soup	Classic	nose
1993	Hollywood Wildcat	Distaff	nose
1992	Fraise	Turf	nose
1988	Personal Ensign	Distaff	nose
1987	Ferdinand	Classic	nose
1987	Epitome	Juvenile Fillies	nose
1985	Tasso	Juvenile	nose
1984	Eillo	Sprint	nose

Nominations, Pre-Entries, Entries, and Starters by Year

Year	Foal Nominations	Pre-Entries	Entries	Starters
2004	15,850	101	93	91
2003	14,927	101	91	90
2002	13,846	104	92	90
2001	15,020	109	98	94
2000	15,760	135	105	103
1999	15,191	128	102	101
1998	14,081	117	85	82
1997	12,751	94	77	76
1996	11,971	90	85	82
1995	10,543	101	84	81
1994	9,738	126	94	91
1993	9,564	103	82	81
1992	9,392	112	92	91

Year	Foal Nominations	Pre-Entries	Entries	Starters
1991	10,056	116	91	90
1990	11,003	110	91	83
1989	11,734	101	89	81
1988	11,276	87	79	75
1987	12,183	106	91	84
1986	11,494	90	79	76
1985	10,907	110	90	82
1984	10,034	77	69	68
1983	7,839			
1982	9,260			

Pre-entries are number of individual horses made eligible. Owners may pre-enter a horse in up to two races.

Average Field Sizes by Race

Race	Average Field	Most Starters	Fewest Starters
Distaff	8.8	14	6
Juvenile Fillies	11.5	14	8
Mile	13.2	14	10
Sprint	13.1	14	9
Filly and Mare Turf	12.7	14	12
Juvenile	11.9	14	8
Turf	11.7	14	8
Classic	11.5	14	8

Average Field Sizes by Year

Year	Site	Starters	Avg. Field
2004	Lone Star Park	91	11.38
2003	Santa Anita Park	90	11.25
2002	Arlington Park	90	11.25
2001	Belmont Park	94	11.75
2000	Churchill Downs	103	12.88
1999	Gulfstream Park	101	12.63
1998	Churchill Downs	82	11.71
1997	Hollywood Park	76	10.86
1996	Woodbine	82	11.71
1995	Belmont Park	81	11.57
1994	Churchill Downs	91	13.00
1993	Santa Anita Park	81	11.57
1992	Gulfstream Park	91	13.00
1991	Churchill Downs	90	12.86
1990	Belmont Park	83	11.86
1989	Gulfstream Park	81	11.57
1988	Churchill Downs	75	10.71
1987	Hollywood Park	84	12.00
1986	Santa Anita Park	76	10.86
1985	Aqueduct	82	11.71
1984	Hollywood Park	68	9.71

Most Pre-Entries for a Breeders' Cup Race

Year	Race	Pre-Entries
2000	Mile	29
1998	Mile	27
1999	Mile	25
1994	Sprint	25
1994	Turf	24
2002	Mile	24
1995	Mile	24
1998	Sprint	24

Largest Breeders' Cup On-Track Attendance

Year	Site	On-Track Attendance
1998	Churchill Downs	80,452
2000	Churchill Downs	76,043
1994	Churchill Downs	71,671
1988	Churchill Downs	71,237
1986	Santa Anita Park	69,155
1991	Churchill Downs	66,204

Smallest Breeders' Cup On-Track Attendance

Year	Site	On-Track Attendance
1995	Belmont Park	37,246
1996	Woodbine	42,243
1985	Aqueduct	42,568
1999	Gulfstream Park	45,124
1992	Gulfstream Park	45,415
2002	Arlington Park	46,118

Largest Breeders' Cup On-Track Wagering

Year	Site	On-Track Wagering
2003	Santa Anita Park	$13,678,118
2000	Churchill Downs	13,579,798
1998	Churchill Downs	13,544,859
1986	Santa Anita Park	12,510,109
2002	Arlington Park	12,143,114
1993	Santa Anita Park	12,142,750

Smallest Breeders' Cup On-Track Betting

Year	Site	On-Track Wagering
1996	Woodbine	$5,925,469
1985	Aqueduct	7,200,175
1995	Belmont Park	7,590,332
1997	Hollywood Park	8,191,459
1984	Hollywood Park	8,443,070
1990	Belmont Park	9,107,270

Shortest-Priced Winners

Year	Horse	Race	Odds
1990	Meadow Star	Juvenile Fillies	0.20-to-1
1994	Flanders	Juvenile Fillies	0.40-to-1*
1985	Life's Magic	Distaff	0.40-to-1*
1988	Personal Ensign	Distaff	0.50-to-1
1986	Lady's Secret	Distaff	0.50-to-1*
1991	Dance Smartly	Distaff	0.50-to-1*

* Part of entry

Longest-Priced Winners

Year	Horse	Race	Odds
1993	Arcangues	Classic	133.60-to-1
2000	Spain	Distaff	55.90-to-1
1984	Lashkari (GB)	Turf	53.40-to-1
1994	One Dreamer	Distaff	47.10-to-1
2000	Caressing	Juvenile Fillies	47.00-to-1
2002	Volponi	Classic	43.50-to-1
1991	Miss Alleged	Turf	42.10-to-1
2003	Adoration	Distaff	40.70-to-1
1986	Last Tycoon (Ire)	Mile	35.90-to-1
1999	Cash Run	Juvenile Fillies	32.50-to-1

History of Breeders' Cup Races
Breeders' Cup Classic

America's classic distance is 1¼ miles on dirt, and the Breeders' Cup Classic (G1) has offered some classic, spine-tingling contests. The race has been the kingmaker among the eight Breeders' Cup races, producing ten Horses of the Year in its first 21 runnings.

Although the year's best horse does not always win the Breeders' Cup Classic, the race has been extremely competitive, with eight of the races decided by less than one length. The only two runaway victories were Volponi's 6½-length upset in the 2002 Classic at Arlington Park and Skip Trial's six-length triumph at Hollywood Park in 1997.

The series began with a classic finish in the 1984 Breeders' Cup at Hollywood Park, with three horses charging together through the final furlong. Longshot supplemental entry Wild Again set the pace and prevailed by a neck on the inside. Gate Dancer bore in on favorite Slew o' Gold nearing the wire, and jockey Angel Cordero Jr. restrained Slew o' Gold through the final yards to protect the eventual champion older male. Gate Dancer finished second, but was disqualified to third, moving up Slew o' Gold to second.

The race did not yield its first Horse of the Year until 1987, when the Breeders' Cup returned to Hollywood and '86 Kentucky Derby (G1) winner Ferdinand met '87 Derby victor Alysheba. They hooked up inside the sixteenth pole and fought to the wire, with even-money favorite Ferdinand prevailing by a nose under jockey Bill Shoemaker. Ferdinand was voted Horse of the Year and champion older male, while Alysheba was honored as champion three-year-old male. The following year, Alysheba won the Classic in near darkness at Churchill Downs's first Breeders' Cup and was voted Horse of the Year.

The 1989 Breeders' Cup Classic reunited Triple Crown rivals Sunday Silence and Easy Goer, and they battled through deep stretch as they had in the Derby and Preakness Stakes (G1) that year. Sunday Silence, who had won both the Derby and Preakness, proved best and won by a neck over Belmont Stakes (G1) victor Easy Goer. Sunday Silence was voted champion three-year-old male and Horse of the Year. After a truncated four-year-old campaign, Sunday Silence was sold for stud duty in Japan, where he became that country's all-time leading sire.

Tiznow, the race's only two-time winner, provided two scintillating finishes, holding off Giant's Causeway in 2000 by a neck at Churchill and then coming back courageously to best Sakhee by a nose in '01 at Belmont Park.

Breeders' Cup Classic

Grade 1, $4-million, three-year-olds and up, 1¼ miles, dirt. Run October 30, 2004, at Lone Star Park with gross value of $3,668,000. First run in 1984. Weights: Northern Hemisphere three-year-olds, 121 pounds; older, 126 pounds. Southern Hemisphere three-year-olds, 116 pounds; older, 126 pounds. Fillies and mares allowed three pounds.

Year	Winner	Jockey	Second	Third	Site	Time	Cond.	1st Purse
2004	**Ghostzapper**, 4	J. Castellano	Roses in May	Pleasantly Perfect	LS	**1:59.02**	ft	$2,080,000
2003	**Pleasantly Perfect**, 5	A. Solis	Medaglia d'Oro	Dynever	SA	1:59.88	ft	2,080,000
2002	**Volponi**, 4	J. Santos	Medaglia d'Oro	Milwaukee Brew	AP	2:01.39	ft	2,080,000
2001	**Tiznow**, 4	C. McCarron	Sakhee	Albert the Great	Bel	2:00.62	ft	2,080,000
2000	**Tiznow**, 3	C. McCarron	Giant's Causeway	Captain Steve	CD	2:00.75	ft	2,480,400
1999	**Cat Thief**, 3	P. Day	Budroyale	Golden Missile	GP	1:59.52	ft	2,080,000
1998	**Awesome Again**, 4	P. Day	Silver Charm	Swain (Ire)	CD	2:02.16	ft	**2,662,400**
1997	**Skip Away**, 4	M. Smith	Deputy Commander	Dowty	Hol	1:59.16	ft	2,288,000
1996	**Alphabet Soup**, 5	C. McCarron	Louis Quatorze	Cigar	WO	2:01.00	ft	2,080,000
1995	**Cigar**, 5	J. Bailey	L'Carriere	Unaccounted For	Bel	1:59.58	my	1,560,000
1994	**Concern**, 3	J. Bailey	Tabasco Cat	Dramatic Gold	CD	2:02.41	ft	1,560,000
1993	**Arcangues**, 5	J. Bailey	Bertrando	Kissin Kris	SA	2:00.83	ft	1,560,000
1992	**A.P. Indy**, 3	E. Delahoussaye	Pleasant Tap	Jolypha	GP	2:00.20	ft	1,560,000
1991	**Black Tie Affair (Ire)**, 5	J. Bailey	Twilight Agenda	Unbridled	CD	2:02.95	ft	1,560,000
1990	**Unbridled**, 3	P. Day	Ibn Bey (GB)	Thirty Six Red	Bel	2:02 1/5	ft	1,350,000
1989	**Sunday Silence**, 3	C. McCarron	Easy Goer	Blushing John	GP	2:00 1/5	ft	1,350,000
1988	**Alysheba**, 4	C. McCarron	Seeking the Gold	Waquoit	CD	2:04 4/5	my	1,350,000
1987	**Ferdinand**, 4	W. Shoemaker	Alysheba	Judge Angelucci	Hol	2:01 2/5	ft	1,350,000
1986	**Skywalker**, 4	L. Pincay Jr.	Turkoman	Precisionist	SA	2:00 2/5	ft	1,350,000
1985	**Proud Truth**, 3	J. Velasquez	Gate Dancer	Turkoman	Aqu	2:00 4/5	ft	1,350,000
1984	**Wild Again**, 4	P. Day	Slew o' Gold	Gate Dancer	Hol	2:03 2/5	ft	1,350,000

1997: Skip Away supplemental entry, Whiskey Wisdom disqualified from third to fourth; 1984: Gate Dancer disqualified from second to third

Three-year-olds have done well in the Classic, winning seven of the first 21 runnings, and two three-year-old winners have become successful sires. The 1990 Classic winner, Derby victor Unbridled, sired winners of the Kentucky Derby and Preakness, as well as two Breeders' Cup Juvenile (G1) victors and a Juvenile Fillies (G1) winner. A.P. Indy, the 1992 winner and Horse of the Year, regularly ranks among North America's leading sires and sired 2001 Juvenile Fillies (G1) winner Tempera. Tiznow was a three-year-old when he won in 2000 and was voted Horse of the Year. Awesome Again, winner of the 1998 Classic, became the first Classic winner to sire a Classic winner when his son Ghostzapper won the 2004 edition.

While the Classic has yielded some classic contests, it also has produced its share of puzzles and one especially bizarre finish. Arcangues won in 1993 at 133.60-to-1, the longest price for any Breeders' Cup winner, and Volponi won at 43.50-to-1 in 2002. The unusual finish came in the 1998 Classic, which featured the best field ever assembled for a Breeders' Cup race. Silver Charm took the lead in the stretch but began to bear out in the final furlong. Swain (Ire), a leading European contender, followed Silver Charm to the far outside under left-handed whipping by his jockey, Frankie Dettori. Awesome Again dashed through the hole they created and won by three-quarters of a length over Silver Charm. Skip Away, the 1.90-to-1 favorite who finished sixth, was voted champion older male and Horse of the Year.

Ghostzapper won the 2004 Classic at Lone Star Park, in 1:59.02, the fastest time ever for the Classic.

Owners by Wins

2 Stronach Stables (Awesome Again, Ghostzapper)
1 Amherst Stable and Spruce Pond Stable (Volponi), Black Chip Stable (Wild Again), Cee's Stable (Tiznow), Michael Cooper and Cecilia Straub-Rubens (Tiznow), Darby Dan Farm (Proud Truth), Diamond A Racing (Pleasantly Perfect), William S. Farish, Harold Goodman, William S. Kilroy, and Tomonori Tsurumaki (A.P. Indy), Frances Genter (Unbridled), Arthur Hancock III, Ernest Gaillard, and Charlie Whittingham (Sunday Silence), Carolyn Hine (Skip Away), Elizabeth Keck (Ferdinand), Robert Meyerhoff (Concern), Oak Cliff Stable (Skywalker), Overbrook Farm (Cat Thief), Allen E. Paulson (Cigar), Ridder Thoroughbred Stable (Alphabet Soup), Dorothy and Pamela Scharbauer (Alysheba), Jeffrey Sullivan (Black Tie Affair [Ire]), Daniel Wildenstein (Arcangues)

Breeders by Wins

2 Oak Cliff Thoroughbreds (Skywalker, Sunday Silence), Cecilia Straub-Rubens (Tiznow [twice]), Frank Stronach/Adena Springs (Ghostzapper, Awesome Again)
1 Allez France Stables (Arcangues), Amherst

Stable (Volponi), **Anna Marie Barnhart** (Skip Away), **Clovelly Farms** (Pleasantly Perfect), **William S. Farish and William S. Kilroy** (A.P. Indy), **Mrs. John W. Galbreath** (Proud Truth), **Howard B. Keck** (Ferdinand), **W. Paul Little** (Wild Again), **Preston Madden** (Alysheba), **Robert Meyerhoff** (Concern), **Overbrook Farm** (Cat Thief), **Allen E. Paulson** (Cigar), **Stephen Peskoff** (Black Tie Affair [Ire]), **Southeast Associates** (Alphabet Soup), **Tartan Farms** (Unbridled)

Trainers by Wins

2 Jay Robbins (Tiznow [twice]), Charlie Whittingham (Ferdinand, Sunday Silence)
1 Patrick Byrne (Awesome Again), Neil Drysdale (A.P. Indy), Andre Fabre (Arcangues), Bobby Frankel (Ghostzapper), Hubert "Sonny" Hine (Skip Away), P. G. Johnson (Volponi), David Hofmans (Alphabet Soup), D. Wayne Lukas (Cat Thief), Richard Mandella (Pleasantly Perfect), Bill Mott (Cigar), Carl Nafzger (Unbridled), Ernie Poulos (Black Tie Affair [Ire]), Richard Small (Concern), Vincent Timphony (Wild Again), Jack Van Berg (Alysheba), John Veitch (Proud Truth), Mike Whittingham (Skywalker)

Jockeys by Wins

5 Chris McCarron (Alphabet Soup, Alysheba, Sunday Silence, Tiznow [twice])
4 Jerry Bailey (Arcangues, Black Tie Affair [Ire], Cigar, Concern), Pat Day (Awesome Again, Cat Thief, Unbridled, Wild Again)
1 Javier Castellano (Ghostzapper), Eddie Delahoussaye (A.P. Indy), Laffit Pincay Jr. (Skywalker), Jose Santos (Volponi), Bill Shoemaker (Ferdinand), Mike Smith (Skip Away), Alex Solis (Pleasantly Perfect), Jorge Velasquez (Proud Truth)

Sires by Wins

2 Cee's Tizzy (Tiznow [twice])
1 Alydar (Alysheba), Awesome Again (Ghostzapper), Broad Brush (Concern), Cozzene (Alphabet Soup), Cryptoclearance (Volponi), Deputy Minister (Awesome Again), Fappiano (Unbridled), Graustark (Proud Truth), Halo (Sunday Silence), Icecapade (Wild Again), Miswaki (Black Tie Affair [Ire]), Nijinsky II (Ferdinand), Palace Music (Cigar), Pleasant Colony (Pleasantly Perfect), Relaunch (Skywalker), Sagace (Arcangues), Seattle Slew (A.P. Indy), Skip Trial (Skip Away), Storm Cat (Cat Thief)

Winners by Place Where Bred

Locality	Winners	Locality	Winners
Kentucky	12	Pennsylvania	1
Maryland	2	Canada	1
California	2	Ireland	1
Florida	2		

Supplemental Entries

Year	Runner	Fee	Finish	Earnings
2001	Tiznow	(credit)	1	$2,080,000
	Gander	(credit)	9	0
2000	Tiznow	$360,000	1	2,480,400

Year	Runner	Fee	Finish	Earnings
	Captain Steve	270,000†	3	562,800
	Gander	360,000	9	0
1998	Silver Charm	480,000	2	1,024,000
	Skip Pal	(credit)	6	0
	Gentlemen (Arg)	800,000	10	0
1997	**Skip Away**	480,000	1	2,288,000
1994	Best Pal	360,000	5	60,000
	Bertrando	360,000	6	0
1993	Bertrando	360,000	2	600,000
	Best Pal	360,000	10	0
1988	Waquoit	360,000	3	324,000
	Cutlass Reality	360,000	7	0
1985	Vanlandingham	360,000	7	0
1984	**Wild Again**	360,000	1	1,350,000

† incl. credit from 1999

Eclipse Award Winners from Race

Year	Runner	Finish	Title
2004	**Ghostzapper**	1	HOY, older male
	Azeri	5	Older female
2003	Funny Cide	9	3yo male
2002	War Emblem	8	3yo male
2001	**Tiznow**	1	Older male
2000	**Tiznow**	1	HOY, 3yo male
	Lemon Drop Kid	5	Older male
1998	Skip Away	6	HOY, older male
1997	**Skip Away**	1	Older male
1996	Cigar	3	HOY, older male
1995	**Cigar**	1	HOY, older male
1993	Bertrando	2	Older male
1992	**A.P. Indy**	1	HOY, 3yo male
1991	**Black Tie Affair (Ire)**	1	HOY, older male
1990	**Unbridled**	1	3yo male
1989	**Sunday Silence**	1	HOY, 3yo male
	Blushing John	3	Older male
1988	**Alysheba**	1	HOY, older male
1987	**Ferdinand**	1	HOY, older male
	Alysheba	2	3yo male
1986	Turkoman	2	Older male
1985	Vanlandingham	7	Older male
1984	Slew o' Gold	2	Older male

HOY = Horse of the Year

Largest Winning Margins

Year	Winner	Margin
2002	Volponi	6½
1997	Skip Away	6
2004	Ghostzapper	3
1995	Cigar	2½
1993	Arcangues	2
1992	A.P. Indy	2

Smallest Winning Margins

Year	Winner	Margin
2001	Tiznow	nose
1996	Alphabet Soup	nose
1987	Ferdinand	nose
1985	Proud Truth	head
1984	Wild Again	head
2000	Tiznow	neck
1994	Concern	neck
1989	Sunday Silence	neck

Shortest-Priced Winners

Year	Winner	Odds
1995	Cigar	0.70-to-1
1987	Ferdinand	1.00-to-1

Year	Horse	Odds
1988	Alysheba	1.50-to-1
1997	Skip Away	1.80-to-1

Longest-Priced Winners

Year	Winner	Odds
1993	Arcangues	133.60-to-1
2002	Volponi	43.50-to-1
1984	Wild Again	31.30-to-1
1996	Alphabet Soup	19.85-to-1
1999	Cat Thief	19.60-to-1

Fastest Winners

Year	Winner	Track	Time	Cond.
2004	Ghostzapper	LS	1:59.02	fast
1997	Skip Away	Hol	1:59.16	fast
1999	Cat Thief	GP	1:59.52	fast
1995	Cigar	Bel	1:59.58	muddy
2003	Pleasantly Perfect	SA	1:59.88	fast
1992	A.P. Indy	GP	2:00.20	fast
1989	Sunday Silence	GP	2:00⅕	fast

Slowest Winners

Year	Winner	Track	Time	Cond.
1988	Alysheba	CD	2:04⅘	muddy
1984	Wild Again	Hol	2:03⅗	fast
1991	Black Tie Affair (Ire)	CD	2:02.95	fast
1994	Concern	CD	2:02.41	fast

Most Starters

Year	Track	Starters
1999	Gulfstream Park	14
1994	Churchill Downs	14
1992	Gulfstream Park	14
1990	Belmont Park	14

Fewest Starters

Year	Track	Starters
1989	Gulfstream Park	8
1985	Aqueduct	8
1984	Hollywood Park	8
1997	Hollywood Park	9
1988	Churchill Downs	9

Winning Post Positions

Post	Starters	Winners	Percent
1	21	2	9.5%
2	21	3	14.3%
3	21	2	9.5%
4	21	1	4.8%
5	21	1	4.8%
6	21	3	14.3%
7	21	0	0.0%
8	21	2	9.5%
9	18	0	0.0%
10	16	2	12.5%
11	14	1	7.1%
12	11	3	27.3%
13	9	0	0.0%
14	4	1	25.0%

Changes in Classic

The only change in the Breeders' Cup Classic was an increase in the purse from $3-million to $4-million beginning in 1996.

Breeders' Cup Turf

The race conditions of the Breeders' Cup Turf (G1), 1½ miles on grass at weight for age, constitute the classic standard of European racing, and as a result, overseas runners have won a majority of the $2-million contests. But they have not been dominant, probably because running in late October or early November—sometimes in tropical conditions—is not part of the European schedule, which traditionally culminates for top horses in early October with the running of the Prix de l'Arc de Triomphe (Fr-G1).

In fact, American owners and trainers have fielded some outstanding grass runners, and they have defeated top-level European competitors over the years. At times, lesser American runners have prevailed because the Europeans were past their best form or did not adapt well to warm weather at Breeders' Cup sites.

Because of its importance on the world racing calendar, the Breeders' Cup Turf has become the definitive North American championship race. In every year except 1984 (John Henry's last championship season) and '89 (when the male title went to Breeders' Cup Mile [G1] winner Steinlen [GB]), a North American turf champion has come out of the Turf.

The 2003 edition featured the first dead heat in any Breeders' Cup race when High Chaparral (Ire) and Johar reached the finish line together. High Chaparral was the first dual Turf winner.

A decade earlier, American-trained Kotashaan (Fr) dominated grass racing in Southern California and scored a half-length victory over fellow Californian Bien Bien in the Turf. With a weak handicap division that year and no dominant three-year-old coming out of the Triple Crown series, Kotashaan was voted both champion turf male and Horse of the Year. He remains the only Turf winner to earn the top North American honor.

Early in the Turf's history, European runners gave indications they would dominate the race. Unheralded Lashkari (GB) won the inaugural running at Hollywood Park in 1984 at 53.40-to-1, the longest winning odds in the race's history. Lashkari, who never duplicated that effort, was bred and owned by the Aga Khan, who also bred back-to-back Turf winners Daylami (Ire), who was leased to Godolphin Racing, and Kalanisi (Ire), also owned by the Aga Khan. In 2001, Godolphin's Fantastic Light won at 7-to-5.

Pebbles (GB) was supplemented to the race in 1985 and scored a hard-fought victory over Strawberry Road (Aus). The Turf in the following year at Santa Anita Park was expected to showcase Dancing Brave, the Arc winner whose only career defeat was a second-place finish in the Epsom Derby (Eng-G1). But Dancing Brave was clearly over the top and tired to finish fourth as Manila stormed to a neck victory over Theatrical (Ire), who would win the Turf the following year.

Breeders' Cup Turf

Grade 1, $2-million, three-year-olds and up, 1½ miles, turf. Run October 30, 2004, at Lone Star Park with gross value $1,834,000. First run in 1984. Weights: Northern Hemisphere three-year-olds, 121 pounds; older, 126 pounds; Southern Hemisphere three-year-olds, 116 pounds; older, 125 pounds. Fillies and mares allowed three pounds.

Year	Winner	Jockey	Second	Third	Site	Time	Cond.	1st Purse
2004	**Better Talk Now**, 5	R. Dominguez	Kitten's Joy	Powerscourt (GB)	LS	2:29.70	yl	$1,040,000
2003	(DH) **High Chaparral**, 4	M. Kinane		Falbrav (Ire)	SA	2:24.24	fm	763,200
	(DH) **Johar**, 4	A. Solis						763,200
2002	**High Chaparral (Ire)**, 3	M. Kinane	With Anticipation	Falcon Flight (Fr)	AP	2:30.14	yl	1,258,400
2001	**Fantastic Light**, 5	L. Dettori	Milan (GB)	Timboroa (GB)	Bel	2:24.36	fm	1,112,800
2000	**Kalinisi (Ire)**, 4	J. Murtagh	Quiet Resolve	John's Call	CD	2:26.96	fm	**1,289,600**
1999	**Daylami (Ire)**, 5	L. Dettori	Royal Anthem	Buck's Boy	GP	2:24.73	gd	1,040,000
1998	**Buck's Boy**, 5	S. Sellers	Yagli	Dushyantor	CD	2:28.74	fm	1,040,000
1997	**Chief Bearhart**, 4	J. Santos	Borgia (Ger)	Flag Down	Hol	**2:23.92**	fm	1,040,000
1996	**Pilsudski (Ire)**, 4	W. Swinburn	Singspiel (Ire)	Swain (Ire)	WO	2:30.20	gd	1,040,000
1995	**Northern Spur (Ire)**, 4	C. McCarron	Freedom Cry (GB)	Carnegie (Ire)	Bel	2:42.07	sf	1,040,000
1994	**Tikkanen**, 3	M. Smith	Hatoof	Paradise Creek	CD	2:26.50	fm	1,040,000
1993	**Kotashaan (Fr)**, 5	K. Desormeaux	Bien Bien	Luazur (Fr)	SA	2:25.16	fm	1,040,000
1992	**Fraise**, 4	P. Valenzuela	Sky Classic	Quest for Fame (GB)	GP	2:24.08	fm	1,040,000
1991	**Miss Alleged**, f, 4	E. Legrix	Itsallgreektome	Quest for Fame (GB)	CD	2:30.95	fm	1,040,000
1990	**In the Wings (GB)**, 4	G. Stevens	With Approval	El Senor	Bel	2:29$\frac{3}{5}$	gd	900,000
1989	**Prized**, 3	E. Delahoussaye	Sierra Roberta (Fr)	Star Lift (GB)	GP	2:28	gd	900,000
1988	**Great Communicator**, 5	R. Sibille	Sunshine Forever	Indian Skimmer	CD	2:35$\frac{1}{5}$	gd	900,000
1987	**Theatrical (Ire)**, 5	P. Day	Trempolino	Village Star (Fr)	Hol	2:24$\frac{4}{5}$	fm	900,000
1986	**Manila**, 3	J. Santos	Theatrical (Ire)	Estrapade	SA	2:25$\frac{3}{5}$	fm	900,000
1985	**Pebbles (GB)**, f, 4	P. Eddery	Strawberry Road (Aus)	Mourjane (Ire)	Aqu	2:27	fm	900,000
1984	**Lashkari (GB)**, 3	Y. Saint-Martin	All Along (Fr)	Raami (GB)	Hol	2:25$\frac{1}{5}$	fm	900,000

2003: Dead heat. 2002, '03: High Chaparral (Ire), supplemental entry. 1985: Pebbles (GB), supplemental entry.

California-based runners Great Communicator and Prized won in 1988 and '89, respectively, and the American home-court advantage appeared to be an important factor in the Turf. But European runners won the following two years and subsequently have performed well. In 1996, overseas interests swept the top four spots as Pilsudski (Ire) finished ahead of Singspiel (Ire), Swain (Ire), and Shantou.

North American runners won the following two years—Canadian-bred Chief Bearhart scored a popular 1.90-to-1 victory in 1997, and Illinois-bred Buck's Boy led a North American sweep of the top spots at Churchill Downs in '98. The European contingent then asserted itself through 2002, with California-based Johar sharing the winner's circle with High Chaparral in 2003. In 2004, Maryland-based Better Talk Now won at 27.90-to-1 over 7-to-10 favorite Kitten's Joy at Lone Star Park.

Owners by Wins

2 **Aga Khan** (Kalanisi [Ire], Lashkari [GB]), **Godolphin Racing** (Daylami [Ire], Fantastic Light), **Susan Magnier and Michael Tabor** (High Chaparral [Ire] [twice]), **Sheikh Mohammed bin Rashid al Maktoum** (In the Wings [GB], Pebbles [GB])

1 **Augustin Stables** (Tikkanen), **Bushwood Racing Partners** (Better Talk Now), **Charles Cella** (Northern Spur [Ire]), **Class Act Stable** (Great Communicator), **Clover Racing Stable and Meadowbrook Farm** (Prized), **Fares Farm** (Miss Alleged), **La Presle Farm** (Kotashaan [Fr]), **Allen Paulson** (Theatrical [Ire]), **Madeleine Paulson** (Fraise), **Quarter B Farm** (Buck's Boy), **Sam-Son Farm** (Chief Bearhart), **Bradley M. "Mike" Shannon** (Manila), **The Thoroughbred Corp.** (Johar), **Lord Arnold Weinstock and executors of Simon Weinstock** (Pilsudski [Ire])

Breeders by Wins

3 **Aga Khan** (Daylami [Ire], Kalanisi [Ire], Lashkari [GB])

2 **Sean Coughlan** (High Chaparral [Ire] [twice])

1 **Ballymacoll Stud** (Pilsudski [Ire]), **Eduardo Cojuangco Jr.** (Manila), **Bertram and Diana Firestone** (Theatrical [Ire]), **Carl M. Freeman** (Miss Alleged), **Gainsborough Farm** (Fantastic Light), **Irish Acres Farm** (Buck's Boy), **Sheikh Mohammed bin Rashid al Maktoum** (In the Wings [GB]), **Richard Maynard** (Chief Bearhart), **Meadowbrook Farm** (Prized), **Allen E. Paulson** (Fraise), **George M. Strawbridge Jr.** (Tikkanen), **Swettenham Stud & Partners** (Northern Spur [Ire]), **The Thoroughbred Corp.** (Johar), **Warren Hill Stud** (Pebbles [GB]), **James B. Watriss** (Great Communicator), **Wertheimer & Frere** (Kotashaan [Fr]), **Wimborne Farm** (Better Talk Now)

Trainers by Wins

2 **Richard Mandella** (Kotashaan [Fr], Johar), **William Mott** (Fraise, Theatrical [Ire]), **Aidan O'Brien** (High Chaparral [Ire] [twice]), **Sir Michael Stoute** (Kalanisi [Ire], Pilsudski [Ire]), **Saeed bin Suroor** (Daylami [Ire], Fantastic Light)

1 **Thad Ackel** (Great Communicator), **Pascal Bary** (Miss Alleged), **Clive Brittain** (Pebbles [GB]), **Neil Drysdale** (Prized), **Andre Fabre** (In the Wings [GB]), **Mark Frostad** (Chief Bearhart), **P. Noel Hickey** (Buck's Boy), **LeRoy Jolley** (Manila), **Ron McAnally** (Northern Spur [Ire]), **H. Graham Motion** (Better Talk Now), **Jonathan Pease** (Tikkanen), **Alain de Royer-Dupre** (Lashkari [GB])

Jockeys by Wins

2 **Lanfranco Dettori** (Daylami [Ire], Fantastic Light), **Michael Kinane** (High Chaparral [Ire] [twice]), **Jose Santos** (Chief Bearhart, Manila)

1 **Pat Day** (Theatrical [Ire]), **Eddie Delahoussaye** (Prized), **Kent Desormeaux** (Kotashaan [Fr]), **Ramon Dominguez** (Better Talk Now), **Pat Eddery** (Pebbles [GB]), **Eric Legrix** (Miss Alleged), **Chris McCarron** (Northern Spur [Ire]), **John Murtagh** (Kalanisi [Ire]), **Yves Saint-Martin** (Lashkari [GB]), **Shane Sellers** (Buck's Boy), **Ray Sibille** (Great Communicator), **Alex Solis** (Johar), **Mike Smith** (Tikkanen), **Gary Stevens** (In the Wings [GB]), **Walter Swinburn** (Pilsudski [Ire]), **Patrick Valenzuela** (Fraise)

Sires by Wins

4 **Sadler's Wells** (High Chaparral [Ire] [twice], In the Wings [GB], Northern Spur [Ire])

2 **Doyoun** (Daylami [Ire], Kalanisi [Ire])

1 **Alleged** (Miss Alleged), **Bucksplasher** (Buck's Boy), **Chief's Crown** (Chief Bearhart), **Cozzene** (Tikkanen), **Darshaan** (Kotashaan [Fr]), **Gone West** (Johar), **Key to the Kingdom** (Great Communicator), **Kris S.** (Prized), **Lyphard** (Manila), **Mill Reef** (Lashkari [GB]), **Nureyev** (Theatrical [Ire]), **Polish Precedent** (Pilsudski [Ire]), **Rahy** (Fantastic Light), **Sharpen Up (GB)** (Pebbles [GB]), **Strawberry Road (Aus)** (Fraise), **Talkin Man** (Better Talk Now)

Winners by Place Where Bred

Locality	Winners	Locality	Winners
Ireland	7	Florida	1
Kentucky	7	France	1
Great Britain	3	Illinois	1
Canada	1	Pennsylvania	1

Supplemental Entries

Year	Runner	Fee	Finish	Earnings
2003	**High Chaparral (Ire)**	(credit)	1	$762,200
	Falbrav (Ire)	$180,000	3	233,200
2002	**High Chaparral (Ire)**	180,000	1	1,258,400
	Falcon Flight (Fr)	180,000	3	290,400
	Golan (Ire)	180,000	6	0
2001	Timboroa (GB)	180,000	3	256,800
2000	John's Call	240,000	3	297,600
	Montjeu (Ire)	180,000	7	0
	Subtle Power (Ire)	180,000	10	0
1986	Estrapade	240,000	3	216,000
1985	**Pebbles (GB)**	240,000	1	900,000
	Greinton (GB)	240,000	7	0

Eclipse Award Winners from Race

Year	Runner	Finish	Title
2004	Kitten's Joy	2	Turf male
2003	High Chaparral (Ire)	1 (dh)	Turf male
2002	High Chaparral (Ire)	1	Turf male
2001	Fantastic Light	1	Turf male
2000	Kalanisi (Ire)	1	Turf male
1999	Daylami (Ire)	1	Turf male
1998	Buck's Boy	1	Turf male
1997	Chief Bearhart	1	Turf male
1996	Singspiel (Ire)	2	Turf male
1995	Northern Spur (Ire)	1	Turf male
1994	Paradise Creek	3	Turf male
1993	Kotashaan (Fr)	1	Horse of the Year, Turf male
1992	Sky Classic	2	Turf male
1991	Miss Alleged	1	Turf female
1988	Sunshine Forever	2	Turf male
1987	Theatrical (Ire)	1	Turf male
1986	Manila	1	Turf male
1985	Pebbles (GB)	1	Turf female

Largest Winning Margins

Year	Winner	Margin
1999	Daylami (Ire)	2½
2004	Better Talk Now	1¾
1994	Tikkanen	1½
2002	High Chaparral (Ire)	1¼
1999	Buck's Boy	1¼
1996	Pilsudski (Ire)	1¼

Smallest Winning Margins

Year	Winner	Margin
2003	High Chaparral (Ire)	Dead heat
	Johar	
1992	Fraise	nose
1989	Prized	head
1995	Northern Spur (Ire)	neck
1986	Manila	neck
1985	Pebbles (GB)	neck
1984	Lashkari (GB)	neck

Shortest-Priced Winners

Year	Winner	Odds
2002	High Chaparral (Ire)	0.90-to-1
2001	Fantastic Light	1.40-to-1
1993	Kotashaan (Fr)	1.50-to-1
1999	Daylami (Ire)	1.60-to-1
1987	Theatrical (Ire)	1.80-to-1

Longest-Priced Winners

Year	Winner	Odds
1984	Lashkari (GB)	53.40-to-1
1991	Miss Alleged	42.10-to-1
2004	Better Talk Now	27.90-to-1
1994	Tikkanen	16.60-to-1
2003	Johar	14.20-to-1
1992	Fraise	14.00-to-1

Odds-On Beaten Favorites in Turf

Year	Favorite	Odds	Finish
2004	Kitten's Joy	7-to-10	2
1994	Paradise Creek	4-to-5	3
1992	Sky Classic	9-to-10	2
1986	Dancing Brave	1-to-2	4

Fastest Winners

Year	Winner	Track	Time	Cond.
1997	Chief Bearhart	Hol	2:23.92	firm
1992	Fraise	GP	2:24.08	firm
2003	(DH) High Chaparral (Ire) (DH) Johar	SA	2:24.24	firm
2001	Fantastic Light	Bel	2:24.36	firm

Slowest Winners

Year	Winner	Track	Time	Cond.
1995	Northern Spur (Ire)	Bel	2:42.07	soft
1988	Great Communicator	CD	2:35⅕	good
1991	Miss Alleged	CD	2:30.95	firm
1996	Pilsudski (Ire)	WO	2:30.20	good
2002	High Chaparral (Ire)	AP	2:30.14	yielding

Most Starters

Year	Track	Starters
1999	Gulfstream Park	14
1996	Woodbine	14
1994	Churchill Downs	14
1993	Santa Anita Park	14
1989	Gulfstream Park	14
1987	Hollywood Park	14
1985	Aqueduct	14

Fewest Starters

Year	Track	Starters
2004	Lone Star Park	8
2002	Arlington Park	8
2003	Santa Anita Park	9
1986	Santa Anita Park	9
1992	Gulfstream Park	10
1988	Churchill Downs	10

Winning Post Positions

Post	Starters	Winners	Percent
1	21	2	9.5%
2	21	5	23.8%
3	21	2	9.5%
4	21	0	0.0%
5	21	3	14.3%
6	21	0	0.0%
7	21	1	4.8%
8	21	1	4.8%
9	19	3	15.8%
10	17	0	0.0%
11	15	0	0.0%
12	11	3	27.3%
13	11	2	18.2%
14	7	0	0.0%

Changes in Turf

No changes have been made in the 1½-mile distance or $2-million purse of the Breeders' Cup Turf.

Breeders' Cup Juvenile

Until a winner of the Breeders' Cup Juvenile (G1) delivers a Kentucky Derby (G1) victory, the $1\frac{1}{16}$-mile race (run at $1\frac{1}{8}$ miles in 2002, and at one mile in 1984, '85, and '87) will be regarded as a measure of two-year-old form—which it obviously is—rather than a reliable yardstick of classic potential.

The race has yet to yield a Derby or Belmont Stakes (G1) winner, and only one classic winner, 1995 Preakness Stakes (G1) victor Timber Country, has won the Juvenile.

With regularity, however, the Derby winner and other classic winners have been in the beaten Juvenile field, implying that classic winners were either not sufficiently precocious to win the Juvenile or found its distance to be too short for their best efforts.

The first Breeders' Cup Juvenile was won by Chief's Crown, who finished second or third in all of the following year's classics, won the Travers Stakes (G1) against three-year-olds, and took the Marlboro Cup Handicap (G1) against older horses. He had the three-year-old title and Horse of the Year honors in his sights until finishing fourth as the favorite in the 1985 Breeders' Cup Classic (G1).

Second to Chief's Crown in the 1984 Juvenile was Tank's Prospect, who won the following year's Preakness. Tiring to finish third, beaten only $1\frac{1}{2}$ lengths, was Spend a Buck, the 1985 Derby winner who was voted champion three-year-old male and Horse of the Year.

The pattern would be repeated in subsequent editions of the Juvenile. Alysheba, third in 1986, won the following year's Derby and Preakness and was voted three-year-old male champion. Bet Twice, who conquered him in the Belmont Stakes (G1), finished fourth in the '86 Juvenile. Pine Bluff was seventh in the 1991 Juvenile but won the Preakness the following year. Sea Hero, seventh in the 1992 Juvenile, won the following year's Derby. Finishing third to Brocco in the 1993 Juvenile was Tabasco Cat, who would become a dual classic winner in '94 for D. Wayne Lukas, the leading trainer of Juvenile winners. Seven years later, Point Given came off a close second-place finish in the Juvenile to win the 2001 Preakness, Belmont, and Travers. Retired with an injury after the Travers, he was voted 2001 Horse of the Year and champion three-year-old male. Afleet Alex, second in the 2004 Juvenile, won the following year's Preakness and Belmont.

Losing a close decision was the best sire of the late 1990s and early 2000s, Storm Cat, who just failed to last the one-mile distance of the Juvenile at Aqueduct in '85. Capote, winner of the '86 Juvenile, never won again but became a successful sire, getting '96 Juvenile winner Boston Harbor.

Perhaps the most memorable running of the Juvenile occurred at Churchill Downs in '91, when French-trained Arazi broke from the outside post position, blew by the field on the final turn, and romped to a five-length victory. Voted two-year-old male champion off that one North American start, Arazi was hampered by knee problems early in his three-year-old season. He finished eighth as the favorite in the '92 Derby.

Another disappointment was Favorite Trick, who was voted '97 Horse of the Year after an overwhelming victory in the Juvenile. He finished eighth in the Derby.

Breeders' Cup Juvenile

Grade 1, \$1.5-million, two-year-old colts and geldings, $1\frac{1}{16}$ miles, dirt. Run on October 30, 2004, at Lone Star Park with gross value of \$1,375,500. First run in 1984. Weights: 122 pounds.

Year	Winner	Jockey	Second	Third	Site	Time	Cond.	1st Purse
2004	**Wilko**	L. Dettori	Afleet Alex	Sun King	LS	1:42.09	ft	**\$780,000**
2003	**Action This Day**	D. Flores	Minister Eric	Chapel Royal	SA	1:43.62	ft	**780,000**
2002	**Vindication**	M. Smith	Kafwain	Hold That Tiger	AP	149.61	ft	556,400
2001	**Johannesburg**	M. Kinane	Repent	Siphonic	Bel	1:42.27	ft	520,000
2000	**Macho Uno**	J. Bailey	Point Given	Street Cry (Ire)	CD	1:42.05	ft	556,400
1999	**Anees**	G. Stevens	Chief Seattle	High Yield	GP	1:42.29	ft	556,400
1998	**Answer Lively**	J. Bailey	Aly's Alley	Cat Thief	CD	1:44	ft	520,000
1997	**Favorite Trick**	P. Day	Dawson's Legacy	Nationalore	Hol	**1:41.47**	ft	520,000
1996	**Boston Harbor**	J. Bailey	Acceptable	Ordway	WO	1:43.40	ft	520,000
1995	**Unbridled's Song**	M. Smith	Hennessy	Editor's Note	Bel	1:41.60	my	520,000
1994	**Timber Country**	P. Day	Eltish	Tejano Run	CD	1:44.55	ft	520,000
1993	**Brocco**	G. Stevens	Blumin Affair	Tabasco Cat	SA	1:42.99	ft	520,000
1992	**Gilded Time**	C. McCarron	It'sali'lknownfact	River Special	GP	1:43.43	ft	520,000
1991	**Arazi**	P. Valenzuela	Bertrando	Snappy Landing	CD	1:44.78	ft	520,000
1990	**Fly So Free**	J. Santos	Take Me Out	Lost Mountain	Bel	1:43$\frac{2}{5}$	ft	450,000
1989	**Rhythm**	C. Perret	Grand Canyon	Slavic	GP	1:43$\frac{3}{5}$	ft	450,000
1988	**Is It True**	L. Pincay Jr.	Easy Goer	Tagel	CD	1:46$\frac{3}{5}$	my	450,000
1987	**Success Express**	J. Santos	Regal Classic	Tejano	Hol	**1:35**$\frac{1}{5}$	ft	450,000
1986	**Capote**	L. Pincay Jr.	Qualify	Alysheba	SA	1:43$\frac{4}{5}$	ft	450,000
1985	**Tasso**	L. Pincay Jr.	Storm Cat	Scat Dancer	Aqu	1:36$\frac{1}{5}$	ft	450,000
1984	**Chief's Crown**	D. MacBeth	Tank's Prospect	Spend a Buck	Hol	1:36$\frac{1}{5}$	ft	450,000

2002: Run at $1\frac{1}{8}$ miles. 1984-'85, 1987: run at one mile. 1985: Tasso supplementary entry.

The following year's Juvenile winner, Answer Lively, ran tenth in the 1999 Derby, and that year's Juvenile victor, Anees, was 13th at Churchill Downs the following May. Macho Uno, the 2000 Juvenile winner, did not make it to the following year's Derby, and '01 Juvenile winner Johannesburg ran eighth in the '02 Derby. Vindication, an easy winner at Arlington Park in 2002, did not start in the Derby. Action This Day, the 2003 Juvenile victor, finished sixth behind Smarty Jones in '04, and Wilko, the 2004 Juvenile winner at Lone Star Park, came home sixth behind Giacomo in the '05 Derby.

Owners by Wins

2   **Eugene V. Klein** (Is It True, Success Express)
1   **Barry A. Beal, Lloyd R. "Bob" French Jr., Eugene V. Klein** (Capote), **Mr. and Mrs. Albert Broccoli** (Brocco), **John Franks** (Answer Lively), **Gainesway Stable, Overbrook Farm, Robert and Beverly Lewis** (Timber Country), **B. Wayne Hughes** (Action This Day), **Joseph LaCombe** (Favorite Trick), **David Milch, Jack and Mark Silverman** (Gilded Time), **Overbrook Farm** (Boston Harbor), **Padua Stables** (Vindication), **Paraneck Stable** (Unbridled's Song), **Allen E. Paulson, Sheikh Mohammed bin Rashid al Maktoum** (Arazi), **Ogden Mills Phipps** (Rhythm), **J. Paul Reddam and Susan Roy** (Wilko), **Gerald Robins** (Tasso), **Stronach Stables** (Macho Uno), **Star Crown Stable** (Chief's Crown), **Michael Tabor and Susan Magnier** (Johannesburg), **The Thoroughbred Corp.** (Anees), **Thomas Valando** (Fly So Free)

Breeders by Wins

1   **Adena Springs** (Macho Uno), **Jaime Carrion (trustee)** (Action This Day), **Farfellow Farms** (Anees), **John Franks** (Answer Lively), **Bruce Hundley and Wayne Garrison** (Fly So Free), **Warner L. Jones** (Is It True), **Lowquest Ltd.** (Timber Country), **Wayne G. Lyster III and Jayeff B Stables** (Johannesburg), **Mandysland Farm** (Unbridled's Song), **Mr. and Mrs. Harry T. Mangurian Jr.** (Gilded Time), **Meadowbrook Farms** (Brocco), **North Ridge Farm** (Capote), **Overbrook Farm** (Boston Harbor), **Rosenda Parra** (Wilko), **Payson Stud** (Vindication), **Ogden Mills Phipps** (Rhythm), **Rosenda Parra** (Wilko), **Gerald L. Robins and Timothy H. Sams** (Tasso), **Carl Rosen** (Chief's Crown), **Tri Star Stable** (Success Express), **Ralph Wilson Jr.** (Arazi), **Mr. and Mrs. M. L. Wood** (Favorite Trick)

Trainers by Wins

5   **D. Wayne Lukas** (Boston Harbor, Timber Country, Is It True, Success Express, Capote)
1   **Bob Baffert** (Vindication), **Bobby Barnett** (Answer Lively), **Francois Boutin** (Arazi), **Patrick Byrne** (Favorite Trick), **Neil Drysdale** (Tasso), **Alex Hassinger Jr.** (Anees), **Roger Laurin** (Chief's Crown), **Richard Mandella** (Action This Day), **Claude R. "Shug" McGaughey III** (Rhythm), **Jeremy Noseda** (Wilko), **Aidan O'Brien** (Johannesburg), **Joseph Orseno** (Macho Uno), **James Ryerson** (Unbridled's Song), **Flint S. "Scotty" Schulhofer** (Fly So Free), **Darrell Vienna** (Gilded Time), **Randy Winick** (Brocco)

Jockeys by Wins

3   **Jerry Bailey** (Macho Uno, Answer Lively, Boston Harbor), **Laffit Pincay Jr.** (Is It True, Capote, Tasso)
2   **Pat Day** (Favorite Trick, Timber Country), **Jose Santos** (Fly So Free, Success Express), **Mike Smith** (Vindication, Unbridled's Song), **Gary Stevens** (Anees, Brocco)
1   **Lanfranco Dettori** (Wilko), **David Flores** (Action This Day), **Michael Kinane** (Johannesburg), **Don MacBeth** (Chief's Crown), **Chris McCarron** (Gilded Time), **Craig Perret** (Rhythm), **Patrick Valenzuela** (Arazi)

Sires by Wins

2   **Kris S.** (Brocco, Action This Day), **Seattle Slew** (Capote, Vindication), **Unbridled** (Anees, Unbridled's Song)
1   **Awesome Again** (Wilko), **Blushing Groom (Fr)** (Arazi), **Capote** (Boston Harbor), **Danzig** (Chief's Crown), **Fappiano** (Tasso), **Hennessy** (Johannesburg), **Hold Your Peace** (Success Express), **Holy Bull** (Macho Uno), **Lively One** (Answer Lively), **Mr. Prospector** (Rhythm), **Phone Trick** (Favorite Trick), **Raja Baba** (Is It True), **Time for a Change** (Fly So Free), **Timeless Moment** (Gilded Time), **Woodman** (Timber Country)

Winners by Place Where Bred

Locality	Winners
Kentucky	18
Florida	3

Supplemental Entries

Year	Runner	Fee	Finish	Earnings
2002	Whywhywhy	$90,000	10	$0
2000	Arabian Light	90,000	5	21,400
1999	Captain Steve	90,000	11	0
1992	Caponostro	120,000	6	0
1991	Bertrando	120,000	2	200,000
	Agincourt	120,000	5	20,000
1990	Best Pal	120,000	6	10,000
1985	**Tasso**	120,000	1	450,000
1984	Spend a Buck	120,000	3	108,000

Eclipse Award Winners from Race

Year	Runner	Finish	Title
2003	**Action This Day**	1	Juvenile male
2002	**Vindication**	1	Juvenile male
2001	**Johannesburg**	1	Juvenile male
2000	**Macho Uno**	1	Juvenile male
1999	**Anees**	1	Juvenile male
1998	**Answer Lively**	1	Juvenile male
1997	**Favorite Trick**	1	Horse of the Year, Juvenile male
1996	**Boston Harbor**	1	Juvenile male
1994	**Timber Country**	1	Juvenile male
1993	Dehere	8	Juvenile male
1992	**Gilded Time**	1	Juvenile male
1991	**Arazi**	1	Juvenile male
1990	**Fly So Free**	1	Juvenile male
1989	**Rhythm**	1	Juvenile male
1988	Easy Goer	2	Juvenile male
1986	**Capote**	1	Juvenile male
1985	**Tasso**	1	Juvenile male
1984	**Chief's Crown**	1	Juvenile male

Largest Winning Margins

Year	Winner	Margin
1997	Favorite Trick	5½
1993	Brocco	5
1991	Arazi	5

Smallest Winning Margins

Year	Winner	Margin
2000	Macho Uno	nose
1985	Tasso	nose
1998	Answer Lively	head

Shortest-Priced Winners

Year	Winner	Odds
1984	Chief's Crown	0.70-to-1
1997	Favorite Trick	1.20-to-1
1990	Fly So Free	1.40-to-1
1992	Gilded Time	2.00-to-1

Longest-Priced Winners

Year	Winner	Odds
1999	Anees	30.30-to-1
2004	Wilko	28.30-to-1
2003	Action This Day	26.80-to-1
1988	Is It True	9.20-to-1
2001	Johannesburg	7.20-to-1
2000	Macho Uno	6.30-to-1

Odds-On Beaten Favorites in Juvenile

Year	Favorite	Odds	Finish
2001	Officer	0.75-to-1	5
1993	Dehere	7-to-10	8
1988	Easy Goer	3-to-10	2

Fastest Winners

Year	Winner	Track	Time	Cond.
1997	Favorite Trick	Hol	1:41.47	fast
1995	Unbridled's Song	Bel	1:41.60	muddy
2000	Macho Uno	CD	1:42.05	fast
2004	Wilko	LS	1:42.09	fast
2001	Johannesburg	Bel	1:42:27	fast

Slowest Winners

Year	Winner	Track	Time	Cond.
1988	Is It True	CD	1:46⅗	muddy
1991	Arazi	CD	1:44.78	fast
1994	Timber Country	CD	1:44.55	fast
1998	Answer Lively	CD	1:44.00	fast

Most Starters

Year	Track	Starters
2000	Churchill Downs	14
1999	Gulfstream Park	14
1991	Churchill Downs	14

Fewest Starters

Year	Track	Starters
2004	Lone Star Park	8
1997	Hollywood Park	8
1996	Woodbine	10
1988	Churchill Downs	10
1984	Hollywood Park	10

Winning Post Positions

Post	Starters	Winners	Percent
1	21	1	4.8%
2	21	2	9.5%
3	21	6	28.6%
4	21	2	9.5%
5	21	2	9.5%
6	21	1	4.8%
7	21	2	9.5%
8	21	2	9.5%
9	19	1	5.3%
10	19	0	0.0%
11	16	1	6.3%
12	14	0	0.0%
13	11	0	0.0%
14	3	1	33.3%

Changes in Juvenile

For the 2003 Juvenile, the purse was increased to $1.5-million. Originally contested at one mile, the distance was changed to 1¹⁄₁₆ miles in 1988. It was contested at 1¹⁄₁₆ miles in 1986 and at 1¼ miles in 2002.

Breeders' Cup Filly and Mare Turf

In July 1998, the Breeders' Cup board of directors voted to fill an obvious gap in its championship lineup by creating the $1-million Breeders' Cup Filly and Mare Turf (G1) at 1¼ miles. Until the first Filly and Mare Turf at Gulfstream Park in 1999, the female turf division had no definitive championship race, and distaffers were forced to race in open company.

The new race for fillies and mares, first run at 1⅜ miles because of Gulfstream's grass course configuration, fulfilled its intended function. Phillips Racing Partnership's Soaring Softly locked up an Eclipse Award as champion turf female with a three-quarter-length victory in 1999.

Breeders' Cup Filly and Mare Turf

Grade 1, $1-million, fillies and mares, three-year-olds and up, 1⅜ miles, turf. Run October 30, 2004, at Lone Star Park with gross value of $1,292,970. First run in 1999. Weights: Northern Hemisphere three-year-olds, 119 pounds; older, 123 pounds; Southern Hemisphere three-year-olds, 113 pounds; older, 123 pounds.

Year	Winner	Jockey	Second	Third	Site	Time	Cond.	1st purse
2004	Ouija Board (GB)	K. Fallon	Film Maker	Wonder Again	LS	2:18.25	yl	**$733,200**
2003	Islington (Ire), 4	K. Fallon	L'Ancresse (Ire)	Yesterday (Ire)	SA	**1:59.15**	fm	551,200
2002	Starine (Fr)	J. Velazquez	Banks Hill (GB	Islington (GB)	AP	2:03.57	yl	665,600
2001	Banks Hill (GB), 3	O. Peslier	Spook Express (SAf)	Spring Oak (GB)	Bel	2:00.36	fm	722,800
2000	Perfect Sting, 4	J. Bailey	Tout Charmant	Catella (Ger)	CD	2:13.07	fm	629,200
1999	Soaring Softly, 4	J. Bailey	Coretta (Ire)	Zomaradah (GB)	GP	2:13.89	gd	556,400

1999-2000, 2004, 1⅜ miles; 2001-'03, 1¼ miles

The following year, Stronach Stable's Perfect Sting won by the same margin over Tout Charmant at Churchill Downs. Perfect Sting was subsequently voted champion turf female. European interests broke through in 2001 when Juddmonte Farms' French-based Banks Hill (GB) won by 5½ lengths at Belmont Park. For the first time in 2001, the Filly and Mare Turf was run at 1¼ miles, its prescribed distance when course configurations permit.

Beginning with Banks Hill, horses bred overseas dominated the Filly and Mare Turf. Horses bred outside North America took the first three finish positions in 2001, the top six spots the following year, the top five positions in '03, and the winning spot in '04, when few European-trained horses made the trip to Lone Star Park.

Juddmonte Farms' Banks Hill, a Danehill filly trained by Andre Fabre for her 2001 triumph, returned in '02 to seek a second victory, this time in the care of Bobby Frankel. She could manage no better than second, beaten 1½ lengths by Starine (Fr), who was owned and trained by Frankel. Islington (Ire) finished third in the 2002 Filly and Mare Turf, and she returned the following year to score a neck victory over L'Ancresse (Ire) in the Filly and Mare Turf at Santa Anita Park. In an unusual pattern to that race, all North American-bred horses finished behind the five top finishers. Irish-breds took the top three spots, followed by two fillies bred in Great Britain.

Britain's honor would be upheld in 2004 when Lord Derby's homebred Ouija Board (GB) invaded and scored a 1½-length victory over Film Maker. Europe's Horse of the Year after her victories in the Epsom Oaks (Eng-G1) and Darley Irish Oaks (Ire-G1), the Cape Cross (Ire) filly also was voted an Eclipse Award as North America's outstanding turf female.

Owners by Wins

1   **Lord Derby** (Ouija Board [GB]), **Estate of Lord Weinstock** (Islington [Ire]), **Robert Frankel** (Starine [Fr]), **Juddmonte Farms** (Banks Hill [GB]), **Phillips Racing Partnership** (Soaring Softly), **Stronach Stables** (Perfect Sting)

Breeders by Wins

1   **Ballymacoll Stud Farm** (Islington [Ire]), **Catherine Dubois** (Starine [Fr]), **Galbreath-Phillips Racing Partnership** (Soaring Softly), **Juddmonte Farms** (Banks Hill [GB]), **Stanley Estate and Stud Co.** (Ouija Board [GB]), **Frank Stronach** (Perfect Sting)

Trainers by Wins

1   **Edward Dunlop** (Ouija Board [GB]), **Andre Fabre** (Banks Hill [GB]), **Robert Frankel** (Starine [Fr]), **Joseph Orseno** (Perfect Sting), **Sir Michael Stoute** (Islington [Ire]), **James J. Toner** (Soaring Softly)

Jockeys by Wins

2   **Jerry Bailey** (Soaring Softly, Perfect Sting), **Kieren Fallon** (Ouija Board [GB], Islington [Ire])
1   **Olivier Peslier** (Banks Hill [GB]), **John Velazquez** (Starine [Fr])

Sires by Wins

1   **Cape Cross (Ire)** (Ouija Board [GB]), **Danehill** (Banks Hill [GB]), **Kris S.** (Soaring Softly), **Mendocino** (Starine [Fr]), **Red Ransom** (Perfect Sting), **Sadler's Wells** (Islington [Ire])

Winners by Place Where Bred

Locality	Winners
Great Britain	2
Kentucky	2
France	1
Ireland	1

Supplemental Entries

Year	Runner	Fee	Finish	Earnings
2004	**Ouija Board (GB)**	$90,000	1	$733,200
	Moscow Burning	90,000	4	80,370
	Super Brand (SAf)	200,000	9	0
	Katdogwan (GB)	90,000	10	0
	Megahertz (GB)	(credit)	11	0
	Aubonne (Ger)	90,000	12	0
2003	**Islington (Ire)**	(credit)	1	551,200
	Megahertz (GB)	90,000	5	31,800
2002	**Starine (Fr)**	(credit)	1	665,600
	Islington (Ire)	90,000	3	153,600
	Golden Apples (Ire)	90,000	4	71,680
	Kazzia (Ger)	90,000	6	0
	Turtle Bow (Fr)	90,000	9	0
2001	Spook Express (SAf)	200,000	2	278,000
	Kalypso Katie (Ire)	200,000	6	0
	Starine (Fr)	90,000	10	0
	England's Legend (Fr)	90,000	11	0
2000	Caffe Latte (Ire)	(credit)	9	0
	Catella (Ger)	90,000	3	145,200
	Colstar	90,000	7	0
	Petrushka (Ire)	90,000	5	24,200
1999	Caffe Latte (Ire)	90,000	4	59,920

Eclipse Award Winners from Race

Year	Runner	Finish	Title
2004	Ouija Board (GB)	1	Turf female
2003	Islington (Ire)	1	Turf female
2002	Golden Apples (Ire)	4	Turf female
2001	Banks Hill (GB)	1	Turf female
2000	Perfect Sting	1	Turf female
1999	Soaring Softly	1	Turf female

Winning Margins

Year	Winner	Margin
2001	Banks Hill (GB)	5½
2004	Ouija Board (GB)	1½
2002	Starine (Fr)	1½
2000	Perfect Sting	¾
1999	Soaring Softly	¾
2003	Islington (Ire)	neck

Beaten Favorites in Filly and Mare Turf

Year	Favorite	Odds	Finish
2002	Golden Apples (Ire)	2.80-to-1	4
2001	Lailani (GB)	2.75-to-1	8
2000	Petrushka (Ire)	7-to-5	5

Odds of Winners

Year	Winner	Odds
2004	Ouija Board (GB)	0.90-to-1
2003	Islington (Ire)	2.90-to-1
2002	Starine (Fr)	13.20-to-1
2001	Banks Hill (GB)	6.00-to-1
2000	Perfect Sting	5.00-to-1
1999	Soaring Softly	3.60-to-1

Winning Times

Year	Winner	Track	Time	Cond.
2004	Ouija Board (GB)	LS	2:18.25	yielding
2003	Islington (Ire)	SA	1:59.13	firm
2002	Starine (Fr)	AP	2:03.57	yielding
2001	Banks Hill (GB)	Bel	2:00.36	firm
2000	Perfect Sting	CD	2:13.07	firm
1999	Soaring Softly	GP	2:13.89	good

Number of Starters

Year	Track	Starters
2004	Lone Star Park	12
2003	Santa Anita Park	12
2002	Arlington Park	12
2001	Belmont Park	12
2000	Churchill Downs	14
1999	Gulfstream Park	14

Winning Post Positions

Post	Starters	Winners	Percent
1	6	0	0.0%
2	6	0	0.0%
3	6	0	0.0%
4	6	1	16.7%
5	6	2	33.3%
6	6	0	0.0%
7	6	0	0.0%
8	6	1	16.7%
9	6	0	0.0%
10	6	0	0.0%
11	6	1	16.7%
12	6	1	16.7%
13	2	0	0.0%
14	2	0	0.0%

Changes in Filly and Mare Turf

No changes in conditions or purse other than the distance have been made since the Filly and Mare Turf was inaugurated in 1999. The race has been held at 1⅜ miles three times rather than its prescribed 1¼ miles due to course configurations.

Breeders' Cup Sprint

Roughly half of all North American races are run at six furlongs, and thus the $1-million Breeders' Cup Sprint (G1) is the prototypical American race. The six-furlong dash has proved to be a competitive contest, principally among North American runners, and in many years it has been a nightmare for handicappers.

As a championship event, the Breeders' Cup Sprint has been especially decisive in years when no horse clearly dominated the division. In 13 of the 21 runnings of the Sprint, the Eclipse Award

for champion sprinter has gone to the winner.

The first Breeders' Cup Sprint in 1984 set the tone for the series, with Eillo desperately holding off Commemorate to win by a nose. Seven runnings of the Breeders' Cup Sprint have been decided by a neck or less. Eillo was favored at 1.30-to-1, and no favorite would again win the Sprint for ten years, until Cherokee Run (2.80-to-1) in 1994. Lit de Justice was a lukewarm 4-to-1 favorite in 1996, Kona Gold won at 1.70-to-1 in 2000, and Orientate prevailed at 2.70-to-1 in '02.

Breeders' Cup Sprint

Grade 1, $1-million, three-year-olds and up, 6 furlongs. Held on October 30, 2004, at Lone Star Park with gross value of $972,020. First run in 1984. Weights: Northern Hemisphere three-year-olds, 123 pounds; older, 126 pounds; Southern Hemisphere three-year-olds, 122 pounds; older, 126 pounds; fillies and mares allowed three pounds.

Year	Winner	Jockey	Second	Third	Site	Time	Cond.	1st Purse
2004	Speightstown	J. Velazquez	Kela	My Cousin Matt	LS	1:08.11	ft	$551,200
2003	Cajun Beat, 3	C. Velasquez	Bluesthestandard	Shake You Down	SA	1:07.95	ft	613,600
2002	Orientate	J. Bailey	Thunderello	Crafty C. T.	AP	1:08.89	ft	592,800
2001	Squirtle Squirt, 3	J. Bailey	Xtra Heat	Caller One	Bel	1:08.41	ft	520,000
2000	Kona Gold, 6	A. Solis	Honest Lady	Bet On Sunshine	CD	1:07.77	ft	520,000
1999	Artax, 4	J. Chavez	Kona Gold	Big Jag	GP	1:07.89	ft	624,000
1998	Reraise, 3	C. Nakatani	Grand Slam	Kona Gold	CD	1:09.07	ft	572,000
1997	Elmhurst, 7	C. Nakatani	Hesabull	Bet On Sunshine	Hol	1:08.01	ft	613,600
1996	Lit de Justice, 6	C. Nakatani	Paying Dues	Honour and Glory	WO	1:08.60	ft	520,000
1995	Desert Stormer, f, 5	K. Desormeaux	Mr. Greeley	Lit de Justice	Bel	1:09.14	my	520,000
1994	Cherokee Run, 4	M. Smith	Soviet Problem	Cardmania	CD	1:09.54	ft	520,000
1993	Cardmania, 7	E. Delahoussaye	Meafara	Gilded Time	SA	1:08.76	ft	520,000
1992	Thirty Slews, 5	E. Delahoussaye	Meafara	Rubiano	GP	1:08.21	ft	520,000
1991	Sheikh Albadou (GB), 3	P. Eddery	Pleasant Tap	Robyn Dancer	CD	1:09.36	ft	520,000
1990	Safely Kept, f, 4	C. Perret	Dayjur	Black Tie Affair (Ire)	Bel	1:09 3/5	ft	450,000
1989	Dancing Spree, 4	A. Cordero Jr.	Safely Kept	Dispersal	GP	1:09.36	ft	450,000
1988	Gulch, 4	A. Cordero Jr.	Play the King	Afleet	CD	1:10 2/5	sy	450,000
1987	Very Subtle, f, 3	P. Valenzuela	Groovy	Exclusive Enough	Hol	1:08 4/5	ft	450,000
1986	Smile, 4	J. Vasquez	Pine Tree Lane	Beside Promise	SA	1:08 2/5	ft	450,000
1985	Precisionist, 4	C. McCarron	Smile	Mt. Livermore	Aqu	1:08 2/5	ft	450,000
1984	Eillo, 4	C. Perret	Commemorate	Fighting Fit	Hol	1:10 1/5	ft	450,000

Between Eillo and Cherokee Run, the Sprint was won by two other champions, Precisionist (1985) and Gulch ('88), who could not be characterized as pure sprinters. Fred Hooper's home-bred Precisionist won the 1¼-mile Charles H. Strub Stakes (G1) the same year he was sprint champion, and Gulch was really best at one mile, winning the Metropolitan Handicap (G1) twice, 1987 and '88, the latter his championship year.

The Sprint in 1990 remains one of the most memorable in Breeders' Cup history. Safely Kept, the prior year's champion sprinter, fought a spirited, head-to-head battle with English invader Dayjur, the 2.40-to-1 favorite. Inside the furlong pole, Dayjur appeared to take command, but 40 yards from the wire he jumped the shadow of Belmont Park's grandstand and briefly lost his action. Those missteps proved sufficient for 12.20-to-1 Safely Kept to regain the lead and hold on for a neck victory.

Although Dayjur failed to become the first overseas horse to win the Sprint, the European contingent broke through the following year when Sheikh Albadou (GB) won at Churchill Downs. At 26.30-to-1, Sheikh Albadou remains the longest-priced winner of the Sprint. Average odds of Sprint winners were a healthy 9.96-to-1.

Kona Gold, the 2000 winner, proved that top-quality sprinters could be durable as well as fast. Carefully managed by co-owner and trainer Bruce Headley, the Java Gold gelding ran third in 1998, second in '99, and finally won at age six. In winning at Churchill Downs, Kona Gold set a track record, 1:07.77, the fastest time ever for the Sprint. Kona Gold was the 7-to-2 favorite when seeking a second straight win in 2001 but finished seventh behind winner Squirtle Squirt. In 2002, his record fifth start in the race, he finished fourth.

Racing Hall of Fame trainer D. Wayne Lukas may be best known for his classic horses, but he collected his second Sprint victory with favored Orientate in 2002 at Arlington Park. The following year, Cajun Beat stormed to a 22.80-to-1 victory over a talented field at Santa Anita Park, and the Eclipse Award went to race favorite Aldebaran, who finished sixth at 2.10-to-1. In 2004, Speightstown secured an Eclipse Award with a 1¼-length victory over Kela.

In the 1980s, the Sprint was a graveyard for one of the era's most talented sprinters, Groovy. He went off at 2-to-5 in the 1986 Sprint and finished fourth, 4¼ lengths behind front-running winner Smile. At Hollywood Park the following year, Groovy went off at 4-to-5 and ran second to another front-runner, Ben Rochelle's filly Very Subtle. Groovy was voted an Eclipse Award as outstanding sprinter in 1987. The only other Sprint starter to lose at odds-on was two-time champion Housebuster, who finished ninth at 2-to-5 odds in 1991.

Owners by Wins

1   **Peter M. Brant** (Gulch), **Jean Couvercelle** (Cardmania), **Crown Stable** (Eillo), **Mitch Degroot, Dutch Masters III, and Mike Pegram** (Thirty Slews), **Craig Dollase, Barry Fey, Moon Han, and Frank Sinatra** (Reraise), **Evergreen Farm** (Lit de Justice), **Evergreen Farm and Jenine Sahadi** (Elmhurst), **Frances Genter Stable** (Smile), **Fred Hooper** (Precisionist), **Bruce Headley, Irwin and Andrew Molasky, and High Tech Stable** (Kona Gold), **Jayeff B Stables and Barry Weisbord** (Safely Kept), **David J. Lanzman** (Squirtle Squirt), **Robert and Beverly Lewis** (Orientate), **Eugene and Laura Melnyk** (Speightstown), **Joanne Nor** (Desert Stormer), **Padua Stable and John and Joseph Iracane** (Cajun Beat), **Paraneck Stable** (Artax), **Ogden Phipps** (Dancing Spree), **Jill Robinson** (Cherokee Run), **Ben Rochelle** (Very Subtle), **Hilal Salem** (Sheikh Albadou [GB])

Breeders by Wins

1   **Peter M. Brant** (Gulch), **Calumet Farm** (Elmhurst), **Carondelet Farm and Vinery** (Artax), **Ollie A. Cohen** (Eillo), **Delta Thoroughbreds** (Cardmania), **Gainesway Thoroughbreds Ltd.** (Orientate), **Frances Genter Stable** (Smile), **Grousemont Farm** (Thirty Slews), **Mr. and Mrs. David Hayden** (Safely Kept), **Highclere Stud** (Sheikh Albadou [GB]), **Fred Hooper** (Precisionist), **Aaron and Marie Jones** (Speightstown), **John T. L. Jones Jr. and H. Smoot Fahlgren** (Cajun Beat), **John Howard King** (Very Subtle), **Audrey Narducci, M.D.** (Squirtle Squirt), **Joanne Nor** (Desert Stormer), **George Onett** (Cherokee Run), **Carlos Perez** (Kona Gold), **Ogden Phipps** (Dancing Spree), **Swettenham Stud and Julian G. Rogers** (Lit de Justice), **Willard Sergent** (Reraise)

Trainers by Wins

2   **D. Wayne Lukas** (Gulch, Orientate), **Jenine Sahadi** (Elmhurst, Lit de Justice)

1   **Louis Albertrani** (Artax), **Frank Alexander** (Cherokee Run), **Bob Baffert** (Thirty Slews), **Craig Dollase** (Reraise), **Ross Fenstermaker** (Precisionist), **Robert Frankel** (Squirtle Squirt), **Alan Goldberg** (Safely Kept), **Bruce Headley** (Kona Gold), **Budd Lepman** (Eillo), **Frank Lyons** (Desert Stormer), **Steve Margolis** (Cajun Beat), **Claude R. "Shug" McGaughey III** (Dancing Spree), **Derek Meredith** (Cardmania), **Todd Pletcher** (Speightstown), **Flint S. "Scotty" Schulhofer** (Smile), **Alexander Scott** (Sheikh Albadou [GB]), **Mel Stute** (Very Subtle)

Jockeys by Wins

3   **Corey Nakatani** (Reraise, Elmhurst, Lit de Justice)

2   **Jerry Bailey** (Squirtle Squirt, Orientate), **Angel Cordero Jr.** (Dancing Spree, Gulch), **Eddie Delahoussaye** (Cardmania, Thirty Slews), **Craig Perret** (Safely Kept, Eillo)

1   **Jorge Chavez** (Artax), **Kent Desormeaux** (Desert Stormer), **Pat Eddery** (Sheikh Albadou [GB]), **Chris McCarron** (Precisionist), **Mike Smith** (Cherokee Run), **Alex Solis** (Kona Gold), **Patrick Valenzuela** (Very Subtle), **Cornelio Velasquez** (Cajun Beat), **John Velazquez** (Speightstown), **Jacinto Vasquez** (Smile)

Sires of Winners

2 **Marquetry** (Artax, Squirtle Squirt), **Mr. Prospector** (Eillo, Gulch)

1 **Cox's Ridge** (Cardmania), **Crozier** (Precisionist), **Danzatore** (Reraise), **El Gran Senor** (Lit de Justice), **Gone West** (Speightstown), **Grand Slam** (Cajun Beat), **Green Desert** (Sheikh Albadou [GB]), **Hoist the Silver** (Very Subtle), **Horatius** (Safely Kept), **In Reality** (Smile), **Java Gold** (Kona Gold), **Mt. Livermore** (Orientate), **Nijinsky II** (Dancing Spree), **Runaway Groom** (Cherokee Run), **Slewpy** (Thirty Slews), **Storm Cat** (Desert Stormer), **Wild Again** (Elmhurst)

Winners by Place Where Bred

Locality	Winners
Kentucky	15
Florida	4
Maryland	1
Great Britain	1

Supplemental Entries

Year	Runner	Fee	Finish	Earnings
2004	Pt's Grey Eagle	$90,000	8	$0
2003	Bluesthestandard	90,000	2	236,000
	Shake You Down	90,000	3	129,800
	Private Horde	90,000	9	0
2002	Disturbingthepeace	90,000	7	0
	Bonapaw	90,000	10	0
1999	Son of a Pistol	120,000	13	0
	Enjoy the Moment	120,000	14	0
1998	**Reraise**	120,000	1	572,000
1997	Men's Exclusive	200,000	6	0
1996	Criollito (Arg)	200,000	12	0
1994	**Cherokee Run**	120,000	1	520,000
	Soviet Problem	120,000	2	200,000
	Exclusive Praline	120,000	9	0
1989	Sewickley	120,000	5	50,000
1987	Zabaleta	120,000	4	70,000
	Zany Tactics	120,000	9	0
1985	Committed	200,000	7	0
1984	Pac Mania	200,000	9	0

Eclipse Award Winners from Race

Year	Runner	Finish	Title
2004	**Speightstown**	1	Sprinter
2003	Aldebaran	6	Sprinter
2002	**Orientate**	1	Sprinter
2001	**Squirtle Squirt**	1	Sprinter
	Xtra Heat	2	3yo filly
2000	**Kona Gold**	1	Sprinter
1999	**Artax**	1	Sprinter
1998	**Reraise**	1	Sprinter
1996	**Lit de Justice**	1	Sprinter
1995	Not Surprising	4	Sprinter
1994	**Cherokee Run**	1	Sprinter
1993	**Cardmania**	1	Sprinter
1992	Rubiano	3	Sprinter
1991	Housebuster	9	Sprinter
1989	Safely Kept	2	Sprinter
1988	**Gulch**	1	Sprinter
1987	Groovy	2	Sprinter
1986	**Smile**	1	Sprinter
1985	**Precisionist**	1	Sprinter
1984	**Eillo**	1	Sprinter

Largest Winning Margins

Year	Winner	Margin
1987	Very Subtle	4
1991	Sheikh Albadou (GB)	3
2003	Cajun Beat	2¼
1998	Reraise	2
2004	Speightstown	1¼
1996	Lit de Justice	1¼
1986	Smile	1¼

Smallest Winning Margins

Year	Winner	Margin
1984	Eillo	nose
1994	Cherokee Run	head
1995	Desert Stormer	neck
1993	Cardmania	neck
1992	Thirty Slews	neck
1990	Safely Kept	neck
1989	Dancing Spree	neck

Shortest-Priced Winners

Year	Winner	Odds
1984	Eillo	1.30-to-1
2000	Kona Gold	1.70-to-1
2002	Orientate	2.70-to-1
1994	Cherokee Run	2.80-to-1
1985	Precisionist	3.40-to-1

Longest-Priced Winners

Year	Winner	Odds
1991	Sheikh Albadou (GB)	26.30-to-1
2003	Cajun Beat	22.80-to-1
1992	Thirty Slews	18.70-to-1
1997	Elmhurst	16.60-to-1
1989	Dancing Spree	16.60-to-1
1987	Very Subtle	16.40-to-1

Odds-On Beaten Favorites in Sprint

Year	Favorite	Odds	Finish
1991	Housebuster	2-to-5	9
1987	Groovy	4-to-5	2
1986	Groovy	2-to-5	4

Fastest Winners

Year	Winner	Track	Time	Cond.
2000	Kona Gold	CD	1:07.77	fast
1999	Artax	GP	1:07.89	fast
2003	Cajun Beat	SA	1:07.95	fast
1997	Elmhurst	Hol	1:08.01	fast

Slowest Winners

Year	Winner	Track	Time	Cond.
1988	Gulch	CD	1:10⅖	sloppy
1984	Eillo	Hol	1:10⅕	fast
1990	Safely Kept	Bel	1:09⅗	fast
1994	Cherokee Run	CD	1:09.54	fast

Most Starters

Year	Track	Starters
2001	Belmont Park	14
2000	Churchill	14
1999	Gulfstream Park	14
1998	Churchill Downs	14
1997	Hollywood Park	14
1994	Churchill Downs	14
1993	Santa Anita Park	14
1992	Gulfstream Park	14
1990	Belmont Park	14
1985	Aqueduct	14

Fewest Starters

Year	Track	Starters
1986	Santa Anita Park	9
1991	Churchill Downs	11
1984	Hollywood Park	11

Winning Post Positions

Post	Starters	Winners	Percent
1	21	1	4.8%
2	21	3	14.3%
3	21	2	9.5%
4	21	2	9.5%
5	21	5	23.8%
6	21	0	0.0%
7	21	0	0.0%
8	21	1	4.8%
9	21	1	4.8%
10	20	3	15.0%
11	20	3	15.0%
12	18	0	0.0%
13	18	0	0.0%
14	10	0	0.0%

Changes in Sprint

No changes have been made in the conditions or purse of the race since its first running in 1984.

Breeders' Cup Mile

In the Breeders' Cup Mile (G1), good things have come in twos. Four Breeders' Cup races have had repeat winners, and the Breeders' Cup Mile has had three horses who have posted two victories each.

Miesque, bred by owner Stavros Niarchos's Flaxman Holdings Ltd., sparkled in the Mile on turf at Hollywood Park in 1987 and conquered a significantly slower surface at Churchill Downs the following year. The remarkable Francois Boutin-trained filly won by 3½ lengths in California and by four lengths in Kentucky—the largest winning margins in the race's history. On the strength of her single North American victories, Miesque was voted champion grass female in 1987 and '88. The Niarchos family also campaigned Mile winners Spinning World (1997), Domedriver (Ire) (2002), and Six Perfections (Fr) ('03) in the name of Flaxman Holdings.

Claiborne Farm's homebred Lure, arguably one of the most accomplished horses never to win an end-of-year championship, also scored two daylight victories, winning by three lengths at Gulfstream Park in 1992 and by 2¼ lengths the following year at Santa Anita Park for trainer Claude R. "Shug" McGaughey III.

Although not necessarily possessing talent to equal Miesque or Lure, Da Hoss became a two-time Mile winner by virtue of his courage and the innovative training regimen of Michael Dickinson. In 1996, Dickinson had his assistant, Joan Wakefield, test the Woodbine turf course in high heels to determine the best path for the Gone West gelding, who won by 1½ lengths. Da Hoss missed the entire following season due to injury and came back to run in the 1998 Mile with only one start in two years. He rallied on a firm Churchill turf course to overtake Hawksley Hill (Ire) and win by a head.

European-based horses have had consistent success in the Mile. Nine of the first 21 winners were based with European trainers prior to their wins.

Breeders' Cup Mile

Grade 1, $1.5-million, three-year-olds and up, 1 mile, turf. Run October 30, 2004, at Lone Star Park with gross value of $1,540,560. First run in 1984. Weights: Northern Hemisphere three-year-olds, 123 pounds; older, 126 pounds. Southern Hemisphere three-year-olds, 119 pounds; older, 126 pounds. Fillies and mares allowed three pounds.

Year	Winner	Jockey	Second	Third	Site	Time	Cond.	1st Purse
2004	**Singletary**	D. Flores	Antonius Pius	Six Perfections (Fr)	LS	1:36.90	yl	**$873,600**
2003	**Six Perfections (Fr)**, 3	J. Bailey	Touch of the Blues (Fr)	Century City (Ire)	SA	1:33.86	ft	780,000
2002	**Domedriver (Ire)**	T. Thulliez	Rock of Gibraltar (Ire)	Good Journey	AP	1:36.92	yl	556,400
2001	**Val Royal (Fr)**, 5	J. Valdivia Jr.	Forbidden Apple	Bach (Ire)	Bel	**1:32.05**	fm	592,800
2000	**War Chant**, 3	G. Stevens	North East Bound	Dansili (GB)	CD	1:34.67	fm	608,400
1999	**Silic (Fr)**, 4	C. Nakatani	Tuzla (Fr)	Docksider	GP	1:34.26	gd	520,000
1998	**Da Hoss**, 6	J. Velazquez	Hawksley Hill (Ire)	Labeeb (GB)	CD	1:35.27	fm	520,000
1997	**Spinning World**, 4	C. Asmussen	Geri	Decorated Hero (GB)	Hol	1:32.77	fm	572,000
1996	**Da Hoss**, 4	G. Stevens	Spinning World	Same Old Wish	WO	1:35.80	gd	520,000
1995	**Ridgewood Pearl (GB)**, f, 3	J. Murtagh	Fastness (Ire)	Sayyedati (GB)	Bel	1:43.65	sf	520,000
1994	**Barathea (Ire)**, 4	L. Dettori	Johann Quatz (Fr)	Unfinished Symph	CD	1:34.50	fm	520,000
1993	**Lure**, 4	M. Smith	Ski Paradise	Fourstars Allstar	SA	1:33.58	fm	520,000
1992	**Lure**, 3	M. Smith	Paradise Creek	Brief Truce	GP	1:32.90	fm	520,000
1991	**Opening Verse**, 5	P. Valenzuela	Val des Bois (Fr)	Star of Cozzene	CD	1:37.59	fm	520,000
1990	**Royal Academy**, 3	L. Piggott	Itsallgreektome	Priolo	Bel	1:35⅕	gd	450,000
1989	**Steinlen (GB)**, 6	J. Santos	Sabona	Most Welcome (GB)	GP	1:37⅕	gd	450,000
1988	**Miesque**, f, 4	F. Head	Steinlen (GB)	Simply Majestic	CD	1:38⅗	gd	450,000
1987	**Miesque**, f, 3	F. Head	Show Dancer	Sonic Lady	Hol	1:32⅘	fm	450,000
1986	**Last Tycoon (Ire)**, 3	Y. Saint-Martin	Palace Music	Fred Astaire	SA	1:35⅕	fm	450,000
1985	**Cozzene**, 5	W. Guerra	Al Mamoon	Shadeed	Aqu	1:35	fm	450,000
1984	**Royal Heroine (Ire)**, f, 4	F. Toro	Star Choice	Cozzene	Hol	1:32⅗	fm	450,000

1985—Palace Music disqualified from second to ninth.

Most remarkable about the Mile has been the domination of the Northern Dancer sire line. Although the great Windfields Farm stallion did not sire a winner himself, six of his sons and two of his grandsons have sired winners, accounting for 12 victories in the first 21 years. His sons Danzig and Nureyev have each sired three winners.

The interests of the late Stavros Niarchos have had unprecedented success in the Mile. Following the victories of Miesque, the Niarchos family's Spinning World won in 1997, and the family recorded back-to-back victories in 2002 and '03, with Domedriver (Ire) and Six Perfections (Fr), respectively.

Owners by Wins

5 **Flaxman Holdings Ltd./Stavros Niarchos** (Domedriver [Ire], Miesque [twice], Six Perfections [Fr], Spinning World)

2 **Claiborne Farm** (Lure [twice]), **Prestonwood Farm and Wall Street Stable** (Da Hoss, [twice])

1 **Classic Thoroughbreds PLC** (Royal Academy), **Anne Coughlan** (Ridgewood Pearl [GB]), **Marjorie and Irving Cowan** (War Chant), **J. Terrence Lanni, Bernard Schiappa, Kenneth Poslosky, et al.** (Silic [Fr]), **Little Red Feather Racing** (Singletary), **David S. Milch** (Val Royal [Fr]), **Sheikh Mohammed bin Rashid al Maktoum and Gerald Leigh** (Barathea [Ire]), **John Nerud** (Cozzene), **Allen E. Paulson** (Opening Verse), **Richard C. Strauss** (Last Tycoon [Ire]), **Robert Sangster** (Royal Heroine [Ire]), **Wildenstein Stable** (Steinlen [GB])

Breeders by Wins

5 **Flaxman Holdings Ltd./Niarchos Family** (Domedriver [Ire], Miesque [twice], Six Perfections [Fr], Spinning World)

2 **Claiborne Farm and Gamely Corp.** (Lure [twice]), **Fares Farm** (Da Hoss [twice])

1 **Allez France Stables Ltd.** (Steinlen [GB]), **Tom Gentry** (Royal Academy), **Sean Coughlan** (Ridgewood Pearl [GB]), **Marjorie and Irving Cowan** (War Chant), **M. Armenio Simoes de Almeida** (Silic [Fr]), **Disler Farms Ltd.** (Singletary), **Kilfrush Stud Ltd.** (Last Tycoon [Ire]), **Jean-Luc Lagardere** (Val Royal [Fr]), **Gerald Leigh** (Barathea [Ire]), **John Nerud** (Cozzene), **B. L. Ryan** (Royal Heroine [Ire]), **Jacques D. Wimpfheimer** (Opening Verse)

Trainers by Wins

2 **Pascal Bary** (Domedriver [Ire], Six Perfections [Fr]), **Francois Boutin** (Miesque [twice]), **Julio Canani** (Silic [Fr], Val Royal [Fr]), **Michael Dickinson** (Da Hoss [twice]), **Claude R. "Shug" McGaughey III** (Lure [twice])

1 **Don Chatlos** (Singletary), **Robert Collet** (Last Tycoon [Ire]), **Luca Cumani** (Barathea [Ire]), **Neil Drysdale** (War Chant), **John Gosden** (Royal Heroine [Ire]), **D. Wayne Lukas** (Steinlen [GB]), **Richard Lundy** (Opening Verse), **Jan Nerud** (Cozzene), **Michael O'Brien** (Royal Academy), **John Oxx** (Ridgewood Pearl [GB]), **Jonathan Pease** (Spinning World)

Jockeys by Wins

2 **Freddie Head** (Miesque [twice]), **Mike Smith** (Lure [twice]), **Gary Stevens** (Da Hoss, War Chant)

1 **Cash Asmussen** (Spinning World), **Jerry Bailey** (Six Perfections [Fr]), **Lanfranco Dettori** (Barathea [Ire]), **David Flores** (Singletary), **Walter Guerra** (Cozzene), **John Murtagh** (Ridgewood Pearl [GB]), **Corey Nakatani** (Silic [Fr]), **Lester Piggott** (Royal Academy), **Yves Saint-Martin** (Last Tycoon [Ire]), **Jose Santos** (Steinlen [GB]), **Thierry Thulliez** (Domedriver [Ire]), **Fernando Toro** (Royal Heroine [Ire]), **Jose Valdivia Jr.** (Val Royal [Fr]), **John Velazquez** (Da Hoss), **Patrick Valenzuela** (Opening Verse)

Sires by Wins

3 **Danzig** (Lure [twice], War Chant), **Nureyev** (Miesque [twice], Spinning World)

2 **Gone West** (Da Hoss [twice]), **Indian Ridge** (Domedriver [Ire], Ridgewood Pearl [GB])

1 **Caro (Ire)** (Cozzene), **Celtic Swing** (Six Perfections [Fr]), **Habitat** (Steinlen [GB]), **Lypheor (GB)** (Royal Heroine [Ire]), **Nijinsky II** (Royal Academy), **Royal Academy** (Val Royal [Fr]), **Sadler's Wells** (Barathea [Ire]), **Sillery** (Silic [Fr]), **Sultry Song** (Singletary), **The Minstrel** (Opening Verse), **Try My Best** (Last Tycoon [Ire])

Winners by Place Where Bred

Locality	Winners
Kentucky	11
Ireland	4
France	3
Great Britain	2
Florida	1

Supplemental Entries

Year	Runner	Fee	Finish	Earnings
2004	Blackdoun (Fr)	$90,000	7	$0
	Mr. O'Brien (Ire)	90,000	9	0
2002	Landseer (GB)	90,000	DNF	0
2001	Val Royal (Fr)	90,000	1	592,800
	Express Tour	90,000	10	0
2000	Ladies Din	120,000	8	0
	Indian Lodge (Ire)	90,000	13	0
1997	Lucky Coin	120,000	4	61,600
1992	Bistro Garden	120,000	14	0
1991	Star of Cozzene	120,000	3	120,000
1986	Hatim	120,000	13	0
	Truce Maker	120,000	14	0
1985	Rousillon	120,000	9	0
1984	Night Mover	120,000	8	0

DNF Did not finish

Eclipse Award Winners from Race

Year	Runner	Finish	Title
1993	Flawlessly	9	Turf female
1991	Tight Spot	9	Turf male
1990	Itsallgreektome	2	Turf male
1989	**Steinlen (GB)**	1	Turf male
1988	**Miesque**	1	Turf female
1987	**Miesque**	1	Turf female
1985	**Cozzene**	1	Turf male
1984	**Royal Heroine (Ire)**	1	Turf female

Largest Winning Margins

Year	Winner	Margin
1988	Miesque	4
1987	Miesque	3½
1994	Barathea (Ire)	3
1992	Lure	3

Smallest Winning Margins

Year	Winner	Margin
1998	Da Hoss	head
1986	Last Tycoon (Ire)	head
2000	War Chant	neck
1999	Silic (Fr)	neck
1990	Royal Academy	neck

Shortest-Priced Winners

Year	Winner	Odds
1993	Lure	1.30-to-1
1984	Royal Heroine (Ire)	1.70-to-1*
1989	Steinlen (GB)	1.80-to-1
1988	Miesque	2.00-to-1*

*Part of entry

Longest-Priced Winners

Year	Winner	Odds
1986	Last Tycoon (Ire)	35.90-to-1
1991	Opening Verse	26.70-to-1
2002	Domedriver (Ire)	26.00-to-1
2004	Singletary	16.50-to-1
1998	Da Hoss	11.60-to-1
1994	Barathea (Ire)	10.40-to-1

Odds-On Beaten Favorites in Mile

Year	Favorite	Odds	Finish
2002	Rock of Gibraltar (Ire)	4-to-5	2
1994	Lure	9-to-10	9

Fastest Winners

Year	Winner	Track	Time	Cond.
2001	Val Royal (Fr)	Bel	1:32.05	firm
1984	Royal Heroine (Ire)	Hol	1:32⅗	firm
1997	Spinning World	Hol	1:32.77	firm
1987	Miesque	Hol	1:32⅘	firm
1992	Lure	GP	1:32.90	firm

Slowest Winners

Year	Winner	Track	Time	Cond.
1995	Ridgewood Pearl (GB)	Bel	1:43.65	soft
1988	Miesque	CD	1:38⅗	good
1991	Opening Verse	CD	1:37.59	firm
1989	Steinlen (GB)	GP	1:37⅕	good

Most Starters

Year	Track	Starters
2004	Lone Star Park	14
2002	Arlington Park	14
2000	Churchill Downs`	14
1999	Gulfstream Park	14
1998	Churchill Downs	14
1996	Woodbine	14
1994	Churchill Downs	14
1992	Gulfstream Park	14
1991	Churchill Downs	14
1987	Hollywood Park	14
1986	Santa Anita	14
1985	Aqueduct	14

Fewest Starters

Year	Track	Starters
1984	Hollywood Park	10
1989	Gulfstream Park	11
2001	Belmont Park	12
1997	Hollywood Park	12
1988	Churchill Downs	12

Winning Post Positions

Post	Starters	Winners	Percent
1	21	3	14.3%
2	21	3	14.3%
3	21	1	4.6%
4	21	2	9.5%
5	21	1	4.6%
6	21	2	9.5%
7	21	1	4.6%
8	21	1	4.6%
9	21	0	0.0%
10	21	2	9.5%
11	20	2	10.0%
12	19	3	15.8%
13	16	0	0.0%
14	12	0	0.0%

Changes in Mile

The purse of the Breeders' Cup Mile was increased to $1.5-million from $1-million in 2003.

Breeders' Cup Juvenile Fillies

One of the most all-American of the Breeders' Cup races, the Breeders' Cup Juvenile Fillies (G1) has produced the most champions in year-end Eclipse Award balloting among Breeders' Cup races. Eighteen of the 21 winners were subsequently voted year-end champions.

The first Breeders' Cup Juvenile Fillies, the second race on the inaugural card in 1984, produced the afternoon's first bit of controversy. In making a winning move at the top of the stretch, Fran's Valentine knocked Pirate's Glow off stride and pushed her into Canadian star Bessarabian. Fran's Valentine held off Outstandingly to reach the finish line first, but stewards disqualified Fran's Valentine to tenth for causing interference. After Outstandingly followed with a win in the Hollywood Starlet Stakes (G1), she was voted an Eclipse Award as champion two-year-old filly, a title that would be earned by all but three of the succeeding Juvenile Fillies winners.

The Juvenile Fillies at Aqueduct in 1985 launched a dominating run by D. Wayne Lukas, who took the first two spots that year with Twilight Ridge and Family Style. Lukas saddled the top three finishers in 1988, with Open Mind the winner. In 1994, he sent out Flanders and Serena's Song to finish one-two. Flanders pulled up lame after the race and subsequently was retired. Serena's Song, second by a head, was champion three-year-old filly the following year and retired as North America's then-leading female earner with $3,283,388. Lukas also won in 1999 with longshot Cash Run.

In addition to Open Mind, who was voted champion at two and three, Juvenile Fillies winners who earned two championship titles were Go for Wand and Silverbulletday. Go for Wand took the two-year-old title with a triumph at Gulfstream Park in 1989 and won an Eclipse Award as champion three-year-old filly posthumously after a fatal breakdown in the 1990 Breeders' Cup Distaff (G1). Silverbulletday scored a half-length victory over stablemate Excellent Meeting in the 1998 Juvenile Fillies and won four Grade 1 races the following year to wrap up the three-year-old filly title.

Ashado, second to Halfbridled in 2003, went on to win the Breeders' Cup Distaff (G1) in '04 and collect an Eclipse Award as champion three-year-old filly.

Even more than the Breeders' Cup Juvenile (G1), the Juvenile Fillies in recent years has been noteworthy for the inability of its winners to maintain their form at age three. Storm Flag Flying, a daughter of 1995 Juvenile Fillies winner My Flag and unbeaten in 2002, failed to win at three, although she was a Grade 1 winner at four in '04 and finished second to Ashado in the '04 Distaff. Halfbridled, also unbeaten at two, failed to win her two starts at three in 2004 and was retired. Sweet Catomine, also an impressive Juvenile Fillies winner and a near-unanimous Eclipse Award champion, won twice at three, including an easy

victory in the Santa Anita Oaks (G1), but was retired after running fifth in the Santa Anita Derby (G1).

The Juvenile Fillies also is notable for its number of odds-on winners. Lukas's three-horse entry was 3-to-5 in 1985, and in '88 his five-horse coupling was 7-to-10. Two years later at Belmont Park, LeRoy Jolley-trained Meadow Star went off at 1-to-5 and breezed home by five lengths. Lukas struck again at Churchill in 1994, when Flanders won at 2-to-5 in an entry with Cat Appeal. Silverbulletday, trained by Bob Baffert, won at 4-to-5 in 1998, and Ogden Mills Phipps's Storm Flag Flying won at 4-to-5 in 2002. The only filly beaten at odds-on was 0.95-to-1 You, who finished fourth in 2001.

Through 2004, only 12 overseas-based fillies have competed in the Juvenile Fillies, with their best finishes a pair of fourths in 1993 and '94. Godolphin Racing won in 2001 with Tempera, who was trained in the United States by Eoin Harty.

Owners by Wins

2 **Eugene V. Klein** (Twilight Ridge, Open Mind)
1 **John A. Bell III** (Epitome), **Buckland Farm** (Pleasant Stage), **Christiana Stable** (Go for Wand), **Dogwood Stable** (Storm Song), **Dolly Green** (Brave Raj), **Godolphin Racing** (Tempera), **Harbor View Farm** (Outstandingly), **Carl Icahn** (Meadow Star), **Richard A. Kaster, Nancy R. Kaster, Nancy A. Kaster, and Donald Propson** (Countess Diana), **Overbrook Farm** (Flanders), **Padua Stables** (Cash Run), **Allen E. Paulson** (Silverbulletday), **Mike Pegram** (Silverbulletday), **Ogden Phipps** (My Flag), **Ogden Mills Phipps** (Storm Flag Flying), **Carl F. Pollard** (Caressing), **Herman Sarkowsky** (Phone Chatter), **Wertheimer Farm** (Halfbridled), **Martin and Pamela Wygod** (Sweet Catomine)

Breeders' Cup Juvenile Fillies

Grade 1, $1-million, two-year-old fillies, 1¹⁄₁₆ miles, dirt. Run on October 30, 2004, at Lone Star Park with gross value of $917,000. First run in 1984. Weights: 119 pounds

Year	Winner	Jockey	Second	Third	Site	Time	Cond.	1st Purse
2004	Sweet Catomine	C. Nakatani	Balletto (UAE)	Runway Model	LS	1:41.65	ft	$520,000
2003	Halfbridled	J. Krone	Ashado	Victory U. S. A.	SA	1:42.75	ft	520,000
2002	Storm Flag Flying	J. Velaquez	Composure	Santa Catarina	AP	1:49.60	gd	520,000
2001	Tempera	D. Flores	Imperial Gesture	Bella Bellucci	Bel	1:41.49	ft	520,000
2000	Caressing	J. Velazquez	Platinum Tiara	She's a Devil Due	CD	1:42.77	ft	592,800
1999	Cash Run	J. Bailey	Chilukki	Surfside	GP	1:43.31	ft	520,000
1998	Silverbulletday	G. Stevens	Excellent Meeting	Three Ring	CD	1:43.68	ft	520,000
1997	Countess Diana	S. Sellers	Career Collection	Primaly	Hol	1:42.11	ft	535,600
1996	Storm Song	C. Perret	Love That Jazz	Critical Factor	WO	1:43.60	ft	520,000
1995	My Flag	J. Bailey	Cara Rafaela	Golden Attraction	Bel	1:42.55	my	520,000
1994	Flanders	P. Day	Serena's Song	Stormy Blues	CD	1:45.28	ft	520,000
1993	Phone Chatter	L. Pincay	Sardula	Heavenly Prize	SA	1:43.08	ft	520,000
1992	Eliza	P. Valenzuela	Educated Risk	Boots 'n Jackie	GP	1:42.93	ft	520,000
1991	Pleasant Stage	E. Delahoussaye	La Spia	Cadillac Women	CD	1:46.48	ft	520,000
1990	Meadow Star	J. Santos	Private Treasure	Dance Smartly	Bel	1:44	ft	450,000
1989	Go for Wand	R. Romero	Sweet Roberta	Stella Madrid	GP	1:44¹⁄₅	ft	450,000
1988	Open Mind	A. Cordero Jr.	Darby Shuffle	Lea Lucinda	CD	1:46³⁄₅	my	450,000
1987	Epitome	P. Day	Jeanne Jones	Dream Team	Hol	1:36²⁄₅	ft	450,000
1986	Brave Raj	P. Valenzuela	Tappiano	Saros Brig	SA	1:43¹⁄₅	ft	450,000
1985	Twilight Ridge	J. Velasquez	Family Style	Steal a Kiss	Aqu	1:35¹⁄₅	ft	450,000
1984	Outstandingly	W. Guerra	Dusty Heart	Fine Spirit	Hol	1:37¹⁄₅	ft	450,000

1984-'85, '87—run at one mile; 1984—Fran's Valentine disqualified from first to tenth.

Breeders by Wins

2 Ogden Phipps (My Flag, Storm Flag Flying)
1 Thomas E. Burrow (Twilight Ridge), Jaime S. Carrion (Meadow Star), Christiana Stable (Go for Wand), Darley Stud Management (Tempera), Due Process Stable (Open Mind), Robert S. Evans (Cash Run), Mrs. Thomas M. Evans (Pleasant Stage), William S. Farish and Ogden Mills Phipps (Storm Song), Harbor View Farm (Outstandingly), Highclere Inc. and Clear Creek (Silverbulletday), Brereton C. Jones (Caressing), Richard A. and Nancy R. Kaster (Countess Diana), Wallace S. Karutz (Brave Raj), Jessica Bell Nicholson and H. Bennett Bell (Epitome), Overbrook Farm (Flanders), Allen E. Paulson (Eliza), Herman Sarkowsky (Phone Chatter), Wertheimer Farm et Frere (Halfbridled), Martin and Pamela Wygod (Sweet Catomine)

Trainers by Wins

4 D. Wayne Lukas (Twilight Ridge, Open Mind, Flanders, Cash Run)
2 Richard Mandella (Halfbridled, Phone Chatter), Claude R. "Shug" McGaughey III (My Flag, Storm Flag Flying)
1 William Badgett (Go for Wand), Bob Baffert (Silverbulletday), Patrick Byrne (Countess Diana), Julio Canani (Sweet Catomine), Eoin Harty (Tempera), Alex Hassinger Jr. (Eliza), Philip Hauswald (Epitome), LeRoy Jolley (Meadow Star), Frank Martin (Outstandingly), Christopher Speckert (Pleasant Stage), Mel Stute (Brave Raj), David Vance (Caressing), Nick P. Zito (Storm Song)

Jockeys by Wins

2 Jerry Bailey (My Flag, Cash Run), Pat Day (Epitome, Flanders), John Velazquez (Caressing, Storm Flag Flying), Patrick Valenzuela (Brave Raj, Eliza)
1 Angel Cordero Jr. (Open Mind), Eddie Delahoussaye (Pleasant Stage), David Flores (Tempera), Walter Guerra (Outstandingly), Julie Krone (Halfbridled), Corey Nakatani (Sweet Catomine), Craig Perret (Storm Song), Laffit Pincay Jr. (Phone Chatter), Randy Romero (Go for Wand), Jose Santos (Meadow Star), Shane Sellers (Countess Diana), Gary Stevens (Silverbulletday), Jorge Velasquez (Twilight Ridge)

Sires by Wins

2 Deputy Minister (Open Mind, Go for Wand), Seeking the Gold (Flanders, Cash Run), Storm Cat (Sweet Catomine, Storm Flag Flying)
1 A.P. Indy (Tempera), Cox's Ridge (Twilight Ridge), Deerhound (Countess Diana), Easy Goer (My Flag), Exclusive Native (Outstandingly), Honour and Glory (Caressing), Meadowlake (Meadow Star), Mt. Livermore (Eliza), Phone Trick (Phone Chatter), Pleasant Colony (Pleasant Stage), Rajab (Brave Raj), Silver Deputy (Silverbulletday), Summer Squall (Storm Song), Summing (Epitome), Unbridled (Halfbridled)

Winners by Place Where Bred

Locality	Winners
Kentucky	16
Florida	3
New Jersey	1
Pennsylvania	1

Supplemental Entries

Year	Runner	Fee	Finish	Earnings
2000	Cindy's Hero	$ 90,000	4	$63,840
	Out of Sync	90,000	9	0
1995	Tipically Irish	120,000	6	0
1994	Post It	120,000	6	0

Eclipse Award Winners from Race

Year	Runner	Finish	Title
2004	Sweet Catomine	1	Juvenile filly
2003	Halfbridled	1	Juvenile filly
2002	Storm Flag Flying	1	Juvenile filly
2001	Tempera	1	Juvenile filly
2000	Caressing	1	Juvenile filly
1999	Chilukki	2	Juvenile filly
1998	Silverbulletday	1	Juvenile filly
1997	Countess Diana	1	Juvenile filly
1996	Storm Song	1	Juvenile filly
1995	Golden Attraction	3	Juvenile filly
1994	Flanders	1	Juvenile filly
1993	Phone Chatter	1	Juvenile filly
1992	Eliza	1	Juvenile filly
1991	Pleasant Stage	1	Juvenile filly
1990	Meadow Star	1	Juvenile filly
1989	Go for Wand	1	Juvenile filly
1988	Open Mind	1	Juvenile filly
1987	Epitome	1	Juvenile filly
1986	Brave Raj	1	Juvenile filly
1985	Family Style	2	Juvenile filly
1984	Outstandingly	1	Juvenile filly

Largest Winning Margins

Year	Winner	Margin
1997	Countess Diana	8½
1986	Brave Raj	5½
1990	Meadow Star	5
1996	Storm Song	4½

Smallest Winning Margins

Year	Winner	Margin
1987	Epitome	nose
1994	Flanders	head
1993	Phone Chatter	head
1991	Pleasant Stage	head

Shortest-Priced Winners

Year	Winner	Odds
1990	Meadow Star	0.20-to-1
1994	Flanders	0.40-to-1*
1985	Twilight Ridge	0.60-to-1*
1988	Open Mind	0.70-to-1*
2002	Storm Flag Flying	0.80-to-1
1998	Silverbulletday	0.80-to-1

*Part of entry

Longest-Priced Winners

Year	Winner	Odds
2000	Caressing	47.00-to-1
1999	Cash Run	32.50-to-1
1987	Epitome	30.40-to-1
1984	Outstandingly	22.80-to-1

Odds-On Beaten Favorites

Year	Favorite	Odds
2001	You	0.95-to-1

Fastest Winners at 1 1/16 Miles

Year	Winner	Track	Time	Cond.
2001	Tempera	Bel	1:41.49	fast
2004	Sweet Catomine	LS	1:41.65	fast
1997	Countess Diana	Hol	1:42.11	fast
1995	My Flag	Bel	1:42.55	muddy
2003	Halfbridled	SA	1:42.75	fast
2000	Caressing	CD	1:42.77	fast
1992	Eliza	GP	1:42.93	fast

Slowest Winners at 1 1/16 Miles

Year	Winner	Track	Time	Cond.
1988	Open Mind	CD	1:46⅗	muddy
1991	Pleasant Stage	CD	1:46.48	fast
1994	Flanders	CD	1:45.28	fast
1989	Go for Wand	GP	1:44⅕	fast

Most Starters

Year	Track	Starters
2003	Santa Anita Park	14
1997	Hollywood Park	14
1991	Churchill Downs	14
1994	Churchill Downs	13
1990	Belmont Park	13

Fewest Starters

Year	Track	Starters
1995	Belmont Park	8
1993	Santa Anita Park	8
2001	Belmont Park	9
1999	Gulfstream Park	9

Winning Post Positions

Post	Starters	Winners	Percent
1	21	1	4.8%
2	21	1	4.8%
3	21	1	4.8%
4	21	3	14.3%
5	21	1	4.8%
6	21	3	14.3%
7	21	0	0.0%
8	21	4	19.0%
9	19	4	21.1%
10	17	0	0.0%
11	15	1	6.7%
12	13	0	0.0%
13	5	0	0.0%
14	3	2	66.7%

Changes in Juvenile Fillies

The only change to the Breeders' Cup Juvenile Fillies over the years has been the distance. Originally at one mile for the 1984 and '85 runnings, the distance was changed to 1 1/16 miles in 1988. It was contested at 1 1/16 miles in 1986 and at 1⅛ miles in 2002.

Breeders' Cup Distaff

Although the Breeders' Cup Distaff (G1) has produced three of the eight highest-priced winners in the event's history, the race for fillies and mares has in fact been one of the most consistent of the original seven races.

That record of consistency began with the inaugural Breeders' Cup Distaff at Hollywood Park in 1984. Princess Rooney, winner of the Vanity Handicap (G1) and Spinster Stakes (G1) in prior starts, went off as the 7-to-10 favorite and rolled to a seven-length victory.

In subsequent editions, the Distaff generally was characterized by dominant winners scoring by open lengths. In fact, Inside Information's 13½-length win in 1995 remains the series' largest winning margin. Azeri waltzed away to a five-

Breeders' Cup Distaff

Grade 1, $2-million, fillies and mares, three-year-olds and up, 1⅛ miles. Run October 30, 2004, at Lone Star Park with gross value of $1,834,000. First run in 1984. Weights: Northern Hemisphere three-year-olds, 120 pounds; older, 123 pounds. Southern Hemisphere three-year-olds, 114 pounds; older, 123 pounds.

Year	Winner	Jockey	Second	Third	Site	Time	Cond.	1st Purse
2004	**Ashado**, 4	J. Velazquez	Storm Flag Flying	Stellar Jayne	LS	1:48.26	ft	$1,080,000
2003	**Adoration**, 4	P. Valenzuela	Elloluv	Got Koko	SA	1:49.17	ft	1,040,000
2002	**Azeri**	M. Smith	Farda Amiga	Imperial Gesture	AP	1:48.64	gd	1,040,000
2001	**Unbridled Elaine**, 3	P. Day	Spain	Two Item Limit	Bel	1:49.21	ft	1,227,200
2000	**Spain**, 3	V. Espinoza	Surfside	Heritage of Gold	CD	1:47.66	ft	**1,227,200**
1999	**Beautiful Pleasure**, 4	J. Chavez	Banshee Breeze	Heritage of Gold	GP	1:47.56	ft	1,040,000
1998	**Escena**, 5	G. Stevens	Banshee Breeze	Keeper Hill	CD	1:49.89	ft	1,040,000
1997	**Ajina**, 3	M. Smith	Sharp Cat	Escena	Hol	1:47.30	ft	520,000
1996	**Jewel Princess**, 4	C. Nakatani	Serena's Song	Different (Arg)	WO	1:48.40	ft	520,000
1995	**Inside Information**, 4	M. Smith	Heavenly Prize	Lakeway	Bel	**1:46.15**	my	520,000
1994	**One Dreamer**, 6	G. Stevens	Heavenly Prize	Miss Dominique	CD	1:50.70	ft	520,000
1993	**Hollywood Wildcat**, 3	E. Delahoussaye	Paseana (Arg)	Re Toss (Arg)	SA	1:48.35	ft	520,000
1992	**Paseana (Arg)**, 5	C. McCarron	Versailles Treaty	Magical Maiden	GP	1:48.17	ft	520,000
1991	**Dance Smartly**, 3	P. Day	Versailles Treaty	Brought to Mind	CD	1:50.95	ft	520,000
1990	**Bayakoa (Arg)**, 6	L. Pincay Jr.	Colonial Waters	Valay Maid	Bel	1:49⅕	ft	450,000
1989	**Bayakoa (Arg)**, 5	L. Pincay Jr.	Gorgeous	Open Mind	GP	1:47⅖	ft	450,000
1988	**Personal Ensign**, 4	R. Romero	Winning Colors	Goodbye Halo	CD	1:52	my	450,000
1987	**Sacahuista**, 3	R. Romero	Clabber Girl	Oueee Bebe	Hol	2:02⅘	ft	450,000
1986	**Lady's Secret**, 4	P. Day	Fran's Valentine	Outstandingly	SA	**2:01⅕**	ft	450,000
1985	**Life's Magic**, 4	A. Cordero Jr.	Lady's Secret	Dontstop Themusic	Aqu	2:02	ft	450,000
1984	**Princess Rooney**, 4	E. Delahoussaye	Life's Magic	Adored	Hol	2:02⅖	ft	450,000

1984-'87—run at 1¼ miles; 1989 and '90—Bayakoa (Arg) supplementary entry; 1992—Paseana (Arg) supplemental entry.

length victory in 2002 to lock up a Horse of the Year title, and Lady's Secret won by 2½ lengths in 1986, her Horse of the Year season. Odds-on favorites have won the race seven times.

The 1988 running remains one of the most memorable of all Breeders' Cup races. Undefeated Personal Ensign, seemingly beaten at the sixteenth pole, closed relentlessly on Winning Colors, that year's Kentucky Derby (G1) winner, and put her nose in front at the wire to close out her career undefeated in 13 starts.

In 14 of 21 years, both the champion three-year-old filly and older female have competed in the Distaff.

Supplemental entries, principally top-quality mares from South America, have had excellent success in the Distaff. Bayakoa (Arg), supplemented for $200,000 in 1989 and '90, won both years. Paseana (Arg), supplemented in 1992 and '93, won in her first try and finished second by a nose to Hollywood Wildcat in '93.

The biggest upset in Distaff history occurred in 2000, when dominant West Coast mare Riboletta (Brz) ran seventh as the 2-to-5 favorite.

Racing Hall of Fame members who have contested the race are Princess Rooney, Lady's Secret, Personal Ensign, Winning Colors, Bayakoa, Go for Wand, Dance Smartly, Paseana, and Serena's Song.

Owners by Wins

2 Allen E. Paulson (Ajina, Escena), **Frank and Janis Whitham** (Bayakoa [Arg] [twice])

1 Amerman Racing Stable (Adoration), **Barry A. Beal and L. R. French Jr.** (Sacahuista), **Irving and Marjorie Cowan** (Hollywood Wildcat), **Sidney Craig** (Paseana [Arg]), **Roger J. Devenport** (Unbridled Elaine), **Glen Hill Farm** (One Dreamer), **Mel Hatley and Eugene V. Klein** (Life's Magic), **Mr. and Mrs. Eugene V. Klein** (Lady's Secret), **John Oxley** (Beautiful Pleasure), **Allen E. Paulson Living Trust** (Azeri), **Ogden Phipps** (Personal Ensign), **Ogden Mills Phipps** (Inside Information), **Sam-Son Farm** (Dance Smartly), **Starlight Stables, Paul Saylor, and Johns Martin** (Ashado), **The Thoroughbred Corp. and Martha and Richard Stephen** (Jewel Princess), **The Thoroughbred Corp.** (Spain), **Paula Tucker** (Princess Rooney)

Breeders by Wins

3 Allen E. Paulson (Ajina, Azeri, Escena)

2 Farnsworth Farms (Beautiful Pleasure, Jewel Princess), **Haras Principal** (Bayakoa [Arg], twice)

1 Lucy G. Bassett (Adoration), **Irving and Marjorie Cowan** (Hollywood Wildcat), **Golden Orb Farm and K. David Schwartz** (Unbridled Elaine), **Haras Vacacion** (Paseana [Arg]), **G. Watts Humphrey and William S. Farish** (Sacahuista), **Aaron and Marie Jones** (Ashado), **Mr. and Mrs. Douglas Parrish and David Parrish III** (Life's Magic), **Ogden Phipps** (Personal Ensign), **Ogden Mills Phipps** (Inside Information), **Ben and Tom Roach** (Princess Rooney), **Sam-Son Farm** (Dance Smartly), **Robert H. Spreen** (Lady's Secret), **The Thoroughbred Corp.** (Spain)

Trainers by Wins

4 D. Wayne Lukas (Lady's Secret, Life's Magic, Sacahuista, Spain)

3 Ron McAnally (Bayakoa [Arg] [twice], Paseana [Arg])

2 Neil Drysdale (Hollywood Wildcat, Princess Rooney), **Claude R. "Shug" McGaughey III** (Inside Information, Personal Ensign), **William I. Mott** (Ajina, Escena)

1 James Day (Dance Smartly), **Laura de Seroux** (Azeri), **Wallace Dollase** (Jewel Princess), **David Hofmans** (Adoration), **Todd Pletcher** (Ashado), **Tom Proctor** (One Dreamer), **Dallas Stewart** (Unbridled Elaine), **John T. Ward Jr.** (Beautiful Pleasure)

Jockeys by Wins

3 Pat Day (Dance Smartly, Lady's Secret, Unbridled Elaine), **Mike Smith** (Azeri, Ajina, Inside Information)

2 Eddie Delahoussaye (Hollywood Wildcat, Princess Rooney), **Laffit Pincay Jr.** (Bayakoa [Arg] [twice]), **Randy Romero** (Personal Ensign, Sacahuista), **Gary Stevens** (Escena, One Dreamer)

1 Jorge Chavez (Beautiful Pleasure), **Angel Cordero** (Life's Magic), **Victor Espinoza** (Spain), **Chris McCarron** (Paseana [Arg]), **Corey Nakatani** (Jewel Princess), **Patrick Valenzuela** (Adoration), **John Velazquez** (Ashado)

Sires by Wins

2 Consultant's Bid (Bayakoa [Arg], twice), **Private Account** (Inside Information, Personal Ensign), **Strawberry Road (Aus)** (Ajina, Escena)

1 Ahmad (Paseana [Arg]), **Cox's Ridge** (Life's Magic), **Danzig** (Dance Smartly), **Honor Grades** (Adoration), **Jade Hunter** (Azeri), **Key to the Mint** (Jewel Princess), **Kris S.** (Hollywood Wildcat), **Maudlin** (Beautiful Pleasure), **Raja Baba** (Sacahuista), **Relaunch** (One Dreamer), **Saint Ballado** (Ashado), **Secretariat** (Lady's Secret), **Thunder Gulch** (Spain), **Unbridled's Song** (Unbridled Elaine), **Verbatim** (Princess Rooney)

Winners by Place Where Bred

Locality	Winners
Kentucky	12
Florida	4
Argentina	3
Oklahoma	1
Ontario	1

Supplemental Entries

Year	Runner	Fee	Finish	Earnings
2001	Miss Linda (Arg)	$400,000	6	$0
2000	Riboletta (Brz)	400,000	7	0
1996	Different (Arg)	200,000	3	120,000
1993	Paseana (Arg)	200,000	2	200,000
1992	Paseana (Arg)	200,000	1	520,000
1990	Bayakoa (Arg)	200,000	1	450,000
1989	Bayakoa (Arg)	200,000	1	450,000
1986	Classy Cathy	120,000	4	70,000
1985	Dontstop Themusic	120,000	3	108,000
	Isayso	120,000	6	10,000

Eclipse Award Winners from Race

Year	Runner	Finish	Title
2004	Ashado	1	3yo filly
2002	Azeri	1	Horse of the Year, Older female
	Farda Amiga	2	3yo filly

Year	Runner	Finish	Title
2000	Surfside	2	3yo filly
	Riboletta (Brz)	7	Older female
1999	**Beautiful Pleasure**	1	Older female
	Silverbulletday	6	3yo filly
1998	**Escena**	1	Older female
	Banshee Breeze	2	3yo filly
1997	**Ajina**	1	3yo filly
	Hidden Lake	7	Older female
1996	**Jewel Princess**	1	Older female
1995	**Inside Information**	1	Older female
	Serena's Song	5	3yo filly
1994	Heavenly Prize	2	3yo filly
	Sky Beauty	9	Older female
1993	**Hollywood Wildcat**	1	3yo filly
	Paseana (Arg)	2	Older female
1992	**Paseana (Arg)**	1	Older female
	Saratoga Dew	12	3yo filly
1991	**Dance Smartly**	1	3yo filly
	Queena	5	Older female
1990	**Bayakoa (Arg)**	1	Older female
	Go for Wand	DNF	3yo filly
1989	**Bayakoa (Arg)**	1	Older female
	Open Mind	3	3yo female
1988	**Personal Ensign**	1	Older female
	Winning Colors	2	3yo filly
1987	**Sacahuista**	1	3yo filly
	North Sider	6	Older female
1986	**Lady's Secret**	1	Horse of the Year, Older female
1985	**Life's Magic**	1	Older female
1984	**Princess Rooney**	1	Older female
	Life's Magic	2	3yo filly

Largest Winning Margins

Year	Winner	Margin
1995	Inside Information	13½
1984	Princess Rooney	7
1990	Bayakoa (Arg)	6¾
1985	Life's Magic	6¼
2002	Azeri	5

Smallest Winning Margins

Year	Winner	Margin
1998	Escena	nose
1993	Hollywood Wildcat	nose
1988	Personal Ensign	nose
1994	One Dreamer	neck

Shortest-Priced Winners

Year	Winner	Odds
1985	Life's Magic	.40-to-1*
1991	Dance Smartly	.50-to-1*
1988	Personal Ensign	.50-to-1*
1986	Lady's Secret	.50-to-1*
1989	Bayakoa (Arg)	.70-to-1
1984	Princess Rooney	.70-to-1

*Part of entry

Longest-Priced Winners

Year	Winner	Odds
2000	Spain	55.90-to-1
1994	One Dreamer	47.10-to-1
2003	Adoration	40.70-to-1
2001	Unbridled Elaine	12.30-to-1
1997	Ajina	4.80-to-1*
1999	Beautiful Pleasure	3.00-to-1

*Part of entry

Odds-On Beaten Favorites

Year	Winner	Odds	Finish
2003	Sightseek	.60-to-1	4
2000	Riboletta (Brz)	.40-to-1	7
1998	Banshee Breeze	.80-to-1	2
1990	Go for Wand	.70-to-1	DNF
1987	Infinidad (Chi)	.70-to-1	4

Fastest Winners at 1⅛ Miles

Year	Winner	Track	Time	Cond.
1995	Inside Information	Bel	1:46.15	muddy
1997	Ajina	Hol	1:47.30	fast
1989	Bayakoa (Arg)	GP	1:47⅗	fast
1999	Beautiful Pleasure	GP	1:47.56	fast
2000	Spain	CD	1:47.66	fast

Slowest Winners at 1⅛ Miles

Year	Winner	Track	Time	Cond.
1988	Personal Ensign	CD	1:52	muddy
1991	Dance Smartly	CD	1:50.95	fast
1994	One Dreamer	CD	1:50.70	fast
1998	Escena	CD	1:49.89	fast
2001	Unbridled Elaine	Bel	1:49.21	fast

Most Starters

Year	Track	Starters
1992	Gulfstream Park	14
1991	Churchill Downs	13
2004	Lone Star Park	11
2001	Belmont Park	11
1995	Belmont Park	10
1989	Gulfstream Park	10

Fewest Starters

Year	Track	Starters
1996	Woodbine	6
1987	Hollywood Park	6
2003	Santa Anita Park	7
1990	Belmont Park	7
1985	Aqueduct	7
1984	Hollywood Park	7

Winning Post Positions

Post	Starters	Winners	Percent
1	21	5	23.8%
2	21	1	4.8%
3	21	0	0.0%
4	21	5	23.8%
5	21	4	19.0%
6	21	3	14.3%
7	19	1	5.3%
8	15	0	0.0%
9	9	0	0.0%
10	6	1	16.7%
11	4	0	0.0%
12	2	0	0.0%
13	2	0	0.0%
14	1	1	100.0%

Changes in Distaff

Two significant changes have occurred in the conditions of the Breeders' Cup Distaff. For the 1988 running, the distance was shortened to 1⅛ miles from 1¼ miles, and in 1998 the purse was increased to $2–million from $1-million.

2004 Classic: Zapping the Demons

Demons seemed to lurk everywhere. From the shedrow of Lone Star Park's Barn B-2, which Bobby Frankel feared was so bustling that his horses would be spooked into nervous anxiety, all the way to the darkest recesses of his mind, gremlins haunted the Racing Hall of Fame trainer. After a blood-red full moon stained the black sprawl of Texas sky two days before the October 30, 2004, Breeders' Cup World Thoroughbred Championships, Frankel could not forget how he had been ambushed so many times before.

On four occasions, including the three previous years, he had tightened the girths on favorites in the $4-million Breeders' Cup Classic (G1) only to see them waylaid on the treacherous 1¼-mile dirt journey and robbed of any chance for the coveted Horse of the Year title. In four other runnings of North America's richest race, he sent out longshots who suffered the same fate. Indeed, his misfortune extended across the history of the entire Breeders' Cup event. From 57 starters since the inaugural 1984 program, including some of the best horses to compete on the continent, he had achieved only two winners prior to 2004.

"It can be depressing," Frankel confided. Stretched out in the deep bedding of his stall, Frankel's Classic hopeful paid no heed to the strain in his master's voice. The diamond-shaped star on his bay forehead gleamed as he dozed peacefully. This was Ghostzapper, and his whimsical name proved to be his destiny.

On October 30, Frankel watched five of his runners fail to hit the board in three earlier Cup races and gloomily pondered never participating again in a Breeders' Cup. Then Frank Stronach's homebred son of 1998 Classic winner Awesome Again burst out of the starting gate on a mission.

Jockey Javier Castellano had his own Breeders' Cup demons to conquer after his only previous assignment, Exogenous, suffered a fatal injury in a freak accident before making it to the starting gate for the Distaff (G1) in 2001. Coolly steered away from his rail position by Castellano, Ghostzapper streaked to the lead. Daring defending Classic winner Pleasantly Perfect, 2002 Horse of the Year Azeri, '03 three-year-old champion and dual classic winner Funny Cide, '04 Belmont (G1) and Travers (G1) Stakes winner Birdstone, and eight others to catch him, Ghostzapper cruised effortlessly around the track, maintaining or widening his advantage at every point of call.

With Castellano pumping his right fist in exultation, the colt spurted under the finish line in a Breeders' Cup record 1:59.02, erasing the previous mark of 1:59.16 set by Skip Away in 1997 at Hollywood Park. In his first career start at 1¼ miles, Ghostzapper had run his last quarter-mile in :23.64, faster than his third (:24.32) and fourth (:24.02) quarter-mile splits, a rarity in an age that values speed over stamina.

Even those who were defeated were amazed. "Ghostzapper is a super horse," said Dale Romans, trainer of runner-up Roses in May, who finished three lengths behind the winner after gamely pressing him the entire trip. "He may be as good as we've seen in a long time. We picked a bad year to have a top horse for the Classic."

"He is a very good horse. Excellent," conceded trainer Richard Mandella, who had hoped Pleasantly Perfect would show he was "one of the great ones" with back-to-back Classic victories but had to settle for third place after the huge six-year-old raced wide and was rank early under Jerry Bailey.

Redemption proved deliciously sweet for Frankel, who, although protesting repeatedly that he is not superstitious, had yanked off his tie before the Classic in hopes of changing his luck. "On the QT, I have told everybody that this is the best horse I ever trained," he said during the winners' press conference. "But he had to come out and show it. That's why I didn't go out publicly and say it because I didn't want to look like a fool."

Yet the outspoken Stronach had not shied away from revealing his own assessment. Calmly stating his philosophy that the race result "had already been written in the stars" on the eve of the Breeders' Cup, Stronach declared then that he thought Ghostzapper could be better than any of his other runners, including 1998 Classic winner Awesome Again, '97 Belmont Stakes winner Touch Gold, 2000 Preakness Stakes (G1) winner Red Bullet, and '00 juvenile champion Macho Uno. He went on to suggest that the colt's versatility makes him virtually unique in the current era of racing.

Backstretch buzz during the week before the Breeders' Cup was all about how the Classic field might be the strongest ever assembled, comparable to the 1998 field that Awesome Again defeated. Hall of Fame trainer D. Wayne Lukas, who leads all his colleagues with 17 wins in Breeders'

Owner-Breeder

Frank Stronach is master of Adena Springs farms in Kentucky, Florida, and Ontario that encompass about 7,300 acres and house more than 470 broodmares. Chairman of Magna International, an autoparts conglomerate, and Magna Entertainment Corp., which owns racetracks, Stronach has bred and raced two Breeders' Cup Classic (G1) winners, Awesome Again (1998) and his son Ghostzapper, the 2004 winner. Stronach earned three Eclipse Awards as outstanding owner from 1998-2000 and as outstanding breeder in 2000 and '04.

Cup races, strode to center stage by entering Azeri in the Classic instead of the Distaff, which she had won easily in 2002. Since the six-year-old Jade Hunter mare had never raced successfully at 1¼ miles or against males, the move seemed beyond daring for even the unorthodox Lukas.

Frankel, a devotee of the Ragozin speed numbers formulated to assess racing performance in a system commonly known as "the sheets," saw the race as purely a three-horse contest. Ghostzapper, Roses in May, and Pleasantly Perfect were the only ones who had a shot based on the numbers they had recently generated, he said. As the race unfolded, he was proved to be right.

With Ghostzapper and Roses in May running first and second the entire way, Pleasantly Per-

fect rallied from tenth early to be third, four lengths behind the runner-up and three-quarters of a length in front of Perfect Drift. Azeri finished fifth.

Ghostzapper arrived at Frankel's barn in 2002 as a plain, medium-sized bay colt who did not stand out in any kind of positive way. He turned around when Frankel added blinkers to his morning drills, however. He flashed brilliance when defeating older horses by 6½ lengths in the 2003 Vosburgh Stakes (G1), speeding through 6½ furlongs in 1:14.72, and he rattled through '04 undefeated, including his gritty win in the Woodward Stakes (G1) and an easy romp in the seven-furlong Tom Fool Handicap (G2) in a blistering 1:20.42.—*Michele MacDonald*

NINTH RACE
Lone Star Park
October 30, 2004

1¼ miles. 21st running of the Breeders' Cup Classic (G1). Purse $4,000,000. 3-year-olds and up. Weights (Northern Hemisphere): 3-year-olds, 121 lbs. Older, 126 lbs. (Southern Hemisphere): 3-year-olds, 116 lbs. Older, 126 lbs. Fillies and mares allowed 3 lbs.

Value of race: $3,668,000. Value to winner: $2,080,000; second: $800,000; third: $440,000; fourth: $228,000; fifth, $120,000. Mutuel Pool $8,498,771.00.

Horse	Wgt.	M/Eqt	PP	St.	¼	½	¾	Str.	Fin.	Jockey	Odds $1
Ghostzapper, 4, c.	126	Lb	1	1hd	1½	1½	11	12	13	J. Castellano	*2.50
Roses in May, 4, c.	126	L	6	2½	2½	21	21	23	24	J. Velazquez	8.70
Pleasantly Perfect, 6, h.	126	Lb	12	9½	10½	10½	5½	3hd	3¾	J. Bailey	2.50
Perfect Drift, 5, g.	126	L	4	6½	6hd	8hd	6hd	4½	42	K. Desormeaux	13.80
Azeri, 6, m.	123	L	3	31	3½	4½	71	52	52	P. Day	15.20
Personal Rush, 3, c.	121	b	8	5½	51	5½	8½	7hd	6¾	L. Dettori	25.10
Birdstone, 3, c.	121	Lb	7	101	91½	92	91	9½	7nk	E. Prado	6.50
Dynever, 4, c.	126	L	13	71	8½	71	3½	6½	8¾	C. Nakatani	15.30
Fantasticat, 3, c.	121	Lb	5	1212	1220	1225	1215	112½	9¾	G. Melancon	59.90
Funny Cide, 4, g.	126	Lb	9	8½	7½	6½	4½	81	10nk	J. Santos	7.70
Bowman's Band, 6, h.	126	L	11	112½	114	113	101	10hd	113	C. Velasquez	61.70
Newfoundland, 4, c.	126	Lb	10	4½	4½	3½	112½	1210	126	E. Coa	38.80
Freefourinternet, 6, h.	126	L	2	13	13	13	13	13	13	G. Kuntzweiler	54.30

OFF AT 4:42. Start: Good. Winner: Drew clear late.
Time: :23.42, :47.00, 1:11.32, 1:35.38, 1:59.02. Weather: Clear. Track: Fast.

$2 Mutuel Prices:	1—GHOSTZAPPER	7.00	4.00	3.60
	6—ROSES IN MAY		8.20	5.20
	12—PLEASANTLY PERFECT			3.00

$2 PICK THREE 8-5-1 PAID $9,884.20
$2 PICK FOUR 5-8-5-1 PAID $46,791.20
$2 PICK SIX 10-2-5-8-5-1 PAID $56,149.60
$2 PICK SIX 13-11-4-2-3/9-2 PAID $2,687,611.60 (6 correct)
$2 DAILY DOUBLE 5-1 PAID $390.40 $2 EXACTA 1-6 PAID $46.60
$2 HEAD2HEAD 7 vs. 9 (WINNER 7) PAID $3.60
$2 SUPERFECTA 1-6-12-4 PAID $1,297.80 $2 TRIFECTA 1-6-12 PAID $164.00

B. h., by Awesome Again—Baby Zip, by Relaunch. Trainer: Bobby Frankel. Owner: Stronach Stables. Bred by Adena Springs Farms (Ky.).

GHOSTZAPPER rushed up along the inside to gain a slim early advantage, set the pace under pressure along the backstretch, opened a clear lead approaching the quarter pole, and drew away under intermittent right-hand encouragement. ROSES IN MAY moved up from outside to contest the early pace, couldn't stay with the winner in upper stretch but continued on well. PLEASANTLY PERFECT raced well back for six furlongs, was brushed a bit at the top of the stretch, and rallied mildly. PERFECT DRIFT was shuffled back on the far turn, swung out on the turn, and failed to threaten while improving his position. AZERI broke at bay slowly, raced in good position just behind the top two while saving ground to the top of the stretch, and weakened in the final eighth. PERSONAL RUSH rushed up after breaking slowly, remained a factor to the turn and gradually tired thereafter. BIRDSTONE raced well back for seven furlongs, advanced four wide nearing the quarter pole, and passed tiring rivals. DYNEVER lodged a brief bid on the turn and flattened out. FANTASTICAT never reached contention. FUNNY CIDE, taken in hand while in traffic nearing the first turn, lodged a mild bid between horses on the far turn and then gave way. BOWMAN'S BAND checked early along the rail and never reached contention. NEWFOUNDLAND raced up close for seven furlongs and gave way. FREEFOURINTERNET never reached contention.

2004 Turf: Tough Talk

For its 2003 and '04 runnings, the Breeders' Cup Turf (G1) was a waiting game. After High Chaparral (Ire) and Johar reached the finish line together in 2003, Santa Anita Park's stewards took 13 minutes before declaring the first dead heat in Breeders' Cup history. The finish of the 2004 Turf, worth $1,834,000, was not close—Better Talk Now finished 1¾ lengths ahead of 7-to-10 favorite Kitten's Joy. But Lone Star Park's stewards flashed the inquiry sign immediately after the finish of the Turf on October 30 and then attempted to sort out a roughly run race. As they reviewed the videotape, the first two finishers walked patient circles on the track and their connections waited nervously for another delayed decision in the Turf.

After a few excruciating minutes, the stewards determined that Bushwood Racing Partners' Better Talk Now had run just straight enough down Lone Star's short homestretch to warrant the victory. Though Better Talk Now had come in a bit, third finisher Powerscourt (GB) had caused most of the problems, especially for Kitten's Joy. "That was a cruel five minutes," said Better Talk Now's trainer, H. Graham Motion, who recorded his first Breeders' Cup triumph.

Jamie Spencer on the big Sadler's Wells four-year-old Powerscourt had attempted to break the race open by surging from last place heading into the turn. He came out of the tight last bend with a two-length lead, but Better Talk Now and Kitten's Joy were closing determinedly, and the combination of Better Talk Now coming in slightly and Powerscourt rolling markedly right left Kitten's Joy with no room to run around the eighth pole.

Owner

Bushwood Stables is a partnership between Brent Johnson (managing partner) of Oakton, Virginia, Karl Barth of Seattle, and Chris Dwyer of Chicago. Johnson, an investment adviser, attended high school with Barth, a lawyer, and met Dwyer in law school. They currently own eight horses in training, all with Graham Motion, in this or other partnerships.

Breeder

Diane Perkins owned Wimborne Farm, in Paris, Kentucky, for nearly 30 years before her dispersal in 2002. Perkins is the daughter of Diana Guest Manning, the Countess de la Valdene, breeder of major European runners Prince Regent, Sea Hawk II, *Pieces of Eight II, and *Roi Dagobert. Manning was the sister of Raymond Guest, owner-breeder of champion and classic winner Tom Rolfe and owner of champion Sir Ivor. Perkins and her late husband, trainer Peter Perkins, bred and raced many stakes winners at Wimborne or at their Argentine farm, Haras San Francisco de Pilar, including prominent sire Lord At War (Arg), Al Mamoon, and Breeders' Cup starters John's Call and Sampras.

Ramon Dominguez, the dominant rider in Maryland and Delaware who broke through for his first Breeders' Cup victory, said: "I just basically held my ground. I had full control of my horse at all times. ... He has lugged in in the past, but not today. ... I have every right to hold my ground, and that's what I did. He [Kitten's Joy] tried to push his way out, but I was in the same path. Johnny [Velazquez on Kitten's Joy] was in a bad spot because he was between horses, but I was just holding my ground. Bouncing was bound to happen at that point." The stewards agreed and let the result stand.

Better Talk Now ran the 1½ miles in 2:29.70 on a turf course rated as yielding, but one that was quite slippery in spots after overnight rains. Velazquez, though, thought Kitten's Joy was not at his best because of the excess moisture in the surface. "He didn't handle the track," Velazquez told trainer Dale Romans and co-owner Ken Ramsey. "The soft going was a lot different here than in New York," [where Kitten's Joy captured the Joe Hirsch Turf Classic Invitational Stakes (G1) on yielding ground in his previous outing]. "That was way, way too much [soft] for him."

"This is a very tricky horse," Motion said later of Bushwood's elegant, almost black five-year-old Talkin Man gelding out of Bendita, by Baldski, who was bred in Kentucky by Wimborne Farm. "We've been through this before with this horse. I wasn't clear what had happened, but, knowing his antics, I was very worried. I've been on the wrong side of so many of these. ... I expect to get taken down more often than not."

Better Talk Now ran only once at two in 2001 and did not win until his fifth start, when he was switched to the grass for the first time at Churchill Downs on July 6, 2002. He failed in his only two attempts in stakes as a three-year-old but improved rapidly as a four-year-old and ended the 2003 season with a half-length win over Del Mar Show in the Knickerbocker Handicap (G2).

The key to Better Talk Now, though, was the addition of a full extension cup on the left side of his blinkers. Somewhere along the way, Better Talk Now had developed the bad habit of lugging in badly at the top of the stretch, and Motion thought it cost him the 2003 Arlington Handicap (G3), when jockey Rene Douglas had to steer instead of riding the horse out when he was beaten a neck by Honor in War.

"We had to do something, and Graham came up with the full extension blinker," said Brent Johnson, who manages Bushwood for his partners, Chris Dwyer and Karl Barth. An investment adviser in northern Virginia, Johnson went to high school with Barth and met Dwyer in law school.

Better Talk Now's first trip to Texas in April 2004 was a disaster when torrential rains hit Sam Houston Race Park during the John B. Connally Breeders' Cup Turf Handicap, and he checked in eighth. It took the gelding a couple races to get over that trip, but he returned to form with a good second to Kicken Kris in Belmont Park's Bowling Green Handicap (G2) in July, and then won the Sword Dancer Invitational Stakes (G1) at Saratoga Race Course in August. After Better Talk Now's disappointing effort in the Man o' War Stakes (G1) behind Magistretti, Motion decided to skip the Joe Hirsch Turf Classic and take a shot at the Breeders' Cup. But a moderate workout on October 22 at Motion's home base at Fair Hill Training Center almost scotched a second trip to Texas. "We were very close to not running," Motion admitted. "He worked very averagely. They recently changed the surface on the wood-chip track at Fair Hill, and he did a very subpar breeze." Better Talk Now perked up, however, and Motion decided to go on October 25.

Kitten's Joy earned his favoritism with the best sophomore season on the turf for any American three-year-old since Sunshine Forever won eight of 12 grass starts in 1988, including the Turf Classic, Budweiser International (G1) at Laurel Park, and Man o' War. Sunshine Forever also finished second in the Breeders' Cup Turf under difficult circumstances, but had done enough to earn an Eclipse Award. Kitten's Joy also had done enough to merit the male turf championship.

Powerscourt again ran erratically on American turf, after throwing away the Arlington Million (G1) by lugging in sharply while running away from rider Jamie Spencer's right-handed whip. Better Talk Now's victory finally broke a five-year skein of Turf wins by Europeans, though Johar managed to win in a dead heat in 2003. It evened the score in the Turf at 11 winners trained in North America and 11 abroad.

—John P. Sparkman

EIGHTH RACE
Lone Star Park
October 30, 2004

1½ miles on turf. 21st running of the Breeders' Cup Turf (G1). Purse $2-million. 3-year-olds and up. Weights (Northern Hemisphere): 3-year-olds, 121 lbs. Older, 126 lbs. (Southern Hemisphere): 3-year-olds, 116 lbs. Older, 125 lbs. Fillies and mares allowed 3 lbs.

Value of race: $1,834,000. Value to winner: $1,040,000; second: $400,000; third: $220,000; fourth: $114,000; fifth, $60,000. Mutuel Pool $3,942,242.

Horse	Wt.	M/Eqt	PP	¼	½	1m	1¼	Str.	Fin.	Jockey	Odds $1
Better Talk Now, 5, g.	126	Lbf	5	8	7^{hd}	$6^{2\frac{1}{2}}$	$4^{\frac{1}{2}}$	$2^{1\frac{1}{2}}$	$1^{1\frac{3}{4}}$	R. Dominguez	27.90
Kitten's Joy, 3, c.	121	L	4	$3^{\frac{1}{2}}$	3^{2}	3^{1}	3^{1}	3^{2}	2^{1}	J. Velazquez	*0.70
Powerscourt (GB), 4, c.	126	Lb	1	6^{2}	$6^{1\frac{1}{2}}$	$2^{\frac{1}{2}}$	1^{2}	1^{hd}	$3^{2\frac{1}{4}}$	J. Spencer	2.90
Magistretti, 4, c.	126	Lb	6	5^{2}	$4^{1\frac{1}{2}}$	5^{2}	2^{hd}	$4^{2\frac{1}{2}}$	$4^{2\frac{3}{4}}$	E. Prado	6.10
Mustanfar, 3, c.	121	Lb	8	7^{hd}	8	8	7^{1}	5^{2}	5^{nk}	J. Santos	23.40
Request for Parole, 5, h.	126	L	2	4^{hd}	5^{hd}	7^{hd}	8	$6^{\frac{1}{2}}$	6^{4}	P. Day	22.20
Strut the Stage, 6, h.	126	Lb	3	2^{2}	2^{2}	$4^{\frac{1}{2}}$	$6^{\frac{1}{2}}$	$7^{\frac{1}{2}}$	$7^{3\frac{3}{4}}$	C. Nakatani	27.40
Star Over the Bay, 6, g.	126	L	7	$1^{3\frac{1}{2}}$	1^{5}	1^{2}	$5^{2\frac{1}{2}}$	8	8	T. Baze	8.10

OFF AT 3:59. Start: Good. Winner: Five-wide move, clear.
Time: :24.90, :49.16, 1:13.96, 1:40.14, 2:04.15, 2:29.70. Weather: Clear. Turf: Yielding.

$2 Mutuel Prices:				
	5—BETTER TALK NOW	**57.80**	**12.40**	**5.20**
	4—KITTEN'S JOY		**2.80**	**2.20**
	1—POWERSCOURT (GB)			**3.00**

$2 PICK THREE 5-8-5 PAID $4,007.40
$2 EXACTA 5-4 PAID $134.80 $2 HEAD2HEAD 1 vs. 4 (WINNER 4) PAID $2.80
$2 SUPERFECTA 5-4-1-6 PAID $1,483.40 $2 TRIFECTA 5-4-1 PAID $492.00

B. g., by Talkin Man—Bendita, by Baldski. Trainer: H. Graham Motion. Owner: Bushwood Racing Partners. Bred by Wimborne Farm, Inc. (Ky.).

BETTER TALK NOW, unhurried for a mile, circled five wide rallying into the stretch, charged to the front while drifting in slightly in midstretch, and then drew away under steady left-hand urging. KITTEN'S JOY launched a rally in the two path on the turn, made a run along the inside to threaten in upper stretch, but was no match for the winner. POWERSCOURT (GB) broke poorly, made a strong middle move along the backstretch, opened a clear advantage on the far turn, brushed with the winner while drifting out in midstretch, and weakened. MAGISTRETTI rallied three wide to reach contention on the far turn, moved up between horses in upper stretch, steadied in traffic nearing the furlong marker, and weakened late. MUSTANFAR was outrun for a mile and failed to threaten. REQUEST FOR PAROLE raced up close for a mile and steadily tired thereafter. STRUT THE STAGE chased the pacesetter to the far turn and faltered. STAR OVER THE BAY was used up setting the early pace. Following a stewards' inquiry into the stretch run, there was no change in the order of finish.

2004 Juvenile: On Target With Wilko

The day that had started out with so much promise was not going well for J. Paul Reddam, and it certainly did not give the impression it was going to get any better with about a quarter-mile left to run in the Breeders' Cup Juvenile (G1) on October 30 at Lone Star Park.

Reddam, who has enjoyed plenty of recent success as a Thoroughbred owner and even more as the founder of the Ditech.com mortgage company, missed the mark with his first three 2004 Breeders' Cup starters, who on paper appeared to have a chance to earn at least minor awards in their respective races. Elloluv was the first one off target (seventh in the Distaff [G1]), then there was Sharp Lisa (sixth in the Juvenile Fillies [G1]), and finally Pt's Grey Eagle (eighth in the Sprint [G1]).

Wilko, a fairly unheralded European-based colt in whom Reddam purchased a 75% interest from owner Susan Roy earlier in the fall, made the day a big success. Wilko not only produced the second-biggest upset in the Juvenile's history but also perhaps the most surprising victory on the 21st World Thoroughbred Championships card.

With Frankie Dettori in the saddle, the son of Awesome Again upset a talented quintet of American-based two-year-olds at odds of 28.30-to-1. Wilko and Dettori rallied in the middle of

the Lone Star stretch to finish three-quarters of a length in front of unlucky Hopeful Stakes (G1) winner Afleet Alex. Sun King was another neck back in third in the 1⅟₁₆-mile Juvenile, which was run in 1:42.09 on a fast track. Wilko's $58.60 winning mutuel was the second largest behind the $62.60 mutuel for Anees in the 1999 Juvenile at Gulfstream Park.

The payout was impressive, but no more so than the fact that Wilko earned the win in his first start on dirt against a field that included the winners of nearly every major American prep for the championship race. The victory was also the first stakes win for Wilko, who had placed in five stakes on the grass in England. Shortly after Wilko made his second career start, a seventh-place finish in a six-furlong race at York racecourse, trainer Jeremy Noseda got the impression the colt would be more effective on dirt. Nine starts later, Wilko got the chance to show he was better suited on the main track and left the talented Juvenile field in tatters.

Among Wilko's opponents were Norfolk Stakes (G2) winner Roman Ruler from trainer Bob Baffert's barn, Champagne Stakes (G1) winner Proud Accolade, and the gritty Afleet Alex, whose only loss from five starts came in the Champagne. The bettors settled on Roman Ruler as the 2-to-1 favorite in the field of eight, with Proud Accolade and Afleet Alex right behind in the wagering at 2.60-to-1 and 3-to-1, respectively. Twice Unbridled, whose only accomplishment in two starts was a third-place finish in a maiden race at Del Mar, was the only member of the field to get less respect than Wilko at 33.20-to-1.

Twice Unbridled would be the Juvenile's early pacesetter as jockey Victor Espinoza sent the son of Unbridled's Song through relatively soft fractions of :23.54 for the opening quarter-mile and :47.49 for the half. Consolidator, winner of the Lane's End Breeders' Futurity (G1), and jockey Rafael Bejarano were just off the pace in the early stages, with Wilko running a surprising third.

Dettori, who had three prior Breeders' Cup wins but never one on the main track from nine attempts, had worked Wilko for Noseda at Newmarket in the weeks leading up to the Juvenile and was also surprised the colt raced up close after his clean start.

Afleet Alex did not enjoy the same luxury; the son of Northern Afleet bobbled slightly at the start and bumped Roman Ruler to the inside and Consolidator to the outside. He eventually recovered but was forced to run four wide around the first turn and was still in sixth after the opening half-mile. Roman Ruler had similar troubles after the break and raced at the back of the pack to the chagrin of Baffert, who had a heated exchange with jockey Corey Nakatani near the winner's cir-

Co-Owners

Susan Roy and her husband, Paul, sprung the biggest upset in Belmont Stakes (G1) history when Sarava denied War Emblem's Triple Crown bid with a victory in the 2002 edition of the American classic at odds of 70.25-to-1. Susan Roy lives in Ascot in Berkshire, England, and has been involved in Thoroughbred ownership since 1997.

A native of Windsor, Ontario, **J. Paul Reddam** earned degrees in psychology and philosophy but made his fortune as the founder of the hugely successful Ditech.com mortgage loan company, which was the first to use television and billboard advertising extensively. A Standardbred owner in the 1980s, Reddam claimed his first Thoroughbred in 1988 and has approximately 40 horses. Top runners campaigned in his purple-and-white colors include Ten Most Wanted, Swept Overboard, Elloluv, and Pt's Grey Eagle.

Breeder

Rosendo "Ro" Parra has made a huge investment in the Thoroughbred industry since claiming his first runner for $5,000 out of 1999 race at Retama Park. Parra has since purchased a Central Kentucky farm, Millennium Farms Kentucky, and has assembled a band of about 150 broodmares and a racing stable that features approximately 60 runners scattered across the country. The senior vice president and general manager of Dell Computers' Public Americas and International Group in Austin, Texas, Parra is a native of Ecuador who moved with his family to Maryland in 1974. Parra has campaigned more than 30 stakes winners, including 2004 Californian Stakes (G2) and Mervyn LeRoy Handicap (G2) winner Even the Score.

cle after the Fusaichi Pegasus colt finished fifth.

While Roman Ruler and Afleet Alex were languishing toward the rear, Edgar Prado guided Sun King down on the inside to snatch a narrow lead after six furlongs in 1:11.25. Sun King battled on gamely from that position just ahead of Consolidator and the steadily progressing Afleet Alex. Wilko had started to retreat while running three wide around the far turn and looked out of the race at the quarter pole. Dettori did not panic as Afleet Alex and Sun King continued to slug it out, tipped Wilko out a bit more in the stretch, and gave the colt an aggressive ride in deep stretch.

Wilko snatched the lead from Afleet Alex with a sixteenth to run and inched close in the end to join Johannesburg and Arazi as European-based winners of the Breeders' Cup Juvenile. "One thing that he does, he always tries," Dettori said. "Around the turn he didn't go anywhere. I switched him back to the outside, and all of a sudden a dream comes true. He started to pick it up, and I knew I was going to win. It was great, absolutely fantastic."

Sun King hung on gamely for third, 1¼ lengths in front of Consolidator. Roman Ruler, Proud Ac-

colade, Twice Unbridled, and Scandinavia completed the field.

Wilko earned $780,000 of the Juvenile's $1,375,500 total purse and improved his record to three wins in 11 career starts and boosted his bankroll to $880,494. The final time of the Juvenile time was the fourth fastest in the race's history but slower than the 1:41.65 clocking turned in by two-year-old filly Sweet Catomine earlier in the Breeders' Cup Juvenile Fillies (G1).

Reddam got his opportunity to land his first Breeders' Cup winner after purchasing a 75% interest in Wilko from Roy in a private transaction just weeks before the Juvenile. The one catch to the transaction forced Noseda to relinquish Wilko's training to the Southern California-based Craig Dollase, who conditions many of Reddam's top runners. Noseda, who previously worked for the Maktoum family's Godolphin Racing operation, said the victory was bittersweet because the Juvenile was his last chance with the colt. Wilko made one start after the Juvenile, in the Hollywood Futurity (G1) on December 18. He finished third, a length behind winner Declan's Moon.

—Tom Law

SEVENTH RACE
Lone Star Park
October 30, 2004

1¹⁄₁₆ miles. 21st running of the Breeders' Cup Juvenile (G1). Purse $1,500,000. Colts and geldings, 2-year-olds. Weight: 122 lbs.

Value of race: $1,375,500. Value to winner: $780,000; second: $300,000; third: $165,000; fourth: $85,500; fifth, $45,000. Mutuel Pool $3,893,107.

Horse	Wt.	M/Eqt	PP	St.	¼	½	¾	Str.	Fin.	Jockey	Odds $1
Wilko, 2, c.	122	L	8	5	3¹	3ʰᵈ	4²½	4²	1¾	L. Dettori	28.30
Afleet Alex, 2, c.	122	L	3	7	8	6¹½	3½	1ʰᵈ	2ⁿᵏ	J. Rose	3.00
Sun King, 2, c.	122	L	1	2	5¹½	4½	1ʰᵈ	2½	3¹¼	E. Prado	6.90
Consolidator, 2, c.	122	L	4	1	2½	2¹	2ʰᵈ	3½	4¹½	R. Bejarano	7.50
Roman Ruler, 2, c.	122	L	2	3	7¹	7ʰᵈ	5½	5²	5¹¼	C. Nakatani	*2.00
Proud Accolade, 2, c.	122	L	6	6	4ʰᵈ	5ʰᵈ	6ʰᵈ	6⁵	6⁹¾	J. Velazquez	2.60
Twice Unbridled, 2, c.	122	b	7	4	1¹½	1¹	7½	7¹	7¹¼	V. Espinoza	33.20
Scandinavia, 2, c.	122	L	5	8	6ʰᵈ	8	8	8	8	J. Spencer	14.50

OFF AT 3:24. Start: Good. Winner: 3-4W, came again, gamely.
Time: :23.54, :47.49, 1:11.25, 1:35.77, 1:42.09. Weather: Clear. Track: Fast.

$2 Mutuel Prices:				
	8—WILKO	58.60	18.20	6.80
	3—AFLEET ALEX		5.00	3.60
	1—SUN KING			5.60

$2 PICK THREE 2-5-8 PAID $1,114.40
$2 EXACTA 8-3 PAID $254.00 $2 EXACTA 8-3 PAID $254.00
$2 HEAD2HEAD 1 vs. 4 (WINNER 1) PAID $3.20
$2 SUPERFECTA 8-3-1-4 PAID $7,150.20 $2 TRIFECTA 8-3-1 PAID $1,424.60

B. c., by Awesome Again—Native Roots (Ire), by Indian Ridge (Ire). Trainer: Jeremy Noseda. Owner: J. Paul Reddam and Susan Roy. Bred by Ro Parra (Ky.).

WILKO settled on the outside, made a four-wide bid leaving the backstretch, dropped back passing the quarter pole, rallied again outside the furlong marker, surged to the lead near the sixteenth pole and inched clear under steady left-hand encouragement. AFLEET ALEX bobbled at the start then bumped with CONSOLIDATOR and ROMAN RULER, engaged the leaders while five wide leaving the backstretch, took the lead passing the quarter pole, and was collared near the sixteenth pole. SUN KING moved through to contest the lead leaving the backstretch, bumped with CONSOLIDATOR in upper stretch, battled gamely into the final sixteenth and weakened slightly. CONSOLIDATOR made a bid between rivals entering the far turn, fought determinedly into the final sixteenth and gave way grudgingly. ROMAN RULER bumped with AFLEET ALEX after the start, steadied off heels approaching the first turn, continued just off heels into the backstretch, angled out sharply near the furlong marker and came up empty. PROUD ACCOLADE moved midway through the turn and failed to respond. TWICE UNBRIDLED set the pace under moderate pressure and stopped. SCANDINAVIA, roused on the far turn, had nothing left.

2004 Filly and Mare Turf: Favorable Signs

Ouija Board (GB) arrived at Lone Star Park as the most celebrated European runner to participate in the 2004 Breeders' Cup World Thoroughbred Championships. In June, the three-year-old daughter of Cape Cross (Ire) won the Epsom Oaks (Eng-G1) by seven lengths. In July, she won the Darley Irish Oaks (Ire-G1) by one length and became the first runner in five years to accomplish the rare double in the 1½-mile races. "Once you find yourself with a classic-winning filly, then that first bit of the dream has been won, and at that point dreams are allowed to take over," said Ouija Board's breeder and owner, Lord Derby.

A winner of one of three races in 2003, Ouija Board began her '04 campaign with a six-length victory in the 1¼-mile Pretty Polly Stakes at Newmarket on May 2 and then collected her two classic wins. Scratched from the Aston Upthorpe Yorkshire Oaks (Eng-G1) on August 18 because of soft ground, Ouija Board had nearly three months off before she ran a strong third behind Bago in the 2,400-meter Prix de l'Arc de Triomphe (Fr-G1) on October 3.

"She was unlucky in the Arc, but that's the nature of the race," said her trainer, Edward Dunlop, the son of 1995 British champion trainer John Dunlop. On October 30, Ouija Board became the shortest-priced winner of the 2004 World Thoroughbred Championships when she scored a 1½-length victory in the Breeders' Cup Filly and Mare Turf (G1) at odds of 9-to-10. The purse reached a stakes-record $1,292,970 due to the appearance of six supplemental entries, including the winner, in the 12-horse field. Ouija Board earned $733,200 to push her career earnings to $1,671,768. She also gave champion jockey Kieren Fallon his second consecutive win in the race, following his score aboard Islington (Ire) at Santa Anita Park that secured

Owner-Breeder

Ouija Board (GB) is a homebred racing for Lord Derby, who carries the most famous name in horse racing. In 1779, the 12th Earl of Derby and Sir Charles Bunbury tossed a coin to determine which of their names would be attached to a new race for three-year-old colts that was designed after the Oaks for fillies. That race was the Epsom Derby (Eng-G1), and the name "Derby" is carried by horse races conducted throughout the world.

The 19th Earl of Derby is Edward Richard William Stanley, who inherited the title on the death of his uncle in 1994. Among the horses the 18th Earl had raced was Teleprompter (GB), who won the 1985 Arlington Million Stakes (G1), Teleprompter is a half brother to Selection Board (GB), Ouija Board's dam. Lord Derby, whose friends call him Teddy, owns Stanley Estate & Stud Co., which includes the 100-acre Stanley House Stud in Newmarket and the Knowsley Safari Park near Liverpool. Lord Derby's brother, Peter Stanley, manages Stanley House Stud.

her the Eclipse Award as champion turf female with only one North American start. Fallon had been aboard Ouija Board in her three victories this year prior to the Arc, in which he instead rode the favorite, North Light, who finished fifth.

Lord Derby pre-entered Ouija Board in both the Filly and Mare Turf and the Breeders' Cup Turf (G1), with the Turf the first preference. "We were thinking about the Turf because the fillies and mares start very close to the turn and we were a bit worried because we like to drop way behind," he said. "So that extra furlong [of the Turf] gave us a bit more on the back straight, but in the end we decided to keep her racing against her sex. It's obviously a very expensive entry [a 9% supplemental fee, or $90,000] to come over and do it, but she's such a fantastic filly. She's just done us so well all year. And it makes it a lot easier if you're reinvesting your prize money to make that decision."

After three years at 1¼ miles, the sixth edition of the Filly and Mare Turf returned to 1⅜ miles, the distance of its first two runnings. At Lone Star, that distance placed the starting gate on the turf course's backstretch just a little more than 100 yards from the far turn, with the configuration requiring the horses to race around three turns. The morning before the race, Fallon took Ouija Board over the surface and was pleased with how relaxed she was.

When the gates opened on a clear afternoon with the temperature at 70°, Grade 2 winner Moscow Burning, an 18.80-to-1 longshot, took the lead from the four post. She opened up a clear advantage over the yielding course as she led the field past the grandstand for the first time. Film Maker, a Grade 1 winner whom trainer Graham Motion had thought might be his best chance to win on Breeders' Cup day (he won the Turf with Better Talk Now), took second. Aubonne (Ger), who also was supplemented to the race, was third, followed by Riskaverse, who had finished sixth in the 2003 race. Fallon tucked Ouija Board into fifth along the inside.

Moscow Burning set slow fractions of :26.42, :52.47, and 1:18.50 for the first six furlongs. "We were just at a high gallop around there," said Jose Valdivia Jr., whose mount was as many as four lengths in front. Meanwhile, Dunlop said he was concerned with how the fractions would affect Ouija Board. "She was coming from 1½ miles [of the Arc de Triomphe] back to 1⅜ miles, and I was afraid that slow pace might get her beat," Fallon said.

Ouija Board continued to rate comfortably down the backstretch and began to advance approaching the final turn. Moscow Burning had picked up the pace, but gave way on the front end, and Ouija Board rallied three wide to take the lead in midstretch. With Fallon urging her on, Ouija Board surged past Film Maker and won by 1½ lengths. Ouija Board's time was 2:18.25. She joined Banks Hill, the 2001 winner, as the only three-year-olds to win the race.

Film Maker held off Grade 1 winner Wonder Again, who broke from the outside post but benefited from a ground-saving ride from Edgar Prado, by a neck for second, and Moscow Burning finished fourth. Yesterday (Ire), who was third in the 2003 race in her North American debut, finished fifth in her second attempt. She was followed by Grade 3 winner Shaconage and multiple West Coast Grade 1 winner Light Jig (GB), the 6.40-to-1 second choice. Grade 1 winner Riskaverse was eighth, followed by Super Brand (SAf), Grade 2 winner Katdogawn (GB), Grade 1 winner Megahertz (GB), who ran fifth

in 2003, and Aubonne. Moscow Burning and Katdogawn, the only runner with a previous start over the track, both are trained by James Cassidy. Bobby Frankel, who won the Breeders' Cup Classic (G1) with Ghostzapper, sent out both Light Jig and Megahertz.

Peter Stanley, Lord Derby's brother and the manager of Stanley House Stud, said he chose to breed Ouija Board's dam, Selection Board (GB), to Cape Cross, who was ninth in the 1998 Breeders' Cup Mile (G1), because of the stallion's commercial appeal. The operation sells its colts and races its fillies. Ouija Board "was like the rest of the family. She was tall and leggy and a little light-boned at birth. ... By the time she was weaned, she was a lovely little filly," he said. "We always had good hopes for her, but we never quite saw her as a dual classic winner and a Breeders' Cup winner. So it's been a dream come true."—*Amy Owens*

SIXTH RACE
Lone Park Park
October 30, 2004

1⅜ miles on turf. 6th running of the Breeders' Cup Filly and Mare Turf (G1). Purse $1,000,000. Fillies and mares 3-year-olds and up. Weights (Northern Hemisphere): 3-year-olds, 118 lbs. Older, 123 lbs. (Southern Hemisphere): 3-year-olds, 113 lbs. Older, 123 lbs.

Value of race: $1,292,970. Value to winner: $733,200; second: $282,000; third: $155,100; fourth: $80,370; fifth, $42,300. Mutuel Pool $4,014,411.

Horse	Wt	M/Eqt	PP	¼	½	¾	1m	Str.	Fin.	Jockey	Odds $1
Ouija Board (GB), 3, f.	118	L	5	6½	5½	4hd	4¹	2½	1¹½	K. Fallon	*0.90
Film Maker, 4, f.	123	Lb	3	2½	2½	2½	2¹½	3¹½	2nk	J. Velazquez	16.50
Wonder Again, 5, m.	123	L	12	11½	11²	112½	10¹	4½	32¾	E. Prado	10.70
Moscow Burning, 4, f.	123	L	4	1²	1⁴	11½	11½	1hd	41¼	J. Valdivia Jr.	18.80
Yesterday (Ire), 4, f.	123	Lb	11	8¹	8¹	71½	6hd	5³	5¹	J. Spencer	9.00
Shaconage, 4, f.	123	L	6	12	12	12	12	7hd	6¾	R. Bejarano	62.40
Light Jig (GB), 4, f.	123	L	7	101½	101	8½	11¹	82½	7½	R. Douglas	6.40
Riskaverse, 5, m.	123	L	9	4½	4hd	5½	5hd	61½	8¹	C. Velasquez	13.70
Super Brand (SAf), 5, m.	123	L	1	7½	7hd	9½	9hd	9hd	95½	P. Day	32.60
Katdogawn (GB), 4, f.	123	L	2	9½	9½	101½	8hd	102½	101	K. Desormeaux	55.40
Megahertz (GB), 5, m.	123	L	10	5hd	6½	6¹	71½	11hd	11nk	C. Nakatani	10.10
Aubonne (Ger), 4, f.	123		8	3¹	3¹	31½	3hd	12	12	J. Bailey	16.80

OFF AT 2:48. Start: Good. Winner: Drew off late.
Time: :26.42, :52.47, 1:18.50, 1:42.36, 2:06.34, 2:18.25. Weather: Clear. Turf: Yielding.

$2 Mutuel Prices:	5—OUIJA BOARD	3.80	3.00	2.80
	3—FILM MAKER		9.00	6.60
	12—WONDER AGAIN			6.60

$2 PICK THREE 10-2-5 PAID $505.80 $2 EXACTA 5-3 PAID $43.40
$2 HEAD2HEAD 3 vs. 10 vs. 11 (WINNER 3) PAID $5.60
$2 SUPERFECTA 5-3-12-4 PAID $3,257.40 $2 TRIFECTA 5-3-12 PAID $364.00

B. f., by Cape Cross (Ire)—Selection Board (GB), by Welsh Pageant (Fr). Trainer: Ed Dunlop. Owner: Lord Derby. Bred by Stanley Estate and Stud Co. (GB).

OUIJA BOARD (GB), taken in hand soon after the start, was rated in good position for a mile, launched a rally three wide leaving the turn, rapidly closed the gap in upper stretch, accelerated to the front inside the furlong marker, and drew clear under steady right-hand encouragement. FILM MAKER raced just off the pace for a mile, made a run to threaten at the quarter pole, but couldn't stay with the winner while holding well for the place. WONDER AGAIN, outrun for six furlongs, gradually worked her way forward on the turn, and rallied belatedly to gain a share. MOSCOW BURNING sprinted well clear in the early stages, fought gamely into midstretch, and weakened. YESTERDAY (Ire) dwelt at the start, rallied inside the winner to threaten nearing the quarter pole, but couldn't sustain her bid. SHACONAGE raced far back to the turn and failed to threaten. LIGHT JIG (GB) failed to mount a serious rally. RISKAVERSE steadied while rank in the early stages, lodged a brief bid on the turn, and faded in the stretch. SUPER BRAND (SAf) swung seven wide leaving the turn and lacked a strong closing response. KATDOGAWN (GB) outrun for a mile, circled six wide entering the stretch and lacked a further response. MEGAHERTZ (GB) raced within striking distance most of the way and faded in the stretch. AUBONNE (Ger), up close while three wide for a mile, dropped back on the turn and steadily tired thereafter.

2004 Sprint: Patience Rewarded

A $2-million yearling purchase usually means at least two things: The horse has a stellar pedigree, and his owner and trainer will be anxious to see a quick return on that investment. Fortunately for Speightstown, his connections were willing to wait nearly five years for him to blossom, and they were rewarded with a resounding triumph in the $972,020 Breeders' Cup Sprint (G1) on October 30 at Lone Star Park.

Until October 2, 2004, the date of the Vosburgh Stakes (G1) at Belmont Park, Speightstown looked invincible, with four dominating stakes victories in as many starts since March. But a poor break in the Vosburgh and a track surface that trainer Todd Pletcher called "dead and cuppy" resulted in a third-place finish behind Pico Central (Brz). Perhaps Speightstown was tailing off, some opined, and others suggested he did not train well after that start. Then the Breeders' Cup post-position draw was not especially kind to the six-year-old son of Gone West, who drew the second post. But the naysayers turned out to be dead wrong, and Speightstown was dead-on perfect.

With John Velazquez in the irons and racing in the colors of Eugene and Laura Melnyk, Speightstown burned up the Lone Star oval with a six-furlong clocking in 1:08.11 as the 3.70-to-1 second choice. "The inside post is tough only because you have everyone from the outside coming

down on you," said Pletcher, who made no secret of his intention to send his horse early. While the break was not perfect for Speightstown, it was decent enough and allowed Velazquez to secure a contending position along the rail just behind speedball Abbondanza, who fired an opening quarter-mile of :21.23 and a half-mile in :43.47, the second-fastest four-furlong time in the Sprint's history.

As Abbondanza hit the wall at the top of the stretch, Speightstown turned on the afterburners and sprinted for the finish line along the inside. Kela made a late run to close the final margin to 1¼ lengths, but the outcome was never in doubt once Speightstown made his move. Midas Eyes, the slight betting favorite at 3.60-to-1, never reached contention from post 13 and finished tenth.

Speightstown, with some right-handed encouragement from Velazquez, earned a first-place check for $551,200. Kela, winner of the Bing Crosby Breeders' Cup Handicap (G1) at Del Mar, took a circuitous tour around the Lone Star turn and rallied seven wide entering the stretch while finishing with good energy under Jerry Bailey. My Cousin Matt, the longest shot in the field at 60.70-to-1, also ran on late to get third for owner Richard Englander and conditioner Jeff Mullins.

The 2004 Sprint did not shape up as a Texas shootout for the title when the connections of Pico Central opted not to supplement him to the Sprint for $200,000. Owned by Gary Tanaka and trained by Paulo Lobo, Pico Central won the seven-furlong Carter Handicap (G1) and the one-mile Metropolitan Handicap (G1) prior to the Vosburgh. He weakened to finish third in Aqueduct's Cigar Mile Handicap (G1) on November 28 and effectively knocked himself out of the championship hunt.

Melnyk, who paid a reported $100-million in 2003 for the Ottawa Senators of the National Hockey League, hooked up with Pletcher in 1996, and in '98 the young trainer prepared Archers Bay—named for a spot in Barbados, as is Speightstown—to win the Queen's Plate Stakes at Woodbine, the first race of the Canadian Triple Crown.

"The Queen's Plate is something I had been going to since I was six or seven years old and that was my very first big stakes win on national television in Canada," Melnyk said. "It was a huge thrill, and my wife was pregnant at the time, so we had a great time." Archers Bay helped to increase Melnyk's interest in racing and also to launch Pletcher into the upper echelon of conditioners. "[Archers Bay] was the very first yearling I ever bought," Melnyk said. "It was just sheer dumb luck. The next thing I know, I got absolutely hooked and now I have over 500 horses."

Speightstown did not start his career like a $2-million Keeneland July selected yearling should; in his lone start at two, he finished last

Owners

Eugene Melnyk, a resident of Barbados, West Indies, with his wife, **Laura**, and two daughters, is the owner of the Ottawa Senators of the National Hockey League and chairman and chief executive of Biovail Corp., a pharmaceutical company based in Toronto, where he was born and raised. The Melnyks raced Archers Bay, winner of the 1998 Queen's Plate Stakes and Canada's champion three-year-old male that year. The couple also campaigned Grade 1 winners Marley Vale, Tweedside, and Harmony Lodge. Other graded stakes winners for the Melnyks include Graeme Hall, Strong Hope, and Pico Teneriffe. The Melnyks in 2001 bought Harry T. Mangurian Jr.'s 1,100-acre Mockingbird Farm in Ocala and renamed it Winding Oaks Farm.

Breeders

Aaron and Marie Jones are the breeders of two 2004 Breeders' Cup race winners, Ashado in the Distaff (G1) and Speightstown in the Sprint. Only two other breeders have duplicated that feat, Frank Stronach (Macho Uno and Perfect Sting in 2000) and the late Allen Paulson (Eliza and Fraise in 1992). Residents of Eugene, Oregon, the Joneses own Seneca Sawmill Co., which Aaron Jones founded in 1953. As owners, the Joneses campaigned Riboletta (Brz), the Eclipse Award winner as top older female in 2000, and Forestry, a Grade 1 winner whom they still own and stand at Taylor Made Farm in Nicholasville, Kentucky. Aaron Jones campaigned homebred champions Lemhi Gold and Tiffany Lass.

of 13 in a Saratoga Race Course maiden race. In his first start as a three-year-old, Speightstown won his maiden victory at Gulfstream Park under the care of trainer Phillip England. The colt showed considerable talent that spring with three consecutive scores at Woodbine and a second in the Amsterdam Stakes (G2) back at Saratoga in early August.

But Speightstown spent his entire four-year-old season on the sidelines after ankle surgery and raced only twice as a five-year-old, then under the tutelage of Pletcher. At age six, he developed into a powerhouse. He opened his 2004 campaign with his first career stakes win in the Artax Handicap at Gulfstream in March. Then he reeled off three straight Grade 2 victories in the Churchill Downs, True North Breeders' Cup, and Alfred G. Vanderbilt Handicaps.

"There are very few owners in this business that would have had the success with Speightstown that Eugene and Laura did because they were patient three times with this horse," Pletcher said. "Every time this horse had a little problem, Eugene said, 'Give this horse time.' He always believed in this horse."

Bred in Kentucky by Aaron and Marie Jones, Speightstown is the only winner from two named foals out of the stakes-winning Storm Cat mare Silken Cat, 1995 Canada champion two-year-old filly.

In September 2004, Melnyk announced that he had sold an interest in the horse to Taylor Made Farm and WinStar Farm. The Breeders' Cup Sprint was Speightstown's last start, and he was retired with ten wins from 16 career starts and earnings of $1,258,256. He entered stud at WinStar in Versailles, Kentucky, in 2005.

—Denis Blake

FIFTH RACE
Lone Star Park
October 30, 2004

6 furlongs. 21st running of the Breeders' Cup Sprint (G1). Purse $1,000,000. 3-year-olds and up. Weights (Northern Hemisphere): 3-year-olds, 123 lbs. Older, 126 lbs. (Southern Hemisphere): 3-year-olds, 121 lbs. Older, 126 lbs. Fillies and mares allowed 3 lbs.

Value of race: $972,020. Value to winner: $551,200; second: $212,000; third: $116,600; fourth: $60,420; fifth, $31,800. Mutuel Pool $4,140,082.

Horse	Wt.	M/Eqt	PP	St.	¼	½	Str.	Fin.	Jockey	Odds $1
Speightstown, 6, h.	126	L	2	8	4^1	3^1	$11^{1/2}$	$11^{1/4}$	J. Velazquez	3.70
Kela, 6, h.	126	Lb	5	10	$101^{1/2}$	10^1	$7^{1/2}$	$2^{3/4}$	J. Bailey	4.00
My Cousin Matt, 5, g.	126	Lf	12	2	$91^{1/2}$	$9^{1/2}$	4^1	$3^{1/2}$	R. Dominguez	60.70
Bwana Charlie, 3, c.	123	L	1	11	$113^{1/2}$	11^3	8^{hd}	$4^{3/4}$	R. Migliore	35.30
Cajun Beat, 4, g.	126	Lb	11	3	$61^{1/2}$	5^1	5^1	5^{hd}	C. Velasquez	14.80
Clock Stopper, 4, g.	126	Lb	7	13	13	13	11^{hd}	6^{hd}	P. Day	7.70
Champali, 4, c.	126	L	3	9	7^{hd}	$8^{1/2}$	$6^{1/2}$	7^{nk}	R. Bejarano	7.30
Pt's Grey Eagle, 3, g.	123	Lb	8	12	12^2	12^2	$101^{1/2}$	8^{nk}	C. Nakatani	23.70
Gold Storm, 4, c.	126	Lb	9	7	3^1	2^{hd}	$2^{1/2}$	$91^{1/2}$	L. Taylor	18.70
Midas Eyes, 4, c.	126	Lb	13	1	8^1	$7^{1/2}$	9^2	$103^{1/2}$	E. Prado	*3.60
Abbondanza, 3, c.	123	Lf	6	6	$1^{1/2}$	1^1	3^{hd}	$111^{1/4}$	E. Coa	25.70
Our New Recruit, 5, h.	126	L	4	5	5^{hd}	6^{hd}	12^{hd}	$128^{1/2}$	T. Baze	8.90
Cuvee, 3, c.	123	L	10	4	2^{hd}	4^1	13	13	R. Albarado	39.20

OFF AT 2:13. Start: Good. Winner: Rail trip, edged clear.
Time: :21.23, :43.47, 55.56, 1:08.11. Weather: Clear. Track: Fast.

$2 Mutuel Prices:	2—SPEIGHTSTOWN	9.40	5.20	4.00
	5—KELA		5.00	4.00
	12—MY COUSIN MATT			15.00

$2 PICK THREE 3/10-10-2 PAID $761.00
$2 PICK FOUR 1-3/10-10-2 PAID $3,130.20 $2 EXACTA 2-5 PAID $41.60
$2 HEAD2HEAD 7 vs. 11 (WINNER 11) PAID $4.20
$2 SUPERFECTA 2-5-12-1 PAID $42,365.20 $2 TRIFECTA 2-5-12 PAID $2,684.20

Ch. h., by Gone West—Silken Cat, by Storm Cat. Trainer: T. Pletcher. Owner: Eugene and Laura Melnyk. Bred by Aaron U. Jones and Marie Jones (Ky.).

SPEIGHTSTOWN, well placed on the inside, slipped through to make a bid at the top of the stretch, edged clear into the final furlong, and held well under strong right-hand urging. KELA, outrun early, swung seven wide leaving the turn, drifted inward in upper stretch and finished well while unable to reach the winner. MY COUSIN MATT settled toward the rear of the field, shifted out near the furlong marker and finished willingly. BWANA CHARLIE lacked early speed, swung eight wide into the stretch, and improved position. CAJUN BEAT vied three to four wide on the turn, lacked room near the sixteenth pole and failed to rally. CLOCK STOPPER, completely devoid of early speed, failed to menace while finishing with some interest. CHAMPALI bumped repeatedly with OUR NEW RECRUIT near the three-sixteenths marker and came up empty. PT'S GREY EAGLE lacked room late and never reached serious contention. GOLD STORM chased the pace on the outside, made a bid near the quarter pole, drifted in while briefly in the lead passing the three-sixteenths marker and tired. MIDAS EYES was forced inward in upper stretch and had nothing left. ABBONDANZA set the pace through quick fractions and faded. OUR NEW RECRUIT steadied repeatedly on the backstretch, bumped repeatedly with CHAMPALI, and stopped in a rough trip. CUVEE was jostled in upper stretch and stopped.

2004 Mile: Singletary's Sack

Before he became a devoted Thoroughbred owner, Bill Koch was a football fan and a passionate supporter of the National Football League's Chicago Bears. Growing up in Southern California, Koch had an affinity for horses as well, an affection that began at an early age when he regularly attended Hollywood Park with his grandfather, the late legendary movie producer Howard Koch.

The two sporting loves of Koch's life blended together on a wild afternoon at Lone Star Park on October 30. The entertaining result was a football-style celebration when Singletary, a horse named after Mike Singletary, a Pro Football Hall of Fame linebacker for his beloved Bears, took an easy lead at the top of the stretch and charged to the wire to capture the $1,540,560 Breeders' Cup Mile (G1) by a half-length over late-running Antonius Pius.

"Those 1985 Bears were my favorite team," said Koch, managing partner of Little Red Feather Racing, the fun-loving partnership that owns the four-year-old son of Sultry Song out of Joiski's Star, by Star de Naskra. For those lacking in football lore, the Bears were world champions in 1985, and fearsome linebacker Mike Singletary was one of the stars of that dominant but slightly off-center team.

The Singletary team of 2004 was no less fun-loving at the sun-splashed Grand Prairie, Texas, track on Breeders' Cup championship day. There was the ownership group and their friends high-fiving fans as they entered and departed the paddock prior to the race. There was the chant: "Single-tary—clap, clap, clap, clap" in the paddock, in the owners' box as the horses entered the gate, and loudest of all, after their hero held off Antonius Pius's charge to win in 1:36.90 on

yielding turf. There was the massive entourage that stormed the interview tent behind the paddock, gleefully interrupting the post-race press conference with raucous cheers midway through answers from Koch, trainer Don Chatlos Jr., and jockey David Flores. Then there was the party that went well into the night at a Dallas hotel. The 1985 Bears would have been proud.

And, of course, there were the distinctive silks, worn by Flores. Adorned with Bears colors and a large "C" on the back in the same script as on the team's helmets, there was no doubt as to the allegiance. The demonstrative scene in the winner's circle was reminiscent of the fun-loving Funny Cide crew that stormed the Churchill Downs presentation stand following the 2003 Kentucky Derby (G1). "We think anybody who does those kinds of things is great for the sport," said Koch, likening the 13 partners in Singletary to Sackatoga Stable, which owns Funny Cide. "And that's why we do this. We want to be good for the sport. We want the sport to grow. That's what we're about. That's why we were out high-fiving in the paddock. We want people to know it's okay to have fun. Too many people think horse racing is all blueblood and Kentucky. ... We're just a bunch of California boys who want to have a good time."

A rousing good time, to be sure. During the week leading up to the race, many of the owners sported Singletary "trucker's hats" in Bears colors and emblazoned with the player's number 50. They patrolled the backstretch in groups, many sporting Singletary football jerseys. "We felt this massive push behind us all week," Koch said. "We were walking around the backstretch one morning, and I got stopped by a security guard, and I got nervous. He put his arm around me and said, 'We're rooting for you guys.'" No wonder; Mike Singletary grew up in Houston and starred at Baylor University in Waco, Texas.

Though Singletary was a $3,200 purchase at the 2001 Keeneland October yearling sale by his original owners, Little Red Feather paid $30,000 in a private transaction for the then-unnamed Kentucky-bred. The return has been phenomenal. With the $873,600 Singletary earned in the Mile, his career earnings swelled to $1,439,732.

Singletary the player was not a racing fan, but he has been kept up to speed on his namesake's exploits by the ownership group. Currently a linebackers coach for the NFL's Baltimore Ravens, Singletary has been in regular contact with the Little Red Feather bunch.

Though he did not inspire widespread support among the worldwide wagering crowd on Breeders' Cup day, Singletary was clearly well prepared for the biggest test of his career. He had not finished worse than third in five races

Owner

Singletary is owned by **Little Red Feather Racing**, a partnership managed by Los Angeles resident Bill Koch, grandson of legendary Hollywood producer Howard Koch. The Singletary partnership has 15 members, including assistant managing partner Marc Madnick and trainer Donald Chatlos Jr. Little Red Feather is named for the fictitious character in the stories Howard Koch told to his grandson. The younger Koch became a Chicago Bears fan while attending Northwestern University. Chatlos is a native of Chicago's South Side.

Breeder

Disler Farms ceased breeding operations in 2002, six years after the death of Loyd Disler, who founded the racing operation in 1972. The family farm is located in Hulbert, Oklahoma, about 40 miles east of Tulsa and is managed by Loyd's son Donald. Loyd Disler's widow, Joy, lives in Tulsa. The farm's major starters descend from Singletary's grandam, Joi'ski, a stakes-winning Key to the Mint mare named for Joy Disler.

in 2004, including a win in the San Fernando Breeders' Cup Handicap (G2) at Bay Meadows Race Course in April and a game second to Designed for Luck in Hollywood's Shoemaker Breeders' Cup Mile Stakes (G1) on May 31. With just one start in the interim—a third-place effort in the Oak Tree Breeders' Cup Mile Stakes (G2) at Santa Anita Park on October 9—Singletary was allowed to escape at odds of 16.50-1.

Breaking from the tenth post position, Singletary left alertly but was reserved nicely by Flores, who settled him into good position. Racing between horses for the opening five furlongs, Flores found a hole as the pace picked up on the final turn, and then urged his mount to charge through it like a running back.

"All he needed was a little hole," Flores said.

"When he sees it and I let him go through it, he just responds." Singletary seized the lead near the three-sixteenths pole, held a length lead over Canadian-based pacesetter Soaring Free at the furlong pole, and then repelled Antonius Pius's late move.

Defending race winner Six Perfections (Fr) rallied for third despite being steadied in traffic on the final turn. "She ran into trouble on the last turn," trainer Pascal Bary said. "[Jockey Jerry Bailey] told me she was squeezed for room, but she made her usual good run at the end." Soaring Free finished fourth in the full field of 14. Artie Schiller, the Mile's lukewarm favorite at 3.80-to-1, showed nothing and finished 12th, a half-length behind second betting choice Nothing to Lose, who was ninth.—*Rob Longley*

FOURTH RACE
Lone Star Park
October 30, 2004

1 mile on turf. 21st running of the Breeders' Cup Mile (G1). Purse $1.5-million. 3-year-olds and up. Weights (Northern Hemisphere): 3-year-olds, 122 lbs. Older, 126 lbs. (Southern Hemisphere): 3-year-olds, 119 lbs. Older, 126 lbs. Fillies and mares allowed 3 lbs.

Value of race: $1,540,560. Value to winner: $873,600; second: $336,000; third: $184,800; fourth: $95,760; fifth, $50,400. Mutuel Pool $4,143,442.

Horse	Wt.	M/Eqt	PP	St.	¼	½	¾	Str.	Fin.	Jockey	Odds $1
Singletary, 4, c.	126	L	10	7	5¹	5½	4ʰᵈ	1¹	1½	D. Flores	16.50
Antonius Pius, 3, c.	122	L	7	10	12¹½	12¹	10ʰᵈ	4¹	2¹½	J. Spencer	31.40
Six Perfections (Fr), 4, f.	123	L	11	11	8¹	8½	7¹	7ʰᵈ	3ⁿᵏ	J. Bailey	5.90
Soaring Free, 5, g.	126	L	4	3	11½	11	1½	2¹	4¾	T. Kabel	10.90
Silver Tree, 4, c.	126	L	2	2	7¹	7½	8½	5ʰᵈ	5ⁿᵏ	E. Prado	21.90
Musical Chimes, 4, f.	123	L	9	9	10ʰᵈ	9½	11ʰᵈ	8ʰᵈ	6ⁿᵏ	K. Desormeaux	22.90
Blackdoun (Fr), 3, c.	122	Lb	13	14	14	14	13¹½	11ʰᵈ	7ⁿᵏ	C. Nakatani	10.60
Diamond Green (Fr), 3, c.	122		8	13	13¹	13ʰᵈ	14	10¹½	8¹	L. Dettori	19.70
Mr O'Brien (Ire), 5, g.	126	L	14	8	6ʰᵈ	6¹	5½	6½	9ⁿᵒ	E. Coa	20.70
Whipper, 3, c.	122	L	1	5	4¹½	4½	2ʰᵈ	3ʰᵈ	10ⁿᵒ	C. Soumillon	7.10
Nothing to Lose, 4, c.	126	Lb	12	12	11ʰᵈ	10½	9ʰᵈ	12¹	11½	J. Velazquez	4.30
Artie Schiller, 3, c.	122	L	6	6	9½	11½	12½	9¹½	12³¾	R. Migliore	*3.80
Special Ring, 7, g.	126	Lb	3	1	3ʰᵈ	2ʰᵈ	3ʰᵈ	13³	13³½	V. Espinoza	8.60
Domestic Dispute, 4, c.	126	L	5	4	2ʰᵈ	3¹	6ʰᵈ	14	14	K. John	53.80

OFF AT 1:37. Start: Good for all. Winner: Swung wide, drew clear.
Time: :24.03, :48.65, 1:12.71, 1:24.77, 1:36.90. Weather: Clear. Turf: Yielding.

$2 Mutuel Prices:	10—SINGLETARY	35.00	15.60	9.80
	7—ANTONIUS PIUS		37.60	13.60
	11—SIX PERFECTIONS (Fr)			5.00

$2 PICK THREE 1-3/10-10 PAID $474.00 $2 EXACTA 10-7 PAID $1,495.60
$2 HEAD2HEAD 11 vs. 12 (WINNER 11) PAID $3.80
$2 SUPERFECTA 10-7-11-4 PAID $107,388.00 $2 TRIFECTA 10-7-11 PAID $12,435.20

B. c., by Sultry Song—Joiski's Star, by Star de Naskra. Trainer: Donald Chatlos. Owner: Little Red Feather Racing. Bred by Disler Farms Ltd. (Ky.).

SINGLETARY waited patiently while gaining on the turn, split horses while angling out at the top of the stretch, took charge at the three-sixteenths pole, opened a clear advantage in midstretch then prevailed under steady right-hand urging. ANTONIUS PIUS, well back early, steadied sharply while in traffic on the turn, lugged in while gaining in midstretch, closed strongly from outside nearing the sixteenth pole, and checked behind the winner while lugging in again in the late stages. SIX PERFECTIONS (Fr) launched a bid between horses on the far turn, steadied in traffic midway on the turn, and rallied belatedly. SOARING FREE, uncontested on the lead for a half, relinquished the lead to the winner in upper stretch, and weakened. SILVER TREE rallied along the rail midway on the turn, was blocked along the inside nearing the quarter pole, lodged a mild bid to reach contention in upper stretch, and flattened out. MUSICAL CHIMES, steadied while trapped between horses on the turn and in upper stretch then lacked a strong closing bid. BLACKDOUN (Fr) steadied sharply in traffic on the turn, swung seven wide entering the stretch, and failed to threaten thereafter. DIAMOND GREEN (Fr) broke slowly, steadied behind a wall of horses on the turn, and failed to threaten while improving his position. MR O'BRIEN (Ire), in the middle of the pack along the backstretch, lodged a mild rally on the turn, and tired. WHIPPER, in close contention along the inside for a half, made a run to challenge on the turn, and tired in the final eighth. NOTHING TO LOSE failed to mount a serious rally. ARTIE SCHILLER rallied briefly along the rail in upper stretch and flattened out. SPECIAL RING, up close for five furlongs, steadied sharply in upper stretch and tired. DOMESTIC DISPUTE showed speed for five furlongs and tired.

2004 Juvenile Fillies: Sweet Victory

To paraphrase the late entertainer Jackie Gleason, how sweet it was for Sweet Catomine. The 21st running of the $917,000 Breeders' Cup Juvenile Fillies (G1) on October 30 belonged totally, completely to the homebred of Pamela and Martin Wygod. Against 11 other two-year-old fillies, she proved too tough, and her victory was something to savor.

She had dominated on the road to the first Breeders' Cup championship day to be held at Lone Star Park, winning a Grade 1 and a Grade 2 race in Southern California. She had dominated in the mornings, first with a dazzling workout at Santa Anita Park and then with her drop-dead good looks during her brief sojourn on Lone Star's backstretch. She went off as the 2.30-to-1 favorite in a good but not great field. If anything, she was an overlay.

And, when it came time to run, she found the right spot behind a fast early pace, overcame a tight position on Lone Star's final turn, and spurted away in the final sixteenth to a dominating 3¾-length victory in North America's premier contest for juvenile females.

The decisive win under Corey Nakatani assured Sweet Catomine an Eclipse Award. The powerfully built Storm Cat filly out of the Wygods' stakes-winning mare Sweet Life also gave trainer Julio Canani his first victory in a Breeders' Cup dirt race after two wins in the Breeders' Cup Mile (G1).

Another Grade 1 winner, Frizette Stakes (G1) victress Balletto (UAE), easily overcame her inside post position and followed Sweet Catomine in deep stretch to take second, with Darley Alcibiades Stakes (G2) winner Runway Model finishing third, another 1¼ lengths back, despite being bothered slightly by Balletto in the lane.

Sis City, who pressed or set the pace past the furlong pole, finished fourth, three-quarters of a length behind Runway Model. Sense of Style, a Grade 1 winner in New York who went off as the 7-to-2 second betting choice, missed the break and never got in the hunt, finishing ninth.

The winner ran the 1¹⁄₁₆ miles of the Juvenile Fillies in 1:41.65 on a fast, wet track; it was the race's second-fastest running after Tempera's 1:41.49 at Belmont Park in 2001. Sweet Catomine became the third consecutive favorite to win the Breeders' Cup Juvenile Fillies, after Storm Flag Flying (4-to-5) at Arlington Park in 2002 and Halfbridled (2.30-to-1) at Santa Anita last year. The Juvenile Fillies has had more winning favorites, 11, than any other Breeders' Cup race.

For the second straight year, the winner emerged from Southern California following consecutive victories in the Del Mar Debutante (G1) and Oak Leaf (G2) Stakes. Both prevailed decisively in the Juvenile Fillies after drawing less than desirable post positions: Halfbridled left from the outside starting position, and Sweet Catomine had the nine hole after the scratch of In the Gold because of a fever.

Sweet Catomine recorded a big speed figure in the Oak Leaf and had so dominated her opponents that only one, fourth-place finisher Culture Clash, opted to oppose her at Lone Star. Precipitating the flood of pre-entries—16 in all—was a poor fifth-place finish by Sense of Style, the queen of the East and the 3-to-5 favorite in the Alcibiades at Keeneland Race Course on October 8. The fluidity of the starting field was such that trainer Richard Dutrow Jr. declared Frizette third-place finisher Sis City from the race on October 23 and then put her back in the hunt three days later.

Sweet Catomine clearly was a champion by the time the sun set over Lone Star on October 30, but only ten weeks earlier she had been regarded as second string in the Wygod stable, to a filly named Proposed. "They came to the track together, and in the mornings Proposed was always finishing ahead of her," Martin Wygod said. "But Proposed was a much more precocious type, whereas Sweet Catomine was relaxed."

Proposed was the favored part of the 8-to-5 Debutante entry but finished a well-beaten seventh and emerged with bone chips in a knee. Sweet Catomine won by three-quarters of a length that day over Souvenir Gift and then captured the Oak Leaf by four lengths on October 2 as the 2-to-1 second choice behind 7-to-5 Splendid Blended.

Canani, who won the Breeders' Cup Mile with Silic (Fr) in 1999 and with Val Royal (Fr) two years later, had one other piece of business to take care of before shipping to Texas. Six days before the Lone Star race, Sweet Catomine drilled five furlongs in :58.80, second-fastest of 130 workouts at the distance on the Santa Anita tab.

Sis City's presence in the field assured an honest pace. Balletto broke on top from the rail, but Mazarine Breeders' Cup Stakes (Can-G2) winner Higher World and Sis City rolled through the first quarter-mile in :22.99 and the half-mile in :46.44, with Higher World leading narrowly at both calls before retiring to the back of the field. Nakatani restrained Sweet Catomine off the hot pace, running seventh through the first six furlongs in 1:10.69.

Sweet Catomine accelerated on the final turn and looked to be making a winning move on the inside. But Balletto drifted into her path, forcing Nakatani to steady his mount.

Sweet Catomine fired again, with both barrels. She settled back into stride, and Nakatani guided her to the outside as the field turned for home. "When I moved outside and set her down, I knew I had the race won," said Nakatani, who notched his sixth Breeders' Cup win and his first in the Juvenile Fillies. Sis City held on until the furlong pole, but the battle was over. Within a few strides, Sweet Catomine had drawn clear, and she bolted away from her opposition in the final 70 yards.

Pam and Martin Wygod scored their first Breeders' Cup victory as both owners and breeders.—*Don Clippinger*

THIRD RACE
Lone Star Park
October 30, 2004

1$\frac{1}{16}$ miles. 21st running of the Breeders' Cup Juvenile Fillies (G1). Purse $1-million. Fillies, 2-year-olds. Weight: 119 lbs.

Value of race: $917,000. Value to winner: $520,000; second: $200,000; third: $110,000; fourth: $57,000; fifth, $30,000. Mutuel Pool $3,452,881.

Horse	Wgt.	M/Eqt	PP	St.	¼	½	¾	Str.	Fin.	Jockey	Odds $1
Sweet Catomine, 2, f.	119	Lb	9	7	$7^{1\frac{1}{2}}$	$7^{\frac{1}{2}}$	$7^{\frac{1}{2}}$	$2^{\frac{1}{2}}$	$1^{\frac{3}{4}}$	C. Nakatani	*2.30
Balletto (UAE), 2, f.	119	L	1	5	$3^{1\frac{1}{2}}$	3^{1}	$2^{\frac{1}{2}}$	$3^{\frac{1}{2}}$	$2^{1\frac{1}{4}}$	J. Bailey	4.10
Runway Model, 2, f.	119	L	3	1	5^{hd}	6^{1}	$6^{\frac{1}{2}}$	$4^{2\frac{1}{2}}$	$3^{\frac{3}{4}}$	R. Bejarano	10.00
Sis City, 2, f.	119	L	6	3	2^{2}	$2^{1\frac{1}{2}}$	$1^{\frac{1}{2}}$	1^{hd}	4^{nk}	J. Velazquez	20.20
Dance Away Capote, 2, f.	119	L	5	9	$9^{\frac{1}{2}}$	$9^{\frac{1}{2}}$	$9^{\frac{1}{2}}$	$5^{\frac{1}{2}}$	$5^{1\frac{1}{4}}$	R. Dominguez	15.70
Sharp Lisa, 2, f.	119	Lf	11	6	$6^{\frac{1}{2}}$	$5^{\frac{1}{2}}$	5^{hd}	6^{1}	$6^{2\frac{1}{4}}$	L. Dettori	12.10
Culinary, 2, f.	119	L	4	2	4^{1}	4^{hd}	3^{hd}	$7^{1\frac{1}{2}}$	7^{hd}	C. Marquez Jr.	7.30
Play With Fire, 2, f.	119	L	12	8	10^{1}	12	12	$9^{\frac{1}{2}}$	8^{3}	P. Day	28.80
Sense of Style, 2, f.	119	L	8	11	$8^{\frac{1}{2}}$	8^{1}	8^{hd}	$8^{1\frac{1}{2}}$	9^{1}	E. Prado	3.50
Culture Clash, 2, f.	119	Lb	10	10	$11^{\frac{1}{2}}$	$10^{\frac{1}{2}}$	10^{2}	10^{2}	$10^{5\frac{1}{4}}$	K. John	61.60
Mona LIsa (GB), 2, f.	119	L	7	12	12	11^{1}	11^{hd}	12	$11^{2\frac{1}{4}}$	J. Spencer	18.50
Higher World, 2, f.	119	L	2	4	$1^{\frac{1}{2}}$	1^{hd}	4^{hd}	$11^{2\frac{1}{2}}$	12	P. Husbands	60.80

In the Gold scratched.

OFF AT 12:56. Start: Good. Winner: Blocked five-sixteenths, checked.
Time: :22.99, :46.44, 1:10.69, 1:35.47, 1:41.65. Weather: Clear. Track: Fast.

$2 Mutuel Prices:				
	10—SWEET CATOMINE	6.60	4.00	3.00
	1—BALLETTO (UAE)		4.80	3.40
	4—RUNWAY MODEL			5.00

$2 PICK THREE 4-1-3/10 PAID $1,629.40
$2 DAILY DOUBLE 1-10 PAID $19.60 $2 EXACTA 10-1 PAID $29.00
$2 HEAD2HEAD 5 vs. 12 vs. 13 (WINNER 12) PAID $5.60
$2 SUPERFECTA 10-1-4-7 PAID $1,561.20 $2 TRIFECTA 10-1-4 PAID $174.20

B. f., by Storm Cat—Sweet Life, by Kris S. Trainer: Julio Canani. Owners: Mr. and Mrs. Martin J. Wygod (Ky.). Bred by Mr. and Mrs. Martin J. Wygod (Ky.).

SWEET CATOMINE, unhurried along the backstretch, launched a rally between horses entering the far turn, steadied sharply while lacking room midway on the turn, swung between horses for clear sailing at the top of the stretch, made a strong run nearing the furlong marker, took control approaching the sixteenth pole, and drew away with authority through the final 70 yards. BALLETTO (UAE) raced just behind the leaders while saving ground along the backstretch, ranged up from outside to challenge on the turn, battled between horses into upper stretch, was in a bit tight while dueling for the lead in midstretch, and then continued on well to best the others. RUNWAY MODEL moved around rivals while rallying on the far turn, lacked room while saving ground at the top of the stretch, steadied in traffic between horses at the eighth pole and again a sixteenth out, and failed to threaten thereafter. SIS CITY pressed the pace from outside for five furlongs, surged to the front on the far turn, and weakened under pressure in the final eighth. DANCE AWAY CAPOTE raced well back for six furlongs, closed the gap midway on the turn, steadied while blocked in traffic at the five-sixteenths pole, made a run to reach contention in upper stretch, and lacked a strong closing response. SHARP LISA lodged a mild bid while being forced six wide at the quarter pole, and then flattened out. CULINARY moved into contention while four wide leaving the backstretch, raced just off the pace while being carried five wide on the turn, and then faded in the stretch. PLAY WITH FIRE failed to mount a serious rally while four wide. SENSE OF STYLE broke in the air, was behind a wall of horses on the turn, and lacked the needed response. CULTURE CLASH was steadied at the start and was never close thereafter. MONA LISA (GB) broke in the air at the start and never reached contention. HIGHER WORLD drifted out while taking the lead on the first turn, dueled along the inside for five furlongs, and gave way.

2004 Distaff: Ashado Rebounds

Ashado's run in the $1,834,000 Breeders' Cup Distaff (G1) was a microcosm of her 2004 season. She contended, she slipped, and she came back again to win with flair. That was, in a nutshell, how she won the Distaff and how she assured herself an Eclipse Award as champion three-year-old filly.

Just as Ashado asserted herself early in the season with victories in the Fair Grounds Oaks (G2) and Kentucky Oaks (G1), the Saint Ballado filly gained a good early position in the 1⅛-mile Breeders' Cup Distaff on October 30, tracking pacesetter Tamweel in third. Ashado got shuffled back to fifth in the middle stages of the race—emblematic of her miscues in the Mother Goose (G1) and Alabama (G1) Stakes, two races she lost as the odds-on favorite.

Ashado regrouped in both instances, however, and when jockey John Velazquez found the perfect opening on the rail, the filly responded with a tremendous burst to win the Distaff by 1¼ lengths over Storm Flag Flying in 1:48.26, which broke Moosekabear's 1997 Lone Star Park track record by 1.43 seconds. Likewise, trainer Todd Pletcher had found the perfect prep race for Ashado to rebound from her Alabama loss in the Cotillion Handicap (G2) on October 2 at Philadelphia Park, and she responded with an effortless win that primed her perfectly for the Distaff.

"The one thing I felt strongly about was that I wanted four weeks between races, and when I looked at the calendar after the Alabama [on August 21], there were really no alternatives that I really liked with the exception of the Cotillion," Pletcher said. "I was a little concerned about shipping to Philadelphia Park, that it was a hand-

icap, but our main focus was the Breeders' Cup Distaff, and we would work our way back. In order to do the very best in the Distaff, we thought the Cotillion was our best option."

Tamweel received one of the race's better trips as she set a brisk but not urgent pace through the first six furlongs with opening splits of :22.93, :46.70, and 1:10.50 before giving way first to Island Fashion, who raced four wide throughout the race, briefly on the far turn. Once the field straightened for home, however, Ashado easily dispatched the early leaders while holding off a late rush from Storm Flag Flying, who came from last at the five-eighths pole to be second, a neck in front of Stellar Jayne, who also encountered traffic problems early in the race after she broke poorly and took a right-hand turn out of the starting gate.

Tamweel finished fourth and was followed by Island Fashion, Indy Groove, Elloluv, Nebraska Tornado, Society Selection, Hollywood Story, and Bare Necessities. Less than 13 lengths separated the field, one of the smallest margins from first to last in the history of the race.

"I had a perfect trip," said John Velazquez, Ashado's regular rider. "I tucked into position on the first turn, and I just had to bide my time following the leaders. When Stellar Jayne went to the outside, a hole opened up for me, and when I asked her, she was there for me. I am grateful I was the one to win for Todd."

Pletcher, who won the Breeders' Cup Sprint (G1) with Speightstown later on the card, called the Distaff victory the biggest in his short, though already illustrious career, not only because he was winless in 12 previous Breeders' Cup attempts and because he is a Dallas native, but also because he trains Ashado for one of his first major clients, Jack and Laurie Wolf's Starlight Stable, which owns the filly in partnership with Paul Saylor and Johns Martin. In their few short years in the game, the Wolfs have campaigned many good runners with Pletcher, including multiple Grade 1 winner Harlan's Holiday and Purge, a multiple Grade 2 winner in 2004.

Barry Berkelhammer, the Wolfs' bloodstock agent, picked out Ashado at the 2002 Keeneland September yearling sale and was thrilled that Starlight Stable was able to buy her for $170,000, which he considered a bargain. Ashado began showing what she could do right from the start. She won her career debut by seven lengths on June 18, 2003, at Belmont Park and followed that performance with victories in the Schuylerville (G2) and Spinaway (G1) Stakes before finishing third behind Society Selection and Victory U. S. A. in the Frizette Stakes (G1) and second behind champion Halfbridled in the Breeders' Cup Juvenile Fillies (G1).

Owners

Paul Saylor, **Johns Martin**, and the **Starlight Stable** of Jack and Laurie Wolf have successfully owned horses on their own, but their joint ownership of Ashado has brought them their biggest success. Saylor resides in Atlanta, where the Wolfs lived when they formed Starlight Stable in 2000. The two got together on the advice of a mutual friend who pointed out that they all lived in Atlanta and loved horses. In addition to Ashado, Martin has partnered with Saylor and Starlight Stable on multiple Grade 2 winner Purge.

Breeders

Aaron and Marie Jones bred two 2004 Breeders' Cup winners, Distaff (G1) winner Ashado and Sprint (G1) victor Speightstown. The husband-and-wife team from Eugene, Oregon, keep 26 broodmares at Taylor Made Farm in Nicholasville, Kentucky, including Ashado's dam, Goulash. The Joneses own the Seneca Sawmill, Seneca Timber, and Seneca Wholesale Cos. in Eugene. Aaron Jones is a world-renowned inventor of sawmill technology. They began buying racehorses in 1971, dispersed in 1990, but returned to the game in the late 1990s.

Ashado then closed out her juvenile season a month later at Aqueduct with a nose victory in the Demoiselle Stakes (G2) before taking 14 weeks off to freshen up for her three-year-old debut in the Fair Grounds Oaks. With Ashado's two-year-old record of four wins from six starts and $610,800 in earnings, her connections were obviously very high on her, and just as they plotted her course backward from the Distaff this year, they circled the Oaks as their early season target and began those preparations with about five weeks of rest at Palm Meadows training center in Florida.

The buzz leading up to the Distaff had more to do with who was not in the race than who was in it, after 2002 Horse of the Year and two-time champion older female Azeri opted for the Breeders' Cup Classic (G1) (she finished fifth) and multiple Grade 1 winner Sightseek was retired following her win in the Beldame Stakes (G1) on October 9 at Belmont Park. Wolf welcomed Azeri's

defection. "Any time you can move a 3-to-5 horse out of the race and become the 2-to-1 favorite. ... I was pretty pleased when she ran with the boys."

Ashado's adversaries for the three-year-old championship were Stellar Jayne, the Mother Goose and Gazelle Handicap (G1) winner, and Society Selection, the Alabama and Test Stakes (G1) winner. Both contested the Distaff, but Society Selection was never in the race, and Stellar Jayne, who has raced within three lengths of the pace in each of her past six starts, was last in the opening quarter-mile. "I was pleased, in light of the way [the race] unfolded," trainer D. Wayne Lukas said of Stellar Jayne's run.

The Distaff was the last race for Storm Flag Flying, the Phipps family's homebred champion juvenile filly of 2002. The Storm Cat filly, a granddaughter of undefeated Personal Ensign, was shipped to Claiborne Farm in Paris, Kentucky, for her career as a broodmare.—*Ed DeRosa*

SECOND RACE
Lone Star Park
October 30, 2004

1⅛ miles, dirt. 21st running of the Breeders' Cup Distaff (G1). Purse $2-million. Fillies and mares 3-year-olds and upward. Weights (Northern Hemisphere): 3-year-olds, 119 lbs. Older, 123 lbs. (Southern Hemisphere): 3-year-olds, 114 lbs. Older, 123 lbs.

Value of race: $1,834,000. Value to winner: $1,040,000; second: $400,000; third: $220,000; fourth: $114,000; fifth, $60,000. Mutuel Pool $3,097,057.

Horse	Wt.	M/Eqt	PP	St.	¼	½	¾	Str.	Fin.	Jockey	Odds $1
Ashado, 3, f.	119	L	1	1	3½	5½	4hnd	1½	1¹¼	J. Velazquez	*2.00
Storm Flag Flying, 4, f.	123	L	7	10	10¹½	11	8½	5²½	2nk	J. Bailey	4.60
Stellar Jayne, 3, f.	119	Lb	11	11	11	10½	6hd	4½	3¹½	R. Albarado	10.30
Tamweel, 4, f.	123	L	3	2	1¹	1½	1½	2¹	4¹¾	R. Douglas	9.00
Island Fashion, 4, f.	123	Lb	10	9	8¹	4½	2hd	3hd	5³¾	K. John	6.60
Indy Groove, 4, f.	123	L	8	5	4¹	3¹	3¹	6²	6¹	M. Guidry	48.80
Elloluv, 4, f.	123	Lb	2	3	5½	7¹	7¹	7²	7nk	C. Nakatani	21.20
Nebraska Tornado, 4, f.	123		5	6	2hd	2hd	5¹	8½	8nk	E. Prado	7.30
Society Selection, 3, f.	119	L	4	8	6hd	6hd	9¹½	9²½	9½	C. Velasquez	5.10
Hollywood Story, 3, f.	119	Lb	6	4	7hd	9hd	11	11	10¹¾	T. Baze	32.40
Bare Necessities, 5, m.	123	L	9	7	9hd	8½	10²	10²	11	J. Valdivia Jr.	57.10

OFF AT 12:21. Start: Good. Winner: Blocked quarter pole, steadied.
Time: :22.93, :46.70, 1:10.50, 1:35.48, 1:48.26. Weather: Clear. Track: Good.

	1—ASHADO	6.00	3.60	2.80
$2 Mutuel Prices:	7—STORM FLAG FLYING	7.00	4.00	
	11—STELLAR JAYNE			4.80

$2 DAILY DOUBLE 4-1 PAID $297.60   **$2 EXACTA 1-7 PAID $34.80**
$2 HEAD2HEAD 1 vs. 7 (WINNER 1) PAID $3.20
$2 SUPERFECTA 1-7-11-3 PAID $1,191.80   **$2 TRIFECTA 1-7-11 PAID $178.00**

Dkbbr. f., by Saint Ballado—Goulash by Mari's Book. Trainer: Todd Pletcher. Owners: Starlight Stables LLC, Paul Saylor, and Johns Martin (Ky.). Bred by Aaron U. and Marie D. Jones (Ky.).

ASHADO, well placed just behind the leaders along the backstretch, waited patiently while saving ground through the turn, checked briefly while awaiting room nearing the quarter pole, split rivals to get clear entering the stretch, surged to the front nearing the furlong marker, and edged clear under strong right-hand encouragement. STORM FLAG FLYING checked slightly when SOCIETY SELECTION angled in on the first turn, was unhurried while saving ground along the backstretch, worked her way forward along the rail midway on the turn, launched a bid along the inside entering the stretch, angled between horses while gaining in midstretch, and finished well. STELLAR JAYNE, unhurried early, menaced at the furlong pole but flattened out. TAMWEEL, bobbled at the start, rushed up along the rail to gain a clear early advantage, dug in when challenged on the turn, battled into midstretch, and weakened. ISLAND FASHION, strung out four wide on the first turn, circled four wide to reach contention on the turn, remained a factor into midstretch, and weakened in the final eighth. INDY GROOVE pressed the pace to the turn, steadied in traffic nearing the quarter pole, and gradually tired. ELLOLUV lodged a mild rally while five wide on the final turn then lacked a further response. NEBRASKA TORNADO pressed the pace along the backstretch and tired. SOCIETY SELECTION raced in the middle of the pack for seven furlongs and steadily tired thereafter. HOLLYWOOD STORY, in tight on the first turn, faded on the far turn. BARE NECESSITIES steadied between horses nearing the far turn and was never close thereafter.

RACING
Review of 2004 Racing Season

If the speed handicappers are to be believed, 2004 was highlighted by two of the fastest horses ever to peer through a bridle. One of them, Smarty Jones, dominated the spring season and the year's headlines. He lost the Belmont Stakes (G1) after romping in the Kentucky Derby (G1) and Preakness Stakes (G1), but his brilliance rivaled some of the finest three-year-olds ever seen in North America.

Smarty Jones was very fast, but the speed handicappers concluded that he was not the year's fastest horse. That designation fell to Ghostzapper, who whirled through a carefully orchestrated season without a defeat, won the year's definitive race in the Breeders' Cup Classic (G1) after Smarty Jones had been whisked off to stud, and was voted Horse of the Year by a substantial margin.

Behind those marquee performers were a supporting cast that eclipsed the racing class of 2003. To be sure, the season had its weak points, and the two-year-old male division was almost as feeble as it had been in 2003. But, as in 2003, the two-year-old filly division had a star who also dazzled the speed handicappers. Unlike Halfbridled before her, Sweet Catomine was not undefeated through her juvenile season, but she won all the races that really mattered with authority and was a near-unanimous choice as champion.

Other divisions offered spirited arguments over which competitor was atop the heap at the end of the season and enlivened a racing season that was both memorable and of high quality.

Two-Year-Old Males

The picture for two-year-old males was so muddled in 2004 that the championship was not decided until after the Eclipse Award ballots were mailed out in early December. Certainly, the 2003 season was even weaker, a mish-mash so unfathomable that the Experimental Free Handicap split highweight honors among three horses. In the end, none of them reached the spring classics. The 2004 season was slightly more definitive, but only in its closing days. In the end, two horses, undefeated Hollywood Futurity (G1) winner Declan's Moon and Wilko, upset winner of the Breeders' Cup Juvenile (G1), shared the Experimental highweight.

Action for two-year-old males grows serious at Del Mar and Saratoga Race Course in the summer. Afleet Alex, owned by the Cash is King stable, made a good case for himself on the East Coast. Trained by Tim Ritchey, the Northern Afleet colt cruised in his first stakes start, the Sanford Stakes (G2) at Saratoga, and then narrowly won Saratoga's centerpiece juvenile race, the Hopeful Stakes (G1). Proud Accolade beat him in the Champagne Stakes (G1) when racing moved to Belmont Park.

At Del Mar, Roman Ruler made a strong early statement with runaway victories in a maiden race and the Best Pal Stakes (G2). The Bob Baffert-trained Fusaichi Pegasus colt looked to be a lock in the Del Mar Futurity (G2) and went off at 1-to-10, but he could not hold off Declan's Moon, at that point an unheralded Maryland-bred gelding with only a maiden victory to his credit. Ron Ellis took a calculated risk and put the son of Malibu Moon away until late November. In October, trainer D. Wayne Lukas sent out Consolidator for a victory in the Lane's End Breeders' Futurity (G1) at Keeneland Race Course.

With Declan's Moon waiting in the wings, the Breeders' Cup Juvenile was a wide-open affair. Roman Ruler, who had come back to win the Norfolk Stakes (G2), was favored at 2-to-1, but he never was a factor, and longshot Wilko overtook 3-to-1 Afleet Alex to win by three-quarters of a length. Wilko, making his first North American start, went off at 28.30-to-1, the longest-priced winner ever in the Breeders' Cup Juvenile, because he had been unable to win against top-level company in England.

Ellis played his cards well in the year's final months. He sent out Declan's Moon to win the Hollywood Prevue Stakes (G2) in late November and brought him back four weeks later for a one-length victory in the Hollywood Futurity, with Wilko in his wake. When the Eclipse ballots were counted at the end of the year, Declan's Moon was voted the champion.

Two-Year-Old Fillies

If two-year-old fillies have a reputation for being flighty and unpredictable, the top juvenile fillies of the past few years have done their very best to bury that stereotype. To be sure, Storm Flag Flying was flighty, but her talents overcame her quirks and made her an undefeated champion in 2002. Halfbridled had no apparent personality abnormalities and soared to a divisional title while undefeated in 2003. While Sweet Catomine lost her maiden start by five lengths, she came back to win three consecutive graded races and assure herself a 2004 championship with only one dissenting vote.

Early in the juvenile filly season, Sense of Style put together a fashionable summer. After winning her maiden victory for owners Derrick Smith and Michael Tabor, the $800,000 Keeneland September yearling purchase rolled to an eye-opening, 6¾-length victory in Saratoga's Spinaway Stakes (G2). Also during the Saratoga season, Richard Dutrow Jr. made one of the year's most clever claims when he took Sis City for $50,000 from a maiden claimer. In her next start, she won Monmouth Park's Mongo Queen Stakes and won back more than half of her purchase price for a partnership that included New York Yankees Manager Joe Torre.

On the West Coast, Sweet Catomine established herself as the division's class when she went from a defeat in her career debut to winning the Del Mar Debutante Stakes (G1) in her second start for her owners and breeders, Martin and Pam Wygod. That three-quarter-length win effectively scared off a lot of her West Coast competition, and she coasted to four-length victory in the Oak Leaf Stakes (G2) in early October.

Sense of Style kicked off her fall campaign with a one-length victory over Balletto (UAE) in the Matron Stakes (G1), but thereafter the two fillies went in different directions. Sense of Style stumbled badly in her first start around two turns in Keeneland's Darley Alcibiades Stakes (G2), finishing fifth behind winner Runway Model. Darley Stable's Balletto remained in New York and won the Frizette Stakes (G1). The stage was set for a competitive race in the Breeders' Cup Juvenile Fillies (G1).

To the amazement of those who had watched her during the week, Sweet Catomine went off as the 2.30-to-1 favorite—many thought her odds should have been much shorter—and was coiled to strike on Lone Star's final turn as Sis City set the pace. But jockey Corey Nakatani found himself in traffic nearing the stretch and had to check his mount. No matter. Sweet Catomine almost immediately resumed running, caught Sis City inside the furlong pole, and won by 3¾ lengths over Balletto. Sense of Style never fired and finished ninth. In the aftermath of the Breeders' Cup race, Runway Model came back to win the Golden Rod Stakes (G2) at Churchill Downs and Sis City took the Demoiselle Stakes (G2) at Aqueduct.

Three-Year-Old Males

Not since Iroquois has a little horse from Pennsylvania created as much excitement as Smarty Jones did in 2004. He had everything: a rags-to-riches story, appealing connections, and a world of speed. His victory in the 2004 Kentucky Derby and Preakness may not have been as epochal as Iroquois's win in the 1881 Epsom Derby (the first by an American-bred horse), but he provided a welcome burst of positive news coverage for Thoroughbred racing.

As the three Experimental Free Handicap co-highweights and other notable horses failed to live up to their form or were injured, new contenders took their places. On the West Coast, Imperialism won the San Rafael Stakes (G2), but Castledale (Ire), sixth in the San Rafael, came back to win the Santa Anita Derby (G1) at 30-to-1, with Imperialism advanced to second on the disqualification of Rock Hard Ten.

East Coast three-year-olds were no less inconsistent. Read the Footnotes narrowly won the Fountain of Youth Stakes (G2) at Gulfstream Park but finished fourth behind 37.40-to-1 Friends Lake in the Florida Derby (G1). Nonetheless, the Florida Derby proved to be a key race for the run-up to the Derby. The Cliff's Edge, the third-place finisher, won the Blue Grass Stakes (G1) at Keeneland, and Tapit, fifth in the Florida Derby, went on to win Aqueduct's Wood Memorial Stakes (G1).

The only model of consistency in the spring was Smarty Jones, and trainer John Servis kept Someday Farm's unbeaten homebred well below the radar of national attention until late April. The diminutive Elusive Quality colt won Aqueduct's Count Fleet Stakes in early January and then embarked on a quest for Oaklawn Park's $5-million centennial bonus. While short of full conditioning, Smarty Jones won the one-mile Southwest Stakes and then easily won the 1¹⁄₁₆-mile Rebel Stakes, the first race in the Oaklawn bonus series. He won the Arkansas Derby (G2) by 1½ lengths but was not convincing enough to be rated as the program-line favorite for the Derby. Nonetheless, a brilliant pre-Derby workout made him the 4.10-to-1 favorite on May 1, and he won by 2¾ lengths over Lion Heart, with Imperialism finishing third.

Smarty Jones faced a similar field in the Preakness and won by a record 11½ lengths. He appeared to be the horse of destiny, the first to wear the Triple Crown mantle since Affirmed in 1978, but it was not to be. He resisted Servis's efforts to mitigate his speed before the Belmont, was too competitive too early, and fell to Birdstone. Syndicated for $39-million, Smarty Jones never raced again. Lion Heart won the Haskell Invitational Handicap (G1), and Birdstone won the Travers Stakes (G1), with Lion Heart far behind him. Birdstone was the only horse with any chance to overtake Smarty Jones for the year-end title, but those hopes evaporated when he finished a well-beaten seventh in the Breeders' Cup Classic (G1).

Three-Year-Old Fillies

While all of 2004's three-year-old males except Smarty Jones were inconsistent, their filly counterparts were much more dependable. At the beginning of the year, Martin and Pam Wygod sent out their homebred Silent Sighs for a victory in the Sunshine Millions Oaks at Gulfstream Park, and Bob and Beverly Lewis's A. P. Adventure won the Santa Ysabel (G3) and Las Virgenes (G1) Stakes at Santa Anita. Silent Sighs won the Santa Anita Oaks (G1) by 1½ lengths over Half-bridled, with A. P. Adventure third.

In Florida, Madcap Escapade rolled through the Gulfstream Park season, winning her first career start there and then taking the Old Hat and Forward Gal (G2) Stakes. Trainer Frank Brothers shipped her to Keeneland, where she met the second-best juvenile filly of 2003, Ashado, in the Ashland Stakes (G1) in early April. Winner of the Fair Grounds Oaks (G2) in March, Ashado ran gamely but could not overtake Madcap Escapade, who won by a half-length. Their efforts set up a rematch in a talent-packed Kentucky Oaks (G1) on April 30. The Oaks's 1⅛-mile distance appeared to help Ashado, who won by 1¼ lengths over Island Sand.

Stellar Jayne, who had finished seventh in the Kentucky Oaks, put together a strong summer. In June, she won Churchill's Dogwood Breeders' Cup Stakes (G3) and then defeated Ashado in the Mother Goose Stakes (G1). Ashado whipped her in the subsequent Coaching Club American Oaks (G1), and Society Selection beat her in the Alabama Stakes (G1), but the Wild Rush filly bounced back from those two second-place finishes to win Belmont's Gazelle Handicap (G1). After her Alabama victory, Society Selection ran second to older mare Sightseek in the Beldame Stakes (G1).

Ashado posed a timing problem for trainer Todd Pletcher after her third-place finish in the Alabama on a sloppy Saratoga track. The trainer wanted one more start for her before the Breeders' Cup Distaff (G1), and he wanted a four-week break before the Lone Star race. The only race that presented the right scenario was Philadelphia Park's Cotillion Handicap (G2), and the Saint Ballado filly won easily as the 124-pound high-weight. She went into the Breeders' Cup Distaff (G1) as the 2-to-1 favorite and vanquished a field of older fillies and mares. She finished 1¼ lengths clear of Storm Flag Flying, the 2002 juvenile filly champion, with Stellar Jayne finishing third. Ashado was voted champion three-year-old filly.

Older Males

With increasing frequency, the competition for North America's older-male title begins halfway around the world in Dubai, and 2004 was no exception. After his 2003 Breeders' Cup Classic (G1) victory, Pleasantly Perfect was pointed toward the $6-million Dubai World Cup (UAE-G1), a race so rich that the winner is guaranteed to be among the leading earners at year-end. Following the big Pleasant Colony horse to the shores

of the Arabian Gulf was Medaglia d'Oro, who had finished second to Pleasantly Perfect in the Breeders' Cup Classic at Santa Anita. Before their duel in the desert, both horses tuned up in the United States. Pleasantly Perfect won the San Antonio Handicap (G2) at the end of January for trainer Richard Mandella, and trainer Bobby Frankel sent Medaglia d'Oro to Gulfstream Park for a commanding victory in the Donn Handicap (G1). The two Americans did not disappoint their backers in the Dubai World Cup on March 27. Medaglia d'Oro seized the lead in the long homestretch at Nad al Sheba racecourse, but Pleasantly Perfect overtook him in the last 100 yards and won by three-quarters of a length.

Back in the United States, the season had a more prosaic beginning. Southern Image, trained by Mike Machowsky, won the Sunshine Millions Classic Stakes, and the Florida-bred Halo's Image colt confirmed that form with a win in a surprisingly weak Santa Anita Handicap (G1). In his next start, Southern Image won the Pimlico Special Handicap (G1). Peace Rules, another member of Frankel's all-star stable, finished fourth in the Sunshine Millions Classic but came back to win the New Orleans (G2) and Oaklawn (G2) Handicaps. Southern Image and Peace Rules met for a second time in the Stephen Foster Handicap (G1) at Churchill Downs, but 62.60-to-1 Colonial Colony upstaged them with a nose victory over Southern Image. Peace Rules finished a well-beaten fourth but came back to win the Suburban Handicap (G1) on July 3.

The following day, the complexion of the 2004 handicap season changed when Ghostzapper made his first start of the year. The Awesome Again colt had shown promise when winning the Vosburgh Stakes (G2) the previous fall, but he was simply awesome in the seven-furlong Tom Fool Handicap (G2), which he won by 4¼ lengths. Yet another member of Frankel's stable, Ghostzapper had proved that he could sprint, and he showed middle-distance ability in winning Monmouth Park's Philip H. Iselin Breeders' Cup Handicap (G3) with a breathtaking speed figure. Still, he had not faced Grade 1 competition, and he had to work for a neck victory over Saint Liam in the Woodward Stakes (G1) in September.

In the meantime, Kentucky trainer Dale Romans was developing a championship contender of his own. Roses in May, owned by Kenneth and Sarah Ramsey, won the Prairie Meadows Cornhusker Breeders' Cup Handicap (G3) and then notched the Whitney Handicap (G1) over Perfect Drift at Saratoga. For his Breeders' Cup Classic tuneup, Romans sent Roses in May out for a four-length victory in Turfway Park's Kentucky Cup Classic Handicap (G2). Pleasantly Perfect returned to the races in the San Diego Handicap (G2) in August but faded to second behind

Choctaw Nation. But he moved forward and won the Pacific Classic Stakes (G1) over Perfect Drift in August.

The speed handicappers declared that the Breeders' Cup Classic was between Ghostzapper and Roses in May, with the edge to Frank Stronach's homebred colt. They were correct. Ghostzapper went to the lead immediately and won by three lengths. Roses in May followed him all the way around the Lone Star track and finished second. Pleasantly Perfect made a modest bid and finished third. At season's end, Stronach's Ghostzapper was rewarded with Eclipse Awards as Horse of the Year and champion older male.

Older Females

Securing an end-of-year championship requires winning on the racetrack, but human management also is crucial in collecting an Eclipse Award. A prime example is the 2004 campaign of Azeri, trained by D. Wayne Lukas, who has won more championships, 28, than any other horseman. As the 2004 season began, Azeri was all but retired and scheduled for the auction ring. For trainer Laura de Seroux, Azeri had been Horse of the Year in 2002 and champion older female in both 2002 and '03. The latter season ended with an injury in her only defeat of the year, and de Seroux recommended that she be retired. Michael Paulson, manager of his late father's Allen E. Paulson Living Trust, disagreed, overcame a challenge to his stewardship of the trust, and placed the Jade Hunter mare with Lukas.

Her quest for a third title was assisted immeasurably by division members who, like her, proved largely unable to string together two consecutive victories. Island Fashion won Santa Anita's seven-furlong Santa Monica Handicap (G1) in late January, with Juddmonte Farms' millionaire Sightseek finishing fourth as the 6-to-5 favorite. Star Parade (Arg) won the Santa Maria Handicap (G1) but fell to 2003 Breeders' Cup Distaff (G1) winner Adoration in the Santa Margarita Invitational Handicap (G1). Trainer Bobby Frankel shipped Sightseek to Florida, where she won Gulfstream's Rampart Handicap (G2) easily against outclassed competition.

Lukas began Azeri's 2004 season with a trip to a familiar locale, Oaklawn Park, where she won the Apple Blossom Handicap (G1) in April for the third straight year. The race was not without incident. Star Parade, who finished second, was bumped sharply by Wild Spirit (Chi) at the quarter pole and was placed ahead of Wild Spirit.

The action then moved to Churchill Downs, where the division's two leaders, Azeri and Sightseek, both were defeated while odds-on in two different races. On a sloppy track in the Louisville Breeders' Cup Handicap (G2), 2-to-5 Sightseek briefly took the lead but faded to fourth behind winner Lead Story, whom she had beaten in the Rampart. Azeri went off at 7-to-10 in the Humana Distaff Handicap (G1) at seven furlongs, but her stretch charge was gamely turned back by Mayo On the Side. Lukas sent Azeri out against males in the Metropolitan Handicap (G1), but she was no match for Pico Central (Brz).

Then began one of the most interesting and competitive summers of distaff racing in recent memory. The division's leaders first met in the Ogden Phipps Handicap (G1) at $1\frac{1}{16}$ miles at Belmont. In a four-horse field, Azeri went to the lead early but tired after six furlongs. Sightseek, who had pressed her modest pace, opened a six-length lead in midstretch and cruised to a $3\frac{1}{4}$-length victory over Storm Flag Flying. Azeri finished last in the Phipps, but she bounced back to win Saratoga's Go for Wand Handicap (G1), with Sightseek second by $1\frac{3}{4}$ lengths. Tried at $1\frac{1}{4}$ miles in Saratoga's Personal Ensign Handicap (G1), Azeri finished second to Storm Flag Flying.

Juddmonte and Frankel chose to close out Sightseek's career at Belmont, where she had never been beaten, and she put together back-to-back Grade 1 victories in the Ruffian Handicap and Beldame Stakes. Back at her preferred $1\frac{1}{8}$-mile distance, Azeri won Keeneland's Overbrook Spinster Stakes (G1). Lukas had a choice of Breeders' Cup races, the Classic (G1) at a $1\frac{1}{4}$-mile distance at which Azeri had never won, and the Distaff (G1) at $1\frac{1}{8}$ miles. He went for the Classic. She could lose the title to Sightseek if she lost the Distaff, but she could win the Eclipse Award if she ran decently in the Classic. Although no match for Ghostzapper, she finished fifth and effectively assured herself the older female title.

Sprinters

Just as good management can help a horse to win a championship, a misstep can turn a contender into an also-ran. The 2004 season, which was not a particularly vintage year for sprinters, came down to two older campaigners, Pico Central and Speightstown.

Pico Central, owned by Gary Tanaka and trained by Paulo Lobo, began the year by being moved up to first via disqualification in a Santa Anita Park optional claiming race and then notched a facile victory in the San Carlos Handicap (G2) at seven furlongs. On the East Coast, trainer Todd Pletcher had two top sprinters, and both were winners at Gulfstream Park's winter meet. Michael Tabor's Lion Tamer won the Richter Scale Breeders' Cup Handicap (G2) over Coach Jimi Lee. Speightstown, owned by Eugene and Laura Melnyk, won the Artax Handicap easily. Moving northward to Kentucky, Lion Tamer added the Commonwealth Breeders' Cup Stakes (G2), and Speightstown won the Churchill Downs Handicap (G2) on Derby day.

Lobo and Tanaka chose a New York path for Pico Central. The Spend a Buck horse won the seven-furlong Carter Handicap (G1) in a very fast time and then took the Metropolitan Handicap (G1) in a modest time. Pletcher gave Speightstown some additional time and brought the Gone West horse back for a 1½-length victory in the True North Breeders' Cup Handicap (G2) on the Belmont Stakes program. Dispatched to Saratoga, he won the Alfred G. Vanderbilt Handicap (G2) in mid-August. Also at Saratoga, Pomeroy won the King's Bishop Stakes (G1), and Midas Eyes scored in the seven-furlong Forego Handicap (G1).

Pico Central was returned to his California base and stubbed his toe in the Pat O'Brien Breeders' Cup Handicap (G2), in which he led early over the Del Mar track and then weakened to finish third behind Kela and Domestic Dispute. He had an opportunity to salvage the title with a head-to-head meeting with Speightstown in the six-furlong Vosburgh Stakes. The race was over early when Speightstown stumbled leaving the gate and Pico Central cruised to a four-length victory. Speightstown finished third.

The Breeders' Cup Sprint (G1) has been a key race in years when the division had no clear-cut leader, and Pletcher put Speightstown on a path to Lone Star Park. Lobo did not. Pico Central had not been nominated to the Breeders' Cup program, and Tanaka decided to pass on the $1-million race. Speightstown jumped back into the title picture with a sparkling 1¼-length victory over Kela at Lone Star. Even after the Sprint, Lobo contended that Pico Central had done enough to warrant the sprint title, and perhaps he had. But Pico Central ran a disappointing race in Aqueduct's Cigar Mile Handicap (G1), in which he set the early pace and faded to third, 1¼ lengths behind winner Lion Tamer. The Eclipse voters went with the Sprint winner and awarded the 2004 title to Speightstown.

Turf Males

In the past several years, winning the Eclipse Award in the turf male division has all but meant a horse based in Europe who won the Breeders' Cup Turf (G1) in a single North American start. Since Illinois-bred Buck's Boy won the Breeders' Cup Turf and the male turf title in 1998, all male grass champions had been based overseas. That pattern was interrupted in 2004, when the Europeans had a relatively weak year on their favored surface and North America produced one of its best turf three-year-olds in a long time.

From the first of the year, Kitten's Joy was a contender in the division. On New Year's Day, Kenneth and Sarah Ramsey's homebred El Prado (Ire) colt celebrated his official third birthday with a facile victory in Calder Race Course's Tropical Park Derby (G3). In February, he added Gulfstream Park's Palm Beach Stakes (G3). On the West Coast, Sweet Return (GB) opened the season with victories in the San Marcos Stakes (G2) and Frank E. Kilroe Mile Handicap (G2), but he failed to win for the remainder of the year. After a fourth-place finish in the San Luis Obispo Handicap (G2), Horizon Stable's Meteor Storm (GB) rolled to victories in the San Luis Rey (G2) and San Juan Capistrano (G2) Handicaps at Santa Anita and then took the Manhattan Handicap (G1) on the Belmont Stakes program. But his streak and his season came to an end when he finished seventh behind Request for Parole in Monmouth Park's United Nations Handicap (G1).

Trained by Dale Romans and named for Sarah Ramsey's nickname, Kitten's Joy worked his way gradually toward the sport's top-ranked races. At his home base, Churchill Downs, Kitten's Joy won the Crown Royal American Turf Stakes (G3) on the Kentucky Oaks (G1) card and then finished second as the 7-to-10 favorite to Prince Arch in the Jefferson Cup Stakes (G3). He bounced back to win the Virginia Derby (G3) at Colonial Downs in July and then collected his first Grade 1 triumph in Arlington Park's Secretariat Stakes (G1) in August. The Secretariat was on the Arlington Million Stakes (G1) card, and in the main event Powerscourt (GB) finished first but was disqualified for running erratically and pushing Bowling Green Handicap (G2) victor Kicken Kris into the rail. After finishing second to Kicken Kris in the Bowling Green at Belmont, Better Talk Now won the Sword Dancer Invitational Handicap (G1) at Saratoga.

While Kitten's Joy was gaining momentum on the East Coast, Leroidesanimaux (Brz) blossomed for Frankel on the West Coast. He won an allowance and an optional claiming race at a mile and then took Hollywood Park's Inglewood Handicap (G3) in May. Designed for Luck, second in the Inglewood, came back to take the Shoemaker Breeders' Cup Mile Stakes (G1) at the end of May, but he did not start again in 2004, and Leroidesanimaux did not reappear until late October, when he won the Morvich Handicap (G3) at Hollywood. In late November, Leroidesanimaux collected his first North American Grade 1 victory in Hollywood's Citation Handicap (G1).

The East Coast's turf battle gained momentum when Michael Tabor's Magistretti, third in the Arlington Million, won the Man o' War Stakes (G1) at Belmont in September, with Better Talk Now disappointing trainer H. Graham Motion with a fourth-place finish. The next stop was the Joe Hirsch Turf Classic Invitational Stakes (G1) in early October, and Kitten's Joy moved to the top of the class with a 2½-length victory over Magistretti.

The Breeders' Cup Turf (G1) attracted many

of the top contenders, including Star Over the Bay, winner of the Clement L. Hirsch Memorial Turf Championship Stakes (G1) in early October. Kitten's Joy found himself in traffic trouble for much of the trip and Better Talk Now rolled to a 1¾-length win over Kitten's Joy, with Powerscourt checking in third after another erratic race. Better Talk Now's bid for the title fell short when the gelding finished off the board on December 4 in the Hollywood Turf Cup Stakes (G1), won by Pellegrino (Brz). Singletary emerged to win the Breeders' Cup Mile (G1), his first Grade 1 score, and Sulamani (Ire) invaded Canada to win the Canadian International Stakes (Can-G1) a week before the Breeders' Cup Turf. Kitten's Joy was voted the Eclipse Award as champion older male on the strength of his two Grade 1 victories and four other graded stakes wins.

Turf Females
Frankel had a barn filled with female turf horses in 2004, but none of them accomplished enough to overcome the brilliance of Ouija Board (GB), a two-time classic winner who sparkled in her one North American appearance in the Breeders' Cup Filly and Mare Turf (G1). Kicking off Frankel's parade of turf winners was Megahertz (GB), who won the San Gorgonio Handicap (G2), was disqualified to seventh after finishing first in the Santa Ana Handicap (G2), and bounced back to take the Santa Barbara Handicap (G2), all at Santa Anita Park. She finished second to Noches De Rosa (Chi) in Hollywood Park's Gamely Breeders' Cup Handicap (G1) and did not reappear until the Breeders' Cup race, in which she tired to finish 11th.

Just as Megahertz was beginning her respite in May, Frankel cranked up Juddmonte Farms' Light Jig (GB), who won the Beverly Hills Handicap (G2) before finishing sixth behind winner Musical Chimes in the John C. Mabee Handicap (G1) at Del Mar. Frankel sent another Juddmonte runner, Intercontinental (GB), on the road, and she won Keeneland's Jenny Wiley Stakes (G3) and the Just a Game Breeders' Cup Handicap (G2) at Belmont. However, the Danehill filly faltered on Saratoga's yielding turf, finishing fifth in the Diana Handicap (G1), won by Wonder Again, with Fox Ridge Farm's Riskaverse taking second. Crimson Palace (SAf), Godolphin Racing's inconsistent mare, shipped into Arlington Park and won the Beverly D. Stakes (G1) over Riskaverse, who finally broke through for her only 2004 victory in the Flower Bowl Handicap (G1) at Belmont. Also in the run-up to the Breeders' Cup race, Musical Chimes won the Oak Tree Breeders' Cup Mile Stakes (G2) over males.

Ouija Board was pre-entered for both the Breeders' Cup Filly and Mare Turf and the Breeders' Cup Turf (G1), and owner Lord Derby decided to keep her in her own division. Winner of the Epsom Oaks (Eng-G1) by a dazzling seven lengths and the Darley Irish Oaks (Ire-G1) by a length, she was a good third in the Prix de l'Arc de Triomphe (Fr-G1) before her trip to Lone Star Park. Sent off at 7-to-10, she won in a cakewalk.

Steeplechasers
American steeplechase racing has three seasons—spring, summer, and fall—and very often the title is determined in the autumn, when the best horses match up in the Breeders' Cup Steeplechase and the Marion duPont Scott Colonial Cup Hurdle Stakes. In 2004, the championship again came down to the last two major races of the year. Reigning champion McDynamo won one of them, the Breeders' Cup Steeplechase, but faltered in the Colonial Cup, allowing Hirapour (Ire) to gain the championship.

Owned by Eldon Farm and trained by P. Douglas Fout, Hirapour raced in the spring and fall but missed the summer season at Saratoga because of sore feet. In his first start of the year, Hirapour gained the lead but faded to finish second to Preemptive Strike in the Carolina Cup Hurdle Stakes at the Springdale Course in Camden, South Carolina. In their next meeting, at Keeneland for the Royal Chase for the Sport of Kings Hurdle Stakes on April 16, Hirapour surged to a 1¾-length victory as the 6-to-5 favorite and set a course record. Preemptive Strike made one further spring start and fell in the three-mile Iroquois Hurdle Stakes.

With the major contenders taking the summer off, the Saratoga season was anticlimactic. Praise the Prince (NZ) won the A. P. Smithwick Memorial Steeplechase Stakes for the second time. Tres Touche won the New York Turf Writers Steeplechase Handicap but finished second to Sur La Tete in the Metcalf Memorial Hurdle Stakes at Monmouth Park in late September.

The Breeders' Cup Steeplechase in Far Hills, New Jersey, on October 23 provided a stellar matchup of the divisional leaders. McDynamo went to the lead in midrace and Hirapour challenged before the final fence, drawing within 1½ lengths of the leader. But McDynamo dug in gamely through the run-in and maintained his margin to the finish line. At Camden for the Colonial Cup, McDynamo was close to the early lead but faded in midrace. Hirapour challenged pacesetter Preemptive Strike before the last fence and drew away to win by 2¾ lengths. Sur La Tete finished third, two lengths behind Preemptive Strike and nine lengths ahead of McDynamo, who finished fourth. Hirapour set a course record in the Colonial Cup, covering 2¾ miles in 5:04.60, which knocked four-fifths of a second off the record set by McDynamo a year earlier.

—Don Clippinger

Richest North American Stakes Races of 2004

Race (Grade)	Purse	Track	Distance (Miles)	Winner	Value to Winner
Breeders' Cup Classic (G1)	$3,668,000	Lone Star Park	1¼	Ghostzapper	$2,080,000
Breeders' Cup Distaff (G1)	1,834,000	Lone Star Park	1⅛	Ashado	1,040,000
Breeders' Cup Turf (G1)	1,834,000	Lone Star Park	1½	Better Talk Now	1,040,000
Breeders' Cup Mile (G1)	1,540,560	Lone Star Park	1	Singletary	873,600
Canadian International S. (G1)	1,500,000	Woodbine	1½	Sulamani (Ire)	900,000
Breeders' Cup Juvenile (G1)	1,375,500	Lone Star Park	1¹⁄₁₆	Wilko	780,000
Breeders' Cup Filly & Mare Turf (G1)	1,292,970	Lone Star Park	1⅜	Ouija Board (GB)	733,200
Kentucky Derby (G1)	1,184,800	Churchill Downs	1¼	Smarty Jones	884,800
Arkansas Derby (G2)	1,000,000	Oaklawn Park	1⅛	Smarty Jones	600,000
Arlington Million S. (G1)	1,000,000	Arlington Park	1¼	Kicken Kris	600,000
Atto Mile (G1)	1,000,000	Woodbine	1	Soaring Free	600,000
Belmont S. (G1)	1,000,000	Belmont Park	1½	Birdstone	600,000
Delta Jackpot S.	1,000,000	Delta Downs	1¹⁄₁₆	Texcess	600,000
Florida Derby (G1)	1,000,000	Gulfstream Park	1⅛	Friends Lake	600,000
Haskell Invitational H. (G1)	1,000,000	Monmouth Park	1⅛	Lion Heart	600,000
Jockey Club Gold Cup S. (G1)	1,000,000	Belmont Park	1¼	Funny Cide	600,000
Pacific Classic S. (G1)	1,000,000	Del Mar	1¼	Pleasantly Perfect	600,000
Preakness S. (G1)	1,000,000	Pimlico	1³⁄₁₆	Smarty Jones	650,000
Queen's Plate S.	1,000,000	Woodbine	1¼	Niigon	600,000
Santa Anita H. (G1)	1,000,000	Santa Anita Park	1¼	Southern Image	600,000
Sunshine Millions Classic S.	1,000,000	Santa Anita Park	1⅛	Southern Image	550,000
Travers S. (G1)	1,000,000	Saratoga	1¼	Birdstone	600,000
Breeders' Cup Sprint (G1)	972,020	Lone Star Park	¾	Speightstown	551,200
Breeders' Cup Juvenile Fillies (G1)	917,000	Lone Star Park	1¹⁄₁₆	Sweet Catomine	520,000
Stephen Foster H. (G1)	810,750	Churchill Downs	1⅛	Colonial Colony	502,665
Delaware H. (G2)	750,900	Delaware Park	1¼	Summer Wind Dancer	450,000
Alabama S. (G1)	750,000	Saratoga	1¼	Society Selection	450,000
American Invitational Oaks (G1)	750,000	Hollywood Park	1¼	Ticker Tape (GB)	450,000
Beverly D. S. (G1)	750,000	Arlington Park	1³⁄₁₆	Crimson Palace (SAf)	450,000
Blue Grass S. (G1)	750,000	Keeneland	1⅛	The Cliff's Edge	465,000
Flower Bowl Invitational H. (G1)	750,000	Belmont Park	1¼	Riskaverse	450,000
Hawthorne Gold Cup H. (G2)	750,000	Hawthorne	1¼	Freefourinternet	450,000
Hollywood Gold Cup S. (G1)	750,000	Hollywood Park	1¼	Total Impact (Chi)	450,000
Joe Hirsch Turf Classic Invitational S. (G1)	750,000	Belmont Park	1½	Kitten's Joy	450,000
Metropolitan H. (G1)	750,000	Belmont Park	1	Pico Central (Brz)	450,000
Pennsylvania Derby (G2)	750,000	Philadelphia Park	1⅛	Love of Money	450,000
Santa Anita Derby (G1)	750,000	Santa Anita Park	1⅛	Castledale (Ire)	450,000
E. P. Taylor S. (G1)	750,000	Woodbine	1¼	Commercante (Fr)	450,000
United Nations S. (G1)	750,000	Monmouth Park	1⅜	Request for Parole	450,000
Whitney H. (G1)	750,000	Saratoga	1⅛	Roses in May	450,000
Wood Memorial S. (G1)	750,000	Aqueduct	1⅛	Tapit	450,000
Beldame S. (G1)	735,000	Belmont Park	1⅛	Sightseek	450,000
Louisiana Derby (G2)	600,000	Fair Grounds	1¹⁄₁₆	Wimbledon	360,000
Shadwell Turf Mile (G1)	600,000	Keeneland	1	Nothing to Lose	372,000
West Virginia Derby (G3)	600,000	Mountaineer Race Track	1⅛	Sir Shackleton	363,000
Kentucky Oaks (G1)	572,000	Churchill Downs	1⅛	Ashado	354,640
Clark H. (G2)	558,000	Churchill Downs	1⅛	Saint Liam	345,960
Indiana Derby (G2)	511,300	Hoosier Park	1¹⁄₁₆	Brass Hat	306,780
Delaware Oaks (G2)	500,900	Delaware Park	1¹⁄₁₆	Yearly Report	300,000
Apple Blossom H. (G1)	500,000	Oaklawn Park	1¹⁄₁₆	Azeri	300,000
Breeders' S.	500,000	Woodbine	1½	A Bit O'Gold	300,000
Champagne S. (G1)	500,000	Belmont Park	1¹⁄₁₆	Proud Accolade	300,000
Coaching Club American Oaks (G1)	500,000	Belmont Park	1¼	Ashado	300,000
Diana H. (G1)	500,000	Saratoga	1⅛	Wonder Again	300,000
Donn H. (G1)	500,000	Gulfstream Park	1⅛	Medaglia d'Oro	300,000
Franks Farm Turf S.	500,000	Gulfstream Park	1⅛	Proud Man	275,000
Frizette S. (G1)	500,000	Belmont Park	1¹⁄₁₆	Balletto (UAE)	300,000
Hollywood Derby (G1)	500,000	Hollywood Park	1¼	Good Reward	300,000
Illinois Derby (G2)	500,000	Hawthorne	1⅛	Pollard's Vision	300,000
Jim Dandy S. (G2)	500,000	Saratoga	1⅛	Purge	300,000

Race (Grade)	Purse	Track	Distance (Miles)	Winner	Value to Winner
Lane's End Breeders' Futurity (G1)	$500,000	Keeneland	1 1/16	Consolidator	$310,000
Lane's End S. (G2)	500,000	Turfway Park	1 1/8	Sinister G	300,000
Man o' War S. (G1)	500,000	Belmont Park	1 3/8	Magistretti	300,000
Massachusetts H. (G2)	500,000	Suffolk Downs	1 1/8	Offlee Wild	300,000
Matriarch S. (G1)	500,000	Hollywood Park	1	Intercontinental (GB)	300,000
Meadowlands Breeders' Cup S. (G2)	500,000	The Meadowlands	1 1/8	Balto Star	300,000
Mervin H. Muniz Jr. Memorial H. (G2)	500,000	Fair Grounds	1 1/8	Mystery Giver	300,000
New Orleans H. (G2)	500,000	Fair Grounds	1 1/8	Peace Rules	300,000
Oaklawn H. (G2)	500,000	Oaklawn Park	1 1/8	Peace Rules	300,000
Ocala Breeders' Sales Distaff S.	500,000	Gulfstream Park	1 1/16	Secret Request	275,000
Overbrook Spinster S. (G1)	500,000	Keeneland	1 1/8	Azeri	310,000
Pimlico Special H. (G1)	500,000	Pimlico	1 3/16	Southern Image	300,000
Prince of Wales S.	500,000	Fort Erie	1 3/16	A Bit O'Gold	300,000
Princess Rooney H. (G2)	500,000	Calder	3/4	Ema Bovary (Chi)	294,000
Queen Elizabeth II Challenge Cup S. (G1)	500,000	Keeneland	1 1/8	Ticker Tape (GB)	310,000
Smile Sprint H. (G3)	500,000	Calder	3/4	Champali	294,000
Suburban H. (G1)	500,000	Belmont Park	1 1/4	Peace Rules	300,000
Sunshine Millions Filly and Mare Turf S.	500,000	Santa Anita Park	1 1/8	Valentine Dancer	275,000
Super Derby (G2)	500,000	Louisiana Downs	1 1/8	Fantasticat	300,000
Sword Dancer Invitational H. (G1)	500,000	Saratoga	1 1/2	Better Talk Now	300,000
Virginia Derby (G3)	500,000	Colonial Downs	1 1/4	Kitten's Joy	300,000
WinStar Derby	500,000	Sunland Park	1 1/16	Hi Teck Man	270,000
WinStar Galaxy S. (G2)	500,000	Keeneland	1 3/16	Stay Forever	310,000
Woodbine Oaks	500,000	Woodbine	1 1/8	Eye of the Sphynx	300,000
Woodward S. (G1)	500,000	Belmont Park	1 1/8	Ghostzapper	300,000
Yellow Ribbon S. (G1)	500,000	Santa Anita Park	1 1/4	Light Jig (GB)	300,000
Vosburgh S. (G1)	490,000	Belmont Park	3/4	Pico Central (Brz)	300,000
Ashland S. (G1)	485,000	Keeneland	1 1/16	Madcap Escapade	310,000
Goodwood Breeders' Cup H. (G2)	480,000	Santa Anita Park	1 1/8	Lundy's Liability (Brz)	300,000
Shoemaker Breeders' Cup Mile S. (G1)	456,000	Hollywood Park	1	Designed for Luck	282,000
Woodford Reserve Turf Classic S. (G1)	453,900	Churchill Downs	1 1/8	Stroll	281,418
Hollywood Futurity (G1)	449,500	Hollywood Park	1 1/16	Declan's Moon	269,700
Fleur de Lis H. (G2)	439,200	Churchill Downs	1 1/8	Adoration	272,304
Swaps Breeders' Cup S. (G2)	409,300	Hollywood Park	1 1/8	Rock Hard Ten	252,780
Indiana Breeders' Cup Oaks (G3)	406,300	Hoosier Park	1 1/16	Daydreaming	243,780
Darley Alcibiades S. (G2)	400,000	Keeneland	1 1/16	Runway Model	248,000
Eddie Read H. (G1)	400,000	Del Mar	1 1/8	Special Ring	240,000
In Reality S.	400,000	Calder	1 1/16	B. B. Best	240,000
John C. Mabee H. (G1)	400,000	Del Mar	1 1/8	Musical Chimes	240,000
Secretariat S. (G1)	400,000	Arlington Park	1 1/4	Kitten's Joy	240,000

Chronology of Richest North American Race

Purse	Race	Track	Year	Winner	Value to Winner
$4,689,920	Breeders' Cup Classic (G1)	Churchill Downs	1998	Awesome Again	$2,662,400
4,030,400	Breeders' Cup Classic (G1)	Hollywood Park	1997	Skip Away	2,288,000
3,664,000	Breeders' Cup Classic (G1)	Woodbine	1996	Alphabet Soup	2,080,000
2,798,000	Breeders' Cup Classic (G1)	Belmont Park	1995	Cigar	1,560,000
2,748,000	Breeders' Cup Classic (G1)	Churchill Downs	1991	Black Tie Affair (Ire)	1,560,000
2,739,000	Breeders' Cup Classic (G1)	Hollywood Park	1984	Wild Again	1,350,000
1,049,725	Hollywood Futurity (G1)	Hollywood Park	1983	Fali Time	549,849
1,000,000	Arlington Million S. (G1)	Arlington Park	1981	John Henry	600,000
549,000	Jockey Club Gold Cup S. (G1)	Belmont Park	1980	Temperence Hill	329,400
500,000	Hollywood Gold Cup H. (G1)	Hollywood Park	1979	Affirmed	275,000
385,350	Arlington-Washington Futurity	Arlington Park	1968	Strong Strong	212,850
367,700	Arlington-Washington Futurity	Arlington Park	1966	Diplomat Way	195,200
357,250	Arlington-Washington Futurity	Arlington Park	1962	Candy Spots	142,250
319,210	Garden State S.	Garden State Park	1956	Barbizon	168,430
282,370	Garden State S.	Garden State Park	1955	Prince John	157,918
269,965	Garden State S.	Garden State Park	1954	Summer Tan	151,096
269,395	Garden State S.	Garden State Park	1953	*Turn-to	151,282
205,700	Santa Anita Maturity	Santa Anita Park	1951	Great Circle	144,325

How American Races Are Graded

At the urging of European racing officials who in 1972 had created the pattern race system to identify and grade the best-quality races in Europe, the Thoroughbred Owners and Breeders Association created the North American Graded Stakes Committee and implemented a similar grading system for the '73 racing season. The gradings were principally designed to assist bloodstock buyers by identifying the North American races that in the recent past had consistently attracted the highest levels of competition. Grade 1 would be the highest level, followed by Grade 2 and Grade 3, the latter being the lowest level of stakes race accorded a grade.

The first North American gradings, totaling 330 races, were announced in January 1973, and the English Jockey Club immediately accepted them. Fasig-Tipton Co. began to publish the gradings in its catalogs in 1975, and

Keeneland Association followed in '76. In 1998, Canadian racing authorities began to grade that nation's races, and the name of the TOBA-led organization was changed to the American Graded Stakes Committee and dealt only with United States stakes races.

Grades of all America's best races are reviewed annually by the American Graded Stakes Committee because stakes programs are dynamic and ever-changing products of conditions. The quality of any race's contestants may differ markedly from one year to the next. When a trend in the quality of the field of a race is established, be it improving or deteriorating, the race is re-evaluated for grading. Members have said that they take a five-year view of each race when considering the gradings.

Committee

The committee has ten voting members: five TOBA members serving five-year terms and five racing official members elected by the TOBA committee members and serving three-year terms. In addition, the committee's grading sessions have guest observers and invited guests. To be considered for membership on the committee, a candidate must have served as a guest observer for at least one grading session.

Members of the committee for the November 30, 2004, sessions at which 2005 gradings were determined:

TOBA: C. Steven Duncker (chairman), John Amerman, Rollin W. Baugh, Dell Hancock, and John Phillips.

Racing official members: Frank C. Gabriel Jr., Michael Harlow, Michael S. Lakow, Thomas S. Robbins, and Robert D. Umphrey.

Guest observers: Rogers Beasley, Dan Doocy, Rick Hammerle, Ben Huffman, Allan Lavin Jr., and Chris Warren.

Invited guests: John Cella, Carl Hamilton, John Roark, David Switzer, and Osamu Yamamoto.

Criteria

To be eligible for grading, a race must meet several criteria for being graded and for retaining its status. Among the criteria are:

Purse: The race must have a minimum purse, excluding state-bred supplements, of: $250,000 for Grade 1, $150,000 for Grade 2, and $100,000 for Grade 3.

Continuity: In general, a race must have two prior runnings under essentially the same conditions to be graded, although in rare circumstances Grade 1 status has been accorded immediately to races of special note, such as the Breeders' Cup races. Races with restrictions

2005 Graded Stakes by Racetrack

Track	G1	G2	G3	Total
Belmont Park	30	21	12	63
Santa Anita Park	13	31	12	56
Hollywood Park	13	13	19	45
Churchill Downs	5	10	20	35
Aqueduct	3	7	21	31
Gulfstream Park	3	12	16	31
Saratoga	12	13	5	30
Keeneland	6	7	14	27
Del Mar	6	11	2	19
Arlington Park	3	2	10	15
Calder Race Course	0	5	10	15
Monmouth Park	2	1	10	13
Pimlico Race Course	2	2	7	11
Oaklawn Park	1	3	6	10
Fair Grounds	0	4	5	9
Bay Meadows	0	1	5	6
Hawthorne	0	2	4	6
Turfway Park	0	2	4	6
Delaware Park	0	2	3	5
Meadowlands	0	1	4	5
Laurel Park	1	2	1	4
Lone Star Park	0	0	4	4
Golden Gate Fields	0	0	3	3
Philadelphia Park	0	2	0	2
Colonial Downs	0	0	2	2
Hoosier Park	0	1	1	2
Prairie Meadows	0	1	1	2
Tampa Bay Downs	0	0	2	2
Delta Downs	0	0	1	1
Ellis Park	0	0	1	1
Emerald Downs	0	0	1	1
Kentucky Downs	0	0	1	1
Louisiana Downs	0	1	0	1
Mountaineer Race Track	0	0	1	1
Suffolk Downs	0	1	0	1
Thistledown	0	1	0	1
Totals	**100**	**159**	**208**	**467**

other than sex or age are not eligible.

Drug testing: Post-race tests must meet or exceed guidelines in the committee's drug testing protocol.

In addition, if track management changes a graded race from dirt to grass, or vice versa, or changes the race's distance by more than one-quarter mile or from less than one mile to more than one mile, or vice versa, the race will be considered a new race and ineligible for grading until it has been run twice under the same conditions. If a race's place on the calendar is changed substantially, such as from July to January, the race's grading may be reviewed.

Seven votes are required to raise any grading, and six votes are needed to downgrade a race.

In determining a grading, the committee considers the quality of its field over the prior five years as measured by several statistical yardsticks. Among the considerations are:

- Points based on number of in-the-money finishes in unrestricted black-type races;
- Percentage of graded stakes winners in the field;
- Quality points assigned to the race based on the number of graded stakes winners in the field; and
- Ratings of the North American Rating Com-

Summary of Grade Changes

	No.	% Graded Stakes	Change from 2003
Grade 1	100	21.3%	0%
Grade 2	159	34.7%	0%
Grade 3	208	44.5%	−5.9%

mittee, a panel composed of racing secretaries that each week assigns a hypothetical weight to every horse running in American black-type races.

Beginning in 1999, graded turf races moved to the main track because of course conditions were automatically downgraded one grade, although the American Graded Stakes Committee reviews each such race within five days of the running and can restore the original grading. The change in grading affects only that year's running and is not considered in the grading process.

The American Graded Stakes Committee notifies racetracks with races in the lowest echelons of their respective gradings that the races may be downgraded, but the race will not be considered for downgrading until it has been run another time.

More graded stakes are offered in the U.S. than all group races throughout Europe, which has evoked criticism among some Europeans who contend that American black type is cheap-

Purse Comparison of Graded and Group Races by Country

Country	Grade 1		Grade 2		Grade 3		Total	
	Races	Average First Money	Races	Average First Money	Races	Average First Money	Races	Average First Money
2003 Racing Season								
Canada*	4	$529,163	11	$181,931	25	$99,728	40	$165,277
Ireland	10	364,350	9	94,640	23	55,865	42	136,785
Great Britain	29	349,753	35	103,734	59	53,072	123	137,437
France	26	245,185	27	72,904	54	41,366	107	98,851
Italy	8	158,769	6	73,777	11	40,239	25	86,261
Germany	7	206,529	14	64,929	24	39,167	45	73,216
United States	101	344,786	148	150,868	213	88,597	462	164,552
2002 Racing Season								
Canada*	5	$456,000	10	$153,000	26	$86,538	41	$147,805
Ireland	10	322,186	5	83,002	23	50,275	38	126,136
Great Britain	28	300,829	29	91,728	54	46,879	111	122,656
France	26	186,720	27	55,834	54	31,680	107	75,456
Italy	8	160,793	6	71,087	11	42,502	25	87,21
Germany	7	187,475	13	63,804	25	38,246	45	68,843
United States	100	343,832	150	152,295	217	87,469	467	$163,187
2001 Racing Season								
Canada*	6	$625,000	10	$200,000	27	$132,000	43	$129,512
Ireland	10	281,507	4	79,860	23	49,913	37	115,743
Great Britain	27	264,092	29	82,646	55	40,604	111	105,914
France	26	153,789	27	45,856	54	29,770	107	63,964
Italy	8	148,306	7	63,741	10	40,968	25	81,692
Germany	7	185,048	14	58,385	23	37,479	44	67,607
United States	98	348,722	157	148,464	207	87,649	462	163,695

*Canada listed in Canadian dollars; all others United States dollars or equivalents

ened by the plentiful graded races. However, less than 1% of all American races are graded, a smaller percentage than Ireland, Great Britain, or France.

2005 Graded Stakes Changes
Upgrades
Grade 2 to Grade 1: Frank E. Kilroe Mile Handicap (Santa Anita Park).

Grade 3 to Grade 2: Carry Back Stakes (Calder Race Course), Comely Stakes (Aqueduct), Prairie Meadows Cornhusker Breeders' Cup Handicap (Prairie Meadows Racetrack), Shirley Jones Handicap (Gulfstream Park), Smile Sprint Handicap (Calder).

Ungraded to Grade 3: Delta Jackpot Stakes (Delta Downs), Frances A. Genter Stakes (Calder), Hirsch Jacobs Stakes (Pimlico Race Course), Hurricane Bertie Handicap (Gulfstream), Jim Murray Memorial Handicap (Hollywood Park), Old Hat Stakes (Gulfstream), Perryville Stakes (Keeneland Race Course), Pocahontas Stakes (Churchill Downs), Providencia Stakes (Santa Anita), Rebel Stakes (Oaklawn Park), Vinery Madison Stakes (Keeneland).

Downgrades
Grade 1 to Grade 2: Milady Breeders' Cup Handicap (Hollywood Park).

Grade 2 to Grade 3: Arlington Classic Stakes (Arlington Park), Knickerbocker Handicap (Aqueduct), Monmouth Breeders' Cup Oaks (Monmouth Park), Schuylerville Stakes (Saratoga Race Course), Silverbulletday Stakes (Fair Grounds).

Grade 3 to Ungraded: Affectionately Handicap (Aqueduct), Anne Arundel Stakes (Laurel Park), Arlington Breeders' Cup Oaks (Arlington), Brown Bess Handicap (Golden Gate Fields), Canadian Turf Handicap (Gulfstream Park), Chaposa Springs Handicap (Calder

Race Course), Cradle Stakes (River Downs), Derby Trial Stakes (Churchill Downs), Donald LeVine Memorial Handicap (Philadelphia Park), Fall Highweight Handicap (Aqueduct), Golden Gate Derby (Golden Gate), Jersey Derby (Monmouth), Ladies Handicap (Aqueduct), Landaluce Stakes (Hollywood), Lawrence Realization Stakes (Belmont), Martha Washington Breeders' Cup Stakes (Pimlico Race Course), Oklahoma Derby (Remington Park), Pebbles Stakes (Belmont Park), San Miguel Stakes (Santa Anita Park), Spectacular Bid Stakes (Gulfstream).

2005 Graded Stakes by State

State	G1	G2	G3	Total
California	32	56	41	129
New York	45	41	38	124
Kentucky	11	19	40	70
Florida	3	17	28	48
Illinois	3	4	14	21
New Jersey	2	2	14	18
Maryland	3	4	8	15
Louisiana	0	5	6	11
Arkansas	1	3	6	10
Delaware	0	2	3	5
Texas	0	0	4	14
Pennsylvania	0	2	0	2
Indiana	0	1	1	2
Iowa	0	1	1	2
Virginia	0	0	2	2
Ohio	0	1	0	1
Massachusetts	0	1	0	1
Washington	0	0	1	1
West Virginia	0	0	1	1
Totals	**100**	**159**	**208**	**467**

Percentages of Best Races by Country

	Total Races	Stakes	Graded Stakes	G1 Stakes
2003 Racing Season				
Canada	5,498	259 (4.7%)	40 (0.7%)	4 (0.1%)
Ireland	850	94 (11.1%)	42 (4.9%)	10 (1.2%)
Great Britain	4,761	281 (5.9%)	1.3 (2.5%)	29 (0.6%)
France	3,981	231 (5.8%)	107 (2.6%)	26 (0.6%)
Italy	4,772	76 (1.6%)	25 (0.5%)	8 (0.2%)
Germany	2,060	108 (5.2%)	45 (2.2%)	7 (0.3%)
United States	53,309	1,923 (3.6%)	462 (0.9%)	101 (0.2%)
2002 Racing Season				
Canada	5,592	267 (4.8%)	41 (0.7%)	5 (0.1%)
Ireland	788	81 (10.3%)	38 (4.8%)	10 (1.2%)
Great Britain	4,572	250 (5.5%)	111 (2.4%)	28 (0.6%)
France	3,901	230 (5.9%)	107 (2.7%)	26 (0.7%)
Italy	4,752	73 (1.5%)	25 (0.5%)	8 (0.2%)
Germany	2,382	103 (4.3%)	45 (1.9%)	7 (0.3%)
United States	54,117	1,970 (3.6%)	467 (0.9%)	100 (0.2%)
2001 Racing Season				
Canada	5,611	252 (4.5%)	43 (0.8%)	6 (0.1%)
Ireland	782	80 (10.2%)	37 (4.7%)	10 (1.3%)
Great Britain	4,435	239 (5.4%)	111 (2.5%)	27 (0.6%)
France	3,853	229 (5.9%)	107 (2.7%)	26 (0.6%)
Italy	4,774	72 (1.5%)	25 (0.5%)	8 (0.2%)
Germany	2,418	109 (4.5%)	44 (1.8%)	7 (0.3%)
United States	55,127	2,125 (3.9%)	462 (0.8%)	98 (0.2%)

American Graded Stakes

Ack Ack Handicap

Grade 3 in 2005. Churchill Downs, three-year-olds and up, 7½ furlongs, dirt. Held October 31, 2004, with a gross value of $165,300. First held in 1991. First graded in 1997. Stakes record 1:28.63 (2001 Illusioned).

Year	Winner	Jockey	Second	Third	Strs	Time	1st Purse
2004	Sir Cherokee, 4, 114	C. H. Borel	Fire Slam, 3, 117	Slate Run, 4, 106	6	1:29.48	$102,486
2003	Cappuchino, 4, 117	J. K. Court	Pass Rush, 4, 116	Twilight Road, 6, 116	7	1:31.66	102,579
2002	Twilight Road, 5, 113	P. Day	Mountain General, 4, 116	Binthebest, 5, 113	9	1:29.39	69,874
2001	Illusioned, 3, 118	P. Day	Strawberry Affair, 3, 112	Fappie's Notebook, 4, 116	11	1:28.63	70,866
2000	Chindi, 6, 113	T. T. Doocy	Smolderin Heart, 5, 113	Millencolin, 3, 113	10	1:29.30	70,494
1999	Littlebitlively, 5, 119	C. H. Borel	Run Johnny, 7, 117	Tactical Cat, 3, 117	11	1:28.97	71,672
1998	Distorted Humor, 5, 120	C. H. Borel	Crafty Friend, 5, 113	Chindi, 4, 113	6	1:29.61	68,262
1997	Cat's Career, 4, 108	W. Martinez	Rare Rock, 4, 112	Victor Cooley, 4, 122	6	1:34.64	69,130
1996	Western Trader, 5, 113	C. H. Borel	Top Account, 4, 117	Strategic Intent, 4, 113	8	1:29.84	70,308
1995	Mystery Storm, 3, 112	C. Gonzalez	I'm Very Irish, 4, 113	Tarzans Blade, 4, 116	10	1:29.10	75,660
1994	Lost Pan, 4, 114	D. M. Barton	Sir Vixen, 6, 112	Groovy Jett, 3, 112	8	1:30.27	54,795
1991	Seven Spades, 4, 108	D. W. Cox	Discover, 3, 114	Senator to Be, 4, 115	12	1:37.62	38,513

Named for Forked Lightning Ranch's 1971 Horse of the Year and '69 Derby Trial winner Ack Ack (1966 c. by Battle Joined). Not held 1992-'93. Equaled track record 1995. Track record 2001.

Acorn Stakes

Grade 1 in 2005. Belmont Park, three-year-olds, fillies, 1 mile, dirt. Held June 4, 2005, with a gross value of $250,000. First held in 1931. First graded in 1973. Stakes record 1:34.05 (2002 You).

Year	Winner	Jockey	Second	Third	Strs	Time	1st Purse
2005	Round Pond, 3, 121	S. Elliott	Smuggler, 3, 121	In the Gold, 3, 121	6	1:35.33	$150,000
2004	Island Sand, 3, 121	T. J. Thompson	Society Selection, 3, 121	Friendly Michelle, 3, 121	8	1:34.89	150,000
2003	Bird Town, 3, 121	E. S. Prado	Lady Tak, 3, 121	Final Round, 3, 121	7	1:35.29	150,000
2002	You, 3, 121	J. D. Bailey	Willa On the Move, 3, 121	Bella Bellucci, 3, 121	5	1:34.05	150,000
2001	Forest Secrets, 3, 121	C. J. McCarron	Victory Ride, 3, 121	Real Cozzy, 3, 121	8	1:34.92	120,000
2000	Finder's Fee, 3, 121	J. R. Velazquez	C'Est L'Amour, 3, 121	Roxelana, 3, 121	10	1:37.38	120,000
1999	Three Ring, 3, 121	J. D. Bailey	Better Than Honour, 3, 121	Madison's Charm, 3, 121	8	1:36.16	120,000
1998	Jersey Girl, 3, 121	M. E. Smith	Santaria, 3, 121	Brave Deed, 3, 121	10	1:36.32	90,000
1997	Sharp Cat, 3, 121	G. L. Stevens	Dixie Flag, 3, 121	Ajina, 3, 121	7	1:34.41	90,000
1996	Star de Lady Ann, 3, 121	M. E. Smith	Yanks Music, 3, 121	Stop Traffic, 3, 121	12	1:34.62	90,000
1995	Cat's Cradle, 3, 121	C. W. Antley	Country Cat, 3, 121	Lucky Lavender Gal, 3, 121	7	1:37.53	90,000
1994	Inside Information, 3, 121	M. E. Smith	Cinnamon Sugar (Ire), 3, 121	Sovereign Kitty, 3, 121	5	1:34.26	90,000
1993	Sky Beauty, 3, 121	M. E. Smith	Educated Risk, 3, 121	In Her Glory, 3, 121	6	1:35.50	90,000
1992	Prospectors Delite, 3, 121	P. Day	Pleasant Stage, 3, 121	Turnback the Alarm, 3, 121	12	1:35.10	113,040
1991	Meadow Star, 3, 121	J. D. Bailey	Versailles Treaty, 3, 121	Dazzle Me Jolie, 3, 121	6	1:37.42	103,680
1990	Stella Madrid, 3, 121	A. T. Cordero Jr.	Danzig's Beauty, 3, 121	Seaside Attraction, 3, 121	7	1:36.00	104,580
1989	Open Mind, 3, 121	A. T. Cordero Jr.	Hot Novel, 3, 121	Triple Strike, 3, 121	11	1:35.40	111,960
1988	Aptostar, 3, 121	R. G. Davis	Topicount, 3, 121	Avie's Gal, 3, 121	9	1:34.80	109,980
1987	Grecian Flight, 3, 121	C. Perret	Fiesta Gal, 3, 121	Bound, 3, 121	13	1:35.20	113,580
1986	Lotka, 3, 121	J. D. Bailey	Dynamic Star, 3, 121	Life At the Top, 3, 121	8	1:35.20	136,080
1985	Mom's Command, 3, 121	A. Fuller	Le l'Argent, 3, 121	Diplomette, 3, 121	8	1:35.80	113,040
1984	Miss Oceana, 3, 121	E. Maple	Life's Magic, 3, 121	Proud Clarioness, 3, 121	9	1:35.80	135,720
1983	Ski Goggle, 3, 121	C. J. McCarron	Princess Rooney, 3, 121	Thirty Flags, 3, 121	9	1:35.00	69,360
1982	Cupecoy's Joy, 3, 121	A. Santiago	Nancy Huang, 3, 121	Vestris, 3, 121	9	1:34.20	51,750
1981	Heavenly Cause, 3, 121	L. A. Pincay Jr.	Dame Mysterieuse, 3, 121	Autumn Glory, 3, 121	7	1:35.20	50,850
1980	Bold 'n Determined, 3, 121	E. J. Delahoussaye	Mitey Lively, 3, 121	Sugar and Spice, 3, 121	8	1:36.80	50,400
1979	Davona Dale, 3, 121	J. Velasquez	Eloquent, 3, 121	Plankton, 3, 121	8	1:36.00	50,130
1978	Tempest Queen, 3, 121	J. Velasquez	Lakeville Miss, 3, 121	White Star Line, 3, 121	6	1:35.40	31,920
1977	Bring Out the Band, 3, 121	D. Brumfield	Your Place Or Mine, 3, 121	Mrs. Warren, 3, 121	11	1:36.80	33,690
1976	Dearly Precious, 3, 121	J. Velasquez	Optimistic Gal, 3, 121	Tell Me All, 3, 121	8	1:35.80	33,390
1975	Ruffian, 3, 121	J. Vasquez	Somethingregal, 3, 121	Gallant Trial, 3, 121	7	1:34.80	33,660
1974	Special Team, 3, 121	M. A. Rivera	Stage Door Betty, 3, 121	Raisela, 3, 121	9	1:35.40	33,960
	Chris Evert, 3, 121	J. Velasquez	Clear Copy, 3, 121	Fiesta Libre, 3, 121	9	1:36.00	33,960
1973	Windy's Daughter, 3, 121	B. Baeza	Poker Night, 3, 121		11	1:35.40	36,540

Named for the phrase, "Great oaks from little acorns grow"; in the past the Acorn immediately preceded the Coaching Club American Oaks. Held at Aqueduct 1960-'67, 1969-'75. Two divisions 1951, 1970, 1974. Dead heat for first 1954, 1956.

Adena Stallions' Miss Preakness Stakes

Grade 3 in 2005. Pimlico, three-year-olds, fillies, 6 furlongs, dirt. Held May 20, 2005, with a gross value of $100,000. First held in 1986. First graded in 2002. Stakes record 1:10 (2000 Lucky Livi).

Year	Winner	Jockey	Second	Third	Strs	Time	1st Purse
2005	Burnish, 3, 118	R. Bejarano	Partners Due, 3, 116	Hot Storm, 3, 122	7	1:12.40	$60,000
2004	Forest Music, 3, 115	R. A. Dominguez	Stephan's Angel, 3, 119	Fall Fashion, 3, 119	11	1:10.97	60,000
2003	Belong to Sea, 3, 117	J. Castellano	Chimichurri, 3, 122	Forever Partners, 3, 119	5	1:11.10	60,000
2002	Vesta, 3, 117	M. G. Pino	Willa On the Move, 3, 117	Shameful, 3, 119	4	1:10.25	60,000
2001	Kimbralata, 3, 117	T. L. Dunkelberger	Carafe, 3, 117	Stormy Pick, 3, 122	5	1:11.20	60,000

Year	Winner	Jockey	Second	Third	Strs	Time	1st Purse
2000	Lucky Livi, 3, 119	R. Wilson	Big Bambu, 3, 117	Swept Away, 3, 119	5	**1:10.00**	$60,000
1999	Hookedonthefeelin, 3, 122	G. L. Stevens	Silent Valay, 3, 122	Paula's Girl, 3, 122	4	1:11.26	60,000
1998	Storm Beauty, 3, 119	C. R. Woods Jr.	Brac Drifter, 3, 115	Hair Spray, 3, 122	5	1:10.81	45,000
1997	Weather Vane, 3, 122	M. G. Pino	Move, 3, 122	Cayman Sunset, 3, 122	8	1:11.94	64,740
1996	Nic's Halo, 3, 117	R. Wilson	Palette Knife, 3, 115	Crafty But Sweet, 3, 122	4	1:11.75	32,655
1995	Lilly Capote, 3, 122	G. L. Stevens	Broad Smile, 3, 122	Norstep, 3, 122	7	1:10.90	32,640
1994	Foolish Kisses, 3, 113	E. S. Prado	Aly's Conquest, 3, 114	Platinum Punch, 3, 113	8	1:12.45	32,730
1993	My Rosa, 3, 113	E. S. Prado	Fighting Jet, 3, 121	Code Blum, 3, 121	5	1:11.33	32,175
1992	Toots La Mae, 3, 113	J. Bravo	Missy White Oak, 3, 118	Jazzy One, 3, 121	6	1:11.97	26,505
1991	Missy's Music, 3, 114	M. G. Pino	Dixie Rouge, 3, 113	Accent Knightly, 3, 113	6	1:11.48	15,975
1990	Love Me a Lot, 3, 115	C. J. McCarron	Dixie Landera, 3, 113	Tabs, 3, 116	6	1:11.40	19,170
1989	Montoya, 3, 118	L. A. Pincay Jr.	dh-Another Boom, 3, 121 dh-Cojinx, 3, 121		7	1:10.60	22,470
1988	Caromine, 3, 115	C. J. McCarron	Light Beat, 3, 118	Saved by Grace, 3, 118	9	1:13.00	24,911
1987	Cutlasee, 3, 116	C. J. McCarron	I'm Out, 3, 114	Pelican Bay, 3, 115	8	1:12.60	21,158
1986	Marion's Madel, 3, 115	C. J. McCarron	Zigbelle, 3, 115	Babbling Brook, 3, 116	8	1:12.80	21,060

Held day before the Preakness S. (G1). Sponsored by Adena Springs, which is owned by Magna Entertainment Corp. Chairman Frank Stronach 2004. Miss Preakness S. 1986-2003. Dead heat for second 1989.

Adirondack Stakes

Grade 2 in 2005. Saratoga Race Course, two-year-olds, fillies, 6½ furlongs, dirt. Held August 11, 2003, with a gross value of $150,000. First held in 1901. First graded in 1973. Stakes record 1:15.16 (2001 You).

Year	Winner	Jockey	Second	Third	Strs	Time	1st Purse
2003	Whoopi Cat, 2, 116	E. S. Prado	Unbridled Beauty, 2, 116	Eye Dazzler, 2, 116	7	1:17.51	$90,000
2002	Awesome Humor, 2, 122	P. Day	Stellar, 2, 116	Holiday Runner, 2, 122	6	1:17.75	90,000
2001	You, 2, 115	E. S. Prado	Cashier's Dream, 2, 122	Magic Storm, 2, 115	7	**1:15.16**	90,000
2000	Raging Fever, 2, 122	J. D. Bailey	Two Item Limit, 2, 117	Secret Lover, 2, 117	6	1:17.47	90,000
1999	Regally Appealing, 2, 114	E. S. Prado	Miss Wineshine, 2, 122	Trump My Heart, 2, 114	6	1:16.86	90,000
1998	Things Change, 2, 114	J. A. Santos	Extended Applause, 2, 117	Brittons Hill, 2, 114	9	1:18.14	90,000
1997	Salty Perfume, 2, 114	S. J. Sellers	Brac Drifter, 2, 114	Joustabout, 2, 114	6	1:17.94	90,000
1996	Storm Song, 2, 113	P. Day	Last Two States, 2, 113	dh- Exclusive Hold, 2, 113 dh- Larkwhistle, 2, 116	9	1:17.60	84,075
1995	Flat Fleet Feet, 2, 113	M. E. Smith	Steady Cat, 2, 112	Western Dreamer, 2, 120	7	1:16.74	65,760
1994	Seeking Regina, 2, 114	J. D. Bailey	Changing Ways, 2, 119	Phone Bird, 2, 114	6	1:18.51	66,600
1993	Astas Foxy Lady, 2, 119	R. P. Romero	Footing, 2, 114	Casa Eire, 2, 119	6	1:10.11	68,520
1992	Sky Beauty, 2, 116	E. Maple	Missed the Storm, 2, 114	Distinct Habit, 2, 121	7	1:10.16	70,560
1991	American Royale, 2, 119	A. T. Gryder	Bless Our Home, 2, 114	Turnback the Alarm, 2, 119	8	1:10.72	71,640
1990	Really Quick, 2, 114	A. T. Cordero Jr.	Devilish Touch, 2, 119	Ferber's Follies, 2, 114	9	1:11.40	54,270
1989	Dance Colony, 2, 116	J. A. Santos	In Full Cry, 2, 114	Saratoga Sizzle, 2, 114	6	1:11.80	52,200
1988	Pat Copelan, 2, 114	P. Day	Channel Three, 2, 116	Premier Playmate, 2, 116	6	1:10.80	66,780
1987	Over All, 2, 121	A. T. Cordero Jr.	Flashy Runner, 2, 114	Careless Flirt, 2, 114	5	1:10.60	64,890
1986	Sacahuista, 2, 119	C. J. McCarron	Collins, 2, 114	Release the Lyd, 2, 116	7	1:11.00	53,280
1985	Nervous Baba, 2, 114	J. Velasquez	Family Style, 2, 114	Steal a Kiss, 2, 114	8	1:09.60	54,450
1984	Contredance, 2, 114	E. Maple	Outstandingly, 2, 114	Oriental, 2, 114	7	1:10.40	53,100
1983	Buzz My Bell, 2, 114	J. Velasquez	Upturning, 2, 116	Mrs. Flagler, 2, 116	6	1:12.40	33,720
1982	Jelly Bean Holiday, 2, 116	J. Fell	Midnight Rapture, 2, 114	Flying Lassie, 2, 114	7	1:10.80	34,920
1981	Thrilld n Delightd, 2, 114	J. Velasquez	Apalachee Honey, 2, 119	Trove, 2, 114	8	1:10.80	35,160
1980	Sweet Revenge, 2, 119	J. Velasquez	Companionship, 2, 114	Honey's Appeal, 2, 114	9	1:10.40	34,080
1979	Smart Angle, 2, 119	S. Maple	Lucky My Way, 2, 114	Andrea F., 2, 114	8	1:11.00	26,835
1978	Whisper Fleet, 2, 119	J. Cruguet	Island Kitty, 2, 114	Golferette, 2, 114	7	1:10.60	22,410
1977	L'Alezane, 2, 121	R. Turcotte	Sunny Bay, 2, 121	Misgivings, 2, 114	7	1:11.00	22,335
1976	Harvest Girl, 2, 114	J. Cruguet	Bonnie Empress, 2, 114	Drama Critic, 2, 119	7	1:11.00	22,545
1975	Optimistic Gal, 2, 120	B. Baeza	Glory Glory, 2, 120	Against all Flags, 2, 120	5	1:11.20	22,515
1974	Laughing Bridge, 2, 120	L. A. Pincay Jr.	Stulcer, 2, 120	Some Swinger, 2, 120	6	1:10.80	16,950
1973	Talking Picture, 2, 120	B. Baeza	In Hot Pursuit, 2, 120	Bedknob, 2, 120	10	1:11.00	17,625

Named for the Adirondack mountain region of New York. Grade 3 1975-'83. Adirondack H. 1901-'45. Held at Belmont Park 1943-'45. Held at Jamaica 1953-'54. Not held 1911-'12, 1946-'52, 1956-'61, 2004. 6 furlongs 1901-'45, 1962-'93. 5½ furlongs 1953-'55. Both sexes 1901-'39. Dead heat for third 1996.

Aegon Turf Sprint Stakes

Grade 3 in 2005. Churchill Downs, three-year-olds and up, 5 furlongs, turf. Held May 6, 2005, with a gross value of $113,500. First held in 1995. First graded in 2001. Stakes record :56.01 (2003 Fiscally Speaking).

Year	Winner	Jockey	Second	Third	Strs	Time	1st Purse
2005	Mighty Beau, 6, 121	P. A. Valenzuela	Chosen Chief, 6, 119	Sgt. Bert, 4, 119	10	:56.18	$70,370
2004	Lydgate, 4, 114	P. Day	Mighty Beau, 5, 117	Banned in Boston, 4, 114	11	:56.56	71,114
2003	Fiscally Speaking, 4, 114	J. K. Court	Morluc, 7, 122	Testify, 6, 122	11	**:56.01**	71,486
2002	Testify, 5, 119	E. J. Delahoussaye	Texas Glitter, 6, 122	Gone Fishin, 6, 116	10	:57.39	75,206
2001	Morluc, 5, 122	R. Albarado	Testify, 4, 119	Texas Glitter, 5, 122	9	:56.60	70,494
2000	Bold Fact, 5, 120	R. Migliore	Howbaddouwantit, 5, 123	Fantastic Finish, 4, 114	12	:56.37	75,330
1999	Howbaddouwantit, 4, 123	M. E. Smith	Mr Festus, 4, 114	Three Card Willie, 4, 118	11	:56.90	71,486

Year	Winner	Jockey	Second	Third	Strs	Time	1st Purse
1998	**Indian Rocket (GB)**, 4, 116	G. L. Stevens	G H's Pleasure, 6, 120	Claire's Honor, 4, 114	12	:57.32	$75,950
1997	**Sandtrap**, 4, 123	A. O. Solis	Appealing Skier, 4, 114	G H's Pleasure, 5, 120	11	:56.51	71,734
1996	**Danjur**, 4, 114	J. D. Bailey	Hello Paradise, 5, 114	Linear, 6, 123	10	:56.09	57,281
1995	**Long Suit**, 4, 114	W. Martinez	Bold n' Flashy, 6, 120	†Scottish Fantasy, 7, 111	11	:56.90	57,086

Sponsored by the AEGON Group N.V. of The Hague, the Netherlands 1999-2005. Churchill Downs Turf Sprint S. 1995-'98. Established course record 1995. Course record 1996, 2003. †Denotes female.

Affirmed Handicap

Grade 3 in 2005. Hollywood Park, three-year-olds, 1¹/₁₆ miles, dirt. Held June 19, 2004, with a gross value of $110,200. First held in 1940. First graded in 1973. Stakes record 1:40.83 (1999 General Challenge).

Year	Winner	Jockey	Second	Third	Strs	Time	1st Purse
2004	**Boomzeeboom**, 3, 115	V. Espinoza	Twice as Bad, 3, 121	Wimplestiltskin, 3, 116	9	1:42.11	$66,120
2003	**Eye of the Tiger**, 3, 119	A. O. Solis	Ministers Wild Cat, 3, 118	Bullistic, 3, 115	4	1:42.30	63,120
2002	**Came Home**, 3, 124	C. J. McCarron	Tracemark, 3, 120	Calkins Road, 3, 117	6	1:41.99	64,500
2001	**Until Sundown**, 3, 117	G. L. Stevens	Top Hit, 3, 114	Bayou the Moon, 3, 118	5	1:43.10	60,000
2000	**Tiznow**, 3, 117	V. Espinoza	Dixie Union, 3, 122	Millencolin, 3, 117	6	1:42.35	80,550
1999	**General Challenge**, 3, 124	D. R. Flores	Desert Hero, 3, 120	Crowning Storm, 3, 116	5	**1:40.83**	75,000
1998	**Old Trieste**, 3, 118	C. J. McCarron	Old Topper, 3, 117	Kraal, 3, 116	4	1:41.84	62,340
1997	**Deputy Commander**, 3, 117	C. S. Nakatani	Hello (Ire), 3, 117	Holzmeister, 3, 121	6	1:42.80	61,500
1996	**Hesabull**, 3, 117	E. J. Delahoussaye	Benton Creek, 3, 116	Semoran, 3, 118	7	1:43.25	61,050
1995	**Mr Purple**, 3, 120	C. S. Nakatani	Pumpkin House, 3, 115	Oncefortheroad, 3, 114	6	1:42.37	77,050
1994	**R Friar Tuck**, 3, 113	J. D. Bailey	Pollock's Luck, 3, 114	Wild Invader, 3, 115	8	1:49.08	96,100
1993	**Codified**, 3, 117	G. L. Stevens	Roman Image, 3, 117	Future Storm, 3, 118	7	1:48.85	94,100
1992	**Natural Nine**, 3, 117	L. A. Pincay Jr.	Prospect for Four, 3, 114	Never Round, 3, 117	8	1:49.42	95,500
1991	**Compelling Sound**, 3, 118	G. L. Stevens	Best Pal, 3, 123	Caliche's Secret, 3, 117	5	1:47.90	91,300
1990	**Stalwart Charger**, 3, 120	L. A. Pincay Jr.	Toby Jug, 3, 112	Kentucky Jazz, 3, 120	5	1:48.40	91,100
1989	**Raise a Stanza**, 3, 115	C. A. Black	Broke the Mold, 3, 112	Prized, 3, 116	12	1:48.40	102,200
1988	**Iz a Saros**, 3, 113	A. T. Gryder	Stalwars, 3, 119	Bel Air Dancer, 3, 115	8	1:49.00	95,900
1987	**Candi's Gold**, 3, 116	G. L. Stevens	On the Line, 3, 116	The Medic, 3, 116	6	1:47.60	93,000
1986	**†Melair**, 3, 115	P. A. Valenzuela	Southern Halo, 3, 113	Snow Chief, 3, 127	12	1:32.80	220,000
1985	**Pancho Villa**, 3, 118	L. A. Pincay Jr.	Proudest Doon, 3, 118	Nostalgia's Star, 3, 118	9	1:33.80	64,050
1984	**Tights**, 3, 119	L. A. Pincay Jr.	M. Double M., 3, 116	Precisionist, 3, 121	6	1:48.60	46,850
1983	**My Habitony**, 3, 115	D. Pierce	Tanks Brigade, 3, 119	Hyperborean, 3, 115	6	1:48.60	47,250
1982	**Journey At Sea**, 3, 122	C. J. McCarron	Cassaleria, 3, 120	Guachan, 3, 112	9	1:46.80	49,600
1981	**Stancharry**, 3, 117	P. A. Valenzuela	Dusty Hula, 3, 116	Seafood, 3, 117	6	1:51.00	47,150
1980	**Score Twenty Four**, 3, 114	D. G. McHargue	dh-First Albert, 3, 116		6	1:48.20	37,200
			dh-Loto Canada, 3, 119				
1979	**Valdez**, 3, 117	L. A. Pincay Jr.	Pole Position, 3, 118	Beau's Eagle, 3, 123	5	1:47.40	37,500
1978	**Radar Ahead**, 3, 123	D. G. McHargue	Double Win, 3, 114	Think Snow, 3, 122	6	1:48.40	38,200
1977	**Text**, 3, 119	D. G. McHargue	Bad 'n Big, 3, 122	Sonny Collins, 3, 118	5	1:47.20	37,000
1976	**L'Heureux**, 3, 119	D. Pierce	Romeo, 3, 115	Crystal Water, 3, 125	7	1:47.40	38,600
1975	**Forceten**, 3, 119	D. Pierce	Sibirri, 3, 114	Larrikin, 3, 121	6	1:48.80	37,300
1974	**Battery E.**, 3, 117	L. A. Pincay Jr.	Stardust Mel, 3, 120	Agitate, 3, 124	5	1:47.80	36,800
1973	**Carry the Banner**, 3, 115	A. Pineda	Rod, 3, 119	Out of the East, 3, 120	8	1:41.20	39,200

Named for Harbor View Farm's 1978, '79 Horse of the Year, '78 Triple Crown winner, and '79 Hollywood Gold Cup H. (G1) winner Affirmed (1975 c. by Exclusive Native). Formerly named in honor of Hollywood's film industry. Formerly named in honor of the Forty-niners ("argonauts") who went west to California in search of gold. Grade 2 1973-'89. Argonaut H. 1940-'60, 1973-'78. Argonaut S. 1961-'72. Silver Screen H. 1979-'92. Held at Santa Anita Park 1949. Not held 1942-'43. 1¹/₁₆ miles 1940, 1944, 1946-'53, 1960-'73. 1 mile 1941, 1945, 1954-'59, 1985-'86. 1¹/₈ miles 1979-'84, 1987-'94. Turf 1968-'72. Four-year-olds and up 1940-'41. Three-year-olds and up 1944-'59, 1986. Two divisions 1963, 1967, 1970. Dead heat for second 1980. †Denotes female.

A Gleam Invitational Handicap

Grade 2 in 2005. Hollywood Park, three-year-olds and up, fillies and mares, 7 furlongs, dirt. Held July 10, 2004, with a gross value of $150,000. First held in 1941. First graded in 1973. Stakes record 1:20.53 (1998 A. P. Assay).

Year	Winner	Jockey	Second	Third	Strs	Time	1st Purse
2004	**Dream of Summer**, 5, 114	M. E. Smith	Tucked Away, 4, 116	Elusive Diva, 3, 112	9	1:21.16	$90,000
2003	**Cee's Elegance**, 6, 116	V. Espinoza	You, 4, 121	Affluent, 5, 119	5	1:21.47	150,000
2002	**Irguns Angel**, 4, 116	E. J. Delahoussaye	Secret Liaison, 4, 116	Kalookan Queen, 6, 122	10	1:22.50	120,000
2001	**Go Go**, 4, 124	E. J. Delahoussaye	Kitty On the Track, 4, 115	Nany's Sweep, 5, 117	5	1:22.19	120,000
2000	**Honest Lady**, 4, 121	K. J. Desormeaux	Seth's Choice, 4, 115	Hookedonthefeelin, 4, 116	5	1:21.47	120,000
1999	**Enjoy the Moment**, 4, 117	D. R. Flores	Snowberg, 4, 115	Woodman's Dancer, 5, 117	6	1:21.35	120,000
1998	**A. P. Assay**, 4, 116	E. J. Delahoussaye	Exotic Wood, 6, 124	Closed Escrow, 5, 114	7	**1:20.53**	150,000
1997	**Toga Toga Toga**, 5, 119	G. L. Stevens	Our Summer Bid, 5, 115	Radu Cool, 5, 115	7	1:22.75	65,040
1996	**Igotrhythm**, 4, 116	E. J. Delahoussaye	Klassy Kim, 5, 116	Cat's Cradle, 4, 118	5	1:21.54	63,840
1995	**Angi Go**, 5, 115	G. L. Stevens	Desert Stormer, 5, 118	Dancing Mirage, 4, 115	6	1:21.45	62,700
1994	**Golden Klair (GB)**, 4, 117	C. J. McCarron	Cargo, 5, 115	Minidar, 4, 117	4	1:22.00	60,400
1993	**Bold Windy**, 4, 115	G. L. Stevens	La Spia, 4, 115	Bountiful Native, 5, 122	9	1:21.62	65,700
1992	**Forest Fealty**, 5, 116	M. A. Pedroza	Brought to Mind, 5, 120	Devil's Orchid, 5, 120	8	1:22.13	64,800
1991	**Survive**, 7, 119	R. A. Baze	Stormy But Valid, 5, 121	Brought to Mind, 4, 117	6	1:22.10	62,400

					Strs	Time	
1990	**Stormy But Valid**, 4, 120	G. L. Stevens	Hot Novel, 4, 118	Tis Juliet, 4, 114	5	1:21.20	$61,300
1989	**Daloma (Fr)**, 5, 115	C. J. McCarron	Survive, 5, 116	Behind the Scenes, 5, 116	7	1:21.60	47,900
1988	**Integra**, 4, 118	G. L. Stevens	Behind the Scenes, 4, 116	Carol's Wonder, 4, 117	5	1:23.00	46,100
1987	**Le l'Argent**, 5, 118	D. G. McHargue	Sari's Heroine, 4, 117	Rare Starlet, 4, 115	8	1:23.00	48,650
1986	**Outstandingly**, 4, 120	G. L. Stevens	Eloquack, 4, 110	Shywing, 4, 120	5	1:21.80	46,100
1985	**Dontstop Themusic**, 5, 121	L. A. Pincay Jr.	Lovlier Linda, 5, 122	Mimi Baker, 4, 110	4	1:21.40	36,500
1984	**Lass Trump**, 4, 116	C. J. McCarron	Pleasure Cay, 4, 116	Angel Savage (Mex), 4, 112	9	1:21.20	39,400
1983	**Matching**, 5, 121	R. Sibille	Sierva (Arg), 5, 116	Bara Lass, 4, 117	7	1:22.40	31,800
1982	**Happy Bride (Ire)**, 4, 113	W. A. Guerra	Lucky Lady Ellen, 3, 117	Jones Time Machine, 3, 112	6	1:08.40	30,700
1981	**She Can't Miss**, 4, 117	P. A. Valenzuela	Cherokee Frolic, 3, 114	Shine High, 5, 122	8	1:09.00	32,050
1980	**Great Lady M.**, 5, 115	P. A. Valenzuela	Double Deceit, 4, 114	Splendid Girl, 4, 122	6	1:08.40	30,550
1979	**Delice**, 4, 116	E. J. Delahoussaye	Great Lady M., 4, 117	Sateen, 3, 111	6	1:08.80	25,100
1978	**Reminiscing**, 4, 124	L. A. Pincay Jr.	Sing Back, 5, 122	Thirteenth Hope, 5, 113	7	1:09.60	25,450
1977	**Just a Kick**, 5, 121	S. Hawley	Cornish Colleen, 4, 113	Winter Solstice, 5, 122	5	1:09.40	18,450
1976	**Winter Solstice**, 4, 119	J. Lambert	Vol Au Vent, 4, 120	Powerful Lady, 4, 118	8	1:09.00	19,700
1975	**Viva La Vivi**, 5, 125	L. A. Pincay Jr.	Modus Vivendi, 4, 122	Fleet Gazelle, 4, 112	6	1:08.40	18,800
1974	**Lt.'s Joy**, 4, 117	L. A. Pincay Jr.	Viva La Vivi, 4, 123	Shadycroft Gal, 5, 115	7	1:09.00	16,000
1973	**Wingo Belle**, 5, 118	R. Nono	Convenience, 5, 126	Veneke, 6, 116	8	1:08.60	19,150

Named for Calumet Farm's 1952, '53 Milady H. winner A Gleam (1949 f. by *Blenheim II). Formerly named for California's redwood, the sequoia. Grade 3 1986-'89. A Gleam H. 1997-2003. Sequoia H. 1959-'78. Not held 1942-'43, 1947-'58. 6 furlongs 1944, 1959-'82. Two-year-olds 1944. Equaled track record 1998.

Alabama Stakes

Grade 1 in 2005. Saratoga Race Course, three-year-olds, fillies, 1¼ miles, dirt. Held August 21, 2004, with a gross value of $750,000. First held in 1872. First graded in 1973. Stakes record 2:00.80 (1990 Go for Wand).

Year	Winner	Jockey	Second	Third	Strs	Time	1st Purse
2004	**Society Selection**, 3, 121	C. H. Velasquez	Stellar Jayne, 3, 121	Ashado, 3, 121	8	2:02.70	$450,000
2003	**Island Fashion**, 3, 121	J. R. Velazquez	Awesome Humor, 3, 121	Spoken Fur, 3, 121	6	2:05.08	450,000
2002	**Farda Amiga**, 3, 121	P. Day	Allamerican Bertie, 3, 121	You, 3, 121	6	2:04.68	450,000
2001	**Flute**, 3, 121	E. S. Prado	Exogenous, 3, 121	Two Item Limit, 3, 121	7	2:01.88	450,000
2000	**Jostle**, 3, 121	M. E. Smith	Secret Status, 3, 121	Spain, 3, 121	8	2:04.72	450,000
1999	**Silverbulletday**, 3, 121	J. D. Bailey	Strolling Belle, 3, 121	Gandria, 3, 121	6	2:02.71	240,000
1998	**Banshee Breeze**, 3, 121	J. D. Bailey	Lu Ravi, 3, 121	Manistique, 3, 121	6	2:03.41	150,000
1997	**Runup the Colors**, 3, 121	J. D. Bailey	Ajina, 3, 121	Tomisue's Delight, 3, 121	6	2:02.28	150,000
1996	**Yanks Music**, 3, 121	J. R. Velazquez	Escena, 3, 121	My Flag, 3, 121	7	2:03.06	150,000
1995	**Pretty Discreet**, 3, 121	M. E. Smith	Friendly Beauty, 3, 121	Rogues Walk, 3, 121	9	2:02.14	120,000
1994	**Heavenly Prize**, 3, 121	M. E. Smith	Lakeway, 3, 121	Sovereign Kitty, 3, 121	7	2:03.25	120,000
1993	**Sky Beauty**, 3, 121	M. E. Smith	Future Pretense, 3, 121	Silky Feather, 3, 121	8	2:03.49	120,000
1992	**November Snow**, 3, 121	C. W. Antley	Saratoga Dew, 3, 121	Pacific Squall, 3, 121	7	2:02.75	120,000
1991	**Versailles Treaty**, 3, 121	A. T. Cordero Jr.	Til Forbid, 3, 121	Designated Dancer, 3, 121	6	2:02.57	120,000
1990	**Go for Wand**, 3, 121	R. P. Romero	Charon, 3, 121	Pampered Star, 3, 121	3	**2:00.80**	130,560
1989	**Open Mind**, 3, 121	A. T. Cordero Jr.	Dearly Loved, 3, 121	Dream Deal, 3, 121	7	2:04.20	139,440
1988	**Maplejinsky**, 3, 121	A. T. Cordero Jr.	Make Change, 3, 121	Willa On the Move, 3, 121	5	2:01.80	136,320
1987	**Up the Apalachee**, 3, 121	J. Velasquez	Without Feathers, 3, 121	Fiesta Gal, 3, 121	7	2:04.00	138,240
1986	**Classy Cathy**, 3, 121	E. Fires	Valley Victory (Ire), 3, 121	Life At the Top, 3, 121	5	2:04.20	138,720
1985	**Mom's Command**, 3, 121	A. Fuller	Fran's Valentine, 3, 121	Foxy Deen, 3, 121	5	2:03.20	84,000
1984	**Life's Magic**, 3, 121	J. Velasquez	Lucky Lucky Lucky, 3, 121	Class Play, 3, 121	5	2:02.60	98,100
1983	**Spit Curl**, 3, 121	J. Cruguet	Lady Norcliffe, 3, 121	Sabin, 3, 121	5	2:02.40	65,880
1982	**Broom Dance**, 3, 121	G. McCarron	Too Chic, 3, 121	Mademoiselle Forli, 3, 121	7	2:02.20	67,680
1981	**Prismatical**, 3, 121	E. Maple	Banner Gala, 3, 121	Discorama, 3, 121	6	2:02.40	66,000
1980	**Love Sign**, 3, 121	R. Hernandez	Weber City Miss, 3, 121	Sugar and Spice, 3, 121	6	2:01.00	65,880
1979	**It's in the Air**, 3, 121	J. Fell	Davona Dale, 3, 121	Mairzy Doates, 3, 121	5	2:01.40	64,980
1978	**White Star Line**, 3, 121	M. Venezia	Summer Fling, 3, 121	Tempest Queen, 3, 121	6	2:04.00	64,920
1977	**Our Mims**, 3, 121	J. Velasquez	Sensational, 3, 121	Cum Laude Laurie, 3, 121	11	2:03.00	66,060
1976	**Optimistic Gal**, 3, 121	E. Maple	‡Javamine, 3, 121	Moontee, 3, 121	7	2:01.60	48,555
1975	**Spout**, 3, 121	J. Cruguet	Aunt Jin, 3, 121	Funalon, 3, 121	10	2:04.00	49,170
1974	**Quaze Quilt**, 3, 121	H. Gustines	Chris Evert, 3, 121	Fiesta Libre, 3, 115	8	2:02.60	33,660
1973	**Desert Vixen**, 3, 119	J. Velasquez	Bag of Tunes, 3, 119	Summer Festival, 3, 116	9	2:04.20	34,620

Named for the home state of Confederate Capt. Cottrill of Mobile, Alabama, the race's originator. Held at Belmont Park 1943-'45. Not held 1893-'96, 1898-1900, 1911-'12. 1⅛ miles 1872-'97, 1904, 1906-'16. 1¹⁄₁₆ miles 1901-'03, 1905.
‡Dona Maya finished second, DQ to fourth, 1976.

Alfred G. Vanderbilt Handicap

Grade 2 in 2005. Saratoga Race Course, three-year-olds and up, 6 furlongs, dirt. Held August 14, 2004, with a gross value of $200,000. First held in 1985. First graded in 1990. Stakes record 1:08.04 (2004 Speightstown).

Year	Winner	Jockey	Second	Third	Strs	Time	1st Purse
2004	**Speightstown**, 6, 120	J. R. Velazquez	Clock Stopper, 4, 115	Gators N Bears, 4, 118	5	**1:08.04**	$120,000
2003	**Private Horde**, 4, 115	J. P. Lumpkins	Mountain General, 5, 118	Mike's Classic, 4, 114	5	1:09.18	120,000
2002	**Orientate**, 4, 121	J. D. Bailey	Say Florida Sandy, 8, 115	Multiple Choice, 4, 112	6	1:09.72	120,000
2001	**Five Star Day**, 5, 117	G. K. Gomez	Delaware Township, 5, 116	Bonapaw, 5, 117	7	1:08.57	120,000

				Strs	Time	1st Purse
2000 ‡Successful Appeal, 4, 118	E. S. Prado	Intidab, 7, 117	Chasin' Wimmin, 5, 112	8	1:09.21	$120,000
1999 Intidab, 6, 113	R. G. Davis	Artax, 4, 117	Yes It's True, 3, 117	7	1:09.03	90,000
1998 Kelly Kip, 4, 122	J. Samyn	Trafalger, 4, 114	Receiver, 5, 113	7	1:09.60	82,545
1997 Royal Haven, 5, 116	R. Migliore	Cold Execution, 6, 116	Punch Line, 7, 120	7	1:09.65	65,220
1996 Prospect Bay, 4, 113	J. D. Bailey	Honour and Glory, 3, 119	Lite the Fuse, 5, 123	7	1:08.29	65,760
1995 Not Surprising, 5, 115	R. G. Davis	Chimes Band, 4, 119	Mining Burrah, 5, 116	10	1:09.60	67,140
1994 Boundary, 4, 117	J. R. Velazquez	Cherokee Run, 4, 120	I Can't Believe, 6, 113	7	1:08.61	65,880
1993 Gold Spring (Arg), 5, 119	P. Day	Friendly Lover, 5, 122	Detox, 4, 115	7	1:09.31	70,680
1992 For Really, 5, 115	P. Day	Burn Fair, 5, 115	Drummond Lane, 5, 122	9	1:08.68	71,520
1991 Kid Russell, 5, 115	R. Mojica Jr.	Mr. Nasty, 4, 122	To Freedom, 3, 117	8	1:09.52	71,400
1990 Prospectors Gamble, 5, 122	J. A. Garcia	Sewickley, 5, 115	Mr. Nickerson, 4, 122	4	1:09.20	50,400
1989 Mr. Nickerson, 3, 112	J. A. Santos	Quick Call, 5, 115	Miami Slick, 4, 119	6	1:08.80	52,650
1988 High Brite, 4, 122	A. T. Cordero Jr.	Abject, 4, 115	Uncle Ho, 5, 115	4	1:10.20	50,400
1987 Banker's Jet, 5, 115	J. L. Vargas	Royal Pennant, 4, 115	Sun Master, 6, 122	6	1:09.20	49,230
1986 Cognizant, 5, 117	P. Day	Royal Pennant, 3, 112	Cullendale, 4, 115	7	1:09.20	33,060
1985 Cognizant, 4, 117	P. Day	Mayanesian, 6, 117	Spender, 4, 117	7	1:09.60	33,360

Named for Alfred Gwynne Vanderbilt (1912-'99), chairman of NYRA, and president of Belmont and Pimlico. Formerly named for Brownell Combs II's 1983 Jim Dandy S. (G3) winner A Phenomenon (1980 c. by Tentam), who broke down while leading in the 1984 Forego H. (G2); A Phenomenon is one of four horses buried on the Saratoga grounds. Grade 3 1992-'94. A Phenomenon S. 1985-'93, 1996-'97. A Phenomenon H. 1994-'95, 1998-'99. A. G. Vanderbilt H. 2000-'02.
‡Intidab finished first, DQ to second, 2000.

All Along Breeders' Cup Stakes

Grade 3 in 2005. Colonial Downs, three-year-olds and up, fillies and mares, 1⅛ miles, turf. Held July 10, 2004, with a gross value of $200,000. First held in 1985. First graded in 1990. Stakes record 1:47.34 (1994 Alice Springs).

Year	Winner	Jockey	Second	Third	Strs	Time	1st Purse
2004	Film Maker, 4, 119	E. S. Prado	Noisette, 4, 119	Lady Linda, 6, 119	7	1:50.08	$120,000
2003	Dress To Thrill (Ire), 4, 117	E. S. Prado	Lady Linda, 5, 117	Lady of the Future, 5, 117	9	1:49.16	120,000
2002	Secret River, 5, 117	H. Karamanos	Golden Corona, 4, 117	Cayman Sunset (Ire), 5, 117	6	1:50.76	90,000
2001	Colstar, 5, 121	J. K. Court	Lucky Lune (Fr), 4, 119	Crystal Sea, 4, 119	8	1:47.53	90,000
2000	Idle Rich, 5, 115	A. T. Gryder	Emanating, 4, 115	Orange Sunset (Ire), 4, 115	11	1:55.95	60,000
1999	Tampico, 6, 122	E. S. Prado	Heavenly Advice, 5, 115	Absolutely Queenie, 6, 115	10	1:47.63	60,000
1998	Bursting Forth, 4, 122	E. S. Prado	The Unforgiven, 4, 117	Be Elusive, 4, 115	8	1:48.01	60,000
1997	Beyrouth, 5, 115	D. Rice	Hero's Pride, 4, 117	Palliser Bay, 5, 122	10	1:49.27	67,830
1996	Another Legend, 4, 115	C. O. Klinger	Brushing Gloom, 4, 119	Short Time, 4, 115	7	1:58.80	60,000
1994	Alice Springs, 4, 120	R. R. Douglas	Via Borghese, 5, 120	Mz. Zill Bear, 5, 116	6	1:47.34	150,000
1993	Lady Blessington (Fr), 5, 116	C. A. Black	Via Borghese, 4, 118	Logan's Mist, 4, 116	5	1:51.58	150,000
1992	Marble Maiden (GB), 3, 114	T. Jarnet	Wedding Ring (Ire), 3, 122	Sheba Dancer (Fr), 3, 114	7	1:49.89	180,000
1991	Sha Tha, 3, 113	M. E. Smith	Julie La Rousse (Ire), 3, 113	Once in My Life (Ire), 3, 114	11	1:52.59	180,000
1990	Foresta, 4, 120	A. T. Cordero Jr.	Miss Josh, 4, 120	Vijaya, 3, 114	10	1:49.40	180,000
1989	Lady Winner (Fr), 3, 112	K. J. Desormeaux	Capades, 3, 116	Betty Lobelia, 4, 116	8	1:53.60	180,000
1988	Ravinella, 3, 120	G. Guignard	Chapel of Dreams, 4, 120	Betty Lobelia, 3, 116	12	1:49.80	150,000
1985	Bug Eyed Betty, 2, 118	V. A. Bracciale Jr.	Cosmic Tiger, 2, 118	Eleanor's Best, 2, 118	7	1:36.60	29,185

Named for Daniel Wildenstein's 1983 Horse of the Year and '83 Washington, D.C. International (G1) winner All Along (Fr) (1979 f. by Targowice). Grade 2 1990-'97. All Along S. 1985, 1988-'94, 1996-2000. Held at Laurel Park 1988-'94, 1996. Held at Delaware Park 1997. Held at Pimlico 1999. Not held 1995, 1986-'87. 1⁷⁄₁₆ miles 2000. Equaled course record 2001.

American Derby

Grade 2 in 2005. Arlington Park, three-year-olds, 1³⁄₁₆ miles, turf. Held July 24, 2004, with a gross value of $250,000. First held in 1884. First graded in 1973. Stakes record 1:54.60 (1955 Swaps).

Year	Winner	Jockey	Second	Third	Strs	Time	1st Purse
2004	Simple Exchange (Ire), 3, 119	P. Smullen	Cool Conductor, 3, 119	Toasted, 3, 123	8	1:54.93	$150,000
2003	Evolving Tactics (Ire), 3, 117	P. Smullen	Californian (GB), 3, 121	Scottago, 3, 116	5	1:59.04	150,000
2002	Mananan McLir, 3, 116	R. R. Douglas	Jazz Beat (Ire), 3, 117	Extra Check, 3, 116	8	1:57.11	135,000
2001	Fan Club's Mister, 3, 121	R. A. Meier	Monsieur Cat, 3, 116	Royal Spy, 3, 123	7	2:03.27	150,000
2000	Pine Dance, 3, 114	E. Ahern	Hymn (Ire), 3, 114	Del Mar Show, 3, 114	4	1:55.46	120,000
1997	Honor Glide, 3, 120	G. K. Gomez	Worldly Ways (GB), 3, 120	Daylight Savings, 3, 114	8	1:55.94	120,000
1996	‡Jaunatxo, 3, 114	J. L. Diaz	Trail City, 3, 120	Marlin, 3, 114	12	1:55.82	180,000
1995	Gold and Steel (Fr), 3, 114	A. T. Gryder	Torrential, 3, 120	Unanimous Vote (Ire), 3, 120	7	1:55.02	180,000
1994	dh- Overbury (Ire), 3, 114	S. J. Sellers		Star Campaigner, 3, 114	10	1:55.29	120,000
	dh- Vaudeville, 3, 114	A. D. Lopez					
1993	Explosive Red, 3, 120	S. J. Sellers	Earl of Barking (Ire), 3, 120	Newton's Law (Ire), 3, 114	9	1:59.92	180,000
1992	The Name's Jimmy, 3, 120	P. Day	Standiford, 3, 114	May I Inquire, 3, 114	14	1:59.41	180,000
1991	Olympio, 3, 126	E. J. Delahoussaye	Discover, 3, 114	Jackie Wackie, 3, 123	8	2:00.99	180,000
1990	Real Cash, 3, 123	P. A. Valenzuela	Home At Last, 3, 123	Adjudicating, 3, 117	6	2:02.00	180,000
1989	Awe Inspiring, 3, 126	C. Perret	Dispersal, 3, 123	Caesar, 3, 114	8	2:02.40	124,500
1987	Fortunate Moment, 3, 118	E. Fires	Fast Forward, 3, 114	Gem Master, 3, 118	9	2:03.80	100,350
1985	Creme Fraiche, 3, 123	E. Maple	Red Attack, 3, 114	Smile, 3, 123	5	2:01.60	96,000
1984	dh- At the Threshold, 3, 126	P. Day		Par Flite, 3, 114	7	2:04.00	46,800
	dh- High Alexander, 3, 120	G. Gallitano					

1983 Play Fellow, 3, 123	P. Day	Le Cou Cou, 3, 114	Brother, 3, 114	8	2:04.40	$65,100
1982 Wolfie's Rascal, 3, 123	R. Hernandez	Dew Line, 3, 114	Northern Majesty, 3, 120	8	2:05.60	65,100
1981 Pocket Zipper, 3, 120	R. Sibille	Fairway Phantom, 3, 123	Double Sonic, 3, 123	11	2:03.80	84,000
1980 Hurry Up Blue, 3, 114	G. Gallitano	Tizon, 3, 114	Spruce Needles, 3, 123	6	2:04.40	83,400
1979 Smarten, 3, 126	S. Maple	Super Hit, 3, 114	Weather Tamer, 3, 114	6	2:05.20	63,600
1978 Nasty and Bold, 3, 114	J. Samyn	Star de Naskra, 3, 114	Beau Sham, 3, 114	13	2:03.40	68,100
1977 Silver Series, 3, 126	L. Snyder	Run Dusty Run, 3, 126	Brach's Hilarious, 3, 112	6	2:02.40	68,880
1976 Fifth Marine, 3, 121	R. Turcotte	Majestic Light, 3, 121	Play the Red, 3, 121	11	1:49.20	93,400
1975 Honey Mark, 3, 116	G. Patterson	High Steel, 3, 112	Go to the Bank, 3, 111	14	1:44.40	93,400
1974 Determined King, 3, 112	D. Montoya	Orders, 3, 114	Sr. Diplomat, 3, 111	13	1:47.80	92,000
1973 Bemo, 3, 117	W. J. Passmore	Golden Don, 3, 115	Buffalo Lark, 3, 109	12	1:49.60	69,400

Formerly sponsored by PrimeCo Communications 1997. Grade 1 1973-'74, 1981-'89. PrimeCo American Derby 1997. Held at Washington Park 1884-1904, 1926-'27, 1929-'57. Held at Hawthorne Race Course 1916. Not held 1895-'97, 1899, 1905-'15, 1917-'25, 1936, 1938-'39, 1986, 1988, 1998-'99. 1½ miles 1884-1904, 1926-'27. 1¼ miles 1916, 1928-'51, 1962-'65, 1977-'91. 1⅛ miles 1952-'54, 1958-'61, 1966-'74, 1976. 1¹⁄₁₆ miles 1975. Dirt 1884-1954, 1958-'69, 1977-'91. Dead heat for first 1984, 1994. ‡Trail City finished first, DQ to second, 1996.

American Handicap

Grade 2 in 2005. Hollywood Park, three-olds and up, 1⅛ miles, turf. Held July 4, 2004, with a gross value of $150,000. First held in 1938. First graded in 1973. Stakes record 1:45.60 (1987 Clever Song).

Year	Winner	Jockey	Second	Third	Strs	Time	1st Purse
2004	Bayamo (Ire), 5, 117	D. R. Flores	Sarafan, 7, 119	Night Patrol, 8, 114	5	1:46.60	$90,000
2003	Candy Ride (Arg), 4, 120	G. L. Stevens	Special Ring, 6, 118	Irish Warrior, 5, 116	5	1:46.20	90,000
2002	The Tin Man, 4, 115	M. E. Smith	Devine Wind, 6, 115	Kappa King, 5, 116	7	1:46.82	90,000
2001	Takarian (Ire), 6, 114	G. K. Gomez	Fighting Falcon, 5, 114	Fateful Dream, 4, 116	7	1:48.19	90,000
2000	Dark Moondancer (GB), 5, 122	C. J. McCarron	Sardaukar (GB), 4, 113	Sunshine Street, 5, 119	6	1:46.74	90,000
1999	Takarian (Ire), 4, 114	G. K. Gomez	Montemiro (Fr), 5, 112	Special Quest (Fr), 4, 115	6	1:47.37	90,000
1998	Magellan, 5, 116	G. L. Stevens	Bonapartiste (Fr), 4, 116	Sharekann (Ire), 6, 112	6	1:47.05	90,000
1997	El Angelo, 5, 118	A. O. Solis	Naninja, 4, 114	Wavy Run (Ire), 6, 117	6	1:46.99	96,360
1996	Labeeb (GB), 4, 119	E. J. Delahoussaye	Gold and Steel (Fr), 4, 118	Earl of Barking (Ire), 6, 116	8	1:45.78	66,120
1995	Silver Wizard, 5, 118	G. L. Stevens	Romarin (Brz), 5, 120	Savinio, 5, 118	5	1:46.02	91,900
1994	Blues Traveller (Ire), 4, 115	C. W. Antley	Gothland (Fr), 5, 119	Johann Quatz (Fr), 5, 116	7	1:46.50	128,000
1993	†Toussaud, 4, 114	K. J. Desormeaux	Man From Eldorado, 5, 115	Journalism, 5, 117	6	1:46.87	126,000
1992	Man From Eldorado, 4, 114	K. J. Desormeaux	Bold Russian (GB), 5, 116	Golden Pheasant, 6, 123	4	1:47.11	122,000
1991	Tight Spot, 4, 123	L. A. Pincay Jr.	Exbourne, 5, 122	Super May, 5, 118	8	1:46.00	129,400
1990	Classic Fame, 4, 117	E. J. Delahoussaye	Steinlen (GB), 7, 125	Pleasant Variety, 6, 116	7	1:47.80	126,800
1989	Mister Wonderful (GB), 6, 115	F. Toro	Steinlen (GB), 6, 121	Pranke (Arg), 5, 117	8	1:47.20	183,600
1988	Skip Out Front, 6, 115	C. J. McCarron	Steinlen (GB), 5, 121	World Court, 5, 113	4	1:46.40	120,800
1987	Clever Song, 5, 118	L. A. Pincay Jr.	Skip Out Front, 5, 114	Barbery, 6, 115	7	1:45.60	127,800
1986	Al Mamoon, 5, 119	P. A. Valenzuela	Truce Maker, 8, 111	Will Dancer (Fr), 4, 114	6	1:39.20	107,000
1985	Tsunami Slew, 4, 117	G. L. Stevens	Al Mamoon, 4, 117	Dahar, 4, 123	7	1:46.20	122,300
1984	Bel Bolide, 6, 121	T. Lipham	Silveyville, 5, 118	Vin St Benet (GB), 5, 118	8	1:46.80	123,600
1983	John Henry, 8, 127	C. J. McCarron	Prince Florimund (SAf), 5, 120	Tonzarun, 5, 114	10	1:47.20	97,100
1982	Spence Bay (Ire), 7, 122	F. Toro	The Bart, 6, 124	Peter Jones, 4, 113	9	1:46.80	100,300
1981	Bold Tropic (SAf), 6, 126	W. Shoemaker	The Bart, 5, 117	Don Roberto, 4, 112	9	1:46.80	98,100
1980	Bold Tropic (SAf), 5, 122	W. Shoemaker	Inkerman, 5, 115	Borzoi, 4, 117	8	1:46.40	65,700
1979	Smoggy (GB), 5, 114	D. G. McHargue	Dom Alaric (Fr), 5, 120	Inkerman, 4, 119	8	1:47.40	65,500
1978	Effervescing, 5, 119	L. A. Pincay Jr.	Diagramatic, 5, 123	April Axe, 3, 113	8	1:47.20	65,500
1977	Hunza Dancer, 5, 120	J. Cruguet	Anne's Pretender, 5, 121	Legendaire, 4, 115	11	1:47.20	68,900
1976	King Pellinore, 4, 121	W. Shoemaker	Riot in Paris, 5, 123	Caucasus, 4, 120	7	1:48.00	48,200
1975	Pass the Glass, 4, 115	F. Toro	Big Band, 5, 116	Against the Snow, 5, 114	11	1:48.20	53,800
	Montmartre, 5, 115	F. Toro	Top Crowd, 4, 115	Ancient Title, 5, 128	9	1:49.60	51,800
1974	Plunk, 4, 117	L. A. Pincay Jr.	Scantling, 4, 115	Mr. Cockatoo, 5, 114	11	1:48.20	51,900
1973	Kentuckian, 4, 114	R. Campas	Life Cycle, 4, 121	Wing Out, 5, 118	9	1:48.00	50,400

Traditionally held during the July 4 holiday. Held at Santa Anita Park 1949. Not held 1942-'43. 1¹⁄₁₆ miles 1945-'46, 1986. 1¼ miles 1950. Dirt 1938-'67. Four-year-olds and up 1945. Two divisions 1975. †Denotes female.

American Invitational Oaks

Grade 1 in 2005. Hollywood Park, three-year-olds (Northern and Southern Hemisphere), fillies, 1¼ miles, turf. Held July 3, 2004, with a gross value of $750,000. First held in 2002. First graded in 2004. Stakes record 1:59.98 (2003 Dimitrova).

Year	Winner	Jockey	Second	Third	Strs	Time	1st Purse
2004	Ticker Tape (GB), 3, 121	K. J. Desormeaux	Dance in the Mood (Jpn), 3, 121	Hollywood Story, 3, 121	13	2:01.54	$450,000
2003	Dimitrova, 3, 121	D. R. Flores	Sand Springs, 3, 121	Atlantic Ocean, 3, 121	14	**1:59.98**	450,000
2002	‡Megahertz (GB), 3, 121	A. O. Solis	Dublino, 3, 121	Alozaina (Ire), 3, 121	14	2:00.46	300,000

Held during the July 4 holiday. ‡Dublino finished first, DQ to second, 2002.

American Turf Stakes

Grade 3 in 2005. Churchill Downs, three-year-olds, 1⅛ miles, turf. Held May 6, 2005, with a gross value of $114,700. First held in 1992. First graded in 1998. Stakes record 1:40.93 (1997 Royal Strand [Ire]).

Year	Winner	Jockey	Second	Third	Strs	Time	1st Purse
2005	Rey de Cafe, 3, 122	J. Castellano	Rush Bay, 3, 116	Guillaume Tell (Ire), 3, 116	9	1:42.00	$71,114
2004	Kitten's Joy, 3, 123	J. D. Bailey	Prince Arch, 3, 123	Capo, 3, 117	9	1:43.31	70,556
2003	Senor Swinger, 3, 117	P. Day	Remind, 3, 117	Foufa's Warrior, 3, 117	10	1:41.38	75,268
2002	Legislator, 3, 116	E. S. Prado	Stage Call (Ire), 3, 123	Orchard Park, 3, 123	10	1:44.43	72,106
2001	Strategic Partner, 3, 116	J. R. Velazquez	Baptize, 3, 123	Dynameaux, 3, 120	6	1:42.89	73,098
2000	King Cugat, 3, 123	J. D. Bailey	Lendell Ray, 3, 116	Go Lib Go, 3, 123	11	1:41.25	73,222
1999	Air Rocket, 3, 120	J. D. Bailey	Haus of Dehere, 3, 116	Conserve, 3, 118	10	1:42.65	71,548
1998	Dernier Croise (Fr), 3, 116	G. L. Stevens	Tenbyssimo (Ire), 3, 123	Silver Lord, 3, 114	10	1:44.28	78,120
1997	Royal Strand (Ire), 3, 116	P. Day	Rob 'n Gin, 3, 118	Deputy Commander, 3, 115	10	1:40.93	71,796
1996	Broadway Beau, 3, 114	C. J. McCarron	Trail City, 3, 123	Gotcha, 3, 114	10	1:41.87	76,375
1995	Unanimous Vote (Ire), 3, 120	G. L. Stevens	Nostra, 3, 116	Native Regent, 3, 123	12	1:42.07	76,700
1994	Jaggery John, 3, 123	M. E. Smith	Milt's Overture, 3, 116	Zuno Star, 3, 116	10	1:45.05	56,453
1993	‡Desert Waves, 3, 118	S. J. Sellers	Compadre, 3, 116	Super Snazzie, 3, 116	5	1:42.64	36,628
1992	Senor Tomas, 3, 118	M. E. Smith	Coaxing Matt, 3, 114	Black Question, 3, 123	8	1:43.10	37,440

Sponsored by the Crown Royal Co. of Stamford, Connecticut 1995-2005. American Turf S. 1992-'94. ‡Compadre finished first, DQ to second, 1993. Course record 1997.

Amsterdam Stakes

Grade 2 in 2005. Saratoga Race Course, three-year-olds, 6 furlongs, dirt. Held August 7, 2004, with a gross value of $150,000. First held in 1901. First graded in 1998. Stakes record 1:08.64 (2003 Zavata).

Year	Winner	Jockey	Second	Third	Strs	Time	1st Purse
2004	Bwana Charlie, 3, 123	S. J. Sellers	Pomeroy, 3, 123	Weigelia, 3, 123	7	1:09.40	$90,000
2003	Zavata, 3, 119	J. D. Bailey	Great Notion, 3, 121	Trust N Luck, 3, 123	7	1:08.64	90,000
2002	Listen Here, 3, 121	P. Day	Boston Common, 3, 123	Bold Truth, 3, 115	8	1:09.58	90,000
2001	City Zip, 3, 123	J. F. Chavez	Speightstown, 3, 118	Smile My Lord, 3, 118	6	1:11.03	81,420
2000	Personal First, 3, 120	P. Day	Disco Rico, 3, 123	Trippi, 3, 123	6	1:09.33	66,000
1999	Successful Appeal, 3, 122	E. S. Prado	Lion Hearted, 3, 114	Silver Season, 3, 119	9	1:10.25	50,340
1998	dh- Mint, 3, 119	E. Coa		Southern Bostonian, 3, 119	8	1:10.28	33,060
	dh- Secret Firm, 3, 117	E. S. Prado					
1997	Oro de Mexico, 3, 117	C. W. Antley	Trafalger, 3, 122	Kelly Kip, 3, 122	7	1:10.58	16,425
1996	Distorted Humor, 3, 115	P. Day	Gold Fever, 3, 121	Stu's Choice, 3, 115	7	1:09.13	32,820
1995	Kings Fiction, 3, 112	P. Day	Lord Carson, 3, 115	Ft. Stockton, 3, 115	5	1:09.75	32,250
1994	Chimes Band, 3, 117	J. D. Bailey	Ledford, 3, 115	Halo's Image, 3, 115	6	1:09.90	32,325
	Mr. Shawklit, 3, 115	W. H. McCauley	Scarlet Rage, 3, 115	Groovy Jett, 3, 117	5	1:10.89	32,325
1993	Evil Bear, 3, 117	J. A. Santos	Punch Line, 3, 122	Digging In, 3, 119	5	1:22.09	28,800

Named for Amsterdam, New York, located in Montgomery County. Formerly named for Flying Zee Stable's G2 SW Screen King (1976 c. by Silent Screen); Screen King broke his maiden at Belmont Park and ended his career at Saratoga in the Travers S. (G1). Grade 3 1998-2000. Screen King S. 1993-'97. Held at Belmont Park 1993. Not held 1911-'12, 1924-'92. 1 mile 1901-'23. 7 furlongs 1993. Three-year-olds and up 1901-'23. Two divisions 1994. Dead heat for first 1998.

Ancient Title Breeders' Cup Handicap

Grade 1 in 2005. Santa Anita Park, three-year-olds and up, 6 furlongs, dirt. Held October 10, 2004, with a gross value of $213,000. First held in 1985. First graded in 1990. Stakes record 1:07.67 (2001 Swept Overboard).

Year	Winner	Jockey	Second	Third	Strs	Time	1st Purse
2004	Pt's Grey Eagle, 3, 109	A. Bisono	Pohave, 6, 118	Hombre Rapido, 7, 114	8	1:08.84	$120,000
2003	Avanzado (Arg), 6, 116	T. Baze	Captain Squire, 4, 117	Bluesthestandard, 6, 115	6	1:08.12	81,375
2002	†Kalookan Queen, 6, 119	A. O. Solis	Crafty C. T., 4, 116	Mellow Fellow, 7, 117	6	1:08.26	125,625
2001	Swept Overboard, 4, 116	E. J. Delahoussaye	Kona Gold, 7, 127	I Love Silver, 3, 116	6	1:07.67	124,260
2000	Kona Gold, 6, 124	A. O. Solis	Regal Thunder, 6, 117	Elaborate, 5, 116	4	1:08.11	123,060
1999	Lexicon, 4, 116	K. J. Desormeaux	Kona Gold, 5, 120	Regal Thunder, 5, 117	8	1:07.84	125,400
1998	Gold Land, 7, 117	K. J. Desormeaux	†A. P. Assay, 4, 116	Swiss Yodeler, 4, 114	8	1:08.50	94,020
1997	Elmhurst, 7, 114	C. S. Nakatani	Swiss Yodeler, 3, 113	Larry the Legend, 5, 115	7	1:08.82	95,000
1996	Lakota Brave, 7, 117	E. J. Delahoussaye	Letthebighossroll, 8, 119	‡Paying Dues, 4, 118	5	1:08.16	93,700
1995	†Track Gal, 4, 116	G. L. Stevens	Siphon (Brz), 4, 117	Forest Gazelle, 4, 116	6	1:08.32	59,150
1994	Saratoga Gambler, 6, 113	M. A. Pedroza	Uncaged Fury, 3, 114	Concept Win, 4, 117	8	1:08.87	62,500
1993	Cardmania, 7, 116	E. J. Delahoussaye	Music Merci, 7, 117	Bahatur, 4, 116	8	1:08.04	61,975
1992	Gray Slewpy, 4, 118	K. J. Desormeaux	Trick Me, 4, 117	Light of Morn, 6, 117	9	1:08.48	59,372
1991	Frost Free, 6, 118	C. J. McCarron	Answer Do, 5, 118	Sir Beaufort, 4, 113	7	1:08.66	61,525
1990	Corwyn Bay (Ire), 4, 118	E. J. Delahoussaye	Sensational Star, 6, 119	Yes I'm Blue, 4, 117	6	1:08.40	61,375
1989	Sam Who, 4, 120	L. A. Pincay Jr.	Sunny Blossom, 4, 116	Don's Irish Melody, 6, 114	5	1:08.00	46,050
1988	Olympic Prospect, 4, 123	L. A. Pincay Jr.	Sebrof, 4, 118	Reconnoitering, 4, 114	6	1:09.00	55,630
1987	Zany Tactics, 6, 123	J. L. Kaenel	On the Line, 3, 116	Carload, 5, 117	3	1:09.00	35,500
1986	Groovy, 3, 123	J. A. Santos	Rosie's K. T., 5, 117	Sun Master, 5, 114	8	1:08.20	49,450
1985	Temerity Prince, 5, 120	W. A. Ward	Debonaire Junior, 4, 124	Bid Us, 5, 115	6	1:09.20	37,150

Named for Kirkland Stable's 1975, '76 Californian S. (G1) winner Ancient Title (1970 g. by Gummo). Grade 3 1990-'98. Grade 2 1999-2000. Ancient Title H. 1985-'89. ‡Criollito (Arg) finished third, DQ to fourth, 1996. Track record 2001.
†Denotes female.

Apple Blossom Handicap

Grade 1 in 2005. Oaklawn Park, four-year-olds and up, fillies and mares, 1¹/₁₆ miles, dirt. Held April 9, 2005, with a gross value of $500,000. First held in 1973. First graded in 1977. Stakes record 1:40.20 (1984 Heatherten).

Year	Winner	Jockey	Second	Third	Strs	Time	1st Purse
2005	Dream of Summer, 6, 117	P. A. Valenzuela	Star Parade (Arg), 6, 116	Shadow Cast, 4, 116	7	1:43.86	$300,000
2004	Azeri, 6, 123	M. E. Smith	‡Star Parade (Arg), 5, 114	Wild Spirit (Chi), 5, 119	6	1:41.24	300,000
2003	Azeri, 5, 123	M. E. Smith	Take Charge Lady, 4, 118	Mandy's Gold, 5, 116	7	1:43.00	300,000
2002	Azeri, 4, 117	M. E. Smith	Affluent, 4, 118	Miss Linda (Arg), 5, 118	5	1:42.75	300,000
2001	Gourmet Girl, 6, 113	C. H. Borel	Lu Ravi, 6, 114	Lazy Slusan, 6, 116	11	1:42.15	300,000
2000	Heritage of Gold, 5, 118	S. J. Sellers	Lu Ravi, 5, 114	Bordelaise (Arg), 5, 113	7	1:42.22	300,000
1999	Banshee Breeze, 4, 122	J. D. Bailey	Sister Act, 4, 114	Silent Eskimo, 4, 112	6	1:41.64	300,000
1998	Escena, 5, 117	J. D. Bailey	Glitter Woman, 4, 119	Toda Una Dama (Arg), 5, 115	7	1:40.95	300,000
1997	Halo America, 7, 117	C. H. Borel	Jewel Princess, 5, 124	Different (Arg), 5, 121	7	1:41.65	300,000
1996	Twice the Vice, 5, 117	C. J. McCarron	Halo America, 6, 115	Serena's Song, 4, 124	7	1:41.71	300,000
1995	Heavenly Prize, 4, 120	P. Day	Halo America, 5, 116	Paseana (Arg), 8, 122	6	1:42.76	300,000
1994	Nine Keys, 4, 116	M. E. Smith	Mamselle Bebette, 4, 116	Re Toss (Arg), 7, 117	10	1:42.15	300,000
1993	Paseana (Arg), 6, 124	C. J. McCarron	Looie Capote, 4, 115	Luv Me Luv Me Not, 4, 114	9	1:41.80	300,000
1992	Paseana (Arg), 5, 124	C. J. McCarron	Fit for a Queen, 6, 121	Slide Out Front, 4, 109	8	1:42.13	300,000
1991	Degenerate Gal, 6, 115	P. Day	Charon, 4, 121	Fit to Scout, 4, 116	6	1:41.25	300,000
1990	Gorgeous, 4, 122	E. J. Delahoussaye	Bayakoa (Arg), 6, 126	Affirmed Classic, 4, 112	4	1:40.60	210,000
1989	Bayakoa (Arg), 5, 120	L. A. Pincay Jr.	Goodbye Halo, 4, 125	Invited Guest (Ire), 5, 116	6	1:41.60	150,000
1988	By Land by Sea, 4, 121	F. Toro	Invited Guest (Ire), 4, 116	Hail a Cab, 5, 113	10	1:41.20	150,000
1987	North Sider, 5, 122	A. T. Cordero Jr.	Family Style, 4, 120	Queen Alexandra, 5, 119	7	1:41.20	162,300
1986	Love Smitten, 5, 119	C. J. McCarron	Lady's Secret, 4, 127	Sefa's Beauty, 7, 122	7	1:40.40	162,180
1985	Sefa's Beauty, 6, 120	P. Day	Heatherten, 6, 127	Life's Magic, 4, 123	7	1:42.20	161,700
1984	Heatherten, 5, 116	S. Maple	Try Something New, 5, 121	Holiday Dancer, 4, 115	10	1:40.20	167,400
1983	Miss Huntington, 6, 118	J. Velasquez	‡Sefa's Beauty, 4, 117	Queen of Song, 4, 114	13	1:44.80	172,620
1982	Track Robbery, 6, 124	E. J. Delahoussaye	Andover Way, 4, 120	Jameela, 6, 123	6	1:45.20	161,040
1981	Bold 'n Determined, 4, 124	E. J. Delahoussaye	La Bonzo, 5, 111	Karla's Enough, 4, 119	7	1:44.20	131,820
1980	Billy Jane, 4, 113	J. L. Lively	Jameela, 4, 118	Miss Baja, 5, 121	11	1:43.60	106,290
1979	Miss Baja, 4, 113	E. Maple	Kit's Double, 6, 114	Navajo Princess, 5, 121	10	1:43.00	106,800
1978	Northernette, 4, 119	D. Brumfield	Taisez Vous, 4, 124	Cum Laude Laurie, 4, 121	9	1:42.00	74,130
1977	Hail Hilarious, 4, 121	D. Pierce	Kittyluck, 4, 112	Summertime Promise, 5, 119	15	1:41.40	82,290
1976	Summertime Promise, 4, 119	D. G. McHargue	Baygo, 7, 114	Costly Dream, 5, 113	9	1:40.60	35,760
1975	Susan's Girl, 6, 124	J. Nichols	Truchas, 6, 116	Matuta, 4, 114	12	1:42.40	36,720
1974	Big Dare, 4, 116	R. N. Ussery	Gallant Davelle, 4, 122	Sixty Sails, 4, 115	13	1:11.80	19,050

Named for the apple trees typically in bloom during the Oaklawn Park meet. Grade 3 1977. Grade 2 1978-'81, 1990-'91. 6 furlongs 1974. 1 mile 70 yards 1975-'79. Three-year-olds and up 1974. ‡Number finished second, DQ to fourth, 1983. ‡Wild Spirit (Chi) finished second, DQ to third on an Arkansas Racing Commission decision, 2004. Held as an overnight handicap 1973.

Appleton Handicap

Grade 3 in 2005. Gulfstream Park, three-year-olds and up, 1 mile, turf. Held February 12, 2005, with a gross value of $100,000. First held in 1952. First graded in 1973. Stakes record 1:32.98 (2005 Mr. Light [Arg]).

Year	Winner	Jockey	Second	Third	Strs	Time	1st Purse
2005	Mr. Light (Arg), 6, 114	C. H. Velasquez	Host (Chi), 5, 119	Millennium Dragon (GB), 6, 120	8	1:32.98	$60,000
2004	Millennium Dragon (GB), 5, 116	R. Migliore	Political Attack, 5, 118	Proud Man, 6, 116	12	1:34.40	90,000
2003	Point Prince, 4, 115	M. R. Cruz	Krieger, 5, 115	Red Sea (GB), 7, 114	9	1:37.84	90,000
2002	Pisces, 5, 113	R. I. Velez	North East Bound, 6, 117	Capsized, 6, 114	10	1:39.41	90,000
2001	Associate, 6, 114	J. F. Chavez	Band Is Passing, 5, 119	El Mirasol, 6, 115	12	1:33.69	90,000
2000	Band Is Passing, 4, 115	E. Coa	Hibernian Rhapsody (Ire), 5, 115	Shamrock City, 5, 114	11	1:40.11	60,000
1999	Behaviour (GB), 7, 113	S. J. Sellers	Notoriety, 6, 112	Legs Galore, 4, 113	6	1:45.77	60,000
1998	Sir Cat, 5, 119	J. D. Bailey	Wild Event, 5, 114	Kingcanrunallday, 5, 116	5	1:42.69	60,000
1997	Montjoy, 5, 116	M. E. Smith	Mighty Forum (GB), 6, 114	Elite Jeblar, 7, 114	12	1:39.88	60,000
1996	The Vid, 6, 122	W. H. McCauley	Dove Hunt, 5, 120	Montreal Red, 4, 114	11	1:41.79	60,000
1995	Dusty Screen, 7, 116	W. H. McCauley	The Vid, 5, 114	Dove Hunt, 4, 114	7	1:42.72	60,000
1994	Paradise Creek, 5, 121	M. E. Smith	Fourstars Allstar, 6, 117	Elite Jeblar, 4, 111	8	1:40.57	60,000
1993	Cigar Toss (Arg), 6, 112	B. G. Moore	Bidding Proud, 4, 113	Archies Laughter, 5, 114	9	1:43.55	60,000
1992	Royal Ninja, 6, 112	J. D. Bailey	Archies Laughter, 4, 114	Native Boundary, 4, 116	12	1:42.49	60,000
1991	Jolie's Halo, 4, 116	R. Platts	Rowdy Regal, 4, 110	Shot Gun Scott, 4, 118	11	1:40.50	60,000
1990	Highland Springs, 6, 118	C. Perret	Prince Randi, 4, 115	Wanderkin, 7, 116	9	1:35.20	60,000
1989	Fabulous Indian, 4, 109	E. O. Nunez	Equalize, 7, 125	Simply Majestic, 5, 121	11	1:35.00	60,000
1988	Yankee Affair, 6, 116	R. P. Romero	Performing Pappy, 4, 114	Kings River (Ire), 6, 114	14	1:35.00	60,000
1987	Regal Flier, 6, 113	J. Vasquez	Wollaston, 5, 112	Hi Ideal, 5, 113	9	1:35.60	27,375
	Racing Star, 5, 111	S. B. Soto	Trubulare, 4, 114	Onyxii, 6, 116	10	1:35.60	27,975
1986	Cool, 5, 116	J. Vasquez	Dr. Schwartzman, 5, 120	Smart and Sharp, 7, 115	11	1:39.60	39,690
1985	Smart and Sharp, 6, 117	M. Russ	Amerilad, 4, 112	Dr. Schwartzman, 4, 117	11	1:34.60	31,740
	Star Choice, 6, 118	J. McKnight	Late Act, 6, 121	Solidified, 4, 114	10	1:34.40	31,440
1984	Super Sunrise (GB), 5, 118	C. Perret	Smart and Sharp, 5, 110	Guston (Arg), 6, 115	11	1:34.40	23,628
	Great Substence, 6, 113	G. St. Leon	Dr. Schwartzman, 3, 109	Rising Raja, 4, 113	10	1:35.00	23,418
1983	Northrop, 4, 116	J. Velasquez	Forkali, 5, 114	North Course, 8, 113	6	1:22.00	26,754

Year	Winner	Jockey	Second	Third	Strs	Time	1st Purse
1982	Gleaming Channel, 4, 116	C. Perret	Double Cadet, 4, 111	Victorian Double, 4, 112	9	1:36.00	$18,375
	King of Mardi Gras, 6, 113	A. Smith Jr.	Some One Frisky, 6, 114	Explosive Bid, 4, 115	9	1:36.40	18,225
1981	North Course, 6, 115	B. Thornburg	Proctor, 4, 120	Royal Centurion, 4, 113	11	1:34.80	23,292
	Drum's Captain (Ire), 6, 114	A. Gilbert	Foretake, 5, 116	Poverty Boy, 6, 114	10	1:35.00	23,082
1980	Morning Frolic, 5, 117	A. T. Cordero Jr.	Match the Hatch, 4, 111	Nar, 5, 113	12	1:35.40	19,365
	Pipedreamer (GB), 5, 113	J. Cruguet	Houdini, 5, 119	Once Over Lightly, 7, 114	10	1:34.40	18,915
1979	Fleet Gar, 4, 114	J. Fell	Romeo, 6, 118	Vic's Magic, 6, 121	11	1:36.40	19,005
	Regal and Royal, 4, 120	J. Fell	North Course, 4, 114	Bob's Dusty, 5, 121	11	1:37.00	19,155
1978	Do Lishus, 4, 110	J. D. Bailey	Haverty, 4, 113	Leader of the Band, 6, 113	11	1:37.20	19,500
	Qui Native, 4, 117	D. MacBeth	All Friends (Ire), 6, 115	Tablao (Chi), 5, 114	10	1:36.40	19,350
1977	Gay Jitterbug, 4, 118	L. Saumell	What a Threat, 5, 110	Riverside Sam, 4, 109	9	1:36.40	16,185
	Cinteelo, 4, 115	B. Thornburg	Commanding Lead, 6, 110	*El Guindo, 6, 111	10	1:36.20	16,335
1976	Step Forward, 4, 114	M. Solomone	Faithful Diplomat, 4, 111	Passionate Pirate, 5, 111	9	1:34.00	20,775
	Improviser, 4, 113	J. Cruguet	Odd Man, 5, 112	Peppy Addy, 4, 113	11	1:35.60	21,195
1975	Duke Tom, 5, 113	P. I. Grimm	Dartsum, 6, 116	Return to Reality, 6, 110	14	1:36.20	17,460
	Beau Bugle, 5, 116	M. Hole	The Grok, 4, 114	Mr. Door, 4, 115	13	1:36.20	16,860
1974	Right On, 5, 112	E. Maple	*Rey Maya, 7, 112	Rapid Sage, 4, 114	13	1:37.80	21,930
1973	Windtex, 4, 113	J. L. Rotz	Getajetholme, 4, 112	Prince of Truth, 5, 114	9	1:35.20	16,140
	Life Cycle, 4, 112	F. Iannelli	Roundhouse, 5, 108	Hope Eternal, 5, 112	10	1:35.40	16,290

Named in honor of Arthur I. Appleton, owner of Bridlewood Farm in Florida. Not graded 1975-'84. Grade 2 1998, 2000-'03. 1¹/₁₆ miles 1952, 1992-2000. 1¹/₈ miles 1953-'64. 7 furlongs 1965-'66, 1972, 1983. 1 mile 70 yards 1991. Dirt 1952-'66, 1972, 1983, 1991, 1993, 1995, 1998-'99. Two divisions 1973, 1975-'82, 1984-'85, 1987.

Aqueduct Handicap

Grade 3 in 2005. Aqueduct, three-year-olds and up, 1¹/₁₆ miles, dirt. Held January 30, 2005, with a gross value of $110,300. First held in 1902. First graded in 1985. Stakes record 1:41.13 (1995 Danzig's Dance).

Year	Winner	Jockey	Second	Third	Strs	Time	1st Purse
2005	Country Be Gold, 8, 114	J. L. Espinoza	Aggadan, 6, 123	Mahzouz, 4, 112	8	1:44.80	$66,180
2004	Seattle Fitz (Arg), 8, 114	A. T. Gryder	Evening Attire, 6, 122	Rogue Agent, 5, 112	8	1:42.13	66,060
2003	Snake Mountain, 5, 120	M. J. Luzzi	Ground Storm, 7, 117	Cat's At Home, 6, 114	5	1:44.17	64,440
2002	Evening Attire, 4, 116	S. Bridgmohan	Ground Storm, 6, 115	Tempest Fugit, 5, 114	7	1:42.69	65,520
2001	Liberty Gold, 7, 115	J. Bravo	Coyote Lakes, 7, 116	Talk's Cheap, 5, 116	7	1:42.20	66,300
2000	Sky Approval, 6, 115	C. H. Velasquez	Parental Pressure, 9, 115	Phone the King, 5, 114	8	1:44.45	49,770
1999	Mr. Sinatra, 5, 118	A. T. Gryder	Brushing Up, 6, 112	Wouldn't We All, 5, 117	5	1:43.11	49,335
1998	Star of Valor, 5, 113	A. T. Gryder	Christian Soldier, 4, 113	Mr. Sinatra, 4, 117	8	1:42.48	49,725
1997	Pacific Fleet, 5, 112	J. Chavez	More to Tell, 6, 116	Admiralty, 5, 116	8	1:43.45	39,924
1996	Mighty Magee, 4, 118	M. J. Luzzi	May I Inquire, 7, 113	More to Tell, 5, 115	8	1:43.89	39,780
1995	Danzig's Dance, 6, 111	J. F. Chavez	Key Contender, 7, 115	Golden Larch, 4, 112	8	**1:41.13**	50,010
1994	As Indicated, 4, 121	R. G. Davis	Primitive Hall, 5, 113	Jacksonport, 5, 112	6	1:45.77	48,690
1993	Shots Are Ringing, 6, 118	J. R. Velazquez	A Call to Rise, 5, 111	Federal Funds, 4, 109	6	1:44.44	52,650
1992	‡Formal Dinner, 4, 112	A. T. Cordero Jr.	Shots Are Ringing, 5, 113	Island Edition, 5, 110	6	1:43.60	51,750
1991	Sports View, 4, 115	J. D. Bailey	I'm Sky High, 5, 115	Lost Opportunity, 5, 112	6	1:43.61	51,750
1990	Congeleur, 5, 116	A. T. Cordero Jr.	Silver Survivor, 4, 118	King's Swan, 10, 116	7	1:44.80	52,020
1989	Lord of the Night, 6, 114	W. H. McCauley	Its Acedemic, 5, 110	True and Blue, 4, 113	6	1:42.80	52,110
1988	‡Clever Secret, 4, 112	E. T. Baird	Proud Debonair, 6, 114	Native Wizard, 5, 112	9	1:45.20	54,810
1987	King's Swan, 7, 118	J. A. Santos	Raja's Revenge, 4, 111	Cost Conscious, 5, 112	8	1:41.80	54,990
1986	Aggressive Bid, 5, 109	M. Venezia	Badwagon Harry, 7, 120	Carjack, 5, 114	6	1:43.80	50,850
1985	Fight Over, 4, 118	A. T. Cordero Jr.	Imp Society, 4, 113	Verbarctic, 5, 112	9	1:42.60	55,260
1984	Moro, 5, 120	J. Samyn	Jacksboro, 5, 120	Ask Muhammad, 5, 117	9	1:43.40	45,120
1983	Fort Monroe, 4, 108	V. H. Molina	Lark Oscillation (Fr), 8, 113	Fabulous Find, 5, 116	6	1:42.40	33,420
1982	Reef Searcher, 5, 114	A. T. Cordero Jr.	Deedee's Deal, 5, 107	Alla Breva, 5, 114	13	1:48.40	35,760
1981	Irish Tower, 4, 114	J. Fell	Dr. Blum, 4, 116	Lark Oscillation (Fr), 6, 108	5	1:44.60	32,760
1980	Charlie Coast, 5, 112	J. J. Miranda	Pole Position, 6, 126	Pirate's Bounty, 5, 112	12	1:44.80	35,400
1978	Wise Philip, 5, 117	J. Vasquez	Gallivantor, 6, 119	*Vanistorio, 6, 112	10	1:43.80	33,060
1977	Magnetizer, 4, 112	A. Santiago	Turn and Count, 4, 126	Due Diligence, 5, 112	6	1:45.40	32,580
1976	Right Mind, 5, 114	R. Turcotte	General Beauregard, 4, 119	Our Hero, 4, 115	5	1:38.80	32,670
1973	Cannonade, 2, 126	P. Anderson	Roger's Dandy, 2, 112	Flip Sal, 2, 116	7	1:51.60	34,080

Aqueduct S. 1962-'65, 1967-'68. Held at Belmont Park 1961. Not held 1910-'16, 1924, 1956-'58, 1969-'72, 1974-'75, 1979. 1¹/₈ miles 1917-'19, 1926-'32, 1961-'73. 1⁹/₁₆ miles 1920-'23. 1 mile 1959-'60, 1976. Two-year-olds 1973. ‡King's Swan finished first, DQ to fourth, 1988. ‡Shots Are Ringing finished first, DQ to second, 1992. Equaled track record 1995.

Arcadia Handicap

Grade 2 in 2005. Santa Anita Park, four-year-olds and up, 1 mile, turf. Held April 9, 2005, with a gross value of $150,000. First held in 1988. First graded in 1990. Stakes record 1:33.21 (1992 Exbourne).

Year	Winner	Jockey	Second	Third	Strs	Time	1st Purse
2005	Singletary, 5, 120	A. O. Solis	Sweet Return (GB), 5, 117	Buckland Manor, 5, 117	5	1:33.52	$90,000
2004	Diplomatic Bag, 4, 116	D. R. Flores	Statement, 6, 114	Seinne (Chi), 7, 115	7	1:47.90	90,000
2003	Century City (Ire), 4, 114	J. Valdivia Jr.	Gondolieri (Chi), 4, 116	Sunday Break (Jpn), 4, 117	9	1:47.84	90,000
2002	Seinne (Chi), 5, 115	C. J. McCarron	Irish Prize, 6, 122	Kerrygold (Fr), 6, 116	9	1:47.16	90,000

Year	Winner	Jockey	Second	Third	Strs	Time	1st Purse
2001	Lazy Lode (Arg), 7, 121	L. A. Pincay Jr.	Night Patrol, 5, 116	Wake the Tiger, 5, 114	5	1:49.74	$90,000
2000	Falcon Flight (Fr), 4, 114	B. Blanc	Bonapartiste (Fr), 6, 118	Otavalo (Ire), 5, 114	7	1:47.88	97,950
1999	Commitisize, 4, 117	D. R. Flores	Majorien (GB), 5, 117	Ladies Din, 4, 119	7	1:48.25	90,000
1998	Hawksley Hill (Ire), 5, 117	G. L. Stevens	Precious Ring, 5, 114	Kirkwall (GB), 4, 117	8	1:49.96	167,350
1997	Labeeb (GB), 5, 120	E. J. Delahoussaye	Talloires, 7, 118	Pinfloron (Fr), 5, 115	5	1:35.80	80,100
1996	Tychonic (GB), 6, 118	G. L. Stevens	Debutant Trick, 6, 117	Savinio, 6, 117	6	1:35.84	80,300
1995	Savinio, 5, 116	C. J. McCarron	River Flyer, 4, 121	Romarin (Brz), 5, 120	7	1:34.74	91,800
1994	Norwich (GB), 7, 117	P. A. Valenzuela	Megan's Interco, 5, 119	Gothland (Fr), 5, 118	5	1:34.14	75,850
1993	Val des Bois (Fr), 7, 118	P. A. Valenzuela	Star of Cozzene, 5, 122	C. Sam Maggio, 7, 113	7	1:35.07	77,750
1992	Exbourne, 6, 122	G. L. Stevens	Repriced, 4, 113	Madjaristan, 6, 115	6	**1:33.21**	95,000
1991	Pharisien (Fr), 4, 113	C. S. Nakatani	Exbourne, 5, 118	Tartas (Fr), 5, 112	11	1:33.30	102,500
1990	Steinlen (GB), 7, 125	J. A. Santos	Bruho, 4, 117	Wonder Dancer, 4, 111	6	1:33.40	63,200
1989	Political Ambition, 5, 121	E. J. Delahoussaye	Patchy Groundfog, 6, 118	Steinlen (GB), 6, 122	5	1:35.60	62,600
1988	Steinlen (GB), 5, 117	G. L. Stevens	Political Ambition, 4, 120	Neshad, 4, 117	9	1:34.80	88,760

Named for Arcadia, California, city in which Santa Anita Park is located. Formerly named for two California land grants called Rancho El Rincon. Grade 3 1990-'94. El Rincon H. 1988-2000. 1¹⁄₈ miles 1998-2004.

Aristides Breeders' Cup Handicap

Grade 3 in 2005. Churchill Downs, three-year-olds and up, 6 furlongs, dirt. Held June 19, 2004, with a gross value of $162,150. First held in 1989. First graded in 1999. Stakes record 1:09.04 (2004 Champali).

Year	Winner	Jockey	Second	Third	Strs	Time	1st Purse
2004	Champali, 4, 116	R. Bejarano	Beau's Town, 6, 121	Battle Won, 4, 114	6	**1:09.04**	$100,533
2003	Mountain General, 5, 116	C. J. Lanerie	Beau's Town, 5, 123	Pass Rush, 4, 118	7	1:16.01	67,580
2002	Orientate, 4, 118	R. Albarado	Binthebest, 5, 114	No Armistice, 5, 116	5	1:14.41	66,650
2001	Bet On Sunshine, 9, 120	C. H. Borel	Alannan, 5, 119	Dash for Daylight, 4, 110	6	1:14.79	67,208
2000	Bet On Sunshine, 8, 119	F. C. Torres	Proven Cure, 6, 111	Sun Bull, 4, 111	7	1:15.11	68,014
1999	Run Johnny, 7, 116	P. Day	Squall Valley, 4, 112	Neon Shadow, 5, 114	8	1:16.27	68,572
1998	Thisnearlywasmine, 4, 115	S. J. Sellers	Partner's Hero, 4, 115	El Amante, 5, 118	7	1:15.72	67,518
1997	High Stakes Player, 5, 119	S. J. Sellers	Trafalger, 3, 106	Bet On Sunshine, 5, 112	7	1:15.85	21,800
1996	Lord Carson, 4, 115	D. M. Barton	Criollito (Arg), 5, 117	Bet On Sunshine, 4, 110	5	1:15.94	70,525
1995	Boone's Mill, 3, 106	D. M. Barton	Ojai, 6, 113	Hot Jaws, 5, 118	7	1:15.90	69,924
1994	Never Wavering, 5, 116	S. J. Sellers	Demaloot Demashoot, 4, 119	American Chance, 5, 117	8	1:16.55	53,479
1993	Gold Spring (Arg), 5, 115	F. A. Arguello Jr.	Take Me Out, 5, 119	In the Zone, 4, 113	6	1:16.43	35,718
1992	Tricky Fun, 4, 113	P. Day	Guns of Cielo, 5, 112	Richman, 4, 118	6	1:16.35	44,720
1991	Bio, 5, 117	B. E. Bartram	Bratt's Choice, 4, 117	Guns of Cielo, 4, 112	6	1:16.62	44,668
1990	Beau Genius, 5, 122	R. D. Lopez	Bio, 4, 113	Launch a Dream, 5, 111	9	1:16.20	45,240
1989	Bet the Pot, 4, 115	C. R. Woods Jr.	Temptation Time, 5, 115	Good Roar, 5, 113	5	1:16.00	33,703

Named for the first winner of the Kentucky Derby, H. P. McGrath's Aristides (1872 c. by *Leamington). Aristides H. 1996-2003. 6¹⁄₂ furlongs 1989-2003. Track record 2000.

Arkansas Derby

Grade 2 in 2005. Oaklawn Park, three-year-olds, 1¹⁄₈ miles, dirt. Held April 16, 2005, with a gross value of $1,000,000. First held in 1936. First graded in 1973. Stakes record 1:46.80 (1984 Althea).

Year	Winner	Jockey	Second	Third	Strs	Time	1st Purse
2005	Afleet Alex, 3, 122	J. Rose	Flower Alley, 3, 122	Andromeda's Hero, 3, 122	10	1:48.80	$600,000
2004	Smarty Jones, 3, 122	S. Elliott	Borrego, 3, 118	Pro Prado, 3, 122	11	1:49.41	600,000
2003	Sir Cherokee, 3, 118	T. J. Thompson	Eugene's Third Son, 3, 118	Christine's Outlaw, 3, 118	12	1:48.39	300,000
2002	Private Emblem, 3, 122	D. J. Meche	Wild Horses, 3, 118	dh- Bay Monster, 3, 118	11	1:52.20	300,000
				dh- Windward Passage, 3, 122			
2001	Balto Star, 3, 122	M. Guidry	Jamaican Rum, 3, 122	Son of Rocket, 3, 122	11	1:49.04	300,000
2000	Graeme Hall, 3, 118	R. Albarado	Snuck In, 3, 122	Impeachment, 3, 118	14	1:49.08	300,000
1999	‡Certain, 3, 122	K. J. Desormeaux	Torrid Sand, 3, 118	Ecton Park, 3, 122	7	1:49.30	300,000
1998	Victory Gallop, 3, 122	A. O. Solis	Hanuman Highway (Ire), 3, 118	Favorite Trick, 3, 122	9	1:49.86	300,000
1997	Crypto Star, 3, 122	P. Day	Phantom On Tour, 3, 122	Pacificbounty, 3, 122	11	1:49.20	300,000
1996	Zarb's Magic, 3, 122	D. R. Ardoin	Grindstone, 3, 122	Halo Sunshine, 3, 122	12	1:49.21	300,000
1995	Dazzling Falls, 3, 122	G. K. Gomez	Flitch, 3, 118	On Target, 3, 122	8	1:50.60	300,000
1994	Concern, 3, 118	G. K. Gomez	Blumin Affair, 3, 118	Silver Goblin, 3, 122	9	1:48.16	300,000
1993	Rockamundo, 3, 118	C. H. Borel	Kissin Kris, 3, 122	Foxtrail, 3, 122	10	1:48.17	300,000
1992	Pine Bluff, 3, 122	J. D. Bailey	Lil E. Tee, 3, 122	Desert Force, 3, 122	6	1:49.49	300,000
1991	Olympio, 3, 122	E. J. Delahoussaye	Corporate Report, 3, 118	Richman, 3, 122	11	1:47.67	300,000
1990	Silver Ending, 3, 122	G. L. Stevens	Real Cash, 3, 122	Power Lunch, 3, 118	13	1:48.00	300,000
1989	Dansil, 3, 121	L. Snyder	Clever Trevor, 3, 126	Advocate Training, 3, 115	11	1:49.20	240,000
1988	Proper Reality, 3, 118	J. D. Bailey	Primal, 3, 115	Sea Trek, 3, 123	8	1:48.40	300,000
1987	Demons Begone, 3, 123	P. Day	Lookinforthebigone, 3, 118	You're No Bargain, 3, 115	14	1:48.20	300,000
1986	Rampage, 3, 118	P. Day	Wheatly Hall, 3, 115	†Family Style, 3, 121	11	1:48.40	300,000
1985	Tank's Prospect, 3, 123	G. L. Stevens	Encolure, 3, 126	Irish Fighter, 3, 115	9	1:48.40	349,650
1984	†Althea, 3, 122	P. A. Valenzuela	Pine Circle, 3, 118	Gate Dancer, 3, 118	11	**1:46.80**	360,150
1983	Sunny's Halo, 3, 126	E. J. Delahoussaye	Caveat, 3, 120	Exile King, 3, 117	14	1:49.40	176,340
1982	Hostage, 3, 117	J. Fell	El Baba, 3, 126	Bold Style, 3, 123	10	1:51.60	170,580
1981	Bold Ego, 3, 123	J. L. Lively	Top Avenger, 3, 120	Woodchopper, 3, 123	9	1:50.40	137,160

1980	**Temperence Hill**, 3, 123	D. Haire	Bold 'n Rulling, 3, 117	Sun Catcher, 3, 120	10	1:50.60	$107,160
1979	**Golden Act**, 3, 126	S. Hawley	Smarten, 3, 120	Strike the Main, 3, 115	10	1:50.00	107,280
1978	**Esops Foibles**, 3, 126	C. J. McCarron	Chief of Dixieland, 3, 117	Special Honor, 3, 120	13	1:52.20	82,470
1977	**Clev Er Tell**, 3, 126	R. Broussard	Kodiack, 3, 117	Best Person, 3, 117	12	1:50.60	80,520
1976	**Elocutionist**, 3, 126	J. L. Lively	New Collection, 3, 117	Klen Klitso, 3, 120	12	1:49.20	81,480
1975	**Promised City**, 3, 126	D. E. Whited	Bold Chapeau, 3, 117	My Friend Gus, 3, 120	14	1:51.80	82,140
1974	**J. R.'s Pet**, 3, 123	D. G. McHargue	Silver Florin, 3, 120	Nick's Folly, 3, 120	17	1:50.60	86,910
1973	**Impecunious**, 3, 126	J. Velasquez	Vodika, 3, 123	Warbucks, 3, 123	10	1:49.60	74,130

Named Arkansas Centennial Derby in honor of the 100th anniversary of the founding of the state of Arkansas in 1936. Grade 1 1981-'88. Not held 1945. Dead heat for third 2002. ‡Valhol finished first, DQ to seventh for jockey's use of an illegal electrical stimulation device, 1999. †Denotes female.

Arlington Classic Stakes

Grade 3 in 2005. Arlington Park, three-olds, 1¹⁄₁₆ miles, turf. Held July 3, 2004, with a gross value of $200,000. First held in 1929. First graded in 1973. Stakes record 1:41.95 (2002 Mr. Mellon).

Year	Winner	Jockey	Second	Third	Strs	Time	1st Purse
2004	**Toasted**, 3, 121	R. R. Douglas	Street Theatre, 3, 119	Cool Conductor, 3, 119	8	1:50.91	$120,000
2003	**Lismore Knight**, 3, 119	R. R. Douglas	Remind, 3, 116	Good Day Too (Ire), 3, 116	10	1:42.73	105,000
2002	**Mr. Mellon**, 3, 121	R. R. Douglas	Doc Holiday (Ire), 3, 121	Seainsky, 3, 116	9	**1:41.95**	105,000
2001	**Baptize**, 3, 121	M. Guidry	Indygo Shiner, 3, 114	Cherokee Kim, 3, 116	6	1:48.80	120,000
2000	**King Cugat**, 3, 123	R. Albarado	Boyum, 3, 114	El Ballezano, 3, 114	5	1:48.16	90,000
1997	**Honor Glide**, 3, 114	G. K. Gomez	Brave Act (GB), 3, 120	Daylight Savings, 3, 114	8	1:47.59	75,000
1996	**Trail City**, 3, 114	P. Day	More Royal, 3, 120	Winter Quarters, 3, 114	5	1:48.61	120,000
1995	**Hawk Attack**, 3, 114	P. Day	Via Lombardia (Ire), 3, 120	Bryntirion, 3, 114	10	1:48.04	120,000
1994	**Eagle Eyed**, 3, 120	C. S. Nakatani	Mr. Angel, 3, 114	Star Campaigner, 3, 114	11	1:48.46	180,000
1993	**Boundlessly**, 3, 120	P. Day	Hegar, 3, 114	Williamstown, 3, 123	13	1:49.89	180,000
1992	**Saint Ballado**, 3, 120	J. A. Krone	Desert Force, 3, 114	Star Recruit, 3, 117	6	1:46.82	180,000
1991	**Whadjathink**, 3, 120	J. Velasquez	Freezing Dock, 3, 114	Character (GB), 3, 120	4	1:49.18	180,000
1990	**Sound of Cannons**, 3, 114	P. Day	Adjudicating, 3, 117	Home At Last, 3, 123	7	1:47.40	150,000
1989	**Clever Trevor**, 3, 126	D. R. Pettinger	Bio, 3, 114	Western Playboy, 3, 126	8	1:49.40	124,500
1987	**Lost Code**, 3, 123	G. St. Leon	Gem Master, 3, 120	Avies Copy, 3, 120	7	1:49.60	99,090
1986	**Sumptious**, 3, 115	R. P. Romero	Glow, 3, 120	Cheapskate, 3, 123	13	1:49.40	96,720
1985	**Smile**, 3, 117	J. Vasquez	Red Attack, 3, 114	Clever Allemont, 3, 123	6	1:51.20	114,000
1984	**At the Threshold**, 3, 126	P. Day	Par Flite, 3, 114	Dugan Knight, 3, 114	8	1:50.20	71,400
1983	**Play Fellow**, 3, 123	P. Day	Bet Big, 3, 114	Passing Base, 3, 114	9	1:49.00	65,400
1982	**Wolfie's Rascal**, 3, 114	A. T. Cordero Jr.	Drop Your Drawers, 3, 114	Dew Line, 3, 114	13	1:49.00	72,600
1981	**Fairway Phantom**, 3, 114	J. L. Lively	Golden Derby, 3, 114	Television Studio, 3, 117	11	1:53.40	84,000
1980	**Spruce Needles**, 3, 114	M. R. Morgan	I'ma Hell Raiser, 3, 114	Stone Manor, 3, 126	6	1:49.20	81,000
1979	**Steady Growth**, 3, 123	B. Swatuk	Private Account, 3, 114	Third and Lex, 3, 114	5	2:00.60	65,400
1978	**Alydar**, 3, 126	J. Fell	Chief of Dixieland, 3, 114	Gordie H., 3, 114	5	2:00.40	63,000
1977	**Private Thoughts**, 4, 117	R. R. Perez	Pay Tribute, 5, 118	Dragset, 6, 114	9	1:59.40	90,000
1973	**Linda's Chief**, 3, 123	B. Baeza	Blue Chip Dan, 3, 114	Golden Don, 3, 114	8	1:44.60	72,200

Formerly sponsored by General Motors Corp. of Detroit, Michigan 1971-'73. Grade 1 1981-'89. Not graded 1977. Classic S. 1929-'45. Pontiac Grand Prix S. 1971-'73. Held at Washington Park 1943-'45. Not held 1974-'76, 1988, 1998-'99. 1¼ miles 1929-'51, 1977-'79. 1 mile 1952-'72. 1⅛ miles 1980-2001. Dirt 1929-'93. Three-year-olds and up 1977. Equaled course record 1997.

Arlington Handicap

Grade 3 in 2005. Arlington Park, three-year-olds and up, 1¼ miles, turf. Held July 24, 2004, with a gross value of $250,000. First held in 1929. First graded in 1973. Stakes record 2:00.40 (1985 Pass the Line).

Year	Winner	Jockey	Second	Third	Strs	Time	1st Purse
2004	**Senor Swinger**, 4, 118	B. Blanc	Mystery Giver, 6, 120	Ballingarry (Ire), 5, 121	7	2:03.38	$150,000
2003	**Honor in War**, 4, 120	D. R. Flores	Better Talk Now, 4, 115	Mystery Giver, 5, 118	10	2:02.71	150,000
2002	**Falcon Flight (Fr)**, 6, 115	R. R. Douglas	Kappa King, 5, 117	Gretchen's Star, 7, 115	10	2:03.13	135,000
2001	**Make No Mistake (Ire)**, 6, 116	R. Albarado	Takarian (Ire), 6, 116	El Gran Papa, 4, 115	7	2:02.53	150,000
2000	**Northern Quest (Fr)**, 5, 113	R. Albarado	Profit Option, 5, 112	Where's Taylor, 4, 114	11	2:02.13	90,000
1997	**Wild Event**, 4, 114	M. Guidry	Storm Trooper, 4, 114	Chorwon, 4, 113	4	2:01.52	90,000
1996	**Torch Rouge (GB)**, 5, 116	M. Guidry	Sentimental Moi, 6, 113	Volochine (Ire), 5, 115	6	2:03.32	120,000
1995	**Manilaman**, 4, 114	R. P. Romero	Snake Eyes, 5, 117	Bluegrass Prince (Ire), 4, 117	7	2:02.82	120,000
1994	**Fanmore**, 6, 119	P. Day	Marastani, 4, 114	Split Run, 6, 114	7	2:01.72	150,000
1993	**Evanescent**, 6, 114	A. T. Gryder	Split Run, 5, 113	Magesterial Cheer, 5, 112	9	2:00.93	150,000
1992	**Sky Classic**, 5, 125	P. Day	‡Duckaroo, 6, 111	Glity, 4, 116	9	2:00.62	150,000
1991	**Filago**, 4, 116	P. A. Valenzuela	Super Abound, 4, 113	Izvestia, 4, 120	12	2:01.40	150,000
1990	**Pleasant Variety**, 6, 115	E. Fires	Double Booked, 5, 114	Ten Keys, 6, 121	7	2:04.00	180,000
1989	**Unknown Quantity (GB)**, 4, 112	J. Velasquez	Frosty the Snowman, 4, 122	Delegant, 5, 113	5	2:11.20	120,000
1987	**Ifrad**, 5, 114	G. Baze	Storm On the Loose, 4, 115	Grey Classic, 4, 114	8	2:12.20	90,360
1986	**Mourjane (Ire)**, 6, 117	J. A. Santos	Will Dancer (Fr), 4, 115	Clever Song, 4, 118	9	2:01.40	112,350
1985	**Pass the Line**, 4, 113	J. L. Diaz	The Noble Player, 5, 118	Executive Pride (Ire), 4, 113	7	**2:00.40**	82,050
1984	**Who's for Dinner**, 5, 109	M. Venezia	Nijinsky's Secret, 6, 127	Star Choice, 5, 112	7	2:04.00	70,800
1983	**Palikaraki (Fr)**, 5, 116	W. Shoemaker	Rossi Gold, 7, 122	Late Act, 4, 113	11	2:35.80	76,200

Year Winner	Jockey	Second	Third	Strs	Time	1st Purse
1982 **Flying Target**, 5, 115	R. W. Cox	Rossi Gold, 6, 125	Don Roberto, 5, 118	8	2:32.40	$71,640
1981 **Spruce Needles**, 4, 115	J. C. Espinoza	Summer Advocate, 4, 117	Sea Chimes (Ire), 5, 116	8	2:35.00	72,060
1980 **Yvonand (Fr)**, 4, 111	E. Beitia	Rossi Gold, 4, 120	Lyphard's Wish (Fr), 4, 121	8	2:31.40	71,700
1979 **Bowl Game**, 5, 124	J. Velasquez	Young Bob, 4, 110	†Liveinthesunshine, 4, 105	14	2:32.20	79,260
1978 **Romeo**, 5, 116	E. Fires	Fluorescent Light, 4, 118	Improviser, 6, 118	9	2:32.00	73,080
1977 **Cunning Trick**, 4, 110	B. Fann	‡*Vadim, 7, 118	No Turning, 4, 118	8	2:33.80	72,480
1976 **Victorian Prince**, 6, 118	R. Platts	Improviser, 4, 118	Bold Roll, 4, 112	12	1:58.20	90,000
1975 **Royal Glint**, 5, 125	J. E. Tejeira	*Zografos, 7, 113	Buffalo Lark, 5, 122	9	1:55.80	87,400
1974 **Buffalo Lark**, 4, 118	L. Snyder	Royal Glint, 4, 112	Spot T V, 7, 111	13	1:54.40	91,800
1973 **Dubassoff**, 4, 117	J. Vasquez	Jogging, 6, 114	Red Reality, 7, 118	14	1:58.60	72,750

Grade 2 1973-'80, 1990-'97. Grade 1 1981-'89. Arlington Park H. 1963, 1972, 1974. Held at Washington Park 1943-'45. Held at Hawthorne Race Course 1985. Not held 1940, 1969-'71, 1988, 1998-'99. 1 1/8 miles 1929, 1952, 1965. 1 3/16 miles 1941, 1953-'62, 1964, 1973-'76. 1 mile 1963, 1966-'67. 7 furlongs 1968. 1 1/2 miles 1972, 1977-'83. Dirt 1929-'39, 1942-'53, 1963, 1965-'72. Originally scheduled on turf 1975. ‡No Turning finished second, DQ to third, 1977. ‡Plate Dancer finished second, DQ to fifth, 1992. Track record 1975. †Denotes female.

Arlington Matron Handicap

Grade 3 in 2005. Arlington Park, three-year-olds and up, fillies and mares, 1 1/8 miles, dirt. Held September 4, 2004, with a gross value of $150,000. First held in 1930. First graded in 1973. Stakes record 1:48.40 (1986 Queen Alexandra, 1989 Between the Hedges).

Year Winner	Jockey	Second	Third	Strs	Time	1st Purse
2004 **Adoration**, 5, 123	V. Espinoza	Tamweel, 4, 116	Indy Groove, 4, 116	7	1:49.75	$90,000
2003 **Take Charge Lady**, 4, 123	S. J. Sellers	Lakenheath, 5, 116	To the Queen, 4, 117	6	1:50.19	90,000
2002 **Lakenheath**, 4, 115	C. A. Emigh	With Ability, 4, 116	Your Out, 4, 115	5	1:50.78	90,000
2001 **Humble Clerk**, 4, 114	L. J. Melancon	Maltese Superb, 4, 115	Lakenheath, 3, 115	7	1:51.53	90,000
2000 **Megans Bluff**, 3, 111	C. R. Woods Jr.	On a Soapbox, 4, 115	Tutorial, 4, 113	6	1:51.41	90,000
1997 **Omi**, 4, 114	M. Guidry	Gold Memory, 4, 115	Trick Attack, 6, 114	6	1:51.93	60,000
1996 **Belle of Cozzene**, 4, 115	D. R. Pettinger	War Thief, 4, 116	Your Ladyship, 6, 116	9	1:49.34	75,000
1995 **Mariah's Storm**, 4, 117	R. N. Lester	Mysteriously, 4, 117	Minority Dater, 4, 114	8	1:50.98	60,000
1994 **Hey Hazel**, 4, 115	M. G. Pino	Passing Vice, 4, 114	Pennyhill Park, 4, 116	8	1:49.58	60,000
1993 **Erica's Dream**, 5, 115	W. Martinez	Pleasant Jolie, 5, 114	Meafara, 4, 123	6	1:50.09	45,000
1992 **Lemhi Go**, 4, 114	E. Fires	Beth Believes, 6, 112	Diamond City, 4, 113	6	1:49.67	45,000
1991 **Lucky Lady Lauren**, 4, 112	J. Velasquez	Beth Believes, 5, 113	Bungalow, 4, 112	6	1:49.21	45,000
1990 **Degenerate Gal**, 5, 115	R. P. Romero	Evangelica, 4, 115	Confirmed Dancer, 4, 113	10	1:49.20	48,555
1989 **Between the Hedges**, 5, 112	P. A. Johnson	Topicount, 4, 116	Stoneleigh's Hope, 4, 114	10	**1:48.40**	65,010
1987 **Family Style**, 4, 123	S. Hawley	Royal Cielo, 3, 113	Tide, 5, 114	7	1:52.20	49,320
1986 **Queen Alexandra**, 4, 122	D. Brumfield	Mr. T.'s Tune, 5, 113	Bessarabian, 4, 121	6	**1:48.40**	92,220
1985 **Heatherten**, 6, 126	R. P. Romero	Solo Skater, 5, 112	Mr. T.'s Tune, 4, 114	8	2:04.00	49,410
1984 **Choose a Partner**, 4, 116	D. Brumfield	First Flurry, 5, 113	Silvered Silk, 4, 117	7	2:04.00	62,595
1983 **May Day Eighty**, 4, 115	J. Vasquez	Sefa's Beauty, 4, 125	Stay a Leader, 4, 113	10	2:04.40	50,355
1982 **Sweetest Chant**, 4, 115	E. Fires	Miss Huntington, 5, 119	Turnablade, 5, 115	7	2:02.60	48,960
1981 **La Bonzo**, 5, 110	J. L. Lively	Wistful, 4, 123	Weber City Miss, 4, 123	8	2:02.60	66,360
1980 **Impetuous Gal**, 5, 115	E. Fires	Salzburg, 5, 112	Liveinthesunshine, 5, 108	10	2:01.40	67,200
1979 **Amerigirl**, 4, 115	B. Swatuk	Frosty Skater, 4, 118	Calderina (Ity), 4, 122	10	1:51.20	52,800
1978 **Rich Soil**, 4, 117	C. H. Silva	Satan's Cheer, 6, 112	Sans Arc, 4, 113	11	1:51.20	38,340
1977 **Javamine**, 4, 119	J. Velasquez	*Star Ball, 5, 119	Ivory Castle, 3, 110	9	1:53.20	52,620
1976 **Nicosia**, 4, 118	W. Gavidia	B. J. King, 4, 111	Hope of Glory, 4, 109	9	1:49.40	45,450
Cycylya Zee, 3, 110	H. Arroyo	Sugar Plum Time, 4, 115	True Reality, 3, 109	9	1:49.60	46,200
1975 ***Polynesienne**, 4, 110	L. Snyder	Princesse Grey, 4, 110	Pass a Glance, 4, 116	9	1:51.80	45,050
Sixty Sails, 5, 114	L. Snyder	Victorian Queen, 4, 118	Princess Ormea, 3, 110	8	1:52.80	45,050
1974 **Sixty Sails**, 4, 121	D. E. Whited	*Protectora, 5, 113	What Will Be, 4, 118	14	1:50.60	46,300
1973 ***Last Home**, 4, 112	F. Alvarez	North Broadway, 3, 115	Ziba Blue, 6, 114	12	1:50.00	35,800

Matron races are traditionally held for older fillies and mares. Grade 2 1973-'89. Matron H. 1964-'83. Held at Washington Park 1943-'45. Held at Hawthorne Race Course 1985. Not held 1933-'36, 1988, 1998-'99. 1 mile 1930-'57. 1 1/4 miles 1980-'85. Turf 1966-'79. Three-year-olds 1952. Fillies 1952. Two divisions 1975-'76.

Arlington Million Stakes

Grade 1 in 2005. Arlington Park, three-year-olds and up, 1 1/4 miles, turf. Held August 14, 2004, with a gross value of $1,000,000. First held in 1981. First graded in 1983. Stakes record 1:58.69 (1995 Awad).

Year Winner	Jockey	Second	Third	Strs	Time	1st Purse
2004 ‡**Kicken Kris**, 4, 126	K. J. Desormeaux	Magistretti, 4, 126	Epalo (Ger), 5, 126	13	2:00.08	$600,000
2003 ‡**Sulamani (Ire)**, 4, 126	D. R. Flores	dh-Kaieteur, 4, 126 dh-Paolini (Ger), 6, 126		13	2:02.29	600,000
2002 **Beat Hollow (GB)**, 5, 126	J. D. Bailey	Sarafan, 5, 126	Forbidden Apple, 7, 126	9	2:02.94	600,000
2001 **Silvano (Ger)**, 5, 126	A. Suborics	Hap, 5, 126	Redattore (Brz), 6, 126	12	2:02.64	600,000
2000 **Chester House**, 5, 126	J. D. Bailey	Manndar (Ire), 4, 126	Mula Gula, 4, 126	7	2:01.37	1,200,000
1997 **Marlin**, 4, 126	G. L. Stevens	Sandpit (Brz), 8, 126	Percutant (GB), 6, 126	8	2:02.54	600,000
1996 **Mecke**, 4, 126	R. G. Davis	Awad, 6, 126	Sandpit (Brz), 7, 126	9	2:00.49	600,000
1995 **Awad**, 5, 126	E. Maple	Sandpit (Brz), 6, 126	The Vid, 5, 126	11	**1:58.69**	600,000
1994 **Paradise Creek**, 5, 126	P. Day	Fanmore, 6, 126	Muhtarram, 5, 126	14	1:59.78	600,000

Year	Winner	Jockey	Second	Third	Strs	Time	1st Purse
1993	Star of Cozzene, 5, 126	J. A. Santos	Evanescent, 6, 126	Johann Quatz (Fr), 4, 126	8	2:07.50	$600,000
1992	Dear Doctor (Fr), 5, 126	C. B. Asmussen	Sky Classic, 5, 126	Golden Pheasant, 6, 126	12	1:59.84	600,000
1991	Tight Spot, 4, 126	L. A. Pincay Jr.	Algenib (Arg), 4, 126	†Kartajana (Ire), 4, 123	10	1:59.55	600,000
1990	Golden Pheasant, 4, 126	G. L. Stevens	With Approval, 4, 126	Steinlen (GB), 7, 126	11	1:59.60	600,000
1989	Steinlen (GB), 6, 126	J. A. Santos	†Lady in Silver, 3, 117	Yankee Affair, 7, 126	13	2:03.60	600,000
1988	Mill Native, 4, 126	C. B. Asmussen	Equalize, 6, 126	Sunshine Forever, 3, 118	14	2:00.00	600,000
1987	Manila, 4, 126	A. T. Cordero Jr.	Sharrood, 4, 126	Theatrical (Ire), 5, 126	8	2:02.40	600,000
1986	†Estrapade, 6, 122	F. Toro	Divulge, 4, 126	Pennine Walk (Ire), 4, 126	14	2:00.80	600,000
1985	Teleprompter (GB), 5, 126	T. A. Ives	Greinton (GB), 4, 126	Flying Pidgeon, 4, 126	13	2:03.40	600,000
1984	John Henry, 9, 126	C. J. McCarron	†Royal Heroine (Ire), 4, 122	Gato Del Sol, 5, 126	12	2:01.40	600,000
1983	Tolomeo (Ire), 3, 118	P. Eddery	John Henry, 8, 126	Nijinsky's Secret, 5, 126	14	2:04.40	600,000
1982	Perrault (GB), 5, 126	L. A. Pincay Jr.	Be My Native, 3, 118	Motavato, 4, 126	14	1:58.80	600,000
1981	John Henry, 6, 126	W. Shoemaker	The Bart, 5, 126	†Madam Gay (GB), 3, 117	12	2:07.60	600,000

First million-dollar Thoroughbred race in North America. Formerly sponsored by the Anheuser-Busch Co. of St. Louis, Missouri 1982-'87. Arlington Million Invitational S. 1981. Budweiser Million S. 1982-'84. Budweiser-Arlington Million 1985-'87. Held at Woodbine Race Course 1989. Not held 1998-'99. Dead heat for second 2003. ‡Powerscourt (GB) finished first, DQ to fourth, 2004. ‡Storming Home (GB) finished first, DQ to fourth, 2003. Course record 1995. †Denotes female.

Arlington-Washington Breeders' Cup Futurity

Grade 3 in 2005. Arlington Park, two-year-olds, 1 mile, dirt. Held September 19, 2004, with a gross value of $200,000. First held in 1927. First graded in 1973. Stakes record 1:35.44 (2003 Cactus Ridge).

Year	Winner	Jockey	Second	Third	Strs	Time	1st Purse
2004	Three Hour Nap, 2, 119	E. Razo Jr.	dh-Elusive Chris, 2, 122 dh-Straight Line, 2, 119		6	1:38.56	$120,000
2003	Cactus Ridge, 2, 122	E. M. Martin Jr.	Glittergem, 2, 117	Texas Deputy, 2, 119	6	1:35.44	90,000
2002	Most Feared, 2, 122	M. Guidry	Anasheed, 2, 122	Unleash the Power, 2, 122	10	1:37.52	90,000
2001	Publication, 2, 122	R. A. Meier	It'sallinthechase, 2, 122	Dubai Squire, 2, 122	7	1:38.78	90,000
2000	Trailthefox, 2, 121	S. J. Sellers	Starbury, 2, 121	Blame It On Ruby, 2, 121	11	1:37.25	90,000
1997	Cowboy Dan, 2, 121	D. Kutz	Captain Maestri, 2, 121	Fiamma, 2, 121	9	1:37.68	90,000
1996	Night in Reno, 2, 121	M. Guidry	Flying With Eagles, 2, 121	Thisnearlywasmine, 2, 121	8	1:36.67	120,000
1994	Evansville Slew, 2, 121	P. Compton	Valid Wager, 2, 121	Mr Purple, 2, 121	9	1:37.84	120,000
1993	Polar Expedition, 2, 121	C. C. Bourque	Gimme Glory, 2, 121	Delicate Cure, 2, 121	6	1:39.28	120,000
1992	Gilded Time, 2, 121	C. J. McCarron	Boundlessly, 2, 121	Rockamundo, 2, 121	6	1:37.84	200,580
1991	Caller I. D., 2, 121	J. D. Bailey	Count the Time, 2, 121	West by West, 2, 121	7	1:36.01	188,880
1990	Hansel, 2, 122	P. Day	Walesa, 2, 122	Discover, 2, 122	7	1:36.40	220,440
1989	Secret Hello, 2, 122	A. T. Gryder	Richard R., 2, 122	Bite the Bullet, 2, 122	6	1:35.80	220,860
1987	Tejano, 2, 122	J. Vasquez	Jim's Orbit, 2, 122	Native Stalwart, 2, 122	7	1:36.20	247,080
1986	Bet Twice, 2, 122	C. Perret	Conquistarose, 2, 122	Jazzing Around, 2, 122	11	1:37.20	300,420
1985	Meadowlake, 2, 122	J. L. Diaz	Bar Tender, 2, 122	Papal Power, 2, 122	6	1:16.80	286,320
1984	Spend a Buck, 2, 122	C. Hussey	Dusty's Darby, 2, 122	Viva Maxi, 2, 122	7	1:38.00	355,320
1983	All Fired Up, 2, 122	R. D. Evans	Holme On Top, 2, 122	Smart n Slick, 2, 122	17	1:27.00	330,135
1982	Total Departure, 2, 122	E. Fires	Coax Me Matt, 2, 122	Highland Park, 2, 122	8	1:23.60	271,515
1981	Lets Dont Fight, 2, 122	J. L. Lively	Tropic Ruler, 2, 122	Music Leader, 2, 122	15	1:29.20	305,385
1980	Well Decorated, 2, 122	L. A. Pincay Jr.	Lord Avie, 2, 122	Fairway Phantom, 2, 122	15	1:23.80	240,885
1979	Execution's Reason, 2, 122	E. J. Delahoussaye	Preemptive, 2, 122	Brent's Trans Am, 2, 122	9	1:22.40	89,790
1978	Jose Binn, 2, 122	A. T. Cordero Jr.	Exuberant, 2, 122	Strike Your Colors, 2, 122	12	1:17.40	120,660
1977	Sauce Boat, 2, 122	S. Cauthen	Gonquin, 2, 122	Forever Casting, 2, 122	14	1:16.60	130,665
1976	Run Dusty Run, 2, 122	D. G. McHargue	Royal Ski, 2, 122	Eagletar, 2, 122	11	1:16.40	120,465
1975	Honest Pleasure, 2, 122	D. G. McHargue	Khyber King, 2, 122	Rule the Ridge, 2, 122	19	1:18.40	140,610
1974	Greek Answer, 2, 122	M. A. Castaneda	Colonel Power, 2, 122	The Bagel Prince, 2, 122	7	1:17.80	122,505
1973	Lover John, 2, 122	R. N. Ussery	Beau Groton, 2, 122	Hula Chief, 2, 122	9	1:11.60	97,470

Merged with old Washington Park Futurity, renamed after closure of Washington Park. Grade 1 1973-'89. Grade 2 1990-2001. American National Futurity 1927-'28. Arlington Futurity 1932-'61. Held at Washington Park 1943-'45. Held at Hawthorne Race Course 1985. Not held 1929-'31, 1970, 1988, 1995, 1998-'99. 6 furlongs 1927-'61, 1971-'73. 7 furlongs 1962-'69, 1979-'83. 6½ furlongs 1974-'78, 1985. Colts and geldings 1973-'83. Dead heat for second 2004.

Arlington-Washington Lassie Stakes

Grade 3 in 2005. Arlington Park, two-year-olds, fillies, 1 mile, dirt. Held September 19, 2004, with a gross value of $100,000. First held in 1929. First graded in 1973. Stakes record 1:36.02 (2003 Zosima).

Year	Winner	Jockey	Second	Third	Strs	Time	1st Purse
2004	Culinary, 2, 116	C. H. Marquez Jr.	Runway Model, 2, 118	Kota, 2, 118	8	1:36.98	$60,000
2003	Zosima, 2, 118	P. Day	Everyday Angel, 2, 116	Cryptos' Best, 2, 118	10	1:36.02	60,000
2002	Moonlight Sonata, 2, 121	S. Laviolette	Parting, 2, 121	Souris, 2, 121	13	1:37.82	60,000
2001	Joanies Bella, 2, 121	M. St. Julien	Brief Bliss, 2, 121	First Again, 2, 121	9	1:39.34	60,000
2000	Thunder Bertie, 2, 119	J. Beasley	Caressing, 2, 119	Zahwah, 2, 119	10	1:36.91	60,000
1997	Silver Maiden, 2, 119	B. S. Laviolette	Arctic Lady, 2, 119	So Generous, 2, 119	6	1:37.54	60,000
1996	Southern Playgirl, 2, 119	R. P. Romero	Leo's Gypsy Dancer, 2, 119	Broad Dynamite, 2, 119	7	1:37.84	60,000
1994	Shining Light, 2, 119	J. L. Diaz	She's a Lively One, 2, 119	Alltheway Bertie, 2, 119	5	1:41.70	90,000
1993	Mariah's Storm, 2, 119	R. N. Lester	Shapely Scrapper, 2, 119	Minority Dater, 2, 119	14	1:38.95	90,000
1992	Eliza, 2, 119	P. A. Valenzuela	Banshee Winds, 2, 119	Tourney, 2, 119	6	1:39.58	134,850
1991	Speed Dialer, 2, 119	P. Day	Cadillac Women, 2, 119	Mystic Hawk, 2, 119	7	1:36.58	141,390

Year	Winner	Jockey	Second	Third	Strs	Time	1st Purse
1990	Through Flight, 2, 120	J. M. Johnson	Good Potential, 2, 120	Wild for Traci, 2, 120	6	1:39.00	$138,870
1989	Trumpet's Blare, 2, 120	L. A. Pincay Jr.	Special Happening, 2, 122	Puffy Doodle, 2, 122	6	1:38.60	128,040
1987	Joe's Tammie, 2, 122	C. Perret	Tomorrow's Child, 2, 122	Pearlie Gold, 2, 122	6	1:25.00	186,840
1986	Delicate Vine, 2, 122	G. L. Stevens	Sacahuista, 2, 122	Ruling Angel, 2, 122	6	1:23.40	165,660
1985	Family Style, 2, 119	L. A. Pincay Jr.	Deep Silver, 2, 119	Pamela Kay, 2, 119	8	1:18.00	250,200
1984	Contredance, 2, 119	P. Day	Tiltalating, 2, 119	Miss Delice, 2, 119	5	1:26.00	211,560
1983	Miss Oceana, 2, 119	E. Maple	Life's Magic, 2, 119	Bottle Top, 2, 119	11	1:23.40	112,146
1982	For Once'n My Life, 2, 119	E. Maple	Some Kinda Flirt, 2, 119	How Clever, 2, 119	8	1:23.40	106,461
1981	Milingo, 2, 119	R. Sibille	Maniches, 2, 119	Justa Little One, 2, 119	15	1:25.20	129,798
1980	Truly Bound, 2, 119	W. Shoemaker	Safe Play, 2, 119	Masters Dream, 2, 119	11	1:25.20	83,022
1979	Sissy's Time, 2, 119	E. Fires	Ellie Milove, 2, 119	Vogue Folks, 2, 119	6	1:11.00	63,399
1978	It's in the Air, 2, 119	E. J. Delahoussaye	Angel Island, 2, 119	Bequa, 2, 119	8	1:09.60	71,394
1977	Stub, 2, 119	R. Turcotte	Rainy Princess, 2, 119	Go Line, 2, 119	13	1:10.40	70,329
1976	Special Warmth, 2, 119	S. Maple	Wavy Waves, 2, 119	Drama Critic, 2, 119	10	1:10.40	68,700
1975	Dearly Precious, 2, 119	M. Hole	Free Journey, 2, 119	Head Spy, 2, 119	12	1:11.20	67,938
1974	Hot n Nasty, 2, 119	D. G. McHargue	Sharm a Sheikh, 2, 119	Mystery Mood, 2, 119	10	1:11.40	64,386
1973	Special Team, 2, 119	A. Pineda	Thirty One Jewels, 2, 119	Two Timing Lass, 2, 119	9	1:11.00	59,574

Merged with old Washington Park Lassie S., renamed after closure of Washington Park. Grade 2 1976-'80, 1990-'97. Grade 1 1981-'89. Lassie S. 1929-'31. Arlington Lassie S. 1932-'62. Held at Washington Park 1943-'45. Not held 1970-'71, 1988, 1995, 1998-'99. 5½ furlongs 1929-'31. 7 furlongs 1932, 1980-'84, 1986-'87. 6 furlongs 1933-'61, 1972-'79. 6½ furlongs 1962-'69, 1985.

Ashland Stakes

Grade 1 in 2005. Keeneland, three-year-olds, fillies, 1 1/16 miles, dirt. Held April 9, 2005, with a gross value of $500,000. First held in 1879. First graded in 1973. Stakes record 1:41.72 (1999 Silverbulletday).

Year	Winner	Jockey	Second	Third	Strs	Time	1st Purse
2005	Sis City, 3, 121	E. S. Prado	Runway Model, 3, 121	Memorette, 3, 121	6	1:46.35	$310,000
2004	Madcap Escapade, 3, 118	R. R. Douglas	Ashado, 3, 123	Last Song, 3, 120	4	1:44.55	310,000
2003	Elloluv, 3, 120	R. Albarado	Lady Tak, 3, 123	Holiday Lady, 3, 116	7	1:43.58	342,085
2002	Take Charge Lady, 3, 123	A. J. D'Amico	Take the Cake, 3, 118	Belterra, 3, 120	8	1:43.29	345,805
2001	Fleet Renee, 3, 116	J. R. Velazquez	Golden Ballet, 3, 123	Latour, 3, 120	11	1:43.77	357,275
2000	Rings a Chime, 3, 116	S. J. Sellers	Zoftig, 3, 116	Circle of Life, 3, 116	6	1:44.43	341,155
1999	Silverbulletday, 3, 123	J. D. Bailey	Marley Vale, 3, 115	Gold From the West, 3, 115	6	1:41.72	337,280
1998	Well Chosen, 3, 115	C. R. Woods Jr.	Let, 3, 115	Banshee Breeze, 3, 120	7	1:43.00	344,410
1997	Glitter Woman, 3, 121	M. E. Smith	Anklet, 3, 121	Storm Song, 3, 121	6	1:43.80	337,125
1996	My Flag, 3, 121	J. D. Bailey	Cara Rafaela, 3, 121	Mackie, 3, 118	5	1:42.69	335,265
1995	Urbane, 3, 115	E. J. Delahoussaye	Conquistadoress, 3, 115	Post It, 3, 121	6	1:43.41	207,483
1994	Inside Information, 3, 121	M. E. Smith	Bunting, 3, 115	Private Status, 3, 118	6	1:46.99	171,198
1993	Lunar Spook, 3, 121	S. J. Sellers	Avie's Shadow, 3, 115	Roamin Rachel, 3, 115	7	1:43.43	171,973
1992	Prospectors Delite, 3, 121	C. Perret	Spinning Round, 3, 121	Luv Me Luv Me Not, 3, 121	10	1:42.65	186,063
1991	Do It With Style, 3, 115	S. J. Sellers	Private Treasure, 3, 121	Til Forbid, 3, 112	7	1:43.67	182,894
1990	Go for Wand, 3, 121	R. P. Romero	Charon, 3, 121	Piper Piper, 3, 112	5	1:43.60	145,665
1989	Gorgeous, 3, 118	E. J. Delahoussaye	Blondeinamotel, 3, 115	Some Romance, 3, 121	13	1:43.20	157,430
1988	Willa On the Move, 3, 118	C. J. McCarron	On to Royalty, 3, 121	Colonial Waters, 3, 121	11	1:45.80	151,125
1987	Chic Shirine, 3, 118	S. Hawley	Buryyourbelief, 3, 112	Our Little Margie, 3, 113	12	1:44.60	117,683
1986	Classy Cathy, 3, 116	E. Fires	She's a Mystery, 3, 116	Patricia J. K., 3, 121	11	1:44.00	116,513
1985	Koluctoo's Jill, 3, 116	R. P. Romero	Lucy Manette, 3, 121	Foxy Deen, 3, 121	7	1:44.40	74,718
1984	Enumerating, 3, 114	D. Brumfield	Miss Oceana, 3, 121	Rose of Ashes, 3, 113	4	1:49.20	88,707
1983	Princess Rooney, 3, 121	J. Vasquez	Shamivor, 3, 114	Decision, 3, 116	6	1:45.40	74,133
1982	Blush With Pride, 3, 118	W. Shoemaker	Exclusive Love, 3, 116	Delicate Ice, 3, 113	10	1:45.00	83,070
1981	Truly Bound, 3, 121	W. Shoemaker	Wayward Lass, 3, 121	Dame Mysterieuse, 3, 121	5	1:44.00	56,778
1980	Flos Florum, 3, 112	R. P. Romero	Cerada Ridge, 3, 114	Lady Taurian Peace, 3, 116	8	1:26.40	41,210
	Sugar and Spice, 3, 113	J. Fell	Nice and Sharp, 3, 114	Satin Ribera, 3, 116	9	1:27.20	41,210
1979	Candy Eclair, 3, 121	A. S. Black	Himalayan, 3, 114	Countess North, 3, 115	7	1:27.00	39,618
1978	Mucchina, 3, 113	J. Amy	Grenzen, 3, 121	Bold Rendezvous, 3, 118	10	1:27.20	40,527
1977	Sound of Summer, 3, 118	F. Toro	Mrs. Warren, 3, 121	Our Mims, 3, 118	9	1:26.80	40,333
1976	Optimistic Gal, 3, 121	B. Baeza	Alvarada, 3, 116	Confort Zone, 3, 113	6	1:26.80	37,895
1975	Sun and Snow, 3, 116	G. Patterson	My Juliet, 3, 116	Red Cross, 3, 114	8	1:26.60	39,488
1974	Maud Muller, 3, 114	D. Brumfield	Clemanna, 3, 113	Irish Sonnet, 3, 119	9	1:27.00	29,834
	Winged Wishes, 3, 116	D. Brumfield	Cherished Moment, 3, 117	Jay Bar Pet, 3, 113	8	1:28.80	29,786
1973	Raging Whirl, 3, 113	W. Soirez	Protest, 3, 116	A Little Lovin, 3, 110	12	1:10.80	23,611

Named for Henry Clay's home, Ashland, located in Lexington. Sponsored by Ashland Inc. of Covington, Kentucky 1996-2005. Grade 3 1973-'78. Grade 2 1979-'85. Ashland Oaks 1879-1932. Held at Kentucky Association 1932. Held at Churchill Downs 1943-'45. Not held 1897-1911, 1933-'35, 1938-'39. 1½ miles 1879-'82. 1¼ miles 1883-'89. 1 mile 1890-1926. 1 mile 70 yards 1932. 6 furlongs 1940-'73. About 7 furlongs 1974-'80. Three-year-olds and up 1936-'37. Fillies and mares 1936-'37. Two divisions 1974, 1980.

Astarita Stakes

Grade 3 in 2005. Belmont Park, two-year-olds, fillies, 6½ furlongs, dirt. Held October 17, 2004, with a gross value of $108,000. First held in 1946. First graded in 1973. Stakes record 1:16.40 (1974 Stulcer).

Year	Winner	Jockey	Second	Third	Strs	Time	1st Purse
2004	Toll Taker, 2, 117	E. Coa	Im a Dixie Girl, 2, 120	Summer Raven, 2, 117	6	1:18.16	$64,800
2003	Spectacular Moon, 2, 117	J. F. Chavez	Feline Story, 2, 120	Smokey Glacken, 2, 117	9	1:17.16	90,000

2002	Humorous Lady, 2, 117	J. D. Bailey	Fast Cookie, 2, 117	Chimichurri, 2, 117	7	1:17.76	$90,000
2001	Bella Bellucci, 2, 117	G. L. Stevens	Forest Heiress, 2, 120	Speed to Burn, 2, 117	4	1:16.67	63,955
2000	Xtra Heat, 2, 117	M. T. Johnston	Gold Mover, 2, 120	Major Wager, 2, 117	8	1:16.71	66,060
1999	Silentlea, 2, 119	R. G. Davis	Valerie's Dream, 2, 119	Lucky Livi, 2, 119	10	1:17.44	67,620
1998	Paved in Gold, 2, 119	J. F. Chavez	Blushing Deed, 2, 119	Paula's Girl, 2, 119	5	1:18.86	63,780
1997	Ninth Inning, 2, 119	R. G. Davis	Salty Perfume, 2, 119	Madam Fireplace, 2, 119	5	1:17.44	64,680
1996	Broad Dynamite, 2, 119	D. W. Cordova	Glitter Woman, 2, 119	Biding Time, 2, 119	4	1:24.02	63,960
1995	Top Secret, 2, 119	M. E. Smith	Plum Country, 2, 119	Mesabi Maiden, 2, 119	8	1:36.79	69,480
1994	Miss Golden Circle, 2, 119	J. A. Krone	Golden Bri, 2, 119	Mistress S., 2, 119	6	1:23.67	64,740
1993	Shapely Scrapper, 2, 119	J. Bravo	Brighter Course, 2, 119	Fashion Maven, 2, 119	4	1:24.02	67,560
1992	Missed the Storm, 2, 119	M. E. Smith	Dispute, 2, 119	Statuette, 2, 119	6	1:24.90	67,920
1991	Easy Now, 2, 112	M. E. Smith	Stolen Beauty, 2, 113	Celeste Cielo, 2, 112	6	1:22.84	69,240
1990	Devilish Touch, 2, 116	C. Perret	Makin Faces, 2, 112	Missy's Mirage, 2, 112	8	1:18.00	71,760
1989	Dance Colony, 2, 119	J. A. Santos	Charging Fire, 2, 114	Trumpet's Blare, 2, 114	6	1:17.80	68,640
1988	Channel Three, 2, 116	C. Barrera	Pat Copelan, 2, 119	Mistaurian, 2, 112	7	1:17.00	83,460
1987	Flashy Runner, 2, 112	J. Vasquez	Tap Your Toes, 2, 112	Galway Song, 2, 112	6	1:16.60	70,560
1986	Cagey Exuberance, 2, 116	J. Nied Jr.	Sea Basque, 2, 112	Maxi Ruler, 2, 112	6	1:18.20	51,300
1985	Guadery, 2, 112	A. T. Cordero Jr.	Musical Lark (Ire), 2, 112	I'm Sweets, 2, 112	6	1:17.00	64,800
1984	Mom's Command, 2, 116	A. Fuller	Self Image, 2, 112	Winters' Love, 2, 112	10	1:17.80	54,900
1983	Tina's Ten, 2, 112	R. Migliore	Masked Barb, 2, 116	Upturning, 2, 114	9	1:19.20	34,740
1982	Wings of Jove, 2, 112	W. H. McCauley	On the Bench, 2, 112	Bammer, 2, 112	5	1:16.80	32,220
1981	Before Dawn, 2, 119	J. Velasquez	Betty Money, 2, 112	Take Lady Anne, 2, 112	5	1:16.60	33,540
1980	Sweet Revenge, 2, 116	J. Velasquez	Expressive Dance, 2, 113	Hagley's Point, 2, 112	9	1:17.20	33,360
1979	Royal Suite, 2, 114	J. Fell	Andrea F., 2, 112	Smart Angle, 2, 116	6	1:17.20	25,815
1978	Fall Aspen, 2, 112	R. I. Velez	Whisper Fleet, 2, 112	Island Kitty, 2, 112	6	1:17.00	25,755
1977	Lakeville Miss, 2, 112	R. Hernandez	Sherry Peppers, 2, 116	Tempermental Pet, 2, 112	6	1:17.80	21,990
1976	Sensational, 2, 112	A. T. Cordero Jr.	Tickle My Toes, 2, 112	Spy Flag, 2, 112	7	1:17.40	22,185
1975	Picture Tube, 2, 113	E. Maple	La Tamborera, 2, 115	Dottie's Doll, 2, 113	11	1:18.40	23,340
1974	Stulcer, 2, 113	A. T. Cordero Jr.	Copernica, 2, 113	But Exclusive, 2, 116	8	1:16.40	17,040
1973	Raisela, 2, 113	R. Turcotte	Nancy G., 2, 113	Quick Cure, 2, 115	10	1:16.80	17,610

Named for Astarita (1900 f. by *Bathampton), first winner of the Astoria S. at Gravesend Park in 1902. Grade 2 1981-2003. New York City Astarita S. 1995. Held at Aqueduct 1946-'55, 1962-'67, 1991-'94, 1996-'97. Not held 1958-'60. 6 furlongs 1946-'56. 7 furlongs 1957-'71, 1991-'94, 1996. 1 mile 1995.

Athenia Handicap

Grade 3 in 2005. Aqueduct, three-year-olds and up, fillies and mares, 1 1/16 miles, turf. Held October 31, 2004, with a gross value of $115,700. First held in 1978. First graded in 1980. Stakes record 1:40.53 (2001 Babae [Chi] [2nd Div.]).

Year	Winner	Jockey	Second	Third	Strs	Time	1st Purse
2004	Finery, 4, 113	P. Fragoso	Madeira Mist (Ire), 5, 118	With Patience, 5, 114	11	1:43.73	$69,420
2003	Caught in the Rain, 4, 115	R. Migliore	Lojo, 4, 114	Coney Kitty (Ire), 5, 113	8	1:47.05	67,800
2002	Babae (Chi), 6, 120	J. F. Chavez	Strawberry Blonde (Ire), 4, 116	Silver Rail, 5, 112	12	1:44.90	70,020
2001	Verruma (Brz), 5, 114	J. R. Velazquez	Siringas (Ire), 3, 112	Freefourracing, 3, 113	8	1:42.09	82,725
	Babae (Chi), 5, 116	J. F. Chavez	Batique, 5, 114	Sweet Prospect (GB), 3, 110	8	1:40.53	82,725
2000	Wild Heart Dancing, 4, 115	J. F. Chavez	Fickle Friends, 4, 114	Silken (GB), 4, 114	8	1:43.40	67,500
1999	Antoniette, 4, 119	J. F. Chavez	Dominique's Joy, 4, 114	Prospectress, 4, 115	8	1:41.89	66,840
1998	Tampico, 5, 114	J. Bravo	Irish Daisy, 5, 113	Rumpipumpy (GB), 5, 115	10	1:42.90	51,210
1997	Rapid Selection, 4, 113	J. Bravo	Dynasty, 4, 114	Preachersnightmare, 4, 111	6	1:47.11	65,940
1996	Sixieme Sens, 4, 116	J. D. Bailey	Rapunzel Runz, 5, 115	Fashion Star, 4, 113	7	1:37.92	66,660
1995	Caress, 4, 114	R. G. Davis	Manila Lila, 5, 116	Vinista, 5, 119	6	1:54.18	68,340
1994	Lady Affirmed, 3, 111	J. F. Chavez	Irving's Girl, 4, 110	Cox Orange, 4, 116	11	1:48.66	52,245
1993	Trampoli, 4, 117	M. E. Smith	Kirov Premiere (GB), 3, 110	Dahlia's Dreamer, 4, 110	8	2:17.16	54,000
1992	Fairy Garden, 4, 112	J. A. Krone	Passagere du Soir (GB), 5, 117	Seewillo, 4, 113	5	2:13.62	52,020
1991	Flaming Torch (Ire), 4, 117	P. A. Valenzuela	Plenty of Grace, 4, 114	Highland Penny, 6, 116	9	2:13.99	55,800
1990	Buy the Firm, 4, 111	J. D. Bailey	Rigamajig, 4, 111	Igmaar (Fr), 4, 111	4	2:18.20	52,650
1989	Capades, 3, 115	A. T. Cordero Jr.	Miss Unnameable, 5, 114	Key Flyer, 3, 110	8	2:13.20	54,360
1988	High Browser, 3, 108	P. Day	Miss Unnameable, 4, 109	Gaily Gaily (Ire), 5, 110	12	2:18.60	57,780
1987	Lead Kindly Light, 4, 110	J. M. Pezua	Barbara's Moment, 3, 111	Spectacular Bev, 3, 114	7	2:23.80	70,920
1986	Dawn's Curtsey, 4, 111	E. Maple	Festivity, 3, 113	Perfect Point, 4, 115	10	2:16.00	55,440
1985	Videogenic, 3, 114	J. Cruguet	Persian Tiara (Ire), 5, 119	Key Witness, 3, 108	13	2:15.40	61,020
1984	Key Dancer, 3, 111	A. T. Cordero Jr.	Surely Georgie's, 3, 107	Rossard (Den), 4, 123	11	2:14.80	56,700
1983	Rose Crescent, 4, 108	R. G. Davis	Lady Norcliffe, 3, 111	Infinite, 3, 112	9	2:22.00	34,380
1982	Mintage (Fr), 3, 114	J. Samyn	Doodle, 3, 119	Street Dance, 3, 112	8	2:17.80	32,790
	Middle Stage, 3, 112	J. J. Miranda	Realms Reason (Ire), 3, 114	Vocal, 3, 115	6	2:17.40	32,790
1981	De La Rose, 3, 125	E. Maple	Noble Damsel, 3, 111	Andover Way, 3, 113	8	2:00.40	51,120
1980	Love Sign, 3, 121	R. Hernandez	Rokeby Rose, 3, 111	Classic Curves, 3, 111	10	2:00.40	50,490
1979	Poppycock, 3, 114	J. Velasquez	Fourdrinier, 3, 114	Six Crowns, 3, 114	10	2:05.60	52,470
1978	Terpsichorist, 3, 114	M. Venezia	Consort, 3, 110	Bonnie Blue Flag, 3, 110	12	2:03.20	33,300

Named for Hal Price Headley's 1946 Ladies H. winner Athenia (1943 f. by *Pharamond II). Held at Belmont Park 1978-'81, 1983-'93, 1996-'97, 2001. 1 1/4 miles 1978-'81. 1 3/8 miles 1982-'93. 1 1/8 miles 1994-'95, 1997. 1 mile 1996. Dirt 1979, 1990, 1995. Three-year-olds 1978-'83. Fillies 1978-'83. Two divisions 1982, 2001.

Azalea Breeders' Cup Stakes

Grade 3 in 2005. Calder Race Course, three-year-olds, fillies, 6 furlongs, dirt. Held July 10, 2004, with a gross value of $300,000. First held in 1972. First graded in 1996. Stakes record 1:10.82 (2003 Ebony Breeze).

Year	Winner	Jockey	Second	Third	Strs	Time	1st Purse
2004	Dazzle Me, 3, 115	S. J. Sellers	Reforest, 3, 114	Boston Express, 3, 114	7	1:11.40	$177,000
2003	Ebony Breeze, 3, 118	C. H. Velasquez	Storm Flag, 3, 116	Crafty Brat, 3, 116	13	1:10.82	176,025
2002	Bold World, 3, 118	C. H. Borel	Willa On the Move, 3, 114	Tchula Miss, 3, 114	10	1:10.86	105,000
2001	Hattiesburg, 3, 116	M. Guidry	Southern Tour, 3, 114	Spanish Glitter, 3, 116	11	1:11.81	150,000
2000	Swept Away, 3, 116	P. Day	Precious Feather, 3, 112	Watchfull, 3, 116	8	1:11.53	120,000
1999	Show Me the Stage, 3, 116	R. J. Courville	Could Be, 3, 116	Exact, 3, 116	9	1:11.91	75,000
1998	Cassidy, 3, 114	J. A. Rivera II	Holy Capote, 3, 114	Fantasy Angel, 3, 118	8	1:11.93	75,000
1997	Little Sister, 3, 116	F. Lovato Jr.	Princess Pietrina, 3, 112	Maggie Auxier, 3, 114	7	1:13.08	120,000
1996	J J'sdream, 3, 118	H. Castillo Jr.	Supah Avalanche, 3, 112	Race Artist, 3, 114	7	1:23.87	65,100
1995	Lucky Lavender Gal, 3, 116	R. R. Douglas	Chaposa Springs, 3, 117	Dancin Renee, 3, 116	6	1:23.50	60,000
1994	Cut the Charm, 3, 121	H. Castillo Jr.	Just a Little Kiss, 3, 114	Tasso Bee, 3, 112	11	1:25.51	60,000
1993	Kimscountrydiamond, 3, 115	J. Vasquez	Nijivision, 3, 113	Hollywood Wildcat, 3, 117	10	1:23.44	60,000
1992	C. C.'s Return, 3, 113	R. J. Thibeau Jr.	Fortune Forty Four, 3, 114	Subtle Dancer, 3, 113	7	1:25.33	30,000
1991	Ranch Ragout, 3, 113	E. O. Nunez	Parisian Flight, 3, 115	Foolishly Wild, 3, 110	8	1:18.53	33,120
1990	Sweet Proud Polly, 3, 115	P. A. Rodriguez	Highway Lady, 3, 115	Bald Cat, 3, 112	7	1:26.20	32,790
1989	Princess Mora, 3, 112	S. Gaffalione	Georgies Doctor, 3, 118	Silk Stocks, 3, 117	7	1:25.60	32,790
1988	Grand Splash, 3, 114	R. N. Lester	Myfavorite Charity, 3, 114	Hi Maudie, 3, 116	8	1:25.60	46,500
1987	My Sweet Replica, 3, 115	S. B. Soto	Shot Gun Bonnie, 3, 114	Ches Pie, 3, 116	10	1:25.20	33,990
1986	Classy Tricks, 3, 112	M. C. Suckie	Janjac, 3, 112	Thirty Zip, 3, 119	13	1:25.40	30,410
1985	Jackie McCleaf, 3, 120	C. Hussey	Nahema, 3, 118	Nyama, 3, 118	10	1:25.80	33,840
1984	Birdie Belle, 3, 120	H. A. Valdivieso	Sugar's Image, 3, 120	Scorched Panties, 3, 120	10	1:25.80	33,990
1983	Current Gal, 3, 112	E. Cardone	Silvered Silk, 3, 115	Paris Roulette, 3, 115	12	1:25.60	17,295
1982	Here's to Peg, 3, 116	J. A. Velez Jr.	Cut, 3, 114	Bad Dancin Rita, 3, 116	10	1:26.00	16,905
1981	Ange Gal, 3, 113	G. Cohen	Float Upstream, 3, 115	Whoop It, 3, 114	8	1:26.00	16,515
	Kaylem Ho, 3, 115	A. Smith Jr.	Toga Toga, 3, 119	Secret Kingdom, 3, 115	8	1:25.80	16,515
1980	She Can't Miss, 3, 122	W. A. Guerra	Nice and Sharp, 3, 115	Karla's Enough, 3, 119	7	1:11.20	16,515
1979	Burn's Return, 3, 115	M. A. Rivera	Solo Haina, 3, 120	Speier's Hope, 3, 115	9	1:24.00	16,860
1978	Lucy Belle, 3, 113	A. Smith Jr.	We Believe in You, 3, 113	Wings of Destiny, 3, 122	8	1:25.20	14,040
1977	Countess Pruner, 3, 116	J. S. Rodriguez	Delphic Oracle, 3, 113	White Goddess, 3, 119	5	1:11.40	13,440
1976	Forty Nine Sunsets, 3, 122	G. St. Leon	Head Spy, 3, 113	Noble Royalty, 3, 113	6	1:11.80	13,560
1975	Solo Royal, 3, 113	G. St. Leon	My Mom Nullah, 3, 119	Finery, 3, 119	11	1:12.40	14,640

Named for the azalea of the rhododendron family common to South Florida. Azalea H. 1972, 1992-'93. Azalea S. 1975-'95. Not held 1973-'74. 1¹⁄₁₆ miles 1972. 7 furlongs 1978-'79, 1981-'90, 1992-'96. Three-year-olds and up 1972. Fillies and mares 1972. Two divisions 1981.

Azeri Breeders' Cup Stakes

Grade 3 in 2005. Oaklawn Park, three-year-olds and up, fillies and mares, 1¹⁄₁₆ miles, dirt. Held March 12, 2005, with a gross value of $175,000. First held in 1987. First graded in 1990. Stakes record 1:42.01 (1999 Sister Act).

Year	Winner	Jockey	Second	Third	Strs	Time	1st Purse
2005	Injustice, 4, 115	L. S. Quinonez	Colony Band, 4, 113	Island Sand, 4, 113	6	1:43.40	$105,000
2004	Golden Sonata, 5, 117	C. H. Marquez Jr.	Keys to the Heart, 5, 117	Mayo On the Side, 5, 113	10	1:44.32	120,000
2003	Bien Nicole, 5, 122	D. R. Pettinger	Red n'Gold, 5, 117	Mandy's Gold, 5, 117	9	1:44.19	120,000
2002	Ask Me No Secrets, 4, 116	M. E. Smith	Red n'Gold, 4, 116	Descapate, 4, 118	5	1:44.56	120,000
2001	Heritage of Gold, 6, 116	R. Albarado	Lu Ravi, 6, 118	Ive Gota Bad Liver, 4, 114	8	1:44.30	120,000
2000	Heritage of Gold, 5, 112	S. J. Sellers	Lu Ravi, 5, 112	Light Line, 5, 112	4	1:44.15	120,000
1999	Sister Act, 4, 113	C. H. Borel	Glitter Woman, 5, 114	Mil Kilates, 6, 114	6	1:42.01	60,000
1998	Turn to the Queen, 5, 112	T. T. Doocy	Danzalert, 4, 112	Leo's Gypsy Dancer, 4, 118	7	1:44.76	90,000
1997	Halo America, 7, 118	C. H. Borel	Gold n Delicious, 4, 112	Capote Belle, 4, 117	6	1:42.18	90,000
1996	Belle of Cozzene, 4, 113	D. R. Pettinger	Halo America, 6, 120	Little May, 6, 115	5	1:43.32	94,350
1995	Halo America, 5, 115	W. T. Cloninger Jr.	Heavenly Prize, 4, 121	Biolage, 6, 111	6	1:42.59	92,700
1994	Morning Meadow, 4, 116	S. P. Romero	Gravette, 4, 113	Her Valentine, 4, 113	10	1:44.60	94,650
1993	Guiza, 6, 118	C. S. Nakatani	Teddy's Top Ten, 4, 113	Fappies Cosy Miss, 5, 112	8	1:44.79	93,600
1992	Cuddles, 4, 118	D. R. Guillory	Rare Guest, 5, 112	Dixie Splash, 4, 113	10	1:43.82	94,500
1991	A Wild Ride, 4, 120	P. Day	Timber Ribbon, 4, 114	Topsa, 4, 107	9	1:42.31	94,770
1990	A Penny Is a Penny, 5, 116	A. T. Gryder	Affirmed Classic, 4, 114	Fit for a Queen, 4, 113	8	1:43.60	95,340
1989	Savannah's Honor, 4, 117	J. D. Bailey	Invited Guest (Ire), 5, 120	Barbara Sue, 5, 114	7	1:45.00	94,920
1988	Ms. Margi, 4, 116	J. D. Bailey	Queen Alexandra, 6, 121	Hail a Cab, 5, 116	7	1:42.20	94,890
1987	North Sider, 5, 121	A. T. Cordero Jr.	Queen Alexandra, 5, 122	Ann's Bid, 4, 123	8	1:42.20	79,872

Named for the Allen E. Paulson Living Trust's 2002 Horse of the Year and 2002, '03, '04 Apple Blossom H. (G1) winner Azeri (1998 m. by Jade Hunter). Not graded 1995-'99. Oaklawn Budweiser Breeders' Cup H. 1987-'91, 1993-'95. Oaklawn Breeders' Cup H. 1992, 1996-'97. Oaklawn Breeders' Cup S. 1998-2004.

Baldwin Stakes

Not graded in 2005. Santa Anita Park, three-year-olds, 6½ furlongs, dirt (originally scheduled at about 6½ furlongs on turf). Held March 5, 2005, with a gross value of $110,450. First held in 1968. First graded in 1973. Stakes record 1:12.56 (2003 Buddy Gil).

Year	Winner	Jockey	Second	Third	Strs	Time	1st Purse
2005	High Standards, 3, 117	E. S. Prado	Talking to John, 3, 117	Run Thruthe Sun, 3, 117	7	1:16.16	$66,270
2004	Seattle Borders, 3, 114	A. O. Solis	Stalking Tiger, 3, 117	Jungle Prince, 3, 114	10	1:14.09	68,010

Year	Winner	Jockey	Second	Third	Strs	Time	1st Purse
2003	Buddy Gil, 3, 117	G. L. Stevens	King Robyn, 3, 116	Flirt With Fortune, 3, 116	11	1:12.56	$68,730
2002	Shuffling Kid (GB), 3, 117	P. A. Valenzuela	Red Briar (Ire), 3, 116	Dark Sorcerer (GB), 3, 114	12	1:13.30	68,640
2001	Skip to the Stone, 3, 117	C. S. Nakatani	Trailthefox, 3, 122	Bills Paid, 3, 114	6	1:16.29	66,000
2000	Fortifier, 3, 114	B. Blanc	Performing Magic, 3, 116	Joopy Doopy, 3, 117	8	1:16.79	66,870
1999	American Spirit, 3, 114	E. Ramsammy	Chomper (Ire), 3, 115	Impressive Grades, 3, 119	13	1:13.93	69,300
1998	Wrekin Pilot (GB), 3, 116	E. J. Delahoussaye	Commitisize, 3, 122	Tenbyssimo (Ire), 3, 117	8	1:13.32	66,240
1997	Latin Dancer, 3, 116	C. A. Black	King of Swing, 3, 116	Swiss Yodeler, 3, 122	11	1:14.48	67,850
1996	Sandtrap, 3, 114	C. S. Nakatani	Strangelove, 3, 115	Benton Creek, 3, 117	6	1:15.03	64,300
1995	Sierra Diablo, 3, 116	E. J. Delahoussaye	Raji, 3, 117	Huge Gator, 3, 116	6	1:15.36	47,300
1994	Silver Music, 3, 114	C. W. Antley	Eagle Eyed, 3, 117	Makinanhonestbuck, 3, 117	8	1:13.76	48,375
1993	Future Storm, 3, 117	K. J. Desormeaux	Concept Win, 3, 119	Siebe, 3, 117	11	1:15.02	51,550
1992	Reckless Ruckus, 3, 116	P. A. Valenzuela	Fabulous Champ, 3, 114	Slerp, 3, 115	8	1:17.28	49,850
1991	What a Spell, 3, 117	D. R. Flores	Broadway's Top Gun, 3, 122	Shining Prince, 3, 114	7	1:16.30	49,875
1990	Farma Way, 3, 115	R. Sibille	Iam the Iceman, 3, 117	Robyn Dancer, 3, 117	12	1:13.80	52,975
1989	Tenacious Tom, 3, 119	E. J. Delahoussaye	Mountain Ghost, 3, 122	Gum, 3, 119	11	1:14.80	51,900
1988	Exclusive Nureyev, 3, 116	E. J. Delahoussaye	Prospectors Gamble, 3, 114	Mehmetski, 3, 114	9	1:14.40	39,162
	Dr. Brent, 3, 117	A. O. Solis	Accomplish Ridge, 3, 117	Glad Music, 3, 114	9	1:15.00	39,262
1987	Chime Time (GB), 3, 116	P. A. Valenzuela	Sweetwater Springs, 3, 117	McKenzie Prince, 3, 114	11	1:15.00	40,750
1986	Jetting Home, 3, 116	D. G. McHargue	Royal Treasure, 3, 114	El Corazon, 3, 114	6	1:17.40	38,350
1985	Knighthood (Fr), 3, 114	G. L. Stevens	Full Honor, 3, 117	Infantryman, 3, 114	8	1:14.80	39,900
1984	Debonaire Junior, 3, 117	C. J. McCarron	Fortunate Prospect, 3, 119	Distant Ryder, 3, 117	11	1:14.40	41,700
1983	Total Departure, 3, 117	L. A. Pincay Jr.	Paris Prince, 3, 117	Morry's Champ, 3, 114	9	1:15.20	40,950
1982	Remember John, 3, 117	E. J. Delahoussaye	Time to Explode, 3, 120	Crystal Star, 3, 114	7	1:15.20	39,200
1981	Descaro, 3, 115	D. G. McHargue	Motivity, 3, 120	Steelinctive (GB), 3, 114	13	1:14.60	36,700
1980	Corvette Chris, 3, 115	F. Toro	Executive Counsel, 3, 114	Moorish Star, 3, 114	10	1:13.60	28,550
1979	To B. Or Not, 3, 114	C. Baltazar	Debonair Roger, 3, 116	Young Driver, 3, 114	7	1:15.60	27,000
1978	B. W. Turner, 3, 117	D. Pierce	O Big Al, 3, 120	Princely Lark, 3, 114	9	1:14.00	27,550
1977	Current Concept, 3, 120	S. Hawley	Bad 'n Big, 3, 114	Text, 3, 120	10	1:13.20	24,900
1976	Gaelic Christian, 3, 114	R. Rosales	El Portugues, 3, 117	Grandaries, 3, 114	9	1:13.60	20,750
1975	Uniformity, 3, 114	S. Hawley	Crumbs, 3, 114	Wine Nipper, 3, 114	7	1:13.20	20,050
1974	Battery E., 3, 116	L. A. Pincay Jr.	Wedge Shot, 3, 117	Ride Off, 3, 117	5	1:14.00	19,150
1973	Bensadream, 3, 115	D. Pierce	Princely Axe, 3, 114	Gold Bag, 3, 115	9	1:14.00	21,350

Named for Elias J. "Lucky" Baldwin (1828-1909), builder of the original Santa Anita Park. Not graded 1974-'94, 2005. 6½ furlongs 1979, 1982-'83, 1986, 1991-'92, 1995, 2000-'01, 2005. Dirt 1979, 1982-'83, 1986, 1991-'92, 1995, 2000-'01, 2005. Colts and geldings 1978-'87. Two divisions 1988.

Ballerina Handicap

Grade 1 in 2005. Saratoga Race Course, three-year-olds and up, fillies and mares, 7 furlongs, dirt. Held August 29, 2004, with a gross value of $250,000. First held in 1979. First graded in 1981. Stakes record 1:21.09 (2004 Lady Tak).

Year	Winner	Jockey	Second	Third	Strs	Time	1st Purse
2004	Lady Tak, 4, 119	J. D. Bailey	My Trusty Cat, 4, 116	Harmony Lodge, 6, 119	7	1:21.09	$150,000
2003	Harmony Lodge, 5, 115	R. Migliore	Shine Again, 6, 120	Gold Mover, 5, 118	8	1:22.23	150,000
2002	Shine Again, 5, 116	J. Samyn	Raging Fever, 4, 121	Mandy's Gold, 4, 118	7	1:22.26	150,000
2001	Shine Again, 4, 113	J. Samyn	Country Hideaway, 5, 118	Dream Supreme, 4, 122	5	1:22.33	150,000
2000	Dream Supreme, 3, 113	P. Day	Country Hideaway, 4, 117	Bourbon Belle, 5, 118	9	1:22.97	150,000
1999	Furlough, 5, 114	M. E. Smith	Bourbon Belle, 4, 117	dh- Catinca, 4, 121	10	1:23.04	120,000
				dh- Hurricane Bertie, 4, 117			
1998	Stop Traffic, 5, 118	S. J. Sellers	Runup the Colors, 4, 116	U Can Do It, 5, 115	6	1:22.23	120,000
1997	Pearl City, 3, 110	J. Bravo	Ashboro, 4, 115	Flashy n Smart, 4, 112	5	1:22.39	90,000
1996	Chaposa Springs, 4, 120	S. J. Sellers	Capote Belle, 3, 117	Broad Smile, 4, 114	6	1:21.88	90,000
1995	Classy Mirage, 5, 119	J. A. Krone	Inside Information, 4, 126	Laura's Pistolette, 4, 112	6	1:22.55	90,000
1994	Roamin Rachel, 4, 118	P. Day	Classy Mirage, 4, 123	Twist Afleet, 3, 113	6	1:21.85	65,040
1993	Spinning Round, 4, 119	J. F. Chavez	November Snow, 4, 119	Apelia, 4, 122	7	1:21.49	69,120
1992	Serape, 4, 116	C. W. Antley	Harbour Club, 5, 116	Nannerl, 5, 122	9	1:21.22	71,160
1991	Queena, 5, 119	M. E. Smith	Missy's Mirage, 3, 111	Dream Touch, 4, 110	9	1:22.00	72,240
1990	Feel the Beat, 5, 119	J. A. Santos	Fantastic Find, 4, 116	Proper Evidence, 5, 119	8	1:22.00	71,880
1989	Proper Evidence, 4, 116	C. W. Antley	Aptostar, 4, 119	Lake Valley, 4, 114	11	1:23.20	73,080
1988	Cadillacing, 4, 116	A. T. Cordero Jr.	Thirty Zip, 5, 116	Ready Jet Go, 3, 111	6	1:21.60	69,000
1987	I'm Sweets, 4, 119	E. Maple	Storm and Sunshine, 4, 116	Pine Tree Lane, 5, 122	5	1:22.60	82,260
1986	Gene's Lady, 5, 119	R. P. Romero	Le Slew, 5, 116	Tea Room, 4, 110	4	1:22.40	81,420
1985	Lady's Secret, 3, 117	D. MacBeth	Mrs. Revere, 4, 116	Solar Halo, 4, 116	9	1:22.60	67,680
1984	Lass Trump, 4, 122	P. Day	Adored, 4, 122	Sultry Sun, 4, 116	5	1:21.80	51,840
1983	Ambassador of Luck, 4, 124	A. Graell	Number, 4, 119	Broom Dance, 4, 122	4	1:22.20	32,640
1982	Expressive Dance, 4, 122	D. MacBeth	Tell a Secret, 5, 114	Sprouted Rye, 5, 113	8	1:22.80	35,160
1981	Love Sign, 4, 119	R. Hernandez	Jameela, 5, 122	Tell a Secret, 4, 113	4	1:22.60	32,400
1980	Davona Dale, 4, 119	J. Velasquez	Misty Gallore, 4, 124	It's in the Air, 4, 119	4	1:22.20	33,780
1979	Blitey, 3, 111	A. T. Cordero Jr.	Shukey, 4, 116	Bold Rendezvous, 4, 116	5	1:23.20	25,770

Named for Howell E. Jackson's Ballerina (1950 f. by Rosemont), first winner of the Maskette S. Grade 3 1981-'83. Grade 2 1984-'87. Ballerina S. 1979-'93. Dead heat for third 1999.

Ballston Spa Breeders' Cup Handicap

Grade 3 in 2005. Saratoga Race Course, three-year-olds and up, fillies and mares, 1¹/₁₆ miles, turf. Held August 30, 2004, with a gross value of $201,000. First held in 1983. First graded in 1994. Stakes record 1:39.47 (1997 Valor Lady).

Year	Winner	Jockey	Second	Third	Strs	Time	1st Purse
2004	Ocean Drive, 4, 119	J. R. Velazquez	Personal Legend, 4, 115	High Court (Brz), 4, 114	10	1:43.92	$128,400
2003	Stylish, 5, 116	J. R. Velazquez	Snow Dance, 5, 117	Cozzy Corner, 5, 112	9	1:41.03	120,000
2002	Surya, 4, 114	J. D. Bailey	Shooting Party, 4, 118	Solvig, 5, 114	3	1:52.29	126,409
2001	Penny's Gold, 4, 118	J. D. Bailey	Babae (Chi), 5, 114	Chaste, 5, 113	6	1:40.69	126,120
2000	License Fee, 5, 116	P. Day	Pico Teneriffe, 4, 116	Hello Soso (Ire), 4, 114	7	1:43.53	125,700
1999	Pleasant Temper, 5, 118	J. D. Bailey	Cuanto Es, 4, 113	Lets Get Cozzy, 5, 114	7	1:41.84	124,680
1998	Memories of Silver, 5, 122	J. D. Bailey	Witchful Thinking, 4, 118	Ashford Castle, 4, 114	7	1:40.93	126,600
1997	Valor Lady, 5, 112	J. R. Velazquez	Antespend, 4, 116	Rumpipumpy (GB), 4, 114	8	**1:39.47**	130,200
1996	Danish (Ire), 5, 115	J. A. Santos	Apolda, 5, 121	dh- Caress, 5, 113	8	1:41.50	126,360
				dh- Upper Noosh, 4, 111			
1995	Weekend Madness (Ire), 5, 117	S. J. Sellers	Irish Linnet, 7, 120	Allez Les Trois, 4, 115	7	1:40.34	93,300
1994	Weekend Madness (Ire), 4, 115	S. J. Sellers	You'd Be Surprised, 5, 120	Heed, 5, 110	8	1:43.77	93,510
1993	One Dreamer, 5, 116	E. Fires	Eenie Meenie Miney, 4, 111	Irish Linnet, 5, 116	10	1:39.38	94,440
1992	Aurora, 4, 114	C. Perret	Olden Rijn, 4, 112	Irish Linnet, 4, 113	7	1:36.94	93,870
1991	Paris Opera, 5, 116	G. L. Stevens	Daring Doone (GB), 8, 114	Le Famo, 5, 114	10	1:37.41	94,470
1990	Fire the Groom, 3, 114	L. Dettori	Sally Rous (Ire), 3, 114	Christiecat, 3, 115	12	1:35.20	95,820
1989	Wakonda, 5, 116	A. T. Cordero Jr.	Foresta, 3, 108	Toll Fee, 4, 111	5	1:33.80	93,900
1983	Subversive Chick, 3, 114	D. J. Murphy	Soft Morning, 4, 119	It Takes Only One, 3, 114	11	1:24.20	22,380

Named for Ballston Spa, New York, located south of Saratoga Springs. Grade 3 1995-2001. Not graded when taken off turf 2002. Aqueduct Breeders' Cup H. 1989-'92. Aqueduct Budweiser Breeders' Cup H. 1993. Saratoga Budweiser Breeders' Cup H. 1994-'95. Saratoga Breeders' Cup H. 1996. Held at Aqueduct 1992-'93. Not held 1984-'88. 1 mile 1989-'93. 1¹/₈ miles 2002. Dirt 1989, 2002. Dead heat for third 1996.

Barbara Fritchie Handicap

Grade 2 in 2005. Laurel Park, three-year-olds and up, fillies and mares, 7 furlongs, dirt. Held February 19, 2005, with a gross value of $200,000. First held in 1952. First graded in 1973. Stakes record 1:21.40 (1989 Tappiano).

Year	Winner	Jockey	Second	Third	Strs	Time	1st Purse
2005	Cativa, 5, 114	E. S. Prado	Sensibly Chic, 5, 115	Silmaril, 4, 114	10	1:23.64	$120,000
2004	Bear Fan, 5, 116	R. Fogelsonger	Gazillion, 5, 116	Bronze Abe, 5, 117	9	1:23.55	120,000
2003	Xtra Heat, 5, 125	R. Wilson	Carson Hollow, 4, 119	Spelling, 4, 113	7	1:24.76	120,000
2002	Xtra Heat, 4, 128	H. Vega	Prized Stamp, 5, 114	Kimbralata, 4, 114	8	1:22.70	120,000
2001	Prized Stamp, 4, 113	T. L. Dunkelberger	Superduper Miss, 5, 114	Tax Affair, 4, 113	6	1:23.74	120,000
2000	Tap to Music, 5, 115	J. Bravo	Her She Kisses, 4, 114	Di's Time, 5, 114	13	1:24.75	120,000
1999	Passeggiata (Arg), 6, 113	M. G. Pino	Catinca, 4, 121	Nothing Special, 5, 108	8	1:23.55	150,000
1998	J J'sdream, 5, 115	L. C. Reynolds	Palette Knife, 5, 113	Stylish Encore, 5, 114	10	1:24.21	150,000
1997	Miss Golden Circle, 5, 118	R. Migliore	Lottsa Talc, 7, 119	Whaleneck, 4, 113	12	1:23.05	120,000
1996	Lottsa Talc, 6, 117	F. T. Alvarado	Up an Eighth, 5, 114	Evil's Pic, 4, 116	14	1:22.61	120,000
1995	Smart 'N Noble, 4, 117	M. G. Pino	Dust Bucket, 4, 114	Gooni Goo Hoo, 5, 110	10	1:24.13	120,000
1994	Mixed Appeal, 6, 111	A. C. Salazar	Known as Nancy, 4, 111	Winka, 4, 115	12	1:23.31	120,000
1993	Moon Mist, 4, 112	T. G. Turner	Ritchie Trail, 5, 113	Femma, 5, 114	9	1:23.50	120,000
1992	Wood So, 5, 115	M. G. Pino	Wide Country, 4, 120	Wait for the Lady, 5, 111	7	1:24.56	120,000
1991	Fappaburst, 4, 114	A. T. Cordero Jr.	Devil's Orchid, 4, 118	Diva's Debut, 5, 116	10	1:23.30	120,000
1990	Amy Be Good, 4, 112	M. E. Smith	Channel Three, 4, 111	Banbury Fair, 5, 110	10	1:23.40	120,000
1989	Tappiano, 5, 123	K. J. Desormeaux	Very Subtle, 5, 114	Tops in Taps, 6, 114	7	**1:21.40**	120,000
1988	Psyched, 5, 113	K. J. Desormeaux	Spring Beauty, 4, 116	Kerygma, 4, 115	10	1:22.60	81,250
1987	Spring Beauty, 4, 115	J. A. Santos	Notches Trace, 4, 110	Pine Tree Lane, 5, 126	12	1:25.40	88,770
1986	Willowy Mood, 4, 115	B. Thornburg	Aerturas (Fr), 5, 116	Alabama Nana (Ire), 5, 119	10	1:25.40	73,840
1985	Dumdedumdedum, 4, 115	D. A. Miller Jr.	Kattegat's Pride, 6, 119	Sharp Little Girl, 4, 110	8	1:25.00	87,993
	Flip's Pleasure, 5, 115	J. Samyn	Applause, 5, 120	Gene's Lady, 4, 109	8	1:24.00	71,793
1984	Pleasure Cay, 4, 115	D. A. Miller Jr.	Kattegat's Pride, 5, 117	Amanti, 5, 117	9	1:22.80	56,325
	Bara Lass, 5, 125	D. A. Miller Jr.	Owned by All, 4, 109	Willamae, 4, 113	7	1:24.00	55,025
1983	Stellarette, 5, 114	A. Delgado	Hoist Emy's Flag, 4, 116	Cheap Seats, 4, 122	10	1:24.40	74,100
1982	Lady Dean, 4, 119	D. A. Miller Jr.	Sweet Revenge, 4, 114	Sinister Queen, 6, 114	10	1:24.20	46,768
	The Wheel Turns, 5, 121	G. McCarron	Island Charm, 5, 122	Up the Flagpole, 4, 119	9	1:23.60	46,118
1981	Skipat, 7, 124	C. B. Asmussen	Whisp'y Lass, 6, 114	Secret Emotion, 4, 113	8	1:23.00	72,865
1980	Misty Gallore, 4, 121	D. MacBeth	Gladiolus, 6, 122	Silver Ice, 5, 116	10	1:23.60	55,770
1979	Skipat, 5, 125	J. W. Edwards	Pearl Necklace, 5, 122	The Very One, 4, 113	8	1:22.40	53,755
1978	Bold Brat, 5, 115	J. W. Moseley	Spot Two, 4, 116	Satin Dancer, 5, 114	7	1:23.40	37,375
1977	Mt. Airy Queen, 4, 114	D. R. Wright	Avum, 4, 109	Forty Nine Sunsets, 4, 118	6	1:23.80	36,270
1976	Donetta, 5, 119	J. W. Moseley	Pinch Pie, 5, 117	Heydairya, 5, 108	11	1:24.60	37,765
1975	Twixt, 6, 126	W. J. Passmore	Crackerfax, 4, 109	Donetta, 4, 112	11	1:25.40	38,350
1974	Twixt, 5, 124	W. J. Passmore	Groton Miss, 5, 112	In the Mattress, 4, 109	10	1:24.40	38,350
1973	First Bloom, 5, 117	A. Gomez	Pas de Nom, 5, 116	Winged Affair, 5, 111	12	1:23.40	38,025

Named for Barbara Fritchie, a 95-year-old woman who, according to legend, waved her Union flag as Confederate General Thomas "Stonewall" Jackson passed through Frederick, Maryland. Grade 3 1973-'91. Held at Bowie 1952-'84. Barbara Fritchie H. 1952-'58. Not held 1960, 1972. 1¹/₁₆ miles 1952-'54. 6 furlongs 1957-'59, 1963. 1 mile 1961. Two divisions 1982, 1984-'85.

Bashford Manor Stakes

Grade 3 in 2005. Churchill Downs, two-year-olds, 6 furlongs, dirt. Held July 5, 2004, with a gross value of $163,200. First held in 1902. First graded in 1991. Stakes record 1:09.68 (2002 Lone Star Sky).

Year	Winner	Jockey	Second	Third	Strs	Time	1st Purse
2004	Lunarpal, 2, 121	S. J. Sellers	Storm Surge, 2, 117	Maximus C, 2, 117	7	1:11.54	$101,184
2003	Limehouse, 2, 121	R. Albarado	First Money, 2, 117	Cuvee, 2, 121	6	1:10.62	100,905
2002	Lone Star Sky, 2, 115	M. Guidry	Posse, 2, 121	Cooper Crossing, 2, 115	7	1:09.68	84,475
2001	Lunar Bounty, 2, 115	F. Lovato Jr.	Binyamin, 2, 115	Storm Passage, 2, 115	5	1:09.90	82,925
2000	Duality, 2, 115	C. H. Borel	Strait Cat, 2, 114	Take Arms, 2, 115	9	1:10.09	86,258
1999	Dance Master, 2, 115	B. Peck	Sky Dweller, 2, 115	Snuck In, 2, 115	8	1:10.38	89,280
1998	Time Bandit, 2, 115	C. R. Woods Jr.	Yes It's True, 2, 121	Haus of Dehere, 2, 115	8	1:10.78	68,262
1997	Favorite Trick, 2, 121	P. Day	Double Honor, 2, 115	Cowboy Dan, 2, 118	8	1:09.92	68,696
1996	Boston Harbor, 2, 115	M. J. Luzzi	Prairie Junction, 2, 115	Nobel Talent, 2, 115	8	1:09.96	72,150
1995	A. V. Eight, 2, 115	A. J. Trosclair	Aggie Southpaw, 2, 115	Seeker's Reward, 2, 115	8	1:11.40	71,630
1994	Hyroglyphic, 2, 116	G. K. Gomez	Boone's Mill, 2, 116	Hobgoblin, 2, 116	13	1:10.25	75,660
1993	†Miss Ra He Ra, 2, 113	W. Martinez	Ramblin Guy, 2, 116	Riverinn, 2, 112	13	1:12.98	76,180
1992	Mountain Cat, 2, 116	C. R. Woods Jr.	Tempered Halo, 2, 121	Storm Flight, 2, 116	7	1:10.62	53,869
1991	Pick Up the Phone, 2, 116	J. C. Espinoza	Sprintmaster, 2, 116	Thanatopsis, 2, 112	7	1:12.08	35,815
1990	To Freedom, 2, 121	J. C. Espinoza	Richman, 2, 121	Discover, 2, 116	7	1:10.20	35,555
1989	Summer Squall, 2, 121	P. Day	Table Limit, 2, 118	Appealing Breeze, 2, 121	6	1:12.20	35,068
1988	Bio, 2, 118	P. A. Johnson	Revive, 2, 112	Curtis John, 2, 114	11	1:11.80	37,148
1987	Blair's Cove, 2, 114	S. J. Sellers	Endurance, 2, 118	Mr. Igloo, 2, 116	11	1:11.80	37,310
1986	Faster Than Sound, 2, 118	C. Perret	Renumeration, 2, 115	Arunti, 2, 121	7	1:11.20	46,648
1985	Tile, 2, 115	L. J. Melancon	Tug, 2, 115	Sir Grandeur, 2, 115	12	1:04.40	30,896
1984	Jerry F., 2, 112	P. Day	Storm Scope, 2, 115	Wet My Whistle, 2, 115	3	1:05.80	17,241
1983	Betwixt n' Between, 2, 115	P. Day	Real Sharp Dancer, 2, 121	Biloxi Indian, 2, 118	13	1:05.00	22,896
1982	Willow Drive, 2, 115	J. Neagle	Stepping E. J., 2, 118	Mindboggling, 2, 115	11	1:05.00	20,264
1981	T. V. Mark, 2, 122	P. Nicolo	Shilling, 2, 122	Good Ole Master, 2, 122	10	:59.60	18,103
1980	Golden Derby, 2, 117	J. C. Espinoza	Wrong Impression, 2, 122	Stubilem, 2, 117	9	:59.00	19,338
1979	Rajohn Greco, 2, 122	J. C. Espinoza	Egg's Dynamite, 2, 122	Native Amber, 2, 122	6	1:00.20	19,451
1978	Spy Charger, 2, 127	G. Mahon	Uncle Fudge, 2, 122	Vennie Redberry, 2, 122	6	:58.40	14,490
1977	Going Investor, 2, 122	B. Sayler	Old Jake, 2, 117	Chwesboken, 2, 122	7	:58.40	14,235
1976	Judge John Boone, 2, 122	E. J. Delahoussaye	Wishem Well, 2, 122	Golden Trade, 2, 117	8	:58.60	14,625
1975	Khyber King, 2, 122	E. J. Delahoussaye	Bold Laddie, 2, 122	Right On Mike, 2, 122	5	:58.60	15,633
1974	Pac Quick, 2, 115	G. Patterson	Paris Dust, 2, 127	Kaanapali, 2, 122	9	:58.60	16,608
1973	Tisab, 2, 122	M. Manganello	No Advance, 2, 122	To the Rescue, 2, 122	9	:58.80	16,965

Named for an old Louisville-area plantation and neighborhood, Bashford Manor. Grade 2 1999-2001. 4½ furlongs 1902-'25. 5 furlongs 1926-'81. 5½ furlongs 1982-'85. Colts and geldings 1940-'81. †Denotes female.

Bayakoa Handicap

Grade 2 in 2005. Hollywood Park, three-year-olds and up, fillies and mares, 1 1/16 miles, dirt. Held December 12, 2004, with a gross value of $150,000. First held in 1981. First graded in 1983. Stakes record 1:41.02 (2003 Star Parade [Arg]).

Year	Winner	Jockey	Second	Third	Strs	Time	1st Purse
2004	Hollywood Story, 3, 115	V. Espinoza	Royally Chosen, 6, 116	A. P. Adventure, 3, 117	7	1:41.11	$90,000
2003	Star Parade (Arg), 4, 112	V. Espinoza	Adoration, 4, 121	Bare Necessities, 4, 119	6	1:41.02	90,000
2002	Starrer, 4, 118	P. A. Valenzuela	Cee's Elegance, 5, 113	Angel Gift, 4, 115	6	1:41.74	90,000
2001	Starrer, 3, 118	J. D. Bailey	Queenie Belle, 4, 118	Tropical Lady (Brz), 4, 115	7	1:42.52	90,000
2000	Feverish, 5, 119	E. J. Delahoussaye	Gourmet Girl, 5, 118	Lazy Slusan, 5, 117	9	1:42.26	90,000
1999	Manistique, 4, 124	C. S. Nakatani	Snowberg, 4, 115	Riboletta (Brz), 4, 116	7	1:43.16	90,000
1998	Manistique, 3, 119	G. L. Stevens	India Divina (Chi), 4, 114	Numero Uno, 4, 115	4	1:42.51	60,000
1997	Sharp Cat, 3, 121	A. O. Solis			1	1:42.68	60,000
1996	Listening, 3, 120	C. J. McCarron	Cat's Cradle, 4, 120	Belle's Flag, 3, 117	5	1:42.66	64,920
1995	Pirate's Revenge, 4, 119	C. W. Antley	Urbane, 4, 120	Ashtabula, 4, 116	5	1:41.80	61,900
1994	Thirst for Peace, 5, 115	A. O. Solis	Glass Ceiling, 4, 117	Dancing Mirage, 3, 119	7	1:42.28	63,500
1993	Golden Klair (GB), 3, 115	C. J. McCarron	Pacific Squall, 4, 118	Cargo, 4, 116	7	1:41.20	63,500
1992	Brought to Mind, 5, 120	P. A. Valenzuela	Re Toss (Arg), 5, 115	Interactive, 3, 112	8	1:42.62	65,200
1991	Paseana (Arg), 4, 117	C. J. McCarron	Damewood, 3, 116	Luna Elegante (Arg), 5, 117	6	1:42.70	62,700
1990	Fantastic Look, 4, 118	C. J. McCarron	Spanish Dior, 3, 112	Tis Juliet, 4, 115	6	1:42.40	62,200
1989	Approved to Fly, 3, 115	A. O. Solis	Saros Brig, 5, 115	Lucky Song, 3, 114	7	1:48.20	63,400
1988	Nastique, 4, 119	W. Shoemaker	Miss Brio (Chi), 4, 116	T. V. of Crystal, 3, 117	9	1:48.00	76,800
1986	Family Style, 3, 115	G. L. Stevens	Infinidad (Chi), 4, 114	Waterside, 4, 113	7	1:50.00	82,700
1985	Love Smitten, 4, 116	C. J. McCarron	Mimi Baker, 4, 115	Dontstop Themusic, 5, 125	5	1:47.80	61,600
1984	Dontstop Themusic, 4, 118	T. Lipham	Paradies (Arg), 4, 114	Fancy Wings, 4, 116	8	1:50.20	64,500
1983	Sweet Diane, 3, 115	R. Sibille	Miss Huntington, 6, 117	Bersid, 5, 117	11	1:48.00	67,900
1982	Sierva (Arg), 4, 117	L. A. Pincay Jr.	Miss Huntington, 5, 117	Plenty O'Toole, 5, 115	11	1:48.20	68,900
1981	Happy Guess (Arg), 5, 117	W. Shoemaker	Track Robbery, 4, 123	Targa, 4, 112	6	1:49.60	62,100

Named for Mr. and Mrs. Frank E. Whitham's 1989, '90 champion older mare and '89 Vanity H. (G1) winner Bayakoa (Arg) (1984 f. by Consultant's Bid). Grade 3 1983-'85. Silver Belles H. 1981-'93. Not held 1987. 1 1/8 miles 1981-'89. Won in a walkover 1997.

Bay Meadows Breeders' Cup Handicap

Grade 3 in 2005. Bay Meadows, three-year-olds and up, 1⅛ miles, turf. Held October 2, 2004, with a gross value of $112,500. First held in 1934. First graded in 1981. Stakes record 1:45.45 (1995 Caesour).

Year	Winner	Jockey	Second	Third	Strs	Time	1st Purse
2004	Needwood Blade (GB), 6, 116	D. Carr	Seinne (Chi), 7, 116	Balestrini (Ire), 4, 117	7	1:46.55	$55,000
2003	Mister Acpen (Chi), 5, 116	R. M. Gonzalez	Fateful Dream, 6, 117	Ninebanks, 5, 118	10	1:46.94	55,000
2002	David Copperfield, 5, 117	J. P. Lumpkins	Ninebanks, 4, 115	Little Ghazi, 6, 115	5	1:48.95	110,000
2001	Super Quercus (Fr), 5, 117	R. A. Baze	Most Likely (Arg), 5, 112	Sign of Hope (GB), 4, 116	6	1:47.50	55,000
2000	Devine Wind, 4, 114	G. K. Gomez	Irish Prize, 4, 115	Deploy Venture (GB), 4, 117	6	1:47.19	110,000
1999	Kirkwall (GB), 5, 114	V. Espinoza	Special Quest (Fr), 4, 115	Game Ploy (Pol), 7, 113	8	1:47.13	110,000
1998	Hawksley Hill (Ire), 5, 120	A. O. Solis	Magellan, 5, 117	Floriselli, 4, 115	5	1:45.49	110,000
1997	El Angelo, 5, 119	A. O. Solis	Via Lombardia (Ire), 5, 115	Dreamer, 5, 115	5	1:45.47	110,000
1996	Gentlemen (Arg), 4, 117	C. S. Nakatani	Party Season (GB), 5, 116	Petit Poucet (GB), 4, 119	5	1:45.90	110,000
1995	Caesour, 5, 115	R. A. Baze	Johann Quatz (Fr), 6, 115	Canaska Dancer (Ire), 4, 113	6	**1:45.45**	110,000
1994	Blues Traveller (Ire), 4, 116	G. L. Stevens	Fastness (Ire), 4, 116	Wharf, 4, 114	6	1:46.03	110,000
1993	Slew of Damascus, 5, 114	T. M. Chapman	Fast Cure, 4, 112	Lissitki (Fr), 4, 112	7	1:45.91	110,000
1992	Forty Niner Days, 5, 115	C. S. Nakatani	Bistro Garden, 4, 116	Luthier Enchanteur, 5, 118	8	1:46.58	137,500
1991	French Seventyfive, 4, 112	G. Boulanger	Forty Niner Days, 4, 115	Batshoof (Ire), 5, 116	9	1:49.40	137,500
1990	Robinski (NZ), 7, 112	J. Velasquez	Sekondi (Fr), 3, 113	Rushing Raj, 4, 113	12	1:50.80	137,500
1989	Ten Keys, 5, 118	K. J. Desormeaux	Colway Rally (GB), 5, 116	Nediym (Ire), 4, 113	12	1:46.60	137,500
1988	Wait Till Monday (Ire), 4, 113	R. E. Dominguez	Miswaki Tern, 3, 113	Skip Out Front, 6, 117	12	1:46.00	137,500
1987	Show Dancer, 5, 113	M. Castaneda	Skip Out Front, 5, 114	Exclusive Partner, 5, 116	10	1:47.80	165,000
1986	Palace Music, 5, 123	F. Toro	Nugget Point (Ire), 4, 113	Barbery, 5, 116	10	1:50.60	165,000
1985	Drumalis (Ire), 5, 116	R. Q. Meza	Silveyville, 7, 121	Talakeno, 5, 115	8	1:47.00	165,000
1984	Scrupules (Ire), 4, 118	E. J. Delahoussaye	Raami (GB), 3, 120	Both Ends Burning, 4, 123	8	2:17.20	178,500
1983	Interco, 3, 115	J. C. Judice	Super Sunrise (GB), 4, 116	Floriano, 4, 114	15	1:55.40	179,200
1982	Super Moment, 5, 120	R. A. Baze	†Buchanette, 3, 113	Les Aspres (Fr), 6, 112	10	1:51.60	132,400
1981	Super Moment, 4, 124	L. A. Pincay Jr.	Tahitian King (Ire), 5, 121	The Bart, 5, 126	8	1:53.60	98,400
1980	Super Moment, 3, 116	F. Toro	Fleet Tempo, 3, 114	Mike Fogarty (Ire), 5, 118	12	1:46.20	68,600
1979	Leonotis (NZ), 6, 118	R. M. Gonzalez	John Henry, 4, 123	Capt. Don, 4, 117	14	1:49.60	69,900
1978	Bywayofchicago, 4, 122	F. Toro	Noble Bronze, 3, 113	As de Copas (Arg), 4, 119	16	1:50.80	72,000
1977	Painted Wagon, 4, 120	M. S. Sellers	Sudanes (Arg), 4, 117	Mark's Place, 5, 123	12	1:41.40	51,000
1976	Life's Hope, 3, 118	D. G. McHargue	Fighting Bill, 3, 113	Podium, 4, 117	7	1:43.40	31,400
1975	Bahia Key, 5, 120	F. Olivares	Fleet Velvet, 3, 120	Holding Pattern, 4, 120	7	1:43.00	31,700
1974	Indefatigable, 4, 117	D. Pierce	Star of Kuwait, 6, 116	Confederate Yankee, 3, 115	8	1:41.40	31,900
1973	Partner's Hope, 4, 117	A. L. Diaz	Ipse, 5, 116	Woodland Breas, 4, 116	6	1:43.20	17,525

Grade 2 1982-'84, 1986-'95. Not graded 1985. Bay Meadows H. 1934-2000. 1¹⁄₁₆ miles 1936-'37, 1939, 1954-'58, 1960, 1962-'69, 1973-'77. 1¹⁄₄ miles 1952. 1³⁄₈ miles 1984. 1¹⁄₈ miles 1934-'35, 1938, 1940-'51, 1953, 1959, 1961, 1970-'72, 1978-'87, 1989, 1993. Dirt 1934-'77, 1980. Two-year-olds and up 1935-'40, 1942, 1947-'50, 1953. Course record 1993, 1995. †Denotes female.

Bay Meadows Breeders' Cup Sprint Handicap

Grade 3 in 2005. Bay Meadows, three-year-olds and up, 6 furlongs, dirt. Held June 19, 2004, with a gross value of $80,000. First held in 1986. First graded in 2000. Stakes record 1:07.94 (2001 Lexicon).

Year	Winner	Jockey	Second	Third	Strs	Time	1st Purse
2004	Court's in Session, 5, 115	R. M. Gonzalez	Debonair Joe, 5, 117	Hombre Rapido, 7, 118	9	1:08.91	$41,250
2003	El Dorado Shooter, 6, 120	C. P. Schvaneveldt	Halo Cat, 5, 118	Radar Contact, 7, 116	6	1:08.61	82,500
2002	Mellow Fellow, 7, 119	R. A. Baze	Explicit, 5, 120	Swept Overboard, 5, 122	6	1:08.35	110,000
2001	Lexicon, 6, 117	R. A. Baze	Swept Overboard, 4, 117	You and You Alone, 4, 115	4	**1:07.94**	82,500
2000	Lexicon, 5, 115	R. A. Baze	Men's Exclusive, 7, 115	Dixie Dot Com, 5, 116	5	1:09.19	110,000
1999	Big Jag, 6, 118	J. Valdivia Jr.	Men's Exclusive, 6, 115	Lexicon, 4, 116	6	1:08.87	110,000
1998	Musafi, 4, 116	D. R. Flores	dh-The Barking Shark, 5, 116		7	1:08.59	110,000
			dh-Mr. Doubledown, 4, 116				
1997	Tres Paraiso, 5, 116	C. S. Nakatani	Mashaka's Pride, 4, 112	Boundless Moment, 5, 117	5	1:07.98	110,000
1996	Boundless Moment, 4, 116	K. J. Desormeaux	Concept Win, 6, 115	Paying Dues, 4, 119	11	1:08.81	110,000
1995	Lucky Forever, 6, 116	G. F. Almeida	Wild Gold, 5, 115	Uncaged Fury, 4, 116	6	1:08.71	117,700
1994	†Soviet Problem, 4, 120	R. A. Baze	Wild Gold, 4, 115	Concept Win, 4, 119	6	1:08.58	31,200
1993	Lucky Forever, 4, 114	A. L. Castanon	Cardmania, 7, 116	Scherando, 4, 115	9	1:08.98	87,750
1992	Superstrike (GB), 3, 114	D. Sorenson	Anjiz, 4, 114	Naevus Star, 6, 111	7	1:08.83	86,950
1991	Robyn Dancer, 4, 119	L. A. Pincay Jr.	Blue Eyed Danny, 5, 115	Letthebighossroll, 3, 116	7	1:09.30	84,728
1990	Earn Your Stripes, 6, 117	P. A. Valenzuela	Frost Free, 5, 116	Just Deeds, 4, 113	6	1:08.40	84,700
1989	Happy Toss (Arg), 4, 115	F. Toro	No Marker, 5, 111	Hot Operator, 4, 113	6	1:39.80	86,250
1988	Good Command, 5, 117	R. A. Baze	Slyly Gifted, 5, 113	Miracle Horse (Fr), 4, 117	5	1:42.00	85,950
1987	Judge Angelucci, 4, 122	G. Baze	He's a Saros, 4, 115	Show Dancer, 5, 117	4	1:48.20	85,350
1986	Hopeful Word, 5, 120	F. Toro	Armin, 5, 116	Bozina, 5, 115	8	1:40.40	87,335

Bay Meadows Budweiser Breeders' Cup H. 1986-'95. 1¹⁄₁₆ miles 1986, 1988-'89. 1¹⁄₈ miles 1987. Dead heat for second 1998. †Denotes female.

Bay Meadows Derby

Grade 3 in 2005. Bay Meadows, three-year-olds, 1 1/8 miles, turf. Held November 6, 2004, with a gross value of $100,000.
First held in 1954. First graded in 1983. Stakes record 1:45.34 (1999 Mula Gula).

Year	Winner	Jockey	Second	Third	Strs	Time	1st Purse
2004	Congressionalhonor, 3, 115	R. A. Baze	Talaris, 3, 116	‡On the Acorn (GB), 3, 116	8	1:48.92	$55,000
2003	Stanley Park, 3, 116	E. Saint-Martin	Bis Repetitas, 3, 118	Kewen, 3, 116	8	1:48.97	55,000
2002	Royal Gem, 3, 119	R. A. Baze	Aly Bubba, 3, 114	Century City (Ire), 3, 122	8	1:48.38	55,000
2001	Blue Steller (Ire), 3, 119	A. O. Solis	Sir Alfred, 3, 116	Sea to See, 3, 116	8	1:46.81	55,000
2000	Walkslikeaduck, 3, 122	E. J. Delahoussaye	Jokerman, 3, 119	Calamari, 3, 115	5	1:46.57	82,500
1999	Mula Gula, 3, 117	R. Q. Meza	†Miss Chryss (Ire), 3, 111	Fighting Falcon, 3, 120	10	1:45.34	82,500
1998	Takarian (Ire), 3, 116	C. A. Black	I. M. Bzy, 3, 115	Prevalence (GB), 3, 114	8	1:46.80	82,500
1997	Shellbacks, 3, 113	R. Q. Meza	Brave Act (GB), 3, 122	Zippersup, 3, 115	7	1:49.01	82,500
1996	†Ocean Queen, 3, 110	J. A. Garcia	Mateo, 3, 115	Mystic Knight (GB), 3, 116	8	1:47.80	110,000
1995	Virginia Carnival, 3, 115	R. J. Warren Jr.	Helmsman, 3, 113	Tabor, 3, 116	10	1:46.17	55,000
1994	Marvin's Faith (Ire), 3, 116	M. Castaneda	Western Trader, 3, 116	Turbo Fan, 3, 115	8	1:48.68	55,000
1993	Ranger (Fr), 3, 114	G. Boulanger	El Atroz, 3, 113	Guide (Fr), 3, 120	9	1:48.90	55,000
1992	Star Recruit, 3, 116	R. D. Hansen	Siberian Summer, 3, 116	Fax News, 3, 115	6	1:49.13	55,000
1991	Bistro Garden, 3, 120	M. Castaneda	Dominion Gold (GB), 3, 116	Fraise, 3, 115	8	1:46.70	82,500
1990	Sekondi (Fr), 3, 114	R. M. Gonzalez	Courtesy Title, 3, 115	†Appealing Missy, 3, 113	12	1:48.80	55,000
1989	Irish, 3, 115	M. A. Espindola	Polar Boy, 3, 115	Two Moccasins, 3, 113	12	1:48.20	55,000
1988	Coax Me Clyde, 3, 118	R. J. Warren Jr.	Gran Judgement, 3, 116	Literati, 3, 117	11	1:49.00	68,500
1987	Hot and Smoggy, 3, 117	J. Vasquez	Wolsey, 3, 116	Lucky Harold H., 3, 115	9	1:48.60	66,400
1986	Le Belvedere, 3, 113	W. Shoemaker	Santella Mac (Ire), 3, 115	Grand Exchange, 3, 116	11	1:47.60	81,300
1985	Minutes Away, 3, 115	C. R. Hummel	Charming Duke (Fr), 3, 124	Lucky n Green (Ire), 3, 115	10	1:51.40	66,800
1984	Mangaki, 3, 115	C. Lamance	Refueled (Ire), 3, 117	Foscarini (Ire), 3, 120	11	1:52.00	68,400
1983	Interco, 3, 116	J. C. Judice	Bang Bang Bang, 3, 112	Baron O'Dublin, 3, 120	6	1:49.60	63,500
1982	Ask Me, 3, 120	F. Toro	Water Bank, 3, 120	Take the Floor, 3, 121	10	1:46.00	66,100
1981	Silveyville, 3, 120	D. Winick	Sunshine Swag, 3, 113	Tempo's Tiger, 3, 117	10	1:48.20	67,000
1980	Fleet Tempo, 3, 114	R. M. Gonzalez	Super Moment, 3, 123	Aliyoun (Ire), 3, 112	9	1:44.60	32,750
1979	Nain Bleu (Fr), 3, 113	C. Baltazar	Bends Me Mind, 3, 118	Gummaka, 3, 115	9	1:45.40	32,300
1978	Quip, 3, 115	T. Lipham	Shagbark, 3, 115	Kamehameha, 3, 123	11	1:45.20	34,250

Bay Meadows Breeders' Cup Derby 1996-2000. Not held 1955-'56, 1958-'77. 1 1/16 miles 1957, 1978-'82. About 1 1/8 miles 1983-'84, 1986, 1988-'91, 1994-'95, 1997-2002. Dirt 1992. ‡Hendrix finished third, DQ to eighth, 2004. †Denotes female.

Bayou Breeders' Cup Handicap

Grade 3 in 2005. Fair Grounds, four-year-olds and up, fillies and mares, about 1 1/8 miles, turf. Held February 19, 2005, with a gross value of $125,000. First held in 1969. First graded in 2004. Stakes record 1:49.32 (2000 Histoire Sainte [Fr]).

Year	Winner	Jockey	Second	Third	Strs	Time	1st Purse
2005	Shadow Cast, 4, 119	R. Albarado	Bijou, 6, 115	Sister Swank, 4, 120	8	1:53.75	$75,000
2004	Bedanken, 5, 121	D. R. Pettinger	Due to Win Again, 6, 118	Lady Linda, 6, 115	10	1:52.74	75,000
2003	Quick Tip, 5, 116	R. Albarado	Histoire Sainte (Fr), 7, 118	Snow Dance, 5, 119	10	1:54.61	90,000
2002	Katy Kat, 4, 116	R. Albarado	Pretty Gale, 4, 113	Temis (Chi), 6, 109	4	1:50.67	90,000
2001	On a Soapbox, 5, 113	M. St. Julien	Always Sure, 5, 115	Lady Tamworth, 6, 111	6	1:53.82	94,770
2000	Histoire Sainte (Fr), 4, 111	S. J. Sellers	Snow Polina, 5, 115	Neptune's Bride, 4, 115	9	1:49.32	65,850
1999	Red Cat, 4, 113	R. D. Ardoin	Swearingen, 5, 117	Justenuffheart, 4, 115	7	1:51.31	95,280
1998	Cuando, 4, 114	W. Martinez	Water Street, 4, 111	B. A. Valentine, 5, 118	8	1:53.60	52,620
1997	Maxzene, 4, 116	J. A. Krone	Flame Valley, 4, 112	Tough Broad, 5, 114	10	1:53.00	91,875
1996	Tough Broad, 4, 110	S. P. LeJeune Jr.	Brushing Gloom, 4, 112	Stellarina, 5, 114	11	1:51.38	91,875
1995	Lismore Lass, 6, 113	J. E. Broussard III	Onceinabluemamoon, 4, 115	Bendel Bonnet, 4, 110	10	1:53.97	36,000
1994	Prominent Feather, 5, 113	R. D. Ardoin	Mystical Path, 5, 112	Forever North, 6, 116	13	1:52.68	47,070
1993	Liz Cee, 5, 114	L. J. Martinez	To Be Dazzling, 5, 115	Trim Cut, 5, 112	14	1:52.20	32,130
1992	Bishops Idea, 4, 113	B. E. Poyadou	Palace Chill, 5, 120	Hero's Love, 4, 110	10	1:53.80	31,545
1991	Phoenix Sunshine, 6, 117	V. L. Smith	Leering, 4, 114	Chore Girl, 5, 113	12	1:52.30	19,755
1990	Phoenix Sunshine, 5, 115	C. J. Woodley	Regal Wonder, 6, 118	Lyphover, 5, 122	11	1:53.00	16,725
1989	How I Wish, 5, 120	C. H. Borel	Factually, 5, 112	Profit Island, 5, 113	12	1:52.00	16,815
1988	How I Wish, 4, 116	E. J. Perrodin	Robertina, 4, 117	Vigorous Market, 4, 112	9	1:48.00	16,575
1987	Sastarda (Chi), 6, 120	K. Bourque	Anadia, 4, 116	Costa Del Sol, 6, 113	10	2:22.40	21,540
1986	Dancing Slippers, 5, 113	J. Samyn	Costa Del Sol, 5, 118	Lock's Dream, 4, 114	11	2:21.40	53,145
1985	Over Your Shoulder, 4, 114	G. St. Leon	Costa Del Sol, 4, 116	Erudite (Fr), 5, 113	12	2:19.00	40,325
1984	Freeway Folly, 5, 122	R. P. Romero	Gabfest, 5, 113	Erudite (Fr), 4, 116	10	2:33.00	39,025
1983	Countess Tully (Ire), 5, 114	D. Brumfield	Full of Reason, 4, 114	Valid Bess, 5, 115	13	2:19.20	42,825
1982	Vibro Vibes, 5, 114	E. J. Perrodin	Lady Offshore, 5, 120	Sweetest Sound, 4, 113	14	2:17.60	40,100
1981	Royal Saint, 4, 118	J. McKnight	La Bonzo, 5, 122	Vibro Vibes, 4, 114	6	2:06.00	32,075
1980	Holy Mount, 4, 117	E. Fires	Salzburg, 5, 118	Fun Worthy, 4, 115	12	2:04.00	35,975
1979	Lily S., 4, 112	D. Montoya	Flaunter, 4, 110	Jevalin, 4, 114	9	2:07.20	28,875
1978	Quid Kit, 4, 115	D. Copling	Famed Princess, 5, 114	La Doree (Arg), 4, 112	12	1:45.40	30,800
1977	Forlana, 4, 118	A. J. Trosclair	Hail to El, 5, 114	Critical Miss, 4, 117	10	1:44.60	20,550
1976	Point in Time, 4, 117	A. J. Trosclair	Hope She Does, 4, 116	Flama Ardiente, 4, 124	14	1:45.00	22,150
1975	Truchas, 6, 115	O. Sanchez	Big Dare, 5, 119	Stylish Genie, 4, 115	9	1:44.60	19,775

| 1974 | **Sixty Sails**, 4, 120 | P. Rubbicco | Sassy Bee, 4, 116 | Knitted Gloves, 4, 117 | 7 | 1:44.40 | $12,050 |
| 1973 | **Neigh Neigh**, 4, 112 | D. Meade Jr. | Lyrs Poker, 4, 115 | Daring Jester, 5, 114 | 10 | 1:46.60 | 11,225 |

Named for the swampy marshes found throughout Louisiana. Bayou H. 1969-'95. 1 mile 70 yards 1969-'72. 1¹/₁₆ miles 1973-'78, 1988. 1¹/₄ miles 1979-'81. 1³/₈ miles 1982-'83, 1985-'87. 1¹/₂ miles 1984. 1¹/₈ miles 1989-'90, 1998, 2001-'02. Dirt 1969-'81, 1998, 2001-'02. Three-year-olds and up 1969-'78.

Bay Shore Stakes

Grade 3 in 2005. Aqueduct, three-year-olds, 7 furlongs, dirt. Held April 9, 2005, with a gross value of $150,000. First held in 1894. First graded in 1973. Stakes record 1:20.54 (1998 Limit Out).

Year	Winner	Jockey	Second	Third	Strs	Time	1st Purse
2005	**Lost in the Fog**, 3, 123	R. A. Baze	White Socks, 3, 116	Big Top Cat, 3, 116	6	1:21.33	$90,000
2004	**Forest Danger**, 3, 116	J. R. Velazquez	Abbondanza, 3, 116	Indian War Dance, 3, 116	8	1:20.67	90,000
2003	**Halo Homewrecker**, 3, 116	J. R. Velazquez	Don Six, 3, 116	Stanislavsky, 3, 116	11	1:23.19	90,000
2002	**Roman Dancer**, 3, 120	K. J. Desormeaux	Warners, 3, 116	Monthir, 3, 116	10	1:22.21	90,000
2001	**Skip to the Stone**, 3, 120	V. Espinoza	Multiple Choice, 3, 116	Friday's a Comin', 3, 120	8	1:22.46	90,000
2000	**Precise End**, 3, 116	J. F. Chavez	Turnofthecentury, 3, 114	Port Herman, 3, 114	7	1:22.27	66,000
1999	**Perfect Score**, 3, 118	E. S. Prado	Royal Ruby, 3, 114	Prince Monty, 3, 116	8	1:22.98	66,120
1998	**Limit Out**, 3, 115	J. Samyn	Good and Tough, 3, 113	Diamond Studs, 3, 113	6	**1:20.54**	65,460
1997	**Hawks Landing**, 3, 114	R. Migliore	Adverse, 3, 113	Standing On Edge, 3, 113	7	1:22.00	66,480
1996	**Jamies First Punch**, 3, 115	J. R. Velazquez	Gold Fever, 3, 115	Firey Jennifer, 3, 115	9	1:22.13	67,200
1995	**Blissful State**, 3, 118	M. J. Luzzi	Northern Ensign, 3, 114	Pat n Jac, 3, 115	6	1:23.92	64,680
1994	**Prank Call**, 3, 113	J. R. Velazquez	Mr. Shawklit, 3, 117	Popol's Gold, 3, 122	7	1:09.84	65,940
1992	**Three Peat**, 3, 114	C. W. Antley	Goldwater, 3, 117	Best Decorated, 3, 114	10	1:21.68	75,600
1991	**Stately Wager**, 3, 119	J. F. Chavez	Mineral Ice, 3, 119	Vouch for Me, 3, 117	7	1:23.95	71,040
1990	**Richard R.**, 3, 117	J. A. Santos	For Really, 3, 114	Cielo, 3, 114	7	1:22.80	70,080
1989	**Houston**, 3, 116	L. A. Pincay Jr.	Mr. Nickerson, 3, 114	Wee Stark, 3, 119	4	1:22.40	69,000
1988	**Perfect Spy**, 3, 119	R. G. Davis	Success Express, 3, 123	Proud and Valid, 3, 117	5	1:22.60	98,460
1987	**Gulch**, 3, 123	J. A. Santos	High Brite, 3, 119	Shawklit Won, 3, 114	9	1:23.20	124,800
1986	**Zabaleta**, 3, 114	D. G. McHargue	Groovy, 3, 117	Belocolus, 3, 114	8	1:22.00	95,250
	Buck Aly, 3, 117	N. Santagata	Landing Plot, 3, 119	Raja's Revenge, 3, 119	8	1:23.80	95,250
1985	**Pancho Villa**, 3, 114	F. Lovato Jr.	El Basco, 3, 114	Spend a Buck, 3, 123	9	1:22.20	97,020
1984	**Secret Prince**, 3, 114	C. Perret	The Wedding Guest, 3, 126	I'm a Rounder, 3, 114	9	1:11.20	95,580
1983	**Strike Gold**, 3, 114	E. Maple	Assault Landing, 3, 114	Chas Conerly, 3, 114	9	1:22.60	34,620
1982	**Shimatoree**, 3, 114	A. T. Cordero Jr.	Big Brave Rock, 3, 114	John's Gold, 3, 114	7	1:23.20	33,000
1981	**Proud Appeal**, 3, 121	J. Fell	Willow Hour, 3, 114	Royal Pavilion, 3, 114	4	1:22.20	32,940
1980	**Colonel Moran**, 3, 121	J. Velasquez	Son of a Dodo, 3, 114	Dunham's Gift, 3, 114	7	1:23.80	34,260
1979	**Belle's Gold**, 3, 114	G. Martens	Screen King, 3, 121	General Assembly, 3, 123	4	1:21.80	32,040
1978	**Piece of Heaven**, 3, 119	R. Hernandez	Just Right Classi, 3, 114	Slap Jack, 3, 114	8	1:11.00	32,460
1977	**Cormorant**, 3, 121	D. R. Wright	Medieval Man, 3, 119	Hey Hey J. P., 3, 114	6	1:10.80	32,460
1976	**Bold Forbes**, 3, 119	A. T. Cordero Jr.	Eustace, 3, 121	Full Out, 3, 124	8	1:20.80	33,780
1975	**Laramie Trail**, 3, 113	M. Venezia	T. V. Charger, 3, 113	Ascetic, 3, 121	5	1:23.60	26,910
	Lefty, 3, 113	R. Turcotte	Tass, 3, 113	Gallant Bob, 3, 119	8	1:23.80	27,360
1974	**Hudson County**, 3, 113	M. Miceli	Frankie Adams, 3, 119	Instead of Roses, 3, 116	11	1:22.60	34,680
1973	**Secretariat**, 3, 126	R. Turcotte	Champagne Charlie, 3, 118	Impecunious, 3, 116	6	1:23.20	16,650

Named for Bay Shore, a resort community located on Long Island, New York. Grade 2 1985-'92. Bayshore S. 1894-1909. Bay Shore H. 1925-'62, 1979-'80. Held at Gravesend 1894-1909. Not held 1910-'24, 1956-'59, 1993. 1¹/₁₆ miles 1894. 1 mile 1895, 1933, 1960-'63. 6 furlongs 1896-'98, 1934-'35, 1977-'78, 1984, 1994. About 6 furlongs 1899-1909. 6¹/₂ furlongs 1936-'39. Three-year-olds and up 1894-1960. Two divisions 1975, 1986.

Beaugay Handicap

Grade 3 in 2005. Aqueduct, three-year-olds and up, fillies and mares, 1¹/₁₆ miles, turf. Held April 30, 2005, with a gross value of $112,800. First held in 1978. First graded in 1986. Stakes record 1:40.16 (1991 Summer Secretary).

Year	Winner	Jockey	Second	Third	Strs	Time	1st Purse
2005	**Finery**, 5, 116	P. Fragoso	Changing World, 5, 118	Asti (Ire), 4, 117	9	1:44.56	$67,680
2004	**Dedication (Fr)**, 5, 118	J. Castellano	Aud, 4, 117	Caught in the Rain, 5, 114	7	1:46.38	66,000
2003	**Delta Princess**, 4, 113	M. J. Luzzi	Wonder Again, 4, 118	Voodoo Dancer, 5, 120	9	1:42.36	67,440
2002	**Voodoo Dancer**, 4, 119	J. D. Bailey	Golden Corona, 4, 115	Babae (Chi), 6, 116	10	1:43.10	67,920
2001	**Gaviola**, 4, 120	J. D. Bailey	Truebreadpudding, 6, 113	Efficient Frontier, 4, 114	6	1:41.74	65,940
2000	**Perfect Sting**, 4, 119	J. D. Bailey	License Fee, 5, 114	Fictitious (GB), 4, 114	7	1:42.30	65,820
1999	**Tampico**, 6, 114	J. R. Velazquez	U R Unforgetable, 5, 115	Shashobegon, 4, 114	7	1:44.32	67,020
1998	**National Treasure**, 5, 117	R. Migliore	Aspiring, 5, 113	Dixie Ghost, 4, 111	7	1:37.94	67,740
1997	**Careless Heiress**, 4, 116	J. Bravo	Song of Africa, 4, 113	Gastronomical, 4, 115	6	1:46.28	65,760
1996	**Christmas Gift**, 4, 118	J. D. Bailey	Caress, 5, 119	Aucilla, 5, 113	9	1:42.89	50,805
1995	**Caress**, 4, 113	R. G. Davis	Shir Dar (Fr), 5, 113	Statuette, 5, 116	8	1:42.06	49,905
1994	**Cox Orange**, 4, 112	J. D. Bailey	Irish Linnet, 6, 116	Statuette, 4, 116	5	1:43.32	49,395
1993	**McKaymackenna**, 4, 113	J. Velasquez	Aurora, 5, 115	Chinese Empress, 4, 114	10	1:44.80	57,240
1992	**Christiecat**, 5, 116	J. Samyn	Metamorphose, 4, 113	Navarra, 4, 109	10	1:46.84	56,520
1991	**Summer Secretary**, 6, 116	J. Velasquez	Virgin Michael, 4, 113	Christiecat, 4, 115	7	**1:40.16**	54,270
1990	**Fieldy (Ire)**, 7, 119	C. Perret	Summer Secretary, 5, 114	Lady Talc, 6, 110	5	1:45.80	52,740
1989	**Summer Secretary**, 4, 109	J. Samyn	Far East, 6, 110	Fieldy (Ire), 6, 116	9	1:43.40	56,880

1988	**Key to the Bridge**, 4, 112	E. Maple	Marimascus, 4, 112	Just Class (Ire), 4, 115	5	1:51.80	$65,160
1987	**Give a Toast**, 4, 111	R. G. Davis	Videogenic, 5, 117	Small Virtue, 4, 113	8	1:44.20	68,940
1986	**Duty Dance**, 4, 115	J. Cruguet	Possible Mate, 5, 124	Lucky Touch, 4, 109	10	1:40.20	55,800
1985	**Possible Mate**, 4, 119	J. Vasquez	Make the Magic, 4, 109	Annie Edge (Ire), 5, 114	8	1:40.60	42,600
1984	**Thirty Flags**, 4, 113	A. T. Cordero Jr.	Jubilous, 4, 114	Nany, 4, 111	12	1:42.00	45,840
1983	**Trevita (Ire)**, 6, 119	J. Velasquez	Beech Island, 5, 108	Top of the Barrel, 5, 105	12	1:47.80	37,020
1982	**Cheap Seats**, 3, 113	A. T. Cordero Jr.	Tina Tina Too, 4, 115	Fancy Naskra, 4, 112	7	1:45.20	33,780
1981	**Andover Way**, 3, 120	A. T. Cordero Jr.	Water Dance, 4, 117	Tournament Star, 3, 109	10	1:44.00	34,440
1980	**Samarta Dancer**, 4, 114	L. Saumell	Plankton, 4, 121	Bien Fait, 4, 109	8	1:43.60	33,540
1979	**Plankton**, 3, 113	R. Hernandez	Miss Baja, 4, 114	Reflection Pool, 5, 112	6	1:46.00	25,612
	Heavenly Ade, 3, 114	M. Solomone	Propitiate, 4, 112	Gladiolus, 5, 122	5	1:45.60	25,613
1978	**Shukey**, 3, 113	J. Velasquez	Sans Critique, 4, 118	Whodatorsay, 4, 109	6	1:45.20	25,755

Named for Maine Chance Farm's 1945 champion two-year-old filly Beaugay (1943 f. by Stimulus). Held at Belmont Park 1983-'92. 1 mile 1998. Dirt 1978-'82, 1998. Two divisions 1979.

Bed o' Roses Breeders' Cup Handicap

Grade 3 in 2005. Aqueduct, three-year-olds and up, fillies and mares, 1 mile, dirt. Held April 23, 2005, with a gross value of $153,200. First held in 1957. First graded in 1973. Stakes record 1:33.60 (1998 Dixie Flag).

Year	Winner	Jockey	Second	Third	Strs	Time	1st Purse
2005	**Pleasant Home**, 4, 114	C. H. Velasquez	Traci Girl, 6, 114	Cativa, 5, 117	7	1:36.72	$95,220
2004	**Passing Shot**, 5, 115	J. A. Santos	Smok'n Frolic, 5, 119	Nonsuch Bay, 5, 116	6	1:35.50	95,040
2003	**Raging Fever**, 5, 119	A. T. Gryder	Smok'n Frolic, 4, 120	Nonsuch Bay, 4, 117	5	1:34.86	93,960
2002	**Raging Fever**, 4, 121	J. R. Velazquez	Atelier, 5, 119	Shiny Band, 4, 112	6	1:34.96	94,980
2001	**Country Hideaway**, 5, 117	J. R. Velazquez	Critical Eye, 4, 115	Jostle, 4, 117	7	1:34.98	95,520
2000	**Ruby Rubles**, 5, 113	C. C. Lopez	Up We Go, 4, 114	Go to the Ink, 4, 111	7	1:36.96	65,580
1999	**Catinca**, 4, 120	R. Migliore	Foil, 4, 113	License Fee, 4, 113	6	1:34.95	94,620
1998	**Dixie Flag**, 4, 117	M. J. Luzzi	Hidden Reserve, 4, 113	U Can Do It, 5, 118	9	**1:33.60**	96,780
1997	**Flat Fleet Feet**, 4, 121	M. E. Smith	Mama Dean, 4, 113	Ashboro, 4, 116	6	1:34.00	95,940
1996	**Punkin Pie**, 6, 110	J. C. Trejo	Incinerate, 6, 115	Lottsa Talc, 6, 121	6	1:35.13	65,220
1995	**Incinerate**, 5, 113	F. Leon	Imah, 5, 114	Beckys Shirt, 4, 113	5	1:35.86	63,960
1994	**Classy Mirage**, 4, 117	R. G. Davis	For all Seasons, 4, 115	Dispute, 4, 122	6	1:34.00	64,680
1993	**Lady d'Accord**, 6, 111	J. F. Chavez	Missy's Mirage, 5, 123	Buck Some Belle, 4, 106	5	1:36.76	67,320
1992	**Nannerl**, 5, 115	J. A. Krone	English Charm, 6, 111	Spy Leader Lady, 4, 115	7	1:37.27	68,100
	Lady d'Accord, 5, 114	J. F. Chavez	My Treasure, 5, 112	Crystal Vous, 4, 112	7	1:37.86	68,580
1991	**Devil's Orchid**, 4, 120	R. A. Baze	Colonial Waters, 6, 119	Sharp Dance, 5, 114	6	1:35.93	68,520
1990	**Survive**, 6, 117	J. A. Santos	Amy Be Good, 4, 114	Warfie, 4, 111	6	1:34.20	68,640
1989	**Banker's Lady**, 4, 118	A. T. Cordero Jr.	Aptostar, 4, 118	Avie's Gal, 4, 114	5	1:35.40	68,400
1988	**Aptostar**, 3, 103	J. A. Krone	Clabber Girl, 5, 117	Psyched, 5, 114	8	1:35.40	70,680
1987	**Ms. Eloise**, 4, 115	R. G. Davis	Spring Beauty, 4, 116	Tricky Squaw, 4, 115	9	1:36.60	84,660
1986	**Chaldea**, 6, 110	J. Samyn	Add Mint, 4, 111	Lady On the Run, 4, 120	9	1:36.00	75,120
1985	**Nany**, 5, 120	J. Vasquez	Flip's Pleasure, 5, 118	Sintrillium, 7, 120	6	1:36.00	50,850
1984	**Pleasure Cay**, 4, 115	R. G. Davis	Sweet Missus, 4, 103	Sintrillium, 6, 113	4	1:42.00	54,090
1983	**Broom Dance**, 4, 118	G. McCarron	Adept, 4, 109	Viva Sec, 5, 112	7	1:35.40	33,420
1982	**Who's to Answer**, 4, 108	E. Beitia	Real Prize, 4, 114	Faisana (Arg), 5, 110	9	1:36.60	33,180
1981	**Chain Bracelet**, 4, 114	F. Lovato Jr.	Lady Oakley (Ire), 4, 116	Contrary Rose, 5, 115	7	1:35.40	33,960
1980	**Misty Gallore**, 4, 125	D. MacBeth	Propitiate, 5, 115	Gueniviere, 4, 111	6	1:36.40	33,600
1979	**One Sum**, 5, 118	J. Fell	Reflection Pool, 5, 113	Pearl Necklace, 5, 121	7	1:37.80	31,980
	Lady Lonsdale, 4, 111	C. B. Asmussen	Hagany, 5, 113	Back to Stay, 4, 107	7	1:36.80	31,980
1978	**Fearless Queen**, 5, 108	M. Venezia	Notably, 5, 110	One Sum, 4, 123	7	1:46.20	25,785
1977	**Shawi**, 4, 109	M. Venezia	Proud Delta, 5, 125	Secret Lanvin, 4, 111	8	1:45.80	25,770
1976	**Imminence**, 4, 115	E. Maple	Spring Is Here, 4, 108	Land Girl, 4, 114	6	1:35.40	23,040
1975	**Shy Dawn**, 4, 121	D. Montoya	Something Super, 5, 118	Flo's Pleasure, 5, 115	7	1:36.20	16,860
1974	**Klepto**, 4, 123	D. Montoya	Ladies Agreement, 4, 112	Summer Guest, 5, 122	6	1:35.40	16,410
1973	**Poker Night**, 3, 108	R. Woodhouse	Numbered Account, 4, 123	Ferly, 5, 114	6	1:35.40	16,605

Named for Alfred G. Vanderbilt's 1949 champion two-year-old filly and '51 champion older mare, Bed o' Roses (1947 f. by Rosemont). Grade 2 1973-'74, 1988-'96. Bed o' Roses H. 1957-'95. Held at Jamaica 1957-'59. 1 1/16 miles 1957-'59, 1977-'78. 1 mile 70 yards 1984. Two divisions 1979, 1992.

Beldame Stakes

Grade 1 in 2005. Belmont Park, three-year-olds and up, fillies and mares, 1 1/8 miles, dirt. Held October 9, 2004, with a gross value of $735,000. First held in 1905. First graded in 1973. Stakes record 1:45.80 (1990 Go for Wand).

Year	Winner	Jockey	Second	Third	Strs	Time	1st Purse
2004	**Sightseek**, 5, 123	J. Castellano	Society Selection, 3, 120	Storm Flag Flying, 4, 123	5	1:49.60	$450,000
2003	**Sightseek**, 4, 123	J. D. Bailey	Bird Town, 3, 120	Buy the Sport, 3, 120	7	1:49.27	450,000
2002	**Imperial Gesture**, 3, 120	J. D. Bailey	Mandy's Gold, 4, 123	Summer Colony, 4, 123	7	1:50.63	450,000
2001	**Exogenous**, 3, 120	J. Castellano	Flute, 3, 120	Spain, 4, 123	8	1:49.20	450,000
2000	**Riboletta (Brz)**, 5, 123	C. J. McCarron	Beautiful Pleasure, 5, 123	Pentatonic, 5, 123	5	1:46.14	450,000
1999	**Beautiful Pleasure**, 4, 123	J. F. Chavez	Silverbulletday, 3, 119	Catinca, 4, 123	5	1:47.74	300,000
1998	**Sharp Cat**, 4, 123	C. S. Nakatani	Tomisue's Delight, 4, 123	Pocho's Dream Girl, 4, 123	7	1:46.20	240,000
1997	**Hidden Lake**, 4, 123	R. Migliore	Ajina, 3, 119	Jewel Princess, 5, 123	8	1:48.26	240,000

Year	Winner	Jockey	Second	Third	Strs	Time	1st Purse
1996	Yanks Music, 3, 119	J. R. Velazquez	Serena's Song, 4, 123	Clear Mandate, 4, 123	6	1:47.02	$240,000
1995	Serena's Song, 3, 119	G. L. Stevens	Heavenly Prize, 4, 123	Lakeway, 4, 123	5	1:48.75	150,000
1994	Heavenly Prize, 3, 119	P. Day	Educated Risk, 4, 123	Classy Mirage, 4, 123	4	1:48.86	150,000
1993	Dispute, 3, 119	J. D. Bailey	Shared Interest, 5, 123	Vivano, 4, 123	6	1:47.22	150,000
1992	Saratoga Dew, 3, 119	W. H. McCauley	Versailles Treaty, 4, 123	Coxwold, 4, 123	5	1:46.99	150,000
1991	Sharp Dance, 5, 123	M. E. Smith	Versailles Treaty, 3, 119	Lady d'Accord, 4, 123	6	1:48.01	150,000
1990	Go for Wand, 3, 119	R. P. Romero	Colonial Waters, 5, 123	Buy the Firm, 4, 123	5	1:45.80	167,700
1989	Tactile, 3, 118	R. Migliore	Colonial Waters, 4, 123	Rose's Cantina, 5, 123	6	2:05.20	170,100
1988	Personal Ensign, 4, 123	R. P. Romero	Classic Crown, 3, 118	Sham Say, 3, 118	5	2:01.20	199,440
1987	Personal Ensign, 3, 118	R. P. Romero	Coup de Fusil, 5, 123	Silent Turn, 3, 118	10	2:04.40	182,100
1986	Lady's Secret, 4, 123	P. Day	Coup de Fusil, 4, 123	Classy Cathy, 3, 118	4	2:01.60	189,600
1985	Lady's Secret, 3, 118	J. Velasquez	Isayso, 6, 123	Kamikaze Rick, 3, 118	5	2:03.60	160,920
1984	Life's Magic, 3, 118	J. Velasquez	Miss Oceana, 3, 118	Key Dancer, 3, 118	4	2:03.20	158,280
1983	Dance Number, 4, 123	A. T. Cordero Jr.	Heartlight No. One, 3, 118	Mochila, 4, 123	7	2:00.60	133,200
1982	Weber City Miss, 5, 123	A. T. Cordero Jr.	Mademoiselle Forli, 3, 118	Love Sign, 5, 123	9	2:04.20	134,100
1981	Love Sign, 4, 123	W. Shoemaker	dh-Glorious Song, 5, 123		7	2:01.20	131,100
			dh-Jameela, 5, 123				
1980	Love Sign, 3, 118	R. Hernandez	Misty Gallore, 4, 123	It's in the Air, 4, 123	4	2:02.80	96,300
1979	Waya (Fr), 5, 123	C. B. Asmussen	Fourdrinier, 3, 118	Kit's Double, 6, 123	7	2:06.20	97,050
1978	Late Bloomer, 4, 123	J. Velasquez	Pearl Necklace, 4, 123	Cum Laude Laurie, 4, 123	4	2:02.20	78,150
1977	Cum Laude Laurie, 3, 118	A. T. Cordero Jr.	What a Summer, 4, 123	Charming Story, 3, 118	7	2:01.80	80,025
1976	Proud Delta, 4, 123	J. Velasquez	Revidere, 3, 118	*Bastonera II, 5, 120	8	1:46.80	64,920
1975	Susan's Girl, 6, 123	B. Baeza	*Tizna, 6, 123	Pass a Glance, 4, 123	9	1:48.40	67,980
1974	Desert Vixen, 4, 123	L. A. Pincay Jr.	Poker Night, 4, 123	*Tizna, 5, 123	9	1:46.60	68,760
1973	Desert Vixen, 3, 118	J. Velasquez	Poker Night, 3, 118	Susan's Girl, 4, 123	7	1:46.20	65,880

Named for August Belmont II's consensus champion racemare and 1904 Carter H. winner Beldame (1901 f. by Octagon). Beldame H. 1905-'59. Held at Aqueduct 1905-'56, 1959, 1962-'68. Not held 1908, 1910-'16, 1933-'38. 5 furlongs 1905-'32. 1 1/16 miles 1939. 1 1/4 miles 1977-'89. Two-year-olds 1905-'32. Fillies 1905-'32. Dead heat for second 1981. Equaled world record 1973. Equaled track record 1973.

Belmont Breeders' Cup Handicap

Grade 2 in 2005. Belmont Park, three-year-olds and up, 1 1/8 miles, turf. Held September 18, 2004, with a gross value of $197,800. First held in 1986. First graded in 1988. Stakes record 1:45.90 (1998 Subordination).

Year	Winner	Jockey	Second	Third	Strs	Time	1st Purse
2004	Senor Swinger, 4, 117	E. S. Prado	Stroll, 4, 120	B. A. Way, 4, 113	4	1:52.72	$124,680
2003	Della Francesca, 4, 114	J. F. Chavez	Rouvres (Fr), 4, 116	Volponi, 5, 119	7	1:47.48	125,760
2002	Startac, 4, 116	J. D. Bailey	Volponi, 4, 117	Dr. Kashnikow, 5, 115	6	1:46.60	125,160
2000	Forbidden Apple, 5, 114	J. A. Santos	Val's Prince, 8, 118	Altibr, 5, 113	6	1:51.73	126,000
1999	With the Flow, 4, 114	J. A. Santos	Comic Strip, 4, 118	Wised Up, 4, 112	9	1:49.39	127,620
1998	Subordination, 4, 121	D. R. Flores	Yagli, 5, 122	Bomfim, 5, 114	9	1:45.90	127,020
1997	Fortitude, 4, 112	R. G. Davis	Green Means Go, 5, 113	Boyce, 6, 118	8	1:38.53	126,600
1996	‡Gentleman Beau, 4, 114	J. A. Santos	Volochine (Ire), 5, 116	Kiri's Clown, 7, 114	7	1:41.18	127,140
1995	Dove Hunt, 4, 121	P. Day	Fly Cry, 4, 116	Unfinished Symph, 4, 122	6	1:40.18	92,970
1994	A in Sociology, 4, 116	J. Samyn	Fourstars Allstar, 6, 119	Home of the Free, 6, 114	10	1:40.19	34,290
1993	Fourstars Allstar, 5, 116	J. A. Santos	Lech, 5, 115	Cleone, 4, 113	6	1:39.88	92,880
1992	Roman Envoy, 4, 113	C. Perret	Lotus Pool, 5, 114	Daarik (Ire), 5, 114	10	1:41.50	34,800
1991	Solar Splendor, 4, 113	W. H. McCauley	Who's to Pay, 5, 118	Jalaajel, 7, 114	7	1:41.16	93,210
1990	Who's to Pay, 4, 113	J. D. Bailey	Jalaajel, 6, 115	Caltech, 4, 120	8	1:46.00	93,570
1989	Highland Springs, 5, 117	K. J. Desormeaux	Maceo, 5, 113	Slew City Slew, 5, 118	6	1:39.20	93,180
1988	Steinlen (GB), 5, 120	P. Day	Iron Courage, 4, 113	Barood, 5, 110	4	1:43.40	93,540
1987	Talakeno, 7, 117	A. T. Cordero Jr.	Lightning Leap, 5, 110	Glaros (Fr), 5, 111	4	1:49.40	93,090
1986	Danger's Hour, 4, 116	J. D. Bailey	‡Salem Drive, 4, 115	Silver Voice, 3, 110	5	1:40.80	95,280

Grade 3 1988-'97. Saratoga Budweiser Breeders' Cup H. 1986-'93. Belmont Budweiser Breeders' Cup H. 1994-'95. Held at Saratoga Race Course 1986-'93. Not held due to World Trade Center attack 2001. 1 1/16 miles 1986-'97. ‡Silver Voice finished second, DQ to third, 1986. DQ to third 1986. ‡Kiri's Clown finished first, DQ to third, 1996. Course record 1997.

Belmont Stakes

Grade 1 in 2005. Belmont Park, three-year-olds, 1 1/2 miles, dirt. Held June 11, 2005, with a gross value of $1,000,000. First held in 1867. First graded in 1924. Stakes record 2:24 (1973 Secretariat [current world and track record]).

(See Triple Crown section for complete history of the Belmont Stakes)

Year	Winner	Jockey	Second	Third	Strs	Time	1st Purse
2005	Afleet Alex, 3, 126	J. Rose	Andromeda's Hero, 3, 126	Nolan's Cat, 3, 126	11	2:28.75	$600,000
2004	Birdstone, 3, 126	E. S. Prado	Smarty Jones, 3, 126	Royal Assault, 3, 126	9	2:27.50	600,000
2003	Empire Maker, 3, 126	J. D. Bailey	Ten Most Wanted, 3, 126	Funny Cide, 3, 126	6	2:28.26	600,000
2002	Sarava, 3, 126	E. S. Prado	Medaglia d'Oro, 3, 126	Sunday Break (Jpn), 3, 126	11	2:29.71	600,000
2001	Point Given, 3, 126	G. L. Stevens	A P Valentine, 3, 126	Monarchos, 3, 126	9	2:26.56	600,000
2000	Commendable, 3, 126	P. Day	Aptitude, 3, 126	Unshaded, 3, 126	11	2:31.19	600,000
1999	Lemon Drop Kid, 3, 126	J. A. Santos	Vision and Verse, 3, 126	Charismatic, 3, 126	12	2:27.88	600,000
1998	Victory Gallop, 3, 126	G. L. Stevens	Real Quiet, 3, 126	Thomas Jo, 3, 126	11	2:29.16	600,000
1997	Touch Gold, 3, 126	C. J. McCarron	Silver Charm, 3, 126	Free House, 3, 126	7	2:28.82	432,600

				Strs	Time	1st Purse
1996 **Editor's Note**, 3, 126	R. R. Douglas	Skip Away, 3, 126	†My Flag, 3, 121	14	2:28.96	$437,880
1995 **Thunder Gulch**, 3, 126	G. L. Stevens	Star Standard, 3, 126	Citadeed, 3, 126	11	2:32.02	415,440
1994 **Tabasco Cat**, 3, 126	P. Day	Go for Gin, 3, 126	Strodes Creek, 3, 126	6	2:26.82	392,280
1993 **Colonial Affair**, 3, 126	J. A. Krone	Kissin Kris, 3, 126	Wild Gale, 3, 126	13	2:29.97	444,540
1992 **A.P. Indy**, 3, 126	E. J. Delahoussaye	My Memoirs (GB), 3, 126	Pine Bluff, 3, 126	11	2:26.13	458,880
1991 **Hansel**, 3, 126	J. D. Bailey	Strike the Gold, 3, 126	Mane Minister, 3, 126	11	2:28.10	1,417,480
1990 **Go and Go (Ire)**, 3, 126	M. J. Kinane	Thirty Six Red, 3, 126	Baron de Vaux, 3, 126	9	2:27.20	411,600
1989 **Easy Goer**, 3, 126	P. Day	Sunday Silence, 3, 126	Le Voyageur, 3, 126	10	2:26.00	413,520
1988 **Risen Star**, 3, 126	E. J. Delahoussaye	Kingpost, 3, 126	Brian's Time, 3, 126	11	2:26.40	1,303,720
1987 **Bet Twice**, 3, 126	C. Perret	Cryptoclearance, 3, 126	Gulch, 3, 126	9	2:28.20	1,329,160
1986 **Danzig Connection**, 3, 126	C. J. McCarron	Johns Treasure, 3, 126	Ferdinand, 3, 126	10	2:29.80	338,640
1985 **Creme Fraiche**, 3, 126	E. Maple	Stephan's Odyssey, 3, 126	Chief's Crown, 3, 126	11	2:27.00	307,740
1984 **Swale**, 3, 126	L. A. Pincay Jr.	Pine Circle, 3, 126	Morning Bob, 3, 126	11	2:27.00	310,020
1983 **Caveat**, 3, 126	L. A. Pincay Jr.	Slew o' Gold, 3, 126	Barberstown, 3, 126	15	2:27.80	215,100
1982 **Conquistador Cielo**, 3, 126	L. A. Pincay Jr.	Gato Del Sol, 3, 126	Illuminate, 3, 126	11	2:28.20	159,720
1981 **Summing**, 3, 126	G. Martens	Highland Blade, 3, 126	Pleasant Colony, 3, 126	11	2:29.00	170,580
1980 **Temperence Hill**, 3, 126	E. Maple	†Genuine Risk, 3, 121	Rockhill Native, 3, 126	10	2:29.80	176,220
1979 **Coastal**, 3, 126	R. Hernandez	Golden Act, 3, 126	Spectacular Bid, 3, 126	8	2:28.60	161,400
1978 **Affirmed**, 3, 126	S. Cauthen	Alydar, 3, 126	Darby Creek Road, 3, 126	5	2:26.80	110,580
1977 **Seattle Slew**, 3, 126	J. Cruguet	Run Dusty Run, 3, 126	Sanhedrin, 3, 126	8	2:29.60	109,080
1976 **Bold Forbes**, 3, 126	A. T. Cordero Jr.	McKenzie Bridge, 3, 126	Great Contractor, 3, 126	10	2:29.00	117,000
1975 **Avatar**, 3, 126	W. Shoemaker	Foolish Pleasure, 3, 126	Master Derby, 3, 126	9	2:28.20	116,160
1974 **Little Current**, 3, 126	M. A. Rivera	Jolly Johu, 3, 126	Cannonade, 3, 126	9	2:29.20	101,970
1973 **Secretariat**, 3, 126	R. Turcotte	Twice a Prince, 3, 126	My Gallant, 3, 126	5	**2:24.00**	90,120

Named for August Belmont I (1816-'90), president of Jerome Park. Belmont H. 1895, 1913. Held at Jerome Park 1867-'89. Held at Morris Park 1890-1904. Held at Aqueduct 1963-'67. Not held 1911-'12. 1⅝ miles 1867-'73. 1¼ miles 1890-'92, 1895, 1904-'05. 1⅛ miles 1893-'94. 1⅜ miles 1896-1903, 1906-'25. Colts and fillies 1919-'56. World record 1973. Track record 1973. †Denotes female. $1,000,000 Triple Crown bonus awarded on a points basis 1987-'88, 1991.

Ben Ali Stakes

Grade 3 in 2005. Keeneland, four-year-olds and up, 1⅛ miles, dirt. Held April 28, 2005, with a gross value of $150,000. First held in 1917. First graded in 1973. Stakes record 1:46.78 (2004 Midway Road).

Year	Winner	Jockey	Second	Third	Strs	Time	1st Purse
2005	**Alumni Hall**, 6, 121	R. Albarado	Pies Prospect, 4, 123	Go Now, 4, 117	8	1:51.29	$93,000
2004	**Midway Road**, 4, 116	R. Albarado	Evening Attire, 6, 116	Sir Cherokee, 4, 120	5	**1:46.78**	93,000
2003	**Mineshaft**, 4, 120	R. Albarado	American Style, 4, 116	Metatron, 4, 116	4	1:48.52	68,386
2002	**Duckhorn**, 4, 116	J. F. Chavez	Parade Leader, 5, 120	Connected, 5, 118	4	1:50.18	66,464
2001	**Broken Vow**, 4, 116	E. S. Prado	Perfect Cat, 4, 116	Jadada, 6, 116	5	1:48.47	66,216
2000	**Midway Magistrate**, 6, 116	S. J. Sellers	Liberty Gold, 6, 116	Early Warning, 5, 118	7	1:49.15	67,518
1999	**Jazz Club**, 4, 115	P. Day	Smile Again, 4, 115	Early Warning, 4, 115	6	1:48.16	67,456
1998	**Storm Broker**, 4, 114	R. Albarado	Delay of Game, 5, 119	Gator Dancer, 5, 114	6	1:48.23	67,208
1997	**Louis Quatorze**, 4, 119	P. Day	Knockadoon, 5, 113	King James, 5, 113	5	1:49.44	66,526
1996	**Knockadoon**, 4, 112	J. D. Bailey	Halo's Image, 5, 117	Thorny Crown, 5, 113	4	1:48.92	66,216
1995	**Wildly Joyous**, 4, 114	M. Walls	Danville, 4, 117	Powerful Punch, 6, 113	7	1:49.68	50,406
1994	**Pistols and Roses**, 5, 123	M. E. Smith	Sunny Sunrise, 7, 119	Compadre, 4, 113	6	1:51.77	50,251
1993	**Sunny Sunrise**, 6, 119	R. Wilson	Conte Di Savoya, 4, 113	Prize Fight, 4, 112	8	1:48.90	50,933
1992	**dh- Loach**, 4, 117	P. A. Valenzuela		Out of Place, 5, 119	6	1:49.95	34,212
	dh- Profit Key, 5, 113	S. J. Sellers					
1991	**Sports View**, 4, 119	C. Perret	Bright Again, 4, 113	Exemplary Leader, 5, 112	6	1:49.67	53,495
1990	**Master Speaker**, 5, 121	J. D. Bailey	Lac Ouimet, 7, 114	Silver Survivor, 4, 119	7	1:49.00	54,893
1989	**Classic Account**, 4, 114	P. Day	Regal Classic, 4, 117	Brian's Time, 4, 121	5	1:50.60	53,885
1988	**Homebuilder**, 4, 119	D. Brumfield	Bet Twice, 4, 126	Blue Buckaroo, 5, 117	4	1:51.40	52,293
1987	**Intrusion**, 5, 111	S. Hawley	Coaxing Mark, 4, 114	Blue Buckaroo, 4, 117	5	1:49.60	34,678
1986	**Czar Nijinsky**, 4, 119	W. H. McCauley	Little Missouri, 4, 117	Minneapple, 4, 117	8	1:50.20	43,542
1985	**Bello**, 4, 116	G. Gallitano	Silent King, 4, 117	Hi Pi, 6, 113	7	1:48.80	35,295
1984	**Aspro**, 6, 116	D. Brumfield	Play Fellow, 4, 123	Jack Slade, 4, 115	5	1:50.80	34,564
1983	**Aspro**, 5, 115	V. A. Bracciale Jr.	Thirty Eight Paces, 5, 115	Rivalero, 7, 121	8	1:49.60	35,588
1982	**Withholding**, 5, 121	L. J. Melancon	Aspro, 4, 122	Swinging Light, 4, 113	4	1:49.60	35,880
1981	**Withholding**, 4, 113	B. Sayler	Summer Advocate, 4, 113	Two's a Plenty, 4, 115	4	1:50.20	34,986
1980	**Architect**, 4, 120	S. A. Spencer	Revivalist, 6, 116	All the More, 7, 116	6	1:48.80	27,999
1979	**Kodiack**, 5, 114	G. Gallitano	Hot Words, 4, 113	Morning Frolic, 4, 115	4	1:49.60	31,054
1978	**Prince Majestic**, 4, 118	E. J. Delahoussaye	Inca Roca, 5, 114	All the More, 5, 122	9	1:41.80	21,824
1977	**Honest Pleasure**, 4, 124	C. Perret	Inca Roca, 4, 118	Packer Captain, 5, 113	9	1:42.40	18,623
1976	**My Friend Gus**, 4, 114	D. G. McHargue	Packer Captain, 4, 116	Dragset, 5, 113	8	1:42.40	18,119
1975	**Navajo**, 5, 122	J. Nichols	L. Grant Jr., 5, 118	Hasty Flyer, 4, 115	12	1:43.80	19,419
1974	**Knight Counter**, 6, 119	E. Fires	Model Husband, 5, 117	Jim's Alibhi, 7, 113	6	1:41.80	17,648
1973	**Knight Counter**, 5, 120	D. Brumfield	‡Guitar Player, 5, 118	Introductivo, 4, 114	12	1:43.00	18,785

Named for James Ben Ali Haggin (1821-1914), native Kentuckian and owner of Elmendorf Farm, and his 1886 Kentucky Derby winner Ben Ali (1883 c. by Virgil). Ben Ali H. 1917-'89. Held at Kentucky Association 1917-'31. Held at Churchill Downs 1943-'45. Not held 1923-'27, 1932-'36. 1¹⁄₁₆ miles 1917-'30, 1937-'53, 1963-'78. About 6 furlongs 1931. About 7 furlongs 1954-'62. Three-year-olds and up 1917-'85. Dead heat for first 1992. ‡Hustlin Greek finished second, DQ to 12th for a positive drug test, 1973. Track record 2004.

Berkeley Handicap

Grade 3 in 2005. Golden Gate Fields, three-year-olds and up, 1¹/₁₆ miles, dirt. Held June 11, 2005, with a gross value of $100,000. First held in 1933. First graded in 2000. Stakes record 1:40.94 (2005 Desert Boom).

Year	Winner	Jockey	Second	Third	Strs	Time	1st Purse
2005	Desert Boom, 5, 113	R. M. Gonzalez	Easy Million, 5, 116	Yougottawanna, 6, 118	7	1:40.94	$55,000
2004	Snorter, 4, 116	R. A. Baze	Yougottawanna, 5, 116	Taste of Paradise, 5, 116	5	1:33.92	55,000
2003	I'madrifter, 5, 115	R. M. Gonzalez	Palmeiro, 5, 117	Skip to the Stone, 5, 116	6	1:35.13	55,000
2002	Irisheyesareflying, 6, 120	J. Valdivia Jr.	Boss Ego, 6, 116	Palmeiro, 4, 116	11	1:35.41	55,000
2001	Blade Prospector (Brz), 6, 116	O. A. Berrio	Dixie Dot Com, 6, 119	Milk Wood (GB), 6, 115	6	1:34.18	55,000
2000	Voice of Destiny, 4, 113	R. Q. Meza	Mr. Doubledown, 6, 115	Twilight Affair, 6, 115	8	1:35.67	75,000
1999	Hal's Pal (GB), 6, 117	B. Blanc	Wild Wonder, 5, 122	Worldly Ways (GB), 5, 115	7	1:34.96	75,000
1998	Wild Wonder, 4, 115	R. A. Baze	General Royal, 4, 115	March of Kings, 5, 116	7	1:35.19	47,700
1996	Houston Fleet M D, 2, 118	D. Carr	Slewp'a Doop, 2, 116	Big Find, 2, 116	5	1:36.67	26,600
1995	Double Jab, 4, 115	R. A. Baze	Corslew, 5, 116	Cleante (Arg), 6, 115	8	1:35.18	49,725
1994	River Special, 4, 115	T. M. Chapman	He's Illustrious, 7, 116	Misty Wind (Ire), 6, 114	8	1:34.33	32,600
1993	Infamous Deed, 5, 115	R. J. Warren Jr.	Misty Wind (Ire), 5, 116	J. F. Williams, 4, 115	7	1:35.67	25,960
1992	Music Prospector, 5, 118	R. D. Hansen	Michael's Flyer, 6, 115	Flying Continental, 6, 124	5	1:35.29	31,450
1991	High Energy, 4, 115	R. J. Warren Jr.	Bold Current, 4, 114	Beau's Alliance, 5, 115	8	1:35.70	32,800
1990	On the Menu, 4, 112	C. L. Davenport	Crackedbell, 5, 116	Ongoing Mister, 5, 117	6	1:34.80	31,600
1989	Ongoing Mister, 4, 114	T. T. Doocy	Present Value, 5, 113	Lucky Harold H., 5, 110	8	1:34.20	33,600
1988	Sanger Chief, 5, 114	T. T. Doocy	Lucky Harold H., 4, 114	Power Forward, 5, 119	7	1:35.60	31,900
1987	Rocky Marriage, 7, 116	R. A. Baze	Dormello (Arg), 6, 115	Bagdad Dawn, 5, 112	7	1:36.80	32,250
1986	Sun Master, 5, 117	M. Castaneda	Beldale Lear, 5, 123	Prairie Breaker, 6, 114	6	1:34.60	25,400
1985	Nak Ack, 4, 114	J. C. Judice	Holmbury, 5, 113	Chum Salmon, 5, 116	9	1:36.20	26,600
1984	Songhay, 5, 114	J. C. Judice	Grand Balcony, 5, 113	The Jandy Man, 4, 113	11	1:35.40	27,300
1983	Pleasant Power, 5, 115	J. R. Anderson	Lord Advocate, 4, 117	Red Crescent, 7, 119	13	1:40.60	27,800
1982	Foyt's Ack, 7, 115	R. M. Gonzalez	Borrego Sun, 5, 118	Pleasant Power, 4, 112	8	1:38.00	25,650
1981	Head Hawk, 5, 111	D. Sorenson	His Honor, 6, 115	Beau Moro, 6, 117	7	1:45.60	25,750
1979	Gustoso, 4, 120	R. Campas	Rassendyll, 5, 113	Rescator, 5, 117	7	1:34.40	20,500
1978	Boy Tike, 5, 114	A. L. Diaz	Dr. Krohn, 5, 120	Miami Sun, 4, 120	7	1:36.20	19,250
1977	Lino, 5, 112	R. Caballero	Crafty Native, 4, 114	Classy Surgeon, 4, 116	7	1:37.40	16,050
1976	Branford Court, 6, 113	A. L. Diaz	Austin Mittler, 4, 117	Carry the Banner, 6, 113	7	1:35.00	15,700
1975	Star of Kuwait, 7, 118	W. Mahorney	Willie Pleasant, 4, 116	Mac's L., 4, 111	10	1:44.80	16,450
1974	*Yvetot, 6, 120	F. Olivares	Sensitive Music, 5, 114	*Larkal II, 6, 113	8	1:43.80	17,800
1973	*Yvetot, 5, 112	V. Tejada	Cabin, 5, 121	Masked, 4, 120	10	1:44.20	18,050

Named for Berkeley, California, located near San Francisco. Berkeley S. 1948. Berkeley H. 1933, 1938, 1949-2003. Held at Tanforan 1933. Held at Bay Meadows 1938. Not held 1934-'37, 1939-'47, 1961-'62, 1980, 1997. About 6 furlongs 1938. 6 furlongs 1938-'50, 1952-'55, 1957-'59. 1 mile 1951, 1956, 1964, 1976-'80, 1982-2004. 1¹/₄ miles 1966-'70. 1¹/₈ miles 1971. Turf 1972-'74, 1976. Originally scheduled on turf 1975. Two-year-olds and up 1933. Two-year-olds and up 1948, 1957, 1996. Three-year-olds 1949-'56, 1958-'65. Four-year-olds and up 1968. Colts and geldings 1948. Fillies 1956-'58, 1964. Nonwinners of a race worth $12,500 to the winner 1973. Nonwinners of a race worth $35,000 to the winner one mile or over 1990, 1992.

Bernard Baruch Handicap

Grade 2 in 2005. Saratoga Race Course, three-year-olds and up, 1¹/₈ miles, turf. Held July 30, 2004, with a gross value of $150,000. First held in 1959. First graded in 1973. Stakes record 1:45.40 (1973 Tentam).

Year	Winner	Jockey	Second	Third	Strs	Time	1st Purse
2004	Silver Tree, 4, 116	J. D. Bailey	Nothing to Lose, 4, 117	Irish Colonial, 5, 113	7	1:49.66	$90,000
2003	Trademark (SAf), 7, 114	R. Migliore	Rouvres (Fr), 4, 116	Slew Valley, 6, 113	7	1:49.06	90,000
2002	Del Mar Show, 5, 120	J. D. Bailey	Volponi, 4, 116	Forbidden Apple, 7, 121	7	1:48.51	90,000
2001	Hap, 5, 121	J. D. Bailey	Royal Strand (Ire), 7, 115	Dr. Kashnikow, 4, 114	7	1:47.06	90,000
2000	Hap, 4, 115	J. D. Bailey	Inexplicable, 5, 116	Draw Shot, 7, 114	13	1:45.82	90,000
1999	Middlesex Drive, 4, 117	S. J. Sellers	Tangazi, 4, 114	Comic Strip, 4, 116	8	1:46.55	90,000
1998	Yagli, 5, 121	J. D. Bailey	Tamhid, 5, 113	Jambalaya Jazz, 6, 115	9	1:46.22	85,380
1997	Sentimental Moi, 7, 112	C. P. DeCarlo	Jambalaya Jazz, 5, 115	Boyce, 6, 120	8	1:46.11	66,480
1996	Volochine (Ire), 5, 113	P. Day	Green Means Go, 4, 116	Compadre, 6, 108	10	1:47.58	68,700
1995	Fourstars Allstar, 7, 120	J. A. Santos	Turk Passer, 5, 116	Compadre, 5, 112	7	1:47.67	66,240
1994	Lure, 5, 125	M. E. Smith	Paradise Creek, 4, 126	Fourstardave, 9, 114	5	1:46.10	64,920
1993	Furiously, 4, 119	J. D. Bailey	Star of Cozzene, 5, 123	Royal Mountain Inn, 4, 114	5	1:45.46	70,320
1992	Fourstars Allstar, 4, 113	M. E. Smith	Lotus Pool, 5, 113	Maxigroom, 4, 114	8	1:46.06	70,680
1991	Double Booked, 6, 122	A. Madrid Jr.	Who's to Pay, 5, 118	Solar Splendor, 4, 113	8	1:49.14	71,400
1990	Who's to Pay, 4, 110	J. Samyn	Steinlen (GB), 7, 126	River of Sin, 6, 115	9	1:48.40	52,920
1989	Steinlen (GB), 6, 121	J. A. Santos	Soviet Lad, 4, 111	Brian's Time, 4, 112	8	1:51.00	73,920
1988	My Big Boy, 5, 113	R. P. Romero	Steinlen (GB), 5, 120	Wanderkin, 5, 115	9	1:46.80	72,600
1987	Talakeno, 7, 115	A. T. Cordero Jr.	Manila, 4, 127	Duluth, 5, 114	4	1:47.40	85,380
1986	Exclusive Partner, 4, 112	J. Velasquez	I'm a Banker, 4, 111	Creme Fraiche, 4, 117	12	1:50.80	82,200
1985	Win, 5, 124	R. Migliore	Cozzene, 5, 120	Sitzmark, 5, 112	9	1:47.00	59,400
1984	Win, 4, 112	A. Graell	Intensify, 4, 113	Cozzene, 4, 114	9	1:47.40	57,510
1983	Tantalizing, 4, 115	J. D. Bailey	Ten Below, 4, 114	Acaroid, 5, 115	9	1:48.80	34,140
	Fray Star (Arg), 5, 114	O. Vergara	Fortnightly, 3, 113	Who's for Dinner, 4, 109	9	1:48.40	34,380
1982	Pair of Deuces, 4, 115	R. Hernandez	Native Courier, 7, 117	McCann, 4, 112	11	1:47.80	36,540
1981	Native Courier, 6, 114	E. Maple	Manguin, 5, 105	Proctor, 4, 118	7	1:47.40	33,450
	Great Neck, 5, 119	A. T. Cordero Jr.	War of Words, 4, 111	Match the Hatch, 5, 114	5	1:47.60	33,690

1980	Premier Ministre, 4, 116	R. I. Encinas	Great Neck, 4, 112	Tiller, 6, 126	11	2:13.60	$35,700
1979	Overskate, 4, 128	R. Platts	Timbo, 3, 108	Native Courier, 4, 115	7	1:51.80	35,610
1978	Dominion (GB), 6, 115	J. Samyn	Bill Brill, 4, 111	Upper Nile, 4, 119	11	1:49.00	24,480
1977	Majestic Light, 4, 126	S. Hawley	Alias Smith, 4, 112	Clout, 5, 114	11	1:46.20	23,175
1976	Intrepid Hero, 4, 123	E. Maple	Modred, 3, 118	Erwin Boy, 5, 126	8	1:50.40	22,530
1975	dh- Salt Marsh, 5, 116	E. Maple		Drollery, 5, 112	8	1:49.80	18,061
	dh- Ward McAllister, 4, 110	D. Montoya					
1974	Golden Don, 4, 113	V. A. Bracciale Jr.	Halo, 5, 119	Scantling, 4, 117	10	1:46.00	23,580
1973	Tentam, 4, 118	J. Velasquez	Scrimshaw, 5, 111	Astray, 4, 114	10	1:45.40	14,265
	Red Reality, 7, 120	J. Velasquez	Tri Jet, 4, 121	Ruritania, 4, 113	9	1:46.60	14,190

Named for Bernard Baruch (1870-1965), avid racing fan and adviser to presidents. Grade 3 1973-'82. Grade 1 1988-'89. Bernard Baruch S. 1959-'60. 1¹/₁₆ miles 1962-'71. 1³/₈ miles 1980. Dirt 1959-'60, 1979. Three-year-olds 1959-'60. Two divisions 1973, 1981, 1983. Dead heat for first 1975. Equaled course record 1993.

Best Pal Stakes

Grade 2 in 2005. Del Mar, two-year-olds, 6¹/₂ furlongs, dirt. Held August 15, 2004, with a gross value of $147,000. First held in 1967. First graded in 1983. Stakes record 1:15.08 (2001 Officer).

Year	Winner	Jockey	Second	Third	Strs	Time	1st Purse
2004	Roman Ruler, 2, 118	C. S. Nakatani	Actxecutive, 2, 118	Slewsbag, 2, 116	5	1:15.93	$90,000
2003	Perfect Moon, 2, 122	P. A. Valenzuela	Capitano, 2, 118	Military Mandate, 2, 118	10	1:16.90	90,000
2002	Kafwain, 2, 117	V. Espinoza	Chief Planner, 2, 117	Outta Here, 2, 117	7	1:17.00	90,000
2001	Officer, 2, 121	V. Espinoza	Metatron, 2, 117	Essence of Dubai, 2, 117	3	1:15.08	90,000
2000	Flame Thrower, 2, 118	C. S. Nakatani	Trailthefox, 2, 121	Legendary Weave, 2, 117	7	1:16.51	90,000
1999	Dixie Union, 2, 121	A. O. Solis	Exchange Rate, 2, 117	Captain Steve, 2, 117	5	1:16.40	90,000
1998	Worldly Manner, 2, 117	G. L. Stevens	Domination, 2, 117	Waki American, 2, 115	8	1:16.78	65,580
1997	Old Topper, 2, 117	A. O. Solis	King of the Wild, 2, 117	Souvenir Copy, 2, 117	8	1:16.57	68,825
1996	Swiss Yodeler, 2, 121	A. O. Solis	Golden Bronze, 2, 117	Deeds Not Words, 2, 117	8	1:16.12	65,550
1995	Cobra King, 2, 117	R. A. Baze	Northern Afleet, 2, 117	Desert Native, 2, 117	8	1:15.89	60,350
1994	Timber Country, 2, 117	A. O. Solis	Desert Mirage, 2, 115	Supremo, 2, 117	7	1:16.60	46,575
1993	Creston, 2, 117	C. A. Black	Troyalty, 2, 121	Flying Sensation, 2, 115	6	1:16.35	45,900
1992	Devil Diamond, 2, 117	K. J. Desormeaux	Wheeler Oil, 2, 119	Crafty, 2, 117	6	1:22.60	45,900
1991	Scherando, 2, 121	F. Mena	Star Recruit, 2, 117	Prince Wild, 2, 119	9	1:22.47	47,625
1990	Best Pal, 2, 119	P. A. Valenzuela	Xray, 2, 117	Sunshine Machine, 2, 117	7	1:22.20	46,575
1989	A. Sir Dancer, 2, 117	E. J. Delahoussaye	Drag Race, 2, 115	†Patches, 2, 113	7	1:23.00	47,550
1988	Rob an Plunder, 2, 119	C. J. McCarron	Mountain Ghost, 2, 117	Pokarito, 2, 117	8	1:23.00	48,050
1987	Purdue King, 2, 121	C. J. McCarron	Accomplish Ridge, 2, 117	Mixed Pleasure, 2, 119	8	1:23.20	38,500
1986	Temperate Sil, 2, 117	W. Shoemaker	Polar Jet, 2, 117	Gold On Green, 2, 115	8	1:23.00	32,250
1985	Swear, 2, 116	E. J. Delahoussaye	Bright Tom, 2, 116	Smokey Orbit, 2, 114	9	1:36.60	32,750
1984	Saratoga Six, 2, 120	A. T. Cordero Jr.	Private Jungle, 2, 117	Indigenous, 2, 116	7	1:36.80	31,650
1983	Party Leader, 2, 116	R. Sibille	Juliet's Pride, 2, 115	Gumboy, 2, 116	7	1:37.20	31,550
1982	Roving Boy, 2, 115	E. J. Delahoussaye	Encourager, 2, 115	Full Choke, 2, 117	5	1:35.40	30,650
1981	The Captain, 2, 117	L. A. Pincay Jr.	Distant Heart, 2, 115	Gato Del Sol, 2, 115	9	1:36.80	26,400
1980	Bold and Gold, 2, 113	D. C. Hall	Splendid Spruce, 2, 115	Sir Dancer, 2, 113	7	1:37.40	22,550
1979	Doonesbury, 2, 113	S. Hawley	Executive Counsel, 2, 115	Defiance, 2, 117	7	1:35.40	19,300
1978	Flying Paster, 2, 117	D. Pierce	Roman Oblisk, 2, 117	Runaway Hit, 2, 114	9	1:35.60	19,500
1977	Spanish Way, 2, 117	L. A. Pincay Jr.	Tampoy, 2, 114	Misrepresentation, 2, 114	10	1:36.00	16,700
1976	Visible, 2, 117	L. A. Pincay Jr.	*Habitony, 2, 114	Replant, 2, 115	8	1:35.80	16,200
1975	Crazy Channon, 2, 115	D. Pierce	Classy Surgeon, 2, 114	Lexington Laugh, 2, 117	9	1:37.20	13,700
1974	Diabolo, 2, 120	W. Shoemaker	Trond Sang, 2, 114	Neat Claim, 2, 114	7	1:35.60	13,050
1973	Battery E., 2, 115	W. Harris	Jenny's Boy, 2, 120	Marchen McTavish, 2, 115	5	1:30.60	12,750

Named for Golden Eagle Farm's multiple Grade 1 SW and 1990 Balboa S. (G3) winner Best Pal (1988 g. by *Habitony); Best Pal retired as the leading California-bred earner. Formerly named for Vasco Nunez de Balboa, first European to see the Pacific Ocean. Grade 3 1983-2002. Balboa S. 1967. Balboa S. 1972-'95. Not held 1968-'71. About 7¹/₂ furlongs 1972-'73. 1 mile 1974-'85. 7 furlongs 1986-'92. Turf 1972-'73. †Denotes female. Nonwinners of a race worth $10,000 to the winner 1974-'75.

Beverly D. Stakes

Grade 1 in 2005. Arlington Park, three-year-olds and up, fillies and mares, 1³/₁₆ miles, turf. Held August 14, 2004, with a gross value of $750,000. First held in 1987. First graded in 1991. Stakes record 1:53.20 (1990 Reluctant Guest).

Year	Winner	Jockey	Second	Third	Strs	Time	1st Purse
2004	Crimson Palace (SAf), 5, 123	L. Dettori	Riskaverse, 5, 123	Necklace (GB), 3, 117	11	1:56.58	$450,000
2003	Heat Haze (GB), 4, 123	J. Valdivia Jr.	Bien Nicole, 5, 123	Riskaverse, 4, 123	7	1:55.94	420,000
2002	Golden Apples (Ire), 4, 123	P. A. Valenzuela	Astra, 6, 123	England's Legend (Fr), 5, 123	6	1:54.86	420,000
2001	England's Legend (Fr), 4, 123	C. S. Nakatani	The Seven Seas, 5, 123	Spook Express (SAf), 7, 123	9	1:56.75	420,000
2000	Snow Polina, 5, 123	J. D. Bailey	Happyanunoit (NZ), 5, 123	Country Garden (GB), 5, 123	10	1:55.87	300,000
1997	Memories of Silver, 4, 123	J. D. Bailey	Maxzene, 4, 123	Dance Design (Ire), 4, 123	6	1:54.38	300,000
1996	Timarida (Ire), 4, 123	J. P. Murtagh	Perfect Arc, 4, 123	Alpride (Ire), 5, 123	11	1:54.06	300,000
1995	Possibly Perfect, 5, 123	C. S. Nakatani	Alice Springs, 5, 123	Alpride (Ire), 4, 123	7	1:54.95	300,000
1994	Hatoof, 5, 123	W. R. Swinburn	Flawlessly, 6, 123	Potridee (Arg), 5, 123	8	1:55.59	300,000
1993	‡Flawlessly, 5, 123	C. J. McCarron	Via Borghese, 4, 123	Let's Elope (NZ), 6, 123	7	1:55.61	300,000

1992	**Kostroma (Ire)**, 6, 123	K. J. Desormeaux	Ruby Tiger (Ire), 5, 123	Dance Smartly, 4, 123	13	1:54.10	$300,000
1991	**Fire the Groom**, 4, 123	G. L. Stevens	Colour Chart, 4, 123	Miss Josh, 5, 123	7	1:53.58	300,000
1990	**Reluctant Guest**, 4, 123	R. G. Davis	Lady Winner (Fr), 4, 123	Royal Touch (Ire), 5, 123	12	**1:53.20**	300,000
1989	**Claire Marine (Ire)**, 4, 123	C. J. McCarron	Capades, 3, 117	Gaily Gaily (Ire), 6, 123	8	2:01.80	300,000
1987	**Dancing On a Cloud**, 4, 114	J. M. Lauzon	Spruce Luck, 6, 114	Caitie Kisses, 4, 112	10	1:55.00	34,650

Named for the late wife of Arlington Park Chairman Richard Duchossois, Beverly Duchossois. Not held 1988, 1998-'99. 1¹/₁₆ miles 1987. ‡Let's Elope (NZ) finished first, DQ to third, 1993.

Beverly Hills Handicap

Grade 2 in 2005. Hollywood Park, three-year-olds and up, fillies and mares, 1¹/₄ miles, turf. Held June 27, 2004, with a gross value of $200,000. First held in 1938. First graded in 1973. Stakes record 1:58.56 (2002 Astra).

Year	Winner	Jockey	Second	Third	Strs	Time	1st Purse
2004	**Light Jig (GB)**, 4, 114	A. O. Solis	Moscow Burning, 4, 117	Noches De Rosa (Chi), 6, 118	6	2:01.52	$120,000
2003	**Voodoo Dancer**, 5, 120	C. S. Nakatani	Dublino, 4, 122	Megahertz (GB), 4, 117	5	2:00.80	120,000
2002	**Astra**, 6, 124	K. J. Desormeaux	Peu a Peu (Ger), 4, 116	Crazy Ensign (Arg), 6, 117	8	**1:58.56**	150,000
2001	**Astra**, 5, 121	K. J. Desormeaux	Happyanunoit (NZ), 6, 122	Kalypso Katie (Ire), 4, 116	5	1:59.61	120,000
2000	**Happyanunoit (NZ)**, 5, 121	B. Blanc	Sweet Life, 4, 115	Polaire (Ire), 4, 116	5	1:59.32	150,000
1999	**Virginie (Brz)**, 5, 118	L. A. Pincay Jr.	Tranquility Lake, 4, 122	Keeper Hill, 4, 118	6	2:00.21	150,000
1998	**Squeak (GB)**, 4, 115	G. L. Stevens	Sixy Saint, 4, 115	Freeport Flight, 4, 114	7	2:01.56	180,000
1997	**Windsharp**, 6, 122	C. S. Nakatani	Different (Arg), 5, 121	Donna Viola (GB), 5, 122	6	2:00.60	180,000
1996	**Different (Arg)**, 4, 117	C. J. McCarron	Bail Out Becky, 4, 118	Flagbird, 5, 118	8	2:00.74	163,800
1995	**Alpride (Ire)**, 4, 115	C. J. McCarron	Possibly Perfect, 5, 124	Wandesta (GB), 4, 119	6	1:46.67	185,000
1994	**Corrazona**, 4, 119	G. L. Stevens	Hollywood Wildcat, 4, 124	Flawlessly, 6, 124	7	1:47.40	188,400
1993	**Flawlessly**, 5, 123	C. J. McCarron	Jolypha, 4, 121	Party Cited, 4, 117	4	1:47.00	180,200
1992	**Flawlessly**, 4, 122	C. J. McCarron	Kostroma (Ire), 6, 124	Alcando (Ire), 6, 113	5	1:47.13	184,000
1991	**Alcando (Ire)**, 5, 113	J. A. Garcia	Fire the Groom, 4, 120	Countus In, 6, 117	8	1:46.50	130,200
1990	dh- **Beautiful Melody**, 4, 115	K. J. Desormeaux		Stylish Star, 4, 116	6	1:47.00	82,300
	dh- **Reluctant Guest**, 4, 116	R. G. Davis					
1989	**Claire Marine (Ire)**, 4, 120	C. J. McCarron	Fitzwilliam Place (Ire), 5, 121	No Review, 4, 116	6	1:47.20	93,100
1988	**Fitzwilliam Place (Ire)**, 4, 119	A. T. Gryder	Ladanum, 4, 114	Chapel of Dreams, 4, 117	9	1:47.20	98,200
1987	**Auspiciante (Arg)**, 6, 117	P. A. Valenzuela	Reloy, 4, 120	Festivity, 4, 114	8	1:46.20	64,600
1986	**Estrapade**, 6, 122	F. Toro	Treizieme, 5, 115	Sauna (Aus), 5, 117	7	1:59.00	63,800
1985	**Johnica**, 4, 115	G. L. Stevens	Estrapade, 4, 125	L'Attrayante (Fr), 5, 118	5	1:48.20	61,900
1984	**Royal Heroine (Ire)**, 4, 123	F. Toro	Adored, 4, 121	Comedy Act, 5, 118	9	1:47.20	93,200
1983	**Absentia**, 4, 115	F. Toro	Latrone, 6, 110	Triple Tipple, 4, 118	11	1:49.00	68,500
1982	**Sangue (Ire)**, 4, 119	W. Shoemaker	Ack's Secret, 6, 123	Miss Huntington, 5, 117	6	1:47.40	63,300
1981	**Track Robbery**, 5, 120	P. A. Valenzuela	Princess Karenda, 4, 121	Save Wild Life, 4, 115	5	1:46.80	61,800
1980	**Country Queen**, 5, 122	L. A. Pincay Jr.	Wishing Well, 5, 122	The Very One, 5, 117	10	1:47.40	50,550
1979	**Giggling Girl**, 5, 117	C. J. McCarron	Country Queen, 4, 123	More So (Ire), 4, 116	9	1:47.60	50,100
1978	**Swingtime**, 6, 119	F. Toro	Grande Brisa, 4, 115	Drama Critic, 4, 118	7	1:48.40	48,000
1977	**Swingtime**, 5, 120	F. Toro	Fortunate Betty, 4, 115	*Bastonera II, 6, 126	6	1:48.40	25,200
1976	***Bastonera II**, 5, 121	L. A. Pincay Jr.	Miss Toshiba, 4, 124	Miss Tokyo, 4, 115	7	1:50.20	38,800
1975	***La Zanzara**, 5, 122	D. Pierce	*Dulcia, 6, 123	Mercy Dee, 4, 110	5	2:14.40	46,500
1974	***La Zanzara**, 4, 120	D. Pierce	Mon Miel, 4, 114	Dogtooth Violet, 4, 116	6	2:14.20	38,000
1973	**Le Cle**, 4, 119	W. Shoemaker	Pallisima, 4, 115	Convenience, 5, 124	9	2:14.80	49,900

Named for Beverly Hills, California. Grade 1 1973-2002. Not held 1940-'67. 1¹/₁₆ miles 1938. 1 mile 1939. 1³/₈ miles 1968-'75. 1¹/₈ miles 1976-'85, 1987-'95. Dirt 1938-'39. Three-year-olds 1939. Both sexes 1939. Dead heat for first 1990. California-breds 1938-'39.

Bewitch Stakes

Grade 3 in 2005. Keeneland, four-year-olds and up, fillies and mares, 1¹/₂ miles, turf. Held April 27, 2005, with a gross value of $109,300. First held in 1962. First graded in 1982. Stakes record 2:27.54 (1999 Bursting Forth).

Year	Winner	Jockey	Second	Third	Strs	Time	1st Purse
2005	**Angara (GB)**, 4, 118	G. L. Stevens	Cape Town Lass, 4, 118	Strike Me Lucky, 4, 118	7	2:36.24	$67,766
2004	**Meridiana (Ger)**, 4, 118	E. S. Prado	Alternate, 5, 116	Binya (Ger), 5, 118	10	2:31.05	70,308
2003	**Lilac Queen (Ger)**, 5, 116	J. D. Bailey	Beyond the Waves, 6, 116	San Dare, 5, 118	10	2:29.70	69,503
2002	**Sweetest Thing**, 4, 120	M. Guidry	Lapuma, 5, 116	Lady Upstage (Ire), 5, 116	9	2:31.97	68,634
2001	**Keemoon (Fr)**, 5, 120	J. D. Bailey	Playact (Ire), 4, 116	Krisada, 5, 116	8	2:30.28	124,000
2000	**The Seven Seas**, 4, 116	A. O. Solis	Innuendo (Ire), 5, 116	Hollywood Baldcat, 4, 116	10	2:29.31	70,122
1999	**Bursting Forth**, 5, 114	J. F. Chavez	Moments of Magic, 4, 114	Pinafore Park, 4, 114	9	**2:27.54**	68,758
1998	**Maxzene**, 5, 113	J. A. Santos	Cuando, 4, 113	Gastronomical, 5, 113	8	2:30.50	69,626
1997	**Cymbala (Fr)**, 4, 113	P. Day	Noble Cause, 4, 113	Last Approach, 5, 113	10	2:28.87	69,130
1996	**Memories (Ire)**, 5, 117	S. J. Sellers	Future Act, 4, 114	Curtain Raiser, 4, 114	5	2:30.14	66,030
1995	**Market Booster**, 6, 119	P. Day	Memories (Ire), 4, 113	Abigailthewife, 6, 114	7	2:29.33	50,732
1994	**Freewheel**, 5, 114	P. Day	Key Chance, 4, 114	Amal Hayati, 4, 119	6	1:50.24	50,871
1993	**Miss Lenora**, 4, 112	J. A. Krone	Hero's Love, 5, 117	Radiant Ring, 5, 119	8	1:50.60	51,367
1992	**La Gueriere**, 4, 114	B. D. Peck	Indian Fashion, 5, 117	Plenty of Grace, 5, 112	10	1:48.37	54,438
1991	**Miss Unnameable**, 7, 112	P. Day	Cheerful Spree, 4, 117	The Caretaker (Ire), 4, 114	10	1:50.02	56,225
1990	**Coolawin**, 4, 122	J. D. Bailey	To the Lighthouse, 4, 114	Ann Alleged, 5, 112	7	1:49.20	54,048
1989	**Gaily Gaily (Ire)**, 6, 122	J. A. Krone	Chez Chez Chez, 5, 114	Blossoming Beauty, 4, 113	6	1:50.00	53,853

1988	**Beauty Cream**, 5, 121	P. Day	Native Mommy, 5, 121	Fraulein Lieber, 4, 113	9	1:51.60	$55,933
1987	**Gerrie Singer**, 6, 113	R. L. Frazier	Innsbruck (GB), 4, 110	Debutant Dancer, 5, 110	10	1:52.60	36,221
1986	**Devalois (Fr)**, 4, 118	E. Maple	Debutant Dancer, 4, 113	Natural Approach, 5, 113	8	1:54.00	35,685
1985	**Sintra**, 4, 119	K. K. Allen	Electric Fanny, 4, 110	Switching Trick, 5, 110	7	1:43.60	43,964
1984	**Heatherten**, 5, 119	S. Maple	Any Spray, 4, 110	Marisma (Chi), 6, 119	10	1:45.80	36,628
1983	**Try Something New**, 4, 110	P. Day	Kattegat's Pride, 4, 119	Number, 4, 119	10	1:44.20	37,001
1982	**Expressive Dance**, 4, 116	D. Brumfield	Mean Martha, 4, 115	Really Royal, 4, 116	10	1:43.40	36,416
1981	**Bold 'n Determined**, 4, 121	E. J. Delahoussaye	Likely Exchange, 7, 113	Save Wild Life, 4, 110	5	1:43.80	38,236
1980	**Jolie Dutch**, 4, 113	R. P. Romero	Miss Baja, 5, 112	Mi Muchacha, 5, 113	9	1:43.00	29,039
1979	**Miss Baja**, 4, 119	E. Maple	Likely Exchange, 5, 110	Plains and Simple, 4, 113	7	1:43.00	23,286
1978	**Twenty One Inch**, 2, 119	E. J. Delahoussaye	All's Well, 2, 119	Satan's Pride, 2, 116	10	:52.60	11,846
1977	**Crystalan**, 2, 119	G. Patterson	No No-Nos, 2, 119	Surprise Trip, 2, 119	11	:53.00	11,947
1976	**Olden**, 2, 116	R. Breen	Bagiorix, 2, 116	Foreverness, 2, 119	6	:51.40	11,030
	Fun and Tears, 2, 119	L. J. Melancon	Miss Cigarette, 2, 119	Every Move, 2, 116	9	:51.40	11,291
1975	**Pink Jade**, 2, 119	E. J. Delahoussaye	Old Goat, 2, 119	T. V. Vixen, 2, 119	12	:51.60	12,139
1974	**Secret's Out**, 2, 119	D. Brumfield	Floral Princess, 2, 116	Ain't Easy, 2, 119	8	:53.20	11,727
	Dancing Home, 2, 121	A. Patterson	Semi Princess, 2, 119	Spark, 2, 116	9	:53.60	11,793
1973	**Me and Connie**, 2, 121	J. Nichols	Lady Bahia, 2, 115	Bundler, 2, 115	8	:52.40	12,604

Named for Calumet Farm's 1947 champion two-year-old filly, '49 champion older mare, and '48 Ashland S. winner Bewitch (1945 f. by Bull Lea). About 4 furlongs 1962-'64. 4¹/₂ furlongs 1965-'78. 1¹/₁₆ miles 1979-'85. 1¹/₈ miles 1986-'94. Dirt 1962-'85. Two-year-olds 1962-'78. Three-year-olds 1980-'85. Fillies 1962-'78. Two divisions 1974, 1976.

Bing Crosby Breeders' Cup Handicap

Grade 1 in 2005. Del Mar, three-year-olds and up, 6 furlongs, dirt. Held July 25, 2004, with a gross value of $244,000. First held in 1946. First graded in 1985. Stakes record 1:07.80 (1962 Crazy Kid; 1968 Pretense; 1969 Kissin' George; 1978 Bad 'n Big).

Year	Winner	Jockey	Second	Third	Strs	Time	1st Purse
2004	**Kela**, 6, 113	T. Baze	Pohave, 6, 118	Hombre Rapido, 7, 115	10	1:08.51	$150,000
2003	**Beau's Town**, 5, 119	P. A. Valenzuela	Captain Squire, 4, 117	Bluesthestandard, 6, 117	9	1:07.96	120,000
2002	**Disturbingthepeace**, 4, 116	V. Espinoza	Freespool, 6, 115	Mellow Fellow, 7, 118	9	1:09.21	90,000
2001	**Kona Gold**, 7, 126	A. O. Solis	Caller One, 4, 124	Swept Overboard, 4, 115	4	1:08.22	120,000
2000	**Kona Gold**, 6, 123	A. O. Solis	Love That Red, 4, 118	Lexicon, 5, 117	6	1:08.50	124,200
1999	**Christmas Boy**, 6, 114	C. S. Nakatani	Son of a Pistol, 7, 123	Expressionist, 4, 116	6	1:08.11	96,360
1998	**Son of a Pistol**, 6, 120	A. O. Solis	Gold Land, 7, 117	Boundless Moment, 6, 116	7	1:08.10	97,200
1997	**First Intent**, 8, 115	R. R. Douglas	Boundless Moment, 5, 118	High Stakes Player, 5, 120	7	1:08.80	102,000
1996	**Lit de Justice**, 6, 121	C. S. Nakatani	Concept Win, 6, 116	Gold Land, 5, 116	6	1:08.19	126,750
1995	**Gold Land**, 4, 116	E. J. Delahoussaye	Lucky Forever, 6, 118	G Malleah, 4, 116	6	1:08.07	89,300
1994	**King's Blade**, 3, 112	C. S. Nakatani	Memo (Chi), 7, 121	Gundaghia, 7, 118	8	1:08.64	62,400
1993	**The Wicked North**, 4, 116	C. A. Black	Thirty Slews, 6, 121	Black Jack Road, 9, 115	6	1:08.52	61,200
1992	**Thirty Slews**, 5, 116	E. J. Delahoussaye	Slerp, 3, 115	Anjiz, 4, 115	10	1:08.20	64,900
1991	**Bruho**, 5, 116	C. S. Nakatani	Thirty Slews, 4, 115	Due to the King, 4, 116	8	1:08.25	62,900
1990	**Sensational Star**, 6, 113	R. Q. Meza	Frost Free, 5, 118	Timeless Answer, 4, 116	5	1:08.00	60,150
1989	**On the Line**, 5, 124	G. L. Stevens	Speedratic, 4, 117	Cresting Water, 4, 115	7	1:08.00	63,800
1988	**Olympic Prospect**, 4, 121	A. O. Solis	Faro, 6, 118	Sebrof, 4, 119	6	1:08.80	59,410
1987	**Zany Tactics**, 6, 120	J. L. Kaenel	Bolder Than Bold, 5, 118	My Favorite Moment, 6, 115	8	1:09.00	38,600
1986	**American Legion**, 6, 119	E. J. Delahoussaye	Bold Brawley, 3, 112	‡Ondarty, 4, 112	7	1:08.20	38,000
1985	**My Favorite Moment**, 4, 116	E. J. Delahoussaye	Rosie's K. T., 4, 116	Fifty Six Ina Row, 4, 119	10	1:09.80	33,350
1984	**Night Mover**, 4, 120	L. E. Ortega	Premiership, 4, 119	Pac Mania, 4, 115	7	1:08.40	31,800
1983	**Chinook Pass**, 4, 125	L. A. Pincay Jr.	Vagabond Song, 4, 116	Haughty But Nice, 5, 115	7	1:08.60	32,000
1982	**Pencil Point (Ire)**, 4, 114	C. J. McCarron	Terresto's Singer, 5, 114	Shanekite, 4, 115	8	1:09.00	32,650
1981	**Syncopate**, 6, 120	E. J. Delahoussaye	Reb's Golden Ale, 6, 119	To B. Or Not, 5, 122	6	1:08.60	31,100
1980	**Reb's Golden Ale**, 5, 117	S. Hawley	Bolger, 4, 114	Bad 'n Big, 6, 118	4	1:08.80	24,400
1979	**Syncopate**, 4, 116	S. Hawley	White Rammer, 5, 122	Fleet Twist, 5, 116	7	1:08.40	22,750
1978	**Bad 'n Big**, 4, 124	W. Shoemaker	Amadevil, 4, 121	Decoded, 4, 115	8	**1:07.80**	19,400
1977	**Cherry River**, 7, 120	L. A. Pincay Jr.	*Leinster House, 4, 111	Mark's Place, 5, 124	7	1:08.40	15,800
1976	**Cherry River**, 6, 120	L. A. Pincay Jr.	Sawtooth, 5, 111	Fast Spot, 6, 115	7	1:09.40	15,900
1975	**Messenger of Song**, 3, 119	J. Lambert	‡Stake House, 5, 114	Century's Envoy, 4, 122	5	1:08.60	12,450
1974	**Rise High**, 4, 113	J. E. Tejeira	Tragic Isle, 5, 121	Against the Snow, 4, 115	8	1:09.00	13,250
1973	**Pataha Prince**, 8, 114	W. Shoemaker	King of Cricket, 6, 114	Rough Night, 5, 120	9	1:08.00	13,700

Named for movie star and singer H. L. "Bing" Crosby (1903-'77), first president of Del Mar Turf Club. Grade 3 1985-'98. Grade 2 1999-2003. Bing Crosby H. 1946-'95. About 7¹/₂ furlongs 1970. Turf 1970. ‡Beira finished second, DQ to fifth, 1975. ‡Triple Sec finished third, DQ to fourth, 1986.

Black-Eyed Susan Stakes

Grade 2 in 2005. Pimlico, three-year-olds, 1¹/₈ miles, dirt. Held May 20, 2005, with a gross value of $200,000. First held in 1919. First graded in 1973. Stakes record 1:47.83 (1999 Silverbulletday).

Year	Winner	Jockey	Second	Third	Strs	Time	1st Purse
2005	**Spun Sugar**, 3, 116	J. R. Velazquez	R Lady Joy, 3, 122	Pleasant Chimes, 3, 116	6	1:53.27	$120,000
2004	**Yearly Report**, 3, 122	J. D. Bailey	Pawyne Princess, 3, 115	Rare Gift, 3, 115	7	1:52.65	120,000
2003	**Roar Emotion**, 3, 122	J. R. Velazquez	Fircroft, 3, 119	Santa Catarina, 3, 117	8	1:52.33	120,000

Year	Winner	Jockey	Second	Third	Strs	Time	1st Purse
2002	Chamrousse, 3, 115	J. D. Bailey	Shop Till You Drop, 3, 117	Autumn Creek, 3, 115	6	1:51.61	$120,000
2001	Two Item Limit, 3, 122	R. Migliore	Indy Glory, 3, 117	Tap Dance, 3, 122	5	1:50.84	120,000
2000	Jostle, 3, 122	K. J. Desormeaux	March Magic, 3, 122	Impending Bear, 3, 122	7	1:52.56	120,000
1999	Silverbulletday, 3, 122	G. L. Stevens	Dreams Gallore, 3, 117	Vee Vee Star, 3, 115	7	**1:47.83**	120,000
1998	Added Gold, 3, 115	J. R. Velazquez	Tappin' Ginger, 3, 115	Hansel's Girl, 3, 117	8	1:49.75	120,000
1997	Salt It, 3, 117	C. H. Marquez Jr.	Buckeye Search, 3, 122	Holiday Ball, 3, 115	7	1:50.52	120,000
1996	Mesabi Maiden, 3, 115	M. E. Smith	Cara Rafaela, 3, 122	Ginny Lynn, 3, 122	8	1:51.00	120,000
1995	Serena's Song, 3, 122	G. L. Stevens	Conquistadoress, 3, 115	Rare Opportunity, 3, 115	7	1:48.45	120,000
1994	Calipha, 3, 114	R. Wilson	Bunting, 3, 114	Golden Braids, 3, 114	13	1:51.12	120,000
1993	Aztec Hill, 3, 122	M. E. Smith	Traverse City, 3, 114	Jacody, 3, 117	10	1:49.78	120,000
1992	Miss Legality, 3, 122	C. J. McCarron	Known Feminist, 3, 114	Diamond Duo, 3, 114	8	1:51.11	150,000
1991	Wide Country, 3, 122	S. N. Chavez	John's Decision, 3, 117	Nalees Pin, 3, 117	9	1:51.26	150,000
1990	Charon, 3, 122	C. Perret	Valay Maid, 3, 122	Bright Candles, 3, 122	9	1:48.40	150,000
1989	Imaginary Lady, 3, 122	G. L. Stevens	Some Romance, 3, 122	Moonlight Martini, 3, 117	9	1:48.20	150,000
1988	Costly Shoes, 3, 121	P. Day	Thirty Eight Go Go, 3, 121	Lost Kitty, 3, 121	6	1:44.80	97,915
1987	Grecian Flight, 3, 121	C. Perret	Bal Du Bois, 3, 121	Arctic Cloud, 3, 121	10	1:44.20	101,750
1986	Family Style, 3, 121	C. J. McCarron	Steel Maiden, 3, 121	Firgie's Jule, 3, 121	8	1:44.60	100,385
1985	Koluctoo's Jill, 3, 121	C. J. McCarron	Denver Express, 3, 116	A Joyful Spray, 3, 121	7	1:43.00	74,295
1984	Lucky Lucky Lucky, 3, 121	A. T. Cordero Jr.	Sintra, 3, 116	Duo Disco, 3, 121	7	1:41.20	100,060
1983	Batna, 3, 121	L. D. Ruch	Lovin Touch, 3, 116	Weekend Surprise, 3, 121	10	1:42.40	75,400
1982	Delicate Ice, 3, 114	D. Brumfield	Trove, 3, 121	Milingo, 3, 121	10	1:44.60	74,945
1981	Dame Mysterieuse, 3, 121	E. Maple	Wayward Lass, 3, 121	Real Prize, 3, 121	7	1:44.20	72,800
1980	Weber City Miss, 3, 118	V. A. Bracciale Jr.	Bishop's Ring, 3, 111	Champagne Star, 3, 114	8	1:44.40	74,620
1979	Davona Dale, 3, 121	J. Velasquez	Phoebe's Donkey, 3, 118	Plankton, 3, 121	6	1:42.60	72,670
1978	Caesar's Wish, 3, 121	D. R. Wright	Jevalin, 3, 116	Miss Baja, 3, 121	8	1:44.20	55,120
1977	Small Raja, 3, 114	A. T. Cordero Jr.	Northern Sea, 3, 121	Enthused, 3, 116	5	1:42.80	54,503
1976	What a Summer, 3, 111	C. J. McCarron	Dearly Precious, 3, 121	Artfully, 3, 114	10	1:42.40	37,895
1975	My Juliet, 3, 116	A. Hill	Gala Lil, 3, 114	Funalon, 3, 121	6	1:44.00	37,635
1974	Blowing Rock, 3, 111	A. Agnello	Heydairya, 3, 111	Shantung Silk, 3, 116	8	1:43.00	22,425
1973	Fish Wife, 3, 111	D. Gargan	Guided Missle, 3, 112	Out Cold, 3, 116	6	1:44.00	22,685

Named for the Maryland state flower. Grade 3 1973-'75. Pimlico Oaks 1937-'49. Black-Eyed Susan H. 1951. Not held 1932-'36, 1950. 1 1/16 miles 1919-'29, 1931, 1937-'49, 1953-'88. 1 mile 70 yards 1930. 1 3/16 miles 1951.

Blue Grass Stakes

Grade 1 in 2005. Keeneland, three-year-olds, 1 1/8 miles, dirt. Held April 16, 2005, with a gross value of $750,000. First held in 1911. First graded in 1973. Stakes record 1:47.29 (1996 Skip Away).

Year	Winner	Jockey	Second	Third	Strs	Time	1st Purse
2005	Bandini, 3, 123	J. R. Velazquez	High Limit, 3, 123	Closing Argument, 3, 123	7	1:50.16	$465,000
2004	The Cliff's Edge, 3, 123	S. J. Sellers	Lion Heart, 3, 123	Limehouse, 3, 123	8	1:49.42	465,000
2003	Peace Rules, 3, 123	E. S. Prado	Brancusi, 3, 123	Offlee Wild, 3, 123	9	1:51.73	465,000
2002	Harlan's Holiday, 3, 123	E. S. Prado	Booklet, 3, 123	Ocean Sound (Ire), 3, 123	6	1:51.51	465,000
2001	Millennium Wind, 3, 123	L. A. Pincay Jr.	Songandaprayer, 3, 123	Dollar Bill, 3, 123	7	1:48.32	465,000
2000	High Yield, 3, 123	P. Day	More Than Ready, 3, 123	Wheelaway, 3, 123	8	1:48.79	465,000
1999	Menifee, 3, 123	P. Day	Cat Thief, 3, 123	Vicar, 3, 123	8	1:48.66	465,000
1998	Halory Hunter, 3, 123	G. L. Stevens	Lil's Lad, 3, 123	Cape Town, 3, 123	5	1:47.98	434,000
1997	Pulpit, 3, 121	S. J. Sellers	Acceptable, 3, 121	Stolen Gold, 3, 121	7	1:49.91	434,000
1996	Skip Away, 3, 121	S. J. Sellers	Louis Quatorze, 3, 121	Editor's Note, 3, 121	7	**1:47.29**	434,000
1995	Wild Syn, 3, 121	R. P. Romero	Suave Prospect, 3, 121	Tejano Run, 3, 121	6	1:49.31	310,000
1994	Holy Bull, 3, 121	M. E. Smith	Valiant Nature, 3, 121	Mahogany Hall, 3, 121	7	1:50.02	310,000
1993	Prairie Bayou, 3, 121	M. E. Smith	Wallenda, 3, 121	Dixieland Heat, 3, 121	9	1:49.62	310,000
1992	Pistols and Roses, 3, 121	J. Vasquez	Conte Di Savoya, 3, 121	Ecstatic Ride, 3, 121	11	1:49.19	325,000
1991	Strike the Gold, 3, 121	C. W. Antley	Fly So Free, 3, 121	Nowork all Play, 3, 121	6	1:48.44	260,520
1990	Summer Squall, 3, 121	P. Day	Land Rush, 3, 121	Unbridled, 3, 121	5	1:48.60	185,006
1989	Western Playboy, 3, 121	R. P. Romero	Dispersal, 3, 121	Tricky Creek, 3, 121	6	1:51.20	185,900
1988	Granacus, 3, 121	J. Vasquez	Intensive Command, 3, 121	Regal Classic, 3, 121	9	1:52.20	190,856
1987	‡War, 3, 121	W. H. McCauley	Leo Castelli, 3, 121	Alysheba, 3, 121	5	1:48.40	148,135
1986	Bachelor Beau, 3, 121	L. J. Melancon	Bolshoi Boy, 3, 121	Bold Arrangement (GB), 3, 121	11	1:51.20	171,290
1985	Chief's Crown, 3, 121	D. MacBeth	Floating Reserve, 3, 121	Banner Bob, 3, 121	4	1:47.60	127,740
1984	Taylor's Special, 3, 121	P. Day	Silent King, 3, 121	Charmed Rook, 3, 121	9	1:52.20	133,883
1983	Play Fellow, 3, 121	J. Cruguet	‡Desert Wine, 3, 121	Copelan, 3, 121	12	1:49.40	121,924
1982	Linkage, 3, 121	W. Shoemaker	Gato Del Sol, 3, 121	Wavering Monarch, 3, 121	9	1:48.00	127,774
1981	Proud Appeal, 3, 121	J. Fell	Law Me, 3, 121	Golden Derby, 3, 121	11	1:51.40	120,559
1980	Rockhill Native, 3, 121	J. Oldham	Super Moment, 3, 121	Gold Stage, 3, 121	11	1:50.00	84,208
1979	Spectacular Bid, 3, 121	R. J. Franklin	Lot o' Gold, 3, 121	Bishop's Choice, 3, 121	4	1:50.00	79,658
1978	Alydar, 3, 121	J. Velasquez	Raymond Earl, 3, 121	Go Forth, 3, 121	9	1:49.60	77,350
1977	For The Moment, 3, 121	A. T. Cordero Jr.	Run Dusty Run, 3, 121	Western Wind, 3, 121	11	1:50.20	77,578
1976	Honest Pleasure, 3, 121	B. Baeza	Certain Roman, 3, 121	Inca Roca, 3, 121	7	1:49.40	73,028
1975	Master Derby, 3, 123	D. G. McHargue	Honey Mark, 3, 117	Prince Thou Art, 3, 123	9	1:49.00	39,878
1974	Judger, 3, 123	L. A. Pincay Jr.	Big Latch, 3, 117	Gold and Myrrh, 3, 114	14	1:49.20	42,608
1973	My Gallant, 3, 117	A. T. Cordero Jr.	Our Native, 3, 123	dh- Impecunious, 3, 126	9	1:49.60	37,765
				dh- Warbucks, 3, 117			

Named for the Bluegrass region of Kentucky. Sponsored by Toyota Motor Manufacturing Co. of Georgetown, Kentucky 1996-2005. Grade 2 1990-'98. Held at Kentucky Association 1911-'36. Held at Churchill Downs 1943-'45. Not held 1915-'18, 1927-'36. 6 furlongs 1964. Dead heat for third 1973. ‡Marfa finished second, DQ to fourth, 1983. ‡Alysheba finished first, DQ to third, 1987.

Boiling Springs Stakes

Not graded in 2005. Monmouth Park, three-year-olds, fillies, 1¹⁄₁₆ miles, dirt (originally scheduled as a Grade 3 on the turf). Held May 29, 2005, with a gross value of $136,500. First held in 1977. First graded in 1980. Stakes record 1:40.09 (1998 Mysterious Moll).

Year	Winner	Jockey	Second	Third	Strs	Time	1st Purse
2005	Toll Taker, 3, 118	A. T. Gryder	Pleasant Lyrics, 3, 116	Ruby Martini, 3, 116	3	1:44.36	$90,000
2004	Seducer's Song, 3, 119	J. Bravo	Go Robin, 3, 117	River Belle (GB), 3, 117	9	1:45.66	90,000
2002	Showlady, 3, 114	R. Migliore	Dreamers Glory, 3, 116	With Patience, 3, 117	9	1:42.27	120,000
2001	Mystic Lady, 3, 120	E. Coa	Shooting Party, 3, 114	Plunderthepeasants, 3, 115	4	1:42.63	120,000
2000	Storm Dream (Ire), 3, 116	J. Samyn	Watch, 3, 117	Lady Dora, 3, 114	11	1:47.09	60,000
1999	Wild Heart Dancing, 3, 116	J. F. Chavez	Confessional, 3, 118	Petunia, 3, 114	8	1:43.08	120,000
1998	Mysterious Moll, 3, 116	J. L. Espinoza	Who Did It and Run, 3, 120	Thunder Kitten, 3, 116	12	**1:40.09**	120,000
1997	Victory Chime, 3, 114	J. A. Santos	Majestic Sunlight, 3, 114	Dancing Water, 3, 115	6	1:41.13	60,000
	Victory Chime, 3, 114	M. E. Smith	Miss Pop Carn, 3, 111	Colonial Play, 3, 113	9	1:41.99	60,000
1996	Careless Heiress, 3, 118	C. Perret	Briarcliff, 3, 114	Dathuil (Ire), 3, 115	9	1:50.54	60,000
1995	Christmas Gift, 3, 116	W. H. McCauley	Ring by Spring, 3, 114	Transient Trend, 3, 114	7	1:43.49	48,000
	Class Kris, 3, 118	R. Wilson	Twilight Encounter, 3, 112	Appointed One, 3, 114	7	1:43.27	48,000
1994	Avie's Fancy, 3, 119	J. C. Ferrer	Teasing Charm, 3, 114	Knocknock, 3, 115	7	1:41.41	45,000
1993	Tribulation, 3, 110	J. Samyn	Exotic Sea, 3, 114	Bright Penny, 3, 115	11	1:42.70	45,000
1992	Captive Miss, 3, 120	J. Bravo	Logan's Mist, 3, 116	Aquilegia, 3, 113	9	1:40.78	45,000
1991	Dance O'My Life, 3, 114	C. W. Antley	Monica Faye, 3, 110	Verbasle, 3, 115	11	1:41.44	45,000
1990	Memories of Pam, 3, 112	J. D. Bailey	Hot Marshmellow, 3, 114	Baltic Chill, 3, 118	8	1:41.00	41,550
	Plenty of Grace, 3, 112	J. D. Bailey	Southern Tradition, 3, 120	Sabina, 3, 114	6	1:42.20	40,950
1989	Darby Shuffle, 3, 116	J. A. Krone	To the Lighthouse, 3, 116	Warranty Applied, 3, 115	9	1:40.60	53,730
1988	Siggebo, 3, 119	R. Wilson	Flashy Runner, 3, 115	Lusty Lady, 3, 113	7	1:43.20	51,930
1987	Rullah Runner, 3, 109	W. A. Guerra	Tappiano, 3, 119	Key Bid, 3, 120	12	1:41.40	35,460
1986	Small Virtue, 3, 114	J. A. Santos	Sweet Velocity, 3, 115	Country Recital, 3, 121	11	1:41.60	47,985
	Spruce Fir, 3, 119	D. B. Thomas	Ala Mahlik (Ire), 3, 116	Spring Innocence, 3, 113	11	1:41.60	47,985
1985	Jolly Saint (Ire), 3, 114	J. A. Santos	Miss Hardwick, 3, 115	Dawn's Curtsey, 3, 115	13	1:41.00	49,620
1984	Possible Mate, 3, 116	D. MacBeth	Distaff Magic, 3, 113	Miss Audimar, 3, 112	13	1:41.80	33,930
1983	Sabin, 3, 124	E. Maple	Aspen Rose, 3, 114	Propositioning, 3, 117	11	1:47.80	33,480
1982	Sunny Sparkler, 3, 113	J. Samyn	Fact Finder, 3, 113	Milingo, 3, 117	10	1:41.40	26,895
	Larida, 3, 119	E. Maple	Doodle, 3, 115	Distinctive Moon, 3, 114	11	1:41.40	27,075
1981	Irish Joy, 3, 114	C. C. Lopez	First Approach, 3, 113	Dance Forth, 3, 114	11	1:42.40	26,925
	Wings of Grace, 3, 112	J. Velasquez	Andover Way, 3, 114	Pukka Princess, 3, 120	8	1:41.40	26,385
1980	Champagne Ginny, 3, 114	J. Velasquez	Qui Royalty, 3, 112	Classic Curves, 3, 111	9	1:42.00	26,505
	Refinish, 3, 113	C. J. McCarron	Keep Off (Ire), 3, 111	Cannon Boy, 3, 113	9	1:41.60	26,505
1979	Jameela, 3, 118	V. A. Bracciale Jr.	Fanny Saperstein, 3, 119	Whydidju, 3, 119	6	1:41.60	27,934
	Gala Regatta, 3, 122	E. Maple	dh-Record Acclaim, 3, 114 dh-Tweak, 3, 113		6	1:41.00	27,934
1978	Key to the Saga, 3, 118	J. Samyn	Terpsichorist, 3, 117	Amerigirl, 3, 112	9	1:41.40	28,519
	Sisterhood, 3, 112	B. Gonzalez	Island Kiss, 3, 108	White Star Line, 3, 122	9	1:41.40	28,519
1977	Council House, 3, 116	C. Perret	Rich Soil, 3, 119	Pressing Date, 3, 115	10	1:42.40	28,633
	Critical Cousin, 3, 119	A. T. Cordero Jr.	Sans Arc, 3, 116	Small Raja, 3, 123	8	1:42.40	28,243

Named for former name of East Rutherford, New Jersey, home of the Meadowlands, the race's original location. Not graded when taken off turf 2001, 2005. Boiling Springs H. 1977-'78, 1981-'97. Boiling Springs Breeders' Cup H. 1998-2002. Held at The Meadowlands 1977-2002. Not held 2003. Dirt 1998, 2001, 2005. Two divisions 1977-'82, 1986, 1990, 1995, 1997. Dead heat for second 1979 (2nd Div.).

Bold Ruler Handicap

Grade 3 in 2005. Belmont Park, three-year-olds and up, 6 furlongs, dirt. Held May 7, 2005, with a gross value of $104,600. First held in 1976. First graded in 1982. Stakes record 1:07.54 (1999 Kelly Kip).

Year	Winner	Jockey	Second	Third	Strs	Time	1st Purse
2005	Uncle Camie, 5, 115	R. Migliore	Don Six, 5, 120	Thunder Touch, 4, 114	5	1:08.67	$63,960
2004	Canadian Frontier, 5, 111	J. Castellano	Key Deputy, 4, 114	First Blush, 4, 113	6	1:08.97	64,620
2003	Shake You Down, 5, 115	M. J. Luzzi	Here's Zealous, 6, 114	Peeping Tom, 6, 117	7	1:08.47	65,040
2002	Left Bank, 5, 121	J. R. Velazquez	Silky Sweep, 6, 114	Say Florida Sandy, 8, 116	4	1:09.30	63,646
2001	Say Florida Sandy, 7, 117	J. Bravo	Delaware Township, 5, 117	Lake Pontchartrain, 6, 113	7	1:08.67	65,520
2000	Brutally Frank, 6, 115	S. Bridgmohan	Kelly Kip, 6, 121	Kashatreya, 6, 115	6	1:08.64	65,880
1999	Kelly Kip, 5, 123	J. Samyn	Artax, 4, 115	Brushed On, 4, 115	5	**1:07.54**	64,440
1998	Kelly Kip, 4, 117	J. Samyn	Say Florida Sandy, 4, 111	Johnny Legit, 4, 114	8	1:07.61	66,120
1997	Punch Line, 7, 122	R. G. Davis	Golden Tent, 8, 111	Blissful State, 5, 116	6	1:08.80	64,980
1996	Lite the Fuse, 5, 119	J. A. Krone	Cold Execution, 5, 115	Splendid Sprinter, 4, 115	5	1:09.51	64,500
1995	Rizzi, 4, 112	D. V. Beckner	Lite the Fuse, 4, 111	Evil Bear, 5, 116	6	1:08.91	64,560
1994	Chief Desire, 4, 117	J. R. Velazquez	Boom Towner, 6, 120	Won Song, 4, 112	8	1:08.76	66,300

1993 **Slerp**, 4, 119	J. A. Santos	Argyle Lake, 7, 121	Big Jewel, 5, 121	8	1:09.17	$70,200
1992 **Jolies Appeal**, 4, 119	W. H. McCauley	Reappeal, 6, 119	Fiercely, 4, 119	5	1:09.29	67,560
1991 **Rousing Past**, 4, 119	N. Santagata	True and Blue, 6, 121	Sunshine Jimmy, 4, 119	6	1:09.96	67,200
1990 **Mr. Nickerson**, 4, 119	C. W. Antley	Dancing Pretense, 5, 119	Diamond Donnie, 4, 119	5	1:09.20	66,240
1989 **Pok Ta Pok**, 4, 121	R. Migliore	Teddy Drone, 4, 119	Claim, 4, 119	6	1:09.80	67,560
1988 **King's Swan**, 8, 123	C. W. Antley	Seattle Knight, 4, 119	Faster Than Sound, 4, 123	7	1:10.20	103,680
1987 †**Pine Tree Lane**, 5, 118	A. T. Cordero Jr.	Love That Mac, 5, 123	Play the King, 4, 121	7	1:09.00	103,680
1986 **Phone Trick**, 4, 123	J. Velasquez	Love That Mac, 4, 119	Rexson's Bishop, 4, 121	7	1:08.80	70,680
1985 **Rocky Marriage**, 5, 119	A. T. Cordero Jr.	Entropy, 5, 121	Majestic Venture, 4, 119	6	1:08.80	51,390
1984 **Top Avenger**, 6, 121	A. Graell	Believe the Queen, 4, 119	Au Point, 4, 123	10	1:09.80	55,350
1983 **Maudlin**, 5, 119	J. D. Bailey	Top Avenger, 5, 123	Singh Tu, 4, 121	4	1:11.60	49,500
1982 **Always Run Lucky**, 4, 123	J. J. Miranda	King's Fashion, 7, 119	Band Practice, 4, 119	4	1:09.40	49,050
1981 **Dave's Friend**, 6, 123	A. S. Black	Naughty Jimmy, 4, 119	Fappiano, 4, 119	6	1:09.60	48,510
1980 **Dave's Friend**, 5, 123	V. A. Bracciale Jr.	Tilt Up, 5, 121	Double Zeus, 5, 121	6	1:09.80	48,690
1979 **Star de Naskra**, 4, 119	J. Fell	Vencedor, 5, 126	Big John Taylor, 5, 119	8	1:09.20	48,420
1978 **Half High**, 5, 115	A. Santiago	Great Above, 6, 121	Cruise On In, 4, 110	6	1:09.40	25,665
1977 **Jaipur's Gem**, 4, 113	J. Samyn	Expletive Deleted, 4, 107	Cojak, 4, 126	7	1:09.60	22,050
1976 **Chief Tamanaco**, 3, 114	A. T. Cordero Jr.	Relent, 5, 114	Jackson Square, 4, 116	4	1:09.80	21,750

Named for Wheatley Stable's 1957 Horse of the Year and eight-time leading North American sire Bold Ruler (1954 c. by *Nasrullah). Grade 2 1985-'89. Bold Ruler S. 1979-'93. Held at Aqueduct 1976-2001. Track record 1998, 1999. †Denotes female.

Bonnie Miss Stakes

Grade 2 in 2005. Gulfstream Park, three-year-olds, fillies, 1¹/₈ miles, dirt. Held March 5, 2005, with a gross value of $150,000. First held in 1971. First graded in 1982. Stakes record 1:49.67 (2002 Dust Me Off).

Year	Winner	Jockey	Second	Third	Strs	Time	1st Purse
2005	**Jill Robin L**, 3, 116	J. D. Bailey	In the Gold, 3, 118	Holy Trinity, 3, 116	7	1:53.12	$90,000
2004	**Last Song**, 3, 118	E. S. Prado	Society Selection, 3, 120	Rare Gift, 3, 116	5	1:50.60	120,000
2003	**Ivanavinalot**, 3, 122	J. R. Velazquez	My Boston Gal, 3, 120	Holiday Lady, 3, 118	7	1:50.72	120,000
2002	**Dust Me Off**, 3, 116	M. Guidry	Nonsuch Bay, 3, 116	Belterra, 3, 120	6	**1:49.67**	150,000
2001	**Tap Dance**, 3, 114	J. D. Bailey	Halo Reality, 3, 117	Unbridled Lassie, 3, 114	7	1:52.05	150,000
2000	**Cash Run**, 3, 119	J. D. Bailey	Deed I Do, 3, 114	Bejoyfulandrejoyce, 3, 114	6	1:44.11	120,000
1999	**Three Ring**, 3, 122	J. R. Velazquez	Olympic Charmer, 3, 117	Marley Vale, 3, 117	5	1:43.75	120,000
1998	**Banshee Breeze**, 3, 114	R. P. Romero	Santaria, 3, 114	Cotton House Bay, 3, 114	8	1:46.57	120,000
1997	**Glitter Woman**, 3, 117	M. E. Smith	Southern Playgirl, 3, 119	Dixie Flag, 3, 114	7	1:43.20	120,000
1996	**My Flag**, 3, 117	J. D. Bailey	Escena, 3, 114	La Rosa, 3, 117	5	1:45.77	120,000
1995	**Mia's Hope**, 3, 117	K. L. Chapman	Minister Wife, 3, 119	Incredible Blues, 3, 117	9	1:44.85	120,000
1994	**Inside Information**, 3, 114	M. E. Smith	Cinnamon Sugar (Ire), 3, 113	Jade Flush, 3, 114	10	1:42.94	120,000
1993	**Dispute**, 3, 114	J. D. Bailey	Sky Beauty, 3, 114	Lunar Spook, 3, 117	6	1:43.67	120,000
1992	**Spectacular Sue**, 3, 114	W. S. Ramos	Spinning Round, 3, 117	Tricky Cinderella, 3, 112	6	1:44.14	120,000
1991	**Withallprobability**, 3, 117	C. Perret	Fancy Ribbons, 3, 117	Outlasting, 3, 114	6	1:43.30	120,000
1990	**Charon**, 3, 121	E. Fires	Trumpet's Blare, 3, 121	De La Devil, 3, 121	7	1:44.20	120,000
1989	**Open Mind**, 3, 121	A. T. Cordero Jr.	Seattle Meteor, 3, 121	Surging, 3, 114	8	1:43.80	120,000
1988	**On to Royalty**, 3, 121	C. Perret	Tomorrow's Child, 3, 121	Make Change, 3, 112	12	1:44.60	120,000
1987	**Mar Mar**, 3, 121	W. A. Guerra	Super Cook, 3, 121	Without Feathers, 3, 118	12	1:44.60	90,000
1986	**Patricia J. K.**, 3, 121	J. A. Santos	Noranc, 3, 121	Family Style, 3, 121	11	1:45.20	135,570
1985	**Lucy Manette**, 3, 121	C. Perret	Outstandingly, 3, 121	Micki Bracken, 3, 121	9	1:44.60	72,240
1984	**Miss Oceana**, 3, 121	E. Maple	Enumerating, 3, 114	Katrinka, 3, 112	9	1:42.40	70,605
1983	**Unaccompanied**, 3, 116	R. Woodhouse	‡Bright Crocus, 3, 114	Dewl Reason, 3, 112	12	1:45.40	58,320
1982	**Christmas Past**, 3, 121	J. Vasquez	Norsan, 3, 113	Our Darling, 3, 112	6	1:44.20	34,830
1981	**Dame Mysterieuse**, 3, 118	J. Samyn	Banner Gala, 3, 113	Heavenly Cause, 3, 121	7	1:44.40	52,335
1980	**Lien**, 3, 112	E. Maple	Wistful, 3, 115	Champagne Ginny, 3, 114	9	1:22.00	18,510
1979	**Davona Dale**, 3, 122	J. Velasquez	Candy Eclair, 3, 122	Prove Me Special, 3, 114	4	1:21.00	17,545
1978	**Jevalin**, 3, 114	M. Solomone	‡Raise a Companion, 3, 110	Sharp Belle, 3, 114	10	1:23.80	18,600
1977	**Herecomesthebride**, 3, 114	L. Saumell	Grand Luxe, 3, 112	Rich Soil, 3, 112	9	1:21.80	20,970
1976	**Get Swinging**, 5, 111	A. Ramos	Twenty Six Girl, 4, 112	North of Boston, 4, 114	8	1:45.80	17,400
1975	**Cheers Marion**, 4, 113	M. Castaneda	Hinterland, 5, 116	Summer Sprite, 5, 114	8	1:42.20	10,207
	Diomedia, 4, 116	M. Castaneda	Gems and Roses, 5, 122	Exclusive Lady, 5, 113	8	1:42.00	10,207
1974	**City Girl**, 3, 112	E. Maple	Maud Muller, 3, 112	Double Bend, 3, 112	12	1:22.60	21,540
1973	**Fan Palace**, 4, 111	E. Fires	Hasty Jude, 4, 119	Viewpoise, 3, 112	12	1:44.40	14,145

Named for Bonnie Donn, daughter of James Donn Jr., president of Gulfstream Park from 1972-'78. Grade 3 1982-'87. Bonnie Miss H. 1976. About 1¹/₁₆ miles 1971. 7 furlongs 1972, 1974, 1977-'80. 1¹/₁₆ miles 1973, 1975-'76, 1981-2000. Turf 1971, 1975-'76. Originally scheduled on turf 1973. Three-year-olds and up 1971, 1973, 1975-'76. Fillies and mares 1971, 1973, 1975-'76. Two divisions 1975. ‡Cornish Queen finished second, DQ to fourth, 1978. ‡Miss Molly finished second, DQ to twelfth, 1983.

Bowling Green Handicap

Grade 2 in 2005. Belmont Park, three-year-olds and up, 1³/₈ miles, turf. Held July 17, 2004, with a gross value of $150,000. First held in 1958. First graded in 1973. Stakes record 2:10.20 (1990 With Approval).

Year	Winner	Jockey	Second	Third	Strs	Time	1st Purse
2004	**Kicken Kris**, 4, 117	E. S. Prado	Better Talk Now, 5, 115	Gigli (Brz), 6, 113	10	2:12.19	$90,000
2003	**Whitmore's Conn**, 5, 116	J. Samyn	Quest Star, 4, 117	Macaw (Ire), 4, 116	9	2:15.92	90,000

Year	Winner	Jockey	Second	Third	Strs	Time	1st Purse
2002	Whitmore's Conn, 4, 112	S. Bridgmohan	Staging Post, 4, 115	Moon Solitaire (Ire), 5, 116	9	2:13.43	$90,000
2001	King Cugat, 4, 119	J. D. Bailey	Slew Valley, 4, 112	Man From Wicklow, 4, 112	7	2:10.62	90,000
2000	Elhayq (Ire), 5, 113	S. Bridgmohan	Yankee Dollar, 4, 110	Carpenter's Halo, 4, 115	9	2:13.81	90,000
1999	Honor Glide, 5, 114	J. A. Santos	Parade Ground, 4, 118	‡Fahris (Ire), 5, 114	6	2:11.07	90,000
1998	Cetewayo, 4, 112	J. R. Velazquez	Officious, 5, 113	Chief Bearhart, 5, 124	6	2:13.45	90,000
1997	Influent, 6, 120	J. Samyn	Flag Down, 7, 118	Notoriety, 4, 108	8	2:11.00	90,000
1996	Flag Down, 6, 118	J. A. Santos	Broadway Flyer, 5, 118	Diplomatic Jet, 4, 119	9	2:13.29	90,000
1995	Sentimental Moi, 5, 111	R. B. Perez	Awad, 5, 121	Proceeded, 4, 108	8	2:15.48	90,000
1994	Turk Passer, 4, 110	J. R. Velazquez	Sea Hero, 4, 117	Fraise, 6, 124	6	2:13.25	90,000
1993	Dr. Kiernan, 4, 114	C. W. Antley	Spectacular Tide, 4, 111	Lomitas (GB), 5, 117	9	2:17.70	90,000
1992	Wall Street Dancer, 4, 114	P. Day	Fraise, 4, 113	Libor, 5, 109	7	2:12.92	120,000
1991	Three Coins Up, 3, 111	J. D. Bailey	Phantom Breeze (Ire), 5, 117	Beyond the Lake (Ire), 5, 115	12	2:10.86	120,000
1990	With Approval, 4, 118	C. Perret	Chenin Blanc, 4, 113	El Senor, 6, 121	9	**2:10.20**	113,280
1989	El Senor, 5, 117	W. H. McCauley	Coeur de Lion (Fr), 5, 121	Pay the Butler, 5, 116	10	2:18.60	144,960
1988	Coeur de Lion (Fr), 4, 117	C. Perret	Pay the Butler, 4, 112	Milesius, 4, 115	13	2:13.40	151,680
1987	Theatrical (Ire), 5, 123	P. Day	Akabir, 6, 116	Dance of Life, 4, 121	10	2:14.00	144,960
1986	Uptown Swell, 4, 114	E. Maple	Palace Panther (Ire), 5, 116	Equalize, 4, 116	13	2:14.80	147,690
1985	Sharannpour (Ire), 5, 114	A. T. Cordero Jr.	Flying Pidgeon, 4, 117	Long Mick (Fr), 4, 121	14	2:18.20	156,300
1984	Hero's Honor, 4, 120	J. D. Bailey	Nassipour, 4, 110	Super Sunrise (GB), 5, 123	11	2:14.00	144,120
1983	Tantalizing, 4, 113	J. Vasquez	Sprink, 5, 113	Majesty's Prince, 4, 122	7	2:14.80	105,120
1982	Open Call, 4, 124	J. Velasquez	Johnny Dance, 4, 114	Baltimore Canyon, 4, 116	10	2:24.80	89,850
1981	Great Neck, 5, 114	A. T. Cordero Jr.	Key to Content, 4, 119	Match the Hatch, 5, 115	8	2:12.00	84,450
1980	Sten, 5, 117	J. Fell	John Henry, 5, 128	Lyphard's Wish (Fr), 4, 120	9	2:13.20	86,550
1979	Overskate, 4, 117	R. Platts	†Waya (Fr), 5, 125	Bowl Game, 5, 123	7	2:11.40	84,525
1978	Tiller, 4, 117	J. Fell	Proud Arion, 4, 111	Bowl Game, 4, 124	10	2:12.40	70,260
1977	Hunza Dancer, 5, 117	J. Cruguet	Improviser, 5, 122	Noble Dancer (GB), 5, 117	13	1:58.80	68,580
1976	Erwin Boy, 5, 120	R. Turcotte	Drollery, 6, 111	Trumpeter Swan, 5, 111	9	2:26.00	34,740
1975	Barcas, 4, 113	M. Castaneda	Drollery, 5, 113	*Telefonico, 4, 124	6	2:32.20	33,240
1974	Take Off, 5, 120	R. Turcotte	†Garland of Roses, 5, 109	Astray, 5, 126	9	2:26.40	34,260
1973	†Summer Guest, 4, 119	J. Vasquez	Red Reality, 7, 124	Astray, 4, 113	9	2:29.20	34,200

Named for the lower tip of Manhattan Island, New York, where there was once a green for lawn bowling. Grade 1 1983-'89. Held at Aqueduct 1963-'67. 1½ miles 1960-'62, 1968-'76. 1⅛ miles 1963-'67. 1¼ miles 1977. Course record 1977. ‡Federal Trial finished third, DQ to fourth, 1999. †Denotes female.

Breeders' Cup Classic

Grade 1 in 2005. Lone Star Park, three-year-olds and up, 1¼ miles, dirt. Held October 30, 2004, with a gross value of $3,668,000. First held in 1984. First graded in 1984. Stakes record 1:59.02 (2004 Ghostzapper).

Year	Winner	Jockey	Second	Third	Strs	Time	1st Purse
2004	Ghostzapper, 4, 126	J. Castellano	Roses in May, 4, 126	Pleasantly Perfect, 6, 126	13	**1:59.02**	$2,080,000
2003	Pleasantly Perfect, 5, 126	A. O. Solis	Medaglia d'Oro, 4, 126	Dynever, 3, 121	10	1:59.88	2,080,000
2002	Volponi, 4, 126	J. A. Santos	Medaglia d'Oro, 3, 121	Milwaukee Brew, 5, 126	12	2:01.39	2,080,000
2001	Tiznow, 4, 126	C. J. McCarron	Sakhee, 4, 126	Albert the Great, 4, 126	13	2:00.62	2,080,000
2000	Tiznow, 3, 122	C. J. McCarron	Giant's Causeway, 3, 122	Captain Steve, 3, 122	13	2:00.75	2,480,400
1999	Cat Thief, 3, 122	P. Day	Budroyale, 6, 126	Golden Missile, 4, 126	14	1:59.52	2,080,000
1998	Awesome Again, 4, 126	P. Day	Silver Charm, 4, 126	Swain (Ire), 6, 126	10	2:02.16	2,662,400
1997	Skip Away, 4, 126	M. E. Smith	Deputy Commander, 3, 122	‡Dowty, 5, 126	9	1:59.16	2,288,000
1996	Alphabet Soup, 5, 126	C. J. McCarron	Louis Quatorze, 3, 121	Cigar, 6, 126	13	2:01.00	2,080,000
1995	Cigar, 5, 126	J. D. Bailey	L'Carriere, 4, 126	Unaccounted For, 4, 126	11	1:59.58	1,560,000
1994	Concern, 3, 122	J. D. Bailey	Tabasco Cat, 3, 122	Dramatic Gold, 3, 122	14	2:02.41	1,560,000
1993	Arcangues, 5, 126	J. D. Bailey	Bertrando, 4, 126	Kissin Kris, 3, 122	13	2:00.83	1,560,000
1992	A.P. Indy, 3, 121	E. J. Delahoussaye	Pleasant Tap, 5, 126	†Jolypha, 3, 118	14	2:00.20	1,560,000
1991	Black Tie Affair (Ire), 5, 126	J. D. Bailey	Twilight Agenda, 5, 126	Unbridled, 4, 126	11	2:02.80	1,560,000
1990	Unbridled, 3, 121	P. Day	Ibn Bey (GB), 6, 126	Thirty Six Red, 3, 121	14	2:02.20	1,350,000
1989	Sunday Silence, 3, 122	C. J. McCarron	Easy Goer, 3, 122	Blushing John, 4, 126	8	2:00.20	1,350,000
1988	Alysheba, 4, 126	C. J. McCarron	Seeking the Gold, 3, 122	Waquoit, 5, 126	9	2:04.80	1,350,000
1987	Ferdinand, 4, 126	W. Shoemaker	Alysheba, 3, 122	Judge Angelucci, 4, 126	12	2:01.40	1,350,000
1986	Skywalker, 4, 126	L. A. Pincay Jr.	Turkoman, 4, 126	Precisionist, 5, 126	11	2:00.40	1,350,000
1985	Proud Truth, 3, 122	J. Velasquez	Gate Dancer, 4, 126	Turkoman, 3, 122	8	2:00.80	1,350,000
1984	Wild Again, 4, 126	P. Day	‡Slew o' Gold, 4, 126	Gate Dancer, 3, 122	8	2:03.40	1,350,000

Sponsored by the Dodge division of DaimlerChrysler of Detroit, Michigan 2003-'04. Held at Hollywood Park 1984, 1987, 1997. Held at Aqueduct 1985. Held at Santa Anita Park 1986, 1993, 2003. Held at Churchill Downs 1988, 1991, 1994, 1998, 2000. Held at Gulfstream Park 1989, 1992, 1999. Held at Belmont Park 1990, 1995, 2001. Held at Woodbine 1996. Held at Arlington Park 2002. Track record 1996. ‡Gate Dancer finished second, DQ to third, 1984. ‡Whiskey Wisdom finished third, DQ to fourth, 1997. †Denotes female.

Breeders' Cup Distaff

Grade 1 in 2005. Lone Star Park, three-year-olds and up, fillies and mares, 1⅛ miles, dirt. Held October 30, 2004, with a gross value of $1,834,000. First held in 1984. First graded in 1984. Stakes record 1:46.15 (1995 Inside Information).

Year	Winner	Jockey	Second	Third	Strs	Time	1st Purse
2004	Ashado, 3, 119	J. R. Velazquez	Storm Flag Flying, 4, 123	Stellar Jayne, 3, 119	11	1:48.26	$1,040,000
2003	Adoration, 4, 123	P. A. Valenzuela	Elloluv, 3, 119	Got Koko, 4, 123	7	1:49.17	1,040,000

Year	Winner	Jockey	Second	Third	Strs	Time	1st Purse
2002	**Azeri**, 4, 123	M. E. Smith	Farda Amiga, 3, 119	Imperial Gesture, 3, 119	8	1:48.64	$1,040,000
2001	**Unbridled Elaine**, 3, 120	P. Day	Spain, 4, 123	Two Item Limit, 3, 120	11	1:49.21	1,227,200
2000	**Spain**, 3, 120	V. Espinoza	Surfside, 3, 120	Heritage of Gold, 5, 123	9	1:47.66	1,227,200
1999	**Beautiful Pleasure**, 4, 123	J. F. Chavez	Banshee Breeze, 4, 123	Heritage of Gold, 4, 123	8	1:47.56	1,040,000
1998	**Escena**, 5, 123	G. L. Stevens	Banshee Breeze, 3, 120	Keeper Hill, 3, 120	8	1:49.89	1,040,000
1997	**Ajina**, 3, 120	M. E. Smith	Sharp Cat, 3, 120	Escena, 4, 123	8	1:47.30	520,000
1996	**Jewel Princess**, 4, 123	C. S. Nakatani	Serena's Song, 4, 123	Different (Arg), 4, 123	6	1:48.40	520,000
1995	**Inside Information**, 4, 123	M. E. Smith	Heavenly Prize, 4, 123	Lakeway, 4, 123	10	**1:46.15**	520,000
1994	**One Dreamer**, 6, 123	G. L. Stevens	Heavenly Prize, 3, 120	Miss Dominique, 5, 123	9	1:50.70	520,000
1993	**Hollywood Wildcat**, 3, 120	E. J. Delahoussaye	Paseana (Arg), 6, 123	Re Toss (Arg), 6, 123	8	1:48.35	520,000
1992	**Paseana (Arg)**, 5, 123	C. J. McCarron	Versailles Treaty, 4, 123	Magical Maiden, 3, 119	14	1:48.17	520,000
1991	**Dance Smartly**, 3, 120	P. Day	Versailles Treaty, 3, 120	Brought to Mind, 4, 123	13	1:50.95	520,000
1990	**Bayakoa (Arg)**, 6, 123	L. A. Pincay Jr.	Colonial Waters, 5, 123	Valay Maid, 3, 119	7	1:49.20	450,000
1989	**Bayakoa (Arg)**, 5, 123	L. A. Pincay Jr.	Gorgeous, 3, 119	Open Mind, 3, 119	10	1:47.40	450,000
1988	**Personal Ensign**, 4, 123	R. P. Romero	Winning Colors, 3, 119	Goodbye Halo, 3, 119	4	1:52.00	450,000
1987	**Sacahuista**, 3, 119	R. P. Romero	Clabber Girl, 4, 123	Queee Bebe, 3, 119	6	2:02.80	450,000
1986	**Lady's Secret**, 4, 123	P. Day	Fran's Valentine, 4, 123	Outstandingly, 4, 123	8	2:01.20	450,000
1985	**Life's Magic**, 4, 123	A. T. Cordero Jr.	Lady's Secret, 3, 119	Dontstop Themusic, 5, 123	7	2:02.00	450,000
1984	**Princess Rooney**, 4, 123	E. J. Delahoussaye	Life's Magic, 3, 119	Adored, 4, 123	7	2:02.40	450,000

Sponsored by Nextel Communications of Reston, Virginia 2004. Held at Hollywood Park 1984, 1987, 1997. Held at Aqueduct 1985. Held at Santa Anita Park 1986, 1993, 2003. Held at Churchill Downs, 1988, 1991, 1994, 1998, 2000. Held at Gulfstream Park 1989, 1992, 1999. Held at Belmont Park 1990, 1995, 2001. Held at Woodbine 1996. Held at Arlington Park 2002. 1 1/4 miles 1984-'87.

Breeders' Cup Filly and Mare Turf

Grade 1 in 2005. Lone Star Park, three-year-olds and up, fillies and mares, 1 3/8 miles, turf. Held October 30, 2004, with a gross value of $1,292,970. First held in 1999. First graded in 1999. Stakes record 2:13.07 (2000 Perfect Sting).

Year	Winner	Jockey	Second	Third	Strs	Time	1st Purse
2004	**Ouija Board (GB)**, 3, 118	K. Fallon	Film Maker, 4, 123	Wonder Again, 5, 123	12	2:18.25	$733,200
2003	**Islington (Ire)**, 4, 123	K. Fallon	L'Ancresse (Ire), 3, 118	Yesterday (Ire), 3, 118	12	1:59.13	551,200
2002	**Starine (Fr)**, 5, 123	J. R. Velazquez	Banks Hill (GB), 4, 123	Islington (Ire), 3, 118	12	2:03.57	665,600
2001	**Banks Hill (GB)**, 3, 119	O. Peslier	Spook Express (SAf), 7, 123	Spring Oak (GB), 3, 119	12	2:00.36	722,800
2000	**Perfect Sting**, 4, 123	J. D. Bailey	Tout Charmant, 4, 123	Catella (Ger), 4, 123	14	**2:13.07**	629,200
1999	**Soaring Softly**, 4, 123	J. D. Bailey	Coretta (Ire), 5, 123	Zomaradah (GB), 4, 123	14	2:13.89	556,400

Sponsored by the Alberto-Culver Co. of Chicago, Illinois 2004. Held at Gulfstream Park 1999. Held at Churchill Downs 2000. Held at Belmont Park 2001. Held at Arlington Park 2002. Held at Santa Anita Park 2003. 1 1/4 miles 2001-'03.

Breeders' Cup Juvenile

Grade 1 in 2005. Lone Star Park, two-year-olds, colts and geldings, 1 1/16 miles, dirt. Held October 30, 2004, with a gross value of $1,375,500. First held in 1984. First graded in 1984. Stakes record 1:41.47 (1997 Favorite Trick).

Year	Winner	Jockey	Second	Third	Strs	Time	1st Purse
2004	**Wilko**, 2, 122	L. Dettori	Afleet Alex, 2, 122	Sun King, 2, 122	8	1:42.09	$780,000
2003	**Action This Day**, 2, 122	D. R. Flores	Minister Eric, 2, 122	Chapel Royal, 2, 122	12	1:43.62	780,000
2002	**Vindication**, 2, 122	M. E. Smith	Kafwain, 2, 122	Hold That Tiger, 2, 122	13	1:49.61	556,400
2001	**Johannesburg**, 2, 122	M. J. Kinane	Repent, 2, 122	Siphonic, 2, 122	12	1:42.27	520,000
2000	**Macho Uno**, 2, 122	J. D. Bailey	Point Given, 2, 122	Street Cry (Ire), 2, 122	14	1:42.05	556,400
1999	**Anees**, 2, 122	G. L. Stevens	Chief Seattle, 2, 122	High Yield, 2, 122	14	1:42.29	556,400
1998	**Answer Lively**, 2, 122	J. D. Bailey	Aly's Alley, 2, 122	Cat Thief, 2, 122	13	1:44.00	520,000
1997	**Favorite Trick**, 2, 122	P. Day	Dawson's Legacy, 2, 122	Nationalore, 2, 122	7	**1:41.47**	520,000
1996	**Boston Harbor**, 2, 122	J. D. Bailey	Acceptable, 2, 122	Ordway, 2, 122	10	1:43.40	520,000
1995	**Unbridled's Song**, 2, 122	M. E. Smith	Hennessy, 2, 122	Editor's Note, 2, 122	13	1:41.60	520,000
1994	**Timber Country**, 2, 122	P. Day	Eltish, 2, 122	Tejano Run, 2, 122	14	1:44.55	520,000
1993	**Brocco**, 2, 122	G. L. Stevens	Blumin Affair, 2, 122	Tabasco Cat, 2, 122	11	1:42.99	520,000
1992	**Gilded Time**, 2, 122	C. J. McCarron	It'sali'lknownfact, 2, 122	River Special, 2, 122	13	1:43.43	520,000
1991	**Arazi**, 2, 122	P. A. Valenzuela	Bertrando, 2, 122	Snappy Landing, 2, 122	14	1:44.78	520,000
1990	**Fly So Free**, 2, 122	J. A. Santos	Take Me Out, 2, 122	Lost Mountain, 2, 122	11	1:43.40	450,000
1989	**Rhythm**, 2, 122	C. Perret	Grand Canyon, 2, 122	Slavic, 2, 122	12	1:43.60	450,000
1988	**Is It True**, 2, 122	L. A. Pincay Jr.	Easy Goer, 2, 122	Tagel, 2, 122	10	1:46.60	450,000
1987	**Success Express**, 2, 122	J. A. Santos	Regal Classic, 2, 122	Tejano, 2, 122	13	1:35.20	450,000
1986	**Capote**, 2, 122	L. A. Pincay Jr.	Qualify, 2, 122	Alysheba, 2, 122	13	1:43.80	450,000
1985	**Tasso**, 2, 122	L. A. Pincay Jr.	Storm Cat, 2, 122	Scat Dancer, 2, 122	13	1:36.20	450,000
1984	**Chief's Crown**, 2, 122	D. MacBeth	Tank's Prospect, 2, 122	Spend a Buck, 2, 122	10	1:36.20	450,000

Sponsored by Bessemer Trust of New York City 2001-'04. Held at Hollywood Park 1984, 1987, 1997. Held at Aqueduct 1985. Held at Santa Anita Park 1986, 1993, 2003. Held at Churchill Downs 1988, 1991, 1994, 1998, 2000. Held at Gulfstream Park 1989, 1992, 1999. Held at Belmont Park 1990, 1995, 2001. Held at Woodbine 1996. Held at Arlington Park 2002. 1 mile 1984-'85, 1987. 1 1/8 miles 2002.

Breeders' Cup Juvenile Fillies

Grade 1 in 2005. Lone Star Park, two-year-olds, fillies, 1¹⁄₁₆ miles, dirt. Held October 30, 2004, with a gross value of $917,000. First held in 1984. First graded in 1984. Stakes record 1:41.49 (2001 Tempera).

Year	Winner	Jockey	Second	Third	Strs	Time	1st Purse
2004	Sweet Catomine, 2, 119	C. S. Nakatani	Balletto (UAE), 2, 119	Runway Model, 2, 119	12	1:41.65	$520,000
2003	Halfbridled, 2, 119	J. A. Krone	Ashado, 2, 119	Victory U. S. A., 2, 119	14	1:42.75	520,000
2002	Storm Flag Flying, 2, 119	J. R. Velazquez	Composure, 2, 119	Santa Catarina, 2, 119	10	1:49.60	520,000
2001	Tempera, 2, 119	D. R. Flores	Imperial Gesture, 2, 119	Bella Bellucci, 2, 119	9	1:41.49	520,000
2000	Caressing, 2, 119	J. R. Velazquez	Platinum Tiara, 2, 119	She's a Devil Due, 2, 119	12	1:42.77	592,800
1999	Cash Run, 2, 119	J. D. Bailey	Chilukki, 2, 119	Surfside, 2, 119	9	1:43.31	520,000
1998	Silverbulletday, 2, 119	G. L. Stevens	Excellent Meeting, 2, 119	Three Ring, 2, 119	10	1:43.68	520,000
1997	Countess Diana, 2, 119	S. J. Sellers	Career Collection, 2, 119	Primaly, 2, 119	14	1:42.11	535,600
1996	Storm Song, 2, 119	C. Perret	Love That Jazz, 2, 119	Critical Factor, 2, 119	12	1:43.60	520,000
1995	My Flag, 2, 119	J. D. Bailey	Cara Rafaela, 2, 119	Golden Attraction, 2, 119	8	1:42.55	520,000
1994	Flanders, 2, 119	P. Day	Serena's Song, 2, 119	Stormy Blues, 2, 119	13	1:45.28	520,000
1993	Phone Chatter, 2, 119	L. A. Pincay Jr.	Sardula, 2, 119	Heavenly Prize, 2, 119	8	1:43.08	520,000
1992	Eliza, 2, 119	P. A. Valenzuela	Educated Risk, 2, 119	Boots 'n Jackie, 2, 119	12	1:42.93	520,000
1991	Pleasant Stage, 2, 119	E. J. Delahoussaye	La Spia, 2, 119	Cadillac Women, 2, 119	14	1:46.48	520,000
1990	Meadow Star, 2, 119	J. A. Santos	Private Treasure, 2, 119	Dance Smartly, 2, 119	13	1:44.00	450,000
1989	Go for Wand, 2, 119	R. P. Romero	Sweet Roberta, 2, 119	Stella Madrid, 2, 119	12	1:44.20	450,000
1988	Open Mind, 2, 119	A. T. Cordero Jr.	Darby Shuffle, 2, 119	Lea Lucinda, 2, 119	12	1:46.60	450,000
1987	Epitome, 2, 119	P. Day	Jeanne Jones, 2, 119	Dream Team, 2, 119	12	1:36.40	450,000
1986	Brave Raj, 2, 119	P. A. Valenzuela	Tappiano, 2, 119	Saros Brig, 2, 119	12	1:43.20	450,000
1985	Twilight Ridge, 2, 119	J. Velasquez	Family Style, 2, 119	Steal a Kiss, 2, 119	12	1:35.80	450,000
1984	‡Outstandingly, 2, 119	W. A. Guerra	Dusty Heart, 2, 119	Fine Spirit, 2, 119	11	1:37.80	450,000

Formerly sponsored by Long John Silver's of Louisville, Kentucky 2002. Held at Hollywood Park 1984, 1987, 1997. Held at Aqueduct 1985. Held at Santa Anita Park 1986, 1993, 2003. Held at Churchill Downs 1988, 1991, 1994, 1998, 2000. Held at Gulfstream Park 1989, 1992, 1999. Held at Belmont Park 1990, 1995, 2001. Held at Woodbine 1996. Held at Arlington Park 2002. 1 mile 1984-'85, 1987. 1¹⁄₈ miles 2002. ‡Fran's Valentine finished first, DQ to tenth, 1984.

Breeders' Cup Mile

Grade 1 in 2005. Lone Star Park, three-year-olds and up, 1 mile, turf. Held October 30, 2004, with a gross value of $1,540,560. First held in 1984. First graded in 1984. Stakes record 1:32.05 (2001 Val Royal [Fr]).

Year	Winner	Jockey	Second	Third	Strs	Time	1st Purse
2004	Singletary, 4, 126	D. R. Flores	Antonius Pius, 3, 122	†Six Perfections (Fr), 4, 123	14	1:36.90	$873,600
2003	†Six Perfections (Fr), 3, 119	J. D. Bailey	Touch of the Blues (Fr), 6, 126	Century City (Ire), 4, 126	13	1:33.86	780,000
2002	Domedriver (Ire), 4, 126	T. Thulliez	Rock of Gibraltar (Ire), 3, 122	Good Journey, 6, 126	14	1:36.92	556,400
2001	Val Royal (Fr), 5, 126	J. Valdivia Jr.	Forbidden Apple, 6, 126	Bach (Ire), 4, 126	12	1:32.05	592,800
2000	War Chant, 3, 123	G. L. Stevens	North East Bound, 4, 126	Dansili (GB), 4, 126	14	1:34.67	608,400
1999	Silic (Fr), 4, 126	C. S. Nakatani	†Tuzla (Fr), 5, 123	Docksider, 4, 126	14	1:34.26	520,000
1998	Da Hoss, 6, 126	J. R. Velazquez	Hawksley Hill (Ire), 5, 126	Labeeb (GB), 6, 126	14	1:35.27	520,000
1997	Spinning World, 4, 126	C. B. Asmussen	Geri, 5, 126	Decorated Hero (GB), 5, 126	12	1:32.77	572,000
1996	Da Hoss, 4, 126	G. L. Stevens	Spinning World, 3, 122	Same Old Wish, 6, 126	14	1:35.80	520,000
1995	†Ridgewood Pearl (GB), 3, 119	J. Murtagh	Fastness (Ire), 5, 126	†Sayyedati (GB), 5, 123	13	1:43.65	520,000
1994	Barathea (Ire), 4, 126	L. Dettori	Johann Quatz (Fr), 5, 126	Unfinished Symph, 3, 123	14	1:34.50	520,000
1993	Lure, 4, 126	M. E. Smith	†Ski Paradise, 3, 120	Fourstars Allstar, 5, 126	14	1:33.58	520,000
1992	Lure, 3, 122	M. E. Smith	Paradise Creek, 3, 122	Brief Truce, 3, 122	14	1:32.90	520,000
1991	Opening Verse, 5, 126	P. A. Valenzuela	Val des Bois (Fr), 5, 126	Star of Cozzene, 3, 123	14	1:37.59	520,000
1990	Royal Academy, 3, 122	L. Piggott	Itsallgreektome, 3, 122	Priolo, 3, 122	13	1:35.20	450,000
1989	Steinlen (GB), 6, 126	J. A. Santos	Sabona, 7, 126	Most Welcome (GB), 5, 126	11	1:37.20	450,000
1988	†Miesque, 4, 123	F. Head	Steinlen (GB), 5, 126	Simply Majestic, 4, 126	14	1:38.60	450,000
1987	†Miesque, 3, 120	F. Head	Show Dancer, 5, 126	†Sonic Lady, 4, 123	14	1:32.80	450,000
1986	Last Tycoon (Ire), 3, 123	Y. Saint-Martin	Palace Music, 5, 126	Fred Astaire, 3, 123	14	1:35.20	450,000
1985	Cozzene, 5, 126	W. A. Guerra	‡Al Mamoon, 4, 126	Shadeed, 3, 123	14	1:35.00	450,000
1984	†Royal Heroine (Ire), 4, 123	F. Toro	Star Choice, 5, 126	Cozzene, 4, 126	10	1:32.60	450,000

Sponsored by NetJets Inc. of Woodbridge, New Jersey 2002-'04. Held at Hollywood Park 1984, 1987, 1997. Held at Aqueduct 1985. Held at Santa Anita Park 1986, 1993, 2003. Held at Churchill Downs 1988, 1991, 1994, 1998, 2000. Held at Gulfstream Park 1989, 1992, 1999. Held at Belmont Park 1990, 1995, 2001. Held at Woodbine Race Course 1996. Held at Arlington Park 2002. ‡Palace Music finished second, DQ to ninth, 1985. Course record 1992, 1994. †Denotes female.

Breeders' Cup Sprint

Grade 1 in 2005. Lone Star Park, three-year-olds and up, 6 furlongs, dirt. Held October 30, 2004, with a gross value of $972,020. First held in 1984. First graded in 1984. Stakes record 1:07.77 (2000 Kona Gold).

Year	Winner	Jockey	Second	Third	Strs	Time	1st Purse
2004	Speightstown, 6, 126	J. R. Velazquez	Kela, 6, 126	My Cousin Matt, 5, 126	13	1:08.11	$551,200
2003	Cajun Beat, 3, 123	C. H. Velasquez	Bluesthestandard, 6, 126	Shake You Down, 5, 126	13	1:07.95	613,600
2002	Orientate, 4, 126	J. D. Bailey	Thunderello, 3, 123	Crafty C. T., 4, 126	13	1:08.89	592,800
2001	Squirtle Squirt, 3, 124	J. D. Bailey	†Xtra Heat, 3, 121	Caller One, 4, 126	14	1:08.41	520,000
2000	Kona Gold, 6, 126	A. O. Solis	†Honest Lady, 4, 123	Bet On Sunshine, 8, 126	14	1:07.77	520,000

Year	Winner	Jockey	Second	Third	Strs	Time	1st Purse
1999	**Artax**, 4, 126	J. F. Chavez	Kona Gold, 5, 126	Big Jag, 6, 126	14	1:07.89	$624,000
1998	**Reraise**, 3, 124	C. S. Nakatani	Grand Slam, 3, 124	Kona Gold, 4, 126	14	1:09.07	572,000
1997	**Elmhurst**, 7, 126	C. S. Nakatani	Hesabull, 4, 126	Bet On Sunshine, 5, 126	14	1:08.01	613,600
1996	**Lit de Justice**, 6, 126	C. S. Nakatani	Paying Dues, 4, 126	Honour and Glory, 3, 123	13	1:08.60	520,000
1995	**†Desert Stormer**, 5, 123	K. J. Desormeaux	Mr. Greeley, 3, 123	Lit de Justice, 5, 126	13	1:09.14	520,000
1994	**Cherokee Run**, 4, 126	M. E. Smith	†Soviet Problem, 4, 123	Cardmania, 8, 126	14	1:09.54	520,000
1993	**Cardmania**, 7, 126	E. J. Delahoussaye	†Meafara, 4, 123	Gilded Time, 3, 124	14	1:08.76	520,000
1992	**Thirty Slews**, 5, 126	E. J. Delahoussaye	†Meafara, 3, 120	Rubiano, 5, 126	14	1:08.21	520,000
1991	**Sheikh Albadou (GB)**, 3, 124	P. Eddery	Pleasant Tap, 4, 126	Robyn Dancer, 4, 126	11	1:09.36	520,000
1990	**†Safely Kept**, 4, 123	C. Perret	Dayjur, 3, 123	Black Tie Affair (Ire), 4, 126	14	1:09.60	450,000
1989	**Dancing Spree**, 4, 126	A. T. Cordero Jr.	†Safely Kept, 3, 121	Dispersal, 3, 124	13	1:09.00	450,000
1988	**Gulch**, 4, 126	A. T. Cordero Jr.	Play the King, 5, 126	Afleet, 4, 126	13	1:10.40	450,000
1987	**†Very Subtle**, 3, 121	P. A. Valenzuela	Groovy, 4, 126	Exclusive Enough, 3, 124	13	1:08.80	450,000
1986	**Smile**, 4, 126	J. Vasquez	†Pine Tree Lane, 4, 123	Bedside Promise, 4, 126	9	1:08.40	450,000
1985	**Precisionist**, 4, 126	C. J. McCarron	Smile, 3, 124	Mt. Livermore, 4, 126	14	1:08.40	450,000
1984	**Eillo**, 4, 126	C. Perret	Commemorate, 3, 124	Fighting Fit, 5, 126	11	1:10.20	450,000

Formerly sponsored by NAPA Auto Parts of Atlanta, Georgia 2002. Formerly sponsored by Penske Auto Center 2001. Held at Hollywood Park 1984, 1987, 1997. Held at Gulfstream Park 1992, 1999. Held at Santa Anita Park 1986, 1993, 2003. Held at Churchill Downs 1988, 1991, 1994, 1998, 2000. Held at Belmont Park 1995, 2001. Held at Woodbine 1996. Held at Arlington Park 2002. Equaled track record 1996, 1999. Track record 2000. †Denotes female.

Breeders' Cup Turf

Grade 1 in 2005. Lone Star Park, three-year-olds and up, 1½ miles, turf. Held October 30, 2004, with a gross value of $1,834,000. First held in 1984. First graded in 1984. Stakes record 2:23.92 (1997 Chief Bearhart).

Year	Winner	Jockey	Second	Third	Strs	Time	1st Purse
2004	**Better Talk Now**, 5, 126	R. A. Dominguez	Kitten's Joy, 3, 121	Powerscourt (GB), 4, 126	8	2:29.70	$1,040,000
2003	**dh- High Chaparral (Ire)**, 4, 126	M. J. Kinane	Falbrav (Ire), 5, 126		9	2:24.24	763,200
	dh- Johar, 4, 126	A. O. Solis					
2002	**High Chaparral (Ire)**, 3, 121	M. J. Kinane	With Anticipation, 7, 126	Falcon Flight (Fr), 6, 126	8	2:30.14	1,258,400
2001	**Fantastic Light**, 5, 126	L. Dettori	Milan (GB), 3, 121	Timboroa (GB), 5, 126	11	2:24.36	1,112,800
2000	**Kalanisi (Ire)**, 4, 126	J. Murtagh	Quiet Resolve, 5, 126	John's Call, 9, 126	13	2:26.96	1,289,600
1999	**Daylami (Ire)**, 5, 126	L. Dettori	Royal Anthem, 4, 126	Buck's Boy, 6, 126	14	2:24.73	1,040,000
1998	**Buck's Boy**, 5, 126	S. J. Sellers	Yagli, 5, 126	Dushyantor, 5, 126	13	2:28.74	1,040,000
1997	**Chief Bearhart**, 4, 126	J. A. Santos	†Borgia (Ger), 3, 119	Flag Down, 7, 126	11	**2:23.92**	1,040,000
1996	**Pilsudski (Ire)**, 4, 126	W. R. Swinburn	Singspiel (Ire), 4, 126	Swain (Ire), 4, 126	14	2:30.20	1,040,000
1995	**Northern Spur (Ire)**, 4, 126	C. J. McCarron	Freedom Cry (GB), 4, 126	Carnegie (Ire), 4, 126	13	2:42.07	1,040,000
1994	**Tikkanen**, 3, 122	M. E. Smith	†Hatoof, 5, 123	Paradise Creek, 5, 126	14	2:26.50	1,040,000
1993	**Kotashaan (Fr)**, 5, 126	K. J. Desormeaux	Bien Bien, 4, 126	Luazur (Fr), 4, 126	14	2:25.16	1,040,000
1992	**Fraise**, 4, 126	P. A. Valenzuela	Sky Classic, 5, 126	Quest for Fame (GB), 5, 126	10	2:24.08	1,040,000
1991	**†Miss Alleged**, 4, 123	E. Legrix	Itsallgreektome, 4, 126	Quest for Fame (GB), 4, 126	13	2:30.95	1,040,000
1990	**In the Wings (GB)**, 4, 126	G. L. Stevens	With Approval, 4, 126	El Senor, 6, 126	11	2:29.60	900,000
1989	**Prized**, 3, 122	E. J. Delahoussaye	†Sierra Roberta (Fr), 3, 119	Star Lift (GB), 5, 126	14	2:28.00	900,000
1988	**Great Communicator**, 5, 126	R. Sibille	Sunshine Forever, 3, 122	†Indian Skimmer, 4, 123	10	2:35.20	900,000
1987	**Theatrical (Ire)**, 5, 126	P. Day	Trempolino, 3, 122	Village Star (Fr), 4, 126	14	2:24.40	900,000
1986	**Manila**, 3, 122	J. A. Santos	Theatrical (Ire), 4, 126	†Estrapade, 6, 123	9	2:25.40	900,000
1985	**†Pebbles (GB)**, 4, 123	P. Eddery	Strawberry Road (Aus), 6, 126	Mourjane (Ire), 5, 126	14	2:27.00	900,000
1984	**Lashkari (GB)**, 3, 122	Y. Saint-Martin	†All Along (Fr), 5, 123	Raami (GB), 3, 122	11	2:25.20	900,000

Sponsored by John Deere & Co. of Moline, Illinois 2002-'04. Held at Hollywood Park 1984, 1987, 1997. Held at Aqueduct 1985. Held at Santa Anita Park 1986, 1993, 2003. Held at Churchill Downs 1988, 1991, 1994, 1998, 2000. Held at Gulfstream Park 1989, 1992, 1999. Held at Belmont Park 1990, 1995, 2001. Held at Woodbine 1996. Held at Arlington Park 2002. Dead heat for first 2003. Course record 1992. †Denotes female.

Brooklyn Handicap

Grade 2 in 2005. Belmont Park, three-year-olds and up, 1⅛ miles, dirt. Held June 11, 2005, with a gross value of $250,000. First held in 1887. First graded in 1973. Stakes record 1:46.21 (1997 Formal Gold).

Year	Winner	Jockey	Second	Third	Strs	Time	1st Purse
2005	**Limehouse**, 4, 115	J. R. Velazquez	Gygistar, 6, 117	‡Royal Assault, 4, 112	9	1:46.69	$150,000
2004	**Seattle Fitz (Arg)**, 5, 116	R. Migliore	Dynever, 4, 117	Newfoundland, 4, 115	6	1:46.30	150,000
2003	**Iron Deputy**, 4, 114	R. Migliore	Volponi, 5, 122	Saarland, 4, 115	5	1:47.84	150,000
2002	**Seeking Daylight**, 4, 113	E. S. Prado	Country Be Gold, 5, 113	Griffinite, 4, 114	8	1:46.35	150,000
2001	**Albert the Great**, 4, 122	J. F. Chavez	Perfect Cat, 4, 115	Top Official, 6, 113	7	1:47.41	150,000
2000	**Lemon Drop Kid**, 4, 120	E. S. Prado	Lager, 6, 114	Down the Aisle, 7, 112	7	1:49.93	150,000
1999	**Running Stag**, 5, 117	S. J. Sellers	Deputy Diamond, 4, 113	Sir Bear, 6, 119	8	1:46.39	210,000
1998	**Subordination**, 4, 114	E. Coa	Sir Bear, 5, 118	Mr. Sinatra, 4, 114	11	1:46.64	180,000
1997	**Formal Gold**, 4, 119	J. D. Bailey	Stephanotis, 4, 116	Circle of Light, 4, 111	8	**1:46.21**	180,000
1996	**Wekiva Springs**, 5, 120	M. E. Smith	Mahogany Hall, 5, 114	Admiralty, 4, 111	7	1:46.78	180,000
1995	**You and I**, 4, 115	J. F. Chavez	Key Contender, 7, 112	Slick Horn, 5, 113	9	1:49.02	150,000
1994	**Devil His Due**, 5, 120	M. E. Smith	Wallenda, 4, 111	Sea Hero, 4, 119	7	1:46.71	150,000
1993	**Living Vicariously**, 3, 111	R. G. Davis	Michelle Can Pass, 5, 116	Jacksonport, 4, 111	8	2:17.80	150,000
1992	**Chief Honcho**, 5, 117	R. P. Romero	‡Valley Crossing, 4, 113	Lost Mountain, 4, 114	11	2:16.91	210,000

1991	Timely Warning, 6, 112	M. J. Luzzi	Chief Honcho, 4, 121	De Roche, 5, 115	8	2:14.03	$210,000
1990	‡Montubio (Arg), 5, 113	J. Vasquez	Mi Selecto, 5, 114	De Roche, 4, 113	7	2:28.60	241,920
1989	Forever Silver, 4, 116	J. Vasquez	Drapeau Tricolore, 4, 112	Jack of Clubs, 6, 112	6	2:28.60	238,560
1988	Waquoit, 5, 121	J. A. Santos	Personal Flag, 5, 120	Creme Fraiche, 6, 118	4	2:28.80	229,740
1987	Waquoit, 4, 123	C. J. McCarron	Bordeaux Bob, 4, 112	Full Courage, 4, 108	9	2:28.40	249,480
1986	Little Missouri, 4, 109	J. Samyn	Roo Art, 4, 118	Creme Fraiche, 4, 118	6	2:26.40	195,900
1985	Bounding Basque, 5, 111	A. Graell	†Life's Magic, 4, 114	Pine Circle, 4, 115	10	2:28.40	207,300
1984	Fit to Fight, 5, 129	J. D. Bailey	Vision, 3, 109	Dew Line, 5, 116	8	2:27.40	201,600
1983	Highland Blade, 5, 117	J. Vasquez	Sing Sing, 5, 118	Silver Supreme, 5, 113	13	2:31.00	172,800
1982	Silver Supreme, 4, 111	A. T. Cordero Jr.	Princelet, 4, 112	Baltimore Canyon, 4, 113	6	2:29.40	131,700
1981	Hechizado (Arg), 5, 116	R. Hernandez	The Liberal Member, 6, 113	Peat Moss, 6, 111	10	2:26.00	138,300
1980	Winter's Tale, 4, 120	J. Fell	State Dinner, 5, 121	Ring of Light, 5, 114	5	2:28.60	130,200
1979	The Liberal Member, 4, 114	R. I. Encinas	Bowl Game, 5, 119	State Dinner, 4, 123	5	2:28.80	99,000
1978	Nasty and Bold, 3, 112	J. Samyn	Father Hogan, 5, 116	Great Contractor, 5, 122	7	2:26.00	63,900
1977	Great Contractor, 4, 112	A. T. Cordero Jr.	Forego, 7, 137	American History, 5, 112	13	2:26.20	66,660
1976	Forego, 6, 134	H. Gustines	Lord Rebeau, 5, 114	Foolish Pleasure, 4, 126	8	2:01.20	67,860
1975	Forego, 5, 132	H. Gustines	Monetary Principle, 5, 109	Stop the Music, 5, 121	8	1:59.80	66,780
1974	Forego, 4, 129	H. Gustines	Billy Come Lately, 4, 114	Arbees Boy, 4, 116	7	1:54.80	66,600
1973	Riva Ridge, 4, 127	R. Turcotte	True Knight, 4, 117	Tentam, 4, 119	7	1:52.40	67,200

Named for Brooklyn borough of New York City. Grade 1 1973-'92. Held at Gravesend Park 1887-1910. Held at Aqueduct 1914-'44, 1946-'55, 1960-'74, 1991-'93. Held at Jamaica 1956-'59. Not held 1911-'12. 1¼ miles 1887-1914, 1940-'55, 1960-'71, 1975-'76. 1³⁄₁₆ miles 1956-'59, 1972-'74. 1⅞ miles 1991-'93. 1½ miles 1977-'90. ‡Mi Selecto finished first, DQ to second, 1990. ‡Lost Mountain finished second, DQ to third, 1992. ‡ Cuba finished third, DQ to fifth, 2005. World record 1973. Track record 1973, 1975. †Denotes female.

Buena Vista Handicap

Grade 3 in 2005. Santa Anita Park, four-year-olds and up, fillies and mares, 1 mile (originally scheduled as a Grade 2 on the turf), dirt. Held February 21, 2005, with a gross value of $150,000. First held in 1988. First graded in 1990. Stakes record 1:33.48 (1992 Gold Fleece [1st Div.]; 1997 Media Nox [GB]).

Year	Winner	Jockey	Second	Third	Strs	Time	1st Purse
2005	Uraib (Ire), 5, 115	J. K. Court	Resplendency, 4, 117	Elusive Diva, 4, 116	5	1:33.72	$90,000
2004	Fun House, 5, 116	G. L. Stevens	Katdogawn (GB), 4, 117	Fudge Fatale, 4, 116	7	1:36.13	90,000
2003	Final Destination (NZ), 5, 115	V. Espinoza	Garden in the Rain (Fr), 6, 115	Embassy Belle (Ire), 5, 116	6	1:35.99	90,000
2002	Blue Moon (Fr), 5, 113	B. Blanc	Queen of Wilshire, 6, 116	Old Money (Aus), 5, 118	7	1:35.54	90,000
2001	Rare Charmer, 6, 115	L. A. Pincay Jr.	Elegant Ridge (Ire), 6, 117	Uncharted Haven (GB), 4, 116	11	1:36.67	90,000
2000	Lexa (Fr), 6, 115	B. Blanc	Here's to You, 4, 114	Sierra Virgen, 5, 114	6	1:36.17	97,290
1999	Tuzla (Fr), 5, 120	C. S. Nakatani	Supercilious, 6, 117	Green Jewel (GB), 5, 116	5	1:35.79	90,000
1998	Dance Parade, 4, 116	K. J. Desormeaux	Shake the Yoke (GB), 5, 116	Donna Viola (GB), 6, 121	10	1:36.03	101,520
1997	Media Nox (GB), 4, 115	C. S. Nakatani	Traces of Gold, 5, 115	Grafin, 6, 116	12	1:33.48	85,250
1996	Matiara, 4, 119	G. L. Stevens	Real Connection, 5, 114	Dirca (Ire), 4, 116	8	1:35.74	81,800
1995	Lyin to the Moon, 6, 116	K. J. Desormeaux	Jacodra's Devil, 4, 115	Exchange, 7, 122	5	1:36.77	61,700
1994	‡Skimble, 5, 118	C. S. Nakatani	Hero's Love, 6, 121	Possibly Perfect, 4, 120	9	1:34.85	66,300
1993	Marble Maiden (GB), 4, 118	K. J. Desormeaux	Suivi, 4, 117	Party Cited, 4, 116	7	1:36.23	65,000
1992	Gold Fleece, 4, 114	A. O. Solis	Elegance, 5, 115	Danzante, 4, 114	9	1:33.48	52,100
	Appealing Missy, 5, 117	C. J. McCarron	Exchange, 4, 120	Re Toss (Arg), 5, 117	9	1:34.25	52,100
1991	Taffeta and Tulle, 5, 120	C. J. McCarron	Bequest, 5, 117	Somethingmerry, 4, 114	9	1:34.30	67,200
1990	Saros Brig, 6, 116	P. A. Valenzuela	Royal Touch (Ire), 5, 123	Nikishka, 5, 118	10	1:34.20	68,400
1989	Annoconnor, 5, 121	C. A. Black	Daring Doone (GB), 6, 112	Daloma (Fr), 5, 116	8	1:36.40	65,800
1988	Davie's Lamb, 4, 117	F. Toro	Sly Charmer, 4, 114	Pen Bal Lady (GB), 4, 119	9	1:39.00	63,050

Named for two 19th-century California ranchos named Buena Vista Rancho; buena vista means "good view." Grade 3 1990-'94. Two divisions 1992. ‡Lady Blessington (Fr) finished first, DQ to ninth, 1994.

Calder Derby

Grade 3 in 2005. Calder Race Course, three-year-olds, 1⅛ miles, turf. Held October 23, 2004, with a gross value of $200,000. First held in 1972. First graded in 1996. Stakes record 1:47.70 (1998 Crowd Pleaser).

Year	Winner	Jockey	Second	Third	Strs	Time	1st Purse
2004	Eddington, 3, 114	E. Coa	Bob's Proud Moment, 3, 116	‡Caballero Negro, 3, 114	12	1:51.25	$120,000
2003	Stroll, 3, 122	J. D. Bailey	Certifiably Crazy, 3, 115	Super Frolic, 3, 119	9	1:48.39	120,000
2002	Union Place, 3, 115	E. Coa	Miesque's Approval, 3, 122	The Judge Sez Who, 3, 122	11	1:47.76	120,000
2001	Western Pride, 3, 122	D. G. Whitney	Tour of the Cat, 3, 113	Built Up, 3, 117	10	1:51.12	120,000
2000	Whata Brainstorm, 3, 122	R. B. Homeister Jr.	Muntej (GB), 3, 122	Womble, 3, 117	12	1:47.80	120,000
1999	Isaypete, 3, 122	J. C. Ferrer	Rhythmean, 3, 117	Phi Beta Doc, 3, 122	12	1:50.01	120,000
1998	Crowd Pleaser, 3, 122	J. Samyn	Stay Sound, 3, 122	The Kaiser, 3, 117	10	1:47.70	120,000
1997	Blazing Sword, 3, 117	G. Boulanger	dh-Royal Tuneup, 3, 117		10	1:53.15	90,000
			dh-Topaz Runner, 3, 117				
1996	Laughing Dan, 3, 117	P. A. Rodriguez	Sea Horse, 3, 117	†Flying Concert, 3, 114	11	1:50.75	66,300
1995	Pineing Patty, 3, 122	L. J. Melancon	Sea Emperor, 3, 122	Mucha Mosca, 3, 117	7	1:51.40	60,000
1994	Halo's Image, 3, 117	G. Boulanger	Honest Colors, 3, 117	Rocky's Halo, 3, 117	10	1:52.38	90,000
1993	Medieval Mac, 3, 113	M. Russ	Raise an Alarm, 3, 117	Fight for Love, 3, 116	9	1:41.79	30,000
1992	Birdonthewire, 3, 112	M. T. Hunter	Shahpour, 3, 113	Ponche, 3, 111	7	1:44.36	30,000

Year	Winner	Jockey	Second	Third	Strs	Time	1st Purse
1991	**Scottish Ice**, 3, 113	R. N. Lester	Chihuahua, 3, 120	Jackie Wackie, 3, 121	9	1:46.10	$33,450
1990	**Zalipour**, 3, 118	D. A. Acevedo	Country Isle, 3, 115	Rowdy Regal, 3, 114	7	1:46.60	32,580
1989	**‡Silver Sunsets**, 3, 114	M. A. Gonzalez	Compuquine, 3, 114	Run for Your Honey, 3, 111	6	1:45.80	32,190
1988	**Frosty the Snowman**, 3, 116	D. Valiente	In the Slammer, 3, 116	Distinctintentions, 3, 112	7	1:44.40	30,750
1987	**Schism**, 3, 117	R. N. Lester	Slewdonza, 3, 112	Fabulous Devotion, 3, 114	6	1:47.20	32,640
1986	**Annapolis John**, 3, 120	J. A. Velez Jr.	Kid Colin, 3, 115	Real Forest, 3, 118	7	1:46.20	28,160
1985	**Gray Haze**, 3, 115	F. A. Pennisi	Alfred, 3, 115	Jeblar, 3, 115	11	1:46.00	33,780
1984	**Opening Lead**, 4, 114	J. A. Santos	Ward Off Trouble, 4, 114	Darn That Alarm, 3, 112	14	1:47.60	34,860
1983	**Opening Lead**, 3, 117	B. Gonzalez	The Cerfer, 3, 112	Neutral Player, 3, 112	12	1:48.20	20,640
1982	**Glorious Past**, 3, 115	A. Smith Jr.	Count Rebeau, 3, 115	Ell's New Canaan, 3, 112	9	1:45.80	19,905
1981	**Poking**, 3, 115	G. Cohen	Yosi Boy, 5, 114	Pair of Deuces, 3, 112	10	1:53.40	23,415
1980	**J. Rodney G.**, 5, 113	F. Verardi	Two's a Plenty, 3, 109	Cherry Pop, 4, 125	8	1:53.20	23,040
1979	**Breezy Fare**, 4, 118	M. A. Rivera	Abba Cap, 5, 115	Selma's Boy, 4, 117	9	1:52.00	16,665
1978	**Ole Wilk**, 4, 114	I. J. Jimenez	America Behave, 4, 110	Classy State, 5, 115	10	1:42.60	18,600
1977	**What a Threat**, 5, 117	R. Gaffalione	†Noble Royalty, 4, 116	Lightning Thrust, 4, 122	8	1:42.60	17,400
1976	**Chilean Chief**, 5, 118	J. Imparato	El Rosillo, 3, 112	L. Grant Jr., 6, 116	9	1:45.80	17,700
1975	dh- ***Rimsky II**, 4, 116	A. Haldar		Plagiarize, 4, 121	12	1:42.20	12,400
	dh- **Strand of Gold**, 5, 112	P. Nicolo					
1974	**‡Amberbee**, 6, 117	J. Garrido	Enchanted Ruler, 3, 112	Seminole Joe, 6, 113	9	1:46.60	14,280
1973	**Willmar**, 5, 122	G. St. Leon	Sea Phantom, 5, 118	†Hickory Gray, 4, 115	8	1:25.20	7,020

Formerly named for Hollywood, Florida, hometown of real-estate developer Stephen Calder, who built Calder Race Course. Not graded 1998-'99. Hollywood H. 1972-'81, 1984, 1987-'93. Hollywood S. 1982-'83, 1985-'86. Calder Breeders' Cup Derby 1996. 7 furlongs 1972-'73. 1¹⁄₁₆ miles 1974-'78, 1982-'92. 1 mile 70 yards 1993. Dirt 1972-'74, 1976, 1979-'97, 2001. Three-year-olds and up 1972-'81, 1984. Dead heat for first 1975. Dead heat for second 1997. ‡Snurb finished first, DQ to seventh, 1974. ‡Big Stanley finished first, DQ to sixth, 1989. ‡Capias finished third, DQ to twelfth, 2004. Track record 1993. †Denotes female.

Californian Stakes

Grade 2 in 2005. Hollywood Park, three-year-olds and up, 1¹⁄₈ miles, dirt. Held June 12, 2004, with a gross value of $250,000. First held in 1954. First graded in 1973. Stakes record 1:45.80 (1980 Spectacular Bid).

Year	Winner	Jockey	Second	Third	Strs	Time	1st Purse
2004	**Even the Score**, 6, 118	D. R. Flores	Total Impact (Chi), 6, 116	Nose The Trade (GB), 6, 116	8	1:47.64	$150,000
2003	**Kudos**, 6, 116	A. O. Solis	Piensa Sonando (Chi), 5, 118	Reba's Gold, 5, 118	7	1:47.91	240,000
2002	**Milwaukee Brew**, 5, 118	K. J. Desormeaux	Bosque Redondo, 5, 118	Momentum, 4, 118	8	1:48.06	300,000
2001	**Skimming**, 5, 116	G. K. Gomez	Futural, 5, 120	Aptitude, 4, 116	8	1:48.12	300,000
2000	**Big Ten (Chi)**, 5, 116	A. O. Solis	Early Pioneer, 5, 118	Mojave Moon, 4, 116	5	1:49.22	150,000
1999	**Old Trieste**, 4, 116	C. J. McCarron	Budroyale, 6, 120	Puerto Madero (Chi), 5, 122	7	1:46.55	180,000
1998	**Mud Route**, 4, 116	C. J. McCarron	Deputy Commander, 4, 122	Worldly Ways (GB), 4, 117	6	1:48.00	150,000
1997	**River Keen (Ire)**, 5, 117	K. J. Desormeaux	Hesabull, 4, 118	Benchmark, 6, 118	6	1:47.38	150,000
1996	**Tinners Way**, 6, 116	E. J. Delahoussaye	Helmsman, 4, 122	Mr Purple, 4, 122	4	1:46.60	151,980
1995	**Concern**, 4, 122	M. E. Smith	Tossofthecoin, 4, 118	Tinners Way, 5, 116	8	1:47.74	160,900
1994	**The Wicked North**, 5, 120	K. J. Desormeaux	Kingdom Found, 4, 116	Slew of Damascus, 6, 116	7	1:46.68	165,000
1993	**Latin American**, 5, 116	G. L. Stevens	Missionary Ridge (GB), 6, 116	Memo (Chi), 6, 118	7	1:46.92	220,000
1992	**Another Review**, 4, 119	K. J. Desormeaux	Defensive Play, 5, 120	Ibero (Arg), 5, 119	7	1:48.11	119,400
1991	**Roanoke**, 4, 116	E. J. Delahoussaye	Anshan (GB), 4, 118	Marquetry, 4, 113	10	1:48.30	175,600
1990	**Sunday Silence**, 4, 126	P. A. Valenzuela	Stylish Winner, 6, 115	Charlatan (Chi), 5, 111	3	1:48.00	168,400
1989	**Sabona**, 7, 115	C. J. McCarron	Blushing John, 4, 124	Lively One, 4, 118	6	1:46.80	185,800
1988	**Cutlass Reality**, 6, 115	C. J. McCarron	Gulch, 4, 126	Judge Angelucci, 5, 126	4	1:47.60	180,200
1987	**Judge Angelucci**, 4, 118	G. Baze	Iron Eyes, 4, 115	Snow Chief, 4, 126	8	1:48.20	193,200
1986	**Precisionist**, 5, 126	C. J. McCarron	Super Diamond, 6, 117	Skywalker, 4, 121	7	1:33.60	188,400
1985	**Greinton (GB)**, 4, 119	L. A. Pincay Jr.	Precisionist, 4, 126	Lord At War (Arg), 5, 126	4	1:32.60	179,600
1984	**Desert Wine**, 4, 121	E. J. Delahoussaye	Interco, 4, 126	Sari's Dreamer, 5, 116	8	1:47.60	193,600
1983	**The Wonder (Fr)**, 5, 119	W. Shoemaker	Prince Spellbound, 4, 122	Poley, 4, 117	8	1:48.40	192,000
1982	**Erins Isle (Ire)**, 4, 117	L. A. Pincay Jr.	It's the One, 4, 128	Major Sport, 5, 118	10	1:48.00	200,200
1981	**Eleven Stitches**, 4, 122	S. Hawley	Temperence Hill, 4, 130	†Kilijaro (Ire), 5, 123	12	1:48.40	207,600
1980	**Spectacular Bid**, 4, 130	W. Shoemaker	Paint King, 4, 115	Caro Bambino (Ire), 5, 118	7	**1:45.80**	184,450
1979	**Affirmed**, 4, 130	L. A. Pincay Jr.	Syncopate, 4, 114	Harry's Love, 4, 117	8	1:41.20	159,900
1978	**J. O.Tobin**, 4, 126	S. Cauthen	Replant, 4, 120	Cox's Ridge, 4, 127	6	1:41.00	124,550
1977	**Crystal Water**, 4, 128	L. A. Pincay Jr.	Mark's Place, 5, 121	Ancient Title, 7, 123	6	1:41.20	65,300
1976	**Ancient Title**, 6, 127	S. Hawley	Pay Tribute, 4, 117	Austin Mittler, 6, 118	6	1:41.20	65,300
1975	**Ancient Title**, 5, 126	L. A. Pincay Jr.	Big Band, 5, 117	Century's Envoy, 4, 117	10	1:40.20	73,100
1974	**Quack**, 5, 126	D. Pierce	Ancient Title, 4, 126	Woodland Pines, 5, 120	9	1:40.20	70,900
1973	**Quack**, 4, 126	D. Pierce	Royal Owl, 4, 125	Tri Jet, 4, 118	6	1:41.40	65,300

Named in honor of the residents of the state of California. Grade 1 1973-'96. 1¹⁄₁₆ miles 1954-'79. †Denotes female.

Cardinal Handicap

Grade 3 in 2005. Churchill Downs, three-year-olds and up, fillies and mares, 1¹⁄₈ miles, turf. Held November 20, 2004, with a gross value of $173,550. First held in 1974. First graded in 1995. Stakes record 1:47.81 (1996 Bail Out Becky [DQ to second]).

Year	Winner	Jockey	Second	Third	Strs	Time	1st Purse
2004	**Aud**, 4, 115	B. Blanc	May Gator, 5, 117	Angela's Love, 4, 114	11	1:53.94	$107,601
2003	**Riskaverse**, 4, 118	C. H. Velasquez	Bien Nicole, 5, 120	Firth of Lorne (Ire), 4, 116	12	1:50.53	108,624

2002	Quick Tip, 4, 114	R. Albarado	San Dare, 4, 114	Bien Nicole, 4, 118	10	1:51.08	$107,322
2001	Watch, 4, 114	C. Perret	Sitka, 4, 111	Gino's Spirits (GB), 5, 118	9	1:49.12	104,997
2000	Illiquidity, 4, 115	J. K. Court	License Fee, 5, 118	Miss of Wales (Chi), 5, 114	12	1:49.72	109,182
1999	Pratella, 4, 114	B. Peck	Mingling Glances, 5, 116	Uanme, 4, 112	9	1:48.88	106,299
1998	B. A. Valentine, 5, 115	J. F. Chavez	Mingling Glances, 4, 112	Cuando, 4, 116	13	1:48.62	111,693
1997	Colcon, 4, 114	J. D. Bailey	Dance Clear (Ire), 4, 112	Sagar Pride (Ire), 4, 113	12	1:51.89	108,903
1996	‡Miss Caerleona (Fr), 4, 114	L. J. Melancon	Bail Out Becky, 4, 121	Striesen, 4, 113	12	**1:47.81**	72,850
1995	Apolda, 4, 114	P. Day	Alive With Hope, 4, 114	Lady Reiko (Ire), 4, 115	11	1:49.59	75,530
1994	Bold Ruritana, 4, 116	P. Day	Eternal Reve, 3, 117	Monaassabaat, 3, 113	11	1:48.25	76,375
1993	River Ball (Arg), 7, 109	J. Parsley	Marshua's River, 6, 112	Logan's Mist, 4, 118	9	1:55.79	74,945
1992	Auto Dial, 4, 115	S. J. Sellers	Radiant Ring, 4, 119	Red Journey, 4, 114	5	1:52.04	71,500
1991	Christiecat, 4, 118	A. T. Cordero Jr.	Super Fan, 4, 115	Screen Prospect, 4, 113	9	1:51.10	75,010
1990	Dance for Lucy, 4, 113	D. Penna	Betty Lobelia, 5, 114	Phoenix Sunshine, 5, 113	10	1:51.80	39,033
	Lady in Silver, 4, 122	P. Day	Coolawin, 4, 121	Splendid Try, 4, 112	8	1:51.40	38,789
1989	Townsend Lass, 4, 114	K. K. Allen	Bangkok Lady, 3, 112	Bearly Cooking, 6, 114	8	1:52.00	57,233
1988	Top Corsage, 5, 118	P. A. Valenzuela	Savannah's Honor, 3, 116	Graceful Darby, 4, 119	8	1:52.40	36,823
1987	Lake Champlain (Ire), 4, 119	P. Day	Marianna's Girl, 4, 113	Shot Gun Bonnie, 3, 119	10	1:46.20	37,440
1986	Oriental, 4, 123	K. K. Allen	Kapalua Butterfly, 5, 112	Glorious View, 4, 120	13	1:45.80	31,281
1985	Mrs. Revere, 4, 112	L. J. Melancon	Wealthy and Wise, 3, 113	My Inheritance, 3, 112	8	1:48.20	22,219
	Mr. T.'s Tune, 4, 118	K. K. Allen	Gerrie Singer, 4, 115	Adaptable, 4, 112	8	1:47.40	22,219
1984	Electric Fanny, 3, 112	J. C. Espinoza	Straight Edition, 4, 115	Mickey's Echo, 5, 120	8	1:48.00	21,271
1983	Charge My Account, 4, 112	P. Day	Heatherten, 4, 123	Etoile Du Matin, 4, 115	10	1:47.20	18,801
1982	Promising Native, 3, 114	S. Maple	What Glitter, 4, 112	Sweetest Chant, 4, 123	13	1:39.60	20,629
	Betty Money, 3, 116	B. Sayler	Raja's Delight, 4, 112	Mezimica, 4, 112	8	1:38.80	20,792
1981	Knights Beauty, 4, 115	T. W. Hightower	Deuces Over Seven, 4, 117	Roger's Turn, 3, 115	15	1:24.80	20,768
	Safe Play, 3, 122	S. A. Spencer	Lillian Russell, 4, 122	La Vue, 4, 119	10	1:24.20	18,330
1980	Vite View, 4, 120	D. Brumfield	Doing It My Way, 4, 120	Jeanie's Fancy, 4, 117	9	1:24.60	19,581
	Champagne Ginny, 3, 119	D. Brumfield	Impetuous Gal, 5, 122	Red Chiffon, 3, 114	9	1:24.60	18,119
1979	Impetuous Gal, 4, 116	E. Fires	Billy Jane, 3, 114	Cookie Puddin, 3, 113	9	1:24.60	18,021
	Gap Axe, 4, 115	D. Brumfield	Unreality, 5, 120	Honey Blonde, 4, 112	8	1:24.80	19,484
1978	Love to Tell, 3, 116	E. J. Delahoussaye	Selari's Choice, 4, 112	Bit of Sunshine, 4, 112	9	1:24.40	17,883
	Unreality, 4, 123	L. P. Suire	Navajo Princess, 4, 123	Irish Agate, 3, 111	9	1:24.20	18,046
1977	Likely Exchange, 3, 114	J. McKnight	My Compliments, 5, 113	My Bold Beauty, 3, 114	8	1:24.60	14,675
	Famed Princess, 4, 113	C. Ledezma	Chatta, 3, 114	Leigh Simms, 4, 113	9	1:24.80	14,836
1976	Hope of Glory, 4, 114	D. Brumfield	Bronze Point, 3, 115	Straight, 4, 116	8	1:25.00	14,666
	Vivacious Meg, 4, 114	R. Breen	Regal Gal, 3, 115	Regal Rumor, 4, 119	8	1:25.40	14,666
1975	Visier, 3, 116	R. Riera Jr.	Slade's Prospect, 3, 116	Ski Run, 3, 116	6	1:45.80	17,225
1974	Cut the Talk, 3, 116	D. Brown	Holding Pattern, 3, 126	Sturdy Steel, 3, 116	7	1:45.20	14,349

Named for Kentucky's state bird. Kentucky Cardinal S. 1974-'75, 1983-'85. Kentucky Cardinal H. 1976-'82. Cardinal S. 1986. 1 1/16 miles 1974-'75, 1983-'87. 7 furlongs 1976-'81. 1 mile 1982. Dirt 1974-'86, 1988, 1992. Three-year-olds 1974-'75. Both sexes 1974-'75. Two divisions 1976-'82, 1985, 1990. ‡Bail Out Becky finished first, DQ to second, 1996.

Carleton F. Burke Handicap

Grade 3 in 2005. Santa Anita Park, three-year-olds and up, 1 1/2 miles, turf. Held October 23, 2004, with a gross value of $100,000. First held in 1969. First graded in 1973. Stakes record 2:24.24 (1996 Dernier Empereur).

Year	Winner	Jockey	Second	Third	Strs	Time	1st Purse
2004	Habaneros, 5, 116	D. R. Flores	Pellegrino (Brz), 5, 116	Gallant (GB), 7, 113	8	2:26.91	$60,000
2003	Runaway Dancer, 4, 112	M. E. Smith	Labirinto, 5, 116	Senor Swinger, 3, 114	9	2:28.38	83,550
2002	Special Matter, 4, 110	T. Baze	Alyzig, 5, 113	Dance Dreamer, 4, 117	5	2:28.47	90,000
2001	Cagney (Brz), 4, 116	M. E. Smith	Kerrygold (Fr), 5, 116	Northern Quest (Fr), 6, 118	9	2:26.10	90,000
2000	Timboroa (GB), 4, 114	D. R. Flores	dh-Kerrygold (Fr), 4, 116		9	2:27.91	84,990
			dh-Res Judicata (GB), 5, 115				
1999	Public Purse, 5, 119	A. O. Solis	Star Performance, 6, 115	Achilles (GB), 4, 115	8	2:25.83	90,000
1998	Perim (Fr), 5, 113	B. Blanc	Single Empire (Ire), 4, 116	Rate Cut, 4, 114	9	2:29.29	75,000
1997	Prussian Blue, 5, 117	K. J. Desormeaux	Embraceable You (Fr), 4, 116	Kessem Power (NZ), 5, 114	7	2:31.37	75,000
1996	Dernier Empereur, 6, 118	C. J. McCarron	Bon Point (GB), 6, 118	Party Season (GB), 5, 116	8	**2:24.24**	98,750
1995	Varadavour (Ire), 6, 115	A. O. Solis	Patio de Naranjos (Chi), 4, 117	Raintrap (GB), 5, 116	7	2:30.27	90,350
1994	Savinio, 4, 114	C. J. McCarron	Square Cut, 5, 114	Sir Mark Sykes (Ire), 5, 117	8	2:02.69	95,700
1993	Know Heights (Ire), 4, 117	K. J. Desormeaux	Fanmore, 5, 116	Myrakalu (Fr), 5, 114	7	2:00.07	96,000
1992	Missionary Ridge (GB), 5, 117	K. J. Desormeaux	Carnival Baby, 4, 112	Myrakalu (Fr), 4, 113	9	2:00.89	98,000
1991	Super May, 5, 117	C. S. Nakatani	Algenib (Arg), 4, 121	Pride of Araby, 5, 112	9	1:58.58	103,700
1990	‡Ultrasonido (Arg), 5, 114	C. J. McCarron	Rial (Arg), 5, 118	Eradicate (GB), 5, 117	8	1:59.80	129,400
1989	Alwuhush, 4, 120	J. A. Santos	Frankly Perfect, 4, 122	Speedratic, 4, 115	10	1:58.00	134,400
1988	Nasr El Arab, 3, 121	G. L. Stevens	Northern Provider, 6, 112	Trokhos, 5, 115	9	2:01.00	133,000
1987	Rivlia, 5, 117	L. A. Pincay Jr.	Captain Vigors, 5, 116	Circus Prince, 4, 115	10	2:03.20	102,500
1986	Louis Le Grand, 4, 115	W. Shoemaker	Schiller, 4, 117	Silveyville, 8, 120	10	2:01.20	133,700
1985	Tsunami Slew, 4, 121	G. L. Stevens	Yashgan (GB), 4, 121	Best of Both, 5, 121	7	1:59.60	78,500
1984	Silveyville, 6, 117	C. J. McCarron	Gordian (GB), 4, 115	Gato Del Sol, 5, 121	7	1:59.60	64,100
1983	Bel Bolide, 5, 122	T. Lipham	Travelling Victor, 4, 118	Bold Run (Fr), 4, 118	7	2:01.20	64,200
1982	Mehmet, 4, 117	E. J. Delahoussaye	Craelius, 3, 114	It's the One, 4, 124	7	1:58.60	63,600
1981	Spence Bay (Ire), 6, 120	F. Toro	Providential (Ire), 4, 121	Super Moment, 4, 121	10	2:00.60	67,200
1980	Bold Tropic (SAf), 5, 125	W. Shoemaker	Balzac, 5, 121	Shagbark, 5, 116	7	1:58.20	49,300

1979	Silver Eagle (Ire), 5, 115	F. Toro	John Henry, 4, 118	Shagbark, 4, 118	9	1:59.20	$50,200
1978	Star of Erin (Ire), 4, 113	W. Shoemaker	Improviser, 6, 115	Mr. Redoy, 4, 118	9	1:59.00	38,400
	Palton (Chi), 5, 122	H. E. Moreno	Star Spangled, 4, 118	Lunar Probe (NZ), 4, 114	9	1:59.00	38,400
1977	Double Discount, 4, 116	F. Mena	No Turning, 4, 118	Vigors, 4, 120	8	1:57.40	33,000
1976	King Pellinore, 4, 124	W. Shoemaker	*Royal Derby II, 7, 116	George Navonod, 4, 115	8	1:57.60	33,300
1975	Top Command, 4, 113	W. Shoemaker	Against the Snow, 5, 116	Top Crowd, 4, 116	6	2:01.20	24,875
	Kirrary, 5, 114	F. Mena	Buffalo Lark, 5, 121	†*Dulcia, 6, 117	6	2:00.40	24,875
1974	†Tallahto, 4, 120	L. A. Pincay Jr.	High Protein, 4, 117	Scantling, 4, 117	6	1:59.00	32,300
1973	‡Kentuckian, 4, 117	D. Pierce	Wing Out, 5, 119	†Le Cle, 4, 116	8	1:59.00	33,400

Named for Carleton F. Burke (1882-1962), first chairman of the California Horse Racing Board. Grade 2 1973-'84, 1990-'97. Grade 1 1985-'89. Carleton F. Burke Invitational H. 1969-'70. 1¼ miles 1969-'94. About 1½ miles 2000. Two divisions 1975, 1978. Dead heat for second 2000. ‡Groshawk finished first, DQ to fifth, 1973. ‡Rial (Arg) finished first, DQ to second, 1990. †Denotes female.

Carry Back Stakes

Grade 2 in 2005. Calder Race Course, three-year-olds, 6 furlongs, dirt. Held July 10, 2004, with a gross value of $300,000. First held in 1970. First graded in 2003. Stakes record 1:09.60 (1970 Ponderosa Jane).

Year	Winner	Jockey	Second	Third	Strs	Time	1st Purse
2004	Weigelia, 3, 117	A. Toribio Jr.	Classy Migration, 3, 112	Bwana Charlie, 3, 119	11	1:10.50	$177,000
2003	Valid Video, 3, 122	J. Bravo	Cajun Beat, 3, 117	Super Fuse, 3, 117	10	1:10.15	177,000
2002	Royal Lad, 3, 117	J. D. Bailey	Captain Squire, 3, 122	Friendly Frolic, 3, 114	9	1:10.73	150,000
2001	Illusioned, 3, 117	J. F. Chavez	Beyond Brilliant, 3, 117	Gallant Frolic, 3, 115	10	1:11.08	150,000
2000	Caller One, 3, 122	C. S. Nakatani	Fappie's Notebook, 3, 115	Malagot, 3, 115	9	1:10.35	120,000
1999	Silver Season, 3, 112	E. Coa	Deep Gold, 3, 117	Night Patrol, 3, 117	9	1:11.32	120,000
1998	Mint, 3, 115	E. Coa	Diamond Studs, 3, 115	Mt. Laurel, 3, 112	8	1:11.38	120,000
1997	Renteria, 3, 115	E. Coa	Red, 3, 122	Willow Skips Trial, 3, 115	11	1:11.28	120,000
1996	Fortunate Review, 3, 117	A. Toribio	Betweenhereorthere, 3, 115	Night Runner, 3, 113	12	1:23.27	60,000
1995	Sonic Signal, 3, 115	R. R. Douglas	Leave'm Inthedark, 3, 117	Too Great, 3, 113	10	1:24.79	60,000
1994	Score a Birdie, 3, 115	H. Castillo Jr.	Fortunate Joe, 3, 112	Ali'lbito'reality, 3, 114	7	1:24.09	60,000
1993	Humbugalous, 3, 112	M. Russ	Signoir Valery, 3, 112	Kassec, 3, 113	8	1:22.74	60,000
1992	Always Silver, 3, 116	M. A. Lee	Appealtothechief, 3, 114	Dr Arne, 3, 114	7	1:25.00	30,000
1991	Ocala Flame, 3, 113	R. N. Lester	Sunny and Pleasant, 3, 113	Jacquelyn's Groom, 3, 113	9	1:19.02	33,180
1990	Country Isle, 3, 114	H. Castillo Jr.	Run Turn, 3, 120	Ultimate Swale, 3, 112	10	1:24.80	33,840
1989	Big Stanley, 3, 120	D. Valiente	Valid Space, 3, 114	Jabotinsky, 3, 117	6	1:23.60	32,490
1988	In the Slammer, 3, 114	M. A. Gonzalez	Lover's Trust, 3, 122	Ashmint, 3, 115	6	1:23.80	32,220
1987	You're No Bargain, 3, 117	O. J. Londono	Right Rudder, 3, 112	Jilsie's Gigalo, 3, 118	9	1:25.60	44,010
1986	Kid Colin, 3, 116	G. St. Leon	Big Jolt, 3, 116	Lucky Rebeau, 3, 116	13	1:25.80	38,610
1985	Smile, 3, 123	J. Vasquez	Paravon, 3, 114	Hickory Hill Flyer, 3, 114	7	1:23.80	46,260
1984	Bowmans Express, 3, 117	O. J. Londono	Mo Exception, 3, 114	No Room, 3, 119	12	1:25.40	19,305
1983	Opening Lead, 3, 112	B. Gonzalez	El Perico, 3, 117	Neutral Player, 3, 112	9	1:25.80	16,785
1982	Rex's Profile, 3, 115	E. Cardone	Libra Moon, 3, 118	Center Cut, 3, 123	7	1:11.40	16,395
1981	Face the Moment, 3, 115	E. Cardone	†Toga Toga, 3, 113	Incredible John, 3, 118	8	1:11.00	16,530
1980	Diplomatic Note, 3, 112	J. D. Bailey	Buckn' Shoe, 3, 115	Fast Fast Freddie, 3, 113	9	1:12.00	16,785
1979	Breezy Fire, 4, 120	M. A. Rivera	Cherry Pop, 3, 113	Noble Heart, 3, 111	9	1:24.60	16,770
1978	Admiral Rix, 2, 116	T. Barrow	Tartan Tam, 2, 116	Cherry Pop, 2, 116	9	1:07.40	14,160
1977	Chwesboken, 2, 119	D. Hidalgo	Noon Time Spender, 2, 122	Ski's Never Bend, 2, 116	5	1:05.40	13,320
1976	Winners Hit, 2, 119	R. Broussard	My Budget, 2, 119	Time for Fun, 2, 116	11	1:07.00	14,640
1975	†Precipitory, 2, 116	J. Salinas	Chic Ruler, 2, 116	Upper Current, 2, 119	10	1:06.80	14,400

Named for Dorchester Farm Stable's 1961 champion three-year-old colt Carry Back (1958 c. by Saggy); Carry Back was the all-time leading Florida-bred earner at his retirement. Carry Back H. 1981-'93. Held at Tropical Park 1970. Not held 1972-'74. 5½ furlongs 1975-'78. 7 furlongs 1979, 1984-'90, 1992-'96. 6½ furlongs 1991. Two-year-olds 1975-'78. Three-year-olds and up 1979. †Denotes female.

Carter Handicap

Grade 1 in 2005. Aqueduct, three-year-olds and up, 7 furlongs, dirt. Held April 9, 2005, with a gross value of $350,000. First held in 1895. First graded in 1973. Stakes record 1:20.04 (1999 Artax).

Year	Winner	Jockey	Second	Third	Strs	Time	1st Purse
2005	Forest Danger, 4, 117	R. Bejarano	Medallist, 4, 117	Don Six, 5, 116	6	1:20.46	$210,000
2004	Pico Central (Brz), 5, 117	A. O. Solis	Strong Hope, 4, 119	Eye of the Tiger, 4, 114	9	1:20.22	210,000
2003	Congaree, 5, 122	G. L. Stevens	Aldebaran, 5, 118	Peeping Tom, 6, 114	5	1:21.48	210,000
2002	Affirmed Success, 8, 119	R. Migliore	Voodoo, 4, 113	Burning Roma, 4, 117	10	1:21.84	210,000
2001	Peeping Tom, 4, 118	S. Bridgmohan	Say Florida Sandy, 7, 116	Hook and Ladder, 4, 118	7	1:21.33	180,000
2000	Brutally Frank, 6, 116	S. Bridgmohan	Western Expression, 4, 113	Affirmed Success, 6, 122	7	1:21.66	120,000
1999	Artax, 4, 114	J. F. Chavez	Affirmed Success, 5, 119	Western Borders, 5, 113	9	1:20.04	120,000
1998	Wild Rush, 4, 117	K. J. Desormeaux	Banker's Gold, 4, 114	Western Borders, 4, 115	10	1:21.16	120,000
1997	Langfuhr, 5, 122	J. F. Chavez	Stalwart Member, 4, 113	Western Winter, 5, 112	9	1:22.99	90,000
1996	Lite the Fuse, 5, 121	J. A. Krone	Flying Chevron, 4, 115	Placid Fund, 5, 114	10	1:20.92	90,000
1995	Lite the Fuse, 4, 111	R. B. Perez	Our Emblem, 4, 114	You and I, 4, 113	9	1:21.48	90,000
1994	Virginia Rapids, 4, 118	J. Samyn	Punch Line, 4, 114	Cherokee Run, 4, 119	11	1:21.45	90,000
1993	Alydeed, 4, 122	C. Perret	Loach, 5, 112	Argyle Lake, 7, 113	10	1:22.70	90,000

1992	**Rubiano**, 5, 118	J. A. Santos	Kid Russell, 6, 112	In Excess (Ire), 5, 122	9	1:21.41	$120,000
1991	**Housebuster**, 4, 122	C. Perret	Black Tie Affair (Ire), 5, 123	Gervazy, 4, 116	8	1:21.31	120,000
1990	**Dancing Spree**, 5, 123	C. W. Antley	Dancing Pretense, 5, 115	Sewickley, 5, 119	7	1:22.00	137,280
1989	**On the Line**, 5, 125	G. L. Stevens	True and Blue, 4, 114	Dr. Carrington, 4, 110	8	1:21.40	140,880
1988	**Gulch**, 4, 124	J. A. Santos	Afleet, 4, 124	Its Acedemic, 4, 108	8	1:20.40	174,300
1987	**†Pine Tree Lane**, 5, 119	R. P. Romero	King's Swan, 7, 123	Zany Tactics, 6, 119	6	1:21.20	170,400
1986	**Love That Mac**, 4, 117	E. Maple	Ziggy's Boy, 4, 118	King's Swan, 6, 120	7	1:21.60	116,460
1985	**Mt. Livermore**, 4, 117	J. D. Bailey	Rocky Marriage, 5, 122	Carr de Naskra, 4, 125	6	1:20.80	83,340
1984	**Bet Big**, 4, 115	J. Samyn	Cannon Shell, 5, 109	A Phenomenon, 4, 126	10	1:21.80	73,200
1983	**Vittorioso**, 4, 113	A. Smith Jr.	Sing Sing, 5, 122	Fit to Fight, 4, 116	9	1:22.80	67,800
1982	**Pass the Tab**, 4, 118	A. Graell	Royal Hierarchy, 5, 115	Maudlin, 4, 114	12	1:22.40	52,110
1981	**Amber Pass**, 4, 114	E. Maple	Guilty Conscience, 5, 111	Dunham's Gift, 4, 116	7	1:23.00	49,410
1980	**Czaravich**, 4, 126	L. Adams	Tanthem, 5, 122	Nice Catch, 6, 120	6	1:21.00	49,050
1979	**Star de Naskra**, 4, 122	J. Fell	Alydar, 4, 126	Sensitive Prince, 4, 126	6	1:21.80	48,690
1978	**Pumpkin Moonshine**, 4, 107	D. A. Borden	Prefontaine, 4, 112	Big John Taylor, 4, 113	6	1:22.20	31,920
	Jaipur's Gem, 5, 115	J. Samyn	Vencedor, 4, 111	Half High, 5, 118	7	1:21.60	32,070
1977	dh- **Gentle King**, 4, 110	D. Montoya		Full Out, 4, 117	8	1:22.00	21,914
	dh- **Quiet Little Table**, 4, 119	E. Maple					
	Soy Numero Uno, 4, 126	R. Broussard	Barrera, 4, 119	Gallant Bob, 5, 116	8	1:22.20	31,770
1976	**Due Diligence**, 4, 111	J. Amy	†Honorable Miss, 6, 122	Amerrico, 4, 112	8	1:22.40	33,540
1975	**Forego**, 5, 134	H. Gustines	Stop the Music, 5, 123	Orders, 4, 114	10	1:21.60	34,860
1974	**Forego**, 4, 129	H. Gustines	Mr. Prospector, 4, 124	Timeless Moment, 4, 113	8	1:22.20	33,900
1973	**King's Bishop**, 4, 114	E. Maple	Onion, 4, 114	Petrograd, 4, 118	10	1:20.40	35,220

Named for Capt. William Carter of Brooklyn, New York, who contributed $500 of the first $600 purse. Grade 2 1973-'87. Held at Belmont Park 1946, 1956-'59, 1968-'69, 1972-'74, 1986, 1994-'96. Not held 1909, 1911-'13. 1 1/4 miles 1895. 1 1/8 miles 1896. 1 1/16 miles 1897. About 7 furlongs 1898. 6 1/2 furlongs 1899-1902. Two divisions 1977-'78. Dead heat for first 1977 (1st Div.). Track record 1973, 1999. †Denotes female. Held as an allowance race 1933-'34.

Champagne Stakes

Grade 1 in 2005. Belmont Park, two-year-olds, 1 1/16 miles, dirt. Held October 9, 2004, with a gross value of $500,000. First held in 1867. First graded in 1973. Stakes record 1:40.59 (1997 Grand Slam).

Year	Winner	Jockey	Second	Third	Strs	Time	1st Purse
2004	**Proud Accolade**, 2, 122	J. R. Velazquez	Afleet Alex, 2, 122	Sun King, 2, 122	8	1:42.30	$300,000
2003	**Birdstone**, 2, 122	J. D. Bailey	Chapel Royal, 2, 122	Dashboard Drummer, 2, 122	7	1:44.05	300,000
2002	**Toccet**, 2, 122	J. F. Chavez	Icecoldbeeratreds, 2, 122	Erinsouthernman, 2, 122	9	1:44.45	300,000
2001	**Officer**, 2, 122	V. Espinoza	Jump Start, 2, 122	Heavyweight Champ, 2, 122	5	1:43.39	300,000
2000	**A P Valentine**, 2, 122	J. F. Chavez	Point Given, 2, 122	Yonaguska, 2, 122	10	1:41.45	300,000
1999	**Greenwood Lake**, 2, 122	J. Samyn	Chief Seattle, 2, 122	High Yield, 2, 122	7	1:43.70	240,000
1998	**The Groom Is Red**, 2, 122	C. S. Nakatani	Lemon Drop Kid, 2, 122	Weekend Money, 2, 122	7	1:42.91	240,000
1997	**Grand Slam**, 2, 122	G. L. Stevens	Lil's Lad, 2, 122	Halory Hunter, 2, 122	8	**1:40.59**	240,000
1996	**Ordway**, 2, 122	J. R. Velazquez	Traitor, 2, 122	Gold Tribute, 2, 122	12	1:42.09	240,000
1995	**Maria's Mon**, 2, 122	R. G. Davis	Diligence, 2, 122	Devil's Honor, 2, 122	8	1:42.39	300,000
1994	**Timber Country**, 2, 122	P. Day	Sierra Diablo, 2, 122	On Target, 2, 122	11	1:44.01	300,000
1993	**Dehere**, 2, 122	C. J. McCarron	Crary, 2, 122	Amathos, 2, 122	6	1:35.91	300,000
1992	**Sea Hero**, 2, 122	J. D. Bailey	Secret Odds, 2, 122	Press Card, 2, 122	10	1:34.87	300,000
1991	**Tri to Watch**, 2, 122	A. T. Cordero Jr.	Snappy Landing, 2, 122	Pine Bluff, 2, 122	15	1:36.61	300,000
1990	**Fly So Free**, 2, 122	J. A. Santos	Happy Jazz Band, 2, 122	Subordinated Debt, 2, 122	13	1:35.60	381,600
1989	**Adjudicating**, 2, 122	J. Vasquez	Rhythm, 2, 122	Senor Pete, 2, 122	6	1:37.60	343,200
1988	**Easy Goer**, 2, 122	P. Day	Is It True, 2, 122	Irish Actor, 2, 122	4	1:34.80	334,200
1987	**Forty Niner**, 2, 122	E. Maple	Parlay Me, 2, 122	Tejano, 2, 122	11	1:36.80	370,800
1986	**Polish Navy**, 2, 122	R. P. Romero	Demons Begone, 2, 122	Bet Twice, 2, 122	7	1:35.20	199,500
1985	**Mogambo**, 2, 122	A. T. Cordero Jr.	Groovy, 2, 122	Mr. Classic, 2, 122	5	1:37.20	194,700
1984	**For Certain Doc**, 2, 122	M. Zuniga	Mighty Appealing, 2, 122	Tank's Prospect, 2, 122	6	1:49.20	171,600
1983	**Devil's Bag**, 2, 122	E. Maple	Dr. Carter, 2, 122	Our Casey's Boy, 2, 122	12	1:34.20	142,200
1982	**Copelan**, 2, 122	J. D. Bailey	Pappa Riccio, 2, 122	El Cubanaso, 2, 122	13	1:37.80	144,000
1981	**Timely Writer**, 2, 122	J. Fell	†Before Dawn, 2, 122	New Discovery, 2, 122	13	1:36.40	90,150
1980	**Lord Avie**, 2, 122	J. Velasquez	Noble Nashua, 2, 122	Sezyou, 2, 122	9	1:37.20	85,350
1979	**Joanie's Chief**, 2, 122	R. Hernandez	Rockhill Native, 2, 122	Googolplex, 2, 122	8	1:38.20	81,750
1978	**Spectacular Bid**, 2, 122	J. Velasquez	General Assembly, 2, 122	Crested Wave, 2, 122	6	1:34.80	80,250
1977	**Alydar**, 2, 122	J. Velasquez	Affirmed, 2, 122	Darby Creek Road, 2, 122	6	1:36.60	80,400
1976	**Seattle Slew**, 2, 122	J. Cruguet	For The Moment, 2, 122	Sail to Rome, 2, 122	10	1:34.40	82,350
1975	**Honest Pleasure**, 2, 122	B. Baeza	Dance Spell, 2, 122	Whatsyourpleasure, 2, 122	14	1:36.40	89,625
1974	**Foolish Pleasure**, 2, 122	J. Vasquez	Harvard Man, 2, 122	Ramahorn, 2, 122	9	1:36.00	86,850
1973	**Holding Pattern**, 2, 122	M. Miceli	Green Gambados, 2, 122	Hosiery, 2, 122	10	1:36.00	55,425
	Protagonist, 2, 122	A. Santiago	Prince of Reason, 2, 122	Cannonade, 2, 122	10	1:36.00	55,425

Named after the Champagne S. (Eng-G2) in England, held at Doncaster. Sponsored by Moet & Chandon Champagne of Epernay, France 1994-'97. Moet Champagne S. 1994-'97. Held at Jerome Park 1867-'89. Held at Morris Park 1890-1904. Held at Aqueduct 1959, 1961, 1963-'67, 1984. Not held 1910-'13, 1956. 1 mile 1867-'70, 1890, 1940-'83, 1985-'93. 6 furlongs 1871-'89. 7 furlongs 1891-1904. About 7 furlongs 1905-'32. 6 1/2 furlongs 1933-'39. 1 1/8 miles 1984. Two divisions 1973. †Denotes female.

Charles Whittingham Memorial Handicap

Grade 1 in 2005. Hollywood Park, three-year-olds and up, 1¼ miles, turf. Held June 11, 2005, with a gross value of $350,000. First held in 1969. First graded in 1973. Stakes record 1:57.75 (1993 Bien Bien).

Year	Winner	Jockey	Second	Third	Strs	Time	1st Purse
2005	Sweet Return (GB), 5, 119	A. O. Solis	Red Fort (Ire), 5, 117	Vangelis, 6, 118	9	2:01.35	$210,000
2004	Sabiango (Ger), 6, 116	T. Baze	Bayamo (Ire), 5, 116	Just Wonder (GB), 4, 116	11	2:01.52	210,000
2003	Storming Home (GB), 5, 124	G. L. Stevens	Mister Acpen (Chi), 5, 115	Cagney (Brz), 6, 114	6	2:00.66	210,000
2002	Denon, 4, 116	G. K. Gomez	Night Patrol, 6, 114	Skipping (GB), 5, 117	9	2:01.47	210,000
2001	Bienamado, 5, 124	C. J. McCarron	Senure, 5, 117	Timboroa (GB), 5, 116	9	1:59.34	210,000
2000	White Heart (GB), 5, 117	K. J. Desormeaux	Self Feeder (Ire), 6, 116	Deploy Venture (GB), 4, 112	6	2:00.83	180,000
1999	River Bay, 6, 119	A. O. Solis	Majorien (GB), 5, 117	Alvo Certo (Brz), 6, 115	9	2:00.66	240,000
1998	Storm Trooper, 5, 117	K. J. Desormeaux	River Bay, 5, 121	Prize Giving (GB), 5, 116	7	2:03.05	240,000
1997	Rainbow Dancer (Fr), 6, 116	A. O. Solis	Sunshack (GB), 6, 118	Marlin, 4, 120	6	2:00.00	240,000
1996	Sandpit (Brz), 7, 120	C. S. Nakatani	Northern Spur (Ire), 5, 123	Awad, 6, 119	6	1:59.52	300,000
1995	Earl of Barking (Ire), 5, 115	G. F. Almeida	Sandpit (Brz), 6, 122	Savinio, 5, 117	10	1:59.78	275,000
1994	Grand Flotilla, 7, 116	G. L. Stevens	Bien Bien, 5, 124	Blues Traveller (Ire), 4, 114	8	1:59.26	275,000
1993	Bien Bien, 4, 119	C. J. McCarron	Best Pal, 5, 122	Leger Cat (Arg), 7, 116	8	1:57.75	275,000
1992	Quest for Fame (GB), 5, 122	G. L. Stevens	Classic Fame, 6, 124	River Traffic, 4, 114	9	1:58.99	275,000
1991	Exbourne, 5, 119	G. L. Stevens	Itsallgreektome, 4, 123	Prized, 5, 123	6	2:00.10	275,000
1990	Steinlen (GB), 7, 124	L. A. Pincay Jr.	Hawkster, 4, 122	Santangelo (Arg), 6, 110	6	2:03.00	275,000
1989	Great Communicator, 6, 123	R. Sibille	Nasr El Arab, 4, 124	Equalize, 7, 124	9	1:59.40	275,000
1988	Political Ambition, 4, 119	E. J. Delahoussaye	Baba Karam (Ire), 4, 116	dh- Great Communicator, 5, 120 dh- Skip Out Front, 6, 115	7	1:58.60	165,000
1987	Rivlia, 5, 117	C. J. McCarron	Great Communicator, 4, 112	Schiller, 5, 116	6	2:24.20	165,000
1986	Flying Pidgeon, 5, 120	S. B. Soto	Dahar, 5, 126	Both Ends Burning, 6, 122	6	2:27.00	165,000
1985	Both Ends Burning, 5, 121	E. J. Delahoussaye	Dahar, 4, 123	Swoon, 7, 114	5	2:25.00	165,000
1984	John Henry, 9, 126	C. J. McCarron	Galant Vert (Fr), 4, 116	Load the Cannons, 4, 120	9	2:25.00	165,000
1983	Erins Isle (Ire), 5, 127	L. A. Pincay Jr.	Exploded, 6, 115	Prince Spellbound, 4, 120	12	2:25.80	165,000
1982	Exploded, 5, 117	L. A. Pincay Jr.	Lemhi Gold, 4, 123	The Bart, 6, 125	6	2:25.20	165,000
1981	John Henry, 6, 130	L. A. Pincay Jr.	Caterman (NZ), 5, 122	Galaxy Libra (Ire), 5, 118	7	2:27.80	110,000
1980	John Henry, 5, 128	D. G. McHargue	Balzac, 5, 120	Go West Young Man, 5, 117	10	2:25.40	137,500
1979	Johnny's Image, 4, 123	S. Hawley	Star Spangled, 5, 122	Dom Alaric (Fr), 5, 119	11	2:25.20	137,500
1978	Exceller, 5, 127	W. Shoemaker	Bowl Game, 4, 123	Noble Dancer (GB), 6, 126	12	2:25.80	110,000
1977	Vigors, 4, 117	J. Lambert	Caucasus, 5, 126	Anne's Pretender, 5, 122	12	2:26.80	120,000
1976	†Dahlia, 6, 117	W. Shoemaker	Caucasus, 4, 119	Pass the Glass, 5, 121	12	2:26.80	120,000
1975	*Barclay Joy, 5, 113	A. L. Diaz	Captain Cee Jay, 5, 117	Chief Hawk Ear, 7, 119	10	2:27.00	75,000
1974	Court Ruling, 4, 117	W. Mahorney	Outdoors, 5, 113	London Company, 4, 123	10	2:27.60	75,000
1973	Life Cycle, 4, 115	L. A. Pincay Jr.	Wing Out, 5, 118	*Cougar II, 7, 130	10	2:25.60	75,000

Named for Racing Hall of Fame trainer Charles Whittingham (1913-'99). Formerly sponsored by Ford Motor Co. of Detroit, Michigan 1971. Hollywood Park Invitational Turf H. 1969-'70, 1972. Ford Pinto Invitational Turf H. 1971. Hollywood Invitational H. 1973-'88. Hollywood Turf H. 1989-'98. Charles Whittingham H. 1999-2002. 1½ miles 1969-'87. Dead heat for third 1988. Equaled course record 1973. Course record 1993. †Denotes female.

Chicago Breeders' Cup Handicap

Grade 3 in 2005. Arlington Park, three-year-olds and up, fillies and mares, 7 furlongs, dirt. Held June 19, 2004, with a gross value of $175,000. First held in 1986. First graded in 1992. Stakes record 1:21.24 (1992 Withallprobability).

Year	Winner	Jockey	Second	Third	Strs	Time	1st Purse
2004	My Trusty Cat, 4, 116	R. R. Douglas	Our Josephina, 4, 112	Smoke Chaser, 5, 116	5	1:23.54	$105,000
2003	For Rubies, 4, 116	C. Perret	Raging Fever, 5, 120	Oglala Sue, 5, 113	8	1:24.21	69,450
2002	Mandy's Gold, 4, 116	R. R. Douglas	Cat and the Hat, 4, 116	Caressing, 4, 115	6	1:22.86	98,664
2001	Trip, 4, 114	C. Perret	Hidden Assets, 4, 115	Rose of Zollern (Ire), 5, 115	7	1:22.18	99,312
2000	Saoirse, 4, 118	D. Clark	The Happy Hopper, 4, 115	Dif a Dot, 5, 114	7	1:23.09	102,195
1997	J J'sdream, 4, 118	M. Guidry	Capote Belle, 4, 120	Eseni, 4, 117	7	1:22.20	101,625
1996	Bunbeg, 4, 114	M. Walls	Morris Code, 4, 118	Rhapsodic, 5, 114	8	1:23.86	102,990
1995	Low Key Affair, 4, 113	A. T. Gryder	Morning Meadow, 5, 115	Marina Park (GB), 5, 120	9	1:24.64	93,840
1994	Minidar, 4, 116	V. Belvoir	Spinning Round, 5, 118	Traverse City, 4, 113	10	1:22.49	93,960
1993	Meafara, 4, 121	J. L. Diaz	Shared Interest, 5, 116	Real Display, 4, 114	11	1:22.12	93,870
1992	Withallprobability, 4, 115	G. K. Gomez	Fit for a Queen, 6, 120	Madam Bear, 4, 114	9	1:21.24	93,450
1991	Safely Kept, 5, 126	C. Perret	Nurse Dopey, 4, 118	Token Dance, 4, 114	7	1:23.05	93,060
1990	Fit for a Queen, 4, 112	P. Day	Channel Three, 4, 113	Sexy Slew, 4, 115	12	1:23.00	94,650
1989	Rose's Record, 5, 114	J. Velasquez	Sunshine Always, 5, 114	‡Daloma (Fr), 5, 116	7	1:24.60	93,120
1987	Lazer Show, 4, 123	P. Day	Very Subtle, 3, 120	Moonbeam McQueen, 4, 111	6	1:22.80	46,275
1986	Lazer Show, 3, 115	P. Day	Balladry, 4, 115	Gene's Lady, 5, 122	8	1:21.40	93,360

Named for the city of Chicago, near suburban Arlington Heights, location of Arlington Park. Chicago Budweiser Breeders' Cup H. 1986-'95. Not held 1988, 1998-'99. ‡Josette finished third, DQ to fourth, 1989.

Churchill Downs Distaff Handicap

Grade 2 in 2005. Churchill Downs, three-year-olds and up, fillies and mares, 1 mile, dirt. Held November 7, 2004, with a gross value of $230,400. First held in 1986. First graded in 1988. Stakes record 1:33.57 (2000 Chilukki).

Year	Winner	Jockey	Second	Third	Strs	Time	1st Purse
2004	Halory Leigh, 4, 115	C. Perret	Lady Tak, 4, 123	Susan's Angel, 3, 115	12	1:35.05	$142,848
2003	Lead Story, 4, 114	C. H. Borel	Awesome Humor, 3, 118	Born to Dance, 4, 113	10	1:36.55	139,748

2002	Softly, 4, 114	J. K. Court	Bare Necessities, 3, 115	Victory Ride, 4, 118	9	1:35.07	$138,632
2001	Nasty Storm, 3, 115	P. Day	Forest Secrets, 3, 113	Trip, 4, 117	8	1:35.30	137,764
2000	Chilukki, 3, 116	G. L. Stevens	Reciclada (Chi), 5, 113	Rose of Zollern (Ire), 4, 114	10	1:33.57	154,008
1999	Let, 4, 113	C. H. Borel	Roza Robata, 4, 114	Dif a Dot, 4, 115	9	1:34.41	138,880
1998	Dream Scheme, 5, 113	C. H. Borel	Sister Act, 3, 111	Beautiful Pleasure, 3, 110	9	1:34.41	139,624
1997	Feasibility Study, 5, 120	R. Albarado	J J'sdream, 4, 113	Mama's Pro, 4, 115	14	1:37.61	146,196
1996	Fast Catch, 4, 109	W. Martinez	Serena's Song, 4, 125	Bedroom Blues, 5, 112	9	1:36.55	139,624
1995	Lakeway, 4, 122	K. J. Desormeaux	Alcovy, 5, 113	Laura's Pistolette, 4, 116	8	1:35.94	137,280
1994	Educated Risk, 4, 118	P. Day	Pennyhill Park, 4, 117	Alcovy, 4, 116	8	1:35.74	138,125
1993	Miss Indy Anna, 3, 111	P. Day	One Dreamer, 5, 115	Deputation, 4, 119	13	1:37.72	141,960
1992	Wilderness Song, 4, 120	C. Perret	Miss Jealski, 3, 110	Dance Colony, 5, 113	11	1:36.22	102,440
1991	Fit for a Queen, 5, 121	R. D. Lopez	Wilderness Song, 3, 118	Summer Matinee, 4, 113	6	1:38.60	100,555
1990	Oh My Jessica Pie, 4, 114	M. A. Gonzalez	Seaside Attraction, 3, 115	Sweet Nostalgia, 3, 111	10	1:36.80	102,993
1989	Classic Value, 3, 114	P. Day	Coastal Connection, 4, 115	Rose's Record, 5, 117	12	1:35.40	102,960
1988	Darien Miss, 3, 116	P. A. Johnson	Sheena Native, 4, 117	Coastal Connection, 3, 112	13	1:36.80	102,928
1987	Bound, 3, 114	E. Maple	Miss Bid, 4, 115	Intently, 4, 114	14	1:37.00	103,253
1986	Lazer Show, 3, 120	C. R. Woods Jr.	Balladry, 4, 116	Mrs. Revere, 5, 120	11	1:22.60	102,473

Races for females are typically referred to as distaff races. Grade 3 1988-'91. Churchill Downs Budweiser Breeders' Cup H. 1986-'91, 1993-'95. 7 furlongs 1986. Track record 2000.

Churchill Downs Handicap

Grade 2 in 2005. Churchill Downs, four-year-olds and up, 7 furlongs, dirt. Held May 7, 2005, with a gross value of $231,000. First held in 1911. First graded in 1992. Stakes record 1:20.50 (2001 Alannan).

Year	Winner	Jockey	Second	Third	Strs	Time	1st Purse
2005	Battle Won, 5, 115	R. A. Dominguez	Level Playingfield, 4, 112	Pomeroy, 4, 118	11	1:20.56	$143,220
2004	Speightstown, 6, 115	J. R. Velazquez	McCann's Mojave, 4, 117	Publication, 5, 116	7	1:21.38	137,516
2003	Aldebaran, 5, 120	J. D. Bailey	Pass Rush, 4, 117	Cappuchino, 4, 115	12	1:21.80	144,956
2002	‡D'wildcat, 4, 115	K. J. Desormeaux	Snow Ridge, 4, 119	Binthebest, 5, 113	10	1:22.37	106,299
2001	Alannan, 5, 116	E. S. Prado	Bonapaw, 5, 116	Exchange Rate, 4, 113	10	1:20.50	111,321
2000	Straight Man, 4, 112	J. F. Chavez	Mula Gula, 4, 114	Patience Game, 4, 114	7	1:21.53	104,904
1999	Rock and Roll, 4, 112	P. Day	Liberty Gold, 5, 114	Run Johnny, 7, 113	7	1:22.81	103,137
1998	Distorted Humor, 5, 119	G. L. Stevens	Gold Land, 7, 116	El Amante, 5, 113	7	1:21.18	103,509
1997	Diligence, 4, 114	M. E. Smith	Victor Cooley, 4, 115	Criollito (Arg), 6, 115	9	1:22.37	70,432
1996	Criollito (Arg), 5, 115	C. J. McCarron	Forty Won, 5, 115	Powis Castle, 5, 114	9	1:22.01	74,620
1995	Goldseeker Bud, 4, 109	W. Martinez	Level Sands, 4, 112	Go for Gin, 4, 115	11	1:21.75	75,225
1994	Honor the Hero, 6, 116	G. K. Gomez	Memo (Chi), 7, 121	Saratoga Gambler, 6, 116	6	1:23.05	71,370
1993	Callide Valley, 5, 116	G. L. Stevens	Furiously, 4, 117	Ojai, 4, 110	11	1:22.01	56,063
1992	Pleasant Tap, 5, 120	E. J. Delahoussaye	Take Me Out, 4, 120	Cantrell Road, 6, 113	9	1:22.32	55,526
1991	Thirty Six Red, 4, 117	J. D. Bailey	Private School, 4, 113	Bratt's Choice, 4, 115	10	1:22.15	37,635
1990	Beau Genius, 5, 119	R. D. Lopez	Traskwood, 4, 113	Learn by Heart, 5, 115	12	1:23.20	37,830
1989	Dancing Spree, 4, 116	P. Day	Carborundum, 5, 117	Broadway Chief, 4, 115	13	1:24.00	38,253
1988	Conquer, 4, 117	G. L. Stevens	Homebuilder, 4, 121	Carborundum, 4, 115	9	1:23.20	36,823
1987	Sovereign's Ace, 5, 117	L. A. Pincay Jr.	Sun Master, 6, 123	Savings, 4, 114	9	1:22.00	21,236
1986	Sovereign's Ace, 4, 117	P. Rubbicco	Artichoke, 5, 120	Clever Wake, 4, 116	9	1:22.60	21,957
1985	Rapid Gray, 6, 120	P. Day	Roxbury Park, 4, 114	Steel Robbing, 5, 115	7	1:24.00	24,391
	Bayou Hebert, 4, 111	J. McKnight	Harry 'n Bill, 5, 117	Never Company, 5, 117	6	1:23.40	24,196
1984	Habitonia, 4, 118	P. Day	Roman Jamboree, 4, 114	Euathlos, 4, 113	5	1:23.00	20,914
1983	Shot n' Missed, 6, 118	L. Moyers	Vodika Collins, 5, 112	Gallant Gentleman, 4, 115	6	1:23.60	21,239
1982	Top Avenger, 4, 114	R. P. Romero	It's a Rerun, 6, 110	Shot n' Missed, 5, 117	9	1:23.00	21,661
	Bayou Black, 6, 119	R. D. Ardoin	Vodika Collins, 4, 118	Prince Crimson, 5, 116	6	1:22.80	23,433
1981	Dreadnought, 4, 112	J. C. Espinoza	Tiger Lure, 7, 113	Turbulence, 5, 119	12	1:23.60	19,874
1980	Dr. Riddick, 6, 114	D. Brumfield	Cregan's Cap, 5, 112	Silent Dignity, 4, 119	8	1:23.20	17,615
1979	Trimlea, 5, 113	J. Velasquez	Dr. Riddick, 5, 119	Cabrini Green, 4, 118	8	1:24.60	19,240
1978	To the Quick, 4, 116	J. Amy	It's Freezing, 6, 120	Prince Majestic, 4, 121	9	1:25.00	14,511
1977	It's Freezing, 5, 120	E. J. Delahoussaye	Buddy Larosa, 4, 112	Silver Hope, 6, 119	4	1:23.40	14,528
1976	Yamanin, 4, 115	G. Patterson	It's Freezing, 4, 117	Easter Island, 4, 115	9	1:23.80	14,495
1975	Navajo, 5, 123	J. Nichols	Silver Hope, 4, 116	Silver Badge, 4, 110	10	1:24.40	14,804
1974	Barbizon Streak, 6, 115	R. Wilson	Grocery List, 5, 117	Jim's Alibhi, 7, 114	11	1:25.40	15,015
1973	Code of Honor, 5, 115	E. Fires	Knight Counter, 6, 122	Hook It Up, 5, 115	10	1:23.00	15,096

Sponsored by W. S. Farish's Lane's End, located near Versailles, Kentucky 2001. Sponsored by Winner Communications, a telecommunications company involved in televised horse racing 2000. Grade 3 1992-'97. Winnercomm H. 2000. Lane's End Churchill Downs H. 2001. Not held 1914-'37. 1⅛ miles 1911-'13. Three-year-olds and up 1911-'13, 1938-'43, 1947-'88. Two divisions 1982, 1985. ‡Snow Ridge finished first, DQ to second, 2002. Track record 1998, 2001.

Cicada Stakes

Grade 3 in 2005. Aqueduct, three-year-olds, fillies, 7 furlongs, dirt. Held March 19, 2005, with a gross value of $109,800. First held in 1975. First graded in 1996. Stakes record 1:22.38 (1994 Our Royal Blue).

Year	Winner	Jockey	Second	Third	Strs	Time	1st Purse
2005	Dixie Talking, 3, 116	A. Garcia	Acey Deucey, 3, 122	Alfonsina, 3, 116	8	1:23.04	$65,880
2004	Bohemian Lady, 3, 116	E. S. Prado	Whoopi Cat, 3, 116	Baldomera, 3, 122	6	1:23.22	65,460

2003 **Cyber Secret**, 3, 122	S. Bridgmohan	Roar Emotion, 3, 116	Boxer Girl, 3, 118	6	1:22.55	$64,980
2002 **Proper Gamble**, 3, 122	J. Castellano	Short Note, 3, 118	Forest Heiress, 3, 120	6	1:23.32	65,160
2001 **Xtra Heat**, 3, 122	R. Wilson	Erin Moor, 3, 116	Chasm, 3, 116	4	1:23.39	63,770
2000 **Finder's Fee**, 3, 118	J. D. Bailey	Apollo Cat, 3, 116	Southern Sandra, 3, 121	6	1:23.07	65,100
1999 **Potomac Bend**, 3, 118	M. T. Johnston	Carleaville, 3, 114	Jane, 3, 112	7	1:23.18	48,915
1998 **Jersey Girl**, 3, 116	R. Migliore	Vienna Blues, 3, 114	Babai Danzig, 3, 116	9	1:22.95	50,175
1997 **Vegas Prospector**, 3, 116	M. J. McCarthy	Ormsby County, 3, 112	Valid Affect, 3, 118	6	1:26.23	48,375
1996 **J J'sdream**, 3, 121	G. Boulanger	Dahl, 3, 114	Mystic Rhythms, 3, 118	9	1:23.44	50,310
1995 **Lucky Lavender Gal**, 3, 114	R. G. Davis	Stormy Blues, 3, 118	Dancin Renee, 3, 116	7	1:23.45	48,870
1994 **Our Royal Blue**, 3, 114	R. Wilson	Sovereign Kitty, 3, 118	Princess Joanne, 3, 113	5	**1:22.38**	48,375
1993 **Personal Bid**, 3, 118	J. A. Santos	Sheila's Revenge, 3, 118	In Excelcis Deo, 3, 116	4	1:23.52	31,800
1988 **Feel the Beat**, 3, 114	J. A. Santos	Bold Lady Anne, 3, 121	Dear Dusty, 3, 114	6	1:11.00	41,220
1983 **May Day Eighty**, 4, 117	J. Fell	Viva Sec, 5, 117	Clever Guest, 4, 117	9	1:42.80	26,430
1982 **Bold Ribbons**, 3, 116	A. T. Cordero Jr.	Cupecoy's Joy, 3, 121	Adept, 3, 114	11	1:11.00	34,980
1981 **In True Form**, 3, 114	A. Santiago	Wading Power, 3, 114	Hawkeye Express, 3, 114	12	1:12.80	34,800
1980 **The Wheel Turns**, 3, 114	M. Venezia	Darlin Momma, 3, 121	Remote Ruler, 3, 118	8	1:11.20	33,180
1979 **Spanish Fake**, 3, 114	J. Amy	Shirley the Queen, 3, 114	Quadrangles Plum, 3, 114	11	1:13.20	32,790
1978 **New Rinkle**, 3, 114	R. Hernandez	Star Gala, 3, 114	Idmon, 3, 114	6	1:13.00	25,440
1977 **Ring O'Bells**, 3, 118	A. T. Cordero Jr.	Shufleur, 3, 114	Maria's Baby, 3, 116	5	1:10.80	21,855
1976 **Tough Elsie**, 3, 116	J. Imparato	Light Frost, 3, 114	Quintas Vicki, 3, 118	13	1:10.20	23,610
1975 **Cast the Die**, 2, 116	R. Turcotte	Artfully, 2, 116	Veroom Maid, 2, 116	9	1:10.40	27,240

Named for Meadow Stable's 1961 champion two-year-old filly, '62 champion three-year-old filly, '62, '63 champion older mare, and '62 Beldame H. winner Cicada (1959 f. by Bryan G.). Held at Belmont Park 1983, 1993. Not held 1984-'87, 1989-'92. 6 furlongs 1975-'82, 1988. 1¹/₁₆ miles 1983. Two-year-olds 1975. Three-year-olds and up 1983. Fillies and mares 1983.

Cigar Mile Handicap

Grade 1 in 2005. Aqueduct, three-year-olds and up, 1 mile, dirt. Held November 27, 2004, with a gross value of $350,000. First held in 1988. First graded in 1990. Stakes record 1:32.80 (1990 Quiet American; 1989 Dispersal).

Year	Winner	Jockey	Second	Third	Strs	Time	1st Purse
2004	**Lion Tamer**, 4, 115	J. A. Santos	Badge of Silver, 4, 115	Pico Central (Brz), 5, 123	8	1:33.46	$210,000
2003	**Congaree**, 5, 124	J. D. Bailey	Midas Eyes, 3, 115	Toccet, 3, 115	7	1:34.30	210,000
2002	**Congaree**, 4, 119	J. D. Bailey	Aldebaran, 4, 116	Crafty C. T., 4, 117	8	1:33.11	210,000
2001	**Left Bank**, 4, 120	J. R. Velazquez	Graeme Hall, 4, 118	Red Bullet, 4, 118	9	1:33.35	210,000
2000	**El Corredor**, 3, 116	J. D. Bailey	Peeping Tom, 3, 111	Affirmed Success, 6, 120	11	1:34.68	210,000
1999	**Affirmed Success**, 5, 118	J. F. Chavez	Adonis, 3, 115	Honorifico (Arg), 5, 113	9	1:34.18	210,000
1998	**Sir Bear**, 5, 116	J. D. Bailey	Affirmed Success, 4, 119	Distorted Humor, 5, 116	8	1:34.05	180,000
1997	**Devious Course**, 5, 112	J. F. Chavez	Lucayan Prince, 4, 114	Basqueian, 6, 115	12	1:34.98	150,000
1996	**Gold Fever**, 3, 115	M. E. Smith	Diligence, 3, 114	Top Account, 4, 117	14	1:34.98	150,000
1995	**Flying Chevron**, 3, 112	R. G. Davis	Wekiva Springs, 4, 117	Dramatic Gold, 4, 120	13	1:34.57	150,000
1994	**Cigar**, 4, 111	J. D. Bailey	Devil His Due, 5, 124	Punch Line, 4, 112	12	1:36.10	150,000
1992	**Ibero (Arg)**, 5, 117	L. A. Pincay Jr.	Irish Swap, 5, 116	Nines Wild, 3, 111	7	1:33.97	300,000
1991	**Rubiano**, 4, 116	J. A. Santos	Sultry Song, 5, 117	Diablo, 4, 112	15	1:33.68	300,000
1990	**Quiet American**, 4, 116	C. J. McCarron	Dancing Spree, 5, 119	Sewickley, 5, 124	12	**1:32.80**	382,800
1989	**Dispersal**, 3, 115	A. T. Cordero Jr.	Sewickley, 4, 120	Speedratic, 4, 117	7	**1:32.80**	348,600
1988	**Forty Niner**, 3, 121	W. I. Fox Jr.	Mawsuff (GB), 5, 115	Precisionist, 7, 124	6	1:34.00	340,200

Named for Allen E. Paulson's 1995, '96 Horse of the Year, '94 NYRA Mile H. (G1) winner, and world's leading earner at his retirement, Cigar (1990 c. by Palace Music). Formerly named for the New York Racing Association. Not held 1993. NYRA Mile H. 1988-'96.

Cinema Breeders' Cup Handicap

Grade 3 in 2005. Hollywood Park, three-year-olds, 1¹/₈ miles, turf. Held June 26, 2004, with a gross value of $153,450. First held in 1946. First graded in 1973. Stakes record 1:46.56 (1994 Unfinished Symph).

Year	Winner	Jockey	Second	Third	Strs	Time	1st Purse
2004	**Greek Sun**, 3, 120	A. O. Solis	Laura's Lucky Boy, 3, 122	Whilly (Ire), 3, 117	7	1:48.40	$97,470
2003	**Just Wonder (GB)**, 3, 117	K. J. Desormeaux	Bis Repetitas, 3, 115	Slew City Citadel, 3, 115	8	1:47.41	98,730
2002	**Inesperado (Fr)**, 3, 116	K. J. Desormeaux	Regiment, 3, 122	Johar, 3, 118	7	1:47.63	97,560
2001	**Sligo Bay (Ire)**, 3, 118	L. A. Pincay Jr.	Learing At Kathy, 3, 117	Marine (GB), 3, 119	7	1:48.40	65,160
2000	**David Copperfield**, 3, 116	V. Espinoza	Duke of Green (GB), 3, 117	Silver Axe, 3, 115	6	1:47.73	64,560
1999	**Fighting Falcon**, 3, 119	B. Blanc	Eagleton, 3, 120	Major Hero, 3, 113	8	1:48.06	66,000
1998	**Commitisize**, 3, 118	D. R. Flores	Killer Image, 3, 115	Lord Smith (GB), 3, 116	7	1:48.03	65,220
1997	**Worldly Ways (GB)**, 3, 115	C. S. Nakatani	P. T. Indy, 3, 118	Brave Act (GB), 3, 120	9	1:48.43	66,180
1996	**Let Bob Do It**, 3, 120	K. J. Desormeaux	Dr. Sardonica, 3, 115	Winter Quarters, 3, 115	7	1:47.58	81,660
1995	**Via Lombardia (Ire)**, 3, 119	E. J. Delahoussaye	Bryntirion, 3, 113	Oncefortheroad, 3, 115	9	1:47.22	65,400
1994	**Unfinished Symph**, 3, 118	G. Baze	Vaudeville, 3, 115	Fumo Di Londra (Ire), 3, 121	7	**1:46.56**	63,100
1993	**Earl of Barking (Ire)**, 3, 121	C. J. McCarron	Manny's Prospect, 3, 115	Minks Law, 3, 113	5	1:47.45	61,100
1992	**Bien Bien**, 3, 113	C. J. McCarron	Fax News, 3, 114	Prospect for Four, 3, 112	9	1:47.10	65,600
1991	**Character (GB)**, 3, 114	G. L. Stevens	River Traffic, 3, 117	Kalgrey (Fr), 3, 114	6	1:47.10	62,600
1990	**Jovial (GB)**, 3, 115	G. L. Stevens	Mehmetori, 3, 113	Itsallgreektome, 3, 117	10	1:47.80	67,400
1989	**‡Raise a Stanza**, 3, 114	G. L. Stevens	Exemplary Leader, 3, 116	Notorious Pleasure, 3, 120	6	1:47.80	62,100

Year	Winner	Jockey	Second	Third	Strs	Time	1st Purse
1988	Peace, 3, 117	A. O. Solis	Blade of the Ball, 3, 113	Roberto's Dancer, 3, 115	8	1:46.80	$78,400
1987	Something Lucky, 3, 119	L. A. Pincay Jr.	The Medic, 3, 117	Savona Tower, 3, 115	6	1:46.80	62,400
1986	Manila, 3, 117	F. Toro	Vernon Castle, 3, 120	Full of Stars, 3, 115	10	1:47.00	80,400
1985	Don't Say Halo, 3, 116	D. G. McHargue	Derby Dawning, 3, 115	Emperdori, 3, 115	9	1:47.60	65,800
1984	Prince True, 3, 117	P. A. Valenzuela	M. Double M., 3, 116	Majestic Shore, 3, 115	7	1:40.20	63,700
1983	Baron O'Dublin, 3, 115	E. J. Delahoussaye	Tanks Brigade, 3, 119	Re Ack, 3, 116	9	1:43.00	66,300
1982	Give Me Strength, 3, 121	J. Samyn	Journey At Sea, 3, 122	Bargain Balcony, 3, 118	8	1:40.60	64,600
1981	Minnesota Chief, 3, 119	C. J. McCarron	Stancharry, 3, 117	Splendid Spruce, 3, 125	12	1:40.60	69,900
1980	First Albert, 3, 113	F. Mena	Big Doug, 3, 115	Kenderboun, 3, 117	12	1:48.00	68,800
1979	Beau's Eagle, 3, 121	S. Hawley	Ibacache (Chi), 3, 122	Paint King, 3, 113	4	1:47.00	64,500
1978	Kamehameha, 3, 120	T. M. Chapman	El Fantastico, 3, 114	Singular, 3, 118	12	1:47.40	102,800
1977	Bad 'n Big, 3, 121	L. A. Pincay Jr.	Iron Constitution, 3, 124	Minnesota Gus, 3, 112	4	1:48.00	96,450
1976	Majestic Light, 3, 121	S. Hawley	L'Heureux, 3, 120	*Bynoderm, 3, 116	10	1:48.20	67,200
1975	Terete, 3, 113	W. Shoemaker	Larrikin, 3, 125	Dusty County, 3, 117	6	1:48.60	46,400
1973	*Amen II, 3, 115	E. Belmonte	Kirrary, 3, 114	†Card Table, 3, 110	12	1:49.00	52,350

Named for Los Angeles's best-known industry. Grade 2 1973-'93. Cinema H. 1946-2001. Held at Santa Anita Park 1949. Not held 1974. 1¹/₁₆ miles 1946-'49, 1951-'55, 1981-'84. 1 mile 1950. Dirt 1946-'67. ‡Notorious Pleasure finished first, DQ to third, 1989. †Denotes female.

Citation Handicap

Grade 1 in 2005. Hollywood Park, three-year-olds and up, 1¹/₁₆ miles, turf. Held November 27, 2004, with a gross value of $400,000. First held in 1977. First graded in 1979. Stakes record 1:39.69 (1999 Brave Act [GB]).

Year	Winner	Jockey	Second	Third	Strs	Time	1st Purse
2004	Leroidesanimaux (Brz), 4, 117	J. K. Court	A to the Z, 4, 115	Three Valleys, 3, 115	10	1:41.36	$240,000
2003	Redattore (Brz), 8, 120	J. A. Krone	Irish Warrior, 5, 117	Mister Acpen (Chi), 5, 116	6	1:40.74	240,000
2002	Good Journey, 6, 123	P. Day	Seinne (Chi), 5, 115	White Heart (GB), 7, 115	10	1:41.45	300,000
2001	Good Journey, 5, 115	C. J. McCarron	Decarchy, 4, 117	Irish Prize, 5, 122	8	1:44.30	300,000
2000	Charge d'Affaires (GB), 5, 116	J. A. Santos	Ladies Din, 5, 122	Native Desert, 7, 116	10	1:40.30	300,000
1999	Brave Act (GB), 5, 119	A. O. Solis	Native Desert, 6, 119	Bouccaneer (Fr), 4, 119	11	1:39.69	300,000
1998	Military, 4, 118	G. K. Gomez	Mr Lightfoot (Ire), 4, 117	Worldly Ways (GB), 4, 114	8	1:50.58	180,000
1997	Geri, 5, 121	J. D. Bailey	Mufattish, 4, 116	Martiniquais (Ire), 4, 116	6	1:48.35	180,000
1996	Gentlemen (Arg), 4, 119	G. L. Stevens	Smooth Runner, 5, 116	Via Lombardia (Ire), 4, 116	7	1:45.55	180,000
1995	Fastness (Ire), 5, 120	G. L. Stevens	Earl of Barking (Ire), 5, 116	Silver Wizard, 5, 117	7	1:44.78	165,000
1994	Southern Wish, 5, 115	C. S. Nakatani	Square Cut, 5, 114	Jeune Homme, 4, 117	7	2:00.20	137,500
1993	Jeune Homme, 3, 114	T. Jarnet	Paradise Creek, 4, 120	Johann Quatz (Fr), 4, 120	8	1:45.84	137,500
1992	Leger Cat (Arg), 6, 114	C. S. Nakatani	†Trishyde, 3, 111	Luthier Enchanteur, 5, 117	8	1:46.48	137,500
1991	Notorious Pleasure, 5, 118	L. A. Pincay Jr.	Somethingdifferent, 4, 114	Classic Fame, 5, 118	8	1:45.80	102,600
	Fly Till Dawn, 5, 119	L. A. Pincay Jr.	Best Pal, 3, 119	Wolf (Chi), 4, 119	8	1:45.86	102,600
1990	Colway Rally (GB), 6, 114	C. A. Black	Exclusive Partner, 8, 117	The Medic, 6, 116	5	1:47.80	62,300
1989	Fair Judgment, 5, 117	E. J. Delahoussaye	Quiet Boy, 4, 113	Skip Out Front, 7, 117	8	1:50.00	63,300
1988	Forlitano (Arg), 7, 118	P. A. Valenzuela	Precisionist, 7, 121	Skip Out Front, 6, 117	11	1:46.60	69,200
1987	Forlitano (Arg), 6, 120	P. A. Valenzuela	Conquering Hero, 4, 115	Ifrad, 5, 115	12	1:47.40	71,500
1986	Al Mamoon, 5, 122	G. L. Stevens	Silveyville, 8, 118	Will Dancer (Fr), 4, 115	8	1:48.00	123,700
1985	Zoffany, 5, 116	E. J. Delahoussaye	Lord At War (Arg), 5, 125	Foscarini (Ire), 4, 119	9	1:44.80	69,100
1984	Lord At War (Arg), 4, 117	W. Shoemaker	Executive Pride (Ire), 3, 116	Prairie Breaker, 4, 116	8	1:50.60	68,300
1983	Beldale Lustre, 4, 113	C. J. McCarron	The Hague, 4, 115	Sir Pele, 4, 114	10	1:49.40	53,000
	Pewter Grey, 4, 115	R. Sibille	Belmont Bay (Ire), 6, 119	Lucence, 4, 115	10	1:49.60	53,500
1982	Caterman (NZ), 6, 121	C. J. McCarron	Cajun Prince, 5, 118	Island Whirl, 4, 123	5	1:41.00	46,700
1981	Tahitian King (Ire), 5, 120	W. Shoemaker	King Go Go, 6, 115	Cajun Prince, 4, 113	11	1:48.00	136,000
1980	Caro Bambino (Ire), 5, 118	P. A. Valenzuela	Life's Hope, 7, 116	Island Sultan, 5, 111	6	1:33.20	36,950
1979	Text, 5, 122	W. Shoemaker	Farnesio (Arg), 5, 117	Bad 'n Big, 5, 119	7	1:40.40	63,600
1978	Effervescing, 5, 120	L. A. Pincay Jr.	Dr. Patches, 4, 116	Text, 4, 122	4	1:40.20	62,700
1977	Painted Wagon, 4, 117	C. Baltazar	Legendaire, 4, 114	Pay Tribute, 5, 118	7	1:41.00	48,500

Named for Calumet Farm's 1948 Horse of the Year, '48 Triple Crown winner, and '51 Hollywood Gold Cup winner Citation (1945 c. by Bull Lea). Grade 3 1979-'80, 1948-'86. Not graded 1981-'83. Grade 2 1987-2003. 1 mile 1980. 1¹/₈ miles 1981, 1983-'84, 1986-'93, 1995-'98. About 1¹/₈ miles 1985. 1¹/₄ miles 1994. Dirt 1977-'82, 1984. Two divisions 1983, 1991. Course record 1995. †Denotes female.

Clark Handicap

Grade 2 in 2005. Churchill Downs, three-year-olds and up, 1¹/₈ miles, dirt. Held November 26, 2004, with a gross value of $558,000. First held in 1875. First graded in 1973. Stakes record 1:48.26 (2001 Ubiquity).

Year	Winner	Jockey	Second	Third	Strs	Time	1st Purse
2004	Saint Liam, 4, 117	E. S. Prado	Seek Gold, 4, 111	Perfect Drift, 5, 118	9	1:50.81	$345,960
2003	‡Quest, 4, 114	J. Castellano	Evening Attire, 5, 118	Aeneas, 4, 114	4	1:52.42	360,840
2002	Lido Palace (Chi), 5, 121	J. F. Chavez	Crafty Shaw, 4, 115	Hero's Tribute, 4, 114	11	1:49.13	283,464
2001	Ubiquity, 4, 113	C. Perret	Include, 4, 120	Mr Ross, 6, 114	10	1:48.26	280,240
2000	†Surfside, 3, 113	P. Day	Guided Tour, 4, 114	Maysville Slew, 4, 113	9	1:48.75	276,272
1999	Littlebitlively, 5, 118	C. H. Borel	Pleasant Breeze, 4, 112	Nite Dreamer, 4, 114	12	1:50.88	284,456
1998	Silver Charm, 4, 124	G. L. Stevens	Littlebitlively, 4, 113	Wild Rush, 4, 117	8	1:49.07	275,776
1997	Concerto, 3, 113	J. D. Bailey	Terremoto, 6, 114	Rod and Staff, 4, 107	11	1:49.72	284,704

Year	Winner	Jockey	Second	Third	Strs	Time	1st Purse
1996	Isitingood, 5, 120	D. R. Flores	Savinio, 6, 119	Coup D' Argent, 4, 110	9	1:48.99	$174,220
1995	Judge T C, 4, 115	J. M. Johnson	Tyus, 5, 113	Alphabet Soup, 4, 117	14	1:49.82	153,140
1994	Sir Vixen, 6, 112	D. Kutz	Danville, 3, 113	Prize Fight, 5, 115	7	1:51.36	143,130
1993	Mi Cielo, 3, 117	M. E. Smith	Take Me Out, 5, 115	Forry Cow How, 5, 115	13	1:51.43	150,540
1992	Zeeruler, 4, 113	G. K. Gomez	Flying Continental, 6, 118	Echelon's Ice Man, 4, 109	13	1:50.11	76,050
1991	Out of Place, 4, 119	W. H. McCauley	Echelon's Ice Man, 3, 110	British Banker, 3, 111	11	1:52.29	74,230
1990	Secret Hello, 3, 115	P. Day	Din's Dancer, 5, 119	De Roche, 4, 121	7	1:50.60	72,410
1989	No Marker, 5, 113	D. W. Cox	Set a Record, 5, 114	Stop the Stage, 4, 111	12	1:51.20	75,205
1988	Balthazar B., 5, 112	K. J. Desormeaux	Clever Secret, 4, 115	Slew City Slew, 4, 123	9	1:51.20	80,835
1987	Intrusion, 5, 114	L. J. Melancon	Savings, 4, 116	Mister C., 4, 116	9	1:51.40	47,655
1986	Come Summer, 4, 112	P. A. Johnson	Taylor's Special, 5, 126	Sumptious, 3, 120	9	1:49.80	47,363
1985	Hopeful Word, 4, 118	P. Day	Dramatic Desire, 4, 113	Big Bobcat, 5, 111	9	1:51.00	49,510
1984	Eminency, 6, 121	P. Day	Jack Slade, 4, 122	Bayou Hebert, 3, 114	10	1:49.00	36,400
1983	Jack Slade, 3, 117	J. McKnight	Northern Majesty, 4, 122	Cad, 5, 118	8	1:49.80	35,912
1982	Hechizado (Arg), 6, 117	R. P. Romero	Withholding, 5, 116	Pleasing Times, 3, 115	10	1:52.40	36,823
1981	Withholding, 4, 121	L. J. Melancon	Recusant, 3, 111	Hard Up, 5, 115	11	1:52.00	37,213
1980	Sun Catcher, 3, 117	D. Brumfield	Belle's Ruler, 5, 116	Withholding, 3, 116	10	1:53.40	35,636
1979	Lot o' Gold, 3, 123	J. C. Espinoza	Poverty Boy, 4, 114	Capital Idea, 6, 114	9	1:50.80	38,383
1978	Bob's Dusty, 4, 116	R. DePass	Kodiack, 4, 114	Raymond Earl, 3, 117	7	1:49.60	34,629
1977	Bob's Dusty, 3, 118	R. DePass	Packer Captain, 5, 116	Almost Grown, 5, 113	12	1:49.80	21,889
1976	Yamanin, 4, 120	G. Patterson	Warbucks, 6, 115	Play Boy, 3, 113	10	1:54.40	21,661
1975	Warbucks, 5, 124	L. J. Melancon	Silver Badge, 4, 118	†Shoo Dear, 4, 111	7	1:54.40	17,761
1974	Mr. Door, 3, 114	W. Gavidia	†Fairway Flyer, 5, 116	Cut the Talk, 3, 115	8	1:52.20	17,989
1973	Golden Don, 3, 122	M. Manganello	Amber Prey, 4, 115	Rastaferian, 4, 118	13	1:52.80	22,392

Named for Meriwether Lewis Clark (1846-'99), founder of the Kentucky Derby. Grade 3 1973-'97. Clark S. 1875-1901. 2 miles 1875-'80. 1¼ miles 1881-'95. 1¹⁄₁₆ miles 1902-'21, 1925-'54. Three-year-olds 1875-1901. ‡Evening Attire finished first, DQ to second, 2003. †Denotes female.

Clement L. Hirsch Handicap

Grade 2 in 2005. Del Mar, three-year-olds and up, fillies and mares, 1¹⁄₁₆ miles, dirt. Held August 8, 2004, with a gross value of $300,000. First held in 1937. First graded in 1983. Stakes record 1:40 (1982 Matching).

Year	Winner	Jockey	Second	Third	Strs	Time	1st Purse
2004	Miss Loren (Arg), 6, 114	J. K. Court	House of Fortune, 3, 113	Royally Chosen, 6, 116	8	1:42.93	$180,000
2003	Azeri, 5, 127	M. E. Smith	Got Koko, 4, 118	Tropical Blossom, 5, 108	5	1:42.12	180,000
2002	Azeri, 4, 126	M. E. Smith	Angel Gift, 4, 114	Se Me Acabo (Chi), 4, 114	5	1:42.66	180,000
2001	Tranquility Lake, 6, 120	E. J. Delahoussaye	Gourmet Girl, 6, 122	Nany's Sweep, 5, 116	4	1:41.78	180,000
2000	Riboletta (Brz), 5, 125	C. J. McCarron	Bordelaise (Arg), 5, 115	Gourmet Girl, 5, 115	5	1:42.06	180,000
1999	A Lady From Dixie, 4, 116	C. W. Antley	Manistique, 4, 124	Yolo Lady, 4, 116	5	1:43.58	180,000
1998	Sharp Cat, 4, 124	C. S. Nakatani	Supercilious, 5, 115	Numero Uno, 4, 116	4	1:42.16	180,000
1997	Radu Cool, 5, 117	C. J. McCarron	Supercilious, 4, 113	Swoon River, 5, 110	4	1:42.66	180,000
1996	Different (Arg), 4, 120	C. J. McCarron	Top Rung, 5, 115	Borodislew, 6, 117	4	1:42.48	189,200
1995	Borodislew, 5, 118	C. J. McCarron	Lakeway, 4, 117	Golden Klair (GB), 5, 118	6	1:41.87	178,100
1994	Paseana (Arg), 7, 123	C. J. McCarron	Exchange, 6, 120	Magical Maiden, 5, 118	4	1:40.59	117,100
1993	Magical Maiden, 4, 120	G. L. Stevens	Vieille Vigne (Fr), 6, 111	Party Cited, 4, 117	8	1:42.68	123,600
1992	Exchange, 4, 120	L. A. Pincay Jr.	Fowda, 4, 120	Brought to Mind, 5, 119	8	1:42.00	123,100
1991	Vieille Vigne (Fr), 4, 116	M. A. Pedroza	Formidable Lady, 5, 113	Lite Light, 3, 121	5	1:42.67	120,300
1990	Bayakoa (Arg), 6, 127	L. A. Pincay Jr.	Fantastic Look, 4, 113	Formidable Lady, 4, 112	5	1:40.60	88,500
1989	Goodbye Halo, 4, 120	C. A. Black	Flying Julia, 6, 112	Kool Arrival, 3, 115	6	1:41.80	77,450
1988	Clabber Girl, 5, 120	C. J. McCarron	Annoconnor, 4, 118	Integra, 4, 119	5	1:41.60	75,100
1987	Infinidad (Chi), 5, 118	C. A. Black	Margaret Booth, 4, 117	Le l'Argent, 5, 117	9	1:41.40	63,540
1986	Fran's Valentine, 4, 117	W. Shoemaker	Cenyak's Star, 4, 116	Dontstop Themusic, 6, 123	5	1:41.40	59,500
1985	Dontstop Themusic, 5, 122	D. G. McHargue	Golden Screen, 5, 112	Lovlier Linda, 5, 119	4	1:41.80	45,650
1984	Princess Rooney, 4, 123	P. A. Valenzuela	Flag de Lune, 4, 115	Moment to Buy, 3, 116	5	1:40.40	60,100
1983	Sangue (Ire), 5, 121	W. Shoemaker	Avigaition, 4, 122	Skillful Joy, 4, 117	5	1:42.20	46,600
1982	Matching, 4, 116	R. Sibille	Miss Huntington, 5, 116	Cat Girl, 4, 117	4	**1:40.00**	45,850
1981	Save Wild Life, 4, 118	C. J. McCarron	Princess Karenda, 4, 120	Track Robbery, 5, 125	6	1:41.60	47,650
1980	Wayside Station, 5, 113	P. A. Valenzuela	Concussion, 6, 117	Mike Fogarty (Ire), 5, 115	6	1:28.80	19,775
	Galaxy Libra (Ire), 4, 118	W. Shoemaker	Wickerr, 5, 117	To B. Or Not, 4, 116	5	1:29.00	19,375
1979	He's Dewan, 4, 119	D. G. McHargue	Caro Bambino (Ire), 4, 119	No No, 4, 115	10	1:29.00	23,950
1978	Nantequos, 5, 120	D. G. McHargue	Lunar Probe (NZ), 4, 118	dh- Around We Go, 5, 117	10	1:29.40	20,250
				dh- Crew of Ocala, 4, 114			
1977	Notably Different, 4, 113	C. Baltazar	Key Account, 5, 114	Pikehall, 3, 109	8	1:29.40	13,375
	Authorization, 5, 113	D. G. McHargue	Cherry River, 7, 112	Mister Dan, 4, 114	7	1:29.20	13,175
1976	Uniformity, 4, 115	R. Campas	White Fir, 4, 118	*Royal Derby II, 7, 119	9	1:28.20	16,900
1975	Bahia Key, 5, 119	W. Harris	Fair Test, 7, 119	Top Command, 4, 117	5	1:34.00	12,750
1974	Bahia Key, 4, 120	A. Pineda	*Trotteur, 4, 117	Soft Victory, 6, 122	9	1:34.20	13,650
1973	Grotonian, 4, 117	W. Shoemaker	Expediter, 4, 115	China Silk, 4, 114	5	1:50.60	12,600

Named for Clement L. Hirsch (1914-2000), an original Del Mar director. Formerly named for the city of Chula Vista, California. Grade 3 1983-'85. Chula Vista H. 1937-'99. Not held 1938-'66, 1968-'72. 5¹⁄₂ furlongs 1937. 1 mile 1967, 1974-'75. 1¹⁄₈ miles 1973. 7¹⁄₂ furlongs 1976-'80. Turf 1973, 1976-'80. Two-year-olds 1937. Both sexes 1973-'80. Two divisions 1977, 1980. Dead heat for third 1978. Nonwinners of a race worth $12,500 to the winner other than claiming 1974. California-breds 1937.

Clement L. Hirsch Memorial Turf Championship Stakes

Grade 1 in 2005. Santa Anita Park, three-year-olds and up, 1 1/4 miles, turf. Held October 3, 2004, with a gross value of $250,000. First held in 1969. First graded in 1973. Stakes record 1:58.48 (1996 Bon Point [GB] [DQ to fifth]).

Year	Winner	Jockey	Second	Third	Strs	Time	1st Purse
2004	Star Over the Bay, 6, 124	T. Baze	Sarafan, 7, 124	Vangelis, 5, 124	7	1:58.70	$150,000
2003	Storming Home (GB), 5, 124	G. L. Stevens	Johar, 4, 124	Irish Warrior, 5, 124	4	2:01.64	150,000
2002	The Tin Man, 4, 124	M. E. Smith	Sarafan, 5, 124	Blue Steller (Ire), 4, 124	6	1:58.93	180,000
2001	Senure, 5, 124	A. O. Solis	White Heart (GB), 6, 124	Cagney (Brz), 4, 124	6	1:59.47	180,000
2000	Mash One (Chi), 6, 124	D. R. Flores	Boatman, 4, 124	Asidero (Arg), 4, 124	6	2:00.67	180,000
1999	Mash One (Chi), 5, 124	D. R. Flores	Lazy Lode (Arg), 5, 124	Bonapartiste (Fr), 5, 124	6	1:59.07	180,000
1998	Military, 4, 124	C. S. Nakatani	Bonapartiste (Fr), 4, 124	River Bay, 5, 124	5	2:02.04	180,000
1997	Rainbow Dancer (Fr), 6, 124	A. O. Solis	‡Lord Jain (Arg), 5, 124	Sandpit (Brz), 8, 124	5	2:01.80	180,000
1996	‡†Admise (Fr), 4, 121	K. J. Desormeaux	Khoraz, 6, 124	Golden Post, 6, 124	5	1:58.48	180,000
1995	Northern Spur (Ire), 4, 124	C. J. McCarron	Sandpit (Brz), 6, 124	Royal Chariot, 5, 124	8	2:02.37	180,000
1994	Sandpit (Brz), 5, 124	C. S. Nakatani	Grand Flotilla, 7, 124	Approach the Bench (Ire), 6, 124	5	2:25.12	180,000
1993	Kotashaan (Fr), 5, 124	K. J. Desormeaux	Luazur (Fr), 4, 124	†Let's Elope (NZ), 6, 121	4	2:25.06	180,000
1992	Navarone, 4, 126	P. A. Valenzuela	Defensive Play, 5, 126	Daros (GB), 3, 121	6	2:24.29	240,000
1991	Filago, 4, 126	P. A. Valenzuela	Missionary Ridge (GB), 4, 126	†Kartajana (Ire), 4, 123	9	2:23.62	300,000
1990	Rial (Arg), 5, 126	R. Q. Meza	Eradicate (GB), 5, 126	Saratoga Passage, 5, 126	11	2:23.80	300,000
1989	Hawkster, 3, 121	R. A. Baze	Pay the Butler, 5, 126	Saratoga Passage, 4, 126	9	2:22.80	300,000
1988	Nasr El Arab, 3, 121	G. L. Stevens	Great Communicator, 5, 126	Circus Prince, 5, 126	8	2:25.20	240,000
1987	Allez Milord, 4, 126	C. J. McCarron	Louis Le Grand, 5, 126	Rivlia, 5, 126	10	2:36.20	240,000
1986	†Estrapade, 6, 123	F. Toro	Theatrical (Ire), 4, 126	Uptown Swell, 4, 126	10	2:26.00	240,000
1985	Yashgan (GB), 4, 126	C. J. McCarron	Both Ends Burning, 5, 126	Cariellor (Fr), 4, 126	10	2:27.20	240,000
1984	Both Ends Burning, 4, 126	R. A. Baze	Gato Del Sol, 5, 126	Raami (GB), 3, 121	12	2:25.40	240,000
1983	†Zalataia (Fr), 4, 123	F. Head	John Henry, 8, 126	Load the Cannons, 3, 122	9	2:29.20	240,000
1982	John Henry, 7, 126	W. Shoemaker	Craelius, 3, 122	Regalberto, 4, 126	7	2:24.00	180,000
1981	John Henry, 6, 126	W. Shoemaker	Spence Bay, 6, 126	The Bart, 5, 126	7	2:23.40	180,000
1980	John Henry, 5, 126	L. A. Pincay Jr.	Balzac, 5, 126	Bold Tropic (SAf), 5, 126	10	2:23.40	120,000
1979	Balzac, 4, 126	C. J. McCarron	†Trillion, 5, 123	Silver Eagle (Ire), 5, 126	9	2:25.40	90,000
1978	Exceller, 5, 126	W. Shoemaker	Star of Erin (Ire), 4, 126	dh- As de Copas (Arg), 5, 126	9	2:24.60	90,000
				dh- Good Lord (NZ), 7, 126			
1977	Crystal Water, 4, 126	W. Shoemaker	Vigors, 4, 126	Ancient Title, 7, 126	10	2:26.40	60,000
1976	King Pellinore, 4, 126	W. Shoemaker	*Royal Derby II, 7, 126	L'Heureux, 3, 121	9	2:31.40	60,000
1975	Top Command, 4, 126	W. Shoemaker	Top Crowd, 4, 126	Buffalo Lark, 5, 126	8	2:26.00	60,000
1974	†Tallahto, 4, 123	L. A. Pincay Jr.	Within Hail, 3, 122	Montmartre, 4, 126	11	2:25.80	60,000
1973	Portentous, 3, 122	J. Ramirez	Groshawk, 3, 122	dh- Kentuckian, 4, 126	8	2:25.60	60,000
				dh- Kirrary, 3, 122			

Named for Clement L. Hirsch (1914-2000), co-founder and first president of Oak Tree Racing Association. The race is held during the Oak Tree meet at Santa Anita Park. Oak Tree S. 1969-'70. Oak Tree Invitational 1971-'95. Oak Tree Turf Championship 1996-'99. Clement L. Hirsch Turf Championship 2000. 1 1/2 miles 1969-'94. Dead heat for third 1973, 1978. ‡Bon Point (GB) finished first, DQ to fifth, 1996. ‡Marlin finished second, DQ to fourth, 1997. †Denotes female.

Cliff Hanger Handicap

Grade 3 in 2005. The Meadowlands, three-year-olds and up, 1 1/16 miles, turf. Held October 15, 2004, with a gross value of $200,000. First held in 1977. First graded in 1985. Stakes record 1:39.40 (1988 Wanderkin).

Year	Winner	Jockey	Second	Third	Strs	Time	1st Purse
2004	Dr. Kashnikow, 7, 116	R. Migliore	Tam's Terms, 6, 116	Host (Chi), 4, 117	8	1:42.41	$120,000
2002	Saint Verre, 4, 113	J. Samyn	Pinky Pizwaanski, 4, 116	Spruce Run, 4, 115	4	1:42.40	90,000
2001	Crash Course, 5, 114	R. Wilson	Solitary Dancer, 5, 114	Union One, 4, 114	10	1:43.14	90,000
2000	North East Bound, 4, 118	J. A. Velez Jr.	Johnny Dollar, 4, 114	Swamp, 4, 120	11	1:41.78	90,000
1999	Virginia Carnival, 7, 114	J. Samyn	Star Connection, 5, 114	Grapeshot, 5, 116	12	1:42.44	90,000
1998	Mi Narrow, 4, 111	J. Bravo	Treat Me Doc, 4, 114	Boyce, 5, 116	6	1:43.58	60,000
1997	Dixie Bayou, 4, 114	J. R. Velazquez	Brave Note (Ire), 6, 115	Joker, 5, 116	10	1:39.45	60,000
1996	Thorny Crown, 5, 115	M. J. Luzzi	Ihtiraz (GB), 6, 114	Winnetou, 6, 112	5	1:44.71	60,000
1995	‡Mighty Forum (GB), 4, 114	W. H. McCauley	Joker, 3, 106	Fourstars Allstar, 7, 120	7	1:41.09	60,000
1994	Binary Light, 5, 114	J. Samyn	Brazany, 4, 112	Burst of Applause, 5, 109	5	1:41.41	45,000
1993	Excellent Tipper, 5, 117	C. Perret	Rinka Das, 5, 115	First and Only, 6, 115	6	1:43.69	45,000
1992	Roman Envoy, 4, 116	C. Perret	Futurist, 4, 116	Royal Ninja, 6, 115	8	1:39.92	45,000
1991	Finder's Choice, 6, 114	R. Aviles	Royal Rue, 5, 113	Great Normand, 6, 117	9	1:40.31	45,000
1990	Chas' Whim, 3, 115	A. T. Stacy	Kali High, 4, 115	Royal Ninja, 4, 115	11	1:46.40	45,000
1989	Ten Keys, 5, 114	K. J. Desormeaux	Wanderkin, 6, 121	Soviet Lad, 4, 112	7	1:42.20	52,290
1988	Wanderkin, 5, 118	R. G. Davis	Salem Drive, 6, 117	San's the Shadow, 4, 117	9	1:39.40	53,730
1987	Foligno, 5, 115	J. A. Santos	Cost Conscious, 5, 116	Air Display, 4, 113	7	1:41.40	46,995
	Silver Comet, 4, 117	W. H. McCauley	Broadway Tommy, 5, 112	Prince Daniel, 4, 114	3	1:43.80	31,831
1986	Explosive Darling, 4, 118	R. P. Romero	Equalize, 4, 115	Lieutenant's Lark, 4, 120	7	1:40.00	48,360
1985	Late Act, 6, 117	J. D. Bailey	Silver Surfer, 4, 116	Pax Nobiscum, 5, 116	7	1:45.00	47,790
1984	Late Act, 5, 113	E. Maple	Sitzmark, 4, 111	Quick Dip, 4, 112	10	1:40.80	46,020
	Cozzene, 4, 115	W. A. Guerra	Ayman, 4, 112	Pin Puller, 5, 114	6	1:40.40	45,300
1983	Erin's Tiger, 5, 112	J. Velasquez	Who's for Dinner, 4, 113	Kentucky River, 5, 112	9	1:41.20	33,450

Year	Winner	Jockey	Second	Third	Strs	Time	1st Purse
1982	Erin's Tiger, 4, 114	J. Velasquez	Santo's Joe, 5, 116	Dew Line, 3, 114	8	1:44.60	$26,295
	Acaroid, 4, 114	A. T. Cordero Jr.	North Course, 7, 114	Thirty Eight Paces, 4, 116	7	1:44.60	26,115
1981	Bill Wheeler, 4, 119	W. H. McCauley	Mannerism, 4, 113	Brahmin, 5, 115	15	1:43.60	33,510
1980	Quality T. V., 3, 114	J. Velasquez	Conservatoire, 3, 109	Bill Wheeler, 3, 112	10	1:43.80	32,640
1979	Exclusively Mine, 3, 114	W. Nemeti	Telly Hill, 5, 126	Picturesque, 3, 116	7	1:44.20	34,678
1978	Mr. Lincroft, 4, 117	V. A. Bracciale Jr.	Telly Hill, 4, 119	†Forbidden Isle, 3, 109	15	1:44.20	36,270
1977	Dan Horn, 5, 125	D. MacBeth	Shore Patrol, 7, 113	Popular Victory, 5, 118	9	1:43.60	34,873

Named to honor the early movie industry in New Jersey, referring to suspenseful silent film serials. Grade 3 1985-2001. Not graded when taken off turf 2002. Cliff Hanger S. 1982. Not held 2003. Dirt 1978-'81, 1985, 1987, 1993, 1996, 1998. Originally scheduled on turf 2002. Two divisions 1982, 1984, 1987. Equaled course record 1997. ‡Joker finished first, DQ to second, 1995. †Denotes female.

Coaching Club American Oaks

Grade 1 in 2005. Belmont Park, three-year-olds, fillies, 1¼ miles, dirt. Held July 24, 2004, with a gross value of $500,000. First held in 1917. First graded in 1973. Stakes record 2:00.40 (1997 Ajina).

Year	Winner	Jockey	Second	Third	Strs	Time	1st Purse
2004	Ashado, 3, 121	J. R. Velazquez	Stellar Jayne, 3, 121	Magical Illusion, 3, 121	6	2:02.43	$300,000
2003	Spoken Fur, 3, 121	J. D. Bailey	Fircroft, 3, 121	Savedbythelight, 3, 121	7	2:31.02	300,000
2002	Jilbab, 3, 121	M. J. Luzzi	Tarnished Lady, 3, 121	Shop Till You Drop, 3, 121	7	2:31.48	210,000
2001	Tweedside, 3, 121	J. R. Velazquez	Exogenous, 3, 121	Unbridled Lassie, 3, 121	8	2:30.70	210,000
2000	Jostle, 3, 121	M. E. Smith	Resort, 3, 121	Secret Status, 3, 121	7	2:29.99	210,000
1999	On a Soapbox, 3, 121	J. D. Bailey	Dreams Gallore, 3, 121	Strolling Belle, 3, 121	8	2:29.31	210,000
1998	Banshee Breeze, 3, 121	J. D. Bailey	Keeper Hill, 3, 121	Best Friend Stro, 3, 121	6	2:31.56	180,000
1997	Ajina, 3, 121	M. E. Smith	Tomisue's Delight, 3, 121	Key Hunter, 3, 121	5	2:00.40	150,000
1996	My Flag, 3, 121	J. D. Bailey	Gold n Delicious, 3, 121	Weekend in Seattle, 3, 121	7	2:04.64	150,000
1995	Golden Bri, 3, 121	J. A. Santos	Serena's Song, 3, 121	Change Fora Dollar, 3, 121	6	2:03.86	150,000
1994	Two Altazano, 3, 121	J. A. Santos	Plenty of Sugar, 3, 121	Sovereign Kitty, 3, 121	7	2:02.88	150,000
1993	Sky Beauty, 3, 121	M. E. Smith	Future Pretense, 3, 121	Silky Feather, 3, 121	5	2:01.56	150,000
1992	Turnback the Alarm, 3, 121	C. W. Antley	Easy Now, 3, 121	Pleasant Stage, 3, 121	6	2:03.53	150,000
1991	Lite Light, 3, 121	C. S. Nakatani	Meadow Star, 3, 121	Car Gal, 3, 121	6	2:00.54	150,000
1990	Charon, 3, 121	C. Perret	Crowned, 3, 121	Paper Money, 3, 121	7	2:02.60	172,500
1989	‡Open Mind, 3, 121	A. T. Cordero Jr.	Nite of Fun, 3, 121	Rose Diamond, 3, 121	6	2:32.40	170,100
1988	Goodbye Halo, 3, 121	J. Velasquez	Aptostar, 3, 121	Make Change, 3, 121	6	2:32.80	170,040
1987	Fiesta Gal, 3, 121	A. T. Cordero Jr.	Mint Cooler, 3, 121	Run Come See, 3, 121	5	2:31.00	172,500
1986	Valley Victory (Ire), 3, 121	R. P. Romero	Life At the Top, 3, 121	Lotka, 3, 121	8	2:28.00	166,680
1985	Mom's Command, 3, 121	A. Fuller	Bessarabian, 3, 121	Foxy Deen, 3, 121	9	2:32.00	142,560
1984	Class Play, 3, 121	J. Cruguet	Life's Magic, 3, 121	Miss Oceana, 3, 121	5	2:29.80	164,520
1983	High Schemes, 3, 121	J. Samyn	Spit Curl, 3, 121	Lady Norcliffe, 3, 121	16	2:30.20	107,460
1982	Christmas Past, 3, 121	J. Vasquez	Cupecoy's Joy, 3, 121	Flying Partner, 3, 121	10	2:28.60	84,900
1981	‡Wayward Lass, 3, 121	C. B. Asmussen	Real Prize, 3, 121	Banner Gala, 3, 121	6	2:28.20	81,750
1980	Bold 'n Determined, 3, 121	E. J. Delahoussaye	Erin's Word, 3, 121	Farewell Letter, 3, 121	5	2:31.80	84,000
1979	Davona Dale, 3, 121	J. Velasquez	Plankton, 3, 121	Croquis, 3, 121	5	2:30.00	79,575
1978	Lakeville Miss, 3, 121	R. Hernandez	Caesar's Wish, 3, 121	Tempest Queen, 3, 121	5	2:29.40	63,540
1977	Our Mims, 3, 121	J. Velasquez	Road Princess, 3, 121	Fia, 3, 121	12	2:29.40	65,880
1976	Revidere, 3, 121	J. Vasquez	Optimistic Gal, 3, 121	No Duplicate, 3, 121	10	2:28.40	68,640
1975	Ruffian, 3, 121	J. Vasquez	Equal Change, 3, 121	Let Me Linger, 3, 121	5	2:27.80	66,700
1974	Chris Evert, 3, 121	J. Velasquez	Fiesta Libre, 3, 121	Maud Muller, 3, 121	10	2:28.80	68,520
1973	Magazine, 3, 121	A. T. Cordero Jr.	Bag of Tunes, 3, 121	Lady Love, 3, 121	13	2:27.80	70,200

Named in honor of the Coaching Club of America, first sponsor of the race. The Coaching Club preserved the aristocratic traditions of driving four-in-hand coaches (a coach driven by four horses with a single rein) socially and in competitions—the ability to drive one of these coaches was a condition of membership. Coaching Club American Oaks H. 1917-'27. Held at Aqueduct 1963-'67. 1⅛ miles 1917. 1½ miles 1942-'43, 1971-'89, 1998-2003. 1⅜ miles 1919-'41, 1944-'58. ‡Real Prize finished first, DQ to second, 1981. ‡Nite of Fun finished first, DQ to second, 1989.

Comely Stakes

Grade 2 in 2005. Aqueduct, three-year-olds, fillies, 1 mile, dirt. Held April 16, 2005, with a gross value of $150,000. First held in 1945. First graded in 1973. Stakes record 1:35.50 (2002 Bella Bellucci).

Year	Winner	Jockey	Second	Third	Strs	Time	1st Purse
2005	Acey Deucey, 3, 118	D. Nelson	Seeking the Ante, 3, 116	Pleasant Chimes, 3, 116	8	1:35.95	$90,000
2004	Society Selection, 3, 122	J. F. Chavez	Bending Strings, 3, 116	Daydreaming, 3, 116	8	1:35.89	67,200
2003	Cyber Secret, 3, 122	S. Bridgmohan	Storm Flag Flying, 3, 122	Bonay, 3, 116	5	1:35.97	64,740
2002	Bella Bellucci, 3, 122	G. L. Stevens	Short Note, 3, 116	Nonsuch Bay, 3, 116	5	1:35.50	64,920
2001	‡Two Item Limit, 3, 122	R. Migliore	Mandy's Gold, 3, 118	It All Adds Up, 3, 116	7	1:36.17	66,060
2000	March Magic, 3, 114	R. Migliore	Jostle, 3, 121	Finder's Fee, 3, 121	6	1:36.79	65,460
1999	Madison's Charm, 3, 112	J. Samyn	Better Than Honour, 3, 121	Oh What a Windfall, 3, 121	7	1:35.54	65,520
1998	Fantasy Angel, 3, 114	J. F. Chavez	Hansel's Girl, 3, 116	Best Friend Stro, 3, 118	12	1:37.44	69,300
1997	Dixie Flag, 3, 114	J. Samyn	Global Star, 3, 114	How About Now, 3, 114	7	1:36.96	66,120
1996	Little Miss Fast, 3, 118	J. F. Chavez	J J'sdream, 3, 118	Stop Traffic, 3, 112	7	1:36.58	65,940
1995	Nappelon, 3, 112	J. F. Chavez	Stormy Blues, 3, 121	Incredible Blues, 3, 114	6	1:36.26	64,440
1994	Dixie Luck, 3, 116	F. Leon	Penny's Reshoot, 3, 116	Our Royal Blue, 3, 112	7	1:37.02	66,240

1993	**Private Light**, 3, 112	R. G. Davis	Russian Bride, 3, 113	True Affair, 3, 118	6	1:44.19	$68,280
1992	**Saratoga Dew**, 3, 114	W. H. McCauley	City Dance, 3, 113	Looking for a Win, 3, 114	7	1:37.22	69,480
1991	**Meadow Star**, 3, 121	C. W. Antley	Do It With Style, 3, 114	I'm a Thriller, 3, 118	5	1:38.02	67,560
1990	**Fappaburst**, 3, 114	J. Vasquez	Miss Spentyouth, 3, 114	Bundle Bits, 3, 118	4	1:21.60	49,770
1989	**Surging**, 3, 118	A. T. Cordero Jr.	Nite of Fun, 3, 112	Luv That Native, 3, 112	6	1:23.00	52,290
1988	**Avie's Gal**, 3, 114	J. Velasquez	Topicount, 3, 116	Ready Jet Go, 3, 114	8	1:22.40	66,780
1987	**Devil's Bride**, 3, 116	R. Q. Meza	Oh So Precious, 3, 116	Valid Line, 3, 114	7	1:23.60	65,790
1986	**Misty Drone**, 3, 112	J. Vasquez	I'm Splendid, 3, 121	Storm and Sunshine, 3, 114	14	1:24.00	59,940
1985	**Mom's Command**, 3, 121	A. Fuller	Majestic Folly, 3, 113	Clocks Secret, 3, 121	9	1:22.20	55,170
1984	**Wild Applause**, 3, 113	P. Day	Suavite, 3, 113	Proud Clarioness, 3, 116	7	1:23.20	52,110
1983	**Able Money**, 3, 113	A. Graell	Stark Drama, 3, 113	Idle Gossip, 3, 113	10	1:23.80	35,580
1982	**Nancy Huang**, 3, 113	J. Velasquez	Broom Dance, 3, 113	Dance Number, 3, 113	10	1:24.40	34,860
1981	**Expressive Dance**, 3, 113	D. MacBeth	Tina Tina Too, 3, 118	Explosive Kingdom, 3, 114	11	1:23.40	35,220
1980	**Cybele**, 3, 113	C. B. Asmussen	Punta Punta, 3, 113	Kashan, 3, 113	7	1:22.60	27,225
1979	**Countess North**, 3, 113	A. T. Cordero Jr.	Palm Hut, 3, 116	Run Cosmic Run, 3, 113	5	1:23.40	25,725
1978	**Mashteen**, 3, 113	R. Hernandez	Tempest Queen, 3, 118	Mucchina, 3, 113	6	1:23.00	25,665
1977	**Bring Out the Band**, 3, 118	D. Brumfield	Cum Laude Laurie, 3, 113	Emmy, 3, 113	10	1:23.60	22,650
1976	**Tell Me All**, 3, 113	J. Ruane	Dearly Precious, 3, 121	Worthyana, 3, 113	5	1:23.20	22,080
1975	**Ruffian**, 3, 113	J. Vasquez	Aunt Jin, 3, 113	Point in Time, 3, 113	5	1:21.20	16,755
1974	**Clear Copy**, 3, 113	D. Montoya	Shy Dawn, 3, 118	Chris Evert, 3, 118	10	1:24.40	17,670
1973	**Java Moon**, 3, 116	A. T. Cordero Jr.	Windy's Daughter, 3, 121	Voler, 3, 116	11	1:22.80	17,610

Named for James Butler's Comely (1912 f. by Disguise); Butler was the owner of Empire City, where the race originated. Grade 2 1988-'95. Comely H. 1945-'53. Held at Jamaica 1945-'51, 1959. Held at Empire City 1952-'53. Held at Belmont Park 1976, 1981, 1984-'85. Not held 1954-'58. 1¹/₁₆ miles 1945-'53, 1993. 5 furlongs 1959. 7 furlongs 1960-'90. Three-year-olds and up 1945-'53. Fillies and mares 1945-'53. Two-year-olds 1959. Both sexes 1959. ‡Mandy's Gold finished first, DQ to second, 2001.

Commonwealth Breeders' Cup Stakes

Grade 2 in 2005. Keeneland, three-year-olds and up, 7 furlongs, dirt. Held April 16, 2005, with a gross value of $424,900. First held in 1987. First graded in 1990. Stakes record 1:20.50 (1998 Distorted Humor).

Year	Winner	Jockey	Second	Third	Strs	Time	1st Purse
2005	**Clock Stopper**, 5, 118	J. D. Bailey	Gators N Bears, 5, 118	Silver Wagon, 4, 118	6	1:22.06	$263,438
2004	**Lion Tamer**, 4, 122	M. E. Smith	Private Horde, 5, 120	Marino Marini, 4, 118	6	1:23.14	167,555
2003	**Smooth Jazz**, 4, 118	E. S. Prado	Crafty C. T., 5, 118	Multiple Choice, 5, 120	7	1:21.73	169,725
2002	**Orientate**, 4, 120	P. Day	Aldebaran, 4, 118	Twilight Road, 5, 118	7	1:21.54	168,640
2001	**Alannan**, 5, 118	E. S. Prado	Valiant Halory, 4, 118	Liberty Gold, 7, 118	8	1:22.39	170,965
2000	**Richter Scale**, 6, 121	R. Migliore	Son's Corona, 5, 117	Deep Gold, 4, 117	6	1:21.07	128,836
1999	**Good and Tough**, 4, 115	S. J. Sellers	Purple Passion, 5, 115	Crucible, 4, 115	5	1:22.09	127,906
1998	**Distorted Humor**, 5, 119	G. L. Stevens	El Amante, 5, 118	Partner's Hero, 4, 121	8	**1:20.50**	130,820
1997	**Victor Cooley**, 4, 114	E. M. Martin Jr.	Western Winter, 5, 112	Appealing Skier, 4, 121	7	1:22.40	129,332
1996	**Afternoon Deelites**, 4, 124	K. J. Desormeaux	Western Winter, 4, 113	Our Emblem, 5, 115	6	1:21.12	131,068
1995	**Golden Gear**, 4, 118	C. Perret	Turkomatic, 4, 112	Lit de Justice, 5, 121	8	1:22.06	130,758
1994	**Memo (Chi)**, 7, 118	P. Atkinson	American Chance, 5, 115	British Banker, 6, 115	10	1:22.32	69,378
1993	**Alydeed**, 4, 115	C. Perret	Binalong, 4, 118	Senor Speedy, 6, 115	6	1:21.43	113,057
1992	**Pleasant Tap**, 5, 116	E. J. Delahoussaye	To Freedom, 4, 115	Run On the Bank, 5, 118	6	1:22.00	118,138
1991	**Black Tie Affair (Ire)**, 5, 124	J. L. Diaz	Housebuster, 4, 124	Exemplary Leader, 5, 115	6	1:21.86	118,625
1990	**Black Tie Affair (Ire)**, 4, 121	M. Guidry	Shaker Knit, 5, 115	Momsfurrari, 6, 118	9	1:22.00	121,111
1989	**Sewickley**, 4, 115	R. P. Romero	Irish Open, 5, 118	Dancing Spree, 4, 115	9	1:22.40	36,368
1988	**Calestoga**, 6, 120	D. Brumfield	You're No Bargain, 4, 117	Carload, 6, 120	10	1:09.40	101,628
1987	**Exclusive Enough**, 3, 111	M. E. Smith	†Lazer Show, 4, 120	High Brite, 3, 120	8	1:08.40	101,010

Named for the Commonwealth of Kentucky. Grade 3 1990-'93. Commonwealth Breeders' Cup H. 1989. 6 furlongs 1987-'88. †Denotes female.

CompUSA Turf Mile Stakes

Grade 3 in 2005. Churchill Downs, three-year-olds and up, fillies and mares, 1 mile, turf. Held May 7, 2005, with a gross value of $112,200. First held in 1983. First graded in 1997. Stakes record 1:33.96 (2003 Heat Haze [GB]).

Year	Winner	Jockey	Second	Third	Strs	Time	1st Purse
2005	**Miss Terrible (Arg)**, 6, 117	A. O. Solis	Sand Springs, 5, 123	Shaconage, 5, 121	7	1:35.89	$69,564
2004	**Shaconage**, 4, 121	B. Blanc	Etoile Montante, 4, 123	Chance Dance, 4, 117	10	1:36.10	70,246
2003	**Heat Haze (GB)**, 4, 123	J. Valdivia Jr.	Quick Tip, 5, 123	Sentimental Value, 4, 121	11	**1:33.96**	72,540
2002	**Stylish**, 4, 123	J. D. Bailey	La Recherche, 4, 123	Dianehill (Ire), 6, 123	10	1:35.72	71,424
2001	**Iftiraas (GB)**, 4, 118	J. D. Bailey	Gino's Spirits (GB), 5, 118	Solvig, 4, 120	7	1:36.69	70,432
2000	**Don't Be Silly**, 5, 116	J. F. Chavez	Really Polish, 5, 114	Pricearose, 4, 116	8	1:34.78	71,548
1999	**Shires Ende**, 4, 118	J. R. Velazquez	Ashford Castle, 5, 120	Sophie My Love, 4, 123	9	1:35.43	74,152
1998	**Witchful Thinking**, 4, 120	S. J. Sellers	Colcon, 5, 123	Swearingen, 4, 123	10	1:37.23	74,896
1997	**B. A. Valentine**, 4, 114	S. J. Sellers	Striesen, 5, 116	Romy, 6, 123	10	1:36.98	71,796
1996	**Apolda**, 5, 123	J. D. Bailey	Country Cat, 4, 123	Bold Ruritana, 5, 123	8	1:36.50	55,283
1995	**Bold Ruritana**, 5, 123	P. Day	Icy Warning, 5, 116	Rapunzel Runz, 4, 114	10	1:34.64	56,111
1994	**Weekend Madness (Ire)**, 4, 123	C. R. Woods Jr.	Russian Bride, 4, 120	Suspect Terrain, 5, 114	9	1:38.58	55,770
1993	**Lady Blessington (Fr)**, 5, 120	P. Day	You'd Be Surprised, 4, 118	Wassifa (GB), 5, 116	9	1:34.96	37,570

Year	Winner	Jockey	Second	Third	Strs	Time	1st Purse
1992	Quilma (Chi), 5, 120	E. J. Delahoussaye	Behaving Dancer, 5, 123	Radiant Ring, 4, 123	10	1:35.36	$38,285
1991	Foresta, 5, 123	A. T. Cordero Jr.	Coolawin, 5, 118	Primetime North, 4, 120	10	1:36.30	38,870
1990	Foresta, 4, 114	A. T. Cordero Jr.	Saros Brig, 6, 123	Bearly Cooking, 7, 114	5	1:37.20	36,205
1989	Classic Account, 4, 116	P. Day	Fast Forward, 5, 116	R. B. McCurry, 4, 112	4	1:51.20	35,132
1988	Buoy, 3, 123	P. Day	Frosty the Snowman, 3, 115	Cougarized, 3, 123	7	1:43.40	36,725
1987	Fast Forward, 3, 115	P. Day	Sooner Showers, 3, 115	Homebuilder, 3, 115	5	1:43.20	36,043
1983	‡Le Cou Cou, 3, 121	D. L. Howard	High Honors, 3, 121	Common Sense, 3, 121	10	1:49.60	34,125

Formerly named for Churchill Downs's most recognized feature (and corporate logo), the twin spires atop its grandstand. Sponsored by CompUSA Management Co. of Dallas, Texas 2005. Formerly sponsored by Argent Mortgage Co. of Orange, California 2004. Formerly sponsored by CITGO Petroleum Corp. of Tulsa, Oklahoma 2001-'03. Formerly sponsored by Ashland Inc. of Covington, Kentucky 1999. Formerly sponsored by AEGON Group N.V. of The Hague, the Netherlands 1998. Formerly sponsored by Providian Corp. of Louisville, 1995-'97. Formerly sponsored by Capital Holding Corp. (predecessor of Providian Corp.) of Louisville 1988-'94. Twin Spires S. 1983-'87. Capital Holding Twin Spires S. 1988. Capital Holding Twin Spires H. 1989. Capital Holding Mile S. 1990-'91, 1993-'94. Capital Holding S. 1992. Providian Mile S. 1995-'97. Aegon Mile S. 1998. Ashland Mile S. 1999. Churchill Downs Distaff Turf Mile S. 2000. CITGO Distaff Turf Mile S. 2001-'03. Argent Mortgage Distaff Turf Mile S. 2004. Not held 1984-'86. 1⅛ miles 1983, 1989. 1¹/₁₆ miles 1987-'88. Dirt 1983-'89. Three-year-olds 1983-'88. Both sexes 1983-'88. ‡High Honors finished first, DQ to second, 1983. Equaled course record 1992. Course record 1993.

Coolmore Lexington Stakes

Grade 2 in 2005. Keeneland, three-year-olds, 1¹/₁₆ miles, dirt. Held April 23, 2005, with a gross value of $325,000. First held in 1936. First graded in 1986. Stakes record 1:41.06 (1999 Charismatic).

Year	Winner	Jockey	Second	Third	Strs	Time	1st Purse
2005	Coin Silver, 3, 117	J. Castellano	Sort It Out, 3, 117	Storm Surge, 3, 117	7	1:45.76	$201,500
2004	Quintons Gold Rush, 3, 116	J. D. Bailey	Fire Slam, 3, 116	Song of the Sword, 3, 116	14	1:43.82	$201,500
2003	Scrimshaw, 3, 116	E. S. Prado	Eye of the Tiger, 3, 116	Domestic Dispute, 3, 116	7	1:45.47	225,479
2002	Proud Citizen, 3, 116	M. E. Smith	Crimson Hero, 3, 116	Easyfromthegitgo, 3, 116	8	1:44.58	226,083
2001	Keats, 3, 116	L. J. Melancon	‡Griffinite, 3, 116	Bay Eagle, 3, 116	10	1:43.54	230,315
2000	Unshaded, 3, 116	S. J. Sellers	Globalize, 3, 120	Harlan Traveler, 3, 116	8	1:43.72	221,588
1999	Charismatic, 3, 115	J. D. Bailey	Yankee Victor, 3, 115	Finder's Gold, 3, 115	12	1:41.06	234,794
1998	Classic Cat, 3, 114	R. Albarado	Voyamerican, 3, 114	Grand Slam, 3, 123	8	1:42.85	228,300
1997	Touch Gold, 3, 115	G. L. Stevens	Smoke Glacken, 3, 118	Deeds Not Words, 3, 112	5	1:43.27	116,963
1996	City by Night, 3, 113	S. J. Sellers	Prince of Thieves, 3, 118	Roar, 3, 118	11	1:42.39	123,473
1995	Star Standard, 3, 115	P. Day	Royal Mitch, 3, 118	Guadalcanal, 3, 115	5	1:45.02	99,882
1994	Southern Rhythm, 3, 118	G. K. Gomez	Soul of the Matter, 3, 118	Ulises, 3, 113	8	1:45.72	85,095
1993	Grand Jewel, 3, 118	J. D. Bailey	El Bakan, 3, 113	Truth of It All, 3, 118	9	1:43.61	87,219
1992	My Luck Runs North, 3, 115	R. D. Lopez	Lure, 3, 118	Agincourt, 3, 115	5	1:44.06	89,083
1991	Hansel, 3, 121	J. D. Bailey	Shotgun Harry J., 3, 115	Speedy Cure, 3, 118	4	1:42.66	86,743
1990	Home At Last, 3, 118	J. D. Bailey	Pleasant Tap, 3, 115	Thirty Slews, 3, 116	9	1:43.40	73,385
1989	Notation, 3, 115	P. Day	Bionic Prospect, 3, 114	Charlie Barley, 3, 118	8	1:44.40	71,663
1988	Risen Star, 3, 118	J. Vasquez	Forty Niner, 3, 121	Stalwars, 3, 118	5	1:42.80	68,673
1987	War, 3, 115	W. H. McCauley	Candi's Gold, 3, 115	Momentus, 3, 118	6	1:44.40	96,843
1986	Wise Times, 3, 112	K. K. Allen	Country Light, 3, 118	Blue Buckaroo, 3, 112	9	1:44.80	71,793
1985	Stephan's Odyssey, 3, 118	L. A. Pincay Jr.	Tajawa, 3, 112	Northern Bid, 3, 112	7	1:42.60	34,775
1984	He is a Great Deal, 3, 118	J. C. Espinoza	Swale, 3, 123	Timely Advocate, 3, 112	5	1:45.40	34,450

Named for the city of Lexington, Kentucky. Sponsored by John and Susan Magnier's Coolmore Stud in County Tipperary, Ireland, 1998-2005. Grade 3 1986-'87. Not held 1938-'83. 6 furlongs 1936-'37. Two-year-olds 1936-'37. ‡Mr. John finished second, DQ to eighth, 2001. Held as overnight handicap 1940.

Cotillion Handicap

Grade 2 in 2005. Philadelphia Park, three-year-olds, fillies, 1¹/₁₆ miles, dirt. Held October 2, 2004, with a gross value of $250,000. First held in 1969. First graded in 1973. Stakes record 1:41.68 (2004 Ashado).

Year	Winner	Jockey	Second	Third	Strs	Time	1st Purse
2004	Ashado, 3, 124	E. Coa	Ender's Sister, 3, 117	My Lordship, 3, 115	7	1:41.68	$150,000
2003	Fast Cookie, 3, 116	N. Santagata	Ladyecho, 3, 116	Savedbythelight, 3, 117	5	1:45.83	150,000
2002	Smok'n Frolic, 3, 118	J. A. Velez Jr.	Pupil, 3, 114	Jilbab, 3, 120	4	1:44.27	150,000
2001	Mystic Lady, 3, 121	E. Coa	Zonk, 3, 117	Celtic Melody, 3, 115	8	1:43.86	150,000
2000	Jostle, 3, 124	M. E. Smith	Gold for My Gal, 3, 112	Prized Stamp, 3, 114	7	1:42.54	120,000
1999	Skipping Around, 3, 114	M. J. McCarthy	Strolling Belle, 3, 120	Waltz, 3, 114	10	1:43.45	120,000
1998	Lu Ravi, 3, 121	W. Martinez	Sister Act, 3, 115	Let, 3, 117	8	1:43.55	90,000
1997	Snit, 3, 116	R. E. Colton	Proud Run, 3, 116	Salt It, 3, 117	9	1:43.91	90,000
1996	Double Dee's, 3, 111	F. Leon	Ginny Lynn, 3, 121	Princess Eloise, 3, 113	5	1:44.69	90,000
1995	Clear Mandate, 3, 113	J. C. Ferrer	Blue Sky Princess, 3, 114	Country Cat, 3, 118	11	1:42.87	98,730
1994	Sovereign Kitty, 3, 118	W. H. McCauley	Cinnamon Sugar (Ire), 3, 120	Cavada, 3, 114	8	1:43.52	97,440
1993	Jacody, 3, 118	T. G. Turner	Aztec Hill, 3, 121	Cearas Dancer, 3, 109	4	1:43.22	95,520
1992	Star Minister, 3, 117	A. J. Seefeldt	Diamond Duo, 3, 121	Squirm, 3, 116	7	1:44.06	80,760
1990	Valay Maid, 3, 119	L. Saumell	Toffeelee, 3, 115	Trumpet's Blare, 3, 116	4	1:43.80	81,600
1989	Sharp Dance, 3, 115	K. Castaneda	Misty Ivor, 3, 113	Tactile, 3, 117	11	1:45.80	81,900
1988	Aquaba, 3, 115	J. Cruguet	Ice Tech, 3, 113	Mother of Eight, 3, 114	8	1:44.40	79,320
1987	‡Silent Turn, 3, 118	R. P. Romero	Sacahuista, 3, 119	Single Blade, 3, 117	8	1:42.80	65,280

Year	Winner	Jockey	Second	Third	Strs	Time	1st Purse
1986	Toes Knows, 3, 119	D. Wright	Life At the Top, 3, 121	I'm Sweets, 3, 119	8	1:42.80	$65,880
1985	Koluctoo's Jill, 3, 119	W. H. McCauley	Overwhelming, 3, 115	Tabayour, 3, 118	8	1:42.80	65,520
1984	Squan Song, 3, 122	R. Z. Hernandez	Given, 3, 122	You're Too Special, 3, 113	9	1:42.80	60,945
	Dowery, 3, 122	V. A. Bracciale Jr.	Duo Disco, 3, 122	Hot Milk, 3, 117	9	1:42.60	60,945
1983	Quixotic Lady, 3, 122	G. McCarron	Lady Hawthorn, 3, 117	Springtime Sharon, 3, 117	8	1:42.80	33,180
1982	Lady Eleanor, 3, 122	C. Perret	Smart Heiress, 3, 122	Glass House, 3, 117	12	1:45.00	34,800
1981	Truly Bound, 3, 121	R. J. Franklin	Pukka Princess, 3, 118	Debonair Dancer, 3, 118	8	1:42.80	33,810
1980	Sugar and Spice, 3, 116	G. Martens	Pepi Wiley, 3, 118	Nijit, 3, 116	8	1:45.00	34,800
1979	Alada, 3, 116	J. Fell	Too Many Sweets, 3, 116	Heavenly Ade, 3, 116	6	1:43.80	33,090
1978	Queen Lib, 3, 121	D. MacBeth	Silken Delight, 3, 116	Sharp Belle, 3, 116	11	1:43.20	28,620
1977	Suede Shoe, 3, 116	A. S. Black	Raise Old Glory, 3, 113	Bafflin Lil, 3, 116	11	1:42.60	27,930
1976	Revidere, 3, 118	J. Vasquez	Critical Miss, 3, 116	Hay Patcher, 3, 116	8	1:44.00	20,190
1975	My Juliet, 3, 116	D. Brumfield	Hot n Nasty, 3, 116	Gala Lil, 3, 118	7	1:43.60	20,160
1974	Honky Star, 3, 121	D. G. McHargue	Special Team, 3, 118	Kudara, 3, 121	7	1:44.00	32,910
1973	Lilac Hill, 3, 113	D. MacBeth	Ladies Agreement, 3, 114	Suzi Sunshine, 3, 114	10	1:43.60	34,590

A cotillion is a traditional dance where debutantes are formally presented to society. Grade 1 1973-'74. Grade 3 1981-'88. Cotillion S. 1975-'84. Held at Liberty Bell 1969-'74. Held at Keystone 1975-'84. Not held 1991. Two divisions 1984. ‡Sacahuista finished first, DQ to second, 1987.

Count Fleet Sprint Handicap

Grade 3 in 2005. Oaklawn Park, four-year-olds and up, 6 furlongs, dirt. Held April 14, 2005, with a gross value of $150,000. First held in 1974. First graded in 1986. Stakes record 1:08.18 (2001 Bonapaw).

Year	Winner	Jockey	Second	Third	Strs	Time	1st Purse
2005	Top Commander, 5, 113	C. Gonzalez	Forest Grove, 4, 114	That Tat, 7, 119	8	1:08.74	$90,000
2004	Shake You Down, 6, 121	R. A. Dominguez	Where's the Ring, 5, 115	Aloha Bold, 6, 114	6	1:09.27	90,000
2003	Beau's Town, 5, 122	J. Theriot	Honor Me, 5, 116	Sand Ridge, 8, 114	6	1:09.01	90,000
2002	Explicit, 5, 116	L. J. Meche	Entepreneur, 5, 115	Junior Deputy, 4, 113	5	1:08.60	90,000
2001	Bonapaw, 5, 118	G. Melancon	Chindi, 7, 114	Bidis, 4, 117	7	1:08.18	75,000
2000	†Show Me the Stage, 4, 116	D. R. Flores	Smolderin Heart, 5, 115	Vinnie's Boy, 4, 114	6	1:09.62	75,000
1999	Reraise, 4, 122	C. S. Nakatani	Run Johnny, 7, 114	E J Harley, 7, 115	6	1:08.59	75,000
1998	Chindi, 4, 113	D. R. Pettinger	E J Harley, 6, 113	Western Fame, 6, 115	8	1:09.77	75,000
1997	High Stakes Player, 5, 120	K. J. Desormeaux	†Capote Belle, 4, 116	Victor Avenue, 4, 116	7	1:08.86	90,000
1996	Concept Win, 6, 116	G. L. Stevens	Roythelittleone, 4, 114	Spiritbound, 4, 113	7	1:09.06	90,000
1995	Hot Jaws, 5, 113	C. H. Borel	Demaloot Demashoot, 5, 116	Mr. Cooperative, 4, 114	9	1:09.49	90,000
1994	Demaloot Demashoot, 4, 115	M. E. Smith	Honor the Hero, 6, 117	Sir Hutch, 4, 118	8	1:08.39	90,000
1993	Approach, 6, 116	P. Day	Ponche, 4, 113	Never Wavering, 4, 110	13	1:09.64	90,000
1992	Gray Slewpy, 4, 117	K. J. Desormeaux	Potentiality, 6, 116	Hidden Tomahawk, 4, 115	7	1:08.97	60,000
1991	Overpeer, 7, 122	P. Day	Silent Reflex, 5, 113	Peaked, 6, 118	7	1:08.87	60,000
1990	Malagra, 4, 117	V. L. Smith	Pentelicus, 6, 115	Sunny Blossom, 5, 120	10	1:08.80	60,000
1989	Twice Around, 4, 116	C. H. Borel	Be a Agent, 5, 117	Never Forgotten, 5, 114	10	1:09.20	60,000
1988	Salt Dome, 5, 116	L. Snyder	Pewter, 4, 113	Bold Pac Man, 4, 112	9	1:08.60	60,000
1987	Sun Master, 6, 117	G. L. Stevens	Rocky Marriage, 7, 116	Chief Steward, 6, 118	3	1:09.40	69,540
1986	Mister Gennaro, 5, 115	F. Olivares	Beveled, 4, 114	Charging Falls, 5, 125	9	1:08.80	71,100
1985	Taylor's Special, 4, 123	R. P. Romero	Mt. Livermore, 4, 119	T. H. Bend, 4, 110	10	1:08.40	98,280
1984	Dave's Friend, 9, 122	E. J. Delahoussaye	†All Sold Out, 5, 114	Lucky Salvation, 4, 113	8	1:09.00	70,260
1983	Dave's Friend, 8, 124	L. Snyder	General Jimmy, 4, 117	Liberty Lane, 5, 113	9	1:10.00	70,320
1982	Sandbagger, 4, 114	D. Haire	Blue Water Line, 4, 117	Lockjaw, 4, 116	10	1:12.00	39,240
1981	General Custer, 5, 111	L. Snyder	Avenging Gossip, 4, 111	Be a Prospect, 4, 112	7	1:10.40	34,470
1980	Silent Dignity, 4, 114	S. Maple	Gustoso, 5, 111	J. Burns, 5, 115	7	1:11.00	34,460
1979	Amadevil, 5, 114	T. G. Greer	Little Reb, 4, 120	Sean's Song, 4, 114	9	1:11.20	34,890
1978	Last Buzz, 5, 120	A. Rini	Best Person, 4, 117	Sucha Pleasure, 4, 118	10	1:11.00	33,390
1977	Silver Hope, 6, 120	R. L. Turcotte	Dr's Enjoy Dollars, 5, 116	Brets Kicker, 6, 113	9	1:10.40	18,480
1976	Brets Kicker, 5, 111	J. D. Bailey	Silver Doctor, 6, 118	Mr. Barb, 4, 110	6	1:10.00	17,640
1975	Prince Astro, 4, 118	D. W. Whited	Silver Doctor, 5, 117	Faneuil Boy, 4, 112	7	1:10.00	18,030
1974	Barbizon Streak, 6, 114	R. Wilson	Pleasure Castle, 4, 120	Pesty Jay, 6, 122	7	1:11.00	17,370

Named for Mrs. John D. Hertz's 1943 Horse of the Year, '43 Triple Crown winner, and '51 leading North American sire Count Fleet (1940 c. by Reigh Count). Grade 2 1988-'89. Count Fleet H. 1974-'82. Three-year-olds and up 1974-'75. †Denotes female.

Dahlia Handicap

Grade 2 in 2005. Hollywood Park, three-year-olds and up, fillies and mares, 1¹/₁₆ miles, dirt (originally scheduled on the turf). Held December 20, 2004, with a gross value of $150,000. First held in 1982. First graded in 1984. Stakes record 1:42.11 (2004 Festival [Jpn]).

Year	Winner	Jockey	Second	Third	Strs	Time	1st Purse
2004	Festival (Jpn), 5, 111	D. Sorenson	Irgunette (Aus), 5, 113	Belle Ange (Fr), 3, 114	5	1:42.11	$90,000
2003	Katdogawn (GB), 3, 116	M. E. Smith	Personal Legend, 3, 115	Betty's Wish, 3, 117	10	1:41.52	90,000
2002	dh-Surya, 4, 118	P. A. Valenzuela		Honestly Darling, 4, 114	9	1:44.55	60,000
	dh-Tout Charmant, 6, 119	A. O. Solis					
2001	Verruma (Brz), 5, 115	G. K. Gomez	Vencera (Fr), 4, 115	Heads Will Roll (GB), 3, 117	8	1:43.24	90,000
2000	Follow the Money, 4, 115	V. Espinoza	Smooth Player, 4, 120	Beautiful Noise, 4, 117	7	1:40.71	90,000
1999	Lady At Peace, 3, 113	G. K. Gomez	Cyrillic, 4, 117	Country Garden (GB), 4, 115	5	1:41.50	90,000

Year	Winner	Jockey	Second	Third	Strs	Time	1st Purse
1998	Tuzla (Fr), 4, 119	C. S. Nakatani	Sonja's Faith (Ire), 4, 118	Curitiba, 4, 115	5	1:41.75	$60,000
1997	Golden Arches (Fr), 3, 117	C. J. McCarron	Sonja's Faith (Ire), 3, 113	Traces of Gold, 5, 116	8	1:41.09	60,000
1996	Sixieme Sens, 4, 116	C. S. Nakatani	Grafin, 5, 116	Admise (Fr), 4, 121	8	1:42.37	66,600
1995	Didina (GB), 3, 115	E. J. Delahoussaye	Dirca (Ire), 3, 113	Rapunzel Runz, 4, 116	10	1:45.20	68,300
1994	Skimble, 5, 118	E. J. Delahoussaye	Queens Court Queen, 5, 118	Shir Dar (Fr), 4, 115	8	1:42.33	66,000
1993	Kalita Melody (GB), 5, 115	C. A. Black	Vinista, 3, 116	Gumpher, 5, 116	7	1:44.73	64,500
1992	Kostroma (Ire), 6, 124	G. L. Stevens	Vijaya, 5, 114	Guiza, 5, 116	8	1:41.40	66,500
1991	Re Toss (Arg), 4, 115	C. S. Nakatani	Elegance, 4, 115	Gaelic Bird (Fr), 4, 114	11	1:40.77	70,400
1990	Petalia, 5, 113	K. J. Desormeaux	Bequest, 4, 117	Island Jamboree, 4, 113	6	1:41.40	48,900
	Little Brianne, 5, 119	J. A. Garcia	Stylish Star, 4, 119	Girl of France (GB), 4, 115	8	1:40.60	50,900
1989	Stylish Star, 3, 116	C. J. McCarron	Ariosa, 3, 113	Sugarplum Gal, 4, 114	9	1:40.40	51,600
	Saros Brig, 5, 114	G. L. Stevens	Nikishka, 4, 120	Beat, 4, 115	7	1:40.40	49,600
1988	Balbonella (Fr), 4, 117	F. Toro	Goodbye Halo, 3, 120	Pen Bal Lady (GB), 4, 117	7	1:42.80	75,100
1987	Top Corsage, 4, 118	J. A. Santos	Any Song (Ire), 4, 116	Aberuschka (Ire), 5, 120	6	1:43.20	48,700
	Invited Guest (Ire), 3, 114	W. Shoemaker	Secuencia (Chi), 5, 115	Smooch (GB), 4, 117	9	1:43.40	71,950
1986	Aberuschka (Ire), 4, 122	P. A. Valenzuela	An Empress, 3, 117	Reloy, 3, 118	7	1:41.60	80,740
1985	Capricorn Belle (GB), 4, 118	C. J. McCarron	Justicara (Ire), 4, 118	Solva (GB), 4, 115	9	1:41.60	66,200
1984	Lina Cavalieri (GB), 4, 117	E. J. Delahoussaye	Pampas (Ire), 4, 115	Salt Spring (Arg), 5, 117	12	1:44.20	53,050
1983	Geraldine's Store, 4, 118	J. Samyn	Northerly Glow, 4, 111	Satin Ribera, 6, 115	8	1:42.40	32,500
	First Advance, 4, 114	T. Lipham	Absentia, 4, 116	Bersid, 5, 122	10	1:42.00	33,500
1982	Sangue (Ire), 4, 122	L. A. Pincay Jr.	Star Pastures (GB), 4, 118	Pat's Joy, 4, 115	7	1:41.40	31,900
	Milingo, 3, 114	T. Lipham	Pink Safir (Fr), 6, 119	Berry Bush, 5, 119	10	1:42.60	33,400

Named for Nelson Bunker Hunt's 1973, '74 English Horse of the Year, '74 North American champion grass horse, and '76 Hollywood Invitational H. (G1) winner Dahlia (1970 f. by *Vaguely Noble). Grade 3 1984-'89. Grade 3 in 2004 when taken off turf. Two divisions 1982-'83, 1987, 1989-'90. Dead heat for first 2002.

Darley Alcibiades Stakes

Grade 2 in 2005. Keeneland, two-year-olds, fillies, 1 1/16 miles, dirt. Held October 8, 2004, with a gross value of $400,000. First held in 1952. First graded in 1973. Stakes record 1:42.24 (1998 Silverbulletday).

Year	Winner	Jockey	Second	Third	Strs	Time	1st Purse
2004	Runway Model, 2, 118	R. Bejarano	Sharp Lisa, 2, 118	In the Gold, 2, 118	10	1:44.31	$248,000
2003	Be Gentle, 2, 118	C. H. Velasquez	Galloping Gal, 2, 118	Deb's Charm, 2, 118	7	1:45.51	248,000
2002	Westerly Breeze, 2, 118	R. Albarado	Ruby's Reception, 2, 118	Final Round, 2, 118	9	1:46.90	276,024
2001	Take Charge Lady, 2, 118	A. J. D'Amico	Never Out, 2, 118	Cunning Play, 2, 118	11	1:46.23	280,736
2000	She's a Devil Due, 2, 118	M. Guidry	Nasty Storm, 2, 118	Cash Deal, 2, 118	9	1:44.86	270,320
1999	Scratch Pad, 2, 118	W. Martinez	Rare Beauty, 2, 118	Cash Run, 2, 118	8	1:44.16	274,288
1998	Silverbulletday, 2, 118	G. L. Stevens	Extended Applause, 2, 118	Grand Deed, 2, 118	11	1:42.24	281,976
1997	Countess Diana, 2, 118	S. J. Sellers	Lily O'Gold, 2, 118	Beautiful Pleasure, 2, 118	6	1:45.39	266,600
1996	Southern Playgirl, 2, 118	R. P. Romero	‡Screamer, 2, 118	Private Pursuit, 2, 118	7	1:46.94	168,330
1995	Cara Rafaela, 2, 118	P. Day	Birr, 2, 118	Gold Sunrise, 2, 118	10	1:44.43	139,252
1994	Post It, 2, 118	S. Maple	Morris Code, 2, 118	Cat Appeal, 2, 118	6	1:46.33	66,650
1993	Stellar Cat, 2, 118	S. J. Sellers	Slew Kitty Slew, 2, 118	Beau Blush, 2, 118	6	1:44.68	122,200
1992	Eliza, 2, 118	P. A. Valenzuela	Avie's Shadow, 2, 118	True Affair, 2, 118	7	1:43.30	122,200
1991	Spinning Round, 2, 118	J. M. Johnson	Queens Court Queen, 2, 118	Midnight Society, 2, 118	5	1:47.38	122,200
1990	Private Treasure, 2, 118	J. D. Bailey	Through Flight, 2, 118	Southern Bar Girl, 2, 118	8	1:43.80	173,420
1989	Special Happening, 2, 118	J. A. Santos	Talltaleday, 2, 118	Fashion Delight, 2, 118	7	1:44.60	141,375
1988	Wonders Delight, 2, 118	G. L. Stevens	Affirmed Classic, 2, 118	Seattle Meteor, 2, 118	7	1:46.40	130,000
1987	Terra Incognita, 2, 118	D. E. Foster	Epitome, 2, 118	Pearlie Gold, 2, 118	8	1:44.60	102,996
1986	Zero Minus, 2, 118	S. Hawley	Bound, 2, 118	Desirous, 2, 118	7	1:45.20	125,567
1985	Silent Account, 2, 118	K. K. Allen	Steal a Kiss, 2, 118	Python, 2, 118	10	1:46.20	132,321
1984	Foxy Deen, 2, 118	D. Montoya	Weekend Delight, 2, 118	Dusty Heart, 2, 118	12	1:45.60	117,224
1983	Lucky Lucky Lucky, 2, 118	J. Vasquez	Flippers, 2, 118	Geevilla, 2, 118	10	1:47.00	119,675
1982	Jelly Bean Holiday, 2, 118	D. Brumfield	Quarrel Over, 2, 118	Issues n' Answers, 2, 118	7	1:45.80	97,825
1981	Apalachee Honey, 2, 118	W. Shoemaker	Chilling Thought, 2, 118	Casual, 2, 118	10	1:45.20	102,034
1980	Sweet Revenge, 2, 118	J. Velasquez	Expressive Dance, 2, 118	Masters Dream, 2, 118	6	1:28.00	99,190
1979	Salud, 2, 118	J. C. Espinoza	Diorama, 2, 118	Sweetest Roman, 2, 118	6	1:28.20	93,503
1978	Angel Island, 2, 119	E. J. Delahoussaye	Terlingua, 2, 119	Too Many Sweets, 2, 119	7	1:26.40	89,619
1977	L'Alezane, 2, 119	R. Turcotte	Robalea, 2, 119	No No-Nos, 2, 119	5	1:27.20	80,990
1976	Sans Supplement, 2, 119	W. Gavidia	Avilion, 2, 119	Resolver, 2, 119	10	1:27.60	89,733
1975	Optimistic Gal, 2, 119	D. G. McHargue	Old Goat, 2, 119	Answer, 2, 119	9	1:28.00	79,593
1974	Hope of Glory, 2, 119	J. Nichols	Funny Cat, 2, 119	Snow Doll, 2, 119	9	1:27.20	54,197
1973	City Girl, 2, 119	E. Fires	Fairway Fable, 2, 119	Quick Cure, 2, 119	8	1:27.80	44,924

Named for Hal Price Headley's 1929 consensus champion two-year-old filly, '30 champion three-year-old filly, and '30 Kentucky Oaks winner Alcibiades (1927 f. by Supremus). Sponsored by Sheikh Mohammed bin Rashid al Maktoum's Darley 2003-'04. Formerly sponsored by Walmac Int'l. of Lexington 1997-2002. Grade 3 1973-'75. About 7 furlongs 1952-'80. ‡Private Pursuit finished second, DQ to third, 1996.

Davona Dale Stakes

Grade 2 in 2005. Gulfstream Park, three-year-olds, fillies, 1 1/8 miles, dirt. Held February 5, 2005, with a gross value of $150,000. First held in 1988. First graded in 1993. Stakes record 1:50.20 (2005 Sis City).

Year	Winner	Jockey	Second	Third	Strs	Time	1st Purse
2005	Sis City, 3, 121	J. R. Velazquez	In the Gold, 3, 117	Jill Robin L, 3, 117	6	1:50.20	$90,000

2004 **Miss Coronado**, 3, 117	C. H. Velasquez	Eye Dazzler, 3, 115	Society Selection, 3, 121	7	1:44.62	$90,000
2003 **Yell**, 3, 117	J. R. Velazquez	Ivanavinalot, 3, 121	Gold Player, 3, 115	5	1:44.96	90,000
2002 **Ms Brookski**, 3, 121	R. B. Homeister Jr.	Colonial Glitter, 3, 117	French Satin, 3, 115	9	1:45.14	60,000
2001 **Latour**, 3, 112	J. R. Velazquez	Gold Mover, 3, 116	Courageous Maiden, 3, 113	7	1:45.51	60,000
2000 **Cash Run**, 3, 118	J. D. Bailey	Regally Appealing, 3, 116	Secret Status, 3, 114	9	1:40.37	60,000
1999 **Three Ring**, 3, 118	J. R. Velazquez	Golden Temper, 3, 113	Gold From the West, 3, 116	5	1:41.53	60,000
1998 **Diamond On the Run**, 3, 112	P. Day	Uanme, 3, 114	Dixie Melody, 3, 113	10	1:42.65	60,000
1997 **Glitter Woman**, 3, 114	M. E. Smith	City Band, 3, 121	Southern Playgirl, 3, 121	6	1:39.31	60,000
1996 **Plum Country**, 3, 118	P. Day	‡My Flag, 3, 118	La Rosa, 3, 118	9	1:42.08	60,000
1995 **Mia's Hope**, 3, 114	K. L. Chapman	Minister Wife, 3, 121	Culver City, 3, 113	6	1:43.26	60,000
1994 **Cut the Charm**, 3, 118	J. D. Bailey	She Rides Tonite, 3, 114	Delightful Bet, 3, 113	8	1:41.44	60,000
1993 **Lunar Spook**, 3, 118	M. Guidry	Boots 'n Jackie, 3, 121	In Her Glory, 3, 112	7	1:42.09	30,000
1992 **Miss Legality**, 3, 116	J. A. Krone	November Snow, 3, 114	Spectacular Sue, 3, 114	8	1:42.00	30,000
1991 **Fancy Ribbons**, 3, 118	C. Perret	Hula Pride, 3, 114	Designated Dancer, 3, 116	9	1:41.10	45,420
1990 **Big Pride**, 3, 112	E. Fires	Crowned, 3, 121	Sonic Gray, 3, 112	6	1:26.00	21,000
1989 **Waggley**, 6, 122	J. Samyn	Plate Queen, 4, 113	Ataentsic, 5, 113	7	1:22.60	20,640
1988 **Charming Tigress**, 5, 115	P. Day	Polar Wind, 4, 117	No Doublet, 5, 115	8	1:24.60	21,069
Cadillacing, 4, 122	R. P. Romero	Easter Mary, 4, 115	Saucey Missy, 5, 117	9	1:23.00	21,429

Named for Calumet Farm's 1979 champion three-year-old filly and '79 Filly Triple Crown winner, and '79 Bonnie Miss S. winner Davona Dale (1976 f. by Best Turn). Grade 3 1993-'97. Davona Dale H. 1988. Davona Dale Breeders' Cup S. 1989, 1991. 7 furlongs 1988-'90. 1 mile 70 yards 1991-2000. Four-year-olds and up 1988. Three-year-olds and up 1989. Fillies and mares 1988, 1989. Two divisions 1988. ‡Rare Blend finished second, DQ to sixth, 1996.

Debutante Stakes

Grade 3 in 2005. Churchill Downs, two-year-olds, fillies, 5½ furlongs, dirt. Held July 4, 2004, with a gross value of $110,800. First held in 1889. First graded in 1996. Stakes record 1:02.52 (2001 Cashier's Dream).

Year	Winner	Jockey	Second	Third	Strs	Time	1st Purse
2004	**Classic Elegance**, 2, 117	P. Day	Paragon Queen, 2, 117	Cool Spell, 2, 117	9	1:04.18	$68,696
2003	**Be Gentle**, 2, 117	C. H. Velasquez	Renaissance Lady, 2, 117	Sweet Jo Jo, 2, 117	8	1:03.96	68,758
2002	**Awesome Humor**, 2, 115	C. H. Borel	Vibs, 2, 115	Attemptress, 2, 115	7	1:03.45	67,890
2001	**Cashier's Dream**, 2, 118	D. J. Meche	Lakeside Cup, 2, 115	Colonial Glitter, 2, 115	8	**1:02.52**	68,510
2000	**Gold Mover**, 2, 121	C. Perret	Princess Belle, 2, 115	Tricky Elaine, 2, 115	9	1:03.79	69,626
1999	**Chilukki**, 2, 121	W. Martinez	Miss Wineshine, 2, 112	Cecilia's Crown, 2, 115	9	1:03.66	69,998
1998	**Silverbulletday**, 2, 115	W. Martinez	The Happy Hopper, 2, 115	Mancari's Rose, 2, 115	9	1:04.70	69,502
1997	**Love Lock**, 2, 115	P. Day	Countess Diana, 2, 115	Quick Lap, 2, 115	13	1:03.84	72,478
1996	**Move**, 2, 121	P. Day	Sarah's Prospector, 2, 115	Live Your Best, 2, 115	10	1:05.66	73,840
1995	**Golden Attraction**, 2, 115	D. M. Barton	Western Dreamer, 2, 121	Tipically Irish, 2, 115	9	1:04.19	70,948
1994	**Chargedupsycamore**, 2, 121	P. Day	Phone Bird, 2, 116	Our Gem, 2, 116	9	1:05.24	54,405
1993	**Fly Love**, 2, 116	B. E. Bartram	Miss Ra He Ra, 2, 116	Astas Foxy Lady, 2, 121	11	1:05.23	37,635
1992	**Hollywood Wildcat**, 2, 116	F. A. Arguello Jr.	Cosmic Speed Queen, 2, 118	Dixie Band, 2, 115	14	1:06.02	38,480
1991	**Greenhaven Lane**, 2, 112	K. Tsuchiya	Moment of Grace, 2, 112	One for Smoke, 2, 116	11	1:06.23	36,953
1990	**Barbara's Nemesis**, 2, 116	J. Deegan	Gracielle, 2, 112	Cosmic Music, 2, 112	10	1:12.00	36,693
1989	**Icy Folly**, 2, 118	K. K. Allen	Hard Freeze, 2, 118	Lucy's Glory, 2, 118	14	1:11.20	37,993
1988	**Seaquay**, 2, 114	R. M. Ehrlinspiel	Weekend Spree, 2, 118	Coax Chelsie, 2, 112	8	1:11.20	35,718
1987	**Bold Lady Anne**, 2, 118	J. Davidson	Over All, 2, 118	Penny's Growl, 2, 114	7	1:11.60	25,773
	Dark Silver, 2, 116	M. McDowell	She's Freezing, 2, 116	Saved by Grace, 2, 116	9	1:12.60	26,260
1986	**Burnished Bright**, 2, 121	P. Day	Before Sundown, 2, 118	Shivering Gal, 2, 115	7	1:11.20	46,810
1985	**Tricky Fingers**, 2, 115	L. J. Melancon	Likker Is Quikker, 2, 118	Time for Honor, 2, 115	12	1:05.20	31,013
1984	**Knot**, 2, 115	K. K. Allen	Don't Joke, 2, 112	Off Shore Breeze, 2, 115	10	1:06.40	22,393
1983	**Arabizon**, 2, 115	L. Moyers	Ark, 2, 115	Starafar, 2, 113	9	1:05.80	22,181
1982	**Ice Fantasy**, 2, 115	P. A. Johnson	Wrong Answer, 2, 115	Fifth Affair, 2, 121	12	1:04.60	20,735
1981	**Pure Platinum**, 2, 119	P. Day	Miss Preakness, 2, 119	Cypress Bay, 2, 119	10	:58.80	19,939
1980	**Excitable Lady**, 2, 119	D. Brumfield	Masters Dream, 2, 119	Bend the Times, 2, 119	7	:58.60	19,484
1979	**Lissy**, 2, 114	M. S. Sellers	Barbizon's Flower, 2, 119	Happy Hollie, 2, 119	13	:59.80	20,426
1978	**Nervous John**, 2, 122	C. J. McCarron	Porpourie, 2, 114	Rainbow Streak, 2, 122	7	:58.40	14,658
1977	**Sweet Little Lady**, 2, 122	R. Turcotte	Sahsie, 2, 119	‡Crystalan, 2, 122	8	:58.00	14,706
1976	**Olden**, 2, 122	R. Breen	Jungle Angel, 2, 119	Every Move, 2, 114	9	:58.80	14,950
1975	**Answer**, 2, 119	M. Hole	Pink Jade, 2, 122	Turn Over, 2, 119	8	:58.20	16,283
1974	**Sun and Snow**, 2, 119	E. Guerin	Floral Princess, 2, 114	Classy Note, 2, 119	13	:59.40	17,794
1973	**Me and Connie**, 2, 124	J. Nichols	Bundler, 2, 119	Shanjar, 2, 114	7	:58.20	16,835

Young women making their first formal appearance in society are known as debutantes. Churchill Downs Debutante S. 1928. Not held 1932-'37. 4 furlongs 1895-1922. 4½ furlongs 1923-'25. 5 furlongs 1926-'81. 6 furlongs 1986-'90. Two divisions 1987. ‡Miss Poodle Pup finished third, DQ to fourth, 1977. Equaled track record 1997, 1999. Track record 2001.

Delaware Handicap

Grade 2 in 2005. Delaware Park, three-year-olds and up, fillies and mares, 1¼ miles, dirt. Held July 18, 2004, with a gross value of $750,900. First held in 1937. First graded in 1973. Stakes record 1:59.80 (1987 Coup de Fusil).

Year	Winner	Jockey	Second	Third	Strs	Time	1st Purse
2004	**Summer Wind Dancer**, 4, 116	V. Espinoza	Roar Emotion, 4, 117	Misty Sixes, 6, 116	8	2:03.63	$450,000
2003	**Wild Spirit (Chi)**, 4, 117	J. D. Bailey	Take Charge Lady, 4, 120	Shiny Sheet, 5, 112	4	2:02.95	450,000
2002	**Summer Colony**, 4, 118	J. R. Velazquez	Your Out, 4, 113	Two Item Limit, 4, 115	9	2:04.52	360,000
2001	**Irving's Baby**, 4, 113	R. A. Dominguez	Under the Rug, 6, 115	Lazy Slusan, 6, 121	6	2:05.21	360,000

Year	Winner	Jockey	Second	Third	Strs	Time	1st Purse
2000	Lu Ravi, 5, 117	P. Day	Tap to Music, 5, 116	Silverbulletday, 4, 119	8	2:02.21	$360,000
1999	Tap to Music, 4, 116	P. Day	Keeper Hill, 4, 120	Unbridled Hope, 5, 114	13	2:02.15	300,000
1998	Amarillo, 4, 110	J. A. Krone	Tuxedo Junction, 5, 115	Timely Broad, 4, 110	9	2:04.37	300,000
1997	Power Play, 5, 114	L. C. Reynolds	Gold n Delicious, 4, 115	Effectiveness, 4, 113	11	2:03.40	210,000
1996	Urbane, 4, 117	A. O. Solis	Alcovy, 6, 117	Shoop, 5, 115	13	2:01.89	180,000
1995	Night Fax, 4, 108	J. D. Carle	Cavada, 4, 113	It's Personal, 5, 114	8	2:02.98	95,070
1994	With a Wink, 4, 114	R. Migliore	Passing Vice, 4, 115	Alphabulous, 5, 111	9	2:03.37	95,130
1993	Green Darlin, 4, 113	M. J. Luzzi	Girl On a Mission, 4, 116	Starry Val, 4, 112	11	2:03.76	96,300
1992	Brilliant Brass, 5, 117	E. S. Prado	Train Robbery, 5, 111	Risen Colony, 4, 113	6	2:03.11	93,780
1991	Crowned, 4, 117	R. Wilson	Maskra's Lady, 4, 114	Tia Juanita, 5, 113	8	2:04.01	69,420
1990	Seattle Dawn, 4, 115	R. E. Colton	Warfie, 4, 112	Thirty Eight Go Go, 5, 115	7	2:03.00	68,160
1989	Nastique, 5, 120	E. Maple	Colonial Waters, 4, 117	Thirty Eight Go Go, 4, 118	4	2:01.20	64,890
1988	Nastique, 4, 116	E. Maple	Ms. Eloise, 5, 117	Lawyer Talk, 4, 112	7	2:07.60	67,410
1987	Coup de Fusil, 5, 114	A. T. Cordero Jr.	Steal a Kiss, 4, 113	Catatonic, 5, 118	8	1:59.80	68,760
1986	Shocker T., 4, 122	G. St. Leon	Endear, 4, 122	Leecoo, 5, 112	6	2:02.20	69,120
1985	Basie, 4, 110	J. Cruguet	Heatherten, 6, 126	Life's Magic, 4, 122	5	2:02.00	93,360
1984	Adored, 4, 120	L. A. Pincay Jr.	Mademoiselle Forli, 5, 114	Weekend Surprise, 4, 111	6	2:03.20	94,680
1983	May Day Eighty, 4, 115	J. Vasquez	Try Something New, 4, 116	Broom Dance, 4, 119	6	2:03.20	66,720
1982	Jameela, 6, 121	J. L. Kaenel	Zvetlana, 4, 111	Love Sign, 5, 125	9	2:02.60	74,523
1981	Relaxing, 5, 119	A. T. Cordero Jr.	Wistful, 4, 121	Lady of Promise, 4, 111	10	2:01.00	75,075
1980	Heavenly Ade, 4, 112	J. D. Bailey	Croquis, 4, 112	Blitey, 4, 113	9	2:00.00	93,893
1979	Likely Exchange, 5, 112	M. S. Sellers	Sans Critique, 5, 111	Plains and Simple, 4, 110	9	2:03.40	73,938
1978	Late Bloomer, 4, 119	J. Velasquez	Dottie's Doll, 5, 117	Cum Laude Laurie, 4, 119	9	2:02.20	73,938
1977	Our Mims, 3, 117	J. Velasquez	Mississippi Mud, 4, 124	Dottie's Doll, 4, 118	5	2:01.00	70,785
1976	Optimistic Gal, 3, 119	E. Maple	T. V. Vixen, 3, 118	Vodka Time, 4, 115	6	2:01.00	65,040
1975	Susan's Girl, 6, 125	R. Broussard	Pass a Glance, 4, 116	Raisela, 4, 117	6	2:01.80	70,915
1974	Krislin, 5, 115	A. T. Cordero Jr.	Twixt, 5, 124	Summer Guest, 5, 114	9	2:01.60	74,555
1973	Susan's Girl, 4, 127	L. A. Pincay Jr.	Summer Guest, 4, 122	Light Hearted, 4, 125	6	2:00.60	71,305

Formerly named for the city of New Castle, Delaware. Grade 1 1973-'89. Grade 3 1996-2002. New Castle H. 1937-'54. Held at Saratoga 1983-'85. Not held 1943. 1¹/₁₆ miles 1937-'50.

Delaware Oaks

Grade 2 in 2005. Delaware Park, three-year-olds, fillies, 1¹/₁₆ miles, dirt. Held July 17, 2004, with a gross value of $500,900. First held in 1938. First graded in 1973. Stakes record 1:42.81 (1998 Nickel Classic).

Year	Winner	Jockey	Second	Third	Strs	Time	1st Purse
2004	Yearly Report, 3, 122	J. D. Bailey	Ender's Sister, 3, 119	A Lula Ofa Menifee, 3, 115	8	1:43.80	$300,000
2003	Island Fashion, 3, 122	I. Puglisi	Awesome Humor, 3, 115	Ladyecho, 3, 115	9	1:44.95	300,000
2002	Allamerican Bertie, 3, 115	L. J. Melancon	Alternate, 3, 117	Pass the Virtue, 3, 119	6	1:43.81	150,000
2001	Zonk, 3, 115	M. J. McCarthy	Mystic Lady, 3, 122	Lady Andromeda, 3, 115	11	1:45.27	151,000
2000	Sincerely, 3, 117	M. J. McCarthy	Trip, 3, 119	Valleydar, 3, 117	5	1:43.83	150,000
1999	Brushed Halory, 3, 115	E. M. Martin Jr.	Gold From the West, 3, 115	Queen's Word, 3, 115	5	1:43.42	150,000
1998	Nickel Classic, 3, 119	C. H. Borel	Lu Ravi, 3, 122	Taffy Davenport, 3, 117	8	1:42.81	120,000
1997	Runup the Colors, 3, 116	P. Day	Timely Broad, 3, 113	City Band, 3, 113	10	1:44.20	90,000
1996	Like a Hawk, 3, 114	R. E. Colton	Mercedes Song, 3, 118	Winter Melody, 3, 118	10	1:37.01	30,000
1982	Lady Eleanor, 3, 115	R. Wilson	Sailing Hour, 3, 112	Milingo, 3, 115	10	1:50.20	38,480
1981	Up the Flagpole, 3, 112	K. D. Black	Stunning Native, 3, 112	Object d'Art, 3, 113	6	1:49.40	53,820
1980	Bishop's Ring, 3, 112	M. G. Pino	Diplomatic Role, 3, 122	Sugar and Spice, 3, 122	7	1:48.60	53,203
1979	It's in the Air, 3, 122	W. Shoemaker	Jameela, 3, 119	Himalayan, 3, 114	6	1:49.40	52,780
1978	White Star Line, 3, 122	J. Fell	Queen Lib, 3, 119	Silken Delight, 3, 114	6	1:52.60	35,230
1977	Cum Laude Laurie, 3, 112	J. Velasquez	Pressing Date, 3, 113	Sweet Alliance, 3, 122	7	1:48.20	35,490
1976	‡Pacific Princess, 3, 111	E. Maple	T. V. Vixen, 3, 125	All Rainbows, 3, 114	9	1:49.60	33,660
1975	Let Me Linger, 3, 117	C. Barrera	dh-Funalon, 3, 123 dh-M'lle. Cyanne, 3, 117		9	1:51.40	36,237
1974	Plantain, 3, 114	G. McCarron	Enchanted Native, 3, 111	Knightly Wooing, 3, 114	14	1:50.40	38,350
1973	Desert Vixen, 3, 121	J. Velasquez	Bag of Tunes, 3, 121	Ladies Agreement, 3, 112	10	1:49.20	37,083

Grade 1 1973-'80. Grade 2 1981-'82. Not graded 1996-'98. Grade 3 1999-2003. Not held 1943, 1983-'95. 1¹/₈ miles 1938-'82. 1 mile 1996. Turf 1996. Dead heat for second 1975. ‡T. V. Vixen finished first, DQ to second, 1976.

Del Mar Breeders' Cup Handicap

Grade 2 in 2005. Del Mar, three-year-olds and up, 1 mile, dirt. Held September 5, 2004, with a gross value of $250,000. First held in 1987. First graded in 1989. Stakes record 1:33.40 (1989 On the Line).

Year	Winner	Jockey	Second	Third	Strs	Time	1st Purse
2004	Supah Blitz, 4, 116	V. Espinoza	Domestic Dispute, 4, 117	During, 4, 117	6	1:35.14	$150,000
2003	Joey Franco, 4, 116	P. A. Valenzuela	Reba's Gold, 6, 116	Grey Memo, 6, 117	7	1:35.70	90,000
2002	Congaree, 4, 119	M. E. Smith	Kela, 4, 117	Reba's Gold, 5, 116	6	1:36.34	150,000
2001	El Corredor, 4, 121	V. Espinoza	Figlio Mio, 4, 113	Performing Magic, 4, 116	6	1:35.24	150,000
2000	El Corredor, 3, 111	V. Espinoza	Cliquot, 4, 117	Literal Prowler, 6, 112	8	1:35.05	158,160
1999	Hollycombe, 5, 116	G. L. Stevens	Flying With Eagles, 5, 115	Old Trieste, 4, 122	8	1:35.46	126,060
1998	Old Trieste, 3, 116	C. J. McCarron	Grajagan (Arg), 4, 111	Stalwart Tsu, 4, 116	4	1:35.35	123,172
1997	Benchmark, 6, 117	E. J. Delahoussaye	Crafty Friend, 4, 118	Northern Afleet, 4, 120	5	1:35.57	126,700

Year	Winner	Jockey	Second	Third	Strs	Time	1st Purse
1996	Dramatic Gold, 5, 118	K. J. Desormeaux	Alphabet Soup, 5, 120	Savinio, 6, 118	5	1:34.78	$125,650
1995	Alphabet Soup, 4, 115	C. J. McCarron	Lykatill Hil, 5, 117	Luthier Fever, 4, 115	9	1:34.33	117,150
1994	Lykatill Hil, 4, 118	E. J. Delahoussaye	D'Hallevant, 4, 117	Stuka, 4, 116	6	1:34.01	62,200
1993	Region, 4, 115	C. S. Nakatani	Lottery Winner, 4, 115	L'Express (Chi), 4, 115	10	1:34.98	122,100
1992	Reign Road, 4, 114	D. R. Flores	Sir Beaufort, 5, 116	Charmonnier, 4, 115	10	1:35.29	122,000
1991	Twilight Agenda, 5, 122	K. J. Desormeaux	Opening Verse, 5, 117	Robyn Dancer, 4, 117	5	1:34.17	116,950
1990	Stalwart Charger, 3, 115	R. M. Gonzalez	Flying Continental, 4, 120	Ruhlmann, 5, 123	4	1:34.60	116,300
1989	On the Line, 5, 124	L. A. Pincay Jr.	Good Taste (Arg), 7, 117	Lively One, 4, 125	4	1:33.40	115,400
1988	Precisionist, 7, 125	C. J. McCarron	Lively One, 3, 114	He's a Saros, 5, 116	4	1:34.60	85,150
1987	Good Command, 4, 114	C. J. McCarron	Stop the Fighting (Ire), 4, 116	Candi's Gold, 3, 113	6	1:34.80	86,250

Grade 3 1989. Del Mar Budweiser Breeders' Cup H. 1987-'95.

Del Mar Debutante Stakes

Grade 1 in 2005. Del Mar, two-year-olds, fillies, 7 furlongs, dirt. Held August 28, 2004, with a gross value of $250,000. First held in 1951. First graded in 1973. Stakes record 1:21.45 (1994 Call Now).

Year	Winner	Jockey	Second	Third	Strs	Time	1st Purse
2004	Sweet Catomine, 2, 114	V. Espinoza	Souvenir Gift, 2, 120	Hello Lucky, 2, 116	9	1:24.18	$150,000
2003	Halfbridled, 2, 116	J. A. Krone	Hollywood Story, 2, 115	Victory U. S. A., 2, 116	6	1:22.20	150,000
2002	Miss Houdini, 2, 116	G. L. Stevens	Santa Catarina, 2, 115	Indy Groove, 2, 115	8	1:23.43	150,000
2001	Habibti, 2, 115	V. Espinoza	Who Loves Aleyna, 2, 116	Tempera, 2, 119	5	1:22.22	150,000
2000	Cindy's Hero, 2, 114	G. K. Gomez	Notable Career, 2, 119	Euro Empire, 2, 119	5	1:22.61	150,000
1999	Chilukki, 2, 121	D. R. Flores	Spain, 2, 115	She's Classy, 2, 116	7	1:23.54	150,000
1998	Excellent Meeting, 2, 115	K. J. Desormeaux	Antahkarana, 2, 115	Colorado Song, 2, 115	9	1:22.34	150,000
1997	Vivid Angel, 2, 115	K. J. Desormeaux	Griselle, 2, 115	Czarina, 2, 117	8	1:24.26	150,000
1996	Sharp Cat, 2, 115	R. R. Douglas	Desert Digger, 2, 119	Broad Dynamite, 2, 116	10	1:23.98	150,000
1995	Batroyale, 2, 119	M. A. Pedroza	Proud Dixie, 2, 117	General Idea, 2, 116	12	1:22.55	137,500
1994	Call Now, 2, 115	A. O. Solis	How So Oiseau, 2, 119	Ski Dancer, 2, 116	9	1:21.45	137,500
1993	Sardula, 2, 116	E. J. Delahoussaye	Phone Chatter, 2, 119	Ballerina Gal, 2, 114	8	1:21.61	137,500
1992	Beal Street Blues, 2, 116	G. L. Stevens	Fit n Fappy, 2, 114	Zoonaqua, 2, 120	10	1:37.17	137,500
1991	La Spia, 2, 114	A. O. Solis	Soviet Sojourn, 2, 120	Wicked Wit, 2, 116	7	1:37.09	161,000
1990	Beyond Perfection, 2, 114	A. O. Solis	Lite Light, 2, 120	Title Bought, 2, 116	7	1:34.80	191,400
1989	Rue de Palm, 2, 115	R. A. Baze	Dominant Dancer, 2, 118	Cheval Volant, 2, 116	9	1:35.00	202,050
1988	‡Lea Lucinda, 2, 114	G. L. Stevens	Approved to Fly, 2, 114	Beware of the Cat, 2, 115	8	1:36.40	193,850
1987	Lost Kitty, 2, 117	G. L. Stevens	Royal Weekend, 2, 113	Hasty Pasty, 2, 117	5	1:36.00	128,850
1986	Brave Raj, 2, 117	C. A. Black	Road to Happiness, 2, 113	Soft Copy, 2, 115	7	1:35.80	125,325
1985	Arewehavingfunyet, 2, 120	P. A. Valenzuela	Python, 2, 117	Wee Lavaliere, 2, 117	6	1:36.00	134,210
1984	Fiesta Lady, 2, 117	L. A. Pincay Jr.	Doon's Baby, 2, 119	Trunk, 2, 115	7	1:38.80	93,050
	Full O Wisdom, 2, 113	C. J. McCarron	Pirate's Glow, 2, 115	Wayward Pirate, 2, 119	5	1:37.40	91,050
1983	Althea, 2, 119	L. A. Pincay Jr.	Diachrony, 2, 113	Victorous Joy, 2, 113	6	1:36.00	126,190
1982	Landaluce, 2, 119	L. A. Pincay Jr.	Issues n' Answers, 2, 116	Granja Reina, 2, 113	6	1:35.60	124,655
1981	Skillful Joy, 2, 113	C. J. McCarron	Marl Lee Ann, 2, 113	A Kiss for Luck, 2, 116	12	1:37.40	138,310
1980	Raja's Delight, 2, 113	C. J. McCarron	Prestigious Lady, 2, 115	Native Fancy, 2, 119	10	1:37.40	110,225
1979	Table Hands, 2, 119	W. Shoemaker	Hazel R., 2, 116	Arcades Ambo, 2, 117	9	1:35.00	106,770
1978	Terlingua, 2, 119	D. G. McHargue	Beauty Hour, 2, 116	Blowin' Wild, 2, 115	8	1:36.20	79,140
1977	Extravagant, 2, 113	M. Castaneda	Foxy Juliana, 2, 115	Honey Jar, 2, 113	12	1:36.40	81,490
1976	Telferner, 2, 116	L. A. Pincay Jr.	Asterisca, 2, 113	Maxine N., 2, 113	7	1:37.20	65,175
1975	Queen to Be, 2, 116	D. G. McHargue	T. V. Terese, 2, 113	Awaken, 2, 113	6	1:36.80	57,805
1974	Bubblewin, 2, 113	W. Shoemaker	Spout, 2, 116	Cut Class, 2, 114	6	1:36.80	57,445
1973	Fleet Peach, 2, 116	D. Pierce	Fresno Star, 2, 113	Divine Grace, 2, 113	8	1:09.60	46,205

Young women making their first formal appearance in society are known as debutantes. Formerly sponsored by Vinery of Lexington 1999. Grade 2 1973-'98. 6 furlongs 1951-'73. 1 mile 1974-'92. Two divisions 1984. ‡Approved to Fly finished first, DQ to second, 1988.

Del Mar Derby

Grade 2 in 2005. Del Mar, three-year-olds, 1⅛ miles, turf. Held September 6, 2004, with a gross value of $400,000. First held in 1945. First graded in 1973. Stakes record 1:46.45 (2003 Fairly Ransom).

Year	Winner	Jockey	Second	Third	Strs	Time	1st Purse
2004	Blackdoun (Fr), 3, 122	C. S. Nakatani	Toasted, 3, 122	Laura's Lucky Boy, 3, 122	10	1:46.75	$240,000
2003	Fairly Ransom, 3, 122	A. O. Solis	Devious Boy (GB), 3, 122	Sweet Return (GB), 3, 122	9	1:46.45	180,000
2002	Inesperado (Fr), 3, 121	C. S. Nakatani	Johar, 3, 121	Rock Opera, 3, 121	9	1:47.49	180,000
2001	Romanceishope, 3, 121	C. J. McCarron	Indygo Shiner, 3, 121	Blue Steller (Ire), 3, 121	10	1:47.93	180,000
2000	Walkslikeaduck, 3, 121	E. J. Delahoussaye	Purely Cozzene, 3, 121	†New Story, 3, 118	10	1:46.66	180,000
1999	Val Royal (Fr), 3, 121	C. S. Nakatani	Fighting Falcon, 3, 121	In Frank's Honor, 3, 121	10	1:48.53	180,000
1998	Ladies Din, 3, 121	K. J. Desormeaux	Expressionist, 3, 121	Scooter Brown, 3, 121	9	1:48.50	180,000
1997	Anet, 3, 121	G. L. Stevens	Brave Act (GB), 3, 121	Worldly Ways (GB), 3, 121	7	1:48.42	180,000
1996	Rainbow Blues (Ire), 3, 122	C. S. Nakatani	The Barking Shark, 3, 122	Mateo, 3, 122	9	1:50.01	180,000
1995	Da Hoss, 3, 122	R. R. Douglas	Lake George, 3, 122	Tabor, 3, 122	9	1:48.49	165,000
1994	Ocean Crest, 3, 122	L. A. Pincay Jr.	Unfinished Symph, 3, 122	‡Powis Castle, 3, 122	10	1:48.74	165,000
1993	Guide (Fr), 3, 122	K. J. Desormeaux	Future Storm, 3, 122	The Real Vaslav, 3, 122	12	1:49.73	165,000
1992	Daros (GB), 3, 122	E. J. Delahoussaye	Smiling and Dancin, 3, 122	Major Impact, 3, 122	12	1:48.80	165,000

Year	Winner	Jockey	Second	Third	Strs	Time	1st Purse
1991	**Eternity Star**, 3, 122	F. T. Alvarado	Stark South, 3, 122	June's Reward, 3, 122	10	1:49.24	$165,000
1990	**Tight Spot**, 3, 122	L. A. Pincay Jr.	Itsallgreektome, 3, 122	Predecessor, 3, 122	10	1:49.60	165,000
1989	**Hawkster**, 3, 121	P. A. Valenzuela	River Master, 3, 119	Lode, 3, 116	9	1:48.00	130,500
1988	**Silver Circus**, 3, 118	R. A. Baze	Perfecting, 3, 118	Roberto's Dancer, 3, 116	8	1:49.00	127,900
1987	**Deputy Governor**, 3, 119	E. J. Delahoussaye	Stately Don, 3, 120	The Medic, 3, 118	9	1:48.40	98,700
1986	**Vernon Castle**, 3, 123	E. J. Delahoussaye	Prince Bobby B., 3, 119	Mazaad (Ire), 3, 119	9	1:48.40	95,500
1985	**First Norman**, 3, 117	G. L. Stevens	Pretensor, 3, 116	Catane, 3, 112	9	1:48.00	82,300
1984	**Tsunami Slew**, 3, 119	E. J. Delahoussaye	Prince True, 3, 119	Majestic Shore, 3, 115	12	1:48.00	99,650
1983	**Tanks Brigade**, 3, 122	R. Q. Meza	Ansuan, 3, 115	Evening M'lord (Ire), 3, 117	11	1:49.00	85,350
1982	**Give Me Strength**, 3, 123	L. A. Pincay Jr.	Water Bank, 3, 117	Take the Floor, 3, 117	13	1:49.00	88,100
1981	**Juan Barrera**, 3, 115	F. Toro	Buen Chico, 3, 114	Rock Softly, 3, 113	10	1:49.00	83,950
1980	**Exploded**, 3, 117	L. A. Pincay Jr.	Aristocratical, 3, 120	Son of a Dodo, 3, 118	10	1:49.60	70,300
1979	**Relaunch**, 3, 121	L. A. Pincay Jr.	Kamalii King, 3, 111	Pole Position, 3, 120	8	1:48.80	51,450
1978	**Misrepresentation**, 3, 119	D. Pierce	Singular, 3, 119	Wayside Station, 3, 115	10	1:49.60	33,450
1977	**Text**, 3, 122	D. G. McHargue	Pay the Toll, 3, 119	Hill Fox, 3, 115	10	1:49.40	32,750
1976	**Montespan**, 3, 115	D. G. McHargue	Dr. Krohn, 3, 117	Today 'n Tomorrow, 3, 118	10	1:48.40	26,550
1975	**Larrikin**, 3, 116	D. Pierce	Messenger of Song, 3, 116	Wood Carver, 3, 115	9	1:48.80	28,900
1974	**Lightning Mandate**, 3, 116	A. Pineda	Within Hail, 3, 113	Prince Petrone, 3, 113	7	1:50.00	27,900
1973	**Right Honorable**, 3, 115	J. Lambert	Groshawk, 3, 119	Dancing Papa, 3, 113	10	1:49.20	28,650

Formerly named for William Quigley, a La Jolla, California, stockbroker and co-founder of the Del Mar Turf Club. Grade 3 1973-'80. Quigley Memorial H. 1945-'47. Del Mar Invitational Derby 1991-'96. 1¹/₁₆ miles 1945-'48. Dirt 1945-'69. Two divisions 1970. ‡Eagle Eyed finished third, DQ to seventh, 1994. Equaled course record 2000. †Denotes female.

Del Mar Futurity

Grade 2 in 2005. Del Mar, two-year-olds, 7 furlongs, dirt. Held September 8, 2004, with a gross value of $245,000. First held in 1948. First graded in 1973. Stakes record 1:21.29 (2004 Declan's Moon).

Year	Winner	Jockey	Second	Third	Strs	Time	1st Purse
2004	**Declan's Moon**, 2, 116	V. Espinoza	Roman Ruler, 2, 120	Swiss Lad, 2, 116	4	**1:21.29**	$150,000
2003	**Siphonizer**, 2, 116	J. A. Krone	Minister Eric, 2, 116	Perfect Moon, 2, 122	5	1:23.10	150,000
2002	**Icecoldbeeratreds**, 2, 119	D. R. Flores	Kafwain, 2, 119	Chief Planner, 2, 116	8	1:22.94	150,000
2001	**Officer**, 2, 121	V. Espinoza	Kamsack, 2, 115	Metatron, 2, 116	5	1:22.33	150,000
2000	**Flame Thrower**, 2, 119	J. D. Bailey	Street Cry (Ire), 2, 116	Arabian Light, 2, 119	8	1:22.00	150,000
1999	**Forest Camp**, 2, 116	D. R. Flores	Dixie Union, 2, 121	Captain Steve, 2, 115	5	1:21.67	150,000
1998	**Worldly Manner**, 2, 119	K. J. Desormeaux	Daring General, 2, 119	Waki American, 2, 114	7	1:23.05	150,000
1997	**Souvenir Copy**, 2, 115	C. J. McCarron	Old Topper, 2, 119	Commitisize, 2, 115	8	1:23.10	150,000
1996	**Silver Charm**, 2, 116	D. R. Flores	Gold Tribute, 2, 115	Swiss Yodeler, 2, 121	7	1:22.88	150,000
1995	**Future Quest**, 2, 115	K. J. Desormeaux	Othello, 2, 115	Cavonnier, 2, 117	8	1:21.81	137,500
1994	**On Target**, 2, 115	A. O. Solis	Supremo, 2, 115	Timber Country, 2, 119	9	1:22.37	137,500
1993	**Winning Pact**, 2, 115	C. S. Nakatani	Ramblin Guy, 2, 119	Ferrara, 2, 116	7	1:22.04	137,500
1992	**River Special**, 2, 115	C. J. McCarron	Sudden Hush, 2, 120	Seattle Sleet, 2, 114	7	1:36.64	137,500
1991	**Bertrando**, 2, 114	A. O. Solis	Zurich, 2, 114	Star Recruit, 2, 115	10	1:36.45	188,500
1990	**Best Pal**, 2, 120	P. A. Valenzuela	Pillaring, 2, 116	Got to Fly, 2, 117	11	1:35.40	231,600
1989	**Drag Race**, 2, 114	F. Olivares	†Rue de Palm, 2, 117	Single Dawn, 2, 114	12	1:35.40	241,600
1988	**Music Merci**, 2, 118	C. J. McCarron	Bruho, 2, 114	Texian, 2, 117	11	1:35.40	229,300
1987	†**Lost Kitty**, 2, 117	L. A. Pincay Jr.	Bold Second, 2, 118	Purdue King, 2, 118	9	1:36.20	174,800
1986	**Qualify**, 2, 114	G. L. Stevens	†Sacahuista, 2, 117	Brevito, 2, 116	9	1:35.60	158,535
1985	**Tasso**, 2, 117	L. A. Pincay Jr.	†Arewehavingfunyet, 2, 117	Snow Chief, 2, 117	6	1:36.00	155,760
1984	**Saratoga Six**, 2, 120	A. T. Cordero Jr.	Indigenous, 2, 114	Lomax, 2, 117	9	1:36.00	173,440
1983	†**Althea**, 2, 117	L. A. Pincay Jr.	Juliet's Pride, 2, 115	Gumboy, 2, 114	5	1:34.80	147,865
1982	**Roving Boy**, 2, 117	E. J. Delahoussaye	Desert Wine, 2, 120	Balboa Native, 2, 114	9	1:38.80	159,945
1981	**Gato Del Sol**, 2, 114	E. J. Delahoussaye	The Captain, 2, 120	Ring Proud, 2, 115	10	1:37.40	160,720
1980	**Bold and Gold**, 2, 114	D. C. Hall	Looks Like Rain, 2, 114	Sir Dancer, 2, 117	12	1:36.20	129,630
1979	**The Carpenter**, 2, 114	C. J. McCarron	Doonesbury, 2, 117	Executive Counsel, 2, 114	6	1:35.20	98,710
1978	**Flying Paster**, 2, 117	D. Pierce	Priority, 2, 117	Roman Oblisk, 2, 117	8	1:34.80	100,040
1977	**Go West Young Man**, 2, 114	F. Olivares	Tampoy, 2, 114	Spanish Way, 2, 117	10	1:35.60	85,845
1976	**Visible**, 2, 117	L. A. Pincay Jr.	*Habitony, 2, 114	Washoe County, 2, 115	10	1:35.60	74,535
1975	**Telly's Pop**, 2, 117	F. Mena	Lexington Laugh, 2, 114	Body Bend, 2, 114	8	1:36.00	66,275
1974	**Diabolo**, 2, 116	W. Shoemaker	George Navonod, 2, 119	Dimaggio, 2, 122	7	1:35.40	67,120
1973	**Such a Rush**, 2, 116	W. Shoemaker	Fast Pappa, 2, 116	The Gay Greek, 2, 115	11	1:29.80	65,740

Grade 1 1984-'89. 6 furlongs 1948-'70. 7¹/₂ furlongs 1971-'73. 1 mile 1974-'92. Turf 1971-'73. Two divisions 1971. †Denotes female.

Del Mar Handicap

Grade 2 in 2005. Del Mar, three-year-olds and up, 1³/₈ miles, turf. Held August 29, 2004, with a gross value of $250,000. First held in 1937. First graded in 1973. Stakes record 2:12.15 (2002 Delta Form [Aus]).

Year	Winner	Jockey	Second	Third	Strs	Time	1st Purse
2004	**Star Over the Bay**, 6, 116	T. Baze	Sarafan, 7, 121	†Moscow Burning, 4, 114	9	2:12.71	$150,000
2003	**Irish Warrior**, 5, 116	A. O. Solis	Continental Red, 7, 117	Continuously, 4, 114	9	2:12.28	150,000
2002	**Delta Form (Aus)**, 6, 115	G. F. Almeida	The Tin Man, 4, 117	Blue Steller (Ire), 4, 117	10	**2:12.15**	150,000
2001	**Timboroa (GB)**, 5, 118	L. A. Pincay Jr.	Northern Quest (Fr), 6, 116	Super Quercus (Fr), 5, 117	7	2:12.59	150,000

Year	Winner	Jockey	Second	Third	Strs	Time	1st Purse
2000	Northern Quest (Fr), 5, 116	C. J. McCarron	‡Perssonet (Chi), 5, 114	Alvo Certo (Brz), 7, 115	8	2:12.65	$150,000
1999	Sayarshan (Fr), 4, 115	B. Blanc	Dancing Place (Chi), 6, 116	Ladies Din, 4, 120	8	2:14.35	150,000
1998	Bonapartiste (Fr), 4, 115	C. J. McCarron	River Bay, 5, 123	Military, 4, 116	6	2:14.18	150,000
1997	Rainbow Dancer (Fr), 6, 118	A. O. Solis	Dowty, 5, 119	Lord Jain (Arg), 5, 114	8	2:13.68	150,000
1996	Dernier Empereur, 6, 118	P. A. Valenzuela	Talloires, 6, 119	Party Season (GB), 5, 117	7	2:13.89	150,000
1995	Royal Chariot, 5, 117	L. A. Pincay Jr.	River Rhythm, 8, 117	Party Season (GB), 4, 116	10	2:13.78	137,500
1994	Navarone, 6, 117	P. A. Valenzuela	Approach the Bench (Ire), 6, 116	Sir Mark Sykes (Ire), 5, 116	8	2:14.37	137,500
1993	Luazur (Fr), 4, 116	P. Day	Kotashaan (Fr), 5, 123	Myrakalu (Fr), 5, 114	7	2:15.11	137,500
1992	Navarone, 4, 117	P. A. Valenzuela	Qathif, 5, 117	Stark South, 4, 117	8	2:15.17	137,500
1991	My Style (Ire), 4, 115	K. J. Desormeaux	Forty Niner Days, 4, 118	Super May, 5, 117	9	2:13.38	165,000
1990	Live the Dream, 4, 118	A. O. Solis	Mehmetori, 3, 107	Soft Machine, 5, 113	12	2:13.00	165,000
1989	Payant (Arg), 5, 118	R. G. Davis	Saratoga Passage, 4, 118	†No Review, 4, 112	9	2:15.20	165,000
1988	Sword Dance (Ire), 4, 114	C. J. McCarron	Great Communicator, 5, 120	Baba Karam (Ire), 4, 115	11	2:15.80	165,000
1987	Swink, 4, 120	W. Shoemaker	Santella Mac (Ire), 4, 116	Skip Out Front, 5, 115	12	2:13.80	165,000
1986	Raipillan (Chi), 4, 114	R. A. Baze	Schiller, 4, 113	Shulich (GB), 5, 113	12	2:14.40	165,000
1985	Barberstown, 5, 117	F. Toro	My Habitony, 5, 118	First Norman, 3, 114	10	1:58.00	137,000
1984	Precisionist, 3, 116	C. J. McCarron	Pair of Deuces, 6, 116	Super Diamond, 4, 117	10	1:56.80	137,000
1983	Bel Bolide, 5, 117	W. Shoemaker	Gato Del Sol, 4, 123	Egg Toss, 6, 117	9	1:58.20	82,500
1982	Muttering, 3, 117	W. Shoemaker	Regalberto, 4, 119	Exploded, 5, 121	9	1:57.00	82,500
1981	Wickerr, 6, 118	C. J. McCarron	Tahitian King (Ire), 5, 121	Galaxy Libra (Ire), 5, 121	7	1:57.40	82,500
1980	Go West Young Man, 5, 123	E. J. Delahoussaye	Relaunch, 4, 118	Balzac, 5, 121	9	1:58.20	75,000
1979	Ardiente, 4, 118	C. J. McCarron	Quick Turnover, 4, 122	Sudanes (Arg), 6, 111	10	1:56.80	75,000
1978	Palton (Chi), 5, 114	H. E. Moreno	Farnesio (Arg), 4, 119	Vic's Magic, 5, 119	8	1:57.40	60,000
1977	Ancient Title, 7, 123	D. G. McHargue	Painted Wagon, 4, 118	†Cascapedia, 4, 117	9	1:55.40	60,000
1976	Riot in Paris, 5, 122	W. Shoemaker	Avatar, 4, 122	Good Report, 6, 115	8	1:57.40	60,000
1975	*Cruiser II, 6, 117	F. Olivares	Top Crowd, 4, 115	Against the Snow, 5, 117	9	2:14.40	60,000
1974	*Redtop III, 5, 115	F. Toro	My Old Friend, 5, 118	Nantwice, 5, 111	10	2:16.00	60,000
1973	Red Reality, 7, 122	B. Baeza	Wing Out, 5, 119	Life Cycle, 4, 124	10	2:17.00	60,000

Del Mar Invitational H. 1973, 1975-'87, 1989-'96. Not held 1942-'44. 1¹⁄₁₆ miles 1937-'48. 1¹⁄₈ miles 1949-'69. 1³⁄₄ miles 1971. About 1¹⁄₄ miles 1976-'85. Dirt 1937-'69, 1976-'85. Two divisions 1972. ‡Alvo Certo (Brz) finished second, DQ to third, 2000. Course record 1975. †Denotes female.

Del Mar Oaks

Grade 1 in 2005. Del Mar, three-year-olds, fillies, 1¹⁄₈ miles, turf. Held August 21, 2004, with a gross value of $300,000. First held in 1957. First graded in 1973. Stakes record 1:46.26 (2004 Amorama [Fr]).

Year	Winner	Jockey	Second	Third	Strs	Time	1st Purse
2004	Amorama (Fr), 3, 122	D. R. Flores	Ticker Tape (GB), 3, 122	Sweet Win, 3, 122	7	**1:46.26**	$180,000
2003	Dessert, 3, 122	C. S. Nakatani	Solar Echo, 3, 122	Personal Legend, 3, 122	8	1:47.04	180,000
2002	Dublino, 3, 121	K. J. Desormeaux	Megahertz (GB), 3, 121	Alozaina (Ire), 3, 121	6	1:47.16	180,000
2001	Golden Apples (Ire), 3, 121	G. K. Gomez	Affluent, 3, 121	Reine de Romance (Ire), 3, 121	8	1:47.98	180,000
2000	No Matter What, 3, 121	V. Espinoza	Theoretically, 3, 121	Premiere Creation (Fr), 3, 121	9	1:50.02	150,000
1999	Tout Charmant, 3, 121	D. R. Flores	Smooth Player, 3, 121	Sweet Ludy (Ire), 3, 121	10	1:48.64	150,000
1998	Sicy d'Alsace (Fr), 3, 121	C. S. Nakatani	‡Adel, 3, 121	Tranquility Lake, 3, 121	10	1:48.26	150,000
1997	Famous Digger, 3, 121	B. Blanc	Golden Arches (Fr), 3, 121	See You Soon (Fr), 3, 121	10	1:49.14	150,000
1996	Antespend, 3, 120	C. W. Antley	Gastronomical, 3, 120	True Flare, 3, 120	8	1:48.93	150,000
1995	Bail Out Becky, 3, 120	S. J. Sellers	Sleep Easy, 3, 120	Top Ruhl, 3, 120	9	1:49.72	137,500
1994	Twice the Vice, 3, 120	G. L. Stevens	Malli Star, 3, 120	Pharma, 3, 120	6	1:47.73	96,250
1993	Hollywood Wildcat, 3, 120	E. J. Delahoussaye	Possibly Perfect, 3, 120	Miami Sands (Ire), 3, 120	10	1:48.31	96,250
1992	Suivi, 3, 120	A. O. Solis	Race the Wild Wind, 3, 120	Alysbelle, 3, 120	8	1:48.60	96,250
1991	Flawlessly, 3, 120	C. J. McCarron	Seattle Symphony, 3, 120	Fowda, 3, 120	6	1:49.50	96,250
1990	Slew of Pearls, 3, 117	C. A. Black	Adorable Emilie (Fr), 3, 115	Annual Reunion, 3, 117	12	1:49.80	97,900
1989	Stylish Star, 3, 115	C. J. McCarron	Darby's Daughter, 3, 119	General Charge (Ire), 3, 119	9	1:48.60	97,500
1988	No Review, 3, 115	R. Q. Meza	Do So, 3, 124	Jungle Gold, 3, 115	7	1:49.00	96,300
1987	Lizzy Hare, 3, 114	G. L. Stevens	Chapel of Dreams, 3, 114	Down Again, 3, 114	13	1:50.40	104,300
1986	Hidden Light, 3, 124	W. Shoemaker	Kraemer, 3, 114	Shotgun Wedding, 3, 119	7	1:47.80	92,700
1985	Savannah Dancer, 3, 119	W. Shoemaker	‡Magnificent Lindy, 3, 122	Queen of Bronze, 3, 115	8	1:48.80	94,250
1984	Fashionably Late, 3, 119	C. J. McCarron	Lucky Lucky Lucky, 3, 124	Auntie Betty, 3, 114	7	1:49.40	92,400
1983	Heartlight No. One, 3, 122	L. A. Pincay Jr.	Foggy Moon, 3, 115	Fabulous Notion, 3, 122	10	1:50.20	84,100
1982	Castilla, 3, 122	R. Sibille	Avigaition, 3, 119	Skillful Joy, 3, 119	8	1:50.20	81,050
1981	French Charmer, 3, 117	D. G. McHargue	Amber Ever, 3, 119	Shimmy, 3, 119	9	1:49.40	82,200
1980	Movin' Money, 3, 114	P. A. Valenzuela	Princess Karenda, 3, 122	Tobin's Rose, 3, 119	11	1:49.40	71,000
1979	Our Suiti Pie, 3, 113	C. J. McCarron	Caline, 3, 121	Ancient Art, 3, 116	9	1:49.80	52,300
1978	Country Queen, 3, 121	F. Toro	B. Thoughtful, 3, 124	Donna Inez, 3, 113	11	1:49.80	33,450
1977	Taisez Vous, 3, 121	D. Pierce	Drama Critic, 3, 114	Giggling Girl, 3, 113	9	1:48.80	31,550
1976	Go March, 3, 116	L. A. Pincay Jr.	Pennygown, 3, 113	Franmari, 3, 116	7	1:49.20	25,700
1975	Snap Apple, 3, 113	F. Mena	Mia Amore, 3, 115	Miss Francesca, 3, 116	8	1:50.00	21,450
1974	Modus Vivendi, 3, 122	D. Pierce	Move Abroad, 3, 116	Heather Road, 3, 115	9	1:50.20	21,850
1973	Sandy Blue, 3, 121	D. Pierce	Sphere, 3, 112	Meilleur, 3, 118	12	1:49.40	20,850

Grade 3 1973-'78, 1988-'91. Grade 2 1979-'87, 1992-'93. Del Mar Invitational Oaks 1992-'94, 1996. 1 mile 1957-'64. Dirt 1957-'64. Two divisions 1966, 1970. ‡Pirate's Glow finished second, DQ to fourth, 1985. ‡Tranquility Lake finished second, DQ to third, 1998.

Delta Jackpot Stakes

Grade 3 in 2005. Delta Downs, two-year-olds, 1 1/16 miles, dirt. Held December 4, 2004, with a gross value of $1,000,000. First held in 2002. First graded in 2005. Stakes record 1:45.34 (2003 Mr. Jester).

Year	Winner	Jockey	Second	Third	Strs	Time	1st Purse
2004	**Texcess**, 2, 119	V. Espinoza	Closing Argument, 2, 119	Anthony J., 2, 117	10	1:48.20	$600,000
2003	**Mr. Jester**, 2, 115	R. Chapa	Fire Slam, 2, 115	Perfect Moon, 2, 115	10	**1:45.34**	600,000
2002	**Outta Here**, 2, 116	K. J. Desormeaux	Comic Truth, 2, 117	Cherokee's Boy, 2, 116	10	1:37.77	300,000

The Delta Jackpot S. (G3) is the second-richest race for juveniles in North America. Sponsored by Boyd's Gaming Corp. of Henderson, Nevada, parent company of Delta Downs 2003-'04.

Demoiselle Stakes

Grade 2 in 2005. Aqueduct, two-year-olds, fillies, 1 1/8 miles, dirt. Held November 27, 2004, with a gross value of $200,000. First held in 1908. First graded in 1973. Stakes record 1:50 (1978 Plankton).

Year	Winner	Jockey	Second	Third	Strs	Time	1st Purse
2004	**Sis City**, 2, 119	J. R. Velazquez	Salute, 2, 115	Winning Season, 2, 115	7	1:50.39	$120,000
2003	**Ashado**, 2, 117	J. D. Bailey	La Reina, 2, 121	Dr. Kathy, 2, 115	7	1:52.88	120,000
2002	**Roar Emotion**, 2, 115	J. R. Velazquez	Savedbythelight, 2, 115	Feisty Step, 2, 115	10	1:51.43	120,000
2001	**Smok'n Frolic**, 2, 121	J. R. Velazquez	Lady Shari, 2, 121	Proxy Statement, 2, 117	7	1:50.57	120,000
2000	**Two Item Limit**, 2, 122	R. Migliore	Sweep Dreams, 2, 116	Kingsland, 2, 116	8	1:52.25	120,000
1999	**Jostle**, 2, 121	S. Elliott	March Magic, 2, 112	Shawnee Country, 2, 121	8	1:51.51	120,000
1998	**‡Better Than Honour**, 2, 113	R. Migliore	Waltz On By, 2, 115	Oh What a Windfall, 2, 121	9	1:52.70	120,000
1997	**Clark Street**, 2, 121	M. E. Smith	Soft Senorita, 2, 114	Mercy Me, 2, 121	8	1:53.98	120,000
1996	**Ajina**, 2, 121	P. Day	Hidden Reserve, 2, 114	Biding Time, 2, 114	9	1:53.74	120,000
1995	**La Rosa**, 2, 114	J. A. Krone	Quiet Dance, 2, 114	Escena, 2, 112	7	1:50.92	120,000
1994	**Minister Wife**, 2, 121	J. D. Bailey	Miss Golden Circle, 2, 118	Special Broad, 2, 121	9	1:53.48	120,000
1993	**Strategic Maneuver**, 2, 116	J. D. Bailey	Sovereign Kitty, 2, 112	‡Princess Tru, 2, 114	6	1:53.62	120,000
1992	**Fortunate Faith**, 2, 112	A. Madrid Jr.	True Affair, 2, 116	Our Tomboy, 2, 112	8	1:53.59	120,000
1991	**Stolen Beauty**, 2, 113	C. W. Antley	Turnback the Alarm, 2, 116	Easy Now, 2, 116	6	1:52.08	120,000
1990	**Debutant's Halo**, 2, 116	C. Perret	Private Treasure, 2, 121	Slept Thru It, 2, 112	7	1:53.80	69,960
1989	**Rootentootenwooten**, 2, 112	J. D. Bailey	Bookkeeper, 2, 113	Why Go On Dreaming, 2, 113	9	1:51.60	109,440
1988	**Open Mind**, 2, 121	A. T. Cordero Jr.	Darby's Daughter, 2, 119	Gild, 2, 115	10	1:52.00	147,120
1987	**Goodbye Halo**, 2, 113	A. T. Cordero Jr.	Tap Your Toes, 2, 112	Galway Song, 2, 119	9	1:53.00	142,080
1986	**Tappiano**, 2, 121	J. Cruguet	Soaring Princess, 2, 112	Graceful Darby, 2, 112	7	1:53.20	131,940
1985	**I'm Sweets**, 2, 121	E. Maple	Family Style, 2, 121	Steal a Kiss, 2, 112	8	1:50.20	98,280
1984	**Diplomette**, 2, 112	R. Hernandez	Golden Silence, 2, 114	Koluctoo's Jill, 2, 112	10	1:54.60	72,360
1983	**Qualique**, 2, 112	M. Venezia	Lucky Lucky Lucky, 2, 121	Buzz My Bell, 2, 121	6	1:51.20	65,160
1982	**Quiet Queens**, 2, 116	M. A. Rivera	Gold Spruce, 2, 113	National Banner, 2, 113	7	1:52.00	49,680
1981	**Snow Plow**, 2, 121	A. T. Cordero Jr.	Larida, 2, 113	Vain Gold, 2, 121	8	1:53.00	50,220
1980	**Rainbow Connection**, 2, 119	A. T. Cordero Jr.	De La Rose, 2, 116	Tina Tina Too, 2, 116	6	1:50.80	48,870
1979	**Genuine Risk**, 2, 116	L. A. Pincay Jr.	Smart Angle, 2, 121	Spruce Pine, 2, 112	7	1:51.20	49,185
1978	**Plankton**, 2, 112	R. Hernandez	Distinct Honor, 2, 113	Belladora, 2, 112	9	**1:50.00**	48,465
1977	**Caesar's Wish**, 2, 116	D. R. Wright	Lakeville Miss, 2, 121	Island Kiss, 2, 114	7	1:50.60	47,565
1976	**Bring Out the Band**, 2, 116	D. Brumfield	Our Mims, 2, 113	Road Princess, 2, 112	12	1:50.80	49,500
1975	**Free Journey**, 2, 117	L. A. Pincay Jr.	Artfully, 2, 112	Dottie's Doll, 2, 114	11	1:50.20	51,210
1974	**Land Girl**, 2, 116	J. Vasquez	Alpine Lass, 2, 121	Funalon, 2, 118	14	1:36.20	35,940
1973	**Chris Evert**, 2, 121	L. A. Pincay Jr.	Amberalero, 2, 116	Khaled's Kaper, 2, 116	11	1:36.40	17,370

Demoiselle in French means young female. Grade 3 1973-'75. Grade 1 1981-'89. Held at Empire City 1908-'14, 1917-'42. Held at Belmont Park 1915-'16, 1958. Held at Jamaica 1944-'53. Not held 1909, 1911-'13, 1933-'35, 1954-'57, 1960-'62. 5 1/2 furlongs 1908-'32. 5 3/4 furlongs 1936-'42. 6 furlongs 1943-'47. 1 1/16 miles 1948-'53. 7 furlongs 1958-'59. 1 mile 1963-'74. ‡Bunting finished third, DQ to fifth, 1993. ‡Tutorial finished first, DQ to fifth, 1998.

Deputy Minister Handicap

Grade 3 in 2005. Gulfstream Park, three-year-olds and up, 6 1/2 furlongs, dirt. Held February 5, 2005, with a gross value of $100,000. First held in 1990. First graded in 2000. Stakes record 1:15.17 (2003 Native Heir).

Year	Winner	Jockey	Second	Third	Strs	Time	1st Purse
2005	**Medallist**, 4, 115	J. A. Santos	Mister Fotis, 4, 113	Kela, 7, 119	6	1:15.62	$60,000
2004	**Alke**, 4, 112	J. R. Velazquez	Cajun Beat, 4, 123	Coach Jimi Lee, 4, 115	7	1:15.80	60,000
2003	**Native Heir**, 5, 114	C. H. Velasquez	Binthebest, 6, 115	Fire and Glory, 4, 114	8	**1:15.17**	60,000
2002	**Fappie's Notebook**, 5, 116	J. F. Chavez	Twilight Road, 5, 116	Binthebest, 5, 114	7	1:16.19	60,000
2001	**Istintaj**, 5, 118	J. D. Bailey	Fappie's Notebook, 4, 113	Fantastic Finish, 5, 114	8	1:16.08	60,000
2000	**Deep Gold**, 4, 112	J. R. Velazquez	Forty One Carats, 4, 116	Klabin's Gold, 5, 114	8	1:15.89	60,000
1999	**Good and Tough**, 4, 115	S. J. Sellers	Western Borders, 5, 113	Mint, 4, 113	7	1:21.63	60,000
1998	**Irish Conquest**, 5, 113	E. Coa	Frisk Me Now, 4, 119	Oro de Mexico, 4, 114	10	1:22.54	60,000
1997	**Templado (Ven)**, 4, 113	J. D. Bailey	Sea Emperor, 5, 114	Punch Line, 7, 119	6	1:09.69	45,000
1996	**Jess C's Whirl**, 6, 115	J. A. Krone	Buffalo Dan, 5, 117	Patton, 5, 114	6	1:10.67	30,000
1995	**Chimes Band**, 4, 120	J. D. Bailey	Distinct Reality, 4, 112	Ponche, 6, 113	6	1:09.16	30,000
1994	**I Can't Believe**, 6, 113	E. Maple	Demaloot Demashoot, 4, 115	Devil On Ice, 5, 115	7	1:08.12	30,000
1993	**Loach**, 5, 114	J. A. Santos	Hidden Tomahawk, 5, 113	British Banker, 5, 114	6	1:22.51	30,000
1992	**Take Me Out**, 4, 118	J. D. Bailey	Drummond Lane, 5, 110	Frozen Runway, 5, 114	9	1:22.78	30,000

					Strs	Time	
1991	**Unbridled**, 4, 119	P. Day	Housebuster, 4, 122	Shuttleman, 5, 114	9	1:21.92	$30,000
1990	**Beau Genius**, 5, 118	C. Perret	The Red Rolls, 6, 112	Joel (Arg), 8, 112	7	1:23.00	30,000

Named for Centurion Farm's, Kinghaven Farm's, and Due Process Stable's 1981 Canadian Horse of the Year, '97, '98 leading North American sire, and '83 Donn H. (G2) winner Deputy Minister (1979 c. by Vice Regent). 7 furlongs 1990-'93, 1998-'99. 6 furlongs 1994-'97. Equaled track record 2003.

Desert Stormer Handicap

Grade 3 in 2005. Hollywood Park, three-year-olds and up, fillies and mares, 6 furlongs, dirt. Held June 5, 2005, with a gross value of $106,400. First held in 1997. First graded in 2001. Stakes record 1:08.09 (2001 Go Go).

Year	Winner	Jockey	Second	Third	Strs	Time	1st Purse
2005	**Puxa Saco**, 5, 116	M. E. Smith	Tucked Away, 5, 116	Ramatuelle (Chi), 5, 115	5	1:09.79	$63,840
2004	**Coconut Girl**, 5, 115	V. Espinoza	Ema Bovary (Chi), 5, 123	Stormica, 4, 115	5	1:08.91	63,600
2003	**Madame Pietra**, 6, 121	P. A. Valenzuela	Bear Fan, 4, 116	Jetinto Houston, 4, 116	6	1:09.71	64,080
2002	**Slewsbox**, 5, 117	L. A. Pincay Jr.	Kalookan Queen, 6, 123	Rolly Polly (Ire), 4, 117	6	1:09.57	64,260
2001	**Go Go**, 4, 122	E. J. Delahoussaye	Kalookan Queen, 5, 117	Wired to Fly, 4, 113	5	**1:08.09**	63,600
2000	**Theresa's Tizzy**, 6, 118	L. A. Pincay Jr.	Hookedonthefeelin, 4, 117	Seth's Choice, 4, 114	7	1:09.30	64,980
1999	**A. P. Assay**, 5, 122	E. J. Delahoussaye	Woodman's Dancer, 5, 116	Corona Lake, 5, 118	5	1:08.69	63,600
1998	**Corona Lake**, 4, 118	E. J. Delahoussaye	Lavender, 4, 118	Grab the Prize, 6, 116	5	1:14.71	64,020
1997	**Advancing Star**, 4, 119	K. J. Desormeaux	Stop Traffic, 4, 118	Tiffany Diamond, 4, 113	5	1:14.21	60,000

Named for Joanne H. Nor's 1995 Breeders' Cup Sprint (G1) winner Desert Stormer (1990 f. by Storm Cat). 6½ furlongs 1997-'98.

Diana Handicap

Grade 1 in 2005. Saratoga Race Course, three-year-olds and up, fillies and mares, 1⅛ miles, turf. Held July 31, 2004, with a gross value of $500,000. First held in 1939. First graded in 1973. Stakes record 1:45.40 (1978 Waya [Fr]).

Year	Winner	Jockey	Second	Third	Strs	Time	1st Purse
2004	**Wonder Again**, 5, 120	E. S. Prado	Riskaverse, 5, 118	Ocean Drive, 4, 118	7	1:48.99	$300,000
2003	**Voodoo Dancer**, 5, 120	C. S. Nakatani	Heat Haze (GB), 4, 118	Pertuisane (GB), 4, 115	8	1:47.98	300,000
2002	**Tates Creek**, 4, 117	J. D. Bailey	Voodoo Dancer, 4, 120	Snow Dance, 4, 117	9	1:48.00	300,000
2001	**Starine (Fr)**, 4, 114	J. R. Velazquez	Babae (Chi), 5, 114	Penny's Gold, 4, 120	9	1:46.17	300,000
2000	**Perfect Sting**, 4, 123	J. D. Bailey	License Fee, 5, 116	Hello Soso (Ire), 4, 113	7	1:47.01	300,000
1999	**Heritage of Gold**, 4, 115	S. J. Sellers	Khumba Mela (Ire), 4, 114	Mossflower, 5, 114	9	1:45.93	180,000
1998	**Memories of Silver**, 5, 123	J. D. Bailey	B. A. Valentine, 5, 114	Auntie Mame, 4, 122	8	1:46.14	180,000
1997	**Rumpipumpy (GB)**, 4, 114	J. A. Santos	B. A. Valentine, 4, 116	Antespend, 4, 117	12	1:48.59	120,000
1996	**Electric Society (Ire)**, 5, 117	M. E. Smith	Powder Bowl, 4, 116	Upper Noosh, 4, 110	9	1:46.56	120,000
1995	**Perfect Arc**, 3, 113	J. R. Velazquez	Danish (Ire), 4, 118	Tiffany's Taylor, 5, 113	9	1:46.85	85,125
1994	**Via Borghese**, 5, 115	J. A. Santos	Blazing Kadie, 4, 110	Coronation Cup, 3, 108	7	1:52.01	83,010
1993	**Ratings**, 5, 110	J. A. Krone	Lady Blessington (Fr), 5, 118	Garendare (GB), 4, 113	8	1:49.80	72,240
1992	**Plenty of Grace**, 5, 114	W. H. McCauley	Ratings, 4, 114	Highland Crystal, 4, 115	12	1:46.66	75,960
1991	**Christiecat**, 4, 117	J. Samyn	Virgin Michael, 4, 112	Senora Tippy, 5, 111	9	1:47.66	75,360
1990	**Foresta**, 4, 113	A. T. Cordero Jr.	To the Lighthouse, 4, 113	Songlines, 4, 111	11	1:48.40	56,790
1989	**‡Glowing Honor**, 4, 115	J. D. Bailey	Wooing, 4, 111	Laugh and Be Merry, 4, 114	9	1:50.20	76,200
1988	**Glowing Honor**, 3, 106	P. Day	Sunny Roberta, 3, 111	Graceful Darby, 4, 112	9	1:49.40	73,680
1987	**Bairullah**, 5, 111	J. Cruguet	Perfect Point, 5, 114	Videogenic, 5, 116	13	1:46.20	91,860
1986	**Duty Dance**, 4, 118	J. Cruguet	Dismasted, 4, 115	Kapalua Butterfly, 5, 112	11	1:49.80	91,380
1985	**Lake Country**, 4, 117	J. Fell	Possible Mate, 4, 118	Key Dancer, 4, 120	11	1:48.40	58,230
1984	**Wild Applause**, 3, 109	W. A. Guerra	Pretty Perfect, 4, 109	Spit Curl, 4, 112	9	1:48.20	70,650
1983	**Geraldine's Store**, 4, 108	J. Samyn	Trevita (Ire), 6, 120	Infinite, 3, 111	8	1:47.20	33,840
	Hush Dear, 5, 123	J. Vasquez	If Winter Comes, 5, 112	First Approach, 5, 118	9	1:48.40	34,080
1982	**Hush Dear**, 4, 109	E. Beitia	Larida, 3, 114	So Pleasantly, 4, 113	11	1:47.40	34,170
	If Winter Comes, 4, 110	E. Beitia	Canaille (Ire), 4, 112	Noble Damsel, 4, 114	10	1:47.40	34,170
1981	**De La Rose**, 3, 114	E. Maple	Rokeby Rose, 4, 115	Euphrosyne, 5, 112	8	1:50.60	36,420
1980	**Just a Game (Ire)**, 4, 123	D. Brumfield	The Very One, 5, 117	Relaxing, 4, 113	9	1:49.00	35,520
1979	**Pearl Necklace**, 5, 124	J. Fell	Island Kiss, 4, 114	Terpsichorist, 4, 119	9	1:48.80	35,010
1978	**Waya (Fr)**, 4, 115	A. T. Cordero Jr.	Pearl Necklace, 4, 125	Fia, 4, 110	12	**1:45.40**	33,240
1977	**Javamine**, 4, 114	A. T. Cordero Jr.	Pearl Necklace, 3, 109	Rich Soil, 3, 114	8	1:48.40	32,640
1976	**Glowing Tribute**, 3, 116	R. Turcotte	Fleet Victress, 4, 117	Nijana, 3, 111	9	1:47.60	32,910
1975	**Heloise**, 4, 113	M. Venezia	Victorian Queen, 4, 118	Princesse Grey, 4, 113	12	1:47.40	35,250
1974	**Fairway Flyer**, 5, 118	J. Velasquez	North Broadway, 4, 117	Brindabella, 4, 113	9	1:47.20	35,070
1973	**Cathy Baby**, 4, 119	J. Velasquez	Something Super, 3, 113	Worldling, 4, 111	8	1:46.60	13,620
	Lightning Lucy, 3, 116	R. Turcotte	Flying Fur, 4, 114	Summer Guest, 4, 122	7	1:46.60	13,545

Named for the mythological Roman goddess of the hunt, Diana. Grade 2 1973-2002. Held at Belmont Park 1943-'45. Dirt 1939-'72. Two divisions 1973, 1982-'83. ‡Wooing finished first, DQ to second, 1989.

Discovery Handicap

Grade 3 in 2005. Aqueduct, three-year-olds and up, 1⅛ miles, dirt. Held October 27, 2004, with a gross value of $110,100. First held in 1945. First graded in 1973. Stakes record 1:47.20 (1973 Forego).

Year	Winner	Jockey	Second	Third	Strs	Time	1st Purse
2004	**Zakocity**, 3, 116	J. Castellano	Stolen Time, 3, 116	Mahzouz, 3, 115	8	1:49.78	$66,060
2003	**During**, 3, 120	J. A. Santos	Unforgettable Max, 3, 114	Inamorato, 3, 114	8	1:51.18	67,080
2002	**Saint Marden**, 3, 117	J. D. Bailey	Regency Park, 3, 115	No Parole, 3, 117	10	1:49.13	68,400

2001	Evening Attire, 3, 111	S. Bridgmohan	Street Cry (Ire), 3, 118	Free of Love, 3, 115	7	1:48.62	$65,580
2000	Left Bank, 3, 119	J. R. Velazquez	Perfect Cat, 3, 114	Open Sesame, 3, 115	4	1:47.30	64,020
1999	Adonis, 3, 118	J. R. Velazquez	Best of Luck, 3, 118	Waddaan, 3, 113	6	1:50.11	64,980
1998	Early Warning, 3, 115	J. F. Chavez	Deputy Diamond, 3, 117	Gulliver, 3, 115	8	1:48.94	50,010
1997	Mr. Sinatra, 3, 116	M. E. Smith	Concerto, 3, 121	Twin Spires, 3, 116	5	1:49.55	64,626
1996	Gold Fever, 3, 121	M. E. Smith	Crafty Friend, 3, 115	Early Echoes, 3, 111	9	1:49.01	66,720
1995	Michael's Star, 3, 112	J. A. Krone	Hunting Hard, 3, 113	Reality Road, 3, 114	10	1:50.34	67,380
1994	Serious Spender, 3, 113	J. F. Chavez	Unaccounted For, 3, 121	Malmo, 3, 112	4	1:51.24	63,540
1993	Prospector's Flag, 3, 114	J. F. Chavez	Virginia Rapids, 3, 118	Living Vicariously, 3, 114	8	1:52.30	70,320
1992	New Deal, 3, 111	R. G. Davis	Offbeat, 3, 114	Dodsworth, 3, 113	11	1:48.08	74,880
1991	Upon My Soul, 3, 112	J. Samyn	Excellent Tipper, 3, 114	Honest Ensign, 3, 110	11	1:49.62	75,960
1990	Sports View, 3, 113	J. A. Santos	Chief Honcho, 3, 117	dh- Killer Diller, 3, 116	7	1:48.60	52,830
				dh- Out of Place, 3, 112			
1989	Tricky Creek, 3, 117	C. Perret	Traskwood, 3, 113	Farewell Wave, 3, 110	9	1:50.00	71,280
1988	Dynaformer, 3, 116	A. T. Cordero Jr.	Star Attitude, 3, 113	Congeleur, 3, 112	7	1:50.00	104,580
1987	Parochial, 3, 117	J. A. Krone	Homebuilder, 3, 112	Forest Fair, 3, 115	11	1:51.20	109,620
1986	Moment of Hope, 3, 108	M. Venezia	Gold Alert, 3, 109	Clear Choice, 3, 112	9	1:49.60	54,000
1985	Proud Truth, 3, 126	J. Velasquez	Important Business, 3, 113	Romancer, 3, 110	6	1:49.20	51,750
1984	Key to the Moon, 3, 120	D. Beckon	Silver Stark, 3, 110	Raja's Shark, 3, 124	6	1:50.00	42,300
1983	Country Pine, 3, 118	J. D. Bailey	Jacque's Tip, 3, 115	Father Don Juan, 3, 112	6	1:49.60	33,420
1982	Trenchant, 3, 113	J. Samyn	Dew Line, 3, 113	Exclusive Era, 3, 112	5	1:50.80	32,880
1981	Princelet, 3, 113	E. Maple	Accipiter's Hope, 3, 118	Pass the Tab, 3, 126	7	1:51.00	33,240
1980	Fappiano, 3, 114	A. T. Cordero Jr.	Reef Searcher, 3, 114	Royal Hierarchy, 3, 111	11	1:50.00	35,280
1979	Belle's Gold, 3, 121	A. T. Cordero Jr.	Smarten, 3, 122	Gallant Best, 3, 115	7	1:48.00	33,270
1978	Sorry Lookin, 3, 110	R. I. Velez	Silent Cal, 3, 115	Judge Advocate, 3, 114	6	1:49.60	31,740
1977	Cox's Ridge, 3, 126	E. Maple	Broadway Forli, 3, 123	Papelote, 3, 107	9	1:48.60	32,670
1976	Wise Philip, 3, 107	D. Montoya	Teddy's Courage, 3, 115	Patriot's Dream, 3, 112	8	1:48.60	32,460
1975	Dr. Emil, 3, 115	B. Baeza	● Rushing Man, 3, 125	Syllabus, 3, 113	7	1:48.60	33,630
1974	Rube the Great, 3, 119	A. T. Cordero Jr.	Holding Pattern, 3, 126	Sharp Gary, 3, 118	8	1:48.20	33,270
	Green Gambados, 3, 120	A. T. Cordero Jr.	Best of It, 3, 116	Jolly Johu, 3, 121	9	1:48.20	33,570
1973	Forego, 3, 127	H. Gustines	My Gallant, 3, 122	‡Arbees Boy, 3, 114	7	1:47.20	33,300

Named for Alfred G. Vanderbilt's 1935 Horse of the Year and three-time Brooklyn H. winner Discovery (1931 c. by Display). Grade 2 1988-'89. Held at Belmont Park 1945-'58, 1960-'61, 1968-'70. Two divisions 1974. Dead heat for third 1990. ‡Key to the Kingdom finished third, DQ to seventh, 1973.

Distaff Breeders' Cup Handicap

Grade 2 in 2005. Aqueduct, three-year-olds and up, fillies and mares, 7 furlongs. Held March 26, 2005, with a gross value of $148,900. First held in 1954. First graded in 1973. Stakes record 1:21.18 (1991 Devil's Orchid).

Year	Winner	Jockey	Second	Third	Strs	Time	1st Purse
2005	Bank Audit, 4, 118	R. Migliore	Sensibly Chic, 5, 117	Travelator, 5, 116	7	1:22.07	$95,040
2004	Randaroo, 4, 121	R. Migliore	Chirimoya, 5, 110	Storm Flag Flying, 4, 118	4	1:22.64	93,240
2003	Carson Hollow, 4, 120	M. J. Luzzi	Raging Fever, 5, 118	Bonefide Reason, 5, 112	6	1:22.42	94,740
2002	Raging Fever, 4, 120	J. R. Velazquez	Prized Stamp, 5, 114	La Galerie (Arg), 6, 115	6	1:21.78	94,680
2001	Dream Supreme, 4, 119	A. T. Gryder	Folly Dollar, 4, 113	Country Hideaway, 5, 118	5	1:23.66	108,960
2000	Honest Lady, 4, 117	B. Blanc	Her She Kisses, 4, 115	Tap to Music, 5, 118	8	1:22.10	111,300
1999	Furlough, 5, 115	H. Castillo Jr.	Catinca, 4, 121	Tomorrows Sunshine, 5, 113	9	1:23.23	112,260
1998	Parlay, 4, 114	R. Migliore	Lucky Marty, 5, 113	Green Light, 4, 114	9	1:24.10	67,260
1997	Miss Golden Circle, 5, 120	R. Migliore	Inquisitive Look, 4, 110	Punkin Pie, 7, 109	6	1:24.47	65,400
1996	Lottsa Talc, 6, 120	F. T. Alvarado	Traverse City, 6, 120	Dust Bucket, 5, 116	7	1:24.04	75,820
1995	Recognizable, 4, 120	M. E. Smith	Beckys Shirt, 4, 113	Kurofune Mystery, 5, 116	8	1:22.94	66,540
1994	Classy Mirage, 4, 114	R. G. Davis	Jill Miner, 4, 114	Air Port Won, 4, 109	8	1:11.37	66,480
1992	Nannerl, 5, 112	M. E. Smith	Missy's Mirage, 4, 119	Withallprobability, 4, 117	6	1:24.68	68,800
1991	Devil's Orchid, 4, 117	R. A. Baze	Your Hope, 6, 112	Fappaburst, 4, 114	5	1:21.18	67,080
1990	Channel Three, 4, 111	J. F. Chavez	Divine Answer, 4, 113	Hedgeabout, 6, 112	10	1:23.20	54,090
1989	Avie's Gal, 4, 112	N. Santagata	Haiati, 4, 111	Topicount, 4, 117	5	1:24.00	51,660
1988	Cadillacing, 4, 112	R. P. Romero	Cagey Exuberance, 4, 118	Bishop's Delight, 5, 111	5	1:22.60	50,670
1987	Pine Tree Lane, 5, 125	A. T. Cordero Jr.	Spring Beauty, 4, 117	Gene's Lady, 6, 117	7	1:22.40	52,650
1986	Ride Sally, 4, 118	W. A. Guerra	Willowy Mood, 4, 116	Clocks Secret, 4, 122	6	1:21.60	54,540
1985	Give Me a Hint, 5, 109	W. A. Ward	Nany, 5, 121	Descent, 5, 106	8	1:20.80	55,080
1984	Am Capable, 4, 125	A. T. Cordero Jr.	Sweet Missus, 4, 104	Fissure, 4, 107	7	1:11.00	52,290
1983	Jones Time Machine, 4, 122	A. T. Cordero Jr.	Fancy Naskra, 5, 113	Adept, 4, 111	6	1:23.20	32,880
1982	Lady Dean, 4, 120	D. A. Miller Jr.	Westport Native, 4, 114	Raise 'n Dance, 4, 107	8	1:23.80	33,000
1981	Lady Oakley (Ire), 4, 114	J. Fell	It's in the Air, 5, 120	Lovin' Lass, 4, 110	8	1:25.40	33,900
1980	Misty Gallore, 4, 124	D. MacBeth	Lady Lonsdale, 5, 114	Spanish Fake, 4, 112	6	1:24.60	33,240
1979	Skipat, 5, 122	J. W. Edwards	Sweet Joyce, 4, 106	Unpossible, 4, 107	10	1:10.40	32,520
1978	Vandy Sue, 4, 112	A. M. Rodriguez	Sea Drone, 4, 108	Dalton Road, 5, 118	7	1:12.00	22,185
1977	What a Summer, 4, 118	E. Maple	Secret Lanvin, 4, 112	Shy Dawn, 6, 120	5	1:11.60	22,590
1976	Shy Dawn, 5, 118	A. T. Cordero Jr.	‡Land Girl, 4, 114	Ladies Agreement, 6, 114	8	1:24.20	22,550
1975	Something Super, 5, 115	J. Cruguet	Shy Dawn, 4, 121	Second Coming, 4, 108	9	1:22.20	16,996
1974	Krislin, 5, 113	V. A. Bracciale Jr.	Batucada, 5, 116	Ladies Agreement, 4, 112	8	1:22.00	16,770
1973	Ferly, 5, 113	R. Turcotte	Wakefield Miss, 5, 115	Twixt, 4, 112	8	1:24.00	16,920

Races for females are typically referred to as distaff races. Grade 3 1973-'88. Distaff H. 1954-'98. Held at Belmont Park 1956-'59. Not held 1993. 6 furlongs 1977-'79, 1984, 1994. ‡Imminence finished second, DQ to fourth, 1976.

Dixie Stakes

Grade 2 in 2005. Pimlico, three-year-olds and up, 1⅛ miles, turf. Held May 21, 2005, with a gross value of $200,000. First held in 1870. First graded in 1973. Stakes record 1:46.34 (2004 Mr O'Brien [Ire]).

Year	Winner	Jockey	Second	Third	Strs	Time	1st Purse
2005	Cool Conductor, 4, 118	C. H. Velasquez	Artie Schiller, 4, 124	Good Reward, 4, 118	5	1:52.79	$120,000
2004	Mr O'Brien (Ire), 4, 117	R. A. Dominguez	Millennium Dragon (GB), 5, 121	Warleigh, 6, 124	11	**1:46.34**	120,000
2003	Dr. Brendler, 5, 117	R. A. Dominguez	Perfect Soul (Ire), 5, 117	Sardaukar (GB), 7, 117	6	1:57.78	120,000
2002	Strut the Stage, 4, 117	R. Albarado	Del Mar Show, 5, 119	Slew the Red, 5, 117	7	1:51.70	120,000
2001	Hap, 5, 119	J. D. Bailey	Make No Mistake (Ire), 6, 119	Cynics Beware, 7, 119	8	1:48.56	120,000
2000	Quiet Resolve, 5, 117	R. Albarado	Haami, 5, 117	Holdithditholdit, 4, 117	9	1:50.42	120,000
1999	Middlesex Drive, 4, 115	P. Day	Sky Colony, 6, 115	Divide and Conquer, 5, 115	10	1:48.64	120,000
1998	Yagli, 5, 121	J. D. Bailey	Sky Colony, 5, 115	Blazing Sword, 4, 115	12	1:51.01	120,000
1997	Ops Smile, 5, 115	E. S. Prado	Brave Note (Ire), 6, 115	Sharp Appeal, 4, 121	8	1:48.20	120,000
1996	Canaveral, 5, 115	S. J. Sellers	Michael's Star, 4, 114	Rugged Bugger, 5, 113	7	1:49.03	120,000
1995	The Vid, 5, 119	J. D. Bailey	Pennine Ridge, 4, 115	Blues Traveller (Ire), 5, 121	6	1:52.25	120,000
1994	Paradise Creek, 5, 124	P. Day	Lure, 5, 124	Astudillo (Ire), 4, 115	5	1:48.51	90,000
1993	Lure, 4, 124	M. E. Smith	Star of Cozzene, 5, 119	Binary Light, 4, 115	8	1:47.60	90,000
1992	Sky Classic, 5, 122	P. Day	Fourstars Allstar, 4, 116	Social Retiree, 5, 112	10	1:47.83	90,000
1991	Double Booked, 6, 118	P. Day	Chas' Whim, 4, 116	Opening Verse, 5, 118	9	1:47.04	90,000
1990	Two Moccasins, 4, 114	R. P. Romero	My Big Boy, 7, 115	Marksmanship, 5, 113	10	2:35.80	90,000
1989	Coeur de Lion (Fr) 5, 121	J. Cruguet	Dance Card Filled, 6, 115	Dynaformer, 4, 118	10	2:38.40	90,000
1988	Kadial (Ire), 5, 112	G. L. Stevens	Top Guest (Ire), 5, 118	Milesius, 4, 120	5	2:45.00	71,045
1987	Akabir, 4, 114	C. Perret	Little Bold John, 5, 117	Vilzak, 4, 113	9	2:28.60	74,360
1986	Uptown Swell, 4, 117	W. A. Guerra	Southern Sultan, 4, 112	†Carlypha (Ire), 5, 108	13	2:27.40	92,445
1985	Nassipour, 5, 115	V. A. Bracciale Jr.	†Persian Tiara (Ire), 5, 113	‡Computer's Choice, 5, 116	8	2:27.80	72,800
1984	†Persian Tiara (Ire), 4, 109	R. L. Shelton	Crazy Moon, 4, 112	Canadian Factor, 4, 118	8	2:41.00	88,675
1983	Khatango, 4, 114	V. A. Bracciale Jr.	London Times, 5, 108	Super Sunrise (GB), 4, 114	10	2:28.60	75,075
1982	Robsphere, 5, 120	J. Velasquez	Present the Colors, 5, 113	Rich and Ready, 6, 115	13	2:30.20	76,960
1981	El Barril (Chi), 5, 116	J. Vasquez	Buckpoint (Fr), 5, 119	Birthday List, 6, 108	9	2:29.80	73,225
1980	Marquee Universal (Ire), 4, 118	H. Pilar	†The Very One, 5, 113	Match the Hatch, 4, 115	14	2:29.60	77,155
1979	†The Very One, 4, 108	C. Cooke	That's a Nice, 5, 116	Fluorescent Light, 5, 124	8	2:28.60	72,995
1978	Bowl Game, 4, 120	J. Velasquez	Oilfield, 5, 110	Trumpeter Swan, 7, 110	9	2:33.40	37,993
	Fluorescent Light, 4, 114	V. A. Bracciale Jr.	That's a Nice, 4, 115	Improviser, 4, 108	7	2:33.20	37,343
1977	Improviser, 5, 120	M. A. Rivera	Grey Beret, 5, 114	Oilfield, 4, 118	12	2:29.40	56,875
1976	Barcas, 5, 112	V. A. Bracciale Jr.	One On the Aisle, 4, 122	Neapolitan Way, 5, 108	9	2:29.60	37,375
1975	Bemo, 5, 114	C. J. McCarron	Outdoors, 6, 115	Drollery, 5, 114	13	2:33.40	39,325
1974	London Company, 4, 122	A. T. Cordero Jr.	Scrimshaw, 6, 110	Mister Diz, 5, 114	9	2:28.80	38,025
1973	Laplander, 6, 111	V. A. Bracciale Jr.	Chrisaway, 5, 112	*Wustenchef, 8, 112	10	2:30.40	38,675

Named for Major Barak G. Thomas's mare Dixie (1859 f. by *Sovereign). Sponsored by Argent Mortgage Co. of Orange, California 2004. Formerly sponsored by CITGO Petroleum Corp. of Tulsa, Oklahoma. Formerly sponsored by Early Times Distillery Co. of Louisville. Named the Reunion Stakes to signify a reunion of the original subscribers to the Dinner Party S. Originally named the Dinner Party S. The name originated with a Saratoga Springs dinner party attended by a group of men whose main topic of conversation was the revival of Baltimore racing after the Civil War; all present agreed to support the inaugural running of the race in 1870. Grade 3 1990-'93. Dinner Party S. 1870. Dixie H. 1871, 1902-'04, 1925-'90, 1991-'94, 1996. Reunion S. 1872-'88. Held at Benning, Washington, D.C. 1902-'04. Not held 1889-1901, 1905-'23. 2 miles 1870-'88. 1¾ miles 1902-'04. 1³⁄₁₆ miles 1924. 1³⁄₁₆ miles 1955-'59. 1½ miles 1960-'90. 1⅛ miles 1988. Dirt 1870-1954, 1988. Three-year-olds 1870-1904. Two divisions 1965, 1978. ‡Pass the Line finished third, DQ to fourth, 1985. Course record 2004. †Denotes female.

Dogwood Breeders' Cup Stakes

Grade 3 in 2005. Churchill Downs, three-year-olds, fillies, 1¹⁄₁₆ miles, dirt. Held June 11, 2005, with a gross value of $162,900. First held in 1975. First graded in 1998. Stakes record 1:42.73 (2002 Take Charge Lady).

Year	Winner	Jockey	Second	Third	Strs	Time	1st Purse
2005	Miss Matched, 3, 116	S. Bridgmohan	Culinary, 3, 120	Catta Pilosa, 3, 116	7	1:43.49	$101,928
2004	Stellar Jayne, 3, 120	R. Albarado	Dynaville, 3, 114	Ender's Sister, 3, 122	5	1:43.14	100,068
2003	Golden Marlin, 3, 115	S. J. Sellers	Double Scoop, 3, 114	Throne, 3, 114	7	1:45.96	67,580
2002	Take Charge Lady, 3, 121	A. J. D'Amico	Charmed Gift, 3, 116	Allamerican Bertie, 3, 114	7	**1:42.73**	67,890
2001	Nasty Storm, 3, 114	L. J. Meche	Love At Noon, 3, 114	Golly Greeley, 3, 116	7	1:43.41	68,014
2000	Welcome Surprise, 3, 112	F. C. Torres	Lady Melesi, 3, 114	Vivid Sunset, 3, 114	7	1:46.80	68,014
1999	Golden Temper, 3, 116	S. J. Sellers	Boom Town Girl, 3, 121	Honey Hill Lil, 3, 116	8	1:43.73	69,068
1998	Really Polish, 3, 116	P. Day	‡Beat the Play, 3, 114	Victorica, 3, 121	5	1:44.78	67,642
1997	Leo's Gypsy Dancer, 3, 116	P. Day	Buckeye Search, 3, 121	Flying Lauren, 3, 118	7	1:44.95	69,006
1996	Ginny Lynn, 3, 121	L. J. Melancon	Everhope, 3, 121	Hidden Lake, 3, 114	7	1:43.22	53,576
1995	Gal in a Ruckus, 3, 121	W. H. McCauley	Country Cat, 3, 116	Naskra Colors, 3, 114	7	1:43.88	53,528
1994	Briar Road, 3, 114	L. J. Melancon	Stella Cielo, 3, 114	Shadow Miss, 3, 121	6	1:44.78	53,186
1993	With a Wink, 3, 114	C. R. Woods Jr.	Lovat's Lady, 3, 112	Unlaced, 3, 116	8	1:44.21	36,010
1992	Hitch, 3, 121	B. E. Baemon	Bionic Soul, 3, 121	Secretly, 3, 114	8	1:47.68	36,075
1991	Be Cool, 3, 121	A. T. Gryder	Barri Mac, 3, 114	Saratoga Dame, 3, 121	8	1:46.46	36,563
1990	Patches, 3, 118	K. K. Allen	Mrs. K., 3, 116	Mirth, 3, 114	4	1:46.60	34,873
1989	Luthier's Launch, 3, 118	P. Day	Motion in Limine, 3, 116	Dreamy Mimi, 3, 121	9	1:45.20	36,465
1988	Darien Miss, 3, 121	D. Brumfield	Stolie, 3, 118	Most Likely, 3, 116	8	1:43.80	35,848

Year Winner	Jockey	Second	Third	Strs	Time	1st Purse
1987 **Lady Gretchen**, 3, 112	M. McDowell	Super Cook, 3, 122	Jonowo, 3, 122	7	1:44.00	$46,193
1986 **Hail a Cab**, 3, 119	P. A. Johnson	Tall Poppy, 3, 111	Marshesseaux, 3, 114	8	1:46.60	46,810
1985 **Foxy Deen**, 3, 118	D. Montoya	Weekend Delight, 3, 120	Clouhalo, 3, 112	8	1:50.00	35,945
1984 **Mrs. Revere**, 3, 121	L. J. Melancon	Rambling Rhythm, 3, 119	Robin's Rob, 3, 115	8	1:51.20	49,510
1983 **Bon Gout**, 3, 117	P. Day	Andthebeatgoeson, 3, 112	Workin Girl, 3, 112	8	1:53.00	36,368
1982 **Amazing Love**, 3, 117	L. J. Melancon	Sefa's Beauty, 3, 117	Bold Siren, 3, 113	8	1:46.60	23,546
1981 **Savage Love**, 3, 116	P. Nicolo	Westport Native, 3, 118	Brian's Babe, 3, 116	6	1:24.80	19,053
Fancy Naskra, 3, 118	J. L. Lively	Contrefaire, 3, 121	Solo Disco, 3, 118	10	1:25.20	17,948
1980 **Quality Corner**, 3, 121	M. S. Sellers	Forever Cordial, 3, 121	No No Nona, 3, 121	8	1:24.00	19,403
1979 **Split the Tab**, 3, 121	D. Haire	Shawn's Gal, 3, 121	Safe, 3, 121	10	1:24.00	19,663
1978 **Bold Rendezvous**, 3, 121	A. Rini	Step in the Circle, 3, 118	Timeforaturn, 3, 118	8	1:23.40	14,446
1977 **Unreality**, 3, 121	M. Fromin	Shady Lou, 3, 121	Time for Pleasure, 3, 118	12	1:25.40	15,031
1976 **T. V. Vixen**, 3, 121	M. Manganello	Sunny Romance, 3, 116	Old Goat, 3, 121	6	1:23.40	14,154
1975 **My Juliet**, 3, 121	A. Hill	Snow Doll, 3, 118	Hope She Does, 3, 118	9	1:24.00	14,999

Named for the dogwood tree, plentiful in Kentucky. Dogwood S. 1975-2003. 7 furlongs 1975-'81. 1⅛ miles 1983-'85. Two divisions 1981. ‡Nickel Classic finished second, DQ to fifth, 1998.

Donn Handicap

Grade 1 in 2005. Gulfstream Park, three-year-olds and up, 1⅛ miles, dirt. Held February 5, 2005, with a gross value of $500,000. First held in 1959. First graded in 1973. Stakes record 1:46.40 (1979 Jumping Hill).

Year Winner	Jockey	Second	Third	Strs	Time	1st Purse
2005 **Saint Liam**, 5, 119	E. S. Prado	Roses in May, 5, 121	Eddington, 4, 114	6	1:48.43	$300,000
2004 **Medaglia d'Oro**, 5, 122	J. D. Bailey	Seattle Fitz (Arg), 5, 113	Funny Cide, 4, 119	8	1:47.68	300,000
2003 **Harlan's Holiday**, 4, 120	J. R. Velazquez	Hero's Tribute, 5, 114	Puzzlement, 4, 114	11	1:49.17	300,000
2002 **Mongoose**, 4, 114	E. S. Prado	‡Kiss a Native, 5, 114	Rize, 6, 114	14	1:49.63	300,000
2001 **Captain Steve**, 4, 120	J. D. Bailey	Albert the Great, 4, 119	Gander, 5, 115	7	1:48.95	300,000
2000 **Stephen Got Even**, 4, 115	S. J. Sellers	Golden Missile, 5, 114	Behrens, 6, 121	10	1:48.50	300,000
1999 **Puerto Madero (Chi)**, 5, 120	K. J. Desormeaux	Behrens, 5, 113	Silver Charm, 5, 126	12	1:48.34	300,000
1998 **Skip Away**, 5, 126	J. D. Bailey	Unruled, 5, 112	Sir Bear, 5, 113	10	1:50.17	180,000
1997 **Formal Gold**, 4, 113	J. Bravo	Skip Away, 4, 123	Mecke, 5, 120	10	1:47.49	180,000
1996 **Cigar**, 6, 128	J. D. Bailey	Wekiva Springs, 5, 117	†Heavenly Prize, 5, 115	8	1:49.12	180,000
1995 **Cigar**, 5, 115	J. D. Bailey	Primitive Hall, 5, 112	Bonus Money (GB), 4, 112	9	1:49.68	180,000
1994 **Pistols and Roses**, 5, 113	H. Castillo Jr.	Eequalsmcsquared, 5, 113	Wallenda, 4, 118	11	1:50.67	180,000
1993 **Pistols and Roses**, 4, 112	H. Castillo Jr.	Irish Swap, 6, 118	Missionary Ridge (GB), 6, 118	9	1:50.10	240,000
1992 **Sea Cadet**, 4, 115	A. O. Solis	Out of Place, 5, 114	Sunny Sunrise, 5, 115	8	1:48.17	300,000
1991 **Jolie's Halo**, 4, 114	R. Platts	Sports View, 4, 116	Secret Hello, 4, 116	12	1:47.50	300,000
1990 **Primal**, 5, 120	E. Fires	Ole Atocha, 5, 111	Western Playboy, 4, 119	8	1:50.00	120,000
1989 **Cryptoclearance**, 5, 121	J. A. Santos	Slew City Slew, 5, 118	Primal, 4, 117	12	1:50.20	120,000
1988 **Jade Hunter**, 4, 112	J. D. Bailey	Cryptoclearance, 4, 123	Personal Flag, 5, 120	8	1:48.80	120,000
1987 **Little Bold John**, 5, 111	M. A. Gonzalez	Skip Trial, 5, 118	Wise Times, 4, 117	7	1:48.80	96,660
1986 **Creme Fraiche**, 4, 122	E. Maple	Skip Trial, 4, 122	Minneapple, 4, 113	13	1:51.20	77,280
1985 **Mo Exception**, 4, 115	R. Breen	Dr. Carter, 4, 120	Key to the Moon, 4, 122	10	1:48.60	74,280
1984 **Play Fellow**, 4, 122	P. Day	Courteous Majesty, 4, 111	Jack Slade, 4, 114	9	1:49.00	53,955
1983 **Deputy Minister**, 4, 122	D. MacBeth	Key Count, 4, 113	Rivalero, 7, 121	16	1:48.60	60,840
1982 **Joanie's Chief**, 5, 111	J. Samyn	Double Sonic, 4, 111	Lord Darnley, 4, 113	12	1:49.00	57,330
1981 **Hurry Up Blue**, 4, 116	C. C. Lopez	Tunerup, 5, 126	Joanie's Chief, 4, 107	5	1:49.00	51,345
1980 **Lot o' Gold**, 4, 119	D. Brumfield	Addison, 5, 111	Going Investor, 5, 112	9	1:48.80	54,600
1979 **Jumping Hill**, 7, 122	J. Fell	Bob's Dusty, 5, 120	Silent Cal, 4, 121	14	**1:46.40**	60,150
1978 **Man's Man**, 4, 115	R. Woodhouse	Intercontinent, 4, 116	Adriatico (Arg), 7, 110	11	1:42.20	39,000
1977 **Legion**, 7, 113	L. Saumell	Logical, 5, 114	Yamanin, 5, 124	7	1:48.80	37,440
1976 **Foolish Pleasure**, 4, 129	B. Baeza	Packer Captain, 4, 114	Home Jerome, 6, 112	10	1:21.40	37,980
1975 **Proud and Bold**, 5, 118	G. St. Leon	Holding Pattern, 4, 121	Arbees Boy, 5, 119	6	1:48.00	35,280
1974 **Forego**, 4, 125	H. Gustines	True Knight, 5, 123	Proud and Bold, 4, 122	5	1:48.60	36,000
1973 **Triumphant**, 4, 114	B. Baeza	Second Bar, 4, 121	Gentle Smoke, 4, 113	7	1:47.80	37,560

Named in honor of James Donn Sr. (1887-1972), founder of modern Gulfstream Park. Grade 3 1973-'74. Grade 2 1975-'87. 1½ miles 1959-'64. 7 furlongs 1976. 1¹⁄₁₆ miles 1978. Turf 1959-'64. ‡Red Bullet finished second, DQ to fourth, 2002. †Denotes female.

Dwyer Stakes

Grade 2 in 2005. Belmont Park, three-year-olds, 1¹⁄₁₆ miles, dirt. Held July 11, 2004, with a gross value of $150,000. First held in 1887. First graded in 1973. Stakes record 1:40.02 (2004 Medallist).

Year Winner	Jockey	Second	Third	Strs	Time	1st Purse
2004 **Medallist**, 3, 121	J. F. Chavez	The Cliff's Edge, 3, 123	Sir Shackleton, 3, 121	6	**1:40.02**	$90,000
2003 **Strong Hope**, 3, 115	J. R. Velazquez	Nacheezmo, 3, 115	Sky Mesa, 3, 119	7	1:41.76	90,000
2002 **Gygistar**, 3, 121	J. R. Velazquez	Nothing Flat, 3, 117	American Style, 3, 115	6	1:42.59	90,000
2001 **E Dubai**, 3, 121	J. D. Bailey	Windsor Castle, 3, 119	Hero's Tribute, 3, 121	4	1:42.38	145,500
2000 **Albert the Great**, 3, 115	R. Migliore	More Than Ready, 3, 119	Red Bullet, 3, 123	4	1:42.62	90,000
1999 **Forestry**, 3, 122	J. D. Bailey	Doneraile Court, 3, 119	Successful Appeal, 3, 122	6	1:41.00	90,000
1998 **Coronado's Quest**, 3, 124	M. E. Smith	Ian's Thunder, 3, 112	Scatmandu, 3, 122	5	1:42.49	90,000

Year	Winner	Jockey	Second	Third	Strs	Time	1st Purse
1997	Behrens, 3, 117	J. D. Bailey	Glitman, 3, 114	Banker's Gold, 3, 122	6	1:42.26	$90,000
1996	Victory Speech, 3, 117	J. D. Bailey	Gold Fever, 3, 119	Robb, 3, 117	6	1:41.53	99,000
1995	Hoolie, 3, 117	R. G. Davis	Reality Road, 3, 112	Western Larla, 3, 119	6	1:42.74	90,000
1994	Holy Bull, 3, 124	M. E. Smith	Twining, 3, 122	Bay Street Star, 3, 119	4	1:41.15	90,000
1993	Cherokee Run, 3, 123	P. Day	Miner's Mark, 3, 123	Silver of Silver, 3, 123	6	1:47.62	120,000
1992	‡Agincourt, 3, 119	J. F. Chavez	Three Peat, 3, 119	Windundermywings, 3, 114	6	1:47.84	120,000
1991	Lost Mountain, 3, 123	C. Perret	Smooth Performance, 3, 114	Fly So Free, 3, 126	7	1:49.20	120,000
1990	Profit Key, 3, 123	J. A. Santos	Rhythm, 3, 123	Graf, 3, 114	4	1:47.40	102,960
1989	Roi Danzig, 3, 114	E. Maple	Contested Colors, 3, 114	Rampart Road, 3, 114	5	1:49.20	133,680
1988	Seeking the Gold, 3, 123	P. Day	Evening Kris, 3, 119	Gay Rights, 3, 123	7	1:48.00	137,040
1987	Gone West, 3, 123	E. Maple	Pledge Card, 3, 114	Polish Navy, 3, 123	6	1:48.40	138,240
1986	Ogygian, 3, 119	W. A. Guerra	Johns Treasure, 3, 114	Personal Flag, 3, 114	4	1:48.40	112,680
1985	Stephan's Odyssey, 3, 123	L. A. Pincay Jr.	Cutlass Reality, 3, 114	Important Business, 3, 126	8	1:49.20	88,500
1984	Track Barron, 3, 119	J. Cruguet	Darn That Alarm, 3, 123	Slew the Coup, 3, 114	7	1:47.80	99,600
1983	Au Point, 3, 114	J. D. Bailey	Potentiate, 3, 114	Intention, 3, 114	10	1:48.20	68,640
1982	Conquistador Cielo, 3, 126	E. Maple	John's Gold, 3, 114	Reinvested, 3, 119	6	1:45.80	67,560
1981	Noble Nashua, 3, 119	C. B. Asmussen	Tap Shoes, 3, 126	Silver Express, 3, 114	10	1:49.20	68,160
1980	Amber Pass, 3, 114	D. MacBeth	Temperence Hill, 3, 129	Comptroller, 3, 119	8	1:49.00	67,440
1979	Coastal, 3, 126	R. Hernandez	Private Account, 3, 114	Quiet Crossing, 3, 119	6	1:47.00	63,840
1978	Junction, 3, 120	J. Fell	Buckaroo, 3, 127	Darby Creek Road, 3, 121	3	1:48.80	47,025
1977	Bailjumper, 3, 116	A. T. Cordero Jr.	Lynn Davis, 3, 112	Iron Constitution, 3, 121	4	1:47.60	48,870
1976	Quiet Little Table, 3, 111	E. Maple	Sir Lister, 3, 116	Dance Spell, 3, 117	8	1:49.00	50,895
1975	Valid Appeal, 3, 110	J. S. Long	Wajima, 3, 118	Hunka Papa, 3, 116	8	1:48.40	50,400
1974	Hatchet Man, 3, 114	R. Turcotte	Rube the Great, 3, 124	Kin Run, 3, 112	9	2:01.20	51,120
1973	Stop the Music, 3, 120	H. Gustines	Arbees Boy, 3, 115	Duc de Flanagan, 3, 111	8	2:02.60	50,625

Named in honor of leading 19th-century owners Mike and Phil Dwyer. Formerly named in honor of the city of Brooklyn, New York. Grade 1 1983-'88. Brooklyn Derby 1887-1917. Dwyer H. 1956-'78. Held at Gravesend Park 1887-1910. Held at Aqueduct 1914-'55, 1960-'74, 1976. Held at Jamaica 1956, 1959. Not held 1911-'12. 1½ miles 1887, 1898-1909, 1926-'34. 1⅛ miles 1888-'97, 1915-'24, 1935-'39, 1975-'93. 1¼ miles 1910-'14, 1940-'55, 1960-'74. 1⁵⁄₁₆ miles 1925. 1³⁄₁₆ miles 1956-'59. ‡Three Peat finished first, DQ to second, 1992.

Eatontown Handicap

Grade 3 in 2005. Monmouth Park, three-year-olds and up, fillies and mares, 1¹⁄₁₆ miles, turf. Held July 10, 2004, with a gross value of $100,000. First held in 1971. First graded in 1996. Stakes record 1:40.40 (1996 Gail's Brush).

Year	Winner	Jockey	Second	Third	Strs	Time	1st Purse
2004	Ocean Drive, 4, 120	E. Coa	Honorable Cat, 5, 114	Fast Cookie, 4, 118	6	1:41.79	$60,000
2003	Stylish, 5, 118	H. Castillo Jr.	Something Ventured, 4, 117	Sweet Deimos (GB), 4, 113	9	1:41.69	60,000
2002	Clearly a Queen, 5, 119	E. Coa	Laurica, 5, 114	Presumed Innocent, 5, 117	9	1:44.02	60,000
2001	Cousin Gigi, 4, 115	R. Wilson	Quidnaskra, 6, 116	Crystal Sea, 4, 113	8	1:47.50	60,000
2000	Reciclada (Chi), 5, 115	A. O. Solis	Mumtaz (Fr), 4, 122	Dominique's Joy, 5, 117	8	1:44.34	60,000
1999	Formal Tango, 4, 113	J. D. Bailey	Proud Owner, 4, 115	Natalie Too, 5, 122	7	1:42.62	60,000
1998	Gastronomical, 5, 115	G. L. Stevens	Tampico, 5, 117	dh- Dance Clear (Ire), 5, 112 dh- Poopsie, 4, 114	10	1:43.39	41,400
1997	B. A. Valentine, 4, 122	C. J. McCarron	Everhope, 4, 112	Vashon, 4, 122	11	1:41.20	41,460
1996	Gail's Brush, 5, 116	G. Boulanger	Plenty of Sugar, 5, 117	Lady Affirmed, 5, 116	7	**1:40.40**	45,000
1995	Symphony Lady, 5, 119	J. Bravo	Cox Orange, 5, 122	Grafin, 4, 119	6	1:43.64	30,000
1994	Verbal Volley, 5, 119	R. E. Colton	Irving's Girl, 4, 114	Uptown Show, 5, 113	8	1:44.71	24,000
1993	Topsa, 6, 113	L. R. Rivera Jr.	Naked Royalty, 4, 115	Suspect Terrain, 4, 115	7	1:46.39	21,000
1992	Red Journey, 4, 115	N. Santagata	Hot Times Are Here, 4, 113	Flashing Eyes, 4, 113	7	1:45.06	21,000
1991	Jacuzzi Boogie, 4, 119	N. Santagata	Hear the Bells, 4, 113	Be Exclusive (Ire), 5, 113	5	1:41.67	21,000
1990	Miss Unnameable, 6, 113	L. Saumell	Lip Service, 5, 116	Perfect Coin, 4, 112	9	1:48.00	34,110
1989	Highland Penny, 4, 112	D. Carr	Starofanera, 4, 113	River Memories, 5, 114	9	1:50.00	34,770
1988	Hear Music, 5, 115	M. Castaneda	Fancy Pan, 5, 112	Antique Mystique, 4, 111	7	1:49.80	34,440
1987	Bailrullah, 5, 111	N. Santagata	Princely Proof, 4, 116	Krotz, 4, 118	10	1:44.00	28,590
	Cadabra Abra, 4, 118	W. H. McCauley	Treasure Map, 5, 115	Spruce Fir, 4, 121	6	1:43.80	28,110
1986	Mazatleca (Mex), 6, 117	C. Perret	Cope of Flowers, 4, 114	Darbrielle, 4, 113	8	1:43.20	27,960
	Bharal, 5, 114	J. Velasquez	Thirteen Keys, 4, 114	Dawn's Curtsey, 4, 118	8	1:43.80	28,200
1985	Agacerie, 4, 118	A. T. Cordero Jr.	Meddlin Maggie, 4, 112	Natural Grace, 4, 114	8	1:44.20	34,830
1984	Jubilous, 4, 118	G. McCarron	Maidenhead, 5, 113	High Schemes, 4, 118	13	1:43.40	36,000
1983	Doodle, 4, 118	J. J. Miranda	Olamic, 4, 110	Bright Choice, 4, 112	12	1:44.00	28,410
1982	Kuja Happa, 4, 114	D. R. Wright	Qui Silent, 4, 113	Suave Princess, 4, 113	10	1:44.80	27,465
1981	Wayward Lassie, 4, 112	D. Montoya	Earlham, 5, 114	Paris Press, 4, 114	7	1:44.60	16,957
	Endicotta, 5, 116	D. Brumfield	Dance Troupe, 4, 115	Farewell Letter, 4, 113	5	1:44.80	16,717
1980	Riddle's Reply, 4, 113	E. Cardone	Sharp Zone, 4, 111	Newmarket Lady, 4, 112	8	1:44.20	20,078
	Nasty Jay, 5, 111	R. E. McKnight	T. V. Highlights, 6, 119	O'Connell Street, 4, 113	9	1:44.00	20,288
1979	The Very One, 4, 116	C. Cooke	Frosty Skater, 4, 120	Municipal Bond, 4, 113	8	1:46.20	25,236
1978	Huggle Duggle, 4, 113	B. Gonzalez	All Biz, 6, 118	Navajo Princess, 4, 114	9	1:42.60	22,116
1977	Jolly Song, 5, 112	J. Nied Jr.	T. V. Genie, 4, 112	All Biz, 5, 117	9	1:47.20	18,590
1976	‡Collegiate, 4, 113	J. W. Edwards	Copano, 4, 119	Double Ack, 3, 114	10	1:43.60	14,950
	Stage Luck, 4, 118	J. W. Edwards	Hinterland, 6, 114	*Deesse Du Val, 5, 121	9	1:43.80	14,788

1975 **Hinterland**, 5, 114	C. Perret	Ringmistress, 5, 114	Kudara, 4, 119	8	1:43.60	$18,135
1974 **Bird Boots**, 5, 119	B. Thornburg	Belle Marie, 4, 117	Shaya, 4, 108	13	1:46.80	19,207
1973 ‡**Telly**, 5, 110	V. A. Bracciale Jr.	Lightning Lucy, 3, 113	Wire Chief, 5, 111	8	1:43.60	14,763
Cathy Baby, 4, 116	M. A. Rivera	Aglimmer, 4, 116	Bold Place, 4, 117	7	1:42.60	14,633

Named for Eatontown, New Jersey, located in Monmouth County. Eatontown S. 1991-'95, 1997-2000. 1¹/₁₆ miles 1988-'90, 2001. Dirt 1974, 1977. Two divisions 1972, 1973, 1976, 1980-'81, 1986-'87. Dead heat for third 1998. ‡Lightning Lucy finished first, DQ to second, 1973 (1st Div.). ‡Copano finished first, DQ to second, 1976 (1st Div.).

Eddie Read Handicap

Grade 1 in 2005. Del Mar, three-year-olds and up, 1¹/₁₆ miles, turf. Held July 25, 2004, with a gross value of $400,000. First graded in 1974. First graded in 1980. Stakes record 1:45.87 (2003 Special Ring).

Year	Winner	Jockey	Second	Third	Strs	Time	1st Purse
2004	**Special Ring**, 7, 118	V. Espinoza	Bayamo (Ire), 5, 119	Sweet Return (GB), 4, 119	10	1:45.90	$240,000
2003	**Special Ring**, 6, 117	D. R. Flores	Decarchy, 6, 117	Irish Warrior, 5, 114	6	**1:45.87**	240,000
2002	**Sarafan**, 5, 117	C. S. Nakatani	Beat Hollow (GB), 5, 122	Redattore (Brz), 7, 118	6	1:46.77	240,000
2001	**Redattore (Brz)**, 6, 115	A. O. Solis	Native Desert, 8, 116	Super Quercus (Fr), 5, 115	6	1:47.16	240,000
2000	**Ladies Din**, 5, 120	K. J. Desormeaux	Chester House, 5, 114	Gold Nugget, 5, 115	8	1:48.64	240,000
1999	**Joe Who (Brz)**, 6, 116	C. W. Antley	Ladies Din, 4, 119	Bouccaneer (Fr), 4, 115	10	1:48.75	240,000
1998	**Subordination**, 4, 117	D. R. Flores	Bonapartiste (Fr), 4, 115	Hawksley Hill (Ire), 5, 120	5	1:47.40	180,000
1997	**Expelled**, 5, 113	J. A. Garcia	El Angelo, 5, 119	Marlin, 4, 122	7	1:48.60	180,000
1996	**Fastness (Ire)**, 6, 124	C. S. Nakatani	Smooth Runner, 5, 114	Gold and Steel (Fr), 4, 118	6	1:47.05	193,000
1995	**Fastness (Ire)**, 5, 115	G. L. Stevens	Romarin (Brz), 5, 119	Northern Spur (Ire), 4, 118	8	1:48.42	182,600
1994	**Approach the Bench (Ire)**, 6, 113	C. S. Nakatani	Fastness (Ire), 4, 114	Johann Quatz (Fr), 5, 116	7	1:48.83	187,250
1993	**Kotashaan (Fr)**, 5, 122	K. J. Desormeaux	Leger Cat (Arg), 7, 116	Rainbow Corner (GB), 4, 114	6	1:48.45	183,750
1992	**Marquetry**, 5, 118	D. R. Flores	Luthier Enchanteur, 5, 116	Leger Cat (Arg), 6, 115	7	1:47.20	187,250
1991	**Tight Spot**, 4, 125	L. A. Pincay Jr.	Val des Bois (Fr), 5, 115	Madjaristan, 5, 116	7	1:47.32	188,500
1990	**Fly Till Dawn**, 4, 112	R. Q. Meza	Classic Fame, 4, 119	Golden Pheasant, 4, 122	8	1:48.20	157,750
1989	**Saratoga Passage**, 4, 116	E. J. Delahoussaye	Skip Out Front, 7, 116	Pasakos, 4, 116	8	1:49.00	162,750
1988	**Deputy Governor**, 4, 120	E. J. Delahoussaye	Santella Mac (Ire), 5, 114	Simply Majestic, 4, 115	12	1:48.80	176,500
1987	**Sharrood**, 4, 120	L. A. Pincay Jr.	Santella Mac (Ire), 4, 115	Skip Out Front, 5, 118	9	1:48.00	133,200
1986	**Al Mamoon**, 5, 121	P. A. Valenzuela	Zoffany, 6, 123	Truce Maker, 8, 115	7	1:46.60	113,400
1985	**Tsunami Slew**, 4, 119	G. L. Stevens	Al Mamoon, 4, 118	Both Ends Burning, 5, 123	7	1:46.80	112,300
1984	**Ten Below**, 5, 117	L. A. Pincay Jr.	Silveyville, 6, 117	Desert Wine, 4, 124	6	1:48.20	96,200
1983	**Prince Spellbound**, 4, 121	C. Lamance	Bel Bolide, 5, 117	Ask Me, 4, 115	11	1:48.80	108,000
1982	**Wickerr**, 7, 119	E. J. Delahoussaye	Spence Bay, 7, 122	Perrault (GB), 5, 129	7	1:48.40	95,300
1981	**Wickerr**, 6, 115	C. J. McCarron	Super Moment, 4, 117	Mike Fogarty (Ire), 6, 114	7	1:49.80	80,750
1980	**Go West Young Man**, 5, 120	E. J. Delahoussaye	The Bart, 4, 118	Bold Tropic (SAf), 5, 124	6	1:47.60	64,250
1979	**Good Lord (NZ)**, 8, 115	W. Shoemaker	Shagbark, 4, 114	True Statement, 5, 115	11	1:49.20	42,450
1978	**Effervescing**, 5, 124	L. A. Pincay Jr.	Text, 4, 123	Bywayofchicago, 4, 117	9	1:48.60	33,050
1977	**No Turning**, 4, 115	F. Toro	Today 'n Tomorrow, 4, 119	†*Star Ball, 5, 111	9	1:48.80	32,400
1976	**Branford Court**, 6, 116	R. Campas	Diode, 4, 114	Austin Mittler, 4, 115	8	1:48.40	26,150
1975	**Blue Times**, 4, 115	J. Lambert	Portentous, 5, 112	Confederate Yankee, 4, 115	11	1:49.20	28,200
1974	**My Old Friend**, 5, 115	A. L. Diaz	Montmartre, 4, 116	War Heim, 7, 121	9	1:49.20	22,100

Named in honor of longtime Del Mar publicity director Eddie Read. Grade 3 1980-'81. Grade 2 1982-'87. Course record 2003. †Denotes female.

El Camino Real Derby

Grade 3 in 2005. Bay Meadows, three-year-olds, 1¹/₁₆ miles, dirt. Held March 12, 2005, with a gross value of $200,000. First held in 1982. First graded in 1986. Stakes record 1:39.40 (1988 Ruhlmann).

Year	Winner	Jockey	Second	Third	Strs	Time	1st Purse
2005	**Uncle Denny**, 3, 117	R. A. Baze	Wannawinemall, 3, 115	Buzzards Bay, 3, 117	10	1:42.22	$110,000
2004	**Kilgowan**, 3, 116	C. J. Rollins	dh-Capitano, 3, 116		10	1:43.87	110,000
			dh-Seattle Borders, 3, 117				
2003	**Ocean Terrace**, 3, 115	M. E. Smith	Ministers Wild Cat, 3, 117	Ten Most Wanted, 3, 115	10	1:42.26	110,000
2002	**Yougottawanna**, 3, 120	J. P. Lumpkins	Danthebluegrassman, 3, 117	Lusty Latin, 3, 115	10	1:43.48	110,000
2001	**Hoovergetthekeys**, 3, 120	R. J. Warren Jr.	Startac, 3, 120	Mo Mon, 3, 115	8	1:40.85	110,000
2000	**Remember Sheikh**, 3, 117	F. T. Alvarado	True Confidence, 3, 116	Country Coast, 3, 115	14	1:43.47	110,000
1999	**Cliquot**, 3, 117	D. R. Flores	Charismatic, 3, 115	No Cal Bread, 3, 117	7	1:43.29	110,000
1998	**Event of the Year**, 3, 115	R. A. Baze	Post a Note, 3, 117	Clover Hunter, 3, 120	5	1:40.27	110,000
1997	**Pacificbounty**, 3, 120	K. J. Desormeaux	Wild Wonder, 3, 115	Carmen's Baby, 3, 117	6	1:41.85	110,000
1996	**Cavonnier**, 3, 115	M. A. Pedroza	Sergeant Stroh, 3, 113	E C's Dream, 3, 116	9	1:43.41	110,000
1995	**Jumron (GB)**, 3, 113	G. F. Almeida	Snow Kidd'n, 3, 113	American Day, 3, 113	8	1:43.73	110,000
1994	**Tabasco Cat**, 3, 113	P. Day	Flying Sensation, 3, 115	Robannier, 3, 115	7	1:42.78	110,000
1993	**El Atroz**, 3, 117	R. Q. Meza	Offshore Pirate, 3, 115	Lykatill Hil, 3, 119	6	1:43.77	110,000
1992	**Casual Lies**, 3, 117	A. Patterson	Seahawk Gold, 3, 115	Silver Ray, 3, 122	11	1:42.00	165,000
1991	**Sea Cadet**, 3, 117	T. M. Chapman	General Meeting, 3, 118	Mizter Interco, 3, 122	9	1:40.70	165,000
1990	**Silver Ending**, 3, 115	G. L. Stevens	Individualist, 3, 115	Single Dawn, 3, 122	8	1:43.00	165,000
1989	**Double Quick**, 3, 115	A. O. Solis	Rob an Plunder, 3, 119	Hawkster, 3, 122	6	1:43.60	165,000
1988	**Ruhlmann**, 3, 117	P. Day	Havanaffair, 3, 117	Chinese Gold, 3, 119	9	**1:39.40**	137,500
1987	**Masterful Advocate**, 3, 120	L. A. Pincay Jr.	Fast Delivery, 3, 120	Hot and Smoggy, 3, 120	11	1:42.40	137,500

Year	Winner	Jockey	Second	Third	Strs	Time	1st Purse
1986	**Snow Chief**, 3, 120	A. O. Solis	Badger Land, 3, 120	Darby Fair, 3, 120	6	1:42.60	$137,500
1985	**Tank's Prospect**, 3, 120	J. Velasquez	Right Con, 3, 120	‡Dan's Diablo, 3, 120	9	1:41.00	151,000
1984	**French Legionaire**, 3, 120	R. A. Baze	Gate Dancer, 3, 120	Heavenly Plain (Ire), 3, 120	11	1:42.40	126,200
1983	**Knightly Rapport**, 3, 120	F. Toro	Croeso, 3, 120	Twilight Career, 3, 120	9	1:44.80	96,700
1982	**Cassaleria**, 3, 120	D. G. McHargue	Crystal Star, 3, 120	Tropic Ruler, 3, 120	9	1:42.80	76,100

Named for the El Camino Real, "the Royal Road" through the California frontier. Held at Golden Gate 2001-'04. Dead heat for second 2004. ‡Skywalker finished third, DQ to fourth, 1985.

El Conejo Handicap

Grade 3 in 2005. Santa Anita Park, four-year-olds and up, 5½ furlongs, dirt. Held January 2, 2005, with a gross value of $110,500. First held in 1975. First graded in 2000. Stakes record 1:01.74 (1999 Kona Gold).

Year	Winner	Jockey	Second	Third	Strs	Time	1st Purse
2005	**Areyoutalkintome**, 4, 114	T. Baze	Hombre Rapido, 8, 116	Woke Up Dreamin, 5, 115	9	1:02.52	$66,300
2004	**Boston Common**, 5, 117	G. L. Stevens	Summer Service, 4, 112	King Robyn, 4, 119	6	1:02.35	64,560
2003	**Kona Gold**, 9, 123	A. O. Solis	Radiata, 6, 115	No Armistice, 6, 116	7	1:02.63	65,280
2002	**Snow Ridge**, 4, 114	M. E. Smith	Explicit, 5, 117	Rio Oro, 7, 115	8	1:03.05	65,700
2000	**Freespool**, 4, 115	C. J. McCarron	Men's Exclusive, 7, 117	Lexicon, 5, 118	7	1:02.50	65,220
	Freespool, 4, 114	C. J. McCarron	Mellow Fellow, 5, 115	Old Topper, 5, 116	6	1:03.33	64,200
1999	**Kona Gold**, 5, 119	A. O. Solis	Big Jag, 6, 117	Mr. Doubledown, 5, 118	6	**1:01.74**	64,380
1998	**The Exeter Man**, 6, 114	G. K. Gomez	Tower Full, 6, 117	Red, 4, 114	5	1:02.23	64,020
1997	**High Stakes Player**, 5, 115	C. S. Nakatani	Kern Ridge, 6, 111	Subtle Trouble, 6, 114	5	1:02.89	63,850
1996	**Lit de Justice**, 6, 119	C. S. Nakatani	A. J. Jett, 4, 112	Fu Man Slew, 5, 116	6	1:01.85	64,250
1995	**Phone Roberto**, 6, 114	C. J. McCarron	‡Lost Pan, 5, 112	Rotsaluck, 4, 117	8	1:02.34	65,000
1994	**Gundaghia**, 7, 116	E. J. Delahoussaye	Sir Hutch, 4, 114	Davy Be Good, 6, 117	8	1:02.01	64,800
1993	**Fabulous Champ**, 4, 113	C. J. McCarron	Arrowtown, 5, 115	Slerp, 4, 117	7	1:02.66	63,800
1992	**Gray Slewpy**, 4, 114	K. J. Desormeaux	Frost Free, 7, 119	Cardmania, 6, 116	5	1:02.01	61,275
1991	**Black Jack Road**, 7, 115	G. L. Stevens	Laurens Quest, 6, 110	Lee's Tanthem, 4, 114	6	1:05.30	61,975
1990	**Frost Free**, 5, 115	C. J. McCarron	Sunny Blossom, 5, 119	Prospectors Gamble, 5, 114	5	1:03.00	45,900
1989	**Sunny Blossom**, 4, 114	F. H. Valenzuela	Sensational Star, 5, 115	Prospectors Gamble, 4, 116	7	1:04.60	47,100
1988	**Sylvan Express (Ire)**, 5, 119	E. J. Delahoussaye	Carload, 6, 117	High Brite, 4, 120	8	1:03.80	48,100
1986	**†Take My Picture**, 4, 119	G. L. Stevens	Rosie's K. T., 5, 119	Five North, 5, 114	5	1:03.00	37,300
1985	**Debonaire Junior**, 4, 126	C. J. McCarron	Much Fine Gold, 4, 112	Fifty Six Ina Row, 4, 119	7	1:02.60	38,950
	Night Mover, 4, 117	R. Q. Meza	Haughty But Nice, 6, 116	Chip o' Lark, 5, 117	7	1:03.40	30,425
1983	**Pompeii Court**, 6, 123	L. A. Pincay Jr.	General Jimmy, 4, 115	†Bara Lass, 5, 117	7	1:03.20	30,525
1982	**To B. Or Not**, 6, 122	C. J. McCarron	Belfort (Fr), 5, 116	Terresto's Singer, 5, 115	8	1:02.20	39,350
1981	**To B. Or Not**, 5, 122	P. A. Valenzuela	Summer Time Guy, 5, 119	Cool Frenchy, 6, 115	11	1:02.40	35,500
1975	**Move Abroad**, 4, 113	S. Hawley	Reputation, 5, 115	Mercy Dee, 4, 121	5	1:49.20	11,375

Named for Rancho El Conejo, located in Ventura, California; conejo means rabbit. Not graded 2000 (January). Not held 1976-'80, 1987, 2001. Four-year-olds and up 1992-2000. Held in January and December 2000. Two divisions 1984. ‡Lit de Justice finished second, DQ to sixth, 1995. Track record 1992, 1996, 1999. †Denotes female.

El Encino Stakes

Grade 2 in 2005. Santa Anita Park, four-year-olds, fillies, 1¹/₁₆ miles, dirt. Held January 16, 2005, with a gross value of $150,000. First held in 1954. First graded in 1980. Stakes record 1:41.20 (1990 Akinemod, 1983 Beautiful Glass, 1982 Edge, 1980 It's in the Air).

Year	Winner	Jockey	Second	Third	Strs	Time	1st Purse
2005	**Girl Warrior**, 4, 115	V. Espinoza	A. P. Adventure, 4, 119	Tarlow, 4, 116	7	1:42.76	$90,000
2004	**Victory Encounter**, 4, 117	M. E. Smith	Personal Legend, 4, 115	Cat Fighter, 4, 115	7	1:42.52	90,000
2003	**Got Koko**, 4, 119	A. O. Solis	Bella Bellucci, 4, 117	Bare Necessities, 4, 119	8	1:42.25	90,000
2002	**Affluent**, 4, 119	E. J. Delahoussaye	Royally Chosen, 4, 117	Sea Reel, 4, 115	6	1:42.60	90,000
2001	**Chilukki**, 4, 119	G. L. Stevens	Spain, 4, 122	Queenie Belle, 4, 119	4	1:42.55	90,000
2000	**Olympic Charmer**, 4, 119	C. J. McCarron	Her She Kisses, 4, 115	Smooth Player, 4, 117	7	1:42.71	97,470
1999	**Manistique**, 4, 119	G. L. Stevens	Gourmet Girl, 4, 117	Magical Allure, 4, 119	3	1:43.10	90,000
1998	**‡Fleet Lady**, 4, 117	G. K. Gomez	Minister's Melody, 4, 117	I Ain't Bluffing, 4, 119	6	1:43.04	96,840
1997	**Belle's Good**, 4, 117	C. S. Nakatani	Housa Dancer (Fr), 4, 115	Listening, 4, 119	9	1:41.61	82,650
1996	**Jewel Princess**, 4, 117	A. O. Solis	Sleep Easy, 4, 119	Urbane, 4, 119	4	1:41.94	78,800
1995	**Klassy Kim**, 4, 117	K. J. Desormeaux	Twice the Vice, 4, 119	Crissy Aya, 4, 115	5	1:42.43	61,400
1994	**Supah Gem**, 4, 117	C. S. Nakatani	Sensational Eyes, 4, 117	Stalcreek, 4, 119	8	1:41.33	64,500
1993	**Pacific Squall**, 4, 119	C. J. McCarron	Avian Assembly, 4, 117	Magical Maiden, 4, 119	7	1:45.67	63,900
1992	**Exchange**, 4, 117	L. A. Pincay Jr.	Grand Girlfriend, 4, 115	Damewood, 4, 115	10	1:43.32	67,000
1991	**A Wild Ride**, 4, 122	C. J. McCarron	Highland Tide, 4, 114	Somethingmerry, 4, 117	5	1:42.50	63,600
1990	**Akinemod**, 4, 119	G. L. Stevens	Luthier's Launch, 4, 117	Kelly, 4, 116	6	**1:41.20**	62,900
1989	**Goodbye Halo**, 4, 124	P. Day	T. V. of Crystal, 4, 117	Savannah's Honor, 4, 114	4	1:41.80	60,200
1988	**By Land by Sea**, 4, 115	F. Toro	Very Subtle, 4, 122	Annoconnor, 4, 114	6	1:41.60	64,300
1987	**Seldom Seen Sue**, 4, 114	W. Shoemaker	Miraculous, 4, 117	Top Corsage, 4, 122	6	1:43.00	61,850
1986	**Lady's Secret**, 4, 124	C. J. McCarron	Shywing, 4, 117	Sharp Ascent, 4, 119	10	1:41.80	65,850
1985	**Mitterand**, 4, 119	E. J. Delahoussaye	Percipient, 4, 117	Allusion, 4, 117	6	1:42.00	61,600
1984	**Lovlier Linda**, 4, 117	W. Shoemaker	Weekend Surprise, 4, 117	Angel Savage (Mex), 4, 114	8	1:42.40	51,250
1983	**Beautiful Glass**, 4, 119	C. J. McCarron	Header Card, 4, 119	Skillful Joy, 4, 122	11	**1:41.20**	50,550
1982	**Edge**, 4, 114	C. B. Asmussen	Safe Play, 4, 119	Northern Fable, 4, 117	12	**1:41.20**	68,000
1981	**Princess Karenda**, 4, 122	E. J. Delahoussaye	Swift Bird, 4, 117	Lisawan, 4, 114	10	1:42.00	49,650
1980	**It's in the Air**, 4, 124	L. A. Pincay Jr.	Prize Spot, 4, 121	‡Glorious Song, 4, 116	8	**1:41.20**	38,750

1979 **B. Thoughtful**, 4, 121	D. Pierce	Queen Yasna, 4, 116	Petron's Love, 4, 114	7	1:41.60	$38,250
1978 **Taisez Vous**, 4, 121	D. Pierce	Little Happiness, 4, 116	Table the Rumor, 4, 121	4	1:41.80	30,200
1977 ***Woodsome**, 4, 115	M. S. Sellers	*Lucie Manet, 4, 115	Granja Sueno, 4, 115	11	1:42.20	27,450
1976 **Fascinating Girl**, 4, 115	S. Hawley	Bold Baby, 4, 115	Just a Kick, 4, 121	6	1:42.40	18,850
1975 **Triggairo**, 6, 119	D. Pierce	*Benson, 6, 116	Lansquinet, 4, 119	7	1:49.40	19,700
1974 **Wild World**, 5, 118	W. Shoemaker	Class A, 6, 115	Proper Escort, 5, 112	10	1:49.80	18,150
1973 **Class A**, 5, 122	D. Tierney	Sitka D., 6, 119	Cabin, 5, 119	10	1:44.60	18,950

Named for Rancho El Encino, one of the original Spanish ranchos located in western Los Angeles County, California. Grade 3 1980-'89. El Encino H. 1954-'57, 1974-'75. El Encino Claiming S. 1968-'73. Not held 1958-'67, 1970. 1 1/16 miles 1955-'57. 1 1/8 miles 1974-'75. Turf 1955-'57. Four-year-olds and up 1954-'75. Both sexes 1954-'75. ‡Terlingua finished third, DQ to fourth, 1980. ‡I Ain't Bluffing finished first, DQ to third, 1998. Starters for a claiming price of $50,000 or less 1974.

Elkhorn Stakes

Grade 3 in 2005. Keeneland, four-year-olds and up, 1 1/2 miles, turf. Held April 29, 2005, with a gross value of $200,000. First held in 1986. First graded in 1988. Stakes record 2:27.84 (1999 African Dancer).

Year	Winner	Jockey	Second	Third	Strs	Time	1st Purse
2005	**Macaw (Ire)**, 6, 118	J. Castellano	European (Ire), 5, 118	Rochester, 9, 118	12	2:32.62	$124,000
2004	**Epicentre**, 5, 116	J. D. Bailey	Rochester, 8, 116	Art Variety (Brz), 6, 116	10	2:31.96	93,000
2003	**Kim Loves Bucky**, 6, 117	K. J. Desormeaux	Man From Wicklow, 6, 123	Williams News, 8, 116	10	2:29.39	93,000
2002	**Kim Loves Bucky**, 5, 116	J. F. Chavez	Rochester, 6, 116	Cetewayo, 8, 118	10	2:32.49	93,000
2001	**Williams News**, 6, 116	R. Albarado	Gritty Sandie, 5, 116	Craigsteel (GB), 6, 116	9	2:29.13	70,308
2000	**Drama Critic**, 4, 116	J. D. Bailey	Craigsteel (GB), 5, 116	Dixie's Crown, 4, 116	10	2:28.03	69,750
1999	**African Dancer**, 7, 114	J. D. Bailey	Magest, 4, 114	Chorwon, 6, 113	8	**2:27.84**	68,138
1998	**African Dancer**, 6, 114	J. D. Bailey	Chief Bearhart, 5, 122	Chorwon, 5, 114	5	2:31.71	66,712
1997	**Chief Bearhart**, 4, 114	J. A. Santos	Snake Eyes, 7, 113	Lassigny, 6, 122	8	2:28.43	68,324
1996	**Vladivostok**, 6, 112	P. Day	Penn Fifty Three, 4, 114	Party Season (GB), 5, 119	7	2:30.83	68,262
1995	**Marvin's Faith (Ire)**, 4, 123	C. Perret	Hasten To Add, 5, 120	Opera Score, 4, 120	10	1:47.10	70,680
1994	**Lure**, 5, 123	M. E. Smith	Buckhar, 6, 120	Pride of Summer, 6, 120	5	1:53.76	66,526
1993	**Coaxing Matt**, 4, 118	P. Day	Cleone, 4, 113	Maxigroom, 5, 118	9	1:47.64	68,603
1992	**Fourstars Allstar**, 4, 118	J. D. Bailey	Slew the Slewor, 5, 120	Rainbows for Life, 4, 120	10	1:47.66	72,995
1991	**Itsallgreektome**, 4, 123	R. A. Baze	Pirate Army, 5, 113	Spark O'Dan, 6, 113	7	1:51.28	71,143
1990	**Ten Keys**, 6, 123	R. P. Romero	Yankee Affair, 8, 123	Maceo, 6, 118	8	1:51.80	71,468
1989	**Exclusive Partner**, 7, 120	F. Toro	Yankee Affair, 7, 120	Pappas Swing, 4, 120	7	1:50.40	54,958
1988	**Yankee Affair**, 6, 123	P. Day	Storm On the Loose, 5, 118	Blazing Bart, 4, 123	10	1:49.60	56,485
1987	**Manila**, 4, 113	J. Vasquez	Lieutenant's Lark, 5, 120	Royal Treasurer, 4, 112	7	1:48.40	35,019
1986	**Lieutenant's Lark**, 4, 113	F. Lovato Jr.	Leprechauns Wish, 4, 115	Majestic Jabot, 5, 115	10	1:54.60	36,351

Sponsored by Fifth Third Bancorp of Cincinnati in 2005. Named for a large local creek, the Elkhorn, long used as a water source by Bluegrass-area farms. Grade 2 1990-'95. 1 1/8 miles 1986-'95. Course record 1995, 1999.

Endine Handicap

Grade 3 in 2005. Delaware Park, three-year-olds and up, fillies and mares, 6 furlongs, dirt. Held September 11, 2004, with a gross value of $200,300. First held in 1971. First graded in 2001. Stakes record 1:08.35 (2003 House Party).

Year	Winner	Jockey	Second	Third	Strs	Time	1st Purse
2004	**Ebony Breeze**, 4, 119	H. Castillo Jr.	Umpateedle, 5, 117	Bronze Abe, 5, 119	6	1:09.73	$120,000
2003	**House Party**, 3, 117	J. A. Santos	Vision in Flight, 4, 114	Mooji Moo, 4, 115	8	**1:08.35**	120,000
2002	**Xtra Heat**, 4, 121	H. Vega	Outstanding Info, 4, 118	Urban Dancer, 4, 118	5	1:10.91	90,000
2001	**Xtra Heat**, 3, 118	R. Wilson	Ivy's Jewel, 4, 118	Big Bambu, 4, 121	5	1:09.64	90,000
2000	**Superduper Miss**, 4, 114	T. G. Turner	Debby d'Or, 5, 119	Cassidy, 5, 119	7	1:10.22	60,000
1999	**Hurricane Bertie**, 4, 117	P. Day	Little Sister, 4, 119	Bourbon Belle, 4, 119	4	1:08.75	60,000
1998	**Soverign Lady**, 4, 119	M. E. Smith	Weather Vane, 4, 122	Little Sister, 4, 117	8	1:09.43	45,000
1997	**Dancin Renee**, 5, 122	J. A. Velez Jr.	Two Punch Lil, 5, 122	Ana Belen (Chi), 4, 113	6	1:10.04	30,000
1996	**Hay Hanne**, 4, 114	J. A. Velez Jr.	Know B's, 4, 116	Ayrial Delight, 4, 122	5	1:10.30	22,770
1982	**Wading Power**, 4, 107	H. Pilar	Bravo Native, 4, 108	Lady Dean, 4, 123	9	1:10.60	14,723
1981	**Veiled Look**, 5, 120	W. J. Passmore	Rejuvanate, 5, 113	Tequila Sheila, 3, 109	7	1:08.80	17,875
1980	**Candy Eclair**, 4, 126	J. D. Bailey	‡Wondrous Me, 4, 108	Grecian Victory, 4, 112	9	1:09.80	29,803
1979	**Quatre Saisons**, 4, 115	V. A. Bracciale Jr.	Shanachie, 4, 112	Order in Court, 6, 115	6	1:12.00	21,580
1978	**Dainty Dotsie**, 4, 127	B. Phelps	Spot Two, 4, 123	Debby's Turn, 4, 113	5	1:09.60	21,450
1977	**My Juliet**, 5, 127	A. S. Black	Debby's Turn, 3, 115	Catabias, 5, 113	4	1:09.60	17,973
1976	**Donetta**, 5, 118	J. W. Moseley	Susie's Last, 4, 112	Crackerfax, 5, 113	10	1:12.00	17,145
1975	**Honky Star**, 4, 119	J. E. Tejeira	Laraka, 5, 117	Sailingon, 4, 114	7	1:11.00	18,655
1974	**Miss Rebound**, 6, 123	B. Baeza	Flo's Pleasure, 4, 116	Gallant Davelle, 4, 116	8	1:10.00	19,045
1973	**Light Hearted**, 4, 118	E. Nelson	Barely Even, 4, 125	Levee Night, 5, 113	7	1:10.40	18,525

Named for Christiana Stable's 1958, '59 Delaware H. winner Endine (1954 f. by *Rico Monte). Endine H. 1971-'82. Not held 1983-'95. ‡She Can't Miss finished second, DQ to fourth, 1980. Equaled track record 2003.

Essex Handicap

Grade 3 in 2005. Oaklawn Park, four-year-olds and up, 1 1/16 miles, dirt. Held February 12, 2005, with a gross value of $100,000. First held in 1976. First graded in 1985. Stakes record 1:41 (1987 Sun Master, 1976 Navajo).

Year	Winner	Jockey	Second	Third	Strs	Time	1st Purse
2005	**Absent Friend**, 5, 112	R. Chapa	Mauk Four, 5, 112	Separato, 4, 113	10	1:43.66	$60,000

Year	Winner	Jockey	Second	Third	Strs	Time	1st Purse
2004	Private Emblem, 5, 113	T. T. Doocy	Pie N Burger, 6, 118	Crafty Shaw, 6, 118	8	1:43.66	$60,000
2003	Colorful Tour, 4, 116	L. S. Quinonez	Ask the Lord, 6, 118	Premeditation, 4, 117	10	1:46.62	60,000
2002	Crafty Shaw, 4, 116	J. Lopez	Kiss of Lion (Arg), 7, 113	Remington Rock, 8, 116	6	1:43.14	45,000
2001	Mr Ross, 6, 117	D. R. Pettinger	Remington Rock, 7, 114	Maysville Slew, 5, 118	7	1:43.59	45,000
2000	Maysville Slew, 4, 115	L. S. Quinonez	Sand Ridge, 5, 112	Mr Ross, 5, 116	7	1:44.12	45,000
1999	Brush With Pride, 7, 116	T. T. Doocy	Littlebitlively, 5, 118	Treat Me Doc, 5, 114	7	1:43.26	45,000
1998	Relic Reward, 4, 113	C. H. Borel	Phantom On Tour, 4, 119	Brush With Pride, 6, 116	7	1:43.92	45,000
1997	No Spend No Glow, 5, 113	R. N. Lester	Illesam, 5, 113	Auggie My Dad, 6, 111	8	1:45.94	45,000
1996	Classic Fit, 6, 114	C. Gonzalez	Judge T C, 5, 122	Juliannus, 7, 113	4	1:42.98	47,700
1995	Silver Goblin, 4, 122	D. W. Cordova	Prince of the Mt., 4, 113	Golden Gear, 4, 113	7	1:42.10	33,150
1994	Greatsilverfleet, 4, 116	G. K. Gomez	Prize Fight, 5, 113	All Gone, 4, 111	5	1:42.08	32,250
1993	Delafield, 4, 113	P. Day	Famed Devil, 5, 117	Yukon Robbery, 4, 116	8	1:42.11	33,900
1992	Allijeba, 6, 118	P. Day	On the Edge, 5, 113	Bedeviled, 5, 116	10	1:43.95	34,500
1991	Greydar, 4, 117	P. Day	Silver Survivor, 5, 120	The Great Carl, 4, 112	8	1:42.08	34,770
1990	Forli Light, 4, 115	D. R. Guillory	Momsfurrari, 6, 115	Traskwood, 4, 115	9	1:42.80	36,930
1989	Proper Reality, 4, 120	J. D. Bailey	Contact Game, 5, 111	Lyphard's Ridge, 6, 112	6	1:44.00	34,530
1988	Savings, 5, 117	P. A. Johnson	Entitled To, 6, 117	Red Attack, 6, 115	7	1:42.60	43,680
1987	Sun Master, 6, 116	R. L. Frazier	Royal Troon, 5, 112	Lyphard's Ridge, 4, 111	9	**1:41.00**	36,750
1986	Double Ready, 6, 113	D. E. Whited	Red Attack, 4, 112	Khozaam, 4, 112	10	1:41.60	51,060
1985	Star Choice, 6, 121	J. McKnight	Plaza Star, 7, 115	Shamtastic, 5, 112	8	1:40.60	49,260
1984	Le Cou Cou, 4, 119	D. L. Howard	Hi Pi, 5, 120	Double Ready, 4, 114	9	1:41.80	36,480
1983	Eminency, 5, 121	W. Nemeti	Dance Pavilion, 4, 113	Majesty's Prince, 4, 125	12	1:42.40	38,670
1982	Plaza Star, 4, 113	R. P. Romero	Vodika Collins, 4, 118	Tally Ho the Fox, 7, 116	11	1:42.80	37,950
1981	Prince Majestic, 7, 118	G. Patterson	Blue Ensign, 4, 114	Uncool, 6, 117	9	1:42.40	34,650
1980	J. Burns, 5, 113	J. McKnight	Convenient, 4, 114	Daring Damascus, 4, 115	10	1:42.80	35,220
1979	Cisk, 5, 117	G. Patterson	Forever Casting, 4, 114	Oui Henry, 5, 117	10	1:42.40	35,850
1978	Mark's Place, 6, 122	R. Ramirez	Yallah Native, 5, 114	Dragset, 7, 118	11	1:41.60	36,570
1977	Go to the Bank, 5, 111	G. Patterson	Romeo, 4, 119	Limited Addition, 4, 114	13	1:42.40	37,260
1976	Navajo, 6, 123	J. Nichols	My Friend Gus, 4, 121	Bold Trap, 4, 113	9	**1:41.00**	34,950

Named for old Essex Park in Hot Springs, Arkansas. 1 mile 70 yards 1976-'86.

Excelsior Breeders' Cup Handicap

Grade 3 in 2005. Aqueduct, three-year-olds and up, 1⅛ miles, dirt. Held April 2, 2005, with a gross value of $196,000. First held in 1903. First graded in 1973. Stakes record 1:47.69 (1997 Ormsby).

Year	Winner	Jockey	Second	Third	Strs	Time	1st Purse
2005	Offlee Wild, 5, 121	R. Bejarano	Rogue Agent, 6, 115	Cuba, 4, 113	5	1:50.41	$120,000
2004	Funny Cide, 4, 120	J. A. Santos	Evening Attire, 6, 119	Host (Chi), 4, 114	5	1:49.57	120,000
2003	Classic Endeavor, 5, 113	C. C. Lopez	Balto Star, 5, 119	Tempest Fugit, 6, 114	5	1:48.10	90,000
2002	John Little, 4, 111	N. Arroyo Jr.	Windsor Castle, 4, 113	Ground Storm, 6, 118	6	1:49.25	120,000
2001	Cat's At Home, 4, 115	F. Leon	Top Official, 6, 113	Boston Party, 5, 115	8	1:48.92	120,000
2000	Lager, 6, 113	H. Castillo Jr.	Best of Luck, 4, 114	Chester House, 5, 117	9	1:49.76	120,000
1999	Smart Coupons, 6, 114	R. R. Douglas	Archers Bay, 4, 118	Pasay, 4, 112	9	1:49.71	120,000
1998	Sir Bear, 5, 117	E. M. Jurado	K. J.'s Appeal, 4, 117	Accelerator, 4, 111	8	1:49.24	120,000
1997	Ormsby, 5, 116	C. C. Lopez	Greatsilverfleet, 7, 112	Circle of Light, 4, 111	9	**1:47.69**	120,000
1996	May I Inquire, 7, 111	J. Bravo	Personal Merit, 5, 114	Ormsby, 4, 115	8	1:50.67	120,000
1995	Iron Gavel, 5, 111	J. R. Martinez Jr.	Electrojet, 6, 114	Danzig's Dance, 6, 115	7	1:49.28	90,000
1994	Colonial Affair, 4, 121	J. A. Santos	Contract Court, 4, 109	West by West, 5, 116	6	1:49.82	90,000
1993	Devil His Due, 4, 117	M. E. Smith	Exotic Slew, 5, 109	Bill Of Rights, 4, 112	10	2:03.05	72,120
1992	Defensive Play, 5, 117	D. R. Flores	Alyten, 4, 111	Will to Reign, 5, 109	5	2:01.95	102,780
1991	Chief Honcho, 4, 117	M. E. Smith	I'm Sky High, 5, 115	Apple Current, 4, 115	6	2:02.69	102,060
1990	Lay Down, 6, 112	C. W. Antley	Lac Ouimet, 7, 113	Doc's Leader, 4, 112	5	2:02.20	100,980
1989	Forever Silver, 4, 111	J. A. Krone	Its Acedemic, 5, 113	Jack of Clubs, 6, 113	5	2:02.60	99,720
1988	Lac Ouimet, 5, 116	J. D. Bailey	Personal Flag, 5, 117	Talinum, 4, 116	9	2:00.20	140,880
1987	Lac Ouimet, 4, 114	E. Maple	Alioth, 4, 113	Proud Debonair, 5, 115	9	2:02.00	106,380
1986	Garthorn, 6, 124	R. Q. Meza	Nordance, 4, 110	Broadway Tommy, 4, 107	5	2:02.40	101,340
1985	Morning Bob, 4, 112	J. Vasquez	Lord of the Manor, 4, 112	Last Turn, 5, 110	8	2:04.20	87,750
1984	Canadian Factor, 4, 117	J. Velasquez	Luv a Libra, 4, 117	Canadian Calm, 4, 108	3	2:03.00	102,150
1983	Fast Gold, 4, 114	J. Samyn	Turn Bold, 4, 107	Sing Sing, 5, 124	7	2:04.00	67,200
1982	Globe, 5, 112	M. Venezia	Accipiter's Hope, 4, 116	Bar Dexter, 5, 118	9	2:03.40	66,480
1981	Irish Tower, 4, 127	J. Fell	Ring of Light, 6, 113	†Relaxing, 5, 125	9	2:00.80	64,680
1980	Ring of Light, 5, 114	C. B. Asmussen	Silent Cal, 5, 122	Rivalero, 4, 118	10	2:01.40	67,560
1979	Special Tiger, 4, 113	G. Martens	Mister Brea (Arg), 5, 125	Coverack, 6, 112	6	2:03.80	63,600
1978	Cox's Ridge, 4, 129	E. Maple	Pumpkin Moonshine, 4, 108	Nearly On Time, 4, 113	7	1:50.60	49,005
1977	Turn and Count, 4, 123	S. Cauthen	Festive Mood, 8, 115	Gabe Benzur, 4, 112	7	1:51.00	48,150
1976	Double Edge Sword, 6, 116	A. T. Cordero Jr.	Northerly, 4, 115	Sharp Gary, 5, 119	9	1:48.20	51,120
1975	Step Nicely, 5, 126	A. T. Cordero Jr.	Monetary Principle, 5, 113	Jolly Johu, 4, 119	5	1:48.40	33,990
1974	*Everton II, 5, 117	M. A. Castaneda	Prince Dantan, 4, 123	Three Or Less, 4, 108	7	1:49.00	33,840
1973	Key to the Mint, 4, 126	R. Turcotte	King's Bishop, 4, 115	North Sea, 4, 120	5	1:47.80	32,640

Named for the state motto of New York, "Excelsior," meaning "upward, ever upward." Grade 2 1973-'97. Excelsior H. 1903-'95. Held at Jamaica 1903-'10, 1915-'59. Not held 1909, 1911-'12, 1914, 1933, 1967. 1 1/16 miles 1903-'59. 1 mile 1960. 1 1/4 miles 1979-'93. †Denotes female.

Fair Grounds Oaks

Grade 2 in 2005. Fair Grounds, three-year-olds, fillies, 1¹/₁₆ miles, dirt. Held March 12, 2005, with a gross value of $300,000. First held in 1966. First graded in 1982. Stakes record 1:42.20 (1997 Blushing K. D.).

Year	Winner	Jockey	Second	Third	Strs	Time	1st Purse
2005	Summerly, 3, 121	J. D. Bailey	Carlea, 3, 121	Runway Model, 3, 121	6	1:43.79	$180,000
2004	Ashado, 3, 121	C. H. Velasquez	Victory U. S. A., 3, 121	Shadow Cast, 3, 121	6	1:43.07	180,000
2003	Lady Tak, 3, 121	D. J. Meche	Atlantic Ocean, 3, 121	Belle of Perintown, 3, 121	6	1:44.36	210,000
2002	Take Charge Lady, 3, 121	A. J. D'Amico	Lake Lady, 3, 121	Chamrousse, 3, 121	8	1:43.30	210,000
2001	Real Cozzy, 3, 121	E. M. Martin Jr.	Mystic Lady, 3, 121	She's a Devil Due, 3, 121	9	1:44.58	210,000
2000	Shawnee Country, 3, 121	D. J. Meche	Eden Lodge, 3, 121	Zoftig, 3, 121	9	1:44.81	210,000
1999	Silverbulletday, 3, 121	G. L. Stevens	Runaway Venus, 3, 112	Brushed Halory, 3, 114	7	1:44.99	223,740
1998	Lu Ravi, 3, 121	W. Martinez	Well Chosen, 3, 112	Silent Eskimo, 3, 112	6	1:43.70	180,000
1997	Blushing K. D., 3, 121	L. J. Meche	Tomisue's Delight, 3, 114	Cozy Blues, 3, 112	5	1:42.20	105,000
1996	Bright Time, 3, 112	L. F. Diaz	Mackie, 3, 121	Proper Dance, 3, 114	9	1:45.98	94,530
1995	Brushing Gloom, 3, 112	J. Brown	Kuda, 3, 118	Legendary Priness, 3, 121	9	1:45.12	90,000
1994	Two Altazano, 3, 112	K. P. LeBlanc	Tricky Code, 3, 121	Minority Dater, 3, 112	6	1:42.50	93,840
1993	Silky Feather, 3, 112	E. J. Perrodin	She's a Little Shy, 3, 121	Sum Runner, 3, 121	7	1:44.60	64,080
1992	Prospectors Delite, 3, 118	P. Day	Glitzi Bj, 3, 118	Desert Radiance, 3, 118	7	1:44.20	63,990
1991	Rare Pick, 3, 112	P. A. Johnson	Nalees Pin, 3, 121	Lady Blockbuster, 3, 118	6	1:46.50	65,640
1990	Pampered Star, 3, 112	S. P. Romero	Windansea, 3, 118	Gayla's Pleasure, 3, 115	9	1:44.60	59,520
1989	Mistaurian, 3, 113	D. Valiente	Affirmed Classic, 3, 121	Exquisite Mistress, 3, 118	6	1:44.80	57,900
1988	Quite a Gem, 3, 115	E. J. Perrodin	False Glitter, 3, 118	Sable Decor, 3, 118	9	1:46.40	59,580
1987	Up the Apalachee, 3, 121	M. R. Torres	Cathy Quick, 3, 118	Out of the Bid, 3, 121	6	1:45.40	60,000
1986	Tiffany Lass, 3, 121	R. L. Frazier	Patricia J. K., 3, 121	Turn and Dance, 3, 112	6	1:45.00	97,400
1985	Marshua's Echelon, 3, 121	R. J. Franklin	Golden Silence, 3, 113	Little Biddy Comet, 3, 118	13	1:44.80	113,400
1984	My Darling One, 3, 112	C. J. McCarron	Texas Cowgirl Nite, 3, 118	Rays Joy, 3, 112	9	1:44.60	101,400
1983	Bright Crocus, 3, 121	S. Hawley	Miss Molly, 3, 118	Shamivor, 3, 115	6	1:45.80	66,100
1982	Before Dawn, 3, 121	J. Velasquez	Girlie, 3, 121	Linda North, 3, 118	7	1:45.40	66,400
1981	Truly Bound, 3, 121	J. Brown	Lou's Dance, 3, 118	‡Sunwonshine, 3, 112	7	1:44.80	61,400
1980	Honest and True, 3, 118	A. Guajardo	Smart Angle, 3, 121	Lady Taurian Peace, 3, 118	8	1:44.40	33,875
1978	La Doree (Arg), 4, 108	B. Fann	Royal Graustark, 4, 114	Burn the Money, 4, 107	10	1:52.40	25,738
	Shadycroft Lady, 3, 109	R. Martinez Jr.	Miss Baja, 3, 117	Belle of Dodge Me, 4, 114	9	1:52.60	25,737
1977	Table the Rumor, 3, 112	W. Shoemaker	La Doree (Arg), 3, 112	Ivory Castle, 3, 118	9	1:52.40	57,800
	Quid Kit, 3, 115	A. J. Trosclair	Royal Graustark, 3, 112	Pay Dust, 3, 112	11	1:45.60	21,025
1976	Bronze Point, 3, 118	H. Arroyo	Little Broadway, 3, 118	Confort Zone, 3, 118	9	1:44.40	20,075
1975	Lucky Leslie, 3, 118	D. Brumfield	Regal Rumor, 3, 121	Decanter, 3, 118	8	1:46.60	19,650
1974	Bold Rosie, 3, 118	P. Rubbicco	Trade Me Later, 3, 112	Kaye's Commander, 3, 118	12	1:46.60	20,625
1973	Knitted Gloves, 3, 118	J. C. Espinoza	Fussy Girl, 3, 121	Westward, 3, 118	11	1:46.00	14,825

Formerly sponsored by Coca-Cola Co. of Atlanta 1989-'90. Grade 3 1982-2000. Coca-Cola Fair Grounds Oaks 1989-'90. Not held 1979. 1¹/₈ miles 1977-'78. Three- and four-year-olds 1978. Two divisions 1978. Run in March and December 1977. ‡Plain Speaking finished third, DQ to fourth, 1981. Equaled track record 1994.

Falls City Handicap

Grade 2 in 2005. Churchill Downs, three-year-olds and up, fillies and mares, 1¹/₈ miles, dirt. Held November 25, 2004, with a gross value of $325,200. First held in 1875. First graded in 1973. Stakes record 1:48.85 (1999 Silent Eskimo).

Year	Winner	Jockey	Second	Third	Strs	Time	1st Purse
2004	Halory Leigh, 4, 116	E. M. Martin Jr.	Susan's Angel, 3, 114	Miss Fortunate, 4, 113	7	1:51.81	$201,624
2003	Lead Story, 4, 116	C. H. Borel	Mayo On the Side, 4, 114	Cloakof Vagueness, 3, 114	9	1:51.23	207,204
2002	Allamerican Bertie, 3, 117	P. Day	Take Charge Lady, 3, 122	Softly, 4, 116	6	1:49.60	167,400
2001	Forest Secrets, 3, 113	C. Perret	Printemps (Chi), 4, 117	Unbridled Elaine, 3, 121	7	1:49.49	169,570
2000	Bordelaise (Arg), 5, 117	P. Day	Spain, 3, 122	On a Soapbox, 4, 116	5	1:50.01	168,020
1999	Silent Eskimo, 4, 117	C. H. Borel	Let, 4, 116	Pleasant Temper, 5, 115	8	1:48.85	171,585
1998	Tomisue's Delight, 4, 121	S. J. Sellers	Top Secret, 5, 115	Silent Eskimo, 3, 113	8	1:51.05	171,740
1997	Feasibility Study, 5, 122	M. E. Smith	Omi, 4, 114	Naskra Colors, 5, 112	7	1:50.65	170,345
1996	Halo America, 6, 118	C. H. Borel	Bedroom Blues, 5, 115	Debit My Account, 4, 113	8	1:49.08	171,120
1995	Mariah's Storm, 4, 120	R. N. Lester	Alcovy, 5, 112	Heavenliness, 5, 112	7	1:51.37	143,390
1994	Alcovy, 4, 114	S. E. Miller	Pennyhill Park, 4, 115	Hey Hazel, 5, 114	7	1:51.16	141,440
1993	Gray Cashmere, 4, 120	P. Day	Avie's Shadow, 3, 110	Princess Polonia, 3, 112	7	1:50.96	142,090
1992	Bungalow, 5, 118	P. Day	Wilderness Song, 4, 123	Auto Dial, 4, 115	7	1:52.03	70,915
1991	Screen Prospect, 4, 117	S. J. Sellers	Fit for a Queen, 5, 124	Bungalow, 4, 112	11	1:51.23	73,580
1990	Screen Prospect, 3, 114	P. Day	Sleek Feet, 3, 110	Degenerate Gal, 5, 119	13	1:51.40	75,920
1989	Degenerate Gal, 4, 116	L. J. Melancon	Luthier's Launch, 3, 113	Blackened, 3, 112	9	1:52.60	72,410
1988	Top Corsage, 5, 121	D. Brumfield	Epitome, 3, 116	Lawyer Talk, 4, 111	14	1:51.80	76,895
1987	Royal Cielo, 3, 114	K. K. Allen	Firgie's Jule, 4, 115	Fantasy Lover, 4, 113	8	1:53.00	47,330
1986	Queen Alexandra, 4, 124	D. Brumfield	Kapalua Butterfly, 5, 113	Gerrie Singer, 5, 116	13	1:51.40	49,248
1985	Donut's Pride, 3, 112	L. J. Melancon	Playful Queen, 4, 114	My Inheritance, 3, 111	8	1:53.20	35,743
	Electric Fanny, 4, 115	J. C. Espinoza	Mrs. Revere, 4, 121	Chattahoochee, 3, 113	10	1:52.60	26,780
1984	Pretty Perfect, 4, 121	G. Gallitano	Electric Fanny, 3, 116	Queen of Song, 5, 122	12	1:50.80	37,115
1983	Narrate, 3, 117	M. S. Sellers	Queen of Song, 4, 116	Promising Native, 4, 116	9	1:51.60	36,335
1982	Mezimica, 4, 112	D. E. Foster	Charge My Account, 3, 111	Shade Miss, 3, 112	10	1:51.40	39,910
	What Glitter, 4, 114	D. Brumfield	Sprite Flight, 4, 114	Betty Money, 3, 118	11	1:52.80	36,823

Year	Winner	Jockey	Second	Third	Strs	Time	1st Purse
1981	Safe Play, 3, 123	S. A. Spencer	Sweetest Chant, 3, 118	Friendly Frolic, 4, 112	13	1:46.20	$37,993
1980	Sweet Audrey, 3, 113	C. R. Woods Jr.	Likely Exchange, 6, 123	Impetuous Gal, 5, 122	11	1:48.20	36,156
1979	Holy Mount, 3, 112	M. R. Morgan	Impetuous Gal, 4, 118	Cup of Honey, 3, 115	11	1:47.60	39,163
1978	Navajo Princess, 4, 123	C. Perret	Love to Tell, 3, 118	Likely Exchange, 4, 120	12	1:45.40	36,043
1977	Time for Pleasure, 3, 115	T. Barrow	Dear Irish, 3, 114	Famed Princess, 4, 115	13	1:46.20	22,084
1976	Hope of Glory, 4, 118	D. Brumfield	Hail to El, 4, 116	Flama Ardiente, 4, 117	12	1:48.20	21,938
1975	Flama Ardiente, 3, 119	B. Fann	Costly Dream, 4, 120	Go On Dreaming, 3, 116	11	1:38.20	18,623
1974	Susan's Girl, 5, 126	W. Gavidia	Crystal Stone, 4, 114	Enchanted Native, 3, 112	9	1:37.40	18,184
1973	Delta Empress, 3, 111	E. Fires	Pig Party, 4, 113	Fine Tuning, 3, 115	12	1:37.40	15,348
	Fairway Flyer, 4, 115	D. E. Whited	Nalees Folly, 4, 118	Knitted Gloves, 3, 113	11	1:37.20	15,185

Named for the early nickname of Louisville, "Falls City." Grade 3 1973-2001. Not held 1878-'81, 1885-'91, 1893-1909, 1928-'40. 1 mile 1875-'55, 1892, 1941-'75. 1½ miles 1882-'83. 1¹⁄₁₆ miles 1884, 1919, 1976-'81. 6 furlongs 1910, 1912-'18. Three-year-olds 1875-'77. Two-year-olds and up 1882-'92. Both sexes 1875-'77, 1882-'92, 1910-'26. Two divisions 1973, 1982, 1985.

Fantasy Stakes

Grade 2 in 2005. Oaklawn Park, three-year-olds, fillies, 1¹⁄₁₆ miles, dirt. Held April 15, 2005, with a gross value of $250,000. First held in 1973. First graded in 1975. Stakes record 1:41.20 (1984 My Darling One).

Year	Winner	Jockey	Second	Third	Strs	Time	1st Purse
2005	Round Pond, 3, 121	S. Elliott	Rugula, 3, 117	R Lady Joy, 3, 121	7	1:43.49	$150,000
2004	House of Fortune, 3, 121	A. O. Solis	Island Sand, 3, 121	Stellar Jayne, 3, 121	11	1:42.62	120,000
2003	Ruby's Reception, 3, 117	T. J. Thompson	Harbor Blues, 3, 121	Go for Glamour, 3, 117	6	1:44.61	120,000
2002	See How She Runs, 3, 121	D. R. Pettinger	Lake Lady, 3, 121	Chamrousse, 3, 117	6	1:43.80	120,000
2001	Mystic Lady, 3, 121	E. Coa	Collect Call, 3, 121	Mysia Jo, 3, 121	10	1:43.32	120,000
2000	Classy Cara, 3, 121	I. Puglisi	Eden Lodge, 3, 117	Gold for My Gal, 3, 117	8	1:43.95	120,000
1999	Excellent Meeting, 3, 121	K. J. Desormeaux	The Happy Hopper, 3, 121	Dreams Gallore, 3, 121	8	1:42.73	150,000
1998	Silent Eskimo, 3, 121	C. Gonzalez	Misty Hour, 3, 121	Came Unwound, 3, 121	8	1:43.84	150,000
1997	Blushing K. D., 3, 121	L. J. Meche	Valid Bonnet, 3, 121	Ajina, 3, 121	5	1:42.60	150,000
1996	Escena, 3, 117	P. Day	Antespend, 3, 121	Ski Trail, 3, 117	7	1:43.93	150,000
1995	Cat's Cradle, 3, 121	C. W. Antley	Forever Cherokee, 3, 117	Humble Eight, 3, 121	8	1:44.29	150,000
1994	Two Altazano, 3, 121	K. P. LeBlanc	Slide Show, 3, 121	Flying in the Lane, 3, 121	11	1:43.64	150,000
1993	Aztec Hill, 3, 121	M. E. Smith	Adorydar, 3, 117	Stalcreek, 3, 117	7	1:44.33	150,000
1992	Race the Wild Wind, 3, 117	C. J. McCarron	Golden Treat, 3, 121	Now Dance, 3, 117	8	1:43.74	150,000
1991	Lite Light, 3, 121	C. S. Nakatani	Withallprobability, 3, 121	Nalees Pin, 3, 121	8	1:41.93	150,000
1990	Silvered, 3, 112	D. L. Howard	Lonely Girl, 3, 114	Fit to Scout, 3, 118	8	1:44.20	150,000
1989	Fantastic Look, 3, 113	C. J. McCarron	Imaginary Lady, 3, 121	Affirmed Classic, 3, 114	7	1:43.20	150,000
1988	Jeanne Jones, 3, 118	W. Shoemaker	Fara's Team, 3, 112	Costly Shoes, 3, 114	7	1:42.20	150,000
1987	‡Very Subtle, 3, 121	C. J. McCarron	Up the Apalachee, 3, 121	Hometown Queen, 3, 116	7	1:42.40	162,780
1986	Tiffany Lass, 3, 121	G. L. Stevens	Lotka, 3, 116	Turn and Dance, 3, 112	8	1:42.00	164,640
1985	Rascal Lass, 3, 118	R. Sibille	Denver Express, 3, 113	Little Biddy Comet, 3, 114	11	1:43.20	169,620
1984	My Darling One, 3, 121	C. J. McCarron	Althea, 3, 121	Personable Lady, 3, 118	6	**1:41.20**	160,440
1983	Brindy Brindy, 3, 115	K. Jones Jr.	Fifth Question, 3, 115	Choose a Partner, 3, 112	11	1:44.60	169,080
1982	Flying Partner, 3, 118	R. Sibille	Skillful Joy, 3, 121	Before Dawn, 3, 121	7	1:47.00	163,020
1981	Heavenly Cause, 3, 121	L. A. Pincay Jr.	Nell's Briquette, 3, 121	Wayward Lass, 3, 121	9	1:43.80	133,890
1980	Bold 'n Determined, 3, 121	E. J. Delahoussaye	Satin Ribera, 3, 115	Honest and True, 3, 118	7	1:45.20	101,940
1979	Davona Dale, 3, 121	J. Velasquez	Caline, 3, 121	Very Special Lady, 3, 110	7	1:44.40	101,610
1978	Equanimity, 3, 110	H. E. Moreno	Ba Ba Bee, 3, 115	Miss Baja, 3, 121	11	1:44.60	77,850
1977	Our Mims, 3, 112	D. Brumfield	Sweet Alliance, 3, 118	Meteor Dancer, 3, 110	15	1:45.00	83,970
1976	T. V. Vixen, 3, 121	B. Walt	Answer, 3, 121	All Rainbows, 3, 112	8	1:43.40	73,170
1975	Hoso, 3, 114	M. Solomone	Luxury, 3, 114	Dancers Countess, 3, 118	6	1:46.00	70,830
1974	Miss Musket, 3, 121	W. Shoemaker	Out to Lunch, 3, 115	Fairway Fable, 3, 118	12	1:44.80	79,740
1973	Knitted Gloves, 3, 121	J. C. Espinoza	Fussy Girl, 3, 121	Westward, 3, 118	14	1:42.60	36,960

Grade 1 1978-'89. 1 mile 70 yards 1973. ‡Up the Apalachee finished first, DQ to second, 1987.

Fayette Stakes

Grade 3 in 2005. Keeneland, three-year-olds and up, 1⅛ miles, dirt. Held October 30, 2004, with a gross value of $161,250. First held in 1959. First graded in 1979. Stakes record 1:46.80 (1987 Good Command).

Year	Winner	Jockey	Second	Third	Strs	Time	1st Purse
2004	Midway Road, 4, 121	C. H. Borel	Total Impact (Chi), 6, 125	Alumni Hall, 5, 119	5	1:50.39	$99,975
2003	M B Sea, 4, 119	C. Perret	Tenpins, 5, 121	dh- Changeintheweather, 4, 119 dh- Seattle Fitz (Arg), 4, 119	7	1:50.30	101,556
2002	Tenpins, 4, 123	C. Perret	X Country, 4, 119	Crafty Shaw, 4, 121	4	1:51.17	99,789
2001	Connected, 4, 119	M. St. Julien	Broken Vow, 4, 123	Outofthebox, 3, 122	9	1:50.05	103,509
2000	Jadada, 5, 116	S. J. Sellers	Mojave Moon, 4, 118	Get Away With It (Ire), 7, 118	5	1:54.92	133,176
1999	Social Charter, 4, 120	M. St. Julien	Master O Foxhounds, 4, 118	Early Warning, 4, 118	4	1:55.28	135,904
1998	Arch, 3, 123	S. J. Sellers	Touch Gold, 4, 115	Wild Tempest, 4, 115	4	1:53.87	98,394
1997	Whiskey Wisdom, 4, 115	W. Martinez	City by Night, 4, 123	Pyramid Peak, 5, 120	6	1:48.64	101,184
1996	Isitingood, 5, 120	D. R. Flores	Distorted Humor, 3, 114	Strawberry Wine, 4, 117	8	1:50.42	120,110
1995	Judge T C, 4, 114	J. M. Johnson	Powerful Punch, 6, 120	Sir Vixen, 7, 114	9	1:49.05	104,625
1994	Sunny Sunrise, 7, 120	J. D. Carle	Key Contender, 6, 117	Powerful Punch, 5, 117	7	1:50.18	67,766

Year	Winner	Jockey	Second	Third	Strs	Time	1st Purse
1993	Grand Jewel, 3, 120	J. D. Bailey	Split Run, 5, 120	Secreto's Hideaway, 4, 114	8	1:46.87	$68,634
1992	Barkerville, 4, 114	S. J. Sellers	Medium Cool, 4, 117	Majesterian, 4, 114	11	1:48.43	70,680
1991	Summer Squall, 4, 122	P. Day	Unbridled, 4, 122	Secret Hello, 4, 115	5	1:48.84	69,810
1990	Lac Ouimet, 7, 119	R. P. Romero	Din's Dancer, 5, 121	Secret Hello, 3, 116	6	1:47.20	70,233
1989	Drapeau Tricolore, 4, 114	J. E. Bruin	Air Worthy, 4, 116	Blue Buckaroo, 6, 118	8	1:48.20	71,695
1988	Homebuilder, 4, 121	D. Brumfield	Blue Buckaroo, 5, 120	Ile de Jinsky, 4, 112	4	1:51.20	68,315
1987	Good Command, 4, 118	D. Brumfield	Minneapple, 5, 120	Savings, 4, 115	12	**1:46.80**	73,921
1986	Harham's Sizzler, 7, 120	R. A. Meier	Derby Wish, 4, 119	Pirate's Skiff, 3, 112	5	1:49.20	34,792
1985	Wop Wop, 3, 112	D. E. Foster	Banner Bob, 3, 117	Exclusive Greer, 4, 114	10	1:51.40	36,530
1984	Star Choice, 5, 112	J. McKnight	Explosive Wagon, 4, 117	Bright Baron, 4, 112	8	1:47.40	47,492
1983	dh- Cad, 5, 116	D. Brumfield		Bold Style, 4, 120	5	1:48.80	22,663
	dh- Frost King, 5, 123	R. Platts					
1982	Rivalero, 6, 115	R. P. Romero	Cad, 4, 114	Recusant, 4, 120	7	1:50.40	35,563
	El Baba, 3, 118	D. Brumfield	Vodika Collins, 4, 120	Hechizado (Arg), 6, 115	7	1:50.20	38,813
1981	Ironworks, 3, 117	P. Day	Two's a Plenty, 4, 116	Sun Catcher, 4, 118	11	1:49.20	39,861
1980	Hurry Up Blue, 3, 112	G. Gallitano	Marcy Road, 3, 111	All the More, 7, 116	10	1:49.00	39,423
1979	Architect, 3, 117	S. A. Spencer	Coverack, 6, 121	Trimlea, 5, 120	8	1:49.60	35,669
1978	‡Silver Series, 4, 121	D. Brumfield	Buckfinder, 4, 121	Romeo, 5, 118	6	1:41.20	20,768
1977	Bob's Dusty, 3, 117	R. DePass	Man's Man, 3, 115	Packer Captain, 5, 118	11	1:42.80	18,395
1976	Silver Badge, 5, 111	G. Patterson	Easy Gallop, 3, 117	Topinabee, 5, 112	9	1:44.60	17,981
	Yamanin, 4, 114	G. Patterson	Run for Clem, 3, 111	Faneuil Boy, 5, 118	8	1:43.20	17,899
1975	Warbucks, 5, 120	J. Nichols	Hasty Flyer, 4, 119	Mr. Door, 4, 114	11	1:44.40	18,460
1974	Jesta Dream Away, 4, 115	A. Rini	Super Sail, 6, 121	Joyous Jester, 4, 112	9	1:41.60	18,119
1973	Chateauvira, 5, 112	G. Gallitano	Grocery List, 4, 116	O So Big, 4, 115	13	1:42.80	19,093

Named for Fayette County, Kentucky, where Keeneland is located. Grade 2 1987-'96. Fayette H. 1959-'91. Fayette Breeders' Cup S. 1999-2000. 1¹⁄₁₆ miles 1963-'78. 1¹⁄₁₆ miles 1998-2000. Turf 1985. Two divisions 1976, 1982. Dead heat for first 1983. Dead heat for third 2003. ‡Buckfinder finished first, DQ to second, 1978. Equaled track record 1993. Track record 1998.

Fifth Season Stakes

Grade 3 in 2005. Oaklawn Park, four-year-olds and up, 1¹⁄₁₆ miles, dirt. Held April 13, 2005, with a gross value of $100,000. First held in 1988. First graded in 1999. Stakes record 1:40.30 (1991 Hang On Slewpy).

Year	Winner	Jockey	Second	Third	Strs	Time	1st Purse
2005	Mauk Four, 5, 113	J. Burningham	Clays Awesome, 5, 117	Absent Friend, 5, 122	8	1:42.89	$60,000
2004	Spanish Empire, 4, 118	E. M. Martin Jr.	Crafty Shaw, 6, 122	No Comprende, 6, 122	8	1:42.50	60,000
2003	Patton's Victory, 5, 117	A. Birzer	Colorful Tour, 4, 122	Makors Mark, 6, 118	7	1:43.26	60,000
2001	Remington Rock, 7, 114	D. E. Simington	Kombat Kat, 4, 114	Da Devil, 6, 114	7	1:43.13	45,000
2000	Mr Ross, 5, 115	E. C. Perner	Relic Reward, 6, 114	Crimson Classic, 6, 114	7	1:42.93	60,000
1999	Truluck, 4, 114	L. J. Melancon	Slide to the Left, 4, 114	Rock and Roll, 4, 114	8	1:42.28	60,000
1998	Acceptable, 4, 117	A. O. Solis	Littlebitlively, 4, 117	Brush With Pride, 6, 124	8	1:42.50	60,000
1997	Krigeorj's Gold, 4, 119	J. Johnson	Bucks Nephew, 7, 117	Prince of the Mt., 6, 116	9	1:43.20	49,050
1996	No Spend No Glow, 4, 117	R. N. Lester	Bucks Nephew, 6, 117	Groovy Jett, 5, 117	7	1:42.96	47,880
1995	Tyus, 5, 114	C. H. Borel	Prince of the Mt., 4, 114	Joseph's Robe, 4, 114	7	1:42.98	26,760
1994	Nelson, 7, 117	S. P. Romero	Punch Line, 4, 117	Senor Tomas, 5, 114	6	1:43.16	41,640
1993	Delafield, 4, 117	J. A. Santos	Far Out Wadleigh, 5, 119	Lanyons Star, 5, 114	11	1:42.43	43,080
1992	Medium Cool, 4, 117	C. S. Nakatani	On the Edge, 5, 114	Hayes G., 5, 117	10	1:43.35	40,500
1991	Hang On Slewpy, 4, 119	D. L. Howard	Greydar, 4, 125	Traskwood, 5, 117	5	**1:40.30**	31,635
1990	Idabel, 4, 119	P. Day	Albert's First, 7, 117	Beirne Station, 4, 112	9	1:42.20	32,115
1989	Smackover Creek, 4, 114	D. L. Howard	Sir Bubby, 6, 114	Sarhilla, 5, 117	9	1:43.20	32,475
1988	Contact Game, 4, 113	J. D. Bailey	General Silver, 4, 113	Itsallinthegame, 5, 114	9	1:42.20	20,280

Named for Hot Springs, Arkansas's "fifth season," the Oaklawn Park race meet. Fifth Season Breeders' Cup S. 1989-2001. Not held 2002. Three-year-olds and up 1989-2001.

Firecracker Breeders' Cup Handicap

Grade 2 in 2005. Churchill Downs, three-year-olds and up, 1 mile, turf. Held July 3, 2004, with a gross value of $287,750. First held in 1983. First graded in 1995. Stakes record 1:33.78 (1995 Jaggery John).

Year	Winner	Jockey	Second	Third	Strs	Time	1st Purse
2004	Quantum Merit, 5, 117	S. J. Sellers	‡Perfect Soul (Ire), 6, 121	Senor Swinger, 4, 117	9	1:34.15	$178,405
2003	Tap the Admiral, 5, 115	J. McKee	Freefourinternet, 5, 114	Package Store, 5, 114	9	1:35.48	178,870
2002	Good Journey, 6, 118	P. Day	Morluc, 6, 114	Even the Score, 4, 114	9	1:34.83	181,350
2001	Irish Prize, 5, 122	G. L. Stevens	‡Aly's Alley, 5, 117	Where's Taylor, 5, 114	7	1:34.68	175,770
2000	Conserve, 4, 116	S. J. Sellers	Riviera (Fr), 6, 115	King Slayer (GB), 5, 115	8	1:35.12	177,940
1999	Joe Who (Brz), 6, 113	R. Albarado	Middlesex Drive, 4, 116	Wild Event, 6, 121	9	1:36.78	132,680
1998	Claire's Honor, 4, 109	A. J. D'Amico	Soviet Line (Ire), 8, 115	Optic Nerve, 5, 113	9	1:35.93	177,630
1997	Soviet Line (Ire), 7, 114	P. Day	Volochine (Ire), 6, 115	Same Old Wish, 7, 118	10	1:37.60	126,077
1996	Rare Reason, 5, 115	P. A. Johnson	Artema (Ire), 5, 114	Wavy Run (Ire), 5, 116	9	1:33.81	131,950
1995	Jaggery John, 4, 113	D. Kutz	Rare Reason, 4, 115	Fly Cry, 4, 119	10	**1:33.78**	74,360
1994	First and Only, 7, 118	T. J. Hebert	†Weekend Madness (Ire), 4, 111	Avid Affection, 5, 112	8	1:35.33	73,580
1993	Cleone, 4, 115	C. Perret	Magesterial Cheer, 5, 113	Harlan, 4, 110	9	1:35.90	74,815

1985	**Rapid Gray**, 6, 122	L. J. Melancon	Silahis, 8, 116	Silver Wraith, 4, 110	5	1:21.20	$35,263
1984	**Turn and Cheer**, 4, 113	J. McKnight	Coax Me Matt, 4, 112	Keep At It, 3, 112	7	1:25.60	35,912
1983	**Shot n' Missed**, 6, 121	L. Moyers	Dave's Friend, 8, 124	Rackensack, 5, 118	4	1:23.20	28,145

Traditionally held during the July 4 holiday. Grade 3 1995-'99. Firecracker H. 1983-'95. Not held 1986-'92. 7 furlongs 1983-'85. Dirt 1983-'85. Course record 1995. ‡Where's Taylor finished second, DQ to third, 2001. ‡Senor Swinger finished second, DQ to third, 2004. †Denotes female.

First Flight Handicap

Grade 2 in 2005. Aqueduct, three-year-olds and up, fillies and mares, 7 furlongs, dirt. Held October 30, 2004, with a gross value of $150,000. First held in 1978. First graded in 1982. Stakes record 1:20.65 (1992 Shared Interest).

Year	Winner	Jockey	Second	Third	Strs	Time	1st Purse
2004	**Bending Strings**, 3, 116	S. Bridgmohan	Smokey Glacken, 3, 115	Passing Shot, 5, 118	6	1:22.13	$90,000
2003	**Randaroo**, 3, 115	H. Castillo Jr.	Shine Again, 6, 121	Zawzooth, 4, 113	8	1:23.65	90,000
2002	**Shine Again**, 5, 117	J. Samyn	Redhead Riot, 3, 112	Raging Fever, 4, 119	5	1:23.75	90,000
2001	**Shine Again**, 4, 116	J. Samyn	Dream Supreme, 4, 121	Kalookan Queen, 5, 119	6	1:23.21	90,000
2000	**Country Hideaway**, 4, 117	J. L. Espinoza	Go to the Ink, 4, 113	Cat Cay, 3, 114	7	1:22.60	90,000
1999	**Country Hideaway**, 3, 114	H. Castillo Jr.	Harpia, 5, 117	Anklet, 5, 114	8	1:23.00	90,000
1998	**Catinca**, 3, 116	R. Migliore	Glitter Woman, 4, 121	Blue Begonia, 5, 115	7	1:22.14	82,260
1997	**Dixie Flag**, 5, 113	M. J. Luzzi	Silent City, 3, 113	Aldiza, 3, 116	4	1:22.84	64,800
1996	**Thunder Achiever**, 3, 112	R. G. Davis	Miss Golden Circle, 4, 117	Call Account, 4, 110	10	1:21.59	81,864
1995	**Twist Afleet**, 4, 121	G. L. Stevens	Igotrhythm, 3, 109	Lottsa Talc, 5, 116	5	1:22.95	66,780
1994	**Twist Afleet**, 3, 117	J. D. Bailey	Ann Dear, 4, 117	Incinerate, 4, 113	8	1:23.02	66,120
1993	**Raise Heck**, 5, 114	R. I. Velez	Regal Victress, 6, 113	Shared Interest, 5, 121	6	1:23.51	69,000
1992	**Shared Interest**, 4, 111	J. D. Bailey	Missy's Mirage, 4, 121	Nannerl, 5, 119	5	**1:20.65**	120,000
1991	**Missy's Mirage**, 3, 113	E. Maple	Makin Faces, 3, 112	Withallprobability, 3, 114	10	1:21.98	74,160
1990	**Queena**, 4, 113	J. D. Bailey	Quick Mischief, 4, 115	A Penny Is a Penny, 5, 122	5	1:22.40	51,480
1989	**Grecian Flight**, 5, 122	C. Perret	Feel the Beat, 4, 121	Dance Teacher, 4, 112	5	1:22.00	51,480
1988	**Cagey Exuberance**, 4, 119	J. Imparato	Nasty Affair, 4, 114	Intently, 5, 111	10	1:24.40	55,350
1987	**Al's Helen**, 4, 112	J. D. Bailey	Girl Powder, 4, 117	Willowy Mood, 5, 118	9	1:21.80	54,180
1986	**Chaldea**, 6, 115	J. Samyn	Le Slew, 5, 114	Gene's Lady, 5, 120	4	1:22.40	53,100
1985	**Alabama Nana (Ire)**, 4, 121	J. Velasquez	Gene's Lady, 4, 115	Paradies (Arg), 5, 119	5	1:22.20	50,040
1984	**Shortley**, 4, 114	M. G. Pino	Quixotic Lady, 4, 116	Rarely Layte, 4, 108	7	1:22.60	42,060
1983	**Pert**, 4, 112	F. Lovato Jr.	Pretty Sensible, 3, 112	Quixotic Lady, 3, 121	8	1:25.20	34,620
1982	**Number**, 3, 112	E. Maple	Lady Dean, 4, 123	Privacy, 4, 113	11	1:22.80	34,500
1981	**Island Charm**, 4, 120	R. Migliore	Tax Holiday, 4, 116	Chain Bracelet, 4, 123	8	1:23.60	33,720
1980	**Samarta Dancer**, 4, 112	C. B. Asmussen	Jedina, 4, 115	Damask Fan, 3, 116	9	1:25.60	33,780
1979	**Gladiolus**, 5, 120	L. A. Pincay Jr.	Imarebel, 4, 117	Plankton, 3, 114	5	1:22.40	25,740
1978	**What a Summer**, 5, 126	J. Fell	Flying Above, 4, 120	Mrs. Warren, 4, 113	5	1:22.20	25,410

Named for C. V. Whitney's 1946 champion two-year-old filly and '46 Futurity S. winner First Flight (1944 f. by *Mahmoud). Grade 3 1982-'89. I Love New York First Flight H. 1995. Held at Belmont Park 1990, 1992, 1995, 2001, 2003.

First Lady Handicap

Grade 3 in 2005. Gulfstream Park, three-year-olds and up, fillies and mares, 6 furlongs, dirt. Held January 22, 2005, with a gross value of $100,000. First held in 1981. First graded in 1993. Stakes record 1:09.21 (2005 Savorthetime).

Year	Winner	Jockey	Second	Third	Strs	Time	1st Purse
2005	**Savorthetime**, 6, 116	J. R. Velazquez	Cology, 5, 117	Ebony Breeze, 5, 116	7	**1:09.21**	$60,000
2004	**Harmony Lodge**, 6, 119	R. Migliore	House Party, 4, 118	Mayo On the Side, 5, 115	9	1:09.64	60,000
2003	**Harmony Lodge**, 5, 113	J. R. Velazquez	Fly Me Crazy, 5, 114	Haunted Lass, 4, 114	7	1:10.31	60,000
2002	**Raging Fever**, 4, 118	J. R. Velazquez	Cat Cay, 5, 118	Mandy's Gold, 4, 116	7	1:10.36	60,000
2001	**Another**, 4, 113	E. S. Prado	Curious Treasures, 4, 114	Dynamite Diablo, 4, 115	11	1:10.41	60,000
2000	**Hurricane Bertie**, 5, 118	P. Day	Marley Vale, 4, 118	Cassidy, 5, 113	7	1:10.22	45,000
1999	**Scotzanna**, 7, 114	R. Migliore	U Can Do It, 6, 118	Foil, 4, 116	8	1:10.17	45,000
1998	**U Can Do It**, 5, 115	S. J. Sellers	Start At Once, 5, 113	Vivace, 5, 118	10	1:09.86	45,000
1997	**Chip**, 4, 113	J. Bravo	Phone the Doctor, 5, 116	Surprising Fact, 4, 113	10	1:09.76	45,000
1996	**Chaposa Springs**, 4, 122	J. D. Bailey	Phone the Doctor, 4, 117	Market Slide, 5, 113	9	1:10.23	45,000
1995	**Recognizable**, 4, 113	M. E. Smith	Insight to Cope, 5, 114	Maison de Reve, 5, 113	10	1:09.74	30,000
1994	**Santa Catalina**, 4, 114	J. D. Bailey	Insight to Cope, 4, 119	Capture the Crown, 5, 113	11	1:11.26	30,000
1993	**Si Si Sezyou**, 5, 112	R. Hernandez	Illeria, 6, 113	Jeano, 5, 114	11	1:10.06	30,000
1992	**Withallprobability**, 4, 118	C. Perret	Christina Czarina, 4, 114	Spirit of Fighter, 9, 114	14	1:11.14	30,000
1991	**Spirit of Fighter**, 8, 118	J. A. Velez Jr.	Mistaurian, 5, 115	Love's Exchange, 5, 128	9	1:11.70	30,000
1990	**Sez Fourty**, 4, 114	M. A. Gonzalez	Classic Value, 5, 118	Fit for a Queen, 4, 114	7	1:11.20	22,764
1989	**Waggley**, 6, 112	J. Samyn	Damality, 6, 113	My Peace, 4, 114	5	1:11.00	27,288
1988	**Funistrada**, 5, 120	W. A. Guerra	Easter Mary, 4, 114	Cadillacing, 4, 113	9	1:10.20	29,232
1987	**One Fine Lady**, 5, 114	R. Danjean	Fleur de Soleil, 4, 112	Sheer Ice, 5, 113	6	1:10.40	24,045
1986	**Sugar's Image**, 5, 115	J. A. Velez Jr.	Summer Mood, 5, 120	Mr. T.'s Tune, 5, 117	10	1:11.20	29,736
1985	**Nany**, 5, 120	G. St. Leon	Mickey's Echo, 6, 118	Birdie Belle, 4, 118	9	1:09.80	29,352
1983	**Prime Prospect**, 5, 118	D. MacBeth	Miss Hitch, 7, 114	Mrs. Roberts, 5, 113	16	1:10.80	24,282
1981	**Island Charm**, 4, 113	J. Velasquez	La Voyageuse, 6, 126	Lacey, 4, 114	11	1:10.60	22,536

Inaugurated in 1981 following a presidential election year and run in mid-January when presidential inaugurations are held, the race is named for the first lady of the United States. First Lady Breeders' Cup H. 1990. Not held 1982, 1984.

Flash Stakes

Grade 3 in 2005. Belmont Park, two-year-olds, 5 furlongs, dirt. Held June 10, 2005, with a gross value of $105,100. First held in 1869. First graded in 2001. Stakes record :56.93 (2001 Buster's Daydream).

Year	Winner	Jockey	Second	Third	Strs	Time	1st Purse
2005	Beacon Shine, 2, 118	J. Castellano	Union Course, 2, 118	Speed of Sound, 2, 118	5	:58.39	$64,260
2004	Primal Storm, 2, 116	S. J. Sellers	Winning Expression, 2, 115	Gold Joy, 2, 115	5	:57.49	63,780
2003	Chapel Royal, 2, 114	J. R. Velazquez	Hasslefree, 2, 114	Juventus, 2, 114	4	:57.02	63,955
2002	Whywhywhy, 2, 114	E. S. Prado	Presence, 2, 115	Down Play, 2, 114	7	:57.10	65,460
2001	Buster's Daydream, 2, 115	E. S. Prado	Harmony Hall, 2, 115	Huber Woods, 2, 115	8	**:56.93**	49,365
2000	Yonaguska, 2, 115	J. D. Bailey	The Goo, 2, 115	City Zip, 2, 115	7	:57.86	49,470
1999	More Than Ready, 2, 119	J. R. Velazquez	Diablo's Addition, 2, 115	Bevo, 2, 115	6	:57.10	49,245
1982	Victorious, 2, 115	J. D. Bailey	Satan's Charger, 2, 119	Great Ending, 2, 119	7	1:04.20	33,420
1981	Ringaro, 2, 119	A. T. Cordero Jr.	Lead Astray, 2, 119	Prince Westport, 2, 115	6	1:04.60	33,300

Held at Saratoga 1869-1942, 1946-'71. Not held 1896, 1899-1900, 1911-'12, 1960, 1972-'80, 1983-'98. 4 furlongs 1869-'97. 5½ furlongs 1902-'68, 1981-'82. 6 furlongs 1969-'71. Colts and geldings 1981-'82.

Fleur de Lis Handicap

Grade 2 in 2005. Churchill Downs, three-year-olds and up, fillies and mares, 1⅛ miles, dirt. Held June 12, 2004, with a gross value of $439,200. First held in 1975. First graded in 1988. Stakes record 1:48.26 (2000 Heritage of Gold).

Year	Winner	Jockey	Second	Third	Strs	Time	1st Purse
2004	Adoration, 5, 122	V. Espinoza	Bare Necessities, 5, 120	La Reason, 4, 110	6	1:52.15	$272,304
2003	You, 4, 119	J. D. Bailey	Printemps (Chi), 6, 114	Nonsuch Bay, 4, 114	6	1:49.12	203,298
2002	Spain, 5, 121	J. F. Chavez	With Ability, 4, 117	Dancethruthedawn, 4, 119	6	1:49.64	204,228
2001	Saudi Poetry, 4, 114	V. Espinoza	Secret Status, 4, 119	Asher, 4, 112	8	1:49.27	206,460
2000	Heritage of Gold, 5, 121	S. J. Sellers	Silverbulletday, 4, 119	Roza Robata, 5, 115	7	**1:48.26**	201,252
1999	Banshee Breeze, 4, 124	R. Albarado	Silent Eskimo, 4, 114	Meadow Vista, 4, 109	4	1:50.02	197,718
1998	Escena, 5, 123	S. J. Sellers	One Rich Lady, 4, 113	Tomisue's Delight, 4, 118	5	1:50.19	199,020
1997	Gold n Delicious, 4, 113	C. H. Borel	Effectiveness, 4, 111	Everhope, 4, 111	10	1:52.87	104,718
1996	Serena's Song, 4, 124	G. L. Stevens	Halo America, 6, 117	Alcovy, 6, 117	9	1:50.30	109,493
1995	Fit to Lead, 5, 117	S. J. Sellers	Pennyhill Park, 5, 118	Low Key Affair, 4, 112	7	1:51.59	107,055
1994	Trishyde, 5, 117	C. J. McCarron	Eskimo's Angel, 4, 115	Ma Guerre, 4, 109	8	1:51.34	107,315
1993	Quilma (Chi), 6, 117	R. P. Romero	Fappies Cosy Miss, 5, 110	Hitch, 4, 112	6	1:50.80	71,240
1992	Bungalow, 5, 114	F. C. Torres	Til Forbid, 4, 113	Beth Believes, 6, 112	12	1:50.87	74,815
1991	Maskra's Lady, 4, 111	J. M. Johnson	Fit for a Queen, 5, 116	Under Oath, 5, 113	10	1:50.46	73,515
1990	A Penny Is a Penny, 5, 120	A. T. Gryder	Stoneleigh's Hope, 5, 115	Lady Hoolihan, 4, 112	7	1:51.20	70,980
1989	Stoneleigh's Hope, 4, 112	J. Deegan	Way It Should Be, 5, 111	Lt. Lao, 5, 116	8	1:52.60	71,435
1988	Lt. Lao, 4, 116	D. Brumfield	Lawyer Talk, 4, 111	She's a Mystery, 5, 111	9	1:49.60	72,215
1987	Infinidad (Chi), 5, 118	M. Solomone	Marianna's Girl, 4, 117	Queen Alexandra, 5, 126	8	1:50.60	64,815
1986	Queen Alexandra, 4, 117	D. Brumfield	Tide, 4, 111	Zenobia Empress, 5, 119	11	1:49.20	66,083
1985	Straight Edition, 5, 113	C. R. Woods Jr.	Dusty Gloves, 4, 110	Del Dun Gee, 5, 110	8	1:50.80	36,108
1984	Heatherten, 5, 124	S. Maple	Satiety, 5, 110	Hotsy Totsy, 4, 112	5	1:51.40	35,233
1983	Try Something New, 4, 121	P. Day	Naskra Magic, 4, 116	Header Card, 4, 114	5	1:51.60	35,328
1982	Classic Ambition, 4, 112	W. Gavidia	Beyond Reproof, 4, 113	Mean Martha, 4, 117	10	1:44.80	36,855
1981	Forever Cordial, 4, 114	D. Haire	Salud, 4, 114	Passolyn, 4, 118	10	1:45.40	23,205
1980	Likely Exchange, 6, 121	M. S. Sellers	Salzburg, 5, 116	Smooth Bore, 4, 115	9	1:45.00	23,026
1979	Table the Rumor, 5, 116	D. E. Whited	Likely Exchange, 5, 123	Pretty Delight, 4, 116	8	1:45.20	22,864
1978	Likely Exchange, 4, 113	J. McKnight	Time for Pleasure, 4, 123	Bold Rendezvous, 3, 114	5	1:45.40	13,894
1977	Go On Dreaming, 5, 115	P. Nicolo	B. J. King, 5, 114	Kittyluck, 4, 117	9	1:43.80	14,381
1976	Pago Hop, 4, 116	H. Arroyo	Flama Ardiente, 4, 122	Precious Proof, 5, 113	6	1:38.40	14,056
1975	Bundler, 4, 120	J. Nichols	Jay Bar Pet, 4, 112	Tappahannock, 4, 116	7	1:39.40	14,511

Named for the fleur de lis ("lily" in French), symbol of the city of Louisville. Grade 3 1998-2001. 1 mile 1975-'76. 1¹/₁₆ miles 1977-'82. Four-year-olds and up 1983-'85, 1987-'89.

Floral Park Handicap

Grade 3 in 2005. Belmont Park, three-year-olds and up, fillies and mares, 6 furlongs, dirt. Held September 18, 2004, with a gross value of $104,400. First held in 1995. First graded in 2002. Stakes record 1:09.20 (1995 Twist Afleet).

Year	Winner	Jockey	Second	Third	Strs	Time	1st Purse
2004	Feline Story, 3, 114	E. S. Prado	Cologny, 4, 115	Travelator, 4, 116	5	1:10.69	$63,840
2003	Bauhauser (Arg), 5, 115	R. Migliore	Shine Again, 6, 120	Literary Light, 4, 113	6	1:10.84	65,100
2002	Carson Hollow, 3, 117	J. R. Velazquez	Gold Mover, 4, 117	Shiny Band, 4, 115	4	1:10.25	63,955
2001	Gold Mover, 3, 118	E. S. Prado	Dat You Miz Blue, 4, 119	Finder's Fee, 4, 115	6	1:10.03	65,040
2000	Big Bambu, 3, 114	R. G. Davis	Tropical Punch, 4, 114	Cash Run, 3, 114	5	1:09.81	64,620
1999	Positive Gal, 3, 113	J. D. Bailey	Final Proposal, 3, 113	Flamingo Way, 5, 113	7	1:09.23	49,125
1998	Blue Begonia, 5, 114	J. F. Chavez	Dixie Flag, 4, 117	Soverign Lady, 4, 116	5	1:10.30	48,570
1997	Creamy Dreamy, 4, 118	R. G. Davis	Silent City, 3, 113	Secret Prospect, 4, 118	5	1:10.56	47,835
1996	Lottsa Talc, 6, 119	F. T. Alvarado	Fresa, 4, 113	Culver City, 4, 113	5	1:10.61	38,736
1995	Twist Afleet, 4, 120	G. L. Stevens	For all Seasons, 5, 115	Regal Solution, 5, 113	6	**1:09.20**	32,490

Named for Floral Park, a community in Nassau County, New York, near Belmont Park.

Florida Derby

Grade 1 in 2005. Gulfstream Park, three-year-olds, 1$\frac{1}{8}$ miles, dirt. Held April 2, 2005, with a gross value of $1,000,000. First held in 1952. First graded in 1973. Stakes record 1:46.80 (1957 Gen. Duke).

Year	Winner	Jockey	Second	Third	Strs	Time	1st Purse
2005	High Fly, 3, 122	J. D. Bailey	Noble Causeway, 3, 122	B. B. Best, 3, 122	9	1:49.43	$600,000
2004	Friends Lake, 3, 122	R. Migliore	Value Plus, 3, 122	The Cliff's Edge, 3, 122	10	1:51.38	600,000
2003	Empire Maker, 3, 122	J. D. Bailey	Trust N Luck, 3, 122	Indy Dancer, 3, 122	7	1:49.05	600,000
2002	Harlan's Holiday, 3, 122	E. S. Prado	Blue Burner, 3, 122	Peekskill, 3, 122	11	1:48.80	600,000
2001	Monarchos, 3, 122	J. F. Chavez	Outofthebox, 3, 122	Invisible Ink, 3, 122	13	1:49.95	600,000
2000	Hal's Hope, 3, 122	R. I. Velez	High Yield, 3, 122	Tahkodha Hills, 3, 122	10	1:51.49	450,000
1999	Vicar, 3, 122	S. J. Sellers	Wondertross, 3, 122	Cat Thief, 3, 122	10	1:50.83	450,000
1998	‡Cape Town, 3, 122	S. J. Sellers	Lil's Lad, 3, 122	Halory Hunter, 3, 122	6	1:49.21	450,000
1997	Captain Bodgit, 3, 122	A. O. Solis	Pulpit, 3, 122	Frisk Me Now, 3, 122	8	1:50.60	300,000
1996	Unbridled's Song, 3, 122	M. E. Smith	Editor's Note, 3, 122	Skip Away, 3, 122	9	1:47.85	300,000
1995	Thunder Gulch, 3, 122	M. E. Smith	Suave Prospect, 3, 122	Mecke, 3, 122	10	1:49.70	300,000
1994	Holy Bull, 3, 122	M. E. Smith	Ride the Rails, 3, 122	Halo's Image, 3, 122	14	1:47.66	300,000
1993	Bull Inthe Heather, 3, 122	W. S. Ramos	Storm Tower, 3, 122	Wallenda, 3, 122	13	1:51.38	300,000
1992	Technology, 3, 122	J. D. Bailey	Dance Floor, 3, 122	Pistols and Roses, 3, 122	12	1:50.72	300,000
1991	Fly So Free, 3, 122	J. A. Santos	Strike the Gold, 3, 118	Hansel, 3, 122	8	1:50.44	300,000
1990	Unbridled, 3, 122	P. Day	Slavic, 3, 122	Run Turn, 3, 122	9	1:52.00	300,000
1989	Mercedes Won, 3, 122	E. Fires	Western Playboy, 3, 118	Big Stanley, 3, 122	11	1:49.60	300,000
1988	Brian's Time, 3, 118	R. P. Romero	Forty Niner, 3, 122	Notebook, 3, 122	10	1:49.80	300,000
1987	Cryptoclearance, 3, 122	J. A. Santos	No More Flowers, 3, 118	Talinum, 3, 122	9	1:49.60	300,000
1986	Snow Chief, 3, 122	A. O. Solis	Badger Land, 3, 122	Mogambo, 3, 122	16	1:51.80	300,000
1985	Proud Truth, 3, 122	J. Velasquez	Irish Sur, 3, 122	Do It Again Dan, 3, 122	11	1:50.00	180,000
1984	Swale, 3, 122	L. A. Pincay Jr.	Dr. Carter, 3, 122	Darn That Alarm, 3, 122	9	1:47.60	180,000
1983	Croeso, 3, 118	F. Olivares	Copelan, 3, 122	Law Talk, 3, 118	13	1:49.80	150,000
1982	Timely Writer, 3, 122	J. Fell	Star Gallant, 3, 122	Our Escapade, 3, 122	7	1:49.60	150,000
1981	Lord Avie, 3, 122	C. J. McCarron	Akureyri, 3, 122	Linnleur, 3, 118	11	1:50.40	147,388
1980	Plugged Nickle, 3, 122	B. Thornburg	Naked Sky, 3, 122	Lord Gallant, 3, 118	8	1:50.20	110,000
1979	Spectacular Bid, 3, 122	R. J. Franklin	Lot o' Gold, 3, 122	Fantasy 'n Reality, 3, 122	7	1:48.80	115,000
1978	Alydar, 3, 122	J. Velasquez	Believe It, 3, 122	Dr. Valeri, 3, 122	7	1:47.00	100,000
1977	Coined Silver, 3, 118	B. Thornburg	Nearly On Time, 3, 122	Fort Prevel, 3, 122	8	1:48.80	68,700
	Ruthie's Native, 3, 122	C. Perret	For The Moment, 3, 122	Sir Sir, 3, 122	10	1:50.20	69,900
1976	Honest Pleasure, 3, 122	B. Baeza	Great Contractor, 3, 122	Proud Birdie, 3, 122	6	1:47.80	91,440
1975	Prince Thou Art, 3, 118	B. Baeza	Sylvan Place, 3, 118	Foolish Pleasure, 3, 122	9	1:50.40	94,440
1974	Judger, 3, 118	L. A. Pincay Jr.	Cannonade, 3, 122	Buck's Bid, 3, 118	16	1:49.00	130,200
1973	Royal and Regal, 3, 122	W. Blum	Forego, 3, 118	Restless Jet, 3, 122	8	1:47.40	78,120

Honoring Gulfstream Park's home state, the race name first was used at Tampa in 1926. After a two-year hiatus, the race was run at Hialeah Park. In 1937, Hialeah's leading three-year-old race was renamed the Flamingo Stakes. ‡Lil's Lad finished first, DQ to second, 1998. Two divisions 1977.

Flower Bowl Invitational Stakes

Grade 1 in 2005. Belmont Park, three-year-olds and up, fillies and mares, 1$\frac{1}{4}$ miles, turf. Held October 2, 2004, with a gross value of $750,000. First held in 1978. First graded in 1980. Stakes record 1:59.33 (1998 Auntie Mame).

Year	Winner	Jockey	Second	Third	Strs	Time	1st Purse
2004	Riskaverse, 5, 118	C. H. Velasquez	Commercante (Fr), 4, 118	Moscow Burning, 4, 120	8	2:04.65	$450,000
2003	Dimitrova, 3, 114	J. D. Bailey	Walzerkoenigin, 4, 120	Heat Haze (GB), 4, 123	7	2:02.74	450,000
2002	Kazzia (Ger), 3, 118	J. F. Chavez	Turtle Bow (Fr), 3, 115	Mot Juste (GB), 4, 118	7	2:05.22	450,000
2001	Lailani (GB), 3, 118	J. D. Bailey	England's Legend (Fr), 4, 123	Starine (Fr), 4, 123	6	2:01.88	450,000
2000	Colstar, 4, 116	J. Samyn	Snow Polina, 5, 121	Pico Teneriffe, 4, 115	5	2:01.78	450,000
1999	Soaring Softly, 4, 118	J. D. Bailey	Coretta (Ire), 5, 118	Mossflower, 5, 115	7	2:01.41	300,000
1998	Auntie Mame, 4, 121	J. R. Velazquez	B. A. Valentine, 5, 114	Bahr (GB), 3, 118	5	1:59.33	240,000
1997	Yashmak, 3, 114	C. S. Nakatani	Maxzene, 4, 123	Memories of Silver, 4, 123	8	1:59.73	240,000
1996	Chelsey Flower, 5, 115	R. G. Davis	Powder Bowl, 4, 116	Electric Society (Ire), 5, 118	10	2:05.96	210,000
1995	Northern Emerald, 5, 117	R. B. Perez	Danish (Ire), 4, 116	Duda, 4, 113	10	2:06.68	120,000
1994	Dahlia's Dreamer, 5, 112	J. F. Chavez	Alywow, 3, 114	Danish (Ire), 3, 113	12	2:05.52	120,000
1993	Far Out Beast, 6, 111	J. Samyn	Dahlia's Dreamer, 4, 110	Lady Blessington (Fr), 5, 118	10	2:03.88	90,000
1992	Christiecat, 5, 116	J. Samyn	Ratings, 4, 114	Plenty of Grace, 5, 115	9	2:01.66	120,000
1991	Lady Shirl, 4, 117	R. Migliore	Franc Argument, 5, 111	Christiecat, 4, 120	12	2:02.43	120,000
1990	Laugh and Be Merry, 5, 115	W. H. McCauley	Foresta, 4, 115	Gaily Gaily (Ire), 7, 117	13	2:00.20	78,840
1989	River Memories, 5, 112	P. Day	Capades, 3, 116	Miss Unnameable, 5, 116	11	2:06.80	74,880
1988	Gaily Gaily (Ire), 5, 109	J. A. Krone	Love You by Heart, 3, 113	Princely Proof, 5, 116	12	2:02.80	76,800
1987	Slew's Exceller, 5, 113	J. A. Santos	Videogenic, 5, 118	Fiesta Gal, 3, 114	9	2:02.20	91,020
1986	dh- Dismasted, 4, 115	J. Samyn		Cope of Flowers, 4, 112	12	2:00.00	52,152
	dh- Scoot, 3, 106	W. Shoemaker					
1985	Dawn's Curtsey, 3, 111	E. Maple	Vers La Caisse, 4, 116	Agacerie, 4, 116	9	2:02.20	87,540
1984	Rossard (Den), 4, 117	L. A. Pincay Jr.	Aspen Rose, 4, 115	Persian Tiara (Ire), 4, 116	9	2:03.40	72,840
1983	First Approach, 5, 117	J. Velasquez	If Winter Comes, 4, 113	Mintage (Fr), 4, 111	8	2:00.20	68,160
1982	Trevita (Ire), 5, 117	R. Hernandez	Hunston (GB), 4, 108	Hush Dear, 4, 112	12	2:01.40	71,880
1981	Rokeby Rose, 4, 114	J. Fell	De La Rose, 3, 116	Euphrosyne, 5, 110	6	2:01.60	67,200

1980	**Just a Game (Ire)**, 4, 124	D. Brumfield	Hey Babe, 4, 114	Euphrosyne, 4, 112	11	2:00.80	$68,640
1979	**Pearl Necklace**, 5, 125	W. Shoemaker	The Very One, 4, 112	Terpsichorist, 4, 118	8	2:02.20	68,160
1978	**Waya (Fr)**, 4, 120	A. T. Cordero Jr.	Magnificence, 4, 108	Leave Me Alone, 5, 108	7	2:00.60	32,490

Named for Brookmeade Stable's 1956 Ladies H. winner Flower Bowl (1952 f. by *Alibhai), dam of champion Bowl of Flowers and leading sires Graustark and His Majesty. Grade 2 1980-'81. Flower Bowl H. 1978-'93. Dirt 1987. Dead heat for first 1986.

Forego Handicap

Grade 1 in 2005. Saratoga Race Course, three-year-olds and up, 7 furlongs, dirt. Held September 4, 2004, with a gross value of $250,000. First held in 1980. First graded in 1983. Stakes record 1:21 (1988 Quick Call).

Year	Winner	Jockey	Second	Third	Strs	Time	1st Purse
2004	**Midas Eyes**, 4, 117	E. S. Prado	Clock Stopper, 4, 114	Gygistar, 5, 114	9	1:22.22	$150,000
2003	**Aldebaran**, 5, 123	J. D. Bailey	Najran, 4, 114	Gygistar, 4, 119	7	1:21.26	150,000
2002	**Orientate**, 4, 122	J. D. Bailey	Aldebaran, 4, 115	Multiple Choice, 4, 114	8	1:15.68	150,000
2001	**Delaware Township**, 5, 116	J. D. Bailey	Left Bank, 4, 115	Alannan, 5, 117	9	1:15.53	150,000
2000	**Shadow Caster**, 4, 113	J. F. Chavez	Intidab, 7, 118	Successful Appeal, 4, 119	10	1:15.00	150,000
1999	**Crafty Friend**, 6, 119	G. L. Stevens	Affirmed Success, 5, 119	Sir Bear, 6, 119	9	1:21.32	150,000
1998	**Affirmed Success**, 4, 115	J. F. Chavez	Receiver, 5, 114	Purple Passion, 4, 114	4	1:21.98	120,000
1997	**Score a Birdie**, 6, 113	W. H. McCauley	Victor Cooley, 4, 120	Royal Haven, 5, 120	8	1:22.47	120,000
1996	**Langfuhr**, 4, 110	J. F. Chavez	Top Account, 4, 115	Lite the Fuse, 5, 121	7	1:21.90	90,000
1995	**Not Surprising**, 5, 121	R. G. Davis	Our Emblem, 4, 113	Lite the Fuse, 4, 123	4	1:21.91	64,200
1994	**American Chance**, 5, 113	P. Day	Evil Bear, 4, 114	Go for Gin, 3, 117	7	1:22.74	66,000
1993	**Birdonthewire**, 4, 117	M. E. Smith	Harlan, 4, 110	Senor Speedy, 6, 117	9	1:21.88	73,080
1992	**Rubiano**, 5, 124	J. A. Krone	Drummond Lane, 5, 115	Diablo, 5, 114	8	1:22.54	70,080
1991	**Housebuster**, 4, 126	C. Perret	Senor Speedy, 4, 112	Clever Trevor, 5, 120	6	1:21.08	69,480
1990	**Lay Down**, 6, 113	C. W. Antley	Quick Call, 6, 120	Traskwood, 4, 112	6	1:21.80	51,840
1989	**Quick Call**, 5, 116	P. Day	Dancing Spree, 4, 117	Sewickley, 4, 119	6	1:21.80	67,920
1988	**Quick Call**, 4, 110	P. Day	Mawsuff (GB), 5, 110	High Brite, 4, 122	6	**1:21.00**	68,520
1987	**Groovy**, 4, 132	A. T. Cordero Jr.	Purple Mountain, 5, 113	Sun Master, 6, 118	6	1:21.80	81,060
1986	**Groovy**, 3, 118	J. A. Santos	Turkoman, 4, 124	Innamorato, 5, 110	8	1:21.20	83,820
1985	**Ziggy's Boy**, 3, 115	A. T. Cordero Jr.	Taylor's Special, 4, 124	Knight of Armor, 5, 112	5	1:21.20	66,510
1984	**Mugatea**, 4, 111	R. G. Davis	Eskimo, 4, 108	I Enclose, 4, 111	6	1:22.40	53,370
1983	**Maudlin**, 5, 119	A. T. Cordero Jr.	Danebo, 4, 115	Singh Tu, 4, 113	6	1:21.60	32,580
1982	**Engine One**, 4, 112	R. Hernandez	Rise Jim, 6, 121	Pass the Tab, 4, 120	5	1:21.20	33,360
1981	**Fappiano**, 4, 119	A. T. Cordero Jr.	Herb Water, 4, 108	Guilty Conscience, 5, 112	5	1:33.80	50,220
1980	**Tanthem**, 5, 114	J. Velasquez	Dr. Patches, 6, 114	Hold Your Tricks, 4, 116	7	1:35.00	51,030

Named for Mrs. Martha Gerry's 1974, '75, '76 Horse of the Year and '74, '75, '76, '77 Woodward H. (G1) winner Forego (1970 g. by *Forli). Grade 3 1983. Grade 2 1984-2000. Held at Belmont Park 1980-'81. 1 mile 1980-'81. 6 furlongs 2000-'02.

Fort Marcy Handicap

Grade 3 in 2005. Aqueduct, three-year-olds and up, 1 1/16 miles, turf. Held April 23, 2005, with a gross value of $107,400. First held in 1975. First graded in 1980. Stakes record 1:40.88 (2000 Spindrift [Ire]).

Year	Winner	Jockey	Second	Third	Strs	Time	1st Purse
2005	**Better Talk Now**, 6, 123	R. A. Dominguez	Remind, 5, 117	Ecclesiastic, 4, 115	5	1:42.74	$65,640
2004	**Chilly Rooster**, 4, 113	S. Uske	Union Place, 5, 113	Slew Valley, 7, 119	8	1:42.47	66,840
2003	**Saint Verre**, 5, 117	J. L. Espinoza	Windsor Castle, 5, 119	Judge's Case, 6, 115	8	1:33.77	70,500
2002	**Pyrus**, 4, 113	E. S. Prado	Proud Man, 4, 116	Capsized, 6, 113	8	1:44.53	67,260
2001	**Strategic Mission**, 6, 118	R. Migliore	Pine Dance, 4, 116	Legal Jousting (Ire), 4, 114	9	1:41.62	67,740
2000	**Spindrift (Ire)**, 5, 115	J. Samyn	Middlesex Drive, 5, 118	Wised Up, 5, 114	9	**1:40.88**	67,680
1999	**Wised Up**, 4, 112	M. J. Luzzi	N B Forrest, 7, 116	La-Faah (Ire), 4, 114	11	1:45.03	69,660
1998	**Subordination**, 4, 118	J. F. Chavez	Fortitude, 5, 116	Crimson Guard, 6, 110	6	1:35.24	67,620
1997	**Influent**, 6, 117	J. Samyn	Slicious (GB), 5, 115	Montjoy, 5, 117	8	1:47.59	67,140
1996	**Warning Glance**, 5, 119	M. E. Smith	Shahid (GB), 4, 115	Grand Continental, 5, 113	10	1:42.48	51,450
1995	**Fourstars Allstar**, 7, 118	J. A. Santos	Chief Master, 5, 112	A in Sociology, 5, 118	8	1:41.69	50,250
1994	**Adam Smith (GB)**, 6, 118	M. E. Smith	Halissee, 4, 113	Nijinsky's Gold, 5, 113	7	1:42.49	49,650
1993	**Adam Smith (GB)**, 5, 112	J. Samyn	Kiri's Clown, 4, 114	Casino Magistrate, 4, 113	11	1:42.30	55,260
1992	**Maxigroom**, 4, 111	J. A. Krone	Colchis Island (Ire), 7, 111	Buchman, 5, 111	6	1:42.66	53,460
1991	**Stage Colony**, 4, 115	C. Perret	Chenin Blanc, 5, 114	Scottish Monk, 8, 116	9	1:42.38	54,630
1990	**Crystal Moment**, 5, 113	S. N. Chavez	Impersonator, 5, 112	Wanderkin, 7, 117	7	1:43.40	53,010
1989	**Arlene's Valentine**, 4, 112	J. A. Krone	Fourstardave, 4, 113	Sunshine Forever, 4, 126	5	1:50.20	52,920
1988	**Equalize**, 6, 115	J. A. Santos	All Hands On Deck, 6, 109	Glaros (Fr), 6, 111	12	1:42.60	89,340
1987	**Dance of Life**, 4, 120	R. P. Romero	Regal Flier, 6, 113	Iroko (GB), 5, 113	7	1:45.00	84,240
	Glaros (Fr), 5, 112	E. Maple	Onyxly, 6, 113	Explosive Dancer, 5, 111	8	1:45.00	85,200
1986	**Onyxly**, 5, 117	J. A. Santos	Equalize, 4, 114	Lieutenant's Lark, 4, 117	9	1:42.20	55,890
1985	**Forzando (GB)**, 4, 120	J. Velasquez	Native Raid, 5, 115	Solidified, 4, 113	7	1:46.00	54,180
1984	**Hero's Honor**, 4, 115	J. D. Bailey	Super Sunrise (GB), 5, 126	Reinvested, 5, 113	9	1:43.60	54,270
1983	**John's Gold**, 4, 108	A. Graell	Acaroid, 5, 115	Beagle (Arg), 5, 105	8	1:47.40	36,600

				Strs	Time	1st Purse
1982 Folge, 4, 110	J. Velasquez	Johnny Dance, 4, 114	St. Brendan, 4, 116	12	1:42.80	$36,060
1981 Masked Marvel (Ire), 5, 112	R. I. Encinas	Blue Ensign, 4, 116	Freeo, 4, 113	8	1:44.80	33,300
Key to Content, 4, 117	J. Fell	Ghazwan (Ire), 4, 114	Contare, 5, 107	7	1:46.00	33,060
1980 Sten, 5, 115	C. B. Asmussen	Native Courier, 5, 126	Told, 4, 113	10	1:44.00	35,460
1979 Uncle Pokey (GB), 5, 113	J. Cruguet	Alias Smith, 6, 114	Proud Arion, 5, 111	7	1:45.60	32,550
1978 True Colors, 4, 114	E. Maple	Proud Arion, 4, 112	Cinteelo, 5, 119	5	1:42.80	25,410
Tiller, 4, 112	J. Fell	Noble Dancer (GB), 6, 127	Arachnoid, 5, 111	5	1:41.80	25,410
1976 Bold Sunrise, 3, 109	R. W. Cox	Lean To, 3, 113	Scrutiny, 3, 112	10	1:37.60	19,500
1975 *Apollo Nine, 8, 110	M. Venezia	Silver Badge, 4, 112	Bold Play, 5, 112	11	1:23.00	24,630
Beau Bugle, 5, 113	J. Cruguet	Ribot Grande, 5, 112	New Alibhai, 7, 112	10	1:22.40	24,510

Named for Rokeby Stable's 1970 Horse of the Year and '70 Man o' War S. winner Fort Marcy (1964 g. by *Amerigo). Held at Belmont Park 1975, 1981, 1987-'88. Not held 1977. 7 furlongs 1975. 1 mile 1998, 2003. Dirt 1998. Originally scheduled on turf 2003. Two divisions 1975, 1978, 1987. Nonwinners of a stakes 1975.

Fountain of Youth Stakes

Grade 2 in 2005. Gulfstream Park, three-year-olds, 1 1/16 miles, dirt. Held March 5, 2005, with a gross value of $300,000. First held in 1945. First graded in 1973. Stakes record 1:49.70 (2005 High Fly).

Year	Winner	Jockey	Second	Third	Strs	Time	1st Purse
2005	High Fly, 3, 120	J. D. Bailey	Bandini, 3, 116	B. B. Best, 3, 120	9	**1:49.70**	$180,000
2004	Read the Footnotes, 3, 122	J. D. Bailey	Second of June, 3, 120	Silver Wagon, 3, 120	8	1:42.71	150,000
2003	Trust N Luck, 3, 122	C. H. Velasquez	Supah Blitz, 3, 120	Midway Cat, 3, 116	8	1:43.33	120,000
2002	Booklet, 3, 122	J. F. Chavez	Harlan's Holiday, 3, 122	Blue Burner, 3, 116	8	1:44.49	120,000
2001	Songandaprayer, 3, 117	E. S. Prado	Outofthebox, 3, 114	City Zip, 3, 117	11	1:43.48	120,000
2000	High Yield, 3, 117	P. Day	Hal's Hope, 3, 117	Elite Mercedes, 3, 117	11	1:42.56	120,000
1999	Vicar, 3, 114	S. J. Sellers	Cat Thief, 3, 119	Certain, 3, 117	10	1:45.64	120,000
1998	Lil's Lad, 3, 112	J. D. Bailey	Coronado's Quest, 3, 119	Halory Hunter, 3, 112	4	1:42.63	120,000
1997	Pulpit, 3, 112	S. J. Sellers	Blazing Sword, 3, 117	Captain Bodgit, 3, 117	9	1:41.86	120,000
1996	Built for Pleasure, 3, 112	G. Boulanger	Unbridled's Song, 3, 119	Victory Speech, 3, 114	9	1:43.64	120,000
1995	Thunder Gulch, 3, 119	M. E. Smith	Suave Prospect, 3, 117	Jambalaya Jazz, 3, 119	12	1:43.21	120,000
1994	Dehere, 3, 119	C. Perret	Go for Gin, 3, 119	Ride the Rails, 3, 117	6	1:44.70	120,000
1993	Duc d'Sligovil, 3, 112	J. A. Krone	Bull Inthe Heather, 3, 113	Silver of Silver, 3, 122	9	1:45.16	113,094
	Storm Tower, 3, 113	R. Wilson	Great Navigator, 3, 117	Kissin Kris, 3, 117	9	1:44.98	113,094
1992	Dance Floor, 3, 122	C. W. Antley	‡Pistols and Roses, 3, 119	Tiger Tiger, 3, 112	11	1:45.32	150,258
1991	Fly So Free, 3, 122	J. A. Santos	Moment of True, 3, 117	Subordinated Debt, 3, 113	10	1:44.30	73,737
1990	Shot Gun Scott, 3, 122	D. Penna	Smelly, 3, 119	Unbridled, 3, 117	13	1:44.60	77,427
1989	Dixieland Brass, 3, 122	R. P. Romero	Mercedes Won, 3, 122	Triple Buck, 3, 112	13	1:44.60	78,000
1988	Forty Niner, 3, 122	E. Maple	Notebook, 3, 122	Buoy, 3, 119	9	1:43.20	98,991
1987	Bet Twice, 3, 122	C. Perret	No More Flowers, 3, 112	Gone West, 3, 114	9	1:43.40	100,482
1986	Ensign Rhythm, 3, 112	J. M. Pezua	Jig's Haven, 3, 113	Regal Dreamer, 3, 117	10	1:45.60	57,210
	My Prince Charming, 3, 112	J. A. Santos	Mykawa, 3, 117	Papal Power, 3, 122	10	1:45.00	78,060
1985	Proud Truth, 3, 112	J. Velasquez	Stephan's Odyssey, 3, 122	Do It Again Dan, 3, 112	14	1:43.60	106,860
1984	Darn That Alarm, 3, 112	M. Venezia	Counterfeit Money, 3, 112	Swale, 3, 122	8	1:43.00	73,200
1983	Highland Park, 3, 122	D. Brumfield	Thalassocrat, 3, 117	Chumming, 3, 114	9	1:44.60	45,338
	Copelan, 3, 122	L. A. Pincay Jr.	Current Hope, 3, 117	Blink, 3, 112	8	1:43.60	44,888
1982	Star Gallant, 3, 117	S. Hawley	Distinctive Pro, 3, 117	Cut Away, 3, 113	9	1:43.20	54,630
1981	Akureyri, 3, 119	E. Maple	Pleasant Colony, 3, 122	Lord Avie, 3, 122	9	1:44.40	47,697
1980	Naked Sky, 3, 112	J. D. Bailey	Joanie's Chief, 3, 122	Gold Stage, 3, 122	8	1:43.80	29,820
1979	Spectacular Bid, 3, 122	R. J. Franklin	Lot o' Gold, 3, 117	Bishop's Choice, 3, 122	6	1:41.20	35,820
1978	Sensitive Prince, 3, 114	M. Solomone	Believe It, 3, 122	Kissing U., 3, 113	11	1:41.00	22,170
1977	Ruthie's Native, 3, 122	C. Perret	‡Steve's Friend, 3, 112	Fort Prevel, 3, 117	15	1:42.00	26,010
1976	Sonkisser, 3, 117	B. Baeza	Proud Birdie, 3, 122	Archie Beamish, 3, 113	7	1:43.80	22,770
1975	Greek Answer, 3, 122	M. Solomone	Decipher, 3, 117	Gatch, 3, 116	8	1:42.80	22,650
1974	Green Gambados, 3, 112	C. Baltazar	Judger, 3, 115	Eric's Champ, 3, 112	15	1:42.40	46,440
1973	Shecky Greene, 3, 122	B. Baeza	Twice a Prince, 3, 117	My Gallant, 3, 112	6	1:43.80	22,590

Named for the legendary spring sought by Spanish explorer Ponce de Leon in Florida. Grade 3 1973-'81. Grade 1 1999-2003. Fountain of Youth 1947-'56, 1958. Not held 1946, 1948, 1952. 1 mile 70 yards 1945, 1947. 6 furlongs 1947. 1 1/16 miles 1949-'51, 1953-2004. Two-year-olds 1945-'47. Two divisions 1983, 1986, 1993. Held in March and December 1947. ‡Fort Prevel finished second, DQ to third, 1977. ‡Careful Gesture finished second, DQ to fifth, 1992.

Fourstardave Handicap

Grade 2 in 2005. Saratoga Race Course, three-year-olds and up, 1 1/16 miles, turf. Held August 28, 2004, with a gross value of $200,000. First held in 1985. First graded in 1988. Stakes record 1:38.91 (1991 Fourstardave).

Year	Winner	Jockey	Second	Third	Strs	Time	1st Purse
2004	Nothing to Lose, 4, 117	J. R. Velazquez	Silver Tree, 4, 117	Royal Regalia, 6, 114	10	1:39.50	$120,000
2003	Trademark (SAf), 7, 118	R. Migliore	Quest Star, 4, 116	Tap the Admiral, 5, 115	11	1:39.29	120,000
2002	Capsized, 6, 115	J. A. Santos	Pure Prize, 4, 119	Pyrus, 4, 113	5	1:50.90	120,000
2001	Dr. Kashnikow, 4, 113	J. R. Velazquez	Tubrok, 4, 113	Aly's Alley, 5, 117	12	1:39.30	120,000
2000	Hap, 4, 118	J. D. Bailey	Altibr, 5, 115	Weatherbird, 5, 112	11	1:40.24	120,000

Year	Winner	Jockey	Second	Third	Strs	Time	1st Purse
1999	Comic Strip, 4, 115	P. Day	Divide and Conquer, 5, 114	Bomfim, 6, 113	11	1:41.76	$90,000
1998	Wild Event, 5, 116	M. Guidry	Bomfim, 5, 114	Rob 'n Gin, 4, 119	11	1:39.25	68,940
1997	Soviet Line (Ire), 7, 118	P. Day	Val's Prince, 5, 114	Outta My Way Man, 5, 114	7	1:39.99	67,500
1996	Da Hoss, 4, 113	J. R. Velazquez	Green Means Go, 4, 113	Rare Reason, 5, 118	13	1:40.54	71,100
1995	Pride of Summer, 7, 115	E. Maple	Fourstars Allstar, 7, 120	Jaggery John, 4, 120	8	1:40.85	69,240
1994	A in Sociology, 4, 115	J. Samyn	Namaqualand, 4, 113	Fourstars Allstar, 6, 120	9	1:41.23	68,340
1993	Lure, 4, 122	M. E. Smith	Fourstardave, 8, 122	Scott the Great, 7, 115	6	1:40.84	72,120
1992	Now Listen, 5, 119	J. R. Velazquez	Crackedbell, 7, 119	Cold Hoist, 4, 115	5	1:36.64	71,640
1991	Fourstardave, 6, 115	M. E. Smith	Who's to Pay, 5, 122	Kate's Valentine, 6, 117	7	1:38.91	71,640
1990	Fourstardave, 5, 115	M. E. Smith	Foreign Survivor, 5, 119	Wanderkin, 7, 119	8	1:41.20	57,150
1989	Steinlen (GB), 6, 122	A. T. Cordero Jr.	Expensive Decision, 3, 117	Sparkling Wit, 3, 110	8	1:41.00	53,955
	Highland Springs, 5, 122	E. S. Prado	Fourstardave, 4, 122	Soviet Lad, 4, 115	7	1:41.60	53,955
1988	San's the Shadow, 4, 115	A. T. Cordero Jr.	My Big Boy, 5, 117	Real Courage, 5, 115	10	1:40.00	56,340
1987	Persian Mews (Ire), 4, 115	J. A. Santos	Island Sun, 5, 115	Explosive Dancer, 5, 115	8	1:42.00	51,120
	Duluth, 5, 117	J. Cruguet	Mourjane (Ire), 7, 115	I'm a Banker, 5, 115	8	1:41.20	51,120
1986	Mourjane (Ire), 6, 119	J. A. Santos	Island Sun, 4, 117	Little Look, 5, 115	6	1:42.80	33,960
1985	Roving Minstrel, 4, 119	A. T. Cordero Jr.	Four Bases, 6, 115	Alev (GB), 6, 117	8	1:45.40	33,540

Named for Richard M. Bomze's local favorite and 1990, '91 Daryl's Joy S. (G3) winner Fourstardave (1985 g. by Compliance); Fourstardave won a race at Saratoga for eight consecutive years and is one of four horses buried on the Saratoga grounds. Formerly named for R. K. C. Goh's multiple SW *Daryl's Joy (1966 c. by Stunning). Grade 3 1988-'99. Downgraded to Grade 3 when taken off turf 2002. Daryl's Joy S. 1985-'93, 1995. Daryl's Joy H. 1994. Fourstardave S. 1996-'97. 1 1/16 miles 1985-'91, 1993-2001. 1 mile 1992. Dirt 1992, 2002. Two divisions 1987, 1989.

Frances A. Genter Stakes

Grade 3 in 2005. Calder Race Course, three-year-olds, fillies, 7 1/2 furlongs, turf. Held November 27, 2004, with a gross value of $100,000. First held in 1993. First graded in 2005. Stakes record 1:27.67 (2003 Changing World).

Year	Winner	Jockey	Second	Third	Strs	Time	1st Purse
2004	R Obsession, 3, 121	M. R. Cruz	Our Exploit, 3, 116	Marina de Chavon, 3, 118	12	1:28.05	$60,000
2003	Changing World, 3, 118	J. Bravo	Campsie Fells (UAE), 3, 121	Formal Miss, 3, 121	12	1:27.67	60,000
2002	Cellars Shiraz, 3, 121	E. Coa	Madeira Mist (Ire), 3, 118	May Gator, 3, 116	12	1:29.45	60,000
2001	Amelia, 3, 118	J. Castellano	Sara's Success, 3, 121	Ing Ing (Fr), 3, 118	12	1:28.56	60,000
2000	Zeiting (Ire), 3, 114	R. R. Douglas	Jemima (GB), 3, 113	Golden Saint, 3, 114	11	1:30.08	45,000
1999	Seducer, 3, 114	J. A. Santos	Crystal Symphony, 3, 119	Talamanca, 3, 113	11	1:28.67	60,000
1998	Justenuffheart, 3, 119	E. Coa	Terreavigne, 3, 114	Robyns Tune, 3, 114	12	1:28.68	60,000
1997	Oh My Butterfly, 3, 114	A. R. Toribio	More Silver, 3, 114	Basse Besogne (Ire), 3, 115	12	1:28.40	60,000
1996	Voy Si No, 3, 113	E. O. Nunez	Courtlin, 3, 113	Victoria Regia (Ire), 3, 114	11	1:28.19	30,000
1995	Majestic Dy, 3, 114	A. Toribio	With a Princess, 3, 114	Reign Dance, 3, 113	10	1:27.90	32,550
1994	Clean Wager, 3, 113	A. Toribio	Sunset Gal, 3, 112	Notable Sword, 3, 114	6	1:39.92	19,710
1993	Putthepowdertoit, 3, 116	R. R. Douglas	Liberada, 3, 116	Tenacious Tiffany, 3, 114	12	1:28.64	20,970

Named for Frances A. Genter (1898-1992), Eclipse Award-winning Florida breeder.

Frank E. Kilroe Mile Handicap

Grade 1 in 2005. Santa Anita Park, four-year-olds and up, 1 mile, turf. Held March 5, 2005, with a gross value of $300,000. First held in 1955. First graded in 1973. Stakes record 1:31.89 (1997 Atticus [course and world record]).

Year	Winner	Jockey	Second	Third	Strs	Time	1st Purse
2005	Leroidesanimaux (Brz), 5, 119	J. K. Court	Buckland Manor, 5, 116	Sweet Return (GB), 5, 117	9	1:33.89	$180,000
2004	Sweet Return (GB), 4, 119	G. L. Stevens	Singletary, 4, 117	Inesperado (Fr), 5, 116	14	1:33.87	210,000
2003	Redattore (Brz), 8, 120	A. O. Solis	Good Journey, 7, 124	Decarchy, 6, 118	11	1:34.94	240,000
2002	Decarchy, 5, 119	K. J. Desormeaux	Sarafan, 5, 116	Designed for Luck, 5, 117	11	1:34.04	180,000
2001	Road to Slew, 6, 117	L. A. Pincay Jr.	Val Royal (Fr), 5, 117	dh- Exchange Rate, 4, 115 dh- Hawksley Hill (Ire), 8, 118	10	1:35.96	240,000
2000	Commitisize, 5, 112	V. Espinoza	Chullo (Arg), 6, 117	Sultry Substitute, 5, 114	6	1:36.61	120,000
1999	Lord Smith (GB), 4, 116	G. K. Gomez	Hawksley Hill (Ire), 6, 122	Ladies Din, 4, 120	6	1:34.53	90,000
1998	Hawksley Hill (Ire), 5, 115	P. Day	Via Lombardia (Ire), 6, 117	A Magician (Fr), 6, 120	10	1:34.84	101,190
1997	Atticus, 5, 117	C. S. Nakatani	Pinfloron (Fr), 5, 115	Rainbow Blues (Ire), 4, 121	6	1:31.89	97,400
1996	Tychonic (GB), 6, 116	G. L. Stevens	Debutant Trick, 6, 117	Silver Wizard, 6, 117	8	1:35.52	99,400
1995	College Town, 4, 117	L. A. Pincay Jr.	Romarin (Brz), 5, 120	Finder's Fortune, 6, 113	5	1:40.62	63,800
1994	Megan's Interco, 5, 118	C. A. Black	Tinners Way, 4, 115	Ibero (Arg), 7, 118	7	1:33.86	64,400
1993	Leger Cat (Arg), 7, 114	C. S. Nakatani	Luthier Enchanteur, 6, 116	The Name's Jimmy, 4, 115	12	1:34.19	70,800
1992	Fly Till Dawn, 6, 120	L. A. Pincay Jr.	Itsallgreektome, 5, 123	Qathif, 6, 115	11	1:34.69	100,200
1991	Madjaristan, 5, 115	E. J. Delahoussaye	Trebizond, 5, 116	Major Moment, 5, 114	13	1:33.30	105,040
1990	Prized, 4, 124	E. J. Delahoussaye	Happy Toss (Arg), 5, 115	On the Menu, 4, 112	9	1:34.40	67,000
1989	Bello Horizonte (Ire), 6, 116	E. J. Delahoussaye	Sarhoob, 4, 120	Patchy Groundfog, 6, 117	7	1:36.20	64,700
1988	Mohamed Abdu (Ire), 4, 118	E. J. Delahoussaye	The Medic, 4, 118	The Scout, 4, 118	10	1:37.00	95,300
1987	Thrill Show, 4, 121	W. Shoemaker	Skywalker, 5, 123	Aventino (Ire), 4, 115	9	1:36.00	92,150
1986	Strawberry Road (Aus), 7, 125	G. L. Stevens	Hail Bold King, 5, 116	Schiller, 4, 115	7	2:03.40	76,800
1985	Fatih, 5, 116	W. Shoemaker	Tsunami Slew, 4, 119	Swoon, 7, 113	8	1:59.60	64,300
1984	Sir Pele, 5, 114	R. Q. Meza	Lucence, 5, 117	Ginger Brink (Fr), 4, 117	6	2:01.20	49,850
1983	Manantial (Chi), 5, 115	K. D. Black	Bohemian Grove, 7, 115	Western, 5, 120	5	2:03.40	46,500
1982	Perrault (GB), 5, 124	L. A. Pincay Jr.	Silveyville, 4, 117	Le Duc de Bar, 5, 111	7	2:04.60	47,700

Year	Winner	Jockey	Second	Third	Strs	Time	1st Purse
1981	Premier Ministre, 5, 117	L. A. Pincay Jr.	Galaxy Libra (Ire), 5, 119	Bold Tropic (SAf), 6, 126	7	2:02.60	$38,350
1980	Henschel, 6, 114	W. Shoemaker	Silver Eagle (Ire), 6, 120	Balzac, 5, 112	11	1:58.80	40,900
1979	Fluorescent Light, 5, 121	L. A. Pincay Jr.	†Waya (Fr), 5, 123	As de Copas (Arg), 6, 118	9	2:03.60	39,650
1978	Exceller, 5, 126	W. Shoemaker	Soldier's Lark, 4, 113	Tacitus, 4, 115	6	2:01.20	31,750
1977	Caucasus, 5, 124	F. Toro	dh-Exact Duplicate, 5, 115		9	2:00.00	33,900
			dh-Victorian Prince, 7, 116				
1976	Ga Hai, 5, 115	F. Olivares	Riot in Paris, 5, 120	Copper Mel, 4, 117	10	2:00.40	34,050
1975	Ga Hai, 4, 114	J. Vasquez	Indefatigable, 5, 115	Gold Standard, 4, 111	8	2:07.00	32,800
1974	Court Ruling, 4, 114	B. Baeza	Scantling, 4, 116	Barrydown, 4, 116	8	2:01.40	32,800
1973	River Buoy, 8, 117	D. Pierce	Wing Out, 5, 116	*Mazus, 5, 121	9	2:02.80	20,875
	Kobuk King, 7, 116	J. Lambert	Triggairo, 4, 114	Presidial, 4, 116	8	2:02.80	20,475

Named in honor of Frank E. "Jimmy" Kilroe (1912-'96), longtime racing secretary and handicapper at Santa Anita Park. Formerly named for Arcadia, California, city in which Santa Anita Park is located. Formerly named for the El Camino Real, "the Royal Road" through the California frontier. Grade 3 1973-'83, 1990-'94, 2000. Camino Real H. 1955-'59. Arcadia H. 1960-2000. 1¼ miles 1955-'71, 1973-'86. About 1¼ miles 1972. Dirt 1975-'76, 1978, 1983, 1995, 2000. Three-year-olds and up 1955-'61. Two divisions 1973. Dead heat for second 1977. Dead heat for third 2001. World record 1997. Course record 1997. †Denotes female.

Frank J. De Francis Memorial Dash Stakes

Grade 1 in 2005. Pimlico, three-year-olds and up, 6 furlongs, dirt. Held November 20, 2004, with a gross value of $300,000. First held in 1990. First graded in 1992. Stakes record 1:07.95 (2000 Richter Scale).

Year	Winner	Jockey	Second	Third	Strs	Time	1st Purse
2004	Wildcat Heir, 4, 119	S. Elliott	Midas Eyes, 4, 123	Clock Stopper, 4, 119	10	1:09.45	$180,000
2003	A Huevo, 7, 119	R. A. Dominguez	Shake You Down, 5, 123	Gators N Bears, 3, 115	10	1:08.90	180,000
2002	D'wildcat, 4, 122	J. F. Chavez	Deer Run, 5, 118	Sassy Hound, 5, 118	8	1:10.81	180,000
2001	Delaware Township, 5, 125	J. D. Bailey	Early Flyer, 3, 115	†Xtra Heat, 3, 117	7	1:09.00	180,000
2000	Richter Scale, 6, 123	R. Migliore	Just Call Me Carl, 5, 119	Falkenburg, 5, 114	4	1:07.95	180,000
1999	Yes It's True, 3, 114	J. D. Bailey	Good and Tough, 4, 123	Storm Punch, 4, 114	6	1:08.67	180,000
1998	Kelly Kip, 4, 121	J. Samyn	Affirmed Success, 4, 114	Partner's Hero, 4, 114	6	1:08.50	180,000
1997	Smoke Glacken, 3, 113	C. Perret	Wise Dusty, 6, 112	†Capote Belle, 4, 110	7	1:09.40	180,000
1996	Lite the Fuse, 5, 117	J. A. Krone	Meadow Monster, 5, 119	Prospect Bay, 4, 114	7	1:08.81	180,000
1995	Lite the Fuse, 4, 119	J. A. Krone	Crafty Dude, 6, 117	Hot Jaws, 5, 119	7	1:08.89	180,000
1994	Cherokee Run, 4, 114	C. Perret	Boom Towner, 6, 119	Fu Man Slew, 3, 107	11	1:08.92	180,000
1993	Montbrook, 3, 112	C. J. Ladner III	Lion Cavern, 4, 117	Flaming Emperor, 7, 114	9	1:08.71	180,000
1992	Superstrike (GB), 3, 112	D. Sorenson	†Parisian Flight, 4, 114	King Corrie, 4, 117	12	1:09.90	180,000
1991	Housebuster, 4, 126	C. Perret	Clever Trevor, 5, 123	†Safely Kept, 5, 121	6	1:08.76	180,000
1990	Northern Wolf, 4, 120	M. J. Luzzi	Glitterman, 5, 124	Sewickley, 5, 126	7	1:09.00	210,000

Named in honor of Frank J. De Francis (1927-'89), president and chairman of Laurel Park and Pimlico Race Course. Grade 3 1992-'93. Grade 2 1994-'98. Held at Laurel Park 1991-2003. Track record 2000. †Denotes female.

Fred W. Hooper Handicap

Grade 3 in 2005. Calder Race Course, three-year-olds and up, 1⅛ miles, dirt. Held December 18, 2004, with a gross value of $100,000. First held in 1938. First graded in 1992. Stakes record 1:46.60 (1960 On-and-On).

Year	Winner	Jockey	Second	Third	Strs	Time	1st Purse
2004	Pies Prospect, 3, 114	E. S. Prado	Twilight Road, 7, 115	Hear No Evil, 4, 112	11	1:50.74	$60,000
2003	Predawn Raid, 4, 112	J. F. Chavez	Best of the Rest, 8, 122	Deeliteful Guy, 4, 112	9	1:52.47	60,000
2002	The Judge Sez Who, 3, 116	C. H. Velasquez	Best of the Rest, 7, 121	Dancing Guy, 7, 112	9	1:50.53	60,000
2001	Kiss a Native, 4, 116	C. H. Velasquez	Hal's Hope, 4, 115	Groomstick Stock's, 5, 113	8	1:51.05	60,000
2000	American Halo, 4, 117	C. Hunt	General Grant, 3, 112	Sir Bear, 7, 118	8	1:51.68	60,000
1999	Dancing Guy, 4, 120	J. C. Ferrer	Wicapi, 7, 118	Loon, 4, 112	8	1:50.83	60,000
1998	Wicapi, 6, 113	J. Bravo	Smuggler's Prize, 4, 111	Best of the Rest, 3, 115	5	1:52.15	60,000
1997	Shrike, 4, 113	J. D. Bailey	Wicapi, 5, 112	Sir Bear, 4, 113	11	1:51.50	60,000
1996	Cimarron Secret, 5, 115	J. A. Velez Jr.	Laughing Dan, 3, 114	Wicapi, 4, 116	8	1:52.70	60,000
1995	Bound by Honor, 4, 112	J. A. Krone	Bay Street Star, 4, 113	Halo's Image, 3, 114	10	1:51.81	60,000
1994	Halo's Image, 3, 117	G. Boulanger	Fight for Love, 4, 114	Migrating Moon, 4, 120	7	1:51.44	60,000
	Take Me Out, 6, 115	M. E. Smith	Migrating Moon, 4, 119	Meena, 6, 114	11	1:51.80	60,000
1993	Barkerville, 5, 114	R. P. Romero	Pistols and Roses, 4, 114	Count the Time, 4, 114	7	1:52.47	45,000
1992	Classic Seven, 4, 110	C. E. Lopez Sr.	Honest Ensign, 4, 111	Le Merle Blanc, 4, 114	13	1:53.01	102,960
1990	Public Account, 5, 117	H. Castillo Jr.	Zalipour, 3, 114	Cefis, 4, 114	9	1:52.60	49,860
1989	Primal, 4, 119	J. A. Velez Jr.	Big Stanley, 3, 122	Falerno (Arg), 7, 111	10	1:51.60	66,960
1988	Creme Fraiche, 6, 118	W. A. Guerra	Fast Forward, 4, 114	Primal, 3, 118	7	1:51.80	65,940
	Creme Fraiche, 6, 118	A. T. Cordero Jr.	Cryptoclearance, 4, 122	All Sincerity, 6, 111	8	2:05.80	131,760
	Homebuilder, 4, 118	L. Saumell	All Sincerity, 6, 111	Silver Comet, 5, 116	8	1:53.20	93,000
1987	Arctic Honeymoon, 4, 114	C. Perret	Smile, 5, 122	Darn That Alarm, 6, 120	6	1:59.60	92,460
1986	Racing Star, 4, 115	E. Fires	Lyphard Line, 3, 114	Show Dancer, 4, 121	12	1:45.20	31,370

Named in honor of Fred W. Hooper (1989-2000), longtime Florida breeder. Formerly named for old Tropical Park, a Miami racetrack that closed in January 1972. Tropical H. 1938-'40, 1942-'58. Tropical Park H. 1941, 1959-'96. Held at Tropical Park 1938-'71. Not held 1943, 1945, 1948, 1951, 1972-'85, 1991. 1¹⁄₁₆ miles 1938-'41, 1946-'49, 1987. 1¼ miles 1988. Turf 1986. Three-year-olds 1944. Four-year-olds and up 1949, 1992. Held in January and December 1986. Held in March (twice) and December 1988. Held in January and December 1994. Track record 1960.

Frizette Stakes

Grade 1 in 2005. Belmont Park, two-year-olds, fillies, 1¹/₁₆ miles, dirt. Held October 9, 2004, with a gross value of $500,000. First held in 1945. First graded in 1973. Stakes record 1:42.47 (1996 Storm Song).

Year	Winner	Jockey	Second	Third	Strs	Time	1st Purse
2004	Balletto (UAE), 2, 120	C. S. Nakatani	Ready's Gal, 2, 120	Sis City, 2, 120	8	1:43.52	$300,000
2003	Society Selection, 2, 120	R. Ganpath	Victory U. S. A., 2, 120	Ashado, 2, 120	8	1:43.95	300,000
2002	Storm Flag Flying, 2, 120	J. R. Velazquez	Santa Catarina, 2, 120	Appleby Gardens, 2, 120	7	1:44.20	300,000
2001	You, 2, 120	E. S. Prado	Cashier's Dream, 2, 120	Riskaverse, 2, 120	5	1:43.94	300,000
2000	Raging Fever, 2, 120	J. D. Bailey	Out of Sync, 2, 120	Western Justice, 2, 120	10	1:43.57	300,000
1999	Surfside, 2, 119	P. Day	Darling My Darling, 2, 119	March Magic, 2, 119	5	1:43.18	240,000
1998	Confessional, 2, 119	J. D. Bailey	Things Change, 2, 119	Pico Teneriffe, 2, 119	5	1:42.88	240,000
1997	Silver Maiden, 2, 119	J. D. Bailey	Diamond On the Run, 2, 119	Brac Drifter, 2, 119	6	1:42.74	240,000
1996	Storm Song, 2, 119	C. Perret	Sharp Cat, 2, 119	Aldiza, 2, 119	7	**1:42.47**	240,000
1995	Golden Attraction, 2, 119	G. L. Stevens	My Flag, 2, 119	Flat Fleet Feet, 2, 119	5	1:42.95	150,000
1994	Flanders, 2, 119	P. Day	Change Fora Dollar, 2, 119	Pretty Discreet, 2, 119	4	1:43.94	150,000
1993	Heavenly Prize, 2, 119	M. E. Smith	Facts of Love, 2, 119	Footing, 2, 119	7	1:35.46	150,000
1992	Educated Risk, 2, 119	J. D. Bailey	Standard Equipment, 2, 119	Beal Street Blues, 2, 119	8	1:36.62	150,000
1991	Preach, 2, 119	J. A. Krone	Vivano, 2, 119	Anh Duong, 2, 119	12	1:37.20	150,000
1990	Meadow Star, 2, 119	J. A. Santos	Champagne Glow, 2, 119	Flawlessly, 2, 119	5	1:35.40	171,000
1989	Stella Madrid, 2, 119	A. T. Cordero Jr.	Go for Wand, 2, 119	Dance Colony, 2, 119	7	1:36.80	176,700
1988	Some Romance, 2, 119	L. A. Pincay Jr.	Open Mind, 2, 119	Ms. Gold Pole, 2, 119	7	1:36.80	209,520
1987	Classic Crown, 2, 119	A. T. Cordero Jr.	Tap Your Toes, 2, 119	Justsayno, 2, 119	9	1:37.20	215,640
1986	Personal Ensign, 2, 119	R. P. Romero	Collins, 2, 119	Flying Katuna, 2, 119	5	1:36.40	161,400
1985	Family Style, 2, 119	L. A. Pincay Jr.	Funistrada, 2, 119	Guadery, 2, 119	7	1:37.20	133,200
1984	Charleston Rag (Ire), 2, 119	D. MacBeth	Tiltalating, 2, 119	Mom's Command, 2, 119	6	1:39.00	130,860
1983	Miss Oceana, 2, 119	E. Maple	Life's Magic, 2, 119	Lucky Lucky Lucky, 2, 119	10	1:36.60	68,040
1982	Princess Rooney, 2, 119	J. Fell	Winning Tack, 2, 119	Weekend Surprise, 2, 119	13	1:39.00	70,080
1981	Proud Lou, 2, 119	D. Beckon	Mystical Mood, 2, 119	Chilling Thought, 2, 119	12	1:38.80	70,920
1980	Heavenly Cause, 2, 119	L. A. Pincay Jr.	Sweet Revenge, 2, 119	Prayers'n Promises, 2, 119	8	1:38.00	66,000
1979	Smart Angle, 2, 119	S. Maple	Royal Suite, 2, 119	Hardship, 2, 119	11	1:38.20	66,240
1978	Golferette, 2, 119	J. Fell	It's in the Air, 2, 119	Terlingua, 2, 119	7	1:35.40	63,780
1977	Lakeville Miss, 2, 119	R. Hernandez	Misgivings, 2, 119	Itsamaza, 2, 119	5	1:36.20	64,680
1976	Sensational, 2, 119	J. Velasquez	Northern Sea, 2, 119	Mrs. Warren, 2, 119	7	1:36.20	64,740
1975	Optimistic Gal, 2, 121	B. Baeza	Artfully, 2, 121	Picture Tube, 2, 121	12	1:36.80	69,360
1974	Molly Ballantine, 2, 121	L. A. Pincay Jr.	Copernica, 2, 121	Mystery Mood, 2, 121	6	1:37.00	67,140
1973	Bundler, 2, 121	J. Vasquez	Chris Evert, 2, 121	I'm a Pleasure, 2, 121	14	1:36.40	72,660

Named for James R. Keene's stakes winner and foundation mare Frizette (1905 f. by Hamburg). Held at Jamaica 1945-'58. Held at Aqueduct 1959-'61, 1963-'67. Not held 1949-'51. 6 furlongs 1945-'47, 1952-'53. 5 furlongs 1948. 1 mile 1959-'93.

Futurity Stakes

Grade 2 in 2005. Belmont Park, two-year-olds, 1 mile, dirt. Held September 19, 2004, with a gross value of $300,000. First held in 1888. First graded in 1973. Stakes record 1:35.12 (1995 Maria's Mon).

Year	Winner	Jockey	Second	Third	Strs	Time	1st Purse
2004	Park Avenue Ball, 2, 120	J. Castellano	Wallstreet Scandal, 2, 120	Evil Minister, 2, 120	6	1:38.84	$180,000
2003	Cuvee, 2, 120	J. D. Bailey	Value Plus, 2, 120	El Prado Rob, 2, 120	6	1:35.75	120,000
2002	Whywhywhy, 2, 120	E. S. Prado	Pretty Wild, 2, 120	Truckle Feature, 2, 120	7	1:36.33	120,000
2000	‡Burning Roma, 2, 122	R. Wilson	City Zip, 2, 122	Scorpion, 2, 122	9	1:37.90	120,000
1999	Bevo, 2, 122	J. Bravo	Greenwood Lake, 2, 122	More Than Ready, 2, 122	8	1:36.16	90,000
1998	Lemon Drop Kid, 2, 122	J. R. Velazquez	Yes It's True, 2, 122	Medievil Hero, 2, 122	6	1:37.50	90,000
1997	Grand Slam, 2, 122	G. L. Stevens	K. O. Punch, 2, 122	Devil's Pride, 2, 122	10	1:35.69	90,000
1996	Traitor, 2, 122	J. R. Velazquez	Night in Reno, 2, 122	Harley Tune, 2, 122	9	1:35.29	90,000
1995	Maria's Mon, 2, 122	R. G. Davis	Louis Quatorze, 2, 122	Honour and Glory, 2, 122	7	**1:35.12**	90,000
1994	Montreal Red, 2, 122	J. A. Santos	Northern Ensign, 2, 122	Wild Escapade, 2, 122	6	1:36.22	66,180
1993	Holy Bull, 2, 122	M. E. Smith	Dehere, 2, 122	Prenup, 2, 122	6	1:23.31	69,360
1992	Strolling Along, 2, 122	C. W. Antley	Fight for Love, 2, 122	Caponostro, 2, 122	9	1:23.67	72,120
1991	Agincourt, 2, 122	J. F. Chavez	Tri to Watch, 2, 122	Pine Bluff, 2, 122	7	1:23.89	73,140
1990	Eastern Echo, 2, 122	J. D. Bailey	Deposit Ticket, 2, 122	Groom's Reckoning, 2, 122	4	1:22.40	69,360
1989	Senor Pete, 2, 122	J. A. Santos	Adjudicating, 2, 122	Dawn Quixote, 2, 122	5	1:23.20	75,360
1988	Trapp Mountain, 2, 122	A. T. Cordero Jr.	Bio, 2, 122	Fast Play, 2, 122	5	1:23.80	74,280
1987	Forty Niner, 2, 122	E. Maple	Tsarbaby, 2, 122	Crusader Sword, 2, 122	5	1:22.60	80,100
1986	Gulch, 2, 122	A. T. Cordero Jr.	Demons Begone, 2, 122	Captain Valid, 2, 122	7	1:22.20	82,920
1985	Ogygian, 2, 122	W. A. Guerra	Groovy, 2, 122	dh- Mr. Classic, 2, 122 dh- Sovereign Don, 2, 122	6	1:22.40	81,600
1984	Spectacular Love, 2, 122	L. A. Pincay Jr.	Chief's Crown, 2, 122	Mugzy's Rullah, 2, 122	8	1:23.20	105,900
1983	Swale, 2, 122	E. Maple	Shuttle Jet, 2, 122	Hail Bold King, 2, 122	5	1:24.00	72,915
1982	Copelan, 2, 122	J. D. Bailey	Satan's Charger, 2, 122	Pax in Bello, 2, 122	6	1:24.20	97,110
1981	Irish Martini, 2, 122	J. Velasquez	Herschelwalker, 2, 122	Timely Writer, 2, 122	8	1:24.40	103,605
1980	Tap Shoes, 2, 122	R. Hernandez	Dash o' Pleasure, 2, 122	McCracken, 2, 122	6	1:23.80	85,605
1979	Rockhill Native, 2, 122	J. Oldham	Sportful, 2, 122	Gold Stage, 2, 122	8	1:22.00	90,150
1978	‡Crested Wave, 2, 122	J. Cruguet	dh-Picturesque, 2, 122 dh-Strike Your Colors, 2, 122		8	1:24.00	75,660

1977	**Affirmed**, 2, 122	S. Cauthen	Alydar, 2, 122	Nasty and Bold, 2, 122	5	1:21.60	$63,570
1976	**For The Moment**, 2, 122	E. Maple	Banquet Table, 2, 122	Western Wind, 2, 122	10	1:23.20	67,353
1975	**Soy Numero Uno**, 2, 122	J. Vasquez	Jackknife, 2, 122	Beau Talent, 2, 122	7	1:17.80	66,408
1974	**Just the Time**, 2, 122	M. A. Castaneda	High Steel, 2, 122	Valid Appeal, 2, 122	12	1:16.40	66,801
1973	**Wedge Shot**, 2, 122	J. Vasquez	‡Protagonist, 2, 122	Judger, 2, 122	10	1:17.00	82,230

Named for the future nominations, before a foal was born, of early futurity races. Held at Sheepshead Bay 1888-1909. Held at Saratoga Race Course 1910, 1913-'14. Held at Aqueduct 1959-'60, 1963-'67. Not held 1911-'12. Not held due to World Trade Center attack 2001. 6 furlongs 1888-'91, 1902-'09. About 6 furlongs 1892-1901. 6½ furlongs 1910-'24, 1934-'75. About 7 furlongs 1925-'33. 7 furlongs 1976-'93. Colts and fillies 1944. Colts and geldings 1977. Dead heat for second 1978. Dead heat for third 1985. ‡Judger finished second, DQ to third, 1973. ‡Fuzzbuster finished first, DQ to fourth, 1978. ‡City Zip finished first, DQ to second, 2000.

Gallant Bloom Handicap

Grade 2 in 2005. Belmont Park, three-year-olds and up, fillies and mares, 6½ furlongs, dirt. Held October 10, 2004, with a gross value of $150,000. First held in 1992. First graded in 1997. Stakes record 1:15.60 (1998 Catinca).

Year	Winner	Jockey	Second	Third	Strs	Time	1st Purse
2004	**Lady Tak**, 4, 122	J. R. Velazquez	Molto Vita, 4, 115	Zawzooth, 5, 115	7	1:16.04	$90,000
2003	**Harmony Lodge**, 5, 117	R. Migliore	House Party, 3, 116	Slews Final Answer, 4, 112	6	1:16.20	90,000
2002	**Nasty Storm**, 4, 114	J. A. Santos	Raging Fever, 4, 120	Shine Again, 5, 118	6	1:17.89	90,000
2001	**Finder's Fee**, 4, 113	J. R. Velazquez	Cedar Knolls, 4, 114	Gold Mover, 3, 115	4	1:17.60	79,928
2000	**Dream Supreme**, 3, 118	P. Day	Finder's Fee, 3, 116	Tropical Punch, 4, 114	5	1:15.86	64,380
1999	**Positive Gal**, 3, 116	J. D. Bailey	Flamingo Way, 5, 114	Torch, 6, 113	6	1:16.86	65,820
1998	**Catinca**, 3, 114	R. Migliore	Dixie Flag, 4, 117	Crab Grass, 4, 114	9	**1:15.60**	50,595
1997	**Top Secret**, 4, 120	J. R. Velazquez	Aldiza, 3, 116	Dixie Flag, 3, 114	7	1:16.00	49,260
1996	**Miss Golden Circle**, 4, 115	R. Migliore	J J'sdream, 3, 119	Nappelon, 4, 117	9	1:16.26	50,040
1995	**Classy Mirage**, 5, 123	J. D. Bailey	Dust Bucket, 4, 114	Fantastic Women, 3, 110	5	1:17.34	48,375
1994	**Vivano**, 5, 116	W. H. McCauley	Ann Dear, 4, 118	Strategic Reward, 5, 113	5	1:10.93	48,255
1992	**Apelia**, 3, 118	L. Attard	Preach, 3, 116	Fretina, 3, 116	8	1:08.97	32,400

Named for King Ranch's 1968 champion two-year-old filly, '69 champion three-year-old filly, '69 champion handicap mare, and '69 Gazelle H. winner Gallant Bloom (1966 f. by *Gallant Man). Grade 3 1997-2000. Not held 1993. 6 furlongs 1994.

Gallorette Handicap

Grade 3 in 2005. Pimlico, three-year-olds and up, fillies and mares, 1 1/16 miles, turf. Held May 21, 2005, with a gross value of $100,000. First held in 1952. First graded in 1973. Stakes record 1:40.85 (2004 Ocean Drive).

Year	Winner	Jockey	Second	Third	Strs	Time	1st Purse
2005	**Film Maker**, 5, 121	J. D. Bailey	Briviesca (GB), 4, 115	Humoristic, 4, 114	9	1:44.29	$60,000
2004	**Ocean Drive**, 4, 117	J. D. Bailey	Film Maker, 4, 120	With Patience, 5, 112	8	**1:40.85**	60,000
2003	**Carib Lady (Ire)**, 4, 116	P. A. Valenzuela	Affirmed Dancer, 4, 113	Lady of the Future, 5, 114	7	1:50.69	60,000
2002	**Quidnaskra**, 7, 116	C. J. McCarron	De Aar, 5, 111	Step With Style, 5, 115	7	1:46.73	60,000
2001	**License Fee**, 6, 118	P. Day	Starine (Fr), 4, 114	Crystal Sea, 4, 113	8	1:42.81	60,000
2000	**Colstar**, 4, 120	A. Delgado	Melody Queen (GB), 4, 115	Terreavigne, 5, 118	10	1:43.60	60,000
1999	**Winfama**, 6, 114	E. S. Prado	Pleasant Temper, 5, 119	Earth to Jackie, 5, 116	8	1:43.31	60,000
1998	**Tresoriere**, 4, 113	J. A. Santos	Bursting Forth, 4, 114	Starry Dreamer, 4, 114	7	1:45.35	60,000
1997	**Palliser Bay**, 5, 111	C. H. Marquez Jr.	Elusive, 5, 114	Sangria, 4, 117	8	1:43.81	60,000
1996	**Aucilla**, 5, 114	M. E. Smith	Julie's Brilliance, 4, 114	Brushing Gloom, 4, 114	4	1:44.96	60,000
1995	**It's Personal**, 5, 112	J. A. Krone	Churchbell Chimes, 4, 112	Open Toe, 5, 113	6	1:43.72	60,000
1994	**Tribulation**, 4, 117	J. Samyn	McKaymackenna, 5, 118	Fleet Broad, 4, 115	6	1:41.66	60,000
1993	**You'd Be Surprised**, 4, 113	J. D. Bailey	Captive Miss, 4, 117	Dior's Angel, 4, 112	12	1:43.54	60,000
1992	**Brilliant Brass**, 5, 113	E. S. Prado	Spanish Dior, 5, 112	Stem the Tide, 4, 112	8	1:44.81	60,000
1991	**Miss Josh**, 5, 121	E. S. Prado	Splendid Try, 5, 113	Highland Penny, 6, 115	6	1:41.91	60,000
1990	**Highland Penny**, 5, 116	R. I. Rojas	Saphaedra, 6, 112	dh- Channel Three, 4, 112	8	1:42.40	60,000
				dh- Double Bunctious, 6, 113			
1989	**Dance Teacher**, 4, 115	J. Samyn	Arcroyal, 5, 114	Fortunate Facts, 5, 118	9	1:44.00	60,000
1988	**Just Class (Ire)**, 4, 115	C. Perret	Landaura, 4, 115	Hangin On a Star, 4, 119	8	1:42.80	54,145
1987	**Scotch Heather**, 5, 113	M. G. Pino	Catatonic, 5, 117	Foot Stone, 4, 113	6	1:44.40	54,600
1986	**Natania**, 4, 114	J. W. Edwards	Scotch Heather, 4, 115	Valid Doge, 5, 108	12	1:45.60	71,448
1985	**La Reine Elaine**, 4, 113	G. W. Hutton	Stufida (GB), 4, 115	Lady Emerald, 4, 107	12	1:41.60	58,013
1984	**Kattegat's Pride**, 5, 118	D. A. Miller Jr.	Amanti, 5, 114	Bright Choice, 5, 110	7	1:42.60	55,770
1983	**Wedding Party**, 4, 119	C. Perret	Sunny Sparkler, 4, 122	Bemissed, 3, 110	8	1:50.00	56,648
1982	**Island Charm**, 5, 110	N. Santagata	Lovely Lei, 4, 112	Vibro Vibes, 5, 115	10	1:46.40	57,168
1981	**Exactly So (Ire)**, 4, 112	G. McCarron	Crimson April, 4, 110	Ernestine, 4, 111	8	1:47.20	55,998
1980	**Jamila Kadir**, 6, 109	M. G. Pino	The Very One, 5, 122	Wild Bidder, 4, 108	10	1:44.40	57,428
1979	**Calderina (Ity)**, 4, 121	C. Perret	Dottie O., 5, 105	Warfever (Fr), 4, 116	10	1:44.60	56,875
1978	**Huggle Duggle**, 4, 113	B. Gonzalez	Council House, 4, 118	Nanticous (Ire), 4, 112	11	1:44.20	37,765
1977	**Summertime Promise**, 5, 121	L. Moyers	Summer Session, 4, 111	Siz Ziz Zit, 4, 112	9	1:43.60	37,050
1976	***Deesse Du Val**, 5, 119	R. Broussard	Dos a Dos, 4, 113	Margravine, 4, 112	8	1:42.20	29,575
		C. H. Marquez	Summertime Promise, 4, 117	Jabot, 4, 114	9	1:42.20	29,835
1975	**Gulls Cry**, 4, 117	E. Maple	Sarah Percy, 7, 115	Twixt, 6, 127	10	1:46.20	37,960
1974	**Sarre Green**, 6, 113	T. Lee	Unknown Heiress, 3, 103	Out Cold, 4, 112	14	1:44.60	22,295

| 1973 | Deb Marion, 3, 107 | A. Agnello | dh- Aglimmer, 4, 115 | | 11 | 1:44.00 | $22,068 |
| | | | dh- Groton Miss, 4, 115 | | | | |

Named for Mrs. M. A. Moore's 1946 champion handicap mare and '45 Pimlico Oaks winner Gallorette (1942 f. by *Challenger II). Gallorette S. 1952-'66. 1⅛ miles 1952-'66. Dirt 1952-'72, 1979-'80, 1984, 1986-'87, 1995-'96. Two divisions 1976. Dead heat for second 1973. Dead heat for third 1990.

Gamely Breeders' Cup Handicap

Grade 1 in 2005. Hollywood Park, three-year-olds and up, fillies and mares, 1⅛ miles, turf. Held May 30, 2005, with a gross value of $441,500. First held in 1939. First graded in 1973. Stakes record 1:45.07 (1993 Toussaud).

Year	Winner	Jockey	Second	Third	Strs	Time	1st Purse
2005	Mea Domina, 4, 115	T. Baze	Solar Echo, 5, 116	Amorama (Fr), 4, 116	9	1:46.47	$276,900
2004	Noches De Rosa (Chi), 6, 115	M. E. Smith	Megahertz (GB), 5, 122	Quero Quero, 4, 115	4	1:48.34	187,500
2003	Tates Creek, 5, 122	P. A. Valenzuela	Dublino, 4, 122	Megahertz (GB), 4, 118	6	1:46.97	263,400
2002	Astra, 6, 123	K. J. Desormeaux	Starine (Fr), 5, 122	Voodoo Dancer, 4, 119	6	1:46.93	300,000
2001	Happyanunoit (NZ), 6, 121	B. Blanc	Tranquility Lake, 6, 124	Beautiful Noise, 5, 116	7	1:47.34	115,710
2000	Astra, 4, 117	K. J. Desormeaux	Happyanunoit (NZ), 5, 121	Tout Charmant, 4, 119	5	1:45.81	157,170
1999	Tranquility Lake, 4, 119	E. J. Delahoussaye	Midnight Line, 4, 117	Green Jewel (GB), 5, 117	5	1:46.04	157,800
1998	Fiji (GB), 4, 123	K. J. Desormeaux	Kool Kat Katie (Ire), 4, 119	Squeak (GB), 4, 116	6	1:47.40	158,880
1997	Donna Viola (GB), 5, 121	G. L. Stevens	Real Connection, 6, 115	Different (Arg), 5, 121	7	1:47.40	120,000
1996	Auriette (Ire), 4, 118	K. J. Desormeaux	Flagbird, 5, 118	Didina (GB), 4, 116	6	1:46.59	128,760
1995	Possibly Perfect, 5, 123	K. J. Desormeaux	Lady Affirmed, 4, 114	Don't Read My Lips, 4, 114	6	1:46.99	92,900
1994	Hollywood Wildcat, 4, 122	E. J. Delahoussaye	Mz. Zill Bear, 5, 114	Flawlessly, 6, 124	6	1:46.55	92,900
1993	Toussaud, 4, 116	K. J. Desormeaux	Gold Fleece, 5, 114	Bel's Starlet, 6, 116	9	**1:45.07**	97,700
1992	Metamorphose, 4, 114	G. L. Stevens	Guiza, 5, 113	Silvered, 5, 116	6	1:46.56	93,300
1991	Miss Josh, 5, 118	L. A. Pincay Jr.	Island Jamboree, 5, 116	Fire the Groom, 4, 120	11	1:47.50	68,000
1990	Double Wedge, 5, 112	R. G. Davis	Stylish Star, 4, 116	Beautiful Melody, 4, 115	6	1:47.80	62,700
1989	Fitzwilliam Place (Ire), 5, 119	C. A. Black	Claire Marine (Ire), 4, 119	Ravinella, 4, 121	7	1:47.80	63,400
1988	Pen Bal Lady (GB), 4, 120	E. J. Delahoussaye	Chapel of Dreams, 4, 117	Galunpe (Ire), 5, 120	3	1:47.00	72,800
1987	Northern Aspen, 5, 119	G. L. Stevens	Reloy, 4, 121	Frau Altiva (Arg), 5, 115	6	1:47.60	89,800
1986	La Koumia (Fr), 4, 118	R. Sibille	Estrapade, 6, 123	Tax Dodge, 5, 115	8	1:45.80	92,400
1985	Estrapade, 5, 124	C. J. McCarron	Johnica, 4, 115	Possible Mate, 4, 116	6	1:46.60	62,500
1984	Sabin, 4, 125	E. Maple	Triple Tipple, 5, 116	Fenny Rough (Ire), 4, 117	8	1:47.40	65,400
1983	Pride of Rosewood (NZ), 5, 115	E. J. Delahoussaye	Sangue (Ire), 5, 123	Mademoiselle Forli, 4, 119	8	1:48.80	64,800
1982	Ack's Secret, 6, 122	L. A. Pincay Jr.	Miss Huntington, 5, 117	Vocalist (GB), 4, 114	9	1:46.80	66,100
1981	Kilijaro (Ire), 5, 127	M. Castaneda	Princess Karenda, 4, 121	Wishing Well, 6, 122	6	1:48.20	62,400
1980	Wishing Well, 5, 119	F. Toro	Country Queen, 5, 123	Image of Reality, 4, 118	12	1:47.80	69,600
1979	Sisterhood, 4, 118	F. Toro	Country Queen, 4, 118	Camarado, 4, 117	11	1:47.80	50,450
1978	*Lucie Manet, 5, 119	D. G. McHargue	Sensational, 4, 120	*Glenaris, 4, 113	7	1:48.20	38,975
	*Star Ball, 6, 122	D. G. McHargue	Up to Juliet, 5, 114	Teisen Lap, 4, 116	7	1:48.80	38,975
1977	Hail Hilarious, 4, 123	D. Pierce	Cascapedia, 4, 118	Swingtime, 5, 119	6	1:49.60	31,250
1976	Katonka, 4, 121	L. A. Pincay Jr.	Fascinating Girl, 4, 117	*Tizna, 7, 126	5	1:50.40	30,750
1975	Susan's Girl, 6, 124	J. E. Tejeira	Bold Ballet, 4, 118	*Dulcia, 6, 121	6	1:48.00	25,200
1974	Sister Fleet, 4, 115	A. Pineda	*La Zanzara, 4, 121	*Tizna, 5, 122	7	1:47.40	25,550
1973	Bird Boots, 4, 115	E. Belmonte	Susan's Girl, 4, 130	Hill Circus, 5, 120	9	1:47.60	32,950

Named for William Haggin Perry's 1967 champion three-year-old filly, '68, '69 champion older mare, and '68 Vanity H. winner Gamely (1964 f. by Bold Ruler). Formerly named for the city of Long Beach, California. Grade 2 1977-'82. Not graded 1976. Long Beach H. 1939-'75. Gamely H. 1976-'97. Not held 1940-'67. 1 mile 1939, 1969. 1¹⁄₁₆ miles 1968, 1970-'72. Dirt 1939-'68, 1978. Both sexes 1968. Two divisions 1978.

Garden City Breeders' Cup Handicap

Grade 1 in 2005. Belmont Park, three-year-olds, fillies, 1⅛ miles, turf. Held September 12, 2004, with a gross value of $264,000. First held in 1904. First graded in 1985. Stakes record 1:47.10 (1998 Pharatta [Ire]).

Year	Winner	Jockey	Second	Third	Strs	Time	1st Purse
2004	Lucifer's Stone, 3, 118	J. A. Santos	Barancella (Fr), 3, 116	Noahs Ark (Ire), 3, 116	7	1:48.88	$180,000
2003	Indy Five Hundred, 3, 113	P. Day	Dimitrova, 3, 122	Campsie Fells (UAE), 3, 116	8	1:48.44	150,000
2002	Wonder Again, 3, 119	E. S. Prado	Riskaverse, 3, 119	Pertuisane (GB), 3, 115	10	1:47.33	150,000
2001	Voodoo Dancer, 3, 120	C. S. Nakatani	Shooting Party, 3, 113	Wander Mom, 3, 116	10	1:47.69	150,000
2000	Gaviola, 3, 123	J. D. Bailey	Flawly (GB), 3, 115	Millie's Quest, 3, 116	8	1:48.89	150,000
1999	Perfect Sting, 3, 120	P. Day	Nordican Inch (GB), 3, 116	Ronda (GB), 3, 121	12	1:49.41	129,900
1998	Pharatta (Ire), 3, 120	C. S. Nakatani	Tenski, 3, 122	Pratella, 3, 115	12	**1:47.10**	129,720
1997	Auntie Mame, 3, 122	J. D. Bailey	Parade Queen, 3, 115	Swearingen, 3, 117	9	1:48.49	128,040
1996	True Flare, 3, 121	G. L. Stevens	Henlopen, 3, 113	Zephyr, 3, 114	9	1:42.58	128,460
1995	Perfect Arc, 3, 122	J. R. Velazquez	Bail Out Becky, 3, 121	Christmas Gift, 3, 118	8	1:42.35	101,070
1994	Jade Flush, 3, 111	R. G. Davis	Lady Affirmed, 3, 117	Saxuality, 3, 117	6	1:46.79	67,140
1993	Sky Beauty, 3, 124	M. E. Smith	Fadetta, 3, 112	For all Seasons, 3, 114	6	1:35.76	68,400
1992	November Snow, 3, 124	C. W. Antley	Vivano, 3, 112	Easy Now, 3, 124	4	1:35.91	66,480
1991	Dazzle Me Jolie, 3, 115	J. A. Santos	Grand Girlfriend, 3, 112	Wide Country, 3, 124	9	1:35.61	72,000
1990	Aishah, 3, 115	J. A. Santos	Screen Prospect, 3, 115	Vitola (GB), 3, 112	11	1:35.40	57,690
1989	Highest Glory, 3, 115	J. A. Santos	Warfie, 3, 118	Tremolos, 3, 112	7	1:37.20	70,440
1988	Topicount, 3, 115	A. T. Cordero Jr.	Toll Fee, 3, 112	Fara's Team, 3, 115	5	1:38.00	82,260

1987 **Personal Ensign**, 3, 115	R. P. Romero	One From Heaven, 3, 118	Key Bid, 3, 118	9	1:36.60	$82,140
1986 **Life At the Top**, 3, 118	C. J. McCarron	Lotka, 3, 118	Funistrada, 3, 115	6	1:34.40	51,210
1985 **Kamikaze Rick**, 3, 118	A. T. Cordero Jr.	Wising Up, 3, 115	Videogenic, 3, 118	5	1:36.00	50,490
1984 **Given**, 3, 118	M. J. Vigliotti	Maharadoon, 3, 112	Recharged, 3, 118	9	1:43.40	42,960
1983 **Pretty Sensible**, 3, 112	A. Smith Jr.	High Schemes, 3, 112	Lovin Touch, 3, 115	8	1:37.80	33,600
1982 **Nafees**, 3, 112	J. Velasquez	Middle Stage, 3, 112	Beau Cougar, 3, 112	7	1:38.40	33,120
1981 **Banner Gala**, 3, 113	A. T. Cordero Jr.	Expressive Dance, 3, 112	In True Form, 3, 118	9	1:33.60	33,900
1980 **Mitey Lively**, 3, 113	J. Velasquez	Rose of Morn, 3, 112	Paintbrush, 3, 112	6	1:36.40	33,480
1979 **Danielle B.**, 3, 113	R. Hernandez	Distinct Honor, 3, 114	Seascape, 3, 118	10	1:45.40	33,000

Named for the community of Garden City, located in the heart of New York's Long Island. Formerly named for George D. Widener's 1949 Fashion S. winner Rare Perfume (1947 f. by Eight Thirty). Grade 3 1985-'86. Grade 2 1987-'98. Garden City S. 1904-'13. Garden City Selling S. 1915-'32. Rare Perfume S. 1979-'95. Rare Perfume Breeders' Cup H. 1996-'97. Not held 1908, 1910-'12, 1914, 1933-'78. 1¹/₁₆ miles 1904-'79, 1994-'96. 1 mile 70 yards 1984. Dirt 1904-'93. Three-year-olds and up 1904-'32.

Gardenia Handicap

Grade 3 in 2005. Ellis Park, three-year-olds and up, fillies and mares, 1¹/₈ miles, dirt. Held August 7, 2004, with a gross value of $200,000. First held in 1982. First graded in 1988. Stakes record 1:47.60 (1988 Lt. Lao).

Year	Winner	Jockey	Second	Third	Strs	Time	1st Purse
2004	**Angela's Love**, 4, 115	M. Guidry	Miss Fortunate, 4, 116	Bare Necessities, 5, 119	6	1:49.54	$120,000
2003	**Bare Necessities**, 4, 119	R. R. Douglas	Desert Gold, 4, 114	So Much More, 4, 115	9	1:50.09	120,000
2002	**Minister's Baby**, 4, 117	C. Perret	Lakenheath, 4, 115	Softly, 4, 114	8	1:49.73	120,000
2001	**Asher**, 4, 115	M. Guidry	Zenith, 4, 112	Royal Fair, 5, 116	8	1:50.16	120,000
2000	**Silent Eskimo**, 5, 116	J. Lopez	Roza Robata, 5, 119	Tap to Music, 5, 120	7	1:50.56	120,000
1999	**Lines of Beauty**, 4, 112	F. Torres	Roza Robata, 4, 113	Castle Blaze, 6, 109	10	1:49.60	120,000
1998	**Meter Maid**, 4, 119	P. A. Johnson	Proper Banner, 4, 114	Three Fanfares, 5, 113	7	1:51.00	120,000
1997	**Three Fanfares**, 4, 113	F. A. Arguello Jr.	Gold n Delicious, 4, 119	Birr, 4, 116	7	1:49.00	120,000
1996	**Country Cat**, 4, 115	D. M. Barton	Bedroom Blues, 4, 111	Alcovy, 6, 116	8	1:49.60	120,000
1995	**Laura's Pistolette**, 4, 115	E. M. Martin Jr.	Sadie's Dream, 5, 112	Cat Appeal, 3, 116	9	1:50.80	120,000
1994	**Alphabulous**, 5, 112	O. Thorwarth	Added Asset, 4, 115	Hey Hazel, 4, 116	10	1:50.00	120,000
1993	**Erica's Dream**, 5, 113	W. Martinez	Fappies Cosy Miss, 5, 111	Hitch, 4, 114	8	1:49.80	120,000
1992	**Bungalow**, 5, 118	F. C. Torres	Forever Fond, 4, 113	Fappies Cosy Miss, 4, 112	11	1:48.60	120,000
1991	**Summer Matinee**, 4, 113	C. A. Black	Blissful Union, 4, 113	Beth Believes, 5, 113	11	1:50.50	90,000
1990	**Evangelical**, 4, 113	L. J. Melancon	Degenerate Gal, 5, 117	Anitas Surprise, 4, 113	10	1:49.80	90,000
1989	**Lawyer Talk**, 5, 114	M. E. Doser	Gallant Ryder, 4, 120	Miss Barbour, 4, 112	10	1:50.00	90,000
1988	**Lt. Lao**, 4, 123	D. Brumfield	Saucy Deb, 4, 118	Silk's Lady, 4, 112	12	**1:47.60**	90,000
1987	**No Choice**, 4, 113	C. R. Woods Jr.	Layovernite, 5, 112	Firgie's Jule, 4, 112	11	1:49.20	94,500
1986	**Queen Alexandra**, 4, 123	D. E. Foster	Fleet Secretariat, 5, 119	Sherizar, 5, 113	7	1:49.20	63,000
1985	**Crimson Orchid**, 3, 114	S. E. Miller	Electric Fanny, 4, 114	Dusty Gloves, 4, 116	14	1:49.80	41,535
1984	**Rambling Rhythm**, 3, 114	L. J. Martinez	Run Tulle Run, 5, 114	Queen of Song, 5, 122	8	1:50.20	39,325
1983	**Migola**, 3, 115	G. Patterson	Kitchen, 4, 117	Run Tulle Run, 4, 113	14	1:51.60	42,315
1982	**Sweetest Chant**, 4, 121	E. Fires	Muriesk, 3, 111	Run Tulle Run, 3, 112	11	1:49.80	43,778

Named for the flower used in the winner's garland. Formerly sponsored by the Coca-Cola Co. of Atlanta 1985-'86. Formerly sponsored by Stroh's Brewery of Minneapolis 1982-'84. Stroh's H. 1982-'84. Coca-Cola Summer Festival H. 1985. Coca-Cola Centennial H. 1986. Gardenia S. 1990, 1997-'98.

Gazelle Handicap

Grade 1 in 2005. Belmont Park, three-year-olds, fillies, 1¹/₈ miles, dirt. Held September 11, 2004, with a gross value of $250,000. First held in 1887. First graded in 1973. Stakes record 1:46.80 (1974 Maud Muller).

Year	Winner	Jockey	Second	Third	Strs	Time	1st Purse
2004	**Stellar Jayne**, 3, 122	R. Albarado	Daydreaming, 3, 115	He Loves Me, 3, 117	6	1:48.25	$150,000
2003	**Buy the Sport**, 3, 113	P. Day	Lady Tak, 3, 121	Spoken Fur, 3, 118	8	1:48.40	150,000
2002	**Imperial Gesture**, 3, 117	J. A. Santos	Take Charge Lady, 3, 121	Bella Bellucci, 3, 118	7	1:47.12	150,000
2001	**Exogenous**, 3, 118	J. Castellano	Two Item Limit, 3, 118	Fleet Renee, 3, 122	6	1:47.68	150,000
2000	**Critical Eye**, 3, 115	M. E. Smith	Plenty of Light, 3, 115	Resort, 3, 116	8	1:48.54	120,000
1999	**Silverbulletday**, 3, 124	J. D. Bailey	Queen's Word, 3, 113	Awful Smart, 3, 115	6	1:47.71	120,000
1998	**Tap to Music**, 3, 112	P. Day	Keeper Hill, 3, 122	French Braids, 3, 115	6	1:49.72	120,000
1997	**Royal Indy**, 3, 113	P. Day	Starry Dreamer, 3, 114	Pearl City, 3, 117	7	1:49.11	120,000
1996	**My Flag**, 3, 121	J. D. Bailey	Escena, 3, 121	Top Secret, 3, 117	6	1:48.08	120,000
1995	**Serena's Song**, 3, 124	G. L. Stevens	Miss Golden Circle, 3, 113	Golden Bri, 3, 121	6	1:47.29	90,000
1994	**Heavenly Prize**, 3, 123	M. E. Smith	Cinnamon Sugar (Ire), 3, 118	Sovereign Kitty, 3, 118	5	1:47.20	90,000
1993	**Dispute**, 3, 120	J. D. Bailey	Silky Feather, 3, 117	In Her Glory, 3, 112	4	1:47.20	90,000
1992	**Saratoga Dew**, 3, 120	W. H. McCauley	Vivano, 3, 114	Tiney Toast, 3, 113	6	1:47.63	103,140
1991	**Versailles Treaty**, 3, 123	A. T. Cordero Jr.	Grand Girlfriend, 3, 115	Immerse, 3, 112	4	1:47.47	105,840
1990	**Highland Talk**, 3, 111	J. Samyn	Dance Colony, 3, 116	She Can, 3, 116	7	1:50.80	69,960
1989	**Tactile**, 3, 114	R. Migliore	Dream Deal, 3, 117	Fantastic Find, 3, 114	5	1:48.40	67,440
1988	**Classic Crown**, 3, 117	R. P. Romero	Willa On the Move, 3, 120	Make Change, 3, 118	6	1:49.80	69,360
1987	**Single Blade**, 3, 113	C. W. Antley	Without Feathers, 3, 121	Silent Turn, 3, 114	5	1:48.20	80,100
1986	**Classy Cathy**, 3, 121	E. Fires	Life At the Top, 3, 118	Dynamic Star, 3, 116	4	1:48.40	66,480
1985	**Kamikaze Rick**, 3, 113	A. T. Cordero Jr.	Overwhelming, 3, 112	Fran's Valentine, 3, 121	7	1:48.60	68,880

1984	**Miss Oceana**, 3, 121	E. Maple	Sintra, 3, 117	Life's Magic, 3, 122	5	1:47.60	$66,840
1983	**High Schemes**, 3, 121	J. Samyn	Lass Trump, 3, 120	Lady Norcliffe, 3, 115	6	1:48.20	66,720
1982	**Broom Dance**, 3, 121	G. McCarron	Number, 3, 113	Mademoiselle Forli, 3, 114	7	1:47.60	33,360
1981	**Discorama**, 3, 117	R. Hernandez	Secrettame, 3, 114	Tina Tina Too, 3, 114	7	1:48.20	33,300
1980	**Love Sign**, 3, 121	R. Hernandez	Sugar and Spice, 3, 117	Kelley's Day, 3, 112	6	1:49.20	32,580
1979	**Himalayan**, 3, 113	E. Maple	Croquis, 3, 113	Fourdrinier, 3, 112	9	1:48.40	32,580
1978	**Tempest Queen**, 3, 117	J. Velasquez	Lulubo, 3, 116	Terpsichorist, 3, 113	5	1:49.80	31,710
1977	**Pearl Necklace**, 3, 111	S. Cauthen	Sensational, 3, 120	Road Princess, 3, 118	5	1:48.00	31,770
1976	**Revidere**, 3, 124	A. T. Cordero Jr.	Pacific Princess, 3, 112	Ancient Fables, 3, 112	5	1:47.80	31,950
1975	**Land Girl**, 3, 114	J. Vasquez	Hooray Hooray, 3, 108	Let Me Linger, 3, 119	8	1:49.40	33,690
1974	**Maud Muller**, 3, 120	A. T. Cordero Jr.	Raisela, 3, 119	Stage Door Betty, 3, 115	7	**1:46.80**	33,900
1973	**Desert Vixen**, 3, 126	J. Velasquez	Bag of Tunes, 3, 117	Poker Night, 3, 120	7	1:47.40	33,780

Named for the speedy hooved mammal, the gazelle. Grade 2 1973-'83. Gazelle S. 1887-1921, 1923-'55. Held at Gravesend Park 1887-1909. Held at Aqueduct 1910-'55, 1960, 1963-'68. Not held 1911-'16, 1933-'35. 1¹/₁₆ miles 1900-'58. 1 mile 1959-'60. Fillies and mares 1917-'20. Three-year-olds and up 1917-'20.

General George Handicap

Grade 2 in 2005. Laurel Park, three-year-olds and up, 7 furlongs, dirt. Held February 21, 2005, with a gross value of $200,000. First held in 1973. First graded in 1991. Stakes record 1:21.96 (1992 Senor Speedy).

Year	Winner	Jockey	Second	Third	Strs	Time	1st Purse
2005	**Saratoga County**, 4, 114	J. Castellano	Don Six, 5, 118	Gators N Bears, 5, 118	9	1:23.43	$120,000
2004	**Well Fancied**, 6, 115	E. S. Prado	Unforgettable Max, 4, 114	Gators N Bears, 4, 116	9	1:22.49	120,000
2003	**My Cousin Matt**, 4, 113	R. A. Dominguez	Peeping Tom, 6, 114	Disturbingthepeace, 5, 118	11	1:22.12	120,000
2002	**Wrangler**, 4, 115	A. T. Gryder	Rusty Spur, 4, 111	Affirmed Success, 8, 121	8	1:22.53	120,000
2001	**Peeping Tom**, 4, 114	S. Bridgmohan	Delaware Township, 5, 120	Disco Rico, 4, 117	7	1:22.00	120,000
2000	**Affirmed Success**, 6, 121	J. F. Chavez	Young At Heart, 6, 114	Badge, 4, 117	9	1:22.02	120,000
1999	**Esteemed Friend**, 5, 116	M. J. Luzzi	Star of Valor, 6, 114	Purple Passion, 5, 117	9	1:22.54	150,000
1998	**Royal Haven**, 6, 122	R. Migliore	Purple Passion, 4, 116	Wire Me Collect, 5, 117	9	1:23.04	150,000
1997	**Why Change**, 4, 113	M. Guidry	Appealing Skier, 4, 118	Le Grande Pos, 6, 111	10	1:22.41	120,000
1996	**Meadow Monster**, 5, 120	R. Wilson	Splendid Sprinter, 4, 113	Cat Be Nimble, 4, 114	9	1:22.11	120,000
1995	**Who Wouldn't**, 6, 119	J. Rocco	Storm Tower, 5, 116	Powis Castle, 4, 118	8	1:22.08	120,000
1994	**Blushing Julian**, 4, 118	R. E. Colton	Chief Desire, 4, 123	Who Wouldn't, 5, 118	12	1:22.91	120,000
1993	**Majesty's Turn**, 4, 118	A. Delgado	Senor Speedy, 6, 118	Ameri Valay, 4, 123	7	1:22.66	120,000
1992	**Senor Speedy**, 5, 126	J. F. Chavez	Sunny Sunrise, 5, 123	Formal Dinner, 4, 123	12	**1:21.96**	120,000
1991	**Star Touch (Fr)**, 5, 118	M. J. Luzzi	Profit Key, 4, 118	Fire Plug, 8, 118	11	1:22.90	120,000
1990	**King's Nest**, 5, 119	M. T. Hunter	Wind Splitter, 4, 117	Notation, 4, 119	12	1:22.00	120,000
1989	**Little Bold John**, 7, 122	D. A. Miller Jr.	Oraibi, 4, 119	Finder's Choice, 4, 117	13	1:22.80	120,000
1988	**Private Terms**, 3, 116	K. J. Desormeaux	Dynaformer, 3, 122	Delightful Doctor, 3, 122	13	1:38.80	74,328
1987	**Templar Hill**, 3, 116	G. W. Hutton	Hay Halo, 3, 118	Win Dusty Win, 3, 114	11	1:44.00	74,620
1986	**Broad Brush**, 3, 122	V. A. Bracciale Jr.	Fast Step, 3, 113	Swallow, 3, 116	7	1:44.20	54,373
	‡**Lil Tyler**, 3, 122	J. Nied Jr.	Fobby Forbes, 3, 116	Fork Union Cadet, 3, 110	6	1:45.60	53,723
1985	**Roo Art**, 3, 122	D. A. Miller Jr.	Joyfull John, 3, 112	I Am the Game, 3, 119	8	1:37.60	55,380
1984	‡**Judge Mc Guire**, 3, 122	C. H. Mendoza	American Artist, 3, 110	S. S. Hot Sauce, 3, 122	9	1:46.60	55,543
1981	**Classic Go Go**, 3, 122	B. Fann	Thirty Eight Paces, 3, 122	Aztec Crown, 3, 115	9	1:23.20	37,115
1980	**Galaxy Road**, 3, 122	G. McCarron	Leader of the Pack, 3, 113	Ashanti Gold, 3, 110	7	1:24.60	36,660
1978	**Ten Ten**, 3, 122	W. J. Passmore	Game Prince, 3, 113	Gala Forecast, 3, 113	8	1:45.80	18,200
1977	**Do the Bump**, 3, 122	C. J. McCarron	John U to Berry, 3, 115	Steel Bandit, 3, 113	6	1:47.20	17,778
1976	**Princely Game**, 3, 119	A. Agnello	On the Sly, 3, 110	Troll By, 3, 116	7	1:44.60	17,940
1975	**Pendulum Sam**, 3, 110	L. Gino	King of Fools, 3, 113	Broadway Reviewer, 3, 110	7	1:48.20	18,005
1974	**Sharp Gary**, 3, 122	C. Barrera	Jolly Johu, 3, 119	Ground Breaker, 3, 110	10	1:46.60	19,045
1973	**Ecole Etage**, 3, 113	G. Cusimano	Big Red L, 3, 113	Select Performance, 3, 110	9	1:44.60	18,265

Named for Gen. George Washington (1731-'99), first President of the United States. General George S. 1973-'94. Held at Bowie 1973-'84. Held at Pimlico 1986. Not held 1979, 1982-'83. 1¹/₁₆ miles 1973-'78, 1984, 1986-'87. 1 mile 1985. Three-year-olds 1973-'88. Two divisions 1986. ‡American Artist finished first, DQ to second, 1984. ‡Fobby Forbes finished first, DQ to second, 1986 (2nd div.).

Generous Stakes

Grade 3 in 2005. Hollywood Park, two-year-olds, 1 mile, turf. Held November 27, 2004, with a gross value of $100,000. First held in 1982. First graded in 1986. Stakes record 1:34.41 (1991 Contested Bid).

Year	Winner	Jockey	Second	Third	Strs	Time	1st Purse
2004	**Dubleo**, 2, 121	C. S. Nakatani	Littlebitofzip, 2, 116	Sunny Sky (Fr), 2, 116	12	1:37.21	$60,000
2003	**Castledale (Ire)**, 2, 116	J. A. Krone	Dealer Choice (Fr), 2, 116	Lucky Pulpit, 2, 116	12	1:35.43	60,000
2002	**Peace Rules**, 2, 118	V. Espinoza	Lismore Knight, 2, 121	Outta Here, 2, 115	9	1:35.49	120,000
2001	**Mountain Rage**, 2, 116	D. R. Flores	Miesque's Approval, 2, 121	National Park (GB), 2, 117	8	1:40.31	120,000
2000	**Startac**, 2, 118	A. O. Solis	Broadway Moon, 2, 116	Deeliteful Irving, 2, 114	9	1:34.76	120,000
1999	**Jokerman**, 2, 118	P. Day	Purely Cozzene, 2, 121	Kleofus, 2, 121	6	1:35.23	120,000
1998	**Incurable Optimist**, 2, 121	J. R. Velazquez	Company Approval, 2, 114	Brave Gun, 2, 117	8	1:37.72	150,000
1997	**Mantles Star (GB)**, 2, 114	C. J. McCarron	F J's Pace, 2, 116	Commitisize, 2, 121	9	1:36.73	150,000
1996	**Hello (Ire)**, 2, 121	C. J. McCarron	Steel Ruhlr, 2, 114	Divine Insight, 2, 114	12	1:34.77	150,000

1995	Old Chapel, 2, 121	G. L. Stevens	Ayrton S, 2, 116	Heza Gone West, 2, 117	10	1:35.11	$137,500
1994	Native Regent, 2, 121	D. Penna	Dangerous Scenario, 2, 116	Claudius, 2, 121	9	1:37.15	137,500
1993	Delineator, 2, 118	R. A. Baze	Devon Port (Fr), 2, 116	Ferrara, 2, 114	8	1:34.73	137,500
1992	Earl of Barking (Ire), 2, 114	A. O. Solis	Devil's Rock, 2, 115	Corby, 2, 118	8	1:34.49	137,500
1991	Silver Ray, 2, 114	M. A. Pedroza	Thinkernot, 2, 115	African Colony, 2, 114	9	1:35.00	74,775
	Contested Bid, 2, 114	C. S. Nakatani	Turbulent Kris, 2, 114	Sevengreenpairs, 2, 114	9	1:34.41	71,775
1990	Satis (Fr), 2, 115	C. A. Black	What a Spell, 2, 114	Ev for Shir, 2, 114	12	1:35.20	67,800
1989	Single Dawn, 2, 114	A. O. Solis	Pleasant Tap, 2, 118	Doyouseewhatisee, 2, 121	12	1:35.60	69,600
1988	Music Merci, 2, 121	G. L. Stevens	Double Quick, 2, 121	Crown Collection, 2, 115	9	1:36.40	58,220
	Shipping Time, 2, 114	C. A. Black	Super May, 2, 115	Past Ages, 2, 116	7	1:37.20	58,220
1987	Purdue King, 2, 121	C. J. McCarron	Chinese Gold, 2, 121	Blade of the Ball, 2, 115	6	1:36.00	47,500
	White Mischief, 2, 115	J. A. Santos	King Alobar, 2, 115	Texas Typhoon, 2, 115	4	1:35.40	68,750
1986	Persevered, 2, 120	G. L. Stevens	Wilderness Bound, 2, 120	Quietly Bold, 2, 115	9	1:41.80	86,050
	†Sweettuc, 2, 113	G. L. Stevens	Savona Tower, 2, 116	Lord Duckworth, 2, 114	9	1:41.60	68,050
1985	Darby Fair, 2, 120	A. L. Castanon	Snow Chief, 2, 120	Acks Lika Ruler, 2, 114	6	1:37.00	119,400
1984	Overtrump, 2, 120	C. J. McCarron	Right Con, 2, 120	Herat, 2, 120	11	1:41.80	123,350
1983	Artichoke, 2, 120	W. Shoemaker	Nagurski, 2, 114	Fortune's Kingdom, 2, 115	8	1:38.40	50,100
	Precisionist, 2, 116	C. J. McCarron	Fali Time, 2, 120	Tights, 2, 115	4	1:37.60	50,100
1982	Fifth Division, 2, 117	L. A. Pincay Jr.	Dominating Dooley, 2, 114	Mezzo, 2, 116	12	1:35.60	33,450

Named for Fahd Salman's 1991 Irish Horse of the Year and dual European classic winner Generous (Ire) (1988 c. by Caerleon [Ire]). Formerly named for Mrs. Stephen C. Clark Jr.'s 1970 champion two-year-old colt and '87 leading brood-mare sire Hoist the Flag (1968 c. by Tom Rolfe). Grade 2 1988-'89. Hoist the Flag S. 1982-'92. 1$\frac{1}{16}$ miles 1984, 1986. Dirt 1985, 1988. Two divisions 1983, 1986-'88, 1991. †Denotes female.

Genuine Risk Handicap

Grade 2 in 2005. Belmont Park, three-year-olds and up, fillies and mares, 6 furlongs, dirt. Held May 14, 2005, with a gross value of $150,000. First held in 1984. First graded in 1986. Stakes record 1:08.40 (1996 Exotic Wood).

Year	Winner	Jockey	Second	Third	Strs	Time	1st Purse
2005	Bank Audit, 4, 117	N. Arroyo Jr.	Sensibly Chic, 5, 115	Forest Music, 4, 115	9	1:09.65	$90,000
2004	Bear Fan, 5, 117	J. R. Velazquez	Harmony Lodge, 6, 120	Kitty Knight, 4, 114	5	1:08.85	90,000
2003	Shine Again, 6, 119	J. Samyn	Carson Hollow, 4, 122	Harmony Lodge, 5, 116	4	1:09.19	90,000
2002	Xtra Heat, 4, 126	H. Vega	Shine Again, 5, 117	La Galerie (Arg), 6, 114	6	1:10.24	90,000
2001	Katz Me If You Can, 4, 113	J. Bravo	Lucky Livi, 4, 114	Shine Again, 4, 115	10	1:09.55	90,000
2000	Imperfect World, 4, 113	R. G. Davis	Gold Princess, 5, 113	Tropical Punch, 4, 115	7	1:10.00	90,000
1999	Foil, 4, 114	J. Samyn	Harpia, 5, 118	Gold Princess, 4, 115	9	1:10.43	90,000
1998	J J'sdream, 5, 118	L. C. Reynolds	Tate, 4, 112	Capote Belle, 5, 118	8	1:10.28	83,310
1997	Miss Golden Circle, 5, 120	R. Migliore	Start At Once, 4, 111	Nappelon, 5, 110	6	1:09.49	65,040
1996	Exotic Wood, 4, 119	M. E. Smith	Lottsa Talc, 6, 118	Miss Golden Circle, 4, 113	6	1:08.40	65,100
1995	Classy Mirage, 5, 122	J. A. Krone	Through the Door, 5, 112	Lottsa Talc, 5, 117	4	1:11.25	64,080
1994	Apelia, 5, 119	L. Attard	Spinning Round, 5, 119	Ann Dear, 4, 114	4	1:09.01	64,680
1993	Apelia, 4, 119	L. Attard	Santa Catalina, 5, 117	Reach for Clever, 6, 117	7	1:10.18	69,600
1992	Parisian Flight, 4, 117	J. A. Santos	Serape, 4, 117	Devil's Orchid, 5, 119	6	1:09.18	70,680
1991	Safely Kept, 5, 122	C. Perret	Missy's Mirage, 3, 109	Token Dance, 4, 117	5	1:10.15	68,400
1990	Safely Kept, 4, 122	C. Perret	Diva's Debut, 4, 119	Levitation, 5, 117	4	1:10.20	49,140
1989	Safely Kept, 3, 114	A. T. Cordero Jr.	Aptostar, 4, 122	Cagey Exuberance, 5, 122	4	1:09.40	49,410
1988	Tappiano, 4, 122	J. Vasquez	Cagey Exuberance, 4, 122	Hedgeabout, 4, 117	4	1:09.00	50,040
1987	Pine Tree Lane, 5, 122	A. T. Cordero Jr.	Silent Account, 4, 117	Royal Tali, 4, 117	4	1:10.20	47,970
1986	Clocks Secret, 4, 122	W. Shoemaker	Le Slew, 5, 119	Liz Taylor, 3, 109	8	1:10.00	48,900
1985	Alabama Nana (Ire), 4, 117	J. Velasquez	Hare Brain, 5, 119	Two Ours, 4, 119	10	1:10.60	49,260
1984	On the Bench, 4, 115	J. Cruguet	Nany, 4, 117	Grateful Friend, 4, 119	6	1:09.60	33,060

Named for Diana Firestone's 1980 champion three-year-old filly and '80 Ruffian H. (G1) winner Genuine Risk (1977 f. by Exclusive Native). Grade 3 1986-'88. Genuine Risk S. 1984-'94.

Glens Falls Handicap

Grade 3 in 2005. Saratoga Race Course, three-year-olds and up, fillies and mares, 1$\frac{3}{8}$ miles, turf. Held September 5, 2004, with a gross value of $110,400. First held in 1996. First graded in 1999. Stakes record 2:12.81 (1999 Idle Rich).

Year	Winner	Jockey	Second	Third	Strs	Time	1st Purse
2004	Humaita (Ger), 4, 114	C. H. Velasquez	Where We Left Off (GB), 4, 116	Savedbythelight, 4, 115	9	2:15.25	$66,240
	Arvada (GB), 4, 112	J. R. Velazquez	Spice Island, 5, 118	Film Maker, 4, 121	8	2:14.12	65,580
2003	Sixty Seconds (NZ), 5, 115	J. A. Santos	Primetimevalentine, 4, 113	Alternate, 4, 116	9	2:13.96	67,860
2002	Owsley, 4, 116	E. S. Prado	Mot Juste (GB), 4, 116	Sunstone (GB), 4, 114	10	2:15.99	68,100
2001	Irving's Baby, 4, 126	J. D. Bailey	New Assembly (Ire), 4, 113	Caveat's Shot, 6, 114	4	2:07.56	65,995
2000	I'm Indy Mood, 5, 116	H. Castillo Jr.	Idle Rich, 5, 114	Cybil, 4, 114	5	2:07.41	66,120
1999	Idle Rich, 4, 115	J. D. Bailey	Adrian, 5, 114	Bundling, 5, 114	7	2:12.81	65,760
1998	Auntie Mame, 4, 120	J. R. Velazquez	Yvecrique (Fr), 4, 115	Makethemostofit, 4, 111	6	2:13.15	66,060
1997	Shemozzle (Ire), 4, 115	J. D. Bailey	Picture Hat, 5, 113	Last Approach, 5, 113	6	2:12.89	64,740
1996	Ampulla, 5, 113	S. J. Sellers	Look Daggers, 4, 118	Electric Society (Ire), 5, 120	8	2:16.49	67,500

Named for Glens Falls, New York, a town about 15 miles north of Saratoga Springs. Not graded when taken off turf 2001. Glens Falls S. 1996-'97. 1$\frac{1}{4}$ miles 2000-'01. Dirt 2000-'01. Two divisions 2004.

Go for Wand Handicap

Grade 1 in 2005. Saratoga Race Course, three-year-olds and up, fillies and mares, 1⅛ miles, dirt. Held August 1, 2004, with a gross value of $245,000. First held in 1954. First graded in 1973. Stakes record 1:47.86 (2004 Azeri).

Year	Winner	Jockey	Second	Third	Strs	Time	1st Purse
2004	Azeri, 6, 120	P. Day	Sightseek, 5, 122	Storm Flag Flying, 4, 117	5	**1:47.86**	$150,000
2003	Sightseek, 4, 121	J. D. Bailey	She's Got the Beat, 4, 112	Nonsuch Bay, 4, 113	6	1:50.92	150,000
2002	Dancethruthedawn, 4, 118	J. D. Bailey	Transcendental, 4, 113	Too Scarlet, 4, 112	7	1:50.21	150,000
2001	Serra Lake, 4, 113	E. S. Prado	Pompeii, 4, 114	March Magic, 4, 114	8	1:49.62	150,000
2000	Heritage of Gold, 5, 123	S. J. Sellers	Beautiful Pleasure, 5, 125	Roza Robata, 5, 114	5	1:49.84	150,000
1999	Banshee Breeze, 4, 124	J. D. Bailey	Beautiful Pleasure, 4, 113	Heritage of Gold, 4, 117	5	1:49.95	150,000
1998	Aldiza, 4, 114	M. E. Smith	Escena, 5, 124	Tomisue's Delight, 4, 116	7	1:49.88	150,000
1997	Hidden Lake, 4, 123	R. Migliore	Flat Fleet Feet, 4, 120	Clear Mandate, 5, 113	6	1:49.60	150,000
1996	Exotic Wood, 4, 115	C. J. McCarron	Shoop, 5, 118	Frolic, 4, 113	8	1:49.44	105,000
1995	Heavenly Prize, 4, 123	P. Day	Forcing Bid, 4, 108	Little Buckles, 4, 111	5	1:49.90	105,000
1994	Sky Beauty, 4, 123	M. E. Smith	Link River, 4, 123	Life Is Delicious, 4, 123	5	1:49.47	90,000
1993	Turnback the Alarm, 4, 123	C. W. Antley	Nannerl, 6, 116	November Snow, 4, 116	4	1:36.02	120,000
1992	Easy Now, 3, 111	J. D. Bailey	‡Train Robbery, 5, 118	Wide Country, 4, 116	5	1:36.13	120,000
1991	Queena, 5, 123	A. T. Cordero Jr.	Fit to Scout, 4, 123	Screen Prospect, 4, 116	6	1:34.89	120,000
1990	Go for Wand, 3, 118	R. P. Romero	Feel the Beat, 5, 123	Mistaurian, 4, 116	6	1:35.60	68,760
1989	Miss Brio (Chi), 5, 116	J. D. Bailey	Proper Evidence, 4, 116	Aptostar, 4, 123	5	1:35.60	67,080
1988	Personal Ensign, 4, 123	R. P. Romero	Winning Colors, 3, 118	Sham Say, 3, 115	4	1:34.20	67,080
1987	North Sider, 5, 123	A. T. Cordero Jr.	Wisla, 4, 116	Funistrada, 4, 116	7	1:35.00	85,500
1986	Lady's Secret, 4, 125	P. Day	Steal a Kiss, 3, 109	Endear, 4, 120	6	1:33.40	81,060
1985	Lady's Secret, 3, 111	J. Velasquez	Dowery, 4, 117	Mrs. Revere, 4, 117	8	1:34.80	85,020
1984	Miss Oceana, 3, 120	E. Maple	Paradies (Arg), 4, 114	Nany, 4, 120	5	1:35.20	70,560
1983	Ambassador of Luck, 4, 116	A. Graell	A Kiss for Luck, 4, 120	Am Capable, 3, 109	6	1:36.40	67,560
1982	Too Chic, 3, 110	R. Hernandez	Ambassador of Luck, 3, 111	Anti Lib, 4, 116	8	1:34.80	67,920
1981	Jameela, 5, 123	J. Vasquez	Love Sign, 4, 123	Island Charm, 4, 116	5	1:35.00	65,280
1980	Bold 'n Determined, 3, 122	E. J. Delahoussaye	Genuine Risk, 3, 118	Love Sign, 3, 120	5	1:35.40	49,140
1979	Blitey, 3, 112	A. T. Cordero Jr.	It's in the Air, 3, 122	Pearl Necklace, 5, 125	5	1:34.80	48,015
1978	Pearl Necklace, 4, 123	R. Hernandez	Ida Delia, 4, 113	Sensational, 4, 117	5	1:33.80	48,195
1977	What a Summer, 4, 126	J. Vasquez	Crab Grass, 5, 114	Harvest Girl, 3, 111	8	1:37.40	32,280
1976	Artfully, 3, 108	P. Day	Snooze, 4, 108	Land Girl, 4, 109	7	1:34.00	25,920
	Sugar Plum Time, 4, 111	J. Imparato	Pacific Princess, 3, 110	Fleet Victress, 4, 115	9	1:34.00	26,220
1975	Let Me Linger, 3, 117	L. A. Pincay Jr.	Honorable Miss, 5, 121	Susan's Girl, 6, 128	8	1:35.20	34,590
1974	‡Ponte Vecchio, 4, 118	J. Vasquez	Poker Night, 4, 116	Twixt, 5, 124	12	1:34.60	35,850
1973	Light Hearted, 4, 116	E. Nelson	Convenience, 5, 121	Krislin, 4, 111	6	1:34.80	17,040

Named for Christiana Stable's 1989 champion two-year-old filly, '90 champion three-year-old filly, and '90 Maskette S. (G1) winner Go for Wand (1987 f. by Deputy Minister). Go for Wand is buried in Saratoga's infield. Formerly named for James R. Keene's 1908 champion two-year-old filly and Futurity S. winner Maskette (1906 f. by Disguise). Maskette H. 1954-'78. Maskette S. 1979-'91. Go for Wand S. 1992-'97. Held at Belmont Park 1954-'58, 1961, 1969-'93. Held at Aqueduct 1959-'60, 1962-'68. 1 mile 1954-'93. ‡Desert Vixen finished first, DQ to twelfth for a positive drug test, 1974. ‡Nannerl finished second, DQ to fifth, 1992.

Golden Rod Stakes

Grade 2 in 2005. Churchill Downs, two-year-olds, fillies, 1¹⁄₁₆ miles, dirt. Held November 27, 2004, with a gross value of $215,400. First held in 1910. First graded in 1973. Stakes record 1:43.82 (2001 Belterra).

Year	Winner	Jockey	Second	Third	Strs	Time	1st Purse
2004	Runway Model, 2, 122	E. M. Martin Jr.	Kota, 2, 118	Summerly, 2, 116	6	1:45.97	$133,548
2003	Be Gentle, 2, 122	J. McKee	Lotta Kim, 2, 116	Dynaville, 2, 116	11	1:45.91	142,600
2002	My Boston Gal, 2, 117	C. H. Borel	Holiday Lady, 2, 115	My Trusty Cat, 2, 115	7	1:45.00	136,152
2001	Belterra, 2, 117	J. K. Court	Take Charge Lady, 2, 122	Lotta Rhythm, 2, 122	5	**1:43.82**	133,424
2000	Miss Pickums, 2, 122	J. J. Vitek	Nasty Storm, 2, 113	My White Corvette, 2, 119	9	1:44.84	138,384
1999	Humble Clerk, 2, 119	J. K. Court	Cash Run, 2, 122	Secret Status, 2, 111	9	1:45.26	138,880
1998	Silverbulletday, 2, 122	G. L. Stevens	Here I Go, 2, 113	Lefty's Dollbaby, 2, 113	4	1:43.87	134,292
1997	Love Lock, 2, 119	R. Albarado	Barefoot Dyana, 2, 119	Grechelle, 2, 111	9	1:44.49	139,996
1996	City Band, 2, 122	S. J. Sellers	Glitter Woman, 2, 113	Water Street, 2, 122	10	1:46.82	139,996
1995	Gold Sunrise, 2, 113	W. Martinez	Birr, 2, 119	Solana, 2, 113	11	1:45.46	97,500
1994	Lilly Capote, 2, 113	D. M. Barton	Morris Code, 2, 113	Cat Appeal, 2, 119	8	1:46.66	97,500
1993	At the Half, 2, 122	P. Day	Spiritofpocahontas, 2, 115	Mystic Union, 2, 111	9	1:46.83	97,500
1992	Boots 'n Jackie, 2, 120	M. A. Lee	Mollie Creek, 2, 115	Dance Account, 2, 113	6	1:47.29	97,500
1991	Vivid Imagination, 2, 115	J. M. Johnson	Met Her Dream, 2, 113	Pennant Fever, 2, 113	8	1:46.38	97,500
1990	Fancy Ribbons, 2, 114	J. E. Bruin	Nice Assay, 2, 115	Til Forbid, 2, 113	8	1:45.40	97,500
1989	De La Devil, 2, 117	J. A. Krone	Crowned, 2, 120	Flew by Em, 2, 117	7	1:44.60	97,500
1988	Born Famous, 2, 120	E. Fires	Coax Chelsie, 2, 120	Darby Shuffle, 2, 120	6	1:48.20	97,500
1987	Darien Miss, 2, 118	P. A. Johnson	Tap Your Toes, 2, 118	Most Likely, 2, 118	7	1:48.20	83,814
1986	Stargrass, 2, 118	K. K. Allen	Zero Minus, 2, 121	Laserette, 2, 113	11	1:46.60	98,358
1985	Slippin n' Slyding, 2, 116	C. R. Woods Jr.	Turn and Dance, 2, 110	Bonded Miss, 2, 113	9	1:46.20	95,693
1984	Kamikaze Rick, 2, 116	R. Migliore	Boldly Dared, 2, 114	Gallant Libby, 2, 118	9	1:47.80	101,156
1983	Flippers, 2, 119	P. Day	Robin's Rob, 2, 116	Mallorca, 2, 116	11	1:47.60	86,158
1982	Weekend Surprise, 2, 119	P. Day	National Banner, 2, 116	Quarrel Over, 2, 116	6	1:47.00	77,701

1981	Betty Money, 2, 119	D. Brumfield	Hoist Emy's Flag, 2, 116	Subdeb, 2, 119	12	1:45.80	$91,669
1980	Mamzelle, 2, 116	M. S. Sellers	Switch Point, 2, 116	Brent's Star, 2, 119	7	1:46.20	83,236
1979	Remote Ruler, 2, 116	S. Maple	Forever Cordial, 2, 116	Peachblow, 2, 116	10	1:25.00	43,095
1978	Angel Island, 2, 119	E. J. Delahoussaye	Safe, 2, 113	Too Many Sweets, 2, 119	8	1:24.20	36,325
1977	Bold Rendezvous, 2, 113	P. Nicolo	Rainy Princess, 2, 116	Silver Spook, 2, 113	10	1:27.00	46,449
1976	Bring Out the Band, 2, 114	D. Brumfield	Shady Lou, 2, 116	Ciao, 2, 113	10	1:25.20	38,688
1975	Old Goat, 2, 119	M. Hole	Confort Zone, 2, 113	Silent Bidder, 2, 114	7	1:24.80	37,941
1974	Mirthful Flirt, 2, 113	W. J. Passmore	Sun and Snow, 2, 119	Yale Coed, 2, 116	10	1:26.60	38,597
1973	Chris Evert, 2, 116	L. A. Pincay Jr.	Bundler, 2, 119	Kiss Me Darlin, 2, 116	13	1:25.20	38,200

Named for the state flower of Kentucky, the goldenrod. Grade 3 1973-'82, 1989-'99. Not graded 1983-'88. Not held 1928-'61. 6 furlongs 1910-'18. 1 mile 1919. 7 furlongs 1920-'27, 1962-'79.

Goodwood Breeders' Cup Handicap

Grade 2 in 2005. Santa Anita Park, three-year-olds and up, 1 1/8 miles, dirt. Held October 2, 2004, with a gross value of $480,000. First held in 1982. First graded in 1982. Stakes record 1:46.72 (1994 Bertrando).

Year	Winner	Jockey	Second	Third	Strs	Time	1st Purse
2004	Lundy's Liability (Brz), 4, 118	D. R. Flores	Total Impact (Chi), 6, 119	Supah Blitz, 4, 117	5	1:48.39	$300,000
2003	Pleasantly Perfect, 5, 116	A. O. Solis	Fleetstreet Dancer, 5, 113	Star Cross (Arg), 6, 110	8	1:48.37	300,000
2002	Pleasantly Perfect, 4, 115	A. O. Solis	Momentum, 4, 119	Reba's Gold, 5, 116	9	1:46.80	300,000
2001	Freedom Crest, 5, 116	K. J. Desormeaux	Skimming, 5, 123	Tiznow, 4, 124	6	1:48.86	300,000
2000	Tiznow, 3, 116	C. J. McCarron	Captain Steve, 3, 117	Euchre, 4, 115	7	1:47.38	240,000
1999	Budroyale, 6, 119	G. K. Gomez	General Challenge, 3, 120	Old Trieste, 4, 120	6	1:48.31	300,000
1998	Silver Charm, 4, 124	G. L. Stevens	Free House, 4, 124	Score Quick, 6, 115	6	1:47.21	262,800
1997	Benchmark, 6, 118	E. J. Delahoussaye	Score Quick, 5, 114	Hesabull, 4, 117	5	1:47.60	158,700
1996	‡Savinio, 6, 117	C. S. Nakatani	Dare and Go, 5, 122	Alphabet Soup, 5, 120	4	1:47.88	189,300
1995	Soul of the Matter, 4, 121	K. J. Desormeaux	Tinners Way, 5, 121	Alphabet Soup, 4, 116	5	1:47.54	144,450
1994	Bertrando, 5, 120	G. L. Stevens	Dramatic Gold, 3, 115	Tossofthecoin, 4, 115	6	1:46.72	124,400
1993	Lottery Winner, 4, 115	K. J. Desormeaux	Region, 4, 116	Pleasant Tango, 3, 115	7	1:47.71	127,200
1992	Reign Road, 4, 116	K. J. Desormeaux	Sir Beaufort, 5, 116	Marquetry, 5, 120	6	1:48.36	125,200
1991	The Prime Minister, 4, 115	C. J. McCarron	Marquetry, 4, 119	Pleasant Tap, 4, 117	6	1:47.99	152,300
1990	Lively One, 5, 120	A. O. Solis	Miserden, 4, 112	Festin (Arg), 4, 116	7	1:48.00	126,800
1989	Present Value, 5, 119	E. J. Delahoussaye	Rahy, 4, 121	Happy Toss (Arg), 4, 116	8	1:47.20	128,800
1988	Cutlass Reality, 6, 124	G. L. Stevens	Lively One, 3, 116	Stylish Winner, 4, 113	8	1:47.20	130,400
1987	Ferdinand, 4, 127	W. Shoemaker	Candi's Gold, 3, 117	Skywalker, 5, 123	5	1:50.80	102,500
1986	Super Diamond, 6, 122	L. A. Pincay Jr.	Epidaurus, 4, 116	Prince Don B., 5, 115	8	1:41.20	65,500
1985	Lord At War (Arg), 5, 125	W. Shoemaker	Matafao, 4, 106	Last Command, 4, 115	6	1:50.20	62,800
1984	Lord At War (Arg), 4, 117	W. Shoemaker	Video Kid, 4, 118	Menswear, 6, 117	6	1:42.00	60,150
1983	Pettrax, 5, 117	K. D. Black	Konewah, 4, 115	Stancharry, 5, 117	6	1:42.60	46,650
1982	Cajun Prince, 5, 115	W. A. Guerra	Caterman (NZ), 6, 122	Rock Softly, 4, 116	6	1:40.20	46,600

Named for Goodwood Race Course in England, the Oak Tree Racing Association's sister track. Grade 3 1982, 1985-'89. Not graded 1983-'84. Goodwood H. 1982-'95. 1 1/16 miles 1982-'84, 1986. ‡Alphabet Soup finished first, DQ to third, 1996.

Gotham Stakes

Grade 3 in 2005. Aqueduct, three-year-olds, 1 mile, dirt. Held March 19, 2005, with a gross value of $150,000. First held in 1953. First graded in 1973. Stakes record 1:32.40 (1989 Easy Goer).

Year	Winner	Jockey	Second	Third	Strs	Time	1st Purse
2005	Survivalist, 3, 116	R. Migliore	‡Galloping Grocer, 3, 120	Naughty New Yorker, 3, 120	9	1:35.61	$90,000
2004	Saratoga County, 3, 116	J. Castellano	Pomeroy, 3, 116	Eddington, 3, 116	8	1:35.53	120,000
2003	Alysweep, 3, 120	R. Migliore	Grey Comet, 3, 120	Spite the Devil, 3, 116	9	1:40.60	120,000
2002	Mayakovsky, 3, 116	E. S. Prado	Saarland, 3, 120	Parade of Music, 3, 116	7	1:34.90	120,000
2001	Richly Blended, 3, 116	R. Wilson	Mr. John, 3, 116	Voodoo, 3, 116	8	1:35.14	120,000
2000	Red Bullet, 3, 113	A. O. Solis	Aptitude, 3, 113	Performing Magic, 3, 114	9	1:34.27	120,000
1999	Badge, 3, 120	S. Bridgmohan	Apremont, 3, 120	Robin Goodfellow, 3, 113	11	1:34.72	90,000
1998	Wasatch, 3, 117	J. D. Bailey	Dr J, 3, 119	Late Edition, 3, 114	10	1:36.56	90,000
1997	Smokin Mel, 3, 112	J. R. Velazquez	Ordway, 3, 122	Wild Wonder, 3, 119	11	1:34.38	120,000
1996	Romano Gucci, 3, 119	J. A. Krone	Tiger Talk, 3, 117	Feather Box, 3, 114	10	1:34.40	120,000
1995	Talkin Man, 3, 122	M. E. Smith	Da Hoss, 3, 117	Devious Course, 3, 117	11	1:34.40	150,000
1994	Irgun, 3, 114	J. D. Bailey	Bit of Puddin, 3, 117	Jesse F, 3, 114	12	1:36.27	150,000
1993	As Indicated, 3, 114	C. V. Bisono	Itaka, 3, 114	Strolling Along, 3, 121	8	1:36.24	120,000
1992	dh- Devil His Due, 3, 114	W. H. McCauley		Best Decorated, 3, 114	8	1:35.63	102,500
	dh- Lure, 3, 114	M. E. Smith					
1991	Kyle's Our Man, 3, 121	A. T. Cordero Jr.	King Mutesa, 3, 118	Another Review, 3, 118	8	1:34.69	150,000
1990	Thirty Six Red, 3, 114	M. E. Smith	Senor Pete, 3, 121	Burnt Hills, 3, 114	10	1:33.80	182,400
1989	Easy Goer, 3, 123	P. Day	Diamond Donnie, 3, 114	Expensive Decision, 3, 118	9	1:32.40	168,300
1988	Private Terms, 3, 126	C. W. Antley	Seeking the Gold, 3, 114	Perfect Spy, 3, 121	4	1:34.80	181,500
1987	Gone West, 3, 114	R. G. Davis	Shawklit Won, 3, 114	Gulch, 3, 123	9	1:34.60	190,200
1986	Mogambo, 3, 121	J. Vasquez	‡Tasso, 3, 123	Zabaleta, 3, 121	9	1:34.60	214,200
1985	Eternal Prince, 3, 114	R. Migliore	Pancho Villa, 3, 121	El Basco, 3, 114	7	1:34.40	147,840
1984	Bear Hunt, 3, 114	D. MacBeth	Lt. Flag, 3, 123	On the Sauce, 3, 114	9	1:40.40	136,440
1983	Assault Landing, 3, 114	V. A. Bracciale Jr.	Bounding Basque, 3, 123	Jacque's Tip, 3, 123	9	1:35.80	50,895
	Chas Conerly, 3, 123	J. Fell	Elegant Life, 3, 123	Law Talk, 3, 114	6	1:36.60	50,535

Year	Winner	Jockey	Second	Third	Strs	Time	1st Purse
1982	Air Forbes Won, 3, 114	M. Venezia	Shimatoree, 3, 123	Big Brave Rock, 3, 114	8	1:35.60	$50,760
1981	Proud Appeal, 3, 123	J. Fell	Cure the Blues, 3, 126	Noble Nashua, 3, 123	6	1:33.60	50,040
1980	Colonel Moran, 3, 123	J. Velasquez	Dunham's Gift, 3, 114	Bucksplasher, 3, 115	12	1:37.00	53,370
1979	General Assembly, 3, 123	J. Vasquez	Belle's Gold, 3, 123	Screen King, 3, 123	8	1:43.60	49,560
1978	Slap Jack, 3, 114	J. Velasquez	Quadratic, 3, 123	Shelter Half, 3, 121	9	1:38.60	33,210
1977	Cormorant, 3, 123	D. R. Wright	Fratello Ed, 3, 121	Papelote, 3, 114	9	1:43.60	32,850
1976	Zen, 3, 116	J. Vasquez	Cojak, 3, 124	Play the Red, 3, 114	10	1:35.60	34,740
1975	Laramie Trail, 3, 121	M. Venezia	Lefty, 3, 121	Kalong, 3, 116	5	1:38.00	27,180
	Singh, 3, 121	A. T. Cordero Jr.	Round Stake, 3, 116	Mr. Duds, 3, 116	8	1:37.00	27,630
1974	Stonewalk, 3, 116	M. A. Rivera	L'Amour Rullah, 3, 116	Wing South, 3, 119	9	1:36.00	27,570
	Rube the Great, 3, 119	M. A. Rivera	Hosiery, 3, 116	Cumulo Nimbus, 3, 116	8	1:35.20	27,420
1973	Secretariat, 3, 126	R. Turcotte	Champagne Charlie, 3, 117	Flush, 3, 117	6	1:33.40	33,330

Named for the unofficial nickname of New York City, "Gotham." Grade 2 1973-'97. Held at Jamaica 1953-'59. 1¹/₁₆ miles 1953-'59, 1977, 1979. 1 mile 70 yards 1984, 2003. Four-year-olds and up 1958. Two divisions 1974-'75, 1983. Dead heat for first 1992. ‡Groovy finished second, DQ to fifth, 1986. Equaled track record 1973.

Gravesend Handicap

Grade 3 in 2005. Aqueduct, three-year-olds and up, 6 furlongs, dirt. Held December 19, 2004, with a gross value of $109,400. First held in 1959. First graded in 1988. Stakes record 1:08.60 (1973 Petrograd).

Year	Winner	Jockey	Second	Third	Strs	Time	1st Purse
2004	Don Six, 4, 114	M. J. Luzzi	Mr. Whitestone, 4, 114	Papua, 5, 114	6	1:08.97	$65,640
2003	Shake You Down, 5, 124	M. J. Luzzi	Way to the Top, 5, 114	Gators N Bears, 3, 115	7	1:09.55	65,400
2002	Multiple Choice, 4, 118	V. Carrero	Sing Me Back Home, 4, 114	Gold I. D., 3, 113	7	1:09.26	65,520
2001	Here's Zealous, 4, 114	E. S. Prado	Peeping Tom, 4, 120	Say Florida Sandy, 7, 120	6	1:10.37	64,740
2000	Say Florida Sandy, 6, 116	J. Bravo	Liberty Gold, 6, 115	Lake Pontchartrain, 5, 116	11	1:09.80	51,450
1999	Cowboy Cop, 5, 115	A. T. Gryder	Brushed On, 4, 112	Unreal Madness, 4, 116	9	1:09.41	50,370
1998	Say Florida Sandy, 4, 117	S. Bridgmohan	Esteemed Friend, 4, 114	Home On the Ridge, 4, 117	8	1:11.17	50,220
1997	dh- Royal Haven, 5, 122	R. Migliore		Laredo, 4, 115	7	1:10.08	32,670
	dh- Stalwart Member, 4, 118	A. T. Gryder					
1996	Victor Avenue, 3, 119	J. F. Chavez	Royal Haven, 4, 117	Stalwart Member, 3, 114	9	1:09.25	50,325
1995	Cold Execution, 4, 116	J. M. Pezua	Crafty Alfel, 7, 117	Golden Tent, 6, 114	10	1:09.50	50,820
1994	Mining Burrah, 4, 111	J. R. Velazquez	Golden Pro, 4, 115	Won Song, 4, 111	9	1:10.85	51,270
1993	Astudillo (Ire), 3, 108	F. A. Arguello Jr.	Fabersham, 5, 113	Ferociously, 3, 110	8	1:11.91	51,300
1992	Hidden Tomahawk, 4, 111	J. F. Chavez	Smart Alec, 4, 113	Miner's Dream, 5, 114	8	1:08.65	52,920
1991	Shuttleman, 5, 113	A. T. Cordero Jr.	Senor Speedy, 4, 120	Gallant Step, 4, 112	8	1:10.24	52,830
1990	Mr. Nasty, 3, 113	J. D. Bailey	Senor Speedy, 3, 114	Dargai, 4, 113	6	1:09.80	41,220
1989	Never Forgotten, 5, 117	A. Madrid Jr.	Proud and Valid, 4, 111	Garemma, 3, 113	5	1:12.60	40,980
1988	High Brite, 4, 122	A. T. Cordero Jr.	King's Swan, 8, 119	Matter of Honor, 3, 111	6	1:10.60	48,540
1987	Vinnie the Viper, 4, 116	J. A. Krone	King's Swan, 7, 122	Best by Test, 5, 117	6	1:09.60	54,360
1986	Comic Blush, 3, 106	A. Graell	King's Swan, 6, 122	Cutlass Reality, 4, 117	6	1:09.40	41,100
1985	Love That Mac, 3, 111	J. Velasquez	Raja's Shark, 4, 126	Aggressive Bid, 4, 110	6	1:11.00	40,860
1984	Elegant Life, 4, 115	J. Velasquez	Tarantara, 5, 120	Top Avenger, 6, 126	8	1:09.40	42,180
1983	Main Stem, 5, 109	V. Lopez	Havagreatdate, 5, 119	In From Dixie, 6, 113	10	1:14.00	34,440
1982	Chan Balum, 3, 108	J. Samyn	Maudlin, 4, 126	In From Dixie, 5, 120	9	1:11.20	34,320
1981	Lines of Power, 4, 116	D. MacBeth	Stiff Sentence, 4, 110	Bayou Black, 5, 115	6	1:09.60	32,760
1980	Clever Trick, 4, 116	J. Velasquez	Rise Jim, 4, 119	Dr. Blum, 3, 114	6	1:09.60	32,460
1979	Shelter Half, 4, 116	S. A. Boulmetis Jr.	Double Zeus, 4, 114	Tanthem, 4, 126	8	1:11.00	26,220
1978	Half High, 5, 113	A. Santiago	Intercontinent, 4, 114	dh- Bold and Stormy, 6, 107	6	1:09.60	25,755
				dh- Fratello Ed, 4, 119			
1977	Full Out, 4, 116	A. T. Cordero Jr.	Great Above, 5, 114	Jackson Square, 5, 114	7	1:10.20	22,065
1976	Christopher R., 4, 131	W. J. Passmore	Mac Corkle, 4, 115	Gallant Bob, 4, 128	8	1:09.80	26,940
1975	†Honorable Miss, 5, 123	J. Vasquez	Queen City Lad, 3, 111	Piamem, 5, 118	7	1:10.00	16,485
1974	Mr. Prospector, 4, 124	J. Vasquez	Infuriator, 4, 112	Lonetree, 4, 119	8	1:09.00	22,830
1973	Petrograd, 4, 120	A. T. Cordero Jr.	Full Pocket, 4, 120	Delta Oil, 4, 111	6	1:08.60	16,635

Named for old Gravesend Park, a racetrack located in the Coney Island section of Brooklyn, New York. Held at Jamaica 1959-'60. Held at Belmont Park 1974. 7 furlongs 1962. Dead heat for third 1978. Dead heat for first 1997. ‡Unreal Madness finished third, DQ to ninth, 1999. Equaled track record 1973, 1992. †Denotes female.

Gulfstream Park Breeders' Cup Handicap

Grade 1 in 2005. Gulfstream Park, three-year-olds and up, 1³/₈ miles, turf. Held March 6, 2005, with a gross value of $230,000. First held in 1986. First graded in 1990. Stakes record 2:10.73 (1999 Yagli).

Year	Winner	Jockey	Second	Third	Strs	Time	1st Purse
2005	Prince Arch, 4, 119	B. Blanc	Gigli (Brz), 7, 114	Mustanfar, 4, 118	11	2:11.44	$150,000
2004	Hard Buck (Brz), 5, 117	E. S. Prado	Balto Star, 6, 122	Kicken Kris, 4, 118	8	2:11.56	90,000
2003	Man From Wicklow, 6, 119	J. D. Bailey	Just Listen, 7, 113	Sardaukar (GB), 7, 114	10	2:11.62	120,000
2002	Cetewayo, 8, 115	C. H. Velasquez	Band Is Passing, 6, 117	Profit Option, 7, 115	12	2:17.44	120,000
2001	Subtle Power (Ire), 4, 113	P. Day	Whata Brainstorm, 4, 113	Stokosky, 5, 114	9	2:13.50	60,000
2000	Royal Anthem, 5, 121	J. D. Bailey	Thesaurus, 6, 112	Band Is Passing, 4, 116	7	2:11.34	120,000
1999	Yagli, 6, 121	J. D. Bailey	Wild Event, 6, 117	Unite's Big Red, 5, 115	6	2:10.73	120,000

Year	Winner	Jockey	Second	Third	Strs	Time	1st Purse
1998	Flag Down, 8, 120	J. A. Santos	Buck's Boy, 5, 115	Copy Editor, 6, 116	12	2:12.59	$120,000
1997	Lassigny, 6, 116	J. D. Bailey	Flag Down, 7, 117	Awad, 7, 119	11	2:11.33	102,840
1996	Celtic Arms (Fr), 5, 114	M. E. Smith	Broadway Flyer, 5, 117	Flag Down, 6, 118	11	2:13.90	101,880
1995	Misil, 7, 119	J. A. Santos	Myrmidon, 4, 113	Star of Manila, 4, 118	11	2:12.41	94,200
1994	Strolling Along, 4, 117	J. D. Bailey	Conveyor, 6, 119	Awad, 4, 112	6	2:05.01	93,150
1993	Stagecraft (GB), 6, 115	J. D. Bailey	Social Retiree, 6, 116	Futurist, 5, 116	8	2:13.24	93,600
1992	†Passagere du Soir (GB), 5, 114	J. D. Bailey	Colchis Island (Ire), 7, 111	Crystal Moment, 7, 116	14	2:15.71	95,130
1991	Shy Tom, 5, 115	C. Perret	Dr. Root, 4, 112	Runaway Raja, 5, 112	13	2:14.70	94,800
1990	Youmadeyourpoint, 4, 112	D. Valiente	Blazing Bart, 6, 118	Iron Courage, 6, 116	10	1:39.60	94,560
1989	Equalize, 7, 124	J. A. Santos	Posen, 4, 115	Nisswa, 4, 111	11	1:41.00	93,210
1988	Salem Drive, 6, 116	G. St. Leon	Equalize, 6, 112	Kings River (Ire), 6, 113	14	1:40.60	94,530
1987	Bolshoi Boy, 4, 116	R. P. Romero	Arctic Honeymoon, 4, 114	Little Bold John, 5, 115	5	1:44.60	80,286
1986	Sondrio (Ire), 5, 113	J. A. Santos	Chief Run Run, 4, 113	Ends Well, 5, 115	10	1:40.60	80,772

Grade 3 1990-'91. Grade 2 1992-'98. Gulfstream Park Budweiser Breeders' Cup H. 1987-'95. 1¹/₁₆ miles 1986-'90. About 1³/₈ miles 1991. 1¹/₄ miles 1994. Dirt 1987, 1994. Course record 1993, 1999. Equaled course record 1997. †Denotes female.

Gulfstream Park Handicap

Grade 2 in 2005. Gulfstream Park, three-year-olds and up, open, 1¹/₈ miles, dirt. Held March 5, 2005, with a gross value of $300,000. First held in 1946. First graded in 1973. Stakes record 1:54.74 (2005 Eddington).

Year	Winner	Jockey	Second	Third	Strs	Time	1st Purse
2005	Eddington, 4, 115	E. Coa	Pies Prospect, 4, 113	Zakocity, 4, 117	8	1:54.74	$180,000
2004	Jackpot, 6, 113	J. Bravo	Newfoundland, 4, 116	The Lady's Groom, 4, 113	6	2:02.80	180,000
2003	Hero's Tribute, 5, 115	E. S. Prado	Aeneas, 4, 115	Puzzlement, 4, 114	8	2:04.24	180,000
2002	Hal's Hope, 5, 113	R. I. Velez	Mongoose, 4, 115	Sir Bear, 9, 117	5	2:02.91	180,000
2001	Sir Bear, 8, 116	E. Coa	Pleasant Breeze, 6, 115	Broken Vow, 4, 114	9	2:02.96	120,000
2000	Behrens, 6, 120	J. F. Chavez	Adonis, 4, 115	With Anticipation, 5, 113	6	2:01.79	210,000
1999	Behrens, 5, 114	J. F. Chavez	Archers Bay, 4, 114	Sir Bear, 6, 118	8	2:01.91	210,000
1998	Skip Away, 5, 127	J. D. Bailey	Unruled, 5, 112	Behrens, 4, 114	6	2:03.21	300,000
1997	Mt. Sassafras, 5, 113	J. D. Bailey	Skip Away, 4, 122	Tejano Run, 5, 114	6	2:02.39	300,000
1996	Wekiva Springs, 5, 117	J. D. Bailey	Star Standard, 4, 112	Powerful Punch, 7, 113	8	2:03.18	300,000
1995	Cigar, 5, 118	J. D. Bailey	Pride of Burkaan, 5, 114	Mahogany Hall, 4, 113	11	2:02.95	300,000
1994	Scuffleburg, 5, 113	C. Perret	Migrating Moon, 4, 114	Wallenda, 4, 117	10	2:00.46	300,000
1993	Devil His Due, 4, 113	W. H. McCauley	Offbeat, 4, 112	Pistols and Roses, 4, 114	9	2:01.33	300,000
1992	Sea Cadet, 4, 119	A. O. Solis	Strike the Gold, 4, 115	Sunny Sunrise, 5, 114	6	2:01.79	180,000
1991	Jolie's Halo, 4, 119	R. Platts	Primal, 6, 117	Chief Honcho, 4, 118	8	2:01.04	180,000
1990	Mi Selecto, 5, 114	J. D. Bailey	Tour d'Or, 8, 118	Lay Down, 6, 113	8	2:03.60	180,000
1989	Slew City Slew, 5, 117	A. T. Cordero Jr.	Bold Midway, 5, 113	Cryptoclearance, 5, 123	7	2:03.20	180,000
1988	Jade Hunter, 4, 113	J. D. Bailey	Cryptoclearance, 4, 122	Creme Fraiche, 6, 120	6	2:01.60	180,000
1987	Skip Trial, 5, 118	R. P. Romero	Creme Fraiche, 5, 120	Snow Chief, 4, 124	4	2:02.80	150,000
1986	Skip Trial, 4, 121	R. P. Romero	Proud Truth, 4, 125	Important Business, 4, 113	5	2:03.20	180,000
1985	Dr. Carter, 4, 119	J. Velasquez	Key to the Moon, 4, 120	Pine Circle, 4, 116	8	2:02.00	171,480
1984	Mat-Boy (Arg), 5, 118	J. Valdivieso	Lord Darnley, 6, 109	Courteous Majesty, 4, 114	7	1:59.00	86,700
1983	†Christmas Past, 4, 117	J. Velasquez	Crafty Prospector, 4, 115	Rivalero, 7, 120	12	2:02.60	111,630
1982	Lord Darnley, 4, 113	M. Russ	Joanie's Chief, 5, 113	Double Sonic, 4, 111	9	2:01.80	91,200
1981	Hurry Up Blue, 4, 119	C. C. Lopez	Yosi Boy, 5, 111	Imperial Dilemma, 4, 113	9	2:03.20	114,888
1980	Private Account, 4, 119	J. Fell	Lot o' Gold, 4, 120	Silent Cal, 5, 118	7	2:01.40	100,000
1979	Sensitive Prince, 4, 120	J. Vasquez	Jumping Hill, 7, 126	Silent Cal, 4, 119	7	1:59.20	100,000
1978	Bowl Game, 4, 112	J. Velasquez	True Statement, 4, 108	Silver Series, 4, 126	11	2:00.60	100,000
1977	Strike Me Lucky, 5, 109	J. D. Bailey	Legion, 7, 115	Yamanin, 5, 122	12	2:00.80	88,200
1976	Hail the Pirates, 6, 116	B. Baeza	Legion, 6, 113	Packer Captain, 4, 113	7	2:01.80	73,560
1975	Gold and Myrrh, 4, 114	W. Blum	Proud and Bold, 5, 120	Buffalo Lark, 5, 117	9	2:01.80	74,520
1974	Forego, 4, 127	H. Gustines	True Knight, 5, 123	Golden Don, 4, 118	6	1:59.80	72,360
1973	West Coast Scout, 5, 116	L. Adams	Super Sail, 5, 110	Freetex, 4, 113	10	2:01.00	80,880

Grade 1 1975-2002. Gulfstream H. 1946, 1968. 1¹/₄ miles 1946-2004. Four-year-olds and up 1946. †Denotes female. Held as an allowance race 1949-'51.

Hal's Hope Handicap

Grade 3 in 2005. Gulfstream Park, three-year-olds and up, 1¹/₈ miles, dirt. Held January 8, 2005, with a gross value of $100,000. First held in 1990. First graded in 1993. Stakes record 1:48.57 (2005 Badge of Silver).

Year	Winner	Jockey	Second	Third	Strs	Time	1st Purse
2005	Badge of Silver, 5, 115	J. D. Bailey	Dynever, 5, 117	Contante (Arg), 5, 114	12	1:48.57	$60,000
2004	Puzzlement, 5, 116	J. F. Chavez	Bowman's Band, 6, 118	Stockholder, 4, 114	7	1:42.39	60,000
2003	Windsor Castle, 5, 115	E. Coa	Saint Verre, 5, 114	Najran, 4, 114	8	1:42.33	60,000
2002	Hal's Hope, 5, 112	R. I. Velez	American Halo, 6, 113	Windsor Castle, 4, 112	9	1:42.40	60,000
2000	Dancing Guy, 4, 120	J. D. Bailey	Yankee Victor, 4, 113	Midway Magistrate, 6, 117	8	1:44.94	45,000
1999	Jazz Club, 4, 114	P. Day	Rock and Roll, 4, 113	Hanarsaan, 6, 113	7	1:42.76	45,000
1998	K. J.'s Appeal, 4, 114	J. R. Velazquez	Powerful Goer, 4, 112	Tour's Big Red, 5, 114	7	1:42.34	45,000
1997	Louis Quatorze, 4, 121	P. Day	Strawberry Wine, 5, 113	Exalto, 6, 108	5	1:43.43	45,000
1996	Geri, 4, 114	J. D. Bailey	Halo's Image, 5, 120	Second Childhood, 4, 113	6	1:41.49	45,000

Year	Winner	Jockey	Second	Third	Strs	Time	1st Purse
1995	Warm Wayne, 4, 112	J. D. Bailey	Meadow Monster, 4, 113	Silent Lake, 5, 113	9	1:43.11	$45,000
1994	Forever Whirl, 4, 113	W. H. McCauley	Northern Trend, 6, 113	Royal n Gold, 5, 113	10	1:41.81	45,000
1993	Classic Seven, 5, 116	C. E. Lopez Sr.	Devil On Ice, 4, 115	Keratoid, 4, 111	10	1:43.49	60,000
1992	Peanut Butter Onit, 6, 114	J. A. Santos	Sunny Sunrise, 5, 117	Honest Ensign, 4, 109	7	1:43.78	45,000
1991	New York Swell, 8, 111	J. O. Alferez	Rhythm, 4, 121	Mercedes Won, 5, 112	5	1:42.50	45,000
1990	Big Sal, 5, 119	E. Fires	Twice Too Many, 5, 117	Groomstick, 4, 119	6	1:24.80	20,340

Named for Harold Rose's 2000 Florida Derby (G1) and '02 Gulfstream Park H. (G1) winner Hal's Hope (1997 c. by Jolie's Halo). Formerly named for Brushwood Stable's 1986 Donn H. (G2) winner Creme Fraiche (1982 g. by Rich Cream). Creme Fraiche S. 1990. Creme Fraiche H. 1991-2002. Not held 2001. 7 furlongs 1990. Four-year-olds and up 1990.

Hanshin Cup Handicap

Grade 3 in 2005. Arlington Park, three-year-olds and up, 1 mile, dirt. Held May 28, 2005, with a gross value of $100,000. First held in 1941. First graded in 1983. Stakes record 1:33.20 (1979 Bask).

Year	Winner	Jockey	Second	Third	Strs	Time	1st Purse
2005	Lord of the Game, 4, 117	E. Razo Jr.	Gouldings Green, 4, 115	Nkosi Reigns, 4, 115	8	1:34.60	$60,000
2004	Crafty Shaw, 6, 119	C. Perret	Apt to Be, 7, 119	Kodema, 5, 116	7	1:35.36	60,000
2003	Apt to Be, 6, 117	E. Razo Jr.	There's Zealous, 5, 114	San Pedro, 5, 116	7	1:34.40	60,000
2002	Bonapaw, 6, 121	G. Melancon	Slider, 4, 115	Discreet Hero, 4, 116	7	1:34.00	60,000
2001	Bright Valour, 5, 115	R. Albarado	Apt to Be, 4, 114	Castlewood, 4, 115	8	1:36.21	60,000
2000	Yankee Victor, 4, 122	H. Castillo Jr.	Bright Valour, 4, 114	Desert Demon, 4, 113	5	1:34.97	60,000
1997	Announce, 5, 116	C. C. Bourque	Victor Cooley, 4, 117	Hunk of Class, 4, 116	7	1:36.95	60,000
1996	Golden Gear, 5, 122	M. Guidry	Exclusive Garth, 4, 113	Prospect for Love, 4, 113	10	1:36.13	105,000
1995	Tarzans Blade, 4, 115	P. Day	Swank, 4, 114	Come On Flip, 4, 114	9	1:35.64	45,000
1994	Slerp, 5, 117	E. Fires	Seattle Morn, 4, 116	Dancing Jon, 6, 113	5	1:35.43	60,000
1993	Split Run, 5, 114	E. Fires	Gee Can He Dance, 4, 114	Danc'n Jake, 4, 114	11	1:34.46	60,000
1992	Katahaula County, 4, 114	C. C. Bourque	The Great Carl, 5, 111	Stalwars, 7, 116	9	1:37.27	45,000
1991	Bright Again, 4, 112	P. Day	Secret Hello, 4, 115	Irish Swap, 4, 112	6	1:35.39	45,000
1990	Black Tie Affair (Ire), 4, 119	J. Velasquez	Bio, 4, 112	New Plymouth, 7, 110	4	1:36.00	47,923
1989	Present Value, 5, 114	F. Olivares	Paramount Jet, 4, 114	Sutter's Prospect, 4, 110	8	1:34.40	50,310
1987	Red Attack, 5, 116	M. E. Smith	Taylor's Special, 6, 127	Come Summer, 5, 114	7	1:34.20	48,570
1986	Smile, 4, 121	J. Vasquez	Taylor's Special, 5, 124	Red Attack, 4, 114	7	1:34.00	69,180
1985	Timeless Native, 5, 122	J. E. Tejeira	Par Flite, 4, 115	Harham's Sizzler, 6, 115	7	1:33.80	49,275
1984	Win Stat, 7, 117	D. Pettinger	Le Cou Cou, 4, 116	Harham's Sizzler, 5, 111	8	1:37.80	49,860
1983	‡Hale Herk, 4, 113	R. D. Evans	Thumbsucker, 4, 116	Spoonful of Honey, 4, 115	14	1:36.00	52,560
1982	Summer Advocate, 5, 117	R. P. Romero	Prince Freddie, 6, 109	Fabulous Find, 4, 110	9	1:36.40	49,860
1981	J. Burns, 6, 115	J. D. Bailey	Summer Advocate, 4, 115	Brent's Trans Am, 4, 114	11	1:35.80	68,340
1980	Prince Majestic, 6, 113	G. Patterson	Sea Ride, 5, 114	Braze and Bold, 5, 118	12	1:39.20	69,300
1979	Bask, 5, 112	M. R. Morgan	Bold Standard, 5, 111	Hold Your Tricks, 4, 120	9	1:33.20	22,605
1976	Visier, 4, 120	R. Riera Jr.	Dare to Command, 4, 118	Auberge, 3, 112	7	1:47.00	31,650
1975	Sr. Diplomat, 4, 113	P. Day	Recaptured, 5, 109	Mike James, 5, 111	10	1:44.40	37,440
1974	Our Pappa Joe, 7, 114	R. Cox	Radnor, 4, 113	We're Ready Now, 4, 116	11	1:36.60	45,000
	Henry Tudor, 5, 121	R. Platts	Recaptured, 4, 108	Sharp Gary, 3, 118	10	1:36.00	45,000
1973	Test Run, 7, 112	J. Keene	Chateauvira, 5, 120	Fame and Power, 4, 120	12	1:38.20	21,037

Named in honor of the Japan Racing Association, which conducts a race in honor of Arlington Park. Formerly named for C. V. Whitney's 1932, '33 Horse of the Year, '42 leading North American sire, and '32 Stars and Stripes H. winner Equipoise (1928 c. by Pennant). Equipoise Mile H. 1941-'97. Hanshin H. 2000. Held at Washington Park 1943-'45. Not held 1977-'78, 1988, 1998-'99. Two divisions 1974. ‡Thumbsucker finished first, DQ to second, 1983. ‡Yankee Victor finished first, DQ to fifth, 2000. Equaled track record 1974 (2nd Div.).

Haskell Invitational Handicap

Grade 1 in 2005. Monmouth Park, three-year-olds, 1⅛ miles, dirt. Held August 8, 2004, with a gross value of $1,000,000. First held in 1885. First graded in 1973. Stakes record 1:47 (1987 Bet Twice; 1976 Majestic Light).

Year	Winner	Jockey	Second	Third	Strs	Time	1st Purse
2004	Lion Heart, 3, 121	J. Bravo	My Snookie's Boy, 3, 116	Pies Prospect, 3, 116	8	1:48.95	$600,000
2003	Peace Rules, 3, 121	E. S. Prado	Sky Mesa, 3, 118	Funny Cide, 3, 123	7	1:49.32	600,000
2002	War Emblem, 3, 124	V. Espinoza	Magic Weisner, 3, 118	Like a Hero, 3, 117	5	1:48.21	600,000
2001	Point Given, 3, 124	G. L. Stevens	Touch Tone, 3, 115	Burning Roma, 3, 119	6	1:49.77	900,000
2000	Dixie Union, 3, 117	A. O. Solis	Captain Steve, 3, 118	Milwaukee Brew, 3, 117	9	1:50.00	600,000
1999	Menifee, 3, 122	P. Day	Cat Thief, 3, 123	Forestry, 3, 118	7	1:48.06	600,000
1998	Coronado's Quest, 3, 124	M. E. Smith	Victory Gallop, 3, 125	Grand Slam, 3, 118	6	1:48.60	600,000
1997	Touch Gold, 3, 125	C. J. McCarron	Anet, 3, 120	Free House, 3, 125	5	1:47.60	850,000
1996	Skip Away, 3, 124	J. A. Santos	Dr. Caton, 3, 115	Victory Speech, 3, 121	7	1:47.73	450,000
1995	†Serena's Song, 3, 118	G. L. Stevens	Pyramid Peak, 3, 120	Citadeed, 3, 118	11	1:48.94	300,000
1994	Holy Bull, 3, 126	M. E. Smith	Meadow Flight, 3, 118	Concern, 3, 118	6	1:48.36	300,000
1993	Kissin Kris, 3, 118	J. A. Santos	Storm Tower, 3, 119	Dry Bean, 3, 113	7	1:49.58	300,000
1992	Technology, 3, 120	J. D. Bailey	Nines Wild, 3, 112	Scudan, 3, 113	9	1:48.78	300,000
1991	Lost Mountain, 3, 118	C. Perret	Corporate Report, 3, 120	Hansel, 3, 126	4	1:48.06	300,000
1990	Restless Con, 3, 118	T. T. Doocy	Baron de Vaux, 3, 117	Rhythm, 3, 121	9	1:49.20	300,000
1989	King Glorious, 3, 123	C. J. McCarron	Music Merci, 3, 120	Shy Tom, 3, 116	10	1:49.80	300,000
1988	Forty Niner, 3, 126	L. A. Pincay Jr.	Seeking the Gold, 3, 125	Primal, 3, 117	5	1:47.60	300,000

1987	**Bet Twice**, 3, 126	C. Perret	Alysheba, 3, 126	Lost Code, 3, 124	5	**1:47.00**	$300,000
1986	**Wise Times**, 3, 114	C. P. DeCarlo	Personal Flag, 3, 114	Danzig Connection, 3, 123	9	1:48.60	180,000
1985	**Skip Trial**, 3, 116	J. Samyn	Spend a Buck, 3, 127	Creme Fraiche, 3, 126	7	1:48.60	180,000
1984	**Big Pistol**, 3, 119	G. Patterson	Birdie's Legend, 3, 115	Locust Bayou, 3, 115	6	1:47.80	120,000
1983	**Deputed Testamony**, 3, 124	W. H. McCauley	Bet Big, 3, 116	Parfaitement, 3, 116	10	1:49.20	120,000
1982	**Wavering Monarch**, 3, 117	R. P. Romero	Aloma's Ruler, 3, 126	Lejoli, 3, 112	7	1:47.80	120,000
1981	**Five Star Flight**, 3, 119	C. Perret	Lord Avie, 3, 126	Ornery Odis, 3, 112	6	1:48.40	120,000
1980	**Thanks to Tony**, 3, 111	C. E. Lopez Sr.	Superbity, 3, 124	Amber Pass, 3, 121	8	1:49.40	90,000
1979	**Coastal**, 3, 127	R. Hernandez	Steady Growth, 3, 120	Worthy Piper, 3, 112	5	1:48.80	65,000
1978	**Delta Flag**, 3, 112	D. Nied	Dave's Friend, 3, 120	Special Honor, 3, 118	7	1:53.20	65,000
1977	**Affiliate**, 3, 117	M. A. Rivera	Don Sebastian, 3, 112	Iron Constitution, 3, 118	7	1:50.60	65,000
1976	**Majestic Light**, 3, 122	S. Hawley	Appassionato, 3, 113	Honest Pleasure, 3, 126	10	**1:47.00**	65,000
1975	**Wajima**, 3, 118	B. Baeza	Intrepid Hero, 3, 115	My Friend Gus, 3, 116	8	1:49.60	65,000
1974	**Holding Pattern**, 3, 117	M. Miceli	Little Current, 3, 127	Better Arbitor, 3, 119	10	1:49.80	65,000
1973	**Our Native**, 3, 123	M. A. Rivera	Annihilate 'em, 3, 118	Aljamin, 3, 118	8	1:48.60	65,000

Named for Amory L. Haskell (1894-1966), former president of Monmouth Park. Formerly sponsored by General Motors Corp. of Detroit 1996-'98. Choice S. 1885-'92, 1946-'67. Monmouth Invitational H. 1968-'80. Buick Haskell Invitational H. 1996-'98. Not held 1893-1945. $1\frac{1}{2}$ miles 1885-'92. $1\frac{1}{4}$ miles 1946-'52. $1\frac{1}{16}$ miles 1958-'67. †Denotes female.

Hawthorne Derby

Grade 3 in 2005. Hawthorne Race Course, three-year-olds, $1\frac{1}{8}$ miles, turf. Held October 16, 2004, with a gross value of $250,000. First held in 1965. First graded in 1973. Stakes record 1:44.70 (1991 Rainbows for Life).

Year	Winner	Jockey	Second	Third	Strs	Time	1st Purse
2004	**Cool Conductor**, 3, 115	J. A. Santos	Bankruptcy Court, 3, 115	Crown Prince, 3, 113	10	1:47.89	$150,000
2003	**False Promises**, 3, 115	C. H. Marquez Jr.	Megoman, 3, 115	Beau Classic, 3, 113	11	1:48.48	150,000
2002	**‡Scooter Roach**, 3, 115	J. M. Campbell	Quest Star, 3, 115	Colorful Tour, 3, 117	7	1:58.88	150,000
2001	**Kalu**, 3, 119	J. A. Santos	Proud Man, 3, 119	Rahy's Secret, 3, 115	7	1:50.49	150,000
2000	**dh- Hymn (Ire)**, 3, 115	L. A. Pincay Jr.		Lonely Place (Ire), 3, 113	10	1:53.79	100,000
	dh- Rumsonontheriver, 3, 115	A. J. Juarez Jr.					
1999	**Minor Wisdom**, 3, 115	R. Zimmerman	Air Rocket, 3, 119	Fred of Gold, 3, 113	12	1:49.06	150,000
1998	**Stay Sound**, 3, 115	A. J. D'Amico	El Mirasol, 3, 111	Yankee Brass, 3, 114	11	1:47.54	150,000
1997	**River Squall**, 3, 119	C. Perret	Honor Glide, 3, 122	Blazing Sword, 3, 115	6	1:48.20	120,000
1996	**Jaunatxo**, 3, 122	J. L. Diaz	Trail City, 3, 122	Canyon Run, 3, 122	11	1:47.18	120,000
1995	**Cuzzin Jeb**, 3, 117	C. C. Lopez	Hawk Attack, 3, 122	Seven n Seven, 3, 114	9	1:48.90	90,000
1994	**Chrysalis House**, 3, 115	M. Guidry	Unfinished Symph, 3, 122	Marvin's Faith (Ire), 3, 122	11	1:51.88	90,000
1993	**Snake Eyes**, 3, 122	G. K. Gomez	Lt. Pinkerton, 3, 117	Ft. Bent, 3, 115	12	1:50.28	90,000
1992	**Bantan**, 3, 117	C. C. Bourque	†Words of War, 3, 114	Gee Can He Dance, 3, 117	11	1:48.05	60,000
1991	**Rainbows for Life**, 3, 122	D. Penna	Drummer Boy, 3, 117	Kiltartan Cross, 3, 115	11	**1:44.70**	65,370
1990	**Tutu Tobago**, 3, 113	P. A. Johnson	Take That Step, 3, 122	Seti I., 3, 115	11	1:53.60	64,710
1989	**Broto**, 3, 115	S. J. Sellers	Joey Jr., 3, 117	Chenin Blanc, 3, 115	10	1:53.00	94,350
1988	**Pappas Swing**, 3, 119	E. S. Prado	Djedar, 3, 115	Foolish Intent, 3, 117	11	1:55.80	94,200
1987	**Zaizoom**, 3, 119	E. Fires	Sir Bask, 3, 114	Rio's Lark, 3, 116	7	2:09.80	89,280
1986	**Autobot**, 3, 120	E. Fires	Spellbound, 3, 117	Son of the Desert, 3, 115	11	2:00.40	96,360
1985	**Derby Wish**, 3, 123	R. P. Romero	Day Shift, 3, 115	Explosive Darling, 3, 123	8	2:00.20	64,320
1984	**Pass the Line**, 3, 117	C. H. Marquez	Mr. Japan, 3, 117	Bet Blind, 3, 115	12	1:57.60	66,750
1983	**St. Forbes**, 3, 117	E. Fires	His Flower, 3, 117	Saverton, 3, 117	14	1:44.40	67,200
1982	**Drop Your Drawers**, 3, 118	P. Day	Harham's Sizzler, 3, 118	Northern Majesty, 3, 118	9	1:42.80	64,830
1981	**Jeremy Jet**, 3, 112	C. H. Silva	Loose Thoughts, 3, 112	Recusant, 3, 112	14	1:45.60	67,200
1980	**Jaklin Klugman**, 3, 121	C. J. McCarron	Summer Advocate, 3, 115	Hurry Up Blue, 3, 121	7	1:40.80	64,440
1979	**Architect**, 3, 115	S. A. Spencer	Incredible Ease, 3, 112	Door King, 3, 112	9	1:44.60	48,360
1978	**Sensitive Prince**, 3, 118	J. Vasquez	Gordie H., 3, 112	Esops Foibles, 3, 124	8	1:39.60	73,680
1977	**Silver Series**, 3, 114	L. Snyder	Courtly Haste, 3, 114	Affiliate, 3, 112	14	1:41.20	100,800
1976	**Wardlaw**, 3, 117	J. E. Tejeira	Practitioner, 3, 112	Hurricane Ed, 3, 117	8	1:42.80	82,200
1975	**Winter Fox**, 3, 109	B. Fann	Intrepid Hero, 3, 125	American History, 3, 117	14	1:49.20	93,800
1974	**Stonewalk**, 3, 123	R. Turcotte	Tytus Casella, 3, 116	Mr. Door, 3, 114	10	1:40.60	63,150
1973	**‡Golden Don**, 3, 116	M. Manganello	Impecunious, 3, 123	Cades Cove, 3, 114	10	1:41.20	40,600

Hawthorne Diamond Jubilee H. 1965-'68. Hawthorne Derby H. 1969-'75. Held at Sportsman's Park 1979. $1\frac{1}{16}$ miles 1965-'74, 1976-'84. $1\frac{3}{16}$ miles 1985-'87. Dirt 1965-'83. Dead heat for first 2000. ‡Impecunious finished first, DQ to second, 1973. ‡Flying Dash (Ger) finished first, DQ to seventh for a positive drug test, 2002. †Denotes female.

Hawthorne Gold Cup Handicap

Grade 2 in 2005. Hawthorne Race Course, three-year-olds and up, $1\frac{1}{4}$ miles, dirt. Held October 2, 2004, with a gross value of $750,000. First held in 1928. First graded in 1973. Stakes record 1:58.80 (1970 Gladwin).

Year	Winner	Jockey	Second	Third	Strs	Time	1st Purse
2004	**Freefourinternet**, 6, 112	G. Kuntzweiler	Perfect Drift, 5, 121	Sonic West, 5, 115	7	2:03.34	$450,000
2003	**Perfect Drift**, 4, 122	P. Day	Tenpins, 5, 119	Aeneas, 4, 114	6	2:03.63	450,000
2002	**Hail The Chief (GB)**, 5, 114	J. F. Chavez	Dollar Bill, 4, 114	Parade Leader, 5, 115	5	2:02.80	300,000
2001	**Duckhorn**, 4, 112	R. A. Meier	Lido Palace (Chi), 4, 114	Guided Tour, 5, 116	7	2:01.61	300,000
2000	**Dust On the Bottle**, 5, 112	T. T. Doocy	Guided Tour, 4, 113	Golden Missile, 5, 121	8	2:03.09	300,000
1999	**Supreme Sound (GB)**, 5, 112	R. A. Meier	Golden Missile, 4, 115	Beboppin Baby, 6, 113	8	2:01.19	300,000
1998	**Awesome Again**, 4, 123	P. Day	Unruled, 5, 114	Muchacho Fino, 4, 114	8	2:02.71	240,000
1997	**Buck's Boy**, 4, 114	M. Guidry	Cairo Express, 5, 115	Beboppin Baby, 4, 115	7	2:00.54	180,000

Year	Winner	Jockey	Second	Third	Strs	Time	1st Purse
1996	Come On Flip, 5, 113	C. A. Emigh	Michael's Star, 4, 114	Mt. Sassafras, 4, 120	10	2:03.40	$180,000
1995	Yourmissinthepoint, 4, 113	M. Guidry	Basqueian, 4, 114	Sky Carr, 5, 112	9	2:01.00	150,000
1994	Recoup the Cash, 4, 117	J. L. Diaz	Run Softly, 3, 114	Kissin Kris, 4, 118	11	2:01.99	240,000
1993	Evanescent, 6, 115	A. T. Gryder	Marquetry, 6, 123	Valley Crossing, 5, 117	7	2:02.19	240,000
1992	Irish Swap, 5, 115	B. E. Poyadou	Sea Cadet, 4, 121	Evanescent, 5, 112	8	2:01.12	240,000
1991	Sunny Sunrise, 4, 114	C. W. Antley	Sports View, 4, 116	Discover, 3, 114	14	2:04.10	309,840
1990	Black Tie Affair (Ire), 4, 116	J. L. Diaz	Mi Selecto, 5, 115	Silver Tower, 3, 112	10	2:03.40	307,800
1989	Cryptoclearance, 5, 122	J. A. Santos	Proper Reality, 4, 120	Classic Account, 4, 112	7	2:00.40	305,730
1988	Cryptoclearance, 4, 117	J. A. Santos	Cutlass Reality, 6, 124	Nostalgia's Star, 6, 113	4	2:00.20	303,690
1987	Nostalgia's Star, 5, 117	F. Toro	Savings, 4, 114	Minneapple, 5, 117	9	2:02.00	277,440
1986	Ends Well, 5, 121	R. P. Romero	Harham's Sizzler, 7, 115	Inevitable Leader, 7, 113	6	2:00.60	182,340
1985	Garthorn, 5, 116	R. Q. Meza	Magic North, 3, 115	Leroy S., 4, 114	10	2:01.80	158,220
1984	Proof, 4, 118	E. J. Delahoussaye	Jack Slade, 4, 119	Bounding Basque, 4, 117	14	2:01.20	160,170
1983	Water Bank, 4, 114	C. Lamance	Cad, 5, 116	Gallant Gentleman, 4, 111	13	2:01.40	130,050
1982	Recusant, 4, 122	R. J. Hirdes Jr.	Harham's Sizzler, 3, 116	Irish Heart (Ire), 4, 115	12	2:01.80	98,760
1981	Spruce Bouquet, 4, 119	K. D. Clark	Lord Gallant, 4, 114	Bill Monroe, 3, 119	16	2:04.20	101,760
1980	Tunerup, 4, 125	J. Vasquez	Pole Position, 4, 120	The Trader Man, 4, 112	9	2:00.60	82,590
1979	Young Bob, 4, 114	R. L. Turcotte	All the More, 6, 113	Architect, 3, 121	7	1:51.00	62,460
1977	On the Sly, 4, 121	G. McCarron	Milwaukee Avenue, 4, 114	Romeo, 4, 111	8	2:01.60	75,072
1976	Almost Grown, 4, 110	M. R. Morgan	Teddy's Courage, 3, 113	Romeo, 3, 113	10	2:01.60	86,720
1975	Royal Glint, 5, 124	J. E. Tejeira	Buffalo Lark, 5, 123	Group Plan, 5, 126	5	2:02.20	74,480
1974	Group Plan, 4, 115	J. Velasquez	Buffalo Lark, 4, 117	Billy Come Lately, 4, 119	5	1:58.80	66,120
1973	Tri Jet, 4, 117	B. Baeza	Golden Don, 3, 113	Cloudy Dawn, 4, 114	9	2:01.40	75,720

Grade 3 1997-2000. Hawthorne Gold Cup S. 1928-'35. Budweiser-Hawthorne Gold Cup H. 1985-'86, 1988-'91. Hawthorne Budweiser Gold Cup H. 1987, 1992. Not held 1934, 1936, 1940-'45, 1978. Held at Sportsman's Park 1979. 1 1/8 miles 1979. Equaled track record 1974.

Hawthorne Handicap

Grade 3 in 2005. Hollywood Park, three-year-olds and up, fillies and mares, 1 1/16 miles, dirt. Held May 7, 2005, with a gross value of $108,300. First held in 1974. First graded in 1982. Stakes record 1:41.12 (1993 Freedom Cry).

Year	Winner	Jockey	Second	Third	Strs	Time	1st Purse
2005	Hollywood Story, 4, 119	V. Espinoza	Siphon Honey, 6, 112	House of Fortune, 4, 117	7	1:42.42	$64,980
2004	Summer Wind Dancer, 4, 116	V. Espinoza	Pesci, 4, 115	Miss Loren (Arg), 6, 116	7	1:41.56	65,160
2003	Keys to the Heart, 4, 115	J. Valdivia Jr.	Rhiana, 6, 116	‡Alexine (Arg), 7, 117	4	1:42.97	63,240
2002	Queen of Wilshire, 6, 115	P. A. Valenzuela	Alexine (Arg), 6, 119	Verruma (Brz), 6, 116	5	1:43.16	63,660
2001	Printemps (Chi), 4, 116	C. J. McCarron	Feverish, 6, 119	Brianda (Ire), 4, 109	4	1:43.21	90,000
2000	Riboletta (Brz), 5, 117	C. J. McCarron	Excellent Meeting, 4, 122	Speaking of Time, 4, 111	5	1:42.33	90,000
1999	Victory Stripes (Arg), 5, 115	C. J. McCarron	Magical Allure, 4, 118	Housa Dancer (Fr), 6, 115	4	1:41.73	90,000
1998	I Ain't Bluffing, 4, 118	C. J. McCarron	Fun in Excess, 4, 116	Tomorrows Sunshine, 4, 115	5	1:41.49	63,720
1997	Twice the Vice, 6, 120	C. J. McCarron	Chile Chatte, 4, 115	Listening, 4, 117	7	1:42.72	64,860
1996	Borodislew, 6, 119	C. S. Nakatani	Jewel Princess, 4, 120	Urbane, 4, 118	6	1:41.28	64,200
1995	Paseana (Arg), 8, 122	C. J. McCarron	Pirate's Revenge, 4, 117	Top Rung, 4, 117	7	1:42.40	63,300
1994	Golden Klair (GB), 4, 118	K. J. Desormeaux	Likeable Style, 4, 119	Andestine, 4, 117	5	1:41.41	60,000
1993	Freedom Cry, 5, 117	A. O. Solis	Vieille Vigne (Fr), 6, 114	Miss High Blade, 5, 114	11	**1:41.12**	67,600
1992	Sacramentala (Chi), 6, 117	K. J. Desormeaux	Brought to Mind, 5, 120	Re Toss (Arg), 5, 116	5	1:43.04	61,600
1991	Brought to Mind, 4, 116	P. A. Valenzuela	Fantastic Look, 5, 118	Fit to Scout, 4, 118	6	1:41.50	62,300
1990	Bayakoa (Arg), 6, 125	L. A. Pincay Jr.	Stormy Bal, 4, 119	Fantastic Look, 4, 115	5	1:34.00	61,400
1989	Bayakoa (Arg), 5, 122	L. A. Pincay Jr.	Goodbye Halo, 4, 123	Behind the Scenes, 5, 114	5	1:32.80	61,400
1988	Integra, 4, 120	G. L. Stevens	Invited Guest (Ire), 4, 118	Behind the Scenes, 4, 117	5	1:33.60	59,400
1987	Seldom Seen Sue, 4, 114	C. J. McCarron	Clabber Girl, 4, 116	Tiffany Lass, 4, 123	5	1:33.60	59,900
1986	Dontstop Themusic, 6, 121	L. A. Pincay Jr.	Till You, 5, 115	Fran's Valentine, 4, 122	6	1:35.40	46,950
1985	Adored, 5, 124	L. A. Pincay Jr.	Mitterand, 4, 122	Her Royalty, 4, 118	4	1:34.80	45,350
1984	Adored, 4, 117	F. Toro	Holiday Dancer, 4, 116	Princess Rooney, 4, 118	5	1:41.80	36,200
1983	Marisma (Chi), 5, 115	K. D. Black	Sierva (Arg), 5, 115	Matching, 5, 121	4	1:44.80	30,700
1982	Weber City Miss, 5, 122	S. Hawley	Miss Huntington, 5, 117	Aduana, 5, 114	7	1:42.40	31,750
1981	Save Wild Life, 4, 113	C. J. McCarron	Princess Karenda, 4, 122	Spiffy Laree, 5, 113	6	1:42.80	37,400
1980	Country Queen, 5, 122	L. A. Pincay Jr.	Devon Ditty (GB), 4, 117	Wishing Well, 5, 121	4	1:40.60	30,800
1979	Country Queen, 4, 118	L. A. Pincay Jr.	Grande Brisa, 5, 113	Sisterhood, 4, 120	9	1:41.20	26,600
1978	Sensational, 4, 119	L. A. Pincay Jr.	Up to Juliet, 5, 114	Grand Luxe, 4, 117	10	1:41.80	27,300
1977	Cascapedia, 4, 123	S. Hawley	*Bastonera II, 6, 124	*Star Ball, 5, 121	10	1:40.80	26,850
1976	Swingtime, 4, 118	W. Shoemaker	Call Me Proper, 4, 116	Tuscarora, 4, 113	5	1:41.80	19,150
	Mia Amore, 4, 116	F. Toro	*Bastonera II, 5, 118	Summertime Promise, 4, 119	7	1:41.80	19,950
1975	*Tizna, 6, 122	J. Lambert	Modus Vivendi, 4, 117	Lucky Spell, 4, 121	7	1:20.60	22,600
1974	Tallahto, 4, 119	L. A. Pincay Jr.	Sister Fleet, 4, 116	Lt.'s Joy, 4, 119	9	1:20.60	23,200

Named for the nearby town of Hawthorne, California. Grade 2 1983-2001. 7 furlongs 1974-'75. 1 mile 1985-'90. Turf 1976-'80. Two divisions 1976. ‡Se Me Acabo finished third, DQ to fourth, 2003.

Herecomesthebride Stakes

Grade 3 in 2005. Gulfstream Park, three-year-olds, fillies, 1 1/8 miles, turf. Held March 19, 2005, with a gross value of $100,000. First held in 1984. First graded in 1998. Stakes record 1:46.40 (1997 Auntie Mame).

Year	Winner	Jockey	Second	Third	Strs	Time	1st Purse
2005	Cape Hope, 3, 119	J. A. Santos	Dynamite Lass, 3, 117	Dansetta Light, 3, 121	8	1:48.28	$60,000
2004	Lucifer's Stone, 3, 117	J. A. Santos	Dynamia, 3, 115	Honey Ryder, 3, 117	12	1:52.78	60,000

Year	Winner	Jockey	Second	Third	Strs	Time	1st Purse
2003	Gal O Gal, 3, 117	C. P. DeCarlo	Formal Miss, 3, 117	Devil At the Wire, 3, 117	8	1:42.38	$60,000
2002	Cellars Shiraz, 3, 117	C. H. Velasquez	August Storm, 3, 121	She's Vested, 3, 115	10	1:43.21	60,000
2001	Mystic Lady, 3, 116	J. D. Bailey	Open Minded, 3, 114	Ruff, 3, 118	7	1:46.73	60,000
2000	Gaviola, 3, 114	J. D. Bailey	Solvig, 3, 121	Are You Up, 3, 114	8	1:47.28	45,000
1999	Pico Teneriffe, 3, 118	J. D. Bailey	European Rose, 3, 112	Wild Heart Dancing, 3, 114	8	1:48.82	45,000
1998	Rashas Warning, 3, 118	M. E. Smith	Quick Lap, 3, 116	Runnaway Dream, 3, 116	7	1:51.44	45,000
1997	Auntie Mame, 3, 114	J. D. Bailey	Witchful Thinking, 3, 116	Classic Approval, 3, 114	7	**1:46.40**	45,000
1996	Lulu's Ransom, 3, 116	J. D. Bailey	Cymbala (Fr), 3, 116	Vashon, 3, 114	9	1:47.55	30,000
1995	Clever Thing, 3, 114	C. Perret	Transient Trend, 3, 114	Palliser Bay, 3, 114	6	1:53.06	30,000
1994	Cut the Charm, 3, 116	W. Ramos	Mynameispanama, 3, 113	Tambien Me Voy, 3, 113	11	1:43.72	30,000
1993	Sigrun, 3, 116	R. R. Douglas	So Say all of Us, 3, 116	Supah Gem, 3, 116	8	1:45.79	30,000
1992	Morriston Belle, 3, 118	D. Penna	Snazzle Dazzle, 3, 113	Miss Jealski, 3, 116	11	1:42.23	30,000
1989	Darby Shuffle, 3, 121	C. Perret	Seattle Meteor, 3, 121	Imago, 3, 112	8	1:42.80	36,510
1988	Topicount, 3, 112	J. Samyn	Aquaba, 3, 116	Above Special, 3, 113	15	1:43.20	40,350
1987	Sum, 3, 121	R. Woodhouse	Easter Mary, 3, 113	Dawandeh, 3, 116	8	1:43.20	25,410
1986	Judy's Red Shoes, 3, 114	G. St. Leon	Tea for Top, 3, 112	Minstress, 3, 121	8	1:43.00	35,790
1985	Debutant Dancer, 3, 113	G. Gallitano	One Fine Lady, 3, 118	Affirmance, 3, 118	11	1:42.80	38,640
1984	Delta Mary, 3, 112	F. A. Pennisi	Vast Domain, 3, 114	Ingot Way, 3, 114	10	1:42.00	14,955
	Oakbrook Lady, 3, 112	J. A. Velez Jr.	Illaka, 3, 112	Rain Devil, 3, 112	8	1:42.60	14,655

Named for Pelican Stable's and Mrs. Warren A. Croll Jr.'s 1977 Bonnie Miss S. winner Herecomesthebride (1974 f. by Al Hattab). Not held 1990-'91. 1¹/₁₆ miles 1984-'89, 1992-'94, 2001-'03. About 1¹/₈ miles 1998. Dirt 1993-'95, 2001. Two divisions 1984. Equaled course record 1997.

Hill Prince Stakes

Grade 3 in 2005. Belmont Park, three-year-olds, 1¹/₈ miles, turf. Held June 10, 2005, with a gross value of $114,700. First held in 1975. First graded in 1981. Stakes record 1:45.69 (1997 Subordination).

Year	Winner	Jockey	Second	Third	Strs	Time	1st Purse
2005	Rey de Cafe, 3, 123	J. Castellano	Prince Rahy, 3, 116	Classic Campaign, 3, 116	9	1:49.25	$68,820
2004	Artie Schiller, 3, 120	R. Migliore	Timo, 3, 122	Big Booster, 3, 114	6	1:50.06	66,000
2003	Happy Trails, 3, 120	S. Bridgmohan	Traffic Chief, 3, 114	Chilly Rooster, 3, 114	6	1:50.13	67,860
2002	Van Minister, 3, 114	M. J. Luzzi	Miesque's Approval, 3, 120	Westcliffe, 3, 114	5	1:54.42	65,580
2001	Proud Man, 3, 122	R. R. Douglas	Package Store, 3, 114	Navesink, 3, 118	10	1:48.25	68,760
2000	Promontory Gold, 3, 119	E. S. Prado	Rob's Spirit, 3, 113	Avezzano (GB), 3, 115	7	1:49.15	66,540
1999	Time Off, 3, 113	J. Samyn	Hoyle, 3, 113	Lenny's Ransom, 3, 113	8	1:47.48	66,720
1998	Recommended List, 3, 119	J. F. Chavez	Daniel My Brother, 3, 119	Availability, 3, 119	5	1:49.28	67,800
1997	Subordination, 3, 113	J. R. Velazquez	Rob 'n Gin, 3, 119	Tekken (Ire), 3, 119	8	**1:45.69**	67,200
1996	Optic Nerve, 3, 114	J. A. Santos	Fortitude, 3, 117	Allied Forces, 3, 119	7	1:39.70	66,420
1995	Green Means Go, 3, 117	J. D. Bailey	Smells and Bells, 3, 114	Debonair Dan, 3, 119	10	1:40.33	68,160
1994	Pennine Ridge, 3, 112	J. D. Bailey	Check Ride, 3, 119	Add the Gold, 3, 114	8	1:39.87	50,925
1993	Halissee, 3, 121	J. A. Krone	Proud Shot, 3, 117	Logroller, 3, 114	5	1:40.91	52,020
1992	‡Free At Last, 3, 126	J. D. Bailey	Casino Magistrate, 3, 123	Kiri's Clown, 3, 114	8	1:41.05	53,190
1991	Young Daniel, 3, 114	A. T. Cordero Jr.	Share the Glory, 3, 119	Lech, 3, 114	13	1:39.87	58,050
1990	Solar Splendor, 3, 119	E. Maple	Divine Warning, 3, 119	Bismarck Hills, 3, 114	13	1:41.20	57,870
1989	Slew the Knight, 3, 121	C. W. Antley	Orange Sunshine, 3, 117	Expensive Decision, 3, 121	10	1:41.00	56,520
1988	Sunshine Forever, 3, 114	A. T. Cordero Jr.	Posen, 3, 117	Kris Green, 3, 114	7	1:41.20	85,620
1987	Forest Fair, 3, 119	J. A. Santos	Kindly Court, 3, 117	First Patriot, 3, 121	7	1:42.80	86,220
1986	Double Feint, 3, 121	J. A. Santos	Glow, 3, 121	Jack of Clubs, 3, 114	7	1:41.40	53,190
1985	Danger's Hour, 3, 119	D. MacBeth	Foundation Plan, 3, 119	Exclusive Partner, 3, 114	13	1:40.60	59,310
1984	A Gift, 3, 114	D. MacBeth	Is Your Pleasure, 3, 126	Jesse's Hope, 3, 117	7	1:48.40	43,680
1983	Domynsky (GB), 3, 114	J. D. Bailey	White Birch, 3, 114	Macho Duck, 3, 114	11	1:48.80	36,660
1982	Majesty's Prince, 3, 114	R. Hernandez	A Real Leader, 3, 114	†Honed Edge, 3, 109	8	1:43.40	33,180
	†Larida, 3, 112	E. Maple	Dew Line, 3, 117	John's Gold, 3, 114	8	1:42.60	33,180
1981	Summing, 3, 114	A. T. Cordero Jr.	Stage Door Key, 3, 114	Sportin' Life, 3, 114	10	1:42.40	35,700
1980	Ben Fab, 3, 126	J. Cruguet	Vatza, 3, 113	Don Daniello, 3, 117	8	1:43.40	34,800
1979	Bends Me Mind, 3, 114	J. Velasquez	Crown Thy Good, 3, 115	T. V. Series, 3, 110	11	1:46.00	34,470
1978	Darby Creek Road, 3, 121	A. T. Cordero Jr.	John Henry, 3, 111	Scythian Gold, 3, 111	9	1:35.20	22,605
1977	Forward Charger, 3, 115	J. Vasquez	Stir the Embers, 3, 112	Winter Wind, 3, 112	7	1:34.40	22,575
1976	Flirt Marine, 3, 126	R. Turcotte	Quick Card, 3, 120	Drover's Dawn, 3, 112	9	1:41.20	27,405
1975	‡Don Jack, 3, 110	G. Martens	Annie's Brat, 3, 115	Rapid Impact, 3, 113	9	2:23.20	34,650

Named for Christopher T. Chenery's 1950 Horse of the Year and '50 Jockey Club Gold Cup winner Hill Prince (1947 c. by *Princequillo). Hill Prince H. 1975-'80. Held at Aqueduct 1979-'80, 1982. 1³/₈ miles 1975. 1¹/₁₆ miles 1976, 1979-'86. 1 mile 1977-'78. Dirt 1998. Two divisions 1982. ‡Annie's Brat finished first, DQ to second, 1975. ‡Casino Magistrate finished first, DQ to second, 1992. Course record 1997. †Denotes female.

Hillsborough Stakes

Grade 3 in 2005. Tampa Bay Downs, four-year-olds and up, fillies and mares, about 1¹/₈ miles, turf. Held March 19, 2005, with a gross value of $125,000. First held in 1999. First graded in 2004. Stakes record 1:48.83 (2004 Coney Kitty (Ire)).

Year	Winner	Jockey	Second	Third	Strs	Time	1st Purse
2005	Rizzi Girl, 7, 116	O. Castillo	Sister Star, 4, 116	Noisette, 5, 116	9	1:52.59	$75,000
2004	Coney Kitty (Ire), 6, 116	J. A. Santos	Madeira Mist (Ire), 5, 122	Alternate, 5, 116	12	**1:48.83**	60,000
2003	Strait From Texas, 4, 118	J. L. Castanon	Dedication (Fr), 4, 118	Stylish, 5, 118	11	1:41.14	60,000
2002	Platinum Tiara, 4, 116	M. R. Cruz	Step With Style, 5, 116	Ioya Two, 7, 116	11	1:41.34	60,000

Year	Winner	Jockey	Second	Third	Strs	Time	1st Purse
2001	Song for Annie, 5, 116	L. J. Melancon	Megans Bluff, 4, 116	Inside Affair, 6, 122	11	1:41.23	$60,000
2000	St Clair Ridge (Ire), 4, 117	P. Day	Office Miss, 6, 122	Royal Bloomer, 5, 115	11	1:41.17	45,000
1999	Pleasant Temper, 5, 117	P. Day	Sandy Gator, 6, 115	Scatter Buy, 4, 115	10	1:42.62	34,800

Named for Hillsborough County, Florida; the city of Tampa is the county seat. Three-year-olds and up 1999-2001. 1¹/₁₆ miles 1999-2003.

Hirsch Jacobs Stakes

Grade 3 in 2005. Pimlico, three-year-olds, 6 furlongs, dirt. Held May 21, 2005, with a gross value of $100,000. First held in 1975. First graded in 2005. Stakes record 1:10.20 (2001 City Zip, 1990 Collegian).

Year	Winner	Jockey	Second	Third	Strs	Time	1st Purse
2004	Abbondanza, 3, 115	R. A. Dominguez	Bwana Charlie, 3, 122	Penn Pacific, 3, 117	9	1:10.72	$60,000
2003	Mt. Carson, 3, 122	R. A. Dominguez	Gators N Bears, 3, 117	Only the Best, 3, 122	8	1:10.85	60,000
2002	True Direction, 3, 117	R. A. Dominguez	Listen Here, 3, 122	It's a Monster, 3, 117	8	1:10.90	45,000
2001	City Zip, 3, 122	J. F. Chavez	Sea of Green, 3, 119	Stake Runner, 3, 117	7	1:10.20	45,000
2000	Max's Pal, 3, 119	R. Wilson	Ultimate Warrior, 3, 119	Stormin Oedy, 3, 119	8	1:10.32	45,000
1999	Erlton, 3, 122	R. Wilson	Jeanies Rob, 3, 122	Jovial Brush, 3, 117	7	1:10.60	45,000
1998	Klabin's Gold, 3, 115	R. Wilson	Carnivorous Habit, 3, 115	Greenspring Willy, 3, 122	7	1:11.51	32,760
1997	Original Gray, 3, 122	C. H. Marquez Jr.	American Champ, 3, 122	Stroke, 3, 122	9	1:10.85	33,585
1996	Viv, 3, 122	M. T. Johnston	Fort Dodge, 3, 122	Big Rut, 3, 115	6	1:12.11	32,805
1995	Ft. Stockton, 3, 115	J. D. Bailey	Splendid Sprinter, 3, 115	Sittin Cool, 3, 115	6	1:10.29	32,265
1994	Foxie G, 3, 114	E. S. Prado	Distinct Reality, 3, 114	Spartan's Hero, 3, 114	7	1:11.51	32,520
1993	Montbrook, 3, 114	M. J. Luzzi	Without Dissent, 3, 122	Mighty Game, 3, 114	7	1:12.10	32,490
1992	Speakerphone, 3, 114	C. J. Ladner III	Coin Collector, 3, 122	Golden Phase, 3, 122	7	1:10.52	26,160
1991	Ameri Run, 3, 119	G. W. Hutton	Exclusive Dove, 3, 114	Nasty Hero, 3, 122	6	1:10.86	25,860
1990	Collegian, 3, 117	H. Vega	Hit the Mahagoney, 3, 117	Bardland, 3, 114	5	1:10.20	26,115
1989	Pulverizing, 3, 122	A. T. Stacy	Jimmy Coggins, 3, 114	Midas, 3, 114	6	1:11.20	32,460
1988	Finder's Choice, 3, 122	J. A. Santos	†Smarter Than, 3, 117	Royal Highlander, 3, 110	4	1:12.20	27,820
1987	Green Book, 3, 122	G. W. Hutton	Judge's Dream, 3, 110	Silano, 3, 122	7	1:11.80	28,730
1986	Super Delight, 3, 122	J. Nied Jr.	Part Dutch, 3, 113	Fun Bunch, 3, 115	8	1:11.80	21,515
1985	Beat Me Daddy, 3, 122	V. A. Bracciale Jr.	Banjo Dancing, 3, 116	Urigo, 3, 119	7	1:11.80	21,775
1984	Mickey Mall, 3, 119	R. Wilson	Moschini, 3, 116	Bold Flunky, 3, 122	5	1:10.80	20,995
1983	Emperial Age, 3, 116	J. Nied Jr.	Unreal Zeal, 3, 116	Zeb's Hel Cat, 3, 116	5	1:10.80	20,963
1982	Mortgage Man, 3, 122	A. S. Black	Woody's Wish, 3, 116	St. Chrisbee, 3, 122	7	1:10.60	21,353
1981	Century Prince, 3, 122	V. A. Bracciale Jr.	J. D. Quill, 3, 116	Irish King, 3, 119	5	1:10.20	21,027
1980	Amber Pass, 3, 116	D. MacBeth	Pickett's Charge, 3, 116	Peace for Peace, 3, 119	8	1:10.80	21,418
1979	Breezing On, 3, 122	W. J. Passmore	Fearless McGuire, 3, 113	Our Gary, 3, 122	8	1:14.80	21,645
1978	Shelter Half, 3, 119	G. Lindberg	Star de Naskra, 3, 122	Game Prince, 3, 116	9	1:11.00	21,645
1977	Iron Derby, 3, 119	D. R. Wright	Jeff's Try, 3, 116	Tiny Monk, 3, 116	7	1:11.20	17,875
1976	Zen, 3, 116	J. Vasquez	Cojak, 3, 122	Greek Victor, 3, 113	4	1:11.40	17,518
1975	Bombay Duck, 3, 122	M. Aristone	Gallant Bob, 3, 122	Ben S., 3, 116	9	1:11.20	18,622

Named for Racing Hall of Fame trainer Hirsch Jacobs (1904-'70); Jacobs was also a leading breeder and owner. Not held 2005. †Denotes female.

Hollywood Breeders' Cup Oaks

Grade 2 in 2005. Hollywood Park, three-year-olds, fillies, 1¹/₁₆ miles, dirt. Held June 12, 2005, with a gross value of $177,500. First held in 1946. First graded in 1973. Stakes record 1:41.55 (2004 House of Fortune).

Year	Winner	Jockey	Second	Third	Strs	Time	1st Purse
2005	Brooke's Halo, 3, 113	V. Espinoza	Memorette, 3, 116	Cee's Irish, 3, 119	8	1:42.80	$111,900
2004	House of Fortune, 3, 119	A. O. Solis	Elusive Diva, 3, 115	Hollywood Story, 3, 119	5	1:41.55	109,725
2003	Santa Catarina, 3, 116	G. L. Stevens	Buffythecenterfold, 3, 113	Princess V., 3, 114	5	1:41.62	127,320
2002	Adoration, 3, 115	G. K. Gomez	Sister Girl Blues, 3, 114	Saint Bernadette, 3, 115	7	1:43.73	160,080
2001	Affluent, 3, 116	E. J. Delahoussaye	Collect Call, 3, 115	Secret of Mecca, 3, 116	5	1:49.20	90,000
2000	Kumari Continent, 3, 117	K. J. Desormeaux	Queenie Belle, 3, 119	Saudi Poetry, 3, 115	5	1:49.13	90,000
1999	Smooth Player, 3, 117	E. J. Delahoussaye	Excellent Meeting, 3, 121	Nany's Sweep, 3, 116	5	1:48.17	90,000
1998	Manistique, 3, 115	G. L. Stevens	Sweet and Ready, 3, 119	Yolo Lady, 3, 116	5	1:48.40	120,000
1997	Sharp Cat, 3, 121	A. O. Solis	Freeport Flight, 3, 121	Really Happy, 3, 121	5	1:49.60	120,000
1996	Listening, 3, 121	C. J. McCarron	Antespend, 3, 121	Ocean View, 3, 121	4	1:48.70	110,640
1995	Sleep Easy, 3, 121	C. S. Nakatani	‡Bello Cielo, 3, 121	Carsona, 3, 121	5	1:50.24	122,400
1994	Lakeway, 3, 121	K. J. Desormeaux	Sardula, 3, 121	Fancy 'n Fabulous, 3, 121	4	1:46.93	120,000
1993	Hollywood Wildcat, 3, 121	E. J. Delahoussaye	Fit to Lead, 3, 121	Adorydar, 3, 121	9	1:48.48	130,400
1992	Pacific Squall, 3, 121	K. J. Desormeaux	Race the Wild Wind, 3, 121	Alysbelle, 3, 121	7	1:48.07	127,200
1991	Fowda, 3, 121	E. J. Delahoussaye	Grand Girlfriend, 3, 121	Masake, 3, 121	7	1:49.70	94,400
1990	Patches, 3, 121	G. L. Stevens	Jefforee, 3, 121	Pampered Star, 3, 121	8	1:49.80	96,100
1989	Gorgeous, 3, 121	E. J. Delahoussaye	Kelly, 3, 121	Lea Lucinda, 3, 121	6	1:47.80	92,700
1988	Pattern Step, 3, 121	C. J. McCarron	Super Avie, 3, 121	Comedy Court, 3, 121	7	1:48.60	94,700
1987	Perchance to Dream, 3, 121	R. Sibille	Sacahuista, 3, 121	Pen Bal Lady (GB), 3, 121	6	1:48.60	93,200
1986	Hidden Light, 3, 121	W. Shoemaker	An Empress, 3, 121	Family Style, 3, 121	4	1:47.80	116,600
1985	Fran's Valentine, 3, 121	C. J. McCarron	Magnificent Lindy, 3, 121	Deal Price, 3, 121	6	1:47.40	120,300
1984	Moment to Buy, 3, 121	T. M. Chapman	Mitterand, 3, 121	Lucky Lucky Lucky, 3, 121	9	1:49.20	97,150
1983	Heartlight No. One, 3, 121	L. A. Pincay Jr.	Preceptress, 3, 121	Ready for Luck, 3, 121	7	1:49.80	63,900

Year	Winner	Jockey	Second	Third	Strs	Time	1st Purse
1982	**Tango Dancer**, 3, 121	L. A. Pincay Jr.	Faneuil Lass, 3, 121	Royal Donna, 3, 121	9	1:49.00	$66,100
1981	**Past Forgetting**, 3, 121	C. J. McCarron	Balletomane, 3, 121	Glitter Hitter, 3, 121	7	1:50.00	64,100
1980	**Princess Karenda**, 3, 121	D. Pierce	Secretarial Queen, 3, 121	Disconiz, 3, 121	10	1:48.20	67,400
1979	**Prize Spot**, 3, 121	S. Hawley	It's in the Air, 3, 121	Variety Queen, 3, 124	7	1:48.20	63,300
1978	**B.Thoughtful**, 3, 121	D. Pierce	Country Queen, 3, 121	Grenzen, 3, 121	9	1:47.60	65,400
1977	***Glenaris**, 3, 116	W. Shoemaker	One Sum, 3, 116	Taisez Vous, 3, 121	11	1:48.80	68,100
1976	**Answer**, 3, 121	D. G. McHargue	Franmari, 3, 116	I Going, 3, 115	9	1:48.40	49,200
1975	**Nicosia**, 3, 121	W. Shoemaker	Snap Apple, 3, 112	Mia Amore, 3, 112	9	1:48.40	49,400
1974	**Miss Musket**, 3, 124	L. A. Pincay Jr.	Lucky Spell, 3, 121	Modus Vivendi, 3, 121	8	1:47.80	49,550
1973	**Sandy Blue**, 3, 121	D. Pierce	Cellist, 3, 121	Jungle Princess, 3, 112	10	1:48.00	50,550

Grade 1 1976-'96. Hollywood Oaks 1946-2001. Held at Santa Anita Park 1949. 1 mile 1946, 1948-'50. 7 furlongs 1947. 1⅛ miles 1954-2001. ‡Predicted Glory finished second, DQ to fifth, 1975.

Hollywood Derby

Grade 1 in 2005. Hollywood Park, three-year-olds, 1¼ miles, turf. Held November 28, 2004, with a gross value of $500,000. First held in 1938. First graded in 1973. Stakes record 2:01.53 (2004 Good Reward).

Year	Winner	Jockey	Second	Third	Strs	Time	1st Purse
2004	**Good Reward**, 3, 122	J. D. Bailey	Fast and Furious (Fr), 3, 122	Imperialism, 3, 122	13	**2:01.53**	$300,000
2003	**Sweet Return (GB)**, 3, 122	J. A. Krone	Fairly Ransom, 3, 122	Kicken Kris, 3, 122	13	2:04.27	360,000
2002	**Johar**, 3, 122	A. O. Solis	Mananan McLir, 3, 122	Royal Gem, 3, 122	9	1:48.70	300,000
2001	**Denon**, 3, 122	C. J. McCarron	Sligo Bay (Ire), 3, 122	Aldebaran, 3, 122	12	1:49.28	300,000
2000	**‡Brahms**, 3, 122	P. Day	David Copperfield, 3, 122	Zentsov Street, 3, 122	12	1:46.73	300,000
1999	**Super Quercus (Fr)**, 3, 122	A. O. Solis	Manndar (Ire), 3, 122	Fighting Falcon, 3, 122	14	1:45.82	300,000
1998	**Vergennes**, 3, 122	J. R. Velazquez	Dixie Dot Com, 3, 122	Lone Bid (Fr), 3, 122	10	1:49.44	300,000
1997	**Subordination**, 3, 122	J. D. Bailey	Lasting Approval, 3, 122	Blazing Sword, 3, 122	13	1:50.00	300,000
1996	**Marlin**, 3, 122	J. R. Velazquez	Rainbow Blues (Ire), 3, 122	Devil's Cup, 3, 122	14	1:46.08	300,000
1995	**Labeeb (GB)**, 3, 122	E. J. Delahoussaye	Helmsman, 3, 122	Da Hoss, 3, 122	13	1:46.42	220,000
1994	**River Flyer**, 3, 122	C. W. Antley	Dare and Go, 3, 122	Fadeyev, 3, 122	13	1:47.48	220,000
1993	**Explosive Red**, 3, 122	C. S. Nakatani	Jeune Homme, 3, 122	Earl of Barking (Ire), 3, 122	14	1:46.88	220,000
1992	**Paradise Creek**, 3, 122	P. Day	Bien Bien, 3, 122	Kitwood, 3, 122	12	1:47.36	220,000
1991	**Eternity Star**, 3, 122	E. J. Delahoussaye	Native Boundary, 3, 122	Perfectly Proud, 3, 122	11	1:47.30	110,000
	Olympio, 3, 124	E. J. Delahoussaye	Bistro Garden, 3, 122	River Traffic, 3, 122	10	1:47.10	110,000
1990	**Itsallgreektome**, 3, 122	C. S. Nakatani	Septieme Ciel, 3, 122	Anshan (GB), 3, 122	12	1:46.60	110,000
1989	**Live the Dream**, 3, 122	A. O. Solis	Charlie Barley, 3, 122	River Master, 3, 122	13	1:47.00	110,000
1988	**Silver Circus**, 3, 122	G. L. Stevens	Raykour (Ire), 3, 122	Dr. Death, 3, 122	14	1:48.40	110,000
1987	**Political Ambition**, 3, 122	E. J. Delahoussaye	The Medic, 3, 122	Light Sabre, 3, 122	7	1:48.20	101,600
	Stately Don, 3, 122	J. Vasquez	Lockton (GB), 3, 122	Noble Minstrel, 3, 122	9	1:47.40	104,600
1986	**Thrill Show**, 3, 122	W. Shoemaker	Air Display, 3, 122	Bold Arrangement (GB), 3, 122	11	1:46.80	146,000
	Spellbound, 3, 122	R. Sibille	Double Feint, 3, 122	Bruiser (GB), 3, 122	12	1:46.80	147,500
1985	**Charming Duke (Fr)**, 3, 122	Y. Saint-Martin	Herat, 3, 122	†La Koumia (Fr), 3, 119	13	1:46.80	171,225
	Slew the Dragon, 3, 122	J. Velasquez	†Savannah Dancer, 3, 119	Catane, 3, 122	12	1:46.40	168,725
1984	**Procida**, 3, 122	C. B. Asmussen	Executive Pride (Ire), 3, 122	†Reine Mathilde, 3, 122	9	1:48.40	139,250
	Foscarini (Ire), 3, 122	D. G. McHargue	Roving Minstrel, 3, 122	Bean Bag, 3, 122	10	1:47.40	140,750
1983	**†Royal Heroine (Ire)**, 3, 119	F. Toro	Interco, 3, 122	Pac Mania, 3, 122	11	1:48.20	87,400
	Ginger Brink (Fr), 3, 122	F. Toro	Fifth Division, 3, 122	Hur Power, 3, 122	10	1:49.20	86,400
1982	**Racing Is Fun**, 3, 122	W. Shoemaker	Prince Spellbound, 3, 122	Uncle Jeff, 3, 122	7	1:47.20	67,150
	Victory Zone, 3, 122	E. J. Delahoussaye	The Hague, 3, 122	Ask Me, 3, 122	9	1:47.80	70,150
1981	**†De La Rose**, 3, 119	E. Maple	High Counsel, 3, 122	Lord Trendy (Ire), 3, 122	8	1:47.60	68,700
	Silveyville, 3, 122	D. Winick	French Sassafras (GB), 3, 122	Waterway Drive, 3, 122	8	1:48.20	68,700
1980	**Codex**, 3, 122	E. J. Delahoussaye	Rumbo, 3, 122	Cactus Road, 3, 122	11	1:47.40	195,250
1979	**Flying Paster**, 3, 122	D. Pierce	Switch Partners, 3, 122	Shamgo, 3, 122	7	1:47.60	166,750
1978	**Affirmed**, 3, 122	S. Cauthen	Think Snow, 3, 122	Radar Ahead, 3, 122	9	1:48.20	174,750
1977	**Steve's Friend**, 3, 122	R. Hernandez	Affiliate, 3, 122	*Habitony, 3, 122	10	1:47.80	140,000
1976	**Crystal Water**, 3, 122	W. Shoemaker	Life's Hope, 3, 122	Double Discount, 3, 122	11	1:48.40	152,750
1975	**Intrepid Hero**, 3, 122	D. Pierce	Terete, 3, 122	Sibirri, 3, 126	7	2:29.00	90,000
1974	**Agitate**, 3, 126	W. Shoemaker	Stardust Mel, 3, 126	Top Crowd, 3, 126	9	2:28.20	90,000
1973	***Amen II**, 3, 126	E. Belmonte	Groshawk, 3, 126	Kirrary, 3, 126	11	2:27.80	90,000

Formerly sponsored by the Crown Royal Co. of Stamford, Connecticut 1995-'96. Formerly sponsored by Early Times Distillery Co. of Louisville 1998-2000. Westerner S. 1948-'58. Held at Santa Anita Park 1949. Not held 1942-'44. 1⅛ miles 1945, 1950, 1976-2002. 1½ miles 1973-'75. Dirt 1938-'72, 1976-'80. Two divisions 1981-'87, 1991. ‡Designed for Luck finished first, DQ to fifth, 2000. †Denotes female.

Hollywood Futurity

Grade 1 in 2005. Hollywood Park, two-year-olds, 1¹⁄₁₆ miles, dirt. Held December 18, 2004, with a gross value of $449,500. First held in 1981. First graded in 1983. Stakes record 1:40.74 (1994 Afternoon Deelites).

Year	Winner	Jockey	Second	Third	Strs	Time	1st Purse
2004	**Declan's Moon**, 2, 121	V. Espinoza	Giacomo, 2, 121	Wilko, 2, 121	7	1:41.63	$269,700
2003	**Lion Heart**, 2, 121	M. E. Smith	St Averil, 2, 121	That's an Outrage, 2, 121	5	1:42.80	225,600
2002	**Toccet**, 2, 121	J. F. Chavez	‡Domestic Dispute, 2, 121	Coax Kid, 2, 121	6	1:41.26	243,900
2001	**Siphonic**, 2, 121	J. D. Bailey	Fonz's, 2, 121	Officer, 2, 121	8	1:42.09	274,050
2000	**Point Given**, 2, 121	G. L. Stevens	Millennium Wind, 2, 121	Golden Ticket, 2, 121	4	1:42.21	204,300

1999	**Captain Steve**, 2, 121	R. Albarado	High Yield, 2, 121	Cosine, 2, 121	6	1:43.27	$245,400
1998	**Tactical Cat**, 2, 121	L. A. Pincay Jr.	Prime Timber, 2, 121	Premier Property, 2, 121	5	1:42.63	235,800
1997	**Real Quiet**, 2, 121	K. J. Desormeaux	Artax, 2, 121	Nationalore, 2, 121	11	1:41.34	282,120
1996	**Swiss Yodeler**, 2, 121	A. O. Solis	Stolen Gold, 2, 121	In Excessive Bull, 2, 121	13	1:42.70	348,510
1995	**Matty G**, 2, 121	A. O. Solis	Odyle, 2, 121	Ayrton S, 2, 121	7	1:41.75	275,000
1994	**Afternoon Deelites**, 2, 121	K. J. Desormeaux	Thunder Gulch, 2, 121	A. J. Jett, 2, 121	5	1:40.74	275,000
1993	**Valiant Nature**, 2, 121	L. A. Pincay Jr.	Brocco, 2, 121	Flying Sensation, 2, 121	6	1:40.78	275,000
1992	**River Special**, 2, 121	L. A. Pincay Jr.	Stuka, 2, 121	Earl of Barking (Ire), 2, 121	6	1:43.27	275,000
1991	**A.P. Indy**, 2, 121	E. J. Delahoussaye	Dance Floor, 2, 121	Casual Lies, 2, 121	14	1:42.85	329,780
1990	**Best Pal**, 2, 121	J. A. Santos	General Meeting, 2, 121	Reign Road, 2, 121	9	1:35.40	495,000
1989	**Grand Canyon**, 2, 121	A. T. Cordero Jr.	Farma Way, 2, 121	Silver Ending, 2, 121	9	1:33.00	495,000
1988	**King Glorious**, 2, 121	C. J. McCarron	Music Merci, 2, 121	Hawkster, 2, 121	10	1:35.60	495,000
1987	**Tejano**, 2, 121	L. A. Pincay Jr.	Purdue King, 2, 121	Regal Classic, 2, 121	8	1:34.60	495,000
1986	**Temperate Sil**, 2, 121	W. Shoemaker	Alysheba, 2, 121	Masterful Advocate, 2, 121	12	1:36.20	495,000
1985	**Snow Chief**, 2, 121	A. O. Solis	Electric Blue, 2, 121	Ferdinand, 2, 121	10	1:34.20	589,600
1984	**Stephan's Odyssey**, 2, 121	E. Maple	First Norman, 2, 121	Right Con, 2, 121	13	1:43.40	627,000
1983	**Fali Time**, 2, 121	S. Hawley	Bold T. Jay, 2, 121	†Life's Magic, 2, 118	12	1:41.60	549,849
1982	**Roving Boy**, 2, 121	E. J. Delahoussaye	Desert Wine, 2, 121	Fifth Division, 2, 121	9	1:41.80	418,770
1981	**Stalwart**, 2, 121	C. J. McCarron	Cassaleria, 2, 121	†Header Card, 2, 118	12	1:47.80	365,805

1 mile 1985-'90. ‡Kafwain finished second, DQ to fourth, 2002. †Denotes female.

Hollywood Gold Cup Handicap

Grade 1 in 2005. Hollywood Park, three-year-olds and up, 1¼ miles, dirt. Held July 10, 2004, with a gross value of $750,000. First held in 1938. First graded in 1973. Stakes record 1:58.20 (1972 Quack).

Year	Winner	Jockey	Second	Third	Strs	Time	1st Purse
2004	**Total Impact (Chi)**, 6, 124	M. E. Smith	Olmodavor, 5, 124	Even the Score, 6, 124	7	2:00.72	$450,000
2003	**Congaree**, 5, 124	J. D. Bailey	Harlan's Holiday, 4, 124	Kudos, 6, 124	7	2:00.48	450,000
2002	**Sky Jack**, 6, 124	L. A. Pincay Jr.	Momentum, 4, 124	Milwaukee Brew, 5, 124	6	2:01.73	450,000
2001	**‡Aptitude**, 4, 124	L. A. Pincay Jr.	Skimming, 5, 124	Futural, 5, 124	5	2:01.79	450,000
2000	**Early Pioneer**, 5, 124	V. Espinoza	General Challenge, 4, 124	David, 4, 124	9	2:01.40	600,000
1999	**Real Quiet**, 4, 124	J. D. Bailey	Budroyale, 6, 124	Malek (Chi), 6, 124	4	1:59.67	600,000
1998	**Skip Away**, 5, 124	J. D. Bailey	Puerto Madero (Chi), 4, 124	Gentlemen (Arg), 6, 124	8	2:00.16	600,000
1997	**Gentlemen (Arg)**, 5, 124	G. L. Stevens	Siphon (Brz), 6, 124	Sandpit (Brz), 8, 124	6	1:59.26	600,000
1996	**Siphon (Brz)**, 5, 117	D. R. Flores	Geri, 4, 118	Helmsman, 4, 120	8	2:00.50	600,000
1995	**Cigar**, 5, 126	J. D. Bailey	Tinners Way, 5, 118	Tossofthecoin, 5, 118	8	1:59.46	550,000
1994	**Slew of Damascus**, 6, 117	G. L. Stevens	Fanmore, 6, 116	Del Mar Dennis, 4, 116	5	2:00.76	412,500
1993	**Best Pal**, 5, 121	C. A. Black	Bertrando, 4, 118	Major Impact, 4, 114	10	2:00.17	412,500
1992	**Sultry Song**, 4, 113	J. D. Bailey	Marquetry, 5, 118	Another Review, 4, 120	8	2:00.23	550,000
1991	**Marquetry**, 4, 110	D. R. Flores	Farma Way, 4, 122	Itsallgreektome, 4, 119	9	1:59.50	550,000
1990	**Criminal Type**, 5, 121	J. A. Santos	Sunday Silence, 4, 126	Opening Verse, 4, 119	7	1:59.80	550,000
1989	**Blushing John**, 4, 122	P. Day	Sabona, 7, 116	Payant (Arg), 5, 116	7	2:00.40	275,000
1988	**Cutlass Reality**, 6, 116	G. L. Stevens	Alysheba, 4, 126	Ferdinand, 5, 125	6	1:59.40	275,000
1987	**Ferdinand**, 4, 124	W. Shoemaker	dh-Judge Angelucci, 4, 118		11	2:00.60	275,000
			dh-Tasso, 4, 115				
1986	**Super Diamond**, 6, 118	L. A. Pincay Jr.	Alphabatim, 5, 120	Precisionist, 5, 127	6	2:00.40	275,000
1985	**Greinton (GB)**, 4, 120	L. A. Pincay Jr.	Precisionist, 4, 125	Kings Island (Ire), 4, 112	6	1:58.40	275,000
1984	**Desert Wine**, 4, 122	E. J. Delahoussaye	John Henry, 9, 125	Sari's Dreamer, 5, 114	8	2:00.40	275,000
1983	**Island Whirl**, 5, 120	E. J. Delahoussaye	Poley, 4, 116	Prince Spellbound, 4, 120	6	1:59.40	275,000
1982	**Perrault (GB)**, 4, 120	L. A. Pincay Jr.	Erins Isle (Ire), 4, 118	It's the One, 4, 125	8	1:59.20	275,000
1981	**‡Eleven Stitches**, 4, 122	S. Hawley	Caterman (NZ), 5, 120	Super Moment, 4, 117	10	2:00.40	275,000
1980	**Go West Young Man**, 5, 116	E. J. Delahoussaye	Balzac, 5, 120	Caro Bambino (Ire), 5, 116	10	1:58.80	220,000
1979	**Affirmed**, 4, 132	L. A. Pincay Jr.	Sirlad (Ire), 5, 120	Text, 5, 119	10	1:58.40	275,000
1978	**Exceller**, 5, 128	W. Shoemaker	Text, 4, 118	Vigors, 5, 129	7	1:59.20	192,500
1977	**Crystal Water**, 4, 129	L. A. Pincay Jr.	†Cascapedia, 4, 116	Caucasus, 5, 124	12	2:00.00	210,000
1976	**Pay Tribute**, 4, 117	M. Castaneda	Avatar, 4, 123	Riot in Paris, 5, 123	8	1:58.80	150,000
1975	**Ancient Title**, 5, 125	L. A. Pincay Jr.	Big Band, 5, 115	*El Tarta, 5, 115	7	1:59.20	90,000
1974	**Tree of Knowledge**, 4, 115	W. Shoemaker	Ancient Title, 4, 125	War Heim, 7, 114	10	1:59.80	90,000
1973	**Kennedy Road**, 5, 120	W. Shoemaker	Quack, 4, 127	*Cougar II, 7, 128	6	1:59.40	90,000

Formerly sponsored by Sempra Energy of San Diego, California 2000. Hollywood Gold Cup H. 1938-'71, 1973, 1976-'96. Hollywood Gold Cup Invitational H. 1972, 1974-'75; Hollywood Gold Cup S. 1997-2004. Held at Santa Anita Park 1949. Not held 1942-'43. Dead heat for second 1987. ‡Caterman (NZ) finished first, DQ to second, 1981. ‡Futural finished first, DQ to third, 2001. †Denotes female.

Hollywood Juvenile Championship Stakes

Grade 3 in 2005. Hollywood Park, two-year-olds, 6 furlongs, dirt. Held July 17, 2004, with a gross value of $104,272. First held in 1938. First graded in 1973. Stakes record 1:08.60 (1974 Dimaggio).

Year	Winner	Jockey	Second	Third	Strs	Time	1st Purse
2004	**Chandtrue**, 2, 120	V. Espinoza	Actxecutive, 2, 117	Commandant, 2, 115	4	1:10.88	$63,840
2003	**Perfect Moon**, 2, 117	P. A. Valenzuela	Blairs Roarin Star, 2, 117	Ruler's Court, 2, 117	5	1:10.39	61,500
2002	**Crowned Dancer**, 2, 120	A. O. Solis	Outta Here, 2, 117	Chief Planner, 2, 117	7	1:10.10	64,980
2001	**Came Home**, 2, 117	C. J. McCarron	Metatron, 2, 117	A Major Pleasure, 2, 117	6	1:09.20	64,440

Year	Winner	Jockey	Second	Third	Strs	Time	1st Purse
2000	Squirtle Squirt, 2, 120	L. A. Pincay Jr.	Legendary Weave, 2, 117	Drumcliff, 2, 117	5	1:09.98	$63,540
1999	Dixie Union, 2, 117	A. O. Solis	Exchange Rate, 2, 117	High Yield, 2, 115	5	1:09.95	63,780
1998	Yes It's True, 2, 120	J. D. Bailey	O'Rey Fantasma, 2, 117	Worldly Manner, 2, 117	7	1:09.58	61,620
1997	K. O. Punch, 2, 120	A. O. Solis	Old Topper, 2, 117	Majorbigtimesheet, 2, 120	9	1:09.80	66,120
1996	Swiss Yodeler, 2, 120	A. O. Solis	Red, 2, 117	Vermilion, 2, 117	5	1:09.77	61,740
1995	Hennessy, 2, 117	G. L. Stevens	Reef Reef, 2, 117	Desert Native, 2, 117	7	1:09.85	57,400
1994	Mr Purple, 2, 117	C. J. McCarron	†Serena's Song, 2, 117	Cyrano, 2, 117	7	1:10.16	57,600
1993	Ramblin Guy, 2, 117	E. J. Delahoussaye	Swift Walker, 2, 117	Individual Style, 2, 117	8	1:10.09	57,600
1992	Altazarr, 2, 117	E. J. Delahoussaye	Tatum Canyon, 2, 117	Just Sid, 2, 117	6	1:10.01	58,700
1991	Scherando, 2, 117	F. Mena	Prince Wild, 2, 117	Burnished Bronze, 2, 120	7	1:09.70	56,400
1990	Deposit Ticket, 2, 117	G. L. Stevens	Avenue of Flags, 2, 117	Stone God, 2, 117	8	1:09.00	56,500
1989	Magical Mile, 2, 117	E. J. Delahoussaye	Forty Niner Days, 2, 117	Willing Worker, 2, 117	7	1:10.00	61,200
1988	King Glorious, 2, 120	C. J. McCarron	Bruho, 2, 117	Mountain Ghost, 2, 117	9	1:08.80	64,200
1987	Mi Preferido, 2, 117	A. O. Solis	Mixed Pleasure, 2, 120	Purdue King, 2, 117	8	1:10.00	75,900
1986	Captain Valid, 2, 117	C. J. McCarron	Qualify, 2, 117	Jazzing Around, 2, 117	12	1:11.60	73,600
1985	Hilco Scamper, 2, 120	G. L. Stevens	Little Red Cloud, 2, 117	Exuberant's Image, 2, 117	9	1:09.80	64,400
1984	Saratoga Six, 2, 117	A. T. Cordero Jr.	Ten Grand, 2, 117	Spectacular Love, 2, 117	11	1:10.20	90,500
1983	†Althea, 2, 117	L. A. Pincay Jr.	Rejected Suitor, 2, 117	Auto Commander, 2, 117	9	1:09.40	66,200
1982	Desert Wine, 2, 116	F. Olivares	Ft. Davis, 2, 117	Full Choke, 2, 120	6	1:09.60	57,900
1981	The Captain, 2, 117	L. A. Pincay Jr.	Remember John, 2, 115	Helen's Beau, 2, 120	12	1:10.40	64,000
1980	Loma Malad, 2, 122	L. A. Pincay Jr.	Motivity, 2, 122	Bold Ego, 2, 122	13	1:10.00	101,150
1979	Parsec, 2, 122	W. Shoemaker	Doonesbury, 2, 122	Encino, 2, 122	8	1:10.00	89,350
1978	†Terlingua, 2, 119	D. G. McHargue	Flying Paster, 2, 122	Exuberant, 2, 122	8	1:08.80	77,000
1977	Affirmed, 2, 122	L. A. Pincay Jr.	He's Dewan, 2, 122	Esops Foibles, 2, 122	8	1:09.20	60,975
	Noble Bronze, 2, 117	S. Hawley	Little Reb, 2, 122	Tally Ho the Fox, 2, 122	10	1:09.80	62,225
1976	Fleet Dragoon, 2, 122	F. Olivares	Grey Moon Runner, 2, 122	Red Sensation, 2, 117	13	1:09.60	103,250
1975	Restless Restless, 2, 122	S. Hawley	Imacornishprince, 2, 122	Telly's Pop, 2, 122	8	1:09.80	79,350
1974	Dimaggio, 2, 122	L. A. Pincay Jr.	The Bagel Prince, 2, 122	George Navonod, 2, 122	12	1:08.60	74,500
1973	Century's Envoy, 2, 122	J. Lambert	Such a Rush, 2, 122	Tinsley's Image, 2, 122	8	1:09.00	78,550

Grade 2 1973-'96. Starlet Sweepstakes 1938-'39. Starlet S. 1940-'58. Held at Santa Anita 1949. Not held 1942-'43. 5½ furlongs 1938. 7 furlongs 1944. 1 1/16 miles 1950. Two divisions 1977. †Denotes female.

Hollywood Prevue Stakes

Grade 3 in 2005. Hollywood Park, two-year-olds, 7 furlongs, dirt. Held November 20, 2004, with a gross value of $100,000. First held in 1981. First graded in 1985. Stakes record 1:20.63 (2003 Lion Heart).

Year	Winner	Jockey	Second	Third	Strs	Time	1st Purse
2004	Declan's Moon, 2, 122	V. Espinoza	Bushwacker, 2, 114	Seize the Day, 2, 117	8	1:21.74	$60,000
2003	Lion Heart, 2, 114	M. E. Smith	Cooperation, 2, 116	Voladero, 2, 113	5	1:20.63	60,000
2002	Roll Hennessy Roll, 2, 119	A. O. Solis	Red Apache, 2, 115	Hell Cat, 2, 114	7	1:22.68	75,000
2001	Fonz's, 2, 117	L. A. Pincay Jr.	Popular, 2, 113	Labamta Babe, 2, 113	7	1:22.03	60,000
2000	Proud Tower, 2, 122	V. Espinoza	Chinook Cat, 2, 116	Yonaguska, 2, 122	6	1:23.01	60,000
1999	Grey Memo, 2, 115	M. S. Garcia	Magical Dragon, 2, 115	Cameron Pass, 2, 116	6	1:24.44	60,000
1998	Premier Property, 2, 119	D. R. Flores	Select Few, 2, 114	American Spirit, 2, 115	7	1:23.29	60,000
1997	Commitisize, 2, 113	D. R. Flores	Buttons N Moes, 2, 122	Search Me, 2, 117	6	1:21.64	60,000
1996	In Excessive Bull, 2, 115	C. S. Nakatani	Thisnearlywasmine, 2, 118	Constant Demand, 2, 116	5	1:21.54	61,020
1994	Afternoon Deelites, 2, 115	K. J. Desormeaux	Valid Wager, 2, 114	Exetera, 2, 116	6	1:21.25	58,800
1993	Individual Style, 2, 121	C. W. Antley	Egayant, 2, 117	Hunt for Missouri, 2, 114	4	1:20.98	57,500
1992	Stuka, 2, 115	P. A. Valenzuela	Codified, 2, 114	Soul of the Matter, 2, 115	6	1:21.17	46,100
1991	Star of the Crop, 2, 114	G. L. Stevens	Seahawk Gold, 2, 121	Salt Lake, 2, 121	5	1:22.30	57,700
1990	Olympio, 2, 116	E. J. Delahoussaye	Barrage, 2, 115	General Meeting, 2, 114	10	1:21.80	62,600
1989	Individualist, 2, 115	R. G. Davis	Top Cash, 2, 122	Tarascon, 2, 115	6	1:22.20	46,600
1988	King Glorious, 2, 122	C. J. McCarron	Past Ages, 2, 116	Shipping Time, 2, 115	7	1:21.20	47,150
1986	Exclusive Enough, 2, 112	W. Shoemaker	Persevered, 2, 122	Gold On Green, 2, 116	8	1:23.00	45,900
1985	Judge Smells, 2, 117	C. J. McCarron	Raised On Stage, 2, 112	Old Bid, 2, 115	8	1:23.00	46,850
1984	First Norman, 2, 112	W. Shoemaker	Teddy Naturally, 2, 112	Dan's Diablo, 2, 122	6	1:22.20	63,700
1983	So Vague, 2, 115	P. J. Cooksey	Country Manor, 2, 115	French Legionaire, 2, 115	16	1:22.20	76,300
1982	Copelan, 2, 122	J. D. Bailey	R. Awacs, 2, 115	Desert Wine, 2, 122	8	1:21.40	62,850
1981	Sepulveda, 2, 112	C. J. McCarron	Gato Del Sol, 2, 122	Desert Envoy, 2, 112	6	1:22.00	44,625

Sponsored by Jack Daniel's Distillery of Lynchburg, Tennessee 2003. Traditionally used as a prep race for the Hollywood Futurity. Hollywood Prevue Breeders' Cup S. 1990-'95. Jack Daniel's Hollywood Prevue S. 2003. Not held 1987.

Hollywood Starlet Stakes

Grade 1 in 2005. Hollywood Park, two-year-olds, fillies, 1 1/16 miles, dirt. Held December 19, 2004, with a gross value of $389,000. First held in 1981. First graded in 1983. Stakes record 1:41.82 (2004 Splendid Blended).

Year	Winner	Jockey	Second	Third	Strs	Time	1st Purse
2004	Splendid Blended, 2, 120	K. J. Desormeaux	Sharp Lisa, 2, 120	Northern Mischief, 2, 120	7	1:41.82	$233,400
2003	Hollywood Story, 2, 120	P. A. Valenzuela	Rahy Dolly, 2, 120	House of Fortune, 2, 120	6	1:42.87	209,700
2002	Elloluv, 2, 120	P. A. Valenzuela	Composure, 2, 120	Summer Wind Dancer, 2, 120	7	1:42.88	213,900
2001	Habibti, 2, 120	V. Espinoza	You, 2, 120	Tali'sluckybusride, 2, 120	5	1:43.12	214,800
2000	I Believe in You, 2, 120	A. O. Solis	Jetin Excess, 2, 120	Whoopddoo, 2, 120	6	1:43.57	205,050
1999	Surfside, 2, 120	P. Day	She's Classy, 2, 120	Abby Girl, 2, 120	5	1:43.51	228,150

1998	Excellent Meeting, 2, 120	K. J. Desormeaux	Lacquaria, 2, 120	Perfect Six, 2, 120	6	1:42.14	$240,000
1997	Love Lock, 2, 120	K. J. Desormeaux	Career Collection, 2, 120	Snowberg, 2, 120	6	1:42.17	174,600
1996	Sharp Cat, 2, 120	C. S. Nakatani	City Band, 2, 120	High Heeled Hope, 2, 120	8	1:44.69	165,600
1995	Cara Rafaela, 2, 120	C. S. Nakatani	Advancing Star, 2, 120	Chile Chatte, 2, 120	5	1:43.10	137,500
1994	Serena's Song, 2, 120	C. S. Nakatani	Urbane, 2, 120	Ski Dancer, 2, 120	5	1:41.96	137,500
1993	Sardula, 2, 120	E. J. Delahoussaye	Princess Mitterand, 2, 120	Viz, 2, 120	5	1:42.34	139,095
1992	Creaking Board (GB), 2, 120	C. S. Nakatani	Passing Vice, 2, 120	Madame l'Enjoleur, 2, 120	9	1:43.73	137,500
1991	Magical Maiden, 2, 120	G. L. Stevens	Looie Capote, 2, 120	Soviet Sojourn, 2, 120	8	1:42.74	138,105
1990	Cuddles, 2, 120	G. L. Stevens	Lite Light, 2, 120	Garden Gal, 2, 120	10	1:36.20	247,500
1989	Cheval Volant, 2, 120	A. O. Solis	Annual Reunion, 2, 120	Special Happening, 2, 120	9	1:35.60	247,500
1988	Stocks Up, 2, 120	A. O. Solis	Fantastic Look, 2, 120	One of a Klein, 2, 120	8	1:35.00	292,325
1987	Goodbye Halo, 2, 120	J. Velasquez	Variety Baby, 2, 120	Jeanne Jones, 2, 120	7	1:36.20	274,505
1986	Very Subtle, 2, 120	P. A. Valenzuela	Sacahuista, 2, 120	Infringe, 2, 120	6	1:36.00	267,025
1985	I'm Splendid, 2, 120	C. J. McCarron	Trim Colony, 2, 120	Twilight Ridge, 2, 120	9	1:36.00	344,217
1984	Outstandingly, 2, 120	W. A. Guerra	Fran's Valentine, 2, 120	Wising Up, 2, 120	16	1:44.00	386,402
1983	Althea, 2, 120	L. A. Pincay Jr.	Life's Magic, 2, 120	Spring Loose, 2, 120	6	1:43.00	261,250
1982	Fabulous Notion, 2, 120	D. Pierce	O'Happy Day, 2, 120	Stephanie Bryn, 2, 120	9	1:42.40	271,618
1981	Skillful Joy, 2, 120	C. J. McCarron	Header Card, 2, 120	Flying Partner, 2, 120	8	1:43.20	221,238

Young actresses in old Hollywood were traditionally known as starlets before reaching full star status. 1 mile 1985-'90.

Hollywood Turf Cup Handicap

Grade 1 in 2005. Hollywood Park, three-year-olds and up, 1½ miles, turf. Held December 4, 2004, with a gross value of $250,000. First held in 1981. First graded in 1983. Stakes record 2:24.80 (1990 Itsallgreektome).

Year	Winner	Jockey	Second	Third	Strs	Time	1st Purse
2004	Pellegrino (Brz), 5, 126	G. L. Stevens	†Megahertz (GB), 5, 123	License To Run (Brz), 4, 126	9	2:29.73	$150,000
2003	‡Continuously, 4, 126	A. O. Solis	Bowman Mill, 5, 126	Epicentre, 4, 126	7	2:29.01	150,000
2002	Sligo Bay (Ire), 4, 126	L. A. Pincay Jr.	Grammarian, 4, 126	Delta Form (Aus), 6, 126	11	2:27.22	150,000
2001	Super Quercus (Fr), 5, 126	A. O. Solis	Bonapartiste (Fr), 7, 126	Blazing Fury, 3, 122	9	2:29.86	150,000
2000	Bienamado, 4, 126	C. J. McCarron	Northern Quest (Fr), 5, 126	Lazy Lode (Arg), 6, 126	8	2:25.98	240,000
1999	Lazy Lode (Arg), 5, 126	L. A. Pincay Jr.	Public Purse, 5, 126	Single Empire (Ire), 5, 126	7	2:25.85	240,000
1998	Lazy Lode (Arg), 4, 126	C. S. Nakatani	Yagli, 5, 126	Ferrari (Ger), 4, 126	10	2:28.36	300,000
1997	River Bay, 4, 126	A. O. Solis	Awad, 7, 126	Flag Down, 7, 126	12	2:26.47	300,000
1996	Running Flame (Fr), 4, 126	C. J. McCarron	Marlin, 3, 122	Talloires, 6, 126	10	2:28.53	300,000
1995	Royal Chariot, 5, 126	A. O. Solis	Talloires, 4, 126	Earl of Barking (Ire), 5, 126	14	2:25.18	275,000
1994	Frenchpark (GB), 4, 126	C. A. Black	Dare and Go, 3, 122	Regency (GB), 4, 126	11	2:25.66	275,000
1993	Fraise, 5, 126	C. J. McCarron	Know Heights (Ire), 4, 126	Explosive Red, 3, 122	6	2:32.34	275,000
1992	‡Bien Bien, 3, 122	C. J. McCarron	Fraise, 4, 126	†Trishyde, 3, 119	4	2:31.28	275,000
1991	†Miss Alleged, 4, 123	C. J. McCarron	Itsallgreektome, 4, 126	Quest for Fame (GB), 4, 126	7	2:30.00	275,000
1990	Itsallgreektome, 3, 122	C. S. Nakatani	Mashkour, 7, 126	Live the Dream, 4, 126	14	2:24.80	275,000
1989	Frankly Perfect, 4, 126	C. J. McCarron	Yankee Affair, 7, 126	Pleasant Variety, 5, 126	10	2:26.60	275,000
1988	Great Communicator, 5, 126	R. Sibille	Putting (Fr), 5, 126	Nasr El Arab, 3, 122	10	2:34.40	275,000
1987	Vilzak, 4, 126	P. Day	Forlitano (Arg), 6, 126	Political Ambition, 3, 122	14	2:27.00	275,000
1986	Alphabatim, 5, 126	W. Shoemaker	Dahar, 5, 126	Theatrical (Ire), 4, 126	8	2:25.80	275,000
1985	Zoffany, 5, 126	E. J. Delahoussaye	Win, 5, 126	Vanlandingham, 4, 126	13	2:28.40	275,000
1984	Alphabatim, 3, 122	C. J. McCarron	Raami (GB), 3, 122	dh- Both Ends Burning, 4, 126 dh- Scrupules (Ire), 4, 126	12	2:15.80	275,000
1983	John Henry, 8, 126	C. J. McCarron	†Zalataia (Fr), 4, 123	Palikaraki (Fr), 5, 126	12	2:16.60	275,000
1982	Prince Spellbound, 3, 122	M. Castaneda	Majesty's Prince, 3, 122	Lithan, 4, 126	11	2:14.00	220,000
	The Hague, 3, 122	F. Toro	Caterman (NZ), 6, 126	It's the One, 4, 126	13	2:13.40	220,000
1981	Providential (Ire), 4, 126	A. Lequeux	†Queen to Conquer, 5, 123	Goldiko (Fr), 4, 126	10	2:26.80	325,500

Hollywood Turf Cup S. 1989, 1991-2002. Hollywood Turf Cup Invitational H. 1986-'87. 1⅜ miles 1982-'84. Two divisions 1982. Dead heat for third 1984. ‡Fraise finished first, DQ to second, 1992. ‡Epicentre finished first, DQ to third, 2003. †Denotes female.

Hollywood Turf Express Handicap

Grade 3 in 2005. Hollywood Park, three-year-olds and up, 5½ furlongs, turf. Held November 26, 2004, with a gross value of $150,000. First held in 1985. First graded in 1994. Stakes record 1:01.40 (1991 Gundaghia [1st Div]; 1991 Answer Do [2nd Div]).

Year	Winner	Jockey	Second	Third	Strs	Time	1st Purse
2004	Cajun Beat, 4, 122	R. A. Dominguez	Geronimo (Chi), 5, 117	Mighty Beau, 5, 117	9	1:02.08	$90,000
2003	King Robyn, 3, 120	T. Baze	Geronimo (Chi), 4, 116	Golden Arrow, 4, 115	9	1:02.08	90,000
2002	Texas Glitter, 6, 119	J. R. Velazquez	Rocky Bar, 4, 114	Malabar Gold, 5, 118	5	1:01.52	120,000
2001	Swept Overboard, 4, 122	E. J. Delahoussaye	Speak in Passing, 4, 117	Blu Air Force (Ire), 4, 118	10	1:01.86	120,000
2000	El Cielo, 6, 122	C. S. Nakatani	Texas Glitter, 4, 117	Full Moon Madness, 5, 121	7	1:01.73	120,000
1999	Mr. Doubledown, 5, 115	V. Espinoza	Howbaddouwantit, 4, 120	Champ's Star, 4, 115	8	1:01.98	120,000
1998	Soldier Field, 3, 117	R. Wilson	Surachai, 5, 118	Bodyguard (GB), 3, 115	10	1:02.19	120,000
1997	†Advancing Star, 4, 119	K. J. Desormeaux	Latin Dancer, 3, 116	Surachai, 4, 117	9	1:02.68	120,000
1996	Sandtrap, 3, 114	A. O. Solis	Cyrano Storme (Ire), 6, 118	Suggest, 4, 114	9	1:01.46	120,000
1995	Cyrano Storme (Ire), 5, 116	R. R. Douglas	Lakota Brave, 6, 118	Pembroke, 5, 121	9	1:01.64	110,000
1994	Rotsaluck, 3, 118	F. H. Valenzuela	†Marina Park (GB), 4, 116	D'Hallevant, 4, 117	11	1:02.27	82,500
1993	Wild Harmony, 4, 117	C. J. McCarron	Robin des Pins, 5, 119	Monde Bleu (GB), 5, 119	8	1:01.88	110,000
1992	Answer Do, 6, 121	E. J. Delahoussaye	Repriced, 4, 118	Gundaghia, 5, 117	11	1:02.14	110,000

Year	Winner	Jockey	Second	Third	Strs	Time	1st Purse
1991	Gundaghia, 4, 114	C. S. Nakatani	Club Champ, 3, 116	†Sun Brandy, 4, 115	9	1:01.40	$61,875
	Answer Do, 5, 120	E. J. Delahoussaye	Apollo, 3, 115	Cardmania, 5, 116	8	1:01.40	61,875
1990	Answer Do, 4, 115	R. A. Baze	Waterscape, 4, 115	Yes I'm Blue, 4, 118	11	1:07.00	51,200
1989	Summer Sale, 3, 114	B. A. Hernandez	Ofanto, 5, 117	Oraibi, 4, 120	9	1:07.80	51,000
1988	On the Line, 4, 121	G. L. Stevens	Little Red Cloud, 5, 115	Faro, 6, 118	6	1:09.20	47,650
1987	Lord Ruckus, 4, 117	L. A. Pincay Jr.	Bundle of Iron, 5, 114	Faro, 5, 115	7	1:08.20	49,600
1986	Zany Tactics, 5, 114	J. L. Kaenel	Bolder Than Bold, 4, 115	Faro, 4, 113	5	1:07.40	46,100
1985	Temerity Prince, 5, 122	W. A. Ward	French Legionaire, 4, 113	Debonaire Junior, 4, 124	5	1:11.40	38,300

Hollywood Turf Sprint Championship 1985. 6 furlongs 1985-'90. Dirt 1985, 1988. Two divisions 1991. †Denotes female.

Holy Bull Stakes

Grade 3 in 2005. Gulfstream Park, three-year-olds, 1 1/8 miles, dirt. Held February 5, 2005, with a gross value of $150,000. First held in 1972. First graded in 1995. Stakes record 1:50.14 (2005 Closing Argument).

Year	Winner	Jockey	Second	Third	Strs	Time	1st Purse
2005	Closing Argument, 3, 120	C. H. Velasquez	Kansas City Boy, 3, 118	High Fly, 3, 122	8	1:50.14	$90,000
2004	Second of June, 3, 122	C. H. Velasquez	Silver Wagon, 3, 120	Friends Lake, 3, 122	9	1:43.00	60,000
2003	Offlee Wild, 3, 116	M. Guidry	Powerful Touch, 3, 116	Bham, 3, 118	13	1:43.00	60,000
2002	Booklet, 3, 122	E. Coa	Harlan's Holiday, 3, 122	Thiscannonsloaded, 3, 116	7	1:46.16	60,000
2001	Radical Riley, 3, 119	E. O. Nunez	Buckle Down Ben, 3, 119	Cee Dee, 3, 117	8	1:46.06	60,000
2000	Hal's Hope, 3, 112	R. I. Velez	Personal First, 3, 117	Megacles, 3, 113	11	1:44.52	60,000
1999	Grits'n Hard Toast, 3, 114	R. G. Davis	Doneraile Court, 3, 119	Mountain Range, 3, 119	7	1:45.32	60,000
1998	Cape Town, 3, 119	J. D. Bailey	Comic Strip, 3, 114	Sweetsouthernsaint, 3, 119	7	1:44.15	60,000
1997	Arthur L., 3, 122	J. R. Velazquez	Acceptable, 3, 114	Captain Bodgit, 3, 119	9	1:42.93	60,000
1996	Cobra King, 3, 117	C. J. McCarron	Editor's Note, 3, 119	Tilden, 3, 114	7	1:43.42	45,000
1995	Suave Prospect, 3, 119	J. D. Bailey	Bullet Trained, 3, 114	Rush Dancer, 3, 112	8	1:44.03	45,000
1994	Go for Gin, 3, 119	J. D. Bailey	Halo's Image, 3, 114	Senor Conquistador, 3, 112	6	1:41.62	45,000
1993	Pride of Burkaan, 3, 112	J. D. Bailey	Kassec, 3, 112	Jetting Along, 3, 114	8	1:44.74	45,000
1992	Waki Warrior, 3, 114	E. Fires	Scream Machine, 3, 112	Careful Gesture, 3, 113	13	1:44.32	78,258
1991	Shoot to Kill, 3, 112	W. S. Ramos	Shotgun Harry J., 3, 114	Cahill Road, 3, 114	5	1:43.54	120,000
1990	Home At Last, 3, 118	J. D. Bailey	Run Turn, 3, 122	Sound of Cannons, 3, 118	12	1:53.20	140,160
1979	Northern Prospect, 3, 112	J. D. Bailey	Duke of Gansvoort, 3, 114	Coup de Chance, 3, 112	8	1:10.60	18,060
1977	Smashing Native, 3, 114	D. Brumfield	Cheeky Cheetah, 3, 113	Caribe Pirate, 3, 111	7	1:12.60	18,480
1974	Real Supreme, 3, 110	M. Miceli	Eric's Champ, 3, 113	Lord Rebeau, 3, 112	11	1:09.20	20,220

Named for Warren A. Croll Jr.'s 1994 Horse of the Year and '94 Florida Derby (G1) winner Holy Bull (1991 c. by Great Above). Once named the Preview S., the race has been a "preview" of or prep for the Florida Derby (G1). Preview S. 1972-'95. Not held 1973, 1975-'76, 1978, 1980-'89. 6 furlongs 1972-'79. 1 1/16 miles 1991-2004. 1 1/8 miles 1990.

Honey Fox Handicap

Grade 3 in 2005. Gulfstream Park, three-year-olds and up, fillies and mares, 1 1/16 miles, turf. Held March 13, 2005, with a gross value of $100,000. First held in 1985. First graded in 1994. Stakes record 1:38.41 (2005 Sand Springs).

Year	Winner	Jockey	Second	Third	Strs	Time	1st Purse
2005	Sand Springs, 5, 115	J. D. Bailey	Potra Fabulous (Arg), 6, 116	Shaconage, 5, 115	11	1:38.41	$60,000
2004	Delmonico Cat, 5, 116	J. D. Bailey	Coney Kitty (Ire), 6, 115	Madeira Mist (Ire), 5, 117	10	1:41.30	60,000
2003	San Dare, 5, 115	M. Guidry	Calista (GB), 5, 118	Laurica, 6, 114	10	1:46.19	60,000
2002	Batique, 6, 117	J. F. Chavez	My Sweet Westly, 6, 115	Silver Bandana, 6, 114	8	1:49.32	60,000
2001	Spook Express (SAf), 7, 115	M. E. Smith	Please Sign In, 5, 116	Lady Dora, 4, 115	12	1:35.60	60,000
2000	Dominique's Joy, 5, 113	J. D. Bailey	Circus Charmer, 5, 114	Pico Teneriffe, 4, 117	7	1:39.91	45,000
1999	Colcon, 6, 119	J. D. Bailey	Lovers Knot (GB), 4, 115	Tampico, 6, 114	10	1:41.71	45,000
1998	Parade Queen, 4, 118	P. Day	Dispersion, 5, 113	Dance Clear (Ire), 5, 114	12	1:42.10	45,000
1997	Rare Blend, 4, 118	J. D. Bailey	Queen Tutta, 5, 114	Hurricane Viv, 4, 121	6	1:44.28	45,000
1996	Apolda, 5, 116	J. D. Bailey	Class Kris, 4, 116	Alice Springs, 6, 121	11	1:41.55	45,000
1995	Regal Joy, 4, 113	D. Penna	Sambacarioca, 6, 119	Sovereign Kitty, 4, 119	6	1:44.79	36,000
1994	Sambacarioca, 5, 121	J. D. Bailey	Tiney Toast, 5, 114	Marshua's River, 7, 114	6	1:43.41	36,000
1993	Hero's Love, 5, 113	E. Fires	Quilma (Chi), 6, 112	Lady Blessington (Fr), 5, 114	14	1:42.90	30,000
1992	Explosive Kate, 5, 113	D. Penna	Indian Fashion, 5, 114	Belleofbasinstreet, 4, 111	14	1:43.37	30,000
1991	Vigorous Lady, 5, 116	M. A. Lee	Joyce Azalene, 4, 112	Stacie's Toy, 4, 115	8	1:40.30	30,000
1990	Fieldy (Ire), 7, 120	J. D. Bailey	Betty Lobelia, 5, 115	Leave It Be, 5, 117	12	1:37.60	30,000
1989	Vana Turns, 4, 113	R. P. Romero	For Kicks, 4, 112	Stolie, 4, 110	9	1:36.00	30,435
	Fieldy (Ire), 6, 114	C. Perret	Miss Unnameable, 5, 110	Aquaba, 4, 116	8	1:35.80	30,135
1988	Allegedum, 5, 114	A. T. Cordero Jr.	Autumn Glitter, 5, 117	Fama, 5, 111	11	1:35.20	31,515
	Shaughnessy Road, 4, 112	J. A. Velez Jr.	Rally for Justice (GB), 5, 112	Fieldy (Ire), 5, 118	10	1:36.00	31,215
1987	Small Virtue, 4, 114	J. Vasquez	Thirty Zip, 4, 113	Chaldea, 7, 118	10	1:37.00	27,915
	Top Socialite, 5, 119	C. Perret	Give a Toast, 4, 113	Judy's Red Shoes, 4, 116	9	1:37.40	27,615
1986	Gypsy Prayer, 5, 110	R. N. Lester	Four Flings, 5, 112	Isayso, 7, 118	6	1:21.00	29,985
	One Fine Lady, 4, 112	J. A. Velez Jr.	Shocker T., 4, 119	Donna's Dolly, 4, 113	5	1:22.00	29,685
1985	Affirmance, 4, 114	E. Maple	Miss Delice, 3, 114	Deceit Dancer, 3, 116	11	1:35.60	19,617
	One Fine Lady, 3, 116	V. H. Molina	Foxy Deen, 3, 116	Boldly Dared, 3, 114	9	1:34.60	19,257

Named for Dr. Jerome S. Torsney's 1981 Orchid H. (G2) winner Honey Fox (1977 f. by Minnesota Mac). Formerly named for NFL Hall of Fame quarterback Joe Namath. Joe Namath H. 1985-2000. 1 mile 1985, 1987-'89, 2001. 7 furlongs 1986. About 1 mile 1990. 1 mile 70 yards 1991. Dirt 1986, 1991, 1994-'95, 1997. Three-year-olds 1985. Fillies 1985. Two divisions 1985-'89.

Honeymoon Breeders' Cup Handicap

Grade 2 in 2005. Hollywood Park, three-year-olds, fillies, 1⅛ miles, turf. Held June 5, 2005, with a gross value of $163,125. First held in 1952. First graded in 1976. Stakes record 1:46.84 (2005 Three Degrees [Ire]).

Year	Winner	Jockey	Second	Third	Strs	Time	1st Purse
2005	Three Degrees (Ire), 3, 117	G. L. Stevens	Thatswhatimean, 3, 116	Isla Cozzene, 3, 117	13	**1:46.84**	$88,275
2004	Lovely Rafaela, 3, 114	V. Espinoza	Western Hemisphere, 3, 114	Sagitta Ra, 3, 116	8	1:49.96	113,355
2003	Quero Quero, 3, 113	T. Baze	Atlantic Ocean, 3, 121	Sharpbill (GB), 3, 0	10	1:49.34	130,170
2002	Megahertz (GB), 3, 120	P. A. Valenzuela	Arabic Song (Ire), 3, 117	High Society (Ire), 3, 116	7	1:51.97	97,830
2001	Innit (Ire), 3, 117	C. J. McCarron	Live Your Dreams, 3, 116	Beefeater Baby, 3, 115	9	2:01.28	120,000
2000	Classy Cara, 3, 122	I. Puglisi	Kumari Continent, 3, 119	Minor Details, 3, 117	9	1:48.05	90,000
1999	Sweet Ludy (Ire), 3, 116	G. L. Stevens	Tout Charmant, 3, 118	Aviate, 3, 118	7	1:48.05	65,160
1998	Country Garden (GB), 3, 120	K. J. Desormeaux	Janine Rose, 3, 113	Chenille (Ire), 3, 114	6	1:48.74	64,080
1997	Famous Digger, 3, 116	B. Blanc	Freeport Flight, 3, 115	Kentucky Kaper, 3, 117	8	1:47.68	65,460
1996	Antespend, 3, 122	C. W. Antley	Clamorosa, 3, 116	Najecam, 3, 113	9	1:47.50	82,410
1995	Auriette (Ire), 3, 117	E. J. Delahoussaye	Artica, 3, 119	Top Shape (Fr), 3, 118	6	1:41.68	62,100
1994	Work the Crowd, 3, 117	C. J. McCarron	Malli Star, 3, 117	Fancy 'n Fabulous, 3, 118	8	1:39.68	64,700
1993	Likeable Style, 3, 122	E. J. Delahoussaye	Adorydar, 3, 114	Vinista, 3, 113	5	1:46.29	62,200
1992	Pacific Squall, 3, 115	K. J. Desormeaux	Miss Turkana, 3, 119	Morriston Belle, 3, 118	10	1:41.02	67,100
1991	Masake, 3, 115	M. A. Pedroza	Haunting, 3, 114	Now Showing, 3, 116	4	1:42.10	60,400
1990	Materco, 3, 117	E. J. Delahoussaye	Annual Reunion, 3, 119	Slew of Pearls, 3, 117	9	1:41.40	65,800
1989	Hot Option, 3, 116	E. J. Delahoussaye	Formidable Lady, 3, 118	Black Stockings, 3, 113	6	1:40.20	62,600
1988	Do So, 3, 118	A. O. Solis	Pattern Step, 3, 119	Jeanne Jones, 3, 120	5	1:41.80	75,400
1987	Pen Bal Lady (GB), 3, 119	E. J. Delahoussaye	Some Sensation, 3, 117	Davie's Lamb, 3, 115	10	1:41.80	80,300
1986	An Empress, 3, 115	P. A. Valenzuela	Top Corsage, 3, 118	Miraculous, 3, 118	10	1:41.80	66,900
1985	Sharp Ascent, 3, 115	E. J. Delahoussaye	Rose Cream, 3, 117	Akamini (Fr), 3, 119	9	1:41.40	79,400
1984	Vagabond Gal, 3, 118	E. J. Delahoussaye	Heartlight, 3, 119	Allusion, 3, 115	8	1:41.40	65,100
1983	Stage Door Canteen, 3, 118	C. J. McCarron	Saucy Bobbie, 3, 117	Hot n Pearly, 3, 115	8	1:42.00	65,200
1982	Castilla, 3, 116	R. Sibille	Tango Dancer, 3, 117	Skillful Joy, 3, 121	5	1:40.60	61,400
1981	Amber Ever, 3, 114	C. J. McCarron	Verbalize, 3, 117	Bee a Scout, 3, 115	10	1:41.60	50,950
1980	Lady Roberta, 3, 116	S. Hawley	Finance Charge, 3, 112	Street Ballet, 3, 123	8	1:41.80	60,050
1979	Variety Queen, 3, 118	R. Rosales	Prize Spot, 3, 117	Whydidju, 3, 121	8	1:41.60	32,550
1978	Country Queen, 3, 114	M. Castaneda	Collect Call, 3, 116	Equanimity, 3, 121	11	1:43.20	33,700
1977	Joyous Ways, 3, 116	L. A. Pincay Jr.	Penny Pueblo, 3, 113	*Glenaris, 3, 119	8	1:43.00	26,150
1976	Cascapedia, 3, 121	W. Shoemaker	Go March, 3, 117	Dream of Spring, 3, 118	10	1:42.20	26,750
1975	Katonka, 3, 123	L. A. Pincay Jr.	Nicosia, 3, 125	Just a Kick, 3, 118	9	1:42.20	33,150
1974	Bednknob, 3, 115	A. Pineda	Bold Tullah, 3, 118	Bold Ballet, 3, 116	11	1:42.20	20,750
1973	Meilleur, 3, 118	D. Pierce	Sphere, 3, 117	Goddess Roman, 3, 116	10	1:42.40	20,350

Named for Louis B. Mayer's 1946 Hollywood Derby winner Honeymoon (1943 f. by *Beau Pere), once the leading California-bred distaff earner. Formerly named in honor of the nearby Pacific Ocean. Sea Breeze S. 1952-'55. Honeymoon S. 1956-'74. Honeymoon H. 1975-2000. Honeymoon Breeders' Cup Invitational H. 2001. Grade 3 1976-'80, 1983-'97. 6 furlongs 1952-'53. 7 furlongs 1954. 1 mile 1955-'67, 1970. 1¹⁄₁₆ miles 1968-'69, 1971-'95. 1¼ miles 2001. Dirt 1952-'72, 1993. Nonwinners of a race worth $12,500 to the winner 1973-'74.

Honorable Miss Handicap

Grade 2 in 2005. Saratoga Race Course, three-year-olds and up, fillies and mares, 6 furlongs, dirt. Held August 6, 2004, with a gross value of $150,000. First held in 1985. First graded in 1996. Stakes record 1:08.93 (2000 Bourbon Belle [2nd Div]).

Year	Winner	Jockey	Second	Third	Strs	Time	1st Purse
2004	My Trusty Cat, 4, 115	P. Day	Ebony Breeze, 4, 115	Smok'n Frolic, 5, 116	8	1:10.37	$90,000
2003	Willa On the Move, 4, 114	E. S. Prado	Shine Again, 6, 120	Smok'n Frolic, 4, 117	6	1:09.92	64,560
2002	Mandy's Gold, 4, 116	E. S. Prado	Shine Again, 5, 116	Dat You Miz Blue, 5, 114	6	1:09.24	65,100
2001	Big Bambu, 4, 118	J. D. Bailey	Country Hideaway, 5, 118	Dat You Miz Blue, 4, 120	4	1:09.64	63,708
2000	Debby d'Or, 5, 114	S. J. Sellers	Tropical Punch, 4, 115	Katz Me If You Can, 3, 113	9	1:10.11	66,450
	Bourbon Belle, 5, 116	W. Martinez	Cassidy, 5, 114	Go to the Ink, 4, 114	8	**1:08.93**	65,850
1999	Bourbon Belle, 4, 116	P. A. Johnson	Gold Princess, 4, 116	License Fee, 4, 114	10	1:09.53	67,560
1998	Furlough, 4, 113	M. E. Smith	Angel's Tearlet, 5, 114	Dixie Flag, 4, 119	6	1:11.32	48,765
1997	Dancin Renee, 5, 116	R. Migliore	Ashboro, 4, 116	Vivace, 4, 113	6	1:09.16	48,465
1996	Twist Afleet, 5, 119	M. E. Smith	Broad Smile, 4, 116	In Conference, 4, 113	8	1:09.91	49,005
1995	Low Key Affair, 4, 115	P. Day	Classy Mirage, 5, 123	Twist Afleet, 4, 120	5	1:09.67	48,195
1994	Classy Mirage, 4, 122	J. A. Krone	Spinning Round, 5, 119	For all Seasons, 4, 117	8	1:09.72	48,675
1993	Nannerl, 6, 117	J. D. Bailey	Vivano, 4, 117	Via Dei Portici, 4, 117	6	1:15.19	29,040
1992	Nice Assay, 4, 115	C. J. McCarron	Madam Bear, 4, 119	Real Irish Hope, 5, 117	4	1:08.97	31,620
1987	Funistrada, 4, 122	R. G. Davis	Tricky Squaw, 4, 122	I'm Sweets, 4, 122	6	1:36.80	33,300
1986	Wisla, 3, 113	J. Vasquez	Cherry Jubilee, 4, 122	Dancing Danzig, 3, 113	4	1:36.40	32,940
1985	Schematic, 3, 114	R. G. Davis	Ripley, 5, 0	Tiltalating, 3, 114	7	1:10.20	51,570

Named for Pen-Y-Bryn Farm's 1975, '76 Fall Highweight H. (G2) winner Honorable Miss (1970 f. by Damascus). 1996-2003 Grade 3. Honorable Miss S. 1992-'97. Not held 1988-'91. 6½ furlongs 1993. Two divisions 2000.

Hopeful Stakes

Grade 1 in 2005. Saratoga Race Course, two-year-olds, 7 furlongs, dirt. Held August 21, 2004, with a gross value of $250,000. First held in 1903. First graded in 1973. Stakes record 1:21.94 (2001 Came Home).

Year	Winner	Jockey	Second	Third	Strs	Time	1st Purse
2004	Afleet Alex, 2, 122	J. Rose	Devils Disciple, 2, 122	Flamenco, 2, 122	7	1:23.58	$150,000
2003	Silver Wagon, 2, 122	J. D. Bailey	Chapel Royal, 2, 122	Notorious Rogue, 2, 122	7	1:23.47	120,000
2002	Sky Mesa, 2, 122	E. S. Prado	Pretty Wild, 2, 122	Zavata, 2, 122	6	1:23.08	120,000
2001	Came Home, 2, 122	C. J. McCarron	Mayakovsky, 2, 122	Thunder Days, 2, 122	7	1:21.94	120,000
2000	dh- City Zip, 2, 122	J. A. Santos		Macho Uno, 2, 122	11	1:24.52	120,000
	dh- Yonaguska, 2, 122	J. D. Bailey					80,000
1999	High Yield, 2, 122	J. D. Bailey	Settlement, 2, 122	Exciting Story, 2, 122	9	1:22.85	120,000
1998	Lucky Roberto, 2, 122	R. G. Davis	Tactical Cat, 2, 122	Time Bandit, 2, 122	7	1:23.81	120,000
1997	Favorite Trick, 2, 122	P. Day	K. O. Punch, 2, 122	Jess M, 2, 122	7	1:23.87	120,000
1996	Smoke Glacken, 2, 122	C. Perret	Ordway, 2, 122	Gun Fight, 2, 122	8	1:23.63	120,000
1995	Hennessy, 2, 122	G. L. Stevens	Louis Quatorze, 2, 122	Maria's Mon, 2, 122	7	1:23.44	120,000
1994	Wild Escapade, 2, 122	J. F. Chavez	Montreal Red, 2, 122	Law of the Sea, 2, 122	6	1:23.24	120,000
1993	Dehere, 2, 122	C. J. McCarron	Slew Gin Fizz, 2, 122	Whitney Tower, 2, 122	7	1:15.97	120,000
1992	Great Navigator, 2, 122	A. T. Gryder	Strolling Along, 2, 122	England Expects, 2, 122	8	1:15.71	120,000
1991	Salt Lake, 2, 122	M. E. Smith	Slew's Ghost, 2, 122	Caller I. D., 2, 122	9	1:17.74	120,000
1990	Deposit Ticket, 2, 122	G. L. Stevens	Hansel, 2, 122	Link, 2, 122	6	1:16.20	139,680
1989	Summer Squall, 2, 122	P. Day	Sir Richard Lewis, 2, 122	Eternal Flight, 2, 122	8	1:16.80	140,400
1988	Mercedes Won, 2, 122	R. G. Davis	Fast Play, 2, 122	Leading Prospect, 2, 122	6	1:16.60	142,320
1987	Crusader Sword, 2, 122	R. P. Romero	Bill E. Shears, 2, 122	Success Express, 2, 122	5	1:18.60	104,580
1986	Gulch, 2, 122	A. T. Cordero Jr.	Persevered, 2, 122	Flying Granville, 2, 122	4	1:16.40	126,720
1985	Papal Power, 2, 122	D. MacBeth	Danny's Keys, 2, 122	Bullet Blade, 2, 122	10	1:18.40	103,320
1984	Chief's Crown, 2, 122	D. MacBeth	Tiffany Ice, 2, 122	Mugzy's Rullah, 2, 122	9	1:16.00	100,440
1983	Capitol South, 2, 122	J. D. Bailey	Don Rickles, 2, 122	Swale, 2, 122	13	1:17.40	72,720
1982	Copelan, 2, 122	J. D. Bailey	Victorious, 2, 122	Aloha Hawaii, 2, 122	9	1:16.60	69,000
1981	Timely Writer, 2, 122	R. Danjean	Out of Hock, 2, 122	Lejoli, 2, 122	8	1:16.20	51,390
1980	Tap Shoes, 2, 122	R. Hernandez	Lord Avie, 2, 122	Well Decorated, 2, 122	9	1:17.00	51,750
1979	‡J. P. Brother, 2, 122	J. Imparato	Gold Stage, 2, 122	Googolplex, 2, 122	12	1:16.40	50,490
1978	General Assembly, 2, 122	D. G. McHargue	Exuberant, 2, 122	Fuzzbuster, 2, 122	6	1:16.40	48,600
1977	Affirmed, 2, 122	S. Cauthen	Alydar, 2, 122	Regal and Royal, 2, 122	5	1:15.40	48,105
1976	Banquet Table, 2, 122	J. Cruguet	Turn of Coin, 2, 122	P. R. Man, 2, 122	13	1:16.20	51,345
1975	Jackknife, 2, 121	J. Cruguet	Ferrous, 2, 121	Whatsyourpleasure, 2, 121	9	1:16.60	41,625
	Eustace, 2, 121	J. Nichols	Iron Bit, 2, 121	Gentle King, 2, 121	9	1:16.40	41,850
1974	The Bagel Prince, 2, 121	A. T. Cordero Jr.	Knightly Sport, 2, 121	Cardinal George, 2, 121	7	1:16.80	40,995
	Foolish Pleasure, 2, 121	B. Baeza	Greek Answer, 2, 121	Our Talisman, 2, 121	8	1:16.00	41,445
1973	Gusty O'Shay, 2, 121	R. Kotenko	Take by Storm, 2, 121	Prince of Reason, 2, 121	7	1:16.40	50,400

As the first major two-year-old race longer than 6 furlongs, owners are "hopeful" their horses will be able to go a classic distance. Held at Belmont Park 1943-'45. Not held 1911-'12. 6 furlongs 1903-'09. 6½ furlongs 1910-'93. Two divisions 1974-'75. Dead heat for first 2000. ‡Rockhill Native finished first, DQ to sixth, 1979.

Humana Distaff Handicap

Grade 1 in 2005. Churchill Downs, four-year-olds and up, fillies and mares, 7 furlongs, dirt. Held May 7, 2005, with a gross value of $281,750. First held in 1987. First graded in 1990. Stakes record 1:20.70 (2001 Dream Supreme).

Year	Winner	Jockey	Second	Third	Strs	Time	1st Purse
2005	My Trusty Cat, 5, 115	J. Castellano	Molto Vita, 5, 115	Puxa Saco, 5, 115	9	1:21.18	$174,685
2004	Mayo On the Side, 5, 114	P. Day	Azeri, 6, 125	Randaroo, 4, 121	4	1:22.78	174,375
2003	Sightseek, 4, 116	J. D. Bailey	Gold Mover, 5, 119	Miss Lodi, 4, 114	8	1:22.12	137,888
2002	‡Celtic Melody, 4, 114	M. Guidry	Gold Mover, 4, 115	Hattiesburg, 4, 115	9	1:22.98	141,360
2001	Dream Supreme, 4, 120	P. Day	La Feminn, 5, 115	Nany's Sweep, 5, 117	5	1:20.70	102,300
2000	Ruby Surprise, 5, 114	J. C. Judice	Honest Lady, 4, 119	Cassidy, 5, 113	7	1:21.25	102,951
1999	Zuppardo Ardo, 5, 114	S. J. Sellers	French Braids, 4, 115	Prospector's Song, 4, 114	9	1:23.40	105,183
1998	Colonial Minstrel, 4, 115	J. R. Velazquez	Stop Traffic, 5, 117	Meter Maid, 4, 114	11	1:22.12	71,300
1997	Capote Belle, 4, 118	J. R. Velazquez	Hidden Lake, 4, 115	J J'sdream, 4, 117	8	1:22.38	70,060
1996	In Conference, 4, 113	M. E. Smith	Supah Jess, 4, 113	Morris Code, 4, 116	8	1:23.30	72,930
1995	Laura's Pistolette, 4, 114	C. S. Nakatani	Morning Meadow, 5, 113	Traverse City, 5, 114	10	1:22.24	74,425
1994	Roamin Rachel, 4, 118	M. E. Smith	Arches of Gold, 5, 121	Glory's Ghost, 4, 113	7	1:23.83	72,345
1993	Court Hostess, 5, 115	C. J. McCarron	Santa Catalina, 5, 115	Ifyoucouldseemenow, 5, 113	12	1:23.18	56,550
1992	Ifyoucouldseemenow, 4, 120	C. Perret	Madam Bear, 4, 114	Magal, 5, 113	10	1:22.22	56,599
1991	Illeria, 4, 112	P. Day	Nurse Dopey, 4, 117	Tipsy Girl, 5, 115	10	1:23.26	37,603
1990	Medicine Woman, 5, 114	P. Day	Lost Lode, 5, 114	Gallant Ryder, 5, 111	9	1:23.40	36,693
1989	Sunshine Always, 5, 113	P. Day	Littlebitapleasure, 7, 115	Lt. Lao, 5, 119	5	1:24.40	35,425
1988	Le l'Argent, 6, 119	P. Day	Lady Gretchen, 4, 113	Intently, 5, 117	7	1:22.80	36,270
1987	Lazer Show, 4, 120	P. Day	Weekend Delight, 5, 123	Ten Thousand Stars, 5, 118	7	1:22.80	26,442

Races for females are typically referred to as distaff races. Sponsored by Humana Inc., a major medical corporation headquartered in Louisville 1995-2005. Formerly sponsored by Brown & Williamson Tobacco Corp., also headquartered in Louisville 1987-'94. Grade 3 1990-'98. Grade 2 1999-2001. Brown & Williamson S. 1987. Brown & Williamson H. 1988-'94. ‡Gold Mover finished first, DQ to second, 2002.

Hurricane Bertie Handicap

Grade 3 in 2005. Gulfstream Park, three-year-olds and up, fillies and mares, 6½ furlongs, dirt. Held March 20, 2005, with a gross value of $100,000. First held in 2001. First graded in 2005. Stakes record 1:15.38 (2002 Gold Mover).

Year	Winner	Jockey	Second	Third	Strs	Time	1st Purse
2005	Lilah, 8, 114	R. Maragh	Forty Moves, 4, 114	Molto Vita, 5, 118	6	1:15.45	$60,000
2004	House Party, 4, 117	J. A. Santos	Mooji Moo, 5, 115	Zawzooth, 5, 113	10	1:15.55	60,000
2003	Gold Mover, 5, 117	E. S. Prado	Harmony Lodge, 5, 116	Belterra, 4, 116	5	1:15.83	60,000
2002	Gold Mover, 4, 116	E. Coa	Celtic Melody, 4, 114	Mandy's Gold, 4, 114	5	1:15.38	60,000
2001	Swept Away, 4, 121	E. S. Prado	Sahara Gold, 4, 115	Lily's Affair, 5, 115	10	1:09.85	48,720

Named for Richard, Bertram, and Elaine Klein's 2000 First Lady H. (G3) winner Hurricane Bertie (1995 f. by Storm Boot).

Hutcheson Stakes

Grade 2 in 2005. Gulfstream Park, three-year-olds, 7½ furlongs, dirt. Held February 5, 2005, with a gross value of $150,000. First held in 1955. First graded in 1973. Stakes record 1:29.90 (2005 Proud Accolade).

Year	Winner	Jockey	Second	Third	Strs	Time	1st Purse
2005	Proud Accolade, 3, 120	J. R. Velazquez	Park Avenue Ball, 3, 120	Vicarage, 3, 118	6	1:29.90	$90,000
2004	Limehouse, 3, 122	J. R. Velazquez	Deputy Storm, 3, 118	Saratoga County, 3, 116	10	1:22.23	90,000
2003	Lion Tamer, 3, 118	J. R. Velazquez	Strength Within, 3, 116	Crafty Guy, 3, 122	6	1:22.60	90,000
2002	Showmeitall, 3, 118	J. F. Chavez	Monthir, 3, 116	Royal Lad, 3, 116	6	1:26.07	90,000
2001	Yonaguska, 3, 119	J. D. Bailey	City Zip, 3, 122	Sparkling Sabre, 3, 112	11	1:22.63	90,000
2000	dh- More Than Ready, 3, 122	J. R. Velazquez		American Bullet, 3, 114	8	1:21.76	60,000
	dh- Summer Note, 3, 113	S. J. Sellers					
1999	Bet Me Best, 3, 122	J. D. Bailey	Texas Glitter, 3, 119	Cat Thief, 3, 119	7	1:22.33	90,000
1998	Time Limit, 3, 119	J. D. Bailey	Coronado's Quest, 3, 122	Zippy Zeal, 3, 114	5	1:22.53	60,000
1997	Frisk Me Now, 3, 112	E. L. King Jr.	Confide, 3, 117	Crown Ambassador, 3, 117	8	1:22.51	60,000
1996	Appealing Skier, 3, 119	R. Wilson	Unbridled's Song, 3, 119	Gold Fever, 3, 117	5	1:24.72	45,000
1995	Valid Wager, 3, 119	M. A. Pedroza	Mr. Greeley, 3, 117	Don Juan A, 3, 114	7	1:23.51	45,000
1994	Holy Bull, 3, 122	M. E. Smith	Patton, 3, 113	You and I, 3, 119	5	1:21.23	45,000
1993	Hidden Trick, 3, 114	R. P. Romero	‡Great Navigator, 3, 119	Forever Whirl, 3, 113	9	1:23.61	54,108
1992	My Luck Runs North, 3, 113	R. D. Lopez	Sneaky Solicitor, 3, 117	Frosted Spy, 3, 117	9	1:24.95	55,008
1991	Fly So Free, 3, 122	J. A. Santos	To Freedom, 3, 119	Sunny and Pleasant, 3, 114	10	1:23.30	55,527
1990	Housebuster, 3, 119	R. P. Romero	Yonder, 3, 122	Stalker, 3, 114	11	1:24.40	56,787
1989	Dixieland Brass, 3, 114	R. P. Romero	Western Playboy, 3, 112	Tricky Creek, 3, 122	12	1:22.80	58,320
1988	Perfect Spy, 3, 114	J. Samyn	Forty Niner, 3, 122	Notebook, 3, 122	7	1:23.00	52,335
1987	Well Selected, 3, 113	J. Vasquez	Gone West, 3, 114	Faster Than Sound, 3, 119	8	1:23.00	53,376
1986	Papal Power, 3, 122	D. MacBeth	Raja's Revenge, 3, 122	Mr. Classic, 3, 112	10	1:23.80	55,440
1985	Banner Bob, 3, 114	K. K. Allen	‡Creme Fraiche, 3, 114	Do It Again Dan, 3, 114	12	1:21.60	45,720
1984	Swale, 3, 122	E. Maple	For Halo, 3, 114	Darn That Alarm, 3, 112	12	1:22.20	38,790
1983	Current Hope, 3, 114	A. O. Solis	Highland Park, 3, 122	Country Pine, 3, 112	13	1:22.80	39,330
1982	Distinctive Pro, 3, 117	J. Velasquez	Center Cut, 3, 114	Real Twister, 3, 114	6	1:22.40	34,650
1981	Lord Avie, 3, 122	C. J. McCarron	Spirited Boy, 3, 114	Linnleur, 3, 114	7	1:23.40	34,080
1980	Plugged Nickle, 3, 122	B. Thornburg	Execution's Reason, 3, 122	One Son, 3, 114	6	1:22.60	17,640
1979	Spectacular Bid, 3, 122	R. J. Franklin	Lot o' Gold, 3, 114	Northern Prospect, 3, 114	4	1:21.40	17,766
1978	Sensitive Prince, 3, 114	M. Solomone	Kissing U., 3, 114	Pipe Major, 3, 114	11	1:20.80	19,890
1977	Silver Series, 3, 112	L. Snyder	Medieval Man, 3, 114	One in a Million, 3, 113	8	1:22.80	20,610
1976	Sonkisser, 3, 116	B. Baeza	Gay Jitterbug, 3, 116	Star of the Sea, 3, 122	7	1:21.00	19,350
1975	Greek Answer, 3, 122	M. Castaneda	Fashion Sale, 3, 113	Rich Sun, 3, 122	11	1:21.60	20,370
1974	Frankie Adams, 3, 114	R. Turcotte	dh-Judger, 3, 110		13	1:22.40	31,845
			dh-Training Table, 3, 113				
1973	Shecky Greene, 3, 122	B. Baeza	Forego, 3, 116	Leo's Pisces, 3, 112	7	1:20.80	19,170

Named for labor leader William Levi Hutcheson (1874-1953), who served as a member of the Gulfstream Park Advisory Board. Formerly sponsored by Danka Office Imaging Co. of St. Petersburg, Florida 1997. Not graded 1975-'81. Hutcheson H. 1955, 1984. Danka Hutcheson S. 1997. 6½ furlongs 1955-'60. Dead heat for second 1974. Dead heat for first 2000. ‡Do It Again Dan finished second, DQ to third, 1985. ‡Demaloot Demashoot finished second, DQ to fourth, 1993. Equaled track record 1973. Held as an allowance race 1954.

Illinois Derby

Grade 2 in 2005. Hawthorne Race Course, three-year-olds, 1⅛ miles, dirt. Held April 9, 2005, with a gross value of $500,000. First held in 1923. First graded in 1973. Stakes record 1:47.51 (1997 Wild Rush).

Year	Winner	Jockey	Second	Third	Strs	Time	1st Purse
2005	Greeley's Galaxy, 3, 122	K. J. Desormeaux	Monarch Lane, 3, 122	Magna Graduate, 3, 122	8	1:49.62	$300,000
2004	Pollard's Vision, 3, 114	E. Coa	Song of the Sword, 3, 116	Suave, 3, 114	11	1:50.80	300,000
2003	Ten Most Wanted, 3, 114	P. Day	Fund of Funds, 3, 114	Foufa's Warrior, 3, 118	10	1:51.47	300,000
2002	War Emblem, 3, 114	L. J. Sterling Jr.	Repent, 3, 124	Fonz's, 3, 117	9	1:49.92	300,000
2001	Distilled, 3, 114	M. E. Smith	Saint Damien, 3, 119	Dream Run, 3, 114	8	1:51.37	300,000
2000	Performing Magic, 3, 119	S. J. Sellers	Country Only, 3, 117	Country Coast, 3, 114	9	1:50.86	300,000
1999	Vision and Verse, 3, 114	H. Castillo Jr.	Prime Directive, 3, 117	Pineaff, 3, 118	10	1:48.47	300,000
1998	Yarrow Brae, 3, 114	W. Martinez	‡One Bold Stroke, 3, 117	Orville N Wilbur's, 3, 124	10	1:51.21	300,000
1997	Wild Rush, 3, 117	K. J. Desormeaux	Anet, 3, 124	Saratoga Sunrise, 3, 119	8	1:47.51	300,000
1996	Natural Selection, 3, 114	R. P. Romero	El Amante, 3, 124	Irish Conquest, 3, 114	13	1:48.60	300,000

Year	Winner	Jockey	Second	Third	Strs	Time	1st Purse
1995	Peaks and Valleys, 3, 124	J. A. Krone	Da Hoss, 3, 117	Western Echo, 3, 117	13	1:48.99	$300,000
1994	Rustic Light, 3, 117	E. Fires	Amathos, 3, 114	Seminole Wind, 3, 114	7	1:51.89	300,000
1993	Antrim Rd., 3, 114	A. T. Gryder	Seattle Morn, 3, 114	Secret Negotiator, 3, 114	13	1:48.68	300,000
1992	Dignitas, 3, 117	J. D. Bailey	American Chance, 3, 112	Straight to Bed, 3, 114	13	1:49.09	320,100
1991	Richman, 3, 124	J. D. Bailey	Doc of the Day, 3, 119	Nowork all Play, 3, 114	14	1:49.36	319,200
1990	Dotsero, 3, 117	A. T. Gryder	Sound of Cannons, 3, 112	Hofre, 3, 112	9	1:50.60	190,290
1989	‡Music Merci, 3, 124	G. L. Stevens	Notation, 3, 119	Endow, 3, 124	7	1:50.20	310,140
1988	Proper Reality, 3, 124	J. D. Bailey	Jim's Orbit, 3, 122	Classic Account, 3, 112	6	1:50.20	321,000
1987	Lost Code, 3, 124	G. St. Leon	Blanco, 3, 119	Valid Prospect, 3, 112	7	1:49.60	188,130
1986	Bolshoi Boy, 3, 118	R. Migliore	Speedy Shannon, 3, 118	Blue Buckaroo, 3, 116	8	1:52.20	189,432
1985	Important Business, 3, 116	J. L. Diaz	Nostalgia's Star, 3, 122	Another Reef, 3, 124	13	1:51.60	192,786
1984	Delta Trace, 3, 124	K. K. Allen	Wind Flyer, 3, 122	Birdie's Legend, 3, 124	10	1:51.80	127,530
1983	Gen'l Practitioner, 3, 126	J. A. Santiago	Passing Base, 3, 114	Aztec Red, 3, 124	10	1:50.40	127,200
1982	Star Gallant, 3, 126	R. Sibille	Drop Your Drawers, 3, 122	Soy Emperor, 3, 119	8	1:52.60	126,420
1981	Paristo, 3, 126	D. C. Ashcroft	Pass the Tab, 3, 126	Bitterrook, 3, 114	13	1:49.60	93,300
1980	Ray's Word, 3, 124	R. DePass	Mighty Return, 3, 114	Stutz Blackhawk, 3, 121	11	1:52.00	92,970
1979	Smarten, 3, 124	S. Maple	Clever Trick, 3, 124	Julie's Dancer, 3, 116	6	1:49.40	91,710
1978	Batonnier, 3, 124	R. J. Hirdes Jr.	Raymond Earl, 3, 121	Silver Nitrate, 3, 124	12	1:51.60	62,820
1977	Flag Officer, 3, 124	L. Ahrens	Time Call, 3, 116	Cisk, 3, 116	11	1:52.20	62,955
1976	Life's Hope, 3, 124	S. Hawley	Wardlaw, 3, 124	New Collection, 3, 116	9	1:51.40	77,295
1975	Colonel Power, 3, 124	P. Rubbicco	Ruggles Ferry, 3, 124	Methdioxya, 3, 124	14	1:50.20	63,360
1974	Sharp Gary, 3, 124	G. J. Gallitano	Sr. Diplomat, 3, 114	Sports Editor, 3, 119	12	1:50.00	63,060
1973	Big Whippendeal, 3, 119	L. Adams	†What Will Be, 3, 121	Golden Don, 3, 126	9	1:50.20	43,491

Named for home state of Hawthorne Race Course. Grade 3 1973-'87. Held at Sportsman's Park 1924-'32, 1939-'98, 2000-'02. Held at Aurora 1933-'38. Not held 1924-'32, 1939-'62, 1970-'71. 1¼ miles 1923. ‡Notation finished first, DQ to second, 1989. ‡Orville N Wilbur's finished second, DQ to third, 1998. Track record 1997. †Denotes female.

Indiana Breeders' Cup Oaks

Grade 3 in 2005. Hoosier Park, three-year-olds, fillies, 1¹⁄₁₆ miles, dirt. Held October 1, 2004, with a gross value of $406,300. First held in 1995. First graded in 2001. Stakes record 1:42.40 (2000 Humble Clerk).

Year	Winner	Jockey	Second	Third	Strs	Time	1st Purse
2004	Daydreaming, 3, 118	J. R. Velazquez	Capeside Lady, 3, 121	Stellar Jayne, 3, 121	7	1:43.65	$243,780
2003	Awesome Humor, 3, 116	R. Albarado	Cloakof Vagueness, 3, 114	Shot Gun Favorite, 3, 114	10	1:45.75	184,140
2002	Bare Necessities, 3, 118	J. Valdivia Jr.	Erica's Smile, 3, 121	Tarnished Lady, 3, 118	9	1:45.83	183,840
2001	Scoop, 3, 121	R. Albarado	Gold Huntress, 3, 115	Caressing, 3, 121	9	1:44.06	123,480
2000	Humble Clerk, 3, 114	L. J. Melancon	Megans Bluff, 3, 121	Miss Seffens, 3, 116	5	1:42.40	92,580
1999	Brushed Halory, 3, 121	E. M. Martin Jr.	The Happy Hopper, 3, 116	Chelsie's House, 3, 116	10	1:44.64	123,330
1998	French Braids, 3, 116	W. Martinez	Remember Ike, 3, 121	Barefoot Dyana, 3, 118	7	1:43.11	124,080
1997	Cotton Carnival, 3, 118	E. M. Martin Jr.	Sheepscot, 3, 116	Valid Bonnet, 3, 121	9	1:43.30	64,440
1996	Princess Eloise, 3, 118	S. T. Saito	Talking Tower, 3, 116	Shuffle Again, 3, 116	6	1:37.00	33,540
1995	Niner's Home, 3, 121	T. J. Hebert	Alltheway Bertie, 3, 118	Graceful Minister, 3, 114	6	1:37.00	24,480

Hoosier Park is located in Anderson, Indiana. Indiana Oaks 1995-'97. 1 mile 1995-'96.

Indiana Derby

Grade 2 in 2005. Hoosier Park, three-year-olds, 1¹⁄₁₆ miles, dirt. Held October 2, 2004, with a gross value of $511,300. First held in 1995. First graded in 2002. Stakes record 1:41.40 (1996 Canyon Run).

Year	Winner	Jockey	Second	Third	Strs	Time	1st Purse
2004	Brass Hat, 3, 124	W. Martinez	Suave, 3, 124	Hasslefree, 3, 115	9	1:44.04	$306,780
2003	Excessivepleasure, 3, 124	J. K. Court	Grand Hombre, 3, 124	Wando, 3, 124	3	1:43.48	247,080
2002	Perfect Drift, 3, 124	J. K. Court	Easyfromthegitgo, 3, 124	Premeditation, 3, 121	12	1:43.50	248,820
2001	Orientate, 3, 115	R. Albarado	Saratoga Games, 3, 121	Trion Georgia, 3, 124	11	1:42.22	188,460
2000	Mister Deville, 3, 119	L. S. Quinonez	Performing Magic, 3, 122	One Call Close, 3, 119	5	1:41.80	184,500
1999	Forty One Carats, 3, 115	J. F. Chavez	Zanetti, 3, 122	First American, 3, 122	12	1:42.24	187,290
1998	One Bold Stroke, 3, 122	R. Albarado	Dixie Dot Com, 3, 117	Da Devil, 3, 122	11	1:43.14	188,700
1997	Dubai Dust, 3, 113	S. P. LeJeune Jr.	Frisk Me Now, 3, 122	Tansit, 3, 119	8	1:44.00	127,440
1996	Canyon Run, 3, 115	F. C. Torres	Broadway Bit, 3, 113	Hunk of Class, 3, 117	10	1:41.40	64,560
1995	Peruvian, 3, 117	D. Kutz	I Still Believe, 3, 117	Mine Inspector, 3, 119	11	1:43.00	66,900

Hoosier Park is located in Anderson, Indiana. Grade 3 2002-'03.

Inglewood Handicap

Grade 3 in 2005. Hollywood Park, three-year-olds and up, 1¹⁄₁₆ miles, turf. Held April 30, 2005, with a gross value of $107,200. First held in 1938. First graded in 1973. Stakes record 1:38.45 (2004 Leroidesanimaux [Brz]).

Year	Winner	Jockey	Second	Third	Strs	Time	1st Purse
2005	King of Happiness, 6, 117	P. A. Valenzuela	Red Fort (Ire), 5, 117	Just Wonder (GB), 5, 116	6	1:40.67	$64,320
2004	Leroidesanimaux (Brz), 4, 114	J. K. Court	Designed for Luck, 7, 118	Devious Boy (GB), 4, 115	9	1:38.45	66,540
2003	Gondolieri (Chi), 4, 116	F. T. Alvarado	Truly a Judge, 6, 114	Freefourinternet, 5, 116	4	1:40.32	63,540
2002	Night Patrol, 6, 113	V. Espinoza	Redattore (Brz), 7, 120	Seinne (Chi), 5, 117	7	1:39.35	65,820
2001	Fateful Dream, 4, 114	D. R. Flores	National Anthem (GB), 5, 115	Casino King (Ire), 6, 115	5	1:41.65	64,260
2000	Montemiro (Fr), 6, 113	V. Espinoza	Bonapartiste (Fr), 6, 118	Takarian (Ire), 5, 118	8	1:40.71	66,300

Year	Winner	Jockey	Second	Third	Strs	Time	1st Purse
1999	Brave Act (GB), 5, 120	G. F. Almeida	Lord Smith (GB), 4, 119	Expressionist, 4, 116	8	1:39.13	$66,420
1998	Fantastic Fellow, 4, 118	C. S. Nakatani	Via Lombardia (Ire), 6, 116	Sharekann (Ire), 6, 113	6	1:38.77	64,740
1997	El Angelo, 5, 115	C. S. Nakatani	Irish Wings (Ire), 5, 114	Tychonic (GB), 7, 118	5	1:40.20	63,900
1996	Fastness (Ire), 6, 122	C. S. Nakatani	Helmsman, 4, 120	Tychonic (GB), 6, 120	5	1:39.54	79,470
1995	Blaze O'Brien, 8, 116	C. A. Black	Savinio, 5, 118	Stoller, 4, 117	7	1:39.53	79,800
1994	Gothland (Fr), 5, 117	C. S. Nakatani	Rapan Boy (Aus), 6, 116	Johann Quatz (Fr), 5, 117	4	1:39.60	60,700
1993	The Tender Track, 6, 116	E. J. Delahoussaye	Journalism, 5, 118	Johann Quatz (Fr), 4, 117	6	1:40.00	62,500
1992	Golden Pheasant, 6, 121	G. L. Stevens	Blaze O'Brien, 5, 114	Native Boundary, 4, 116	7	1:39.86	64,900
1991	Tight Spot, 4, 121	L. A. Pincay Jr.	Somethingdifferent, 4, 116	Razeen, 4, 114	6	1:40.30	63,400
1990	Mohamed Abdu (Ire), 6, 117	G. L. Stevens	Peace, 5, 117	Classic Fame, 4, 117	7	1:39.40	64,800
1989	Steinlen (GB), 6, 120	G. L. Stevens	Pasakos, 4, 115	Mi Preferido, 4, 117	7	1:39.60	63,400
1988	Steinlen (GB), 5, 119	G. L. Stevens	Deputy Governor, 4, 120	†Galunpe (Ire), 5, 115	9	1:40.40	66,200
1987	Le Belvedere, 4, 113	W. Shoemaker	Sharrood, 4, 118	Barbery, 6, 114	8	1:40.40	65,100
1986	Zoffany, 6, 121	E. J. Delahoussaye	Palace Music, 5, 124	Truce Maker, 8, 112	6	1:45.60	63,300
1985	Al Mamoon, 4, 116	E. J. Delahoussaye	The Noble Player, 5, 118	Swoon, 7, 114	6	1:40.20	62,900
1984	†Royal Heroine (Ire), 4, 116	F. Toro	Bel Bolide, 6, 120	Vin St Benet (GB), 5, 118	13	1:40.20	71,500
1983	Bold Style, 4, 115	P. Day	Noalto (GB), 5, 115	Western, 5, 116	6	1:41.40	65,400
1982	Maipon (Chi), 5, 112	D. G. McHargue	Spence Bay (Ire), 7, 122	Wickerr, 7, 116	11	1:40.00	68,900
1981	Bold Tropic (SAf), 6, 124	W. Shoemaker	The Bart, 5, 117	Adraan (GB), 4, 117	11	1:40.00	52,300
1980	Red Crescent, 4, 112	C. J. McCarron	Henschel, 6, 118	Numa Pompilius, 6, 115	7	1:40.60	31,300
1979	Johnny's Image, 4, 117	C. J. McCarron	Rich Cream, 4, 117	Smoggy (GB), 5, 112	8	1:40.60	26,875
	Star Spangled, 5, 119	L. A. Pincay Jr.	Bywayofchicago, 5, 118	As de Copas (Arg), 6, 121	6	1:40.00	25,875
1978	Star Spangled, 4, 116	A. T. Cordero Jr.	Bad 'n Big, 4, 122	No Turning, 5, 116	8	1:39.80	26,800
	Star of Erin (Ire), 4, 117	W. Shoemaker	Landscaper, 6, 113	Life's Hope, 5, 117	7	1:40.60	26,300
1977	Today 'n Tomorrow, 4, 117	S. Hawley	Anne's Pretender, 5, 122	Sir Jason, 6, 118	7	1:41.00	32,300
1976	Riot in Paris, 5, 121	J. Lambert	Absent Minded, 4, 114	Passionate Pirate, 5, 113	6	1:41.60	25,750
	King Pellinore, 4, 118	W. Shoemaker	Antique, 5, 114	Big Band, 6, 117	7	1:42.00	26,250
1975	*El Botija, 5, 116	J. E. Tejeira	Kirrary, 5, 115	Against the Snow, 5, 117	8	1:41.60	25,475
	†Gay Style, 5, 120	W. Shoemaker	Out of the East, 5, 116	June's Love, 4, 116	10	1:41.40	26,475
1974	Shirley's Champion, 3, 118	H. Grant	Rocket Review, 3, 117	Such a Rush, 3, 121	9	1:14.80	20,100
1973	Ancient Title, 3, 122	F. Toro	Groshawk, 3, 122	Pontoise, 3, 114	8	1:21.00	32,550

Named for the city of Inglewood, California, location of Hollywood Park. Formerly sponsored by the Miller Brewing Co. of Milwaukee 1972. Grade 2 1973-'74, 1987-'94. Not graded 1975-'81. Not graded when taken off the turf 2003. Inglewood Mile H. 1938-'39. Miller High Life Inglewood H. 1972. Held at Santa Anita Park 1949. Not held 1942-'44. 1 mile 1938-'39. 7 furlongs 1945-'47, 1973. 6 furlongs 1948. 1¹⁄₈ miles 1950, 1968-'72. 6½ furlongs 1974. Dirt 1983-'66, 1968-'74. Originally scheduled on turf 2003. Three-year-olds 1973-'74. Two divisions 1975-'76, 1978-'79. Course record 1998, 2004. †Denotes female.

Iowa Oaks

Grade 3 in 2005. Prairie Meadows, three-year-olds, fillies, 1¹⁄₁₆ miles, dirt. Held July 2, 2004, with a gross value of $125,000. First held in 1989. First graded in 2004. Stakes record 1:41.64 (2003 Wildwood Royal).

Year	Winner	Jockey	Second	Third	Strs	Time	1st Purse
2004	He Loves Me, 3, 118	J. Z. Santana	Prospective Saint, 3, 115	Home Court, 3, 115	8	1:42.80	$75,000
2003	Wildwood Royal, 3, 121	S. Danush	Golden Reputashn, 3, 112	Tulupai, 3, 112	8	1:41.64	75,000
2002	Lost At Sea, 3, 115	T. J. Thompson	See How She Runs, 3, 121	Don't Ruffle Me, 3, 115	6	1:42.27	90,000
2001	Unbridled Elaine, 3, 115	P. Day	Supreme Song, 3, 115	Sharky's Review, 3, 118	6	1:43.88	90,000
2000	Trip, 3, 121	W. Martinez	Lady Melesi, 3, 118	Fiesty Countess, 3, 118	7	1:43.56	90,000
1999	Golden Temper, 3, 121	S. J. Sellers	Undermine, 3, 118	Sweeping Story, 3, 121	6	1:42.95	75,000
1998	Shardona, 3, 114	K. Shino	Danzig Foxxy Woman, 3, 118	Lady Tamworth, 3, 121	10	1:46.94	43,305
1997	Bon Ami, 3, 116	G. W. Corbett	Windy City Raja, 3, 114	Quick n Steady, 3, 121	9	1:44.73	37,317
1996	Vaguely Who, 3, 121	V. L. Warhol	Swiss Saphire, 3, 118	Dee's Anny, 3, 117	11	1:43.63	24,439
1995	Our Gaggy, 3, 118	D. R. Bickel	Don't Tary Stalker, 3, 115	Melinda Jo, 3, 114	6	1:41.80	17,184
1994	Punkerdoo, 3, 121	D. Schroeck	Maria Badria, 3, 118	Chateau Queen, 3, 114	7	1:44.00	9,555
1993	Medical History, 3, 114	V. L. Warhol	Millie's Key, 3, 118	Fashioncense, 3, 119	5	1:42.40	8,950
1992	Giggles Up, 3, 120	G. A. Schaefer	Chelle Rae, 3, 120	Cobilion, 3, 120	9	1:46.02	10,120
1991	Chocolate Tuesday, 3, 121	C. G. Lowrance	Proudest Royal, 3, 121	Amdors Love, 3, 115	7	1:43.10	8,266
1990	Sixmo, 3, 118	V. L. Warhol	Dance for the Gold, 3, 115	Pay Her in Gold, 3, 116	12	1:46.60	11,069
1989	Clickety Click, 3, 119	K. M. Murray	She's Due Black, 3, 117	Hurry Home, 3, 115	9	1:38.80	15,450

Prairie Meadows is located in Altoona, Iowa. Held at Canterbury Park 1992. 1 mile 1989. 1 mile 70 yards 1990-'98.

Iroquois Stakes

Grade 3 in 2005. Churchill Downs, two-year-olds, 1 mile, dirt. Held November 6, 2004, with a gross value of $109,600. First held in 1982. First graded in 1990. Stakes record 1:35.01 (2001 Harlan's Holiday).

Year	Winner	Jockey	Second	Third	Strs	Time	1st Purse
2004	Straight Line, 2, 122	B. Blanc	Social Probation, 2, 120	Greater Good, 2, 122	7	1:36.62	$67,952
2003	The Cliff's Edge, 2, 117	S. J. Sellers	Korbyn Gold, 2, 121	Grand Score, 2, 117	9	1:35.57	70,494
2002	Champali, 2, 118	P. Day	Alke, 2, 116	What a Bad Day, 2, 118	10	1:37.06	70,804
2001	Harlan's Holiday, 2, 121	A. J. D'Amico	Request for Parole, 2, 121	Gold Dollar, 2, 116	10	1:35.01	70,184
2000	Meetyouathebrig, 2, 118	G. L. Stevens	Hero's Tribute, 2, 114	Keats, 2, 112	13	1:35.24	77,066
1999	Mighty, 2, 112	M. St. Julien	Ifitstobesuptome, 2, 113	Nature, 2, 114	7	1:35.88	68,758
1998	Exploit, 2, 115	C. J. McCarron	Crowning Storm, 2, 114	Olympic Journey, 2, 114	8	1:36.26	71,114

						Strs	Time	1st Purse
1997	**Keene Dancer**, 2, 121	P. Day	Yarrow Brae, 2, 113	Dawn Exodus, 2, 113		7	1:37.84	$68,882
1996	**Global View**, 2, 112	K. Bourque	Partner's Hero, 2, 112	Haint, 2, 121		6	1:36.49	68,200
1995	**Ide**, 2, 121	C. Perret	El Amante, 2, 116	City by Night, 2, 114		8	1:36.89	73,645
1994	**Peruvian**, 2, 121	J. A. Santos	Our Gatsby, 2, 116	Super Jeblar, 2, 116		11	1:36.68	77,025
1993	**Tarzans Blade**, 2, 121	B. E. Bartram	Dove Hunt, 2, 121	Amathos, 2, 114		11	1:37.00	74,945
1992	**Shoal Creek**, 2, 114	B. E. Bartram	Saw Mill, 2, 116	Demaloot Demashoot, 2, 116		13	1:37.51	76,375
1991	**Portroe**, 2, 114	M. E. Smith	Walkie Talker, 2, 121	Richard of England, 2, 121		11	1:37.96	76,570
1990	**Richman**, 2, 121	P. Day	Speedy Cure, 2, 114	Honor Grades, 2, 116		8	1:36.60	36,628
1989	**Insurrection**, 2, 116	P. A. Johnson	Bite the Bullet, 2, 121	Silent Generation, 2, 116		10	1:36.80	37,375
1988	**Dansil**, 2, 118	L. A. Pincay Jr.	Western Playboy, 2, 114	Lorenzoni, 2, 116		9	1:38.20	36,498
1987	**Buoy**, 2, 116	K. K. Allen	Key Voyage, 2, 118	Delightful Doctor, 2, 116		12	1:37.80	32,285
1986	**Icetrain**, 2, 117	M. E. Smith	Grantley, 2, 117	Authentic Hero, 2, 117		12	1:40.20	34,263
1985	**Tile**, 2, 122	P. Day	Bachelor Beau, 2, 117	Dance to the Wire, 2, 117		11	1:37.20	36,062
1984	**Banner Bob**, 2, 117	K. K. Allen	Nordic Scandal, 2, 114	Tasheen, 2, 117		8	1:37.60	18,078
1983	**Taylor's Special**, 2, 117	D. Brumfield	Bello, 2, 119	At the Threshold, 2, 114		9	1:37.20	19,858
1982	**Highland Park**, 2, 122	D. Brumfield	Coax Me Matt, 2, 114	White Fig, 2, 117		8	1:38.20	19,907

Named for the Iroquois Park area of the city of Louisville. Colts and geldings 1982.

Jaipur Handicap

Grade 3 in 2005. Belmont Park, three-year-olds and up, 7 furlongs, turf. Held May 29, 2005, with a gross value of $111,600. First held in 1984. First graded in 1986. Stakes record 1:20.06 (1994 Nijinsky's Gold [1st Div.]).

Year	Winner	Jockey	Second	Third	Strs	Time	1st Purse
2005	**Ecclesiastic**, 4, 118	C. H. Velasquez	Old Forester, 4, 124	Gulch Approval, 5, 120	7	1:20.71	$66,960
2004	**Multiple Choice**, 6, 113	J. Castellano	†Dedication (Fr), 5, 114	Geronimo (Chi), 5, 118	8	1:22.32	67,320
2003	**Garnered**, 5, 116	V. Carrero	Speightstown, 5, 121	Whitewaterspritzer, 6, 115	5	1:23.49	67,260
2002	**Shibboleth**, 5, 116	J. D. Bailey	Malabar Gold, 5, 121	†Cozzy Corner, 4, 111	7	1:20.08	67,140
2001	**Affirmed Success**, 7, 123	J. D. Bailey	Texas Glitter, 5, 116	Bought in Dixie, 5, 114	3	1:21.69	66,475
2000	**Gone Fishin**, 4, 114	J. R. Velazquez	Weatherbird, 5, 113	French Envoy, 4, 113	12	1:21.73	52,290
1999	**Notoriety**, 6, 115	J. L. Espinoza	Optic Nerve, 6, 116	Cryptic Rascal, 4, 117	12	1:21.35	52,335
1998	**Elusive Quality**, 5, 115	J. D. Bailey	Bristling, 6, 111	Optic Nerve, 5, 115	11	1:20.99	51,750
1997	**Atraf (GB)**, 4, 116	J. R. Velazquez	Mighty Forum (GB), 6, 115	Play Smart, 5, 112	4	1:23.64	49,635
1996	**Grand Continental**, 5, 114	R. Migliore	Inside the Beltway, 5, 115	Goldmine (Fr), 5, 111	10	1:23.78	51,720
1995	**Inside the Beltway**, 4, 114	J. F. Chavez	Gabr (GB), 5, 117	Golden Cloud, 7, 114	5	1:21.23	49,245
	Mighty Forum (GB), 4, 117	G. L. Stevens	Dominant Prospect, 5, 117	City Nights (Ire), 4, 114	9	1:21.12	49,995
1994	**A in Sociology**, 4, 119	E. Maple	Roman Envoy, 6, 114	Halissee, 4, 113	7	1:20.38	34,905
	Nijinsky's Gold, 5, 114	J. A. Santos	Dominant Prospect, 4, 114	Home of the Free, 6, 122	7	1:20.06	34,905
1993	**Home of the Free**, 5, 117	J. D. Bailey	Wind Symbol (GB), 4, 117	Fourstardave, 8, 117	8	1:20.69	55,080
1992	**To Freedom**, 4, 117	J. A. Krone	Fourstardave, 7, 122	Smart Alec, 4, 117	5	1:22.83	55,710
1991	**Kanatiyr (Ire)**, 5, 117	J. D. Bailey	Senor Speedy, 4, 117	Fourstardave, 6, 122	9	1:23.96	54,630
1990	**Fourstardave**, 5, 122	M. E. Smith	Harperstown, 4, 117	Wanderkin, 7, 119	9	1:21.00	57,240
1989	**Harp Islet**, 4, 117	C. Perret	Fourstardave, 4, 119	†Down Again, 5, 114	10	1:27.00	57,150
1988	**Real Courage**, 5, 114	J. Vasquez	Tinchen's Prince, 5, 117	Spectacularphantom, 4, 117	14	1:22.00	60,570
1987	**Raja's Revenge**, 4, 117	M. Venezia	Trubulare, 4, 117	†Give a Toast, 4, 114	11	1:25.20	52,200
1986	**Basket Weave**, 5, 117	R. Migliore	Alev (GB), 7, 117	Judge Costa, 5, 117	4	1:22.80	48,330
	Red Wing Dream, 5, 117	J. D. Bailey	Creme Fraiche, 4, 122	Roy, 3, 109	5	1:23.60	48,510
1985	**Mt. Livermore**, 4, 114	J. Velasquez	Main Top, 6, 117	Cozzene, 5, 117	7	1:09.20	49,020
1984	**Cannon Shell**, 5, 115	D. J. Murphy	Chan Balum, 5, 115	Believe the Queen, 4, 115	12	1:09.20	35,280

Named for George D. Widener's 1962 champion three-year-old colt and '62 Belmont S. winner Jaipur (1959 c. by *Nasrullah). Not graded 1990-'91, 2001. Not graded when taken off turf 2003. Jaipur S. 1984-'95. 6 furlongs 1984-'85. Dirt 1984-'86, 1992, 1997, 2001. Two divisions 1986, 1994-'95. Course record 1993, 1994 (1st Div.). †Denotes female.

Jamaica Handicap

Grade 2 in 2005. Belmont Park, three-year-olds, 1⅛ miles, turf. Held September 26, 2004, with a gross value of $200,000. First held in 1929. First graded in 1978. Stakes record 1:45.50 (2004 Artie Schiller).

Year	Winner	Jockey	Second	Third	Strs	Time	1st Purse
2004	**Artie Schiller**, 3, 123	R. Migliore	Rousing Victory, 3, 113	Icy Atlantic, 3, 120	6	1:45.50	$120,000
2003	**Stroll**, 3, 121	J. D. Bailey	Kicken Kris, 3, 121	Joe Bear (Ire), 3, 117	7	1:46.02	120,000
2002	**Finality**, 3, 116	J. R. Velazquez	Union Place, 3, 115	Chiselling, 3, 121	9	1:46.66	120,000
2001	**Navesink**, 3, 118	E. S. Prado	Strategic Partner, 3, 118	Baptize, 3, 123	8	1:51.53	120,000
2000	**King Cugat**, 3, 123	J. D. Bailey	Mandarin Marsh, 3, 114	Parade Leader, 3, 115	8	1:49.63	120,000
1999	**Monarch's Maze**, 3, 117	J. Bravo	Killer Joe, 3, 112	Monkey Puzzle, 3, 118	5	1:51.66	90,000
1998	**Vergennes**, 3, 115	J. R. Velazquez	Tangazi, 3, 114	Middlesex Drive, 3, 114	10	1:50.42	90,000
1997	**Subordination**, 3, 120	J. F. Chavez	Premier Krischief, 3, 113	Skybound, 3, 121	12	1:49.00	90,000
1996	**Allied Forces**, 3, 119	R. Migliore	Cliptomania, 3, 116	Lite Approval, 3, 114	11	1:40.91	86,325
1994	**Pennine Ridge**, 3, 118	J. R. Velazquez	Holy Mountain, 3, 116	I'm Very Irish, 3, 113	7	1:35.13	66,540
1993	**Mi Cielo**, 3, 116	M. E. Smith	Prospector's Flag, 3, 113	Cherokee Run, 3, 120	7	1:35.20	70,440
1992	**West by West**, 3, 113	J. Samyn	Offbeat, 3, 110	Portroe, 3, 111	7	1:34.27	70,320
1991	**Sultry Song**, 3, 113	C. W. Antley	Honest Ensign, 3, 110	Take Me Out, 3, 116	7	1:34.44	70,320
1990	**Confidential Talk**, 3, 111	J. F. Chavez	Rubiano, 3, 112	Sunshine Jimmy, 3, 114	7	1:35.60	52,470
1989	**Domasca Dan**, 3, 116	S. Hawley	Garemma, 3, 114	Is It True, 3, 120	5	1:35.40	70,920
1988	**Ruhlmann**, 3, 113	G. L. Stevens	Teddy Drone, 3, 112	Din's Dancer, 3, 112	8	1:35.40	84,540

					Strs	Time	1st Purse
1987	Stacked Pack, 3, 110	R. P. Romero	Gulch, 3, 123	Homebuilder, 3, 112	8	1:34.80	$67,770
1986	Waquoit, 3, 112	R. Migliore	Mogambo, 3, 119	‡Moment of Hope, 3, 110	8	1:34.20	53,280
1985	Don's Choice, 3, 114	D. MacBeth	I Enrich, 3, 110	Easton, 3, 109	6	1:36.00	53,010
1984	Raja's Shark, 3, 112	R. Migliore	Is Your Pleasure, 3, 116	Leroy S., 3, 117	6	1:36.60	52,560
1983	Bounding Basque, 3, 115	G. McCarron	A Phenomenon, 3, 120	Bet Big, 3, 115	8	1:34.00	51,480
1982	John's Gold, 3, 113	A. T. Cordero Jr.	Lord Lister, 3, 111	Estoril, 3, 114	5	1:37.00	33,180
1981	Pass the Tab, 3, 112	J. Velasquez	Spirited Boy, 3, 117	Counter Espionage, 3, 112	7	1:35.20	33,300
1980	Far Out East, 3, 113	C. B. Asmussen	Dunham's Gift, 3, 112	Settlement Day, 3, 111	12	1:34.00	35,100
1979	Belle's Gold, 3, 118	L. A. Pincay Jr.	Lean Lad, 3, 107	Gallant Best, 3, 113	10	1:33.60	33,180
1978	Regal and Royal, 3, 116	J. Fell	Squire Ambler, 3, 111	Roman Reasoning, 3, 112	8	1:35.00	32,460
1977	Affiliate, 3, 124	A. T. Cordero Jr.	Buckfinder, 3, 113	Proud Arion, 3, 115	12	1:35.20	33,660
1976	Dance Spell, 3, 119	R. Hernandez	Cojak, 3, 119	Quiet Little Table, 3, 114	9	1:34.00	33,330
1975	Funalon, 3, 113	V. A. Bracciale Jr.	Busy Saxon, 3, 114	Precious Elaine, 3, 113	10	1:35.80	34,140

Named for the Jamaica neighborhood of Queens, New York. Jamaica racetrack was located there until it was closed in 1959. Grade 3 1978-'87. Held at Jamaica 1929-'59. Held at Aqueduct 1960-'77, 1979-'81, 1987. Not held 1933-'35, 1955-'56, 1961-'74, 1995. 6 furlongs 1929-'53, 1957-'60. 1 mile 1975-'94. 1¹⁄₁₆ miles 1996. Dirt 1929-'93. Three-year-olds and up 1929-'44, 1949-'54, 1960. Fillies 1975. ‡Midnight Call finished third, DQ to fourth, 1986.

Jefferson Cup Stakes

Grade 3 in 2005. Churchill Downs, three-year-olds, 1¹⁄₈ miles, turf. Held June 12, 2004, with a gross value of $226,200. First held in 1977. First graded in 2001. Stakes record 1:47.27 (2000 King Cugat).

Year	Winner	Jockey	Second	Third	Strs	Time	1st Purse
2004	Prince Arch, 3, 120	B. Blanc	Kitten's Joy, 3, 122	Cool Conductor, 3, 116	9	1:50.61	$140,244
2003	Senor Swinger, 3, 120	R. Albarado	Remind, 3, 116	Rapid Proof, 3, 120	7	1:47.54	136,772
2002	Orchard Park, 3, 119	M. Guidry	Mr. Mellon, 3, 112	Quest Star, 3, 113	8	1:48.53	172,050
2001	Indygo Shiner, 3, 113	L. J. Meche	Strategic Partner, 3, 119	Fast City, 3, 114	9	1:48.81	175,150
2000	King Cugat, 3, 122	R. Albarado	Four On the Floor, 3, 122	Field Cat, 3, 122	10	**1:47.27**	177,940
1999	Special Coach, 3, 115	C. H. Velasquez	Silver Chadra, 3, 119	Air Rocket, 3, 122	12	1:49.82	180,110
1998	Buff, 3, 122	C. H. Borel	Keene Dancer, 3, 122	Ladies Din, 3, 122	7	1:50.80	175,770
1997	Greed Is Good, 3, 115	W. Martinez	Royal Strand (Ire), 3, 122	Crimson Classic, 3, 117	5	1:49.47	69,068
1996	Unruled, 3, 119	C. Perret	Broadway Beau, 3, 122	Trail City, 3, 122	6	1:50.07	54,210
1995	Ago, 3, 115	S. J. Sellers	Michael's Star, 3, 119	Lemon Drop, 3, 113	11	1:49.48	56,550
1994	Milt's Overture, 3, 112	P. Day	Jaggery John, 3, 122	Camptown Dancer, 3, 117	6	1:48.21	53,528
1993	Lt. Pinkerton, 3, 115	T. J. Hebert	Snake Eyes, 3, 119	Mi Cielo, 3, 117	6	1:48.27	35,555
1992	Senor Tomas, 3, 122	P. Day	Coaxing Matt, 3, 112	Black Question, 3, 122	7	1:49.80	35,945
1991	Hanging Curve, 3, 119	J. M. Johnson	Wall Street Dancer, 3, 119	Air Force, 3, 112	8	1:50.89	36,368
1990	Divine Warning, 3, 117	J. Deegan	Super Abound, 3, 115	Bioblast, 3, 110	4	1:52.20	36,238
1989	Shy Tom, 3, 120	E. Fires	Captain Savy, 3, 116	Ruszhinka, 3, 114	4	1:49.20	52,114
1988	Stop the Stage, 3, 115	M. McDowell	Cold Cathode, 3, 114	Bates Fay, 3, 115	9	1:51.60	62,310
1987	Fast Forward, 3, 120	R. L. Frazier	Unleavened, 3, 118	Gretna Green, 3, 112	5	1:50.00	63,109
1986	Buffalo Beau, 3, 110	J. McKnight	Clear Choice, 3, 124	Sumptious, 3, 113	7	1:52.80	53,040
1985	Avey's Brother, 3, 110	D. Montoya	La Marseillaise, 3, 110	Hollywood Hackett, 3, 113	10	1:50.00	50,420
1984	Coax Me Chad, 3, 119	W. H. McCauley	Fairly Straight, 3, 114	Last Command, 3, 110	7	1:50.60	48,958
1983	Pron Regard, 3, 116	C. R. Woods Jr.	Le Cou Cou, 3, 125	Whitesburg Lark, 3, 112	9	1:51.60	36,303
1982	Wavering Monarch, 3, 111	R. P. Romero	Forli's Jet, 3, 117	Noted, 3, 111	6	1:44.20	23,026
1981	Talent Town, 2, 122	B. Sayler	Helen's Tip, 2, 122	Ken's Revenge, 2, 122	11	1:05.40	19,858
1980	Golden Derby, 2, 125	J. C. Espinoza	†Plain Speaking, 2, 119	Bold Tyson, 2, 125	7	1:04.20	19,256
1979	Rockhill Native, 2, 122	J. Oldham	Earl of Odessa, 2, 122	Egg's Dynamite, 2, 122	9	1:05.20	19,581
1978	Future Hope, 2, 122	A. Rini	Backstabber, 2, 125	Amber White, 2, 117	6	1:05.20	14,073
1977	Old Jake, 2, 122	J. C. Espinoza	Bolero's Orphan, 2, 122	Set in My Ways, 2, 122	7	1:04.80	14,219

Named for Jefferson County, Kentucky, home of Churchill Downs. 5¹⁄₂ furlongs 1977-'81. 1¹⁄₁₆ miles 1982. Dirt 1977-'87. Two-year-olds 1977-'81. †Denotes female.

Jenny Wiley Stakes

Grade 3 in 2005. Keeneland, four-year-olds and up, fillies and mares, 1¹⁄₁₆ miles, turf. Held April 17, 2005, with a gross value of $200,000. First held in 1989. First graded in 1995. Stakes record 1:40.78 (1996 Apolda).

Year	Winner	Jockey	Second	Third	Strs	Time	1st Purse
2005	Intercontinental (GB), 5, 123	J. D. Bailey	Delta Princess, 6, 117	Sister Swank, 4, 117	7	1:41.89	$124,000
2004	Intercontinental (GB), 4, 116	J. D. Bailey	Ocean Drive, 4, 116	Madeira Mist (Ire), 5, 118	8	1:41.41	68,386
2003	Sea of Showers, 4, 116	J. D. Bailey	Magic Mission (GB), 5, 116	Snow Dance, 5, 116	10	1:41.69	70,246
2002	Tates Creek, 4, 116	K. J. Desormeaux	Snow Dance, 4, 123	Step With Style, 5, 116	10	1:42.27	70,432
2001	Penny's Gold, 4, 116	J. A. Santos	License Fee, 6, 118	Solvig, 4, 116	9	1:40.93	70,618
2000	Astra, 4, 118	C. S. Nakatani	Pratella, 5, 118	Ronda (GB), 4, 116	8	1:42.48	69,688
1999	Pleasant Temper, 5, 117	J. D. Bailey	Mingling Glances, 5, 114	Red Cat, 4, 117	8	1:40.93	70,246
1998	Maxzene, 5, 114	J. A. Santos	Parade Queen, 4, 121	Rumpipumpy (GB), 5, 114	7	1:42.82	69,192
1997	Thrilling Day (GB), 4, 115	W. Martinez	Romy, 6, 118	Gastronomical, 4, 115	7	1:41.16	68,634
1996	Apolda, 5, 121	J. D. Bailey	Mediation (Ire), 4, 118	Luzette (Brz), 6, 121	9	**1:40.78**	69,006
1995	Romy, 4, 118	F. C. Torres	Weekend Madness (Ire), 5, 121	Bold Ruritana, 5, 121	9	1:43.32	52,173
1994	Misspitch, 4, 118	M. E. Smith	Park Dream (Ire), 5, 112	Sh Bang, 5, 118	10	1:43.83	34,658
1993	Lady Blessington (Fr), 5, 118	P. Day	Radiant Ring, 5, 118	Super Fan, 6, 118	6	1:42.59	34,844

Year	Winner	Jockey	Second	Third	Strs	Time	1st Purse
1992	Indian Fashion, 5, 115	J. A. Santos	Spanish Parade, 4, 121	Radiant Ring, 4, 121	10	1:41.26	$36,514
1991	Foresta, 5, 121	A. T. Cordero Jr.	Dance for Lucy, 5, 121	The Caretaker (Ire), 4, 115	10	1:43.88	37,115
1990	Regal Wonder, 6, 121	R. D. Lopez	Majestic Legend, 5, 121	Phoenix Sunshine, 5, 115	8	1:46.20	36,043
1989	Native Mommy, 6, 121	C. Perret	Blossoming Beauty, 4, 113	Here's Your Silver, 4, 115	8	1:43.60	35,864

Named for Eastern Kentucky heroine Jenny Wiley (1760-1831), a pioneer woman who was captured by Indians and escaped to return to her family. About 1¹/₁₆ miles 1991. Course record 1992, 1996.

Jerome Handicap

Grade 2 in 2005. Belmont Park, three-year-olds, 1 mile, dirt. Held September 18, 2004, with a gross value of $150,000. First held in 1866. First graded in 1973. Stakes record 1:33.20 (1981 Noble Nashua).

Year	Winner	Jockey	Second	Third	Strs	Time	1st Purse
2004	Teton Forest, 3, 116	S. Bridgmohan	Ice Wynnd Fire, 3, 116	Mahzouz, 3, 112	7	1:35.74	$90,000
2003	During, 3, 118	J. A. Santos	Tafaseel, 3, 114	Pretty Wild, 3, 116	9	1:36.32	90,000
2002	Boston Common, 3, 118	J. F. Chavez	Vinemeister, 3, 115	No Parole, 3, 115	7	1:36.12	90,000
2001	Express Tour, 3, 115	J. R. Velazquez	Illusioned, 3, 117	Burning Roma, 3, 120	5	1:34.57	90,000
2000	Fusaichi Pegasus, 3, 124	K. J. Desormeaux	El Corredor, 3, 117	Albert the Great, 3, 120	6	1:34.07	90,000
1999	Doneraile Court, 3, 117	C. W. Antley	Vicar, 3, 120	Badger Gold, 3, 115	7	1:35.63	90,000
1998	Limit Out, 3, 117	J. Samyn	Grand Slam, 3, 120	Scatmandu, 3, 115	5	1:36.22	90,000
1997	Richter Scale, 3, 118	S. J. Sellers	Trafalger, 3, 117	Smokin Mel, 3, 115	8	1:35.88	90,000
1996	Why Change, 3, 112	C. C. Lopez	Distorted Humor, 3, 115	Diligence, 3, 117	10	1:34.22	90,000
1995	French Deputy, 3, 113	G. L. Stevens	Mr. Greeley, 3, 117	Top Account, 3, 115	6	1:33.53	120,000
1994	Prenup, 3, 113	J. D. Bailey	Ulises, 3, 112	End Sweep, 3, 118	8	1:34.59	120,000
1993	Schossberg, 3, 113	J. D. Bailey	Williamstown, 3, 118	Mi Cielo, 3, 116	5	1:35.53	120,000
1992	Furiously, 3, 113	J. D. Bailey	Colony Light, 3, 111	Dixie Brass, 3, 122	6	1:34.20	120,000
1991	Scan, 3, 117	J. A. Santos	Excellent Tipper, 3, 113	King Mutesa, 3, 113	8	1:34.09	120,000
1990	Housebuster, 3, 126	C. Perret	Citidancer, 3, 114	D'Parrot, 3, 112	5	1:34.00	102,060
1989	De Roche, 3, 108	D. Carr	Fast Play, 3, 116	I'm Influential, 3, 111	6	1:34.40	134,880
1988	Evening Kris, 3, 119	J. D. Bailey	dh-Din's Dancer, 3, 113		7	1:37.80	176,400
			dh-Parlay Me, 3, 113				
1987	Afleet, 3, 115	G. Stahlbaum	Stacked Pack, 3, 109	Templar Hill, 3, 117	9	1:33.80	107,640
1986	Ogygian, 3, 126	W. A. Guerra	Mogambo, 3, 119	Moment of Hope, 3, 111	5	1:34.00	127,620
1985	Creme Fraiche, 3, 124	E. Maple	Pancho Villa, 3, 119	El Basco, 3, 114	9	1:34.60	109,260
1984	Is Your Pleasure, 3, 114	D. MacBeth	Track Barron, 3, 124	Concorde Bound, 3, 115	9	1:35.20	109,080
1983	A Phenomenon, 3, 116	A. T. Cordero Jr.	Desert Wine, 3, 124	Copelan, 3, 118	8	1:35.00	104,940
1982	Fit to Fight, 3, 112	J. D. Bailey	John's Gold, 3, 115	Lord Lister, 3, 107	6	1:35.40	101,880
1981	Noble Nashua, 3, 120	C. B. Asmussen	Maudlin, 3, 112	Sing Sing, 3, 109	11	1:33.20	69,000
1980	Jaklin Klugman, 3, 122	C. J. McCarron	Fappiano, 3, 114	Plugged Nickle, 3, 124	6	1:34.20	67,320
1979	Czaravich, 3, 122	J. Cruguet	Valdez, 3, 122	Gallant Best, 3, 112	10	1:35.20	65,580
1978	Sensitive Prince, 3, 118	J. Vasquez	Darby Creek Road, 3, 122	Sorry Lookin, 3, 112	5	1:36.00	62,940
1977	‡Broadway Forli, 3, 111	P. Day	‡To the Quick, 3, 112	Affiliate, 3, 120	10	1:36.20	66,360
1976	Dance Spell, 3, 117	R. Hernandez	Soy Numero Uno, 3, 117	Clean Bill, 3, 112	10	1:35.00	66,600
1975	Guards Up, 3, 114	C. C. Lopez	Valid Appeal, 3, 119	Great Above, 3, 114	7	1:34.20	33,720
1974	Stonewalk, 3, 126	A. T. Cordero Jr.	Best of It, 3, 117	Heir to the Line, 3, 113	9	1:34.00	34,470
1973	Step Nicely, 3, 118	A. T. Cordero Jr.	Forego, 3, 124	Linda's Chief, 3, 126	10	1:34.00	34,800

Named for Leonard Jerome (1817-'91), builder of Jerome Park and president of Coney Island Jockey Club. Jerome was also the maternal grandfather of Sir Winston Churchill. Grade 1 1984-'94. Jerome S. 1866, 1872-'92. Champion S. 1867-'71. Held at Jerome Park 1866-'89. Held at Morris Park 1890-1904. Held at Aqueduct 1960, 1962-'67, 1972-'74. Not held 1910-'13. One mile heats 1866-'70. Two miles 1871-'77. 1³/₄ miles 1878-'89. 1⁵/₁₆ miles 1890-'91, 1903-'09. 1¹/₂ miles 1892. 1¹/₄ miles 1893-'94, 1896, 1914. 1¹/₈ miles 1895. Dead heat for second 1988. ‡Affiliate finished second, DQ to third, 1977.

Jersey Shore Breeders' Cup Stakes

Grade 3 in 2005. Monmouth Park, three-year-olds, 6 furlongs, dirt. Held June 26, 2004, with a gross value of $95,000. First held in 1992. First graded in 1994. Stakes record 1:08.53 (1997 Smoke Glacken).

Year	Winner	Jockey	Second	Third	Strs	Time	1st Purse
2004	Pomeroy, 3, 113	J. Bravo	Gotaghostofachance, 3, 115	Midnight Express, 3, 113	5	1:09.07	$60,000
2003	Gators N Bears, 3, 115	C. C. Lopez	Mt. Carson, 3, 122	Don Six, 3, 115	6	1:09.80	60,000
2002	Boston Common, 3, 117	E. M. Martin Jr.	Listen Here, 3, 117	It's a Monster, 3, 115	6	1:09.35	60,000
2001	City Zip, 3, 119	J. C. Ferrer	Sea of Green, 3, 117	Songandaprayer, 3, 122	5	1:09.02	60,000
2000	Disco Rico, 3, 115	J. Bravo	Max's Pal, 3, 122	Stormin Oedy, 3, 117	6	1:09.05	60,000
1999	Yes It's True, 3, 122	J. D. Bailey	Erlton, 3, 122	Flying Griffoni, 3, 112	4	1:08.59	60,000
1998	Good and Tough, 3, 115	W. H. McCauley	Klabin's Gold, 3, 117	El Mirasol, 3, 112	6	1:10.01	45,000
1997	Smoke Glacken, 3, 122	C. Perret	Partner's Hero, 3, 115	King Buck, 3, 115	4	1:08.53	45,000
1996	Swing and Miss, 3, 112	T. G. Turner	Seacliff, 3, 119	Dixie Connection, 3, 115	6	1:10.00	60,000
1995	Ft. Stockton, 3, 115	J. Bravo	Jealous Crusader, 3, 115	Gala Knockout, 3, 115	6	1:22.64	64,050
1994	End Sweep, 3, 114	M. E. Smith	Meadow Flight, 3, 122	Foxie G, 3, 115	5	1:21.20	63,450
1993	Montbrook, 3, 122	C. J. Ladner III	Evil Bear, 3, 114	Shu Fellow, 3, 114	7	1:21.04	63,420
1992	Surely Six, 3, 112	R. Wilson	Superstrike (GB), 3, 122	Salt Lake, 3, 119	8	1:21.94	64,230

Monmouth Park is located on the coast of New Jersey. Jersey Shore Budweiser Breeders' Cup S. 1992-'95. Held at Atlantic City 1992-'96. 7 furlongs 1992-'95.

Jim Dandy Stakes

Grade 2 in 2005. Saratoga Race Course, three-year-olds, 1⅛ miles, dirt. Held August 8, 2004, with a gross value of $500,000. First held in 1964. First graded in 1973. Stakes record 1:47.26 (1996 Louis Quatorze).

Year	Winner	Jockey	Second	Third	Strs	Time	1st Purse
2004	Purge, 3, 121	J. R. Velazquez	The Cliff's Edge, 3, 123	‡Niigon, 3, 117	6	1:47.56	$300,000
2003	Strong Hope, 3, 121	J. R. Velazquez	Empire Maker, 3, 123	Congrats, 3, 115	6	1:48.10	300,000
2002	Medaglia d'Oro, 3, 121	J. D. Bailey	‡Gold Dollar, 3, 115	Essence of Dubai, 3, 121	9	1:47.82	300,000
2001	Scorpion, 3, 114	J. D. Bailey	Free of Love, 3, 114	Congaree, 3, 123	6	1:48.90	360,000
2000	Graeme Hall, 3, 120	J. D. Bailey	Curule, 3, 114	Unshaded, 3, 120	7	1:48.95	240,000
1999	Ecton Park, 3, 116	A. O. Solis	Lemon Drop Kid, 3, 124	Badger Gold, 3, 114	7	1:49.52	180,000
1998	Favorite Trick, 3, 119	P. Day	Deputy Diamond, 3, 114	Raffie's Majesty, 3, 114	7	1:50.00	150,000
1997	Awesome Again, 3, 116	M. E. Smith	Glitman, 3, 114	Affirmed Success, 3, 114	9	1:51.00	150,000
1996	Louis Quatorze, 3, 124	P. Day	Will's Way, 3, 114	Secreto de Estado, 3, 114	8	**1:47.26**	90,000
1995	Composer, 3, 112	J. D. Bailey	Malthus, 3, 112	Pat n Jac, 3, 112	7	1:51.13	82,575
1994	Unaccounted For, 3, 112	J. A. Santos	Tabasco Cat, 3, 126	Ulises, 3, 114	5	1:49.69	80,820
1993	Miner's Mark, 3, 117	C. J. McCarron	Virginia Rapids, 3, 121	Colonial Affair, 3, 126	8	1:49.01	90,000
1992	Thunder Rumble, 3, 117	W. H. McCauley	Dixie Brass, 3, 126	Devil His Due, 3, 126	8	1:47.53	108,000
1991	Fly So Free, 3, 126	J. A. Santos	Upon My Soul, 3, 114	Strike the Gold, 3, 128	8	1:48.88	107,820
1990	Chief Honcho, 3, 114	M. E. Smith	Senator to Be, 3, 114	Paradise Found, 3, 114	4	1:51.60	67,680
1989	Is It True, 3, 121	J. A. Santos	Fast Play, 3, 114	Roi Danzig, 3, 126	4	1:48.40	99,180
1988	Brian's Time, 3, 126	A. T. Cordero Jr.	Evening Kris, 3, 114	Din's Dancer, 3, 114	10	1:48.20	109,980
1987	Polish Navy, 3, 117	P. Day	Pledge Card, 3, 117	Cryptoclearance, 3, 126	7	1:48.00	106,740
1986	Lac Ouimet, 3, 114	E. Maple	Moment of Hope, 3, 114	Wayar, 3, 114	5	1:48.00	69,360
1985	Stephan's Odyssey, 3, 123	L. A. Pincay Jr.	Don's Choice, 3, 114	Government Corner, 3, 121	9	1:48.80	73,080
1984	Carr de Naskra, 3, 114	E. Maple	Slew the Coup, 3, 114	Raja's Shark, 3, 114	10	1:47.40	75,720
1983	A Phenomenon, 3, 114	A. T. Cordero Jr.	Timeless Native, 3, 126	Head of the House, 3, 114	8	1:49.40	33,900
1982	Conquistador Cielo, 3, 128	E. Maple	Lejoli, 3, 114	No Home Run, 3, 114	4	1:48.60	32,700
1981	Willow Hour, 3, 117	E. Maple	Lemhi Gold, 3, 117	Silver Supreme, 3, 114	8	1:49.20	34,200
1980	Plugged Nickle, 3, 128	J. Fell	Current Legend, 3, 121	Herb Water, 3, 114	8	1:49.40	34,140
1979	Private Account, 3, 114	J. Fell	Instrument Landing, 3, 126	Pianist, 3, 114	5	1:47.80	22,155
1978	Affirmed, 3, 128	S. Cauthen	Sensitive Prince, 3, 119	Bound Green, 3, 114	10	1:50.40	22,830
1977	Music of Time, 3, 114	M. Venezia	Sanhedrin, 3, 114	Super Joy, 3, 114	10	1:50.00	22,830
1976	Father Hogan, 3, 114	M. Venezia	Dance Spell, 3, 121	El Portugues, 3, 114	10	1:48.80	22,410
1975	Forceten, 3, 126	D. Pierce	Prince Thou Art, 3, 123	Northerly, 3, 114	6	1:48.40	25,725
1974	Sea Songster, 3, 114	A. T. Cordero Jr.	‡Hatchet Man, 3, 120	Bobby Murcer, 3, 114	7	1:50.60	22,860
1973	Cheriepe, 3, 117	E. Belmonte	Arbees Boy, 3, 120	Bemo, 3, 123	9	1:50.20	17,310

Named for 100-to-1 1930 Travers S. winner Jim Dandy (1927 g. by Jim Gaffney), who upset heavily favored rivals Gallant Fox and Whichone. Grade 3 1973-'83. Grade 1 2001. 1 mile 1964-'70. 7 furlongs 1971. ‡T. V. Newscaster finished second, DQ to fourth, 1974. ‡Quest finished second, DQ to eighth, 2002. ‡Eddington finished third, DQ to fourth, 2004.

Jim Murray Memorial Handicap

Grade 3 in 2005. Hollywood Park, three-year-olds and up, 1½ miles, turf. Held May 14, 2005, with a gross value of $350,000. First held in 1990. First graded in 2005. Stakes record 2:25.31 (2003 Storming Home [GB]).

Year	Winner	Jockey	Second	Third	Strs	Time	1st Purse
2005	Runaway Dancer, 6, 115	G. K. Gomez	Vangelis, 6, 117	Exterior, 4, 117	8	2:26.75	$210,000
2004	Rhythm Mad (Fr), 4, 116	A. O. Solis	Continental Red, 8, 117	Gassan Royal, 4, 113	8	2:26.73	210,000
2003	Storming Home (GB), 5, 122	G. L. Stevens	Denon, 5, 122	Ballingarry (Ire), 4, 120	8	**2:25.31**	240,000
2002	Skipping (GB), 5, 116	K. J. Desormeaux	Startac, 4, 120	Our Main Man, 4, 114	7	2:26.23	46,485
2001	Kudos, 4, 117	E. J. Delahoussaye	Indigo Myth, 4, 115	Piranesi (Ire), 5, 113	4	2:26.74	45,900
2000	Bienamado, 4, 121	C. J. McCarron	Casino King (Ire), 5, 117	Adcat, 5, 116	8	1:58.93	47,070
1999	Lazy Lode (Arg), 5, 122	C. S. Nakatani	Musgrave, 4, 116	Astarabad, 5, 121	7	2:01.44	42,690
1998	Cote d'Azur (Ire), 4, 114	C. S. Nakatani	Belgravia (GB), 4, 113	Kaafih Homm (Ire), 7, 115	5	2:30.23	42,990
1997	Percutant (GB), 6, 120	G. L. Stevens	Seaborg (Arg), 6, 119	Big Sky Jim, 5, 116	7	2:26.10	43,800
1996	Polish Admiral (GB), 5, 117	B. Blanc	Big Sky Jim, 4, 116	Bedivere, 4, 115	6	2:26.13	40,500
1995	Jahafil (GB), 7, 117	C. J. McCarron	Talloires, 5, 119	Exalto, 4, 116	7	2:25.45	63,700
1994	Mashaallah, 6, 119	L. A. Pincay Jr.	Marfamatic, 5, 114	Samourzakan (Ire), 5, 116	5	2:25.37	46,600
1993	Toulon (GB), 5, 117	E. J. Delahoussaye	Beyton, 4, 118	Super Chief, 4, 111	4	2:26.67	45,850
1992	Berillon (GB), 5, 115	C. S. Nakatani	Single Dawn, 5, 112	Carnival Baby, 4, 114	7	2:26.80	48,900
1991	Sahib's Light, 5, 116	G. L. Stevens	Black Monday (GB), 5, 114	Razeen, 4, 117	12	2:25.90	52,150
1990	Shotiche, 4, 114	C. A. Black	Record Boom, 4, 114	Kaboi, 4, 115	12	2:00.60	50,450

Named for Pulitzer Prize-winning Los Angeles *Times* sports columnist Jim Murray (1919-'98).

Jockey Club Gold Cup Stakes

Grade 1 in 2005. Belmont Park, three-year-olds and up, 1¼ miles, dirt. Held October 2, 2004, with a gross value of $1,000,000. First held in 1919. First graded in 1973. Stakes record 1:58.89 (1997 Skip Away).

Year	Winner	Jockey	Second	Third	Strs	Time	1st Purse
2004	Funny Cide, 4, 126	J. A. Santos	Newfoundland, 4, 126	The Cliff's Edge, 3, 122	7	2:02.44	$600,000
2003	Mineshaft, 4, 126	R. Albarado	Quest, 4, 126	Evening Attire, 5, 126	5	2:00.25	600,000

Year	Winner	Jockey	Second	Third	Strs	Time	1st Purse
2002	Evening Attire, 4, 126	S. Bridgmohan	Lido Palace (Chi), 5, 126	Harlan's Holiday, 3, 122	8	1:59.58	$600,000
2001	Aptitude, 4, 126	J. D. Bailey	Generous Rosi (GB), 6, 126	Country Be Gold, 4, 126	7	2:01.49	600,000
2000	Albert the Great, 3, 122	J. F. Chavez	Gander, 4, 126	Vision and Verse, 4, 126	7	1:59.24	600,000
1999	River Keen (Ire), 7, 126	C. W. Antley	Behrens, 5, 126	Almutawakel (GB), 4, 126	8	2:01.40	600,000
1998	Wagon Limit, 4, 126	R. G. Davis	Gentlemen (Arg), 6, 126	Skip Away, 5, 126	6	2:00.62	600,000
1997	Skip Away, 4, 126	J. D. Bailey	Instant Friendship, 4, 126	Wagon Limit, 3, 121	7	1:58.89	600,000
1996	Skip Away, 3, 121	S. J. Sellers	Cigar, 6, 126	Louis Quatorze, 3, 121	6	2:00.70	600,000
1995	Cigar, 5, 126	J. D. Bailey	Unaccounted For, 4, 126	Star Standard, 3, 121	7	2:01.29	450,000
1994	Colonial Affair, 4, 126	J. A. Santos	Devil His Due, 5, 126	Flag Down, 4, 126	8	2:02.19	450,000
1993	Miner's Mark, 3, 121	C. J. McCarron	Colonial Affair, 3, 121	Brunswick, 4, 126	5	2:02.79	510,000
1992	Pleasant Tap, 5, 126	G. L. Stevens	Strike the Gold, 4, 126	A.P. Indy, 3, 121	7	1:58.95	510,000
1991	Festin (Arg), 5, 126	E. J. Delahoussaye	Chief Honcho, 4, 126	Strike the Gold, 3, 121	5	2:00.69	510,000
1990	Flying Continental, 4, 126	C. A. Black	De Roche, 4, 126	Izvestia, 3, 121	6	2:00.60	503,100
1989	Easy Goer, 3, 121	P. Day	Cryptoclearance, 5, 126	Forever Silver, 4, 126	7	2:29.20	659,400
1988	Waquoit, 5, 126	J. A. Santos	Personal Flag, 5, 126	Easy N Dirty, 5, 126	4	2:27.60	637,800
1987	Creme Fraiche, 5, 126	L. A. Pincay Jr.	Java Gold, 3, 121	Easy N Dirty, 4, 126	6	2:30.80	650,400
1986	Creme Fraiche, 4, 126	R. P. Romero	Turkoman, 4, 126	Danzig Connection, 3, 121	6	2:28.00	510,300
1985	Vanlandingham, 4, 126	P. Day	Gate Dancer, 4, 126	Creme Fraiche, 3, 121	7	2:27.00	516,600
1984	Slew o' Gold, 4, 126	A. T. Cordero Jr.	Hail Bold King, 3, 121	Bounding Basque, 4, 126	5	2:28.80	1,350,400
1983	Slew o' Gold, 3, 121	A. T. Cordero Jr.	Highland Blade, 5, 126	Bounding Basque, 3, 121	11	2:26.20	342,000
1982	Lemhi Gold, 4, 126	C. J. McCarron	Silver Supreme, 4, 126	†Christmas Past, 3, 118	10	2:31.20	337,800
1981	John Henry, 6, 126	W. Shoemaker	Peat Moss, 6, 126	†Relaxing, 5, 123	11	2:28.40	340,800
1980	Temperence Hill, 3, 121	E. Maple	John Henry, 5, 126	Ivory Hunter, 6, 126	7	2:30.20	329,400
1979	Affirmed, 4, 126	L. A. Pincay Jr.	Spectacular Bid, 3, 121	Coastal, 3, 121	4	2:27.40	225,000
1978	Exceller, 5, 126	W. Shoemaker	Seattle Slew, 4, 126	Great Contractor, 5, 126	6	2:27.20	193,080
1977	On the Sly, 4, 126	G. McCarron	Great Contractor, 4, 126	Cox's Ridge, 3, 121	13	2:28.20	208,080
1976	Great Contractor, 3, 121	P. Day	Appassionato, 3, 121	†Revidere, 3, 118	10	2:28.80	201,360
1975	Group Plan, 5, 124	J. Velasquez	Wajima, 3, 119	Outdoors, 6, 124	4	3:23.20	95,850
1974	Forego, 4, 124	H. Gustines	*Copte, 4, 124	Group Plan, 4, 124	8	3:21.20	67,140
1973	Prove Out, 4, 124	J. Velasquez	Loud, 6, 124	Twice a Prince, 3, 119	8	3:20.00	66,060

Named for the Jockey Club, keeper of the *American Stud Book* and registrar of North American Thoroughbreds. Jockey Club S. 1919-'20. Held at Aqueduct 1959-'61, 1963-'67, 1969-'74. 1½ miles 1919-'20, 1976-'89. 2 miles 1921-'75. Colts and fillies 1944. †Denotes female. Winner's purse includes $1,000,000 bonus for winning the Woodward S. (G1), Marlboro Cup (G1), and Jockey Club Gold Cup (G1) 1984.

Joe Hirsch Turf Classic Invitational Stakes

Grade 1 in 2005. Belmont Park, three-year-olds and up, 1½ miles, turf. Held October 2, 2004, with a gross value of $750,000. First held in 1977. First graded in 1979. Stakes record 2:24.50 (1992 Sky Classic).

Year	Winner	Jockey	Second	Third	Strs	Time	1st Purse
2004	Kitten's Joy, 3, 121	J. R. Velazquez	Magistretti, 4, 126	Tycoon (GB), 3, 121	7	2:29.97	$450,000
2003	Sulamani (Ire), 4, 126	J. D. Bailey	Deeliteful Irving, 5, 126	Balto Star, 5, 126	7	2:27.51	450,000
2002	Denon, 4, 126	E. S. Prado	Blazing Fury, 4, 126	Delta Form (Aus), 6, 126	8	2:28.47	450,000
2001	Timboroa (GB), 5, 126	E. S. Prado	King Cugat, 4, 126	Cetewayo, 7, 126	6	2:29.43	450,000
2000	John's Call, 9, 126	J. Samyn	Craigsteel (GB), 5, 126	†Ela Athena (GB), 4, 123	12	2:28.58	450,000
1999	Val's Prince, 7, 126	J. F. Chavez	Dream Well (Fr), 4, 126	Fahris (Ire), 5, 126	7	2:28.63	360,000
1998	Buck's Boy, 4, 126	S. J. Sellers	Cetewayo, 4, 126	Lazy Lode (Arg), 4, 126	6	2:33.25	300,000
1997	Val's Prince, 5, 126	M. E. Smith	Flag Down, 7, 126	Ops Smile, 5, 126	5	2:28.92	300,000
1996	Diplomatic Jet, 4, 126	J. F. Chavez	Awad, 6, 126	Marlin, 3, 121	10	2:27.51	300,000
1995	Turk Passer, 5, 126	J. R. Velazquez	Hernando (Fr), 5, 126	Celtic Arms (Fr), 4, 126	8	2:36.63	300,000
1994	Tikkanen, 3, 121	C. B. Asmussen	Vaudeville, 3, 121	†Yenda (GB), 3, 118	5	2:25.88	300,000
1993	Apple Tree (Fr), 4, 126	M. E. Smith	Solar Splendor, 6, 126	George Augustus, 5, 126	5	2:28.31	300,000
1992	Sky Classic, 5, 126	P. Day	Fraise, 4, 126	Solar Splendor, 6, 126	6	**2:24.50**	300,000
1991	Solar Splendor, 4, 126	W. H. McCauley	Dear Doctor (Fr), 4, 126	‡Fortune's Wheel (Ire), 3, 121	9	2:27.89	300,000
1990	Cacoethes, 4, 126	R. Cochrane	Alwuhush, 5, 126	With Approval, 4, 126	6	2:25.00	360,000
1989	Yankee Affair, 7, 126	J. A. Santos	El Senor, 5, 126	My Big Boy, 6, 126	7	2:27.20	392,550
1988	Sunshine Forever, 3, 121	A. T. Cordero Jr.	My Big Boy, 5, 126	Most Welcome (GB), 4, 126	9	2:33.80	360,000
1987	Theatrical (Ire), 5, 126	P. Day	†River Memories, 3, 116	Talakeno, 7, 126	6	2:29.20	360,000
1986	Manila, 3, 119	J. A. Santos	Damister, 4, 126	Danger's Hour, 4, 126	6	2:27.80	423,150
1985	Noble Fighter, 3, 119	A. Lequeux	Win, 5, 126	Strawberry Road (Aus), 6, 126	12	2:25.40	431,100
1984	John Henry, 9, 126	C. J. McCarron	Win, 4, 126	Majesty's Prince, 5, 126	6	2:25.20	375,150
1983	†All Along (Fr), 4, 123	W. R. Swinburn	Thunder Puddles, 4, 126	Erins Isle (Ire), 5, 126	10	2:34.00	351,420
1982	†April Run (Ire), 4, 123	C. B. Asmussen	Naskra's Breeze, 5, 126	Bottled Water, 4, 126	7	2:29.80	286,080
1981	†April Run (Ire), 3, 118	P. Paquet	Galaxy Libra (Ire), 5, 126	†The Very One, 6, 123	9	2:31.20	180,000
1980	†Anifa, 4, 123	A. Gilbert	Golden Act, 4, 126	John Henry, 5, 126	8	2:39.60	180,000
1979	Bowl Game, 5, 126	J. Velasquez	†Trillion, 5, 123	Native Courier, 4, 126	7	2:28.20	150,000
1978	†Waya (Fr), 4, 123	A. T. Cordero Jr.	Tiller, 4, 126	†Trillion, 4, 123	6	2:26.80	130,000
1977	Johnny D., 3, 122	S. Cauthen	Majestic Light, 4, 126	Crow (Fr), 4, 126	9	2:33.20	130,000

Named in honor of Joe Hirsch, retired executive columnist of *Daily Racing Form* and dean of American Turf writers 2004. Turf Classic Invitational S. 1977-2003. Held at Aqueduct 1977-'79, 1981-'83. ‡Spinning (Ire) finished third, DQ to fourth, 1991. Course record 1992. †Denotes female.

John C. Mabee Handicap

Grade 1 in 2005. Del Mar, three-year-olds and up, fillies and mares, 1⅛ miles, turf. Held July 24, 2004, with a gross value of $400,000. First held in 1945. First graded in 1973. Stakes record 1:47.09 (2004 Musical Chimes).

Year	Winner	Jockey	Second	Third	Strs	Time	1st Purse
2004	Musical Chimes, 4, 116	K. J. Desormeaux	Moscow Burning, 4, 117	Notting Hill (Brz), 5, 113	6	**1:47.09**	$240,000
2003	Megahertz (GB), 4, 116	A. O. Solis	dh- Dublino, 4, 121		5	1:49.09	240,000
			dh- Golden Apples (Ire), 5, 122				
			dh- Tates Creek, 5, 123				
2002	Affluent, 4, 118	E. J. Delahoussaye	Golden Apples (Ire), 4, 120	Janet (GB), 5, 118	7	1:48.37	240,000
2001	Janet (GB), 4, 116	D. R. Flores	Tranquility Lake, 6, 123	Minor Details, 4, 112	6	1:48.20	240,000
2000	Caffe Latte (Ire), 4, 117	B. Blanc	Tout Charmant, 4, 120	Alexine (Arg), 4, 115	7	1:47.16	240,000
1999	Tuzla (Fr), 5, 121	D. R. Flores	Happyanunoit (NZ), 4, 115	Spanish Fern, 4, 115	10	1:47.66	240,000
1998	See You Soon (Fr), 4, 114	C. S. Nakatani	Sonja's Faith (Ire), 4, 113	Fiji (GB), 4, 125	8	1:47.40	180,000
1997	Escena, 4, 115	P. Day	Real Connection, 6, 115	Different (Arg), 5, 121	7	1:49.80	180,000
1996	Matiara, 4, 118	C. S. Nakatani	Alpride (Ire), 5, 119	Pourquoi Pas (Ire), 4, 114	6	1:49.28	193,500
1995	Possibly Perfect, 5, 123	C. S. Nakatani	Morgana, 4, 115	Yearly Tour, 4, 116	7	1:49.98	180,600
1994	Flawlessly, 6, 124	C. J. McCarron	Hollywood Wildcat, 4, 124	Skimble, 5, 116	5	1:48.25	181,000
1993	Flawlessly, 5, 125	C. J. McCarron	Heart of Joy, 6, 118	Let's Elope (NZ), 6, 118	7	1:48.38	186,500
1992	Flawlessly, 4, 123	C. J. McCarron	Re Toss (Arg), 5, 115	Polemic, 4, 116	7	1:50.00	187,500
1991	Campagnarde (Arg), 4, 115	J. A. Garcia	Bequest, 5, 118	Somethingmerry, 4, 118	10	1:49.41	196,250
1990	Double Wedge, 5, 114	R. G. Davis	Reluctant Guest, 4, 117	Nikishka, 5, 116	8	1:49.00	158,000
1989	Brown Bess, 7, 117	J. L. Kaenel	Daring Doone (GB), 6, 117	Galunpe (Ire), 6, 118	7	1:48.40	157,750
1988	Annoconnor, 4, 116	C. A. Black	Chapel of Dreams, 4, 118	Short Sleeves (GB), 6, 121	10	1:48.40	134,000
1987	Short Sleeves (GB), 5, 116	E. J. Delahoussaye	Festivity, 4, 117	Auspiciante (Arg), 6, 120	9	1:50.20	97,900
1986	Auspiciante (Arg), 5, 114	G. L. Stevens	Justicara (Ire), 5, 116	Sauna (Aus), 5, 119	9	1:48.20	81,600
1985	Daily Busy (Fr), 4, 115	W. Shoemaker	Eastland, 4, 114	Envie de Rire (Fr), 4, 116	7	1:48.20	93,500
1984	Flag de Lune, 4, 115	F. Olivares	Royal Heroine (Ire), 4, 126	Salt Spring (Arg), 5, 115	9	1:48.40	97,200
1983	Sangue (Ire), 5, 123	W. Shoemaker	Castilla, 4, 121	First Advance, 4, 115	8	1:48.80	83,900
1982	Honey Fox, 5, 122	M. Castaneda	Sangue (Ire), 4, 112	French Charmer, 4, 115	10	1:48.80	84,000
1981	Queen to Conquer, 5, 120	M. Castaneda	Amber Ever, 3, 112	Track Robbery, 5, 123	13	1:49.40	74,050
1980	Queen to Conquer, 4, 115	W. Shoemaker	A Thousand Stars, 4, 118	Wishing Well, 5, 122	10	1:48.60	69,500
1979	Country Queen, 4, 121	L. A. Pincay Jr.	More So (Ire), 4, 119	Prize Spot, 3, 116	10	1:49.20	47,500
1978	Drama Critic, 4, 120	D. G. McHargue	Country Queen, 3, 113	B. Thoughtful, 3, 115	8	1:49.20	37,150
1977	Dancing Femme, 4, 122	D. G. McHargue	Up to Juliet, 4, 113	Swingtime, 5, 121	11	1:48.40	34,550
1976	Vagabonda, 5, 115	S. Hawley	*Stravina, 5, 115	Miss Tokyo, 4, 116	8	1:51.00	34,550
1975	*Dulcia, 6, 122	W. Shoemaker	*Tizna, 6, 123	Charger's Star, 5, 115	7	1:48.80	33,550
1974	*Tizna, 5, 120	W. Shoemaker	Modus Vivendi, 3, 118	*La Zanzara, 4, 122	11	1:49.20	29,800
1973	Minstrel Miss, 6, 122	D. Pierce	Le Cle, 4, 123	Pallisima, 4, 118	8	1:49.40	19,750

Named for John C. Mabee (1921-2002), owner of Golden Eagle Farm, located in Ramona, and longtime chairman of Del Mar Turf Club. Formerly named for the town of Ramona, California. Grade 3 1973-'79. Grade 2 1980-'83. Ramona H. 1945-2001. John C. Mabee Ramona H. 2002. Not held 1946-'58. 1 mile 1945. Dirt 1945-'69. Dead heat for second 2003.

Just a Game Breeders' Cup Handicap

Grade 2 in 2005. Belmont Park, three-year-olds and up, fillies and mares, 1 mile, turf. Held June 11, 2005, with a gross value of $300,000. First held in 1992. First graded in 1997. Stakes record 1:32.53 (1995 Caress).

Year	Winner	Jockey	Second	Third	Strs	Time	1st Purse
2005	Sand Springs, 5, 117	J. R. Velazquez	Intercontinental (GB), 5, 123	Wonder Again, 6, 121	9	1:33.05	$180,000
2004	Intercontinental (GB), 4, 118	J. D. Bailey	Vanguardia (Arg), 6, 113	Etoile Montante, 4, 121	8	1:33.33	150,000
2003	Mariensky, 4, 116	J. A. Santos	Riskaverse, 4, 119	Wonder Again, 4, 119	8	1:43.28	128,700
2002	Babae (Chi), 6, 115	J. F. Chavez	Tates Creek, 4, 117	Stylish, 4, 116	8	1:34.57	67,920
2001	License Fee, 6, 118	P. Day	Shopping for Love, 4, 114	Veil of Avalon, 4, 115	11	1:32.62	114,780
2000	Perfect Sting, 4, 121	J. D. Bailey	Ronda (GB), 4, 116	Snow Polina, 5, 116	7	1:34.48	111,180
1999	Cozy Blues, 5, 112	J. F. Chavez	U R Unforgetable, 5, 114	Mysterious Moll, 4, 115	7	1:33.33	94,620
1998	Witchful Thinking, 4, 118	C. J. McCarron	Sopran Mariduff (GB), 4, 117	Dixie Ghost, 4, 111	9	1:33.45	95,745
1997	Memories of Silver, 4, 120	J. D. Bailey	Dynasty, 4, 113	Elusive, 5, 115	7	1:32.80	95,370
1996	‡Caress, 5, 117	R. G. Davis	Class Kris, 4, 122	Upper Noosh, 4, 112	7	1:33.30	94,890
1995	Caress, 4, 119	R. G. Davis	Coronation Cup, 4, 119	Grafin, 4, 117	5	1:32.53	49,320
1994	Elizabeth Bay, 4, 114	M. E. Smith	Tiffany's Taylor, 5, 117	Statuette, 4, 119	5	1:32.85	33,330
1992	Lady Lear, 5, 115	G. Brocklebank	Flaming Torch (Ire), 5, 119	Totemic, 3, 116	5	2:15.90	47,340

Named for Peter M. Brant's 1980 champion grass female and '80 Flower Bowl H. (G2) winner Just a Game (Ire) (1976 f. by Tarboosh). Just a Game S. 1992-'95. Not held 1993. Grade 3 1997-2003. Equaled course record 1995. ‡Class Kris finished first, DQ to second, 1996.

Kelso Breeders' Cup Handicap

Grade 2 in 2005. Belmont Park, three-year-olds and up, 1 mile, turf. Held October 9, 2004, with a gross value of $270,000. First held in 1980. First graded in 1984. Stakes record 1:32.40 (1990 Expensive Decision).

Year	Winner	Jockey	Second	Third	Strs	Time	1st Purse
2004	Mr O'Brien (Ire), 5, 119	E. Coa	Millennium Dragon (GB), 5, 119	Gulch Approval, 4, 114	8	1:32.69	$150,000
2003	Freefourinternet, 5, 113	J. L. Espinoza	Proud Man, 5, 114	Rouvres (Fr), 4, 115	10	1:34.73	210,000

Year	Winner	Jockey	Second	Third	Strs	Time	1st Purse
2002	Green Fee, 6, 113	J. R. Velazquez	Forbidden Apple, 7, 121	Moon Solitaire (Ire), 5, 117	7	1:33.83	$210,000
2001	Forbidden Apple, 6, 118	J. A. Santos	Sarafan, 4, 114	City Zip, 3, 112	9	1:36.77	150,000
2000	Forbidden Apple, 5, 116	J. Samyn	Affirmed Success, 6, 120	Johnny Dollar, 4, 113	9	1:34.39	150,000
1999	Middlesex Drive, 4, 117	S. J. Sellers	Divide and Conquer, 5, 114	Wised Up, 4, 113	10	1:35.45	150,000
1998	Dixie Bayou, 5, 112	J. F. Chavez	Sahm, 4, 115	Let Goodtimes Roll, 5, 112	6	1:36.21	120,000
1997	Lucky Coin, 4, 119	R. G. Davis	Hawksley Hill (Ire), 4, 115	†Colcon, 4, 112	12	1:33.72	120,000
1996	Same Old Wish, 6, 113	S. J. Sellers	Da Hoss, 4, 120	Volochine (Ire), 5, 116	10	1:34.42	105,000
1995	Mighty Forum (GB), 4, 115	E. J. Delahoussaye	Fastness (Ire), 5, 119	Dowty, 3, 112	14	1:39.58	120,000
1994	Nijinsky's Gold, 5, 114	J. A. Santos	Lure, 5, 128	A in Sociology, 4, 117	7	1:34.18	120,000
1993	Lure, 4, 125	M. E. Smith	Paradise Creek, 4, 120	Daarik (Ire), 6, 112	10	1:35.86	120,000
1992	Roman Envoy, 4, 117	C. Perret	Lure, 3, 111	Val des Bois (Fr), 6, 118	9	1:36.39	120,000
1991	Star of Cozzene, 3, 114	J. A. Santos	Known Ranger (GB), 5, 113	Fourstardave, 6, 117	6	1:33.37	69,720
1990	Expensive Decision, 4, 112	J. Samyn	Who's to Pay, 4, 115	Great Commotion, 4, 113	9	**1:32.40**	57,420
1989	I Rejoice, 6, 114	J. D. Bailey	Quick Call, 5, 113	Wanderkin, 6, 118	9	1:36.40	75,360
1988	San's the Shadow, 4, 116	C. W. Antley	Posen, 3, 117	Tinchen's Prince, 5, 114	7	1:42.00	72,240
1987	I'm a Banker, 5, 107	A. Graell	Tertiary Zone, 3, 113	Island Sun, 5, 112	11	2:10.80	76,920
1986	I'm a Banker, 4, 111	A. Graell	Duluth, 4, 113	Premier Mister (Mor), 6, 113	9	2:03.20	54,720
1985	Mourjane (Ire), 5, 114	R. Migliore	Cool, 4, 116	Palace Panther (Ire), 4, 116	9	2:02.00	70,560
1984	Who's for Dinner, 5, 115	W. A. Guerra	Pin Puller, 5, 112	Norwick, 5, 109	11	2:01.20	71,100
1982	Worthy Too, 4, 109	J. Samyn	Nice Pirate, 4, 112	Jadosa Star, 5, 113	12	3:24.40	69,840
1981	Peat Moss, 6, 126	F. Lovato Jr.	Field Cat, 4, 114	Birthday List, 6, 114	8	3:20.80	66,240
1980	Peat Moss, 5, 108	F. Lovato Jr.	Ivory Hunter, 6, 114	Ring of Light, 5, 117	10	3:24.60	68,160

Named for Bohemia Stable's 1960, '61, '62, '63, '64 Horse of the Year and '60, '61, '62, '63, '64 Jockey Club Gold Cup winner Kelso (1957 g. by Your Host); Kelso is the only five-time Horse of the Year. Grade 3 1984-'96. Held at Aqueduct 1980-'82. Not held 1983. 2 miles 1980-'82. 1¼ miles 1984-'87. Dirt 1980-'82. †Denotes female.

Kent Breeders' Cup Stakes

Grade 3 in 2005. Delaware Park, three-year-olds, 1⅛ miles, turf. Held June 26, 2004, with a gross value of $250,900. First held in 1937. First graded in 1973. Stakes record 1:47.44 (2003 Foufa's Warrior).

Year	Winner	Jockey	Second	Third	Strs	Time	1st Purse
2004	Timo, 3, 117	R. Migliore	Icy Atlantic, 3, 117	Commendation, 3, 115	8	1:55.75	$150,000
2003	Foufa's Warrior, 3, 115	R. A. Dominguez	Remind, 3, 115	Lismore Knight, 3, 119	7	**1:47.44**	150,000
2002	Miesque's Approval, 3, 115	J. D. Bailey	Regal Sanction, 3, 115	dh- Coco's Madness, 3, 115	8	1:48.81	150,000
				dh- Quest Star, 3, 115			
2001	Navesink, 3, 115	R. A. Dominguez	Bowman Mill, 3, 115	Harrisand (Fr), 3, 115	10	1:49.98	151,000
2000	Three Wonders, 3, 115	P. Day	Field Cat, 3, 117	Dawn of the Condor, 3, 115	8	1:48.95	150,000
1999	North East Bound, 3, 114	J. A. Velez Jr.	Courtside, 3, 113	Swamp, 3, 119	8	1:51.93	150,000
1998	Keene Dancer, 3, 117	P. Day	Red Reef, 3, 115	Danielle's Gray, 3, 117	10	1:50.65	120,000
1997	Royal Strand (Ire), 3, 122	P. Day	Subordination, 3, 122	Broad Choice, 3, 113	7	1:48.00	90,000
1996	Sir Cat, 3, 113	J. D. Bailey	Optic Nerve, 3, 122	Fortitude, 3, 116	5	1:52.93	60,000
1982	Cagey Cougar, 3, 114	V. A. Bracciale Jr.	King's Dusty, 3, 113	Big Shot (Fr), 3, 113	7	1:43.20	14,495
1979	T. V. Series, 3, 116	C. Barrera	Bear Arms, 3, 113	Buck's Chief, 3, 114	11	1:43.60	22,978
1976	Improve It, 3, 117	L. Saumell	Return of a Native, 3, 120	Impeccable, 3, 120	7	1:38.00	12,795
	*King Streaker, 3, 111	H. Pilar	Chati, 3, 117	Parade to Glory, 3, 111	7	1:38.40	12,795
1975	Talc, 3, 117	R. Broussard	King of Fools, 3, 117	Leader of the Band, 3, 111	10	1:39.20	15,503
	Grey Beret, 3, 120	J. Canessa	My Friend Gus, 3, 117	Too Easy, 3, 111	10	1:39.40	15,503
1974	Splitting Headache, 3, 120	R. Woodhouse	Malaga Bay, 3, 114	Clyde William, 3, 117	12	1:40.80	20,475
1973	Shane's Prince, 3, 117	E. Maple	*Amen II, 3, 117	My Darling Boy, 3, 117	12	1:37.60	21,352

Named for Kent County, Delaware. Kent H. 1937-'41. Kent S. 1942-'82. Not held 1943, 1977-'78, 1980-'81, 1983-'95. 1¹⁄₁₆ miles 1937-'68, 1979, 1982. 1 mile 1969-'76. Dirt 1937-'68. Two divisions 1975-'76. Dead heat for third 2002. Course record 1997, 2003.

Kentucky Breeders' Cup Stakes

Grade 3 in 2005. Churchill Downs, two-year-olds, 5½ furlongs, dirt. Held June 5, 2004, with a gross value of $132,088. First held in 1988. First graded in 1999. Stakes record 1:03.11 (2001 Leelanau).

Year	Winner	Jockey	Second	Third	Strs	Time	1st Purse
2004	Lunarpal, 2, 121	S. J. Sellers	Consolidator, 2, 115	Smoke Warning, 2, 117	4	1:04.07	$86,025
2003	Cuvee, 2, 117	L. J. Meche	First Money, 2, 117	Exploit Lad, 2, 117	6	1:04.45	109,554
2002	Posse, 2, 115	D. J. Meche	Del Diablo, 2, 115	Blackjack Boy, 2, 115	8	1:03.73	102,300
2001	Leelanau, 2, 115	J. K. Court	Gygistar, 2, 115	†Lakeside Cup, 2, 112	6	**1:03.11**	100,812
2000	†Gold Mover, 2, 113	C. Perret	City Zip, 2, 115	Unbridled Time, 2, 115	6	1:03.67	101,091
1999	†Chilukki, 2, 112	R. Albarado	Barrier, 2, 115	Sky Dweller, 2, 115	7	1:04.01	106,485
1998	Yes It's True, 2, 121	S. J. Sellers	Tactical Cat, 2, 115	Alannan, 2, 115	8	1:03.61	85,948
1997	Favorite Trick, 2, 121	P. Day	Jess M, 2, 115	†Cutie Luttie, 2, 112	8	1:04.80	68,882
1996	†Move, 2, 113	S. J. Sellers	Prairie Junction, 2, 115	†Live Your Best, 2, 112	7	1:05.74	71,175
1995	†Miraloma, 2, 112	D. M. Barton	Great Southern, 2, 114	A. V. Eight, 2, 112	9	1:04.04	68,933
1994	My My, 2, 116	S. J. Sellers	Wise Affair, 2, 116	Hyroglyphic, 2, 116	11	1:05.96	37,310
1993	†Astas Foxy Lady, 2, 118	T. J. Hebert	Dish It Out, 2, 116	Riverinn, 2, 116	9	1:05.51	68,738
1992	Tempered Halo, 2, 121	P. A. Johnson	‡Mountain Cat, 2, 116	†Secret Bundle, 2, 113	7	1:05.39	50,326
1991	Hippomenes, 2, 112	P. Day	Cold Gate, 2, 118	It's Chemistry, 2, 113	9	1:06.30	50,716

1990	**To Freedom**, 2, 118	J. C. Espinoza	St. Alegis, 2, 112	Maxwell Street, 2, 112	5	1:05.00	$17,647
1989	**Summer Squall**, 2, 118	C. R. Woods Jr.	Dr. Bobby A., 2, 118	Wink Road, 2, 118	7	1:05.00	50,294
1988	**†Island Escape**, 2, 115	C. R. Woods Jr.	One That Got Away, 2, 121	Papa Leonard, 2, 114	7	1:04.60	50,456

Churchill Downs is located in Louisville. Kentucky Budweiser Breeders' Cup S. 1988-'95. Not run in 2005. Track record 1998, 2001. ‡Exclusive Zone finished second, DQ to fourth, 1992. †Denotes female.

Kentucky Cup Classic Handicap

Grade 2 in 2005. Turfway Park, three-year-olds and up, 1 1/8 miles, dirt. Held September 18, 2004, with a gross value of $350,000. First held in 1994. First graded in 1996. Stakes record 1:47.43 (1996 Atticus).

Year	Winner	Jockey	Second	Third	Strs	Time	1st Purse
2004	**Roses in May**, 4, 118	J. R. Velazquez	Pie N Burger, 6, 117	Sonic West, 5, 113	6	1:49.13	$221,500
2003	**Perfect Drift**, 4, 120	P. Day	Congaree, 5, 124	Crafty Shaw, 5, 115	5	1:50.43	221,500
2002	**Pure Prize**, 4, 115	M. E. Smith	Dollar Bill, 4, 117	Hero's Tribute, 4, 113	8	1:51.24	254,000
2001	**Guided Tour**, 5, 119	L. J. Melancon	Balto Star, 3, 114	A Fleets Dancer, 6, 115	6	1:47.90	254,000
2000	**Captain Steve**, 3, 115	S. J. Sellers	Golden Missile, 5, 121	Early Pioneer, 5, 120	6	1:49.95	314,500
1999	**Da Devil**, 4, 112	C. H. Borel	Social Charter, 4, 115	Cat Thief, 3, 117	8	1:50.54	314,500
1998	**dh- Silver Charm**, 4, 123	G. L. Stevens	Acceptable, 4, 117		5	1:47.48	143,500
	dh- Wild Rush, 4, 117	P. Day					
1997	**Semoran**, 4, 116	K. J. Desormeaux	Distorted Humor, 4, 116	Coup D' Argent, 5, 114	8	1:48.08	217,000
1996	**Atticus**, 4, 115	C. S. Nakatani	Judge T C, 5, 116	Isitingood, 5, 114	10	**1:47.43**	325,000
1995	**Thunder Gulch**, 3, 121	G. L. Stevens	Judge T C, 4, 112	Bound by Honor, 4, 113	6	1:49.42	260,000
1994	**Tabasco Cat**, 3, 120	P. Day	Mighty Avanti, 4, 115	Best Pal, 6, 115	6	1:50.32	260,000

Turfway Park is located in Florence, Kentucky. Grade 3 1996-'98. Kentucky Cup Classic S. 1994. Dead heat for first 1998.

Kentucky Cup Juvenile Stakes

Grade 3 in 2005. Turfway Park, two-year-olds, 1 1/16 miles, dirt. Held September 18, 2004, with a gross value of $100,000. First held in 1986. First graded in 1989. Stakes record 1:42.89 (1996 Boston Harbor).

Year	Winner	Jockey	Second	Third	Strs	Time	1st Purse
2004	**Greater Good**, 2, 114	J. McKee	Magna Graduate, 2, 114	Norainonthisparty, 2, 114	6	1:44.96	$62,000
2003	**‡Mr. Jester**, 2, 118	R. Bejarano	The Cliff's Edge, 2, 114	Pomeroy, 2, 116	8	1:46.61	62,000
2002	**Vindication**, 2, 116	M. E. Smith	Private Gold, 2, 118	Tito's Beau, 2, 114	8	1:46.70	62,750
2001	**Repent**, 2, 114	A. J. D'Amico	French Assault, 2, 118	Gold Dollar, 2, 114	7	1:43.78	62,750
2000	**Point Given**, 2, 114	S. J. Sellers	Holiday Thunder, 2, 114	The Goo, 2, 116	11	1:47.01	62,600
1999	**Millencolin**, 2, 114	P. Day	Personal First, 2, 114	Deputy Warlock, 2, 118	10	1:47.02	62,600
1998	**Aly's Alley**, 2, 118	P. A. Johnson	Time Bandit, 2, 120	Mac's Rule, 2, 116	9	1:45.63	62,600
1997	**Laydown**, 2, 114	M. E. Smith	Time Limit, 2, 118	Da Devil, 2, 114	7	1:43.17	62,600
1996	**Boston Harbor**, 2, 120	D. M. Barton	Play Waki for Me, 2, 118	Dr. Spine, 2, 112	8	**1:42.89**	65,000
1995	**Editor's Note**, 2, 115	G. L. Stevens	Devil's Honor, 2, 118	Never to Squander, 2, 110	8	1:45.07	65,000
1994	**Tejano Run**, 2, 120	J. D. Bailey	Gold Miner, 2, 120	Bick, 2, 120	7	1:46.10	65,000
1993	**Bibury Court**, 2, 120	S. T. Saito	Moving Van, 2, 120	Durham, 2, 120	11	1:47.75	81,250
1992	**Mountain Cat**, 2, 120	C. R. Woods Jr.	Saw Mill, 2, 120	Shoal Creek, 2, 120	10	1:43.50	97,500
1991	**Star Recruit**, 2, 120	R. D. Lopez	Pick Up the Phone, 2, 120	Battenburg, 2, 120	9	1:45.68	97,500
1990	**Fire in Ice**, 2, 120	A. J. Garcia	Wall Street Dancer, 2, 120	Gold Shoulder, 2, 120	10	1:46.60	81,250
1989	**Fighting Fantasy**, 2, 120	D. W. Cox	Top Snob, 2, 120	Hardburly, 2, 120	9	1:48.40	81,250
1988	**Light Crude**, 2, 120	R. L. Frazier	Bravoure, 2, 120	Revive, 2, 120	8	1:44.80	81,250
1987	**Jim's Orbit**, 2, 120	P. Day	Kingpost, 2, 120	Delightful Doctor, 2, 120	11	1:37.80	81,250
1986	**Rainbow East**, 2, 120	O. B. Aviles	Alysheba, 2, 120	David L.'s Rib, 2, 120	11	1:37.20	78,500

Turfway Park is located in Florence, Kentucky. Formerly sponsored by James McIngvale's Gallery Furniture Co. of Houston, Texas 1998. Formerly named for Dorothy and Pam Scharbauer's 1988 Horse of the Year Alysheba (1984 c. by Alydar); Alysheba placed second in the 1986 In Memoriam S. Formerly named for 1923 champion three-year-old colt and '23 Latonia Championship S. winner In Memoriam (1920 c. by *McGee). In Memoriam S. 1986-'88. Alysheba S. 1989-'93. 1 mile 1986-'87. ‡Pomeroy finished first, DQ to third, 2003.

Kentucky Cup Sprint Stakes

Grade 3 in 2005. Turfway Park, three-year-olds, 6 furlongs, dirt. Held September 18, 2004, with a gross value of $100,000. First held in 1994. First graded in 1996. Stakes record 1:08.24 (1996 Appealing Skier).

Year	Winner	Jockey	Second	Third	Strs	Time	1st Purse
2004	**Level Playingfield**, 3, 116	J. McKee	Cuvee, 3, 116	Swift Attraction, 3, 116	5	1:09.76	$62,000
2003	**Cajun Beat**, 3, 122	C. H. Velasquez	Clock Stopper, 3, 116	Champali, 3, 122	11	1:09.54	62,000
2002	**Day Trader**, 3, 118	P. Day	Premier Performer, 3, 114	Ecstatic, 3, 114	11	1:10.01	94,500
2001	**Snow Ridge**, 3, 114	P. Day	City Zip, 3, 122	Dream Run, 3, 117	5	1:09.22	94,500
2000	**Caller One**, 3, 120	K. J. Desormeaux	Millencolin, 3, 116	Kings Command, 3, 116	6	1:09.46	93,750
1999	**Successful Appeal**, 3, 122	E. S. Prado	Five Star Day, 3, 114	American Spirit, 3, 118	6	1:09.40	74,400
1998	**Reraise**, 3, 116	C. S. Nakatani	Copelan Too, 3, 114	Mr Bert, 3, 114	7	1:08.50	93,900
1997	**Partner's Hero**, 3, 114	P. Day	Oro de Mexico, 3, 116	Prosong, 3, 114	6	1:09.00	74,400
1996	**Appealing Skier**, 3, 118	M. E. Smith	†Capote Belle, 3, 119	Delay of Game, 3, 114	9	**1:08.24**	97,500
1995	**Lord Carson**, 3, 116	M. E. Smith	Ft. Stockton, 3, 122	Evansville Slew, 3, 116	10	1:08.60	97,500
1994	**End Sweep**, 3, 120	C. J. McCarron	Exclusive Praline, 3, 122	Chimes Band, 3, 122	7	1:09.99	97,500

Turfway Park is located in Florence, Kentucky. Grade 2 1996-2001. Equaled track record 1995. †Denotes female.

Kentucky Cup Turf Handicap

Grade 3 in 2005. Kentucky Downs, three-year-olds and up, $1\frac{1}{2}$ miles, turf. Held September 25, 2004, with a gross value of $200,000. First held in 1998. First graded in 2001. Stakes record 2:27.60 (1998 Yaqthan [Ire]).

Year	Winner	Jockey	Second	Third	Strs	Time	1st Purse
2004	Sabiango (Ger), 6, 119	B. Blanc	Rochester, 8, 117	Gottabeachboy, 4, 115	6	2:33.70	$124,000
2003	‡Rochester, 7, 116	E. M. Martin Jr.	Quest Star, 4, 116	Art Variety (Brz), 5, 111	8	2:31.39	124,000
2002	Rochester, 6, 115	E. M. Martin Jr.	Nowrass (GB), 6, 112	Continental Red, 6, 117	11	2:38.28	186,000
2001	Chorwon, 8, 113	J. K. Court	The Knight Sky, 5, 114	Man From Wicklow, 4, 114	7	2:28.68	186,000
2000	Down the Aisle, 7, 117	R. Albarado	Crowd Pleaser, 5, 113	Royal Strand (Ire), 6, 115	8	2:27.70	186,000
1999	Fahris (Ire), 5, 116	S. J. Sellers	Yaqthan (Ire), 9, 116	Royal Strand (Ire), 5, 114	12	2:29.60	186,000
1998	Yaqthan (Ire), 8, 115	B. Peck	Perim (Fr), 5, 114	Chorwon, 5, 116	8	**2:27.60**	186,000

Established course record 1998. ‡Art Variety (Brz) finished first, DQ to third, 2003.

Kentucky Derby

Grade 1 in 2005. Churchill Downs, three-year-olds, $1\frac{1}{4}$ miles, dirt. Held May 7, 2005, with a gross value of $2,399,600. First held in 1875. First graded in 1973. Stakes record 1:59.40 (1973 Secretariat).

(See Triple Crown section for complete history of the Kentucky Derby)

Year	Winner	Jockey	Second	Third	Strs	Time	1st Purse
2005	Giacomo, 3, 126	M. E. Smith	Closing Argument, 3, 126	Afleet Alex, 3, 126	20	2:02.75	$1,639,600
2004	Smarty Jones, 3, 126	S. Elliott	Lion Heart, 3, 126	Imperialism, 3, 126	18	2:04.06	5,854,800
2003	Funny Cide, 3, 126	J. A. Santos	Empire Maker, 3, 126	Peace Rules, 3, 126	16	2:01.19	800,200
2002	War Emblem, 3, 126	V. Espinoza	Proud Citizen, 3, 126	Perfect Drift, 3, 126	18	2:01.13	1,875,000
2001	Monarchos, 3, 126	J. F. Chavez	Invisible Ink, 3, 126	Congaree, 3, 126	17	1:59.97	812,000
2000	Fusaichi Pegasus, 3, 126	K. J. Desormeaux	Aptitude, 3, 126	Impeachment, 3, 126	19	2:01.12	1,038,400
1999	Charismatic, 3, 126	C. W. Antley	Menifee, 3, 126	Cat Thief, 3, 126	19	2:03.29	886,200
1998	Real Quiet, 3, 126	K. J. Desormeaux	Victory Gallop, 3, 126	Indian Charlie, 3, 126	15	2:02.38	700,000
1997	Silver Charm, 3, 126	G. L. Stevens	Captain Bodgit, 3, 126	Free House, 3, 126	13	2:02.44	700,000
1996	Grindstone, 3, 126	J. D. Bailey	Cavonnier, 3, 126	Prince of Thieves, 3, 126	19	2:01.06	869,800
1995	Thunder Gulch, 3, 126	G. L. Stevens	Tejano Run, 3, 126	Timber Country, 3, 126	19	2:01.27	707,400
1994	Go for Gin, 3, 126	C. J. McCarron	Strodes Creek, 3, 126	Blumin Affair, 3, 126	14	2:03.72	628,800
1993	Sea Hero, 3, 126	J. D. Bailey	Prairie Bayou, 3, 126	Wild Gale, 3, 126	19	2:02.42	735,900
1992	Lil E. Tee, 3, 126	P. Day	Casual Lies, 3, 126	Dance Floor, 3, 126	18	2:03.04	724,800
1991	Strike the Gold, 3, 126	C. W. Antley	Best Pal, 3, 126	Mane Minister, 3, 126	16	2:03.08	655,800
1990	Unbridled, 3, 126	C. Perret	Summer Squall, 3, 126	Pleasant Tap, 3, 126	15	2:02.00	581,000
1989	Sunday Silence, 3, 126	P. A. Valenzuela	Easy Goer, 3, 126	Awe Inspiring, 3, 126	15	2:05.00	574,200
1988	†Winning Colors, 3, 121	G. L. Stevens	Forty Niner, 3, 126	Risen Star, 3, 126	17	2:02.20	611,200
1987	Alysheba, 3, 126	C. J. McCarron	Bet Twice, 3, 126	Avies Copy, 3, 126	17	2:03.40	618,600
1986	Ferdinand, 3, 126	W. Shoemaker	Bold Arrangement (GB), 3, 126	Broad Brush, 3, 126	16	2:02.80	609,400
1985	Spend a Buck, 3, 126	A. T. Cordero Jr.	Stephan's Odyssey, 3, 126	Chief's Crown, 3, 126	13	2:00.20	406,800
1984	Swale, 3, 126	L. A. Pincay Jr.	Coax Me Chad, 3, 126	At the Threshold, 3, 126	20	2:02.40	537,400
1983	Sunny's Halo, 3, 126	E. J. Delahoussaye	Desert Wine, 3, 126	Caveat, 3, 126	20	2:02.20	426,000
1982	Gato Del Sol, 3, 126	E. J. Delahoussaye	Laser Light, 3, 126	Reinvested, 3, 126	19	2:02.40	428,850
1981	Pleasant Colony, 3, 126	J. Velasquez	Woodchopper, 3, 126	Partez, 3, 126	21	2:02.00	317,200
1980	†Genuine Risk, 3, 121	J. Vasquez	Rumbo, 3, 126	Jaklin Klugman, 3, 126	13	2:02.00	250,550
1979	Spectacular Bid, 3, 126	R. J. Franklin	General Assembly, 3, 126	Golden Act, 3, 126	10	2:02.40	228,650
1978	Affirmed, 3, 126	S. Cauthen	Alydar, 3, 126	Believe It, 3, 126	11	2:01.20	186,900
1977	Seattle Slew, 3, 126	J. Cruguet	Run Dusty Run, 3, 126	Sanhedrin, 3, 126	15	2:02.20	214,700
1976	Bold Forbes, 3, 126	A. T. Cordero Jr.	Honest Pleasure, 3, 126	Elocutionist, 3, 126	9	2:01.60	165,200
1975	Foolish Pleasure, 3, 126	J. Vasquez	Avatar, 3, 126	Diabolo, 3, 126	15	2:02.00	209,600
1974	Cannonade, 3, 126	A. T. Cordero Jr.	Hudson County, 3, 126	Agitate, 3, 126	23	2:04.00	274,000
1973	Secretariat, 3, 126	R. Turcotte	Sham, 3, 126	Our Native, 3, 126	13	**1:59.40**	155,050

The Kentucky Derby was named for the Derby S. (Eng-G1) in England, commonly known as the Epsom Derby, its predecessor and model. Churchill Downs is located in Louisville. $1\frac{1}{2}$ miles 1875-'95. Track record 1973. †Denotes female. Winner's purse includes $1,000,000 bonus for winning the Illinois Derby (G2) and the Kentucky Derby (G1) 2002. Winner's purse includes $5,000,000 bonus from Oaklawn Park 2004.

Kentucky Jockey Club Stakes

Grade 2 in 2005. Churchill Downs, two-year-olds, $1\frac{1}{16}$ miles, dirt. Held November 27, 2004, with a gross value of $223,200. First held in 1920. First graded in 1973. Stakes record 1:43.14 (1999 Captain Steve).

Year	Winner	Jockey	Second	Third	Strs	Time	1st Purse
2004	Greater Good, 2, 122	J. McKee	Rush Bay, 2, 116	Wild Desert, 2, 118	9	1:45.14	$138,384
2003	The Cliff's Edge, 2, 122	S. J. Sellers	Gran Prospect, 2, 116	Proper Prado, 2, 118	8	1:45.50	137,764
2002	Soto, 2, 117	L. J. Melancon	Ten Cents a Shine, 2, 115	Most Feared, 2, 122	12	1:44.67	143,344
2001	Repent, 2, 122	A. J. D'Amico	Request for Parole, 2, 117	High Star, 2, 115	6	1:44.42	134,540
2000	Dollar Bill, 2, 113	C. H. Borel	Holiday Thunder, 2, 113	Gift of the Eagle, 2, 113	6	1:47.18	135,656
1999	Captain Steve, 2, 122	R. Albarado	Mighty, 2, 122	Personal First, 2, 119	12	**1:43.14**	143,840
1998	Exploit, 2, 122	C. J. McCarron	Vicar, 2, 113	Grits'n Hard Toast, 2, 113	11	1:44.16	140,740
1997	Cape Town, 2, 113	W. Martinez	Time Limit, 2, 119	Real Quiet, 2, 116	11	1:43.97	142,228

Year	Winner	Jockey	Second	Third	Strs	Time	1st Purse
1996	Concerto, 2, 119	C. H. Marquez Jr.	Celtic Warrior, 2, 113	Carmen's Baby, 2, 122	11	1:46.91	$142,104
1995	Ide, 2, 122	C. Perret	Editor's Note, 2, 119	El Amante, 2, 113	5	1:44.31	97,500
1994	Jambalaya Jazz, 2, 113	S. Maple	You're the One, 2, 112	Peaks and Valleys, 2, 119	7	1:46.46	97,500
1993	War Deputy, 2, 112	G. K. Gomez	Tarzans Blade, 2, 122	Rustic Light, 2, 119	11	1:46.75	97,500
1992	Wild Gale, 2, 116	S. J. Sellers	Mi Cielo, 2, 116	Shoal Creek, 2, 121	11	1:45.64	105,918
1991	Dance Floor, 2, 121	C. W. Antley	Waki Warrior, 2, 116	Choctaw Ridge, 2, 116	10	1:45.21	104,891
1990	Richman, 2, 121	P. Day	Discover, 2, 116	Honor Grades, 2, 116	10	1:45.40	107,718
1989	Grand Canyon, 2, 121	A. T. Cordero Jr.	Insurrection, 2, 121	Dusty's Command, 2, 118	6	1:44.60	95,550
1988	Tricky Creek, 2, 118	L. J. Melancon	Western Playboy, 2, 116	Revive, 2, 118	10	1:45.40	106,083
1987	‡Notebook, 2, 122	J. A. Santos	Buoy, 2, 122	Hey Pat, 2, 119	6	1:47.40	74,701
1986	Mt. Pleasant, 2, 116	K. K. Allen	Mondulick, 2, 113	Funny Tunes, 2, 113	11	1:46.40	93,561
1985	Mustin Lake, 2, 116	P. Day	Bachelor Beau, 2, 116	Regal Dreamer, 2, 122	10	1:46.80	87,432
1984	Fuzzy, 2, 114	D. Brumfield	Banner Bob, 2, 119	Nordic Scandal, 2, 113	13	1:45.00	106,902
1983	Biloxi Indian, 2, 119	G. Patterson	Country Manor, 2, 119	Taylor's Special, 2, 119	7	1:46.20	71,721
1982	Highland Park, 2, 122	D. Brumfield	Coax Me Matt, 2, 116	Caveat, 2, 122	5	1:47.00	75,869
1981	El Baba, 2, 119	R. P. Romero	Crown the King, 2, 116	Talent Town, 2, 119	9	1:45.20	85,888
1980	Television Studio, 2, 119	D. Brumfield	Linnleur, 2, 119	Bear Creek Dam, 2, 116	8	1:47.00	73,226
1979	King Neptune, 2, 116	D. Brumfield	Royal Sporan, 2, 119	Silver Shears, 2, 116	7	1:37.80	37,001
1978	Lot o' Gold, 2, 119	R. DePass	Arctic Action, 2, 116	Uncle Fudge, 2, 119	12	1:37.80	37,645
1977	Going Investor, 2, 116	R. DePass	Jaycean, 2, 119	Silver Nitrate, 2, 116	7	1:38.20	36,121
1976	Run Dusty Run, 2, 122	D. G. McHargue	Get the Axe, 2, 116	Silver Series, 2, 116	8	1:37.20	34,831
1975	Play Boy, 2, 116	D. Brumfield	Khyber King, 2, 119	Please Find John, 2, 116	9	1:36.80	30,492
	Pastry, 2, 116	B. R. Feliciano	Bold Laddie, 2, 119	Bid to Fame, 2, 116	8	1:36.80	30,329
1974	Circle Home, 2, 116	M. Hole	Master Derby, 2, 122	Ruggles Ferry, 2, 116	9	1:36.00	36,748
1973	Cannonade, 2, 119	P. Anderson	Satan's Hills, 2, 116	Don't Be Late Jim, 2, 116	15	1:36.80	49,510

Churchill Downs is located in Louisville. Formerly sponsored by Brown & Williamson Tobacco Corp. of Louisville 1987-'93, 1996-2000. Grade 3 1973-'82, 1984-'86, 1989-'97. Not graded 1983. Held at Old Latonia 1931-'33. Not held 1939-'45. 1 mile 1920-'79. Two divisions 1975. ‡Buoy finished first, DQ to second, 1987.

Kentucky Oaks

Grade 1 in 2005. Churchill Downs, three-year-olds, fillies, 1 1/16 miles, dirt. Held May 6, 2005, with a gross value of $554,400. First held in 1875. First graded in 1973. Stakes record 1:48.64 (2003 Bird Town).

Year	Winner	Jockey	Second	Third	Strs	Time	1st Purse
2005	Summerly, 3, 121	J. D. Bailey	In the Gold, 3, 121	Gallant Secret, 3, 121	7	1:50.23	$343,728
2004	Ashado, 3, 121	J. R. Velazquez	Island Sand, 3, 121	Madcap Escapade, 3, 121	11	1:50.81	354,640
2003	Bird Town, 3, 121	E. S. Prado	Santa Catarina, 3, 121	Yell, 3, 121	12	**1:48.64**	355,756
2002	Farda Amiga, 3, 121	C. J. McCarron	Take Charge Lady, 3, 121	Habibti, 3, 121	9	1:50.41	348,502
2001	Flute, 3, 121	J. D. Bailey	Real Cozzy, 3, 121	Collect Call, 3, 121	13	1:48.85	377,704
2000	Secret Status, 3, 121	P. Day	Rings a Chime, 3, 121	Classy Cara, 3, 121	14	1:50.30	378,696
1999	Silverbulletday, 3, 121	G. L. Stevens	Dreams Gallore, 3, 121	Sweeping Story, 3, 121	7	1:49.92	341,620
1998	Keeper Hill, 3, 121	D. R. Flores	Banshee Breeze, 3, 121	Really Polish, 3, 121	13	1:52.06	375,410
1997	Blushing K. D., 3, 121	L. J. Meche	Tomisue's Delight, 3, 121	‡Storm Song, 3, 121	9	1:50.29	362,514
1996	Pike Place Dancer, 3, 121	C. S. Nakatani	Escena, 3, 121	Cara Rafaela, 3, 121	6	1:49.88	325,000
1995	Gal in a Ruckus, 3, 121	W. H. McCauley	Urbane, 3, 121	Sneaky Quiet, 3, 121	8	1:50.09	235,040
1994	Sardula, 3, 121	E. J. Delahoussaye	Lakeway, 3, 121	Dianes Halo, 3, 121	7	1:51.16	184,340
1993	Dispute, 3, 121	J. D. Bailey	Eliza, 3, 121	Quinpool, 3, 121	11	1:52.47	191,230
1992	Luv Me Luv Me Not, 3, 121	F. A. Arguello Jr.	Pleasant Stage, 3, 121	Prospectors Delite, 3, 121	6	1:51.41	182,455
1991	Lite Light, 3, 121	C. S. Nakatani	Withallprobability, 3, 121	Til Forbid, 3, 121	10	1:48.83	207,285
1990	Seaside Attraction, 3, 121	C. J. McCarron	Go for Wand, 3, 121	Bright Candles, 3, 121	10	1:52.80	156,910
1989	Open Mind, 3, 121	A. T. Cordero Jr.	Imaginary Lady, 3, 121	Blondeinamotel, 3, 121	5	1:50.60	150,540
1988	Goodbye Halo, 3, 121	P. Day	Jeanne Jones, 3, 121	Willa On the Move, 3, 121	10	1:50.40	156,715
1987	Buryyourbelief, 3, 121	J. A. Santos	Hometown Queen, 3, 121	Super Cook, 3, 121	8	1:50.40	155,415
1986	Tiffany Lass, 3, 121	G. L. Stevens	Life At the Top, 3, 121	Family Style, 3, 121	12	1:50.60	122,103
1985	Fran's Valentine, 3, 121	P. A. Valenzuela	Foxy Deen, 3, 121	Rascal Lass, 3, 121	9	1:50.00	118,365
1984	Lucky Lucky Lucky, 3, 121	A. T. Cordero Jr.	Miss Oceana, 3, 121	My Darling One, 3, 121	6	1:51.80	112,710
1983	Princess Rooney, 3, 121	J. Vasquez	Bright Crocus, 3, 121	Bemissed, 3, 121	7	1:50.80	116,968
1982	Blush With Pride, 3, 121	W. Shoemaker	Before Dawn, 3, 121	Flying Partner, 3, 121	7	1:50.20	126,133
1981	Heavenly Cause, 3, 121	L. A. Pincay Jr.	De La Rose, 3, 121	Wayward Lass, 3, 121	6	1:43.80	79,300
1980	Bold 'n Determined, 3, 121	E. J. Delahoussaye	Mitey Lively, 3, 121	Honest and True, 3, 121	8	1:44.80	83,915
1979	Davona Dale, 3, 121	J. Velasquez	Himalayan, 3, 121	Prize Spot, 3, 121	6	1:47.20	83,590
1978	White Star Line, 3, 121	E. Maple	Grenzen, 3, 121	Bold Rendezvous, 3, 121	11	1:45.20	60,889
1977	Sweet Alliance, 3, 121	C. J. McCarron	Our Mims, 3, 121	Mrs. Warren, 3, 121	12	1:43.60	60,889
1976	Optimistic Gal, 3, 121	B. Baeza	Confort Zone, 3, 121	Carmelita Gibbs, 3, 121	7	1:44.60	40,186
1975	Sun and Snow, 3, 121	G. Patterson	Funalon, 3, 121	Funny Cat, 3, 121	11	1:44.60	42,315
1974	Quaze Quilt, 3, 121	W. Gavidia	Special Team, 3, 121	Kaye's Commander, 3, 121	14	1:46.60	43,631
1973	Bag of Tunes, 3, 121	D. Gargan	La Prevoyante, 3, 121	Coraggioso, 3, 121	13	1:44.20	43,648

Named for the Oaks S. (Eng-G1), commonly known as the Epsom Oaks, its prototype in England. Churchill Downs is located in Louisville. Grade 2 1973-'77. 1 1/2 miles 1875-'90. 1 1/4 miles 1891-'95. 1 1/16 miles 1896-1919, 1942-'81. ‡Sharp Cat finished third, DQ to eighth, 1997.

King's Bishop Stakes

Grade 1 in 2005. Saratoga Race Course, three-year-olds, 7 furlongs, dirt. Held August 28, 2004, with a gross value of $250,000. First held in 1984. First graded in 1987. Stakes record 1:20.99 (2004 Pomeroy).

Year	Winner	Jockey	Second	Third	Strs	Time	1st Purse
2004	**Pomeroy**, 3, 121	E. S. Prado	Weigelia, 3, 121	Ice Wynnd Fire, 3, 117	8	**1:20.99**	$150,000
2003	**Valid Video**, 3, 121	J. Bravo	Great Notion, 3, 117	Ghostzapper, 3, 117	13	1:22.14	120,000
2002	**Gygistar**, 3, 124	J. R. Velazquez	Boston Common, 3, 121	Thunder Days, 3, 115	8	1:22.85	120,000
2001	**Squirtle Squirt**, 3, 121	J. D. Bailey	Illusioned, 3, 119	City Zip, 3, 124	8	1:21.97	120,000
2000	**More Than Ready**, 3, 124	P. Day	Valiant Halory, 3, 114	Millencolin, 3, 121	6	1:22.49	120,000
1999	**Forestry**, 3, 124	C. W. Antley	Five Star Day, 3, 115	Successful Appeal, 3, 124	12	1:21.00	120,000
1998	**Secret Firm**, 3, 121	E. S. Prado	Mint, 3, 121	Scatmandu, 3, 116	8	1:22.78	120,000
1997	**Tale of the Cat**, 3, 114	J. A. Krone	Oro de Mexico, 3, 116	Trafalgar, 3, 121	6	1:21.71	90,000
1996	**Honour and Glory**, 3, 123	J. A. Santos	Elusive Quality, 3, 112	Distorted Humor, 3, 115	6	1:21.78	64,920
1995	**Top Account**, 3, 112	P. Day	Ft. Stockton, 3, 120	Excelerate, 3, 113	10	1:22.50	68,100
1994	**Chimes Band**, 3, 117	J. D. Bailey	End Sweep, 3, 122	Halo's Image, 3, 117	7	1:21.82	65,700
1993	**Mi Cielo**, 3, 115	M. E. Smith	Williamstown, 3, 122	Schossberg, 3, 115	11	1:21.73	74,280
1992	**Salt Lake**, 3, 117	M. E. Smith	Binalong, 3, 115	Agincourt, 3, 122	10	1:21.53	73,440
1991	**Take Me Out**, 3, 115	M. E. Smith	Joey the Student, 3, 115	To Freedom, 3, 119	10	1:21.73	74,400
1990	**Housebuster**, 3, 122	C. Perret	Poppiano, 3, 115	Sunshine Jimmy, 3, 115	9	1:21.80	54,090
1989	**Houston**, 3, 119	P. Day	Fast Play, 3, 117	Fierce Fighter, 3, 115	6	1:22.00	51,930
1988	**King's Nest**, 3, 115	C. J. McCarron	Tejano, 3, 117	Parlay Me, 3, 115	8	1:21.80	53,280
1987	**Templar Hill**, 3, 119	C. J. McCarron	Mister S. M., 3, 119	Homebuilder, 3, 115	8	1:23.00	51,660
1985	**Pancho Villa**, 3, 122	D. G. McHargue	El Basco, 3, 119	Cullendale, 3, 115	9	1:22.20	33,540
1984	**Commemorate**, 3, 119	F. Lovato Jr.	All Fired Up, 3, 122	Raja's Shark, 3, 115	8	1:22.60	33,900

Named for Bohemia Stable's 1973 Carter H. (G2) winner King's Bishop (1969 c. by Round Table). Grade 3 1987-'91. Grade 2 1992-'98. Not held 1986.

Knickerbocker Handicap

Grade 3 in 2005. Aqueduct, three-year-olds and up, 1 1/8 miles, turf. Held October 30, 2004, with a gross value of $150,000. First held in 1960. First graded in 1973. Stakes record 1:48.69 (1998 Sahm).

Year	Winner	Jockey	Second	Third	Strs	Time	1st Purse
2004	**Host (Chi)**, 4, 115	C. P. DeCarlo	Evening Attire, 6, 114	Sailaway, 4, 113	9	1:49.95	$90,000
2003	**Better Talk Now**, 4, 116	E. S. Prado	Del Mar Show, 6, 116	Millennium Dragon (GB), 4, 115	12	1:50.53	90,000
2002	**Dawn of the Condor**, 5, 114	J. F. Chavez	Serial Bride, 5, 114	Polish Miner, 5, 114	9	1:52.54	90,000
2001	**Sumitas (Ger)**, 5, 115	E. S. Prado	Manndar (Ire), 5, 116	Crash Course, 5, 115	11	2:02.55	90,000
2000	**Charge d'Affaires (GB)**, 5, 115	J. A. Santos	Devine Wind, 4, 116	Understood, 4, 111	7	1:49.01	90,000
1999	**Charge d'Affaires (GB)**, 4, 114	J. A. Santos	Comic Strip, 4, 119	Nat's Big Party, 5, 113	7	1:49.06	66,480
1998	**Sahm**, 4, 116	J. R. Velazquez	Glok, 4, 113	Let Goodtimes Roll, 5, 112	8	**1:48.69**	67,440
1997	**Sir Cat**, 4, 115	M. E. Smith	Tarnhid, 4, 114	Outta My Way Man, 5, 114	5	1:50.02	69,060
1996	**Mr. Bluebird**, 5, 113	M. E. Smith	Devil's Cup, 3, 107	Ops Smile, 4, 116	12	1:49.21	69,660
1995	**Diplomatic Jet**, 3, 113	M. E. Smith	Flag Down, 5, 114	Easy Miner, 4, 110	11	2:04.97	87,870
1994	**Kiri's Clown**, 5, 114	M. J. Luzzi	River Majesty, 5, 117	Red Earth, 3, 111	12	1:49.38	52,335
1993	**River Majesty**, 4, 115	M. E. Smith	Daarik (Ire), 6, 114	Home of the Free, 5, 118	6	1:54.54	52,920
1992	**Binary Light**, 3, 111	J. Cruguet	Share the Glory, 4, 110	Turkey Point, 7, 113	7	1:52.70	56,160
1991	**Home of the Free**, 3, 110	J. R. Velazquez	Turkey Point, 6, 114	Fourstars Allstar, 3, 113	7	1:48.73	56,070
1990	**Who's to Pay**, 4, 115	J. D. Bailey	Yankee Affair, 8, 120	Green Line Express, 4, 121	8	1:49.20	57,240
1989	**Trans Banner**, 4, 112	J. Samyn	Soviet Lad, 4, 112	Impersonator, 4, 114	12	1:53.60	58,770
1988	**Jimmy's Bronco**, 4, 112	J. Cruguet	Coeur de Lion (Fr), 4, 118	†Gai Minois (Fr), 6, 113	11	1:54.60	58,590
1987	**Laser Lane**, 4, 113	J. A. Santos	Yankee Affair, 6, 116	Wanderkin, 4, 112	12	1:51.60	73,260
1986	**Duluth**, 4, 113	J. Cruguet	Dance of Life, 3, 122	Broadway Tommy, 4, 109	8	2:20.80	55,710
1985	**Putting Green**, 5, 112	E. Maple	Domynsky (GB), 5, 113	Capricorn Son (Ire), 3, 109	7	2:23.80	54,405
	Rocamadour (Ire), 6, 109	J. Cruguet	‡Sondrio (Ire), 4, 115	He's Vivacious, 5, 110	7	2:23.80	54,405
1984	**He's Vivacious**, 4, 108	R. G. Davis	Nassipour, 4, 109	Lucky Scott (GB), 3, 107	12	2:26.00	46,440
1983	**Four Bases**, 4, 105	R. J. Thibeau Jr.	Moon Spirit, 3, 114	Ask Me, 4, 117	10	2:17.80	34,230
	Piling, 5, 114	E. Maple	Chem, 4, 116	Charging Through, 3, 110	8	2:19.00	34,470
1982	**Half Iced**, 3, 114	D. MacBeth	No Neck, 7, 109	Erin's Tiger, 4, 113	8	2:18.20	33,330
	†**If Winter Comes**, 4, 108	M. Venezia	Ten Below, 3, 113	Forkali, 4, 112	8	2:19.60	33,330
1981	†**Euphrosyne**, 5, 110	R. Migliore	Our Captain Willie, 3, 115	Naskra's Breeze, 4, 115	8	2:18.40	33,300
	Ghazwan (Ire), 4, 110	C. Hernandez	Wicked Will (GB), 3, 108	†Hunston (GB), 3, 107	7	2:20.60	33,540
1980	**Foretake**, 4, 112	J. Ruane	El Barril (Chi), 4, 113	Ministrel (Fr), 4, 109	9	2:22.20	33,450
	Lobsang (Ire), 4, 111	M. Venezia	Match the Hatch, 4, 115	King Crimson (Fr), 5, 111	7	2:23.60	33,450
1979	**French Colonial**, 4, 114	J. Vasquez	T. V. Series, 3, 113	Golden Reserve, 5, 112	12	2:21.40	35,880
1978	**Fluorescent Light**, 4, 115	J. Cruguet	Banquet Table, 4, 109	Scythian Gold, 3, 110	10	2:14.20	34,560
1977	**Dance d'Espoir**, 5, 112	J. Cruguet	Java Rajah, 4, 106	Diagramatic, 4, 112	5	2:05.00	26,010
	Keep the Promise, 5, 112	J. Cruguet	Soldier's Lark, 3, 110	Star Spangled, 3, 114	8	2:04.40	26,460
1976	†**Javamine**, 3, 111	J. Velasquez	*Recupere, 6, 112	Banghi, 3, 118	9	2:20.60	26,400
	Oilfield, 3, 112	S. Hawley	Royal Mission, 3, 111	Trumpeter Swan, 5, 112	7	2:22.60	26,100
1975	**Shady Character**, 4, 113	A. T. Cordero Jr.	Blue Times, 4, 115	*Yvetot, 7, 113	8	2:16.20	33,900

1974 **Shady Character**, 3, 115	A. T. Cordero Jr.	John Drew, 3, 111	Crafty Khale, 5, 126	5 2:41.40	$33,690
1973 **Astray**, 4, 112	C. Baltazar	Triangular, 6, 114	*Yvetot, 5, 112	11 2:39.80	34,710

Named for a Washington Irving fictional character, Diedrich Knickerbocker; in the 19th century, New Yorkers were often called "Knickerbockers." Grade 3 1973-'97. Held at Belmont Park 1962, 1975, 1995, 2001. 1⅝ miles 1960-'61, 1970-'74. 1⅜ miles 1962, 1975-'76, 1978-'86. 1³/₁₆ miles 1963-'69. 1¼ miles 1977, 1995, 2001. Dirt 1977, 1992, 1997. Two divisions 1976-'77, 1980-'83, 1985. ‡He's Vivacious finished second, DQ to third, 1985 (2nd Div.). †Denotes female.

La Brea Stakes

Grade 1 in 2005. Santa Anita Park, three-year-olds, fillies, 7 furlongs, dirt. Held December 27, 2004, with a gross value of $250,000. First held in 1974. First graded in 1983. Stakes record 1:20.45 (1993 Mamselle Bebette).

Year	Winner	Jockey	Second	Third	Strs	Time	1st Purse
2004	**Alphabet Kisses**, 3, 117	M. E. Smith	Bending Strings, 3, 121	Elusive Diva, 3, 119	10	1:21.38	$150,000
2003	**Island Fashion**, 3, 123	K. J. Desormeaux	Randaroo, 3, 119	Buffythecenterfold, 3, 119	10	1:21.79	150,000
2002	**Got Koko**, 3, 117	A. O. Solis	Spring Meadow, 3, 119	Erica's Smile, 3, 117	10	1:22.57	120,000
2001	**Affluent**, 3, 121	E. J. Delahoussaye	Royally Chosen, 3, 119	Love At Noon, 3, 117	12	1:21.29	120,000
2000	**Spain**, 3, 123	V. Espinoza	Cover Gal, 3, 119	Serenita (Arg), 3, 115	6	1:22.27	120,000
1999	**Hookedonthefeelin**, 3, 119	D. R. Flores	Olympic Charmer, 3, 119	Kalookan Queen, 3, 119	8	1:21.84	120,000
1998	**Magical Allure**, 3, 121	G. L. Stevens	Gourmet Girl, 3, 117	Tranquility Lake, 3, 116	7	1:22.06	120,000
1997	**I Ain't Bluffing**, 3, 119	E. J. Delahoussaye	Minister's Melody, 3, 119	Praviana (Chi), 3, 115	9	1:21.23	120,000
1996	**Hidden Lake**, 3, 115	C. J. McCarron	Belle's Flag, 3, 119	Tiffany Diamond, 3, 115	7	1:22.00	80,900
1995	**Exotic Wood**, 3, 119	C. J. McCarron	Evil's Pic, 3, 119	Jewel Princess, 3, 119	6	1:21.57	80,250
1994	**Top Rung**, 3, 115	G. L. Stevens	Klassy Kim, 3, 119	Twice the Vice, 3, 119	7	1:21.84	63,700
1993	**Mamselle Bebette**, 3, 115	C. S. Nakatani	Desert Stormer, 3, 116	Island Orchid, 3, 115	9	**1:20.45**	65,900
1992	**Arches of Gold**, 3, 115	E. J. Delahoussaye	Race the Wild Wind, 3, 121	Terre Haute, 3, 117	8	1:21.28	64,800
1991	**D'Or Ruckus**, 3, 115	C. J. McCarron	Good Potential, 3, 119	Garden Gal, 3, 117	6	1:22.05	48,800
	Teresa Mc, 3, 119	P. A. Valenzuela	Remarkably Easy, 3, 119	Suziqcute, 3, 119	6	1:23.05	48,800
1990	**Brought to Mind**, 3, 117	A. O. Solis	A Wild Ride, 3, 119	Mama Simba, 3, 114	8	1:21.60	65,000
	Akinemod, 4, 117	G. L. Stevens	Fantastic Look, 4, 122	Reluctant Guest, 4, 117	8	1:21.60	62,650
1989	**Variety Baby**, 4, 117	C. A. Black	T. V. of Crystal, 4, 117	Forewarning, 4, 117	8	1:21.60	49,050
1988	**Very Subtle**, 4, 124	P. A. Valenzuela	Saros Brig, 4, 114	Fold the Flag, 4, 117	6	1:21.60	60,300
1987	**Family Style**, 4, 122	G. L. Stevens	Sari's Heroine, 4, 119	Winter Treasure, 3, 119	6	1:22.60	46,700
1985	**Savannah Slew**, 3, 119	W. Shoemaker	Lady's Secret, 3, 124	Ambra Ridge, 3, 114	7	1:22.40	39,150
	Mitterand, 4, 117	E. J. Delahoussaye	Percipient, 4, 119	Lady Trilby, 4, 117	9	1:21.80	39,950
1983	**Lovlier Linda**, 3, 114	W. Shoemaker	Angel Savage (Mex), 3, 115	Fabulous Notion, 3, 124	9	1:22.20	40,700
1982	**Beautiful Glass**, 3, 114	C. J. McCarron	Skillful Joy, 3, 122	Header Card, 3, 119	11	1:21.00	42,450
	Nell's Briquette, 4, 122	C. J. McCarron	Bannockburn, 4, 115	Bee a Scout, 4, 117	6	1:25.80	40,150
1981	**Dynanite**, 4, 114	W. Shoemaker	Bold 'n Determined, 4, 125	Pachena, 4, 114	5	1:21.40	31,750
1980	**Terlingua**, 4, 121	D. G. McHargue	Glorious Song, 4, 116	Prize Spot, 4, 121	4	1:20.80	31,350
1979	**Great Lady M.**, 4, 117	L. A. Pincay Jr.	dh-B. Thoughtful, 4, 121		11	1:22.60	35,850
			dh-Queen Yasna, 4, 114				
1978	**Taisez Vous**, 4, 121	D. Pierce	Ida Delia, 4, 114	Sound of Summer, 4, 121	7	1:22.80	26,700
1976	**Kirby Lane**, 3, 117	L. A. Pincay Jr.	Tregillick, 3, 116	Missing Marbles, 3, 116	9	1:45.20	23,750
1975	**Featherfoot**, 3, 114	W. Shoemaker	Banyan Road, 3, 120	Graham Heagney, 3, 114	5	1:43.20	13,025
	Big Destiny, 3, 114	S. Hawley	Bending Away, 3, 120	Mark's Place, 3, 120	6	1:42.80	13,325
	Bobby Murcer, 4, 120	E. Belmonte	Bold Clarion, 4, 120	Roger's Dandy, 4, 117	11	1:43.40	20,800
1974	**Niner Power**, 4, 117	S. Valdez	First Majesty, 4, 117	Handsome Native, 4, 117	10	1:43.80	20,350

Named for Rancho La Brea in Los Angeles County, California; brea means "tar." Grade 2 1994-'96. Not held 1977, 1984, 1986. 1¹/₁₆ miles 1974-'76. Four-year-olds 1974, 1975 (January), 1978-'81, 1982 (January), 1985 (January), 1987-'89, 1990 (January). Both sexes 1974-'76. Two divisions 1991. Held in January and December 1975, 1982, 1985, 1990. Dead heat for second 1979. Nonwinners of a race worth $10,000 to the winner 1974. Nonwinners of a race worth $12,500 to the winner 1975.

La Canada Stakes

Grade 2 in 2005. Santa Anita Park, four-year-olds, fillies, 1⅛ miles, dirt. Held February 12, 2005, with a gross value of $200,000. First held in 1975. First graded in 1977. Stakes record 1:47.60 (1980 Glorious Song).

Year	Winner	Jockey	Second	Third	Strs	Time	1st Purse
2005	**Tarlow**, 4, 117	P. A. Valenzuela	Sweet Lips, 4, 121	A. P. Adventure, 4, 118	5	1:48.64	$120,000
2004	**Cat Fighter**, 4, 115	A. O. Solis	Fencelineneighbor, 4, 116	Tangle (Ire), 4, 116	8	1:50.41	120,000
2003	**Got Koko**, 4, 121	A. O. Solis	Sightseek, 4, 118	Bella Bellucci, 4, 118	5	1:48.41	120,000
2002	**Summer Colony**, 4, 119	G. L. Stevens	Azeri, 4, 115	Ask Me No Secrets, 4, 115	6	1:49.26	120,000
2001	**Spain**, 4, 122	V. Espinoza	Chilukki, 4, 119	Letter of Intent, 4, 116	5	1:49.74	120,000
2000	**Scholars Studio**, 4, 116	C. S. Nakatani	Smooth Player, 4, 119	The Seven Seas, 4, 116	5	1:49.14	120,000
1999	**Manistique**, 4, 119	G. L. Stevens	Magical Allure, 4, 119	Gourmet Girl, 4, 117	7	1:48.81	120,000
1998	**Fleet Lady**, 4, 119	G. K. Gomez	Minister's Melody, 4, 117	I Ain't Bluffing, 4, 117	7	1:48.59	120,000
1997	**Belle's Flag**, 4, 119	C. S. Nakatani	Chile Chatte, 4, 115	Housa Dancer (Fr), 4, 115	8	1:48.26	133,200
1996	**Jewel Princess**, 4, 119	A. O. Solis	Dixie Pearl, 4, 116	Privity, 4, 117	6	1:49.42	129,900
1995	**Dianes Halo**, 4, 115	C. S. Nakatani	Twice the Vice, 4, 119	Klassy Kim, 4, 119	6	1:49.35	123,800
1994	**Stalcreek**, 4, 119	G. L. Stevens	Alyshena, 4, 115	Hollywood Wildcat, 4, 122	4	1:48.85	120,000
1993	**Alysbelle**, 4, 116	E. J. Delahoussaye	Pacific Squall, 4, 119	Interactive, 4, 117	9	1:49.85	130,850
1992	**Exchange**, 4, 119	L. A. Pincay Jr.	Winglet, 4, 117	Damewood, 4, 116	8	1:49.96	128,250

1991	**Fit to Scout**, 4, 120	J. A. Garcia	Vieille Vigne (Fr), 4, 116	A Wild Ride, 4, 121	7	1:48.50	$126,700
1990	**Gorgeous**, 4, 125	E. J. Delahoussaye	Luthier's Launch, 4, 117	Kelly, 4, 116	5	1:50.00	122,000
1989	**Goodbye Halo**, 4, 126	P. Day	Seattle Smooth, 4, 117	Savannah's Honor, 4, 115	7	1:54.40	125,300
1988	**Hollywood Glitter**, 4, 117	L. A. Pincay Jr.	By Land by Sea, 4, 119	Very Subtle, 4, 126	5	1:49.20	94,200
1987	**Family Style**, 4, 122	G. L. Stevens	Winter Treasure, 4, 117	Sari's Heroine, 4, 121	6	1:49.60	94,800
1986	**Lady's Secret**, 4, 126	C. J. McCarron	Shywing, 4, 119	North Sider, 4, 118	6	1:49.80	120,200
1985	**Mitterand**, 4, 121	E. J. Delahoussaye	Percipient, 4, 117	Life's Magic, 4, 126	5	1:48.80	90,700
1984	**Sweet Diane**, 4, 120	R. Sibille	Weekend Surprise, 4, 115	Lovlier Linda, 4, 120	4	1:49.20	117,200
1983	**Avigaition**, 4, 117	E. J. Delahoussaye	Elusive, 4, 115	Etoile Du Matin, 4, 116	11	1:49.80	101,900
1982	**Safe Play**, 4, 119	D. Brumfield	Rainbow Connection, 4, 121	Native Plunder, 4, 117	11	**1:47.60**	100,800
1981	**Summer Siren**, 4, 117	M. Castaneda	Miss Huntington, 4, 115	Tobin's Rose, 4, 118	10	1:48.60	86,250
1980	**Glorious Song**, 4, 118	C. J. McCarron	Prize Spot, 4, 119	It's in the Air, 4, 125	7	**1:47.60**	80,350
1979	**B. Thoughtful**, 4, 119	D. Pierce	Petron's Love, 4, 117	Island Kiss, 4, 115	8	1:48.80	69,900
1978	**Taisez Vous**, 4, 120	D. Pierce	Drama Critic, 4, 116	Table the Rumor, 4, 117	5	1:49.80	65,000
1977	***Lucie Manet**, 4, 115	W. Shoemaker	Hail Hilarious, 4, 121	Up to Juliet, 4, 115	7	1:48.20	68,300
1976	**Raise Your Skirts**, 4, 119	W. Shoemaker	Fascinating Girl, 4, 117	Our First Delight, 4, 117	8	1:48.40	50,150
1975	**Chris Evert**, 4, 128	J. Velasquez	Mercy Dee, 4, 116	Lucky Spell, 4, 119	7	1:41.60	35,400

Named for Rancho La Canada where the city of La Crescenta, California, is located; canada means "glen" or "dell." Grade 1 1978-'89. 1 1/16 miles 1975.

Lady's Secret Breeders' Cup Handicap

Grade 2 in 2005. Santa Anita Park, three-year-olds and up, fillies and mares, 1 1/16 miles, dirt. Held October 3, 2004, with a gross value of $235,000. First held in 1993. First graded in 1995. Stakes record 1:40.61 (1994 Hollywood Wildcat).

Year	Winner	Jockey	Second		Strs	Time	1st Purse
2004	**Island Fashion**, 4, 120	K. John	Miss Loren (Arg), 6, 116	Elloluv, 4, 118	7	1:43.43	$150,000
2003	**Got Koko**, 4, 118	A. O. Solis	‡Azeri, 5, 128	Adoration, 4, 115	6	1:42.92	180,000
2002	**Azeri**, 4, 127	M. E. Smith	Starrer, 4, 115	Mystic Lady, 4, 116	7	1:41.10	130,500
2001	**Queenie Belle**, 4, 116	B. Blanc	Letter of Intent, 4, 116	Nany's Sweep, 5, 116	4	1:43.64	126,240
2000	**Smooth Player**, 4, 116	E. J. Delahoussaye	Speaking of Time, 4, 109	Bordelaise (Arg), 5, 116	4	1:42.27	126,360
1999	**Manistique**, 4, 123	C. S. Nakatani	Cookin Vickie, 4, 111	Kalosca (Fr), 5, 114	5	1:42.39	125,100
1998	**Magical Allure**, 3, 116	D. R. Flores	Victory Stripes (Arg), 4, 114	Housa Dancer (Fr), 5, 117	8	1:42.55	110,280
1997	**Sharp Cat**, 3, 117	A. O. Solis	Twice the Vice, 6, 122	Minister's Melody, 3, 115	5	1:41.40	109,400
1996	**Top Rung**, 5, 116	E. Fires	Jewel Princess, 4, 122	Sleep Easy, 4, 116	5	1:41.84	109,450
1995	**Borodislew**, 5, 120	G. L. Stevens	Top Rung, 4, 116	Golden Klair (GB), 5, 117	6	1:41.61	74,000
1994	**Hollywood Wildcat**, 4, 124	E. J. Delahoussaye	Exchange, 6, 121	Dancing Mirage, 3, 113	6	**1:40.61**	61,400
1993	**Hollywood Wildcat**, 3, 117	E. J. Delahoussaye	Re Toss (Arg), 6, 117	Wedding Ring (Ire), 4, 113	5	1:41.05	61,700

Named for Mr. and Mrs. Eugene V. Klein's 1986 Horse of the Year and '86 Breeders' Cup Distaff (G1) (at Santa Anita Park) winner Lady's Secret (1982 f. by Secretariat). Grade 3 1995. Lady's Secret H. 1993-'95. ‡Elloluv finished second, DQ to fourth, 2003.

Lafayette Stakes

Grade 3 in 2005. Keeneland, three-year-olds, 6 furlongs, dirt. Held April 10, 2005, with a gross value of $103,887. First held in 1937. First graded in 1990. Stakes record 1:09.88 (2005 More Smoke).

Year	Winner	Jockey	Second	Third	Strs	Time	1st Purse
2005	**More Smoke**, 3, 119	C. L. Potts	Crimson Stag, 3, 123	Razor, 3, 119	4	**1:09.88**	$66,402
2004	**Bwana Charlie**, 3, 117	S. J. Sellers	Quick Action, 3, 116	Tales of Glory, 3, 116	6	1:24.73	67,890
2003	**Posse**, 3, 118	C. J. Lanerie	Roll Hennessy Roll, 3, 118	Bossanova, 3, 116	6	1:23.14	66,898
2002	**Cashel Castle**, 3, 116	P. Day	Governor Hickel, 3, 116	Sky Terrace, 3, 116	6	1:24.47	69,006
2001	**Griffinite**, 3, 116	J. A. Santos	Sam Lord's Castle, 3, 118	Yonaguska, 3, 123	7	1:22.61	68,820
2000	**Caller One**, 3, 120	R. G. Davis	Sun Cat, 3, 116	Littleexpectations, 3, 120	9	1:21.73	70,370
1999	**Yes It's True**, 3, 123	J. D. Bailey	Trickey Crew, 3, 118	Fort La Roca, 3, 115	5	1:22.15	66,340
1998	**Dontletthebigonego**, 3, 114	W. Martinez	Flashing Tammany, 3, 114	Swear by Dixie, 3, 114	6	1:23.15	67,394
1997	**Trafalger**, 3, 113	J. D. Bailey	Open Forum, 3, 118	Muchacho Fino, 3, 113	4	1:21.68	67,456
1996	**Wire Me Collect**, 3, 112	K. L. Chapman	Appealing Skier, 3, 121	Irish Conquest, 3, 112	9	1:21.82	69,192
1995	**Mr. Greeley**, 3, 121	J. A. Krone	Peaks and Valleys, 3, 118	Tethra, 3, 121	7	1:21.43	51,429
1994	**Exclusive Praline**, 3, 121	J. A. Santos	Dynamic Asset, 3, 115	End Sweep, 3, 113	5	1:23.82	49,321
1993	**Cherokee Run**, 3, 118	P. Day	Poverty Slew, 3, 112	Williamstown, 3, 121	8	**1:21.25**	52,297
1992	**American Chance**, 3, 118	P. Day	Capitalimprovement, 3, 118	Mon Capitan, 3, 114	7	1:22.16	53,365
1991	**To Freedom**, 3, 121	C. W. Antley	Romiano, 3, 112	Broadway's Top Gun, 3, 113	7	1:22.83	54,958
1990	**Housebuster**, 3, 121	C. Perret	Sacra Hoxen, 3, 114	Critical Choice, 3, 113	3	1:22.80	52,215
1989	**Belek**, 3, 112	S. P. Romero	Notation, 3, 118	Mr. Sea Sanders, 3, 118	6	1:23.00	35,051
1988	**Forty Niner**, 3, 121	P. Day	Buoy, 3, 122	Aloha Prospector, 3, 121	8	1:22.00	46,306
1987	**Trick Card**, 3, 118	D. A. Miller Jr.	War, 3, 118	Contractor's Tune, 3, 112	6	1:23.80	35,084
1986	**Numero Uno Pass**, 3, 113	C. Perret	Color Me Smart, 3, 121	Friendly Blue, 3, 112	8	1:23.60	35,945
1985	**Proudest Hour**, 3, 121	R. P. Romero	Felter On the Quay, 3, 112	Don't Hesitate, 3, 121	7	1:10.80	35,133
1984	**Delta Trace**, 3, 118	K. K. Allen	Patch of Sun, 3, 112	Soybean Trader, 3, 112	14	1:10.40	37,488
1983	**Freezing Rain**, 3, 118	D. Brumfield	Harry 'n Bill, 3, 118	Hamlet, 3, 112	11	1:11.20	36,546
1982	**Jungle Blade**, 3, 115	J. Neagle	Talk of the Times, 3, 118	Baraco, 3, 112	12	1:10.20	40,544
1981	**Grey Bucket**, 2, 119	J. Oldham	Talent Town, 2, 116	†Lady Ann's Key, 2, 116	10	:53.20	15,356
1980	**Firm Boss**, 2, 122	M. R. Morgan	†Bend the Times, 2, 116	Silver Dollar Boy, 2, 122	7	:53.00	14,723

1979	**Raised Socially**, 2, 119	M. R. Morgan	Native Moment, 2, 119	Landing Stripes, 2, 119	8	:52.20	$16,380
1978	**Spy Charger**, 2, 122	G. Mahon	It's a Rerun, 2, 119	Trip Over, 2, 116	8	:53.20	11,278
1977	**‡Fiddle Faddle**, 2, 116	W. Gavidia	Old Crony, 2, 119	Bye Bye Bud, 2, 116	8	:52.80	11,356
1976	**United Holme**, 2, 119	W. Gavidia	Marve, 2, 119	Golden Gossip, 2, 119	5	:52.00	11,125
1975	**Inca Roca**, 2, 116	T. Warner	Joseph Daniel, 2, 116	Khyber King, 2, 119	11	:52.80	11,928
1974	**Paris Dust**, 2, 122	C. Perret	Commercial Pilot, 2, 119	‡Master Derby, 2, 119	7	:51.80	12,379
1973	**Mr. A. Z.**, 2, 118	R. N. Ussery	Hudson County, 2, 115	Best of It, 2, 116	10	:52.60	12,808

Named for the Marquis de Lafayette, French hero of the American Revolutionary War. Held at Churchill Downs 1943-'44. Not held 1945. About 4 furlongs 1946-'64. 4½ furlongs 1943-'44, 1965-'81. 7 furlongs 1937-'42, 1986-2004. Colts and geldings 1937-'78. ‡Idle Cadet finished third, DQ to fourth, 1974. ‡Forever Casting finished first, DQ to eighth, 1977. Equaled track record 1993. †Denotes female.

La Jolla Handicap

Grade 2 in 2005. Del Mar, three-year-olds, 1¹⁄₁₆ miles, turf. Held August 14, 2004, with a gross value of $150,000. First held in 1937. First graded in 1973. Stakes record 1:40.39 (2003 Singletary).

Year	Winner	Jockey	Second	Third	Strs	Time	1st Purse
2004	**Blackdoun (Fr)**, 3, 120	C. S. Nakatani	Semi Lost, 3, 116	Bedmar (GB), 3, 113	7	1:41.03	$90,000
2003	**Singletary**, 3, 118	P. A. Valenzuela	Devious Boy (GB), 3, 117	Senor Swinger, 3, 120	7	**1:40.39**	90,000
2002	**Inesperado (Fr)**, 3, 118	E. J. Delahoussaye	Regiment, 3, 121	Mountain Rage, 3, 119	4	1:43.92	90,000
2001	**Marine (GB)**, 3, 117	C. S. Nakatani	Romanceishope, 3, 118	Mister Approval, 3, 113	8	1:41.72	90,000
2000	**Purely Cozzene**, 3, 120	D. R. Flores	Duke of Green (GB), 3, 117	Sign of Hope (GB), 3, 115	9	1:41.50	90,000
1999	**Eagleton**, 3, 119	I. D. Enriquez	In Frank's Honor, 3, 117	Zanetti, 3, 117	9	1:41.89	90,000
1998	**Ladies Din**, 3, 120	G. L. Stevens	Success and Glory (Ire), 3, 116	Lucayan Indian (Ire), 3, 116	7	1:41.94	80,670
1997	**Fantastic Fellow**, 3, 118	A. O. Solis	Worldly Ways (GB), 3, 119	Falkenham (GB), 3, 115	7	1:43.43	85,450
1996	**Ambivalent**, 3, 116	R. R. Douglas	The Barking Shark, 3, 114	Caribbean Pirate, 3, 117	10	1:43.34	82,850
1995	**Petionville**, 3, 120	C. S. Nakatani	Private Interview, 3, 115	Beau Temps (GB), 3, 115	7	1:44.26	74,600
1994	**Marvin's Faith (Ire)**, 3, 114	C. W. Antley	Unfinished Symph, 3, 120	Ocean Crest, 3, 114	7	1:42.38	62,800
1993	**Manny's Prospect**, 3, 115	C. J. McCarron	Golden Slewpy, 3, 116	Hawk Spell, 3, 116	9	1:42.12	64,700
1992	**Blacksburg**, 3, 119	K. J. Desormeaux	Free At Last, 3, 121	Fax News, 3, 114	9	1:41.60	64,700
1991	**Track Monarch**, 3, 116	P. A. Valenzuela	Soweto (Ire), 3, 116	Persianalli (Ire), 3, 115	6	1:41.91	61,400
1990	**Tight Spot**, 3, 118	E. J. Delahoussaye	Itsallgreektome, 3, 119	Music Prospector, 3, 118	6	1:41.80	62,100
1989	**River Master**, 3, 115	C. J. McCarron	Tokatee, 3, 113	Art Work, 3, 114	8	1:42.60	65,100
1988	**Perfecting**, 3, 116	G. L. Stevens	Roberto's Dancer, 3, 115	Prove Splendid, 3, 115	8	1:41.60	64,800
1987	**The Medic**, 3, 116	C. J. McCarron	Something Lucky, 3, 120	Savona Tower, 3, 117	11	1:42.20	66,250
1986	**Vernon Castle**, 3, 120	E. J. Delahoussaye	Tripoli Shores, 3, 117	Marvin's Policy, 3, 116	12	1:35.20	64,650
1985	**Floating Reserve**, 3, 117	P. A. Valenzuela	First Norman, 3, 116	Derby Dawning, 3, 119	9	1:34.60	62,750
1984	**Tights**, 3, 120	C. J. McCarron	Ocean View, 3, 113	Refueled (Ire), 3, 115	6	1:35.60	59,150
1983	**Tanks Brigade**, 3, 120	E. J. Delahoussaye	Dr. Daly, 3, 121	Pair of Aces, 3, 116	7	1:35.80	50,150
1982	**Hugabay**, 3, 115	K. D. Black	Bargain Balcony, 3, 118	The Captain, 3, 118	8	1:35.60	33,050
	Take the Floor, 3, 115	C. J. McCarron	Craelius, 3, 116	Sword Blade, 3, 115	8	1:35.60	33,050
1981	**Minnesota Chief**, 3, 122	C. J. McCarron	High Counsel, 3, 117	Stancharry, 3, 124	11	1:35.20	40,950
1980	**Aristocratical**, 3, 117	C. J. McCarron	Son of a Dodo, 3, 117	Exploded, 3, 117	9	1:36.20	32,850
1979	**Relaunch**, 3, 117	L. A. Pincay Jr.	Hyannis Port, 3, 122	Pole Position, 3, 124	7	1:35.40	25,600
1978	**Singular**, 3, 114	D. G. McHargue	Misrepresentation, 3, 119	Sea Ride, 3, 114	9	1:35.80	23,150
1977	**Stone Point**, 3, 114	M. Castaneda	Pay the Toll, 3, 114	Windy Dancer, 3, 114	6	1:35.80	18,850
1976	**Today 'n Tomorrow**, 3, 114	D. Pierce	Noble Envoy, 3, 114	Wood Green, 3, 115	8	1:35.20	19,400
1975	**Larrikin**, 3, 123	D. Pierce	Wood Carver, 3, 115	Sibirri, 3, 119	9	1:35.00	16,850
1974	**Lightning Mandate**, 3, 125	A. Pineda	Within Hail, 3, 120	Sea Aglo, 3, 113	6	1:34.40	15,800
1973	**Groshawk**, 3, 125	W. Shoemaker	Dancing Papa, 3, 115	Expression, 3, 123	6	1:34.20	16,300

Named for the resort community of La Jolla, California, located in the San Diego area. La Jolla Mile H. 1937-'65, 1982-'86. La Jolla Mile S. 1977-'81. Grade 3 1973-2003. Not held 1939, 1942-'44. 1 mile 1938-'86. Dirt 1937-'74. Three-year-olds and up 1937-'38, 1945-'46, 1949-'50. Two divisions 1982. Course record 1975.

Lake George Stakes

Grade 3 in 2005. Saratoga Race Course, three-year-olds, fillies, 1¹⁄₁₆ miles, turf. Held August 2, 2004, with a gross value of $113,900. First held in 1996. First graded in 1998. Stakes record 1:40.11 (1999 Nani Rose).

Year	Winner	Jockey	Second	Third	Strs	Time	1st Purse
2004	**Seducer's Song**, 3, 115	J. D. Bailey	Venturi (GB), 3, 119	Fortunate Damsel, 3, 117	10	1:42.01	$68,340
2003	**Film Maker**, 3, 115	E. S. Prado	Ocean Drive, 3, 119	Gal O Gal, 3, 122	11	1:41.80	68,700
2002	**Nunatall (GB)**, 3, 115	J. F. Chavez	Guana (Fr), 3, 117	Mariensky, 3, 117	11	1:40.71	69,000
2001	**Light Dancer**, 3, 117	M. Guidry	Owsley, 3, 117	Cozzy Corner, 3, 115	9	1:41.06	67,050
	Voodoo Dancer, 3, 122	J. D. Bailey	Sadler's Sarah, 3, 117	O K to Dance, 3, 122	9	1:41.45	67,350
2000	**Millie's Quest**, 3, 114	J. R. Velazquez	Shopping for Love, 3, 117	Battenkill, 3, 114	9	1:44.52	70,080
1999	**Nani Rose**, 3, 122	S. J. Sellers	Perfect Sting, 3, 122	Intrigued, 3, 122	8	**1:40.11**	67,680
1998	**Caveat Competor**, 3, 116	J. R. Velazquez	Mysterious Moll, 3, 114	Recording, 3, 121	10	1:41.05	50,760
	Tenski, 3, 114	R. Migliore	Pratella, 3, 114	Camella, 3, 114	8	1:40.86	50,070
1997	**Auntie Mame**, 3, 115	J. D. Bailey	Crab Grass, 3, 114	Innovate, 3, 116	9	1:42.80	51,120
1996	**Memories of Silver**, 3, 112	J. D. Bailey	Clamorosa, 3, 118	Captive Number, 3, 113	10	1:42.98	33,780
	Dynasty, 3, 112	J. D. Bailey	River Antoine, 3, 113	Vashon, 3, 116	8	1:42.26	33,630

Named for a favorite summertime resort in upstate New York, just north of Saratoga Springs. Lake George H. 1999. Two divisions 1996, 1998, 2001.

Lake Placid Handicap

Grade 2 in 2005. Saratoga Race Course, three-year-olds, fillies, 1 1/16 miles, turf. Held August 23, 2004, with a gross value of $150,000. First held in 1984. First graded in 1986. Stakes record 1:46.33 (1998 Tenski).

Year	Winner	Jockey	Second	Third	Strs	Time	1st Purse
2004	Spotlight (GB), 3, 116	J. D. Bailey	Mambo Slew, 3, 120	Fortunate Damsel, 3, 116	7	1:50.54	$90,000
2003	Sand Springs, 3, 121	M. Guidry	Indy Five Hundred, 3, 114	Film Maker, 3, 119	10	1:49.03	90,000
2002	Wonder Again, 3, 114	E. S. Prado	Riskaverse, 3, 120	Miss Marcia, 3, 114	9	1:49.24	90,000
2001	Snow Dance, 3, 116	R. Migliore	Wander Mom, 3, 116	Mystic Lady, 3, 117	12	1:47.42	90,000
2000	Gaviola, 3, 122	J. D. Bailey	Good Game, 3, 117	Millie's Quest, 3, 117	11	1:48.04	90,000
1999	Badouizm, 3, 113	R. G. Davis	Confessional, 3, 115	Emanating, 3, 115	8	1:46.44	90,000
1998	Tenski, 3, 119	R. Migliore	Naskra's de Light, 3, 117	Caveat Competor, 3, 118	12	1:46.33	90,000
1997	Witchful Thinking, 3, 123	S. J. Sellers	Miss Huff n' Puff, 3, 114	Majestic Sunlight, 3, 114	12	1:47.65	90,000
1996	Memories of Silver, 3, 115	J. D. Bailey	Unify, 3, 113	Henlopen, 3, 112	9	1:47.80	68,640
1995	Class Kris, 3, 112	P. Day	In a Daydream, 3, 112	Shocking Pleasure, 3, 113	9	1:40.90	67,380
	Bail Out Becky, 3, 115	S. J. Sellers	Fashion Star, 3, 112	Grand Charmer, 3, 120	9	1:41.87	67,680
1994	Alywow, 3, 121	M. E. Smith	Irish Forever, 3, 121	Knocknock, 3, 114	9	1:43.81	66,660
	Coronation Cup, 3, 114	J. D. Bailey	Stretch Drive, 3, 114	Golden Tajniak (Ire), 3, 118	7	1:43.88	65,760
1993	Amal Hayati, 3, 121	J. D. Bailey	Eloquent Silver, 3, 114	Irving's Girl, 3, 114	10	1:40.97	56,940
	Statuette, 3, 114	M. E. Smith	Icy Warning, 3, 114	Dispute, 3, 118	8	1:41.58	55,980
1992	Shannkara (Ire), 3, 114	M. E. Smith	Tiney Toast, 3, 116	Favored Lady, 3, 114	11	1:41.84	73,380
	Heed, 3, 114	M. E. Smith	Captive Miss, 3, 116	Mystic Hawk, 3, 114	10	1:40.98	72,420
1991	Jinski's World, 3, 121	J. A. Santos	Belleofbasinstreet, 3, 114	Verbasle, 3, 114	11	1:41.01	59,760
	Grab the Green, 3, 114	A. T. Cordero Jr.	Shareefa, 3, 121	Irish Linnet, 3, 114	11	1:40.20	59,280
1990	Jefforee, 3, 114	J. A. Santos	Toffeefee, 3, 114	Colonial Runner, 3, 114	9	1:49.00	60,030
1989	Capades, 3, 121	A. T. Cordero Jr.	To the Lighthouse, 3, 116	Vanities, 3, 114	8	1:41.00	55,620
1988	Betty Lobelia, 3, 116	J. A. Santos	Curlew, 3, 114	‡Costly Shoes, 3, 121	8	1:41.60	66,780
	Love You by Heart, 3, 114	R. P. Romero	Another Paddock, 3, 116	Flashy Runner, 3, 114	8	1:41.60	66,780
1987	Graceful Darby, 3, 116	J. D. Bailey	Spectacular Bev, 3, 114	Token Gift, 3, 114	7	1:41.40	50,760
1986	An Empress, 3, 121	J. A. Santos	Fama, 3, 116	Spring Innocence, 3, 114	11	1:42.00	52,200
1985	Videogenic, 3, 114	R. G. Davis	My Regrets (Ire), 3, 114	Forever Command, 3, 116	9	1:41.80	33,720
1984	Possible Mate, 3, 114	D. MacBeth	Proud Nova, 3, 114	Miss Audimar, 3, 114	6	1:50.00	26,070

Named for the popular Adirondack mountain resort that has hosted the Winter Olympics twice. Formerly named for Cragwood Stable's 1975 Schuylerville S. (G3) winner Nijana (1973 f. by Nijinsky II). Grade 3 1991-'98. Nijana S. 1984-'97. 1 1/16 miles 1984-'89, 1991-'95. Dirt 1990. Two divisions 1988, 1991-'95. ‡Tunita finished third, DQ to fourth, 1988 (1st Div.).

Lane's End Breeders' Futurity

Grade 1 in 2005. Keeneland, two-year-olds, 1 1/16 miles, dirt. Held October 9, 2004, with a gross value of $500,000. First held in 1910. First graded in 1973. Stakes record 1:42.23 (1993 Polar Expedition).

Year	Winner	Jockey	Second	Third	Strs	Time	1st Purse
2004	Consolidator, 2, 121	R. Bejarano	Patriot Act, 2, 121	Diamond Isle, 2, 121	10	1:43.67	$310,000
2003	Eurosilver, 2, 121	J. Castellano	Tiger Hunt, 2, 121	Limehouse, 2, 121	11	1:43.42	248,000
2002	Sky Mesa, 2, 121	E. S. Prado	Lone Star Sky, 2, 121	Truckle Feature, 2, 121	6	1:46.78	269,576
2001	Siphonic, 2, 121	C. J. McCarron	Harlan's Holiday, 2, 121	Metatron, 2, 121	11	1:43.79	281,728
2000	Arabian Light, 2, 121	S. J. Sellers	Dollar Bill, 2, 121	Holiday Thunder, 2, 121	10	1:43.18	279,744
1999	Captain Steve, 2, 121	G. K. Gomez	Graeme Hall, 2, 121	Millencolin, 2, 121	8	1:42.59	274,040
1998	Cat Thief, 2, 121	P. Day	Answer Lively, 2, 121	Yes It's True, 2, 121	8	1:44.17	272,552
1997	Favorite Trick, 2, 121	P. Day	Time Limit, 2, 121	Laydown, 2, 121	5	1:43.36	265,112
1996	Boston Harbor, 2, 121	J. D. Bailey	Blazing Sword, 2, 121	Haint, 2, 121	5	1:45.31	1,166,005
1995	Honour and Glory, 2, 121	P. Day	City by Night, 2, 121	Blushing Jim, 2, 121	10	1:43.33	139,252
1994	Tejano Run, 2, 121	J. D. Bailey	Cinch, 2, 121	Gold Miner, 2, 121	11	1:44.71	71,548
1993	Polar Expedition, 2, 121	C. C. Bourque	Goodbye Doeny, 2, 121	Solly's Honor, 2, 121	8	1:42.23	122,200
1992	Mountain Cat, 2, 121	P. Day	Living Vicariously, 2, 121	Boundlessly, 2, 121	4	1:45.42	1,122,200
1991	Dance Floor, 2, 121	C. R. Woods Jr.	Star Recruit, 2, 121	Count the Time, 2, 121	7	1:44.37	122,200
1990	Sir Bordeaux, 2, 121	W. S. Ramos	Wall Street Dancer, 2, 121	Fire in Ice, 2, 121	6	1:44.40	145,925
1989	Slavic, 2, 121	J. A. Santos	Top Snob, 2, 121	Harry, 2, 121	4	1:44.60	159,770
1988	Fast Play, 2, 121	A. T. Cordero Jr.	Lorenzoni, 2, 121	Bio, 2, 121	6	1:45.20	129,350
1987	Forty Niner, 2, 121	E. Maple	Hey Pat, 2, 121	Sea Trek, 2, 121	7	1:43.80	104,868
1986	Orono, 2, 121	S. Hawley	Alysheba, 2, 121	Pledge Card, 2, 121	10	1:45.20	116,711
1985	Tasso, 2, 121	L. A. Pincay Jr.	Regal Dreamer, 2, 121	Thundering Force, 2, 121	11	1:46.00	122,424
1984	Crater Fire, 2, 121	D. Montoya	Nickel Back, 2, 121	Cullendale, 2, 121	8	1:45.80	110,474
1983	Swale, 2, 121	E. Maple	Spender, 2, 121	Back Bay Barrister, 2, 121	8	1:44.00	108,631
1982	Highland Park, 2, 121	J. L. Lively	Caveat, 2, 121	Bright Baron, 2, 121	12	1:43.60	97,825
1981	D'Accord, 2, 121	D. G. McHargue	Lets Dont Fight, 2, 121	Shooting Duck, 2, 121	10	1:44.40	94,575
1980	Fairway Phantom, 2, 121	J. L. Lively	Total Pleasure, 2, 121	Quick Ice, 2, 121	10	1:28.80	94,575
1979	Gold Stage, 2, 121	D. Brumfield	Degenerate Jon, 2, 121	Tonka Wakhan, 2, 121	5	1:26.80	81,608
1978	Strike Your Colors, 2, 122	E. J. Delahoussaye	Lot o' Gold, 2, 122	Uncle Fudge, 2, 122	13	1:26.20	92,284
1977	Gonquin, 2, 122	F. Olivares	Sunny Songster, 2, 122	Jaycean, 2, 122	7	1:28.00	83,866
1976	Run Dusty Run, 2, 122	D. G. McHargue	Banquet Table, 2, 122	Get the Axe, 2, 122	10	1:27.40	84,695

1975 **Harbor Springs**, 2, 122	E. Maple	Best Bee, 2, 122	‡Scrutiny, 2, 122	10	1:27.00	$82,046
1974 **Packer Captain**, 2, 122	D. Brumfield	Master Derby, 2, 122	Ruggles Ferry, 2, 122	11	1:25.80	53,277
1973 **Provante**, 2, 122	M. Manganello	Training Table, 2, 122	Wage Raise, 2, 122	10	1:27.20	48,327

Sponsored by W. S. Farish's Lane's End, located near Versailles, Kentucky 1997-2004, and in honor of Kentucky breeders. Grade 3 1973-'75. Grade 2 1976-2003. Held at Kentucky Association 1910-'30. Held at Old Latonia 1931-'33. Held at Churchill Downs 1943-'45. Not held 1934-'37. 4 furlongs 1910-'11. 4¹/₂ furlongs 1912. 5 furlongs 1913-'16. About 6 furlongs 1917-'33. 6 furlongs 1938-'49. 7 furlongs 1950-'55. About 7 furlongs 1956-'80. ‡Vuelo finished third, DQ to fourth, 1975. Winner's purse includes $1,000,000 bonus from the Kentucky Thoroughbred Development Fund 1992, 1996.

Lane's End Stakes

Grade 2 in 2005. Turfway Park, three-year-olds, 1¹/₈ miles, dirt. Held March 26, 2005, with a gross value of $500,000. First held in 1972. First graded in 1984. Stakes record 1:46.70 (1991 Hansel).

Year	Winner	Jockey	Second	Third	Strs	Time	1st Purse
2005	**Flower Alley**, 3, 121	J. F. Chavez	Wild Desert, 3, 121	Mr Sword, 3, 121	9	1:50.33	$300,000
2004	**Sinister G**, 3, 121	P. R. Toscano	Tricky Taboo, 3, 121	Little Matth Man, 3, 121	11	1:50.71	300,000
2003	**New York Hero**, 3, 121	N. Arroyo Jr.	Eugene's Third Son, 3, 121	Champali, 3, 121	9	1:50.68	300,000
2002	**Perfect Drift**, 3, 121	E. J. Delahoussaye	Azillion (Ire), 3, 121	Request for Parole, 3, 121	8	1:48.83	300,000
2001	**Balto Star**, 3, 121	M. Guidry	Halo's Stride, 3, 121	Mongoose, 3, 121	9	1:47.23	360,000
2000	**Globalize**, 3, 121	F. C. Torres	Elite Mercedes, 3, 121	Rollin With Nolan, 3, 121	10	1:49.16	360,000
1999	**Stephen Got Even**, 3, 121	S. J. Sellers	K One King, 3, 121	Epic Honor, 3, 121	8	1:49.03	450,000
1998	**Event of the Year**, 3, 121	R. A. Baze	Yarrow Brae, 3, 121	Truluck, 3, 121	10	1:47.12	360,000
1997	**Concerto**, 3, 121	C. H. Marquez Jr.	Jack Flash, 3, 121	Shammy Davis, 3, 121	10	1:48.23	360,000
1996	**Roar**, 3, 121	M. E. Smith	Ensign Ray, 3, 121	Victory Speech, 3, 121	9	1:49.70	360,000
1995	†**Serena's Song**, 3, 116	C. S. Nakatani	Tejano Run, 3, 121	Mecke, 3, 121	8	1:49.65	360,000
1994	**Polar Expedition**, 3, 121	C. C. Bourque	Powis Castle, 3, 121	Chimes Band, 3, 121	11	1:49.03	360,000
1993	**Prairie Bayou**, 3, 121	C. J. McCarron	Proudest Romeo, 3, 121	Miner's Mark, 3, 121	9	1:50.97	360,000
1992	**Lil E. Tee**, 3, 121	P. Day	Vying Victor, 3, 121	Treekster, 3, 121	11	1:53.44	300,000
1991	**Hansel**, 3, 121	J. D. Bailey	Richman, 3, 121	Wilder Than Ever, 3, 121	11	**1:46.70**	300,000
1990	**Summer Squall**, 3, 121	P. Day	Bright Again, 3, 121	Yonder, 3, 121	10	1:49.40	300,000
1989	**Western Playboy**, 3, 121	P. Day	Feather Ridge, 3, 121	Mercedes Won, 3, 121	12	1:49.00	300,000
1988	**Kingpost**, 3, 121	E. J. Sipus Jr.	Stalwars, 3, 121	Brian's Time, 3, 121	11	1:50.80	300,000
1987	**J.T.'s Pet**, 3, 121	P. Day	Faster Than Sound, 3, 121	Homebuilder, 3, 121	12	1:42.80	300,000
1986	**Broad Brush**, 3, 121	V. A. Bracciale Jr.	Miracle Wood, 3, 121	Bachelor Beau, 3, 121	12	1:44.20	210,000
1985	**Banner Bob**, 3, 121	K. K. Allen	Image of Greatness, 3, 121	Roo Art, 3, 121	10	1:42.00	227,500
1984	**At the Threshold**, 3, 121	P. Day	Bold Southerner, 3, 121	The Wedding Guest, 3, 121	12	1:42.80	195,000
1983	**Marfa**, 3, 120	J. Velasquez	Noble Home, 3, 120	Hail to Rome, 3, 120	12	1:42.40	151,515
1982	**Good n' Dusty**, 3, 120	M. T. Moran	Fast Gold, 3, 120	Cupecoy's Joy, 3, 115	12	1:44.60	125,450
1981	**Mythical Ruler**, 3, 114	K. B. Wirth	Classic Go Go, 3, 122	Iron Gem, 3, 115	10	1:38.00	33,210
1980	**Major Run**, 3, 116	M. S. Sellers	Ray's Word, 3, 122	Misty Bell, 3, 113	8	1:37.60	18,740
	Spruce Needles, 3, 116	J. C. Espinoza	Avenger M., 3, 122	Summer Advocate, 3, 113	6	1:36.20	18,440
1979	**Lot o' Gold**, 3, 122	D. Brumfield	Julie's Dancer, 3, 113	Will Henry, 3, 113	6	1:37.60	29,030
1978	**Five Star General**, 3, 113	J. C. Espinoza	As in Elbow, 3, 113	Doc's Rock, 3, 119	9	1:37.80	12,900
	Raymond Earl, 3, 113	J. C. Espinoza	Washington County, 3, 119	Shake Rattl'n Fly, 3, 113	10	1:38.80	12,960
1977	**Smiley's Dream**, 3, 114	W. Destefano	Lighten the Load, 3, 111	Vestry's Best, 3, 111	9	1:39.40	12,788
	Bob's Dusty, 3, 122	J. C. Espinoza	A Letter to Harry, 3, 116	John Washington, 3, 116	9	1:38.80	12,817
1976	**Inca Roca**, 3, 122	W. Nemeti	Here Comes Jo, 3, 116	Brentwood Prince, 3, 116	6	1:37.40	18,780
1975	**Naughty Jake**, 3, 119	G. Vasquez	Promenade Left, 3, 114	Jim Dan Bob, 3, 112	8	1:40.00	15,840
	Ambassador's Image, 3, 122	E. Snell	Clarence Henry, 3, 116	Upper Need, 3, 116	8	1:38.40	15,870
1974	**King of Rome**, 3, 112	K. Wirth	Consigliori, 3, 112	Aroyoport, 3, 116	8	1:44.60	12,204
	Aglorite, 3, 119	J. Beech Jr.	Joint Agreement, 3, 116	Robard, 3, 112	8	1:45.40	12,236
1973	**Jacks Chevron**, 3, 117	B. Phelps	Trip Stop, 3, 116	Mr. Champ, 3, 116	9	1:42.00	9,785
	Bootlegger's Pet, 3, 116	M. Solomone	Out Ahead, 3, 117	Babingtons Image, 3, 113	8	1:41.00	9,720

Sponsored by W. S. Farish's Lane's End, located in Versailles, Kentucky 2002-'04. Formerly sponsored by James B. Beam Distilling Co. of Clermont, Kentucky 1982-'98. Formerly sponsored by James McIngvale's Gallery Furniture Co. of Houston, Texas 1999. Originally designed as a prep race that "spiraled up" to the Blue Grass S. (G1) and the Kentucky Derby (G1). Spiral S. 1972-'81. Jim Beam Spiral S. 1982-'83. Jim Beam S. 1984-'98. Gallery Furniture.com S. 1999. Turfway Spiral S. 2000-'01. Lane's End Spiral S. 2002. Host track known as Latonia Race Course 1972-'85. 1 mile 1972-'81. 1¹/₁₆ miles 1982-'87. Two divisions 1973-'75, 1977-'78, 1980. †Denotes female.

La Prevoyante Handicap

Grade 2 in 2005. Calder Race Course, three-year-olds and up, fillies and mares, 1¹/₂ miles, turf. Held December 18, 2004, with a gross value of $200,000. First held in 1976. First graded in 1982. Stakes record 2:25.20 (1988 Singular Bequest).

Year	Winner	Jockey	Second	Third	Strs	Time	1st Purse
2004	**Arvada (GB)**, 4, 117	E. S. Prado	Humaita (Ger), 4, 119	Honey Ryder, 3, 113	11	2:27.19	$120,000
2003	**Volga (Ire)**, 5, 119	R. Migliore	Lady Annaliese (NZ), 4, 116	Lost Appeal, 5, 115	11	2:26.13	120,000
2002	**New Economy**, 4, 113	R. B. Homeister Jr.	Jennasietta, 4, 112	Tweedside, 4, 114	12	2:28.55	120,000
2001	**Krisada**, 5, 115	P. Day	Sweetest Thing, 3, 115	Great Fever (Fr), 4, 113	10	2:26.63	90,000
2000	**Prospectress**, 5, 114	J. D. Bailey	Innuendo (Ire), 5, 114	Orange Sunset (Ire), 4, 114	10	2:26.97	90,000

Year	Winner	Jockey	Second	Third	Strs	Time	1st Purse
1999	**Coretta (Ire)**, 5, 120	J. A. Santos	Idle Rich, 4, 116	St. Bernadette (Per), 3, 114	8	2:27.27	$90,000
1998	**Coretta (Ire)**, 4, 117	J. A. Santos	Starry Dreamer, 4, 114	dh- Cuando, 4, 115	12	2:26.67	90,000
				dh- Tedarshana (GB), 4, 113			
1997	**Last Approach**, 5, 110	J. A. Krone	Flying Concert, 4, 118	Grey Way, 4, 110	6	2:39.13	90,000
1996	**Ampulla**, 5, 122	S. J. Sellers	Miss Caerleona (Fr), 4, 114	Electric Society (Ire), 5, 117	8	2:27.50	90,000
1995	**Interim (GB)**, 4, 116	C. S. Nakatani	Northern Emerald, 5, 116	Caromana, 4, 114	10	2:26.38	90,000
1994	**Abigailthewife**, 5, 114	J. A. Santos	Trampoli, 5, 118	Market Booster, 5, 118	14	2:28.91	90,000
	Trampoli, 5, 120	M. E. Smith	Putthepowdertoit, 4, 115	Adoryphar, 5, 112	14	2:28.14	90,000
1993	**Lemhi Go**, 5, 112	M. A. Gonzalez	Indian Chris (Brz), 6, 112	Silvered, 6, 118	6	2:37.53	60,000
1992	**Sardaniya (Ire)**, 4, 113	J. Cruguet	Flaming Torch (Ire), 5, 112	Expensiveness, 4, 111	9	2:29.62	90,000
1991	**Rigamajig**, 5, 114	J. F. Chavez	Roseate Tern (GB), 5, 117	Ahead (GB), 4, 112	11	2:26.10	60,000
1990	**Yestday's Kisses**, 4, 113	W. H. McCauley	Black Tulip (Fr), 5, 115	Coolawin, 4, 116	11	2:30.80	60,000
1989	**Judy's Red Shoes**, 6, 120	D. Valiente	Gaily Gaily (Ire), 6, 111	Beauty Cream, 6, 118	14	2:26.40	90,000
1988	**Singular Bequest**, 5, 115	E. Fires	Autumn Glitter, 5, 114	Green Oasis (Fr), 6, 114	9	**2:25.20**	120,000
1987	**Lotka**, 4, 121	E. Maple	Bonne Ile (GB), 6, 116	After Party, 5, 112	13	2:36.00	120,000
1986	**Powder Break**, 5, 116	J. A. Santos	Shocker T., 4, 119	Devalois (Fr), 4, 118	9	2:30.40	120,000
1985	**Persian Tiara (Ire)**, 5, 120	J. Terry	Dictina (Fr), 4, 117	Silver in Flight, 5, 115	11	2:28.80	85,335
	Sabin, 5, 126	D. Brumfield	Key Dancer, 4, 118	Burst of Colors, 5, 117	11	2:27.40	72,285
1984	**Bolt From the Blue**, 4, 113	J. Samyn	Bezique (Ire), 7, 112	Gabfest, 5, 110	9	2:33.40	51,960
	Sabin, 4, 120	E. Maple	Grunip (GB), 5, 113	Pat's Joy, 6, 118	10	2:32.80	52,260
1983	**London Lil**, 4, 117	A. Smith Jr.	Dana Calqui (Arg), 5, 114	Middle Stage, 4, 116	14	1:47.40	54,680
	Fact Finder, 4, 115	A. T. Cordero Jr.	Sunny Sparkler, 4, 122	Seaholme, 5, 112	11	1:48.00	53,780
	Canaille (Ire), 5, 118	A. T. Cordero Jr.	Castle Royale, 5, 115	Genuine Diamond, 4, 113	13	1:46.60	54,380
1982	**Judgable Gypsy**, 4, 114	J. O'Driscoll	Castle Royale, 4, 110	Imayrrahtoo, 5, 110	12	1:50.20	42,165
	Just a Game (Ire), 6, 123	A. T. Cordero Jr.	Sweetest Chant, 4, 115	Irish Joy, 4, 114	9	1:50.40	41,655
1981	**Mairzy Doates**, 5, 121	O. B. Aviles	Champagne Ginny, 4, 118	Knightly Noble, 4, 110	11	1:47.20	41,670
	Deuces Over Seven, 4, 114	G. Gallitano	Little Bonny (Ire), 4, 121	Quick as Lightning, 4, 119	8	1:48.00	40,950
1980	**Impetuous Gal**, 5, 113	E. Fires	Tangerine Doll, 4, 118	Highland Gypsy, 4, 116	5	1:52.20	23,775
	Jolie Dutch, 4, 116	B. Thornburg	Reina Del Rulo (Arg), 7, 116	Behave Taurian, 4, 108	4	1:54.60	23,925
1979	**Unreality**, 5, 119	J. D. Bailey	Excitable, 4, 117	Sans Arc, 5, 117	12	1:48.20	37,200
1978	**Len's Determined**, 4, 114	A. Smith Jr.	Regal Gal, 5, 120	Carolina Moon, 6, 114	12	1:48.40	37,200
1976	**Forty Nine Sunsets**, 3, 116	C. H. Marquez	Cycylya Zee, 3, 121	Satan's Cheer, 4, 116	14	1:46.00	27,510
	Redundancy, 5, 117	A. Haldar	Katonka, 4, 125	Yes Dear Maggy, 4, 121	12	1:41.60	26,040

Named for Jean-Louis Levesque's 1972 Canadian Horse of the Year La Prevoyante (1970 f. by Buckpasser). Grade 3 1982-'87. La Prevoyante Invitational H. 1986-'93. Not held 1977. $1\frac{1}{16}$ miles 1976. About $1\frac{1}{8}$ miles 1978-'79, 1981-'83. $1\frac{1}{8}$ miles 1980. About $1\frac{1}{2}$ miles 1992. Dirt 1980, 1987, 1990, 1993, 1997. Two divisions 1980-'82, 1984-'85. Three divisions 1983. Held in January and December 1976, 1994. Dead heat for third 1998. ‡Silvered finished fourth, DQ to fifth, 1992.

Las Cienegas Handicap

Grade 3 in 2005. Santa Anita Park, four-year-olds and up, fillies and mares, about $6\frac{1}{2}$ furlongs, turf. Held April 10, 2005, with a gross value of $111,100. First held in 1974. First graded in 1992. Stakes record 1:11.66 (2005 Elusive Diva).

Year	Winner	Jockey	Second	Third	Strs	Time	1st Purse
2005	**Elusive Diva**, 4, 117	P. A. Valenzuela	Quero Quero, 5, 116	Winendynme, 4, 116	9	**1:11.66**	$66,660
2004	**Etoile Montante**, 4, 121	J. Santiago	Dedication (Fr), 5, 118	Any for Love (Arg), 6, 115	9	1:13.32	$67,680
2003	**Heat Haze (GB)**, 4, 114	J. Valdivia Jr.	Icantgoforthat, 4, 114	Paga (Arg), 6, 116	8	1:13.11	66,000
2002	**Rolly Polly (Ire)**, 4, 119	K. J. Desormeaux	Penny Marie, 6, 119	Twin Set (Ger), 5, 116	7	1:12.55	65,100
2001	**Go Go**, 4, 118	E. J. Delahoussaye	Separata (Chi), 5, 118	Dianehill (Ire), 5, 116	8	1:13.54	65,700
2000	**Evening Promise (GB)**, 4, 114	D. Sorenson	La Madame (Chi), 5, 116	Reciclada (Chi), 5, 113	5	1:13.66	63,840
1999	**Desert Lady (Ire)**, 4, 118	C. S. Nakatani	Hula Queen, 5, 112	Bella Chiarra, 4, 115	7	1:13.55	65,640
1998	**Dance Parade**, 4, 119	K. J. Desormeaux	Advancing Star, 5, 121	Imroz, 4, 115	6	1:13.60	64,800
1997	**Advancing Star**, 4, 116	G. L. Stevens	Ski Dancer, 5, 118	Grab the Prize, 5, 116	6	1:12.50	96,550
1996	**Ski Dancer**, 4, 117	G. L. Stevens	Klassy Kim, 5, 117	Igotrhythm, 4, 117	6	1:14.59	64,300
1995	**Marina Park (GB)**, 5, 119	A. O. Solis	Pirate's Revenge, 4, 116	Rabiadella, 4, 118	9	1:13.77	63,175
1994	**Mamselle Bebette**, 4, 120	C. J. McCarron	Cool Air, 4, 122	Bel's Starlet, 7, 122	5	1:13.05	45,975
1993	**Glen Kate (Ire)**, 6, 121	C. A. Black	Heart of Joy, 6, 121	Worldly Possession, 5, 115	6	1:12.71	61,225
1992	**Heart of Joy**, 5, 123	C. J. McCarron	Sheltered View, 4, 114	Crystal Gazing, 4, 119	9	1:12.72	63,475
1991	**Flower Girl (GB)**, 4, 116	E. J. Delahoussaye	Mahaska, 4, 117	Survive, 7, 117	8	1:13.30	49,650
1990	**Stylish Star**, 4, 117	C. J. McCarron	‡Hot Novel, 4, 118	Warning Zone, 5, 116	6	1:13.40	47,100
1989	**Imperial Star (GB)**, 5, 115	R. G. Davis	Down Again, 5, 117	Serve n' Volley (GB), 5, 115	10	1:15.60	50,450
1988	**Hairless Heiress**, 5, 117	G. L. Stevens	Chick Or Two, 5, 115	Aromacor, 5, 113	12	1:15.00	52,050
1987	**Lichi (Chi)**, 7, 115	G. Baze	An Empress, 4, 119	Aromacor, 4, 112	7	1:14.40	38,150
1986	**Shywing**, 4, 120	L. A. Pincay Jr.	Reigning Countess, 4, 114	Her Royalty, 5, 121	4	1:18.00	37,550
1985	**Danzadar**, 4, 114	D. A. Lozoya	Pampas (Ire), 4, 120	Natural Summit, 4, 116	5	1:14.00	37,250
1984	**Tangent (NZ)**, 4, 120	G. Barrera	Irish O'Brien, 6, 118	Frieda Frame, 6, 118	4	1:15.00	39,600
1983	**Faneuil Lass**, 4, 120	L. A. Pincay Jr.	Queen of Song, 4, 115	Waving, 4, 117	9	1:17.40	41,200
1982	**Excitable Lady**, 4, 119	E. J. Delahoussaye	‡Peppy's Lucky Girl, 5, 117	Glitter Hitter, 4, 119	7	1:14.40	37,450
1981	**Wishing Well**, 6, 122	F. Toro	Back At Two, 4, 114	Peppy's Lucky Girl, 4, 113	9	1:13.40	34,250
1980	**Great Lady M.**, 5, 116	P. A. Valenzuela	Wishing Well, 5, 120	Billie Bets, 4, 115	10	1:14.80	28,100
1979	**Pressing Date**, 5, 114	A. T. Cordero Jr.	Country Queen, 4, 121	Critic, 5, 114	8	1:16.40	27,550
1978	**Drama Critic**, 4, 119	D. G. McHargue	Perils of Pauline, 4, 118	Little Happiness, 4, 120	10	1:14.00	27,800

Year	Winner	Jockey	Second	Third	Strs	Time 1st Purse
1977	**Dancing Femme**, 4, 117	W. Shoemaker	Winter Solstice, 5, 123	Katonka, 5, 120	4	1:13.60 $24,600
1976	**Life's Hope**, 3, 116	L. A. Pincay Jr.	Sure Fire, 3, 119	Private Signal, 3, 114	7	1:09.40 20,100
1974	**Woodland Pines**, 5, 120	D. Pierce	Pataha Prince, 9, 122	dh- Pontoise, 4, 116	9	1:13.00 18,650
				dh- Single Agent, 6, 116		

Named for Rancho Las Cienegas in southwestern Los Angeles County, California; las cienegas means "the swamps." Las Cienegas S. 1976. Las Cienegas Breeders' Cup H. 1992-'95. Not held 1975. 6 furlongs 1976. 6½ furlongs 1979, 1982-'83, 1986. Dirt 1976, 1979, 1982-'83, 1986. Three-year-olds 1976. Both sexes 1974-'76. Dead heat for third 1974. ‡Queen of Cornwall finished second, DQ to sixth, 1982. ‡Stormy But Valid finished second, DQ to fifth, 1990.

Las Flores Handicap

Grade 3 in 2005. Santa Anita Park, four-year-olds and up, fillies and mares, 6 furlongs, dirt. Held February 27, 2005, with a gross value of $109,600. First held in 1951. First graded in 1973. Stakes record 1:08.02 (2004 Ema Bovary [Chi]).

Year	Winner	Jockey	Second	Third	Strs	Time 1st Purse
2005	**Miss Terrible (Arg)**, 6, 116	A. O. Solis	Puxa Saco, 5, 115	Mazella, 4, 113	8	1:09.47 $65,760
2004	**Ema Bovary (Chi)**, 5, 121	R. M. Gonzalez	Buffythecenterfold, 4, 117	Coconut Girl, 5, 113	6	**1:08.02** $64,380
2003	**Spring Meadow**, 4, 117	C. S. Nakatani	Brisquette, 5, 116	dh- September Secret, 4, 116	7	1:10.20 81,300
				dh- Wild Tickle, 5, 117		
2002	**Above Perfection**, 4, 117	C. S. Nakatani	Kalookan Queen, 6, 122	Enchanted Woods, 5, 117	4	1:08.65 78,642
2001	**Go Go**, 4, 116	E. J. Delahoussaye	La Feminn, 5, 120	Cover Gal, 4, 119	6	1:08.83 80,400
2000	**Show Me the Stage**, 4, 118	K. J. Desormeaux	Theresa's Tizzy, 6, 117	Woodman's Dancer, 6, 115	6	1:08.54 79,440
1999	**Enjoy the Moment**, 4, 117	L. A. Pincay Jr.	Tomorrows Sunshine, 5, 114	Closed Escrow, 6, 116	5	1:08.55 78,720
1998	**Funallover**, 4, 114	A. O. Solis	Advancing Star, 5, 122	Zenda's Diablo, 4, 109	7	1:09.10 79,800
1997	**Our Summer Bid**, 5, 114	J. Silva	Track Gal, 6, 120	Advancing Star, 4, 116	6	1:09.15 80,100
1996	**Igotrhythm**, 4, 115	C. S. Nakatani	Miss L Attack, 6, 115	Little Blue Sheep, 4, 115	7	1:08.88 81,100
1995	**Desert Stormer**, 5, 117	K. J. Desormeaux	Velvet Tulip, 5, 114	Flying in the Lane, 4, 114	5	1:08.49 59,725
1994	**Mamselle Bebette**, 4, 118	C. S. Nakatani	Arches of Gold, 5, 120	Aspasante, 5, 114	7	1:08.32 47,475
1993	**Bountiful Native**, 5, 121	P. A. Valenzuela	Freedom Cry, 5, 119	Forest Fealty, 6, 112	6	1:09.42 60,325
1992	**Forest Fealty**, 5, 116	M. A. Pedroza	Middlefork Rapids, 4, 118	Phil's Illusion, 5, 113	9	1:08.87 49,350
1991	**Classic Value**, 5, 116	G. L. Stevens	Devil's Orchid, 4, 116	Hasty Pasty, 6, 116	6	1:10.30 60,325
1990	**Stormy But Valid**, 4, 117	E. J. Delahoussaye	Survive, 6, 117	Warning Zone, 5, 119	7	1:08.20 47,850
1989	**Very Subtle**, 5, 124	L. A. Pincay Jr.	Sadie B. Fast, 4, 113	Comical Cat, 4, 116	3	1:08.60 44,350
1987	**Flying Julia**, 4, 112	F. Olivares	Pine Tree Lane, 5, 122	Le l'Argent, 5, 119	9	1:10.20 48,850
	Pine Tree Lane, 5, 124	A. T. Cordero Jr.	Rangoon Ruby (Ire), 5, 117	Her Royalty, 6, 120	8	1:09.80 38,350
1986	**Baroness Direct**, 5, 120	E. J. Delahoussaye	Her Royalty, 5, 113	Aerturas (Fr), 5, 113	7	1:08.40 38,850
1985	**Foggy Nation**, 5, 117	L. A. Pincay Jr.	Lovlier Linda, 5, 124	Tangent (NZ), 5, 122	5	1:09.60 37,250
1984	**Bara Lass**, 5, 122	P. A. Valenzuela	Champagne Isle, 4, 116	Bally Knockan, 5, 114	9	1:09.40 40,100
1983	**Matching**, 5, 122	L. A. Pincay Jr.	Bara Lass, 4, 115	Past Forgetting, 5, 122	7	1:09.00 38,650
1982	**Back At Two**, 5, 117	C. J. McCarron	Abisinia (Ven), 5, 116	Excitable Lady, 4, 120	5	1:12.40 37,750
1981	**Shine High**, 5, 114	T. Lipham	Image of Reality, 5, 119	Parsley, 5, 117	7	1:08.60 32,600
1979	**Terlingua**, 3, 121	D. G. McHargue	Powder Room, 4, 113	Ideal Exchange, 3, 116	7	1:08.40 32,800
1978	**Sweet Little Lady**, 3, 117	D. G. McHargue	Grenzen, 3, 122	Great Lady M., 3, 114	8	1:09.00 33,200
1977	**Winter Solstice**, 5, 120	D. G. McHargue	Squander, 3, 114	Don's Music, 3, 115	6	1:11.80 26,100
	My Juliet, 5, 128	A. S. Black	Just a Kick, 5, 121	Juliana F., 4, 115	7	1:10.20 26,750
1976	**Just a Kick**, 4, 114	E. Munoz	Raise Your Skirts, 4, 121	Mismoyola, 6, 115	9	1:09.20 21,550
1975	**Lucky Spell**, 4, 120	J. E. Tejeira	‡*Tizna, 6, 123	Impressive Style, 6, 122	8	1:09.60 21,700
1973	**Sandy Blue**, 3, 120	D. Pierce	Market Again, 5, 112	Impressive Style, 4, 120	10	1:08.60 22,150

Named for the 1844 land grant of Rancho Las Flores, located in Tehama County, California; flores means "flowers." Not graded 1975-'84. Not graded 1975-'84. Las Flores Breeders' Cup H. 1990-'95. Not held 1953, 1969, 1971, 1974, 1980, 1988. Three-year-olds and up 1951-'52, 1956-'68, 1970, 1977 (December), 1978, 1987 (December). Two-year-olds and up 1972 (December), 1973, 1983. Held in January and December 1977, 1987. Dead heat for third 2003. ‡Modus Vivendi finished second, DQ to fourth, 1975.

Las Palmas Handicap

Grade 2 in 2005. Santa Anita Park, three-year-olds and up, fillies and mares, 1⅛ miles, turf. Held October 31, 2004, with a gross value of $150,000. First held in 1969. First graded in 1973. Stakes record 1:43.92 (1991 Kostroma [Ire]).

Year	Winner	Jockey	Second	Third	Strs	Time 1st Purse
2004	**Theater R. N.**, 4, 114	R. R. Douglas	Lots of Hope (Brz), 4, 117	Good Student (Arg), 4, 114	7	1:47.81 $90,000
2002	**Tates Creek**, 4, 120	J. D. Bailey	Voodoo Dancer, 4, 115	Magic Mission (GB), 4, 113	8	1:47.69 120,000
2001	**Golden Apples (Ire)**, 3, 115	G. K. Gomez	Dancingonice, 5, 113	Janet (GB), 4, 120	9	1:46.61 150,000
2000	**Smooth Player**, 4, 117	E. J. Delahoussaye	Beautiful Noise, 4, 115	Happyanunoit (NZ), 5, 121	10	1:46.99 105,000
1999	**Sapphire Ring (GB)**, 4, 118	G. L. Stevens	Cyrillic, 4, 117	Country Garden (GB), 4, 113	11	1:48.20 150,000
1998	**Sonja's Faith (Ire)**, 4, 115	E. Ramsammy	See You Soon (Fr), 4, 116	Idealistic Cause, 4, 113	6	1:48.92 90,000
1997	**Real Connection**, 6, 115	G. F. Almeida	Toda Una Dama (Arg), 4, 114	Luna Wells (Ire), 4, 119	9	1:47.60 75,000
1996	**Wandesta (GB)**, 5, 120	C. S. Nakatani	Real Connection, 5, 113	Alpride (Ire), 5, 120	5	1:46.72 79,700
1995	**Onceinabluemamoon**, 4, 116	B. Blanc	Yearly Tour, 4, 117	Don't Read My Lips, 4, 117	9	1:50.34 76,400
1994	**Aube Indienne (Fr)**, 4, 115	K. J. Desormeaux	Queens Court Queen, 5, 115	Skimble, 5, 116	5	1:49.62 61,300
1993	**Miatuschka**, 5, 114	C. A. Black	Skimble, 4, 115	Potridee (Arg), 4, 115	6	1:47.98 62,600
1992	**Super Staff**, 4, 116	K. J. Desormeaux	Flawlessly, 4, 124	Re Toss (Arg), 5, 115	7	1:46.89 77,750
1991	**Kostroma (Ire)**, 5, 117	K. J. Desormeaux	Kikala (GB), 5, 113	Campagnarde (Arg), 4, 118	6	**1:43.92** 80,750
1990	**Little Brianne**, 5, 115	J. A. Garcia	Double Wedge, 5, 117	Reluctant Guest, 4, 121	5	1:46.80 93,200

Year	Winner	Jockey	Second		Strs	Time	1st Purse
1989	Nikishka, 4, 116	E. J. Delahoussaye	No Review, 4, 117	Agirlfromars, 3, 111	7	1:46.60	$96,800
1988	Annoconnor, 4, 120	C. A. Black	No Review, 3, 114	Goodbye Halo, 3, 120	7	1:47.00	97,800
1987	Autumn Glitter, 4, 116	P. Day	Galunpe (Ire), 4, 119	Festivity, 4, 117	8	1:50.40	91,800
1986	Outstandingly, 4, 118	G. L. Stevens	Shywing, 4, 118	Justicara (Ire), 5, 118	6	1:47.60	63,400
1985	Estrapade, 5, 124	W. Shoemaker	L'Attrayante (Fr), 5, 118	Johnica, 4, 118	11	1:47.20	69,100
1984	Fenny Rough (Ire), 4, 118	K. D. Black	Comedy Act, 5, 117	Pride of Rosewood (NZ), 6, 115	8	1:47.40	78,800
1983	Castilla, 4, 121	C. J. McCarron	Night Fire, 4, 113	Berry Bush, 6, 117	7	1:49.20	64,300
1982	Berry Bush, 5, 115	M. Castaneda	Satin Ribera, 5, 115	Northern Fable, 4, 115	13	1:47.40	70,400
1981	Ack's Secret, 5, 119	D. G. McHargue	Queen to Conquer, 5, 123	Berry Bush, 4, 118	9	1:47.00	50,500
1980	Ack's Secret, 4, 114	P. A. Valenzuela	A Thousand Stars, 5, 119	Princess Toby, 5, 117	9	1:46.00	40,400
1979	High Pheasant, 4, 114	F. Olivares	Prize Spot, 3, 119	Axe Me Dear, 5, 114	7	1:54.00	39,700
1978	Grenzen, 3, 119	L. A. Pincay Jr.	Country Queen, 3, 119	Drama Critic, 4, 123	8	1:48.40	39,400
1977	Swingtime, 5, 119	F. Toro	Theia (Fr), 4, 113	Summertime Promise, 5, 118	6	1:47.20	25,650
1976	Vagabonda, 5, 118	O. Vergara	*Bastonera II, 5, 122	*Accra II, 4, 115	12	1:48.60	34,500
1975	Charger's Star, 5, 116	W. Shoemaker	*Tizna, 6, 126	Hinterland, 5, 116	8	1:47.20	26,000
1974	Lucky Spell, 3, 117	J. E. Tejeira	Bold Ballet, 3, 117	Fresh Pepper, 4, 112	10	1:47.40	26,750
1973	Minstrel Miss, 6, 123	D. Pierce	*Cruz de Roble, 6, 113	Veiled Desire, 4, 111	10	1:47.80	27,100

Named for Las Palmas (1929 f. by Bon Homme), winner of the first race run at Santa Anita Park on December 25, 1934. Grade 3 1973-'82. Not held 2003. 1¹⁄₁₆ miles 1969, 1982. Dirt 1969, 1979.

Las Virgenes Stakes

Grade 1 in 2005. Santa Anita Park, three-year-olds, fillies, 1 mile, dirt. Held February 12, 2005, with a gross value of $250,000. First held in 1983. First graded in 1985. Stakes record 1:35.14 (1994 Lakeway).

Year	Winner	Jockey	Second	Third	Strs	Time	1st Purse
2005	Sharp Lisa, 3, 119	C. S. Nakatani	Memorette, 3, 119	Charming Colleen, 3, 117	6	1:35.64	$150,000
2004	A. P. Adventure, 3, 118	A. O. Solis	Hollywood Story, 3, 120	Friendly Michelle, 3, 116	8	1:36.50	150,000
2003	Composure, 3, 120	J. D. Bailey	Elloluv, 3, 122	Watching You, 3, 116	6	1:36.13	120,000
2002	You, 3, 122	J. D. Bailey	Habibti, 3, 122	Tali'sluckybusride, 3, 120	6	1:36.84	120,000
2001	Golden Ballet, 3, 122	C. J. McCarron	Two Item Limit, 3, 120	Affluent, 3, 114	7	1:36.89	120,000
2000	Surfside, 3, 122	P. Day	Spain, 3, 115	Rings a Chime, 3, 116	4	1:37.00	120,000
1999	Excellent Meeting, 3, 122	K. J. Desormeaux	Tout Charmant, 3, 116	Weekend Squall, 3, 115	5	1:35.35	120,000
1998	Keeper Hill, 3, 114	D. R. Flores	Star of Broadway, 3, 116	Occhi Verdi (Ire), 3, 116	9	1:36.94	120,000
1997	Sharp Cat, 3, 122	C. S. Nakatani	High Heeled Hope, 3, 118	Demon Acquire, 3, 116	8	1:35.52	98,800
1996	Antespend, 3, 120	C. W. Antley	Cara Rafaela, 3, 122	Hidden Lake, 3, 116	6	1:36.45	96,900
1995	Serena's Song, 3, 122	C. S. Nakatani	Cat's Cradle, 3, 118	Urbane, 3, 116	7	1:35.46	92,700
1994	Lakeway, 3, 117	K. J. Desormeaux	Fancy 'n Fabulous, 3, 114	Princess Mitterand, 3, 116	8	1:35.14	93,600
1993	Likeable Style, 3, 117	G. L. Stevens	Incindress, 3, 117	Blue Moonlight, 3, 119	6	1:36.67	91,000
1992	Magical Maiden, 3, 121	G. L. Stevens	Golden Treat, 3, 115	Red Bandana, 3, 115	10	1:36.23	96,800
1991	Lite Light, 3, 121	C. S. Nakatani	Garden Gal, 3, 121	Nice Assay, 3, 119	8	1:35.70	93,800
1990	Cheval Volant, 3, 123	A. O. Solis	Nasers Pride, 3, 119	Bright Candles, 3, 119	7	1:38.00	78,150
1989	Kool Arrival, 3, 121	L. A. Pincay Jr.	Some Romance, 3, 123	Fantastic Look, 3, 115	7	1:37.20	77,200
1988	Goodbye Halo, 3, 123	J. Velasquez	Winning Colors, 3, 119	Sadie B. Fast, 3, 115	5	1:36.80	74,750
1987	Timely Assertion, 3, 114	G. L. Stevens	Very Subtle, 3, 121	My Turbulent Beau, 3, 114	5	1:36.80	74,900
1986	Life at the Top, 3, 114	R. Q. Meza	Twilight Ridge, 3, 121	An Empress, 3, 117	7	1:36.20	77,050
1985	Fran's Valentine, 3, 121	P. A. Valenzuela	Rascal Lass, 3, 121	Wising Up, 3, 121	7	1:36.40	77,150
1984	Althea, 3, 124	L. A. Pincay Jr.	Vagabond Gal, 3, 117	My Darling One, 3, 114	6	1:37.00	50,500
1983	Saucy Bobbie, 3, 114	L. A. Pincay Jr.	A Lucky Sign, 3, 121	Little Hailey, 3, 114	9	1:36.20	50,100

Named for Rancho Las Virgenes, an 1837 land grant located in Los Angeles County, California. Grade 3 1985-'86. Grade 2 1987.

La Troienne Stakes

Grade 3 in 2005. Churchill Downs, three-year-olds, fillies, 7¹⁄₂ furlongs, dirt. Held May 5, 2005, with a gross value of $114,200. First held in 1956. First graded in 1998. Stakes record 1:28.26 (2004 Friendly Michelle).

Year	Winner	Jockey	Second	Third	Strs	Time	1st Purse
2005	Seek a Star, 3, 116	J. F. Chavez	Cool Spell, 3, 116	Hot Storm, 3, 122	9	1:28.75	$70,804
2004	Friendly Michelle, 3, 118	A. O. Solis	Ender's Sister, 3, 122	Bohemian Lady, 3, 122	7	1:28.26	69,564
2003	Final Round, 3, 116	J. D. Bailey	Lovely Sage, 3, 116	Fast Cookie, 3, 118	6	1:22.13	69,316
2002	Cashier's Dream, 3, 121	D. J. Meche	Shameful, 3, 113	Colonial Glitter, 3, 121	5	1:24.83	69,812
2001	Caressing, 3, 121	P. Day	Sweet Nanette, 3, 121	Golly Greeley, 3, 116	9	1:22.90	75,020
2000	Roxelana, 3, 116	L. J. Melancon	Magicalmysterycat, 3, 121	Watchfull, 3, 116	7	1:21.97	70,308
1999	Sapphire n' Silk, 3, 113	P. Day	English Bay, 3, 116	Grand Deed, 3, 121	6	1:23.85	69,936
1998	Sister Act, 3, 113	C. H. Borel	Bourbon Belle, 3, 118	Marie J, 3, 114	6	1:24.46	69,874
1997	Star of Goshen, 3, 115	A. O. Solis	Pearl City, 3, 115	Flying Lauren, 3, 116	8	1:22.75	70,370
1996	Rare Blend, 3, 121	P. Day	Ruby Baby, 3, 113	Prissy One, 3, 113	9	1:23.75	55,624
1995	Dixieland Gold, 3, 121	D. Penna	Daylight Ridge, 3, 113	Ivorilla, 3, 121	7	1:22.74	55,088
1994	Packet, 3, 113	J. M. Johnson	Golden Braids, 3, 113	Miss Ra He Ra, 3, 121	6	1:24.14	55,770
1993	Traverse City, 3, 116	J. A. Krone	Added Asset, 3, 113	Bellewood, 3, 113	10	1:24.38	38,075
1992	Bell Witch, 3, 111	J. A. Krone	Take the Cure, 3, 116	Meadow Storm, 3, 121	6	1:24.35	36,497
1991	Exclusive Bird, 3, 116	J. D. Bailey	Wilderness Song, 3, 121	Through Flight, 3, 121	8	1:23.64	36,953
1990	Screen Prospect, 3, 121	P. Day	Hard Freeze, 3, 116	Windansea, 3, 116	7	1:24.60	37,018
1989	Top of My Life, 3, 122	P. Day	Seaquay, 3, 122	Exquisite Mistress, 3, 122	7	1:23.80	36,595
1988	Gerri n Jo Go, 3, 122	P. Day	Raging Lady, 3, 114	Whitesburg Express, 3, 114	7	1:25.40	36,205

Year	Winner	Jockey	Second	Third	Strs	Time	1st Purse
1987	**Footy**, 3, 122	C. J. McCarron	Sheena Native, 3, 117	Only a Glance, 3, 122	11	1:23.80	$38,025
1986	**Lazer Show**, 3, 121	P. Day	Miss Bid, 3, 115	In Full View, 3, 121	6	1:23.60	24,817
1985	**Magnificent Lindy**, 3, 118	E. J. Delahoussaye	Turn to Wilma, 3, 115	Sewing Classic, 3, 115	8	1:23.40	21,824
1984	**Sintra**, 3, 115	K. K. Allen	Robin's Rob, 3, 121	Tah Dah, 3, 121	7	1:23.20	23,855
1983	**How Clever**, 3, 121	G. Gallitano	Super Belle, 3, 115	Weekend Surprise, 3, 121	8	1:25.40	24,245
1982	**Betty Money**, 3, 121	L. J. Melancon	Avadewan, 3, 112	All Sold Out, 3, 112	9	1:26.20	23,774
	Hoist Emy's Flag, 3, 118	P. Day	Plucky Hussy, 3, 121	Jay Birdie, 3, 115	8	1:26.20	23,579
1981	**Heavenly Cause**, 3, 121	P. Day	Fiddleatune, 3, 121	Roger's Turn, 3, 121	6	1:24.00	17,030
1980	**Ribbon**, 3, 121	R. D. Ardoin	Tilly's Curve, 3, 121	Noble Appeal, 3, 121	12	1:26.60	19,435
1979	**Justa Reflection**, 3, 118	A. L. Fernandez	Hand Creme, 3, 115	Disco Diane, 3, 115	11	1:25.80	17,680
1978	**White Star Line**, 3, 121	E. Maple	Unconscious Doll, 3, 121	Miss Mary Deb, 3, 121	4	1:25.20	13,520
1977	**Sweet Alliance**, 3, 121	C. J. McCarron	Like Ducks, 3, 121	La Lonja, 3, 118	10	1:25.20	14,300
1976	**Moreland Hills**, 3, 121	A. Rini	Thunder Lady, 3, 115	Three Colors, 3, 118	6	1:26.60	13,780
1975	**High Estimate**, 3, 121	E. J. Delahoussaye	Hoso, 3, 121	My Juliet, 3, 121	6	1:25.60	13,780
1974	**‡Shantung Silk**, 3, 121	A. T. Cordero Jr.	Clemanna, 3, 118	Irish Sonnet, 3, 118	11	1:25.40	14,430
1973	**La Prevoyante**, 3, 121	J. O. LeBlanc	Old Goldie, 3, 115	Coraggioso, 3, 118	8	1:23.80	14,040

Named for Idle Hour Stock Farm's great foundation mare *La Troienne (1926 f. by *Teddy). Formerly held as a prep race for the Kentucky Oaks (G1). Oaks Prep S. 1956-'66. 6 furlongs 1956-'60. 7 furlongs 1961-2003. Two divisions 1982. ‡Clemanna finished first, DQ to second, 1974.

Laurel Futurity

Grade 3 in 2005. Pimlico, two-year-olds, 1 1/16 miles, dirt. Held November 20, 2004, with a gross value of $100,000. First held in 1921. First graded in 1973. Stakes record 1:41.60 (1978 Spectacular Bid).

Year	Winner	Jockey	Second	Third	Strs	Time	1st Purse
2004	**Defer**, 2, 122	J. D. Bailey	Funk, 2, 122	Woody'a Apache, 2, 122	5	1:45.48	$60,000
2003	**Tapit**, 2, 122	R. A. Dominguez	Polish Rifle, 2, 122	Ghost Mountain, 2, 122	7	1:43.81	60,000
2002	**Toccet**, 2, 122	J. F. Chavez	Ironton, 2, 122	Cherokee's Boy, 2, 122	7	1:46.10	60,000
2000	**Buckle Down Ben**, 2, 122	M. J. McCarthy	Gift of the Eagle, 2, 122	Niner's Echo, 2, 122	8	1:51.93	60,000
1999	**Scottish Halo**, 2, 122	T. G. Turner	Un Fino Vino, 2, 122	Grundlefoot, 2, 122	8	1:49.35	60,000
1998	**Millions**, 2, 122	E. S. Prado	Raire Standard, 2, 122	More Better, 2, 122	6	1:51.52	60,000
1997	**Fight for M'lady**, 2, 122	C. H. Marquez Jr.	Victory Gallop, 2, 122	Essential, 2, 122	6	1:53.63	60,000
1996	**Captain Bodgit**, 2, 122	F. G. Douglas	Concerto, 2, 122	Carrolls Favorite, 2, 122	10	1:49.53	60,000
1995	**Appealing Skier**, 2, 122	R. Wilson	Liberty Road, 2, 122	Pirate Performer, 2, 122	8	1:30.70	60,000
1994	**Western Echo**, 2, 122	E. S. Prado	Old Tascosa, 2, 122	Shimmering Prince, 2, 122	10	1:30.82	60,000
1993	**Dove Hunt**, 2, 122	R. G. Davis	Lotsa Chile, 2, 122	‡Thrilla in Manila, 2, 122	8	1:49.03	81,000
1992	**Lord of the Bay**, 2, 122	R. Wilson	Glorieux Dancer (Fr), 2, 122	Halissee, 2, 122	11	1:45.54	120,000
1991	**Smiling and Dancin**, 2, 122	R. Migliore	Free At Last, 2, 122	Older But Smarter, 2, 122	8	1:48.77	120,000
1990	**River Traffic**, 2, 122	C. B. Asmussen	Fourstars Allstar, 2, 122	Share the Glory, 2, 122	13	1:44.80	180,000
1989	**Go and Go (Ire)**, 2, 122	C. Perret	Robyn Dancer, 2, 122	Super Cholo, 2, 122	9	1:44.00	180,000
1988	**Luge (GB)**, 2, 122	J. A. Santos	Ringerman, 2, 122	Downtown Davey, 2, 122	10	1:45.20	150,000
1987	**Antiqua**, 2, 122	C. B. Asmussen	Mister Modesty, 2, 122	Kohen Witha K., 2, 122	14	1:46.00	150,000
1986	**Bet Twice**, 2, 122	C. Perret	Pledge Card, 2, 122	Grand Rol, 2, 122	5	1:45.00	146,145
1985	**Southern Appeal**, 2, 122	J. Davidson	Papal Power, 2, 122	Miracle Wood, 2, 122	6	1:44.20	130,770
1984	**Mighty Appealing**, 2, 122	G. P. Smith	Cutlass Reality, 2, 122	Rhoman Rule, 2, 122	12	1:43.00	169,485
1983	**Devil's Bag**, 2, 122	E. Maple	Hail Bold King, 2, 122	Pied A' Tierre, 2, 122	5	1:42.20	138,150
1982	**Cast Party**, 2, 122	J. Velasquez	Pax in Bello, 2, 122	Primitive Pleasure, 2, 122	11	1:45.00	145,293
1981	**Deputy Minister**, 2, 122	D. MacBeth	Laser Light, 2, 122	‡Majesty's Prince, 2, 122	8	1:44.60	110,190
1980	**Cure the Blues**, 2, 122	R. L. Turcotte	Matching Gift, 2, 122	Kan Reason, 2, 122	7	1:44.40	91,116
1979	**Plugged Nickle**, 2, 122	B. Thornburg	Gold Stage, 2, 122	New Regent, 2, 122	8	1:43.80	108,630
1978	**Spectacular Bid**, 2, 122	R. J. Franklin	General Assembly, 2, 122	Clever Trick, 2, 122	4	**1:41.60**	84,237
1977	**Affirmed**, 2, 122	S. Cauthen	Alydar, 2, 122	Star de Naskra, 2, 122	4	1:44.20	82,290
1976	**Royal Ski**, 2, 122	J. Kurtz	For The Moment, 2, 122	Medieval Man, 2, 122	8	1:44.00	86,046
1975	**Honest Pleasure**, 2, 122	B. Baeza	Whatsyourpleasure, 2, 122	Dance Spell, 2, 122	7	1:42.80	91,662
1974	**L'Enjoleur**, 2, 122	S. Hawley	Wajima, 2, 122	Bombay Duck, 2, 122	3	1:42.60	75,564
1973	**Protagonist**, 2, 122	A. Santiago	Hasty Flyer, 2, 122	Prince of Reason, 2, 122	5	1:43.20	79,911

Pimlico Futurity 1921-'66. Pimlico-Laurel Futurity 1967-'71. Grade 1 1973-'88. Grade 2 1989. Held at Pimlico Race Course 1921-'65, 1979. Not held 1933-'34, 2001. 1 mile 1921-'28. 7 1/2 furlongs 1994-'95. 1 1/8 miles 1996-2000. Turf 1987-'88, 1990-'93. ‡Cagey Cougar finished third, DQ to fourth, 1981. ‡Linkatariat finished third, DQ to fourth, 1993.

Lazaro S. Barrera Memorial Stakes

Grade 2 in 2005. Hollywood Park, three-year-olds, 7 furlongs, dirt. Held May 21, 2005, with a gross value of $150,000. First held in 1953. First graded in 2001. Stakes record 1:20.42 (2001 Early Flyer).

Year	Winner	Jockey	Second	Third	Strs	Time	1st Purse
2005	**Storm Wolf**, 3, 116	A. O. Solis	Dover Dere, 3, 115	Ransom Demanded, 3, 115	6	1:22.26	$90,000
2004	**Twice as Bad**, 3, 116	A. O. Solis	Wimplestiltskin, 3, 116	Don'tsellmeshort, 3, 123	8	1:21.57	90,000
2003	**Blazonry**, 3, 115	M. E. Smith	Fly to the Wire, 3, 116	Jimmy O, 3, 116	9	1:22.19	90,000
2002	**Captain Squire**, 3, 123	C. J. Rollins	Fonz's, 3, 123	Kamsack, 3, 117	5	1:21.95	90,000
2001	**Early Flyer**, 3, 123	C. J. McCarron	Squirtle Squirt, 3, 123	Top Hit, 3, 118	7	**1:20.42**	65,160
2000	**Caller One**, 3, 122	C. S. Nakatani	Dixie Union, 3, 122	Swept Overboard, 3, 122	4	1:21.10	60,960
1999	**Love That Red**, 3, 122	G. K. Gomez	Apremont, 3, 118	O'Rey Fantasma, 3, 118	4	1:20.81	56,910
1998	**Reraise**, 3, 116	E. J. Delahoussaye	Souvenir Copy, 3, 122	Full Moon Madness, 3, 118	6	1:08.51	39,930

1996 **Future Quest**, 3, 122	K. J. Desormeaux	Slews Royal Son, 3, 119	Tiger Talk, 3, 120	8	1:15.17	$35,100
1995 **Flying Standby**, 3, 115	C. W. Antley	Desert Pirate, 3, 119	Boundless Moment, 3, 116	6	1:09.09	40,200

Named for Racing Hall of Fame and Eclipse Award-winning trainer Lazaro Barrera (1924-'91), trainer of 1978 Triple Crown winner Affirmed. Formerly named for the city of Playa del Rey, California. Grade 3 2001. Playa del Rey S. 1953-'54, 1995-'96, 1998. Not held 1955-'94, 1997. 6 furlongs 1954, 1995, 1998. 6¹/₂ furlongs 1996.

Lecomte Stakes

Grade 3 in 2005. Fair Grounds, three-year-olds, 1 mile, dirt. Held January 15, 2005, with a gross value of $100,000. First held in 1943. First graded in 2003. Stakes record 1:37.60 (1993 Dixieland Heat).

Year	Winner	Jockey	Second	Third	Strs	Time	1st Purse
2005	**Storm Surge**, 3, 122	R. Albarado	Smooth Bid, 3, 122	Kansas City Boy, 3, 114	5	1:39.34	$60,000
2004	**Fire Slam**, 3, 119	S. J. Sellers	Shadowland, 3, 118	Two Down Automatic, 3, 117	7	1:38.48	60,000
2003	**Saintly Look**, 3, 122	S. J. Sellers	Call Me Lefty, 3, 122	Winning Fans, 3, 114	11	1:37.62	60,000
2002	**Easyfromthegitgo**, 3, 114	D. J. Meche	Sky Terrace, 3, 119	It'sallinthechase, 3, 122	11	1:37.98	60,000
2001	**Sam Lord's Castle**, 3, 122	R. Albarado	Wild Hits, 3, 122	Mc Mahon, 3, 119	10	1:37.98	60,000
2000	**Noble Ruler**, 3, 114	L. J. Melancon	Mighty, 3, 122	Peninsula, 3, 114	10	1:39.11	60,000
1999	**Some Actor**, 3, 114	E. M. Martin Jr.	Desert Demon, 3, 114	Silver Chadra, 3, 114	14	1:38.59	60,000
1998	**Western City**, 3, 112	R. Albarado	Captain Maestri, 3, 116	Slick Report, 3, 112	6	1:37.84	60,000
1997	**Cash Deposit**, 3, 120	R. D. Ardoin	Stroke, 3, 114	Kalispell, 3, 113	5	1:37.97	36,000
1996	**Boomerang**, 3, 116	E. M. Martin Jr.	Commanders Palace, 3, 116	Playing to Win, 3, 115	8	1:39.49	25,845
1995	**Moonlight Dancer**, 3, 112	L. J. Melancon	Beavers Nose, 3, 114	Timeless Honor, 3, 120	8	1:40.13	25,725
1994	**Fly Cry**, 3, 119	R. D. Ardoin	Smilin Singin Sam, 3, 114	Sweet Wager, 3, 115	12	1:39.29	19,905
1993	**Dixieland Heat**, 3, 116	E. J. Perrodin	Apprentice, 3, 117	Masters Windfall, 3, 112	13	1:37.60	19,995
1992	**Line In The Sand**, 3, 112	S. P. Romero	Greinton's Dancer, 3, 113	Best Boy's Jade, 3, 116	7	1:39.80	19,215
1991	**Big Courage**, 3, 116	T. L. Fox	Near the Limit, 3, 118	Slick Groom, 3, 111	11	1:48.30	19,725
1990	**Martha's Buck**, 3, 113	B. J. Walker Jr.	Axe It, 3, 115	Arrowhead Al, 3, 112	7	1:47.00	16,050
1989	**Majesty's Imp**, 3, 116	S. R. Rydowski	Nooo Problema, 3, 119	Esker Island, 3, 113	10	1:45.60	16,455
1988	**Pastourelles**, 3, 113	B. J. Walker Jr.	Risen Star, 3, 122	Run Paul Run, 3, 114	9	1:46.60	16,275
1987	**One Tough Cat**, 3, 114	K. P. LeBlanc	Authentic Hero, 3, 118	French 'n Irish, 3, 113	8	1:46.20	17,250
1986	**Timely Albert**, 3, 109	P. Rubbicco	Irish Irish, 3, 114	New Plymouth, 3, 117	9	1:45.60	34,200
1985	**Encolure**, 3, 114	R. D. Ardoin	Northern Bid, 3, 119	Ten Times Ten, 3, 116	11	1:45.80	33,450
1984	**Silent King**, 3, 115	C. Mueller	Taylor's Special, 3, 122	Fairly Straight, 3, 111	4	1:45.20	24,150
1983	**Explosive Wagon**, 3, 116	C. Mueller	Found Pearl Harbor, 3, 116	Pronto Forli, 3, 120	11	1:45.00	26,900
1982	**Linkage**, 3, 116	G. P. Smith	Soy Emperor, 3, 113	Mid Yell, 3, 109	7	1:45.00	23,350
1981	**Law Me**, 3, 113	J. McKnight	Brazen Ruler, 3, 119	Corsicana, 3, 114	10	1:46.40	24,500
1980	**Withholding**, 3, 108	B. Fann	Brent's Trans Am, 3, 120	Bold Source, 3, 107	10	1:44.20	23,650
1979	**Fuego Seguro**, 3, 116	M. R. Morgan	Bo, 3, 114	Will Henry, 3, 116	12	1:46.60	21,175
1978	**Dragon Tamer**, 3, 118	R. Sibille	Batonnier, 3, 110	Traffic Warning, 3, 114	14	1:44.60	22,050
1977	**Clev Er Tell**, 3, 119	R. Broussard	A Letter to Harry, 3, 118	Sea Defier, 3, 110	8	1:44.80	16,725
1976	**Tudor Tambourine**, 3, 117	D. Copling	Glassy Dip, 3, 112	Go East Young Man, 3, 117	12	1:46.00	18,000
1975	**Colonel Power**, 3, 123	P. Rubbicco	Davey Dan, 3, 113	Rustic Ruler, 3, 119	13	1:40.60	18,625
1974	**Crimson Ruler**, 3, 119	K. LeBlanc	Don't Be Late Jim, 3, 116	Heavy Mayonnaise, 3, 120	11	1:43.80	17,650
1973	**Vodika**, 3, 119	T. Barrow	Navajo, 3, 120	Rocket Pocket, 3, 123	14	1:46.00	15,825

Named for Gen. T. J. Wells's Lecomte (1850 c. by Boston); Lecomte was the only horse to defeat Lexington, in a match race at Metairie Race Course near New Orleans.

Leonard Richards Stakes

Grade 3 in 2005. Delaware Park, three-year-olds, 1¹/₁₆ miles, dirt. Held July 18, 2004, with a gross value of $250,600. First held in 1937. First graded in 1973. Stakes record 1:42.41 (2001 Burning Roma).

Year	Winner	Jockey	Second	Third	Strs	Time	1st Purse
2004	**Pollard's Vision**, 3, 122	J. D. Bailey	Britt's Jules, 3, 116	Pies Prospect, 3, 115	7	1:43.85	$150,000
2003	**Awesome Time**, 3, 115	A. S. Black	Christine's Outlaw, 3, 115	Cherokee's Boy, 3, 122	8	1:43.26	150,000
2002	**Running Tide**, 3, 115	R. A. Dominguez	Nothing Flat, 3, 115	The Sewickley Kid, 3, 115	8	1:45.10	150,000
2001	**Burning Roma**, 3, 122	R. Wilson	Marciano, 3, 122	Bay Eagle, 3, 115	5	1:42.41	120,000
2000	**Grundlefoot**, 3, 113	T. L. Dunkelberger	Perfect Cat, 3, 114	Mercaldo, 3, 114	8	1:44.04	120,000
1999	**Stellar Brush**, 3, 114	M. J. McCarthy	Smart Guy, 3, 115	Successful Appeal, 3, 122	8	1:42.78	120,000
1998	**Scatmandu**, 3, 114	R. Migliore	Hot Wells, 3, 115	True Silver, 3, 113	7	1:42.43	90,000
1997	**Leestown**, 3, 116	J. A. Velez Jr.	Universe, 3, 113	Bleu Madura, 3, 116	8	1:43.46	90,000
1982	**Northrop**, 3, 113	L. Moyers	Majesty's Prince, 3, 126	Victory Zone, 3, 113	6	1:50.00	14,755
1981	**Sportin' Life**, 3, 116	K. D. Black	Main Stem, 3, 116	Aspro, 3, 113	7	1:49.00	18,801
1980	**Proctor**, 3, 113	V. A. Bracciale Jr.	Poor Dad, 3, 122	Colossal Apostle, 3, 113	12	1:50.20	30,778
1979	**Lucy's Axe**, 3, 126	R. B. Gilbert	Buck's Chief, 3, 114	Idle Jack, 3, 113	8	1:50.80	21,450
1978	**Mac Diarmida**, 3, 122	J. Cruguet	Prince Misko, 3, 122	Strange Proposal, 3, 113	10	1:46.80	22,653
1977	**True Colors**, 3, 113	S. Cauthen	Singleton, 3, 113	Best Person, 3, 113	13	1:43.20	19,663
1976	**Cinteelo**, 3, 117	B. Thornburg	Chati, 3, 117	Babas Fables, 3, 114	12	1:43.40	28,500
1975	**My Friend Gus**, 3, 117	B. Fann	Talc, 3, 120	Too Easy, 3, 114	10	1:42.20	30,290
1974	**Silver Florin**, 3, 122	R. Wilson	Ground Breaker, 3, 116	Clyde William, 3, 116	12	1:47.40	34,450
1973	**London Company**, 3, 122	C. Barrera	Berno, 3, 119	Warbucks, 3, 119	8	1:47.80	41,798

Named for Leonard P. Richards, second chairman of the Delaware Racing Commission. Formerly named for the Delaware state nickname, the Diamond State. Grade 2 1973-'74. Not graded 1980-'82, 1997-2001. Diamond State S. 1937-'47. Not held 1943, 1983-'96. 1¹/₈ miles 1937-'68, 1979-'82. Turf 1970-'80.

Lexington Stakes

Grade 3 in 2005. Belmont Park, three-year-olds, 1¼ miles, turf. Held July 18, 2004, with a gross value of $111,100. First held in 1961. First graded in 1973. Stakes record 1:58.93 (2001 Sharp Performance).

Year	Winner	Jockey	Second	Third	Strs	Time	1st Purse
2004	‡Mustanfar, 3, 114	J. A. Santos	Icy Atlantic, 3, 122	Second Performance, 3, 118	8	2:01.15	$66,660
2003	Sharp Impact, 3, 114	R. Migliore	Hidden Truth, 3, 118	Urban King (Ire), 3, 114	6	2:02.62	90,000
2002	Chiselling, 3, 114	J. D. Bailey	Finality, 3, 114	Irish Colonial, 3, 114	8	2:00.42	90,000
2001	Sharp Performance, 3, 114	J. R. Velazquez	Package Store, 3, 114	Whitmore's Conn, 3, 114	8	**1:58.93**	90,000
2000	Rob's Spirit, 3, 113	J. D. Bailey	Plato, 3, 113	Rumsonontheriver, 3, 115	6	2:02.87	90,000
1999	Mythical Gem, 3, 117	J. F. Chavez	Monkey Puzzle, 3, 113	Bugatti, 3, 114	11	2:01.21	90,000
1998	Parade Ground, 3, 117	M. E. Smith	Ay Rouge, 3, 113	La Reine's Terms, 3, 113	8	2:00.55	84,060
1997	Private Buck Trout, 3, 119	J. F. Chavez	Red Castle, 3, 112	Renewed, 3, 112	10	2:01.29	90,000
1996	Ok by Me, 3, 122	J. F. Chavez	Value Investor, 3, 117	Alzeus (Ire), 3, 113	10	2:03.58	68,160
1995	Green Means Go, 3, 119	J. D. Bailey	Nostra, 3, 112	Flitch, 3, 112	9	2:01.69	66,960
1994	Holy Mountain, 3, 112	J. R. Velazquez	Islefaxyou, 3, 112	Check Ride, 3, 117	10	1:59.74	50,850
1993	Llandaff, 3, 123	J. A. Krone	Strolling Along, 3, 114	Eastern Memories (Ire), 3, 114	7	2:02.93	52,380
1992	Spectacular Tide, 3, 114	J. A. Krone	Preferences, 3, 121	Casino Magistrate, 3, 123	6	2:02.20	69,120
1991	Lech, 3, 114	A. T. Cordero Jr.	Fourstars Allstar, 3, 123	Lucky Mathieu, 3, 114	7	1:59.55	71,160
1990	Solar Splendor, 3, 123	E. Maple	Rouse the Louse, 3, 123	Apple Current, 3, 114	8	2:01.80	56,640
1989	Coosaragga, 3, 114	R. Migliore	Valid Ordinate, 3, 114	Orange Sunshine, 3, 119	8	2:00.80	69,720
1988	Sunshine Forever, 3, 123	A. T. Cordero Jr.	Hodges Bay, 3, 114	Ask Not, 3, 114	8	2:03.00	85,500
1987	Milesius, 3, 114	E. Maple	Yucca, 3, 117	Rio's Lark, 3, 114	10	2:03.20	89,580
1986	Manila, 3, 126	J. A. Santos	Glow, 3, 123	Dance Card Filled, 3, 114	10	2:03.60	88,980
1985	Danger's Hour, 3, 123	J. D. Bailey	Foundation Plan, 3, 123	Exclusive Partner, 3, 114	14	2:00.40	71,370
1984	Onyxly, 3, 114	J. D. Bailey	Dr. Schwartzman, 3, 126	Vision, 3, 126	13	2:01.20	58,770
1983	Kilauea, 3, 114	J. Cruguet	Fortnightly, 3, 126	Top Competitor, 3, 114	10	2:00.60	34,800
1982	Majesty's Prince, 3, 126	E. Maple	Lamerok, 3, 114	Flamingo Two, 3, 114	8	2:03.00	50,310
	‡Royal Roberto, 3, 126	J. Fell	Otter Slide, 3, 117	‡Royal Ring, 3, 114	6	2:01.80	50,310
1981	Acaroid, 3, 117	C. B. Asmussen	†De La Rose, 3, 121	Wicked Will (GB), 3, 117	11	2:00.20	52,380
1980	‡Good Bid, 3, 112	J. Samyn	Proctor, 3, 116	Don Daniello, 3, 122	8	2:01.00	50,310
1979	Virilly, 3, 108	R. I. Velez	T. V. Series, 3, 113	Crown Thy Good, 3, 114	11	2:02.40	50,895
1978	Mac Diarmida, 3, 126	J. Cruguet	John Henry, 3, 112	Ashikaga, 3, 110	9	1:41.00	34,110
1977	Swoon Swept, 3, 112	L. J. Melancon	Stir the Embers, 3, 112	Lynn Davis, 3, 116	8	1:41.20	32,400
	Johnny D., 3, 113	A. T. Cordero Jr.	‡Forward Charger, 3, 117	Best Person, 3, 112	6	1:41.00	32,100
1976	Fabled Monarch, 3, 114	J. Vasquez	‡Fighting Bill, 3, 113	Effervescing, 3, 112	8	1:50.00	27,450
	Modred, 3, 117	C. Perret	Dream 'n De Lucky, 3, 112	Spanish Dagger, 3, 110	7	1:49.40	27,300
1975	Dr. Emil, 3, 109	M. Venezia	Martial Law, 3, 109	Le Cypriote, 3, 112	7	2:07.00	27,270
	Brian Boru, 3, 116	B. Baeza	Rapid Invader, 3, 111	Clout, 3, 113	7	2:07.60	27,270
1974	Jack Sprat, 3, 112	R. Turcotte	Kin Run, 3, 115	Never Explain, 3, 116	9	1:56.40	28,020
	Hasty Tudor, 3, 112	V. A. Bracciale Jr.	R. Tom Can, 3, 115	Splitting Headache, 3, 118	9	1:56.80	27,870
1973	London Company, 3, 125	L. A. Pincay Jr.	Rapid Sage, 3, 112	Bold Nix, 3, 116	13	1:56.00	35,760

Named for champion and leading sire Lexington (1850 c. by Boston). Grade 2 1973-'89. Lexington H. 1961-'80. Held at Aqueduct 1961-'76. 1⅝ miles 1961. 1 mile 1962. 1¹/₁₆ miles 1963-'70, 1977-'78. 1³/₁₆ miles 1971-'74. 1¼ miles 1976. Dirt 1962. Two divisions 1970, 1974-'77, 1982. ‡Effervescing finished second, DQ to third, 1976 (1st Div.). ‡True Colors finished second, DQ to sixth, 1977 (2nd Div.). ‡Proctor finished first, DQ to second, 1980. ‡Dew Line finished first, DQ to fifth; Reinvested finished third, DQ to fourth, 1982. ‡Icy Atlantic finished first, DQ to second, 2004. †Denotes female.

Locust Grove Handicap

Grade 3 in 2005. Churchill Downs, three-year-olds and up, fillies and mares, 1⅛ miles, turf. Held June 26, 2004, with a gross value of $165,750. First held in 1982. First graded in 1998. Stakes record 1:46.75 (2004 Shaconage).

Year	Winner	Jockey	Second	Third	Strs	Time	1st Purse
2004	Shaconage, 4, 116	B. Blanc	Halory Leigh, 4, 111	Sand Springs, 4, 119	6	**1:46.75**	$102,765
2003	Ipi Tombe (Zim), 5, 123	P. Day	⋅ Kiss the Devil, 5, 116	Quick Tip, 5, 117	6	1:47.70	101,928
2002	Voodoo Dancer, 4, 120	J. A. Santos	Blue Moon (Fr), 5, 116	Solvig, 5, 116	9	1:46.91	104,718
2001	Colstar, 5, 121	J. K. Court	Solvig, 4, 115	Megans Bluff, 4, 119	11	1:48.79	107,136
2000	Colstar, 4, 121	A. Delgado	Pricearose, 4, 113	Histoire Sainte (Fr), 4, 113	6	1:47.44	102,300
1999	Shires Ende, 4, 117	W. Martinez	Formal Tango, 4, 116	Uanme, 4, 112	11	1:49.11	107,508
1998	Colcon, 5, 118	S. J. Sellers	Leo's Gypsy Dancer, 4, 113	Mingling Glances, 4, 112	6	1:48.53	103,974
1997	Romy, 6, 121	F. Torres	Yokama, 4, 112	Cymbala (Fr), 4, 116	6	1:48.89	68,634
1996	Bail Out Becky, 4, 121	C. Perret	Ms. Isadora, 4, 113	Memories (Ire), 5, 117	6	1:47.38	72,670
1995	Memories (Ire), 4, 112	S. J. Sellers	Market Booster, 6, 120	Thread, 4, 115	7	1:47.48	71,760
1994	Life Is Delicious, 4, 113	J. R. Martinez Jr.	Eurostorm, 4, 113	Obtain, 4, 112	4	1:53.87	70,850
1993	Lady Blessington (Fr), 5, 121	C. A. Black	Gone Seeking, 4, 109	Crusie, 4, 115	4	1:50.16	74,425
1992	Behaving Dancer, 5, 111	D. L. Howard	Firm Stance, 4, 118	Olden Rijn, 4, 112	10	1:47.27	74,750
1991	Nice Serve, 4, 111	J. M. Johnson	Super Fan, 4, 118	Behaving Dancer, 4, 113	9	1:51.30	73,840
1990	Dibs, 4, 111	A. T. Gryder	City Crowds (Ire), 4, 111	Phillipa Rush (NZ), 4, 116	6	1:50.60	71,435
1989	Jungle Gold, 4, 111	C. R. Woods Jr.	Here's Your Silver, 4, 116	Heretic, 4, 115	7	1:43.20	53,381
1988	Chez Chez Chez, 4, 111	J. J. Garcia	Lt. Lao, 4, 115	How I Wish, 4, 113	10	1:45.20	55,575

1987	**Luckiest Girl**, 4, 114	D. J. Soto	Slippin n' Slyding, 4, 111	Marianna's Girl, 4, 120	9	1:51.60	$36,465
1986	**Glorious View**, 4, 113	C. R. Woods Jr.	Zenobia Empress, 5, 120	Tide, 4, 112	9	1:44.00	36,693
1985	**Sintra**, 4, 123	K. K. Allen	Sweet Missus, 5, 112	Switching Trick, 5, 112	6	1:43.40	21,076
1984	**Heatherten**, 5, 122	S. Maple	Mickey's Echo, 5, 110	Forest Maiden, 4, 113	6	1:43.00	26,462
1983	**Try Something New**, 4, 117	P. Day	Kitchen, 4, 114	Naskra Magic, 4, 117	6	1:45.20	23,156
1982	**Excitable Lady**, 4, 120	D. G. McHargue	Dawn's Beginning, 4, 111	Sweetest Fantasy, 4, 111	9	1:37.20	24,310

Named for the historic landmark Locust Grove, a house once owned by the brother-in-law and surveying partner of George Rogers Clark. Locust Grove S. 1982-'85, 1988. 1 mile 1988. $1\frac{1}{16}$ miles 1983-'86, 1988-'89. About $1\frac{1}{8}$ miles 1990. Dirt 1982-'86, 1994. Four-year-olds and up 1983-'89.

Lone Star Park Handicap

Grade 3 in 2005. Lone Star Park, three-year-olds and up, $1\frac{1}{16}$ miles, dirt. Held May 30, 2005, with a gross value of $300,000. First held in 1997. First graded in 2000. Stakes record 1:40.53 (2001 Dixie Dot Com).

Year	Winner	Jockey	Second	Third	Strs	Time	1st Purse
2005	**Supah Blitz**, 5, 118	J. K. Court	Cryptograph, 4, 116	Absent Friend, 5, 115	10	1:41.90	$180,000
2004	**Yessirgeneralsir**, 4, 114	O. Figueroa	Sonic West, 5, 117	Spanish Empire, 4, 117	6	1:41.29	180,000
2003	**Pie N Burger**, 5, 117	J. Theriot	dh-Bluesthestandard, 6, 120		8	1:42.03	180,000
			dh-Maysville Slew, 7, 114				
2002	**Congaree**, 4, 119	P. Day	Prince Iroquois, 5, 115	Mercenary, 4, 115	12	1:42.96	180,000
2001	**Dixie Dot Com**, 6, 118	D. R. Flores	Fan the Flame, 4, 113	Big Numbers, 4, 114	8	**1:40.53**	180,000
2000	**Luftikus**, 4, 114	D. R. Flores	Nite Dreamer, 5, 118	Sultry Substitute, 5, 114	11	1:40.87	180,000
1999	**Mocha Express**, 5, 116	M. St. Julien	Littlebitlively, 5, 118	Nite Dreamer, 4, 113	7	1:43.36	183,300
1998	**Mocha Express**, 4, 114	M. St. Julien	Prince of the Mt., 7, 114	Dickey Rickey, 5, 114	5	1:42.17	123,000
1997	**Connecting Terms**, 4, 112	L. J. Melancon	Humble Seven, 5, 112	Isitingood, 6, 122	7	1:41.97	120,000

The track and the race are named for Texas's (Lone Star Park's home state) nickname, the Lone Star State. Equaled track record 2000. Track record 2001. Dead heat for second 2003.

Longacres Mile Handicap

Grade 3 in 2005. Emerald Downs, three-year-olds and up, 1 mile, dirt. Held August 22, 2004, with a gross value of $250,000. First held in 1935. First graded in 1975. Stakes record 1:33 (2003 Sky Jack).

Year	Winner	Jockey	Second	Third	Strs	Time	1st Purse
2004	**Adreamisborn**, 5, 116	R. A. Baze	Demon Warlock, 4, 114	Mr. Makah, 4, 112	12	1:34.80	$137,500
2003	**Sky Jack**, 7, 123	R. A. Baze	Poker Brad, 5, 116	Lord Nelson, 6, 116	10	**1:33.00**	137,500
2002	**Sabertooth**, 4, 114	N. J. Chaves	Moonlight Meeting, 7, 119	San Nicolas, 4, 115	12	1:34.60	137,500
2001	**Irisheyesareflying**, 5, 117	I. Puglisi	Handy N Bold, 6, 119	Makors Mark, 4, 118	10	1:35.40	137,500
2000	**Edneator**, 4, 111	G. V. Mitchell	Big Ten (Chi), 5, 119	Crafty Boy, 5, 114	11	1:33.20	137,500
1999	**Budroyale**, 6, 119	G. K. Gomez	Mike K, 5, 117	Kid Katabatic, 6, 116	8	1:34.60	137,500
1998	**Wild Wonder**, 4, 121	E. J. Delahoussaye	Mocha Express, 4, 115	Hal's Pal (GB), 5, 117	9	1:33.20	110,000
1997	**Kid Katabatic**, 4, 113	C. Loseth	Hesabull, 4, 119	Liberty Road, 4, 114	7	1:34.20	110,000
1996	**Isitingood**, 5, 117	D. R. Flores	Cleante (Arg), 7, 121	Humpty's Hoedown, 6, 114	10	1:35.60	110,000
1995	**L. J. Express**, 5, 119	M. Allen	Funboy, 4, 121	Secret Damascus, 5, 114	10	1:34.60	50,350
1994	**Want a Winner**, 4, 119	V. Belvoir	Sneakin Jake, 5, 118	Forgotten Days, 8, 114	8	1:35.20	48,250
1993	**Adventuresome Love**, 7, 117	G. Baze	Sneakin Jake, 6, 118	For the Children, 3, 115	8	1:34.60	48,050
1992	**Bolulight**, 4, 114	R. D. Hansen	Ibero (Arg), 5, 122	Charmonnier, 4, 118	12	1:34.00	181,300
1991	**Louis Cyphre (Ire)**, 5, 120	G. L. Stevens	Captain Condo, 9, 116	Ever Steady, 4, 113	11	1:36.10	178,500
1990	**Snipledo**, 5, 115	J. R. Corral	Adventuresome Love, 4, 114	dh- Captain Condo, 8, 116	14	1:35.60	187,700
				dh- Kent Green, 7, 112			
1989	**Simply Majestic**, 5, 122	R. D. Hansen	Crystal Run, 5, 114	Harmony Creek, 3, 113	9	1:34.20	154,000
1988	**Simply Majestic**, 4, 116	R. A. Baze	Kent Green, 5, 113	Chan's Dragon, 4, 113	9	1:33.80	147,800
1987	**Judge Angelucci**, 4, 121	G. Baze	Leading Hour, 4, 111	Slyly Gifted, 4, 117	8	1:34.20	150,000
1986	**Skywalker**, 4, 123	L. A. Pincay Jr.	Bedside Promise, 4, 120	Sir Macamillion, 7, 116	7	1:34.60	177,000
1985	**Chum Salmon**, 5, 122	G. Baze	Dear Rick, 4, 120	M. Double M., 4, 123	9	1:34.60	150,000
1984	**Travelling Victor**, 5, 123	C. Loseth	Night Mover, 4, 121	Iron Billy, 5, 114	10	1:34.80	115,000
1983	**Chinook Pass**, 4, 125	L. A. Pincay Jr.	Travelling Victor, 4, 118	Earthquack, 4, 119	14	1:35.60	115,000
1982	**Pompeii Court**, 5, 121	S. Hawley	Chinook Pass, 3, 118	Police Inspector, 5, 119	11	1:35.60	100,000
1981	**Trooper Seven**, 5, 126	G. Baze	Reb's Golden Ale, 6, 121	Loto Canada, 4, 117	13	1:35.40	100,650
1980	**Trooper Seven**, 4, 123	G. Baze	Island Sultan, 5, 125	Tilt the Balance, 5, 121	10	1:34.40	78,200
1979	**Always Gallant**, 5, 127	D. G. McHargue	Tilt the Balance, 4, 119	Bad 'n Big, 5, 127	13	1:33.80	79,500
1978	**Bad 'n Big**, 4, 128	W. Shoemaker	Smiley's Dream, 4, 118	Run'n Prince, 4, 111	8	1:34.00	75,000
1977	**Theologist**, 4, 118	B. B. Cooper	Ben Adhem, 5, 116	Detrimental, 6, 120	13	1:38.40	65,000
1976	**Yu Wipi**, 4, 123	S. Hawley	Holding Pattern, 5, 121	Ben Adhem, 4, 124	10	1:34.80	55,500
1975	**Jim**, 5, 118	A. Cuthbertson	Times Rush, 7, 121	Whoa Boy, 4, 116	12	1:37.00	39,500
1974	**Times Rush**, 6, 119	B. Frazier	Red Eye Express, 5, 123	Red Wind, 6, 120	13	1:35.20	38,400
1973	**Silver Maverick**, 5, 122	L. Pierce	Pataha Prince, 8, 118	Reluctant Lord, 4, 120	10	1:34.00	30,250

Named for Longacres Park in Renton, Washington; Longacres closed in 1992. Formerly named for Mt. Rainier, which is located in Washington State. Grade 2 1982-'89. Rainier Mile H. 1991. Budweiser Mile H. 1993. Emerald Budweiser Mile H. 1994-'95. Held at Longacres Park 1935-'92. Held at Yakima Meadows 1993-'95. Not held 1943. Four-year-olds and up 1970. Dead heat for third 1990. Established track record 1996. Track record 1998, 2003. Equaled track record 2000.

Long Branch Breeders' Cup Stakes

Grade 3 in 2005. Monmouth Park, three-year-olds, 1¹/₁₆ miles, dirt. Held July 17, 2004, with a gross value of $100,000. First held in 1878. First graded in 1973. Stakes record 1:41 (1956 Skipper Bill).

Year	Winner	Jockey	Second	Third	Strs	Time	1st Purse
2004	Lion Heart, 3, 116	J. Bravo	My Snookie's Boy, 3, 115	Royal Assault, 3, 122	7	1:43.51	$60,000
2003	Max Forever, 3, 113	J. C. Ferrer	Christine's Outlaw, 3, 115	Chilly Rooster, 3, 112	6	1:43.56	60,000
2002	Puck, 3, 122	M. Aguilar	Shah Jehan, 3, 114	Stephentown, 3, 114	6	1:44.35	60,000
2001	Burning Roma, 3, 122	R. Wilson	This Fleet Is Due, 3, 114	Thunder Blitz, 3, 122	7	1:43.28	60,000
2000	Thistyranthasclass, 3, 114	J. A. Velez Jr.	Graeme Hall, 3, 120	Summinitup, 3, 112	9	1:43.60	60,000
1999	Ghost Story, 3, 112	R. G. Davis	Unbridled Jet, 3, 114	Clever Gem, 3, 114	6	1:42.64	60,000
1998	Favorite Trick, 3, 116	P. Day	Tomorrows Cat, 3, 113	Arctic Sweep, 3, 114	6	1:43.10	60,000
1997	Jules, 3, 114	A. T. Gryder	Leestown, 3, 120	Capture the Gold, 3, 114	4	1:42.40	60,000
1996	Dr. Caton, 3, 112	J. Bravo	Devil's Honor, 3, 122	Clash by Night, 3, 114	5	1:41.89	45,000
1995	Pyramid Peak, 3, 120	W. H. McCauley	Suave Prospect, 3, 120	Mighty Magee, 3, 118	5	1:44.09	47,250
1994	Meadow Flight, 3, 120	J. Bravo	Red Tazz, 3, 114	Don's Sho, 3, 114	5	1:43.92	47,370
1993	Bert's Bubbleator, 3, 120	E. L. King Jr.	P. J. Higgins, 3, 120	Signoir Valery, 3, 112	5	1:45.92	32,310
1992	Scudan, 3, 114	N. Santagata	Pistols and Roses, 3, 122	Munch n' Nosh, 3, 114	8	1:42.18	39,300
1991	Sultry Song, 3, 120	N. Santagata	Arrowtown, 3, 114	Zig n' Zag, 3, 116	7	1:42.38	33,630
1990	Tees Prospect, 3, 112	R. Wilson	Sir Richard Lewis, 3, 116	Big Ted K., 3, 114	8	1:42.40	33,660
1989	Orange Sunshine, 3, 120	E. L. King Jr.	Slew the Knight, 3, 120	Currently Red, 3, 113	7	1:36.60	34,740
1988	Mi Selecto, 3, 120	C. Perret	Blew by Em, 3, 114	Master Speaker, 3, 115	7	1:35.80	40,380
1987	I'm So Bad, 3, 112	N. Santagata	Marine Command, 3, 115	Saratoga Sun, 3, 112	6	1:37.40	34,680
1986	Lyphard Line, 3, 120	K. Castaneda	Laser Lane, 3, 112	A Blend of Six, 3, 114	8	1:39.20	34,080
1985	Bea Quality, 3, 116	C. W. Antley	Sport Jet, 3, 118	Ice and Fire, 3, 114	9	1:38.80	34,980
1984	Dr. Schwartzman, 3, 118	C. Perret	Stay the Course, 3, 112	For Halo, 3, 114	8	1:35.00	34,260
1983	Smart Style, 3, 120	A. O. Solis	Rocky Marriage, 3, 112	American Diabolo, 3, 114	8	1:36.60	27,855
	Princilian, 3, 113	J. Vasquez	Silent Landing, 3, 113	Northern Ice, 3, 120	6	1:35.60	27,375
1982	Prince Westport, 3, 120	D. Brumfield	Cagey Cougar, 3, 114	Our Escapade, 3, 114	10	1:38.40	27,825
	Play for Love, 3, 114	D. Brumfield	†Larida, 3, 115	Colorful Leader, 3, 112	9	1:38.00	27,645
1981	†De La Rose, 3, 117	E. Maple	Century Banker, 3, 114	Victorian Double, 3, 114	9	1:35.60	34,410
1980	No Bend, 3, 114	W. Nemeti	Dressage, 3, 118	Peaslee, 3, 114	12	1:35.80	27,810
1979	Commadore C., 3, 114	R. Wilson	Quiet Crossing, 3, 124	Durham Ranger, 3, 124	7	1:36.80	21,629
1978	Mac Diarmida, 3, 124	J. Cruguet	Noon Time Spender, 3, 118	Morning Frolic, 3, 116	8	1:42.20	21,921
1977	P. R. Man, 3, 118	C. Perret	Prince Hagley, 3, 114	Ver-E-Sharp, 3, 114	6	1:37.00	18,298
1976	Pastry, 3, 118	M. Solomone	Modred, 3, 114	Noble Surviver, 3, 114	10	1:37.20	18,753
1975	Lee Gary, 3, 114	P. I. Grimm	Bombay Duck, 3, 121	Designated Hitter, 3, 114	7	1:36.80	19,143
1974	Silver Florin, 3, 124	R. Wilson	I'm On Top, 3, 116	R. Tom Can, 3, 114	10	1:36.60	15,258
	Hat Full, 3, 114	C. Barrera	To the Rescue, 3, 116	Never Explain, 3, 114	9	1:38.00	15,161
1973	Bemo, 3, 116	W. J. Passmore	Warbucks, 3, 118	Hey Rube, 3, 116	10	1:36.80	18,753

Named for a popular seaside resort of the 1880s, Long Branch, New Jersey; Long Branch is near Oceanport, Monmouth Park's current location. Not graded 1989-2001. Long Branch H. 1878-1958. Long Branch S. 1963-'91, 1996-'97. Not held 1894-1946, 1959-'62. 1¹/₄ miles 1878-'93. 6 furlongs 1963. 1 mile 1964-'70, 1972-'89. Turf 1963-'69, 1971-'74, 1976, 1978-'82, 1984, 1986, 1988-'89. Originally scheduled on turf 1975. Three-year-olds and up 1947-'58. Two divisions 1974, 1982-'83. †Denotes female.

Long Island Handicap

Grade 2 in 2005. Aqueduct, three-year-olds and up, fillies and mares, 1¹/₂ miles, turf. Held November 6, 2004, with a gross value of $150,000. First held in 1956. First graded in 1973. Stakes record 2:29.04 (1992 Villandry).

Year	Winner	Jockey	Second	Third	Strs	Time	1st Purse
2004	Eleusis, 3, 115	J. A. Santos	Literacy, 4, 114	Arvada (GB), 4, 117	7	2:31.51	$90,000
2003	Spice Island, 4, 117	V. Carrero	Volga (Ire), 5, 120	Banyu Dewi (Ger), 4, 114	11	2:32.58	90,000
2002	Uriah (Ger), 3, 112	N. Arroyo Jr.	Sunstone (GB), 4, 114	Mot Juste (GB), 4, 119	11	2:42.48	90,000
2001	Queue, 4, 115	J. L. Espinoza	Sweetest Thing, 3, 115	Lady Dora, 4, 114	13	2:29.36	90,000
2000	Moonlady (Ger), 3, 114	C. P. DeCarlo	Playact (Ire), 3, 114	La Ville Rouge, 4, 118	11	2:17.94	90,000
1999	Midnight Line, 4, 120	J. D. Bailey	Win for Us (Ger), 3, 116	Horatia (Ire), 3, 112	10	2:29.67	90,000
1998	Coretta (Ire), 4, 114	J. A. Santos	Starry Dreamer, 4, 115	Dixie Ghost, 4, 114	11	2:29.73	60,000
	Yokama, 5, 120	J. D. Bailey	Moments of Magic, 3, 113	Bristol Channel (GB), 3, 114	11	2:31.03	60,000
1997	Sweetzie, 5, 115	J. F. Chavez	Sweet Sondra, 4, 114	Scenic Point, 4, 120	6	2:16.66	90,000
1996	Ampulla, 5, 121	S. J. Sellers	Wandering Star, 3, 118	Beyrouth, 4, 113	12	2:30.70	87,270
1995	Yenda (GB), 4, 113	C. S. Nakatani	Windsharp, 4, 111	Market Booster, 6, 118	10	2:37.15	86,400
1994	Market Booster, 5, 115	M. J. Luzzi	Tiffany's Taylor, 5, 114	Lady Affirmed, 3, 113	12	2:31.95	87,495
1993	Trampoli, 4, 119	M. E. Smith	Bright Generation (Ire), 3, 114	Northern Emerald, 3, 108	5	2:31.57	68,760
1992	Villandry, 4, 115	M. E. Smith	Ratings, 4, 116	Gina Romantica, 4, 113	8	2:29.04	71,160
1991	Shaima, 3, 115	L. Dettori	Highland Penny, 6, 116	Franc Argument, 5, 111	9	2:31.48	73,560
1990	Rigamajig, 4, 110	J. F. Chavez	Narwala (Ire), 3, 115	Roberto's Hope, 3, 112	10	2:29.60	72,120
	Peinture Bleue, 3, 115	J. A. Santos	Franc Argument, 4, 113	Roseate Tern (GB), 4, 119	10	2:29.80	72,600
1989	Warfie, 3, 111	W. H. McCauley	River Memories, 4, 113	Noble Links, 4, 111	6	2:14.40	72,480
1988	Dancing All Night, 4, 108	J. J. Vazquez	Casey (GB), 3, 113	Gaily Gaily (Ire), 5, 111	10	2:34.20	112,320
1987	Stardusk, 3, 109	J. Cruguet	Spruce Fir, 4, 121	Videogenic, 5, 118	13	2:30.40	115,740
1986	Dismasted, 4, 120	J. Samyn	Dawn's Curtsey, 4, 113	Anka Germania (Ire), 4, 114	13	2:30.40	115,560
1985	Videogenic, 3, 116	J. Cruguet	Duty Dance, 3, 114	Mariella, 3, 110	9	2:29.20	92,175
	Faburola (Fr), 4, 114	E. Legrix	Halloween Queen, 4, 107	Easy to Copy, 4, 114	9	2:29.40	105,675

Year	Winner	Jockey	Second	Third	Strs	Time	1st Purse
1984	Heron Cove, 4, 114	J. Cruguet	Key Dancer, 3, 115	Secret Sharer, 4, 110	13	2:32.80	$109,650
1983	Hush Dear, 5, 125	J. Samyn	Mintage (Fr), 4, 111	If Winter Comes, 5, 113	13	2:34.60	70,920
1982	Hush Dear, 4, 111	E. Beitia	Canaille (Ire), 4, 112	Mintage (Fr), 3, 111	14	2:31.40	71,160
1981	Euphrosyne, 5, 110	R. Migliore	Mairzy Doates, 5, 120	Noble Damsel, 3, 112	12	2:33.00	70,440
1980	The Very One, 5, 120	J. Velasquez	Relaxing, 4, 113	Proud Barbara, 3, 113	5	2:35.20	68,400
1979	Flitalong, 3, 107	R. I. Encinas	Terpsichorist, 4, 122	Catherine's Bet, 4, 114	10	2:31.40	52,245
1978	Terpsichorist, 3, 116	A. T. Cordero Jr.	Leave Me Alone, 5, 109	Proud Event, 4, 113	9	2:34.00	48,555
1977	Pearl Necklace, 3, 123	R. Hernandez	Javamine, 4, 121	Leave Me Alone, 4, 113	7	1:43.80	32,430
1976	Javamine, 3, 113	J. Velasquez	Nijana, 3, 115	Fun Forever, 3, 112	11	1:41.60	33,270
1975	Slip Screen, 3, 115	G. P. Intelisano Jr.	Fleet Victress, 3, 115	Jabot, 3, 115	6	1:42.80	33,930
1974	D. O. Lady, 3, 115	M. A. Rivera	Speak Action, 3, 113	Gulls Cry, 3, 116	10	1:43.20	28,080
	Lie Low, 3, 114	J. Velasquez	Victorian Queen, 3, 120	Markhimoff, 3, 115	10	1:42.00	28,080
1973	Tuerta, 3, 116	J. Vasquez	North of Venus, 3, 117	Spring in the Air, 3, 118	12	1:43.80	17,850

Named for the largest island in the continental United States, Long Island, New York; Aqueduct is located on Long Island. Grade 3 1973-'80. Held at Jamaica 1956-'58. Held at Belmont Park 1960, 1962, 1968-'69, 1975-'76, 1990-'98, 1995. 1⅝ miles 1956-'58. 1³⁄₁₆ miles 1959, 1961, 1963-'67, 1970-'71. 1³⁄₈ miles 1960, 1962, 1968-'69, 2000. 1 mile 1972. 1¹⁄₁₆ miles 1973-'77. Dirt 1956-'58, 1961, 1972, 1989, 1997, 2000. Originally scheduled on turf 1975. Three-year-olds 1972-'76. Both sexes 1956-'71. Fillies 1972-'76. Two divisions 1959, 1962, 1966-'70, 1972, 1974, 1985, 1990, 1998.

Los Angeles Times Handicap

Grade 3 in 2005. Hollywood Park, three-year-olds and up, 6 furlongs, dirt. Held May 8, 2004, with a gross value of $150,000. First held in 1938. First graded in 1973. Stakes record 1:07.90 (1995 Forest Gazelle).

Year	Winner	Jockey	Second	Third	Strs	Time	1st Purse
2005	Forest Grove, 4, 117	C. S. Nakatani	Areyoutalkintome, 4, 117	Woke Up Dreamin, 5, 115	6	1:08.57	$90,000
2004	Pohave, 6, 114	J. K. Court	Marino Marini, 4, 119	Summer Service, 4, 117	9	1:08.12	90,000
2003	Hombre Rapido, 6, 116	J. Valdivia Jr.	Publication, 4, 116	Giovannetti, 4, 116	8	1:08.49	120,000
2002	Kona Gold, 8, 125	A. O. Solis	No Armistice, 4, 116	Komax, 4, 114	6	1:08.72	64,500
2001	Caller One, 4, 124	C. S. Nakatani	Stormy Jack, 4, 115	Rapidough, 6, 115	6	1:08.35	64,380
2000	Highland Gold, 5, 115	C. J. McCarron	Mellow Fellow, 5, 113	Your Halo, 5, 114	6	1:09.11	64,260
1999	Son of a Pistol, 7, 122	A. O. Solis	Men's Exclusive, 6, 118	Ray of Sunshine (Ire), 4, 118	4	1:08.17	63,300
1998	Gold Land, 7, 116	K. J. Desormeaux	Mr. Doubledown, 4, 119	The Exeter Man, 6, 114	7	1:08.06	64,800
1997	Men's Exclusive, 4, 117	L. A. Pincay Jr.	‡First Intent, 8, 117	Gold Land, 6, 115	7	1:08.80	80,970
1996	dh- Abaginone, 5, 119	G. L. Stevens		Score Quick, 4, 115	6	1:08.33	53,480
	dh- Paying Dues, 4, 115	C. W. Antley					
1995	Forest Gazelle, 4, 117	K. J. Desormeaux	Lucky Forever, 6, 114	Cardmania, 9, 119	10	1:07.90	83,650
1994	J. F. Williams, 5, 115	C. J. McCarron	Gundaghia, 7, 117	Thirty Slews, 7, 120	6	1:09.03	61,900
1993	Star of the Crop, 4, 119	G. L. Stevens	Fabulous Champ, 4, 115	Wild Harmony, 4, 116	7	1:08.78	63,300
1992	Cardmania, 6, 118	E. J. Delahoussaye	Gray Slewpy, 4, 119	Robyn Dancer, 5, 119	5	1:08.73	61,200
1991	Black Jack Road, 7, 117	R. A. Baze	Sunny Blossom, 6, 121	Tanker Port, 6, 116	6	1:09.10	62,000
1990	Timeless Answer, 4, 114	R. G. Davis	Prospectors Gamble, 5, 116	Sam Who, 5, 120	8	1:08.80	64,500
1989	Sam Who, 4, 118	L. A. Pincay Jr.	Prospectors Gamble, 4, 114	Mi Preferido, 4, 119	5	1:09.40	46,200
1988	Olympic Prospect, 4, 116	A. O. Solis	Happy in Space, 4, 113	Sylvan Express (Ire), 5, 119	7	1:08.80	47,700
1987	Bedside Promise, 5, 126	G. L. Stevens	Bolder Than Bold, 5, 117	Lincoln Park, 5, 115	5	1:08.40	46,200
1986	Rosie's K. T., 5, 116	P. A. Valenzuela	Mane Magic, 4, 116	Much Fine Gold, 5, 112	6	1:10.00	47,050
1985	Charging Falls, 4, 114	W. Shoemaker	Fifty Six Ina Row, 4, 117	Premiership, 5, 115	8	1:08.60	48,650
1984	Night Mover, 4, 116	E. J. Delahoussaye	Debonaire Junior, 3, 113	Croeso, 4, 117	6	1:08.40	47,150
1983	Mr. Prime Minister, 7, 115	M. A. Pedroza	Poley, 4, 118	Unreal Zeal, 3, 107	4	1:09.80	45,550
1982	Terresto's Singer, 5, 118	P. A. Valenzuela	Remember Joon, 4, 115	Petro D. Jay, 6, 116	7	1:09.20	47,800
1981	Doonesbury, 4, 121	S. Hawley	Reb's Golden Ale, 6, 115	Summer Time Guy, 5, 122	7	1:08.70	37,900
1980	Beau's Eagle, 4, 123	L. A. Pincay Jr.	Real Soul, 4, 116	Minstrel Grey, 6, 114	8	1:08.20	32,400
1979	Hawkin's Special, 4, 117	D. G. McHargue	White Rammer, 5, 117	Whatsyourpleasure, 6, 117	6	1:08.40	31,350
1978	J. O. Tobin, 4, 130	S. Cauthen	Maheras, 5, 125	Drapier (Arg), 6, 121	4	1:21.40	30,200
1977	Beat Inflation, 4, 120	D. G. McHargue	Full Out, 4, 117	Mark's Place, 5, 126	5	1:20.20	30,500
1976	Century's Envoy, 5, 123	S. Hawley	Home Jerome, 6, 116	Sporting Goods, 6, 120	7	1:20.80	31,950
1975	Big Band, 5, 117	L. A. Pincay Jr.	Century's Envoy, 4, 121	Shirley's Champion, 4, 120	8	1:20.60	32,300
1974	Ancient Title, 4, 126	L. A. Pincay Jr.	Woodland Pines, 5, 118	Soft Victory, 6, 118	8	1:20.40	32,200
1973	Soft Victory, 4, 118	D. Pierce	Crusading, 5, 124	‡Convenience, 5, 117	7	1:21.00	31,850

Named for the Los Angeles *Times*, daily newspaper of Los Angeles. Formerly named for the city of Los Angeles. Grade 2 1973-'79. 1938-2002 Los Angeles H. Not held 1940-'54. 1¹⁄₁₆ miles 1938-'39. 7 furlongs 1957-'78. Dead heat for first 1996. ‡Surachai finished second, DQ to sixth, 1997. Track record 1995. †Denotes female.

Louisiana Derby

Grade 2 in 2005. Fair Grounds, three-year-olds, 1¹⁄₁₆ miles, dirt. Held March 12, 2005, with a gross value of $600,000. First held in 1894. First graded in 1973. Stakes record 1:42.60 (1997 Crypto Star).

Year	Winner	Jockey	Second	Third	Strs	Time	1st Purse
2005	High Limit, 3, 122	R. A. Dominguez	Vicarage, 3, 122	Storm Surge, 3, 122	9	1:42.74	$360,000
2004	Wimbledon, 3, 122	J. Santiago	Borrego, 3, 122	Pollard's Vision, 3, 122	11	1:42.71	360,000
2003	Peace Rules, 3, 122	E. S. Prado	‡Funny Cide, 3, 122	Lone Star Sky, 3, 122	10	1:42.67	450,000
2002	Repent, 3, 122	J. D. Bailey	Easyfromthegitgo, 3, 122	It'sallinthechase, 3, 122	7	1:43.86	450,000

2001 **Fifty Stars**, 3, 122	D. J. Meche	Millennium Wind, 3, 122	Hero's Tribute, 3, 122	9	1:44.78	$450,000
2000 **Mighty**, 3, 122	S. J. Sellers	More Than Ready, 3, 122	Captain Steve, 3, 122	10	1:43.29	450,000
1999 **Kimberlite Pipe**, 3, 122	R. Albarado	Answer Lively, 3, 122	Ecton Park, 3, 122	8	1:43.56	384,000
1998 **Comic Strip**, 3, 122	S. J. Sellers	Nite Dreamer, 3, 122	Captain Maestri, 3, 122	10	1:43.36	300,000
1997 **Crypto Star**, 3, 118	P. Day	Stop Watch, 3, 118	Smoke Glacken, 3, 122	9	**1:42.60**	240,000
1996 **Grindstone**, 3, 118	J. D. Bailey	Zarb's Magic, 3, 122	Commanders Palace, 3, 118	8	1:42.79	222,000
1995 **Petionville**, 3, 122	C. W. Antley	In Character (GB), 3, 118	Moonlight Dancer, 3, 122	11	1:42.96	210,000
1994 **Kandaly**, 3, 118	C. Perret	Game Coin, 3, 118	Argolid, 3, 118	10	1:42.86	195,750
1993 **Dixieland Heat**, 3, 117	R. P. Romero	Offshore Pirate, 3, 117	Tossofthecoin, 3, 115	13	1:44.80	180,000
1992 ‡**Line In The Sand**, 3, 117	P. Day	Hill Pass, 3, 117	Colony Light, 3, 112	9	1:43.40	120,000
1991 **Richman**, 3, 122	P. Day	Near the Limit, 3, 114	Far Out Wadleigh, 3, 122	11	1:44.50	120,000
1990 **Heaven Again**, 3, 113	C. S. Nakatani	Big E. Z., 3, 113	Very Formal, 3, 113	9	1:43.80	100,440
1989 **Dispersal**, 3, 118	J. A. Santos	Majesty's Imp, 3, 118	Dansil, 3, 123	9	1:43.60	100,560
1988 **Risen Star**, 3, 120	S. P. Romero	Word Pirate, 3, 118	Pastourelles, 3, 118	7	1:43.20	98,520
1987 **J. T.'s Pet**, 3, 115	P. Day	Authentic Hero, 3, 118	Plumcake, 3, 115	8	1:51.00	70,260
1986 **Country Light**, 3, 123	P. Day	Bolshoi Boy, 3, 118	Lightning Touch, 3, 118	13	1:50.40	112,000
1985 **Violado**, 3, 115	J. Vasquez	Creme Fraiche, 3, 120	Irish Fighter, 3, 113	11	1:50.20	112,000
1984 **Taylor's Special**, 3, 118	S. Maple	Silent King, 3, 120	Fight Over, 3, 123	7	1:49.60	112,000
1983 **Balboa Native**, 3, 118	J. Velasquez	Found Pearl Harbor, 3, 113	Slewpy, 3, 123	8	1:50.60	112,000
1982 **El Baba**, 3, 123	D. Brumfield	Linkage, 3, 120	Spoonful of Honey, 3, 113	8	1:50.60	112,000
1981 **Woodchopper**, 3, 113	J. Velasquez	A Run, 3, 123	Beau Rit, 3, 126	13	1:50.80	125,800
1980 **Prince Valiant**, 3, 115	M. A. Gonzalez	Native Uproar, 3, 118	Brent's Trans Am, 3, 123	10	1:50.40	97,150
1979 **Golden Act**, 3, 123	S. Hawley	Rivalero, 3, 115	Incredible Ease, 3, 120	9	1:51.20	100,750
1978 **Esops Foibles**, 3, 118	C. J. McCarron	Quadratic, 3, 123	Batonnier, 3, 120	10	1:50.80	79,750
1977 **Clev Er Tell**, 3, 120	R. Broussard	Run Dusty Run, 3, 123	A Letter to Harry, 3, 115	9	1:48.80	61,000
1976 **Johnny Appleseed**, 3, 118	M. Castaneda	Glassy Dip, 3, 113	Gay Jitterbug, 3, 118	15	1:49.80	61,000
1975 **Master Derby**, 3, 123	D. G. McHargue	Colonel Power, 3, 120	Honey Mark, 3, 118	11	1:49.60	61,000
1974 **Sellout**, 3, 118	M. A. Castaneda	Buck's Bid, 3, 115	Beau Groton, 3, 120	12	1:51.20	55,800
1973 **Leo's Pisces**, 3, 115	R. Breen	Navajo, 3, 120	Angle Light, 3, 118	11	1:51.60	50,000

Name honors Fair Grounds's home state. Grade 3 1985-'98. Held at Crescent City 1894-1908. Held at Jefferson Park 1920-'31. Not held 1895-'97, 1909-'19, 1921-'22, 1940-'42, 1945. 1 mile 1894. 1¹/₈ miles 1898-1987. ‡Colony Light finished first, DQ to third, 1992. ‡Kafwain finished second, DQ to tenth for a positive drug test, 2003.

Louisville Breeders' Cup Handicap

Grade 2 in 2005. Churchill Downs, three-year-olds and up, fillies and mares, 1¹/₁₆ miles, dirt. Held May 6, 2005, with a gross value of $339,300. First held in 1986. First graded in 1988. Stakes record 1:42.43 (2005 Shadow Cast).

Year	Winner	Jockey	Second	Third	Strs	Time	1st Purse
2005	**Shadow Cast**, 4, 116	R. Albarado	Island Sand, 4, 115	Storm's Darling, 4, 115	9	**1:42.43**	$210,366
2004	**Lead Story**, 5, 116	C. H. Borel	Yell, 4, 114	Cat Fighter, 4, 116	6	1:44.37	202,740
2003	**You**, 4, 118	J. D. Bailey	Fly Borboleta, 4, 111	Seven Four Seven, 5, 113	5	1:43.21	201,810
2002	**Spain**, 5, 118	J. D. Bailey	Mystic Lady, 4, 118	De Bertie, 5, 115	6	1:43.93	207,204
2001	**Saudi Poetry**, 4, 112	V. Espinoza	Royal Fair, 5, 113	Dreams Gallore, 5, 114	8	1:42.53	172,980
2000	**Heritage of Gold**, 5, 119	S. J. Sellers	Roza Robata, 5, 112	Bella Chiarra, 5, 116	6	1:42.99	170,655
1999	**Silent Eskimo**, 4, 113	C. H. Borel	Lu Ravi, 4, 118	Leo's Gypsy Dancer, 5, 112	6	1:43.82	169,415
1998	**Escena**, 5, 119	J. D. Bailey	One Rich Lady, 4, 113	Three Fanfares, 5, 109	10	1:44.84	178,405
1997	**Halo America**, 7, 120	C. H. Borel	Escena, 4, 116	Rare Blend, 4, 116	7	1:42.78	138,012
1996	**Jewel Princess**, 4, 118	C. J. McCarron	Serena's Song, 4, 123	Naskra Colors, 4, 113	6	1:42.50	143,000
1995	**Fit to Lead**, 5, 113	K. J. Desormeaux	Jade Flush, 4, 115	Teewinot, 4, 109	9	1:43.46	138,125
1994	**One Dreamer**, 6, 113	G. L. Stevens	Kalita Melody (GB), 6, 117	Added Asset, 4, 114	7	1:43.73	136,630
1993	**Quilma (Chi)**, 6, 113	J. A. Santos	Looie Capote, 4, 118	Hitch, 4, 113	12	1:44.61	37,570
1992	**Fowda**, 4, 117	P. A. Valenzuela	Dance Colony, 5, 114	Fit for a Queen, 6, 120	7	1:44.16	100,750
1991	**Fit for a Queen**, 5, 113	J. D. Bailey	Crowned, 4, 115	Topsa, 4, 109	8	1:43.13	101,530
1990	**Connie's Gift**, 4, 111	P. Day	Affirmed Classic, 4, 115	Barbarika, 5, 115	6	1:45.80	100,425
1989	**Darien Miss**, 4, 115	P. A. Johnson	Savannah's Honor, 4, 119	Miss Barbour, 4, 109	4	1:46.00	100,750
1988	**By Land by Sea**, 4, 124	F. Toro	Bound, 4, 115	Bestofbothworlds, 4, 113	5	1:43.20	100,198
1987	**Queen Alexandra**, 5, 117	D. Brumfield	Infinidad (Chi), 5, 116	I'm Sweets, 4, 116	6	1:42.80	100,295
1986	**Hopeful Word**, 5, 119	P. Day	Little Missouri, 4, 116	Czar Nijinsky, 4, 121	4	1:49.40	99,808

Named for the city of Louisville, home of Churchill Downs. Grade 3 1988-'89. Louisville Budweiser Breeders' Cup H. 1987-'95. 1¹/₈ miles 1986. Both sexes 1986.

Louisville Handicap

Grade 3 in 2005. Churchill Downs, three-year-olds and up, 1³/₈ miles, turf. Held May 30, 2005, with a gross value of $110,400. First held in 1895. First graded in 2002. Stakes record 2:14.09 (2003 Kim Loves Bucky).

Year	Winner	Jockey	Second	Third	Strs	Time	1st Purse
2005	**Silverfoot**, 5, 117	R. Albarado	Rochester, 9, 115	Epicentre, 6, 116	7	2:18.77	$68,448
2004	**Silverfoot**, 4, 114	R. Albarado	Rochester, 8, 116	Ballingarry (Ire), 5, 120	9	2:17.63	69,688
2003	**Kim Loves Bucky**, 6, 117	S. J. Sellers	Rochester, 7, 117	Dr. Kashnikow, 6, 117	8	**2:14.09**	69,440
2002	‡**dh- Classic Par**, 4, 114	D. J. Meche		Red Mountain, 5, 114	9	2:15.82	47,355
	‡**dh- Pisces**, 5, 116	R. Albarado					
2001	**With Anticipation**, 6, 112	J. K. Court	Profit Option, 6, 112	Gritty Sandie, 5, 115	6	2:16.28	68,138

Year	Winner	Jockey	Second	Third	Strs	Time	1st Purse
2000	Buff, 5, 113	F. C. Torres	Williams News, 5, 116	Royal Strand (Ire), 6, 115	11	2:14.31	$71,734
1999	Chorwon, 6, 114	C. H. Borel	Buff, 4, 114	Keats and Yeats, 5, 110	8	2:14.15	69,812
1998	Chorwon, 5, 114	P. Day	African Dancer, 6, 117	Thesaurus, 4, 115	5	2:17.10	67,890
1997	Chorwon, 4, 113	C. H. Borel	Down the Aisle, 4, 111	Snake Eyes, 7, 116	5	2:19.45	67,952
1996	Nash Terrace (Ire), 4, 105	D. M. Barton	Vladivostok, 6, 117	Hawkeye Bay, 5, 110	6	2:18.82	71,760
1995	Lindon Lime, 5, 114	C. Perret	Caesour, 5, 116	Snake Eyes, 5, 116	8	1:48.12	72,800
1994	L'Hermine (GB), 5, 110	L. J. Melancon	Llandaff, 4, 116	Snake Eyes, 4, 118	5	1:48.36	70,525
1993	Stark South, 5, 116	R. P. Romero	Cleone, 4, 115	Coaxing Matt, 4, 116	5	1:48.88	71,955
1992	Lotus Pool, 5, 115	C. R. Woods Jr.	Buchman, 5, 114	Magesterial Cheer, 4, 111	8	1:47.69	74,230
1991	Chenin Blanc, 5, 118	J. A. Krone	Tees Prospect, 4, 109	Cameroon, 4, 113	4	1:52.21	55,120
	Allijeba, 5, 115	D. Kutz	Tutu Tobago, 4, 115	Alaqua, 5, 114	9	1:51.59	55,770
1990	Silver Medallion, 4, 114	P. A. Johnson	Spark O'Dan, 5, 113	Mr. Adorable, 4, 111	8	1:50.40	73,125
1989	El Clipper, 5, 113	L. J. Melancon	Set a Record, 5, 113	Pollenate (GB), 5, 113	10	1:50.00	55,478
1988	First Patriot, 4, 116	E. Fires	Rio's Lark, 4, 118	Uncle Cam, 4, 114	9	1:51.80	54,698
1987	Icy Groom, 4, 117	M. McDowell	Niccolo Polo, 4, 108	Blandford Park, 4, 114	9	1:37.80	36,595
1986	Ten Times Ten, 4, 114	K. K. Allen	Little Missouri, 4, 114	Fuzzy, 4, 120	11	1:43.60	25,402
1985	Big Pistol, 4, 114	P. Day	Hopeful Word, 4, 111	Big Mav, 7, 111	5	1:48.60	35,100
1984	Le Cou Cou, 4, 114	D. L. Howard	Big Mav, 6, 111	Jack Slade, 4, 111	5	1:50.80	34,872
1983	Big Mav, 5, 111	P. A. Johnson	Eminency, 5, 123	Diverse Dude, 5, 114	6	1:53.80	35,393
1982	Bobrobbery, 4, 114	R. P. Romero	Swinging Light, 4, 114	Boys Nite Out, 4, 111	7	1:51.40	38,968
1981	Dreadnought, 4, 115	T. Meyers	Oil City, 4, 115	Withholding, 4, 116	5	1:44.60	22,393
1980	Dr. Riddick, 6, 117	D. Brumfield	Incredible Ease, 4, 117	King Celebrity, 4, 113	7	1:44.00	20,703
1979	Hot Words, 4, 114	J. McKnight	Prince Majestic, 5, 124	Dr. Riddick, 5, 119	8	1:45.00	22,750
1978	It's Freezing, 6, 119	L. J. Melancon	To the Quick, 4, 119	Prince Majestic, 4, 120	6	1:45.40	14,105
1977	Amano, 4, 112	L. J. Melancon	‡Inca Roca, 4, 120	Buddy Larosa, 4, 114	8	1:43.80	14,381
1976	Ski Run, 4, 115	G. Patterson	Dragset, 5, 117	Yamanin, 4, 117	7	1:44.00	14,203
1975	Navajo, 5, 125	J. Nichols	Silver Badge, 4, 110	Vodika, 5, 115	8	1:43.20	14,463
1974	List, 6, 115	R. Breen	Royal Knight, 4, 122	Model Husband, 5, 116	12	1:44.40	15,129
1973	Knight Counter, 5, 122	D. Brumfield	‡List, 5, 121	Sipin Whiskey, 4, 110	9	1:43.00	14,771

Named for the city of Louisville, home of Churchill Downs. Formerly held as a "special" race; special races are traditionally "winner takes all." Churchill Downs Special 1946. Louisville S. 1982-'86. Not held 1897, 1900-'06, 1914-'37, 1939-'45, 1953-'56. 1¹/₁₆ miles 1895-'99, 1938, 1957-'81, 1986. 6 furlongs 1907-'13. 1¹/₈ miles 1946-'52, 1982-'85, 1988-'95. 1 mile 1987. Dirt 1895-1986. Four-year-olds and up 1986-'87. Two divisions 1991. Dead heat for first 2002. ‡Sipin Whiskey finished second, DQ to third, 1973. ‡Buddy Larosa finished second, DQ to third, 1977. ‡Two Point Two Mill finished first, DQ to eighth, 2002.

Mac Diarmida Handicap

Grade 3 in 2005. Gulfstream Park, three-year-olds and up, 1³/₈ miles, turf. Held January 30, 2005, with a gross value of $100,000. First held in 1995. First graded in 1997. Stakes record 2:12.14 (2000 Unite's Big Red).

Year	Winner	Jockey	Second	Third	Strs	Time	1st Purse
2005	Host, 5, 114	J. Castellano	Navesink River, 4, 112	Burning Sun, 6, 118	12	2:12.83	$60,000
2004	Request for Parole, 5, 115	J. A. Santos	Slew Valley, 7, 117	Sir Brian's Sword, 6, 113	12	2:12.58	60,000
2003	Riddlesdown (Ire), 6, 113	R. I. Velez	Macaw (Ire), 4, 114	Just Listen, 7, 113	12	2:14.75	60,000
2002	Crash Course, 6, 114	J. D. Bailey	Unite's Big Red, 8, 112	Eltawaasul, 6, 113	12	2:16.27	60,000
2000	Unite's Big Red, 6, 113	J. F. Chavez	Thesaurus, 4, 115	Carpenter's Halo, 4, 113	8	2:12.14	60,000
1999	Panama City, 5, 114	J. D. Bailey	The Kaiser, 4, 113	Notoriety, 6, 111	5	2:20.65	60,000
1998	Copy Editor, 6, 114	J. D. Bailey	Inkatha (Fr), 4, 114	Lafitte the Pirate (GB), 5, 112	12	2:16.72	60,000
1997	Mecke, 5, 123	J. D. Bailey	Fabulous Frolic, 6, 112	Spicilege, 5, 113	4	2:05.80	45,000
1996	A Real Zipper, 3, 114	A. T. Gryder	Tour's Big Red, 3, 114	Shananie's Finale, 3, 114	12	1:42.66	30,000
1995	Kings Course, 3, 112	R. G. Davis	Ops Smile, 3, 113	Mecke, 3, 119	10	1:43.12	30,000

Named for Dr. Jerome M. Torsney's 1978 champion turf horse and '78 Golden Grass H. winner Mac Diarmida (1975 c. by Minnesota Mac). Mac Diarmida S. 1995-'96. Not held 2001. 1 mile 70 yards 1995. 1¹/₁₆ miles 1996. 1¹/₄ miles 1997. About 1³/₈ miles 1999. Dirt 1995, 1997. Three-year-olds 1995-'96.

Maker's Mark Mile Stakes

Grade 2 in 2005. Keeneland, four-year-olds and up, 1 mile, turf. Held April 15, 2005, with a gross value of $250,000. First held in 1989. First graded in 1991. Stakes record 1:33.54 (2004 Perfect Soul [Ire]).

Year	Winner	Jockey	Second	Third	Strs	Time	1st Purse
2005	Artie Schiller, 4, 121	E. S. Prado	Gulch Approval, 5, 117	Good Reward, 4, 123	10	1:34.09	$155,000
2004	Perfect Soul (Ire), 6, 116	E. S. Prado	Burning Roma, 6, 116	Royal Spy, 6, 116	10	1:33.54	124,000
2003	Royal Spy, 5, 118	R. Albarado	Miesque's Approval, 4, 118	Touch of the Blues (Fr), 6, 117	9	1:35.82	124,000
2002	Touch of the Blues (Fr), 5, 116	K. J. Desormeaux	Pisces, 5, 123	Boastful, 4, 116	10	1:35.02	124,000
2001	North East Bound, 5, 120	J. A. Velez Jr.	Brahms, 4, 123	Strategic Mission, 6, 116	8	1:34.44	140,492
2000	Conserve, 4, 116	S. J. Sellers	Marquette, 4, 120	Inkatha (Fr), 6, 116	9	1:35.08	105,927
1999	Soviet Line (Ire), 9, 115	J. R. Velazquez	Trail City, 6, 115	Rob 'n Gin, 5, 120	8	1:35.37	68,696
1998	Lasting Approval, 4, 122	R. Albarado	Soviet Line (Ire), 8, 113	Same Old Wish, 8, 122	10	1:35.57	70,060
1997	Influent, 6, 116	J. Samyn	Chief Bearhart, 4, 114	Foolish Pole, 4, 113	9	1:34.59	69,936
1996	Tejano Run, 4, 113	J. D. Bailey	Sandpit (Brz), 7, 116	Dove Hunt, 5, 116	10	1:35.03	70,618
1995	Dove Hunt, 4, 113	J. A. Santos	Road of War, 5, 114	Night Silence, 5, 116	10	1:35.95	53,196
1994	First and Only, 7, 116	T. J. Hebert	The Name's Jimmy, 5, 113	Pride of Summer, 6, 116	7	1:36.63	50,685

1993	**Ganges**, 5, 113	J. D. Bailey	Bidding Proud, 4, 119	Rocket Fuel, 6, 114	10	1:35.40	$52,731
1992	**Shudanz**, 4, 114	C. Perret	To Freedom, 4, 113	Cudas, 4, 116	9	1:36.52	55,283
1991	**Opening Verse**, 5, 113	J. D. Bailey	Jalaajel, 7, 113	Buchman, 4, 113	8	1:36.17	53,138
1990	**Charlie Barley**, 4, 119	R. Platts	Known Ranger (GB), 4, 113	Careafolie (Ire), 5, 113	10	1:35.80	36,790
1989	**Yankee Affair**, 7, 119	R. P. Romero	Jalaajel, 5, 114	Pollenate (GB), 5, 114	10	1:43.60	36,693

Sponsored by Maker's Mark Distillery of Loretto, Kentucky 1997-2005. Formerly named for Fort Harrod, located in present-day Harrodsburg, Kentucky, first permanent settlement west of the Allegheny Mountains. Grade 3 1991-'99. Fort Harrod S. 1989-'96. About 1 1/16 miles 1989. Course record 2004.

Malibu Stakes

Grade 1 in 2005. Santa Anita Park, three-year-olds, 7 furlongs, dirt. Held December 26, 2004, with a gross value of $250,000. First held in 1952. First graded in 1973. Stakes record 1:20 (1980 Spectacular Bid).

Year	Winner	Jockey	Second	Third	Strs	Time	1st Purse
2004	**Rock Hard Ten**, 3, 121	G. L. Stevens	Lava Man, 3, 115	Harvard Avenue, 3, 115	10	1:21.89	$150,000
2003	**Southern Image**, 3, 115	V. Espinoza	Marino Marini, 3, 115	Midas Eyes, 3, 119	12	1:22.65	150,000
2002	**Debonair Joe**, 3, 119	J. A. Krone	Total Limit, 3, 117	American System, 3, 117	11	1:22.40	120,000
2001	**Mizzen Mast**, 3, 117	K. J. Desormeaux	Giant Gentleman, 3, 115	I Love Silver, 3, 117	13	1:22.13	120,000
2000	**Dixie Union**, 3, 121	A. O. Solis	Caller One, 3, 119	Wooden Phone, 3, 116	6	1:21.62	120,000
1999	**Love That Red**, 3, 119	G. K. Gomez	Straight Man, 3, 118	Cat Thief, 3, 123	7	1:22.06	120,000
1998	**Run Man Run**, 3, 115	M. J. Luzzi	Artax, 3, 119	Event of the Year, 3, 121	10	1:21.51	120,000
1997	**Lord Grillo (Arg)**, 3, 119	E. J. Delahoussaye	Silver Charm, 3, 121	Swiss Yodeler, 3, 115	9	1:21.46	120,000
1996	**King of the Heap**, 3, 116	K. J. Desormeaux	Hesabull, 3, 118	Northern Afleet, 3, 116	9	1:21.84	134,300
1995	**Afternoon Deelites**, 3, 120	K. J. Desormeaux	Score Quick, 3, 120	High Stakes Player, 3, 116	9	1:21.73	100,000
1994	**Powis Castle**, 3, 117	P. A. Valenzuela	Ferrara, 3, 116	Numerous, 3, 118	8	1:20.96	64,300
1993	**Diazo**, 3, 120	L. A. Pincay Jr.	Concept Win, 3, 116	Mister Jolie, 3, 116	8	1:21.17	64,700
1992	**Star of the Crop**, 3, 118	G. L. Stevens	The Wicked North, 3, 116	Bertrando, 3, 120	11	1:20.67	67,850
1991	**Olympio**, 3, 122	E. J. Delahoussaye	Charmonnier, 3, 120	Apollo, 3, 118	10	1:21.28	66,850
1990	**Pleasant Tap**, 3, 117	A. O. Solis	Bedeviled, 3, 120	Due to the King, 3, 117	10	1:21.60	67,600
1989	**Music Merci**, 3, 123	L. A. Pincay Jr.	Exemplary Leader, 3, 117	Doncareer, 3, 114	11	1:21.60	67,300
1988	**Oraibi**, 3, 117	L. A. Pincay Jr.	Perceive Arrogance, 3, 120	Speedratic, 3, 120	13	1:21.60	70,550
1987	**On the Line**, 3, 117	A. T. Cordero Jr.	Temperate Sil, 3, 126	Candi's Gold, 3, 123	9	1:21.00	66,550
1986	**Ferdinand**, 3, 123	W. Shoemaker	Snow Chief, 3, 126	Don B. Blue, 3, 114	12	1:21.60	72,300
1985	**Banner Bob**, 3, 123	G. Baze	Encolure, 3, 120	Carload, 3, 114	9	1:21.00	71,600
1984	**Precisionist**, 3, 126	C. J. McCarron	Bunker, 3, 117	Milord, 3, 115	7	1:21.40	66,700
	Glacial Stream, 4, 120	C. J. McCarron	Total Departure, 4, 120	Hula Blaze, 4, 117	8	1:22.20	43,150
	Pac Mania, 4, 115	P. A. Valenzuela	Retsina Run, 4, 114	Desert Wine, 4, 123	8	1:22.60	43,150
1983	**Time to Explode**, 4, 117	L. A. Pincay Jr.	Prince Spellbound, 4, 123	Wavering Monarch, 4, 123	8	1:21.00	52,550
1982	**Island Whirl**, 4, 123	L. A. Pincay Jr.	Shanekite, 4, 120	It's the One, 4, 120	8	1:26.00	64,000
1981	**Doonesbury**, 4, 117	S. Hawley	Roper, 4, 114	Unalakleet, 4, 114	9	1:20.40	44,100
	Raise a Man, 4, 120	L. A. Pincay Jr.	Just Right Mike, 4, 114	Aristocratical, 4, 117	9	1:20.40	44,400
1980	**Spectacular Bid**, 4, 126	W. Shoemaker	Flying Paster, 4, 123	Rosie's Seville, 4, 117	5	**1:20.00**	47,800
1979	**Little Reb**, 4, 120	F. Olivares	Radar Ahead, 4, 123	Affirmed, 4, 126	5	1:21.00	38,200
1978	**J. O. Tobin**, 4, 123	S. Cauthen	Bad 'n Big, 4, 120	Eagle Ki, 4, 114	9	1:23.00	35,050
1977	**Cojak**, 4, 117	W. Shoemaker	Double Discount, 4, 117	Little Riva, 4, 114	6	1:23.00	26,050
	Romantic Lead, 4, 114	W. Shoemaker	Maheras, 4, 120	Life's Hope, 4, 124	6	1:22.40	24,800
1976	**Forceten**, 4, 123	D. Pierce	Messenger of Song, 4, 120	†My Juliet, 4, 115	8	1:21.20	35,450
1975	**Lightning Mandate**, 4, 120	A. Pineda	Rocket Review, 4, 117	Century's Envoy, 4, 120	8	1:20.60	28,525
	Princely Native, 4, 117	B. Baeza	First Back, 4, 115	Holding Pattern, 4, 123	7	1:20.80	27,775
1974	**Ancient Title**, 4, 120	F. Toro	Linda's Chief, 4, 126	Dancing Papa, 4, 120	7	1:22.80	34,800
1973	**Bicker**, 4, 117	G. Brogan	Royal Owl, 4, 120	Tri Jet, 4, 117	13	1:21.40	39,300

Named for Topanga Malibu Sequit Rancho in Los Angeles County, California. Grade 2 1973-'94. Malibu Sequet S. 1952-'57. Not held 1959, 1964, 1967, 1970. Four-year-olds 1955 (January), 1960 (January), 1965, 1966 (January), 1968-'75, 1977-'83, 1984 (January). Four-year-olds and up 1976. Two divisions 1975, 1977, 1981. Held January (two divisions) and December 1984. Equaled track record 1975. Track record 1980. †Denotes female.

Manhattan Handicap

Grade 1 in 2005. Belmont Park, three-year-olds and up, 1 1/4 miles, turf. Held June 11, 2005, with a gross value of $400,000. First held in 1896. First graded in 1973. Stakes record 1:57.79 (1994 Paradise Creek).

Year	Winner	Jockey	Second	Third	Strs	Time	1st Purse
2005	**Good Reward**, 4, 117	J. D. Bailey	Relaxed Gesture (Ire), 4, 116	Artie Schiller, 4, 122	11	2:00.69	$240,000
2004	**Meteor Storm (GB)**, 5, 117	J. Valdivia Jr.	Millennium Dragon (GB), 5, 116	Mr O'Brien (Ire), 5, 116	9	1:59.34	240,000
2003	**Denon**, 5, 122	J. D. Bailey	Requete (GB), 4, 116	Dr. Brendler, 5, 116	10	2:14.16	240,000
2002	**Beat Hollow (GB)**, 5, 118	A. O. Solis	Forbidden Apple, 7, 118	Strut the Stage, 4, 117	8	2:01.29	240,000
2001	**Forbidden Apple**, 6, 117	C. S. Nakatani	King Cugat, 4, 120	Tijiyr (Ire), 5, 115	10	2:00.77	240,000
2000	**Manndar (Ire)**, 4, 117	C. S. Nakatani	Boatman, 4, 113	Spindrift (Ire), 5, 116	8	1:59.61	240,000
1999	**Yagli**, 6, 122	J. D. Bailey	Federal Trial, 4, 116	Middlesex Drive, 4, 116	10	1:58.48	180,000
1998	**Chief Bearhart**, 5, 122	J. A. Santos	Devonwood, 4, 113	Buck's Boy, 5, 117	9	1:58.25	150,000
1997	**Ops Smile**, 5, 116	R. G. Davis	Flag Down, 7, 118	Always a Classic, 4, 121	8	1:59.08	120,000
1996	**Diplomatic Jet**, 4, 117	J. F. Chavez	Flag Down, 6, 119	Kiri's Clown, 7, 121	12	2:00.14	120,000
1995	**Awad**, 5, 121	E. Maple	Blues Traveller (Ire), 5, 119	Kiri's Clown, 6, 115	12	1:58.57	120,000
1994	**Paradise Creek**, 5, 124	P. Day	Solar Splendor, 7, 112	River Majesty, 5, 113	7	**1:57.79**	275,000
1993	**Star of Cozzene**, 5, 118	J. A. Santos	Lure, 4, 124	Solar Splendor, 6, 112	8	1:58.99	190,000

1992	Sky Classic, 5, 123	P. Day	Roman Envoy, 4, 111	Leger Cat (Arg), 6, 116	11	2:02.42	$252,860
1991	Academy Award, 5, 117	A. Madrid Jr.	Three Coins Up, 3, 110	Tarsho (Ire), 5, 113	10	1:59.78	111,600
1990	Phantom Breeze (Ire), 4, 113	M. E. Smith	Green Barb, 5, 111	Milesius, 6, 116	6	2:02.60	52,110
1989	Milesius, 5, 115	R. Migliore	Salem Drive, 7, 115	My Big Boy, 6, 114	8	2:00.00	73,440
1988	Milesius, 4, 112	C. W. Antley	My Big Boy, 5, 114	Maceo, 4, 111	5	2:04.40	71,760
1987	Silver Voice, 4, 109	J. M. Pezua	Talakeno, 7, 118	Duluth, 5, 113	9	2:01.40	86,220
1986	Danger's Hour, 4, 117	J. D. Bailey	Premier Mister (Mor), 6, 111	Exclusive Partner, 4, 115	8	2:02.60	87,300
1985	Cool, 4, 112	J. Vasquez	Win, 5, 126	Sondrio (Ire), 4, 110	13	2:02.00	77,280
1984	Win, 4, 114	A. Graell	Fortnightly, 4, 112	Norwick, 5, 110	12	2:00.60	77,520
1983	Acaroid, 5, 114	A. T. Cordero Jr.	Craelius, 4, 109	Half Iced, 4, 119	12	2:00.00	72,240
1982	Sprink, 4, 113	J. J. Miranda	Naskra's Breeze, 5, 119	Native Courier, 7, 116	8	2:01.00	51,570
1981	Match the Hatch, 5, 114	J. Samyn	†Mrs. Penny, 4, 117	Native Courier, 6, 115	8	2:03.00	52,470
1980	Morold (Fr), 5, 113	E. Maple	Match the Hatch, 4, 111	Foretake, 4, 113	13	2:00.20	53,910
1979	Fluorescent Light, 5, 121	J. Fell	Tiller, 5, 124	Native Courier, 4, 122	8	2:04.80	51,615
1978	Fabulous Time, 4, 112	A. T. Cordero Jr.	Bill Brill, 4, 109	Tiller, 4, 127	8	2:01.40	48,690
1977	Gentle King, 4, 111	S. Cauthen	Double Quill, 8, 105	Keep the Promise, 5, 112	6	2:28.40	32,220
	Gallivantor, 5, 112	S. Cauthen	Gallapiat, 4, 112	Togus, 4, 112	5	2:28.00	32,070
1976	Caucasus, 4, 120	F. Toro	Trumpeter Swan, 5, 113	*Kamaraan II, 5, 116	13	2:14.40	33,930
1975	Salt Marsh, 5, 115	E. Maple	Drollery, 5, 109	London Company, 5, 118	7	2:16.60	33,600
	*Snow Knight, 4, 123	J. Velasquez	Shady Character, 4, 113	One On the Aisle, 3, 114	3	2:16.20	33,900
1974	Golden Don, 4, 119	J. Cruguet	Anono, 4, 112	R. Tom Can, 3, 114	10	2:19.80	35,970
1973	London Company, 3, 116	L. A. Pincay Jr.	Big Spruce, 4, 120	Triangular, 6, 110	13	2:15.60	36,120

Named for the borough of Manhattan, principal borough of New York City. Sponsored by Early Times Distillery Co. of Louisville 1991-'96. Grade 2 1973-'83, 1990-'93. Early Times Manhattan H. 1991-'92. Early Times Manhattan S. 1991-'96. Held at Morris Park 1896-1904. Held at Aqueduct 1959, 1961, 1963-'67. Not held 1897, 1909-'13. 6 furlongs 1898-1908. 7 furlongs 1914-'15. 1 mile 1916-'32. 1½ miles 1933-'58, 1960, 1962-'64, 1968-'69, 1977. 1⅛ miles 1959, 1965-'67. 1⁵⁄₁₆ miles 1961. 1⅜ miles 1970-'76. Dirt 1896-1969, 1977, 1988. Two divisions 1975, 1977. Course record 1994. †Denotes female.

Man o' War Stakes

Grade 1 in 2005. Belmont Park, three-year-olds and up, 1⅜ miles, turf. Held September 11, 2004, with a gross value of $500,000. First held in 1959. First graded in 1973. Stakes record 2:11.69 (1997 Influent).

Year	Winner	Jockey	Second	Third	Strs	Time	1st Purse
2004	Magistretti, 4, 126	E. S. Prado	Epalo (Ger), 5, 126	King's Drama (Ire), 4, 126	8	2:14.65	$300,000
2003	Lunar Sovereign, 4, 126	R. Migliore	Slew Valley, 6, 126	Denon, 5, 126	8	2:17.99	300,000
2002	With Anticipation, 7, 126	P. Day	Balto Star, 4, 126	Man From Wicklow, 5, 126	8	2:15.05	300,000
2001	With Anticipation, 6, 126	P. Day	Silvano (Ger), 5, 126	†Ela Athena (GB), 5, 123	8	2:15.11	300,000
2000	Fantastic Light, 4, 126	J. D. Bailey	†Ela Athena (GB), 4, 123	Drama Critic, 4, 126	8	2:17.44	300,000
1999	Val's Prince, 7, 126	J. F. Chavez	Single Empire (Ire), 5, 126	Federal Trial, 4, 126	7	2:16.69	300,000
1998	Daylami (Ire), 4, 126	J. D. Bailey	Buck's Boy, 5, 126	Indy Vidual, 4, 126	9	2:13.18	240,000
1997	Influent, 6, 126	J. D. Bailey	Val's Prince, 5, 126	Awad, 7, 126	10	2:11.69	240,000
1996	Diplomatic Jet, 4, 126	J. F. Chavez	Mecke, 4, 126	Marlin, 3, 120	8	2:14.37	240,000
1995	Millkom (GB), 4, 126	G. L. Stevens	Kaldounevees (Fr), 4, 126	Signal Tap, 4, 126	12	2:12.80	240,000
1994	Royal Mountain Inn, 5, 126	J. A. Krone	Flag Down, 4, 126	Fraise, 6, 126	9	2:11.75	240,000
1993	Star of Cozzene, 5, 126	J. A. Santos	Serrant, 5, 126	Dr. Kiernan, 4, 126	8	2:23.14	240,000
1992	Solar Splendor, 5, 126	W. H. McCauley	Dear Doctor (Fr), 5, 126	Spinning (Ire), 5, 126	8	2:12.45	240,000
1991	Solar Splendor, 4, 126	W. H. McCauley	Dear Doctor (Fr), 4, 126	Beau Sultan, 3, 120	9	2:12.01	240,000
1990	Defensive Play, 3, 120	P. Eddery	Shy Tom, 4, 126	†Ode, 4, 123	7	2:17.80	284,160
1989	Yankee Affair, 7, 126	J. A. Santos	My Big Boy, 6, 126	Alwuhush, 4, 126	8	2:20.80	282,240
1988	Sunshine Forever, 3, 120	A. T. Cordero Jr.	Pay the Butler, 4, 126	My Big Boy, 5, 126	9	2:14.40	357,600
1987	Theatrical (Ire), 5, 126	P. Day	Le Glorieux (GB), 3, 121	Midnight Cousins, 4, 126	8	2:15.40	351,000
1986	Dance of Life, 3, 121	P. Day	†Duty Dance, 4, 123	Pillaster, 3, 121	7	2:14.40	201,000
1985	Win, 5, 126	R. Migliore	Bob Back, 4, 126	Baillamont, 3, 121	8	2:15.40	183,600
1984	Majesty's Prince, 5, 126	V. A. Bracciale Jr.	Win, 4, 126	Cozzene, 4, 126	9	2:14.60	214,200
1983	Majesty's Prince, 4, 126	E. Maple	Erins Isle, 4, 126	L'Emigrant, 3, 121	11	2:23.60	176,700
1982	Naskra's Breeze, 5, 126	J. Samyn	Sprink, 4, 126	Thunder Puddles, 3, 121	9	2:13.00	103,860
1981	Galaxy Libra (Ire), 5, 126	W. Shoemaker	Match the Hatch, 5, 126	‡Great Neck, 5, 126	6	2:14.80	99,180
1980	French Colonial, 5, 126	J. Vasquez	†Just a Game (Ire), 4, 123	Golden Act, 4, 126	5	2:15.40	84,300
1979	Bowl Game, 5, 126	J. Velasquez	Native Courier, 4, 126	Czaravich, 3, 121	4	2:19.00	82,425
1978	†Waya (Fr), 4, 123	A. T. Cordero Jr.	Tiller, 4, 126	Mac Diarmida, 3, 121	5	2:16.20	79,725
1977	Majestic Light, 4, 126	S. Hawley	Exceller, 4, 126	Johnny D., 3, 121	8	2:27.60	67,860
1976	Effervescing, 3, 121	A. T. Cordero Jr.	Banghi, 3, 121	‡dh- Erwin Boy, 5, 126	13	2:31.20	67,500
				‡dh- Rouge Sang, 4, 126			
1975	‡*Snow Knight, 4, 126	J. Velasquez	One On the Aisle, 3, 121	Drollery, 5, 126	8	2:29.20	68,400
1974	†Dahlia, 4, 123	R. Turcotte	Crafty Khale, 5, 126	London Company, 4, 126	13	2:26.60	71,700
1973	Secretariat, 3, 121	R. Turcotte	Tentam, 4, 126	Big Spruce, 4, 126	7	2:24.80	68,160

Named for Samuel D. Riddle's 1920 Horse of the Year, '20 Belmont S. winner, and '26 leading North American sire Man o' War (1917 c. by Fair Play). Man o' War H. 1959, 1961. Held at Aqueduct 1959, 1961, 1963-'67, 1987. 1½ miles 1959-'60, 1962, 1968-'77. 1⅛ miles 1961, 1963-'67. Dead heat for third 1976. ‡One On the Aisle finished first, DQ to second, 1975. ‡Crackle finished third, DQ to fifth, 1976. ‡Native Courier finished third, DQ to fourth, 1981. Course record 1973. †Denotes female.

Maryland Breeders' Cup Handicap

Grade 3 in 2005. Pimlico, three-year-olds and up, 6 furlongs, dirt. Held May 21, 2005, with a gross value of $189,000.
First held in 1987. First graded in 1994. Stakes record 1:09.07 (1996 Forest Wildcat).

Year	Winner	Jockey	Second	Third	Strs	Time	1st Purse
2005	Willy o'the Valley, 4, 114	E. S. Prado	With Distinction, 4, 115	Take Achance On Me, 7, 114	8	1:09.95	$120,000
2004	Gators N Bears, 4, 117	C. C. Lopez	Highway Prospector, 7, 114	Sassy Hound, 7, 115	9	1:10.84	120,000
2003	Pioneer Boy, 5, 113	J. Rose	Sassy Hound, 6, 113	dh- Highway Prospector, 6, 115	7	1:10.35	60,000
				dh- Tasty Caberneigh, 5, 114			
2002	Snow Ridge, 4, 120	M. E. Smith	Smile My Lord, 4, 113	Clever Gem, 6, 116	7	1:10.06	120,000
2001	Disco Rico, 4, 118	H. Vega	Flame Thrower, 3, 114	Istintaj, 5, 116	6	1:10.40	120,000
2000	Dr. Max, 4, 113	S. J. Sellers	Moon Over Prospect, 4, 114	Crucible, 5, 113	7	1:10.91	60,000
1999	Yes It's True, 3, 113	J. D. Bailey	The Trader's Echo, 5, 109	Purple Passion, 5, 114	8	1:09.20	120,000
1998	Richter Scale, 4, 117	J. D. Bailey	Trafalger, 4, 115	Original Gray, 4, 112	7	1:09.45	120,000
1997	Cat Be Nimble, 5, 118	J. Rocco	Political Whit, 4, 116	Excelerate, 5, 112	7	1:10.12	127,560
1996	Forest Wildcat, 5, 109	J. Bravo	Kayrawan, 4, 113	Demaloot Demashoot, 6, 115	9	1:09.07	129,720
1995	Commanche Trail, 4, 113	M. E. Smith	Goldminer's Dream, 6, 116	Marry Me Do, 6, 114	6	1:09.35	92,850
1994	Secret Odds, 4, 119	E. S. Prado	Honor the Hero, 6, 117	Linear, 4, 119	10	1:10.38	93,615
1993	Senor Speedy, 6, 117	J. D. Bailey	He Is Risen, 5, 115	Who Wouldn't, 4, 113	7	1:09.69	93,390
1992	Potentiality, 6, 117	P. Day	Smart Alec, 4, 114	Boom Towner, 4, 117	9	1:10.25	93,300
1991	Jeweler's Choice, 6, 115	C. J. McCarron	Shuttleman, 5, 116	Hadif, 5, 118	5	1:10.38	92,610
1990	Norquestor, 4, 115	C. Perret	Kechi, 4, 115	Amerrico's Bullet, 4, 112	9	1:09.40	93,540
1989	King's Nest, 4, 120	J. Rocco	Silano, 5, 115	Regal Intention, 4, 119	6	1:09.60	92,760
1988	Fire Plug, 5, 116	J. F. Hampshire Jr.	Harriman, 4, 117	High Brite, 4, 121	6	1:10.60	35,620
1987	Purple Mountain, 5, 111	E. Ortiz Jr.	Little Bold John, 5, 120	Berngoo, 5, 106	6	1:24.40	100,100

Maryland Budweiser Breeders' Cup H. 1987-'95. Held at Laurel Park 1987. 7 furlongs 1987. Dead heat for third 2003.

Massachusetts Handicap

Grade 2 in 2005. Suffolk Downs, three-year-olds and up, 1 1/8 miles, dirt. Held June 19, 2004, with a gross value of
$500,000. First held in 1935. First graded in 1973. Stakes record 1:47.27 (1998 Skip Away).

Year	Winner	Jockey	Second	Third	Strs	Time	1st Purse
2004	Offlee Wild, 4, 111	E. S. Prado	Funny Cide, 4, 117	The Lady's Groom, 4, 116	9	1:49.14	$300,000
2002	Macho Uno, 4, 117	G. L. Stevens	Evening Attire, 4, 114	Include, 5, 120	9	1:50.52	300,000
2001	Include, 4, 118	J. D. Bailey	Sir Bear, 8, 117	Broken Vow, 4, 116	7	1:48.61	300,000
2000	Running Stag, 6, 116	J. R. Velazquez	Out of Mind (Brz), 5, 116	David, 4, 113	8	1:49.45	400,000
1999	Behrens, 5, 118	J. F. Chavez	Running Stag, 5, 113	Real Quiet, 4, 121	6	1:49.14	400,000
1998	Skip Away, 5, 130	J. D. Bailey	Puerto Madero (Chi), 4, 116	K. J.'s Appeal, 4, 113	5	1:47.27	500,000
1997	Skip Away, 4, 119	S. J. Sellers	Formal Gold, 4, 114	Will's Way, 4, 114	6	1:47.92	500,000
1996	Cigar, 6, 130	J. D. Bailey	Personal Merit, 5, 111	Prolanzier, 6, 112	6	1:49.63	400,000
1995	Cigar, 5, 124	J. D. Bailey	Poor But Honest, 5, 107	Double Calvados, 5, 113	6	1:48.74	650,000
1989	Private Terms, 4, 119	K. J. Desormeaux	Granacus, 4, 113	Simply Majestic, 5, 120	8	1:49.40	180,000
1988	Lost Code, 4, 127	C. Perret	Waquoit, 5, 122	Afleet, 4, 123	5	1:50.20	154,108
1987	Waquoit, 4, 117	C. J. McCarron	Broad Brush, 4, 126	Tour d'Or, 5, 114	6	1:49.00	124,560
1986	Skip Trial, 4, 123	J. Samyn	Creme Fraiche, 4, 121	El Basco, 4, 118	11	1:49.80	128,040
1985	Bounding Basque, 5, 110	A. Graell	Dr. Carter, 4, 122	Hail Bold King, 4, 120	10	1:47.60	124,560
1984	Dixieland Band, 4, 115	D. J. Murphy	Ward Off Trouble, 4, 113	Vigumand, 3, 107	13	1:52.00	126,300
1983	Let Burn, 4, 115	J. C. Penney	Space Mountain, 4, 110	Bemedalled, 4, 112	11	1:48.80	98,220
1982	Silver Supreme, 4, 111	E. Beitia	Reef Searcher, 5, 117	Frost King, 4, 127	13	1:48.80	100,740
1981	Soldier Boy, 5, 114	R. Danjean	Niteange, 7, 108	Driving Home, 4, 114	9	1:49.40	97,200
1980	Ring of Light, 5, 121	F. Lovato Jr.	Crow's Nest, 4, 114	Niteange, 6, 110	10	1:50.40	68,400
1979	Island Sultan, 4, 110	J. Ruane	Western Front, 4, 113	Quiet Jay, 4, 115	13	1:48.60	70,140
1978	Big John Taylor, 4, 112	J. Vasquez	Giboulee, 4, 114	Buckfinder, 4, 114	9	1:48.60	67,200
1977	Blue Times, 6, 113	A. T. Cordero Jr.	Pension Plan, 7, 109	Nearly On Time, 3, 106	9	1:49.40	42,930
	Swinging Hal, 4, 110	S. R. Pagano	El Pitirre, 5, 113	‡Gentle King, 4, 108	10	1:49.20	43,410
1976	Dancing Champ, 4, 118	C. J. McCarron	Rushing Man, 4, 114	El Pitirre, 4, 117	10	1:49.20	60,000
1975	Stonewalk, 4, 117	R. Turcotte	Group Plan, 5, 118	Mongongo, 6, 115	10	1:48.60	60,000
1974	Billy Come Lately, 4, 109	D. MacBeth	Forage, 5, 114	North Sea, 5, 111	7	1:48.60	45,000
1973	Riva Ridge, 4, 125	R. Turcotte	Crafty Khale, 4, 112	Loud, 6, 113	7	1:48.20	36,432

Grade 3 1980-'82, 1997-'98. Not graded 1995-'96. Not held 1990-'94, 2003. 1 1/4 miles 1948-'69. About 1 1/2 miles 1970-
'71. Turf 1970-'71. Equaled track record 1973. Two divisions 1977. ‡Coverack finished third, DQ to fourth, 1977 (2nd
Div.). Track record 1998.

Matchmaker Handicap

Grade 3 in 2005. Monmouth Park, three-year-olds and up, fillies and mares, 1 1/8 miles, turf. Held August 8, 2004, with
a gross value of $100,000. First held in 1967. First graded in 1973. Stakes record 1:46.19 (2001 Batique).

Year	Winner	Jockey	Second	Third	Strs	Time	1st Purse
2004	Where We Left Off (GB), 4, 118	C. S. Nakatani	Mrs. M, 5, 118	Spin Control, 4, 116	9	1:48.80	$60,000
2003	Volga (Ire), 5, 116	J. Bravo	Something Ventured, 4, 117	Cocktailsandreams, 6, 115	10	1:48.22	60,000
2002	Clearly a Queen, 5, 115	E. Coa	Siringas (Ire), 4, 116	Platinum Tiara, 4, 115	7	1:47.76	60,000
2001	Batique, 5, 113	J. C. Ferrer	Melody Queen (GB), 5, 114	Lucky Lune (Fr), 4, 114	8	1:46.19	60,000
2000	Horatia (Ire), 4, 114	J. A. Santos	Camella, 5, 120	Champagne Royal, 6, 114	11	1:47.52	60,000

1999	**Natalie Too**, 5, 116	J. Bravo	Saralea (Fr), 4, 116	U R Unforgetable, 5, 120	6	1:46.81	$60,000
1998	**Bursting Forth**, 4, 116	M. E. Verge	French Buster, 4, 116	Gastronomical, 5, 113	9	1:48.46	60,000
1997	**Fleur de Nuit**, 4, 113	J. A. Krone	Flame Valley, 4, 113	Overcharger, 5, 113	7	1:48.97	60,000
1996	**Powder Bowl**, 4, 113	D. S. Rice	Class Kris, 4, 120	Turkish Tryst, 5, 114	6	1:54.71	60,000
1995	**Avie's Fancy**, 4, 113	W. H. McCauley	Plenty of Sugar, 4, 118	Northern Emerald, 5, 113	8	1:54.19	60,000
1994	**Alice Springs**, 4, 118	J. A. Krone	Hero's Love, 6, 118	Cox Orange, 4, 118	8	1:55.21	60,000
1993	**Fairy Garden**, 5, 120	M. E. Smith	Saratoga Source, 4, 118	Logan's Mist, 4, 118	8	1:57.81	60,000
1992	**Radiant Ring**, 4, 115	R. E. Colton	Highland Crystal, 4, 118	La Gueriere, 4, 118	8	1:55.92	60,000
1991	**Miss Josh**, 5, 123	L. A. Pincay Jr.	Whip Cream, 5, 113	Le Famo, 5, 113	7	1:54.18	90,000
1990	**Capades**, 4, 120	A. T. Cordero Jr.	Gaily Gaily (Ire), 7, 115	Summer Secretary, 5, 115	7	1:55.60	90,000
1989	**Spruce Fir**, 6, 113	D. B. Thomas	Ravinella, 4, 120	Native Mommy, 6, 120	8	1:53.40	90,000
1988	**Magdelaine (NZ)**, 5, 120	E. Maple	Spruce Fir, 5, 115	Carotene, 5, 120	7	1:56.20	60,000
1987	**Carotene**, 4, 118	D. J. Seymour	Spruce Fir, 4, 115	Cadabra Abra, 4, 120	10	1:56.60	73,500
1986	**Lake Country**, 5, 118	V. A. Bracciale Jr.	Capo Di Monte (Ire), 4, 120	Top Socialite, 4, 120	11	1:54.60	60,000
1985	**Key Dancer**, 4, 118	J. D. Bailey	Forest Maiden, 5, 118	Dictina (Fr), 4, 115	7	2:02.40	30,000
1984	**Sabin**, 4, 123	E. Maple	Doblique, 5, 113	Virgin Bride, 4, 113	8	1:53.80	30,000
1983	**Luminaire**, 4, 113	B. Thornburg	Vestris, 4, 113	Lonely Balladier, 5, 113	8	1:56.80	25,000
1982	**Hunston (GB)**, 4, 113	J. Samyn	Trevita (Ire), 5, 118	Kuja Happa, 4, 115	9	1:58.60	35,000
1981	**Mairzy Doates**, 5, 120	C. B. Asmussen	Honey Fox, 4, 120	Little Bonny (Ire), 4, 120	7	1:56.00	35,000
1980	**Just a Game (Ire)**, 4, 120	D. Brumfield	La Soufriere, 5, 115	Record Acclaim, 4, 115	10	1:57.60	25,000
1979	**Warfever (Fr)**, 4, 113	J. Samyn	Smooth Journey, 3, 106	La Soufriere, 4, 118	10	2:03.20	25,000
1978	**Queen Lib**, 3, 112	D. MacBeth	Debby's Turn, 4, 114	Dottie's Doll, 5, 117	8	1:54.60	25,000
1977	**Mississippi Mud**, 4, 119	J. E. Tejeira	Vodka Time, 5, 114	*Lucie Manet, 4, 124	8	1:54.20	30,000
1976	**Dancers Countess**, 4, 119	C. J. McCarron	Vodka Time, 4, 114	Garden Verse, 4, 119	8	1:56.00	20,000
1975	**Susan's Girl**, 6, 121	R. Broussard	Aunt Jin, 3, 114	Pink Tights, 4, 114	6	1:54.20	20,000
1974	**Desert Vixen**, 4, 123	L. A. Pincay Jr.	Coraggioso, 4, 115	Twixt, 5, 123	9	1:55.20	30,000
1973	**Alma North**, 5, 118	F. Lovato	Light Hearted, 4, 121	Susan's Girl, 4, 125	9	1:55.20	30,000

The first three finishers of this race are awarded future breeding seasons; named for "matchmaking" between stallions and mares. Formerly sponsored by Vinery of Lexington 1996, 1998-2001. Formerly sponsored by Gainesway of Lexington 1997. Grade 1 1973-'79. Grade 2 1980-'96. Matchmaker S. 1967-2001. Held at Atlantic City Race Course 1967-'96. 1³/₁₆ miles 1967-'96. Dirt 1967-'78, 1983. Track record 1975. Course record 2001.

Matriarch Stakes

Grade 1 in 2005. Hollywood Park, three-year-olds and up, fillies and mares, 1 mile, turf. Held November 28, 2004, with a gross value of $500,000. First held in 1981. First graded in 1983. Stakes record 1:34.43 (2003 Heat Haze [GB]).

Year	Winner	Jockey	Second	Third	Strs	Time	1st Purse
2004	**Intercontinental (GB)**, 4, 123	J. D. Bailey	Etoile Montante, 4, 123	Ticker Tape (GB), 3, 120	9	1:35.87	$300,000
2003	**Heat Haze (GB)**, 4, 123	J. R. Velazquez	Musical Chimes, 3, 120	Dedication (Fr), 4, 123	14	**1:34.43**	300,000
2002	**Dress To Thrill (Ire)**, 3, 120	P. Smullen	Golden Apples (Ire), 4, 123	Magic Mission (GB), 4, 123	6	1:48.31	300,000
2001	**Starine (Fr)**, 4, 123	J. R. Velazquez	Lethals Lady (GB), 3, 120	Golden Apples (Ire), 3, 120	12	1:50.16	300,000
2000	**Tout Charmant**, 4, 123	C. J. McCarron	Tranquility Lake, 5, 123	Happyanunoit (NZ), 5, 123	9	1:46.06	300,000
1999	**Happyanunoit (NZ)**, 4, 123	B. Blanc	Tuzla (Fr), 5, 123	Spanish Fern, 4, 123	9	1:46.30	300,000
1998	**Squeak (GB)**, 4, 123	A. O. Solis	Real Connection, 7, 123	Green Jewel (GB), 4, 123	8	2:05.08	420,000
1997	**Ryafan**, 3, 120	A. O. Solis	Maxzene, 4, 123	Yokama, 4, 120	8	2:05.80	420,000
1996	**Wandesta (GB)**, 5, 123	C. S. Nakatani	Windsharp, 5, 123	Memories of Silver, 3, 120	12	2:00.14	420,000
1995	**Duda**, 4, 123	J. D. Bailey	Angel in My Heart (Fr), 3, 120	Wandesta (GB), 4, 123	14	2:00.37	385,000
1994	**Exchange**, 6, 123	L. A. Pincay Jr.	Aube Indienne (Fr), 4, 123	Wandesta (GB), 3, 120	8	1:49.42	220,000
1993	**Flawlessly**, 5, 123	C. J. McCarron	Toussaud, 4, 123	Skimble, 4, 123	7	1:46.78	220,000
1992	**Flawlessly**, 4, 123	C. J. McCarron	Super Staff, 4, 123	Kostroma (Ire), 6, 123	9	1:46.14	220,000
1991	**Flawlessly**, 3, 120	C. J. McCarron	Fire the Groom, 4, 123	Free At Last (GB), 4, 123	14	1:46.60	110,000
1990	**Countus In**, 5, 123	C. S. Nakatani	Taffeta and Tulle, 4, 123	Little Brianne, 5, 123	14	1:46.20	110,000
1989	**Claire Marine (Ire)**, 4, 123	C. J. McCarron	General Charge (Ire), 3, 120	Royal Touch (Ire), 4, 123	7	1:47.40	110,000
1988	**Nastique**, 4, 123	W. Shoemaker	Annoconnor, 4, 123	White Mischief (GB), 4, 123	10	1:47.00	110,000
1987	**Asteroid Field**, 4, 123	A. T. Gryder	Nashmeel, 3, 120	Any Song (Ire), 4, 123	10	1:51.00	110,000
1986	**Auspiciante (Arg)**, 5, 123	C. B. Asmussen	Aberuschka (Ire), 4, 123	Reloy, 3, 120	12	1:48.00	110,000
1985	**Fact Finder**, 6, 123	S. Hawley	Tamarinda (Fr), 4, 123	Possible Mate, 4, 123	10	1:48.20	137,000
1984	**Royal Heroine (Ire)**, 4, 123	F. Toro	Reine Mathilde, 3, 120	Sabin, 4, 123	6	1:49.40	164,000
1983	**Sangue (Ire)**, 5, 123	W. Shoemaker	Castilla, 4, 123	Geraldine's Store, 4, 123	10	1:49.40	110,000
1982	**Pale Purple**, 4, 123	R. Sibille	Berry Bush, 5, 123	Ticketed, 3, 120	9	1:48.60	104,600
	Castilla, 3, 120	R. Sibille	Sangue (Ire), 4, 123	Star Pastures (GB), 4, 123	9	1:47.40	104,600
1981	**Kilijaro (Ire)**, 5, 123	L. A. Pincay Jr.	Glorious Song, 5, 123	Bersid, 3, 120	9	1:47.00	131,600

Older women are sometimes known as "matriarchs." Matriarch Invitational S. 1983-'87. 1¹/₈ miles 1981-'94, 1999-2002. 1¹/₄ miles 1995-'98. Two divisions 1982.

Matron Stakes

Grade 1 in 2005. Belmont Park, two-year-olds, fillies, 1 mile, dirt. Held September 19, 2004, with a gross value of $300,000. First held in 1892. First graded in 1973. Stakes record 1:35.16 (1994 Flanders [DQ to sixth]).

Year	Winner	Jockey	Second	Third	Strs	Time	1st Purse
2004	**Sense of Style**, 2, 119	E. S. Prado	Balletto (UAE), 2, 119	Play With Fire, 2, 119	6	1:37.67	$180,000

Year	Winner	Jockey	Second	Third	Strs	Time	1st Purse
2003	**Marylebone**, 2, 119	E. S. Prado	Lokoya, 2, 119	Eye Dazzler, 2, 119	8	1:38.02	$120,000
2002	**Storm Flag Flying**, 2, 119	J. R. Velazquez	Wild Snitch, 2, 119	Fircroft, 2, 119	7	1:38.52	120,000
2000	**Raging Fever**, 2, 120	J. D. Bailey	Dancinginmydreams, 2, 120	Ilusoria, 2, 120	5	1:38.20	120,000
1999	**Finder's Fee**, 2, 119	H. Castillo Jr.	Darling My Darling, 2, 119	Circle of Life, 2, 119	7	1:36.68	90,000
1998	**Oh What a Windfall**, 2, 119	S. J. Sellers	Arrested Dreams, 2, 119	Marley Vale, 2, 119	6	1:39.29	90,000
1997	**Beautiful Pleasure**, 2, 119	J. D. Bailey	Diamond On the Run, 2, 119	Carrielle, 2, 119	11	1:35.71	90,000
1996	**Sharp Cat**, 2, 119	J. D. Bailey	Storm Song, 2, 119	Fabulously Fast, 2, 119	6	1:36.19	90,000
1995	**Golden Attraction**, 2, 119	G. L. Stevens	Cara Rafaela, 2, 119	My Flag, 2, 119	8	1:36.33	90,000
1994	**‡Stormy Blues**, 2, 119	J. A. Santos	Pretty Discreet, 2, 119	Phone Caller, 2, 119	6	**1:35.16**	64,740
1993	**Strategic Maneuver**, 2, 119	J. A. Santos	Astas Foxy Lady, 2, 119	Sovereign Kitty, 2, 119	8	1:23.84	70,680
1992	**Sky Beauty**, 2, 119	E. Maple	Educated Risk, 2, 119	Family Enterprize, 2, 119	9	1:23.32	72,480
1991	**Anh Duong**, 2, 119	A. T. Cordero Jr.	Miss Iron Smoke, 2, 119	Vivano, 2, 119	9	1:23.47	81,300
1990	**Meadow Star**, 2, 119	J. A. Santos	Verbasle, 2, 119	Clark Cotton, 2, 119	6	1:22.80	93,240
1989	**Stella Madrid**, 2, 119	A. T. Cordero Jr.	Golden Reef, 2, 119	Miss Cox's Hat, 2, 119	7	1:24.40	72,720
1988	**Some Romance**, 2, 119	G. L. Stevens	Seattle Meteor, 2, 119	Dreamy Mimi, 2, 119	3	1:24.80	68,580
1987	**Over All**, 2, 119	A. T. Cordero Jr.	Justsayno, 2, 119	Flashy Runner, 2, 119	6	1:24.80	82,140
1986	**Tappiano**, 2, 119	J. Cruguet	Sea Basque, 2, 119	Daytime Princess, 2, 119	5	1:23.40	72,000
1985	**Musical Lark (Ire)**, 2, 119	D. MacBeth	Family Style, 2, 119	I'm Sweets, 2, 119	5	1:24.00	66,240
1984	**Fiesta Lady**, 2, 119	L. A. Pincay Jr.	Tiltalating, 2, 119	Contredance, 2, 119	4	1:24.80	57,060
1983	**Lucky Lucky Lucky**, 2, 119	A. T. Cordero Jr.	Miss Oceana, 2, 119	Buzz My Bell, 2, 119	9	1:23.60	76,590
1982	**Wings of Jove**, 2, 119	W. H. McCauley	Share the Fantasy, 2, 119	Weekend Surprise, 2, 119	5	1:24.00	72,600
1981	**Before Dawn**, 2, 119	J. Velasquez	Arabian Dancer, 2, 119	Mystical Mood, 2, 119	9	1:23.20	81,210
1980	**Prayers'n Promises**, 2, 119	A. T. Cordero Jr.	Heavenly Cause, 2, 119	Sweet Revenge, 2, 119	8	1:24.60	70,725
1979	**Smart Angle**, 2, 119	S. Maple	Royal Suite, 2, 119	Nuit d'Amour, 2, 119	5	1:23.80	69,075
1978	**Fall Aspen**, 2, 119	R. I. Velez	Fair Advantage, 2, 119	Island Kitty, 2, 119	4	1:23.80	58,980
1977	**Lakeville Miss**, 2, 119	R. Hernandez	Stub, 2, 119	Akita, 2, 119	10	1:22.80	49,335
1976	**Mrs. Warren**, 2, 119	E. Maple	Negotiator, 2, 119	Resolver, 2, 119	7	1:24.60	51,162
1975	**Optimistic Gal**, 2, 119	B. Baeza	Pacific Princess, 2, 119	Prowess, 2, 119	8	1:23.00	51,132
1974	**Alpine Lass**, 2, 119	A. T. Cordero Jr.	Copernica, 2, 119	Spring Is Here, 2, 119	13	1:23.00	52,674
1973	**Talking Picture**, 2, 119	R. Turcotte	Dancealot, 2, 119	Raisela, 2, 119	9	1:23.20	64,050

Held at Morris Park 1892-1904. Held at Pimlico 1910. Held at Aqueduct 1960, 1964-'68. Not held 1895-'98, 1911-'13, 1915-'22. Not held due to World Trade Center attack 2001. 6 furlongs 1892-1971. 7 furlongs 1973-'93. Colts and fillies 1892-1901. Colt and filly divisions 1902-'14. ‡Flanders finished first, DQ to sixth, 1994.

Meadowlands Breeders' Cup Stakes

Grade 2 in 2005. The Meadowlands, three-year-olds, 1⅛ miles, dirt. Held October 8, 2004, with a gross value of $500,000. First held in 1977. First graded in 1979. Stakes record 1:46.06 (1998 K. J.'s Appeal).

Year	Winner	Jockey	Second	Third	Strs	Time	1st Purse
2004	**Balto Star**, 6, 123	J. R. Velazquez	Dynever, 4, 119	Gygistar, 5, 119	8	1:48.68	$300,000
2003	**Bowman's Band**, 5, 119	R. A. Dominguez	Dynever, 3, 120	‡Volponi, 5, 123	6	1:46.84	240,000
2002	**Burning Roma**, 4, 115	E. Coa	Volponi, 4, 116	Windsor Castle, 4, 112	9	1:46.95	240,000
2001	**Gander**, 5, 114	J. R. Velazquez	Broken Vow, 4, 119	Include, 4, 121	5	1:47.11	300,000
2000	**North East Bound**, 4, 116	J. A. Velez Jr.	Lord Sterling, 4, 115	Where's Taylor, 4, 113	10	1:48.84	240,000
1999	**Pleasant Breeze**, 4, 110	J. F. Chavez	Jazz Club, 4, 118	Vision and Verse, 3, 112	8	1:47.17	300,000
1998	**K. J.'s Appeal**, 4, 118	J. R. Velazquez	Hal's Pal (GB), 5, 116	Sir Bear, 5, 119	8	**1:46.06**	300,000
1996	**Dramatic Gold**, 5, 119	K. J. Desormeaux	Formal Gold, 3, 112	Mt. Sassafras, 4, 114	11	1:48.02	450,000
1995	**Peaks and Valleys**, 3, 116	J. A. Krone	Poor But Honest, 5, 116	Concern, 4, 122	6	1:48.07	300,000
1994	**Conveyor**, 6, 113	M. E. Smith	Personal Merit, 3, 109	Bruce's Mill, 3, 114	11	1:47.96	300,000
1993	**Marquetry**, 6, 120	K. J. Desormeaux	Michelle Can Pass, 5, 110	Northern Trend, 5, 112	9	1:47.21	300,000
1992	**Sea Cadet**, 4, 120	A. O. Solis	Valley Crossing, 4, 111	American Chance, 3, 109	10	1:48.19	300,000
1991	**Twilight Agenda**, 5, 121	C. J. McCarron	Scan, 3, 116	Sea Cadet, 3, 115	9	1:46.63	300,000
1990	**Great Normand**, 5, 113	C. E. Lopez Sr.	Norquestor, 4, 116	Beau Genius, 5, 122	10	1:47.20	300,000
1989	**Mi Selecto**, 4, 115	J. A. Santos	Make the Most, 4, 110	dh- Master Speaker, 4, 114	8	2:00.20	300,000
				dh- Slew City Slew, 5, 116			
1988	**Alysheba**, 4, 127	C. J. McCarron	Slew City Slew, 4, 116	Pleasant Virginian, 4, 114	5	1:58.80	360,000
1987	**Creme Fraiche**, 5, 123	L. A. Pincay Jr.	Afleet, 3, 118	Cryptoclearance, 3, 120	7	2:01.80	300,000
1986	**Broad Brush**, 3, 117	A. T. Cordero Jr.	Skip Trial, 4, 122	Little Missouri, 4, 116	10	2:01.60	300,000
1985	**Bounding Basque**, 5, 113	R. G. Davis	Wild Again, 5, 120	Al Mamoon, 4, 115	11	2:00.40	300,000
1984	**Wild Again**, 4, 115	R. Migliore	Canadian Factor, 4, 114	Inevitable Leader, 5, 116	9	2:00.60	300,000
1983	**Slewpy**, 3, 116	A. T. Cordero Jr.	Deputy Minister, 4, 118	Water Bank, 4, 117	9	2:02.40	240,000
1982	**Mehmet**, 4, 118	E. J. Delahoussaye	Thirty Eight Paces, 4, 113	John Henry, 7, 129	9	2:01.40	240,000
1981	**Princelet**, 3, 110	W. Nemeti	Niteange, 7, 114	Peat Moss, 6, 121	14	2:02.40	202,080
1980	**Tunerup**, 4, 117	J. Vasquez	Dr. Patches, 6, 116	Dewan Keys, 5, 115	12	2:00.40	196,500
1979	**Spectacular Bid**, 3, 126	W. Shoemaker	Smarten, 3, 120	Valdez, 3, 121	5	2:01.20	234,650
1978	**Dr. Patches**, 4, 119	A. T. Cordero Jr.	Do Tell George, 5, 114	Niteange, 4, 115	7	2:01.60	104,878
1977	**Pay Tribute**, 5, 117	A. T. Cordero Jr.	Father Hogan, 4, 112	Super Boy, 4, 110	11	2:02.60	114,920

Formerly sponsored by General Motors Corp. of Detroit 1996. Grade 1 1983-'98. Meadowlands Cup H. 1977-'95, 1996-2002. Buick Meadowlands Cup H. 1996. Not held 1997. 1¼ miles 1977-'89. Dead heat for third 1989. ‡Unforgettable Max finished third, DQ to fourth, 2003. Track record 1998.

Memorial Day Handicap

Grade 3 in 2005. Calder Race Course, three-year-olds and up, 1¹/₁₆ miles, dirt. Held May 30, 2005, with a gross value of $100,000. First held in 1971. First graded in 2002. Stakes record 1:44.60 (1985 Rexson's Hope).

Year	Winner	Jockey	Second	Third	Strs	Time	1st Purse
2005	Twilight Road, 8, 119	P. Teator	Whos Crying Now, 5, 115	Hear No Evil, 5, 114	8	1:47.71	$60,000
2004	Twilight Road, 7, 111	P. Teator	Hear No Evil, 4, 115	Gold Dollar, 5, 112	12	1:45.99	60,000
2003	Dancing Guy, 8, 113	R. I. Velez	Shotgun Fire, 5, 110	High Ideal, 5, 113	7	1:45.56	60,000
2002	Best of the Rest, 7, 123	C. H. Velasquez	High Ideal, 4, 112	Hal's Hope, 5, 117	4	1:44.75	60,000
2001	Hal's Hope, 4, 115	R. I. Velez	American Halo, 5, 115	Tahkodha Hills, 4, 118	7	1:45.81	45,000
2000	Dancing Guy, 5, 121	J. C. Ferrer	Reporter, 5, 111	Groomstick Stock's, 4, 111	9	1:46.28	45,000
1999	Wicapi, 7, 116	E. Coa	Dancing Guy, 4, 114	Golf Game, 4, 112	8	1:46.79	45,000
1998	Born Mighty, 4, 114	J. A. Rivera II	Hard Rock Ridge, 5, 113	Auroral, 6, 114	7	1:40.96	30,000
1997	Vilhelm, 5, 114	J. C. Ferrer	‡Sir Bear, 4, 113	Donthelumbertrader, 4, 118	9	1:40.80	30,000
1996	Marcie's Ensign, 4, 115	E. Coa	Derivative, 5, 114	Halo Bird (Arg), 5, 110	9	1:50.02	30,000
1995	Mr. Light Tres (Arg), 6, 113	K. L. Chapman	Fabulous Frolic, 4, 112	Flying American, 6, 116	11	1:47.17	30,000
1994	Final Sunrise, 4, 113	P. A. Rodriguez	Crucial Trial, 4, 114	Bill Mooney, 4, 112	4	1:51.86	30,000
1993	Boots 'n Buck, 4, 116	M. Russ	Yankee Axe, 6, 113	Darian's Reason, 5, 113	10	1:53.82	30,000
1992	Jodi's Sweetie, 4, 114	J. C. Duarte Jr.	Scottish Ice, 4, 114	Bidding Proud, 3, 113	9	1:44.21	30,000
1991	S. W. Wildcard, 5, 116	P. A. Rodriguez	So Dashing, 4, 113	Bold Circle, 5, 114	9	1:46.92	34,110
1990	Primal, 5, 122	H. Castillo Jr.	Eagle Watch, 6, 116	Public Account, 5, 113	7	1:47.40	33,180
1989	Hooting Star, 4, 116	J. A. Velez Jr.	Val d'Enchere, 6, 116	Bright Balloon, 5, 111	8	1:41.00	33,300
1988	Billie Osage, 4, 116	G. St. Leon	Fabulous Devotion, 4, 110	Engrupido II (Uru), 6, 114	7	1:46.20	33,150
1985	Rexson's Hope, 4, 113	G. W. Bain	Brother Liam, 5, 121	Ameriilad, 4, 115	10	**1:44.60**	33,660
1983	Bolivar (Chi), 6, 116	S. B. Soto	Dallas Express, 5, 114	Grey Adorn, 5, 115	11	1:46.00	23,700
1982	Two's a Plenty, 5, 122	A. Smith Jr.	Catch That Pass, 4, 114	Poking, 6, 117	7	1:45.40	19,470
1980	Poverty Boy, 5, 119	M. Fromin	J. Rodney G., 5, 115	Irish Swords, 4, 117	11	1:45.60	20,565
1979	Great Sound (Ire), 5, 115	W. A. Guerra	Raymond Earl, 4, 123	Prince Misko, 4, 116	10	1:45.40	20,835
1978	One Moment, 5, 114	J. Giovanni	Out Door Johnny, 4, 115	Haverty, 4, 112	8	1:52.20	21,242
1977	‡Lightning Thrust, 4, 121	G. St. Leon	Jatski, 3, 110	What a Threat, 5, 116	10	1:45.80	21,780
1976	Freepet, 6, 117	R. Broussard	Chilean Chief, 5, 119	Rastaferian, 7, 112	7	1:53.80	20,700
1974	Snurb, 4, 121	G. St. Leon	Stairway to Stars, 5, 113	Somewhat Striking, 4, 113	8	1:46.20	14,040
1973	*Correntoso, 6, 116	R. Danjean	Great Divide, 5, 121	*Asher, 5, 104	9	1:47.80	10,620

Traditionally held during Memorial Day weekend. Not held 1981, 1984, 1986-'87. 1 mile 1971. 1¹/₈ miles 1976, 1978, 1993-'96. About 1¹/₈ miles 1977, 1992. Turf 1977, 1989, 1992, 1995, 1997-'98. ‡What a Threat finished first, DQ to third, 1977. ‡Donthelumbertrader finished second, DQ to third, 1997.

Mervin H. Muniz Jr. Memorial Handicap

Grade 2 in 2005. Fair Grounds, four-year-olds and up, about 1¹/₈ miles, turf. Held March 19, 2005, with a gross value of $500,000. First held in 1992. First graded in 1996. Stakes record 1:48.29 (2004 Mystery Giver).

Year	Winner	Jockey	Second	Third	Strs	Time	1st Purse
2005	‡A to the Z, 5, 121	V. Espinoza	America Alive, 4, 116	Honor in War, 6, 117	11	1:50.99	$300,000
2004	Mystery Giver, 6, 120	R. Albarado	Herculated, 4, 116	Skate Away, 5, 117	10	**1:48.29**	300,000
2003	Candid Glen, 6, 114	E. J. Perrodin	Rouvres (Fr), 4, 115	Freefourinternet, 5, 115	11	1:51.15	390,000
2002	Sarafan, 5, 116	C. S. Nakatani	Beat Hollow (GB), 5, 115	Even the Score, 4, 116	14	1:48.88	420,000
2001	Tijiyr (Ire), 5, 110	R. Albarado	Northcote Road, 6, 115	King Cugat, 4, 121	13	1:50.72	360,000
2000	Brave Act (GB), 6, 121	C. B. Asmussen	Where's Taylor, 4, 113	Chester House, 5, 114	13	1:48.98	360,000
1999	Lord Smith (GB), 4, 117	G. K. Gomez	Hawksley Hill (Ire), 6, 122	Chorwon, 6, 116	12	1:51.27	398,160
1998	Joyeux Danseur, 5, 121	R. Albarado	Martiniquais (Ire), 5, 118	Hollie's Chief, 7, 113	9	1:49.30	223,980
1997	Always a Classic, 4, 114	E. M. Martin Jr.	Rainbow Blues (Ire), 4, 120	Snake Eyes, 7, 118	7	1:54.83	131,970
1996	Kazabaiyn, 6, 113	K. J. Desormeaux	Party Season (GB), 5, 116	Coaxing Matt, 7, 112	10	1:50.80	93,195
1995	Earl of Barking (Ire), 5, 115	G. F. Almeida	Kazabaiyn, 5, 114	Coaxing Matt, 6, 113	11	1:52.01	93,375
1994	Snake Eyes, 4, 115	B. E. Bartram	Yukon Robbery, 4, 115	dh- Cozzene's Prince, 7, 122	8	1:49.41	76,305
				dh- Dipotamos, 6, 111			
	Pride of Summer, 6, 113	R. J. King Jr.	Alpine Choice, 4, 114	Empire Pool (GB), 4, 116	10	1:49.59	76,425
1993	Coaxing Matt, 4, 114	E. M. Martin Jr.	Dixie Poker Ace, 6, 120	Spending Record, 6, 114	12	1:50.80	47,010
1992	‡Slick Groom, 4, 112	K. P. LeBlanc	Little Bro Lantis, 4, 113	Brownsboro, 8, 117	10	1:52.60	31,590

Named for longtime Fair Grounds racing secretary Mervin H. Muniz Jr., who died in 2003. Formerly named for Hawksworth Farm's 1984 Louisiana H. winner Explosive Bid (1978 c. by Explodent). Grade 3 1996-2000. Explosive Bid S. 1992-'94. Explosive Bid H. 1995-2003. Two divisions 1994. Dead heat for third 1994 (2nd Div.). ‡City Ballet finished first, DQ to sixth, 1992; Rapid Proof finished first, DQ to 11th, due to a positive drug test 2005. Course record 2004.

Mervyn LeRoy Handicap

Grade 2 in 2005. Hollywood Park, three-year-olds and up, 1¹/₁₆ miles, dirt. Held May 14, 2005, with a gross value of $150,000. First held in 1980. First graded in 1980. Stakes record 1:40.20 (1989 Ruhlmann).

Year	Winner	Jockey	Second	Third	Strs	Time	1st Purse
2005	Ace Blue (Brz), 5, 116	D. R. Flores	Ender's Shadow, 5, 116	Borrego, 4, 119	7	1:41.45	$90,000
2004	Even the Score, 6, 116	D. R. Flores	Ender's Shadow, 4, 113	Total Impact (Chi), 6, 116	8	1:40.81	90,000
2003	Total Impact (Chi), 5, 114	M. E. Smith	Fleetstreet Dancer, 5, 114	Piensa Sonando (Chi), 5, 115	8	1:40.88	90,000
2002	Sky Jack, 6, 117	L. A. Pincay Jr.	Bosque Redondo, 5, 117	Devine Wind, 6, 114	6	1:41.36	90,000

Year	Winner	Jockey	Second	Third	Strs	Time	1st Purse
2001	**Futural**, 5, 117	C. J. McCarron	Skimming, 5, 119	Moonlight Charger, 6, 114	5	1:42.02	$90,000
2000	**Out of Mind (Brz)**, 5, 116	E. J. Delahoussaye	Early Pioneer, 5, 116	Skimming, 4, 111	7	1:41.82	90,000
1999	**Budroyale**, 6, 118	G. K. Gomez	Moore's Flat, 5, 107	Wild Wonder, 5, 120	6	1:42.12	90,000
1998	**Wild Wonder**, 4, 116	E. J. Delahoussaye	Budroyale, 5, 116	Flick (GB), 6, 117	7	1:40.92	64,320
1997	**Hesabull**, 4, 116	G. F. Almeida	Region, 8, 112	Kingdom Found, 7, 116	5	1:41.30	63,720
1996	**Siphon (Brz)**, 5, 117	D. R. Flores	Del Mar Dennis, 6, 119	Dramatic Gold, 5, 117	4	1:40.44	61,500
1995	**Tossofthecoin**, 5, 118	C. S. Nakatani	Ferrara, 4, 114	Polar Route, 5, 116	8	1:40.70	64,600
1994	**Del Mar Dennis**, 4, 115	S. Gonzalez Jr.	Tinners Way, 4, 114	Hill Pass, 5, 115	6	1:40.48	93,300
1993	**Marquetry**, 6, 117	K. J. Desormeaux	Potrillon (Arg), 5, 117	Lottery Winner, 4, 115	6	1:49.10	92,800
1992	**Another Review**, 4, 116	K. J. Desormeaux	Sir Beaufort, 5, 116	Marquetry, 5, 119	5	1:41.38	87,900
1991	**Louis Cyphre (Ire)**, 5, 114	J. A. Santos	Warcraft, 4, 115	Anshan (GB), 4, 116	6	1:40.90	110,600
1990	**Super May**, 4, 116	R. G. Davis	Charlatan (Chi), 5, 110	Lively One, 5, 122	12	1:40.80	121,600
1989	**Ruhlmann**, 4, 121	L. A. Pincay Jr.	Sabona, 7, 114	Perfec Travel, 7, 115	5	**1:40.20**	122,800
1988	**Judge Angelucci**, 5, 123	E. J. Delahoussaye	Simply Majestic, 4, 118	Mark Chip, 5, 117	8	1:40.80	129,600
1987	**Zabaleta**, 4, 117	L. A. Pincay Jr.	Nostalgia's Star, 5, 116	Sabona, 5, 114	7	1:34.80	127,000
1986	**Skywalker**, 4, 117	L. A. Pincay Jr.	Sabona, 4, 113	Al Mamoon, 5, 120	8	1:34.80	123,600
1985	**Precisionist**, 4, 126	C. J. McCarron	Greinton (GB), 4, 121	My Habitony, 5, 115	5	1:32.80	118,700
1984	**Sari's Dreamer**, 5, 112	R. Q. Meza	Fighting Fit, 5, 120	Ancestral (Ire), 4, 115	7	1:34.20	95,000
1983	**Fighting Fit**, 4, 115	W. Shoemaker	Island Whirl, 5, 122	Kangroo Court, 6, 116	7	1:35.80	63,600
1982	**Mehmet**, 4, 116	S. Hawley	A Run, 4, 112	Major Sport, 5, 112	6	1:34.60	63,100
1981	**Eleven Stitches**, 4, 115	S. Hawley	†Glorious Song, 5, 121	Summer Time Guy, 5, 114	8	1:36.40	97,100
1980	**Spectacular Bid**, 4, 132	W. Shoemaker	Peregrinator (Ire), 5, 119	Beau's Eagle, 4, 121	6	1:40.40	120,400

Named for Mervyn LeRoy (1900-'87), one of the organizers of Hollywood Park and its president until 1985; LeRoy was a leading Hollywood producer and director. Grade 1 1988-'91. 1 mile 1981-'87. 1⅛ miles 1993. †Denotes female.

Metropolitan Handicap

Grade 1 in 2005. Belmont Park, three-year-olds and up, 1 mile, dirt. Held May 30, 2005, with a gross value of $750,000. First held in 1891. First graded in 1973. Stakes record 1:32.81 (1996 Honour and Glory).

Year	Winner	Jockey	Second	Third	Strs	Time	1st Purse
2005	**Ghostzapper**, 5, 123	J. Castellano	Silver Wagon, 4, 115	Sir Shackleton, 4, 116	6	1:33.29	$450,000
2004	**Pico Central (Brz)**, 5, 119	A. O. Solis	Bowman's Band, 6, 114	Strong Hope, 4, 119	9	1:35.47	450,000
2003	**Aldebaran**, 5, 119	J. D. Bailey	Saarland, 4, 114	Peeping Tom, 6, 114	8	1:34.15	450,000
2002	**Swept Overboard**, 5, 117	J. F. Chavez	Aldebaran, 4, 115	Crafty C. T., 4, 116	10	1:33.34	450,000
2001	**Exciting Story**, 4, 115	P. Husbands	Peeping Tom, 4, 119	Alannan, 5, 118	10	1:37.14	450,000
2000	**Yankee Victor**, 4, 117	H. Castillo Jr.	†Honest Lady, 4, 112	Sir Bear, 7, 117	8	1:34.64	450,000
1999	**Sir Bear**, 6, 117	J. R. Velazquez	Crafty Friend, 6, 114	Liberty Gold, 5, 114	8	1:34.55	300,000
1998	**Wild Rush**, 4, 119	J. D. Bailey	Banker's Gold, 4, 115	Accelerator, 4, 113	9	1:33.50	300,000
1997	**Langfuhr**, 5, 122	J. F. Chavez	Western Winter, 5, 115	Northern Afleet, 4, 117	10	1:33.11	240,000
1996	**Honour and Glory**, 3, 110	J. R. Velazquez	dh-Afternoon Deelites, 4, 123	Timeless Moment, 4, 109	9	**1:32.81**	240,000
			dh-Lite the Fuse, 5, 122				
1995	**You and I**, 4, 112	J. F. Chavez	Lite the Fuse, 4, 113	Our Emblem, 4, 114	9	1:34.63	300,000
1994	**Holy Bull**, 3, 112	M. E. Smith	Cherokee Run, 4, 118	Devil His Due, 5, 122	10	1:33.98	300,000
1993	**Ibero (Arg)**, 6, 119	L. A. Pincay Jr.	Bertrando, 4, 121	Alydeed, 4, 124	9	1:34.29	300,000
1992	**Dixie Brass**, 3, 107	J. M. Pezua	Pleasant Tap, 5, 119	In Excess (Ire), 5, 121	11	1:33.68	300,000
1991	**In Excess (Ire)**, 4, 117	P. A. Valenzuela	Rubiano, 4, 111	Gervazy, 4, 114	14	1:35.45	300,000
1990	**Criminal Type**, 5, 120	J. A. Santos	Housebuster, 3, 113	Easy Goer, 4, 127	9	1:34.40	357,000
1989	**Proper Reality**, 4, 117	J. D. Bailey	Seeking the Gold, 4, 126	Dancing Spree, 4, 113	8	1:34.00	353,440
1988	**Gulch**, 4, 125	J. A. Santos	Afleet, 4, 124	Stacked Pack, 4, 110	8	1:34.60	351,600
1987	**Gulch**, 3, 110	P. Day	King's Swan, 7, 121	Broad Brush, 4, 128	9	1:34.80	360,900
1986	**Garthorn**, 6, 124	R. Q. Meza	Love That Mac, 4, 117	†Lady's Secret, 4, 120	8	1:33.60	179,750
1985	**Forzando (GB)**, 4, 118	D. MacBeth	Mo Exception, 4, 113	Track Barron, 4, 125	8	1:34.40	207,600
1984	**Fit to Fight**, 5, 124	J. D. Bailey	A Phenomenon, 4, 126	Moro, 5, 116	10	1:34.00	209,100
1983	**Star Choice**, 4, 113	J. Velasquez	Tough Critic, 4, 110	John's Gold, 4, 111	13	1:33.80	145,200
1982	**Conquistador Cielo**, 3, 111	E. Maple	Silver Buck, 4, 111	Star Gallant, 3, 111	14	1:33.00	91,800
1981	**Fappiano**, 4, 115	A. T. Cordero Jr.	Irish Tower, 4, 127	Amber Pass, 4, 115	7	1:33.80	85,650
1980	**Czaravich**, 4, 126	L. A. Pincay Jr.	State Dinner, 5, 117	Silent Cal, 5, 120	8	1:35.80	83,850
1979	**State Dinner**, 4, 115	C. J. McCarron	Dr. Patches, 5, 118	Sorry Lookin, 4, 113	9	1:34.00	64,980
1978	**Cox's Ridge**, 4, 130	E. Maple	Buckfinder, 4, 112	Quiet Little Table, 5, 118	9	1:34.60	66,180
1977	**Forego**, 7, 133	W. Shoemaker	Co Host, 5, 111	Full Out, 4, 115	12	1:34.80	68,640
1976	**Forego**, 6, 130	H. Gustines	Master Derby, 4, 126	Lord Rebeau, 5, 119	6	1:34.80	66,660
1975	**Gold and Myrrh**, 4, 121	W. Blum	Stop the Music, 5, 124	Forego, 5, 136	7	1:33.60	66,840
1974	**Arbees Boy**, 4, 112	E. Maple	Forego, 4, 134	Timeless Moment, 4, 109	8	1:34.40	67,200
1973	**Tentam**, 4, 116	J. Velasquez	Key to the Mint, 4, 127	King's Bishop, 4, 118	8	1:35.00	68,580

Held at Morris Park 1891-1904. Held at Aqueduct 1960-'67, 1969, 1975. Not held 1891, 1911-'12. 1⅛ miles 1891-'96. Dead heat for second 1996. †Denotes female.

Miami Mile Breeders' Cup Handicap

Grade 3 in 2005. Calder Race Course, three-year-olds and up, 1 mile, turf. Held September 11, 2004, with a gross value of $150,000. First held in 1987. First graded in 1989. Stakes record 1:33.75 (2001 Mr. Livingston).

Year	Winner	Jockey	Second	Third	Strs	Time	1st Purse
2004	**Twilight Road**, 7, 114	P. Teator	Gold Dollar, 5, 114	Paradise Dancer, 4, 115	9	1:39.56	$90,000
2003	**Tour of the Cat**, 5, 115	A. Cabassa Jr.	Last Stand, 4, 113	Lavender's Lad, 5, 114	10	1:38.65	90,000

Year	Winner	Jockey	Second	Third	Strs	Time	1st Purse
2002	Band Is Passing, 6, 117	C. H. Velasquez	Pisces, 5, 116	Doowaley (Ire), 6, 113	8	1:37.78	$90,000
2001	Mr. Livingston, 4, 115	A. Castellano Jr.	Honorable Pic, 4, 114	Pisces, 4, 112	8	1:33.75	90,000
2000	Band Is Passing, 4, 120	E. Coa	Hurrahy, 7, 115	Tiger Shark, 4, 112	9	1:37.28	90,000
1999	Sharp Appeal, 6, 114	J. Castellano	Shamrock City, 4, 114	Hurrahy, 6, 115	10	1:35.70	135,000
1998	Unite's Big Red, 4, 115	E. O. Nunez	Fig Fest, 5, 113	dh- Copy Editor, 6, 117	10	1:36.62	120,000
				dh- Ensign Ray, 5, 113			
1997	Vilhelm, 5, 114	J. C. Ferrer	Marcie's Ensign, 5, 114	Elite Jeblar, 7, 113	11	1:36.67	120,000
1996	Satellite Nealski, 3, 112	J. C. Ferrer	Marcie's Ensign, 4, 115	Copy Editor, 4, 117	10	1:47.63	95,805
1995	Elite Jeblar, 5, 113	E. Fires	Myrmidon, 4, 117	Fabulous Frolic, 4, 114	10	1:47.67	94,200
1994	The Vid, 4, 114	R. R. Douglas	Mr. Angel, 3, 118	Carterista, 5, 116	9	1:48.28	94,350
1993	Carterista, 4, 117	M. A. Lee	Wild Forest, 4, 112	Mr. Explosive, 5, 112	13	1:47.51	95,610
1992	Jodi's Sweetie, 4, 115	J. D. Bailey	‡Walkie Talker, 3, 114	‡Futurist, 4, 117	10	1:43.94	94,140
1991	Run Turn, 4, 111	G. St. Leon	Scottish Ice, 3, 118	Hidden Tomahawk, 3, 111	6	1:52.96	93,150
1990	Public Account, 5, 115	P. A. Rodriguez	Bold Circle, 4, 112	Primal, 5, 126	8	1:52.00	93,300
1989	Simply Majestic, 5, 117	H. Castillo Jr.	Maceo, 5, 113	Bold Circle, 3, 110	8	1:48.60	93,510
1988	Simply Majestic, 4, 117	J. D. Bailey	Val d'Enchere, 5, 116	Racing Star, 6, 115	8	1:43.60	93,900
1987	Blazing Bart, 3, 117	J. A. Santos	Silver Voice, 4, 115	New Colony, 4, 114	9	1:44.20	93,630

Named for the city of Miami. Miami Budweiser Breeders' Cup H. 1987-'95. Miami Breeders' Cup H. 1996-'98. About 1¹/₈ miles 1987-'89, 1992-'93. 1¹/₁₆ miles 1990-'91, 1994-'96. Dirt 1990-'91. Dead heat for third 1998. ‡Futurist finished second, DQ to third; Say Dance finished third, DQ to fourth, 1992.

Miesque Stakes

Grade 3 in 2005. Hollywood Park, two-year-olds, fillies, 1 mile, turf. Held November 26, 2004, in two divisions, with a gross value of $75,000 for each division. First held in 1990. First graded in 1995. Stakes record 1:34.30 (1995 Antespend).

Year	Winner	Jockey	Second	Third	Strs	Time	1st Purse
2004	Louvain (Ire), 2, 115	R. A. Dominguez	Royal Copenhagen (Fr), 2, 114	La Maitresse (Ire), 2, 114	8	1:37.19	$45,000
	Paddy's Daisy, 2, 121	C. S. Nakatani	Conveyor's Angel, 2, 118	Kenza, 2, 116	8	1:36.92	45,000
2003	Mambo Slew, 2, 116	M. E. Smith	Ticker Tape (GB), 2, 116	Winendynme, 2, 116	11	1:36.17	60,000
2002	Atlantic Ocean, 2, 121	D. R. Flores	Tangle (Ire), 2, 114	Major Idea, 2, 121	8	1:34.63	120,000
2001	Forty On Line (GB), 2, 117	C. S. Nakatani	Riskaverse, 2, 121	Daisyago, 2, 118	10	1:36.38	120,000
2000	Fantastic Filly (Fr), 2, 116	G. K. Gomez	Smart Timing, 2, 115	Eminent, 2, 118	11	1:35.11	120,000
1999	Prairie Princess, 2, 116	A. O. Solis	She's Classy, 2, 118	Mary Kies, 2, 121	6	1:37.30	120,000
1998	Here's to You, 2, 116	E. J. Delahoussaye	Sweet Ludy (Ire), 2, 118	Nausicaa, 2, 116	7	1:36.57	120,000
1997	Star's Proud Penny, 2, 116	G. K. Gomez	Superlative, 2, 121	Ransom the Dreamer, 2, 121	9	1:37.42	120,000
1996	Ascutney, 2, 116	E. J. Delahoussaye	Wealthy, 2, 116	Clever Pilot, 2, 118	8	1:35.16	120,000
1995	Antespend, 2, 121	C. W. Antley	Wheatly Special, 2, 121	Platinum Blonde, 2, 121	10	1:34.30	110,000
1994	Bail Out Becky, 2, 121	K. J. Desormeaux	Miss Union Avenue, 2, 121	Makin Whopee (Fr), 2, 117	10	1:37.26	110,000
1993	Tricky Code, 2, 116	C. S. Nakatani	Irish Forever, 2, 121	Roget's Fact, 2, 114	6	1:35.15	137,500
1992	Creaking Board (GB), 2, 115	K. J. Desormeaux	Ask Anita, 2, 117	Zoonaqua, 2, 121	10	1:35.62	137,500
1991	More Than Willing, 2, 118	E. J. Delahoussaye	Stormagain, 2, 115	Looie Capote, 2, 114	8	1:35.51	61,875
	Hopeful Amber, 2, 114	D. R. Flores	Storm Ring, 2, 115	Crownette, 2, 114	8	1:36.72	61,875
1990	Dead Heat, 3, 114	J. A. Garcia	Bel's Starlet, 3, 114	Somethingmerry, 3, 114	7	1:41.00	35,650

Named for Flaxman Holding's English and French champion, '87, '88 North American champion grass mare, and '87 Breeders' Cup Mile (at Hollywood Park) winner Miesque (1984 f. by Nureyev). 1¹/₁₆ miles 1990. Three-year-olds 1990. Two divisions 1991, 2004.

Milady Breeders' Cup Handicap

Grade 2 in 2005. Hollywood Park, three-year-olds and up, fillies and mares, 1¹/₁₆ miles, dirt. Held June 4, 2005, with a gross value of $205,150. First held in 1952. First graded in 1973. Stakes record 1:40.20 (1980 Image of Reality).

Year	Winner	Jockey	Second	Third	Strs	Time	1st Purse
2005	Andujar, 4, 117	C. S. Nakatani	Hollywood Story, 4, 121	Star Parade (Arg), 6, 115	7	1:41.59	$127,290
2004	Star Parade (Arg), 5, 116	V. Espinoza	Quero Quero, 4, 115	Pesci, 4, 114	5	1:41.83	125,670
2003	Azeri, 5, 125	M. E. Smith	Enjoy, 4, 114	Tropical Blossom, 5, 111	4	1:41.87	127,080
2002	Azeri, 4, 122	M. E. Smith	Affluent, 4, 119	Collect Call, 4, 115	6	1:42.02	126,840
2001	Lazy Slusan, 6, 119	V. Espinoza	Lady Melesi, 4, 116	Feverish, 6, 118	4	1:42.25	157,980
2000	Riboletta (Brz), 5, 120	C. J. McCarron	Bordelaise (Arg), 5, 117	Excellent Meeting, 4, 121	6	1:42.01	112,860
1999	Gourmet Girl, 4, 115	E. J. Delahoussaye	Yolo Lady, 4, 115	Victory Stripes (Arg), 5, 117	5	1:40.97	112,440
1998	I Ain't Bluffing, 4, 120	C. J. McCarron	Fleet Lady, 4, 119	Real Connection, 7, 112	6	1:42.16	158,640
1997	Listening, 4, 116	A. O. Solis	Chile Chatte, 4, 114	Exotic Wood, 5, 118	5	1:41.20	95,220
1996	Twice the Vice, 5, 120	C. J. McCarron	Jewel Princess, 4, 120	Urbane, 4, 117	5	1:40.96	110,100
1995	Pirate's Revenge, 4, 116	C. W. Antley	Paseana (Arg), 8, 123	Private Persuasion, 4, 116	5	1:41.57	91,000
1994	Andestine, 4, 116	C. J. McCarron	Golden Klair (GB), 4, 119	Zarani Sidi Anna, 4, 116	7	1:41.40	94,900
1993	Paseana (Arg), 6, 125	C. J. McCarron	Bold Windy, 4, 114	Re Toss (Arg), 6, 116	7	1:41.67	94,500
1992	Paseana (Arg), 5, 125	C. J. McCarron	Re Toss (Arg), 5, 115	Fowda, 4, 119	7	1:41.46	94,200
1991	Brought to Mind, 4, 118	P. A. Valenzuela	Luna Elegante (Arg), 5, 114	Vieille Vigne (Fr), 4, 117	8	1:41.70	95,800
1990	Bayakoa (Arg), 6, 127	L. A. Pincay Jr.	Fantastic Look, 4, 113	Kelly, 4, 110	4	1:41.20	89,700
1989	Bayakoa (Arg), 5, 124	L. A. Pincay Jr.	Flying Julia, 6, 113	Carita Tostada (Chi), 5, 115	5	1:42.00	91,500
1988	By Land by Sea, 4, 124	F. Toro	Invited Guest (Ire), 4, 114	Integra, 4, 121	4	1:43.60	89,200
1987	Seldom Seen Sue, 4, 117	C. J. McCarron	Tiffany Lass, 4, 120	Frau Altiva (Arg), 5, 114	7	1:48.20	95,000
1986	Dontstop Themusic, 6, 122	D. G. McHargue	Magnificent Lindy, 4, 117	Truffles, 5, 110	4	1:48.80	63,500

1985 **Adored**, 5, 125	L. A. Pincay Jr.	Lovlier Linda, 5, 120	Mitterand, 4, 120	4	1:33.60	$73,500
1984 **Adored**, 4, 119	L. A. Pincay Jr.	Princess Rooney, 4, 122	Lass Trump, 4, 117	7	1:41.00	63,800
1983 **Marisma (Chi)**, 5, 118	K. D. Black	A Kiss for Luck, 4, 113	Sangue (Ire), 5, 123	7	1:42.20	63,100
1982 **Cat Girl**, 4, 114	C. J. McCarron	Track Robbery, 6, 124	Ack's Secret, 6, 123	6	1:41.60	62,500
1981 **Save Wild Life**, 4, 115	C. J. McCarron	Princess Karenda, 4, 120	Swift Bird, 4, 115	9	1:42.80	65,700
1980 **Image of Reality**, 4, 117	D. G. McHargue	It's in the Air, 4, 122	Fondre, 5, 113	5	**1:40.20**	36,050
1979 **Innuendo**, 5, 113	D. Pierce	It's in the Air, 3, 112	Country Queen, 4, 121	9	1:41.20	32,700
1978 **Taisez Vous**, 4, 127	D. Pierce	Drama Critic, 4, 118	Sensational, 4, 121	8	1:41.80	32,150
1977 **Cascapedia**, 4, 126	S. Hawley	Rocky Trip, 5, 115	Just a Kick, 5, 118	6	1:40.80	31,250
1976 ***Bastonera II**, 5, 117	L. A. Pincay Jr.	Swingtime, 4, 120	Just a Kick, 4, 121	6	1:42.00	31,600
1975 **Modus Vivendi**, 4, 121	D. Pierce	*Tizna, 6, 124	Mercy Dee, 4, 111	6	1:42.00	32,100
1974 **Twixt**, 5, 123	W. J. Passmore	Tallahto, 4, 121	*La Zanzara, 4, 121	10	1:41.00	33,900
1973 **Minstrel Miss**, 6, 118	D. Pierce	Susan's Girl, 4, 128	Pallisima, 4, 115	6	1:41.80	38,000

Grade 1 1973-2004. Milady H. 1952-'95. 7 furlongs 1952-'53. 1 mile 1954, 1958-'66, 1970-'72, 1985. 6 furlongs 1955-'57. 1⅛ miles 1986-'87.

Mineshaft Handicap

Grade 3 in 2005. Fair Grounds, four-year-olds and up, 1¹/₁₆ miles, dirt. Held February 12, 2005, with a gross value of $100,000. First held in 1973. First graded in 2003. Stakes record 1:42.55 (1994 Cool Quaker).

Year	Winner	Jockey	Second	Third	Strs	Time	1st Purse
2005	**Wanderin Boy**, 4, 113	L. J. Melancon	Pollard's Vision, 4, 121	‡Gigawatt, 5, 115	9	1:43.08	$60,000
2004	**Olmodavor**, 5, 121	C. J. Lanerie	Spanish Empire, 4, 118	Almuhathir, 6, 114	9	1:45.59	60,000
2003	**Balto Star**, 5, 118	E. M. Martin Jr.	Mineshaft, 4, 116	Bonapaw, 7, 115	8	1:43.74	75,000
2002	**Valhol**, 6, 115	R. Albarado	Parade Leader, 5, 115	Fight for Ally, 5, 113	10	1:42.94	75,000
2001	**Include**, 4, 112	L. J. Meche	Connected, 4, 112	Kombat Kat, 4, 113	8	1:44.01	75,000
2000	**Take Note of Me**, 6, 118	R. Albarado	Crimson Classic, 6, 114	Nite Dreamer, 5, 116	6	1:42.94	75,000
1999	**Precocity**, 5, 117	E. M. Martin Jr.	Prory, 7, 114	Take Note of Me, 5, 117	5	1:43.42	75,000
1998	**Moonlight Dancer**, 6, 114	C. C. Bourque	Precocity, 4, 117	Hot Brush, 4, 113	7	1:44.34	75,000
1997	**Byars**, 4, 114	C. C. Bourque	Bucks Nephew, 7, 117	Clash by Night, 4, 113	7	1:44.47	60,000
1996	**Bucks Nephew**, 6, 116	C. Perret	Prory, 4, 114	Vast Joy, 4, 114	9	1:43.40	38,025
1995	**Adhocracy**, 5, 112	L. J. Melancon	Dynamic Brush, 5, 111	Cool Quaker, 6, 113	7	1:43.10	31,530
1994	**Cool Quaker**, 5, 114	E. M. Martin Jr.	Dixie Poker Ace, 7, 121	Dixieland Heat, 4, 114	6	**1:42.55**	31,005
1993	**West by West**, 4, 117	J. Samyn	Place Dancer, 4, 112	Genuine Meaning, 6, 113	5	1:43.80	18,885
1992	**Irish Swap**, 5, 118	B. E. Poyadou	Jarraar, 5, 113	Wild and Tingley, 5, 113	6	1:43.00	18,975
1985	**Rapid Gray**, 6, 122	R. P. Romero	Hopeful Word, 4, 113	Silver Diplomat, 4, 118	6	1:43.00	19,250

Named for W. S. Farish's 2003 Horse of the Year and '03 New Orleans H. (G2) winner Mineshaft. Formerly named for Calumet Farm's 1941, '42 Horse of the Year, '41 Triple Crown winner, and '42 Louisiana H. winner Whirlaway (1938 c. by *Blenheim II). Whirlaway H. 1985, 1992, 1998-2004. Whirlaway S. 1993-'97. Not held 1978-'80, 1982-'84, 1986-'91. 1 mile 40 yards 1973-'81. ‡Alumni Hall finished third, DQ to ninth for a positive drug test. Overnight handicap 1973-'77, 1981.

Mint Julep Handicap

Grade 3 in 2005. Churchill Downs, three-year-olds and up, fillies and mares, 1¹/₁₆ miles, turf. Held June 4, 2005, with a gross value of $110,100. First held in 1977. First graded in 2001. Stakes record 1:40.98 (1994 Words of War).

Year	Winner	Jockey	Second	Third	Strs	Time	1st Purse
2005	**Delta Princess**, 6, 117	R. Albarado	Shaconage, 5, 116	Erhu, 4, 112	7	1:42.43	$68,262
2004	**Stay Forever**, 7, 116	E. Castro	Sand Springs, 4, 120	Eternal Melody (NZ), 4, 115	9	1:42.66	104,346
2003	**Kiss the Devil**, 5, 115	L. J. Meche	Quick Tip, 5, 119	Cellars Shiraz, 4, 120	9	1:41.73	104,346
2002	**Megans Bluff**, 5, 118	C. Perret	Cozy Island, 4, 112	Solvig, 5, 117	8	1:42.87	69,998
2001	**Megans Bluff**, 4, 118	C. Perret	Sitka, 5, 109	Good Game, 4, 116	10	1:42.88	70,432
2000	**Pratella**, 5, 118	L. J. Melancon	Silver Comic, 4, 115	Histoire Sainte (Fr), 4, 113	8	1:43.08	69,378
1999	**Mingling Glances**, 5, 113	L. J. Melancon	Formal Tango, 4, 115	Red Cat, 4, 116	11	1:42.59	70,928
1998	**B. A. Valentine**, 5, 116	F. Torres	Lordy Lordy, 5, 113	Mingling Glances, 4, 112	9	1:41.42	70,804
1997	‡**Valor Lady**, 5, 114	R. Albarado	My Secret, 5, 114	Everhope, 4, 112	11	1:41.20	71,238
1996	**Bail Out Becky**, 4, 118	C. Perret	Country Cat, 4, 117	Fluffkins, 4, 115	8	1:41.86	54,698
1995	**Romy**, 4, 118	J. L. Diaz	Olden Lek, 5, 114	Memories (Ire), 4, 113	6	1:42.69	54,941
1994	**Words of War**, 5, 117	C. H. Marquez Jr.	Freewheel, 5, 116	Eurostorm, 4, 112	10	**1:40.98**	55,673
1993	**Classic Reign**, 4, 115	F. A. Arguello Jr.	Tap Routine, 4, 113	Liz Cee, 5, 114	10	1:42.84	37,375
1992	**Lady Shirl**, 5, 123	P. A. Johnson	Topsa, 5, 112	Behaving Dancer, 5, 119	10	1:41.41	37,083
1991	**Dance for Lucy**, 5, 116	L. J. Melancon	Welsh Muffin (Ire), 4, 113	Super Fan, 4, 118	10	1:43.07	37,148
1990	**Tunita**, 5, 114	R. J. Thibeau Jr.	Port St. Mary (GB), 4, 111	Flags Waving, 4, 112	8	1:43.80	25,821
	Phoenix Sunshine, 5, 116	J. Deegan	Vana Turns, 5, 111	Carousel Baby, 4, 111	8	1:43.20	31,476
1989	**Here's Your Silver**, 4, 115	M. McDowell	Lt. Lao, 5, 117	Danzig's Bride, 4, 114	10	1:50.40	37,115
1988	**How I Wish**, 4, 113	E. Fires	Gaily Gaily (Ire), 5, 113	No Choice, 5, 114	10	1:51.00	36,660
1987	**Thunderdome**, 4, 119	S. H. Bass	Acquire, 5, 119	No Choice, 4, 119	8	1:37.80	26,240
	Innsbruck (GB), 4, 114	S. Hawley	Fantasy Lover, 4, 114	Marianna's Girl, 4, 122	8	1:38.00	21,470
1986	**Zenobia Empress**, 5, 120	E. Fires	Donut's Pride, 4, 120	Ante, 5, 117	7	1:35.80	28,418
1985	**Stave**, 4, 117	C. R. Woods Jr.	Gerrie Singer, 4, 120	Switching Trick, 5, 117	10	1:35.00	21,694
1984	**Lass Trump**, 4, 111	G. Patterson	Lady Hawthorn, 4, 114	Delhousie, 4, 111	7	1:37.00	26,267
1983	**Naskra Magic**, 4, 114	P. Rubbicco	Excitable Lady, 5, 120	Charge My Account, 4, 112	6	1:36.60	23,433
1982	**Kate's Cabin**, 4, 115	E. Snell	Mean Martha, 4, 112	Forever Cordial, 5, 112	8	1:25.20	23,855
1981	**Lillian Russell**, 4, 118	R. J. Hirdes Jr.	Run Ky. Run, 4, 121	Salud, 4, 114	9	1:23.20	19,468

1980	**Likely Exchange**, 6, 118	D. E. Whited	Nauti Lass, 5, 119	Dearyouloveme, 4, 117	11	1:24.40	$19,728
1979	**Bold Rendezvous**, 4, 115	A. L. Fernandez	Likely Exchange, 5, 116	Popped Corn, 4, 116	10	1:25.00	17,908
1978	**Time for Pleasure**, 4, 120	T. Barrow	Don't Cry Barbi, 4, 119	Dear Irish, 4, 119	10	1:23.40	14,609
1977	**Satan's Cheer**, 5, 115	M. Manganello	Confort Zone, 4, 117	Decided Lady, 4, 115	7	1:24.00	14,300

Named for the traditional bourbon drink served at the Kentucky Derby. Sponsored by Early Times Distillery Co. of Louisville 2001-'05. Mint Julep S. 1982-'87, 1995-'96, 1998. 7 furlongs 1977-'82. 1 mile 1983-'87. 1⅛ miles 1988-'89. Three-year-olds and up 1988. Two divisions 1987, 1990. ‡Romy finished first, DQ to fourth, 1997. Course record 1992, 1994.

Modesty Handicap

Grade 3 in 2005. Arlington Park, three-year-olds and up, fillies and mares, 1³/₁₆ miles, turf. Held July 24, 2004, with a gross value of $150,000. First held in 1942. First graded in 1985. Stakes record 1:55 (1985 Kapalua Butterfly).

Year	Winner	Jockey	Second	Third	Strs	Time	1st Purse
2004	**Bedanken**, 5, 119	D. R. Pettinger	Aud, 4, 116	Shaconage, 4, 118	8	1:57.00	$90,000
2003	**Owsley**, 5, 120	R. R. Douglas	Bien Nicole, 5, 119	Beret, 4, 115	7	1:55.06	90,000
2002	**England's Legend (Fr)**, 5, 121	R. R. Douglas	Quick Tip, 4, 114	Innit (Ire), 4, 116	8	1:55.69	90,000
2001	**Ioya Two**, 6, 115	M. Guidry	Megans Bluff, 4, 118	Solvig, 4, 116	11	1:55.47	90,000
2000	**Wade for Me**, 5, 116	C. A. Emigh	Candleinthedark, 5, 113	Wild Heart Dancing, 4, 115	10	1:57.06	60,000
1997	**War Thief**, 5, 116	S. J. Sellers	My Secret (Jpn), 5, 114	Bog Wild, 4, 117	8	1:57.40	60,000
1996	**Belle of Cozzene**, 4, 114	D. R. Pettinger	Trick Attack, 5, 112	Naskra Colors, 4, 113	6	1:58.24	60,000
1994	**‡Assert Oneself**, 4, 115	F. H. Valenzuela	One Dreamer, 6, 117	Seventies, 4, 112	9	1:56.01	60,000
1993	**Hero's Love**, 5, 120	E. Fires	Villandry, 5, 114	Silvered, 6, 120	10	1:55.31	60,000
1992	**Tango Charlie**, 3, 114	A. G. Sorrows Jr.	Alcando (Ire), 6, 114	Hero's Love, 4, 117	13	1:58.79	45,000
1991	**Lady Shirl**, 4, 120	S. J. Sellers	Lyphover, 6, 114	Country Casual, 4, 114	10	1:56.53	45,000
1990	**Gaily Gaily (Ire)**, 7, 114	M. E. Smith	Coolawin, 4, 123	Marsha's Dancer, 4, 114	11	1:55.40	51,405
1989	**Gaily Gaily (Ire)**, 6, 123	J. A. Krone	Baba Cool (Ire), 4, 117	Coolawin, 3, 115	13	1:58.20	52,740
1987	**Spruce Luck**, 6, 114	D. Brumfield	Dancing On a Cloud, 4, 120	Autumn Glitter, 4, 114	9	1:51.60	34,080
1986	**Zenobia Empress**, 5, 118	E. Fires	Navarchus, 4, 112	Flying Girl (Fr), 4, 118	11	1:44.00	53,580
1985	**Kapalua Butterfly**, 4, 115	D. G. McHargue	Trinado, 4, 116	Another Penny, 4, 111	11	**1:55.00**	44,265
1984	**Jay's Sue**, 5, 123	P. Day	Dictina (Fr), 3, 109	Pretty Perfect, 4, 113	9	2:01.20	43,719
1983	**Dana Calqui (Arg)**, 5, 114	F. Lovato Jr.	Unknown Lady, 4, 113	Sarah's a Beauty, 5, 115	12	2:01.40	34,470
1982	**Office Wife**, 5, 113	E. Fires	Sprite Flight, 4, 112	Touch of Glamour, 4, 117	9	1:58.20	33,750
1981	**Innocent Victim**, 3, 108	R. W. Cox	Passolyn, 4, 113	Touch of Glamour, 3, 112	13	1:59.00	35,040
1980	**Allisons' Gal**, 4, 112	M. R. Morgan	La Bonzo, 4, 112	Jolie Dutch, 4, 114	14	2:01.20	35,160

Named for Modesty (1881 f. by War Dance), first female winner of the American Derby. Modesty S. 1942-'50, 1991-'93. Held at Washington Park 1942-'45, 1958-'61. Held at Hawthorne Race Course 1985. Not held 1969-'79, 1988, 1995, 1998-'99. 1 mile 1942, 1944-'46, 1952, 1966. 7 furlongs 1943, 1963-'65. 6 furlongs 1947-'51, 1953-'54, 1959-'62. 1¹/₁₆ miles 1955-'58, 1967-'68. 1⅛ miles 1987. Dirt 1942-'54, 1959-'65, 1996. Three-year-olds 1942. ‡Aube Indienne (Fr) finished first, DQ to seventh, 1994.

Molly Pitcher Breeders' Cup Handicap

Grade 2 in 2005. Monmouth Park, three-year-olds and up, fillies and mares, 1⅛ miles, dirt. Held July 4, 2004, with a gross value of $300,000. First held in 1946. First graded in 1973. Stakes record 1:48.63 (2002 Atelier).

Year	Winner	Jockey	Second	Third	Strs	Time	1st Purse
2004	**La Reason**, 4, 111	C. C. Lopez	Yell, 4, 114	Bare Necessities, 5, 119	7	1:51.00	$180,000
2003	**Summer Colony**, 5, 120	G. L. Stevens	She's Got the Beat, 4, 112	Call an Audible, 4, 110	4	1:51.83	180,000
2002	**Atelier**, 5, 115	E. Coa	Summer Colony, 4, 119	Spain, 5, 122	5	**1:48.63**	180,000
2001	**March Magic**, 4, 113	M. J. Luzzi	Vivid Sunset, 4, 112	Shine Again, 4, 113	7	1:43.79	180,000
2000	**Lu Ravi**, 5, 116	P. Day	Silverbulletday, 4, 118	Bella Chiarra, 5, 116	7	1:43.17	180,000
1999	**Heritage of Gold**, 4, 114	C. T. Lambert	Harpia, 5, 116	Tap to Music, 4, 116	6	1:41.76	180,000
1998	**Relaxing Rhythm**, 4, 116	P. Day	Minister's Melody, 4, 117	Glitter Woman, 4, 120	6	1:42.30	120,000
1997	**Rare Blend**, 4, 116	M. E. Smith	Top Secret, 4, 116	Chip, 4, 115	5	1:43.60	120,000
1996	**Halo America**, 6, 117	P. Day	Rogues Walk, 4, 116	Why Be Normal, 8, 112	6	1:41.75	120,000
1995	**Inside Information**, 4, 124	M. E. Smith	Jade Flush, 4, 115	Halo America, 5, 118	5	1:43.81	90,000
1994	**Hey Hazel**, 4, 114	R. C. Landry	Ann Dear, 4, 113	Future of Gold, 4, 110	6	1:46.41	120,000
1993	**Wilderness Song**, 5, 119	D. Clark	Quilma (Chi), 6, 117	Looie Capote, 4, 116	6	1:44.79	90,000
1992	**Versailles Treaty**, 4, 120	M. E. Smith	Quick Mischief, 6, 115	Cozzene's Wish, 5, 113	6	1:43.18	90,000
1991	**Valay Maid**, 4, 116	M. Castaneda	Train Robbery, 4, 112	Toffeefee, 4, 116	8	1:43.88	90,000
1990	**A Penny Is a Penny**, 5, 120	A. T. Gryder	Leave It Be, 5, 116	Bodacious Tatas, 5, 117	9	1:43.40	90,000
1989	**Bodacious Tatas**, 4, 111	R. Wilson	Make Change, 4, 112	Grecian Flight, 5, 122	5	1:42.40	90,000
1988	**Personal Ensign**, 4, 125	R. P. Romero	Grecian Flight, 4, 119	Le l'Argent, 6, 117	5	1:41.80	90,000
1987	**Reel Easy**, 4, 112	W. H. McCauley	Lady's Secret, 5, 125	Catatonic, 5, 117	8	1:42.00	99,300
1986	**Lady's Secret**, 4, 126	P. Day	Chaldea, 6, 114	Key Witness, 4, 112	4	1:41.20	95,610
1985	**Sefa's Beauty**, 6, 119	P. Day	Mitterand, 4, 119	Dowery, 4, 115	11	1:42.60	69,090
1984	**Sultry Sun**, 4, 116	M. Solomone	Quixotic Lady, 4, 118	Nany, 4, 114	10	1:41.60	68,640
1983	**Ambassador of Luck**, 4, 117	A. Graell	Kattegat's Pride, 4, 122	Dance Number, 4, 115	8	1:41.20	67,830
1982	**Jameela**, 6, 120	J. L. Kaenel	Pukka Princess, 4, 114	Prismatical, 4, 117	8	1:42.60	67,620
1981	**Weber City Miss**, 4, 119	R. Hernandez	Jameela, 5, 118	Wistful, 4, 121	6	1:44.00	49,455
1980	**Plankton**, 4, 120	V. A. Bracciale Jr.	Doing It My Way, 4, 114	Whose Bid, 4, 113	12	1:44.20	34,950
1979	**Navajo Princess**, 5, 120	C. Perret	Frosty Skater, 4, 121	Water Malone, 5, 116	9	1:43.40	36,335
1978	**Creme Wave**, 4, 114	D. MacBeth	Pearl Necklace, 4, 123	Flame Lily, 4, 110	8	1:45.20	36,530

1977	**Dottie's Doll**, 4, 113	C. Perret	Proud Delta, 5, 123	Mississippi Mud, 4, 115	11	1:41.80	$37,180
1976	**Garden Verse**, 4, 112	F. Lovato Sr.	Spring Is Here, 4, 111	Vodka Time, 4, 112	8	1:46.00	36,433
1975	**Honky Star**, 4, 123	J. E. Tejeira	Twixt, 6, 126	Bundler, 4, 119	9	1:43.00	36,156
1974	**Lady Love**, 4, 117	M. Hole	Ponte Vecchio, 4, 116	Belle Marie, 4, 117	8	1:43.80	28,908
1973	**Light Hearted**, 4, 120	E. Nelson	Wanda, 4, 118	Alma North, 5, 121	7	1:41.40	28,259

Named for Molly Pitcher, a woman who is renowned for handling a cannon during the Battle of Monmouth, New Jersey, during the Revolutionary War. Molly Pitcher H. 1946-'95. 1¹/₁₆ miles 1946-2001.

Monmouth Breeders' Cup Oaks

Grade 3 in 2005. Monmouth Park, three-year-olds, fillies, 1¹/₁₆ miles, dirt. Held August 15, 2004, with a gross value of $200,000. First held in 1871. First graded in 1973. Stakes record 1:41.92 (1997 Blushing K. D.).

Year	Winner	Jockey	Second	Third	Strs	Time	1st Purse
2004	**Capeside Lady**, 3, 115	C. P. DeCarlo	Hopelessly Devoted, 3, 118	Habiboo, 3, 115	6	1:42.18	$120,000
2002	**Magic Storm**, 3, 112	E. L. King Jr.	Alternate, 3, 114	Bronze Autumn, 3, 114	5	1:51.17	150,000
2001	**Unbridled Elaine**, 3, 121	E. Coa	Unrestrained, 3, 112	Indy Glory, 3, 114	7	1:51.02	150,000
2000	**Spain**, 3, 114	J. A. Velez Jr.	North Lake Jane, 3, 116	Prized Stamp, 3, 114	7	1:42.78	150,000
1999	**Silverbulletday**, 3, 121	J. D. Bailey	Boom Town Girl, 3, 121	Bag Lady Jane, 3, 116	4	1:43.03	150,000
1998	**Kirby's Song**, 3, 121	T. Kabel	Santaria, 3, 114	Brave Deed, 3, 112	6	1:43.31	120,000
1997	**Blushing K. D.**, 3, 121	L. J. Meche	Holiday Ball, 3, 116	Snowy Apparition, 3, 121	7	**1:41.92**	120,000
1996	**Top Secret**, 3, 114	J. Bravo	Yanks Music, 3, 121	Mesabi Maiden, 3, 115	5	1:42.33	120,000
1995	**Kathie's Colleen**, 3, 112	J. McAleney	Gal in a Ruckus, 3, 121	Country Cat, 3, 121	5	1:51.50	90,000
1994	**Two Altazano**, 3, 121	C. Perret	Stellarina, 3, 118	Cavada, 3, 121	5	1:52.19	90,000
1993	**Jacody**, 3, 121	T. G. Turner	Deputy Jane West, 3, 121	Sheila's Revenge, 3, 114	5	1:50.77	90,000
1992	**Diamond Duo**, 3, 121	T. G. Turner	dh-C. C.'s Return, 3, 114		8	1:51.40	90,000
			dh-Secretly, 3, 112				
1991	**Fowda**, 3, 121	R. Migliore	Shared Interest, 3, 114	Nalees Pin, 3, 116	5	1:50.48	90,000
1990	**Pampered Star**, 3, 121	J. C. Ferrer	Valay Maid, 3, 121	Jefforee, 3, 112	9	1:52.40	90,000
1989	**Dream Deal**, 3, 114	C. Perret	Some Romance, 3, 121	Top of My Life, 3, 121	9	1:49.20	90,000
1988	**Maplejinsky**, 3, 113	C. W. Antley	Make Change, 3, 114	Mother of Eight, 3, 114	6	1:53.60	102,000
1987	**Without Feathers**, 3, 116	C. W. Antley	Single Blade, 3, 121	Grecian Flight, 3, 121	8	1:48.00	66,240
1986	**Fighter Fox**, 3, 114	W. H. McCauley	Toes Knows, 3, 114	Dynamic Star, 3, 118	12	1:49.60	97,170
1985	**Golden Horde**, 3, 116	W. H. McCauley	Koluctoo's Jill, 3, 121	Tabayour, 3, 118	9	1:48.00	94,380
1984	**Life's Magic**, 3, 121	J. Velasquez	Flippers, 3, 118	Cassowary, 3, 112	10	1:50.00	94,050
1983	**Quixotic Lady**, 3, 116	E. Maple	Am Capable, 3, 114	Pop Rock, 3, 116	5	1:50.40	64,770
1982	**Christmas Past**, 3, 121	J. Vasquez	Milingo, 3, 119	Mademoiselle Forli, 3, 112	9	1:49.40	67,050
1981	**Prismatical**, 3, 117	D. Brumfield	Stunning Native, 3, 112	Privacy, 3, 117	7	1:49.80	49,500
1980	**Rose of Morn**, 3, 114	D. Brumfield	Weber City Miss, 3, 121	Sami Sutton, 3, 117	7	1:50.40	33,030
1979	**Burn's Return**, 3, 117	J. Vasquez	Heavenly Ade, 3, 114	Dominant Dream, 3, 114	8	1:48.80	35,718
1978	**Sharp Belle**, 3, 117	D. B. Thomas	Mucchina, 3, 119	Jevalin, 3, 117	8	1:52.40	35,783
1977	**Small Raja**, 3, 121	M. Solomone	Herecomesthebride, 3, 117	Suede Shoe, 3, 116	8	1:49.60	35,978
1976	**Revidere**, 3, 121	J. Vasquez	Javamine, 3, 112	Quacker, 3, 114	9	1:50.60	36,238
1975	**Aunt Jin**, 3, 119	C. H. Marquez	Let Me Linger, 3, 112	Sarsar, 3, 121	6	1:49.20	35,295
1974	**Honky Star**, 3, 117	W. Blum	Kudara, 3, 117	Raisela, 3, 117	14	1:49.40	38,642
1973	**Desert Vixen**, 3, 114	M. Hole	Ladies Agreement, 3, 111	Lady Love, 3, 111	11	1:49.00	37,473

Monmouth Oaks 1871-'75, 1977-'95. Held at Jerome Park 1891. Not held 1878, 1894-1945, 2003. 1¹/₂ miles 1871-'77. 1¹/₄ miles 1879-'93. 1¹/₈ miles 1953-'95, 2001-'03. Dead heat for second 1992.

Monrovia Handicap

Grade 3 in 2005. Santa Anita Park, three-year-olds and up, fillies and mares, 6¹/₂ furlongs, dirt (originally scheduled as a Grade 3 on the turf). Held December 31, 2004, with a gross value of $113,550. First held in 1968. First graded in 1973. Stakes record 1:15.34 (2004 Resplendency).

Year	Winner	Jockey	Second	Third	Strs	Time	1st Purse
2004	**Resplendency**, 3, 112	C. Fusilier	Puxa Saco, 4, 115	Market Garden, 4, 115	9	**1:15.34**	$68,130
2003	**Icantgoforthat**, 4, 114	T. Baze	Polygreen (Fr), 4, 116	Spring Star (Fr), 4, 119	6	1:13.07	65,580
2002	**Lil Sister Stich**, 5, 117	L. A. Pincay Jr.	Pina Colada (GB), 3, 115	I'm the Business (NZ), 5, 116	12	1:13.81	68,820
2001	**Paga (Arg)**, 4, 117	M. E. Smith	Twin Set (Ger), 4, 115	Impeachable, 4, 115	13	1:15.09	70,890
2000	**Evening Promise (GB)**, 4, 120	K. J. Desormeaux	Squall Linda, 4, 113	New Heaven (Arg), 6, 119	12	1:15.22	68,640
1999	**Show Me the Stage**, 3, 117	K. J. Desormeaux	Chichim, 4, 116	Honest Lady, 3, 114	4	1:15.14	64,140
	Desert Lady (Ire), 4, 117	C. S. Nakatani	Sweet Mazarine (Ire), 5, 118	Supercilious, 6, 119	7	1:14.59	65,100
1998	**Madame Pandit**, 5, 118	E. J. Delahoussaye	Ski Dancer, 6, 115	Dixie Pearl, 6, 117	7	1:15.80	65,700
1997	**Grab the Prize**, 5, 116	A. O. Solis	Finite E. F., 4, 111	Evil's Pic, 5, 116	7	1:16.89	66,900
1996	**Klassy Kim**, 5, 116	G. F. Almeida	Ski Dancer, 4, 116	Baby Diamonds, 5, 114	8	1:14.48	65,650
1995	**Rabiadella**, 4, 117	P. A. Valenzuela	Dezibelle's Star, 4, 113	Las Meninas (Ire), 4, 120	5	1:14.92	47,450
1994	**Mamselle Bebette**, 4, 117	C. S. Nakatani	Shugglesown, 4, 116	Kalita Melody (GB), 6, 117	6	1:15.35	49,650
1993	**Glen Kate (Ire)**, 6, 118	C. A. Black	Bel's Starlet, 6, 122	Heart of Joy, 6, 121	7	1:12.89	48,650
1992	**Middlefork Rapids**, 4, 116	P. A. Valenzuela	Remarkably Easy, 4, 115	Crystal Gazing, 4, 121	11	1:12.55	51,150
1991	**Wedding Bouquet (Ire)**, 4, 115	K. J. Desormeaux	Linda Card, 5, 118	Flower Girl (GB), 4, 116	11	1:13.90	51,875
1990	**Down Again**, 6, 117	C. A. Black	Sexy Slew, 4, 111	Hot Novel, 4, 116	9	1:13.00	50,200
1989	**Daloma (Fr)**, 5, 117	F. H. Valenzuela	Valdemosa (Arg), 5, 116	Sadie B. Fast, 4, 116	8	1:16.20	49,550
1988	**Aberuschka (Ire)**, 6, 121	G. L. Stevens	Pen Bal Lady (GB), 4, 118	Aberuschka (Ire), 5, 124	10	1:14.60	50,050
1987	**Sari's Heroine**, 4, 117	P. A. Valenzuela	Lichi (Chi), 7, 116	Aberuschka (Ire), 5, 124	7	1:15.00	38,400

1986	Water Crystals, 5, 116	G. L. Stevens	Baroness Direct, 5, 120	Solva (GB), 5, 116	8	1:15.60	$40,100
1985	Lina Cavalieri (GB), 5, 121	E. J. Delahoussaye	Air Distingue, 5, 117	Tangent (NZ), 5, 121	8	1:14.00	39,650
1984	Tangent (NZ), 4, 117	J. A. Garcia	Irish O'Brien, 6, 115	Frieda Frame, 6, 119	10	1:14.60	41,750
1983	Matching, 5, 123	R. Sibille	Irish O'Brien, 5, 115	Night Fire, 4, 115	9	1:13.20	40,600
1982	Cat Girl, 4, 117	C. J. McCarron	Excitable Lady, 4, 122	Chateau Dancer, 4, 117	10	1:14.60	41,250
1981	Kilijaro (Ire), 5, 127	M. Castaneda	Love You Dear, 5, 115	She Can't Miss, 4, 119	10	1:12.40	34,950
1980	Fondre, 5, 118	F. Olivares	Powder Room, 5, 117	Celine, 4, 118	8	1:15.20	27,500
1979	Camarado, 4, 119	W. Shoemaker	Pet Label, 6, 115	Sister Julie, 6, 115	11	1:15.40	22,900
	Palmistry, 4, 114	C. J. McCarron	Sing Back, 6, 113	Pressing Date, 5, 114	10	1:15.20	22,500
1978	Little Happiness, 4, 116	L. A. Pincay Jr.	Perils of Pauline, 4, 115	Harvest Girl, 4, 119	6	1:16.00	26,200
1977	Winter Solstice, 5, 119	M. S. Sellers	Nana Lee, 5, 116	Olive Wreath, 4, 113	9	1:13.60	27,600
1976	Winter Solstice, 4, 117	J. Lambert	Miss Tokyo, 4, 121	Exotic Age, 5, 115	7	1:17.60	20,300
1975	‡Special Goddess, 4, 119	S. Hawley	Charger's Star, 5, 115	Miss Musket, 4, 124	8	1:13.80	20,700
1974	Viva La Vivi, 4, 118	D. Pierce	Impressive Style, 5, 120	Charger's Star, 4, 113	9	1:15.00	17,800
1973	*Tizna, 4, 119	F. Toro	Generous Portion, 5, 120	‡Soul Mate, 4, 120	11	1:13.80	22,700

Named for railroad pioneer W. N. Monroe (1841-1935), founder of the city of Monrovia, California. Not graded 1975-'89. Not graded when taken off turf 2004. 6½ furlongs 1969-'70, 1976, 1978, 1980, 1989, 1994, 1997-'99. Dirt 1969-'70, 1976, 1978, 1980, 1989, 1994, 1997-'99. Originally scheduled on turf 2004. Four-year-olds and up 1968-'98, 1999 (January). Two divisions 1979. Held in January and December 1999. ‡*Rich Return II finished third, DQ to fourth, 1973. ‡Viva La Vivi finished first, DQ to eighth, 1975.

Morvich Handicap

Grade 3 in 2005. Santa Anita Park, three-year-olds and up, about 6½ furlongs, turf. Held October 30, 2004, with a gross value of $100,000. First held in 1974. First graded in 1999. Stakes record 1:11.46 (2001 El Cielo).

Year	Winner	Jockey	Second	Third	Strs	Time	1st Purse
2004	Leroidesanimaux (Brz), 4, 117	J. K. Court	De Valmont (Aus), 7, 115	Cayoke (Fr), 7, 116	6	1:11.76	$60,000
2003	King Robyn, 3, 117	A. O. Solis	Medecis (GB), 4, 116	Geronimo (Chi), 4, 115	9	1:13.22	66,480
2002	Master Belt (NZ), 4, 114	T. Baze	I Love Silver, 4, 116	Kachamandi (Chi), 5, 117	10	1:12.26	67,020
2001	El Cielo, 7, 123	J. Valdivia Jr.	Speak in Passing, 4, 116	Islander, 6, 115	6	1:11.46	64,680
2000	El Cielo, 6, 119	J. Valdivia Jr.	Kahal (GB), 6, 119	Montemiro (Fr), 6, 116	10	1:12.00	67,020
1999	‡Riviera (Fr), 5, 118	B. Blanc	Kahal (GB), 5, 114	Howbaddouwantit, 4, 121	10	1:12.99	66,840
1998	Musafi, 4, 117	G. K. Gomez	Fabulous Guy (Ire), 4, 114	Expelled, 6, 119	8	1:14.54	60,000
1997	Reality Road, 5, 115	C. S. Nakatani	Latin Dancer, 3, 116	Torch Rouge (GB), 6, 115	7	1:13.60	60,000
1996	Comininalittlehot, 5, 117	K. J. Desormeaux	Wild Zone, 6, 116	Wavy Run (Ire), 5, 116	7	1:11.57	65,100
1995	Score Quick, 3, 113	G. F. Almeida	Dramatic Gold, 4, 120	Fu Man Slew, 4, 114	7	1:14.64	60,700
1994	Rotsaluck, 3, 115	F. H. Valenzuela	D'Hallevant, 4, 118	Didyme, 4, 115	7	1:13.66	47,925
1993	†Western Approach, 4, 115	K. J. Desormeaux	†Yousefia, 4, 116	Exemplary Leader, 7, 115	6	1:12.12	47,025
1992	Regal Groom, 5, 118	M. A. Pedroza	Bailarin, 5, 112	Repriced, 4, 118	8	1:16.88	45,150
1991	Waterscape, 5, 119	K. J. Desormeaux	Hollywood Reporter, 5, 113	Anjiz, 3, 115	6	1:11.95	47,250
1990	Yes I'm Blue, 4, 116	D. R. Flores	Waterscape, 4, 115	Oraibi, 5, 118	9	1:12.40	49,350
1989	Basic Rate, 4, 113	R. Q. Meza	Patchy Groundfog, 6, 118	Major Current, 5, 116	12	1:12.20	52,125
1988	Dr. Brent, 3, 115	F. Toro	†Serve n' Volley (GB), 4, 115	Caballo de Oro, 4, 114	12	1:15.80	51,350
1987	Sabona, 5, 117	C. J. McCarron	†Aberuschka (Ire), 5, 117	Deputy Governor, 3, 118	8	1:14.80	38,900
1986	River Drummer, 4, 121	G. L. Stevens	Prince Sky (Ire), 4, 118	Perfec Travel, 4, 116	11	1:13.80	69,700
1985	Dear Rick, 4, 118	C. J. McCarron	Champagne Bid, 6, 121	Hegemony (Ire), 4, 121	8	1:14.20	38,650
1984	Tsunami Slew, 3, 119	E. J. Delahoussaye	Night Mover, 4, 121	Debonaire Junior, 3, 120	8	1:14.00	39,000
1983	Kangroo Court, 6, 119	J. J. Steiner	Shanekite, 5, 120	Dave's Friend, 8, 121	7	1:16.00	38,350
1982	Shanekite, 4, 115	S. Hawley	Remember John, 3, 120	Smokite, 6, 117	7	1:12.80	37,050
1981	Forlion, 5, 116	M. Castaneda	Aristocratical, 4, 117	Syncopate, 6, 122	8	1:13.80	32,800
1980	To B. Or Not, 4, 118	M. Castaneda	Someonenoble, 5, 115	†Great Lady M., 5, 119	9	1:13.80	32,200
1979	Arachnoid, 6, 119	D. Pierce	He's Dewan, 4, 118	Bywayofchicago, 5, 120	6	1:12.60	25,150
1978	Impressive Luck, 5, 119	F. Toro	Bad 'n Big, 4, 126	Eagle in Flight, 7, 114	6	1:13.20	25,250
1977	Impressive Luck, 4, 118	F. Toro	Jumping Hill, 5, 120	Key Account, 5, 115	9	1:13.60	19,650
1976	Cherry River, 6, 120	L. A. Pincay Jr.	Mark's Place, 4, 119	Uniformity, 4, 117	10	1:13.40	20,400
1975	Century's Envoy, 4, 125	J. Lambert	Sir Jason, 4, 117	Cherry River, 5, 123	6	1:13.40	15,900
1974	Palladium, 5, 115	A. Pineda	Against the Snow, 4, 118	Soft Victory, 6, 119	6	1:16.20	15,800

Named for Benjamin Block's 1921 champion two-year-old colt and '22 Kentucky Derby winner Morvich (1919 c. by Runnymede); Morvich was the race's first California-bred winner. 6½ furlongs 1983, 1992, 1995. Dirt 1983, 1992, 1995. Two-year-olds and up 1974-'92. ‡Kahal (GB) finished first, DQ to second, 1999. †Denotes female.

Mother Goose Stakes

Grade 1 in 2005. Belmont Park, three-year-olds, fillies, 1⅛ miles, dirt. Held June 26, 2004, with a gross value of $300,000. First held in 1957. First graded in 1965. Stakes record 1:46.58 (1994 Lakeway).

Year	Winner	Jockey	Second	Third	Strs	Time	1st Purse
2004	Stellar Jayne, 3, 121	R. Albarado	Ashado, 3, 121	Island Sand, 3, 121	6	1:48.13	$180,000
2003	Spoken Fur, 3, 121	J. D. Bailey	Yell, 3, 121	Final Round, 3, 121	6	1:50.41	180,000
2002	Nonsuch Bay, 3, 121	J. D. Bailey	Chamrousse, 3, 121	Seba (GB), 3, 121	4	1:49.09	150,000
2001	Fleet Renee, 3, 121	J. R. Velazquez	Real Cozzy, 3, 121	Exogenous, 3, 121	10	1:47.19	150,000
2000	Secret Status, 3, 121	P. Day	Jostle, 3, 121	Finder's Fee, 3, 121	7	1:48.03	150,000
1999	Dreams Gallore, 3, 121	R. Albarado	Oh What a Windfall, 3, 121	Better Than Honour, 3, 121	6	1:48.69	150,000

1998	**Jersey Girl**, 3, 121	M. E. Smith	Keeper Hill, 3, 121	Banshee Breeze, 3, 121	11	1:47.77	$120,000
1997	**Ajina**, 3, 121	M. E. Smith	Sharp Cat, 3, 121	Tomisue's Delight, 3, 121	6	1:48.40	120,000
1996	**Yanks Music**, 3, 121	J. R. Velazquez	Escena, 3, 121	Cara Rafaela, 3, 121	7	1:47.90	120,000
1995	**Serena's Song**, 3, 121	G. L. Stevens	Golden Bri, 3, 121	Forested, 3, 121	6	1:50.37	120,000
1994	**Lakeway**, 3, 121	K. J. Desormeaux	Cinnamon Sugar (Ire), 3, 121	Inside Information, 3, 121	6	**1:46.58**	120,000
1993	**Sky Beauty**, 3, 121	M. E. Smith	Dispute, 3, 121	Silky Feather, 3, 121	4	1:49.69	120,000
1992	**Turnback the Alarm**, 3, 121	C. W. Antley	Easy Now, 3, 121	Queen of Triumph, 3, 121	7	1:48.80	120,000
1991	**Meadow Star**, 3, 121	J. D. Bailey	Lite Light, 3, 121	Nalees Pin, 3, 121	4	1:48.92	120,000
1990	**Go for Wand**, 3, 121	R. P. Romero	Charon, 3, 121	Stella Madrid, 3, 121	6	1:48.80	136,560
1989	**Open Mind**, 3, 121	A. T. Cordero Jr.	Gorgeous, 3, 121	Nite of Fun, 3, 121	5	1:47.40	136,320
1988	**Goodbye Halo**, 3, 121	J. Velasquez	Make Change, 3, 121	Aptostar, 3, 121	9	1:49.80	142,320
1987	**Fiesta Gal**, 3, 121	A. T. Cordero Jr.	Grecian Flight, 3, 121	Chic Shirine, 3, 121	12	1:50.20	150,240
1986	**Life At the Top**, 3, 121	J. A. Santos	Dynamic Star, 3, 121	Family Style, 3, 121	8	1:49.60	132,300
1985	**Mom's Command**, 3, 121	A. Fuller	Le l'Argent, 3, 121	Willowy Mood, 3, 121	11	1:49.60	109,800
1984	**Life's Magic**, 3, 121	J. Velasquez	Miss Oceana, 3, 121	Wild Applause, 3, 121	5	1:48.80	127,620
1983	**Able Money**, 3, 121	A. Graell	High Schemes, 3, 121	Far Flying, 3, 121	7	1:49.20	84,150
1982	**Cupecoy's Joy**, 3, 121	A. Santiago	Christmas Past, 3, 121	Blush With Pride, 3, 121	12	1:48.40	69,120
1981	**Wayward Lass**, 3, 121	C. B. Asmussen	Heavenly Cause, 3, 121	Banner Gala, 3, 121	8	1:48.80	66,720
1980	**Sugar and Spice**, 3, 121	J. Fell	Bold 'n Determined, 3, 121	Erin's Word, 3, 121	8	1:49.60	68,040
1979	**Davona Dale**, 3, 121	J. Velasquez	Eloquent, 3, 121	Plankton, 3, 121	6	1:48.80	63,960
1978	**Caesar's Wish**, 3, 121	D. R. Wright	Lakeville Miss, 3, 121	Tempest Queen, 3, 121	8	1:47.60	48,600
1977	**Road Princess**, 3, 121	J. Cruguet	Mrs. Warren, 3, 121	Cum Laude Laurie, 3, 121	16	1:48.80	51,840
1976	**Girl in Love**, 3, 121	J. Cruguet	Optimistic Gal, 3, 121	Ancient Fables, 3, 121	5	1:48.80	48,510
1975	**Ruffian**, 3, 121	J. Vasquez	Sweet Old Girl, 3, 121	Sun and Snow, 3, 121	7	1:47.80	50,220
1974	**Chris Evert**, 3, 121	J. Velasquez	Maud Muller, 3, 121	Quaze Quilt, 3, 121	14	1:48.60	53,775
1973	**Windy's Daughter**, 3, 121	E. Belmonte	Lady Love, 3, 121	North Broadway, 3, 121	10	1:48.40	52,965

Named for Harry Payne Whitney's consensus 1924 champion two-year-old filly and '24 Fashion S. winner Mother Goose (1922 f. by *Chicle). Held at Aqueduct 1963-'67, 1969, 1975. 1¹/₁₆ miles 1957-'58.

Mr. Prospector Handicap

Grade 3 in 2005. Gulfstream Park, three-year-olds and up, 6 furlongs, dirt. Held January 8, 2005, with a gross value of $100,000. First held in 1946. First graded in 1999. Stakes record 1:08.45 (1997 Punch Line).

Year	Winner	Jockey	Second	Third	Strs	Time	1st Purse
2005	Saratoga County, 4, 112	J. Castellano	Limehouse, 4, 116	All Hail Stormy, 4, 113	10	1:08.99	$60,000
2004	Cajun Beat, 4, 121	C. H. Velasquez	Gygistar, 5, 118	Deer Lake, 5, 115	6	1:09.06	60,000
2003	Baileys Edge, 6, 114	G. Boulanger	Friendly Frolic, 4, 114	Out of Fashion, 7, 115	6	1:09.95	60,000
2002	Hook and Ladder, 5, 116	J. R. Velazquez	Kipperscope, 5, 114	Red's Honor, 4, 114	8	1:09.69	60,000
2001	Istintaj, 5, 116	J. D. Bailey	Miners Gamble, 5, 115	Smokin Pete, 4, 115	13	1:09.63	60,000
2000	Mountain Top, 5, 115	J. A. Santos	Lifeisawhirl, 4, 112	Silver Season, 4, 115	6	1:10.80	45,000
1999	Cowboy Cop, 5, 114	P. Day	Good and Tough, 4, 115	Mint, 4, 115	6	1:09.65	45,000
1998	Rare Rock, 5, 116	P. Day	Heckofaralph, 5, 115	Banjo, 4, 114	8	1:08.67	45,000
1997	Punch Line, 7, 116	P. Day	Appealing Skier, 4, 119	Constant Escort, 5, 115	8	**1:08.45**	45,000
1996	Meadow Monster, 5, 114	R. Wilson	Lord Carson, 4, 119	Ponche, 7, 118	8	1:09.47	30,000
1995	Sweet Beast, 5, 118	M. E. Smith	Exclusive Praline, 4, 119	Distinct Reality, 4, 113	5	1:09.36	30,000
1994	Binalong, 5, 116	J. D. Bailey	I Can't Believe, 6, 113	Golden Pro, 4, 113	12	1:09.68	30,000
1993	Surely Six, 4, 113	R. Wilson	Groomstick, 7, 114	Poulain d'Or, 4, 117	9	1:21.85	30,000
1992	Take Me Out, 4, 115	J. D. Bailey	Gizmo's Fortune, 4, 111	Ocala Flame, 4, 113	10	1:23.75	30,000
1991	Stalker, 4, 114	C. Perret	Secret Hello, 4, 117	Shuttleman, 5, 114	11	1:22.50	30,000
1990	Beau Genius, 5, 117	W. Shoemaker	The Red Rolls, 6, 112	Norquestor, 4, 116	6	1:23.20	30,000
1989	Miami Slick, 4, 112	J. D. Bailey	Dancing Spree, 4, 114	The Red Rolls, 5, 112	6	1:09.20	34,200
1988	Jato D'Agua (Brz), 6, 110	W. A. Guerra	Banbury Cross, 5, 111	Our Happy Warrior, 4, 110	11	1:09.80	37,560
1987	Uncle Ho, 4, 111	J. A. Santos	Splendid Catch, 5, 113	Mugatea, 7, 114	7	1:22.60	27,984
1986	Fortunate Prospect, 5, 118	R. I. Velez	It's a Done Deal, 4, 113	Basket Weave, 5, 115	8	1:10.40	28,608
1985	For Halo, 4, 120	B. Fann	Northern Trader, 4, 115	Rupert's Wing, 4, 111	11	1:09.60	37,620
1984	D. White, 3, 112	A. O. Solis	Mo Exception, 3, 112	Reach for More, 3, 117	7	1:44.40	24,276
1983	Chan Balum, 4, 111	J. Samyn	Center Cut, 4, 118	Royal Hierarchy, 6, 114	10	1:10.00	25,683
1982	Noble Warrior, 6, 119	O. J. Londono	Morold (Fr), 7, 114	San Sal, 4, 110	9	2:27.20	18,585
1980	Archie Beamish, 7, 111	W. A. Guerra	Proud Manner, 6, 114	Foretake, 4, 115	7	2:27.20	14,970
1978	Practitioner, 5, 121	J. A. Santiago	Unilateral, 4, 110	Odd Man, 7, 113	8	3:18.20	14,520

Named for Aisco Stable's 1987, '88 leading North American sire Mr. Prospector (1970 c. by Raise a Native), who set a six-furlong track record at Gulfstream Park in 1973. Formerly named for Hallandale, Florida, location of Gulfstream Park. Hallandale H. 1946-2000. Not held 1949, 1957-'77, 1979, 1981. 1¹/₁₆ miles 1946, 1984. 1¹/₈ miles 1947-'56. About 2 miles 1978. 1¹/₂ miles 1980, 1982. 7 furlongs 1987, 1990-'93. Turf 1978-'82. Three-year-olds 1946, 1984. Four-year-olds and up 1947. Held as an allowance race 1950-'55.

Mrs. Revere Stakes

Grade 2 in 2005. Churchill Downs, three-year-olds, fillies, 1¹/₁₆ miles, turf. Held November 13, 2004, with a gross value of $171,150. First held in 1991. First graded in 1995. Stakes record 1:42.86 (2001 Snow Dance).

Year	Winner	Jockey	Second	Third	Strs	Time	1st Purse
2004	River Belle (GB), 3, 120	K. Fallon	Lenatareese, 3, 120	Cape Town Lass, 3, 114	10	1:44.59	$106,113
2003	Hoh Buzzard (Ire), 3, 120	R. Fogelsonger	Aud, 3, 120	Gamble to Victory, 3, 116	12	1:45.01	108,903

Year	Winner	Jockey	Second	Third	Strs	Time	1st Purse
2002	Caught in the Rain, 3, 119	E. L. King Jr.	Glia, 3, 119	Bedanken, 3, 122	11	1:46.25	$107,694
2001	Snow Dance, 3, 122	C. Perret	Stylish, 3, 115	Cozy Island, 3, 111	10	1:42.86	106,950
2000	Megans Bluff, 3, 122	M. Guidry	Uncharted Haven (GB), 3, 119	Impending Bear, 3, 119	12	1:43.37	107,973
1999	Silver Comic, 3, 115	L. J. Melancon	St Clair Ridge (Ire), 3, 119	Circle of Gold (Ire), 3, 119	12	1:45.13	108,345
1998	Anguilla, 3, 119	P. Day	Darling Alice, 3, 119	White Beauty, 3, 119	11	1:45.67	107,601
1997	Parade Queen, 3, 122	P. Day	Mystery Code, 3, 117	Starry Dreamer, 3, 122	11	1:45.46	108,624
1996	Maxzene, 3, 117	J. A. Krone	Fasta, 3, 117	Turkappeal, 3, 119	12	1:43.78	72,354
1995	Petrouchka, 3, 122	D. Penna	Christmas Gift, 3, 122	Ms. Isadora, 3, 117	11	1:44.20	75,725
1994	Mariah's Storm, 3, 122	R. N. Lester	Avie's Fancy, 3, 119	Bear Truth, 3, 119	10	1:43.99	75,400
1993	Weekend Madness (Ire), 3, 117	C. R. Woods Jr.	Flower Circle, 3, 117	Amal Hayati, 3, 122	10	1:46.32	74,685
1992	McKaymackenna, 3, 119	J. Velasquez	Spinning Round, 3, 122	Aquilegia, 3, 117	10	1:45.04	56,209
1991	Spanish Parade, 3, 117	P. Day	Liz Cee, 3, 117	Savethelastdance, 3, 117	10	1:46.19	37,408

Named for Dr. Hiram Polk Jr.'s and Dr. David Richardson's 1984 Dogwood, Edgewood, and Regret S. winner Mrs. Revere (1981 f. by Silver Series). Grade 3 1995-'97.

My Charmer Handicap

Grade 3 in 2005. Calder Race Course, three-year-olds and up, fillies and mares, 1 1/8 miles, turf. Held December 4, 2004, with a gross value of $100,000. First held in 1984. First graded in 1998. Stakes record 1:44.74 (1992 Lady Shirl).

Year	Winner	Jockey	Second	Third	Strs	Time	1st Purse
2004	Something Ventured, 5, 115	J. R. Velazquez	Snowdrops (GB), 4, 115	Changing World, 4, 117	12	1:46.79	$60,000
2003	New Economy, 5, 115	R. B. Homeister Jr.	Something Ventured, 4, 114	Ivanavinalot, 3, 113	12	1:46.90	60,000
2002	Wander Mom, 4, 114	E. Coa	Strawberry Blonde (Ire), 4, 114	Babae (Chi), 6, 121	10	1:48.43	60,000
2001	Batique, 5, 116	J. F. Chavez	Please Sign In, 5, 114	Wander Mom, 3, 114	12	1:49.85	60,000
2000	‡Wild Heart Dancing, 4, 116	J. F. Chavez	Megans Bluff, 3, 116	Orange Sunset (Ire), 4, 114	12	1:47.58	60,000
1999	Crystal Symphony, 3, 114	C. H. Velasquez	Winfama, 6, 114	Khumba Mela (Ire), 4, 120	11	1:47.65	60,000
1998	Colcon, 5, 118	J. D. Bailey	Cuando, 4, 117	Winfama, 5, 117	12	1:50.51	60,000
1997	Overcharger, 5, 116	J. A. Rivera II	Dance Clear (Ire), 4, 113	Hero's Pride (Fr), 4, 116	12	1:48.18	60,000
1996	Romy, 5, 114	F. C. Torres	Delta Love, 3, 114	Ms. Mostly, 3, 115	7	1:47.33	60,000
1995	Danish (Ire), 4, 116	J. A. Santos	Cox Orange, 5, 119	Alice Springs, 5, 123	11	1:46.40	60,000
1994	Caress, 3, 114	R. G. Davis	Putthepowdertoit, 4, 114	Cox Orange, 4, 116	12	1:50.63	60,000
1993	Chickasha, 4, 115	R. D. Lopez	Marshua's River, 6, 113	Always Nettie, 4, 114	14	1:47.36	30,000
1992	Explosive Kate, 5, 118	D. Penna	Mia Bird Too, 3, 113	Kiwi Mint, 4, 114	9	1:46.58	30,000
	Julie La Rousse (Ire), 4, 120	J. D. Bailey	Marshua's River, 4, 114	Highland Crystal, 4, 115	10	1:45.78	30,000
	Lady Shirl, 5, 120	E. Fires	Ratings, 4, 115	Seaquay, 6, 111	11	1:44.74	51,150
1990	Primetime North, 3, 112	W. S. Ramos	Igmaar (Fr), 4, 112	Be Exclusive (Ire), 4, 113	11	1:45.60	27,825
1989	Princess Mora, 3, 111	M. A. Gonzalez	Coolawin, 3, 118	Yestday's Kisses, 3, 115	13	1:47.60	36,000
1988	Sunny Issues, 3, 109	W. A. Guerra	Beauty Cream, 5, 119	Miss Unnameable, 4, 112	10	1:45.40	28,830
	Judy's Red Shoes, 5, 117	D. Valiente	Orange Motiff, 3, 113	Chores At Dawn, 4, 113	13	1:45.60	29,130
	Princely Proof, 5, 113	R. Breen	Fraulein Lieber, 4, 112	Judy's Red Shoes, 4, 113	8	1:46.20	33,870
	Fama, 5, 111	J. M. Pezua	Singular Bequest, 5, 116	Ladanum, 4, 115	9	1:44.80	24,570
1986	Donna's Dolly, 4, 112	M. A. Lee	Fritzie Bey, 4, 113	Thirty Zip, 3, 117	6	1:55.00	31,010
1985	Powder Break, 4, 116	J. A. Santos	Duty Dance, 3, 117	Dictina (Fr), 4, 117	10	1:47.80	20,555
	Shocker T., 3, 119	G. St. Leon	Erin's Dunloe, 3, 119	Spruce Luck, 4, 112	12	1:48.80	20,675
1984	Our Reverie, 3, 114	G. St. Leon	Id Am Fac, 3, 114	Break In, 3, 110	13	1:47.60	13,927
	Burst of Colors, 4, 116	J. A. Santos	Ava Romance, 3, 111	Cosmic Sea Queen, 4, 115	13	1:47.60	13,928

Named for Ben S. Castleman's SW My Charmer (1969 f. by Poker), dam of 1977 Horse of the Year and '77 Triple Crown winner Seattle Slew. Not held 1987, 1991. Two divisions 1984-'85. Held in March (two divisions) and December (two divisions) 1988. Held in April and December (two divisions) 1992. About 1 1/8 miles 1984-'85, 1988-'93. Dirt 1986. ‡Megans Bluff finished first, DQ to second, 2000.

Nashua Stakes

Grade 3 in 2005. Aqueduct, two-year-olds, 1 mile, dirt. Held November 2, 2004, with a gross value of $109,500. First held in 1975. First graded in 1982. Stakes record 1:35.40 (1977 Quadratic).

Year	Winner	Jockey	Second	Third	Strs	Time	1st Purse
2004	Rockport Harbor, 2, 118	S. Elliott	Defer, 2, 116	Better Than Bonds, 2, 116	6	1:36.67	$65,700
2003	Read the Footnotes, 2, 118	J. D. Bailey	Paddington, 2, 120	Who Is Chris G., 2, 116	9	1:36.48	67,860
2002	Added Edge, 2, 122	P. Husbands	Outer Reef, 2, 116	Boston Bull, 2, 122	7	1:36.77	65,820
2001	Listen Here, 2, 117	J. D. Bailey	Monthir, 2, 115	Thunder Days, 2, 115	6	1:37.61	65,580
2000	Ommadon, 2, 115	A. T. Gryder	Windsor Castle, 2, 117	Griffinite, 2, 115	10	1:36.74	67,920
1999	Mass Market, 2, 117	M. E. Smith	Polish Miner, 2, 114	Parade Leader, 2, 117	9	1:38.60	67,020
1998	Doneraile Court, 2, 115	J. D. Bailey	Successful Appeal, 2, 122	Exiled Groom, 2, 113	8	1:36.17	66,600
1997	Coronado's Quest, 2, 122	M. E. Smith	Not Tricky, 2, 117	Dice Dancer, 2, 119	5	1:37.06	65,100
1996	Jules, 2, 114	J. A. Santos	Shammy Davis, 2, 114	Sal's Driver, 2, 114	9	1:36.89	68,340
1994	Devious Course, 2, 114	F. T. Alvarado	Mighty Magee, 2, 112	Old Tascosa, 2, 122	7	1:37.50	65,580
1993	Popol's Gold, 2, 114	W. H. McCauley	Personal Merit, 2, 117	Sonny's Bruno, 2, 114	11	1:46.68	74,400
1992	Dalhart, 2, 114	M. E. Smith	Rohwer, 2, 114	Peace Baby, 2, 114	11	1:44.60	74,640
1991	Pine Bluff, 2, 124	C. Perret	Speakerphone, 2, 114	Best Decorated, 2, 114	11	1:46.14	75,960
1990	Kyle's Our Man, 2, 114	J. D. Bailey	Oregon, 2, 114	Vouch for Me, 2, 117	11	1:45.40	55,980
1989	Champagneforashley, 2, 119	J. Vasquez	Armed for Peace, 2, 114	Flathorn, 2, 114	4	1:45.20	66,480
1988	Traskwood, 2, 117	A. T. Cordero Jr.	Doc's Leader, 2, 119	Triple Buck, 2, 117	10	1:45.20	63,240

Year	Winner	Jockey	Second	Third	Strs	Time	1st Purse
1987	Cougarized, 2, 117	J. A. Santos	Blew by Em, 2, 119	Chicot County, 2, 117	12	1:46.00	$104,160
1986	Bold Summit, 2, 114	C. W. Antley	Drachma, 2, 114	Perdition's Son, 2, 114	8	1:45.00	72,360
1985	Raja's Revenge, 2, 117	R. G. Davis	Royal Doulton, 2, 117	Bordeaux Bob, 2, 114	12	1:44.40	56,610
1984	Stone White, 2, 119	R. G. Davis	Banner Bob, 2, 117	Old Main, 2, 114	12	1:38.20	71,550
1983	Don Rickles, 2, 114	A. T. Cordero Jr.	Arabian Gift, 2, 114	Raja's Shark, 2, 114	9	1:38.40	34,800
1982	I Enclose, 2, 114	R. Hernandez	Loose Cannon, 2, 114	Moment of Joy, 2, 114	11	1:37.60	35,460
1981	Our Escapade, 2, 114	D. MacBeth	John's Gold, 2, 114	Hostage, 2, 114	10	1:36.80	35,280
1980	‡A Run, 2, 114	C. J. McCarron	Copper Mine, 2, 114	Triocala, 2, 114	12	1:37.20	35,460
1979	Googolplex, 2, 117	L. A. Pincay Jr.	Thanks to Tony, 2, 114	Comptroller, 2, 114	8	1:36.40	32,550
1978	Instrument Landing, 2, 114	J. Fell	Miroman, 2, 114	Bold Ruckus, 2, 117	12	1:37.00	26,520
1977	Quadratic, 2, 119	E. Maple	No Sir, 2, 114	Quip, 2, 114	5	1:35.40	21,975
1976	Nearly On Time, 2, 114	J. Vasquez	Ruthie's Native, 2, 114	Upper Nile, 2, 114	5	1:35.60	22,005
1975	Lord Henribee, 2, 115	E. Maple	Cojak, 2, 120	Expletive Deleted, 2, 115	6	1:35.80	33,030

Named for Belair Stud's 1955 Horse of the Year and '55 Belmont S. winner Nashua (1952 c. by *Nasrullah). Grade 2 1986-'88. Held at Belmont Park 2001. Not held 1995. 1 mile 70 yards 1985. 1¹/₁₆ miles 1986-'93. ‡Willow Hour finished first, DQ to twelfth, 1980.

Nassau County Breeders' Cup Stakes

Grade 2 in 2005. Belmont Park, three-year-olds, fillies, 7 furlongs, dirt. Held May 7, 2005, with a gross value of $192,000. First held in 1996. First graded in 1998. Stakes record 1:22.19 (1996 Star de Lady Ann).

Year	Winner	Jockey	Second	Third	Strs	Time	1st Purse
2005	Seeking the Ante, 3, 116	M. J. Luzzi	Slew Motion, 3, 116	Exit to Heaven, 3, 116	7	1:22.86	$120,000
2004	Bending Strings, 3, 116	J. D. Bailey	Grey Traffic, 3, 116	A Lulu Ofa Menifee, 3, 116	6	1:22.70	120,000
2003	House Party, 3, 122	J. A. Santos	Cyber Secret, 3, 122	City Sister, 3, 116	4	1:23.28	120,000
2002	Nonsuch Bay, 3, 116	J. Castellano	Wopping, 3, 116	Wilzada, 3, 116	8	1:23.90	120,000
2001	Cat Chat, 3, 114	J. R. Velazquez	Xtra Heat, 3, 122	Shooting Party, 3, 114	6	1:23.02	90,000
2000	C'Est L' Amour, 3, 115	E. S. Prado	Tugger, 3, 114	Miss Inquistive, 3, 119	6	1:23.46	90,000
1999	Oh What a Windfall, 3, 118	M. E. Smith	Paved in Gold, 3, 118	Things Change, 3, 118	8	1:23.59	66,480
1998	Jersey Girl, 3, 121	M. E. Smith	Countess Diana, 3, 118	Foil, 3, 114	4	1:22.63	48,831
1997	Alyssum, 3, 116	J. A. Santos	Screamer, 3, 121	Sinclara, 3, 112	7	1:22.90	49,065
1996	Star de Lady Ann, 3, 114	J. F. Chavez	Stop Traffic, 3, 114	J J'sdream, 3, 121	8	1:22.19	49,590

Named for Nassau County, Long Island, New York, where Belmont Park is located. Grade 3 1998-'99. Nassau County S. 1996-2001.

National Jockey Club Handicap

Grade 3 in 2005. Hawthorne Race Course, three-year-olds and up, 1¹/₈ miles, dirt. Held April 23, 2005, with a gross value of $242,500. First held in 1956. First graded in 1984. Stakes record 1:47.60 (1999 Baytown).

Year	Winner	Jockey	Second	Third	Strs	Time	1st Purse
2005	Pollard's Vision, 4, 118	J. R. Velazquez	Badge of Silver, 5, 120	Lord of the Game, 4, 117	4	1:49.12	$150,000
2004	Ten Most Wanted, 4, 121	D. R. Flores	Colonial Colony, 6, 113	New York Hero, 4, 113	6	1:49.54	150,000
2003	Fight for Ally, 6, 116	E. Razo Jr.	Colonial Colony, 5, 114	Parrott Bay, 6, 115	8	1:53.46	150,000
2002	Hail The Chief (GB), 5, 114	J. F. Chavez	E Z Glory, 5, 115	Ubiquity, 5, 115	7	1:51.72	120,000
2001	Chicago Six, 6, 117	A. J. Juarez Jr.	Guided Tour, 5, 118	Glacial, 6, 114	5	1:48.28	120,000
2000	Take Note of Me, 6, 120	R. Albarado	Glacial, 5, 113	Nite Dreamer, 5, 118	8	1:49.91	120,000
1999	Baytown, 5, 114	M. Guidry	Precocity, 5, 120	Fred Bear Claw, 5, 116	7	1:47.60	120,000
1998	Polar Expedition, 7, 117	M. Guidry	Bucks Nephew, 8, 115	Shed Some Light, 6, 114	9	1:49.91	120,000
1997	Bucks Nephew, 7, 118	G. K. Gomez	Natural Selection, 4, 114	Gotha, 5, 112	8	1:49.87	120,000
1996	‡Prory, 4, 113	C. H. Silva	Polar Expedition, 5, 116	Shed Some Light, 4, 114	9	1:50.83	150,000
1995	Dusty Screen, 7, 116	E. Maple	Come On Flip, 4, 114	Adhocracy, 5, 113	8	1:51.57	150,000
1994	Recoup the Cash, 4, 113	J. L. Diaz	Dread Me Not, 4, 114	Danc'n Jake, 5, 112	7	1:49.03	150,000
1993	Stalwars, 8, 118	J. L. Diaz	Count the Time, 4, 115	Richman, 5, 119	8	1:49.46	150,000
1992	Stalwars, 7, 115	M. Guidry	Richman, 4, 122	Sunny Prince, 5, 113	6	1:48.15	156,300
1991	Allijeba, 5, 116	S. J. Sellers	Whiz Along, 6, 110	Sound of Cannons, 4, 115	8	1:50.43	157,680
1990	Dual Elements, 4, 114	J. L. Diaz	Tricky Creek, 4, 120	Blue Buckaroo, 7, 115	11	1:49.60	143,730
1989	Present Value, 5, 112	W. Shoemaker	Super Roberto, 4, 113	Honor Medal, 8, 121	9	1:49.20	126,510
1988	Lost Code, 4, 129	C. Perret	Honor Medal, 7, 122	Outlaws Sham, 5, 114	7	1:49.60	125,640
1987	Honor Medal, 6, 118	L. E. Ortega	Blue Buckaroo, 4, 115	Coffer Dam, 6, 113	9	1:49.80	95,490
1986	Magic North, 4, 117	J. L. Diaz	Rocky Knave, 6, 121	Tuner Jr., 4, 113	8	1:50.00	65,220
1985	Norwick, 6, 117	K. Skinner	Harham's Sizzler, 6, 121	Badwagon Harry, 6, 115	9	1:51.20	67,440
1984	Prince Forli, 4, 118	R. A. Meier	Full Flame, 8, 119	Spare Card, 4, 117	8	1:52.60	64,080
1983	Determined Bidder, 4, 114	C. H. Silva	Thumbsucker, 4, 117	John's Gold, 4, 115	9	1:52.00	64,710
1982	Frost King, 4, 127	R. Platts	Dusky Duke, 6, 114	Recusant, 4, 115	12	1:49.80	66,150
1981	Dusky Duke, 5, 118	G. E. Louviere	Boyne Valley (Ire), 5, 119	Good and Early, 5, 120	6	1:49.00	46,350
1980	All the More, 7, 119	L. Snyder	Hold Your Tricks, 4, 114	Young Bob, 5, 117	9	1:46.20	46,890
1979	Once Over Lightly, 6, 113	S. A. Spencer	‡Batonnier, 4, 114	Hold Your Tricks, 4, 114	8	1:45.60	46,800
1978	Auberge, 5, 112	O. Sanchez	Bill Bonbright, 5, 121	Brown Cabildo, 4, 116	9	1:41.00	19,305
1977	Yallah Native, 4, 112	J. P. Powell	Dare to Command, 5, 119	Brown Cabildo, 3, 109	8	1:37.80	31,860
1976	Honey Mark, 4, 124	R. Sibille	Heathen Ways, 6, 114	Chateauvira, 8, 111	7	1:46.80	46,680

1975 ***Zografos**, 7, 120	H. Arroyo	Sr. Diplomat, 4, 116	‡Sharp Gary, 4, 118	6	1:44.20	$34,410
1974 **Tom Tulle**, 4, 120	L. Snyder	Smooth Dancer, 4, 111	Chateauvira, 6, 117	8	1:43.40	37,800
1973 **Fame and Power**, 4, 118	A. Rini	Full Pocket, 4, 122	Chateauvira, 5, 113	9	1:37.80	21,285

Named for the National Jockey Club, parent company of Sportsman's Park until 2002, when it merged with Hawthorne Race Course to become Hawthorne National LLC. Held at Sportsman's Park 1956-'98, 2000-'02. 1¹/₁₆ miles 1956-'71, 1974-'76, 1979-'80. 6¹/₂ furlongs 1972. 1 mile 1973, 1977-'78. Four-year-olds and up 1984-2002. ‡Christopher R. finished third, DQ to fourth, 1975. ‡Hold Your Tricks finished second, DQ to third, 1979. ‡Bucks Nephew finished first, DQ to fourth, 1996. Track record 1992, 1993.

National Museum of Racing Hall of Fame Handicap

Grade 2 in 2005. Saratoga Race Course, three-year-olds, 1¹/₈ miles, turf. Held August 9, 2004, with a gross value of $150,000. First held in 1985. First graded in 1992. Stakes record 1:46.65 (1992 Paradise Creek).

Year	Winner	Jockey	Second	Third	Strs	Time	1st Purse
2004	**Artie Schiller**, 3, 122	R. Migliore	Mustanfar, 3, 122	Good Reward, 3, 115	8	1:47.71	$90,000
2003	**Stroll**, 3, 117	J. D. Bailey	Urban King (Ire), 3, 115	Saint Stephen, 3, 115	11	1:49.34	90,000
2002	**Quest Star**, 3, 117	P. Day	Union Place, 3, 115	Patrol, 3, 120	5	1:49.66	90,000
2001	**Baptize**, 3, 122	J. D. Bailey	Strategic Partner, 3, 120	Saint Verre, 3, 113	7	1:47.94	90,000
2000	**Turnofthecentury**, 3, 118	A. T. Gryder	Aldo, 3, 118	Polish Miner, 3, 123	5	1:52.35	90,000
1999	**Marquette**, 3, 119	J. D. Bailey	Phi Beta Doc, 3, 118	Good Night, 3, 118	13	1:49.33	90,000
1998	**Parade Ground**, 3, 120	S. J. Sellers	Vergennes, 3, 115	Stay Sound, 3, 115	8	1:47.82	90,000
1997	**Rob 'n Gin**, 3, 120	J. D. Bailey	River Squall, 3, 114	Subordination, 3, 120	6	1:42.09	66,000
1996	**Sir Cat**, 3, 113	J. D. Bailey	Fortitude, 3, 113	Optic Nerve, 3, 120	9	1:40.46	68,340
1995	**Flitch**, 3, 113	M. E. Smith	Diplomatic Jet, 3, 120	Nostra, 3, 112	8	1:48.08	83,700
1994	**Islefaxyou**, 3, 113	E. Maple	Jaggery John, 3, 122	dh- Lahint, 3, 115	13	1:48.61	70,200
				dh- Mr. Impatience, 3, 119			
1993	**A in Sociology**, 3, 115	C. W. Antley	Strolling Along, 3, 117	Palashall, 3, 117	10	1:48.81	73,080
1992	**Paradise Creek**, 3, 115	M. E. Smith	Smiling and Dancin, 3, 119	Spectacular Tide, 3, 122	4	**1:46.65**	72,600
1991	**Lech**, 3, 122	A. T. Cordero Jr.	Sultry Song, 3, 117	Fourstars Allstar, 3, 122	10	1:49.02	73,920
1990	**Social Retiree**, 3, 115	M. E. Smith	Go Dutch, 3, 115	Divine Warning, 3, 119	7	1:48.20	54,720
1989	**Orange Sunshine**, 3, 117	J. Cruguet	Fast 'n' Gold, 3, 115	Expensive Decision, 3, 122	10	1:49.00	55,980
1988	**Posen**, 3, 122	J. D. Bailey	‡Blew by Em, 3, 119	Harp Islet, 3, 115	9	1:47.00	55,710
1987	**Drachma**, 3, 115	R. G. Davis	Crown the Leader, 3, 115	Major Beard, 3, 115	8	1:49.80	51,480
1986	**Dance of Life**, 3, 115	J. D. Bailey	Southjet, 3, 115	Dance Card Filled, 3, 115	6	1:52.20	49,860
1985	**Duluth**, 3, 115	J. Cruguet	Explosive Dancer, 3, 115	Equalize, 3, 122	8	1:47.60	51,570

Named for the National Museum of Racing and Hall of Fame located in Saratoga Springs, New York. Formerly named for Ralph Lowe's 1957 Travers S. winner *Gallant Man (1954 c. by *Migoli). Gallant Man S. 1985-'91. National Museum of Racing Hall of Fame S. 1992-'97. 1³/₁₆ miles 1991. 1¹/₁₆ miles 1996-'97. Dirt 2000. Three-year-olds and up 1991. Fillies and mares 1991. Dead heat for third 1994. ‡Fourstardave finished second, DQ to fourth, 1988.

Native Diver Handicap

Grade 3 in 2005. Hollywood Park, three-year-olds and up, 1¹/₈ miles, dirt. Held December 11, 2004, with a gross value of $100,000. First held in 1979. First graded in 1979. Stakes record 1:45.35 (1996 Gentlemen [Arg]).

Year	Winner	Jockey	Second	Third	Strs	Time	1st Purse
2004	**Truly a Judge**, 6, 115	M. A. Pedroza	Dynever, 4, 119	Calkins Road, 5, 116	8	1:47.06	$60,000
2003	**Olmodavor**, 4, 117	A. O. Solis	Nose The Trade (GB), 5, 115	Chinkapin, 7, 118	5	1:49.16	60,000
2002	**Piensa Sonando (Chi)**, 4, 117	L. A. Pincay Jr.	Fleetstreet Dancer, 4, 112	Nose The Trade (GB), 4, 116	8	1:48.43	60,000
2001	**Momentum**, 3, 117	C. S. Nakatani	Euchre, 5, 121	Last Parade (Arg), 5, 117	7	1:48.24	60,000
2000	**Sky Jack**, 4, 118	L. A. Pincay Jr.	Lethal Instrument, 4, 116	Grey Memo, 3, 113	8	1:46.81	60,000
1999	**General Challenge**, 3, 123	C. J. McCarron	Moore's Flat, 5, 117	Koslanin (Arg), 5, 113	6	1:49.07	60,000
1998	**Puerto Madero (Chi)**, 4, 121	K. J. Desormeaux	Musical Gambler, 4, 117	River Keen (Ire), 6, 114	5	1:48.43	60,000
1997	**Refinado Tom (Arg)**, 4, 119	G. L. Stevens	Steel Ruhlr, 3, 112	Boggle, 5, 114	8	1:47.84	60,000
1996	**Gentlemen (Arg)**, 4, 121	G. L. Stevens	Dramatic Gold, 5, 122	Don't Blame Rio, 3, 113	5	**1:45.35**	63,840
1995	**Alphabet Soup**, 4, 117	C. W. Antley	El Florista (Arg), 5, 118	Regal Rowdy, 6, 116	5	1:47.03	61,400
1994	**Best Pal**, 6, 121	C. J. McCarron	Tossofthecoin, 4, 117	Royal Chariot, 4, 114	7	1:48.44	64,000
1993	**Slew of Damascus**, 5, 118	C. S. Nakatani	Lottery Winner, 4, 117	L'Express (Chi), 4, 115	7	1:47.46	63,300
1992	**Sir Beaufort**, 5, 119	C. J. McCarron	Memo (Chi), 5, 115	Berillon (GB), 5, 115	5	1:47.88	61,700
1991	**Twilight Agenda**, 5, 124	C. J. McCarron	Ibero (Arg), 4, 117	Cobra Classic, 4, 117	4	1:49.00	60,600
1990	**Warcraft**, 4, 117	C. J. McCarron	Pleasant Tap, 3, 115	Go and Go (Ire), 3, 115	7	1:47.40	63,500
1989	**Ruhlmann**, 4, 121	C. J. McCarron	Lively One, 4, 122	Stylish Winner, 5, 116	7	1:48.00	63,100
1988	**Cutlass Reality**, 6, 124	G. L. Stevens	Precisionist, 7, 123	Payant (Arg), 4, 116	7	1:48.60	63,700
1987	**Epidaurus**, 5, 116	P. A. Valenzuela	Midwest King, 4, 116	He's a Saros, 4, 116	8	1:47.60	91,200
1986	**Hopeful Word**, 5, 117	L. A. Pincay Jr.	Epidaurus, 4, 115	Nostalgia's Star, 4, 118	7	1:47.80	90,800
1985	**Innamorato**, 4, 107	S. Hawley	Beldale Lear, 4, 116	Lord At War (Arg), 5, 125	4	1:33.40	87,900
1984	**Lord At War (Arg)**, 4, 120	W. Shoemaker	Fighting Fit, 5, 118	Video Kid, 4, 118	6	1:35.40	62,700
1983	**Menswear**, 5, 115	F. Toro	Fighting Fit, 4, 117	Major Sport, 6, 115	6	1:42.40	63,200
1982	**Native Tactics**, 4, 116	E. J. Delahoussaye	Belfort (Fr), 5, 116	Rock Softly, 4, 115	10	1:41.60	67,000
1981	**Syncopate**, 6, 117	C. J. McCarron	King Go Go, 6, 115	Wickerr, 6, 121	6	1:38.80	63,500
1980	**Replant**, 6, 111	W. Shoemaker	Relaunch, 4, 120	Flying Paster, 4, 124	6	1:34.20	63,000
1979	**Life's Hope**, 6, 117	L. A. Pincay Jr.	Hawkin's Special, 4, 117	White Rammer, 5, 116	6	1:35.00	31,500

Named for Mr. and Mrs. L. K. Shapiro's 1965, '66, and '67 Hollywood Gold Cup winner Native Diver (1959 g. by Imbros); Native Diver won 33 stakes, second only to Exterminator. Grade 2 1979. 1 mile 1979-'81, 1984-'85. 1¹/₁₆ miles 1982-'83.

New Orleans Handicap

Grade 2 in 2005. Fair Grounds, four-year-olds and up, 1⅛ miles, dirt. Held March 12, 2005, with a gross value of $500,000. First held in 1918. First graded in 1973. Stakes record 1:48.13 (1998 Phantom On Tour).

Year	Winner	Jockey	Second	Third	Strs	Time	1st Purse
2005	Badge of Silver, 5, 118	J. D. Bailey	Limehouse, 4, 115	Second of June, 4, 115	9	1:48.78	$300,000
2004	Peace Rules, 4, 119	J. D. Bailey	Saint Liam, 4, 114	Funny Cide, 4, 118	8	1:48.61	300,000
2003	Mineshaft, 4, 115	R. Albarado	Olmodavor, 4, 117	Strive, 4, 114	11	1:48.92	300,000
2002	Parade Leader, 5, 115	C. J. Lanerie	Graeme Hall, 5, 116	Keats, 4, 113	9	1:50.44	300,000
2001	Include, 4, 114	J. D. Bailey	Nite Dreamer, 6, 112	Valhol, 5, 116	5	1:49.18	300,000
2000	Allen's Oop, 5, 112	W. Martinez	Take Note of Me, 6, 116	Ecton Park, 4, 117	8	1:48.80	300,000
1999	Precocity, 5, 118	E. M. Martin Jr.	Real Quiet, 4, 122	Allen's Oop, 4, 108	6	1:49.17	320,640
1998	Phantom On Tour, 4, 114	L. J. Melancon	Precocity, 4, 114	Lord Cromby (Ire), 4, 110	8	1:48.13	300,000
1997	Isitingood, 6, 121	D. R. Flores	Western Trader, 6, 114	Scott's Scoundrel, 5, 113	7	1:48.43	180,000
1996	Scott's Scoundrel, 4, 116	R. D. Ardoin	Knockadoon, 4, 113	Patio de Naranjos (Chi), 5, 114	9	1:49.97	162,540
1995	Concern, 4, 125	M. E. Smith	Fly Cry, 4, 118	Tossofthecoin, 5, 117	7	1:49.40	120,000
1994	Brother Brown, 4, 118	P. Day	Far Out Wadleigh, 6, 112	Eequalsmcsquared, 5, 116	10	1:48.83	120,000
1993	Latin American, 5, 112	G. K. Gomez	Delafield, 4, 115	West by West, 4, 119	12	1:49.20	90,000
1992	Jarraar, 5, 112	B. J. Walker Jr.	Irish Swap, 4, 120	Bayou Reality, 4, 113	8	1:48.80	60,000
1991	Silver Survivor, 5, 120	L. J. Melancon	El Zorzal (Arg), 5, 110	Sangria Time, 4, 115	9	1:50.10	60,000
1990	Festive, 5, 117	B. J. Walker Jr.	Majesty's Imp, 4, 116	De Roche, 4, 116	8	1:50.40	60,000
1989	Galba, 5, 115	A. L. Castanon	Honor Medal, 8, 123	Position Leader, 4, 116	9	1:51.20	60,000
1988	Honor Medal, 7, 121	P. Day	New York Swell, 5, 114	Manzotti, 5, 115	12	1:50.00	60,000
1987	Honor Medal, 6, 116	R. A. Baze	Dramatic Desire, 6, 117	Inevitable Leader, 8, 116	10	1:52.20	71,040
1986	Herat, 4, 116	R. Q. Meza	Hopeful Word, 5, 120	Kamakura (GB), 4, 108	11	2:01.80	112,000
1985	Westheimer, 4, 112	L. Snyder	Inevitable Leader, 6, 116	Vornorco, 4, 108	9	2:01.80	112,000
1984	Wild Again, 4, 112	P. Day	Explosive Bid, 6, 112	Crazy Moon, 4, 110	10	2:02.00	112,000
1983	Listcapade, 4, 121	E. J. Perrodin	Bold Style, 4, 113	Aspro, 5, 114	9	2:03.20	112,000
1982	It's the One, 4, 124	W. A. Guerra	Boys Nite Out, 4, 116	Aspro, 4, 113	11	2:01.80	112,000
1981	Sun Catcher, 4, 123	A. Guajardo	Prince Majestic, 7, 118	Yosi Boy, 5, 112	7	2:03.40	103,550
1980	Pool Court, 5, 111	R. D. Ardoin	Five Star General, 5, 112	Book of Kings, 6, 113	7	2:04.60	84,500
1979	A Letter to Harry, 5, 126	E. J. Delahoussaye	Prince Majestic, 5, 114	Johnny's Image, 4, 112	6	2:02.60	84,050
1978	Life's Hope, 5, 112	C. J. McCarron	Silver Series, 4, 125	Inca Roca, 5, 111	10	2:20.20	77,550
1977	Tudor Tambourine, 4, 112	A. J. Trosclair	Inca Roca, 4, 113	Soy Numero Uno, 4, 127	11	1:49.80	65,000
1976	Master Derby, 4, 121	D. G. McHargue	Hatchet Man, 5, 118	‡Promised City, 4, 116	9	1:50.00	61,000
1975	Lord Rebeau, 4, 116	C. H. Marquez	Warbucks, 5, 113	Diamond Black, 6, 110	16	1:50.60	61,000
1974	Smooth Dancer, 4, 116	L. Adams	*Trupan, 7, 108	Rastaferian, 5, 115	12	1:50.60	56,300
1973	Combat Ready, 4, 111	L. Moyers	Hustlin Greek, 4, 111	Guitar Player, 5, 114	9	1:51.00	50,000

Named for New Orleans, home of Fair Grounds. Grade 3 1973-'80, 1990-2000. Not held 1919-'23, 1941-'42, 1945. 1¹⁄₁₆ miles 1918, 1925-'31, 1933, 1936, 1938-'39, 1943-'53. 1 mile 1924, 1935, 1937. 1 mile 70 yards 1940. 1¼ miles 1978-'86. Three-year-olds and up 1918-'36, 1939-'78. Three-year-olds 1937-'38. ‡*Zografos finished third, DQ to ninth, 1976. Track record 1997, 1998. Equaled track record 1992, 1994.

New York Handicap

Grade 2 in 2005. Belmont Park, three-year-olds and up, fillies and mares, 1¼ miles, turf. Held July 5, 2004, with a gross value of $250,000. First held in 1940. First graded in 1977. Stakes record 1:58.40 (1990 Capades).

Year	Winner	Jockey	Second	Third	Strs	Time	1st Purse
2004	Wonder Again, 5, 115	E. S. Prado	Stay Forever, 7, 115	Spice Island, 5, 118	7	2:05.60	$150,000
2003	Snow Dance, 5, 116	R. Migliore	Pertuisane (GB), 4, 115	Riskaverse, 4, 119	8	1:59.63	150,000
2002	Owsley, 4, 114	E. S. Prado	Volga (Ire), 4, 116	Janet (GB), 5, 119	7	1:59.81	150,000
2001	England's Legend (Fr), 4, 115	C. S. Nakatani	Gaviola, 4, 119	Spook Express (SAf), 7, 116	7	1:59.63	150,000
2000	Perfect Sting, 4, 122	J. D. Bailey	Snow Polina, 5, 116	Pico Teneriffe, 4, 115	6	2:05.36	150,000
1999	Soaring Softly, 4, 117	M. E. Smith	Tampico, 6, 116	Anguilla, 4, 119	6	2:02.25	150,000
1998	Auntie Mame, 4, 118	J. R. Velazquez	Tresoriere, 4, 115	Cuando, 4, 113	8	1:59.50	120,000
1997	Maxzene, 4, 120	M. E. Smith	Memories of Silver, 4, 122	Shemozzle (Ire), 4, 114	6	1:59.80	120,000
1996	Electric Society (Ire), 5, 115	J. F. Chavez	Danish (Ire), 5, 115	Chelsey Flower, 5, 116	7	2:03.79	90,000
1995	Irish Linnet, 7, 118	J. R. Velazquez	Danish (Ire), 4, 116	Market Booster, 6, 119	5	1:59.92	65,520
1994	You'd Be Surprised, 5, 118	J. D. Bailey	Dahlia's Dreamer, 5, 112	Aquilegia, 5, 115	6	1:59.69	65,520
1993	Aquilegia, 4, 114	J. A. Krone	Via Borghese, 4, 117	Ginny Dare, 5, 108	11	1:59.05	74,760
1992	Plenty of Grace, 5, 111	J. A. Krone	Dancing Devlette, 5, 111	Flaming Torch (Ire), 5, 115	9	2:00.74	72,720
1991	Foresta, 5, 121	A. T. Cordero Jr.	Crockadore, 4, 112	Flaming Torch (Ire), 4, 110	8	1:59.38	72,360
1990	Capades, 4, 119	A. T. Cordero Jr.	Laugh and Be Merry, 5, 114	Key Flyer, 4, 109	7	1:58.40	71,640
1989	Miss Unnameable, 5, 108	R. I. Rojas	‡Love You by Heart, 4, 119	Gaily Gaily (Ire), 6, 113	8	2:05.80	72,000
1988	Beauty Cream, 5, 119	P. Day	Antique Mystique, 4, 109	Key to the Bridge, 4, 114	8	2:03.00	70,200
1987	Anka Germania (Ire), 5, 117	C. Perret	Videogenic, 5, 117	Lead Kindly Light, 4, 109	7	2:01.00	83,580
1986	Possible Mate, 5, 123	J. Samyn	Lucky Touch, 4, 110	Perfect Point, 4, 113	5	2:02.40	51,750
1985	Powder Break, 4, 115	J. D. Bailey	Annie Edge (Ire), 5, 112	Pull the Wool, 5, 107	4	2:03.60	53,280
1984	Annie Edge (Ire), 4, 112	J. Velasquez	Thirty Flags, 4, 114	Geraldine's Store, 5, 121	11	2:02.20	58,950
1983	Sabin, 3, 111	E. Maple	If Winter Comes, 5, 113	Doodle, 4, 115	12	2:01.00	53,010
1982	Noble Damsel, 4, 114	J. Velasquez	Office Wife, 5, 113	Castle Royale, 4, 111	8	2:07.00	34,620
1981	Mairzy Doates, 5, 120	A. T. Cordero Jr.	Love Sign, 4, 114	Wayward Lassie, 4, 107	6	2:04.00	33,960
1980	Just a Game (Ire), 4, 121	D. Brumfield	Poppycock, 4, 112	Please Try Hard, 4, 113	6	2:00.40	33,720

1979	**La Soufriere**, 4, 111	J. Cruguet	Navajo Princess, 5, 118	Emerald Hill (Brz), 5, 120	8	1:41.20	$33,600
1978	**Pearl Necklace**, 4, 122	R. Hernandez	Waya (Fr), 4, 116	Dottie's Doll, 5, 118	7	1:40.00	33,360
	Late Bloomer, 4, 115	J. Velasquez	Island Kiss, 3, 108	Fia, 4, 113	9	1:41.20	33,810
1977	**Fleet Victress**, 5, 115	R. Hernandez	Lady Singer (Ire), 4, 113	*Welsh Pearl, 5, 119	9	1:39.20	33,330
1976	**Sugar Plum Time**, 4, 113	A. T. Cordero Jr.	‡*Deesse Du Val, 5, 120	Dos a Dos, 4, 111	9	2:03.20	33,780

Named for New York City, home of Belmont Park. Grade 3 1977-'82. Held at Aqueduct 1940-'60, 1963-'72. Not held 1957, 1973-'75. 2¼ miles 1940-'50. 1⅛ miles 1951-'54, 1959-'60. 1⅜ miles 1955-'58, 1961. 1¹/₁₆ miles 1963, 1968-'71. 1¹/₁₆ miles 1965-'67, 1977-'79. 7 furlongs 1972. Dirt 1940-'54, 1972. Three-year-olds 1972. Both sexes 1940-'62. Fillies 1972. Two divisions 1978. ‡Carolerno finished second, DQ to ninth, 1976. ‡Laugh and Be Merry finished second, DQ to fourth, 1989.

Next Move Handicap

Grade 3 in 2005. Aqueduct, three-year-olds and up, fillies and mares, 1⅛ miles, dirt. Held March 25, 2005, with a gross value of $110,000. First held in 1975. First graded in 1977. Stakes record 1:48.96 (1999 Diggins).

Year	Winner	Jockey	Second	Third	Strs	Time	1st Purse
2005	**Daydreaming**, 4, 119	E. S. Prado	Saintliness, 5, 117	Rare Gift, 4, 116	8	1:50.77	$66,000
2004	**Smok'n Frolic**, 5, 119	R. Migliore	Stake, 4, 112	U K Trick, 4, 110	7	1:51.55	65,040
2003	**Smok'n Frolic**, 4, 120	J. R. Velazquez	Ellie's Moment, 5, 116	Pupil, 4, 113	6	1:49.11	64,800
2002	**With Ability**, 4, 113	J. Castellano	Irving's Baby, 5, 117	Diversa, 4, 113	7	1:49.88	65,160
2001	**Atelier**, 4, 117	E. S. Prado	Pompeii, 4, 117	Tax Affair, 4, 114	4	1:50.65	64,264
2000	**Biogio's Rose**, 6, 117	N. Arroyo Jr.	Up We Go, 4, 115	Perlinda (Arg), 5, 114	7	1:51.32	49,875
1999	**Diggins**, 5, 113	J. L. Espinoza	Biogio's Rose, 5, 116	Powerful Nation, 5, 114	7	**1:48.96**	48,915
1998	**Panama Canal**, 4, 113	S. Bridgmohan	Endowment, 4, 110	Dewars Rocks, 4, 116	8	1:51.37	49,455
1997	**Full and Fancy**, 5, 115	R. Migliore	Shoop, 6, 117	Prophet's Warning, 4, 117	8	1:51.12	49,500
1996	**Madame Adolphe**, 4, 110	F. Leon	Shoop, 5, 114	Lotta Dancing, 5, 122	9	1:51.39	49,080
1995	**Restored Hope**, 4, 118	M. J. Luzzi	Cherokee Wonder, 4, 114	Sterling Pound, 4, 114	6	1:52.26	48,975
1994	**Groovy Feeling**, 5, 123	M. J. Luzzi	Broad Gains, 4, 116	Megaroux, 4, 112	7	1:59.79	63,735
1993	**Low Tolerance**, 4, 120	M. E. Smith	Hilbys Brite Flite, 4, 112	Lady Lear, 6, 114	8	1:55.93	67,470
1992	**Spy Leader Lady**, 4, 112	M. E. Smith	Haunting, 4, 117	Grecian Pass, 5, 115	6	2:00.26	67,560
1991	**Buy the Firm**, 5, 119	W. H. McCauley	Overturned, 4, 115	Won Scent, 4, 112	6	1:56.57	65,850
1990	**Bold Wench**, 5, 117	J. Velasquez	Buy the Firm, 4, 112	Dactique, 4, 113	8	1:58.40	53,280
1989	**Rose's Cantina**, 5, 118	E. Maple	To the Hunt, 4, 111	No Butter, 5, 108	4	1:59.80	49,950
1988	**Triple Wow**, 5, 116	R. Migliore	With a Twist, 5, 112	Cuantalamera, 5, 104	5	1:57.60	66,120
1987	**Tricky Squaw**, 4, 110	C. W. Antley	Ms. Eloise, 4, 115	Videogenic, 5, 121	9	1:58.40	70,440
1986	**Cherry Jubilee**, 4, 110	C. H. Marquez Jr.	Madame Called, 4, 109	Lady On the Run, 4, 121	11	1:56.00	68,220
1985	**Flip's Pleasure**, 5, 112	J. Samyn	Sintrillium, 7, 121	Emphatic, 5, 104	7	1:58.20	52,380
1984	**Adept**, 5, 109	M. Venezia	Far Flying, 4, 120	Chieftain's Command, 5, 123	8	1:57.80	67,860
1983	**Chieftain's Command**, 4, 116	A. Smith Jr.	Noble Damsel, 5, 115	Pert, 4, 113	6	1:53.20	32,880
1982	**Andover Way**, 4, 122	J. Velasquez	Autumn Glory, 4, 111	Who's to Answer, 4, 109	8	1:50.20	50,940
1981	**Plankton**, 5, 123	R. Hernandez	Nalee's Fantasy, 4, 107	Ms. Balding, 5, 109	6	1:53.40	50,130
1980	**Water Lily (Fr)**, 4, 113	M. Castaneda	Plankton, 4, 121	Propitiate, 5, 116	7	1:51.00	49,410
1979	**One Sum**, 5, 116	R. Hernandez	Kit's Double, 6, 111	Municipal Bond, 4, 111	7	1:53.00	48,105
1978	**One Sum**, 4, 121	R. Hernandez	Crab Grass, 6, 121	Sweet Bernice, 5, 114	10	1:52.80	48,690
1977	**Forty Nine Sunsets**, 4, 116	J. Vasquez	Double Quester, 4, 115	Shark's Jaws, 4, 116	9	1:51.00	48,915
1976	**Yes Dear Maggy**, 4, 119	R. Hernandez	Pass a Glance, 5, 115	Mary Queenofscots, 5, 119	8	1:49.40	48,360
1975	**My Juliet**, 3, 125	D. G. McHargue	Channelette, 3, 117	Spring Is Here, 3, 113	7	1:35.60	33,660

Named for Alfred G. Vanderbilt's 1950 champion three-year-old filly, '52 champion older mare, and '50, '52 Beldame H. winner Next Move (1947 f. by Bull Lea). Next Move Breeders' Cup H. 1990-'95. 1 mile 1975. 1³/₁₆ miles 1984-'94. Three-year-olds 1975. Fillies 1975.

Noble Damsel Handicap

Grade 3 in 2005. Belmont Park, three-year-olds and up, fillies and mares, 1 mile, turf. Held September 25, 2004, with a gross value of $150,000. First held in 1985. First graded in 1988. Stakes record 1:32.79 (2002 Tates Creek).

Year	Winner	Jockey	Second	Third	Strs	Time	1st Purse
2004	**Ocean Drive**, 4, 120	J. R. Velazquez	High Court (Brz), 4, 115	Hour of Justice, 4, 116	9	1:34.71	$90,000
2003	**Wonder Again**, 4, 117	E. S. Prado	Dancal (Ire), 5, 114	Something Ventured, 4, 115	11	1:33.07	90,000
2002	**Tates Creek**, 4, 119	J. D. Bailey	Amonita (GB), 4, 117	Dat You Miz Blue, 5, 114	8	**1:32.79**	68,640
2001	**Tugger**, 4, 119	J. D. Bailey	Shine Again, 4, 123	Tippity Witch, 4, 113	6	1:35.18	68,280
2000	**Gino's Spirits (GB)**, 4, 114	E. S. Prado	La Ville Rouge, 4, 115	Solar Bound, 4, 114	8	1:36.61	66,720
1999	**Khumba Mela (Ire)**, 4, 118	J. A. Santos	Uanme, 4, 114	Cyrillic, 4, 116	8	1:35.50	67,740
1998	**Oh Nellie**, 4, 116	J. R. Velazquez	Heaven's Command (GB), 4, 116	Irish Daisy, 5, 114	7	1:32.80	50,400
1997	**Colcon**, 4, 113	J. D. Bailey	Antespend, 4, 118	Tiffany's Taylor, 8, 113	11	1:32.80	69,360
1996	**Perfect Arc**, 4, 125	J. R. Velazquez	Fashion Star, 4, 112	Tough Broad, 4, 112	7	1:42.41	60,160
1995	**Irish Linnet**, 7, 121	J. R. Velazquez	Caress, 4, 120	Weekend Madness (Ire), 5, 120	7	1:40.67	60,048
1994	**Irish Linnet**, 6, 117	J. R. Velazquez	Statuette, 4, 113	Cox Orange, 4, 117	10	1:39.59	50,790
1993	**McKaymackenna**, 4, 120	C. W. Antley	La Piaf (Fr), 4, 116	Heed, 4, 116	10	1:43.74	55,620
1992	**Miss Otis**, 5, 115	A. Madrid Jr.	Big Big Affair, 5, 115	Tiney Toast, 3, 115	4	1:43.64	53,460
1991	**Highland Penny**, 6, 116	A. T. Cordero Jr.	Southern Tradition, 4, 116	Virgin Michael, 4, 116	8	1:40.21	50,850
1990	**Christiecat**, 3, 112	E. Maple	Aldbourne (Ire), 4, 120	To the Lighthouse, 4, 116	7	1:43.40	54,090
1989	**Miss Unnameable**, 5, 120	R. I. Rojas	High Browser, 4, 116	Highland Penny, 4, 116	9	1:40.60	55,080

1988	**Glowing Honor**, 3, 115	P. Day	Love You by Heart, 3, 115	Fieldy (Ire), 5, 116	8	1:42.00	$55,350
1987	**Fieldy (Ire)**, 4, 116	A. T. Cordero Jr.	Perfect Point, 5, 120	Bailrullah, 5, 123	9	1:43.40	34,500
1986	**Slew's Exceller**, 4, 115	J. Samyn	Tri Argo, 4, 115	Chinguetti (Fr), 4, 115	6	1:42.20	32,460
	Fama, 3, 113	R. P. Romero	Tax Dodge, 5, 119	Anka Germania (Ire), 4, 115	7	1:41.00	32,580
1985	**Alabama Nana (Ire)**, 4, 115	P. A. Valenzuela	Paradies (Arg), 5, 115	Nany, 5, 115	8	1:35.20	34,800

Named for G. Watts Humphrey Jr.'s 1982 New York H. (G3) winner Noble Damsel (1978 f. by *Vaguely Noble). Leixable S. 1985-'88. Noble Damsel S. 1989-'93. 1⁄16 miles 1988-'96. Dirt 1992, 2001. Two divisions 1986.

Norfolk Stakes

Grade 2 in 2005. Santa Anita Park, two-year-olds. Held October 3, 2004, with a gross value of $196,000. First held in 1970. First graded in 1973. Stakes record 1:41.27 (2003 Ruler's Court).

Year	Winner	Jockey	Second	Third	Strs	Time	1st Purse
2004	**Roman Ruler**, 2, 120	C. S. Nakatani	Boston Glory, 2, 120	Littlebitofzip, 2, 120	4	1:44.27	$120,000
2003	**Ruler's Court**, 2, 120	A. O. Solis	Capitano, 2, 120	Perfect Moon, 2, 120	9	**1:41.27**	150,000
2002	**Kafwain**, 2, 120	V. Espinoza	Bull Market, 2, 120	Listen Indy, 2, 120	7	1:42.75	120,000
2001	**Essence of Dubai**, 2, 118	A. O. Solis	Ibn Al Haitham (GB), 2, 118	‡Ecstatic, 2, 118	6	1:37.16	150,000
2000	**Flame Thrower**, 2, 118	V. Espinoza	Street Cry (Ire), 2, 118	Mr Freckles, 2, 118	8	1:34.86	120,000
1999	**Dixie Union**, 2, 118	A. O. Solis	Forest Camp, 2, 118	Anees, 2, 118	6	1:35.79	120,000
1998	**Buck Trout**, 2, 118	E. J. Delahoussaye	Eagleton, 2, 118	Daring General, 2, 118	9	1:37.55	120,000
1997	**Souvenir Copy**, 2, 118	G. L. Stevens	Old Trieste, 2, 118	Double Honor, 2, 118	7	1:36.00	120,000
1996	**Free House**, 2, 118	K. J. Desormeaux	Zippersup, 2, 118	Swiss Yodeler, 2, 118	7	1:43.54	120,000
1995	**Future Quest**, 2, 118	K. J. Desormeaux	Odyle, 2, 118	Exetera, 2, 118	7	1:43.31	120,000
1994	**Supremo**, 2, 118	G. L. Stevens	Desert Mirage, 2, 118	Strong Ally, 2, 118	9	1:43.48	120,000
1993	**Shepherd's Field**, 2, 118	C. J. McCarron	Ramblin Guy, 2, 118	Ferrara, 2, 118	7	1:43.11	120,000
1992	**River Special**, 2, 118	K. J. Desormeaux	Imperial Ridge, 2, 118	Devil Diamond, 2, 118	5	1:43.58	120,000
1991	**Bertrando**, 2, 118	A. O. Solis	Zurich, 2, 118	Bag, 2, 118	9	1:42.87	164,820
1990	**Best Pal**, 2, 118	P. A. Valenzuela	Pillaring, 2, 118	Formal Dinner, 2, 118	12	1:42.80	178,620
1989	**Grand Canyon**, 2, 118	C. J. McCarron	Single Dawn, 2, 118	Due to the King, 2, 118	7	1:43.20	166,440
1988	**Hawkster**, 2, 118	P. A. Valenzuela	Bold Bryn, 2, 118	Double Quick, 2, 118	9	1:43.40	187,740
1987	**Saratoga Passage**, 2, 118	J. J. Steiner	Purdue King, 2, 118	Bold Second, 2, 118	7	1:45.00	181,140
1986	**Capote**, 2, 118	L. A. Pincay Jr.	Gulch, 2, 118	Gold On Green, 2, 118	6	1:45.20	193,680
1985	**Snow Chief**, 2, 118	A. O. Solis	Lord Allison, 2, 118	Darby Fair, 2, 118	9	1:44.60	167,340
1984	**Chief's Crown**, 2, 118	D. MacBeth	Matthew T. Parker, 2, 118	Viva Maxi, 2, 118	6	1:42.40	201,960
1983	**Fali Time**, 2, 118	S. Hawley	†Life's Magic, 2, 117	Artichoke, 2, 118	10	1:44.20	168,930
1982	**Roving Boy**, 2, 118	E. J. Delahoussaye	Desert Wine, 2, 118	Aguila, 2, 118	9	1:41.60	181,110
1981	**Stalwart**, 2, 118	C. J. McCarron	Racing Is Fun, 2, 118	Gato Del Sol, 2, 118	9	1:42.60	140,790
1980	**Sir Dancer**, 2, 118	F. Olivares	Chiaroscuro, 2, 118	Partez, 2, 118	8	1:43.80	100,980
	High Counsel, 2, 118	L. M. Gilligan	Regalberto, 2, 118	Cogency, 2, 118	7	1:42.80	99,780
1979	**The Carpenter**, 2, 118	C. J. McCarron	Rumbo, 2, 118	Idyll, 2, 118	8	1:41.60	119,280
1978	**Flying Paster**, 2, 118	D. Pierce	Golden Act, 2, 118	Knights Choice, 2, 118	6	1:42.00	118,860
1977	**Balzac**, 2, 118	W. Shoemaker	Misrepresentation, 2, 118	Noble Bronze, 2, 118	10	1:45.40	157,230
1976	***Habitony**, 2, 118	W. Shoemaker	Replant, 2, 118	Hey Hey J. P., 2, 118	11	1:40.20	79,290
1975	**Telly's Pop**, 2, 118	F. Mena	Imacornishprince, 2, 118	Thermal Energy, 2, 118	8	1:43.60	74,295
1974	**George Navonod**, 2, 118	D. Pierce	Diabolo, 2, 118	Fleet Velvet, 2, 118	9	1:42.20	77,370
1973	**Money Lender**, 2, 118	J. Lambert	Merry Fellow, 2, 118	Holding Pattern, 2, 118	7	1:42.60	58,050

Named for Theodore Winter's undefeated Norfolk (1861 c. by Lexington), member of the great "triumvirate" of Lexington sons, with Asteroid and Kentucky. Grade 1 1980-'92. 1 mile 1997-2001. Two divisions 1980. ‡Roman Dancer finished third, DQ to fourth, 2001. †Denotes female.

Northern Dancer Stakes

Grade 3 in 2005. Churchill Downs, three-year-olds, 1⁄16 miles, dirt. Held June 12, 2004, with a gross value of $232,400. First held in 1998. First graded in 2004. Stakes record 1:44.50 (2004 Suave).

Year	Winner	Jockey	Second	Third	Strs	Time	1st Purse
2004	**Suave**, 3, 114	R. Bejarano	J Town, 3, 114	Ecclesiastic, 3, 114	12	**1:44.50**	$144,000
2003	**Champali**, 3, 122	P. Day	Lone Star Sky, 3, 120	During, 3, 114	8	1:34.69	68,882
2002	**Danthebluegrassman**, 3, 119	J. D. Bailey	Stephentown, 3, 113	Sky Terrace, 3, 119	7	1:35.04	67,890

Named for E. P. Taylor's 1964 Canadian Horse of the Year and '64 Kentucky Derby winner Northern Dancer (1961 c. by Nearctic). 1 mile 2002-'03. Run as an overnight handicap 1998-2001.

Oaklawn Handicap

Grade 2 in 2005. Oaklawn Park, four-year-olds and up, 1⁄8 miles, dirt. Held April 9, 2005, with a gross value of $490,000. First held in 1946. First graded in 1973. Stakes record 1:46.60 (1987 Snow Chief).

Year	Winner	Jockey	Second	Third	Strs	Time	1st Purse
2005	**Grand Reward**, 4, 112	J. McKee	Second of June, 4, 117	Eddington, 4, 117	5	1:49.54	$300,000
2004	**Peace Rules**, 4, 120	J. D. Bailey	Ole Faunty, 5, 116	Saint Liam, 4, 114	6	1:48.26	300,000
2003	**Medaglia d'Oro**, 4, 122	J. D. Bailey	Slider, 5, 112	Kudos, 6, 117	5	1:47.66	300,000
2002	**Kudos**, 5, 117	E. J. Delahoussaye	Bowman's Band, 4, 114	Dollar Bill, 4, 114	8	1:48.34	300,000
2001	**Traditionally**, 4, 112	P. Day	Mr Ross, 6, 117	Wooden Phone, 4, 118	7	1:48.15	360,000
2000	**K One King**, 4, 113	C. H. Borel	Almutawakel (GB), 5, 117	Cat Thief, 4, 118	6	1:48.02	360,000
1999	**Behrens**, 5, 116	J. F. Chavez	Littlebitlively, 5, 112	Precocity, 5, 119	7	1:47.77	450,000
1998	**Precocity**, 4, 114	C. Gonzalez	Frisk Me Now, 4, 117	Phantom On Tour, 4, 117	7	1:48.28	450,000

Year	Winner	Jockey	Second	Third	Strs	Time	1st Purse
1997	Atticus, 5, 114	S. J. Sellers	Isitingood, 6, 120	Tejano Run, 5, 115	8	1:48.20	$450,000
1996	Geri, 4, 115	J. D. Bailey	Wekiva Springs, 5, 119	Scott's Scoundrel, 4, 113	7	1:47.52	450,000
1995	Cigar, 5, 120	J. D. Bailey	Silver Goblin, 4, 119	Concern, 4, 122	7	1:47.22	450,000
1994	The Wicked North, 5, 119	K. J. Desormeaux	Devil His Due, 5, 120	Brother Brown, 4, 116	12	1:47.86	450,000
1993	Jovial (GB), 6, 117	E. J. Delahoussaye	Lil E. Tee, 4, 123	Best Pal, 5, 123	10	1:48.63	450,000
1992	Best Pal, 4, 125	K. J. Desormeaux	Sea Cadet, 4, 120	Twilight Agenda, 6, 123	7	1:48.10	300,000
1991	Festin (Arg), 5, 115	E. J. Delahoussaye	Primal, 6, 115	Jolie's Halo, 4, 120	8	1:48.71	300,000
1990	Opening Verse, 4, 118	C. J. McCarron	De Roche, 4, 114	Silver Survivor, 4, 116	8	1:47.20	300,000
1989	Slew City Slew, 5, 118	A. T. Cordero Jr.	Stalwars, 4, 113	Homebuilder, 5, 115	8	1:49.00	240,000
1988	Lost Code, 4, 126	C. Perret	Cryptoclearance, 4, 122	Gulch, 4, 120	8	1:47.00	300,000
1987	Snow Chief, 4, 123	A. O. Solis	Red Attack, 5, 112	Vilzak, 4, 108	7	1:46.60	163,020
1986	Turkoman, 4, 123	C. J. McCarron	Gate Dancer, 5, 123	Red Attack, 4, 114	4	1:47.40	159,180
1985	Imp Society, 4, 125	P. Day	Strength in Unity, 4, 109	Pine Circle, 4, 118	11	1:48.40	168,540
1984	Wild Again, 4, 115	P. Day	Win Stat, 7, 114	Dew Line, 5, 118	14	1:46.80	173,940
1983	Bold Style, 4, 113	P. Day	Eminency, 5, 123	Listcapade, 4, 123	8	1:43.00	165,180
1982	Eminency, 4, 116	P. Day	Reef Searcher, 5, 117	Thirty Eight Paces, 4, 120	9	1:44.00	166,740
1981	Temperence Hill, 4, 126	E. Maple	Sun Catcher, 4, 123	Uncool, 6, 114	5	1:43.40	128,310
1980	Uncool, 5, 116	J. Velasquez	Hold Your Tricks, 5, 111	Braze and Bold, 5, 118	8	1:44.40	103,110
1979	San Juan Hill, 4, 114	D. Brumfield	Alydar, 4, 127	A Letter to Harry, 5, 125	7	1:43.60	101,730
1978	Cox's Ridge, 4, 128	E. Maple	Prince Majestic, 4, 115	All the More, 5, 120	11	1:43.20	80,190
1977	Soy Numero Uno, 4, 123	R. Broussard	Romeo, 4, 119	Dragset, 6, 114	13	1:42.40	80,610
1976	Master Derby, 4, 125	D. G. McHargue	Royal Glint, 6, 128	Dragset, 5, 113	6	1:41.60	70,890
1975	Warbucks, 5, 121	D. Gargan	Hey Rube, 5, 112	Eastern Pageant, 4, 115	10	1:42.80	37,380
1974	Royal Knight, 4, 123	I. Valenzuela	Crimson Falcon, 4, 122	Visualizer, 4, 121	11	1:43.40	38,070
1973	Prince Astro, 4, 116	D. W. Whited	Herbalist, 6, 116	Gage Line, 7, 118	8	1:43.60	34,470

Grade 3 1973-'76. Grade 1 1988-2002. Not held 1955-'62. 1¹/₁₆ miles 1946-'83. Three-year-olds and up 1946-'76.

Oak Leaf Stakes

Grade 2 in 2005. Santa Anita Park, two-year-olds, fillies, 1¹/₁₆ miles, dirt. Held October 2, 2004, with a gross value of $200,000. First held in 1969. First graded in 1973. Stakes record 1:41.20 (1978 It's in the Air).

Year	Winner	Jockey	Second	Third	Strs	Time	1st Purse
2004	Sweet Catomine, 2, 119	C. S. Nakatani	Splendid Blended, 2, 119	Memorette, 2, 119	9	1:42.98	$120,000
2003	Halfbridled, 2, 119	J. A. Krone	Tarlow, 2, 119	Hollywood Story, 2, 119	7	1:43.72	150,000
2002	Composure, 2, 119	M. E. Smith	Buffythecenterfold, 2, 119	Sea Jewel, 2, 119	6	1:42.65	120,000
2001	Tali'sluckybusride, 2, 117	J. Valdivia Jr.	Imperial Gesture, 2, 117	Ms Louisett, 2, 117	6	1:37.77	150,000
2000	Notable Career, 2, 118	D. R. Flores	Euro Empire, 2, 118	Cindy's Hero, 2, 118	7	1:36.34	120,000
1999	Chilukki, 2, 118	D. R. Flores	Abby Girl, 2, 118	Spain, 2, 118	5	1:36.12	120,000
1998	Excellent Meeting, 2, 115	K. J. Desormeaux	Antahkarana, 2, 115	Stylish Talent, 2, 115	7	1:37.71	120,000
1997	Vivid Angel, 2, 116	E. J. Delahoussaye	Love Lock, 2, 116	Balisian Beauty, 2, 115	9	1:37.33	120,000
1996	City Band, 2, 115	J. A. Garcia	Clever Pilot, 2, 115	Wealthy, 2, 115	8	1:44.57	120,000
1995	Tipically Irish, 2, 117	L. A. Pincay Jr.	Ocean View, 2, 115	Gastronomical, 2, 117	7	1:42.60	120,000
1994	Serena's Song, 2, 115	C. S. Nakatani	Call Now, 2, 115	Mama Mucci, 2, 115	5	1:41.83	120,000
1993	Phone Chatter, 2, 117	L. A. Pincay Jr.	Sardula, 2, 116	Tricky Code, 2, 115	6	1:41.78	120,000
1992	Zoonaqua, 2, 115	C. J. McCarron	Turkstand, 2, 115	Madame l'Enjoleur, 2, 115	10	1:43.91	120,000
1991	Pleasant Stage, 2, 116	E. J. Delahoussaye	Soviet Sojourn, 2, 116	La Spia, 2, 115	5	1:43.53	156,540
1990	Lite Light, 2, 115	R. A. Baze	Garden Gal, 2, 115	Beyond Perfection, 2, 115	4	1:42.80	148,320
1989	Dominant Dancer, 2, 116	E. J. Delahoussaye	Bel's Starlet, 2, 115	Materco, 2, 115	7	1:44.60	153,870
1988	One of a Klein, 2, 115	C. J. McCarron	Stocks Up, 2, 115	Lady Lister, 2, 115	8	1:44.00	168,090
1987	Dream Team, 2, 115	C. J. McCarron	Lost Kitty, 2, 117	Tomorrow's Child, 2, 115	6	1:44.40	158,910
1986	Sacahuista, 2, 115	C. J. McCarron	Silk's Lady, 2, 115	Delicate Vine, 2, 115	7	1:44.60	187,050
1985	Arewehavingfunyet, 2, 115	P. A. Valenzuela	Trim Colony, 2, 115	Laz's Joy, 2, 115	8	1:44.60	192,420
1984	Folk Art, 2, 117	L. A. Pincay Jr.	Pirate's Glow, 2, 115	Wayward Pirate, 2, 115	6	1:42.60	186,540
1983	Life's Magic, 2, 115	C. J. McCarron	Althea, 2, 117	Percipient, 2, 115	9	1:44.40	164,310
1982	Landaluce, 2, 117	L. A. Pincay Jr.	Sophisticated Girl, 2, 115	Granja Reina, 2, 115	7	1:41.80	155,610
1981	Header Card, 2, 115	D. G. McHargue	A Kiss for Luck, 2, 117	Model Ten, 2, 115	9	1:43.00	144,390
1980	Astrious, 2, 115	T. Lipham	Irish Arrival, 2, 115	Bee a Scout, 2, 115	8	1:43.80	90,180
1979	Bold 'n Determined, 2, 115	A. T. Cordero Jr.	Hazel R., 2, 115	Arcades Ambo, 2, 115	8	1:46.20	82,440
1978	It's in the Air, 2, 115	E. J. Delahoussaye	Caline, 2, 115	Spiffy Laree, 2, 115	8	1:41.20	75,570
1977	B.Thoughtful, 2, 115	D. G. McHargue	Grenzen, 2, 115	High Pheasant, 2, 117	9	1:43.80	73,530
1976	Any Time Girl, 2, 115	R. Schacht	Lady T. V., 2, 115	*Glenaris, 2, 115	8	1:44.00	73,140
1975	Answer, 2, 115	M. Hole	Queen to Be, 2, 115	Awaken, 2, 115	12	1:44.20	84,720
1974	Cut Class, 2, 115	F. Toro	Double You Lou, 2, 115	Sweet Old Girl, 2, 115	13	1:42.80	84,300
1973	Divine Grace, 2, 115	S. Valdez	Chalk Face, 2, 115	Round Rose, 2, 115	6	1:43.60	59,940

Run at Santa Anita Park's fall Oak Tree Racing Association meet. Grade 1 1980-'89, 1992-2001. 1 mile 1997-2001.

Oak Tree Breeders' Cup Mile Stakes

Grade 2 in 2005. Santa Anita Park, three-year-olds and up, 1 mile, turf. Held October 9, 2004, with a gross value of $246,000. First held in 1986. First graded in 1989. Stakes record 1:32.44 (1996 Urgent Request [Ire]).

Year	Winner	Jockey	Second	Third	Strs	Time	1st Purse
2004	†Musical Chimes, 4, 118	K. J. Desormeaux	Buckland Manor, 4, 119	Singletary, 4, 119	6	1:33.29	$150,000
2003	Designed for Luck, 6, 119	P. A. Valenzuela	Sarafan, 6, 119	Century City (Ire), 4, 119	8	1:32.61	180,000
2002	Night Patrol, 6, 119	J. Valdivia Jr.	Kachamandi (Chi), 5, 119	Nicobar (GB), 5, 119	8	1:32.93	150,000

Year	Winner	Jockey	Second	Third	Strs	Time	1st Purse
2001	**Val Royal (Fr)**, 5, 119	J. Valdivia Jr.	Thady Quill, 4, 119	I've Decided, 4, 119	6	1:33.21	$120,000
2000	**War Chant**, 3, 117	G. L. Stevens	Road to Slew, 5, 119	Sharan (GB), 5, 119	8	1:33.75	172,050
1999	**Silic (Fr)**, 4, 121	C. S. Nakatani	Bouccaneer (Fr), 4, 119	Brave Act (GB), 5, 119	7	1:33.76	150,000
1998	**Hawksley Hill (Ire)**, 5, 123	A. O. Solis	Mr Lightfoot (Ire), 4, 119	Magellan, 5, 119	5	1:36.72	166,200
1997	**Fantastic Fellow**, 3, 115	A. O. Solis	Magellan, 4, 119	Taiki Blizzard, 6, 123	8	1:36.23	165,000
1996	**Urgent Request (Ire)**, 6, 115	C. J. McCarron	Megan's Interco, 7, 119	Felon (Ire), 4, 116	6	**1:32.44**	110,300
1995	**Ventiquattrofogli (Ire)**, 5, 116	G. F. Almeida	Megan's Interco, 6, 119	Debutant Trick, 5, 115	8	1:35.30	76,850
1994	**Bon Point (GB)**, 4, 116	E. J. Delahoussaye	Journalism, 6, 120	Johann Quatz (Fr), 5, 117	5	1:33.86	62,050
1993	**Johann Quatz (Fr)**, 4, 119	E. J. Delahoussaye	Myrakalu (Fr), 5, 114	The Tender Track, 6, 117	5	1:36.28	62,350
1992	**Twilight Agenda**, 6, 120	C. J. McCarron	Luthier Enchanteur, 5, 117	Bourgogne (GB), 4, 115	8	1:33.36	65,300
1991	**Ibero (Arg)**, 4, 115	A. O. Solis	Val des Bois (Fr), 5, 118	Tokatee, 5, 116	9	1:33.77	67,000
1990	**Notorious Pleasure**, 4, 117	L. A. Pincay Jr.	Kanatiyr (Ire), 4, 114	Fly Till Dawn, 4, 116	11	1:33.00	68,700
1989	**Political Ambition**, 5, 122	E. J. Delahoussaye	Mister Wonderful (GB), 6, 118	Sabona, 7, 117	10	1:33.40	67,800
1988	**Mohamed Abdu (Ire)**, 4, 120	G. L. Stevens	Mazilier, 4, 116	Deputy Governor, 4, 121	7	1:34.40	65,550
1987	**Double Feint**, 4, 117	F. Toro	Deputy Governor, 3, 118	Vilzak, 4, 115	10	1:37.00	64,810
1986	**Palace Music**, 5, 122	G. L. Stevens	‡Skywalker, 4, 122	Mangaki, 5, 116	6	1:35.00	59,350

Run at Santa Anita Park's fall Oak Tree Racing Association meet. Formerly named for Col. F. W. Koester, general manager of the California Thoroughbred Breeders' Association. Grade 3 1989, 1996-'99. Col. F. W. Koester H. 1986-'95. Col. F. W. Koester Breeders' Cup H. 1996. Oak Tree Breeders' Cup Mile H. 1997-'98. Course record 1996. ‡Mangaki finished second, DQ to third, 1986. †Denotes female.

Oak Tree Derby

Grade 2 in 2005. Santa Anita Park, three-year-olds, 1⅛ miles, turf. Held October 17, 2004, with a gross value of $150,000. First held in 1969. First graded in 1974. Stakes record 1:45.80 (1989 Seven Rivers).

Year	Winner	Jockey	Second	Third	Strs	Time	1st Purse
2004	**Greek Sun**, 3, 118	E. S. Prado	Laura's Lucky Boy, 3, 118	Hendrix, 3, 118	9	1:48.08	$90,000
2003	**Devious Boy (GB)**, 3, 118	J. A. Krone	Sweet Return (GB), 3, 118	Urban King (Ire), 3, 118	5	1:48.82	90,000
2002	**Johar**, 3, 118	A. O. Solis	Rock Opera, 3, 118	Mananan McLir, 3, 120	8	1:46.00	90,000
2001	**No Slip (Fr)**, 3, 118	K. J. Desormeaux	Sligo Bay (Ire), 3, 118	Romanceishope, 3, 122	9	1:46.56	90,000
2000	**Sign of Hope (GB)**, 3, 118	A. O. Solis	David Copperfield, 3, 118	El Gran Papa, 3, 118	5	1:47.71	150,000
1999	**Mula Gula**, 3, 118	G. L. Stevens	Eagleton, 3, 118	Super Quercus (Fr), 3, 118	9	1:46.67	150,000
1998	**Ladies Din**, 3, 120	G. L. Stevens	Dr Fong, 3, 120	Bouccaneer (Fr), 3, 118	7	1:50.24	150,000
1997	**Lasting Approval**, 3, 118	A. O. Solis	Voyagers Quest, 3, 118	Early Colony, 3, 118	7	1:50.84	150,000
1996	**Odyle**, 3, 117	C. J. McCarron	Lago, 3, 115	Rainbow Blues (Ire), 3, 117	6	1:46.83	80,250
1995	**Helmsman**, 3, 115	C. J. McCarron	Virginia Carnival, 3, 118	Mr Purple, 3, 121	8	1:48.98	75,650
1994	**Run Softly**, 3, 117	L. A. Pincay Jr.	Alphabet Soup, 3, 114	Powis Castle, 3, 118	8	1:49.96	64,800
1993	**Eastern Memories (Ire)**, 3, 113	J. D. Bailey	Cigar, 3, 117	Snake Eyes, 3, 120	9	1:48.03	66,800
1992	**Blacksburg**, 3, 118	A. O. Solis	Siberian Summer, 3, 117	Star Recruit, 3, 115	10	1:48.12	67,700
1991	**General Meeting**, 3, 116	K. J. Desormeaux	Dominion Gold (GB), 3, 115	Eternity Star, 3, 120	12	1:46.78	69,500
1990	**In Excess (Ire)**, 3, 117	G. L. Stevens	Warcraft, 3, 118	Barton Dene (Ire), 3, 113	8	1:46.60	65,300
1989	**Seven Rivers**, 3, 115	R. G. Davis	Bruho, 3, 117	Raise a Stanza, 3, 121	9	**1:45.80**	66,100
1988	**Coax Me Clyde**, 3, 116	P. A. Valenzuela	Bel Air Dancer, 3, 117	Undercut, 3, 120	11	1:48.40	81,500
1987	**The Medic**, 3, 119	S. Hawley	Temperate Sil, 3, 122	Hot and Smoggy, 3, 115	9	1:47.80	63,800
1986	**Air Display**, 3, 114	G. L. Stevens	Armada (GB), 3, 117	Vernon Castle, 3, 124	8	1:48.00	64,700
1985	**Justoneoftheboys**, 3, 115	A. O. Solis	Floating Reserve, 3, 118	Schiller, 3, 113	7	1:47.60	65,000
1984	**Tights**, 3, 121	C. J. McCarron	Tsunami Slew, 3, 122	Blind Spot, 3, 115	8	1:46.60	65,500
1983	**Mamaison**, 3, 117	C. J. McCarron	Sunny's Halo, 3, 117	Fifth Division, 3, 118	6	1:49.80	63,900
1982	**Lamerok**, 3, 117	L. A. Pincay Jr.	Craelius, 3, 118	Sari's Dreamer, 3, 113	9	1:46.20	66,300
1981	**dh- Seafood**, 3, 118	M. Castaneda		High Counsel, 3, 117	11	1:49.00	33,350
	dh- Waterway Drive, 3, 120	J. D. Bailey					
1980	**Pocketful in Vail**, 3, 115	F. Toro	Son of a Dodo, 3, 118	Always Best, 3, 117	8	1:47.80	39,400
1979	**Hyannis Port**, 3, 118	W. Shoemaker	Red Crescent, 3, 115	Relaunch, 3, 126	7	1:47.60	32,300
1978	**Wayside Station**, 3, 117	L. A. Pincay Jr.	April Axe, 3, 120	John Henry, 3, 122	11	1:47.80	34,600
1977	**Kulak**, 3, 123	W. Shoemaker	Hill Fox, 3, 114	Kaskee, 3, 110	4	1:46.80	19,800
1976	**Today 'n Tomorrow**, 3, 121	L. A. Pincay Jr.	Pocket Park, 3, 115	Kings Cliffe, 3, 115	8	1:46.80	19,450
1975	**Messenger of Song**, 3, 119	J. Lambert	Larrikin, 3, 123	Forceten, 3, 125	6	1:46.80	25,450
1974	**Within Hail**, 3, 124	W. Shoemaker	Orders, 3, 117	Chief Pronto, 3, 113	11	1:48.40	27,250

Run at Santa Anita Park's fall Oak Tree Racing Association meeting. Formerly named for Elias J. "Lucky" Baldwin's American Derby winner Volante, one of four horses whose gravesites were moved to the entrance of the paddock gardens at Santa Anita Park from their original location on Baldwin's ranch across the street from the track. Grade 3 1974-'87, 1990-'95. Volante H. 1969-'96. Not held 1973. Dead heat for first 1981.

Oceanport Handicap

Grade 3 in 2005. Monmouth Park, three-year-olds and up, 1¹/₁₆ miles, turf. Held August 8, 2004, with a gross value of $100,000. First held in 1947. First graded in 1973. Stakes record 1:39.40 (1999 Mi Narrow).

Year	Winner	Jockey	Second	Third	Strs	Time	1st Purse
2004	**Gulch Approval**, 4, 117	P. Day	Kathir, 7, 116	Stormy Roman, 5, 115	10	1:42.31	$60,000
2003	**Runspastum**, 6, 113	J. Pimentel	Balto Star, 5, 119	Saint Verre, 5, 118	6	1:42.31	60,000

Year	Winner	Jockey	Second	Third	Strs	Time	1st Purse
2002	Tempest Fugit, 5, 115	J. A. Velez Jr.	Runspastum, 5, 112	One Eyed Joker, 4, 114	3	1:42.72	$60,000
2001	Key Lory, 7, 111	C. C. Lopez	North East Bound, 5, 121	Crash Course, 5, 115	13	1:40.39	60,000
2000	North East Bound, 4, 114	J. A. Velez Jr.	Rize, 4, 112	Selective, 7, 114	6	1:44.70	60,000
1999	Mi Narrow, 5, 113	J. Bravo	Hurrahy, 6, 114	Forbidden Apple, 4, 111	8	**1:39.40**	60,000
1998	Daylight Savings, 4, 115	H. Castillo Jr.	Mi Narrow, 4, 112	Rob 'n Gin, 4, 120	8	1:42.31	60,000
1997	Boyce, 6, 118	J. A. Krone	Foolish Pole, 4, 113	Jambalaya Jazz, 5, 116	7	1:40.20	60,000
1995	Boyce, 4, 114	A. S. Black	Myrmidon, 4, 117	Rocket City, 4, 112	9	1:40.91	45,000
1994	Nijinsky's Gold, 5, 120	R. G. Davis	Winnetou, 4, 116	Marco Bay, 4, 115	5	1:41.66	45,000
1993	Furiously, 4, 119	J. D. Bailey	Adam Smith (GB), 5, 120	Rocket Fuel, 6, 114	5	1:39.60	45,000
1992	Maxigroom, 4, 113	R. G. Davis	Rocket Fuel, 5, 112	Go Dutch, 5, 112	9	1:41.77	45,000
1991	Fiftysevenvette, 4, 113	J. C. Ferrer	Great Normand, 6, 118	Thunder Regent, 4, 112	6	1:44.94	45,000
1990	Bill E. Shears, 5, 118	R. Wilson	Pete the Chief, 4, 115	Timely Warning, 5, 113	9	1:42.80	53,910
1989	Yankee Affair, 7, 121	P. Day	River of Sin, 5, 116	Primino (Fr), 4, 110	7	1:43.40	51,870
1988	Feeling Gallant, 6, 119	C. W. Antley	Copper Cup, 5, 111	Sovereign Song, 6, 107	8	1:45.20	41,820
1987	Sovereign Song, 5, 106	J. A. Krone	Feeling Gallant, 5, 120	Spellbound, 4, 117	8	1:41.60	35,100
1986	Salem Drive, 4, 115	D. B. Thomas	Exclusive Partner, 4, 114	Pine Belt, 4, 113	10	1:42.60	34,650
1985	Cozzene, 5, 121	W. A. Guerra	Stay the Course, 4, 119	Roving Minstrel, 4, 118	9	1:42.40	34,470
1984	World Appeal, 4, 120	C. Perret	Rocca Reale, 5, 109	Castle Guard, 5, 120	8	1:42.80	34,950
1983	Fray Star (Arg), 5, 114	O. Vergara	Domynsky (GB), 3, 112	And More, 5, 117	12	1:43.40	35,190
1982	McCann, 4, 114	J. Fell	Sprink, 4, 108	Lord Carnavon, 4, 111	9	1:43.60	27,555
	Erin's Tiger, 4, 114	K. Skinner	Dom Menotti (Fr), 5, 111	War of Words, 5, 114	9	1:43.00	27,555
1981	Winds of Winter, 4, 113	G. McCarron	Foretake, 5, 116	No Bend, 4, 115	12	1:43.40	24,225
1980	North Course, 5, 114	B. Thornburg	Horatius, 5, 119	Lucy's Axe, 4, 116	11	1:44.00	24,210
1979	Revivalist, 5, 117	W. Nemeti	Horatius, 4, 117	Gristle, 4, 113	10	1:38.00	18,866
	Alias Smith, 6, 114	M. Solomone	Qui Native, 5, 114	Fed Funds, 5, 114	9	1:38.00	18,671
1978	Mr. Red Wing, 4, 110	W. H. McCauley	Chati, 5, 118	Dan Horn, 6, 116	15	1:43.20	23,514
1977	Quick Card, 4, 115	M. Solomone	Bemo, 7, 115	Star of the Sea, 4, 115	12	1:42.60	19,516
1976	Toujours Pret, 7, 114	J. W. Edwards	Hat Full, 5, 114	Our Hermis, 5, 113	10	1:43.00	15,072
	Break Up the Game, 5, 114	E. J. Delahoussaye	Expropriate, 6, 120	Leader of the Band, 4, 118	6	1:44.20	14,682
1975	R. Tom Can, 4, 115	D. Brumfield	Prod, 4, 117	Royal Glint, 5, 119	11	1:49.80	15,291
	Haraka, 5, 113	J. Velasquez	London Company, 5, 124	East Sea, 4, 115	9	1:49.80	15,096
1974	Mo Bay, 5, 118	W. Tichenor	Shane's Prince, 4, 118	Barbizon Streak, 6, 116	10	1:42.40	18,541
1973	Lexington Park, 6, 118	J. Imparato	Prince of Truth, 5, 116	Halo, 4, 117	9	1:45.20	15,056
	Dartsum, 4, 112	M. Cedeno	Dundee Marmalade, 5, 114	Return to Reality, 4, 111	8	1:46.20	14,893

Monmouth Park is located in Oceanport, New Jersey. Grade 3 1984-2001. Not graded when taken off turf 2002. Not held 1996. 6 furlongs 1947-'63. 5 furlongs 1964-'67. 1 mile 1968-'72, 1979. Dirt 1947-'63, 1970, 1984, 1990-'91, 2000. Originally scheduled on turf 2002. Two divisions 1973, 1975-'76, 1979, 1982. Course record 1993, 1999.

Ogden Phipps Handicap

Grade 1 in 2005. Belmont Park, three-year-olds and up, fillies and mares, 1¹/₁₆ miles, dirt. Held June 19, 2004, with a gross value of $285,000. First held in 1961. First graded in 1973. Stakes record 1:39.90 (1998 Mossflower).

Year	Winner	Jockey	Second	Third	Strs	Time	1st Purse
2004	Sightseek, 5, 120	J. D. Bailey	Storm Flag Flying, 4, 117	Passing Shot, 5, 116	4	1:41.46	$180,000
2003	Sightseek, 4, 118	J. D. Bailey	Take Charge Lady, 4, 119	Mandy's Gold, 5, 118	5	1:40.89	180,000
2002	Raging Fever, 4, 120	J. R. Velazquez	Transcendental, 4, 113	Two Item Limit, 4, 114	9	1:41.75	180,000
2001	Critical Eye, 4, 115	M. J. Luzzi	Jostle, 4, 117	Apple of Kent, 5, 117	7	1:42.18	150,000
2000	Beautiful Pleasure, 5, 124	J. F. Chavez	Pentatonic, 5, 112	Roza Robata, 5, 115	6	1:41.54	150,000
1999	Sister Act, 4, 117	P. Day	Beautiful Pleasure, 4, 112	Catinca, 4, 122	6	1:40.79	150,000
1998	Mossflower, 4, 114	R. G. Davis	Glitter Woman, 4, 120	Colonial Minstrel, 4, 118	6	**1:39.90**	150,000
1997	Hidden Lake, 4, 117	R. Migliore	Twice the Vice, 6, 121	Jewel Princess, 5, 124	9	1:40.87	150,000
1996	Serena's Song, 4, 125	J. D. Bailey	Shoop, 5, 115	Restored Hope, 5, 114	8	1:41.63	120,000
1995	Heavenly Prize, 4, 122	P. Day	Little Buckles, 4, 111	Sky Beauty, 5, 124	4	1:43.37	90,000
1994	Sky Beauty, 4, 128	M. E. Smith	You'd Be Surprised, 5, 118	Schway Baby Sway, 4, 109	5	1:47.48	90,000
1993	Turnback the Alarm, 4, 119	C. W. Antley	Deputation, 4, 117	You'd Be Surprised, 4, 112	6	1:48.14	90,000
1992	Missy's Mirage, 4, 118	E. Maple	Harbour Club, 5, 110	Versailles Treaty, 4, 117	6	1:47.03	120,000
1991	A Wild Ride, 4, 115	M. E. Smith	Fit to Scout, 4, 115	Buy the Firm, 5, 121	6	1:49.09	120,000
1990	Fantastic Find, 4, 113	C. Perret	Mistaurian, 4, 113	Dreamy Mimi, 4, 113	8	1:50.00	139,680
1989	Rose's Cantina, 5, 117	J. Cruguet	Make Change, 4, 111	Colonial Waters, 4, 114	6	1:48.60	135,120
1988	Personal Ensign, 4, 123	R. P. Romero	Hometown Queen, 4, 109	Clabber Girl, 5, 118	5	1:47.60	131,760
1987	Catatonic, 5, 116	D. A. Miller Jr.	Ms. Eloise, 4, 118	Steal a Kiss, 4, 111	7	1:50.00	137,520
1986	Endear, 4, 115	E. Maple	Lady's Secret, 4, 128	Ride Sally, 4, 124	5	1:48.60	97,650
1985	Heatherten, 6, 124	R. P. Romero	Life's Magic, 4, 122	Sefa's Beauty, 6, 120	6	1:48.80	84,300
1984	Heatherten, 5, 118	S. Maple	Quixotic Lady, 4, 115	Thirty Flags, 4, 114	10	1:49.20	92,400
1983	Number, 4, 117	E. Maple	Dance Number, 4, 114	Broom Dance, 4, 121	4	1:48.40	65,880
1982	Love Sign, 5, 123	R. Hernandez	Anti Lib, 4, 116	Jameela, 6, 122	4	1:48.00	65,280
1981	Wistful, 4, 119	D. Brumfield	Chain Bracelet, 4, 119	Love Sign, 4, 115	5	1:49.80	64,200
1980	Misty Gallore, 4, 125	D. MacBeth	Blitey, 4, 115	What'll I Do, 4, 110	6	1:48.80	32,760
1979	Pearl Necklace, 5, 122	J. Fell	Miss Baja, 4, 115	Sweet Woodruff, 4, 108	5	1:48.60	31,470
1978	Dottie's Doll, 5, 115	J. Vasquez	One Sum, 4, 123	Water Malone, 4, 119	6	1:47.60	32,040
1977	Pacific Princess, 4, 112	E. Maple	Mississippi Mud, 4, 114	Fleet Victress, 5, 113	10	1:49.20	32,700

1976 **Proud Delta**, 4, 124	J. Velasquez	Garden Verse, 4, 111	Let Me Linger, 4, 114	8	1:48.40	$33,690
1975 **Raisela**, 4, 114	E. Maple	Pass a Glance, 4, 114	Sarsar, 3, 115	7	1:49.20	33,510
1974 **Poker Night**, 4, 114	J. Velasquez	Krislin, 5, 115	Fairway Flyer, 5, 117	8	1:48.60	33,300
1973 **Light Hearted**, 4, 123	E. Nelson	Inca Queen, 5, 116	Blessing Angelica, 5, 117	6	1:48.80	32,880

Named for Ogden Phipps (1908-2002), former chairman of the Jockey Club and New York Racing Association. Formerly named for Hempstead, New York, located in Nassau County, home of Belmont Park. Grade 2 1973-'83. Hempstead H. 1961-2001. Held at Aqueduct 1973-'74. Not held 1910-'60, 1962-'69. 6 furlongs 1970-'71. 1¹⁄₂ miles 1961. 1¹⁄₈ miles 1972-'94. Both sexes 1961.

Ohio Derby

Grade 2 in 2005. Thistledown, three-year-olds, 1¹⁄₈ miles, dirt. Held June 12, 2004, with a gross value of $350,000. First held in 1876. First graded in 1973. Stakes record 1:47.40 (1979 Smarten).

Year	Winner	Jockey	Second	Third	Strs	Time	1st Purse
2004	**Brass Hat**, 3, 115	W. Martinez	Pollard's Vision, 3, 121	Trieste's Honor, 3, 115	9	1:49.50	$210,000
2003	**Wild and Wicked**, 3, 114	S. J. Sellers	Hackendiffy, 3, 112	Midway Road, 3, 114	7	1:50.08	180,000
2002	**Magic Weisner**, 3, 116	R. Migliore	Wiseman's Ferry, 3, 120	The Judge Sez Who, 3, 114	4	1:49.96	195,000
2001	**Western Pride**, 3, 119	D. G. Whitney	Woodmoon, 3, 113	Macho Uno, 3, 119	6	1:48.66	180,000
2000	**Milwaukee Brew**, 3, 116	M. J. McCarthy	Brave Quest, 3, 113	Kiss a Native, 3, 116	10	1:50.58	180,000
1999	**Stellar Brush**, 3, 119	M. J. McCarthy	Ecton Park, 3, 116	Valhol, 3, 114	13	1:49.22	180,000
1998	**Classic Cat**, 3, 122	S. J. Sellers	One Bold Stroke, 3, 118	Hot Wells, 3, 118	10	1:49.92	180,000
1997	**Frisk Me Now**, 3, 122	E. L. King Jr.	Anet, 3, 122	Mr. Groush, 3, 118	7	1:48.28	180,000
1996	**Skip Away**, 3, 122	J. A. Santos	Victory Speech, 3, 118	Clash by Night, 3, 118	10	1:47.86	180,000
1995	**Petionville**, 3, 122	P. Day	Dazzling Falls, 3, 124	Is Sveikatas, 3, 116	6	1:48.93	180,000
1994	**Exclusive Praline**, 3, 118	W. Martinez	Concern, 3, 122	Smilin Singin Sam, 3, 122	8	1:48.54	180,000
1993	**Forever Whirl**, 3, 122	A. Toribio	Boundlessly, 3, 120	Mighty Avanti, 3, 114	10	1:49.44	180,000
1992	**Majestic Sweep**, 3, 117	E. Fires	Technology, 3, 126	Always Silver, 3, 117	8	1:50.07	180,000
1991	**Private Man**, 3, 114	J. R. Velazquez	Richman, 3, 126	Shudanz, 3, 114	9	1:50.30	180,000
1990	**Private School**, 3, 120	J. Vasquez	Restless Con, 3, 123	Real Cash, 3, 123	15	1:51.20	180,000
1989	**King Glorious**, 3, 120	C. J. McCarron	Roi Danzig, 3, 114	Caesar, 3, 114	10	1:50.40	180,000
1988	**Jim's Orbit**, 3, 123	S. P. Romero	Primal, 3, 114	Intensive Command, 3, 114	8	1:50.60	150,000
1987	**Lost Code**, 3, 126	G. St. Leon	Proudest Duke, 3, 117	Homebuilder, 3, 114	9	1:50.60	150,000
1986	**Broad Brush**, 3, 126	G. L. Stevens	Bolshoi Boy, 3, 123	Forty Kings, 3, 114	9	1:51.20	150,000
1985	**Skip Trial**, 3, 114	J. Samyn	Encolure, 3, 123	Jacque l'Heureux, 3, 114	8	1:49.00	120,000
1984	**At the Threshold**, 3, 123	G. Patterson	Biloxi Indian, 3, 123	Perfect Player, 3, 120	7	1:49.60	120,000
1983	**Pax Nobiscum**, 3, 120	R. Platts	Bet Big, 3, 114	Fightin Hill, 3, 114	9	1:50.20	90,000
1982	**Spanish Drums**, 3, 123	J. Vasquez	Air Forbes Won, 3, 126	Lejoli, 3, 114	9	1:49.60	90,000
1981	**Pass the Tab**, 3, 120	A. Graell	Paristo, 3, 123	Classic Go Go, 3, 123	9	1:49.20	90,000
1980	**Stone Manor**, 3, 123	P. Day	Colonel Moran, 3, 123	Hillbizon, 3, 114	13	1:52.00	90,000
1979	**Smarten**, 3, 124	S. Maple	Bold Ruckus, 3, 115	Picturesque, 3, 122	12	1:47.40	90,000
1978	**Special Honor**, 3, 115	R. Breen	Batonnier, 3, 122	Star de Naskra, 3, 120	10	1:47.80	90,000
1977	**Silver Series**, 3, 122	L. Snyder	Cormorant, 3, 122	Pruneplum, 3, 115	12	1:49.20	90,000
1976	**Return of a Native**, 3, 115	G. Patterson	Cojak, 3, 122	Dream 'n Be Lucky, 3, 115	14	1:49.80	75,000
1975	**Brent's Prince**, 3, 115	B. R. Feliciano	Sylvan Place, 3, 112	Canvasser, 3, 115	11	1:49.40	66,780
1974	**Stonewalk**, 3, 120	M. A. Rivera	Better Arbitor, 3, 122	Sharp Gary, 3, 122	9	1:53.20	63,000
1973	**Our Native**, 3, 122	A. Rini	Hearts of Lettuce, 3, 112	Arbees Boy, 3, 115	12	1:50.20	63,882

Thistledown is located in North Randall, Ohio. Held at Chester Park 1876-'83. Held at Maple Heights 1924-'26. Held at Bainbridge Park 1928-'35. Held at Cranwood Park 1952. Held at Randall Park 1961-'62. Not held 1884-1923, 1927, 1933-'34, 1936-'51. 1¹⁄₂ miles 1876-'83. 1¹⁄₁₆ miles 1960-'64.

Old Hat Stakes

Grade 3 in 2005. Gulfstream Park, three-year-olds, fillies, 6¹⁄₂ furlongs, dirt. Held February 5, 2005, with a gross value of $100,000. First held in 1976. First graded in 2005. Stakes record 1:16.31 (2005 Maddalena).

Year	Winner	Jockey	Second	Third	Strs	Time	1st Purse
2005	**Maddalena**, 3, 115	J. R. Velazquez	Alfonsina, 3, 119	Holy Trinity, 3, 115	7	**1:16.31**	$60,000
2004	**Madcap Escapade**, 3, 115	R. R. Douglas	Sweet Vision, 3, 115	Smokey Glacken, 3, 119	9	1:08.85	60,000
2003	**House Party**, 3, 115	J. A. Santos	Chimichurri, 3, 119	Glorious Miss, 3, 115	5	1:10.81	60,000
2002	**A New Twist**, 3, 115	E. S. Prado	Forest Heiress, 3, 119	French Satin, 3, 115	7	1:10.61	60,000
2000	**Swept Away**, 3, 112	E. Coa	Petite Deputy, 3, 113	Sabre Dance, 3, 118	10	1:09.96	45,000
1999	**Belle's Appeal**, 3, 114	R. Migliore	Extended Applause, 3, 112	Preciosa V., 3, 112	7	1:11.59	45,000
1998	**Evening Hush**, 3, 114	R. G. Davis	Cotton House Bay, 3, 116	Argos Appeal, 3, 116	7	1:10.63	45,000
1997	**Cupids Revenge**, 3, 112	E. Coa	Supah Syble, 3, 112	Witchful Thinking, 3, 116	6	1:09.47	45,000
1996	**J J'sdream**, 3, 116	M. E. Smith	Mindy Gayle, 3, 112	Nic's Halo, 3, 113	8	1:10.60	30,000
1995	**Bluff's Dividend**, 3, 116	J. A. Santos	Mackenzie Slew, 3, 114	Twist a Lime, 3, 112	9	1:10.82	30,000
1994	**Pagofire**, 3, 112	J. D. Bailey	Deaf Power, 3, 116	Vivance, 3, 113	11	1:10.32	30,000
1993	**Sum Runner**, 3, 116	E. Fires	Best in Sale, 3, 114	Hidden Fire, 3, 114	9	1:10.25	30,000
1992	**Super Doer**, 3, 114	R. R. Douglas	Ravensmoor, 3, 114	Miss Valid Pache, 3, 116	7	1:10.99	30,000
1991	**My Own True Love**, 3, 114	H. Castillo Jr.	Flashing Eyes, 3, 116	Parisian Flight, 3, 114	7	1:10.30	30,000
1990	**dh- Sun Luck**, 3, 112	M. A. Gonzalez		Miss Cox's Hat, 3, 113	9	1:12.00	14,000
	dh- Traki Traki, 3, 114	E. Fires					

1989 **Surging**, 3, 114	C. Perret	Royal Snub, 3, 112	Coax Chelsie, 3, 121	6	1:10.40	$27,528
1988 **On to Royalty**, 3, 113	J. Vasquez	Willing'n Waiting, 3, 114	Level, 3, 112	9	1:11.40	28,848
1987 **Sheer Ice**, 5, 113	R. Woodhouse	Grand Creation, 5, 110	One Fine Lady, 5, 115	7	1:23.80	20,862
1986 **Noranc**, 3, 112	W. H. McCauley	Spirit of Fighter, 3, 114	Bespeak, 3, 112	15	1:11.00	31,776
1985 **Glorious Glory**, 3, 112	B. Zoppo-Bundy	Sheer Ice, 3, 116	Golden Silence, 3, 112	14	1:11.60	31,752
1984 **Flip for Luck**, 4, 114	G. St. Leon	Pretty as Patty, 4, 115	Amber's Desire, 4, 113	11	1:23.40	13,572
1983 **Unaccompanied**, 3, 112	R. Woodhouse	Lisa's Capital, 3, 114	Masked Romance, 3, 112	11	1:10.80	22,518
1981 **Dame Mysterieuse**, 3, 118	E. Maple	Masters Dream, 3, 112	Irish Joy, 3, 112	9	1:10.20	21,906
1976 **Anne Campbell**, 3, 114	M. Solomone	Veroom Maid, 3, 114	Jet Set Jennifer, 3, 113	8	1:09.80	9,960

Named for Stanley Conrad's 1964, '65 champion older mare and '63, '65 Suwannee River H. winner Old Hat (1959 f. by Boston Doge). Not held 1977-'80, 1982, 2001. Dead heat for first 1990.

Orchid Handicap

Grade 2 in 2005. Gulfstream Park, three-year-olds and up, fillies and mares, 1½ miles, turf. Held April 2, 2005, with a gross value of $150,000. First held in 1954. First graded in 1973. Stakes record 2:23.85 (1999 Coretta [Ire]).

Year	Winner	Jockey	Second	Third	Strs	Time	1st Purse
2005	**Honey Ryder**, 4, 116	J. R. Velazquez	Ellieonthemarch, 4, 114	Pretty Jane, 4, 114	7	2:27.15	$90,000
2004	**Meridiana (Ger)**, 4, 114	E. S. Prado	Savedbythelight, 4, 114	Miss Hellie, 5, 114	10	2:26.99	120,000
2003	**Tweedside**, 5, 116	R. R. Douglas	San Dare, 5, 119	Hi Tech Honeycomb, 4, 115	7	2:32.36	120,000
2002	**Julie Jalouse**, 4, 114	J. A. Santos	Sweetest Thing, 4, 115	Refugee, 4, 110	9	2:25.89	120,000
2001	**Innuendo (Ire)**, 6, 116	J. D. Bailey	Windsong, 4, 113	Aiglonne, 4, 114	4	2:25.24	120,000
2000	**Lisieux Rose (Ire)**, 5, 114	J. A. Santos	Champagne Royal, 6, 114	Fly for Avie, 5, 114	10	2:25.64	120,000
1999	**Coretta (Ire)**, 5, 118	J. A. Santos	Delilah (Ire), 5, 117	Almost Skint (Ire), 5, 113	11	2:23.85	120,000
1998	**Colonial Play**, 4, 113	R. G. Davis	Almost Skint (Ire), 4, 114	Gastronomical, 5, 113	11	2:24.75	120,000
1997	**Golden Pond (Ire)**, 4, 116	W. H. McCauley	Tocopilla (Arg), 7, 115	Miss Caerleona (Fr), 5, 114	11	2:26.80	120,000
1996	**Memories (Ire)**, 5, 114	J. A. Santos	Caromana, 5, 112	Curtain Raiser, 4, 113	11	2:31.51	120,000
1995	**Exchange**, 7, 120	L. A. Pincay Jr.	Market Booster, 6, 116	Northern Emerald, 5, 115	10	2:29.02	120,000
1994	**Trampoli**, 5, 121	M. E. Smith	Good Morning Smile, 6, 110	Northern Emerald, 4, 113	7	2:25.42	120,000
1993	**Fairy Garden**, 5, 115	W. S. Ramos	Rougeur, 4, 115	Trampoli, 4, 115	14	2:25.79	120,000
1992	**Crockadora**, 5, 115	M. E. Smith	Indian Fashion, 5, 112	Sardaniya (Ire), 4, 114	10	2:28.32	120,000
1991	**Star Standing**, 4, 114	C. W. Antley	Coolawin, 5, 118	Peinture Bleue, 4, 119	9	2:25.02	120,000
1990	**Coolawin**, 4, 112	J. D. Bailey	Laugh and Be Merry, 5, 113	Gaily Gaily (Ire), 7, 121	10	2:24.20	120,000
1989	**Gaily Gaily (Ire)**, 6, 110	J. A. Krone	Anka Germania (Ire), 7, 120	Laugh and Be Merry, 4, 110	13	2:26.80	120,000
1988	**Beauty Cream**, 5, 115	P. Day	Ladanum, 4, 112	Green Oasis (Fr), 6, 112	14	2:28.40	120,000
1987	**Anka Germania (Ire)**, 5, 117	C. Perret	Singular Bequest, 4, 116	Ivor's Image, 4, 119	14	2:31.40	90,000
1986	**Videogenic**, 4, 121	R. G. Davis	Powder Break, 5, 118	Devalois (Fr), 4, 117	14	2:27.20	118,440
1985	**Pretty Perfect**, 5, 120	G. Gallitano	Early Lunch, 4, 113	Trinado, 4, 112	13	1:41.60	61,980
	Aspen Rose, 5, 116	J. Velasquez	Over Your Shoulder, 4, 114	Dictina (Fr), 4, 117	14	1:42.00	63,180
1984	**Sabin**, 4, 125	E. Maple	Jubilous, 4, 114	Sulemeif, 4, 115	7	1:41.40	70,680
1983	**Sweetest Chant**, 5, 116	E. Fires	Betty Money, 4, 114	Norsan, 4, 115	8	1:43.60	53,040
	Larida, 4, 118	E. Maple	Syrianna, 4, 116	Promising Native, 4, 115	8	1:44.80	53,640
1982	**Blush**, 4, 112	J. Vasquez	Pine Flower, 4, 114	Honey Fox, 5, 125	12	1:41.00	76,500
1981	**Honey Fox**, 4, 115	J. Vasquez	The Very One, 6, 125	Solo Haina, 5, 114	16	1:41.20	88,530
1980	**Just a Game (Ire)**, 4, 119	D. Brumfield	La Soufriere, 5, 115	La Rouquine (GB), 4, 114	10	1:40.40	80,340
1979	**Sans Arc**, 5, 116	E. Fires	‡Terpsichorist, 4, 122	Time for Pleasure, 5, 119	13	1:41.40	86,093
1978	**Time for Pleasure**, 4, 115	T. Barrow	Late Bloomer, 4, 113	Rich Soil, 4, 116	11	1:41.00	37,800
1977	**Copano**, 5, 122	M. Solomone	Jabot, 5, 117	Carolina Moon, 5, 114	13	1:41.40	43,500
1976	***Deesse Du Val**, 5, 116	C. H. Marquez	Redundancy, 5, 120	K D Princess, 5, 114	12	1:41.80	28,785
1975	***Protectora**, 6, 114	H. Gustines	Zippy Do, 6, 118	Lorraine Edna, 5, 116	7	1:41.20	26,100
1974	**Dogtooth Violet**, 4, 113	D. Brumfield	Dove Creek Lady, 4, 124	Shearwater, 5, 115	8	1:41.00	39,420
1973	**Deb Marion**, 3, 116	F. Iannelli	Tico's Donna, 5, 113	Barely Even, 4, 125	6	1:42.60	27,240

James Donn Sr., Gulfstream Park founder, was a world-renowned florist who developed a special breed of orchid in honor of his wife. Grade 3 1973-'80. Orchid S. 1954-'66. Not held 1955-'64. 6 furlongs 1954. 1¹⁄₁₆ miles 1965-'66, 1969-'85. 1 mile 1967-'68. About 1½ miles 1992. Dirt 1954-'66, 1983-'84. Originally scheduled at about 1½ miles on turf 2003. Three-year-olds 1954-'66. Two divisions 1983, 1985. ‡Time for Pleasure finished second, DQ to third, 1979. Course record 1992.

Overbrook Spinster Stakes

Grade 1 in 2005. Keeneland, three-year-olds and up, fillies and mares, 1⅛ miles, dirt. Held October 10, 2004, with a gross value of $500,000. First held in 1956. First graded in 1973. Stakes record 1:47 (1990 Bayakoa [Arg]).

Year	Winner	Jockey	Second	Third	Strs	Time	1st Purse
2004	**Azeri**, 6, 123	P. Day	Tamweel, 4, 123	Mayo On the Side, 5, 123	7	1:49.74	$310,000
2003	**Take Charge Lady**, 4, 123	E. S. Prado	You, 4, 123	Miss Linda (Arg), 6, 123	6	1:49.57	310,000
2002	**Take Charge Lady**, 3, 120	E. S. Prado	You, 3, 120	Printemps (Chi), 5, 123	7	1:49.90	338,520
2001	**Miss Linda (Arg)**, 4, 123	R. Migliore	Starrer, 3, 120	Printemps (Chi), 4, 123	10	1:49.79	348,440
2000	**Plenty of Light**, 3, 120	G. K. Gomez	Spain, 3, 120	Roza Robata, 4, 123	6	1:48.18	336,970
1999	**Keeper Hill**, 4, 123	K. J. Desormeaux	Banshee Breeze, 4, 123	A Lady From Dixie, 4, 123	9	1:47.19	344,410
1998	**Banshee Breeze**, 3, 119	R. Albarado	Runup the Colors, 4, 123	Aldiza, 4, 123	8	1:47.04	341,930
1997	**Clear Mandate**, 5, 123	P. Day	Feasibility Study, 5, 123	Naskra Colors, 5, 123	7	1:50.47	336,350

Year	Winner	Jockey	Second	Third	Strs	Time	1st Purse
1996	**Different (Arg)**, 4, 123	C. J. McCarron	Top Secret, 3, 119	Belle of Cozzene, 4, 123	6	1:49.74	$336,040
1995	**Inside Information**, 4, 123	M. E. Smith	Jade Flush, 4, 123	Mariah's Storm, 4, 123	4	1:50.01	198,276
1994	**Dispute**, 4, 123	P. Day	Lets Be Alert, 3, 119	Miss Dominique, 5, 123	8	1:48.91	204,414
1993	**Paseana (Arg)**, 6, 123	C. J. McCarron	Gray Cashmere, 4, 123	Jacody, 3, 119	9	1:48.46	205,902
1992	**Fowda**, 4, 123	P. A. Valenzuela	Paseana (Arg), 5, 123	Meadow Star, 4, 123	10	1:49.91	209,994
1991	**Wilderness Song**, 3, 119	P. Day	Screen Prospect, 4, 123	Til Forbid, 3, 119	14	1:49.69	226,980
1990	**Bayakoa (Arg)**, 6, 123	L. A. Pincay Jr.	Gorgeous, 4, 123	Luthier's Launch, 4, 123	8	**1:47.00**	174,606
1989	**Bayakoa (Arg)**, 5, 123	L. A. Pincay Jr.	Goodbye Halo, 4, 123	Sharp Dance, 3, 119	6	1:47.80	172,413
1988	**Hail a Cab**, 5, 123	J. Vasquez	Willa On the Move, 3, 119	Integra, 4, 123	5	1:51.00	171,600
1987	**Sacahuista**, 3, 119	R. P. Romero	Ms. Margi, 3, 119	Tall Poppy, 4, 123	13	1:48.60	148,395
1986	**Top Corsage**, 3, 119	S. Hawley	Endear, 4, 123	Life At the Top, 3, 119	8	1:48.20	142,610
1985	**Dontstop Themusic**, 5, 123	L. A. Pincay Jr.	Life's Magic, 4, 123	Dowery, 4, 123	11	1:50.40	110,419
1984	**Princess Rooney**, 4, 123	E. J. Delahoussaye	Lucky Lucky Lucky, 3, 119	Heatherten, 5, 123	9	1:50.40	123,840
1983	**Try Something New**, 4, 123	P. Day	Dance Number, 4, 123	Miss Huntington, 6, 123	9	1:49.80	107,689
1982	**Track Robbery**, 6, 123	P. A. Valenzuela	Blush With Pride, 3, 119	Our Darling, 3, 119	9	1:47.80	110,517
1981	**Glorious Song**, 5, 123	R. Platts	Truly Bound, 3, 119	Safe Play, 3, 119	7	1:49.20	106,567
1980	**Bold 'n Determined**, 3, 119	E. J. Delahoussaye	Love Sign, 3, 119	Likely Exchange, 6, 123	6	1:49.20	114,660
1979	**Safe**, 3, 119	E. Fires	Spark of Life, 4, 123	Miss Baja, 4, 123	11	1:49.20	79,852
1978	**Tempest Queen**, 3, 119	J. Velasquez	Northernette, 4, 123	Likely Exchange, 4, 123	10	1:49.00	72,865
1977	**Cum Laude Laurie**, 3, 119	A. T. Cordero Jr.	Mississippi Mud, 4, 123	Ivory Wand, 4, 123	10	1:48.40	54,974
1976	**Optimistic Gal**, 3, 119	C. Perret	Ivory Wand, 3, 119	Rocky Trip, 4, 123	8	1:51.60	53,008
1975	**Susan's Girl**, 6, 123	L. A. Pincay Jr.	Flama Ardiente, 3, 119	Costly Dream, 4, 123	7	1:49.80	37,830
1974	**Summer Guest**, 5, 123	D. Montoya	Desert Vixen, 4, 123	Coraggioso, 4, 123	5	1:48.40	36,953
1973	**Susan's Girl**, 4, 123	B. Baeza	Light Hearted, 4, 123	Coraggioso, 3, 119	6	1:48.80	38,090

A spinster is an unmarried woman beyond the traditional marriage age, hence an appropriate name for a race for females still racing in the fall. Sponsored by the Young family's Overbrook Farm, located in Lexington 2001-'04. Formerly sponsored by Robert N. Clay's Three Chimneys Farm, located in Midway, Kentucky 1996-2000. Spinster S. 1956-'95. Three, four, and five-year-olds 1956-'63.

Pacific Classic Stakes

Grade 1 in 2005. Del Mar, three-year-olds and up, 1¼ miles, dirt. Held August 22, 2004, with a gross value of $1,000,000. First held in 1991. First graded in 1993. Stakes record 1:59.11 (2003 Candy Ride [Arg]).

Year	Winner	Jockey	Second	Third	Strs	Time	1st Purse
2004	**Pleasantly Perfect**, 6, 124	J. D. Bailey	Perfect Drift, 5, 124	Total Impact (Chi), 6, 124	8	2:01.17	$600,000
2003	**Candy Ride (Arg)**, 4, 124	J. A. Krone	Medaglia d'Oro, 4, 124	Fleetstreet Dancer, 5, 124	4	**1:59.11**	600,000
2002	**Came Home**, 3, 117	M. E. Smith	Momentum, 4, 124	Milwaukee Brew, 5, 124	14	2:01.45	600,000
2001	**Skimming**, 5, 124	G. K. Gomez	Dixie Dot Com, 6, 124	Dig for It, 6, 124	6	1:59.96	600,000
2000	**Skimming**, 4, 124	G. K. Gomez	Tiznow, 3, 117	Ecton Park, 4, 124	7	2:01.22	600,000
1999	**General Challenge**, 3, 117	D. R. Flores	River Keen (Ire), 7, 124	Barter Town, 4, 124	8	2:00.57	700,000
1998	**Free House**, 4, 124	C. J. McCarron	Gentlemen (Arg), 6, 124	Pacificbounty, 4, 124	9	2:00.29	600,000
1997	**Gentlemen (Arg)**, 5, 124	G. L. Stevens	Siphon (Brz), 6, 124	Crafty Friend, 4, 124	5	2:00.56	600,000
1996	**Dare and Go**, 5, 124	A. O. Solis	Cigar, 6, 124	Siphon (Brz), 5, 124	6	1:59.85	600,000
1995	**Tinners Way**, 5, 124	E. J. Delahoussaye	Soul of the Matter, 4, 124	Blumin Affair, 4, 124	6	1:59.63	550,000
1994	**Tinners Way**, 4, 124	E. J. Delahoussaye	Best Pal, 6, 124	Dramatic Gold, 3, 117	9	1:59.43	550,000
1993	**Bertrando**, 4, 124	G. L. Stevens	Missionary Ridge (GB), 6, 124	Best Pal, 5, 124	7	1:59.55	550,000
1992	**Missionary Ridge (GB)**, 5, 124	K. J. Desormeaux	Defensive Play, 5, 124	Claret (Ire), 4, 124	7	2:00.87	550,000
1991	**Best Pal**, 3, 116	P. A. Valenzuela	Twilight Agenda, 5, 124	Unbridled, 4, 124	8	1:59.86	550,000

Named for the Pacific Ocean, where Del Mar's "turf meets the surf." Track record 1993-'94, 2003.

Palm Beach Stakes

Grade 3 in 2005. Gulfstream Park, three-year-olds, 1⅛ miles, turf. Held March 26, 2005, with a gross value of $100,000. First held in 1987. First graded in 1990. Stakes record 1:47.12 (2005 Interpatation).

Year	Winner	Jockey	Second	Third	Strs	Time	1st Purse
2005	**Interpatation**, 3, 116	T. G. Turner	Tadreeb, 3, 118	Fishy Advice, 3, 118	8	**1:47.12**	$60,000
2004	**Kitten's Joy**, 3, 122	J. D. Bailey	Prince Arch, 3, 118	Pa Pa Da, 3, 118	12	1:48.76	60,000
2003	**Nothing to Lose**, 3, 122	J. D. Bailey	White Cat, 3, 118	Imitation, 3, 118	12	1:48.28	60,000
2002	**Orchard Park**, 3, 118	J. D. Bailey	Lord Juban, 3, 118	Red's Top Gun, 3, 116	12	1:49.80	60,000
2001	**Proud Man**, 3, 119	R. R. Douglas	One Eyed Joker, 3, 114	Strategic Partner, 3, 112	12	1:48.32	90,000
2000	**Mr. Livingston**, 3, 114	S. J. Sellers	Powerful Appeal, 3, 114	Gateman (GB), 3, 117	11	1:48.04	45,000
1999	**Swamp**, 3, 114	R. Migliore	Marquette, 3, 114	Valid Reprized, 3, 119	12	1:48.38	45,000
1998	**Cryptic Rascal**, 3, 119	M. E. Smith	The Kaiser, 3, 113	American Odyssey, 3, 114	8	1:55.01	45,000
1997	**Unite's Big Red**, 3, 117	R. A. Hernandez	Trample, 3, 112	Tekken (Ire), 3, 117	7	1:47.32	45,000
1996	**Harrowman**, 3, 114	M. E. Smith	A Real Zipper, 3, 117	Ok by Me, 3, 119	6	1:49.22	45,000
1995	**Admiralty**, 3, 114	J. A. Krone	Nostra, 3, 114	Smells and Bells, 3, 114	4	1:51.03	30,000
1994	**Mr. Angel**, 3, 112	W. H. McCauley	Clint Essential, 3, 114	Fabulous Frolic, 3, 119	9	1:44.66	30,000
1993	**Kissin Kris**, 3, 112	D. Penna	Pride Prevails, 3, 112	Awad, 3, 119	10	1:46.41	38,760
1992	**Preferences**, 3, 114	J. C. Duarte Jr.	Doo You, 3, 112	Stress Buster, 3, 114	12	1:42.64	38,940
1991	**Magic Interlude**, 3, 114	C. W. Antley	Island Delay, 3, 117	Explosive Jeff, 3, 114	11	1:43.10	38,310
1990	**Dawn Quixote**, 3, 119	C. Perret	Rowdy Regal, 3, 119	Always Running, 3, 115	9	1:23.40	30,000
1989	**Shy Tom**, 3, 113	R. P. Romero	Verbatree, 3, 114	Group Process, 3, 114	8	1:37.20	29,835
	Storm Predictions, 3, 119	S. Gaffalione	Mercedes Won, 3, 122	Ocean Mistery, 3, 113	10	1:36.20	30,735

| 1988 | Tanzanid, 3, 115 | D. Valiente | Cefis, 3, 113 | Denomination (GB), 3, 113 | 12 | 1:35.60 | $39,420 |
| 1987 | Racing Star, 5, 114 | S. B. Soto | Explosive Darling, 5, 118 | New Colony, 4, 109 | 9 | 1:34.80 | 36,390 |

Named for West Palm Beach and Palm Beach County, Florida. Palm Beach H. 1987. 1 mile 1987-'89. 7 furlongs 1990. 1¹/₁₆ miles 1991-'93. About 1¹/₁₆ miles 1994. About 1¹/₈ miles 1998. Dirt 1990, 1993, 1995. Three-year-olds and up 1987. Two divisions 1989.

Palomar Breeders' Cup Handicap

Grade 2 in 2005. Del Mar, three-year-olds and up, fillies and mares, 1¹/₁₆ miles, turf. Held September 4, 2004, with a gross value of $180,000. First held in 1945. First graded in 1981. Stakes record 1:40.59 (2004 Etoile Montante).

Year	Winner	Jockey	Second	Third	Strs	Time	1st Purse
2004	Etoile Montante, 4, 120	J. Valdivia Jr.	Katdogawn (GB), 4, 117	Tangle (Ire), 4, 117	7	1:40.59	$120,000
2003	Spring Star (Fr), 4, 116	A. O. Solis	Magic Mission (GB), 5, 117	Garden in the Rain (Fr), 6, 114	5	1:40.78	120,000
2002	Voodoo Dancer, 4, 120	K. J. Desormeaux	I'm the Business (NZ), 5, 114	Skywriting, 4, 114	7	1:41.56	90,000
2001	Tranquility Lake, 6, 123	E. J. Delahoussaye	La Ronge, 4, 116	Al Desima (GB), 4, 113	6	1:41.94	90,000
2000	Tranquility Lake, 5, 121	E. J. Delahoussaye	Tout Charmant, 4, 121	Miss of Wales (Chi), 5, 114	7	1:41.01	82,170
1999	Happyanunoit (NZ), 4, 113	B. Blanc	Tuzla (Fr), 5, 123	Isle de France, 4, 118	6	1:41.28	80,520
1998	Tuzla (Fr), 4, 117	C. S. Nakatani	Ecoute, 5, 114	Call Me (GB), 5, 116	7	1:42.28	80,970
1997	Blushing Heiress, 5, 117	C. J. McCarron	Traces of Gold, 5, 115	Listening, 4, 120	6	1:43.32	83,200
1996	Yearly Tour, 5, 116	C. J. McCarron	Slewvera, 4, 115	Real Connection, 5, 114	8	1:42.56	81,350
1995	Morgana, 4, 118	G. L. Stevens	Yearly Tour, 4, 118	Lady Affirmed, 4, 117	7	1:42.41	74,450
1994	Shir Dar (Fr), 4, 114	C. S. Nakatani	Baby Diamonds, 3, 110	Prying (Arg), 6, 117	7	1:42.95	63,600
1993	Heart of Joy, 6, 119	D. R. Flores	Kalita Melody (GB), 5, 114	Amal Hayati, 3, 114	8	1:42.07	63,000
1992	Super Staff, 4, 114	C. J. McCarron	Odalea (Arg), 6, 114	Only Yours (GB), 4, 115	10	1:42.20	64,900
1991	Guiza, 4, 114	G. L. Stevens	Agirlfromars, 5, 114	Run to Jenny (Ire), 5, 113	8	1:42.11	49,300
	Somethingmerry, 4, 117	L. A. Pincay Jr.	Countus In, 6, 117	Sweet Roberta (Fr), 7, 115	7	1:41.84	48,800
1990	Jabalina Brown (Arg), 5, 112	J. A. Garcia	Stylish Star, 4, 116	Nikishka, 5, 117	8	1:42.60	64,200
1989	Claire Marine (Ire), 4, 122	R. G. Davis	Galunpe (Ire), 4, 115	Daring Doone (GB), 6, 116	8	1:43.20	64,800
1988	Chapel of Dreams, 4, 117	E. J. Delahoussaye	Short Sleeves (GB), 6, 121	Davie's Lamb, 4, 117	7	1:42.60	78,000
1987	Festivity, 4, 115	A. O. Solis	Adorable Micol, 4, 117	Secuencia (Chi), 5, 117	9	1:35.80	64,850
1986	Aberuschka (Ire), 4, 118	P. A. Valenzuela	Sauna (Aus), 5, 118	Fran's Valentine, 4, 119	9	1:34.40	62,750
1985	Capichi, 5, 116	R. A. Baze	L'Attrayante (Fr), 5, 119	Gala Event (Ire), 4, 115	8	1:35.20	50,150
1984	‡Moment to Buy, 3, 115	T. M. Chapman	L'Attrayante (Fr), 4, 120	Royal Heroine (Ire), 4, 125	8	1:35.20	50,550
1983	Triple Tipple, 4, 118	C. J. McCarron	Castilla, 4, 121	First Advance, 4, 115	10	1:35.60	52,050
1982	Northern Fable, 4, 114	S. Hawley	Sangue (Ire), 4, 114	Princess Gayle (Ire), 4, 116	8	1:35.20	33,500
	Star Pastures (GB), 4, 117	W. Shoemaker	Honey Fox, 5, 122	Cannon Boy, 5, 111	9	1:35.40	34,000
1981	Kilijaro (Ire), 5, 129	M. Castaneda	Lisawan, 4, 115	Satin Ribera, 4, 118	9	1:35.40	40,700
1980	A Thousand Stars, 5, 115	E. J. Delahoussaye	Wishing Well, 5, 121	Devon Ditty (GB), 4, 120	9	1:34.80	34,150
1979	More So (Ire), 4, 115	W. Shoemaker	Giggling Girl, 5, 119	Wishing Well, 4, 118	8	1:35.60	34,150
1978	Drama Critic, 4, 118	D. Pierce	Afifa, 4, 119	Fact (Arg), 5, 115	9	1:36.40	26,550
1977	Dancing Femme, 4, 120	D. Pierce	Swingtime, 5, 121	Dacani (Ire), 4, 115	12	1:35.60	17,250
1976	Just a Kick, 4, 120	L. A. Pincay Jr.	Our First Delight, 4, 114	Effusive, 5, 113	5	1:29.40	15,900
1975	Modus Vivendi, 4, 122	F. Toro	Move Abroad, 4, 113	*Tizna, 6, 124	10	1:28.80	14,100
1974	Sphere, 4, 114	S. Valdez	Lt.'s Joy, 4, 121	Modus Vivendi, 3, 122	10	1:28.40	14,050
1973	Meilleur, 3, 114	D. Pierce	Lady Debbie, 5, 116	Probation, 4, 113	9	1:28.60	10,775
	Belle Marie, 3, 114	W. Shoemaker	Best Go, 5, 115	Chargerette, 4, 116	5	1:28.80	9,975

Named for Palomar and Mt. Palomar, California, located near San Diego, California; Mt. Palomar was once the site of the world's largest telescope. Grade 3 1981-'84, 1997-2000. 6 furlongs 1945-'69. 7¹/₂ furlongs 1970-'76. 1 mile 1977-'87. Dirt 1945-'69. Two divisions 1973, 1982, 1991. ‡Royal Heroine (Ire) finished first, DQ to third, 1984.

Palos Verdes Handicap

Grade 2 in 2005. Santa Anita Park, four-year-olds and up, 6 furlongs, dirt. Held January 23, 2005, with a gross value of $150,000. First held in 1951. First graded in 1973. Stakes record 1:07.20 (1989 Sunny Blossom).

Year	Winner	Jockey	Second	Third	Strs	Time	1st Purse
2005	Saint Afleet, 4, 117	P. A. Valenzuela	Hombre Rapido, 8, 116	Bluesthestandard, 8, 116	8	1:09.15	$90,000
2004	Bluesthestandard, 7, 117	M. E. Smith	Marino Marini, 4, 115	Our New Recruit, 5, 114	7	1:08.13	90,000
2003	Avanzado (Arg), 6, 116	T. Baze	Mellow Fellow, 8, 117	Disturbingthepeace, 5, 120	6	1:07.85	90,000
2002	Snow Ridge, 4, 116	M. E. Smith	Squirtle Squirt, 4, 122	Ceeband, 5, 117	6	1:07.70	90,000
2001	Men's Exclusive, 8, 116	L. A. Pincay Jr.	Big Jag, 8, 120	Freespool, 5, 116	6	1:08.33	120,000
2000	Kona Gold, 6, 121	A. O. Solis	Big Jag, 7, 121	Freespool, 4, 115	5	1:08.85	120,000
1999	Big Jag, 6, 116	J. Valdivia Jr.	Kona Gold, 5, 121	Swiss Yodeler, 4, 115	5	1:08.05	120,000
1998	Funontherun, 4, 113	G. F. Almeida	Red, 4, 116	Elmhurst, 8, 119	9	1:08.93	120,000
1997	High Stakes Player, 5, 118	C. S. Nakatani	Rotsaluck, 6, 114	Larry the Legend, 5, 116	7	1:08.44	131,600
1996	Lit de Justice, 6, 122	E. J. Delahoussaye	Siphon (Brz), 5, 119	Lakota Brave, 7, 115	9	1:08.88	135,100
1995	D'Hallevant, 5, 117	C. S. Nakatani	Cardmania, 9, 120	Subtle Trouble, 4, 115	10	1:08.44	94,400
1994	Concept Win, 4, 115	G. L. Stevens	J. F. Williams, 5, 117	Scherando, 5, 116	6	1:07.71	62,100
1993	Music Merci, 7, 114	D. R. Flores	Star of the Crop, 4, 119	Cardmania, 7, 117	7	1:08.82	63,700
1992	Individualist, 5, 117	L. A. Pincay Jr.	High Energy, 5, 114	Rushmore, 5, 114	9	1:08.66	65,600
1990	Frost Free, 5, 119	C. J. McCarron	Valiant Pete, 4, 117	Kipper Kelly, 3, 112	5	1:08.60	61,400
1989	Sunny Blossom, 4, 115	G. L. Stevens	Olympic Prospect, 5, 123	Sam Who, 4, 122	6	1:07.20	62,400
1988	On the Line, 4, 124	G. L. Stevens	Claim, 3, 118	Basic Rate, 3, 115	6	1:07.60	62,700

Year	Winner	Jockey	Second	Third	Strs	Time	1st Purse
1987	High Brite, 3, 116	G. L. Stevens	Hilco Scamper, 4, 117	Zany Tactics, 6, 123	6	1:09.00	$62,500
1986	Bedside Promise, 4, 123	G. L. Stevens	Bolder Than Bold, 4, 116	Rocky Marriage, 6, 115	6	1:08.40	60,000
1985	Phone Trick, 3, 121	L. A. Pincay Jr.	Five North, 4, 112	Debonaire Junior, 4, 123	6	1:08.00	50,100
1984	Debonaire Junior, 3, 120	C. J. McCarron	Charging Falls, 3, 112	Premiership, 4, 117	7	1:10.20	51,700
1983	Fighting Fit, 4, 122	E. J. Delahoussaye	Expressman, 3, 115	Gemini Dreamer, 3, 117	5	1:09.00	38,150
1982	Chinook Pass, 3, 120	L. A. Pincay Jr.	General Jimmy, 3, 112	Unpredictable, 3, 122	8	1:07.60	40,050
1981	I'm Smokin, 5, 119	P. A. Valenzuela	To B. Or Not, 5, 121	Solo Guy, 3, 119	7	1:08.00	39,200
1980	To B. Or Not, 4, 121	M. Castaneda	Unalakleet, 3, 115	Syncopate, 5, 123	9	1:08.20	34,000
1979	Beau's Eagle, 3, 122	S. Hawley	Always Gallant, 5, 124	‡Charley Sutton, 5, 115	7	1:10.00	32,750
1978	Little Reb, 3, 116	F. Olivares	Crash Program, 3, 112	Bad 'n Big, 4, 125	9	1:08.60	33,900
1977	Impressive Luck, 4, 119	S. Hawley	Maheras, 4, 120	Current Concept, 3, 117	6	1:10.40	26,000
1976	Maheras, 3, 119	L. A. Pincay Jr.	Sure Fire, 3, 116	Ancient Title, 6, 126	13	1:08.60	29,400
1975	Messenger of Song, 3, 125	J. Lambert	Willmar, 7, 115	Rise High, 5, 118	6	1:08.60	19,800
1974	Ancient Title, 4, 121	L. A. Pincay Jr.	Princely Native, 3, 116	King of the Blues, 5, 113	8	1:08.80	20,900
1973	Woodland Pines, 4, 115	D. Pierce	Tragic Isle, 4, 117	Ancient Title, 3, 122	8	1:09.00	20,800

Named for the 1824 California land grant named Los Palos Verdes Ranchos; palos verdes means "green trees." Grade 3 1973-'74, 1988-'97. Not held 1969-'70, 1991. Three-year-olds and up 1951-'66, 1971 (January). Two-year-olds and up 1967-'68, 1971 (December) 1972-'89. ‡Grand Alliance finished third, DQ to fourth, 1979.

Pan American Handicap

Grade 2 in 2005. Gulfstream Park, three-year-olds and up, 1½ miles, turf. Held April 2, 2005, with a gross value of $150,000. First held in 1962. First graded in 1973. Stakes record 2:23.15 (1999 Unite's Big Red).

Year	Winner	Jockey	Second	Third	Strs	Time	1st Purse
2005	Navesink River, 4, 114	J. R. Velazquez	Quest Star, 6, 114	Deputy Lad, 5, 115	8	2:25.95	$90,000
2004	Quest Star, 5, 114	P. Day	Request for Parole, 5, 115	Megantic, 6, 112	7	2:26.46	120,000
2003	Quest Star, 4, 113	E. S. Prado	Man From Wicklow, 6, 122	Reduit (GB), 5, 114	9	2:28.45	120,000
2002	Deeliteful Irving, 4, 113	C. P. DeCarlo	Cetewayo, 8, 118	Mr. Livingston, 5, 114	9	2:24.14	120,000
2001	Whata Brainstorm, 4, 114	J. R. Velazquez	Subtle Power (Ire), 4, 115	Craigsteel (GB), 6, 114	7	2:23.75	150,000
2000	Buck's Boy, 7, 120	E. S. Prado	Thesaurus, 6, 113	‡Epistolaire (Ire), 5, 114	7	2:24.80	150,000
1999	Unite's Big Red, 5, 114	M. E. Smith	African Dancer, 7, 116	Panama City, 5, 116	7	2:23.15	150,000
1998	Buck's Boy, 5, 115	E. Fires	African Dancer, 6, 115	Royal Strand (Ire), 4, 114	9	2:23.43	150,000
1997	Flag Down, 7, 117	J. A. Santos	Lassigny, 6, 117	Awad, 7, 117	6	2:27.00	180,000
1996	Celtic Arms (Fr), 5, 115	M. E. Smith	Broadway Flyer, 5, 116	Flag Down, 6, 117	7	2:25.71	180,000
1995	Awad, 5, 114	E. Maple	Misil, 7, 120	Frenchpark (GB), 5, 117	9	2:29.44	180,000
1994	Fraise, 6, 124	M. E. Smith	Summer Ensign, 5, 113	†Fairy Garden, 6, 115	10	2:24.65	180,000
1993	Fraise, 5, 124	P. A. Valenzuela	Stagecraft (GB), 6, 117	Futurist, 5, 114	8	2:32.86	180,000
1992	Wall Street Dancer, 4, 114	J. Velasquez	†Passagere du Soir (GB), 5, 116	Missionary Ridge (GB), 5, 115	14	2:25.53	210,000
1991	Phantom Breeze (Ire), 5, 116	J. A. Krone	Dr. Root, 4, 114	Runaway Raja, 5, 111	11	2:29.55	180,000
1990	My Big Boy, 7, 112	H. Castillo Jr.	Marksmanship, 5, 113	Turfah, 7, 115	12	2:29.20	180,000
1989	Mi Selecto, 4, 114	J. A. Santos	Pay the Butler, 5, 121	Fabulous Indian, 4, 112	8	2:01.60	180,000
1988	†Carotene, 5, 115	D. J. Seymour	†Ladanum, 4, 110	Salem Drive, 6, 117	13	2:25.00	180,000
1987	Iroko (GB), 5, 112	E. Fires	Akabir, 6, 113	Glaros (Fr), 5, 112	13	2:26.40	150,000
1986	†Powder Break, 5, 112	S. B. Soto	Uptown Swell, 4, 116	Flying Pidgeon, 5, 118	11	2:25.00	180,000
1985	Selous Scout, 4, 112	R. Platts	Norclin, 5, 111	Nassipour, 5, 115	13	2:25.20	185,280
1984	Tonzarun, 6, 112	W. H. McCauley	Ayman, 4, 114	Nassipour, 4, 110	9	2:26.80	109,275
1983	Highland Blade, 5, 121	J. Vasquez	Tonzarun, 5, 108	Dhausli (Fr), 6, 113	10	2:29.20	80,295
	Field Cat, 6, 110	J. Samyn	Pin Puller, 4, 112	Santo's Joe, 6, 109	11	2:29.60	82,095
1982	Robsphere, 5, 117	J. Velasquez	Come Rain Or Shine, 5, 110	The Bart, 6, 126	16	2:26.00	102,150
1981	†Little Bonny (Ire), 4, 114	E. Maple	Lobsang (Ire), 5, 115	Buckpoint (Fr), 5, 124	12	2:32.40	121,030
1980	†Flitalong, 4, 110	R. I. Encinas	Morning Frolic, 5, 119	Novel Notion, 5, 117	12	2:28.40	100,000
1979	Noble Dancer (GB), 7, 129	J. Vasquez	Fleet Gar, 4, 116	†Warfever (Fr), 4, 113	9	2:25.20	100,000
1978	Bowl Game, 4, 117	J. Velasquez	That's a Nice, 4, 116	Court Open, 4, 112	10	2:30.20	100,000
1977	Gravelines (Fr), 5, 124	J. D. Bailey	Le Cypriote, 5, 110	Gay Jitterbug, 4, 124	9	2:24.80	80,400
1976	Improviser, 4, 114	J. Cruguet	Green Room, 6, 109	Pampered Jabneh, 6, 113	13	2:26.60	86,880
1975	Buffalo Lark, 5, 120	L. Snyder	London Company, 5, 123	Duke Tom, 5, 115	6	2:27.60	84,120
1974	London Company, 4, 119	A. T. Cordero Jr.	Outdoors, 5, 112	*Bush Fleet, 5, 113	12	2:26.40	84,720
1973	Lord Vancouver, 5, 112	W. Blum	Life Cycle, 4, 118	Windtex, 4, 116	11	2:26.60	83,520

Named in honor of the multicultural heritage of South Florida's residents. Formerly sponsored by the Crown Royal Co. of Stamford, Connecticut 1996. Grade 1 1983-'89. Crown Royal Pan American H. 1996. 1⅛ miles 1989. About 1½ miles 1993, 2003. Dirt 1962-'64, 1975, 1989. Two divisions 1983. ‡Beautiful Dancer finished third, DQ to sixth, 2000. Track record 1975. Course record 1989. †Denotes female.

Pat O'Brien Breeders' Cup Handicap

Grade 2 in 2005. Del Mar, three-year-olds and up, 7 furlongs, dirt. Held August 15, 2004, with a gross value of $194,000. First held in 1986. First graded in 1994. Stakes record 1:20.06 (1995 Lit de Justice).

Year	Winner	Jockey	Second	Third	Strs	Time	1st Purse
2004	Kela, 6, 116	T. Baze	Domestic Dispute, 4, 116	Pico Central (Brz), 5, 122	5	1:21.17	$120,000
2003	Disturbingthepeace, 5, 116	V. Espinoza	Rushin' to Altar, 4, 117	Full Moon Madness, 8, 119	10	1:21.53	90,000
2002	Disturbingthepeace, 4, 119	V. Espinoza	Hot Market, 4, 115	I Love Silver, 4, 117	5	1:21.89	90,000
2001	El Corredor, 4, 119	V. Espinoza	Swept Overboard, 4, 117	Ceeband, 4, 114	7	1:20.42	90,000

Year	Winner	Jockey	Second	Third	Strs	Time	1st Purse
2000	Love That Red, 4, 118	C. S. Nakatani	Cliquot, 4, 117	Son of a Pistol, 8, 117	5	1:21.89	$90,000
1999	Regal Thunder, 5, 116	C. W. Antley	Christmas Boy, 6, 118	Bet On Sunshine, 7, 116	9	1:21.13	90,000
1998	Old Topper, 3, 116	E. J. Delahoussaye	Son of a Pistol, 6, 123	Uncaged Fury, 7, 115	5	1:21.51	95,220
1997	Tres Paraiso, 5, 115	G. L. Stevens	High Stakes Player, 5, 119	Gold Land, 6, 114	7	1:21.45	68,200
1996	Alphabet Soup, 5, 118	C. W. Antley	Boundless Moment, 4, 116	Lit de Justice, 6, 123	8	1:20.79	65,450
1995	Lit de Justice, 5, 118	C. S. Nakatani	D'Hallevant, 5, 117	Pembroke, 5, 119	7	1:20.06	60,400
1994	D'Hallevant, 4, 115	C. S. Nakatani	Minjinsky, 4, 115	J. F. Williams, 5, 117	5	1:20.25	59,725
1993	Slerp, 4, 117	A. D. Lopez	Portoferraio (Arg), 5, 114	Cardmania, 7, 116	7	1:21.36	47,850
1992	Light of Morn, 6, 116	E. J. Delahoussaye	Three Peat, 3, 116	Slerp, 3, 114	12	1:20.65	66,025
1991	Bruho, 5, 118	C. S. Nakatani	Burn Annie, 6, 115	Due to the King, 4, 116	5	1:21.45	46,350
1990	Sensational Star, 6, 116	R. Q. Meza	Frost Free, 5, 116	Earn Your Stripes, 6, 116	9	1:20.60	49,275
1989	Olympic Native, 4, 116	R. G. Davis	On the Line, 5, 126	Sam Who, 4, 121	4	1:20.20	44,850
1988	Sebrof, 4, 116	G. L. Stevens	Synastry, 5, 116	Epidaurus, 6, 119	9	1:20.40	39,350
1987	Zany Tactics, 6, 123	J. L. Kaenel	Bold Smoocher, 5, 114	Bolder Than Bold, 5, 120	7	1:21.20	31,750
1986	Bold Brawley, 3, 115	P. A. Valenzuela	First Norman, 4, 115	American Legion, 6, 121	5	1:20.40	30,850

Named in honor of actor Pat O'Brien (1899-1983), co-founder with Bing Crosby of the Del Mar Turf Club. Grade 3 1994-'98. Pat O'Brien H. 1986-'89, 1996-2003.

Pegasus Stakes

Grade 3 in 2005. The Meadowlands, three-year-olds, 1⅛ miles, dirt. Held October 1, 2004, with a gross value of $300,000. First held in 1980. First graded in 1983. Stakes record 1:45.50 (1999 Forty One Carats).

Year	Winner	Jockey	Second	Third	Strs	Time	1st Purse
2004	Pies Prospect, 3, 118	E. S. Prado	Eddington, 3, 118	Zakocity, 3, 118	8	1:48.57	$180,000
2002	Regal Sanction, 3, 115	J. A. Santos	No Parole, 3, 117	This Guns for Hire, 3, 115	6	1:49.87	210,000
2001	Volponi, 3, 114	S. Bridgmohan	Burning Roma, 3, 119	Giant Gentleman, 3, 116	6	1:46.55	150,000
2000	Kiss a Native, 3, 119	M. K. Walls	Cool N Collective, 3, 115	Pine Dance, 3, 121	7	1:48.33	150,000
1999	Forty One Carats, 3, 120	J. F. Chavez	Unbridled Jet, 3, 116	Talk's Cheap, 3, 118	6	1:45.50	240,000
1998	Tomorrows Cat, 3, 113	J. Bravo	Limit Out, 3, 115	Comic Strip, 3, 119	6	1:46.95	300,000
1997	Behrens, 3, 117	J. D. Bailey	Anet, 3, 120	Frisk Me Now, 3, 119	4	1:46.61	600,000
1996	Allied Forces, 3, 116	R. Migliore	Lite Approval, 3, 112	Defacto, 3, 116	9	1:47.19	120,000
1995	Flying Chevron, 3, 112	R. G. Davis	Da Hoss, 3, 122	Ghostly Moves, 3, 113	4	1:40.27	120,000
1994	Brass Scale, 3, 114	E. S. Prado	Hello Chicago, 3, 114	Serious Spender, 3, 111	9	1:49.27	120,000
1993	Diazo, 3, 117	L. A. Pincay Jr.	Press Card, 3, 116	Schossberg, 3, 116	7	1:47.18	150,000
1992	Scuffleburg, 3, 111	J. A. Krone	Nines Wild, 3, 113	Agincourt, 3, 115	11	1:49.09	300,000
1991	Scan, 3, 119	J. A. Santos	Sea Cadet, 3, 119	Sultry Song, 3, 114	8	1:46.53	180,000
1990	Silver Ending, 3, 119	E. J. Delahoussaye	Music Prospector, 3, 116	Runaway Stream, 3, 113	12	1:47.20	180,000
1989	Norquestor, 3, 114	J. A. Krone	Rampart Road, 3, 113	Fast Play, 3, 116	12	1:49.60	180,000
1988	Brian's Time, 3, 121	A. T. Cordero Jr.	Festive, 3, 110	Congeleur, 3, 112	14	1:47.00	180,000
1987	Cryptoclearance, 3, 122	J. A. Santos	Lost Code, 3, 122	Templar Hill, 3, 118	8	1:48.60	180,000
1986	Danzig Connection, 3, 122	P. Day	Broad Brush, 3, 122	Oygian, 3, 124	5	1:49.00	180,000
1985	Skip Trial, 3, 123	J. Samyn	Stephan's Odyssey, 3, 123	Violado, 3, 117	7	1:51.00	200,040
1984	Hail Bold King, 3, 115	J. Velasquez	Carr de Naskra, 3, 118	dh- Jyp, 3, 115	8	1:49.20	131,040
				dh- Morning Bob, 3, 119			
1983	World Appeal, 3, 114	A. Graell	Hyperborean, 3, 118	Bounding Basque, 3, 115	10	1:46.60	135,360
1982	Fast Gold, 3, 110	J. Samyn	Muttering, 3, 120	Exclusive One, 3, 116	8	1:49.00	131,160
1981	Summing, 3, 122	G. Martens	Johnny Dance, 3, 114	Maudlin, 3, 112	11	1:51.00	133,620
1980	Dr. Blum, 3, 115	R. Hernandez	Bill Wheeler, 3, 115	Peace for Peace, 3, 115	7	1:11.00	15,150

Named for the winged horse of Greek mythology. Formerly sponsored by the General Motors Corp. of Detroit 1997-'98. Grade 1 1987-'93. Pegasus H. 1981-'95, 1997-2002. Pegasus Breeders' Cup H. 1996. Buick Pegasus H. 1997-'98. Not held 2003. 6 furlongs 1980. 1¹/₁₆ miles 1995-'96. Turf 1996. Dead heat for third 1984. Track record 1999.

Pennsylvania Derby

Grade 2 in 2005. Philadelphia Park, three-year-olds, 1⅛ miles, dirt. Held September 6, 2004, with a gross value of $750,000. First held in 1979. First graded in 1981. Stakes record 1:47.60 (1989 Western Playboy).

Year	Winner	Jockey	Second	Third	Strs	Time	1st Purse
2004	Love of Money, 3, 116	R. Albarado	Pollard's Vision, 3, 122	Swingforthefences, 3, 119	12	1:48.42	$450,000
2003	Grand Hombre, 3, 114	J. Bravo	Gimmeawink, 3, 122	Ashmore, 3, 114	10	1:49.03	450,000
2002	Harlan's Holiday, 3, 122	E. S. Prado	Essence of Dubai, 3, 122	Make the Bend, 3, 119	5	1:51.10	300,000
2001	Macho Uno, 3, 116	G. L. Stevens	†Unbridled Elaine, 3, 119	Touch Tone, 3, 122	6	1:49.69	300,000
2000	Pine Dance, 3, 122	M. J. McCarthy	Mass Market, 3, 122	Cherokeeinthehills, 3, 114	10	1:49.03	180,000
1999	Smart Guy, 3, 119	R. E. Colton	Ghost Ring, 3, 114	Pineaff, 3, 122	10	1:49.40	180,000
1998	Rock and Roll, 3, 114	H. Castillo Jr.	Tomorrows Cat, 3, 114	Black Blade, 3, 119	11	1:47.69	150,000
1997	Frisk Me Now, 3, 122	E. L. King Jr.	Envy of the Crown, 3, 114	Christian Soldier, 3, 114	8	1:48.14	120,000
1996	Devil's Honor, 3, 122	A. S. Black	Formal Gold, 3, 117	Clash by Night, 3, 119	7	1:48.58	120,000
1995	Pineing Patty, 3, 122	L. J. Melancon	Royal Haven, 3, 117	Tenants Harbor, 3, 117	12	1:48.05	120,000
1994	Meadow Flight, 3, 122	J. Bravo	Red Tazz, 3, 117	Kandaly, 3, 122	9	1:49.08	120,000
1993	Wallenda, 3, 114	W. H. McCauley	Press Card, 3, 117	Saintly Prospector, 3, 122	9	1:49.33	120,000
1992	Thelastcrusade, 3, 114	V. H. Molina	Ecstatic Ride, 3, 114	Nines Wild, 3, 117	10	1:49.47	90,000
1991	Valley Crossing, 3, 119	A. J. Seefeldt	Gala Spinaway, 3, 122	Riflery, 3, 117	11	1:50.10	90,000
1990	Summer Squall, 3, 122	P. Day	Challenge My Duty, 3, 122	Sports View, 3, 122	9	1:48.20	180,000

1989	**Western Playboy**, 3, 122	K. D. Clark	Roi Danzig, 3, 122	Tricky Creek, 3, 122	12	**1:47.60**	$180,000
1988	**Cefis**, 3, 122	L. Saumell	Congeleur, 3, 119	Ballindaggin, 3, 122	10	1:49.60	180,000
1987	**Afleet**, 3, 122	G. Stahlbaum	Lost Code, 3, 122	Homebuilder, 3, 119	8	1:48.20	180,000
1986	**Broad Brush**, 3, 122	A. T. Cordero Jr.	Sumptious, 3, 122	Glow, 3, 122	7	1:50.80	180,000
1985	**Skip Trial**, 3, 122	J. Samyn	El Basco, 3, 122	Jacque l'Heureux, 3, 119	13	1:50.20	180,000
1984	**Morning Bob**, 3, 122	G. McCarron	At the Threshold, 3, 122	dh- Biloxi Indian, 3, 122	7	1:49.40	132,240
				dh- Raja's Shark, 3, 122			
1983	**Dixieland Band**, 3, 122	W. J. Passmore	Jacque's Tip, 3, 122	Intention, 3, 122	9	1:49.40	136,500
1982	**Spanish Drums**, 3, 122	J. Vasquez	Air Forbes Won, 3, 122	A Magic Spray, 3, 122	11	1:49.00	101,460
1981	**Summing**, 3, 122	G. Martens	Sportin' Life, 3, 122	Classic Go Go, 3, 122	9	1:49.00	100,380
1980	**Lively King**, 3, 122	C. J. Baker	Mutineer, 3, 122	Stutz Blackhawk, 3, 122	7	1:48.80	99,480
1979	**Smarten**, 3, 122	S. Maple	Incredible Ease, 3, 122	Incubator, 3, 122	6	1:49.20	68,880

Philadelphia Park is located in Bensalem, Pennsylvania. Grade 3 1981-'84, 1996-2003. Dead heat for third 1984. †Denotes female.

Perryville Stakes

Grade 3 in 2005. Keeneland, three-year-olds, about 7 furlongs, dirt. Held October 14, 2004, with a gross value of $112,600. First held in 1999. First graded in 2005. Stakes record 1:25.19 (2004 Commentator).

Year	Winner	Jockey	Second	Third	Strs	Time	1st Purse
2004	**Commentator**, 3, 117	R. Bejarano	Eurosilver, 3, 123	Weigelia, 3, 123	7	**1:25.19**	$69,812
2003	**Clock Stopper**, 3, 117	R. Albarado	Ballado Chieftan, 3, 117	Champali, 3, 123	6	1:25.33	67,146
2002	**Najran**, 3, 118	P. Day	Flying Free, 3, 118	Premier Performer, 3, 118	9	1:26.00	52,127
2001	**Dream Run**, 3, 118	P. Day	Strawberry Affair, 3, 118	Solingen, 3, 120	5	1:27.25	50,360
2000	**Smokin Pete**, 3, 118	S. J. Sellers	Classic Appeal, 3, 120	Chervy, 3, 118	6	1:25.38	44,020
1999	**National Saint**, 3, 118	R. Albarado	Moon Over Prospect, 3, 118	Hidden City, 3, 120	6	1:25.21	36,674

Named for Perryville, Kentucky. The largest Civil War battle in the state was fought there on October 8, 1862.

Personal Ensign Handicap

Grade 1 in 2005. Saratoga Race Course, three-year-olds and up, fillies and mares, 1¼ miles, dirt. Held August 27, 2004, with a gross value of $392,000. First held in 1948. First graded in 1973. Stakes record 2:02.57 (1999 Beautiful Pleasure).

Year	Winner	Jockey	Second	Third	Strs	Time	1st Purse
2004	**Storm Flag Flying**, 4, 116	J. R. Velazquez	Azeri, 6, 122	Nevermore, 4, 114	5	2:03.63	$240,000
2003	**Passing Shot**, 4, 114	J. A. Santos	Wild Spirit (Chi), 4, 122	Miss Linda (Arg), 6, 114	5	2:03.33	240,000
2002	**Summer Colony**, 4, 120	J. R. Velazquez	Transcendental, 4, 114	Dancethruthedawn, 4, 120	6	2:03.15	240,000
2001	**Pompeii**, 4, 117	R. Migliore	Beautiful Pleasure, 6, 117	Irving's Baby, 4, 117	7	2:04.60	240,000
2000	**Beautiful Pleasure**, 5, 124	J. F. Chavez	‡Heritage of Gold, 5, 124	Pentatonic, 5, 113	5	2:03.77	240,000
1999	**Beautiful Pleasure**, 4, 113	J. F. Chavez	Banshee Breeze, 4, 124	Keeper Hill, 4, 118	6	**2:02.57**	240,000
1998	**Tomisue's Delight**, 4, 115	P. Day	Tuzia, 4, 114	One Rich Lady, 4, 114	8	2:04.08	240,000
1997	**Clear Mandate**, 5, 115	M. E. Smith	Shoop, 6, 111	Power Play, 5, 117	6	2:03.71	210,000
1996	**Urbane**, 4, 119	A. O. Solis	Shoop, 5, 114	Frolic, 4, 113	8	2:03.05	180,000
1995	**Heavenly Prize**, 4, 127	P. Day	Forcing Bid, 4, 108	Cinnamon Sugar (Ire), 4, 114	8	2:04.16	120,000
1994	**Link River**, 4, 114	J. A. Krone	You'd Be Surprised, 5, 120	Dispute, 4, 119	7	1:50.46	120,000
1993	**You'd Be Surprised**, 4, 115	J. D. Bailey	Avian Assembly, 4, 111	Gray Cashmere, 4, 114	8	1:48.59	90,000
1992	**Quick Mischief**, 6, 113	C. Perret	Versailles Treaty, 4, 122	Shared Interest, 4, 111	7	1:47.96	120,000
1991	**Fit to Scout**, 4, 114	C. W. Antley	Train Robbery, 4, 112	Her She Shawklit, 4, 111	7	1:50.30	120,000
1990	**Personal Business**, 4, 111	C. W. Antley	Buy the Firm, 4, 112	Lady Hoolihan, 4, 110	8	1:51.20	70,200
1989	**Colonial Waters**, 4, 116	A. T. Cordero Jr.	Topicount, 4, 116	Rose's Cantina, 5, 119	5	1:50.00	67,080
1988	**Rose's Cantina**, 4, 111	J. A. Santos	Ms. Eloise, 5, 118	Clabber Girl, 5, 120	4	1:49.80	67,080
1987	**Coup de Fusil**, 5, 116	A. T. Cordero Jr.	Clabber Girl, 4, 113	I'm Sweets, 4, 118	7	1:49.20	83,700
1986	**Shocker T.**, 4, 124	G. St. Leon	Bharal, 5, 113	Natania, 4, 115	5	1:50.00	66,840
1985	**Lady On the Run**, 3, 115	A. T. Cordero Jr.	Verbality, 3, 112	Halloween Queen, 4, 112	6	1:52.00	51,210
1984	**Solar Halo**, 3, 110	R. G. Davis	It's Fine, 4, 109	Quixotic Lady, 4, 115	8	1:49.20	53,640
1983	**Chieftan's Command**, 4, 117	A. T. Cordero Jr.	Adept, 4, 110	Sintrillium, 5, 116	7	1:51.60	34,440
1982	**Number**, 3, 114	E. Maple	Sintrillium, 4, 112	Norsan, 3, 112	5	1:51.40	32,340
1981	**Tina Tina Too**, 3, 114	D. MacBeth	Explorare, 4, 114	Office Wife, 4, 113	8	1:51.00	33,060
1980	**Relaxing**, 4, 118	J. Velasquez	Sugar and Spice, 3, 115	Plankton, 4, 121	8	1:49.20	33,540
1979	**Catherine's Bet**, 4, 113	D. Montoya	Water Malone, 5, 117	Miss Baja, 4, 114	9	1:50.20	32,340
1978	**Mrs. Warren**, 4, 113	J. Velasquez	Water Malone, 4, 121	One Sum, 4, 121	7	1:51.40	32,190
1977	**Water Malone**, 3, 121	J. Samyn	Northernette, 3, 120	Sweet Bernice, 4, 113	8	1:50.40	32,280
1976	**Sugar Plum Time**, 4, 113	A. T. Cordero Jr.	Ten Cents a Dance, 3, 110	Quacker, 3, 111	9	1:51.00	32,610
1975	**Lie Low**, 4, 115	J. Velasquez	Princesse Grey, 4, 114	Carolerno, 4, 112	12	2:15.20	35,910
1974	**Lie Low**, 3, 116	J. Velasquez	Aglimmer, 5, 116	D. O. Lady, 3, 115	8	1:49.00	27,840
	Twixt, 5, 121	W. J. Passmore	Garland of Roses, 5, 114	Fairway Flyer, 5, 124	10	1:49.80	28,290
1973	**Aglimmer**, 4, 115	M. Venezia	Garland of Roses, 4, 111	Cathy Baby, 4, 120	13	1:49.40	36,150

Named for Ogden Phipps's undefeated 1988 champion older mare, '96 Broodmare of the Year, and '88 Whitney H. (G1) winner Personal Ensign (1984 f. by Private Account). Formerly named for John A. Morris (1892-1985), former president of the Thoroughbred Racing Association and Jamaica racetrack. Formerly named for James Ben Ali Haggin's multiple SW Firenze (1884 f. by Glenelg). Grade 2 1983-'86. Firenze H. 1948-'85. John A. Morris H. 1986-'97. Held at Jamaica 1948-'57. Held at Aqueduct 1958-'74, 1976-'85. Held at Belmont Park 1975. 1¹⁄₁₆ miles 1948-'51, 1958. 1¹⁄₈ miles 1952-'57, 1959, 1962-'74, 1976-'94. 1 mile 1960-'61. 1³⁄₈ miles 1975. Turf 1972-'75. Two divisions 1974. ‡Back in Shape finished second, DQ to fourth, 2000.

Peter Pan Stakes

Grade 2 in 2005. Belmont Park, three-year-olds, 1 1/8 miles, dirt. Held May 28, 2005, with a gross value of $200,000. First held in 1940. First graded in 1978. Stakes record 1:46.35 (2005 Oratory).

Year	Winner	Jockey	Second	Third	Strs	Time	1st Purse
2005	Oratory, 3, 116	J. D. Bailey	Reverberate, 3, 116	Golden Man, 3, 116	8	**1:46.35**	$120,000
2004	Purge, 3, 115	J. R. Velazquez	Swingforthefences, 3, 115	Master David, 3, 115	10	1:47.98	120,000
2003	Go Rockin' Robin, 3, 117	S. Bridgmohan	Alysweep, 3, 123	Supervisor, 3, 115	6	1:48.47	120,000
2002	Sunday Break (Jpn), 3, 121	G. L. Stevens	Puzzlement, 3, 115	Deputy Dash, 3, 115	7	1:48.10	120,000
2001	Hero's Tribute, 3, 117	J. F. Chavez	E Dubai, 3, 123	Dayton Flyer, 3, 115	7	1:47.47	120,000
2000	Postponed, 3, 113	E. S. Prado	Unshaded, 3, 123	Globalize, 3, 123	9	1:49.71	120,000
1999	Best of Luck, 3, 113	J. Samyn	Treasure Island, 3, 114	Lemon Drop Kid, 3, 120	9	1:47.94	90,000
1998	Grand Slam, 3, 120	J. D. Bailey	Rubiyat, 3, 113	Parade Ground, 3, 120	7	1:49.14	90,000
1997	Banker's Gold, 3, 113	E. Maple	Zede, 3, 120	Prince Giustino, 3, 114	4	1:48.60	90,000
1996	Jamies First Punch, 3, 118	J. R. Velazquez	Unbridled's Song, 3, 123	Diligence, 3, 118	5	1:47.32	90,000
1995	Citadeed, 3, 112	E. Maple	Pat n Jac, 3, 113	Treasurer (GB), 3, 115	10	1:50.03	90,000
1994	Twining, 3, 122	J. A. Santos	Lahint, 3, 112	Gash, 3, 119	5	1:49.11	90,000
1993	Virginia Rapids, 3, 114	E. Maple	Colonial Affair, 3, 117	Itaka, 3, 114	6	1:48.48	90,000
1992	A.P. Indy, 3, 126	E. J. Delahoussaye	Colony Light, 3, 114	Berkley Fitz, 3, 114	7	1:47.49	106,380
1991	Lost Mountain, 3, 114	C. Perret	Man Alright, 3, 114	Scan, 3, 126	6	1:49.47	106,380
1990	Profit Key, 3, 117	J. A. Santos	Country Day, 3, 114	Paradise Found, 3, 114	8	1:47.20	106,560
1989	Imbibe, 3, 117	A. T. Cordero Jr.	Irish Actor, 3, 126	Pro Style, 3, 117	9	1:48.60	110,160
1988	Seeking the Gold, 3, 120	P. Day	Tejano, 3, 126	Gay Rights, 3, 117	7	1:47.60	140,880
1987	Leo Castelli, 3, 114	J. A. Santos	Gone West, 3, 126	Shawklit Won, 3, 114	9	1:48.00	132,360
1986	Danzig Connection, 3, 117	P. Day	Clear Choice, 3, 123	Parade Marshal, 3, 117	8	1:48.40	85,380
1985	Proud Truth, 3, 126	J. Velasquez	Cutlass Reality, 3, 114	Salem Drive, 3, 114	7	1:47.60	67,050
1984	Back Bay Barrister, 3, 117	D. MacBeth	Gallant Hour, 3, 114	Romantic Tradition, 3, 114	9	1:50.00	57,330
1983	Slew o' Gold, 3, 126	A. T. Cordero Jr.	I Enclose, 3, 123	Foyt, 3, 117	5	1:46.80	34,380
1982	Wolfie's Rascal, 3, 120	A. T. Cordero Jr.	John's Gold, 3, 114	Illuminate, 3, 117	6	1:48.80	34,020
1981	Tap Shoes, 3, 126	R. Hernandez	Willow Hour, 3, 117	West On Broad, 3, 120	7	1:48.40	34,080
1980	Comptroller, 3, 114	R. I. Encinas	Bar Dexter, 3, 117	Suzanne's Star, 3, 114	9	1:49.20	34,080
1979	Coastal, 3, 120	R. Hernandez	Lucy's Axe, 3, 123	Pianist, 3, 117	6	1:47.00	32,820
1978	Buckaroo, 3, 114	J. Velasquez	Darby Creek Road, 3, 117	Star de Naskra, 3, 123	8	1:48.00	32,520
1977	Spirit Level, 3, 114	A. Graell	Sanhedrin, 3, 114	Lynn Davis, 3, 114	9	1:49.20	32,910
1976	Sir Lister, 3, 114	J. Velasquez	‡Jamming, 3, 117	El Portugues, 3, 114	9	1:36.00	34,620
1975	Singh, 3, 114	E. Maple	Majestic One, 3, 114	Sir Paulus, 3, 115	8	1:35.20	33,420

Named for James R. Keene's champion and 1907 Belmont S. winner Peter Pan (1904 c. by Commando). Grade 3 1978-'82. Grade 1 1984-'86. Peter Pan H. 1940-'60. Held at Aqueduct 1940-'43, 1945-'49, 1952-'55, 1958-'60, 1975. Not held 1961-'74. 1 mile 1975-'76. Three-year-olds and up 1979. ‡El Portugues finished second, DQ to third, 1976.

Philip H. Iselin Breeders' Cup Handicap

Grade 3 in 2005. Monmouth Park, three-year-olds and up, 1 1/8 miles, dirt. Held August 21, 2004, with a gross value of $194,000. First held in 1884. First graded in 1973. Stakes record 1:46.80 (1992 Jolie's Halo; 1985 Spend a Buck).

Year	Winner	Jockey	Second	Third	Strs	Time	1st Purse
2004	Ghostzapper, 4, 120	J. Castellano	Presidentialaffair, 5, 117	Zoffinger, 4, 115	4	1:47.66	$120,000
2003	Tenpins, 5, 119	R. Albarado	Aeneas, 4, 114	Jersey Giant, 4, 115	9	1:50.35	120,000
2002	Cat's At Home, 5, 116	J. A. Velez Jr.	Bowman's Band, 4, 117	Runspastum, 5, 114	7	1:49.10	210,000
2001	Broken Vow, 4, 119	R. A. Dominguez	First Lieutenant, 4, 115	Sir Bear, 8, 117	5	1:49.55	210,000
2000	Rize, 4, 112	J. C. Ferrer	Sir Bear, 7, 118	Talk's Cheap, 4, 114	6	1:48.42	210,000
1999	Frisk Me Now, 5, 117	E. L. King Jr.	Call Me Mr. Vain, 5, 110	Black Cash, 4, 112	6	1:49.00	210,000
1998	Skip Away, 5, 113	J. D. Bailey	Stormin Fever, 4, 113	‡Devil's Fire, 6, 113	7	1:47.33	300,000
1997	Formal Gold, 4, 121	K. J. Desormeaux	Skip Away, 4, 124	Distorted Humor, 4, 115	4	1:40.20	250,000
1996	Smart Strike, 4, 115	C. Perret	Eltish, 4, 116	†Serena's Song, 4, 115	7	1:41.59	180,000
1995	Schossberg, 5, 118	D. Penna	Poor But Honest, 5, 115	Mickeray, 4, 114	10	1:49.22	180,000
1994	Taking Risks, 4, 115	M. T. Johnston	Valley Crossing, 6, 117	Proud Shot, 4, 112	9	1:48.33	150,000
1993	Valley Crossing, 5, 113	C. W. Antley	Devil His Due, 4, 123	Bertrando, 4, 119	8	1:49.20	300,000
1992	Jolie's Halo, 5, 116	E. S. Prado	Out of Place, 5, 113	Valley Crossing, 4, 111	11	**1:46.80**	300,000
1991	Black Tie Affair (Ire), 5, 119	P. Day	Farma Way, 4, 122	Chief Honcho, 4, 115	8	1:47.80	300,000
1990	Beau Genius, 5, 122	R. D. Lopez	Tricky Creek, 4, 112	De Roche, 4, 115	10	1:48.20	150,000
1989	Proper Reality, 4, 119	J. D. Bailey	Bill E. Shears, 4, 112	Mi Selecto, 4, 114	9	1:48.00	150,000
1988	Alysheba, 4, 124	C. J. McCarron	Bet Twice, 4, 123	Gulch, 4, 122	6	1:47.80	300,000
1987	Bordeaux Bob, 4, 115	C. W. Antley	Silver Comet, 4, 114	Lost Code, 3, 117	8	1:48.20	163,920
1986	Roo Art, 4, 117	W. Shoemaker	Precisionist, 5, 125	†Lady's Secret, 4, 120	5	1:48.80	188,280
1985	Spend a Buck, 3, 118	L. A. Pincay Jr.	Carr de Naskra, 4, 120	‡Valiant Lark, 5, 115	6	**1:46.80**	162,180
1984	Believe the Queen, 4, 120	D. A. Miller Jr.	World Appeal, 4, 121	Bet Big, 4, 117	9	1:48.20	194,040
1983	Bates Motel, 4, 124	T. Lipham	Island Whirl, 5, 124	Linkage, 4, 115	9	1:47.20	167,520
1982	Mehmet, 4, 115	E. J. Delahoussaye	†Pukka Princess, 4, 108	Summer Advocate, 5, 117	13	1:48.20	174,240
1981	Amber Pass, 4, 117	C. B. Asmussen	Joanie's Chief, 4, 117	Ring of Light, 6, 114	10	1:47.40	170,580
1980	Spectacular Bid, 4, 132	W. Shoemaker	†Glorious Song, 4, 117	The Cool Virginian, 4, 112	8	1:48.00	158,160
1979	‡Text, 5, 118	W. Shoemaker	Cox's Ridge, 4, 120	Silent Cal, 4, 115	6	1:47.40	70,948
1978	Life's Hope, 5, 115	C. Perret	Wise Philip, 5, 114	Father Hogan, 5, 115	7	2:03.20	72,183
1977	Majestic Light, 4, 124	S. Hawley	Capital Idea, 4, 108	Peppy Addy, 5, 116	6	2:00.40	71,143

1976 **Hatchet Man**, 5, 112	V. A. Bracciale Jr.	Intrepid Hero, 4, 119	Forego, 6, 136	8	2:00.60	$71,793
1975 **Royal Glint**, 5, 121	C. Perret	Proper Bostonian, 5, 118	Stonewalk, 4, 121	6	2:00.60	70,948
1974 **True Knight**, 5, 124	M. A. Rivera	Ecole Etage, 4, 112	Hey Rube, 4, 111	9	2:02.00	72,215
1973 **West Coast Scout**, 5, 114	L. Adams	Tentam, 4, 118	Windtex, 4, 113	11	2:01.20	74,295

Named for Philip H. Iselin (1902-'76), president and chairman of the board of Monmouth Park (1966-'77). Formerly named for Amory L. Haskell (1894-1966), former president of Monmouth Park. Grade 1 1973-'96. Monmouth H. 1884-'93, 1946-'66, 1981-'85. Amory L. Haskell H. 1967-'80. Not held 1894-1945. 1½ miles 1884-'93. 1¼ miles 1956-'78. 1¹⁄₁₆ miles 1996-'97. Two-year-olds and up 1884-'86. ‡Cox's Ridge finished first, DQ to second, 1979. ‡Rumptious finished third, DQ to sixth, 1985. ‡Testafly finished third, DQ to seventh for a positive drug test, 1998. Track record 1974. Equaled track record 1992. †Denotes female.

Phoenix Breeders' Cup Stakes

Grade 3 in 2005. Keeneland, three-year-olds and up, 6 furlongs, dirt. Held October 8, 2004, with a gross value of $271,250. First held in 1831. First graded in 2000. Stakes record 1:07.78 (1993 Anjiz).

Year	Winner	Jockey	Second	Third	Strs	Time	1st Purse
2004	**Champali**, 4, 122	R. Bejarano	Gold Storm, 4, 118	Clock Stopper, 4, 118	11	1:08.72	$168,175
2003	**Najran**, 4, 122	J. Castellano	Ethan Man, 4, 118	Take Achance On Me, 5, 118	8	1:08.32	169,880
2002	**†Xtra Heat**, 4, 123	H. Vega	Day Trader, 3, 120	Touch Tone, 4, 119	5	1:10.13	155,000
2001	**Bet On Sunshine**, 9, 123	C. H. Borel	Robin de Nest, 4, 121	Erlton, 5, 119	5	1:09.65	166,470
2000	**Five Star Day**, 4, 119	G. K. Gomez	Istintaj, 4, 119	Bet On Sunshine, 8, 123	6	1:07.90	167,245
1999	**Richter Scale**, 5, 117	K. J. Desormeaux	Bet On Sunshine, 7, 117	Vicar, 3, 121	6	1:08.40	166,780
1998	**Partner's Hero**, 4, 117	C. H. Borel	Pyramid Peak, 6, 117	High Stakes Player, 6, 123	6	1:09.25	100,533
1997	**Bet On Sunshine**, 5, 123	F. Torres	Receiver, 4, 117	Valid Expectations, 4, 117	5	1:08.70	97,464
1996	**Forest Wildcat**, 5, 121	J. Bravo	Valid Expectations, 3, 119	Bet On Sunshine, 4, 115	10	1:09.57	101,246
1995	**Golden Gear**, 4, 124	C. Perret	Hello Paradise, 4, 115	Mississippi Chat, 3, 113	4	1:08.96	67,456
1994	**Lost Pan**, 4, 114	D. M. Barton	Pacific West, 4, 112	Fort Chaffee, 4, 116	5	1:09.45	33,728
1993	**Anjiz**, 5, 114	D. A. Miller Jr.	Gold Spring (Arg), 4, 124	Friendly Lover, 5, 121	9	**1:07.78**	50,251
1992	**British Banker**, 4, 114	D. Kutz	Megas Vukefalos, 4, 124	Binalong, 3, 113	6	1:09.20	49,693
1991	**Deposit Ticket**, 3, 114	P. Day	Tom Cobbley, 5, 114	Hammocker, 7, 113	6	1:10.38	51,838
1990	**Hadif**, 4, 120	D. Penna	Fighting Fantasy, 3, 115	Raise a Tradition, 4, 114	11	1:09.40	52,796
1989	**Momsfurrari**, 5, 114	M. E. Smith	Hammocker, 5, 114	Irish Open, 5, 118	9	1:10.60	36,319
1988	**Carload**, 6, 114	E. Fires	Conquer, 4, 117	Carborundum, 4, 117	8	1:09.80	45,275
1987	**Diapason**, 7, 112	P. A. Johnson	Hail the Ruckus, 4, 116	Dr. Koch, 5, 114	9	1:09.80	35,783
1986	**Lucky North**, 5, 115	P. Day	Clever Wake, 4, 114	Fortunate Prospect, 5, 121	5	1:11.00	34,613
1985	**Harry 'n Bill**, 5, 115	M. Russ	Irish Freeze, 4, 116	Diapason, 5, 113	9	1:09.60	35,913
1984	**Timeless Native**, 4, 121	D. Brumfield	Euathlos, 4, 116	Runderbar, 4, 112	10	1:10.80	36,286
1983	**Shot n' Missed**, 6, 115	L. Moyers	Gallant Gentleman, 4, 114	†Excitable Lady, 5, 115	6	1:09.00	35,214
1982	**Golden Derby**, 4, 115	J. C. Espinoza	Shot n' Missed, 5, 117	Aristocratical, 5, 119	13	1:10.00	40,853
1981	**Turbulence**, 5, 115	J. C. Espinoza	Final Tribute, 5, 114	It's a Rerun, 5, 114	9	1:09.40	35,783
	Zuppardo's Prince, 5, 116	J. C. Espinoza	Convenient, 5, 118	Done Well, 4, 116	8	1:09.40	38,870
1980	**Zuppardo's Prince**, 4, 116	J. C. Espinoza	Cregan's Cap, 5, 111	Cabrini Green, 5, 116	9	1:09.00	35,165
1979	**Shelter Half**, 4, 116	S. A. Boulmetis Jr.	Cabrini Green, 4, 114	Going Innocent, 4, 115	12	1:09.20	29,494
1978	**Amadevil**, 4, 117	S. Maple	It's Freezing, 6, 121	See the U. S. A., 8, 118	11	1:09.40	22,539
1977	**It's Freezing**, 5, 118	E. Maple	Harbor Springs, 4, 114	Dixmart, 5, 113	13	1:09.60	19,143
1976	**Gallant Bob**, 4, 126	D. Brumfield	Real Value, 4, 120	Amerrico, 4, 115	12	1:08.40	18,736
1975	**Delta Oil**, 6, 118	R. Breen	Jazziness, 5, 117	Hasty Flyer, 4, 116	12	1:09.40	19,468
1974	**Penholder**, 5, 116	B. Thornburg	List, 6, 118	Grocery List, 5, 118	12	1:09.40	18,330
1973	**Honey Jay**, 5, 123	J. C. Espinoza	Three Martinis, 5, 116	Mighty Mackie, 4, 110	12	1:11.40	18,493

Named for the old Phoenix Hotel in Lexington; oldest recognized race in North America. The race has also been known as the Brennan, Chiles, Association, and Phoenix Hotel S. Not held 1898-1904, 1906-'10, 1914-'16, 1929, 1931-'36. Phoenix H. 1937-'80. Phoenix Breeders' Cup H. 1990-'91. Phoenix S. 1994-'95. Held at Kentucky Association 1831-1930. Held at Churchill Downs 1943-'45. Two divisions 1981. Track record 1993. †Denotes female. Held as a heat race 1831-'77.

Pimlico Breeders' Cup Distaff Handicap

Grade 3 in 2005. Pimlico, three-year-olds and up, fillies and mares, 1¹⁄₁₆ miles, dirt. Held May 20, 2005, with a gross value of $107,400. First held in 1992. First graded in 1994. Stakes record 1:42.90 (2002 Summer Colony).

Year	Winner	Jockey	Second	Third	Strs	Time	1st Purse
2005	**Silmaril**, 4, 115	R. Fogelsonger	Ashado, 4, 123	Friel's for Real, 5, 114	4	1:44.87	$60,000
2004	**Friel's for Real**, 4, 115	A. Castellano Jr.	Saintly Action, 5, 114	Nonsuch Bay, 5, 116	4	1:45.03	90,000
2003	**Mandy's Gold**, 5, 117	J. D. Bailey	Summer Colony, 5, 121	Stormy Frolic, 4, 114	4	1:46.32	90,000
2002	**Summer Colony**, 4, 119	J. R. Velazquez	Dancethruthedawn, 4, 119	Happily Unbridled, 4, 119	7	**1:42.90**	90,000
2001	**Serra Lake**, 4, 112	P. Day	Jostle, 4, 119	Prized Stamp, 4, 114	6	1:50.22	120,000
2000	**Roza Robata**, 5, 114	P. Day	Bella Chiarra, 5, 118	On a Soapbox, 4, 116	8	1:49.82	120,000
1999	**Mil Kilates**, 6, 113	S. J. Sellers	Merengue, 4, 121	Unbridled Hope, 5, 116	8	1:49.05	120,000
1998	**Ajina**, 4, 120	J. D. Bailey	Naskra Colors, 6, 112	Pocho's Dream Girl, 4, 113	8	1:48.70	120,000
1997	**Rare Blend**, 4, 114	J. D. Bailey	Scenic Point, 4, 114	Aileen's Countess, 5, 114	5	1:51.51	120,000
1996	**Serena's Song**, 4, 123	G. L. Stevens	Shoop, 5, 116	Churchbell Chimes, 5, 114	4	1:49.75	120,000
1995	**Pennyhill Park**, 5, 115	M. E. Smith	Halo America, 5, 117	Calipha, 4, 121	6	1:49.32	120,000

1994	Double Sixes, 4, 112	E. S. Prado	Broad Gains, 4, 118	Mz. Zill Bear, 5, 118	6	1:51.19	$120,000
1993	Deputation, 4, 114	C. W. Antley	D. Theatrical Gal, 4, 112	Low Tolerance, 4, 115	6	1:49.12	120,000
1992	Wilderness Song, 4, 121	C. Perret	Harbour Club, 5, 110	Brilliant Brass, 5, 117	7	1:49.06	150,000

Races for females are typically referred to as distaff races. Pimlico Distaff H. 1992-2001. 1 1/8 miles 1992-2001.

Pimlico Special Handicap

Grade 1 in 2005. Pimlico, four-year-olds and up, 1 3/16 miles, dirt. Held May 20, 2005, with a gross value of $500,000. First held in 1937. First graded in 1990. Stakes record 1:52.55 (1991 Farma Way).

Year	Winner	Jockey	Second	Third	Strs	Time	1st Purse
2005	Eddington, 4, 116	E. Coa	Pollard's Vision, 4, 117	Presidentialaffair, 6, 115	7	1:58.05	$300,000
2004	Southern Image, 4, 120	V. Espinoza	Midway Road, 4, 116	Bowman's Band, 6, 114	6	1:55.89	300,000
2003	Mineshaft, 4, 121	R. Albarado	Western Pride, 5, 116	Judge's Case, 6, 113	9	1:56.16	400,000
2001	Include, 4, 114	J. D. Bailey	Albert the Great, 4, 121	Pleasant Breeze, 6, 114	6	1:55.61	450,000
2000	Golden Missile, 5, 116	K. J. Desormeaux	Pleasant Breeze, 5, 111	Lemon Drop Kid, 4, 120	6	1:54.65	450,000
1999	Real Quiet, 4, 120	G. L. Stevens	Free House, 5, 124	Fred Bear Claw, 5, 113	5	1:54.31	300,000
1998	Skip Away, 5, 128	J. D. Bailey	Precocity, 4, 115	Hot Brush, 4, 113	5	1:54.26	450,000
1997	Gentlemen (Arg), 5, 122	G. L. Stevens	Skip Away, 4, 119	Tejano Run, 5, 114	8	1:53.03	360,000
1996	Star Standard, 4, 111	P. Day	Key of Luck, 5, 120	Geri, 4, 118	4	1:54.46	360,000
1995	Cigar, 5, 122	J. D. Bailey	Devil His Due, 6, 121	Concern, 4, 121	6	1:53.72	360,000
1994	As Indicated, 4, 120	R. G. Davis	Devil His Due, 5, 121	Valley Crossing, 6, 113	6	1:55.08	360,000
1993	Devil His Due, 4, 120	W. H. McCauley	Valley Crossing, 5, 112	Pistols and Roses, 4, 114	6	1:55.53	510,000
1992	Strike the Gold, 4, 114	C. Perret	Fly So Free, 4, 116	Twilight Agenda, 6, 122	7	1:54.86	420,000
1991	Farma Way, 4, 119	G. L. Stevens	Summer Squall, 4, 120	Jolie's Halo, 4, 119	7	**1:52.55**	450,000
1990	Criminal Type, 5, 117	J. A. Santos	Ruhlmann, 5, 124	De Roche, 4, 114	10	1:53.00	600,000
1989	Blushing John, 4, 117	P. Day	Proper Reality, 4, 118	Granacus, 4, 113	12	1:53.20	420,000
1988	Bet Twice, 4, 124	C. Perret	Lost Code, 4, 126	Cryptoclearance, 4, 121	6	1:54.20	425,000

In the past, "special" races were "winner takes all" (the winner got all of the purse money). Not held 1959-'87, 2002. Three-year-olds 1937, 1954. Four-year-olds and up 1988-'97. Winner's share included mid-series bonus of $150,000 from ACRS 1993.

Pocahontas Stakes

Grade 3 in 2005. Churchill Downs, two-year-olds, fillies, 1 mile, dirt. Held November 6, 2004, with a gross value of $109,500. First held in 1969. First graded in 2005. Stakes record 1:34.82 (2000 Unbridled Elaine).

Year	Winner	Jockey	Second	Third	Strs	Time	1st Purse
2004	Punch Appeal, 2, 122	P. Day	Holy Trinity, 2, 118	Kota, 2, 122	7	1:37.77	$67,890
2003	Stellar Jayne, 2, 119	C. H. Velasquez	Turn to Lass, 2, 119	Sister Star, 2, 117	9	1:38.97	69,626
2002	Belle of Perintown, 2, 116	M. Guidry	Star of Atticus, 2, 116	Souris, 2, 121	8	1:36.52	68,882
2001	Lotta Rhythm, 2, 116	M. St. Julien	Cunning Play, 2, 116	Joanies Bella, 2, 121	8	1:37.96	69,130
2000	Unbridled Elaine, 2, 113	S. J. Sellers	Ilusoria, 2, 112	Gold Mover, 2, 121	8	**1:34.82**	70,060
1999	Crown of Crimson, 2, 112	R. Albarado	Maddie's Promise, 2, 121	Dance for Dixie, 2, 114	8	1:37.81	69,812
1998	The Happy Hopper, 2, 119	W. Martinez	Tutorial, 2, 112	Gold From the West, 2, 112	9	1:37.73	70,556
1997	Mission Park, 2, 113	C. H. Borel	Rave, 2, 113	So Generous, 2, 112	10	1:38.55	70,432
1996	Water Street, 2, 112	C. Perret	Cotton Carnival, 2, 114	Private Pursuit, 2, 114	9	1:36.90	69,936
1995	Birr, 2, 112	P. Day	Gold Sunrise, 2, 116	Classy 'n' Bold, 2, 114	8	1:36.84	73,580
1994	Minister Wife, 2, 116	P. Day	Valor Lady, 2, 114	Musical Cat, 2, 114	6	1:38.64	73,385
1993	At the Half, 2, 121	S. J. Sellers	Footing, 2, 116	Mystic Union, 2, 112	12	1:38.13	75,660
1992	Coni Bug, 2, 121	S. J. Sellers	Sock City, 2, 121	Far Out Countess, 2, 114	8	1:37.85	54,698
1991	Fretina, 2, 116	J. E. Bruin	Pleasant Baby, 2, 116	Vivid Imagination, 2, 116	10	1:40.25	55,478
1990	Middlefork Rapids, 2, 116	R. M. Gonzalez	Dark Stage, 2, 116	Til Forbid, 2, 114	10	1:38.00	37,700
1989	Crowned, 2, 116	M. E. Smith	Charitable Gift, 2, 114	Truly My Style, 2, 114	6	1:39.80	36,010
1988	Solid Eight, 2, 121	R. P. Romero	Box Office Gold, 2, 114	Northern Wife, 2, 114	6	1:40.60	36,270
1987	Epitome, 2, 114	P. Day	Darien Miss, 2, 114	Cushion Cut, 2, 118	9	1:38.20	34,589
1986	Bestofbothworlds, 2, 112	P. J. Cooksey	Laserette, 2, 114	Combative, 2, 117	12	1:42.60	34,649
1985	Prime Union, 2, 119	D. E. Foster	Northern Maiden, 2, 112	Whirl Series, 2, 117	8	1:38.40	22,133
1984	Gallant Libby, 2, 119	P. Day	Off Shore Breeze, 2, 117	Gallants Gem, 2, 122	10	1:41.80	18,460
1983	Geevilla, 2, 114	P. Day	Robin's Rob, 2, 119	Sintra, 2, 114	11	1:40.20	18,403
	Flippers, 2, 117	P. Day	Shelbiana, 2, 114	Jay Paree, 2, 117	8	1:39.80	19,703
1982	Brindy Brindy, 2, 117	J. C. Espinoza	Roberto's Doll, 2, 119	Issues n' Answers, 2, 122	7	1:38.20	19,500
	Weekend Surprise, 2, 122	D. Brumfield	Decision, 2, 119	Quarrel Over, 2, 117	9	1:37.80	19,663
1981	Majestic Gold, 2, 118	J. C. Espinoza	I See Spring, 2, 112	Golden Try, 2, 112	15	1:26.80	20,768
	Taylor Park, 2, 121	J. McKnight	Ecole d'Humanite, 2, 118	Dreamtide, 2, 112	14	1:26.40	20,605
1980	Kathy T., 2, 118	L. J. Melancon	Silver Doll, 2, 115	Fleet Pocket, 2, 114	10	1:27.60	18,476
	Masters Dream, 2, 118	G. Gallitano	Taralina, 2, 118	Singing Rockett, 2, 118	11	1:27.40	20,101
1979	Dancing Blade, 2, 121	A. S. Black	Champagne Ginny, 2, 115	Ribbon, 2, 115	13	1:26.80	17,258
1978	Starclock, 2, 121	R. DePass	Silver Oaks, 2, 114	Sensuous Sinnamon, 2, 115	9	1:25.40	14,820
	Safe, 2, 118	E. Fires	Sexy, 2, 115	Fair Advantage, 2, 114	10	1:25.60	14,983
1977	Rainy Princess, 2, 118	L. Snyder	Silver Spook, 2, 121	Irish Agate, 2, 118	8	1:25.20	14,909
	Plains and Simple, 2, 118	A. L. Fernandez	Salzburg, 2, 118	She's Debonair, 2, 112	6	1:26.20	14,909
1976	Ciao, 2, 121	W. Gavidia	Shady Lou, 2, 121	Every Move, 2, 112	9	1:27.00	14,812
	Sweet Alliance, 2, 115	C. J. McCarron	Pocket Princess, 2, 115	My Bold Beauty, 2, 118	8	1:25.60	14,649

1975	**Alvarada**, 2, 118	D. Brumfield	Confort Zone, 2, 121	Bells and Blades, 2, 121	11	1:27.60	$15,941
1974	**My Juliet**, 2, 121	A. Hill	Channelette, 2, 115	Yale Coed, 2, 121	12	1:23.60	15,941
1973	**Shoo Dear**, 2, 121	D. Brumfield	Escrolla, 2, 118	Snow Peak, 2, 115	10	1:27.80	15,308
	Fairway Fable, 2, 118	D. E. Whited	Clemanna, 2, 121	Passing Look, 2, 118	9	1:26.00	15,308

Named for Pocahontas (1837 f. by *Glencoe), one of the great foundation mares of all time and ancestress of numerous American classic winners. Two divisions 1973, 1976-'78, 1980-'83. Nonwinners of a stakes worth $7,500 to the winner 1973. Nonwinners of a stakes 1975.

Poker Handicap

Grade 3 in 2005. Belmont Park, three-year-olds and up, 1 mile, turf. Held July 10, 2004, with a gross value of $112,600. First held in 1983. First graded in 1988. Stakes record 1:31.63 (1998 Elusive Quality [current course and world record]).

Year	Winner	Jockey	Second	Third	Strs	Time	1st Purse
2004	**Christine's Outlaw**, 4, 113	S. Bridgmohan	Millennium Dragon (GB), 5, 120	Silver Tree, 4, 117	9	1:32.46	$67,560
2003	**War Zone**, 4, 117	J. Castellano	Trademark (SAf), 7, 114	Saint Verre, 5, 112	11	1:32.81	69,720
2002	**Volponi**, 4, 115	S. Bridgmohan	Saint Verre, 4, 112	Navesink, 4, 117	7	1:32.24	66,720
2001	**Affirmed Success**, 7, 121	J. D. Bailey	In Frank's Honor, 5, 114	Union One, 4, 114	6	1:34.60	66,240
2000	**Affirmed Success**, 6, 117	J. F. Chavez	Rabi (Ire), 5, 114	Weatherbird, 5, 113	10	1:34.06	68,280
1999	**Rob 'n Gin**, 5, 118	J. F. Chavez	Bomfim, 6, 115	Wised Up, 4, 115	8	1:32.81	69,120
1998	**Elusive Quality**, 5, 117	J. D. Bailey	Za-Im (GB), 4, 114	Fortitude, 5, 114	9	**1:31.63**	51,240
1997	**Draw Shot**, 4, 118	C. W. Antley	Val's Prince, 5, 114	Fortitude, 4, 112	10	1:33.08	51,345
1996	**Smooth Runner**, 5, 113	J. A. Krone	Mighty Forum (GB), 5, 116	Da Hoss, 4, 119	10	1:33.62	51,600
1995	**†Caress**, 4, 117	R. G. Davis	Fourstars Allstar, 7, 119	Pennine Ridge, 4, 119	8	1:34.35	51,030
1994	**Dominant Prospect**, 4, 114	J. F. Chavez	Fourstardave, 9, 114	Nijinsky's Gold, 5, 114	8	1:32.69	49,905
1993	**Fourstardave**, 8, 117	R. Migliore	Adam Smith (GB), 5, 122	Lech, 5, 117	7	1:33.02	53,190
1992	**Scott the Great**, 6, 117	J. Samyn	Kate's Valentine, 7, 117	Cigar Toss (Arg), 5, 117	7	1:33.27	54,810
1991	**Who's to Pay**, 5, 117	J. D. Bailey	Scott the Great, 5, 117	Senor Speedy, 4, 117	10	1:33.55	56,160
1990	**Scottish Monk**, 7, 117	A. T. Cordero Jr.	Quick Call, 6, 117	Yankee Affair, 8, 122	5	1:33.40	52,110
1989	**Fourstardave**, 4, 117	J. A. Santos	Feeling Gallant, 7, 117	Valid Fund, 4, 117	9	1:33.20	56,610
1988	**Wanderkin**, 5, 122	J. A. Santos	Kings River (Ire), 6, 122	dh- My Prince Charming, 5, 117	7	1:35.60	54,720
				dh- Silver Voice, 5, 117			
1987	**Double Feint**, 4, 117	J. A. Santos	Onyxly, 6, 117	Island Sun, 5, 117	8	1:35.20	34,320
1986	**Island Sun**, 4, 119	R. Migliore	Divulge, 4, 119	Equalize, 4, 119	10	2:02.40	33,300
1985	**Mr. Chromacopy**, 4, 119	J. Cruguet	Roving Minstrel, 4, 121	Regal Humor, 4, 119	6	1:42.40	33,420
1983	**Freon**, 6, 115	R. G. Davis	Nadasdy (Ire), 3, 113	Kentucky River, 5, 117	5	2:03.20	24,870

Named for Ogden Phipps's 1967 Bowling Green H. winner Poker (1963 c. by Round Table), broodmare sire of Seattle Slew and Silver Charm. Poker S. 1985-'95. Not held 1984. Dead heat for third 1988. Course record 1998. World record 1998. †Denotes female.

Potrero Grande Breeders' Cup Handicap

Grade 2 in 2005. Santa Anita Park, four-year-olds and up, 6½ furlongs, dirt. Held April 3, 2005, with a gross value of $194,000. First held in 1983. First graded in 1988. Stakes record 1:13.71 (1998 Son of a Pistol).

Year	Winner	Jockey	Second	Third	Strs	Time	1st Purse
2005	**Harvard Avenue**, 4, 115	G. K. Gomez	Rushin' to Altar, 6, 116	Roi Charmant, 4, 114	9	1:16.12	$120,000
2004	**McCann's Mojave**, 4, 116	J. Valdivia Jr.	Unfurl the Flag, 4, 114	Bluesthestandard, 7, 118	5	1:15.60	66,840
2003	**Bluesthestandard**, 6, 115	M. E. Smith	Joey Franco, 4, 116	Kona Gold, 9, 121	7	1:14.86	72,000
2002	**†Kalookan Queen**, 6, 116	A. O. Solis	Ceeband, 5, 116	Elaborate, 7, 115	8	1:15.31	130,620
2001	**Kona Gold**, 7, 126	A. O. Solis	dh-Explicit, 4, 116		5	1:15.03	123,000
			dh-Hollycombe, 7, 114				
2000	**Kona Gold**, 6, 122	A. O. Solis	Old Topper, 5, 116	Your Halo, 5, 116	4	1:14.75	123,060
1999	**Big Jag**, 6, 119	J. Valdivia Jr.	‡Gold Land, 8, 117	Son of a Pistol, 7, 120	5	1:15.09	123,720
1998	**Son of a Pistol**, 6, 114	G. K. Gomez	White Bronco, 4, 114	Gold Land, 7, 115	9	**1:13.71**	66,420
1997	**First Intent**, 8, 114	R. R. Douglas	Hesabull, 4, 117	Northern Afleet, 4, 118	6	1:14.60	64,250
1996	**Abaginone**, 5, 115	G. L. Stevens	Dramatic Gold, 5, 117	Kingdom Found, 6, 118	6	1:14.59	124,400
1995	**Lit de Justice**, 5, 115	C. S. Nakatani	Cardmania, 9, 119	Phone Roberto, 6, 116	6	1:14.65	63,000
1994	**Sir Hutch**, 4, 117	P. A. Valenzuela	Concept Win, 4, 117	Furiously, 5, 117	5	1:14.48	61,100
1993	**Gray Slewpy**, 5, 118	K. J. Desormeaux	Cardmania, 7, 117	Star of the Crop, 4, 119	8	1:14.91	64,700
1992	**Cardmania**, 6, 117	E. J. Delahoussaye	Frost Free, 7, 117	Answer Do, 6, 123	6	1:17.16	60,200
1991	**Jacodra**, 4, 111	C. S. Nakatani	Answer Do, 5, 118	Bruho, 5, 117	6	1:15.10	62,300
1990	**Olympic Prospect**, 6, 121	P. A. Valenzuela	Raise a Stanza, 4, 118	Doncareer, 4, 114	6	1:14.20	60,400
1989	**On the Line**, 5, 125	G. L. Stevens	Ron Bon, 4, 116	Jamoke, 5, 114	10	1:14.00	66,500
1988	**Gulch**, 4, 117	E. J. Delahoussaye	†Very Subtle, 4, 120	Gallant Sailor, 5, 111	3	1:15.00	44,050
1987	**Zabaleta**, 4, 117	L. A. Pincay Jr.	Zany Tactics, 6, 120	Bedside Promise, 5, 125	4	1:15.00	44,850
1986	**Halo Folks**, 5, 124	C. J. McCarron	Bozina, 5, 111	American Legion, 6, 112	5	1:15.60	43,050
1985	**Fifty Six Ina Row**, 4, 117	L. A. Pincay Jr.	Hula Blaze, 5, 120	Coyotero, 7, 114	6	1:15.40	44,650
1984	**Honeyland**, 5, 117	W. Shoemaker	American Legion, 4, 113	Shecky Blue, 4, 116	9	1:15.40	40,450
1983	**Chinook Pass**, 4, 123	L. A. Pincay Jr.	Haughty But Nice, 5, 115	The Captain, 4, 114	5	1:14.60	37,050

Named for Potrero Grande Rancho, near present-day El Monte, California; potrero grande means "big pasture." Grade 3 1988-'96. Potrero Grande H. 1983-'95. Dead heat for second 2001. ‡Early Pioneer finished second, DQ to fourth, 1999. Track record 1998. †Denotes female.

Prairie Meadows Cornhusker Breeders' Cup Handicap

Grade 2 in 2005. Prairie Meadows, three-year-olds and up, 1⅛ miles, dirt. Held July 3, 2004, with a gross value of $300,000. First held in 1966. First graded in 1973. Stakes record 1:46.62 (1998 Beboppin Baby).

Year	Winner	Jockey	Second	Third	Strs	Time	1st Purse
2004	Roses in May, 4, 115	M. Guidry	Perfect Drift, 5, 119	Crafty Shaw, 6, 117	6	1:46.63	$180,000
2003	Tenpins, 5, 118	R. Albarado	Bowman's Band, 5, 116	Woodmoon, 5, 116	6	1:48.39	210,000
2002	Mr. John, 4, 114	M. Guidry	Unshaded, 5, 115	Fajardo, 5, 113	10	1:47.97	240,000
2001	Euchre, 5, 116	G. K. Gomez	Dixie Dot Com, 6, 119	Sure Shot Biscuit, 5, 115	7	1:47.72	240,000
2000	Sir Bear, 7, 116	E. Coa	Skimming, 4, 111	Ecton Park, 4, 117	5	1:48.49	240,000
1999	Nite Dreamer, 4, 113	R. Albarado	Mocha Express, 5, 117	Worldly Ways (GB), 5, 116	7	1:48.85	231,000
1998	Beboppin Baby, 5, 114	J. Campbell	Acceptable, 4, 116	Pacificbounty, 4, 113	8	1:46.62	150,000
1997	Semoran, 4, 117	D. R. Flores	Mister Fire Eyes (Ire), 5, 115	Come On Flip, 6, 114	9	1:48.40	120,000
1995	Powerful Punch, 6, 115	C. C. Bourque	All Gone, 5, 115	Glaring, 5, 116	8	1:49.80	90,000
1994	Zeeruler, 6, 116	R. N. Lester	Powerful Punch, 5, 118	Dancing Jon, 6, 114	8	1:50.20	75,000
1993	Link, 5, 114	R. D. Ardoin	Rapid World, 5, 115	Flying Continental, 7, 117	9	1:50.40	75,000
1992	Irish Swap, 5, 117	B. E. Poyadou	Zeeruler, 4, 115	Stalwars, 7, 116	11	1:47.80	75,000
1991	Black Tie Affair (Ire), 5, 124	P. Day	Bedeviled, 4, 117	Whodam, 6, 113	5	1:48.70	75,000
1990	Dispersal, 4, 122	J. Velasquez	No More Cash, 4, 114	Protect Yourself, 8, 113	9	1:50.00	90,000
1989	Blue Buckaroo, 6, 115	S. J. Sellers	Henbane, 4, 115	Advancing Ensign, 4, 112	10	1:49.40	120,000
1988	Palace March (Ire), 4, 118	J. A. Krone	Outlaws Sham, 5, 114	Galba, 4, 112	9	1:49.00	120,000
1987	Bolshoi Boy, 4, 117	C. W. Antley	Forkintheroad, 5, 112	Honor Medal, 6, 119	10	1:48.40	120,000
1986	Gourami, 4, 116	T. T. Doocy	Honor Medal, 5, 114	Smile, 4, 120	7	1:49.40	150,000
1985	Gate Dancer, 4, 126	C. J. McCarron	Badwagon Harry, 6, 114	Eminency, 7, 119	8	1:48.60	100,800
1984	Timeless Native, 4, 122	D. Brumfield	‡Inevitable Leader, 5, 120	Wild Again, 4, 121	12	1:49.40	90,000
1983	Win Stat, 6, 111	D. Pettinger	†Bersid, 5, 116	Aspro, 5, 121	11	1:53.20	92,978
1982	Recusant, 4, 118	R. J. Hirdes Jr.	Plaza Star, 4, 121	Vodika Collins, 4, 118	10	1:51.60	92,895
1981	Summer Advocate, 4, 118	K. Jones Jr.	Sun Catcher, 4, 121	Brent's Trans Am, 4, 116	11	1:48.20	93,143
1980	Hold Your Tricks, 5, 116	D. Pettinger	Overskate, 5, 126	Daring Damascus, 4, 117	10	1:49.20	88,688
1979	Star de Naskra, 4, 125	J. Fell	Prince Majestic, 5, 119	Quiet Jay, 4, 117	13	1:48.40	90,613
1978	True Statement, 4, 118	B. Fann	Big John Taylor, 4, 115	Giboulee, 4, 116	9	1:48.20	60,913
1977	Private Thoughts, 4, 118	R. R. Perez	Latimer, 5, 114	Dragset, 6, 113	12	1:48.00	62,782
1976	Dragset, 5, 112	S. Maple	Sharp Gary, 5, 113	Methdioxya, 4, 114	7	1:49.00	60,500
1975	Stonewalk, 4, 120	R. Turcotte	Sharp Gary, 4, 115	Rooter, 5, 114	14	1:48.40	59,290
1974	Blazing Gypsey, 5, 114	S. Burgos	Tom Tulle, 4, 122	Super Sail, 6, 117	10	1:49.60	57,963
1973	Joey Bob, 5, 118	L. Moyers	Haveago, 6, 121	Prince Astro, 4, 114	12	1:42.80	30,828

The Cornhusker Handicap was formerly held at AK-Sar-Ben in Nebraska, the "Cornhusker State." Cornhusker H. 1966-'72, 1985-'95. Ak-Sar-Ben Cornhusker H. 1973-'84. Prairie Meadows Cornhusker H. 1997. Held at AK-Sar-Ben 1966-'95. Not held 1996. 1¹/₁₆ miles 1966-'73. ‡Pron Regard finished second, DQ to sixth, 1984. Track record 1998. †Denotes female.

Preakness Stakes

Grade 1 in 2005. Pimlico, three-year-olds, 1³/₁₆ miles, dirt. Held May 21, 2005, with a gross value of $1,000,000. First held in 1873. First graded in 1973. Stakes record 1:53.40 (1985 Tank's Prospect).

(See Triple Crown section for complete history of the Preakness Stakes)

Year	Winner	Jockey	Second	Third	Strs	Time	1st Purse
2005	Afleet Alex, 3, 126	J. Rose	Scrappy T, 3, 126	Giacomo, 3, 126	14	1:55.04	$650,000
2004	Smarty Jones, 3, 126	S. Elliott	Rock Hard Ten, 3, 126	Eddington, 3, 126	10	1:55.59	650,000
2003	Funny Cide, 3, 126	J. A. Santos	Midway Road, 3, 126	Scrimshaw, 3, 126	10	1:55.61	650,000
2002	War Emblem, 3, 126	V. Espinoza	Magic Weisner, 3, 126	Proud Citizen, 3, 126	13	1:56.36	650,000
2001	Point Given, 3, 126	G. L. Stevens	A P Valentine, 3, 126	Congaree, 3, 126	11	1:55.51	650,000
2000	Red Bullet, 3, 126	J. D. Bailey	Fusaichi Pegasus, 3, 126	Impeachment, 3, 126	8	1:56.04	650,000
1999	Charismatic, 3, 126	C. W. Antley	Menifee, 3, 126	Badge, 3, 126	13	1:55.32	650,000
1998	Real Quiet, 3, 126	K. J. Desormeaux	Victory Gallop, 3, 126	Classic Cat, 3, 126	10	1:54.75	650,000
1997	Silver Charm, 3, 126	G. L. Stevens	Free House, 3, 126	Captain Bodgit, 3, 126	10	1:54.84	488,150
1996	Louis Quatorze, 3, 126	P. Day	Skip Away, 3, 126	Editor's Note, 3, 126	12	1:53.43	458,120
1995	Timber Country, 3, 126	P. Day	Oliver's Twist, 3, 126	Thunder Gulch, 3, 126	11	1:54.45	446,810
1994	Tabasco Cat, 3, 126	P. Day	Go for Gin, 3, 126	Concern, 3, 126	10	1:56.47	447,720
1993	Prairie Bayou, 3, 126	M. E. Smith	Cherokee Run, 3, 126	El Bakan, 3, 126	12	1:56.61	471,835
1992	Pine Bluff, 3, 126	C. J. McCarron	Alydeed, 3, 126	Casual Lies, 3, 126	14	1:55.60	484,120
1991	Hansel, 3, 126	J. D. Bailey	Corporate Report, 3, 126	Mane Minister, 3, 126	8	1:54.05	432,770
1990	Summer Squall, 3, 126	P. Day	Unbridled, 3, 126	Mister Frisky, 3, 126	9	1:53.60	445,900
1989	Sunday Silence, 3, 126	P. A. Valenzuela	Easy Goer, 3, 126	Rock Point, 3, 126	8	1:53.80	438,230
1988	Risen Star, 3, 126	E. J. Delahoussaye	Brian's Time, 3, 126	†Winning Colors, 3, 121	9	1:56.20	413,700
1987	Alysheba, 3, 126	C. J. McCarron	Bet Twice, 3, 126	Cryptoclearance, 3, 126	9	1:55.80	421,100
1986	Snow Chief, 3, 126	A. O. Solis	Ferdinand, 3, 126	Broad Brush, 3, 126	7	1:54.80	411,900
1985	Tank's Prospect, 3, 126	P. Day	Chief's Crown, 3, 126	Eternal Prince, 3, 126	11	1:53.40	423,200
1984	Gate Dancer, 3, 126	A. T. Cordero Jr.	Play On, 3, 126	Fight Over, 3, 126	10	1:53.60	243,600
1983	Deputed Testamony, 3, 126	D. A. Miller Jr.	Desert Wine, 3, 126	High Honors, 3, 126	12	1:55.40	251,200
1982	Aloma's Ruler, 3, 126	J. L. Kaenel	Linkage, 3, 126	Cut Away, 3, 126	7	1:55.40	209,900
1981	Pleasant Colony, 3, 126	J. Velasquez	Bold Ego, 3, 126	Paristo, 3, 126	13	1:54.60	200,800
1980	Codex, 3, 126	A. T. Cordero Jr.	†Genuine Risk, 3, 121	Colonel Moran, 3, 126	8	1:54.20	180,600
1979	Spectacular Bid, 3, 126	R. J. Franklin	Golden Act, 3, 126	Screen King, 3, 126	5	1:54.20	165,300

1978 **Affirmed**, 3, 126	S. Cauthen	Alydar, 3, 126	Believe It, 3, 126	7	1:54.40	$136,200
1977 **Seattle Slew**, 3, 126	J. Cruguet	Iron Constitution, 3, 126	Run Dusty Run, 3, 126	9	1:54.40	138,600
1976 **Elocutionist**, 3, 126	J. L. Lively	Play the Red, 3, 126	Bold Forbes, 3, 126	6	1:55.00	129,700
1975 **Master Derby**, 3, 126	D. G. McHargue	Foolish Pleasure, 3, 126	Diabolo, 3, 126	10	1:56.40	158,100
1974 **Little Current**, 3, 126	M. A. Rivera	Neapolitan Way, 3, 126	Cannonade, 3, 126	13	1:54.60	156,500
1973 **Secretariat**, 3, 126	R. Turcotte	Sham, 3, 126	Our Native, 4, 126	6	1:54.40	129,900

Named for M. H. Sanford's Preakness (1867 c. by Lexington), first winner of the Dinner Party S. (now the Dixie S. [G2]) at Pimlico. Held at Morris Park, New York, 1890. Held at Gravesend Park, New York, 1894-1908. Not held 1891-'93. 1½ miles 1894. 1¼ miles 1889. 1¹/₁₆ miles 1894-1900, 1908. 1 mile 70 yards 1901-'07. 1 mile 1909-'10. 1⅛ miles 1911-'24. ‡Dancer's Image finished third, DQ to eighth, 1968. †Denotes female. *Daily Racing Form* reported the time as 1:53.40, a track and stakes record 1973; official time is recorded as 1:54.40.

Princess Rooney Handicap

Grade 2 in 2005. Calder Race Course, three-year-olds and up, fillies and mares, 6 furlongs, dirt. Held July 10, 2004, with a gross value of $500,000. First held in 1985. First graded in 1999. Stakes record 1:10.12 (1998 U Can Do It).

Year	Winner	Jockey	Second	Third	Strs	Time	1st Purse
2004	**Ema Bovary (Chi)**, 5, 119	R. M. Gonzalez	Bear Fan, 5, 122	Lady Tak, 4, 119	6	1:10.81	$294,000
2003	**Gold Mover**, 5, 118	J. D. Bailey	Vision in Flight, 4, 113	Harmony Lodge, 5, 116	8	1:11.31	294,000
2002	**Gold Mover**, 4, 115	J. D. Bailey	Xtra Heat, 4, 127	Fly Me Crazy, 4, 112	6	1:10.21	240,000
2001	**Dream Supreme**, 4, 122	P. Day	Hidden Assets, 4, 114	Sugar N Spice, 6, 114	9	1:10.48	240,000
2000	**Hurricane Bertie**, 5, 117	P. Day	Bourbon Belle, 5, 116	Cassidy, 5, 115	7	1:11.43	240,000
1999	**Princess Pietrina**, 5, 114	R. B. Homeister Jr.	Hurricane Bertie, 4, 118	U Can Do It, 6, 119	8	1:10.49	180,000
1998	**U Can Do It**, 5, 118	E. Coa	Closed Escrow, 5, 117	Colonial Minstrel, 4, 118	9	1:10.12	150,000
1997	**Vivace**, 4, 117	R. P. Romero	Ashboro, 4, 119	Special Request, 4, 115	9	1:10.94	150,000
1996	**Chaposa Springs**, 4, 126	L. A. Pincay Jr.	Reign Dance, 4, 113	Supah Jess, 4, 113	6	1:23.54	60,000
1995	**Miss Gibson County**, 4, 115	G. Boulanger	Goldarama, 5, 113	Sigrun, 5, 116	7	1:23.18	60,000
1994	**Roamin Rachel**, 4, 119	W. S. Ramos	Sigrun, 4, 113	Goldarama, 4, 110	10	1:24.01	60,000
1993	**Lady Sonata**, 4, 115	M. A. Lee	Fortune Forty Four, 4, 112	Treasured, 6, 112	5	1:23.00	30,000
1992	**Magal**, 5, 117	R. Hernandez	Fortune Forty Four, 3, 111	My Own True Love, 4, 116	8	1:23.60	30,000
1991	**Magal**, 4, 112	R. Hernandez	Joyce Azalene, 4, 110	Wekive Run, 3, 112	7	1:24.62	32,550
1990	**Sweet Proud Polly**, 3, 112	P. A. Rodriguez	Legend One, 4, 110	Love's Exchange, 4, 117	6	1:25.00	32,040
1989	**Ana T.**, 4, 113	R. N. Lester	‡Ells Once Again, 5, 111	My Sweet Replica, 5, 112	8	1:24.80	48,990
1988	**Spirit of Fighter**, 5, 121	O. J. Londono	Stanleys Run, 3, 111	Sheer Ice, 6, 117	7	1:24.60	32,550
1987	**Classy Tricks**, 4, 115	M. C. Suckie	Sheer Ice, 5, 117	Spirit of Fighter, 4, 123	5	1:25.00	32,040
1986	**Classy Tricks**, 3, 112	R. N. Lester	Fleur de Soleil, 8, 113	Southern Velvet, 5, 113	6	1:25.00	28,130
1985	**Birdie Belle**, 4, 121	J. A. Santiago	Private Secretary, 4, 119	T. V. Snow, 5, 118	8	1:24.40	33,240

Named for Paula J. Tucker's 1984 champion older mare and '82 Melaleuca S. winner Princess Rooney (1980 f. by Verbatim). Grade 3 1999-2001. 7 furlongs 1985-'96. ‡Spirit of Fighter finished second, DQ to fifth, 1989.

Prioress Stakes

Grade 1 in 2005. Belmont Park, three-year-olds, fillies, 6 furlongs, dirt. Held July 3, 2004, with a gross value of $250,000. First held in 1948. First graded in 1973. Stakes record 1:08.26 (2001 Xtra Heat).

Year	Winner	Jockey	Second	Third	Strs	Time	1st Purse
2004	**Friendly Michelle**, 3, 119	C. S. Nakatani	Feline Story, 3, 121	Forest Music, 3, 119	9	1:09.09	$150,000
2003	**House Party**, 3, 121	J. A. Santos	Chimichurri, 3, 119	Princess V., 3, 115	8	1:09.45	120,000
2002	**Carson Hollow**, 3, 114	J. R. Velazquez	Spring Meadow, 3, 121	Proper Gamble, 3, 121	7	1:08.79	120,000
2001	**Xtra Heat**, 3, 121	R. Wilson	Above Perfection, 3, 116	Harmony Lodge, 3, 116	7	1:08.26	120,000
2000	**I'm Brassy**, 3, 113	M. J. Luzzi	Dat You Miz Blue, 3, 114	Lucky Livi, 3, 121	9	1:09.53	90,000
1999	**Sapphire n' Silk**, 3, 121	P. Day	Marley Vale, 3, 112	Confessional, 3, 118	8	1:09.55	90,000
1998	**Hurricane Bertie**, 3, 121	P. Day	Catinca, 3, 114	Foil, 3, 114	11	1:08.85	68,220
1997	**Pearl City**, 3, 118	J. D. Bailey	Alyssum, 3, 121	Vegas Prospector, 3, 121	5	1:09.40	64,680
1996	**Capote Belle**, 3, 112	J. R. Velazquez	Flat Fleet Feet, 3, 118	Miss Maggie, 3, 116	10	1:08.81	67,200
1995	**Scotzanna**, 3, 121	R. Platts	Culver City, 3, 116	Miss Golden Circle, 3, 118	9	1:10.61	66,840
1994	**Penny's Reshoot**, 3, 116	J. R. Velazquez	Heavenly Prize, 3, 117	Beckys Shirt, 3, 114	6	1:09.07	64,500
1993	**Classy Mirage**, 3, 114	J. A. Krone	Missed the Storm, 3, 118	Educated Risk, 3, 118	5	1:08.89	67,680
1992	**American Royale**, 3, 118	J. A. Santos	Debra's Victory, 3, 121	Preach, 3, 118	6	1:09.36	68,280
1991	**Zama Hummer**, 3, 114	G. L. Stevens	Missy's Mirage, 3, 114	Devilish Touch, 3, 118	10	1:09.98	74,760
1990	**Token Dance**, 3, 114	E. Maple	Stella Madrid, 3, 121	Charging Fire, 3, 114	4	1:09.40	49,770
1989	**Safely Kept**, 3, 118	A. T. Cordero Jr.	Cojinx, 3, 114	The Way It's Binn, 3, 114	5	1:11.60	49,770
1988	**Fara's Team**, 3, 114	J. D. Bailey	Lake Valley, 3, 112	Raging Lady, 3, 114	8	1:10.20	65,700
1987	**Firey Challenge**, 3, 114	R. Migliore	Up the Apalachee, 3, 118	Monogram, 3, 114	12	1:10.60	69,300
1986	**Religiously**, 3, 112	J. A. Santos	Fighter Fox, 3, 112	Tromphe de Naskra, 3, 114	8	1:11.00	54,450
1985	**Clocks Secret**, 3, 115	J. Nied Jr.	Lady's Secret, 3, 118	Ride Sally, 3, 112	8	1:10.00	53,010
1984	**Proud Clarioness**, 3, 115	J. Samyn	Dumdedumdedum, 3, 112	Suavite, 3, 112	6	1:10.40	41,400
1983	**Able Money**, 3, 112	A. Graell	Quixotic Lady, 3, 118	Captivating Grace, 3, 118	10	1:11.00	34,440
1982	**Trove**, 3, 118	M. Venezia	Larida, 3, 114	Dearly Too, 3, 112	8	1:10.00	34,380
1981	**Tina Tina Too**, 3, 118	C. B. Asmussen	Sweet Revenge, 3, 121	Ruler's Dancer, 3, 112	8	1:11.20	33,420
1980	**Lien**, 3, 115	E. Maple	Cybele, 3, 112	Nuit d'Amour, 3, 115	10	1:11.00	27,390

1979	Fall Aspen, 3, 121	R. I. Velez	Spanish Fake, 3, 118	Too Many Sweets, 3, 115	7	1:11.40	$25,740
1978	Tempest Queen, 3, 118	J. Velasquez	Sweet Joyce, 3, 112	Silver Ice, 3, 115	5	1:11.40	25,320
1977	Ring O'Bells, 3, 116	A. T. Cordero Jr.	Road Princess, 3, 118	Pearl Necklace, 3, 116	10	1:10.40	22,410
1976	Dearly Precious, 3, 121	B. Baeza	Old Goat, 3, 118	Answer, 3, 118	4	1:09.80	22,110
1975	Sarsar, 3, 118	W. Shoemaker	Stulcer, 3, 114	Gallant Trial, 3, 114	8	1:10.80	17,070
1974	Clear Copy, 3, 115	D. Montoya	Heartful, 3, 118	Talking Picture, 3, 115	12	1:10.20	17,745
1973	Windy's Daughter, 3, 121	B. Baeza	Voler, 3, 115	Waltz Fan, 3, 115	9	1:10.20	17,355

Named for the first American Thoroughbred ever to win a race in England, Prioress (1853 f. by *Sovereign). Grade 3 1973-'74, 1985-'87. Not graded 1975-'84. Grade 2 1988-2000. Held at Jamaica 1948-'59. Held at Aqueduct 1960-'86.

Providencia Stakes

Grade 3 in 2005. Santa Anita Park, three-year-olds, fillies, 1⅛ miles, turf. Held April 9, 2005, with a gross value of $111,600. First held in 1981. First graded in 2005. Stakes record 1:47 (1982 Phaedra).

Year	Winner	Jockey	Second	Third	Strs	Time	1st Purse
2005	Berbatim, 3, 116	A. O. Solis	Royal Copenhagen (Fr), 3, 117	Thatswhatimean, 3, 119	10	1:47.66	$66,960
2004	Ticker Tape (GB), 3, 118	K. J. Desormeaux	Amorama (Fr), 3, 114	Winendynme, 3, 115	12	1:34.55	68,220
2003	Star Vega (GB), 3, 114	M. E. Smith	Makeup Artist, 3, 115	Shapes and Shadows, 3, 115	6	1:47.89	90,000
2002	Megahertz (GB), 3, 118	A. O. Solis	La Martina (GB), 3, 118	Ayzal (GB), 3, 114	7	1:47.34	48,690
2001	Dynamous, 3, 114	V. Espinoza	Heads Will Roll (GB), 3, 114	Little Firefly (Ire), 3, 116	7	1:50.13	48,915
2000	Kumari Continent, 3, 116	D. R. Flores	Minor Details, 3, 116	Velvet Morning, 3, 115	5	1:48.37	47,790
1999	Sweet Life, 3, 118	A. O. Solis	Lady At Peace, 3, 116	Smittenby (Ire), 3, 116	6	1:49.85	48,375
1998	Country Garden (GB), 3, 118	K. J. Desormeaux	Star's Proud Penny, 3, 120	Marie J, 3, 115	8	1:50.84	49,050
1997	Famous Digger, 3, 114	B. Blanc	Cerita, 3, 114	Clever Pilot, 3, 114	7	1:49.85	48,160
1996	Gastronomical, 3, 116	K. J. Desormeaux	Wish You, 3, 114	Staffin (GB), 3, 114	6	1:50.40	47,880
1995	Artica, 3, 117	L. A. Pincay Jr.	Kindred Soul, 3, 114	One Hot Mama, 3, 115	6	1:49.36	46,725
1994	Fancy 'n Fabulous, 3, 114	A. O. Solis	Rabiadella, 3, 117	Espadrille, 3, 117	7	1:49.02	47,700
1993	On the Catwalk (Ire), 3, 116	E. J. Delahoussaye	Amal Hayati, 3, 118	Voluptuous, 3, 114	6	1:50.35	46,650
1992	Miss Turkana, 3, 115	A. L. Castanon	Red Bandana, 3, 114	More Than Willing, 3, 120	7	1:47.32	47,475
1991	Fantastic Ways, 3, 115	C. J. McCarron	Island Shuffle, 3, 114	Saucy Lady B, 3, 115	9	1:49.50	49,425
1990	Materco, 3, 120	E. J. Delahoussaye	Somethingmerry, 3, 120	Nijinsky's Lover, 3, 120	9	1:47.40	48,900
1989	Formidable Lady, 3, 117	G. L. Stevens	General Charge (Ire), 3, 117	Kelly, 3, 117	10	1:50.60	49,350
1988	Pattern Step, 3, 120	C. J. McCarron	Do So, 3, 117	Twice Titled, 3, 117	8	1:48.00	48,000
1987	Some Sensation, 3, 117	L. A. Pincay Jr.	Davie's Lamb, 3, 113	Pink Slipper, 3, 113	7	1:48.20	37,950
1986	Miraculous, 3, 113	G. L. Stevens	Top Corsage, 3, 116	Roberto's Key, 3, 115	8	1:47.80	38,350
1985	Soft Dawn, 3, 113	W. Shoemaker	Rose Cream, 3, 114	Charming Susan, 3, 117	7	1:49.60	37,850
1984	Class Play, 3, 117	L. A. Pincay Jr.	Pronto Miss, 3, 115	Powder Break, 3, 113	7	1:50.20	37,850
1983	Spruce Song, 3, 115	S. Hawley	Yours Or Mine, 3, 114	Stage Door Canteen, 3, 115	10	1:47.40	39,850
1982	Phaedra, 3, 117	L. A. Pincay Jr.	Northern Style, 3, 115	Carry a Tune, 3, 115	10	1:47.00	39,800
1981	Flying Baton, 3, 113	T. Lipham	Ice Princess, 3, 115	Bee a Scout, 3, 115	11	1:47.60	34,050

Named for an 1843 California land grant, Rancho Providencia, located near present-day Burbank; providencia means "providence" or "foresight." 1 mile 2004.

Pucker Up Stakes

Grade 3 in 2005. Arlington Park, three-year-olds, fillies, 1⅛ miles, turf. Held September 18, 2004, with a gross value of $200,000. First held in 1961. First graded in 1973. Stakes record 1:47.58 (1991 Jinski's World).

Year	Winner	Jockey	Second	Third	Strs	Time	1st Purse
2004	Ticker Tape (GB), 3, 122	K. J. Desormeaux	Spotlight (GB), 3, 122	Sister Swank, 3, 116	11	1:48.63	$120,000
2003	Aud, 3, 118	B. D. Peck	Hail Hillary, 3, 116	Julie's Prize, 3, 120	12	1:49.16	105,000
2002	Little Treasure (Fr), 3, 122	R. R. Douglas	Cellars Shiraz, 3, 122	Kathy K D, 3, 116	11	1:49.92	90,000
2001	Snow Dance, 3, 122	C. Perret	Kiss the Devil, 3, 116	Twilite Tryst, 3, 116	12	1:47.93	90,000
2000	Solvig, 3, 121	P. Day	Zoftig, 3, 118	Impending Bear, 3, 118	6	1:52.40	90,000
1997	Witchful Thinking, 3, 118	G. K. Gomez	Swearingen, 3, 116	Cozy Blues, 3, 116	8	1:48.80	75,000
1996	Ms. Mostly, 3, 114	R. P. Romero	Mountain Affair, 3, 116	Clamorosa, 3, 121	9	1:51.18	90,000
1995	Grand Charmer, 3, 116	P. Day	Upper Noosh, 3, 116	Set Me Straight, 3, 114	8	1:49.59	60,000
1994	Work the Crowd, 3, 118	A. T. Gryder	Irish Forever, 3, 116	Looking for Heaven, 3, 116	14	1:49.32	60,000
1993	Amal Hayati, 3, 113	W. S. Ramos	Warside, 3, 113	Future Starlet, 3, 111	11	1:53.39	60,000
1992	Ziggy's Act, 3, 116	G. Boulanger	Bernique, 3, 116	Luv Me Luv Me Not, 3, 121	10	1:48.79	60,000
1991	Jinski's World, 3, 111	A. Madrid Jr.	Ms. Aerosmith, 3, 116	Radiant Ring, 3, 121	9	1:47.58	60,000
1990	Southern Tradition, 3, 116	E. Fires	Virgin Michael, 3, 116	Slew of Pearls, 3, 116	11	1:49.20	70,140
1989	Oczy Czarnie, 3, 112	C. A. Black	Adira, 3, 112	Vanities, 3, 115	9	1:55.00	67,680
1987	Sum, 3, 118	E. Fires	Spectacular Bev, 3, 118	Lucie's Bower, 3, 113	10	1:51.80	47,790
1986	Top Corsage, 3, 120	S. Hawley	Marianna's Girl, 3, 115	Innsbruck (GB), 3, 114	10	1:44.20	34,620
1985	Itsagem, 3, 118	K. K. Allen	Miss Ultimo, 3, 121	Tide, 3, 112	7	1:57.60	35,520
1984	Witwatersrand, 3, 112	E. Fires	Madam Flutterby, 3, 118	Mr. T.'s Tune, 3, 112	9	1:52.40	48,885
	Dictina (Fr), 3, 112	J. L. Diaz	Nettie Cometti, 3, 121	Princess Moran, 3, 116	7	1:51.40	48,285
1983	Decision, 3, 121	E. Fires	Narrate, 3, 118	Won'tyoucomehome, 3, 116	15	1:51.20	35,310
1982	Rose Bouquet, 3, 121	R. P. Romero	Stay a Leader, 3, 116	Smart Heiress, 3, 121	11	1:53.60	34,710
1981	Melanie Frances, 3, 116	R. Sibille	Safe Play, 3, 121	Touch of Glamour, 3, 116	9	1:51.80	33,660

1980	**Ribbon**, 3, 114	P. Day	Satin Ribera, 3, 121	Cannon Boy, 3, 113	14	1:52.20	$35,250
1979	**Allisons' Gal**, 3, 112	M. R. Morgan	Safe, 3, 121	Cup of Honey, 3, 116	12	2:00.40	34,500
1978	**Key to the Saga**, 3, 119	J. Samyn	Pretty Delight, 3, 119	Xandu, 3, 122	13	1:51.40	34,650
1977	**Rich Soil**, 3, 122	M. A. Rivera	New Scent, 3, 114	Ivory Castle, 3, 122	12	1:50.40	34,530
1976	**T. V. Vixen**, 3, 122	M. Manganello	Three Colors, 3, 119	True Reality, 3, 113	8	1:48.40	36,600
1975	**Kissapotamus**, 3, 118	D. Stover	Miami Game, 3, 118	Be Victorious, 3, 113	11	1:45.60	21,400
1974	**Tappahannock**, 3, 113	W. Gavidia	Pot Roast Billie, 3, 112	Miss Indian Chief, 3, 115	13	1:47.60	22,350
1973	**Eleven Pleasures**, 3, 112	H. Arroyo	Princess Doubleday, 3, 121	Guided Missle, 3, 112	9	1:37.60	16,150

Named for Mrs. Ada L. Rice's 1957 champion older mare and '57 Washington Park H. winner Pucker Up (1953 f. by Olympia). Not graded 1979. Grade 2 1996-'97. Pucker Up H. 1961, 1963-'73. Held at Hawthorne Race Course 1985. Not held 1988, 1998-'99. 1 mile 1961, 1966-'73. 1¹/₁₆ miles 1962-'65, 1974-'75, 1986. 1³/₁₆ miles 1979. Originally scheduled at 1¹/₈ miles on turf 1973. Originally scheduled at 1¹/₁₆ miles on turf 1974. Dirt 1961-'74, 1976. Two divisions 1984.

Queen Elizabeth II Challenge Cup Stakes

Grade 1 in 2005. Keeneland, three-year-olds, fillies, 1¹/₈ miles, turf. Held October 16, 2004, with a gross value of $500,000. First held in 1984. First graded in 1986. Stakes record 1:45.81 (1996 Memories of Silver).

Year	Winner	Jockey	Second	Third	Strs	Time	1st Purse
2004	**Ticker Tape (GB)**, 3, 121	K. J. Desormeaux	Barancella (Fr), 3, 121	River Belle (GB), 3, 121	7	1:51.35	$310,000
2003	**Film Maker**, 3, 121	E. S. Prado	Maiden Tower (GB), 3, 121	Casual Look, 3, 121	10	1:47.82	310,000
2002	**Riskaverse**, 3, 121	M. Guidry	Zenda (GB), 3, 121	Lush Soldier, 3, 121	9	1:49.84	310,000
2001	**Affluent**, 3, 121	E. J. Delahoussaye	Golden Apples (Ire), 3, 121	Snow Dance, 3, 121	10	1:50.03	310,000
2000	**Collect the Cash**, 3, 121	S. J. Sellers	Blue Moon (Fr), 3, 121	Theoretically, 3, 121	9	1:47.94	310,000
1999	**Perfect Sting**, 3, 121	P. Day	Tout Charmant, 3, 121	Wannabe Grand (Ire), 3, 121	9	1:50.66	310,000
1998	**Tenski**, 3, 121	R. Migliore	Shires Ende, 3, 121	Sierra Virgen, 3, 121	9	1:48.54	248,000
1997	**Ryafan**, 3, 121	A. O. Solis	Auntie Mame, 3, 121	Golden Arches (Fr), 3, 121	8	1:46.64	248,000
1996	**Memories of Silver**, 3, 121	R. G. Davis	Shake the Yoke (GB), 3, 121	Antespend, 3, 121	10	1:45.81	248,000
1995	**Perfect Arc**, 3, 121	J. R. Velazquez	Auriette (Ire), 3, 121	Country Cat, 3, 121	8	1:49.84	155,000
1994	**Danish (Ire)**, 3, 121	J. A. Krone	Eternal Reve, 3, 121	Avie's Fancy, 3, 121	10	1:48.89	124,000
1993	**Tribulation**, 3, 121	J. Samyn	Miami Sands (Ire), 3, 121	Possibly Perfect, 3, 121	9	1:53.62	124,000
1992	**Captive Miss**, 3, 121	J. A. Krone	Suivi, 3, 121	Trampoli, 3, 121	10	1:48.66	124,000
1991	**La Gueriere**, 3, 121	B. D. Peck	Satin Flower, 3, 121	Radiant Ring, 3, 121	9	1:49.86	130,000
1990	**Plenty of Grace**, 3, 121	J. D. Bailey	Christiecat, 3, 121	My Girl Jeannie, 3, 121	10	1:51.40	65,000
1989	**Coolawin**, 3, 121	J. A. Velez Jr.	To the Lighthouse, 3, 121	Songlines, 3, 121	8	1:43.20	65,000
1988	**Love You by Heart**, 3, 121	R. P. Romero	Siggebo, 3, 121	Glowing Honor, 3, 121	8	1:44.80	65,000
1987	**Graceful Darby**, 3, 121	J. D. Bailey	Shot Gun Bonnie, 3, 121	Sum, 3, 121	10	1:47.20	65,000
1986	**Lotka**, 3, 121	W. A. Guerra	Minstress, 3, 121	Top Corsage, 3, 121	9	1:50.00	65,000
1985	**Contredance**, 3, 112	E. Maple	Debutant Dancer, 3, 115	Folk Art, 3, 120	10	1:47.00	55,608
1984	**Sintra**, 3, 112	K. K. Allen	Solar Halo, 3, 112	Mr. T.'s Tune, 3, 112	12	1:43.40	69,644

Named in honor of the 1984 visit of Queen Elizabeth II of England to Central Kentucky; she presented the first winner's trophy. Grade 3 1986-'87. Grade 2 1988-'90. 1¹/₁₆ miles 1987. Dirt 1984-'86.

Queens County Handicap

Grade 3 in 2005. Aqueduct, three-year-olds and up, 1⁹/₁₆ miles, dirt. Held December 4, 2004, with a gross value of $112,100. First held in 1902. First graded in 1973. Stakes record 1:54.40 (1972 Sunny and Mild).

Year	Winner	Jockey	Second	Third	Strs	Time	1st Purse
2004	**Classic Endeavor**, 6, 117	A. T. Gryder	Evening Attire, 6, 123	Colita, 4, 115	9	1:57.13	$67,260
2003	**Thunder Blitz**, 5, 114	J. F. Chavez	Evening Attire, 5, 123	Seattle Fitz (Arg), 4, 115	6	1:55.90	64,980
2002	**Snake Mountain**, 4, 117	J. A. Santos	Docent, 4, 115	Cat's At Home, 5, 115	7	1:56.84	66,000
2001	**Evening Attire**, 3, 113	S. Bridgmohan	Balto Star, 3, 118	Top Official, 6, 113	8	1:55.08	67,140
2000	**Boston Party**, 4, 117	N. Arroyo Jr.	Talk's Cheap, 4, 115	Turnofthecentury, 3, 116	9	1:56.32	50,340
1999	**Early Warning**, 4, 116	J. F. Chavez	Doc Martin, 4, 112	Yankee Victor, 3, 114	7	1:55.03	49,230
1998	**Fire King**, 5, 113	F. Lovato Jr.	Las Vegas Fever, 4, 112	Mr. Sinatra, 4, 119	7	1:56.88	49,140
1997	**Mr. Sinatra**, 3, 115	R. Migliore	Delay of Game, 4, 118	Draw, 4, 113	8	1:55.68	49,725
1996	**Topsy Robsy**, 4, 111	P. Keim-Bruno	More to Tell, 5, 114	Colonial Secretary, 4, 116	5	1:55.30	48,705
1995	**Aztec Empire**, 5, 113	J. Samyn	Mighty Magee, 3, 115	More to Tell, 4, 115	9	1:55.56	50,340
1994	**Federal Funds**, 5, 112	D. Carr	Jacksonport, 5, 110	Contract Court, 4, 116	8	1:56.42	49,665
1993	**Repletion**, 4, 111	M. E. Smith	Dibbs n' Dubbs, 5, 111	Primitive Hall, 4, 113	8	1:44.35	53,010
1992	**Shots Are Ringing**, 5, 117	J. R. Velazquez	A Call to Rise, 4, 111	Jacksonport, 3, 111	6	1:54.90	51,120
1991	**Nome**, 5, 112	E. Maple	Runaway Stream, 4, 116	Challenge My Duty, 4, 114	5	1:56.18	51,390
1990	**Sports View**, 3, 114	C. Perret	I'm Sky High, 4, 115	dh- Killer Diller, 3, 115	8	1:57.00	53,550
				dh- Lost Opportunity, 4, 112			
1989	**Its Acedemic**, 5, 115	J. D. Bailey	Homebuilder, 5, 113	Ole Atocha, 4, 113	7	1:58.00	52,290
1988	**Lay Down**, 4, 109	J. Samyn	Nostalgia's Star, 6, 113	Pleasant Virginian, 4, 113	6	1:57.20	64,980
1987	**Personal Flag**, 4, 115	R. P. Romero	Easy N Dirty, 4, 113	Gold Alert, 4, 114	5	1:59.00	64,170
1986	**Pine Belt**, 4, 111	E. Maple	Scrimshaw, 3, 108	Cost Conscious, 4, 111	6	1:57.20	55,260
1985	**Late Act**, 6, 118	E. Maple	Lightning Leap, 3, 110	Morning Bob, 4, 113	8	1:55.40	52,380
1984	**Puntivo**, 4, 114	R. G. Davis	High Honors, 4, 114	Moro, 5, 121	9	1:58.00	44,640
1983	**Country Pine**, 3, 118	J. D. Bailey	Count Normandy, 4, 108	Megaturn, 3, 113	8	1:58.00	33,240

1982 **Bar Dexter**, 5, 112	J. Fell	Castle Knight, 4, 111	Nice Pirate, 4, 110	5	1:58.20	$32,880
1981 **French Cut**, 4, 112	D. MacBeth	Bar Dexter, 4, 110	Alla Breva, 4, 109	11	1:56.40	35,040
1980 **Fool's Prayer**, 5, 112	J. Velasquez	Ring of Light, 5, 115	Picturesque, 4, 114	7	1:56.00	33,360
1979 **Dewan Keys**, 4, 112	E. Maple	Mr. International, 6, 108	Gallant Best, 3, 116	8	1:56.80	32,940
1978 †**Cum Laude Laurie**, 4, 114	A. T. Cordero Jr.	Wise Philip, 5, 112	Do Tell George, 5, 112	8	1:55.80	32,580
1977 **Cox's Ridge**, 3, 126	E. Maple	Father Hogan, 4, 111	Popular Victory, 5, 115	7	1:55.80	32,670
1976 **It's Freezing**, 4, 113	J. Vasquez	Distant Land, 4, 111	Nalees Rialto, 4, 108	8	1:56.60	32,640
1975 **Hail the Pirates**, 5, 111	R. Turcotte	‡Sharp Gary, 4, 110	Herculean, 4, 111	10	1:55.60	34,560
1974 **Free Hand**, 4, 109	J. Amy	Arbees Boy, 4, 121	Group Plan, 4, 123	8	1:55.00	33,780
1973 **True Knight**, 4, 126	A. T. Cordero Jr.	Triangular, 6, 110	North Sea, 4, 117	12	1:55.00	35,070

Named for Queens County, New York, in which Aqueduct is located. Grade 2 1973-'74. Not graded 1980. Held at Belmont Park 1946. Held at Jamaica 1956-'58. Not held 1909, 1911-'13. 1 mile 70 yards 1902-'03. 1 mile 1904-'39, 1959-'62. 1¹/₁₆ miles 1940-'58, 1993. 1¹/₈ miles 1963-'71. Dead heat for third 1990. ‡Festive Mood finished second, DQ to tenth, 1975. †Denotes female.

Railbird Stakes

Grade 3 in 2005. Hollywood Park, three-year-olds, fillies, 7 furlongs, dirt. Held May 1, 2005, with a gross value of $109,700. First held in 1963. First graded in 1973. Stakes record 1:20.60 (1979 Eloquent).

Year	Winner	Jockey	Second	Third	Strs	Time	1st Purse
2005	**Short Route**, 3, 118	P. A. Valenzuela	Inspiring, 3, 123	Off the Richter, 3, 115	8	1:22.99	$65,820
2004	**Elusive Diva**, 3, 118	P. A. Valenzuela	M. A. Fox, 3, 116	Speedy Falcon, 3, 123	8	1:21.36	65,760
2003	**Buffythecenterfold**, 3, 123	V. Espinoza	Honest Answer, 3, 117	Dash for Money, 3, 115	6	1:22.54	64,320
2002	**September Secret**, 3, 118	P. A. Valenzuela	Affairs of State, 3, 118	Fun House, 3, 118	5	1:22.95	63,780
2001	**Golden Ballet**, 3, 123	C. J. McCarron	Starrer, 3, 115	Pretty 'n Smart, 3, 115	6	1:21.57	90,000
2000	‡**Cover Gal**, 3, 122	L. A. Pincay Jr.	Wired to Fly, 3, 122	Classic Olympio, 3, 122	5	1:22.57	90,000
1999	**Olympic Charmer**, 3, 115	C. J. McCarron	Dianehill (Ire), 3, 115	Fee Fi Foe, 3, 116	9	1:21.18	90,000
1998	**Brulay**, 3, 115	G. L. Stevens	Gourmet Girl, 3, 119	Unreal Squeal, 3, 116	6	1:20.84	64,260
1997	**I Ain't Bluffing**, 3, 118	E. J. Delahoussaye	Really Happy, 3, 121	Montecito, 3, 114	7	1:22.60	65,100
1996	**Supercilious**, 3, 121	C. S. Nakatani	Tiffany Diamond, 3, 118	Raw Gold, 3, 121	6	1:22.55	64,260
1995	**Sleep Easy**, 3, 113	C. S. Nakatani	Texinadress, 3, 118	Laguna Seca, 3, 115	8	1:22.42	64,600
1994	**Sportful Snob**, 3, 118	P. A. Valenzuela	Pirate's Revenge, 3, 121	Accountable Lady, 3, 116	5	1:21.94	61,400
1993	**Afto**, 3, 114	P. Atkinson	Fit to Lead, 3, 121	Nijivision, 3, 113	8	1:22.48	64,500
1992	**She's Tops**, 3, 114	K. J. Desormeaux	Race the Wild Wind, 3, 121	Magical Maiden, 3, 121	9	1:22.78	66,500
1991	**Suziqcute**, 3, 119	C. J. McCarron	Zama Hummer, 3, 117	Ifyoucouldseemenow, 3, 122	6	1:21.90	62,800
1990	**Forest Fealty**, 3, 114	J. A. Garcia	Patches, 3, 122	Golden Reef, 3, 122	6	1:21.60	48,950
1989	**Imaginary Lady**, 3, 122	G. L. Stevens	Kiwi, 3, 114	Stormy But Valid, 3, 122	7	1:21.40	47,800
1988	**Sheesham**, 3, 122	L. A. Pincay Jr.	Affordable Price, 3, 114	Super Avie, 3, 116	9	1:22.60	49,700
1987	**Very Subtle**, 3, 122	W. Shoemaker	Joey the Trip, 3, 117	Sacahuista, 3, 122	4	1:22.60	45,750
1986	**Melair**, 3, 122	P. A. Valenzuela	Comparability, 3, 119	Silent Arrival, 3, 122	7	1:22.40	48,600
1985	**Reigning Countess**, 3, 122	G. L. Stevens	Window Seat, 3, 122	Charming Susan, 3, 115	6	1:22.40	38,300
1984	**Mitterand**, 3, 115	E. J. Delahoussaye	Gene's Lady, 3, 122	Lucky Lucky Lucky, 3, 122	10	1:22.20	40,000
1983	**Ski Goggle**, 3, 122	C. J. McCarron	Madam Forbes, 3, 115	Gatita, 3, 117	9	1:23.40	33,150
1982	**Faneuil Lass**, 3, 117	T. Lipham	Jones Time Machine, 3, 119	Hasty Hannah, 3, 119	8	1:23.20	32,400
1981	**Cherokee Frolic**, 3, 119	G. Cohen	Strangeways, 3, 114	Terra Miss, 3, 115	6	1:22.20	32,400
1980	**Cinegita**, 3, 114	T. Lipham	Thundertee, 3, 122	Back At Two, 3, 119	6	1:20.80	31,450
1979	**Eloquent**, 3, 122	D. Pierce	Celine, 3, 122	Joy's Jewel, 3, 114	9	**1:20.60**	26,800
1978	**Eximious**, 3, 119	W. Shoemaker	B. Thoughtful, 3, 122	Joe's Bee, 3, 114	7	1:22.60	25,550
1977	**Taisez Vous**, 3, 115	F. Toro	Wavy Waves, 3, 122	Silent Wisdom, 3, 114	8	1:22.60	22,650
1976	**Hail Hilarious**, 3, 114	D. Pierce	Doc Shah's Siren, 3, 119	I Going, 3, 115	10	1:21.40	20,550
1975	**Raise Your Skirts**, 3, 118	W. Mahorney	Miss Tokyo, 3, 117	Fascinating Girl, 3, 119	7	1:20.80	19,350
1974	**Modus Vivendi**, 3, 121	D. Pierce	Fleet Peach, 3, 118	Fresno Star, 3, 118	9	1:21.60	19,800
1973	**Sandy Blue**, 3, 118	D. Pierce	Sphere, 3, 113	Goddess Roman, 3, 113	9	1:21.80	20,250

Named for racing fans who watch races from along the rail, known as "railbirds." Grade 2 1988, 1991-2001. Railbird H. 1963-'64. Both sexes 1963. ‡Abby Girl finished first, DQ to fifth for a positive drug test, 2001.

Rampart Handicap

Grade 2 in 2005. Gulfstream Park, three-year-olds and up, fillies and mares, 1¹/₈ miles, dirt. Held March 26, 2005, with a gross value of $200,000. First held in 1976. First graded in 1986. Stakes record 1:47.92 (2003 Allamerican Bertie).

Year	Winner	Jockey	Second	Third	Strs	Time	1st Purse
2005	**D'Wildcat Speed**, 5, 113	M. R. Cruz	Isola Piu Bella (Chi), 5, 118	Pampered Princess, 5, 116	5	1:48.92	$120,000
2004	**Sightseek**, 5, 121	J. D. Bailey	Redoubled Miss, 5, 113	Lead Story, 5, 117	4	1:51.07	120,000
2003	**Allamerican Bertie**, 4, 122	J. R. Velazquez	Smok'n Frolic, 4, 118	Softly, 5, 115	6	**1:47.92**	120,000
2002	**Forest Secrets**, 4, 117	P. Day	Summer Colony, 4, 118	Happily Unbridled, 4, 114	6	1:49.83	120,000
2001	**De Bertie**, 4, 116	J. F. Chavez	Apple of Kent, 5, 114	Scratch Pad, 4, 116	7	1:50.48	120,000
2000	**Bella Chiarra**, 5, 116	S. J. Sellers	Lines of Beauty, 5, 114	Up We Go, 4, 113	8	1:43.27	120,000
1999	**Banshee Breeze**, 4, 122	J. D. Bailey	Glitter Woman, 5, 119	Timely Broad, 5, 114	5	1:42.83	120,000
1998	**Dance for Thee**, 4, 113	J. Bravo	Escena, 5, 119	Glitter Woman, 4, 121	6	1:44.73	120,000
1997	**Chip**, 4, 114	J. Bravo	Rare Blend, 4, 122	Hurricane Viv, 4, 116	9	1:42.51	120,000

1996 **Investalot**, 5, 114	S. J. Sellers	Queen Tutta, 4, 113	Alcovy, 6, 117	9	1:43.99	$120,000
1995 **Educated Risk**, 5, 126	M. E. Smith	Recognizable, 4, 117	Jade Flush, 4, 113	5	1:43.09	120,000
1994 **Nine Keys**, 4, 113	M. E. Smith	Educated Risk, 4, 120	Traverse City, 4, 113	6	1:42.12	120,000
1993 **Girl On a Mission**, 4, 112	J. D. Bailey	‡Luv Me Luv Me Not, 4, 116	Haunting, 5, 114	8	1:45.47	120,000
1992 **Fit for a Queen**, 6, 119	J. D. Bailey	Firm Stance, 4, 111	Nannerl, 5, 113	12	1:43.66	120,000
1991 **Charon**, 4, 121	C. Perret	Wortheroatsingold, 4, 112	Train Robbery, 4, 113	8	1:43.10	120,000
1990 **Barbarika**, 5, 113	C. Perret	Fit for a Queen, 4, 112	Natala, 4, 112	11	1:44.20	120,000
1989 **Colonial Waters**, 4, 112	W. H. McCauley	Savannah's Honor, 4, 113	Haiati, 4, 112	12	1:44.80	120,000
1988 **By Land by Sea**, 4, 118	F. Toro	Queen Alexandra, 6, 120	Bound, 4, 113	10	1:43.80	120,000
1987 **Life At the Top**, 4, 122	R. P. Romero	I'm Sweets, 4, 119	Natania, 5, 113	7	1:44.00	97,440
1986 **Endear**, 4, 113	E. Maple	Isayso, 7, 118	Natania, 4, 112	11	1:45.80	103,080
1985 **Isayso**, 6, 113	E. Maple	Pretty Perfect, 5, 122	Basie, 4, 114	7	1:44.20	70,080
1984 **Thinghatab**, 4, 118	C. Perret	National Banner, 4, 117	Vestris, 5, 112	10	1:43.80	36,870
1983 **Flag Waver**, 4, 108	A. O. Solis	Prime Prospect, 5, 118	Our Darling, 4, 112	13	1:44.00	57,960
1982 **Sweetest Chant**, 4, 117	E. Fires	Deby's Willing, 5, 115	Pretorienne (Fr), 6, 114	10	1:43.40	25,662
1981 **Wistful**, 4, 117	D. Brumfield	Lillian Russell, 4, 109	Deby's Willing, 4, 112	9	1:44.60	54,180
1976 **Moon Glitter**, 4, 110	E. Fires	Regal Quillo, 3, 112	K D Princess, 5, 111	8	1:22.20	9,960

Named for Mrs. H. Haggerty's 1948 Gulfstream Park H. winner Rampart (1942 f. by Trace Call); Rampart was the race's first female winner. Formerly sponsored by Johnnie Walker Scotch Whisky 1989-'90. Grade 3 1986-'87. Johnnie Walker Black Classic H. 1989-'90. Not held 1977-'80. 7 furlongs 1976. 1¹/₁₆ miles 1981-2000. ‡Now Dance finished second, DQ to fifth, 1993.

Rancho Bernardo Handicap

Grade 3 in 2005. Del Mar, three-year-olds and up, fillies and mares, 6¹/₂ furlongs, dirt. Held August 21, 2004, with a gross value of $150,000. First held in 1967. First graded in 1988. Stakes record 1:14.28 (1995 Track Gal).

Year	Winner	Jockey	Second	Third	Strs	Time	1st Purse
2004	**Dream of Summer**, 5, 118	M. E. Smith	Barbara Orr, 4, 113	Cyber Slew, 4, 117	7	1:15.85	$90,000
2003	**Secret Liaison**, 5, 116	C. S. Nakatani	Lacie Girl, 4, 116	Spring Meadow, 4, 117	8	1:15.53	90,000
2002	**Kalookan Queen**, 6, 123	A. O. Solis	Warren's Whistle, 4, 116	Fancee Bargain, 6, 112	5	1:16.40	90,000
2001	**Kalookan Queen**, 5, 119	A. O. Solis	Go Go, 4, 115	Warren's Whistle, 3, 111	6	1:15.52	90,000
2000	**Theresa's Tizzy**, 6, 117	L. A. Pincay Jr.	Nany's Sweep, 4, 117	Hookedonthefeelin, 4, 119	6	1:16.23	90,000
1999	**Enjoy the Moment**, 4, 119	D. R. Flores	Snowberg, 4, 117	Stop Traffic, 6, 121	6	1:15.97	90,000
1998	**Advancing Star**, 5, 120	C. J. McCarron	Closed Escrow, 5, 115	Tiffany Diamond, 5, 116	6	1:14.64	64,140
1997	**Track Gal**, 6, 120	G. L. Stevens	Madame Pandit, 4, 118	Advancing Star, 4, 116	8	1:15.64	69,125
1996	**Track Gal**, 5, 122	C. J. McCarron	Tricky Code, 5, 116	Evil's Pic, 4, 117	5	1:14.64	63,550
1995	**Track Gal**, 4, 118	C. J. McCarron	Desert Stormer, 5, 119	Lakeway, 4, 122	5	**1:14.28**	58,650
1994	**Desert Stormer**, 4, 116	E. J. Delahoussaye	Magical Maiden, 5, 120	Booklore, 4, 117	9	1:14.81	62,800
1993	**Knight Prospector**, 4, 119	K. J. Desormeaux	Interactive, 4, 119	Bountiful Native, 5, 120	5	1:16.14	45,675
1992	**Bountiful Native**, 4, 117	P. A. Valenzuela	Devil's Orchid, 5, 120	She's Tops, 3, 114	9	1:15.30	63,400
1991	**Cascading Gold**, 5, 117	L. A. Pincay Jr.	Survive, 7, 120	Suziqcute, 3, 114	5	1:15.42	60,100
1990	**Hot Novel**, 4, 118	K. J. Desormeaux	Sexy Slew, 4, 116	Down Again, 6, 115	9	1:14.60	62,875
1989	**Kool Arrival**, 3, 117	L. A. Pincay Jr.	Super Avie, 4, 117	Survive, 5, 116	7	1:15.20	47,625
1988	**Clabber Girl**, 5, 120	L. A. Pincay Jr.	Queen Forbes, 4, 113	Behind the Scenes, 4, 117	8	1:14.60	38,750
1987	**Julie the Flapper**, 3, 114	C. J. McCarron	Clabber Girl, 4, 117	Sari's Heroine, 4, 119	10	1:15.00	33,200
1986	**Bold n Special**, 3, 115	C. J. McCarron	Rangoon Ruby (Ire), 4, 116	Eloquack, 4, 117	5	1:14.60	30,850
1985	**Take My Picture**, 3, 114	F. Olivares	Sales Bulletin, 4, 118	Mimi Baker, 4, 112	10	1:09.20	33,200
1984	**Pleasure Cay**, 4, 121	L. A. Pincay Jr.	Lovlier Linda, 4, 120	Pride of Rosewood (NZ), 6, 115	8	1:08.60	32,250
1983	**Bara Lass**, 4, 120	C. J. McCarron	Excitable Lady, 5, 124	Milingo, 4, 115	7	1:09.40	31,800
1982	**Lucky Lady Ellen**, 3, 117	L. A. Pincay Jr.	Glitter Hitter, 4, 118	Excitable Lady, 4, 125	4	1:08.60	31,850
1981	**Forluvofiv**, 4, 108	E. J. Delahoussaye	Untamed Spirit, 4, 122	Ack's Secret, 5, 118	8	1:09.40	31,400
1980	**Great Lady M.**, 5, 121	L. A. Pincay Jr.	Sal's High, 4, 118	Western Hand, 3, 110	8	1:08.60	25,800
1979	**Fantastic Girl**, 3, 112	W. Shoemaker	Happy Holme, 5, 120	Delice, 4, 122	8	1:09.20	22,850
1978	**Happy Holme**, 4, 120	C. J. McCarron	Telferner, 4, 117	Dallas Deb, 3, 114	5	1:13.00	18,200
1977	**Lullaby Song**, 4, 120	L. A. Pincay Jr.	Miss Rising Market, 4, 113	Honeyhugger, 4, 117	7	1:09.00	16,550
1976	**Mama Kali**, 5, 117	L. A. Pincay Jr.	Mismoyola, 6, 119	Vol Au Vent, 4, 120	6	1:09.20	16,400
1975	**Mama Kali**, 4, 120	J. Lambert	Hooley Ruley, 5, 117	Modus Vivendi, 4, 124	8	1:08.40	17,050
1974	**Impressive Style**, 5, 117	R. Rosales	Fleet Peach, 3, 115	Lt.'s Joy, 4, 120	10	1:08.60	16,300
1973	**Fairly Certain**, 4, 121	S. Valdez	Tannyhill, 4, 117	Normandy Grey, 4, 115	8	1:42.80	10,400
	dh -D. B. Carm, 4, 119	F. Toro		Dr. Kerlan, 4, 118	5	1:43.20	6,400
	dh- Dollar Discount, 4, 119	S. Valdez					

Named for the city of Rancho Bernardo, California. Rancho Bernardo Breeders' Cup H. 1990-'95. Not held 1968-'72. 1 mile 1967. 1¹/₁₆ miles 1973. 6 furlongs 1974-'85. Turf 1973. Both sexes 1967-'73. Two divisions 1973. Dead heat for first 1973 (2nd Div.). Nonwinners of a race worth $10,000 to the winner 1973.

Raven Run Stakes

Grade 2 in 2005. Keeneland, three-year-olds, fillies, 7 furlongs, dirt. Held October 15, 2004, with a gross value of $224,200. First held in 1999. First graded in 2002. Stakes record 1:20.88 (2000 Darling My Darling).

Year	Winner	Jockey	Second	Third	Strs	Time	1st Purse
2004	**Josh's Madelyn**, 3, 118	J. Shepherd	Vision of Beauty, 3, 116	Feline Story, 3, 118	10	1:22.86	$139,004
2003	**Yell**, 3, 123	P. Day	Ebony Breeze, 3, 123	Tina Bull, 3, 117	12	1:21.75	108,159

Year	Winner		Jockey	Second		Third		Strs	Time	1st Purse
2002	**Sightseek**, 3, 117		J. D. Bailey	Miss Lodi, 3, 123		Respectful, 3, 117		12	1:23.98	$106,578
2001	**Nasty Storm**, 3, 123		P. Day	Hattiesburg, 3, 123		Forest Secrets, 3, 123		7	1:23.30	68,138
2000	**Darling My Darling**, 3, 117		M. E. Smith	Surfside, 3, 123		Cat Cay, 3, 117		6	**1:20.88**	51,104
1999	**Dreamy Maiden**, 3, 117		P. Day	Golden Illusion, 3, 117		Cosmic Wing, 3, 117		6	1:22.64	37,076

Named for the Raven Run nature sanctuary located outside Lexington. Grade 3 2002-'03.

Razorback Breeders' Cup Handicap

Grade 3 in 2005. Oaklawn Park, four-year-olds and up, $1\frac{1}{16}$ miles, dirt. Held March 13, 2005, with a gross value of $125,000. First held in 1976. First graded in 1978. Stakes record 1:40.40 (1988 Lost Code).

Year	Winner	Jockey	Second	Third	Strs	Time	1st Purse
2005	**Added Edge**, 5, 115	L. S. Quinonez	Mauk Four, 5, 112	Absent Friend, 5, 115	10	1:43.88	$75,000
2004	**Sonic West**, 5, 113	W. Martinez	Crafty Shaw, 6, 117	Pie N Burger, 6, 119	7	1:43.56	60,000
2003	**Colorful Tour**, 4, 118	L. S. Quinonez	Crafty Shaw, 5, 114	Windward Passage, 4, 118	7	1:43.53	60,000
2002	**Mr Ross**, 7, 120	D. R. Pettinger	Remington Rock, 8, 115	Big Numbers, 5, 116	8	1:44.13	60,000
2001	**Mr Ross**, 6, 119	D. R. Pettinger	Graeme Hall, 4, 120	Maysville Slew, 5, 117	9	1:42.60	75,000
2000	**Well Noted**, 5, 112	T. T. Doocy	Crimson Classic, 6, 115	Mr Ross, 5, 119	7	1:43.21	75,000
1999	**Desert Air**, 4, 113	C. J. Lanerie	Magnify, 6, 113	Black Tie Dinner, 6, 112	7	1:44.75	75,000
1998	**Brush With Pride**, 6, 115	T. T. Doocy	Littlebitlively, 4, 112	Krigeorj's Gold, 5, 115	7	1:43.55	75,000
1997	**No Spend No Glow**, 5, 115	R. N. Lester	Illesam, 5, 114	Come On Flip, 6, 115	8	1:43.20	90,000
1996	**Juliannus**, 7, 113	R. Albarado	Judge T C, 5, 121	Dazzling Falls, 4, 118	5	1:43.37	90,000
1995	**Silver Goblin**, 4, 124	D. W. Cordova	Joseph's Robe, 4, 111	Wooden Ticket, 5, 115	6	1:42.79	120,000
1994	**Prize Fight**, 5, 113	P. A. Johnson	Brother Brown, 4, 120	Country Store, 4, 113	8	1:43.70	90,000
1993	**Lil E. Tee**, 4, 123	P. Day	Zeeruler, 5, 115	Senor Tomas, 4, 114	7	1:41.55	90,000
1992	**Tokatee**, 6, 115	G. K. Gomez	On the Edge, 5, 112	Total Assets, 7, 110	9	1:42.87	90,000
1991	**Bedeviled**, 4, 115	D. L. Howard	Din's Dancer, 6, 117	Black Tie Affair (Ire), 5, 118	7	1:42.50	90,000
1990	**Opening Verse**, 4, 116	P. Day	Primal, 5, 121	Silver Survivor, 4, 118	7	1:41.40	90,000
1989	**Blushing John**, 4, 117	P. Day	Lyphard's Ridge, 6, 111	Proper Reality, 4, 123	5	1:43.00	60,000
1988	**Lost Code**, 4, 123	C. Perret	Red Attack, 6, 112	Demons Begone, 4, 121	7	**1:40.40**	73,500
1987	**Bolshoi Boy**, 4, 119	R. P. Romero	Lyphard's Ridge, 4, 110	Sun Master, 6, 119	7	1:40.80	86,520
1986	**Red Attack**, 4, 111	L. Snyder	Vanlandingham, 5, 125	Inevitable Leader, 7, 111	9	1:42.00	96,900
1985	**Imp Society**, 4, 126	P. Day	Introspective, 4, 113	Strength in Unity, 4, 109	10	1:42.60	97,740
1984	**Dew Line**, 5, 116	S. Maple	Passing Base, 4, 112	Win Stat, 7, 115	14	1:41.60	74,520
1983	**Eminency**, 5, 120	P. Day	Cassaleria, 4, 115	Bold Style, 4, 113	10	1:43.60	70,740
1982	**Eminency**, 4, 111	P. Day	Reef Searcher, 5, 119	Tally Ho the Fox, 7, 115	15	1:45.20	76,200
1981	**Temperence Hill**, 4, 124	E. Maple	Blue Ensign, 4, 113	Belle's Ruler, 6, 112	6	1:44.20	66,660
1980	**All the More**, 7, 114	L. Snyder	Prince Majestic, 6, 116	Breaker Breaker, 4, 117	11	1:45.40	56,400
1979	**Cisk**, 5, 120	G. Patterson	Droll's Reason, 4, 113	Prince Majestic, 5, 121	8	1:45.40	53,700
1978	**Cox's Ridge**, 4, 125	E. Maple	Dr. Riddick, 4, 116	Mark's Place, 6, 124	12	1:43.00	37,110
1977	**Dragset**, 6, 111	J. Kunitake	Romeo, 4, 120	Last Buzz, 4, 115	9	1:44.40	35,910
1976	**Royal Glint**, 6, 126	J. E. Tejeira	Marauding, 4, 115	Heaven Forbid, 5, 112	8	1:42.40	35,550

Named for the unofficial state animal and University of Arkansas mascot, the razorback hog. Grade 2 1985-'96. Razorback H. 1976-2004.

Rebel Stakes

Grade 3 in 2005. Oaklawn Park, three-year-olds, $1\frac{1}{16}$ miles, dirt. Held March 19, 2005, with a gross value of $250,000. First held in 1976. First graded in 1990. Stakes record 1:41 (1984 Vanlandingham).

Year	Winner	Jockey	Second	Third	Strs	Time	1st Purse
2005	**Greater Good**, 3, 122	J. McKee	Rockport Harbor, 3, 119	Batson Challenge, 3, 117	6	1:44.92	$150,000
2004	**Smarty Jones**, 3, 122	S. Elliott	Purge, 3, 117	Pro Prado, 3, 117	9	1:42.07	120,000
2003	**Crowned King**, 3, 115	C. R. Rennie	Great Notion, 3, 119	Comic Truth, 3, 117	7	1:44.00	75,000
2002	**Windward Passage**, 3, 116	D. J. Meche	Ocean Sound (Ire), 3, 114	Dusty Spike, 3, 114	8	1:45.06	60,000
2001	**Crafty Shaw**, 3, 113	J. M. Johnson	Arctic Boy, 3, 114	Strike It Smart, 3, 114	9	1:43.82	60,000
2000	**Snuck In**, 3, 119	C. B. Asmussen	Big Numbers, 3, 114	Fan the Flame, 3, 113	12	1:42.99	60,000
1999	**Etbauer**, 3, 112	M. E. Smith	Desert Demon, 3, 119	Kutsa, 3, 112	11	1:44.02	75,000
1998	**Victory Gallop**, 3, 119	E. Coa	Robinwould, 3, 114	Whataflashyactor, 3, 114	10	1:44.72	75,000
1997	**Phantom On Tour**, 3, 117	L. J. Melancon	Direct Hit, 3, 119	River Squall, 3, 117	12	1:42.80	75,000
1996	**Ide**, 3, 122	C. Perret	Blow Out, 3, 112	Bunker Hill Road, 3, 113	7	1:44.10	60,000
1995	**Mystery Storm**, 3, 122	C. Perret	Rich Man's Gold, 3, 112	Valid Advantage, 3, 113	7	1:44.41	75,000
1994	**Judge T C**, 3, 119	J. M. Johnson	Concern, 3, 114	Milt's Overture, 3, 114	11	1:44.14	75,000
1993	**Dalhart**, 3, 122	M. E. Smith	Foxtrail, 3, 122	Mi Cielo, 3, 114	8	1:42.31	75,000
1992	**Pine Bluff**, 3, 122	J. D. Bailey	Desert Force, 3, 117	Looks Like Money, 3, 113	7	1:42.83	75,000
1991	**Quintana**, 3, 112	D. R. Guillory	Corporate Report, 3, 114	Far Out Wadleigh, 3, 119	8	1:42.70	60,000
1990	**Nuits St. Georges**, 3, 114	J. E. Bruin	Maverick Miner, 3, 114	Tarascon, 3, 122	11	1:46.00	60,000
1989	**Manastash Ridge**, 3, 119	A. L. Castanon	Big Stanley, 3, 122	Double Quick, 3, 122	14	1:43.00	60,000
1988	**Sea Trek**, 3, 112	P. A. Johnson	Din's Dancer, 3, 114	Notebook, 3, 114	10	1:42.60	73,500
1987	**Demons Begone**, 3, 119	P. Day	Fast Forward, 3, 114	You're No Bargain, 3, 112	6	1:41.40	86,520
1986	**Rare Brick**, 3, 119	M. E. Smith	Clear Choice, 3, 112	The Flats, 3, 114	8	1:43.20	68,760
1985	**Clever Allemont**, 3, 119	P. Day	Bonham, 3, 113	Proper Native, 3, 114	7	1:44.40	95,100
1984	**Vanlandingham**, 3, 115	P. Day	Wind Flyer, 3, 118	Leavesumdouble, 3, 112	10	**1:41.00**	70,740
1983	**Sunny's Halo**, 3, 121	L. Snyder	Sligh Jet, 3, 117	Le Cou Cou, 3, 115	11	1:42.20	68,850

1982 **Bold Style**, 3, 116	L. Snyder	Majesty's Prince, 3, 115	Lost Creek, 3, 114	8	1:43.80	$51,420
1981 **Bold Ego**, 3, 122	J. L. Lively	Catch That Pass, 3, 117	Chapel Creek, 3, 112	10	1:41.40	35,580
1980 **Temperence Hill**, 3, 114	D. Haire	Royal Sporan, 3, 111	Be a Prospect, 3, 123	15	1:42.80	38,430
1979 **Lucy's Axe**, 3, 121	E. Maple	Tunerup, 3, 115	Arctic Action, 3, 118	8	1:42.80	35,070
1978 **Chop Chop Tomahawk**, 3, 116	L. Snyder	Abidan, 3, 114	Forever Casting, 3, 124	10	1:42.40	36,150
1977 **United Holme**, 3, 120	J. E. Tejeira	J. J. Battle, 3, 124	Tinsley's Affair, 3, 115	12	1:42.20	36,810
1976 **Riverside Sam**, 3, 113	G. Patterson	Elocutionist, 3, 121	Klen Klitso, 3, 113	14	1:41.60	37,710

Named for the nickname of Southerners, "rebels"; the nickname is derived from the South's rebellion against the United States during the Civil War. Rebel H. 1976-'83. Not graded 2003-'04.

Red Bank Handicap

Grade 3 in 2005. Monmouth Park, three-year-olds and up, 1 mile, turf. Held May 28, 2005, with a gross value of $150,000. First held in 1974. First graded in 1986. Stakes record 1:33.34 (1991 Double Booked).

Year	Winner	Jockey	Second	Third	Strs	Time	1st Purse
2005	**American Freedom**, 7, 115	J. A. Velez Jr.	Spruce Run, 7, 113	Royal Affirmed, 7, 112	8	1:43.12	$90,000
2004	**Burning Roma**, 6, 120	J. L. Castanon	Remind, 4, 117	American Freedom, 6, 115	11	1:34.73	60,000
2003	**Just Le Facts**, 4, 111	J. Bravo	Saint Verre, 5, 118	Runspastum, 6, 114	4	1:37.73	20,000
2002	**Key Lory**, 8, 117	H. Vega	Sardaukar (GB), 6, 113	Spruce Run, 4, 113	8	1:35.92	60,000
2001	**Pavillon (Brz)**, 7, 112	J. Bravo	Western Summer, 4, 114	Runspastum, 4, 114	10	1:36.38	90,000
2000	**Mi Narrow**, 6, 114	C. H. Velasquez	Deep Gold, 4, 114	Inkatha (Fr), 6, 117	9	1:34.84	90,000
1999	**Inkatha (Fr)**, 5, 114	H. Castillo Jr.	Rob 'n Gin, 5, 119	Soviet Line (Ire), 9, 118	8	1:33.95	90,000
1998	**Statesmanship**, 4, 117	J. A. Santos	Rob 'n Gin, 4, 120	Bomfim, 5, 114	11	1:35.00	60,000
1997	**Basqueian**, 6, 118	R. Wilson	Wild Night Out, 5, 111	Jambalaya Jazz, 5, 117	6	1:35.20	60,000
1996	**Joker**, 4, 113	J. A. Velez Jr.	Rare Reason, 5, 118	Diplomatic Jet, 4, 116	8	1:35.90	60,000
1995	**Dove Hunt**, 4, 118	W. H. McCauley	Rare Reason, 4, 115	Winnetou, 5, 113	9	1:33.95	45,000
1994	**Adam Smith (GB)**, 6, 120	J. A. Krone	Discernment, 5, 113	Fourstardave, 9, 118	8	1:34.43	45,000
1993	**Adam Smith (GB)**, 5, 116	J. A. Krone	Fourstars Allstar, 5, 116	Rinka Das, 5, 115	8	1:34.39	45,000
1992	**Daarik (Ire)**, 5, 114	L. Saumell	Leger Cat (Arg), 6, 116	Kate's Valentine, 7, 114	8	1:34.07	45,000
1991	**Double Booked**, 6, 122	J. C. Ferrer	Great Normand, 6, 118	Now Listen, 4, 112	10	**1:33.34**	45,000
1990	**Norquestor**, 4, 118	J. Samyn	Master Speaker, 5, 120	Grande Jette, 5, 111	5	1:36.00	52,980
1989	**Arlene's Valentine**, 4, 115	J. C. Ferrer	Yankee Affair, 7, 121	Alwasmi, 5, 114	6	1:40.20	52,290
1988	**Iron Courage**, 4, 113	W. H. McCauley	Spellbound, 5, 112	Ioskeha, 5, 113	7	1:35.40	42,210
1987	**Castelets**, 6, 115	C. W. Antley	Hi Ideal, 5, 114	Racing Star, 5, 117	5	1:37.20	35,610
1986	†**Mazatleca (Mex)**, 6, 112	C. W. Antley	Feeling Gallant, 4, 114	Hi Ideal, 4, 113	8	1:35.80	34,800
1985	**Castelets**, 5, 117	V. A. Bracciale Jr.	Evzone, 4, 117	Gothic Revival, 4, 112	8	1:37.00	27,885
	Ends Well, 4, 116	M. R. Morgan	Domynsky (GB), 5, 117	Bold Southerner, 4, 115	9	1:35.60	28,065
1984	**Tough Mickey**, 4, 118	K. Skinner	Fortnightly, 4, 117	Roman Bend, 4, 108	9	1:36.40	28,470
	Castle Guard, 5, 118	J. C. Ferrer	Super Sunrise (GB), 4, 123	Fray Star (Arg), 6, 117	10	1:35.80	28,530
1983	**Sun and Shine (GB)**, 4, 115	J. Terry	St. Brendan, 5, 116	Mr. Dreamer, 6, 113	11	1:36.60	24,480
1982	**Alhambra Joe**, 5, 111	W. Nemeti	Pepper's Segundo, 5, 117	Timely Counsel, 4, 112	5	1:38.60	23,265
1981	**Colonel Moran**, 4, 116	G. W. Donahue	Dan Horn, 9, 115	Contare, 5, 108	12	1:35.20	24,570
1980	**Horatius**, 5, 117	D. MacBeth	Pipedreamer (GB), 5, 116	North Course, 5, 114	11	1:35.00	24,495
1979	**Navajo Princess**, 5, 122	J. Vasquez	La Soufriere, 4, 116	Sans Arc, 5, 115	10	1:43.20	22,441
1978	**Love Jenny**, 4, 108	M. A. Gomez	Table Hopper, 5, 111	Chanctonbury, 4, 114	9	1:46.20	28,308
1977	**Playin' Footsie**, 4, 110	R. D. Ardoin	Desiree, 4, 110	Artfully, 4, 112	10	1:44.40	29,510
1976	**Collegiate**, 4, 116	J. W. Edwards	Show Me How, 4, 110	Four Bells, 5, 114	11	1:40.20	25,919
1975	**Kudara**, 4, 118	D. MacBeth	Enchanted Native, 4, 111	Twixt, 6, 121	11	1:42.20	18,850
1974	‡**Mystery Mood**, 2, 115	J. E. Tejeira	Molly Ballantine, 2, 121	Lucky Leslie, 2, 117	11	1:45.20	18,672

Named for the town of Red Bank, New Jersey. Not graded when taken off turf 2003. Red Bank S. 1974. 1¹⁄₁₆ miles 1974-'75, 1977-'79. 1 mile 70 yards 1976. Dirt 1974-'78, 1982, 1987, 1990, 1997. Originally scheduled on turf 2003. Two-year-olds 1974. Fillies and mares 1975-'79. Two divisions 1984-'85. ‡Molly Ballantine finished first, DQ to second, 1974. Course record 1999. †Denotes female.

Red Smith Handicap

Grade 2 in 2005. Aqueduct, three-year-olds and up, 1³⁄₈ miles, turf. Held November 20, 2004, with a gross value of $150,000. First held in 1960. First graded in 1973. Stakes record 2:14.44 (1999 Monarch's Maze).

Year	Winner	Jockey	Second	Third	Strs	Time	1st Purse
2004	**Dreadnaught**, 4, 115	J. Samyn	Certifiably Crazy, 4, 112	Alost (Fr), 4, 116	10	2:18.87	$90,000
2003	**Balto Star**, 5, 120	J. R. Velazquez	Macaw (Ire), 4, 118	Cetewayo, 9, 116	11	2:18.86	90,000
2002	**Evening Attire**, 4, 126	S. Bridgmohan	Fisher Pond, 3, 116	Pleasant Breeze, 7, 120	6	2:14.81	90,000
2001	**Mr. Pleasentfar (Brz)**, 4, 115	J. A. Santos	Eltawaasul, 5, 114	Regal Dynasty, 5, 113	12	2:16.94	90,000
2000	**Cetewayo**, 6, 114	R. Migliore	Understood, 4, 113	Val's Prince, 8, 118	13	2:17.93	90,000
1999	**Monarch's Maze**, 4, 113	J. Bravo	Williams News, 4, 114	Gritty Sandie, 3, 114	14	**2:14.44**	90,000
1998	**Musical Ghost**, 6, 115	J. R. Velazquez	Rice, 6, 115	Plato's Love, 3, 109	12	2:15.53	90,000
1997	**Instant Friendship**, 4, 123	J. R. Velazquez	Demi's Brett, 4, 117	Trample, 3, 112	5	2:17.08	150,000
1996	**Mr. Bluebird**, 5, 114	M. E. Smith	Ops Smile, 4, 116	Raintrap (GB), 6, 117	13	2:15.35	87,750
1995	**Flag Down**, 5, 114	J. A. Santos	‡Party Season (GB), 4, 116	Proceeded, 4, 110	11	2:22.03	69,900
1994	**Franchise Player**, 5, 109	D. V. Beckner	Red Bishop, 6, 119	Same Old Wish, 4, 112	14	2:20.53	72,120
1993	**Royal Mountain Inn**, 4, 110	J. A. Krone	Spectacular Tide, 4, 113	Share the Glory, 5, 111	8	1:59.82	71,760
1992	**Montserrat**, 4, 118	J. A. Krone	Preferences, 3, 110	First Rate (Ire), 7, 111	7	2:00.32	70,920

Year	Winner	Jockey	Second	Third	Strs	Time	1st Purse
1991	Who's to Pay, 5, 117	J. D. Bailey	Simili (Fr), 5, 114	Solar Splendor, 4, 114	8	1:58.18	$71,160
1990	Yankee Affair, 8, 122	J. A. Santos	Hodges Bay, 5, 116	Phantom Breeze (Ire), 4, 112	7	2:00.20	70,560
1989	Rambo Dancer, 5, 113	J. A. Santos	El Senor, 5, 117	Salem Drive, 7, 116	8	2:01.00	72,360
1988	Pay the Butler, 4, 110	R. G. Davis	Equalize, 6, 116	Yankee Affair, 6, 120	15	2:01.40	118,620
1987	Theatrical (Ire), 5, 122	P. Day	Dance of Life, 4, 122	Equalize, 5, 112	11	2:00.80	116,460
1986	Divulge, 4, 116	J. Cruguet	Tri for Size, 5, 113	Island Sun, 4, 118	9	1:59.00	88,950
	Equalize, 4, 114	W. A. Guerra	Palace Panther (Ire), 5, 116	Entitled To, 4, 112	8	2:02.20	103,650
1985	Sharannpour (Ire), 5, 112	A. T. Cordero Jr.	Inevitable Leader, 6, 116	Cold Feet (Fr), 4, 110	13	2:04.20	114,600
1984	Hero's Honor, 4, 117	J. D. Bailey	Win, 4, 114	Eskimo, 4, 112	5	2:02.20	102,900
1983	Super Sunrise (GB), 4, 117	C. Perret	Mariacho (Ire), 5, 116	Field Cat, 6, 111	7	2:06.80	67,200
	Thunder Puddles, 4, 117	J. Samyn	John's Gold, 4, 112	Open Call, 5, 124	7	2:06.40	67,200
1982	Highland Blade, 4, 124	J. Vasquez	Dom Menotti (Fr), 5, 109	Open Call, 4, 125	8	2:06.40	69,000
1981	Match the Hatch, 5, 114	K. Skinner	Passing Zone, 4, 108	Great Neck, 5, 114	9	1:59.60	68,160
1980	Marquee Universal (Ire), 4, 121	H. Pilar	Match the Hatch, 4, 114	Lyphard's Wish (Fr), 4, 122	8	1:58.80	67,680
1978	Tiller, 4, 114	J. Fell	True Colors, 4, 116	Tacitus, 4, 113	8	2:00.20	33,960
1977	Clout, 5, 114	G. Martens	Chati, 4, 117	Gay Jitterbug, 4, 122	8	1:40.00	25,927
	Quick Card, 4, 112	A. T. Cordero Jr.	Bemo, 7, 115	Noble Dancer (GB), 5, 119	6	1:39.60	25,687
1976	Erwin Boy, 5, 116	R. Turcotte	Clout, 4, 111	Quick Card, 3, 110	10	2:01.20	28,110
1975	*Telefonico, 4, 120	C. Perret	Drollery, 5, 114	Barcas, 4, 114	9	2:03.00	17,400
1974	Take Off, 5, 117	R. Turcotte	Jogging, 7, 112	Red Reality, 8, 112	7	2:00.40	23,070
1973	Red Reality, 7, 122	J. Velasquez	Malwak, 5, 114	New Hope, 4, 113	5	2:13.20	16,890

Named in honor of Walter "Red" Smith, Pulitzer Prize-winning sports columnist. Formerly named for Edgemere, New York, a Queens neighborhood. Grade 3 1973-'80, 2002. Downgraded to Grade 3 when taken off turf 2002. Edgemere H. 1960-'73, 1976-'81. Edgemere S. 1974-'75. Held at Belmont Park 1960-'62, 1968-'78, 1980-'93. Not held 1979. $1\frac{1}{16}$ miles 1963-'67. $1\frac{1}{4}$ miles 1972-'76, 1978, 1980-'93. $1\frac{1}{16}$ miles 1977. Dirt 1960-'64, 1984, 1997. Originally scheduled on turf 2002. Two divisions 1977, 1983, 1986. ‡Boyce finished second, DQ to eleventh, 1995.

Regret Stakes

Grade 3 in 2005. Churchill Downs, three-year-olds, fillies, $1\frac{1}{8}$ miles, turf. Held June 12, 2004, with a gross value of $221,800. First held in 1970. First graded in 1999. Stakes record 1:48.78 (2003 Sand Springs).

Year	Winner	Jockey	Second	Third	Strs	Time	1st Purse
2004	Sister Star, 3, 116	B. Blanc	Western Ransom, 3, 120	Jinny's Gold, 3, 118	7	1:51.40	$137,516
2003	Sand Springs, 3, 118	M. Guidry	Personal Legend, 3, 116	Achnasheen, 3, 116	12	1:48.78	143,220
2002	Distant Valley (GB), 3, 119	J. D. Bailey	Peace River Lady, 3, 115	Stylelistick, 3, 122	9	1:42.95	104,811
2001	Casual Feat, 3, 115	L. J. Melancon	Amaretta, 3, 117	La Vida Loca (Ire), 3, 119	8	1:42.75	103,695
2000	Solvig, 3, 122	P. Day	Trip, 3, 117	Miss Chief, 3, 115	9	1:42.95	104,439
1999	Nani Rose, 3, 115	S. J. Sellers	Solar Bound, 3, 122	Suffragette, 3, 115	8	1:42.40	104,439
1998	Formal Tango, 3, 115	C. R. Woods Jr.	Adel, 3, 122	Pratella, 3, 112	10	1:48.73	105,927
1997	Starry Dreamer, 3, 122	W. Martinez	Cozy Blues, 3, 115	Swearingen, 3, 122	8	1:42.77	69,378
1996	Daylight Come, 3, 117	C. C. Bourque	Fleur de Nuit, 3, 112	Esquive (GB), 3, 115	9	1:45.72	55,526
1995	Christmas Gift, 3, 122	C. R. Woods Jr.	Bail Out Becky, 3, 122	Grand Charmer, 3, 117	7	1:45.00	54,210
1994	Packet, 3, 117	J. M. Johnson	Thread, 3, 122	Slew Kitty Slew, 3, 112	7	1:42.14	54,551
1993	Lovat's Lady, 3, 112	B. D. Peck	Warside, 3, 122	Mari's Key, 3, 112	8	1:42.95	36,595
1992	Tiney Toast, 3, 122	S. P. Payton	Shes Just Super, 3, 122	Riverjinsky, 3, 115	10	1:42.06	37,440
1991	Maria Balastiere, 3, 117	A. T. Gryder	Savethelastdance, 3, 119	Lady Be Great, 3, 119	7	1:44.40	35,718
1990	Secret Advice, 3, 119	B. E. Bartram	Super Fan, 3, 122	Screen Prospect, 3, 119	6	1:44.40	35,815
1989	Justice Will Come, 3, 119	S. H. Bass	Luthier's Launch, 3, 119	Motion in Limine, 3, 117	10	1:46.20	36,693
1988	Lets Do Lunch, 3, 114	K. K. Allen	Stolie, 3, 119	Lucky Lydia, 3, 117	8	1:45.60	44,208
1987	Jonowo, 3, 119	M. McDowell	Lt. Lao, 3, 122	Sum, 3, 119	10	1:39.20	37,115
1986	Rosemont Risk, 3, 114	P. Day	Prime Union, 3, 122	Hail a Cab, 3, 122	8	1:36.80	25,090
1985	Weekend Delight, 3, 122	J. McKnight	Gallants Gem, 3, 122	Turn to Wilma, 3, 117	6	1:35.60	21,028
1984	Mrs. Revere, 3, 111	L. J. Melancon	Dusty Gloves, 3, 119	Robin's Rob, 3, 122	6	1:36.60	21,873
1983	Rosy Spectre, 3, 112	J. McKnight	Princesse Rapide, 3, 119	Fiesty Belle, 3, 111	8	1:37.80	19,939
1982	Amazing Love, 3, 116	L. J. Melancon	Jay Birdie, 3, 113	Noon Balloon, 3, 116	7	1:37.00	19,289
	Sefa's Beauty, 3, 119	M. S. Sellers	Mystical Mood, 3, 115	Smooth Fleet, 3, 113	5	1:37.60	19,143
1981	Contrefaire, 3, 121	T. Barrow	Solo Disco, 3, 121	Sweet Granny, 3, 118	13	1:11.60	16,705
1980	Forever Cordial, 3, 118	R. DePass	Missile Masquerade, 3, 118	Sweetladyroll, 3, 118	10	1:12.00	15,966
	No No Nona, 3, 115	M. A. Holland	Cerada Ridge, 3, 121	Romper, 3, 122	7	1:12.00	15,575
1979	Fearless Dame, 3, 121	R. DePass	Im for Joy, 3, 121	Shawn's Gal, 3, 121	10	1:10.80	16,120
1978	Unconscious Doll, 3, 121	E. J. Delahoussaye	Swervy, 3, 118	White Song, 3, 121	11	1:10.60	14,853
1977	‡Shady Lou, 3, 121	E. J. Delahoussaye	Time for Pleasure, 3, 121	Welsung, 3, 121	8	1:10.60	14,528
1976	Carmelita Gibbs, 3, 121	R. Breen	Sunny Romance, 3, 118	Island Venture, 3, 121	8	1:12.80	14,504
	Confort Zone, 3, 121	J. C. Espinoza	Rough Girl, 3, 121	My Fair Maid, 3, 115	6	1:12.80	14,114
1975	Red Cross, 3, 121	D. Brumfield	Flama Ardiente, 3, 121	Jill the Terrible, 3, 121	10	1:09.60	15,243
1974	Clemanna, 3, 121	J. C. Espinoza	Sarah Babe, 3, 121	Quick Sea, 3, 121	9	1:11.20	14,763
	Mary Dugan, 3, 121	J. McKnight	Princess Teamiga, 3, 118	Miss Orevent, 3, 121	12	1:10.40	15,153
1973	Juke Joint, 3, 118	W. Soirez	La Gentillesse, 3, 118	Never Ask, 3, 121	12	1:11.80	15,535

Named for Harry Payne Whitney's 1915 champion three-year-old filly and '15 Kentucky Derby winner Regret (1912 f. by Broomstick); Regret was the first filly to win the Derby. 6 furlongs 1970-'81. 1 mile 1982-'87. $1\frac{1}{16}$ miles 1988-2002. Dirt 1970-'86. Two divisions 1974, 1976, 1980, 1982. ‡Time for Pleasure finished first, DQ to second, 1977. Nonwinners of a stakes worth $7,500 to the winner 1973-'75.

Remsen Stakes

Grade 2 in 2005. Aqueduct, two-year-olds, 1⅛ miles, dirt. Held November 27, 2004, with a gross value of $200,000. First held in 1904. First graded in 1973. Stakes record 1:47.80 (1977 Believe It).

Year	Winner	Jockey	Second	Third	Strs	Time	1st Purse
2004	Rockport Harbor, 2, 120	S. Elliott	Galloping Grocer, 2, 120	Killenaule, 2, 120	6	1:48.88	$120,000
2003	Read the Footnotes, 2, 122	J. D. Bailey	Master David, 2, 116	West Virginia, 2, 116	11	1:50.62	120,000
2002	Toccet, 2, 122	J. F. Chavez	Bham, 2, 116	Empire Maker, 2, 116	8	1:50.40	120,000
2001	Saarland, 2, 116	J. R. Velazquez	Nokoma, 2, 116	Silent Fred, 2, 116	9	1:51.28	120,000
2000	Windsor Castle, 2, 116	R. G. Davis	Ommadon, 2, 122	Buckle Down Ben, 2, 122	8	1:51.92	120,000
1999	Greenwood Lake, 2, 122	J. Samyn	Un Fino Vino, 2, 113	Polish Miner, 2, 113	8	1:50.63	120,000
1998	Comeonmom, 2, 113	J. Bravo	Millions, 2, 122	Wondertross, 2, 113	9	1:49.84	120,000
1997	Coronado's Quest, 2, 122	M. E. Smith	Halory Hunter, 2, 115	Brooklyn Nick, 2, 115	7	1:52.27	120,000
1996	The Silver Move, 2, 114	R. Migliore	Jules, 2, 122	Accelerator, 2, 122	6	1:53.54	120,000
1995	Tropicool, 2, 112	J. F. Chavez	Skip Away, 2, 112	Crafty Friend, 2, 113	11	1:50.30	170,000
1994	Thunder Gulch, 2, 115	G. L. Stevens	Western Echo, 2, 119	Mighty Magee, 2, 114	10	1:53.80	120,000
1993	Go for Gin, 2, 117	J. D. Bailey	Arrovente, 2, 113	Linkatariat, 2, 113	7	1:52.79	120,000
1992	Silver of Silver, 2, 122	J. Vasquez	Dalhart, 2, 115	Wild Gale, 2, 115	11	1:50.25	120,000
1991	Pine Bluff, 2, 113	C. Perret	Offbeat, 2, 113	Cheap Shades, 2, 113	8	1:50.80	120,000
1990	Scan, 2, 119	J. D. Bailey	Subordinated Debt, 2, 115	Kyle's Our Man, 2, 113	8	1:52.40	106,560
1989	Yonder, 2, 115	E. Maple	Roanoke, 2, 122	Armed for Peace, 2, 113	10	1:51.20	145,680
1988	Fast Play, 2, 122	A. T. Cordero Jr.	Fire Maker, 2, 115	Silver Sunsets, 2, 122	15	1:50.60	197,400
1987	Batty, 2, 113	J. A. Santos	Old Stories, 2, 115	Three Engines, 2, 113	8	1:52.40	176,400
1986	Java Gold, 2, 113	P. Day	Talinum, 2, 115	Drachma, 2, 113	8	1:49.60	172,680
1985	Pillaster, 2, 119	A. T. Cordero Jr.	Mr. Classic, 2, 113	Dance of Life, 2, 113	10	1:49.00	175,800
1984	‡Mighty Appealing, 2, 122	G. P. Smith	Hot Debate, 2, 117	Bolting Holme, 2, 115	11	1:53.20	178,680
1983	Dr. Carter, 2, 113	J. Velasquez	Secret Prince, 2, 117	Hail Bold King, 2, 113	8	1:49.00	134,700
1982	Pax in Bello, 2, 113	J. Fell	Chumming, 2, 115	Primitive Pleasure, 2, 113	11	1:50.20	141,300
1981	Laser Light, 2, 113	E. Maple	Real Twister, 2, 115	Wolfie's Rascal, 2, 113	11	1:50.80	103,500
1980	‡Pleasant Colony, 2, 116	V. A. Bracciale Jr.	Foolish Tanner, 2, 113	Akureyri, 2, 117	8	1:50.20	67,920
1979	Plugged Nickle, 2, 122	B. Thornburg	Googolplex, 2, 117	Proctor, 2, 113	8	1:50.40	64,560
1978	Instrument Landing, 2, 119	J. Fell	Lucy's Axe, 2, 117	Picturesque, 2, 117	9	1:50.20	48,375
1977	Believe It, 2, 122	E. Maple	Alydar, 2, 122	Quadratic, 2, 116	5	1:47.80	48,015
1976	Royal Ski, 2, 122	J. Kurtz	Nostalgia, 2, 122	Hey Hey J. P., 2, 116	9	1:50.40	49,545
1975	Hang Ten, 2, 116	L. A. Pincay Jr.	Dance Spell, 2, 113	Play the Red, 2, 113	12	1:49.20	52,290
1974	El Pitirre, 2, 112	M. Venezia	Bombay Duck, 2, 118	Circle Home, 2, 115	10	1:49.40	34,380
1973	Heavy Mayonnaise, 2, 112	C. Baltazar	Hegemony, 2, 112	Flip Sal, 2, 112	13	1:51.40	17,925

Named for Col. Joremus Remsen (1735–'90), leader of the Revolutionary forces at the battle of Long Island, New York. Grade 1 1981–'88. Remsen H. 1904–'53. Held at Jamaica 1904–'58. Not held 1908, 1910–'17, 1951. 5½ furlongs 1904–'09. 6 furlongs 1918–'45, 1949–'50. 1¹⁄₁₆ miles 1946–'47, 1952–'58. 5 furlongs 1948. 1 mile 1959–'72. Colts 1954–'57. Colts and geldings 1958–'60. ‡Akureyri finished first, DQ to third, 1990. ‡Stone White finished first, DQ to eleventh, 1984.

Richter Scale Breeders' Cup Sprint Championship Handicap

Grade 2 in 2005. Gulfstream Park, three-year-olds and up, 7 furlongs, dirt. Held March 12, 2005, with a gross value of $200,000. First held in 1972. First graded in 1996. Stakes record 1:21.15 (2003 Tour of the Cat).

Year	Winner	Jockey	Second	Third	Strs	Time	1st Purse
2005	Sir Shackleton, 4, 116	J. Castellano	Lion Tamer, 5, 119	Clock Stopper, 5, 117	6	1:21.64	$120,000
2004	Lion Tamer, 4, 116	J. R. Velazquez	Coach Jimi Lee, 4, 115	Wacky for Love, 4, 114	7	1:21.52	120,000
2003	Tour of the Cat, 5, 116	A. Cabassa Jr.	Burning Roma, 5, 116	Highway Prospector, 6, 114	8	1:21.15	120,000
2002	Dream Run, 4, 113	P. Day	Binthebest, 5, 114	Burning Roma, 4, 118	8	1:22.30	120,000
2001	Hook and Ladder, 4, 115	R. Migliore	Trippi, 4, 115	Rollin With Nolan, 4, 116	6	1:21.85	120,000
2000	Richter Scale, 6, 118	R. Migliore	Forty One Carats, 4, 116	Kelly Kip, 6, 120	10	1:23.30	120,000
1999	Frisk Me Now, 5, 117	E. L. King Jr.	Young At Heart, 5, 113	Good and Tough, 4, 115	6	1:22.86	60,000
1998	Rare Rock, 5, 117	P. Day	Irish Conquest, 5, 114	Frisco View, 5, 118	7	1:22.00	120,000
1997	Frisco View, 4, 116	J. D. Bailey	El Amante, 4, 114	Templado (Ven), 4, 114	7	1:23.14	98,160
1996	Patton, 5, 113	R. G. Davis	Forty Won, 5, 115	Our Emblem, 5, 115	10	1:21.81	100,140
1995	Cherokee Run, 5, 122	M. E. Smith	Waldoboro, 4, 115	Evil Bear, 5, 116	6	1:21.70	60,000
1994	I Can't Believe, 6, 113	E. Maple	American Chance, 5, 114	British Banker, 6, 114	8	1:22.55	60,000
1993	Binalong, 4, 112	J. D. Bailey	Loach, 5, 114	Richman, 5, 113	6	1:22.35	60,000
1992	Groomstick, 6, 112	W. S. Ramos	Ocala Flame, 4, 111	Cold Digger, 5, 113	9	1:23.98	60,000
1991	Gervazy, 4, 115	W. S. Ramos	Shuttleman, 5, 114	Swedaus, 4, 110	7	1:21.46	60,000
1990	‡Dancing Spree, 5, 126	A. T. Cordero Jr.	Pentelicus, 6, 114	Shuttleman, 4, 111	7	1:10.00	30,000
1989	Claim, 4, 115	C. Perret	Position Leader, 4, 117	Prospector's Halo, 5, 115	7	1:23.40	41,904
1988	Royal Pennant, 5, 113	J. A. Santos	dh-Grantley, 4, 112		12	1:23.20	45,612
			dh-Real Forest, 5, 113				
1987	Dwight D., 5, 116	R. N. Lester	Splendid Catch, 5, 113	Uncle Ho, 4, 112	7	1:10.80	27,816
1986	Hot Cop, 4, 115	J. Samyn	Dwight D., 4, 114	Opening Lead, 6, 115	12	1:22.80	45,324
1985	Key to the Moon, 4, 122	R. Platts	For Halo, 4, 123	Northern Ocean, 5, 112	8	1:22.60	42,552
1984	Number One Special, 4, 116	E. Fires	Ward Off Trouble, 4, 116	El Perico, 4, 114	6	1:21.80	23,793
1983	Deputy Minister, 4, 122	D. MacBeth	Wipe 'em Out, 4, 109	Center Cut, 4, 118	12	1:22.80	38,040
1981	King's Fashion, 6, 122	J. Samyn	Jaklin Klugman, 4, 124	Joanie's Chief, 4, 108	7	1:22.60	34,920
1977	Yamanin, 5, 122	W. Gavidia	Full Out, 4, 119	Rexson, 4, 114	6	1:22.80	37,860

1974 **Cheriepe**, 4, 115   J. Velasquez   Shecky Greene, 4, 127   Gay Pierre, 5, 112   4   1:22.40 $25,236
Named for Wafare Farm's and Richard S. and Nancy Kaster's 2000 Gulfstream Park Breeders' Cup Sprint Championship H. (G2) winner Richter Scale (1994 c. by *Habitony). Grade 3 1996-'98. Sprint Championship H. 1972, 1974, 1977, 1981. Gulfstream Sprint Championship H. 1983-'90. Gulfstream Park Sprint Championship H. 1991-'93. Gulfstream Park Sprint H. 1994-'95. Gulfstream Park Breeders' Cup Sprint Championship H. 1996-2002. Richter Scale Breeders' Cup H. 2004. Not held 1973, 1975-'76, 1978-'80, 1982. 6 furlongs 1987, 1990. Dead heat for second 1988. ‡Pentelicus finished first, DQ to second, 1990.

Risen Star Stakes

Grade 3 in 2005. Fair Grounds, three-year-olds, 1 1/16 miles, dirt. Held February 12, 2005, with a gross value of $150,000. First held in 1988. First graded in 2002. Stakes record 1:42.98 (1996 Zarb's Magic).

Year	Winner	Jockey	Second	Third	Strs	Time	1st Purse
2005	Scipion, 3, 117	G. L. Stevens	Real Dandy, 3, 118	Storm Surge, 3, 122	11	1:44.54	$90,000
2004	Gradepoint, 3, 116	R. Albarado	Mr. Jester, 3, 122	Nightlifeatbigblue, 3, 118	6	1:45.36	90,000
2003	Badge of Silver, 3, 116	R. Albarado	Lone Star Sky, 3, 122	Defrere's Vixen, 3, 114	12	1:42.99	90,000
2002	Repent, 3, 122	A. J. D'Amico	Bob's Image, 3, 115	Easyfromthegitgo, 3, 122	9	1:43.17	90,000
2001	Dollar Bill, 3, 122	C. J. McCarron	Gracie's Dancer, 3, 114	Rahy's Secret, 3, 122	10	1:43.45	75,000
2000	Exchange Rate, 3, 119	C. S. Nakatani	Mighty, 3, 122	Ifitstobeitsuptome, 3, 114	8	1:44.25	75,000
1999	Ecton Park, 3, 114	S. J. Sellers	Answer Lively, 3, 122	Kimberlite Pipe, 3, 122	12	1:44.83	75,000
1998	Comic Strip, 3, 119	S. J. Sellers	Captain Maestri, 3, 122	Time Limit, 3, 122	7	1:44.27	75,000
1997	Open Forum, 3, 117	D. M. Barton	Crypto Star, 3, 117	Cash Deposit, 3, 122	5	1:44.20	60,000
1996	Zarb's Magic, 3, 122	E. J. Perrodin	Imminent First, 3, 114	Palikar, 3, 122	9	**1:42.98**	37,950
1995	Knockadoon, 3, 114	W. Martinez	Key to Malagra, 3, 114	Scott's Scoundrel, 3, 122	9	1:45.44	31,882
	Beavers Nose, 3, 117	K. Bourque	Moonlight Dancer, 3, 122	Fuzzy Me, 3, 114	8	1:45.22	31,792
1994	Fly Cry, 3, 122	R. D. Ardoin	Smilin Singin Sam, 3, 122	Little Jazz Boy, 3, 122	7	1:43.02	31,155
1993	Dixieland Heat, 3, 119	R. P. Romero	O'Star, 3, 114	Gold Angle, 3, 114	7	1:43.20	16,080
	Dry Bean, 3, 117	A. T. Gryder	Apprentice, 3, 119	Grand Jewel, 3, 114	6	1:43.80	16,020
1992	Line In The Sand, 3, 119	S. P. Romero	Hill Pass, 3, 119	Sheik to Sheik, 3, 114	11	1:45.00	19,635
1991	Big Courage, 3, 119	T. L. Fox	Slick Groom, 3, 114	Denizen, 3, 115	4	1:46.70	19,230
1990	Genuine Meaning, 3, 122	J. Hirdes	Very Formal, 3, 114	Diamond Prospector, 3, 114	12	1:40.80	16,740
1989	Nooo Problema, 3, 117	S. P. Romero	Alota Strawberry, 3, 114	Majesty's Imp, 3, 119	8	1:42.40	13,163
	Dispersal, 3, 114	B. J. Walker Jr.	Island Alibi, 3, 114	Major Prospect, 3, 114	8	1:42.20	13,103
1988	Risen Star, 3, 120	S. P. Romero	Pastourelles, 3, 115	Jim's Orbit, 3, 122	12	1:40.00	13,890

Named for Lamarque Racing Stable's and Louie J. Roussel III's 1988 champion three-year-old male and '88 Louisiana Derby (G3) winner Risen Star (1985 c. by Secretariat). Louisiana Derby Trial S. 1988. 1 mile 40 yards 1988-'90. Two divisions 1989, 1993, 1995.

Riva Ridge Breeders' Cup Stakes

Grade 2 in 2005. Belmont Park, three-year-olds, 7 furlongs, dirt. Held June 11, 2005, with a gross value of $170,000. First held in 1985. First graded in 1988. Stakes record 1:20.33 (1994 You and I).

Year	Winner	Jockey	Second	Third	Strs	Time	1st Purse
2005	Lost in the Fog, 3, 123	E. S. Prado	Egg Head, 3, 119	Middle Earth, 3, 116	8	1:21.54	$90,000
2004	Fire Slam, 3, 123	P. Day	Teton Forest, 3, 115	Abbondanza, 3, 123	7	1:20.94	120,000
2003	Posse, 3, 123	C. J. Lanerie	Midas Eyes, 3, 123	Halo Homewrecker, 3, 123	8	1:22.03	120,000
2002	Gygistar, 3, 119	P. Day	Draw Play, 3, 115	True Direction, 3, 119	9	1:22.61	120,000
2001	Put It Back, 3, 120	N. A. Wynter	Flame Thrower, 3, 120	Touch Tone, 3, 123	6	1:21.76	90,000
2000	Trippi, 3, 123	J. D. Bailey	Bevo, 3, 120	Sun Cat, 3, 116	6	1:23.68	90,000
1999	Yes It's True, 3, 123	J. D. Bailey	Lion Hearted, 3, 114	Silver Season, 3, 113	8	1:22.35	90,000
1998	Coronado's Quest, 3, 123	M. E. Smith	Mellow Roll, 3, 113	Flashing Tammany, 3, 120	7	1:22.50	82,050
1997	Smoke Glacken, 3, 123	C. Perret	Trafalger, 3, 123	Wild Wonder, 3, 120	6	1:20.98	66,060
1996	Gold Fever, 3, 118	M. E. Smith	Gameel, 3, 114	Bright Launch, 3, 120	9	1:23.30	67,620
1995	Western Larla, 3, 119	G. L. Stevens	Mr. Greeley, 3, 122	Blu Tusmani, 3, 122	8	1:24.24	66,960
1994	You and I, 3, 122	C. J. McCarron	End Sweep, 3, 114	Slew Gin Fizz, 3, 122	9	**1:20.33**	67,080
1993	Montbrook, 3, 117	C. J. Ladner III	As Indicated, 3, 122	Forever Whirl, 3, 122	10	1:23.34	74,160
1992	Superstrike (GB), 3, 115	J. A. Santos	Three Peat, 3, 122	Windundermywings, 3, 115	7	1:22.41	70,560
1991	Fly So Free, 3, 122	J. D. Bailey	Formal Dinner, 3, 122	Dodge, 3, 122	11	1:23.13	74,040
1990	Adjudicating, 3, 122	J. Vasquez	Silent Generation, 3, 115	Bayou Blur, 3, 115	7	1:23.80	68,040
1989	Is It True, 3, 122	C. W. Antley	Mr. Nickerson, 3, 115	Fierce Fighter, 3, 115	8	1:22.20	70,200
1988	Evening Kris, 3, 117	L. A. Pincay Jr.	Perfect Spy, 3, 122	King's Nest, 3, 115	7	1:22.80	69,120
1987	Jazzing Around, 3, 115	J. A. Santos	dh-High Brite, 3, 119		7	1:22.40	48,240
			dh-Polish Navy, 3, 122				
1986	Ogygian, 3, 122	W. A. Guerra	Wayar, 3, 115	Landing Plot, 3, 115	5	1:23.40	48,900
1985	Ziggy's Boy, 3, 115	A. T. Cordero Jr.	Tiffany Ice, 3, 115	Huddle Up, 3, 115	6	1:22.20	48,960

Named for Meadow Stable's 1971 champion two-year-old male, '73 champion older horse, and '72 Belmont S. winner Riva Ridge (1969 c. by First Landing). Grade 3 1988-'97. Dead heat for second 1987. Track record 1994.

River City Handicap

Grade 3 in 2005. Churchill Downs, three-year-olds and up, 1 1/8 miles, turf. Held November 21, 2004, with a gross value of $174,300. First held in 1978. First graded in 1996. Stakes record 1:47.90 (2001 Dr. Kashnikow).

Year	Winner	Jockey	Second	Third	Strs	Time	1st Purse
2004	G P Fleet, 4, 115	J. R. Martinez Jr.	Cloudy's Knight, 4, 115	Ay Caramba (Brz), 4, 115	12	1:51.26	$108,066

2003	Hard Buck (Brz), 4, 118	B. Blanc	Warleigh, 5, 117	Rowans Park, 3, 114	10	1:51.60	$107,136
2002	Dr. Kashnikow, 5, 116	R. Albarado	Foster's Landing, 4, 109	Roxinho (Brz), 4, 115	11	1:51.44	108,903
2001	Dr. Kashnikow, 4, 116	R. Albarado	Tijiyr (Ire), 5, 117	Strategic Mission, 6, 115	8	1:47.90	109,926
2000	Brahms, 3, 112	P. Day	Vergennes, 5, 115	Super Quercus (Fr), 4, 116	9	1:48.09	111,879
1999	Comic Strip, 4, 119	P. Day	Keats and Yeats, 5, 112	Aboriginal Apex, 6, 114	10	1:50.71	106,113
1998	Wild Event, 5, 116	S. J. Sellers	Buff, 3, 113	Floriselli, 4, 114	13	1:49.18	116,436
1997	Same Old Wish, 7, 117	S. J. Sellers	Aboriginal Apex, 4, 113	Joyeux Danseur, 4, 114	9	1:50.90	106,578
1996	Same Old Wish, 6, 119	S. J. Sellers	Jet Freighter, 5, 113	Franchise Player, 7, 111	7	1:49.21	70,122
1995	Homing Pigeon, 5, 113	R. P. Romero	Hawk Attack, 3, 115	Dusty Asher, 5, 111	8	1:51.00	73,320
1994	Lindon Lime, 4, 113	S. J. Sellers	Torch Rouge (GB), 3, 114	Jaggery John, 3, 115	11	1:49.30	75,660
1993	Secreto's Hideaway, 4, 110	W. Martinez	Little Bro Lantis, 5, 115	Ganges, 5, 113	5	1:53.83	72,670
1992	Cozzene's Prince, 5, 117	D. Penna	Lotus Pool, 5, 118	Stagecraft (GB), 5, 114	8	1:49.31	73,060
1991	Spending Record, 4, 114	P. Day	Stage Colony, 4, 113	Silver Medallion, 5, 118	10	1:50.34	75,075
1990	Silver Medallion, 4, 118	C. Perret	Blair's Cove, 5, 114	Rushing Raj, 4, 114	10	1:50.80	56,550
1989	Spark O'Dan, 4, 113	J. M. Johnson	Exclusive Greer, 8, 115	Air Worthy, 4, 118	10	1:50.80	55,429
1988	Ile de Jinsky, 4, 113	E. J. Sipus Jr.	Stop the Stage, 3, 114	Herakles, 5, 117	7	1:53.20	44,618
1987	Kings River (Ire), 5, 114	M. E. Smith	Lord Grundy (Ire), 5, 119	Boulder Run, 4, 117	10	1:45.40	37,148
1986	Taylor's Special, 5, 123	P. Day	Doonesbear, 3, 116	Sumptious, 3, 121	8	1:36.20	30,007
1985	Banner Bob, 3, 118	K. K. Allen	Rapid Gray, 6, 123	Cullendale, 3, 116	6	1:36.60	29,348
1984	Eminency, 6, 115	P. Day	Thumbsucker, 5, 123	Bayou Hebert, 3, 116	8	1:38.40	18,103
1983	Northern Majesty, 4, 120	S. Maple	Shot n' Missed, 6, 123	Straight Flow, 5, 115	8	1:37.00	18,249
1982	Pleasing Times, 3, 110	P. Day	Hechizado (Arg), 6, 115	Rackensack, 4, 118	13	1:38.20	20,719
1981	Suliman, 4, 113	L. Snyder	Tiger Lure, 7, 121	Senate Chairman, 3, 113	12	1:10.60	20,199
1980	Tinsley's Hope, 6, 113	J. C. Espinoza	Go With the Times, 4, 122	Withholding, 3, 114	6	1:11.00	19,208
1979	Go With the Times, 3, 120	G. Gallitano	Cossett Charlie, 6, 112	Bask, 5, 117	7	1:10.20	19,435
1978	Inca Roca, 5, 118	J. C. Espinoza	Perplext, 4, 114	Raymond Earl, 3, 115	10	1:10.40	17,859

Named for one of the nicknames of Louisville: the "River City." River City S. 1983-'86. 6 furlongs 1978-'81. 1 mile 1982-'86. 1 1/16 miles 1987. Dirt 1978-'86, 1988, 1993.

Robert F. Carey Memorial Handicap

Grade 3 in 2005. Hawthorne Race Course, three-year-olds and up, 1 mile, turf. Held October 9, 2004, with a gross value of $150,000. First held in 1983. First graded in 1986. Stakes record 1:33.40 (1998 Soviet Line [Ire]).

Year	Winner	Jockey	Second	Third	Strs	Time	1st Purse
2004	Scooter Roach, 5, 115	J. M. Campbell	Gin and Sin, 4, 116	Cloudy's Knight, 4, 116	9	1:34.51	$90,000
2003	Wiggins, 3, 117	E. Razo Jr.	Scooter Roach, 4, 116	Baker Road, 6, 121	11	1:43.89	71,610
	Mystery Giver, 5, 120	C. H. Marquez Jr.	Al's Dearly Bred, 6, 118	Major Rhythm, 4, 116	8	1:34.70	90,000
2002	Kimberlite Pipe, 6, 115	C. A. Emigh	Aslaaf, 4, 114	Major Omansky, 6, 115	10	1:35.94	90,000
2001	Galic Boy, 6, 115	R. Sibille	Where's Taylor, 5, 121	Good Journey, 5, 115	10	1:35.10	90,000
2000	Where's Taylor, 4, 117	C. J. Lanerie	Dernier Croise (Fr), 5, 113	Associate, 5, 115	11	1:36.31	90,000
1999	Ray's Approval, 6, 114	E. Fires	Stay Sound, 4, 115	Inkatha (Fr), 5, 115	10	1:37.01	90,000
1998	Soviet Line (Ire), 8, 115	S. J. Sellers	Fun to Run, 5, 110	Wild Event, 5, 115	10	1:33.40	90,000
1997	Trail City, 4, 119	J. D. Bailey	Power of Opinion, 4, 113	Da Bull, 5, 114	8	1:36.04	90,000
1996	Homing Pigeon, 6, 114	R. Albarado	Joker, 4, 115	Why Change, 3, 115	12	1:36.58	90,000
1995	Homing Pigeon, 5, 114	R. Albarado	Gilder, 4, 113	Rare Reason, 4, 119	9	1:38.09	60,000
1994	Recoup the Cash, 4, 119	J. L. Diaz	Road of War, 4, 115	Glenfiddich Lad, 5, 114	7	1:40.91	60,000
1993	High Habitation, 5, 114	G. C. Retana	Beau Fasa, 7, 114	Glenfiddich Lad, 4, 114	12	1:35.33	60,000
1992	Double Booked, 7, 115	J. C. Ferrer	Evanescent, 5, 113	That's Sunny, 7, 114	11	1:39.82	60,000
1991	Slew the Slewor, 4, 114	G. K. Gomez	Jalaajel, 7, 118	The Great Carl, 4, 118	9	1:38.72	96,090
1990	Allijeba, 4, 118	K. D. Clark	Wave Wise, 4, 114	Expensive Decision, 4, 118	9	1:39.20	86,070
1989	Iron Courage, 5, 121	R. R. Pena	Saint Oxford, 5, 112	Do Loop, 6, 109	10	1:47.00	94,080
1988	New Colony, 5, 114	R. R. Douglas	Rio's Lark, 4, 115	Bank Fast, 4, 111	9	1:47.60	93,900
1987	The Sassman, 4, 115	K. D. Clark	Zaizoom, 3, 115	Zuppardo's Love, 6, 111	6	2:05.40	89,130
1986	Pass the Line, 5, 117	J. L. Diaz	Explosive Darling, 4, 117	Salem Drive, 4, 116	8	2:01.00	94,500
1985	River Lord, 6, 111	R. A. Meier	Harham's Sizzler, 6, 118	Attaway to Go, 4, 111	4	2:06.20	63,370
1984	Ronbra, 4, 115	C. H. Marquez	Grazie, 4, 115	Bold Run (Fr), 5, 115	12	2:03.80	66,540
1983	Sir Pele, 4, 112	O. Vergara	John's Gold, 4, 120	Energetic King, 4, 111	7	1:55.00	64,800

Named for Robert F. Carey (1904-'80), managing director of Hawthorne Race Course (1947-'80). Formerly sponsored by United Airlines of Chicago 1995. Not graded 1990-'97. Robert F. Carey H. 1984-'85. 1 3/16 miles 1983. 1 1/4 miles 1984-'87. 1 1/8 miles 1988-'89. 1 mile 70 yards 1994. Dirt 1985, 1994. Two divisions 2003.

Royal Heroine Stakes

Grade 3 in 2005. Hollywood Park, three-year-olds and up, fillies and mares, 1 mile, turf. Held July 3, 2004, with a gross value of $109,700. First held in 1998. First graded in 2001. Stakes record 1:33.98 (2000 Tranquility Lake).

Year	Winner	Jockey	Second	Third	Strs	Time	1st Purse
2004	Janeian (NZ), 6, 121	K. J. Desormeaux	Katdogawn (GB), 4, 123	Makeup Artist, 4, 121	6	1:34.79	$65,820
2003	Magic Mission (GB), 5, 115	C. S. Nakatani	Little Treasure (Fr), 4, 121	Belleski, 4, 115	9	1:34.25	67,320
2002	Surya, 4, 117	K. J. Desormeaux	Angel Gift, 4, 117	Reine de Romance (Ire), 4, 121	12	1:34.73	68,880
2001	Kalatiara (Aus), 4, 114	C. J. McCarron	Dianehill (Ire), 5, 119	Al Desima (GB), 4, 116	7	1:34.41	65,940
2000	Tranquility Lake, 5, 121	E. J. Delahoussaye	Dianehill (Ire), 4, 119	Reciclada (Chi), 5, 119	6	1:33.98	46,590
1999	Tuzla (Fr), 5, 123	C. S. Nakatani	Isle de France, 4, 119	Chime After Chime, 4, 113	5	1:34.32	42,240

| 1998 | Tuzla (Fr), 4, 115 | C. S. Nakatani | Sonja's Faith (Ire), 4, 119 | Plus (Chi), 5, 115 | 6 | 1:34.33 | $42,990 |

Named for Robert E. Sangster's 1984 champion grass mare and '84 Breeders' Cup Mile (at Hollywood Park) winner Royal Heroine (Ire) (1980 f. by Lypheor [GB]).

Ruffian Handicap

Grade 1 in 2005. Belmont Park, three-year-olds and up, fillies and female, 1¹/₁₆ miles, dirt. Held September 19, 2004, with a gross value of $294,000. First held in 1976. First graded in 1976. Stakes record 1:40.35 (2000 Riboletta [Brz]).

Year	Winner	Jockey	Second	Third	Strs	Time	1st Purse
2004	Sightseek, 5, 122	J. R. Velazquez	Pocus Hocus, 6, 114	Miss Loren (Arg), 6, 117	5	1:41.51	$180,000
2003	Wild Spirit (Chi), 4, 121	J. D. Bailey	You, 4, 118	Passing Shot, 4, 115	6	1:41.23	180,000
2002	Mandy's Gold, 4, 116	J. A. Santos	You, 3, 117	Shine Again, 5, 117	5	1:42.57	180,000
2000	Riboletta (Brz), 5, 125	C. J. McCarron	Gourmet Girl, 5, 114	Country Hideaway, 4, 114	7	1:40.35	150,000
1999	Catinca, 4, 119	J. D. Bailey	Furlough, 5, 116	Keeper Hill, 4, 118	5	1:41.94	150,000
1998	Sharp Cat, 4, 124	C. S. Nakatani	Furlough, 4, 115	Stop Traffic, 5, 119	8	1:42.48	150,000
1997	Tomisue's Delight, 3, 113	J. D. Bailey	Clear Mandate, 5, 119	Mil Kilates, 4, 114	9	1:44.43	150,000
1996	Yanks Music, 3, 116	J. R. Velazquez	Serena's Song, 4, 126	Head East, 4, 108	6	1:41.84	150,000
1995	Inside Information, 4, 125	M. E. Smith	Unlawful Behavior, 5, 110	Incinerate, 5, 112	6	1:40.98	120,000
1994	Sky Beauty, 4, 130	M. E. Smith	Dispute, 4, 117	Educated Risk, 4, 114	5	1:41.79	120,000
1993	Shared Interest, 5, 114	R. G. Davis	Dispute, 3, 115	Turnback the Alarm, 4, 123	5	1:41.92	120,000
1992	Versailles Treaty, 4, 120	M. E. Smith	Quick Mischief, 6, 116	Nannerl, 5, 119	6	1:41.41	120,000
1991	Queena, 5, 120	A. T. Cordero Jr.	Sharp Dance, 5, 114	Lady d'Accord, 4, 113	7	1:41.65	120,000
1990	Quick Mischief, 4, 111	R. I. Rojas	Personal Business, 4, 113	Mistaurian, 4, 115	9	1:42.80	144,480
1989	Bayakoa (Arg), 5, 125	L. A. Pincay Jr.	Colonial Waters, 4, 118	Open Mind, 3, 120	6	1:48.40	135,840
1988	Sham Say, 3, 113	J. Vasquez	Classic Crown, 3, 115	Make Change, 3, 114	11	1:48.00	146,400
1987	‡Coup de Fusil, 5, 117	A. T. Cordero Jr.	Clabber Girl, 4, 112	Sacahuista, 3, 114	12	1:48.60	149,760
1986	Lady's Secret, 4, 129	P. Day	Steal a Kiss, 3, 109	Endear, 4, 119	6	1:46.60	165,240
1985	Lady's Secret, 3, 116	J. Velasquez	Isayso, 6, 115	Sintrillium, 7, 118	4	1:47.40	128,880
1984	Heatherten, 5, 118	R. P. Romero	Miss Oceana, 3, 119	Adored, 4, 123	7	1:48.20	103,320
1983	Heartlight No. One, 3, 117	L. A. Pincay Jr.	Mochila, 4, 113	Try Something New, 4, 116	12	1:47.20	103,140
1982	Christmas Past, 3, 117	J. Vasquez	Mademoiselle Forli, 3, 112	Love Sign, 5, 123	8	1:48.60	100,080
1981	Relaxing, 5, 123	A. T. Cordero Jr.	Love Sign, 4, 120	Jameela, 5, 122	4	1:47.60	97,020
1980	Genuine Risk, 3, 118	J. Vasquez	Misty Gallore, 4, 124	It's in the Air, 4, 118	6	1:49.20	81,900
1979	It's in the Air, 3, 122	L. A. Pincay Jr.	Blitey, 3, 113	Waya (Fr), 5, 126	4	1:47.40	79,875
1978	Late Bloomer, 4, 122	J. Velasquez	Pearl Necklace, 4, 124	Tempest Queen, 5, 117	9	1:47.00	64,860
1977	Cum Laude Laurie, 3, 114	A. T. Cordero Jr.	Mississippi Mud, 4, 123	Cascapedia, 4, 128	12	1:52.20	66,480
1976	Revidere, 3, 118	J. Vasquez	*Bastonera II, 5, 123	Optimistic Gal, 3, 118	5	2:01.00	79,425

Named for Locust Hill Farm's 1974 champion two-year-old filly, '75 champion three-year-old filly, and '75 Filly Triple Crown winner Ruffian (1972 f. by Reviewer); Ruffian is buried in the Belmont infield. Ruffian S. 1976. Not held due to World Trade Center attack 2001. 1¹/₄ miles 1976. 1¹/₈ miles 1977-'89. ‡Sacahuista finished first, DQ to third, 1987.

Sabin Handicap

Grade 3 in 2005. Gulfstream Park, three-year-olds and up, fillies and mares, 1¹/₈ miles, dirt. Held February 26, 2005, with a gross value of $100,000. First held in 1991. First graded in 1994. Stakes record 1:50.68 (2005 Isola Piu Bella [Chi]).

Year	Winner	Jockey	Second	Third	Strs	Time	1st Purse
2005	Isola Piu Bella (Chi), 5, 116	J. R. Velazquez	Pampered Princess, 5, 117	Adobe Gold, 4, 116	5	1:50.68	$60,000
2004	Roar Emotion, 4, 116	J. R. Velazquez	Nonsuch Bay, 5, 115	Lead Story, 5, 119	9	1:43.32	60,000
2003	Allamerican Bertie, 4, 120	J. D. Bailey	Small Promises, 5, 112	Redoubled Miss, 4, 114	11	1:42.49	60,000
2002	Miss Linda (Arg), 5, 119	R. Migliore	Forest Secrets, 4, 117	Tap Dance, 4, 113	12	1:42.61	60,000
2001	De Bertie, 4, 115	J. F. Chavez	Royal Fair, 5, 113	Frankly My Dear, 4, 116	8	1:44.74	60,000
2000	Brushed Beauty, 4, 115	M. E. Smith	Roza Robata, 5, 115	Mop Squeezer, 4, 113	5	1:41.84	45,000
1999	Timely Broad, 5, 115	N. J. Petro	Highfalutin, 5, 116	Mudslinger, 4, 116	9	1:42.50	45,000
1998	Radiant Megan, 5, 113	J. A. Krone	Escena, 5, 119	Biding Time, 4, 113	7	1:41.25	45,000
1997	Rare Blend, 4, 120	J. D. Bailey	Golden Gale, 4, 113	Termly, 4, 112	7	1:41.28	45,000
1996	Lindsay Frolic, 4, 117	P. Day	Investalot, 5, 114	Queen Tutta, 4, 113	8	1:43.70	45,000
1995	Recognizable, 4, 115	M. E. Smith	Jade Flush, 4, 113	Sambacarioca, 6, 118	8	1:42.50	45,000
1994	Hunzinga, 5, 113	J. E. Felix	Nine Keys, 4, 114	Pleasant Jolie, 6, 112	9	1:39.57	45,000
1993	Now Dance, 4, 113	M. Guidry	Spinning Round, 4, 115	Luv Me Luv Me Not, 4, 117	10	1:41.68	30,000
1992	Lemhi Go, 4, 113	R. N. Lester	Trumpet's Blare, 5, 114	Tappanzee, 4, 114	8	1:44.79	45,000
1991	Fit for a Queen, 5, 114	J. D. Bailey	Trumpet's Blare, 4, 114	Express Star, 5, 116	9	1:42.50	46,020

Named for Henryk de Kwiatkowski's 1984 Orchid H. (G2) winner Sabin (1980 f. by Lyphard). Sabin Breeders' Cup H. 1991. 1 mile 70 yards 1993-2000. 1¹/₁₆ miles 1991-'92, 2001-'04.

Safely Kept Breeders' Cup Stakes

Grade 3 in 2005. Pimlico, three-year-olds, fillies, 6 furlongs, dirt. Held October 2, 2004, with a gross value of $143,000. First held in 1986. First graded in 1990. Stakes record 1:09.21 (1999 Godmother).

Year	Winner	Jockey	Second	Third	Strs	Time	1st Purse
2004	Bending Strings, 3, 119	H. Karamanos	Smokey Glacken, 3, 119	Then She Laughs, 3, 117	6	1:10.11	$90,000

2003	Randaroo, 3, 119	H. Castillo Jr.	Follow Me Home, 3, 117	Awesome Charm, 3, 115	8	1:10.54	$90,000
2002	Miss Lodi, 3, 117	R. Fogelsonger	For Rubies, 3, 117	Wilzada, 3, 117	8	1:11.20	60,000
2000	Swept Away, 3, 122	J. Beasley	Another, 3, 115	Cat Cay, 3, 117	8	1:09.51	60,000
1999	Godmother, 3, 117	M. G. Pino	Superduper Miss, 3, 117	Rills, 3, 113	7	1:09.21	60,000
1998	Hair Spray, 3, 117	J. A. Velez Jr.	Expensive Issue, 3, 115	Ninth Inning, 3, 119	8	1:10.67	66,390
1997	Weather Vane, 3, 119	M. G. Pino	Vegas Prospector, 3, 117	Requesting More, 3, 115	7	1:10.21	64,800
1996	J J'sdream, 3, 122	M. G. Pino	Flat Fleet Feet, 3, 119	Rare Blend, 3, 122	5	1:09.45	60,000
1995	Broad Smile, 3, 117	J. Brown	Scotzanna, 3, 122	Shebatim's Trick, 3, 115	7	1:10.30	60,000
1994	Twist Afleet, 3, 117	D. Carr	Penny's Reshoot, 3, 117	Our Royal Blue, 3, 114	7	1:10.88	60,000
1993	Miss Indy Anna, 3, 113	D. B. Thomas	Ann Dear, 3, 113	Lily of the North, 3, 113	7	1:10.12	60,000
1992	Meafara, 3, 119	B. Swatuk	Squirm, 3, 122	Super Doer, 3, 122	6	1:10.55	60,000
1991	Missy's Mirage, 3, 119	W. H. McCauley	Withallprobability, 3, 122	Corporate Fund, 3, 114	5	1:10.53	60,000
1990	Voodoo Lily, 3, 117	K. J. Desormeaux	Miss Spentyouth, 3, 119	Catchamenot, 3, 114	8	1:10.60	60,000
1989	Safely Kept, 3, 122	C. Perret	Cojinx, 3, 119	Kathleen the Queen, 3, 117	5	1:11.20	60,000
1988	Clever Power, 3, 120	J. A. Krone	Lake Valley, 3, 120	Ready Jet Go, 3, 120	8	1:16.40	65,000
1987	Endless Surprise, 4, 118	K. J. Desormeaux	Bea Quality, 5, 120	Miracle Wood, 4, 111	7	1:17.40	28,340
1986	Debtor's Prison, 5, 108	D. Byrnes	Night Above, 4, 117	Bea Quality, 4, 114	6	1:11.40	28,178

Named for Jayeff "B" Stables's and Barry Weisbord's 1989 champion sprinter and '89 Columbia S. winner Safely Kept (1986 f. by Horatius). Formerly named for the nearby city of Columbia, Maryland. Columbia H. 1986-'87. Columbia S. 1988-'95. Held at Laurel Park 1988, 1990, 1998-2000. Held at Colonial Downs 1997. Not held 2001. 6½ furlongs 1988.

Salvator Mile Handicap

Grade 3 in 2005. Monmouth Park, three-year-olds and up, 1 mile, dirt. Held July 25, 2004, with a gross value of $100,000. First held in 1894. First graded in 1973. Stakes record 1:34.46 (1991 Peanut Butter Onit).

Year	Winner	Jockey	Second	Third	Strs	Time	1st Purse
2004	Presidentialaffair, 5, 117	S. Elliott	Unforgettable Max, 4, 117	Roaring Fever, 4, 115	5	1:35.27	$60,000
2003	Vinemeister, 4, 114	J. A. Velez Jr.	Jersey Giant, 4, 117	Highway Prospector, 6, 113	6	1:35.89	60,000
2002	‡Sea of Tranquility, 6, 120	J. C. Ferrer	Free of Love, 4, 117	First Lieutenant, 5, 114	8	1:36.12	60,000
2001	Sea of Tranquility, 5, 115	J. C. Ferrer	Knock Again, 4, 112	Hal's Hope, 4, 117	7	1:36.74	90,000
2000	Leave It to Beezer, 7, 120	R. E. Alvarado Jr.	Delaware Township, 4, 112	Prime Directive, 4, 114	5	1:37.29	90,000
1999	Truluck, 4, 115	J. Bravo	Rock and Roll, 4, 119	Siftaway, 4, 114	6	1:35.18	90,000
1998	El Amante, 5, 119	J. A. Krone	Stormin Fever, 4, 117	Gold Token, 5, 114	8	1:34.95	60,000
1997	Distorted Humor, 4, 114	J. A. Krone	Wild Deputy, 4, 114	Smooth the Loot, 4, 113	4	1:36.03	60,000
1996	Smart Strike, 4, 113	S. Hawley	Cozy Drive, 4, 113	November Sunset, 4, 115	10	1:36.28	60,000
1995	Schossberg, 5, 116	D. Penna	Cast Iron, 4, 110	Relentless Star, 5, 109	9	1:35.86	45,000
1994	Storm Tower, 4, 119	R. Wilson	Cold Digger, 7, 113	Koluctoo Jimmy Al, 4, 114	6	1:36.26	45,000
1993	Dusty Screen, 5, 117	E. L. King Jr.	Count New York, 4, 112	Root Boy, 5, 118	8	1:35.86	45,000
1992	Peanut Butter Onit, 6, 120	A. T. Gryder	Root Boy, 4, 114	He Is Risen, 4, 118	7	1:36.21	45,000
1991	Peanut Butter Onit, 5, 115	W. S. Ramos	Private School, 4, 114	Runaway Stream, 4, 116	8	1:34.46	45,000
1990	Shy Tom, 4, 115	J. A. Krone	Bill E. Shears, 5, 121	Pete the Chief, 4, 115	5	1:36.00	49,020
1989	Bill E. Shears, 4, 112	R. Hernandez	Festive, 4, 110	Mi Selecto, 4, 117	6	1:35.40	49,890
1988	Slew City Slew, 4, 116	M. Castaneda	Bet Twice, 4, 125	Matthews Keep, 4, 116	5	1:35.00	38,880
1987	Moment of Hope, 4, 118	M. Venezia	Owens Troupe, 4, 117	Entitled To, 5, 116	6	1:34.60	33,270
1986	Jyp, 5, 115	J. Rocco	Minneapple, 4, 119	Valiant Lark, 6, 117	8	1:35.80	33,300
1985	Valiant Lark, 5, 116	V. A. Bracciale Jr.	Pat's Addition, 5, 115	Rumptious, 5, 116	10	1:36.00	33,990
1984	Rumptious, 4, 115	W. H. McCauley	English Master, 4, 112	World Appeal, 4, 122	10	1:34.60	34,260
1983	Naughty Jimmy, 6, 114	L. Saumell	Castle Guard, 4, 115	Star Gallant, 4, 120	7	1:37.00	33,510
1982	Count His Fleet, 4, 116	W. Nemeti	Explosive Bid, 4, 117	Accipiter's Hope, 4, 116	12	1:35.40	35,070
1981	Colonel Moran, 4, 117	C. Perret	Sun Catcher, 4, 120	Pikotazo (Mex), 4, 117	12	1:35.60	35,190
1980	Convenient, 4, 114	V. A. Bracciale Jr.	Tunerup, 4, 113	Foretake, 4, 113	8	1:36.60	26,640
1979	‡Revivalist, 5, 122	D. MacBeth	Horatius, 4, 120	Nice Catch, 5, 120	9	1:35.40	25,578
1978	Do Tell George, 5, 113	B. Mize	Buckfinder, 4, 118	Get Permission, 5, 114	5	1:36.40	17,664
1977	Peppy Addy, 5, 120	B. Phelps	Resound, 5, 115	Break Up the Game, 6, 117	8	1:36.00	18,168
1976	Royal Glint, 6, 126	J. E. Tejeira	Talc, 4, 113	Peppy Addy, 4, 118	9	1:35.20	18,395
1975	Proper Bostonian, 5, 117	M. Miceli	Rastaferian, 6, 113	Orbit Round, 4, 110	8	1:36.20	14,576
	Mongongo, 6, 119	B. Thornburg	Good John, 5, 114	Silver Hope, 4, 116	8	1:36.20	14,576
1974	Okavango, 4, 112	W. Blum	Hey Rube, 4, 114	Escaped, 5, 113	9	1:35.80	18,265
1973	Prince of Truth, 5, 117	W. Blum	Windtex, 4, 116	New Alibhai, 5, 115	7	1:35.80	17,761

Named for James Ben Ali Haggin's 1890 Monmouth Cup winner Salvator (1886 c. by *Prince Charlie); in 1890 he set an American record for one mile at Monmouth Park that stood for 28 years. Salvator Mile S. 1957, 1997. Two divisions 1975. ‡Nice Catch finished first, DQ to third, 1979. ‡First Lieutenant finished first, DQ to third, 2002.

San Antonio Handicap

Grade 2 in 2005. Santa Anita Park, four-year-olds and up, 1⅛ miles, dirt. Held February 6, 2005, with a gross value of $250,000. First held in 1935. First graded in 1973. Stakes record 1:46.20 (1978 Vigors).

Year	Winner	Jockey	Second	Third	Strs	Time	1st Purse
2005	Lundy's Liability (Brz), 5, 119	D. R. Flores	Truly a Judge, 7, 118	Congrats, 5, 116	9	1:49.05	$150,000
2004	Pleasantly Perfect, 6, 121	A. O. Solis	Star Cross (Arg), 7, 114	Fleetstreet Dancer, 6, 116	4	1:47.25	150,000
2003	Congaree, 5, 123	J. D. Bailey	Milwaukee Brew, 6, 120	Pleasantly Perfect, 5, 117	6	1:47.60	150,000

Year	Winner	Jockey	Second	Third	Strs	Time	1st Purse
2002	Redattore (Brz), 7, 116	A. O. Solis	Euchre, 6, 119	Irisheyesareflying, 6, 117	7	1:48.66	$150,000
2001	Guided Tour, 5, 115	L. J. Melancon	Lethal Instrument, 5, 116	Moonlight Charger, 6, 113	8	1:48.70	180,000
2000	Budroyale, 7, 121	G. K. Gomez	Cat Thief, 4, 120	Elaborate, 5, 116	5	1:48.70	180,000
1999	Free House, 5, 123	C. J. McCarron	Malek (Chi), 6, 119	Dramatic Gold, 8, 116	4	1:48.54	180,000
1998	Gentlemen (Arg), 6, 124	G. L. Stevens	Da Bull, 6, 115	Refinado Tom (Arg), 5, 120	5	1:47.60	180,000
1997	Gentlemen (Arg), 5, 122	G. L. Stevens	Alphabet Soup, 6, 122	Kingdom Found, 7, 116	5	1:47.38	180,300
1996	Alphabet Soup, 5, 119	C. W. Antley	Soul of the Matter, 5, 121	Dare and Go, 5, 119	5	1:49.96	184,900
1995	Best Pal, 7, 121	C. J. McCarron	Slew of Damascus, 7, 119	Tossofthecoin, 5, 117	10	1:47.43	148,500
1994	The Wicked North, 5, 116	K. J. Desormeaux	‡Region, 5, 117	Hill Pass, 5, 116	9	1:47.48	155,500
1993	Marquetry, 6, 117	E. J. Delahoussaye	Sir Beaufort, 6, 120	Reign Road, 5, 116	6	1:48.96	155,500
1992	Ibero (Arg), 5, 115	A. O. Solis	In Excess (Ire), 5, 123	Cobra Classic, 5, 114	8	1:47.05	189,750
1991	Farma Way, 4, 118	G. L. Stevens	Anshan (GB), 4, 116	dh- Festin (Arg), 5, 116	9	1:47.30	196,750
				dh- Louis Cyphre (Ire), 5, 111			
1990	Criminal Type, 5, 117	A. O. Solis	Stylish Winner, 6, 113	Ruhlmann, 5, 122	7	1:49.00	190,500
1989	Super Diamond, 9, 121	L. A. Pincay Jr.	Frankly Perfect, 4, 116	Cherokee Colony, 4, 120	7	1:48.80	159,600
1988	Judge Angelucci, 5, 122	E. J. Delahoussaye	Ferdinand, 5, 118	Crimson Slew, 4, 115	6	1:48.60	156,700
1987	Bedside Promise, 5, 121	G. L. Stevens	Hopeful Word, 6, 118	Bruiser (GB), 4, 114	9	1:47.20	129,600
1986	Hatim, 5, 117	L. A. Pincay Jr.	Right Con, 4, 117	Nostalgia's Star, 4, 118	8	1:47.40	128,700
1985	Lord At War (Arg), 5, 122	W. Shoemaker	Al Mamoon, 4, 114	Hail Bold King, 4, 122	7	1:48.20	125,200
1984	Poley, 5, 120	C. J. McCarron	Water Bank, 5, 117	Danebo, 5, 119	5	1:48.00	156,900
1983	Bates Motel, 4, 114	T. Lipham	Time to Explode, 4, 121	It's the One, 5, 124	10	1:47.00	132,300
1982	Score Twenty Four, 5, 115	P. A. Valenzuela	Super Moment, 5, 124	High Counsel, 4, 114	6	1:47.80	124,200
1981	Flying Paster, 5, 126	C. J. McCarron	‡Doonesbury, 4, 121	King Go Go, 6, 119	5	1:46.60	91,700
1980	Beau's Eagle, 4, 121	D. Pierce	Relaunch, 4, 117	Double Discount, 7, 114	6	1:48.40	79,650
1979	Tiller, 5, 121	A. T. Cordero Jr.	Painted Wagon, 6, 114	‡Life's Hope, 6, 120	6	1:47.00	65,800
1978	Vigors, 5, 121	D. G. McHargue	Ancient Title, 8, 120	Double Discount, 5, 116	7	**1:46.20**	67,100
1977	Ancient Title, 7, 119	S. Hawley	Double Discount, 4, 115	Properantes, 4, 114	10	1:47.80	72,500
1976	Lightning Mandate, 5, 118	A. T. Cordero Jr.	Dancing Papa, 6, 117	Messenger of Song, 4, 122	10	1:48.20	54,350
1975	Cheriepe, 5, 120	A. Santiago	First Back, 4, 117	Ancient Title, 5, 128	9	1:46.80	52,850
1974	Prince Dantan, 4, 116	L. A. Pincay Jr.	Forage, 5, 119	Dancing Papa, 4, 116	8	1:47.60	51,550
1973	Kennedy Road, 5, 119	D. Pierce	Crusading, 5, 119	Big Spruce, 4, 117	5	1:47.60	49,400

Named for seven California land grants, each of which was called Rancho San Antonio; two were in Los Angeles County, one is now Beverly Hills. Grade 1 1983–'89. San Antonio S. 1968–'82. Not held 1941–'45. 1¹/₁₆ miles 1940. Three-year-olds and up 1946, 1948, 1950–'52, 1956, 1958, 1960. Dead heat for third 1991. ‡Mr. Redoy finished third, DQ to sixth, 1979. ‡King Go Go finished second, DQ to third, 1981. ‡Hill Pass finished second, DQ to third, 1994.

San Carlos Handicap

Grade 2 in 2005. Santa Anita Park, four-year-olds and up, 7 furlongs, dirt. Held February 26, 2005, with a gross value of $150,000. First held in 1935. First graded in 1973. Stakes record 1:20.20 (1981 Flying Paster).

Year	Winner	Jockey	Second	Third	Strs	Time	1st Purse
2005	Hasty Kris, 8, 115	R. R. Douglas	Harvard Avenue, 4, 115	Perfect Moon, 4, 117	8	1:21.42	$90,000
2004	Pico Central (Brz), 5, 116	D. R. Flores	Publication, 5, 116	Pohave, 6, 112	10	1:21.16	90,000
2003	Aldebaran, 5, 116	J. Valdivia Jr.	Crafty C. T., 5, 116	Grey Memo, 6, 116	6	1:21.53	120,000
2002	Snow Ridge, 4, 118	M. E. Smith	Alyzig, 5, 112	Grey Memo, 5, 114	6	1:22.02	90,000
2001	Kona Gold, 7, 125	A. O. Solis	Blade Prospector (Brz), 6, 113	Grey Memo, 4, 115	7	1:21.35	90,000
2000	Son of a Pistol, 8, 117	G. K. Gomez	Kona Gold, 6, 122	Old Topper, 5, 116	6	1:22.11	96,930
1999	Big Jag, 6, 118	J. Valdivia Jr.	Kona Gold, 5, 120	Dramatic Gold, 8, 117	5	1:21.18	90,000
1998	Reality Road, 6, 116	C. J. McCarron	Gold Land, 7, 116	Son of a Pistol, 6, 114	10	1:21.62	100,530
1997	Northern Afleet, 4, 117	C. J. McCarron	Hesabull, 4, 117	High Stakes Player, 5, 120	7	1:21.45	97,700
1996	Kingdom Found, 6, 116	C. J. McCarron	Lakota Brave, 7, 114	Lit de Justice, 6, 123	9	1:22.23	98,850
1995	Softshoe Sure Shot, 9, 113	A. O. Solis	Ferrara, 4, 115	Subtle Trouble, 4, 113	7	1:21.46	91,600
1994	Cardmania, 8, 122	E. J. Delahoussaye	The Wicked North, 5, 117	Portoferraio (Arg), 6, 115	7	1:21.23	63,900
1993	Sir Beaufort, 6, 120	C. J. McCarron	Cardmania, 7, 117	Excavate, 5, 114	6	1:22.22	62,900
1992	Answer Do, 6, 120	G. L. Stevens	Individualist, 5, 115	Media Plan, 4, 116	7	1:21.23	63,700
1991	Farma Way, 4, 115	G. L. Stevens	Yes I'm Blue, 5, 117	Tanker Port, 6, 117	7	1:21.50	63,500
1990	Raise a Stanza, 4, 117	R. A. Baze	Oraibi, 5, 119	Tanker Port, 5, 117	7	1:21.60	64,500
1989	Cherokee Colony, 4, 119	R. Q. Meza	On the Line, 5, 126	Happy in Space, 5, 116	6	1:20.60	62,800
1988	Epidaurus, 6, 117	P. A. Valenzuela	Super Diamond, 8, 125	Lord Ruckus, 5, 118	7	1:22.00	63,500
1987	Zany Tactics, 6, 118	J. L. Kaenel	Bolder Than Bold, 5, 116	Epidaurus, 5, 115	8	1:22.40	65,600
1986	Phone Trick, 4, 120	L. A. Pincay Jr.	Temerity Prince, 6, 122	My Habitony, 6, 117	6	1:20.80	78,200
1985	Debonaire Junior, 4, 125	C. J. McCarron	Tennessee Rite, 4, 112	Fifty Six Ina Row, 4, 116	6	1:21.60	64,300
1984	Danebo, 5, 117	L. A. Pincay Jr.	Pac Mania, 4, 118	Poley, 5, 119	7	1:21.00	54,900
1983	Kangroo Court, 6, 118	J. J. Steiner	Dave's Friend, 8, 117	Shanekite, 5, 118	6	1:21.00	49,550
1982	Solo Guy, 4, 118	W. Shoemaker	‡Smokite, 6, 116	King Go Go, 7, 119	8	1:20.80	60,700
1981	Flying Paster, 5, 124	C. J. McCarron	To B. Or Not, 5, 123	Double Discount, 8, 115	8	**1:20.20**	51,550
1980	Handsomeness, 4, 118	L. A. Pincay Jr.	Relaunch, 4, 121	Beau's Eagle, 4, 125	5	1:24.00	49,100
1979	O Big Al, 4, 120	D. G. McHargue	Maheras, 6, 122	Bad 'n Big, 5, 124	7	1:22.20	40,800
1978	Double Discount, 5, 117	F. Mena	Impressive Luck, 5, 120	Romantic Lead, 5, 117	6	1:22.00	32,650
1977	Uniformity, 5, 115	F. Toro	†My Juliet, 5, 123	Messenger of Song, 5, 122	7	1:21.60	34,050
1976	No Bias, 6, 120	L. A. Pincay Jr.	Century's Envoy, 5, 126	Bahia Key, 6, 120	5	1:21.80	32,200
1975	Ancient Title, 5, 128	L. A. Pincay Jr.	dh-Bahia Key, 5, 117 dh-Hudson County, 4, 116		12	1:21.20	37,750

1974 **Royal Owl**, 5, 117	L. A. Pincay Jr.	Soft Victory, 6, 116	Against the Snow, 4, 112	9	1:23.40	$35,600
1973 ‡**Crusading**, 5, 119	F. Toro	Kennedy Road, 5, 117	*Figonero, 8, 114	8	1:20.80	33,850

Named for Rancho El Potrero de San Carlos in Monterey County, California. Grade 1 2001-'03. Not held 1942-'45, 1960. 1¹⁄₁₆ miles 1935-'39. Three-year-olds and up 1946, 1949-'52, 1954-'59. Dead heat for second 1975. ‡Kennedy Road finished first, DQ to second, 1973. ‡King Go Go finished second, DQ to third, 1982. †Denotes female.

San Clemente Handicap

Grade 2 in 2005. Del Mar, three-year-olds, fillies, 1 mile, turf. Held July 31, 2004, with a gross value of $150,000. First held in 1950. First graded in 1994. Stakes record 1:33.62 (2003 Katdogawn [GB]).

Year	Winner	Jockey	Second	Third	Strs	Time	1st Purse
2004	**Sweet Win**, 3, 114	V. Espinoza	Miss Vegas (Ire), 3, 121	Victory U. S. A., 3, 119	5	1:34.11	$90,000
2003	**Katdogawn (GB)**, 3, 116	J. A. Krone	Atlantic Ocean, 3, 120	Buffythecenterfold, 3, 118	9	**1:33.62**	90,000
2002	**Little Treasure (Fr)**, 3, 117	K. J. Desormeaux	Pina Colada (GB), 3, 115	Arabic Song (Ire), 3, 118	9	1:33.97	90,000
2001	**Reine de Romance (Ire)**, 3, 116	E. J. Delahoussaye	Gabriellina Giof (GB), 3, 116	La Vida Loca (Ire), 3, 116	8	1:34.88	90,000
2000	**Uncharted Haven (GB)**, 3, 116	A. O. Solis	Automated, 3, 117	Islay Mist (GB), 3, 118	10	1:35.13	90,000
1999	**Sweet Ludy (Ire)**, 3, 118	C. S. Nakatani	Caffe Latte (Ire), 3, 115	Sweet Life, 3, 117	10	1:35.02	90,000
1998	**Sicy d'Alsace (Fr)**, 3, 115	C. S. Nakatani	Miss Hot Salsa, 3, 117	Tranquility Lake, 3, 114	10	1:34.97	67,500
1997	**Famous Digger**, 3, 120	B. Blanc	Cozy Blues, 3, 116	Really Happy, 3, 119	10	1:36.00	71,725
1996	**True Flare**, 3, 116	C. S. Nakatani	Gastronomical, 3, 119	Najecam, 3, 114	10	1:35.59	67,200
1995	**Jewel Princess**, 3, 115	C. J. McCarron	Auriette (Ire), 3, 119	Scratch Paper, 3, 119	6	1:36.12	59,650
1994	**Work the Crowd**, 3, 120	C. J. McCarron	Pharma, 3, 116	Dancing Mirage, 3, 115	8	1:36.47	48,550
1993	**Hollywood Wildcat**, 3, 120	E. J. Delahoussaye	Miami Sands (Ire), 3, 116	Beal Street Blues, 3, 117	10	1:34.89	49,950
1992	**Golden Treat**, 3, 121	K. J. Desormeaux	Morriston Belle, 3, 118	Alysbelle, 3, 118	8	1:35.20	49,350
1991	**Flawlessly**, 3, 120	C. J. McCarron	Gold Fleece, 3, 114	Miss High Blade, 3, 117	9	1:34.88	64,600
1990	**Nijinsky's Lover**, 3, 118	G. L. Stevens	Bimbo (GB), 3, 113	Slew of Pearls, 3, 116	9	1:36.40	50,300
	Lonely Girl, 3, 116	P. A. Valenzuela	Bel's Starlet, 3, 114	Bidder Cream, 3, 113	9	1:36.20	50,300
1989	**Darby's Daughter**, 3, 116	G. L. Stevens	Sticky Wile, 3, 117	Bel Darling, 3, 116	9	1:36.60	66,000
1988	**Do So**, 3, 121	A. O. Solis	Affordable Price, 3, 115	Variety Baby, 3, 117	8	1:35.80	50,650
1987	**Davie's Lamb**, 3, 115	F. Toro	Develop, 3, 114	Wild Manor, 3, 116	7	1:42.80	25,500
	Future Bright, 3, 114	P. A. Valenzuela	Chapel of Dreams, 3, 114	Down Again, 3, 116	7	1:44.60	25,300
1986	**Our Sweet Sham**, 3, 114	S. B. Soto	Mille Et Une, 3, 115	T. V. Residual, 3, 115	10	1:43.20	33,450
1985	**Mint Leaf**, 3, 122	C. J. McCarron	Queen of Bronze, 3, 115	Stakes to Win, 3, 117	10	1:42.60	33,650
1984	**Fashionably Late**, 3, 117	C. J. McCarron	Auntie Betty, 3, 117	Patricia James, 3, 114	8	1:43.20	32,800
1983	**Eastern Bettor**, 3, 113	R. Q. Meza	Nice 'n Proper, 3, 117	Olympic Bronze, 3, 116	9	1:44.00	25,875
	Lituya Bay, 3, 121	L. A. Pincay Jr.	Corselette, 3, 116	Capitalization, 3, 115	8	1:43.80	25,375
1982	**Northern Style**, 3, 114	M. Castaneda	Mama Tia, 3, 116	Marl Lee Ann, 3, 115	7	1:43.40	32,200
1981	**French Charmer**, 3, 118	D. G. McHargue	Tap Dancer (Fr), 3, 113	I Got Speed, 3, 121	9	1:44.20	26,850
1980	**Plenty O'Toole**, 3, 116	T. Lipham	Potter, 3, 115	Swift Bird, 3, 113	10	1:44.20	27,050
1979	**Ancient Art**, 3, 121	F. Toro	Our Suiti Pie, 3, 116	Double Deceit, 3, 117	9	1:44.20	23,550
1978	**Miss Magnetic**, 3, 117	M. Castaneda	Secala, 3, 112	Agree, 3, 114	9	1:44.40	13,550
	Joe's Bee, 3, 120	L. A. Pincay Jr.	Fairy Dance, 3, 117	Carrie's Angel, 3, 115	7	1:44.40	13,150
1977	**Teisen Lap**, 3, 113	D. G. McHargue	Goldfilled, 3, 112	Lullaby, 3, 120	8	1:44.80	12,850
1976	**Go March**, 3, 114	D. Pierce	Granja Sueno, 3, 112	I Going, 3, 115	8	1:42.80	13,150
1975	**Miss Francesca**, 3, 113	D. G. McHargue	Summer Evening, 3, 115	Bradley's Pago, 3, 113	8	1:43.20	10,475
	‡**Princess Papulee**, 3, 121	F. Toro	Mia Amore, 3, 121	Miracolo, 3, 113	8	1:43.80	10,275
1974	**Bold Ballet**, 3, 121	F. Toro	Shah's Envoy, 3, 121	Sweet Ramblin Rose, 3, 116	9	1:44.60	13,350
1973	**Button Top**, 3, 112	S. Valdez	Merry Madeleine, 3, 120	Gourmet Lark, 3, 117	5	1:43.80	12,750

Named for San Clemente, California, located in Orange County. Grade 3 1994-'95. Not held 1951-'69. 1¹⁄₁₆ miles 1950, 1970-'87. Dirt 1950. Two divisions 1975, 1978, 1983, 1987, 1990. ‡Mia Amore finished first, DQ to second, 1975. Nonwinners of a race worth $10,000 to the winner 1973-'74. Nonwinners of a race worth $12,500 to the winner 1975.

San Diego Handicap

Grade 2 in 2005. Del Mar, three-year-olds and up, 1¹⁄₁₆ miles, dirt. Held August 1, 2004, with a gross value of $250,000. First held in 1937. First graded in 1983. Stakes record 1:40 (1965 Native Diver).

Year	Winner	Jockey	Second	Third	Strs	Time	1st Purse
2004	**Choctaw Nation**, 4, 114	V. Espinoza	Pleasantly Perfect, 6, 124	During, 4, 118	7	1:42.32	$150,000
2003	**Taste of Paradise**, 4, 113	V. Espinoza	Gondolieri (Chi), 4, 117	Reba's Gold, 6, 116	8	1:42.62	150,000
2002	**Grey Memo**, 5, 116	E. J. Delahoussaye	Euchre, 6, 116	Congaree, 4, 120	8	1:43.48	150,000
2001	**Skimming**, 5, 120	G. K. Gomez	Futural, 5, 120	Captain Steve, 4, 122	7	1:41.62	150,000
2000	**Skimming**, 4, 117	G. K. Gomez	Prime Timber, 4, 116	National Saint, 4, 117	7	1:41.06	150,000
1999	**Mazel Trick**, 4, 117	C. J. McCarron	River Keen (Ire), 7, 116	Tibado, 5, 116	4	1:40.68	150,000
1998	**Mud Route**, 4, 117	C. J. McCarron	Hal's Pal (GB), 5, 113	Benchmark, 7, 117	5	1:41.11	150,300
1997	**Northern Afleet**, 4, 118	C. J. McCarron	Benchmark, 6, 117	New Century, 5, 114	9	1:41.80	100,300
1996	**Savinio**, 6, 116	C. W. Antley	Misnomer, 4, 114	Nonproductiveasset, 6, 118	6	1:40.82	95,350
1995	**Blumin Affair**, 4, 116	C. J. McCarron	Rapan Boy (Aus), 7, 115	Luthier Fever, 4, 115	4	1:41.29	87,200
1994	**Kingdom Found**, 4, 116	C. J. McCarron	Tossofthecoin, 4, 117	Rapan Boy (Aus), 6, 115	6	1:41.21	75,850
1993	**Fanatic Boy (Arg)**, 6, 115	C. J. McCarron	Memo (Chi), 6, 116	Missionary Ridge (GB), 6, 116	5	1:48.59	74,450
1992	**Another Review**, 4, 120	L. A. Pincay Jr.	Claret (Ire), 4, 116	Quintana, 4, 114	6	1:47.00	76,050
1991	**Twilight Agenda**, 5, 118	C. S. Nakatani	Roanoke, 4, 118	Louis Cyphre (Ire), 5, 118	7	1:47.65	90,900
1990	**Quiet American**, 4, 115	K. J. Desormeaux	†Bayakoa (Arg), 6, 122	Bosphorus (Arg), 5, 112	6	1:40.40	89,800
1989	**Lively One**, 4, 120	R. G. Davis	Mi Preferido, 4, 115	Hot Operator, 4, 114	5	1:40.80	76,200

1988 **Cutlass Reality**, 6, 123	G. L. Stevens	Simply Majestic, 4, 115	Nostalgia's Star, 6, 116	7	1:41.40	$63,700
1987 **Super Diamond**, 7, 123	L. A. Pincay Jr.	Nostalgia's Star, 5, 116	Good Command, 4, 114	7	1:40.80	48,050
1986 **Skywalker**, 4, 121	L. A. Pincay Jr.	Nostalgia's Star, 4, 118	Epidaurus, 4, 113	13	1:40.80	65,350
1985 **Super Diamond**, 5, 115	R. Q. Meza	M. Double M., 4, 119	French Legionaire, 4, 115	7	1:41.40	48,550
1984 **Ancestral (Ire)**, 4, 116	E. J. Delahoussaye	Retsina Run, 4, 117	Slew's Royalty, 4, 117	8	1:41.20	60,550
1983 **Bates Motel**, 4, 122	T. Lipham	The Wonder (Fr), 5, 123	Runaway Groom, 4, 117	6	1:41.00	47,650
1982 **Wickerr**, 7, 117	E. J. Delahoussaye	Cajun Prince, 5, 117	Drouilly (Fr), 6, 114	9	1:41.40	50,350
1981 **Summer Time Guy**, 5, 115	S. Hawley	Shamgo, 5, 117	Exploded, 4, 115	7	1:41.00	48,550
1980 **Island Sultan**, 5, 114	M. Castaneda	Summer Time Guy, 4, 116	Borzoi, 4, 120	6	1:41.80	38,000
1979 **Always Gallant**, 5, 118	D. G. McHargue	Bad 'n Big, 5, 120	Blondie's Dancer, 4, 117	6	1:41.00	33,050
1978 **Vic's Magic**, 5, 116	F. Toro	Mr. Redoy, 4, 119	Clout, 6, 117	6	1:40.20	25,300
1977 **Mark's Place**, 5, 124	W. Shoemaker	Austin Mittler, 5, 113	Confederate Yankee, 6, 114	5	1:40.60	18,450
1976 **‡Good Report**, 6, 116	L. A. Pincay Jr.	Austin Mittler, 4, 117	Holding Pattern, 5, 115	7	1:42.40	19,000
1975 **Chesapeake**, 6, 116	F. Olivares	Top Command, 4, 116	Against the Snow, 5, 123	6	1:40.60	16,800
1974 ***Matun**, 5, 121	W. Shoemaker	Chesapeake, 5, 113	Imaginative, 8, 115	4	1:40.60	16,150
1973 **Kennedy Road**, 5, 126	W. Shoemaker	Imaginative, 7, 117	New Prospect, 4, 120	5	1:41.40	15,700

Named for the city of San Diego; the track is located in the nearby town of Del Mar, which means "by the sea." Grade 3 1983-2000. Not held 1939-'40, 1942-'44. 6 furlongs 1937, 1945-'47. 1 mile 1941. 1⅛ miles 1991-'93. ‡Mark's Place finished first, DQ to seventh, 1976. †Denotes female.

Sands Point Stakes

Grade 3 in 2005. Belmont Park, three-year-olds, fillies, 1⅛ miles, turf. Held June 5, 2005, with a gross value of $111,200. First held in 1995. First graded in 1998. Stakes record 1:46.65 (1997 Auntie Mame).

Year	Winner	Jockey	Second	Third	Strs	Time	1st Purse
2005	**Melhor Ainda**, 3, 123	J. R. Velazquez	Laurafina, 3, 115	My Typhoon (Ire), 3, 121	7	1:47.50	$66,720
2004	**Mambo Slew**, 3, 122	E. S. Prado	Lucifer's Stone, 3, 122	Vous, 3, 119	10	1:47.24	68,880
2003	**Savedbythelight**, 3, 115	R. Migliore	Virgin Voyage, 3, 117	Little Bonnet, 3, 115	5	1:49.18	68,760
2002	**Riskaverse**, 3, 119	R. G. Davis	Cyclorama, 3, 115	She's Vested, 3, 115	11	1:51.63	69,660
2001	**Tweedside**, 3, 119	R. Migliore	Owsley, 3, 114	Platinum Tiara, 3, 122	4	1:50.43	66,674
2000	**Gaviola**, 3, 121	J. D. Bailey	Shopping for Love, 3, 121	Millie's Quest, 3, 113	8	1:47.77	66,780
1999	**Perfect Sting**, 3, 118	P. Day	Pico Teneriffe, 3, 121	Illiquidity, 3, 113	6	1:46.99	65,160
1998	**Recording**, 3, 113	J. F. Chavez	Royal Ransom, 3, 114	Naskra's de Light, 3, 116	11	1:48.93	69,600
1997	**Auntie Mame**, 3, 121	J. D. Bailey	Hoochie Coochie, 3, 114	Sagasious, 3, 113	8	**1:46.65**	66,720
1996	**Merit Wings**, 3, 120	R. G. Davis	Unify, 3, 113	Turkappeal, 3, 117	10	1:45.83	51,885
1995	**Perfect Arc**, 3, 117	J. R. Velazquez	Miss Union Avenue, 3, 123	Transient Trend, 3, 110	5	1:43.14	49,395

Named for the community of Sands Point, New York, located on Long Island. Not graded when taken off turf 2001, 2003. Sands Point H. 1995-'98, 2000, 2003. 1¹⁄₁₆ miles 1995-'96. Originally scheduled on turf 2001, 2003.

San Felipe Stakes

Grade 2 in 2005. Santa Anita Park, three-year-olds, 1¹⁄₁₆ miles, dirt. Held March 19, 2005, with a gross value of $250,000. First held in 1935. First graded in 1973. Stakes record 1:40.11 (2005 Consolidator).

Year	Winner	Jockey	Second	Third	Strs	Time	1st Purse
2005	**Consolidator**, 3, 116	R. Bejarano	Giacomo, 3, 116	Don't Get Mad, 3, 116	8	**1:40.11**	$150,000
2004	**Preachinatthebar**, 3, 116	J. Santiago	St Averil, 3, 122	Harvard Avenue, 3, 116	9	1:42.87	150,000
2003	**Buddy Gil**, 3, 119	G. L. Stevens	Atswhatimtalknbout, 3, 116	Brancusi, 3, 116	10	1:43.64	150,000
2002	**Medaglia d'Oro**, 3, 116	L. A. Pincay Jr.	U S S Tinosa, 3, 116	Siphonic, 3, 122	6	1:41.95	150,000
2001	**Point Given**, 3, 122	G. L. Stevens	I Love Silver, 3, 116	Jamaican Rum, 3, 119	8	1:41.94	150,000
2000	**Fusaichi Pegasus**, 3, 116	K. J. Desormeaux	The Deputy (Ire), 3, 122	Anees, 3, 119	7	1:42.66	150,000
1999	**Prime Timber**, 3, 116	D. R. Flores	Exploit, 3, 122	High Wire Act, 3, 116	7	1:42.16	150,000
1998	**Artax**, 3, 122	C. J. McCarron	Real Quiet, 3, 119	Prosperous Bid, 3, 116	5	1:41.73	150,000
1997	**Free House**, 3, 119	D. R. Flores	Silver Charm, 3, 122	King Crimson, 3, 116	9	1:42.49	152,400
1996	**Odyle**, 3, 116	C. S. Nakatani	Smithfield, 3, 116	Cavonnier, 3, 122	7	1:42.43	152,400
1995	**Afternoon Deelites**, 3, 119	K. J. Desormeaux	Timber Country, 3, 122	Lake George, 3, 116	4	1:42.11	117,240
1994	**Soul of the Matter**, 3, 116	K. J. Desormeaux	Brocco, 3, 119	Valiant Nature, 3, 119	5	1:44.68	118,500
1993	**Corby**, 3, 116	C. J. McCarron	Personal Hope, 3, 116	Devoted Brass, 3, 122	6	1:42.11	121,100
1992	**Bertrando**, 3, 122	A. O. Solis	Arp, 3, 116	Hickman Creek, 3, 116	6	1:42.76	120,800
1991	**Sea Cadet**, 3, 119	C. J. McCarron	Scan, 3, 119	Compelling Sound, 3, 116	8	1:41.90	124,200
1990	**Real Cash**, 3, 113	A. O. Solis	Warcraft, 3, 117	Music Prospector, 3, 117	12	1:42.00	102,600
1989	**Sunday Silence**, 3, 119	P. A. Valenzuela	Flying Continental, 3, 118	Music Merci, 3, 124	5	1:42.60	91,800
1988	**Mi Preferido**, 3, 119	C. J. McCarron	Purdue King, 3, 119	Tejano, 3, 122	8	1:42.20	96,300
1987	**Chart the Stars**, 3, 116	E. J. Delahoussaye	Alysheba, 3, 122	Temperate Sil, 3, 122	8	1:43.00	107,450
1986	**Variety Road**, 3, 120	C. J. McCarron	Big Play, 3, 114	Dancing Pirate, 3, 116	5	1:45.40	75,350
1985	**Image of Greatness**, 3, 120	L. A. Pincay Jr.	Skywalker, 3, 120	Nostalgia's Star, 3, 117	9	1:43.20	106,350
1984	**Fali Time**, 3, 122	S. Hawley	Gate Dancer, 3, 117	Commemorate, 3, 117	6	1:42.60	103,450
1983	**‡Desert Wine**, 3, 124	C. J. McCarron	Naevus, 3, 115	Fifth Division, 3, 120	6	1:41.60	62,900
1982	**Advance Man**, 3, 117	C. J. McCarron	Gato Del Sol, 3, 118	Cassaleria, 3, 123	4	1:42.20	77,550
1981	**Stancharry**, 3, 118	F. Toro	Splendid Spruce, 3, 119	Flying Nashua, 3, 121	12	1:42.00	69,900
1980	**Raise a Man**, 3, 119	W. Shoemaker	The Carpenter, 3, 123	Rumbo, 3, 119	7	1:41.60	64,300
1979	**Pole Position**, 3, 119	S. Hawley	Switch Partners, 3, 114	Flying Paster, 3, 127	7	1:41.20	48,500
1978	**Affirmed**, 3, 126	S. Cauthen	Chance Dancer, 3, 117	Tampoy, 3, 118	6	1:42.60	38,100
1977	**Smasher**, 3, 115	S. Hawley	*Habitony, 3, 122	Miami Sun, 3, 115	5	1:42.60	32,850

414   Racing — Graded Stakes

1976	**Crystal Water**, 3, 117	W. Shoemaker	Beau Talent, 3, 117	Double Discount, 3, 113	6	1:42.60	$34,000
1975	**Fleet Velvet**, 3, 120	F. Toro	George Navonod, 3, 122	Diabolo, 3, 124	6	1:42.40	33,200
1974	**Aloha Mood**, 3, 118	D. Pierce	Money Lender, 3, 124	Triple Crown, 3, 124	10	1:42.40	43,700
1973	**Linda's Chief**, 3, 126	B. Baeza	Ancient Title, 3, 120	Out of the East, 3, 115	9	1:41.80	42,700

Named for the Rancho Valle de San Felipe located in present-day San Diego County, California. Grade 1 1984-'88. San Felipe H. 1935-'41, 1952-'90. Not held 1942-'44. 1 mile 1935-'36. 7 furlongs 1937, 1941, 1947-'51. 6 furlongs 1938-'40, 1945-'46. Three-year-olds and up 1935-'40. Colts and geldings 1935-'51. ‡Naevus finished first, DQ to second, 1983.

San Fernando Breeders' Cup Stakes

Grade 2 in 2005. Santa Anita Park, four-year-olds, 1 1/16 miles, dirt. Held January 15, 2005, with a gross value of $198,000. First held in 1952. First graded in 1973. Stakes record 1:41.06 (1999 Dixie Dot Com).

Year	Winner	Jockey	Second	Third	Strs	Time	1st Purse
2005	**Minister Eric**, 4, 116	R. R. Douglas	Mass Media, 4, 118	Skipaslew, 4, 116	9	1:42.14	$120,000
2004	**During**, 4, 120	D. R. Flores	Toccet, 4, 116	Touch the Wire, 4, 117	10	1:41.63	134,280
2003	**Pass Rush**, 4, 116	C. S. Nakatani	Tracemark, 4, 116	Tizbud, 4, 116	8	1:42.37	131,760
2002	**Western Pride**, 4, 122	G. K. Gomez	Orientate, 4, 120	Fancy As, 4, 120	10	1:41.30	134,640
2001	**Tiznow**, 4, 122	C. J. McCarron	Walkslikeaduck, 4, 120	Wooden Phone, 4, 116	6	1:42.05	98,880
2000	**Saint's Honor**, 4, 117	K. J. Desormeaux	Cat Thief, 4, 122	Mr. Broad Blade, 4, 118	7	1:41.94	190,200
1999	**Dixie Dot Com**, 4, 116	D. R. Flores	Event of the Year, 4, 122	Old Topper, 4, 118	8	**1:41.06**	190,800
1998	**Silver Charm**, 4, 122	G. L. Stevens	Mud Route, 4, 116	Lord Grillo (Arg), 4, 120	4	1:41.94	125,520
1997	**Northern Afleet**, 4, 116	C. J. McCarron	Ambivalent, 4, 116	Ready to Order, 4, 116	9	1:48.59	194,000
1996	**Helmsman**, 4, 118	C. J. McCarron	Gold and Steel (Fr), 4, 120	The Key Rainbow (Ire), 4, 116	9	1:48.87	134,500
1995	**Wekiva Springs**, 4, 118	K. J. Desormeaux	Dramatic Gold, 4, 120	Dare and Go, 4, 116	7	1:48.59	126,800
1994	**Zignew**, 4, 116	C. J. McCarron	Nonproductiveasset, 4, 116	Pleasant Tango, 4, 116	12	1:47.87	135,400
1993	**Bertrando**, 4, 120	C. J. McCarron	Star Recruit, 4, 120	The Wicked North, 4, 116	8	1:51.22	127,800
1992	**Best Pal**, 4, 122	K. J. Desormeaux	Olympio, 4, 122	Dinard, 4, 120	9	1:48.25	130,000
1991	**In Excess (Ire)**, 4, 126	G. L. Stevens	Warcraft, 4, 120	Go and Go (Ire), 4, 123	9	1:46.70	128,800
1990	**Flying Continental**, 4, 120	C. A. Black	Splurger, 4, 114	Secret Slew, 4, 114	4	1:47.20	128,600
1989	**Mi Preferido**, 4, 123	C. J. McCarron	Speedratic, 4, 120	Perceive Arrogance, 4, 120	12	1:47.40	138,200
1988	**On the Line**, 4, 120	J. A. Santos	Candi's Gold, 4, 123	Grand Vizier, 4, 114	5	1:49.00	122,400
1987	**Variety Road**, 4, 123	L. A. Pincay Jr.	Broad Brush, 4, 126	Snow Chief, 4, 126	8	1:49.00	96,300
1986	**Right Con**, 4, 117	R. Q. Meza	Nostalgia's Star, 4, 120	Fast Account, 4, 114	10	1:48.40	101,800
1985	**Precisionist**, 4, 126	C. J. McCarron	Greinton (GB), 4, 120	Gate Dancer, 4, 126	7	1:47.40	123,350
1984	**Interco**, 4, 123	P. A. Valenzuela	Desert Wine, 4, 123	Paris Prince, 4, 120	12	1:48.60	92,850
1983	**Wavering Monarch**, 4, 123	E. J. Delahoussaye	Water Bank, 4, 120	Prince Spellbound, 4, 126	9	1:50.00	88,400
1982	**It's the One**, 4, 120	W. A. Guerra	Princelet, 4, 123	Rock Softly, 4, 114	9	1:47.60	84,650
1981	**Doonesbury**, 4, 120	S. Hawley	Raise a Man, 4, 120	Idyll, 4, 117	11	1:47.00	74,300
1980	**Spectacular Bid**, 4, 126	W. Shoemaker	Flying Paster, 4, 126	Relaunch, 4, 120	4	1:48.00	63,300
1979	**Radar Ahead**, 4, 123	D. G. McHargue	Affirmed, 4, 126	Little Reb, 4, 120	8	1:48.00	69,200
1978	**Text**, 4, 120	F. Toro	J. O. Tobin, 4, 123	Centennial Pride, 4, 114	5	1:49.40	65,500
1977	**Kirby Lane**, 4, 120	L. A. Pincay Jr.	Double Discount, 4, 117	Rajab, 4, 114	10	1:47.60	39,000
	‡Pocket Park, 4, 114	S. Cauthen	Properantes, 4, 114	Crystal Water, 4, 123	9	1:48.60	38,500
1976	**Messenger of Song**, 4, 120	J. Lambert	Avatar, 4, 123	Larrikin, 4, 120	11	1:48.20	54,350
1975	**Stardust Mel**, 4, 120	W. Shoemaker	Century's Envoy, 4, 120	Princely Native, 4, 120	8	1:48.60	36,700
	First Back, 4, 114	J. Vasquez	Lightning Mandate, 4, 120	Confederate Yankee, 4, 117	9	1:46.80	37,700
1974	**Ancient Title**, 4, 120	L. A. Pincay Jr.	Linda's Chief, 4, 123	*Mariache II, 4, 114	7	1:47.60	50,250
1973	**Bicker**, 4, 120	G. Brogan	Royal Owl, 4, 120	Commoner, 4, 114	14	1:48.20	58,350

Named for San Fernando, California, west of Santa Anita Park. Grade 1 1981-'89. San Fernando S. 1952-'96. Not held 1970. 1 1/8 miles 1960-'97. Four-year-olds and up 1981. Two divisions 1975, 1977. ‡Properantes finished first, DQ to second, 1977 (2nd Div.).

Sanford Stakes

Grade 2 in 2005. Saratoga Race Course, two-year-olds, 6 furlongs, dirt. Held July 29, 2004, with a gross value of $150,000. First held in 1913. First graded in 1973. Stakes record 1:09.32 (2004 Afleet Alex).

Year	Winner	Jockey	Second	Third	Strs	Time	1st Purse
2004	**Afleet Alex**, 2, 120	J. Rose	Flamenco, 2, 122	Consolidator, 2, 118	11	**1:09.32**	$90,000
2003	**Chapel Royal**, 2, 122	J. R. Velazquez	Blushing Indian, 2, 118	Flushing Meadows, 2, 118	7	1:10.74	90,000
2002	**Whywhywhy**, 2, 122	E. S. Prado	Wildcat Heir, 2, 118	Spite the Devil, 2, 118	9	1:10.40	90,000
2001	**Buster's Daydream**, 2, 122	J. R. Velazquez	Seeking the Money, 2, 117	Heavyweight Champ, 2, 117	6	1:10.55	64,680
2000	**City Zip**, 2, 119	J. A. Santos	Yonaguska, 2, 119	Scorpion, 2, 114	7	1:10.69	65,220
1999	**More Than Ready**, 2, 122	J. R. Velazquez	Mighty, 2, 114	Bulling, 2, 114	5	1:09.65	64,560
1998	**Time Bandit**, 2, 119	P. Day	Prime Directive, 2, 117	Texas Glitter, 2, 117	9	1:11.59	66,480
1997	**Polished Brass**, 2, 116	P. Day	Double Honor, 2, 116	Jigadee, 2, 116	7	1:10.23	65,520
1996	**Kelly Kip**, 2, 118	J. Samyn	Boston Harbor, 2, 118	Say Florida Sandy, 2, 115	8	1:10.31	66,840
1995	**Maria's Mon**, 2, 115	R. G. Davis	Seeker's Reward, 2, 115	Frozen Ice, 2, 112	11	1:10.80	64,540
1994	**Montreal Red**, 2, 115	J. A. Santos	Boone's Mill, 2, 115	De Niro, 2, 122	5	1:10.56	64,620
1993	**Dehere**, 2, 122	C. J. McCarron	Prenup, 2, 115	Distinct Reality, 2, 122	6	1:10.48	68,520
1992	**Mountain Cat**, 2, 119	P. Day	‡Satellite Signal, 2, 115	Rule Sixteen, 2, 122	10	1:10.62	73,440
1991	**Caller I. D.**, 2, 122	J. D. Bailey	Pick Up the Phone, 2, 119	Money Run, 2, 115	6	1:10.92	69,000
1990	**Formal Dinner**, 2, 115	J. A. Santos	Beaudaspic, 2, 115	Link, 2, 117	10	1:10.20	55,260

1989	**Bite the Bullet**, 2, 115	J. A. Santos	Graf, 2, 115	For Really, 2, 113	9	1:09.80	$54,720
1988	**Mercedes Won**, 2, 119	R. G. Davis	Leading Prospect, 2, 115	Fire Maker, 2, 115	11	1:10.00	55,440
1987	**Forty Niner**, 2, 115	E. Maple	Once Wild, 2, 115	Velvet Fog, 2, 115	6	1:10.00	65,340
1986	**Persevered**, 2, 115	A. T. Cordero Jr.	Perdition's Son, 2, 115	Bucks Best, 2, 115	5	1:10.60	51,120
1985	**Sovereign Don**, 2, 122	J. Velasquez	Roy, 2, 115	Cause for Pause, 2, 119	9	1:10.60	54,000
1984	**Tiffany Ice**, 2, 115	G. McCarron	Vindaloo, 2, 115	Fortunate Dancer, 2, 113	4	1:10.80	51,300
1983	**Big Walt**, 2, 115	J. Fell	Fill Ron's Pockets, 2, 122	Agile Jet, 2, 115	8	1:11.00	34,260
1982	**Copelan**, 2, 115	J. D. Bailey	Smart Style, 2, 115	Safe Ground, 2, 117	5	1:10.40	33,660
1981	**Mayanesian**, 2, 115	J. Vasquez	Shipping Magnate, 2, 115	Lejoli, 2, 115	10	1:11.20	35,280
1980	**Tap Shoes**, 2, 115	R. Hernandez	Triocala, 2, 115	Painted Shield, 2, 117	10	1:10.00	34,260
1979	**I Speedup**, 2, 122	J. Fell	Muckraker, 2, 122	My Pal Jeff, 2, 117	7	1:10.40	26,175
1978	**Fuzzbuster**, 2, 115	J. Velasquez	Make a Mess, 2, 115	Turnbuckle, 2, 115	6	1:10.80	22,230
1977	**Affirmed**, 2, 124	S. Cauthen	Tilt Up, 2, 122	Jet Diplomacy, 2, 124	6	1:09.60	22,290
1976	**Turn of Coin**, 2, 122	A. T. Cordero Jr.	Hey Hey J. P., 2, 115	Super Joy, 2, 115	7	1:10.20	22,395
1975	**Turn to Turia**, 2, 121	E. Maple	Iron Bit, 2, 121	Gentle King, 2, 121	5	1:10.80	22,575
1974	**Ramahorn**, 2, 121	C. Baltazar	Prop Man, 2, 121	Knightly Sport, 2, 121	8	1:11.00	17,205
1973	**Az Igazi**, 2, 121	M. Venezia	Prince of Reason, 2, 121	Totheend, 2, 121	6	1:10.60	16,680

Named for the Sanford family, owners of Hurricane Stud in Amsterdam, New York. Grade 3 1990-'98. Sanford Memorial S. 1913-'26. Held at Belmont Park 1943-'45. Not held 1961. 5½ furlongs 1962-'68. ‡Thirty Two Slew finished second, DQ to fourth, 1992.

San Francisco Breeders' Cup Mile Handicap

Grade 2 in 2005. Bay Meadows, three-year-olds and up, 1 mile, turf. Held April 23, 2005, with a gross value of $111,250. First held in 1948. First graded in 1987. Stakes record 1:33.40 (1980 Don Alberto).

Year	Winner	Jockey	Second	Third	Strs	Time	1st Purse
2005	**Castledale (Ire)**, 4, 118	R. R. Douglas	Adreamisborn, 6, 119	Aly Bubba, 6, 116	9	1:37.40	$55,000
2004	**Singletary**, 4, 119	J. Valdivia Jr.	Captain Squire, 5, 116	Gold Ruckus, 6, 116	7	1:35.16	82,500
2003	**Ninebanks**, 5, 117	R. J. Warren Jr.	Nicobar (GB), 6, 116	National Anthem (GB), 7, 116	8	1:37.20	110,000
2002	**Suances (GB)**, 5, 116	D. R. Flores	Decarchy, 5, 121	The Tin Man, 4, 116	4	1:35.19	110,000
2001	**Redattore (Brz)**, 6, 115	J. P. Lumpkins	Hawksley Hill (Ire), 8, 119	Kerrygold (Fr), 5, 116	9	1:35.14	137,500
2000	**Ladies Din**, 5, 120	K. J. Desormeaux	Fighting Falcon, 4, 116	Self Feeder (Ire), 6, 116	10	1:35.46	150,000
1999	**†Tuzla (Fr)**, 5, 112	B. Blanc	Poteen, 5, 116	Rob 'n Gin, 5, 117	10	1:35.46	180,000
1998	**Hawksley Hill (Ire)**, 5, 119	G. L. Stevens	Fantastic Fellow, 4, 121	Uncaged Fury, 7, 117	6	1:34.33	120,000
1997	**Wavy Run (Ire)**, 6, 116	B. Blanc	Savinio, 7, 118	Romarin (Brz), 7, 118	7	1:37.11	120,000
1996	**Gold and Steel (Fr)**, 4, 114	A. O. Solis	Savinio, 6, 115	Debutant Trick, 6, 117	7	1:35.07	120,000
1995	**Unfinished Symph**, 4, 118	C. W. Antley	Vaudeville, 4, 119	Torch Rouge (GB), 4, 115	9	1:34.14	110,000
1994	**Gothland (Fr)**, 5, 115	C. S. Nakatani	Emerald Jig, 5, 113	The Tender Track, 7, 116	11	1:35.46	110,000
1993	**Norwich (GB)**, 6, 114	K. J. Desormeaux	Qathif, 6, 115	Luthier Enchanteur, 6, 117	8	1:35.57	137,500
1992	**Tight Spot**, 5, 125	L. A. Pincay Jr.	Notorious Pleasure, 6, 116	Forty Niner Days, 5, 116	9	1:35.57	110,000
1991	**Forty Niner Days**, 4, 112	T. T. Doocy	Exbourne, 5, 116	Blaze O'Brien, 4, 116	6	1:38.90	110,000
1990	**Colway Rally (GB)**, 6, 116	C. A. Black	River Master, 4, 115	Miswaki Tern, 5, 117	10	1:35.80	110,000
1989	**Patchy Groundfog**, 6, 116	F. Olivares	No Commitment, 4, 113	Mazilier, 5, 115	7	1:38.20	82,500
1988	**Ifrad**, 6, 115	T. M. Chapman	The Medic, 4, 118	Blanco, 4, 117	9	1:36.40	82,500
1987	**Dormello (Arg)**, 6, 113	A. L. Diaz	Air Display, 4, 116	Barbery, 6, 115	8	1:36.20	82,500
1986	**Hail Bold King**, 5, 117	M. Castaneda	Right Con, 4, 119	Lucky n Green (Ire), 4, 114	12	1:36.40	69,900
1985	**Truce Maker**, 7, 112	J. A. Garcia	†Lina Cavalieri (GB), 5, 115	Baron O'Dublin, 5, 116	11	1:35.20	69,500
1984	**Drumalis (Ire)**, 4, 117	E. J. Delahoussaye	Silveyville, 6, 117	Ten Below, 5, 115	8	1:35.60	43,275
	Icehot, 4, 115	M. Castaneda	Major Sport, 7, 117	Otter Slide, 5, 114	8	1:35.40	34,275
1983	**King's County (Ire)**, 4, 112	E. Munoz	Police Inspector, 6, 118	Silveyville, 5, 121	12	1:37.60	48,950
1982	**Silveyville**, 4, 121	D. Winick	Visible Pole, 4, 110	A Sure Hit, 4, 113	10	1:36.80	51,050
1981	**Opus Dei (Fr)**, 6, 119	F. Olivares	Drouilly (Fr), 5, 116	His Honor, 6, 117	13	1:34.80	41,850
1980	**Don Alberto**, 5, 114	R. M. Gonzalez	Saboulard (Fr), 5, 116	Capt. Don, 5, 121	10	1:33.40	33,300
1979	**Struttin' George**, 5, 117	T. M. Chapman	Crafty Native, 6, 111	Foreign Power, 5, 115	8	1:37.40	32,950
1978	**Jumping Hill**, 6, 121	J. Lambert	Boy Tike, 5, 115	Dr. Henry K., 4, 109	6	1:38.40	32,500
1977	**Crafty Native**, 4, 112	M. James	Cojak, 4, 122	Money Lender, 6, 119	8	1:38.40	26,350
1975	**Whoa Boy**, 4, 113	G. Baze	Ocala Boy, 5, 113	Star of Kuwait, 7, 116	7	1:39.00	18,100
1974	**Visualizer**, 4, 114	F. Mena	Roka Zaca, 4, 117	*Larkal II, 6, 110	10	1:38.00	21,900
1973	**New Prospect**, 4, 118	J. Sellers	Masked, 4, 116	Rock Bath, 5, 113	6	1:43.20	22,150

Named for the city of San Francisco. Grade 3 1987-'93. San Francisco Mile H. 1948-'98. Held at Golden Gate Fields 1948-2000. Not held 1960, 1976. Dirt 1948-'65. Originally scheduled on turf 1974. Four-year-olds and up 1968. Two divisions 1984. †Denotes female.

San Gabriel Handicap

Grade 3 in 2005. Santa Anita Park, four-year-olds and up, 1⅛ miles, dirt (originally scheduled as a Grade 2 on the turf). Held January 1, 2005, with a gross value of $150,000. First held in 1935. First graded in 1973. Stakes record 1:47.40 (1988 Simply Majestic).

Year	Winner	Jockey	Second	Third	Strs	Time	1st Purse
2005	**Truly a Judge**, 7, 116	M. A. Pedroza	Star Cross (Arg), 8, 112	Continental Red, 9, 116	6	1:48.90	$90,000
2003	**Redattore (Brz)**, 8, 122	A. O. Solis	Continental Red, 7, 116	Denied, 5, 116	9	1:48.17	90,000
2002	**Grammarian**, 4, 117	J. Valdivia Jr.	David Copperfield, 5, 117	Decarchy, 5, 119	9	1:48.12	90,000

Year	Winner	Jockey	Second	Third	Strs	Time	1st Purse
2001	Irish Prize, 5, 121	G. L. Stevens	Sligo Bay (Ire), 3, 117	El Gran Papa, 4, 114	11	1:50.56	$90,000
	Irish Prize, 5, 117	K. J. Desormeaux	Manndar (Ire), 5, 121	Here Comes Big C, 6, 110	8	1:47.88	90,000
2000	Brave Act (GB), 6, 120	A. O. Solis	Native Desert, 7, 116	Manndar (Ire), 4, 116	6	1:49.25	97,470
1998	Brave Act (GB), 4, 118	G. F. Almeida	Mash One (Chi), 4, 116	Fabulous Guy (Ire), 4, 113	8	1:46.78	90,000
1997	Martiniquais (Ire), 4, 116	C. S. Nakatani	Bienvenido (Arg), 4, 115	Da Bull, 5, 115	8	1:48.42	99,180
	Rainbow Blues (Ire), 4, 119	G. L. Stevens	River Deep, 6, 116	Via Lombardia (Ire), 5, 116	7	1:46.89	81,500
1996	Romarin (Brz), 6, 119	C. S. Nakatani	Virginia Carnival, 4, 116	Silver Wizard, 6, 117	8	1:49.69	82,050
1995	Romarin (Brz), 5, 119	C. S. Nakatani	Inner City (Ire), 6, 117	Ianomami (Ire), 5, 116	6	1:49.36	62,900
1994	Earl of Barking (Ire), 4, 118	C. J. McCarron	Fanmore, 6, 116	Navarone, 6, 119	8	1:48.64	65,300
1993	Star of Cozzene, 5, 118	G. L. Stevens	Bistro Garden, 5, 114	Leger Cat (Arg), 7, 115	9	1:48.33	66,100
1992	Classic Fame, 6, 118	E. J. Delahoussaye	Super May, 6, 119	Defensive Play, 5, 116	6	1:46.69	64,300
1990	In Excess (Ire), 3, 117	G. L. Stevens	Rouvignac (Fr), 4, 113	Kanatiyr (Ire), 4, 115	11	1:47.20	68,100
1989	Wretham (GB), 4, 117	L. A. Pincay Jr.	Patchy Groundfog, 6, 117	In Extremis, 4, 117	10	1:46.20	67,700
1988	Simply Majestic, 4, 120	J. D. Bailey	Payant (Arg), 4, 118	Dr. Death, 3, 115	8	**1:47.40**	66,100
	Conquering Hero, 5, 115	G. L. Stevens	Hot and Smoggy, 4, 117	Ten Keys, 4, 116	9	1:50.60	66,500
1987	Nostalgia's Star, 5, 118	L. A. Pincay Jr.	Inevitable Leader, 8, 112	Spellbound, 4, 116	5	1:51.20	61,550
1986	Yashgan (GB), 5, 124	C. J. McCarron	Tights, 5, 118	Rivlia, 4, 116	8	1:49.60	51,800
1985	Dahar, 4, 120	F. Toro	Paris Prince, 5, 116	Massera (Chi), 7, 116	7	1:47.60	50,750
1984	Prince Florimund (SAf), 6, 118	P. A. Valenzuela	Ten Below, 5, 113	Ginger Brink (Fr), 4, 118	8	1:48.20	40,225
	Beldale Lustre, 5, 118	L. A. Pincay Jr.	I'll See You (GB), 6, 112	Color Bearer, 6, 111	7	1:48.80	39,425
1983	Greenwood Star (GB), 6, 119	D. Pierce	Tell Again, 5, 118	Western, 5, 115	12	1:47.20	51,450
1981	The Bart, 5, 125	E. J. Delahoussaye	Irish Heart (Ire), 3, 115	Forlion, 5, 114	7	1:48.00	48,050
1980	Premier Ministre, 4, 113	L. A. Pincay Jr.	Galaxy Libra (Ire), 4, 117	Fast, 4, 118	7	1:48.20	38,250
	John Henry, 5, 123	D. G. McHargue	Smasher, 6, 111	As de Copas (Arg), 7, 117	9	1:49.80	39,300
1979	Fluorescent Light, 5, 118	A. T. Cordero Jr.	As de Copas (Arg), 6, 118	Tiller, 5, 127	7	1:47.60	32,200
1978	Mr. Redoy, 4, 110	S. Hawley	Dr. Krohn, 5, 116	Papelote, 4, 113	9	1:48.40	33,100
1977	Riot in Paris, 6, 125	W. Shoemaker	Distant Land, 5, 115	Ribot Grande, 7, 113	7	1:50.00	34,000
1975	Zanthe, 6, 117	S. Hawley	Copper Mel, 3, 115	Riot in Paris, 4, 124	9	**1:47.40**	26,550
1974	Fair Test, 6, 113	A. Santiago	Indefatigable, 4, 118	Montmartre, 4, 118	6	1:50.60	25,750
1973	Astray, 4, 115	J. Vasquez	Golden Doc Ray, 3, 114	Kirrary, 3, 117	8	1:48.20	26,250
	Kentuckian, 4, 114	J. Lambert	Artaxerxes, 5, 113	Harkville, 5, 112	10	1:47.60	26,950

Named for the nearby city of San Gabriel, California; the city is named for a Spanish mission. Grade 3 1983-'93. Downgraded to a Grade 3 when taken off turf 2005. Not held 1936, 1939-'44, 1947-'51, 1970, 1976, 1982, 1991, 1999, 2004. 3 furlongs 1935-'38. 6 furlongs 1945-'46. 7 furlongs 1952-'54. 1 1/4 miles 1955-'59. Dirt 1935-'54, 1965, 1972, 1974, 1977, 1987. Originally scheduled on turf 2005. Two-year-olds 1935-'38. Three-year-olds and up 1945-'46, 1975-'77, 1981, 1988-'90, 1997-'98, 2001-'02. Three-year-olds 1952-'54. Two divisions 1984. Held in January and December 1973, 1980, 1988, 1997, 2001.

San Gorgonio Handicap

Grade 3 in 2005. Santa Anita Park, four-year-olds and up, fillies and mares, 1 1/8 miles, dirt (originally scheduled as Grade 2 on the turf). Held January 8, 2005, with a gross value of $150,000. First held in 1968. First graded in 1983. Stakes record 1:48.70 (1995 Queens Court Queen).

Year	Winner	Jockey	Second	Third	Strs	Time	1st Purse
2005	Fencelineneighbor, 5, 115	L. H. Jauregui	Uraib (Ire), 5, 115	Dolly Wells (Arg), 5, 113	5	1:49.82	$90,000
2004	Megahertz (GB), 5, 119	A. O. Solis	Garden in the Rain (Fr), 7, 116	Firth of Lorne (Ire), 5, 116	4	1:49.51	90,000
2003	Tates Creek, 5, 121	P. A. Valenzuela	Megahertz (GB), 4, 117	Double Cat, 5, 114	7	1:46.91	90,000
2002	Tout Charmant, 6, 120	C. J. McCarron	Janet (GB), 5, 119	Vencera (Fr), 5, 115	8	1:47.22	90,000
2001	Uncharted Haven (GB), 4, 115	A. O. Solis	Brianda (Ire), 4, 110	Beautiful Noise, 5, 116	12	1:50.02	90,000
2000	Lady At Peace, 4, 115	G. K. Gomez	Spanish Fern, 5, 119	Riboletta (Brz), 5, 116	5	1:48.75	90,000
1999	See You Soon (Fr), 5, 118	K. J. Desormeaux	Sonja's Faith (Ire), 5, 118	Verinha (Brz), 5, 115	6	1:49.14	90,000
1998	Golden Arches (Fr), 4, 120	C. J. McCarron	Ecoute, 5, 115	‡Real Connection, 7, 116	6	1:49.42	96,870
1997	Sixieme Sens, 5, 116	C. S. Nakatani	Alpride (Ire), 6, 120	Grafin, 6, 116	9	1:47.16	82,950
1996	Wandesta (GB), 5, 119	C. S. Nakatani	Matiara, 4, 118	Yearly Tour, 5, 117	6	1:49.13	80,550
1995	Queens Court Queen, 4, 117	C. S. Nakatani	Wende, 5, 116	Vinista, 5, 115	5	**1:48.70**	62,000
1994	Hero's Love, 6, 119	L. A. Pincay Jr.	Skimble, 5, 118	Miss Turkana, 5, 118	10	1:47.65	66,800
1993	Southern Truce, 5, 114	C. S. Nakatani	Laura Ly (Arg), 7, 114	Lite Light, 5, 115	5	1:51.24	67,100
1992	Paseana (Arg), 5, 118	C. J. McCarron	Laura Ly (Arg), 6, 112	Reluctant Guest, 6, 117	4	1:53.88	77,250
1991	Royal Touch (Ire), 6, 118	C. J. McCarron	Countus In, 6, 119	Marsha's Dancer, 5, 113	10	1:47.90	83,850
1990	Invited Guest (Ire), 6, 117	R. A. Baze	White Mischief (GB), 6, 115	Oeilladine (Fr), 4, 115	10	1:46.40	83,750
1989	No Review, 4, 117	R. Q. Meza	Annoconnor, 5, 122	White Mischief (GB), 5, 116	6	1:48.80	79,950
1988	Miss Alto, 5, 116	E. J. Delahoussaye	Top Corsage, 5, 119	My Virginia Reel, 6, 115	6	1:49.20	63,200
1987	Frau Altiva (Arg), 5, 117	L. A. Pincay Jr.	Auspicante (Arg), 6, 122	Solva (GB), 5, 119	7	1:50.20	63,100
1986	Mountain Bear (GB), 5, 118	E. J. Delahoussaye	Royal Regatta (NZ), 7, 115	Justicara (Ire), 5, 117	8	1:48.40	67,150
1985	Fact Finder, 6, 118	F. Toro	Capichi, 5, 118	Comedy Act, 6, 119	7	1:48.20	62,500
1984	First Advance, 5, 115	M. Castaneda	Avigaition, 5, 120	L'Attrayante (Fr), 4, 121	11	1:48.80	53,950
1983	Castilla, 4, 122	C. J. McCarron	Star Pastures (GB), 5, 119	Cat Girl, 5, 115	11	1:46.40	50,800
1982	Track Robbery, 6, 123	E. J. Delahoussaye	Rainbow Connection, 4, 117	Targa, 5, 114	5	1:52.60	45,050
1981	Kilijaro (Ire), 5, 128	W. Shoemaker	Queen to Conquer, 5, 122	Refinish, 4, 117	4	1:49.20	36,300
1980	Miss Magnetic, 5, 111	L. E. Ortega	Maytide, 4, 112	Persona, 4, 113	9	1:50.00	39,700
1979	Via Maris (Fr), 4, 113	A. T. Cordero Jr.	Drama Critic, 5, 122	Donna Inez, 4, 114	10	1:52.60	33,550
1977	*Lucie Manet, 4, 121	W. Shoemaker	Theia (Fr), 4, 116	Claire Valentine (Ire), 4, 114	4	1:54.00	30,250
	*Merry Lady III, 5, 119	L. A. Pincay Jr.	Our First Delight, 5, 117	*Pacara, 5, 114	10	1:50.80	36,200

				Strs	Time	1st Purse
1976 *Tizna, 7, 132	F. Alvarez	Miss Tokyo, 4, 120	Charger's Star, 6, 121	8	1:47.20	$25,800
1975 *Madison Palace, 7, 119	D. Pierce	Grotonian, 6, 115	At the Dance, 6, 115	9	1:48.40	21,400
1974 Margum, 5, 115	W. Shoemaker	Harbor Point, 6, 117	Expediter, 5, 115	10	1:50.60	22,500
1973 Extra Hand, 7, 118	L. A. Pincay Jr.	Timoteo, 5, 122	Dundee Marmalade, 5, 115	8	1:49.00	23,200

Named for San Gorgonio Mountain, highest mountain in Southern California. Grade 3 1983-'84. Downgraded to a Grade 3 when taken off turf 2005. San Gorgonio Claiming S. 1969-'75. Not held 1970, 1978. 6½ furlongs 1968. Dirt 1969-'71, 1973-'74, 1977-'80, 1982, 1988-'89, 1992-'93, 1995. Originally scheduled on turf 1973, 2005. Three-year-olds and up 1977. Both sexes 1968-'75. Held in January and December 1977. ‡Escabiosa (Arg) finished third, DQ to fourth, 1998.

San Juan Capistrano Invitational Handicap

Grade 2 in 2005. Santa Anita Park, four-year-olds and up, about 1¾ miles, turf. Held April 16, 2005, with a gross value of $250,000. First held in 1935. First graded in 1973. Stakes record 2:42.96 (2001 Bienamado).

Year Winner	Jockey	Second	Third	Strs	Time	1st Purse
2005 T. H. Approval, 4, 115	R. R. Douglas	Exterior, 4, 116	Fitz Flag (Arg), 5, 113	8	2:45.02	$150,000
2004 Meteor Storm (GB), 5, 116	J. Valdivia Jr.	Rhythm Mad (Fr), 4, 115	Runaway Dancer, 5, 115	9	2:45.98	150,000
2003 Passinetti, 7, 111	B. Blanc	All the Boys, 6, 115	Champion Lodge (Ire), 6, 117	9	2:46.97	240,000
2002 Ringaskiddy, 6, 116	E. J. Delahoussaye	Staging Post, 4, 115	Continental Red, 6, 117	8	2:44.49	240,000
2001 Bienamado, 5, 122	C. J. McCarron	Persianlux (GB), 5, 114	Blueprint (Ire), 6, 116	11	**2:42.96**	240,000
2000 Sunshine Street, 5, 115	J. D. Bailey	Single Empire (Ire), 6, 118	Chelsea Barracks (GB), 4, 109	5	2:49.06	240,000
1999 Single Empire (Ire), 5, 118	K. J. Desormeaux	Le Paillard (Ire), 5, 115	Lucayan Indian (Ire), 4, 113	9	2:45.93	240,000
1998 Amerique, 4, 116	E. J. Delahoussaye	Star Performance, 5, 115	Kessem Power (NZ), 6, 116	10	2:47.08	240,000
1997 Marlin, 4, 119	E. J. Delahoussaye	dh- African Dancer, 5, 114 dh- Sunshack (GB), 6, 118		7	2:44.56	240,000
1996 Raintrap (GB), 6, 115	A. O. Solis	†Windsharp, 5, 116	Awad, 6, 120	8	2:48.40	240,000
1995 Red Bishop, 7, 119	M. E. Smith	Special Price, 6, 116	Liyoun (Ire), 7, 112	8	2:48.02	220,000
1994 Bien Bien, 5, 122	C. J. McCarron	Grand Flotilla, 7, 116	Alex the Great (GB), 5, 114	9	2:46.69	220,000
1993 Kotashaan (Fr), 5, 121	K. J. Desormeaux	Bien Bien, 4, 119	Fraise, 5, 123	5	2:45.00	220,000
1992 Fly Till Dawn, 6, 121	P. A. Valenzuela	†Miss Alleged, 5, 118	Wall Street Dancer, 4, 114	9	2:46.53	275,000
1991 Mashkour, 8, 115	C. J. McCarron	River Warden, 5, 115	Aksar, 4, 116	11	2:47.70	275,000
1990 Delegant, 6, 115	K. J. Desormeaux	Valdali (Ire), 4, 114	Hawkster, 4, 123	7	2:46.60	275,000
1989 Nasr El Arab, 4, 123	P. A. Valenzuela	Pleasant Variety, 5, 117	Academic (Ire), 4, 113	8	2:51.40	220,000
1988 Great Communicator, 5, 119	R. Sibille	Fiction, 4, 118	†Carotene, 5, 115	7	2:51.60	220,000
1987 Rosedale, 4, 117	L. A. Pincay Jr.	Wylfa (GB), 6, 115	Rivlia, 5, 115	6	2:49.00	220,000
1986 Dahar, 5, 124	A. O. Solis	†Mountain Bear (GB), 5, 115	Jupiter Island (GB), 7, 123	10	2:48.20	220,000
1985 Prince True, 4, 124	C. J. McCarron	†Estrapade, 5, 120	Swoon, 7, 117	7	2:26.40	180,000
1984 Load the Cannons, 4, 119	L. A. Pincay Jr.	Jenkins Ferry, 4, 114	Norwick, 5, 115	9	2:48.00	180,000
1983 Erins Isle (Ire), 5, 125	L. A. Pincay Jr.	Wolver Heights (Ire), 5, 118	Victory Zone, 4, 115	12	2:48.60	180,000
1982 Lemhi Gold, 4, 121	W. A. Guerra	Exploded, 5, 118	Perrault (GB), 5, 129	9	2:45.60	180,000
1981 Obraztsovy, 6, 121	P. A. Valenzuela	Exploded, 4, 115	Singularity, 4, 115	9	2:50.40	120,000
1980 John Henry, 5, 126	D. G. McHargue	Fiestero (Chi), 5, 114	†The Very One, 5, 113	11	2:46.80	120,000
1979 Tiller, 5, 126	A. T. Cordero Jr.	Exceller, 6, 127	Noble Dancer (GB), 7, 128	11	2:48.00	120,000
1978 Exceller, 5, 126	W. Shoemaker	Noble Dancer (GB), 6, 125	Xmas Box, 4, 115	11	2:51.00	120,000
1977 Properantes, 4, 120	D. G. McHargue	Top Crowd, 6, 118	Caucasus, 5, 128	8	2:47.60	85,000
1976 One On the Aisle, 4, 119	S. Hawley	*Elaborado, 5, 113	Top Crowd, 5, 121	10	2:50.00	75,000
1975 †*La Zanzara, 5, 114	D. Pierce	Astray, 6, 125	Stardust Mel, 4, 126	12	2:52.20	75,000
1974 Astray, 5, 124	J. Vasquez	*El Rey, 6, 113	Big Spruce, 5, 125	6	2:45.40	75,000
1973 Queen's Hustler, 4, 115	R. Rosales	Big Spruce, 4, 119	*Cougar II, 7, 127	7	2:46.40	75,000

Named for San Juan Capistrano, California, which took its name from the mission. San Juan Capistrano H. 1935-'64. Grade 1 1973-2003. Not held 1942-'44, 1947-'48. 1⅛ miles 1935-'38. 1½ miles 1939, 1941, 1945-'46, 1949, 1954. 1⁷⁄₁₆ miles 1940. 1¾ miles 1950-'53. Dirt 1935-'53. Three-year-olds and up 1935-'39, 1941-'67. Three-year-olds 1940. Dead heat for second 1997. Course record 1993, 2001. †Denotes female.

San Luis Obispo Handicap

Grade 2 in 2005. Santa Anita Park, four-year-olds and up, 1½ miles, dirt (originally scheduled on turf). Held February 19, 2005, with a gross value of $150,000. First held in 1952. First graded in 1973. Stakes record 2:23.80 (1974 Captain Cee Jay).

Year Winner	Jockey	Second	Third	Strs	Time	1st Purse
2005 License To Run (Brz), 5, 117	P. A. Valenzuela	Californian (GB), 5, 114	T. H. Approval, 4, 115	8	2:28.72	$90,000
2004 Puerto Banus, 5, 115	V. Espinoza	Continuously, 5, 116	Continental Red, 8, 117	12	2:28.00	120,000
2003 The Tin Man, 5, 116	M. E. Smith	Special Matter, 5, 113	Harrisand (Fr), 5, 116	5	2:31.22	120,000
2002 Nazirali (Ire), 5, 112	B. Blanc	Continental Red, 6, 116	Bonapartiste (Fr), 8, 114	7	2:26.09	120,000
2001 Persianlux (GB), 5, 113	T. Baze	Devon Deputy, 5, 114	Falcon Flight (Fr), 5, 116	10	2:27.70	120,000
2000 Dark Moondancer (GB), 5, 120	C. J. McCarron	The Fly (GB), 6, 115	Casino King (Ire), 5, 116	5	2:39.61	120,000
1999 Kessem Power (NZ), 7, 115	G. L. Stevens	Brave Act (GB), 5, 121	Lazy Lode (Arg), 5, 120	7	2:28.02	120,000
1998 Bienvenida (Arg), 5, 115	C. J. McCarron	Prize Giving (GB), 5, 116	Callisthene (Fr), 6, 115	6	2:29.34	120,000
1997 Shanawi (Ire), 5, 111	B. Blanc	Rainbow Dancer (Fr), 6, 117	Bon Point (GB), 7, 115	7	2:24.51	120,000
1996 †Windsharp, 5, 115	E. J. Delahoussaye	†Wandesta, 5, 114	Virginia Carnival, 4, 115	6	2:30.33	130,800
1995 Square Cut, 6, 114	C. W. Antley	Ianomami (Ire), 5, 115	River Rhythm, 8, 111	10	2:26.04	133,200
1994 Fanmore, 6, 116	K. J. Desormeaux	Bien Bien, 5, 124	Navire (Fr), 5, 114	9	2:27.03	131,400

Year Winner	Jockey	Second	Third	Strs	Time	1st Purse
1993 **Kotashaan (Fr)**, 5, 114	K. J. Desormeaux	Carnival Baby, 5, 112	The Name's Jimmy, 4, 115	8	2:27.64	$129,600
1992 **Quest for Fame (GB)**, 5, 121	G. L. Stevens	Cool Gold Mood, 5, 114	†Miss Alleged, 5, 121	9	2:28.79	158,500
1991 **Rial (Arg)**, 6, 118	J. Velasquez	Intelligently, 5, 113	Royal Reach, 5, 113	9	2:24.10	163,400
1990 **Frankly Perfect**, 5, 124	C. J. McCarron	Delegant, 6, 116	Just as Lucky, 5, 114	12	2:28.00	171,100
1989 **Great Communicator**, 6, 124	R. Sibille	Vallotton (Fr), 4, 117	Roberto's Dancer, 4, 114	5	2:30.20	122,800
1988 **Great Communicator**, 5, 117	R. Sibille	Trokhos, 5, 116	†Ivor's Image, 5, 114	10	2:27.60	133,800
1987 **Louis Le Grand**, 5, 118	W. Shoemaker	Zoffany, 7, 125	Schiller, 5, 115	8	2:28.40	96,600
1986 **Talakeno**, 6, 115	P. A. Valenzuela	Foscarini (Ire), 5, 117	Strawberry Road (Aus), 7, 126	12	2:33.20	123,750
1985 **Western**, 7, 114	G. L. Stevens	Scrupules (Ire), 5, 121	Strong Dollar (Ire), 5, 115	5	2:26.00	89,250
1984 **Sir Pele**, 5, 118	R. Q. Meza	Lucence, 5, 118	Debonair Herc, 4, 114	9	2:27.40	79,375
1983 **Pelerin (Fr)**, 6, 116	W. Shoemaker	Western, 5, 118	Massera (Chi), 5, 118	10	2:24.60	67,200
1982 **Regal Bearing (GB)**, 6, 114	J. J. Steiner	Le Duc de Bar, 5, 114	Goldiko (Fr), 5, 119	10	2:27.20	80,450
1981 **John Henry**, 6, 127	L. A. Pincay Jr.	Galaxy Libra (Ire), 5, 119	Zor, 8, 115	6	2:24.00	62,800
1980 **Silver Eagle (Ire)**, 6, 120	W. Shoemaker	Balzac, 5, 123	Friuli (Arg), 7, 114	8	2:30.20	65,100
1979 **Fluorescent Light**, 5, 124	L. A. Pincay Jr.	As de Copas (Arg), 6, 118	dh- Alpha Boy, 5, 112	8	2:28.20	48,950
			dh- Nostalgia, 5, 112			
1978 **Copper Mel**, 6, 115	S. Hawley	Avodire, 5, 110	Tacitus, 4, 115	11	2:28.00	42,300
1977 ***Royal Derby II**, 8, 126	W. Shoemaker	Gallivantor, 5, 115	Anne's Pretender, 5, 123	10	2:24.80	41,700
1976 **Announcer**, 4, 118	F. Toro	Top Crowd, 5, 123	Zanthe, 7, 121	6	2:30.80	38,200
1975 ***Madison Palace**, 7, 120	L. A. Pincay Jr.	Toujours Pret, 6, 121	*Barclay Joy, 5, 118	8	2:30.20	40,100
1974 **Captain Cee Jay**, 4, 113	F. Alvarez	Court Ruling, 4, 112	*El Rey, 6, 112	8	**2:23.80**	28,150
Astray, 5, 118	J. Vasquez	Scantling, 4, 112	Wichita Oil, 6, 115	8	2:24.40	28,150
1973 **Queen's Hustler**, 4, 112	R. Rosales	China Silk, 4, 115	River Buoy, 8, 117	9	2:27.20	40,800

Named for St. Louis of Toulouse, a Franciscan bishop and Catholic saint. Formerly named in honor of George Washington's birthday; the race was held on that holiday. Grade 3 1990-'91. Washington's Birthday H. 1952-'62. Not held 1963-'67. 7 furlongs 1952-'53. 1¼ miles 1954, 1970. About 1½ miles 1968, 1972. Dirt 1952-'53, 1973, 1980. Two divisions 1974. Dead heat for third 1979. Track record 1973. †Denotes female.

San Luis Rey Handicap

Grade 2 in 2005. Santa Anita Park, four-year-olds and up, 1½ miles, turf. Held March 27, 2005, with a gross value of $200,000. First held in 1952. First graded in 1973. Stakes record 2:23 (1980 John Henry; 1970 Fiddle Isle).

Year Winner	Jockey	Second	Third	Strs	Time	1st Purse
2005 **Stanley Park**, 5, 116	G. L. Stevens	Meteor Storm (GB), 6, 118	Epicentre, 6, 115	10	2:24.45	$120,000
2004 **Meteor Storm (GB)**, 5, 115	J. Valdivia Jr.	Labirinto, 6, 114	Gene de Campeao (Brz), 5, 114	10	2:26.03	120,000
2003 **Champion Lodge (Ire)**, 6, 116	A. O. Solis	Special Matter, 5, 113	Adminniestrador, 6, 116	7	2:33.48	150,000
2002 **Continental Red**, 6, 116	P. A. Valenzuela	†Keemoon (Fr), 6, 115	Speedy Pick, 4, 112	8	2:26.81	150,000
2001 **Blueprint (Ire)**, 6, 116	G. L. Stevens	Devon Deputy, 5, 114	Kerrygold (Fr), 5, 116	8	2:28.57	150,000
2000 **Dark Moondancer (GB)**, 5, 122	C. J. McCarron	Single Empire (Ire), 6, 122	Bonapartiste (Fr), 6, 122	6	2:26.00	150,000
1999 **Single Empire (Ire)**, 5, 122	K. J. Desormeaux	Kessem Power (NZ), 7, 122	Alvo Certo (Brz), 6, 122	7	2:27.97	150,000
1998 **Kessem Power (NZ)**, 6, 122	L. Dettori	Storm Trooper, 5, 122	Star Performance, 5, 122	12	2:28.40	150,000
1997 **Marlin**, 4, 122	C. J. McCarron	Sunshack (GB), 6, 122	Peckinpah's Soul (Fr), 5, 122	10	2:28.14	166,600
1996 **†Windsharp**, 5, 117	E. J. Delahoussaye	†Wandesta (GB), 5, 117	Silver Wizard, 6, 122	7	2:27.91	161,900
1995 **Sandpit (Brz)**, 6, 124	C. S. Nakatani	River Rhythm, 8, 124	Square Cut, 6, 124	7	2:27.15	155,000
1994 **Bien Bien**, 5, 124	C. J. McCarron	Navire (Fr), 5, 124	Grand Flotilla, 7, 124	5	2:26.65	149,500
1993 **Kotashaan (Fr)**, 5, 124	K. J. Desormeaux	Bien Bien, 4, 124	Fast Cure, 4, 124	4	2:23.91	148,250
1992 **Fly Till Dawn**, 6, 124	L. A. Pincay Jr.	Provins, 4, 124	Quest for Fame (GB), 5, 124	6	2:27.26	179,000
1991 **Pleasant Variety**, 7, 126	G. L. Stevens	Royal Reach, 5, 126	Mashkour, 8, 126	10	2:24.50	188,250
1990 **Prized**, 4, 126	E. J. Delahoussaye	Hawkster, 4, 126	Frankly Perfect, 5, 126	6	2:25.20	180,000
1989 **Frankly Perfect**, 4, 126	E. J. Delahoussaye	Great Communicator, 6, 126	Payant (Arg), 5, 126	5	2:32.80	152,400
1988 **Rivlia**, 6, 126	C. J. McCarron	Great Communicator, 6, 126	Swink, 5, 126	7	2:27.20	158,400
1987 **Zoffany**, 7, 126	E. J. Delahoussaye	Louis Le Grand, 5, 126	Long Mick (Fr), 6, 126	5	2:25.20	121,200
1986 **Dahar**, 5, 126	A. O. Solis	Strawberry Road (Aus), 7, 126	Alphabatim, 5, 126	7	2:26.40	148,600
1985 **Prince True**, 4, 126	C. J. McCarron	Western, 7, 126	Dahar, 4, 126	6	2:25.40	147,300
1984 **Interco**, 4, 126	P. A. Valenzuela	Gato Del Sol, 5, 126	John Henry, 9, 126	10	2:26.80	127,200
1983 **Erins Isle (Ire)**, 5, 126	L. A. Pincay Jr.	Prince Spellbound, 4, 126	Majesty's Prince, 4, 126	9	2:26.20	120,900
1982 **Perrault (GB)**, 5, 126	L. A. Pincay Jr.	Exploded, 5, 126	John Henry, 7, 126	5	2:24.00	116,200
1981 **John Henry**, 6, 126	L. A. Pincay Jr.	Obraztsovy, 6, 126	Fiestero (Chi), 6, 126	6	2:25.20	93,900
1980 **John Henry**, 5, 126	D. G. McHargue	Relaunch, 4, 126	Silver Eagle (Ire), 6, 126	7	**2:23.00**	94,800
1979 **Noble Dancer (GB)**, 7, 126	J. Vasquez	Tiller, 5, 126	Good Lord (NZ), 8, 126	7	2:34.60	95,300
1978 **Noble Dancer (GB)**, 6, 126	S. Cauthen	Properantes, 5, 126	Text, 4, 126	7	2:24.00	64,400
1977 **Caucasus**, 5, 126	F. Toro	King Pellinore, 5, 126	Top Crowd, 6, 126	7	2:25.60	64,400
1976 **Avatar**, 4, 126	L. A. Pincay Jr.	‡Top Crowd, 5, 126	Top Command, 5, 126	7	2:24.80	64,300
1975 **Trojan Bronze**, 4, 126	J. E. Tejeira	Okavango, 5, 126	Montmartre, 5, 126	6	2:29.60	63,500
1974 **Astray**, 5, 126	J. Vasquez	Big Spruce, 5, 126	Quack, 5, 126	10	2:24.40	67,000
1973 **Big Spruce**, 4, 126	D. Pierce	*Cicero's Court, 4, 126	*Cougar II, 7, 126	10	2:27.60	66,800

Named for the San Luis Rey Mission; the California mission was named in honor of King and Catholic St. Louis IX of France. Grade 1 1973-'96. San Luis Rey S. 1952-'53, 1973-2000. 7 furlongs 1952. 6 furlongs 1953. 1 mile 1954. Dirt 1952-'54, 1962. Originally scheduled on turf 1975. Three-year-olds and up 1958-'59. ‡Ga Hai finished second, DQ to fourth, 1976. †Denotes female. California-breds 1952-'54.

San Marcos Stakes

Grade 2 in 2005. Santa Anita Park, four-year-olds and up, 1¼ miles, turf. Held January 22, 2005, with a gross value of $150,000. First held in 1952. First graded in 1973. Stakes record 1:57.92 (2003 Johar).

Year	Winner	Jockey	Second	Third	Strs	Time	1st Purse
2005	Whilly (Ire), 4, 117	F. F. Martinez	Puppeteer (GB), 5, 116	T. H. Approval, 4, 117	6	2:00.68	$90,000
2004	Sweet Return (GB), 4, 121	G. L. Stevens	Nothing to Lose, 4, 116	Blue Steller (Ire), 6, 116	9	1:58.82	90,000
2003	Johar, 4, 120	A. O. Solis	The Tin Man, 5, 122	Grammarian, 5, 122	7	1:57.92	90,000
2002	Irish Prize, 6, 122	G. L. Stevens	Continental Red, 6, 116	Cagney (Brz), 5, 119	6	2:01.27	90,000
2001	Bienamado, 5, 122	C. J. McCarron	Kerrygold (Fr), 5, 116	Northern Quest (Fr), 6, 122	7	2:02.75	90,000
2000	Public Purse, 6, 119	A. O. Solis	Dark Moondancer (GB), 5, 120	The Fly (GB), 6, 114	7	1:59.58	98,280
1999	Brave Act (GB), 5, 120	G. F. Almeida	Ferrari (Ger), 5, 117	Native Desert, 6, 117	7	2:04.25	90,000
1998	Prize Giving (GB), 5, 114	A. O. Solis	Bienvenido (Arg), 5, 115	Martiniquais (Ire), 5, 118	6	2:04.41	97,380
1997	Sandpit (Brz), 8, 123	C. S. Nakatani	River Deep, 6, 116	‡Shanawi (Ire), 5, 112	8	2:00.61	99,000
1996	Urgent Request (Ire), 6, 115	C. W. Antley	Bon Point (GB), 6, 114	Virginia Carnival, 4, 116	6	2:02.26	97,000
1995	River Flyer, 4, 118	C. W. Antley	Silver Wizard, 5, 117	Savinio, 5, 116	7	2:05.61	92,200
1994	Bien Bien, 5, 122	L. A. Pincay Jr.	Explosive Red, 4, 116	Myrakalu (Fr), 6, 113	6	2:00.55	75,850
1993	Star of Cozzene, 5, 120	G. L. Stevens	Kotashaan (Fr), 5, 116	Carnival Baby, 5, 112	7	2:01.71	77,650
1992	Classic Fame, 6, 120	E. J. Delahoussaye	Fly Till Dawn, 6, 120	French Seventyfive, 5, 115	6	1:58.02	90,600
1991	Fly Till Dawn, 5, 120	L. A. Pincay Jr.	Vaguely Hidden, 4, 115	The Medic, 7, 115	8	1:58.70	97,350
1990	Putting (Fr), 7, 114	C. A. Black	Colway Rally (GB), 6, 115	Live the Dream, 4, 119	13	1:58.20	105,600
1989	Trokhos, 6, 117	L. A. Pincay Jr.	Vallotton (Fr), 4, 117	Roberto's Dancer, 4, 113	8	2:02.00	97,200
1988	Great Communicator, 5, 115	R. Sibille	Schiller, 6, 113	Bello Horizonte (Ire), 5, 113	10	2:02.60	100,400
1987	Zoffany, 7, 123	E. J. Delahoussaye	Louis Le Grand, 5, 117	Strawberry Road (Aus), 8, 122	8	2:00.80	64,100
1986	Silveyville, 8, 120	C. J. McCarron	Strawberry Road (Aus), 7, 125	Nasib (Ire), 4, 116	7	2:00.80	63,200
1985	Dahar, 4, 121	F. Toro	Scrupules (Ire), 5, 122	Alphabatim, 4, 124	6	2:01.20	61,900
1984	Lucence, 5, 114	P. A. Valenzuela	Ginger Brink (Fr), 4, 117	Sir Pele, 5, 114	11	2:01.80	54,200
1983	Western, 5, 116	C. J. McCarron	Handsome One, 5, 116	Tell Again, 5, 117	7	2:04.00	47,950
1982	Super Moment, 5, 125	L. A. Pincay Jr.	Forlion, 6, 114	Le Duc de Bar, 5, 111	5	2:00.60	45,900
1981	Galaxy Libra (Ire), 5, 116	A. T. Cordero Jr.	Bold Tropic (SAf), 6, 127	Mike Fogarty (Ire), 6, 115	9	2:00.20	40,300
1980	John Henry, 5, 124	D. G. McHargue	El Fantastico, 5, 113	Conmemorativo, 5, 110	5	2:01.60	37,350
1979	Tiller, 5, 126	A. T. Cordero Jr.	Palton (Chi), 6, 121	How Curious, 5, 112	6	1:58.80	37,700
1978	Vigors, 5, 121	D. G. McHargue	Pay Tribute, 6, 122	Jumping Hill, 6, 123	9	1:46.60	33,350
1977	*Royal Derby II, 8, 124	W. Shoemaker	Anne's Pretender, 5, 123	Teddy's Courage, 4, 116	10	1:58.20	34,150
1976	Announcer, 4, 115	F. Toro	Zanthe, 7, 122	Top Crowd, 5, 123	9	1:58.40	32,800
1975	Trojan Bronze, 4, 117	W. Shoemaker	Indefatigable, 5, 115	*El Botija, 5, 0	11	1:59.80	34,550
1974	Triangular, 7, 118	D. Pierce	Big Spruce, 5, 124	Kentuckian, 5, 118	9	2:04.80	33,000
1973	*Tuqui II, 6, 114	L. A. Pincay Jr.	*Soudard, 5, 115	Aggressively, 6, 114	9	2:02.20	27,000

Named for Rancho San Marcos, which was located in Santa Barbara County, California. Grade 3 1973-'92. San Marcos H. 1952-2000. Not held 1970. 1 mile 1952-'53. 1⅛ miles 1978. Dirt 1952-'53, 1956, 1962, 1969, 1973, 1975, 1978-'83, 1996. Originally scheduled on turf 1973. Three-year-olds and up 1955-'59. ‡Marlin finished third, DQ to fifth, 1997.

San Pasqual Handicap

Grade 2 in 2005. Santa Anita Park, four-year-olds and up, 1¹⁄₁₆ miles, dirt. Held January 8, 2005, with a gross value of $150,000. First held in 1935. First graded in 1973. Stakes record 1:40.20 (1980 Valdez, 1978 Ancient Title).

Year	Winner	Jockey	Second	Third	Strs	Time	1st Purse
2005	Congrats, 5, 114	T. Baze	Total Impact (Chi), 7, 120	Sigfreto, 7, 111	5	1:41.97	$90,000
2004	Star Cross (Arg), 7, 113	V. Espinoza	Nose The Trade (GB), 6, 115	Olmodavor, 5, 118	7	1:42.22	90,000
2003	Congaree, 5, 121	J. D. Bailey	Kudos, 6, 119	Hot Market, 5, 116	9	1:41.04	90,000
2002	Wooden Phone, 5, 119	D. R. Flores	Euchre, 6, 120	Red Eye, 6, 112	7	1:41.83	120,000
2001	Freedom Crest, 5, 108	G. L. Stevens	Bosque Redondo, 4, 114	Sultry Substitute, 6, 114	8	1:41.94	120,000
2000	Dixie Dot Com, 5, 118	P. A. Valenzuela	Budroyale, 7, 122	Six Below, 5, 116	5	1:40.95	120,000
1999	Silver Charm, 5, 125	G. L. Stevens	Malek (Chi), 6, 119	Crafty Friend, 6, 118	5	1:41.78	120,000
1998	Hal's Pal (GB), 5, 113	B. Blanc	Malek (Chi), 5, 116	Flick (GB), 6, 116	9	1:41.89	120,000
1997	Kingdom Found, 7, 115	G. L. Stevens	Savinio, 7, 117	Eltish, 5, 113	4	1:40.74	122,200
1996	Alphabet Soup, 5, 118	C. W. Antley	Luthier Fever, 5, 115	Cezind, 6, 114	9	1:41.66	130,100
1995	Del Mar Dennis, 5, 118	A. O. Solis	Slew of Damascus, 7, 120	Tossofthecoin, 5, 116	6	1:41.23	116,100
1994	Hill Pass, 5, 113	C. J. McCarron	Best Pal, 6, 122	Lottery Winner, 5, 116	7	1:41.00	87,800
1993	Jovial (GB), 6, 115	M. Walls	‡Marquetry, 6, 118	Provins, 5, 115	7	1:41.94	91,400
1992	Twilight Agenda, 6, 125	K. J. Desormeaux	Ibero (Arg), 5, 116	Answer Do, 6, 118	5	1:42.32	89,000
1991	Farma Way, 4, 116	G. L. Stevens	Flying Continental, 5, 122	Stylish Stud, 5, 114	9	1:40.90	93,100
1990	Criminal Type, 5, 114	C. J. McCarron	Lively One, 5, 122	Present Value, 6, 121	8	1:42.40	96,300
1989	On the Line, 5, 123	G. L. Stevens	Mark Chip, 6, 114	Stylish Winner, 5, 115	6	1:41.00	93,300
1988	Super Diamond, 8, 125	L. A. Pincay Jr.	Judge Angelucci, 5, 122	He's a Saros, 5, 114	5	1:43.00	92,300
1987	Epidaurus, 5, 116	G. Baze	Ascension, 5, 114	Nostalgia's Star, 5, 120	7	1:42.40	90,800
1986	Precisionist, 5, 126	C. J. McCarron	Bare Minimum, 5, 113	My Habitony, 6, 116	5	1:41.20	96,000
1985	Hula Blaze, 5, 117	P. A. Valenzuela	Video Kid, 5, 117	Tennessee Rite, 4, 112	11	1:42.00	95,300
1984	Danebo, 5, 112	L. A. Pincay Jr.	Water Bank, 5, 118	Honeyland, 5, 116	8	1:41.80	91,900
1983	Regal Falcon, 5, 115	E. J. Delahoussaye	Time to Explode, 4, 121	West On Broad, 5, 113	7	1:43.20	63,900
1982	Five Star Flight, 4, 120	L. A. Pincay Jr.	Tahitian King (Ire), 6, 122	King Go Go, 7, 119	8	1:41.80	65,000
1981	Flying Paster, 5, 127	C. J. McCarron	King Go Go, 6, 117	Fiestero (Chi), 6, 113	6	1:41.20	47,150
1980	Valdez, 4, 125	L. A. Pincay Jr.	Prenotion, 5, 111	Balzac, 5, 122	4	1:40.20	46,350

1979	Mr. Redoy, 5, 117	A. T. Cordero Jr.	Life's Hope, 6, 116	Big John Taylor, 5, 115	8	1:42.20	$38,900
1978	Ancient Title, 8, 124	D. G. McHargue	Mark's Place, 6, 120	Double Discount, 5, 120	4	**1:40.20**	30,250
1977	Uniformity, 5, 117	F. Toro	Distant Land, 5, 116	*Pisistrato, 5, 117	8	1:41.00	35,500
1976	Lightning Mandate, 5, 118	S. Hawley	Guards Up, 4, 113	Ga Hai, 5, 116	5	1:48.40	32,250
1975	Okavango, 5, 114	F. Toro	†Tallahto, 5, 118	Cheriepe, 5, 114	12	1:41.40	38,400
1974	Tri Jet, 5, 121	W. Shoemaker	Forage, 5, 121	†Susan's Girl, 5, 119	10	1:41.40	36,550
1973	Single Agent, 5, 119	J. Lambert	Kennedy Road, 5, 119	Autobiography, 5, 125	6	1:41.80	33,850

Named for El Rancho San Pasqual, which encompassed almost all of what is now the Pasadena, California, area. Not held 1942–'44. 6 furlongs 1935–'36. 7 furlongs 1938. 1¹⁄₈ miles 1939–'41. 1¹⁄₄ miles 1955. Three-year-olds 1935–'36. Three-year-olds and up 1937–'53, 1958. ‡Best Pal finished second, DQ to fifth, 1993. †Denotes female.

San Rafael Stakes

Grade 2 in 2005. Santa Anita Park, three-year-olds, 1 mile, dirt. Held January 15, 2005, with a gross value of $150,000. First held in 1975. First graded in 1983. Stakes record 1:34.40 (1982 Prince Spellbound).

Year	Winner	Jockey	Second	Third	Strs	Time	1st Purse
2005	Spanish Chestnut, 3, 116	G. L. Stevens	Iced Out, 3, 115	Texcess, 3, 116	5	1:36.69	$90,000
2004	Imperialism, 3, 118	V. Espinoza	Lion Heart, 3, 121	Consecrate, 3, 115	10	1:36.11	120,000
2003	Rojo Toro, 3, 115	J. D. Bailey	Spensive, 3, 118	Crowned Dancer, 3, 118	7	1:35.89	120,000
2002	Came Home, 3, 118	C. J. McCarron	Easy Grades, 3, 116	Werblin, 3, 115	7	1:36.24	120,000
2001	Crafty C.T., 3, 116	E. J. Delahoussaye	Palmeiro, 3, 117	Early Flyer, 3, 118	9	1:35.79	120,000
2000	War Chant, 3, 116	K. J. Desormeaux	Archer City Slew, 3, 118	Cocky, 3, 115	6	1:36.45	120,000
1999	Desert Hero, 3, 116	C. S. Nakatani	Prime Timber, 3, 115	Capsized, 3, 115	9	1:36.45	120,000
1998	Orville N Wilbur's, 3, 115	C. S. Nakatani	Souvenir Copy, 3, 121	Futuristic, 3, 115	6	1:35.96	120,000
1997	Funontherun, 3, 115	G. F. Almeida	Inexcessivelygood, 3, 116	Hello (Ire), 3, 121	10	1:36.01	121,800
1996	Honour and Glory, 3, 121	G. L. Stevens	Halo Sunshine, 3, 115	Matty G, 3, 121	8	1:36.45	122,000
1995	Larry the Legend, 3, 118	K. J. Desormeaux	Fandarel Dancer, 3, 118	Timber Country, 3, 121	5	1:37.61	88,600
1994	Tabasco Cat, 3, 117	P. Day	Powis Castle, 3, 115	Shepherd's Field, 3, 121	5	1:36.39	89,700
1993	Devoted Brass, 3, 115	K. J. Desormeaux	Union City, 3, 115	Stuka, 3, 118	6	1:35.13	90,000
1992	A.P. Indy, 3, 121	E. J. Delahoussaye	Treekster, 3, 116	Prince Wild, 3, 118	5	1:35.41	90,300
1991	Dinard, 3, 118	C. J. McCarron	Apollo, 3, 118	Best Pal, 3, 121	5	1:35.90	91,900
1990	Mister Frisky, 3, 115	G. L. Stevens	Tight Spot, 3, 115	Land Rush, 3, 115	7	1:36.60	80,300
1989	Music Merci, 3, 121	G. L. Stevens	Manastash Ridge, 3, 118	Past Ages, 3, 118	5	1:34.80	76,300
1988	What a Diplomat, 3, 115	G. L. Stevens	Flying Victor, 3, 121	Success Express, 3, 121	9	1:38.00	79,350
1987	Masterful Advocate, 3, 122	L. A. Pincay Jr.	Chart the Stars, 3, 116	Hot and Smoggy, 3, 116	7	1:35.80	90,500
1986	Variety Road, 3, 116	C. J. McCarron	Ferdinand, 3, 116	Jetting Home, 3, 116	9	1:35.60	68,300
1985	Smarten Up, 3, 122	R. Q. Meza	Fast Account, 3, 122	Stan's Bower, 3, 118	9	1:36.20	94,500
1984	Precisionist, 3, 120	C. J. McCarron	Fali Time, 3, 122	Commemorate, 3, 118	6	1:35.00	91,600
1983	Desert Wine, 3, 119	C. J. McCarron	Naevus, 3, 114	Balboa Native, 3, 116	7	1:35.60	65,900
1982	Prince Spellbound, 3, 119	M. Castaneda	Muttering, 3, 121	Unpredictable, 3, 119	9	**1:34.40**	68,200
1981	Johnlee n' Harold, 3, 119	M. Castaneda	Minnesota Chief, 3, 115	A Run, 3, 119	10	1:36.00	51,500
1978	Little Happiness, 4, 116	S. Cauthen	*Merry Lady III, 6, 114	Up to Juliet, 5, 118	7	1:35.40	16,975
1976	Vagabonda, 5, 114	W. Shoemaker	*Bastonera II, 5, 117	Mia Amore, 4, 117	9	1:48.20	16,825
1975	Donna B Quick, 4, 114	W. Shoemaker	In Prosperity, 5, 115	Take Powder, 5, 122	10	1:09.60	11,300

Named for Rancho San Rafael, a 1785 land grant where Burbank, Glendale, and Montrose, California, are now located. Grade 3 1983. Not held 1977, 1979–'80. 6 furlongs 1975. 1¹⁄₈ miles 1976. Turf 1976. Four-year-olds and up 1975–'78. Fillies and mares 1975–'78.

San Simeon Handicap

Grade 3 in 2005. Santa Anita Park, four-year-olds and up, 6¹⁄₂ furlongs, turf. Held April 18, 2005, with a gross value of $107,000. First held in 1968. First graded in 1973. Stakes record 1:11.46 (2004 Glick).

Year	Winner	Jockey	Second	Third	Strs	Time	1st Purse
2005	Shadow of Illinois, 5, 116	M. Guidry	Geronimo (Chi), 6, 117	Golden Arrow, 6, 116	6	1:12.62	$64,200
2004	Glick, 8, 117	A. O. Solis	Cayoke (Fr), 7, 116	Summer Service, 4, 117	6	**1:11.46**	64,380
2003	Speak in Passing, 6, 118	D. R. Flores	Spinelessjellyfish, 7, 115	Rocky Bar, 5, 116	8	1:12.87	82,500
2002	Malabar Gold, 5, 117	C. J. McCarron	Astonished (GB), 6, 117	Nuclear Debate, 7, 118	9	1:11.73	82,825
2001	Lake William, 5, 114	V. Espinoza	Macward, 5, 117	Touch of the Blues (Fr), 4, 116	6	1:12.34	80,175
2000	El Cielo, 6, 117	J. Valdivia Jr.	King Slayer (GB), 5, 116	Scooter Brown, 5, 117	6	1:12.66	79,440
1999	Naninja, 6, 115	C. J. McCarron	Expressionist, 4, 116	Indian Rocket (GB), 5, 119	7	1:13.32	65,220
1998	Labeeb (GB), 6, 120	K. J. Desormeaux	Surachai, 5, 118	Captain Collins (Ire), 4, 115	11	1:12.94	67,860
1997	Sandtrap, 4, 117	A. O. Solis	‡Daggett Peak, 6, 113	Tychonic (GB), 5, 119	6	1:12.50	96,850
1996	†Ski Dancer, 4, 114	G. L. Stevens	Daggett Peak, 5, 115	Boulderdash Bay, 6, 118	6	1:13.98	64,200
1995	Finder's Fortune, 6, 117	P. A. Valenzuela	Rotsaluck, 4, 117	Pembroke, 5, 117	7	1:13.65	64,550
1994	Rapan Boy (Aus), 6, 114	G. L. Stevens	The Berkeley Man, 4, 115	Artistic Reef (GB), 5, 116	7	1:13.16	63,100
1993	Exemplary Leader, 7, 113	M. A. Pedroza	Prince Ferdinand (GB), 4, 119	Wild Harmony, 4, 117	8	1:13.98	64,300
1992	†Heart of Joy, 5, 119	C. J. McCarron	Regal Groom, 5, 115	Time Gentlemen (GB), 4, 117	10	1:12.94	69,600
1991	Forest Glow, 4, 116	J. A. Garcia	Answer Do, 5, 116	‡Shirkee, 6, 117	9	1:12.50	63,900
1990	Coastal Voyage, 6, 118	A. O. Solis	Patchy Groundfog, 7, 117	Raise a Stanza, 4, 119	4	1:12.20	60,000
1989	Mazilier, 5, 116	P. A. Valenzuela	†Imperial Star (GB), 5, 112	Caballo de Oro, 6, 116	6	1:13.80	48,750
1988	Caballo de Oro, 4, 112	R. Q. Meza	Gallant Sailor, 5, 112	Sylvan Express (Ire), 5, 121	5	1:15.40	46,700
1987	Bolder Than Bold, 5, 117	G. Baze	Prince Bobby B., 4, 122	†Lichi (Chi), 7, 112	9	1:13.60	49,800
1986	Estate, 7, 114	A. L. Castanon	Will Dancer (Fr), 4, 118	Exclusive Partner, 4, 116	8	1:13.80	52,150

1985 **Champagne Bid**, 6, 121	R. Sibille	Forzando (GB), 4, 122	Smart and Sharp, 6, 118	8	1:13.60	$52,150
1984 **Champagne Bid**, 5, 121	R. Sibille	Retsina Run, 4, 115	Famous Star (GB), 5, 115	9	1:14.40	53,350
1983 **Chinook Pass**, 4, 124	L. A. Pincay Jr.	Shanekite, 5, 118	Earthquack, 4, 121	7	1:15.40	39,100
1982 **Shagbark**, 7, 122	L. A. Pincay Jr.	Shanekite, 4, 118	Belfort (Fr), 5, 116	8	1:13.00	39,850
1981 **Syncopate**, 6, 119	D. Pierce	Parsec, 4, 116	Matsadoon's Honey, 4, 115	4	1:16.40	31,450
1980 **Dragon Command (NZ)**, 6, 115	E. J. Delahoussaye	Numa Pompilius, 6, 115	Bywayofchicago, 6, 115	11	1:12.60	29,050
1979 **Bywayofchicago**, 5, 120	D. G. McHargue	Maheras, 6, 118	Whatsyourpleasure, 6, 117	9	1:21.80	33,850
1978 **Maheras**, 5, 122	L. A. Pincay Jr.	dh-Bad 'n Big, 4, 119		6	1:22.80	25,650
		dh-Yu Wipi, 6, 114				
1977 **Mark's Place**, 5, 122	S. Hawley	Maheras, 4, 124	Painted Wagon, 4, 114	7	1:21.00	26,250
1976 **Pay Tribute**, 4, 118	L. A. Pincay Jr.	Against the Snow, 6, 118	King Pellinore, 4, 122	6	1:35.20	25,650
1975 **Century's Envoy**, 4, 121	J. E. Tejeira	First Back, 4, 121	Rocket Review, 4, 120	5	1:22.40	19,700
1974 ***Matun**, 5, 118	S. Valdez	‡Selecting, 5, 115	Forage, 5, 123	8	1:21.20	21,200
1973 **Soft Victory**, 5, 115	D. Pierce	Selecting, 4, 115	dh- Andrew Feeney, 4, 116	12	1:21.40	23,050
			dh- Goalie, 4, 113			

Named for Rancho San Simeon, California, originally attached to the San Miguel Mission. Not graded 1975-'83. 7 furlongs 1968-'75, 1977-'79. 1 mile 1976. 6¹/₂ furlongs 1980-'85, 1987-'90. Dirt 1968-'79, 1981, 1983, 1988. Dead heat for third 1973. Dead heat for second 1978. ‡Forage finished second, DQ to third, 1974. ‡Coastal Voyage finished third, DQ to fourth, 1991. ‡Destiny's Venture finished second, DQ to fourth, 1997. Course record 2004. †Denotes female.

Santa Ana Handicap

Grade 2 in 2005. Santa Anita Park, four-year-olds and up, fillies and mares, 1¹/₈ miles, turf. Held March 20, 2005, with a gross value of $150,000. First raced in 1968. First graded in 1981. Stakes record 1:46.23 (1993 Exchange).

Year	Winner	Jockey	Second	Third	Strs	Time	1st Purse
2005	**Megahertz (GB)**, 6, 122	A. O. Solis	Katdogawn (GB), 5, 117	Valentine Dancer, 5, 117	7	1:47.95	$90,000
2004	‡**Katdogawn (GB)**, 4, 117	M. E. Smith	Fun House, 5, 118	Arabic Song (Ire), 5, 117	7	1:47.36	90,000
2003	**Noches De Rosa (Chi)**, 5, 115	M. E. Smith	Garden in the Rain (Fr), 6, 116	Megahertz (GB), 4, 117	8	1:48.31	90,000
2002	**Golden Apples (Ire)**, 4, 119	G. K. Gomez	Starine (Fr), 5, 122	Astra, 6, 122	9	1:47.05	90,000
2001	**Beautiful Noise**, 5, 115	C. J. McCarron	High Walden, 4, 114	Matiere Grise (Fr), 4, 113	12	1:47.27	90,000
2000	**Spanish Fern**, 5, 119	V. Espinoza	Virginie (Brz), 6, 120	Country Garden (GB), 5, 116	7	1:49.30	97,830
1999	**See You Soon (Fr)**, 5, 119	K. J. Desormeaux	Blending Element (Ire), 6, 116	La Madame (Chi), 4, 116	6	1:49.46	90,000
1998	**Fiji (GB)**, 4, 115	K. J. Desormeaux	Shake the Yoke (GB), 5, 116	Golden Arches (Fr), 4, 120	6	1:49.85	96,480
1997	**Windsharp**, 6, 121	E. J. Delahoussaye	Wheatly Special, 4, 113	Donna Viola (GB), 5, 120	7	1:49.47	97,750
1996	**Pharma**, 5, 116	C. J. McCarron	Angel in My Heart (Fr), 4, 120	Matiara, 4, 120	5	1:49.14	95,650
1995	**Wandesta (GB)**, 4, 115	C. S. Nakatani	Yearly Tour, 4, 116	Aube Indienne (Fr), 5, 120	7	1:50.18	90,700
1994	**Possibly Perfect**, 4, 119	K. J. Desormeaux	Hero's Love, 6, 120	‡Lady Blessington (Fr), 6, 120	7	1:51.05	91,000
1993	**Exchange**, 5, 120	L. A. Pincay Jr.	Party Cited, 4, 115	Villandry, 5, 116	5	**1:46.23**	89,700
1992	**Gravieres (Fr)**, 4, 116	G. L. Stevens	Appealing Missy, 5, 117	Explosive Ele, 5, 119	8	1:47.75	94,900
1991	dh- **Annual Reunion**, 4, 116	G. L. Stevens		Bequest, 5, 115	8	1:46.70	63,400
	dh- **Noble and Nice**, 5, 113	K. J. Desormeaux					
1990	**Annoconnor**, 6, 119	C. A. Black	Royal Touch (Ire), 5, 121	Brown Bess, 8, 123	7	1:47.80	94,500
1989	**Maria Jesse (Fr)**, 4, 116	G. L. Stevens	Fieldy (Ire), 6, 117	Claire Marine (Ire), 4, 115	8	1:47.20	97,100
1988	‡**Pen Bal Lady (GB)**, 4, 118	E. J. Delahoussaye	Fitzwilliam Place (Ire), 4, 119	Galunpe (Ire), 5, 119	10	1:47.20	94,900
1987	**Reloy**, 4, 116	W. Shoemaker	Northern Aspen, 5, 119	North Sider, 5, 120	7	1:48.00	91,300
1986	**Videogenic**, 4, 120	R. G. Davis	Capichi, 6, 118	Water Crystals, 5, 114	6	1:48.40	62,800
1985	**Estrapade**, 5, 123	F. Toro	Fact Finder, 6, 119	Air Distingue, 5, 116	10	1:47.00	67,100
1984	**Avigaition**, 5, 118	W. Shoemaker	Pride of Rosewood (NZ), 6, 116	L'Attrayante (Fr), 4, 122	9	1:48.40	93,600
1983	**Happy Bride (Ire)**, 5, 116	C. J. McCarron	Avigaition, 4, 121	Miss Huntington, 6, 115	6	1:47.80	63,400
1982	**Track Robbery**, 6, 123	E. J. Delahoussaye	Manzanera (Arg), 6, 117	Ack's Secret, 6, 123	8	1:47.20	65,100
1981	**Queen to Conquer**, 5, 121	L. A. Pincay Jr.	Track Robbery, 5, 119	Ack's Secret, 5, 123	7	1:48.00	46,900
1980	**The Very One**, 5, 117	C. Cooke	Sisterhood, 5, 118	Mairzy Doates, 4, 115	8	1:48.40	37,300
1979	**Waya (Fr)**, 5, 127	A. T. Cordero Jr.	Amazer, 4, 123	Shua, 4, 115	10	1:48.40	38,450
1978	**Kittyluck**, 5, 115	F. Toro	Innuendo, 4, 111	‡Belle o' Reason, 5, 120	9	1:53.00	26,750
1977	**Up to Juliet**, 4, 120	L. A. Pincay Jr.	Quintas Fannie, 4, 114	Belle o' Reason, 4, 115	11	1:48.00	27,550
1976	**Sun Festival**, 7, 116	D. Pierce	Quaze Quilt, 5, 122	Cut Class, 4, 117	9	1:48.40	25,450
1975	**Move Abroad**, 4, 115	S. Hawley	Joli Vert, 4, 114	Bold Ballet, 4, 122	6	1:51.40	19,500
1974	**Belle Marie**, 4, 118	W. Shoemaker	Grasping, 5, 114	Flying Fur, 5, 115	12	1:46.60	26,800
1973	**Bird Boots**, 4, 115	E. Belmonte	Best Go, 5, 119	Resolutely, 6, 115	9	1:47.00	15,600
	Minstrel Miss, 6, 119	D. Pierce	*Rich Return II, 6, 118	Hill Circus, 5, 124	8	1:46.80	15,300

Named for the Rancho Santa Ana, located in present-day Ventura County, California. Grade 3 1981. Grade 1 1984-'96. 1¹/₁₆ miles 1971. Dirt 1981-'83, 1986. Two divisions 1973. Dead heat for first 1991. ‡Ida Delia finished third, DQ to fifth, 1978. ‡Fitzwilliam Place (GB) finished first, DQ to second, 1988. ‡Waitryst (NZ) finished third, DQ to seventh, 1994. ‡Megahertz (GB) finished first, DQ to seventh, 2004. Nonwinners of a race worth $12,500 the winner 1973.

Santa Anita Derby

Grade 1 in 2005. Santa Anita Park, three-year-olds, 1¹/₈ miles, dirt. Held April 9, 2005, with a gross value of $750,000. First held in 1935. First graded in 1973. Stakes record 1:47 (1998 Indian Charlie; 1973 Sham; 1965 Lucky Debonair).

Year	Winner	Jockey	Second	Third	Strs	Time	1st Purse
2005	**Buzzards Bay**, 3, 122	M. Guidry	General John B, 3, 122	Wilko, 3, 122	11	1:49.18	$450,000
2004	**Castledale (Ire)**, 3, 122	J. Valdivia Jr.	‡Imperialism, 3, 122	Rock Hard Ten, 3, 122	7	1:49.24	450,000

2003	**Buddy Gil**, 3, 122	G. L. Stevens	Indian Express, 3, 122	Kafwain, 3, 122	9	1:49.36	$450,000
2002	**Came Home**, 3, 122	C. J. McCarron	Easy Grades, 3, 122	Lusty Latin, 3, 122	8	1:50.02	450,000
2001	**Point Given**, 3, 122	G. L. Stevens	Crafty C. T., 3, 122	I Love Silver, 3, 122	6	1:47.77	450,000
2000	**The Deputy (Ire)**, 3, 120	C. J. McCarron	War Chant, 3, 120	Captain Steve, 3, 120	6	1:49.08	600,000
1999	**General Challenge**, 3, 120	G. L. Stevens	Prime Timber, 3, 120	Desert Hero, 3, 120	8	1:48.92	450,000
1998	**Indian Charlie**, 3, 120	G. L. Stevens	Real Quiet, 3, 120	Artax, 3, 120	7	**1:47.00**	450,000
1997	**Free House**, 3, 120	K. J. Desormeaux	Silver Charm, 3, 120	Hello (Ire), 3, 120	10	1:47.60	450,000
1996	**Cavonnier**, 3, 120	C. J. McCarron	‡Honour and Glory, 3, 120	Corker, 3, 120	8	1:48.81	600,000
1995	**Larry the Legend**, 3, 122	G. L. Stevens	Afternoon Deelites, 3, 122	Jumron (GB), 3, 122	8	1:47.99	385,000
1994	**Brocco**, 3, 122	G. L. Stevens	Tabasco Cat, 3, 122	Strodes Creek, 3, 122	6	1:48.33	275,000
1993	**Personal Hope**, 3, 122	G. L. Stevens	Union City, 3, 122	†Eliza, 3, 117	7	1:49.03	275,000
1992	**A.P. Indy**, 3, 122	E. J. Delahoussaye	Bertrando, 3, 122	Casual Lies, 3, 122	7	1:49.25	275,000
1991	**Dinard**, 3, 122	C. J. McCarron	Best Pal, 3, 122	Sea Cadet, 3, 122	9	1:48.10	275,000
1990	**Mister Frisky**, 3, 122	G. L. Stevens	Video Ranger, 3, 122	Warcraft, 3, 122	8	1:49.00	275,000
1989	**Sunday Silence**, 3, 122	P. A. Valenzuela	Flying Continental, 3, 122	Music Merci, 3, 122	6	1:47.60	275,000
1988	†**Winning Colors**, 3, 117	G. L. Stevens	Lively One, 3, 122	Mi Preferido, 3, 122	9	1:47.80	275,000
1987	**Temperate Sil**, 3, 122	W. Shoemaker	Masterful Advocate, 3, 122	Something Lucky, 3, 122	6	1:49.00	278,250
1986	**Snow Chief**, 3, 122	A. O. Solis	Icy Groom, 3, 122	Ferdinand, 3, 122	7	1:48.60	275,000
1985	**Skywalker**, 3, 122	L. A. Pincay Jr.	Fast Account, 3, 122	Nostalgia's Star, 3, 122	9	1:48.40	219,500
1984	**Mighty Adversary**, 3, 120	E. J. Delahoussaye	Precisionist, 3, 120	Prince True, 3, 120	8	1:49.00	189,700
1983	**Marfa**, 3, 120	J. Velasquez	My Habitony, 3, 120	Naevus, 3, 120	10	1:49.40	198,000
1982	**Muttering**, 3, 120	L. A. Pincay Jr.	Prince Spellbound, 3, 120	Journey At Sea, 3, 120	9	1:47.60	188,800
1981	**Splendid Spruce**, 3, 120	D. G. McHargue	Johnlee n' Harold, 3, 120	Hoedown's Day, 3, 120	13	1:49.00	180,600
1980	**Codex**, 3, 120	P. A. Valenzuela	Rumbo, 3, 120	Bic's Gold, 3, 120	9	1:47.60	117,200
1979	**Flying Paster**, 3, 120	D. Pierce	Beau's Eagle, 3, 120	Switch Partners, 3, 120	10	1:48.00	124,900
1978	**Affirmed**, 3, 120	L. A. Pincay Jr.	Balzac, 3, 120	Think Snow, 3, 120	12	1:48.00	127,300
1977	*****Habitony**, 3, 120	W. Shoemaker	For The Moment, 3, 120	Steve's Friend, 3, 120	15	1:48.20	131,000
1976	**An Act**, 3, 120	L. A. Pincay Jr.	Double Discount, 3, 120	Life's Hope, 3, 120	9	1:48.00	97,700
1975	**Avatar**, 3, 120	J. E. Tejeira	Rock of Ages, 3, 120	Diabolo, 3, 120	7	1:47.60	82,900
1974	**Destroyer**, 3, 120	I. Valenzuela	Aloha Mood, 3, 120	Agitate, 3, 120	8	1:48.80	85,200
1973	**Sham**, 3, 120	L. A. Pincay Jr.	Linda's Chief, 3, 120	Out of the East, 3, 120	6	**1:47.00**	79,400

The race and the track are both named in honor of Rancho Santa Anita, the name of the land when it was purchased by E. J. "Lucky" Baldwin. Not held 1942-'44. 1 1/16 miles 1935-'37. 1 1/4 miles 1947. ‡Alyrob finished second, DQ to eighth, 1996. ‡Rock Hard Ten finished second, DQ to third, 2004. †Denotes female.

Santa Anita Handicap

Grade 1 in 2005. Santa Anita Park, four-year-olds and up, 1 1/4 miles, dirt. Held March 5, 2005, with a gross value of $1,000,000. First held in 1935. First graded in 1973. Stakes record 1:58.60 (1979 Affirmed).

Year	Winner	Jockey	Second	Third	Strs	Time	1st Purse
2005	**Rock Hard Ten**, 4, 119	G. L. Stevens	Congrats, 5, 115	Borrego, 4, 115	11	2:01.20	$600,000
2004	**Southern Image**, 4, 118	V. Espinoza	†Island Fashion, 4, 115	Saint Buddy, 4, 111	8	2:01.64	600,000
2003	**Milwaukee Brew**, 6, 119	E. S. Prado	Congaree, 5, 124	Kudos, 6, 117	6	1:59.80	600,000
2002	**Milwaukee Brew**, 5, 115	K. J. Desormeaux	Western Pride, 4, 116	Kudos, 5, 116	14	2:01.02	600,000
2001	**Tiznow**, 4, 122	C. J. McCarron	Wooden Phone, 4, 117	Tribunal, 4, 116	12	2:01.55	600,000
2000	**General Challenge**, 4, 121	C. S. Nakatani	Budroyale, 7, 122	Puerto Madero (Chi), 6, 118	8	2:01.49	600,000
1999	**Free House**, 5, 123	C. J. McCarron	Event of the Year, 4, 119	Silver Charm, 5, 124	6	2:00.67	600,000
1998	**Malek (Chi)**, 5, 115	A. O. Solis	Bagshot, 4, 113	Don't Blame Rio, 5, 117	4	2:02.26	600,000
1997	**Siphon (Brz)**, 6, 120	D. R. Flores	Sandpit (Brz), 8, 121	Gentlemen (Arg), 5, 123	11	2:00.23	600,000
1996	**Mr Purple**, 4, 116	E. J. Delahoussaye	Luthier Fever, 5, 114	Just Java, 5, 114	11	2:02.04	600,000
1995	**Urgent Request (Ire)**, 5, 116	G. L. Stevens	Best Pal, 7, 122	Dare and Go, 4, 120	10	1:59.25	550,000
1994	‡**Stuka**, 4, 115	C. W. Antley	Bien Bien, 5, 120	Myrakalu (Fr), 6, 114	8	2:00.17	550,000
1993	**Sir Beaufort**, 6, 119	P. A. Valenzuela	Star Recruit, 4, 117	Major Impact, 4, 114	11	2:00.55	550,000
1992	**Best Pal**, 4, 124	K. J. Desormeaux	Twilight Agenda, 6, 124	Defensive Play, 5, 115	7	1:59.08	550,000
1991	**Farma Way**, 4, 120	G. L. Stevens	Festin (Arg), 5, 115	Pleasant Tap, 4, 115	10	2:00.30	550,000
1990	**Ruhlmann**, 5, 121	G. L. Stevens	Criminal Type, 5, 119	Flying Continental, 4, 121	10	2:01.20	550,000
1989	**Martial Law**, 4, 113	M. A. Pedroza	Triteamtri, 4, 116	Stylish Winner, 5, 113	11	1:58.80	550,000
1988	**Alysheba**, 4, 126	C. J. McCarron	Ferdinand, 5, 127	Super Diamond, 8, 124	4	1:59.80	550,000
1987	**Broad Brush**, 4, 122	A. T. Cordero Jr.	Ferdinand, 4, 125	Hopeful Word, 6, 117	9	2:00.60	550,000
1986	**Greinton (GB)**, 5, 122	L. A. Pincay Jr.	Herat, 4, 112	Hatim, 5, 115	13	2:00.00	689,500
1985	**Lord At War (Arg)**, 5, 125	W. Shoemaker	Greinton (GB), 4, 120	Gate Dancer, 4, 125	7	2:00.60	275,660
1984	**Interco**, 4, 121	P. A. Valenzuela	Journey At Sea, 5, 117	Gato Del Sol, 5, 117	12	2:00.60	298,650
1983	**Bates Motel**, 4, 118	T. Lipham	It's the One, 5, 123	Wavering Monarch, 4, 121	17	1:59.60	317,350
1982	‡**John Henry**, 7, 130	W. Shoemaker	Perrault (GB), 4, 126	It's the One, 4, 120	11	1:59.00	318,800
1981	**John Henry**, 6, 128	L. A. Pincay Jr.	King Go Go, 6, 117	Exploded, 4, 115	11	1:59.40	238,150
1980	**Spectacular Bid**, 4, 130	W. Shoemaker	Flying Paster, 4, 123	Beau's Eagle, 4, 122	5	2:00.60	190,000
1979	**Affirmed**, 4, 128	L. A. Pincay Jr.	Tiller, 5, 127	dh- Exceller, 6, 127	8	**1:58.60**	192,800
				dh- Painted Wagon, 6, 115			
1978	**Vigors**, 5, 127	D. G. McHargue	Mr. Redoy, 4, 120	Jumping Hill, 6, 115	10	2:01.20	180,000
1977	**Crystal Water**, 4, 122	L. A. Pincay Jr.	Faliraki (Ire), 4, 114	King Pellinore, 5, 130	13	1:59.20	173,550
1976	**Royal Glint**, 6, 124	J. E. Tejeira	Ancient Title, 6, 124	Lightning Mandate, 5, 120	15	2:00.40	155,900
1975	**Stardust Mel**, 4, 123	W. Shoemaker	Out of the East, 5, 112	Okavango, 5, 116	8	2:06.40	105,000

1974 **Prince Dantan**, 4, 119	R. Turcotte	Ancient Title, 4, 125	Big Spruce, 5, 122	11	2:03.60	$105,000
1973 ***Cougar II**, 7, 126	L. A. Pincay Jr.	Kennedy Road, 5, 119	Cabin, 5, 110	10	2:00.00	105,000

The race and the track are both named in honor of Rancho Santa Anita, the name of the land when it was purchased by E. J. "Lucky" Baldwin. Not held 1942-'44. Three-year-olds and up 1935-'68. Dead heat for third 1979. ‡Perrault (GB) finished first, DQ to second, 1982. ‡The Wicked North finished first, DQ to fourth, 1994. †Denotes female.

Santa Anita Oaks

Grade 1 in 2005. Santa Anita Park, three-year-olds, fillies, 1¹/₁₆ miles, dirt. Held March 13, 2005, with a gross value of $300,000. First held in 1935. First graded in 1973. Stakes record 1:41.20 (1980 Bold 'n Determined).

Year	Winner	Jockey	Second	Third	Strs	Time	1st Purse
2005	**Sweet Catomine**, 3, 121	C. S. Nakatani	Memorette, 3, 121	She Sings, 3, 121	7	1:44.44	$180,000
2004	**Silent Sighs**, 3, 117	D. R. Flores	Halfbridled, 3, 117	A. P. Adventure, 3, 117	7	1:42.84	180,000
2003	**Composure**, 3, 117	J. D. Bailey	Elloluv, 3, 117	Go for Glamour, 3, 117	5	1:43.34	180,000
2002	**You**, 3, 117	J. D. Bailey	Habibti, 3, 117	Ile de France, 3, 117	9	1:42.70	180,000
2001	**Golden Ballet**, 3, 117	C. J. McCarron	Flute, 3, 117	Affluent, 3, 117	8	1:41.83	180,000
2000	**Surfside**, 3, 117	P. Day	Kumari Continent, 3, 117	Classy Cara, 3, 117	5	1:44.03	180,000
1999	**Excellent Meeting**, 3, 117	K. J. Desormeaux	Tout Charmant, 3, 117	Gleefully, 3, 117	6	1:43.26	150,000
1998	**Hedonist**, 3, 117	K. J. Desormeaux	Keeper Hill, 3, 117	Nijinsky's Passion, 3, 117	7	1:44.14	150,000
1997	**Sharp Cat**, 3, 117	C. S. Nakatani	Queen of Money, 3, 117	Double Park (Fr), 3, 117	5	1:42.22	128,800
1996	**Antespend**, 3, 117	C. W. Antley	Cara Rafaela, 3, 117	Hidden Lake, 3, 117	5	1:43.04	128,600
1995	**Serena's Song**, 3, 117	C. S. Nakatani	Urbane, 3, 117	Mari's Sheba, 3, 117	5	1:42.71	121,600
1994	**Lakeway**, 3, 117	K. J. Desormeaux	Dianes Halo, 3, 117	Flying in the Lane, 3, 117	6	1:41.66	122,800
1993	**Eliza**, 3, 117	P. A. Valenzuela	Stalcreek, 3, 117	Dance for Vanny, 3, 117	9	1:42.97	129,200
1992	**Golden Treat**, 3, 117	K. J. Desormeaux	Magical Maiden, 3, 117	Queens Court Queen, 3, 117	8	1:43.20	129,300
1991	**Lite Light**, 3, 117	C. S. Nakatani	Garden Gal, 3, 117	Ifyoucouldseemenow, 3, 117	5	1:42.50	122,100
1990	**Hail Atlantis**, 3, 117	G. L. Stevens	Bright Candles, 3, 117	Fit to Scout, 3, 117	6	1:43.00	122,800
1989	**Imaginary Lady**, 3, 117	G. L. Stevens	Some Romance, 3, 117	Kool Arrival, 3, 117	7	1:43.40	125,400
1988	**Winning Colors**, 3, 117	G. L. Stevens	Jeanne Jones, 3, 117	Goodbye Halo, 3, 117	4	1:42.00	89,900
1987	**Timely Assertion**, 3, 117	G. L. Stevens	Buryyourbelief, 3, 117	Very Subtle, 3, 117	7	1:43.60	95,100
1986	**Hidden Light**, 3, 117	W. Shoemaker	Twilight Ridge, 3, 117	An Empress, 3, 117	6	1:42.40	120,200
1985	**Fran's Valentine**, 3, 117	P. A. Valenzuela	Rascal Lass, 3, 117	Wising Up, 3, 117	7	1:42.40	122,100
1984	**Althea**, 3, 117	L. A. Pincay Jr.	Personable Lady, 3, 115	Life's Magic, 3, 115	5	1:43.60	118,500
1983	**Fabulous Notion**, 3, 115	D. Pierce	Capichi, 3, 115	O'Happy Day, 3, 115	6	1:43.60	93,900
1982	**Blush With Pride**, 3, 115	W. Shoemaker	Skillful Joy, 3, 115	Carry a Tune, 3, 115	10	1:45.80	100,400
1981	**Nell's Briquette**, 3, 115	W. Shoemaker	Bee a Scout, 3, 115	Ice Princess, 3, 115	8	1:42.80	82,550
1980	**Bold 'n Determined**, 3, 115	E. J. Delahoussaye	Street Ballet, 3, 115	Table Hands, 3, 115	7	**1:41.20**	67,100
1979	**Caline**, 3, 115	W. Shoemaker	Terlingua, 3, 115	It's in the Air, 3, 117	4	1:41.60	69,000
1978	**Grenzen**, 3, 115	D. G. McHargue	Equanimity, 3, 115	Mashteen, 3, 115	7	1:43.80	47,800
1977	**Sound of Summer**, 3, 115	F. Toro	Wavy Waves, 3, 115	Lady T. V., 3, 115	9	1:42.20	33,200
1976	**Girl in Love**, 3, 115	F. Toro	I'm a Charmer, 3, 115	Queen to Be, 3, 115	8	1:43.20	32,700
1975	**Sarsar**, 3, 115	W. Shoemaker	Double You Lou, 3, 115	Fascinating Girl, 3, 115	8	1:42.80	33,100
1974	**Miss Musket**, 3, 115	W. Shoemaker	Out to Lunch, 3, 115	Special Team, 3, 115	7	1:47.00	32,800
1973	**Belle Marie**, 3, 115	L. A. Pincay Jr.	Tallahto, 3, 115	Waltz Fan, 3, 115	6	1:41.80	31,800

The race and the track are both named in honor of Rancho Santa Anita, the name of the land when it was purchased by E. J. "Lucky" Baldwin. Formerly named for the community of Santa Susana, California. Santa Susana S. 1951-'85. Grade 2 1973-'78. Not held 1936, 1942-'44, 1955. 3 furlongs 1935. 6 furlongs 1937-'38, 1946. 7 furlongs 1939-'45, 1947-'51, 1956. 1 mile 1954, 1957. Two-year-olds 1935.

Santa Barbara Handicap

Grade 2 in 2005. Santa Anita Park, four-year-olds and up, fillies and mares, 1¹/₄ miles, turf. Held April 17, 2005, with a gross value of $200,000. First held in 1935. First graded in 1973. Stakes record 1:57.50 (1991 Bequest).

Year	Winner	Jockey	Second	Third	Strs	Time	1st Purse
2005	**Megahertz (GB)**, 6, 123	A. O. Solis	Nadeszhda (GB), 5, 114	Hoh Buzzard (Ire), 5, 117	7	1:59.76	$120,000
2004	**Megahertz (GB)**, 5, 121	A. O. Solis	Noches De Rosa (Chi), 6, 116	Mandela (Ger), 4, 111	5	2:00.71	120,000
2003	**Megahertz (GB)**, 4, 117	A. O. Solis	Trekking, 4, 115	Noches De Rosa (Chi), 5, 117	5	2:00.08	150,000
2002	**Astra**, 6, 121	K. J. Desormeaux	Golden Apples (Ire), 4, 121	Polaire (Ire), 6, 115	6	2:01.48	150,000
2001	**Astra**, 5, 118	K. J. Desormeaux	Beautiful Noise, 5, 116	Uncharted Haven (GB), 4, 116	7	2:01.33	150,000
2000	**Caffe Latte (Ire)**, 4, 116	C. S. Nakatani	Happyanunoit (NZ), 5, 121	Country Garden (GB), 5, 116	6	2:00.51	150,000
1999	**Tranquility Lake**, 4, 116	E. J. Delahoussaye	Virginie (Brz), 5, 118	Midnight Line, 4, 118	7	2:01.06	150,000
1998	**Fiji (GB)**, 4, 119	K. J. Desormeaux	Pomona (GB), 5, 115	Ecoute, 5, 114	5	2:00.35	150,000
1997	**Donna Viola (GB)**, 5, 120	G. L. Stevens	Fanjica (Ire), 5, 114	Windsharp, 6, 122	8	1:59.85	197,200
1996	**Auriette (Ire)**, 4, 116	K. J. Desormeaux	Angel in My Heart (Fr), 4, 119	Wandesta (GB), 5, 121	5	2:02.10	190,900
1995	**Wandesta (GB)**, 4, 118	C. S. Nakatani	Yearly Tour, 4, 116	Morgana, 4, 116	7	2:01.77	126,400
1994	**Possibly Perfect**, 4, 121	K. J. Desormeaux	Pracer, 4, 115	Waitryst (NZ), 5, 114	5	2:00.56	122,800
1993	**Exchange**, 5, 121	L. A. Pincay Jr.	Trishyde, 4, 120	Revasser, 4, 118	4	2:02.26	120,400
1992	**Kostroma (Ire)**, 6, 121	K. J. Desormeaux	Miss Alleged, 5, 124	Free At Last (GB), 5, 117	6	1:59.63	152,700
1991	**Bequest**, 5, 117	E. J. Delahoussaye	Noble and Nice, 5, 114	Annual Reunion, 4, 117	6	**1:57.50**	126,400
1990	**Brown Bess**, 8, 123	J. L. Kaenel	Royal Touch (Ire), 5, 121	Double Wedge, 5, 111	5	1:58.40	122,000
1989	**No Review**, 4, 116	E. J. Delahoussaye	Galunpe (Ire), 6, 117	Annoconnor, 5, 121	8	2:02.60	128,800
1988	**Pen Bal Lady (GB)**, 4, 119	E. J. Delahoussaye	Carotene, 5, 121	Galunpe (Ire), 5, 119	8	1:59.60	95,800

Year	Winner	Jockey	Second	Third	Strs	Time	1st Purse
1987	Reloy, 4, 120	W. Shoemaker	Northern Aspen, 5, 119	Ivor's Image, 4, 119	9	2:00.00	$97,600
1986	Mountain Bear (GB), 5, 119	C. J. McCarron	Estrapade, 6, 124	Royal Regatta (NZ), 7, 116	8	2:01.00	119,300
1985	Fact Finder, 6, 118	G. L. Stevens	Love Smitten, 4, 117	Salt Spring (Arg), 6, 114	6	2:01.60	116,600
1984	Comedy Act, 5, 116	C. J. McCarron	L'Attrayante (Fr), 4, 122	Lido Isle, 4, 114	10	2:00.40	121,200
1983	Avigaition, 4, 121	E. J. Delahoussaye	Happy Bride (Ire), 5, 120	Comedy Act, 4, 116	8	1:59.80	78,650
1982	Ack's Secret, 6, 122	L. A. Pincay Jr.	Landresse (Fr), 4, 116	Plenty O'Toole, 5, 114	8	2:00.60	78,550
1981	The Very One, 6, 122	J. Velasquez	Mairzy Doates, 5, 117	Ack's Secret, 5, 121	9	2:01.20	65,900
1980	Sisterhood, 5, 118	L. A. Pincay Jr.	Petron's Love, 5, 114	Relaxing, 4, 118	10	2:00.40	67,600
1979	Waya (Fr), 5, 131	A. T. Cordero Jr.	Petron's Love, 4, 117	Island Kiss, 4, 111	8	2:01.00	49,350
1978	Kittyluck, 5, 116	L. A. Pincay Jr.	Countess Fager, 4, 117	Sensational, 4, 120	9	2:00.60	40,400
1977	Desiree, 4, 110	V. Centeno	Swingtime, 5, 120	Charger's Star, 7, 113	6	2:02.60	38,100
1976	*Stravina, 5, 109	W. Shoemaker	Katonka, 4, 122	*Tizna, 7, 127	7	1:59.60	38,600
1975	Gay Style, 5, 125	W. Shoemaker	Move Abroad, 4, 113	*La Zanzara, 5, 117	6	2:01.40	31,600
1974	Tallahto, 4, 118	L. A. Pincay Jr.	*La Zanzara, 4, 120	*Tizna, 5, 122	8	1:59.20	39,600
1973	Susan's Girl, 4, 129	L. A. Pincay Jr.	Veiled Desire, 4, 110	Gray Mirage, 4, 112	5	2:03.60	37,600

Named for Santa Barbara, California, where an 1841 tax was the first on racing wagers. Grade 1 1973-'95. Not held 1939-'40, 1942-'45, 1947-'51, 1959-'61. 3 furlongs 1935-'41. 7 furlongs 1946-'52. 6 furlongs 1953-'54, 1958. 1¹⁄₁₆ miles 1955-'57. About 1¹⁄₄ miles 1968. Dirt 1935-'58, 1973, 1977, 1982. Originally scheduled on turf 1973. Two-year-olds 1937-'41. Three-year-olds 1952-'54. Three-year-olds and up 1955-'65. California-breds 1935-'54.

Santa Catalina Stakes

Grade 2 in 2005. Santa Anita Park, three-year-olds, 1¹⁄₁₆ miles, dirt. Held March 5, 2005, with a gross value of $200,000. First held in 1935. First graded in 1998. Stakes record 1:41.40 (1981 Minnesota Chief).

Year	Winner	Jockey	Second	Third	Strs	Time	1st Purse
2005	Declan's Moon, 3, 122	V. Espinoza	Going Wild, 3, 122	Spanish Chestnut, 3, 122	6	1:42.41	$120,000
2004	St Averil, 3, 113	T. Baze	Lucky Pulpit, 3, 115	Master David, 3, 113	9	1:41.62	90,000
2003	Domestic Dispute, 3, 113	D. R. Flores	Our Bobby V., 3, 113	Scrimshaw, 3, 115	8	1:42.20	90,000
2002	Labamta Babe, 3, 115	K. J. Desormeaux	Siphonic, 3, 123	Cottonwood Cowboy, 3, 115	6	1:42.50	90,000
2001	Millennium Wind, 3, 114	C. J. McCarron	Palmeiro, 3, 117	Denied, 3, 116	6	1:42.38	64,620
2000	The Deputy (Ire), 3, 115	C. J. McCarron	High Yield, 3, 117	Captain Steve, 3, 123	6	1:43.04	64,380
1999	General Challenge, 3, 117	G. L. Stevens	Buck Trout, 3, 120	Brilliantly, 3, 115	5	1:42.93	63,900
1998	Artax, 3, 114	C. J. McCarron	Souvenir Copy, 3, 120	Allen's Oop, 3, 117	6	1:42.32	64,320
1997	Hello (Ire), 3, 120	C. J. McCarron	Bagshot, 3, 116	Carmen's Baby, 3, 120	8	1:42.60	65,950
1996	Prince of Thieves, 3, 113	G. L. Stevens	Smithfield, 3, 116	Matty G, 3, 124	6	1:42.94	64,250
1995	Larry the Legend, 3, 117	K. J. Desormeaux	In Character (GB), 3, 115	Awesome Thought, 3, 119	5	1:42.93	45,975
1994	Wekiva Springs, 3, 121	K. J. Desormeaux	Gracious Ghost, 3, 116	Dream Trapp, 3, 117	5	1:41.94	45,900
1993	Art of Living, 3, 115	G. L. Stevens	Tossofthecoin, 3, 115	Glowing Crown, 3, 115	5	1:43.48	45,900
1992	Vying Victor, 3, 115	C. A. Black	Turbulent Kris, 3, 114	Al Sabin, 3, 117	11	1:44.33	51,000
1991	Mane Minister, 3, 114	D. R. Flores	Conveyor, 3, 114	Famed Devil, 3, 114	8	1:42.70	48,375
1990	Music Prospector, 3, 114	F. Olivares	Senegalaise, 3, 114	Tsu's Dawning, 3, 120	6	1:43.60	46,950
1989	Flying Continental, 3, 117	L. A. Pincay Jr.	Very Personably, 3, 114	Morlando, 3, 114	9	1:43.60	48,750
1988	Lively One, 3, 120	W. Shoemaker	Stalwars, 3, 114	Havanaffair, 3, 114	9	1:43.40	48,650
1987	Stylish Winner, 3, 114	G. L. Stevens	Prince Sassafras, 3, 117	Barb's Relic, 3, 116	7	1:43.80	38,250
1986	Ferdinand, 3, 114	W. Shoemaker	Variety Road, 3, 114	Grand Allegiance, 3, 117	8	1:43.00	38,750
1985	Floating Reserve, 3, 117	L. A. Pincay Jr.	Brecons Charge, 3, 117	Bolder Than Bold, 3, 114	11	1:42.60	40,450
1984	Tights, 3, 120	R. Q. Meza	Prince True, 3, 117	Gate Dancer, 3, 120	10	1:43.60	40,150
1983	Fast Passage, 3, 116	E. J. Delahoussaye	Hyperborean, 3, 114	My Habitony, 3, 114	8	1:42.60	38,900
1982	Water Bank, 3, 115	D. G. McHargue	Bargain Balcony, 3, 117	Crystal Star, 3, 115	8	1:42.40	38,850
1981	‡Stancharry, 3, 117	L. A. Pincay Jr.	Minnesota Chief, 3, 120	Litigator, 3, 120	8	**1:41.40**	31,900
1980	Super Moment, 3, 115	D. Pierce	Executive Counsel, 3, 117	Decent Davey, 3, 120	7	1:44.40	20,075
	Rumbo, 3, 117	W. Shoemaker	Idyll, 3, 114	Bold 'n Rulling, 3, 117	6	1:44.60	19,675
1979	Pole Position, 3, 120	C. J. McCarron	Grand Alliance, 3, 114	Shamgo, 3, 115	8	1:42.00	26,100
1978	Johnny's Image, 3, 115	S. Hawley	Kamehameha, 3, 115	Go Forth, 3, 115	8	1:44.00	26,350
1977	Text, 3, 118	D. Pierce	Cuzwrong, 3, 118	Nordic Prince, 3, 118	9	1:42.00	24,600
1976	An Act, 3, 118	L. A. Pincay Jr.	Life's Hope, 3, 118	First Return, 3, 118	8	1:42.00	20,800
1975	Kinalmeaky, 3, 118	W. Shoemaker	Rock of Ages, 3, 118	Looks Impressive, 3, 118	10	1:42.80	22,400
1974	Rube the Great, 3, 118	A. Santiago	Aloha Mood, 3, 118	L'Amour Rullah, 3, 118	10	1:43.00	18,700
1973	Sham, 3, 118	L. A. Pincay Jr.	Out of the East, 3, 118	Scantling, 3, 118	5	1:45.00	19,800

Named for Rancho Santa Catalina Island, which occupied the entire island of Santa Catalina off the California coast. Grade 3 1998. Santa Catalina H. 1935, 1941-'63, 1997. Santa Catalina California-bred Championship 1937-'39. Santa Catalina Nursery S. 1940. Not held 1936, 1942-'44. 1 mile 1935. 1¹⁄₈ miles 1939, 1947-'52, 1954-'63. 3 furlongs 1940. 7 furlongs 1970. Three-year-olds and up 1937-'38, 1941-'46, 1991. Two-year-olds 1940. Four-year-olds and up 1947-'63. Two divisions 1980. ‡Minnesota Chief finished first, DQ to second, 1981. Nonwinners of a race worth $12,500 to the winner 1973-'75. Nonwinners of a race worth $25,000 to the winner 1990, 1992.

Santa Margarita Invitational Handicap

Grade 1 in 2005. Santa Anita Park, four-year-olds and up, fillies and mares, 1¹⁄₈ miles, dirt. Held March 12, 2005, with a gross value of $300,000. First held in 1935. First graded in 1973. Stakes record 1:47 (1986 Lady's Secret; 1954 Cerise Reine).

Year	Winner	Jockey	Second	Third	Strs	Time	1st Purse
2005	Tarlow, 4, 117	P. A. Valenzuela	Dream of Summer, 6, 116	Miss Loren (Arg), 7, 118	9	1:49.41	$180,000

Year	Winner	Jockey	Second	Third	Strs	Time	1st Purse
2004	Adoration, 5, 118	M. E. Smith	Star Parade (Arg), 5, 115	Bare Necessities, 5, 118	5	1:48.85	$180,000
2003	Starrer, 5, 121	P. A. Valenzuela	Sightseek, 4, 116	Bella Bellucci, 4, 116	5	1:48.20	180,000
2002	Azeri, 4, 115	M. E. Smith	Spain, 5, 118	Printemps (Chi), 5, 116	7	1:49.01	180,000
2001	Lazy Slusan, 6, 116	D. R. Flores	Spain, 4, 122	Critikola (Arg), 6, 116	7	1:48.59	180,000
2000	Riboletta (Brz), 5, 115	C. S. Nakatani	Bordelaise (Arg), 5, 114	Snowberg, 5, 114	5	1:50.40	180,000
1999	Manistique, 4, 122	G. L. Stevens	Magical Allure, 4, 118	India Divina (Chi), 5, 116	4	1:48.31	180,000
1998	Toda Una Dama (Arg), 5, 114	G. F. Almeida	Exotic Wood, 6, 123	Praviana (Chi), 4, 114	10	1:48.87	180,000
1997	Jewel Princess, 5, 125	C. S. Nakatani	Top Rung, 6, 116	Hidden Lake, 4, 114	6	1:49.30	180,000
1996	Twice the Vice, 5, 117	C. J. McCarron	Sleep Easy, 4, 115	Jewel Princess, 4, 119	8	1:49.53	180,000
1995	Queens Court Queen, 6, 120	C. S. Nakatani	Paseana (Arg), 8, 123	Klassy Kim, 4, 116	5	1:48.81	180,000
1994	Paseana (Arg), 7, 123	C. J. McCarron	Kalita Melody (GB), 6, 117	Stalcreek, 4, 119	9	1:49.12	180,000
1993	Southern Truce, 5, 115	C. S. Nakatani	Paseana (Arg), 6, 125	Guiza, 6, 114	9	1:49.46	180,000
1992	Paseana (Arg), 5, 122	C. J. McCarron	Laramie Moon (Arg), 5, 116	Colour Chart, 5, 118	5	1:47.48	180,000
1991	Little Brianne, 6, 119	J. A. Garcia	Bayakoa (Arg), 7, 126	A Wild Ride, 4, 119	7	1:48.50	180,000
1990	Bayakoa (Arg), 6, 127	C. J. McCarron	Gorgeous, 4, 125	Luthier's Launch, 4, 113	4	1:48.40	180,000
1989	Bayakoa (Arg), 5, 118	L. A. Pincay Jr.	Goodbye Halo, 4, 125	No Review, 4, 117	7	1:48.40	180,000
1988	Flying Julia, 5, 114	F. Olivares	Hollywood Glitter, 4, 118	Clabber Girl, 5, 118	10	1:50.40	180,000
1987	North Sider, 5, 117	A. T. Cordero Jr.	Winter Treasure, 4, 115	Frau Altiva (Arg), 5, 117	12	1:48.80	180,000
1986	Lady's Secret, 4, 125	J. Velasquez	Johnica, 5, 120	Dontstop Themusic, 6, 122	9	1:47.00	180,000
1985	Lovlier Linda, 5, 119	C. J. McCarron	Mitterand, 4, 123	Percipient, 4, 116	8	1:48.00	180,000
1984	Adored, 4, 114	F. Toro	High Haven, 5, 118	Weekend Surprise, 4, 114	11	1:48.60	150,000
1983	Marimbula (Chi), 5, 119	S. Hawley	Avigaition, 4, 120	Sintrillium, 5, 114	11	1:48.20	150,000
1982	Ack's Secret, 6, 118	L. A. Pincay Jr.	Track Robbery, 6, 123	Past Forgetting, 4, 122	10	1:47.60	150,000
1981	Princess Karenda, 4, 118	L. A. Pincay Jr.	Glorious Song, 5, 130	Ack's Secret, 5, 122	10	1:47.20	120,000
1980	Glorious Song, 4, 120	C. J. McCarron	The Very One, 5, 116	Kankam (Arg), 5, 125	11	1:48.40	82,500
1979	Sanedtki (Ire), 5, 124	W. Shoemaker	‡Surera (Arg), 6, 115	Ida Delia, 5, 117	11	1:47.80	75,000
1978	Taisez Vous, 4, 120	D. Pierce	Sensational, 4, 118	*Merry Lady III, 6, 114	11	1:49.00	60,000
1977	*Lucie Manet, 4, 119	D. G. McHargue	*Bastonera II, 6, 126	Hope of Glory, 5, 114	9	1:48.40	60,000
1976	Fascinating Girl, 4, 115	F. Toro	Summertime Promise, 4, 114	Charger's Star, 6, 114	9	1:49.40	60,000
1975	*Tizna, 6, 120	D. Pierce	Susan's Girl, 6, 123	Gay Style, 5, 125	12	1:48.60	60,000
1974	*Tizna, 5, 117	F. Toro	Penny Flight, 4, 113	Tallahto, 4, 119	12	1:50.80	60,000
1973	Susan's Girl, 4, 127	L. A. Pincay Jr.	Convenience, 5, 123	Minstrel Miss, 6, 115	8	1:47.80	60,000

Named for the 1841 California land grant Rancho Santa Margarita y Las Flores. Santa Margarita H. 1935-'67. Not held 1942-'44. 7 furlongs 1935-'36. 6 furlongs 1937. 1¹/₁₆ miles 1938-'48, 1953-'54. Three-year-olds and up 1935-'40, 1945-'60. Both sexes 1935-'37. ‡Queen Yasna finished second, DQ to seventh, 1979.

Santa Maria Handicap

Grade 1 in 2005. Santa Anita Park, four-year-olds and up, fillies and mares, 1¹/₁₆ miles, dirt. Held February 13, 2005, with a gross value of $250,000. First held in 1934. First graded in 1973. Stakes record 1:40.95 (1998 Exotic Wood).

Year	Winner	Jockey	Second	Third	Strs	Time	1st Purse
2005	Miss Loren (Arg), 7, 117	J. Valdivia Jr.	Good Student (Arg), 5, 114	Hollywood Story, 4, 117	8	1:42.42	$150,000
2004	Star Parade (Arg), 5, 114	V. Espinoza	Bare Necessities, 5, 118	La Tour (Chi), 5, 115	6	1:43.87	150,000
2003	Starrer, 5, 119	P. A. Valenzuela	You, 4, 118	Rhiana, 6, 112	6	1:42.75	120,000
2002	Favorite Funtime, 5, 116	G. L. Stevens	Verruma (Brz), 6, 114	Printemps (Chi), 5, 116	7	1:44.15	120,000
2001	Lovellon (Arg), 5, 116	G. L. Stevens	Feverish, 6, 119	Critikola (Arg), 6, 115	5	1:43.37	120,000
2000	Manistique, 5, 125	C. S. Nakatani	Snowberg, 5, 114	Gourmet Girl, 5, 116	8	1:42.60	120,000
1999	India Divina (Chi), 5, 114	G. K. Gomez	Victory Stripes (Arg), 5, 115	Belle's Flag, 6, 117	5	1:42.71	120,000
1998	Exotic Wood, 6, 121	C. J. McCarron	Toda Una Dama (Arg), 5, 115	Tuxedo Junction, 5, 115	5	1:40.95	120,000
1997	Jewel Princess, 5, 123	C. S. Nakatani	Cat's Cradle, 5, 118	Top Rung, 6, 117	7	1:41.72	97,900
1996	Serena's Song, 4, 124	G. L. Stevens	Twice the Vice, 5, 118	Real Connection, 5, 114	5	1:42.21	95,800
1995	Queens Court Queen, 6, 118	C. S. Nakatani	Paseana (Arg), 8, 123	Key Phrase, 4, 117	5	1:41.61	89,300
1994	Supah Gem, 4, 116	C. S. Nakatani	Paseana (Arg), 7, 124	Alysbelle, 5, 116	7	1:41.83	90,700
1993	Race the Wild Wind, 4, 117	K. J. Desormeaux	Paseana (Arg), 6, 126	Southern Truce, 5, 116	6	1:41.27	90,500
1992	Paseana (Arg), 5, 120	C. J. McCarron	Colour Chart, 5, 118	Campagnarde (Arg), 5, 117	5	1:41.94	89,100
1991	Little Brianne, 6, 117	J. A. Garcia	Luna Elegante (Arg), 5, 114	Somethingumm, 4, 114	4	1:41.70	89,700
1990	Bayakoa (Arg), 6, 126	C. J. McCarron	Nikishka, 5, 117	Carita Tostada (Chi), 6, 112	4	1:43.00	90,200
1989	Miss Brio (Chi), 5, 119	E. J. Delahoussaye	Bayakoa (Arg), 5, 118	Annoconnor, 5, 122	7	1:41.00	79,000
1988	Mausie (Arg), 6, 114	G. L. Stevens	Miss Alto, 5, 118	Novel Sprite, 5, 115	7	1:43.60	63,800
1987	Fran's Valentine, 5, 121	P. A. Valenzuela	North Sider, 5, 118	Infinidad (Chi), 5, 113	4	1:42.60	91,700
1986	Love Smitten, 5, 120	C. J. McCarron	Johnica, 5, 121	North Sider, 4, 118	9	1:44.60	65,600
1985	Adored, 5, 124	L. A. Pincay Jr.	Dontstop Themusic, 5, 121	Lovlier Linda, 5, 122	5	1:42.40	88,800
1984	Marisma (Chi), 6, 117	L. A. Pincay Jr.	Brindy Brindy, 4, 114	Sierva, 6, 118	7	1:44.20	69,850
	High Haven, 5, 116	R. Sibille	Castilla, 5, 122	Avigaition, 5, 120	8	1:42.40	50,600
1983	Star Pastures (GB), 5, 119	W. Shoemaker	Sintrillium, 5, 116	Viga (Chi), 6, 112	7	1:42.60	49,650
	Sangue (Ire), 5, 124	L. A. Pincay Jr.	Cat Girl, 5, 115	Happy Bride (Ire), 5, 116	8	1:41.00	50,650
1982	Targa, 5, 114	F. Olivares	Jameela, 6, 114	Track Robbery, 6, 114	8	1:42.60	65,100
1981	Glorious Song, 5, 127	C. J. McCarron	Track Robbery, 5, 117	Miss Huntington, 4, 113	4	1:43.20	45,450
1980	Kankam (Arg), 5, 123	E. J. Delahoussaye	Flaming Leaves, 5, 123	Miss Magnetic, 5, 117	5	1:41.80	47,400
1979	Grenzen, 4, 124	L. A. Pincay Jr.	Ida Delia, 5, 118	Drama Critic, 5, 122	6	1:47.20	37,650
1978	Swingtime, 6, 122	F. Toro	Winter Solstice, 6, 124	Granja Sueno, 5, 113	6	1:41.40	37,500
1977	Hail Hilarious, 4, 122	D. Pierce	Swingtime, 5, 120	*Bastonera II, 6, 126	10	1:42.00	36,050
1976	Gay Style, 6, 127	D. Pierce	Raise Your Skirts, 4, 120	*Tizna, 7, 127	9	1:41.40	35,100

1975 **Gay Style**, 5, 122	W. Shoemaker	*Tizna, 6, 120	Susan's Girl, 6, 124	8	1:42.00	$34,650
1974 **Convenience**, 6, 121	L. A. Pincay Jr.	*Tizna, 5, 117	Tallahto, 4, 119	8	1:42.80	34,750
1973 **Susan's Girl**, 4, 125	L. A. Pincay Jr.	Convenience, 5, 123	Hill Circus, 5, 119	6	1:42.00	32,900

Named for the city of Santa Maria, California, located in Santa Barbara County. Grade 2 1973-'89. Santa Maria S. 1934-'47. Not held 1937, 1942-'45, 1948-'51. 6 furlongs 1934-'60. 3 furlongs 1941. 1 mile 1946-'53. 7 furlongs 1954-'56. Two-year-olds and up 1934-'35. Three-year-olds 1936-'40, 1946-'47. Two-year-olds 1941. Three-year-olds and up 1952-'59. Fillies 1936-'47. Two divisions 1983-'84. California-breds 1941.

Santa Monica Handicap

Grade 1 in 2005. Santa Anita Park, four-year-olds and up, fillies and mares, 7 furlongs, dirt. Held January 30, 2005, with a gross value of $250,000. First held in 1957. First graded in 1973. Stakes record 1:20.60 (1982 Past Forgetting).

Year	Winner	Jockey	Second	Third	Strs	Time	1st Purse
2005	**Salt Champ (Arg)**, 5, 116	G. L. Stevens	Island Fashion, 5, 120	Resplendency, 4, 114	9	1:22.14	$150,000
2004	**Island Fashion**, 4, 120	K. J. Desormeaux	Buffythecenterfold, 4, 114	Got Koko, 5, 119	6	1:21.37	150,000
2003	**Affluent**, 5, 119	A. O. Solis	Sightseek, 4, 115	Secret of Mecca, 5, 110	7	1:22.17	120,000
2002	**Kalookan Queen**, 6, 119	A. O. Solis	Leading Light, 7, 115	Spain, 5, 120	5	1:22.37	120,000
2001	**Nany's Sweep**, 5, 117	K. J. Desormeaux	Serenita (Arg), 4, 115	Surfside, 4, 121	7	1:22.50	120,000
2000	**Honest Lady**, 4, 114	C. S. Nakatani	Kalookan Queen, 4, 116	Enjoy the Moment, 5, 118	9	1:21.45	132,840
1999	**Stop Traffic**, 6, 120	C. A. Black	Belle's Flag, 6, 118	Closed Escrow, 6, 116	8	1:22.17	120,000
1998	**Exotic Wood**, 6, 121	C. J. McCarron	Madame Pandit, 5, 119	Advancing Star, 5, 121	8	1:21.07	120,000
1997	**Toga Toga Toga**, 5, 114	J. A. Garcia	Ski Dancer, 5, 117	Grab the Prize, 5, 116	6	1:23.27	96,750
1996	**Serena's Song**, 4, 123	G. L. Stevens	Exotic Wood, 4, 118	Klassy Kim, 5, 116	6	1:21.56	96,800
1995	**Key Phrase**, 4, 116	C. W. Antley	Flying in the Lane, 4, 114	Desert Stormer, 5, 117	9	1:22.82	93,100
1994	**Southern Truce**, 6, 116	G. L. Stevens	Arches of Gold, 5, 119	Mamselle Bebette, 4, 115	9	1:21.44	93,100
1993	**Freedom Cry**, 5, 114	A. O. Solis	Devil's Orchid, 6, 119	Mama Simba, 6, 114	7	1:21.78	91,200
1992	**Laramie Moon (Arg)**, 5, 116	E. J. Delahoussaye	D'Or Ruckus, 4, 114	Ifyoucouldseemenow, 4, 118	10	1:22.66	94,700
1991	**Devil's Orchid**, 4, 116	R. A. Baze	‡Stormy But Valid, 5, 121	Classic Value, 5, 118	7	1:21.90	90,800
1990	**Stormy But Valid**, 4, 119	G. L. Stevens	Survive, 6, 118	Hot Novel, 4, 117	5	1:22.40	61,300
1989	**Miss Brio (Chi)**, 5, 117	E. J. Delahoussaye	Valdemosa (Arg), 5, 116	Josette, 4, 115	8	1:21.60	64,800
1988	**Pine Tree Lane**, 6, 121	G. L. Stevens	Fairly Old, 5, 115	Le l'Argent, 6, 120	6	1:23.00	60,000
1987	**Pine Tree Lane**, 5, 125	A. T. Cordero Jr.	Balladry, 5, 116	Her Royalty, 6, 119	6	1:21.80	58,140
1986	**Her Royalty**, 5, 120	C. J. McCarron	North Sider, 4, 119	Take My Picture, 4, 115	8	1:21.60	51,300
1985	**Lovlier Linda**, 5, 123	W. Shoemaker	Dontstop Themusic, 5, 123	Foggy Nation, 5, 119	6	1:22.80	48,900
1984	**Bara Lass**, 5, 124	W. A. Guerra	Holiday Dancer, 4, 117	Bally Knockan, 5, 113	9	1:22.00	52,250
1983	**Past Forgetting**, 5, 123	C. J. McCarron	‡Sierva (Arg), 5, 119	Bara Lass, 4, 115	10	1:23.40	49,850
1982	**Past Forgetting**, 4, 122	W. Shoemaker	Nell's Briquette, 4, 118	In True Form, 4, 117	9	1:20.60	49,250
1981	**Parsley**, 5, 116	A. T. Cordero Jr.	Ack's Secret, 4, 125	Splendid Girl, 5, 118	7	1:23.40	40,050
1980	**Flack Flack**, 5, 117	W. Shoemaker	Shine High, 4, 115	Flaming Leaves, 5, 123	6	1:23.80	39,100
1979	**Grenzen**, 4, 122	L. A. Pincay Jr.	Dottie's Doll, 6, 116	Bidding Bold, 4, 116	4	1:21.60	40,600
1978	**Winter Solstice**, 6, 123	D. G. McHargue	Little Happiness, 4, 115	Splendid Size, 4, 117	7	1:21.20	27,200
1977	**Hail Hilarious**, 4, 119	D. Pierce	*Bastonera II, 6, 125	Modus Vivendi, 6, 121	8	1:22.60	28,150
1976	**Gay Style**, 6, 125	D. Pierce	Raise Your Skirts, 4, 123	*Tizna, 7, 129	6	1:22.00	26,650
1975	**Sister Fleet**, 5, 117	W. Shoemaker	Susan's Girl, 5, 125	Modus Vivendi, 4, 123	13	1:21.40	31,250
1974	***Tizna**, 5, 116	F. Toro	Susan's Girl, 5, 127	Impressive Style, 5, 118	7	1:24.00	28,050
1973	**Chou Croute**, 5, 128	J. L. Rotz	Generous Portion, 5, 114	Minstrel Miss, 6, 115	7	1:23.60	27,800

Named for the city of Santa Monica, California. Grade 2 1973-'83, 1988-'89. Grade 3 1984-'87. Not held 1970. Three-year-olds and up 1957-'59. ‡Marimbula (Chi) finished second, DQ to sixth, 1983. ‡Classic Value finished second, DQ to third, 1991.

Santa Ynez Stakes

Grade 2 in 2005. Santa Anita Park, three-year-olds, fillies, 7 furlongs, dirt. Held January 17, 2005, with a gross value of $150,000. First held in 1952. First graded in 1973. Stakes record 1:21.11 (2004 Yearly Report).

Year	Winner	Jockey	Second	Third	Strs	Time	1st Purse
2005	**Sharp Lisa**, 3, 114	T. Baze	No Bull Baby, 3, 121	Hot Attraction, 3, 114	7	1:23.10	$90,000
2004	**Yearly Report**, 3, 114	J. D. Bailey	House of Fortune, 3, 121	Papa to Kinzie, 3, 115	8	**1:21.11**	90,000
2003	**Elloluv**, 3, 121	P. A. Valenzuela	Watching You, 3, 116	Himalayan, 3, 116	5	1:23.03	90,000
2002	**Dancing (GB)**, 3, 116	G. L. Stevens	Respectful, 3, 116	Lady George, 3, 115	8	1:23.07	90,000
2001	**Golden Ballet**, 3, 123	C. J. McCarron	Affluent, 3, 114	Warren's Whistle, 3, 116	9	1:22.30	90,000
2000	**Penny Blues**, 3, 118	E. J. Delahoussaye	Classic Olympio, 3, 121	Mean Imogene, 3, 117	5	1:23.38	63,600
1999	**Honest Lady**, 3, 115	K. J. Desormeaux	Rayelle, 3, 118	Controlled, 3, 123	4	1:21.67	63,240
1998	**Nijinsky's Passion**, 3, 121	C. A. Black	Well Chosen, 3, 115	Vivid Angel, 3, 123	7	1:23.15	64,980
1997	**Queen of Money**, 3, 116	D. R. Flores	Goodnight Irene, 3, 116	High Heeled Hope, 3, 121	6	1:22.55	65,650
1996	**Raw Gold**, 3, 121	C. W. Antley	Pareja, 3, 121	Hidden Lake, 3, 116	6	1:22.66	64,550
1995	**Serena's Song**, 3, 123	C. S. Nakatani	Cat's Cradle, 3, 121	Call Now, 3, 113	5	1:21.45	59,800
1994	**Tricky Code**, 3, 121	C. S. Nakatani	Fancy 'n Fabulous, 3, 114	Sophisticatedcielo, 3, 116	5	1:22.16	59,575
1993	**Fit to Lead**, 3, 116	C. S. Nakatani	Nijivision, 3, 114	Booklore, 3, 115	8	1:22.55	62,500
1992	**Looie Capote**, 3, 114	K. J. Desormeaux	Icy Eyes, 3, 118	Soviet Sojourn, 3, 121	7	1:23.42	61,450
1991	**Brazen**, 3, 121	C. J. McCarron	Fowda, 3, 116	Ifyoucouldseemenow, 3, 121	5	1:23.70	46,050
1990	**Fit to Scout**, 3, 118	C. J. McCarron	Bright Candles, 3, 114	Heaven for Bid, 3, 116	6	1:23.80	60,625
1989	**Hot Novel**, 3, 123	E. J. Delahoussaye	Fantastic Look, 3, 114	Agotaras, 3, 121	6	1:22.80	46,950
1988	**Goodbye Halo**, 3, 123	J. Velasquez	Bolchina, 3, 116	Floral Magic, 3, 114	8	1:23.40	47,900
1987	**Very Subtle**, 3, 122	W. Shoemaker	Chic Shirine, 3, 119	Young Flyer, 3, 122	5	1:22.60	46,200

Year	Winner	Jockey	Second	Third	Strs	Time	1st Purse
1986	Sari's Heroine, 3, 119	A. O. Solis	An Empress, 3, 117	Life At the Top, 3, 115	8	1:23.40	$52,000
1985	Wising Up, 3, 119	E. J. Delahoussaye	Rascal Lass, 3, 122	Reigning Countess, 3, 119	9	1:23.40	52,700
1984	Gene's Lady, 3, 117	L. A. Pincay Jr.	Kennedy Express, 3, 115	Natural Summit, 3, 117	9	1:23.80	41,600
	Boo La Boo, 3, 122	L. A. Pincay Jr.	Personable Lady, 3, 122	Costly Array, 3, 117	7	1:23.20	39,900
1983	A Lucky Sign, 3, 121	C. J. McCarron	Sophisticated Girl, 3, 116	Fabulous Notion, 3, 124	8	1:23.40	49,050
1982	Flying Partner, 3, 114	R. Sibille	Skillful Joy, 3, 124	Carry a Tune, 3, 114	8	1:23.40	49,300
1981	Past Forgetting, 3, 119	S. Hawley	Rosie Doon, 3, 119	Nell's Briquette, 3, 121	11	1:22.40	41,800
1980	Table Hands, 3, 117	W. Shoemaker	Street Ballet, 3, 119	Hazel R., 3, 119	7	1:22.40	38,700
1979	Terlingua, 3, 121	L. A. Pincay Jr.	Caline, 3, 119	It's in the Air, 3, 121	5	1:21.20	37,900
1978	Grenzen, 3, 119	D. G. McHargue	Extravagant, 3, 121	Happy Kin, 3, 114	9	1:22.20	27,600
1977	Wavy Waves, 3, 121	L. A. Pincay Jr.	Don's Music, 3, 119	Any Time Girl, 3, 121	11	1:22.80	29,550
1976	Daisy Do, 3, 114	S. Hawley	Girl in Love, 3, 115	Windy Welcome, 3, 117	6	1:22.40	20,300
1975	Raise Your Skirts, 3, 117	W. Mahorney	Fascinating Girl, 3, 115	Miss Francesca, 3, 117	13	1:22.40	23,350
1974	Modus Vivendi, 3, 119	D. Pierce	Donna Chere, 3, 114	Special Team, 3, 121	9	1:22.40	28,500
1973	Tallahto, 3, 117	J. E. Tejeira	Waltz Fan, 3, 117	Windy's Daughter, 3, 121	5	1:21.40	25,800

Named for the city of Santa Ynez, California, which takes its name from an 1804 mission. Grade 3 1975-'80, 1984-'98. Santa Ynez Breeders' Cup S. 1990-'95. Not held 1953. 6 furlongs 1952, 1956-'57. 6½ furlongs 1958-'66. Two-year-olds 1952 (December). Two divisions 1984.

Santa Ysabel Stakes

Grade 3 in 2005. Santa Anita Park, three-year-olds, fillies, 1¹/₁₆ miles, dirt. Held January 16, 2005, with a gross value of $108,000. First held in 1968. First graded in 1998. Stakes record 1:41.34 (1997 Sharp Cat).

Year	Winner	Jockey	Second	Third	Strs	Time	1st Purse
2005	Sweet Catomine, 3, 124	D. R. Flores	Pussycat Doll, 3, 115	On London Time, 3, 115	5	1:43.77	$64,800
2004	A. P. Adventure, 3, 115	A. O. Solis	Salty Romance, 3, 120	Wildwood Flower, 3, 115	6	1:44.27	64,080
2003	Atlantic Ocean, 3, 120	D. R. Flores	Sea Jewel, 3, 115	Summer Wind Dancer, 3, 120	6	1:43.25	66,540
2002	Bella Bella Bella, 3, 115	C. J. McCarron	Tamarack Bay, 3, 116	No Turbulence, 3, 116	4	1:44.14	64,550
2001	Collect Call, 3, 115	A. O. Solis	Irguns Angel, 3, 115	Eminent, 3, 115	8	1:44.69	65,580
2000	Surfside, 3, 123	P. Day	Rings a Chime, 3, 115	She's Classy, 3, 118	4	1:43.53	62,880
1999	Holywood Picture, 3, 115	O. Vergara	Exbourne Free, 3, 115	Gleefully, 3, 116	7	1:43.48	64,860
1998	‡Nonies Dancer Ali, 3, 114	G. K. Gomez	Mamaison Miss, 3, 116	Continental Lea, 3, 113	5	1:44.14	63,660
1997	Sharp Cat, 3, 120	C. S. Nakatani	Clever Pilot, 3, 115	Guthrie, 3, 116	6	1:41.34	64,300
1996	Antespend, 3, 120	C. W. Antley	Dancing Prism, 3, 114	Rumpipumpy (GB), 3, 116	6	1:43.87	64,950
1995	Ski Dancer, 3, 115	K. J. Desormeaux	Dixie Pearl, 3, 117	Wilga, 3, 115	5	1:44.24	45,750
1994	Princess Mitterand, 3, 119	C. J. McCarron	Dianes Halo, 3, 115	Jacodra's Devil, 3, 115	4	1:43.25	44,925
1993	Likeable Style, 3, 115	G. L. Stevens	Fit to Lead, 3, 117	Amandari, 3, 117	5	1:44.74	45,900
1992	Crownette, 3, 116	P. A. Valenzuela	Golden Treat, 3, 114	Looie Capote, 3, 114	6	1:44.33	48,975
1991	Nice Assay, 3, 117	L. A. Pincay Jr.	Assombrie, 3, 117	Ms. Aerosmith, 3, 115	9	1:43.70	49,275
1990	Bright Candles, 3, 114	G. L. Stevens	Heaven for Bid, 3, 117	Annual Reunion, 3, 117	7	1:45.60	47,175
1989	Gorgeous, 3, 116	E. J. Delahoussaye	My Glamorous One, 3, 117	April Mon, 3, 114	6	1:42.40	46,450
1988	Jeanne Jones, 3, 114	W. Shoemaker	Pattern Step, 3, 120	Affordable Price, 3, 116	8	1:43.60	48,100
1987	Perchance to Dream, 3, 117	R. Sibille	Buryyourbelief, 3, 115	My Turbulent Beau, 3, 114	7	1:43.40	37,900
1986	Trim Colony, 3, 117	G. L. Stevens	Fashion Book, 3, 115	Top Corsage, 3, 117	5	1:44.80	36,900
1985	Savannah Dancer, 3, 120	W. Shoemaker	Pink Sapphire, 3, 115	Ed's Bold Lady (Ire), 3, 117	6	1:44.20	37,350
1984	Sales Bulletin, 3, 115	C. J. McCarron	Spring Loose, 3, 115	Agitated Miss, 3, 115	9	1:44.00	39,300
1983	Ski Goggle, 3, 115	C. J. McCarron	Sophisticated Girl, 3, 116	Saucy Bobbie, 3, 115	7	1:41.60	38,100
1982	Avigaition, 3, 115	E. J. Delahoussaye	Blush With Pride, 3, 117	Carry a Tune, 3, 114	10	1:42.40	39,750
1981	Lovely Robbery, 3, 117	L. A. Pincay Jr.	Bee a Scout, 3, 117	Ice Princess, 3, 117	10	1:44.20	33,350
1980	Back At Two, 3, 117	F. Toro	Thundertee, 3, 117	Regretfully, 3, 114	4	1:45.20	24,250
1979	Maytide, 3, 114	A. T. Cordero Jr.	Smile On Me, 3, 117	Smaller Bicker, 3, 114	7	1:44.00	19,875
	Top Soil, 3, 115	D. Pierce	Reporting Act, 3, 114	To the Top, 3, 114	9	1:44.00	20,675
1978	Palmistry, 3, 115	W. Shoemaker	Equanimity, 3, 115	My Buck, 3, 115	8	1:44.40	26,050
1977	Geothermal, 3, 116	M. Castaneda	*Glenaris, 3, 116	Sound of Summer, 3, 116	8	1:43.00	23,550
1976	Flunsa, 3, 116	S. Hawley	Girl in Love, 3, 116	Go March, 3, 116	7	1:43.80	20,100
1975	Double You Lou, 3, 116	S. Hawley	Fascinating Girl, 3, 116	Miss Francesca, 3, 116	10	1:44.80	21,300
1974	Miss Musket, 3, 116	W. Shoemaker	Acknowledge Me, 3, 116	Lucky Spell, 3, 116	9	1:41.80	17,800
1973	Belle Marie, 3, 116	L. A. Pincay Jr.	Wind Gap, 3, 116	Flo's Pleasure, 3, 116	7	1:45.40	20,800

Named for two California land grants called Rancho Santa Ysabel, home of the Santa Ysabel mission. 7 furlongs 1970. Two divisions 1979. ‡Love Lock finished first, DQ to fifth for a positive drug test, 1998. Nonwinners of a race worth $12,500 to the winner 1973. Nonwinners of a race worth $25,000 to the winner 1992.

San Vicente Stakes

Grade 2 in 2005. Santa Anita Park, three-year-olds, 7 furlongs, dirt. Held February 13, 2005, with a gross value of $147,000. First held in 1935. First graded in 1973. Stakes record 1:21 (1973 Ancient Title).

Year	Winner	Jockey	Second	Third	Strs	Time	1st Purse
2005	Fusaichi Rock Star, 3, 116	D. R. Flores	Don't Get Mad, 3, 115	Kirkendahl, 3, 116	4	1:22.59	$90,000
2004	Imperialism, 3, 116	V. Espinoza	Hosco, 3, 120	Consecrate, 3, 116	6	1:22.34	90,000
2003	Kafwain, 3, 123	V. Espinoza	Sum Trick, 3, 120	Southern Image, 3, 117	5	1:21.12	90,000
2002	Came Home, 3, 123	C. J. McCarron	Jack's Silver, 3, 116	Werblin, 3, 116	6	1:21.92	90,000

Year	Winner	Jockey	Second	Third	Strs	Time	1st Purse
2001	Early Flyer, 3, 114	C. J. McCarron	Lasersport, 3, 120	D'wildcat, 3, 117	5	1:21.51	$90,000
2000	Archer City Slew, 3, 117	K. J. Desormeaux	Joopy Doopy, 3, 116	Gibson County, 3, 120	6	1:22.18	90,000
1999	Exploit, 3, 123	C. J. McCarron	Aristotle, 3, 116	Yes It's True, 3, 123	3	1:22.00	90,000
1998	Sea of Secrets, 3, 116	K. J. Desormeaux	Late Edition, 3, 115	Pleasant Drive, 3, 116	5	1:22.00	64,080
1997	Silver Charm, 3, 120	C. J. McCarron	Free House, 3, 120	Funontherun, 3, 114	9	1:21.07	66,400
1996	Afleetaffair, 3, 116	C. S. Nakatani	Honour and Glory, 3, 123	Ready to Order, 3, 120	5	1:22.28	63,850
1995	Afternoon Deelites, 3, 120	K. J. Desormeaux	Mr Purple, 3, 116	Fandarel Dancer, 3, 117	5	1:21.35	59,725
1994	Fly'n J. Bryan, 3, 114	C. A. Black	Gracious Ghost, 3, 114	Cois Na Tine (Ire), 3, 116	6	1:22.32	60,700
1993	Yappy, 3, 116	P. A. Valenzuela	Denmars Dream, 3, 118	Devoted Brass, 3, 116	9	1:22.33	63,100
1992	Mineral Wells, 3, 116	P. A. Valenzuela	Star of the Crop, 3, 116	Prince Wild, 3, 118	7	1:21.28	61,450
1991	Olympio, 3, 120	E. J. Delahoussaye	Dinard, 3, 118	Scan, 3, 123	6	1:21.50	61,075
1990	Mister Frisky, 3, 118	G. L. Stevens	Tarascon, 3, 120	Top Cash, 3, 120	6	1:22.60	47,325
1989	Gum, 3, 117	L. A. Pincay Jr.	Yes I'm Blue, 3, 120	Roman Avie, 3, 114	7	1:22.40	47,600
1988	Mi Preferido, 3, 120	A. O. Solis	No Commitment, 3, 120	Success Express, 3, 123	5	1:22.60	45,900
1987	Stylish Winner, 3, 119	G. L. Stevens	Prince Sassafras, 3, 116	Mount Laguna, 3, 116	6	1:23.80	46,750
1986	Grand Allegiance, 3, 114	R. Hernandez	Royal Treasure, 3, 114	Dancing Pirate, 3, 119	7	1:23.20	51,050
1985	The Rogers Four, 3, 124	C. J. McCarron	Teddy Naturally, 3, 119	Michadilla, 3, 122	5	1:22.80	49,400
1984	Fortunate Prospect, 3, 119	D. Pierce	Precisionist, 3, 122	Tights, 3, 117	5	1:22.80	49,700
1983	Shecky Blue, 3, 114	S. Hawley	Full Choke, 3, 117	Naevus, 3, 115	7	1:22.40	48,200
1982	Unpredictable, 3, 122	E. J. Delahoussaye	Prince Spellbound, 3, 122	Sepulveda, 3, 119	10	1:21.20	50,700
1981	Flying Nashua, 3, 114	A. T. Cordero Jr.	Minnesota Chief, 3, 117	Torso, 3, 117	9	1:23.40	40,450
1980	Raise a Man, 3, 114	W. Shoemaker	Super Moment, 3, 114	Bold 'n Rulling, 3, 117	8	1:21.40	39,550
1979	Flying Paster, 3, 124	D. Pierce	Oats and Corn, 3, 119	Infusive, 3, 122	8	1:21.20	37,300
1978	Chance Dancer, 3, 122	R. Culberson	O Big Al, 3, 122	Reb's Golden Ale, 3, 114	6	1:22.20	25,600
1977	Replant, 3, 117	D. G. McHargue	Current Concept, 3, 122	Smasher, 3, 122	8	1:21.20	29,750
1976	Thermal Energy, 3, 117	W. Shoemaker	Stained Glass, 3, 122	Bold Forbes, 3, 119	7	1:21.80	20,200
1975	Boomie S., 3, 114	S. Hawley	George Navonod, 3, 122	Udonegood, 3, 114	8	1:22.00	21,350
1974	Triple Crown, 3, 114	B. Baeza	El Espanoleto, 3, 114	Destroyer, 3, 114	8	1:22.00	28,000
1973	Ancient Title, 3, 122	F. Toro	Linda's Chief, 3, 122	Out of the East, 3, 114	9	1:21.00	28,150

Named for El Rancho San Vicente, California; early horse races were held there on a mesa. Grade 3 1973-'82, 1984-'97. San Vicente H. 1956-'66. San Vicente Breeders' Cup S. 1990-'95. Not held 1942-'44, 1949-'51, 1970. 6 furlongs 1935-'36, 1952-'54. 1 mile 1940-'46. 1 1/16 miles 1947-'48. Three-year-olds and up 1935-'36. Colts and geldings 1935-'53.

Sapling Stakes

Grade 3 in 2005. Monmouth Park, two-year-olds, 6 furlongs, dirt. Held August 28, 2004, with a gross value of $100,000. First held in 1883. First graded in 1973. Stakes record 1:07.84 (1992 Gilded Time).

Year	Winner	Jockey	Second	Third	Strs	Time	1st Purse
2004	Evil Minister, 2, 120	J. Pimentel	Park Avenue Ball, 2, 120	Upscaled, 2, 120	8	1:11.21	$60,000
2003	Dashboard Drummer, 2, 120	J. C. Ferrer	Deputy Storm, 2, 120	Charming Jim, 2, 120	7	1:10.84	60,000
2002	Valid Video, 2, 120	C. C. Lopez	Farno, 2, 120	Boston Park, 2, 120	8	1:09.88	60,000
2001	Pure Precision, 2, 120	E. Coa	Truman's Raider, 2, 120	Wild Navigator, 2, 120	8	1:10.82	90,000
2000	Shooter, 2, 120	J. Bravo	Snow Ridge, 2, 119	T P Louie, 2, 119	7	1:10.63	120,000
1999	Dont Tell the Kids, 2, 122	J. E. Tejeira	Outrigger, 2, 122	House Burner, 2, 122	6	1:10.18	120,000
1998	Yes It's True, 2, 122	S. J. Sellers	Erlton, 2, 122	Heroofthegame, 2, 122	7	1:10.09	120,000
1997	Double Honor, 2, 122	J. Bravo	Jigadee, 2, 122	E Z Line, 2, 122	8	1:09.75	120,000
1996	Smoke Glacken, 2, 122	C. Perret	Harley Tune, 2, 122	Country Rainbow, 2, 122	10	1:10.16	120,000
1995	Hennessy, 2, 122	D. M. Barton	Built for Pleasure, 2, 122	Cashier Coyote, 2, 122	7	1:10.84	120,000
1994	Boone's Mill, 2, 122	P. Day	Enlighten, 2, 122	Western Echo, 2, 122	8	1:10.46	120,000
1993	Sacred Honour, 2, 122	C. E. Lopez Sr.	Meadow Flight, 2, 122	Solly's Honor, 2, 117	6	1:11.19	120,000
1992	Gilded Time, 2, 122	C. J. McCarron	Wild Zone, 2, 122	Great Navigator, 2, 122	8	**1:07.84**	120,000
1991	Big Sur, 2, 122	R. Migliore	Never Wavering, 2, 122	Dr Fountainstein, 2, 122	8	1:10.92	120,000
1990	Deposit Ticket, 2, 122	G. L. Stevens	Alaskan Frost, 2, 122	Hansel, 2, 122	9	1:11.00	120,000
1989	Carson City, 2, 122	J. A. Krone	Mr. Nasty, 2, 122	Adjudicating, 2, 122	7	1:10.40	120,000
1988	Bio, 2, 120	P. A. Johnson	Truely Colorful, 2, 122	Light My Fuse, 2, 122	8	1:10.40	111,660
1987	Tejano, 2, 122	J. Vasquez	Unzipped, 2, 122	Jim's Orbit, 2, 122	8	1:09.00	111,600
1986	Bet Twice, 2, 122	C. W. Antley	Faster Than Sound, 2, 122	Homebuilder, 2, 122	5	1:10.20	120,000
1985	Hilco Scamper, 2, 122	G. L. Stevens	Danny's Keys, 2, 122	Mr. Spiffy, 2, 122	8	1:10.80	114,555
1984	Doubly Clear, 2, 122	J. R. Garcia	†Tiltalating, 2, 119	Do It Again Dan, 2, 122	10	1:10.40	120,150
1983	Smart n Slick, 2, 122	D. A. Miller Jr.	Tonto, 2, 122	Triple Sec, 2, 122	9	1:10.80	120,615
1982	O. K. by You, 2, 122	C. Perret	Willow Drive, 2, 122	Love to Laugh, 2, 122	8	1:10.80	82,032
1981	Out of Hock, 2, 122	D. Brumfield	T. Dykes, 2, 122	What a Wabbit, 2, 122	9	1:10.20	90,591
1980	Travelling Music, 2, 122	C. Perret	Lord Avie, 2, 122	Timeless Event, 2, 122	8	1:11.00	78,438
1979	Rockhill Native, 2, 122	J. Oldham	Antique Gold, 2, 122	Gold Stage, 2, 122	7	1:08.60	75,366
1978	Tim the Tiger, 2, 122	J. Fell	Groton High, 2, 122	Spartan Emperor, 2, 116	7	1:11.80	86,682
1977	Alydar, 2, 122	E. Maple	Noon Time Spender, 2, 122	Dominant Ruler, 2, 122	5	1:10.60	65,829
1976	Ali Oop, 2, 122	L. Saumell	Ahoy Mate, 2, 122	First Ambassador, 2, 122	10	1:09.80	84,636
1975	Full Out, 2, 122	B. Thornburg	Riverside Sam, 2, 116	Eustace, 2, 122	13	1:11.60	82,227
1974	Foolish Pleasure, 2, 122	J. Vasquez	The Bagel Prince, 2, 122	Bombay Duck, 2, 122	15	1:10.40	86,997
1973	Tisab, 2, 122	W. Blum	Wedge Shot, 2, 122	Go for Love, 2, 122	11	1:10.20	77,721

Young trees are referred to as saplings. Grade 1 1973-'83. Grade 2 1984-'96. Not held 1894-1945. 5 1/2 furlongs. Track record 1992. †Denotes female.

Saranac Handicap

Grade 3 in 2005. Saratoga Race Course, three-year-olds, 1 9/16 miles, turf. Held September 6, 2004, with a gross value of $108,200. First held in 1901. First graded in 1973. Stakes record 1:51.61 (1999 Phi Beta Doc).

Year	Winner	Jockey	Second	Third	Strs	Time	1st Purse
2004	Prince Arch, 3, 123	J. Castellano	Mustanfar, 3, 121	Catch the Glory, 3, 115	6	1:53.89	$64,920
2003	Shoal Water, 3, 116	J. R. Velazquez	Urban King (Ire), 3, 115	Sharp Impact, 3, 116	6	1:55.43	65,280
2002	Ibn Al Haitham (GB), 3, 114	R. Migliore	Finality, 3, 116	Irish Colonial, 3, 115	9	1:55.30	66,900
2001	Blazing Fury, 3, 113	J. Castellano	Fast City, 3, 114	Rapid Ryan, 3, 114	9	1:54.88	67,500
2000	Rob's Spirit, 3, 120	J. D. Bailey	Whata Brainstorm, 3, 117	Dawn of the Condor, 3, 117	9	1:55.47	68,280
1999	Phi Beta Doc, 3, 118	R. A. Dominguez	Monarch's Maze, 3, 114	Big Rascal, 3, 113	8	1:51.61	67,020
1998	Crowd Pleaser, 3, 115	J. Samyn	Parade Ground, 3, 122	Reformer Rally, 3, 115	7	1:53.42	66,060
1997	River Squall, 3, 114	C. Perret	Daylight Savings, 3, 114	Inkatha (Fr), 3, 114	10	1:52.82	68,460
1996	Harghar, 3, 113	P. Day	Sir Cat, 3, 123	Defacto, 3, 115	11	1:48.58	69,180
1995	Debonair Dan, 3, 112	J. F. Chavez	Crimson Guard, 3, 122	Treasurer (GB), 3, 114	7	1:33.65	50,400
1994	†Casa Eire, 3, 114	J. Bravo	Warn Me (GB), 3, 114	Presently, 3, 117	8	1:34.67	66,480
1993	Halissee, 3, 114	J. A. Krone	Forest Wind, 3, 117	Compadre, 3, 114	9	1:34.34	74,280
1992	Casino Magistrate, 3, 120	E. Maple	Restless Doctor, 3, 114	Smiling and Dancin, 3, 117	10	1:39.37	76,440
1991	Club Champ, 3, 114	A. T. Cordero Jr.	Share the Glory, 3, 117	Young Daniel, 3, 114	15	1:34.34	81,480
1990	Rouse the Louse, 3, 114	J. D. Bailey	†My Girl Jeannie, 3, 118	V. J.'s Honor, 3, 114	12	1:37.00	78,600
1989	Expensive Decision, 3, 114	J. Samyn	Ninety Years Young, 3, 114	Valid Ordinate, 3, 114	8	1:36.00	55,140
	Slew the Knight, 3, 114	J. Samyn	Verbatree, 3, 114	Luge (GB), 3, 123	8	1:36.00	55,620
1988	Posen, 3, 123	D. Brumfield	Sunshine Forever, 3, 114	Blew by Em, 3, 114	8	1:38.40	73,560
1987	Lights and Music, 3, 114	E. Maple	Forest Fair, 3, 114	First Patriot, 3, 117	10	1:34.80	73,560
1986	Glow, 3, 114	E. Maple	Manila, 3, 114	Pillaster, 3, 120	11	1:34.60	72,270
1985	Equalize, 3, 114	R. G. Davis	Verification, 3, 114	Danger's Hour, 3, 114	9	1:39.00	71,820
1984	Is Your Pleasure, 3, 114	A. T. Cordero Jr.	Onyxly, 3, 114	Loft, 3, 123	12	1:35.20	61,470
1983	†Sabin, 3, 113	E. Maple	Fortnightly, 3, 117	Domynsky (GB), 3, 123	10	1:39.60	36,600
1982	Prince Westport, 3, 114	J. D. Bailey	Four Bases, 3, 114	A Real Leader, 3, 114	8	1:39.00	35,040
1981	†De La Rose, 3, 112	E. Maple	Stage Door Key, 3, 114	Color Bearer, 3, 114	7	1:34.40	35,400
1980	Key to Content, 3, 114	G. Martens	Current Legend, 3, 114	Ben Fab, 3, 123	13	1:33.80	36,300
1979	Told, 3, 114	J. Cruguet	Crown Thy Good, 3, 114	Quiet Crossing, 3, 123	10	1:34.40	35,250
1978	Buckaroo, 3, 123	J. Velasquez	Junction, 3, 123	Quadratic, 3, 123	5	1:35.00	31,950
1977	Bailjumper, 3, 114	A. T. Cordero Jr.	Lynn Davis, 3, 114	Gift of Kings, 3, 114	9	1:35.20	32,910
1976	Dance Spell, 3, 114	A. T. Cordero Jr.	Zen, 3, 123	Quiet Little Table, 3, 114	6	1:34.20	33,030
1975	Bravest Roman, 3, 114	E. Maple	Wajima, 3, 114	Valid Appeal, 3, 114	9	1:34.80	34,380
1974	Accipiter, 3, 123	A. Santiago	Best of It, 3, 117	Hosiery, 3, 117	11	1:36.40	34,980
1973	Linda's Chief, 3, 126	B. Baeza	Step Nicely, 3, 123	Illberightback, 3, 117	4	1:34.00	33,150

Named for an Adirondack mountain village in Clinton County, New York. Grade 2 1973-'89. Saranac S. 1901-'97. Held at Jamaica 1948-'56. Held at Aqueduct 1957-'61, 1963-'67, 1972-'74, 1976. Held at Belmont Park 1962, 1968-'71, 1975, 1977-'95. Not held 1911-'12, 1944, 1946-'47. 1 1/8 miles 1901-'08, 1996-'97. 1 mile 1909, 1913-'42, 1960-'95. 1 1/16 miles 1948-'59. Dirt 1901-'79. Two divisions 1989. †Denotes female. Held as an allowance race 1943, 1945.

Saratoga Breeders' Cup Handicap

Grade 2 in 2005. Saratoga Race Course, three-year-olds and up, 1 1/4 miles, dirt. Held August 22, 2004, with a gross value of $250,000. First held in 1865. First graded in 1996. Stakes record 2:00.83 (2004 Evening Attire).

Year	Winner	Jockey	Second	Third	Strs	Time	1st Purse
2004	Evening Attire, 6, 115	C. H. Velasquez	Funny Cide, 4, 118	Bowman's Band, 6, 116	7	2:00.83	$150,000
2003	Puzzlement, 4, 113	J. F. Chavez	Volponi, 5, 122	Iron Deputy, 4, 115	8	2:03.54	180,000
2002	Evening Attire, 4, 115	S. Bridgmohan	Abreeze, 7, 113	Dollar Bill, 4, 117	10	2:02.95	180,000
2001	Aptitude, 4, 122	J. D. Bailey	Perfect Cat, 4, 115	A Fleets Dancer, 6, 115	7	2:01.55	180,000
2000	Pleasant Breeze, 5, 116	J. F. Chavez	Catienus, 6, 114	Gander, 4, 114	7	2:02.17	180,000
1999	Running Stag, 5, 122	S. J. Sellers	Catienus, 5, 115	Golden Missile, 4, 115	8	2:01.11	180,000
1998	Awesome Again, 4, 120	P. Day	Concerto, 4, 114	Early Warning, 3, 110	7	2:03.14	180,000
1997	Cairo Express, 5, 111	J. Samyn	Golden Larch, 6, 111	Instant Friendship, 4, 108	9	2:03.99	180,000
1996	L'Carriere, 5, 114	J. F. Chavez	Peaks and Valleys, 4, 121	Mahogany Hall, 5, 116	8	2:01.67	130,000
1995	L'Carriere, 4, 113	J. D. Bailey	Yourmissinthepoint, 4, 108	Unaccounted For, 4, 120	6	2:02.87	120,000
1994	Thunder Rumble, 5, 112	R. Migliore	West by West, 5, 113	Wallenda, 4, 117	8	1:48.52	150,000

The race and the track are named for the town of Saratoga Springs, New York. Grade 3 1996-'97. Saratoga Cup H. 1865-'96. Held at Belmont Park 1943-'45. Not held 1887-'90, 1892-1900, 1908, 1911-'12, 1956-'62, 1964-'93. 2 1/4 miles 1865-'86. 2 miles 1891. 1 5/8 miles 1901, 1963. 1 3/4 miles 1902-'55. 1 1/8 miles 1994.

Saratoga Special Stakes

Grade 2 in 2005. Saratoga Race Course, two-year-olds, 6 1/2 furlongs, dirt. Held August 13, 2003, with a gross value of $150,000. First held in 1901. First graded in 1973. Stakes record 1:15.97 (2003 Cuvee).

Year	Winner	Jockey	Second	Third	Strs	Time	1st Purse
2003	Cuvee, 2, 122	J. D. Bailey	Pomeroy, 2, 118	Limehouse, 2, 122	8	1:15.97	$90,000
2002	Zavata, 2, 122	J. D. Bailey	Lone Star Sky, 2, 122	Spite the Devil, 2, 116	5	1:17.65	90,000
2001	Jump Start, 2, 115	P. Day	Heavyweight Champ, 2, 115	Booklet, 2, 117	6	1:17.35	90,000
2000	City Zip, 2, 122	J. A. Santos	Scorpion, 2, 114	Standard Speed, 2, 117	8	1:16.88	90,000
1999	Bevo, 2, 117	E. S. Prado	Afternoon Affair, 2, 114	Settlement, 2, 114	6	1:17.78	90,000

Year	Winner	Jockey	Second	Third	Strs	Time	1st Purse
1998	Prime Directive, 2, 114	J. F. Chavez	Silk Broker, 2, 114	Tactical Cat, 2, 117	4	1:17.18	$90,000
1997	Favorite Trick, 2, 122	P. Day	Case Dismissed, 2, 114	K. O. Punch, 2, 119	5	1:17.15	90,000
1996	All Chatter, 2, 113	J. F. Chavez	Gray Raider, 2, 114	Just a Cat, 2, 113	10	1:16.37	84,375
1995	Bright Launch, 2, 112	J. A. Santos	Devil's Honor, 2, 114	Severe Clear, 2, 113	8	1:17.98	66,540
1994	Montreal Red, 2, 122	J. A. Santos	Flitch, 2, 115	Law of the Sea, 2, 115	5	1:17.96	64,800
1993	Dehere, 2, 117	E. Maple	Slew Gin Fizz, 2, 117	Whitney Tower, 2, 117	9	1:09.92	71,760
1992	Tactical Advantage, 2, 117	J. A. Krone	Strolling Along, 2, 117	Mi Cielo, 2, 117	10	1:10.59	72,600
1991	Caller I. D., 2, 117	J. D. Bailey	Pick Up the Phone, 2, 122	Coin Collector, 2, 122	8	1:09.55	71,040
1990	To Freedom, 2, 124	A. T. Cordero Jr.	Fighting Affair, 2, 117	Eugene Eugene, 2, 117	6	1:11.40	52,740
1989	Summer Squall, 2, 124	P. Day	Dr. Bobby A., 2, 117	Graf, 2, 117	8	1:09.80	53,370
1988	Trapp Mountain, 2, 117	J. D. Bailey	Bio, 2, 122	Leading Prospect, 2, 117	7	1:10.80	66,240
1987	Crusader Sword, 2, 117	R. G. Davis	Tejano, 2, 117	Endurance, 2, 119	8	1:10.20	66,420
1986	Gulch, 2, 122	A. T. Cordero Jr.	Jazzing Around, 2, 117	Java Gold, 2, 117	10	1:10.00	54,990
1985	Sovereign Don, 2, 122	J. Velasquez	Hagley Mill, 2, 117	Bullet Blade, 2, 117	9	1:11.40	43,200
1984	Chief's Crown, 2, 117	D. MacBeth	Do It Again Dan, 2, 117	Sky Command, 2, 122	6	1:10.20	42,060
1983	Swale, 2, 117	E. Maple	Shuttle Jet, 2, 117	Big Walt, 2, 117	7	1:12.60	33,720
1982	Victorious, 2, 122	A. T. Cordero Jr.	Pappa Riccio, 2, 124	Safe Ground, 2, 119	7	1:10.60	33,960
1981	Conquistador Cielo, 2, 117	E. Maple	Herschelwalker, 2, 117	Timely Writer, 2, 122	10	1:10.60	33,900
1980	Well Decorated, 2, 117	M. Venezia	Tap Shoes, 2, 117	Motivity, 2, 119	10	1:10.20	34,320
1979	J. P. Brother, 2, 122	E. Maple	Native Moment, 2, 117	Muckraker, 2, 122	5	1:12.00	25,365
1978	General Assembly, 2, 117	D. G. McHargue	‡Turnbuckle, 2, 117	Make a Mess, 2, 117	8	1:09.00	22,350
1977	Darby Creek Road, 2, 117	A. T. Cordero Jr.	Jet Diplomacy, 2, 122	Quadratic, 2, 122	10	1:10.00	22,470
1976	Banquet Table, 2, 122	J. Vasquez	Turn of Coin, 2, 122	May I Rule, 2, 117	9	1:11.60	22,455
1975	Bold Forbes, 2, 120	J. Velasquez	Family Doctor, 2, 117	Gentle King, 2, 120	5	1:09.80	22,680
1974	Our Talisman, 2, 117	M. Venezia	Valid Appeal, 2, 117	Knightly Sport, 2, 120	10	1:10.40	17,430
1973	Az Igazi, 2, 117	M. Venezia	Gusty O'Shay, 2, 117	Lakeville, 2, 117	8	1:11.00	17,025

The race and the track are named for the town of Saratoga Springs, New York. In the past, "special" races were "winner takes all." Saratoga Special Sweepstakes 1901-'58. Held at Belmont Park 1943-'45. Not held 1911-'12, 2004. 5½ furlongs 1901-'05. 6 furlongs 1906-'93. ‡Smarten finished second, DQ to eighth, 1978.

Schuylerville Stakes

Grade 3 in 2005. Saratoga Race Course, two-year-olds, fillies, 6 furlongs, dirt. Held July 28, 2004, with a gross value of $150,000. First held in 1918. First graded in 1973. Stakes record 1:09.80 (1988 Wonders Delight; 1974 Laughing Bridge [2nd Div.]).

Year	Winner	Jockey	Second	Third	Strs	Time	1st Purse
2004	Classic Elegance, 2, 122	P. Day	Angel Trumpet, 2, 118	Wild Chick, 2, 118	10	1:12.48	$90,000
2003	Ashado, 2, 118	E. S. Prado	Maple Syrple, 2, 122	Hermione's Magic, 2, 118	7	1:12.12	90,000
2002	Freedom's Daughter, 2, 118	J. R. Velazquez	Miss Mary Apples, 2, 118	Mymich, 2, 116	7	1:12.14	90,000
2001	Touch Love, 2, 119	J. F. Chavez	Lakeside Cup, 2, 117	Lost Expectations, 2, 117	6	1:11.12	65,460
2000	Gold Mover, 2, 122	C. Perret	Seeking It All, 2, 114	Miss Doolittle, 2, 114	5	1:10.33	64,920
1999	Magicalmysterycat, 2, 122	P. Day	Circle of Life, 2, 114	Regally Appealing, 2, 114	7	1:10.91	65,700
1998	Call Me Up, 2, 117	J. F. Chavez	Brittons Hill, 2, 117	Fantasy Lake, 2, 117	8	1:12.89	66,060
1997	Countess Diana, 2, 116	S. J. Sellers	Love Lock, 2, 119	Sequence, 2, 116	6	1:10.39	64,800
1996	How About Now, 2, 115	R. Migliore	Exclusive Hold, 2, 115	City College, 2, 115	11	1:12.37	68,220
1995	Golden Attraction, 2, 121	D. M. Barton	Daylight Come, 2, 112	Western Dreamer, 2, 121	8	1:10.84	65,940
1994	Changing Ways, 2, 114	M. E. Smith	Unacceptable, 2, 119	Artic Experience, 2, 114	10	1:12.66	67,980
1993	Strategic Maneuver, 2, 114	J. A. Santos	Astas Foxy Lady, 2, 114	She Rides Tonite, 2, 114	11	1:11.15	73,560
1992	Distinct Habit, 2, 119	J. D. Bailey	Tourney, 2, 114	Lily La Belle, 2, 114	9	1:11.03	72,480
1991	Turnback the Alarm, 2, 114	D. Carr	Speed Dialer, 2, 119	Teddy's Top Ten, 2, 114	13	1:12.04	76,200
1990	Meadow Star, 2, 119	C. W. Antley	Garden Gal, 2, 119	Prayerful Miss, 2, 114	7	1:11.20	53,010
1989	Golden Reef, 2, 114	J. A. Santos	Lucy's Glory, 2, 119	Miss Cox's Hat, 2, 114	10	1:10.40	54,360
1988	Wonders Delight, 2, 114	J. A. Santos	Coax Chelsie, 2, 114	Attu, 2, 112	9	1:09.80	67,680
1987	Over All, 2, 119	A. T. Cordero Jr.	Joe's Tammie, 2, 119	Flashy Runner, 2, 119	10	1:10.60	68,850
1986	Sacahuista, 2, 114	C. J. McCarron	Our Little Margie, 2, 114	Collins, 2, 114	9	1:10.60	54,540
1985	I'm Splendid, 2, 114	A. T. Cordero Jr.	Musical Lark (Ire), 2, 114	Famous Speech, 2, 114	6	1:10.80	41,820
1984	Weekend Delight, 2, 119	C. R. Woods Jr.	Resembling, 2, 114	Winters' Love, 2, 114	8	1:11.60	42,840
1983	Bottle Top, 2, 114	D. Brumfield	Officer's Ball, 2, 114	Ark, 2, 114	7	1:11.40	34,020
1982	Weekend Surprise, 2, 114	J. Velasquez	Share the Fantasy, 2, 116	Flying Lassie, 2, 114	7	1:11.00	34,620
1981	Mystical Mood, 2, 114	J. Vasquez	Aga Pantha, 2, 114	Trove, 2, 116	8	1:11.80	34,320
1980	Sweet Revenge, 2, 114	J. Velasquez	Companionship, 2, 114	Heavenly Cause, 2, 114	11	1:10.40	34,980
1979	Damask Fan, 2, 116	E. Maple	Jet Rating, 2, 114	Lovin' Lass, 2, 112	4	1:10.20	25,860
1978	Palm Hut, 2, 121	R. I. Velez	Hermanville, 2, 114	Please Try Hard, 2, 114	8	1:10.40	22,215
1977	L'Alezane, 2, 121	R. Turcotte	Akita, 2, 114	Lakeville Miss, 2, 114	8	1:11.80	22,350
1976	Mrs. Warren, 2, 114	E. Maple	Tickle My Toes, 2, 116	Spy Flag, 2, 114	12	1:11.80	22,980
1975	Nijana, 2, 112	J. Velasquez	Future Tense, 2, 116	Crown Treasure, 2, 116	7	1:12.20	22,680
1974	Our Dancing Girl, 2, 116	V. A. Bracciale Jr.	Secret's Out, 2, 119	But Exclusive, 2, 116	7	1:11.20	16,575
	Laughing Bridge, 2, 117	B. Baeza	Molly Ballantine, 2, 114	Fair Wind, 2, 119	7	1:09.80	16,500
1973	Talking Picture, 2, 116	B. Baeza	Imajoy, 2, 116	Celestial Lights, 2, 119	10	1:10.80	17,760

Named for a town located 12 miles east of Saratoga Springs in upstate New York. Grade 3 1975-'86. Held at Belmont Park 1943-'45. Held at Jamaica 1952. 5½ furlongs 1918-'59, 1962-'68. Two divisions 1974.

Seabiscuit Breeders' Cup Handicap

Grade 3 in 2005. Bay Meadows, four-year-olds and up, $1\frac{1}{16}$ miles, dirt. Held February 5, 2005, with a gross value of $86,250. First held in 1968. First graded in 1985. Stakes record 1:40.08 (2004 Yougottawanna).

Year	Winner	Jockey	Second	Third	Strs	Time	1st Purse
2005	Yougottawanna, 6, 118	J. P. Lumpkins	Jake Skate, 5, 119	Adreamisborn, 6, 119	7	1:41.42	$41,250
2004	Yougottawanna, 5, 116	R. A. Baze	Gold Ruckus, 5, 116	Snorter, 4, 118	5	**1:40.08**	41,250
2003	Reba's Gold, 6, 118	C. J. Rollins	Free Corona, 5, 116	Truly a Judge, 5, 117	6	1:41.63	55,000
2002	Palmeiro, 4, 115	J. P. Lumpkins	Moonlight Meeting, 7, 116	Prodigious, 5, 116	9	1:42.31	82,500
2001	Euchre, 5, 118	J. P. Lumpkins	Irisheyesareflying, 5, 118	Moonlight Charger, 6, 115	8	1:41.69	82,500
2000	Peach Flat, 6, 114	J. Valdivia Jr.	Boss Ego, 4, 115	Casey Griffin, 4, 115	5	1:42.48	75,000
1999	Worldly Ways (GB), 5, 116	R. A. Baze	Barter Town, 4, 112	dh- Highland Gold, 4, 115	8	1:40.62	60,000
				dh- Scooter Brown, 4, 114			
1998	Wild Wonder, 4, 121	R. A. Baze	Crypto Star, 4, 118	General Royal, 4, 115	6	1:41.33	60,000
1997	Mister Fire Eyes (Ire), 5, 115	R. J. Warren Jr.	Region, 8, 115	Tolemeo, 4, 113	6	1:41.28	60,000
1996	Tzar Rodney (Fr), 4, 114	T. M. Chapman	Joy of Glory, 7, 115	Opera Score, 5, 115	6	1:49.74	60,000
1995	Bluegrass Prince (Ire), 4, 114	T. M. Chapman	Lord Shirldor (SAf), 6, 116	Kinema Red, 5, 113	7	1:49.01	68,750
1994	Slew of Damascus, 6, 122	T. M. Chapman	Fast Cure, 5, 114	The Tender Track, 7, 116	6	1:43.75	55,000
1993	Never Black, 6, 115	C. S. Nakatani	Stark South, 5, 115	Daros (GB), 4, 114	6	1:42.53	55,000
1992	Gum, 6, 112	G. Boulanger	Forty Niner Days, 5, 116	Prudent Manner (Ire), 5, 115	7	1:41.73	55,000
1991	Forty Niner Days, 4, 115	T. T. Doocy	Neptuno (Arg), 5, 116	Trebizond, 5, 115	6	1:42.70	55,000
1990	River Master, 4, 116	R. G. Davis	Miswaki Tern, 5, 116	Exclusive Partner, 8, 117	8	1:43.20	55,000
1989	Simply Majestic, 5, 121	R. D. Hansen	Ongoing Mister, 4, 113	Astronaut Prince, 5, 115	6	1:42.40	55,000
1988	Ifrad, 6, 117	T. M. Chapman	Stop the Fighting (Ire), 5, 115	Nickle Band, 4, 113	7	1:43.40	55,000
1987	Mangaki, 6, 115	T. T. Doocy	Barbery, 6, 116	Santella Mac (Ire), 4, 115	12	1:34.40	84,410
1986	Clever Song, 4, 122	F. Toro	Truce Maker, 8, 114	Ocean View, 5, 117	7	1:28.00	63,000
1985	Hegemony (Ire), 4, 121	D. G. McHargue	Champion Pilot, 4, 121	Nak Ack, 4, 117	5	1:28.40	71,740
1984	Ancestral (Ire), 4, 115	R. Sibille	Otter Slide, 5, 116	dh- Famous Star (GB), 5, 115	10	1:29.20	49,750
				dh- Silveyville, 6, 124			
1983	Major Sport, 6, 115	T. M. Chapman	Aristocratical, 6, 114	Take the Floor, 4, 115	11	1:29.40	50,300
1982	Crews Hill (GB), 6, 118	R. A. Baze	Shagbark, 7, 122	Hallowed Envoy, 5, 116	7	1:29.40	64,800
1981	Borrego Sun, 4, 114	R. A. Baze	Prenotion, 6, 116	Kane County, 4, 113	7	1:29.60	25,550
1980	California Express, 5, 110	J. Aragon	Kamehameha, 6, 121	Miami Sun, 6, 120	7	1:29.60	19,000
1979	Struttin' George, 5, 122	T. M. Chapman	Don Alberto, 4, 119	Charley Sutton, 5, 114	8	1:28.00	13,100
1978	Maheras, 5, 132	W. Mahorney	Charley Sutton, 4, 115	Oriental Magic, 6, 113	5	:56.20	15,550
1977	L'Natural, 4, 114	R. Caballero	Maheras, 4, 126	Sporting Goods, 7, 122	7	:56.00	15,800
1976	Shirley's Champion, 5, 114	F. Olivares	King Charly, 6, 113	Oriental Magic, 4, 114	7	:56.80	15,800
1975	Cherry River, 5, 126	W. Mahorney	El Potrero, 4, 115	Black Tornado, 5, 116	9	:56.80	16,200
1974	Tragic Isle, 5, 124	F. Mena	Prince Rameses, 5, 113	Times Rush, 6, 113	6	1:08.80	15,000
1973	Selecting, 4, 112	R. Yaka	I'm Ed, 4, 111	Goalie, 4, 120	7	1:09.00	15,150

Named for Charles S. Howard's 1938 Horse of the Year and '37, '38 Bay Meadows H. winner Seabiscuit (1933 c. by Hard Tack). Renamed in 2003 to coincide with the release of the movie *Seabiscuit*. Was formerly a traditional Memorial Day weekend race. All-American H. 1968-2002. Held at Golden Gate Fields 1968-2000. 6 furlongs 1968-'74. 5 furlongs 1975-'78. $7\frac{1}{2}$ furlongs 1979-'86. 1 mile 1987. $1\frac{1}{8}$ miles 1995-'96. Turf 1975-'96. Dead heat for third 1984, 1999.

Secretariat Stakes

Grade 1 in 2005. Arlington Park, three-year-olds, $1\frac{1}{4}$ miles, turf. Held August 14, 2004, with a gross value of $400,000. First held in 1974. First graded in 1975. Stakes record 1:59.65 (2004 Kitten's Joy).

Year	Winner	Jockey	Second	Third	Strs	Time	1st Purse
2004	Kitten's Joy, 3, 123	J. D. Bailey	Greek Sun, 3, 121	Moscow Ballet (Ire), 3, 119	7	**1:59.65**	$240,000
2003	Kicken Kris, 3, 116	J. Castellano	Joe Bear (Ire), 3, 116	Lismore Knight, 3, 121	11	2:02.53	240,000
2002	Chiselling, 3, 123	K. J. Desormeaux	Jazz Beat (Ire), 3, 117	Extra Check, 3, 116	7	2:04.16	240,000
2001	Startac, 3, 121	A. O. Solis	Strut the Stage, 3, 123	Sharp Performance, 3, 121	11	2:04.91	240,000
2000	Ciro, 3, 120	M. J. Kinane	King Cugat, 3, 120	Guillamou City (Fr), 3, 117	8	2:01.64	240,000
1997	Honor Glide, 3, 123	G. K. Gomez	Casey Tibbs (Ire), 3, 116	Glok, 3, 114	9	2:02.74	240,000
1996	Marlin, 3, 114	S. J. Sellers	Trail City, 3, 126	Dancing Fred, 3, 114	10	2:01.09	300,000
1995	Hawk Attack, 3, 120	P. Day	Mecke, 3, 117	Petit Poucet (GB), 3, 114	10	2:00.17	240,000
1994	Vaudeville, 3, 123	G. L. Stevens	Dare and Go, 3, 114	Jaggery John, 3, 120	13	2:01.11	240,000
1993	Awad, 3, 120	J. Velasquez	Explosive Red, 3, 123	Brazany, 3, 114	14	2:08.74	240,000
1992	Ghazi, 3, 114	R. G. Davis	Paradise Creek, 3, 123	†Tango Charlie, 3, 117	10	2:01.18	180,000
1991	Jackie Wackie, 3, 123	P. Day	Olympio, 3, 126	Sultry Song, 3, 114	8	2:01.27	180,000
1990	Super Abound, 3, 114	R. P. Romero	Unbridled, 3, 126	†Super Fan, 3, 117	8	2:01.60	150,000
1989	Hawkster, 3, 123	P. A. Valenzuela	Chenin Blanc, 3, 114	Ninety Years Young, 3, 114	8	2:04.00	150,000
1987	Stately Don, 3, 113	J. Vasquez	The Medic, 3, 120	Zaizoom, 3, 120	11	2:04.60	103,590
1986	Southjet, 3, 113	J. A. Santos	Glow, 3, 120	Tripoli Shores, 3, 115	10	2:02.00	102,510
1985	Derby Wish, 3, 114	R. P. Romero	‡Day Shift, 3, 114	Duluth, 3, 123	12	2:01.00	146,880
1984	Vision, 3, 114	G. McCarron	Mr. Japan, 3, 114	Pine Circle, 3, 114	8	2:38.40	117,240
1983	Fortnightly, 3, 117	P. Day	Jack Slade, 3, 114	Reap, 3, 114	13	2:32.40	102,360
1982	Half Iced, 3, 114	D. MacBeth	Dew Line, 3, 114	Continuing, 3, 114	8	2:31.20	90,000
1981	Sing Sing, 3, 114	M. Venezia	Television Studio, 3, 117	Jungle Tough, 3, 114	11	2:53.60	96,240
1980	Spruce Needles, 3, 123	J. C. Espinoza	Proctor, 3, 120	The Messanger, 3, 123	6	2:40.80	99,960
1979	Golden Act, 3, 126	S. Hawley	Smarten, 3, 120	Flying Dad, 3, 120	6	2:32.80	91,080

Year	Winner	Jockey	Second	Third	Strs	Time	1st Purse
1978	**Mac Diarmida**, 3, 120	J. Cruguet	April Axe, 3, 120	The Liberal Member, 3, 114	11	2:29.80	$99,600
1977	**Text**, 3, 120	M. Castaneda	Run Dusty Run, 3, 126	Flag Officer, 3, 123	7	1:42.00	73,140
1976	**Joachim**, 3, 123	S. Maple	Romeo, 3, 112	L'Heureux, 3, 117	10	1:50.80	88,400
1975	**Intrepid Hero**, 3, 123	A. T. Cordero Jr.	Gab Bag, 3, 117	Larrikin, 3, 117	14	1:49.80	94,000
1974	**Glossary**, 3, 114	A. Santiago	Stonewalk, 3, 123	Talkative Turn, 3, 117	13	1:42.80	96,400

Named for Meadow Stable's 1972, '73 Horse of the Year and '73 Triple Crown winner Secretariat (1970 c. by Bold Ruler); he made his first start after the Belmont S. (G1) in a stakes race at Arlington Park. Grade 2 1975-'83. Held at Hawthorne Race Course 1985. Not held 1988, 1998-'99. 1 1/16 miles 1974, 1977. 1 1/8 miles 1975-'76. 1 1/2 miles 1978-'84. Dirt 1977. ‡Racing Star finished second, DQ to fourth, 1985. †Denotes female.

Senator Ken Maddy Handicap

Grade 3 in 2005. Santa Anita Park, three-year-olds and up, fillies and mares, about 6 1/2 furlongs, turf. Held September 29, 2004, with a gross value of $100,000. First held in 1969. First graded in 1973. Stakes record 1:11.63 (1992 Bel's Starlet).

Year	Winner	Jockey	Second	Third	Strs	Time	1st Purse
2004	**Belleski**, 5, 118	C. S. Nakatani	Intercontinental (GB), 4, 120	Acago, 4, 116	9	1:12.86	$60,000
2003	**Belleski**, 4, 117	V. Espinoza	Buffythecenterfold, 3, 116	Icantgoforthat, 4, 115	10	1:12.37	67,200
2002	**Rolly Polly (Ire)**, 4, 119	P. A. Valenzuela	I'm the Business (NZ), 5, 117	Nanogram, 5, 113	12	1:12.86	68,460
2001	**A La Reine**, 4, 115	A. O. Solis	Nanogram, 4, 111	Global, 4, 113	8	1:13.27	66,240
2000	**Evening Promise (GB)**, 4, 118	K. J. Desormeaux	Strawberry Way, 5, 114	Southern House (Ire), 4, 114	10	1:13.05	67,020
1999	**Hula Queen**, 5, 116	A. O. Solis	Desert Lady (Ire), 4, 121	Ecudienne, 5, 117	11	1:13.05	67,740
1998	**Dance Parade**, 4, 120	K. J. Desormeaux	Advancing Star, 5, 121	Green Jewel (GB), 4, 116	8	1:13.87	60,000
1997	**Madame Pandit**, 4, 118	E. J. Delahoussaye	Advancing Star, 4, 120	Highest Dream (Ire), 4, 116	10	1:13.82	60,000
1996	**Dixie Pearl**, 4, 116	E. J. Delahoussaye	Ski Dancer, 4, 119	Cat's Cradle, 4, 118	9	1:12.33	66,400
1995	**Denim Yenem**, 3, 115	C. J. McCarron	Miss L Attack, 5, 116	Jacodra's Devil, 4, 116	7	1:14.92	60,400
1994	**Starolamo**, 5, 117	K. J. Desormeaux	Sophisticatedcielo, 3, 114	Beautiful Gem, 3, 115	6	1:16.07	47,475
1993	**Toussaud**, 4, 122	K. J. Desormeaux	Best Dress, 3, 113	Yousefia, 4, 116	6	1:14.32	46,950
1992	**Bel's Starlet**, 5, 120	K. J. Desormeaux	Glen Kate (Ire), 5, 117	Brisa de Mar, 4, 117	9	1:11.63	49,575
1991	**Bel's Starlet**, 4, 115	K. J. Desormeaux	Sun Brandy, 4, 117	Bright Asset, 5, 115	12	1:11.89	52,125
1990	**Stylish Star**, 4, 118	E. J. Delahoussaye	Tasteful T. V., 3, 115	Linda Card, 4, 113	11	1:12.00	51,525
1989	**Warning Zone**, 4, 119	R. Q. Meza	Down Again, 5, 119	Stormy But Valid, 3, 116	11	1:12.80	51,675
1988	**Jeanne Jones**, 3, 118	A. T. Gryder	Native Paster, 4, 116	Serve n' Volley (GB), 4, 116	14	1:14.80	53,100
1987	**Aberuschka (Ire)**, 5, 120	P. A. Valenzuela	Luisant (Arg), 5, 118	Down Again, 3, 113	11	1:14.80	41,050
1986	**Lichi (Chi)**, 6, 115	G. Baze	Tax Dodge, 5, 119	Outstandingly, 4, 120	7	1:14.60	29,875
	Shywing, 4, 120	L. A. Pincay Jr.	Her Royalty, 5, 119	Water Crystals, 5, 119	9	1:14.80	31,075
1985	**Love Smitten**, 4, 119	G. L. Stevens	Danzadar, 4, 116	Sales Bulletin, 4, 117	7	1:15.40	29,725
1984	**Irish O'Brien**, 6, 116	J. J. Steiner	Mel's Whisper, 4, 111	Foggy Nation, 4, 116	11	1:14.60	32,200
	Lina Cavalieri (GB), 4, 116	E. J. Delahoussaye	Betty Money, 5, 115	Percipient, 3, 116	8	1:14.40	30,400
1983	**Matching**, 5, 122	R. Sibille	Excitable Lady, 5, 123	Nan's Dancer, 4, 113	6	1:17.00	37,850
1982	**Maple Tree**, 4, 115	E. J. Delahoussaye	Northern Fable, 4, 116	A Kiss for Luck, 3, 115	7	1:15.60	30,650
	Jones Time Machine, 3, 117	L. A. Pincay Jr.	Rosy Cloud, 5, 115	Manzanera (Arg), 6, 117	9	1:16.00	31,950
1981	**Kilijaro (Ire)**, 5, 120	L. A. Pincay Jr.	Ack's Secret, 5, 118	Miss Huntington, 4, 110	9	1:13.80	28,650
	Save Wild Life, 4, 121	M. Castaneda	Disconiz, 4, 115	I Got Speed, 3, 112	11	1:14.20	29,750
1980	**Great Lady M.**, 5, 122	P. A. Valenzuela	Evyostling, 5, 115	Conveniently, 4, 117	11	1:13.60	29,400
1979	**Palmistry**, 4, 115	C. J. McCarron	Splendid Size, 5, 116	Terresto's Dream, 4, 113	10	1:12.80	22,325
	Wishing Well, 4, 117	F. Toro	Great Lady M., 4, 116	Habeebti (GB), 5, 115	8	1:12.60	21,425
1978	**Happy Holme**, 4, 118	C. J. McCarron	Stellar Envoy, 4, 114	Pet Label, 5, 116	10	1:14.20	22,300
	‡Country Queen, 3, 118	F. Toro	Sweet Little Lady, 3, 116	Rich Soil, 4, 119	9	1:14.20	21,900
1977	**Dancing Femme**, 4, 125	D. G. McHargue	Lullaby Song, 4, 117	Swingtime, 5, 121	12	1:13.20	22,250
1976	**If You Prefer**, 5, 118	L. A. Pincay Jr.	*Accra II, 4, 115	Vagabonda, 5, 121	7	1:13.00	15,750
	Dancing Liz, 4, 114	W. Shoemaker	Miss Tokyo, 4, 120	Lucky Spell, 5, 113	8	1:12.40	16,050
1975	***Tizna**, 6, 125	D. Pierce	Mama Kali, 4, 121	Modus Vivendi, 4, 122	9	1:12.80	17,700
1974	**Impressive Style**, 5, 123	R. Rosales	Modus Vivendi, 3, 121	*Tizna, 5, 124	12	1:13.80	19,150
1973	***New Moon II**, 6, 116	W. Shoemaker	Minstrel Miss, 6, 124	Meilleur, 3, 116	11	1:13.20	19,200

Named for California state Sen. Kenneth L. Maddy (1935-2000), a longtime racing enthusiast. The race is held during the autumn Oak Tree Racing Association meet at Santa Anita Park. Autumn Days S. 1969. Autumn Days H. 1970-'98. 6 1/2 furlongs 1983, 1994. Dirt 1983, 1994. Two-year-olds and up 1975, 1988-'89. Both sexes 1969-'70. Two divisions 1976, 1978-'79, 1981-'82, 1984, 1986. ‡Sweet Little Lady finished first, DQ to second, 1978.

Senorita Stakes

Grade 3 in 2005. Hollywood Park, three-year-olds, fillies, 1 mile, turf. Held May 8, 2005, with a gross value of $111,900. First held in 1968. First graded in 1990. Stakes record 1:33.66 (1992 Charm a Gendarme).

Year	Winner	Jockey	Second	Third	Strs	Time	1st Purse
2005	**Virden**, 3, 119	O. Figueroa	Three Degrees (Ire), 3, 116	Thatswhatimean, 3, 117	10	1:35.37	$67,140
2004	**Miss Vegas (Ire)**, 3, 115	A. O. Solis	Ticker Tape (GB), 3, 121	Amorama (Fr), 3, 116	7	1:34.25	65,340
2003	**Makeup Artist**, 3, 117	V. Espinoza	Rutters Renegade (Ire), 3, 117	Shapes and Shadows, 3, 117	7	1:36.54	68,100
2002	**Adoration**, 3, 117	A. O. Solis	High Society (Ire), 3, 116	Nunatall (GB), 3, 115	6	1:34.91	64,380
2001	**Fantastic Filly (Fr)**, 3, 123	G. K. Gomez	Innit (Ire), 3, 115	Blushing Bride (GB), 3, 115	8	1:35.13	65,880
2000	**Islay Mist (GB)**, 3, 116	D. R. Flores	Fire Sale Queen, 3, 118	Miss Pixie, 3, 114	10	1:34.16	67,080
1999	**Coracle**, 3, 116	K. J. Desormeaux	Aviate, 3, 118	Dianehill (Ire), 3, 115	11	1:34.04	67,740

Year	Winner	Jockey	Second	Third	Strs	Time	1st Purse
1998	Dancing Rhythm, 3, 117	K. J. Desormeaux	Phone Alex (Ire), 3, 115	Star's Proud Penny, 3, 122	7	1:35.39	$64,860
1997	Kentucky Kaper, 3, 114	R. R. Douglas	Ascutney, 3, 120	Ava Knowsthecode, 3, 115	10	1:34.74	66,780
1996	To B. Super, 3, 118	C. W. Antley	Gastronomical, 3, 118	Ribot's Secret (Ire), 3, 116	13	1:34.36	68,940
1995	Top Shape (Fr), 3, 114	C. S. Nakatani	Artica, 3, 118	Auriette (Ire), 3, 116	10	1:34.79	63,900
1994	Rabiadella, 3, 118	L. A. Pincay Jr.	Magical Avie, 3, 116	Fancy 'n Fabulous, 3, 118	6	1:34.84	60,800
1993	Likeable Style, 3, 121	K. J. Desormeaux	Adorydar, 3, 113	Icy Warning, 3, 118	7	1:34.56	61,250
1992	Charm a Gendarme, 3, 116	R. Q. Meza	Moonlight Elegance, 3, 116	Morriston Belle, 3, 118	13	**1:33.66**	67,250
1991	Paula Revere, 3, 117	J. A. Santos	Shy Trick, 3, 114	Island Shuffle, 3, 119	7	1:35.50	61,850
1990	Brought to Mind, 3, 114	A. O. Solis	Tasteful T. V., 3, 119	She's a V. P., 3, 117	8	1:34.40	62,600
1989	Reluctant Guest, 3, 114	C. J. McCarron	Formidable Lady, 3, 119	General Charge (Ire), 3, 117	9	1:34.00	50,200
1988	Do So, 3, 117	A. O. Solis	Pattern Step, 3, 119	Sheesham, 3, 117	4	1:34.20	45,950
1987	Pen Bal Lady (GB), 3, 117	E. J. Delahoussaye	Sweettuc, 3, 119	Davie's Lamb, 3, 115	6	1:35.40	61,350
1986	Nature's Way, 3, 117	C. J. McCarron	An Empress, 3, 115	Miraculous, 3, 119	7	1:42.60	39,200
1985	Akamini (Fr), 3, 117	F. Toro	Charming Susan, 3, 115	Sharp Ascent, 3, 114	6	1:35.40	32,250
	Shywing, 3, 117	T. Lipham	Delaware Ginny, 3, 117	Savannah Dancer, 3, 119	8	1:35.60	33,450
1984	Heartlight, 3, 117	L. A. Pincay Jr.	Table Ten, 3, 115	Dear Carrie, 3, 115	8	1:35.60	38,900
1983	Stage Door Canteen, 3, 114	C. J. McCarron	I'm Prestigious, 3, 116	O'Happy Day, 3, 115	6	1:35.60	25,675
	Preceptress, 3, 115	M. Castaneda	Madam Forbes, 3, 114	Toga, 3, 116	6	1:36.60	25,675
1982	Skillful Joy, 3, 119	C. J. McCarron	Phaedra, 3, 122	Faneuil Lass, 3, 122	5	1:34.00	31,050
1981	Shimmy, 3, 114	P. A. Valenzuela	Queen of Prussia (Ire), 3, 117	Bee a Scout, 3, 114	6	1:36.20	37,450
1980	Ballare, 3, 117	C. J. McCarron	Street Ballet, 3, 122	Cinegita, 3, 114	6	1:35.00	31,600
1979	Variety Queen, 3, 117	R. Rosales	Top Soil, 3, 119	Whydidju, 3, 122	7	1:37.00	25,850
1978	Blue Blood, 3, 117	D. Pierce	Equanimity, 3, 122	Eximious, 3, 119	6	1:37.00	25,000
1977	*Glenaris, 3, 114	W. Shoemaker	Countess Fager, 3, 119	Shop Windows, 3, 114	7	1:36.00	19,300
1976	Now Pending, 3, 117	D. Pierce	Cascapedia, 3, 115	Queen to Be, 3, 119	11	1:36.00	20,650
1975	Raise Your Skirts, 3, 119	W. Mahorney	Fresno Flyer, 3, 117	Vol Au Vent, 3, 117	7	1:36.40	19,050
1973	Cellist, 3, 119	J. L. Rotz	Jungle Princess, 3, 120	Meilleur, 3, 119	10	1:42.20	20,250

Young, unmarried women are known as senoritas in Spanish. Senorita Breeders' Cup S. 1992-'95. Not held 1974. 1 1/16 miles 1973, 1986. Dirt 1973. Two divisions 1983, 1985. Nonwinners of a race worth $10,000 to the winner 1973.

Shadwell Turf Mile Stakes

Grade 1 in 2005. Keeneland, three-year-olds and up, 1 mile, turf. Held October 9, 2004, with a gross value of $600,000. First held in 1986. First graded in 1988. Stakes record 1:33.72 (2000 Altibr).

Year	Winner	Jockey	Second	Third	Strs	Time	1st Purse
2004	Nothing to Lose, 4, 126	R. Albarado	Honor in War, 5, 126	Silver Tree, 4, 126	9	1:35.55	$372,000
2003	Perfect Soul (Ire), 5, 126	E. S. Prado	Honor in War, 4, 126	Touch of the Blues (Fr), 6, 126	10	1:36.01	372,000
2002	Landseer (GB), 3, 123	E. S. Prado	Touch of the Blues (Fr), 5, 126	Beat Hollow (GB), 5, 126	8	1:35.55	372,000
2001	Hap, 4, 126	J. D. Bailey	Where's Taylor, 5, 126	Aly's Alley, 5, 126	9	**1:33.72**	279,744
2000	Altibr, 5, 126	R. Migliore	Strategic Mission, 6, 126	Quiet Resolve, 5, 126	9	1:33.72	279,744
1999	Kirkwall (GB), 5, 126	V. Espinoza	Delay of Game, 6, 126	Ladies Din, 4, 126	10	1:37.96	281,232
1998	Favorite Trick, 3, 123	P. Day	Soviet Line (Ire), 8, 126	Wild Event, 5, 126	5	1:35.00	168,795
1997	Wild Event, 4, 126	M. Guidry	Trail City, 4, 126	Soviet Line (Ire), 7, 126	10	1:34.66	134,075
1996	Dumaani, 5, 126	J. A. Krone	Desert Waves, 6, 126	Dove Hunt, 5, 126	9	1:35.68	133,843
1995	Dumaani, 4, 126	J. A. Krone	Holy Mountain, 4, 126	Mr Purple, 3, 123	10	1:38.78	116,514
1994	†Weekend Madness (Ire), 4, 123	S. J. Sellers	†Words of War, 5, 123	Pennine Ridge, 3, 123	10	1:38.73	116,328
1993	Coaxing Matt, 4, 126	E. M. Martin Jr.	Adam Smith (GB), 5, 126	Mr. Light Tres (Arg), 4, 126	9	1:53.16	116,421
1992	Lotus Pool, 5, 126	C. R. Woods Jr.	Thunder Regent, 5, 126	Chenin Blanc, 6, 126	6	1:48.36	114,902
1991	Itsallgreektome, 4, 126	J. Velasquez	Opening Verse, 5, 126	Super Abound, 4, 126	6	1:48.42	119,600
1990	Silver Medallion, 4, 126	C. Perret	Shot Gun Scott, 3, 122	†Coolawin, 4, 123	9	1:52.20	121,973
1989	Steinlen (GB), 6, 126	J. A. Santos	Crystal Moment, 4, 126	Posen, 4, 126	10	1:52.40	122,103
1988	Niccolo Polo, 5, 126	D. Brumfield	Pollenate (GB), 4, 126	Eve's Error (Ire), 5, 126	10	1:53.00	101,823
1987	Storm On the Loose, 4, 126	J. C. Espinoza	Uptown Swell, 5, 126	Vilzak, 4, 126	9	1:52.60	101,855
1986	Leprechauns Wish, 4, 126	J. D. Bailey	Ingot's Ruler, 4, 126	Wop Wop, 4, 126	7	1:51.80	100,848

Sponsored by Sheikh Hamdan bin Rashid al Maktoum's Shadwell Farm, located a short distance from Keeneland in Lexington. Grade 3 1991-'97. Grade 2 1998-2001. Keeneland Breeders' Cup S. 1991-'95. Keeneland Breeders' Cup Mile S. 1996-'98. 1 1/8 miles 1991-'93. †Denotes female.

Shakertown Stakes

Grade 3 in 2005. Keeneland, three-year-olds and up, 5 1/2 furlongs, turf. Held April 16, 2005, with a gross value of $113,300. First held in 1995. First graded in 2003. Stakes record 1:01.78 (2004 Soaring Free).

Year	Winner	Jockey	Second	Third	Strs	Time	1st Purse
2005	Soaring Free, 6, 121	J. D. Bailey	Mighty Beau, 6, 121	Parker Run, 4, 119	11	1:02.22	$70,246
2004	Soaring Free, 5, 120	S. J. Sellers	Chosen Chief, 5, 118	Banned in Boston, 4, 118	12	**1:01.78**	71,362
2003	No Jacket Required, 6, 118	B. Blanc	Testify, 6, 120	Aberdian (Ire), 6, 120	10	1:03.25	70,494
2002	Morluc, 6, 118	R. Albarado	Mighty Beau, 3, 116	Grangeville, 7, 118	10	1:03.25	52,731
2001	Airbourne Command, 6, 118	J. F. Chavez	Final Row (GB), 4, 118	Grangeville, 6, 118	10	1:02.71	52,824
2000	Bold Fact, 5, 115	R. Migliore	Howbaddouwantit, 5, 118	Claire's Honor, 6, 115	10	1:02.61	46,800
1999	Prankster, 6, 115	S. J. Sellers	Tyaskin, 6, 120	Howbaddouwantit, 4, 123	10	1:02.43	43,850
1998	Sesaro, 6, 123	S. J. Sellers	Brave Pancho, 4, 114	Claire's Honor, 4, 114	9	1:02.35	43,850
1997	G H's Pleasure, 5, 114	J. A. Santos	Louie the Lucky, 6, 114	Parklo, 5, 117	10	1:03.00	34,410

1995 **Cinch**, 3, 112 R. P. Romero Hollywood Flash, 3, 115 Ikickedthehabit, 3, 112 4 1:47.69 $38,168

Named for Shakertown, a Shaker village located at Pleasant Hill, Kentucky, near Harrodsburg. Formerly named for Robert E. Sangster's 1977 English Horse of the Year The Minstrel (1974 c. by Northern Dancer). The Minstrel S. 1995, 1997. Not held 1996. Course record 1997, 1998.

Sheepshead Bay Handicap

Grade 2 in 2005. Belmont Park, three-year-olds and up, fillies and mares, 1⅜ miles, turf. Held May 22, 2005, with a gross value of $150,000. First held in 1959. First graded in 1973. Stakes record 2:11.57 (1997 Maxzene).

Year	Winner	Jockey	Second	Third	Strs	Time	1st Purse
2005	Sauvage (Fr), 4, 115	J. Castellano	Angara (GB), 4, 118	Barancella (Fr), 4, 116	8	2:15.65	$90,000
2004	Moscow Burning, 4, 114	M. E. Smith	Spice Island, 5, 119	Meridiana (Ger), 4, 119	7	2:18.24	90,000
2003	Mariensky, 4, 114	J. R. Velazquez	Owsley, 5, 119	Silent Crystal, 4, 112	8	2:28.19	90,000
2002	Tweedside, 4, 114	J. R. Velazquez	Sweetest Thing, 4, 119	Golden Corona, 4, 114	10	2:13.63	90,000
2001	Critical Eye, 4, 122	M. J. Luzzi	Playact (Ire), 4, 115	Janet (GB), 4, 116	5	2:18.18	90,000
2000	Lisieux Rose (Ire), 5, 116	J. A. Santos	Melody Queen (GB), 4, 113	La Ville Rouge, 4, 113	7	2:14.16	90,000
1999	Soaring Softly, 4, 114	M. E. Smith	Starry Dreamer, 5, 114	Pinafore Park, 4, 113	6	2:15.11	90,000
1998	Maxzene, 5, 121	J. A. Santos	Sweetzie, 6, 111	Colonial Play, 4, 115	6	2:14.17	90,000
1997	Maxzene, 4, 117	M. E. Smith	Fanjica (Ire), 5, 117	Future Act, 5, 112	8	**2:11.57**	90,000
1996	Chelsey Flower, 5, 114	R. G. Davis	Look Daggers, 4, 114	Transient Trend, 4, 113	10	2:12.64	67,320
1995	Duda, 4, 112	J. D. Bailey	Danish (Ire), 4, 116	Chelsey Flower, 4, 112	7	2:13.69	65,700
1994	Market Booster, 5, 114	J. A. Santos	Irish Linnet, 6, 115	Fairy Garden, 6, 120	9	2:11.69	66,960
1993	Trampoli, 4, 116	M. E. Smith	Aquilegia, 4, 116	Revasser, 4, 114	4	2:14.08	67,680
1992	Ratings, 4, 112	J. Cruguet	Ristna (GB), 4, 110	Dancing Devlette, 5, 113	12	2:15.14	75,000
1991	Crockadore, 4, 112	M. E. Smith	Rigamajig, 5, 114	Star Standing, 4, 114	8	2:14.95	71,760
1990	Destiny Dance, 4, 111	J. A. Santos	Key Flyer, 4, 108	Yestday's Kisses, 4, 112	5	2:19.20	55,080
1989	Love You by Heart, 4, 118	J. Cruguet	Nastique, 5, 117	Laugh and Be Merry, 4, 112	10	2:12.60	72,480
1988	Nastique, 4, 111	R. G. Davis	Princely Proof, 5, 115	Anka Germania (Ire), 6, 124	9	2:16.40	71,040
1987	Steal a Kiss, 4, 111	E. Maple	Videogenic, 5, 117	Graceful Darby, 3, 112	5	2:23.80	87,180
1986	Possible Mate, 5, 124	J. Samyn	Tremulous, 4, 112	Dawn's Curtsey, 4, 113	9	2:14.00	75,480
1985	Persian Tiara (Ire), 5, 116	J. Velasquez	Key Dancer, 4, 118	Dictina (Fr), 4, 112	10	2:16.00	86,820
1984	Sabin, 4, 125	E. Maple	Thirty Flags, 4, 114	Double Jeux, 4, 111	9	2:12.80	71,880
1983	Sabin, 3, 112	E. Maple	First Approach, 5, 118	Mintage (Fr), 4, 114	9	2:13.80	67,920
1982	Castle Royale, 4, 110	J. J. Miranda	Trevita (Ire), 5, 118	So Pleasantly, 4, 113	6	2:13.00	66,060
	Dana Calqui (Arg), 4, 110	A. T. Cordero Jr.	If Winter Comes, 4, 110	Noble Damsel, 4, 115	7	2:14.20	66,060
1981	Love Sign, 4, 114	R. Hernandez	Rokeby Rose, 4, 115	Mairzy Doates, 5, 122	8	2:13.00	67,680
1980	The Very One, 5, 116	C. Cooke	Euphrosyne, 4, 114	Baby Sister, 5, 115	15	2:13.00	71,520
1979	Terpsichorist, 4, 117	E. Maple	Late Bloomer, 5, 123	Warfever (Fr), 4, 110	10	2:01.60	67,200
1978	Late Bloomer, 4, 118	J. Velasquez	Waya (Fr), 4, 115	Pearl Necklace, 4, 124	11	2:01.00	68,880
1977	Glowing Tribute, 4, 118	J. Velasquez	Fleet Victress, 5, 119	Dottie's Doll, 4, 116	6	1:59.60	65,700
1976	Glowing Tribute, 3, 110	P. Day	Bubbling, 4, 119	Carmelize, 4, 109	6	1:49.20	50,700
	Fleet Victress, 4, 115	P. Day	‡Redundancy, 5, 123	Summertime Promise, 4, 119	8	1:49.60	51,600
1975	Gems and Roses, 5, 112	M. Venezia	Hinterland, 5, 113	Carolerno, 4, 110	11	2:01.60	34,740
1974	North Broadway, 4, 116	A. T. Cordero Jr.	Lorraine Edna, 4, 117	Gnome Home, 4, 109	10	1:56.20	35,190
1973	Shearwater, 4, 112	A. T. Cordero Jr.	Inca Queen, 4, 118	Aglimmer, 4, 115	13	1:59.80	35,610

Named for the old Brooklyn, New York, racetrack Sheepshead Bay, which closed in 1911 with the ban of racing in New York and never reopened. Grade 3 1991-'94. Held at Jamaica 1959. Held at Aqueduct 1960-'74, 1976. 1¹/₁₆ miles 1959, 1963-'64. 1¹/₈ miles 1960-'61, 1976. 1 mile 1962. 1³/₁₆ miles 1965-'74. 1¹/₄ miles 1975, 1977-'79. Dirt 1959, 1962, 1974, 1990, 2001. Both sexes 1959-'61. Two divisions 1976, 1982. ‡Summertime Promise finished second, DQ to third, 1976 (2nd Div.). Course record 1997.

Shirley Jones Handicap

Grade 2 in 2005. Gulfstream Park, three-year-olds and up, fillies and mares, 7 furlongs, dirt. Held February 19, 2005, with a gross value of $150,000. First held in 1976. First graded in 1988. Stakes record 1:21.42 (2004 Randaroo).

Year	Winner	Jockey	Second	Third	Strs	Time	1st Purse
2005	Madcap Escapade, 4, 118	J. D. Bailey	Alix M, 5, 115	D'Wildcat Speed, 5, 114	7	1:22.06	$90,000
2004	Randaroo, 4, 118	J. R. Velazquez	Harmony Lodge, 6, 121	Halory Leigh, 4, 114	8	**1:21.42**	60,000
2003	Harmony Lodge, 5, 114	J. R. Velazquez	Gold Mover, 5, 117	Nonsuch Bay, 4, 117	6	1:22.35	60,000
2002	Cat Cay, 5, 118	P. Day	Raging Fever, 4, 120	Vague Memory, 5, 112	7	1:22.31	60,000
2001	Hidden Assets, 4, 114	J. D. Bailey	Another, 4, 115	Dream Supreme, 4, 120	6	1:22.40	60,000
2000	Marley Vale, 4, 118	J. R. Velazquez	Cassidy, 5, 113	Class On Class, 5, 113	8	1:22.24	60,000
1999	Harpia, 5, 118	R. Migliore	Scotzanna, 7, 115	Memories of Gold, 4, 113	5	1:22.17	60,000
1998	U Can Do It, 5, 116	S. J. Sellers	Glitter Woman, 4, 123	Flashy n Smart, 5, 118	8	1:23.33	60,000
1997	Chip, 4, 114	J. Bravo	Steady Cat, 4, 113	Flat Fleet Feet, 4, 117	7	1:22.24	60,000
1996	Dust Bucket, 5, 112	R. G. Davis	Russian Flight (Ire), 4, 110	Culver City, 4, 115	5	1:25.97	60,000
1995	Educated Risk, 5, 120	M. E. Smith	Elizabeth Bay, 5, 115	Clever Act, 4, 114	5	1:22.94	60,000
1994	Santa Catalina, 6, 115	P. Day	Jeano, 6, 113	Traverse City, 4, 113	11	1:21.94	60,000
1993	Jeano, 5, 113	S. J. Sellers	Santa Catalina, 5, 115	Miss Jealski, 4, 113	13	1:23.56	39,060
1992	Nannerl, 5, 111	J. A. Krone	Withallprobability, 4, 120	Fit for a Queen, 6, 119	10	1:23.23	36,600
1991	Love's Exchange, 5, 126	H. Castillo Jr.	Peach of It, 5, 116	Tipsy Girl, 5, 114	8	1:23.30	35,820
1990	Love's Exchange, 4, 112	E. Fires	Fantastic Find, 4, 113	Fit for a Queen, 4, 112	9	1:23.60	36,720
1989	Social Pro, 4, 110	J. F. Chavez	Haiati, 4, 113	Costly Shoes, 4, 114	8	1:23.60	35,640

1988 **Tappiano**, 4, 115	J. Cruguet	Cadillacing, 4, 111	Bound, 4, 115	13	1:23.00	$52,110
1987 **Life At the Top**, 4, 121	R. P. Romero	I'm Sweets, 4, 120	Jose's Bomb, 4, 112	8	1:22.80	35,640
1986 **Soli**, 4, 113	J. D. Bailey	Bessarabian, 4, 123	Nany, 6, 117	14	1:23.80	39,390
1985 **Mickey's Echo**, 6, 117	W. A. Guerra	Sugar's Image, 4, 117	Nany, 5, 122	10	1:23.60	37,110
1984 **Chic Belle**, 4, 114	C. Perret	Promising Native, 5, 114	First Flurry, 5, 115	9	1:22.40	25,578
1983 **Meringue Pie**, 5, 115	J. Velasquez	Cherokee Frolic, 5, 118	Mara Mia, 5, 109	8	1:24.20	24,717
Secrettame, 5, 116	J. Vasquez	Prime Prospect, 5, 120	Miss Hitch, 7, 114	9	1:23.60	25,158
1982 **Bushmaid**, 4, 112	J. D. Bailey	Expressive Dance, 4, 124	Sweetest Chant, 4, 117	11	1:23.20	19,470
1981 **Sober Jig**, 4, 112	J. P. Souter	‡Likely Exchange, 7, 116	Island Charm, 4, 115	12	1:23.20	27,153
1979 **Candy Eclair**, 3, 122	A. S. Black	Davona Dale, 3, 122	Drop Me a Note, 3, 114	4	1:08.60	17,766
1976 **Regal Quillo**, 3, 114	C. Baltazar	Forty Nine Sunsets, 3, 112	Tristana, 3, 112	10	1:42.20	10,200

Named for James V. Tigani's stakes winner Shirley Jones (1956 f. by Double Jay); Shirley Jones, the horse, was named for the actress. Not held 1977-'78, 1980. 1 1/16 miles 1976. 6 furlongs 1979. Two divisions 1983. ‡Cherry Berry finished second, DQ to fourth, 1981.

Shoemaker Breeders' Cup Mile Stakes

Grade 1 in 2005. Hollywood Park, three-year-olds and up, 1 mile, turf. Held May 30, 2005, with a gross value of $369,000. First held in 1938. First graded in 1973. Stakes record 1:32.64 (1994 Megan's Interco).

Year Winner	Jockey	Second	Third	Strs	Time	1st Purse
2005 **Castledale (Ire)**, 4, 124	R. R. Douglas	King of Happiness, 6, 124	Fast and Furious (Fr), 4, 124	7	1:33.17	$205,800
2004 **Designed for Luck**, 7, 124	P. A. Valenzuela	Singletary, 4, 124	Tsigane (Fr), 5, 124	8	1:32.81	282,000
2003 **Redattore (Brz)**, 8, 124	A. O. Solis	Special Ring, 6, 124	Touch of the Blues (Fr), 6, 124	9	1:33.37	225,000
2002 **Ladies Din**, 7, 124	P. A. Valenzuela	Redattore (Brz), 7, 124	Spinelessjellyfish, 6, 124	10	1:33.39	240,000
2001 **Irish Prize**, 5, 124	G. L. Stevens	Touch of the Blues (Fr), 4, 124	Brahms, 4, 124	9	1:33.68	285,000
2000 **Silic (Fr)**, 5, 124	C. S. Nakatani	Ladies Din, 5, 124	Sharan (GB), 5, 124	11	1:33.36	304,800
1999 **Silic (Fr)**, 4, 124	C. S. Nakatani	Ladies Din, 4, 124	Hawksley Hill (Ire), 6, 124	8	1:32.95	280,200
1998 **Labeeb (GB)**, 6, 124	K. J. Desormeaux	Fantastic Fellow, 4, 124	Hawksley Hill (Ire), 5, 124	7	1:33.29	319,200
1997 **Pinfloron (Fr)**, 5, 124	D. R. Flores	Surachai, 4, 124	Helmsman, 5, 124	14	1:34.40	353,400
1996 **Fastness (Ire)**, 6, 124	C. S. Nakatani	Romarin (Brz), 6, 124	Atticus, 4, 124	7	1:32.74	420,000
1995 **Unfinished Symph**, 4, 121	C. W. Antley	Rapan Boy (Aus), 7, 115	Journalism, 7, 117	9	1:33.14	98,400
1994 **Megan's Interco**, 5, 119	C. A. Black	Furiously, 5, 116	Rapan Boy (Aus), 6, 115	6	**1:32.64**	63,200
1993 **Journalism**, 5, 114	A. O. Solis	Lomitas (GB), 5, 118	Brief Truce, 4, 122	7	1:32.89	63,800
1991 **Exbourne**, 5, 118	G. L. Stevens	Super May, 5, 117	Dansil, 5, 111	7	1:33.50	65,300
1990 **Shining Steel (GB)**, 4, 114	C. J. McCarron	Super May, 4, 117	Brave Capade, 5, 111	5	1:34.00	63,000
1989 **Peace**, 4, 115	W. Shoemaker	Steinlen (GB), 6, 121	Political Ambition, 5, 122	8	1:33.00	65,700
1988 **Steinlen (GB)**, 5, 119	G. L. Stevens	Siyah Kalem, 6, 115	Neshad, 4, 115	8	1:33.20	80,200
1987 **Clever Song**, 5, 119	F. Toro	Al Mamoon, 6, 122	Le Belvedere, 4, 114	5	1:41.20	61,900
1986 **Clever Song**, 4, 116	F. Toro	Poly Test (Fr), 6, 115	Both Ends Burning, 6, 124	7	1:38.80	49,400
1985 dh- **Capture Him**, 4, 120	C. J. McCarron		Val Danseur, 5, 113	8	1:33.40	26,500
dh- **Retsina Run**, 5, 116	E. J. Delahoussaye					
Native Charmer (GB), 4, 113	S. Hawley	Gato Del Sol, 6, 120	Both Ends Burning, 5, 123	8	1:33.60	41,000
1984 **Massera (Chi)**, 6, 115	E. J. Delahoussaye	Sari's Dreamer, 5, 112	Barberstown, 4, 119	7	1:34.20	33,350
Drumalis (Ire), 4, 119	E. J. Delahoussaye	Bel Bolide, 6, 122	Hula Blaze, 4, 114	8	1:33.80	33,950
1980 **Peregrinator (Ire)**, 5, 119	C. J. McCarron	Dragon Command (NZ), 6, 117	Life's Hope, 7, 117	7	1:41.60	31,850
1979 **Farnesio (Arg)**, 5, 119	W. Shoemaker	Harry's Love, 4, 114	Star Spangled, 5, 120	5	1:41.60	31,100
1978 **J. O. Tobin**, 4, 125	S. Cauthen	Mr. Redoy, 4, 121	Miami Sun, 4, 115	5	1:41.40	30,600
1977 **Barrera**, 4, 119	L. A. Pincay Jr.	Beat Inflation, 4, 120	Maheras, 4, 124	5	1:07.40	24,650
1976 **Sporting Goods**, 6, 115	F. Toro	Century's Envoy, 5, 124	Money Lender, 5, 115	10	1:08.20	20,500
1975 **Rise High**, 5, 116	S. Hawley	‡Selecting, 6, 117	Money Lender, 4, 115	6	1:09.00	18,900
1974 **Beira**, 5, 115	W. Mahorney	Woodland Pines, 5, 119	Linda's Chief, 4, 124	8	1:07.80	19,700
1973 **Diplomatic Agent**, 5, 115	R. Rosales	Rough Night, 5, 111	Selecting, 4, 116	9	1:09.00	20,150

Named for Racing Hall of Fame jockey William Shoemaker (1931-2003), who retired as leading rider by number of wins. Formerly named in honor of Hollywood's turf industry. Formerly sponsored by the Miller Brewing Co. of Milwaukee, Wisconsin 1971. Grade 3 1987-'89. Not graded 1975-'86. Grade 2 1990-'99. Hollywood Premiere H. 1938-'63. Premiere H. 1964-'70, 1972-'80, 1984-'89. Miller High Life Premiere H. 1971. Shoemaker H. 1990-'95. Held at Santa Anita Park 1949. Not held 1942-'43, 1948, 1981-'83, 1992. 6 furlongs 1938-'49, 1951-'77. 7 furlongs 1950. 1 1/16 miles 1978-'80, 1986-'87. Dirt 1938-'80. Two-year-olds and up 1944. Two divisions 1984-'85. Dead heat for first 1985. ‡Shirley's Champion finished second, DQ to fourth, 1975. Equaled track record 1940. Equaled course record 1993, 1996. Course record 1994.

Shuvee Handicap

Grade 2 in 2005. Belmont Park, three-year-olds and up, fillies and mares, 1 mile, dirt. Held May 21, 2005, with a gross value of $196,000. First held in 1976. First graded in 1978. Stakes record 1:34.23 (2005 Society Selection).

Year Winner	Jockey	Second	Third	Strs	Time	1st Purse
2005 **Society Selection**, 4, 118	E. Coa	Daydreaming, 4, 119	Bohemian Lady, 4, 114	5	**1:34.23**	$120,000
2004 **Storm Flag Flying**, 4, 116	J. R. Velazquez	Passing Shot, 5, 117	Roar Emotion, 4, 117	6	1:36.10	120,000
2003 **Wild Spirit (Chi)**, 4, 115	J. Castellano	Smok'n Frolic, 4, 119	You, 4, 115	6	1:34.51	120,000
2002 **Shiny Band**, 4, 113	R. G. Davis	Raging Fever, 4, 121	Victory Ride, 4, 118	5	1:34.95	120,000
2001 **Apple of Kent**, 5, 114	R. Migliore	March Magic, 4, 113	Country Hideaway, 5, 118	5	1:35.16	120,000
2000 **Beautiful Pleasure**, 5, 122	J. F. Chavez	Biogio's Rose, 6, 115	Up We Go, 4, 114	5	1:35.65	120,000
1999 **Catinca**, 4, 121	R. Migliore	Sister Act, 4, 117	Tap to Music, 4, 115	6	1:34.38	90,000

Year	Winner	Jockey	Second	Third	Strs	Time	1st Purse
1998	Colonial Minstrel, 4, 117	J. R. Velazquez	Dixie Flag, 4, 120	Hidden Reserve, 4, 113	5	1:36.20	$90,000
1997	Hidden Lake, 4, 115	R. Migliore	Flat Fleet Feet, 4, 120	Escena, 4, 116	9	1:35.27	90,000
1996	Clear Mandate, 4, 111	J. A. Krone	Smooth Charmer, 4, 111	Restored Hope, 5, 115	7	1:35.01	90,000
1995	Inside Information, 4, 119	J. A. Santos	Sky Beauty, 5, 126	Restored Hope, 4, 115	4	1:35.10	80,220
1994	Sky Beauty, 4, 125	M. E. Smith	For all Seasons, 4, 113	Looie Capote, 5, 112	4	1:40.60	90,000
1993	Turnback the Alarm, 4, 117	C. W. Antley	Shared Interest, 5, 113	Vivano, 4, 112	9	1:43.11	90,000
1992	Missy's Mirage, 4, 116	E. Maple	Harbour Club, 5, 110	Versailles Treaty, 4, 119	6	1:40.74	102,960
1991	A Wild Ride, 4, 119	M. E. Smith	Buy the Firm, 5, 122	Degenerate Gal, 6, 117	6	1:42.52	103,140
1990	Tis Juliet, 4, 113	R. Migliore	Survive, 6, 119	Dreamy Mimi, 4, 114	7	1:43.00	102,780
1989	Banker's Lady, 4, 122	A. T. Cordero Jr.	Rose's Cantina, 5, 117	Grecian Flight, 5, 117	7	1:40.80	104,580
1988	Personal Ensign, 4, 121	R. P. Romero	Clabber Girl, 5, 118	Bishop's Delight, 5, 111	6	1:41.60	102,060
1987	Ms. Eloise, 4, 117	R. G. Davis	North Sider, 5, 120	Clemanna's Rose, 6, 114	10	1:41.80	107,820
1986	Lady's Secret, 4, 126	P. Day	Endear, 4, 115	Ride Sally, 4, 125	6	1:41.80	81,780
1985	Life's Magic, 4, 122	J. Velasquez	Heatherten, 6, 126	Some for All, 4, 109	7	1:42.40	83,820
1984	Queen of Song, 5, 117	S. Maple	Try Something New, 5, 121	Narrate, 4, 116	10	1:43.00	86,340
1983	Dance Number, 4, 113	A. T. Cordero Jr.	Number, 4, 117	May Day Eighty, 4, 116	4	1:40.40	49,500
1982	Anti Lib, 4, 113	J. Vasquez	Tina Tina Too, 4, 112	Funny Bone, 4, 108	7	1:41.60	33,420
1981	Chain Bracelet, 4, 117	R. Hernandez	Weber City Miss, 4, 118	Wistful, 4, 120	5	1:42.80	32,700
1980	Alada, 4, 115	J. Fell	Lady Lonsdale, 5, 115	Blitey, 4, 116	5	1:43.00	32,460
1979	Pearl Necklace, 5, 121	J. Fell	Tingle Stone, 4, 120	Kit's Double, 6, 109	8	1:41.40	32,280
1978	One Sum, 4, 121	R. Hernandez	Sparkling Topaz, 4, 107	Charming Story, 4, 113	5	1:44.00	31,830
1977	‡Mississippi Mud, 4, 113	J. Vasquez	Sweet Bernice, 4, 109	Secret Lanvin, 4, 111	10	1:43.60	32,760
1976	Proud Delta, 4, 122	J. Velasquez	Snooze, 4, 108	Let Me Linger, 4, 115	8	1:35.00	33,810

Named for Mrs. Whitney Stone's 1970, '71 champion older female and '69 Coaching Club American Oaks winner Shuvee (1966 f. by Nashua). Grade 1 1986-'96. 1 1/16 miles 1977-'94. ‡Secret Lanvin finished first, DQ to third, 1977.

Silverbulletday Stakes

Grade 3 in 2005. Fair Grounds, three-year-olds, fillies, 1 1/16 miles, dirt. Held February 12, 2005, with a gross value of $150,000. First held in 1982. First graded in 1999. Stakes record 1:42.09 (2002 Take Charge Lady).

Year	Winner	Jockey	Second	Third	Strs	Time	1st Purse
2005	Summerly, 3, 118	D. J. Meche	Eyes On Eddy, 3, 112	Enduring Will, 3, 122	9	1:43.79	$90,000
2004	Shadow Cast, 3, 116	R. Albarado	Quick Temper, 3, 113	Sister Swank, 3, 117	6	1:46.82	90,000
2003	Belle of Perintown, 3, 122	C. H. Borel	Afternoon Dreams, 3, 112	Rebridled Dreams, 3, 117	8	1:44.48	90,000
2002	Take Charge Lady, 3, 122	J. K. Court	Charmed Gift, 3, 119	Chamrousse, 3, 115	5	1:42.09	90,000
2001	Lakenheath, 3, 119	C. J. Lanerie	Morning Sun, 3, 112	Beloved by All, 3, 114	5	1:46.00	75,000
2000	Shawnee Country, 3, 122	D. J. Meche	Chilukki, 3, 122	Humble Clerk, 3, 122	9	1:45.11	75,000
1999	Silverbulletday, 3, 122	G. L. Stevens	Brushed Halory, 3, 114	On a Soapbox, 3, 119	8	1:44.36	75,000
1998	Cool Dixie, 3, 122	R. D. Ardoin	Lu Ravi, 3, 114	Silent Eskimo, 3, 112	9	1:43.38	75,000
1997	Blushing K. D., 3, 122	L. J. Meche	Tomisue's Delight, 3, 119	Morelia, 3, 122	6	1:42.48	60,000
1996	Up Dip, 3, 114	C. C. Bourque	Brush With Tequila, 3, 113	Not Likely, 3, 122	8	1:44.61	37,635
1995	Legendary Priness, 3, 113	C. A. Emigh	Broad Smile, 3, 122	Hero's Valor, 3, 114	9	1:44.42	25,875
1994	Playcaller, 3, 119	R. D. Ardoin	Two Altazano, 3, 112	Briar Road, 3, 112	7	1:44.31	31,095
1993	Bright Penny, 3, 114	R. D. Ardoin	She's a Little Shy, 3, 114	Wakerup, 3, 112	7	1:44.80	19,095
1992	Prospectors Delite, 3, 117	B. J. Walker Jr.	Royal Med, 3, 112	Glitzi Bj, 3, 119	7	1:43.80	19,020
1991	Nalees Pin, 3, 122	K. Bourque	Oxford Screen, 3, 112	Lady Blockbuster, 3, 119	7	1:46.50	19,065
1990	Windansea, 3, 112	R. P. Romero	Everlasting Lady, 3, 119	A Hula, 3, 114	11	1:46.40	16,560
1989	Exquisite Mistress, 3, 114	C. H. Borel	Jewel Bid, 3, 117	Lunar Princess, 3, 112	6	1:46.80	16,065
1988	False Glitter, 3, 114	S. P. Romero	Part Native, 3, 117	Quite a Gem, 3, 114	10	1:47.40	16,710
1987	Out of the Bid, 3, 112	K. Bourque	Trapped, 3, 115	Quick Closing, 3, 122	7	1:47.20	25,170
1986	Tiffany Lass, 3, 122	R. L. Frazier	Super Set, 3, 122	Port of Departure, 3, 117	10	1:46.00	25,200
1985	Marshua's Echelon, 3, 122	R. J. Franklin	Turn to Wilma, 3, 114	Not Again Debbie, 3, 114	8	1:45.20	19,150
1984	Texas Cowgirl Nite, 3, 122	K. Bourque	Only Bid, 3, 114	Runny Nose, 3, 114	8	1:42.00	18,950
1983	Duped, 3, 122	J. C. Espinoza	Shamivor, 3, 117	Juliet's Pet, 3, 117	5	1:43.00	14,100
1982	Linda North, 3, 122	R. J. Franklin	‡Mickey's Echo, 3, 117	Rose Bouquet, 3, 122	9	1:42.80	13,950

Named for Mike Pegram's 1998 champion two-year-old filly, '99 champion three-year-old filly, and '99 Davona Dale S. (G3) winner Silverbulletday (1996 f. by Silver Deputy). Formerly named for Calumet Farm's 1979 champion three-year-old filly Davona Dale (1976 f. by Best Turn). Davona Dale S. 1982-2000. 1 mile 40 yards 1982-'84. ‡Avadewan finished second, DQ to fifth, 1982.

Sixty Sails Handicap

Grade 3 in 2005. Hawthorne Race Course, three-year-olds and up, fillies and mares, 1 1/8 miles, dirt. Held April 23, 2005, with a gross value of $250,000. First held in 1976. First graded in 1984. Stakes record 1:46.69 (1999 Crafty Oak).

Year	Winner	Jockey	Second	Third	Strs	Time	1st Purse
2005	Isola Piu Bella (Chi), 5, 118	J. R. Velazquez	Rare Gift, 4, 115	Ghostly Gate, 4, 117	7	1:49.58	$150,000
2004	Allspice, 4, 115	C. A. Emigh	Bare Necessities, 5, 122	Mavoreen, 4, 114	6	1:50.66	150,000
2003	Bare Necessities, 4, 118	R. R. Douglas	Jaramar Rain, 4, 114	Lakenheath, 5, 114	9	1:52.84	150,000
2002	With Ability, 4, 115	J. Castellano	Lakenheath, 4, 115	Katy Kat, 4, 116	7	1:51.37	180,000
2001	License Fee, 6, 116	L. J. Melancon	Lady Melesi, 4, 116	Megans Bluff, 4, 116	8	1:49.11	180,000
2000	Lu Ravi, 5, 116	P. Day	Tap to Music, 5, 120	Batuka, 4, 116	8	1:49.15	180,000
1999	Crafty Oak, 5, 114	R. Sibille	Highfalutin, 5, 115	Lines of Beauty, 4, 114	7	1:46.69	180,000
1998	Glitter Woman, 4, 118	G. L. Stevens	Top Secret, 5, 115	dh- Im Out First, 5, 112	7	1:50.49	180,000
				dh- Tuxedo Junction, 5, 115			

1997	Top Secret, 4, 115	C. Perret	Hurricane Viv, 4, 119	Gold n Delicious, 4, 114	9	1:49.71	$180,000
1996	Alcovy, 6, 119	W. Martinez	Shoop, 5, 118	Lotta Dancing, 5, 120	13	1:50.70	180,000
1995	Eskimo's Angel, 6, 114	M. Guidry	Little Buckles, 4, 113	Norfolk Lavender, 4, 112	13	1:51.53	180,000
1994	Princess Polonia, 4, 113	W. S. Ramos	Eskimo's Angel, 5, 115	Joyous Melody, 4, 113	8	1:51.88	180,000
1993	Pleasant Baby, 4, 112	J. L. Diaz	Miss Jealski, 4, 113	Steff Graf (Brz), 5, 115	9	1:49.30	180,000
1992	Peach of It, 6, 114	E. T. Baird	Bungalow, 5, 115	Zend to Aiken, 4, 113	13	1:51.28	162,090
1991	Balotra, 4, 112	R. A. Meier	Charon, 4, 122	Beth Believes, 5, 113	8	1:50.98	157,860
1990	Leave It Be, 5, 119	H. A. Sanchez	Anitas Surprise, 4, 114	Degenerate Gal, 5, 116	8	1:53.40	156,510
1989	Valid Vixen, 4, 116	J. L. Diaz	Scorned Lass, 5, 115	Arcroyal, 5, 116	8	1:52.60	156,480
1988	Top Corsage, 5, 118	P. A. Valenzuela	Yukon Dolly, 4, 114	Inspiracion (Uru), 7, 110	6	1:52.00	125,010
1987	Queen Alexandra, 5, 123	D. Brumfield	My Gallant Duchess, 5, 116	Happy Hollow Miss, 4, 113	7	1:49.60	126,330
1986	Sefa's Beauty, 7, 124	R. P. Romero	Flying Heat, 4, 122	Farer Belle Lee, 7, 118	10	1:50.00	112,290
1985	Sefa's Beauty, 6, 122	P. Day	Farer Belle Lee, 6, 115	Princess Moran, 4, 113	12	1:52.60	113,580
1984	Queen of Song, 5, 122	R. J. Hirdes Jr.	Frosty Tail, 4, 120	Herb Wine, 5, 118	11	1:46.60	97,710
1983	Queen of Song, 4, 115	R. J. Hirdes Jr.	Bersid, 5, 121	Sefa's Beauty, 4, 120	9	1:43.80	96,630
1982	Targa, 5, 116	R. D. Evans	Really Royal, 4, 115	Knights Beauty, 5, 115	12	1:45.00	98,040
1981	Karla's Enough, 4, 120	E. Fires	Favorite Prospect, 4, 117	Romantic Mood, 4, 113	9	1:37.60	46,890
	Gold Treasure, 4, 118	J. L. Diaz	Sissy's Time, 4, 120	Satin Ribera, 4, 120	10	1:38.00	47,040
1980	Doing It My Way, 4, 115	R. J. Hirdes Jr.	Powerless, 4, 118	Cookie Puddin, 4, 116	8	1:40.20	40,335
	Conga Miss, 4, 118	G. Gallitano	Century Type, 6, 120	Royal Villa, 3, 115	7	1:40.20	40,215
1979	Strate Sunshine, 5, 113	R. Lindsay	Timeforaturn, 4, 114	Century Type, 5, 112	9	1:40.80	46,830
1978	Drop the Pigeon, 4, 118	J. L. Diaz	Evelyn's Time, 5, 113	Creation, 5, 119	11	1:39.40	16,320
1977	Kissapotamus, 5, 115	G. Baze	Kittyluck, 4, 116	Lady B. Gay, 4, 116	10	1:38.80	22,470
1976	Enchanted Native, 5, 115	L. Snyder	Honky Star, 5, 121	Regal Rumor, 4, 118	11	1:40.00	31,650

Named for John J. Petre's and Chris Vodanovich's 1974 Louis S. Meen Memorial H. winner Sixty Sails (1970 f. by Creme dela Creme). Held at Sportsman's Park 1976-'89, 2000-'02. 1 mile 1976-'81. 1 1/16 miles 1982-'84. Four-year-olds and up 1984-'87. Two divisions 1980-'81. Dead heat for third 1998. Track record 1993. Equaled track record 1999.

Skip Away Handicap

Grade 3 in 2005. Gulfstream Park, three-year-olds and up, open, 1 1/8 miles, dirt. Held April 2, 2005, with a gross value of $100,000. First held in 1987. First graded in 1992. Stakes record 1:48.10 (1991 Chief Honcho).

Year	Winner	Jockey	Second	Third	Strs	Time	1st Purse
2005	Eurosilver, 4, 113	J. Castellano	Twilight Road, 8, 114	Zakocity, 4, 117	10	1:49.29	$60,000
2004	Newfoundland, 4, 116	J. R. Velazquez	Supah Blitz, 4, 114	Bowman's Band, 6, 117	10	1:43.26	60,000
2003	Best of the Rest, 8, 121	E. Coa	Consistency, 4, 114	Roger E, 4, 114	5	1:42.72	60,000
2002	Sir Bear, 9, 116	E. S. Prado	Red Bullet, 5, 118	Hal's Hope, 5, 114	8	1:43.98	60,000
2001	American Halo, 5, 114	R. G. Davis	Vision and Verse, 5, 114	Pleasant Breeze, 6, 118	10	1:42.31	60,000
2000	Horse Chestnut (SAf), 5, 117	M. E. Smith	Isaypete, 4, 116	Rock and Roll, 5, 120	6	1:42.78	60,000
1999	Sir Bear, 6, 119	J. D. Bailey	Behrens, 5, 113	Hanarsaan, 6, 110	8	1:43.66	60,000
1998	Sir Bear, 5, 112	E. M. Jurado	Black Forest, 4, 113	Kiridashi, 6, 116	7	1:43.27	60,000
1997	Crafty Friend, 4, 114	M. E. Smith	Diligence, 4, 116	Ghostly Moves, 5, 114	8	1:42.27	45,000
1996	Halo's Image, 5, 119	P. Day	Wekiva Springs, 5, 119	Flying Chevron, 4, 116	7	1:42.71	45,000
1995	Fight for Love, 5, 113	J. D. Bailey	‡Danville, 4, 113	Pride of Burkaan, 5, 113	7	1:43.98	45,000
1994	Devil His Due, 5, 121	M. E. Smith	Migrating Moon, 4, 116	Northern Trend, 6, 111	8	1:43.17	45,000
1993	Technology, 4, 118	J. D. Bailey	Barkerville, 5, 117	Bidding Proud, 4, 114	8	1:42.47	45,000
1992	Honest Ensign, 4, 109	J. Cruguet	Peanut Butter Onit, 6, 114	Strike the Gold, 4, 117	7	1:49.41	45,000
1991	Primal, 5, 120	M. E. Smith	No Marker, 7, 113	Barkada, 5, 114	8	**1:48.10**	45,000
1990	Chief Honcho, 4, 116	E. Fires	Ole Atocha, 5, 113	Wonderloaf, 4, 113	10	1:43.40	60,000
1987	Big Blowup, 3, 115	C. Baltazar	Micanopy Boy, 3, 113	Jim Bowie, 3, 113	4	1:44.40	34,290

Named for Carolyn Hine's 1998 Horse of the Year and '98 Donn H. (G1) winner Skip Away (1993 c. by Skip Trial). Formerly named for Broward County, Florida, location of Gulfstream Park. Broward H. 1987-2000. Not held 1988-'89. 1 1/16 miles 1987, 1993-2004. Turf 1987. Three-year-olds 1987. ‡Northern Trend finished second, DQ to fifth, 1995.

Smile Sprint Handicap

Grade 2 in 2005. Calder Race Course, three-year-olds and up, 6 furlongs, dirt. Held July 10, 2004, with a gross value of $500,000. First held in 1958. First graded in 2003. Stakes record 1:08.95 (2000 Forty One Carats).

Year	Winner	Jockey	Second	Third	Strs	Time	1st Purse
2004	Champali, 4, 117	J. D. Bailey	Clock Stopper, 4, 115	Built Up, 6, 114	10	1:10.14	$294,000
2003	Shake You Down, 5, 119	M. J. Luzzi	Private Horde, 4, 113	My Cousin Matt, 4, 116	13	1:10.03	294,000
2002	Orientate, 4, 119	M. E. Smith	Echo Eddie, 5, 117	Crafty C. T., 4, 117	7	1:09.98	240,000
2001	Fappie's Notebook, 4, 116	J. F. Chavez	Thrillin Discovery, 6, 112	Salty Glance, 6, 115	12	1:09.89	120,000
2000	Forty One Carats, 4, 116	J. Castellano	Personal First, 3, 114	Alice's Notebook, 4, 111	7	**1:08.95**	180,000
1999	Silver Season, 3, 112	E. Coa	Son of a Pistol, 7, 119	My Jeff's Mombo, 5, 116	7	1:10.03	180,000
1998	Heckofaralph, 5, 115	W. Ramos	Thunder Breeze, 4, 113	Nicholas Ds, 4, 115	13	1:11.48	180,000
1997	†Vivace, 4, 114	R. P. Romero	Score a Birdie, 6, 113	Valid Expectations, 4, 117	9	1:10.65	150,000
1996	Constant Escort, 4, 114	E. O. Nunez	Honest Colors, 5, 114	Excelerate, 4, 113	10	1:21.82	60,000
1995	Request a Star, 4, 119	A. Toribio	Thats Our Buck, 5, 113	Halo's Image, 4, 118	11	1:23.69	60,000
1994	Exclusive Praline, 3, 117	W. S. Ramos	Migrating Moon, 4, 118	Fortunate Joe, 3, 114	10	1:22.29	60,000
1993	Song of Ambition, 4, 116	R. D. Lopez	Coolin It, 4, 113	Daniel's Boy, 5, 117	12	1:22.52	45,000
1992	My Luck Runs North, 3, 114	R. D. Lopez	Groomstick, 6, 119	Cigar Toss (Arg), 5, 112	9	1:17.57	45,000

Year	Winner	Jockey	Second	Third	Strs	Time	1st Purse
1991	**Greg At Bat**, 6, 114	J. Vasquez	Sunny and Pleasant, 3, 113	Perfection, 4, 115	11	1:24.26	$51,105
1990	**Groomstick**, 4, 113	P. A. Rodriguez	Country Isle, 3, 113	Medieval Victory, 5, 119	7	1:24.20	49,170
1989	**Glitterman**, 4, 119	W. A. Guerra	Doddle Bug Mel, 4, 112	Proud and Valid, 4, 112	7	1:10.40	32,970
1988	**Position Leader**, 3, 112	D. Valiente	Medieval Victory, 3, 112	Hooting Star, 3, 113	9	1:24.80	49,635
1987	**Princely Lad**, 4, 110	B. Green	Rilial, 6, 113	Ward Off Trouble, 7, 114	6	1:23.80	32,580
1986	**Jeblar**, 4, 123	J. A. Velez Jr.	Power Plan, 4, 116	Mugatea, 6, 115	9	1:24.80	32,790
1985	**Opening Lead**, 5, 117	J. M. Pezua	Rexson's Hope, 4, 121	King of Bridlewood, 5, 115	7	1:24.00	32,760
1984	**I Really Will**, 4, 120	G. St. Leon	Mo Exception, 3, 120	El Kaiser, 4, 112	11	1:12.00	33,840
1978	**J. Burns**, 3, 114	N. B. Navarro	Jungle Adam, 4, 113	Forward Charger, 4, 114	8	1:45.20	17,400
1977	**Ilefetchit**, 5, 115	M. A. Rivera	‡Super Boy, 4, 110	Coverack, 4, 121	9	1:44.60	17,700
1974	**Canvasser**, 2, 116	M. Solomone	Hunka Papa, 2, 120	What a Threat, 2, 112	12	1:47.60	14,880
1973	**Tai G.T.**, 2, 117	R. Hernandez	Mr. Sad, 2, 118	Neapolitan Way, 2, 118	12	1:46.40	14,880

Named for Frances A. Genter's 1986 champion sprinter and '85 Carry Back S. winner Smile (1982 c. by In Reality). Formerly named for the city of Miami Beach, Florida. City of Miami Beach S. 1958-'62. City of Miami Beach H. 1963-'69, 1978. Miami Beach H. 1970-'77, 1984-'93. Miami Beach Sprint H. 1994-'98. Not held 1975-'76, 1979-'83. 7 furlongs 1985-'88, 1990-'91, 1993-'96. 1¹/₁₆ miles 1958-'60. 6¹/₂ furlongs 1992. Two divisions 1958, 1961. ‡Coverack finished second, DQ to third, 1977. †Denotes female.

Sorrento Stakes

Grade 3 in 2005. Del Mar, two-year-olds, fillies, 6¹/₂ furlongs, dirt. Held August 7, 2004, with a gross value of $150,000. First held in 1967. First graded in 1986. Stakes record 1:15.26 (1995 Batroyale).

Year	Winner	Jockey	Second	Third	Strs	Time	1st Purse
2004	**Inspiring**, 2, 118	D. R. Flores	Souvenir Gift, 2, 122	Hello Lucky, 2, 118	8	1:18.29	$90,000
2003	**Tizdubai**, 2, 118	D. R. Flores	Dirty Diana, 2, 122	Solar Fire, 2, 118	8	1:17.15	90,000
2002	**Buffythecenterfold**, 2, 121	M. S. Garcia	Tricks Her, 2, 115	Indy Groove, 2, 117	8	1:17.39	90,000
2001	**Tempera**, 2, 117	D. R. Flores	Respectful, 2, 115	Roaring Blaze, 2, 117	8	1:16.13	90,000
2000	**Give Praise**, 2, 116	L. A. Pincay Jr.	Sea Reel, 2, 115	Fort Lauderdale, 2, 117	7	1:17.88	90,000
1999	**Chilukki**, 2, 121	D. R. Flores	November Slew, 2, 117	She's Classy, 2, 117	6	1:16.40	90,000
1998	**Silverbulletday**, 2, 121	G. L. Stevens	Excellent Meeting, 2, 117	Colorado Song, 2, 117	7	1:17.56	64,980
1997	**Career Collection**, 2, 121	C. S. Nakatani	Griselle, 2, 117	Bent Creek City, 2, 121	7	1:17.83	67,825
1996	**Desert Digger**, 2, 116	E. J. Delahoussaye	Silken Magic, 2, 117	Montecito, 2, 117	9	1:16.03	65,950
1995	**Batroyale**, 2, 119	G. L. Stevens	Cosmic Fire, 2, 117	Waycross, 2, 117	6	**1:15.26**	59,200
1994	**How So Oiseau**, 2, 117	P. A. Valenzuela	Ski Dancer, 2, 117	Serena's Song, 2, 121	8	1:15.89	47,100
1993	**Phone Chatter**, 2, 117	L. A. Pincay Jr.	Rhapsodic, 2, 121	Noassemblyrequired, 2, 117	6	1:16.23	45,900
1992	**Zoonaqua**, 2, 117	E. J. Delahoussaye	Eliza, 2, 117	Medici Bells, 2, 117	11	1:22.67	49,125
1991	**Soviet Sojourn**, 2, 121	C. S. Nakatani	La Spia, 2, 117	She's Tops, 2, 117	4	1:22.38	44,475
1990	**Lite Light**, 2, 115	R. A. Baze	Beyond Perfection, 2, 117	Dragonetta, 2, 117	8	1:22.00	47,100
1989	**Cheval Volant**, 2, 117	L. A. Pincay Jr.	Breezing Dixie, 2, 115	Dancing Jamie, 2, 115	6	1:23.80	46,575
1988	**Stocks Up**, 2, 117	G. L. Stevens	Approved to Fly, 2, 116	Lea Lucinda, 2, 117	8	1:23.40	49,100
1987	**Hasty Pasty**, 2, 121	L. A. Pincay Jr.	Lost Kitty, 2, 121	Torch the Track, 2, 117	6	1:23.00	37,200
1986	**Brave Raj**, 2, 117	P. A. Valenzuela	Breech, 2, 117	Footy, 2, 121	10	1:22.60	33,250
1985	**Arewehavingfunyet**, 2, 120	P. A. Valenzuela	Life At the Top, 2, 116	Python, 2, 117	11	1:37.00	34,250
1984	**Wayward Pirate**, 2, 114	W. Shoemaker	Doon's Baby, 2, 120	Trunk, 2, 116	6	1:37.20	31,350
1983	**Leading Ladybug**, 2, 115	P. A. Valenzuela	Bright Orphan, 2, 118	Lapidist, 2, 116	6	1:40.20	31,150
1982	**Time of Sale**, 2, 113	W. Shoemaker	Sharili Brown, 2, 117	Infantes, 2, 115	8	1:38.40	32,300
1981	**First Advance**, 2, 113	W. Shoemaker	Merry Sport, 2, 115	Skillful Joy, 2, 113	8	1:38.60	26,100
1980	**Native Fancy**, 2, 117	L. A. Pincay Jr.	Raja's Delight, 2, 115	Wedding Reception, 2, 114	8	1:38.80	22,950
1979	**Hazel R.**, 2, 117	C. J. McCarron	Arcades Ambo, 2, 113	Princess Karenda, 2, 114	6	1:35.80	19,100
1978	**Beauty Hour**, 2, 114	M. Castaneda	Hand Creme, 2, 117	Top Soil, 2, 114	8	1:37.00	19,150
1977	**My Little Maggie**, 2, 114	W. Shoemaker	Extravagant, 2, 114	Short Stanza, 2, 114	6	1:36.40	16,150
1976	**Telferner**, 2, 114	L. A. Pincay Jr.	Lullaby, 2, 117	Asterisca, 2, 114	9	1:36.60	16,150
1975	**Queen to Be**, 2, 113	D. G. McHargue	T. V. Terese, 2, 114	Pet Label, 2, 116	8	1:36.80	13,350
1974	**Spout**, 2, 115	A. Pineda	Just a Kick, 2, 115	Cut Class, 2, 113	11	1:36.80	14,000
1973	**Fleet Peach**, 2, 113	D. Pierce	Calaki, 2, 116	Poona's Double, 2, 116	5	1:09.20	12,600

Named for Sorrento, California, and the Sorrento Valley region. Grade 2 1994-2003. Not held 1968-'69. About 7¹/₂ furlongs 1967. 6 furlongs 1970-'73. 1 mile 1974-'85. 7 furlongs 1986-'92. Turf 1967. Nonwinners of a race worth $10,000 to the winner 1974-'75.

Spend a Buck Handicap

Grade 3 in 2005. Calder Race Course, three-year-olds and up, 1¹/₁₆ miles, dirt. Held October 23, 2004, with a gross value of $100,000. First held in 1991. First graded in 2003. Stakes record 1:42.59 (2001 Best of the Rest).

Year	Winner	Jockey	Second	Third	Strs	Time	1st Purse
2004	**Built Up**, 6, 115	E. Coa	Super Frolic, 4, 117	Gold Dollar, 5, 115	11	1:45.86	$60,000
2003	**Tour of the Cat**, 5, 116	A. Cabassa Jr.	Best of the Rest, 8, 122	Dancing Guy, 8, 116	8	1:46.30	60,000
2002	**Pay the Preacher**, 4, 114	C. H. Velasquez	Best of the Rest, 7, 121	Built Up, 4, 112	8	1:44.91	60,000
2001	**Best of the Rest**, 6, 116	E. Coa	Dancing Guy, 6, 117	Sir Bear, 8, 117	7	**1:42.59**	60,000
2000	**Groomstick Stock's**, 4, 111	R. B. Homeister Jr.	Reporter, 5, 113	Broadway Tune, 4, 113	8	1:44.82	60,000
1999	**Best of the Rest**, 4, 114	E. Coa	Dancing Guy, 4, 113	High Security (Ven), 4, 114	10	1:44.67	60,000
1998	**Unruled**, 5, 116	G. Boulanger	Sir Bear, 5, 124	Laughing Dan, 5, 113	6	1:45.68	60,000

1997	Derivative, 6, 116	J. C. Ferrer	Shan's Ready, 6, 114	Sur Irish's Secret, 4, 114	8	1:45.65	$30,000
1996	King Rex, 4, 116	R. D. Lopez	Derivative, 5, 113	Leave'm Inthedark, 4, 114	6	1:52.92	48,945
1995	Pride of Burkaan, 5, 119	R. R. Douglas	Crafty Chris, 5, 114	Dauntless Gem, 5, 114	10	1:51.96	60,000
1994	Daniel's Boy, 6, 111	P. A. Rodriguez	It'sali'lknownfact, 4, 110	Aggressive Chief, 4, 115	8	1:52.68	60,000
1991	Higgler, 3, 112	D. Nied	Jodi's Sweetie, 3, 115	Treblestaff, 3, 112	9	1:48.38	50,505

Named for Hunter Farm's 1985 Horse of the Year Spend a Buck (1982 c. by Buckaroo); Spend a Buck broke his maiden at Calder. Spend a Buck Breeders' Cup H. 1996. Not held 1993. 1⅛ miles 1994-'96. Three-year-olds 1991. Held as an overnight handicap 1992.

Spinaway Stakes

Grade 2 in 2005. Saratoga Race Course, two-year-olds, fillies, 7 furlongs, dirt. Held August 20, 2004, with a gross value of $250,000. First held in 1881. First graded in 1973. Stakes record 1:23.18 (1994 Flanders).

Year	Winner	Jockey	Second	Third	Strs	Time	1st Purse
2004	Sense of Style, 2, 121	E. S. Prado	Miss Matched, 2, 121	Play With Fire, 2, 121	7	1:23.83	$150,000
2003	Ashado, 2, 121	E. S. Prado	Be Gentle, 2, 121	Daydreaming, 2, 121	6	1:24.08	120,000
2002	Awesome Humor, 2, 121	P. Day	Forever Partners, 2, 121	Midnight Cry, 2, 121	12	1:24.36	120,000
2001	Cashier's Dream, 2, 121	D. J. Meche	Smok'n Frolic, 2, 121	Magic Storm, 2, 121	7	1:23.47	120,000
2000	Stormy Pick, 2, 121	J. C. Ferrer	Nasty Storm, 2, 121	Seeking It All, 2, 121	9	1:24.33	120,000
1999	Circle of Life, 2, 121	J. R. Velazquez	Surfside, 2, 121	Miss Wineshine, 2, 121	6	1:23.25	120,000
1998	Things Change, 2, 121	J. A. Santos	Extended Applause, 2, 121	Miss Jennifer Lynn, 2, 121	7	1:24.82	120,000
1997	Countess Diana, 2, 121	S. J. Sellers	Brac Drifter, 2, 121	Aunt Anne, 2, 121	5	1:24.17	120,000
1996	Oath, 2, 121	S. J. Sellers	Pearl City, 2, 121	Fabulously Fast, 2, 121	9	1:23.71	120,000
1995	Golden Attraction, 2, 121	G. L. Stevens	Flat Fleet Feet, 2, 121	Western Dreamer, 2, 121	8	1:23.85	120,000
1994	Flanders, 2, 119	P. Day	Sea Breezer, 2, 119	Stormy Blues, 2, 119	6	**1:23.18**	120,000
1993	Strategic Maneuver, 2, 119	J. A. Santos	Astas Foxy Lady, 2, 119	Delta Lady, 2, 119	9	1:10.34	120,000
1992	‡Family Enterprize, 2, 119	P. Day	Standard Equipment, 2, 119	‡Sky Beauty, 2, 119	5	1:09.82	120,000
1991	Miss Iron Smoke, 2, 119	M. A. Pedroza	Turnback the Alarm, 2, 119	Preach, 2, 119	10	1:10.68	120,000
1990	Meadow Star, 2, 119	J. A. Santos	Garden Gal, 2, 119	Good Potential, 2, 119	8	1:10.20	143,040
1989	Stella Madrid, 2, 119	A. T. Cordero Jr.	Golden Reef, 2, 119	Saratoga Sizzle, 2, 119	7	1:10.40	141,840
1988	Seattle Meteor, 2, 119	R. P. Romero	Love and Affection, 2, 119	Moonlight Martini, 2, 119	6	1:12.60	141,120
1987	Over All, 2, 119	A. T. Cordero Jr.	Bold Lady Anne, 2, 119	Flashy Runner, 2, 119	4	1:11.00	101,340
1986	Tappiano, 2, 119	J. Cruguet	Our Little Margie, 2, 119	Daytime Princess, 2, 119	4	1:11.40	130,680
1985	Family Style, 2, 119	D. MacBeth	Musical Lark (Ire), 2, 119	Nervous Baba, 2, 119	7	1:12.00	97,680
1984	Tiltalating, 2, 119	A. T. Cordero Jr.	Sociable Duck, 2, 119	Contredance, 2, 119	7	1:11.00	85,380
1983	Buzz My Bell, 2, 119	J. Velasquez	Demetria, 2, 119	Bottle Top, 2, 119	10	1:13.20	52,740
1982	Share the Fantasy, 2, 119	J. Fell	Singing Susan, 2, 119	Midnight Rapture, 2, 119	6	1:09.80	50,040
1981	Before Dawn, 2, 119	G. McCarron	Betty Money, 2, 119	Take Lady Anne, 2, 119	9	1:09.40	52,920
1980	Prayers'n Promises, 2, 119	A. T. Cordero Jr.	Fancy Naskra, 2, 119	Companionship, 2, 119	9	1:11.00	50,850
1979	Smart Angle, 2, 119	S. Maple	Jet Rating, 2, 119	Marathon Girl, 2, 119	9	1:10.60	48,510
1978	Palm Hut, 2, 119	R. I. Velez	Himalayan, 2, 119	Golferette, 2, 119	5	1:10.60	31,770
1977	Sherry Peppers, 2, 119	A. T. Cordero Jr.	Akita, 2, 119	Stub, 2, 119	4	1:10.80	32,340
1976	Mrs. Warren, 2, 119	E. Maple	Exerene, 2, 119	Sensational, 2, 119	10	1:10.40	33,060
1975	Dearly Precious, 2, 119	M. Hole	Optimistic Gal, 2, 119	Quintas Vicki, 2, 119	6	1:10.60	47,880
1974	Ruffian, 2, 120	V. A. Bracciale Jr.	Laughing Bridge, 2, 120	Scottish Melody, 2, 120	4	1:08.60	33,060
1973	Talking Picture, 2, 120	R. Turcotte	Special Team, 2, 120	Raisela, 2, 120	10	1:10.00	35,040

Named for 1880 consensus champion two-year-old filly Spinaway (1878 f. by *Leamington). Held at Belmont Park 1943-'45. Not held 1892-1900, 1911-'12. 5 furlongs 1881-'91. 5½ furlongs 1901-'22. 6 furlongs 1923-'93. ‡Sky Beauty finished first, DQ to third; Try in the Sky finished third, DQ to fourth, 1992.

Sport Page Handicap

Grade 3 in 2005. Aqueduct, three-year-olds and up, 7 furlongs, dirt. Held October 31, 2004, with a gross value of $111,200. First held in 1953. First graded in 1984. Stakes record 1:21.10 (2004 Mass Media).

Year	Winner	Jockey	Second	Third	Strs	Time	1st Purse
2004	Mass Media, 3, 113	J. Castellano	Lion Tamer, 4, 118	Gygistar, 5, 120	9	1:21.10	$66,720
2003	Voodoo, 5, 114	J. F. Chavez	Bowman's Band, 5, 120	Highway Prospector, 6, 114	9	1:22.18	67,620
2002	Multiple Choice, 4, 113	V. Carrero	Bowman's Band, 4, 118	‡Gold I. D., 3, 112	8	1:23.28	66,840
2001	Yonaguska, 3, 116	C. J. McCarron	Silky Sweep, 5, 116	Big E E, 4, 114	6	1:15.54	65,640
2000	Stalwart Member, 7, 117	N. Arroyo Jr.	Istintaj, 4, 117	Mister Tricky (GB), 5, 112	6	1:21.97	48,690
1999	Scatmandu, 4, 115	A. T. Gryder	Aristotle, 3, 114	Watchman's Warning, 4, 112	8	1:22.68	50,250
1998	Stormin Fever, 4, 120	R. Migliore	Olympic Cat, 4, 113	Adverse, 4, 113	9	1:21.49	50,115
1997	Stalwart Member, 4, 114	A. T. Gryder	Basquelan, 6, 116	Why Change, 4, 115	10	1:22.15	68,640
1996	Valid Expectations, 3, 117	C. B. Asmussen	Diligence, 3, 116	Blissful State, 4, 117	8	1:21.80	68,040
1995	Siphon (Brz), 4, 117	K. J. Desormeaux	In Case, 5, 113	Ft. Stockton, 5, 116	13	1:22.08	71,460
1994	Man's Hero, 4, 111	M. J. Luzzi	Itaka, 4, 117	Storm Tower, 4, 118	10	1:22.10	51,045
1993	Boom Towner, 5, 114	F. Lovato Jr.	†Raise Heck, 5, 115	Fabersham, 5, 113	9	1:10.62	53,730
1992	R. D. Wild Whirl, 4, 114	R. G. Davis	Senor Speedy, 5, 114	Burn Fair, 5, 114	6	1:09.93	51,570
1991	Senor Speedy, 4, 119	J. F. Chavez	Shuttleman, 5, 113	Gallant Step, 4, 113	9	1:09.34	55,080
1990	Senor Speedy, 3, 113	A. Santiago	Brave Adventure, 4, 116	Dargai, 4, 115	8	1:10.00	53,190
1989	Garemma, 3, 111	J. F. Chavez	Proud and Valid, 4, 111	Born to Shop, 5, 117	6	1:10.20	51,120

Year	Winner	Jockey	Second	Third	Strs	Time	Purse
1988	**High Brite**, 4, 120	A. T. Cordero Jr.	Proud and Valid, 3, 109	Matter of Honor, 3, 112	7	1:09.60	$64,980
1987	**Vinnie the Viper**, 4, 115	J. A. Krone	King's Swan, 7, 123	Banker's Jet, 5, 118	10	1:10.40	67,500
1986	**Best by Test**, 4, 112	F. Lovato Jr.	King's Swan, 6, 118	Sun Master, 5, 117	7	1:08.80	66,870
1985	**Raja's Shark**, 4, 120	A. T. Cordero Jr.	Love That Mac, 3, 110	Whoop Up, 5, 115	6	1:09.60	51,120
1984	**Tarantara**, 5, 117	R. Migliore	Muskoka Wyck, 5, 114	New Connection, 3, 113	13	1:10.80	46,140
1983	**Fast as the Breeze**, 4, 110	M. Toro	Maudlin, 5, 120	Swelegant, 5, 117	8	1:10.60	33,180
1982	**Maudlin**, 4, 115	J. D. Bailey	‡Top Avenger, 4, 115	Duke Mitchell, 3, 115	11	1:09.40	34,200
1981	**Well Decorated**, 3, 117	R. Hernandez	Engine One, 3, 116	Guilty Conscience, 5, 126	6	1:10.60	32,760
1980	**Dave's Friend**, 5, 126	V. A. Bracciale Jr.	Tilt Up, 5, 114	Hawkin's Special, 5, 114	8	1:08.20	34,380
1979	**Amadevil**, 5, 113	W. H. McCauley	Tanthem, 4, 123	Dave's Friend, 4, 119	7	1:09.40	32,580
1978	**Topsider**, 4, 109	M. Venezia	†What a Summer, 5, 124	Affiliate, 4, 118	6	1:10.20	32,400
1977	**Affiliate**, 3, 124	A. T. Cordero Jr.	Intercontinent, 3, 112	Gitche Gumee, 5, 117	4	1:10.00	31,560
1976	**Amerrico**, 4, 111	S. Hawley	†Honorable Miss, 6, 115	Relent, 5, 113	9	1:09.80	32,610
1975	**Lonetree**, 5, 122	E. Maple	Petrograd, 6, 119	Piamem, 5, 114	8	1:09.40	26,805
1974	**Startahemp**, 4, 114	J. Velasquez	Nostrum, 3, 114	Frankie Adams, 3, 121	7	1:09.60	22,950
1973	**Timeless Moment**, 3, 116	B. Baeza	Tap the Tree, 4, 122	North Sea, 4, 124	5	1:09.20	16,350

Named for Royce Martin's 1948 East View S. winner Sport Page (1946 c. by Our Boots). Held at Jamaica 1953-'58. Held at Aqueduct 1959-'67, 1969-'70, 1972-'94, 1996-2000, 2002. 6 furlongs 1953-'93. 6½ furlongs 2001. Two-year-olds and up 1953-'58. ‡King's Fashion finished second, DQ to fifth, 1982. ‡Sing Me Back Home finished third, DQ to eighth for a positive drug test, 2002. †Denotes female.

Stanford Breeders' Cup Handicap

Grade 3 in 2005. Bay Meadows, three-year-olds and up, 1 1/16 miles, turf. Held March 19, 2005, with a gross value of $113,750. First held in 1934. First graded in 1981. Stakes record 1:46.28 (2005 Adreamisborn).

Year	Winner	Jockey	Second	Third	Strs	Time	1st Purse
2005	**Adreamisborn**, 6, 117	R. A. Baze	Night Bokbel (Ire), 6, 116	Fantastic Spain, 5, 112	8	1:46.28	$68,750
2004	**Tronare (Chi)**, 4, 115	R. M. Gonzalez	Soud, 6, 118	Aly Bubba, 5, 116	9	1:48.48	41,250
2003	**Ninebanks**, 5, 116	R. J. Warren Jr.	Surprise Halo, 5, 115	Royal Gem, 4, 118	4	1:50.07	82,500
2002	**No Slip (Fr)**, 4, 117	K. J. Desormeaux	Kerrygold (Fr), 6, 116	Sumitas (Ger), 6, 119	5	1:49.41	82,500
2001	**Northern Quest (Fr)**, 6, 118	V. Espinoza	Eagleton, 5, 114	Entorchado (Ire), 4, 115	6	1:58.58	137,500
2000	**Deploy Venture (GB)**, 4, 115	R. A. Baze	Single Empire (Ire), 6, 121	Bonapartiste (Fr), 6, 119	8	2:19.12	120,000
1999	**Sayarshan (Fr)**, 4, 112	B. Blanc	Alvo Certo (Brz), 6, 117	Plicck (Ire), 4, 115	6	2:15.56	120,000
1998	**Dushyantor**, 5, 118	C. S. Nakatani	Eternity Range, 5, 114	Star Performance, 5, 116	6	2:15.26	150,000
1997	**Irish Wings (Ire)**, 5, 114	D. Carr	Savinio, 7, 117	Mufattish, 4, 114	7	1:49.60	120,000
1996	**Time Star**, 5, 116	C. A. Black	Sand Reef (GB), 5, 116	Bon Point (GB), 6, 117	5	2:16.37	120,000
1995	**Special Price**, 6, 122	E. J. Delahoussaye	Bluegrass Prince (Ire), 4, 122	Sans Ecocide (GB), 4, 122	6	2:15.14	110,000
1994	**Alex the Great (GB)**, 5, 118	P. A. Valenzuela	Fanmore, 6, 117	Emerald Jig, 5, 113	8	2:15.11	165,000
1993	**Val des Bois (Fr)**, 7, 119	P. A. Valenzuela	Norwich (GB), 6, 116	Never Black, 6, 116	5	1:48.21	165,000
1992	**Algenib (Arg)**, 5, 120	L. A. Pincay Jr.	Missionary Ridge (GB), 5, 114	Never Black, 5, 113	7	2:13.96	220,000
1991	**Forty Niner Days**, 4, 115	R. Q. Meza	Aksar, 4, 115	Missionary Ridge (GB), 4, 114	9	2:17.30	220,000
1990	**†Petite Ile (Ire)**, 4, 113	C. A. Black	Valdali (Ire), 4, 114	Pleasant Variety, 6, 116	11	2:15.60	220,000
1989	**Frankly Perfect**, 4, 122	E. J. Delahoussaye	Pleasant Variety, 5, 114	†Brown Bess, 7, 114	7	2:15.00	165,000
1988	**Great Communicator**, 5, 120	R. Sibille	Putting (Fr), 5, 117	Rivlia, 6, 120	5	2:15.40	165,000
1987	**Rivlia**, 5, 116	C. J. McCarron	Air Display, 4, 115	Reco (Fr), 5, 113	8	2:14.20	165,000
1986	**dh- Le Solaret (Fr)**, 4, 113	M. Castaneda		Complice (Fr), 5, 115	5	2:16.40	113,875
	dh- Val Danseur, 6, 117	G. L. Stevens					
1985	**Fatih**, 5, 119	T. Lipham	†Fact Finder, 6, 115	dh- Nak Ack, 4, 115	9	2:15.40	171,770
				dh- Semillero (Chi), 5, 115			
1984	**John Henry**, 9, 125	C. J. McCarron	Silveyville, 6, 117	Lucence, 5, 116	6	2:13.00	184,200
1983	**Silveyville**, 5, 115	D. Winick	Ask Me, 4, 115	Majesty's Prince, 4, 122	9	2:14.60	165,800
1982	**Regal Bearing (GB)**, 6, 117	R. A. Baze	Visible Pole, 4, 110	Score Twenty Four, 5, 121	5	1:46.00	73,900
1981	**Caterman (NZ)**, 5, 123	M. Castaneda	Opus Dei (Fr), 6, 121	His Honor, 6, 118	9	1:41.40	77,000
1980	**Eagle Toast**, 6, 113	P. A. Valenzuela	Daranstone, 5, 108	Saboulard (Fr), 5, 116	7	1:41.00	63,200
1979	**As de Copas (Arg)**, 6, 120	H. E. Moreno	True Statement, 5, 117	Bywayofchicago, 5, 123	6	1:43.40	62,600
1978	**Bad 'n Big**, 4, 120	A. L. Diaz	Effervescing, 5, 123	Jumping Hill, 6, 124	9	1:44.80	65,500
1977	**Announcer**, 5, 115	M. Castaneda	The Fop, 4, 114	Sir Jason, 6, 116	14	1:40.40	71,700
1976	**Pass the Glass**, 5, 119	F. Olivares	Willie Pleasant, 5, 111	Barrydown, 6, 117	6	1:41.40	31,250
1975	**Pass the Glass**, 4, 115	F. Olivares	Confederate Yankee, 4, 116	Ga Hai, 4, 118	10	1:41.80	33,150
1974	**Acclimatization**, 6, 119	S. Valdez	*Yvetot, 6, 118	Wild World, 5, 111	9	2:27.80	46,350
1973	**Wing Out**, 5, 124	R. Schacht	Fair Test, 5, 116	*Yvetot, 5, 116	7	1:43.80	30,800

Named for Stanford University, located in nearby Palo Alto, California. Grade 2 1982-'84, 1986-'95. Not graded 1985. Bay Meadows H. 1934-2000. Bay Meadows Breeders' Cup H. 2001-'04. 1 1/8 miles 1934-'35, 1938, 1940-'51, 1953, 1959, 1961, 1970-'72, 1978-'83, 1985-2004. 1 1/4 miles 1952. 1 3/8 miles 1984. Dirt 1934-'77, 1980. Two-year-olds and up 1935-'40, 1942, 1947-'50, 1953. Course record 1993, 1995. †Denotes female.

Stars and Stripes Breeders' Cup Turf Handicap

Grade 3 in 2005. Arlington Park, three-year-olds and up, 1 1/2 miles, turf. Held July 4, 2004, with a gross value of $200,000. First held in 1929. First graded in 1973. Stakes record 2:27.50 (2002 Cetewayo).

Year	Winner	Jockey	Second	Third	Strs	Time	1st Purse
2004	**Ballingarry (Ire)**, 5, 120	R. R. Douglas	‡Grey Beard, 5, 117	Art Variety (Brz), 6, 116	8	2:36.30	$120,000
2003	**Ballingarry (Ire)**, 4, 121	R. R. Douglas	Dr. Brendler, 5, 118	Jack's Own Time, 4, 112	9	2:28.30	131,520
2002	**Cetewayo**, 8, 118	R. R. Douglas	Private Son, 4, 115	Pisces, 5, 117	9	2:27.50	137,475

2001	**Falcon Flight (Fr)**, 5, 114	R. R. Douglas	Langston, 4, 114	Williams News, 6, 116	11	2:27.86	$96,300
2000	**Williams News**, 5, 115	R. Albarado	Profit Option, 5, 110	Buff, 5, 114	12	2:31.22	148,425
1997	**Lakeshore Road**, 4, 114	C. H. Borel	Chief Bearhart, 4, 119	Awad, 7, 119	9	2:29.57	140,025
1996	**Vladivostok**, 6, 116	C. Perret	Raintrap (GB), 6, 118	Special Price, 7, 118	8	2:30.23	138,075
1995	**Snake Eyes**, 5, 116	R. Albarado	Coaxing Matt, 6, 115	Bucks Nephew, 5, 114	7	1:56.46	45,000
1994	**Marastani**, 4, 113	A. T. Gryder	‡Snake Eyes, 4, 117	The Vid, 4, 113	12	1:54.64	60,000
1993	**Little Bro Lantis**, 5, 114	C. C. Bourque	Stark South, 5, 119	Coaxing Matt, 4, 115	12	1:56.92	60,000
1992	**Plate Dancer**, 7, 114	E. Fires	Little Bro Lantis, 4, 114	Stark South, 4, 114	9	1:55.00	60,000
1991	**Blair's Cove**, 6, 115	G. K. Gomez	Opening Verse, 5, 118	Cameroon, 4, 112	9	1:55.95	60,000
1990	**Mister Sicy (Fr)**, 4, 114	C. A. Black	Silver Medallion, 4, 115	Careafolie (Ire), 5, 113	12	1:54.40	69,900
1989	**Salem Drive**, 7, 116	P. Day	Green Barb, 4, 115	Delegant, 5, 115	10	1:55.20	69,660
1987	**Sharrood**, 4, 120	F. Toro	Explosive Darling, 5, 121	Santella Mac (Ire), 4, 115	11	1:56.20	52,080
1986	**Explosive Darling**, 4, 115	E. Fires	Clever Song, 4, 120	Forkintheroad, 4, 113	13	1:48.40	70,560
1985	**Drumalis (Ire)**, 5, 118	P. Day	Best of Both, 5, 116	Lofty (Ire), 5, 117	13	1:42.20	91,920
1984	**Tough Mickey**, 4, 119	J. Samyn	Fortnightly, 4, 115	Jack Slade, 4, 113	15	1:41.40	80,460
1983	**Rossi Gold**, 7, 122	P. Day	Who's for Dinner, 4, 110	Lucence, 4, 115	7	1:48.80	70,860
1982	**Rossi Gold**, 6, 124	P. Day	Johnny Dance, 4, 115	Don Roberto, 5, 118	7	1:46.00	70,560
1981	**‡dh- Ben Fab**, 4, 122	G. Stahlbaum		Opus Dei (Fr), 6, 116	8	1:43.80	48,600
	‡dh- Rossi Gold, 5, 123	P. Day					
1980	**Told**, 4, 114	J. Samyn	Rossi Gold, 4, 111	Overskate, 5, 130	8	1:43.00	72,960
1979	**Overskate**, 4, 125	R. Platts	That's a Nice, 5, 119	Bold Standard, 5, 111	8	1:44.00	33,360
1978	**Old Frankfort**, 6, 112	R. Turcotte	Capt. Stevens, 8, 114	That's a Nice, 4, 122	10	1:50.20	34,380
1977	**Quick Card**, 4, 118	M. Solomone	dh-Emperor Rex, 6, 116		14	1:43.00	35,640
			dh-Proponent, 5, 116				
1976	**Passionate Pirate**, 5, 114	H. Arroyo	Improviser, 4, 122	*Zografos, 8, 115	11	1:43.00	39,500
1975	**Buffalo Lark**, 5, 121	L. Snyder	*Kuryakin, 5, 111	‡*Zografos, 7, 115	7	1:43.00	40,600
1974	***Zografos**, 6, 113	W. Gavidia	Smooth Dancer, 4, 111	Fun Co K., 5, 109	10	1:50.80	45,600
1973	**Triumphant**, 4, 119	A. Rini	Super Sail, 5, 116	Vegas Vic, 5, 114	11	1:34.80	36,400

Traditionally held during the July 4 holiday, celebrating the birth of the United States and its flag, the "stars and stripes." Grade 2 1973-'89. Stars and Stripes H. 1929-'95. Stars and Stripes Breeders' Cup H. 2000-'01. Held at Washington Park 1958-'59. Not held 1988, 1998-'99. $1\frac{1}{8}$ miles 1929-'41, 1943-'72, 1974-'75, 1986. $1\frac{3}{16}$ miles 1942, 1987-'95. 1 mile 1973. $1\frac{1}{16}$ miles 1976-'85. Dirt 1929-'49, 1956-'58, 1960-'64, 1968-'74. Originally scheduled at $1\frac{1}{16}$ miles on the turf 1973. Originally scheduled at $1\frac{1}{8}$ miles on the turf 1974. Three-year-olds 1958. Dead heat for second 1977. Dead heat for first 1981. ‡*Nevermore II finished third, DQ to seventh, 1975. ‡Key to Content finished first, DQ to fourth, 1981. ‡Kazabaiyn finished second, DQ to fifth, 1994. ‡Silverfoot finished second, DQ to fourth, 2004.

Stephen Foster Handicap

Grade 1 in 2005. Churchill Downs, three-year-olds and up, $1\frac{1}{8}$ miles, dirt. Held June 12, 2004, with a gross value of $810,750. First held in 1982. First graded in 1988. Stakes record 1:47.28 (1999 Victory Gallop).

Year	Winner	Jockey	Second	Third	Strs	Time	1st Purse
2004	**Colonial Colony**, 6, 111	R. Bejarano	Southern Image, 4, 122	Perfect Drift, 5, 119	6	1:50.40	$502,665
2003	**Perfect Drift**, 4, 115	P. Day	Mineshaft, 4, 123	Aldebaran, 5, 120	10	1:47.55	531,030
2002	**Street Cry (Ire)**, 4, 120	J. D. Bailey	Dollar Bill, 4, 114	Tenpins, 4, 115	8	1:47.84	516,615
2001	**Guided Tour**, 5, 113	L. J. Melancon	Captain Steve, 4, 123	Brahms, 4, 114	8	1:47.74	515,220
2000	**Golden Missile**, 5, 118	K. J. Desormeaux	Ecton Park, 4, 114	Cat Thief, 4, 117	6	1:49.56	502,200
1999	**Victory Gallop**, 4, 120	J. D. Bailey	Nite Dreamer, 4, 110	Littlebitlively, 5, 115	7	**1:47.28**	512,895
1998	**Awesome Again**, 4, 113	P. Day	Silver Charm, 4, 127	Semoran, 5, 114	7	1:48.61	495,690
1997	**City by Night**, 4, 113	S. J. Sellers	Victor Cooley, 4, 115	Semoran, 4, 113	6	1:50.40	101,649
1996	**Tenants Harbor**, 4, 112	F. C. Torres	Pleasant Tango, 6, 113	Mt. Sassafras, 4, 115	8	1:49.94	107,933
1995	**Recoup the Cash**, 5, 119	A. T. Gryder	Tyus, 5, 114	Powerful Punch, 6, 114	9	1:49.39	109,298
1994	**Recoup the Cash**, 4, 112	J. L. Diaz	Taking Risks, 4, 113	Dignitas, 5, 113	7	1:49.46	106,275
1993	**Root Boy**, 5, 113	T. G. Turner	Discover, 5, 114	Flying Continental, 7, 117	11	1:50.80	74,100
1992	**Discover**, 4, 116	B. E. Bartram	Barkerville, 4, 113	Classic Seven, 4, 113	13	1:50.14	75,335
1991	**Black Tie Affair (Ire)**, 5, 119	J. L. Diaz	Private School, 4, 114	Greydar, 4, 115	5	1:49.81	70,915
1990	**No Marker**, 6, 115	A. T. Gryder	Western Playboy, 4, 117	Lucky Peach, 5, 114	10	1:49.80	72,930
1989	**Air Worthy**, 4, 115	D. J. Soto	J. T.'s Pet, 5, 115	Present Value, 5, 114	9	1:49.60	73,255
1988	**Honor Medal**, 7, 123	L. E. Ortega	Outlaws Sham, 5, 115	Momsfurrari, 4, 109	10	1:50.60	82,655
1987	**Red Attack**, 5, 119	J. L. Kaenel	Sir Naskra, 5, 116	Blue Buckaroo, 4, 117	9	1:51.20	65,254
1986	**Hopeful Word**, 5, 123	K. K. Allen	Dramatic Desire, 5, 114	Ten Gold Pots, 5, 122	7	1:49.40	64,133
1985	**Vanlandingham**, 4, 121	P. Day	Manantial (Chi), 7, 112	Sovereign Exchange, 4, 113	7	1:48.80	35,263
1984	**Mythical Ruler**, 6, 117	J. McKnight	Fairly Straight, 3, 114	Le Cou Cou, 4, 121	5	1:49.60	34,808
1983	**Vodika Collins**, 5, 118	L. Moyers	Mythical Ruler, 5, 120	Northern Majesty, 4, 114	7	1:49.20	35,588
1982	**Vodika Collins**, 4, 116	T. Barrow	Mythical Ruler, 4, 113	Two's a Plenty, 5, 115	7	1:51.80	38,610

Named for composer Stephen Foster (1826-'64), who wrote Kentucky's state song, "My Old Kentucky Home." Grade 3 1988-'94. Grade 2 1995-2001. Four-year-olds and up 1983, 1985-'87. Track record 1999.

Stonerside Beaumont Stakes

Grade 2 in 2005. Keeneland, three-year-olds, fillies, about 7 furlongs, dirt. Held April 14, 2005, with a gross value of $250,000. First held in 1986. First graded in 1990. Stakes record 1:25.61 (1999 Swingin On Ice).

Year	Winner	Jockey	Second	Third	Strs	Time	1st Purse
2005	**In the Gold**, 3, 117	R. Bejarano	Holy Trinity, 3, 117	Hot Storm, 3, 119	5	1:26.04	$155,000
2004	**Victory U. S. A.**, 3, 118	J. D. Bailey	Halfbridled, 3, 123	Wildwood Flower, 3, 118	8	1:27.06	155,000

Year	Winner	Jockey	Second	Third	Strs	Time	1st Purse
2003	My Boston Gal, 3, 120	P. Day	Bird Town, 3, 118	Midnight Cry, 3, 118	9	1:26.87	$155,000
2002	Proper Gamble, 3, 118	J. Castellano	Respectful, 3, 116	Vicki Vallencourt, 3, 118	7	1:28.79	155,000
2001	Xtra Heat, 3, 120	R. Wilson	Mountain Bird, 3, 116	Raging Fever, 3, 123	5	1:27.86	155,000
2000	Sahara Gold, 3, 123	J. D. Bailey	Swept Away, 3, 118	Darling My Darling, 3, 116	6	1:26.58	84,847
1999	Swingin On Ice, 3, 115	R. Albarado	Secret Hills, 3, 115	Appealing Phylly, 3, 123	7	1:25.61	83,917
1998	Star of Broadway, 3, 119	P. Day	Santaria, 3, 119	Bourbon Belle, 3, 119	12	1:26.67	91,140
1997	dh- Make Haste, 3, 112	P. Day		Move, 3, 121	7	1:28.08	57,042
	dh- Screamer, 3, 112	R. Albarado					
1996	Golden Gale, 3, 115	M. E. Smith	Birr, 3, 115	Bright Time, 3, 115	7	1:26.10	84,398
1995	Dixieland Gold, 3, 118	D. Penna	Niner's Home, 3, 113	Conquistadoress, 3, 118	10	1:27.42	69,874
1994	Her Temper, 3, 112	P. Day	Lotta Dancing, 3, 113	Term Limits, 3, 121	6	1:28.41	67,456
1993	Roamin Rachel, 3, 122	C. W. Antley	Added Asset, 3, 114	Fit to Lead, 3, 122	10	1:26.48	69,998
1992	Fluttery Danseur, 3, 122	S. J. Sellers	Miss Iron Smoke, 3, 119	Spinning Round, 3, 122	8	1:27.46	53,918
1991	Ifyoucouldseemenow, 3, 122	M. A. Pedroza	Versailles Treaty, 3, 114	Ever a Lady, 3, 114	6	1:27.01	54,275
1990	Go for Wand, 3, 122	R. P. Romero	Trumpet's Blare, 3, 119	Seaside Attraction, 3, 119	6	1:26.40	53,983
1989	Exquisite Mistress, 3, 117	D. Brumfield	Love's Exchange, 3, 114	Up, 3, 114	10	1:28.60	36,774
1988	On to Royalty, 3, 121	C. Perret	Plate Queen, 3, 121	Tilt My Halo, 3, 121	9	1:26.60	46,680
1987	Fold the Flag, 3, 113	S. Hawley	Bound, 3, 113	Arctic Cloud, 3, 118	6	1:28.20	43,428
1986	Classy Cathy, 3, 112	E. Fires	She's a Mystery, 3, 119	Close Tolerance, 3, 112	13	1:27.60	37,408

Named for Hal Price Headley's Beaumont Farm; Headley was one of Keeneland's founders and the track's first president. Sponsored by Robert and Janice McNair's Stonerside Stables of Paris, Kentucky 2000-'05. Grade 3 1990-'92. Beaumont S. 1986-'99. Dead heat for first 1997.

Stonerside Forward Gal Stakes

Grade 2 in 2005. Gulfstream Park, three-year-olds, fillies, 7 furlongs, dirt. Held March 5, 2005, with a gross value of $150,000. First held in 1981. First graded in 1986. Stakes record 1:21.76 (1997 Glitter Woman).

Year	Winner	Jockey	Second	Third	Strs	Time	1st Purse
2005	Letgomyecho, 3, 115	J. Castellano	Little Money Down, 3, 115	Hot Storm, 3, 121	7	1:23.24	$90,000
2004	Madcap Escapade, 3, 121	J. D. Bailey	La Reina, 3, 121	Frenchglen, 3, 115	5	1:22.97	90,000
2003	Midnight Cry, 3, 117	E. S. Prado	Final Round, 3, 117	Chimichurri, 3, 121	8	1:22.55	60,000
2002	Take the Cake, 3, 117	R. R. Douglas	A New Twist, 3, 121	Cherokee Girl, 3, 117	7	1:25.47	60,000
2001	Gold Mover, 3, 121	J. D. Bailey	Hazino, 3, 114	Thunder Bertie, 3, 118	5	1:22.43	60,000
2000	Miss Inquisitive, 3, 114	T. G. Turner	Swept Away, 3, 118	Regally Appealing, 3, 118	9	1:22.25	45,000
1999	China Storm, 3, 114	P. Day	Three Ring, 3, 121	Extended Applause, 3, 112	5	1:23.69	45,000
1998	Uanme, 3, 113	S. J. Sellers	Diamond On the Run, 3, 114	Holy Capote, 3, 112	7	1:24.56	45,000
1997	Glitter Woman, 3, 114	M. E. Smith	City Band, 3, 121	Southern Playgirl, 3, 121	6	1:21.76	45,000
1996	Mindy Gayle, 3, 112	J. A. Krone	Marfa's Finale, 3, 113	Supah Jen, 3, 114	7	1:24.54	45,000
1995	Chaposa Springs, 3, 114	H. Castillo Jr.	Culver City, 3, 113	Mackenzie Slew, 3, 114	7	1:24.18	44,580
1994	Mynameispanama, 3, 113	M. Castaneda	Frigid Coed, 3, 116	Wonderlan, 3, 114	9	1:22.97	45,960
1993	Sum Runner, 3, 118	R. P. Romero	Boots'n Jackie, 3, 121	Lunar Spook, 3, 118	9	1:23.67	45,270
1992	Spinning Round, 3, 118	J. A. Santos	Patty's Princess, 3, 116	Super Doer, 3, 118	5	1:24.85	44,550
1991	Withallprobability, 3, 114	C. Perret	Private Treasure, 3, 118	Far Out Nurse, 3, 112	8	1:22.50	48,240
1990	Charon, 3, 112	E. Fires	Trumpet's Blare, 3, 121	De La Devil, 3, 121	8	1:24.80	36,180
1989	Open Mind, 3, 121	A. T. Cordero Jr.	Surging, 3, 114	Georgies Doctor, 3, 118	9	1:24.20	36,780
1988	On to Royalty, 3, 114	C. Perret	Social Pro, 3, 122	Most Likely, 3, 112	10	1:23.20	37,020
1987	Added Elegance, 3, 121	J. Vasquez	Beau Love Flowers, 3, 112	Easter Mary, 3, 112	11	1:24.60	37,380
1986	Noranc, 3, 116	W. H. McCauley	Dancing Danzig, 3, 112	I'm Sweets, 3, 121	8	1:23.80	36,000
1985	Lucy Manette, 3, 114	C. Perret	Grand Glory, 3, 112	Boldly Dared, 3, 112	13	1:23.40	39,690
1984	Miss Oceana, 3, 121	E. Maple	Katrinka, 3, 112	Scorched Panties, 3, 121	5	1:22.40	24,108
1983	Unaccompanied, 3, 114	R. Woodhouse	Lisa's Capital, 3, 114	Quixotic Lady, 3, 113	15	1:23.40	28,203
1982	Trove, 3, 116	L. Saumell	Here's to Peg, 3, 112	Wendy's Ten, 3, 113	8	1:22.80	17,828
	All Manners, 3, 116	O. J. Londono	Acharmer, 3, 114	Smart Heiress, 3, 112	9	1:23.00	17,978
1981	Dame Mysterieuse, 3, 118	J. Samyn	Heavenly Cause, 3, 121	Masters Dream, 3, 113	10	1:22.20	26,040

Named for Aisco Stable's 1970 Florida-bred champion two-year-old filly Forward Gal (1968 f. by Native Charger). Sponsored by Robert and Janice McNair's Stonerside Stables of Paris, Kentucky 2003-'04. Grade 3 1986-'90, 1997-2003. Forward Gal Breeders' Cup S. 1991-'95. Forward Gal S. 1996-2002. Two divisions 1982.

Strub Stakes

Grade 2 in 2005. Santa Anita Park, four-year-olds, 1 1/8 miles, dirt. Held February 5, 2005, with a gross value of $300,000. First held in 1948. First graded in 1973. Stakes record 1:47.25 (2002 Mizzen Mast).

Year	Winner	Jockey	Second	Third	Strs	Time	1st Purse
2005	Rock Hard Ten, 4, 121	G. L. Stevens	Imperialism, 4, 119	Love of Money, 4, 123	9	1:49.24	$180,000
2004	Domestic Dispute, 4, 117	K. J. Desormeaux	During, 4, 121	Buckland Manor, 4, 117	11	1:49.08	180,000
2003	Medaglia d'Oro, 4, 123	J. D. Bailey	Olmodavor, 4, 117	Tracemark, 4, 117	6	1:48.04	240,000
2002	Mizzen Mast, 4, 121	K. J. Desormeaux	Giant Gentleman, 4, 117	Fancy As, 4, 119	11	1:47.25	240,000
2001	Wooden Phone, 4, 117	C. S. Nakatani	Tiznow, 4, 123	Jimmy Z, 4, 117	6	1:48.43	300,000
2000	General Challenge, 4, 123	C. S. Nakatani	Luftikus, 4, 117	Saint's Honor, 4, 121	4	1:48.81	300,000
1999	Event of the Year, 4, 119	C. S. Nakatani	Dr Fong, 4, 121	Hanuman Highway (Ire), 4, 117	7	1:47.65	300,000
1998	Silver Charm, 4, 123	G. L. Stevens	Mud Route, 4, 117	Bagshot, 4, 117	6	1:47.27	300,000

1997	Victory Speech, 4, 124	J. D. Bailey	The Barking Shark, 4, 118	Ambivalent, 4, 118	9	2:01.50	$300,000
1996	Helmsman, 4, 122	C. J. McCarron	Afternoon Deelites, 4, 120	Mr Purple, 4, 118	9	2:02.76	300,000
1995	Dare and Go, 4, 118	A. O. Solis	Dramatic Gold, 4, 124	Wekiva Springs, 4, 122	5	2:00.15	275,000
1994	Diazo, 4, 120	L. A. Pincay Jr.	Nonproductiveasset, 4, 118	Stuka, 4, 118	11	2:00.33	275,000
1993	Siberian Summer, 4, 118	C. S. Nakatani	Bertrando, 4, 122	Major Impact, 4, 118	8	2:00.78	275,000
1992	Best Pal, 4, 124	K. J. Desormeaux	Dinard, 4, 120	Reign Road, 4, 118	8	1:59.95	275,000
1991	Defensive Play, 4, 122	J. A. Santos	My Boy Adam, 4, 117	In Excess (Ire), 4, 121	7	2:00.90	275,000
1990	Flying Continental, 4, 119	C. A. Black	Quiet American, 4, 114	Hawkster, 4, 126	10	2:01.40	275,000
1989	Nasr El Arab, 4, 123	P. A. Valenzuela	Perceive Arrogance, 4, 117	Silver Circus, 4, 120	7	2:02.20	275,000
1988	Alysheba, 4, 126	C. J. McCarron	Candi's Gold, 4, 117	On the Line, 4, 119	6	2:00.40	275,000
1987	Snow Chief, 4, 126	P. A. Valenzuela	Ferdinand, 4, 126	Broad Brush, 4, 126	8	2:00.00	291,750
1986	Nostalgia's Star, 4, 116	F. Toro	Roo Art, 4, 117	Fast Account, 4, 115	12	2:03.60	314,250
1985	Precisionist, 4, 125	C. J. McCarron	Greinton (GB), 4, 117	Gate Dancer, 4, 126	5	2:00.20	189,300
1984	Desert Wine, 4, 117	E. J. Delahoussaye	Load the Cannons, 4, 115	Silent Fox, 4, 114	11	2:02.20	221,400
1983	Swing Till Dawn, 4, 115	P. A. Valenzuela	Wavering Monarch, 4, 121	Water Bank, 4, 117	10	2:02.00	178,000
1982	It's the One, 4, 118	W. A. Guerra	Dorcaro (Fr), 4, 115	Rock Softly, 4, 115	8	2:00.40	172,700
1981	Super Moment, 4, 116	F. Toro	Exploded, 4, 116	Doonesbury, 4, 118	10	2:01.20	145,000
1980	Spectacular Bid, 4, 126	W. Shoemaker	Flying Paster, 4, 121	Valdez, 4, 121	4	1:57.80	124,500
1979	Affirmed, 4, 126	L. A. Pincay Jr.	Johnny's Image, 4, 115	Quip, 4, 115	9	2:01.00	142,500
1978	Mr. Redoy, 4, 116	D. G. McHargue	Text, 4, 121	J. O. Tobin, 4, 122	9	2:01.00	140,200
1977	Kirby Lane, 4, 118	S. Hawley	Properantes, 4, 114	Double Discount, 4, 115	14	2:00.40	90,900
1976	George Navonod, 4, 115	F. Toro	Larrikin, 4, 118	Dancing Gun, 4, 115	8	2:12.00	76,900
1975	Stardust Mel, 4, 120	W. Shoemaker	Confederate Yankee, 4, 116	Rube the Great, 4, 122	9	2:04.20	86,300
1974	Ancient Title, 4, 121	L. A. Pincay Jr.	Dancing Papa, 4, 116	Prince Dantan, 4, 115	9	2:00.80	85,200
1973	Royal Owl, 4, 116	J. Sellers	Big Spruce, 4, 117	New Prospect, 4, 117	10	2:04.00	82,800

Originally named for Charles H. Strub (1884-1958), founder of the modern Santa Anita Park. Race name shortened in 1993 to also honor Robert P. Strub (1919-'93), his son and former track president. Formerly the Santa Anita Maturity; maturities are typically for four-year-old and older horses. Grade 1 1973-'97. Santa Anita Maturity 1948-'62. Charles H. Strub S. 1963-'93. 1¼ miles 1948-'69, 1971-'97.

Stuyvesant Handicap

Grade 3 in 2005. Aqueduct, three-year-olds and up, 1⅛ miles, dirt. Held November 13, 2004, with a gross value of $109,900. First held in 1916. First graded in 1973. Stakes record 1:47 (1973 Riva Ridge).

Year	Winner	Jockey	Second	Third	Strs	Time	1st Purse
2004	Classic Endeavor, 6, 114	E. S. Prado	Colita, 4, 115	Snake Mountain, 6, 115	7	1:49.70	$65,940
2003	Presidentialaffair, 4, 115	R. Migliore	Thunder Blitz, 5, 114	Gander, 7, 115	8	1:50.86	66,180
2002	Snake Mountain, 4, 114	J. A. Santos	Windsor Castle, 4, 115	Docent, 4, 115	10	1:50.56	68,040
2001	Graeme Hall, 4, 119	J. R. Velazquez	Country Be Gold, 4, 115	Cat's At Home, 4, 114	6	1:47.95	64,620
2000	Lager, 6, 116	H. Castillo Jr.	Top Official, 5, 113	Fire King, 7, 115	6	1:50.03	64,860
1999	Best of Luck, 3, 114	M. E. Smith	Wild Imagination, 5, 115	Durmiente (Chi), 5, 113	9	1:49.77	67,200
1998	Mr. Sinatra, 4, 115	A. T. Gryder	Rock and Roll, 3, 114	Accelerator, 4, 115	5	1:48.16	65,280
1997	Delay of Game, 4, 114	J. Samyn	Concerto, 3, 118	Mr. Sinatra, 3, 117	8	1:47.72	66,060
1996	Poor But Honest, 6, 116	J. F. Chavez	Flitch, 4, 115	Admiralty, 4, 117	8	1:49.44	66,480
1995	Silver Fox, 4, 113	M. E. Smith	Yourmissinthepoint, 4, 111	Earth Colony, 4, 114	7	1:48.03	68,940
1994	Wallenda, 4, 118	W. H. McCauley	Lost Soldier, 4, 109	Pistols and Roses, 5, 117	6	1:50.69	64,560
1993	Michelle Can Pass, 5, 115	J. R. Velazquez	Key Contender, 5, 115	Primitive Hall, 4, 113	8	1:51.07	70,200
1992	Shots Are Ringing, 5, 114	J. R. Velazquez	Key Contender, 4, 111	Timely Warning, 7, 115	7	1:49.36	69,120
1991	Montubio (Arg), 6, 110	J. M. Pezua	Mountain Lore, 4, 112	Timely Warning, 6, 114	9	1:48.30	72,480
1990	I'm Sky High, 4, 111	M. E. Smith	Silver Survivor, 4, 113	Lost Opportunity, 4, 111	7	1:48.20	71,760
1989	Its Acedemic, 5, 110	J. D. Bailey	Congeleur, 4, 115	Homebuilder, 5, 114	8	1:48.80	70,560
1988	Talinum, 4, 112	M. Castaneda	Nostalgia's Star, 6, 113	Pleasant Virginian, 4, 113	9	1:51.20	111,240
1987	Moment of Hope, 4, 118	M. Venezia	Wind Chill, 4, 110	I Rejoice, 4, 111	9	1:49.60	109,080
1986	Little Missouri, 4, 116	R. G. Davis	Waquoit, 3, 115	Let's Go Blue, 5, 118	10	1:50.00	125,280
1985	Garthorn, 5, 112	R. Q. Meza	Morning Bob, 4, 114	Waitlist, 6, 118	7	1:48.40	70,320
1984	Valiant Lark, 4, 112	V. A. Bracciale Jr.	Puntivo, 4, 113	Bounding Basque, 4, 117	8	1:51.40	70,080
1983	Fit to Fight, 4, 117	J. D. Bailey	Deputy Minister, 4, 119	Sing Sing, 5, 115	7	1:49.00	68,280
1982	Engine One, 4, 123	R. Hernandez	Bar Dexter, 5, 112	Fit to Fight, 3, 118	4	1:49.60	67,200
1981	Idyll, 4, 114	C. B. Asmussen	Spoils of War, 4, 113	Silver Buck, 3, 112	12	1:48.80	68,280
1980	Plugged Nickle, 3, 122	C. B. Asmussen	Dr. Patches, 6, 115	Ring of Light, 5, 116	10	1:50.20	68,880
1979	Music of Time, 5, 114	J. Fell	What a Gent, 5, 111	Dewan Keys, 4, 112	6	1:50.40	65,220
1978	Seattle Slew, 4, 134	A. T. Cordero Jr.	Jumping Hill, 6, 115	Wise Philip, 5, 113	5	1:47.40	62,310
1977	Cox's Ridge, 3, 124	E. Maple	Wise Philip, 4, 114	Gentle King, 4, 112	8	1:48.40	32,760
1976	Distant Land, 4, 111	H. Gustines	Blue Times, 5, 114	It's Freezing, 4, 115	9	1:49.00	32,610
1975	Festive Mood, 6, 115	H. Hinojosa	‡Step Nicely, 5, 124	Stonewalk, 4, 122	6	1:48.40	33,210
1974	Crafty Khale, 5, 121	J. Cruguet	Stop the Music, 4, 120	True Knight, 5, 121	10	1:48.00	34,848
1973	Riva Ridge, 4, 130	E. Maple	Forage, 4, 116	True Knight, 4, 122	9	**1:47.00**	34,470

Named for the Bedford-Stuyvesant neighborhood in the borough of Brooklyn, New York. Held at Jamaica 1916-'24, 1937-'39. Held at Belmont Park 1990, 1995, 2001. Not held 1925-'36, 1940-'62. 6 furlongs 1916-'17. 1 mile 1919-'24, 1965-'72, 1988. Three-year-olds 1916-'24. ‡Herculean finished second, DQ to sixth, 1975.

Suburban Handicap

Grade 1 in 2005. Belmont Park, three-year-olds and up, 1¼ miles, dirt. Held July 3, 2004, with a gross value of $500,000. First held in 1884. First graded in 1973. Stakes record 1:58.33 (1991 In Excess [Ire]).

Year	Winner	Jockey	Second	Third	Strs	Time	1st Purse
2004	Peace Rules, 4, 120	J. D. Bailey	Newfoundland, 4, 114	Funny Cide, 4, 117	8	1:59.52	$300,000
2003	Mineshaft, 4, 121	R. Albarado	Volponi, 5, 121	Dollar Bill, 5, 115	8	2:01.57	300,000
2002	E Dubai, 4, 116	J. R. Velazquez	Lido Palace (Chi), 5, 119	Macho Uno, 4, 119	7	2:00.95	300,000
2001	Albert the Great, 4, 123	J. F. Chavez	Lido Palace (Chi), 4, 115	Include, 4, 122	6	2:00.39	300,000
2000	Lemon Drop Kid, 4, 122	E. S. Prado	Behrens, 6, 122	Lager, 6, 113	6	1:58.97	300,000
1999	Behrens, 5, 121	J. F. Chavez	Catienus, 5, 113	Social Charter, 4, 113	8	2:01.06	240,000
1998	Frisk Me Now, 4, 118	E. L. King Jr.	Ordway, 4, 110	Sir Bear, 5, 117	8	2:00.45	210,000
1997	Skip Away, 4, 122	S. J. Sellers	Will's Way, 4, 116	Formal Gold, 4, 120	6	2:02.39	210,000
1996	Wekiva Springs, 5, 122	M. E. Smith	Mahogany Hall, 5, 114	L'Carriere, 5, 118	7	2:02.78	300,000
1995	Key Contender, 7, 115	J. D. Bailey	Kissin Kris, 5, 113	Federal Funds, 6, 107	10	2:02.30	210,000
1994	Devil His Due, 5, 124	M. E. Smith	Valley Crossing, 6, 113	Federal Funds, 5, 110	5	2:02.52	210,000
1993	Devil His Due, 4, 121	W. H. McCauley	Pure Rumor, 4, 110	West by West, 4, 116	8	2:01.25	180,000
1992	Pleasant Tap, 5, 119	E. J. Delahoussaye	Strike the Gold, 4, 119	Defensive Play, 5, 115	7	2:00.33	337,500
1991	In Excess (Ire), 4, 119	G. L. Stevens	Chief Honcho, 4, 115	Killer Diller, 4, 113	7	1:58.33	300,000
1990	Easy Goer, 4, 126	P. Day	De Roche, 4, 113	Montubio (Arg), 5, 113	7	2:00.00	239,400
1989	Dancing Spree, 4, 114	A. T. Cordero Jr.	Forever Silver, 4, 116	Easy N Dirty, 6, 114	12	2:02.40	258,720
1988	Personal Flag, 5, 117	P. Day	Waquoit, 5, 121	Bet Twice, 4, 126	4	2:01.40	228,060
1987	Broad Brush, 4, 126	A. T. Cordero Jr.	Set Style (Chi), 4, 112	Bordeaux Bob, 4, 112	5	2:03.00	232,260
1986	Roo Art, 4, 116	P. Day	Proud Truth, 4, 121	Creme Fraiche, 4, 121	6	2:01.20	197,700
1985	Vanlandingham, 4, 115	D. MacBeth	Carr de Naskra, 4, 120	Dramatic Desire, 4, 109	9	2:01.00	180,600
1984	Fit to Fight, 5, 126	J. D. Bailey	Canadian Factor, 4, 116	Wild Again, 4, 116	7	2:00.60	201,300
1983	Winter's Tale, 7, 120	J. Fell	Sing Sing, 5, 119	Highland Blade, 5, 119	8	2:01.60	168,600
1982	Silver Buck, 4, 111	D. MacBeth	It's the One, 4, 124	Aloma's Ruler, 3, 112	4	1:59.60	100,620
1981	Temperence Hill, 4, 127	D. MacBeth	Ring of Light, 6, 115	Highland Blade, 3, 113	8	2:02.00	100,620
1980	Winter's Tale, 4, 114	J. Fell	State Dinner, 5, 117	Czaravich, 4, 127	7	2:00.60	97,920
1979	State Dinner, 4, 118	J. Velasquez	Mister Brea (Arg), 5, 120	Alydar, 4, 126	5	2:01.60	79,125
1978	Upper Nile, 4, 113	J. Velasquez	Nearly On Time, 4, 109	Great Contractor, 5, 114	6	2:01.80	63,840
1977	Quiet Little Table, 4, 114	E. Maple	Forego, 7, 138	Nearly On Time, 3, 104	6	2:03.00	63,840
1976	Foolish Pleasure, 4, 125	E. Maple	Forego, 6, 134	Lord Rebeau, 5, 114	4	1:55.40	65,280
1975	Forego, 5, 134	H. Gustines	Arbees Boy, 5, 118	Loud, 8, 114	7	2:27.80	66,840
1974	True Knight, 5, 127	A. T. Cordero Jr.	Plunk, 4, 114	Forego, 4, 131	10	2:01.40	68,880
1973	Key to the Mint, 4, 126	B. Baeza	True Knight, 4, 118	Cloudy Dawn, 4, 113	6	2:00.80	65,700

Named after the City and Suburban Handicap in England, won by Parole, one of the first American horses to win a major English stakes race. 1997-2002 Grade 2. Held at Sheepshead Bay 1884-1910. Held at Aqueduct 1961-'74, 1976. Not held 1911-'12, 1914. 1½ miles 1975. 1³⁄₁₆ miles 1976.

Sunset Handicap

Grade 2 in 2005. Hollywood Park, three-year-olds and up, 1½ miles, turf. Held July 18, 2004, with a gross value of $150,000. First held in 1938. First graded in 1973. Stakes record 2:23.55 (1996 Talloires).

Year	Winner	Jockey	Second	Third	Strs	Time	1st Purse
2004	Star Over the Bay, 6, 113	T. Baze	Continuously, 5, 116	Leprechaun Kid, 5, 114	7	2:26.47	$90,000
2003	Puerto Banus, 4, 113	V. Espinoza	Cagney (Brz), 6, 116	Continental Red, 7, 116	8	2:26.95	90,000
2002	Grammarian, 4, 112	B. Blanc	Continental Red, 6, 116	Lord Flasheart, 5, 115	7	2:26.59	150,000
2001	Blueprint (Ire), 6, 116	G. L. Stevens	Kudos, 4, 116	Northern Quest (Fr), 6, 116	5	2:26.16	120,000
2000	Bienamado, 4, 122	C. J. McCarron	Deploy Venture (GB), 4, 115	Single Empire (Ire), 6, 120	5	2:25.06	150,000
1999	Pllcck (Ire), 4, 116	D. R. Flores	River Bay, 6, 121	Lazy Lode (Arg), 5, 120	8	2:26.97	150,000
1998	River Bay, 5, 121	A. O. Solis	Lazy Lode (Arg), 4, 115	Devonwood, 4, 114	6	2:27.40	210,000
1997	Marlin, 4, 120	D. R. Flores	Flyway (Fr), 4, 117	Percutant (GB), 6, 118	6	2:25.20	240,000
1996	Talloires, 6, 116	K. J. Desormeaux	Awad, 6, 117	Sandpit (Brz), 7, 125	7	2:23.55	420,000
1995	Sandpit (Brz), 6, 124	C. S. Nakatani	Special Price, 6, 122	Liyoun (Ire), 7, 115	5	2:25.50	464,700
1994	Grand Flotilla, 7, 119	G. L. Stevens	Semillon (GB), 4, 116	Emerald Jig, 5, 115	7	2:26.35	158,000
1993	Bien Bien, 4, 122	C. J. McCarron	Emerald Jig, 4, 114	Beyton, 4, 116	6	2:26.72	154,300
1992	Qathif, 5, 114	A. O. Solis	Seven Rivers, 6, 114	Stark South, 4, 114	6	2:26.72	153,600
1991	Black Monday (GB), 5, 112	C. S. Nakatani	Super May, 5, 117	Razeen, 4, 116	6	2:26.10	158,400
1990	†Petite Ile (Ire), 4, 115	C. A. Black	Live the Dream, 4, 116	Soft Machine, 5, 110	9	2:25.60	163,600
1989	Pranke (Arg), 5, 117	P. A. Valenzuela	Frankly Perfect, 4, 123	Pleasant Variety, 5, 117	7	2:28.00	157,200
1988	Roi Normand, 5, 114	F. Toro	Putting (Fr), 5, 117	Circus Prince, 5, 114	11	2:24.60	170,000
1987	Swink, 4, 112	W. Shoemaker	Forlitano (Arg), 6, 122	Rivlia, 5, 116	10	2:25.00	165,300
1986	Zoffany, 6, 122	E. J. Delahoussaye	Dahar, 5, 125	Flying Pidgeon, 5, 121	8	2:24.40	161,500
1985	Kings Island (Ire), 4, 116	F. Toro	Greinton (GB), 4, 122	Val Danseur, 5, 114	5	2:25.80	148,800
1984	John Henry, 9, 126	C. J. McCarron	Load the Cannons, 4, 118	Pair of Deuces, 6, 113	9	2:24.80	129,800
1983	Craelius, 4, 118	C. J. McCarron	Palikaraki (Fr), 5, 115	Decadrachm, 4, 115	12	2:26.40	137,600
1982	Erins Isle (Ire), 4, 118	A. T. Cordero Jr.	Don Roberto, 5, 117	Exploded, 5, 119	8	2:25.60	129,600
1981	Galaxy Libra (Ire), 5, 119	W. Shoemaker	Caterman (NZ), 5, 122	The Bart, 5, 117	11	2:25.80	136,050
1980	Inkerman, 5, 115	W. Shoemaker	Balzac, 5, 120	Obraztsovy, 5, 121	7	2:24.40	94,700
1979	Sirlad (Ire), 5, 122	D. G. McHargue	Ardiente, 4, 115	Inkerman, 4, 119	12	2:24.00	102,000

1978	**Exceller**, 5, 130	W. Shoemaker	Diagramatic, 5, 122	Effervescing, 5, 122		8	2:27.00	$96,600
1977	**Today 'n Tomorrow**, 4, 116	W. Shoemaker	Hunza Dancer, 5, 122	Copper Mel, 5, 117		13	2:27.60	104,450
1976	**Caucasus**, 4, 121	F. Toro	King Pellinore, 4, 124	Riot in Paris, 5, 123		10	2:26.40	81,350
1975	***Barclay Joy**, 5, 117	W. Shoemaker	Captain Cee Jay, 5, 118	Top Crowd, 4, 115		8	2:26.80	50,450
	***Cruiser II**, 6, 114	F. Olivares	Pass the Glass, 4, 119	Kirrary, 5, 116		7	2:27.00	49,450
1974	***Greco II**, 5, 113	W. Shoemaker	Big Whippendeal, 4, 120	Scantling, 4, 118		12	2:27.00	69,600
1973	***Cougar II**, 7, 128	W. Shoemaker	Life Cycle, 4, 120	Rock Bath, 5, 114		7	2:26.00	80,100

The Sunset is traditionally one of the last races run at the Hollywood Park spring meeting. Formerly sponsored by Caesars International's hotel, Caesars Palace 1995-'96. Formerly named for the Hawaiian word for "goodbye," aloha. Grade 1 1973-'89. Aloha H. 1938-'39. Caesars Palace Turf Championship H. 1995-'96. Held at Santa Anita Park 1949. Not held 1942-'45. 1 1/8 miles 1938, 1950. 1 5/8 miles 1941-'49, 1952, 1955-'59, 1961-'66. 2 miles 1969-'72. Dirt 1938-'66. Two divisions 1975. Course record 1996. †Denotes female.

Super Derby

Grade 2 in 2005. Louisiana Downs, three-year-olds, 1 1/8 miles, dirt. Held September 25, 2004, with a gross value of $500,000. First held in 1980. First graded in 1982. Stakes record 1:49.43 (2002 Essence of Dubai).

Year	Winner	Jockey	Second	Third	Strs	Time	1st Purse
2004	**Fantasticat**, 3, 124	G. Melancon	Borrego, 3, 124	Britt's Jules, 3, 124	9	1:51.40	$300,000
2003	**Ten Most Wanted**, 3, 124	P. Day	Soto, 3, 124	Crowned King, 3, 124	6	1:50.77	300,000
2002	**Essence of Dubai**, 3, 124	J. F. Chavez	Walk in the Snow, 3, 124	A. P. Five Hundred, 3, 124	8	**1:49.43**	300,000
2001	**Outofthebox**, 3, 124	L. J. Meche	E Dubai, 3, 124	Quadrophonic Sound, 3, 124	9	2:06.20	300,000
2000	**Tiznow**, 3, 124	C. J. McCarron	Commendable, 3, 124	Mass Market, 3, 124	6	1:59.84	300,000
1999	**Ecton Park**, 3, 126	A. O. Solis	Menifee, 3, 124	Pineaff, 3, 126	8	2:00.59	300,000
1998	**Arch**, 3, 126	C. S. Nakatani	Classic Cat, 3, 126	Sir Tiff, 3, 126	9	2:01.51	300,000
1997	**Deputy Commander**, 3, 126	C. J. McCarron	Precocity, 3, 126	Blazing Sword, 3, 126	6	2:00.80	300,000
1996	**Editor's Note**, 3, 126	G. L. Stevens	The Barking Shark, 3, 126	Devil's Honor, 3, 126	11	2:02.37	450,000
1995	**Mecke**, 3, 126	J. D. Bailey	Pineing Patty, 3, 126	Scott's Scoundrel, 3, 126	12	2:00.34	450,000
1994	**Soul of the Matter**, 3, 126	K. J. Desormeaux	Concern, 3, 126	Bay Street Star, 3, 126	6	2:03.57	450,000
1993	**Wallenda**, 3, 126	W. H. McCauley	Saintly Prospector, 3, 126	Peteski, 3, 126	12	2:02.71	450,000
1992	**Senor Tomas**, 3, 126	A. T. Gryder	Count the Time, 3, 126	Orbit's Revenge, 3, 126	14	2:04.09	450,000
1991	**Free Spirit's Joy**, 3, 126	C. H. Borel	Olympio, 3, 126	Zeeruler, 3, 126	7	2:00.96	600,000
1990	**Home At Last**, 3, 126	J. D. Bailey	Unbridled, 3, 126	Cee's Tizzy, 3, 126	9	2:02.00	600,000
1989	**Sunday Silence**, 3, 126	P. A. Valenzuela	‡Awe Inspiring, 3, 126	Dispersal, 3, 126	8	2:03.20	600,000
1988	**Seeking the Gold**, 3, 126	P. Day	Happyasalark Tomas, 3, 126	Lively One, 3, 126	9	2:03.80	600,000
1987	**Alysheba**, 3, 126	C. J. McCarron	Candi's Gold, 3, 126	Parochial, 3, 126	8	2:03.20	600,000
1986	**Wise Times**, 3, 126	E. Maple	dh-Cheapskate, 3, 126		7	2:04.00	300,000
			dh-Southern Halo, 3, 126				
1985	**Creme Fraiche**, 3, 126	E. Maple	Encolure, 3, 126	Government Corner, 3, 126	8	2:02.80	300,000
1984	**Gate Dancer**, 3, 126	L. A. Pincay Jr.	Precisionist, 3, 126	Big Pistol, 3, 126	8	2:00.20	300,000
1983	**Sunny's Halo**, 3, 126	L. A. Pincay Jr.	Play Fellow, 3, 126	My Habitony, 3, 126	6	2:01.60	300,000
1982	**Reinvested**, 3, 126	J. Velasquez	El Baba, 3, 126	Drop Your Drawers, 3, 126	10	2:01.60	300,000
1981	**Island Whirl**, 3, 126	L. A. Pincay Jr.	Summing, 3, 126	Willow Hour, 3, 126	12	2:03.20	300,000
1980	**Temperence Hill**, 3, 126	E. Maple	First Albert, 3, 126	Cactus Road, 3, 126	8	2:06.60	300,000

Formerly sponsored by the Isle of Capri Casino in Bossier City, Louisiana, location of Louisiana Downs 1995-'96. Super Derby Invitational 1980-'86. Grade 1 1983-2001. Isle of Capri Casino Super Derby 1995-'96. 1 1/4 miles 1980-2001. Dead heat for second 1986. ‡Big Earl finished second, DQ to eighth, 1989.

Suwannee River Handicap

Grade 3 in 2005. Gulfstream Park, three-year-olds and up, fillies and mares, 1 1/8 miles, turf. Held February 12, 2005, with a gross value of $100,000. First held in 1947. First graded in 1973. Stakes record 1:46.40 (2005 Snowdrops [GB]).

Year	Winner	Jockey	Second	Third	Strs	Time	1st Purse
2005	**Snowdrops (GB)**, 5, 116	E. S. Prado	Angela's Love, 5, 117	High Court (Brz), 5, 116	10	**1:46.40**	$60,000
2004	**Wishful Splendor**, 5, 114	J. A. Santos	May Gator, 5, 113	Mymich, 4, 113	5	1:54.86	60,000
2003	**Amonita (GB)**, 5, 117	J. Samyn	What a Price, 5, 114	Calista (GB), 5, 118	9	1:47.90	60,000
2002	**Snow Dance**, 4, 119	P. Day	Step With Style, 5, 114	Windsong, 5, 113	6	1:49.04	60,000
2001	**Spook Express (SAf)**, 7, 120	M. E. Smith	Gaviola, 4, 120	Windsong, 4, 113	8	1:47.28	60,000
2000	**Pico Teneriffe**, 4, 115	J. F. Chavez	Dominique's Joy, 5, 114	Crystal Symphony, 4, 115	8	1:47.83	45,000
1999	**Winfama**, 6, 114	R. Migliore	Circus Charmer, 4, 113	Colcon, 6, 120	10	1:52.38	45,000
1998	**Seebe**, 4, 114	D. Rice	Colcon, 5, 115	Parade Queen, 4, 119	10	1:47.58	45,000
1997	**Golden Pond (Ire)**, 4, 115	J. D. Bailey	Rumpipumpy (GB), 4, 114	Elusive, 5, 113	11	1:47.87	45,000
1996	**Class Kris**, 4, 116	P. Day	Apolda, 5, 118	Majestic Dy, 4, 113	5	1:49.17	45,000
1995	**Cox Orange**, 5, 116	J. D. Bailey	Irving's Girl, 5, 113	Alice Springs, 5, 120	7	1:47.43	45,000
1994	**Marshua's River**, 7, 114	J. A. Santos	Sheila's Revenge, 4, 118	Icy Warning, 4, 115	12	1:46.68	45,000
1993	**Via Borghese**, 4, 116	J. D. Bailey	Marshua's River, 6, 113	Blue Daisy, 5, 114	14	1:48.22	40,230
1992	**Julie La Rousse (Ire)**, 4, 115	J. D. Bailey	Christiecat, 5, 117	Grab the Green, 4, 120	11	1:48.48	38,670
1991	**Vigorous Lady**, 5, 117	M. A. Lee	Yen for Gold, 5, 111	Premier Question, 4, 116	5	1:45.10	36,120
1990	**Princess Mora**, 4, 111	M. A. Gonzalez	Fieldy (Ire), 7, 121	Northling, 6, 113	12	1:41.20	38,970
1989	**Love You by Heart**, 4, 117	R. P. Romero	Native Mommy, 6, 118	Aquaba, 4, 115	10	1:41.60	37,275
	Fieldy (Ire), 6, 116	C. Perret	Summer Secretary, 4, 110	Chapel of Dreams, 5, 122	9	1:41.60	36,975

Year	Winner	Jockey	Second	Third	Strs	Time	1st Purse
1988	Go Honey Go (Ire), 5, 110	J. M. Pezua	Princely Proof, 5, 115	Fieldy (Ire), 5, 119	11	1:41.80	$38,490
	Anka Germania (Ire), 6, 122	C. Perret	Sum, 4, 114	Fama, 5, 112	12	1:41.80	39,090
1987	dh- Fama, 4, 114	R. P. Romero		Navarchus, 5, 114	8	1:44.20	17,810
	dh- Fieldy (Ire), 4, 114	C. Perret					
	Singular Bequest, 4, 114	E. Fires	Cadabra Abra, 4, 114	Duckweed, 5, 112	7	1:43.60	26,415
1986	Chesire Kitten, 4, 112	J. Samyn	Chaldea, 6, 111	Four Flings, 5, 113	10	1:44.80	30,990
	Videogenic, 4, 120	R. G. Davis	Contredance, 4, 117	Verbality, 4, 112	9	1:44.60	30,690
1985	Early Lunch, 4, 112	W. A. Guerra	Eva G., 5, 114	Maidenhead, 6, 111	11	1:35.60	28,521
	Sherizar, 4, 113	J. McKnight	Madam Flutterby, 4, 114	Melanie Frances, 7, 115	12	1:36.40	28,820
	Burst of Colors, 5, 117	J. A. Santos	Queen of Song, 6, 121	Silver in Flight, 5, 115	12	1:35.60	28,820
1984	Sulemeif, 4, 113	J. D. Bailey	Jubilous, 4, 115	Melanie Frances, 6, 113	13	1:36.80	39,330
1983	Norsan, 4, 113	J. D. Bailey	Dana Calqui (Arg), 5, 114	Colatina, 4, 111	12	1:38.20	28,890
	Syrianna, 4, 114	J. Vasquez	Meringue Pie, 5, 115	Plenty O'Toole, 6, 114	8	1:24.20	27,390
	Promising Native, 4, 113	D. MacBeth	Avowal, 4, 117	Our Darling, 4, 112	7	1:23.80	27,060
1982	Pine Flower, 4, 113	C. Perret	Sweetest Chant, 4, 116	Fair Davina (Ire), 6, 110	9	1:35.40	27,000
	Teacher's Pet (GB), 5, 114	C. H. Marquez	Shark Song (GB), 4, 114	Blush, 4, 113	9	1:35.20	27,300
1981	Honey Fox, 4, 111	J. Samyn	Racquette (Ire), 4, 115	Pompoes (Den), 4, 110	9	1:35.20	22,568
	Exactly So (Ire), 4, 109	J. Samyn	Draw In, 5, 114	Champagne Ginny, 4, 118	9	1:35.80	22,568
1980	Ouro Verde, 4, 112	R. I. Encinas	No Disgrace (Ire), 4, 110	Anna Yrrah D., 4, 112	10	1:37.20	18,870
	Just a Game (Ire), 4, 117	D. Brumfield	La Soufriere, 5, 113	La Voyageuse, 5, 120	10	1:35.20	18,870
1979	Navajo Princess, 5, 124	C. Perret	La Soufriere, 4, 119	Unreality, 5, 121	13	1:35.20	19,650
	Calderina (Ity), 4, 117	J. Fell	Terpsichorist, 4, 122	She Can Dance, 4, 113	11	1:36.20	19,200
1978	Len's Determined, 4, 119	J. Cruguet	What a Summer, 5, 122	Late Bloomer, 4, 113	9	1:35.60	19,260
1977	Bronze Point, 4, 120	H. Arroyo	Funny Peculiar, 5, 114	Collegiate, 5, 114	7	1:24.20	21,390
1976	Jabot, 4, 112	H. Gustines	Redundancy, 5, 114	*Deesse Du Val, 5, 117	14	1:34.60	21,330
1975	*Deesse Du Val, 4, 115	M. Hole	North of Venus, 5, 118	Lorraine Edna, 5, 118	11	1:35.40	20,400
1974	Dove Creek Lady, 4, 121	M. A. Rivera	North Broadway, 4, 120	North of Venus, 4, 119	13	1:36.40	21,960
1973	Ziba Blue, 6, 110	M. Miceli	Cathy Baby, 4, 113	dh- Barely Even, 4, 127	13	1:35.80	21,270
				dh- Tico's Donna, 5, 114			

Named for river that runs from Okefenokee Swamp to the Gulf of Mexico. Not graded 1979-'81. Downgraded when taken off turf 2004. Not held 1949. 7 furlongs 1947, 1961-'66, 1977, 1983 (two divisions). 6 furlongs 1948. 1¹/₁₆ miles 1953-'60, 1967-'68, 1986-'91. 1 mile 1969-'76, 1978-'79, 1981-'82, 1983 (one division), 1984-'85. About 1¹/₈ miles 1999. Dirt 1965-'66, 1977, 1983 (two divisions), 1986, 1991. Originally scheduled on turf 2004. Four-year-olds and up 1994. Two divisions 1979-'82, 1986-'89. Three divisions 1983, 1985. Dead heat for third 1973. Dead heat for first 1987. Equaled course record 1992. Held as an overnight handicap 1950-'52.

Swale Stakes

Grade 2 in 2005. Gulfstream Park, three-year-olds, 7 furlongs, dirt. Held March 5, 2005, with a gross value of $150,000. First held in 1985. First graded in 1990. Stakes record 1:21.06 (2003 Midas Eyes).

Year	Winner	Jockey	Second	Third	Strs	Time	1st Purse
2005	Lost in the Fog, 3, 120	R. A. Baze	Around the Cape, 3, 116	More Smoke, 3, 118	10	1:22.21	$90,000
2004	Wynn Dot Comma, 3, 120	E. S. Prado	Eurosilver, 3, 120	Dashboard Drummer, 3, 120	5	1:22.87	90,000
2003	Midas Eyes, 3, 116	J. D. Bailey	Posse, 3, 120	Whywhywhy, 3, 122	8	**1:21.06**	90,000
2002	Ethan Man, 3, 116	P. Day	Listen Here, 3, 120	Governor Hickel, 3, 116	5	1:22.29	90,000
2001	D'wildcat, 3, 116	C. S. Nakatani	Tarek, 3, 112	Yonaguska, 3, 122	6	1:22.25	90,000
2000	Trippi, 3, 113	J. D. Bailey	Ultimate Warrior, 3, 117	Harlan Traveler, 3, 114	5	1:23.43	60,000
1999	Yes It's True, 3, 122	J. D. Bailey	Texas Glitter, 3, 117	Lucky Roberto, 3, 119	5	1:22.29	60,000
1998	Favorite Trick, 3, 122	P. Day	Good and Tough, 3, 114	Dice Dancer, 3, 113	9	1:22.86	60,000
1997	Confide, 3, 117	M. E. Smith	Country Rainbow, 3, 112	The Silver Move, 3, 119	9	1:23.35	45,000
1996	Roar, 3, 113	M. E. Smith	Gomtuu, 3, 119	Dixie Connection, 3, 112	6	1:22.46	45,000
1995	Mr. Greeley, 3, 114	J. A. Krone	Devious Course, 3, 119	Pyramid Peak, 3, 114	7	1:22.18	45,000
1994	Arrival Time, 3, 115	C. J. McCarron	Senor Conquistador, 3, 113	Meadow Monster, 3, 112	7	1:22.53	45,000
1993	Premier Explosion, 3, 114	D. Penna	Demaloot Demashoot, 3, 113	Cherokee Run, 3, 114	8	1:23.23	53,520
1992	D. J. Cat, 3, 114	J. D. Bailey	Binalong, 3, 118	Always Silver, 3, 112	10	1:23.39	71,250
1991	Chihuahua, 3, 112	J. O. Alferez	To Freedom, 3, 119	Greek Costume, 3, 114	6	1:23.47	51,060
1990	Housebuster, 3, 122	C. Perret	Summer Squall, 3, 122	Thirty Six Red, 3, 113	6	1:22.20	34,350
1989	Easy Goer, 3, 122	P. Day	Trion, 3, 122	Tricky Creek, 3, 122	6	1:22.20	34,290
1988	Seeking the Gold, 3, 114	R. P. Romero	Above Normal, 3, 114	Perfect Spy, 3, 122	7	1:21.60	35,100
1986	One Magic Moment, 3, 113	D. MacBeth	Admiral's Image, 3, 122	Two Punch, 3, 113	11	1:25.40	31,230
1985	Chief's Crown, 3, 122	D. MacBeth	Creme Fraiche, 3, 117	Cherokee Fast, 3, 113	9	1:22.40	30,792

Named for Claiborne Farm's 1984 champion three-year-old male and '84 Florida Derby (G1) winner Swale (1981 c. by Seattle Slew). Grade 3 1990-2004. Not held 1987.

Swaps Breeders' Cup Stakes

Grade 2 in 2005. Hollywood Park, three-year-olds, 1¹/₈ miles, dirt. Held July 10, 2004, with a gross value of $409,300. First held in 1974. First graded in 1975. Stakes record 1:45.80 (1997 Free House).

Year	Winner	Jockey	Second	Third	Strs	Time	1st Purse
2004	Rock Hard Ten, 3, 116	C. S. Nakatani	Suave, 3, 120	Boomzeeboom, 3, 118	6	1:47.47	$252,780
2003	During, 3, 115	J. D. Bailey	Ten Most Wanted, 3, 122	dh- Eye of the Tiger, 3, 118	6	1:49.38	240,000
				dh- Outta Here, 3, 120			

2002	Came Home, 3, 122	M. E. Smith	Like a Hero, 3, 114	Fonz's, 3, 116	7	1:48.28	$300,000
2001	Congaree, 3, 122	G. L. Stevens	Until Sundown, 3, 118	Jamaican Rum, 3, 118	6	1:48.61	300,000
2000	Captain Steve, 3, 120	C. S. Nakatani	Tiznow, 3, 118	Spacelink, 3, 118	6	1:48.01	300,000
1999	Cat Thief, 3, 120	P. Day	General Challenge, 3, 122	Walk That Walk, 3, 117	4	1:47.87	300,000
1998	Old Trieste, 3, 118	C. J. McCarron	Grand Slam, 3, 120	Old Topper, 3, 117	6	1:47.00	300,000
1997	Free House, 3, 122	K. J. Desormeaux	Deputy Commander, 3, 118	Wild Rush, 3, 122	6	1:45.80	300,000
1996	Victory Speech, 3, 118	J. D. Bailey	Prince of Thieves, 3, 118	Hesabull, 3, 118	5	1:48.28	300,000
1995	Thunder Gulch, 3, 126	G. L. Stevens	Da Hoss, 3, 118	Petionville, 3, 120	7	1:49.09	275,000
1994	Silver Music, 3, 119	C. W. Antley	Dramatic Gold, 3, 119	Valiant Nature, 3, 121	6	2:00.76	123,800
1993	Devoted Brass, 3, 123	L. A. Pincay Jr.	Future Storm, 3, 119	Codified, 3, 123	6	2:00.64	124,000
1992	Bien Bien, 3, 119	C. J. McCarron	Treekster, 3, 123	Sevengreenpairs, 3, 119	5	2:02.91	123,400
1991	Best Pal, 3, 116	P. A. Valenzuela	Corporate Report, 3, 114	Compelling Sound, 3, 123	4	2:00.70	120,000
1990	Jovial (GB), 3, 120	G. L. Stevens	Silver Ending, 3, 126	Stalwart Charger, 3, 126	4	2:01.20	120,000
1989	Prized, 3, 120	E. J. Delahoussaye	Sunday Silence, 3, 126	Endow, 3, 123	5	2:01.80	232,400
1988	Lively One, 3, 120	W. Shoemaker	Blade of the Ball, 3, 114	Iz a Saros, 3, 123	9	2:01.00	131,200
1987	Temperate Sil, 3, 123	W. Shoemaker	Candi's Gold, 3, 123	Pledge Card, 3, 115	6	2:02.20	124,400
1986	Clear Choice, 3, 120	C. J. McCarron	Southern Halo, 3, 114	Jota, 3, 116	9	2:03.60	137,000
1985	Padua, 3, 115	P. A. Valenzuela	Turkoman, 3, 115	Don't Say Halo, 3, 120	8	2:01.40	123,500
1984	Precisionist, 3, 123	C. J. McCarron	Prince True, 3, 120	Majestic Shore, 3, 114	7	1:59.80	121,300
1983	Hyperborean, 3, 115	F. Toro	My Habitony, 3, 120	Tanks Brigade, 3, 120	9	2:01.00	97,500
1982	Journey At Sea, 3, 120	C. J. McCarron	West Coast Native, 3, 114	Cassaleria, 3, 123	5	2:00.20	91,300
1981	Noble Nashua, 3, 123	L. A. Pincay Jr.	Dorcaro (Fr), 3, 115	Stancharry, 3, 123	4	2:01.20	127,000
1980	First Albert, 3, 123	F. Mena	Amber Pass, 3, 123	Mr. Mud, 3, 114	11	2:00.80	162,200
1979	Valdez, 3, 120	L. A. Pincay Jr.	Shamgo, 3, 114	Paint King, 3, 114	6	1:59.40	124,250
1978	Radar Ahead, 3, 120	D. G. McHargue	Batonnier, 3, 123	Poppy Popowich, 3, 115	10	2:00.00	133,300
1977	J. O. Tobin, 3, 120	W. Shoemaker	Affiliate, 3, 117	Text, 3, 120	7	1:58.60	194,900
1976	Majestic Light, 3, 114	S. Hawley	Crystal Water, 3, 123	Double Discount, 3, 115	9	1:59.20	98,200
1975	Forceten, 3, 120	D. Pierce	Sibirri, 3, 114	Diabolo, 3, 123	8	1:59.80	119,800
1974	Agitate, 3, 123	W. Shoemaker	Stardust Mel, 3, 120	Master Music, 3, 114	9	1:59.60	66,300

Named for Rex Ellsworth's 1956 Horse of the Year and '56 Hollywood Gold Cup H. winner Swaps (1952 c. by *Khaled). Grade 1 1975-'88, 1999-2001. 1¼ miles 1974-'94. Dead heat for third 2003.

Sword Dancer Invitational Handicap

Grade 1 in 2005. Saratoga Race Course, three-year-olds and up, 1½ miles, turf. Held August 14, 2004, with a gross value of $500,000. First held in 1975. First graded in 1981. Stakes record 2:23.20 (1997 Awad).

Year	Winner	Jockey	Second	Third	Strs	Time	1st Purse
2004	Better Talk Now, 5, 118	R. A. Dominguez	Request for Parole, 5, 123	Balto Star, 6, 120	6	2:28.49	$300,000
2003	Whitmore's Conn, 5, 115	J. Samyn	Macaw (Ire), 4, 114	Slew Valley, 6, 114	11	2:28.14	300,000
2002	With Anticipation, 7, 120	P. Day	Denon, 4, 118	Volponi, 4, 115	11	2:24.06	300,000
2001	With Anticipation, 6, 114	P. Day	King Cugat, 4, 120	Slew Valley, 4, 114	9	2:26.41	300,000
2000	John's Call, 9, 114	J. Samyn	Aly's Alley, 4, 114	Single Empire (Ire), 6, 119	8	2:32.17	300,000
1999	Honor Glide, 5, 116	J. A. Santos	Val's Prince, 7, 115	Chorwon, 6, 114	7	2:28.23	240,000
1998	Cetewayo, 4, 115	J. R. Velazquez	Val's Prince, 6, 113	Dushyantor, 5, 119	6	2:29.56	180,000
1997	Awad, 7, 117	P. Day	Fahim (GB), 4, 110	Val's Prince, 5, 112	10	2:23.20	150,000
1996	Broadway Flyer, 5, 118	M. E. Smith	Kiri's Clown, 7, 113	Flag Down, 6, 119	9	2:32.08	150,000
1995	Kiri's Clown, 6, 114	M. J. Luzzi	Awad, 5, 121	King's Theatre (Ire), 4, 113	13	2:25.45	150,000
1994	Alex the Great (GB), 5, 118	P. A. Valenzuela	Kiri's Clown, 5, 112	L'Hermine (GB), 5, 112	10	2:28.66	150,000
1993	Spectacular Tide, 4, 112	J. A. Krone	Square Cut, 4, 112	Dr. Kiernan, 4, 117	9	2:30.39	120,000
1992	Fraise, 4, 113	J. D. Bailey	Wall Street Dancer, 4, 116	Montserrat, 4, 112	8	2:25.88	150,000
1991	Dr. Root, 4, 109	J. Samyn	Karmani, 6, 113	El Senor, 7, 116	7	2:25.43	150,000
1990	El Senor, 6, 119	A. T. Cordero Jr.	With Approval, 4, 124	Hodges Bay, 5, 114	7	2:28.00	140,440
1989	El Senor, 5, 118	W. H. McCauley	Nediym (Ire), 4, 113	My Big Boy, 6, 115	7	2:27.00	139,920
1988	†Anka Germania (Ire), 6, 117	C. Perret	Sunshine Forever, 3, 114	†Carotene, 5, 114	7	2:32.20	141,120
1987	‡Theatrical (Ire), 5, 124	P. Day	Dance of Life, 4, 122	Akabir, 6, 114	4	2:26.00	133,080
1986	Southern Sultan, 4, 109	R. G. Davis	Talakeno, 6, 114	Tri for Size, 5, 111	8	2:39.40	143,460
1985	Tri for Size, 4, 110	R. J. Thibeau Jr.	Talakeno, 5, 124	†Persian Tiara (Ire), 5, 113	9	2:33.20	151,320
1984	Majesty's Prince, 5, 124	E. Maple	Nassipour, 4, 109	Four Bases, 5, 112	11	2:31.00	176,820
1983	Majesty's Prince, 4, 120	E. Maple	‡Thunder Puddles, 4, 118	Erins Isle (Ire), 5, 128	9	2:34.40	141,600
1982	Lemhi Gold, 4, 126	C. J. McCarron	Erins Isle (Ire), 4, 126	Field Cat, 5, 126	9	2:26.00	99,000
1981	John Henry, 6, 126	W. Shoemaker	Passing Zone, 4, 126	Peat Moss, 5, 126	5	2:26.80	97,380
1980	Tiller, 6, 126	R. Hernandez	John Henry, 5, 126	Sten, 5, 126	4	2:25.20	96,660
1979	Darby Creek Road, 4, 119	A. T. Cordero Jr.	John Henry, 4, 119	Poison Ivory, 4, 119	8	1:41.60	34,320
1978	True Colors, 4, 114	M. Venezia	Bill Brill, 4, 107	Blue Baron, 4, 114	12	1:41.00	34,020
1977	Effervescing, 4, 117	A. T. Cordero Jr.	Gentle King, 4, 110	Cinteelo, 4, 116	9	1:39.60	33,690
1976	Arabian Law, 3, 112	J. Vasquez	Full Out, 3, 118	Half High, 3, 111	7	1:10.60	26,535
1975	Gallant Bob, 3, 126	G. Gallitano	Our Hero, 3, 113	Due Diligence, 3, 113	9	1:09.60	27,630

Named for Brookmeade Stable's 1959 Horse of the Year and '59 Jockey Club Gold Cup winner Sword Dancer (1956 c. by Sunglow). Grade 3 1981. Grade 2 1982-'83. Sword Dancer H. 1975-'78, 1983-'93. Sword Dancer S. 1979-'82. Held at Aqueduct 1975-'76. Held at Belmont Park 1977-'91. 6 furlongs 1975-'76. 1¹⁄₁₆ miles 1977-'79. Dirt 1975-'76. Three-year-olds 1975-'76. ‡‡Hush Dear finished second, DQ to fourth, 1983. ‡Dance of Life finished first, DQ to second, 1987. †Denotes female.

Sycamore Breeders' Cup Stakes

Grade 3 in 2005. Keeneland, three-year-olds and up, 1½ miles, turf. Held October 9, 2004, with a gross value of $152,300. First held in 1995. First graded in 2003. Stakes record 2:29.55 (2003 Sharbayan [Ire]).

Year	Winner	Jockey	Second	Third	Strs	Time	1st Purse
2004	Mustanfar, 3, 118	J. A. Santos	Deputy Strike, 6, 120	Rochester, 8, 122	9	2:30.88	$100,626
2003	Sharbayan (Ire), 5, 120	P. Day	Cetewayo, 9, 122	Deputy Strike, 5, 120	10	2:29.55	73,904
2002	Rochester, 6, 125	P. Day	Roxinho (Brz), 4, 120	Lord Flasheart, 5, 120	7	2:30.48	101,928
2001	Rochester, 5, 119	P. Day	Chorwon, 8, 125	Regal Dynasty, 5, 119	7	2:31.29	103,044
2000	Crowd Pleaser, 5, 118	C. H. Borel	Dixie's Crown, 4, 122	Kim Loves Bucky, 3, 114	7	2:44.00	44,439
1999	Royal Strand (Ire), 5, 117	P. Day	Arizona Storm, 4, 117	Magest, 4, 117	6	2:38.68	42,315
1998	Royal Strand (Ire), 4, 116	S. J. Sellers	Thesaurus, 4, 116	Lakeshore Road, 5, 116	5	2:41.93	33,015
1997	Gleaming Key, 5, 116	S. J. Sellers	Double Leaf (GB), 4, 116	Seattle Blossom, 4, 116	5	2:45.86	33,015
1996	Gleaming Key, 4, 114	R. Albarado	Nash Terrace (Ire), 4, 120	Hawkeye Bay, 5, 114	4	2:44.49	32,860
1995	Lindon Lime, 5, 123	C. Perret	Hyper Shu, 5, 114	Lordly Prospect, 6, 114	9	2:42.11	39,098

Named for the sycamore tree at the entrance to Keeneland's walking ring. Sycamore S. 1995-2000.

Tampa Bay Derby

Grade 3 in 2005. Tampa Bay Downs, three-year-olds, 1¹⁄₁₆ miles, dirt. Held March 19, 2005, with a gross value of $250,000. First held in 1981. First graded in 1984. Stakes record 1:43.66 (2002 Equality).

Year	Winner	Jockey	Second	Third	Strs	Time	1st Purse
2005	Sun King, 3, 116	E. S. Prado	Forever Wild, 3, 116	Global Trader, 3, 116	7	1:43.98	$150,000
2004	Limehouse, 3, 118	P. Day	Mustanfar, 3, 116	Swingforthefences, 3, 116	8	1:43.99	150,000
2003	Region of Merit, 3, 120	E. Coa	Aristocat, 3, 118	Hear No Evil, 3, 123	8	1:44.61	150,000
2002	Equality, 3, 118	R. A. Dominguez	Tails of the Crypt, 3, 123	Political Attack, 3, 123	9	1:43.66	120,000
2001	Burning Roma, 3, 123	R. Migliore	American Prince, 3, 123	Paging, 3, 116	11	1:44.30	120,000
2000	Wheelaway, 3, 116	R. Migliore	Impeachment, 3, 116	Perfect Cat, 3, 116	10	1:43.90	90,000
1999	Pineaff, 3, 122	J. A. Santos	Menifee, 3, 120	Doneraile Court, 3, 122	6	1:45.33	90,000
1998	Parade Ground, 3, 118	P. Day	Middlesex Drive, 3, 118	Rock and Roll, 3, 116	8	1:44.20	90,000
1997	Zede, 3, 118	J. D. Bailey	Brisco Jack, 3, 116	Favorable Regard, 3, 118	12	1:44.80	90,000
1996	Thundering Storm, 3, 118	J. A. Guerra	El Amante, 3, 118	Natural Selection, 3, 116	10	1:43.80	90,000
1995	Gadzook, 3, 116	G. Boulanger	Composer, 3, 116	Bet Your Bucks, 3, 116	10	1:45.20	90,000
1994	Prix de Crouton, 3, 120	M. Walls	Able Buck, 3, 120	Parental Pressure, 3, 122	7	1:46.60	90,000
1993	Marco Bay, 3, 120	R. D. Allen Jr.	Thriller Chiller, 3, 116	Tunecke Charlie, 3, 118	12	1:44.40	90,000
1992	Careful Gesture, 3, 118	R. N. Lester	Chief Speaker, 3, 116	Clipper Won, 3, 116	12	1:45.93	120,000
1991	Speedy Cure, 3, 118	R. D. Lopez	Link, 3, 118	Shudanz, 3, 116	9	1:46.26	90,000
1990	Champagneforashley, 3, 122	J. Vasquez	Slew of Angels, 3, 120	Always Running, 3, 116	10	1:44.60	90,000
1989	Storm Predictions, 3, 120	S. Gaffalione	With Approval, 3, 120	Mercedes Won, 3, 122	11	1:43.80	90,000
1988	Cefis, 3, 116	E. Maple	Buck Forbes, 3, 118	Twice Too Many, 3, 118	9	1:44.40	90,000
1987	Phantom Jet, 3, 122	K. K. Allen	Homebuilder, 3, 116	You're No Bargain, 3, 116	10	1:43.80	90,000
1986	My Prince Charming, 3, 122	C. Perret	Lucky Rebeau, 3, 120	Major Moran, 3, 116	13	1:46.60	98,100
1985	Regal Remark, 3, 122	J. Fell	Verification, 3, 122	Sport Jet, 3, 118	14	1:46.80	95,400
1984	Bold Southerner, 3, 116	W. Crews	Rexson's Hope, 3, 122	Stickler, 3, 120	13	1:44.60	95,400
1983	Morganmorganmorgan, 3, 118	W. Rodriguez	Slew o' Gold, 3, 118	Quick Dip, 3, 118	14	1:47.20	60,000
1982	Reinvested, 3, 114	R. D. Luhr	Stage Reviewer, 3, 120	Real Twister, 3, 120	12	1:45.20	40,140
1981	Paristo, 3, 112	D. C. Ashcroft	Bravestofall, 3, 120	Darby Gillic, 3, 122	14	1:45.40	43,560

The race and the track are named for the city of Tampa, Florida, and the bay on which it is located. Sponsored by Budweiser 1981-'86. Not graded 1990-2001. Budweiser Tampa Bay Derby 1981-'86.

Tempted Stakes

Grade 3 in 2005. Aqueduct, two-year-olds, fillies, 1 mile, dirt. Held November 2, 2004, with a gross value of $104,600. First held in 1975. First graded in 1980. Stakes record 1:35.40 (1975 Secret Lanvin).

Year	Winner	Jockey	Second	Third	Strs	Time	1st Purse
2004	Summer Raven, 2, 115	S. Elliott	K. D's Shady Lady, 2, 115	Salute, 2, 115	5	1:36.09	$63,960
2003	La Reina, 2, 115	J. R. Velazquez	Eye Dazzler, 2, 115	Sisti's Pride, 2, 115	8	1:36.15	66,420
2002	Chimichurri, 2, 119	J. R. Velazquez	Reheat, 2, 115	Bonay, 2, 115	8	1:37.52	66,240
2001	Smok'n Frolic, 2, 119	J. R. Velazquez	Saintly Action, 2, 115	Wopping, 2, 117	8	1:37.77	66,900
2000	Two Item Limit, 2, 117	R. Migliore	Celtic Melody, 2, 115	Twining Star, 2, 115	6	1:38.53	65,520
1999	Shawnee Country, 2, 116	J. F. Chavez	To Marquet, 2, 114	Marigalante, 2, 116	5	1:38.60	65,460
1998	Oh What a Windfall, 2, 121	J. D. Bailey	La Ville Rouge, 2, 114	Honour a Bull, 2, 114	8	1:39.84	66,120
1997	Dancing With Ruth, 2, 118	T. G. Turner	Soft Senorita, 2, 118	Aunt Anne, 2, 116	6	1:37.40	65,340
1996	Ajina, 2, 112	J. D. Bailey	Glitter Woman, 2, 114	Aldiza, 2, 114	7	1:36.59	66,240
1994	Special Broad, 2, 114	J. A. Krone	Carson Creek, 2, 114	Golden Bri, 2, 114	7	1:37.20	66,000
1993	Sovereign Kitty, 2, 112	J. R. Velazquez	Seeking the Circle, 2, 112	Her Temper, 2, 112	8	1:46.84	69,720
1992	True Affair, 2, 121	J. Bravo	Broad Gains, 2, 121	Touch of Love, 2, 114	6	1:47.48	68,520
1991	Deputation, 2, 114	D. W. Lidberg	Turnback the Alarm, 2, 121	Bless Our Home, 2, 114	9	1:46.74	72,600
1990	Flawlessly, 2, 121	J. D. Bailey	Debutant's Halo, 2, 121	Slept Thru It, 2, 114	12	1:46.60	56,250
1989	Worth Avenue, 2, 113	R. P. Romero	Crown Quest, 2, 119	Voodoo Lily, 2, 114	6	1:46.80	69,480
1988	Box Office Gold, 2, 116	J. A. Santos	Dreamy Mimi, 2, 116	Surging, 2, 116	5	1:46.20	57,600
1987	Thirty Eight Go Go, 2, 121	K. J. Desormeaux	Best Number, 2, 114	Dangerous Type, 2, 116	9	1:44.60	100,920

1986	**Silent Turn**, 2, 119	C. W. Antley	Grecian Flight, 2, 119	Chase the Dream, 2, 119	11	1:46.20	$74,400
1985	**Cosmic Tiger**, 2, 121	E. Maple	Tracy's Espoir, 2, 114	Roses for Avie, 2, 114	10	1:46.80	68,580
1984	**Willowy Mood**, 2, 121	J. Velasquez	Koluctoo's Jill, 2, 114	Easy Step, 2, 116	12	1:46.20	57,330
1983	**Surely Georgie's**, 2, 113	R. Hernandez	Baroness Direct, 2, 114	Dumdedumdedum, 2, 114	8	1:39.60	34,320
1982	**Only Queens**, 2, 114	M. A. Rivera	Future Fun, 2, 113	Blue Garter, 2, 114	6	1:37.00	33,180
1981	**Choral Group**, 2, 121	J. Velasquez	Michelle Mon Amour, 2, 114	Middle Stage, 2, 113	7	1:38.00	33,000
1980	**Tina Tina Too**, 2, 114	C. B. Asmussen	Prayers'n Promises, 2, 121	Explosive Kingdom, 2, 114	6	1:38.40	32,580
1979	**Genuine Risk**, 2, 114	J. Vasquez	Street Ballet, 2, 117	Tell a Secret, 2, 114	9	1:36.00	33,060
1978	**Whisper Fleet**, 2, 119	A. T. Cordero Jr.	Run Cosmic Run, 2, 114	Distinct Honor, 2, 113	6	1:36.20	25,665
1977	**Caesar's Wish**, 2, 116	G. McCarron	Itsamaza, 2, 116	Lucinda Lea, 2, 114	13	1:36.20	22,635
1976	**Pearl Necklace**, 2, 114	A. T. Cordero Jr.	Our Mims, 2, 113	Road Princess, 2, 115	10	1:39.60	22,380
1975	**Secret Lanvin**, 2, 113	J. Cruguet	Free Journey, 2, 121	Imaflash, 2, 113	9	**1:35.40**	33,600

Named for Mrs. Philip duPont's 1959 champion older mare and '59 Ladies H. winner Tempted (1955 f. by *Half Crown). Grade 2 1981-'82, 1988. Held at Belmont Park 2001. Not held 1995. 1¹/₁₆ miles 1984-'93.

Test Stakes

Grade 1 in 2005. Saratoga Race Course, three-year-olds, fillies, 7 furlongs, dirt. Held July 31, 2004, with a gross value of $250,000. First held in 1922. First graded in 1973. Stakes record 1:20.83 (2003 Lady Tak).

Year	Winner	Jockey	Second	Third	Strs	Time	1st Purse
2004	**Society Selection**, 3, 120	E. S. Prado	Bending Strings, 3, 120	Forest Music, 3, 118	12	1:23.69	$150,000
2003	**Lady Tak**, 3, 122	J. D. Bailey	Bird Town, 3, 122	House Party, 3, 122	7	**1:20.83**	150,000
2002	**You**, 3, 123	J. D. Bailey	Carson Hollow, 3, 120	Spring Meadow, 3, 120	7	1:22.84	150,000
2001	**Victory Ride**, 3, 116	E. S. Prado	Xtra Heat, 3, 123	Nasty Storm, 3, 120	8	1:21.72	150,000
2000	**Dream Supreme**, 3, 115	P. Day	Big Bambu, 3, 118	Finder's Fee, 3, 123	11	1:22.66	150,000
1999	**Marley Vale**, 3, 114	J. R. Velazquez	Awful Smart, 3, 114	Emanating, 3, 114	11	1:22.77	150,000
1998	**Jersey Girl**, 3, 123	M. E. Smith	Brave Deed, 3, 114	Catinca, 3, 114	11	1:23.02	120,000
1997	**Fabulously Fast**, 3, 114	J. D. Bailey	Aldiza, 3, 114	Pearl City, 3, 117	9	1:21.65	90,000
1996	**Capote Belle**, 3, 115	J. R. Velazquez	Flat Fleet Feet, 3, 115	J J'sdream, 3, 123	8	1:21.08	90,000
1995	**Chaposa Springs**, 3, 120	J. D. Bailey	Miss Golden Circle, 3, 114	Daijin, 3, 123	9	1:21.81	90,000
1994	**Twist Afleet**, 3, 114	J. D. Bailey	Penny's Reshoot, 3, 118	Heavenly Prize, 3, 121	8	1:22.08	90,000
1993	**Missed the Storm**, 3, 114	M. E. Smith	Miss Indy Anna, 3, 114	Educated Risk, 3, 114	5	1:22.12	90,000
1992	**November Snow**, 3, 116	C. W. Antley	Meafara, 3, 114	Preach, 3, 116	8	1:21.33	105,480
1991	**Versailles Treaty**, 3, 114	A. T. Cordero Jr.	Ifyoucouldseemenow, 3, 121	‡Classy Women, 3, 116	7	1:22.85	104,040
1990	**Go for Wand**, 3, 124	R. P. Romero	Screen Prospect, 3, 118	Token Dance, 3, 118	10	1:21.00	73,440
1989	**Safely Kept**, 3, 121	C. Perret	Fantastic Find, 3, 114	Cojinx, 3, 116	5	1:21.40	101,520
1988	**Fara's Team**, 3, 121	J. D. Bailey	Lake Valley, 3, 114	Classic Crown, 3, 121	10	1:22.60	109,980
1987	**Very Subtle**, 3, 121	P. A. Valenzuela	Up the Apalachee, 3, 121	Silent Turn, 3, 121	14	1:21.00	116,280
1986	**Storm and Sunshine**, 3, 118	C. Perret	Classy Cathy, 3, 121	I'm Sweets, 3, 121	7	1:22.80	103,500
1985	**Lady's Secret**, 3, 121	J. Velasquez	Mom's Command, 3, 124	Majestic Folly, 3, 118	10	1:21.60	99,600
1984	**Sintra**, 3, 116	K. K. Allen	Wild Applause, 3, 121	Lucky Lucky Lucky, 3, 124	9	1:22.60	101,040
1983	**Lass Trump**, 3, 114	P. Day	Medieval Moon, 3, 121	Chic Belle, 3, 114	9	1:22.20	34,380
1982	**Gold Beauty**, 3, 116	D. Brumfield	Ambassador of Luck, 3, 121	Number, 3, 114	12	1:22.80	35,940
1981	**Cherokee Frolic**, 3, 121	G. Cohen	Maddy's Tune, 3, 114	Discorama, 3, 118	6	1:23.20	34,140
1980	**Love Sign**, 3, 116	A. T. Cordero Jr.	Weber City Miss, 3, 124	Andrea F., 3, 114	7	1:22.20	33,900
1979	**Blitey**, 3, 114	A. T. Cordero Jr.	Jameela, 3, 118	Spanish Fake, 3, 121	10	1:22.60	25,987
	Clef d'Argent, 3, 114	R. Hernandez	Alada, 3, 114	Syncopating Lady, 3, 114	10	1:22.20	25,988
1978	**White Star Line**, 3, 121	J. Fell	Silken Delight, 3, 114	Zerelda, 3, 116	7	1:21.40	22,095
	Tingle Stone, 3, 114	R. Hernandez	Mucchina, 3, 121	Summer Fling, 3, 116	7	1:22.00	22,020
1977	**Small Raja**, 3, 124	M. Solomone	Pressing Date, 3, 114	Pearl Necklace, 3, 116	9	1:21.80	22,275
	Northern Sea, 3, 121	J. Velasquez	Northernette, 3, 121	Flying Above, 3, 114	8	1:22.40	22,200
1976	**Ivory Wand**, 3, 114	P. Day	Doc Shah's Siren, 3, 116	Pacific Princess, 3, 114	10	1:23.00	22,500
1975	**Hot n Nasty**, 3, 122	J. E. Tejeira	A Charm, 3, 113	Alpine Lass, 3, 116	7	1:22.00	19,665
	My Juliet, 3, 116	J. Vasquez	Slip Screen, 3, 113	‡Funalon, 3, 113	7	1:22.00	19,590
1974	**Quaze Quilt**, 3, 121	J. Vasquez	Maud Muller, 3, 113	Clear Copy, 3, 121	11	1:22.40	20,385
	Maybellene, 3, 116	D. Meade Jr.	Raisela, 3, 116	Stage Door Betty, 3, 121	11	1:23.60	20,385
1973	**Desert Vixen**, 3, 121	J. Velasquez	Full of Hope, 3, 118	Clandenita, 3, 118	5	1:23.00	13,470
	Waltz Fan, 3, 118	J. Velasquez	Gallant Davelle, 3, 116	Tuerta, 3, 116	7	1:23.60	13,545

Sometimes used as a prep or "test" for the Alabama S. (G1) later in the meet. Grade 2 1973-'74, 1979-'87. Grade 3 1975-'78. Held at Belmont Park 1943-'45. Not held 1923-'25, 1961. 1¹/₄ miles 1922. Two divisions 1973-'75, 1977-'79. ‡Fleet Victress finished third, DQ to fourth, 1975 (2nd Div.). ‡Zama Hummer finished third, DQ to sixth, 1991.

Texas Mile Stakes

Grade 3 in 2005. Lone Star Park, three-year-olds and up, 1 mile, dirt. Held April 30, 2005, with a gross value of $300,000. First held in 1997. First graded in 1999. Stakes record 1:34.44 (1997 Isitingood).

Year	Winner	Jockey	Second	Third	Strs	Time	1st Purse
2005	**High Strike Zone**, 5, 118	R. J. Faul	Supah Blitz, 5, 120	Twilight Road, 8, 118	6	1:35.34	$185,000
2004	**Kela**, 6, 119	D. C. Nuesch	Supah Blitz, 4, 116	Yessirgeneralsir, 4, 114	8	1:35.64	175,000
2003	**Bluesthestandard**, 6, 120	M. A. Pedroza	Bonapaw, 7, 116	Compendium, 5, 116	9	1:35.68	170,000
2002	**Unrullah Bull**, 5, 116	A. J. Lovato	Reba's Gold, 5, 118	Compendium, 4, 116	9	1:37.78	170,000

2001	**Dixie Dot Com**, 6, 116	D. R. Flores	Mr Ross, 6, 120	Five Straight, 4, 115	7	1:34.72	$180,000
2000	**Sir Bear**, 7, 116	E. Coa	Lexington Park, 4, 118	Luftikus, 4, 118	9	1:35.98	170,000
1999	**Littlebitlively**, 5, 116	C. Gonzalez	Real Quiet, 4, 116	Allen's Oop, 4, 113	8	1:35.65	145,000
1998	**Littlebitlively**, 4, 118	C. Gonzalez	Anet, 4, 116	Scott's Scoundrel, 6, 118	5	1:37.07	160,000
1997	**Isitingood**, 6, 123	D. R. Flores	Spiritbound, 5, 116	Skip Away, 4, 116	7	**1:34.44**	150,000

Texas is the home state of Lone Star Park.

The Very One Handicap

Grade 3 in 2005. Gulfstream Park, three-year-olds and up, fillies and mares, 1⅜ miles, turf. Held March 6, 2005, with a gross value of $100,000. First held in 1987. First graded in 1996. Stakes record 2:11.71 (2005 Honey Ryder).

Year	Winner	Jockey	Second	Third	Strs	Time	1st Purse
2005	**Honey Ryder**, 4, 114	J. R. Velazquez	Briviesca (GB), 4, 114	Vous, 4, 113	10	**2:11.71**	$60,000
2004	**Binya (Ger)**, 5, 114	J. R. Velazquez	Ocean Silk, 4, 115	Boana (Ger), 6, 114	12	2:19.65	60,000
2003	**San Dare**, 5, 116	M. Guidry	Tweedside, 5, 115	Hi Tech Honeycomb, 4, 113	12	2:13.76	60,000
2002	**Moon Queen (Ire)**, 4, 118	J. D. Bailey	Jennasietta, 4, 114	Sweetest Thing, 4, 115	6	2:18.38	60,000
2001	**Innuendo (Ire)**, 6, 115	J. D. Bailey	Lucky Lune (Fr), 4, 114	Silver Bandana, 5, 114	10	2:13.62	60,000
2000	**My Sweet Westly**, 4, 110	P. Day	I'm Indy Mood, 5, 114	Manoa, 5, 114	6	2:06.79	45,000
1999	**Delilah (Ire)**, 5, 116	J. D. Bailey	Starry Dreamer, 5, 114	Justenuffheart, 4, 113	8	2:13.45	45,000
1998	**Shemozzle (Ire)**, 5, 114	J. R. Velazquez	Turkappeal, 5, 114	Yokama, 5, 119	8	2:19.06	45,000
1997	**Tocopilla (Arg)**, 7, 114	B. D. Peck	Ampulla, 6, 123	Beyrouth, 5, 113	6	2:14.35	45,000
1996	**Electric Society (Ire)**, 5, 113	M. E. Smith	Northern Emerald, 6, 117	Chelsey Flower, 5, 114	13	2:15.23	30,000
1995	**P J Floral**, 6, 113	S. J. Sellers	Trampoli, 6, 118	Memories (Ire), 4, 113	6	2:14.44	30,000
1994	**Russian Tango**, 4, 112	J. D. Bailey	Maxamount, 6, 116	Camiunch, 5, 112	6	2:02.58	30,000
1993	**Fairy Garden**, 5, 113	W. S. Ramos	Trampoli, 4, 115	Tango Charlie, 4, 114	11	2:14.67	30,000
1992	**Bungalow**, 5, 112	S. J. Sellers	Raffinierte (Ire), 4, 110	Lover's Quest, 4, 109	7	2:05.79	30,000
1991	**Rigamajig**, 5, 116	R. P. Romero	Star Standing, 4, 114	Ahead (GB), 4, 112	11	2:15.10	30,000
1990	**Storm of Glory**, 6, 113	J. D. Bailey	Tukwila, 4, 110	Topicount, 5, 113	8	1:25.00	30,000
1987	**First Prediction**, 5, 114	J. M. Pezua	Thirty Zip, 4, 113	Lady of the North, 4, 110	11	1:35.20	37,620

Named for Mrs. Helen M. Polinger's 1981 Orchid H. (G2) winner The Very One (1975 f. by One for All). Not graded 2000. Not held 1988-'89. 1 mile 1987. 7 furlongs 1990. 1¼ miles 1992, 1994, 2000. About 1⅜ miles 1998, 2002. Dirt 1990, 1992, 1994, 2000. Four-year-olds and up 1996.

Thoroughbred Club of America Stakes

Grade 3 in 2005. Keeneland, three-year-olds and up, fillies and mares, 6 furlongs, dirt. Held October 17, 2004, with a gross value of $125,000. First held in 1981. First graded in 1988. Stakes record 1:08.70 (1998 Bourbon Belle).

Year	Winner	Jockey	Second	Third	Strs	Time	1st Purse
2004	**Molto Vita**, 4, 122	R. Bejarano	My Trusty Cat, 4, 124	My Boston Gal, 4, 118	6	1:09.92	$77,500
2003	**Summer Mis**, 4, 122	R. R. Douglas	Don't Countess Out, 4, 122	Born to Dance, 4, 122	10	1:09.77	77,500
2002	**French Riviera**, 3, 116	D. J. Meche	Don't Countess Out, 3, 120	Away, 5, 122	10	1:09.75	77,500
2001	**Cat Cay**, 4, 118	P. Day	Spanish Glitter, 3, 120	Another, 4, 124	7	1:09.24	67,580
2000	**Katz Me If You Can**, 3, 115	J. F. Chavez	Hurricane Bertie, 5, 123	My Alibi, 4, 117	6	1:09.42	67,394
1999	**‡Cinemine**, 4, 120	E. M. Martin Jr.	Bourbon Belle, 4, 122	Lucky Again, 3, 114	5	1:08.86	62,000
1998	**Bourbon Belle**, 3, 111	W. Martinez	J J'sdream, 5, 121	Meter Maid, 4, 121	8	**1:08.70**	62,000
1997	**Sky Blue Pink**, 3, 111	P. Day	Bluffing Girl, 3, 114	Mama's Pro, 4, 116	6	1:10.06	62,000
1996	**Surprising Fact**, 3, 110	P. Day	Morris Code, 4, 118	Mama's Pro, 3, 113	9	1:10.14	62,000
1995	**Cat Appeal**, 3, 116	D. M. Barton	Russian Flight (Ire), 3, 113	Traverse City, 5, 118	9	1:10.02	46,500
1994	**Tenacious Tiffany**, 4, 113	C. Perret	Roamin Rachel, 4, 120	Jeano, 6, 120	7	1:11.00	46,500
1993	**Jeano**, 5, 120	P. Day	Apelia, 4, 117	Fluttery Danseur, 4, 120	6	1:09.39	46,500
1992	**Ifyoucouldseemenow**, 4, 120	C. Perret	Harbour Club, 5, 117	Madam Bear, 4, 117	8	1:09.67	48,750
1991	**Avie Jane**, 7, 117	C. Perret	Amen, 4, 114	Hoga, 5, 114	6	1:10.24	48,750
1990	**Safely Kept**, 4, 123	C. Perret	Volterra, 5, 112	Medicine Woman, 5, 117	5	1:10.40	48,750
1989	**Plate Queen**, 4, 117	R. P. Romero	Degenerate Gal, 4, 114	Social Pro, 4, 113	8	1:11.20	48,750
1988	**Tappiano**, 4, 123	J. Vasquez	Bound, 4, 117	Pine Tree Lane, 6, 123	7	1:10.20	48,750
1987	**‡There Are Rainbows**, 7, 120	R. Fletcher	Weekend Delight, 5, 123	Ten Thousand Stars, 5, 120	7	1:11.00	32,500
1986	**Zenobia Empress**, 5, 117	E. Fires	Endear, 4, 120	Weekend Delight, 4, 123	11	1:11.80	32,500
1985	**Boldara**, 4, 114	P. Rubbicco	Shamrock Boat, 4, 114	Space Angel, 5, 120	8	1:10.80	32,500
1984	**Bids and Blades**, 3, 114	D. Brumfield	Lass Trump, 4, 123	Grecian Comedy, 4, 123	8	1:11.60	32,500
1983	**Excitable Lady**, 5, 111	P. Day	Wendy's Ten, 4, 114	A Status Symbol, 4, 111	4	1:09.80	31,250
1982	**Excitable Lady**, 4, 123	D. G. McHargue	Privacy, 4, 117	Arbutus Toehold, 4, 114	10	1:09.20	27,350
1981	**Gold Treasure**, 4, 111	M. S. Sellers	Sweet Revenge, 3, 109	Weber City Miss, 4, 114	8	1:10.20	21,250

Named for the Thoroughbred Club of America, whose headquarters is a short distance from Keeneland. Thoroughbred Club Dinner S. 1981-'82. ‡Zigbelle finished first, DQ to fourth, 1987. ‡Bourbon Belle finished first, DQ to second, 1999.

Toboggan Handicap

Grade 3 in 2005. Aqueduct, three-year-olds and up, 6 furlongs. Held March 12, 2005, with a gross value of $107,100. First held in 1890. First graded in 1973. Stakes record 1:09.09 (2003 Affirmed Success).

Year	Winner	Jockey	Second	Third	Strs	Time	1st Purse
2005	**Primary Suspect**, 4, 115	P. Fragoso	Shake You Down, 7, 122	Houston's Prayer, 5, 115	6	1:09.47	$64,260
2004	**Well Fancied**, 6, 118	E. Coa	Gators N Bears, 4, 115	Don Six, 4, 113	10	1:22.06	67,320

Year	Winner	Jockey	Second	Third	Strs	Time	1st Purse
2003	**Affirmed Success**, 9, 118	R. Migliore	Peeping Tom, 6, 117	Captain Red, 6, 115	6	**1:09.09**	$65,460
2002	**Affirmed Success**, 8, 119	R. Migliore	Vodka, 5, 114	Multiple Choice, 4, 111	6	1:22.87	64,920
2001	**Peeping Tom**, 4, 118	S. Bridgmohan	Say Florida Sandy, 7, 117	Lake Pontchartrain, 6, 113	6	1:21.25	64,380
2000	**Brutally Frank**, 6, 114	S. Bridgmohan	Master O Foxhounds, 5, 114	Watchman's Warning, 5, 113	8	1:20.77	49,410
1999	**Wouldn't We All**, 5, 114	R. Migliore	Brushed On, 4, 115	Esteemed Friend, 5, 120	7	1:20.95	48,900
1998	**Home On the Ridge**, 4, 114	W. H. McCauley	Wire Me Collect, 5, 118	King Roller, 7, 116	7	1:23.01	49,650
1997	**Royal Haven**, 5, 115	R. Migliore	Jamies First Punch, 4, 115	Cold Execution, 6, 113	6	1:22.40	48,600
1996	**Placid Fund**, 4, 112	J. F. Chavez	Valid Wager, 4, 116	Pat n Jac, 4, 112	12	1:22.92	51,480
1995	**Boom Towner**, 7, 117	F. Lovato Jr.	Virginia Rapids, 5, 113	Won Song, 5, 112	6	1:23.77	49,080
1994	**Blare of Trumpets**, 5, 112	D. Carr	Preporant, 5, 117	Fabersham, 6, 115	6	1:09.70	49,200
1993	**Argyle Lake**, 7, 109	D. Carr	The Great M. B., 4, 111	Regal Conquest, 5, 110	12	1:10.11	55,530
1992	**Boom Towner**, 4, 115	D. Nelson	Real Minx, 5, 112	Gallant Step, 5, 114	8	1:10.03	52,740
1991	**Bravely Bold**, 5, 115	M. E. Smith	True and Blue, 6, 116	Proud and Valid, 6, 110	6	1:10.71	52,020
1990	**Sunny Blossom**, 5, 117	E. Maple	Diamond Donnie, 4, 111	Once Wild, 5, 123	6	1:09.60	51,300
1989	**Lord of the Night**, 6, 114	J. Velasquez	Teddy Drone, 4, 117	Vinnie the Viper, 6, 115	7	1:10.40	52,290
1988	**Afleet**, 4, 123	G. Stahlbaum	Pinecutter, 4, 115	Vinnie the Viper, 5, 122	4	1:09.20	66,480
1987	**Play the King**, 4, 112	R. Hernandez	Comic Blush, 4, 117	Best by Test, 5, 124	6	1:09.60	50,400
1986	**Rexson's Bishop**, 4, 114	R. R. Baez	Green Shekel, 4, 126	Cullendale, 5, 116	6	1:11.40	50,760
1985	**Fighting Fit**, 6, 123	R. Migliore	Entropy, 5, 123	Shadowmar, 6, 107	6	1:09.60	51,210
1984	**Top Avenger**, 6, 120	A. Graell	Main Stem, 6, 109	Elegant Life, 4, 116	9	1:10.40	43,080
1983	**Mouse Corps**, 5, 111	R. X. Alvarado Jr.	Top Avenger, 5, 123	Prince Valid, 4, 115	7	1:09.40	33,000
1982	**Always Run Lucky**, 4, 110	J. J. Miranda	Swelegant, 4, 113	In From Dixie, 5, 125	7	1:10.00	33,180
1981	**Dr. Blum**, 4, 123	R. Hernandez	Guilty Conscience, 5, 115	Dunham's Gift, 4, 118	4	1:11.20	32,340
1980	**Tilt Up**, 5, 116	J. Fell	Ardaluan (Ire), 4, 111	Double Zeus, 5, 123	5	1:11.00	33,660
1979	**Vencedor**, 5, 127	M. A. Rivera	Jet Diplomacy, 4, 113	Al Battah, 4, 125	8	1:10.00	32,280
1978	**Barrera**, 5, 126	R. Hernandez	Pumpkin Moonshine, 4, 106	Fratello Ed, 4, 121	5	1:08.80	31,890
1977	**Great Above**, 5, 112	S. Cauthen	Full Out, 4, 117	Patriot's Dream, 4, 126	9	1:09.40	32,490
1976	**Due Diligence**, 4, 111	J. Velasquez	*Pompini, 6, 113	Gallant Bob, 4, 129	11	1:10.20	34,740
1975	†**Honorable Miss**, 5, 117	J. Vasquez	Frankie Adams, 4, 116	Startahemp, 5, 121	6	1:09.00	16,350
1974	**Mike John G.**, 4, 112	V. A. Bracciale Jr.	Tap the Tree, 5, 115	Delta Champ, 4, 113	6	1:08.60	16,575
1973	**Tentam**, 4, 122	J. Velasquez	Spanish Riddle, 4, 115	Tap the Tree, 4, 118	7	1:09.00	16,710

Originally the Toboggan Slide H., held on the downhill course at Old Morris Park in the Bronx, New York. Not graded 1975-'83, 1996-2002. Toboggan Slide H. 1890-'94. Held at Morris Park 1890-'94. Held at Belmont Park 1896-1961. Not held 1891, 1895, 1911-'12. 7 furlongs 1896-1909, 1995-2002, 2004. †Denotes female.

Tokyo City Handicap

Grade 3 in 2005. Santa Anita Park, four-year-olds and up, 1⅛ miles, dirt. Held April 2, 2005, with a gross value of $106,000. First held in 1957. First graded in 1973. Stakes record 1:45.80 (1979 Star Spangled, 1975 Royal Glint).

Year	Winner	Jockey	Second	Third	Strs	Time	1st Purse
2005	**Supah Blitz**, 5, 116	V. Espinoza	Outta Here, 5, 116	Ender's Shadow, 5, 114	5	1:48.90	$63,600
2004	**Dynever**, 4, 117	C. S. Nakatani	Total Impact (Chi), 6, 116	Even the Score, 6, 116	7	1:48.07	66,360
	Diplomatic Bag, 4, 116	D. R. Flores	Statement, 6, 114	Seinne (Chi), 7, 115	7	1:47.90	90,000
2003	**Western Pride**, 5, 116	P. A. Valenzuela	Total Impact (Chi), 5, 113	Fleetstreet Dancer, 5, 112	8	1:48.56	90,000
2002	**Bosque Redondo**, 5, 114	C. J. McCarron	Mysterious Cat, 4, 111	Freedom Crest, 6, 116	6	1:49.11	90,000
2001	**Futural**, 5, 114	G. K. Gomez	Irisheyesareflying, 5, 117	Tribunal, 4, 117	5	1:47.87	90,000
2000	**Early Pioneer**, 5, 113	M. S. Garcia	David, 4, 113	General Challenge, 4, 123	5	1:49.08	95,490
1999	**Classic Cat**, 4, 122	G. L. Stevens	Budroyale, 6, 119	Klinsman (Ire), 5, 115	4	1:47.77	90,000
1998	**Budroyale**, 5, 112	M. S. Garcia	Don't Blame Rio, 5, 114	Bagshot, 4, 116	10	1:48.48	100,530
1997	**Benchmark**, 6, 114	C. J. McCarron	Kingdom Found, 7, 115	Private Song, 4, 112	7	1:48.26	97,650
1996	**Del Mar Dennis**, 6, 118	K. J. Desormeaux	Just Java, 5, 116	Regal Rowdy, 7, 115	6	1:48.37	96,650
1995	**Del Mar Dennis**, 5, 117	C. W. Antley	Wharf, 5, 113	Stoller, 4, 115	8	1:47.27	130,000
1994	**Del Mar Dennis**, 4, 112	S. Gonzalez Jr.	Hill Pass, 5, 115	Tinners Way, 4, 115	8	1:48.36	129,400
1993	**Memo (Chi)**, 6, 114	P. Atkinson	Charmonnier, 5, 117	Marquetry, 6, 118	7	1:47.49	125,860
1992	**Another Review**, 4, 114	K. J. Desormeaux	Defensive Play, 5, 115	Loach, 4, 116	11	1:47.33	163,100
1991	**Anshan (GB)**, 4, 115	C. S. Nakatani	Louis Cyphre (Ire), 5, 112	Pleasant Tap, 4, 116	9	1:47.10	158,900
1990	**Ruhlmann**, 5, 123	G. L. Stevens	Criminal Type, 5, 119	Stylish Winner, 6, 113	6	1:47.20	240,800
1989	**Ruhlmann**, 4, 119	L. A. Pincay Jr.	Lively One, 4, 120	Saratoga Passage, 4, 116	6	1:47.20	185,600
1988	**Alysheba**, 4, 127	C. J. McCarron	Ferdinand, 5, 127	Good Taste (Arg), 6, 113	4	1:47.20	350,000
1987	**Judge Angelucci**, 4, 115	W. Shoemaker	Iron Eyes, 4, 116	Grecian Wonder, 4, 113	4	1:48.40	129,400
1986	**Precisionist**, 5, 126	C. J. McCarron	Greinton (GB), 5, 126	Encolure, 4, 116	4	1:47.60	148,200
1985	**Greinton (GB)**, 4, 120	L. A. Pincay Jr.	Precisionist, 4, 127	Al Mamoon, 4, 115	6	1:47.00	117,300
1984	**Journey At Sea**, 5, 123	W. A. Guerra	My Habitony, 4, 118	Fighting Fit, 5, 121	5	1:48.00	102,050
1983	**The Wonder (Fr)**, 5, 122	W. Shoemaker	Konewah, 4, 112	Swing Till Dawn, 4, 119	6	1:49.20	62,500
1982	**Super Moment**, 5, 124	C. J. McCarron	Mehmet, 4, 116	It's the One, 4, 126	5	1:48.60	75,450
1981	**Borzoi**, 5, 118	W. Shoemaker	Shamgo, 5, 117	King Go Go, 6, 122	8	1:46.20	64,700
1980	**Peregrinator (Ire)**, 5, 115	C. J. McCarron	Lunar Probe (NZ), 6, 116	Henschel, 6, 120	6	1:47.80	65,300
1979	**Star Spangled**, 5, 117	L. A. Pincay Jr.	Farnesio (Arg), 5, 118	State Dinner, 4, 118	6	**1:45.80**	46,900
1978	**J. O. Tobin**, 4, 123	S. Cauthen	Henschel, 4, 115	Riot in Paris, 7, 119	6	1:47.80	31,950
1977	**Today 'n Tomorrow**, 4, 112	S. Hawley	Exact Duplicate, 5, 115	Rajab, 4, 114	9	1:46.40	35,300
1976	**Zanthe**, 7, 118	S. Hawley	Riot in Paris, 5, 121	Mateor, 5, 114	6	1:45.80	34,300
1975	**Royal Glint**, 5, 120	W. Shoemaker	Against the Snow, 5, 115	June's Love, 4, 115	8	**1:45.80**	34,800

1974	**Court Ruling**, 4, 117	B. Baeza	Captain Cee Jay, 4, 119	Acclimatization, 6, 115	8	1:48.40	$25,900
	Wichita Oil, 6, 116	L. A. Pincay Jr.	*Madison Palace, 6, 117	Woodland Pines, 5, 118	8	1:47.60	25,800
1973	**Quack**, 4, 125	D. Pierce	River Bayou, 8, 119	Curious Course, 4, 112	8	1:49.00	36,500

Named for Tokyo City Racecourse in Japan, one of Santa Anita's sister racetracks. Formerly named for Rancho San Bernardino, location of the present-day city of San Bernardino, California. San Bernardino H. 1957-2004. Not graded 1978. Grade 2 1973-'77, 1979-2000. 1¹/₁₆ miles 1957-'66, 1974. Turf 1957-'72, 1974-'78. Originally scheduled on turf 1973. Three-year-olds 1957. Three-year-olds and up 1958-'67. Two divisions 1974, 2004. Equaled course record 1975.

Tom Fool Handicap

Grade 2 in 2005. Belmont Park, three-year-olds and up, 7 furlongs, dirt. Held July 4, 2004, with a gross value of $142,500. First held in 1975. First graded in 1981. Stakes record 1:20.17 (2002 Left Bank).

Year	Winner	Jockey	Second	Third	Strs	Time	1st Purse
2004	**Ghostzapper**, 4, 119	J. Castellano	Aggadan, 5, 114	Unforgettable Max, 4, 114	4	1:20.42	$90,000
2003	**Aldebaran**, 5, 122	J. D. Bailey	Peeping Tom, 6, 117	State City, 4, 118	7	1:22.54	90,000
2002	**Left Bank**, 5, 121	J. R. Velazquez	Affirmed Success, 8, 120	Summer Note, 5, 113	6	**1:20.17**	90,000
2001	**Exchange Rate**, 4, 114	J. D. Bailey	Say Florida Sandy, 7, 117	Here's Zealous, 4, 112	5	1:21.24	90,000
2000	**Trippi**, 3, 112	J. D. Bailey	Cornish Snow, 7, 113	Sailor's Warning, 4, 111	6	1:21.69	90,000
1999	**Crafty Friend**, 6, 116	R. Migliore	Affirmed Success, 5, 119	Artax, 4, 117	5	1:20.62	90,000
1998	**Banker's Gold**, 4, 115	J. F. Chavez	Boundless Moment, 6, 115	Partner's Hero, 4, 114	6	1:21.04	90,000
1997	**Diligence**, 4, 116	J. A. Santos	Royal Haven, 5, 118	Elusive Quality, 4, 114	7	1:22.40	90,000
1996	**Kayrawan**, 4, 113	R. Migliore	Cold Execution, 5, 112	Lite the Fuse, 5, 122	5	1:22.95	64,860
1995	**Lite the Fuse**, 4, 117	J. A. Krone	Our Emblem, 4, 115	Evil Bear, 5, 118	6	1:21.72	65,220
1994	**Virginia Rapids**, 4, 124	J. Samyn	Cherokee Run, 4, 121	Boundary, 4, 119	5	1:22.27	64,380
1993	**Birdonthewire**, 4, 119	C. Perret	Fly So Free, 5, 119	Take Me Out, 5, 119	5	1:20.93	67,680
1992	**Rubiano**, 5, 126	J. A. Krone	Take Me Out, 4, 119	Arrowtown, 4, 119	8	1:21.70	70,920
1991	**Mr. Nasty**, 4, 119	A. T. Cordero Jr.	Rubiano, 4, 121	Senor Speedy, 4, 119	4	1:21.79	67,800
1990	**Quick Call**, 6, 119	J. F. Chavez	Sewickley, 5, 123	Traskwood, 4, 119	5	1:21.40	52,680
1989	**Sewickley**, 4, 119	R. P. Romero	Houston, 3, 114	Crusader Sword, 4, 119	6	1:24.00	67,920
1988	**King's Swan**, 8, 128	A. T. Cordero Jr.	Gulch, 4, 128	Abject, 4, 119	4	1:22.40	100,980
1987	**Groovy**, 4, 128	A. T. Cordero Jr.	Sun Master, 6, 121	Moment of Hope, 4, 119	6	1:22.40	81,900
1986	**Groovy**, 3, 112	J. A. Santos	Phone Trick, 4, 126	Basket Weave, 5, 119	5	1:21.60	80,460
1985	**Track Barron**, 4, 123	A. T. Cordero Jr.	Mt. Livermore, 4, 126	Cannon Shell, 6, 126	6	1:22.40	82,260
1984	**Believe the Queen**, 4, 126	J. Velasquez	A Phenomenon, 4, 119	Cannon Shell, 5, 121	6	1:22.40	70,680
1983	**Deputy Minister**, 4, 126	D. MacBeth	Fit to Fight, 4, 119	Maudlin, 5, 126	9	1:22.20	52,020
1982	**Rise Jim**, 6, 119	A. T. Cordero Jr.	Maudlin, 4, 119	And More, 4, 119	5	1:23.80	32,940
1981	**Rise Jim**, 5, 119	A. T. Cordero Jr.	Proud Appeal, 3, 121	Rivalero, 5, 119	6	1:21.20	32,820
1980	**Plugged Nickle**, 3, 121	J. Fell	Dr. Patches, 6, 119	Isella, 5, 119	5	1:22.20	33,060
1979	**Cox's Ridge**, 5, 119	E. Maple	Nice Catch, 5, 121	Tilt Up, 4, 119	5	1:22.20	25,500
1978	**J. O. Tobin**, 4, 129	J. Fell	White Rammer, 4, 119	It's Freezing, 6, 116	8	1:20.80	25,950
1977	**Mexican General**, 4, 115	C. Perret	Full Out, 4, 119	Sticky Situation, 4, 110	9	1:22.00	22,605
1976	**El Pitirre**, 4, 114	A. T. Cordero Jr.	Nalees Knight, 5, 110	†Honorable Miss, 6, 118	6	1:24.40	26,550
1975	**Kinsman Hope**, 5, 116	J. Ruane	Lonetree, 5, 125	Right Mind, 4, 113	9	1:21.40	26,925

Named for Greentree Stable's 1953 Horse of the Year and '53 Carter H. winner Tom Fool (1949 c. by Menow). Grade 3 1981. Tom Fool S. 1979-'95. Held at Aqueduct 1975-'76. †Denotes female.

Top Flight Handicap

Grade 2 in 2005. Aqueduct, three-year-olds and up, fillies and mares, 1 mile, dirt. Held November 26, 2004, with a gross value of $150,000. First held in 1940. First graded in 1973. Stakes record 1:34.96 (1994 Educated Risk).

Year	Winner	Jockey	Second	Third	Strs	Time	1st Purse
2004	**Daydreaming**, 3, 117	J. D. Bailey	Bending Strings, 3, 118	Roar Emotion, 4, 116	6	1:35.29	$90,000
2003	**Randaroo**, 3, 116	H. Castillo Jr.	Beauty Halo (Arg), 4, 115	Pocus Hocus, 5, 116	12	1:36.49	90,000
2002	**Sightseek**, 3, 113	J. D. Bailey	Zonk, 4, 116	Nasty Storm, 4, 116	9	1:35.46	90,000
2001	**Cat Cay**, 4, 117	J. R. Velazquez	Tugger, 4, 116	Atelier, 4, 120	9	1:35.45	90,000
2000	**Reciclada (Chi)**, 5, 116	J. D. Bailey	Country Hideaway, 4, 120	Critical Eye, 3, 120	8	1:35.54	90,000
1999	**Belle Cherie**, 3, 113	J. R. Velazquez	dh-Furlough, 5, 118		7	1:35.46	90,000
			dh-Harpia, 4, 117				
1998	**Catinca**, 3, 119	R. Migliore	Furlough, 4, 115	Glitter Woman, 4, 120	5	1:35.81	90,000
1997	**Dixie Flag**, 3, 117	M. J. Luzzi	Aldiza, 3, 114	Mil Kilates, 4, 117	9	1:35.34	90,000
1996	**Flat Fleet Feet**, 3, 116	M. E. Smith	Queen Tutta, 4, 114	Miss Golden Circle, 4, 116	9	1:37.00	90,000
1995	**Twist Afleet**, 4, 123	M. E. Smith	Chaposa Springs, 3, 118	Lotta Dancing, 4, 114	8	1:35.26	90,000
1994	**Educated Risk**, 4, 120	M. E. Smith	Triumph At Dawn, 4, 111	Imah, 4, 111	8	**1:34.96**	90,000
1993	**You'd Be Surprised**, 4, 112	J. D. Bailey	Looie Capote, 4, 115	Shared Interest, 5, 114	7	1:48.82	90,000
1992	**Firm Stance**, 4, 114	P. Day	Haunting, 4, 112	Lady d'Accord, 5, 117	14	1:50.55	120,000
1991	**Buy the Firm**, 5, 119	J. A. Krone	Colonial Waters, 6, 118	Sharp Dance, 5, 113	5	1:52.30	120,000
1990	**Dreamy Mimi**, 4, 111	J. D. Bailey	She Can, 3, 108	Survive, 6, 120	7	1:50.40	136,800
1989	**Banker's Lady**, 4, 121	A. T. Cordero Jr.	Colonial Waters, 4, 114	Aptostar, 4, 117	5	1:51.20	133,680
1988	**Clabber Girl**, 5, 117	J. A. Santos	Psyched, 5, 114	Cadillacing, 4, 113	7	1:49.40	141,840
1987	**Ms. Eloise**, 4, 116	R. G. Davis	Beth's Song, 5, 111	Clemanna's Rose, 6, 115	8	1:50.20	138,480
1986	**Ride Sally**, 4, 123	W. A. Guerra	Squan Song, 5, 124	Leecoo, 5, 107	6	1:49.20	148,140
1985	**Flip's Pleasure**, 5, 117	J. Samyn	Sintrillium, 7, 119	Some for All, 4, 110	5	1:51.00	101,160

1984	**Sweet Missus**, 4, 103	R. J. Thibeau Jr.	Lady Norcliffe, 4, 115	Adept, 5, 110	7	1:50.20	$104,040
1983	**Adept**, 4, 109	K. L. Rogers	Broom Dance, 4, 122	Dance Number, 4, 115	6	1:50.00	65,160
1982	**Andover Way**, 4, 121	J. Velasquez	Anti Lib, 4, 113	Discorama, 4, 116	9	1:50.00	66,360
1981	**Chain Bracelet**, 4, 115	R. Hernandez	Lady Oakley (Ire), 4, 115	Weber City Miss, 4, 118	5	1:49.60	64,680
1980	**Glorious Song**, 4, 123	J. Velasquez	Misty Gallore, 4, 126	Blitey, 4, 117	7	1:49.60	66,360
1979	**Waya (Fr)**, 5, 128	A. T. Cordero Jr.	Pearl Necklace, 5, 120	Island Kiss, 4, 112	8	1:50.80	64,680
1978	**Northernette**, 4, 121	J. Fell	One Sum, 4, 121	Dottie's Doll, 5, 116	8	1:49.40	48,330
1977	**Shawi**, 4, 111	M. Venezia	Proud Delta, 5, 124	Mississippi Mud, 4, 114	9	1:49.80	48,285
1976	**Proud Delta**, 4, 120	J. Velasquez	Let Me Linger, 4, 116	Spring Is Here, 4, 108	7	1:49.00	49,455
1975	**Twixt**, 6, 125	W. J. Passmore	Heloise, 4, 109	Something Super, 5, 116	8	1:50.60	33,240
1974	**Lady Love**, 4, 114	E. Maple	Krislin, 5, 111	Penny Flight, 4, 115	7	1:48.60	33,120
1973	**Poker Night**, 3, 110	R. Woodhouse	Summer Guest, 4, 123	Roba Bella, 4, 113	7	1:48.20	33,420

Named for C. V. Whitney's 1931 champion two-year-old filly, '32 champion three-year-old filly, and '32 Coaching Club American Oaks winner Top Flight (1929 f. by *Dis Donc). Sponsored by Delta Airlines of Atlanta 1996-2000, 2003. Grade 1 1973-'96. Delta Top Flight H. 1996-2000, 2003. Held at Belmont Park 1940-'61, 1993. 1¹/₁₆ miles 1940-'60. 1¹/₈ miles 1961-'93. Four-year-olds and up 1988, 1990. Dead heat for second 1999.

Transylvania Stakes

Grade 3 in 2005. Keeneland, three-year-olds, 1 mile, turf. Held April 8, 2005, with a gross value of $150,000. First held in 1989. First graded in 2003. Stakes record 1:34.65 (1998 Dog Watch [GB]).

Year	Winner	Jockey	Second	Third	Strs	Time	1st Purse
2005	**Chattahoochee War**, 3, 121	J. D. Bailey	Guillaume Tell (Ire), 3, 117	Rey de Cafe, 3, 121	8	1:35.28	$93,000
2004	**Timo**, 3, 123	E. S. Prado	Mr. J. T. L., 3, 116	America Alive, 3, 116	9	1:36.52	70,308
2003	**White Cat**, 3, 116	S. J. Sellers	Deep Shadow, 3, 118	Christmas Away, 3, 116	9	1:34.98	62,000
2002	**Flying Dash (Ger)**, 3, 116	J. D. Bailey	Back Packer, 3, 116	Political Attack, 3, 120	8	1:35.69	62,000
2001	**Baptize**, 3, 120	J. D. Bailey	Dynameaux, 3, 116	Act of Reform, 3, 116	9	1:35.28	70,556
2000	**Field Cat**, 3, 116	M. E. Smith	Lendell Ray, 3, 116	Go Lib Go, 3, 123	9	1:35.19	70,618
1999	**Good Night**, 3, 114	S. J. Sellers	Air Rocket, 3, 114	Make Your Mark, 3, 114	10	1:35.00	70,308
1998	**Dog Watch (GB)**, 3, 116	R. G. Davis	Reformer Rally, 3, 118	American Odyssey, 3, 114	10	**1:34.65**	45,781
1997	**Near the Bank**, 3, 118	P. Day	Daylight Savings, 3, 114	Song for James, 3, 113	6	1:36.40	44,249
1996	**More Royal**, 3, 112	J. A. Krone	Defacto, 3, 121	Rough Opening, 3, 121	5	1:35.92	43,202
1995	**‡Crimson Guard**, 3, 118	M. E. Smith	Dixie Dynasty, 3, 114	‡Nostra, 3, 118	9	1:44.04	42,259
1994	**Star of Manila**, 3, 121	S. J. Sellers	Prix de Crouton, 3, 118	Carpet, 3, 118	6	1:42.87	33,635
1993	**Proud Shot**, 3, 118	W. H. McCauley	Explosive Red, 3, 121	Awad, 3, 121	7	1:44.17	34,364
1992	**Casino Magistrate**, 3, 121	R. D. Lopez	Coaxing Matt, 3, 112	Trans Caribbean, 3, 115	7	1:46.62	35,636
1991	**Eastern Dude**, 3, 121	S. J. Sellers	Magic Interlude, 3, 121	January Man, 3, 112	10	1:42.94	36,514
1990	**Izvestia**, 3, 112	R. P. Romero	Scattered, 3, 115	Divine Warning, 3, 112	9	1:43.80	36,043
1989	**Shy Tom**, 3, 121	R. P. Romero	Once Over Knightly, 3, 118	Ringerman, 3, 121	6	1:50.00	35,133

Named for Transylvania University, the oldest college west of the Allegheny Mountains, founded in 1780 in Lexington. Sponsored by Central Bank of Lexington 2005. 1¹/₁₆ miles 1989-'95. ‡Ops Smile finished first, DQ to eighth; Hawk Attack finished third, DQ to seventh, 1995.

Travers Stakes

Grade 1 in 2005. Saratoga Race Course, three-year-olds, 1¹/₄ miles, dirt. Held August 28, 2004, with a gross value of $1,000,000. First held in 1864. First graded in 1973. Stakes record 2:00 (1979 General Assembly).

Year	Winner	Jockey	Second	Third	Strs	Time	1st Purse
2004	**Birdstone**, 3, 126	E. S. Prado	The Cliff's Edge, 3, 126	Eddington, 3, 126	7	2:02.45	$600,000
2003	**Ten Most Wanted**, 3, 126	P. Day	Peace Rules, 3, 126	Strong Hope, 3, 126	6	2:02.14	600,000
2002	**Medaglia d'Oro**, 3, 126	J. D. Bailey	Repent, 3, 126	Nothing Flat, 3, 126	9	2:02.53	600,000
2001	**Point Given**, 3, 126	G. L. Stevens	E Dubai, 3, 126	Dollar Bill, 3, 126	9	2:01.40	600,000
2000	**Unshaded**, 3, 126	S. J. Sellers	Albert the Great, 3, 126	Commendable, 3, 126	9	2:02.59	600,000
1999	**Lemon Drop Kid**, 3, 126	J. A. Santos	Vision and Verse, 3, 126	Menifee, 3, 126	8	2:02.19	600,000
1998	**Coronado's Quest**, 3, 126	M. E. Smith	Victory Gallop, 3, 126	Raffie's Majesty, 3, 126	7	2:03.40	450,000
1997	**Deputy Commander**, 3, 126	C. J. McCarron	Behrens, 3, 126	Awesome Again, 3, 126	8	2:04.08	450,000
1996	**Will's Way**, 3, 126	J. F. Chavez	Louis Quatorze, 3, 126	Skip Away, 3, 126	7	2:02.55	450,000
1995	**Thunder Gulch**, 3, 126	G. L. Stevens	Pyramid Peak, 3, 126	Malthus, 3, 126	7	2:03.70	450,000
1994	**Holy Bull**, 3, 126	M. E. Smith	Concern, 3, 126	Tabasco Cat, 3, 126	5	2:02.03	450,000
1993	**Sea Hero**, 3, 126	J. D. Bailey	Kissin Kris, 3, 126	Miner's Mark, 3, 126	11	2:01.95	600,000
1992	**Thunder Rumble**, 3, 126	W. H. McCauley	Devil His Due, 3, 126	Dance Floor, 3, 126	10	2:00.99	600,000
1991	**Corporate Report**, 3, 126	C. J. McCarron	Hansel, 3, 126	Fly So Free, 3, 126	6	2:01.20	600,000
1990	**Rhythm**, 3, 126	C. Perret	Shot Gun Scott, 3, 126	Sir Richard Lewis, 3, 126	13	2:02.60	707,100
1989	**Easy Goer**, 3, 126	P. Day	Clever Trevor, 3, 126	Shy Tom, 3, 126	6	2:00.80	653,100
1988	**Forty Niner**, 3, 126	C. J. McCarron	Seeking the Gold, 3, 126	Brian's Time, 3, 126	6	2:01.40	653,100
1987	**Java Gold**, 3, 126	P. Day	Cryptoclearance, 3, 126	Polish Navy, 3, 126	9	2:02.00	673,800
1986	**Wise Times**, 3, 126	J. D. Bailey	‡Danzig Connection, 3, 126	Personal Flag, 3, 126	7	2:03.40	203,700
1985	**Chief's Crown**, 3, 126	A. T. Cordero Jr.	Turkoman, 3, 126	Skip Trial, 3, 126	7	2:01.20	202,800
1984	**Carr de Naskra**, 3, 126	L. A. Pincay Jr.	Pine Circle, 3, 126	Morning Bob, 3, 126	9	2:02.60	211,500
1983	**Play Fellow**, 3, 126	P. Day	Slew o' Gold, 3, 126	Hyperborean, 3, 126	7	2:01.00	135,000
1982	**Runaway Groom**, 3, 126	J. Fell	Aloma's Ruler, 3, 126	Conquistador Cielo, 3, 126	5	2:02.60	132,900
1981	**Willow Hour**, 3, 126	E. Maple	Pleasant Colony, 3, 126	Lord Avie, 3, 126	10	2:03.80	135,600
1980	**Temperence Hill**, 3, 126	E. Maple	First Albert, 3, 126	Amber Pass, 3, 126	9	2:02.80	100,980

1979 **General Assembly**, 3, 126	J. Vasquez	Smarten, 3, 126	Private Account, 3, 126	7	**2:00.00**	$80,850
1978 ‡**Alydar**, 3, 126	J. Velasquez	Affirmed, 3, 126	Nasty and Bold, 3, 126	4	2:02.00	62,880
1977 ‡**Jatski**, 3, 126	S. Maple	Run Dusty Run, 3, 126	Silver Series, 3, 126	14	2:01.60	68,160
1976 **Honest Pleasure**, 3, 126	C. Perret	Romeo, 3, 126	Dance Spell, 3, 126	8	2:00.20	65,040
1975 **Wajima**, 3, 126	B. Baeza	Media, 3, 126	Prince Thou Art, 3, 126	5	2:02.00	65,220
1974 **Holding Pattern**, 3, 121	M. Miceli	Little Current, 3, 126	†Chris Evert, 3, 121	11	2:05.20	69,660
1973 **Annihilate 'em**, 3, 120	R. Turcotte	Stop the Music, 3, 122	See the Jaguar, 3, 120	8	2:01.60	68,280

Named for the first president of Saratoga Race Course, William R. Travers; he won the inaugural running with Kentucky. Travers Midsummer Derby 1927-'32. Held at Belmont Park 1943-'45. Not held 1896, 1898, 1900, 1911-'12. 1³/₄ miles 1864-'89. 1¹/₂ miles 1890-'92. 1¹/₈ miles 1895, 1901-'03. ‡Run Dusty Run finished first, DQ to second, 1977. ‡Affirmed finished first, DQ to second, 1978. ‡Broad Brush finished second, DQ to fourth, 1986. †Denotes female.

Triple Bend Breeders' Cup Invitational Handicap

Grade 1 in 2005. Hollywood Park, three-year-olds and up, 7 furlongs, dirt. Held July 3, 2004, with a gross value of $300,000. First held in 1952. First graded in 1988. Stakes record 1:19.40 (1980 Rich Cream).

Year	Winner	Jockey	Second	Third	Strs	Time	1st Purse
2004	**Pohave**, 6, 116	V. Espinoza	Rojo Toro, 4, 115	Revello, 6, 110	13	1:21.06	$180,000
2003	**Joey Franco**, 4, 118	P. A. Valenzuela	Publication, 4, 116	‡Primerica, 5, 113	9	1:21.56	180,000
2002	**Disturbingthepeace**, 4, 113	V. Espinoza	D'wildcat, 4, 115	Mellow Fellow, 7, 120	9	1:21.09	180,000
2001	**Ceeband**, 4, 110	M. S. Garcia	Squirtle Squirt, 3, 114	Elaborate, 6, 118	10	1:21.17	180,000
2000	**Elaborate**, 5, 114	V. Espinoza	Cliquot, 4, 116	Lexicon, 5, 117	10	1:21.19	180,000
1999	**Mazel Trick**, 4, 115	C. J. McCarron	Christmas Boy, 6, 111	Regal Thunder, 5, 115	8	1:19.97	180,000
1998	**Son of a Pistol**, 6, 118	A. O. Solis	The Exeter Man, 6, 114	Benchmark, 7, 118	11	1:20.81	120,000
1997	**Score Quick**, 5, 113	G. F. Almeida	Elmhurst, 7, 115	First Intent, 8, 116	11	1:21.00	100,980
1996	**Letthebighossroll**, 8, 116	C. J. McCarron	Score Quick, 4, 116	Comininalittlehot, 5, 116	7	1:21.43	125,460
1995	**Concept Win**, 5, 118	P. A. Valenzuela	Gold Land, 4, 116	Lucky Forever, 6, 119	6	1:21.09	63,100
1994	**Memo (Chi)**, 7, 120	P. Atkinson	Minjinsky, 4, 115	Slerp, 5, 119	6	1:20.52	62,400
1993	**Now Listen**, 6, 116	K. J. Desormeaux	Cardmania, 7, 116	Star of the Crop, 4, 120	10	1:20.83	66,400
1992	**Slew the Surgeon**, 4, 111	M. G. Linares	Softshoe Sure Shot, 6, 114	Record Boom, 6, 112	8	1:21.44	64,600
1991	**Robyn Dancer**, 4, 118	L. A. Pincay Jr.	Bruho, 4, 117	Black Jack Road, 7, 118	6	1:21.10	62,700
1990	**Prospectors Gamble**, 5, 114	J. A. Garcia	Raise a Stanza, 4, 117	Hot Operator, 5, 113	8	1:21.40	64,200
1989	**Sensational Star**, 5, 114	R. Q. Meza	Oraibi, 4, 120	Hot Operator, 4, 113	9	1:21.40	49,700
1988	**Perfec Travel**, 6, 115	C. A. Black	Reconnoitering, 4, 115	Don's Irish Melody, 5, 115	9	1:22.20	49,600
1987	**Bedside Promise**, 5, 124	R. Q. Meza	Zabaleta, 4, 118	Bolder Than Bold, 5, 118	5	1:21.00	46,500
1986	**Sabona**, 4, 114	C. J. McCarron	Innamorato, 5, 113	Michadilla, 4, 115	6	1:21.00	47,150
1985	**Fifty Six Ina Row**, 4, 117	L. A. Pincay Jr.	Premiership, 5, 115	French Legionaire, 4, 117	7	1:20.80	38,500
1984	**Debonaire Junior**, 3, 114	C. J. McCarron	Croeso, 4, 116	Night Mover, 4, 120	7	1:21.20	37,980
1983	**Regal Falcon**, 5, 117	E. J. Delahoussaye	Island Whirl, 5, 123	Kangroo Court, 6, 118	5	1:23.40	30,700
1982	**Never Tabled**, 5, 112	C. J. McCarron	Shanekite, 4, 117	Pompeii Court, 5, 116	7	1:21.00	31,750
1981	**Summer Time Guy**, 5, 118	C. J. McCarron	Back'n Time, 4, 118	Life's Hope, 8, 115	4	1:21.20	37,400
1980	**Rich Cream**, 5, 118	W. Shoemaker	I'm Smokin, 4, 115	Dragon Command (NZ), 6, 116	10	**1:19.40**	32,250
1979	**White Rammer**, 5, 120	W. Shoemaker	Arachnoid, 6, 124	Bad 'n Big, 5, 122	5	1:21.20	24,650
1978	**Drapier (Arg)**, 6, 120	F. Toro	Voy Por Uno (Mex), 5, 114	Prince of Saron, 5, 115	4	1:21.20	24,200
1977	**Painted Wagon**, 4, 115	C. Baltazar	Beat Inflation, 4, 122	L'Natural, 4, 115	7	1:20.20	25,750
1976	**Home Jerome**, 6, 115	M. Castaneda	Shirley's Champion, 5, 116	Money Lender, 5, 116	6	1:21.20	25,050
1975	**Messenger of Song**, 3, 115	J. Lambert	Century's Envoy, 4, 122	Chesapeake, 6, 115	10	1:20.60	26,650
1974	**Woodland Pines**, 5, 119	L. A. Pincay Jr.	Soft Victory, 6, 118	Finalista, 5, 123	8	1:20.60	19,800
1973	**Briartic**, 5, 122	W. Shoemaker	New Prospect, 4, 121	Silver Mallet, 5, 115	8	1:20.60	25,950

Named for Frank McMahon's 1972 Los Angeles H. winner Triple Bend (1968 c. by Never Bend). Formerly named for Hollywood Park's nickname, "The Track of Lakes and Flowers." Grade 3 1988-'97. Grade 2 1998-2002. Lakes and Flowers H. 1952-'78. Triple Bend H. 1979-'95. Triple Bend Breeders' Cup H. 1996-'97. 6 furlongs 1956-'72. Equaled track record 1993. Track record 1994, 1999. ‡Bluesthestandard finished third, DQ to sixth, 2003.

Tropical Park Derby

Grade 3 in 2005. Calder Race Course, three-year-olds, 1¹/₈ miles, turf. Held January 1, 2005, with a gross value of $100,000. First held in 1976. First graded in 1978. Stakes record 1:46.60 (2000 Go Lib Go; 1985 Irish Sur; 1983 My Mac).

Year	Winner	Jockey	Second	Third	Strs	Time	1st Purse
2005	**Lord Robyn**, 3, 117	E. Coa	Fire Path, 3, 114	Crown Point, 3, 119	12	1:47.18	$60,000
2004	**Kitten's Joy**, 3, 119	J. D. Bailey	Broadway View, 3, 112	Soverign Honor, 3, 117	11	1:46.95	60,000
2003	**Nothing to Lose**, 3, 115	J. D. Bailey	Millennium Storm, 3, 119	Supah Blitz, 3, 115	12	1:50.45	60,000
2002	**Political Attack**, 3, 119	M. Guidry	The Judge Sez Who, 3, 115	Deeliteful Guy, 3, 119	8	1:51.71	60,000
2001	**Proud Man**, 3, 115	R. R. Douglas	Mr Notebook, 3, 119	Cee Dee, 3, 119	11	1:47.95	60,000
2000	**Go Lib Go**, 3, 119	J. A. Santos	Mr. Livingston, 3, 115	Granting, 3, 115	12	**1:46.60**	60,000
1999	**Valid Reprized**, 3, 115	J. Castellano	Mr. Roark, 3, 115	Wertz, 3, 119	12	1:53.58	60,000
1998	**Draw Again**, 3, 117	J. Bravo	Buddha's Delight, 3, 115	Daddy's Dream, 3, 117	11	1:51.28	60,000
1997	**Arthur L.**, 3, 119	E. Coa	Unite's Big Red, 3, 117	Keep It Strait, 3, 117	12	1:46.93	60,000
1996	**Ok by Me**, 3, 117	J. D. Bailey	Darn That Erica, 3, 114	Tour's Big Red, 3, 117	12	1:47.25	60,000
1995	**Mecke**, 3, 117	H. Castillo Jr.	Val's Prince, 3, 112	Claudius, 3, 119	14	1:51.12	60,000
1994	**Fabulous Frolic**, 3, 112	J. Cruguet	Wake Up Alarm, 3, 117	Gator Back, 3, 119	14	1:46.99	60,000
1993	**Summer Set**, 3, 112	M. A. Gonzalez	Duc d'Sligovil, 3, 112	Silver of Silver, 3, 122	10	1:53.87	60,000
1992	**Technology**, 3, 119	J. D. Bailey	Majestic Sweep, 3, 114	Always Silver, 3, 114	10	1:53.01	134,160

1991	Jackie Wackie, 3, 119	H. Castillo Jr.	Gizmo's Fortune, 3, 119	Paulrus, 3, 114	13	1:51.90	$69,120
1990	Run Turn, 3, 117	E. Fires	Country Day, 3, 112	Shot Gun Scott, 3, 119	8	1:52.40	66,420
1989	Big Stanley, 3, 114	J. Vasquez	Appealing Pleasure, 3, 114	Prized, 3, 114	8	1:52.40	100,170
1988	Digress, 3, 117	E. Maple	Intensive Command, 3, 117	Granacus, 3, 117	11	1:54.60	176,460
1987	Baldski's Star, 3, 117	C. Perret	Manhattan's Woody, 3, 112	Schism, 3, 117	13	1:54.80	139,920
1986	Strong Performance, 3, 117	J. Cruguet	Dr. Dan Eyes, 3, 114	Real Forest, 3, 117	12	1:54.40	143,760
1985	Irish Sur, 3, 121	J. A. Santos	Artillerist, 3, 121	Banner Bob, 3, 121	16	1:46.60	107,370
1984	Morning Bob, 3, 121	E. Maple	‡Don Rickles, 3, 121	Papa Koo, 3, 121	15	1:46.00	89,310
1983	My Mac, 3, 121	D. MacBeth	Caveat, 3, 121	Blink, 3, 121	11	1:46.60	100,350
1982	Victorian Line, 3, 121	A. Smith Jr.	North Cat, 3, 121	Sandy Bee's Baby, 3, 121	10	1:45.40	68,280
1981	Double Sonic, 3, 121	A. Smith Jr.	Akureyri, 3, 121	Might Be Home, 3, 121	14	1:46.40	70,740
1980	Superbity, 3, 121	J. Vasquez	Ray's Word, 3, 121	Irish Tower, 3, 121	11	1:45.60	69,600
1979	Bishop's Choice, 3, 111	D. MacBeth	Lot o' Gold, 3, 119	Smarten, 3, 119	12	1:44.20	74,400
1978	Dr. Valeri, 3, 116	R. Riera Jr.	Quadratic, 3, 119	Galimore, 3, 119	11	1:45.20	73,200
1977	Ruthie's Native, 3, 112	L. Saumell	Fort Prevel, 3, 121	Dreaming of Moe, 3, 112	12	1:44.40	55,800
1976	Star of the Sea, 3, 115	C. Perret	Controller Ike, 3, 114	Great Contractor, 3, 121	12	1:44.00	55,800

Named for the old Tropical Park racetrack in Miami, which closed in 1972. Grade 2 1983-'89. 1 1/16 miles 1976-'85. About 1 1/8 miles 1994. Dirt 1978-'93, 2002. ‡Rexson's Hope finished second, DQ to fifth, 1984.

Tropical Turf Handicap

Grade 3 in 2005. Calder Race Course, three-year-olds and up, 1 1/8 miles, turf. Held December 4, 2004, with a gross value of $100,000. First held in 1935. First graded in 1981. Stakes record 1:44.95 (1993 Carterista).

Year	Winner	Jockey	Second	Third	Strs	Time	1st Purse
2004	Host (Chi), 4, 118	J. R. Velazquez	Silver Tree, 4, 118	Demeteor, 5, 114	12	1:45.74	$60,000
2003	Political Attack, 4, 116	R. R. Douglas	Millennium Dragon (GB), 4, 116	Sforza (Fr), 4, 115	12	1:45.81	60,000
2002	Krieger, 4, 113	E. Coa	Stokosky, 6, 113	Serial Bride, 5, 114	12	1:47.02	60,000
2001	Band Is Passing, 5, 118	C. Gonzalez	Crash Course, 5, 116	Groomstick Stock's, 5, 114	12	1:46.90	60,000
2000	Stokosky, 4, 114	C. A. Hernandez	dh- Band Is Passing, 4, 113		11	1:48.77	60,000
			dh- Special Coach, 4, 114				
1999	Hibernian Rhapsody (Ire), 4, 114	R. R. Douglas	Garbu, 5, 117	Shamrock City, 4, 114	12	1:46.17	60,000
1998	Unite's Big Red, 4, 115	E. O. Nunez	N B Forrest, 6, 115	Glok, 4, 115	8	1:48.96	60,000
1997	Sir Cat, 4, 116	J. A. Rivera II	Foolish Pole, 4, 115	Written Approval, 5, 112	6	1:54.08	60,000
1996	Mecke, 4, 124	R. G. Davis	Satellite Nealski, 3, 113	Elite Jeblar, 6, 114	10	1:46.51	60,000
1995	The Vid, 5, 120	W. H. McCauley	Elite Jeblar, 5, 114	Scannapieco, 5, 113	12	1:44.99	60,000
1994	The Vid, 4, 116	R. R. Douglas	Country Coy, 4, 113	Gone for Real, 3, 113	10	1:49.06	60,000
1993	Carterista, 4, 121	W. S. Ramos	Rinka Das, 5, 113	Daarik (Ire), 6, 114	12	1:44.95	45,000
1992	Carterista, 3, 112	M. A. Lee	Rinka Das, 4, 114	Pidgeon's Promise, 3, 110	11	1:46.35	30,000
	Bidding Proud, 3, 115	J. A. Santos	Buckhar, 4, 118	Plate Dancer, 7, 116	7	1:46.02	30,000
1990	Stolen Rolls, 4, 112	P. A. Rodriguez	Gay's Best Boy, 4, 111	Seasabb, 3, 111	13	1:45.20	35,700
1989	Vaguely Double, 4, 118	W. A. Guerra	Mr. Adorable, 3, 113	Highland Springs, 5, 120	14	1:48.80	35,490
1988	Equalize, 6, 122	J. A. Santos	Val d'Enchere, 5, 116	Racing Star, 6, 114	10	1:45.00	35,010
1986	Arctic Honeymoon, 3, 111	R. N. Lester	Lover's Cross, 3, 121	Darn That Alarm, 5, 122	7	1:54.00	32,550
1985	Ban the Blues, 6, 114	G. St. Leon	Jim Bracken, 4, 112	Bold Southerner, 4, 112	11	1:53.20	34,140
1984	Biloxi Indian, 3, 114	B. Fann	Key to the Moon, 3, 122	Di Roma Feast, 3, 114	7	1:54.00	32,700
1983	‡Eminency, 5, 122	P. Day	World Appeal, 3, 118	Ready to Prove, 3, 110	13	1:51.20	34,770
1982	Rivalero, 6, 120	J. Vasquez	Current Blade, 4, 115	In all Honesty, 3, 110	9	1:53.60	33,270
1981	The Liberal Member, 6, 115	J. D. Bailey	Jayme G., 5, 116	Recusant, 3, 112	14	1:51.80	35,130
1980	Yosi Boy, 4, 111	A. Smith Jr.	Two's a Plenty, 3, 120	Von Clausewitz, 5, 119	8	1:51.80	33,180
1979	Lot o' Gold, 3, 123	D. Brumfield	King Celebrity, 3, 117	J. Rodney G., 4, 114	8	1:52.60	33,330
1975	Proud Birdie, 2, 117	J. Fieselman	Controller Ike, 2, 117	†Noble Royalty, 2, 115	13	1:47.00	18,900
1974	L. Grant Jr., 4, 121	J. Combest	Super Sail, 6, 118	El Tordillo, 4, 115	11	1:45.80	18,300
1973	Proud and Bold, 3, 121	R. Woodhouse	Outatholme, 4, 116	Seminole Joe, 5, 112	7	1:45.60	17,100

Named for the old Tropical Park racetrack in Miami; it closed in 1972. Formerly run on or about December 25. Christmas H. 1935-'71. Christmas Day H. 1972-'92. Held at Tropical Park 1935-'71. Not held 1939-'45, 1947, 1950-'51, 1976-'78, 1987, 1991. 1 mile 1935-'36. 6 furlongs 1949. 1 1/16 miles 1960-'75. 1 mile 70 yards 1971. About 1 1/8 miles 1988-'93, 2003. Dirt 1972-'86, 1997. Two-year-olds and up 1935-'36. Two-year-olds 1975. Two divisions 1964, 1967, 1969, 1992. Dead heat for second 2000. ‡World Appeal finished first, DQ to second, 1983. †Denotes female.

True North Breeders' Cup Handicap

Grade 2 in 2005. Belmont Park, three-year-olds and up, 6 furlongs, dirt. Held June 11, 2005, with a gross value of $212,900. First held in 1979. First graded in 1983. Stakes record 1:07.80 (1987 Groovy).

Year	Winner	Jockey	Second	Third	Strs	Time	1st Purse
2005	Woke Up Dreamin, 5, 116	M. E. Smith	Voodoo, 7, 113	Mass Media, 4, 117	10	1:08.38	$128,220
2004	Speightstown, 6, 119	J. R. Velazquez	Cat Genius, 4, 116	Pohave, 6, 117	9	1:08.04	126,840
2003	Shake You Down, 5, 118	M. J. Luzzi	Highway Prospector, 6, 115	Vodka, 6, 114	6	1:09.59	90,000
2002	Explicit, 5, 119	L. J. Meche	Entepreneur, 5, 115	Late Carson, 6, 114	7	1:09.98	150,000
2001	Say Florida Sandy, 7, 116	A. T. Gryder	Wake At Noon, 4, 117	Explicit, 4, 115	8	1:08.77	90,000
2000	Intidab, 7, 117	R. G. Davis	Brutally Frank, 6, 119	Oro de Mexico, 6, 113	7	1:10.22	90,000
1999	Kashatreya, 5, 110	J. Samyn	Artax, 4, 119	The Trader's Echo, 5, 111	9	1:09.63	90,000
1998	Richter Scale, 4, 119	J. D. Bailey	Trafalger, 4, 114	Kelly Kip, 4, 122	8	1:08.83	83,160
1997	Punch Line, 7, 122	R. G. Davis	Cold Execution, 6, 112	Jamies First Punch, 4, 116	7	1:08.96	66,180
1996	Not Surprising, 6, 121	R. G. Davis	Prospect Bay, 4, 113	Forest Wildcat, 5, 114	8	1:09.17	66,720

Year Winner	Jockey	Second	Third	Strs	Time	1st Purse
1995 **Waldoboro**, 4, 112	E. Maple	Corma Ray, 5, 111	Mining Burrah, 5, 117	8	1:09.62	$66,300
1994 **Friendly Lover**, 6, 114	R. Wilson	Boundary, 4, 117	Birdonthewire, 5, 119	9	1:09.65	67,380
1993 **Lion Cavern**, 4, 116	J. A. Krone	Arrowtown, 5, 115	Codys Key, 4, 111	9	1:10.33	69,120
1992 **Shining Bid**, 4, 112	E. Maple	Arrowtown, 4, 113	To Freedom, 4, 117	9	1:08.28	71,880
1991 **Diablo**, 4, 112	J. A. Krone	Sunny Blossom, 6, 120	Bravely Bold, 5, 119	7	1:08.24	69,720
1990 **Mr. Nickerson**, 4, 119	C. W. Antley	Sewickley, 5, 117	Dancing Spree, 5, 123	4	1:10.40	51,360
1989 **Dancing Spree**, 4, 113	A. T. Cordero Jr.	Dr. Carrington, 4, 109	Pok Ta Pok, 4, 118	6	1:09.40	68,160
1988 **High Brite**, 4, 120	A. T. Cordero Jr.	Irish Open, 4, 115	King's Swan, 8, 122	6	1:10.00	81,300
1987 **Groovy**, 4, 123	A. T. Cordero Jr.	King's Swan, 7, 120	Sun Master, 6, 117	4	**1:07.80**	78,780
1986 **Phone Trick**, 4, 127	J. Velasquez	Love That Mac, 4, 117	Cullendale, 4, 111	5	1:09.00	66,480
1985 **Cannon Shell**, 6, 114	D. J. Murphy	Basket Weave, 4, 114	Mt. Livermore, 4, 126	6	1:10.80	52,200
1984 **Believe the Queen**, 4, 114	J. Velasquez	Muskoka Wyck, 5, 112	Cannon Shell, 5, 115	6	1:09.80	52,110
1983 **†Gold Beauty**, 4, 121	D. Brumfield	Singh Tu, 4, 111	Fit to Fight, 4, 113	8	1:10.40	50,760
1982 **Shimatoree**, 3, 117	M. G. Pino	Pass the Tab, 4, 121	Will of Iron, 4, 112	8	1:08.60	49,590
1981 **Joanie's Chief**, 4, 109	J. Samyn	Proud Appeal, 3, 117	Guilty Conscience, 5, 113	7	1:09.00	33,480
1980 **Syncopate**, 5, 120	L. A. Pincay Jr.	Isella, 5, 117	Double Zeus, 5, 116	6	1:09.20	33,000
1979 **Moleolus**, 4, 110	J. Samyn	Jet Diplomacy, 4, 118	Northern Prospect, 3, 116	7	1:10.40	25,335

Named for Derring Howe's 1945 Fall Highweight H. winner True North (1940 g. by Only One). Grade 3 1983-'84. †Denotes female.

Turfway Breeders' Cup Stakes

Grade 3 in 2005. Turfway Park, three-year-olds and up, fillies and mares, 1 1/16 miles, dirt. Held September 18, 2004, with a gross value of $175,000. First held in 1986. First graded in 1991. Stakes record 1:41.67 (1995 Mariah's Storm).

Year	Winner	Jockey	Second	Third	Strs	Time	1st Purse
2004	**Susan's Angel**, 3, 116	R. Bejarano	Mayo On the Side, 5, 120	Angela's Love, 4, 122	6	1:44.21	$108,500
2003	**Smok'n Frolic**, 4, 122	E. S. Prado	Awesome Humor, 3, 112	So Much More, 4, 118	9	1:44.98	108,500
2002	**Trip**, 5, 116	P. Day	Mystic Lady, 4, 118	Red n'Gold, 4, 118	9	1:43.01	125,500
2001	**Trip**, 4, 118	C. Perret	Precious Feather, 4, 114	Spain, 4, 122	7	1:42.47	125,500
2000	**Spain**, 3, 118	P. Day	Ruby Surprise, 5, 118	Undermine, 4, 118	9	1:44.85	156,500
1999	**Ruby Surprise**, 4, 118	W. Martinez	Let, 4, 118	French Braids, 4, 114	8	1:44.95	162,886
1998	**Biding Time**, 4, 117	C. S. Nakatani	Meter Maid, 4, 121	Dancing Gulch, 4, 119	7	1:43.13	162,266
1997	**Feasibility Study**, 5, 119	M. E. Smith	City Band, 3, 114	Gold n Delicious, 4, 121	5	1:42.50	161,522
1996	**Golden Attraction**, 3, 114	G. L. Stevens	Bedroom Blues, 5, 117	Betty Van, 4, 119	8	1:42.53	205,920
1995	**Mariah's Storm**, 4, 117	R. N. Lester	Serena's Song, 3, 119	Alcovy, 5, 117	5	**1:41.67**	116,415
1994	**Pennyhill Park**, 4, 123	C. J. McCarron	Roamin Rachel, 4, 123	Hey Hazel, 4, 123	10	1:44.20	118,073
1993	**Gray Cashmere**, 4, 117	D. Kutz	Deputation, 4, 120	November Snow, 4, 113	8	1:43.39	117,130
1992	**Fit for a Queen**, 6, 123	R. D. Lopez	Auto Dial, 4, 120	Hitch, 3, 112	9	1:43.30	117,975
1991	**Fit for a Queen**, 5, 123	R. D. Lopez	Til Forbid, 3, 118	Screen Prospect, 4, 114	8	1:43.22	117,358
1990	**Barbarika**, 5, 123	A. T. Gryder	Colonial Waters, 5, 114	Luthier's Launch, 4, 112	11	1:44.00	119,015
1989	**Winning Colors**, 4, 115	C. J. McCarron	Grecian Flight, 5, 123	Lawyer Talk, 5, 123	7	1:44.80	101,368
1988	**Darien Miss**, 3, 115	P. A. Johnson	Integra, 4, 123	Ms. Eloise, 5, 120	9	1:43.60	101,758
1987	**In Neon**, 5, 111	M. McDowell	Northern Maiden, 4, 122	Just Barely Able, 5, 113	7	1:45.20	50,180
1986	**Gypsy Prayer**, 5, 111	M. W. Bryan	Queen Alexandra, 4, 114	Donut's Pride, 4, 111	10	1:43.20	19,180

Grade 2 1992-'98. Latonia Breeders' Cup S. 1986. Turfway Park Budweiser Breeders' Cup S. 1987-'88, 1991-'95. Turfway Park Breeders' Cup H. 1989-'90. Held at Latonia Race Course 1986.

Turfway Park Fall Championship Stakes

Grade 3 in 2005. Turfway Park, three-year-olds and up, 1 mile, dirt. Held October 2, 2004, with a gross value of $100,000. First held in 1919. First graded in 1997. Stakes record 1:36.89 (2003 Crafty Shaw).

Year	Winner	Jockey	Second	Third	Strs	Time	1st Purse
2004	**Cappuchino**, 5, 115	D. A. Sarvis	Crafty Shaw, 6, 122	Added Edge, 4, 119	7	1:37.19	$62,000
2003	**Crafty Shaw**, 5, 117	C. Perret	Cat Tracker, 5, 117	Cappuchino, 4, 119	8	**1:36.89**	62,000
2002	**Crafty Shaw**, 4, 117	J. Lopez	Rock Slide, 4, 117	Deferred Comp, 4, 115	7	1:52.29	62,750
2001	**Generous Rosi (GB)**, 6, 115	L. J. Meche	Storm Day, 4, 117	Jadada, 4, 117	6	1:49.83	46,500
2000	**Mount Lemon**, 6, 117	R. Albarado	Unloosened, 5, 114	Phil the Grip, 6, 117	7	1:51.14	62,600
1999	**Phil the Grip**, 5, 112	R. Albarado	Part the Waters, 5, 111	Metatonia, 4, 110	5	1:52.15	49,600
1998	**Acceptable**, 4, 116	C. Perret	Magnify, 5, 114	Muchacho Fino, 4, 112	6	1:51.95	62,600
1997	**Tejano Run**, 5, 122	W. Martinez	Short Stay, 5, 114	Thesaurus, 3, 112	7	1:49.44	46,950
1996	**Strawberry Wine**, 4, 114	B. D. Peck	Kiridashi, 4, 121	Prospect for Love, 4, 114	8	1:50.15	65,000
1995	**Bound by Honor**, 4, 113	R. P. Romero	Lord Gordon, 5, 113	Lordly Prospect, 6, 112	6	1:51.54	48,750
1994	**Meena**, 6, 114	W. Martinez	Powerful Punch, 5, 122	It'sali'lknownfact, 4, 111	4	1:52.92	27,284
1993	**Powerful Punch**, 4, 116	C. C. Bourque	Medium Cool, 5, 114	Benburb, 4, 121	7	1:50.51	41,048
1992	**Flying Continental**, 6, 122	J. Velasquez	Alyten, 4, 116	Regal Affair, 6, 113	5	1:48.67	27,511
1991	**Allijeba**, 5, 116	J. E. Bruin	D. C. Tenacious, 4, 113	Discover, 3, 116	9	1:49.63	41,421
1990	**Aly Mar**, 4, 112	D. Kutz	Cefis, 5, 120	Cantrell Road, 4, 116	9	1:49.20	34,531
1989	**Currentsville Lane**, 4, 112	J. Neagle	Air Worthy, 4, 121	Loyal Pal, 6, 118	8	1:51.60	28,031
1988	**Mr. Odie**, 4, 110	S. Neff	Boyish Charm, 5, 116	Government Corner, 6, 114	11	1:52.40	28,795
1987	**Lord Glacier**, 4, 114	M. Solomone	Aggies Best, 5, 117	Ten Times Ten, 5, 115	12	1:43.60	28,860
1986	**Big Pistol**, 5, 123	L. J. Melancon	Exit Five B., 5, 119	Something Cool, 4, 117	6	1:42.80	19,565
1985	**Country Hick**, 4, 113	J. C. Espinoza	Turn Here, 4, 114	McShane, 6, 117	10	1:43.00	20,215
1984	**Immediate Reaction**, 4, 118	M. McDowell	Fairly Straight, 3, 120	Never Company, 4, 113	9	1:43.80	18,541

					Strs	Time	1st Purse
1983 **Cad**, 5, 115	D. Brumfield	His Flower, 3, 113	Noted, 4, 112		9	1:44.00	$18,444
1982 **Leader Jet**, 4, 117	C. R. Woods Jr.	Rock Steady, 3, 113	Diverse Dude, 4, 118		10	1:44.00	13,680
1981 **Exterminate**, 4, 114	D. E. Foster	Kentucky Scout, 4, 119	Withholding, 4, 120		9	1:44.40	13,080
1980 **Silver Shears**, 3, 110	R. R. Matias	Penalty Declined, 6, 119	One Lucky Devil, 6, 124		9	1:43.20	12,975
1979 **†Lotta Honey**, 4, 116	J. C. Espinoza	Penalty Declined, 5, 113	One Lucky Devil, 5, 114		12	1:42.40	18,005
1978 **†Likely Exchange**, 4, 114	M. S. Sellers	Pirogue, 4, 113	Mr. Pitty Pat, 5, 110		8	1:45.60	16,020
1977 **Certain Roman**, 4, 111	M. McDowell	*The Pepe, 5, 114	Payne Street, 4, 120		9	1:44.80	12,855
1976 **Brustigert**, 6, 113	A. F. Herrera	Faneuil Boy, 5, 118	Visier, 4, 120		12	1:45.40	13,155
1975 **Eager Wish**, 6, 119	C. Bramble	*Zografos, 7, 124	†Princess Jillo, 4, 106		6	1:44.40	12,765
1974 **Bootlegger's Pet**, 4, 116	G. Solomon	Lester's Jester, 5, 113	Babingtons Image, 4, 111		8	1:47.60	13,878
1973 **Knight Counter**, 5, 123	D. Brumfield	Divorce Trial, 4, 114	On the Money, 5, 116		10	1:46.80	9,962

Traditionally held during Turfway Park's fall meet. Latonia Championship S. 1919-'33, 1964-'86. Turfway Championship S. 1987-'90. Turfway Championship H. 1991-'95, 1997. Kentucky Cup Classic Preview H. 1996, 1998-'99. Turfway Park Fall Championship H. 2000. Held at Old Latonia 1919-'33. Held at Latonia 1964-'86. Not held 1934-'63, 1972. 1¹/₈ miles 1913-'18, 1934-'63, 1988-2002. 1³/₄ miles 1919-'33. 1¹/₁₆ miles 1964-'87. Three-year-olds 1919-'33. †Denotes female.

Turnback the Alarm Handicap

Grade 3 in 2005. Aqueduct, three-year-olds and up, fillies and mares, 1¹/₈ miles, dirt. Held November 6, 2004, with a gross value of $110,700. First held in 1995. First graded in 1999. Stakes record 1:48.89 (1995 Incinerate).

Year	Winner	Jockey	Second	Third	Strs	Time	1st Purse
2004	**Personal Legend**, 4, 115	J. D. Bailey	Roar Emotion, 4, 117	Fast Cookie, 4, 114	9	1:51.27	$66,420
2003	**Pocus Hocus**, 5, 114	J. A. Santos	Nonsuch Bay, 4, 115	Miss Linda (Arg), 6, 118	6	1:50.67	64,500
2002	**Svea Dahl**, 5, 114	R. Migliore	Mystic Lady, 4, 119	Critical Eye, 5, 115	5	1:50.42	64,800
2001	**Rochelle's Terms**, 4, 113	R. G. Davis	Resort, 4, 113	Strolling Belle, 5, 118	6	1:51.19	65,100
2000	**Atelier**, 3, 113	E. S. Prado	Tap to Music, 5, 119	Pentatonic, 5, 115	10	1:48.95	67,920
1999	**Belle Cherie**, 3, 112	J. R. Velazquez	Brushed Halory, 3, 114	Sweet Misty, 5, 116	8	1:50.03	66,600
1998	**Snit**, 4, 117	J. R. Velazquez	Manoa, 3, 112	Shoop, 7, 114	8	1:51.30	49,740
1997	**Mil Kilates**, 4, 116	J. Bravo	Radiant Megan, 4, 110	Shoop, 6, 114	5	1:49.40	48,330
1996	**Shoop**, 5, 121	J. D. Bailey	Queen Tutta, 4, 116	Madame Adolphe, 4, 113	4	1:51.35	48,420
1995	**Incinerate**, 5, 115	F. Leon	Lotta Dancing, 4, 115	Pretty Discreet, 3, 110	7	**1:48.89**	49,005

Named for Valley View Farm's and Dr. Richard Coburn's 1992 Coaching Club American Oaks (G1) winner Turnback the Alarm (1989 f. by Darn That Alarm).

United Nations Handicap

Grade 1 in 2005. Monmouth Park, three-year-olds and up, 1³/₈ miles, turf. Held July 3, 2004, with a gross value of $750,000. First held in 1953. First graded in 1973. Stakes record 2:12.78 (2003 Balto Star).

Year	Winner	Jockey	Second	Third	Strs	Time	1st Purse
2004	**Request for Parole**, 5, 118	E. S. Prado	Mr O'Brien (Ire), 5, 120	Nothing to Lose, 4, 118	11	2:13.37	$450,000
2003	**Balto Star**, 5, 117	J. A. Velez Jr.	The Tin Man, 5, 121	Lunar Sovereign, 4, 112	7	**2:12.78**	450,000
2002	**With Anticipation**, 7, 119	P. Day	Denon, 4, 115	Sarafan, 5, 117	7	2:12.81	300,000
2001	**‡Senure**, 5, 116	R. G. Davis	With Anticipation, 6, 113	Gritty Sandie, 5, 112	8	2:13.56	300,000
2000	**Down the Aisle**, 7, 114	R. G. Davis	Aly's Alley, 4, 111	Honor Glide, 6, 116	7	2:13.63	210,000
1999	**Yagli**, 6, 124	J. D. Bailey	Supreme Sound (GB), 5, 113	Amerique, 5, 115	6	2:16.02	150,000
1997	**Influent**, 6, 117	J. Samyn	Geri, 5, 113	Flag Down, 7, 118	4	1:53.72	240,000
1996	**Sandpit (Brz)**, 7, 122	C. S. Nakatani	Diplomatic Jet, 4, 117	Northern Spur (Ire), 5, 122	8	1:55.71	300,000
1995	**Sandpit (Brz)**, 6, 122	C. S. Nakatani	Celtic Arms (Fr), 4, 118	†Alice Springs, 5, 115	9	1:57.25	300,000
1994	**Lure**, 5, 123	M. E. Smith	Fourstars Allstar, 6, 117	Star of Cozzene, 6, 121	5	1:52.66	300,000
1993	**Star of Cozzene**, 5, 120	J. A. Santos	Lure, 4, 123	Finder's Choice, 8, 113	7	1:53.22	300,000
1992	**Sky Classic**, 5, 123	P. Day	Chenin Blanc, 6, 115	Lotus Pool, 5, 114	9	1:52.53	300,000
1991	**Exbourne**, 5, 122	J. D. McCarron	Forty Niner Days, 4, 116	Goofalik, 4, 114	7	1:52.75	300,000
1990	**Steinlen (GB)**, 7, 124	J. A. Santos	†Capades, 4, 112	Alwuhush, 5, 121	9	1:52.00	300,000
1989	**Yankee Affair**, 7, 121	P. Day	Salem Drive, 7, 117	Simply Majestic, 5, 119	5	1:53.20	120,000
1988	**Equalize**, 6, 116	J. A. Santos	Wanderkin, 5, 115	Bet Twice, 4, 124	9	1:52.60	120,000
1987	**Manila**, 4, 124	J. Vasquez	Racing Star, 5, 115	Air Display, 4, 110	5	1:58.80	90,000
1986	**Manila**, 3, 114	J. A. Santos	Uptown Swell, 4, 115	Lieutenant's Lark, 4, 121	8	1:52.60	104,040
1985	**Ends Well**, 4, 114	M. R. Morgan	Who's for Dinner, 6, 116	Cool, 4, 110	11	1:54.60	107,820
1984	**Hero's Honor**, 4, 123	J. D. Bailey	Cozzene, 4, 114	Who's for Dinner, 5, 110	11	1:54.00	106,200
1983	**Acaroid**, 5, 113	A. T. Cordero Jr.	†Trevita (Ire), 6, 116	Majesty's Prince, 4, 120	13	1:53.40	90,000
1982	**Naskra's Breeze**, 5, 117	J. Samyn	Acaroid, 4, 115	Don Roberto, 5, 116	10	1:55.60	90,000
1981	**Key to Content**, 4, 115	G. Martens	Ben Fab, 4, 123	Quality T. V., 4, 110	9	1:52.80	82,500
1980	**Lyphard's Wish (Fr)**, 4, 118	A. T. Cordero Jr.	Match the Hatch, 4, 115	Scythian Gold, 5, 111	9	1:53.80	82,500
1979	**Noble Dancer (GB)**, 7, 125	J. Vasquez	Dom Alaric (Fr), 5, 120	Overskate, 4, 128	6	1:56.60	75,000
1978	**Noble Dancer (GB)**, 6, 127	S. Cauthen	Upper Nile, 4, 118	Dan Horn, 6, 117	5	1:56.40	81,250
1977	**Bemo**, 7, 116	D. Brumfield	Quick Card, 4, 124	Alias Smith, 4, 112	5	1:54.00	65,000
1976	**Intrepid Hero**, 4, 125	S. Hawley	Improviser, 4, 116	Break Up the Game, 5, 120	8	1:53.40	65,000
1975	**Royal Glint**, 5, 120	J. E. Tejeira	Stonewalk, 4, 120	R. Tom Can, 4, 116	9	1:57.00	65,000
1974	**Halo**, 5, 118	J. Velasquez	London Company, 4, 123	Scantling, 4, 115	10	1:56.80	65,000
1973	**Tentam**, 4, 123	J. Velasquez	Star Envoy, 5, 116	Return to Reality, 4, 117	12	1:54.60	75,000

Named for the United Nations, headquartered in New York City. Formerly sponsored by Caesars Palace Hotel of Atlantic City, New Jersey 1990-'97. Grade 2 1990-'93. United Nations Invitational H. 1953-'81. Caesars International H. 1990-'97. Held at Atlantic City 1953-'97. Not held 1998. 1³/₁₆ miles 1953-'97. Dirt 1969. ‡With Anticipation finished first, DQ to second, 2001. Equaled course record 1999. Course record 2000, 2003. †Denotes female.

Vagrancy Handicap

Grade 2 in 2005. Belmont Park, three-year-olds and up, fillies and mares, 6½ furlongs, dirt. Held June 12, 2005, with a gross value of $150,000. First held in 1948. First graded in 1973. Stakes record 1:14.46 (2004 Bear Fan).

Year	Winner	Jockey	Second	Third	Strs	Time	1st Purse
2005	Sensibly Chic, 5, 116	J. R. Velazquez	Bank Audit, 4, 120	Ender's Sister, 4, 116	9	1:16.31	$90,000
2004	Bear Fan, 5, 121	J. R. Velazquez	Smok'n Frolic, 5, 117	Aspen Gal, 3, 109	9	1:14.46	90,000
2003	Shawklit Mint, 4, 115	R. Migliore	Shine Again, 6, 121	Gold Mover, 5, 118	3	1:15.38	90,000
2002	Xtra Heat, 4, 127	H. Vega	Gold Mover, 4, 115	Shine Again, 5, 117	5	1:16.44	90,000
2001	Dat You Miz Blue, 4, 116	J. R. Velazquez	Dream Supreme, 4, 122	Katz Me If You Can, 4, 115	5	1:15.32	64,080
2000	Country Hideaway, 4, 117	J. D. Bailey	Hurricane Bertie, 5, 118	Imperfect World, 4, 115	7	1:17.05	65,640
1999	‡Gold Princess, 4, 114	J. R. Velazquez	Hurricane Bertie, 4, 114	Delta Music, 4, 113	5	1:16.57	63,840
1998	Chip, 5, 115	J. Bravo	Furlough, 4, 114	Parlay, 4, 115	6	1:15.69	48,945
1997	Inquisitive Look, 4, 111	J. F. Chavez	Flat Fleet Feet, 4, 123	Mama Dean, 4, 114	6	1:22.07	64,800
1996	Twist Afleet, 5, 122	J. A. Krone	Smooth Charmer, 4, 111	Lottsa Talc, 6, 120	8	1:20.94	66,300
1995	Sky Beauty, 5, 125	M. E. Smith	Aly's Conquest, 4, 114	Through the Door, 5, 110	4	1:21.56	47,865
1994	Sky Beauty, 4, 122	M. E. Smith	For all Seasons, 4, 114	Pamzig, 4, 107	6	1:21.67	48,855
1993	Spinning Round, 4, 112	J. F. Chavez	Reach for Clever, 6, 114	Nannerl, 6, 118	8	1:24.52	52,740
1992	Nannerl, 5, 116	J. A. Santos	Serape, 4, 115	Makin Faces, 4, 112	6	1:22.55	51,210
1991	Queena, 5, 115	M. E. Smith	Missy's Mirage, 3, 109	Gottagetitdone, 6, 111	10	1:22.07	55,080
1990	Mistaurian, 4, 113	W. H. McCauley	Feel the Beat, 5, 118	Fantastic Find, 4, 116	5	1:25.20	50,040
1989	Aptostar, 4, 118	A. T. Cordero Jr.	Toll Fee, 4, 110	Lambros, 4, 109	7	1:22.80	51,570
1988	Grecian Flight, 4, 121	C. Perret	Nasty Affair, 4, 114	Tappiano, 4, 123	7	1:20.80	66,240
1987	North Sider, 5, 121	A. T. Cordero Jr.	Storm and Sunshine, 4, 117	Funistrada, 4, 114	6	1:24.20	64,440
1986	Le Slew, 5, 113	J. A. Santos	Clocks Secret, 4, 121	Willowy Mood, 4, 114	8	1:23.80	54,630
1985	Nany, 5, 121	J. Velasquez	Sugar's Image, 4, 120	Brindy Brindy, 5, 113	6	1:23.80	52,020
1984	Grateful Friend, 4, 114	A. T. Cordero Jr.	Pleasure Cay, 4, 118	Sweet Laughter, 7, 108	7	1:24.00	52,470
1983	Broom Dance, 4, 121	G. McCarron	Syrianna, 4, 114	Sprouted Rye, 6, 115	7	1:22.80	33,480
1982	Westport Native, 4, 115	J. Velasquez	Tell a Secret, 5, 115	Raise 'n Dance, 4, 113	6	1:22.60	32,580
1981	Island Charm, 4, 110	R. Migliore	Contrary Rose, 5, 114	The Wheel Turns, 4, 114	5	1:23.60	32,520
1980	Lady Lonsdale, 5, 114	L. Saurnell	Peaceful Banner, 4, 108	Worthy Poise, 6, 112	6	1:24.40	32,700
1979	Frosty Skater, 4, 119	D. MacBeth	Hagany, 5, 114	Skipat, 5, 126	10	1:23.20	33,240
1978	Dainty Dotsie, 4, 124	B. Phelps	What a Summer, 5, 127	Navajo Princess, 4, 110	6	1:21.80	32,160
1977	Shy Dawn, 6, 119	A. T. Cordero Jr.	Reasonable Win, 5, 118	Secret Lanvin, 4, 111	5	1:23.80	31,590
1976	My Juliet, 4, 127	J. Velasquez	Shy Dawn, 5, 119	Kudara, 5, 116	5	1:22.00	32,790
1975	Honorable Miss, 5, 120	J. Vasquez	Viva La Vivi, 5, 126	Coraggioso, 5, 121	8	1:22.20	34,020
1974	Coraggioso, 4, 119	D. Brumfield	Ponte Vecchio, 4, 114	‡Lady Love, 4, 118	14	1:22.40	35,940
1973	Krislin, 4, 113	M. A. Castaneda	Numbered Account, 4, 120	Fairway Flyer, 4, 115	8	1:22.60	16,845

Named for Belair Stud's 1942 champion three-year-old filly, '42 champion handicap mare, and '42 Beldame H. winner Vagrancy (1939 f. by *Sir Gallahad III). Held at Aqueduct 1948-'55, 1960, 1963-'67, 1975, 1977-'86, 1997. Not held 1949-'51. 1¹/₁₆ miles 1948-'52. 7 furlongs 1953-'97. ‡Wanda finished third, DQ to fourteenth, 1974. ‡Hurricane Bertie finished first, DQ to second, 1999.

Valley Stream Stakes

Grade 3 in 2005. Aqueduct, two-year-olds, fillies, 6 furlongs, dirt. Held November 7, 2004, with a gross value of $101,500. First held in 1995. First graded in 2001. Stakes record 1:08.66 (2001 Forest Heiress).

Year	Winner	Jockey	Second	Third	Strs	Time	1st Purse
2004	Megascape, 2, 122	J. R. Velazquez	Alfonsina, 2, 118	More Moonlight, 2, 118	5	1:10.38	$63,900
2003	Smokey Glacken, 2, 118	J. A. Santos	Baldomera, 2, 118	Stoic, 2, 118	9	1:11.18	67,320
2002	Randaroo, 2, 116	J. R. Velazquez	House Party, 2, 116	Fast Cookie, 2, 116	8	1:09.46	66,780
2001	Forest Heiress, 2, 122	R. Migliore	A New Twist, 2, 116	On Parade, 2, 116	6	1:08.66	48,465
2000	Astrapi, 2, 116	D. Nelson	Major Wager, 2, 116	Look of the Lynx, 2, 118	5	1:10.66	48,570
1999	Magicalmysterycat, 2, 121	M. E. Smith	Sahara Gold, 2, 121	Silentlea, 2, 121	7	1:10.53	49,815
1998	Paula's Girl, 2, 116	J. R. Velazquez	President's Girl, 2, 114	Godmother, 2, 121	5	1:11.99	38,700
1997	Cotton House Bay, 2, 114	J. F. Chavez	Foil, 2, 116	Kate Again, 2, 114	10	1:10.11	33,990
1996	Dixie Flag, 2, 116	J. Samyn	Alyssum, 2, 114	Nimble Tread, 2, 114	6	1:10.13	32,490
1995	Oxford Scholar, 2, 112	J. D. Bailey	Zee Lady, 2, 120	Stormy Krissy, 2, 112	5	1:12.13	32,430

Named for Valley Stream, a Long Island town in Nassau County, New York. Held at Belmont Park 1995.

Valley View Stakes

Grade 3 in 2005. Keeneland, three-year-olds, fillies, 1¹/₁₆ miles, turf. Held October 23, 2004, with a gross value of $116,300. First held in 1991. First graded in 1999. Stakes record 1:41.51 (1992 Spinning Round).

Year	Winner	Jockey	Second	Third	Strs	Time	1st Purse
2004	Sister Swank, 3, 116	P. Day	Jinny's Gold, 3, 116	Shadow Cast, 3, 119	12	1:46.75	$72,106
2003	Dyna Da Wyna, 3, 119	P. Day	Mexican Moonlight, 3, 116	Derrianne, 3, 123	10	1:43.54	69,998
2002	Bedanken, 3, 119	D. R. Pettinger	Mariensky, 3, 119	High Maintenance (GB), 3, 119	10	1:44.24	71,734
2001	dh- Chausson Poire, 3, 119	R. W. Woolsey		Quick Tip, 3, 123	10	1:42.93	46,576
	dh- Cozzy Corner, 3, 119	L. J. Meche					
2000	Good Game, 3, 119	P. Day	Impending Bear, 3, 119	Soccory, 3, 119	10	1:45.69	71,176
1999	Gimmeakissee, 3, 115	P. J. Cooksey	The Happy Hopper, 3, 119	Celestialbutterfly, 3, 119	9	1:42.05	70,122
1998	White Beauty, 3, 113	C. H. Borel	Shires Ende, 3, 117	Leaveemlaughing, 3, 117	8	1:43.09	56,591
1997	Mingling Glances, 3, 117	J. Bravo	Majestic Sunlight, 3, 113	Fluid Move, 3, 113	9	1:44.51	52,592
1996	Turkappeal, 3, 117	D. M. Barton	Inner Circle, 3, 113	Mariuka, 3, 117	9	1:46.10	52,126

1995	Country Cat, 3, 121	D. M. Barton	Appointed One, 3, 121	Petrouchka, 3, 121	10	1:44.88	$51,150
1994	Pharma, 3, 121	C. W. Antley	Mariah's Storm, 3, 121	Thread, 3, 121	9	1:42.48	50,747
1993	Weekend Madness (Ire), 3, 121	C. R. Woods Jr.	Life Is Delicious, 3, 121	Augusta Springs, 3, 121	10	1:43.06	23,870
1992	Spinning Round, 3, 121	F. A. Arguello Jr.	Shes Just Super, 3, 121	Enticed, 3, 121	9	**1:41.51**	23,870
1991	La Gueriere, 3, 121	B. D. Peck	Dance O'My Life, 3, 121	Spanish Parade, 3, 121	9	1:43.49	29,250

Named for the Valley View ferry, Kentucky's oldest recorded commerical business. Valley View Breeders' Cup S. 1994-'95. Dead heat for first 2001.

Vanity Handicap

Grade 1 in 2005. Hollywood Park, three-year-olds and up, fillies and mares, 1 1/8 miles, dirt. Held May 9, 2004, with a gross value of $245,000. First held in 1940. First graded in 1973. Stakes record 1:46.20 (1984 Princess Rooney).

Year	Winner	Jockey	Second	Third	Strs	Time	1st Purse
2004	Victory Encounter, 4, 116	A. O. Solis	Adoration, 5, 122	Star Parade (Arg), 5, 117	4	1:48.28	$150,000
2003	Azeri, 5, 127	M. E. Smith	Sister Girl Blues, 4, 111	Bare Necessities, 4, 118	7	1:48.48	150,000
2002	Azeri, 4, 125	M. E. Smith	Affluent, 4, 119	dh- Collect Call, 4, 115	5	1:48.88	150,000
				dh- Starrer, 4, 117			
2001	Gourmet Girl, 6, 119	G. L. Stevens	Lazy Slusan, 6, 122	Setareh, 4, 114	5	1:49.21	150,000
2000	Riboletta (Brz), 5, 123	C. J. McCarron	Speaking of Time, 4, 108	Excellent Meeting, 4, 120	6	1:48.54	180,000
1999	Manistique, 4, 122	C. J. McCarron	Yolo Lady, 4, 115	Bella Chiarra, 4, 116	6	1:48.06	240,000
1998	Escena, 5, 124	J. D. Bailey	Housa Dancer (Fr), 5, 115	Different (Arg), 6, 119	7	1:48.13	210,000
1997	Twice the Vice, 6, 121	K. J. Desormeaux	Real Connection, 6, 114	Jewel Princess, 5, 123	5	1:46.40	240,000
1996	Jewel Princess, 4, 120	C. S. Nakatani	Serena's Song, 4, 125	Top Rung, 5, 116	6	1:47.17	150,000
1995	Private Persuasion, 4, 114	G. L. Stevens	Top Rung, 4, 116	Wandesta (GB), 4, 119	7	1:48.30	165,000
1994	Potridee (Arg), 5, 114	A. O. Solis	Exchange, 6, 118	Golden Klair (GB), 4, 119	8	1:48.08	165,000
1993	Re Toss (Arg), 6, 116	E. J. Delahoussaye	Paseana (Arg), 6, 126	Guiza, 6, 114	8	1:47.92	165,000
1992	Paseana (Arg), 5, 127	C. J. McCarron	Fowda, 4, 118	Re Toss (Arg), 5, 115	6	1:48.06	165,000
1991	Brought to Mind, 4, 120	P. A. Valenzuela	Fit to Scout, 4, 115	Luna Elegante (Arg), 5, 114	6	1:48.50	110,000
1990	Gorgeous, 4, 124	E. J. Delahoussaye	Fantastic Look, 4, 112	Kelly, 4, 110	5	1:48.20	110,000
1989	Bayakoa (Arg), 5, 125	L. A. Pincay Jr.	Flying Julia, 6, 112	Goodbye Halo, 4, 122	6	1:47.20	110,000
1988	Annoconnor, 4, 114	C. A. Black	Pen Bal Lady (GB), 4, 119	Abloom (Arg), 4, 113	7	1:49.20	110,000
1987	Infinidad (Chi), 5, 113	C. A. Black	North Sider, 5, 121	Clabber Girl, 4, 115	7	2:00.60	110,000
1986	Magnificent Lindy, 4, 116	C. J. McCarron	Dontstop Themusic, 6, 124	Outstandingly, 4, 118	5	2:02.00	137,000
1985	Dontstop Themusic, 5, 118	A. T. Cordero Jr.	Salt Spring (Arg), 6, 114	Estrapade, 5, 119	7	1:47.80	110,000
1984	Princess Rooney, 4, 122	E. J. Delahoussaye	Adored, 4, 120	Salt Spring (Arg), 5, 113	7	**1:46.20**	150,500
1983	A Kiss for Luck, 4, 114	C. J. McCarron	Try Something New, 4, 118	Sangue (Ire), 5, 122	11	1:49.20	110,000
1982	Sangue (Ire), 4, 120	W. Shoemaker	Track Robbery, 6, 123	Cat Girl, 4, 117	7	1:48.00	110,000
1981	Track Robbery, 4, 120	P. A. Valenzuela	Princess Karenda, 4, 118	Save Wild Life, 4, 117	7	1:47.00	110,000
1980	It's in the Air, 4, 120	L. A. Pincay Jr.	Conveniently, 4, 111	Image of Reality, 4, 119	7	1:47.00	94,600
1979	It's in the Air, 3, 113	W. Shoemaker	Country Queen, 4, 121	Innuendo, 5, 116	8	1:47.40	77,950
1978	Afifa, 4, 113	W. Shoemaker	Drama Critic, 4, 117	Dottie's Doll, 5, 117	7	1:46.40	77,050
1977	Cascapedia, 4, 129	S. Hawley	*Bastonera II, 6, 122	Swingtime, 5, 117	9	1:47.60	65,500
1976	Miss Toshiba, 4, 120	F. Toro	*Bastonera II, 5, 121	Bold Baby, 4, 115	11	1:48.00	67,200
1975	*Dulcia, 6, 118	W. Shoemaker	Susan's Girl, 6, 123	*La Zanzara, 5, 120	11	1:47.40	67,500
1974	Tallahto, 4, 126	L. A. Pincay Jr.	*La Zanzara, 4, 120	Dogtooth Violet, 4, 118	10	1:47.00	66,500
1973	Convenience, 5, 121	J. L. Rotz	Minstrel Miss, 6, 121	Susan's Girl, 4, 127	8	1:47.80	64,500

Vanity Invitational H. 1981-'96, 1998. Held at Santa Anita Park 1949. Not held 1942-'43. 1 mile 1940. 1 1/16 miles 1941-'53. 1 1/4 miles 1986-'87. Dead heat for third 2002.

Vernon O. Underwood Stakes

Grade 3 in 2005. Hollywood Park, three-year-olds and up, 6 furlongs, dirt. Held December 5, 2004, with a gross value of $100,000. First held in 1981. First graded in 1984. Stakes record 1:08.04 (2004 Taste of Paradise).

Year	Winner	Jockey	Second	Third	Strs	Time	1st Purse
2004	Taste of Paradise, 5, 122	J. Valdivia Jr.	Watchem Smokey, 4, 116	My Master (Arg), 5, 116	7	**1:08.04**	$60,000
2003	Watchem Smokey, 3, 112	J. A. Krone	Our New Recruit, 4, 114	Hasty Kris, 6, 116	6	1:08.93	60,000
2002	Debonair Joe, 3, 112	J. A. Krone	F J's Pace, 7, 116	American System, 3, 116	9	1:09.17	60,000
2001	Men's Exclusive, 8, 120	L. A. Pincay Jr.	Tavasco, 4, 114	Caller One, 4, 124	7	1:09.04	60,000
2000	Men's Exclusive, 7, 116	L. A. Pincay Jr.	Love All the Way, 5, 117	Lexicon, 5, 122	7	1:09.02	60,000
1999	Five Star Day, 3, 120	A. O. Solis	Your Halo, 4, 122	Son of a Pistol, 7, 122	5	1:09.91	60,000
1998	†Love That Jazz, 4, 117	K. J. Desormeaux	Peyrano (Arg), 6, 116	Swiss Yodeler, 4, 120	8	1:08.79	60,000
1997	Tower Full, 5, 118	C. S. Nakatani	Trafalger, 3, 118	Swiss Yodeler, 3, 114	4	1:08.17	60,000
1996	Paying Dues, 4, 114	P. Day	Men's Exclusive, 3, 114	Kern Ridge, 5, 114	7	1:08.24	64,860
1995	Powis Castle, 4, 114	G. L. Stevens	Lucky Forever, 6, 122	Plenty Zloty, 5, 116	8	1:08.40	62,300
1994	Wekiva Springs, 3, 118	K. J. Desormeaux	Cardmania, 8, 120	Gundaghia, 7, 120	9	1:08.37	63,750
1993	†Meafara, 4, 119	G. L. Stevens	†Arches of Gold, 4, 121	Davy Be Good, 5, 116	6	1:10.01	60,900
1992	Gundaghia, 5, 116	G. L. Stevens	Gray Slewpy, 4, 124	Cardmania, 6, 124	5	1:09.33	61,300
1991	Individualist, 4, 114	K. J. Desormeaux	Thirty Slews, 4, 117	Cardmania, 5, 120	4	1:08.86	64,500
1990	Frost Free, 5, 116	C. J. McCarron	Timebank, 3, 117	Sam Who, 5, 114	9	1:08.20	65,300
1989	Olympic Prospect, 5, 120	A. O. Solis	Sam Who, 4, 122	Order, 4, 122	4	1:08.80	60,200
1988	Gallant Sailor, 5, 116	F. Olivares	Reconnoitering, 4, 116	†Very Subtle, 4, 117	7	1:09.60	63,400
1987	Hilco Scamper, 4, 114	C. A. Black	Reconnoitering, 3, 112	Zabaleta, 4, 122	6	1:09.60	62,800
1986	Bedside Promise, 4, 122	G. L. Stevens	Bolder Than Bold, 4, 114	†Pine Tree Lane, 4, 117	10	1:08.80	127,200
	Nasib (Ire), 4, 116	E. J. Delahoussaye	Will Dancer (Fr), 4, 116	Barbery, 5, 115	8	1:40.40	66,900

1985	Pancho Villa, 3, 122	L. A. Pincay Jr.	Charging Falls, 4, 122	Temerity Prince, 5, 122	6	1:08.80	$121,900
1984	Fifty Six Ina Row, 3, 112	S. Hawley	Debonaire Junior, 3, 120	Charging Falls, 3, 112	11	1:09.40	91,975
	†Lovlier Linda, 4, 121	W. Shoemaker	Sonrie Jorge (Arg), 4, 116	Fali Time, 3, 122	9	1:10.00	89,475
1983	Fighting Fit, 4, 120	E. J. Delahoussaye	Expressman, 3, 112	†Matching, 5, 119	10	1:09.60	101,950
1982	Mad Key, 5, 116	E. J. Delahoussaye	Shanekite, 4, 120	Dave's Friend, 7, 114	9	1:08.20	70,600
	Unpredictable, 3, 120	K. D. Black	Remember John, 3, 120	Chinook Pass, 3, 112	8	1:08.60	69,100
1981	Shanekite, 3, 114	S. Hawley	Syncopate, 6, 122	Big Presentation, 5, 114	8	1:08.20	50,500
	Smokite, 5, 116	D. C. Hall	I'm Smokin, 5, 120	Stand Pat, 6, 114	8	1:08.60	50,500

Named for Vernon O. Underwood, chief executive officer and chairman of the board of Hollywood Park (1972-'85). National Sprint Championship S. 1981-'89. Vernon O. Underwood Breeders' Cup S. 1993-'95. Two divisions 1981-'82, 1984, 1986. †Denotes female.

Vinery Madison Stakes

Grade 3 in 2005. Keeneland, four-year-olds and up, fillies and mares, 7 furlongs, dirt. Held April 13, 2005, with a gross value of $200,000. First held in 2002. First graded in 2005. Stakes record 1:23.33 (2005 Madcap Escapade).

Year	Winner	Jockey	Second	Third	Strs	Time	1st Purse
2005	Madcap Escapade, 4, 123	J. D. Bailey	My Trusty Cat, 5, 117	Molto Vita, 5, 119	7	1:23.33	$124,000
2004	Ema Bovary (Chi), 5, 120	R. M. Gonzalez	Harmony Lodge, 6, 123	Yell, 4, 116	6	1:23.41	108,500
2003	A New Twist, 4, 116	P. Day	Flaxen Flyer, 4, 116	Forest Secrets, 5, 116	4	1:24.32	84,863
2002	Victory Ride, 4, 116	E. S. Prado	Celtic Melody, 4, 116	Away, 5, 116	7	1:23.70	69,006

Named for Madison County, Kentucky. Sponsored by Vinery of Lexington 2004-'05.

Violet Handicap

Grade 3 in 2005. The Meadowlands, three-year-olds and up, fillies and mares, 1¹/₁₆ miles, turf. Held October 22, 2004, with a gross value of $200,000. First held in 1977. First graded in 1983. Stakes record 1:39.60 (1989 Gather The Clan [Ire]).

Year	Winner	Jockey	Second	Third	Strs	Time	1st Purse
2004	Changing World, 4, 113	P. Fragoso	High Court (Brz), 4, 117	Ocean Drive, 4, 121	7	1:41.53	$120,000
2003	Dancal (Ire), 5, 116	J. Castellano	Madeira Mist (Ire), 4, 116	Something Ventured, 4, 116	8	1:43.69	90,000
2002	Babae (Chi), 6, 119	J. F. Chavez	Platinum Tiara, 4, 115	Stylish, 4, 119	10	1:41.17	90,000
2001	Clearly a Queen, 4, 115	J. F. Chavez	Queue, 4, 115	Paga (Arg), 4, 117	12	1:43.56	90,000
2000	Follow the Money, 4, 116	C. J. McCarron	Melody Queen (GB), 4, 116	Fickle Friends, 4, 114	7	1:42.65	90,000
1999	Tookin Down, 4, 113	E. S. Prado	Proud Run, 5, 115	Darling Alice, 4, 113	7	1:42.39	90,000
1998	Heaven's Command (GB), 4, 115	R. Migliore	Maxzene, 5, 123	Oh Nellie, 4, 116	7	1:40.71	60,000
1997	Sangria, 4, 114	R. Wilson	Fasta, 4, 11	Shemozzle (Ire), 4, 117	8	1:42.02	60,000
1996	Plenty of Sugar, 5, 117	R. E. Colton	Brushing Gloom, 4, 121	Hello Mom, 4, 115	6	1:48.62	60,000
1995	Symphony Lady, 5, 116	J. Bravo	Kira's Dancer, 6, 115	Irish Linnet, 7, 122	8	1:45.48	60,000
1994	It's Personal, 4, 111	J. R. Velazquez	Carezza, 5, 115	Artful Pleasure, 5, 109	11	1:42.61	45,000
1993	Mz. Zill Bear, 4, 113	E. S. Prado	Vivano, 4, 115	Topsa, 6, 113	4	1:44.55	45,000
1992	Highland Crystal, 4, 116	E. S. Prado	Irish Actress, 5, 116	Navarra, 4, 111	7	1:41.26	45,000
1991	Southern Tradition, 4, 116	J. A. Santos	Songlines, 5, 115	Memories of Pam, 4, 114	7	1:43.68	45,000
1990	Miss Josh, 4, 116	M. G. Pino	Summer Secretary, 5, 117	Leave It Be, 5, 118	13	1:40.00	54,750
1989	Gather The Clan (Ire), 4, 117	C. Perret	Sweet Blow Pop, 5, 119	Summer Secretary, 4, 117	10	1:39.60	55,260
1988	Just Class (Ire), 4, 117	C. W. Antley	Shadowfay, 5, 109	Flying Katuna, 4, 115	8	1:40.20	53,400
	Graceful Darby, 4, 115	R. P. Romero	Mystical Lass, 4, 112	Kim Kimmie, 5, 111	10	1:41.00	42,900
1987	Videogenic, 5, 118	J. Cruguet	Spruce Fir, 4, 119	Cadabra Abra, 4, 120	7	1:42.00	45,180
	Dismasted, 5, 118	J. Samyn	Small Virtue, 4, 118	Country Recital, 4, 113	6	1:41.60	44,790
1986	Lake Country, 5, 118	V. A. Bracciale Jr.	Duckweed, 4, 111	Anka Germania (Ire), 4, 114	8	1:41.20	68,310
1985	Possible Mate, 4, 119	J. Samyn	Eastern Dawn, 4, 112	Carlypha (Ire), 4, 116	9	1:42.20	52,665
	Vers La Caisse, 4, 116	R. Migliore	Cato Double, 5, 117	Forest Maiden, 5, 117	10	1:43.00	63,240
1984	Rash But Royal, 4, 114	J. L. Kaenel	High Schemes, 4, 115	Candlelight Affair, 3, 110	8	1:42.20	49,020
	Aspen Rose, 4, 114	J. Velasquez	It's Fine, 4, 112	If Winter Comes, 6, 113	8	1:42.00	49,020
1983	Twosome, 4, 117	J. D. Bailey	Princess Roberta, 5, 115	Svarga, 4, 112	8	1:41.20	26,535
	Geraldine's Store, 4, 117	J. Samyn	Maidenhead, 4, 110	Mistretta (Fr), 4, 116	7	1:40.60	26,355
1982	Pat's Joy, 4, 114	J. D. Bailey	Prismatical, 4, 119	Kuja Happa, 4, 113	9	1:42.20	26,670
	Dearly Too, 3, 114	J. Samyn	Tableaux, 4, 112	Dance Troupe, 5, 114	9	1:42.20	26,670
1981	Honey Fox, 4, 120	J. Samyn	Adlibber, 4, 117	Hemlock, 4, 116	11	1:41.40	33,690
1980	Producer, 4, 119	J. Fell	Champagne Ginny, 3, 116	Cannon Boy, 3, 113	8	1:41.60	26,325
	The Very One, 5, 117	J. Velasquez	Hey Babe, 4, 115	Poppycock, 4, 113	7	1:42.40	26,145
1979	Terpsichorist, 4, 122	M. Venezia	Spark of Life, 4, 111	Sisterhood, 4, 117	11	1:43.20	36,010
1978	Navajo Princess, 4, 115	C. Perret	Pressing Date, 4, 114	Fun Forever, 5, 118	6	1:44.00	35,360
1977	Lady Singer (Ire), 4, 113	A. T. Cordero Jr.	Sans Arc, 3, 111	Jolly Song, 5, 112	6	1:48.40	35,035

Named for New Jersey's state flower, the common violet. Formerly sponsored by the Sheraton Meadowlands in East Rutherford, New Jersey 1995. Sheraton Meadowlands Violet H. 1995. Dirt 1977, 1993, 1999. Two divisions 1980, 1982-'85, 1987-'88.

Virginia Derby

Grade 3 in 2005. Colonial Downs, three-year-olds and up, 1¹/₄ miles, turf. Held July 10, 2004, with a gross value of $500,000. First held in 1998. First graded in 2004. Stakes record 1:59.97 (1999 Phi Beta Doc).

Year	Winner	Jockey	Second	Third	Strs	Time	1st Purse
2004	Kitten's Joy, 3, 117	E. S. Prado	Artie Schiller, 3, 117	Prince Arch, 3, 119	8	2:01.22	$300,000
2003	Silver Tree, 3, 115	E. S. Prado	Kicken Kris, 3, 115	King's Drama (Ire), 3, 115	8	2:01.11	300,000

Year	Winner	Jockey	Second	Third	Strs	Time	1st Purse
2002	Orchard Park, 3, 119	E. S. Prado	Flying Dash (Ger), 3, 119	Touring England, 3, 115	6	2:03.10	$300,000
2001	Potaro (Ire), 3, 115	B. E. Bartram	Bay Eagle, 3, 115	Confucius Say, 3, 115	9	2:02.17	120,000
2000	Lightning Paces, 3, 115	G. W. Hutton	Sunspot, 3, 115	Blaze and Blues, 3, 115	10	2:02.18	120,000
1999	Phi Beta Doc, 3, 117	R. A. Dominguez	Passinetti, 3, 115	North East Bound, 3, 119	13	1:59.97	120,000
1998	Crowd Pleaser, 3, 117	J. Samyn	Distant Mirage (Ire), 3, 115	Errant Escort, 3, 115	10	2:00.28	150,000

Colonial Downs is located in Virginia.

Vosburgh Stakes

Grade 1 in 2005. Belmont Park, three-year-olds and up, 6 furlongs, dirt. Held October 2, 2004, with a gross value of $490,000. First held in 1940. First graded in 1973. Stakes record 1:09.74 (2004 Pico Central [Brz]).

Year	Winner	Jockey	Second	Third	Strs	Time	1st Purse
2004	Pico Central (Brz), 5, 124	V. Espinoza	Voodoo, 6, 124	Speightstown, 6, 124	5	1:09.74	$300,000
2003	Ghostzapper, 3, 123	J. Castellano	Aggadan, 4, 126	Posse, 3, 123	10	1:14.72	300,000
2002	Bonapaw, 6, 126	G. Melancon	Aldebaran, 4, 126	Voodoo, 4, 126	6	1:22.34	180,000
2001	Left Bank, 4, 126	J. R. Velazquez	Squirtle Squirt, 3, 123	Big E E, 4, 126	6	1:20.73	180,000
2000	Trippi, 3, 123	J. D. Bailey	More Than Ready, 3, 123	One Way Love, 5, 126	10	1:21.66	180,000
1999	Artax, 4, 126	J. F. Chavez	Stormin Fever, 5, 126	Mountain Top, 4, 126	6	1:21.65	150,000
1998	Affirmed Success, 4, 126	J. F. Chavez	Stormin Fever, 4, 126	Tale of the Cat, 4, 126	7	1:21.99	150,000
1997	Victor Cooley, 4, 126	J. F. Chavez	Score a Birdie, 6, 126	Tale of the Cat, 3, 122	12	1:22.05	150,000
1996	Langfuhr, 4, 126	J. F. Chavez	Honour and Glory, 3, 122	Lite the Fuse, 5, 126	8	1:21.25	120,000
1995	Not Surprising, 5, 126	R. G. Davis	You and I, 4, 126	Our Emblem, 4, 126	13	1:22.48	120,000
1994	Harlan, 5, 126	J. D. Bailey	American Chance, 5, 126	Cherokee Run, 4, 126	10	1:21.82	120,000
1993	Birdonthewire, 4, 126	M. E. Smith	Take Me Out, 5, 126	Lion Cavern, 4, 126	6	1:22.28	120,000
1992	Rubiano, 5, 126	J. A. Krone	Sheikh Albadou (GB), 4, 126	Salt Lake, 3, 123	8	1:22.80	120,000
1991	Housebuster, 4, 126	C. Perret	Senator to Be, 4, 126	Sunshine Jimmy, 4, 126	6	1:21.85	120,000
1990	Sewickley, 5, 126	A. T. Cordero Jr.	Sunshine Jimmy, 3, 122	Glitterman, 5, 126	9	1:21.00	142,080
1989	Sewickley, 4, 126	R. P. Romero	Once Wild, 4, 126	Mr. Nickerson, 3, 123	5	1:23.00	135,120
1988	Mining, 4, 126	R. P. Romero	Gulch, 4, 126	High Brite, 4, 126	4	1:22.40	133,920
1987	Groovy, 4, 126	A. T. Cordero Jr.	Moment of Hope, 4, 126	Sun Master, 6, 126	8	1:22.60	139,680
1986	King's Swan, 6, 126	J. A. Santos	Love That Mac, 4, 126	Cutlass Reality, 4, 126	8	1:21.80	141,840
1985	Another Reef, 3, 124	N. Santagata	Pancho Villa, 3, 124	Whoop Up, 5, 126	6	1:21.80	102,420
1984	Track Barron, 3, 123	A. T. Cordero Jr.	Timeless Native, 4, 126	Raja's Shark, 3, 123	9	1:22.00	109,800
1983	A Phenomenon, 3, 123	A. T. Cordero Jr.	Fit to Fight, 4, 126	Deputy Minister, 3, 126	8	1:21.00	69,000
1982	Engine One, 4, 126	R. Hernandez	‡‡Gold Beauty, 3, 120	Maudlin, 4, 126	6	1:23.80	65,760
1981	Guilty Conscience, 5, 126	C. B. Asmussen	Rise Jim, 5, 126	Well Decorated, 3, 123	8	1:22.00	67,920
1980	Plugged Nickle, 3, 123	C. B. Asmussen	Jaklin Klugman, 3, 123	Dave's Friend, 5, 126	9	1:21.40	67,440
1979	General Assembly, 3, 123	J. Vasquez	Dr. Patches, 5, 126	Syncopate, 4, 126	6	1:21.00	48,195
1978	Dr. Patches, 4, 117	A. T. Cordero Jr.	†What a Summer, 5, 124	Sorry Lookin, 3, 109	8	1:21.00	48,960
1977	Affiliate, 3, 114	C. Perret	Broadway Forli, 3, 118	Great Above, 5, 112	8	1:21.00	49,905
1976	†My Juliet, 4, 120	A. S. Black	‡It's Freezing, 4, 113	Bold Forbes, 3, 126	6	1:21.80	31,980
1975	No Bias, 5, 116	A. Santiago	Step Nicely, 5, 126	Lonetree, 5, 117	11	1:22.80	34,590
1974	Forego, 4, 131	H. Gustines	Stop the Music, 4, 118	Prince Dantan, 4, 119	12	1:21.60	35,550
1973	Aljamin, 3, 118	A. T. Cordero Jr.	Highbinder, 5, 115	Timeless Moment, 3, 112	8	1:21.20	33,660

Named for Walter S. Vosburgh (1855-1938), official handicapper for the Jockey Club and various racing associations. Grade 2 1973-'79. Vosburgh H. 1940-'78. Held at Aqueduct 1959, 1961-'74, 1976-'77, 1979-'83, 1985-'86. 7 furlongs 1940-2002. Two-year-olds and up 1940-'57. ‡Bold Forbes finished second, DQ to third, 1976. ‡Duke Mitchell finished second, DQ to fourth, 1982. †Denotes female.

Walmac Lone Star Derby

Grade 3 in 2005. Lone Star Park, three-year-olds, 1 1/16 miles, dirt. Held May 14, 2005, with a gross value of $300,000. First held in 1997. First graded in 2002. Stakes record 1:40.88 (1997 Anet).

Year	Winner	Jockey	Second	Third	Strs	Time	1st Purse
2005	Southern Africa, 3, 122	J. K. Court	Shamoan (Ire), 3, 122	Real Dandy, 3, 122	11	1:41.92	$165,000
2004	Pollard's Vision, 3, 122	J. R. Velazquez	Cryptograph, 3, 122	Flamethrowintexan, 3, 122	12	1:42.10	150,000
2003	Dynever, 3, 122	E. S. Prado	Most Feared, 3, 122	Commander's Affair, 3, 122	12	1:50.43	277,500
2002	Wiseman's Ferry, 3, 122	J. F. Chavez	Tracemark, 3, 122	Peekskill, 3, 122	14	1:49.92	277,500
2001	Percy Hope, 3, 122	J. K. Court	Fifty Stars, 3, 122	Gift of the Eagle, 3, 122	8	1:50.27	292,500
2000	Tahkodha Hills, 3, 122	E. Coa	Jeblar Sez Who, 3, 122	Big Numbers, 3, 122	7	1:44.05	180,000
1999	T. B. Track Star, 3, 122	E. M. Martin Jr.	Desert Demon, 3, 122	Congratulate, 3, 122	11	1:42.92	165,000
1998	Smolderin Heart, 3, 122	T. T. Doocy	Shot of Gold, 3, 122	Troy's Play, 3, 122	8	1:46.29	145,000
1997	Anet, 3, 122	D. R. Flores	Frisk Me Now, 3, 122	Holzmeister, 3, 122	9	1:40.88	140,000

Sponsored by John T.L. Jones III's and Bobby Trussell's Walmac Farm of Lexington 2004. The track and the race are named for Texas's (Lone Star Park's home state) nickname, the Lone Star state. Lone Star Derby 1997-2003. 1 1/16 miles 1997-2000.

Washington Park Handicap

Grade 2 in 2005. Arlington Park, three-year-olds and up, 1 3/16 miles, dirt. Held July 31, 2004, with a gross value of $350,000. First held in 1926. First graded in 1973. Stakes record 1:55.07 (2002 Tenpins).

Year	Winner	Jockey	Second	Third	Strs	Time	1st Purse
2004	Eye of the Tiger, 4, 116	E. Razo Jr.	Olmodavor, 5, 121	Congrats, 4, 116	5	1:56.87	$210,000

2003	Perfect Drift, 4, 120	P. Day	Aeneas, 4, 115	Flatter, 4, 114	5	1:55.49	$240,000
2002	Tenpins, 4, 116	R. Albarado	Generous Rosi (GB), 7, 115	Bonus Pack, 4, 115	5	**1:55.07**	240,000
2001	Guided Tour, 5, 116	L. J. Melancon	A Fleets Dancer, 6, 115	Duckhorn, 4, 114	5	2:00.76	240,000
2000	Blazing Sword, 6, 113	J. A. Rivera II	Mula Gula, 4, 114	Nite Dreamer, 5, 116	8	1:50.59	150,000
1997	Beboppin Baby, 4, 112	G. K. Gomez	City by Night, 4, 116	Stephanotis, 4, 118	5	1:49.00	90,000
1996	Polar Expedition, 5, 115	M. Guidry	Knockadoon, 4, 115	Tejano Run, 4, 117	8	1:49.97	120,000
1994	Brother Brown, 4, 117	P. Day	Eequalsmcsquared, 5, 113	Antrim Rd., 4, 113	11	1:49.77	120,000
1993	Powerful Punch, 4, 114	C. C. Bourque	Memo (Chi), 6, 115	Northern Trend, 5, 113	13	1:50.19	120,000
1992	Irish Swap, 5, 118	B. E. Poyadou	Clever Trevor, 6, 119	Barkerville, 4, 113	7	1:47.83	90,000
1991	Black Tie Affair (Ire), 5, 120	S. J. Sellers	Summer Squall, 4, 119	Secret Hello, 4, 114	4	1:49.45	150,000
1990	Lay Down, 6, 115	W. H. McCauley	Sir Wesley, 6, 112	Mercedes Won, 4, 112	6	1:48.40	64,680
1989	Blushing John, 4, 124	P. Day	Grantley, 5, 112	Paramount Jet, 4, 113	5	1:50.80	48,030
1987	Taylor's Special, 6, 118	J. L. Lively	Blue Buckaroo, 4, 120	Fuzzy, 5, 114	6	1:51.60	61,965
1985	Par Flite, 4, 112	E. Fires	Big Pistol, 4, 122	Timeless Native, 5, 122	6	1:47.60	78,300
1984	Thumbsucker, 5, 115	S. Maple	Timeless Native, 4, 122	Le Cou Cou, 4, 122	10	1:48.60	80,940
1983	Harham's Sizzler, 4, 112	J. L. Diaz	Listcapade, 4, 122	Stage Reviewer, 4, 112	9	1:49.80	67,620
1982	Summer Advocate, 5, 115	P. Day	Mythical Ruler, 4, 112	Law Me, 4, 112	6	1:49.80	64,920
1981	Rossi Gold, 5, 119	P. Day	John's Monster, 4, 112	Lord Gallant, 4, 114	7	1:48.60	81,870
1980	Spectacular Bid, 4, 130	W. Shoemaker	Hold Your Tricks, 5, 119	Architect, 4, 119	6	1:46.20	155,880
1979	That's a Nice, 5, 117	I. J. Jimenez	†Calderina (Ity), 4, 113	Me Good Man, 5, 112	10	1:50.00	52,320
1978	That's a Nice, 4, 116	D. Richard	Court Open, 4, 115	Improviser, 6, 117	9	1:50.60	53,160
1977	Majestic Light, 4, 120	M. Venezia	Fifth Marine, 4, 122	Improviser, 5, 122	10	1:48.00	54,180
1976	Double Edge Sword, 6, 116	V. A. Bracciale Jr.	*Zografos, 8, 113	Proponent, 4, 109	5	1:48.20	70,400
1975	Hasty Flyer, 4, 115	H. Arroyo	Group Plan, 5, 116	Yaki King, 4, 113	6	1:48.60	38,100
1974	Super Sail, 6, 118	W. Gavidia	Smooth Dancer, 4, 112	Jesta Dream Away, 4, 111	7	2:03.00	38,300
1973	Burning On, 5, 114	D. Richard	New Hope, 4, 113	Vegas Vic, 5, 109	7	2:02.20	32,800

Named for the old Washington Park racetrack near Chicago. Grade 3 1973-'81. Washington H. 1964. Held at Washington Park 1926-'57. Not held 1928, 1937, 1986, 1988, 1995, 1998-'99. 1¼ miles 1926, 1935-'36, 1940-'50, 1973-'74, 2001. 6 furlongs 1927-'34, 1938. 1 mile 1939, 1951-'58, 1960-'62, 1965-'72. 1⅛ miles 1959, 1963-'64, 1975-2000. Turf 1977-'79. †Denotes female.

Westchester Handicap

Grade 3 in 2005. Belmont Park, three-year-olds and up, 1 mile, dirt. Held May 4, 2005, with a gross value of $109,500. First held in 1918. First graded in 1973. Stakes record 1:32.24 (2003 Najran [track record and equaled American record]).

Year	Winner	Jockey	Second	Third	Strs	Time	1st Purse
2005	Gygistar, 6, 118	J. Castellano	Swingforthefences, 4, 115	Value Plus, 4, 117	7	1:33.50	$65,700
2004	Gygistar, 5, 115	J. Bravo	Saarland, 5, 114	Black Silk (GB), 8, 113	7	1:35.89	65,700
2003	Najran, 4, 113	E. S. Prado	Saarland, 4, 114	Justification, 6, 113	7	**1:32.24**	65,820
2002	Free of Love, 4, 114	J. D. Bailey	Dayton Flyer, 4, 112	Country Be Gold, 5, 114	9	1:35.56	67,500
2001	Cat's At Home, 4, 113	F. Leon	Little Hans, 4, 113	Milwaukee Brew, 4, 117	6	1:33.60	64,920
2000	Yankee Victor, 4, 115	H. Castillo Jr.	Golden Missile, 5, 116	Watchman's Warning, 5, 113	7	1:34.37	66,000
1999	Mr. Sinatra, 5, 116	C. C. Lopez	Laredo, 6, 114	Brushing Up, 6, 113	4	1:35.04	64,202
1998	Wagon Limit, 4, 114	J. Samyn	Draw, 5, 113	Lucayan Prince, 5, 116	8	1:34.06	66,420
1997	Pacific Fleet, 5, 114	F. T. Alvarado	Circle of Light, 4, 110	Stalwart Member, 4, 114	7	1:33.80	65,940
1996	Valid Wager, 4, 115	J. M. Pezua	Pat n Jac, 4, 111	More to Tell, 5, 118	7	1:34.74	66,240
1995	Mr. Shawklit, 4, 112	M. J. Luzzi	Devil His Due, 6, 124	Our Emblem, 4, 112	4	1:34.66	65,760
1994	Virginia Rapids, 4, 116	J. Samyn	Colonial Affair, 4, 121	Cherokee Run, 4, 119	7	1:34.52	65,640
1993	Bill Of Rights, 4, 110	J. Samyn	Fly So Free, 5, 118	Loach, 5, 114	10	1:34.69	72,720
1992	Rubiano, 5, 117	J. A. Santos	Out of Place, 5, 115	Wild Away, 5, 111	6	1:34.83	68,880
1991	Rubiano, 4, 111	J. D. Bailey	Senor Speedy, 4, 113	Killer Diller, 4, 115	9	1:34.94	71,520
1990	Once Wild, 5, 121	A. T. Cordero Jr.	dh-Its Acedemic, 6, 116		5	1:35.00	67,800
			dh-King's Swan, 10, 113				
1989	Lord of the Night, 6, 115	J. Velasquez	Dancing Spree, 4, 112	Congeleur, 4, 112	8	1:35.60	71,040
1988	Faster Than Sound, 4, 113	J. A. Krone	Ron Stevens, 4, 111	King's Swan, 8, 133	9	1:34.40	108,000
1987	King's Swan, 7, 122	J. A. Santos	Cutlass Reality, 5, 114	Landing Plot, 4, 115	6	1:36.20	69,120
1986	Garthorn, 6, 120	R. Q. Meza	Ends Well, 5, 115	Grand Rivulet, 5, 110	11	1:33.80	75,240
1985	Verbarctic, 5, 114	G. McCarron	Moro, 6, 122	Fighting Fit, 6, 124	7	1:36.60	53,460
1984	Jacque's Tip, 4, 114	A. T. Cordero Jr.	Minstrel Glory, 4, 107	Havagreatdate, 6, 111	4	1:41.80	55,440
1983	Singh Tu, 4, 109	J. Samyn	Master Digby, 4, 114	Fabulous Find, 5, 114	10	1:35.20	33,780
1982	John Casey, 5, 114	J. Fell	Brasher Doubloon, 4, 111	Accipiter's Hope, 4, 120	9	1:38.00	33,090
	Fabulous Find, 4, 109	J. O. Cintron	In From Dixie, 5, 122	Princelet, 4, 126	7	1:38.00	33,330
1981	Dunham's Gift, 4, 115	M. Venezia	Ring of Light, 6, 114	Dr. Blum, 4, 124	5	1:33.00	33,000
1980	Nice Catch, 6, 120	J. Fell	Ardaluan (Ire), 4, 119	Lark Oscillation (Fr), 5, 115	8	1:36.80	34,020
1979	Vencedor, 5, 114	R. Hernandez	Don Aronow, 5, 108	Coverack, 6, 114	10	1:44.00	33,060
1978	Pumpkin Moonshine, 4, 105	D. A. Borden	Lynn Davis, 4, 115	Sharpstone, 4, 111	7	1:44.40	32,250
1977	Cinteelo, 4, 113	E. Maple	Turn and Count, 4, 124	Cojak, 4, 120	9	1:43.40	33,090
1976	Double Edge Sword, 6, 116	A. T. Cordero Jr.	Dr. Emil, 4, 116	Bold and Fancy, 5, 111	8	1:33.40	34,170
1975	Step Nicely, 4, 126	J. Velasquez	*Tambac, 5, 116	Onion, 6, 119	9	1:34.00	33,900
1974	Dundee Marmalade, 6, 113	M. Hole	Infuriator, 4, 113	Prove Out, 5, 126	6	1:36.00	32,940

1973 **North Sea**, 4, 117   R. C. Smith   Forage, 4, 116   †Summer Guest, 4, 118   9   1:33.60 $33,990
Named for Westchester County, New York, located to the north of the Bronx. Formerly named in honor of the Allied victory in World War I and the signing of the Versailles Peace Treaty in 1919. Formerly named for Yorktown, New York, a community located in Westchester County. Grade 2 1973-'79. Yorktown H. 1918, 1920-'39. Victory H. 1919. Westchester S. 1953-'71. Held at Empire City 1918-'42. Held at Jamaica 1943-'59. Held at Aqueduct 1960-2001. Not held 1932-'33, 1954-'58. 1⅛ miles 1918, 1922-'39, 1951-'53. 1¼ miles 1919-'21. 1³⁄₁₆ miles 1940-'50. 1¹⁄₁₆ miles 1977-'79. 1 mile 70 yards 1984. Four-year-olds and up 1959-'71. Two divisions 1982. Dead heat for second 1990. Track record 2003. American record 2003. †Denotes female.

West Virginia Derby

Grade 3 in 2005. Mountaineer Race Track, three-year-olds, 1⅛ miles, dirt. Held August 7, 2004, with a gross value of $600,000. First held in 1958. First graded in 2002. Stakes record 1:46.29 (2003 Soto).

Year	Winner	Jockey	Second	Third	Strs	Time	1st Purse
2004	**Sir Shackleton**, 3, 117	R. Bejarano	Pollard's Vision, 3, 119	Britt's Jules, 3, 115	7	1:49.16	$363,000
2003	**Soto**, 3, 111	R. A. Dominguez	Dynever, 3, 117	Colita, 3, 111	9	**1:46.29**	360,000
2002	**Wiseman's Ferry**, 3, 122	J. F. Chavez	The Judge Sez Who, 3, 115	Captain Squire, 3, 115	9	1:49.63	360,000
2001	**Western Pride**, 3, 113	D. G. Whitney	Saratoga Games, 3, 115	Thunder Blitz, 3, 119	9	1:47.20	300,000
2000	**Mass Market**, 3, 115	R. Wilson	Hal's Hope, 3, 122	Bet On Red, 3, 122	10	1:49.94	180,000
1999	**Stellar Brush**, 3, 122	J. V. Stokes	American Spirit, 3, 113	Harry's Halo, 3, 119	11	1:49.02	150,000
1998	**Da Devil**, 3, 113	J. K. Court	One Bold Stroke, 3, 122	Jess M, 3, 115	12	1:48.84	120,000
1990	**Challenge My Duty**, 3, 113	I. B. Ayarza	My Other Brother, 3, 115	Gay's Best Boy, 3, 115	8	1:49.60	60,000
1989	**Doc's Leader**, 3, 114	W. I. Fox Jr.	Halo Hansom, 3, 117	Downtown Davey, 3, 117	7	1:50.00	60,000
1988	**Old Stories**, 3, 114	R. Hernandez	Viva Deputy, 3, 117	Rising Colors, 3, 112	10	1:52.20	60,000
1981	**Park's Policy**, 3, 115	J. S. Lloyd	Diverse Dude, 3, 115	Iron Gem, 3, 115	9	1:49.60	22,750
	Johnny Dance, 3, 115	F. Lovato Jr.	Master Tommy, 3, 115	Amasham, 3, 115	8	1:47.80	22,750
1980	**Summer Advocate**, 3, 115	W. L. Floyd	Lucky Pluck, 3, 115	Foolish Move, 3, 115	11	1:50.80	32,500
1979	**Architect**, 3, 115	S. A. Spencer	Sir Prince P., 3, 115	Lt. Bert, 3, 115	11	1:51.00	32,500
1978	**Beau Sham**, 3, 115	P. Day	Silent Cal, 3, 115	Morning Frolic, 3, 115	9	1:48.60	32,500
1977	**Best Person**, 3, 115	V. A. Bracciale Jr.	Swoon Swept, 3, 115	A Letter to Harry, 3, 115	9	1:48.60	32,500
1976	**Wardlaw**, 3, 115	J. E. Tejeira	American Trader, 3, 115	Joachim, 3, 121	7	1:47.60	32,500
1975	**At the Front**, 3, 117	A. Santiago	My Friend Gus, 3, 117	Packer Captain, 3, 117	10	1:48.60	32,500
1974	**Park Guard**, 3, 124	B. M. Feliciano	Sea Songster, 3, 126	Sahib Nearco, 3, 124	11	1:47.40	32,500
1973	**Blue Chip Dan**, 3, 118	M. Solomone	Dr. Pantano, 3, 121	Double Edge Sword, 3, 124	8	1:49.20	20,930

Mountaineer Race Track is located in Chester, West Virginia. Held at Wheeling Downs 1958-'61. Held at Waterford Park 1963-'81. Not held 1960, 1962, 1982-'87, 1991-'97. Two divisions 1981. Track record 2001, 2003.

Whitney Handicap

Grade 1 in 2005. Saratoga Race Course, three-year-olds and up, 1⅛ miles, dirt. Held August 7, 2004, with a gross value of $750,000. First held in 1928. First graded in 1973. Stakes record 1:47 (1974 Tri Jet, 2002 Left Bank).

Year	Winner	Jockey	Second	Third	Strs	Time	1st Purse
2004	**Roses in May**, 4, 114	E. S. Prado	Perfect Drift, 5, 117	Bowman's Band, 6, 114	9	1:48.54	$450,000
2003	**Medaglia d'Oro**, 4, 123	J. D. Bailey	Volponi, 5, 120	Evening Attire, 5, 118	7	1:47.69	450,000
2002	**Left Bank**, 5, 118	J. R. Velazquez	Street Cry (Ire), 4, 123	Lido Palace (Chi), 5, 119	6	**1:47.04**	450,000
2001	**Lido Palace (Chi)**, 4, 115	J. D. Bailey	Albert the Great, 4, 124	Gander, 5, 113	7	1:47.94	540,000
2000	**Lemon Drop Kid**, 4, 123	E. S. Prado	Cat Thief, 4, 117	Behrens, 6, 122	6	1:48.30	680,000
1999	**Victory Gallop**, 4, 123	J. D. Bailey	Behrens, 5, 123	Catienus, 5, 113	8	1:48.66	360,000
1998	**Awesome Again**, 4, 117	P. Day	Tale of the Cat, 4, 114	Crypto Star, 4, 116	8	1:49.71	240,000
1997	**Will's Way**, 4, 117	J. D. Bailey	Formal Gold, 4, 120	Skip Away, 4, 125	6	1:48.37	210,000
1996	**Mahogany Hall**, 5, 113	J. A. Santos	†Serena's Song, 4, 116	Peaks and Valleys, 4, 121	9	1:48.65	210,000
1995	**Unaccounted For**, 4, 114	P. Day	L'Carriere, 4, 111	Silver Fox, 4, 112	9	1:49.29	210,000
1994	**Colonial Affair**, 4, 117	J. A. Santos	Devil His Due, 5, 125	West by West, 5, 113	7	1:48.61	210,000
1993	**Brunswick**, 4, 112	M. E. Smith	West by West, 4, 115	Devil His Due, 4, 122	7	1:47.41	150,000
1992	**Sultry Song**, 4, 115	J. D. Bailey	Out of Place, 5, 115	Chief Honcho, 5, 116	9	1:47.29	150,000
1991	**In Excess (Ire)**, 4, 121	G. L. Stevens	Chief Honcho, 4, 115	Killer Diller, 4, 112	7	1:48.01	150,000
1990	**Criminal Type**, 5, 126	G. L. Stevens	Dancing Spree, 5, 121	Mi Selecto, 5, 117	6	1:48.60	140,640
1989	**Easy Goer**, 3, 119	P. Day	Forever Silver, 4, 120	Cryptoclearance, 5, 122	6	1:47.40	172,500
1988	**†Personal Ensign**, 4, 117	R. P. Romero	Gulch, 4, 124	King's Swan, 8, 123	3	1:47.80	162,300
1987	**Java Gold**, 3, 113	P. Day	Gulch, 3, 117	Broad Brush, 4, 127	7	1:48.40	173,100
1986	**†Lady's Secret**, 4, 119	P. Day	Ends Well, 5, 116	Fuzzy, 4, 110	7	1:49.80	202,500
1985	**Track Barron**, 4, 124	A. T. Cordero Jr.	Carr de Naskra, 4, 120	Vanlandingham, 4, 124	5	1:47.60	160,680
1984	**Slew o' Gold**, 4, 126	A. T. Cordero Jr.	Track Barron, 3, 117	Thumbsucker, 5, 115	3	1:48.60	165,744
1983	**Island Whirl**, 5, 125	E. J. Delahoussaye	Bold Style, 4, 114	Sunny's Halo, 3, 116	9	1:48.40	103,860
1982	**Silver Buck**, 4, 115	D. MacBeth	Winter's Tale, 6, 119	Tap Shoes, 4, 113	6	1:47.80	99,000
1981	**Fio Rito**, 6, 113	L. Hulet	Winter's Tale, 5, 121	Ring of Light, 6, 114	8	1:48.00	105,300
1980	**State Dinner**, 5, 120	R. Hernandez	Dr. Patches, 6, 114	Czaravich, 4, 123	8	1:48.20	99,540
1979	**Star de Naskra**, 4, 120	J. Fell	Cox's Ridge, 5, 117	The Liberal Member, 4, 120	6	1:47.60	65,040
1978	**Alydar**, 3, 123	J. Velasquez	Buckaroo, 3, 112	Father Hogan, 5, 114	9	1:47.40	49,545
1977	**Nearly On Time**, 3, 103	S. Cauthen	American History, 5, 112	Dancing Gun, 5, 112	5	1:49.40	49,545
1976	**Dancing Gun**, 4, 108	R. I. Velez	American History, 4, 109	Erwin Boy, 5, 116	7	1:50.00	48,825

1975	**Ancient Title**, 5, 128	S. Hawley	Group Plan, 5, 115	Arbees Boy, 5, 118	3	1:48.20	$50,085
1974	**Tri Jet**, 5, 123	L. A. Pincay Jr.	Infuriator, 4, 120	Stop the Music, 4, 120	6	**1:47.00**	33,390
1973	**Onion**, 4, 119	J. Vasquez	Secretariat, 3, 119	Rule by Reason, 6, 119	5	1:49.20	32,310

Named for the Whitney family, one of the most influential families of 20th-century American racing. Grade 2 1973-'80. Whitney S. 1928-'53, 1955-'59, 1961-'65, 1967-'74, 1978-'80. Held at Belmont Park 1943-'45. 1¼ miles 1928-'54. Four-year-olds and up 1957-'69. Colts and fillies 1928-'40. †Denotes female.

William Donald Schaefer Handicap

Grade 3 in 2005. Pimlico, three-year-olds and up, 1⅛ miles, dirt. Held May 21, 2005, with a gross value of $100,000. First held in 1994. First graded in 2001. Stakes record 1:48.19 (1995 Tidal Surge).

Year	Winner	Jockey	Second	Third	Strs	Time	1st Purse
2005	**Zakocity**, 4, 117	J. D. Bailey	Clays Awesome, 5, 114	Royal Assault, 4, 112	8	1:49.19	$60,000
2004	**Seattle Fitz (Arg)**, 5, 116	R. Migliore	The Lady's Groom, 4, 115	Roaring Fever, 4, 114	8	1:49.43	60,000
2003	**Windsor Castle**, 5, 117	J. A. Santos	Changeintheweather, 4, 113	Tempest Fugit, 6, 116	8	1:50.08	60,000
2002	**Tenpins**, 4, 114	R. Albarado	Bowman's Band, 4, 117	Tactical Side, 5, 113	7	1:50.20	60,000
2001	**Perfect Cat**, 4, 115	J. D. Bailey	Rize, 5, 115	Judge's Case, 4, 115	8	1:49.55	60,000
2000	**Ecton Park**, 4, 116	P. Day	The Groom Is Red, 4, 111	Crosspatch, 6, 116	4	1:49.21	60,000
1999	**Perfect to a Tee**, 7, 112	A. C. Cortez	Allen's Oop, 4, 113	Smile Again, 4, 114	7	1:49.20	60,000
1998	**Acceptable**, 4, 118	J. D. Bailey	Littlebitlively, 4, 118	Testafly, 4, 114	8	1:48.76	60,000
1997	**Western Echo**, 5, 116	E. S. Prado	Suave Prospect, 5, 114	Mary's Buckaroo, 6, 120	5	1:49.41	60,000
1996	**Canaveral**, 5, 115	S. J. Sellers	Michael's Star, 4, 114	Rugged Bugger, 5, 113	7	1:49.03	45,000
1995	**Tidal Surge**, 5, 112	J. D. Carle	Mary's Buckaroo, 4, 113	Ameri Valay, 6, 119	5	**1:48.19**	60,000
1994	**Taking Risks**, 4, 117	M. T. Johnston	Frottage, 5, 115	Super Memory, 4, 112	6	1:49.53	45,000

Named for William Donald Schaefer, governor of Maryland (1987-'95) and mayor of Baltimore (1971-'86).

Will Rogers Stakes

Grade 3 in 2005. Hollywood Park, three-year-olds, 1 mile, turf. Held May 28, 2005, with a gross value of $109,900. First held in 1938. First graded in 1973. Stakes record 1:33.45 (2004 Laura's Lucky Boy).

Year	Winner	Jockey	Second	Third	Strs	Time	1st Purse
2005	**Osidy**, 3, 116	A. O. Solis	Willow O Wisp, 3, 119	Eastern Sand, 3, 117	8	1:34.67	$65,940
2004	**Laura's Lucky Boy**, 3, 119	P. A. Valenzuela	Toasted, 3, 121	Street Theatre, 3, 117	8	**1:33.45**	65,640
2003	**Private Chef**, 3, 115	V. Espinoza	Banshee King, 3, 115	Singletary, 3, 117	6	1:35.57	67,560
2002	**Doc Holiday (Ire)**, 3, 116	D. R. Flores	Johar, 3, 119	Golden Arrow, 3, 115	5	1:34.64	63,900
2001	dh- **Dr. Park**, 3, 117	T. Baze		Learing At Kathy, 3, 116	8	1:35.10	43,920
	dh- **Media Mogul (GB)**, 3, 116	A. O. Solis					
2000	**Purely Cozzene**, 3, 120	V. Espinoza	Duke of Green (GB), 3, 116	Silver Axe, 3, 115	8	1:34.67	66,000
1999	**Eagleton**, 3, 118	C. A. Black	Hidden Magic (GB), 3, 115	Mr. Reignmaker, 3, 115	11	1:34.38	67,800
1998	**Magical (GB)**, 3, 114	R. R. Douglas	Commitisize, 3, 119	Son's Corona, 3, 114	8	1:33.98	65,820
1997	**Brave Act (GB)**, 3, 117	C. J. McCarron	P.T. Indy, 3, 118	Without Doubt (Ire), 3, 116	12	1:34.01	68,520
1996	**Let Bob Do It**, 3, 118	K. J. Desormeaux	Nightcapper, 3, 114	Dr. Sardonica, 3, 116	10	1:34.05	67,140
1995	**Via Lombardia (Ire)**, 3, 117	E. J. Delahoussaye	Mr Purple, 3, 119	Bee El Tee, 3, 117	9	1:34.15	63,650
1994	**Unfinished Symph**, 3, 116	G. Baze	Silver Music, 3, 118	Valiant Nature, 3, 122	8	1:34.60	64,600
1993	**Future Storm**, 3, 116	K. J. Desormeaux	Lykatill Hil, 3, 119	Earl of Barking (Ire), 3, 122	12	1:34.01	68,900
1992	**The Name's Jimmy**, 3, 116	D. Sorenson	Bold Assert, 3, 117	Prospect for Four, 3, 114	7	1:40.99	63,600
1991	**Compelling Sound**, 3, 119	P. A. Valenzuela	Stark South, 3, 116	Persianalli (Ire), 3, 117	9	1:40.70	66,100
1990	**Itsallgreektome**, 3, 114	C. S. Nakatani	Warcraft, 3, 120	Balla Cove (Ire), 3, 116	9	1:40.20	66,500
1989	**Notorious Pleasure**, 3, 117	L. A. Pincay Jr.	Advocate Training, 3, 115	First Play, 3, 116	10	1:40.20	66,900
1988	**Word Pirate**, 3, 119	E. J. Delahoussaye	Perfecting, 3, 115	Roberto's Dancer, 3, 116	9	1:40.60	50,400
1987	**Something Lucky**, 3, 117	L. A. Pincay Jr.	The Medic, 3, 115	Persevered, 3, 119	9	1:43.00	49,600
1986	‡**Mazaad (Ire)**, 3, 120	W. Shoemaker	Autobot, 3, 119	He's a Saros, 3, 115	7	1:42.40	48,800
1985	**Pine Belt**, 3, 113	R. Q. Meza	Rich Earth, 3, 119	Academy Road, 3, 115	10	1:41.00	40,700
1984	**Tsunami Slew**, 3, 119	L. A. Pincay Jr.	Swinging Scobie (GB), 3, 115	Tights, 3, 122	6	1:39.80	37,550
1983	**Barberstown**, 3, 116	F. Toro	Lover Boy Leslie, 3, 117	Tanks Brigade, 3, 114	13	1:41.40	35,200
1982	**Give Me Strength**, 3, 116	J. Samyn	Ask Me, 3, 115	Accoustical, 3, 113	8	1:40.60	26,500
	Sword Blade, 3, 112	D. G. McHargue	Art Director, 3, 113	Lucky Ship, 3, 114	7	1:41.80	26,050
1981	**Splendid Spruce**, 3, 123	D. G. McHargue	Seafood, 3, 116	Surprise George, 3, 115	8	1:41.40	38,900
1980	**Stiff Diamond**, 3, 113	T. Lipham	Naked Sky, 3, 117	Big Doug, 3, 115	11	1:41.40	34,300
1979	**Ibacache (Chi)**, 3, 118	D. G. McHargue	Beau's Eagle, 3, 121	David's Gotcha (Ire), 3, 111	8	1:40.80	32,550
1978	**April Axe**, 3, 115	C. J. McCarron	Poppy Popowich, 3, 115	He's Dewan, 3, 117	9	1:41.60	33,100
1977	**Nordic Prince**, 3, 117	S. Hawley	Sonny Collins, 3, 119	Bad 'n Big, 3, 123	10	1:41.40	33,950
1976	**Madera Sun**, 3, 115	L. A. Pincay Jr.	An Act, 3, 126	‡Today 'n Tomorrow, 3, 115	7	1:42.00	32,100
1975	**Uniformity**, 3, 115	W. Shoemaker	Dusty County, 3, 117	Exact Duplicate, 3, 115	8	1:42.00	32,150
1974	**Stardust Mel**, 3, 120	F. Toro	Agitate, 3, 122	El Seetu, 3, 114	8	1:40.80	32,800
1973	**Groshawk**, 3, 123	W. Shoemaker	Ancient Title, 3, 124	dh- Mug Punter, 3, 113	10	1:35.60	33,600
				dh- Out of the East, 3, 118			

Named for actor and American humorist Will Rogers (1879-1935); Rogers was killed in a plane crash in Alaska. Grade 2 1973-'82, 1998-'99. Will Rogers Memorial H. 1938-'40. Will Rogers H. 1941-'51, 1979-'94, 1996-2000. Will Rogers Breeders' Cup H. 1995. Held at Santa Anita Park 1949. Not held 1942-'43, 1950. 7 furlongs 1938-'44, 1946-'47. 6 furlongs 1948-'54. 1 1/16 miles 1974-'94. Dirt 1938-'68. Three-year-olds and up 1938, 1944. Colts and geldings 1953-'73. Two divisions 1982. Dead heat for third 1973. Dead heat for first 2001. ‡Sure Fire finished third, DQ to fourth, 1976. ‡Sovereign Don finished first, DQ to fifth, 1986.

Wilshire Handicap

Grade 3 in 2005. Hollywood Park, three-year-olds and up, fillies and mares, 1 mile, turf. Held April 23, 2005, with a gross value of $109,600. First held in 1953. First graded in 1975. Stakes record 1:33.41 (2004 Spring Star [Fr]).

Year	Winner	Jockey	Second	Third	Strs	Time	1st Purse
2005	Pickle (GB), 4, 114	J. K. Court	Makeup Artist, 5, 114	Amorama (Fr), 4, 117	8	1:33.85	$65,760
2004	Spring Star (Fr), 5, 117	A. O. Solis	Quero Quero, 4, 115	Dublino, 5, 120	9	1:33.41	66,540
2003	Dublino, 4, 120	K. J. Desormeaux	Southern Oasis, 5, 116	Final Destination (NZ), 5, 118	9	1:33.62	66,600
2002	Eurolink Raindance (Ire), 5, 115	C. J. McCarron	Crazy Ensign (Arg), 6, 118	Impeachable, 5, 115	5	1:34.31	63,960
2001	Tranquility Lake, 6, 123	E. J. Delahoussaye	Dianehill (Ire), 5, 116	Out of Reach (GB), 4, 117	7	1:34.69	65,160
2000	Tout Charmant, 4, 121	C. J. McCarron	Penny Marie, 4, 117	Perfect Copy, 4, 117	6	1:33.86	64,740
1999	Sapphire Ring (GB), 4, 119	G. L. Stevens	Bella Chiarra, 4, 116	Green Jewel (GB), 5, 118	7	1:33.86	65,160
1998	Shake the Yoke (GB), 5, 118	E. J. Delahoussaye	Traces of Gold, 6, 116	Cozy Blues, 4, 115	9	1:34.10	66,240
1997	Blushing Heiress, 5, 115	C. J. McCarron	Real Connection, 6, 115	De Puntillas (GB), 5, 117	7	1:40.80	65,040
1996	Pharma, 5, 118	C. S. Nakatani	Didina (GB), 4, 116	Matiara, 4, 120	5	1:40.96	79,770
1995	Possibly Perfect, 5, 121	K. J. Desormeaux	Morgana, 4, 116	Aube Indienne (Fr), 5, 119	5	1:40.37	76,600
1994	Skimble, 5, 118	E. J. Delahoussaye	Bel's Starlet, 7, 117	Miami Sands (Ire), 4, 116	6	1:41.39	62,800
1993	Toussaud, 4, 116	K. J. Desormeaux	Visible Gold, 5, 117	Wedding Ring (Ire), 4, 115	7	1:40.14	63,500
1992	Kostroma (Ire), 6, 123	K. J. Desormeaux	Danzante, 4, 114	Appealing Missy, 5, 116	6	1:41.35	62,600
1991	Fire the Groom, 4, 118	G. L. Stevens	Odalea (Arg), 5, 115	Agirlfromars, 5, 114	6	1:40.10	63,000
1990	Reluctant Guest, 4, 114	R. G. Davis	Beautiful Melody, 4, 115	Estrella Fuega, 4, 114	6	1:39.40	62,400
1989	Claire Marine (Ire), 4, 117	C. J. McCarron	Fitzwilliam Place (Ire), 5, 119	Galunpe (Ire), 6, 119	6	1:39.00	62,700
1988	Chapel of Dreams, 4, 115	G. L. Stevens	Fitzwilliam Place (Ire), 4, 119	Invited Guest (Ire), 4, 116	8	1:39.40	64,700
1987	Galunpe (Ire), 4, 118	F. Toro	Top Socialite, 5, 119	Perfect Match (Fr), 5, 116	6	1:41.00	75,900
1986	Outstandingly, 4, 117	G. L. Stevens	La Kournia (Fr), 4, 118	Estrapade, 6, 124	5	1:41.60	75,600
1985	Johnica, 4, 114	C. J. McCarron	Tamarinda (Fr), 4, 119	Salt Spring (Arg), 6, 113	6	1:40.60	63,100
1984	Triple Tipple, 5, 114	L. A. Pincay Jr.	Comedy Act, 5, 121	Nan's Dancer, 5, 116	7	1:41.20	48,900
1983	Mademoiselle Forli, 4, 118	P. A. Valenzuela	Night Fire, 4, 117	Nan's Dancer, 4, 115	5	1:44.80	47,300
1982	Miss Huntington, 5, 115	P. A. Valenzuela	Mi Quimera (Arg), 5, 114	French Charmer, 4, 116	10	1:41.40	51,250
1981	Track Robbery, 5, 118	P. A. Valenzuela	Luth Music (Fr), 4, 115	Save Wild Life, 4, 116	5	1:40.80	47,550
1980	Wishing Well, 5, 120	F. Toro	Sisterhood, 5, 119	Love You Dear, 4, 113	9	1:41.60	38,500
1979	Country Queen, 4, 121	L. A. Pincay Jr.	Giggling Girl, 5, 116	Camarado, 4, 119	8	1:40.40	33,100
1978	*Lucie Manet, 5, 119	C. J. McCarron	Swingtime, 6, 118	Drama Critic, 4, 119	6	1:49.00	30,950
1977	Now Pending, 4, 114	R. Campas	Swingtime, 5, 116	Up to Juliet, 4, 116	10	1:48.80	33,550
1976	Miss Toshiba, 4, 117	F. Toro	Charger's Star, 6, 116	Swingtime, 4, 120	8	1:49.20	32,300
1975	*Tizna, 6, 123	J. Lambert	Susan's Girl, 6, 123	*Dulcia, 6, 120	10	1:48.60	33,300
1974	Tallahto, 4, 121	L. A. Pincay Jr.	Ready Wit, 4, 113	Dogtooth Violet, 4, 119	11	1:47.60	33,650
1973	Balcony's Babe, 5, 116	J. Lambert	Ground Song, 4, 118	Dating, 6, 111	8	1:48.60	17,250
	Convenience, 5, 124	J. L. Rotz	Pallisima, 4, 120	Veiled Desire, 4, 109	7	1:49.00	16,900

Named for Wilshire, a historic district of Los Angeles. Grade 2 1983-'97. Wilshire S. 1953, 1970-'72. Not held 1954-'62. 7 furlongs 1963-'69. 1¹/₈ miles 1970-'78. 1¹/₁₆ miles 1979-'97. Dirt 1953-'69, 1983. Three-year-olds 1953, 1970. Four-year-olds and up 1971-'72. Fillies 1953, 1970. Two divisions 1973. Nonwinners of a race worth $10,000 to the winner 1973.

WinStar Distaff Handicap

Grade 3 in 2005. Lone Star Park, three-year-olds and up, fillies and mares, 1 mile, turf. Held May 31, 2004, with a gross value of $200,000. First held in 2003. First graded in 2003. Stakes record 1:35.98 (2004 Academic Angel).

Year	Winner	Jockey	Second	Third	Strs	Time	1st Purse
2005	Katdogawn (GB), 5, 120	J. D. Bailey	Valentine Dancer, 5, 120	Voz De Colegiala (Chi), 6, 115	11	1:39.53	$120,000
2004	Academic Angel, 5, 111	S. J. Sellers	Janeian (NZ), 6, 119	Katdogawn (GB), 4, 120	12	1:35.98	120,000
2003	Eagle Lake, 5, 116	G. Melancon	Little Treasure (Fr), 4, 117	Magic Mission, 5, 116	9	1:43.02	120,000
2002	Queen of Wilshire, 6, 117	D. R. Flores	Pleasant State, 7, 115	Blushing Bride (GB), 4, 115	12	1:38.96	120,000
2001	Voladora, 6, 114	M. C. Berry	Dyna Likes Bingo, 6, 109	Iftiraas (GB), 4, 118	10	1:42.23	120,000
2000	Mumtaz (Fr), 4, 113	V. Espinoza	Evening Promise (GB), 4, 117	Really Polish, 5, 114	9	1:37.28	120,000
1999	Heritage of Gold, 4, 114	C. T. Lambert	Red Cat, 4, 116	Nalynn, 5, 114	10	1:37.75	90,000

Races for females are typically referred to as distaff races. Sponsored by Bill Casner's and Kenny Troutt's WinStar Farm of Versailles, Kentucky 2000-'05. Formerly sponsored by Prestonwood Farm (predecessor of WinStar Farm) of Versailles, Kentucky. Prestonwood Distaff H. 1999.

WinStar Galaxy Stakes

Grade 2 in 2005. Keeneland, three-year-olds and up, fillies and mares, 1³/₁₆ miles, turf. Held October 10, 2004, with a gross value of $500,000. First held in 1998. First graded in 2000. Stakes record 1:53.91 (1999 Happyanunoit [NZ]).

Year	Winner	Jockey	Second	Third	Strs	Time	1st Purse
2004	Stay Forever, 7, 121	E. Castro	Super Brand (SAf), 5, 119	Shaconage, 4, 121	9	1:57.08	$310,000
2003	Bien Nicole, 5, 121	D. R. Pettinger	Approach (GB), 3, 116	New Economy, 5, 121	6	1:55.87	310,000
2002	Owsley, 4, 122	E. S. Prado	Snow Dance, 4, 120	Surya, 4, 118	6	1:56.72	337,590
2001	Spook Express (SAf), 7, 120	M. E. Smith	Solvig, 4, 118	Veil of Avalon, 4, 118	9	1:54.24	349,370
2000	Tout Charmant, 4, 119	C. J. McCarron	Perfect Sting, 4, 120	License Fee, 5, 119	7	1:54.74	343,480
1999	Happyanunoit (NZ), 4, 119	B. Blanc	Pleasant Temper, 5, 119	Fiji (GB), 5, 117	9	1:53.91	346,270
1998	Witchful Thinking, 4, 115	C. J. McCarron	Memories of Silver, 5, 120	Starry Dreamer, 4, 115	6	1:54.24	169,415

Sponsored by Bill Casner's and Kenny Troutt's WinStar Farm of Versailles, Kentucky 2000-'04. Formerly sponsored by Vinery of Lexington 1998-'99. Grade 3 2000. Vinery First Lady S. 1998-'99.

Withers Stakes

Grade 3 in 2005. Aqueduct, three-year-olds, 1 mile, dirt. Held April 30, 2005, with a gross value of $150,000. First held in 1874. First graded in 1973. Stakes record 1:32.79 (1993 Williamstown).

Year	Winner	Jockey	Second	Third	Strs	Time	1st Purse
2005	Scrappy T, 3, 120	N. Arroyo Jr.	Park Avenue Ball, 3, 120	War Plan, 3, 116	7	1:35.74	$90,000
2004	Medallist, 3, 116	J. F. Chavez	Forest Danger, 3, 123	Two Down Automatic, 3, 120	5	1:34.49	90,000
2003	Spite the Devil, 3, 116	L. Chavez	Alysweep, 3, 123	Stanislavsky, 3, 116	8	1:35.89	90,000
2002	Fast Decision, 3, 116	J. A. Santos	Shah Jehan, 3, 118	Listen Here, 3, 120	5	1:36.41	90,000
2001	Richly Blended, 3, 123	R. Wilson	Le Grande Danseur, 3, 120	Telescam, 3, 116	7	1:35.66	90,000
2000	Big E E, 3, 116	H. Castillo Jr.	Precise End, 3, 123	Port Herman, 3, 116	8	1:35.69	90,000
1999	Successful Appeal, 3, 120	J. L. Espinoza	Best of Luck, 3, 116	Treasure Island, 3, 116	8	1:35.18	90,000
1998	Dice Dancer, 3, 123	J. F. Chavez	Rubiyat, 3, 123	Limit Out, 3, 123	7	1:34.48	90,000
1997	Statesmanship, 3, 123	W. H. McCauley	Cryp Too, 3, 123	Stormin Fever, 3, 123	7	1:35.30	67,140
1996	Appealing Skier, 3, 123	R. Wilson	Jamies First Punch, 3, 123	Roar, 3, 123	5	1:35.02	66,120
1995	Blu Tusmani, 3, 123	J. A. Santos	Pat n Jac, 3, 123	‡Slice of Reality, 3, 123	9	1:35.19	67,260
1994	Twining, 3, 123	J. A. Santos	Able Buck, 3, 123	Presently, 3, 123	8	1:34.75	67,140
1993	Williamstown, 3, 124	C. Perret	Virginia Rapids, 3, 124	Farmonthefreeway, 3, 124	12	**1:32.79**	76,800
1992	Dixie Brass, 3, 126	J. M. Pezua	Big Sur, 3, 126	Superstrike (GB), 3, 126	8	1:33.71	73,080
1991	Subordinated Debt, 3, 126	J. A. Krone	Scan, 3, 126	Kyle's Our Man, 3, 126	9	1:34.03	73,920
1990	Housebuster, 3, 126	C. Perret	Profit Key, 3, 126	Sunny Serve, 3, 126	6	1:34.80	71,040
1989	Fire Maker, 3, 126	J. D. Bailey	Imbibe, 3, 126	Manastash Ridge, 3, 126	6	1:36.40	73,800
1988	Once Wild, 3, 126	P. Day	Tejano, 3, 126	Perfect Spy, 3, 126	5	1:35.20	69,360
1987	Gone West, 3, 126	E. Maple	High Brite, 3, 126	Mister S. M., 3, 126	6	1:36.40	82,620
1986	Clear Choice, 3, 126	J. Velasquez	Tasso, 3, 126	Landing Plot, 3, 126	10	1:35.60	71,550
1985	El Basco, 3, 126	J. Vasquez	Another Reef, 3, 126	Concert, 3, 126	12	1:36.60	72,990
1984	Play On, 3, 126	J. Samyn	Morning Bob, 3, 126	Back Bay Barrister, 3, 126	10	1:36.40	69,750
1983	Country Pine, 3, 126	J. D. Bailey	I Enclose, 3, 126	Megaturn, 3, 126	10	1:35.60	52,380
1982	Aloma's Ruler, 3, 126	J. L. Kaenel	Spanish Drums, 3, 126	John's Gold, 3, 126	6	1:35.40	33,300
1981	Spirited Boy, 3, 126	A. T. Cordero Jr.	Willow Hour, 3, 126	A Run, 3, 126	7	1:36.80	33,600
1980	Colonel Moran, 3, 126	J. Velasquez	Temperence Hill, 3, 126	J. P. Brother, 3, 126	6	1:34.40	34,200
1979	Czaravich, 3, 126	J. Cruguet	Instrument Landing, 3, 126	Strike the Main, 3, 126	9	1:35.60	33,330
1978	Junction, 3, 126	M. Solomone	Star de Naskra, 3, 126	Buckaroo, 3, 126	8	1:36.80	32,520
1977	Iron Constitution, 3, 126	J. Velasquez	Cormorant, 3, 126	Affiliate, 3, 126	8	1:37.00	33,360
1976	Sonkisser, 3, 126	B. Baeza	El Portugues, 3, 126	Full Out, 3, 126	6	1:35.00	32,760
1975	†Sarsar, 3, 121	W. Shoemaker	Laramie Trail, 3, 126	Ramahorn, 3, 126	13	1:34.60	36,360
1974	Accipiter, 3, 126	A. Santiago	Best of It, 3, 126	Hosiery, 3, 126	12	1:35.60	36,240
1973	Linda's Chief, 3, 126	J. Velasquez	Stop the Music, 3, 126	Forego, 3, 126	6	1:34.80	33,120

Named for David Dunham Withers (1821-'72), a founder of Jerome Park and president of Monmouth Park. Grade 2 1973-'99. Held at Jerome Park 1874-'89. Held at Morris Park 1890-1904. Held at Belmont Park 1905-'55, 1957-'59, 1972-'74, 1976, 1981, 1984-'85, 1987-'96. Held at Jamaica 1956. Not held 1911-'12. 1¹/₁₆ miles 1956. Colts and fillies 1944. ‡Northern Ensign finished third, DQ to ninth, 1995. Track record 1993. †Denotes female.

W. L. McKnight Handicap

Grade 2 in 2005. Calder Race Course, three-year-olds and up, 1¹/₂ miles, turf. Held December 18, 2004, with a gross value of $200,000. First held in 1973. First graded in 1975. Stakes record 2:24.11 (1995 Flag Down).

Year	Winner	Jockey	Second	Third	Strs	Time	1st Purse
2004	Dreadnaught, 4, 116	J. Samyn	Demetero, 5, 112	Scooter Roach, 5, 115	12	2:26.60	$120,000
2003	Balto Star, 5, 121	J. R. Velazquez	Continuously, 4, 116	Rowans Park, 5, 114	11	2:24.87	120,000
2002	Man From Wicklow, 5, 118	J. D. Bailey	Serial Bride, 5, 114	Rochester, 6, 117	12	2:28.05	120,000
2001	Profit Option, 6, 115	M. Guidry	Deeliteful Irving, 3, 113	Eltawaasul, 5, 114	12	2:27.95	90,000
2000	A Little Luck, 6, 114	M. E. Smith	Stokosky, 4, 115	Whata Brainstorm, 3, 113	12	2:29.01	90,000
1999	‡Wicapi, 7, 114	C. H. Velasquez	Special Coach, 3, 114	King's Jewel, 3, 112	12	2:26.28	90,000
1998	Wild Event, 5, 116	S. J. Sellers	N B Forrest, 6, 114	Glok, 4, 114	8	2:26.93	90,000
1997	Panama City, 3, 117	P. Day	Slicious (GB), 5, 114	Skillington, 4, 113	12	2:27.19	90,000
1996	Diplomatic Jet, 4, 123	J. F. Chavez	Marcie's Ensign, 4, 113	dh- Identity, 4, 114	12	2:24.20	90,000
				dh- Lassigny, 5, 116			
1995	Flag Down, 5, 116	J. A. Santos	Mecke, 3, 118	Green Means Go, 3, 115	12	**2:24.11**	90,000
1994	Star of Manila, 3, 116	C. Perret	Spectacular Tide, 5, 114	Kissin Kris, 4, 117	13	2:28.43	90,000
	Cobblestone Road, 5, 113	J. C. Ferrer	Daarik (Ire), 7, 113	Fraise, 6, 126	12	2:27.89	90,000
1993	Antartic Wings, 5, 113	R. R. Douglas	Cigar Toss (Arg), 6, 112	Luv U. Jodi, 6, 110	9	2:33.44	60,000
1992	Bye Union Ave., 6, 113	R. R. Douglas	†Crockadore, 5, 113	Skate On Thin Ice, 5, 111	9	2:27.23	90,000
1991	Stolen Rolls, 5, 115	P. A. Rodriguez	Runaway Raja, 5, 112	Gallant Mel, 6, 110	13	2:27.10	60,000
1990	Drum Taps, 4, 114	J. A. Santos	†Black Tulip (Fr), 5, 112	Turfah, 7, 115	12	2:29.80	60,000
1989	Mataji, 5, 113	D. Valiente	Mi Selecto, 4, 118	Creme Fraiche, 7, 118	13	2:25.60	90,000
1988	All Sincerity, 6, 111	C. Hernandez	Blazing Bart, 4, 118	Creme Fraiche, 6, 118	8	2:25.40	120,000
1987	Creme Fraiche, 5, 115	E. Maple	Flying Pidgeon, 6, 120	Akabir, 6, 113	10	2:27.00	120,000
1986	Flying Pidgeon, 5, 117	J. A. Santos	Creme Fraiche, 4, 115	Amerilad, 5, 112	7	2:39.60	120,000
1985	Jack Slade, 5, 120	G. Gallitano	Rake (Fr), 5, 116	Rilial, 4, 120	9	2:26.20	69,900
	Flying Pidgeon, 4, 114	J. A. Santos	Pass the Line, 4, 114	Selous Scout, 4, 110	10	2:25.80	70,800
1984	Open Call, 6, 120	J. Velasquez	Dom Cimarosa (Ire), 5, 114	Bold Frond, 5, 113	10	2:30.20	63,075
	Nijinsky's Secret, 6, 124	J. A. Velez Jr.	Dom Menotti (Fr), 7, 112	Four Bases, 5, 114	11	2:31.20	63,675

1983	Current Blade, 5, 114	J. D. Bailey	Half Iced, 4, 122	Leader Jet, 5, 115	12	2:29.20	$70,020
1982	Ghazwan (Ire), 5, 120	C. Hernandez	Gleaming Channel, 4, 116	Beyond Recall, 5, 110	11	2:28.80	61,920
	Russian George (Fr), 6, 114	M. A. Rivera	†Euphrosyne, 6, 117	Nar, 7, 113	10	2:29.80	61,920
1981	El Barril (Chi), 5, 118	J. Vasquez	Lord Bawlmer, 5, 115	Lobsang (Ire), 5, 117	9	2:28.40	51,630
	Buckpoint (Fr), 5, 122	J. D. Bailey	Scythian Gold, 6, 116	Proud Manner, 7, 112	10	2:28.00	52,230
1980	Old Crony, 5, 117	D. Brumfield	Once Over Lightly, 7, 114	Houdini, 5, 125	11	1:48.40	35,565
	Drum's Captain (Ire), 5, 118	J. Fell	Lot o' Gold, 4, 125	Scythian Gold, 5, 116	9	1:48.00	34,875
1979	Bob's Dusty, 5, 119	R. DePass	Prince Misko, 4, 116	Bridewell, 4, 112	12	1:48.00	55,800
1978	Practitioner, 5, 118	J. S. Rodriguez	Fort Prevel, 4, 111	Bob's Dusty, 4, 118	12	1:48.80	56,250
1977	Hall of Reason, 4, 119	M. Solomone	Visier, 5, 120	Lightning Thrust, 4, 116	8	1:47.20	52,200
1976	Toonerville, 5, 119	G. St. Leon	Ameri Flyer, 4, 117	Emperor Rex, 5, 115	12	1:44.60	55,800
1975	Snurb, 5, 119	G. St. Leon	Buffalo Lark, 5, 121	Lord Rebeau, 4, 116	13	1:46.00	37,800
1974	Shane's Prince, 4, 116	E. Maple	Star Envoy, 6, 125	Return to Reality, 5, 119	9	1:46.00	35,700
1973	Getajetholme, 4, 121	J. Imparato	Daring Young Man, 4, 120	Outdoors, 4, 0	14	1:47.20	38,700

Named for William L. McKnight (1881-1978), co-founder of Calder Race Course and founder of Tartan Farms. Grade 3 1976-'81. W. L. McKnight Invitational H. 1986-'93. 1$\frac{1}{8}$ miles 1973-'75, 1977-'80. About 1$\frac{1}{8}$ miles 1976. Dirt 1993. Two divisions 1980-'82, 1984-'85. Held in January and December 1994. Dead heat for third 1996. ‡Just Listen finished first, DQ to ninth, 1999. Course record 1976. †Denotes female.

Woodford Reserve Turf Classic Stakes

Grade 1 in 2005. Churchill Downs, three-year-olds and up, 1$\frac{1}{8}$ miles, turf. Held May 7, 2005, with a gross value of $470,400. First held in 1987. First graded in 1989. Stakes record 1:46.34 (1993 Lure).

Year	Winner	Jockey	Second	Third	Strs	Time	1st Purse
2005	America Alive, 4, 117	R. Albarado	Meteor Storm (GB), 6, 119	Quest Star, 6, 115	10	1:47.34	$291,648
2004	Stroll, 4, 121	J. D. Bailey	Sweet Return (GB), 4, 123	Mystery Giver, 6, 123	11	1:53.00	281,418
2003	Honor in War, 4, 116	D. R. Flores	Requete (GB), 4, 116	Patrol, 4, 114	8	1:46.67	276,086
2002	Beat Hollow (GB), 5, 115	A. O. Solis	With Anticipation, 7, 123	Hap, 6, 123	10	1:47.35	280,550
2001	White Heart (GB), 6, 116	G. L. Stevens	King Cugat, 4, 123	Brahms, 4, 123	8	1:48.75	216,938
2000	Manndar (Ire), 4, 114	C. S. Nakatani	Falcon Flight (Fr), 4, 118	Yagli, 7, 120	8	1:47.91	217,310
1999	Wild Event, 6, 120	S. J. Sellers	Garbu, 5, 116	Hawksley Hill (Ire), 6, 120	7	1:47.25	206,646
1998	Joyeux Danseur, 5, 123	R. Albarado	Lasting Approval, 4, 120	Hawksley Hill (Ire), 5, 120	8	1:48.14	174,282
1997	Always a Classic, 4, 120	J. D. Bailey	Labeeb (GB), 5, 118	Down the Aisle, 4, 114	8	1:49.29	145,328
1996	Mecke, 4, 123	P. Day	Petit Poucet (GB), 4, 116	Winged Victory, 6, 116	11	1:49.48	165,230
1995	Romarin (Brz), 5, 118	C. S. Nakatani	Blues Traveller (Ire), 5, 120	Hasten To Add, 5, 120	12	1:46.86	160,095
1994	Paradise Creek, 5, 118	P. Day	Lure, 5, 123	Yukon Robbery, 5, 116	7	1:48.34	152,068
1993	Lure, 4, 123	M. E. Smith	Star of Cozzene, 5, 118	Cleone, 4, 116	8	1:46.34	117,683
1992	Cudas, 4, 117	P. A. Valenzuela	Sky Classic, 5, 123	Fourstars Allstar, 4, 118	12	1:46.56	124,703
1991	Opening Verse, 5, 116	C. J. McCarron	Itsallgreektome, 4, 123	Pedro the Cool, 5, 112	11	1:47.22	125,060
1990	Ten Keys, 6, 120	K. J. Desormeaux	Yankee Affair, 8, 120	Stellar Rival, 7, 113	5	1:50.80	110,435
1989	Equalize, 7, 118	J. A. Santos	Yankee Affair, 7, 116	Gallant Mel, 4, 114	8	1:51.40	114,140
1988	Yankee Affair, 6, 118	P. Day	Yucca, 4, 112	First Patriot, 4, 112	10	1:50.00	121,225
1987	Manila, 4, 120	J. Vasquez	Vilzak, 4, 112	Lieutenant's Lark, 5, 120	4	1:48.80	110,045

Sponsored by Woodford Reserve Distillery of Versailles, Kentucky 2000-'05. Sponsored by Early Times Distillery of Louisville 1987-'99. Grade 3 1989-'93. Grade 2 1994-'95. Early Times Turf Classic S. 1987-'99. Four-year-olds and up 1987-'91. Course record 1992, 1993.

Wood Memorial Stakes

Grade 1 in 2005. Aqueduct, three-year-olds and up, 1$\frac{1}{8}$ miles, dirt. Held April 9, 2005, with a gross value of $750,000. First held in 1925. First graded in 1973. Stakes record 1:47.16 (2005 Bellamy Road).

Year	Winner	Jockey	Second	Third	Strs	Time	1st Purse
2005	Bellamy Road, 3, 123	J. Castellano	Survivalist, 3, 123	Scrappy T, 3, 123	7	1:47.16	$450,000
2004	Tapit, 3, 123	R. A. Dominguez	Master David, 3, 123	Eddington, 3, 123	11	1:49.70	450,000
2003	Empire Maker, 3, 123	J. D. Bailey	Funny Cide, 3, 123	Kissin Saint, 3, 123	8	1:48.70	450,000
2002	Buddha, 3, 123	P. Day	Medaglia d'Oro, 3, 123	Sunday Break (Jpn), 3, 123	8	1:48.61	450,000
2001	Congaree, 3, 123	V. Espinoza	Monarchos, 3, 123	Richly Blended, 3, 123	6	1:47.96	450,000
2000	Fusaichi Pegasus, 3, 123	K. J. Desormeaux	Red Bullet, 3, 123	Aptitude, 3, 123	12	1:47.92	450,000
1999	Adonis, 3, 123	J. F. Chavez	Best of Luck, 3, 123	Cliquot, 3, 123	11	1:47.71	360,000
1998	Coronado's Quest, 3, 123	R. G. Davis	Dice Dancer, 3, 123	Parade Ground, 3, 123	11	1:47.47	300,000
1997	Captain Bodgit, 3, 123	A. O. Solis	Accelerator, 3, 123	Smokin Mel, 3, 123	10	1:48.39	300,000
1996	Unbridled's Song, 3, 123	M. E. Smith	In Contention, 3, 123	Romano Gucci, 3, 123	6	1:49.80	300,000
1995	Talkin Man, 3, 123	S. J. Sellers	‡Is Sveikatas, 3, 123	Candy Cone, 3, 123	8	1:49.24	300,000
1994	Irgun, 3, 123	G. L. Stevens	Go for Gin, 3, 123	Shiprock, 3, 123	9	1:49.07	300,000
1993	Koluccio Jimmy Al, 3, 116	P. Day	Too Wild, 3, 113	Bounding Daisy, 3, 116	8	1:48.09	49,140
	Storm Tower, 3, 126	R. Wilson	Tossofthecoin, 3, 126	Marked Tree, 3, 126	12	1:48.50	300,000
1992	Devil His Due, 3, 126	M. E. Smith	West by West, 3, 126	Rokeby (GB), 3, 126	12	1:49.32	300,000
	Al Sabin, 3, 117	K. J. Desormeaux	Justfortherecord, 3, 117	Jay Gee, 3, 117	8	1:49.24	49,086
1991	Cahill Road, 3, 126	C. Perret	Lost Mountain, 3, 126	Happy Jazz Band, 3, 126	10	1:48.44	300,000
1990	Thirty Six Red, 3, 126	M. E. Smith	Burnt Hills, 3, 126	Champaignforashley, 3, 126	10	1:50.40	362,400
1989	Easy Goer, 3, 126	P. Day	Rock Point, 3, 126	Triple Buck, 3, 126	6	1:50.60	340,800

Year	Winner	Jockey	Second	Third	Strs	Time	1st Purse
1988	**Private Terms**, 3, 126	C. W. Antley	Seeking the Gold, 3, 126	Cherokee Colony, 3, 126	10	1:47.20	$359,400
1987	**Gulch**, 3, 126	J. A. Santos	Gone West, 3, 126	Shawklit Won, 3, 126	8	1:49.00	354,300
1986	**Broad Brush**, 3, 126	V. A. Bracciale Jr.	Mogambo, 3, 126	Groovy, 3, 126	7	1:50.60	178,500
1985	**Eternal Prince**, 3, 126	R. Migliore	Proud Truth, 3, 126	Rhoman Rule, 3, 126	6	1:48.80	204,900
1984	**Leroy S.**, 3, 126	J. Cruguet	Raja's Shark, 3, 126	Bear Hunt, 3, 126	7	1:51.40	207,000
1983	**Bounding Basque**, 3, 126	G. McCarron	Country Pine, 3, 126	Aztec Red, 3, 126	8	1:51.40	100,980
	Slew o' Gold, 3, 126	E. Maple	Parfaitement, 3, 126	High Honors, 3, 126	7	1:51.00	101,700
1982	**Air Forbes Won**, 3, 126	A. T. Cordero Jr.	Shimatoree, 3, 126	Laser Light, 3, 126	10	1:51.00	105,120
1981	**Pleasant Colony**, 3, 126	J. Fell	Highland Blade, 3, 126	Cure the Blues, 3, 126	6	1:49.60	98,280
1980	**Plugged Nickle**, 3, 126	B. Thornburg	Colonel Moran, 3, 126	†Genuine Risk, 3, 121	11	1:50.80	87,300
1979	**Instrument Landing**, 3, 126	A. T. Cordero Jr.	Screen King, 3, 126	Czaravich, 3, 126	10	1:49.20	85,650
1978	**Believe It**, 3, 126	E. Maple	Darby Creek Road, 3, 126	Track Reward, 3, 126	11	1:49.80	65,940
1977	**Seattle Slew**, 3, 126	J. Cruguet	Sanhedrin, 3, 126	Catalan, 3, 126	7	1:49.60	66,180
1976	**Bold Forbes**, 3, 126	A. T. Cordero Jr.	On the Sly, 3, 126	Sonkisser, 3, 126	7	1:47.40	67,560
1975	**Foolish Pleasure**, 3, 126	J. Vasquez	Bombay Duck, 3, 126	Media, 3, 126	15	1:48.80	72,840
1974	**Flip Sal**, 3, 126	A. T. Cordero Jr.	Triple Crown, 3, 126	Sharp Gary, 3, 126	11	1:51.40	69,360
	Rube the Great, 3, 126	M. A. Rivera	Friendly Bee, 3, 126	Hudson County, 3, 126	11	1:49.60	69,660
1973	**Angle Light**, 3, 126	J. Vasquez	Sham, 3, 126	Secretariat, 3, 126	8	1:49.80	68,940

Named for Eugene D. Wood (d. 1924), a founder of Jamaica racetrack. Grade 2 1995-2001. Wood S. 1925-'26. Wood Memorial Invitational S. 1984-'93. Held at Jamaica 1925-'59. 1 mile 70 yards 1925-'39. 1⅛ miles 1940-'51. Two divisions 1974, 1983, 1992-'93. ‡Knockadoon finished second, DQ to eighth, 1995. †Denotes female.

Woodward Stakes

Grade 1 in 2005. Belmont Park, three-year-olds and up, 1⅛ miles, dirt. Held September 11, 2004, with a gross value of $500,000. First held in 1954. First graded in 1973. Stakes record 1:45.80 (1990 Dispersal; 1976 Forego).

Year	Winner	Jockey	Second	Third	Strs	Time	1st Purse
2004	**Ghostzapper**, 4, 126	J. Castellano	Saint Liam, 4, 126	Bowman's Band, 6, 126	7	1:46.38	$300,000
2003	**Mineshaft**, 4, 126	R. Albarado	Hold That Tiger, 3, 122	Puzzlement, 4, 126	5	1:46.21	300,000
2002	**Lido Palace (Chi)**, 5, 126	J. F. Chavez	Gander, 6, 126	Express Tour, 4, 126	6	1:47.75	300,000
2001	**Lido Palace (Chi)**, 4, 126	J. D. Bailey	Albert the Great, 4, 126	Tiznow, 4, 126	5	1:47.42	300,000
2000	**Lemon Drop Kid**, 4, 126	E. S. Prado	Behrens, 6, 126	Gander, 4, 126	5	1:50.53	300,000
1999	**River Keen (Ire)**, 7, 126	C. W. Antley	Almutawakel (GB), 4, 126	Stephen Got Even, 3, 121	7	1:46.85	300,000
1998	**Skip Away**, 5, 126	J. D. Bailey	Gentlemen (Arg), 6, 126	Running Stag, 4, 126	5	1:47.80	300,000
1997	**Formal Gold**, 4, 126	K. J. Desormeaux	Skip Away, 4, 126	Will's Way, 4, 126	5	1:47.51	300,000
1996	**Cigar**, 6, 126	J. D. Bailey	L'Carriere, 5, 126	Golden Larch, 5, 126	5	1:47.06	300,000
1995	**Cigar**, 5, 126	J. D. Bailey	Star Standard, 3, 126	Golden Larch, 4, 126	6	1:47.07	300,000
1994	**Holy Bull**, 3, 121	M. E. Smith	Devil His Due, 5, 126	Colonial Affair, 4, 126	8	1:46.89	300,000
1993	**Bertrando**, 4, 126	G. L. Stevens	Devil His Due, 5, 126	Valley Crossing, 5, 126	6	1:47.00	525,000
1992	**Sultry Song**, 4, 126	J. D. Bailey	Pleasant Tap, 5, 126	Out of Place, 5, 126	8	1:47.05	300,000
1991	**In Excess (Ire)**, 4, 126	G. L. Stevens	Farma Way, 4, 126	Festin (Arg), 5, 126	6	1:46.33	300,000
1990	**Dispersal**, 4, 123	C. W. Antley	Quiet American, 4, 117	Rhythm, 3, 120	8	**1:45.80**	354,000
1989	**Easy Goer**, 3, 122	P. Day	Its Acedemic, 5, 109	Forever Silver, 4, 119	5	2:01.00	485,400
1988	**Alysheba**, 4, 126	C. J. McCarron	Forty Niner, 3, 119	Waquoit, 5, 122	8	1:59.40	498,600
1987	**Polish Navy**, 3, 116	R. P. Romero	Gulch, 3, 118	Creme Fraiche, 5, 119	9	1:47.00	357,000
1986	**Precisionist**, 5, 126	C. J. McCarron	†Lady's Secret, 4, 121	Personal Flag, 3, 110	5	1:46.00	199,200
1985	**Track Barron**, 4, 123	A. T. Cordero Jr.	Vanlandingham, 4, 123	Chief's Crown, 3, 121	4	1:46.60	200,400
1984	**Slew o' Gold**, 4, 126	A. T. Cordero Jr.	Shifty Sheik, 5, 116	Bet Big, 4, 116	6	1:47.80	175,200
1983	**Slew o' Gold**, 3, 118	A. T. Cordero Jr.	Bates Motel, 4, 123	Sing Sing, 5, 119	10	1:46.60	138,900
1982	**Island Whirl**, 4, 123	A. T. Cordero Jr.	Silver Buck, 4, 126	Silver Supreme, 4, 126	7	1:46.80	136,500
1981	**Pleasant Colony**, 3, 123	A. T. Cordero Jr.	Amber Pass, 4, 126	Herb Water, 4, 116	9	1:47.20	137,400
1980	**Spectacular Bid**, 4, 126	W. Shoemaker			1	2:02.40	73,300
1979	**Affirmed**, 4, 126	L. A. Pincay Jr.	Coastal, 3, 120	Czaravich, 3, 120	5	2:01.60	114,600
1978	**Seattle Slew**, 4, 126	A. T. Cordero Jr.	Exceller, 5, 126	It's Freezing, 6, 126	5	2:00.00	97,800
1977	**Forego**, 7, 133	W. Shoemaker	Silver Series, 3, 114	Great Contractor, 4, 115	10	1:48.00	105,000
1976	**Forego**, 6, 135	W. Shoemaker	Dance Spell, 3, 115	dh- Honest Pleasure, 3, 121	10	**1:45.80**	103,250
				dh- Stumping, 6, 109			
1975	**Forego**, 5, 126	H. Gustines	Wajima, 3, 119	Group Plan, 5, 126	6	2:27.20	64,920
1974	**Forego**, 4, 126	H. Gustines	Arbees Boy, 4, 126	Group Plan, 4, 126	11	2:27.40	69,240
1973	**Prove Out**, 4, 126	J. Velasquez	Secretariat, 3, 119	*Cougar II, 7, 126	5	2:25.80	64,920

Named for William Woodward (1876-1953), chairman of the Jockey Club from 1930-'50; owned Belair Stud. Woodward H. 1955, 1976-'77, 1988-'90. Held at Aqueduct 1959-'60, 1962-'67. 1 mile 1954. 1¼ miles 1956-'71, 1978-'80, 1988-'89. 1½ miles 1972-'75. Dead heat for third 1976. †Denotes female. Won in a walkover 1980.

Yellow Ribbon Stakes

Grade 1 in 2005. Santa Anita Park, three-year-olds and up, fillies and mares, 1¼ miles, turf. Held October 2, 2004, with a gross value of $500,000. First held in 1977. First graded in 1979. Stakes record 1:57.60 (1989 Brown Bess).

Year	Winner	Jockey	Second	Third	Strs	Time	1st Purse
2004	**Light Jig (GB)**, 4, 123	R. R. Douglas	Tangle (Ire), 4, 123	Katdogawn (GB), 4, 123	10	1:59.28	$300,000
2003	**Tates Creek**, 5, 123	P. A. Valenzuela	Musical Chimes, 3, 118	Crazy Ensign (Arg), 7, 123	8	2:00.77	300,000

Year	Winner	Jockey	Second	Third	Strs	Time	1st Purse
2002	Golden Apples (Ire), 4, 123	P. A. Valenzuela	Voodoo Dancer, 4, 123	Banks Hill (GB), 4, 123	6	1:59.72	$300,000
2001	Janet (GB), 4, 123	D. R. Flores	Tranquility Lake, 6, 123	Al Desima (GB), 4, 123	8	1:58.64	300,000
2000	Tranquility Lake, 5, 123	E. J. Delahoussaye	Spanish Fern, 5, 123	Polaire (Ire), 4, 123	6	2:02.98	300,000
1999	Spanish Fern, 4, 123	C. J. McCarron	Caffe Latte (Ire), 3, 118	Shabby Chic, 3, 118	7	1:59.52	300,000
1998	Fiji (GB), 4, 122	K. J. Desormeaux	‡Sonja's Faith (Ire), 4, 122	Pomona (GB), 5, 122	10	2:05.23	300,000
1997	Ryafan, 3, 118	A. O. Solis	Fanjica (Ire), 5, 122	Memories of Silver, 4, 122	8	2:03.89	300,000
1996	Donna Viola (GB), 4, 122	G. L. Stevens	Real Connection, 5, 122	Dixie Pearl, 4, 122	8	2:00.62	360,000
1995	Alpride (Ire), 4, 122	C. J. McCarron	Angel in My Heart (Fr), 3, 118	Bold Ruritana, 5, 122	12	2:01.68	360,000
1994	Aube Indienne (Fr), 4, 122	K. J. Desormeaux	Fondly Remembered, 4, 122	Zoonaqua, 4, 122	11	2:02.32	240,000
1993	Possibly Perfect, 3, 118	C. S. Nakatani	Tribulation, 3, 118	Miatuschka, 5, 122	13	2:02.91	240,000
1992	Super Staff, 4, 123	K. J. Desormeaux	Flawlessly, 4, 123	Campagnarde (Arg), 5, 123	9	1:59.36	240,000
1991	Kostroma (Ire), 5, 123	K. J. Desormeaux	Flawlessly, 3, 119	Fire the Groom, 4, 123	13	2:01.01	240,000
1990	Plenty of Grace, 3, 119	W. H. McCauley	Petite Ile (Ire), 4, 123	Royal Touch (Ire), 5, 123	13	1:58.40	240,000
1989	Brown Bess, 7, 123	J. L. Kaenel	Darby's Daughter, 3, 119	Colorado Dancer (Ire), 3, 119	11	1:57.60	240,000
1988	Delighter, 3, 119	C. J. McCarron	Nastique, 4, 123	No Review, 3, 119	12	2:02.40	240,000
1987	Carotene, 4, 123	J. A. Santos	Nashmeel, 3, 119	Khariyda (Fr), 3, 119	12	2:03.80	240,000
1986	Bonne Ile (GB), 5, 123	F. Toro	Top Corsage, 3, 118	Carotene, 3, 118	12	2:01.40	240,000
1985	Estrapade, 5, 123	W. Shoemaker	Alydar's Best, 3, 118	La Koumia (Fr), 3, 118	11	2:00.40	240,000
1984	Sabin, 4, 123	E. Maple	Grise Mine (Fr), 3, 118	Estrapade, 4, 123	8	2:00.00	240,000
1983	Sangue (Ire), 5, 123	W. Shoemaker	L'Attrayante (Fr), 3, 119	Infinite, 3, 119	12	2:02.20	240,000
1982	‡Castilla, 3, 119	R. Sibille	Avigaition, 3, 119	Sangue (Ire), 4, 123	12	1:58.60	180,000
1981	Queen to Conquer, 5, 123	M. Castaneda	Star Pastures (GB), 3, 119	Ack's Secret, 5, 123	11	1:58.60	180,000
1980	Kilijaro (Ire), 4, 123	A. Lequeux	Ack's Secret, 4, 123	Queen to Conquer, 4, 123	10	1:59.20	120,000
1979	Country Queen, 4, 123	L. A. Pincay Jr.	Prize Spot, 3, 119	Giggling Girl, 5, 123	10	2:00.20	90,000
1978	Amazer, 3, 119	W. Shoemaker	Drama Critic, 4, 123	Surera (Arg), 5, 123	9	1:59.20	90,000
1977	*Star Ball, 5, 123	H. Grant	Swingtime, 5, 123	Theia (Fr), 4, 123	11	2:02.60	60,000

Named for the song, "Tie a Yellow Ribbon." Yellow Ribbon Invitational S. 1979-'87, 1989-'94. ‡Avigaition finished first, DQ to second, 1982. ‡See You Soon (Fr) finished second, DQ to fourth, 1998.

Yerba Buena Breeders' Cup Handicap

Grade 3 in 2005. Golden Gate Fields, three-year-olds and up, fillies and mares, 1 1/16 miles, turf. Held May 21, 2005, with a gross value of $80,625. First held in 1973. First graded in 1978. Stakes record 1:41.72 (2005 Pickle [GB]).

Year	Winner	Jockey	Second	Third	Strs	Time	1st Purse
2005	Pickle (GB), 4, 118	R. A. Baze	Marla Bay, 4, 116	Midwife, 4, 117	6	1:41.72	$41,250
2004	A B Noodle, 5, 116	J. M. Castro	Marwood, 4, 116	Hooked On Niners, 5, 116	6	1:46.66	68,750
2003	Chiming (Ire), 5, 116	C. S. Nakatani	Noches De Rosa (Chi), 5, 119	Lindsay Jean, 5, 118	7	1:45.41	55,000
2002	Peu a Peu (Ger), 4, 115	R. A. Baze	Janet (GB), 5, 122	Racene, 5, 115	6	2:16.39	55,000
2001	Janet (GB), 4, 115	D. R. Flores	Keemoon (Fr), 4, 121	Alexine (Arg), 5, 119	4	2:17.09	82,500
2000	Gleefully, 4, 113	R. Q. Meza	Country Garden (GB), 5, 116	Marie de Bayeux (Fr), 4, 113	8	2:15.99	110,000
1999	Blending Element (Ire), 6, 117	G. K. Gomez	Queen Douna (Fr), 6, 113	Midnight Line, 4, 117	6	2:17.26	120,000
1998	Miss Universal (Ire), 5, 114	P. Mercado	Proud Fillie (Fr), 4, 115	Squeak (GB), 4, 118	12	2:15.72	75,000
1997	De Puntillas (GB), 5, 116	V. Espinoza	Dynatar, 5, 117	Tricky Code, 6, 116	11	1:46.71	60,000
1996	Fanjica (Ire), 4, 114	D. Carr	Nimble Mind, 4, 115	Dynatar, 4, 113	8	2:17.42	60,000
1995	Work the Crowd, 4, 123	R. A. Baze	Late Sailing, 5, 116	Ask Anita, 5, 117	5	1:49.27	68,750
1994	Ask Anita, 4, 116	V. Belvoir	Miami Sands (Ire), 4, 115	Oxava (Fr), 4, 115	7	2:15.55	55,000
1993	Party Cited, 4, 117	R. J. Warren Jr.	Silvered, 6, 115	Rougeur, 4, 115	6	2:15.11	55,000
1992	Flaming Torch (Ire), 5, 114	R. A. Baze	Indian Chris (Brz), 5, 116	Silvered, 5, 114	8	2:16.26	82,500
1991	Free At Last (GB), 4, 120	R. D. Hansen	Noble and Nice, 5, 117	Louve Bleue, 4, 113	6	2:15.10	82,500
1990	Petite Ile (Ire), 4, 118	C. A. Black	Double Wedge, 5, 112	Brown Bess, 8, 124	5	2:15.60	82,500
1989	Brown Bess, 7, 119	J. L. Kaenel	Carmanetta, 5, 114	Flattering News, 4, 111	10	2:15.60	82,500
1988	Magdelaine (NZ), 5, 113	T. T. Doocy	Sweet Roberta (Fr), 4, 116	Top Corsage, 5, 118	7	2:14.40	82,500
1987	Ivor's Image, 4, 119	C. J. McCarron	Micenas (Arg), 5, 115	Royal Regatta (NZ), 8, 114	5	2:29.60	82,500
1986	Scythe (GB), 5, 113	T. M. Chapman	Heat Spell, 4, 115	Lock's Dream, 4, 114	11	2:32.20	85,000
1985	Salt Spring (Arg), 6, 115	T. M. Chapman	High Spruce, 5, 111	L'Attrayante (Fr), 5, 120	7	2:30.20	95,800
1984	Fact Finder, 5, 115	M. Castaneda	Lido Isle, 4, 114	Her Decision, 5, 115	7	2:30.20	107,200
1983	Dilmoun (Ire), 4, 111	J. J. Steiner	Latrone, 6, 112	Berry Bush, 6, 119	10	2:31.60	82,350
1982	Sangue (Ire), 4, 117	T. M. Chapman	Berry Bush, 5, 119	Mademoiselle Ivor, 4, 112	10	2:16.40	78,400
1981	Mairzy Doates, 5, 120	F. Mena	Princess Karenda, 4, 123	Princess Toby, 6, 117	10	2:16.40	78,550
1980	Mairzy Doates, 4, 116	F. Mena	Sisterhood, 5, 121	Smaller Bicker, 4, 113	11	2:15.00	66,900
1978	*Star Ball, 6, 124	D. G. McHargue	Up to Juliet, 5, 114	Surera (Arg), 5, 112	8	2:13.60	63,800
1977	*Star Ball, 5, 121	J. L. Vargas	*Bastonera II, 6, 124	Up to Juliet, 4, 117	8	2:14.80	48,350
1976	Our First Delight, 4, 120	E. Munoz	Graceful Banner, 4, 112	Larking Party, 4, 113	11	2:16.40	33,400
1975	Joli Vert, 4, 115	F. Olivares	Lucky Spell, 4, 122	Gentleweave, 4, 106	6	2:16.80	31,000
1974	Merry Madeleine, 4, 113	F. Mena	Hurry Countess, 4, 110	Hum Dum, 6, 111	9	2:31.40	17,625
1973	*Live Forever, 4, 112	J. T. Gonzalez	Fleet Ahead, 6, 112	Homespun, 4, 111	9	2:19.60	12,050

Named for Yerba Buena Island in San Francisco Bay, California. Grade 2 1982-'83. Not graded 1990-'92. Yerba Buena H. 1973-'98. Held at Bay Meadows 2001-'04. 1⅜ miles 1973, 1975-'82, 1988-'94, 1996, 1998-2002. 1½ miles 1974, 1983-'87. 1⅛ miles 1995. About 1⅛ miles 2003-'04.

Previously Graded Stakes

Race	Last Grade	Track	Year Last Graded
Affectionately H.	G3	Aqueduct	2004
Ak-Sar-Ben Oaks	G3	Ak-Sar-Ben	1997
Alabama Derby	G3	Louisiana Downs	1997
Alibhai H.	G3	Santa Anita Park	1985
Allegheny S.	G3	Keystone	1977
Anne Arundel S.	G3	Pimlico	2004
Anoakia S.	G3	Santa Anita Park	1987
Ark-La-Tex H.	G3	Louisiana Downs	1999
Arlington Breeders' Cup Oaks	G3	Arlington Park	2004
Ascot H.	G3	Bay Meadows	2002
Assault H.	G3	Aqueduct	1997
Astoria Breeders' Cup S.	G3	Belmont Park	1994
Bahamas S.	G3	Hialeah	1974
Baltimore Breeders' Cup H.	G3	Pimlico	2003
Bay Meadows Oaks	G3	Bay Meadows	1998
Bel Air H.	G2	Hollywood Park	2001
Benjamin Franklin H.	G3	Garden State	1974
Best Turn S.	G3	Aqueduct	1996
Betsy Ross H.	G3	Garden State	1995
Black Helen H.	G2	Hialeah	2001
Board of Governors' H.	G3	Ak-Sar-Ben	1993
Boardwalk S.	G3	Atlantic City	1975
Bold Reason H.	G3	Saratoga	1988
Bougainvillea H.	G3	Hialeah	2001
Brandywine Turf H.	G3	Delaware Park	1973
Brighton Beach H.	G3	Belmont Park	1983
Brown Bess H.	G3	Golden Gate Fields	2004
Bryn Mawr S.	G3	Keystone	1975
Budweiser H.	G3	Fairmount Park	1989
Busher S.	G3	Aqueduct	1998
Caballero H.	G3	Hollywood Park	1978
Cabrillo H.	G3	Del Mar	1990
California Derby	G3	Golden Gate Fields	1999
California Jockey Club H.	G3	Bay Meadows	1996
California Juvenile S.	G3	Bay Meadows	2000
Camden H.	G3	Garden State	1974
Canadian Turf H.	G3	Gulfstream Park	2004
Canterbury Oaks	G3	Canterbury	1989
Carousel H.	G3	Laurel Park	1992
Chaposa Springs H.	G3	Calder Race Course	2004
Cherry Hill Mile S.	G3	Garden State	1996
Chesapeake H.	G3	Bowie	1975
Choice H.	G3	Monmouth	1995
Chrysanthemum H.	G3	Laurel Park	1989
Coaltown Breeders' Cup H.	G3	Aqueduct	1995
Colin S.	G3	Belmont Park	1994
Colleen S.	G3	Monmouth	1974
Colonial H.	G3	Garden State	1976
Columbiana H.	G3	Hialeah	1989
Correction H.	G3	Aqueduct	1982
Countess Fager H.	G3	Golden Gate Fields	1994
Cowdin S.	G3	Belmont Park	2002
Cradle S.	G3	River Downs	2004
Cygnet S.	G3	Hollywood Park	1974
Dade Turf Classic	G3	Calder Race Course	1975
De La Rose H.	G3	Gulfstream Park	2002
Delaware Valley H.	G3	Garden State	1974
Derby Trial S.	G3	Churchill Downs	2004
Display H.	G3	Aqueduct	1989
Donald LeVine Memorial H.	G3	Philadelphia Park	2004
Donald P. Ross H.	G3	Delaware Park	1981
Dover S.	G3	Delaware Park	1974
Dragoon S.	G3	Liberty Bell	1974
El Camino Real S.	G3	Bay Meadows	1984
El Dorado H.	G3	Hollywood Park	1981
Endurance S.	G3	Meadowlands	1995
Everglades S.	G3	Hialeah	2001
Fair Grounds Classic	G3	Fair Grounds	1987
Fairmount Derby	G3	Fairmount Park	1995
Fall Highweight H.	G3	Aqueduct	2004
Fashion S.	G3	Belmont Park	1974
Fastness H.	G3	Hollywood Park	2001
Federico Tesio S.	G3	Pimlico	1997
Finger Lakes Breeders' Cup S.	G3	Finger Lakes	1999
Flamingo S.	G3	Hialeah	2001
Flintlock S.	G3	Keystone	1974
Flirtation S.	G3	Pimlico	1974
Florida Oaks	G3	Tampa Bay Downs	2003
Florida Turf Cup H.	G3	Calder Race Course	1989
Forerunner S.	G3	Keeneland	1998
Forest Hills H.	G2	Belmont Park	2002
Ft. Lauderdale H.	G3	Gulfstream Park	2002
Gallant Fox H.	G3	Aqueduct	2002
Garden State Breeders' Cup H.	G3	Garden State	1995
Garden State S.	G3	Garden State	1994
Golden Gate Derby	G3	Golden Gate Fields	2004
Golden Harvest H.	G3	Louisiana Downs	1993
Golden Poppy H.	G3	Golden Gate Fields	1994
Gold Rush Futurity	G3	Arapahoe Park	1984
Governor's S.	G1	Belmont Park	1975
Governor's Cup H.	G3	Bowie	1985
Governor's Cup H.	G3	Arlington Park	1974
Great American S.	G3	Aqueduct	1974
Grey Lag H.	G3	Aqueduct	1999
Haggin S.	G3	Hollywood Park	1974
Hall of Fame Breeders' Cup H.	G3	Thistledown	2000
Harold C. Ramser Sr. H.	G3	Santa Anita Park	1989
Hawthorne Breeders' Cup H.	G3	Hawthorne	1993
Hawthorne Juvenile S.	G3	Hawthorne	1982
Heirloom H.	G3	Liberty Bell	1974
Heritage S.	G2	Keystone	1978
Hessian H.	G3	Keystone	1974
Hialeah Turf Cup H.	G2	Hialeah	2001
Hibiscus S.	G3	Hialeah	1973
Hillsborough H.	G3	Bay Meadows	2000
Hobson H.	G2	Keystone	1977
Hollywood Express H.	G3	Hollywood Park	1974
Honey Bee H.	G3	Meadowlands	2001
Honeybee S.	G3	Oaklawn Park	2002
Indian Maid H.	G3	Hawthorne	1978
Interborough H.	G3	Aqueduct	2000
Island Whirl H.	G3	Louisiana Downs	1989
Jasmine S.	G3	Hialeah	1974
Jersey Belle H.	G3	Garden State	1977
Jersey Derby	G3	Monmouth Park	2004
John B. Campbell H.	G3	Pimlico	1999
John Henry H.	G2	Hollywood Park	1994
Junior League S.	G3	Hollywood Park	1974
Junior Miss S.	G3	Del Mar	1992
Juvenile S.	G3	Ak-Sar-Ben	1988
Kelly-Olympic H.	G3	Atlantic City	1979
Keystone H.	G3	Liberty Bell	1974
Kindergarten S.	G3	Liberty Bell	1974
Ladies H.	G3	Aqueduct	2004
Lady Canterbury H.	G3	Canterbury	1991
Lakeside H.	G2	Hollywood Park	1980
Lamplighter H.	G3	Monmouth Park	1998
Laurance Armour H.	G3	Arlington Park	1996

Race	Last Grade	Track	Year Last Graded
Laurel Dash S.	G3	Laurel Park	2000
Laurel Turf Cup S.	G3	Laurel Park	2000
Lazaro S. Barrera H.	G3	Hollywood Park	1998
Letellier Memorial H.	G3	Fair Grounds	1974
Linda Vista H.	G3	Santa Anita Park	1996
Little Silver H.	G3	Monmouth Park	1988
Longacres Derby	G3	Longacres	1988
Longfellow H.	G3	Monmouth Park	1997
Long Look Breeders' Cup H.	G3	Meadowlands	1997
Louisiana Downs H.	G3	Louisiana Downs	1996
Louis R. Rowan H.	G3	Santa Anita Park	1998
Magnolia S.	G3	Oaklawn Park	1974
Margate H.	G3	Atlantic City	1978
Maria H.	G3	Garden State	1996
Marlboro Cup Invitational H.	G1	Belmont Park	1987
Marylander H.	G3	Pimlico	1981
Mermaid S.	G3	Atlantic City	1975
Michigan Mile and One-Eighth H.	G2	Detroit	1993
Militia S.	G3	Keystone	1975
Mimosa S.	G3	Hialeah	1973
Minnesota Derby S.	G2	Canterbury	1991
Minuteman H.	G3	Keystone	1978
Miss America H.	G3	Golden Gate Fields	1996
Miss Grillo S.	G3	Belmont Park	2000
Miss Woodford S.	G3	Monmouth Park	1974
Monmouth Park Breeders' Cup H.	G3	Monmouth Park	1992
Morven S.	G3	Meadowlands	1987
Nassau County H.	G1	Belmont Park	1993
New Hampshire Sweepstakes H.	G3	Rockingham	2002
New Hope S.	G3	Keystone	1975
New Jersey Turf Classic S.	G3	Meadowlands	1993
Norristown H.	G3	Philadelphia Park	1993
Oil Capitol H.	G3	Hawthorne	1975
Oklahoma Derby	G3	Remington Park	2004
Omaha Gold Cup S.	G3	Ak-Sar-Ben	1994
Open Fire S.	G3	Delaware Park	1978
Pageant S.	G3	Atlantic City	1975
Pasadena S.	G3	Santa Anita Park	1974
Paterson H.	G3	Meadowlands	1995
Patriot S.	G3	Keystone	1978
Paumonok H.	G3	Aqueduct	1978
Pebbles H.	G3	Belmont Park	2004
Pennsylvania Governor's Cup H.	G3	Penn National	1989
Philadelphia H.	G3	Monmouth Park	1974
Phoenix Gold Cup S.	G3	Turf Paradise	1997
Pilgrim S.	G3	Belmont Park	2000
Pimlico Oaks	G3	Pimlico	1991
Pimlico S.	G3	Pimlico	1974
Poinsettia S.	G3	Hialeah	1989
Polynesian H.	G3	Pimlico	1994
Post-Deb S.	G2	Monmouth Park	1993
President's Cup S.	G3	Ak-Sar-Ben	1988
Princess S.	G2	Hollywood Park	2001
Princeton S.	G3	Garden State	1974
Quaker H.	G3	Liberty Bell	1974
Queen Charlotte H.	G3	Monmouth Park	1992
Queen's H.	G3	Ak-Sar-Ben	1993
Rare Treat H.	G3	Aqueduct	2002
Reeve Schley Jr. S.	G3	Monmouth Park	2001
Regret H.	G3	Monmouth Park	1974
Riggs H.	G3	Pimlico	1992
River Cities Breeders' Cup S.	G3	Louisiana Downs	1998
Roamer H.	G3	Aqueduct	1983
Rolling Green H.	G3	Golden Gate Fields	1994
Roseben H.	G3	Belmont Park	1995
Rosemont S.	G2	Delaware Park	1976
Round Table S.	G3	Arlington Park	2001
Royal Palm H.	G3	Hialeah	1999
Rutgers H.	G3	Meadowlands	1996
Ruthless S.	G3	Aqueduct	1982
San Jacinto S.	G2	Santa Anita Park	1977
San Miguel S.	G3	Santa Anita Park	2004
Santa Anita Breeders' Cup H.	G3	Santa Anita Park	1995
Santa Paula S.	G3	Santa Anita Park	1974
Saul Silberman H.	G3	Calder	1979
Schuylkill S.	G3	Liberty Bell	1974
Sea O Erin H.	G3	Arlington Park	1994
Seashore H.	G3	Atlantic City	1973
Select H.	G3	Monmouth Park	1974
Selima S.	G3	Laurel	1999
Seminole H.	G2	Hialeah Park	1989
Seneca H.	G3	Saratoga	1997
Sentinel S.	G3	Liberty Bell	1974
Sheridan S.	G3	Arlington Park	1996
Sierra Madre H.	G3	Santa Anita Park	1990
Sierra Nevada H.	G3	Santa Anita Park	1985
Signature S.	G3	Keystone	1976
Snow Goose H.	G3	Laurel	1996
Sorority S.	G3	Monmouth Park	2003
Southwest S.	G3	Oaklawn Park	1999
Spicy Living H.	G3	Rockingham	1994
Spotlight Breeders' Cup H.	G3	Hollywood Park	1994
Stymie S.	G3	Aqueduct	2002
Suffolk Downs Sprint H.	G3	Suffolk Downs	1988
Sunny Slope S.	G3	Santa Anita	1984
Sunrise H.	G3	Atlantic City	1973
Super Bowl S.	G3	Gulfstream Park	1997
Susquehanna H.	G3	Keystone	1978
Sussex Turf H.	G3	Delaware Park	1975
Sweetest Chant S.	G3	Gulfstream Park	2000
Swift S.	G3	Aqueduct	1989
Swoon's Son H.	G3	Arlington Park	1996
Tanforan H.	G3	Golden Gate Fields	2002
Thanksgiving Day H.	G3	Bay Meadows	1979
Thomas D. Nash Memorial H.	G3	Sportsman's Park	1993
Tidal H.	G2	Belmont Park	1993
Tremont S.	G3	Belmont Park	2003
Trenton H.	G3	Garden State	1994
Tyro S.	G3	Monmouth Park	1974
Valley Forge H.	G3	Garden State	1974
Ventnor H.	G3	Monmouth Park	1975
Villager S.	G3	Keystone	1977
Vineland H.	G3	Garden State	1996
Virginia Belle S.	G3	Bowie	1974
Washington, D.C., International H.	G1	Laurel Park	1994
Week of Fame Fortune H.	G3	Fair Grounds	1990
What a Pleasure S.	G3	Calder	2000
Whitemarsh H.	G3	Keystone	1977
Widener H.	G3	Hialeah	2001
William du Pont Jr. H.	G3	Delaware Park	1981
William P. Kyne H.	G3	Bay Meadows	1999
Windy City H.	G3	Sportsman's Park	1973
Woodlawn S.	G3	Pimlico	1988
World's Playground S.	G3	Atlantic City	1979
Young America Breeders' Cup S.	G3	Meadowlands	1995
Youthful S.	G3	Belmont Park	1974

2004 North American Stakes Races

Accordant H. (R), The Meadowlands, Oct. 30, $60,000, 3&up, New Jersey-bred, 6f, 1:09.58, OUR WILDCAT, Jay's Wish, Trueamericanspirit, 8 started.

Achievement H. (R), Woodbine, July 1, $159,900, 3yo, Canadianbred, 6f, 1:08.99, TWISTED WIT, Cut and Shoot, Dashing Admiral, 5 started.

Ack Ack H., Hollywood Park, May 31, $81,225, 3&up, 7^1/$_2$f, 1:28.02, TASTE OF PARADISE, Buddy Gil, Black Bart, 8 started.

ACK ACK H.-G3, Churchill Downs, Oct. 31, $165,300, 3&up, 7^1/$_2$f, 1:29.48, SIR CHEROKEE, Fire Slam, Slate Run, 6 started.

A. C. Kemp H., The Downs at Albuquerque, Sept. 22, $33,750, 2yo, 7f, 1:25.02, RAILROAD, Time to Divorce, Takin Issue, 9 started.

ACORN S.-G1, Belmont Park, June 4, $250,000, 3yo, f, 1m, 1:34.89, ISLAND SAND, Society Selection, Friendly Michelle, 8 started.

Adena Springs Matchmaker S., Fort Erie, June 13, $77,000, 3&up, f&m, 5fT, :58.55, DRESSED FOR ACTION, Soon to Be Single, Leading Role, 10 started.

Adena Springs Matchmaker S., Remington Park, Aug. 8, $40,000, 3&up, f&m, 5fT, :57.72, FLEETA DIF, Queen of Mecca, My Golden Tripp, 12 started.

ADENA STALLIONS' MISS PREAKNESS S.-G3, Pimlico, May 14, $100,000, 3yo, f, 6f, 1:10.97, FOREST MUSIC, Stephan's Angel, Fall Fashion, 11 started.

Adesa Auto Glass H., Marquis Downs, June 25, $5,000, 3&up, f&m, 6f, 1:12.53, RED PARKA MARY, Brite Steel, She's Nifty, 6 started.

AFFECTIONATELY H.-G3, Aqueduct, Jan. 17, $109,600, 3&up, f&m, 1^1/$_8$m, 1:44.02, AUSTIN'S MOM, Golden Damsel, Consort Music, 8 started.

AFFIRMED H.-G3, Hollywood Park, June 19, $110,200, 3yo, 1^1/$_16$m, 1:42.11, BOOMZEEBOOM, Twice as Bad, Wimplestiltskin, 9 started.

Affirmed S. (R), Calder Race Course, Sept. 6, $125,000, 2yo, progeny of eligible Florida stallions, 7f, 1:26, PRECOCIOUS UNITY, Favre, B. B. Best, 7 started.

Afleet S. (R), Woodbine, May 29, $106,000, 3yo, Canadian-bred, 6f, 1:10.20, CUT AND SHOOT, Imperial Alydeed, Langburg, 6 started.

African Prince S. (R), Suffolk Downs, June 5, $40,000, 3yo, Massachusetts-bred, 6f, 1:11.88, SENOR LADD, Strongestsovereign, Episode On Tour, 8 started.

Agassiz S. (R), Assiniboia Downs, Aug. 21, $39,200, 3&up, c&g, Manitoba-bred, 1m, 1:39.20, GUS AGAIN, Minus Three, His Money, 5 started.

A GLEAM INVITATIONAL H.-G2, Hollywood Park, July 10, $150,000, 3&up, f&m, 7f, 1:21.16, DREAM OF SUMMER, Tucked Away, Elusive Diva, 9 started.

Ahwatukee Express S., Turf Paradise, Oct. 23, $40,000, 3yo, f, 6f, 1:08.32, WIND FLOW, Muir Beach, Forward Glance, 6 started.

Airline S., Louisiana Downs, June 5, $50,000, 3yo, 6f, 1:09.63, SOUTH AFRICA, Smalltown Slew, Britt's Jules, 7 started.

A. J. Foyt S. (R), Indiana Downs, June 20, $44,650, 3&up, Indianabred, 1^1/$_16$mT, 1:42.67, RED'S HONOR, Gottabeachboy, If I Were You, 9 started.

Alabama Belle S. (R), Louisiana Downs, Sept. 10, $55,000, 3&up, f&m, Alabama-bred, 6f, 1:10.72, COMALAGOLD, She's a Punter, Bama Belle, 11 started.

ALABAMA S.-G1, Saratoga Race Course, Aug. 21, $750,000, 3yo, f, 1^1/$_4$m, 2:02.70, SOCIETY SELECTION, Stellar Jayne, Ashado, 8 started.

Alameda County Fillies and Mares H., Pleasanton, July 5, $50,595, 3&up, f&m, 1^1/$_16$m, 1:40.04, MARWOOD, Guidebook, Marty's Zee, 7 started.

Alamedan H., Pleasanton, July 11, $50,680, 3&up, 1^1/$_16$m, 1:40.14, ADREAMISBORN, Surprise Halo, Gold Ruckus, 8 started.

Albany S. (R), Saratoga Race Course, Aug. 25, $170,250, 3yo, New York-bred, 1^1/$_8$m, 1:50.42, WEST VIRGINIA, Everydayissaturday, Work With Me, 11 started.

Alberta Bred S. (R), Lethbridge, July 4, $12,050, 3&up, c&g, Albertabred, a6f, 1:09.80, ROYAL DEAL, Super Issue, Arctic Horizon, 7 started.

Alberta Bred S. (R), Lethbridge, July 4, $11,900, 3&up, f&m, Albertabred, 5^1/$_2$f, 1:07.40, GUILTYBYSUPISCION, Coco Mocha, Winsome Weekend, 6 started.

Alberta Bred S. (R), Lethbridge, Oct. 3, $11,900, 2yo, Alberta-bred, 5f, 1:03.60, SCRUFFY, It's Ali's Time, Cool N Cautious, 6 started.

Alberta Breeders' H. (R), Northlands Park, Sept. 25, $75,000, 3&up, Alberta-bred, 1^1/$_16$m, 1:45, BEAU BRASS, Candid Remark, Parlay's Prospect, 7 started.

Alberta Derby, Stampede Park, June 19, $100,000, 3yo, 1^1/$_16$m, 1:45, FLY ESTEEM, Lord Samarai, Tamingo, 11 started.

Alberta Oaks (R), Northlands Park, Sept. 25, $50,000, 3yo, f, Albertabred, 1m, 1:39.80, WEEKEND CEILIDH, The Cashew Queen, Robyn's Request, 10 started.

Alberta Premier's Futurity (R), Northlands Park, Sept. 25, $50,000, 2yo, Alberta-bred, 1m, 1:41.80, FOREVER RASCAL, Magic for Six, Bear Picasso, 9 started.

Alberta Railnet S., Grand Prairie, Aug. 14, $6,905, 3&up, f&m, 6^1/$_2$f, 1:20.20, REAL STERLING, Silver Request, Chaste Fondness, 6 started.

Albert Dominguez Memorial H. (R), Sunland Park, Dec. 19, $104,300, 3&up, New Mexico-bred, 1^1/$_16$m, 1:42.31, ROCKY GULCH, Cattleman Prospect, Casperino, 10 started.

Albuquerque Derby, The Downs at Albuquerque, Sept. 19, $34,300, 3yo, 1^1/$_16$m, 1:45.46, MR. TRIESTE, Western Ridge, Spirit Gulch, 9 started.

Alex M. Robb H. (R), Aqueduct, Dec. 31, $84,000, 3&up, New York-bred, 1^1/$_16$m, 1:44.67, LORD LANGFUHR, Rogue Agent, Halo Malone, 10 started.

ALFRED G. VANDERBILT H.-G2, Saratoga Race Course, Aug. 14, $200,000, 3&up, 6f, 1:08.04, SPEIGHTSTOWN, Clock Stopper, Gators N Bears, 6 started.

Algoma S. (R), Woodbine, Sept. 5, $125,625, 3&up, f&m, Canadianbred foals that passed through the sales ring as yearlings at any 2002 or previous sale conducted by Canadian Breeders' Sales or Woodbine Sales, 1^1/$_16$m, 1:43.54, ONE FOR ROSE, Winning Chance, Kissed by a Prince, 4 started.

ALL ALONG BREEDERS' CUP S.-G3, Colonial Downs, July 10, $200,000, 3&up, f&m, 1^1/$_8$mT, 1:50.08, FILM MAKER, Noisette, Lady Linda, 7 started.

All Brandy S. (R), Pimlico, Aug. 14, $72,750, 3&up, f&m, Marylandbred, 1^1/$_8$mT, 1:53.01, TRUE SENSATION, River Cruise, Grace Bay, 4 started.

Allen Bogan Memorial S. (R), Lone Star Park, Oct. 23, $75,000, 3&up, f&m, Texas-bred, 1m, 1:37.46, NATIVE ANNIE, Jester Rahab, Slewpy's Storm, 9 started.

All Sold Out S. (R), Fairmount Park, Aug. 24, $35,800, 2yo, f, Illinoisbred, f, 1:12.80, CART'S TURN, Denoun N Deverb, Royal Riley, 8 started.

Alma North S. (R), Timonium, Sept. 4, $50,000, 3&up, f&m, Marylandbred, a6^1/$_2$f, 1:16.41, RIBBON CANE, Spirited Game, Glory of Love, 8 started.

A. L. "Red" Erwin S. (R), Louisiana Downs, Aug. 8, $54,400, 3yo, Louisiana-bred, 7f, 1:23.53, NITRO CHIP, Walk This Way, Brandon's Marfa, 7 started.

Al Swihart Memorial H., Fonner Park, May 1, $25,000, 3&up, f&m, 6^1/$_2$f, 1:18.20, SOUTHERN ALERT, Burning Memories, Missy Can Do, 10 started.

Alysheba Breeders' Cup S., Lone Star Park, Oct. 2, $67,000, 3yo, 6f, 1:09.73, CHARMING SOCIALITE, Bwana Charlie, Danieltown, 10 started.

Alysheba S., Churchill Downs, April 30, $113,600, 3&up, 1^1/$_16$m, 1:44.31, CONGRATS, Perfect Drift, Kodema, 8 started.

Alysheba S., The Meadowlands, Oct. 29, $65,000, 3&up, 1^1/$_16$m, 1:41.83, ROARING FEVER, Long Term Success, Last Intention, 6 started.

Alyssa H. (R), Beulah Park, May 1, $15,000, 3&up, f&m, starters at Beulah Park in 2004, 6f, 1:10.81, JACKIE'S HOPE, Milady's Honor, Deliver the Gold, 10 started.

Alywow S., Woodbine, June 13, $112,000, 3yo, f, 6^1/$_2$fT, 1:14.97, SWEET PROBLEM, Emerald Earrings, Royal Liverpool, 11 started.

Amadevil H. (R), Columbus Races, Aug. 8, $15,700, 3&up, Nebraskabred, 6f, 1:13.60, WHAT ABOUT DAVID, Watch Me Dazzle, Irish Flyer, 7 started.

Ambassador of Luck H. (R), Philadelphia Park, Sept. 4, $50,000, 3&up, f&m, Pennsylvania-bred, 7f, 1:23.35, A VISION IN GRAY, Unique Opportunity, Valley of the Gods, 8 started.

Amelia Peabody S. (R), Suffolk Downs, Nov. 17, $40,000, 2yo, f, Massachusetts-bred, 6f, 1:14.34, BRANDED IN GOLD, Strawberry Patch, Sundance Shamrock, 7 started.

American Beauty S., Oaklawn Park, Feb. 7, $50,000, 4&up, f&m, 6f, 1:10.99, ETERNAL CUP, Holiday Runner, Emily Ring, 7 started.

AMERICAN DERBY-G2, Arlington Park, July 24, $250,000, 3yo, 1³/₁₆mT, 1:54.93, SIMPLE EXCHANGE (Ire), Cool Conductor, Toasted, 8 started.

AMERICAN H.-G2, Hollywood Park, July 4, $150,000, 3&up, 1¹/₈mT, 1:46.60, BAYAMO (Ire), Sarafan, Night Patrol, 5 started.

AMERICAN INVITATIONAL OAKS-G1, Hollywood Park, July 3, $750,000, 3&up, f&m, 1¹/₄mT, 2:01.54, TICKER TAPE (GB), Dance in the Mood (Jpn), Hollywood Story, 13 started.

AMERICAN TURF S.-G3, Churchill Downs, April 30, $113,800, 3yo, 1¹/₁₆mT, 1:43.31, KITTEN'S JOY, Prince Arch, Capo, 9 started.

AMSTERDAM S.-G2, Saratoga Race Course, Aug. 7, $150,000, 3yo, 6f, 1:09.40, BWANA CHARLIE, Pomeroy, Weigelia, 7 started.

Anark Millwrighting Mechanical S., Grand Prairie, Aug. 15, $4,000, 3&up, 7f, 1:25.40, LAFLEUR, Prosperity Rose, Roomtwothirtyeight, 5 started.

ANCIENT TITLE BREEDERS' CUP H.-G1, Santa Anita Park, Oct. 10, $213,000, 3&up, 6f, 1:08.84, PT'S GREY EAGLE, Pohave, Hombre Rapido, 8 started.

Anderson Fowler S., Monmouth Park, July 25, $55,000, 3yo, 5fT, :57.16, QUICK ACTION, Little Red Rocket, War's Prospect, 10 started.

Angenora S. (R), Thistledown, April 24, $40,000, 3&up, f&m, Ohiobred, 6f, 1:11, GABRIELES PRINCESS, Ashwood C C, Mercer's Launch, 10 started.

Angie C. S., Emerald Downs, July 11, $48,000, 2yo, f, 6f, 1:10.80, CHARMING COLLEEN, Nu Rays Arabella, Wind and Wine, 8 started.

Angi Go S. (R), Les Bois Park, June 23, $10,965, 3yo, f, Idahobred, 7f, 1:26, PARADISE WILD, Sheza Cats Meow, Hey Robbie, 8 started.

Anka Germania S., Calder Race Course, July 19, $40,000, 3&up, f&m, 1³/₈mT, 2:24.53, IOWA'S IMAGE, Sweet Little Avie, Harts Gap, 7 started.

Anna M. Fisher Debutante S., Ellis Park, Aug. 21, $83,750, 2yo, f, 7f, 1:25, KOTA, Angel Trumpet, Patience Pays, 8 started.

Ann Arbor S. (R), Great Lakes Downs, Aug. 13, $40,000, 3yo, f, Michigan-bred, 1m, 1:46.41, GOLD GINNY, Deb's Favoite Gift, Lunes Grito, 7 started.

ANNE ARUNDEL S.-G3, Pimlico, Nov. 20, $100,000, 3yo, f, 1¹/₁₆m, 1:49.37, ESSENCE, Rare Gift, Family Business, 11 started.

Ann Owens Distaff H. (R), Turf Paradise, April 24, $40,000, 3&up, f&m, Arizona-bred, 6f, 1:08.96, SAUCEONSIDE, Lakesville, Reatta Pass, 6 started.

Anoakia S., Santa Anita Park, Oct. 24, $85,350, 2yo, f, 6f, 1:10, HELLO LUCKY, No Bull Baby, Bulita, 10 started.

Answer Do S., Turf Paradise, May 7, $21,700, 3yo, 6¹/₂f, 1:16.34, KING JUSTIN, Frosty Event, Zal's Pal, 7 started.

Anthony Fair H., Anthony Downs, July 25, $4,600, 3&up, 6¹/₂f, 1:21.54, MARLIN'S RULER, Sunset Cruise, Fly Tricky, 7 started.

Anthony Thoroughbred Futurity, Anthony Downs, July 25, $20,000, 2yo, 5f, 1:01.83, SLEWS IN OZ NOW, Lady Legend, Baby Van, 8 started.

Appalachian S., Keeneland, April 14, $113,500, 3yo, f, 1mT, 1:37.58, LUCIFER'S STONE, Western Ransom, Honey Ryder, 9 started.

APPLE BLOSSOM H.-G1, Oaklawn Park, April 3, $500,000, 4&up, f&m, 1¹/₁₆m, 1:41.24, AZERI, Star Parade (Arg), Wild Spirit (Chi), 6 started.

APPLETON H.-G3, Gulfstream Park, Jan. 4, $150,000, 3&up, 1mT, 1:34.40, MILLENNIUM DRAGON (GB), Political Attack, Proud Man, 12 started.

AQUEDUCT H.-G3, Aqueduct, Jan. 17, $110,100, 3&up, 1¹/₁₆m, 1:42.13, SEATTLE FITZ (Arg), Evening Attire, Rogue Agent, 8 started.

Arapahoe Park Sprint H., Arapahoe Park, July 11, $27,825, 3&up, 6f, 1:08.20, ABSOLUTELY TRUE, Perfect Fit, Lukfata Louis, 10 started.

ARCADIA H.-G2, Santa Anita Park, April 3, $150,000, 4&up, 1¹/₈mT, 1:47.90, DIPLOMATIC BAG, Statement, Senene (Chi), 7 started.

Arcadia S. (R), Louisiana Downs, June 13, $50,000, 3yo, Louisianabred, 6f, 1:11.43, SKYMEISTER, Brandon's Marfa, Walk This Way, 8 started.

Arctic Queen H. (R), Finger Lakes, June 20, $50,000, 3&up, f&m, New York-bred, 6f, 1:10.15, TRAVELATOR, A Smart Punch, Cologny, 7 started.

ARISTIDES BREEDERS' CUP H.-G3, Churchill Downs, June 19, $162,150, 3&up, 6f, 1:09.04, CHAMPALI, Beau's Town, Battle Won, 6 started.

Arizona Breeders' Derby (R), Turf Paradise, April 24, $48,987, 3yo, Arizona-bred, 1¹/₁₆m, 1:44.78, OVERLAND ROAD, Samurai Nanao, Swiss Mocha, 7 started.

Arizona Breeders' Futurity (R), Turf Paradise, Dec. 4, $42,384, 2yo, c&g, Arizona-bred, 6f, 1:10.67, DESERT PROSPECTOR, Buck's Wine, Free Will E, 11 started.

Arizona Breeders' Futurity (R), Turf Paradise, Dec. 4, $40,213, 2yo, f, Arizona-bred, 6f, 1:11.23, MISSINGRBUENO, Cuttin In, Kideeakey, 11 started.

Arizona County Fair Distance Series S., Mohave County Fair, May 16, $2,359, 3&up, 1¹/₁₆m, 1:45.20, OIL MAN, Chehalis, Grand Canyon, 4 started.

Arizona County Fair Speed S., Santa Cruz County Fair, May 2, $2,504, 3&up, 5f, :59.60, GOLD FEVERS GIFT, Jack Dugan, High Riser, 8 started.

Arizona County Fair Speed Series S., Mohave County Fair, May 16, $2,409, 3&up, 6f, 1:13.80, HIGH RISER, Riverboat Party, Gold Fevers Gift, 4 started.

Arizona Juvenile S., Turf Paradise, Dec. 26, $50,000, 2yo, 6¹/₂f, 1:13.55, LOST IN THE FOG, Scottsbluff, Lead for Speed, 10 started.

Arizona Oaks, Turf Paradise, Feb. 7, $75,000, 3yo, f, 1¹/₁₆m, 1:43.67, VERY VEGAS, Coke's Melody, Muir Beach, 6 started.

Arizona Stallion S. (R), Turf Paradise, April 9, $35,944, 3yo, progeny of eligible Arizona stallions, 7¹/₂fT, 1:31.69, OVERLAND ROAD, Bradford, Hollywood Robber, 8 started.

ARKANSAS DERBY-G2, Oaklawn Park, April 10, $1,000,000, 3yo, 1¹/₈m, 1:49.41, SMARTY JONES, Borrego, Pro Prado, 11 started.

Ark-La-Tex H., Louisiana Downs, June 20, $47,500, 3&up, 1¹/₁₆m, 1:45.16, PIE N BURGER, Meteor Impact, Record Assembly, 4 started.

ARLINGTON BREEDERS' CUP OAKS-G3, Arlington Park, Aug. 21, $150,000, 3yo, f, 1¹/₁₆m, 1:51.06, dh-LOVELY AFTERNOON, dh-CATBOAT, My Time Now, 10 started.

Arlington Breeders' Cup Sprint H., Arlington Park, Aug. 28, $147,000, 3&up, 6f, 1:08.65, GOLD STORM, Super Fuse, Champali, 5 started.

ARLINGTON CLASSIC S.-G2, Arlington Park, July 3, $200,000, 3yo, 1¹/₁₆mT, 1:50.91, TOASTED, Street Theatre, Cool Conductor, 8 started.

ARLINGTON H.-G3, Arlington Park, July 24, $250,000, 3&up, 1¹/₄mT, 2:03.38, SENOR SWINGER, Mystery Giver, Ballingarry (Ire), 7 started.

ARLINGTON MATRON H.-G3, Arlington Park, Sept. 4, $150,000, 3&up, f&m, 1¹/₈m, 1:49.75, ADORATION, Tamweel, Indy Groove, 7 started.

ARLINGTON MILLION S.-G1, Arlington Park, Aug. 14, $1,000,000, 3&up, 1¹/₄mT, 2:00.08, KICKEN KRIS, Magistretti, Epalo (Ger), 13 started.

ARLINGTON-WASHINGTON BREEDERS' CUP FUTURITY-G3, Arlington Park, Sept. 19, $200,000, 2yo, 1m, 1:38.56, THREE HOUR NAP, dh-Straight Line, dh-Elusive Chris, 6 started.

ARLINGTON-WASHINGTON LASSIE S.-G3, Arlington Park, Sept. 19, $100,000, 2yo, f, 1m, 1:36.98, CULINARY, Runway Model, Kota, 8 started.

Artax H., Gulfstream Park, March 27, $100,000, 3&up, 7f, 1:22.03, SPEIGHTSTOWN, Pretty Wild, Wacky for Love, 9 started.

Arthur I. Appleton Juvenile Turf S. (R), Calder Race Course, Nov. 13, $100,000, 2yo, Florida-bred, 1¹/₁₆mT, 1:43.03, TURK'S RANSOM, Eastern Sand, Raleigh Express, 8 started.

Ascot Graduation S., Hastings Race Course, Nov. 13, $112,800, 2yo, 1¹/₁₆m, 1:46.26, ALABAMA RAIN, Notis Otis, Western Writer, 6 started.

ASHLAND S.-G1, Keeneland, April 3, $485,000, 3yo, f, 1¹/₁₆m, 1:44.55, MADCAP ESCAPADE, Ashado, Last Song, 4 started.

Ashley T. Cole H. (R), Belmont Park, Sept. 25, $111,700, 3&up, New York-bred, 1¹/₄m, 1:46.43, PROVINCETOWN, Certifiably Crazy, Irish Colonial, 9 started.

Aspen Cup S., Ruidoso Downs, June 26, $25,000, 3&up, f, 6f, 1:10, MISS NOTEWORTHY, Culpeper Moon, Rama Lassie, 5 started.

Aspen H. (R), Arapahoe Park, Aug. 28, $31,000, 3&up, c&g, Colorado-bred, 6f, 1:09.20, DEBATABLE, Sir Debon Aire, Mullen, 8 started.

Aspidistra H., Calder Race Course, Aug. 21, $100,000, 3&up, f&m, 1mT, 1:37.70, TEAK TOTEM, Iowa's Image, Harts Gap, 8 started.

Aspirant S. (R), Finger Lakes, Aug. 21, $112,733, 2yo, New York-bred, 6f, 1:10.86, CARIBBEAN CRUISER, Big Apple Daddy, You Willgo Broke, 5 started.

Assault S. (R), Lone Star Park, Oct. 23, $100,000, 3&up, Texas-bred, 1¹/₁₆m, 1:43.21, GOOSEY MOOSE, Desert Darby, Oncearoundtwice, 11 started.

Assiniboia Oaks, Assiniboia Downs, Sept. 12, $40,000, 3yo, f, 1¹/₁₆m, 1:48, ERICKA'S LASS, Victory Thrill, Strike an Image, 5 started.

ASTARITA S.-G3, Belmont Park, Oct. 17, $108,000, 2yo, f, 6¹/₂f, 1:18.16, TOLL TAKER, Im a Dixie Girl, Summer Raven, 6 started.

Astoria S., Belmont Park, June 27, $107,700, 2yo, f, 5¹/₂f, 1:04.41, BROADWAY GOLD, Lady Glade, Comocina, 6 started.

ATBA Fall Sales S. (R), Turf Paradise, Oct. 16, $72,741, 2yo, f, consigned to the 2003 ATBA sale, 6f, 1:10.94, LADY BERTRANDO, Missingrbueno, O K Topless, 12 started.

ATBA Fall Sales S. (R), Turf Paradise, Oct. 16, $59,840, 2yo, c&g, consigned to the 2003 ATBA sale, 6f, 1:10.56, POWER WAVE, Night Dash, Tudor Needed, 11 started.

ATBA Spring Sales S. (R), Turf Paradise, May 16, $60,282, 2yo, ATBA fall sales graduates, 5f, :56.65, POWER WAVE, Tudor Needed, Royal B, 9 started.

Atchison, Topeka & Santa Fe H., The Woodlands, Oct. 9, $20,000, 3&up, 6f, 1:11.20, ROBIN ZEE, Magic Doe, Ww Conquistador, 7 started.

ATHENIA H.-G3, Aqueduct, Oct. 31, $115,700, 3&up, f&m, 1¹/₁₆mT, 1:43.73, FINERY, Madeira Mist (Ire), With Patience, 11 started.

ATTO MILE-G1, Woodbine, Sept. 19, $1,000,000, 3&up, 1mT, 1:32.72, SOARING FREE, Perfect Soul (Ire), Royal Regalia, 11 started.

Auburn S., Emerald Downs, May 2, $40,000, 3yo, c&g, 6f, 1:09, CRIMSON DESIGN, Random Memo, Spanish Highway, 9 started.

Audrey B. Kenis S., Hollywood Park, Nov. 7, $62,725, 3yo, f, 1¹/₁₆mT, 1:51.40, PENNY'S FORTUNE, Seeking the Heart, Sweet Win, 7 started.

Audubon Oaks, Ellis Park, July 31, $75,000, 3yo, f, 1¹/₁₆mT, 1:41.51, LENATAREESE, Key to the Cat, Lady Offense, 12 started.

Au Revior H., Les Bois Park, Aug. 15, $6,300, 3&up, 1¹/₄m, 2:06.60, FIND MY HALTER, Mystic Man (Arg), El Patron Grande, 6 started.

Autotote Derby, Lethbridge, Oct. 31, $16,600, 3yo, 1¹/₁₆m, 1:48.40, STREAK A ROANI, Easter Weekend, Bizzyweekend, 8 started.

Autumn Classic S. (R), Remington Park, Nov. 7, $40,000, 3&up, Oklahoma-bred, 6¹/₂f, 1:16.80, HERECOMESTHEMANNOW, Zee Oh Six, Medium Rare, 8 started.

Autumn Daze H., Yellowstone Downs, Sept. 6, $4,100, 3&up, 1m 70y, 1:49.60, BOBBY NAZ, Staged Reality, Streak a Roani, 7 started.

Autumn Leaves H., Bay Meadows, Sept. 4, $55,412, 3&up, f&m, 1mT, 1:35.20, MARWOOD, Cat Alert, Sea Jewel, 7 started.

Autumn Leaves S., Mountaineer Race Track, Sept. 28, $75,000, 3&up, f&m, 1¹/₁₆m, 1:45.02, INDY GROOVE, Clouds of Gold, Chance Dance, 5 started.

Autumn S. (R), Charles Town Races, Nov. 27, $51,550, 3&up, f&m, starters at Charles Town the most times in last four starts, 7f, 1:27.06, LETS JUST DO IT, Smokin' Greida, Shesanothergrump, 10 started.

Aventura S., Gulfstream Park, April 3, $250,000, 3yo, 1¹/₁₆m, 1:44.67, KAUFY MATE, Humorously, Baronage, 8 started.

AZALEA BREEDERS' CUP S.-G3, Calder Race Course, July 10, $300,000, 3yo, f, 6f, 1:11.40, DAZZLE ME, Reforest, Boston Express, 7 started.

Azalea S. (R), Delta Downs, March 19, $50,000, 3yo, f, Louisiana-bred, 5f, 1:00.54, VON BRAUN, Derby's Hellraiser, I'mavikingprincess, 7 started.

Aztec Oaks S., SunRay Park, Nov. 2, $71,000, 3yo, f, New Mexico-bred, 6¹/₂f, 1:17.80, LATENITE SPECIAL, Rylie Cheyenne, Vipervapor, 10 started.

Bachman S., Fonner Park, Feb. 28, $10,775, 3yo, 4f, :45.40, TEE TIMES TWO, Rough Neck, Kerosene Prospect, 8 started.

BALDWIN S.-G3, Santa Anita Park, Feb. 28, $113,350, 3yo, a6¹/₂fT, 1:14.09, SEATTLE BORDERS, Stalking Tiger, Jungle Prince, 10 started.

Ballade S. (R), Woodbine, June 30, $127,875, 3&up, f&m, progeny of eligible Ontario stallions, 6f, 1:09.08, BRASS IN POCKET, Regal 'n Bold, Boldest of All, 5 started.

BALLERINA BREEDERS' CUP S.-G3, Hastings Race Course, Oct. 16, $180,637, 3&up, f&m, 1¹/₈m, 1:51.42, SEE ME THROUGH, Summer Symphony, You and Nelly, 11 started.

BALLERINA H.-G1, Saratoga Race Course, Aug. 29, $250,000, 3&up, f&m, 7f, 1:21.09, LADY TAK, My Trusty Cat, Harmony Lodge, 7 started.

BALLSTON SPA BREEDERS' CUP H.-G3, Saratoga Race Course, Aug. 30, $201,000, 3&up, f&m, 1¹/₁₆mT, 1:43.92, OCEAN DRIVE, Personal Legend, High Court (Brz), 10 started.

Bangles and Beads S., Fairplex Park, Sept. 21, $58,200, 3&up, f&m, 6¹/₂f, 1:15.42, MADRINGA, Mazella, Honeypenny, 6 started.

Banshee Breeze H., Gulfstream Park, April 4, $75,000, 3&up, f&m, 1¹/₁₆m, 1:44.62, NONSUCH BAY, D' Wildcat Speed, Pampered Princess, 11 started.

Bara Lass S. (R), Sam Houston Race Park, Nov. 20, $50,000, 2yo, f, Texas-bred, 7f, 1:25.56, SNIPPER LOU, Tuned In, Rhome Magic, 11 started.

BARBARA FRITCHIE H.-G2, Laurel Park, Feb. 14, $200,000, 3&up, f&m, 7f, 1:23.55, BEAR FAN, Gazillion, Bronze Abe, 9 started.

Barbara Shinpoch S. (R), Emerald Downs, Aug. 28, $55,000, 2yo, f, progeny of eligible Washington stallions, 1m, 1:36.20, A CLASSIC LIFE, Charming Colleen, Have'n a Lark, 8 started.

Barb's Dancer S. (R), Calder Race Course, July 13, $40,000, 3&up, f&m, nonwinners of $15,000 since February 1 or nonwinners of four races other than maiden, claiming, or starter, 6f, 1:11.60, PETRINA ABOVE, Really Royal, Sea Span, 6 started.

Barksdale H., Louisiana Downs, May 31, $50,000, 3&up, 1mT, 1:36.25, WAUPACA, Storybook Kid, Sea Dub, 6 started.

Barona Cup H., Del Mar, Aug. 22, $76,105, 3yo, f, 1mT, 1:35.04, SHAKE OFF, John's Kinda Girl, Bonaire (GB), 7 started.

Barretts Debutante S. (R), Fairplex Park, Sept. 18, $118,800, 2yo, f, passed through the ring at a Barretts Equine Ltd. sale, 6¹/₂f, 1:18.18, LUNAR FLIGHT, Bernstein's Babe, High Note Treasure, 10 started.

Barretts Juvenile S. (R), Fairplex Park, Sept. 19, $108,927, 2yo, c&g, passed through the ring at a Barretts Equine Ltd. sale, 6¹/₂f, 1:18.29, BEAT THE CHALK, Texcess, Dover Dere, 7 started.

BASHFORD MANOR S.-G3, Churchill Downs, July 5, $163,200, 2yo, 6f, 1:11.54, LUNARPAL, Storm Surge, Maximus C, 7 started.

Bassinet S., River Downs, Sept. 4, $100,000, 2yo, f, 6f, 1:10.60, IM A DIXIE GIRL, Runway Model, Gallant Secret, 11 started.

Battlefield S., Monmouth Park, June 12, $60,000, 3&up, 1¹/₈mT, 1:48, MEGANTIC, Better Talk Now, Del Mar Show, 6 started.

Battler Star H. (R), Fair Grounds, March 7, $75,000, 3yo, f, Louisiana-bred, 6f, 1:10.69, PLACID STAR, Von Braun, Dear Alicia, 10 started.

Baxter S., Fonner Park, March 20, $16,600, 3yo, 6¹/₂f, 1:20.60, MORTRUMP, Rough Neck, Temptors Prospect, 8 started.

BAYAKOA H.-G2, Hollywood Park, Dec. 12, $150,000, 3&up, f&m, 1¹/₁₆m, 1:41.11, HOLLYWOOD STORY, Royally Chosen, A. P. Adventure, 7 started.

Bayakoa S., Oaklawn Park, April 4, $75,000, 4&up, f&m, 1¹/₁₆m, 1:43.68, LA REASON, Pampered, Sue's Good News, 7 started.

BAY MEADOWS BREEDERS' CUP H.-G3, Bay Meadows, Oct. 2, $112,500, 3&up, a1¹/₈mT, 1:46.55, NEEDWOOD BLADE (GB), Seinne (Chi), Balestrini (Ire), 7 started.

BAY MEADOWS BREEDERS' CUP SPRINT H.-G3, Bay Meadows, June 19, $90,000, 3&up, 6f, 1:08.91, COURT'S IN SESSION, Debonair Joe, Hombre Rapido, 9 started.

BAY MEADOWS DERBY-G3, Bay Meadows, Nov. 6, $100,000, 3yo, a1¹/₈mT, 1:48.92, CONGRESSIONAL HONOR, Talaris, On the Acorn (GB), 8 started.

Bay Meadows Oaks H., Bay Meadows, June 12, $79,950, 3yo, f, 1¹/₁₆mT, 1:43.83, CROZET, Kurlicue (Ire), Lost Bride, 5 started.

BAYOU BREEDERS' CUP H.-G3, Fair Grounds, Feb. 28, $113,500, 4&up, f&m, a1¹/₈mT, 1:52.74, BEDANKEN, Due to Win Again, Lady Linda, 10 started.

Bayou State S. (R), Delta Downs, March 5, $50,000, 4&up, Louisiana-bred, 7f, 1:26.34, SPRITELY WALKER, Zarb's Luck, Prince Slew, 6 started.

BAY SHORE S.-G3, Aqueduct, April 10, $150,000, 3yo, 7f, 1:20.67, FOREST DANGER, Abbondanza, Indian War Dance, 6 started.

B. B. "Sixty" Rayburn S. (R), Evangeline Downs, May 22, $40,000, 3yo, c&g, Louisiana-bred, 1m, 1:41.40, OLD LEE, Brandon's Marfa, Valid Faith, 8 started.

"B" Cup S., Lethbridge, Oct. 16, $11,750, 2yo, f, a6f, 1:13.80, I GIVE UP, Reality Belle, It's Ali's Time, 5 started.

"B" Cup S., Lethbridge, Oct. 16, $11,900, 2yo, a6f, 1:13.60, ITSA-NINETYNINER, V R Blue, Bold Charge, 6 started.

"B" Cup S., Lethbridge, Oct. 16, $12,050, 3yo, f, a6f, 1:11.40, SPECIAL ERA, Wild County, Easter Weekend, 7 started.

"B" Cup S., Lethbridge, Oct. 16, $12,200, 3yo, a6f, 1:12, BIZZYWEEKEND, Streak a Roani, Ezee Target, 8 started.

"B" Cup S., Lethbridge, Oct. 16, $12,050, 3&up, f&m, 5¹/₂f, 1:08.80, IRISH INTRIGUE, Her Brilliancy, Royal Shyann, 7 started.
"B" Cup S., Lethbridge, Oct. 16, $12,200, 3&up, f&m, 7f, 1:27.60, GAME PRINCESS, Flying Lady Cue, Temptor Cielo, 8 started.
"B" Cup S., Lethbridge, Oct. 16, $12,050, 3&up, 7f, 1:28.40, SILVER SKY, Seattle Cue, Lafleur, 7 started.
Beau Brummel S., Fairplex Park, Sept. 14, $58,200, 2yo, c&g, 6¹/₂f, 1:19.20, FOREVER FOXY, Fallfree, Lotta Loot, 6 started.
Beaufort S. (R), Northlands Park, Sept. 25, $50,000, 3yo, Alberta-bred, 1¹/₁₆m, 1:46.60, ROYALTY BOY, Curious Gamble, Ozzie's J J, 10 started.
BEAUGAY H.-G3, Aqueduct, May 1, $110,000, 3&up, f&m, 1¹/₁₆mT, 1:46.38, DEDICATION (Fr), Aud, Caught in the Rain, 7 started.
Beautiful Day S., Delaware Park, July 12, $54,100, 3yo, f, 6f, 1:10.55, HUMOR ME MOLLY, Perilous Night, Xtra Tough, 6 started.
BED O'ROSES BREEDERS' CUP H.-G3, Aqueduct, April 17, $156,900, 3&up, f&m, 1m, 1:35.50, PASSING SHOT, Smok'n Frolic, Nonsuch Bay, 6 started.
BELDAME S.-G1, Belmont Park, Oct. 9, $735,000, 3&up, f&m, 1¹/₈m, 1:49.60, SIGHTSEEK, Society Selection, Storm Flag Flying, 5 started.
Belle Geste S. (R), Woodbine, Oct. 10, $104,000, 3&up, f&m, Canadian-bred, 1¹/₈mT, 1:48.10, MONA ROSE, Heyahohowdy, First Quarter, 7 started.
Belle Mahone S., Woodbine, July 18, $107,000, 3&up, f&m, 1¹/₁₆m, 1:45.27, WINNING CHANCE, One for Rose, Raylene, 7 started.
Belle Roberts S. (R), Emerald Downs, Sept. 19, $49,000, 3&up, f&m, Washington-bred, 1¹/₁₆m, 1:42.20, AUNT SOPHIE, Gettheparty-started, Ruby Dawn, 7 started.
BELMONT BREEDERS' CUP H.-G2, Belmont Park, Sept. 18, $197,800, 3&up, 1¹/₈m, 1:52.72, SENOR SWINGER, Stroll, B. A. Way, 4 started.
BELMONT S.-G1, Belmont Park, June 5, $1,000,000, 3yo, 1¹/₂m, 2:27.50, BIRDSTONE, Smarty Jones, Royal Assault, 9 started.
BEN ALI S.-G3, Keeneland, April 22, $150,000, 4&up, 1¹/₁₆m, 1:46.78, MIDWAY ROAD, Evening Attire, Sir Cherokee, 5 started.
Ben Cohen S., Pimlico, May 22, $50,000, 3&up, 5fT, :56.32, GOVERNOR'S PRIDE, Take Achance On Me, Rudirudy, 10 started.
Bergen County S., The Meadowlands, Oct. 16, $55,000, 3yo, 5fT, :57.55, ALL HAIL STORMY, Anaf, Exploit Lad, 6 started.
BERKELEY H.-G3, Golden Gate Fields, March 27, $94,375, 3&up, 1m, 1:33.92, SNORTER, Yougottawanna, Taste of Paradise, 5 started.
BERNARD BARUCH H.-G2, Saratoga Race Course, July 30, $150,000, 3&up, 1¹/₁₆mT, 1:49.66, SILVER TREE, Nothing to Lose, Irish Colonial, 7 started.
Bernie Dowd H. (R), Monmouth Park, July 18, $60,000, 3&up, New Jersey-bred, 6f, 1:09.83, SOMETHING SMITH, Dixie Two Thousand, Trueamericanspirit, 6 started.
Bersid S., Turf Paradise, Oct. 17, $21,600, 3&up, f&m, 1m, 1:36.75, ARCH LADY, Moonlit Maddie, Friendofthefamily, 5 started.
Bertram F. Bongard S. (R), Belmont Park, Oct. 3, $109,700, 2yo, New York-bred, 7f, 1:24.63, UP LIKE THUNDER, Freddy the Cap, Accurate, 8 started.
BESSARABIAN H.-G3, Woodbine, Nov. 28, $164,250, 3&up, f&m, 7f, 1:23.21, MISS GRINDSTONE, El Prado Essence, Surprised Humor, 6 started.
Best of Ohio Distaff S. (R), Thistledown, Oct. 9, $50,000, 3&up, f&m, Ohio-bred, 1¹/₁₆m, 1:53.76, WHITEWATER WAY, Oh So Easy, Ashwood C C, 12 started.
Best of Ohio Endurance S. (R), Thistledown, Oct. 9, $75,000, 3&up, Ohio-bred, 1¹/₁₆m, 2:06.10, REAL ECHO, Cat Singer, Xtra Jack, 11 started.
Best of Ohio Juvenile S. (R), Thistledown, Oct. 9, $60,000, 2yo, Ohio-bred, 1¹/₁₆m, 1:48.30, FIERCE CAT, Bug Hunter, Cast No Shadow, 14 started.
Best of Ohio Sprint S. (R), Thistledown, Oct. 9, $50,000, 3&up, Ohio-bred, 6f, 1:09.94, BEN'S REFLECTION, Reggie's Winner, Whitermorn, 7 started.
Best of the Rest S., Calder Race Course, July 18, $40,000, 3&up, 1¹/₁₆m, 1:45.78, SUPER FROLIC, Island Skipper, Aeneas, 7 started.
BEST PAL S.-G2, Del Mar, Aug. 15, $147,000, 2yo, 6¹/₂f, 1:15.93, ROMAN RULER, Actxecutive, Slewsbag, 5 started.
Best Turn S., Aqueduct, Feb. 21, $81,825, 3yo, 6f, 1:09.82, RED-SKIN WARRIOR, Scary Bob, Matsui, 7 started.

Betsy Ross S., Monmouth Park, July 4, $60,000, 3&up, f&m, 5fT, :55.93, MELODY OF COLORS, Hidden Ransom, Chez Audra, 8 started.
Better Bee S., Arlington Park, July 3, $40,050, 3&up, 6f, 1:10.09, WITHOUT A DOUBT, Truman's Raider, Chindi, 4 started.
Bettie Bullock Memorial Derby, Wyoming Downs, Aug. 22, $5,600, 3yo, 5¹/₂f, 1:05.57, CLOSELY HELD, New Hey, Splendid High, 8 started.
Bettors Invitational H., Grants Pass, June 26, $3,760, 3&up, 6¹/₂f, 1:18.20, THE LORD IS EAGER, Theycallmecolonel, Jesse Gee, 6 started.
BEVERLY D. S.-G1, Arlington Park, Aug. 14, $750,000, 3&up, f&m, 1³/₁₆mT, 1:56.58, CRIMSON PALACE (SAf), Riskaverse, Necklace (GB), 11 started.
BEVERLY HILLS H.-G2, Hollywood Park, June 27, $200,000, 3&up, f&m, 1¹/₄mT, 2:01.52, LIGHT JIG (GB), Moscow Burning, Noches De Rosa (Chi), 6 started.
BEWITCH S.-G3, Keeneland, April 21, $113,400, 4&up, f&m, 1¹/₂mT, 2:31.05, MERIDIANA (Ger), Alternate, Binya (Ger), 10 started.
Bien Bien S. (R), Hollywood Park, Nov. 6, $63,325, 3yo, nonwinners of $60,000 at one mile or over, 1mT, 1:36.23, WHILLY (Ire), Perfect Moon, We All Love Aleyna, 5 started.
Bienvenidos S., Turf Paradise, Oct. 1, $22,000, 3&up, 1m, 1:37.07, CUT OF MUSIC, No Toro, Instantly, 10 started.
Big Country 93.1 XX FM Futurity, Grand Prairie, Aug. 21, $5,540, 2yo, 5¹/₂f, 1:10, JOHN'S MAGIC, Scruffy, Ding Dong Dandy, 8 started.
Big Jag H., Bay Meadows, Oct. 3, $54,125, 3&up, 6f, 1:08.71, ONEBADSHARK, My Captain, Halo Cat, 4 started.
Big Red Mile H. (R), Lincoln State Fair, May 31, $15,900, 3&up, Nebraska-bred, 1m, 1:41.80, GRAYGLEN, Death Trappe, My Man, 9 started.
Big Sky H., Great Falls, Aug. 1, $7,550, 3&up, 1m 70y, 1:46.20, CABREO, Lovers Son, Excellenceinmotion, 7 started.
Bill Callihan H., Columbus Races, Sept. 5, $10,600, 3&up, f&m, 6¹/₂f, 1:22.60, MISSY CAN DO, Miss Guts, Gotta Jiboo, 5 started.
Bill Thomas Memorial H., Sunland Park, March 6, $54,825, 3&up, 6¹/₂f, 1:14.29, BANG, Haitian Hit, Streak of Royalty, 11 started.
Bill Wheeler H. (R), The Meadowlands, Oct. 8, $60,000, 3&up, New Jersey-bred, 1m 70y, 1:41.62, UPTURN, Trueamericanspirit, Whopaho, 6 started.
Bill Wineberg S. (R), Portland Meadows, Nov. 13, $20,330, 2yo, c&g, Oregon-bred, 6f, 1:13.35, CASCADIANSASQUATCH, Truth Buster, Eighty Eighty, 9 started.
Billy Powell Claiming H. (R), The Downs at Albuquerque, July 5, $17,350, 3&up, starters for a claiming price of $5,000, 1¹/₂m, 2:34.34, HAMMERIN, Prince Hadif, Wolf's Honor, 11 started.
Billy the Kid Distance Series Final S., Ruidoso Downs, Sept. 6, $16,900, 3&up, 1¹/₄m, 2:09.40, FIN ENTERTAINMENT, Security Comet, Masakado Kid, 6 started.
BING CROSBY BREEDERS' CUP H.-G1, Del Mar, July 25, $244,000, 3&up, 6f, 1:08.51, KELA, Pohave, Hombre Rapido, 10 started.
Birdcatcher S., Northlands Park, Sept. 6, $50,000, 2yo, c&g, 6¹/₂f, 1:19.60, ONE SPECIAL HOSS, Golden Hunt, Poor Iggy, 10 started.
Bird of Pay S., Northlands Park, Sept. 4, $50,000, 2yo, f, 6¹/₂f, 1:18.60, MISS VENTUROUS, Speedy Gone Sally, Montero, 7 started.
Birdonthewire S., Calder Race Course, Oct. 23, $75,000, 2yo, 6f, 1:12.66, G P'S BLACK KNIGHT, Kohut, Lucky Frolic, 8 started.
Birmingham Maiden S. (R), River Downs, June 12, $22,500, 3&up, Alabama-bred, 6f, 1:14.40, HEATMONEY, Tootoo, Out Late, 9 started.
Bison City S. (R), Fort Erie, July 4, $250,000, 3yo, f, Canadian-bred, 1¹/₁₆m, 1:45.57, TOUCHNOW, Eye of the Sphynx, My Vintage Port, 6 started.
BK Disposal S., Grand Prairie, Aug. 14, $4,340, 3&up, 6f, 1:14.60, BIZZYWEEKEND, Hunkahunkamango, Bright Appeal, 8 started.
BLACK-EYED SUSAN S.-G2, Pimlico, May 14, $200,000, 3yo, f, 1¹/₁₆m, 1:52.65, YEARLY REPORT, Pawyne Princess, Rare Gift, 7 started.
Black Gold H., Fair Grounds, Jan. 10, $60,000, 3yo, a7¹/₂fT, 1:32.51, SHILOH BOUND, Bachelor Blues, Bogangles, 9 started.
Black Mesa S. (R), Remington Park, Oct. 24, $40,000, 3&up, f&m, Oklahoma-bred, 6f, 1:10.03, RACING SUNDOWN, Rammers Best, Star's Kandi Kane, 8 started.
Black Swan S., Fairplex Park, Sept. 22, $58,200, 2yo, f, 1¹/₁₆m, 1:46.96, KACHINA DREAM, Irish Mafia, Burning Affair, 6 started.

Black Tie Affair H., Arlington Park, July 10, $75,000, 3&up, 1¹/₈m, 1:49.46, ALUMNI HALL, Wiggins, Stratostar, 7 started.

Blair's Cove S. (R), Canterbury Park, July 3, $40,000, 3&up, c&g, Minnesota-bred, 1¹/₁₆mT, 1:44.45, ADROITLY SUPERB, Winter Trick, Big Sand, 8 started.

Blaze O'Brien S., Turf Paradise, March 15, $21,800, 3&up, 1¹/₁₆mT, 1:41.35, BLACK BART, Cut of Music, Hero's Pleasure, 7 started.

Blazing Sevens S. (R), Fort Erie, Aug. 15, $46,000, 3&up, starters at Fort Erie at least three times in 2004, a7fT, 1:26.54, BALTIC PRINCE, Long Term Success, Black Tie Justice, 8 started.

Bloom N Character S., Turf Paradise, Feb. 10, $21,900, 4&up, 1¹/₈mT, 1:50.85, EXPRESSIONATOR, Pittsburgh Star, 6 started.

Bluebonnet S., Lone Star Park, Oct. 31, $100,000, 3&up, f&m, 1¹/₁₆mT, 1:45.19, MY MISTY PRINCESS, Queena Corrina, Bonnie J., 8 started.

Bluegrass H., Lincoln State Fair, June 5, $10,250, 3&up, f&m, 6f, 1:12.40, MISSY CAN DO, Irish Flyer, Annie Flo, 5 started.

BLUE GRASS S.-G1, Keeneland, April 10, $750,000, 3yo, 1¹/₈m, 1:49.42, THE CLIFF'S EDGE, Limehouse, Lion Heart, 8 started.

Blue Hen S., Delaware Park, Oct. 23, $100,000, 2yo, f, 1¹/₁₆m, 1:45.99, BUZZ SONG, Secrets Galore, Trickle of Gold, 5 started.

Blue Mountain Juvenile S. (R), Penn National Race Course, Nov. 12, $53,000, 2yo, f, Pennsylvania-bred, 6f, 1:13.91, NITA CHIQUITA, Webers Drive In, Rhythmically, 6 started.

Blue Norther S., Santa Anita Park, Jan. 14, $76,300, 3yo, f, 1mT, 1:34.68, MAMBO SLEW, Ticker Tape (GB), Yingyingying, 8 started.

Blue Skies H., Louisiana Downs, July 25, $50,000, 3&up, 1¹/₁₆m, 1:44.23, AKANTI (Ire), Crowned King, Guaranteed Sweep, 9 started.

Bobbie Bricker Memorial H. (R), Beulah Park, Oct. 31, $40,000, 3&up, f&m, Ohio-accredited, 1¹/₁₆m, 1:47.38, IMAHONEYTOO, Joann's Joy, Bubble Bourbon, 6 started.

Bob Bryant S. (R), Prairie Meadows, May 22, $50,000, 3yo, f, Iowa-bred, 6f, 1:10.55, HOLLYWOOD AND WINE, Joe Miss, This One for Abbey, 7 started.

Bob Harding S., Monmouth Park, Sept. 5, $60,000, 3&up, 1mT, 1:36.98, STORMY ROMAN, Green Line (GB), Burning Roma, 8 started.

Bob Johnson Memorial S., Lone Star Park, July 3, $75,000, 3&up, 1m, 1:36.18, RARE CURE, Pie N Burger, Lights On Broadway, 6 started.

Bob Slater S., Gulfstream Park, April 17, $50,000, 3&up, f&m, 5fT, :57.01, MELODY OF COLORS, Desirable Moment, Formada (Arg), 9 started.

Boeing H., Emerald Downs, July 24, $40,000, 3&up, f&m, 1¹/₁₆m, 1:42.40, CASCADE CORONA, Hanselina, Aunt Sophie, 7 started.

BOILING SPRINGS S.-G3, Monmouth Park, Sept. 12, $150,000, 3yo, f, 1¹/₁₆mT, 1:45.66, SEDUCER'S SONG, Go Robin, River Belle (GB), 9 started.

Boise Fillies and Mares H., Les Bois Park, Aug. 14, $6,200, 3&up, f&m, 5f, :57.40, DANCE FOR FUN, Mini Me, Bills Proud Mary, 6 started.

Boise Fillies and Mares H., Les Bois Park, Aug. 15, $6,350, 3&up, f&m, 7¹/₂f, 1:32.80, NEVER BEEN CAUGHT, Opal's Song, Mode of the World, 6 started.

Boise Thoroughbred 3,200 Claiming H., Les Bois Park, Aug. 14, $6,650, 3&up, 7¹/₂f, 1:33, HARD HITTER, Hair Jordan, Aer Afrik, 7 started.

Boise Thoroughbred Derby, Les Bois Park, Aug. 11, $6,050, 3yo, 1m, 1:38.80, SILENT SNOW, Fanteria, Royal Stage, 7 started.

Boise Thoroughbred Maiden Derby, Les Bois Park, June 13, $12,510, 3yo, 6¹/₂f, 1:19, WESTERN DROUILLY, Game Master, Royal Stage, 8 started.

Bold Accent H., Fonner Park, Feb. 14, $11,150, 3&up, f&m, 4f, :45.20, MISSY CAN DO, Real Intrusion, Flaming Night, 7 started.

Bold Ego H., Sunland Park, Jan. 3, $53,950, 3&up, f&m, 5¹/₂f, 1:03.63, INOX (Arg), Gimme a Clue, City Sleeper, 8 started.

Bold Ruckus S. (R), Woodbine, June 16, $133,125, 3yo, progeny of eligible Ontario stallions, 6fT, 1:09.33, DASHING ADMIRAL, Archers Bow, Imperial Alydeed, 8 started.

BOLD RULER H.-G3, Belmont Park, May 8, $107,700, 3&up, 6f, 1:08.97, CANADIAN FRONTIER, Key Deputy, First Blush, 6 started.

Bold Venture H., Woodbine, July 11, $141,250, 3&up, 6¹/₂f, 1:15.69, I'M THE TIGER, Twisted Wit, I Thee Wed, 10 started.

Bonnie Heath Turf Cup H. (R), Calder Race Course, Nov. 13, $150,000, 3&up, Florida-bred, 1¹/₈mT, 1:47.22, FINAL PROPHECY, Gin and Sin, Grafton, 9 started.

BONNIE MISS S.-G2, Gulfstream Park, March 6, $200,000, 3yo, f, 1¹/₁₆m, 1:50.60, LAST SONG, Society Selection, Rare Gift, 5 started.

Boomer S. (R), Fair Meadows at Tulsa, July 3, $49,075, 3&up, f&m, Oklahoma-bred, 5¹/₂f, 1:05.80, FRILLY FUN, Racing Sundown, Miss French, 7 started.

Boots 'n Jackie S., Calder Race Course, May 24, $40,000, 3&up, f&m, 1¹/₁₆m, 1:48.30, GENTILLE ALOUETTE, Pampered Princess, Never Fail, 8 started.

Border Cup S. (R), Fort Erie, Aug. 2, $48,000, 3&up, f&m, starters at Fort Erie at least three times in 2004, 1¹/₁₆m, 1:44.34, OLYMPIC ADVICE, Anthonia, Orientalspringhope, 5 started.

Borderland Derby, Sunland Park, Feb. 29, $105,450, 3yo, 1m, 1:37.87, GO KITTY GO, Rocky Gulch, Hi Teck Man, 11 started.

Bossier City H., Louisiana Downs, July 31, $50,000, 3yo, 1¹/₁₆mT, 1:44.46, ALPHA CAPO, Social King, No Place Like It, 6 started.

Bourbon County S., Keeneland, Oct. 29, $112,200, 2yo, 1¹/₁₆mT, 1:42.90, REY DE CAFE, Dubleo, Ready Ruler, 10 started.

Bourbonette Breeders' Cup S., Turfway Park, March 20, $150,000, 3yo, f, 1m, 1:37.98, CLASS ABOVE, Susan's Angel, Native Annie, 6 started.

Bouwerie S. (R), Belmont Park, May 16, $113,600, 3yo, f, New York-bred, 7f, 1:23.07, RODEO LICIOUS, Mistda, Capeside Lady, 11 started.

BOWLING GREEN H.-G2, Belmont Park, July 17, $150,000, 3&up, 1³/₈mT, 2:12.19, KICKEN KRIS, Better Talk Now, Gigli (Brz), 10 started.

Brandywine H., Delaware Park, June 12, $100,600, 3&up, 1¹/₁₆m, 1:43.35, LOVING (Brz), Private Lap, Donald's Pride, 7 started.

Brave Raj S., Calder Race Course, Oct. 2, $100,000, 2yo, f, 1m 70y, 1:49.09, DANSETTA LIGHT, Frosty Royalty, Leona's Knight, 6 started.

BREEDERS' CUP CLASSIC-G1, Lone Star Park, Oct. 30, $3,668,000, 3&up, 1¹/₄m, 1:59.02, GHOSTZAPPER, Roses in May, Pleasantly Perfect, 13 started.

BREEDERS' CUP DISTAFF-G1, Lone Star Park, Oct. 30, $1,834,000, 3&up, f&m, 1¹/₈m, 1:48.26, ASHADO, Storm Flag Flying, Stellar Jayne, 11 started.

BREEDERS' CUP FILLY AND MARE TURF-G1, Lone Star Park, Oct. 30, $1,292,970, 3&up, f&m, 1³/₈mT, 2:18.25, OUIJA BOARD (GB), Film Maker, Wonder Again, 12 started.

BREEDERS' CUP JUVENILE-G1, Lone Star Park, Oct. 30, $1,375,500, 2yo, c&g, 1¹/₁₆m, 1:42.09, WILKO, Afleet Alex, Sun King, 8 started.

BREEDERS' CUP JUVENILE FILLIES-G1, Lone Star Park, Oct. 30, $917,000, 2yo, f, 1¹/₁₆m, 1:41.65, SWEET CATOMINE, Balletto (UAE), Runway Model, 12 started.

BREEDERS' CUP MILE-G1, Lone Star Park, Oct. 30, $1,540,560, 3&up, 1mT, 1:36.90, SINGLETARY, Antonius Pius, Six Perfections (Fr), 14 started.

BREEDERS' CUP SPRINT-G1, Lone Star Park, Oct. 30, $972,020, 3&up, 6f, 1:08.11, SPEIGHTSTOWN, Kela, My Cousin Matt, 13 started.

BREEDERS' CUP TURF-G1, Lone Star Park, Oct. 30, $1,834,000, 3&up, 1¹/₂mT, 2:29.70, BETTER TALK NOW, Kitten's Joy, Powerscourt (GB), 8 started.

Breeders' S. (R), Woodbine, Aug. 8, $500,000, 3yo, Canadian-bred, 1¹/₈mT, 2:27.15, A BIT O'GOLD, Burst of Fire, Silver Ticket, 11 started.

Breeders' Special Fillies S. (R), Lincoln State Fair, July 3, $15,600, 3yo, f, Nebraska-bred, 6f, 1:13.60, SHESO, Jitterbug Joy, Shawklit Premiere, 6 started.

Brent's Princess S. (R), Thistledown, May 22, $40,000, 3&up, f&m, Ohio-bred, 6f, 1:11.66, MERCER'S LAUNCH, Kiosk, Nachen, 8 started.

Brickyard S. (R), Hoosier Park, Oct. 24, $40,000, 3&up, Indiana-bred, 6f, 1:10.35, MR. MINK, Donnies Pick, Call Roy, 10 started.

Brighouse Belles H., Hastings Race Course, June 19, $42,914, 3&up, f&m, 1¹/₁₆m, 1:44.71, VICTOR'S SECRET, Shelby Madison, Defrere's Image, 4 started.

BRITISH COLUMBIA BREEDERS' CUP OAKS-G3, Hastings Race Course, Sept. 25, $174,087, 3yo, f, 1¹/₁₆m, 1:51.08, SUMMER SYMPHONY, Socorro County, See Me Through, 9 started.

British Columbia Cup Classic H. (R), Hastings Race Course, Aug. 2, $72,436, 3&up, British Columbia-bred, 1¹/₈m, 1:49.69, ILLUSIVE FORCE, Lord Nelson, Steady Smiler, 6 started.

British Columbia Cup Debutante S. (R), Hastings Race Course, Aug. 2, $54,465, 2yo, f, British Columbia-bred, 6¹/₂f, 1:19.21, BACKSEAT BECKA, Mandi Tambi, After the Knight, 8 started.

British Columbia Cup Distaff H. (R), Hastings Race Course, Aug. 2, $55,720, 3&up, f&m, British Columbia-bred, 1¹/₈m, 1:50.91, DANCEWITHAVIXEN, Famous Spirit, Victor's Secret, 6 started.

British Columbia Cup Nursery S. (R), Hastings Race Course, Aug. 2, $54,836, 2yo, c&g, British Columbia-bred, 6¹/₂f, 1:19.39, NOTIS OTIS, Speed Victor, Run On, 7 started.

British Columbia Cup Sprint H. (R), Hastings Race Course, Aug. 2, $55,590, 3&up, British Columbia-bred, 6¹/₂f, 1:16.37, FIVE POINT STAR, Silver Donn, Bold 'n Keen, 7 started.

British Columbia Cup Stallion H. (R), Hastings Race Course, Aug. 2, $55,590, 3yo, c&g, British Columbia-bred, 1¹/₁₆m, 1:45.36, LORD SAMARAI, Louie Downtown, Joyride, 7 started.

British Columbia Cup Stallion H. (R), Hastings Race Course, Aug. 2, $55,655, 3yo, f, British Columbia-bred, 1¹/₁₆m, 1:44.65, REGAL RED, She's a Bombshell, Bullseye Bess, 6 started.

BRITISH COLUMBIA DERBY-G3, Hastings Race Course, Sept. 26, $325,500, 3yo, 1¹/₈m, 1:49.58, FLAMETHROWINTEXAN, Lord Samarai, Strike Em Hard, 12 started.

British Columbia Lottery Corp. H., Kin Park, Aug. 1, $10,000, 3&up, a1¹/₁₆m, 1:45.84, TENDER OFFER (Ire), Dawns Ben, Sideline Duchess, 5 started.

British Columbia Lottery Corp. H., Kamloops, Aug. 15, $12,200, 3&up, a1m, 1:38.45, TENDER OFFER (Ire), Bullinsky, Chief Swan, 6 started.

Broadway H. (R), Aqueduct, March 13, $84,125, 3&up, f&m, New York-bred, 7f, 1:24.31, SENSIBLY CHIC, Taghkanic, Beautiful America, 9 started.

BROOKLYN H.-G2, Belmont Park, June 12, $250,000, 3&up, 1¹/₈m, 1:46.30, SEATTLE FITZ (Arg), Dynever, Newfoundland, 6 started.

Brookmeade S. (R), Colonial Downs, July 4, $50,000, 3&up, f&m, Virginia-bred and/or -sired, 1¹/₁₆mT, 1:44.96, BLUFFIE SLEW, Little Miss Pamela, Saints and Sages, 6 started.

Brooks Fields S., Canterbury Park, June 12, $40,000, 3&up, 1m, 1:35.41, NATIVE HAWK, Colorful Tour, Adroitly Superb, 10 started.

Brother Brown S., Remington Park, Oct. 17, $40,300, 3&up, 5fT, :56.64, THE NINER ACCOUNT, Silver Phone, April's Lucky Boy, 11 started.

BROWN BESS H.-G3, Golden Gate Fields, Jan. 31, $100,000, 4&up, f&m, 1¹/₁₆mT, 1:46.01, RED RIOJA (Ire), Hooked On Niners, A B Noodle, 11 started.

Bruce G. Smith Memorial S., Suffolk Downs, Sept. 4, $40,000, 3&up, a1¹/₁₆mT, 1:46.66, FINAL PROPHECY, Milky Way Guy, Jini's Jet, 7 started.

B. Thoughtful S. (R), Hollywood Park, April 24, $150,000, 4&up, f&m, California-bred, 7f, 1:21.43, ROYALLY CHOSEN, Summer Wind Dancer, Tucked Away, 8 started.

Bucharest S., Sam Houston Race Park, Jan. 31, $30,000, 3yo, 6f, 1:11.89, JIMMY CRACKED CORN, Foxtrot Oscar, Polish Navigator, 6 started.

Buckeye Native S. (R), River Downs, Aug. 15, $40,000, 3&up, Ohio-bred, 1¹/₁₆mT, 1:43.60, HANK'S RIB, Brent's Challanger, Woodburner, 10 started.

Buckland S., Colonial Downs, July 3, $50,000, 3&up, f&m, 5¹/₂fT, 1:03.68, SPRING KITTEN, Our Mariah, Glowing Breeze, 9 started.

Buckpasser S., Fairmount Park, Sept. 6, $25,600, 2yo, c&g, 6f, 1:13.60, YUKON'S GAMBLER, Kahok, Bailer Twine, 6 started.

BUENA VISTA H.-G2, Santa Anita Park, Feb. 21, $150,000, 4&up, f&m, 1mT, 1:36.13, FUN HOUSE, Katdogawn (GB), Fudge Fatale, 7 started.

Bueno S., Turf Paradise, Dec. 17, $22,100, 3yo, f, 6f, 1:10.48, CORONA DEL HIELO, Society Cat, Lightning Lydia, 8 started.

Buffalo Bayou S., Sam Houston Race Park, Nov. 27, $40,000, 3&up, 1¹/₁₆mT, 1:46.57, SEA DUB, Payasito, Run to the Border, 7 started.

Buffalo S. (R), Assiniboia Downs, Sept. 26, $41,000, 2yo, Manitoba-bred, 1m, 1:40.20, GOLD STRIKE, Whiskey Drive, Your Excellence, 5 started.

Bull Page S. (R), Woodbine, Oct. 9, $131,625, 2yo, progeny of eligible Ontario stallions, 6f, 1:11.22, WHOLELOTTABOURBON, Enough Is Enough, Quick in Deed, 9 started.

Bullys Futurity, Lethbridge, Oct. 30, $12,200, 2yo, a6f, 1:12.60, IT-SANINETYNINER, Bold Charge, I Give Up, 7 started.

Bungalow H. (R), Fairmount Park, Aug. 24, $35,700, 3&up, f&m, Illinois-bred, 1m, 1:38.60, PRINCESS PASTER, Samantha B., Becky B Mine, 6 started.

Bunty Lawless S. (R), Woodbine, Oct. 31, $146,750, 3&up, progeny of eligible Ontario stallions, 1mT, 1:39.07, MILLFLEET, Tusayan, Obliquity, 14 started.

Burnaby Breeders' Cup H., Hastings Race Course, July 1, $65,872, 3yo, f, 1m, 1:45.25, TOBE SUAVE, Future Flash, Cariboo Prospector, 10 started.

Busanda S., Aqueduct, Jan. 25, $84,375, 3yo, f, 1m 70y, 1:43.04, ISLAND SAND, Tempting Note, Fait Accompli, 10 started.

Busher S., Aqueduct, Feb. 28, $81,600, 3yo, f, 1¹/₁₆m, 1:44.93, FOND, Taittinger Rose, Showmesomelove, 7 started.

Bustles and Bows S., Fairplex Park, Sept. 16, $58,200, 2yo, f, 6¹/₂f, 1:18.06, KASH KLIP, Timeintown, High Zone, 6 started.

Buttons and Bows H., Sun Downs, April 11, $3,050, 3&up, f&m, 4f, :47.40, RAISE A DAUGHTER, Move On Slew, Crissy's Cricket, 5 started.

Caballos del Sol H., Turf Paradise, Oct. 9, $40,000, 3&up, 6f, 1:08.76, NEWARK, Palmerton, Grimm, 5 started.

Cab Calloway S. (R), Saratoga Race Course, Aug. 4, $250,000, 3yo, progeny of eligible New York stallions, 1¹/₈m, 1:50.99, CHOWDER'S FIRST, West Virginia, Pay Attention, 8 started.

Cactus Cup S., Turf Paradise, March 12, $40,000, 3yo, f, 6¹/₂f, 1:16.90, SAUCEONSIDE, Muir Beach, Coke's Melody, 9 started.

Cactus Flower H., Turf Paradise, April 10, $40,000, 3&up, f&m, 6f, 1:09.34, PRINCESS V., Channing Way, Oriana's Magic, 8 started.

Caesar Rodney H., Delaware Park, June 16, $200,000, 3&up, 1¹/₈mT, 1:53.43, B. A. WAY, Gran Cesare (Arg), Foufa's Warrior, 5 started.

Caesar's Wish S. (R), Pimlico, April 24, $72,750, 3yo, f, Maryland-bred, 1¹/₁₆m, 1:44.78, HE LOVES ME, Plata, Dance Fee, 4 started.

Cajun Express S. (R), Delta Downs, March 27, $40,000, 4&up, Louisiana-bred, 5f, :58.53, ZARB'S LUCK, Fine Stormy, Believe Im Special, 6 started.

Cajun S. (R), Louisiana Downs, Oct. 23, $54,300, 3&up, Louisiana-bred, 6f, 1:09.22, ZARB'S DAHAR, Lac Laronge, Patrick's Talent, 9 started.

Calcasieu S. (R), Delta Downs, Nov. 13, $50,000, 2yo, Louisiana-bred, 5f, 1:00.50, MR. EXCELLENT, Robbeau, Wade Away, 7 started.

CALDER DERBY-G3, Calder Race Course, Oct. 23, $200,000, 3yo, 1¹/₈mT, 1:51.25, EDDINGTON, Bob's Proud Moment, Caballero Negro, 12 started.

Calder Oaks, Calder Race Course, Oct. 23, $200,000, 3yo, f, 1¹/₈mT, 1:51.46, HOPELESSLY DEVOTED, Vous, Skip Command, 12 started.

Calder Turf Sprint H., Calder Race Course, July 10, $100,000, 3&up, 5fT, :55.40, WHENTHEDOVEFLIES, Swift Replica, Bishop Court Hill, 11 started.

California Breeders' Champion S. (R), Santa Anita Park, Dec. 26, $138,625, 2yo, California-bred, 7f, 1:22.73, UNCLE DENNY, Iced Out, Lucky J. H., 8 started.

California Breeders' Champion S. (R), Santa Anita Park, Dec. 27, $140,875, 2yo, f, California-bred, 7f, 1:22.66, MEMORETTE, Lady Betrando, Kohar, 11 started.

California Cup Classic H. (R), Santa Anita Park, Oct. 16, $250,000, 3&up, California-bred, 1¹/₈m, 1:47.70, COZY GUY, Lava Man, Anziyan Royalty, 10 started.

California Cup Distaff H. (R), Santa Anita Park, Oct. 16, $150,000, 3&up, f&m, California-bred, a6¹/₂fT, 1:12.63, OUR MANGO, Western Hemisphere, Market Garden, 8 started.

California Cup Distance H. (R), Santa Anita Park, Oct. 16, $100,000, 3&up, California-bred, 1¹/₄mT, 2:01.19, TEST THE WATERS, Shalini, Tucked Away, 7 started.

California Cup Juvenile Fillies S. (R), Santa Anita Park, Oct. 16, $125,000, 2yo, f, California-bred, 1¹/₁₆m, 1:45.22, LADY TRUFFLES, Cee's Irish, Home Ice, 12 started.

California Cup Juvenile S. (R), Santa Anita Park, Oct. 16, $125,000, 2yo, c&g, California-bred, 1¹/₁₆m, 1:44.02, TEXCESS, Generalist, Tizmanian Devil, 6 started.

California Cup Matron H. (R), Santa Anita Park, Oct. 16, $150,000, 3&up, f&m, California-bred, 1¹/₁₆m, 1:42.36, DREAM OF SUMMER, Yearly Report, Summer Wind Dancer, 8 started.

California Cup Mile H. (R), Santa Anita Park, Oct. 16, $175,000, 3&up, California-bred, 1mT, 1:33.44, A TO THE Z, Hemet Thought, Stage Player, 7 started.

California Cup Sprint H. (R), Santa Anita Park, Oct. 16, $150,000, 3&up, California-bred, 6f, 1:08.84, AREYOUTALKINTOME, Full Moon Madness, Green Team, 12 started.

California Cup Starter H. (R), Santa Anita Park, Oct. 16, $50,000, 3&up, California-bred starters for a claiming price of $40,000 or less in 2004, 1¹/₈mT, 2:26.61, RING OF FRIENDSHIP, Noble Kinsman, Gobi Dan, 10 started.

California Cup Starter Sprint H. (R), Santa Anita Park, Oct. 16, $50,000, 3&up, California-bred starters for a claiming price of $32,000 or less in 2004, 6f, 1:09.48, ATA OLYMPIO, Four Checker, Mysterious Cat, 8 started.

California Derby, Bay Meadows, April 17, $100,000, 3yo, 1¹/₈m, 1:47.95, TRIESTE'S HONOR, Capitano, Dream Place, 7 started.

CALIFORNIAN S.-G2, Hollywood Park, June 12, $250,000, 3&up, 1¹/₈m, 1:47.64, EVEN THE SCORE, Total Impact (Chi), Nose The Trade (GB), 4 started.

California Oaks, Golden Gate Fields, March 6, $77,025, 3yo, f, 1¹/₁₆m, 1:41.71, HOUSE OF FORTUNE, Church Editor, Secret Corsage, 4 started.

California Sprint Championship H. (R), Bay Meadows, Sept. 11, $100,000, 3&up, California-bred, 6f, 1:07.41, GREEN TEAM, Areyoutalkintome, Revello, 5 started.

California Thoroughbred Breeders' Association S. (R), Del Mar, July 23, $125,000, 2yo, f, California-bred, 5¹/₂f, 1:04.21, STERLING CAT, Miss January, Proposed, 7 started.

California Turf Championship H. (R), Bay Meadows, Sept. 6, $100,000, 3&up, California-bred, 1mT, 1:35.84, STAGE PLAYER, Ninebanks, Blue Afleet, 6 started.

Caltech S., Gulfstream Park, March 20, $67,700, 3yo, 1¹/₈mT, 1:48.13, SHAKESPEARE, Prince Arch, Prepster, 11 started.

Camelia S. (R), Delta Downs, Jan. 9, $50,000, 4&up, f&m, Louisiana-bred, 6¹/₂f, 1:20.77, FUSE IT, Prized Amberpro, Light Fling, 7 started.

Canada Day S. (R), Fort Erie, July 1, $96,000, 3&up, Canadian-bred, 6f, 1:10.26, KRZ RUCKUS, Barbeau Ruckus, Mulligan the Great, 4 started.

Canada Day S., Assiniboia Downs, July 1, $40,000, 3&up, f&m, 1m, 1:40.20, PETE'S SURPRISE, I B Right Back, Remiewaterbluz, 9 started.

Canad Construction S., Grand Prairie, July 11, $5,175, 3&up, 1m, 1:43.80, GOMKA, Petro Pete, Moe Boots, 8 started.

CANADIAN DERBY-G3, Northlands Park, Aug. 28, $250,000, 3yo, 1³/₈m, 2:22.60, ORGAN GRINDER, Controlled Meeting, dh-Bonspiel, dh-Cariboo Prospector, 11 started.

CANADIAN H.-G2, Woodbine, Sept. 19, $327,500, 3&up, f&m, a1¹/₈mT, 1:43.59, CLASSIC STAMP, Inish Glora, Heyahohowdy, 9 started.

CANADIAN INTERNATIONAL S.-G1, Woodbine, Oct. 24, $1,500,000, 3&up, 1¹/₂mT, 2:28.64, SULAMANI (Ire), Simonas (Ire), Brian Boru (GB), 10 started.

Canadian Juvenile S., Northlands Park, Oct. 11, $75,000, 2yo, 1¹/₁₆m, 1:48.40, POOR IGGY, Nessarose, Magic for Six, 7 started.

CANADIAN TURF H.-G3, Gulfstream Park, Jan. 31, $100,000, 3&up, 1¹/₁₆m, 1:44.90, NEWFOUNDLAND, Millennium Dragon (GB), Everything to Gain, 6 started.

Candy Eclair S., Monmouth Park, Sept. 6, $55,000, 3yo, f, 5fT, :57.04, AMBITION UNBRIDLED, Whatsmineisyours, Very Vegas, 10 started.

Canterbury Park Juvenile S., Canterbury Park, July 11, $40,000, 2yo, 5¹/₂f, 1:05.43, SMOKE SMOKE SMOKE, Still Guilty, El Grande Seville, 7 started.

Canterbury Park Lassie S., Canterbury Park, July 11, $40,000, 2yo, f, 5¹/₂f, 1:06.81, BERBATIM, Tuff Justice, Neeranjanie, 6 started.

Cape Henlopen S., Delaware Park, July 18, $48,139, 3&up, 1¹/₂m, 2:35.73, CHOPPER WON, Spanish Spur (GB), My Request, 3 started.

Capital City H. (R), Penn National Race Course, Aug. 20, $40,900, 3&up, Pennsylvania-bred, 1¹/₁₆mT, 1:42.49, MIXED UP, Sir Echo, Yo, 8 started.

Capitol City Futurity, Lincoln State Fair, June 27, $10,250, 2yo, 4¹/₂f, :52.40, SLOTSFAN, Big Red Fantasy, Gacky, 10 started.

Capote Belle S. (R), Aqueduct, April 21, $59,350, 4&up, f&m, nonwinners of a graded stakes, 6f, 1:10.43, KITTY KNIGHT, Elegant Mercedes, Actcellent, 5 started.

Captain Condo S. (R), Emerald Downs, Sept. 19, $40,000, 2yo, c&g, Washington-bred, 6f, 1:09, SEATTLES BEST JOE, Magna Tice, Tomorrow's Turn, 8 started.

Captain Stanley Harrison H., Marquis Downs, July 2, $5,000, 3yo, f, 6f, 1:15.36, DANZIG BALLERINA, Allourwishes, Guest Table, 5 started.

Capt. Billy Boogie S., Turf Paradise, May 9, $21,700, 3&up, 1m, 1:36.23, REAL CREEK, Lure of the Links, Cut of Music, 6 started.

CARDINAL H.-G3, Churchill Downs, Nov. 20, $173,550, 3&up, f&m, 1¹/₈mT, 1:53.94, AUD, May Gator, Angela's Love, 11 started.

Cardinal H. (R), Arlington Park, June 26, $84,650, 3&up, Illinois-conceived and/or -foaled, 1¹/₁₆mT, 1:44.46, RUNAWAY VICTOR, Colorful Tour, Home of Stars, 7 started.

Caressing H., Churchill Downs, Nov. 20, $71,700, 2yo, f, 1¹/₁₆mT, 1:47.51, SWEET TALKER, Dynamist, Dianne's Debut, 7 started.

CARLETON F. BURKE H.-G3, Santa Anita Park, Oct. 23, $100,000, 3&up, 1¹/₂mT, 2:26.91, HABANEROS, Pellegrino (Brz), Gallant (GB), 8 started.

Carl G. Rose Classic H. (R), Calder Race Course, Nov. 13, $200,000, 3&up, Florida-bred, 1¹/₈m, 1:52.51, SUPAH BLITZ, Hear No Evil, Bob's Proud Moment, 7 started.

Carlos Salazar S. (R), The Downs at Albuquerque, June 12, $45,000, 3&up, f&m, New Mexico-bred, 7f, 1:23.38, SHEMOVES-LIKEAGHOST, Ghost Chatter, Spirit de Azure, 7 started.

Carmel H., Bay Meadows, Sept. 12, $57,825, 3yo, f, 1mT, 1:37.01, PENNY'S FORTUNE, Dawn's Angel, Go Ask Daisy, 6 started.

Carol Wilson Memorial S., Grants Pass, June 20, $3,689, 3&up, f&m, 6¹/₂f, 1:19.40, SOUP N' CRACKERS, Kiznitti, Crown of Pearls, 5 started.

Carotene S. (R), Woodbine, Oct. 9, $165,600, 3yo, f, Canadian-bred, 1¹/₈mT, 1:48.18, BLACK ROCK ROAD, Velvet Snow, Charming Proposal, 9 started.

Carousel S., Oaklawn Park, March 27, $49,000, 4&up, f&m, 6f, 1:10.82, ETERNAL CUP, Surf N Sand, See How She Runs, 6 started.

CARRY BACK S.-G3, Calder Race Course, July 10, $300,000, 3yo, 6f, 1:10.50, WEIGELIA, Classy Migration, Bwana Charlie, 11 started.

Carson Hollow S., Aqueduct, Feb. 22, $59,050, 4&up, f&m, 6f, 1:11.13, FIT PERFORMER, Lavender Lass, Chirimoya, 5 started.

CARTER H.-G1, Aqueduct, April 10, $350,000, 3&up, 7f, 1:20.22, PICO CENTRAL (Brz), Strong Hope, Eye of the Tiger, 9 started.

Carterista H., Calder Race Course, May 8, $75,000, 3&up, 1¹/₁₆mT, 1:40.55, MR. LIVINGSTON, Believe I Can Fly, Marco's Word, 9 started.

Carter McGregor Jr. Memorial S. (R), Lone Star Park, May 31, $50,000, 3&up, Texas-bred, 6f, 1:08.60, TERM SHEET, Aledo Pass, Won C C, 7 started.

Casey Darnell H. (R), The Downs at Albuquerque, July 4, $43,400, 3yo, New Mexico-bred, 7f, 1:22.39, ROCKY GULCH, Sand Spirit, Devon's Diamond, 7 started.

Cassidy S., Calder Race Course, Oct. 23, $75,000, 2yo, f, 6f, 1:12.32, RUNNING BOBCATS, Lady in Pink, Snug Harbour, 6 started.

Castlebrook S., Calder Race Course, May 21, $40,000, 3yo, f, 1¹/₁₆m, 1:48.49, SPECIAL REPORT, Alarkandadove, American Miss, 6 started.

Catcharisingstar S., Calder Race Course, Sept. 6, $40,000, 2yo, f, 5f, 1:00.63, RAGTIME HOPE, Lucky Colleen, Inrightclassitime, 10 started.

Cat's Cradle H. (R), Hollywood Park, Nov. 14, $88,500, 3&up, f&m, California-bred, 7¹/₂f, 1:27.94, ROYALLY CHOSEN, Cyber Slew, Tucked Away, 5 started.

Cavonnier Juvenile S., Santa Rosa, Aug. 8, $53,695, 2yo, 5¹/₂f, 1:04.46, THRESHER, Glassy Acet, Dino Camino, 7 started.

Cavonnier S. (R), Santa Anita Park, Sept. 30, $77,396, 2yo, c&g, California-bred, 7f, 1:23.14, SWISS LAD, Generalist, Johnny High Brite, 4 started.

Centennial H., Anthony Downs, July 24, $10,476, 3&up, a5f, 1:05.31, D D DOT COMM, King Ruler, Missy Can Do, 4 started.

Central Iowa S., Prairie Meadows, Sept. 11, $43,840, 3&up, f&m, 1¹/₁₆m, 1:44.59, CASUAL ATTITUDE, Switch Lanes, Sharky's Review, 6 started.

Centre Stage Anne S. (R), Fort Erie, Sept. 6, $60,000, 3&up, f&m, starters at Fort Erie at least three times in 2004, 1¹/₁₆mT, 1:43.90, CLUBAY, Simply Precious, Orientalspringhope, 8 started.

CERF H. (R), Del Mar, Sept. 8, $81,550, 3&up, f&m, non-winners of a stakes of $50,000 in 2004, 6f, 1:10.40, LADY SABRINA, Jetinto Houston, Papa to Kinzie, 5 started.

Challedon S. (R), Pimlico, Nov. 6, $75,000, 3&up, Maryland-bred, 6f, 1:10.03, AGGADAN, Private Opening, Crossing Point, 6 started.

Challenger S., Tampa Bay Downs, March 6, $75,000, 4&up, 1¹/₁₆m, 1:44.46, ATTACK THE BOOKS, Native Hawk, Burning Roma, 10 started.

Chamisa S., The Downs at Albuquerque, May 16, $45,100, 3&up, f&m, 7f, 1:22.27, SUMMER STAR, Yet Anothernatalie, G. Starr, 11 started.

CHAMPAGNE S.-G1, Belmont Park, Oct. 9, $500,000, 2yo, 1^1/$_16$m, 1:42.30, PROUD ACCOLADE, Afleet Alex, Sun King, 8 started.

Chandler S., Turf Paradise, Nov. 19, $40,000, 3yo, f, 7^1/$_2$fT, 1:29.76, MUIR BEACH, Madison Meadows, Coke's Melody, 10 started.

Chantilly S., Assiniboia Downs, June 12, $40,000, 3yo, f, 6f, 1:12.60, ERICKA'S LASS, Miz Mitzie, Warmnfuzzyfeelin, 8 started.

Chapel Belle S., Louisiana Downs, May 22, $50,000, 3yo, f, a1mT, 1:36.15, TOPANGO, Yoursmineours, Smokey Diplomacy, 8 started.

CHAPOSA SPRINGS H.-G3, Calder Race Course, Dec. 31, $100,000, 3&up, f&m, 7f, 1:23.66, EXPECT AN ANGEL, Alix M, Habiboo, 7 started.

Chariot Chaser H., Northlands Park, July 4, $40,000, 3yo, f, 6^1/$_2$f, 1:19.60, KELLYS GUEST, Miz Mitzie, Ericka's Lass, 6 started.

Charles H. Hadry S., Pimlico, Nov. 20, $100,000, 3&up, 1^1/$_16$m, 1:43.30, IRISH COLONY, Bowman's Band, Last Intention, 8 started.

Charles H. Russell H., Bay Meadows, Sept. 26, $64,475, 3&up, f&m, 6f, 1:10.27, JETINTO HOUSTON, Christmas Time, Pheiffer, 6 started.

Charles Taylor Derby, The Downs at Albuquerque, July 3, $42,550, 3yo, 1^1/$_16$m, 1:44.85, SPIRIT GULCH, Samurai Nanao, Skip and Go, 6 started.

Charles Town Dash H., Charles Town Races, July 4, $100,000, 3&up, 4^1/$_2$f, :51.70, FINE STORMY, Not for Sam, Anthony Soprano, 9 started.

CHARLES WHITTINGHAM MEMORIAL H.-G1, Hollywood Park, June 12, $350,000, 3&up, 1^1/$_4$mT, 2:01.52, SABIANGO (Ger), Bayamo (Ire), Just Wonder (GB), 11 started.

Charlie Barley S., Woodbine, June 27, $108,000, 3yo, 1mT, 1:33.02, DALAVIN, Burst of Fire, Bachelor Blues, 8 started.

Charlie Iles Mile S., The Downs at Albuquerque, May 23, $44,200, 3&up, 1m, 1:35.84, WOLFWITHINTEGRITY, Socko, Pleasant Bend, 9 started.

Charlie Palmer H. (R), Ferndale, Aug. 14, $7,435, 3&up, f&m, starters for a claiming price of $12,500 or less in 2004, 6^1/$_2$f, 1:19.50, IN LOVE WITH LOOT, In Gold We Trust, Mom Liked You Best, 7 started.

Charon S., Gulfstream Park, April 16, $53,500, 3yo, f, 7f, 1:23.61, FALL FASHION, Intrueflight, Special Report, 7 started.

Checkered Flag S., Indiana Downs, May 31, $42,400, 3yo, 1mT, 1:37.40, COLD WATER, Tanner Danner, Jamian, 6 started.

Chenery S., Colonial Downs, July 24, $50,000, 2yo, 5^1/$_2$fT, 1:05.71, DUBLEO, Black Tie, Tip City, 5 started.

Cherokee River Stables Turf Classic S., Tampa Bay Downs, April 4, $84,900, 4&up, a1^1/$_16$mT, 1:49.24, RESTAGE, Final Prophecy, Drink a Toast, 10 started.

Cherokee Run H., Churchill Downs, Nov. 14, $63,780, 3&up, 5fT, :57.69, WORLDWIND ROMANCE, Western Roar, Chosen Chief, 12 started.

Cheval S., Delta Downs, Jan. 31, $40,000, 4&up, 5f, :59.90, JOYFUL TUNE, Spin Zone, Taxicat, 8 started.

CHICAGO BREEDERS' CUP H.-G3, Arlington Park, June 19, $175,000, 3&up, f&m, 7f, 1:23.54, MY TRUSTY CAT, Our Josephina, Smoke Chaser, 5 started.

Chicagoland H. (R), Hawthorne Race Course, April 10, $91,175, 4&up, Illinois-conceived and/or -foaled, 6f, 1:10.78, SHANDY, Silver Bid, Out of My Way, 7 started.

Chick Lang Jr. Memorial S., Retama Park, Aug. 21, $40,000, 3&up, 7^1/$_2$fT, 1:28.77, HONORABLE PIC, Fly Slama Jama, Late Expectations, 12 started.

Chief Bearhart S., Woodbine, Oct. 30, $108,000, 3&up, 1^1/$_4$mT, 2:09.67, LAST ANSWER, Rainbows for Luck, Control Tower, 10 started.

Chief Narbona S. (R), The Downs at Albuquerque, June 12, $45,000, 3yo, f, New Mexico-bred, 6f, 1:10.53, LATENITE SPECIAL, Icy Lane, Vipervapor, 6 started.

China Doll S., Santa Anita Park, March 18, $75,800, 3yo, f, 1mT, 1:36.22, TICKER TAPE (GB), Mambo Slew, Amorama (Fr), 10 started.

CHINESE CULTURAL CENTRE S.-G2, Woodbine, July 25, $333,300, 3&up, 1^3/$_8$mT, 2:12.37, SHOAL WATER, Mobil, Strut the Stage, 8 started.

Chinook Pass Sprint S. (R), Emerald Downs, Sept. 19, $37,000, 3&up, Washington-bred, 6f, 1:08, SLEWICIDE CRUISE, Jade Green, Road Afleet, 5 started.

Chipiski S., Calder Race Course, July 23, $40,000, 2yo, f, 6f, 1:12.82, PUNCH APPEAL, Yes It's Gold, Leona's Knight, 7 started.

Chippewa Downs Open Thoroughbred Futurity S., Chippewa Downs, June 27, $2,700, 2yo, 5f, :59.40, PEACEFULL SAMMY, Private Night, Howard's Fool, 6 started.

Chippewa Downs Open Thoroughbred S., Chippewa Downs, June 27, $2,700, 4&up, 1m 70y, 1:51.80, STILAFERD, Grand Mister, Leaping Leroy, 7 started.

Chippewa Downs Thoroughbred Derby, Chippewa Downs, June 26, $2,001, 3yo, 6^1/$_2$f, 1:24, HARBOUR AXE, Natalia's Secret, Little Big Foot, 3 started.

Choice S., Monmouth Park, July 10, $60,000, 3yo, 1^1/$_16$mT, 1:40.27, WAR TRACE, Mosman Bay, Grand Heritage, 6 started.

Chou Croute H., Fair Grounds, Feb. 21, $100,000, 4&up, f&m, 1^1/$_16$m, 1:43.55, SPECTACULAR LISA, Tropical Blossom, Princess Pelona, 7 started.

Chris Christian Futurity, Les Bois Park, July 2, $14,175, 2yo, 5f, 1:00.40, SHAD, Muley Tune, Gal's Hunter, 10 started.

Chris Thomas Turf Classic S., Tampa Bay Downs, May 1, $60,000, 3&up, a1^1/$_8$mT, 1:48.03, RESTAGE, Coahoma, Milky Way Guy, 9 started.

Christmas S., Mountaineer Race Track, Dec. 26, $75,000, 3&up, 6f, 1:10.38, HIGH BLITZ, Danieltown, Bocca Al Lupo, 7 started.

Chrystal Gail S., Turf Paradise, Jan. 12, $21,700, 4&up, f&m, 5^1/$_2$f, 1:03.10, CHANNING WAY, Miss Pixie, Knoll Lake, 6 started.

Chuck Taliaferro Memorial S., Remington Park, Aug. 15, $40,510, 3&up, 6f, 1:09.80, EXPLOSIVE COUNT, Abbi's Choice, Silver Phone, 6 started.

CHURCHILL DOWNS DISTAFF H.-G2, Churchill Downs, Nov. 7, $230,400, 3&up, f&m, 1m, 1:35.05, HALORY LEIGH, Lady Tak, Susan's Angel, 12 started.

CHURCHILL DOWNS H.-G2, Churchill Downs, May 1, $221,800, 4&up, 7f, 1:21.38, SPEIGHTSTOWN, McCann's Mojave, Publication, 7 started.

CICADA S.-G3, Aqueduct, March 20, $109,100, 3yo, f, 7f, 1:23.22, BOHEMIAN LADY, Whoopi Cat, Baldomera, 6 started.

CIGAR MILE H.-G1, Aqueduct, Nov. 27, $350,000, 3&up, 1m, 1:33.46, LION TAMER, Badge of Silver, Pico Central (Brz), 8 started.

Cigar S., Arlington Park, Aug. 14, $53,000, 3&up, 1m, 1:36.62, SILVER ZIPPER, Apt to Be, Discreet Hero, 7 started.

Cincinnatian S. (R), River Downs, July 5, $40,000, 3yo, f, Ohio-bred, 1^1/$_16$mT, 1:43, HAPPY ENDINGS TOO, Imahoneytoo, Raking in the Gold, 7 started.

Cincinnati Trophy S., Turfway Park, Jan. 17, $49,500, 3yo, f, 6^1/$_2$f, 1:19.67, STONEWAY, Beau Watch, Plumlake Lady, 10 started.

Cinderella S., Hollywood Park, June 6, $85,350, 2yo, f, 5^1/$_2$f, 1:04.80, SOUVENIR GIFT, Fortunate Event, Swiss Please, 6 started.

CINEMA BREEDERS' CUP H.-G3, Hollywood Park, June 26, $153,450, 3yo, 1^1/$_8$mT, 1:49, GREEK SUN, Laura's Lucky Boy, Whilly (Ire), 7 started.

CITATION H.-G1, Hollywood Park, Nov. 27, $400,000, 3&up, 1^1/$_16$mT, 1:41.36, LEROIDESANIMAUX (Brz), A to the Z, Three Valleys, 10 started.

City Centre Bingo H., Marquis Downs, Sept. 10, $5,000, 3yo, f, 1m, 1:40.75, ALLOURWISHES, Lucky in the Lead, Six Hour Wait, 6 started.

City of Anderson S. (R), Hoosier Park, Oct. 1, $40,000, 2yo, f, Indiana-bred, 5^1/$_2$f, 1:05.25, FREE BONUS, Join the Crusade, Corydon's Forloon, 8 started.

City of Bridges Sophomore S. (R), Marquis Downs, Aug. 7, $6,500, 3yo, c&g, Saskatchewan-bred, 1m, 1:41.35, STEEL COPY, Stage Whisper, Astapay, 7 started.

City of Edmonton Distaff H., Northlands Park, Aug. 28, $75,000, 3&up, f&m, 1^1/$_16$m, 1:45.40, ICE GIRL, Think Fast, Sweet Monarch, 6 started.

City of Las Cruces H. (R), Sunland Park, March 20, $103,800, 3&up, f&m, New Mexico-bred, 1m, 1:37.69, LORD IMAJONES, Scarzane, Ghost Chatter, 8 started.

City of Phoenix H., Turf Paradise, Oct. 2, $40,000, 3&up, f&m, 6f, 1:09.27, MUIR BEACH, Arch Lady, Friendofthefamily, 7 started.

City of Roses H., Portland Meadows, Dec. 26, $10,000, 3&up, f&m, 1m, 1:40.23, PETE'S DOLLY, Callie Mae, Chancy Chancy, 8 started.

City of Vancouver H. (R), Hastings Race Course, May 24, $44,472, 3yo, British Columbia-bred, 6^1/$_2$f, 1:16.19, MARK OF DIABLO, Louie Downtown, Lord Samarai, 7 started.

City Zip S., Monmouth Park, Sept. 18, $60,000, 3yo, 6f, 1:09.76, KNIGHT OF DARKNESS, Bola Soup, Frisky Spider, 6 started.

City Zip S. (R), Aqueduct, Dec. 18, $50,650, 2yo, non-winners of a stakes, 6f, 1:10.75, PAVO, Benjamin Baby, Lieutenant Danz, 6 started.

Civic Holiday S. (R), Fort Erie, Aug. 2, $48,000, 3&up, starters at Fort Erie at least three times in 2004, 1¹/₁₆m, 1:44.29, ELEGANT HUNTER, Ardent Eddy, Open Lock, 7 started.

C. J. Hindley Humboldt County Marathon H. (R), Ferndale, Aug. 22, $12,545, 3&up, starters for a claiming price of $12,500 or less in 2004, 1⅝m, 2:47.04, CLIP, Potri Cacho (Arg), Dandi Candi, 5 started.

Claiming Crown Emerald S. (R), Canterbury Park, July 17, $125,000, 3&up, starters for a claiming price of $20,000 or less, 1¹/₁₆mT, 1:42.20, STAGE PLAYER, Bristolville, He Flies, 14 started.

Claiming Crown Express S. (R), Canterbury Park, July 17, $47,000, 3&up, starters for a claiming price of $7,500 or less, 6f, 1:10.10, CHISHOLM, Setthehook, Devil's Con, 8 started.

Claiming Crown Glass Slipper S. (R), Canterbury Park, July 17, $70,500, 3&up, f&m, starters for a claiming price of $12,500 or less, 6¹/₂f, 1:17.29, BANISHED LOVER, Moving Fever, Flaming Night, 8 started.

Claiming Crown Iron Horse S. (R), Canterbury Park, July 17, $48,500, 3&up, starters for a claiming price of $5,000 or less, 1¹/₁₆m, 1:44.26, SUPERMAN CAN, Rough Draft, Gram's Folly, 11 started.

Claiming Crown Jewel S. (R), Canterbury Park, July 17, $145,500, 3&up, starters for a claiming price of $25,000 or less, 1¹/₁₆m, 1:49.62, INTELLIGENT MALE, Musique Toujours, Rize, 11 started.

Claiming Crown Rapid Transit S. (R), Canterbury Park, July 17, $94,000, 3&up, starters for a claiming price of $16,000 or less, 6¹/₂f, 1:15.56, HEROIC SIGHT, Quote Me Later, Satan's Code, 8 started.

Claire Marine S., Arlington Park, Sept. 5, $52,800, 3&up, f&m, 1¹/₂mT, 2:35.36, DELICATESSA, Tamarack Bay, Lifting the Veil, 6 started.

Clarendon S. (R), Woodbine, July 18, $158,700, 2yo, Canadian-foaled, 5¹/₂f, 1:05.91, MOONSHINE JUSTICE, Da Cardinal, Castle Prospect, 4 started.

Clark County S., Keeneland, Oct. 21, $84,450, 3&up, f&m, 5¹/₂fT, 1:03.32, DYNA DAWYNA, Speedy Sonata, Black Escort, 10 started.

CLARK H.-G2, Churchill Downs, Nov. 26, $558,000, 3&up, 1¹/₈m, 1:50.81, SAINT LIAM, Seek Gold, Perfect Drift, 9 started.

Classic "B" Cup S., Lethbridge, Oct. 16, $13,200, 3&up, 1¹/₁₆m, 1:57.40, CANDID REMARK, Tata Pantoja, Ta Keel, 8 started.

Classy 'n Smart S. (R), Woodbine, Dec. 1, $129,000, 3&up, f&m, progeny of eligible Ontario stallions, 1¹/₁₆m, 1:46.02, BRASS IN POCKET, Bay Sweetie Babe, Roman Romance, 6 started.

CLEMENT L. HIRSCH H.-G2, Del Mar, Aug. 8, $300,000, 3&up, f&m, 1¹/₁₆m, 1:42.93, MISS LOREN (Arg), House of Fortune, Royally Chosen, 8 started.

CLEMENT L. HIRSCH MEMORIAL TURF CHAMPIONSHIP S.-G1, Santa Anita Park, Oct. 3, $250,000, 3&up, 1¹/₄mT, 1:58.70, STAR OVER THE BAY, Sarafan, Vangelis, 7 started.

Cleveland Gold Cup S. (R), Thistledown, July 4, $75,000, 3yo, Ohio-bred, 1¹/₈m, 1:54.12, CRYPTO'S PROSPECT, Xtra Jack, Oh Oleg, 12 started.

Cleveland Kindergarten S. (R), Thistledown, Aug. 14, $40,000, 2yo, Ohio-bred, 6f, 1:12.58, RUBIUS, Fierce Cat, Bug Hunter, 11 started.

CLIFF HANGER H.-G3, The Meadowlands, Oct. 15, $200,000, 3&up, 1¹/₁₆mT, 1:42.41, DR. KASHNIKOW, Tam's Terms, Host (Chile), 8 started.

Club House Special S., Columbus Races, Aug. 22, $11,100, 2yo, 6f, 1:15.80, S C KING, The Straw Man, Fine Dreams, 9 started.

Cluff Sprint S., Western Montana Fair, Aug. 13, $4,625, 3&up, 5f, :59.60, SEATTLE CUE, Restrictions Apply, Slew Design, 6 started.

Clyde B. Stephens S. (R), Delta Downs, March 20, $50,000, 3yo, Louisiana-bred, 5f, :59.42, KIM'S GEM, Honey Hit, Smokin Forty Won, 6 started.

COACHING CLUB AMERICAN OAKS-G1, Belmont Park, July 24, $500,000, 3yo, f, 1¹/₄m, 2:02.43, ASHADO, Stellar Jayne, Magical Illusion, 6 started.

Cocodrie S. (R), Delta Downs, Dec. 17, $40,000, 3&up, Louisiana-bred nonwinners of a stakes, 6¹/₂f, 1:22.10, VALID FAITH, Cort's P. B., Mister Ajax, 10 started.

Colin S., Woodbine, July 31, $134,000, 2yo, 6f, 1:11.19, WHOLELOTTABOURBON, Quite a Ruckus, Killenaule, 5 started.

Colleen S., Monmouth Park, Aug. 7, $60,000, 2yo, f, 5¹/₂f, 1:04.76, IM A DIXIE GIRL, Elke, Joyous Song, 10 started.

Col. E. R. Bradley H., Fair Grounds, Jan. 3, $60,000, 4&up, a1¹/₁₆mT, 1:45.04, SKATE AWAY, Warleigh, Great Bloom, 9 started.

College of New Jersey S., The Meadowlands, Nov. 13, $60,000, 3&up, f&m, 1m 70y, 1:40.48, PAISLEY PARK, Twist and Pop, Totally Precious, 8 started.

Colonel Power H., Fair Grounds, Jan. 11, $60,000, 4&up, 6f, 1:09.99, ALOHA BOLD, Ole Rebel, El Ruller, 8 started.

Colorado Derby, Arapahoe Park, Aug. 15, $26,650, 3yo, 1¹/₁₆m, 1:43.40, SKIP AND GO, Nick Missed, Spirit Gulch, 6 started.

Colts Neck H. (R), Monmouth Park, Aug. 29, $100,000, 3&up, New Jersey-bred, 6f, 1:10.16, QUIET DESPERATION, Our Wildcat, Upturn, 8 started.

Columbia River S., Portland Meadows, Nov. 27, $10,000, 2yo, 6f, 1:13.51, TYPHOON AARON, Tomorrow's Turn, Top Toad, 9 started.

Columbine H., Arapahoe Park, Aug. 22, $27,075, 3&up, f&m, 1¹/₁₆m, 1:45, SIDEWAYS, Humble Roannie, Bar Bailey, 6 started.

Columbus Breeders' Special H. (R), Columbus Races, Aug. 29, $13,200, 3yo, f, Nebraska-bred, 6¹/₂f, 1:21.40, SHESO, Shantac, Jitterbug Joy, 7 started.

Columbus Debutante S. (R), Columbus Races, Sept. 12, $13,000, 2yo, f, Nebraska-bred, 6f, 1:18.20, CARISSA'S SHINE, Nurse Alice, Dabney, 5 started.

Columbus Futurity (R), Columbus Races, Sept. 12, $13,100, 2yo, c&g, Nebraska-bred, 6f, 1:16.20, CORK THE BARBER, Buzzaway, The Straw Man, 6 started.

COMELY S.-G3, Aqueduct, April 9, $112,000, 3yo, f, 1m, 1:35.89, SOCIETY SELECTION, Bending Strings, Daydreaming, 8 started.

Come Summer S., Canterbury Park, June 26, $50,000, 3yo, a1mT, 1:36.06, VAZANDAR, It's Lucky, Sultan of Spin, 8 started.

Comet S., The Meadowlands, Oct. 15, $60,000, 2yo, 6f, 1:09.43, FAVALORA, Who's the Cowboy, Doctor Voodoo, 8 started.

COMMONWEALTH BREEDERS' CUP S.-G2, Keeneland, April 10, $250,250, 3&up, 7f, 1:23.14, LION TAMER, Private Horde, Marino Marini, 8 started.

Commonwealth Turf S., Churchill Downs, Nov. 14, $171,150, 3yo, 1¹/₁₆mT, 1:44.75, BROADWAY VIEW, America Alive, Capo, 10 started.

Con Jackson Claiming H., The Downs at Albuquerque, Sept. 26, $15,000, 3&up, 1 13/16m, 3:10.04, MEGAN'S MAN, Barron Dan, Iron Cloud, 7 started.

CONNAUGHT CUP S.-G3, Woodbine, May 30, $164,400, 4&up, 1¹/₁₆mT, 1:40.24, SLEW VALLEY, Le Cinquieme Essai, Shoal Water, 6 started.

Connie's Magic S., Calder Race Course, Dec. 13, $40,000, 3&up, f&m, 6¹/₂f, 1:18.12, ALIX M, D' Wildcat Speed, Slews Final Answer, 9 started.

Conniver S. (R), Laurel Park, March 7, $72,750, 4&up, f&m, Maryland-bred, 7f, 1:23.75, BRONZE ABE, Search for a Cure, In Love, 4 started.

Conroe S., Sam Houston Race Park, Dec. 11, $40,000, 3yo, 6f, 1:09.66, TWO DOWN AUTOMATIC, Charming Socialite, Governor of Spain, 7 started.

Continental Mile S., Monmouth Park, Sept. 5, $55,000, 2yo, 1mT, 1:38.63, DUBLEO, United, Arcturus, 10 started.

Cool Air S., Calder Race Course, May 23, $40,000, 3&up, f&m, 5fT, :54.78, WHENTHEDOVEFLIES, Peace Symbol, Dazzling Deelite, 9 started.

Coolbythepool S., Calder Race Course, June 11, $40,000, 3&up, f&m, 1m, 1:41.91, DAKOTA LIGHT, Firm Reality, Romanesque, 6 started.

COOLMORE LEXINGTON S.-G2, Keeneland, April 17, $325,000, 3yo, 1¹/₁₆m, 1:43.82, QUINTONS GOLD RUSH, Fire Slam, Song of the Sword, 14 started.

Coors Starter Allowance S. (R), Fonner Park, May 8, $11,250, 3&up, starters for a claiming price of $5,000 or less in 2003-'04, 1¹/₈m, 1:52.40, J. R. HONOR, Up Jump the Devil, Kes Kat, 10 started.

Copper Top Futurity (R), Sunland Park, April 11, $186,384, 2yo, New Mexico-bred, 4¹/₂f, :54.16, OSOTRICKY, Ring of the Run, Smartlildevil, 10 started.

Cordially S., Delaware Park, Sept. 27, $51,410, 3&up, f&m, 1m, 1:38.23, THERMAL ABLASION, Misty Sixes, Shiny Sheet, 4 started.

Cormorant S. (R), Aqueduct, Nov. 7, $100,000, 3&up, c&g, progeny of eligible New York stallions, 1mT, 1:37.65, PA PA DA, Thanasi, Unnerving, 9 started.

Cornucopia H., Louisiana Downs, Oct. 9, $39,200, 3&up, f&m, 1¹/₁₆mT, 1:49.12, DUE TO WIN, Boomboomgirl, Dyna Del, 5 started.

Coronation Futurity (R), Woodbine, Nov. 13, $250,000, 2yo, Canadian-foaled, 1¹/₈m, 1:55.24, ABLO, Nikey Missile, Feather Bed Lane, 7 started.

Correction H., Aqueduct, Jan. 31, $82,875, 3&up, f&m, 6f, 1:10.14, SHE'S ZEALOUS, Fit Performer, Balmy, 9 started.

Corte Madera S., Golden Gate Fields, Dec. 19, $60,400, 2yo, f, 1m, 1:36.94, CEE'S IRISH, Island Escape, On London Time, 7 started.

COTILLION H.-G2, Philadelphia Park, Oct. 2, $250,000, 3yo, f, 1¹/₁₆m, 1:41.68, ASHADO, Ender's Sister, My Lordship, 7 started.

Count Fleet S., Aqueduct, Jan. 3, $81,225, 3yo, 1m 70y, 1:41.42, SMARTY JONES, Risky Trick, Mr. Spock, 7 started.

COUNT FLEET SPRINT H.-G3, Oaklawn Park, April 8, $150,000, 4&up, 6f, 1:09.27, SHAKE YOU DOWN, Where's the Ring, Aloha Bold, 6 started.

Count Lathum H., Northlands Park, Aug. 7, $40,000, 3yo, 1 5/16m, 2:12.60, KAT KOOL, Tamingo, Ol Fifty, 5 started.

Courtship S., Bay Meadows, Oct. 10, $67,725, 2yo, f, 6f, 1:12.17, TENSE WAGER, Crisane, Fairy Tale Dream, 5 started.

Cover Gal S. (R), Santa Anita Park, Sept. 29, $81,825, 2yo, f, California-bred, 7f, 1:23.20, SHORT ROUTE, Lady Truffles, Home Ice, 6 started.

Cover Girl H., Hastings Race Course, Sept. 5, $41,414, 3&up, f&m, 6¹/₂f, 1:16.96, STORMENTED, Famous Spirit, April Foolish, 9 started.

Cowdin S., Belmont Park, Oct. 17, $78,988, 2yo, 6¹/₂f, 1:17.20, FLAMENCO, Better Than Bonds, Upscaled, 5 started.

Coyote H., Turf Paradise, Feb. 21, $40,000, 4&up, 6f, 1:07.42, TA-IASLEW, Boston Common, Palmerton, 7 started.

CRADLE S.-G3, River Downs, Sept. 6, $200,000, 2yo, 1¹/₁₆m, 1:45, BELLAMY ROAD, Diamond Isle, Scipion, 8 started.

Crank It Up S., Monmouth Park, June 6, $55,000, 3yo, f, 5fT, :56.90, FOREST MUSIC, Schedule (GB), Forty Moves, 7 started.

Creme de la Creme S. (R), Delta Downs, Nov. 12, $50,000, 2yo, f, Louisiana-bred, 5f, 1:00.08, INDIGO GIRL, Forty Babes, Finest Gold, 7 started.

Crescent City Derby (R), Fair Grounds, Jan. 17, $75,000, 3yo, Louisiana-bred, 1¹/₁₆m, 1:48.84, ARCUS, Walk This Way, Old Lee, 11 started.

Criterium S., Calder Race Course, July 3, $100,000, 2yo, 5¹/₂f, 1:04.88, DEVILS DISCIPLE, Magic Speed, Cherokee Chase, 8 started.

Crystal Water H. (R), Santa Anita Park, March 13, $109,000, 4&up, California-bred, 1mT, 1:34.91, LENNYFROMALIBU, Spinelessjellyfish, Ringaskiddy, 7 started.

CTBA Breeders' Oaks (R), Arapahoe Park, Aug. 7, $27,550, 3yo, f, Colorado-bred, 1m 70y, 1:42.80, VANNACIDE, Kranky Karol, Campo Ridge, 8 started.

CTBA Derby (R), Arapahoe Park, Sept. 4, $29,025, 3yo, Colorado-bred, 1¹/₁₆m, 1:43.60, DA BOXER, My Mega Man, C K Jett, 8 started.

CTBA Futurity (R), Arapahoe Park, Aug. 8, $33,325, 2yo, Colorado-bred, 6f, 1:09.40, CAJUN PEPPER, Run Do Run, R W Jett, 9 started.

CTBA Lassie S. (R), Arapahoe Park, Sept. 6, $30,600, 2yo, f, Colorado-bred, 6f, 1:11.20, JAVA JOLENE, Mandera Ridge, Baby Van, 10 started.

CTBA Marian S. (R), Fairplex Park, Sept. 20, $57,000, 3yo, f, California-bred, 1¹/₁₆m, 1:46.04, DROUGHT BREAKER, Coke's Melody, Little Foxy Baby, 5 started.

CTHS Evergreen Farm S., Grand Prairie, July 23, $5,837, 3&up, 6f, N/A, HY NICK, Highland Road, Onastar, 5 started.

CTHS Sales S. (R), Assiniboia Downs, Sept. 6, $40,000, 2yo, c&g, sold at a CTHS sale, 6f, 1:14, YOUR EXCELLENCE, Icelandic Conquest, Gogogadget, 7 started.

CTHS Sales S. (R), Assiniboia Downs, Sept. 6, $40,000, 2yo, f, sold at a CTHS sale, 6f, 1:15, DANGER PAY, Trick Question, One More Turn, 6 started.

CTHS Sales S. (R), Hastings Race Course, Sept. 11, $66,396, 2yo, f, Canadian-bred sold at a CTHS sale, 6¹/₂f, 1:18.62, BACKSEAT BECKA, After the Knight, Astromaticat, 9 started.

CTHS Sales S. (R), Hastings Race Course, Sept. 11, $66,396, 2yo, c&g, Canadian-bred sold at a CTHS sale, 6¹/₂f, 1:18.84, RUN ON, Forecastor, Alabama Rain, 9 started.

Cub Klahr H., Les Bois Park, June 16, $4,800, 3&up, 7f, 1:25.60, FIND MY HALTER, Quiet Syns, Neil's Advice, 5 started.

Cup and Saucer S. (R), Woodbine, Oct. 17, $250,000, 2yo, Canadian-foaled, 1¹/₁₆mT, 1:44.14, SLEW'S SAGA, Kalyptic, Area Limits, 10 started.

Curribot H., Sunland Park, Feb. 7, $54,576, 3&up, 1¹/₁₆m, 1:42.78, FACE THE BAND, Fame Ina Minute, Streak of Royalty, 10 started.

Cut the Charm S., Calder Race Course, May 7, $40,000, 3&up, f&m, 1¹/₁₆m, 1:47.14, SECRET REQUEST, Sniffles, Grab Bag, 8 started.

C. W. "Doc" Pardee Starter Allowance S. (R), Turf Paradise, April 24, $15,000, 3&up, f&m, Arizona-bred starters for a claiming price of $8,000 or less since September 25, 2003, and have not won for more since that date, 1m, 1:37.71, SI YA DANCING, Lucky Autum, Strawberry Ice, 5 started.

Cyclones H. (R), Prairie Meadows, June 19, $70,000, 3&up, c&g, Iowa-bred, 1¹/₁₆m, 1:43.01, RUBIANOS IMAGE, Take Me Up, Cowboy Stuff, 10 started.

Cy-Fair S., Sam Houston Race Park, Dec. 18, $40,000, 3yo, f, 6f, 1:11.29, INJUSTICE, So Sorry, Shons Secret, 11 started.

Cypress S. (R), Delta Downs, Jan. 2, $50,000, 4&up, Louisiana-bred, 6¹/₂f, 1:19.21, PRINCE SLEW, Zarb's Luck, Bet Me Best, 5 started.

Czaria H., Sunland Park, Feb. 8, $53,500, 3&up, f&m, 6f, 1:09, BIG SCORE, Hacienda Del Mar, City Sleeper, 8 started.

DadeTurf Classic S., Ellis Park, Sept. 4, $75,000, 3&up, f&m, 1¹/₁₆mT, 1:39.98, MAY GATOR, Wildwood Royal, Playa Maya, 8 started.

DAHLIA H.-G3, Hollywood Park, Dec. 20, $150,000, 3&up, f&m, 1¹/₁₆mT, 1:42.11, FESTIVAL (Jpn), Irgunette (Aus), Belle Ange (Fr), 5 started.

Da Hoss S., Colonial Downs, June 26, $50,000, 3&up, 1mT, 1:35.07, MT. CARSON, Duvalier, Access Approved, 5 started.

Da Hoss S., Turf Paradise, April 10, $22,000, 3yo, 7¹/₂fT, 1:30.48, ZAL'S PAL, Plum Red, It's a Shortcut, 9 started.

Daisycutter H., Del Mar, July 30, $96,825, 3&up, f&m, 5fT, :55.95, ICANTGOFORTHAT, Market Garden, Lady General, 8 started.

Dallas Turf Cup S., Lone Star Park, June 19, $200,000, 3&up, 1¹/₄mT, 1:49.89, MAYSVILLE SLEW, Star Over the Bay, A to the Z, 7 started.

Damon Runyon S. (R), Aqueduct, Dec. 12, $85,725, 2yo, New York-bred, 1¹/₁₆m, 1:44.48, NAUGHTY NEW YORKER, Sort It Out, Summerland, 12 started.

DANCE SMARTLY H.-G3, Woodbine, July 17, $209,450, 3&up, f&m, 1¹/₄mT, 1:48.18, MONA ROSE, Inish Glora, Classic Stamp, 4 started.

Dancing Count S., Laurel Park, Jan. 1, $43,400, 3yo, 6f, 1:11.40, KIOWA PRINCE, Basketball Court, Hands On, 5 started.

Daniel Van Clief S. (R), Colonial Downs, July 17, $50,000, 3&up, Virginia-bred and/or -sired, 1¹/₁₆mT, 1:45.31, BAY EAGLE, Jaki's Magic, Rahy's Chance, 8 started.

Danville H., Golden Gate Fields, March 20, $59,312, 3&up, 6f, 1:08.94, MORE CRAFTY, Green Team, K O Love, 8 started.

Danzig S. (R), Penn National Race Course, May 14, $41,400, 3yo, Pennsylvania-bred, 6f, 1:10.06, SALTY PUNCH, Prince Joseph, Hey Rube, 5 started.

DARLEY ALCIBIADES S.-G2, Keeneland, Oct. 8, $400,000, 2yo, f, 1¹/₁₆m, 1:44.31, RUNWAY MODEL, Sharp Lisa, In the Gold, 10 started.

Darrell Ost Memorial S., Western Montana Fair, Aug. 12, $5,100, 3&up, f&m, 6¹/₂f, 1:23.40, A STEP BEYOND, Rosy Ran, Truly Exclusive, 8 started.

Daryl Wells Sr. Memorial S. (R), Fort Erie, July 4, $100,000, 3&up, f&m, Canadian-bred, 6f, 1:11.30, ROMAN ROMANCE, Spanish Decree, Ontheqt, 6 started.

Dave Feldman S., Gulfstream Park, Jan. 18, $66,300, 3yo, 1¹/₁₆m, 1:45.99, TAP DAY, Zakocity, Commendation, 8 started.

DAVONA DALE S.-G2, Gulfstream Park, Feb. 7, $150,000, 3yo, f, 1¹/₁₆m, 1:44.62, MISS CORONADO, Eye Dazzler, Society Selection, 7 started.

Daytona H., Santa Anita Park, Feb. 15, $71,000, 4&up, a6¹/₂fT, 1:12.49, TSIGANE (Fr), Glick, Cayoke (Fr), 6 started.

Dearly Precious S., Aqueduct, Feb. 14, $81,425, 3yo, f, 6f, 1:11.60, AMONG MY SOUVENIRS, Bohemian Lady, Baldomera, 6 started.

Dearly Precious S., Monmouth Park, June 27, $60,000, 3yo, f, 6f, 1:10.28, CHERISH DESTINY, Schedule (GB), Dreamadreamforme, 7 started.

Dear Murray S., Calder Race Course, July 25, $40,000, 2yo, 6f, 1:11.63, DEVILS DISCIPLE, Magic Speed, Hal's Image, 7 started.

Deauville S., Calder Race Course, Dec. 22, $40,000, 3&up, f&m, 7¹/₂fT, 1:28.89, FORMAL MISS, Our Exploit, Far Afield, 6 started.

Debutante S., Assiniboia Downs, July 18, $40,000, 2yo, f, 5¹/₂f, 1:06.20, GOLD STRIKE, Maid for Speed, Rich Rubies, 7 started.

DEBUTANTE S.-G3, Churchill Downs, July 4, $110,800, 2yo, f, 5¹/₂f, 1:04.18, CLASSIC ELEGANCE, Paragon Queen, Cool Spell, 9 started.

Decathlon S., Monmouth Park, Aug. 14, $60,000, 3&up, 5fT, :56.34, SING ME BACK HOME, Choctaw Ridge, Mr. Whitestone, 8 started.

Decoration Day H., Mountaineer Race Track, May 31, $75,000, 3&up, f&m, 1m, 1:41.03, SALZURITA (Arg), Chef's Choice, Strike Rate, 6 started.

De La Rose S. (1st Div.) (R), Saratoga Race Course, Aug. 11, $66,800, 4&up, f&m, nonwinners of $50,000 on the turf in 2003-'04, 1m, 1:36.63, PERSONAL LEGEND, Lentil, Vespers, 8 started.

De La Rose S. (2nd Div.) (R), Saratoga Race Course, Aug. 11, $67,000, 4&up, f&m, nonwinners of $50,000 on the turf in 2003-'04, 1m, 1:37.31, FAST COOKIE, Snowdrops (GB), Super Brand (SAf), 10 started.

DELAWARE H.-G2, Delaware Park, July 18, $750,900, 3&up, f&m, 1¹/₁₆m, 2:03.63, SUMMER WIND DANCER, Roar Emotion, Misty Sixes, 8 started.

DELAWARE OAKS-G2, Delaware Park, July 17, $500,900, 3yo, f, 1¹/₁₆m, 1:43.80, YEARLY REPORT, Ender's Sister, A Lulu Ofa Menifee, 8 started.

Delaware Park NATC Futurity (R), Delaware Park, Sept. 4, $201,640, 2yo, cataloged during 2004 and paid '04 advertising fund fee, 6f, 1:10.78, CLOSING ARGUMENT, Alexandersrun, Mikethegeneral, 7 started.

Delaware Park NATC Sorority (R), Delaware Park, Sept. 4, $200,000, 2yo, f, cataloged during 2004 and paid 2004 advertising fund fee, 6f, 1:11.92, SWITHER, Elke, , 8 started.

DEL MAR BREEDERS' CUP H.-G2, Del Mar, Sept. 5, $250,000, 3&up, 1m, 1:35.14, SUPAH BLITZ, Domestic Dispute, During, 6 started.

DEL MAR DEBUTANTE S.-G1, Del Mar, Aug. 28, $250,000, 2yo, f, 7f, 1:24.18, SWEET CATOMINE, Souvenir Gift, Hello Lucky, 9 started.

DEL MAR DERBY-G2, Del Mar, Sept. 6, $400,000, 3yo, 1¹/₈mT, 1:46.75, BLACKDOUN (Fr), Toasted, Laura's Lucky Boy, 10 started.

DEL MAR FUTURITY-G2, Del Mar, Sept. 8, $245,000, 2yo, 7f, 1:21.29, DECLAN'S MOON, Roman Ruler, Swiss Lad, 4 started.

DEL MAR H.-G2, Del Mar, Aug. 29, $250,000, 3&up, 1³/₈mT, 2:12.71, STAR OVER THE BAY, Sarafan, Moscow Burning, 9 started.

DEL MAR OAKS-G1, Del Mar, Aug. 21, $300,000, 3yo, f, 1¹/₈mT, 1:46.26, AMORAMA (Fr), Ticker Tape (GB), Sweet Win, 7 started.

Delta Beau S., Delta Downs, Nov. 26, $40,000, 2yo, 5f, :59.57, BLAZING EXPLOIT, Camsdancer, Got Myself a Gun, 5 started.

Delta Belle S., Delta Downs, Nov. 20, $40,000, 2yo, f, 5f, 1:00.94, CORONADO ROSE, True Tails, Ketchmewhereyoucan, 6 started.

Delta Colleen H., Hastings Race Course, Sept. 26, $40,446, 3&up, f&m, 1¹/₁₆m, 1:45.13, LA BELLE FLEUR, Stormented, Secret Bullet, 10 started.

Delta Jackpot S., Delta Downs, Dec. 4, $1,000,000, 2yo, 1¹/₁₆m, 1:48.20, TEXCESS, Closing Argument, Anthony J., 10 started.

Delta Mile S., Delta Downs, Feb. 21, $50,000, 4&up, 1m, 1:40.09, KODEMA, Parrott Bay, Mr. Archibald, 6 started.

Delta Princess S., Delta Downs, Dec. 4, $250,000, 2yo, f, 1m, 1:40.42, PUNCH APPEAL, Summer Raven, Snipper Lou, 6 started.

DEMOISELLE S.-G2, Aqueduct, Nov. 27, $200,000, 2yo, f, 1¹/₁₆m, 1:50.39, SIS CITY, Salute, Winning Season, 7 started.

Dempsey Gibbons Thoroughbred H., Marias Fair, July 24, $2,725, 3&up, 7f, 1:25.80, LOST AGAIN, E Mail Trail, Sarah Oteka, 6 started.

Denise Rhudy Memorial S., Delaware Park, July 10, $76,500, 3yo, f, a1¹/₁₆mT, 1:52.38, CUYAHOGA, Gijima, Dancing Colors (Ire), 10 started.

Deputed Testamony S. (R), Pimlico, June 5, $75,000, 3yo, Maryland-bred, 1¹/₁₆m, 1:46.73, JANE'S LUCK, Andiamo, Water Cannon, 6 started.

DEPUTY MINISTER H.-G3, Gulfstream Park, Feb. 7, $100,000, 3&up, 6¹/₂f, 1:15.80, ALKE, Cajun Beat, Coach Jimi Lee, 7 started.

Deputy Minister S. (R), Woodbine, Oct. 20, $132,500, 3yo, progeny of eligible Ontario stallions, 7f, 1:23.65, MILLFLEET, Dashing Admiral, Willie Dunn, 8 started.

Derby Trial S., Assiniboia Downs, July 11, $40,000, 3yo, 1¹/₁₆m, 1:44.60, SHANGHIED, Skipper, Stonewall Harris, 8 started.

Derby Trial S., Fairplex Park, Sept. 13, $58,800, 3yo, 1¹/₁₆m, 1:43.04, LAVA MAN, Last Time in Town, Lindero, 7 started.

DERBY TRIAL S.-G3, Churchill Downs, April 24, $110,800, 3yo, 1m, 1:37.61, SIR SHACKLETON, Courageous Act, Bwana Charlie, 5 started.

Desert Rose H., Ruidoso Downs, Aug. 15, $30,000, 3&up, f&m, 6f, 1:11.60, YET ANOTHERNATALIE, Inox (Arg), Sexy Boots, 8 started.

Desert Sky H. (R), Turf Paradise, May 1, $40,000, 3&up, f&m, starters at the 2003-'04 Turf Paradise meet, 1mT, 1:35.05, MAGNIFICENT VAL, Aspen Hill, Frisco Belle, 6 started.

DESERT STORMER H.-G3, Hollywood Park, June 5, $106,000, 3&up, f&m, 6f, 1:08.91, COCONUT GIRL, Ema Bovary (Chi), Stormica, 5 started.

Desert Vixen S. (R), Calder Race Course, Aug. 14, $75,000, 2yo, f, progeny of eligible Florida stallions, 6f, 1:12.37, ACLASSYSASSY-LASSY, Cut the Mustard, Yes It's Gold, 12 started.

Dessie & Fern Sawyer Futurity (R), The Downs at Albuquerque, Sept. 26, $62,810, 2yo, f, New Mexico-bred, 6f, 1:10.53, HUSH'S GOLD, Hollywood Gone, Last Danz, 11 started.

Devil's Honor H. (R), Philadelphia Park, Sept. 4, $50,000, 3&up, Pennsylvania-bred, 7f, 1:22.80, HERO'S GLOW, Valleyman, Bay of Love, 7 started.

Diamondback S. (R), Yavapai Downs, June 27, $10,200, 3&up, Arizona-bred, 6f, 1:08.80, RED SPARK, Jakes Corner, Instantly, 7 started.

DIANA H.-G1, Saratoga Race Course, July 31, $500,000, 3&up, f&m, 1¹/₈mT, 1:48.99, WONDER AGAIN, Riskaverse, Ocean Drive, 7 started.

Diane Kem H., Portland Meadows, Oct. 23, $10,000, 3&up, f&m, 6f, 1:11.08, QUIZ THE MAID, Breakin My Heart, Charlie's Charmer, 9 started.

Diane Kem S. (R), Emerald Downs, Sept. 19, $40,000, 2yo, f, Washington-bred, 6f, 1:10.20, M K BECK, Queenledo, No Fences, 9 started.

Dine S. (R), SunRay Park, Nov. 2, $69,000, 3yo, c&g, New Mexico-bred, 6¹/₂f, 1:17.40, MACHO MILLER, Tietjen, Jonnygetachex, 6 started.

DISCOVERY H.-G3, Aqueduct, Oct. 27, $110,100, 3yo, 1¹/₈m, 1:49.78, ZAKOCITY, Stolen Time, Mahzouz, 8 started.

Display S., Woodbine, Nov. 21, $137,500, 2yo, 1¹/₁₆mT, 1:47.92, ONE SMOOTH RIDE, Radical Right, Accountforthegold, 5 started.

DISTAFF BREEDERS' CUP H.-G2, Aqueduct, March 27, $147,900, 3&up, f&m, 7f, 1:22.64, RANDAROO, Chirimoya, Storm Flag Flying, 4 started.

Distaff H., Blue Ribbon Downs, May 1, $9,475, 3&up, f&m, 7¹/₂f, 1:34.59, BLONDE OKIE, Miss Time, Party Island, 8 started.

DISTAFF H.-G1, Churchill Downs, May 1, $272,813, 4&up, f&m, 7f, 1:22.78, MAYO ON THE SIDE, Azeri, Randaroo, 4 started.

Distaff S. (R), Assiniboia Downs, Sept. 6, $40,000, 3&up, f&m, Manitoba-bred, 1m, 1:41.60, TAMORNS BLADE, Pete's Surprise, All We Have, 5 started.

DISTAFF TURF MILE S.-G3, Churchill Downs, May 1, $113,300, 3&up, f&m, 1mT, 1:36.10, SHACONAGE, Etoile Montante, Chance Dance, 10 started.

Distance Series Final S., Yavapai Downs, Aug. 9, $11,300, 3&up, 1¹/₄m, 2:06.40, PAPA'S GOT GIN, Longview Legend, Herb's Birthday, 6 started.

Distorted Humor H., Churchill Downs, Nov. 27, $71,680, 3&up, 6¹/₂f, 1:16.44, STRENGTH AND HONOR, Coach Jimi Lee, Level Playingfield, 10 started.

Dixie Belle S., Oaklawn Park, Jan. 23, $50,000, 3yo, f, 6f, 1:11.10, SALTWATER RUNNER, Movant, Yoursmineours, 11 started.

Dixie Miss S., Louisiana Downs, June 12, $50,000, 3yo, f, 6f, 1:09.25, BOSTON EXPRESS, Injustice, Movant, 8 started.

Dixie Poker Ace H. (R), Fair Grounds, Feb. 29, $75,000, 4&up, Louisiana-bred, a7¹/₂fT, 1:32.38, BEBE GARCON, Love Mountain, Rail Rose, 7 started.

DIXIE S.-G2, Pimlico, May 15, $200,000, 3&up, 1¹/₈mT, 1:46.34, MR O'BRIEN (Ire), Millennium Dragon (GB), Warleigh, 11 started.

DOGWOOD BREEDERS' CUP S.-G3, Churchill Downs, June 5, $161,400, 3yo, f, 1¹/₁₆m, 1:43.14, STELLAR JAYNE, Dynaville, Ender's Sister, 5 started.

DOMINION DAY H.-G3, Woodbine, July 1, $217,200, 3&up, 1¹/₄m, 2:03.34, MOBIL, Mark One, The Judge Sez Who, 7 started.

DONALD LEVINE MEMORIAL H.-G3, Philadelphia Park, May 29, $100,000, 3&up, a6f, 1:11.05, PEEPING TOM, Highway Prospector, Richierichierich, 7 started.

Don Bernhardt S., Ellis Park, July 24, $97,500, 3&up, 6¹/₂f, 1:16.91, FIRE SLAM, Unbridled America, Cat Genius, 4 started.

Don Juan De Onate S. (R), The Downs at Albuquerque, June 12, $45,000, 3yo, New Mexico-bred, 6f, 1:09.10, ROCKY GULCH, Sand Spirit, Youareaggravatin', 6 started.

Donna Jensen H., Portland Meadows, April 10, $10,000, 4&up, f&m, 1¹/₁₆m, 1:49.46, LASTING KISS, Little Pursuit, Stately's Choice, 6 started.

Donna Reed S. (R), Prairie Meadows, Aug. 28, $78,600, 4&up, f&m, Iowa-bred, 1m 70y, 1:41.99, SWITCH LANES, Gamblers Passion, One Fine Shweetie, 6 started.

DONN H.-G1, Gulfstream Park, Feb. 7, $500,000, 4&up, 1¹/₈m, 1:47.63, MEDAGLIA D'ORO, Seattle Fitz (Arg), Funny Cide, 8 started.

Donnie Wilhite Memorial H., Louisiana Downs, Sept. 25, $50,000, 3yo, 1$^1/_{16}$mT, 1:45.32, SOCIAL KING, Alpha Capo, Northern Scene, 12 started.

Double Delta S., Arlington Park, June 20, $42,500, 3yo, f, 1mT, 1:38.18, SAHMKINDAWONDERFUL, Chic Dancer, Humorous Miss, 10 started.

Doubledogdare S., Keeneland, April 16, $122,300, 4&up, f&m, 1$^1/_{16}$m, 1:43.92, MAYO ON THE SIDE, Cat Fighter, Roar Emotion, 8 started.

Double Your Flavor S. (R), Sam Houston Race Park, March 27, $40,000, 4&up, f&m, Texas-bred, 7f, 1:24.39, LADY SONYA, Coastalota, Expecting Sugar, 8 started.

Dover S., Delaware Park, Oct. 9, $100,000, 2yo, 1$^1/_{16}$m, 1:46.91, KIL-LENAULE, Wild Desert, Lord Salvatore, 5 started.

Dowd Mile H., Fonner Park, April 10, $30,450, 3&up, 1m, 1:40.60, GETAWAY HOLME, Giant Slam, Intervene, 7 started.

Dowling S. (R), Great Lakes Downs, Aug. 14, $40,000, 3yo, c&g, Michigan-bred, 1m, 1:46.21, ROCKEM SOCKEM, Exclusivenjoyment, Do the Impossible, 9 started.

Down the Isle S., Turf Paradise, March 1, $21,900, 4&up, 1m, 1:33.68, BLACK BART, Real Creek, Alena's Tornado, 9 started.

Dr. A. B. Leggio Memorial H., Fair Grounds, Jan. 18, $60,000, 4&up, f&m, a5$^1/_8$fT, 1:04.14, PUT ME IN, Leslie's Love, Brown Eyed Beauty, 11 started.

Draw In S., Calder Race Course, June 27, $40,000, 3&up, f&m, 1$^1/_{16}$m, 1:47.35, FIRM REALITY, Secret Request, Clandestine, 6 started.

Dream Supreme H., Churchill Downs, Nov. 26, $71,400, 3&up, f&m, 6$^1/_2$f, 1:16.94, SAVORTHETIME, Hippogator, Souris, 6 started.

Dr. Ernest Benner S. (R), Charles Town Races, Sept. 26, $41,350, 2yo, West Virginia-bred, 6$^1/_2$f, 1:22.97, WILD REMARKS, Mr. Bondsman, Shenandoah Harley, 10 started.

Dr. Fager S. (R), Calder Race Course, Aug. 14, $75,000, 2yo, progeny of eligible Florida stallions, 6f, 1:11.93, B. B. BEST, Favre, Hostile Witness, 8 started.

Dr. Fager S., Arlington Park, Sept. 15, $43,625, 3&up, 7$^1/_2$f, 1:28.81, APT TO BE, Arbitrate, Silver Zipper, 6 started.

Dr. Haskell and Dr. Ray Feature S. (R), Rillito Park, Jan. 31, $4,228, 3&up, nonwinners of a race other than open, maiden, or claiming in 2003, 1$^1/_{16}$m, 1:45.80, REALIGNMENT, Screaming Willy, Oil Man, 6 started.

Dr. James Penny Memorial H., Philadelphia Park, July 3, $100,000, 3&up, f&m, 1$^1/_{16}$mT, 1:43.80, LADY OF THE FUTURE, Where We Left Off (GB), Caught in the Rain, 10 started.

Dr. O. G. Fischer Memorial H., SunRay Park, Aug. 28, $31,900, 3&up, f&m, 7f, 1:22.80, MISS NOTEWORTHY, Russian Bonus, Hava Peer, 6 started.

Drumtop S., Suffolk Downs, Aug. 14, $40,000, 3&up, f&m, 1$^1/_{16}$m, 1:46.74, LADY BEELZEBUB, Picture Gallery, Sarah Jade, 10 started.

D. S. "Shine" Young Memorial Futurity (R), Evangeline Downs, July 3, $100,000, 2yo, Louisiana-bred, 5f, :59, SMILIN FINE, Mr. Excellent, Malanato, 11 started.

DTHA Owners' Day H. (R), Delaware Park, Sept. 11, $75,000, 3&up, starters at Delaware Park in 2004, 1$^1/_8$m, 1:48.43, LOVING (Brz), Distinct Vision, Country Be Gold, 5 started.

Duchess of York S., Stampede Park, June 12, $37,200, 3&up, f&m, 1$^1/_{16}$m, 1:44.40, RAYLENE, Northern Neechitoo, A Shaky Start, 3 started.

DUCHESS S.-G3, Woodbine, Aug. 21, $206,150, 3yo, f, 7f, 1:23.26, BLONDE EXECUTIVE, Silver Bird, Search the Church, 5 started.

Duncan Hopeful S., Greenlee County Fair, March 21, $5,696, 3&up, 5$^1/_2$f, 1:06, TWO TIMING PAUL, Big Bad Bagdad, Dine At Tiffany, 7 started.

DURHAM CUP H.-G3, Woodbine, Oct. 16, $159,450, 3&up, 1$^1/_8$m, 1:51.56, NORFOLK KNIGHT, Mobil, Sky Diamond, 5 started.

Dust Commander S., Turfway Park, Feb. 21, $50,000, 4&up, 1m, 1:37.38, ASK THE LORD, Doc D, Twin Talk, 6 started.

Dwight D. Patterson H. (R), Turf Paradise, April 24, $40,000, 3&up, Arizona-bred, 1$^1/_{16}$mT, 1:42.83, IMDABOSSAU, Nice Choice, Road Grader, 11 started.

DWYER S.-G2, Belmont Park, July 11, $150,000, 3yo, 1$^1/_8$m, 1:40.02, MEDALLIST, The Cliff's Edge, Sir Shackleton, 6 started.

Earlene McCabe Derby (R), Sacramento, Aug. 29, $52,095, 3yo, California-bred, 6f, 1:08.60, JET WEST, Bailey's Yodeler, Razen Hazen, 7 started.

Early's Farm and Garden Centre H., Marquis Downs, June 26, $5,000, 3&up, 6f, 1:12.06, DOUBLE TIME, Britts Xpress, Stop the Act, 4 started.

East View S. (R), Aqueduct, Dec. 5, $80,750, 2yo, f, New York-bred, 1$^1/_{16}$m, 1:47.01, SUCCESSFULLY SWEET, Seeking the Ante, Pelham Bay, 6 started.

EATONTOWN H.-G3, Monmouth Park, July 10, $100,000, 3&up, f&m, 1$^1/_{16}$mT, 1:41.79, OCEAN DRIVE, Honorable Cat, Fast Cookie, 6 started.

E. B. Johnston S., Fairplex Park, Sept. 12, $57,000, 3&up, f&m, 1$^1/_{16}$m, 1:44.14, SHEZSOSPIRITUAL, Victory Encounter, Lucky in Love, 5 started.

ECLIPSE S.-G3, Woodbine, May 24, $163,350, 4&up, 1$^1/_8$m, 1:46.70, MARK ONE, Open Concert, Rock Again, 5 started.

EDDIE READ H.-G1, Del Mar, July 25, $400,000, 3&up, 1$^1/_8$mT, 1:45.90, SPECIAL RING, Bayamo (Ire), Sweet Return (GB), 11 started.

Edgewood S., Churchill Downs, April 30, $116,700, 3yo, f, 1$^1/_{16}$mT, 1:43, GALLOPING GAL, Gingham and Lace, Dynaville, 11 started.

Edmonton Juvenile S., Northlands Park, July 30, $40,000, 2yo, c&g, 6f, 1:13.20, POOR IGGY, Golden Hunt, , 8 started.

Edward Babst Memorial H. (R), Beulah Park, April 10, $40,000, 3&up, Ohio-bred, 6f, 1:08.32, DEVIL TIME, Your Abc's, Casino Red, 7 started.

Edward J. DeBartolo Sr. Memorial Breeders' Cup H., Remington Park, Sept. 6, $125,000, 3&up, 1$^1/_8$m, 1:46.22, MAJOR RHYTHM, Maysville Slew, Slew Slayer, 7 started.

Eight Thirty S., Delaware Park, May 31, $48,503, 3&up, 1$^1/_{16}$m, 1:52.50, PRIVATE LAP, My Man Ryan, White Buck, 3 started.

E. K. Rolfson Mile H. (R), North Dakota Horse Park, Sept. 6, $5,335, 4&up, North Dakota-bred, 1m, 1:41.40, MADDIES BLUES, Rileys Silver, Nice Cat, 4 started.

E. K. Rolfson Sprint H. (R), North Dakota Horse Park, Aug. 21, 4&up, North Dakota-bred, 5$^1/_2$f, 1:06.60, MADDIES BLUES, My Friend Frank, Activado's Image, 4 started.

El Cajon S. (R), Del Mar, Sept. 3, $79,550, 3yo, non-winners of a stakes of $50,000 at one mile or over in 2004, 1m, 1:35.09, PERFECT MOON, Borrego, Courageous Act, 7 started.

EL CAMINO REAL DERBY-G3, Golden Gate Fields, March 13, $200,000, 3yo, 1$^1/_8$m, 1:43.87, KILGOWAN, dh-Capitano, dh-Seattle Borders, 10 started.

El Cielo H., Santa Anita Park, March 21, $75,520, 4&up, a6$^1/_2$fT, 1:11.64, CAYOKE (Fr), Just Wonder (GB), Hemet Thought, 5 started.

EL CONEJO H.-G3, Santa Anita Park, Jan. 1, $107,600, 4&up, 5$^1/_2$f, 1:02.35, BOSTON COMMON, Summer Service, King Robyn, 6 started.

Electric City Sprint S., Great Falls, July 30, $3,000, 3&up, 5f, :59.60, ROGAN SLEW, King of Adventure, Kid Slew, 6 started.

EL ENCINO S.-G2, Santa Anita Park, Jan. 18, $150,000, 4yo, f, 1$^1/_{16}$m, 1:42.52, VICTORY ENCOUNTER, Personal Legend, Cat Fighter, 7 started.

Eleven North H. (R), Monmouth Park, Aug. 29, $100,000, 3&up, f&m, New Jersey-bred, 6f, 1:11.18, TOTALLY PRECIOUS, Eastern Gale, Whoop's Ah Daisy, 7 started.

E. L. Gaylord Memorial S., Remington Park, Nov. 26, $40,000, 2yo, f, 6$^1/_2$f, 1:18.04, HONOR THE FLAG, Wind Twister, Proper Wildcat, 11 started.

Elge Rasberry S. (R), Louisiana Downs, Aug. 7, $51,400, 3yo, f, Louisiana-bred, 7f, 1:24.09, HAPPY TICKET, Catlaan, Shes Dixies Eskimo, 6 started.

Elgin S. (R), Woodbine, Sept. 5, $134,125, 3&up, Canadian-bred, 1$^1/_{16}$m, 1:44.56, JUST IN CASE JIMMY, Cool N Collective, Peef, 6 started.

Elie Destruel H., Santa Rosa, Aug. 9, $51,895, 3&up, f&m, 6f, 1:09.32, OUR MANGO, Pheiffer, Channing Way, 7 started.

El Joven S., Retama Park, Sept. 4, $100,000, 2yo, 1mT, 1:36.74, READY RULER, Malanato, Reno Bob, 12 started.

ELKHORN S.-G3, Keeneland, April 23, $150,000, 4&up, 1$^1/_2$mT, 2:31.96, EPICENTRE, Rochester, Art Variety (Brz), 10 started.

Elko Thoroughbred Derby, Elko County Fair, Sept. 5, $13,650, 3yo, 7f, 1:26.60, FANTERIA, Hey Robbie, B. C's Hero, 8 started.

Elko Thoroughbred Futurity, Elko County Fair, Sept. 6, $20,300, 2yo, 5$^1/_2$f, 1:07.20, HANDSOMCHAMP, Spicey N Hot, Gal's Hunter, 8 started.

Elkwood S. (1st Div.), Monmouth Park, July 17, $60,000, 3&up, 1$^1/_{16}$mT, 1:43.39, GULCH APPROVAL, Royal Affirmed, Stormy Ray, 9 started.

Elkwood S. (2nd Div.), Monmouth Park, July 17, $60,000, 3&up, 1$^1/_{16}$mT, 1:43.90, SPRUCE RUN, Stormy Roman, First Lieutenant, 6 started.

Ellis Park Breeders' Cup H., Ellis Park, Aug. 14, $103,700, 3&up, f&m, 6¹/₂f, 1:17.18, MOLTO VITA, Tina Bull, Smoke Chaser, 7 started.

Elmer Heubeck Distaff H. (R), Calder Race Course, Nov. 13, $200,000, 3&up, f&m, Florida-bred, 1¹/₁₆m, 1:45.79, HOPELESSLY DEVOTED, Alix M, Shady Woman, 6 started.

El Paso Times H., Sunland Park, Feb. 14, $54,100, 3yo, f, 6¹/₂f, 1:16.07, SPEEDY FALCON, Spoiled, Ona Rampage, 8 started.

Elusive Quality S. (R), Belmont Park, Oct. 6, $61,100, 4&up, nonwinners of a stakes on the turf in 2003-'04, 1mT, 1:34.33, L'OISEAU D'ARGENT, Mogador, No Parole, 8 started.

Emerald Breeders' Cup Distaff H., Emerald Downs, Aug. 22, $84,375, 3&up, f&m, 1m, 1:36.20, AUNT SOPHIE, Cascade Corona, Hippogator, 8 started.

Emerald Downs Breeders' Cup Derby, Emerald Downs, Sept. 6, $96,250, 3yo, 1¹/₈m, 1:47.40, MY CREED, Flamethrowintexan, Random Memo, 7 started.

Emerald Downs H., Hastings Race Course, June 13, $44,259, 3yo, f, 6¹/₂f, 1:17.66, REGAL RED, Skyhyla, Bullseye Bess, 5 started.

Emerald Express S. (R), Emerald Downs, July 17, $48,000, 2yo, c&g, progeny of eligible Washington stallions, 6f, 1:10, SEATTLES BEST JOE, Sky Harbor, Positive Prize, 7 started.

Emerald H., Emerald Downs, June 20, $75,000, 3&up, 1m, 1:34.40, DEMON WARLOCK, Poker Brad, Briartic Gold, 8 started.

Emerald Necklace S. (R), Thistledown, Sept. 18, $40,000, 2yo, f, Ohio-bred, 6f, 1:13.58, NOON WIN, S R Queenforaday, Marketable, 7 started.

Emergency Nurse S., Calder Race Course, Sept. 19, $40,000, 3&up, f&m, 1¹/₁₆m, 1:47.54, MARIA'S IMAGE, Pampered Princess, Dakota Light, 9 started.

Empire Classic H. (R), Belmont Park, Oct. 23, $250,000, 3&up, New York-bred, 1¹/₈m, 1:50.23, SPITE THE DEVIL, West Virginia, Mr. Determined, 14 started.

Endeavour S., Tampa Bay Downs, Feb. 10, $100,000, 4&up, f&m, 1¹/₁₆mT, 1:44.97, MADEIRA MIST (Ire), Something Ventured, Coney Kitty (Ire), 12 started.

ENDINE H.-G3, Delaware Park, Sept. 11, $200,300, 3&up, f&m, 6f, 1:09.73, EBONY BREEZE, Umpateedle, Bronze Abe, 6 started.

E.P. TAYLOR S.-G1, Woodbine, Oct. 24, $750,000, 3&up, f&m, 1¹/₄mT, 2:04.02, COMMERCANTE (Fr), Punctilious (GB), Classic Stamp, 8 started.

Ernest Finley H., Santa Rosa, July 31, $42,930, 3&up, 6f, 1:07.93, HALO CAT, My Captain, Newark, 8 started.

Ernie Samuel Memorial S. (R), Fort Erie, July 18, $100,000, 3&up, f&m, Canadian-foaled, 1¹/₁₆mT, 1:49.11, GINGER GOLD, Clubay, Robotica, 4 started.

Escondido H. (R), Del Mar, Aug. 4, $79,000, 3&up, non-winners of a stakes of $50,000 at one mile or over in 2004, 1³/₈mT, 2:12.92, SARAFAN, Gene de Campeao (Brz), Outta Here, 6 started.

ESSEX H.-G3, Oaklawn Park, Feb. 21, $100,000, 4&up, 1¹/₁₆m, 1:43.66, PRIVATE EMBLEM, Pie N Burger, Crafty Shaw, 8 started.

Estrapade H., Arlington Park, June 12, $75,000, 3&up, f&m, 1¹/₈m, 1:50.54, CHANCE DANCE, Julie's Prize, It's Spooky, 6 started.

Eternal Search S. (R), Woodbine, Sept. 1, $131,125, 3yo, f, progeny of eligible Ontario stallions, 1¹/₁₆mT, 1:43.98, MY VINTAGE PORT, Bay Sweetie Babe, El Tara, 7 started.

E.T. Springer S. (R), The Downs at Albuquerque, Sept. 11, $32,700, 3&up, New Mexico-bred, 7f, 1:22.39, NINETY NINE JACK, Sharethetime, Jonnygetachex, 5 started.

Eureka Down Thoroughbred Futurity, Eureka Downs, June 20, $3,952, 2yo, 4f, :48.06, SLEWS IN OZ NOW, Jennies Song, S C King, 8 started.

Evangeline Mile H., Evangeline Downs, Aug. 14, $100,000, 3&up, 1m, 1:37.80, PIE N BURGER, Meteor Impact, Akanti (Ire), 9 started.

Evan Shipman H. (R), Belmont Park, July 25, $108,100, 3&up, New York-bred, 1¹/₁₆m, 1:41.89, SPITE THE DEVIL, Sherpa Guide, Mr. Determined, 6 started.

Evanston Mayor's Derby, Wyoming Downs, July 10, $3,800, 3&up, 6f, 1:14.38, SPLENDID HIGH, J. J. Cant Wag, Doclange, 7 started.

Evanston Speed S., Wyoming Downs, July 10, $3,600, 3&up, 4¹/₂f, :52.49, POPESCU (Brz), Forever Jan, Restrictions Apply, 10 started.

Everett Nevin Alameda County Futurity (R), Pleasanton, July 4, $53,465, 2yo, California-bred, 5f, :56.20, WIND WATER, Johnny High Brite, Thresher, 9 started.

Excalibur S., Louisiana Downs, June 26, $50,000, 3yo, 1m 70y, 1:42.46, BRITT'S JULES, Mr. Devious, Foxtrot Oscar, 10 started.

EXCELSIOR BREEDERS' CUP H.-G3, Aqueduct, April 3, $196,000, 3&up, 1¹/₈m, 1:49.57, FUNNY CIDE, Evening Attire, Host (Chi), 5 started.

Excess Energy S., Turf Paradise, Nov. 26, $22,000, 3&up, f&m, 5¹/₂f, 1:02.93, FRIENDOFTHEFAMILY, Corona Del Hielo, Marva Jean, 9 started.

Exogenous S. (R), Aqueduct, Dec. 11, $60,750, 3yo, f, non-winners of a stakes, 1m 70y, 1:43.75, OUR RITE OF SPRING, Strategy, Take Me There, 6 started.

Expedite Plus S. (R), Fort Erie, June 6, $60,000, 3&up, starters at Fort Erie at least three times in 2003-'04, 5f, :59.18, LUCKY TEC, Rundle, Pinedale Star, 7 started.

Express H., The Downs at Albuquerque, May 15, $44,650, 3&up, 5¹/₂f, 1:02.78, BANG, Ninety Nine Jack, Proper Prospect, 9 started.

Express S., Lone Star Park, May 8, $75,000, 3&up, 6f, 1:07.89, BEAU'S TOWN, That Tat, Gold Storm, 6 started.

Fain Road S., Yavapai Downs, Sept. 7, $9,900, 3&up, 4¹/₂f, :50.20, RED SPARK, Flarions Flame, Bobaway, 9 started.

Fairfield S., Solano County Fair, July 24, $43,565, 3yo, f, 6f, 1:10.65, YEREVAN STAR, Favorite Times, Runnin Ute, 9 started.

Fair Grounds Breeders' Cup S., Fair Grounds, Jan. 31, $119,500, 4&up, a1¹/₈mT, 1:51.77, MYSTERY GIVER, Skate Away, Great Bloom, 9 started.

FAIR GROUNDS OAKS-G2, Fair Grounds, March 6, $300,000, 3yo, f, 1¹/₁₆m, 1:43.07, ASHADO, Victory U.S.A., Shadow Cast, 6 started.

Fair Grounds Sales S. (R), Fair Grounds, Feb. 8, $69,000, 3yo, Fair Grounds sales graduates, 1m, 1:39.21, OUTRIGHT BUCK, Silver Indy, Caroline's Prince, 6 started.

Fair Lady S. (R), Hastings Race Course, May 2, $44,368, 3yo, f, British Columbia-bred, 6¹/₂f, 1:17.45, REGAL RED, Crystal Gala, Socorro County, 8 started.

Fair Manager's H., Western Montana Fair, Aug. 13, $4,500, 3&up, 6¹/₂f, 1:23.40, NORTHERN MASTER, Lost Again, Fruit Rapport, 6 started.

Fair Queen H., The Downs at Albuquerque, Sept. 17, $33,200, 3yo, f, 6¹/₂f, 1:16.02, FORWARD GLANCE, Ona Rampage, Paradise Wild, 7 started.

Fairway Fun S., Turfway Park, March 27, $43,000, 4&up, f&m, 1¹/₁₆m, 1:40.85, ANGELA'S LOVE, Secondary School, Jaramar Rain, 7 started.

Fall Classic Distaff H. (R), Northlands Park, Sept. 25, $75,000, 3&up, f&m, Alberta-bred, 1¹/₁₆m, 1:46.20, A SHAKY START, Braetta, Northern Neechitoo, 7 started.

FALL HIGHWEIGHT H.-G3, Aqueduct, Nov. 28, $111,600, 3&up, 6f, 1:09.83, THUNDER TOUCH, Papua, Eavesdropper, 9 started.

Fall Open S., Lethbridge, Sept. 6, $11,200, 3&up, 7f, 1:26.40, dh-LAFLEUR, dh-ROYAL GROUP, Fruit Rapport, 8 started.

Fall S., Lethbridge, Sept. 11, $11,200, 3&up, f&m, a6f, 1:11.80, REAL STERLING, Guiltybysupiscion, Alibi Expert, 8 started.

Fall S., Mountaineer Race Track, Sept. 21, $75,000, 3&up, 1¹/₈m, 1:52.58, TOUR THE HIVE, Wiggins, Woodmoon, 5 started.

Falls Amiss H. (R), Horsemen's Park, July 16, $29,200, 4&up, f&m, Nebraska-bred, 1m, 1:41.60, RUN AROUND SUE, Irish Flyer, Bright Flame, 7 started.

FALLS CITY H.-G2, Churchill Downs, Nov. 25, $325,200, 3&up, f&m, 1¹/₈m, 1:51.81, HALORY LEIGH, Susan's Angel, Miss Fortunate, 7 started.

Fall Sprint S., Lethbridge, Sept. 5, $11,200, 3&up, 5¹/₂f, 1:07.40, HIGHLAND ROAD, Seattle Cue, Royal Deal, 8 started.

Fanfreluche S. (R), Woodbine, Nov. 7, $165,900, 2yo, f, Canadian-foaled, 6f, 1:12.41, SIMPLY LOVELY, Silver Impulse, Susur, 8 started.

Fantango Lady S. (R), Horsemen's Park, July 15, $30,400, 3yo, f, Nebraska-bred, 1m, 1:42.80, JITTERBUG JOY, Sheso, Shantac, 9 started.

Fantasia S. (R), Louisiana Downs, May 23, $50,000, 3yo, f, Louisiana-bred, 6f, 1:10.28, SHES DIXIES ESKIMO, Placid Star, Just Plain Vanilla, 7 started.

Fantasy S., Hastings Race Course, Oct. 23, $62,095, 2yo, f, 1¹/₁₆m, 1:48.50, COUNTRY KAT, Sugar Pine, Honky Tonk Pat, 8 started.

FANTASY S.-G2, Oaklawn Park, April 9, $200,000, 3yo, f, 1¹/₁₆m, 1:42.62, HOUSE OF FORTUNE, Island Sand, Stellar Jayne, 11 started.

Fappie's Notebook S. (R), Calder Race Course, June 13, $40,000, 3&up, nonwinners of $15,000 once since February 1 or nonwinners of four races other than maiden, claiming, or starter, 6¹/₂f, 1:18.75, GOLD DOLLAR, Just Say the Word, Lawbook, 10 started.

Farer Belle Lee H. (R), Great Lakes Downs, Sept. 3, $50,000, 3&up, f&m, Michigan-bred, 1¹/₁₆m, 1:50.97, DANCIN FOR GOLD, Circle the Globe, Charlies Indian, 7 started.

Fashion S., Belmont Park, June 3, $80,625, 2yo, f, 5f, :57.86, CHOCOLATE BROWN, Limited Entry, Western Princess, 6 started.

Fasig-Tipton Turf Dash S., Calder Race Course, Sept. 6, $50,000, 2yo, 5f, 1:00.84, MONTI'S LAD, Kohut, G P's Black Knight, 7 started.

FAYETTE S.-G3, Keeneland, Oct. 30, $161,250, 3&up, 1¹/₈m, 1:50.39, MIDWAY ROAD, Total Impact (Chi), Alumni Hall, 5 started.

Federal Way H., Emerald Downs, May 16, $40,000, 3yo, f, 6¹/₂f, 1:15.80, SARIANO, Sandia's Flicka, Overact, 9 started.

Federico Tesio S., Pimlico, April 17, $100,000, 3yo, 1¹/₁₆m, 1:50.50, WATER CANNON, Pawyne Princess, Irish Laddie, 7 started.

Fern Sawyer H., Ruidoso Downs, July 4, $25,000, 3&up, f&m, 1m, 1:38.40, RUBIN'S GIRL, Hava Peer, Yet Anothernatalie, 7 started.

Fieldy S. (R), Belmont Park, July 2, $62,300, 3yo, f, non-winners of an open stakes, 1mT, 1:33.36, FORTUNATE DAMSEL, Seducer's Song, Jinny's Gold, 7 started.

Fiesta Mile S. (R), Retama Park, Sept. 18, $40,000, 3&up, f&m, Texas-bred, 1mT, 1:35.98, LADY MALLORY, Hay Madison, Leo's Baroness, 11 started.

Fifth Avenue S. (R), Aqueduct, Nov. 7, $125,000, 2yo, f, progeny of eligible New York stallions, 6f, 1:10.94, INDY WOODS, Avery Hall, Brassy Boots, 8 started.

FIFTH SEASON S.-G3, Oaklawn Park, April 7, $100,000, 4&up, 1¹/₁₆m, 1:42.50, SPANISH EMPIRE, Crafty Shaw, No Comprende, 8 started.

Find H. (R), Pimlico, Aug. 21, $75,000, 3&up, Maryland-bred, 1¹/₈mT, 1:50.11, FOUFA'S WARRIOR, Cherokee's Boy, Irish Colony, 5 started.

Finger Lakes Juvenile Fillies S., Finger Lakes, Oct. 2, $50,000, 2yo, f, 6f, 1:12.90, ROVING ANGEL, Red Boa, A Rose for Chris, 11 started.

Finger Lakes Juvenile S., Finger Lakes, Oct. 23, $50,000, 2yo, 6f, 1:13.04, BOSTON RAIDER, A Rose for Chris, Millibrook, 7 started.

FIRECRACKER BREEDERS' CUP H.-G2, Churchill Downs, July 3, $287,750, 3&up, 1mT, 1:34.15, QUANTUM MERIT, Perfect Soul (Ire), Senor Swinger, 9 started.

Firecracker H., Mountaineer Race Track, July 4, $75,000, 3&up, f&m, 1mT, 1:36.42, PASSIONATE BIRD, River Flower, May Gator, 6 started.

Fire Plug S., Pimlico, April 10, $48,500, 3&up, 6f, 1:10.11, SASSY HOUND, Out of Fashion, Cherokee's Boy, 4 started.

First Episode S. (R), Suffolk Downs, Aug. 7, $40,000, 3&up, f&m, Massachusetts-bred, 1¹/₁₆m, 1:48.50, AFRICAN PRINCESS, Cindarullah, Sunlit Ridge, 6 started.

FIRST FLIGHT H.-G2, Aqueduct, Oct. 30, $150,000, 3&up, f&m, 7f, 1:22.13, BENDING STRINGS, Smokey Glacken, Passing Shot, 6 started.

First Lady H., Ruidoso Downs, June 19, $30,000, 3&up, f&m, 6f, 1:09.60, YET ANOTHERNATALIE, Jewels for a Lady, Oriana's Magic, 8 started.

FIRST LADY H.-G3, Gulfstream Park, Jan. 11, $100,000, 3&up, f&m, 6f, 1:09.64, HARMONY LODGE, House Party, Mayo On the Side, 9 started.

First Snowbound S., Yavapai Downs, Aug. 23, $9,800, 3&up, f&m, 5¹/₂f, 1:03.60, DANCE FOR GOLD, Mamacafe, Sunny Loves Sallie, 8 started.

Fit for a Queen S., Arlington Park, May 15, $41,875, 3&up, f&m, 6f, 1:10.65, SMOKE CHASER, Tina Bull, Youcan'ttakeme, 7 started.

Flaming Page S., Woodbine, Sept. 25, $109,000, 3&up, f&m, 1¹/₈mT, 2:28.82, MY PAL LANA, Faswiga, Flashy Thunder, 10 started.

Flashaway Overnight H., Portland Meadows, April 10, $6,500, 3&up, 5f, :59.28, STAR OF ELTTAES, City Parkway, Donnys Dimund Slew, 5 started.

FLASH S.-G3, Belmont Park, June 4, $104,300, 2yo, 5f, :57.49, PRIMAL STORM, Winning Expression, Gold Joy, 5 started.

Flawlessly S., Arlington Park, Sept. 12, $44,375, 3&up, f&m, 1mT, 1:36.66, MYMICH, One Fine Shweetie, dh-Beautiful Bets, dh-Brunilda (Arg), 9 started.

Flawlessly S., Hollywood Park, July 3, $109,700, 3yo, f, 1mT, 1:34.78, MISS VEGAS, Fine Nickels, Shake Off, 8 started.

Fleet Treat S. (R), Del Mar, July 24, $100,000, 3yo, f, California-bred, 7f, 1:22.78, WESTERN HEMISPHERE, Alphabet Kisses, Marie's Rose, 9 started.

FLEUR DE LIS H.-G2, Churchill Downs, June 12, $439,200, 3&up, f&m, 1¹/₈m, 1:52.15, ADORATION, Bare Necessities, La Reason, 6 started.

Fleur de Lis S., Louisiana Downs, May 30, $50,000, 3&up, f&m, 1m 70y, 1:42.52, DUE TO WIN, Southern Surprise, Blue Guru, 6 started.

Fling Ding S., Turf Paradise, Dec. 28, $21,900, 3yo, f, 1m, 1:37.22, SOCIETY CAT, Darling Silver, Marquetryinmotion, 9 started.

Floor Show S., Delaware Park, June 22, $55,300, 3yo, 1¹/₁₆m, 1:43.93, PIES PROSPECT, Gmork, Zakocity, 8 started.

FLORAL PARK H.-G3, Belmont Park, Sept. 18, $104,400, 3&up, f&m, 6f, 1:10.69, FELINE STORY, Cologny, Travelator, 5 started.

Florence Henderson S. (R), Indiana Downs, June 19, $40,000, 3&up, f&m, Indiana-bred, 1¹/₁₆mT, 1:42.45, ELLENS LUCKY STAR, Such a Lady, Speedy Tiffany, 8 started.

Florida Breeders' Distaff S., Ocala Training Center, March 15, $40,000, 3&up, f&m, 1¹/₁₆m, 1:44.20, DOC'S DOLL, Kiss Me Twice, Joyful Ballad, 7 started.

Florida Cup Sprint S., Tampa Bay Downs, April 4, $81,350, 4&up, 6f, 1:10.70, SCRUBS, Rock County, Built Up, 7 started.

FLORIDA DERBY-G1, Gulfstream Park, March 13, $1,000,000, 3yo, 1¹/₈m, 1:51.38, FRIENDS LAKE, Value Plus, The Cliff's Edge, 10 started.

Florida Oaks, Tampa Bay Downs, March 14, $150,000, 3yo, f, 1¹/₁₆m, 1:45.66, ENDER'S SISTER, Menifeeque, America America, 9 started.

Florida Thoroughbred Charities S., Ocala Training Center, March 15, $40,000, 3&up, 5f, :57.80, VISION IN FLIGHT, Winnie's Pooh Bear, Max a Million, 11 started.

FLOWER BOWL INVITATIONAL H.-G1, Belmont Park, Oct. 2, $750,000, 3&up, f&m, 1¹/₄m, 2:04.65, RISKAVERSE, Commercante (Fr), Moscow Burning, 8 started.

Flying Concert S. (R), Calder Race Course, Dec. 31, $40,000, 3&up, f&m, nonwinners of a stakes worth $25,000 or more to the winner, 1¹/₈m, 1:53.78, VESPERS, Gamble to Victory, Cloud Counting, 6 started.

Flying Lark S., Portland Meadows, Jan. 31, $10,000, 3yo, 6f, 1:13.79, MYTHICAL ROAD, Keep On Turkin, Might E Man, 6 started.

Flying Pidgeon H., Calder Race Course, Oct. 9, $100,000, 3&up, 1¹/₈mT, 1:50.61, KEEP COOL, Twilight Road, Unbridels King, 11 started.

Fly So Free S., Belmont Park, Sept. 12, $59,350, 3yo, 6f, 1:08.92, MASS MEDIA, Smokume, All Hail Stormy, 5 started.

Folklore H., Louisiana Downs, Aug. 21, $49,000, 3&up, 6¹/₂f, 1:16.85, OLE REBEL, Dash for Daylight, That Tat, 5 started.

Fonner Park Special S. (R), Fonner Park, April 17, $30,800, 3yo, c&g, Nebraska-bred, 6f, 1:13.60, THUNDERING VERZY, Cassanova Kid, Sunday Trigger, 8 started.

Fonner Park Special S. (R), Fonner Park, April 18, $30,900, 3yo, f, Nebraska-bred, 6f, 1:14.80, SHESAIDSHEKNOWSYA, Very Dark Shades, Jitterbug Joy, 8 started.

Foolish Pleasure S., Calder Race Course, Oct. 2, $100,000, 2yo, 1m 70y, 1:46.30, PRECOCIOUS UNITY, D'court's Speed, Hal's Image, 8 started.

Fool the Experts S., Turf Paradise, Nov. 22, $21,900, 2yo, 6f, 1:10.59, WALKER, Lead for Speed, Night Dash, 8 started.

Foothill S., Fairplex Park, Sept. 10, $58,800, 3yo, 6¹/₂f, 1:16.45, LAST MINUTE DETAIL, Pt's Grey Eagle, Trish's Diamond, 7 started.

Forego H., Fairmount Park, July 31, $30,600, 4&up, c&g, 1m 70y, 1:42.20, MOE B DICK, Beabasque, Canyon de Oro, 6 started.

FOREGO H.-G1, Saratoga Race Course, Sept. 4, $250,000, 3&up, 7f, 1:22.22, MIDAS EYES, Clock Stopper, Gygistar, 9 started.

Forego S., Turfway Park, Jan. 24, $50,000, 4&up, 6¹/₂f, 1:17.64, DOC D, Founding Chairman, Mr Bassett, 8 started.

Forerunner S., Keeneland, April 15, $111,100, 3yo, 1¹/₁₆mT, 1:48.64, PRINCE ARCH, Brass Hat, Big Booster, 8 started.

Formal Gold S., Monmouth Park, Sept. 11, $65,000, 3&up, 1¹/₁₆m, 1:44.01, LION TAMER, One Nice Cat, Weston Field, 6 started.

Fort Bend County S. (R), Sam Houston Race Park, April 3, $40,000, 3yo, Texas-bred, 7f, 1:24.23, MR. DEVIOUS, Goosey Moose, Once-aroundtwice, 11 started.

FORT MARCY H.-G3, Aqueduct, April 24, $111,400, 3&up, 1¹/₁₆mT, 1:42.47, CHILLY ROOSTER, Union Place, Slew Valley, 8 started.

Fort Monmouth S., Monmouth Park, May 30, $60,000, 3&up, f&m, 1mT, 1:36.10, HIGH COURT (Brz), Delta Princess, Mrs. M, 11 started.

Forty-Niner H., Golden Gate Fields, Nov. 26, $82,650, 3&up, 1¹/₁₆m, 1:42.16, YOUGOTTAWANNA, Adreamisborn, My Creed, 9 started.

Forty One Carats S. (R), Calder Race Course, Aug. 20, $40,000, 3&up, nonwinners of $15,000 once since February 1 or nonwinners of four races other than maiden, claiming, or starter, 6¹/₂f, 1:17.24, MODEL HOME, Just Say the Word, Love That Moon, 6 started.

Forward Pass S., Arlington Park, Aug. 14, $52,600, 3yo, 7f, 1:24.51, NEBRASKA MOON, Caiman, Elegant Fame, 6 started.

Foster City H., Bay Meadows, June 20, $65,387, 3&up, 1¹/₁₆mT, 1:42.73, NINEBANKS, Adreamisborn, Handyman Bill, 8 started.

FOUNTAIN OF YOUTH S.-G2, Gulfstream Park, Feb. 14, $250,000, 3yo, 1¹/₁₆m, 1:42.71, READ THE FOOTNOTES, Second of June, Silver Wagon, 8 started.

Four Seasons H., Blue Ribbon Downs, Nov. 7, $9,300, 3&up, 1m, 1:39.78, ROYAL CHALICE, Rein Man, Directaccess, 5 started.

FOURSTARDAVE H.-G2, Saratoga Race Course, Aug. 28, $200,000, 3&up, 1¹/₁₆mT, 1:39.50, NOTHING TO LOSE, Silver Tree, Royal Regalia, 10 started.

Fox Sports Net H., Emerald Downs, May 23, $40,000, 3&up, 6¹/₂f, 1:14.40, WILLIE THE CAT, Slewicide Cruise, Demon Warlock, 10 started.

Foxy J. G. S. (R), Philadelphia Park, July 17, $53,500, 3yo, f, Pennsylvania-bred, 7f, 1:23.48, DEFRERE'S VENTURE, Nash's Valay, Prudencia, 8 started.

Frances A. Genter S., Calder Race Course, Nov. 27, $100,000, 3yo, f, 7¹/₂fT, 1:28.05, R OBSESSION, Our Exploit, Marina de Chavon, 12 started.

Frances Genter S. (R), Canterbury Park, July 10, $41,250, 3yo, f, Minnesota-bred, 6f, 1:10.63, SHAKOPEE, Bleu's Apparition, Lilstarshines, 9 started.

Frances Slocum S. (R), Hoosier Park, Nov. 13, $40,000, 3&up, f&m, Indiana-bred, 1¹/₁₆m, 1:44.81, SENORITA ZIGGY, Ellens Lucky Star, Speedy Tiffany, 10 started.

Francis "Jock" LaBelle Memorial S., Delaware Park, May 1, $75,300, 3yo, 6f, 1:11.16, FRISKY SPIDER, Snub the Devil, Xtreamotion, 6 started.

Frank A. "Buddy" Abadie Memorial S. (R), Evangeline Downs, June 5, $40,000, 3yo, f, Louisiana-bred, 1m, 1:39.60, PLACID STAR, Shes Dixies Eskimo, Madison's Music, 6 started.

Frank Arnason Sire S. (R), Assiniboia Downs, July 31, $40,000, 2yo, Canadian-bred, 6f, 1:14.40, YOUR EXCELLENCE, Danger Pay, Gogogadget, 7 started.

FRANK E. KILROE MILE H.-G2, Santa Anita Park, March 6, $350,000, 4&up, 1mT, 1:33.87, SWEET RETURN (GB), Singletary, Inesperado (Fr), 14 started.

Frank Gall Memorial H. (R), Charles Town Races, Aug. 28, $76,550, 3&up, West Virginia-bred, 7f, 1:30.47, EARTH POWER, Longfield Spud, Tienneman Square, 10 started.

FRANK J. DE FRANCIS MEMORIAL DASH S.-G1, Pimlico, Nov. 20, $300,000, 3&up, 6f, 1:09.45, WILDCAT HEIR, Midas Eyes, Clock Stopper, 10 started.

Franks Farm Turf S. (R), Gulfstream Park, Jan. 24, $500,000, 4&up, California- or Florida-bred, 1¹/₁₆mT, 1:45.69, PROUD MAN, Hear No Evil, Special Matter, 11 started.

Fran's Valentine S. (R), Hollywood Park, April 24, $150,000, 4&up, f&m, California-bred, 1¹/₁₆mT, 1:39.34, MOSCOW BURNING, Super High, Sweet Frippery, 7 started.

Fred "Cappy" Capossela S., Aqueduct, Jan. 19, $81,225, 3yo, 6f, 1:13.92, QUICK ACTION, Risky Trick, Scary Bob, 7 started.

Fred Drysdale Memorial S., Grand Prairie, Aug. 21, $5,500, 3&up, f&m, 6¹/₂f, 1:20.80, GUILTYBYSUPISCION, Prosperity Rose, Jaylo J G, 7 started.

Fred Mendel Memorial H., Marquis Downs, July 23, $5,000, 3&up, 1m, 1:39.53, BEAU RING, Stop the Act, Double Time, 7 started.

FRED W. HOOPER H.-G3, Calder Race Course, Dec. 18, $100,000, 3&up, 1¹/₈m, 1:50.74, PIES PROSPECT, Twilight Road, Hear No Evil, 11 started.

Freedom of the City S., Northlands Park, Oct. 9, $40,000, 2yo, f, 1m, 1:40, KATHERN'S CAT, Rumbeau Ruckus, Speedy Gone Sally, 6 started.

Free Press S., Assiniboia Downs, June 20, $40,000, 3&up, 6f, 1:11.60, IWOODIFICOULD, Smoked Em, Fancy As, 9 started.

Free Spirits S., Ruidoso Downs, June 27, $30,000, 3&up, 6f, 1:10, THIS CHRIS, Perfect Fit, Mr. Zach Man, 9 started.

Friendly Lover H. (R), Monmouth Park, Sept. 19, $60,000, 3&up, New Jersey-bred, 6f, 1:10.10, UPTURN, Trueamericanspirit, Dixie Two Thousand, 7 started.

Frisk Me Now S., Monmouth Park, May 30, $70,000, 3&up, 1m, 1:35.29, PRETTY WILD, First Lieutenant, Cool N Collective, 5 started.

FRIZETTE S.-G1, Belmont Park, Oct. 9, $500,000, 2yo, f, 1¹/₁₆m, 1:43.52, BALLETTO (UAE), Ready's Gal, Sis City, 8 started.

Frontier H. (R), Great Lakes Downs, Sept. 4, $50,000, 3&up, Michiganbred, 1¹/₁₆m, 2:01.28, CATCH THE DEW, Secret Romeo, O. B. Quiet, 7 started.

Front Range H., Arapahoe Park, Aug. 1, $26,875, 3&up, 7f, 1:21.40, PERSONAL BEAU, Spirit Gulch, Debatable, 4 started.

Frost King S. (R), Woodbine, Oct. 27, $132,750, 2yo, progeny of eligible Ontario stallions, 7f, 1:25.29, ENOUGH IS ENOUGH, Quick in Deed, Loving It, 7 started.

Frosty Gardiner Honorary Thoroughbred Championship H., Wyoming Downs, Aug. 22, $5,500, 3&up, 1m, 1:38.53, QUIET SYNS, Kerrygold (Fr), On the Bill Daily, 8 started.

Funallover S., Turf Paradise, May 15, $22,100, 3&up, f&m, 6¹/₂f, 1:15.62, LAKESVILLE, Slew City Lily, Arch Lady, 9 started.

Funallover S., Turf Paradise, Dec. 27, $21,800, 2yo, f, 6¹/₂f, 1:17.15, LITE WRITE, O K Topless, Virden, 7 started.

Funistrada S., Belmont Park, June 12, $60,650, 3yo, f, 6f, 1:10.65, SHE'S A MUGS, Feline Story, Capeside Lady, 6 started.

Furl Sail H., Fair Grounds, Dec. 23, $60,000, 3&up, f&m, a1¹/₁₆mT, 1:47.29, CHANCE DANCE, Fun House, Kitty's Legend, 7 started.

Fury S. (R), Woodbine, May 9, $163,200, 3yo, f, Canadian-bred, 7f, 1:23.32, EYE OF THE SPHYNX, Silver Bird, My Vintage Port, 7 started.

FUTURITY S.-G2, Belmont Park, Sept. 19, $300,000, 2yo, 1m, 1:38.84, PARK AVENUE BALL, Wallstreet Scandal, Evil Minister, 6 started.

Gala Lil S., Laurel Park, March 20, $57,250, 4&up, f&m, 1¹/₁₆m, 1:50.12, FRIEL'S FOR REAL, Undercover, City Fire, 6 started.

GALLANT BLOOM H.-G2, Belmont Park, Oct. 10, $150,000, 3&up, f&m, 6¹/₂f, 1:16.04, LADY TAK, Molto Vita, Zawzooth, 7 started.

Gallant Bob H., Philadelphia Park, Oct. 2, $100,000, 3yo, 6f, 1:08.11, ABBONDANZA, Primary Suspect, Knight of Darkness, 6 started.

Gallant Fox H., Aqueduct, Dec. 29, $82,700, 3&up, 1⅜m, 2:43.95, TAMBURELLO (Chi), Colita, Hydrogen, 8 started.

GALLORETTE H.-G3, Pimlico, May 15, $100,000, 3&up, f&m, 1¹/₁₆mT, 1:40.85, OCEAN DRIVE, Film Maker, With Patience, 8 started.

GAMELY BREEDERS' CUP H.-G1, Hollywood Park, May 31, $324,250, 3&up, f&m, 1¹/₄mT, 1:48.34, NOCHES DE ROSA (Chi), Megahertz (GB), Quero Quero, 4 started.

GARDEN CITY BREEDERS' CUP S.-G1, Belmont Park, Sept. 12, $264,000, 3yo, f, 1¹/₈mT, 1:48.88, LUCIFER'S STONE, Barancella (Fr), Noahs Ark (Ire), 7 started.

Garden City Futurity, Western Montana Fair, Aug. 13, $4,800, 2yo, a5f, 1:07, SECRET VICTORY, Perry's Option, V R Blue, 4 started.

Garden City S. (R), Fort Erie, Aug. 29, $58,000, 3&up, starters at Fort Erie at least three times in 2004, 6f, 1:10.97, LUCKY TEC, Krz Ruckus, Expected Hour, 5 started.

GARDENIA H.-G3, Ellis Park, Aug. 7, $200,000, 3&up, f&m, 1¹/₁₆m, 1:49.54, ANGELA'S LOVE, Miss Fortunate, Bare Necessities, 6 started.

Gardenia S. (R), Delta Downs, Dec. 10, $40,000, 3&up, f&m, Louisianabred nonwinners of a stakes, 6¹/₂f, 1:22.29, MISTY GLO, Sheza Diva, Notrestraintable, 10 started.

Garden Saint S., Calder Race Course, Oct. 10, $40,000, 3&up, f&m, 1¹/₁₆mT, 1:44.08, FORMAL MISS, Iowa's Image, Alix M, 8 started.

Garland of Roses H., Aqueduct, Dec. 11, $80,900, 3&up, f&m, 6f, 1:10.64, TRAVELATOR, Sensibly Chic, Forest Music, 6 started.

Gasparilla S., Tampa Bay Downs, Jan. 31, $52,500, 3yo, f, 7f, 1:26.81, CRAFTY TEARS, Wild Speed, Ladyinareddress, 7 started.

Gate Dancer S., Delaware Park, Aug. 21, $54,100, 3&up, 1¹/₁₆m, 1:43, COUNTRY BE GOLD, Donald's Pride, Lyracist, 9 started.

Gateway to Glory S., Fairplex Park, Sept. 23, $58,200, 2yo, 1¹/₁₆m, 1:47.32, THIS WIZARD ROCKS, Cowboy Badgett, Arch Stanton, 6 started.

Gaviola S. (R), Belmont Park, Oct. 8, $61,250, 4&up, f&m, nonwinners of a stakes on the turf in 2003-'04, 1mT, 1:35.50, NOISETTE, Lentil, Vespers, 8 started.

GAZELLE H.-G1, Belmont Park, Sept. 11, $250,000, 3yo, f, 1¹/₈m, 1:48.25, STELLAR JAYNE, Daydreaming, He Loves Me, 6 started.

GCFA Texas-Bred S. (R), Gillespie County Fairgrounds, Aug. 29, $16,800, 3&up, Texas-bred, 7f, 1:29.61, VICTORY DAY, Dust Pebble, Irish Mountain, 5 started.

Geisha H. (R), Pimlico, Dec. 11, $100,000, 3&up, f&m, Marylandbred, 1¹/₁₆m, 1:53.89, SILMARIL, Pour It On, Chrusciki, 9 started.

Gena Stanley Memorial H., Blue Ribbon Downs, April 10, $10,350, 3&up, 5f, :59.23, CARTERS BOY, Nevasayneva, Canrock, 11 started.

Gene Francis and Associate H. (1st Div.), Anthony Downs, July 24, $4,250, 3&up, 1^1/$_1$₆mi, 1:59.23, MY SILVER DOLLAR, Clever Red, Who Devil Who, 5 started.

Gene Francis and Associate H. (2nd Div.), Anthony Downs, July 24, $5,190, 3&up, 1^1/$_1$₆mi, 1:53.42, OVERPRINT, Silver Town, Coupdeville Jack, 5 started.

General Douglas MacArthur H. (R), Belmont Park, Sept. 10, $105,100, 3&up, New York-bred, 7f, 1:21.58, CLEVER ELECTRICIAN, Top Shoter, Mr. Determined, 5 started.

GENERAL GEORGE H.-G2, Laurel Park, Feb. 16, $200,000, 3&up, 7f, 1:22.49, WELL FANCIED, Unforgettable Max, Gators N Bears, 9 started.

Generous Portion S. (R), Del Mar, Sept. 1, $100,000, 2yo, f, California-bred, 6f, 1:10.64, COASTAL STRIKE, Memorette, Excessively Nice, 6 started.

GENEROUS S.-G3, Hollywood Park, Nov. 27, $100,000, 2yo, 1mT, 1:37.21, DUBLEO, Littlebitofzip, Sunny Sky (Fr), 12 started.

Genesee Valley Breeders' H. (R), Finger Lakes, Sept. 6, $50,000, 3&up, New York-bred, 1^1/$_1$₆mi, 1:44.53, HALO MALONE, Sherpa Guide, Grillhouse, 6 started.

Genesis S., Delta Downs, Jan. 3, $40,000, 3yo, f, 5f, :58.41, WACKY PATTY, Clever Melody, Simply Jolie, 8 started.

Gentilly H. (R), Fair Grounds, March 20, $100,000, 3yo, Louisiana-bred, a1mT, 1:37.39, WALK THIS WAY, Old Lee, Peggy's Promise, 10 started.

GENUINE RISK H.-G2, Belmont Park, May 9, $147,000, 3&up, f&m, 6f, 1:08.85, BEAR FAN, Harmony Lodge, Kitty Knight, 5 started.

Genuine Risk S., Fairmount Park, July 17, $30,800, 3yo, f, 1m 70y, 1:45.60, LADY RISS, Hello Miami, Defuhr, 5 started.

George Lewis Memorial S. (R), Thistledown, July 30, $45,000, 3&up, Ohio-bred, 1^1/$_1$₆mi, 1:52.18, MAJESTIC DINNER, Real Echo, Forest Picnic, 10 started.

George Maloof Futurity (R), The Downs at Albuquerque, Sept. 26, $70,046, 2yo, c&g, New Mexico-bred, 6f, 1:10.03, LEON'S BULL, Mojo Mundo, Bluffen Go, 9 started.

George Rosenberger Memorial S. (R), Delaware Park, Sept. 11, $75,600, 3&up, f&m, starters at Delaware Park in 2004, 1^1/$_1$₆mT, 1:42.35, MYSTERY ITSELF, Misty Sixes, Lady Cheyne, 7 started.

George Royal S., Hastings Race Course, May 2, $44,576, 3&up, 6^1/$_2$f, 1:16.79, LORD NELSON, Commodore Craig, Irish Pleasure, 6 started.

George W. Barker S., Finger Lakes, May 31, $50,000, 3&up, New York-bred, 6f, 1:09.70, TOP SHOTER, Impeachthepro, Go Rockin' Robin, 9 started.

Georgia Debutante S. (R), Calder Race Course, Dec. 12, $50,000, 2yo, f, progeny of sires with a donated season to the 2005 GTOBA stallion auction, 1^1/$_1$₆mT, 1:42.37, DANSETTA LIGHT, Aclassysassylassy, Stavinsky's Gal, 7 started.

Georgia Peaches S. (R), Calder Race Course, Aug. 1, $50,000, 3&up, f&m, progeny of sires that have a donated season to the 2005 GTBOA stallion auction, 1mT, 1:37.62, ALL THE HONOR, Formal Miss, Arab Miss, 8 started.

Gerry Howard Inaugural H., Yavapai Downs, May 29, $17,500, 3&up, 6f, 1:09.80, TOP BOOT, Red Spark, Ripley, 9 started.

Gerry Howard Memorial S., Turf Paradise, May 2, $21,700, 3&up, 6f, 1:08.75, EXPERT, Dan's Groovy, Unyielding, 5 started.

Gilded Time S., Monmouth Park, May 29, $55,000, 3yo, 5fT, :58.26, SMOKUME, War's Prospect, Frisky Spider, 7 started.

Ginger Welch H., Les Bois Park, July 2, $6,350, 3&up, f&m, 1m, 1:40.40, NEVER BEEN CAUGHT, Opal's Song, Mode of the World, 6 started.

Girl Powder H. (R), Monmouth Park, Sept. 25, $60,000, 3&up, f&m, New Jersey-bred, 6f, 1:10.94, EASTERN GALE, Totally Precious, Cowboy Chili, 5 started.

Glacial Princess H. (R), Beulah Park, Nov. 27, $40,000, 2yo, f, Ohio-bred, 1m 70y, 1:49.92, MARKETABLE, Cloud Forty Nine, Liberty Mill, 8 started.

Glendale H., Turf Paradise, Feb. 14, $50,000, 4&up, f&m, 1^1/$_1$₆mT, 1:42.89, MAGNIFICENT VAL, Fanzoca, Moonlit Maddie, 11 started.

GLENS FALLS H. (1st Div.)-G3, Saratoga Race Course, Sept. 5, $110,400, 3&up, f&m, 1^3/$_8$mi, 2:15.25, HUMAITA (Ger), Where We Left Off (GB), Savedbythelight, 9 started.

GLENS FALLS H. (2nd Div.)-G3, Saratoga Race Course, Sept. 5, $109,300, 3&up, f&m, 1^3/$_8$mi, 2:14.12, ARVADA (GB), Spice Island, Film Maker, 8 started.

Glorious Song S., Woodbine, Nov. 21, $136,875, 2yo, f, 7f, 1:25.65, SHOUT TO THE NORTH, Canadian Gem, Roving Angel, 7 started.

Goddess S., Delta Downs, March 26, $75,000, 4&up, f&m, 1m, 1:38.25, HANDPAINTED, Salty Farma, Blue Guru, 6 started.

GO FOR WAND H.-G1, Saratoga Race Course, Aug. 1, $245,000, 3&up, f&m, 1^1/$_8$mi, 1:47.86, AZERI, Sightseek, Storm Flag Flying, 5 started.

Go for Wand S., Delaware Park, May 29, $100,600, 3yo, f, 1^1/$_1$₆mi, 1:46.66, PILFER, Hopelessly Devoted, From Away, 7 started.

Goldarama S., Calder Race Course, May 2, $40,000, 3&up, f&m, 6f, 1:11.08, MARY MURPHY, Whenthedoveflies, Crafty Brat, 6 started.

Gold Breeders' Cup S., Assiniboia Downs, Oct. 3, $63,750, 3&up, 1^1/$_8$mi, 1:52.60, DEPUTY COUNTRY, Indy Lead, Smoked Em, 7 started.

Gold Cup S. (R), Delta Downs, Nov. 13, $100,000, 3&up, Louisiana-bred, 1m, 1:40.55, WITT ANTE, Walk in the Snow, Nitro Chip, 8 started.

Golden Boy S., Assiniboia Downs, June 11, $40,000, 3yo, 6f, 1:11.60, SHANGHIED, Skipper, Stonewall Harris, 9 started.

Golden Circle S., Prairie Meadows, April 17, $50,000, 3yo, 6f, 1:09.20, DANIELTOWN, Jimmy Cracked Corn, Ruba Dub Dub, 10 started.

Golden Eagle Farm S. (R), Hollywood Park, April 24, $70,000, 3&up, California-bred, 7f, 1:21.80, THROW ME A CURVE, Bilo, Fairly Crafty, 13 started.

GOLDEN GATE BREEDERS' CUP H.-G3, Golden Gate Fields, March 14, $90,000, 3&up, 1^1/$_8$mT, 1:48.48, TRONARE (Chi), Soud, Aly Bubba, 9 started.

GOLDEN GATE DERBY-G3, Golden Gate Fields, Jan. 10, $100,000, 3yo, 1^1/$_1$₆mi, 1:41.84, SKIPASLEW, O. K. Mikie, Bensquito, 5 started.

Golden Gull Chris Brown Memorial S. (R), Charles Town Races, Sept. 26, $41,400, 2yo, f, West Virginia-bred, 4f, :48.77, WESHAAM LUCK, Tide City, Standing Safe, 10 started.

Golden Horseshoe S. (R), Fort Erie, Aug. 8, $58,000, 3&up, f&m, starters at Fort Erie at least three times in 2004, a7fT, 1:26.68, ANTHONIA, Kirlan, Silks N Roses, 10 started.

Golden Or S., Calder Race Course, Aug. 29, $40,000, 3&up, f&m, 6f, 1:12.61, TCHULA MISS, Sea Span, Letussojupiseyou, 10 started.

Golden Or S. (R), Calder Race Course, Dec. 19, $40,000, 3&up, f&m, non-winners of a stakes worth $25,000 or more to the winner, 1^1/$_1$₆mT, 1:41.48, LENTIL, Sniffles, Krasnaya, 7 started.

Golden Pond S. (R), Calder Race Course, Dec. 17, $40,000, 3yo, f, nonwinners of a stakes worth $25,000 or more to the winner, 1^1/$_1$₆mT, 1:46.56, PATH OF THUNDER, Coquinerie, Stormy Kitty, 6 started.

Golden Poppy H., Bay Meadows, Oct. 23, $55,550, 3&up, f&m, 1m, 1:35.09, MARWOOD, Beaucette, Devil Dancing, 8 started.

GOLDEN ROD S.-G2, Churchill Downs, Nov. 27, $215,400, 2yo, f, 1^1/$_1$₆mi, 1:45.97, RUNWAY MODEL, Kota, Summerely, 6 started.

Golden State Mile S., Golden Gate Fields, Feb. 8, $83,175, 3yo, 1m, 1:37.49, O. K. MIKIE, Bending Strings, Point Dume, 8 started.

Golden Sylvia H., Mountaineer Race Track, June 15, $75,000, 3&up, f&m, 1m, 1:38.60, TWO MILE HILL, Banished Lover, Ashwood C C, 6 started.

Golden Triangle S., Delta Downs, Oct. 22, $50,000, 3&up, f&m, 1m, 1:40.47, BAILEYS AFFAIR, Took Out, Miss Confusion, 8 started.

Goldfinch H. (R), Monmouth Park, June 26, $60,000, 3&up, f&m, New Jersey-bred, 1m 70y, 1:42.88, FIRECARD, Cigno d'Oro, Eastern Gale, 8 started.

Goldfinch S., Prairie Meadows, April 16, $49,000, 3yo, f, 6f, 1:09.66, SALTWATER RUNNER, Miss Elsie, Riverbrook, 5 started.

Gold Rush Futurity, Arapahoe Park, Sept. 5, $54,000, 2yo, 6f, 1:10.40, RAILROAD, Shesa Private I, Debs Diamond, 8 started.

Gold Rush S., Golden Gate Fields, Dec. 18, $54,800, 2yo, 1m, 1:36.55, DOVER DERE, Booming Along, Krovitz, 7 started.

GOODWOOD BREEDERS' CUP H.-G2, Santa Anita Park, Oct. 2, $480,000, 3&up, 1^1/$_8$mi, 1:48.39, LUNDY'S LIABILITY (Brz), Total Impact (Chi), Supah Blitz, 5 started.

Goss L. Stryker S. (R), Laurel Park, Feb. 7, $75,000, 3yo, Maryland-bred, 7f, 1:24.22, WHITE MOUNTAIN BOY, Hands On, Thiruvengadam, 5 started.

GOTHAM S.-G3, Aqueduct, March 20, $200,000, 3yo, 1m, 1:35.53, SARATOGA COUNTY, Pomeroy, Eddington, 8 started.

Gottstein Futurity (R), Emerald Downs, Sept. 19, $100,000, 2yo, progeny of eligible Washington stallions, 1^1/$_1$₆mi, 1:41.40, POSITIVE PRIZE, Charming Colleen, No Shouting, 7 started.

Governor's Buckeye Cup S. (R), Thistledown, Sept. 6, $75,000, 3&up, Ohio-bred, 1^1/$_4$m, 2:05.36, REAL ECHO, Chuckie's in Love, Xtra Jack, 11 started.

Governor's Cup H., Fairplex Park, Sept. 15, $59,400, 3&up, 6^1/$_2$f, 1:16.53, COURT'S IN SESSION, My Master (Arg), Excess Summer, 8 started.

Governor's Cup H., Wyoming Downs, July 10, $4,000, 3&up, 1m, 1:40.81, DOWNTOWN KID, On the Bill Daily, Cherokee Raid, 10 started.

Governor's H., Elko County Fair, Sept. 5, $3,696, 3&up, 7f, 1:25, QUIET SYNS, On the Bill Daily, dh-Cheese Puff, dh-Silent Snow, 4 started.

Governor's H., Ellis Park, Aug. 28, $75,000, 3&up, 1m, 1:35.34, ADDED EDGE, Discreet Hero, Roar of the Tiger, 10 started.

Governor's H., Emerald Downs, Aug. 8, $40,000, 3&up, 6^1/$_2$f, 1:14.60, SALT GRINDER, Best On Tap, Cody to Reggie, 6 started.

Governor's H., Les Bois Park, May 26, $6,250, 3&up, 7f, 1:25.20, FIND MY HALTER, Neil's Advice, Better Choice, 6 started.

Governor's H., Ruidoso Downs, July 18, $25,000, 3&up, 6f, 1:08.80, NINETY NINE JACK, Pacer, Mr. Zach Man, 7 started.

Governor's H., Sacramento, Aug. 28, $60,595, 3&up, 1^1/$_8$m, 1:48.37, YOUGOTTAWANNA, Sanger, Snoopy Cat, 7 started.

Governor's Lady H. (R) Hawthorne Race Course, April 10, $91,325, 4&up, f&m, Illinois-conceived and/or -foaled, 6f, 1:11.03, SUMMER MIS, Ravalli Girl, Cashmere Miss, 7 started.

Governor's S. (R), Indiana Downs, May 31, $42,400, 3yo, Indianabred, 7^1/$_2$fT, 1:30.63, EDGERRIN, Darn That Cobra, Liepers Fork, 9 started.

Governor's Speed S., Portland Meadows, March 27, $10,000, 4&up, 6f, 1:10.73, STAR OF ELTTAES, Yesss, City Parkway, 5 started.

Gowell S., Turfway Park, Dec. 26, $50,000, 2yo, f, 6f, 1:09.62, ANGEL TRUMPET, Coronado Rose, Im a Dixie Girl, 8 started.

Graceful Klinchit Distaff H., Marquis Downs, Aug. 27, $5,000, 3&up, f&m, 1^1/$_16$m, 1:47.35, SHE'S NIFTY, Picture the Answer, Argyl Rose, 4 started.

Graduation S. (R), Del Mar, July 28, $125,000, 2yo, California-bred, 5^1/$_2$f, 1:04.90, SENOR FANGO, Fallfree, Senske Lad, 8 started.

Grand Canyon H., Churchill Downs, Nov. 21, $70,420, 2yo, 1^1/$_16$mT, 1:46.84, EXCEPTIONAL RIDE, Rey de Cafe, Stormin Eddie, 8 started.

Grand Canyon H. (R), Turf Paradise, April 24, $15,000, 3&up, Arizonabred starters for a claiming price of $8,000 or less since September 25, 2003 and non-winners for more since that date, 6f, 1:10.12, PERFECT FIT, Coolidge, All American Chris, 11 started.

Grand Prairie Turf Challenge S., Lone Star Park, April 24, $75,000, 3yo, 1mT, 1:38.62, CRYPTOGRAPH, Mr. Devious, Rollicking Caller, 10 started.

Grants Pass Sprint Championship H., Grants Pass, June 13, $3,660, 3&up, 4^1/$_2$f, :55, I'M YER HUCKLEBERY, City Parkway, Condo Bob, 6 started.

Grants Pass Three-Year-Old Sprint H., Grants Pass, June 6, $3,541, 3yo, 5^1/$_2$f, 1:05.20, PRIMECAT, Sun Son, Im in the Soup, 5 started.

Grasmick H., Fonner Park, Feb. 21, $10,875, 3&up, 4f, 45.20, TONIGHT RAINBOW, Herewegoagain, Tate's Way, 8 started.

GRAVESEND H.-G3, Aqueduct, Dec. 19, $109,400, 3&up, 6f, 1:08.97, DON SIX, Mr. Whitestone, Papua, 6 started.

Grays Lake S. (R), Prairie Meadows, May 30, $57,123, 3yo, c&g, Iowa-bred, 6f, 1:09.68, WILD WILD WEST, Plum Sober, Cross Canyon, 6 started.

Great White Way S. (R), Aqueduct, Nov. 7, $125,000, 2yo, c&g, progeny of eligible New York stallions, 6f, 1:11.22, ACCURATE, Summerland, Distinctive Trick, 9 started.

Green Carpet S. (R), River Downs, May 29, $45,000, 3yo, Ohio-bred, 1^1/$_16$mT, 1:49.60, FLOATER, Dawn's Revenge, Thinksheshot, 6 started.

Green Flash H., Del Mar, Aug. 18, $76,350, 3&up, 5fT, :55.15, GERONIMO (Chi), Glick, Gray Jag, 6 started.

Green Oaks H., Delta Downs, Feb. 27, $50,000, 3yo, f, 7f, 1:28.02, CRYPTOS' BEST, Simply Jolie, Road to Mandalay, 5 started.

Greenwood Cup H., Philadelphia Park, June 5, $100,000, 3&up, 1^1/$_2$mT, 2:33.32, IN HAND, Host, Monkey Puzzle, 10 started.

GREY BREEDERS' CUP S.-G2, Woodbine, Oct. 11, $261,750, 2yo, 1^1/$_16$mT, 1:47.79, DANCE WITH RAVENS, Accountforthegold, Criminal Mind, 6 started.

Groomstick H., Calder Race Course, July 31, $75,000, 3&up, 6^1/$_2$f, 1:18.48, GOLD DOLLAR, Formal Charade, My Last Chance (Arg), 9 started.

Groovy S. (R), Sam Houston Race Park, Nov. 20, $50,000, 2yo, Texas-bred, 7f, 1:24.99, EXPECT WILL, Super Itron, Cat Tourn, 10 started.

Gulf Coast Classic S., Delta Downs, March 27, $100,000, 4&up, 1^1/$_16$m, 1:45, KODEMA, Spritely Walker, Prince Slew, 8 started.

GULFSTREAM PARK BREEDERS' CUP H.-G1, Gulfstream Park, Feb. 22, $190,000, 3&up, 1^3/$_16$mT, 2:11.56, HARD BUCK (Brz), Balto Star, Kicken Kris, 8 started.

GULFSTREAM PARK H.-G2, Gulfstream Park, April 3, $300,000, 3&up, 1^1/$_4$m, 2:02.80, JACKPOT, Newfoundland, The Lady's Groom, 6 started.

Gus Fonner S., Fonner Park, April 24, $100,000, 3&up, 1^1/$_16$m, 1:46.80, SONIC WEST, Dusty Spike, Tonight Rainbow, 9 started.

Gus Grissom S. (R), Hoosier Park, Oct. 3, $40,000, 3&up, Indianabred and/or -sired, 1^1/$_16$m, 1:47.61, SIR TRAVER, Whenthesmokeclears, Dollar for Dollar, 10 started.

Haggin S., Hollywood Park, June 20, $80,025, 2yo, 5^1/$_2$f, 1:04.02, CHANDTRUE, Gentleman Count, Fallfree, 6 started.

H. A. Hindmarsh S., Fort Erie, July 10, $75,000, 3&up, f&m, 1^1/$_16$m, 1:44.65, KISSED BY A PRINCE, Royal Dalliance, Miss Grindstone, 5 started.

Hail the Ruckus Dating Game S., Lethbridge, Oct. 30, $12,200, 3&up, f&m, 7f, 1:25.80, TEMPTOR CIELO, Guiltybysupiscion, Special Era, 8 started.

Hallowed Dreams S. (R), Louisiana Downs, Aug. 15, $49,000, 3&up, f&m, Louisiana-bred, 6f, 1:11.39, LESLIE'S LOVE, Forty Dolls, Scottish Heritage, 5 started.

Halo America S., Calder Race Course, July 6, $40,000, 3yo, f, 1^1/$_16$m, 1:47.32, ADOBE GOLD, Najibes Acre, Tiz a Dancer, 6 started.

HAL'S HOPE H.-G3, Gulfstream Park, Jan. 3, $100,000, 3&up, 1^1/$_16$m, 1:42.39, PUZZLEMENT, Bowman's Band, Stockholder, 7 started.

Halton S. (R), Woodbine, Sept. 5, $128,750, 3&up, Canadian-bred which passed through the sales ring as a yearling at any 2002 or sale conducted by Canadian Breeders' Sales, Woodbine Sales, or Fasig-Tipton Canada, 1^1/$_8$mT, 1:46.97, MOBIL, Lenny the Lender, Jambalar, 4 started.

Hancock County H., Mountaineer Race Track, May 11, $75,000, 3&up, f&m, 5f, :59.01, GABRIELES PRINCESS, Idadidit, Nattitude, 7 started.

Hank Mills Memorial H., Wyoming Downs, Aug. 21, $4,300, 3&up, f&m, 5f, :56.77, CHEESE PUFF, Forever Jan, Never Been Caught, 8 started.

Hansel S., Turfway Park, March 20, $42,500, 3yo, 6f, 1:11.17, MARLEY'S REVENGE, Danieltown, Wulpe, 7 started.

HANSHIN CUP H.-G3, Arlington Park, May 29, $100,000, 3&up, 1m, 1:35.36, CRAFTY SHAW, Apt to Be, Kodema, 7 started.

Harold C. Ramser Sr. H., Santa Anita Park, Oct. 11, $100,000, 3yo, f, 1mT, 1:33.90, MEA DOMINA, Penny's Fortune, Costume Designer, 9 started.

Harold V. Goodman Memorial S. (R), Lone Star Park, May 31, $50,000, 3yo, Texas-bred, 6^1/$_2$f, 1:14.94, CANADIAN RIVER, Mr. Devious, Late Expectations, 8 started.

Harper County H., Anthony Downs, July 18, $4,000, 3&up, a5f, 1:01.72, SUNSET CRUISE, Fly Tricky, Saintemerald, 5 started.

Harrison E. Johnson Memorial H., Laurel Park, March 13, $67,750, 4&up, 1^1/$_8$m, 1:49.51, JORGIE STOVER, Your Bluffing, Last Intention, 8 started.

Harry F. Brubaker H. (R), Del Mar, Aug. 20, $77,200, 3&up, non-winners of a stakes of $45,000 other than state-bred at one mile or over since March 1, 1^1/$_16$mT, 1:39.93, CAYOKE (Fr), Buddy Gil, King of Happiness, 9 started.

Harry Henson S., Hollywood Park, April 21, $78,075, 3yo, 5^1/$_2$f, 1:01.62, STORMIN' LYON, Wimplestiltskin, Tunder Ponche, 5 started.

Harry Jeffrey S., Assiniboia Downs, Aug. 29, $40,000, 3yo, 1^1/$_16$m, 1:51.80, SHANGHIED, Picador Kat, Stonewall Harris, 5 started.

Harry W. Henson H., Sunland Park, April 4, $105,400, 3&up, f&m, 1m, 1:36.83, ACADEMIC ANGEL, Sideways, Blue Guru, 9 started.

Harvest Futurity, Fresno, Oct. 10, $40,017, 2yo, 6f, 1:08.95, AIR JULIE, Longer Walk, Wind Water, 8 started.

Harvest H., The Downs at Albuquerque, April 17, $44,400, 3yo, 5^1/$_2$f, 1:02.94, OCEAN SYMPHONY, No Term Limit, John Coffee, 11 started.

Harvey Arneault Memorial H., Mountaineer Race Track, Aug. 7, $85,000, 3&up, 6f, 1:09.57, EAVESDROPPER, Frankie R's Winner, Crossing Point, 8 started.

HASKELL INVITATIONAL H.-G1, Monmouth Park, Aug. 8, $1,000,000, 3yo, 1¹/₈m, 1:48.95, LION HEART, My Snookie's Boy, Pies Prospect, 8 started.

Hasta La Vista H., Turf Paradise, May 16, $50,000, 3&up, 1⅛mT, 3:11.97, FADE TO BLUE, Golden Approval, Paladin Power, 10 started.

Hastings Park H., Emerald Downs, May 9, $40,000, 3&up, f&m, 6¹/₂f, 1:15, LASTING CODE, Aunt Sophie, Marva Jean, 11 started.

Hastings Speed H., Hastings Race Course, Aug. 21, $43,619, 3&up, 6¹/₂f, 1:16.31, FIVE POINT STAR, Nineleventurbo, Silver Donn, 6 started.

Hatoof S., Arlington Park, Aug. 28, $54,000, 3yo, f, 1¹/₁₆mT, 1:50.09, HUMOROUS MISS, Code of Ethics, Sean's Baby, 8 started.

Hawkeyes H. (R), Prairie Meadows, June 26, $68,600, 3&up, f&m, Iowa-bred, 1¹/₁₆m, 1:45.62, SHARKY'S REVIEW, One Fine Shweetie, O U Bet, 5 started.

HAWTHORNE DERBY-G3, Hawthorne Race Course, Oct. 16, $250,000, 3yo, 1¹/₄mT, 1:47.89, COOL CONDUCTOR, Bankruptcy Court, Crown Prince, 10 started.

HAWTHORNE GOLD CUP H.-G2, Hawthorne Race Course, Oct. 2, $750,000, 3&up, 1¹/₄m, 2:03.34, FREEFOURINTERNET, Perfect Drift, Sonic West, 7 started.

HAWTHORNE H.-G3, Hollywood Park, June 6, $108,600, 3&up, f&m, 1¹/₁₆m, 1:41.56, SUMMER WIND DANCER, Pesci, Miss Loren (Arg), 7 started.

HBPA and WVRC S. (R), Charles Town Races, July 18, $51,300, 3&up, starters at Charles Town the most times in last four starts, 1¹/₈m, 1:52.95, CHEROKEE'S BOY, Rakeen's Reward, High Wire Glory, 8 started.

HBPA Au Revoir H., Grants Pass, July 5, $4,060, 3&up, 6¹/₂f, 1:18.20, NEVETS, Tiger Town, In Gold We Trust, 5 started.

HBPA City of Charles Town H., Charles Town Races, Oct. 8, $51,200, 3&up, 4f, :44.86, CHOCTAW RIDGE, Ian's Rocket, Tender Toes, 6 started.

HBPA City of Ranson H., Charles Town Races, Oct. 8, $51,475, 3&up, f&m, 7f, 1:27.79, LETS JUST DO IT, City Fire, Miss Hamma, 8 started.

HBPA Dash S. (R), Charles Town Races, July 18, $51,250, 3&up, starters at Charles Town the most times in last four starts, 4¹/₂f, :51.36, NOT FOR SAM, Calisthenic, Anthony Soprano, 7 started.

HBPA Governor's Cup H., Charles Town Races, July 10, $51,175, 3&up, 1¹/₁₆m, 1:58.19, NOMOREBILLS, Trumpets Delight, Last Intention, 8 started.

HBPA H., Ellis Park, July 10, $75,000, 3&up, f&m, 1m, 1:37.24, MISS FORTUNATE, Mayo On the Side, There Runs Hattie, 8 started.

HBPA H., Grants Pass, June 6, $3,450, 3&up, 5¹/₂f, 1:04.80, JESSE GEE, Tee Tommy Slew, City Parkway, 4 started.

HBPA Horsemen's S. (R), Charles Town Races, July 18, $51,200, 3&up, f&m, starters at Charles Town the most times in last four starts, 4¹/₂f, :52.32, UMPATEEDLE, Pompamento, French Republic, 7 started.

HBPA Sagebrush Downs Derby, Kamloops, Aug. 22, $5,250, 3yo, a6¹/₂f, 1:25.24, MARGO DUKE, Shuswap Road, Patchtomatch, 5 started.

HBPA West Virginia S. (R), Charles Town Races, July 18, $51,400, 3&up, f&m, starters at Charles Town the most times in last four starts, 7f, 1:26.30, RIBBON CANE, Lets Just Do It, Experts Only, 9 started.

Heavenly Cause S. (R), Pimlico, Oct. 30, $75,000, 2yo, f, Maryland-bred, 6f, 1:11.94, GOLDEN MALIBU, Take a Check, Lisaized, 6 started.

Helen Anthony Memorial S., Yavapai Downs, Aug. 8, $12,500, 3yo, f, 6f, 1:09.80, DIAMONDSRBUENO, Solly's Dolly, P R Royal Princess, 8 started.

HENDRIE H.-G3, Woodbine, May 16, $174,250, 4&up, f&m, 6¹/₂f, 1:16.76, WINTER GARDEN, Spanish Decree, Handpainted, 5 started.

Henry S. Clark S., Pimlico, May 1, $50,000, 3&up, 1mT, 1:35.80, MR O'BRIEN (Ire), Spruce Run, Tam's Terms, 8 started.

Herald Gold Plate H., Stampede Park, June 13, $50,000, 3&up, 1¹/₁₆m, 1:46.20, BUBBLEGUM KID, Rindanica, Code Name Fred, 10 started.

HERECOMESTHEBRIDE S.-G3, Gulfstream Park, Feb. 28, $100,000, 3yo, f, 1¹/₈mT, 1:52.78, LUCIFER'S STONE, Dynamia, Honey Ryder, 12 started.

Hermosa Beach H., Hollywood Park, Nov. 25, $65,110, 3&up, f&m, 1¹/₈mT, 2:29.40, URAIB (Ire), Nadeszhda (GB), Test the Waters, 8 started.

Hidden Light S. (R), Santa Anita Park, Oct. 27, $78,400, 2yo, f, nonwinners of a stakes at one mile or over, 1mT, 1:38.02, CONVEYOR'S ANGEL, Zain Lass, , 6 started.

High Alexander H. (R), Hawthorne Race Course, Nov. 13, $96,275, 3&up, Illinois-conceived and/or -foaled, 1¹/₁₆m, 1:45.22, HOME OF STARS, Magic Doe, Wiggins, 11 started.

HIGHLANDER H.-G3, Woodbine, June 27, $219,000, 3&up, 6fT, 1:08.72, SOARING FREE, Open Concert, Take Achance On Me, 7 started.

Hildene S. (R), Delaware Park, Oct. 30, $50,300, 2yo, f, Virginia-bred and/or -sired, 6f, 1:11.50, JOYOUS SONG, Partners Due, Toosmartsweetheart, 6 started.

Hill 'n' Dale S., Woodbine, July 3, $109,500, 3yo, f, 1¹/₁₆m, 1:43.63, MY LORDSHIP, Sweet Problem, Pandora's Secret, 5 started.

HILL PRINCE S.-G3, Belmont Park, June 6, $110,000, 3yo, 1¹/₁₆m, 1:50.06, ARTIE SCHILLER, Timo, Big Booster, 6 started.

Hillsborough H., Bay Meadows, Sept. 25, $55,800, 3&up, f&m, 1¹/₁₆mT, 1:42.33, URAIB (Ire), Cat Alert, A B Noodle, 7 started.

HILLSBOROUGH S.-G3, Tampa Bay Downs, March 14, $100,000, 4&up, f&m, a1¹/₈mT, 1:48.83, CONEY KITTY (Ire), Madeira Mist (Ire), Alternate, 12 started.

Hillsdale S. (R), Hoosier Park, Oct. 2, $40,000, 2yo, c&g, Indiana-bred, 5¹/₂f, 1:05.74, BRUCE ON THE LOOSE, Faith in God, Snack, 12 started.

Hilltop S., Pimlico, May 8, $50,000, 3yo, f, 1¹/₁₆mT, 1:43.22, WESTERN RANSOM, Art Fan, Star of Anziyan, 11 started.

Hirsch Jacobs S., Pimlico, May 15, $100,000, 3yo, 6f, 1:10.72, ABBONDANZA, Bwana Charlie, Penn Pacific, 9 started.

H. J. Addison Jr. S. (R), Fort Erie, July 11, $75,000, 3&up, sold at a CTHS or CBS sale, 1¹/₁₆m, 1:45.86, DOMASCAS CONSORT, Forever Grand, Nowyouseeit, 3 started.

Hoist Her Flag S., Canterbury Park, May 29, $40,000, 3&up, f&m, 6f, 1:10.85, BURNING MEMORIES, Sarah Jade, Prime Step, 6 started.

Holiday Inaugural S., Turfway Park, Dec. 4, $49,500, 3&up, f&m, 6f, 1:09.27, REVOLUTIONARY ACT, Golden Marlin, Class Above, 10 started.

Hollie Hughes H. (R), Aqueduct, Feb. 15, $80,175, 3&up, New York-bred, 6f, 1:10.59, PAPUA, A One Rocket, Love Less, 6 started.

Holly S., The Meadowlands, Oct. 23, $60,000, 2yo, f, 6f, 1:10.06, MORE MOONLIGHT, Ruby Be Mine, Galactic Cat, 9 started.

HOLLYWOOD BREEDERS' CUP OAKS-G2, Hollywood Park, June 12, $182,875, 3yo, f, 1¹/₁₆m, 1:41.55, HOUSE OF FORTUNE, Elusive Diva, Hollywood Story, 5 started.

HOLLYWOOD DERBY-G1, Hollywood Park, Nov. 28, $500,000, 3yo, 1¹/₄mT, 2:01.53, GOOD REWARD, Fast and Furious (Fr), Imperialism, 13 started.

HOLLYWOOD FUTURITY-G1, Hollywood Park, Dec. 18, $449,500, 2yo, 1¹/₁₆m, 1:41.63, DECLAN'S MOON, Giacomo, Wilko, 7 started.

HOLLYWOOD GOLD CUP S.-G1, Hollywood Park, July 10, $750,000, 3&up, 1¹/₄m, 2:00.72, TOTAL IMPACT (Chi), Olmodavor, Even the Score, 7 started.

HOLLYWOOD JUVENILE CHAMPIONSHIP S.-G3, Hollywood Park, July 17, $104,272, 2yo, 6f, 1:10.88, CHANDTRUE, Actxecutive, Commandant, 4 started.

HOLLYWOOD PREVUE S.-G3, Hollywood Park, Nov. 20, $100,000, 2yo, 7f, 1:21.74, DECLAN'S MOON, Bushwacker, Seize the Day, 8 started.

HOLLYWOOD STARLET S.-G1, Hollywood Park, Dec. 19, $389,000, 2yo, f, 1¹/₁₆m, 1:41.82, SPLENDID BLENDED, Sharp Lisa, Northern Mischief, 7 started.

HOLLYWOOD TURF CUP H.-G1, Hollywood Park, Dec. 4, $250,000, 3&up, 1¹/₂mT, 2:29.73, PELLEGRINO (Brz), Megahertz (GB), License To Run (Brz), 9 started.

HOLLYWOOD TURF EXPRESS H.-G3, Hollywood Park, Nov. 26, $150,000, 3&up, 5¹/₂fT, 1:02.08, CAJUN BEAT, Geronimo (Chi), Mighty Beau, 8 started.

Hollywood Wildcat Breeders' Cup H., Calder Race Course, May 1, $150,000, 3&up, 1¹/₁₆mT, 1:42, STAY FOREVER, Mrs. M, Sweettrickydancer, 11 started.

HOLY BULL S.-G3, Gulfstream Park, Jan. 17, $100,000, 3yo, 1¹/₁₆m, 1:43, SECOND OF JUNE, Silver Wagon, Friends Lake, 9 started.

Honest Pleasure S., Arlington Park, Aug. 1, $52,600, 2yo, 5¹/₂f, 1:04.65, STRAIGHT LINE, Toliver, Smoke Smoke Smoke, 6 started.

Honeybee S., Oaklawn Park, March 6, $75,000, 3yo, f, 1¹/₁₆m, 1:45.14, YOURSMINEOURS, Stephan's Angel, Solitary Emerald, 7 started.

Honey Bee S., The Meadowlands, Nov. 5, $60,000, 3yo, f, 1¹/₁₆m, 1:42.66, EMERALD EARRINGS, Richetta, From Away, 6 started.

HONEY FOX H.-G3, Gulfstream Park, Jan. 3, $100,000, 3&up, f&m, 1¹/₁₆mT, 1:41.30, DELMONICO CAT, Coney Kitty (Ire), Madeira Mist (Ire), 10 started.

Honey Jay H. (R), Beulah Park, Sept. 19, $40,000, 3&up, Ohio-bred, 6f, 1:11.14, BEN'S REFLECTION, Cayenne Red, Cat Singer, 6 started.

HONEYMOON BREEDERS' CUP H.-G2, Hollywood Park, June 5, $184,925, 3yo, f, 1¹/₈mT, 1:49.96, LOVELY RAFAELA, Western Hemisphere, Sagitta Ra, 8 started.

Honeymoon S., Louisiana Downs, May 15, $50,000, 3&up, f&m, 1mT, 1:36.94, DUE TO WIN AGAIN, Titia, Tincan Too, 10 started.

Hong Kong Jockey Club Sprint H., Hastings Race Course, May 23, $44,160, 3&up, 6¹/₂f, 1:16.14, LORD NELSON, Commodore Craig, Dancewithavixen, 10 started.

HONORABLE MISS H.-G2, Saratoga Race Course, Aug. 6, $150,000, 3&up, f&m, 6f, 1:10.37, MY TRUSTY CAT, Ebony Breeze, Smok'n Frolic, 8 started.

Honor the Hero Express S., Canterbury Park, May 31, $40,000, 3&up, 5fT, :57.11, TONIGHT RAINBOW, Classy Sheikh, Win the Crowd, 9 started.

Honor the Hero S., Turf Paradise, Jan. 18, $21,800, 3yo, 1m, 1:37.29, OZONED, Thundering Verzy, Cincinnati Jay, 8 started.

Hoofprint On My Heart H., Stampede Park, May 30, $40,000, 3yo, 1m, 1:39.40, KAT KOOL, Royalty Boy, Saw Grass Sabre, 10 started.

Hoosier Silver Cup S. (R), Hoosier Park, Oct. 17, $40,000, 2yo, c&g, Indiana-bred, 6f, 1:14.15, UNFORGOTTENPROMISE, Hebe's Express, Dakota North, 7 started.

Hoosier Silver Cup S. (R), Hoosier Park, Oct. 17, $40,000, 2yo, f, Indiana-bred, 6f, 1:13.30, SLIM JUSTICE, Stephie's Cat, Join the Crusade, 6 started.

Hoover S., Laurel Park, Jan. 24, $52,750, 4&up, 6f, 1:10.14, GATORS N BEARS, My Good Trick, Sassy Hound, 10 started.

Hoover S. (R), River Downs, July 18, $40,000, 2yo, Ohio-bred, 5¹/₂f, 1:07, BUG HUNTER, Brooks Blach, Me Son, 9 started.

HOPEFUL S.-G1, Saratoga Race Course, Aug. 21, $250,000, 2yo, 7f, 1:23.58, AFLEET ALEX, Devils Disciple, Flamenco, 7 started.

Horatius S., Laurel Park, March 21, $41,800, 3yo, 6f, 1:10.95, BASKETBALL COURT, Matsui, Snow Eagle, 8 started.

Horizon S. (R), River Downs, July 25, $40,000, 3yo, Ohio-bred, 1¹/₁₆mT, 1:44, BEST BIRD, Child of Light, Benewin, 9 started.

Hot Springs S., Oaklawn Park, March 21, $49,000, 4&up, 6f, 1:09.22, SKEET, That Tat, dh-Cowboy Stuff, dh-Saint Waki, 5 started.

Howard B. Noonan S. (R), Beulah Park, March 27, $40,000, 3yo, Ohio-bred, 6f, 1:11.14, CAYENNE RED, Floater, Oh Oleg, 12 started.

H. Steward Mitchell S., Pimlico, Dec. 4, $40,000, 2yo, 6f, 1:12.70, SEEYOUBYCHANCE, Monster Chaser, Late Night Lover, 6 started.

Hubbard Museum Middle Distance Final S., Ruidoso Downs, Aug. 7, $20,100, 3&up, 7¹/₂f, 1:32.40, HIGHLY SUSPECT, Wolf's Honor, Masakado Kid, 9 started.

Hudson H. (R), Belmont Park, Oct. 23, $125,000, 3&up, New York-bred, 6f, 1:09.49, FRIENDLY ISLAND, Clever Electrician, Papua, 7 started.

Humphrey S. Finney S. (R), Pimlico, Sept. 11, $75,000, 3yo, Maryland-bred, 1¹/₈mT, 1:49.95, CLASS CONCERN, Please Smile, Richetta, 6 started.

Huntington S., Aqueduct, Nov. 14, $82,950, 2yo, 6f, 1:10.17, MAGOO'S MAGIC, Storm Creek Rising, Tani Maru, 9 started.

Hurricane Bertie H., Gulfstream Park, March 7, $100,000, 3&up, f&m, 6¹/₂f, 1:15.55, HOUSE PARTY, Mooji Moo, Zawzooth, 10 started.

HUTCHESON S.-G2, Gulfstream Park, Feb. 14, $150,000, 3yo, 7f, 1:22.23, LIMEHOUSE, Deputy Storm, Saratoga County, 10 started.

Icecapade S., Monmouth Park, Sept. 6, $60,000, 3&up, 6f, 1:09.24, WILDCAT HEIR, Sing Me Back Home, Here's Zealous, 7 started.

I. C. Light Memorial Day H., Mountaineer Race Track, May 31, $75,000, 3&up, 1m, 1:37.74, GIN AND SIN, Doc D, Horrible Evening, 5 started.

Idaho Bred Sophomore Distaff S. (R), Les Bois Park, June 5, $8,805, 3yo, f, Idaho-bred, 6¹/₂f, 1:20, PARADISE WILD, Sheza Cats Meow, Just So Ya No, 7 started.

Idaho Bred Sophomore S. (R), Les Bois Park, June 5, $9,075, 3yo, c&g, Idaho-bred, 6¹/₂f, 1:20.80, ROBS COIN, Heza Spazz, Best Caper, 8 started.

Idaho Cup Claiming S. (R), Les Bois Park, July 31, $12,078, 3&up, Idaho-bred, 7f, 1:24.80, SHERROYAL, J. D. for Shur, Chilly Charlie, 9 started.

Idaho Cup Classic S. (R), Les Bois Park, July 31, $32,099, 4&up, Idaho-bred, 1m, 1:38, CROOKED KEY, Quiet Syns, Jazzing Jack, 7 started.

Idaho Cup Derby (R), Les Bois Park, July 31, $35,582, 3yo, c&g, Idaho-bred, 1m, 1:38.20, SILENT SNOW, Northern Buck, Moab, 10 started.

Idaho Cup Distaff Derby (R), Les Bois Park, July 31, $37,323, 3yo, f, Idaho-bred, 1m, 1:38, PARADISE WILD, Hey Robbie, Petite Motion, 9 started.

Idaho Cup Distaff Maturity (R), Les Bois Park, July 31, $28,656, 4&up, f&m, Idaho-bred, 1m, 1:38.60, THRILL AFTER DARK, Somer Wonders, Shine Along, 7 started.

Idaho Cup Futurity (R), Les Bois Park, July 31, $36,797, 2yo, Idaho-bred, 5f, :59.40, BLUE JULIE, Valid Sex Appeal, Spicey N Hot, 10 started.

Idaho Cup Sprint S. (R), Les Bois Park, July 31, $14,796, 3&up, Idaho-bred, 5f, :57.40, DUN RINGILL, Justifiable Cause, Mini Me, 4 started.

Illini Princess H. (R), Hawthorne Race Course, Nov. 13, $99,000, 3&up, f&m, Illinois-conceived and/or-foaled, 1¹/₁₆m, 1:46.09, CASHMERE MISS, Arsen Annie, Ms. Lydonia, 14 started.

ILLINOIS DERBY-G2, Hawthorne Race Course, April 3, $500,000, 3yo, 1¹/₈m, 1:50.80, POLLARD'S VISION, Song of the Sword, Suave, 11 started.

I'm Smokin S. (R), Del Mar, Sept. 6, $98,000, 2yo, California-bred, 6f, 1:09.28, TOP MONEY, Fallfree, Proud Tower Too, 4 started.

Inaugural H., Evangeline Downs, April 3, $50,000, 3yo, 6f, 1:10.60, SMALLTOWN SLEW, Britt's Jules, Brandon's Marfa, 8 started.

Inaugural H., Les Bois Park, May 1, $6,950, 3&up, 6¹/₂f, 1:18, BETTER CHOICE, Nighthunter, Find My Halter, 8 started.

Inaugural H., Portland Meadows, Oct. 16, $10,000, 3&up, 6f, 1:09.76, SLEWICIDE CRUISE, Yesss, Ten Across, 8 started.

Inaugural H., SunRay Park, Aug. 2, $32,500, 3&up, 6¹/₂f, 1:16.80, SWIFT FOR SURE, Cheyenne Breeze, Pleasant Bend, 7 started.

Inaugural H., Wyoming Downs, June 26, $4,225, 3&up, 6f, 1:12.74, RESTRICTIONS APPLY, Fire Ball John, Better Choice, 11 started.

Inaugural S., Arapahoe Park, July 3, $30,475, 3yo, 6f, 1:09.80, C K JETT, Lissa's Lad, Nakayama Jazz, 9 started.

Inaugural S., Columbus Races, July 23, $11,200, 3yo, f, 6f, 1:15, SHESO, Kerosene Prospect, Shawklit Premiere, 7 started.

Inaugural S., Delta Downs, Oct. 1, $40,000, 3&up, 5f, :59.37, BELIEVE IM SPECIAL, Joyful Tune, Nitro Chip, 9 started.

Inaugural S., Grants Pass, May 15, $4,026, 3&up, 5¹/₂f, 1:06.30, CITY PARKWAY, Jesse Gee, Slewper Sport, 8 started.

Inaugural S., Great Falls, July 3, $2,950, 3&up, 5f, 1:00, SLEW DESIGN, Fruit Rapport, King of Adventure, 5 started.

Inaugural S., Tampa Bay Downs, Dec. 11, $57,500, 2yo, 6f, 1:12.23, HOSTILE WITNESS, Sounds Impossible, Captain Lindsay, 10 started.

Incredible Revenge S., The Meadowlands, Oct. 9, $60,000, 3&up, f&m, 5fT, :56.43, TIGHT SPIN, Melody of Colors, The Rodeo Express, 10 started.

Independence Day H., Emerald Downs, July 4, $40,000, 3&up, 1¹/₁₆m, 1:41.40, BRIARTIC GOLD, Metatron, Mr. Makah, 8 started.

Independence Day H., Mountaineer Race Track, July 4, $75,000, 3&up, 1mT, 1:36.12, MISSME, Ask the Lord, Horrible Evening, 5 started.

Independence H., Louisiana Downs, July 4, $75,000, 3&up, 1¹/₁₆mT, 1:45.19, SEA DUB, Virginia Pride, Waupaca, 7 started.

INDIANA BREEDERS' CUP OAKS-G3, Hoosier Park, Oct. 2, $406,300, 3yo, f, 1¹/₁₆m, 1:43.65, DAYDREAMING, Capeside Lady, Stellar Jayne, 7 started.

INDIANA DERBY-G2, Hoosier Park, Oct. 2, $511,300, 3yo, 1¹/₁₆m, 1:44.04, BRASS HAT, Suave, Hasslefree, 9 started.

Indiana First Lady S. (R), Indiana Downs, May 29, $40,000, 3yo, f, Indiana-bred, 7¹/₂fT, 1:30.07, SPEEDY TIFFANY, Tee's Pearl, Oro's Sugar, 8 started.

Indiana Futurity (R), Hoosier Park, Nov. 7, $40,000, 2yo, Indiana-bred, 6f, 1:13.60, SNACK, Bruce On the Loose, Moros Destiny, 11 started.

Indiana Stallion S. (R), Hoosier Park, Nov. 20, $40,000, 2yo, f, Indiana-bred and/or -sired, 6f, 1:13.44, FREE BONUS, Slim Justice, Black Eyed Susie, 11 started.

Indiana Stallion S. (R), Hoosier Park, Nov. 21, $40,000, 2yo, c&g, Indiana-bred and/or -sired, 6f, 1:12.72, BRUCE ON THE LOOSE, Earl Cruz, Moros Destiny, 9 started.

Indian Maid Breeders' Cup H., Hawthorne Race Course, Oct. 2, $122,500, 3&up, f&m, 1¹/₁₆mT, 1:43.44, BERET, Delicatessa, Golden Trevally, 10 started.

INGLEWOOD H.-G3, Hollywood Park, May 1, $110,900, 3&up, 1¹/₁₆mT, 1:38.45, LEROIDESANIMAUX (Brz), Designed for Luck, Devious Boy (GB), 9 started.

Ingrid Knotts H. (R), Arapahoe Park, July 3, $26,575, 3&up, f&m, Colorado-bred, 6f, 1:10.20, SHE'S FINDING TIME, Sara Margaret, Tricky Transaction, 6 started.

In Reality S. (R), Calder Race Course, Oct. 23, $400,000, 2yo, progeny of eligible Florida stallions, 1¹/₁₆m, 1:47.66, B. B. BEST, Anthony J., Closing Argument, 13 started.

Instant Racing Breeders' Cup S., Oaklawn Park, April 10, $73,750, 3yo, f, 1m, 1:39.20, TEE'S PEARL, Pilfer, Cedar Summer, 8 started.

Interborough H., Aqueduct, Jan. 1, $81,600, 3&up, f&m, 6f, 1:10.76, FIT PERFORMER, Drexel Memorial, Elegant Designer, 7 started.

International Turf Club S. (R), Fort Erie, July 18, $100,000, 3&up, Canadian-bred, 1¹/₁₆m, 1:45.57, LE CINQUIEME ESSAI, Just Watch Me, Longship, 6 started.

Iowa Breeders' Derby (R), Prairie Meadows, Aug. 28, $77,530, 3yo, c&g, Iowa-bred, 1¹/₁₆m, 1:43.05, ROAROFVICTORY, Wild Wild West, Devils Wild, 9 started.

Iowa Breeders' Oaks (R), Prairie Meadows, Aug. 28, $76,300, 3yo, f, Iowa-bred, 1m 70y, 1:42.66, THIS ONE FOR ABBEY, Dis Miss, Butter Crunch, 8 started.

Iowa Cradle S. (R), Prairie Meadows, Aug. 28, $75,130, 2yo, c&g, Iowa-bred, 6f, 1:11.51, MINGO MOHAWK, Dance With Legend, Five Rubies, 10 started.

Iowa Derby, Prairie Meadows, July 2, $250,000, 3yo, 1¹/₁₆m, 1:43.31, SWINGFORTHEFENCES, Courageous Act, Cryptograph, 6 started.

Iowa Distaff Breeders' Cup S., Prairie Meadows, July 3, $122,500, 3&up, f&m, 1¹/₁₆m, 1:41.61, WILDWOOD ROYAL, Chance Dance, Cat Fighter, 5 started.

IOWA OAKS-G3, Prairie Meadows, July 2, $125,000, 3yo, f, 1¹/₁₆m, 1:42.80, HE LOVES ME, Prospective Saint, Home Court, 8 started.

Iowa Sorority S. (R), Prairie Meadows, Aug. 28, $79,630, 2yo, f, Iowa-bred, 6f, 1:11.80, QUEANSCO, Bad Little Bernie, Raiderette, 8 started.

Iowa Sprint H., Prairie Meadows, July 4, $122,500, 3&up, 6f, 1:07.85, COACH JIMI LEE, Cat Genius, Honor Me, 5 started.

Iowa Stallion Futurity (R), Prairie Meadows, Aug. 14, $61,880, 2yo, progeny of eligible Iowa stallions, 6f, 1:12.67, OKIE DOZER, Boxer, Nothing But Cat, 10 started.

Iowa Stallion S. (R), Prairie Meadows, July 24, $63,206, 3yo, progeny of eligible Iowa stallions, 1m 70y, 1:41.32, VAZANDAR, Plum Sober, Indian Village, 12 started.

Iowa State Fair S., Prairie Meadows, Aug. 21, $40,000, 3&up, f&m, 6f, 1:09.47, SUE'S GOOD NEWS, Synco Peach, Goldleafed Mirror, 8 started.

Irish Day H. (R), Emerald Downs, June 13, $47,425, 3yo, f, progeny of eligible Washington stallions, 1m, 1:37.60, SWINGN' NOTES, Time for Magic, Strong Faith, 9 started.

Irish O'Brien S. (R), Santa Anita Park, March 17, $110,300, 4&up, f&m, California-bred, a6¹/₂fT, 1:12.63, BEAR FAN, Super High, Bold Roberta, 9 started.

Irish Sonnet S., Delaware Park, Sept. 25, $54,350, 2yo, f, 1m, 1:39.84, DANCE AWAY CAPOTE, Secrets Galore, Northern Babe, 7 started.

Iroquois H. (R), Philadelphia Park, July 24, $52,950, 3&up, Pennsylvania-bred, 1¹/₁₆m, 1:43.31, PRINCE JOSEPH, Valleyman, Yo, 6 started.

Iroquois H. (R), Belmont Park, Oct. 23, $125,000, 3&up, f&m, New York-bred, 7f, 1:23.10, SUGAR PUNCH, Beautiful America, Distinctive Kitten, 9 started.

IROQUOIS S.-G3, Churchill Downs, Nov. 6, $109,600, 2yo, 1m, 1:36.62, STRAIGHT LINE, Social Probation, Greater Good, 7 started.

Irving Distaff S., Lone Star Park, April 17, $75,000, 3&up, f&m, 7¹/₂fT, 1:28.24, JANEIAN (NZ), Cat's Cat, Bedanken, 8 started.

Isaac Murphy H. (R), Arlington Park, June 26, $85,750, 3&up, f&m, Illinois-conceived and/or -foaled, 6f, 1:10.28, DHARMA GIRL, Jaguar City, Cashmere Miss, 10 started.

Isadorable S. (R), Suffolk Downs, June 19, $40,000, 3&up, f&m, Massachusetts-bred, 6f, 1:11.05, GLORY BE GOOD, Sunlit Ridge, African Princess, 6 started.

Isi Newborn Memorial S., Thistledown, June 12, $45,000, 3&up, 6f, 1:09.78, CAT SINGER, Herve, Lord de Ville, 13 started.

Island Whirl H., Louisiana Downs, July 18, $50,000, 3&up, 6f, 1:10.45, THAT TAT, Ole Rebel, Taxicat, 7 started.

ITBOA Sales Futurity (R), Prairie Meadows, July 17, $42,662, 2yo, graduates of the 2004 ITBOA two-year-olds in training sale, 5¹/₂f, 1:06.09, LORDSLEGACY, Direct Shot, Musicdemi, 6 started.

Izvestia S. (R), Woodbine, Aug. 21, $104,000, 3&up, Canadian-foaled, 1¹/₁₆m, 1:44.85, REFUSE TO BEND, Ide Be Gone, Norfolk Knight, 7 started.

Jack Betta Be Rite S. (R), Finger Lakes, Aug. 28, $50,000, 3&up, f&m, New York-bred, 1¹/₁₆m, 1:47.24, FRENCH HIDEAWAY, S'more Smoke, Market Guru, 8 started.

Jack Diamond Futurity (R), Hastings Race Course, Oct. 2, $107,728, 2yo, c&g, Canadian-foaled, 6¹/₂f, 1:18.31, NOTIS OTIS, Singin Devil, Run On, 9 started.

Jack Dudley Sprint H. (R), Calder Race Course, Nov. 13, $150,000, 3&up, Florida-bred, 6f, 1:10.21, WEIGELIA, Onebadshark, Love That Moon, 10 started.

Jack Hammer Memorial H., Blue Ribbon Downs, Aug. 7, $8,825, 3&up, 5f, :59.68, CARTERS BOY, Shari Bank, G. T. Crusader, 5 started.

Jack Hardy S., Assiniboia Downs, Aug. 2, $40,000, 3yo, f, 1m, 1:39.60, VICTORY THRILL, Southern Spring, Ericka's Lass, 8 started.

Jackie Wackie S., Calder Race Course, July 24, $40,000, 3&up, 1¹/₁₆mT, 1:43.69, CERVELO, Gin Rummy Champ, Silversandsoftime, 8 started.

Jack Price Juvenile S. (R), Calder Race Course, Nov. 13, $150,000, 2yo, Florida-bred, 7f, 1:24.76, FLAMENCO, Closing Argument, Dover Dere, 9 started.

Jack Shoemaker Memorial S., Rillito Park, Feb. 21, $3,726, 3&up, f&m, 5¹/₂f, 1:06.20, CYBER MOVE, Yarnell, Lillian West, 8 started.

Jacques Cartier S., Woodbine, April 17, $135,750, 4&up, 6f, 1:08.75, CHRIS'S BAD BOY, I'm the Tiger, Slim Dusty, 7 started.

JAIPUR H.-G3, Belmont Park, May 30, $112,200, 3&up, 7fT, 1:22.32, MULTIPLE CHOICE, Dedication (Fr), Geronimo (Chi), 8 started.

JAMAICA H.-G2, Belmont Park, Sept. 26, $200,000, 3yo, 1¹/₈m, 1:45.50, ARTIE SCHILLER, Rousing Victory, Icy Atlantic, 6 started.

Jameela S. (R), Laurel Park, Feb. 15, $75,000, 3yo, f, Maryland-bred, 7f, 1:24.84, SILMARIL, Forestier, She's a Rebel Too, 6 started.

James B. Moseley Breeders' Cup H., Suffolk Downs, June 19, $200,000, 3&up, 6f, 1:09.24, GATORS N BEARS, Valid Video, My Cousin Matt, 8 started.

James C. Ellis Juvenile S., Ellis Park, Aug. 22, $98,750, 2yo, 7f, 1:23.81, ELUSIVE CHRIS, Winsomemoneyhoney, Norainonthisparty, 9 started.

James F. Lyttle Memorial H., Santa Rosa, Aug. 6, $46,245, 3yo, 1¹/₁₆m, 1:42.87, MY CREED, Apollo King, A Gallant Discover, 7 started.

James Leakos Sophomore S. (R), Marquis Downs, Aug. 6, $6,500, 3yo, f, Saskatchewan-bred, 1m, 1:43.27, LUCKY IN THE LEAD, Rock n' Romance, Allourwishes, 5 started.

Jammed Lovely S. (R), Woodbine, Nov. 14, $160,350, 3yo, f, Canadian-foaled, 7f, 1:23.12, FINANCINGAVAILABLE, Flashy Anna, Hong Kong Dancer, 6 started.

Jane Driggers Debutante S. (R), Portland Meadows, Dec. 11, $10,000, 2yo, f, Oregon-bred, 6f, 1:13.29, ONE TUFT WOEMAN, Gordys Sweet Jordy, One Fast Cowgirl, 9 started.

Janet Wineberg S. (R), Portland Meadows, Nov. 6, $20,780, 2yo, f, Oregon-bred, 6f, 1:13.41, ONE FAST COWGIRL, Miss Bliss, Wice O Kat, 9 started.

Jatski S., Calder Race Course, Aug. 22, $40,000, 3&up, 1¹/₈m, 1:51.04, KRISTINE'S KING, Island Skipper, Dustys Birthday, 5 started.

Jean Lafitte S., Delta Downs, Nov. 6, $100,000, 2yo, 1m, 1:40.61, LEAVING ON MY MIND, Rubialedo, My Parade, 8 started.

JEFFERSON CUP S.-G3, Churchill Downs, June 12, $226,200, 3yo, 1¹/₈mT, 1:50.61, PRINCE ARCH, Kitten's Joy, Cool Conductor, 9 started.

JEH Stallion Station S. (R), Lone Star Park, May 15, $50,000, 3&up, f&m, Texas-bred, 6¹/₂f, 1:16.16, FLEETA DIF, Leona's Lies, Sly Kona, 12 started.

Jennings H. (R), Pimlico, Dec. 18, $100,000, 3&up, Maryland-bred, 1¹/₁₆m, 1:52.80, AGGADAN, Irish Colony, New York Hero, 7 started.

Jenny Wade H., Penn National Race Course, Aug. 6, $50,000, 3&up, f&m, 5fT, :58.35, DESIRABLE MOMENT, Nicole's Dream, Hostility, 8 started.

JENNY WILEY S.-G3, Keeneland, April 18, $110,300, 4&up, f&m, 1¹/₁₆mT, 1:41.41, INTERCONTINENTAL (GB), Ocean Drive, Madeira Mist (Ire), 8 started.

JEROME H.-G2, Belmont Park, Sept. 18, $150,000, 3yo, 1m, 1:35.74, TETON FOREST, Ice Wynnd Fire, Mahzouz, 7 started.

Jerry and Eileen Towslee Memorial H., Tillamook County Fair, Aug. 14, $3,500, 3&up, a5f, 1:04, LARRON, Rocky Moment, City Parkway, 6 started.

Jersey Breeders' Turf Highweight H. (R), Monmouth Park, Aug. 29, $100,000, 3&up, New Jersey-bred, 1¹/₁₆mT, 1:43.16, AMERICAN FREEDOM, Freedom's Honor, Catechol, 12 started.

JERSEY DERBY-G3, Monmouth Park, May 31, $100,000, 3yo, 1¹/₁₆mT, 1:44.51, ICY ATLANTIC, Commendation, Grand Heritage, 7 started.

Jersey Girl H. (R), Monmouth Park, Aug. 29, $100,000, 3&up, f&m, New Jersey-bred, 1m 70y, 1:44.39, UPHILL SKIER, Cigno d'Oro, Sonia's Song, 11 started.

Jersey Girl S. (R), Belmont Park, May 26, $59,400, 3yo, f, nonwinners of an open stakes, 6f, 1:10.44, FRENCHGLEN, Why You, Lovethatlegend, 5 started.

Jersey Lilly S., Sam Houston Race Park, April 10, $40,000, 4&up, f&m, 1¹/₁₆mT, 1:47.65, SOUND OF GOLD, Tyger River, Tiva's Little Sis, 8 started.

JERSEY SHORE BREEDERS' CUP S.-G3, Monmouth Park, June 26, $95,000, 3yo, 6f, 1:09.07, POMEROY, Gotaghostofachance, Midnight Express, 5 started.

Jersey Village S. (R), Sam Houston Race Park, Feb. 21, $40,000, 4&up, Texas-bred, 1¹/₁₆m, 1:44.53, DESERT DARBY, Record Assembly, Sandburr, 6 started.

Jessamine County S., Keeneland, Oct. 28, $112,600, 2yo, f, 1¹/₁₆mT, 1:44.33, PADDY'S DAISY, Berbatim, Jules Best, 10 started.

Jim Coleman Province H., Hastings Race Course, July 18, $41,005, 3yo, 1¹/₁₆m, 1:44.62, TREASURED FRIEND, Lord Samarai, Tobe Suave, 8 started.

JIM DANDY S.-G2, Saratoga Race Course, Aug. 8, $500,000, 3yo, 1¹/₈m, 1:47.56, PURGE, The Cliff's Edge, Niigon, 6 started.

Jim Edgar Illinois Futurity (R), Hawthorne Race Course, Dec. 18, $115,350, 2yo, c&g, Illinois-conceived and/or -foaled, 1¹/₁₆m, 1:47.10, WIN ME OVER, Humor At Last, Fear of Secrets, 14 started.

Jim McKay Breeders' Cup H., Pimlico, April 17, $150,000, 3&up, 1¹/₈m, 1:48.23, THE LADY'S GROOM, Unforgettable Max, Irish Colony, 7 started.

Jim Murray Memorial H., Hollywood Park, May 8, $350,000, 3&up, 1¹/₂mT, 2:26.73, RHYTHM MAD (Fr), Continental Red, Gassan Royal, 7 started.

Jim Rasmussen Memorial S., Prairie Meadows, May 29, $50,000, 3&up, 1¹/₁₆m, 1:43.10, RIVER MOUNTAIN RD, Dusty Spike, Robin Zee, 9 started.

J J'sdream S., Calder Race Course, June 26, $100,000, 2yo, f, 5¹/₂f, 1:06.95, PUNCH APPEAL, Aclassysassylassy, Spinning Jolie, 9 started.

JOCKEY CLUB GOLD CUP S.-G1, Belmont Park, Oct. 2, $1,000,000, 3&up, 1¹/₄m, 2:02.44, FUNNY CIDE, Newfoundland, The Cliff's Edge, 7 started.

JOE HIRSCH TURF CLASSIC INVITATIONAL S.-G1, Belmont Park, Oct. 2, $750,000, 3&up, 1¹/₂mT, 2:29.97, KITTEN'S JOY, Magistretti, Tycoon (GB), 7 started.

Joe O'Farrell Juvenile Fillies S. (R), Calder Race Course, Nov. 13, $150,000, 2yo, f, Florida-bred, 7f, 1:25.52, ACLASSYSASSYLASSY, Running Bobcats, Frosty Royalty, 6 started.

John and Kitty Fletcher S. (R), Emerald Downs, Sept. 19, $40,000, 3yo, f, Washington-bred, 1m, 1:35.60, ARCO IRIS, Time for Magic, Amanda Marie, 9 started.

John Battaglia Memorial S., Turfway Park, Feb. 28, $100,000, 3yo, 1¹/₁₆m, 1:44.79, SILVER MINISTER, Little Matth Man, White Mountain Boy, 11 started.

John B. Campbell Breeders' Cup H., Laurel Park, Feb. 14, $150,000, 4&up, 1¹/₈m, 1:49.05, OLE FAUNTY, Evening Attire, Rogue Agent, 8 started.

John B. Connally Breeders' Cup Turf H., Sam Houston Race Park, April 10, $222,000, 3&up, 1¹/₂mT, 1:53.01, WARLEIGH, Skate Away, Gentlemen J J, 11 started.

John Bullit S., Canterbury Park, Aug. 7, $50,000, 3&up, 1¹/₁₆mT, 1:43.53, DONTBOTHERKNOCKING, Al's Dearly Bred, Missme, 6 started.

JOHN C. MABEE H.-G1, Del Mar, July 24, $400,000, 3&up, f&m, 1¹/₈mT, 1:47.09, MUSICAL CHIMES, Moscow Burning, Notting Hill (Brz), 6 started.

John D. Schapiro Memorial Breeders' Cup H., Pimlico, Sept. 18, $148,500, 3&up, 1¹/₄mT, 1:49, LUSTY LATIN, Foufa's Warrior, Pay the Preacher, 5 started.

John Franks Juvenile Fillies Turf S. (R), Calder Race Course, Nov. 13, $100,000, 2yo, f, Florida-bred, 1¹/₁₆mT, 1:41.41, RICH IN SPIRIT, Dansetta Light, Yes It's Gold, 12 started.

John Franks Memorial S. (R), Louisiana Downs, May 14, $50,000, 3&up, Louisiana-bred, 1mT, 1:36.38, ROSECOLOREDGLASSES, Rail Rose, Witt Ante, 10 started.

John Franks Memorial Sales S. (R), Evangeline Downs, July 31, $40,000, 2yo, sold at the Evangeline Downs March sale, 5f, :59.40, GRANDE DIABLO, A Galloping Ghost, Miss Excavate, 8 started.

John Henry H., Evangeline Downs, May 1, $50,000, 3&up, 1¹/₁₆mT, 1:46, KISS A NATIVE, Witt Ante, Prince Slew, 7 started.

John Henry S., Arlington Park, Sept. 18, $44,500, 3&up, 1¹/₁₆mT, 1:42.57, CLOUDY'S KNIGHT, Gin and Sin, Honor in War, 10 started.

John Henry S., The Meadowlands, Oct. 29, $60,000, 3&up, 1³/₈mT, 2:14.20, MACAW (Ire), Dreadnaught, Revved Up, 11 started.

Johnie L. Jamison S. (R), Sunland Park, Nov. 27, $132,250, 3&up, New Mexico-bred, 6¹/₂f, 1:14.82, ROCKY GULCH, Values of the Hunt, dh-Some Ghost, dh-B. G. Tiger, 10 started.

John J. Reilly H. (R), Monmouth Park, May 29, $60,000, 3&up, New Jersey-bred, 6f, 1:10.74, TRUEAMERICANSPIRIT, Something Smith, N J Devil, 10 started.

John J. Shumaker H. (R), Penn National Race Course, July 30, $40,850, 3&up, Pennsylvania-bred, 6f, 1:09.79, LONE TRAVELER, R B's Boy, Volley Ball, 8 started.

John Kirby S. (R), Suffolk Downs, Nov. 20, $40,000, 3yo, Massachusetts-bred, 1m 70y, 1:43.50, ASK QUEENIE, Senor Ladd, Episode On Tour, 7 started.

John Longden 6000 H., Hastings Race Course, June 12, $49,540, 3&up, 1¹/₁₆m, 1:43.99, ROSCOE PITO, Dancewithavixen, Commodore Craig, 10 started.

John McSorley S., Monmouth Park, July 11, $60,000, 3&up, 5fT, :55.69, dh-SHADES OF SUNNY, dh-QUEST OF FATE, dh-Tricky Storm, dh-Scattering Breezes, 9 started.

John Morrissey S. (R), Saratoga Race Course, Aug. 19, $66,600, 3&up, New York-bred nonwinners of a stakes in 2004, 6¹/₂f, 1:15.92, CLEVER ELECTRICIAN, Uncle Camie, Traffic Chief, 7 started.

John Patrick H., Northlands Park, July 23, $40,000, 3&up, f&m, 1m, 1:38.80, A SHAKY START, Sly Lady, Rum Candi, 7 started.

John's Call S. (R), Saratoga Race Course, Aug. 16, $67,300, 4&up, nonwinners of a graded stakes in 2003-'04, 1⅜mT, 2:46.29, SPANISH SPUR (GB), Cottage (Arg), Host, 11 started.

John Wayne S. (R), Prairie Meadows, May 15, $60,000, 3&up, c&g, Iowa-bred, 6f, 1:10.37, TAKE ME UP, Country Warrior, Cmego, 8 started.

John W. Galbreath Memorial S. (R), Thistledown, Oct. 9, $60,000, 2yo, f, Ohio-bred, 1¹/₁₆mT, 1:49.80, BOLD PASSAGE, Perfect Connection, Marketable, 11 started.

John W. Rooney H., Delaware Park, June 5, $100,300, 3&up, f&m, 1¹/₄mT, 1:53.28, SHINY SHEET, Aztec Pearl, Jaramar Rain, 6 started.

Joseph A. Gimma S. (R), Belmont Park, Oct. 3, $113,400, 2yo, f, New York-bred, 7f, 1:25.83, MEGASCAPE, Social Virtue, Royal Fudge, 10 started.

Josephine County S., Grants Pass, May 31, $3,800, 3yo, f, 5¹/₂f, 1:05.20, HARVEY'S DELIGHT, Teri Time, Moon Witch, 4 started.

Joseph T. Grace H., Santa Rosa, Aug. 7, $97,840, 3&up, 1¹/₁₆m, 1:41.29, CALKINS ROAD, Yougottawanna, Peteski's Charm, 4 started.

Journal H., Northlands Park, June 26, $40,000, 3&up, 6¹/₂f, 1:17.80, DEPUTY COUNTRY, Rindanica, Sixthirtyjoe, 5 started.

Journal Star H., Lincoln State Fair, May 23, $10,750, 3yo, 6f, 1:12.80, THUNDERING VERZY, Bevys Boy, Sunday Trigger, 5 started.

JRA Fillies and Mares H., Pimlico, Oct. 23, $50,000, 3&up, f&m, 1¹/₁₆mT, 1:50.83, WITH AFFECTION, Lady of the Future, Feisty Bull, 8 started.

J. R. Straus Memorial S., Retama Park, July 23, $40,000, 3&up, 6f, 1:10.20, GOLD STORM, High Strike Zone, The Niner Account, 9 started.

Juan Gonzalez Memorial S., Pleasanton, July 3, $47,450, 2yo, f, 5f, :57.17, TIMEINTOWN, Kelly's Princess, Welcome Queen, 10 started.

Judy's Red Shoes S., Calder Race Course, Sept. 11, $75,000, 3yo, f, 1¹/₁₆mT, 1:47.03, R OBSESSION, Coquinerie, Shorey Village, 10 started.

Junior Champion S., Monmouth Park, Aug. 22, $55,000, 2yo, f, 1m, 1:41.70, SPEEDY DEEDY, By Grace Alone, Northern Babe, 9 started.

JUST A GAME BREEDERS' CUP H.-G2, Belmont Park, June 5, $226,333, 3&up, f&m, 1mT, 1:33.33, INTERCONTINENTAL (GB), Vanguardia (Arg), Etoile Montante, 8 started.

Justakiss S., Delaware Park, Oct. 25, $55,300, 3&up, f&m, 1¹/₁₆m, 1:45.10, FLOWER FOREST, Thermal Ablasion, True Sensation, 8 started.

Just Smashing S., Monmouth Park, Sept. 26, $60,000, 3yo, f, 6f, 1:10.65, MYSTERY'S JULES, Storm Minstrel, Humor Me Molly, 7 started.

Juvenile Mile S., Portland Meadows, Dec. 26, $21,550, 2yo, 1m, 1:40.57, TYPHOON AARON, Tomorrow's Turn, Solid Gold Bar, 10 started.

Juvenile S., Louisiana Downs, Sept. 25, $75,000, 2yo, 1mT, 1:39.82, MAJOR LEAGUE, Zarb's Music Man, Reno Bob, 9 started.

Juvenile S. (R), Fort Erie, Sept. 4, $75,000, 2yo, f, passed through the ring as a yearling in the 2003 Fasig-Tipton open Canadian-bred yearling sale or the 2003 Canadian Thoroughbred Horse Society mixed sale, 6f, 1:12.21, WISDOMISGOLD, Lady Actor, Cold Hard Dash, 5 started.

Juvenile S. (R), Fort Erie, Sept. 5, $75,000, 2yo, c&g, passed through the ring as a yearling at the 2003 Fasig-Tipton open Canadian-bred yearling sale or the 2003 Canadian Thoroughbred Horse Society mixed sale, 6f, 1:12.53, HIGHLAND WARRIOR, Chasing the Fox, Wolly Bully, 5 started.

Juvenile S. (R), Thistledown, Oct. 9, $60,000, 2yo, Ohio-bred, 1¹/₁₆m, 1:48.30, FIERCE CAT, Bug Hunter, Cast No Shadow, 14 started.

J. William "Bill" Petro Memorial H. (R), Thistledown, June 12, $45,000, 3yo, f, Ohio-bred, 1¹/₁₆m, 1:45.14, BARNSY, Spring Cat, Happy Endings Too, 9 started.

J.W. Sifton S. (R), Assiniboia Downs, Sept. 19, $41,000, 3yo, Manitoba-bred, 1m, 1:56.60, COAL SMUDGE, Stonewall Harris, Shrike One, 8 started.

Kachina H., Turf Paradise, Jan. 10, $40,000, 4&up, f&m, 1m, 1:37.68, MOONLIT MADDIE, Darting Dot, No Turbulence, 8 started.

Kalispell Thoroughbred Northwest Montana Fair H., Kalispell, Aug. 22, $2,700, 3&up, 7f, 1:29.60, E MAIL TRAIL, Regal Hit, French Rascal, 4 started.

Kansas Bred Centennial H., Anthony Downs, July 24, $10,476, 3&up, a5f, 1:05.31, D D DOT COMM, King Ruler, Missy Can Do, 4 started.

Kansas Oaks, The Woodlands, Oct. 23, $25,000, 3yo, f, 1m 70y, 1:44, LADY RISS, Reprized Angel, Vannacide, 7 started.

Karl Flaman Memorial S., Yorkton Exh. Assoc., July 10, $2,000, 3&up, 1m, 1:44.60, MAKEWAYFORBIGHOSS, Mr. Talisman, Hez Scott, 5 started.

Katy S., Sam Houston Race Park, Dec. 4, $40,000, 3&up, f&m, 1¹/₁₆mT, 1:47.95, KEY TO THE CAT, Lady Mallory, Fun House, 11 started.

Keddies Tack & Western Wear S., Grand Prairie, Aug. 1, $4,000, 3&up, f&m, 5¹/₂f, 1:07.60, IRISH INTRIGUE, Guiltybysupiscion, Chaste Fondness, 5 started.

Kelly Kip S. (R), Belmont Park, May 14, $60,850, 3yo, nonwinners of a graded stakes, 6¹/₂f, 1:16.13, INDIAN WAR DANCE, Smokume, Knight of Darkness, 8 started.

KELSO BREEDERS' CUP H.-G2, Belmont Park, Oct. 9, $270,000, 3&up, 1mT, 1:32.69, MR O'BRIEN (Ire), Millennium Dragon (GB), Gulch Approval, 8 started.

Kelso H., Delaware Park, Oct. 2, $100,300, 3&up, 1³/₁₆m, 1:57.73, LYRACIST, Spicy Stuff, Ouagadougou, 6 started.

Kendal Pipeline & Oilfield Services S., Grand Prairie, Aug. 13, $6,500, 3&up, 6¹/₂f, 1:20, HY NICK, Captain Carter, Gomka, 8 started.

Ken Kendrick Memorial S., SunRay Park, Oct. 11, $32,200, 2yo, f, 6¹/₂f, 1:18.80, GONE WESTERN, Time to Divorce, Pumkin Cat, 7 started.

Ken Maddy Sprint H. (R), Golden Gate Fields, Feb. 21, $100,000, 3&up, California-bred, 6f, 1:08.49, GIOVANNETTI, Green Team, Debonair Joe, 9 started.

Kenny Noe Jr. H., Calder Race Course, Dec. 18, $100,000, 3&up, 7f, 1:22.62, MEDALLIST, Paradise Dancer, Hasty Kris, 10 started.

Kenora S. (R), Woodbine, Sept. 5, $131,375, 3&up, Canadian-bred which passed through the sales ring as a yearling at any 2002 or previous sale conducted by Canadian Breeders' Sales or Woodbine Sales, 6f, 1:09.72, FOREVER GRAND, Shaws Creek, Crease Infraction, 7 started.

Ken Pearson Memorial H., Stampede Park, May 24, $39,200, 3&up, f&m, 1m, 1:40.60, RAYLENE, Northern Neechitoo, A Shaky Start, 4 started.

KENT BREEDERS' CUP S.-G3, Delaware Park, June 26, $250,900, 3yo, 1¹/₁₆mT, 1:55.75, TIMO, Erlic Atlantic, Commendation, 8 started.

Kent H., Emerald Downs, July 18, $40,000, 3yo, f, 1¹/₁₆m, 1:43.20, SWINGN' NOTES, Karis Makaw, Overact, 8 started.

KENTUCKY BREEDERS' CUP S.-G3, Churchill Downs, June 5, $132,088, 2yo, 5¹/₂f, 1:04.07, LUNARPAL, Consolidator, Smoke Warning, 4 started.

KENTUCKY CUP CLASSIC H.-G2, Turfway Park, Sept. 18, $350,000, 3&up, 1¹/₈m, 1:49.13, ROSES IN MAY, Pie N Burger, Sonic West, 6 started.

Kentucky Cup Juvenile Fillies S., Turfway Park, Sept. 18, $100,000, 2yo, f, 1m, 1:38.04, PUNCH APPEAL, Carmandia, Winning Season, 7 started.

KENTUCKY CUP JUVENILE S.-G3, Turfway Park, Sept. 18, $100,000, 2yo, 1¹/₁₆m, 1:44.96, GREATER GOOD, Magna Graduate, Norainonthisparty, 6 started.

Kentucky Cup Ladies Turf S., Kentucky Downs, Sept. 25, $100,000, 3&up, f&m, 1mT, 1:36.88, SAND SPRINGS, Wildwood Royal, Omeya (Chi), 9 started.

Kentucky Cup Mile S., Kentucky Downs, Sept. 25, $100,000, 3&up, 1mT, 1:37.13, MISSME, Gretchen's Star, Banned in Boston, 6 started.

KENTUCKY CUP SPRINT S.-G3, Turfway Park, Sept. 18, $100,000, 3yo, 6f, 1:09.76, LEVEL PLAYINGFIELD, Cuvee, Swift Attraction, 5 started.

Kentucky Cup Turf Dash S., Kentucky Downs, Sept. 25, $100,000, 3&up, 6fT, 1:10.86, BATTLE WON, Draw Fire, Abderian (Ire), 7 started.

KENTUCKY CUP TURF H.-G3, Kentucky Downs, Sept. 25, $200,000, 3&up, 1¹/₂mT, 2:33.70, SABIANGO (Ger), Rochester, Gottabeachboy, 6 started.

KENTUCKY DERBY-G1, Churchill Downs, May 1, $1,154,800, 3yo, 1¹/₄m, 2:04.06, SMARTY JONES, Lion Heart, Imperialism, 18 started.

KENTUCKY JOCKEY CLUB S.-G2, Churchill Downs, Nov. 27, $223,200, 2yo, 1¹/₁₆m, 1:45.14, GREATER GOOD, Rush Bay, Wild Desert, 9 started.

KENTUCKY OAKS-G1, Churchill Downs, April 30, $572,000, 3yo, f, 1¹/₈m, 1:50.81, ASHADO, Island Sand, Madcap Escapade, 11 started.

Kingarvie S. (R), Woodbine, Dec. 12, $134,875, 2yo, progeny of eligible Ontario stallions, 1¹/₁₆m, 1:46.06, ENOUGH IS ENOUGH, Dave the Knave, El Gran Andre, 8 started.

King Cotton S., Oaklawn Park, Jan. 31, $50,000, 4&up, 6f, 1:09.38, SKEET, Wacky for Love, Chindi, 8 started.

King County H., Emerald Downs, June 26, $40,000, 3&up, f&m, 1m, 1:36.20, CASCADE CORONA, Lasting Code, Aunt Sophie, 9 started.

KING EDWARD BREEDERS' CUP H.-G2, Woodbine, June 19, $324,300, 3&up, 1¹/₈mT, 1:48.42, SLEW VALLEY, Shoal Water, Surging River, 6 started.

KING'S BISHOP S.-G1, Saratoga Race Course, Aug. 28, $250,000, 3yo, 7f, 1:20.99, POMEROY, Weigelia, Ice Wynnd Fire, 8 started.

Kings Court S., Louisiana Downs, May 29, $49,000, 3&up, 6f, 1:09.74, OLE REBEL, I'm Majestic, Aloha Bold, 5 started.

Kings Point H. (R), Aqueduct, May 2, $80,975, 3&up, New York-bred, 1¹/₁₆m, 1:52.31, GANDER, Levendis, Trial Prep, 6 started.

Kingston H. (R), Belmont Park, May 23, $114,300, 3&up, New York-bred, 1¹/₄m, 1:47, QUANTUM MERIT, Forevermess, Golden Commander, 10 started.

KLAQ H., Sunland Park, Nov. 7, $53,700, 3&up, 5¹/₂f, 1:02.74, DAY TRADER, Cheyenne Breeze, Cat Buster, 7 started.

Klassy Briefcase S., Monmouth Park, July 31, $60,000, 3&up, f&m, 5f, :57.38, TANGIER SOUND, Our Mariah, Melody of Colors, 6 started.

Klondike H., Hastings Race Course, June 12, $41,830, 3yo, 6¹/₂f, 1:17.08, MAXWELL, Lord Samarai, Nihilator, 5 started.

Klondike H., Northlands Park, July 31, $40,000, 3&up, 1¹/₁₆m, 1:45.40, RINDANICA, Nugrayonthblock, After the Run, 6 started.

KNICKERBOCKER H.-G2, Aqueduct, Oct. 30, $150,000, 3&up, 1¹/₈mT, 1:49.95, HOST (Chi), Evening Attire, Sailaway, 9 started.

KTA Derby S. (R), The Woodlands, Oct. 2, $16,900, 3yo, c&g, sired by eligible Kansas stallions, 1m 70y, 1:46.60, NICK MISSED, Storminthedesert, Billyjack, 5 started.

Kudzu Juvenile S. (R), Fair Grounds, Dec. 10, $50,000, 2yo, Alabama-bred, 5¹/₂f, 1:08.13, POPS RETURN, Deb Pixum, French Coach, 10 started.

Ky Alta H., Northlands Park, July 24, $40,000, 3yo, 1¹/₁₆m, 1:46.80, CONTROLLED MEETING, Kat Kool, Ol Fifty, 7 started.

Labeeb S., Woodbine, Nov. 7, $106,000, 3&up, 1mT, 1:38.83, LE CINQUIEME ESSAI, Silver Ticket, Tusayan, 9 started.

Labor Day H., Columbus Races, Sept. 6, $11,475, 3&up, 6¹/₂f, 1:20.80, THUNDERING VERZY, Watch Me Dazzle, Hez Comin Thru, 6 started.

Labor Day H., Mountaineer Race Track, Sept. 6, $75,000, 3&up, 1mT, 1:34.13, FREEFOURINTERNET, La Reine's Terms, Sterling Gold, 8 started.

LA BREA S.-G1, Santa Anita Park, Dec. 27, $250,000, 3yo, f, 7f, 1:21.38, ALPHABET KISSES, Bending Strings, Elusive Diva, 10 started.

LA CANADA S.-G2, Santa Anita Park, Feb. 14, $200,000, 4yo, f, 1¹/₈m, 1:50.41, CAT FIGHTER, Fencelineneighbor, Tangle (Ire), 8 started.

La Coneja S. (R), Sunland Park, Dec. 11, $131,250, 3yo, f, New Mexico-bred, 5¹/₂f, 1:03.94, HAT CREEK, Latenite Special, Janna's Gold, 10 started.

LADIES H.-G3, Aqueduct, Dec. 18, $109,400, 3&up, f&m, 1¹/₄m, 2:05.51, RARE GIFT, Board Elligible, Miss Fortunate, 8 started.

Ladnesian S., Hastings Race Course, July 17, $42,483, 2yo, 6¹/₂f, 1:19.16, NOTIS OTIS, Promise One, Poundmaker, 4 started.

Lady Angela S. (R), Woodbine, May 29, $133,250, 3yo, f, progeny of eligible Ontario stallions, 7f, 1:22.97, BLONDE EXECUTIVE, My Vintage Port, Ashlee's Bella, 8 started.

Lady Canterbury Breeders' Cup S., Canterbury Park, June 20, $70,000, 3&up, f&m, 1mT, 1:35.55, BE MY FRIEND, Cat's Cat, Border Blues, 9 started.

Lady Finger S. (R), Finger Lakes, Aug. 21, $126,133, 2yo, f, New York-bred, 6f, 1:11.34, REDDY FOR RUBYS, Party Maker, Carlow, 13 started.

Lady Hallie S. (R), Hawthorne Race Course, April 10, $96,350, 3yo, f, Illinois-conceived and/or -foaled, 6f, 1:12.37, SLEWVILLE, Wish for Gold, Lady Laverne, 10 started.

Lady Luck S., Louisiana Downs, Oct. 17, $50,000, 2yo, f, a1mT, 1:38.86, CASH COUNTER, Ready to Live, Tocha, 8 started.

Lady Razorback Futurity (R), Louisiana Downs, Oct. 16, $40,000, 2yo, f, Arkansas-bred, 6f, 1:13.41, HALF A STORM, Doll and a Half, Swinging Siberian, 6 started.

Lady Slipper S. (R), Canterbury Park, May 16, $40,000, 3&up, f&m, Minnesota-bred, 6f, 1:11.73, SWASTI, Maywood's Jill, Ashley's Affair, 11 started.

LADY'S SECRET BREEDERS' CUP H.-G2, Santa Anita Park, Oct. 3, $235,000, 3&up, f&m, 1¹/₁₆m, 1:43.43, ISLAND FASHION, Miss Loren (Arg), Elloluv, 7 started.

Lady's Secret H., Fairmount Park, Aug. 7, $30,700, 4&up, f&m, 1m 70y, 1:44.60, MOON SHINE TIME, Strike Rate, Princess Paster, 5 started.

Lady's Secret H., Les Bois Park, May 23, $6,900, 3&up, f&m, 7f, 1:25.40, THRILL AFTER DARK, Opal's Song, Gail's Melody, 9 started.

Lady's Secret S., Monmouth Park, Aug. 8, $100,000, 3&up, f&m, 1¹/₁₆mT, 1:44.03, CHRUSCIKI, Misty Sixes, Sanctity Action, 8 started.

Lady's Secret S., Remington Park, Dec. 5, $40,000, 3&up, f&m, 7f, 1:22.45, CASUAL ATTITUDE, Storm Breaking, Angelica Slew, 14 started.

Lafayette H., Golden Gate Fields, Jan. 1, $81,000, 4&up, 1m, 1:34.53, GOLD RUCKUS, Truly a Judge, Bring Home Thegold, 6 started.

Lafayette S., Evangeline Downs, Sept. 6, $75,000, 2yo, 6f, 1:12, MY PARADE, Favorite Mint, J. D.'s Blue Bayou, 10 started.

LAFAYETTE S.-G3, Keeneland, April 4, $109,500, 3yo, 7f, 1:24.73, BWANA CHARLIE, Quick Action, Tales of Glory, 6 started.

La Fiesta H., The Downs at Albuquerque, April 9, $43,250, 3yo, f, 5¹/₂f, 1:02.56, DAYJURETTE, Lil Easy, Ona Rampage, 7 started.

La Habra S., Santa Anita Park, Feb. 29, $111,350, 3yo, f, a6¹/₂fT, 1:13.99, VERY VEGAS, Aspen Gal, Fortunately (Britain), 9 started.

LA JOLLA H.-G2, Del Mar, Aug. 14, $150,000, 3yo, 1¹/₁₆mT, 1:41.03, BLACKDOUN (Fr), Semi Lost, Bedmar (GB), 7 started.

LAKE GEORGE S.-G3, Saratoga Race Course, Aug. 2, $113,900, 3yo, f, 1¹/₁₆mT, 1:42.01, SEDUCER'S SONG, Venturi (GB), Fortunate Damsel, 10 started.

LAKE PLACID H.-G2, Saratoga Race Course, Aug. 23, $150,000, 3yo, f, 1¹/₈mT, 1:50.54, SPOTLIGHT (GB), Mambo Slew, Fortunate Damsel, 7 started.

Lakeway S., Retama Park, Aug. 7, $40,000, 3yo, f, 7f, 1:24.82, WACKY PATTY, Hay Madison, Bluegrass Sara, 8 started.

La Lorgnette S., Woodbine, Sept. 18, $144,147, 3yo, f, 1¹/₁₆m, 1:45.14, PAIOTA FALLS, Touchnow, My Vintage Port, 4 started.

Lamplighter S., Monmouth Park, Aug. 28, $60,000, 3yo, 1m 70y, 1:40.82, GOTAGHOSTOFACHANCE, Tap Day, Stolen Time, 6 started.

LANDALUCE S.-G3, Hollywood Park, July 5, $106,800, 2yo, f, 6f, 1:09.75, SOUVENIR GIFT, Bella Banissa, My Miss Storm Cat, 11 started.

Land of Enchantment S. (R), Ruidoso Downs, Aug. 1, $45,000, 3&up, New Mexico-bred, 7¹/₂f, 1:31.40, NINETY NINE JACK, Local Case, Casperino, 7 started.

Land of Jazz S. (R), Ferndale, Aug. 20, $6,575, 3&up, starters for a claiming price of $12,500 or less in 2004, 7f, 1:25.45, RED SEATTLE, Biometal, Alnaabadancer, 4 started.

Land of Lincoln S. (R), Hawthorne Race Course, April 10, $94,350, 3yo, Illinois-conceived and/or -foaled, 6f, 1:13.10, PRAIRIE KING, Jaguar Friend, Medicine Eyes, 11 started.

LANE'S END BREEDERS' FUTURITY-G1, Keeneland, Oct. 9, $500,000, 2yo, 1¹/₁₆m, 1:43.67, CONSOLIDATOR, Patriot Act, Diamond Isle, 10 started.

LANE'S END S.-G2, Turfway Park, March 20, $500,000, 3yo, 1¹/₈m, 1:50.71, SINISTER G, Tricky Taboo, Little Matth Man, 11 started.

Lansing S. (R), Great Lakes Downs, May 29, $40,000, 3yo, c&g, Michigan-bred, 6f, 1:15.34, ROCKEM SOCKEM, Heza Mountain Man, Express Enjoyment, 7 started.

La Paz S., Turf Paradise, Nov. 21, $21,800, 2yo, f, 6¹/₂f, 1:17.36, ESTACADA, O K Topless, Lady Bertrando, 8 started.

LA PREVOYANTE H.-G2, Calder Race Course, Dec. 18, $200,000, 3&up, f&m, 1¹/₂mT, 2:27.19, ARVADA (GB), Humaita (Ger), Honey Ryder, 11 started.

La Prevoyante S. (R), Woodbine, Sept. 26, $132,250, 3yo, f, progeny of eligible Ontario stallions, 1mT, 1:34.68, BLONDE EXECUTIVE, Financingavailable, Gladiator Queen, 7 started.

La Puente S., Santa Anita Park, April 10, $110,500, 3yo, 1mT, 1:34.18, TOASTED, Erewhon, Seattle Borders, 9 started.

La Quinta S., Turf Paradise, Jan. 19, $21,800, 4&up, 1m, 1:36.17, PITTSBURGH STAR, Captured, Brazen n' Bold, 8 started.

Larkspur H. (R), Great Lakes Downs, June 11, $40,000, 3&up, f&m, Michigan-bred, 6f, 1:15.49, CHARLIES INDIAN, Midway Girl, Pass Bye, 10 started.

Larry R. Riviello President's Cup S., Philadelphia Park, Aug. 14, $100,000, 3yo, 1m 70y, 1:41.93, SEPARATO, Gadace's Khamseh, Prince Joseph, 10 started.

LAS CIENEGAS H.-G3, Santa Anita Park, April 4, $112,800, 4&up, f&m, a6¹/₂fT, 1:13.32, ETOILE MONTANTE, Dedication (Fr), Any for Love (Arg), 9 started.

La Senora H. (R), Sunland Park, Jan. 24, $131,250, 3yo, f&m, New Mexico-bred, 6f, 1:11.87, ICY LANE, Devil Lace, Vipervapor, 10 started.

La Senorita S., Retama Park, Sept. 4, $100,000, 2yo, f, 1mT, 1:36.76, MALIKA'S GOLD, Ready to Live, Kristin's Charm, 11 started.

LAS FLORES H.-G3, Santa Anita Park, Feb. 22, $107,300, 4&up, f&m, 6f, 1:08.02, EMA BOVARY (Chi), Buffythecenterfold, Coconut Girl, 6 started.

Las Madrinas H., Fairplex Park, Sept. 24, $98,000, 3&up, f&m, 1¹/₁₆m, 1:43.92, TALE OF A DREAM, Lady Thatcher (Chi), Shezsospiritual, 7 started.

LAS PALMAS H.-G2, Santa Anita Park, Oct. 31, $150,000, 3&up, f&m, 1¹/₈mT, 1:47.81, THEATER R. N., Lots of Hope (Brz), Good Student (Arg), 7 started.

Lassie H., Hastings Race Course, Aug. 22, $43,833, 2yo, f, 6¹/₂f, 1:19.08, SLEWPAST, Mandi Tambi, Ms. Sarah Vye, 9 started.

Lassie S., Portland Meadows, Nov. 20, $10,000, 2yo, f, 5f, 1:00.81, BULLISHDEMANDS, One Fast Cowgirl, Cool Blast, 8 started.

Last Chance Derby, Turf Paradise, Dec. 31, $22,000, 3yo, 1¹/₁₆m, 1:47.90, AZA, His Way, Western Ridge, 6 started.

Last Dance S. (R), Suffolk Downs, July 5, $38,000, 3&up, Massachusetts-bred, 1^1/$_{16}$m, 1:44.96, JINI'S JET, Stylish Sultan, Puddle Time, 4 started.

Last Don B. S., Turf Paradise, Feb. 6, $21,800, 4&up, 6^1/$_2$f, 1:14.71, ICY TOBIN, Alena's Tornado, Grimm, 6 started.

LAS VIRGENES S.-G1, Santa Anita Park, Feb. 15, $250,000, 3yo, f, 1m, 1:36.50, A. P. ADVENTURE, Hollywood Story, Friendly Michelle, 8 started.

LA TROIENNE S.-G3, Churchill Downs, April 29, $112,200, 3yo, f, 7^1/$_2$f, 1:28.26, FRIENDLY MICHELLE, Ender's Sister, Bohemian Lady, 7 started.

LAUREL FUTURITY-G3, Pimlico, Nov. 20, $100,000, 2yo, 1^1/$_{16}$m, 1:45.48, DEFER, Funk, Woody's Apache, 5 started.

Laurel Lane S. (R), Louisiana Downs, Oct. 23, $53,600, 2yo, f, Louisiana-bred, 6f, 1:10.53, THE BETER MAN CAN, Equestrian Girls, Sweet Macaroni, 7 started.

La Verendrye S., Assiniboia Downs, June 13, $40,000, 3&up, f&m, 6f, 1:13.60, REMIEWATERBLUZ, Dark Rapids, Siberian Falstaff, 8 started.

LAWRENCE REALIZATION S.-G3, Belmont Park, Oct. 16, $110,100, 3yo, 1^1/$_4$mT, 2:29.91, GUNNING FOR, Rousing Victory, Second Performance, 7 started.

La Zanzara H., Santa Anita Park, Feb. 13, $70,875, 4&up, f&m, 1^1/$_4$mT, 2:00.03, LADY ANNALIESE (NZ), Mer de Corail (Ire), Go On Baby, 6 started.

LAZARO BARRERA MEMORIAL S.-G2, Hollywood Park, May 29, $150,000, 3yo, 7f, 1:21.57, TWICE AS BAD, Wimplestiltskin, Don't-sellmeshort, 8 started.

Leader of the Band S., Delaware Park, Aug. 28, $54,300, 3&up, 1^1/$_{16}$mT, 1:41.84, TAM'S TERMS, Dr. Kashnikow, Change Course, 6 started.

LECOMTE S.-G3, Fair Grounds, Jan. 24, $100,000, 3yo, 1m, 1:38.48, FIRE SLAM, Shadowland, Two Down Automatic, 7 started.

Left the Latch S., Turf Paradise, May 15, $21,800, 3yo, f, 6^1/$_2$f, 1:16.38, SWAIN'S GOLD, Bettor Knot, Rockin On, 6 started.

Legacy Chase S., Shawan Downs, Sept. 25, $23,250, 4&up, 2^1/$_4$mT, 4:21.60, PARADISE'S BOSS, Irish Prince (NZ), The Editor's Son, 6 started.

Legal Light S., Delaware Park, April 24, $75,000, 3yo, f, 6f, 1:12.19, FELINE STORY, She's a Mugs, Wild Berry, 7 started.

Lenta S., Calder Race Course, April 30, $40,000, 3yo, f, 1^1/$_{16}$m, 1:47.93, SPECIAL REPORT, Cute Connie, Tiz a Dancer, 8 started.

LEONARD RICHARDS S.-G3, Delaware Park, July 18, $250,600, 3yo, 1^1/$_{16}$m, 1:43.85, POLLARD'S VISION, Britt's Jules, Pies Prospect, 7 started.

Les Mackin H., Yavapai Downs, June 21, $12,500, 3&up, 1m, 1:38, REAL CREEK, Prickly Pirate, Cut of Music, 8 started.

Les Mademoiselle S., Ferndale, Aug. 21, $11,220, 3&up, f&m, 1^1/$_{16}$m, 1:46.67, SCATTERING, In Love With Loot, Mom Liked You Best, 8 started.

Lethbridge Filly and Mare S., Lethbridge, June 12, $11,050, 3&up, f&m, a6f, 1:11.80, CHOICE SLEW, Guiltybysupiscion, Taylor's a Trip, 7 started.

Lethbridge Oaks, Lethbridge, Oct. 2, $12,200, 3yo, f, a6f, 1:10.60, SPECIAL ERA, Easter Weekend, Shirley Patch, 8 started.

Lewis and Clark Derby, Great Falls, Aug. 1, $7,750, 3yo, 7f, 1:26.40, STREAK A ROANI, Shouldbevictory, Tahoe's Gem, 7 started.

LEXINGTON S.-G3, Belmont Park, July 18, $111,100, 3yo, 1^1/$_8$m, 2:01.15, MUSTANFAR, Icy Atlantic, Second Performance, 8 started.

Liberada S., Calder Race Course, May 15, $40,000, 3&up, f&m, 1^1/$_{16}$mT, 1:40.57, FORMAL MISS, Improvised, Sweettrickydancer, 8 started.

Liberation H. (R), Hastings Race Course, July 1, $44,106, 3yo, f, British Columbia-bred and/or -owned, 1^1/$_{16}$m, 1:43.73, REGAL RED, Bullseye Bess, Socorro County, 8 started.

Light Hearted H., Delaware Park, July 18, $91,000, 3&up, f&m, 6f, 1:10.94, NICLIE, Bronze Abe, Our Josephina, 3 started.

Lighthouse S., Monmouth Park, Sept. 19, $65,000, f&m, 1^1/$_{16}$m, 1:43.62, TWIST AND POP, Paisley Park, Chrusciki, 6 started.

Lightning Jet H. (R), Hawthorne Race Course, Nov. 13, $100,875, 3&up, Illinois-conceived and/or -foaled, 6f, 1:10.56, SILVER BID, Big Bold Sweep, Shandy, 6 started.

Lilac H., Stampede Park, June 4, $40,000, 3yo, f, 1m, 1:39.60, SHY LIL, Down to Dixie, Cypriata, 9 started.

Lil E. Tee S. (R), Philadelphia Park, Sept. 4, $50,000, 3yo, Pennsylvania-bred, 1^1/$_{16}$m, 1:45.26, PRINCE JOSEPH, Isle of Mirth, Nittany Express, 5 started.

Lincoln H. (R), Ruidoso Downs, Aug. 1, $45,000, 4&up, f&m, New Mexico-bred, 6f, 1:10.40, SHEMOVESLIKEAGHOST, Scarzane, Betsy N, 8 started.

Lincoln Heritage H. (R), Arlington Park, June 26, $85,850, 3&up, f&m, Illinois-conceived and/or -foaled, 1^1/$_{16}$mT, 1:44.39, LIGHT-HOUSE LIL, I Can Fan Fan, Samantha B., 10 started.

Lincroft H. (R), Monmouth Park, June 20, $60,000, 3&up, New Jersey-bred, 1m, 1:38.02, TRUEAMERICANSPIRIT, N J Devil, Brave Joe, 11 started.

Lindsay Frolic S., Calder Race Course, Sept. 6, $50,000, 2yo, f, 1m, 1:44.07, DANSETTA LIGHT, Frosty Royalty, Halo Jamerica, 9 started.

Lineage S. (R), The Downs at Albuquerque, June 12, $45,000, 3&up, New Mexico-bred, 1^1/$_{16}$m, 1:44.24, CIENTO, April Baby, I'm Not Bluffin, 8 started.

Little Everglades S., Little Everglades, March 7, $37,200, 4&up, 2^3/$_4$mT, 3:46.80, PREEMPTIVE STRIKE, El Guardaespalda (Chi), Raise A Storm (Ire), 4 started.

Little Ones S. (R), Great Lakes Downs, Aug. 28, $45,000, 2yo, c&g, Michigan-bred, 6f, 1:16.11, PER CURIAM, Circus Marquee, Demagoguery, 9 started.

Little Silver S., Monmouth Park, July 5, $60,000, 3yo, f, 1^1/$_{16}$mT, 1:42.27, CAPESIDE LADY, Really American, Legendary Journey, 6 started.

Little Sister S., Calder Race Course, Aug. 9, $40,000, 3&up, f&m, 7f, 1:25.61, SILVER LACE, Sniffles, Petrina Above, 6 started.

Live the Dream H., Del Mar, Sept. 8, $76,900, 3&up, 1mT, 1:34.29, STATEMENT, Cayoke (Fr), Tsigane (Fr), 10 started.

Local Thriller S., Delaware Park, June 21, $54,300, 3&up, f&m, 6f, 1:09.58, BRONZE ABE, Valley of the Gods, Undercover, 6 started.

LOCUST GROVE H.-G3, Churchill Downs, June 26, $165,750, 3&up, f&m, 1^1/$_8$mT, 1:46.75, SHACONAGE, Halory Leigh, Sand Springs, 6 started.

London Lil S., Calder Race Course, Dec. 30, $40,000, 3yo, f, 1^1/$_{16}$mT, 1:42.35, HIGH SPEED ACCESS, Sparkling Humor, Present Danger, 10 started.

Lone Star Oaks, Lone Star Park, July 4, $100,000, 3yo, f, 1^1/$_{16}$mT, 1:43.96, AMERICA AMERICA, Topango, Dancing Meg, 9 started.

LONE STAR PARK H.-G3, Lone Star Park, May 31, $300,000, 3&up, 1^1/$_{16}$m, 1:41.29, YESSIRGENERALSIR, Sonic West, Spanish Empire, 6 started.

Lone Star Park Juvenile Fillies S., Lone Star Park, Oct. 28, $50,000, 2yo, f, 6f, 1:09.74, TRUE TAILS, Ketchmewhereyoucan, Dressed for Succes, 8 started.

Lone Star Park Juvenile S., Lone Star Park, Oct. 30, $100,000, 2yo, 7f, 1:22.41, STORM SURGE, Spanish Chestnut, City Code, 8 started.

LONGACRES MILE H.-G3, Emerald Downs, Aug. 22, $250,000, 3&up, 1m, 1:34.80, ADREAMISBORN, Demon Warlock, Mr. Makah, 12 started.

LONG BRANCH BREEDERS' CUP S.-G3, Monmouth Park, July 17, $100,000, 3yo, 1^1/$_{16}$m, 1:43.51, LION HEART, My Snookie's Boy, Royal Assault, 7 started.

Longfellow S., Monmouth Park, July 3, $65,000, 3&up, 6f, 1:08.98, CANADIAN FRONTIER, Highway Prospector, Richierichierich, 5 started.

LONG ISLAND H.-G2, Aqueduct, Nov. 6, $150,000, 3&up, f&m, 1^1/$_2$mT, 2:31.51, ELEUSIS, Literacy, Arvada (GB), 7 started.

Lord Juban S., Calder Race Course, June 5, $40,000, 3&up, 1m, 1:39.62, R. ASSOCIATE, Unbridels King, Marco's Word, 6 started.

Lorelei S., Louisiana Downs, June 27, $50,000, 3yo, f, 1^1/$_{16}$m, 1:46.96, YOURSMINEOURS, Josie G., Lucky Tunnel, 7 started.

LOS ANGELES TIMES H.-G3, Hollywood Park, May 8, $150,000, 3&up, 6f, 1:08.12, POHAVE, Marino Marini, Summer Service, 9 started.

Lost Code Breeders' Cup S., Hawthorne Race Course, April 3, $109,500, 3yo, 6f, 1:11, WILDCAT SHOES, Danieltown, Wild Eventure, 5 started.

Louise Kimball S. (R), Suffolk Downs, Nov. 6, $40,000, 3yo, f, Massachusetts-bred, 1m 70y, 1:46.45, ASK QUEENIE, Cindarullah, Pasta's Dream, 7 started.

Louisiana Breeders' Derby (R), Louisiana Downs, Oct. 23, $81,700, 3yo, Louisiana-bred, 1^1/$_{16}$m, 1:44.17, NITRO CHIP, Walk This Way, Diggy Fresh, 11 started.

Louisiana Breeders' Oaks (R), Louisiana Downs, Oct. 23, $82,600, 3yo, f, Louisiana-bred, 1¹/₁₆m, 1:44.32, HAPPY TICKET, Shes Dixies Eskimo, Dulciana, 12 started.

Louisiana Champions Day Classic S. (R), Fair Grounds, Dec. 11, $150,000, 3&up, Louisiana-bred, 1¹/₈m, 1:52, WITT ANTE, Screen Idol, Spritely Walker, 7 started.

Louisiana Champions Day Juvenile S. (R), Fair Grounds, Dec. 11, $100,000, 2yo, Louisiana-bred, 6f, 1:10.76, CRIMSON STAG, Robbeau, St. Roch, 10 started.

Louisiana Champions Day Ladies H. (R), Fair Grounds, Dec. 11, $100,000, 3&up, f&m, Louisiana-bred, 1¹/₁₆m, 1:45.29, HAPPY TICKET, Destiny Calls, Legs O'Neal, 6 started.

Louisiana Champions Day Lassie S. (R), Fair Grounds, Dec. 11, $100,000, 2yo, f, Louisiana-bred, 6f, 1:11.78, EQUESTRIAN GIRLS, Indigo Girl, Sweet Macaroni, 9 started.

Louisiana Champions Day Sprint H. (R), Fair Grounds, Dec. 11, $100,000, 3&up, Louisiana-bred, 6f, 1:10.63, ARCHEVAL, Lac Laronge, Sidebuster B, 11 started.

Louisiana Champions Day Starter H. (R), Fair Grounds, Dec. 11, $50,000, 3&up, Louisiana-bred starters for a claiming price of $20,000 or less in 2004, 1¹/₁₆m, 1:45.86, SETEMUP JOE, Cat Ante, Sunny Brick, 11 started.

Louisiana Champions Day Turf S. (R), Fair Grounds, Dec. 11, $100,000, 3&up, Louisiana-bred, a1¹/₁₆mT, 1:43.86, MR. SULU, Little Happy, Spruce's Prince, 13 started.

LOUISIANA DERBY-G2, Fair Grounds, March 7, $600,000, 3yo, 1¹/₁₆m, 1:42.71, WIMBLEDON, Borrego, Pollard's Vision, 11 started.

Louisiana Downs Breeders' Cup H., Louisiana Downs, Sept. 26, $150,000, 3&up, 1¹/₁₆mT, 1:43.51, WARLEIGH, Waupaca, Gentlemen J J, 9 started.

Louisiana Futurity (R), Fair Grounds, Dec. 26, $86,430, 2yo, c&g, Louisiana-bred, 6f, 1:12.98, WITNESS TO A FIGHT, Smilin Fine, Betnow, 9 started.

Louisiana Futurity (R), Fair Grounds, Dec. 26, $85,230, 2yo, f, Louisiana-bred, 6f, 1:12.42, THE BETER MAN CAN, Lil Cream Puff, Pale Satin, 8 started.

Louisiana H., Fair Grounds, Jan. 2, $60,000, 4&up, 1¹/₁₆m, 1:43.58, SPANISH EMPIRE, Tenpins, Cometic Truth, 7 started.

Louisiana H., Fair Grounds, Dec. 31, $60,000, 3&up, 1¹/₁₆m, 1:43.58, GIGAWATT, Alumni Hall, Kodema, 7 started.

Louisiana Premier Night Bon Temps Starter S. (R), Delta Downs, Feb. 7, $50,000, 4&up, f&m, Louisiana-bred starters for a claiming price of $10,000 or less in 2003-'04, 5f, 1:00.40, AUNTIE'S BAG, My Lee Lee, Miss Proper West, 7 started.

Louisiana Premier Night Championship S. (R), Delta Downs, Feb. 7, $200,000, 4&up, Louisiana-bred, 1¹/₁₆m, 1:46.71, SPRITELY WALKER, Mr. Archibald, Prince Slew, 7 started.

Louisiana Premier Night Distaff S. (R), Delta Downs, Feb. 7, $150,000, 4&up, f&m, Louisiana-bred, 1m, 1:40.29, DESTINY CALLS, Legs O'Neal, Cute N Noble, 7 started.

Louisiana Premier Night Gentlemen Starter S. (R), Delta Downs, Feb. 7, $50,000, 4&up, Louisiana-bred starters for a claiming price of $10,000 or less in 2003-'04, 1¹/₁₆m, 1:47.51, MASTER JON, Strike for Richard, Jack of Slades, 8 started.

Louisiana Premier Night Ladies Starter S. (R), Delta Downs, Feb. 7, $50,000, 4&up, f&m, Louisiana-bred starters for a claiming price of $10,000 or less in 2003-'04, 1m, 1:42.38, WITCH REVIVAL, Upper Class, Rich'n Restless, 7 started.

Louisiana Premier Night Matron S. (R), Delta Downs, Feb. 7, $100,000, 4&up, f&m, Louisiana-bred, 5f, :59.61, LESLIE'S LOVE, Fuse It, Kool K. J., 6 started.

Louisiana Premier Night Prince S. (R), Delta Downs, Feb. 7, $125,000, 3yo, Louisiana-bred, 7f, 1:27.96, OLD LEE, Brandon's Marfa, Arcus, 10 started.

Louisiana Premier Night Ragin Cajun Starter S. (R), Delta Downs, Feb. 7, $50,000, 4&up, Louisiana-bred starters for a claiming price of $10,000 or less in 2003-'04, 5f, 1:00.06, SPIRIT OF MALAGRA, Bear Force Won, Screamin Demon, 9 started.

Louisiana Premier Night Sprint S. (R), Delta Downs, Feb. 7, $100,000, 4&up, Louisiana-bred, 5f, :58.76, ZARB'S LUCK, Believe Im Special, Toby's Success, 6 started.

Louisiana Premier Night Starlet S. (R), Delta Downs, Feb. 7, $125,000, 3yo, f, Louisiana-bred, 7f, 1:28.50, PLACID STAR, Commanding Lady, Dmitrilynne, 7 started.

LOUISVILLE BREEDERS' CUP H.-G2, Churchill Downs, April 30, $327,000, 3&up, f&m, 1¹/₁₆m, 1:44.37, LEAD STORY, Yell, Cat Fighter, 6 started.

LOUISVILLE H.-G3, Churchill Downs, May 31, $112,400, 3&up, 1³/₁₆mT, 2:17.63, SILVERFOOT, Rochester, Ballingarry (Ire), 9 started.

Loyalty S. (R), Thistledown, Sept. 5, $40,000, 2yo, Ohio-bred, 6f, 1:11.42, FIERCE CAT, Brooks Blach, Smacker, 6 started.

LT. GOVERNORS' H.-G3, Hastings Race Course, July 1, $103,598, 3&up, 1¹/₈m, 1:49.08, ROYAL PLACE, Lord Nelson, Roscoe Pito, 8 started.

Luther Burbank H., Santa Rosa, Aug. 1, $43,010, 3&up, f&m, 1¹/₁₆m, 1:44.21, MARWOOD, Hippogator, Gonetorule, 6 started.

Lyman Sprint Championship S. (R), Philadelphia Park, June 5, $54,700, 3&up, Pennsylvania-bred, 7f, 1:22.77, DOCENT, Presidentialaffair, Senor Charismatic, 8 started.

Lyrique H., Louisiana Downs, Sept. 4, $50,000, 3yo, f, 1¹/₁₆mT, 1:43.20, OUTRIGHT BUCK, Merry Me in Spring, Topango, 10 started.

MAC DIARMIDA H.-G3, Gulfstream Park, Jan. 25, $100,000, 3³/₈mT, 2:12.58, REQUEST FOR PAROLE, Slew Valley, Sir Brian's Sword, 12 started.

Mac Diarmida S. (R), Belmont Park, June 27, $61,800, 3yo, non-winners of a stakes on the turf, 1¹/₈m, 1:48.76, SECOND PERFORMANCE, Good Reward, Dealer Choice (Fr), 8 started.

Mack Hall Starter H. (R), Turf Paradise, Oct. 16, $20,000, 3&up, consigned to and passed through the sales ring at any ATBA sales and starters for a claiming price of $8,000 or less since September 25, 2003, 6¹/₂f, 1:16.87, FLEETING ALLIANCE, Charm Attack, Credit Call, 9 started.

Mackinac H. (R), Great Lakes Downs, Sept. 18, $50,000, 3yo, c&g, Michigan-bred, 1¹/₁₆m, 1:51.99, DOTHEIMPOSSIBLE, Exclusivenjoyment, Kid Attitude, 8 started.

Madamoiselle S., Northlands Park, Aug. 13, $40,000, 3&up, f&m, 1¹/₁₆m, 1:44.80, SWEET MONARCH, A Shaky Start, Rum Candi, 7 started.

Mademoiselle H., Marquis Downs, July 24, $5,000, 3&up, f&m, 1m, 1:39.63, PICTURE THE ANSWER, Princess Briartic, Queen of Cash, 5 started.

Mademoiselle S. (R), Delta Downs, March 26, $40,000, 4&up, f&m, Louisiana-bred, 5f, :59.03, LIGHT FLING, Notrestraintable, Scottish Heritage, 8 started.

Magali Farms S. (R), Hollywood Park, April 24, $60,000, 3&up, f&m, California-bred, 6¹/₂f, 1:16.26, ALPHABET KISSES, Powerful Sister, Dancing Event, 9 started.

Magic City Classic S. (R), River Downs, June 12, $55,000, 3&up, Alabama-bred, 6f, 1:12.20, CHIEFTUDOR, Sun Block, Pokey Aaron, 9 started.

Magnolia S. (R), Delta Downs, Nov. 12, $75,000, 3&up, f&m, Louisiana-bred, 7f, 1:25.86, HAPPY TICKET, Kylers Midge, Agree to Disagree, 8 started.

Magnolia State H. (R), Fair Grounds, March 28, $31,000, 3&up, Mississippi-owned, 6f, 1:10.36, MONSTER MOVE, Biloxi Pride, Appealing Grades, 10 started.

Maid of the Mist S. (R), Belmont Park, Oct. 23, $100,000, 2yo, f, New York-bred, 1m, 1:39.40, PELHAM BAY, Indy Woods, Social Virtue, 9 started.

Majestic Prince S., Monmouth Park, Sept. 11, $60,000, 3yo, 1¹/₁₆mT, 1:46.20, VICTORY ALLEGED, Honorable Buck, Dashboard Drummer, 7 started.

Majorette H., Louisiana Downs, Oct. 30, $40,000, 3&up, f&m, 5fT, :56.05, OUR LOVE, Countryfide, Comalagold, 9 started.

MAKER'S MARK MILE S.-G2, Keeneland, April 9, $200,000, 4&up, 1mT, 1:33.54, PERFECT SOUL (Ire), Burning Roma, Royal Spy, 10 started.

Malcolm Anderson S., Bay Meadows, June 13, $71,512, 2yo, 4¹/₂f, :51.81, WHATSTHENAMEMAN, Questionable World, Wind Water, 10 started.

MALIBU S.-G1, Santa Anita Park, Dec. 26, $250,000, 3yo, 7f, 1:21.89, ROCK HARD TEN, Lava Man, Harvard Avenue, 10 started.

Mamie Eisenhower S. (R), Prairie Meadows, May 8, $60,000, 3&up, f&m, Iowa-bred, 6f, 1:09.79, ONLY AT NIGHT, Sharky's Review, One Fine Shweetie, 6 started.

Mamzelle S., Churchill Downs, April 29, $117,700, 3&up, f&m, 5fT, :56.40, NICOLE'S DREAM, Tangier Sound, Big Score, 9 started.

Manatee S., Tampa Bay Downs, Jan. 31, $60,000, 4&up, f&m, 7f, 1:26.64, MARY MURPHY, Really Royal, Cherry Tree Hill, 13 started.

Manhattan Beach S., Hollywood Park, May 30, $79,950, 3yo, f, 5¹/₂fT, 1:01.72, WINENDYNME, Very Vegas, Allswellthatnswell, 7 started.

Manhattan H. (R), The Woodlands, Sept. 25, $25,000, 3&up, f&m, Kansas-bred, 6f, 1:11.60, DISCREETLY IRISH, Emy Sue, Noble Delight, 10 started.

MANHATTAN H.-G1, Belmont Park, June 5, $400,000, 3&up, $1\frac{1}{4}$mT, 1:59.34, METEOR STORM (GB), Millennium Dragon (GB), Mr O'Brien (Ire), 9 started.

Manila S. (R), Aqueduct, Nov. 4, $60,850, 3yo, non-winners of a stakes in 2004, 1mT, 1:36.59, INFINITE GLORY, Cherokee Rap, Kennel Up, 6 started.

Manitoba Derby, Assiniboia Downs, Aug. 2, $100,000, 3yo, $1\frac{1}{8}$m, 1:52, ROYALTY BOY, Skipper, Shanghied, 7 started.

Manitoba Maturity S. (R), Assiniboia Downs, July 10, $41,000, 4yo, Manitoba-bred, $1\frac{1}{16}$m, 1:47.20, FANCY BRU, Pete's Surprise, Tarrango, 7 started.

Manitoba S. (R), Assiniboia Downs, June 26, $40,000, 3yo, c&g, Manitoba-bred, 1m, 1:41.60, COAL SMUDGE, Stonewall Harris, Shrike One, 8 started.

Manor Downs Thoroughbred Futurity (1st Div.), Manor Downs, April 25, $10,000, 2yo, $4\frac{1}{2}$f, :53.91, SUMMER CLAIM, Blake B., Beccas' Shoulder, 7 started.

Manor Downs Thoroughbred Futurity (2nd Div.), Manor Downs, April 25, $10,000, 2yo, $4\frac{1}{2}$f, :54.23, KATE'S STORM, Misty Fling, Fly Little Totum, 7 started.

MAN O'WAR S.-G1, Belmont Park, Sept. 11, $500,000, 3&up, $1\frac{3}{8}$mT, 2:14.65, MAGISTRETTI, Epalo (Ger), King's Drama (Ire), 8 started.

MAPLE LEAF S.-G3, Woodbine, Nov. 13, $218,850, 3&up, f&m, $1\frac{1}{4}$m, 2:04.87, ONE FOR ROSE, Clouds of Gold, Raylene, 5 started.

Marathon Series Final S., Turf Paradise, Feb. 29, $24,900, 4&up, $1\frac{5}{8}$m, 2:44.40, SWELTER, Stormie Britches, Foretell, 12 started.

Marathon Series First Leg S., Lethbridge, Oct. 2, $11,200, 3&up, $1\frac{1}{16}$m, 1:49.40, SILVER SKY, Prosperity Rose, Cielo's Honour, 7 started.

Marathon Series Second Leg S., Lethbridge, Oct. 31, $11,200, 3&up, $1\frac{1}{8}$m, 1:52.20, CANDID REMARK, Silver Sky, Cabreo, 8 started.

March Madness Starter H. (R), Santa Anita Park, March 27, $46,450, 4&up, f&m, starters for a claiming price of $40,000 or less in 2003-'04, 1mT, 1:34.35, LA SORPRESA (Arg), Shezsospiritual, Deputy Tombe, 7 started.

Mardi Gras H., Fair Grounds, Feb. 24, $50,000, 4&up, 1m, 1:37.12, MAJESTIC THIEF, Skate Away, One Nice Cat, 6 started.

Marfa S., Turfway Park, Sept. 25, $74,250, 3&up, $6\frac{1}{2}$f, 1:16.18, PRIVATE HORDE, Mountain General, Sterling Gold, 6 started.

Margarita Breeders' Cup H., Retama Park, July 24, $47,750, 3&up, f&m, $1\frac{1}{16}$mT, 1:43.99, CHERYLVILLE SLEW, Mexican Moonlight, Kristina's Wish, 11 started.

Mariah's Storm S., Arlington Park, Aug. 13, $52,400, 3&up, f&m, $1\frac{1}{8}$m, 1:50.99, TAMWEEL, Casual Attitude, Julie's Prize, 6 started.

Marie G. Krantz Memorial H., Fair Grounds, March 13, $75,000, 4&up, f&m, 6f, 1:09.96, PUT ME IN, Savorthetime, Tina Bull, 8 started.

Marie P. DeBartolo Oaks Breeders' Cup H., Louisiana Downs, Sept. 25, $93,750, 3yo, f, $1\frac{1}{16}$mT, 1:45.24, MERRY ME IN SPRING, Outright Buck, Key to the Cat, 6 started.

MARINE S.-G3, Woodbine, May 22, $164,100, 3yo, $1\frac{1}{16}$m, 1:45.96, JUDITHS WILD RUSH, Organ Grinder, Honolua Storm, 6 started.

Marluel's Troy S. (R), Fairmount Park, Aug. 24, $35,800, 2yo, c&g, Illinois-bred, 6f, 1:12.80, REBEL ARMY, Yukon's Gambler, Native Shore, 5 started.

Marshland S., Delta Downs, Oct. 30, $50,000, 3&up, 1m, 1:39.56, HIGH STRIKE ZONE, Monty Man, Dusty Spike, 8 started.

Marshua S., Laurel Park, Jan. 3, $45,200, 3yo, f, 6f, 1:11.20, AMONG MY SOUVENIRS, Forestier, Ask Queenie, 7 started.

Marshua's River S., Gulfstream Park, March 13, $67,350, 3&up, f&m, 1mT, 1:37.87, DEDICATION (Fr), Ocean Drive, Vespers, 9 started.

Martanza S. (R), Sam Houston Race Park, Nov. 20, $75,000, 3&up, f&m, Texas-bred, 1m, 1:37.78, NATIVE ANNIE, Lady Sonya, Jester Rahab, 10 started.

MARTHA WASHINGTON BREEDERS' CUP S.-G3, Pimlico, Sept. 25, $148,500, 3yo, f, $1\frac{1}{16}$mT, 1:43.26, WESTERN RANSOM, Plenty, With Affection, 12 started.

Martha Washington S., Oaklawn Park, Feb. 16, $50,000, 3yo, f, 1m, 1:41.93, TURN TO LASS, All Electric, Yoursmineours, 11 started.

Mary Goldblatt S. (R), Portland Meadows, March 6, $10,000, 3yo, f, Oregon-bred, 1m, 1:41.64, SO HAPPY TOGETHER, Ms Lady Palace, Kya Jo, 5 started.

MARYLAND BREEDERS' CUP H.-G3, Pimlico, May 15, $186,000, 3&up, 6f, 1:10.84, GATORS N BEARS, Highway Prospector, Sassy Hound, 9 started.

Maryland Juvenile Championship S. (R), Pimlico, Dec. 31, $100,000, 2yo, Maryland-bred, $1\frac{1}{16}$m, 1:46.21, LEGAL CONTROL, Monster Chaser, Prideland, 7 started.

Maryland Juvenile Filly Championship S. (R), Pimlico, Dec. 30, $100,000, 2yo, f, Maryland-bred, $1\frac{1}{16}$m, 1:47.71, DIXIE TALKING, Take a Check, Sweetsoutherndessa, 8 started.

Maryland Million Classic S. (R), Pimlico, Oct. 9, $190,000, 3&up, progeny of eligible Maryland stallions, $1\frac{3}{16}$m, 1:55.58, PRESIDENTIALAFFAIR, Aggadan, Irish Colony, 8 started.

Maryland Million Distaff H. (R), Pimlico, Oct. 9, $95,000, 3&up, f&m, progeny of eligible Maryland stallions, 6f, 1:10.67, MERRYLAND MISSY, Spirited Game, A Vision in Gray, 9 started.

Maryland Million Distaff Starter H. (R), Pimlico, Oct. 9, $47,500, 3&up, f&m, Maryland-bred starters for a claiming price of $12,500 or less since October 11, 2003, $1\frac{1}{16}$m, 1:45.72, HUNCA MUNCA, Breezy Bri, Sarah Beaner, 9 started.

Maryland Million Ladies S. (R), Pimlico, Oct. 9, $95,000, 3&up, f&m, progeny of eligible Maryland stallions, $1\frac{1}{8}$mT, 1:51.09, HAIL HILLARY, Rowdy, Love Match, 11 started.

Maryland Million Lassie S. (R), Pimlico, Oct. 9, $95,000, 2yo, f, progeny of eligible Maryland stallions, 6f, 1:11.61, HEAR US ROAR, Partners Due, Golden Malibu, 11 started.

Maryland Million Nursery S. (R), Pimlico, Oct. 9, $95,000, 2yo, progeny of eligible Maryland stallions, 6f, 1:11.72, WHAT'S UP LONELY, Monster Chaser, Late Night Lover, 12 started.

Maryland Million Oaks (R), Pimlico, Oct. 9, $95,000, 3yo, f, progeny of eligible Maryland stallions, $1\frac{1}{16}$m, 1:43.98, SILMARIL, Blind Canyon, Richetta, 9 started.

Maryland Million Sprint H. (R), Pimlico, Oct. 9, $95,000, 3&up, progeny of eligible Maryland stallions, 6f, 1:10.13, MY POKER PLAYER, Crossing Point, Ameri Brilliance, 8 started.

Maryland Million Sprint Starter H. (R), Pimlico, Oct. 9, $23,750, 3&up, Maryland-bred starters for a claiming price of $7,500 or less since October 11, 2003, 6f, 1:11.58, DRUM ROLL PLEASE, In C C's Honor, Deliver Hope, 7 started.

Maryland Million Starter H. (R), Pimlico, Oct. 9, $47,500, 3&up, Maryland-bred starters for a claiming price of $12,500 or less since October 11, 2003, $1\frac{1}{8}$m, 1:51.89, DIXIE COLONY, Proud Punch, Mr Song and Dance, 10 started.

Maryland Million Turf S. (R), Pimlico, Oct. 9, $95,000, 3&up, progeny of eligible Maryland stallions, $1\frac{1}{8}$mT, 1:50.96, DR DETROIT, Private Scandal, La Reine's Terms, 6 started.

Maryland Million Turf Sprint H. (R), Pimlico, Oct. 9, $95,000, 3&up, progeny of eligible Maryland stallions, 5fT, :57.22, NAMEQUEST, Shades of Sunny, Quest of Fate, 11 started.

Maryland Racing Media H., Laurel Park, Feb. 21, $75,000, 4&up, f&m, $1\frac{1}{8}$m, 1:52.91, UNDERCOVER, Friel's for Real, Database, 5 started.

MASSACHUSETTS H.-G2, Suffolk Downs, June 19, $500,000, 3&up, $1\frac{1}{8}$m, 1:49.14, OFFLEE WILD, Funny Cide, The Lady's Groom, 9 started.

Matchmaker H. (R), Lincoln State Fair, June 19, $15,700, 3&up, f&m, Nebraska-bred, 1m, 1:41.60, IRISH FLYER, Bright Flame, Flaming Night, 7 started.

MATCHMAKER H.-G3, Monmouth Park, Aug. 8, $100,000, 3&up, f&m, $1\frac{1}{8}$mT, 1:48.80, WHERE WE LEFT OFF (GB), Mrs. M, Spin Control, 9 started.

MATRIARCH S.-G1, Hollywood Park, Nov. 28, $500,000, 3&up, f&m, 1mT, 1:35.87, INTERCONTINENTAL (GB), Etoile Montante, Ticker Tape (GB), 9 started.

Matron Breeders' Cup S., Assiniboia Downs, Oct. 2, $44,250, 3&up, f&m, $1\frac{1}{8}$m, 1:55.20, REMIEWATERBLUZ, Pete's Surprise, Victory Thrill, 9 started.

Matron H., Evangeline Downs, Sept. 4, $50,000, 3&up, f&m, 1m, 1:39.40, DUE TO WIN, Native Brick, Miss Confusion, 11 started.

MATRON S.-G1, Belmont Park, Sept. 19, $300,000, 2yo, f, 1m, 1:37.67, SENSE OF STYLE, Balletto (UAE), Play With Fire, 6 started.

Matt Winn S., Churchill Downs, May 8, $103,499, 3yo, 6f, 1:09.64, FIRE SLAM, Cuvee, Hasslefree, 4 started.

Maxine M. Piggott S. (R), Turf Paradise, April 24, $40,000, 3yo, f, Arizona-bred, $6\frac{1}{2}$f, 1:15.19, MISS NOTEWORTHY, Rockin On, Lil Easy, 7 started.

Maxxam Gold Cup H., Sam Houston Race Park, Jan. 17, $100,000, 4&up, $1\frac{1}{8}$m, 1:51.76, SIR CHEROKEE, Freefourinternet, Dusty Spike, 8 started.

MAZARINE BREEDERS' CUP S.-G2, Woodbine, Oct. 3, $278,750, 2yo, f, 1^1/₁₆m, 1:47.99, HIGHER WORLD, Didycheatamandhowe, Dancehall Deelites, 9 started.

McFadden Memorial H. (R), Portland Meadows, Feb. 21, $10,000, 3yo, c&g, Oregon-bred, 1^1/₁₆m, 1:50.45, NORTHERN BAQUERO, Mythical Road, Might E Man, 7 started.

MEADOWLANDS BREEDERS' CUP S.-G2, The Meadowlands, Oct. 8, $500,000, 3&up, 1^1/₈m, 1:48.68, BALTO STAR, Dynever, Gygistar, 8 started.

Meafara S., Hawthorne Race Course, April 3, $42,800, 3yo, f, 6f, 1:11.98, PREVALENT, Clever Maid, Stoneway, 7 started.

Mecke H., Calder Race Course, July 4, $100,000, 3&up, 1^1/₁₆mT, 1:47.30, UNBRIDELS KING, Coahoma, Classic Par, 8 started.

Melair S. (R), Hollywood Park, April 24, $200,000, 3yo, f, California-bred, 1^1/₁₆m, 1:41.70, YEARLY REPORT, Western Hemisphere, Nicole and Ben, 8 started.

Mel's Hope S., Calder Race Course, Nov. 28, $40,000, 3&up, 1^1/₁₆m, 1:46.04, SUPER FROLIC, Dustys Birthday, Nightmare Affair, 7 started.

MEMORIAL DAY H.-G3, Calder Race Course, May 31, $100,000, 3&up, 1^1/₁₆m, 1:45.79, TWILIGHT ROAD, Hear No Evil, Gold Dollar, 12 started.

Merrillville S. (R), Hoosier Park, Oct. 23, $40,000, 3&up, f&m, Indiana-bred, 6f, 1:10.94, SENORITA ZIGGY, My Sweet Sug, Ellens Lucky Star, 8 started.

Merry Time S. (R), Thistledown, June 19, $45,000, 3&up, f&m, Ohio-bred, 1^1/₁₆m, 1:46.10, GOLDEN TOUR, Oh So Easy, Whitewater Way, 9 started.

MERVIN H. MUNIZ JR. MEMORIAL H.-G2, Fair Grounds, March 21, $500,000, 4&up, a1^1/₁₆mT, 1:48.29, MYSTERY GIVER, Herculated, Skate Away, 10 started.

MERVYN LEROY H.-G2, Hollywood Park, May 8, $150,000, 3&up, 1^1/₁₆m, 1:40.81, EVEN THE SCORE, Ender's Shadow, Total Impact (Chi), 8 started.

Mesa H., Turf Paradise, Dec. 18, $40,000, 3&up, f&m, 6^1/₂f, 1:15.02, MUIR BEACH, Friendofthefamily, Arch Lady, 7 started.

Metcalf Memorial S. (R), Monmouth Park, Sept. 26, $75,000, 4&up, nonwinners over hurdles prior to June 1, 2003, a2^1/₂mT, 4:38.61, SUR LA TETE, Tres Touche, Santenay (Fr), 7 started.

Metroplex Mile S., Lone Star Park, Oct. 30, $100,000, 3&up, 1m, 1:35.41, WISHINGITWAS, Seek Gold, During, 11 started.

METROPOLITAN H.-G1, Belmont Park, May 31, $750,000, 3&up, 1m, 1:35.47, PICO CENTRAL (Brz), Bowman's Band, Strong Hope, 9 started.

MIAMI MILE BREEDERS' CUP H.-G3, Calder Race Course, Sept. 11, $150,000, 3&up, 1mT, 1:39.56, TWILIGHT ROAD, Gold Dollar, Paradise Dancer, 9 started.

Mia's Hope S., Calder Race Course, Aug. 2, $40,000, 3yo, f, 1^1/₁₆mT, 1:46.59, ADOBE GOLD, Najibes Acre, Special Report, 8 started.

Michael G. Schaefer Mile S., Hoosier Park, Nov. 13, $103,100, 3&up, 1m, 1:35.85, ADDED EDGE, Coach Jimi Lee, Perfect Cut, 9 started.

Michigan Breeders' Cup H. (R), Great Lakes Downs, July 17, $40,000, 3&up, Michigan-bred, 1^1/₈m, 1:50.29, ROCKEM SOCKEM, Catch the Dew, Above the Wind, 5 started.

Michigan Futurity (R), Great Lakes Downs, Oct. 26, $82,500, 2yo, c&g, Michigan-bred, 7f, 1:28.12, ITS HIS TIME, Starlits Mission, Per Curiam, 11 started.

Michigan Juvenile Fillies S. (R), Great Lakes Downs, Oct. 25, $79,450, 2yo, f, Michigan-bred, 7f, 1:30.12, MUSICAL FACTOR, Everglide, Foolininthemeadow, 9 started.

Michigan Oaks (R), Great Lakes Downs, Sept. 17, $50,000, 3yo, f, Michigan-bred, 1^1/₁₆m, 1:49.95, CATS COPY, Lunes Grito, Textbook Tillie, 7 started.

Michigan Sire S. (R), Great Lakes Downs, Oct. 9, $137,262, 2yo, c&g, progeny of eligible Michigan sires, 6f, 1:13.64, DEMAGOGUERY, It's a Ego Thing, Boogie After Dark, 9 started.

Michigan Sire S. (R), Great Lakes Downs, Oct. 9, $136,462, 2yo, f, progeny of eligible Michigan sires, 6f, 1:15.66, FOOLININTHE-MEADOW, Loot Tooten Trudy, Everglide, 9 started.

Michigan Sire S. (R), Great Lakes Downs, Oct. 9, $136,462, 3yo, c&g, progeny of eligible Michigan sires, 1^1/₁₆m, 1:50.73, EXCLU-SIVENJOYMENT, Stormy Fellow, Coin Maker, 10 started.

Michigan Sire S. (R), Great Lakes Downs, Oct. 9, $136,662, 3yo, f, progeny of eligible Michigan sires, 1^1/₁₆m, 1:50.48, CIRCUS DU JOY, Deb's Favoite Gift, Ima Bender Boo, 10 started.

Michigan Sire S. (R), Great Lakes Downs, Oct. 9, $136,262, 4&up, c&g, progeny of eligible Michigan sires, 1^1/₁₆m, 1:58.10, TIMELY FACTOR, Lite Up, Tank's Lil Brother, 9 started.

Michigan Sire S. (R), Great Lakes Downs, Oct. 9, $132,462, 4&up, f&m, progeny of eligible Michigan sires, 1^1/₁₆m, 1:57.63, Pebbett, DANCIN FOR GOLD, Circle the Globe, 6 started.

Middleground Breeders' Cup S., Lone Star Park, Oct. 3, $94,500, 2yo, 1m, 1:39.12, LEAVING ON MY MIND, Ready Ruler, Rubialedo, 8 started.

MIESQUE S. (1st Div.)-G3, Hollywood Park, Nov. 26, $75,000, 2yo, f, 1mT, 1:37.19, LOUVAIN (Ire), Royal Copenhagen (Fr), La Maitresse (Ire), 8 started.

MIESQUE S. (2nd Div.)-G3, Hollywood Park, Nov. 26, $75,000, 2yo, f, 1mT, 1:36.92, PADDY'S DAISY, Conveyor's Angel, Kenza, 8 started.

Mike Lee S. (R), Belmont Park, June 26, $113,900, 3yo, New York-bred, 7f, 1:22.56, MULTIPLICATION, Work With Me, Swinging Ghost, 10 started.

Mike Rowland Memorial H. (R), Thistledown, May 8, $40,000, 3&up, Ohio-bred, 6f, 1:11.64, HANK'S RIB, Wirebender, Clever Jimmy C, 8 started.

MILADY BREEDERS' CUP H.-G1, Hollywood Park, July 11, $228,450, 3&up, f&m, 1^1/₁₆m, 1:41.83, STAR PARADE (Arg), Quero Quero, Pesci, 5 started.

Mile Hi H., Yavapai Downs, Aug. 31, $17,500, 3&up, 1^1/₁₆m, 1:44.60, ROYAL GROOVE, Real Creek, Instantly, 10 started.

Miles City Thoroughbred Maiden S., Cow Capital Turf Club, May 15, $5,300, 3&up, 5^1/₂f, 1:10, OLD COYOTE, Road Wager, K T Wantsafastone, 7 started.

Millard Harrell Memorial S. (R), Charles Town Races, Sept. 11, $41,250, 3yo, West Virginia-bred, 7f, 1:28.59, SHECKATOO, Brigader, Take the Plunge, 11 started.

Millarville Derby, Millarville, July 1, $5,500, 3&up, 1^1/₁₆m, 1:54.80, DIAMOND PASSER, Larry the Longshot, Sagreeno, 5 started.

Miller Lite S., Lone Star Park, June 26, $50,000, 3&up, f&m, 5fT, :58.06, FLEETA DIF, Leslie's Love, Big Score, 8 started.

Milwaukee Avenue H. (R), Hawthorne Race Course, April 10, $92,150, 3&up, Illinois-conceived and/or -foaled, 1^1/₁₆m, 1:46.57, SCOOTER ROACH, Wiggins, Act of War, 5 started.

Minaret S., Tampa Bay Downs, Jan. 3, $60,000, 4&up, f&m, 6f, 1:10.42, SEA SPAN, Mooji Moo, Diablosangeleyes, 10 started.

Minnesota Classic Championship S. (R), Canterbury Park, Aug. 22, $40,000, 3&up, Minnesota-bred, 1^1/₁₆m, 1:41.74, WALLY'S CHOICE, Adroitly Superb, Blue Dancer, 6 started.

Minnesota Derby (R), Canterbury Park, July 31, $62,100, 3yo, Minnesota-bred, 1m 70y, 1:42.61, WALLY'S CHOICE, Lt. Sampson, Carl, 10 started.

Minnesota Distaff Classic Championship S. (R), Canterbury Park, Aug. 22, $40,000, 3&up, f&m, Minnesota-bred, 1^1/₁₆m, 1:43.51, A. CATERINA, Pandorasconnection, Poco Doc, 8 started.

Minnesota Distaff Sprint Championship S. (R), Canterbury Park, Aug. 22, $40,000, 3&up, f&m, Minnesota-bred, 6f, 1:09.96, SWASTI, Shakopee, Demiparfait, 8 started.

Minnesota HBPA Mile S., Canterbury Park, July 5, $40,000, 3&up, f&m, 1mT, 1:36.92, SOUND OF GOLD, Ghostly Gate, Phone the Diva, 9 started.

Minnesota HBPA Sprint S., Canterbury Park, July 5, $40,000, 3&up, 6f, 1:10.43, SILVER ZIPPER, Crocrock, Aces of Gold, 5 started.

Minnesota Oaks (R), Canterbury Park, July 31, $62,250, 3yo, f, Minnesota-bred, 1m 70y, 1:45.52, NILINI, Mrs. Beerman, Bleu's Apparition, 12 started.

Minnesota Sprint Championship S. (R), Canterbury Park, Aug. 22, $40,000, 3&up, Minnesota-bred, 6f, 1:09.30, CROCROCK, Vasant, Lt. Sampson, 8 started.

Minnesota Turf Championship S. (R), Canterbury Park, Aug. 22, $40,000, 3&up, Minnesota-bred, 1mT, 1:35.55, NOW PLAYING, Vazandar, Winter Trick, 9 started.

MINT JULEP H.-G3, Churchill Downs, May 29, $168,300, 4&up, f&m, 1^1/₁₆mT, 1:42.66, STAY FOREVER, Sand Springs, Eternal Melody (NZ), 9 started.

Mint S., Calder Race Course, Dec. 27, $40,000, 3&up, 5^1/₂f, 1:04.50, ALL HAIL STORMY, Swift Replica, Weigelia, 6 started.

Miracle Wood S., Laurel Park, Feb. 28, $40,000, 3yo, 1^1/₁₆m, 1:45.29, WATER CANNON, Eastern Bay, Wanaka, 7 started.

Miss America H., Bay Meadows, April 10, $83,775, 3&up, f&m, 1^1/₁₆mT, 1:41.46, HIPPOGATOR, Marwood, A B Noodle, 10 started.

Miss California S., Golden Gate Fields, Jan. 17, $64,650, 3yo, f, 6f, 1:09.92, HEAVENLY HUMOR, Smoke Break, Uppity Kitty, 6 started.

Miss Gibson County S., Turf Paradise, Dec. 10, $21,700, 2yo, f, 5^1/$_2$f, 1:06.13, LADY BERTRANDO, Estacada, Tall Pines, 7 started.

Miss Grillo S., Belmont Park, Oct. 24, $82,200, 2yo, f, 1^1/$_16$m, 1:51.28, MELHOR AINDA, Gemilli, Accretion, 6 started.

Miss Indiana S. (R), Hoosier Park, Nov. 6, $40,000, 2yo, f, Indiana-bred, 6f, 1:13.06, FREE BONUS, Slim Justice, Join the Crusade, 6 started.

Miss Indy Anna S., Suffolk Downs, May 1, $40,000, 3&up, f&m, 6f, 1:12.10, QUICK SMOKE, But Mommy, Ginas Girl, 7 started.

Mississippi Futurity (R), Fair Grounds, Dec. 4, $27,100, 2yo, Mississippi-owned, 6f, 1:15.09, HEART TO HEART, Lexy's Taxi-ano, Valentino Man, 8 started.

Miss Kansas City H., The Woodlands, Oct. 10, $25,000, 3&up, f&m, 1^1/$_16$m, 1:45, WILDWOOD ROYAL, Switch Lanes, Market's Best, 7 started.

Miss Liberty S., The Meadowlands, Oct. 15, $60,000, 3yo, f, 1m 70yT, 1:37.90, SCHEDULE (GB), Irish Melody, Tigi, 6 started.

Miss Meadowlark Futurity (R), The Woodlands, Oct. 17, $18,500, 2yo, f, progeny of eligible Kansas stallions, 5^1/$_2$f, 1:05.80, WIND TWISTER, Jennies Song, Rumors Wild, 8 started.

Miss Medallion S. (R), Calder Race Course, Aug. 27, $40,000, 3&up, f&m, nonwinners of $15,000 once since February 1 or nonwinners of four races other than maiden, claiming, or starter, 1^1/$_16$m, 1:47.94, ADOBE GOLD, Najibes Acre, Sniffles, 9 started.

Miss Ohio S. (R), Thistledown, Aug. 28, $40,000, 2yo, f, Ohio-bred, 6f, 1:13.48, NOON WIN, Pyrite Bonds, Annabarr, 7 started.

Miss Woodford S., Monmouth Park, Aug. 22, $60,000, 3yo, f, 6f, 1:10.03, THEN SHE LAUGHS, Forty Moves, Absolute Nectar, 6 started.

Missy Good S. (R), Penn National Race Course, July 9, $41,050, 3&up, f&m, Pennsylvania-bred, 6f, 1:10.14, FLAME OF LOVE, May's Pride, A Vision in Gray, 9 started.

Mister Diz S. (R), Pimlico, Aug. 7, $75,000, 3&up, Maryland-bred, 5fT, :58.75, YANKEE WILDCAT, Nortouch, Quest of Fate, 8 started.

Mister Gus S., Arlington Park, May 31, $42,375, 3&up, 1m, 1:35.97, INTERN, Missme, Stormy Impact, 8 started.

Mo Bay S., Delaware Park, July 3, $51,022, 3&up, 6f, 1:10.07, DON SIX, True Direction, Sassy Hound, 4 started.

Moccasin S., Hollywood Park, Nov. 21, $100,000, 2yo, f, 7f, 1:23.06, NO BULL BABY, Short Route, Binasuccess, 7 started.

Mocha Express S. (R), Lone Star Park, Oct. 23, $50,000, 2yo, Texas-bred, 6^1/$_2$f, 1:17.02, LEAVING ON MY MIND, Expect Will, Dixie Meister, 8 started.

Mockingbird S., Gulfstream Park, April 24, $42,375, 2yo, 3f, :33.38, SHOCKING DUNN, Memories of Pa, Joyous Song, 9 started.

MODESTY H.-G3, Arlington Park, July 24, $150,000, 3&up, f&m, 1^3/$_16$mT, 1:57, BEDANKEN, Aud, Shaconage, 8 started.

Mohawk H. (R), Belmont Park, Oct. 23, $150,000, 3&up, New York-bred, 1^1/$_8$m, 1:48.96, IRISH COLONIAL, Certifiably Crazy, No Parole, 12 started.

Molly Brown H., Arapahoe Park, July 25, $27,625, 3&up, f&m, 6f, 1:09.60, SHE'S FINDING TIME, Humble Roannie, Dixie Witch, 9 started.

MOLLY PITCHER BREEDERS' CUP H.-G2, Monmouth Park, July 4, $300,000, 3&up, f&m, 1^1/$_8$m, 1:51.10, LA REASON, Yell, Bare Necessities, 7 started.

Mongo Queen S., Monmouth Park, Sept. 12, $60,000, 2yo, f, 1m 70y, 1:42.18, SIS CITY, By Grace Alone, Our Miss Jones, 7 started.

Monmouth Beach S., Monmouth Park, June 13, $70,000, 3&up, f&m, 1^1/$_16$m, 1:44.32, POCUS HOCUS, Chrusciki, Final Round, 6 started.

MONMOUTH BREEDERS' CUP OAKS-G2, Monmouth Park, Aug. 15, $200,000, 3yo, f, 1^1/$_16$m, 1:42.18, CAPESIDE LADY, Hopelessly Devoted, Habiboo, 6 started.

Monrovia H., Santa Anita Park, Dec. 31, $113,550, 3&up, f&m, 6^1/$_2$f, 1:15.34, RESPLENDENCY, Puxa Saco, Market Garden, 9 started.

Montauk H. (R), Aqueduct, Nov. 20, $83,275, 3&up, f&m, New York-bred, 1^1/$_8$m, 1:51.07, BOARD ELLIGIBLE, South Wing, Bundle of Roses, 8 started.

Montclair State University S., The Meadowlands, Nov. 13, $60,000, 3&up, f&m, 6f, 1:09.17, COLOGNY, Slews Final Answer, Travelator, 7 started.

Moonbeam H. (R), Great Lakes Downs, July 16, $40,000, 3&up, f&m, Michigan-bred, 1m, 1:46.77, CLEVER MOON, Charlies Indian, Dancin for Gold, 8 started.

Moonsplash Futurity (R), The Woodlands, Oct. 17, $16,000, 2yo, c&g, progeny of eligible Kansas stallions, 5^1/$_2$f, 1:06.80, dh-MAKES-YOURHEADSPIN, dh-SCARLET JEFF, C'Mon Kreed, 9 started.

Moonsplash S., Turf Paradise, Dec. 12, $21,800, 3&up, 4^1/$_2$fT, :50.52, WESTERN RIDGE, King Justin, Leather N Lace, 8 started.

MORVICH H.-G3, Santa Anita Park, Oct. 30, $100,000, 3&up, a6^1/$_2$fT, 1:11.76, LEROIDESANIMAUX (Brz), De Valmont (Aus), Cayoke (Fr), 6 started.

MOTHER GOOSE S.-G1, Belmont Park, June 26, $300,000, 3yo, f, 1^1/$_8$m, 1:48.13, STELLAR JAYNE, Ashado, Island Sand, 6 started.

Mountaineer Mile H., Mountaineer Race Track, Nov. 13, $100,000, 3&up, 1m, 1:40.36, DISCREET HERO, Sonic West, Frankie R's Winner, 5 started.

Mountain State H., Mountaineer Race Track, July 4, $75,000, 3&up, 6f, 1:11, CROSSING POINT, Top Shoter, Frankie R's Winner, 5 started.

Mountain Valley S., Oaklawn Park, Jan. 24, $50,000, 3yo, 6f, 1:11.92, PRO PRADO, Wildcat Shoes, Hawkish, 6 started.

Mount Elbert H., Arapahoe Park, Aug. 14, $26,575, 3&up, c&g, Colorado-bred, 1^1/$_16$m, 1:42.20, RUN AT NIGHT, Personal Beau, D's Valentine, 5 started.

Mount Royal H., Stampede Park, May 16, $40,000, 3yo, f, 6f, 1:12.60, ERICKA'S LASS, Alta Aire, Shy Lil, 8 started.

Mount Vernon H. (1st Div.) (R), Belmont Park, June 20, $83,700, 3&up, f&m, New York-bred, 1^1/$_16$mT, 1:48.67, BIG TEASE, Beebe Lake, Raffie's Dream, 8 started.

Mount Vernon H. (2nd Div.), Belmont Park, June 20, $84,600, 3&up, f&m, 1^1/$_16$mT, 1:49.56, BRANDALA, Lady Libby, On the Bus, 10 started.

M. R. Jenkins Memorial H., Stampede Park, May 9, $40,000, 4&up, f&m, 6f, 1:11.80, A SHAKY START, Raylene, Northern Neechitoo, 8 started.

MR. PROSPECTOR H.-G3, Gulfstream Park, Jan. 3, $100,000, 3&up, 6f, 1:09.06, CAJUN BEAT, Gygistar, Deer Lake, 6 started.

Mrs. Penny S. (R), Philadelphia Park, Sept. 4, $50,000, 3&up, f&m, Pennsylvania-bred, 1^1/$_16$mT, 1:45.61, CAUGHT IN THE RAIN, Hereafter, Air Adair, 10 started.

Mrs. Revere S., Churchill Downs, Nov. 13, $171,150, 3yo, f, 1^1/$_16$mT, 1:44.59, RIVER BELLE (GB), Lenatareese, Cape Town Lass, 9 started.

Ms. S., Portland Meadows, Feb. 7, $10,000, 3yo, f, 6f, 1:13.67, QUIZ THE MAID, Kya Jo, Ogygian's Rose, 8 started.

Ms. Southern Ohio S. (R), River Downs, Aug. 8, $40,000, 3&up, f&m, Ohio-bred, 1^1/$_16$mT, 1:48, OH SO EASY, Glorado, Bubble Dourbon, 7 started.

MTA Stallion Auction Laddie S. (R), Canterbury Park, Sept. 6, $42,592, 3yo, progeny of stallion seasons sold at the 1999 MTA stallion auction, 6^1/$_2$f, 1:18.39, VASANT, Sahab, Gopher This One, 4 started.

MTA Stallion Auction Lassie S. (R), Canterbury Park, Sept. 6, $45,160, 3yo, f, progeny of stallion seasons sold at the 1999 MTA stallion auction, 6^1/$_2$f, 1:18.18, NISHANI, Gracious Halo, Grand Rapids Miss, 7 started.

Mt. Rainier Breeders' Cup H., Emerald Downs, July 25, $77,500, 3&up, 1^1/$_16$m, 1:46.60, POKER BRAD, Mr. Makah, Demon Warlock, 9 started.

Mt. Sassafras S. (R), Woodbine, Nov. 13, $103,000, 3&up, Canadian-foaled, 7f, 1:23.63, WANDO, Twisted Wit, Millfleet, 5 started.

Mt. St. Helens S., Portland Meadows, March 27, $10,000, 3yo, f, 1m, 1:41.38, QUIZ THE MAID, Ms Lady Palace, Kya Jo, 10 started.

M.Tyson Gilpin S. (R), Delaware Park, Oct. 30, $50,300, 2yo, Virginia-bred and/or -sired, 6f, 1:11.48, SMOKIN FOREST, Feverish Affair, Java Warrior, 6 started.

Muscogee (Creek) Nation S., Fair Meadows at Tulsa, July 24, $42,910, 3&up, f&m, 6^1/$_2$f, 1:20.40, GOLDLEAFED MIRROR, Frilly Fun, Nikki's Growl, 7 started.

Muskoka S. (R), Woodbine, Sept. 5, $136,000, 2yo, f, Canadian-bred that passed through the sales ring as a yearling at a sale conducted by Canadian Breeders' Sales, 7f, 1:25.36, SIMPLY LOVELY, Victorious Ami, Silver Impulse, 8 started.

MY CHARMER H.-G3, Calder Race Course, Dec. 4, $100,000, 3&up, f&m, 1^1/$_8$mT, 1:46.79, SOMETHING VENTURED, Snowdrops (GB), Changing World, 12 started.

My Charmer S., Turfway Park, Dec. 11, $49,500, 3&up, f&m, 1^1/$_16$m, 1:44.40, TWO MILE HILL, Red Cell, Dick's Chick, 11 started.

My Dear Girl S. (R), Calder Race Course, Oct. 23, $400,000, 2yo, f, progeny of eligible Florida stallions, 1^1/$_16$m, 1:48.31, ACLASSYSASSY-LASSY, Babaganush, Yes It's Gold, 10 started.

My Dear S., Woodbine, July 4, $142,125, 2yo, f, 5f, :58.12, QUITE A RUCKUS, Sweet Solairo, Coconut Popsicle, 6 started.

My Fair Lady S., Suffolk Downs, June 12, $40,000, 3&up, f&m, a1m 70yT, 1:44.19, WHERE WE LEFT OFF (GB), Laredo Lil, Haley's Classic, 9 started.

My Frenchman S. (1st Div.), The Meadowlands, Oct. 8, $60,000, 3&up, 5fT, :56.18, MANOFGLORY, Cumby Texas, Rudirudy, 9 started.

My Frenchman S. (2nd Div.), The Meadowlands, Oct. 8, $60,000, 3&up, 5fT, :56.11, WORLDWIND ROMANCE, Western Roar, Sport d'Hiver, 11 started.

My Juliet S., Philadelphia Park, June 26, $100,000, 3&up, f&m, 6f, 1:10.62, EBONY BREEZE, She Is Raging, Balmy, 5 started.

My Lady's Manor S., Monkton, April 10, $25,000, 5&up, 3mT, 6:15, ASKIM (NZ), Joe At Six, Sam Sullivan, 12 started.

My Melanie S., Calder Race Course, Dec. 10, $40,000, 3&up, f&m, 1$^{1}/_{16}$m, 1:45.81, REDOUBLED MISS, Pampered Princess, Menifeeque, 8 started.

Mystery Jet S. (R), Suffolk Downs, July 31, $40,000, 3yo, f, Massachusetts-bred, 6f, 1:14, D D RUBY, Ask Queenie, Cindarullah, 7 started.

Naked Greed S., Calder Race Course, June 18, $40,000, 3yo, 5fT, :56.28, GIN RUMMY CHAMP, Bourbon N Blues, Misguided Left, 8 started.

Nanaimo H., Hastings Race Course, July 18, $42,951, 3yo, f, 1$^{1}/_{16}$m, 1:45.25, SOCORRO COUNTY, Gold Accent, Stole One, 7 started.

Nancy's Glitter H., Calder Race Course, July 17, $75,000, 3&up, f&m, 1$^{1}/_{16}$m, 1:47.69, SECRET REQUEST, Chase Gap, Dakota Light, 7 started.

Nandi S. (R), Woodbine, Aug. 8, $131,750, 2yo, f, progeny of eligible Ontario stallions, 6f, 1:11.77, BOSSKIRI, Coastal Fortress, Wisdomisgold, 7 started.

NASHUA S.-G3, Aqueduct, Nov. 2, $109,500, 2yo, 1m, 1:36.67, ROCKPORT HARBOR, Defer, Better Than Bonds, 6 started.

NASSAU COUNTY BREEDERS' CUP S.-G2, Belmont Park, May 8, $195,000, 3yo, f, 7f, 1:22.70, BENDING STRINGS, Grey Traffic, A Lulu Ofa Menifee, 6 started.

NASSAU S.-G3, Woodbine, June 5, $310,750, 3&up, f&m, 1$^{1}/_{16}$mT, 1:40.38, INISH GLORA, Ocean Drive, Classic Stamp, 6 started.

NATALMA S.-G3, Woodbine, Sept. 12, $177,300, 2yo, f, 1mT, 1:34.99, FEARLESS FLYER (Ire), Sweet Solairo, Little Hussy, 11 started.

NATIONAL JOCKEY CLUB H.-G3, Hawthorne Race Course, April 17, $250,000, 3&up, 1$^{1}/_{8}$m, 1:49.54, TEN MOST WANTED, Colonial Colony, New York Hero, 6 started.

NATIONAL MUSEUM OF RACING HALL OF FAME S.-G2, Saratoga Race Course, Aug. 9, $150,000, 3yo, 1$^{1}/_{8}$mT, 1:47.71, ARTIE SCHILLER, Mustanfar, Good Reward, 8 started.

Native Dancer S., Arlington Park, June 27, $41,500, 3yo, 1m, 1:36.18, AVID SKIER, Pure American, Roll Your Own, 6 started.

NATIVE DIVER H.-G3, Hollywood Park, Dec. 11, $100,000, 3&up, 1$^{1}/_{8}$m, 1:47.06, TRULY A JUDGE, Dynever, Calkins Road, 8 started.

Navajo Princess S., The Meadowlands, Oct. 1, $60,000, 3&up, f&m, 1$^{1}/_{16}$mT, 1:44.63, DELTA PRINCESS, Something Ventured, Coney Kitty (Ire), 6 started.

NEARCTIC H.-G2, Woodbine, Oct. 24, $282,750, 3&up, 6fT, 1:09.36, I THEE WED, Chris's Bad Boy, Hour of Justice, 10 started.

Nebraska Derby, Fonner Park, May 8, $25,625, 3yo, 1m, 1:38.80, OKIE STYLE, Thundering Verzy, Val Rah, 7 started.

Needles S., Calder Race Course, Aug. 28, $75,000, 3yo, 1$^{1}/_{16}$mT, 1:44.50, SOVERIGN HONOR, Cervelo, Nightmare Affair, 9 started.

Nellie Morse S., Laurel Park, Jan. 31, $50,000, 4&up, f&m, 1$^{1}/_{16}$m, 1:43.76, CITY FIRE, Sweet Dynamite, Undercover, 10 started.

Never Miss T. V. Overnight S., Yavapai Downs, Aug. 10, $10,000, 3&up, 4$^{1}/_{2}$f, :51.80, FLARIONS FLAME, Madigan, Gold Fevers Gift, 10 started.

New Braunfels S., Retama Park, Aug. 28, $40,000, 3&up, f&m, 6f, 1:10.83, ANGELICA SLEW, Wacky Patty, Antartida (Arg), 7 started.

New Jersey Futurity (R), The Meadowlands, Nov. 5, $66,067, 2yo, c&g, New Jersey-bred, 6f, 1:10.36, PUNCH THE ODDS, Who's the Cowboy, Sonawho, 5 started.

New Jersey Futurity (R), The Meadowlands, Nov. 5, $76,481, 2yo, f, New Jersey-bred, 6f, 1:09.66, I'MTOOGOODTOBETRUE, Big City Danse, Patty Girl, 6 started.

New Mexico Breeders' Association H (R), SunRay Park, Aug. 16, $67,600, 3&up, New Mexico-bred, 1m, 1:37.40, CIENTO, Local Case, Sharethetime, 7 started.

New Mexico Breeders' Derby (R), Sunland Park, March 28, $102,950, 3yo, New Mexico-bred, 1m, 1:37.91, JONNYGETACHEX, Youareaggravatin', Some Ghost, 7 started.

New Mexico Breeders' Distaff H. (R), SunRay Park, Aug. 21, $67,500, 3&up, f&m, New Mexico-bred, 6$^{1}/_{2}$f, 1:18.40, SCARZANE, Shemoveslikeaghost, Flipsider, 8 started.

New Mexico Racing Commission H. (R), Sunland Park, Nov. 13, $130,400, 3&up, f&m, New Mexico-bred, 6f, 1:09.83, SHEMOVESLIKEAGHOST, Hat Creek, Scarzane, 9 started.

New Mexico State Fair H., The Downs at Albuquerque, Sept. 26, $35,000, 3&up, 1$^{1}/_{8}$m, 1:49.30, LATENITE TRICK, Fin Entertainment, Long Range, 8 started.

New Mexico State Fair Thoroughbred Derby (R), The Downs at Albuquerque, Sept. 25, $46,773, 3yo, New Mexico-bred, 1$^{1}/_{16}$m, 1:46.17, JONNYGETACHEX, M D Twenty Twenty, Macho Miller, 7 started.

New Mexico State University S. (R), Sunland Park, Jan. 25, $131,150, 4&up, New Mexico-bred, 1m, 1:37.06, CIENTO, Hesa Bad Cat, Casperino, 8 started.

NEW ORLEANS H.-G2, Fair Grounds, Feb. 29, $500,000, 4&up, 1$^{1}/_{8}$m, 1:48.61, PEACE RULES, Saint Liam, Funny Cide, 8 started.

New Providence S. (R), Woodbine, May 15, $134,750, 3&up, progeny of eligible Ontario stallions, 6f, 1:10.19, BARBEAU RUCKUS, Choreography, Norfolk Knight, 9 started.

New Westminster H., Hastings Race Course, Aug. 22, $44,338, 2yo, 6$^{1}/_{2}$f, 1:18.78, ALABAMA RAIN, Speed Victor, C J Come Home, 7 started.

New Year's Eve S., Mountaineer Race Track, Dec. 28, $75,000, 3&up, f&m, 6f, 1:10.53, WALLOP, Glorious Again, Huntingthetruth, 8 started.

New York Breeders' Futurity (R), Finger Lakes, Sept. 6, $217,359, 2yo, New York-bred, 6f, 1:10.77, CARIBBEAN CRUISER, Big Apple Daddy, Urban Conquest, 6 started.

New York Derby (R), Finger Lakes, July 17, $164,000, 3yo, New York-bred, 1$^{1}/_{16}$m, 1:44.76, DON CORLEONE, Seven Come Eleven, Work With Me, 10 started.

NEW YORK H.-G2, Belmont Park, July 5, $250,000, 3&up, f&m, 1$^{1}/_{4}$m, 2:05.60, WONDER AGAIN, Stay Forever, Spice Island, 7 started.

New York Oaks (R), Finger Lakes, Sept. 6, $75,000, 3yo, f, New York-bred, 1$^{1}/_{16}$m, 1:45.40, SO SWEET A CAT, Mother's Sacrifice, Judy Soda, 9 started.

NEXT MOVE H.-G3, Aqueduct, March 14, $108,400, 3&up, f&m, 1$^{1}/_{8}$m, 1:51.55, SMOK'N FROLIC, Stake, U K Trick, 7 started.

NIAGARA BREEDERS' CUP H.-G2, Woodbine, Sept. 6, $324,000, 3&up, 1$^{3}/_{8}$mT, 2:25.87, STRUT THE STAGE, Colorful Judgement, Mark One, 6 started.

Niagara Falls S. (R), Fort Erie, June 27, $60,000, 3&up, starters at Fort Erie at least three times in 2003-'04, 6f, 1:11.77, LUCKY TEC, Rare Friends, Rundle, 5 started.

Niagara S. (R), Finger Lakes, July 4, $50,000, 3yo, f, New York-bred, 6f, 1:11.45, CAMP ON WOOD, So Sweet a Cat, Star Celebrity, 7 started.

Nick Shuk Memorial S., Delaware Park, June 6, $75,300, 3yo, 1$^{1}/_{16}$mT, 1:45.10, COINED FOR SUCCESS, Wanaka, Paddington, 6 started.

Nicole S., Hawthorne Race Course, May 8, $43,800, 4&up, f&m, 1$^{1}/_{16}$mT, 1:41.85, BLUE SKY BABY, Romantic Comedy, Chilling Effect, 9 started.

Nijana S. (R), Aqueduct, Feb. 11, $60,950, 3yo, f, nonwinners of an open stakes, 1$^{1}/_{16}$m, 1:47.28, EXCLUSIVELY WILD, Tempting Note, Taittinger Rose, 9 started.

NOBLE DAMSEL H.-G3, Belmont Park, Sept. 25, $150,000, 3&up, f&m, 1mT, 1:34.71, OCEAN DRIVE, High Court (Brz), Hour of Justice, 9 started.

NORFOLK S.-G2, Santa Anita Park, Oct. 3, $196,000, 2yo, 1$^{1}/_{16}$m, 1:44.27, ROMAN RULER, Boston Glory, Littlebitofzip, 4 started.

Norgor Derby, Ruidoso Downs, Aug. 14, $25,000, 3yo, 6f, 1:10.20, JO DEE WHO, Southern Twilight, Samurai Nanao, 7 started.

Norman Hall S. (R), Suffolk Downs, Nov. 27, $40,000, 2yo, Massachusetts-bred, 6f, 1:12.29, REPRIZED STRIKE, Strawberry Patch, Spectacular Orage, 11 started.

Northampton S. (R), Northampton Fair, Sept. 5, $15,000, 3&up, Massachusetts-bred, a6$^{1}/_{2}$f, 1:23.02, ABIT ERATIC, Jill's Jumpshot, Distinctly Carotic, 6 started.

Northbound Pride S., Canterbury Park, June 19, $40,000, 3yo, f, 1$^{1}/_{16}$mT, 1:41.89, GHOSTLY GATE, Southern Spring, Platinum Ballet, 8 started.

North Dakota Bred Thoroughbred Derby (R), North Dakota Horse Park, Sept. 5, $25,000, 3yo, North Dakota-bred, 1m, 1:42.60, DAKOTA DIXIE, Strike an Image, Princess Brooke, 8 started.

North Dakota Derby, Assiniboia Downs, July 4, $20,000, 3yo, 1m, 1:41, STRIKE AN IMAGE, Dakota Dixie, Mercedes High, 8 started.

North Dakota First Lady's Cup S. (R), North Dakota Horse Park, Sept. 6, $12,400, 4&up, f&m, North Dakota-bred, 7f, 1:28.60, MY STATUE, Sweetest Tour, Run Around Sue, 6 started.

North Dakota Futurity, Assiniboia Downs, Sept. 5, $25,000, 2yo, 6f, 1:15.40, NORTHRNIMPROVEMENT, Could've Been Mine, Pistol Wind, 7 started.

North Dakota Horse Park Thoroughbred Futurity (R), North Dakota Horse Park, Aug. 8, $25,000, 2yo, North Dakota-bred, 6f, 1:18.60, NORTHRNIMPROVEMENT, Peacefull Sammy, Buffalo Alice, 10 started.

North Dakota Horse Park Thoroughbred Inaugural H., North Dakota Horse Park, Aug. 7, $9,400, 3&up, 6f, 1:13.80, MADDIES BLUES, Halo's Echo, Scarlet Lad, 5 started.

North Dakota Open Thoroughbred S., North Dakota Horse Park, Sept. 6, $8,200, 4&up, 1m, 1:42.20, LITTLE ABNER, Scarlet Lad, Cielo's Honour, 4 started.

North Dakota Stallion S. (R), Assiniboia Downs, July 30, $20,000, 3yo, progeny of eligible North Dakota stallions, 1 1/16m, 1:49, STRIKE AN IMAGE, Dakota Dixie, Made in America, 7 started.

North Dakota Stallion S., Assiniboia Downs, Aug. 22, $30,000, 2yo, progeny of eligible North Dakota stallions, 6f, 1:14.40, DODDLES, Your Excellence, My Pink Panther, 8 started.

Northern Dancer S. (R), Pimlico, Nov. 27, $100,000, 3yo, Maryland-bred, 1 1/8m, 1:52.34, PLAY BINGO, Water Cannon, Hastego, 7 started.

NORTHERN DANCER S.-G3, Churchill Downs, June 12, $232,400, 3yo, 1 1/16m, 1:44.50, SUAVE, J Town, Ecclesiastic, 12 started.

Northern Lights Debutante S. (R), Canterbury Park, Aug. 22, $56,800, 2yo, f, Minnesota-bred, 6f, 1:11.82, WA WA WINDY, Saveeta, Masqued Monarch, 11 started.

Northern Lights Futurity (R), Canterbury Park, Aug. 22, $55,300, 2yo, c&g, Minnesota-bred, 6f, 1:10.77, CARELESS NAVIGATOR, Roust About, Steak House, 8 started.

Northern Spur Breeders' Cup S., Oaklawn Park, April 10, $73,750, 3yo, 1m, 1:37.37, TWO DOWN AUTOMATIC, Proper Prado, Level Playingfield, 6 started.

Northlands Oaks, Northlands Park, July 25, $40,000, 3yo, f, 1m, 1:40.80, SHY LIL, Sounce a Silence, This Crime Pays, 8 started.

North Randall S. (R), Thistledown, Aug. 7, $40,000, 3yo, Ohio-bred, 6f, 1:09.66, CAYENNE RED, Xtra Jack, Floater, 7 started.

Northwest Stallion Knights Choice S. (R), Emerald Downs, Aug. 1, $50,000, 2yo, f, progeny of eligible stallions, 6 1/2f, 1:18.40, QUEEN-LEDO, Nu Rays Arabella, T's So Shy, 7 started.

Northwest Stallion Strong Ruler S. (R), Emerald Downs, Aug. 7, $40,000, 2yo, c&g, progeny of eligible stallions, 6 1/2f, 1:18.80, IN-DIAN WEAVER, Kaptnwice, Smilodon, 7 started.

Numbered Account S. (R), Aqueduct, March 13, $60,700, 4&up, f&m, nonwinners of an open stakes, 1 1/8m, 1:52.55, OUR TUNE, Board Elligible, Hot Golden Jet, 7 started.

Nursery S., Hollywood Park, May 16, $83,850, 2yo, f, 5f, :58.06, DOU-BLE D APPEAL, Bella Banissa, Kelly's Princess, 9 started.

Oakland H., Golden Gate Fields, Dec. 11, $58,850, 3&up, 6f, 1:07.77, GREEN TEAM, Bluesthestandard, Onebadshark, 7 started.

OAKLAWN BREEDERS' CUP S.-G3, Oaklawn Park, March 13, $200,000, 3&up, f&m, 1 1/16m, 1:44.32, GOLDEN SONATA, Keys to the Heart, Mayo On the Side, 10 started.

OAKLAWN H.-G2, Oaklawn Park, April 3, $500,000, 4&up, 1 1/8m, 1:48.26, PEACE RULES, Ole Faunty, Saint Liam, 6 started.

OAK LEAF S.-G2, Santa Anita Park, Oct. 2, $200,000, 2yo, f, 1 1/16m, 1:42.98, SWEET CATOMINE, Splendid Blended, Memorette, 9 started.

Oakley S. (R), Colonial Downs, June 20, $50,000, 3yo, f, Virginia-bred and/or -sired, 1 1/16mT, 1:46.48, COBBLEY'S JEWEL, After the Tone, Vermont Mary, 8 started.

Oaks Preview H., Hastings Race Course, Sept. 5, $43,101, 3yo, f, 1 1/8m, 1:44.68, SOCORRO COUNTY, Gold Accent, Bullseye Bess, 8 started.

OAK TREE BREEDERS' CUP MILE S.-G2, Santa Anita Park, Oct. 9, $246,000, 3&up, 1mT, 1:33.29, MUSICAL CHIMES, Buckland Manor, Singletary, 6 started.

OAK TREE DERBY-G2, Santa Anita Park, Oct. 17, $150,000, 3yo, 1 1/8mT, 1:48.08, GREEK SUN, Laura's Lucky Boy, Hendrix, 9 started.

Obeah H., Delaware Park, June 19, $100,300, 3&up, f&m, 1 1/8m, 1:51.23, MISTY SIXES, Redoubled Miss, Nonsuch Bay, 6 started.

OBS Sprint S., Ocala Training Center, March 15, $50,000, 3yo, f, 6f, 1:11.20, VALID MOVE, I's a Fact, Gimme Some Love, 14 started.

Ocala Breeders' Sales Championship S. (R), Ocala Training Center, March 15, $100,000, 3yo, c&g, sold at an OBS sale, 1 1/16m, 1:44.20, HUMOROUSLY, It's Lucky, Cheetah Speed, 7 started.

Ocala Breeders' Sales Championship S. (R), Ocala Training Center, March 15, $100,000, 3yo, f&m, sold at an OBS sale, 1 1/16m, 1:45, TINGWITHASTING, Special Report, Runaway Rizzi, 10 started.

Ocala Breeders' Sales Distaff S. (R), Gulfstream Park, Jan. 24, $500,000, 4&up, f&m, California- or Florida-bred, 1 1/16m, 1:45.16, SECRET REQUEST, Smok'n Frolic, Scapade, 12 started.

Ocala Breeders' Sales Sprint S. (R), Ocala Training Center, March 15, $50,000, 3yo, c&g, sold at an OBS sale, 6f, 1:10.60, BARON-AGE, Kipper's Night, Golden Gator, 9 started.

Ocala Breeders' Sales Sprint S. (R), Ocala Training Center, March 15, $50,000, 3yo, f&m, sold at an OBS sale, 6f, 1:11.20, VALID MOVE, I's a Fact, Gimme Some Love, 14 started.

Ocean Place Resort S., Monmouth Park, Aug. 8, $100,000, 3yo, 1mT, 1:36.78, FOREST GROVE, Wasabi Cat, Grand Heritage, 10 started.

OCEANPORT H.-G3, Monmouth Park, Aug. 8, $100,000, 3&up, 1 1/16mT, 1:42.31, GULCH APPROVAL, Kathir, Stormy Roman, 10 started.

Oceanside S. (1st Div.) (R), Del Mar, July 21, $85,950, 3yo, nonwinners of a stakes of $50,000 in 2004, 1mT, 1:34.56, WILD BABE, Semi Lost, Hippocrates, 8 started.

Oceanside S. (2nd Div.) (R), Del Mar, July 21, $85,450, 3yo, nonwinners of a stakes of $50,000 in 2004, 1mT, 1:33.54, BLACKDOUN (Fr), Terroplane (Fr), Lucky Pulpit, 8 started.

Office Queen S., Calder Race Course, June 12, $100,000, 3yo, f, 1 1/16m, 1:48.75, LADYINAREDDRESS, Alarkandadove, American Miss, 6 started.

Ogataul H. (R), Fonner Park, March 13, $25,950, 3&up, Nebraska-bred, 6f, 1:11.60, DEATH TRAPPE, Doug's Shadow, Harvey Bengal, 9 started.

OGDEN PHIPPS H.-G1, Belmont Park, June 19, $285,000, 3&up, f&m, 1 1/16m, 1:41.46, SIGHTSEEK, Storm Flag Flying, Passing Shot, 4 started.

Ogygian S. (R), Belmont Park, July 9, $61,200, 3yo, non-winners of a graded stakes in 2004, 5 1/2f, 1:02.71, SMOKUME, Quick Action, War's Prospect, 6 started.

Ohio Debutante H. (R), Thistledown, Sept. 4, $40,000, 3yo, f, Ohio-bred, 6f, 1:11.04, ANNA EM, The Great Tyler, Thesmellofhoney, 7 started.

OHIO DERBY-G2, Thistledown, June 12, $350,000, 3yo, 1 1/8m, 1:49.50, BRASS HAT, Pollard's Vision, Trieste's Honor, 9 started.

Ohio Freshman S. (R), Beulah Park, Nov. 14, $40,000, 2yo, Ohio-accredited, 1m, 1:42.90, OPENING WAGER, Willen, Circulator, 7 started.

Ohio Valley H., Mountaineer Race Track, June 1, $75,000, 3&up, f&m, 6f, 1:11.78, OUR JOSEPHINA, Alicita My Love, La Femme Galante, 6 started.

Oilfield H., Marias Fair, July 25, $3,200, 3&up, 1m 70y, 1:48.60, NEIGHBORHOOD BULLY, Clever Legend, Lucky Bounty, 5 started.

Oklahoma Classics Day Classic S. (R), Remington Park, Sept. 25, $75,000, 3&up, Oklahoma-bred, 1 1/16m, 1:43.11, GEORGE TAY-LOR, Zee Oh Six, Proper Prospect, 9 started.

Oklahoma Classics Day Distaff S. (R), Remington Park, Sept. 25, $40,000, 3&up, f&m, Oklahoma-bred, 1m 70y, 1:42.66, RACING SUNDOWN, Ms Bessie, Randi Brandy, 8 started.

Oklahoma Classics Day Filly and Mare Turf S. (R), Remington Park, Sept. 25, $40,000, 3&up, f&m, Oklahoma-bred, 7 1/2fT, 1:30.28, WEE OKIE, Tamara's Babe, Motel Gossip, 10 started.

Oklahoma Classics Day Juvenile S. (R), Remington Park, Sept. 25, $40,000, 2yo, Oklahoma-bred, 6f, 1:11.44, SOONER PRIDE, Yabba Dabba You, Regal Okie, 9 started.

Oklahoma Classics Day Lassie S. (R), Remington Park, Sept. 25, $40,000, 2yo, f, Oklahoma-bred, 6f, 1:11.38, D FINE OKIE, Shiloah, Tickin' Okie, 10 started.

Oklahoma Classics Day Sprint S. (R), Remington Park, Sept. 25, $40,000, 3&up, Oklahoma-bred, 6f, 1:09.26, CHEYENNE BREEZE, Medium Rare, Shiloh Billy, 6 started.

Oklahoma Classics Day Turf S. (R), Remington Park, Sept. 25, $40,000, 3&up, Oklahoma-bred, 1mT, 1:35.66, DANCE AND DAZZLE, April's Lucky Boy, Red Hawkeye, 10 started.

OKLAHOMA DERBY-G3, Remington Park, Nov. 21, $167,250, 3yo, 1¹/₈m, 1:50.26, WALLY'S CHOICE, Golden Glen, Cryptograph, 11 started.

Old Hat S., Gulfstream Park, Feb. 14, $100,000, 3yo, f, 6f, 1:08.85, MADCAP ESCAPADE, Sweet Vision, Smokey Glacken, 9 started.

Old Ironsides S., Suffolk Downs, June 19, $40,000, 3&up, a1m 70yT, 1:42.75, GRAN CESARE (Arg), Milky Way Guy, Jini's Jet, 10 started.

Old Line Policy S., Turf Paradise, Feb. 13, $21,800, 3yo, 6f, 1:09.73, KING JUSTIN, Ozoned, Gato Bob, 7 started.

Old South H., Louisiana Downs, June 19, $50,000, 3&up, f&m, a1¹/₁₆mT, 1:47.15, MEXICAN MOONLIGHT, Due to Win Again, Blue Guru, 8 started.

Old Timers S., Grand Prairie, Aug. 15, $4,405, 9&up, 7f, 1:26.80, ARAN ISLAND, Pick the Best, Crown Butte, 6 started.

Oliver S., Indiana Downs, June 20, $44,750, 3yo, f, 1mT, 1:36.63, RICH FIND, America America, Papa Sids Girl, 9 started.

Omaha S., Horsemen's Park, July 18, $100,000, 3&up, 1m, 1:38.60, STORMY IMPACT, Kodema, Magic Doe, 10 started.

Omnibus S., Monmouth Park, Aug. 28, $60,000, 3&up, f&m, 1¹/₁₆mT, 1:43.23, CONEY KITTY (Ire), With Patience, Constant Touch, 11 started.

Ontario Colleen H., Woodbine, Sept. 4, $143,250, 3yo, f, 1mT, 1:33.40, EMERALD EARRINGS, Faswiga, Jinny's Gold, 11 started.

Ontario County S. (R), Finger Lakes, June 20, $50,000, 3yo, New York-bred, 6f, 1:12.18, HOUSE KEY, H. M. S. Majestic, Fiddlers Pride, 9 started.

Ontario Damsel S. (R), Woodbine, July 10, $161,400, 3yo, f, Canadian-bred, 6¹/₂fT, 1:16.40, VELVET SNOW, Financingavailable, Moment of Peace, 5 started.

Ontario Debutante S., Woodbine, Aug. 22, $175,750, 2yo, f, 6f, 1:11.81, SOUTH BAY COVE, Active Bases, Wise Tommy, 8 started.

Ontario Derby, Woodbine, Oct. 10, $160,050, 3yo, 1¹/₈m, 1:53.18, A BIT O'GOLD, Organ Grinder, Alleged Ruler, 5 started.

Ontario Fashion H., Woodbine, Nov. 6, $137,750, 3&up, f&m, 6f, 1:10.35, WINTER GARDEN, El Prado Essence, Big Cheque, 8 started.

Ontario Jockey Club S. (R), Woodbine, July 24, $107,000, 3&up, Canadian-bred, 7fT, 1:19.38, SOARING FREE, Super Case, Awesome Action, 6 started.

Ontario Lassie S. (R), Woodbine, Dec. 5, $163,350, 2yo, f, Canadian-foaled, 1¹/₁₆m, 1:47.46, SILVER IMPULSE, Simply Again, Good as Gold, 6 started.

Ontario Matron H., Woodbine, June 20, $131,250, 3&up, f&m, 1¹/₁₆m, 1:44.22, ONE FOR ROSE, Winning Chance, Handpainted, 4 started.

On Trust H. (R), Hollywood Park, Nov. 13, $89,200, 3&up, California-bred, 7¹/₂f, 1:27.30, ANZIYAN ROYALTY, Lava Man, Jack's Silver, 8 started.

Opening Verse H., Churchill Downs, June 12, $110,900, 3&up, 1¹/₁₆mT, 1:45.82, SENOR SWINGER, Hard Buck (Brz), Majestic Thief, 7 started.

Open Mind H. (R), Monmouth Park, June 5, $60,000, 3&up, f&m, New Jersey-bred, 6f, 1:09.99, WHOOP'S AH DAISY, Eastern Gale, Primary Colors, 10 started.

Open Mind S., Churchill Downs, May 15, $112,300, 3yo, f, 5fT, :57.22, ANNA EM, Movant, Victoire Bataille, 9 started.

Open S., Lethbridge, June 19, $11,200, 3&up, 7f, 1:24.40, FRUIT RAPPORT, Lovers Son, dh-Prineville, dh-Chief Joseph, 8 started.

ORCHID H.-G2, Gulfstream Park, March 21, $200,000, 3&up, f&m, 1¹/₂mT, 2:26.99, MERIDIANA (Ger), Savedbythelight, Miss Hellie, 10 started.

Oregon Derby, Portland Meadows, April 3, $20,000, 3yo, 1¹/₈m, 1:57.43, SANTIAM TOP JAZZ, Mothers Day Bandit, Might E Man, 9 started.

Oregon HBPA Invitational H., Portland Meadows, Nov. 13, $7,000, 3&up, f&m, 6f, 1:12.34, QUIZ THE MAID, Valentine Surprise, Breakin My Heart, 8 started.

Oregon Hers S. (R), Portland Meadows, Dec. 11, $10,000, 3yo, f, Oregon-bred, 1m, 1:39.69, AMERICAS PRIDE, Kya Jo, Run Irene Run, 7 started.

Oregon His S. (R), Portland Meadows, Dec. 11, $10,000, 3yo, c&g, Oregon-bred, 1¹/₁₆m, 1:47.19, MIGHT E MAN, Treasure Booty, Ack of Congress, 9 started.

Oregon Oaks, Portland Meadows, April 17, $10,000, 3yo, f, 1¹/₁₆m, 1:49.86, KYA JO, Quiz the Maid, So Happy Together, 6 started.

Orinda H., Golden Gate Fields, Jan. 24, $62,600, 4&up, f&m, 6f, 1:08.59, EMA BOVARY (Chi), Christmas Time, Pheiffer, 7 started.

Orphan Kist H. (R), Fonner Park, March 6, $25,900, 3&up, f&m, Nebraska-bred, 6f, 1:14.40, FLAMING NIGHT, Cassa's Affair, Magic Trump, 9 started.

Osunitas H. (R), Del Mar, Aug. 11, $82,850, 3&up, f&m, nonwinners of a stakes of $50,000 at one mile or over in 2004, 1¹/₁₆mT, 1:41.15, VOZ DE COLEGIALA (Chi), Makeup Artist, Shalini, 8 started.

OS West Oregon Futurity (R), Portland Meadows, Dec. 11, $43,880, 2yo, Oregon-bred, 1m, 1:41.83, WICE O KAT, A Colt Named Sue, Abtastic, 8 started.

OTBA Sales S. (R), Portland Meadows, Oct. 30, $7,450, 2yo, passed through the OTBA sales ring, 6f, 1:12.87, EIGHTY EIGHTY, Cascadiansasquatch, Gold Relaunch, 7 started.

OTBA Stallion S. (R), Portland Meadows, June 3, $9,750, 3yo, progeny of eligible Oregon stallions, 6f, 1:13.34, KYA JO, Reignsofire, Treasure Booty, 4 started.

Our Dear Peggy S. (R), Calder Race Course, Dec. 28, $40,000, 3yo, f, nonwinners of a stakes worth $25,000 or more to the winner, 6¹/₂f, 1:17.70, GIVEMEMORE (Brz), Miracle Runner, Forestier, 6 started.

OVERBROOK SPINSTER S.-G1, Keeneland, Oct. 10, $500,000, 3&up, f&m, 1¹/₈m, 1:49.74, AZERI, Tamweel, Mayo On the Side, 7 started.

Overskate S. (R), Woodbine, July 21, $133,000, 3&up, progeny of eligible Ontario stallions, 7f, 1:23.06, BARATH, Choreography, Barbeau Ruckus, 8 started.

Ozark Hills H., Blue Ribbon Downs, March 14, $9,000, 3&up, 4f, :46.13, AS DE ORO, Doctor Free, Oklahoma Homer, 7 started.

Pacifica H., Bay Meadows, Oct. 31, $69,475, 3&up, 1¹/₁₆mT, 1:44.35, NINEBANKS, Motel Staff, Gold Ruckus, 9 started.

PACIFIC CLASSIC S.-G1, Del Mar, Aug. 22, $1,000,000, 3&up, 1¹/₄m, 2:01.17, PLEASANTLY PERFECT, Perfect Drift, Total Impact (Chi), 8 started.

Padua Stables Sophomore S., Tampa Bay Downs, April 4, $83,300, 3yo, 7f, 1:24.45, WEIGELIA, And Skier, Spirit of Montreal, 10 started.

Pago Hop S., Fair Grounds, Dec. 18, $60,000, 3yo, f, a1mT, 1:37.83, SHADOW CAST, Code of Ethics, Sister Swank, 14 started.

PALM BEACH S.-G3, Gulfstream Park, Feb. 21, $100,000, 3yo, 1¹/₈mT, 1:48.76, KITTEN'S JOY, Prince Arch, Pa Pa Da, 12 started.

Palo Alto H., Bay Meadows, Oct. 9, $58,325, 3yo, f, 1¹/₁₆mT, 1:43.33, MIDWIFE, Secret Corsage, Go Ask Daisy, 9 started.

PALOMAR BREEDERS' CUP H.-G2, Del Mar, Sept. 4, $180,000, 3&up, f&m, 1¹/₁₆mT, 1:40.59, ETOILE MONTANTE, Katdogawn (GB), Tangle (Ire), 7 started.

PALOS VERDES H.-G2, Santa Anita Park, Feb. 1, $150,000, 4&up, 6f, 1:08.13, BLUESTHESTANDARD, Marino Marini, Our New Recruit, 7 started.

Palo Verde H., Turf Paradise, Feb. 28, $40,000, 3yo, 6¹/₂f, 1:15.39, BOLD MERIT, Bradford, King Justin, 6 started.

PAN AMERICAN H.-G2, Gulfstream Park, March 20, $200,000, 3&up, 1¹/₂mT, 2:26.46, QUEST STAR, Request for Parole, Megantic, 7 started.

Panhandle H., Mountaineer Race Track, May 1, $75,000, 3&up, 5f, :58.54, RUN ZEAL RUN, Crossing Point, Ex Who, 7 started.

Panthers S., Prairie Meadows, June 5, $50,000, 3yo, f, 1m, 1:36.01, JOSH'S MADELYN, Platinum Ballet, Defuhr, 7 started.

Pan Zareta S., Fair Grounds, Feb. 7, $60,000, 4&up, f&m, 6f, 1:10.23, HANDPAINTED, Tina Bull, Raymond's Dream, 6 started.

Pappa Riccio S. (R), Monmouth Park, Aug. 29, $75,000, 3yo, New Jersey-bred, 1m, 1:37.14, WAR'S PROSPECT, Professor Biggs, Carrots Only, 7 started.

Paradise Creek S., Arlington Park, Sept. 11, $44,375, 3yo, 1¹/₁₆mT, 1:42.62, EXPLOITED STORM, Knox, Gwaihir (Ire), 9 started.

Paradise Mile H., Turf Paradise, Jan. 3, $50,000, 4&up, 1mT, 1:36.75, R. BAGGIO, Expresso Bay, Our Best Man, 8 started.

Paradise Valley H., Turf Paradise, Nov. 20, $40,000, 3yo, 7¹/₂fT, 1:29.12, COCOA LATTE, Azara, Pure, 10 started.

Park Avenue S. (R), Aqueduct, April 25, $150,000, 3yo, f, progeny of eligible New York stallions, 1m, 1:39.93, IHAVEADATE, Judy Soda, Priscilla's Flag, 6 started.

Parkland Heritage S. (R), Marquis Downs, Aug. 21, $10,000, 3yo, f, Saskatchewan-bred, 1¹/₁₆m, 1:47.35, MEGAN'S WAY, Allourwishes, Rock n' Romance, 7 started.

Parnitha S. (R), Fort Erie, July 25, $52,000, 3&up, starters at Fort Erie at least three times in 2004, 5fT, 58.12, MAJOR ZEE, Baltic Prince, Reverse Psychology, 7 started.

Pasadena S., Santa Anita Park, March 17, $77,850, 3yo, 1mT, 1:34.88, UNRIVALLED (GB), Erewhon, Four Song Limit, 11 started.

Pasco S., Tampa Bay Downs, Jan. 17, $60,000, 3yo, 7f, 1:25.94, MIS-GUIDED LEFT, Wire Bound, Bourbon N Blues, 9 started.

Paseana H., Santa Anita Park, Jan. 16, $76,050, 4&up, f&m, 1^1/$_{16}$m, 1:42.58, REAL NECESSITIES, Angel Gift, La Tour (Chi), 5 started.

Passing Mood S. (R), Woodbine, July 28, $131,500, 3yo, f, progeny of eligible stallions, 7fT, 1:22.78, BLONDE EXECUTIVE, Flashy Anna, Lovely Lola, 7 started.

Patchy Groundfog S., Turf Paradise, Nov. 22, $21,900, 3&up, 1m, 1:38.63, REAL CREEK, Cut of Music, Expressionator, 7 started.

Paterson S. (1st Div.), The Meadowlands, Oct. 8, $60,000, 3yo, 1^1/$_{16}$mT, 1:42.34, FOREST GROVE, Commendation, Gunning For, 8 started.

Paterson S. (2nd Div.), The Meadowlands, Oct. 8, $60,000, 3yo, 1^1/$_{16}$mT, 1:43.12, GRAND HERITAGE, Honorable Buck, Dont Knock America, 9 started.

PAT O'BRIEN BREEDERS' CUP H.-G2, Del Mar, Aug. 15, $194,000, 3&up, 7f, 1:21.17, KELA, Domestic Dispute, Pico Central (Brz), 5 started.

Patrick Wood S. (R), Great Lakes Downs, Sept. 21, $50,000, 2yo, c&g, Michigan-bred, 6f, 1:16.25, HONORABLE CLASS, Ernie Cat, Demagoguery, 9 started.

Pat Whitworth Illinois Debutante S. (R), Hawthorne Race Course, Dec. 11, $116,175, 2yo, f, Illinois-conceived and/or -foaled, 1^1/$_{16}$m, 1:45.92, MEADOW BRIDE, You Heard Me Cart, Capistrano, 12 started.

Paul Cacci Eel River Sprint S. (R), Ferndale, Aug. 15, $6,270, 3&up, starters for a claiming price of $12,500 or less in 2004, 5f, :58.29, RED SEATTLE, Truly a Runner, Pedaltothemetal, 6 started.

Paumonok H., Aqueduct, Jan. 24, $83,025, 3&up, 6f, 1:10.44, PEEP-ING TOM, Don Six, Super Fuse, 9 started.

Peach of It H. (R), Hawthorne Race Course, April 10, $86,250, 3&up, f&m, Illinois-conceived and/or -foaled, 1^1/$_{16}$m, 1:45.76, JULIE'S PRIZE, Rathleen, Invader, 7 started.

Peapack Hurdle S., Far Hills, Oct. 23, $50,000, 3&up, f&m, 2^1/$_8$mT, 4:07, GOLD MITTEN, Feeling So Pretty, Classic Gale, 7 started.

Pearl Necklace S. (R), Pimlico, May 31, $75,000, 3yo, f, Maryland-bred, 1^1/$_{16}$mT, 1:44.15, HE LOVES ME, Hi Five Raven, Pour It On, 8 started.

PEBBLES H.-G3, Belmont Park, Oct. 11, $112,300, 3yo, f, 1^1/$_8$m, 1:48.80, FORTUNATE DAMSEL, Venturi (GB), Delta Sensation, 8 started.

PEGASUS S.-G3, The Meadowlands, Oct. 1, $300,000, 3yo, 1^1/$_8$m, 1:48.57, PIES PROSPECT, Eddington, Zakocity, 8 started.

Pelleteri Breeders' Cup H., Fair Grounds, March 14, $125,000, 4&up, 6f, 1:08.83, CAT GENIUS, Mountain General, Aloha Bold, 7 started.

PENNSYLVANIA DERBY-G2, Philadelphia Park, Sept. 6, $750,000, 3yo, 1^1/$_8$m, 1:48.42, LOVE OF MONEY, Pollard's Vision, Swing-forthefences, 12 started.

Pennsylvania Governor's Cup H., Penn National Race Course, July 31, $50,000, 3&up, 5fT, :57.82, RUDIRUDY, Hawkwatch, La Maquina, 9 started.

Pennsylvania Nursery S. (R), Philadelphia Park, Nov. 20, $55,100, 2yo, c&g, Pennsylvania-bred, 7f, 1:23.42, UNITED, Bigboybdancing, No Passing Zone, 10 started.

Pennsylvania Oaks, Philadelphia Park, Sept. 6, $100,000, 3yo, f, 1m 70y, 1:41.35, dh-REFOREST, dh-TAITTINGER ROSE, Grinch, 7 started.

Penny Ridge S., Stampede Park, June 20, $39,200, 3yo, f, 1^1/$_{16}$m, 1:48.20, CYPRIATA, Classa Red Wine, Waikoloa, 4 started.

Pent Up Kiss H., Churchill Downs, Nov. 13, $67,600, 3&up, f&m, 5fT, :58.02, MOCHA QUEEN, Black Escort, Dyna Da Wyna, 11 started.

Pepper Oaks Farm S., Hollywood Park, April 24, $60,000, 3&up, 6^1/$_2$f, 1:15.52, BRAND NAME, Irish Ty, Perfect Mode, 14 started.

Peppy Addy S. (R), Philadelphia Park, June 19, $53,250, 3yo, Pennsylvania-bred, 7f, 1:25.20, PRINCE JOSEPH, Hey Rube, De Magic Moment, 9 started.

Pepsi-Cola H., Emerald Downs, May 31, $40,000, 3yo, c&g, 6^1/$_2$f, 1:13.80, NORTHWEST ATTITUDE, Pool Boy, Spanish Highway, 9 started.

Pepsi-Cola H. (R), Sunland Park, Jan. 17, $128,600, 3yo, New Mexico-bred, 6f, 1:09.16, ROCKY GULCH, Youareaggravatin', Jonnygetachex, 6 started.

Pepsi S., Fonner Park, April 3, $15,900, 3yo, f, 6f, 1:13.60, COME ON PRECIOUS, Second Tam Around, Shawklit Premiere, 7 started.

Perfect Arc S. (R), Aqueduct, Nov. 7, $100,000, 3&up, f&m, progeny of eligible New York stallions, 1mT, 1:37.04, KEVIN'S DECISION, Expect Nothing, South Wing, 10 started.

Perryville S., Keeneland, Oct. 14, $112,600, 3yo, a7f, 1:25.19, COM-MENTATOR, Eurosilver, Weigelia, 7 started.

PERSONAL ENSIGN H.-G1, Saratoga Race Course, Aug. 27, $392,000, 3&up, f&m, 1^1/$_4$m, 2:03.63, STORM FLAG FLYING, Azeri, Nevermore, 5 started.

Pete Axthelm S., Calder Race Course, Dec. 11, $100,000, 3yo, 7^1/$_2$f, 1:27.90, WIRE BOUND, Caballero Negro, More Bourb, 12 started.

Pete Condellone H. (R), Fairmount Park, Aug. 24, $35,900, 3&up, c&g, Illinois-bred, 1m, 1:38.60, ROAD TOWN, Moe B Dick, Medlin Road, 9 started.

PETER PAN S.-G2, Belmont Park, May 22, $200,000, 3yo, 1^1/$_8$m, 1:47.98, PURGE, Swingforthefences, Master David, 10 started.

P. G. Johnson S. (1st Div.), The Meadowlands, Oct. 23, $55,000, 3yo, f, 5fT, :56.58, MS. TRICK OR TREAT, Very Vegas, Datttsdawayilikeit, 9 started.

P. G. Johnson S. (2nd Div.), The Meadowlands, Oct. 23, $55,000, 3yo, f, 5fT, :56.63, AMBITION UNBRIDLED, Sheer Numbers, Humor Me Molly, 7 started.

Phil D. Shepherd S., Fairplex Park, Sept. 11, $58,800, 3&up, 1^1/$_{16}$m, 1:42.48, VERKADE, Anziyan Royalty, Sigfreto, 7 started.

PHILIP H. ISELIN BREEDERS' CUP H.-G3, Monmouth Park, Aug. 21, $194,000, 3&up, 1^1/$_{16}$m, 1:47.66, GHOSTZAPPER, Presidentialaffair, Zoffinger, 4 started.

PHOENIX BREEDERS' CUP S.-G3, Keeneland, Oct. 8, $271,250, 3&up, 6f, 1:08.72, CHAMPALI, Gold Storm, Clock Stopper, 11 started.

Phoenix Gold Cup H., Turf Paradise, March 13, $100,000, 3&up, 6f, 1:08.48, IRON HALO (Arg), R. Baggio, Taiaslew, 7 started.

Piedra Foundation H. (R), Del Mar, Sept. 2, $76,000, 3&up, f&m, nonwinners of a stakes of $50,000 at one mile or over since February 1, 1m, 1:35.78, ELLOLUV, Letra de Cambio (Brz), Saintly Persuasion, 7 started.

Pilgrim S., Belmont Park, Oct. 24, $82,875, 2yo, 1^1/$_8$m, 1:50.31, CROWN POINT, Wallstreet Scandal, Drum Major, 8 started.

PIMLICO BREEDERS' CUP DISTAFF H.-G3, Pimlico, May 14, $150,000, 3&up, f&m, 1^1/$_{16}$m, 1:45.03, FRIEL'S FOR REAL, Saintly Action, Nonsuch Bay, 8 started.

PIMLICO SPECIAL H.-G1, Pimlico, May 14, $500,000, 4&up, 1^3/$_{16}$m, 1:55.89, SOUTHERN IMAGE, Midway Road, Bowman's Band, 6 started.

Pinjara S. (R), Santa Anita Park, Oct. 29, $80,250, 2yo, nonwinners of a stakes at one mile or over, 1mT, 1:36.24, VEILED SPEED, Lucky Bid, Littlebitofzip, 7 started.

Pin Oak Stud USA S., Lone Star Park, May 31, $200,000, 3yo, 1^1/$_{16}$mT, 1:44.40, NO PLACE LIKE IT, Silent Picture, Rollicking Caller, 9 started.

Pinon H. (R), The Downs at Albuquerque, April 18, $43,000, 3&up, f&m, New Mexico-bred, 6^1/$_2$f, 1:15.58, SHEMOVESLIKEAGHOST, Jackie Jan, Lord Imajones, 8 started.

Pioneer S., Louisiana Downs, July 10, $50,000, 2yo, 5^1/$_2$f, 1:05.01, CRAWFISH KING, Secret Tunnel, Reno Bob, 8 started.

Pio Pico S. (R), Fairplex Park, Sept. 17, $54,600, 3&up, f&m, California-bred, 6^1/$_2$f, 1:16.07, MARKET GARDEN, Bold Roberta, Icantgoforthat, 4 started.

Pippin S., Oaklawn Park, Feb. 14, $50,000, 4&up, f&m, 1^1/$_{16}$m, 1:47.20, DREXEL MONORAIL, There Runs Hattie, Due to Win, 6 started.

Pirate's Bounty H. (R), Del Mar, Sept. 6, $76,325, 3&up, nonwinners of a stakes of $50,000 since April 1, 6f, 1:08.25, OUR NEW RE-CRUIT, Bluesthestandard, Newark, 8 started.

Pistol Packer H. (R), Philadelphia Park, Aug. 7, $54,600, 3&up, f&m, Pennsylvania-bred, 1^1/$_{16}$m, 1:45.86, CAUGHT IN THE RAIN, Golddigger Beware, Mint to Kiss, 9 started.

Plate Trial S. (R), Woodbine, June 6, $166,500, 3yo, Canadian-bred, 1^1/$_8$m, 1:51.74, A BIT O'GOLD, Niigon, Little Bentley, 8 started.

PLAY THE KING H.-G3, Woodbine, Aug. 28, $173,400, 3&up, 7fT, 1:20.97, SOARING FREE, Frank's Selection, Dancin Joey, 12 started.

Pleasant Temper S., Kentucky Downs, Sept. 18, $40,000, 3&up, f&m, 1mT, 1:40.49, BEAU WATCH, Honorable Cat, Spring Season, 11 started.

Plymouth S. (R), Great Lakes Downs, July 2, $40,000, 3yo, f, Michigan-bred, 7f, 1:27.72, GOLD GINNY, Cats Copy, Lunes Grito, 8 started.

Pocahontas S., Churchill Downs, Nov. 6, $109,500, 2yo, f, 1m, 1:37.77, PUNCH APPEAL, Holy Trinity, Kota, 7 started.

Pocahontas S., Calder Race Course, Nov. 25, $40,000, 3&up, f&m, 6¹/₂f, 1:17.51, D'WILDCAT SPEED, Kuanyan, Crafty Brat, 8 started.

POKER H.-G3, Belmont Park, July 10, $112,600, 3&up, 1mT, 1:32.46, CHRISTINE'S OUTLAW, Millennium Dragon (GB), Silver Tree, 9 started.

Politely S., Monmouth Park, June 20, $60,000, 3&up, f&m, 1¹/₁₆mT, 1:40.65, SNOWDROPS (GB), Noisette, Lojo, 9 started.

Politely S. (R), Pimlico, Nov. 13, $75,000, 3yo, f, Maryland-bred, 6f, 1:11.96, TWO PUNCH GAL, Sea of Promises, Free Dip, 5 started.

Pollys Jet S., Delaware Park, Aug. 7, $53,500, 3yo, f, 6f, 1:10.64, BALDOMERA, Gilded Gold, Spirited Game, 6 started.

Pomona Derby, Fairplex Park, Sept. 25, $99,000, 3yo, a1¹/₁₆m, 1:48.95, SEMI LOST, Cozy Guy, Lava Man, 8 started.

Ponche H., Calder Race Course, May 29, $75,000, 3&up, 6f, 1:11.10, BUILT UP, Weigelia, Bernard's Candy, 5 started.

Pony Express S. (R), The Downs at Albuquerque, June 12, $45,000, 3&up, New Mexico-bred, 5¹/₂f, 1:02.73, NINETY NINE JACK, B. G. Tiger, J J Mystique, 8 started.

Portland Meadows Invitational H., Portland Meadows, Nov. 6, $6,000, 3&up, 6f, 1:11.80, STAR OF REHAAN, Zip the Bright, My Friend Dave, 6 started.

Portland Meadows Mile H., Portland Meadows, April 10, $40,000, 3&up, 1m, 1:38.89, LETHAL GRANDE, Poker Brad, Court's in Session, 7 started.

Possibly Perfect S., Arlington Park, July 5, $41,875, 3&up, f&m, a1¹/₁₆mT, 1:55.79, BEDANKEN, Cat's Cat, Delicatessa, 6 started.

Potomac S. (R), Charles Town Races, April 10, $41,250, 3&up, West Virginia-bred, 7f, 1:27.79, EARTH POWER, Longfield Spud, Coolmars, 8 started.

POTRERO GRANDE BREEDERS' CUP H.-G2, Santa Anita Park, March 28, $122,488, 4&up, 6¹/₂f, 1:15.60, MCCANN'S MOJAVE, Unfurl the Flag, Bluesthestandard, 5 started.

Powerless H. (R), Hawthorne Race Course, Nov. 13, $101,700, 3&up, f&m, Illinois-conceived and/or -foaled, 6f, 1:11.19, SYNCO PEACH, Jaguar City, Fighting Fever, 7 started.

Prairie Bayou S., Turfway Park, Dec. 18, $50,000, 3&up, 1¹/₈m, 1:47.52, DISCREET HERO, Doc D, Mr. Krisley, 7 started.

Prairie Express S., Prairie Meadows, May 1, $50,000, 3&up, 5¹/₂f, 1:03.65, PIE'S LIL BROTHER, Coach Jimi Lee, Sand Ridge, 8 started.

Prairie Gold Juvenile S., Prairie Meadows, July 1, $50,750, 2yo, 5f, :52.10, DEPARTING NOW, Bigeyelittleyou, Foxie's Boy, 8 started.

Prairie Gold Lassie S., Prairie Meadows, July 1, $51,500, 2yo, f, 5f, :57.02, PANORAMA VALLEY, Midnight Miss, Camela Carson, 7 started.

Prairie Lily Sales S. (R), Marquis Downs, Sept. 4, $22,500, 2yo, sold at a CTHS sale, 7f, 1:28.35, BLEU ROYALE, Rumbeau Ruckus, North Park, 10 started.

PRAIRIE MEADOWS CORNHUSKER BREEDERS' CUP H.-G3, Prairie Meadows, July 3, $300,000, 3&up, 1¹/₈m, 1:46.63, ROSES IN MAY, Perfect Drift, Crafty Shaw, 6 started.

Prairie Meadows Debutante S., Prairie Meadows, Sept. 4, $40,000, 2yo, f, 6f, 1:11.48, MY THREE SISTERS, Galactic Cat, Fast Baby, 8 started.

Prairie Meadows Derby, Prairie Meadows, Sept. 25, $76,125, 3yo, 1¹/₁₆m, 1:43.78, GAMBLIN, Knox, Thermostat, 6 started.

Prairie Meadows Freshman S., Prairie Meadows, Sept. 6, $41,200, 2yo, 6f, 1:11.29, CITY CODE, Raving Rocket, Five Rubies, 7 started.

Prairie Meadows H., Prairie Meadows, July 31, $77,250, 3&up, 1¹/₈m, 1:49.60, TRICKY MOCHA, Patton's Victory, Rubianos Image, 7 started.

Prairie Meadows Oaks, Prairie Meadows, Sept. 18, $77,250, 3yo, f, 1¹/₁₆m, 1:44.43, MISS MOSES, My Time Now, Platinum Ballet, 7 started.

Prairie Meadows Sprint S., Prairie Meadows, Aug. 7, $50,000, 3&up, 6f, 1:09.70, SHANDY, Honor Me, Chindi, 9 started.

Prairie Mile S., Prairie Meadows, May 31, $50,000, 3yo, 1m, 1:36.77, PROPER PRADO, It's Lucky, Ruba Dub Dub, 6 started.

Prairie Rose S., Prairie Meadows, April 24, $50,875, 3&up, f&m, 6f, 1:10.22, SURF N SAND, Caviar Emptor, Captain's Daughter, 7 started.

Prank Call S., Calder Race Course, May 31, $40,000, 3yo, 5fT, :56.65, BOURBON N BLUES, Sami's Majic, Silver Rapt, 9 started.

PREAKNESS S.-G1, Pimlico, May 15, $1,000,000, 3yo, 1³/₁₆m, 1:55.59, SMARTY JONES, Rock Hard Ten, Eddington, 10 started.

Precious Feather S., Calder Race Course, Aug. 6, $40,000, 3&up, f&m, 1¹/₁₆m, 1:46.63, PAMPERED PRINCESS, Dakota Light, Firm Reality, 6 started.

Prelude S., Louisiana Downs, Aug. 28, $60,000, 3yo, 1¹/₁₆m, 1:43.98, SOUTH AFRICA, Fantasticat, Britt's Jules, 10 started.

Premiere S. (R), Lone Star Park, April 15, $50,000, 3&up, Texas-bred, 1m, 1:37.81, AGRIVATING GENERAL, Desert Darby, Lights On Broadway, 10 started.

PREMIER'S H.-G3, Hastings Race Course, Oct. 17, $128,590, 3&up, 1³/₁₆m, 2:19.64, BLOWIN IN THE WIND, Illusive Force, Royal Place, 10 started.

President's H., Stampede Park, May 15, $40,000, 3yo, c&g, 6f, 1:13.20, SAW GRASS SABRE, Ol Fifty, Dupes Delight, 6 started.

Preview S., Portland Meadows, March 13, $10,000, 3yo, 1¹/₁₆m, 1:48.69, MIGHT E MAN, Santiam Top Jazz, Mythical Road, 12 started.

Prime Rewards S., Delta Downs, Jan. 23, $38,800, 4&up, f&m, 5f, :58.71, RAYMOND'S DREAM, Fuse It, Lauren Lynn, 4 started.

Prime Rewards S. (R), Delta Downs, Dec. 31, $40,000, 3&up, f&m, nonwinners of a stakes race, 1m, 1:40.71, MISS CONFUSION, Mini Brush, Ballroom Deputy, 8 started.

Primonetta S., Pimlico, April 3, $50,000, 3&up, f&m, 6f, 1:11.02, UMPATEEDLE, Balmy, Bronze Abe, 6 started.

Prince of Wales S. (R), Fort Erie, July 18, $500,000, 3yo, Canadian-bred, 1³/₁₆m, 1:57.69, A BIT O'GOLD, Niigon, His Smoothness, 7 started.

Princess Elaine S. (R), Canterbury Park, July 4, $40,000, 3yo, f, Minnesota-bred, 1¹/₁₆m, 1:47.77, PANDORASCONNECTION, More Hot Gossip, Desert Star, 8 started.

Princess Elizabeth S. (R), Woodbine, Oct. 23, $250,000, 2yo, f, Canadian-foaled, 1¹/₁₆m, 1:48.44, VICTORIOUS AMI, Smartest Thing, Dancehall Deelites, 10 started.

Princess H., Sunland Park, Nov. 6, $52,550, 2yo, f, 6f, 1:09.71, CORONADO ROSE, Time to Divorce, Star of Gold Fever, 6 started.

Princess Margaret S., Northlands Park, Aug. 1, $40,000, 2yo, f, 6f, 1:12, MISS VENTUROUS, Speedy Gone Sally, Nessarose, 7 started.

Princess Mora S., Calder Race Course, Nov. 20, $40,000, 3&up, f&m, 1¹/₈mT, 1:48.27, HONEY RYDER, Path of Thunder, Spring Season, 11 started.

Princess of Palms H. (R), Turf Paradise, Jan. 31, $40,000, 4&up, f&m, starters at the 2003-'04 Turf Paradise meet, 6f, 1:08.48, ALMOST FOOLED, Miss Pixie, Friendofthefamily, 7 started.

PRINCESS ROONEY H.-G2, Calder Race Course, July 10, $500,000, 3&up, f&m, 6f, 1:10.81, EMA BOVARY (Chi), Bear Fan, Lady Tak, 6 started.

Princess S., Lincoln State Fair, May 15, $10,200, 3yo, f, 6f, 1:12.60, KEROSENE PROSPECT, dh-Peek N Tell, dh-Shesaidsheknowsya, 8 started.

Princeton S., The Meadowlands, Nov. 12, $60,000, 3yo, 1¹/₁₆m, 1:44.32, TAP DAY, Separato, Sonny and Rose, 8 started.

PRIORESS S.-G1, Belmont Park, July 3, $250,000, 3yo, f, 6f, 1:09.09, FRIENDLY MICHELLE, Feline Story, Forest Music, 9 started.

Private Terms S., Laurel Park, March 27, $60,000, 3yo, 1¹/₁₆m, 1:45.42, WATER CANNON, Acclimate, Major Tanner, 6 started.

Pro Or Con H. (R), Santa Anita Park, Feb. 15, $108,000, 4&up, f&m, California-bred, 1mT, 1:35.35, SUPER HIGH, Moscow Burning, Calzada Kid, 7 started.

Prospector's Gamble H., Arapahoe Park, Aug. 29, $27,075, 3&up, 1¹/₁₆m, 1:50.80, PERSONAL BEAU, Run At Night, Cut of Music, 7 started.

Proud Puppy H., Finger Lakes, July 17, $50,000, 3&up, f&m, 6f, 1:10.55, BORDER BOUND, A Smart Punch, Diablosangeleyes, 6 started.

Providencia S., Santa Anita Park, April 11, $113,700, 3yo, f, 1mT, 1:34.55, TICKER TAPE (GB), Amorama (Fr), Winendynme, 12 started.

PUCKER UP S.-G3, Arlington Park, Sept. 18, $200,000, 3yo, f, 1¹/₈mT, 1:48.63, TICKER TAPE (GB), Spotlight (GB), Sister Swank, 11 started.

Punch Line S.(R), Colonial Downs, June 12, $48,500, 3&up, Virginia-bred and/or -sired, 5fT, :58.14, NATIVE HEIR, Satan's Code, Oxford Tea Party, 4 started.

Purple Violet S. (R), Arlington Park, June 26, $85,850, 3yo, f, Illinois-conceived and/or-foaled, 1m, 1:37.43, SLEWVILLE, Wish for Gold, Barrel Racer, 10 started.

Puss N Boots S. (R), Fort Erie, Sept. 6, $58,000, 3&up, starters at Fort Erie at least three times in 2004, 1¹/₁₆mT, 1:43.92, A NICE SPLASH, Moonlight Duel, Baltic Prince, 11 started.

Queen City Oaks (R), River Downs, July 31, $75,000, 3yo, f, Ohio-bred, 1¹/₁₆m, 1:54, BARNSY, Precocious, Happy Endings Too, 7 started.

QUEEN ELIZABETH II CHALLENGE CUP S.-G1, Keeneland, Oct. 16, $500,000, 3yo, f, 1¹/₁₆mT, 1:51.35, TICKER TAPE (GB), Barancella (Fr), Riskaverse (GB), 7 started.

Queen Lib H. (R), The Meadowlands, Oct. 16, $60,000, 3&up, f&m, New Jersey-bred, 1m 70y, 1:40.53, PICNIC THEME, Totally Precious, Uphill Skier, 6 started.

Queen of the Green H., Turf Paradise, Nov. 27, $50,000, 3&up, f&m, 1mT, 1:36.19, VERY VEGAS, Muir Beach, dh-Cal's Baby, dh-Shezsospiritual, 8 started.

Queen S., Turfway Park, March 20, $50,000, 4&up, f&m, 6f, 1:10.28, GLORIOUS MISS, Ebony Breeze, Air Marshall, 6 started.

QUEENS COUNTY H.-G3, Aqueduct, Dec. 4, $112,100, 3&up, 1³/₁₆m, 1:57.13, CLASSIC ENDEAVOR, Evening Attire, Colita, 9 started.

Queen's H., Horsemen's Park, July 17, $40,000, 3&up, f&m, 1m, 1:38.80, CASUAL ATTITUDE, Switch Lanes, Burning Memories, 6 started.

Queen's Plate S.(R), Woodbine, June 27, $1,000,000, 3yo, Canadian-bred, 1¹/₄m, 2:04.72, NIIGON, A Bit O'Gold, Will He Crow, 13 started.

Queenston S. (R), Woodbine, May 8, $166,350, 3yo, Canadian-bred, 7f, 1:23.38, TWISTED WIT, A Bit O'Gold, Nyuk Nyuk Nyuk, 7 started.

Quick Card S., Delaware Park, May 8, $53,700, 3&up, 1m, 1:36.62, MAX FOREVER, Private Lap, Country Be Gold, 7 started.

Quicken Tree S. (R), Hollywood Park, June 13, $76,800, 4&up, California-bred, 1¹/₂mT, 2:28.05, BLACK BART, Remonte, Ringaskiddy, 6 started.

Quill S., Delaware Park, Oct. 11, $54,500, 3&up, f&m, 1¹/₁₆mT, 1:51.47, MADEIRA MIST (Ire), Mystery Itself, Natalie Beach (Arg), 6 started.

Raging Fever S. (R), Aqueduct, Dec. 17, $49,550, 2yo, f, nonwinners of a stakes race, 1m 70y, 1:43.65, WINNING SEASON, Shebelongstoyou, Perfectly Quiet, 5 started.

RAILBIRD S.-G3, Hollywood Park, May 2, $109,600, 3yo, f, 7f, 1:21.36, ELUSIVE DIVA, M. A. Fox, Speedy Falcon, 8 started.

Rainbow Connection S. (R), Fort Erie, July 25, $125,000, 3&up, f&m, progeny of eligible Ontario stallions, 5fT, :58.55, BOLD ARTIC ICE, Spanish Decree, Dressed for Action, 9 started.

Rainbow Miss S. (R), Oaklawn Park, March 28, $50,000, 3yo, f, Arkansas-bred, 6f, 1:11.79, K J'S GIRL, Chene Rouge, Time for Etbauer, 9 started.

Rainbow S.(R), Oaklawn Park, March 28, $50,000, 3yo, c&g, Arkansas-bred, 6f, 1:11.32, BOLD MERIT, Will's a Player, Gun Town, 8 started.

Ralph Hayes S. (R), Prairie Meadows, Aug. 28, $82,200, 4&up, c&g, Iowa-bred, 1¹/₁₆m, 1:42.82, CMEGO, Royalty of Iowa, Buzzle Ways, 12 started.

Ralph M. Hinds Pomona Invitational H., Fairplex Park, Sept. 26, $99,000, 3&up, a1¹/₁₆m, 1:49.60, HOTEL HALL (Ire), Nose The Trade (GB), Kristine's King, 8 started.

Ralph Taylor/Vance Davenport Memorial S. (R), Les Bois Park, Aug. 8, $4,400, 3&up, f&m, starters for $2,500 or less at the Les Bois Park meeting, 7¹/₂f, 1:33.60, CAM'S CAT, Larkwood, Crystal Cinders, 8 started.

RAMPART H.-G2, Gulfstream Park, March 14, $194,000, 3&up, f&m, 1¹/₁₆m, 1:51.07, SIGHTSEEK, Redoubled Miss, Lead Story, 4 started.

RANCHO BERNARDO H.-G3, Del Mar, Aug. 21, $150,000, 3&up, f&m, 6¹/₂f, 1:15.85, DREAM OF SUMMER, Barbara Orr, Cyber Slew, 7 started.

Randy Bailey Memorial H., Blue Ribbon Downs, Feb. 22, $8,425, 3&up, 7¹/₂f, 1:33.95, DOC SENTER, Square Expectation, Idontneedone, 6 started.

Rare Treat H., Aqueduct, Feb. 16, $81,600, 3&up, f&m, 1¹/₈m, 1:52.67, AUSTIN'S MOM, U K Trick, Biogio's Beauty, 7 started.

Rattlesnake S., Turf Paradise, Jan. 18, $40,000, 3yo, 1m, 1:36.81, KISSIN TY, Samurai Nanao, Plum Red, 7 started.

RAVEN RUN S.-G2, Keeneland, Oct. 15, $224,200, 3yo, f, 7f, 1:22.86, JOSH'S MADELYN, Vision of Beauty, Feline Story, 10 started.

Razorback Futurity (R), Louisiana Downs, Oct. 16, $40,000, 2yo, c&g, Arkansas-bred, 6f, 1:11.30, STORMY BUT CRAFTY, Leon's Best, Wild Shivers, 10 started.

RAZORBACK H.-G3, Oaklawn Park, March 14, $100,000, 4&up, 1¹/₁₆m, 1:43.56, SONIC WEST, Crafty Shaw, Pie N Burger, 7 started.

R. C. Anderson S. (R), Assiniboia Downs, July 3, $40,000, 3yo, f, Manitoba-bred, 1m, 1:43.20, POPPO'S SONG, Beauty and Glory, Circulating Sziget, 7 started.

Ready Jet Go S., The Meadowlands, Oct. 2, $60,000, 3&up, f&m, 6f, 1:09.23, SLEWS FINAL ANSWER, Lavender Lass, Umpateedle, 7 started.

Real Good Deal S. (R), Del Mar, Aug. 6, $100,000, 3yo, California-bred, 7f, 1:21.71, AREYOUTALKINTOME, Never Surrender, Jet West, 5 started.

Reappeal S., Calder Race Course, Oct. 3, $40,000, 3&up, 6¹/₂f, 1:17.82, LOVE THAT MOON, Black Mambo, Lawbook, 9 started.

Rebel S., Louisiana Downs, July 3, $49,000, 2yo, f, 5¹/₂f, 1:06.98, READY TO LIVE, Sassy Gal, Cathouse Saint, 5 started.

Rebel S., Oaklawn Park, March 20, $200,000, 3yo, 1¹/₁₆m, 1:42.07, SMARTY JONES, Purge, Pro Prado, 9 started.

RED BANK H.-G3, Monmouth Park, May 29, $100,000, 3&up, 1mT, 1:34.73, BURNING ROMA, Remind, American Freedom, 11 started.

Red Camelia H. (R), Fair Grounds, March 28, $97,000, 4&up, f&m, Louisiana-bred, a1mT, 1:37.05, DESTINY CALLS, Fuse It, K Brown, 4 started.

Red Cross S., Monmouth Park, July 18, $65,000, 3&up, f&m, 6f, 1:10.19, FINAL ROUND, Whoop's Ah Daisy, Cupid Season, 6 started.

Red Diamond Express H. (R), Northlands Park, Sept. 25, $50,000, 3&up, Alberta-bred, 6¹/₂f, 1:17.60, SIXTHIRTYJOE, Winspear, Smooth Cruiser, 7 started.

Red Hedeman Mile H. (R), Sunland Park, Nov. 21, $131,500, 2yo, New Mexico-bred, 1m, 1:42.20, SANDIAS PEPPERMINT, Mojo Mundo, Smooth Ghost, 10 started.

RED SMITH H.-G2, Aqueduct, Nov. 20, $150,000, 3&up, 1³/₈mT, 2:18.87, DREADNAUGHT, Certifiably Crazy, Alost (Fr), 10 started.

Regaey Island S., Ellis Park, July 17, $75,000, 3yo, 1m, 1:37.34, KNOX, Big City Spender, Cold Water, 6 started.

Regret S. (R), Great Lakes Downs, May 28, $40,000, 3yo, f, Michigan-bred, 6f, 1:16.14, CATS COPY, Stylish Factor, Zosia's Genius, 8 started.

Regret S., Monmouth Park, Aug. 8, $100,000, 3&up, f&m, 6f, 1:10.01, TRAVELATOR, Cupid Season, Hidden Ransom, 9 started.

REGRET S.-G3, Churchill Downs, June 12, $221,800, 3yo, f, 1¹/₈mT, 1:51.40, SISTER STAR, Western Ransom, Jinny's Gold, 7 started.

Remington Green S., Remington Park, Nov. 21, $51,040, 3&up, 1¹/₁₆mT, 1:43.95, ZEE OH SIX, George Taylor, No More Chads, 9 started.

Remington MEC Mile S., Remington Park, Nov. 21, $84,000, 3yo, 1m, 1:39.69, SMOOTH BID, Silver Haze, City Code, 12 started.

Remington Park Oaks, Remington Park, Nov. 21, $40,000, 3yo, f, 1mT, 1:39.19, ROAD TO MANDALAY, Platinum Ballet, High Pioneer, 9 started.

REMSEN S.-G2, Aqueduct, Nov. 27, $200,000, 2yo, 1¹/₈m, 1:48.88, ROCKPORT HARBOR, Galloping Grocer, Killenaule, 6 started.

Restoration S., Monmouth Park, June 19, $60,000, 3yo, 1mT, 1:33.95, FRISKY SPIDER, Nooligan, Musical Native, 8 started.

Retama Park Turf Breeders' Cup H., Retama Park, July 31, $31,500, 3&up, 1¹/₁₆mT, 1:41.97, FLY SLAMA JAMA, Virginia Pride, Classoffiftyseven, 8 started.

Revidere S., Monmouth Park, June 12, $60,000, 3yo, f, 1m, 1:36.94, MISTDA, Menifeeque, Hall Fashion, 5 started.

Rex's Profile S. (R), Calder Race Course, Dec. 29, $40,000, 3yo, nonwinners of a stakes worth $25,000 or more to the winner, 6¹/₂f, 1:18.37, MR. PEE VEE, Heart of Jules, Marshon, 7 started.

Rhododendron S., Charles Town Races, May 15, $51,200, 3yo, f, 7f, 1:28.19, PASS ME THE SALT, Strawberry Line, Icy Cat, 8 started.

Ribbons and Lace H., Sun Downs, April 25, $3,200, 3&up, f&m, 6f, 1:16.40, RAISE A DAUGHTER, Noble Endeavor, Lady Lilith, 6 started.

Richard King H. (R), Sam Houston Race Park, Nov. 20, $50,000, 3&up, Texas-bred, 1¹/₈mT, 1:56.38, LATE EXPECTATIONS, Kid Halo, Classoffiftyseven, 8 started.

Richmond Derby Trial H., Hastings Race Course, Sept. 6, $41,005, 3yo, 1¹/₁₆m, 1:43.95, RULES OF WAR, Future Flash, Victory Light, 8 started.

Richmond H., Golden Gate Fields, Feb. 14, $57,300, 3&up, f&m, 6f, 1:09.16, PHEIFFER, Goldy Rock, Christmas Time, 7 started.

Richmond S. (R), Hoosier Park, Oct. 2, $40,000, 3&up, f&m, Indiana-bred and/or -sired, $1^1/_{16}$m, 1:46.74, ELLENS LUCKY STAR, One Eyed Jackie, Oro's Sugar, 8 started.

RICHTER SCALE BREEDERS' CUP H.-G2, Gulfstream Park, March 6, $200,000, 3&up, 7f, 1:21.52, LION TAMER, Coach Jimi Lee, Wacky for Love, 7 started.

Ricks Memorial S., Remington Park, Sept. 5, $40,000, 3&up, f&m, 1mT, 1:34.93, CHERYLVILLE SLEW, Queena Corrina, Kristina's Wish, 9 started.

Riley Allison Futurity, Sunland Park, Dec. 26, $161,331, 2yo, $6^1/_2$f, 1:15.15, CAJUN PEPPER, Voronin, Leverage, 10 started.

Rio Grande Senor Futurity (R), Ruidoso Downs, Aug. 1, $104,670, 2yo, c&g, New Mexico-bred, $5^1/_2$f, 1:04.60, LEON'S BULL, Trickey Todd, Bluffen Go, 8 started.

Rio Grande Senorita Futurity (R), Ruidoso Downs, Aug. 1, $100,207, 2yo, f, New Mexico-bred, $5^1/_2$f, 1:05.60, HUSH'S GOLD, Bay View Sue, Hollywood N Divine, 9 started.

Rise Jim S. (R), Suffolk Downs, May 29, $40,000, 3&up, Massachu-setts-bred, 6f, 1:11.72, STYLISH SULTAN, Jini's Jet, Moosup Val-ley, 6 started.

RISEN STAR S.-G3, Fair Grounds, Feb. 15, $150,000, 3yo, $1^1/_{16}$m, 1:45.36, GRADEPOINT, Mr. Jester, Nightlifeatbigblue, 6 started.

Ritz Cafe S., Grand Prairie, Aug. 22, $4,405, 3&up, f&m, $5^1/_2$f, 1:07.60, MISS COMBO, Coco Mocha, Cool Boots, 5 started.

RIVA RIDGE BREEDERS' CUP S.-G2, Belmont Park, June 5, $200,000, 3yo, 7f, 1:20.94, FIRE SLAM, Teton Forest, Abbondanza, 7 started.

River Cities S., Louisiana Downs, Sept. 11, $60,000, 3&up, f&m, a$1^1/_{16}$mT, 1:41.38, DUE TO WIN AGAIN, Dyna Del, Gilded Wings, 7 started.

RIVER CITY H.-G3, Churchill Downs, Nov. 21, $174,300, 3&up, $1^1/_8$mT, 1:51.26, G P FLEET, Cloudy's Knight, Ay Caramba (Brz), 12 started.

River Memories S., Woodbine, Nov. 6, $112,000, 3&up, f&m, 1mT, 1:39.48, MY PAL LANA, Ginger Gold, Always Awesome, 11 started.

R. J. Speers S., Assiniboia Downs, Sept. 11, $40,000, 3&up, $1^1/_{16}$m, 1:45.40, DEPUTY COUNTRY, Smoked Em, Indy Lead, 10 started.

Road Runner H. (R), Ruidoso Downs, Aug. 1, $45,000, 3yo, c&g, New Mexico-bred, $5^1/_2$f, 1:02.80, ROCKY GULCH, Jonnygetachex, Zaire, 7 started.

ROBERT F. CAREY MEMORIAL H.-G3, Hawthorne Race Course, Oct. 9, $150,000, 3&up, 1mT, 1:34.51, SCOOTER ROACH, Gin and Sin, Cloudy's Knight, 9 started.

Robert G. Dick Memorial Breeders' Cup H., Delaware Park, July 17, $151,500, 3&up, f&m, $1^3/_8$mT, 2:20.07, ALTERNATE, Lady of the Future, Primetimevalentine, 10 started.

Robert G. Leavitt Memorial H. (R), Charles Town Races, July 24, $76,500, 3yo, West Virginia-bred, 7f, 1:26.95, BRIGADER, Sheck-atoo, Five Star Account, 10 started.

Robert R. Hilton Memorial S. (R), Charles Town Races, Sept. 11, $41,250, 3&up, West Virginia-bred, 7f, 1:28.32, GINGER ALE, Long-field Spud, Slew's Smile, 9 started.

Robert W. Camac Memorial S. (R), Philadelphia Park, Sept. 4, $50,000, 3&up, Pennsylvania-bred, 5fT, :58.58, NAMEQUEST, Shades of Sunny, Sir Echo, 10 started.

Rocket Bar S., Turf Paradise, Dec. 20, $21,700, 3yo, 6f, 1:08.12, COCOA LATTE, Chief Mtn, U Betcha Joe, 7 started.

Rocket Man S., Calder Race Course, July 10, $50,000, 2&up, 2f, :21.65, PEMBROKE HALL, Love My Mountain, Caller One, 10 started.

Rockhill Native S., Monmouth Park, Sept. 22, $60,000, 2yo, 6f, 1:10.95, DOCTOR VOODOO, Who's the Cowboy, We Love Rocky, 7 started.

Roger Van Hoozer Memorial S. (R), Charles Town Races, Sept. 26, $40,650, 3&up, f&m, West Virginia-bred, 7f, 1:28.74, SIMON SLEW, Fancy Buckles, Marthamountainmama, 6 started.

Rollicking S. (R), Pimlico, Oct. 30, $75,000, 2yo, Maryland-bred, 6f, 1:12.50, MONSTER CHASER, Bank On the Champ, Maddy's Lion, 5 started.

Roman Colonel S., Fairmount Park, June 26, $30,800, 3yo, c&g, 6f, 1:13.60, PUNCH BAG, Chipotle, Matthew's Blessing, 8 started.

Rood and Riddle Dowager S., Keeneland, Oct. 24, $150,000, 3&up, f&m, $1^1/_2$mT, 2:33.28, HUMAITA (Ger), Aud, Literacy, 7 started.

Rose Blossom H., Western Montana Fair, Aug. 14, $5,500, 3&up, f&m, $1^1/_{16}$m, 1:52.20, SARAH OTEKA, A Tempting Light, Snow-bound Star, 5 started.

Rose City S., Fort Erie, June 20, $60,000, 3&up, f&m, 6f, 1:12.17, CLUBAY, Alittlebitgrumpy, Low Key Affair, 6 started.

Rose DeBartolo Memorial S. (R), Thistledown, July 17, $75,000, 3&up, f&m, Ohio-bred, $1^1/_8$m, 1:53.24, OH SO EASY, Ashwood C C, Whitewater Way, 6 started.

Rossi Gold S., Arlington Park, Sept. 4, $53,800, 3&up, $1^1/_2$mT, 2:33.71, ON THE COURSE, Sharbayan (Ire), False Promises, 8 started.

Round Table S., Arlington Park, July 17, $100,000, 3yo, $1^1/_8$m, 1:51.53, CRYPTOGRAPH, Fantasticat, Chippewa Trail, 9 started.

Route 66 S., Fair Meadows at Tulsa, July 17, $49,875, 3&up, $6^1/_2$f, 1:18.80, HERECOMESTHEMANNOW, Dance and Dazzle, Mar-lukin, 10 started.

ROYAL HEROINE S.-G3, Hollywood Park, July 3, $109,700, 3&up, f&m, 1mT, 1:34.79, JANEIAN (NZ), Katdogawn (GB), Makeup Artist, 6 started.

ROYAL NORTH H.-G3, Woodbine, Aug. 2, $170,550, 3&up, f&m, 6fT, 1:07.83, HOUR OF JUSTICE, With Patience, Boozin' Susan, 9 started.

Royal North S. (R), Beulah Park, April 3, $40,000, 3yo, f, Ohio-bred, 6f, 1:11.91, SALVESTER, Royal Cup, Barnsy, 11 started.

R. R. M. Carpenter Jr. Memorial H., Delaware Park, July 17, $100,300, 3&up, $1^1/_{16}$m, 1:43.48, ANGELIC AURA, The Lady's Groom, Supah Blitz, 6 started.

Rudy Baez S., Suffolk Downs, July 17, $40,000, 3yo, 1m 70y, 1:42.96, SENOR LADD, Isitdustybackthere, Anger, 7 started.

RUFFIAN H.-G1, Belmont Park, Sept. 19, $294,000, 3&up, f&m, $1^1/_{16}$m, 1:41.51, SIGHTSEEK, Pocus Hocus, Miss Loren (Arg), 5 started.

Ruffian S., Fairmount Park, June 19, $30,800, 3yo, f, 6f, 1:13.60, VALIDA, Cart's Maybe So, Hello Miami, 8 started.

Ruff/Kirchberg Memorial H. (R), Beulah Park, Nov. 21, $40,000, 3&up, Ohio-accredited, $1^1/_4$m, 2:06.18, COUNT ON MY WORD, Brent's Challanger, Quiet Soul, 8 started.

Ruidoso Mile H., Ruidoso Downs, Aug. 7, $30,000, 3&up, 1m, 1:40.40, SOCKO, dh-Stone Canyon, dh-Beyond Brilliant, 10 started.

Ruidoso Oaks, Ruidoso Downs, July 31, $25,000, 3yo, f, 6f, 1:10.40, MISS NOTEWORTHY, Strawberry Pet, Rama Lassie, 6 started.

Ruidoso Overnight S., Ruidoso Downs, July 17, $17,500, 2yo, $5^1/_2$f, 1:04.60, SANDIAS PEPPERMINT, C. G's Dollar, Beccas' Shoul-der, 8 started.

Ruidoso Thoroughbred Championship H., Ruidoso Downs, Sept. 6, $42,700, 3&up, $1^1/_{16}$m, 1:46.80, STONE CANYON, Latenite Trick, Mr. Zach Man, 9 started.

Ruidoso Thoroughbred Derby, Ruidoso Downs, Sept. 5, $30,000, 3yo, $1^1/_{16}$m, 1:44.40, SOUTHERN TWILIGHT, Mr. Trieste, Jo Dee Who, 9 started.

Ruidoso Thoroughbred Overnight S., Ruidoso Downs, June 13, $15,500, 3yo, $7^1/_2$f, 1:32.40, SAMURAI NANAO, Go Kitty Go, No Term Limit, 3 started.

Ruidoso Thoroughbred Overnight S., Ruidoso Downs, July 24, $15,800, 3yo, 6f, 1:10.80, TOUGH PILGRIM, Sharm, Samurai Nanao, 7 started.

Ruidoso Thoroughbred Sales Futurity (R), Ruidoso Downs, June 19, $92,742, 2yo, New Mexico-bred, 5f, :58, TRICKY TACTICS, Bay View Sue, Sandias Peppermint, 9 started.

Rumson S., Monmouth Park, Aug. 14, $60,000, 3yo, 6f, 1:08.67, WAR'S PROSPECT, Abbondanza, Gotaghostofachance, 8 started.

Runza H., Fonner Park, April 10, $16,075, 3&up, f&m, 6f, 1:12.60, BURNING MEMORIES, Missy Can Do, Flaming Night, 5 started.

Rushaway S., Turfway Park, March 20, $100,000, 3yo, $1^1/_{16}$m, 1:44.36, BRASS HAT, Tales of Glory, Gamblin, 10 started.

Rushing Man S., Thoroughbreds, Nov. 6, $60,000, 3yo, 6f, 1:09.43, CHOOSE, Wimplestiltskin, Knight of Darkness, 6 started.

Ruth C. Funkhouser S. (R), Charles Town Races, Sept. 26, $41,250, 3yo, f, West Virginia-bred, 7f, 1:30.45, WHITE ICE, Petes Hick Chick, Crafty Carni, 9 started.

Ruthless S., Aqueduct, Jan. 4, $78,375, 3yo, f, 6f, 1:13.93, BAL-DOMERA, High Peaks, Prudencia, 5 started.

SABIN H.-G3, Gulfstream Park, Feb. 15, $100,000, 3&up, f&m, $1^1/_{16}$m, 1:43.32, ROAR EMOTION, Nonsuch Bay, Lead Story, 9 started.

Sabin S. (R), Belmont Park, May 12, $60,800, 4&up, f&m, nonwin-ners of a graded stakes, $1^1/_4$m, 2:04.56, HUMAITA (Ger), Noisette, Primetimevalentine, 7 started.

Sadie Diamond Futurity (R), Hastings Race Course, Oct. 2, $106,818, 2yo, f, Canadian-foaled, $6^1/_2$f, 1:18.43, AVENGING KAT, Backseat Becka, All Round Cowgirl, 10 started.

Sadie Hawkins H. (R), Charles Town Races, July 31, $76,400, 3&up, f&m, West Virginia-bred, 7f, 1:27.38, FANCY BUCKLES, Miss Roberson, Who's Ya Mama, 9 started.

SAFELY KEPT BREEDERS' CUP S.-G3, Pimlico, Oct. 2, $143,000, 3yo, f, 6f, 1:10.11, BENDING STRINGS, Smokey Glacken, Then She Laughs, 6 started.

Safely Kept H., Fairmount Park, July 10, $30,900, 4&up, f&m, 6f, 1:12.20, MOON SHINE TIME, Run Willa Run, Ft. Mann, 7 started.

Safely Kept S., Arlington Park, Sept. 6, $52,600, 3&up, f&m, 6f, 1:10.25, SOURIS, Smoke Chaser, Summer Mis, 6 started.

Safely Kept S. (R), Aqueduct, Nov. 20, $61,050, 3yo, f, nonwinners of $50,000, 6f, 1:11.13, STORM MINSTREL, Then She Laughs, Dreamadreamforme, 9 started.

Saguaro S., Turf Paradise, Oct. 30, $40,000, 3yo, 6f, 1:08.83, COCOA LATTE, Snowbound Writer, Aza, 7 started.

Sail On By S., Turf Paradise, Nov. 2, $21,800, 2yo, 6f, 1:10.14, LEAD FOR SPEED, Thresher, Fuzzyheadedlizard, 7 started.

Salem County S., The Meadowlands, Oct. 2, $55,000, 2yo, f, 1m 70yT, 1:43.64, PADDY'S DAISY, K. D.'s Shady Lady, Elke, 6 started.

Sales H. (R), Northlands Park, Oct. 15, $50,000, 4&up, f&m, Canadian-bred sold at a CTHS sale, 1m, 1:39.20, A SHAKY START, O Howrude, Jadebquick, 5 started.

Sales H. (R), Northlands Park, Oct. 16, $49,000, 4&up, c&g, Canadian-bred sold at a CTHS sale, 1m, 1:39.60, PARLAY'S PROSPECT, Topwynson, Code Name Fred, 7 started.

SALVATOR MILE H.-G3, Monmouth Park, July 25, $100,000, 3&up, 1m, 1:35.27, PRESIDENTIALAFFAIR, Unforgettable Max, Roaring Fever, 5 started.

Sam F. Davis S., Tampa Bay Downs, Feb. 21, $100,000, 3yo, 1¹/₁₆m, 1:44.60, KAUFY MARE, The Cliff's Edge, Zakocity, 11 started.

Sam Houston Distaff H., Sam Houston Race Park, Jan. 17, $40,000, 4&up, f&m, 1¹/₁₆m, 1:45.88, SPECTACULAR LISA, Cheryllvile Slew, Reason to Talk, 10 started.

Sam Houston Oaks, Sam Houston Race Park, March 13, $30,000, 3yo, f, 1m, 1:40.29, JOSIE G., Olympic Emblem, Perennial Favorite, 8 started.

Sam Houston Sprint H., Sam Houston Race Park, Jan. 17, $40,000, 4&up, 7f, 1:23.96, ZEE OH SIX, Term Sheet, Won C C, 6 started.

Sam Houston Texan Juvenile S., Sam Houston Race Park, Nov. 20, $150,000, 2yo, 1¹/₁₆m, 1:44.99, BOGGY CREEK, Major League, Leaving On My Mind, 8 started.

Sam Houston Turf Sprint Cup H., Sam Houston Race Park, April 10, $40,000, 4&up, 5fT, :58.94, BOLD REPLY, Clever Pancho, Gold Storm, 6 started.

Sam J. Whiting Memorial H., Pleasanton, July 10, $50,595, 3&up, 6f, 1:08.14, ONEBADSHARK, El Dorado Shooter, Twentythreejaybird, 7 started.

Sam's Town S., Delta Downs, Dec. 4, $75,000, 3&up, 7f, 1:27.64, INTELLIGENT MALE, Demon's Prince, Shaky Town, 7 started.

Samuel H. (R), Beulah Park, Dec. 18, $25,000, 3&up, starters at the 2004 Beulah Park fall meet, 6f, 1:12.56, JUST MICHEL, Mercer's Launch, Brent's Challanger, 10 started.

SAN ANTONIO H.-G2, Santa Anita Park, Jan. 31, $245,000, 4&up, 1¹/₈m, 1:47.25, PLEASANTLY PERFECT, Star Cross (Arg), Fleetstreet Dancer, 4 started.

SAN BERNARDINO H.-G3, Santa Anita Park, April 3, $110,600, 4&up, 1¹/₈m, 1:48.07, DYNEVER, Total Impact (Chi), Even the Score, 7 started.

San Carlos H., Golden Gate Fields, Feb. 28, $55,500, 3&up, 1m, 1:34.75, JETS FAN, Gold Ruckus, Smile n Wildcat, 5 started.

SAN CARLOS H.-G2, Santa Anita Park, March 7, $150,000, 4&up, 7f, 1:21.16, PICO CENTRAL (Brz), Publication, Pohave, 10 started.

SAN CLEMENTE H.-G2, Del Mar, July 31, $150,000, 3yo, f, 1mT, 1:34.11, SWEET WIN, Miss Vegas (Ire), Victory U. S. A., 5 started.

Sandia H., The Downs at Albuquerque, Sept. 18, $33,100, 3&up, 5¹/₂f, 1:02.84, BEYOND BRILLIANT, Appleton (Mex), This Chris, 7 started.

SAN DIEGO H.-G2, Del Mar, Aug. 1, $250,000, 3&up, 1¹/₁₆m, 1:42.32, CHOCTAW NATION, Pleasantly Perfect, During, 7 started.

Sandpiper S., Tampa Bay Downs, Jan. 10, $60,000, 3yo, f, 6f, 1:11.93, WILD SPEED, Crafty Tears, Atti Girl Fergie, 12 started.

Sandra Hall Grand Canyon H. (R), Turf Paradise, April 24, $40,000, 3&up, Arizona-bred, 6f, 1:08.69, NEWARK, Komax, Red Spark, 8 started.

SANDS POINT S.-G3, Belmont Park, June 13, $114,800, 3yo, f, 1¹/₁₆mT, 1:47.24, MAMBO SLEW, Lucifer's Stone, Vous, 10 started.

SAN FELIPE S.-G2, Santa Anita Park, March 14, $250,000, 3yo, 1¹/₁₆m, 1:42.87, PREACHINATTHEBAR, St Averil, Harvard Avenue, 9 started.

SAN FERNANDO BREEDERS' CUP S.-G2, Santa Anita Park, Jan. 10, $221,800, 4yo, 1¹/₈m, 1:41.63, DURING, Toccet, Touch the Wire, 10 started.

SANFORD S.-G2, Saratoga Race Course, July 29, $150,000, 2yo, 6f, 1:09.32, AFLEET ALEX, Flamenco, Consolidator, 11 started.

SAN FRANCISCO BREEDERS' CUP MILE-G2, Bay Meadows, April 24, $148,750, 3&up, 1mT, 1:35.16, SINGLETARY, Captain Squire, Gold Ruckus, 7 started.

SAN GORGONIO H.-G2, Santa Anita Park, Jan. 10, $147,000, 4&up, f&m, 1¹/₈mT, 1:49.51, MEGAHERTZ (GB), Garden in the Rain (Fr), Firth of Lorne (Ire), 4 started.

Sangue H., Louisiana Downs, Aug. 14, $50,000, 3&up, f&m, a7¹/₂fT, 1:30.44, CHERYLVILLE SLEW, Outright Buck, Due to Win Again, 10 started.

San Jacinto S. (R), Sam Houston Race Park, Nov. 20, $50,000, 3&up, f&m, Texas-bred, 1¹/₁₆mT, 1:50.80, MARFA'S TAXES, Nancibegood, Hay Madison, 10 started.

San Jose S., Bay Meadows, May 15, $59,113, 3yo, f, 1¹/₁₆mT, 1:43.07, HEAVENLY HUMOR, Secret Corsage, Eight Karat, 7 started.

SAN JUAN CAPISTRANO INVITATIONAL H.-G2, Santa Anita Park, April 18, $250,000, 4&up, a1³/₄mT, 2:45.98, METEOR STORM (GB), Rhythm Mad (Fr), Runaway Dancer, 9 started.

San Juan County Commissioners H., SunRay Park, Nov. 2, $52,100, 3&up, 1¹/₈m, 1:50.40, PLEASANT BEND, Long Range, Mydak, 6 started.

SAN LUIS OBISPO H.-G2, Santa Anita Park, Feb. 16, $200,000, 4&up, 1¹/₂mT, 2:28, PUERTO BANUS, Continuously, Continental Red, 12 started.

SAN LUIS REY H.-G2, Santa Anita Park, March 20, $200,000, 4&up, 1¹/₂mT, 2:26.03, METEOR STORM (GB), Labirinto, Gene de Campeao (Brz), 10 started.

SAN MARCOS S.-G2, Santa Anita Park, Jan. 19, $150,000, 4&up, 1¹/₄mT, 1:58.82, SWEET RETURN (GB), Nothing to Lose, Blue Steller (Ire), 9 started.

San Mateo S., Bay Meadows, Sept. 18, $66,075, 2yo, 6f, 1:09.93, WIND WATER, Danny Dingle, Boston Glory, 6 started.

SAN MIGUEL S.-G3, Santa Anita Park, Jan. 11, $108,100, 3yo, 6f, 1:09.36, HOSCO, Roi Charmant, Gethsemani, 7 started.

SAN PASQUAL H.-G2, Santa Anita Park, Jan. 3, $150,000, 4&up, 1¹/₁₆m, 1:42.22, STAR CROSS (Arg), Nose The Trade (GB), Olmodavor, 7 started.

San Pedro S., Santa Anita Park, March 27, $83,625, 3yo, 6¹/₂f, 1:16.13, COURAGEOUS ACT, Wimplestiltskin, Stalking Tiger, 6 started.

SAN RAFAEL S.-G2, Santa Anita Park, March 6, $200,000, 3yo, 1m, 1:36.11, IMPERIALISM, Lion Heart, Consecrate, 10 started.

SAN SIMEON H.-G3, Santa Anita Park, April 18, $107,300, 4&up, a6¹/₂fT, 1:11.46, GLICK, Cayoke (Fr), Summer Service, 6 started.

SANTA ANA H.-G2, Santa Anita Park, March 27, $150,000, 4&up, f&m, 1¹/₈mT, 1:47.36, KATDOGAWN (GB), Fun House, Arabic Song (Ire), 7 started.

SANTA ANITA DERBY-G1, Santa Anita Park, April 3, $750,000, 3yo, 1¹/₈m, 1:49.24, CASTLEDALE (Ire), Imperialism, Rock Hard Ten, 7 started.

SANTA ANITA H.-G1, Santa Anita Park, March 6, $1,000,000, 4&up, 1¹/₄m, 2:01.64, SOUTHERN IMAGE, Island Fashion, Saint Buddy, 8 started.

SANTA ANITA OAKS-G1, Santa Anita Park, March 13, $300,000, 3yo, f, 1¹/₁₆m, 1:42.84, SILENT SIGHS, Halfbridled, A. P. Adventure, 7 started.

SANTA BARBARA H.-G2, Santa Anita Park, April 17, $200,000, 4&up, 1¹/₄mT, 2:00.71, MEGAHERTZ (GB), Noches De Rosa (Chi), Mandela (Ger), 5 started.

SANTA CATALINA S.-G2, Santa Anita Park, Jan. 17, $150,000, 3yo, 1¹/₁₆m, 1:41.62, ST AVERIL, Lucky Pulpit, Master David, 9 started.

Santa Clara H., Bay Meadows, May 29, $58,175, 3&up, f&m, 1m, 1:34.94, GONETORULE, A B Noodle, Bartok's Blithe, 6 started.

Santa Claus S., Calder Race Course, Dec. 26, $40,000, 3yo, 1¹/₁₆mT, 1:41.47, OLD FORESTER, Ecclesiastic, New Science, 10 started.

Santa Lucia H. (R), Santa Anita Park, April 4, $85,725, 4&up, f&m, nonwinners of a stakes at one mile or over in 2004, 1¹/₁₆m, 1:43.42, HOPE RISES, Summer Wind Dancer, Pesci, 7 started.

SANTA MARGARITA INVITATIONAL H.-G1, Santa Anita Park, March 14, $300,000, 4&up, f&m, 1¹/₈m, 1:48.85, ADORATION, Star Parade (Arg), Bare Necessities, 5 started.

SANTA MARIA H.-G1, Santa Anita Park, Feb. 16, $250,000, 4&up, f&m, 1^1/₁₆m, 1:43.87, STAR PARADE (Arg), Bare Necessities, La Tour (Chi), 6 started.

SANTA MONICA H.-G1, Santa Anita Park, Jan. 25, $250,000, 4&up, f&m, 7f, 1:21.37, ISLAND FASHION, Buffythecenterfold, Got Koko, 6 started.

Santa Paula S., Santa Anita Park, March 21, $82,500, 3yo, f, 6^1/₂f, 1:17.34, FRIENDLY MICHELLE, Lyin Goddess, Very Vegas, 5 started.

Santa Teresa H., Sunland Park, March 14, $54,050, 3&up, f&m, 6^1/₂f, 1:17.89, BIG SCORE, Aurora Guadalupe, Ona Rampage, 9 started.

SANTA YNEZ S.-G2, Santa Anita Park, Jan. 19, $150,000, 3yo, f, 7f, 1:21.11, YEARLY REPORT, House of Fortune, Papa to Kinzie, 8 started.

SANTA YSABEL S.-G3, Santa Anita Park, Jan. 4, $106,800, 3yo, f, 1^1/₁₆m, 1:44.27, A. P. ADVENTURE, Salty Romance, Wildwood Flower, 6 started.

SAN VICENTE S.-G2, Santa Anita Park, Feb. 7, $150,000, 3yo, 7f, 1:22.34, IMPERIALISM, Hosco, Consecrate, 6 started.

SAPLING S.-G3, Monmouth Park, Aug. 28, $100,000, 2yo, 6f, 1:11.21, EVIL MINISTER, Park Avenue Ball, Upscaled, 8 started.

Sarah Lane's Oates H. (R), Fair Grounds, March 27, $100,000, 3yo, f, Louisiana-bred, a1mT, 1:38.14, PLACID STAR, Young Emotions, Merry Mary, 13 started.

SARANAC H.-G3, Saratoga Race Course, Sept. 6, $108,200, 3yo, 1^3/₁₆mT, 1:53.89, PRINCE ARCH, Mustanfar, Catch the Glory, 6 started.

SARATOGA BREEDERS' CUP H.-G2, Saratoga Race Course, Aug. 22, $250,000, 3&up, 1^1/₄m, 2:00.83, EVENING ATTIRE, Funny Cide, Bowman's Band, 7 started.

Saratoga Dew S. (R), Saratoga Race Course, Sept. 1, $66,400, 3&up, f&m, New York-bred, 1^1/₄m, 1:52.48, FAIT ACCOMPLI, Leedle Dee, Cat's Roar, 7 started.

Saratoga H., Bay Meadows, May 22, $67,512, 3&up, 6f, 1:09.10, ONEBIGBAG, R. Baggio, Debonair Joe, 9 started.

Saskatchewan Derby, Marquis Downs, Sept. 11, $15,000, 3yo, 1^1/₁₆m, 1:45.45, NOBLE DANE, Cool Lad, Astapay, 6 started.

Saskatchewan Futurity (R), Marquis Downs, July 31, $17,800, 2yo, Canadian-bred and/or -owned, 6f, 1:16.34, FARGO FORBES, Lambrose, Royal Reblar, 8 started.

Saskatoon H., Marquis Downs, July 3, $5,000, 3yo, 6f, 1:14.55, STEEL COPY, Signal to Go, Devil's Nugget, 7 started.

Saylorville S., Prairie Meadows, July 4, $98,000, 3&up, f&m, 6f, 1:08.68, SUMMER MIS, Savorthetime, Clear in the West, 5 started.

Scarlet and Gray H. (R), Beulah Park, Nov. 7, $40,000, 3&up, f&m, Ohio-bred, 6f, 1:10.43, MERCER'S LAUNCH, Scioto Bootski, Heavenly Jet, 11 started.

Scarlet Carnation S., Thistledown, June 12, $40,000, 3&up, f&m, 6f, 1:11.10, CODES PRESHISONE, Whatever I Want, Sarah Jade, 7 started.

Schenectady H. (R), Belmont Park, Sept. 26, $107,700, 3&up, f&m, New York-bred, 6f, 1:09.46, SUGAR PUNCH, Cologny, Beautiful America, 6 started.

SCHUYLERVILLE S.-G2, Saratoga Race Course, July 28, $150,000, 2yo, f, 6f, 1:12.48, CLASSIC ELEGANCE, Angel Trumpet, Wild Chick, 10 started.

Scottsdale H., Turf Paradise, March 27, $40,000, 3yo, f, 1mT, 1:37.13, CHURCH EDITOR, Muir Beach, Choose the Right, 6 started.

Scott's Scoundrel S. (R), Louisiana Downs, Sept. 6, $50,000, 3yo, Louisiana-bred, 1^1/₁₆mT, 1:42.73, SPRUCE'S PRINCE, Old Lee, Nitro Chip, 6 started.

Scotzanna S. (R), Belmont Park, July 16, $61,200, 4&up, f&m, nonwinners of a graded stakes in 2003-'04, 6f, 1:09.29, COLOGNY, Travelator, Beautiful America, 6 started.

SEABISCUIT BREEDERS' CUP H.-G3, Bay Meadows, May 31, $86,250, 3&up, 1^1/₁₆m, 1:40.08, YOUGOTTAWANNA, Gold Ruckus, Snorter, 5 started.

Seacliff S., Calder Race Course, Sept. 6, $50,000, 2yo, 1m, 1:42.27, CHEROKEE CHASE, D'court's Speed, El Batallon, 9 started.

Sea Emperor S. (R), Calder Race Course, Sept. 9, $40,000, 3&up, nonwinners of $15,000 once since February 1 or nonwinners of four races other than maiden, claiming, or starter, 7f, 1:24.70, SWIFT REPLICA, Nightmare Affair, Love That Moon, 9 started.

Seagram Cup S., Woodbine, Aug. 7, $136,750, 3&up, 1^1/₁₆m, 1:44.34, ONE FOR ROSE, Mark One, Hydrogen, 7 started.

Sea O Erin Breeders' Cup Mile H., Arlington Park, Aug. 7, $150,000, 3&up, 1mT, 1:36.48, HERCULATED, False Promises, Major Rhythm, 10 started.

Seattle H., Emerald Downs, April 25, $40,000, 3&up, 6f, 1:07.80, WILLIE THE CAT, Best On Tap, Illusive Force, 5 started.

Seattle Slew Breeders' Cup H., Emerald Downs, July 31, $64,375, 3yo, c&g, 1^1/₁₆m, 1:42.80, FLAMETHROWINTEXAN, Pure American, Soccer Dan, 9 started.

Seattle Slew H., Fairmount Park, July 3, $30,500, 4&up, c&g, 6f, 1:10.40, LIVING A DREAM, Moe B Dick, Medlin Road, 5 started.

SEAWAY S.-G3, Woodbine, Sept. 11, $178,000, 3&up, f&m, 7f, 1:22.26, BRASS IN POCKET, Winter Garden, El Prado Essence, 7 started.

Secretariat Memorial S., Santa Cruz County Fair, May 1, $5,054, 3&up, 6f, 1:11.80, OCCUPIED, Speed Pocket, Bolero Type, 7 started.

SECRETARIAT S.-G1, Arlington Park, Aug. 14, $400,000, 3yo, 1^1/₄mT, 1:59.65, KITTEN'S JOY, Greek Sun, Moscow Ballet (Ire), 7 started.

Seeking The Gold S. (R), Belmont Park, July 22, $61,500, 4&up, nonwinners of a graded stakes in 2003-'04, 1^1/₁₆m, 1:42.08, FREE OF LOVE, Personal Touch, Conservation, 7 started.

SELENE S.-G2, Woodbine, May 23, $275,000, 3yo, f, 1^1/₁₆m, 1:48.28, EYE OF THE SPHYNX, Silver Bird, Sweet Problem, 6 started.

Selima S., Pimlico, Nov. 20, $100,000, 2yo, f, 1^1/₁₆m, 1:46.24, HEAR US ROAR, Take a Check, Gotta Rush, 8 started.

Selma S. (R), Retama Park, Sept. 18, $40,000, 3yo, f, Texas-bred, 5fT, :56.04, SENECA SONG, Tee Pee Tomahawk, Geri Kelly, 8 started.

Senate Appointee H., Hastings Race Course, July 11, $41,096, 3&up, f&m, 1^1/₄m, 1:51.47, HANSELINA, dh-Defrere's Image, dh-Dancewithavixen, 7 started.

SENATOR KEN MADDY H.-G3, Santa Anita Park, Sept. 29, $100,000, 3&up, f&m, a6^1/₂fT, 1:12.86, BELLESKI, Intercontinental (GB), Acago, 9 started.

Seneca S. (R), Louisiana Downs, Sept. 18, $50,000, 3yo, f, Louisiana-bred, a1^1/₁₆mT, 1:43.03, HAPPY TICKET, Katlin's Rocket, Catlaan, 8 started.

Senorita S., Louisiana Downs, July 24, $50,000, 3yo, f, 1^1/₁₆mT, 1:42.66, TOPANGO, Merry Me in Spring, Dancing Meg, 8 started.

SENORITA S.-G3, Hollywood Park, May 15, $108,900, 3yo, f, 1mT, 1:34.25, MISS VEGAS (Ire), Ticker Tape (GB), Amorama (Fr), 7 started.

Sensational Star H. (R), Santa Anita Park, Feb. 14, $109,900, 4&up, California-bred, a6^1/₂fT, 1:12.34, MCCANN'S MOJAVE, Lennyfromalibu, Hemet Thought, 8 started.

Serena's Song S., Monmouth Park, July 24, $60,000, 3yo, f, 1m 70y, 1:41.14, SUSAN'S ANGEL, Schedule (GB), Taittinger Rose, 10 started.

Seton Hall University S., The Meadowlands, Nov. 13, $60,000, 3yo, f, 6f, 1:09.81, FOREST MUSIC, Feline Story, Itsayatessthing, 7 started.

SHADWELL TURF MILE S.-G1, Keeneland, Oct. 9, $600,000, 3&up, 1mT, 1:35.55, NOTHING TO LOSE, Honor in War, Silver Tree, 9 started.

Shady Well S. (R), Woodbine, July 24, $160,350, 2yo, f, Canadian-bred, 5^1/₂f, 1:06.26, SOUTH BAY COVE, Edith Prickley, Dancehall Deelites, 9 started.

SHAKERTOWN S.-G3, Keeneland, April 10, $115,100, 3&up, 5^1/₂fT, 1:01.78, SOARING FREE, Chosen Chief, Banned in Boston, 12 started.

Sham S. (R), Santa Anita Park, Feb. 8, $81,400, 3yo, nonwinners of $50,000 at one mile or over, 1^1/₁₆m, 1:49.20, MASTER DAVID, Borrego, Preachinatthebar, 7 started.

Shecky Greene S., Delaware Park, Nov. 6, $54,500, 3&up, 1^1/₁₆m, 1:43.02, UNFORGETTABLE MAX, Hydrogen, Spicy Stuff, 7 started.

SHEEPSHEAD BAY H.-G2, Belmont Park, May 29, $150,000, 3&up, f&m, 1^3/₈mT, 2:18.24, MOSCOW BURNING, Spice Island, Meridiana (Ger), 10 started.

Shelby County S. (R), Indiana Downs, May 1, $40,000, 3&up, f&m, Indiana-sired, 6f, 1:12.22, ELLENS LUCKY STAR, One Eyed Jackie, Fe Fe's Spirits, 7 started.

Shepperton S. (R), Woodbine, Aug. 14, $133,000, 3&up, progeny of eligible Ontario stallions, 6^1/₂f, 1:16.37, KRZ RUCKUS, Dillinger, Mister Coop, 8 started.

SHIRLEY JONES H.-G3, Gulfstream Park, Feb. 8, $100,000, 3&up, f&m, 7f, 1:21.42, RANDAROO, Harmony Lodge, Halory Leigh, 8 started.

Shiskabob S. (R), Louisiana Downs, Oct. 23, $84,350, 3&up, Louisiana-bred, 1^1/₁₆mT, 1:43.09, SCREEN IDOL, Witt Ante, Little Happy, 13 started.

Shocker T. H., Calder Race Course, Oct. 23, $100,000, 3&up, f&m, 1^1/₁₆m, 1:47.30, REDOUBLED MISS, Maria's Image, Sniffles, 7 started.

SHOEMAKER BREEDERS' CUP MILE S.-G1, Hollywood Park, May 31, $456,000, 3&up, 1mT, 1:32.81, DESIGNED FOR LUCK, Singletary, Tsigane (Fr), 8 started.

Shortgrass Heritage S. (R), Marquis Downs, Aug. 21, $10,000, 3yo, c&g, Saskatchewan-bred, 1¹/₁₆m, 1:48.35, SIGNAL TO GO, Stage Whisper, Astapay, 5 started.

Showtime Deb S. (R), Hawthorne Race Course, Nov. 13, $97,400, 2yo, f, Illinois-conceived and/or -foaled, 6f, 1:12.34, BLUESBDANCING, Meadow Bride, Cart's Turn, 11 started.

SHUVEE H.-G2, Belmont Park, May 15, $200,000, 3&up, f&m, 1m, 1:36.10, STORM FLAG FLYING, Passing Shot, Roar Emotion, 6 started.

Shuvee S., Fairmount Park, Sept. 14, $26,000, 2yo, f, 6f, 1:13.80, DENOUN N DEVERB, Stef's Inheritance, Quarter Irish, 10 started.

Sickles Image S. (R), Great Lakes Downs, Sept. 20, $50,000, 2yo, f, Michigan-bred, 6f, 1:16.32, FOOLININTHEMEADOW, Musical Factor, Everglide, 6 started.

Side Bar S., Calder Race Course, Aug. 15, $40,000, 3&up, 1mT, 1:38.12, CLASS OF SEVENTY, Paradise Dancer, Unbridels King, 12 started.

Sierra Starlet S. (R), Ruidoso Downs, Aug. 1, $45,000, 3yo, f, New Mexico-bred, 1', 1:04, LATENITE SPECIAL, Janna's Gold, Excessive Reign, 7 started.

Silk Stockings S., Yavapai Downs, June 12, $9,600, 3yo, f, 6f, 1:10, SOLLY'S DOLLY, Swain's Gold, Diamondsrbueno, 5 started.

Silverado S. (R), The Downs at Albuquerque, May 2, $42,550, 3&up, New Mexico-bred, 6f, 1:08.44, NINETY NINE JACK, B. G. Tiger, Sharethetime, 6 started.

Silver Bells S. (R), Calder Race Course, Dec. 24, $40,000, 3&up, f&m, nonwinners of a stakes worth $25,000 or more to the winner, 7f, 1:24.51, DOUBLE SCOOP, dh-Tuscany Light, dh-Adobe Gold, 6 started.

SILVERBULLETDAY S.-G2, Fair Grounds, Feb. 14, $150,000, 3yo, f, 1¹/₁₆m, 1:46.82, SHADOW CAST, Quick Temper, Sister Swank, 6 started.

Silver Cup Futurity (R), Arapahoe Park, Aug. 15, $25,000, 2yo, passed through the sales ring at the Silver Cup Sale, 5¹/₂f, 1:04.40, RUN DO RUN, Class in Action, Woody's Dream, 8 started.

Silver Deputy S., Woodbine, Sept. 6, $106,000, 2yo, 6¹/₂f, 1:18.14, WHOLELOTTABOURBON, The Finagler, What's Up Dude, 7 started.

Silver Maiden S., Arlington Park, July 31, $54,600, 2yo, f, 5¹/₂f, 1:06.19, PANORAMA VALLEY, Kota, Mary Alex, 11 started.

Silver Season S., Calder Race Course, Aug. 7, $40,000, 3yo, 7f, 1:25.07, CABALLERO NEGRO, Nightmare Affair, Frolic for Joy, 6 started.

Silver Spur Breeders' Cup S., Lone Star Park, Oct. 1, $100,000, 2yo, f, 1m, 1:39.49, ENDURING WILL, Kristin's Charm, Berdelia, 9 started.

Simcoe S. (R), Woodbine, Sept. 5, $136,125, 2yo, Canadian-bred, 7f, 1:24.68, MOONSHINE JUSTICE, Olympia Fields, Galaxy, 9 started.

Simply Majestic S., Calder Race Course, May 22, $75,000, 3yo, 1¹/₁₆mT, 1:39.74, WIRE BOUND, Gin Rummy Champ, Capias, 9 started.

Sir Barton S. (1st Div.), Pimlico, May 15, $100,000, 3yo, 1¹/₁₆m, 1:41.86, ARTIE SCHILLER, Lipan, Timo, 11 started.

Sir Barton S. (2nd Div.), Pimlico, May 15, $100,000, 3yo, 1¹/₁₆m, 1:45.63, ROYAL ASSAULT, Dashboard Drummer, Humorously, 8 started.

Sir Barton S. (R), Woodbine, Dec. 8, $126,375, 3yo, c&g, progeny of eligible Ontario stallions, 1¹/₁₆m, 1:45.04, ARCH HALL, Cabriolass, Kent Ridge, 9 started.

Sir Beaufort S., Santa Anita Park, Dec. 26, $112,700, 3yo, 1mT, 1:34.60, WHILLY (Ire), We All Love Aleyna, Cozy Guy, 9 started.

Sir Omni S., Calder Race Course, Sept. 25, $40,000, 3yo, 1¹/₁₆mT, 1:45.76, WIRE BOUND, Cervelo, Frolic for Joy, 7 started.

Sir Winston Churchill H., Hastings Race Course, Sept. 25, $41,616, 3&up, 1¹/₈m, 1:49.28, METATRON, Shacane, Illusive Force, 8 started.

Sissy Woolums Memorial Virginia/South Carolina S. (R), Colonial Downs, July 18, $40,000, 3&up, progeny of stallion seasons donated to the 2004 Virginia Stallion Season Auction and the 2004 South Carolina Season Auction or registered Virginia-bred/-sired or South Carolina-bred, 6f, 1:08.83, OUTSTANDER, Native Heir, Standing Room Only, 5 started.

SIXTY SAILS H.-G3, Hawthorne Race Course, April 24, $250,000, 3&up, f&m, 1¹/₈m, 1:50.66, ALLSPICE, Bare Necessities, Mavoreen, 6 started.

Skipat S., Pimlico, May 29, $50,000, 3&up, f&m, 6f, 1:11.59, LOVE YOU MADLY, Wallop, Leavn Ona Jetplane, 6 started.

SKIP AWAY H.-G3, Gulfstream Park, March 13, $100,000, 3&up, 1¹/₈m, 1:43.26, NEWFOUNDLAND, Supah Blitz, Bowman's Band, 10 started.

Skip Away S., Monmouth Park, July 5, $70,000, 3&up, 1m 70y, 1:38.85, PRESIDENTIALAFFAIR, Donald's Pride, Regal Sanction, 6 started.

Ski Roundtop Timber S., Shawan Downs, Sept. 25, $23,260, 4&up, 3³/₄mT, 7:17.20, DARNTIPALARM, Bubble Economy, Romantic Virginian, 5 started.

Skunktail S. (R), Horsemen's Park, July 18, $29,800, 3yo, c&g, Nebraska-bred, 1m, 1:40.60, MORTRUMP, Thundering Verzy, Cassanova Kid, 8 started.

SKY CLASSIC H.-G2, Woodbine, Oct. 2, $275,250, 3&up, 1³/₈mT, 2:16.19, COLORFUL JUDGEMENT, Lenny the Lender, Longship, 7 started.

Sleepy Hollow S. (R), Belmont Park, Oct. 23, $100,000, 2yo, New York-bred, 1m, 1:37.34, GALLOPING GROCER, Naughty New Yorker, Carminooch, 6 started.

Slight in the Rear S. (R), Fairmount Park, Aug. 24, $35,600, 3yo, f, Illinois-bred, 6f, 1:11.40, MISS OUTRAGEOUS, Lady Riss, Buckle Up Cart, 8 started.

Slipton Fell H., Mountaineer Race Track, June 5, $75,000, 3&up, 1m 70y, 1:42.25, ASK THE LORD, Eagle Time, Sir Cherokee, 4 started.

Smart Deb S., Arlington Park, Aug. 14, $52,200, 3yo, f, 6f, 1:11, QUESTIONABLE PAST, Bad Kitty, Silver Crown, 5 started.

Smart Halo S., Pimlico, April 4, $50,000, 3yo, f, 6f, 1:12.67, SPIRITED GAME, Highgate Park, But Mommy, 9 started.

SMILE SPRINT H.-G3, Calder Race Course, July 10, $500,000, 3&up, 6f, 1:10.14, CHAMPALI, Clock Stopper, Built Up, 10 started.

Snow Chief S. (R), Hollywood Park, April 24, $250,000, 3yo, California-bred, 1¹/₈m, 1:48.78, CHEIRON, Don'tsellmeshort, Southern Outlaw, 8 started.

Snow White S., Charles Town Races, Dec. 11, $51,500, 2yo, f, 7f, 1:29.90, SMOKING WISE, Bluesbdancing, Ellajean, 10 started.

Snurb S., Calder Race Course, Aug. 8, $40,000, 3yo, f, 7f, 1:25.12, FORMAT, Family Favorite, Clandestine, 5 started.

Soaring Softly S. (R), Aqueduct, Nov. 11, $61,000, 3yo, f, nonwinners of a stakes in 2004, 1mT, 1:38.04, RIGHT THIS WAY, Humoristic, Tuesday Prayer, 10 started.

Soft Parade S. (1st Div.), Calder Race Course, Nov. 6, $40,000, 3&up, f&m, 1¹/₁₆mT, 1:43.63, FORMAL MISS, Krasnaya, Cute Connie, 9 started.

Soft Parade S. (2nd Div.), Calder Race Course, Nov. 6, $40,000, 3&up, f&m, 1¹/₁₆mT, 1:44.13, BEEBE LAKE, Love Sting, Derrianne, 11 started.

Solana Beach H. (R), Del Mar, Sept. 5, $125,000, 3&up, f&m, California-bred, 1mT, 1:34.92, TUCKED AWAY, Test the Waters, Ran for the Dough, 7 started.

Solano County Juvenile Filly S. (R), Solano County Fair, July 25, $53,400, 2yo, f, California-bred, 5¹/₂f, 1:04.64, KELLY'S PRINCESS, Tense Wager, Point Reyes, 10 started.

Solo Haina S., Calder Race Course, June 22, $40,000, 3&up, f&m, 1mT, 1:41.48, PAMPERED PRINCESS, Tuscany Light, Sierra Lady, 6 started.

Somethingroyal S. (R), Colonial Downs, June 19, $50,000, 3&up, f&m, Virginia-bred and/or -sired, 5¹/₂fT, 1:03.99, WITH PATIENCE, Bright Gold, Key Wi Miss, 11 started.

Sonny Hine S., Pimlico, Oct. 16, $50,000, 3yo, 6f, 1:10.59, MOVE TO STRIKE, Wimplestiltskin, On Thin Ice, 7 started.

Sonoma S., Northlands Park, Aug. 14, $100,000, 3yo, f, 1¹/₁₆m, 1:45.80, OVERACT, Socorro County, Sounce a Silence, 7 started.

Sophomore Sprint Championship S., Mountaineer Race Track, Nov. 23, $75,000, 3yo, 6f, 1:10.07, DANIELTOWN, Nebraska Moon, Elegant Fame, 8 started.

Sophomore Turf S., Tampa Bay Downs, April 4, $85,300, 3yo, 1¹/₁₆mT, 1:42.58, KEYSTONE POINT, Indigo Flyer, Soldier of Fame, 12 started.

Sorority S., Monmouth Park, Sept. 4, $97,000, 2yo, f, 6f, 1:11.73, QUEENS PLAZA, Dance Away Capote, Bold Outlook, 4 started.

SORRENTO S.-G3, Del Mar, Aug. 7, $150,000, 2yo, f, 6¹/₂f, 1:18.29, INSPIRING, Souvenir Gift, Hello Lucky, 8 started.

Southern Beau S. (R), Louisiana Downs, Aug. 29, $50,000, 2yo, Louisiana-bred, 5¹/₂f, 1:05.20, FAVORITE MINIT, Saucey Tiger, Z Storm, 6 started.

Southern Belle S., Grants Pass, May 23, 3&up, f&m, 5¹/₂f, 1:06.10, SOUP N' CRACKERS, Crown of Pearls, Whistle Tester, 6 started.

Southern Belle S. (R), Louisiana Downs, Aug. 22, $50,000, 2yo, f, Louisiana-bred, 5¹/₂f, 1:07.37, MAID IN CHINA, Sweet Macaroni, Equestrian Girls, 8 started.

Southern Oregon Race Horse Association S., Grants Pass, July 3, $3,290, 3&up, 5f, :58.20, PRIMECAT, Whistle Tester, Jehosaphat, 5 started.

South Mississippi Owners and Breeders S. (R), Fair Grounds, Feb. 6, $43,800, 3yo, Mississippi-owned and/or -bred, 6f, 1:12.50, TEN TIMES BETTER, Sonic Eagle, Sutter's Galaxy, 13 started.

South Ocean S. (R), Woodbine, Nov. 10, $134,500, 2yo, f, progeny of eligible Ontario stallions, 1¹/₁₆m, 1:48.89, COASTAL FORTRESS, Go Dancer Go, I'm a Cheetah, 9 started.

Southwest S., Oaklawn Park, Feb. 28, $100,000, 3yo, 1m, 1:37.57, SMARTY JONES, Two Down Automatic, Pro Prado, 9 started.

Soviet Problem S., Golden Gate Fields, March 21, $55,400, 3&up, f&m, 6f, 1:09.33, CHRISTMAS TIME, Annabelly, Devil Dancing, 5 started.

Spangled Jimmy H., Northlands Park, July 10, $40,000, 3&up, 1m, 1:39.40, DEPUTY COUNTRY, Rindanica, Sixthirtyjoe, 10 started.

Spartan S. (R), Great Lakes Downs, July 3, $40,000, 3yo, c&g, Michigan-bred, 7f, 1:27.90, ROCKEM SOCKEM, Exclusivenjoyment, Monetary Dancer, 7 started.

Spectacular Bid S., Arlington Park, Aug. 29, $52,800, 2yo, 7f, 1:23.90, ROCKY RIVER, Santana Strings, Departing Now, 7 started.

SPECTACULAR BID S.-G3, Gulfstream Park, Jan. 10, $100,000, 3yo, 6f, 1:10.60, WYNN DOT COMMA, Saratoga County, Ghost Mountain, 7 started.

Speed H., Lincoln State Fair, May 22, $10,000, 3&up, 4¹/₂f, :50.60, JACK BLACK AND ICE, Classy Sheikh, Festive Fellow, 7 started.

Speed H., Louisiana Downs, Oct. 2, $40,000, 3&up, 6f, 1:09.67, OLE REBEL, That Tat, Nuttyboom, 7 started.

Speed Sprint S., Lethbridge, June 5, $11,200, 3&up, 5¹/₂f, 1:07, LOVERS SON, dh-Arctic Horizon, dh-Royal Deal, 8 started.

Speed to Spare Championship S., Northlands Park, Sept. 11, $100,000, 3&up, 1³/₁₆m, 2:20.20, BEAU BRASS, Illusive Force, Bubblegum Kid, 11 started.

SPEND A BUCK H.-G3, Calder Race Course, Oct. 23, $100,000, 3&up, 1¹/₁₆m, 1:45.86, BUILT UP, Super Frolic, Gold Dollar, 11 started.

Spend a Buck S., Fairmount Park, July 24, $30,900, 3yo, c&g, 1m 70y, 1:43.40, IT'S LUCKY, Warned, Tanner Danner, 9 started.

Spicy H. (R), Arapahoe Park, Sept. 5, $26,725, 3&up, f&m, Colorado-bred, 1¹/₁₆m, 1:42.80, SHE'S FINDING TIME, Tricky Transaction, Bar Bailey, 6 started.

SPINAWAY S.-G2, Saratoga Race Course, Aug. 20, $250,000, 2yo, f, 7f, 1:23.83, SENSE OF STYLE, Miss Matched, Play With Fire, 7 started.

Spirit of Texas S. (R), Sam Houston Race Park, Nov. 20, $50,000, 3&up, Texas-bred, 6f, 1:10.09, CHARMING SOCIALITE, Czech Mate, Term Sheet, 8 started.

Sport City H., Louisiana Downs, Sept. 5, $50,000, 3&up, 1¹/₁₆mT, 1:42.01, NORTHERN SCENE, Rockchalk Jayhawk, Gentlemen J J, 7 started.

Sport of Queens Filly and Mare Hurdle S., Camden, Nov. 21, $30,000, 3&up, f&m, a2¹/₄mT, 4:28, FEELING SO PRETTY, Amazing Truth, Polly Everafter, 6 started.

SPORT PAGE H.-G3, Aqueduct, Oct. 31, $111,200, 3&up, 7f, 1:21.10, MASS MEDIA, Lion Tamer, Gygistar, 9 started.

Sportsman's Paradise S., Delta Downs, March 13, $48,500, 3yo, 7f, 1:26.94, BRITT'S JULES, Every Advantage, There Goes Rocket, 4 started.

Spring Fever S., Oaklawn Park, March 7, $50,000, 4&up, f&m, 5¹/₂f, 1:04.70, SURF N SAND, Eternal Cup, See How She Runs, 6 started.

Springfield S. (R), Arlington Park, June 26, $88,050, 3yo, Illinois-conceived and/or -foaled, 1m, 1:36.31, FORT PRADO, Jaguar Friend, Prairie King, 12 started.

Spring S. (R), Sam Houston Race Park, March 20, $40,000, 4&up, Texas-bred, 7f, 1:22.56, CATALISSA, Won C C, Term Sheet, 7 started.

Springtime S. (R), Charles Town Races, April 24, $51,550, 3&up, starters at Charles Town the most times in last four starts, 7f, 1:25.46, GREAT COMMANDER, Ginger Ale, North Broad, 10 started.

Sprint Series Final S., Yavapai Downs, Aug. 9, $11,500, 3&up, 6f, 1:10.40, PADRE MURPHY, Grand Canyon, Jack Dugan, 6 started.

Spruce Fir H. (R), Monmouth Park, July 24, $60,000, 3&up, f&m, New Jersey-bred, 1mT, 1:38.50, UPHILL SKIER, Smart N Classy, Eastern Gale, 11 started.

Squan Song S. (R), Pimlico, Dec. 26, $50,000, 3&up, f&m, Maryland-bred nonwinners of a stakes, 6f, 1:13.05, PERILOUS NIGHT, Sea of Promises, Free Dip, 10 started.

Stampede Park Sprint Championship H., Stampede Park, May 8, $40,000, 4&up, 6f, 1:11.60, DANCE ME FREE, Rindanica, They Call Me Cody, 7 started.

Standard Auto Glass S., Grand Prairie, July 16, $4,000, 3&up, 5¹/₂f, 1:07.60, LAFLEUR, Bullinsky, Onastar, 5 started.

Stanford S., Bay Meadows, April 18, $68,137, 3yo, f, 6f, 1:09.21, ALLSWELLTHATNSWELL, I'mbethtoo, Madrone, 5 started.

Stanton S., Delaware Park, Sept. 6, $55,100, 3yo, 1¹/₁₆mT, 1:49.93, GUNNING FOR, Commendation, Minnamana, 7 started.

Star Ball H., Golden Gate Fields, Nov. 14, $51,875, 3&up, f&m, 1¹/₁₆mT, 1:45.28, FRISCO BELLE, Stormica, Shezsospiritual, 7 started.

Star de Naskra S. (R), Pimlico, April 25, $75,000, 3yo, Maryland-bred, 6f, 1:11.30, MOVE TO STRIKE, Known Back Home, Hands On, 6 started.

Stardust S. (R), Louisiana Downs, Oct. 23, $56,200, 2yo, Louisiana-bred, 6f, 1:10.88, MALANATO, Robbeau, Z Storm, 11 started.

Star of Texas S. (R), Sam Houston Race Park, Nov. 20, $100,000, 3&up, Texas-bred, 1¹/₁₆mT, 1:43.74, GOOSEY MOOSE, Catalissa, Lights On Broadway, 9 started.

STARS AND STRIPES BREEDERS' CUP TURF H.-G3, Arlington Park, July 4, $200,000, 3&up, 1¹/₄mT, 2:36.30, BALLINGARRY (Ire), Grey Beard, Art Variety (Brz), 8 started.

Stars and Stripes H., Les Bois Park, July 4, $6,550, 3&up, 7¹/₂f, 1:31.80, RENO BOUND, Find My Halter, Quiet Syns, 6 started.

Star Shoot S., Woodbine, April 25, $182,375, 3yo, f, 6f, 1:11.72, ON-THEQT, Nashinda, Dana's Lucky Lady, 5 started.

State Fair Board H., Lincoln State Fair, July 5, $13,563, 3&up, 1m 70y, 1:45.60, GRAYGLEN, Secret Banker, Flyin Brian, 6 started.

State Fair Breeders' Special S. (R), Lincoln State Fair, June 12, $15,600, 3yo, Nebraska-bred, 1m, 1:38.80, THUNDERING VERZY, Cassanova Kid, Sunday Trigger, 6 started.

State Fair Derby, Lincoln State Fair, June 26, $12,813, 3yo, 1m, 1:39, METTS REWARD, Cassanova Kid, Speedy Halo, 6 started.

State Fair Futurity (R), Lincoln State Fair, July 11, $15,700, 2yo, Nebraska-bred, 4¹/₂f, :52.80, BIG RED FANTASY, Yah Sure, Stetson, 7 started.

Statue of Liberty S. (R), Saratoga Race Course, Aug. 5, $250,000, 3yo, f, progeny of eligible New York stallions, 1¹/₄m, 1:51.67, SO SWEET A CAT, South Wing, Cat's Roar, 12 started.

Steady Growth S. (R), Woodbine, June 12, $129,375, 3&up, progeny of eligible Ontario stallions, 1¹/₁₆m, 1:44.54, NORFOLK KNIGHT, Hot Pepper Hill, Barath, 6 started.

Stefanita S., Pimlico, Nov. 20, $50,000, 3&up, f&m, 6f, 1:10.58, SENSIBLY CHIC, Wallop, Thermal Ablasion, 8 started.

STEPHEN FOSTER H.-G1, Churchill Downs, June 12, $810,750, 3&up, 1¹/₈m, 1:50.40, COLONIAL COLONY, Southern Image, Perfect Drift, 6 started.

Steve Van Buren H., Philadelphia Park, Sept. 6, $75,000, 3&up, f&m, 7f, 1:22.60, SMOOTH MANEUVERS, Thermal Ablasion, Ladyecho, 9 started.

St. Georges Overnight S., Delaware Park, June 15, $52,089, 3yo, f, 1¹/₁₆m, 1:45.52, BECKY IN PINK, Via Sacra, Cape Trafalgar (Ire), 4 started.

St. Nick S., Charles Town Races, Dec. 26, $51,150, 2yo, 7f, 1:26.75, MALIBU MOONSHINE, Sueno Del Mar, Wild Remarks, 6 started.

Stonehedge Farm South Sophomore Fillies S., Tampa Bay Downs, April 4, $85,100, 3yo, f, 7f, 1:26.73, CHENIA, Bird Chatter, Runaway Rizzi, 13 started.

STONERSIDE BEAUMONT S.-G2, Keeneland, April 8, $250,000, 3yo, f, a7f, 1:27.06, VICTORY U.S. A., Halfbridled, Wildwood Flower, 8 started.

STONERSIDE FORWARD GAL S.-G2, Gulfstream Park, March 13, $150,000, 3yo, f, 7f, 1:22.97, MADCAP ESCAPADE, La Reina, Frenchglen, 5 started.

Stonerside S., Lone Star Park, Oct. 29, $150,000, 3yo, f, 7f, 1:20.67, YEARLY REPORT, Homemaker, Angelica Slew, 8 started.

Storm Cat S., Keeneland, Oct. 10, $110,600, 3yo, 1mT, 1:36.50, GOOD REWARD, Fort Prado, Silver Ticket, 8 started.

Storm Cat S., The Meadowlands, Oct. 30, $60,000, 2yo, 1 $1/16$m, 1:45.04, KILLENAULE, Elusive Thunder, Diamond Clip, 5 started.

St. Paul S., Canterbury Park, June 5, $40,000, 3yo, 6f, 1:08.94, JIMMY CRACKED CORN, Mississippi Rain, Notonetoquit, 6 started.

Stravinsky S., Keeneland, April 17, $85,575, 3&up, f&m, 5 $1/2$fT, 1:02.63, DYNA DA WYNA, Boozin' Susan, Put Me In, 12 started.

Strawberry Morn S., Hastings Race Course, April 17, $43,340, 3&up, f&m, 6 $1/2$f, 1:19.28, DANCEWITHAVIXEN, Secret Bullet, Shelby Madison, 4 started.

STRUB S.-G2, Santa Anita Park, Feb. 7, $300,000, 4yo, 1 $1/8$m, 1:49.08, DOMESTIC DISPUTE, During, Buckland Manor, 11 started.

Sturgeon River S. (R), Northlands Park, Sept. 25, $50,000, 2yo, f, Alberta-bred, 1m, 1:40.60, SPEEDY GONE SALLY, R Lucinda, Saucy Ciano, 5 started.

STUYVESANT H.-G3, Aqueduct, Nov. 13, $109,900, 3&up, 1 $1/8$m, 1:49.70, CLASSIC ENDEAVOR, Colita, Snake Mountain, 7 started.

Stymie H., Aqueduct, March 6, $81,625, 3&up, 1 $1/8$m, 1:50.92, GROUND STORM, Big Sid's Party, Nothing Flat, 6 started.

Subtle Dancer S., Calder Race Course, Oct. 17, $40,000, 3&up, f&m, 6f, 1:11.90, REALLY ROYAL, Tchula Miss, Crafty Brat, 6 started.

SUBURBAN H.-G1, Belmont Park, July 3, $500,000, 3&up, 1 $1/4$m, 1:59.52, PEACE RULES, Newfoundland, Funny Cide, 8 started.

Suffolk Downs Oaks, Suffolk Downs, July 3, $40,000, 3yo, f, a1m 70yT, 1:45.98, CHENIA, Yingyingying, dh-Casa Nekia, dh-Lady Beelzebub, 9 started.

Sugar Bowl S., Fair Grounds, Dec. 24, $60,000, 2yo, 6f, 1:10.69, STORM SURGE, Santana Strings, Razor, 6 started.

Sugar n Spice S., Calder Race Course, May 30, $40,000, 3&up, f&m, 6f, 1:11.50, MARY MURPHY, Crafty Brat, Splasha, 6 started.

Summer Classic S., Charles Town Races, June 5, $51,050, 3&up, 1 $1/8$m, 1:53.73, CHEROKEE'S BOY, Prince Benjamin, Jackyscrafty-chance, 6 started.

Summer Distaff S., Charles Town Races, June 19, $51,400, 3&up, f&m, 1 $1/16$m, 1:47.19, RIBBON CANE, Lets Just Do It, Grace Bay, 9 started.

Summer Finale H., Mountaineer Race Track, Sept. 6, $75,000, 3&up, f&m, 1mT, 1:34.09, CHANCE DANCE, Passionate Bird, Tempus Fugit, 7 started.

Summer King S., Delaware Park, May 22, $52,700, 3&up, f&m, 1 $1/16$m, 1:45.51, MISTY SIXES, Gelli, Worldly Pleasure, 5 started.

SUMMER S.-G2, Woodbine, Sept. 19, $277,750, 2yo, 1mT, 1:34.69, DUBLEO, Dance With Ravens, Go to the Sun, 8 started.

Summertime Promise S., Hawthorne Race Course, Oct. 23, $43,600, 3yo, f, 1 $1/16$m, 1:45.32, CODE OF ETHICS, Ms. Lydonia, Dancing Liebling, 7 started.

Sumter S., Calder Race Course, Sept. 26, $40,000, 3&up, 1 $1/16$m, 1:46.27, TOUR OF THE CAT, Built Up, Super Frolic, 9 started.

Sun City H., Turf Paradise, March 13, $40,000, 3&up, f&m, 1mT, 1:35.61, ASPEN HILL, Magnificent Val, Frisco Belle, 7 started.

Suncoast S., Tampa Bay Downs, Feb. 21, $60,000, 3yo, f, 1 $1/16$m, 1:47.16, ENDER'S SISTER, Fall Fashion, Ladyinareddress, 10 started.

Sun Devil S., Turf Paradise, Jan. 17, $40,000, 3yo, f, 1m, 1:37.51, COKE'S MELODY, Very Vegas, Fun'ngames Toknite, 10 started.

Sunflower H., The Woodlands, Sept. 26, $25,000, 3&up, c&g, Kansas-bred, 6f, 1:10.60, POLAR BARRON, Mr Ammo, Clever Red, 10 started.

Sun H., Hastings Race Course, May 1, $44,576, 3&up, f&m, 6 $1/2$f, 1:17.04, DANCEWITHAVIXEN, Victor's Secret, Elana d'Amour, 6 started.

Sunland Park Fall Thoroughbred Derby, Sunland Park, Nov. 14, $53,100, 3yo, 6 $1/2$f, 1:15.87, TWO DOWN AUTOMATIC, Russian Elite, Rollicking Caller, 7 started.

Sunland Park H., Sunland Park, April 10, $107,950, 3&up, 1 $1/4$m, 1:53.41, A TO THE Z, Pleasant Bend, Wishingitwas, 12 started.

Sunny's Halo S. (R), Woodbine, Nov. 27, $104,000, 2yo, Canadian-bred, 6 $1/2$f, 1:17.96, DAVE THE KNAVE, Out From Africa, Nikey Missile, 9 started.

Sunny Slope S., Santa Anita Park, Oct. 23, $86,025, 2yo, 6f, 1:09.82, SEATTLES BEST JOE, Chips Are Down, Senor Fango, 6 started.

Sun Power S. (R), Hawthorne Race Course, Nov. 13, $90,225, 2yo, c&g, Illinois-conceived and/or -foaled, 6f, 1:11.70, HUMOR AT LAST, Stormy Afternoon, Win Me Over, 9 started.

SunRay Park and Casino H., SunRay Park, Aug. 9, $32,000, 3yo, 6 $1/2$f, 1:18, RUSSIAN ELITE, Western Ridge, Please Louie, 4 started.

Sunset Gun S. (R), Suffolk Downs, Sept. 6, $40,000, 3&up, f&m, Massachusetts-bred, a1 $1/16$mT, 1:48.88, SUNLIT RIDGE, Ask Queenie, Deerwood Lass, 9 started.

SUNSET H.-G2, Hollywood Park, July 18, $150,000, 3&up, 1 $1/2$mT, 2:26.47, STAR OVER THE BAY, Continuously, Leprechaun Kid, 7 started.

Sunshine Millions Classic S. (R), Santa Anita Park, Jan. 24, $1,000,000, 4&up, California- or Florida-bred, 1 $1/8$m, 1:47.67, SOUTHERN IMAGE, Excess Summer, The Judge Sez Who, 12 started.

Sunshine Millions Dash S. (R), Santa Anita Park, Jan. 24, $250,000, 3yo, California- or Florida-bred, 6f, 1:08.68, SAINT AFLEET, Cheiron, Ice Wynnd Fire, 10 started.

Sunshine Millions Filly and Mare Sprint S. (R), Santa Anita Park, Jan. 24, $300,000, 4&up, f&m, California- or Florida-bred, 6f, 1:09.34, MOOJI MOO, Bold Roberta, dh-Bear Fan, dh-Channing Way, 10 started.

Sunshine Millions Filly and Mare Turf S. (R), Santa Anita Park, Jan. 24, $500,000, 4&up, f&m, California- or Florida-bred, 1 $1/8$mT, 1:46.31, VALENTINE DANCER, Moscow Burning, Bartok's Blithe, 11 started.

Sunshine Millions Oaks (R), Gulfstream Park, Jan. 24, $250,000, 3yo, f, California- or Florida-bred, 6f, 1:10.82, SILENT SIGHS, Wacky Patty, Dixie High, 6 started.

Sunshine Millions Sprint S. (R), Gulfstream Park, Jan. 24, $300,000, 4&up, California- or Florida-bred, 6f, 1:09.18, SHAKE YOU DOWN, Green Team, Valid Video, 7 started.

Sun Sprint Championship S., Northlands Park, Aug. 2, $50,000, 3&up, 6 $1/2$f, 1:17.20, DEPUTY COUNTRY, Sixthirtyjoe, Catalone, 6 started.

Super Bowl S., Sam Houston Race Park, Jan. 24, $29,100, 3yo, f, 6f, 1:11.85, LUCKY TUNNEL, Rare Glitter, Cookin's Cast, 4 started.

SUPER DERBY-G2, Louisiana Downs, Sept. 25, $500,000, 3yo, 1 $1/8$m, 1:51.40, FANTASTICAT, Borrego, Britt's Jules, 9 started.

Supernaturel H., Hastings Race Course, May 24, $43,440, 3yo, f, 6 $1/2$f, 1:17, REGAL RED, Socorro County, Princess Alex, 4 started.

Super S., Tampa Bay Downs, Jan. 24, $50,000, 4&up, 7f, 1:23.78, ABOVE THE WIND, Scrubs, Attack the Books, 14 started.

Susan B. Anthony H. (R), Finger Lakes, May 31, $50,000, 3&up, f&m, New York-bred, 6f, 1:10.94, COLOGNY, Travelator, Serenity's Smile, 9 started.

Susan's Girl Breeders' Cup S., Delaware Park, June 19, $175,900, 3yo, f, 1 $1/16$m, 1:44.90, HOPELESSLY DEVOTED, From Away, Richetta, 8 started.

Susan's Girl S. (R), Calder Race Course, Sept. 6, $125,000, 2yo, f, progeny of eligible Florida stallions, 7f, 1:27.74, ACLASSYSASSY-LASSY, Cut the Mustard, Yes It's Gold, 7 started.

Sussex H., Delaware Park, Sept. 18, $91,000, 3&up, 1 $1/16$mT, 1:43.91, PRIVATE LAP, Run to Victory, American Freedom, 3 started.

Suthern Accent S., Louisiana Downs, June 6, $47,500, 3&up, f&m, 6f, 1:11.23, LESLIE'S LOVE, Joyce Ann, Cielo Girl, 4 started.

Suwannee River H., Gulfstream Park, Jan. 31, $100,000, 3&up, f&m, 1 $1/8$m, 1:54.86, WISHFUL SPLENDOR, May Gator, Mymich, 5 started.

SWALE S.-G3, Gulfstream Park, March 13, $150,000, 3yo, 7f, 1:22.87, WYNN DOT COMMA, Eurosilver, Dashboard Drummer, 5 started.

SWAPS BREEDERS' CUP S.-G2, Hollywood Park, July 10, $409,300, 3yo, 1 $1/8$m, 1:47.47, ROCK HARD TEN, Suave, Boomzeeboom, 6 started.

Sweet Briar Too S., Woodbine, June 6, $108,000, 3&up, f&m, 7f, 1:23.82, WINTER GARDEN, Spanish Decree, Miss Santa Anita, 7 started.

Sweetest Chant S., Arlington Park, July 30, $54,000, 3yo, f, 1m, 1:36.97, FLY AWAY ANGEL, Catboat, Miss Moses, 10 started.

Sweetheart S., Portland Meadows, Feb. 14, $10,000, 4&up, f&m, 1 $1/16$m, 1:46.88, STATELY'S CHOICE, Little Pursuit, Blue Atlantis, 7 started.

Sweetheart S., Delta Downs, Feb. 14, $50,000, 4&up, f&m, 7f, 1:30.46, CIELO GIRL, dh-Bloody Liz, dh-Fuse It, 8 started.

Sweet n Sassy H., Delaware Park, May 15, $75,300, 3&up, f&m, 6f, 1:10.53, BRONZE ABE, Umpateedle, Rebecca's Charm, 6 started.

Swift S. (R), Turf Paradise, Jan. 24, $40,000, 4&up, starters at the 2003-'04 Turf Paradise meet, 5 $1/2$f, 1:02.83, PALMERTON, Captain's Maneuver, Toast for Mr. Expo, 7 started.

SWORD DANCER INVITATIONAL H.-G1, Saratoga Race Course, Aug. 14, $500,000, 3&up, 1 $1/2$mT, 2:28.49, BETTER TALK NOW, Request for Parole, Balto Star, 6 started.

S. W. Randall Plate H., Hastings Race Course, Sept. 6, $43,085, 3&up, 1¹/₁₆m, 1:49.98, LORD NELSON, Blowin in the Wind, Metatron, 7 started.

Swynford S., Woodbine, Sept. 25, $136,000, 2yo, 7f, 1:24.67, WHAT'S UP DUDE, The Finagler, Pack Lightly, 5 started.

SYCAMORE BREEDERS' CUP S.-G3, Keeneland, Oct. 9, $152,300, 3&up, 1¹/₂mT, 2:30.88, MUSTANFAR, Deputy Strike, Rochester, 9 started.

Sydney Gendelman Memorial H.(R), River Downs, June 20, $45,000, 3&up, Ohio-bred, 1¹/₁₆mT, 1:42.40, BRENT'S CHALLANGER, Brent's Victory, Ben's Reflection, 11 started.

Tacoma H., Emerald Downs, June 27, $42,250, 3yo, c&g, 1m, 1:35.80, RANDOM MEMO, Pool Boy, Jablunkov Pass, 8 started.

Tah Dah S. (R), River Downs, Aug. 1, $40,000, 2yo, f, Ohio-bred, 5¹/₂f, 1:07, NOON WIN, Cloud Forty Nine, Melissa Rocks, 8 started.

Taking Risks S., Timonium, Sept. 6, $50,000, 3&up, Maryland-bred, 1¹/₁₆m, 1:46.65, CAPTAIN CHESSIE, Polish Pride, Conservation, 5 started.

Tampa Bay Breeders' Cup S., Tampa Bay Downs, Feb. 14, $100,000, 3&up, 1¹/₁₆mT, 1:41.68, BURNING ROMA, Remind, Native Hawk, 12 started.

TAMPA BAY DERBY-G3, Tampa Bay Downs, March 14, $250,000, 3yo, 1¹/₁₆m, 1:43.99, LIMEHOUSE, Mustanfar, Swingforthefences, 8 started.

Tanforan H., Golden Gate Fields, Feb. 7, $84,900, 4&up, 1¹/₁₆mT, 1:45.35, WIXOE EXPRESS (Ire), Aly Bubba, Gold Ruckus, 10 started.

Taylor's Special H., Fair Grounds, Feb. 22, $75,000, 4&up, 6f, 1:09.57, OUT OF MY WAY, Cat Genius, Aloha Bold, 8 started.

Taylor's Special S., Arlington Park, Sept. 19, $44,125, 3&up, 5¹/₂fT, 1:02.44, MARLEY'S REVENGE, Chosen Chief, Miners Gamble, 8 started.

Teddy Drone S., Monmouth Park, Aug. 8, $100,000, 3&up, 6f, 1:09.14, CANADIAN FRONTIER, Wildcat Heir, Here's Zealous, 7 started.

Ted Theibert Memorial Marathon S., Western Montana Fair, Aug. 14, $3,450, 3&up, 1 5/8m, 2:57.20, NEIGHBORHOOD BULLY, Moe Boots, Slick Decision, 6 started.

Teeworth Plate H., Stampede Park, May 23, $40,000, 3&up, 1m, 1:40.20, DEPUTY COUNTRY, Rindanica, Code Name Fred, 10 started.

Tejano Run S., Turfway Park, March 13, $50,000, 4&up, 1¹/₁₆mT, 1:49.82, ASK THE LORD, Collateral Damage, Play It Out, 7 started.

Tejas S. (R), Retama Park, Sept. 18, $40,000, 3yo, Texas-bred, 5fT, :56.23, CHARMING SOCIALITE, Oncearoundtwice, Aggie Grit, 8 started.

Tellike H., Evangeline Downs, May 29, $40,000, 3&up, f&m, 6f, 1:11.20, KYLERS MIDGE, Light Fling, Power of Dreams, 7 started.

Tempe H., Turf Paradise, March 20, $40,000, 3yo, 1mT, 1:36.14, dh-SPANISH HIGHWAY, dh-WESTERN RIDGE, Thundering Verzy, 10 started.

TEMPTED S.-G3, Aqueduct, Nov. 2, $104,600, 2yo, f, 1m, 1:36.09, SUMMER RAVEN, K. D.'s Shady Lady, Salute, 5 started.

Temptress S. (R), Great Lakes Downs, Aug. 27, $45,000, 2yo, f, Michigan-bred, 6f, 1:17.20, FOOLININTHEMEADOW, Everglide, Holidaisy, 8 started.

Tenacious H., Fair Grounds, Dec. 4, $60,000, 3&up, 1¹/₁₆m, 1:45.48, MIDWAY ROAD, Pie N Burger, Kodema, 8 started.

Ten Thousand Lakes S. (R), Canterbury Park, May 15, $40,000, 3&up, c&g, Minnesota-bred, 6f, 1:11.19, CROCROCK, Adroitly Superb, Timberwolf Power, 10 started.

Terpsichorist S. (R), Belmont Park, May 27, $61,000, 3yo, f, nonwinners of a stakes, 1¹/₁₆mT, 1:45.29, DELTA SENSATION, Savage Beauty, Art Fan, 10 started.

TEST S.-G1, Saratoga Race Course, July 31, $250,000, 3yo, f, 7f, 1:23.69, SOCIETY SELECTION, Bending Strings, Forest Music, 12 started.

Testum S. (R), Les Bois Park, June 23, $13,958, 3yo, c&g, Idaho-bred, 7f, 1:25.60, ROBS COIN, Game Master, Northern Buck, 10 started.

Texas Heritage S., Sam Houston Race Park, March 6, $30,000, 3yo, 1m, 1:38.72, FOXTROT OSCAR, Sling Shot, Goosey Moose, 12 started.

Texas Horse Racing Hall of Fame S. (R), Retama Park, Sept. 18, $100,000, 3&up, Texas-bred, 1¹/₁₆mT, 1:42.24, RARE CURE, Shakethemhatersoff, Desert Deputy, 7 started.

TEXAS MILE S.-G3, Lone Star Park, April 24, $300,000, 3&up, 1m, 1:35.64, KELA, Supah Blitz, Yessirgeneralsir, 8 started.

Texas Stallion S. (R), Lone Star Park, July 10, $125,000, 2yo, f, progeny of eligible Texas stallions, 5¹/₂f, 1:04.70, BERDELIA, Rockin Regent, Timber Jones, 8 started.

Texas Stallion S. (R), Lone Star Park, July 11, $125,000, 2yo, c&g, progeny of eligible Texas stallions, 5¹/₂f, 1:04.28, EXPECT WILL, Leaving On My Mind, Expect Wings, 9 started.

Texas Stallion S. (R), Retama Park, Sept. 18, $125,000, 2yo, progeny of eligible Texas stallions, 6f, 1:11.89, LEAVING ON MY MIND, Expect Will, Dixie Meister, 7 started.

Texas Stallion S. (R), Retama Park, Sept. 18, $125,000, 2yo, f, progeny of eligible Texas stallions, 6f, 1:13.05, TUNED IN, Rockin Regent, Butterfly Bloom, 9 started.

Texas Stallion S. (R), Sam Houston Race Park, Feb. 14, $75,000, 3yo, f, progeny of eligible Texas stallions, 1¹/₁₆m, 1:48.84, NATIVE ANNIE, Marxie, Expect a Surprise, 7 started.

Texas Stallion S. (R), Sam Houston Race Park, Feb. 14, $75,000, 3yo, c&g, progeny of eligible Texas stallions, 1¹/₁₆m, 1:47.64, THERE GOES ROCKET, Sling Shot, Woodmeister, 6 started.

Texas Turf S., Lone Star Park, Oct. 30, $100,000, 3&up, 1¹/₁₆mT, 1:51.96, ROYAL REGALIA, Kathir, Xirius, 12 started.

Tex's Zing S. (R), Fairmount Park, Aug. 24, $35,600, 3yo, c&g, Illinois-bred, 6f, 1:11.20, MATTHEW'S BLESSING, Jaygar Dancer, Kemp, 6 started.

Thanksgiving H., Fair Grounds, Nov. 25, $60,000, 3&up, 6f, 1:10.38, OLE REBEL, Wildcat Shoes, Beau's Town, 7 started.

Thanksgiving H., Portland Meadows, Nov. 26, $10,000, 3&up, 1m, 1:39.41, TABLE ME N SAROS, Yesss, Zip the Bright, 12 started.

Thats Our Buck S. (1st Div.), Calder Race Course, April 26, $40,000, 3&up, 7f, 1:24.35, SEA OF TRANQUILITY, Built Up, Scrubs, 8 started.

Thats Our Buck S. (2nd Div.), Calder Race Course, April 26, $40,000, 3&up, 7f, 1:24.51, TWILIGHT ROAD, Super Frolic, Patriotic Flame, 9 started.

The Downs at Albuquerque H., The Downs at Albuquerque, July 5, $65,900, 3&up, 1¹/₁₆m, 1:49.75, SOCKO, Wolfwithintegrity, Pleasant Bend, 9 started.

Thelma S., Fair Grounds, Jan. 3, $60,000, 3yo, f, 6f, 1:11.27, MOVANT, Sister Swank, Turn to Lass, 5 started.

THE VERY ONE H.-G3, Gulfstream Park, Feb. 28, $100,000, 3&up, f&m, 1³/₈mT, 2:19.65, BINYA (Ger), Ocean Silk, Boana (Ger), 12 started.

The Very One S., Pimlico, May 14, $75,000, 3&up, f&m, 5fT, :56.02, GO GO BABY GO, Oh Say Vicki, Boozin' Susan, 9 started.

Thomas Edison S., The Meadowlands, Nov. 5, $60,000, 3&up, 5fT, :56.37, CUMBY TEXAS, Blue Skies Ahead, Rudirudy, 5 started.

Thomas F. Moran S. (R), Suffolk Downs, Aug. 21, $39,200, 3&up, Massachusetts-bred, 1¹/₁₆mT, 1:46.37, JINI'S JET, Stylish Sultan, Monsterous Mitch, 5 started.

Thomas J. Malley S., Monmouth Park, May 31, $60,000, 3&up, f&m, 5fT, :56.93, HOSTILITY, Hidden Ransom, Umpateedle, 6 started.

THOROUGHBRED CLUB OF AMERICA S.-G3, Keeneland, Oct. 17, $125,000, 3&up, f&m, 6f, 1:09.92, MOLTO VITA, My Trusty Cat, My Boston Gal, 6 started.

Thoroughbred Overnight S. (R), Ruidoso Downs, Aug. 20, $15,000, 3&up, New Mexico-bred, 5f, :57.80, HECAMEFROMACLAIM, Urlacher, Classic Ryder, 6 started.

Thoroughbred Overnight S., Ruidoso Downs, Sept. 6, $15,800, 3&up, f&m, 7¹/₂f, 1:34.80, INOX (Arg), Perty Gerty, Hava Peer, 8 started.

Three Chimneys Juvenile S., Churchill Downs, May 1, $115,400, 2yo, 5f, :57.98, LUNARPAL, Gallant Secret, Classic Elegance, 5 started.

Three Ring S., Calder Race Course, Dec. 4, $100,000, 2yo, f, 1¹/₁₆mT, 1:49.32, LEONA'S KNIGHT, Smuggler, Southern Serenity, 6 started.

Three-Year-Old Filly Sales S. (R), Northlands Park, Sept. 10, $49,000, 3yo, f, Canadian-bred sold at a CTHS sale, 1m, 1:41.60, VIEW HALLOO, The Cashew Queen, Wintuition, 8 started.

Three-Year-Old Sales S. (R), Northlands Park, Sept. 12, $50,000, 3yo, c&g, Canadian-bred sold at a CTHS sale, 1m, 1:42, DURACAT, Private Issue, Laskeek Bay, 7 started.

Thunder Road H., Santa Anita Park, Feb. 11, $71,350, 4&up, 1mT, 1:34.42, SINGLETARY, Inesperado (Fr), Apache Wings, 8 started.

Ticonderoga H. (R), Belmont Park, Oct. 23, $150,000, 3&up, f&m, New York-bred, 1¹/₈mT, 1:50.14, ON THE BUS, Sabellina, Little Buttercup, 12 started.

Tiffany Lass S., Fair Grounds, Jan. 25, $100,000, 3yo, f, 1m, 1:38.88, LOTTA KIM, Josie G., Love Power, 13 started.

Timber Music S. (R), Hastings Race Course, July 17, $44,008, 2yo, f, British Columbia-bred and/or -owned, 6¹/₂f, 1:19.10, FUCHSIA GOLD, Slewpast, Mandi Tambi, 9 started.

Timeless Prince S. (R), Canterbury Park, Aug. 7, $40,000, 2yo, Minnesota-bred, 5¹/₂f, 1:05.13, CARELESS NAVIGATOR, George L Brown, Bigeyelittleyou, 6 started.

Times Square S. (R), Aqueduct, April 25, $150,000, 3yo, progeny of eligible New York stallions, 1m, 1:39.04, WEST VIRGINIA, Pay Attention, Chowder's First, 11 started.

Tiny Toast Derby (R), The Woodlands, Oct. 3, $20,000, 3yo, f, sired by eligible Kansas stallions, 1m 70y, 1:47.20, GROOMS MOKA, Grace Line, Ama Missprint, 6 started.

Tippett S., Colonial Downs, July 25, $50,000, 2yo, f, 5¹/₂fT, 1:05.76, NORTHERN BABE, Heartful Hero, Madison Dollie, 7 started.

Tiznow S. (R), Hollywood Park, April 24, $150,000, 4&up, California-bred, 7¹/₂f, 1:27.52, BEAU SOLEIL, Excessivepleasure, Ride and Shine, 9 started.

TOBOGGAN H.-G3, Aqueduct, March 13, $112,200, 3&up, 7f, 1:22.06, WELL FANCIED, Gators N Bears, Don Six, 10 started.

Toddler S., Pimlico, Dec. 4, $38,800, 2yo, f, 6f, 1:13.23, GOLDEN MALIBU, Flashy Three (GB), Hanalei Bay, 4 started.

Tokyo City H., Santa Anita Park, March 13, $75,300, 4&up, 1m, 1:35.80, ENDER'S SHADOW, Total Impact (Chi), Gift of the Eagle, 9 started.

Tomball S. (R), Sam Houston Race Park, Feb. 7, $40,000, 4&up, f&m, Texas-bred, 1¹/₁₆m, 1:46.95, PROM DATE, Coastalota, Lady Mallory, 7 started.

Tomboy S. (R), River Downs, May 15, $45,000, 3yo, f, Ohio-bred, 1¹/₁₆mT, 1:49.40, OUTRAGEOUS QUEEN, Westward Miss, Royal Cup, 9 started.

TOM FOOL H.-G2, Belmont Park, July 4, $142,500, 3&up, 7f, 1:20.42, GHOSTZAPPER, Aggdan, Unforgettable Max, 4 started.

To Much Coffee S. (R), Hoosier Park, Nov. 14, $40,000, 3&up, Indiana-bred, 1¹/₁₆m, 1:46.51, TIN MAN COMMIN, Call Roy, Dollar for Dollar, 12 started.

Tondi H., Fonner Park, March 27, $25,000, 3&up, 6f, 1:12.60, ABBI'S CHOICE, Getaway Holme, Tonight Rainbow, 8 started.

Tony Sanchez Memorial Mile S., Manor Downs, April 25, $18,000, 3&up, 1m, 1:39.84, FOREGONE, Oro Mountain, Latexo, 10 started.

Toon's H., Marquis Downs, Aug. 28, $5,000, 3&up, 1¹/₁₆m, 1:48.75, ROUGE ROYALE, Beau Ring, Stop the Act, 7 started.

TOP FLIGHT H.-G2, Aqueduct, Nov. 26, $150,000, 3&up, f&m, 1m, 1:35.29, DAYDREAMING, Bending Strings, Roar Emotion, 6 started.

Top Hat S., Yavapai Downs, June 8, $9,700, 3yo, 6f, 1:10, SWISS BOUNTY, It's a Shortcut, Imdabossau, 7 started.

Topsider S., Suffolk Downs, Sept. 6, $40,000, 3&up, 6f, 1:11.49, SENOR LADD, On the Game, Beat the Traffic, 8 started.

TORONTO CUP H.-G3, Woodbine, July 17, $168,600, 3yo, 1¹/₁₆mT, 1:47.35, SILVER TICKET, Bachelor Blues, Burst of Fire, 10 started.

Torrey Pines S. (R), Del Mar, Sept. 4, $81,450, 3yo, f, nonwinners of a stakes of $50,000 at one mile or over in 2004, 1m, 1:37.98, MUIR BEACH, Resplendency, Alphabet Kisses, 6 started.

Totah Futurity (R), SunRay Park, Oct. 26, $92,663, 2yo, New Mexico-bred, 6¹/₂f, 1:19.40, GEIGER GOLD, Metalurgist, Devil's Justice, 9 started.

Total Rewards S., Louisiana Downs, Oct. 31, $40,000, 3&up, a5fT, :55.75, BEAU'S TOWN, G. W.'s Deputy, Aloha Bold, 8 started.

TRANSYLVANIA S.-G3, Keeneland, April 2, $113,400, 3yo, 1mT, 1:36.52, TIMO, Mr. J. T. L., America Alive, 9 started.

TRAVERS S.-G1, Saratoga Race Course, Aug. 28, $1,000,000, 3yo, 1¹/₄m, 2:02.45, BIRDSTONE, The Cliff's Edge, Eddington, 7 started.

Treasure Chest S., Delta Downs, Dec. 4, $75,000, 3&up, f&m, 7f, 1:27.26, SO MUCH MORE, Cat's Cat, Miss Confusion, 10 started.

Treasure State Futurity, Great Falls, July 31, $8,250, 2yo, 5f, 1:02, SECRET VICTORY, V R Blue, Apolo Leah, 8 started.

Tremont S., Belmont Park, June 26, $99,900, 2yo, 5¹/₂f, 1:04.89, GOLD JOY, Winning Expression, Primal Storm, 4 started.

Trenton S., Monmouth Park, Aug. 1, $55,000, 3yo, f, 5fT, :57.59, SMOKEY GLACKEN, Silver Wench, Absolute Nectar, 8 started.

TRIPLE BEND BREEDERS' CUP INVITATIONAL H.-G1, Hollywood Park, July 3, $300,000, 3&up, 7f, 1:21.06, POHAVE, Rojo Toro, Revello, 13 started.

Triple Sec S., Delta Downs, Jan. 17, $40,000, 3yo, 5f, :59.03, BRITT'S JULES, Next Bandit, Iron Expectations, 5 started.

Trippi S., Calder Race Course, May 16, $40,000, 3&up, 5fT, :55.86, CALLTHESHERIFF, Simmer, True Love's Secret, 8 started.

Tri-State Futurity (R), Charles Town Races, Oct. 23, $72,300, 2yo, Maryland-, Virginia- or West Virginia-bred, 7f, 1:29.24, JAZZY J J, Mr. Bondsman, Wild Remarks, 3 started.

Tri-State H., Ellis Park, Sept. 6, $75,000, 3&up, 1¹/₁₆mT, 1:39.22, G P FLEET, Flying Jazz, Gretchen's Star, 9 started.

Trooper Seven S. (R), Emerald Downs, Sept. 19, $40,000, 3yo, c&g, Washington-bred, 1m, 1:35.20, JAZZINAROUNNIGHTLY, dh-Fairly Honest, dh-No Giveaway, 9 started.

TROPICAL PARK DERBY-G3, Calder Race Course, Jan. 1, $100,000, 3yo, 1¹/₈mT, 1:46.95, KITTEN'S JOY, Broadway View, Soverign Honor, 11 started.

Tropical Park Oaks, Calder Race Course, Jan. 1, $100,000, 3yo, 1¹/₁₆mT, 1:42.09, BOBBIE USE, Cold Wynnter, Last Waltz, 12 started.

TROPICAL TURF H.-G3, Calder Race Course, Dec. 4, $100,000, 3&up, 1¹/₈mT, 1:45.74, HOST (Chi), Silver Tree, Demeteor, 12 started.

Troy S. (R), Saratoga Race Course, Sept. 3, $66,800, 4&up, nonwinners of an open stakes on the turf in 2003-'04, 1m, 1:34.49, WILLARD STRAIGHT, Little Jim (Arg), Golden Commander, 9 started.

TRUE NORTH BREEDERS' CUP H.-G2, Belmont Park, June 5, $210,830, 3&up, 6f, 1:08.04, SPEIGHTSTOWN, Cat Genius, Pohave, 9 started.

Truly Bound H., Fair Grounds, Jan. 4, $60,000, 4&up, f&m, 1¹/₁₆m, 1:45.25, GOLDEN SONATA, Spirited Maiden, Whiletheiron'shot, 11 started.

TTA Sales Futurity (R), Lone Star Park, June 12, $118,570, 2yo, c&g, passed through the ring at a TTA sale, 5f, :58.69, EXPECT WILL, Expect Wings, Leaving On My Mind, 11 started.

TTA Sales Futurity (R), Lone Star Park, June 12, $129,830, 2yo, f, passed through the ring at a TTA sale, 5f, :58.79, BERDELIA, Glitter Sexy, Miss Know It All, 11 started.

Tulsa Dash S., Fair Meadows at Tulsa, June 19, $43,400, 3&up, 4f, :44.60, ABBI'S CHOICE, Frilly Fun, Jack Black and Ice, 9 started.

TURF CLASSIC S.-G1, Churchill Downs, May 1, $453,900, 3&up, 1¹/₈mT, 1:53, STROLL, Sweet Return (GB), Mystery Giver, 11 started.

Turf Distaff S., Tampa Bay Downs, April 4, $84,950, 4&up, f&m, 1¹/₁₆mT, 1:42.12, SKIP TO SAVANNAH, Formal Miss, Mrs. M, 11 started.

Turf Distance Series Final S., Turf Paradise, April 26, $36,350, 3&up, 1³/₈mT, 2:16.61, SARGARI (Ire), Adjutant (GB), Mr Wensleydale (GB), 11 started.

Turf Monster H., Philadelphia Park, May 31, $100,000, 3&up, 5fT, :57.53, ABDERIAN (Ire), Testify, Shades of Sunny, 10 started.

Turf Paradise Breeders' Cup H., Turf Paradise, Feb. 7, $150,000, 3&up, 1¹/₁₆mT, 1:40.89, IRISH WARRIOR, Black Bart, Rock N Rosh, 9 started.

Turf Paradise Derby, Turf Paradise, Feb. 7, $100,000, 3yo, 1¹/₁₆m, 1:42.07, MAMBO TRAIN, Perfect Moon, Bradford, 5 started.

TURF SPRINT S.-G3, Churchill Downs, April 30, $114,700, 3&up, 5fT, :56.56, LYDGATE, Mighty Beau, Banned in Boston, 11 started.

Turf Sprint S., Lone Star Park, May 31, $100,000, 3&up, 5fT, :56.33, MIGHTY BEAU, Grifter, Joe Move, 9 started.

TURFWAY BREEDERS' CUP S.-G3, Turfway Park, Sept. 18, $175,000, 3&up, f&m, 1¹/₁₆m, 1:44.21, SUSAN'S ANGEL, Mayo On the Side, Angela's Love, 6 started.

TURFWAY PARK FALL CHAMPIONSHIP S.-G3, Turfway Park, Oct. 2, $100,000, 3&up, 1m, 1:37.19, CAPPUCHINO, Crafty Shaw, Added Edge, 7 started.

Turfway Prevue S., Turfway Park, Jan. 3, $50,000, 3yo, 6¹/₂f, 1:17.87, SILVER MINISTER, Degenerate Gambler, Rayvo's Beau, 7 started.

TURNBACK THE ALARM H.-G3, Aqueduct, Nov. 6, $110,700, 3&up, f&m, 1¹/₈m, 1:51.27, PERSONAL LEGEND, Roar Emotion, Fast Cookie, 9 started.

Tuzla H., Santa Anita Park, Jan. 28, $76,850, 4&up, f&m, 1mT, 1:34.40, FUDGE FATALE, Polygreen (Fr), Fun House, 9 started.

TVG Khaled S. (R), Hollywood Park, April 24, $150,000, 4&up, California-bred, 1¹/₁₆mT, 1:47.68, BLACK BART, dh-Continental Red, dh-Lennyfromalibu, 7 started.

Twilight Oilfield Derby, Grand Prairie, Aug. 14, $11,080, 3yo, 1m, 1:40.60, EZEE TARGET, Regal Laddie, Chief Victor, 9 started.

Twin Lights S., Monmouth Park, Aug. 21, $60,000, 3yo, f, 1¹/₈mT, 1:51.77, RICHETTA, Grinch, Skip Power, 5 started.

Twixt S. (R), Pimlico, July 31, $100,000, 3yo, f, Maryland-bred, 1¹/₈m, 1:51.12, HE LOVES ME, Richetta, Pour It On, 9 started.

Tyro S., Monmouth Park, July 31, $60,000, 2yo, 5^1/$_2$f, 1:05.02, PARK AVENUE BALL, Doctor Voodoo, On the Porch, 8 started.

U Can Do It H., Calder Race Course, Sept. 18, $75,000, 3&up, f&m, 6^1/$_2$f, 1:19, PETRINA ABOVE, Really Royal, Family Favorite, 10 started.

Unbridled S., Calder Race Course, June 19, $100,000, 3yo, 1^1/$_16$m, 1:48.46, MISTER FOTIS, Nightmare Affair, Caballero Negro, 7 started.

Union Avenue S. (R), Saratoga Race Course, Aug. 26, $66,500, 3&up, f&m, New York-bred, 6f, 1:09.81, SUGAR PUNCH, Beautiful America, Cologny, 7 started.

Unique Type S. (R), Calder Race Course, Aug. 13, $40,000, 3&up, f&m, nonwinners of $15,000 once since February 1 or nonwinners of four races other than maiden, claiming, or starter, 5^1/$_2$f, 1:05.02, SEA SPAN, Beautiful Honor, Crafty Brat, 6 started.

UNITED NATIONS S.-G1, Monmouth Park, July 3, $750,000, 3&up, 1^3/$_8$mT, 2:13.37, REQUEST FOR PAROLE, Mr O'Brien (Ire), Nothing to Lose, 11 started.

U. S. Bank S., Emerald Downs, April 18, $40,000, 3yo, f, 6f, 1:09.20, SANDIA'S FLICKA, Melba Jewel, Sariano, 11 started.

Vacaville H., Solano County Fair, July 17, $50,510, 3&up, f&m, 6f, 1:10.10, PHEIFFER, Christmas Time, Summer Lass, 6 started.

VAGRANCY H.-G2, Belmont Park, June 5, $150,000, 3&up, f&m, 6^1/$_2$f, 1:14.46, BEAR FAN, Smok'n Frolic, Aspen Gal, 9 started.

Vague Memory S. (R), Calder Race Course, June 14, $40,000, 3&up, f&m, nonwinners of $15,000 once since February 1 or nonwinners of four races other than maiden, claiming, or starter, 6f, 1:12.28, FRENCH VILLAGE, Petrina Above, Crafty Brat, 7 started.

Valdale S., Turfway Park, Feb. 21, $43,500, 3yo, f, 1m, 1:37.87, SLEWPY'S STORM, Plumlake Lady, Tarrah Trick, 7 started.

Valedictory H., Woodbine, Dec. 12, $137,375, 3&up, 1^3/$_4$m, 3:03.52, DADDY COOL, Jambalar, Solihull, 7 started.

Valid Expectations S., Lone Star Park, May 31, $100,000, 3&up, f&m, 6f, 1:07.82, SAVORTHETIME, Clear in the West, Leona's Lies, 8 started.

Valid Leader S., Turf Paradise, Oct. 26, $21,700, 3&up, f&m, 6^1/$_2$f, 1:15.66, ARCH LADY, Friendofthefamily, Strictly Legit, 6 started.

VALLEY STREAM S.-G3, Aqueduct, Nov. 21, $101,500, 2yo, f, 6f, 1:10.38, MEGASCAPE, Alfonsina, More Moonlight, 5 started.

VALLEY VIEW S.-G3, Keeneland, Oct. 23, $116,300, 3yo, f, 1^1/$_16$mT, 1:46.75, SISTER SWANK, Jinny's Gold, Shadow Cast, 12 started.

Valor Farm S. (R), Lone Star Park, Oct. 23, $50,000, 2yo, f, Texas-bred, 6^1/$_2$f, 1:18.64, MS SENECA ROCK, Martys Expectation, Tuned In, 11 started.

Vandal S. (R), Woodbine, Aug. 15, $164,550, 2yo, Canadian-bred, 6f, 1:12.73, MOONSHINE JUSTICE, Galaxy, Handlebar Hank, 8 started.

VANITY H.-G1, Hollywood Park, May 9, $245,000, 3&up, f&m, 1^1/$_8$m, 1:48.28, VICTORY ENCOUNTER, Adoration, Star Parade (Arg), 4 started.

Vector Communications S., Grand Prairie, July 30, $4,300, 3&up, 6^1/$_2$f, 1:20.20, LAFLEUR, Bullinsky, Prosperity Rose, 6 started.

Vernon Cup H., Kin Park, Aug. 1, $4,830, 3&up, a1^1/$_16$m, 1:45.62, EAGER LEE, Quick to Sin, R Ruby Rae, 3 started.

VERNON O. UNDERWOOD S.-G3, Hollywood Park, Dec. 5, $100,000, 3&up, 6f, 1:08.04, TASTE OF PARADISE, Watchem Smokey, My Master (Arg), 7 started.

Via Borghese S., Gulfstream Park, March 21, $68,050, 3yo, f, 1^1/$_16$mT, 1:40.94, MINGE COVE, Vous, Soul of the Cat, 11 started.

Vice Regent S. (R), Woodbine, Aug. 29, $131,625, 3yo, progeny of eligible Ontario stallions, 1mT, 1:40.83, ARCHERS BOW, Chemistry Class, Dashing Admiral, 7 started.

Victoria H. (R), Louisiana Downs, Oct. 23, $53,950, 3&up, f&m, Louisiana-bred, 6f, 1:10.31, DESTINY CALLS, Kylers Midge, Fuse It, 7 started.

Victoriana S. (R), Woodbine, Aug. 14, $133,250, 3&up, f&m, progeny of eligible Ontario stallions, 1^1/$_16$mT, 1:41.97, INISH GLORA, Heyahohowdy, Rosharon, 8 started.

Victorian Queen S. (R), Woodbine, Oct. 6, $134,500, 2yo, f, progeny of eligible Ontario stallions, 6f, 1:11.97, SIMPLY LOVELY, Wisdomisgold, Coastal Fortress, 9 started.

Victoria Park S., Woodbine, June 13, $140,375, 3yo, 1^1/$_8$m, 1:51.55, ORGAN GRINDER, Copper Trail, Tobe Suave, 9 started.

Victoria S., Woodbine, June 26, $139,875, 2yo, 5f, :57.90, FLAMENCO, Wholelottabourbon, Da Cardinal, 9 started.

Victor S. Myers Jr. S. (R), Canterbury Park, July 10, $40,600, 3yo, Minnesota-bred, 6f, 1:09.70, LT. SAMPSON, Vazandar, Sir Tricky, 6 started.

Victory Ride S., Saratoga Race Course, Aug. 28, $76,800, 3yo, f, 6f, 1:09.64, SMOKEY GLACKEN, Grand Prayer, Feline Story, 7 started.

VIGIL H.-G3, Woodbine, May 1, $160,800, 4&up, 7f, 1:21.81, MOBIL, Chris's Bad Boy, Awesome Action, 5 started.

Vincent A. Moscarelli Memorial H., Delaware Park, July 24, $100,000, 3&up, 6f, 1:09.97, HIGHWAY PROSPECTOR, Don Six, Sing Me Back Home, 5 started.

Vinery Madison S., Keeneland, April 7, $175,000, 4&up, f&m, 7f, 1:23.41, EMA BOVARY (Chi), Harmony Lodge, Yell, 6 started.

VIOLET H.-G3, The Meadowlands, Oct. 22, $200,000, 3&up, f&m, 1^1/$_16$mT, 1:41.53, CHANGING WORLD, High Court (Brz), Ocean Drive, 7 started.

VIRGINIA DERBY-G3, Colonial Downs, July 10, $500,000, 3yo, 1^1/$_4$mT, 2:01.22, KITTEN'S JOY, Artie Schiller, Prince Arch, 8 started.

Virginia Oaks, Colonial Downs, July 10, $200,000, 3yo, f, 1^1/$_8$mT, 1:50.41, ART FAN, Galloping Gal, Vous, 6 started.

Visa Truck Rentals Maturity, Grand Prairie, Aug. 13, $5,025, 4yo, 7f, 1:27.60, MR. ALYBRO, Lettucerace, Hodaruki, 7 started.

Vivacious H. (R), River Downs, Aug. 22, $45,000, 3&up, f&m, Ohio-bred, 1^1/$_16$mT, 1:44, OH SO EASY, Always Dreaming, Rhythm in Shoes, 12 started.

Voodoo Dancer S. (R), Belmont Park, Sept. 12, $61,450, 3&up, f&m, nonwinners of an open stakes on the turf in 2003-'04, 1mT, 1:34.66, WITH PATIENCE, Something Ventured, Fast Cookie, 12 started.

VOSBURGH S.-G1, Belmont Park, Oct. 2, $490,000, 3&up, 6f, 1:09.74, PICO CENTRAL (Brz), Voodoo, Speightstown, 5 started.

Vulcan S. (R), Fair Grounds, March 26, $50,000, 3yo, Alabama-bred, 6f, 1:13.10, SCOTTIES ABITY, Valid's Beauty, Royal Man, 13 started.

Wade Snapp Memorial Starter S., Les Bois Park, June 5, $9,700, 3&up, 7f, 1:24.20, THE LORD IS EAGER, Sport N Light, Key Runner, 10 started.

Wadsworth Memorial H., Finger Lakes, July 4, $50,000, 3&up, 1^1/$_8$m, 1:53.63, DULCE DE LECHE, Doc D, On the Fan, 7 started.

Wafare Farm S., Lone Star Park, May 22, $50,000, 3yo, f, 6f, 1:08.85, EVERHEART, Boston Express, Bluegrass Sara, 6 started.

Wagon Yard S., Grand Prairie, July 31, 3&up, 5^1/$_2$f, 1:08.40, CAPTAIN CARTER, Lettucerace, Wee Wonder, 8 started.

Waldo Williams/W. O. Edwards Memorial Thoroughbred Invitational H., Western Montana Fair, Aug. 15, $4,850, 3&up, 1^1/$_8$m, 1:55.40, STAGED REALITY, Excellenceinmotion, Cabreo, 4 started.

Walmac Farm Matchmaker H. (R), Louisiana Downs, Oct. 23, $80,750, 3&up, f&m, Louisiana-bred, 1^1/$_16$mT, 1:44.18, KATLIN'S ROCKET, Intractabie, Cheerful Bag, 8 started.

WALMAC LONE STAR DERBY-G3, Lone Star Park, Oct. 29, $250,000, 3yo, 1^1/$_16$m, 1:42.10, POLLARD'S VISION, Cryptograph, Flamethrowintexan, 12 started.

Walter R. Cluer Memorial H., Turf Paradise, Nov. 6, $40,000, 3&up, 7^1/$_2$fT, 1:27.54, BLACK BART, Paladin Power, Adroitly Superb, 9 started.

Warren's Thoroughbreds S. (R), Hollywood Park, April 24, $70,000, 3&up, f&m, California-bred, 7f, 1:22.83, THE YELLOW SHEET, Madam General, Secret Caper, 12 started.

Washington Breeders' Cup Oaks, Emerald Downs, Aug. 21, $100,000, 3yo, f, 1^1/$_8$m, 1:48.80, BIANCONI BABY, Karis Makaw, Sariano, 9 started.

Washington Cup Classic S. (R), Emerald Downs, Sept. 19, $50,000, 3&up, Washington-bred, 1^1/$_16$m, 1:40.60, DEMON WARLOCK, Dark Intent, Alfurune, 8 started.

WASHINGTON PARK H.-G2, Arlington Park, July 31, $350,000, 3&up, 1^3/$_16$m, 1:56.87, EYE OF THE TIGER, Olmodavor, Congrats, 5 started.

Washington State Legislators H., Emerald Downs, June 6, $40,000, 3&up, f&m, 6^1/$_2$f, 1:15.60, AUNT SOPHIE, Marva Jean, Lasting Code, 7 started.

Washington Thoroughbred Breeders' Association Lads S. (R), Emerald Downs, Aug. 29, $54,000, 2yo, c&g, progeny of eligible Washington stallions, 1m, 1:36.40, POSITIVE PRIZE, Indian Weaver, Sky Harbor, 8 started.

Waterford Park H., Mountaineer Race Track, May 15, $75,000, 3&up, 6f, 1:09.85, CAT GENIUS, Private Horde, Secret Romeo, 6 started.

Waya S. (R), Saratoga Race Course, Aug. 13, $65,700, 4&up, f&m, nonwinners of a graded stakes in 2004, 1^3/$_16$m, 1:58.51, BOUNDING CHARM, Savedbythelight, Bluffie Slew, 5 started.

Wayward Lass S., Tampa Bay Downs, Feb. 28, $60,000, 4&up, f&m, 1¹/₁₆m, 1:45.77, PAMPERED PRINCESS, Crimson and Roses, Dakota Light, 12 started.

WEBN S., Turfway Park, Feb. 7, $50,000, 3yo, 1m, 1:41.98, SILVER MINISTER, Revolver Six, Dollar a Dip, 8 started.

Weekend Delight S., Turfway Park, Sept. 11, $75,000, 3&up, f&m, 6f, 1:10.46, PUT ME IN, Golden Marlin, There Runs Hattie, 8 started.

Wende S., Turf Paradise, April 20, $21,900, 3yo, f, 7¹/₂fT, 1:29.66, SOUTHERN SPRING, Muir Beach, Solly's Dolly, 9 started.

Wende S., Turf Paradise, Nov. 8, $21,900, 3&up, f&m, 1m, 1:39.43, ARCH LADY, Royal Again, Cal's Baby, 6 started.

WESTCHESTER H.-G3, Belmont Park, May 5, $109,500, 3&up, 1m, 1:35.89, VOLPONINO, Saarland, Black Silk (GB), 7 started.

Western Borders S., Calder Race Course, May 9, $40,000, 3yo, 6f, 1:09.64, WEIGELIA, Classy Migration, Baronage, 6 started.

Western Canada H., Northlands Park, July 1, $40,000, 3yo, 6¹/₂f, 1:18.40, CHIEF MTN, Controlled Meeting, Ol Fifty, 7 started.

Westerner S., Northlands Park, Aug. 22, $40,000, 3&up, 1⅝m, 2:15.40, ILLUSIVE FORCE, After the Run, Regal Ability, 9 started.

Western Heritage S. (R), Marquis Downs, Aug. 21, $10,000, 2yo, c&g, Saskatchewan-bred, 6¹/₂f, 1:22.45, FARGO FORBES, Lambrose, North Park, 5 started.

Western Montana Fair Thoroughbred Maiden Derby, Western Montana Fair, Aug. 10, $4,200, 3yo, a5¹/₄f, 1:07.60, FLYING CATMAN, Government News, Perry Road Joy, 6 started.

West Long Branch S., Monmouth Park, June 19, $65,000, 3&up, f&m, 6f, 1:10.86, OUR ROYAL DANCER, Whoop's Ah Daisy, Fit Performer, 6 started.

West Mesa H., The Downs at Albuquerque, Sept. 24, $33,950, 3&up, f&m, 7f, 1:22.11, ANGELICA SLEW, Yet Anothernatalie, Sexy Boots, 6 started.

West Point H. (R), Saratoga Race Course, Aug. 15, $114,700, 3&up, New York-bred, 1¹/₈mT, 1:48.85, GOLDEN COMMANDER, Foreverness, Irish Colonial, 12 started.

West Virginia Breeders' Classic S. (R), Charles Town Races, Oct. 9, $300,000, 3&up, West Virginia-bred, -sired, or -raised, 1¹/₈m, 1:53.65, A HUEVO, Tienneman Square, Longfield Spud, 10 started.

West Virginia Breeders' Classic S. (R), Charles Town Races, Oct. 9, $75,000, 2yo, f, West Virginia-bred, -sired, or -raised, 4f, :47.43, WESHAAM LUCK, Melissa's Melody, Bravura, 9 started.

West Virginia Cavada Breeders' Classic S. (R), Charles Town Races, Oct. 9, $250,000, 3&up, f&m, West Virginia-bred, -sired, or -raised, 7f, 1:29.11, ORIGINAL GOLD, Marthamountainmama, Fancy Buckles, 10 started.

West Virginia Dash for Cash Breeders' Classic S. (R), Charles Town Races, Oct. 9, $75,000, 3&up, West Virginia-bred, -sired, or -raised, 4f, :45.89, NOT FOR SAM, Brieanna's Boy, Hushaby Babe, 7 started.

WEST VIRGINIA DERBY-G3, Mountaineer Race Track, Aug. 7, $600,000, 3yo, 1¹/₈m, 1:49.16, SIR SHACKLETON, Pollard's Vision, Britt's Jules, 7 started.

West Virginia Division of Tourism Breeders' Classic S. (R), Charles Town Races, Oct. 9, $75,000, 3yo, f, West Virginia-bred, -sired, or -raised, 7f, 1:30.75, ALASKA ASH, Crafty Carni, Our Queen Rules, 10 started.

West Virginia Futurity (1st Div.) (R), Charles Town Races, Nov. 13, $52,475, 2yo, West Virginia-bred and/or -sired, 7f, 1:32.01, BRAVURA, I'm Sure Fancy, Good Humored, 7 started.

West Virginia Futurity (2nd Div.) (R), Charles Town Races, Nov. 13, $53,325, 2yo, West Virginia-bred and/or -sired, 7f, 1:28.11, WILD REMARKS, Cielo's Edge, Miss Angel, 7 started.

West Virginia Governor's H., Mountaineer Race Track, Aug. 7, $100,000, 3&up, 1¹/₁₆m, 1:43.37, WIGGINS, Ask the Lord, Cherokee's Boy, 9 started.

West Virginia House of Delegates Speaker's Cup H., Mountaineer Race Track, Aug. 7, $85,000, 3&up, 1mT, 1:34.97, GIN AND SIN, Spruce Run, Glitter Mean, 11 started.

West Virginia Legislature Chairman's Cup H., Mountaineer Race Track, Aug. 7, $85,000, 3&up, 4¹/₂f, :50.16, AMERI BRILLIANCE, Danieltown, Run Zeal Run, 6 started.

West Virginia Lottery Breeders' Classic S. (R), Charles Town Races, Oct. 9, $75,000, 3yo, West Virginia-bred, -sired, or -raised, 7f, 1:27.58, FIVE STAR ACCOUNT, Sheckatoo, Take the Plunge, 10 started.

West Virginia Onion Juice Breeders' Classic S. (R), Charles Town Races, Oct. 9, $75,000, 3&up, c&g, West Virginia-bred, -sired, or -raised, 7f, 1:28.10, EARTH POWER, Slew's Smile, Shark Eye, 9 started.

West Virginia Secretary of State H., Mountaineer Race Track, Aug. 7, $85,000, 3&up, f&m, 6f, 1:09.62, PUT ME IN, Banished Lover, Our Josephina, 9 started.

West Virginia Senate President's Cup H., Mountaineer Race Track, Aug. 7, $85,000, 3&up, f&m, 1mT, 1:35.62, LADY OF THE FUTURE, Chance Dance, Passionate Bird, 12 started.

West Virginia Vincent Moscarelli Memorial Breeders' Classic S. (R), Charles Town Races, Oct. 9, $75,000, 2yo, West Virginia-bred, -sired, or -raised, 6¹/₂f, 1:21.63, MR. BONDSMAN, Wild Remarks, Bryceslittlesecret, 10 started.

What a Pleasure S., Calder Race Course, Dec. 4, $100,000, 2yo, 1¹/₁₆m, 1:48.90, BETTER THAN BONDS, G P's Black Knight, Cherokee Chase, 6 started.

What a Summer S., Laurel Park, Jan. 17, $73,500, 4&up, f&m, 6f, 1:10.53, BRONZE ABE, Bamba, Gazillion, 7 started.

Wheat City S., Assiniboia Downs, Aug. 2, $40,000, 3&up, 1m, 1:38.20, NORTHERN AFFAIR, Smoked Em, Icy Tobin, 7 started.

Whimsical S., Woodbine, April 18, $139,000, 4&up, f&m, 6f, 1:10.70, HOLY BUBBETTE, Winter Garden, Mille Feville, 6 started.

WHIRLAWAY H.-G3, Fair Grounds, Feb. 1, $100,000, 4&up, 1¹/₁₆m, 1:45.59, OLMODAVOR, Spanish Empire, Almuhathir, 9 started.

Whirlaway S., Aqueduct, Feb. 7, $82,875, 3yo, 1¹/₁₆m, 1:45.78, LITTLE MATTH MAN, Risky Trick, Quick Action, 7 started.

White Carnation S. (R), Belmont Park, June 5, $70,950, 4&up, f&m, nonwinners of an open stakes, 1¹/₁₆m, 1:42.08, BOARD ELLIGIBLE, Princess Dixie, Saintly Action, 9 started.

White Oak H. (R), Arlington Park, June 26, $83,650, 3&up, Illinois-conceived and/or -foaled, 6f, 1:09.70, SILVER BID, Manitowish, Wiggins, 8 started.

WHITNEY H.-G1, Saratoga Race Course, Aug. 7, $750,000, 3&up, 1¹/₈m, 1:48.54, ROSES IN MAY, Perfect Drift, Bowman's Band, 9 started.

Who Doctor Who H. (R), Horsemen's Park, July 17, $31,000, 4&up, Nebraska-bred, 1m, 1:39.80, DEATH TRAPPE, Grayglen, J. R. Honor, 10 started.

Wickerr H. (R), Del Mar, July 31, $76,325, 3&up, nonwinners of $40,000 other than closed, claiming, or starter at one mile or over since May 1, 1mT, 1:33.35, STATEMENT, Seinne (Chi), Golden Arrow, 7 started.

Wide Country S., Laurel Park, March 6, $40,000, 3yo, f, 1¹/₁₆m, 1:47.27, HE LOVES ME, Via Sacra, Pawyne Princess, 8 started.

Wildcat H., Turf Paradise, April 25, $40,000, 3&up, 1³/₈mT, 2:16.12, BRISTOLVILLE, Pittsburgh Star, Brazen n' Bold, 7 started.

Wild Flower S., Lone Star Park, Oct. 16, $50,000, 3&up, f&m, 5fT, :56.09, NICOLE'S DREAM, Leslie's Love, Seneca Song, 12 started.

Wild Rose H., Northlands Park, July 3, $40,000, 3&up, f&m, 6¹/₂f, 1:19, SLY LADY, A Shaky Start, Sister Brass, 4 started.

Wild Rose S., Prairie Meadows, June 12, $50,000, 3&up, f&m, 1¹/₁₆m, 1:41.44, WILDWOOD ROYAL, Miss Fortunate, Casual Attitude, 7 started.

Willard L. Proctor Memorial S. (R), Hollywood Park, May 23, $79,125, 2yo, nonwinners of two races, 5f, :58.24, CHANDTRUE, Dance Thief, Gentleman Count, 8 started.

William Almy Jr. S., Suffolk Downs, May 15, $40,000, 3&up, 6f, 1:10.28, ON THE GAME, Crypto Dixie, Goodbar, 8 started.

WILLIAM DONALD SCHAEFER H.-G3, Pimlico, May 15, $100,000, 3&up, 1¹/₈m, 1:49.43, SEATTLE FITZ (Arg), The Lady's Groom, Roaring Fever, 8 started.

William Henry Harrison S. (R), Indiana Downs, May 2, $40,000, 3&up, Indiana-sired, 6f, 1:11.15, LIEPERS FORK, Whenthesmokeclears, Mo Steely, 9 started.

William Kyne H. (R), Portland Meadows, Jan. 24, $10,000, 4&up, 1¹/₈m, 1:53.36, YESSS, Mt. Vista, Bon to Run, 7 started.

Willowbrook S., Sam Houston Race Park, Feb. 28, $30,000, 4&up, f&m, 5fT, :57.96, SOUND OF GOLD, Leslie's Love, Fleeta Dif, 11 started.

Willow Lake H., Yavapai Downs, July 24, $12,500, 3&up, f&m, 1m, 1:36.80, SIDEWAYS, Hula Hottie, Mamacafe, 9 started.

WILL ROGERS S.-G3, Hollywood Park, May 22, $109,400, 3yo, 1mT, 1:33.45, LAURA'S LUCKY BOY, Toasted, Street Theatre, 8 started.

Willy Fiddle Memorial S. (R), Les Bois Park, July 14, $11,235, 3&up, Idaho-bred, 7¹/₂f, 1:34.40, QUIET SYNS, Crooked Key, Two Star Story, 8 started.

WILSHIRE H.-G3, Hollywood Park, April 25, $110,900, 3&up, f&m, 1mT, 1:33.41, SPRING STAR (Fr), Quero Quero, Dublino, 9 started.

Windsor Ford S., Grand Prairie, Aug. 22, $7,537, 3&up, 1¹/₁₆m, 1:55, MOE BOOTS, Chief Joseph, Gomka, 5 started.

Wine Country H. (R), Finger Lakes, Aug. 21, $50,000, 3&up, New York-bred, 6f, 1:09.02, TOP SHOTER, Seeking the Money, Wild Bill Hiccup, 4 started.

Winning Colors H., Churchill Downs, May 22, $108,600, 3&up, f&m, 6f, 1:08.87, LADY TAK, Put Me In, Ebony Breeze, 7 started.

Winning Colors S. (R), Les Bois Park, June 9, $10,245, 3&up, f&m, Idaho-bred, 7f, 1:26.20, THRILL AFTER DARK, Crossfire Trail, Eyes Sucha Delight, 7 started.

Winnipeg Futurity S., Assiniboia Downs, Aug. 2, $40,000, 2yo, 6f, 1:13.40, TUFF JUSTICE, Maid for Speed, El Grande Seville, 7 started.

Winnipeg Sun S., Assiniboia Downs, Aug. 1, $40,000, 3&up, f&m, 1¹/₁₆m, 1:48.40, MAUI MONEY, Pete's Surprise, Rainbows Forever, 8 started.

Winsham Lad H., Sunland Park, Jan. 10, $55,250, 3&up, 1m, 1:35.56, STREAK OF ROYALTY, Komax, Personal Beau, 11 started.

WinStar Derby, Sunland Park, March 28, $500,000, 3yo, 1¹/₁₆m, 1:43.20, HI TECK MAN, Consecrate, Rocky Gulch, 10 started.

WINSTAR DISTAFF H.-G3, Lone Star Park, May 31, $200,000, 3&up, f&m, 1mT, 1:35.98, ACADEMIC ANGEL, Janeian (NZ), Katdogawn (GB), 12 started.

WINSTAR GALAXY S.-G2, Keeneland, Oct. 10, $500,000, 3&up, f&m, 1³/₁₆mT, 1:57.08, STAY FOREVER, Super Brand (SAf), Shaconage, 9 started.

WinStar Sunland Park Oaks, Sunland Park, March 27, $260,193, 3yo, f, 1m, 1:36.57, SPEEDY FALCON, Sister Swank, Skyladysky, 9 started.

Wintergreen H. (R), Beulah Park, May 1, $45,000, 3yo, Ohio-bred, 1¹/₁₆m, 1:46.08, FLOATER, Another Freddy, Crypto's Prospect, 6 started.

Wintergreen S., Turfway Park, March 12, $50,000, 4&up, f&m, 1m, 1:36.87, STRIKE RATE, River Flower, Mariaworth, 8 started.

Wishing Well S., Turfway Park, Jan. 10, $50,000, 4&up, f&m, 6f, 1:10.33, SARATOGA HUMOR, Emily Ring, Ballado's Halo, 10 started.

Witches' Brew S., The Meadowlands, Oct. 30, $60,000, 3&up, f&m, 5fT, :57.33, KISS ME KATIE, Tight Spin, Ambition Unbridled, 12 started.

With Approval S. (R), Woodbine, Aug. 8, $104,000, 3&up, Canadian-bred, a1¹/₁₆mT, 1:42.87, SURGING RIVER, Le Cinquieme Essai, Tusayan, 6 started.

Without Feathers S., Monmouth Park, Sept. 25, $60,000, 3yo, f, 1m 70y, 1:42.77, GRAND PRAYER, Emerald Earrings, From Away, 6 started.

W. L. MCKNIGHT H.-G2, Calder Race Course, Dec. 18, $200,000, 3&up, 1¹/₂mT, 2:26.60, DREADNAUGHT, Demeteor, Scooter Roach, 12 started.

W. Meredith Bailes Memorial S. (R), Colonial Downs, June 27, $50,000, 3&up, Virginia-bred and/or -sired, 6f, 1:08.48, SATAN'S CODE, Halo Homewrecker, Standing Room Only, 5 started.

Wolf Hill S., Monmouth Park, June 5, $60,000, 3&up, 5fT, :56.04, RUDIRUDY, Manofglory, Blackjack, 10 started.

Wolverine S. (R), Great Lakes Downs, June 12, $40,000, 3&up, Michigan-bred, 6f, 1:12.65, ABOVE THE WIND, Rockem Sockem, O. B. Quiet, 7 started.

Wonders Delight S. (R), Penn National Race Course, June 11, $41,400, 3yo, f, Pennsylvania-bred, 6f, 1:11.12, DEFRERE'S VENTURE, Financial Risk, Linda's Future, 7 started.

Wonder Where S. (R), Woodbine, Aug. 1, $250,000, 3yo, f, Canadian-bred, 1¹/₈mT, 2:05.08, MY VINTAGE PORT, Eye of the Sphynx, Sheer Enchantment, 8 started.

Woodbine Oaks (R), Woodbine, June 13, $500,000, 3yo, f, Canadian-bred, 1¹/₈m, 1:53.11, EYE OF THE SPHYNX, Touchnow, My Vintage Port, 5 started.

WOODBINE SLOTS CUP H.-G3, Woodbine, Nov. 20, $157,950, 3&up, 1¹/₁₆m, 1:45, MARK ONE, A Bit O'Gold, Norfolk Knight, 4 started.

Woodford County S., Keeneland, Oct. 22, $84,675, 3&up, 5¹/₂fT, 1:02.70, BATTLE WON, Sgt. Bert, Chosen Chief, 10 started.

Woodland Heritage S. (R), Marquis Downs, Aug. 21, $10,000, 2yo, f, Saskatchewan-bred, 6¹/₂f, 1:24.45, SHEEN SKY, Arctic Taliyah, Fractious Sue, 6 started.

Woodlands Derby, The Woodlands, Oct. 24, $25,000, 3yo, 1¹/₁₆m, 1:45.60, WALLY'S CHOICE, Roarofvictory, Nick Missed, 7 started.

Woodlands H., The Woodlands, Oct. 30, $25,000, 3&up, 1¹/₁₆m, 1:45.40, MAGIC DOE, Luckymata, Robin Zee, 9 started.

Woodlands Juvenile S., The Woodlands, Oct. 31, $20,000, 2yo, 6f, 1:11.80, WIND TWISTER, Yeah Buddy, Silent World, 11 started.

Woodlawn S., Pimlico, May 15, $100,000, 3yo, 1¹/₁₆mT, 1:41.86, ARTIE SCHILLER, Lipan, Timo, 13 started.

WOOD MEMORIAL S.-G1, Aqueduct, April 10, $750,000, 3yo, 1¹/₈m, 1:49.70, TAPIT, Master David, Eddington, 11 started.

Woodside H., Bay Meadows, May 2, $56,738, 3&up, f&m, 6f, 1:09.43, CHRISTMAS TIME, Stormica, Coconut Girl, 7 started.

Woodstock S., Woodbine, April 24, $137,375, 3yo, 6f, 1:09.64, NYUK NYUK NYUK, Estevan, Imperial Alydeed, 5 started.

WOODWARD S.-G1, Belmont Park, Sept. 11, $500,000, 3&up, 1¹/₈m, 1:46.38, GHOSTZAPPER, Saint Liam, Bowman's Band, 7 started.

Work the Crowd H. (R), Golden Gate Fields, Jan. 3, $100,000, 4&up, f&m, California-bred, 1m, 1:36.09, SUPER HIGH, Amber Hills, Fancee Bargain, 6 started.

Work the Crowd H. (R), Golden Gate Fields, Dec. 26, $100,000, 3&up, f&m, California-bred, 1mT, 1:37.82, SCROFA, Shalini, Bartok's Blithe, 9 started.

World Appeal S., The Meadowlands, Oct. 1, $55,000, 2yo, 1m 70yT, 1:45.70, ELUSIVE THUNDER, United, Dixie Slew, 8 started.

Wynn Dot Comma S., Calder Race Course, June 6, $40,000, 2yo, 5f, :58.89, B. B. BEST, Devils Disciple, Lookin for Biscuit, 7 started.

Yaddo H. (R), Saratoga Race Course, Aug. 18, $114,800, 3&up, f&m, New York-bred, 1¹/₁₆mT, 1:53.06, SABELLINA, On the Bus, Lady Libby, 11 started.

Yankee Affair S., Gulfstream Park, April 11, $50,000, 3&up, 5fT, :53.85, TRUE LOVE'S SECRET, Take Achance On Me, Ghostly Numbers, 7 started.

Yankee Affair S. (R), Philadelphia Park, Oct. 9, $55,100, 3&up, Pennsylvania-bred, 1¹/₁₆mT, 1:47.70, CAUGHT IN THE RAIN, Yo, I'ma a Fax, 7 started.

Yaqthan S., Kentucky Downs, Sept. 18, $40,000, 3&up, 1mT, 1:39.73, DOC D, Salute the Count, Sell to Survive, 8 started.

Yavapai Classic H., Yavapai Downs, June 6, $12,500, 3&up, f&m, 6f, 1:10, PEGALEE, She's Finding Time, Dance for Gold, 8 started.

Yavapai County Arizona Breeders' Futurity (R), Yavapai Downs, June 27, $24,943, 2yo, Arizona-bred, 5f, :57.80, COVER NOW, Rowdy Creek, Hollywood Payday, 8 started.

Yavapai Downs Derby, Yavapai Downs, Aug. 23, $17,500, 3yo, 1¹/₁₆m, 1:46.20, HIS WAY, Imdabossau, Swiss Bounty, 7 started.

Yavapai Downs H., Yavapai Downs, July 13, $12,500, 3&up, 5¹/₂f, 1:03.60, JAKES CORNER, Flarions Flame, Red Spark, 7 started.

Yavapai Downs Thoroughbred Futurity, Yavapai Downs, Sept. 6, $34,000, 2yo, 6f, 1:11, FABULOUS FEY, Clear to the Top, Fleeting Riverman, 9 started.

Yearling Filly Sales S. (R), Northlands Park, Aug. 21, $60,000, 2yo, f, Canadian-bred sold at the CTHS sale, 6¹/₂f, 1:22, R LUCINDA, Saucy Ciano, Speedy Gone Sally, 8 started.

Yearling Sales S. (R), Northlands Park, Aug. 21, $60,000, 2yo, c&g, Canadian-bred sold at the CTHS sale, 6¹/₂f, 1:21.40, BLINKAN-HESGONE, Northtown Will, Cinderchance, 6 started.

YELLOW RIBBON S.-G1, Santa Anita Park, Oct. 2, $500,000, 3&up, f&m, 1¹/₄mT, 1:59.28, LIGHT JIG (GB), Tangle (Ire), Katdogawn (GB), 10 started.

Yellow Rose Breeders' Cup S., Lone Star Park, Oct. 3, $92,250, 3&up, f&m, 1¹/₁₆mT, 1:48.41, AUD, Janeian (NZ), Queena Corrina, 8 started.

Yellow Rose S. (R), Sam Houston Race Park, Nov. 20, $50,000, 3&up, f&m, Texas-bred, 6f, 1:10.40, COUNTRYFIDE, Angelic Jewel, Cookin's Cast, 7 started.

Yellowstone Downs Thoroughbred Futurity, Yellowstone Downs, Sept. 26, $15,000, 2yo, 5¹/₂f, 1:02.40, DEADLY TALONS, Dc Carleysprospect, Man At Arms, 5 started.

YERBA BUENA BREEDERS' CUP H.-G3, Bay Meadows, May 8, $113,750, 3&up, f&m, a1¹/₁₆mT, 1:46.66, A B NOODLE, Marwood, Hooked On Niners, 6 started.

Zadracarta S. (R), Woodbine, June 20, $108,000, 3&up, f&m, Canadian-bred, 6fT, 1:09.59, HEYAHOHOWDY, Whistling Maid, Miss Crissy, 8 started.

Zip Pocket S., Turf Paradise, Nov. 1, $21,600, 3&up, 5¹/₂f, 1:02.70, NEWARK, Flying Supercon, Red Spark, 6 started.

Zydeco S., Delta Downs, Oct. 9, $40,000, 3&up, f&m, 5f, :59.51, FUSE IT, Miss Smart Strike, Ice Forest, 5 started.

Oldest Stakes Races

Although horse racing in North America dates from the Colonial period, stakes races did not become popular until the mid-1800s.

The oldest continually run stakes in North America—meaning that it has been run every year since its inception—is the Queen's Plate Stakes at Woodbine. First run in 1860, the race was named for Queen Victoria, then in the 23rd year of her 64-year reign, and was for horses of all ages foaled in the province of Ontario. The winner of that first Queen's Plate was Don Juan, a five-year-old Sir Tatton Sykes gelding. (Another Queen's Plate, restricted to horses foaled in Quebec, dated from 1836 and was discontinued after World War II.) From 1902 through '51, the race was known as the King's Plate, for a succession of English male monarchs.

North America's oldest stakes race still in existence is the Phoenix Breeders' Cup Stakes (G3), first run in 1831 at the Kentucky Association track in Lexington. Known at various times as the Phoenix Hotel S., Phoenix S., Brennan S., Chiles S., Association S., and the Phoenix H., the race was discontinued in 1930. It was revived with the first spring race meeting of Keeneland Race Course in 1937.

Oldest Continuously Run Stakes

Race	Track	First Running	First Winner
Queen's Plate	Woodbine	1860	Don Juan
Kentucky Derby	Churchill	1875	Aristides
Kentucky Oaks	Churchill	1875	Vinaigrette
Clark H.	Churchill	1875	Voltigeur
Bashford Manor S.	Churchill	1902	Von Rouse
Fall Highweight H.	Aqueduct	1914	Comely
Coaching Club American Oaks	Belmont	1917	Wistful
Schuylerville S.	Saratoga	1918	Tuscaloosa
Jockey Club Gold Cup S.	Belmont	1919	Purchase
Cowdin S.	Belmont	1923	Mr. Mutt
Wood Memorial S.	Aqueduct	1925	Backbone
Selima S.	Laurel	1926	Fair Star
Whitney H.	Saratoga	1928	Black Maria
Canadian Derby	Northlands	1930	Jack Whittier

Oldest Stakes Races

Race	Track	First Running	First Winner

PHOENIX BREEDERS' CUP S. **Keeneland** **1831** **McDonough**
1831-'77, run as a heat race; 1898-1904,1906-'10, 1914-'16, 1929, 1931-'36, not run; before 1937, held at the Kentucky Association track; 1943-'45, held at Churchill Downs; 1972, 1981, run in two divisions; before 1989, held during the spring meeting; inaugurated in 1831 as the Phoenix Hotel S.; has also been run as Brennan S., Chiles S., Phoenix S., Association S., and Phoenix H.

QUEEN'S PLATE S. **Woodbine** **1860** **Don Juan**
Before 1887, run at 1½ miles; 1924-'56, run at 1⅛ miles; before 1938, for three-year-olds and up; 1938, for three- and four-year-olds; 1902-'51, run as the King's Plate; before 1956, held at Old Woodbine; before 1959, for three-year-olds bred and owned in Canada

TRAVERS S. **Saratoga** **1864** **Kentucky**
1943, 1944, 1945, held at Belmont Park; 1896, 1898, 1899, 1900, 1911, 1912, not run; before 1890, run at 1¾ miles; 1890-'92, run at 1½ miles; 1895, 1901-'03, run at 1⅛ miles; 1927-'32, run as the Travers Midsummer Derby

JEROME H. **Belmont** **1866** **Watson**
1866-'89, held at Jerome Park; 1890-1905, held at Morris Park; 1960, 1962-'67, held at Aqueduct; 1910-'13, not run; 1866-'70, run in two divisions; 1871-'77, run at two miles; 1878-'89, run at 1¾ miles; 1890, 1891, 1903, run at 1$\frac{5}{16}$ miles; 1892, run at 1½ miles; 1893, 1894, 1896-1909, run at 1¼ miles; 1895, run at 1⅛ miles

BELMONT S. **Belmont** **1867** **Ruthless**
1867-'89, held at Jerome Park; 1890-1904, held at Morris Park; 1963-'67, held at Aqueduct; 1911-'12, not run; 1867-'73, run at 1⅝ miles; 1890-'92, 1895, 1904-'05, run at 1¼ miles; 1893-'94, run at 1⅛ miles; 1896-1903, 1906-'25, run at 1⅜ miles; 1895, 1913, run as a handicap stakes

CHAMPAGNE S. **Belmont** **1867** **Sarah B.**
Before 1890, held at Jerome Park; 1890-1905, held at Morris Park; 1959, 1963-'67, 1984, held at Aqueduct; 1910-'13, 1956, not run; 1871-'80, run at six furlongs; 1891-1904, run at seven furlongs; 1905-'32, run on the Widener course (165 feet less than seven furlongs); 1933-'39, run on the Widener course at 6½ furlongs; 1940-'83, 1985-'93, run at one mile; 1984, run at 1⅛ miles; 1973, run in two divisions

LADIES H. **Aqueduct** **1868** **Bonnie Braes**
Before 1913, for three-year-old fillies; 1931-'34,1940-2001, for fillies and mares all ages, three-year-olds and up; before 1890, held at Jerome Park; 1890-1904, held at Morris Park; 1950-'58, 1960, held at Belmont Park; 1895, 1911, 1912, not run; before 1874, run at 1⅝ miles; 1889, 1892, run at 1⅛ miles; 1890, 1891, run at 1,400 yards; 1893, 1894, run at 1$\frac{1}{16}$ miles; 1896-1939, run at one mile; 1961, 1962, run at 1$\frac{5}{16}$ miles; 1874-'85, 1940-'58, 1960, 1963, 1964, run at 1½ miles.

FLASH S. **Belmont** **1869** **Remorseless**
1869-1942, 1946-'71, held at Saratoga; 1943-'45, held at Belmont Park on the Widener course; 1981, 1982, held at Belmont Park; 1896, 1898-1900, 1911, 1912, 1960, 1972-'80, 1983-'98, not run; before 1901, run at four furlongs; 1901, run at five furlongs; 1969-'71, run at six furlongs; 1981, 1982, run at 5½ furlongs

DIXIE S. **Pimlico** **1870** **Preakness**
1870, run as Dinner Party S.; 1871, run as Reunion S.; 1903-'04, held at Benning, Washington, D.C., at 1¾ miles for three-year-olds; 1870-'88, run at two miles for three-year-olds; 1924-'52, run at 1$\frac{3}{16}$ miles; 1960-'87, 1989, 1990, run at 1½ miles; 1955-'59, run at 1⅜ miles; 1988, run at 1⅝ miles; before 1955, 1988, run on dirt; 1889-1901, 1905-'23, not run; 1965-'78, run in two divisions

MONMOUTH PARK BREEDERS' CUP OAKS **Monmouth** **1871** **Salina**
1871-'77, run at 1½ miles; 1879-'93, run at 1¼ miles; 1946-'52, 1996-2001, run at 1$\frac{1}{16}$ miles; 1953-'95, run at 1⅛ miles; 1891, held at Jerome Park; 1878, 1894-1945, 2003, not run; 1976, run as Monmouth Bicentennial Oaks

ALABAMA S. **Saratoga** **1872** **Woodbine**
1943-'45, held at Belmont Park; 1893-'96, 1898-1900, 1911, 1912, not run; before 1901, 1904, 1906-'16, run at

Race	Track	First Running	First Winner

1⅛ miles; 1901-'03, run at 1 1/16 miles; 1903, run on turf; 1905, run at 1 5/16 miles

CALIFORNIA DERBY Bay Meadows 1873 Camilla Urso
1897-1909, run at 1¼ miles; 1923, run at 1½ miles; 1936-'48, 1976-'81, run at 1 1/16 miles; 1874, 1891-'96, 1900, 1911-'22, 1924-'34, 1939, 1940, 1942, 1943, 1945, 1947, 1949-'53, 1957, not run; 1873-1959, 1962, held at Tanforan; 1961, 1964-2000, held at Golden Gate Fields

PREAKNESS S. Pimlico 1873 Survivor
Before 1894, run at 1½ miles; 1889, run at 1¼ miles; 1894-1900, 1908, run at 1 1/16 miles; 1901-'07, run at one mile and 70 yards; 1909, 1910, run at one mile; 1911-'24, run at 1⅛ miles; 1891-'93, not run; 1890, for three-year-olds and up; 1890, held at Morris Park, New York; 1894-1908, held at Gravesend, New York; 1918, run in two divisions

WITHERS S. Aqueduct 1874 Dublin
1847-'89, held at Jerome Park; 1890-1904, held at Morris Park; 1956, held at Jamaica; 1984-'96, held at Belmont Park; 1911, 1912, not run; 1956, run at 1 1/16 miles

CLARK H. Churchill 1875 Voltigeur
1875-1901, run as three-year-old stakes; 1902-2001, run as a handicap for three-year-olds and up; 1875-'80, run at two miles; 1881-'95, run at 1¼ miles; 1902-'21, 1925-'54, run at 1 1/16 miles; 1953, run in two divisions

KENTUCKY DERBY Churchill 1875 Aristides
Before 1896, run at 1½ miles

KENTUCKY OAKS Churchill 1875 Vinaigrette
1875-'90, run at 1½ miles; 1891-'95, run at 1¼ miles; 1896-1919, 1942-'81, run at 1 1/16 miles

Fastest Times of 2004

Dirt

Dist.	Time	Winner, Age, Sex	Track	Date	Cond.
2f	:20.71	Pensglitter, 7 h.	Penn National Race Course	Oct. 9	ft
2½f	:27.00	Flutter Butterfly, 2 f.	Evangeline Downs	July 10	ft
3f	:32.86	Desert Wolf Girl, 5 m.	Remington Park	Aug. 7	ft
3½f	:39.40	Love's Conquest, 2 g.	Northlands Park	July 24	ft
4f	:44.00	Dance Me Free, 5 g.	Stampede Park	April 3	ft
4½f	:50.16	Ameri Brilliance, 5 g.	Mountaineer Race Track	Aug. 7	ft
5f	:55.90	Jimmy Jones, 7 g.	Sunland Park	Feb. 7	ft
5¼f	1:02.40	Deadly Talons, 2 g.	Yellowstone Downs	Sept. 26	ft
		Chevron Fleet, 5 g.	Great Falls	Aug. 1	ft
5½f	1:01.20	Willie the Cat, 5 g.	Emerald Downs	April 16	ft
		Swingnlisa, 8 m.	Emerald Downs	Oct. 9	ft
6f	1:07.41	Green Team, 5 g.	Bay Meadows	Sept. 11	ft
6½f	1:13.55	Lost in the Fog, 2 c.	Turf Paradise	Dec. 26	ft
7f	1:20.11	Unfurl the Flag, 4 g.	Santa Anita Park	Feb. 21	ft
7½f	1:27.30	Anziyan Royalty, 4 c.	Hollywood Park	Nov. 13	ft
1m	1:33.46	Lion Tamer, 4 c.	Aqueduct	Nov. 27	ft
1m 40y	1:38.53	Yessirgeneralsir, 4 g.	Fair Grounds	March 4	ft
1m 70y	1:37.90	Schedule (GB), 3 f.	The Meadowlands	Oct. 15	my
1 1/16m	1:40.02	Medallist, 3 c.	Belmont Park	July 11	ft
1⅛m	1:46.30	Seattle Fitz (Arg), 5 h.	Belmont Park	June 12	ft
1 3/16m	1:55.58	Presidentialaffair, 5 g.	Pimlico	Oct. 9	ft
1¼m	1:59.02	Ghostzapper, 4 c.	Lone Star Park	Oct. 30	ft
1 5/16m	2:09.63	Angelic Aura, 4 g.	Aqueduct	April 10	ft
1⅜m	2:17.34	Sigfreto, 6 g.	Fairplex Park	Sept. 26	ft
1½m	2:27.50	Birdstone, 3 c.	Belmont Park	June 5	ft
1 9/16m	2:46.86	Golden Foil, 7 h.	Delta Downs	March 27	ft
1⅝m	2:43.95	Tamburello (Chi), 5 g.	Aqueduct	Dec. 29	ft
1¾m	2:59.47	Sea Navigator, 6 h.	Hastings Race Course	Oct. 2	ft
1 13/16m	3:10.04	Megan's Man, 4 g.	The Downs at Albuquerque	Sept. 26	ft
1⅞m	3:19.50	Mr. Perpetuity, 7 g.	Woodbine	Dec. 12	my
2m	3:22.60	Horatio, 5 g.	Emerald Downs	Sept. 20	ft
2m 70y	3:40.05	Attonotauto, 5 g.	Fort Erie	Sept. 5	ft
2¼m	4:02.17	Calliehadaprenup, 6 g.	Beulah Park	May 1	my

Turf

Dist.	Time	Winner, Age, Sex	Track	Date	Cond.
4½f	:50.23	Long Star, 5 h.	Mountaineer Race Track	June 21	fm
5f	:54.78	Whenthedoveflies, 4 f.	Calder Race Course	May 23	fm
5½f	1:00.60	King Robyn, 4 g.	Hollywood Park	April 23	fm
6f	1:07.83	Hour of Justice, 4 f.	Woodbine	Aug. 2	fm
6½f	1:14.27	Chris's Bad Boy, 7 g.	Woodbine	Aug. 7	fm
7f	1:19.38	Soaring Free, 5 g.	Woodbine	July 24	fm
7½f	1:27.46	Foreign Justice, 3 g.	Remington Park	Aug. 27	fm
1m	1:31.84	Royal Regalia, 6 g.	Woodbine	July 1	fm
1m 70y	1:39.63	Proven Promise, 4 f.	Penn National Race Course	July 9	fm
1 1/16m	1:38.45	Leroidesanimaux (Brz), 4 c.	Hollywood Park	May 1	fm
1⅛m	1:45.50	Artie Schiller, 3 c.	Belmont Park	Sept. 26	fm
1 3/16m	1:53.11	Governor Brown, 4 c.	Saratoga Race Course	Aug. 28	fm
1¼m	1:58.70	Star Over the Bay, 6 g.	Santa Anita Park	Oct. 3	fm
1⅜m	2:11.37	Parisky, 7 g.	Indiana Downs	June 20	fm
1½m	2:25.87	Strut the Stage, 6 h.	Woodbine	Sept. 6	fm
1⅝m	2:46.29	Spanish Spur (GB), 6 g.	Saratoga Race Course	Aug. 16	yl
1¾m	2:55.11	Pleasant Company, 5 g.	Mountaineer Race Track	Aug. 15	fm
1⅞m	3:10.35	Pleasant Company, 5 g.	Mountaineer Race Track	Sept. 6	fm

North American Track Records

Dirt

Dist.	Time	Winner, Age Sex	Track	Date
2f	:20.71	Pensglitter, 7 h.	Penn National Race Course	10/9/2004
2½f	:26.53	Yes He Will, 4 g.	Lone Star Park	11/7/1997
3f	:31.20	Raisable Adversary, 11 g.	Remington Park	8/29/1999
3½f	:38.00	Primero Del Anno, 5 g.	Flagstaff	7/4/1998
4f	:43.10	Slewofrainbows, 7 g.	Mohave County Fair	5/23/1999
4½f	:49.20	Valiant Pete, 4 c.	Los Alamitos	8/11/1990
5f	:55.20	Chinook Pass, 3 c.	Longacres	9/17/1982
5½f	1:01.10	Plenty Zloty, 5 g.	Turf Paradise	4/18/1998
6f	1:06.60	G Malleah, 4 g.	Turf Paradise	4/8/1995
6¼f	1:15.80	Montanic, 4 g.	Washington Park	7/20/1901
6½f	1:13.24	Lucky Forever, 6 g.	Hollywood Park	5/20/1995
7f	1:19.40	Rich Cream, 5 h.	Hollywood Park	5/28/1980
		Time to Explode, 3 c.	Hollywood Park	6/26/1982
7½f	1:26.26	Awesome Daze, 5 g.	Hollywood Park	11/23/1997
1m	1:32.20	Dr. Fager, 4 c.	Arlington Park	8/24/1968
	1:32.24	Najran, 4 c.	Belmont Park	5/7/2003
1m 20y	1:39.00	Froglegs, 4 c.	Churchill Downs	5/13/1913
1m 40y	1:38.20	Zaffarancho (Arg), 5 h.	Rockingham	6/19/1987
1m 70y	1:37.90	Schedule (GB), 3 f.	The Meadowlands	10/15/2004
1m 100y	1:43.80	Old Honesty, 3 c.	Empire City	8/20/1907
1¹⁄₁₆m	1:38.40	Hoedown's Day, 5 h.	Bay Meadows Race Course	10/23/1983
1⅛m	1:45.00	Simply Majestic, 4 c.	Golden Gate Fields	4/2/1988
1³⁄₁₆m	1:52.40	Riva Ridge, 4 c.	Aqueduct	7/4/1973
1¼m	1:57.80	Spectacular Bid, 4 c.	Santa Anita Park	2/3/1980
1⁵⁄₁₆m	2:07.32	Gold Star Deputy, 5 g.	Aqueduct	4/10/1999
1⅜m	2:12.31	Demi's Bret, 4 g.	Aqueduct	10/26/1997
1⁷⁄₁₆m	2:23.00	Who's In Command, 5 h.	Hastings Race Course	8/10/1987
1½m	2:24.00	Secretariat, 3 c.	Belmont Park	6/9/1973
1⁹⁄₁₆m	2:35.77	Well Lit, 5 g.	Sportsman's Park	4/25/1992
1⅝m	2:38.20	Swaps, 4 c.	Hollywood Park	7/25/1956
1¾m	2:52.60	Major Pots, 5 g.	Woodbine	12/8/1994
1⅞m	3:11.56	Asserche, 6 g.	Laurel Park	3/20/1994
2m	3:19.20	Kelso, 7 g.	Aqueduct	10/31/1964
2¼m	3:47.00	Fenelon, 4 c.	Belmont Park	10/4/1941
2½m	4:14.60	*Miss Grillo, 6 m.	Pimlico Race Course	11/12/1948

Turf

Dist.	Time	Winner, Age	Track	Date
4f	:46.60	Fine Tassles, 5 m.	Rillito	1/30/1994
4½f	:49.26	Dan's Groovy, 7 g.	Turf Paradise	4/13/2003
5f	:54.60	General Express, 5 g.	Monmouth Park	7/8/2000
5½f	1:00.46	Pembroke, 5 h.	Hollywood Park	7/15/1995
6f	1:07.00	Answer Do, 4 c.	Hollywood Park	12/15/1990
6½f	1:14.20	Key Twenty Two, 6 g.	Woodbine	6/4/1992
about 6½f	1:11.13	Lennyfromalibu, 5 g.	Santa Anita Park	1/22/2004
7f	1:19.38	Soaring Free, 5 g.	Woodbine	7/24/2004
7½f	1:26.54	Court Lark, 6 g.	Calder Race Course	7/16/1994
1m	1:31.63	Elusive Quality, 5 h.	Belmont Park	7/4/1998
1m 40y	1:38.08	Castaneto (Arg), 7 g.	Atlantic City	6/28/1991
1m 70y	1:37.20	Aborigine, 6 h.	Penn National Race Course	8/20/1978
1¹⁄₁₆m	1:38.00	Told, 4 c.	Penn National Race Course	9/14/1980
1⅛m	1:43.92	Kostroma (Ire), 5 m.	Santa Anita Park	10/20/1991
1³⁄₁₆m	1:51.40	Toonerville, 4 g.	Hialeah Park	2/7/1976
1¼m	1:57.40	Double Discount, 4 c.	Santa Anita Park	10/9/1977
1⁵⁄₁₆m	2:06.00	Ruff Mack, 5 m.	Mountaineer Race Track	8/25/1962
1⅜m	2:10.20	With Approval, 4 c.	Belmont Park	6/17/1990
1⁷⁄₁₆m	2:25.00	Dina's Playmate, 11 g.	River Downs	8/30/1969
1½m	2:22.80	Hawkster, 3 c.	Santa Anita Park	10/14/1989
1⁹⁄₁₆m	2:40.26	To the Floor, 7 g.	Fair Grounds	3/29/1999
1⅝m	2:37.00	Tom Swift, 5 h.	Saratoga Race Course	8/23/1978
1¾m	2:55.11	Pleasant Company, 5 g.	Mountaineer Race Track	8/15/2004
1⅞m	3:08.23	Code's Best, 6 g.	Mountaineer Race Track	9/4/2000
2m	3:18.00	*Petrone, 5 h.	Hollywood Park	7/23/1969
2¼m	3:48.40	Buteo, 6 g.	River Downs	9/3/1990

Progression of Fastest Times on Dirt
Six Furlongs

Time	Horse	YOB, Sex, Sire	Date	Track	Weight
1:06.60	G Malleah	1991 g., Fool the Experts	4/8/1995	Turf Paradise	120
1:06 4/5	Zany Tactics	1981 h., Zanthe	3/8/1987	Turf Paradise	126
1:07 1/5	Petro D. Jay	1976 h., *Grey Tudor	5/9/1982	Turf Paradise	120
1:07 1/5	Grey Papa	1967 g., Grey Eagle	9/4/1972	Longacres	116
1:07 2/5	Vale of Tears	1963 h., *Royal Vale	6/7/1969	Ak-Sar-Ben	120
1:07 2/5	Zip Pocket	1964 h., Nantallah	12/4/1966	Turf Paradise	126
1:07 4/5	Admirably	1962 m., *Oceanus II	4/7/1965	Golden Gate Fields	118
1:07 4/5	Crazy Kid	1958 h., Krakatao	8/18/1962	Del Mar	118
1:08	*Dumpty Humpty	1953 h., Stalino	11/2/1957	Golden Gate Fields	115
1:08 1/5	Bolero	1946 h., Eight Thirty	5/27/1950	Golden Gate Fields	122
1:08 2/5	*Fair Truckle	1943 h., Fair Trial	10/4/1947	Golden Gate Fields	119
1:09 1/5	Polynesian	1942 h., Unbreakable	9/16/1946	Atlantic City	126
1:09 1/5	*Mafosta	1942 h., Fair Trial	7/14/1946	Longacres	116
1:09 1/5	Clang	1932 g., Stimulus	10/12/1935	Coney Island (Oh.)	110
1:09 3/5	Iron Mask	1908 g., Disguise	1/4/1914	Juarez (Mex)	115
1:10 4/5	Orb	1911 h., Luck and Charity	12/9/1913	Juarez (Mex)	90
1:10 4/5	Leochares	1910 g., Broomstick	10/3/1913	Douglas Park	109
1:10 4/5	Iron Mask	1908 g., Disguise	9/23/1913	Douglas Park	127
1:11	Priscillian	1905 g., Hastings	6/19/1911	Hamilton (Can)	113
1:11	Prince Ahmed	1904 h., King Hanover	7/29/1909	Empire City	117
1:11	Chapultepec	1905 h., *Gerolstein	12/28/1908	Santa Anita (old)	112
1:11 3/5	Col. Bob	1905 h., Cesarion	12/27/1907	Santa Anita (old)	92
1:11 3/5	Roseben	1901 g., *Ben Strome	10/6/1905	Belmont Park	147
1:11 4/5	Ivan the Terrible	1902 h., *Pirate of Penzance	10/27/1904	Worth (Il.)	92
1:11 4/5	Dick Welles	1900 h., King Eric	6/30/1903	Washington Park	109
1:12	*Lux Casta	1899 m., Donovan	7/23/1902	Brighton Beach	111
1:12	Bummer II	1896 h., Register	10/17/1900	Kinloch (Mo.)	80
1:12 1/5	*Voter	1894 h., Friar's Balsam	7/6/1900	Brighton Beach	123
1:12 1/4	Mary Black	1895 m., *Islington	7/16/1898	Washington Park	93
1:12 1/4	Flora Louise	1895 m., *Florist	9/30/1897	Harlem (Il.)	88
1:12 1/4	O'Connell	1890 g., Harry o' Fallon	7/18/1895	Oakley (Oh.)	121
1:13	Tom Hood	1884 h., Virgil	9/19/1888	Louisville	115
1:13	Force	1878 h., West Roxbury	9/24/1883	Louisville	121
1:14	Monarch	1879 h., Monarchist	8/22/1882	Saratoga	91
1:14	Knight Templar	1877 g., Fellowcraft	9/18/1880	Gravesend	77
1:14	Barrett	1878 h., *Bonnie Scotland	8/14/1880	Monmouth Park	110
1:15	First Chance	1871 g., Baywood	10/17/1876	Philadelphia	110
1:15 1/2	Bill Bruce	1872 h., Enquirer	5/12/1776	Lexington (Ky.)	108
1:15 3/4	Madge	1871 m., *Australian	8/21/1874	Saratoga	87
1:16	Alarm	1869 h., *Eclipse	7/15/1872	Saratoga	90
1:16 3/4	Tom Bowling	1870 h., Lexington	8/6/1872	Long Branch (N.J.)	100

Seven Furlongs

Time	Horse	YOB, Sex, Sire	Date	Track	Weight
1:19 2/5	Time to Explode	1979 h., Explodent	6/26/1982	Hollywood Park	117
1:19 2/5	Rich Cream	1975 h., Creme dela Crème	5/28/1980	Hollywood Park	118
1:19 4/5	Triple Bend	1968 h., Never Bend	5/6/1972	Hollywood Park	123
1:20	Native Diver	1959 g., Imbros	5/22/1965	Hollywood Park	126
1:20	El Drag	1951 h., *Khaled	5/21/1955	Hollywood Park	115
1:20 3/5	Imbros	1950 h., Polynesian	1/2/1954	Santa Anita Park	118
1:21	Bolero	1946 h., Eight Thirty	1/1/1951	Santa Anita Park	121
1:21 2/5	Ky. Colonel	1946 h., Balladier	8/10/1949	Washington Park	116
1:21 4/5	Buzfuz	1942 g., Zacaweista	6/20/1947	Hollywood Park	120
1:21 4/5	Honeymoon	1943 m., *Beau Pere	6/3/1947	Hollywood Park	114
1:22	High Resolve	1941 g., Zacaweista	10/17/1945	Hollywood Park	126
1:22	Clang	1932 g., Stimulus	7/19/1935	Arlington Park	105
1:22	Roseben	1901 g., *Ben Strome	10/16/1906	Belmont Park	126
1:25	The Musketeer	1898 h., *Masetto	8/18/1902	Saratoga	108
1:25 2/5	Clifford	1890 h., Bramble	8/29/1894	Sheepshead Bay	127
1:26 2/5	Britannic	1884 h., Plevna	9/5/1889	Sheepshead Bay	110
1:27 1/4	Kingston	1884 h., Spendthrift	9/1/1887	Sheepshead Bay	118
1:28 1/2	Joe Murray	1879 h., Rebel	7/17/1884	Chicago	117
1:28 3/4	Little Phil	1878 h., Enquirer	7/3/1882	Monmouth Park	111
1:30	Brambaletta	1878 m., *Bonnie Scotland	9/24/1881	Brighton Beach	92
1:30	Reporter	1877 g., King Ernest	8/13/1881	Brighton Beach	95

One Mile

Time	Horse	YOB, Sex, Sire	Date	Track	Weight
1:32 1/5	Dr. Fager	1964 h., Rough 'n Tumble	8/24/1968	Arlington Park	134
1:32 3/5	Buckpasser	1963 h., Tom Fool	6/25/1966	Arlington Park	125
1:33 1/5	Hedevar	1962 h., Count of Honor	6/18/1966	Arlington Park	116
1:33 1/5	Pia Star	1961 h., Olympia	6/19/1965	Arlington Park	112

Time	Horse	YOB, Sex, Sire	Date	Track	Weight
1:33 1/5	Intentionally	1956 h., Intent	6/27/1959	Washington Park	121
1:33 1/5	Swaps	1952 h., *Khaled	6/9/1956	Hollywood Park	128
1:33 3/5	Citation	1945 h., Bull Lea	6/3/1950	Golden Gate Fields	128
1:34	Coaltown	1945 h., Bull Lea	8/20/1949	Washington Park	130
1:34 2/5	Prevaricator	1943 g., Omaha	10/2/1948	Golden Gate Fields	118
1:34 2/5	Equipoise	1928 h., Pennant	6/30/1932	Arlington Park	128
1:34 4/5	Roamer	1911 g., Knight Errant	8/21/1918	Saratoga	110
1:36 1/5	*Sun Briar	1915 h., Sundridge	8/6/1918	Saratoga	113
1:36 1/4	Amalfi	1908 g., The Scribe	9/3/1914	Syracuse (N.Y.)	107
1:36 4/5	Christophine	1911 m., Plaudit	3/11/1914	Juarez (Mex.)	102
1:37	Bonne Chance	1909 g., Orsini	1/18/1914	Juarez	98
1:37 1/5	Vested Rights	1910 g., Abe Frank	12/25/1913	Juarez	105
1:37 1/5	Manasseh	1909 f., *Star Shoot	12/12/1913	Juarez	93
1:37 1/5	Centre Shot	1905 f., *Sain	12/22/1908	Santa Anita (old)	105
1:37 2/5	Kiamesha	1902 f., *Esher	10/9/1905	Belmont Park	104
1:37 2/5	Dick Welles	1900 h., King Eric	8/14/1903	Harlem (Il.)	112
1:37 3/5	Alan-a-Dale	1899 h., Halma	7/1/1903	Washington Park	110
1:37 4/5	Brigadier	1897 g., *Rayon d'Or	6/22/1901	Sheepshead Bay	112
1:38	Orimar	1894 h., Sir Dixon	7/21/1900	Washington Park	109
1:38	*Voter	1894 h., Friar's Balsam	7/17/1900	Brighton Beach	122
1:38 3/4	Libertine	1891 h., Leonatus	10/24/1894	Harlem (Il.)	90
1:39	Arab	1886 g., *Dalnacardoch	6/11/1894	Morris Park	93
1:39 1/4	Chorister	1890 h., Falsetto	6/1/1893	Morris Park	112
1:39 1/2	Racine	1887 h., Bishop	6/28/1890	Washington Park	107
1:39 3/4*	Ten Broeck	1872 h., *Phaeton	5/24/1877	Louisville	110
1:41 1/4	Kadi	1870 g., Lexington	9/2/1875	Hartford (Ct.)	90
1:41 3/5	Searcher	1872 h., Enquirer	5/13/1875	Lexington (Ky.)	90
1:42 1/2*	Grey Planet	1869 h., Planet	8/13/1874	Saratoga	110
1:42 3/4	Springbok	1870 h., *Australian	6/25/1874	Utica (N.Y.)	108
1:42 3/4	Alarm	1869 h., *Eclipse	7/17/1872	Saratoga	90
1:43 1/2	Herzog	1866 h., Vandal	5/25/1869	Cincinnati	—

*Against time

1⅛ Miles

Time	Horse	YOB, Sex, Sire	Date	Track	Weight
1:45	Simply Majestic	1984 h., Majestic Light	4/2/1988	Golden Gate Fields	114
1:45 2/5	Secretariat	1970 h., Bold Ruler	9/15/1973	Belmont Park	124
1:46 1/5	Canonero II	1968 h., *Pretendre	9/20/1972	Belmont Park	110
1:46 1/5	*Figonero	1965 h., Idle Hour	9/1/1969	Del Mar	124
1:46 2/5	Ole Bob Bowers	1963 h., Prince Blessed	10/12/1968	Bay Meadows	114
1:46 2/5	Quicken Tree	1963 g., Royal Orbit	9/2/1968	Del Mar	120
1:46 2/5	*Colorado King	1959 h., *Grand Rapids II	7/4/1964	Hollywood Park	119
1:46 2/5	Bug Brush	1955 m., *Nasrullah	2/14/1959	Santa Anita Park	113
1:46 4/5	Round Table	1954 h., *Princequillo	2/25/1958	Santa Anita Park	130
1:46 4/5	Gen. Duke	1954 h., Bull Lea	3/30/1957	Gulfstream Park	122
1:46 4/5	Swaps	1952 h., *Khaled	7/4/1956	Hollywood Park	130
1:46 4/5	Alidon	1951 g., *Alibhai	7/4/1955	Hollywood Park	116
1:46 4/5	*Noor	1945 h., *Nasrullah	6/17/1950	Golden Gate Fields	123
1:47 3/5	Coaltown	1945 h., Bull Lea	2/14/1949	Hialeah	114
1:47 3/5	*Shannon II	1941 h., Midstream	10/9/1948	Golden Gate Fields	124
1:47 3/5	Indian Broom	1933 h., Brooms	4/11/1936	Tanforan	94
1:48 1/5	Discovery	1931 h., Display	6/22/1935	Aqueduct	123
1:48 2/5	Blessed Event	1930 g., Happy Argo	3/10/1934	Hialeah	111
1:48 2/5	Hot Toddy	1926 g., Ed Crump	9/13/1929	Belmont Park	110
1:48 3/5	Peanuts	1922 h., *Ambassador IV	9/18/1926	Aqueduct	114
1:48 4/5	Chilhowee	1921 h., Ballot	10/14/1924	Latonia	115
1:49	Grey Lag	1918 h., *Star Shoot	7/7/1921	Aqueduct	123
1:49	*Goaler	1916 h., Duke Michael	6/10/1921	Belmont Park	94
1:49 1/5	Man o' War	1917 h., Fair Play	7/10/1920	Aqueduct	126
1:49 2/5	Boots	1911 g., *Hessian	7/7/1917	Aqueduct	127
1:49 2/5	Borrow	1908 g., Hamburg	6/25/1917	Aqueduct	117
1:49 3/5	Roamer	1911 g., Knight Errant	10/10/1914	Laurel Park	124
1:50	Vox Populi	1904 h., *Voter	12/19/1908	Santa Anita (old)	110
1:50 3/5	Charles Edward	1904 h., *Golden Garter	7/10/1907	Brighton Beach	126
1:51	Bonnibert	1898 h., *Albert	7/30/1902	Brighton Beach	120
1:51 1/5	Roehampton	1898 h., *Bathampton	7/26/1901	Brighton Beach	94
1:51 1/5	Watercure	1897 g., *Watercress	6/18/1900	Brighton Beach	100
1:51 1/2	Tristan	1885 h., *Glenelg	6/2/1891	Morris Park	114
1:53	Terra Cotta	1884 h., Harry o' Fallon	6/23/1888	Sheepshead Bay	124
1:53 1/4	Grover Cleveland	1883 h., Monday	10/12/1887	Los Angeles	118
1:53 1/4	Spalding	1882 g., *Billet	7/1/1886	Washington Park	97
1:53 1/4	Rosalie	1877 m., *Leamington	8/13/1881	Brighton Beach	80
1:54	Bob Woolley	1872 h., *Leamington	9/6/1875	Lexington	90
1:56	Fadladeen	1867 h., War Dance	8/19/1874	Saratoga	101
1:56	Picolo	1871 h., Concord	8/15/1874	Saratoga	83
1:56 1/2	Fanny Ludlow	1865 m., *Eclipse	8/10/1869	Saratoga	105

All-Time Leading
North American-Raced Earners

Horse, YOB, Sex, Sire	Years Raced	Starts	Wins	Stakes Wins	Earnings
Cigar, 1990 h., by Palace Music	4	33	19	15	$9,999,815
Skip Away, 1993 h., by Skip Trial	4	38	18	16	9,616,360
Fantastic Light, 1996 h., by Rahy	4	25	12	10	8,486,957
Pleasantly Perfect, 1998 h., by Pleasant Colony	4	18	9	6	7,789,880
Smarty Jones, 2001 c., by Elusive Quality	2	9	8	7	7,613,155
Silver Charm, 1994 h., by Silver Buck	4	24	12	11	6,944,369
Captain Steve, 1997 h., by Fly So Free	3	25	9	8	6,828,356
Alysheba, 1984 h., by Alydar	3	26	11	10	6,679,242
John Henry, 1975 g., by Ole Bob Bowers	8	83	39	30	6,591,860
Tiznow, 1997 h., by Cee's Tizzy	2	15	8	7	6,427,830
Singspiel (Ire), 1992 h., by In the Wings (GB)	4	20	9	8	5,952,825
Falbrav (Ire), 1998 h., by Fairy King	4	26	13	8	5,825,517
Medaglia d'Oro, 1999 h., by El Prado (Ire)	4	17	8	7	5,754,720
Best Pal, 1988 g., by *Habitony	7	47	18	17	5,668,245
Taiki Blizzard, 1991 h., by Seattle Slew	4	23	6	3	5,523,549
High Chaparral (Ire), 1999 h., by Sadler's Wells	3	13	10	9	5,331,231
Sulamani (Ire), 1999 h., by Hernando (Fr)	3	17	9	8	5,252,368
Street Cry (Ire), 1998 h., by Machiavellian	3	12	5	3	5,150,837
Jim and Tonic (Fr), 1994 g., by Double Bed (Fr)	7	39	13	9	4,975,807
Sunday Silence, 1986 h., by Halo	3	14	9	7	4,968,554
Easy Goer, 1986 h., by Alydar	3	20	14	12	4,873,770
Daylami (Ire), 1994 h., by Doyoun	4	21	11	8	4,614,762
Behrens, 1994 h., by Pleasant Colony	4	27	9	7	4,563,500
Unbridled, 1987 h., by Fappiano	3	24	8	5	4,489,475
Awesome Again, 1994 h., by Deputy Minister	2	12	9	7	4,374,590
Moon Ballad (Ire), 1999 h., by Singspiel (Ire)	3	14	5	4	4,364,791
Spend a Buck, 1982 h., by Buckaroo	2	15	10	7	4,220,689
Pilsudski (Ire), 1992 h., by Polish Precedent	4	22	10	8	4,080,297
Azeri, 1998 m., by Jade Hunter	4	24	17	14	4,079,820
Creme Fraiche, 1982 g., by Rich Cream	6	64	17	14	4,024,727
Seeking the Pearl, 1994 m., by Seeking the Gold	4	21	8	7	4,021,716
Point Given, 1998 h., by Thunder Gulch	2	13	9	8	3,968,500
Cat Thief, 1996 h., by Storm Cat	3	30	4	3	3,951,012
Devil His Due, 1989 h., by Devil's Bag	4	41	11	9	3,920,405
Sandpit (Brz), 1989 h., by Baynoun (Ire)	7	40	14	12	3,812,597
Swain (Ire), 1992 h., by Nashwan	4	22	10	7	3,797,566
Ferdinand, 1983 h., by Nijinsky II	4	29	8	7	3,777,978
Almutawakel (GB), 1995 h., by Machiavellian	5	19	4	2	3,643,021
Harlan's Holiday, 1999 h., by Harlan	3	22	9	8	3,632,664
Gentlemen (Arg), 1992 h., by Robin des Bois	5	24	13	11	3,608,558
Spain, 1997 m., by Thunder Gulch	4	35	9	7	3,540,542
Slew o' Gold, 1980 h., by Seattle Slew	3	21	12	8	3,533,534
Victory Gallop, 1995 h., by Cryptoclearance	3	17	9	7	3,505,895
War Emblem, 1999 c., by Our Emblem	2	13	7	4	3,491,000
Precisionist, 1981 h., by Crozier	5	46	20	17	3,485,398
Strike the Gold, 1988 h., by Alydar	4	31	6	4	3,457,026
Lando (Ger), 1990 h., by Acatenango	4	24	10	8	3,438,727
Paradise Creek, 1989 h., by Irish River (Fr)	4	25	14	10	3,401,416
Snow Chief, 1983 h., by Reflected Glory	3	24	13	12	3,383,210
Chief Bearhart, 1993 h., by Chief's Crown	4	26	12	9	3,381,557
Cryptoclearance, 1984 h., by Fappiano	4	44	12	9	3,376,327
Black Tie Affair (Ire), 1986 h., by Miswaki	4	45	18	13	3,370,694
Agnes World, 1995 h., by Danzig	4	20	8	5	3,365,680
Sky Classic, 1987 h., by Nijinsky II	4	29	15	13	3,320,398
Paseana (Arg), 1987 m., by Ahmad	6	36	19	17	3,317,427
Bet Twice, 1984 h., by Sportin' Life	3	26	10	7	3,308,599
Steinlen (GB), 1983 h., by Habitat	5	45	20	16	3,297,169
Serena's Song, 1992 m., by Rahy	3	38	18	17	3,283,388
Real Quiet, 1995 h., by Quiet American	3	20	6	5	3,271,802
Awad, 1990 h., by Caveat	7	70	14	11	3,270,131
Congaree, 1998 h., by Arazi	5	25	12	10	3,267,490
Dance Smartly, 1988 m., by Danzig	3	17	12	10	3,263,835
Paolini (Ger), 1997 h., by Lando (Ger)	6	28	5	4	3,253,469
Sakhee, 1997 h., by Bahri	4	14	8	5	3,253,253
Lemon Drop Kid, 1996 h., by Kingmambo	3	24	10	7	3,245,370
Caller One, 1997 g., by Phone Trick	5	21	10	8	3,190,000
Volponi, 1998 h., by Cryptoclearance	4	31	7	4	3,187,232
Bertrando, 1989 h., by Skywalker	4	24	9	8	3,185,610
Free House, 1994 h., by Smokester	4	22	9	8	3,178,971
Montjeu (Ire), 1996 h., by Sadler's Wells	3	16	11	10	3,178,177
Funny Cide, 2000 g., by Distorted Humor	3	21	8	6	3,174,485

Horse, YOB, Sex, Sire	Years Raced	Starts	Wins	Stakes Wins	Earnings
Perfect Drift, 1999 g., by Dynaformer	4	27	9	7	$3,168,963
Siphon (Brz), 1991 h., by Itajara	5	25	12	9	3,136,428
Gulch, 1984 h., by Mr. Prospector	3	32	13	11	3,095,521
Silverbulletday, 1996 m., by Silver Deputy	3	23	15	14	3,093,207
Peace Rules, 2000 c., by Jules	3	19	9	8	3,084,278
Concern, 1991 h., by Broad Brush	3	30	7	4	3,079,350
Giant's Causeway, 1997 h., by Storm Cat	2	13	9	8	3,078,989
Lady's Secret, 1982 m., by Secretariat	4	45	25	22	3,021,325
Albert the Great, 1997 h., by Go for Gin	2	22	8	5	3,012,490
Ghostzapper, 2000 h., by Awesome Again	3	10	8	5	2,996,120
Alphabet Soup, 1991 h., by Cozzene	4	24	10	7	2,990,270
A.P. Indy, 1989 h., by Seattle Slew	2	11	8	6	2,979,815
Escena, 1993 m., by Strawberry Road (Aus)	4	29	11	7	2,962,639
Theatrical (Ire), 1982 h., by Nureyev	4	22	10	8	2,940,036
Hansel, 1988 h., by Woodman	2	14	7	6	2,936,586
Dance in the Mood (Jpn), 2001 f., by Sunday Silence	2	10	4	2	2,931,889
Sea Hero, 1990 h., by Polish Navy	3	24	6	3	2,929,869
Great Communicator, 1983 g., by Key to the Kingdom	6	56	14	9	2,922,615
Thunder Gulch, 1992 h., by Gulch	2	16	9	8	2,915,086
Farma Way, 1987 h., by Marfa	3	23	8	6	2,897,175
Milwaukee Brew, 1997 h., by Wild Again	4	24	8	5	2,879,612
General Challenge, 1996 g., by General Meeting	4	21	9	8	2,877,178
Ashado, 2001 f., by Saint Ballado	2	14	9	8	2,870,440
With Approval, 1986 h., by Caro (Ire)	3	23	13	9	2,863,540
Bayakoa (Arg), 1984 m., by Consultant's Bid	6	39	21	17	2,861,701
Rough Habit (NZ), 1986 g., by Roughcast	7	66	28	21	2,861,579
Marquetry, 1987 h., by Conquistador Cielo	5	36	10	7	2,857,886
Budroyale, 1993 g., by Cee's Tizzy	7	52	17	7	2,840,810
Kotashaan (Fr), 1988 h., by Darshaan	4	22	10	8	2,812,114
Banshee Breeze, 1995 m., by Unbridled	3	18	10	8	2,784,798
Spectacular Bid, 1976 h., by Bold Bidder	3	30	26	23	2,781,608
Symboli Rudolf (Jpn), 1981 h., by Partholon	4	16	13	10	2,764,980
Buck's Boy, 1993 g., by Bucksplasher	5	30	16	9	2,750,148
Beautiful Pleasure, 1995 m., by Maudlin	5	25	10	7	2,734,078
Forty Niner, 1985 h., by Mr. Prospector	2	19	11	9	2,726,000
Pleasant Tap, 1987 h., by Pleasant Colony	4	32	9	6	2,721,169
Lido Palace (Chi), 1997 h., by Rich Man's Gold	4	23	11	8	2,705,865
Izvestia, 1987 h., by Icecapade	3	21	11	10	2,702,527
Manila, 1983 h., by Lyphard	3	18	12	10	2,692,799
With Anticipation, 1995 g., by Relaunch	8	48	15	8	2,660,543
Broad Brush, 1983 h., by Ack Ack	3	27	14	12	2,656,793
Trinycarol (Ven), 1979 m., by Velvet Cap	4	29	18	0	2,644,392
Fraise, 1988 h., by Strawberry Road (Aus)	4	34	10	6	2,613,105
Sarafan, 1997 g., by Lear Fan	6	44	10	6	2,588,671
Flawlessly, 1988 m., by Affirmed	5	28	16	15	2,572,536
Dramatic Gold, 1991 g., by Slew o' Gold	6	39	9	4	2,567,630
Wando, 2000 c., by Langfuhr	3	19	11	8	2,543,229
Sir Bear, 1993 g., by Sir Leon	8	71	19	11	2,538,422
Let's Elope (NZ), 1987 m., by Nassipour	5	26	11	8	2,528,902
Lure, 1989 h., by Danzig	4	25	14	10	2,515,289
Gate Dancer, 1981 h., by Sovereign Dancer	4	28	7	4	2,501,705
Holy Bull, 1991 h., by Great Above	3	16	13	11	2,481,760
Take Charge Lady, 1999 m., by Dehere	3	22	11	9	2,480,377
Mecke, 1992 h., by Maudlin	4	40	12	9	2,470,550
Golden Pheasant, 1986 h., by Caro (Ire)	4	22	7	5	2,453,958
Marlin, 1993 h., by Sword Dance (Ire)	3	26	9	6	2,448,880
Sightseek, 1999 m., by Distant View	3	20	12	10	2,445,216
Affirmed, 1975 h., by Exclusive Native	3	29	22	19	2,393,818
Xtra Heat, 1998 m., by Dixieland Heat	4	35	26	25	2,389,635
Malek (Chi), 1993 h., by Mocito Guapo	6	23	10	7	2,382,623
Heritage of Gold, 1995 m., by Gold Legend	4	28	16	11	2,381,762
Evening Attire, 1998 g., by Black Tie Affair (Ire)	5	39	11	7	2,373,010
Balto Star, 1998 g., by Glitterman	5	38	12	7	2,363,780
Criminal Type, 1985 h., by Alydar	4	24	10	6	2,351,274
Tabasco Cat, 1991 h., by Storm Cat	2	18	8	6	2,347,671
Quiet Resolve, 1995 g., by Affirmed	5	31	10	5	2,346,768
Bien Bien, 1989 h., by Manila	3	26	9	8	2,331,975
Fly So Free, 1988 h., by Time for a Change	4	33	12	8	2,330,954
Silvano (Ger), 1996 h., by Lomitas (GB)	4	18	7	5	2,321,024
Triptych, 1982 m., by Riverman	5	41	14	12	2,318,946
Star of Cozzene, 1988 h., by Cozzene	5	38	14	9	2,308,923
Seeking the Gold, 1985 h., by Mr. Prospector	3	15	8	4	2,307,000
Soul of the Matter, 1991 h., by Private Terms	4	16	7	4	2,302,818

Horse, YOB, Sex, Sire	Years Raced	Starts	Stakes Wins	Wins	Earnings
Kona Gold, 1994 g., by Java Gold	6	30	14	11	2,293,384
Skimming, 1996 h., by Nureyev	4	20	8	5	2,286,601
Affirmed Success, 1994 g., by Affirmed	7	42	17	10	2,285,315
Mineshaft, 1999 h., by A.P. Indy	2	18	10	7	2,283,402
Yankee Affair, 1982 h., by Northern Fling	5	55	22	15	2,282,156
Polish Summer (GB), 1997 h., by Polish Precedent	6	27	6	4	2,277,871
Prized, 1986 h., by Kris S.	4	17	9	6	2,262,555
Festin (Arg), 1986 h., by Mat-Boy (Arg)	4	24	9	4	2,256,295
Pine Bluff, 1989 h., by Danzig	2	13	6	5	2,255,884
Life's Magic, 1981 m., by Cox's Ridge	3	33	8	7	2,255,218
Galileo (Ire) 1998 h., by Sadler's Wells	2	8	6	5	2,245,373
Skywalker, 1982 h., by Relaunch	4	20	8	5	2,226,750
Waquoit, 1983 h., by Relaunch	4	30	19	13	2,225,360
Wild Again, 1980 h., by Icecapade	4	28	8	4	2,204,829
Perfect Sting, 1996 m., by Red Ransom	4	21	14	11	2,202,042
Proud Truth, 1982 h., by Graustark	3	21	10	6	2,198,895
Golden Missile, 1995 h., by A.P. Indy	4	25	7	5	2,194,510
Safely Kept, 1986 m., by Horatius	4	31	24	22	2,194,206
Chief's Crown, 1982 h., by Danzig	2	21	12	10	2,191,168
Twilight Agenda, 1986 h., by Devil's Bag	5	32	13	9	2,174,529
Nostalgia's Star, 1982 h., by Nostalgia	5	59	9	7	2,154,827
Kalanisi (Ire), 1996 h., by Doyoun	3	11	6	4	2,148,836
Turkoman, 1982 h., by Alydar	3	22	8	5	2,146,924
Caitano (GB), 1994 h., by Niniski	7	44	9	7	2,137,459
All Along (Fr), 1979 h., by Targowice	4	21	9	7	2,125,828
Daliapour (Ire), 1996 h., by Sadler's Wells	5	26	7	5	2,123,763
Val's Prince, 1992 g., by Eternal Prince	7	52	13	4	2,118,785
You, 1999 m., by You and I	3	23	9	8	2,101,353
Say Florida Sandy, 1994 h., by Personal Flag	8	98	33	19	2,085,408
Lost Code, 1984 h., by Codex	3	27	15	12	2,085,396
Sunshine Forever, 1985 h., by Roberto	3	23	8	5	2,084,800
Hernando (Fr), 1990 h., by Niniski	3	20	7	6	2,081,978
Majesty's Prince, 1979 h., by His Majesty	4	43	12	9	2,077,796
Miesque, 1984 m., by Nureyev	3	16	12	11	2,070,163
Louis Quatorze, 1993 h., by Sovereign Dancer	3	18	7	4	2,054,434
Adoration, 1999 m., by Honor Grades	3	20	8	7	2,051,160
Coronado's Quest, 1995 h., by Forty Niner	2	17	10	8	2,046,190
Charismatic, 1996 h., by Summer Squall	2	17	5	3	2,038,064
Sharp Cat, 1994 m., by Storm Cat	3	22	15	14	2,032,575
Risen Star, 1985 h., by Secretariat	2	11	8	6	2,029,845
Essence of Dubai, 1999 c., by Pulpit	3	13	5	4	2,001,058
Itsallgreektome, 1987 g., by Sovereign Dancer	5	29	8	7	1,994,618
Fusaichi Pegasus, 1997 h., by Mr. Prospector	2	9	6	4	1,994,400
Empire Maker, 2000 c., by Unbridled	2	8	4	3	1,985,800
Arcangues, 1988 h., by Sagace (Fr)	5	19	6	5	1,981,423
Kelso, 1957 g., by Your Host	8	63	39	31	1,977,896
Ladies Din, 1995 g., by Din's Dancer	7	37	12	9	1,966,754
Aptitude, 1997 h., by A.P. Indy	3	15	5	3	1,965,410
Guided Tour, 1996 g., by Hansel	4	31	12	7	1,964,253
Little Bold John, 1982 g., by John Alden	9	105	38	25	1,956,406
Storm Flag Flying, 2000 m., by Storm Cat	3	14	7	4	1,951,828
Chester House, 1995 h., by Mr. Prospector	4	21	6	4	1,944,545
Greinton (GB), 1981 h., by Green Dancer	4	22	10	7	1,943,605
Forego, 1970 g., by *Forli	6	57	34	24	1,938,957
Estrapade, 1980 m., by *Vaguely Noble	4	30	12	10	1,937,142
Boston Harbor, 1994 h., by Capote	2	8	6	5	1,934,605

Progression of Leading Earner

North America

Because of the paucity and unreliability of published records of Thoroughbred racing before the Civil War, the earliest leading North American earner whose record can be reliably verified is the great American Eclipse, who became an American popular hero in the 1820s. More than 20 years later, the baton was handed on to the giant filly Peytona, who collected the largest purse on the continent to that date, $41,000, for her victory in the Peyton Stakes at Nashville, Tennessee, in 1843. Her owner

promptly changed her name from the unwieldy Glumdalclitch and named her after her most famous win.

The pace of change on the leading earner list has quickened since antebellum days. Perhaps the most exciting exchange occurred in 1947, when Racing Hall of Fame members Assault, Armed, and Stymie batted Whirlaway's previous record around like a badminton shuttlecock. Stymie's durability finally outlasted the other two, and he ended his career with earnings of $918,485. Citation, who became the leading earner in 1950, moved the mark above $1-million the following year.

The great two-year-old and epochal sire Domino held the torch for the longest period, 27 years, from 1893 until supplanted by Man o' War in 1920. Assault and Stymie each held the title for the shortest period, seven days, during their duel in 1947. The only stallion to sire two leading North American money earners is Bull Lea. Peytona and Miss Woodford are the only females to hold the title.

International racing has always complicated the issue. Parole's record earnings include about $20,000 earned on his sojourn in England in 1879-'80. Cigar's earnings similarly include the $2.4-million earned in his Dubai World Cup victory.

Chronology of Leading American Money Winners

1823—American Eclipse, 1814 ch. h., Duroc—Millers Damsel, by Messenger. 8-8-0-0, **$56,700.**

1845—Peytona, 1839 ch. f., *Glencoe—Giantess, by *Leviathan. 8-6-1-0, **$62,400.**

1861—Planet, 1855 ch. h., Revenue—Nina, by Boston. 31-27-4-0, **$69,700.**

1881—Hindoo, 1878 b. h., Virgil—Florence, by Lexington. 35-30-3-2, **$71,875.**

1881—Parole, 1873 br. h., *Leamington—Maiden, by Lexington. 129-59-22-16, **$82,816.**

1885—Miss Woodford, 1880 br. f., *Billet—Fancy Jane, by Neil Robinson. 48-37-7-2, **$118,270.**

1889—Hanover, 1884 ch. h., Hindoo—Bourbon Belle, by *Bonnie Scotland. 50-32-14-2, **$118,887.**

1892—Kingston, 1884 dk. b. or br. h., Spendthrift—*Kapanga, by Victorious. 138-89-33-12, **$138,917.**

1893—Domino, 1891 br. h., Himyar—Mannie Gray, by Enquirer. 25-19-3-1, **$193,550.**

1920—Man o' War, 1917 ch. h., Fair Play—Mahubah, by *Rock Sand. 21-20-1-0, **$249,465.**

1923—Zev, 1920 dk. b. or br. h., The Finn—Miss Kearney, by *Planudes. 43-23-8-5, **$313,639.**

1930—Gallant Fox, 1927 b. h., *Sir Gallahad III—Marguerite, by Celt. 17-11-3-2, **$328,165.**

1931—Sun Beau, 1925 b. h., *Sun Briar—Beautiful Lady, by Fair Play. 74-33-12-10, **$376,744.**

1940—Seabiscuit, 1933 b. h., Hard Tack—Swing On, by Whisk Broom II. 89-33-15-13, **$437,730.**

1942—Whirlaway, 1938 ch. h., *Blenheim II—Dustwhirl, by Sweep. 60-32-15-9, **$561,161.**

1947 (June 21)—Assault, 1943 ch. h., Bold Venture—Igual, by Equipoise. 42-18-6-7, **$576,670.**

1947 (July 5)—Stymie, 1941 ch. h., Equestrian—Stop Watch, by On Watch. 131-35-33-28, **$595,510.**

1947 (July 12)—Assault, $613,370 (career $675,470).

1947 (July 19)—Stymie, $678,510.

1947 (October 9)—Armed, 1941 dk. b. or br. g., Bull Lea—Armful, by Chance Shot. 81-41-20-10, **$761,500 (career $817,475).**

1947 (October 25)—Stymie $816,060 (career $918,485).

1950—Citation, 1945 b. h., Bull Lea—*Hydroplane II, by Hyperion. 45-32-10-2, **$1,085,760.**

1956—Nashua, 1952 b. h., *Nasrullah—Segula, by Johnstown. 30-22-4-1, **$1,288,565.**

1958—Round Table, 1954 b. h., *Princequillo—*Knight's Daughter, by Sir Cosmo. 66-43-8-5, **$1,749,869.**

1965—Kelso, 1957 dk. b. or br. g., Your Host—Maid of Flight, by Count Fleet. 63-39-12-2, **$1,977,896.**

1979—Affirmed, 1975 ch. h., Exclusive Native—Won't Tell You, by Crafty Admiral. 29-22-5-1, **$2,393,818.**

1980—Spectacular Bid, 1976 gr. h., Bold Bidder—Spectacular, by Promised Land. 30-26-2-1, **$2,781,608.**

1981—John Henry, 1975 b. g., Ole Bob Bowers—Once Double, by Double Jay. 83-39-15-9, **$6,591,860.**

1988—Alysheba, 1984 b. h., Alydar—Bel Sheba, by Lt. Stevens. 26-11-8-2, **$6,679,242.**

1996—Cigar, 1990 b. h., Palace Music—Solar Slew, by Seattle Slew. 33-19-4-5, **$9,999,815.**

International

In the 20th century, America became so accustomed to being the home of the world's leading money-winning racehorse that it did not even notice when Japanese-bred and -trained Oguri Cap soared past American leader Alysheba in 1990.

Since organized Thoroughbred racing originated in England in the early 18th century, it is obvious that the earliest leading earners must have resided there as well. Determining the first world's richest Thoroughbred is all but impossible because early records are nonexistent or unclear on purse awards.

English record-keepers recorded that in 1889 Donovan broke the record previously held by the French-bred Gladiateur. In turn, Gladiateur had broken the previous record of England's The Flying Dutchman.

The earliest horse who can reliably be accorded the palm of world's leading earner is the undefeated Highflyer, who was foaled in 1774. Based on the exchange rate of $5 to £1 that prevailed in the 19th century (America was still a British colony in 1774), Highflyer earned the equivalent of $38,395 by winning all 12 of his races.

By that standard, American Eclipse surpassed Highflyer, but 1830 Epsom Derby winner *Priam

earned more money by the same exchange rate. The title remained in Europe until 1923, when Zev's victory over *Papyrus propelled him past Isinglass, who remained England's leading earner for more than 60 years.

Zev began a 67-year reign for American horses at the same time the American economy began to dominate the world. Only the huge increases in Japanese purses beginning in the 1980s changed that equation. As shown by the accompanying list of the world's current leading earners, the earnings of T.M.Opera O far exceed any American horse.

Chronology of Leading International Money Winners

1780—Highflyer, 1774 b.h., Herod—Rachel, by Blank. 12-12-0-0, **$38,395.**

1823—American Eclipse, 1814 ch.h., Duroc—Miller's Damsel, by *Messenger. 8-8-0-0, **$56,700.**

1830—*Priam, 1827 br. h., Emilius—Cressida, by Whiskey. 16-14-1-1, **$65,100.**

1850—The Flying Dutchman, 1846 b. h., Bay Middleton—Barbelle, by Sandbeck. 15-14-1-0, **$93,900.**

1865—Gladiateur, 1862 b. h., Monarque—Miss Gladiator, by Gladiator. 19-16-0-1, **$236,537.**

1889—Donovan, 1886 b. h., Galopin—Mowerina, by The Scottish Chief. 21-18-2-1, **$275,775.**

1895—Isinglass, 1890 b. h., Isonomy—Dead Lock, by Wenlock. 12-11-1-0, **$287,275.**

1923—Zev, 1920 dk. b. or br. h., The Finn—Miss Kearney, by *Planudes. 43-23-8-5, **$313,639.**

1930—Gallant Fox, 1927 b. h., *Sir Gallahad III—Marguerite, by Celt. 17-11-3-2, **$328,165.**

1931—Sun Beau, 1925 b. h., *Sun Briar—Beautiful Lady, by Fair Play. 74-33-12-10, **$376,744.**

1940—Seabiscuit, 1933 b.h., Hard Tack—Swing On, by Whisk Broom II. 89-33-15-13, **$437,730.**

1942—Whirlaway, 1938 ch. h., *Blenheim II—Dustwhirl, by Sweep. 60-32-15-9, **$561,161.**

1947 (June 21)—Assault, 1943 ch.h., Bold Venture—Igual, by Equipoise. 42-18-6-7, **$576,670.**

1947 (July 5)—Stymie, 1941 ch. h., Equestrian—Stop Watch, by On Watch. 131-35-33-28, **$595,510.**

1947 (July 12)—Assault, $613,370 (career $675,470).

1947 (July 19)—Stymie, $678,510.

1947 (October 9)—Armed, 1941 dk. b. or br. g., Bull Lea—Armful, by Chance Shot. 81-41-20-10, **$761,500 (career $817,475).**

1947 (October 25)—Stymie $816,060 (career $918,485).

1950—Citation, 1945 b. h., Bull Lea—*Hydroplane II, by Hyperion. 45-32-10-2, **$1,085,760.**

1956—Nashua, 1952 b. h., *Nasrullah—Segula, by Johnstown. 30-22-4-1, **$1,288,565.**

1958—Round Table, 1954 b.h., *Princequillo—*Knight's Daughter, by Sir Cosmo. 66-43-8-5, **$1,749,869.**

1965—Kelso, 1957 dk. b. or br. g., Your Host—Maid of Flight, by Count Fleet. 63-39-12-2, **$1,977,896.**

1979—Affirmed, 1975 ch. h., Exclusive Native—Won't Tell You, by Crafty Admiral. 29-22-5-1, **$2,393,818.**

1980—Spectacular Bid, 1976 gr. h., Bold Bidder—Spectacular, by Promised Land. 30-26-2-1, **$2,781,608.**
1981—John Henry, 1975 b. g., Ole Bob Bowers—Once Double, by Double Jay. 83-39-15-9, **$6,591,860.**
1988—Alysheba, 1984 b. h., Alydar—Bel Sheba, by Lt. Stevens. 26-11-8-2, **$6,679,242.**
1990—Oguri Cap, 1985 gr. h., Dancing Cap—White Narubi, by *Silver Shark. 32-22-6-1, **$6,919,201.**

1993—Mejiro McQueen, 1987 gr. h., Mejiro Titan—Mejiro Aurola, by Remand. 14-9-3-0, **$7,618,803.**
1995—Narita Brian, 1991 dk b. or br. h., Brian's Time—Pacificus, by Northern Dancer. 21-12-3-1, **$9,296,552.**
1996—Cigar, 1990 b. h., Palace Music—Solar Slew, by Seattle Slew. 33-19-4-5, **$9,999,815.**
2000—T.M.Opera O, 1996 ch. h., Opera House (GB)—Once Wed, by Blushing Groom (Fr). 26-14-6-3, **$16,200,337.**

World's Leading Earners

Through February 27, 2005

Rank	Horse	YOB, Color, Sex, Pedigree	Country	Earnings (in Dollars)
1.	T.M.Opera O	1996 ch. h., Opera House (GB)—Once Wed, by Blushing Groom (Fr)	Jpn	$16,200,337
2.	Cigar	1990 b. h., Palace Music—Solar Slew	USA	9,999,815
3.	Skip Away	1993 gr. h., Skip Trial—Ingot Way, by Diplomat Way	USA	9,616,360
4.	Special Week	1995 dk. b. or br. h., Sunday Silence—Campaign Girl, by Maruzensky	Jpn	9,346,435
5.	Narita Brian	1991 dk. b. or br. h., Brian's Time—Pacificus, by Northern Dancer	Jpn	9,296,552
6.	Zenno Rob Roy	2000 dk. b. or br. h., Sunday Silence—Roamin Rachel, by Mining	Jpn	8,994,210
7.	Tap Dance City	1997 b. h., Pleasant Tap—All Dance, by Northern Dancer	Jpn	8,986,709
8.	Stay Gold	1994 dk. b. or br. h., Sunday Silence—Golden Sash, by Dictus	Jpn	8,682,142
9.	Fantastic Light	1996 b. h., Rahy—Jood, by Nijinsky II	GB	8,486,957
10.	Symboli Kris S	1999 dk. b. or br. h., Kris S.—Tee Kay, by Gold Meridian	Jpn	8,401,282
11.	Narita Top Road	1996 ch. h., Soccer Boy—Floral Magic, by Affirmed	Jpn	8,389,594
12.	Hokuto Vega	1990 b. m., Nagurski—Takeno Falcon, by Philip of Spain	Jpn	8,300,301
13.	Agnes Digital	1997 ch. h., Crafty Prospector—Chancey Squaw, by Chief's Crown	Jpn	8,095,160
14.	Meisho Doto	1996 b. h., Bigstone (Ire)—Princess Reema, by Affirmed	Jpn	8,088,202
15.	Pleasantly Perfect	1998 b. h., Pleasant Colony—Regal State, by Affirmed	USA	7,789,880
16.	Admire Don	1999 b. h., Timber Country—Vega, by Tony Bin	Jpn	7,655,421
17.	Mejiro Mc Queen	1987 gr. h., Mejiro Titan—Mejiro Aurola, by Remand	Jpn	7,618,803
18.	Smarty Jones	2001 dk. c., Elusive Quality—I'll Get Along, by Smile	USA	7,613,155
19.	Biwa Hayahide	1990 gr. h., Sharrood—Pacificus, by Northern Dancer	Jpn	7,555,480
20.	Mayano Top Gun	1992 ch. h., Brian's Time—Alp Me Please, by Blushing Groom (Fr)	Jpn	7,463,557
21.	Eishin Preston	1997 dk. b. or br. h., Green Dancer—Warranty Applied, by Monteverdi (Ire)	Jpn	7,408,086
22.	Hishi Amazon	1991 dk. b. or br. m., Theatrical (Ire)—Katies (Ire), by Nonoalco	Jpn	6,981,102
23.	Silver Charm	1994 gr. h., Silver Buck—Bonnie's Poker, by Poker	USA	6,944,369
24.	Oguri Cap	1985 gr. h., Dancing Cap—White Narubi, by *Silver Shark	Jpn	6,919,201
25.	Mejiro Bright	1994 b. h., Mejiro Ryan—Reru du Temps, by Maruzensky	Jpn	6,848,423
26.	Air Groove	1993 b. m., Tony Bin—Dyna Carle, by Northern Taste	Jpn	6,832,242
27.	Captain Steve	1997 ch. h., Fly So Free—Sparkling Delite, by Vice Regent	USA	6,828,356
28.	Alysheba	1984 b. h., Alydar—Bel Sheba, by Lt. Stevens	USA	6,679,242
29.	Sunline	1995 b. m., Desert Sun (GB)—Songline, by Western Symphony	Aus	6,625,105
30.	John Henry	1975 b. g., Ole Bob Bowers—Once Double, by Double Jay	USA	6,591,860
31.	Tiznow	1997 b. h., Cee's Tizzy—Cee's Song, by Seattle Song	USA	6,427,830
32.	Wing Arrow	1995 b. h., Assatis—Sanyo Arrow, by Mr C B	Jpn	6,273,733
33.	Mejiro Dober	1994 b. m., Mejiro Ryan—Mejiro Beauty, by Partholon	Jpn	6,240,681
34.	Rice Shower	1989 dk. b. or br. h., Real Shadai—Lilac Point, by Maruzensky	Jpn	6,070,429
35.	Grass Wonder	1995 ch. h., Silver Hawk—Ameriflora, by Danzig	Jpn	5,987,405
36.	Dance Partner (Jpn)	1992 b. m., Sunday Silence—Dancing Key, by Nijinsky II	Jpn	5,973,652
37.	Singspiel (Ire)	1992 b. h., In the Wings (GB)—Glorious Song, by Halo	GB	5,952,825
38.	Fast Friend	1994 ch. m., Ines Fujin—The Last Word, by Northern Taste	Jpn	5,896,693
39.	Falbrav (Ire)	1998 b. h., Fairy King—Gift of the Night, by Slewpy	GB	5,825,517
40.	Jungle Pocket	1998 b. h., Tony Bin—Dance Charmer, by Nureyev	Jpn	5,788,198
41.	Medaglia d'Oro	1999 dk. b. or br. h., El Prado (Ire)—Cappucino Bay, by Bailjumper	USA	5,754,720
42.	Sakura Laurel	1991 b. h., Rainbow Quest—Lola Lola, by Saint Cyrien	Jpn	5,751,390
43.	Black Hawk (GB)	1994 b. h., Nureyev—Silver Lane, by Silver Hawk	Jpn	5,750,386
44.	Best Pal	1988 b. g., *Habitony—Ubetshedid, by King Pellinore	USA	5,668,245
45.	Kyoto City	1991 b. h., Soccer Boy—Mountain Queen, by Nizon	Jpn	5,622,437
46.	Taiki Blizzard	1991 dk. b. or br. h., Seattle Slew—Tree of Knowledge (Ire), by Sassafras (Fr)	Jpn	5,523,549
47.	Genuine	1992 dk. b. or br. h., Sunday Silence—Croupier Lady, by What Luck	Jpn	5,455,575
48.	High Chaparral (Ire)	1999 b. h., Sadler's Wells—Kasora, by Darshaan	Ire	5,331,231
49.	Marvelous Sunday	1992 ch. h., Sunday Silence—Momiji Dancer, by Viceregal	Jpn	5,305,340
50.	To the Victory	1996 b. m., Sunday Silence—Fairy Doll, by Nureyev	Jpn	5,303,281

Leading North American Earners by Year

North American Racing Only

Year	Horse, YOB, Sex, Pedigree	Earnings
2004	Smarty Jones, 2001 c., Elusive Quality—I'll Get Along, by Smile	$7,563,535
2003	Pleasantly Perfect, 1998 h., Pleasant Colony—Regal State, by Affirmed	2,470,000
2002	War Emblem, 1999 c., Our Emblem—Sweetest Lady, by Lord At War (Arg)	3,455,000
2001	Point Given, 1998 c., Thunder Gulch—Turko's Turn, by Turkoman	3,350,000
2000	Tiznow, 1997 c., Cee's Tizzy—Cee's Song, by Seattle Song	3,445,950
1999	Cat Thief, 1996 c., Storm Cat—Train Robbery, by Alydar	3,020,500
1998	Awesome Again, 1994 c., Deputy Minister—Primal Force, by Blushing Groom (Fr)	3,845,990
1997	Skip Away, 1993 c., Skip Trial—Ingot Way, by Diplomat Way	4,089,000
1996	Skip Away, 1993 c., Skip Trial—Ingot Way, by Diplomat Way	2,699,280
1995	Cigar, 1990 h., Palace Music—Solar Slew, by Seattle Slew	4,819,800
1994	Concern, 1991 c., Broad Brush—Fara's Team, by Tunerup	2,541,670
1993	Sea Hero, 1990 c., Polish Navy—Glowing Tribute, by Graustark	2,484,190
1992	A.P. Indy, 1989 c., Seattle Slew—Weekend Surprise, by Secretariat	2,622,560
1991	Dance Smartly, 1988 f., Danzig—Classy 'n Smart, by Smarten	2,876,821
1990	Unbridled, 1987 c., Fappiano—Gana Facil, by *Le Fabuleux	3,718,149
1989	Sunday Silence, 1986 c., Halo—Wishing Well, by Understanding	4,578,454
1988	Alysheba, 1984 c., Alydar—Bel Sheba, by Lt. Stevens	3,808,600
1987	Alysheba, 1984 c., Alydar—Bel Sheba, by Lt. Stevens	2,511,156
1986	Snow Chief, 1983 c., Reflected Glory—Miss Snowflake, by *Snow Sporting	1,875,200
1985	Spend a Buck, 1982 c., Buckaroo—Belle de Jour, by Speak John	3,552,704
1984	Slew o' Gold, 1980 c., Seattle Slew—Alluvial, by Buckpasser	2,627,944
1983	Sunny's Halo, 1980 c., Halo—Mostly Sunny, by Sunny	1,011,962
1982	Perrault (GB), 1977 h., Djakao—Innocent Air, by *Court Martial	1,197,400
1981	John Henry, 1975 g., Ole Bob Bowers—Once Double, by Double Jay	1,798,030
1980	Temperence Hill, 1977 c., Stop the Music—Sister Shannon, by Etonian	1,130,452
1979	Spectacular Bid, 1976 c., Bold Bidder—Spectacular, by Promised Land	1,279,334
1978	Affirmed, 1975 c., Exclusive Native—Won't Tell You, by Crafty Admiral	901,541
1977	Seattle Slew, 1974 c., Bold Reasoning—My Charmer, by Poker	641,370
1976	Forego, 1970 g., *Forli—Lady Golconda, by Hasty Road	491,701
1975	Foolish Pleasure, 1972 c., What a Pleasure—Fool-Me-Not, by Tom Fool	716,278
1974	Chris Evert, 1971 f., Swoon's Son—Miss Carmie, by T. V. Lark	551,063
1973	Secretariat, 1970 c., Bold Ruler—Somethingroyal, by *Princequillo	860,404
1972	Droll Role, 1968 c., Tom Rolfe—*Pradella, by Preciptic	471,633
1971	Riva Ridge, 1969 c., First Landing—Iberia, by *Heliopolis	503,263
1970	Personality, 1967 c., Hail to Reason—Affectionately, by Swaps	444,049
1969	Arts and Letters, 1966 c., *Ribot—All Beautiful, by Battlefield	555,604
1968	Forward Pass, 1965 c., On-and-On—Princess Turia, by *Heliopolis	546,674
1967	Damascus, 1964 c., Sword Dancer—Kerala, by *My Babu	817,941
1966	Buckpasser, 1963 c., Tom Fool—Busanda, by War Admiral	669,078
1965	Buckpasser, 1963 c., Tom Fool—Busanda, by War Admiral	568,096
1964	Gun Bow, 1960 c., Gun Shot—Ribbons and Bows, by War Admiral	580,100
1963	Candy Spots, 1960 c., *Nigromante—Candy Dish, by *Khaled	604,481
1962	Never Bend, 1960 c., *Nasrullah—Lalun, by *Djeddah	402,969
1961	Carry Back, 1958 c., Saggy—Joppy, by Star Blen	565,349
1960	Bally Ache, 1957 c., *Ballydam—Celestial Blue, by Supremus	455,045
1959	Sword Dancer, 1956 c., Sunglow—Highland Fling, by By Jimminy	537,004
1958	Round Table, 1954 c., *Princequillo—*Knight's Daughter, by Sir Cosmo	662,780
1957	Round Table, 1954 c., *Princequillo—*Knight's Daughter, by Sir Cosmo	600,383
1956	Needles, 1953 c., Ponder—Noodle Soup, by Jack High	440,850
1955	Nashua, 1952 c., *Nasrullah—Segula, by Johnstown	752,550
1954	Determine, 1951 c., *Alibhai—Koubis, by *Mahmoud	328,700
1953	Native Dancer, 1950 c., Polynesian—Geisha, by Discovery	513,425
1952	Crafty Admiral, 1948 c., Fighting Fox—Admiral's Lady, by War Admiral	277,225
1951	Counterpoint, 1948 c., Count Fleet—Jabot, by *Sickle	250,525
1950	*Noor, 1945 h., *Nasrullah—Queen of Baghdad, by *Bahram	346,940
1949	Ponder, 1946 c., Pensive—Miss Rushin, by *Blenheim II	321,825
1948	Citation, 1945 c., Bull Lea—*Hydroplane II, by Hyperion	709,470
1947	Armed, 1941 g., Bull Lea—Armful, by Chance Shot	376,325
1946	Assault, 1943 c., Bold Venture—Igual, by Equipoise	424,195
1945	Busher, 1942 f., War Admiral—Baby League, by Bubbling Over	273,735
1944	Pavot, 1942 c., Case Ace—Coquelicot, by Man o' War	179,040
1943	Count Fleet, 1940 c., Reigh Count—Quickly, by Haste	174,055
1942	Shut Out, 1939 c., Equipoise—Goose Egg, by *Chicle	238,972
1941	Whirlaway, 1938 c., *Blenheim II—Dustwhirl, by Sweep	272,386
1940	Bimelech, 1937 c., Black Toney—*La Troienne, by *Teddy	110,005
1939	Challedon, 1936 c., *Challenger II—Laura Gal, by *Sir Gallahad III	184,535
1938	Stagehand, 1935 c., *Sickle—Stagecraft, by Fair Play	189,710
1937	Seabiscuit, 1933 c., Hard Tack—Swing On, by Whisk Broom II	168,580
1936	Granville, 1933 c., Gallant Fox—Gravita, by *Sarmatian	110,295
1935	Omaha, 1932 c., Gallant Fox—Flambino, by *Wrack	142,255
1934	Cavalcade, 1931 c., *Lancegaye—*Hastily, by Hurry On	111,235
1933	Singing Wood, 1931 c., *Royal Minstrel—Glade, by Touch Me Not	88,050
1932	Gusto, 1929 c., American Flag—Daylight Saving, by *Star Shoot	145,940
1931	Top Flight, 1929 f., *Dis Donc—Flyatit, by Peter Pan	219,000
1930	Gallant Fox, 1927 c., *Sir Gallahad III—Marguerite, by Celt	308,275

Leading Earners in North America
North American Racing Only

Horse, YOB, Sex, Sire	Wins	SWs	Earnings
Skip Away, 1993 h., by Skip Trial	18	16	$9,616,360
Smarty Jones, 2001 c., by Elusive Quality	8	7	7,613,155
Cigar, 1990 h., by Palace Music	18	14	7,599,815
Alysheba, 1984 h., by Alydar	11	10	6,679,242
John Henry, 1975 g., by Ole Bob Bowers	39	30	6,591,860
Tiznow, 1997 h., by Cee's Tizzy	8	7	6,427,830
Best Pal, 1988 g., by *Habitony	18	17	5,668,245
Sunday Silence, 1986 h., by Halo	9	7	4,968,554
Easy Goer, 1986 h., by Alydar	14	12	4,873,770
Medaglia d'Oro, 1999 c., by El Prado (Ire)	8	7	4,554,720
Unbridled, 1987 h., by Fappiano	8	5	4,489,475
Silver Charm, 1994 h., by Silver Buck	11	10	4,444,369
Awesome Again, 1994 h., by Deputy Minister	9	7	4,374,590
Spend a Buck, 1982 h., by Buckaroo	10	7	4,220,689
Pleasantly Perfect, 1998 h., by Pleasant Colony	8	5	4,189,880
Azeri, 1998 m., by Jade Hunter	17	14	4,079,820
Creme Fraiche, 1982 g., by Rich Cream	17	14	4,024,727
Point Given, 1998 h., by Thunder Gulch	9	8	3,968,500
Cat Thief, 1996 h., by Storm Cat	4	3	3,951,012
Devil His Due, 1989 h., by Devil's Bag	11	9	3,920,405
Ferdinand, 1983 h., by Nijinsky II	8	7	3,777,978
Spain, 1997 m., by Thunder Gulch	9	7	3,540,542
Slew o' Gold, 1980 h., by Seattle Slew	12	8	3,533,534
War Emblem, 1999 c., by Our Emblem	7	4	3,491,000
Precisionist, 1981 h., by Crozier	20	17	3,485,398
Strike the Gold, 1988 h., by Alydar	6	4	3,457,026
Snow Chief, 1983 h., by Reflected Glory	13	12	3,383,210
Cryptoclearance, 1984 h., by Fappiano	12	9	3,376,327
Gentlemen (Arg), 1992 h., by Robin des Bois	9	8	3,374,890
Black Tie Affair (Ire), 1986 h., by Miswaki	18	13	3,370,694
Sky Classic, 1987 h., by Nijinsky II	15	13	3,320,398
Bet Twice, 1984 h., by Sportin' Life	10	7	3,308,599
Serena's Song, 1992 m., by Rahy	18	17	3,283,388
Real Quiet, 1995 h., by Quiet American	6	5	3,271,802
Congaree, 1998 h., by Arazi	12	10	3,267,490
Dance Smartly, 1988 m., by Danzig	12	10	3,263,835
Lemon Drop Kid, 1996 h., by Kingmambo	10	7	3,245,370
Behrens, 1994 h., by Pleasant Colony	9	7	3,243,500
Steinlen (GB), 1983 h., by Habitat	16	14	3,229,752
Captain Steve, 1997 h., by Fly So Free	8	7	3,228,356
Chief Bearhart, 1993 h., by Chief's Crown	12	9	3,219,017
Volponi, 1998 h., by Cryptoclearance	7	4	3,187,232
Bertrando, 1989 h., by Skywalker	9	8	3,185,610
Free House, 1994 h., by Smokester	9	8	3,178,971
Funny Cide, 2000 g., by Distorted Humor	8	6	3,174,485
Perfect Drift, 1999 g., by Dynaformer	9	7	3,168,963
Sandpit (Brz), 1989 h., by Baynoun (Ire)	9	8	3,147,973
Paseana (Arg), 1987 m., by Ahmad	14	14	3,111,292
Gulch, 1984 h., by Mr. Prospector	13	11	3,095,521
Silverbulletday, 1996 m., by Silver Deputy	15	14	3,093,207
Peace Rules, 2000 h., by Jules	9	8	3,084,278
Concern, 1991 h., by Broad Brush	7	4	3,079,350
Lady's Secret, 1982 m., by Secretariat	25	22	3,021,325
Albert the Great, 1997 h., by Go for Gin	8	5	3,012,490
Victory Gallop, 1995 h., by Cryptoclearance	9	7	3,005,895
Ghostzapper, 2000 h., by Awesome Again	8	5	2,996,120
Alphabet Soup, 1991 h., by Cozzene	10	7	2,990,270
A.P. Indy, 1989 h., by Seattle Slew	8	6	2,979,815
Escena, 1993 m., by Strawberry Road (Aus)	11	7	2,962,639
Awad, 1990 h., by Caveat	14	11	2,949,179
Hansel, 1988 h., by Woodman	7	6	2,936,586
Sea Hero, 1990 h., by Polish Navy	6	3	2,929,869
Great Communicator, 1983 h., by Key to the Kingdom	14	9	2,922,615
Thunder Gulch, 1992 h., by Gulch	9	8	2,915,086
Farma Way, 1987 h., by Marfa	8	6	2,897,175
Milwaukee Brew, 1997 h., by Wild Again	8	5	2,879,612
General Challenge, 1996 g., by General Meeting	9	8	2,877,178
Ashado, 2001 f., by Saint Ballado	9	8	2,870,440
With Approval, 1986 h., by Caro (Ire)	13	9	2,863,540
Marquetry, 1987 h., by Conquistador Cielo	9	7	2,844,942
Budroyale, 1993 g., by Cee's Tizzy	17	7	2,840,810
Theatrical (Ire), 1982 h., by Nureyev	7	7	2,840,500
Bayakoa (Arg), 1984 m., by Consultant's Bid	18	16	2,785,259
Banshee Breeze, 1995 m., by Unbridled	10	8	2,784,798
Spectacular Bid, 1976 h., by Bold Bidder	26	23	2,781,608
Buck's Boy, 1993 g., by Bucksplasher	16	9	2,750,148

Horse, YOB, Sex, Sire	Wins	SWs	Earnings
Beautiful Pleasure, 1995 m., by Maudlin	10	7	$2,734,078
Forty Niner, 1985 h., by Mr. Prospector	11	9	2,726,000
Pleasant Tap, 1987 h., by Pleasant Colony	9	6	2,721,169
Izvestia, 1987 h., by Icecapade	11	10	2,702,527
Manila, 1983 h., by Lyphard	12	10	2,692,799
Paradise Creek, 1989 h., by Irish River (Fr)	14	10	2,687,514
With Anticipation, 1995 g., by Relaunch	15	8	2,660,543
Broad Brush, 1983 h., by Ack Ack	14	12	2,656,793
Fraise, 1988 h., by Strawberry Road (Aus)	10	6	2,613,105
Flawlessly, 1988 m., by Affirmed	16	15	2,572,536
Dramatic Gold, 1991 g., by Slew o' Gold	9	4	2,567,630
Wando, 2000 c., by Langfuhr	11	8	2,543,229
Sir Bear, 1993 g., by Sir Leon	19	11	2,538,422
Lure, 1989 h., by Danzig	14	10	2,515,289
Fantastic Light, 1996 h., by Rahy	2	2	2,507,400
Gate Dancer, 1981 h., by Sovereign Dancer	7	4	2,501,705

North American Leaders by Graded Stakes Earnings
North American Racing Only

Horse, YOB, Sex, Sire	Years Raced	Graded Stakes Wins	Graded Stakes Earnings
Skip Away, 1993 h., by Skip Trial	4	16	$9,548,100
Smarty Jones, 2001 c., by Elusive Quality	2	3	7,334,800
Alysheba, 1984 h., by Alydar	3	10	6,616,417
Tiznow, 1997 h., by Cee's Tizzy	2	7	6,382,830
Cigar, 1990 h., by Palace Music	4	11	5,695,000
John Henry, 1975 g., by Ole Bob Bowers	8	25	4,953,417
Sunday Silence, 1986 h., by Halo	3	7	4,929,254
Easy Goer, 1986 h., by Alydar	3	10	4,775,280
Best Pal, 1988 g., by *Habitony	7	12	4,713,795
Medaglia d'Oro, 1999 c., by El Prado (Ire)	4	7	4,535,000
Silver Charm, 1994 h., by Silver Buck	4	10	4,416,619
Unbridled, 1987 h., by Fappiano	3	3	4,105,529
Pleasantly Perfect, 1998 h., by Pleasant Colony	4	5	4,070,000
Awesome Again, 1994 h., by Deputy Minister	3	6	4,065,590
Azeri, 1998 m., by Jade Hunter	4	14	3,999,420
Point Given, 1998 h., by Thunder Gulch	2	8	3,930,900
Cat Thief, 1996 h., by Storm Cat	3	3	3,909,952
Devil His Due, 1989 h., by Devil's Bag	4	9	3,895,265
Spend a Buck, 1982 h., by Buckaroo	2	4	3,809,004
Creme Fraiche, 1982 g., by Rich Cream	6	11	3,689,091
Ferdinand, 1983 h., by Nijinsky II	4	5	3,619,978
Spain, 1997 m., by Thunder Gulch	4	7	3,490,307
Slew o' Gold, 1980 h., by Seattle Slew	3	8	3,454,694
War Emblem, 1999 c., by Our Emblem	2	4	3,425,000
Strike the Gold, 1988 h., by Alydar	4	4	3,391,210
Gentlemen (Arg), 1992 h., by Robin des Bois	3	8	3,324,140
Serena's Song, 1992 m., by Rahy	3	17	3,260,353
Behrens, 1994 h., by Pleasant Colony	4	6	3,204,500
Real Quiet, 1995 h., by Quiet American	3	5	3,195,740
Lemon Drop Kid, 1996 h., by Kingmambo	3	7	3,168,900
Cryptoclearance, 1984 h., by Fappiano	4	8	3,162,157
Snow Chief, 1983 h., by Reflected Glory	3	9	3,162,110
Free House, 1994 h., by Smokester	4	8	3,153,021
Precisionist, 1981 h., by Crozier	5	13	3,136,608
Black Tie Affair (Ire), 1986 h., by Miswaki	4	11	3,132,547
Bertrando, 1989 h., by Skywalker	5	7	3,131,320
Paseana (Arg), 1987 m., by Ahmad	5	14	3,074,292
Sandpit (Brz), 1989 h., by Baynoun (Ire)	4	7	3,066,480
Captain Steve, 1997 h., by Fly So Free	3	6	3,050,756
Gulch, 1984 h., by Mr. Prospector	3	11	3,049,671
Volponi, 1998 h., by Cryptoclearance	4	4	3,042,852
Perfect Drift, 1999 g., by Dynaformer	4	6	3,023,490
Funny Cide, 2000 g., by Distorted Humor	3	4	3,010,700
Concern, 1991 h., by Broad Brush	3	4	3,004,530
Silverbulletday, 1996 m., by Silver Deputy	3	13	2,998,073
A.P. Indy, 1989 h., by Seattle Slew	2	6	2,952,340
Sky Classic, 1987 h., by Nijinsky II	4	9	2,942,152
Steinlen (GB), 1983 h., by Habitat	4	6	2,935,042
Hansel, 1988 h., by Woodman	2	6	2,926,986
Peace Rules, 2000 h., by Jules	3	7	2,914,288
Albert the Great, 1997 h., by Go for Gin	2	5	2,913,620
Ghostzapper, 2000 h., by Awesome Again	3	5	2,912,000
Escena, 1993 m., by Strawberry Road (Aus)	4	7	2,884,039
Victory Gallop, 1995 h., by Cryptoclearance	3	5	2,874,615
Alphabet Soup, 1991 h., by Cozzene	4	6	2,858,560

North American Leaders by Grade 1 Earnings
North American Racing Only

Horse, YOB, Sex, Sire	Years Raced	Grade 1 Stakes Wins	Grade 1 Stakes Earnings
Skip Away, 1993 h., by Skip Trial	4	10	$7,310,920
Smarty Jones, 2001 c., by Elusive Quality	2	2	6,734,800
Alysheba, 1984 h., by Alydar	3	9	6,230,506
Tiznow, 1997 h., by Cee's Tizzy	2	4	5,815,400
Cigar, 1990 h., by Palace Music	4	11	5,660,000
Sunday Silence, 1986 h., by Halo	3	6	4,757,454
Easy Goer, 1986 h., by Alydar	3	9	4,606,980
John Henry, 1975 g., by Ole Bob Bowers	8	16	4,125,680
Unbridled, 1987 h., by Fappiano	3	3	4,039,360
Best Pal, 1988 g., by *Habitony	7	6	3,841,870
Point Given, 1998 h., by Thunder Gulch	2	6	3,718,300
Medaglia d'Oro, 1999 c., by El Prado (Ire)	4	3	3,545,000
Devil His Due, 1989 h., by Devil's Bag	4	5	3,466,000
Slew o' Gold, 1980 h., by Seattle Slew	3	7	3,420,314
Azeri, 1998 m., by Jade Hunter	4	11	3,408,920
Cat Thief, 1996 h., by Storm Cat	3	2	3,366,500
Ferdinand, 1983 h., by Nijinsky II	4	3	3,326,678
Pleasantly Perfect, 1998 h., by Pleasant Colony	4	2	3,240,000
War Emblem, 1999 c., by Our Emblem	2	3	3,125,000
Awesome Again, 1994 h., by Deputy Minister	2	2	2,999,900
Real Quiet, 1995 h., by Quiet American	3	5	2,920,920
Creme Fraiche, 1982 g., by Rich Cream	6	7	2,897,068
Strike the Gold, 1988 h., by Alydar	4	2	2,800,876
Paseana (Arg) 1987 m., by Ahmad	5	10	2,753,942
A.P. Indy, 1989 h., by Seattle Slew	2	4	2,725,660
Theatrical (Ire), 1982 h., by Nureyev	3	6	2,724,040
Silver Charm, 1994 h., by Silver Buck	4	2	2,716,350
Ghostzapper, 2000 h., by Awesome Again	3	3	2,702,000
Gulch, 1984 h., by Mr. Prospector	3	7	2,683,496
Sea Hero, 1990 h., by Polish Navy	3	2	2,635,900
Lemon Drop Kid, 1996 h., by Kingmambo	3	5	2,630,400
Gentlemen (Arg), 1992 h., by Robin des Bois	3	3	2,610,000
Bet Twice, 1984 h., by Sportin' Life	3	4	2,573,337
Bertrando, 1989 h., by Skywalker	5	3	2,554,820
Funny Cide, 2000 g., by Distorted Humor	3	3	2,532,700
Fantastic Light, 1996 h., by Rahy	2	2	2,507,400
Spain, 1997 m., by Thunder Gulch	4	2	2,499,900
Beautiful Pleasure, 1995 m., by Maudlin	5	6	2,467,500
Volponi, 1998 h., by Cryptoclearance	4	1	2,406,000
Sandpit (Brz) 1989 h., by Baynoun (Ire)	4	5	2,396,000
Concern, 1991 h., by Broad Brush	3	2	2,375,780
Bayakoa (Arg), 1984 m., by Consultant's Bid	4	12	2,345,509
Farma Way, 1987 h., by Marfa	3	2	2,340,000
Chief Bearhart, 1993 h., by Chief's Crown	4	3	2,321,000
Cryptoclearance, 1984 h., by Fappiano	4	4	2,317,732
Lady's Secret, 1982 m., by Secretariat	4	11	2,314,731
Banshee Breeze, 1995 m., by Unbridled	3	5	2,311,680
Ashado, 2001 f., by Saint Ballado	2	4	2,304,640
Daylami (Ire), 1994 h., by Doyoun	2	2	2,280,000
With Anticipation, 1995 g., by Relaunch	8	5	2,246,859
Serena's Song, 1992 m., by Rahy	3	11	2,244,400
Albert the Great, 1997 h., by Go for Gin	2	1	2,237,120
Free House, 1994 h., by Smokester	4	3	2,229,361
Hansel, 1988 h., by Woodman	2	2	2,226,466
Precisionist, 1981 h., by Crozier	5	6	2,207,810
Snow Chief, 1983 h., by Reflected Glory	3	6	2,181,590
Escena, 1993 m., by Strawberry Road (Aus)	4	4	2,172,000
Great Communicator, 1983 g., by Key to the Kingdom	6	4	2,162,000
Affirmed, 1975 h., by Exclusive Native	3	14	2,158,031
Gate Dancer, 1981 h., by Sovereign Dancer	4	2	2,137,245
Flawlessly, 1988 m., by Affirmed	5	9	2,130,900
Manila, 1983 h., by Lyphard	3	5	2,117,190
General Challenge, 1996 g., by General Meeting	4	3	2,110,000
Pleasant Tap, 1987 h., by Pleasant Colony	4	2	2,090,000
Milwaukee Brew, 1997 h., by Wild Again	4	2	2,087,500
Alphabet Soup, 1991 h., by Cozzene	4	1	2,080,000
Chief's Crown, 1982 h., by Danzig	2	8	2,075,158
Thunder Gulch, 1992 h., by Gulch	2	4	2,064,080
Life's Magic, 1981 m., by Cox's Ridge	3	5	2,060,998
Congaree, 1998 h., by Arazi	5	3	2,059,000
Black Tie Affair (Ire), 1986 h., by Miswaki	4	2	2,025,728

North American Leading Males by Turf Earnings
North American Racing Only

Horse, YOB, Sex, Sire	Years Raced	Turf Wins	Turf Earnings
John Henry, 1975 g., by Ole Bob Bowers	8	30	$5,269,212
Steinlen (GB), 1983 h., by Habitat	4	16	3,229,752
Sky Classic, 1987 h., by Nijinsky II	4	14	3,176,638
Chief Bearhart, 1993 h., by Chief's Crown	4	11	3,164,509
Great Communicator, 1983 g., by Key to the Kingdom	6	13	2,908,485
Awad, 1990 h., by Caveat	7	13	2,871,645
Theatrical (Ire), 1982 h., by Nureyev	3	7	2,840,500
Sandpit (Brz) 1989 h., by Baynoun (Ire)	4	9	2,752,973
Manila, 1983 h., by Lyphard	3	11	2,676,299
Paradise Creek, 1989 h., by Irish River (Fr)	4	14	2,675,514
Fraise, 1988 h., by Strawberry Road (Aus)	4	10	2,613,105
Fantastic Light, 1996 h., by Rahy	2	2	2,507,400
Buck's Boy, 1993 g., by Bucksplasher	5	10	2,493,520
Lure, 1989 h., by Danzig	4	11	2,348,839
Quiet Resolve, 1995 g., by Affirmed	5	10	2,346,768
With Anticipation, 1995 g., by Relaunch	8	7	2,332,512
Daylami (Ire), 1994 h., by Doyoun	2	2	2,280,000
Marlin, 1993 h., by Sword Dance (Ire)	3	8	2,262,255
Yankee Affair, 1982 h., by Northern Fling	5	18	2,204,524
Sunshine Forever, 1985 h., by Roberto	3	8	2,083,700
High Chaparral (Ire), 1999 c., by Sadler's Wells	3	2	2,021,600
Kotashaan (Fr), 1988 h., by Darshaan	2	7	2,017,050
Star of Cozzene, 1988 h., by Cozzene	5	11	2,015,039
Sulamani (Ire), 1999 h., by Hernando (Fr)	2	3	2,013,600
Bien Bien, 1989 h., by Manila	3	8	1,998,725
Majesty's Prince, 1979 h., by His Majesty	4	11	1,942,922
Ladies Din, 1995 g., by Din's Dancer	7	11	1,894,710
Itsallgreektome, 1987 g., by Sovereign Dancer	5	7	1,821,893
El Senor, 1984 h., by Valdez	5	12	1,767,245
Better Talk Now, 1999 g., by Talkin Man	4	8	1,728,077
Soaring Free, 1999 g., by Smart Strike	3	9	1,723,962
Good Journey, 1996 h., by Nureyev	5	7	1,722,965
Yagli, 1993 h., by Jade Hunter	5	10	1,702,121
Kitten's Joy, 2001 c., by El Prado (Ire)	2	8	1,695,361
Denon, 1998 h., by Pleasant Colony	3	8	1,647,269
Val's Prince, 1992 g., by Eternal Prince	7	10	1,585,940
Da Hoss, 1992 g., by Gone West	4	8	1,559,780
Sarafan, 1997 g., by Lear Fan	6	6	1,549,463
John's Call, 1991 g., by Lord At War (Arg)	7	14	1,542,130
Redattore (Brz), 1995 h., by Roi Normand	6	8	1,536,927
Fly Till Dawn, 1986 h., by Swing Till Dawn	5	9	1,536,150
Native Desert, 1993 g., by Desert Classic	8	14	1,532,834
Perfect Soul (Ire), 1998 h., by Sadler's Wells	3	7	1,527,764
Mecke, 1992 h., by Maudlin	4	6	1,522,080

North American Leading Females by Turf Earnings
North American Racing Only

Horse, YOB, Sex, Sire	Years Raced	Turf Starts Wins	Turf Earnings
Flawlessly, 1988 m., by Affirmed	5	14	$2,459,250
Perfect Sting, 1996 m., by Red Ransom	4	13	2,163,673
Estrapade, 1980 m., by *Vaguely Noble	3	8	1,789,600
Golden Apples (Ire), 1998 m., by Pivotal	3	5	1,652,346
Riskaverse, 1999 f., by Dynaformer	4	7	1,631,576
Tout Charmant, 1996 m., by Slewvescent	5	7	1,607,219
Starine (Fr), 1997 m., by Mendocino	2	4	1,560,189
Miss Alleged, 1987 m., by Alleged	2	2	1,532,500
Happyanunoit (NZ), 1995 m., by Yachtie	3	6	1,481,892
Tates Creek, 1998 m., by Rahy	3	11	1,470,834
Megahertz (GB), 1999 f., by Pivotal	4	9	1,457,160
Memories of Silver, 1993 m., by Silver Hawk	3	9	1,435,140
Voodoo Dancer, 1998 m., by Kingmambo	4	11	1,427,952
Tranquility Lake, 1995 m., by Rahy	4	9	1,420,770
Astra, 1996 m., by Theatrical (Ire)	4	11	1,378,424
Possibly Perfect, 1990 m., by Northern Baby	3	11	1,367,050
All Along (Fr), 1979 m., by Targowice	2	5	1,337,146
Tuzla (Fr), 1994 m., by Panoramic (GB)	4	11	1,266,079
Carotene, 1983 m., by Great Nephew	4	10	1,242,126
Brown Bess, 1982 m., by *Petrone	6	13	1,224,265

Horse, YOB, Sex, Sire	Years Raced	Turf Starts Wins	Turf Wins Earnings
Soaring Softly, 1995 m., by Kris S.	3	7	$1,193,450
Irish Linnet, 1988 m., by Seattle Song	6	18	1,191,980
Windsharp, 1991 m., by Lear Fan	3	6	1,191,600
Fieldy (Ire), 1983 m., by Northfields	4	18	1,182,530
Ticker Tape (GB), 2001 f., by Royal Applause (GB)	2	5	1,179,075
Wandesta (GB), 1991 m., by Nashwan	3	6	1,170,650
Heat Haze (GB), 1999 m., by Green Desert	2	5	1,135,660
Royal Heroine (Ire), 1980 m., by Lypheor (GB)	2	5	1,110,900
Wonder Again, 1999 m., by Silver Hawk	3	7	1,106,842
Bold Ruritana, 1990 m., by Bold Ruckus	6	14	1,102,790
Kostroma (Ire), 1986 m., by Caerleon	3	7	1,093,275
Banks Hill (GB), 1998 m., by Danehill	2	1	1,068,800
Maxzene, 1993 m., by Cozzene	3	11	1,067,587
Volga (Ire), 1998 m., by Caerleon	3	4	1,067,320
Colstar, 1996 m., by Opening Verse	4	11	1,053,056
Dimitrova, 2000 f., by Swain (Ire)	2	2	1,045,404
Janet, 1987 m., by Emperor Jones	3	7	1,004,585
Sabin, 1980 m., by Lyphard	4	15	998,235
Capades, 1986 m., by Overskate	3	9	991,516
Sangue (Ire), 1978 m., by Lyphard	3	8	974,900
Ryafan, 1994 m., by Lear Fan	1	3	968,000
Six Perfections (Fr), 2000 f., by Celtic Swing	2	1	964,800
Auntie Mame, 1994 m., by Theatrical (Ire)	3	10	961,480
Real Connection, 1991 m., by Vigors	5	5	956,438
Hatoof, 1989 m., by Irish River (Fr)	3	2	950,960
Spook Express (SAf), 1994 m., by Comic Blush	3	5	932,270
Film Maker, 2000 f., by Dynaformer	3	5	927,650
Bien Nicole, 1998 m., by Bien Bien	3	9	917,570
England's Legend (Fr), 1997 m., by Lure	2	4	917,480
Gaily Gaily (Ire), 1983 m., by Cure the Blues	4	11	914,939
Stay Forever, 1997 m., by Stack	4	10	910,399
Anka Germania (Ire), 1982 m., by Malinowski	4	11	903,554
Miesque, 1984 m., by Nureyev	2	2	900,000
Pebbles (GB), 1981 m., by Sharpen Up (GB)	1	1	900,000
Snow Dance, 1998 m., by Forest Wildcat	4	7	894,457
The Very One, 1975 m., by One for All	5	18	888,523
Fiji (GB), 1994 m., by Rainbow Quest	3	6	871,410
Lady Shirl, 1987 m., by That's a Nice	6	14	863,973
Sweetest Thing, 1998 m., by Candy Stripes	2	6	857,094
Sarah Lane's Oates, 1994 m., by Sunshine Forever	7	20	855,834
Inish Glora, 1998 m., by Regal Classic	5	6	830,101
Fact Finder, 1979 m., by Staff Writer	6	9	822,669
Snow Polina, 1995 m., by Trempolino	2	4	816,143
Owsley, 1998 m., by Harlan	3	7	811,964
Witchful Thinking, 1994 m., by Lord Avie	4	9	806,358
Ocean Drive, 2000 m., by Belong to Me	3	9	803,986
Donna Viola (GB), 1992 m., by Be My Chief	3	3	799,504
Alpride (Ire), 1991 m., by Alzao	3	2	795,000
Moscow Burning, 2000 m., by Moscow Ballet	2	6	793,810
Solvig, 1997 m., by Caerleon	4	7	777,484
Claire Marine (Ire), 1985 m., by What A Guest	1	6	777,215
Hero's Love, 1988 m., by Hero's Honor	4	7	768,480
Skimble, 1989 m., by Lyphard	3	7	758,695
Christiecat, 1987 m., by Majestic Light	4	9	747,095
Coretta (Ire), 1994 m., by Caerleon	2	6	746,900
Exchange, 1988 m., by Explodent	5	9	743,125

Horse, YOB, Sex, Sire	Starts	Wins	Stakes Wins	Earnings
Roving Boy, 1980 h., by Olden Times	7	5	4	$800,425
Macho Uno, 1998 h., by Holy Bull	4	3	2	768,803
Tasso, 1983 h., by Fappiano	7	5	3	761,534
Toccet, 2000 c., by Awesome Again	8	6	4	755,610
Fali Time, 1981 h., by Faliraki (Ire)	7	3	2	748,829
Captain Steve, 1997 h., by Fly So Free	8	4	3	744,880
Officer, 1999 c., by Bertrando	8	5	4	740,010
Success Express, 1985 h., by Hold Your Peace	8	4	3	737,207
Mr. Jester, 2001 c., by Silver Deputy	6	4	3	730,800
Texcess, 2002 g., by In Excess (Ire)	4	3	2	725,427
Siphonic, 1999 c., by Siphon (Brz)	4	3	2	703,978
Easy Goer, 1986 h., by Alydar	6	4	2	697,500
Answer Lively, 1996 h., by Lively One	7	4	2	695,296
Bet Twice, 1984 h., by Sportin' Life	7	5	3	690,565
Vindication, 2000 c., by Seattle Slew	4	4	2	680,950
Afleet Alex, 2002 c., by Northern Afleet	6	4	2	680,800
Spend a Buck, 1982 h., by Buckaroo	8	5	2	667,985
River Special, 1990 h., by Riverman	6	3	3	663,900
Capote, 1984 h., by Seattle Slew	4	3	2	654,680
Brocco, 1991 h., by Kris S.	4	3	1	653,550
Stephan's Odyssey, 1982 h., by Danzig	4	3	1	651,100
King Glorious, 1986 h., by Naevus	5	5	4	646,100
Forty Niner, 1985 h., by Mr. Prospector	6	5	4	634,908
Point Given, 1998 h., by Thunder Gulch	6	3	2	618,500
Swiss Yodeler, 1994 h., by Eastern Echo	9	6	5	617,200
Rhythm, 1987 h., by Mr. Prospector	5	3	1	612,920
Anees, 1997 h., by Unbridled	4	2	1	609,200
Music Merci, 1986 g., by Stop the Music	9	5	3	607,220
Is It True, 1986 h., by Raja Baba	6	2	1	605,342
Dehere, 1991 h., by Deputy Minister	7	5	4	595,912
Hennessy, 1993 h., by Storm Cat	9	4	3	580,400
Bertrando, 1989 h., by Skywalker	4	3	2	570,865
Buckpasser, 1963 h., by Tom Fool	11	9	6	568,096
Unbridled's Song, 1993 h., by Unbridled	3	2	1	568,000
Storm Cat, 1983 h., by Storm Bird	6	3	1	557,080
Temperate Sil, 1984 h., by Temperence Hill	5	3	2	549,625
Kafwain, 2000 c., by Cherokee Run	8	3	2	535,848
Sir Oscar, 2001 c., by Halo's Image	6	6	5	528,800
Stalwart, 1979 h., by Hoist the Flag	5	4	2	528,595
Johannesburg, 1999 c., by Hennessy	1	1	1	520,000
Arazi, 1989 h., by Blushing Groom (Fr)	1	1	1	520,000
Declan's Moon, 2002 g., by Malibu Moon	4	4	3	507,300
Adjudicating, 1987 h., by Danzig	8	4	2	506,232
Riva Ridge, 1969 h., by First Landing	9	7	5	503,263
Maria's Mon, 1993 h., by Wavering Monarch	5	4	3	498,340
Sadair, 1962 h., by *Petare	12	8	5	498,216
Swale, 1981 h., by Seattle Slew	7	5	4	491,950
Purdue Boy, 1985 h., by Dimaggio	10	5	4	489,730
Chapel Royal, 2001 c., by Montbrook	6	3	2	484,755
Consolidator, 2002 c., by Storm Cat	7	2	1	480,260
Shot Gun Scott, 1987 h., by Exuberant	7	4	2	469,640
Yes It's True, 1996 h., by Is It True	9	5	4	464,120
Naked Greed, 1989 g., by Naked Sky	8	5	3	459,132

Leading Two-Year-Old Male by North American Earnings
North American Racing Only

Horse, YOB, Sex, Sire	Starts	Wins	Stakes Wins	Earnings
Boston Harbor, 1994 h., by Capote	7	6	5	$1,928,605
Mountain Cat, 1990 h., by Storm Cat	8	6	5	1,460,627
Favorite Trick, 1995 h., by Phone Trick	8	8	7	1,231,998
Tejano, 1985 h., by Caro (Ire)	10	5	4	1,177,189
Best Pal, 1988 g., by *Habitony	8	6	5	1,026,195
Grand Canyon, 1987 h., by Fappiano	8	4	4	1,019,540
Snow Chief, 1983 h., by Reflected Glory	9	5	4	935,740
Timber Country, 1992 h., by Woodman	7	4	3	928,590
Chief's Crown, 1982 h., by Danzig	9	6	5	920,890
Fly So Free, 1990 h., by Time for a Change	6	4	2	872,580
Gilded Time, 1990 h., by Timeless Moment	4	4	3	855,980
Wilko, 2002 c., by Awesome Again	2	1	1	833,580
Action This Day, 2001 c., by Kris S.	3	2	1	817,200
Regal Classic, 1985 h., by Vice Regent	8	4	4	812,500

Leading Two-Year-Old Females by North American Earnings
North American Racing Only

Horse, YOB, Sex, Sire	Starts	Wins	Stakes Wins	Earnings
Silverbulletday, 1996 m., by Silver Deputy	7	6	5	$1,114,110
Countess Diana, 1995 m., by Deerhound	6	5	4	1,019,785
Meadow Star, 1988 m., by Meadowlake	7	7	6	992,250
Storm Flag Flying, 2000 f., by Storm Cat	4	4	3	967,000
Brave Raj, 1984 m., by Rajab	9	6	5	933,650
Storm Song, 1994 m., by Summer Squall	7	4	3	898,205
Outstandingly, 1982 m., by Exclusive Native	6	3	2	867,872
Halfbridled, 2001 f., by Unbridled	4	4	3	849,400
Eliza, 1990 m., by Mt. Livermore	5	4	3	808,000
Family Style, 1983 m., by State Dinner	10	4	3	805,809
Flanders, 1992 m., by Seeking the Gold	5	4	3	805,000
Sweet Catomine, 2002 f., by Storm Cat	4	3	3	799,800
Excellent Meeting, 1996 m., by General Meeting	8	4	3	773,824
Chilukki, 1997 m., by Cherokee Run	7	6	5	762,723
Phone Chatter, 1991 m., by Phone Trick	6	4	3	753,500
Open Mind, 1986 m., by Deputy Minister	6	4	3	724,064

Horse, YOB, Sex, Sire	Starts	Wins	Stakes Wins	Earnings
Althea, 1981 m., by Alydar	9	5	4	$692,625
Caressing, 1998 m., by Honour and Glory	5	3	2	690,642
Pleasant Stage, 1989 m., by Pleasant Colony	4	2	2	687,240
Surfside, 1997 m., by Seattle Slew	6	4	2	677,350
Golden Attraction, 1993 m., by Mr. Prospector	8	6	5	675,588
Tempera, 1999 f., by A.P. Indy	5	3	2	670,240
Cash Run, 1997 m., by Seeking the Gold	6	3	1	653,352
Twilight Ridge, 1983 m., by Cox's Ridge	5	3	2	617,808
My Flag, 1993 m., by Easy Goer	6	2	1	614,614
Balletto (UAE), 2002 f., by Timber Country	5	3	1	614,000
Ashado, 2001 f., by Saint Ballado	6	4	3	610,800
Raging Fever, 1998 m., by Storm Cat	6	5	4	598,500
Serena's Song, 1992 m., by Rahy	10	4	3	597,335
Runway Model, 2002 f., by Petionville	10	4	2	580,598
Boots 'n Jackie, 1990 m., by Major Moran	12	4	3	579,820
Tappiano, 1984 m., by Fappiano	5	4	3	572,820
Sacahuista, 1984 m., by Raja Baba	9	4	3	564,965
I'm Splendid, 1983 m., by Our Native	7	4	3	560,857
Go for Wand, 1987 m., by Deputy Minister	4	3	1	548,390
Cara Rafaela, 1993 m., by Quiet American	9	3	2	546,962
You, 1999 f., by You and I	6	3	2	540,440
Life's Magic, 1981 m., by Cox's Ridge	7	2	1	537,259
Epitome, 1985 m., by Summing	8	3	2	534,805
Sardula, 1991 m., by Storm Cat	5	3	2	532,545
Be Gentle, 2001 f., by Tale of the Cat	7	4	3	523,078
Stella Madrid, 1987 m., by Alydar	7	4	3	519,096
Sharp Cat, 1994 m., by Storm Cat	7	4	3	505,950
Lost Kitty, 1985 m., by Magesterial	11	4	3	499,038
Aclassysassylassy, 2002 f., by Wild Event	7	5	4	498,800
She's a Devil Due, 1998 m., by Devil His Due	5	4	2	495,320
Love Lock, 1995 m., by Silver Ghost	9	4	3	483,122
Career Collection, 1995 m., by General Meeting	8	4	3	482,005
Arewehavingfunyet, 1983 m., by Sham	9	5	4	475,730
Nancy's Glitter, 1995 m., by Glitterman	8	5	4	464,460
Lea Lucinda, 1986 m., by Secreto	9	3	2	459,962
Three Ring, 1996 m., by Notebook	5	3	2	458,440
Private Treasure, 1988 m., by Explodent	8	3	2	457,242
Tiltalating, 1982 m., by Tilt Up	10	4	3	454,944
Numbered Account, 1969 m., by Buckpasser	10	8	7	446,594
Ruling Angel, 1984 m., by Vice Regent	9	6	5	433,952
Goodbye Halo, 1985 m., by Halo	4	3	2	431,585
Composure, 2000 f., by Touch Gold	6	2	1	431,300
La Spia, 1989 m., by Capote	7	2	1	428,008
Stocks Up, 1986 m., by Kris S.	6	3	2	418,751
Ivananinalot, 2000 f., by West Acre	6	5	3	418,300
La Prevoyante, 1970 m., by Buckpasser	12	12	10	417,109
Sweet Roberta, 1987 m., by Roberto	3	2	1	415,800
Sez Fourty, 1986 m., by Sezyou	11	5	3	414,678
Dominant Dancer, 1987 m., by Moscow Ballet	9	5	4	412,470
Skillful Joy, 1979 m., by Nodouble	8	4	2	411,312
Over All, 1985 m., by Mr. Prospector	10	6	5	406,500
Stormy Blues, 1992 m., by Cure the Blues	6	4	3	403,740
Collins, 1984 m., by Majestic Light	7	3	2	400,806
Strategic Maneuver, 1991 m., by Cryptoclearance	6	5	4	398,340
Educated Risk, 1990 m., by Mr. Prospector	5	2	1	396,256
Habibti, 1999 f., by Tabasco Cat	4	3	2	393,000
Delicate Vine, 1984 m., by Knights Choice	5	4	3	390,370
Punch Appeal, 2002 f., by Successful Appeal	9	6	5	389,840
Darby Shuffle, 1986 m., by Darby Creek Road	10	3	2	389,627
Special Happening, 1987 m., by Relaunch	6	3	2	386,455
Cicada, 1959 m., by Bryan G.	16	11	8	384,676
Chatter Chatter, 2001 f., by Lost Soldier	7	3	2	383,470
Cheval Volant, 1987 m., by Kris S.	7	3	2	379,762
Fabulous Notion, 1980 m., by Somethingfabulous	5	5	3	378,368

Horse, YOB, Sex, Sire	Starts	Wins	Stakes Wins	Earnings
Easy Goer, 1986 h., by Alydar	11	8	8	$3,837,150
Unbridled, 1987 h., by Fappiano	11	4	3	3,718,149
Spend a Buck, 1982 h., by Buckaroo	7	5	5	3,552,704
War Emblem, 1999 c., by Our Emblem	10	5	4	3,455,000
Tiznow, 1997 h., by Cee's Tizzy	9	5	4	3,445,950
Point Given, 1998 h., by Thunder Gulch	7	6	6	3,350,000
Cat Thief, 1996 h., by Storm Cat	13	2	2	3,020,500
Skip Away, 1993 h., by Skip Trial	12	6	5	2,699,280
Thunder Gulch, 1992 h., by Gulch	10	7	7	2,644,080
A.P. Indy, 1989 h., by Seattle Slew	7	5	5	2,622,560
Hansel, 1988 h., by Woodman	9	4	4	2,565,680
Concern, 1991 h., by Broad Brush	14	3	2	2,541,670
Alysheba, 1984 h., by Alydar	10	3	3	2,511,156
Izvestia, 1987 h., by Icecapade	11	8	8	2,486,667
Sea Hero, 1990 h., by Polish Navy	9	2	2	2,484,190
Medaglia d'Oro, 1999 c., by El Prado (Ire)	9	4	3	2,260,600
Tabasco Cat, 1991 h., by Storm Cat	12	5	5	2,164,334
Seeking the Gold, 1985 h., by Mr. Prospector	12	6	4	2,145,620
Holy Bull, 1991 h., by Great Above	10	8	8	2,095,000
Forty Niner, 1985 h., by Mr. Prospector	13	6	5	2,091,092
Sunshine Forever, 1985 h., by Roberto	12	8	5	2,032,636
Wando, 2000 c., by Langfuhr	8	5	5	2,017,323
Charismatic, 1996 h., by Summer Squall	10	4	3	2,007,404
Fusaichi Pegasus, 1997 h., by Mr. Prospector	8	6	4	1,987,800
Victory Gallop, 1995 h., by Cryptoclearance	8	3	3	1,981,720
Pine Bluff, 1989 h., by Danzig	6	3	3	1,970,896
Funny Cide, 2000 g., by Distorted Humor	8	2	2	1,963,200
Risen Star, 1985 h., by Secretariat	8	6	5	1,958,368
Empire Maker, 2000 c., by Unbridled	6	3	3	1,936,200
Proud Truth, 1982 h., by Graustark	11	7	5	1,926,327
Bet Twice, 1984 h., by Sportin' Life	9	3	3	1,922,642
Prized, 1986 h., by Kris S.	7	4	4	1,888,705
Captain Steve, 1997 h., by Fly So Free	11	3	3	1,882,276
Snow Chief, 1983 h., by Reflected Glory	9	6	6	1,875,200
Louis Quatorze, 1993 h., by Sovereign Dancer	12	4	2	1,854,908
Peace Rules, 2000 h., by Jules	7	3	3	1,850,000
Deputy Commander, 1994 h., by Deputy Minister	10	4	3	1,849,440
Manila, 1983 h., by Lyphard	10	8	6	1,814,729
Real Quiet, 1995 h., by Quiet American	6	2	2	1,788,800
With Approval, 1986 h., by Caro (Ire)	10	6	5	1,772,150
Coronado's Quest, 1995 h., by Forty Niner	11	5	5	1,739,950
Monarchos, 1998 h., by Maria's Mon	7	4	2	1,711,600
Menifee, 1996 h., by Harlan	9	3	2	1,695,400
General Challenge, 1996 g., by General Meeting	11	6	6	1,658,100
Silver Charm, 1994 h., by Silver Buck	7	3	3	1,638,750
Kitten's Joy, 2001 c., by El Prado (Ire)	8	6	6	1,625,796
Came Home, 1999 c., by Gone West	8	6	6	1,624,500
Java Gold, 1984 h., by Key to the Mint	8	6	4	1,621,300
Harlan's Holiday, 1999 c., by Harlan	10	3	3	1,606,000
Ten Most Wanted, 2000 c., by Deputy Commander	10	4	3	1,544,860
Touch Gold, 1994 h., by Deputy Minister	7	4	3	1,522,313
Strike the Gold, 1988 h., by Alydar	12	2	2	1,443,850
Broad Brush, 1983 h., by Ack Ack	14	7	7	1,409,778
Prairie Bayou, 1990 g., by Little Missouri	8	5	5	1,405,521
Cryptoclearance, 1984 h., by Fappiano	15	4	4	1,367,150
Lemon Drop Kid, 1996 h., by Kingmambo	9	3	2	1,349,400
Kissin Kris, 1990 h., by Kris S.	12	2	2	1,341,292
Tikkanen, 1991 h., by Cozzene	2	2	2	1,340,000
Free House, 1994 h., by Smokester	10	3	3	1,336,910
Peaks and Valleys, 1992 h., by Mt. Livermore	8	5	4	1,323,750
Gulch, 1984 h., by Mr. Prospector	14	3	3	1,297,171

Leading Three-Year-Old Males by North American Earnings in Single Season
North American Racing Only

Horse, YOB, Sex, Sire	Starts	Wins	Stakes Wins	Earnings
Smarty Jones, 2001 c., by Elusive Quality	7	6	6	$7,563,535
Sunday Silence, 1986 h., by Halo	9	7	6	4,578,454

Leading Three-Year-Old Females by North American Earnings in Single Season
North American Racing Only

Horse, YOB, Sex, Sire	Starts	Wins	Stakes Wins	Earnings
Dance Smartly, 1988 m., by Danzig	8	8	8	$2,876,821
Ashado, 2001 f., by Saint Ballado	8	5	5	2,259,640
Spain, 1997 m., by Thunder Gulch	13	5	4	1,979,500
Silverbulletday, 1996 m., by Silver Deputy	11	8	8	1,707,640

Horse, YOB, Sex, Sire	Starts	Wins	Stakes Wins	Earnings
Unbridled Elaine, 1998 m., by Unbridled's Song	8	4	3	$1,663,175
Serena's Song, 1992 m., by Rahy	13	9	9	1,524,920
Banshee Breeze, 1995 m., by Unbridled	10	6	4	1,425,980
Take Charge Lady, 1999 f., by Dehere	10	6	6	1,388,635
Winning Colors, 1985 m., by Caro (Ire)	10	4	4	1,347,746
Farda Amiga, 1999 f., by Broad Brush	6	3	2	1,248,902
Ticker Tape (GB), 2001 f., by Royal Applause (GB)	10	5	5	1,159,075
Surfside, 1997 m., by Seattle Slew	7	4	4	1,147,637
Open Mind, 1986 m., by Deputy Minister	11	8	8	1,120,308
Island Fashion, 2000 f., by Petionville	10	4	4	1,112,970
Flute, 1998 m., by Seattle Slew	7	4	2	1,094,104
Dancethruthedawn, 1998 m., by Mr. Prospector	6	3	2	1,045,039
Xtra Heat, 1998 m., by Dixieland Heat	13	9	9	1,012,040
Lady's Secret, 1982 m., by Secretariat	17	10	10	994,349
Stellar Jayne, 2001 f., by Wild Rush	13	3	3	992,169
Ajina, 1994 m., by Strawberry Road (Aus)	9	3	3	979,175
Elloluv, 2000 f., by Gilded Time	8	2	2	978,775
Jostle, 1997 m., by Brocco	9	4	4	975,570
Ryafan, 1994 m., by Lear Fan	3	3	3	968,000
Dimitrova, 2000 f., by Swain (Ire)	4	2	2	950,000
Keeper Hill, 1995 m., by Deputy Minister	8	3	2	949,410
Very Subtle, 1984 m., by Hoist the Silver	12	6	6	947,135
My Flag, 1993 m., by Easy Goer	10	4	4	933,043
Society Selection, 2001 f., by Coronado's Quest	9	3	3	929,700
Sharp Cat, 1994 m., by Storm Cat	11	7	7	911,300
Exogenous, 1998 m., by Unbridled	7	4	2	901,500
Hollywood Wildcat, 1990 m., by Kris S.	9	5	5	893,330
You, 1999 f., by You and I	9	4	4	883,805
Life's Magic, 1981 m., by Cox's Ridge	12	4	4	873,956
Imperial Gesture, 1999 f., by Langfuhr	5	3	2	873,600
Blushing K. D., 1994 m., by Blushing John	8	6	6	845,040
Secret Status, 1997 m., by A.P. Indy	9	5	3	842,796
Go for Wand, 1987 m., by Deputy Minister	9	7	7	824,948
Life At the Top, 1983 m., by Seattle Slew	18	6	5	821,349
Bird Town, 2000 f., by Cape Town	8	3	3	815,976
Lite Light, 1988 m., by Majestic Light	9	5	5	804,685
Goodbye Halo, 1985 m., by Halo	11	5	5	789,117
Yearly Report, 2001 f., by General Meeting	7	5	5	787,500
Six Perfections (Fr), 2000 f., by Celtic Swing	1	1	1	780,000
Mystic Lady, 1998 m., by Thunder Gulch	11	6	6	775,000
Yanks Music, 1993 m., by Air Forbes Won	7	5	4	751,000
Dispute, 1990 m., by Danzig	11	6	4	750,226
Ouija Board (GB), 2001 f., by Cape Cross (Ire)	1	1	1	733,200
Affluent, 1998 m., by Affirmed	10	4	4	725,200
Sacahuista, 1984 m., by Raja Baba	9	2	2	724,857
Banks Hill (GB), 1998 m., by Danehill	1	1	1	722,800

Leading Males Four or Older by North American Earnings in Single Season

North American Racing Only

Horse, YOB, Sex, Sire	Age	Starts	Wins	Stakes Wins	Earnings
Cigar, 1990 h., by Palace Music	5	10	10	9	$4,819,800
Skip Away, 1993 h., by Skip Trial	4	11	4	4	4,089,000
Awesome Again, 1994 h., by Deputy Minister	4	6	6	5	3,845,990
Alysheba, 1984 h., by Alydar	4	9	7	7	3,808,600
Tiznow, 1997 h., by Cee's Tizzy	4	6	3	3	2,981,880
Skip Away, 1993 h., by Skip Trial	5	9	7	7	2,740,000
Slew o' Gold, 1980 h., by Seattle Slew	4	6	5	4	2,627,944
Farma Way, 1987 h., by Marfa	4	11	5	5	2,598,350
Ghostzapper, 2000 h., by Awesome Again	4	4	4	4	2,590,000
Alphabet Soup, 1991 h., by Cozzene	5	7	4	4	2,536,450
Cigar, 1990 h., by Palace Music	6	7	4	4	2,510,000
Black Tie Affair (Ire), 1986 h., by Miswaki	5	10	7	7	2,483,540
Pleasantly Perfect, 1998 h., by Pleasant Colony	5	4	2	2	2,470,000
Volponi, 1998 h., by Cryptoclearance	4	8	3	2	2,389,200
John Henry, 1975 g., by Ole Bob Bowers	9	9	6	6	2,336,650
Silver Charm, 1994 h., by Silver Buck	4	8	5	5	2,296,506
Criminal Type, 1985 h., by Alydar	5	11	7	6	2,270,290
Theatrical (Ire), 1982 h., by Nureyev	5	9	7	7	2,235,500
Bertrando, 1989 h., by Skywalker	4	9	3	3	2,217,800
Mineshaft, 1999 h., by A.P. Indy	4	9	7	7	2,209,686
Ferdinand, 1983 h., by Nijinsky II	4	10	4	4	2,185,150
Gentlemen (Arg), 1992 h., by Robin des Bois	5	6	4	4	2,125,300

Horse, YOB, Sex, Sire	Age	Starts	Wins	Stakes Wins	Earnings
Fantastic Light, 1996 h., by Rahy	5	1	1	1	$2,112,800
Wild Again, 1980 h., by Icecapade	4	16	6	4	2,054,409
Daylami (Ire), 1994 h., by Doyoun	5	1	1	1	2,040,000
Great Communicator, 1983 g., by Key to the Kingdom	5	11	6	6	2,017,950
Chief Bearhart, 1993 h., by Chief's Crown	4	7	5	5	2,011,259
Festin (Arg), 1986 h., by Mat-Boy (Arg)	5	11	3	3	2,003,250
Medaglia d'Oro, 1999 h., by El Prado (Ire)	4	5	3	3	1,990,000
Kotashaan (Fr), 1988 h., by Darshaan	5	9	6	6	1,984,100
Pleasant Tap, 1987 h., by Pleasant Colony	5	10	4	4	1,959,914
Devil His Due, 1989 h., by Devil's Bag	4	11	4	4	1,939,120
Paradise Creek, 1989 h., by Irish River (Fr)	5	10	8	8	1,920,872
Strike the Gold, 1988 h., by Alydar	4	13	2	2	1,920,176
Buck's Boy, 1993 g., by Bucksplasher	5	10	6	6	1,874,020
Skywalker, 1982 h., by Relaunch	4	9	4	4	1,811,400
John Henry, 1975 g., by Ole Bob Bowers	6	10	8	8	1,798,030
Albert the Great, 1997 h., by Go for Gin	4	9	3	3	1,740,000
Budroyale, 1993 g., by Cee's Tizzy	6	11	4	4	1,735,640
Sky Classic, 1987 h., by Nijinsky II	5	9	5	5	1,735,482
Behrens, 1994 h., by Pleasant Colony	5	9	4	4	1,735,000
Roses in May, 2000 h., by Devil His Due	4	6	5	3	1,723,277
Lemon Drop Kid, 1996 h., by Kingmambo	4	9	5	4	1,673,900
Best Pal, 1988 g., by *Habitony	4	5	4	4	1,672,000
Star of Cozzene, 1988 h., by Cozzene	5	11	6	6	1,620,744
Southern Image, 2000 h., by Halo's Image	4	4	3	3	1,612,150
Congaree, 1998 h., by Arazi	5	9	5	5	1,608,000
Milwaukee Brew, 1997 h., by Wild Again	5	7	2	2	1,590,000
Twilight Agenda, 1986 h., by Devil's Bag	5	11	6	5	1,563,600
Arcangues, 1988 h., by Sagace (Fr)	5	1	1	1	1,560,000
Fraise, 1988 h., by Strawberry Road (Aus)	4	10	5	2	1,534,720
Turkoman, 1982 h., by Alydar	4	8	4	4	1,531,664
Marlin, 1993 h., by Sword Dance (Ire)	4	10	4	4	1,521,600
Steinlen (GB), 1983 h., by Habitat	6	11	7	6	1,521,378
With Anticipation, 1995 g., by Relaunch	7	8	3	3	1,507,700
Perfect Drift, 1999 g., by Dynaformer	4	8	5	4	1,505,388
Waquoit, 1983 h., by Relaunch	5	7	3	3	1,441,444
Beat Hollow (GB), 1997 h., by Sadler's Wells	4	9	5	5	1,437,150
Include, 1997 h., by Broad Brush	4	9	5	4	1,435,400
Orientate, 1998 h., by Mt. Livermore	4	10	6	6	1,412,970
Chester House, 1995 h., by Mr. Prospector	5	6	1	1	1,408,500
Better Talk Now, 1999 g., by Talkin Man	5	8	2	2	1,407,000
Guided Tour, 1996 g., by Hansel	5	8	4	4	1,384,220
Gulch, 1984 h., by Mr. Prospector	4	11	5	4	1,360,840
Sandpit (Brz), 1989 h., by Baynoun (Ire)	6	8	4	3	1,342,700
Yankee Affair, 1982 h., by Northern Fling	7	13	5	5	1,333,813
Evening Attire, 1998 g., by Black Tie Affair (Ire)	4	9	5	4	1,332,720
Skimming, 1996 h., by Nureyev	5	6	3	3	1,330,000
In Excess (Ire), 1987 h., by Siberian Express	4	8	5	5	1,328,800
Creme Fraiche, 1982 g., by Rich Cream	5	14	4	4	1,323,666

Leading Females Four and Older by North American Earnings in a Single Season

North American Racing Only

Horse, YOB, Sex, Sire	Age	Starts	Wins	Stakes Wins	Earnings
Azeri, 1998 m., by Jade Hunter	4	9	8	7	$2,181,540
Escena, 1993 m., by Strawberry Road (Aus)	5	9	5	5	2,032,425
Lady's Secret, 1982 m., by Secretariat	4	15	10	10	1,871,053
Beautiful Pleasure, 1995 m., by Maudlin	4	7	4	3	1,716,404
Paseana (Arg), 1987 m., by Ahmad	5	9	7	7	1,518,290
Bayakoa (Arg), 1984 m., by Consultant's Bid	5	11	9	8	1,406,403
Riboletta (Brz), 1995 m., by Roi Normand	5	11	7	7	1,384,860
Perfect Sting, 1996 m., by Red Ransom	4	8	6	5	1,367,000
Banshee Breeze, 1995 m., by Unbridled	4	7	4	4	1,358,818
Miss Alleged, 1987 m., by Alleged	4	3	2	2	1,345,000
Heritage of Gold, 1995 m., by Gold Legend	5	8	5	5	1,332,282
Bayakoa (Arg), 1984 m., by Consultant's Bid	6	10	7	7	1,234,406
Personal Ensign, 1984 m., by Private Account	4	7	7	7	1,202,640
Soaring Softly, 1995 m., by Kris S.	4	8	7	5	1,193,450
Estrapade, 1980 m., by *Vaguely Noble	6	9	3	3	1,184,800
Sightseek, 1999 m., by Distant View	4	8	4	4	1,171,888
Serena's Song, 1992 m., by Rahy	4	15	5	5	1,161,133
Adoration, 1999 m., by Honor Grades	4	9	5	2	1,160,750
Inside Information, 1991 m., by Private Account	4	8	7	6	1,160,408
Jewel Princess, 1992 m., by Key to the Mint	4	9	5	5	1,150,800

Horse, YOB, Sex, Sire	Age	Starts	Wins	Stakes Wins	Earnings
Golden Apples (Ire), 1998 m., by Pivotal	4	7	3	3	$1,111,680
Heat Haze (GB), 1999 m., by Green Desert	4	7	4	4	1,101,460
Tout Charmant, 1996 m., by Slewvescent	4	7	3	3	1,089,044
Azeri, 1998 m., by Jade Hunter	6	8	3	3	1,035,000
Royal Heroine (Ire), 1980 m., by Lypheor (GB)	4	8	4	4	1,023,500
Sightseek, 1999 m., by Distant View	5	7	4	4	1,011,350
Summer Colony, 1998 m., by Summer Squall	4	8	4	4	992,500
Storm Flag Flying, 2000 m., by Storm Cat	4	8	3	2	963,248
Safely Kept, 1986 m., by Horatius	4	10	8	7	959,280
Paseana (Arg), 1987 m., by Ahmad	6	8	3	3	950,402
Manistique, 1995 m., by Unbridled	4	9	6	6	935,100
Lu Ravi, 1995 m., by A.P. Indy	5	8	3	3	918,200
Pebbles (GB), 1981 m., by Sharpen Up (GB)	4	1	1	1	900,000
Heavenly Prize, 1991 m., by Seeking the Gold	4	4	4	4	895,900
Tuzla (Fr), 1994 m., by Panoramic (GB)	5	8	4	4	889,080
Flawlessly, 1988 m., by Affirmed	5	5	4	4	886,700
Spook Express (SAf), 1994 m., by Comic Blush	7	8	3	3	866,870
Happyanunoit (NZ), 1995 m., by Yachtie	4	8	4	3	862,792
Princess Rooney, 1980 m., by Verbatim	4	9	6	5	854,791
Heritage of Gold, 1995 m., by Gold Legend	4	10	6	5	853,680
North Sider, 1982 m., by Topsider	5	17	7	6	847,107
Life's Magic, 1981 m., by Cox's Ridge	4	13	2	2	844,003
Different (Arg), 1992 m., by Candy Stripes	4	5	4	3	839,290
One Dreamer, 1988 m., by Relaunch	6	8	4	4	837,730
Spain, 1997 m., by Thunder Gulch	4	9	1	1	837,705
Wild Spirit (Chi), 1999 m., by Hussonet	4	4	3	3	830,000
Starine (Fr), 1997 m., by Mendocino	5	4	1	1	820,600
Azeri, 1998 m., by Jade Hunter	5	5	4	4	817,080
All Along (Fr), 1979 m., by Targowice	4	3	3	3	813,631
Fiji (GB), 1994 m., by Rainbow Quest	4	7	6	4	805,560
Claire Marine (Ire), 1985 m., by What A Guest	4	12	7	6	801,565

Winningest Horses of All Time
North American Racing Only
Through 2004

Horse, YOB, Sex, Sire	Starts	Wins	Earnings
Kingston, 1884 h., by Spendthrift	138	89	$140,195
Bankrupt, 1883 h., by Spendthrift	348	86	41,260
King Crab, 1885 g., by Kingfisher	310	85	55,682
Little Minch, 1880 h., by Glenelg	222	85	58,225
Hiblaze, 1935 h., by Blazes	406	79	32,647
Tippity Witchet, 1915 g., by Broomstick	265	78	88,241
Pan Zareta, 1910 m., by Abe Frank	151	76	39,082
Badge, 1885 h., by *Ill-Used	167	70	73,253
Raceland, 1885 g., by *Billet	130	70	116,391
Geraldine, 1885 f., by Grinstead	185	69	43,020
Care Free, 1918 g., by Colin	227	67	59,873
Welsh Lad, 1934 g., by Prince of Wales	329	67	25,317
Shot One, 1941 g., by Shoeless Joe	360	65	29,982
Worthowning, 1935 g., by *Longworth	339	63	41,830
Back Bay, 1908 g., by Rubicon	289	62	40,377
Banquet, 1887 g., by *Rayon d'Or	166	62	118,872
Ed R., 1948 g., by Donnay	248	62	63,552
Imp, 1894 f., by *Wagner	171	62	70,069
Leochares, 1910 g., by Broomstick	175	62	68,867
Seth's Hope, 1924 h., by Seth	327	62	74,341
Vantime, 1939 g., by Playtime	295	62	46,290
Brandon Prince, 1929 g., by *Axenstein	280	61	47,287
Irene's Bob, 1929 h., by The Turk	237	61	58,010
Kenilworth, 1898 h., by *Sir Modred	163	61	31,270
Molasses Bill, 1933 g., by *Challenger II	262	61	50,699
Mucho Gusto, 1932 h., by Marvin May	217	61	101,880
Shuchor, 1936 g., by Haste	261	61	33,607
Vantryst, 1936 h., by Tryster	334	61	31,971
Frank Fogarty, 1918 g., by Wrack	270	60	47,651
George de Mar, 1922 h., by *Colonel Vennie	333	60	69,091
Indiantown, 1930 h., by Trojan	224	60	55,455
Lewis A. D., 1947 h., by Galway	212	60	65,482
Noah's Pride, 1929 g., by Noah	317	60	41,507
Parole, 1873 g., by Leamington	127	59	82,111
Strathmeath, 1888 g., by Strathmore	133	59	114,958
Charlie Boy, 1955 h., by Graphic	241	58	207,642
Flag Bearer, 1926 h., by *Porte Drapeau	222	58	37,683
Golden Arrow, 1961 h., by Fort Salonga	176	58	167,264
Top o' the Morning, 1912 c., by Peep o'Day	217	58	48,120

Horse, YOB, Sex, Sire	Starts	Wins	Earnings
Columcille, 1948 h., by Alaking	182	57	$89,665
El Puma, 1929 h., by *Spanish Prince II	242	57	44,807
End of Street, 1963 h., by Bunty's Flight	202	57	67,686
Bulwark, 1933 h., by *Bull Dog	252	56	65,125
Matchup, 1936 h., by Misstep	229	55	58,528
Tommy Whelan, 1936 g., by Enoch	233	55	33,279
Vote Boy, 1932 g., by Torchilla	304	55	39,240
Argos, 1937 g., by *Happy Argo	215	54	37,507
Bee Golly, 1942 m., by Bee Line	183	53	54,544
Crying for More, 1965 h., by I'm For More	192	53	183,685
Door Prize, 1952 g., by Eight Thirty	131	53	109,920
Hamburger Jim, 1928 h., by Whiskaway	212	53	24,383
Onus, 1933 g., by Jack High	344	53	32,039
Post War Style, 1941 m., by Burgoo King	179	53	52,600
Agrarian-U, 1942 g., by Agrarian	236	52	199,345
Alviso, 1932 h., by *Hand Grenade	193	52	41,898
Billy Brier, 1953 g., by Bunty Lawless	231	52	83,168
Cloudy Weather, 1934 g., by Mud	294	52	53,487
Fleet Argo, 1947 g., by *Happy Argo	243	52	149,000
Float Away, 1936 g., by Whiskaway	265	52	61,365
My Blaze, 1930 h., by Big Blaze	338	52	32,707
Old Kickapoo, 1924 h., by Runnymede	217	52	35,827
Port Conway Lane, 1969 h., by Bold Commander	242	52	431,593
Air Patrol, 1941 h., by Sun Teddy	146	51	163,100
Blenweed, 1938 g., by *Blenheim II	202	51	105,415
Commendable, 1935 g., by Insco	163	51	30,583
Dr. Johnson, 1940 h., by *Boswell	256	51	54,422
Estin, 1923 g., by Westy Hogan	205	51	46,901
Gay Parisian, 1924 g., by *Parisian Diamond	209	51	49,197
Sagely, 1970 h., by Sage and Sand	124	51	116,196
Small Change, 1930 h., by Aromatic	200	51	18,495
Talked About, 1934 h., by The Porter	235	51	49,447
Big Devil, 1963 h., by Call Over	237	50	222,715
Brownskin, 1946 h., by Martinus	224	50	77,913
Exterminator, 1915 g., by *McGee	100	50	221,227
Frosty Admiral, 1961 h., by Ace Admiral	151	50	166,305
Go Lite, 1960 h., by Go Lightly	211	50	96,938
Live One, 1928 g., by Sweep On	218	50	38,965
Misty Eye, 1938 m., by Dunlin	220	50	25,236
The Break, 1928 h., by Star Master	264	50	31,030
Time to Bid, 1975 h., by Jig Time	179	50	241,247
Ahba's Bull, 1949 h., by Bull Reigh	157	49	97,057
Candle Wood, 1949 h., by Easy Mon	253	49	171,127
Cruising, 1930 h., by Whiskalong	222	49	38,857
Golden Fate, 1930 h., by *The Satrap	216	49	42,570
Imahead, 1955 h., by *Beau Gem	246	49	69,884

Most Wins by Decade by Year of Birth
North American Racing Only
1931-1940

Horse, YOB, Sex, Sire	Yrs. Raced	Starts	Wins	Earnings
Hiblaze, 1935 h., by Blazes	14	406	79	$32,647
Welsh Lad, 1934 g., by Prince of Wales	13	329	67	25,317
Worthowning, 1935 g., by *Longworth	14	339	63	41,830
Vantime, 1939 g., by Playtime	13	295	62	46,290
Molasses Bill, 1933 g., by *Challenger II	13	262	61	50,699
Mucho Gusto, 1932 h., by Marvin May	9	217	61	101,880
Shuchor, 1936 g., by Haste	13	261	61	33,607
Vantryst, 1936 h., by Tryster	13	334	61	31,971
Bulwark, 1933 h., by *Bull Dog	14	252	56	65,125
Matchup, 1936 h., by Misstep	12	229	55	58,528

1941-1950

Horse, YOB, Sex, Sire	Yrs. Raced	Starts	Wins	Earnings
Shot One, 1941 g., by Shoeless Joe	13	360	65	$29,982
Ed R., 1948 g., by Donnay	14	248	62	63,552
Lewis A. D., 1947 h., by Galway	12	212	60	65,482
Columcille, 1948 h., by Alaking	11	182	57	89,665
Bee Golly, 1942 m., by Bee Line	11	183	53	54,544
Post War Style, 1941 m., by Burgoo King	10	179	53	52,600
Agrarian-U, 1942 g., by Agrarian	12	236	53	199,345
Fleet Argo, 1947 g., by *Happy Argo	12	243	52	149,000
Air Patrol, 1941 h., by Sun Teddy	10	146	51	163,100
Brownskin, 1946 h., by Martinus	10	224	50	77,913

1951-1960

Horse, YOB, Sex, Sire	Yrs. Raced	Starts	Wins	Earnings
Charlie Boy, 1955 h., by Graphic	11	241	58	$207,642
Door Prize, 1952 g., by Eight Thirty	10	131	53	109,920
Billy Brier, 1953 g., by Bunty Lawless	12	231	52	83,168
Go Lite, 1960 h., by Go Lightly	11	211	50	96,938
Imahead, 1955 h., by *Beau Gem	13	246	49	69,884
Apple, 1958 g., by *Ambiorix	15	195	48	102,385
Bill Pac, 1951 h., by Billings	10	272	48	73,374
Annette G., 1951 m., by Holdall	10	237	47	68,932
Aquanotte, 1960 h., by Decathlon	10	142	47	80,603
Grand Wizard, 1956 g., by Poised	13	220	47	222,312

1961-1970

Horse, YOB, Sex, Sire	Yrs. Raced	Starts	Wins	Earnings
Golden Arrow, 1961 h., by Fort Salonga	16	176	58	$167,264
End of Street, 1963 h., by Bunty's Flight	11	202	57	67,686
Crying for More, 1965 h., by I'm For More	11	192	53	183,685
Port Conway Lane, 1969 h., by Bold Commander	13	242	52	431,593
Sagely, 1970 h., by Sage and Sand	14	124	51	116,196
Big Devil, 1963 h., by Call Over	12	237	50	222,715
Frosty Admiral, 1961 h., by Ace Admiral	9	151	50	166,305
Bayou Teche, 1961 g., by Bryan G.	12	281	48	107,577
Flyingphere, 1961 g., by Mr. Hemisphere	14	213	48	85,683
Saturnina, 1967 m., by *Ballydonnell	5	107	47	392,195

1971-1980

Horse, YOB, Sex, Sire	Yrs. Raced	Starts	Wins	Earnings
Time to Bid, 1975 h., by Jig Time	12	179	50	$241,247
Dot the T., 1972 h., by *Notable II	12	261	48	227,033
Dobi's Knight, 1971 g., by Dobi Deenar	12	219	45	178,996
Guy, 1974 h., by Golden Ruler	11	161	45	281,085
Chrystal Gail, 1973 m., by Special Dunce	11	137	43	154,910
Flying Hitch, 1972 h., by Double Hitch	8	125	43	124,352
Kintla's Folly, 1972 g., by Run Like Mad	10	130	43	397,761
Norman Prince, 1974 h., by Skookum	11	161	43	169,947
Missouri Brave, 1972 h., by *Indian Chief II	13	137	42	116,717
Moxeytown, 1977 h., by L'Aiglon	10	116	41	216,652

1981-1990

Horse, YOB, Sex, Sire	Yrs. Raced	Starts	Wins	Earnings
Win Man, 1985 g., by Con Man	9	178	48	$416,316
Jilsie's Gigalo, 1984 g., by Gallant Knave	11	136	45	315,456
Boca Ratony, 1988 g., by Boca Rio	12	139	41	133,715
Best Boy's Jade, 1989 g., by Raja's Best Boy	12	175	40	223,983
Last Don B., 1987 g., by Don B.	9	104	40	471,461
Noble But Nasty, 1981 g., by Nasty and Bold	11	200	40	325,588
Sawmill Run, 1988 g., by It's Freezing	12	160	40	253,744
Inspector Moomaw, 1987 g., by Entropy	10	179	38	269,052
Little Bold John, 1982 g., by John Alden	9	105	38	1,956,406
The Hive Five, 1983 g., by Raja Baba	10	159	38	178,907

1991-2000

Horse, YOB, Sex, Sire	Yrs. Raced	Starts	Wins	Earnings
Bandit Bomber, 1991 h., by Prosperous	5	15	39	$471,445
Shotgun Pro, 1993 g., by Shot Gun Scott	9	137	39	250,862
Oh So Fabulous, 1992 g., by Singular	10	125	38	286,339
Secret Service Man, 1992 g., by Shot Gun Scott	9	132	37	364,263
Lightning Al, 1993 h., by Fortunate Prospect	7	63	36	680,146
Maybe Jack, 1993 g., by Classic Account	9	121	35	534,265
J V Bennett, 1993 g., by Key to the Mint	10	100	34	429,790
Say Florida Sandy, 1994 h., by Personal Flag	8	98	33	2,085,408
King Kenny Roberts, 1991 g., by Slew Machine	9	107	32	166,306
Mahrally, 1991 g., by Ballydoyle	11	154	32	168,440

2001-2004

Horse, YOB, Sex, Sire	Yrs. Raced	Starts	Wins	Earnings
Rocky Gulch, 2001 g., by Dry Gulch	2	15	10	$541,088
Ashado, 2001 f., by Saint Ballado	2	14	9	2,870,440
Diligent Gambler, 2001 c., by Diligence	2	18	9	204,020
Danieltown, 2001 g., by Pioneering	2	25	8	310,406
Dorst, 2001 g., by Dance Brightly	2	21	8	144,385
Good as Silver, 2001 g., by Good and Tough	2	22	8	142,280
Kitten's Joy, 2001 c., by El Prado (Ire)	2	12	8	1,705,911
Mystery's Jules, 2001 f., by Jules	2	22	8	182,850
Smarty Jones, 2001 c., by Elusive Quality	2	9	8	7,613,155
We All Love Aleyna, 2001 g., by Nines Wild	2	25	8	219,540

Most Consecutive Victories

Camarero, an unfamiliar name to almost all racing fans, holds the record for the most consecutive victories by a Thoroughbred. His 56 straight wins were not registered in the sport's sometimes murky and poorly documented distant past, however. He raced in the 1950s, going undefeated until his 57th career start. All of his races were in Puerto Rico and were against other Puerto Rican-bred horses. Camarero broke the win mark set by undefeated Kincsem, a Hungarian-bred mare who raced in the late 19th century. Boston made the list of most consecutive wins twice, with 19 wins from 1839-'42 and 17 straight wins from 1836-'38.

Citation and Cigar share the modern record for most consecutive victories, 16, along with Louisiana-bred mare Hallowed Dreams, who won many of her races against overmatched state-breds. Citation and Cigar competed at the highest level of the sport in North America while compiling their win skeins.

Cons. Wins	Horse	YOB	Where Raced
56	Camarero	1951	Puerto Rico
54	Kincsem	1874	Hungary, England
39	Galgo Jr.	1928	Puerto Rico
23	Leviathan	1793	United States
22	Miss Petty	1981	Australia
	Pooker T.	1957	Puerto Rico
21	Bond's First Consul	1798	United States
	Lottery	1803	United States
	Meteor	1783	England
	Picnic In The Park	1979	Australia
20	Filch	1773	Ireland
	Fashion	1837	United States
	Kentucky	1861	United States
19	Boston	1833	United States
	Skiff	1821	Scotland
18	Hindoo	1878	United States
	Karayel	1970	Turkey
17	Alice Hawthorn	1838	England
	Beeswing	1835	United States
	Boston	1833	United States
	Careless	1751	England
	Dudley	1914	England
	Gradisco	1957	Venezuela
	Harkaway	1834	Ireland
	Hanover	1884	United States
	Mainbrace	1947	New Zealand
	Sir Ken	1947	England
16	Cigar	1990	United States
	Citation	1945	United States
	Hallowed Dreams	1997	United States
	Luke Blackburn	1877	United States
	Master Bagot	1787	Ireland
	Minimo	1968	Turkey
	Miss Woodford	1880	United States
	Mister Frisky	1987	Puerto Rico, United States
	*Ormonde	1883	England
	Prestige	1903	France
	*Ribot	1952	Europe
	The Bard	1883	England
15	Bayardo	1906	England
	*Bernborough	1939	Australia
	Brigadier Gerard	1968	England
	Buckpasser	1963	United States
	Carbine	1885	New Zealand, Australia
	Colin	1905	United States
	Macon	1922	Argentina
	Pretty Polly	1901	England, France
	Rattler	1816	United States

Cons. Wins	Horse	YOB	Where Raced
15	Squanderer	1973	India
	Thebais	1878	England
	Vander Pool	1928	United States
14	Friponnier	1864	England
	Harry Bassett	1868	United States
	Lucifer	1813	Scotland
	Man o' War	1917	United States
	Nearco	1935	Europe
	*Phar Lap	1926	New Zealand, Australia, Mexico
	*Prince Charlie	1869	England
	Springfield	1873	England
13	Dungannon	1780	England
	Effie Deans	1815	England
	Grano de Oro	1937	Ireland, Venezuela
	Hippolitus	1767	Ireland
	Kingston	1884	United States
	Limerick	1923	New Zealand, Australia
	Personal Ensign	1984	United States
	Phenomenom	1780	England
	Planet	1855	United States
	Polar Star	1904	England
	Rockingham	1781	England
	Sweet Wall	1925	Ireland
	The Flying Dutchman	1846	England
	Timoleon	1814	United States
	Tremont	1884	United States
	Weimar	1968	Italy

Leading Unbeaten Racehorses

A rare breed indeed is the racehorse that completes its career without a defeat on its record. No modern horse can ever expect to equal the record of Kincsem, who went unbeaten in 54 starts over five racing seasons in Hungary. Although her pedigree was largely English, she was bred in Hungary; her name derives from the Magyar "kincs," which means treasure or jewel. The word itself means "my treasure," and she indeed was a jewel.

Following are some of the best-known horses who have retired unbeaten after careers at the top levels of their divisions. Eclipse's record, in particular, is worth noting because 18th-century records are unreliable. He is attributed in various sources with anywhere from ten to 18 victories. In this listing, he is assigned the highest number, and the one fact for certain is that he never was beaten.

54   **Kincsem,** 1874 m., Cambuscan—Waternymph, by Cotswold
18   **Eclipse,** 1764 h., Marske—Spiletta, by Regulus
16   ***Ormonde,** 1883 h., Bend Or—Lily Agnes, by Macaroni
       *Ribot, 1952 h., Tenerani—Romanella, by El Greco
15   **Colin,** 1905 h., Commando—*Pastorella, by Springfield
14   **Nearco,** 1935 h., Pharos—Nogara, by Havresac II
13   **Personal Ensign,** 1984 m., Private Account—Grecian Banner, by Hoist the Flag
       Tremont, 1884 h., Virgil—Ann Fief, by Alarm
12   **Asteroid,** 1861 h., Lexington—Nebula, by *Glencoe
       Barcaldine, 1878 h., Solon—Ballyroe, by Belladrum
       Crucifix, 1837 m., *Priam—Octaviana, by Octavian
9   ***Bahram,** 1932 h., Blandford—Friar's Daughter, by Friar Marcus
       St. Simon, 1881 h., Galopin—St. Angela, by King Tom
8   **American Eclipse,** 1814 h., Duroc—Millers Damsel, by *Messenger

       Rare Brick, 1983 h., Rare Performer—Windy Brick, by Mr. Brick
       Sensation, 1877, h., *Leamington—Susan Beane, by Lexington
7   **El Rio Rey,** 1887 h., Norfolk—Marian, by Malcolm
       Regulus, 1739 h., Godolphin Arabian—Grey Robinson, by Bald Galloway
       The Tetrarch, 1911 h., Roi Herode—Vahren, by Bona Vista
5   **Ajax,** 1901 h., Flying Fox—Amie, by Clamart
       Bay Middleton, 1833 h., Sultan—Cobweb, by Phantom
       Landaluce, 1980 f., Seattle Slew—Strip Poker, by Bold Bidder
       Norfolk, 1861 h., Lexington—Novice, by *Glencoe
4   **Golden Fleece,** 1979 h., Nijinsky II—Exotic Treat, by *Vaguely Noble
       Lammtarra, 1992 h., Nijinsky II—Snow Bride, by Blushing Groom (Fr)
       Raise a Native, 1961 h., Native Dancer—Raise You, by Case Ace

Leading Winners of Million-Dollar Races in North America

Horse, YOB, Sex	Starts in $1-M Races	Wins in $1-M Races	Earnings in $1 M Races
Skip Away, 1993 h.	8	5	$4,798,000
Point Given, 1998 h.	5	4	2,750,000
Smarty Jones, 2001 h.	4	3	7,304,800
Tiznow, 1997 h.	4	3	5,360,400
Cigar, 1990 h.	6	3	3,740,000
Easy Goer, 1986 h.	4	3	2,401,020
Funny Cide, 2000 g.	7	3	2,360,200
Lemon Drop Kid, 1996 h.	8	3	2,035,400
Sunday Silence, 1986 h.	4	2	3,301,624
Pleasantly Perfect, 1998 h.	5	2	3,240,000
Alysheba, 1984 h.	5	2	2,657,916
War Emblem, 1999 h.	5	2	2,525,000
Best Pal, 1988 g.	11	2	2,237,000
Chief Bearhart, 1993 h.	6	2	2,162,000
A.P. Indy, 1989 r.	3	2	2,048,880
High Chaparral (Ire), 1999 h.	2	2	2,021,600
Milwaukee Brew, 1997 h.	7	2	1,900,000
Gentlemen (Arg), 1992 h.	7	2	1,840,000
Izvestia, 1987 h.	5	2	1,813,600
Dance Smartly, 1988 m.	2	2	1,782,140
Siphon (Brz), 1991 h.	6	2	1,780,000
Bertrando, 1989 h.	6	2	1,675,000
Charismatic, 1996 h.	3	2	1,646,200
Prized, 1986 h.	5	2	1,565,940
Sulamani (Ire), 1999 h.	3	2	1,563,600
General Challenge, 1996 g.	6	2	1,560,000
Real Quiet, 1995 h.	3	2	1,550,000
Monarchos, 1998 h.	4	2	1,522,000
Manila, 1983 h.	3	2	1,500,000
Free House, 1994 h.	4	2	1,385,000
Empire Maker, 2000 h.	3	2	1,370,000
Criminal Type, 1985 h.	3	2	1,350,000
Tinners Way, 1990 h.	7	2	1,330,000
Snow Chief, 1983 h.	3	2	1,214,600
Birdstone, 2001 h.	4	2	1,200,000
John Henry, 1975 g.	2	2	1,200,000
Skimming, 1996 h.	3	2	1,200,000
Southern Image, 2000 h.	2	2	1,150,000

Leading Winners of Grade 1 Races in North America

Horse, YOB, Sex	Wins	G1 SWs	SWs	Earnings
John Henry, 1975 g.	39	16	30	$6,591,860
Affirmed, 1975 h.	22	14	19	2,393,818

Horse, YOB, Sex	Wins	G1 SWs	SWs	Earnings
Forego, 1970 g.	34	14	24	$1,938,957
Spectacular Bid, 1976 h.	26	13	23	2,781,608
Bayakoa (Arg), 1984 m.	18	12	16	2,785,259
Azeri, 1998 m.	17	11	14	4,079,820
Cigar, 1990 h.	18	11	14	7,599,815
Lady's Secret, 1982 m.	25	11	22	3,021,325
Serena's Song, 1992 m.	18	11	17	3,283,388
Paseana (Arg), 1987 m.	14	10	14	3,111,292
Skip Away, 1993 h.	18	10	16	9,616,360
Alysheba, 1984 h.	11	9	10	6,679,242
Easy Goer, 1986 h.	14	9	12	4,873,770
Flawlessly, 1988 h.	16	9	15	2,572,536
Sky Beauty, 1990 m.	15	9	13	1,336,000
Chief's Crown, 1982 h.	12	8	10	2,191,168
Heavenly Prize, 1991 m.	9	8	8	1,825,940
Personal Ensign, 1984 m.	13	8	10	1,679,880
Seattle Slew, 1974 h.	14	8	9	1,208,726
Susan's Girl, 1969 m.	29	8	24	1,251,668
Creme Fraiche, 1982 g.	17	7	14	4,024,727
Exceller, 1973 h.	8	7	8	1,125,772
Foolish Pleasure, 1972 h.	16	7	12	1,216,705
Go for Wand, 1987 m.	10	7	8	1,373,338
Goodbye Halo, 1985 m.	11	7	10	1,706,702
Gulch, 1984 h.	13	7	11	3,095,521
Honest Pleasure, 1973 h.	12	7	9	839,997
Open Mind, 1986 m.	12	7	11	1,844,372
Sharp Cat, 1994 m.	15	7	14	2,032,575
Sightseek, 1999 m.	12	7	10	2,445,216
Slew o' Gold, 1980 h.	12	7	8	3,533,534
Alydar, 1975 h.	14	6	11	957,195
Beautiful Pleasure, 1995 m.	10	6	7	2,734,078
Best Pal, 1988 g.	18	6	17	5,668,245
Bold 'n Determined, 1977 m.	16	6	11	949,599
Desert Vixen, 1970 m.	13	6	9	421,538
Holy Bull, 1991 h.	13	6	11	2,481,760
Inside Information, 1991 m.	14	6	9	1,641,806
Meadow Star, 1988 m.	11	6	10	1,445,740
Miss Oceana, 1981 m.	11	6	9	1,010,385
Optimistic Gal, 1973 m.	13	6	10	686,861
Point Given, 1998 h.	9	6	8	3,968,500
Possibly Perfect, 1990 m.	11	6	8	1,367,050
Precisionist, 1981 h.	20	6	17	3,485,398
Snow Chief, 1983 h.	13	6	12	3,383,210
Sunday Silence, 1986 h.	9	6	7	4,968,554
Theatrical (Ire), 1982 h.	7	6	7	2,840,500

Leading Winners of Graded Stakes in North America

Horse, YOB, Sex	Wins	Graded SWs	SWs	Earnings
John Henry, 1975 g.	39	25	30	$6,591,860
Forego, 1970 g.	34	23	24	1,938,957
Spectacular Bid, 1976 h.	26	21	23	2,781,608
Affirmed, 1975 h.	22	18	19	2,393,818
Ancient Title, 1970 h.	24	17	20	1,252,791
Serena's Song, 1992 m.	18	17	17	3,283,388
Skip Away, 1993 h.	18	16	16	9,616,360
Bayakoa (Arg), 1984 m.	18	15	16	2,785,259
Lady's Secret, 1982 m.	25	15	22	3,021,325
Azeri, 1998 m.	17	14	14	4,079,820
Paseana (Arg), 1987 m.	14	14	14	3,111,292
Flawlessly, 1988 h.	16	13	15	2,572,536
Precisionist, 1981 h.	20	13	17	3,485,398
Silverbulletday, 1996 m.	15	13	14	3,093,207
Sky Beauty, 1990 m.	15	13	13	1,336,000
Best Pal, 1988 g.	18	12	17	5,668,245
Sabin, 1980 m.	18	12	14	1,098,341
Safely Kept, 1986 h.	24	12	22	2,194,206
Sharp Cat, 1994 m.	15	12	14	2,032,575

Horse, YOB, Sex	Wins	Graded SWs	SWs	Earnings
Steinlen (GB), 1983 h.	16	12	14	$3,229,752
Susan's Girl, 1969 m.	29	12	24	1,251,668
Black Tie Affair (Ire), 1986 h.	18	11	13	3,370,694
Cigar, 1990 h.	18	11	14	7,599,815
Creme Fraiche, 1982 g.	17	11	14	4,024,727
Foolish Pleasure, 1972 h.	16	11	12	1,216,705
Gulch, 1984 h.	13	11	11	3,095,521
Housebuster, 1987 h.	15	11	14	1,229,696
Royal Glint, 1970 h.	21	11	15	1,004,816
Xtra Heat, 1998 m.	26	11	25	2,389,635
Alysheba, 1984 h.	11	10	10	6,679,242
Congaree, 1998 h.	12	10	10	3,267,490
Easy Goer, 1986 h.	14	10	12	4,873,770
Goodbye Halo, 1985 m.	11	10	10	1,706,702
King's Swan, 1980 g.	31	10	12	1,924,845
Kona Gold, 1994 g.	14	10	11	2,293,384
Lure, 1989 h.	14	10	10	2,515,289
Optimistic Gal, 1973 m.	13	10	10	686,861
Personal Ensign, 1984 m.	13	10	10	1,679,880
Sightseek, 1999 m.	12	10	10	2,445,216
Silver Charm, 1994 h.	11	10	10	4,444,369
Sir Bear, 1993 g.	19	10	11	2,538,422

Leading Winners of Stakes Races in North America

Horse, YOB, Sex	Wins	Graded SWs	SWs	Earnings
Exterminator, 1915 g.	50	0	34	$221,227
Native Diver, 1959 h.	37	0	34	1,026,500
Miss Woodford, 1880 m.	37	0	33	118,270
Firenze, 1884 m.	47	0	32	112,451
Round Table, 1954 h.	43	0	32	1,749,869
Kelso, 1957 g.	39	0	31	1,977,896
Kingston, 1884 h.	89	0	31	140,195
John Henry, 1975 g.	39	25	30	6,591,860
Hanover, 1884 h.	32	0	27	118,887
Roamer, 1911 g.	39	0	27	98,828
Seabiscuit, 1933 h.	33	0	27	437,730
Who Doctor Who, 1983 g.	33	1	26	813,870
Hindoo, 1878 h.	30	0	25	71,875
Little Bold John, 1982 g.	38	5	25	1,956,406
Stymie, 1941 h.	35	0	25	918,485
Xtra Heat, 1998 m.	26	11	25	2,389,635
Equipoise, 1928 h.	29	0	24	338,610
Forego, 1970 g.	34	23	24	1,938,957
Susan's Girl, 1969 m.	29	12	24	1,251,668
Whirlaway, 1938 h.	32	0	24	561,161
Citation, 1945 h.	32	0	23	1,085,760
Spectacular Bid, 1976 h.	26	21	23	2,781,608
Curribot, 1977 g.	37	0	22	491,527
Discovery, 1931 h.	27	0	22	195,287
Lady's Secret, 1982 m.	25	15	22	3,021,325
Royal Harmony, 1964 h.	38	0	22	587,164
Safely Kept, 1986 h.	24	12	22	2,194,206
Swoon's Son, 1953 h.	30	0	22	970,605
Armed, 1941 g.	41	0	21	817,475
Buckpasser, 1963 h.	25	0	21	1,462,014
Frost King, 1978 h.	26	2	21	1,033,260
Rosy Way, 1989 g.	28	0	21	97,389
Amadevil, 1974 h.	33	0	20	653,534
Ancient Title, 1970 h.	24	17	20	1,252,791
Chilcoton Blaze, 1980 h.	31	0	20	490,862
Hidden Treasure, 1980 h.	24	0	20	187,734
Judy's Red Shoes, 1983 m.	25	1	20	1,085,668
Sarazen, 1921 g.	27	0	20	225,000
Affirmed, 1975 h.	22	18	19	2,393,818
Alsab, 1939 h.	25	0	19	350,015
Ben Brush, 1893 h.	25	0	19	65,217
Decathlon, 1953 h.	25	0	19	269,530

Horse, YOB, Sex	Wins	Graded SWs	SWs	Earnings
Delta Colleen, 1985 m.	23	0	19	$810,798
Man o' War, 1917 h.	20	0	19	249,465
Nashua, 1952 h.	22	0	19	1,288,565
Police Inspector, 1977 h.	25	1	19	713,707
Rapido Dom, 1978 h.	25	0	19	466,974
Say Florida Sandy, 1994 h.	33	5	19	2,085,408
Scott's Scoundrel, 1992 h.	22	2	19	1,270,052
Spirit of Fighter, 1983 m.	33	0	19	847,454
Affectionately, 1960 m.	28	0	18	546,659
Arctic Laur, 1988 h.	21	0	18	634,809
Cicada, 1959 m.	23	0	18	783,674
Copper Case, 1977 g.	33	0	18	365,374
Devil Diver, 1939 h.	22	0	18	261,064
Dixie Poker Ace, 1987 g.	27	0	18	850,126
Energetic King, 1979 h.	35	0	18	765,776
Fantango Lady, 1994 m.	22	0	18	279,295
Grey Lag, 1918 h.	25	0	18	136,715
In Rem, 1975 g.	21	0	18	307,742
Leaping Plum, 1991 g.	29	0	18	371,584
Orphan Kist, 1984 m.	28	0	18	631,997
Overskate, 1975 h.	24	3	18	791,634
Parole, 1873 g.	59	0	18	82,111
Polynesian, 1942 h.	27	0	18	310,410
Timely Ruckus, 1993 g.	25	0	18	618,004
Tom Fool, 1949 h.	21	0	18	570,165
Twixt, 1969 h.	26	7	18	619,141
Victorian Era, 1962 h.	23	0	18	198,410
Best Pal, 1988 g.	18	12	17	5,668,245
Bewitch, 1945 m.	20	0	17	462,605
Bold Ruler, 1954 h.	23	0	17	764,204
Cagey Exuberance, 1984 m.	18	3	17	765,017
Challedon, 1936 h.	20	0	17	334,660
Coaltown, 1945 h.	23	0	17	415,675
Damascus, 1964 h.	21	0	17	1,176,781
Dance Trainer, 1983 g.	27	0	17	276,262
Dave's Friend, 1975 g.	35	2	17	1,079,915
Foncier, 1976 h.	29	0	17	323,515
Full Pocket, 1969 h.	27	1	17	424,031
Gallant Bob, 1972 g.	23	2	17	489,992
Glacial Princess, 1981 m.	27	0	17	542,792
Hallowed Dreams, 1997 m.	25	0	17	740,144
Henry of Navarre, 1891 h.	29	0	17	68,985
Imp, 1894 m.	62	0	17	70,119
Isadorable, 1983 m.	19	0	17	415,018
My Juliet, 1972 m.	24	6	17	548,859
Native Dancer, 1950 h.	21	0	17	785,240
Precisionist, 1981 h.	20	13	17	3,485,398
Secret Romeo, 1998 h.	23	0	17	865,790
Sefa's Beauty, 1979 m.	25	5	17	1,171,628
Serena's Song, 1992 m.	18	17	17	3,283,388
Special Intent, 1981 h.	30	0	17	438,558
Spicy, 1955 m.	33	0	17	135,233
Sun Beau, 1925 h.	33	0	17	376,744
Tosmah, 1961 m.	23	0	17	612,588

Most Stakes Wins by Decade by Year of Birth

1931-1940

Horse, YOB, Sex, Sire	Yrs. Raced	Starts	Wins	Stk. Wins	Earnings
Seabiscuit, 1933 h., by Hard Tack	6	89	33	27	$437,730
Whirlaway, 1938 h., by *Blenheim II	4	60	32	24	561,161
Discovery, 1931 h., by Display	4	63	27	22	195,287
Alsab, 1939 h., by Good Goods	4	51	25	19	350,015
Devil Diver, 1939 h., by *St. Germans	5	47	22	18	261,064
Challedon, 1936 h., by *Challenger II	5	44	20	17	334,660
War Admiral, 1934 h., by Man o' War	4	26	21	15	273,240
Eight Thirty, 1936 h., by Pilate	4	27	16	13	155,475
Marriage, 1936 h., by *Strolling Player	8	99	35	12	216,090
Parasang, 1937 h., by Halcyon	10	134	29	12	102,627

1941-1950

Horse, YOB, Sex, Sire	Yrs. Raced	Starts	Wins	Stk. Wins	Earnings
Stymie, 1941 h., by Equestrian	7	131	35	25	$918,485
Citation, 1945 h., by Bull Lea	4	45	32	23	1,085,760
Armed, 1941 g., by Bull Lea	7	81	41	21	817,475
Polynesian, 1942 h., by Unbreakable	4	58	27	18	310,410
Tom Fool, 1949 h., by Menow	3	30	21	18	570,165
Bewitch, 1945 m., by Bull Lea	5	55	20	17	462,605
Coaltown, 1945 h., by Bull Lea	4	39	23	17	415,675
Native Dancer, 1950 h., by Polynesian	3	22	21	17	785,240
Delegate, 1944 g., by Maeda	9	134	31	16	277,530
My Request, 1945 h., by Requested	4	52	22	16	385,495

1951-1960

Horse, YOB, Sex, Sire	Yrs. Raced	Starts	Wins	Stk. Wins	Earnings
Native Diver, 1959 h., by Imbros	7	81	37	34	$1,026,500
Round Table, 1954 h., by *Princequillo	4	66	43	32	1,749,869
Kelso, 1957 g., by Your Host	8	63	39	31	1,977,896
Swoon's Son, 1953 h., by The Doge	4	51	30	22	970,605
Hidden Treasure, 1957 h., by Dark Star	5	65	24	20	187,734
Decathlon, 1953 h., by Olympia	3	42	25	19	269,530
Nashua, 1952 h., by *Nasrullah	3	30	22	19	1,288,565
Affectionately, 1960 m., by Swaps	4	52	28	18	546,659
Cicada, 1959 m., by Bryan G.	4	42	23	18	783,674
Bold Ruler, 1954 h., by *Nasrullah	3	33	23	17	764,204
Spicy, 1955 m., by Provocative	7	97	33	17	135,233

1961-1970

Horse, YOB, Sex, Sire	Yrs. Raced	Starts	Wins	Stk. Wins	Earnings
Forego, 1970 g., by *Forli	6	57	34	24	$1,938,957
Susan's Girl, 1969 m., by Quadrangle	5	63	29	24	1,251,668
Royal Harmony, 1964 h., by Royal Note	6	105	36	22	587,164
Buckpasser, 1963 h., by Tom Fool	3	31	25	21	1,462,014
Ancient Title, 1970 h., by Gummo	7	57	24	20	1,252,791
Twixt, 1969 m., by Restless Native	4	70	26	18	619,141
Victorian Era, 1962 h., by Victoria Park	4	48	23	18	198,410
Damascus, 1964 h., by Sword Dancer	3	32	21	17	1,176,781
Full Pocket, 1969 h., by Olden Times	4	47	27	17	424,031
Tosmah, 1961 m., by Tim Tam	4	39	23	17	612,588

1971-1980

Horse, YOB, Sex, Sire	Yrs. Raced	Starts	Wins	Stk. Wins	Earnings
John Henry, 1975 g., by Ole Bob Bowers	8	83	39	30	$6,591,860
Spectacular Bid, 1976 h., by Bold Bidder	3	30	26	23	2,781,608
Curribot, 1977 g., by Little Current	12	139	37	22	491,527
Frost King, 1978 h., by Ruritania	4	55	27	21	1,196,954
Amadevil, 1974 h., by Jungle Savage	7	93	33	20	653,534
Chilcoton Blaze, 1980 h., by Victorian Host	10	83	31	20	490,862
Affirmed, 1975 h., by Exclusive Native	3	29	22	19	2,393,818
Police Inspector, 1977 h., by Police Car	6	71	25	19	713,707
Rapido Dom, 1978 h., by Sir Dom	8	105	25	19	466,974
Copper Case, 1977 g., by Hopeful Venture	9	92	33	18	365,374
Energetic King, 1979 h., by On the Sly	10	106	35	18	765,776
In Rem, 1975 g., by El Patio	4	33	21	18	307,742
Overskate, 1975 h., by Nodouble	4	42	24	18	791,634

1981-1990

Horse, YOB, Sex, Sire	Yrs. Raced	Starts	Wins	Stk. Wins	Earnings
Who Doctor Who, 1983 g., by Doctor Stat	8	64	33	26	$813,870
Little Bold John, 1982 g., by John Alden	9	105	38	25	1,956,406
Lady's Secret, 1982 m., by Secretariat	4	45	25	22	3,021,325
Safely Kept, 1986 m., by Horatius	4	31	24	22	2,194,206
Rosy Way, 1989 m., by Lord Avie	8	51	28	21	97,389
Judy's Red Shoes, 1983 m., by Hold Your Tricks	6	83	25	20	1,085,086
Delta Colleen, 1985 m., by Golden Reserve	7	71	23	19	810,798
Spirit of Fighter, 1983 m., by Gallant Knave	8	72	33	19	847,454
Arctic Laur, 1988 m., by Son of Briartic	7	60	21	18	634,809
Dixie Poker Ace, 1987 g., by Patriotically	8	86	27	18	850,126
Orphan Kist, 1984 m., by Fort Prevel	8	100	28	18	631,997

1991-2000

Horse, YOB, Sex, Sire	Yrs. Raced	Starts	Wins	Stk. Wins	Earnings
Xtra Heat, 1998 f., by Dixieland Heat	4	35	26	25	$2,389,635
Say Florida Sandy, 1994 h., by Personal Flag	8	98	33	19	2,085,408
Scott's Scoundrel, 1992 h., by L'Enjoleur	6	50	22	19	1,270,052
Fantango Lady, 1994 m., by Lytrump	5	55	22	18	279,295
Timely Ruckus, 1993 g., by Bold Executive	8	68	25	18	618,004
Hallowed Dreams, 1997 m., by Malagra	4	30	25	17	740,144
Leaping Plum, 1991 g., by Lightning Leap	12	66	29	17	371,584
Secret Romeo, 1998 h., by Service Stripe	5	55	23	17	865,790
Serena's Song, 1992 m., by Rahy	3	38	18	17	3,283,388
Incredible Revenge, 1992 m., by Raja's Revenge	6	57	26	16	638,578
Lottsa Talc, 1990 m., by Talc	6	65	21	16	1,206,248
Skip Away, 1993 h., by Skip Trial	4	38	18	16	9,616,360
Valid Leader, 1995 m., by Valid Appeal	5	57	21	16	411,618

2001-2004

Horse, YOB, Sex, Sire	Yrs. Raced	Starts	Wins	Stk. Wins	Earnings
Ashado, 2001 f., by Saint Ballado	2	14	9	8	$2,870,440
Rocky Gulch, 2001 g., by Dry Gulch	2	15	10	8	541,088
Rockem Sockem, 2001 g., by Ulises	2	14	7	7	249,651
Smarty Jones, 2001 c., by Elusive Quality	2	9	8	7	7,613,155
Kitten's Joy, 2001 c., by El Prado (Ire)	2	12	8	6	1,705,911
Thundering Verzy, 2001 g., by Verzy	2	18	7	6	80,632
A Bit O'Gold, 2001 g., by Gold Fever	2	11	7	5	1,290,819
Blonde Executive, 2001 f., by Bold Executive	2	13	8	5	610,591
He Loves Me, 2001 f., by Not For Love	2	14	7	5	343,250
Sir Oscar, 2001 c., by Halo's Image	1	6	6	5	528,800

Horse, YOB, Sex	Wins	Stakes Wins	Stakes Placings	Earnings
Honor Medal, 1981 h.	19	9	22	$1,347,073
Judy's Red Shoes, 1983 h.	25	20	22	1,085,668
Lucky Salvation, 1980 h.	22	5	22	467,891
Ruler's Whirl, 1966 h.	27	8	22	116,354
Say Florida Sandy, 1994 h.	33	19	22	2,085,408
Sir Bear, 1993 g.	19	11	22	2,538,422
Susan's Girl, 1969 m.	29	24	22	1,251,668
Adventuresome Love, 1986 h.	16	9	21	436,244
Bye and Near, 1963 h.	21	10	21	202,040
Charlie Chalmers, 1985 g.	9	6	21	378,715
Dixie Poker Ace, 1987 g.	27	18	21	850,126
First Fiddle, 1939 h.	23	10	21	398,610
Fort Marcy, 1964 g.	21	16	21	1,109,791
Kent Green, 1983 g.	13	8	21	395,469
King's Swan, 1980 h.	31	12	21	1,924,845
Pongo Boy, 1992 g.	22	12	21	776,184

North American Leading Runners by Most Stakes Placings

Horse, YOB, Sex	Wins	Stakes Wins	Stakes Placings	Earnings
Find, 1950 g.	22	13	38	$803,615
Stymie, 1941 h.	35	25	38	918,485
Pampas Host, 1972 h.	19	13	32	310,922
Major Presto, 1963 g.	24	12	30	125,694
Tick Tock, 1953 g.	20	10	30	386,951
Alerted, 1948 h.	20	12	29	440,485
Orphan Kist, 1984 m.	28	18	28	631,997
Talent Show, 1955 g.	16	7	28	507,038
Exterminator, 1915 g.	50	34	27	221,227
Gene's Lady, 1981 m.	14	10	27	946,190
Royal Harmony, 1964 h.	38	22	27	587,164
Ruhe, 1948 g.	11	6	27	294,490
Gallorette, 1942 m.	21	13	26	445,535
Love Your Host, 1966 h.	22	16	26	160,683
*Grey Monarch, 1955 h.	13	7	25	216,146
Creme Fraiche, 1982 g.	17	14	25	4,024,727
Delegate, 1944 g.	31	15	25	277,530
Delta Colleen, 1985 m.	23	19	25	810,798
Military Hawk, 1987 g.	18	12	25	686,128
Nostalgia's Star, 1982 h.	9	7	25	2,154,827
Special Intent, 1981 h.	30	17	25	438,558
Stranglehold, 1949 g.	25	9	25	289,190
Fiftieth Star, 1972 h.	19	6	24	167,035
Armed, 1941 g.	41	19	23	817,475
Double B Express, 1975 g.	31	13	23	246,013
Eddie Schmidt, 1953 h.	20	12	23	526,292
Fourstardave, 1985 g.	21	13	23	1,636,737
In the Curl, 1984 m.	26	10	23	749,891
Ky Alta, 1977 h.	14	9	23	313,885
On Trust, 1944 h.	23	11	23	554,145
Straight Deal, 1962 m.	21	13	23	733,020
Arctic Laur, 1988 h.	21	18	22	634,809
Buzfuz, 1942 g.	35	11	22	286,740
Chompion, 1965 h.	14	10	22	604,401
Foncier, 1976 h.	29	17	22	323,515
Homebuilder, 1984 h.	11	8	22	1,172,153

North American Leading Runners by Most Stakes Placings Without a Stakes Win

Horse, YOB, Sex, Sire	Years Raced	Starts	Wins	Stakes Plcgs	Earnings
Guadalcanal, 1958 h., by Citation	8	91	7	13	$243,337
Stunning Native, 1978 m., by Our Native	3	35	3	13	155,312
Grand Galop, 1962 g., by Victoria Park	7	119	20	12	115,744
Big Numbers, 1997 h., by Numerous	6	54	5	11	342,904
Blue Trumpeter, 1949 h., by Thumbs Up	6	106	15	11	120,912
Gat's Girl, 1975 m., by Lurullah	5	70	6	11	119,242
Milk Wood (GB), 1995 g., by Zafonic	5	39	7	11	315,990
Mistress Fletcher, 1992 m., by Sovereign Don	6	71	9	11	260,638
Aces Court, 1981 m., by Know Your Aces	6	75	8	10	112,740
Behind the Scenes, 1984 m., by Hurry Up Blue	4	41	7	10	331,095
Dance Play, 1988 m., by Sovereign Dancer	3	42	4	10	168,431
Distinctive Moon, 1979 m., by Distinctive	3	36	4	10	124,086
Hold the Beans, 1977 h., by Northern Fling	10	186	18	10	175,528
Ladies Agreement, 1970 m., by Royal Union	5	68	14	10	295,193
Little Buckles, 1991 m., by Buckley Boy	5	43	9	10	466,755
Lonny's Secret, 1966 h., by Terrang	4	38	6	10	107,542
Lotta Tike, 1974 m., by Skin Head	5	58	10	10	91,760
March of Kings, 1993 g., by River of Kings (Ire)	9	95	17	10	497,643
Patti L., 1987 m., by Lyphard's Wish (Fr)	5	55	9	10	211,995
Phyxius, 1999 f., by Broad Brush	3	32	3	10	220,146
Rule by Reason, 1967 h., by Hail to Reason	5	91	15	10	263,547
Sharethetime, 1998 h., by Local Time	4	46	6	10	208,011
Sweets, 1985 g., by Mr. Redoy	8	85	8	10	196,524
Vaunted Vamp, 1992 m., by Racing Star	6	78	21	10	419,641
A Call to Rise, 1988 g., by Poles Apart	8	124	18	9	600,441
Beth Believes, 1986 m., by Believe It	5	44	10	9	357,936
Cup o' Shine, 1977 m., by Raise a Cup	4	77	9	9	95,556
Dance Card Filled, 1983 h., by Dance Bid	5	71	10	9	398,706
Dewans Mischief, 1984 m., by Dewan	4	55	18	9	256,399
Dusty Heather, 1996 m., by M. Double M.	4	42	5	9	464,887
*Elegant Heir, 1965 h., by Pharamond	5	93	23	9	163,435
Fappies Cosy Miss, 1988 m., by Fappiano	3	35	4	9	304,885
Habby's Stuff, 1995 m., by Habitonia	6	68	7	9	212,343
Intensitivo, 1986 h., by *Sensitivo	9	143	25	9	292,535
Iron Becky, 1977 m., by Iron Anthony	4	61	6	9	85,781
Judy's Joe, 1964 h., by *Ben Lomond	5	78	10	9	34,102
Naskra Colors, 1992 m., by Star de Naskra	5	28	5	9	411,437
Princess Tiree, 1989 m., by Main Debut	6	59	10	9	87,601
River Bank Kid, 1989 m., by Eskimo	5	40	6	9	142,865
Runaway Magic, 1997 m., by Runaway Groom	3	18	3	9	131,305
Sensitive Music, 1969 h., by *Sensitivo	5	68	10	9	159,111
Sentosa, 1991 g., by Northern Supremo	12	93	13	9	54,879
Shed Some Light, 1992 g., by Homebuilder	9	105	20	9	569,638
She's Content, 1983 m., by Restivo	4	47	9	9	225,501
Shuttered, 1993 m., by Wild Again	4	26	7	9	226,918
Todd's Orphan, 1966 m., by Ambehaving	6	86	6	9	60,809
Treachery, 1960 m., by Promised Land	5	105	11	9	182,071
Whiz Along, 1985 h., by Cormorant	6	80	9	9	581,115

Losingest Horses of All Time
(Without a Win)

Thrust, a chestnut gelding by Bold Salute out of Stitching, by Sting, had very little thrust and lost 105 consecutive races before being retired from the field of battle in 1956.

Thrust finished second five times and was third on seven occasions, with career earnings of $8,180.

Zippy Chippy, a foal of 1991, is notable for the length of time he tried and failed to win. He raced his 11th season in 2004, a longer career than any other horse with more than 58 defeats. He was retired at the end of that year with 100 consecutive losses. Following is a list of the sport's leading losers from 1930 through 2004.

Losses	Horse, YOB	Years Raced	Earnings
105	Thrust, 1950	5	$8,180
100	Zippy Chippy, 1991	11	30,834
92	Star Time, 1943	5	7,215
89	Good Get, 1940	5	2,805
86	Fagrace, 1943	5	6,200
85	Maker of Trouble, 1922	4	565
84	Western Holiday, 1929	5	620
83	City Limit, 1934	5	1,105
82	Giant's Heel, 1943	6	1,560
	Master Mark, 1941	6	290
81	Jibberty Bell, 1955	4	4,802
79	Arvella, 1957	4	2,531
	Omashane, 1942	5	1,475
77	Fred Whitham, 1925	7	1,100
	Space, 1942	5	3,070
76	Prima Whisk, 1936	4	670
	Sure Its Legal, 1988	5	9,772
75	War Bull, 1980	4	10,568
73	*Cafre II, 1951	7	2,339
	Gray Leaves, 1961	4	1,424
73	Judgaville, 1981	3	12,965
72	Lattanzio, 1991	5	19,163
	Winnie's Pride, 1988	6	6,790
71	Lady Jule, 1925	3	1,095
	Ninon, 1923	3	1,360
	Roman Sandal, 1924	4	990
	Stark Mad, 1946	4	2,950
70	Red Alley Cat, 1990	6	7,610
69	Buddugie, 1920	4	1,865
	Tuff Nuggets, 1980	4	8,120
68	Buck Flares, 1955	4	6,100
	Lucky Change, 1941	4	3,930
68	Right Chief, 1961	4	3,689

Losses	Horse, YOB	Years Raced	Earnings
67	Bengal Dancer, 1954	4	$5,240
	Jimmy What, 1987	6	14,036
	Tchadar, 1924	6	480
66	Dominate'em, 1978	4	5,860
	Doug's Dame, 1965	4	3,558
	Filly Gumbo, 1970	3	4,667
	Really Rushing, 1995	5	17,184
	Rosette, 1926	4	243
	Unclebuck, 1939	7	730
65	Alpha's Star, 1990	6	12,530
	Amarushka, 1981	5	24,336
	Brill Lon, 1956	4	1,420
	Flashy Lark, 1981	5	14,510
	Goodyear, 1927	5	20
	Icy Ethel, 1948	5	3,215
	Jacinto's Arky, 1980	4	4,536
	Petulant, 1928	4	690
	Sam's Tip, 1975	4	14,344
	Tarbucket, 1932	3	945
64	Able Archer, 1957	3	1,847
	Clay K., 1965	6	2,570
	Dawn's Debbie, 1982	3	7,292
	Gosport, 1936	5	465
	Junior T., 1948	4	1,160
	Pacific Star, 1946	7	1,000
	Truckin, 1936	5	865
63	Bell's Luck, 1961	4	867
	Castle Rock, 1927	4	625
	Double Our Flag, 1994	5	22,175
	Dusky Boy, 1928	5	1,310
	Mail Plane, 1948	3	1,805
	Performance Critic, 1996	4	16,475
	Ruby's Crystal, 1980	4	5,575
	Sweet Bernice, 1935	8	995
62	Colonel Titus, 1939	9	605
	Indiana Spa, 1935	5	635
	Kitty Leon, 1939	7	595
	Navy Bean Soup, 1952	4	3,705
	Rebel Girl, 1951	4	4,005
	Suspended Star, 1954	3	3,040
	War O'Gold, 1966	3	4,313
	White Hoops, 1928	6	350
61	Dengee, 1936	4	200
	El Toro Rey, 1943	5	300
	Grimsby, 1957	5	1,114
	Jackson Better, 1982	3	5,572
	Last Ditch, 1971	4	4,344
	Total Mayhem, 1992	4	12,735
	West River, 1959	4	4,765

Leading Horses of All Time By Starts

Horse, YOB, Sex, Sire	Years Raced	Starts	Wins	2nds	3rds	Stakes Wins	Earnings
Hiblaze, 1935 h., by Blazes	14	406	79	73	52	0	$32,647
*Galley Sweep, 1933 g., by Aga Khan	14	399	19	34	46	0	10,677
Shot One, 1941 g., by Shoeless Joe	13	360	65	65	68	0	29,982
Onus, 1933 g., by Jack High	15	344	53	58	63	0	32,039
Worthowning, 1935 g., by *Longworth	14	339	63	62	64	0	41,830
Agreed, 1950 g., by Revoked	14	338	39	50	49	0	68,004
My Blaze, 1930 h., by Big Blaze	11	338	52	35	51	1	32,707
Marabou, 1925 h., by *Hourless	10	337	41	61	44	0	27,458
Vantryst, 1936 h., by Tryster	13	334	61	78	48	0	31,971
George de Mar, 1922 h., by *Colonel Vennie	13	333	60	54	64	0	69,091
Buffoon, 1937 h., by St. Brideaux	10	329	37	36	45	0	11,538
Welsh Lad, 1934 g., by Prince of Wales	13	329	67	54	49	0	25,317
Panjab, 1937 g., by *Kiev	11	327	21	32	44	0	17,929
Seth's Hope, 1924 h., by Seth	11	327	62	51	50	0	74,341
Copin, 1937 h., by Mate	13	323	42	40	53	0	27,926
Commission, 1935 h., by Banstar	13	319	41	36	39	0	25,626
Golden Sweep, 1923 h., by Flittergold	10	318	46	47	58	0	32,285
Higher Bracket, 1936 h., by *Rolls Royce	11	318	37	50	51	0	15,661

Horse, YOB, Sex, Sire	Years Raced	Starts	Wins	2nds	3rds	Stakes Wins	Earnings
Noah's Pride, 1929 g., by Noah	12	317	60	50	61	1	$41,507
Bee's Little Man, 1961 h., by *Iceberg II	12	315	42	32	31	0	108,675
Champ Sorter, 1952 h., by Four Freedoms	12	315	35	43	51	0	62,747
Appease Not, 1946 g., by King Cole	13	314	42	44	46	0	122,802
Easiest Way, 1931 g., by *Waygood	11	311	27	38	44	0	24,375
Mister Snow Man, 1959 g., by *Iceberg II	14	310	43	37	36	0	104,074
Shannon's Hope, 1956 h., by *Shannon II	12	309	29	36	43	0	39,848
Port o' Play, 1926 h., by The Porter	9	308	44	47	34	1	39,234
Behavin Jerry, 1964 h., by Ambehaving	14	307	38	25	48	0	72,259
Star Soldier, 1934 g., by Son o' Battle	11	305	37	22	50	0	8,307
Dr. Jillson, 1930 h., by *Kiev	12	304	27	42	37	0	12,522
It's No Use, 1950 h., by *Basileus II	11	304	25	40	52	0	68,326
Vote Boy, 1932 g., by Torchilla	11	304	55	37	48	1	39,240
Chronology, 1935 g., by *Donnacona	13	302	44	41	46	0	14,632
Mr. Minx, 1952 h., by *Mafosta	12	302	36	48	34	0	87,072
Bull Market, 1932 g., by Happy Time	14	301	28	49	39	0	19,275
Call Mac, 1965 g., by Loukenmac	13	301	13	61	58	0	82,664
Mantados, 1932 h., by Rock Man	14	299	32	47	50	0	19,840

Most Starts by Decade by Year of Birth

1931-1940

Horse, YOB, Sex, Sire	Yrs. Raced	Starts	Wins	Earnings
Hiblaze, 1935 h., by Blazes	14	406	79	$32,647
*Galley Sweep, 1933 g., by Aga Khan	14	399	19	10,677
Onus, 1933 g., by Jack High	15	344	53	32,039
Worthowning, 1935 g., by *Longworth	14	339	63	41,830
Vantryst, 1936 h., by Tryster	13	334	61	31,971
Buffoon, 1937 h., by St. Brideaux	10	329	37	11,538
Welsh Lad, 1934 g., by Prince of Wales	13	329	67	25,317
Panjab, 1937 g., by *Kiev	11	327	21	17,929
Copin, 1937 h., by Mate	13	323	42	27,926
Commission, 1935 h., by Banstar	13	319	41	25,626

1941-1950

Horse, YOB, Sex, Sire	Yrs. Raced	Starts	Wins	Earnings
Shot One, 1941 g., by Shoeless Joe	13	360	65	$29,982
Agreed, 1950 g., by Revoked	14	338	39	68,004
Appease Not, 1946 g., by King Cole	13	314	42	122,802
It's No Use, 1950 h., by *Basileus II	11	304	25	68,326
Bobs Ace, 1947 g., by War Jeep	10	286	31	56,957
Eagle Speed, 1946 g., by Sun Again	12	284	40	66,337
Shadow Shot, 1944 h., by Chance Shot	11	279	35	88,585
Royal Bones, 1947 g., by Mr. Bones	8	274	33	70,670
Quatrefoil, 1945 h., by *Quatre Bras II	10	273	18	46,994
Bee Lee Tee, 1947 h., by Roy T.	12	270	47	104,805

1951-1960

Horse, YOB, Sex, Sire	Yrs. Raced	Starts	Wins	Earnings
Champ Sorter, 1952 h., by Four Freedoms	12	315	35	$62,747
Mister Snow Man, 1959 g., by *Iceberg II	14	310	43	104,074
Shannon's Hope, 1956 h., by *Shannon II	12	309	29	39,848
Mr. Minx, 1952 h., by *Mafosta	12	302	36	87,072
Ole Sarge, 1956 g., by Carrara Marble	12	296	24	36,373
Easy Knight, 1955 g., by Easy Mon	12	294	22	48,099
Asking, 1952 h., by Pry	12	287	27	46,442
Black Jet, 1957 h., by Lord Boswell	12	281	21	51,077
Knight-King, 1957 g., by Tuscany	12	277	26	79,141
Bell's Range, 1954 g., by Ramillies	13	274	41	65,100

1961-1970

Horse, YOB, Sex, Sire	Yrs. Raced	Starts	Wins	Earnings
Bee's Little Man, 1961 h., by *Iceberg II	12	315	42	$108,675
Behavin Jerry, 1964 h., by Ambehaving	14	307	38	72,259
Call Mac, 1965 g., by Loukenmac	13	301	13	82,664
Royal Doctor, 1961 g., by *Royal Vale	12	286	21	50,793
Bayou Teche, 1961 g., by Bryan G.	12	281	48	107,577
Dandier, 1961 h., by Mohammedan	11	278	31	74,523
Pin Pan Dan, 1966 h., by Pan Dancer	12	278	33	86,330
Wild Wink, 1969 h., by Quickasawink	13	275	44	129,004
Bucket O'Suds, 1965 h., by Rattle Dancer	13	273	38	158,017
Candy Top, 1964 g., by Top Double	13	273	35	94,990

1971-1980

Horse, YOB, Sex, Sire	Yrs. Raced	Starts	Wins	Earnings
Dot the T., 1972 h., by *Notable II	12	261	48	$227,033
Legrand, 1974 h., by Delta Judge	11	255	13	104,322
Mr. Turnabout, 1971 h., by Reverse	11	252	25	89,061
Magic Flash, 1971 g., by *Babieca II	10	250	22	63,175
Catch Poppy, 1973 h., by Poppy Jay	12	246	30	122,346
Arrowsmith, 1976 h., by Briartic	12	243	20	166,106
One Purpose, 1978 g., by Sinister Purpose	13	242	13	145,894
Dan Dan, 1975 g., by Turniga	11	238	29	171,438
Troy Knight, 1973 h., by Nashwood	12	235	38	143,287
Uhrich Enzurich, 1972 g., by *Semillant	13	234	21	60,247

1981-1990

Horse, YOB, Sex, Sire	Yrs. Raced	Starts	Wins	Earnings
Z. Z. Quickfoot, 1982 g., by Master Derby	12	266	27	$122,752
Sharon Caper, 1983 g., by Cartesian	13	244	33	109,685
Passive Loss, 1987 m., by Highland Blade	13	225	22	121,356
Side Winding, 1985 g., by Shananie	12	218	26	121,648
Our Legal Eagle, 1990 g., by Exuberant	13	217	10	100,892
Valley Cat, 1985 g., by Valdez	14	216	29	123,612
Wicked Wike, 1982 g., by Olden Times	11	212	11	318,561
Callisto, 1987 g., by Nasty and Bold	11	210	28	329,002
Playing Politics, 1982 g., by In Reality	15	203	25	187,639
Noble But Nasty, 1981 g., by Nasty and Bold	11	200	40	325,588

1991-2000

Horse, YOB, Sex, Sire	Yrs. Raced	Starts	Wins	Earnings
Smart And Regal, 1991 g., by Regal Classic	11	188	21	$148,253
Talc of Dreams, 1992 g., by Talc	11	172	11	110,421
He Makes Cents, 1992 g., by Narcotics Squad	9	171	7	99,747
Mr. Butterscotch, 1992 g., by Compliance	10	161	12	116,614
Lindapinda, 1992 m., by Unite	7	158	14	104,473
Mahrally, 1991 g., by Ballydoyle	11	154	32	168,440
Indomable, 1992 g., by Blue Ensign	11	153	14	190,799
Miron's Gentleman, 1991 g., by Cutlass	11	153	14	196,353
Jimini C. Dues, 1991 g., by Closing Fast	12	152	24	202,142
Theodore's Devil, 1994 g., by Tasso	9	152	22	179,721

2001-2004

Horse, YOB, Sex, Sire	Yrs. Raced	Starts	Wins	Earnings
Dandy Belle, 2001 f., by Boone's Mill	2	35	1	$25,543
Smart Confidence, 2001 g., by Confide	2	35	3	48,920
Calling Mary Mac, 2001 f., by Family Calling	2	32	1	11,865
D. L. Renzo, 2001 c., by Diligence	2	32	6	114,365
Run N Coke, 2001 c., by Line In The Sand	2	32	5	85,260
Tactical Power, 2001 c., by Tactical Advantage	2	32	2	40,590
All American Ernie, 2001 g., by Halos and Horns	2	31	4	38,627
B Onefifty, 2001 g., by Mr. Greeley	2	31	1	15,125
Compassionate Girl, 2001 f., by Tactical Advantage	2	31	2	31,562
John David, 2001 c., by Is It True	2	31	2	34,480

All-Time Leading Earners by Deflated Dollars

Comparing horses of different eras is always an entertaining exercise. Was Secretariat a better racehorse than Citation? That question will never be answered definitively because they never met on the track, so comparing horses of one era to another is subjective.

Earnings are one measure of performance, though that yardstick also has its drawbacks because the purses of yesteryear do not compare to the purses of today. There is a way to use earnings as a measure of productivity, however, by deflating the earnings; that is, adjusting earnings to account for the effects of inflation.

In the tables presented on this page and the following two pages are deflated earnings of the all-time leaders in Thoroughbred racing since 1929. Considered for inclusion on the list is any horse that started at least once in North America. Horses that raced at least once in North America and also raced overseas have all their earnings included, all being converted

to United States dollars and then deflated by racing year.

All-time leading money winner adjusted for inflation is two-time Horse of the Year John Henry, who raced 83 times from 1977 through '84. The durable gelding won the first $1-million Thoroughbred race in the U.S., the 1981 Arlington Million Stakes (G1), and his career ended the year in which the Breeders' Cup was inaugurated. Second on the list is two-time Horse of the Year Cigar, the all-time leading earner in North America in current dollars.

The deflator used to convert all earnings is the Gross Domestic Product implicit price deflator published by the U.S. Bureau of Economic Analysis.

On the first two pages are the all-time leaders by deflated dollars regardless of sex. On the third page is a list of the all-time leading female earners by deflated dollars. Statistics are through December 31, 2004.

All-Time Leading Earners by Deflated Dollars

Horse, YOB, Sex, Sire	Yrs. Raced	Starts	1st	2nd	3rd	Nominal Earnings	Deflated Earnings
John Henry, 1975 g., by Ole Bob Bowers	8	83	39	15	9	$6,591,860	$11,659,061
Cigar, 1990 h., by Palace Music	4	33	19	4	5	9,999,815	11,651,374
Skip Away, 1993 h., by Skip Trial	4	38	18	10	6	9,616,360	10,928,087
Kelso, 1957 g., by Your Host	8	63	39	12	2	1,977,896	9,903,226
Alysheba, 1984 h., by Alydar	3	26	11	8	2	6,679,242	9,704,457
Round Table, 1954 h., by *Princequillo	4	66	43	8	5	1,749,869	9,307,233
Fantastic Light, 1996 h., by Rahy	4	25	12	5	3	8,486,957	9,101,869
Pleasantly Perfect, 1998 h., by Pleasant Colony	4	18	9	3	2	7,789,880	7,860,856
Silver Charm,1994 h., by Silver Buck	4	24	12	7	2	6,944,369	7,809,509
Smarty Jones, 2001 c., by Elusive Quality	2	9	8	1	0	7,613,155	7,614,198
Nashua, 1952 h., by *Nasrullah	3	30	22	4	1	1,288,565	7,393,745
Captain Steve, 1997 h., by Fly So Free	3	25	9	3	7	6,828,356	7,302,225
Citation, 1945 h., by Bull Lea	4	45	32	10	2	1,085,760	7,153,398
Best Pal, 1988 g., by *Habitony	7	47	18	11	4	5,668,245	7,118,736
Stymie, 1941 h., by Equestrian	7	131	35	33	28	918,485	7,036,886
Tiznow, 1997 h., by Cee's Tizzy	2	15	8	4	2	6,427,830	6,881,778
Buckpasser, 1963 h., by Tom Fool	3	31	25	4	1	1,462,014	6,871,184
Sunday Silence, 1986 h., by Halo	3	14	9	5	0	4,968,554	6,827,395
Singspiel (Ire), 1992 h., by In the Wings (GB)	4	20	9	8	0	5,952,825	6,815,324
Easy Goer, 1986 h., by Alydar	3	20	14	5	1	4,873,770	6,733,516
Spend a Buck, 1982 h., by Buckaroo	2	15	10	3	2	4,220,689	6,583,957
Taiki Blizzard, 1991 h., by Seattle Slew	4	23	6	8	2	5,523,549	6,416,247
Carry Back, 1958 h., by Saggy	4	62	21	11	11	1,241,165	6,298,886
Creme Fraiche, 1982 g., by Rich Cream	6	64	17	12	13	4,024,727	6,068,689
Armed, 1941 g., by Bull Lea	7	81	41	20	10	817,475	6,067,452
Spectacular Bid, 1976 h., by Bold Bidder	3	30	26	2	1	2,781,608	5,942,276
Unbridled, 1987 h., by Fappiano	3	24	8	6	6	4,489,475	5,937,304
Medaglia d'Oro, 1999 h., by El Prado (Ire)	4	17	8	7	0	5,754,720	5,886,563
Slew o' Gold, 1980 h., by Seattle Slew	3	21	12	5	1	3,533,534	5,708,348
Whirlaway, 1938 h., by *Blenheim II	4	60	32	15	9	561,161	5,698,920
Ferdinand, 1983 h., by Nijinsky II	4	29	8	9	6	3,777,978	5,617,772
Forego, 1970 g., by *Forli	6	57	34	9	7	1,938,957	5,603,687
High Chaparral (Ire), 1999 h., by Sadler's Wells	3	13	10	1	2	5,331,231	5,513,959
Affirmed, 1975 h., by Exclusive Native	3	29	22	5	1	2,393,818	5,511,146
Jim and Tonic (Fr), 1994 g., by Double Bed (Fr)	7	39	13	13	4	4,975,807	5,402,864
Street Cry (Ire), 1998 h., by Machiavellian	3	12	5	6	1	5,150,837	5,376,244
Swoon's Son, 1953 h., by The Doge	4	51	30	10	3	970,605	5,363,112
Precisionist, 1981 h., by Crozier	5	46	20	10	4	3,485,398	5,355,868
Damascus, 1964 h., by Sword Dancer	3	32	21	7	3	1,176,781	5,272,234
Snow Chief, 1983 h., by Reflected Glory	3	24	13	3	5	3,383,210	5,147,193
Daylami (Ire), 1994 h., by Doyoun	4	21	11	3	4	4,614,762	5,127,695
Assault, 1943 h., by Bold Venture	6	42	18	6	7	675,470	5,046,305

Horse, YOB, Sex, Sire	Yrs. Raced	Starts	1st	2nd	3rd	Nominal Earnings	Deflated Earnings
Behrens, 1994 h., by Pleasant Colony	4	27	9	8	3	$4,563,500	$5,033,032
Awesome Again, 1994 h., by Deputy Minister	2	12	9	0	2	4,374,590	4,914,159
Bet Twice, 1984 h., by Sportin' Life	3	26	10	6	4	3,308,599	4,885,977
Native Diver, 1959 h., by Imbros	7	81	37	7	12	1,026,500	4,880,385
Cryptoclearance, 1984 h., by Fappiano	4	44	12	10	7	3,376,327	4,841,850
Swaps, 1952 h., by *Khaled	3	25	19	2	2	848,900	4,824,634
Seabiscuit, 1933 h., by Hard Tack	6	89	33	15	13	437,730	4,790,423
Devil His Due, 1989 h., by Devil's Bag	4	41	11	12	3	3,920,405	4,783,596
Dahlia, 1970 m., by *Vaguely Noble	5	48	15	3	7	1,489,105	4,682,950
Native Dancer, 1950 h., by Polynesian	3	22	21	1	0	785,240	4,672,863
Pilsudski (Ire), 1992 h., by Polish Precedent	4	22	10	6	2	4,080,297	4,663,266
T. V. Lark, 1957 h., by *Indian Hemp	4	72	19	13	6	902,194	4,629,943
Lady's Secret, 1982 m., by Secretariat	4	45	25	9	3	3,021,325	4,627,520
Fort Marcy, 1964 g., by *Amerigo	6	75	21	18	14	1,109,791	4,619,512
Roman Brother, 1961 g., by Third Brother	4	42	16	10	5	943,473	4,606,471
Secretariat, 1970 h., by Bold Ruler	2	21	16	3	1	1,316,808	4,561,168
Seeking the Pearl, 1994 m., by Seeking the Gold	4	21	8	2	3	4,021,716	4,545,941
Steinlen (GB), 1983 h., by Habitat	5	45	20	10	7	3,297,169	4,545,523
Gulch, 1984 h., by Mr. Prospector	3	32	13	8	4	3,095,521	4,528,236
Trinycarol (Ven), 1979 m., by Velvet Cap	4	29	18	3	1	2,644,392	4,517,872
Dr. Fager, 1964 h., by Rough'n Tumble	3	22	18	2	1	1,002,642	4,482,007
Find, 1950 g., by Discovery	8	110	22	27	27	803,615	4,459,116
Sandpit (Brz), 1989 h., by Baynoun (Ire)	7	40	14	11	6	3,812,597	4,430,519
Theatrical (Ire), 1982 h., by Nureyev	4	22	10	4	2	2,940,036	4,378,208
Black Tie Affair (Ire), 1986 h., by Miswaki	4	45	18	9	6	3,370,694	4,373,117
Strike the Gold, 1988 h., by Alydar	4	31	6	8	5	3,457,026	4,371,797
Symboli Rudolf (Jpn), 1981 h., by Partholon	4	16	13	1	1	2,764,980	4,370,407
Cat Thief, 1996 h., by Storm Cat	3	30	4	9	8	3,951,012	4,364,397
Sword Dancer, 1956 h., by Sunglow	3	39	15	7	4	829,610	4,314,013
Swain (Ire), 1992 h., by Nashwan	4	22	10	4	6	3,797,566	4,306,821
Sulamani (Ire), 1999 h., by Hernando (Fr)	2	11	5	2	1	4,215,365	4,270,096
Sky Classic, 1987 h., by Nijinsky II	4	29	15	6	1	3,320,398	4,248,658
*Cougar II, 1966 h., by Tale of Two Cities	6	50	20	7	17	1,172,625	4,236,008
Point Given, 1998 h., by Thunder Gulch	2	13	9	3	0	3,968,500	4,210,909
Dance Smartly, 1988 m., by Danzig	3	17	12	2	3	3,263,835	4,187,101
Azeri, 1998 m., by Jade Hunter	4	24	17	4	0	4,079,820	4,186,275
Great Communicator, 1983 h., by Key to the Kingdom	6	56	14	10	7	2,922,615	4,169,704
Susan's Girl, 1969 m., by Quadrangle	5	63	29	14	11	1,251,668	4,160,011
Bold Ruler, 1954 h., by *Nasrullah	3	33	23	4	2	764,204	4,127,021
Exceller, 1973 h., by *Vaguely Noble	5	33	15	5	6	1,674,587	4,119,402
Paradise Creek, 1989 h., by Irish River (Fr)	4	25	14	7	1	3,401,416	4,116,639
Paseana (Arg), 1987 m., by Ahmad	6	36	19	10	2	3,317,427	4,110,294
Gentlemen (Arg), 1992 h., by Robin des Bois	5	24	13	4	2	3,608,558	4,099,552
Lando (Ger), 1990 h., by Acatenango	4	24	10	3	1	3,438,727	4,096,987
Candy Spots, 1960 h., by *Nigromante	3	22	12	5	1	824,718	4,092,973
First Landing, 1956 h., by *Turn-to	3	37	19	9	2	779,577	4,070,898
Mongo, 1959 h., by *Royal Charger	4	46	22	10	4	820,766	4,063,843
Manila, 1983 h., by Lyphard	3	18	12	5	0	2,692,799	4,055,529
Allez France, 1970 m., by *Sea-Bird	4	21	13	3	1	1,262,801	4,039,520
Almutawakel (GB), 1995 h., by Machiavellian	4	19	4	4	1	3,643,021	4,027,266
Riva Ridge, 1969 h., by First Landing	3	30	17	3	1	1,111,497	4,025,769
Crimson Satan, 1959 h., by Spy Song	4	58	18	9	9	796,077	3,993,596
Broad Brush, 1983 h., by Ack Ack	3	27	14	5	5	2,656,793	3,988,336
Cicada, 1959 m., by Bryan G.	4	42	23	8	6	783,674	3,953,269
Gate Dancer, 1981 h., by Sovereign Dancer	4	28	7	8	7	2,501,705	3,937,511
Bertrando, 1989 h., by Skywalker	5	24	9	6	2	3,185,610	3,936,061
Forty Niner, 1985 h., by Mr. Prospector	2	19	11	5	0	2,726,000	3,928,569
Bally Ache, 1957 h., by *Ballydam	2	31	16	9	4	758,522	3,923,331
Victory Gallop, 1995 h., by Cryptoclearance	3	17	9	5	1	3,505,895	3,912,210
With Approval, 1986 h., by Caro (Ire)	3	23	13	5	1	2,863,540	3,894,077
Gun Bow, 1960 h., by Gun Shot	3	42	17	8	4	798,722	3,893,484
Bayakoa (Arg), 1984 m., by Consultant's Bid	6	39	21	9	0	2,861,701	3,884,733
Social Outcast, 1950 g., by Shut Out	5	58	18	9	6	668,300	3,878,664
Serena's Song, 1992 m., by Rahy	3	38	18	11	3	3,283,388	3,847,014
Awad, 1990 h., by Caveat	7	70	14	10	11	3,270,131	3,839,808
Chief Bearhart, 1993 h., by Chief's Crown	4	26	12	5	3	3,381,557	3,833,035
Moon Ballad (Ire), 1999 h., by Singspiel (Ire)	3	14	5	3	1	4,364,791	3,797,986
Spain, 1997 m., by Thunder Gulch	4	35	9	9	7	3,540,542	3,790,169
Hansel, 1988 h., by Woodman	2	14	7	2	3	2,936,586	3,780,247
On Trust, 1944 h., by *Alibhai	7	88	23	19	13	554,145	3,756,275
Harlan's Holiday, 1999 h., by Harlan	3	22	9	6	1	3,632,664	3,751,393

Female All-Time Leading Earners by Deflated Dollars

Horse, YOB, Sex, Sire	Yrs. Raced	Starts	1st	2nd	3rd	Nominal Earnings	Deflated Earnings
Dahlia, 1970 m., by *Vaguely Noble	5	48	15	3	7	$1,489,105	$4,682,950
Lady's Secret, 1982 m., by Secretariat	4	45	25	9	3	3,021,325	4,627,520
Seeking the Pearl, 1994 m., by Seeking the Gold	4	21	8	2	3	4,021,716	4,545,941
Trinycarol (Ven), 1979 m., by Velvet Cap	4	29	18	3	1	2,644,392	4,517,872
Dance Smartly, 1988 m., by Danzig	3	17	12	2	3	3,263,835	4,187,101
Azeri, 1998 m., by Jade Hunter	4	24	17	4	0	4,079,820	4,186,275
Susan's Girl, 1969 m., by Quadrangle	5	63	29	14	11	1,251,668	4,160,011
Paseana (Arg), 1987 m., by Ahmad	6	36	19	10	2	3,317,427	4,110,394
Allez France, 1970 m., by *Sea-Bird	4	21	13	3	1	1,262,801	4,039,520
Cicada, 1959 m., by Bryan G.	4	42	23	8	6	783,674	3,953,269
Bayakoa (Arg), 1984 m., by Consultant's Bid	6	39	21	9	9	2,861,701	3,884,733
Serena's Song, 1992 m., by Rahy	3	38	18	11	3	3,283,388	3,847,014
Spain, 1997 m., by Thunder Gulch	4	35	9	9	7	3,540,542	3,790,169
Shuvee, 1966 m., by Nashua	4	44	16	10	6	890,445	3,620,609
Life's Magic, 1981 m., by Cox's Ridge	3	32	8	11	6	2,255,218	3,600,023
All Along (Fr), 1979 m., by Targowice	4	21	9	4	2	2,125,809	3,516,117
Triptych, 1982 m., by Riverman	5	41	14	5	11	2,318,946	3,456,143
Silverbulletday, 1996 m., by Silver Deputy	3	23	15	3	1	3,093,207	3,432,009
Straight Deal, 1962 m., by Hail to Reason	6	99	21	21	9	733,020	3,374,558
Gallorette, 1942 m., by *Challenger II	5	72	21	20	13	445,535	3,369,534
Escena, 1993 m., by Strawberry Road (Aus)	4	29	11	9	3	2,962,639	3,345,940
Let's Elope (NZ), 1987 m., by Nassipour	5	26	11	0	5	2,528,902	3,230,711
Flawlessly, 1988 m., by Affirmed	5	28	16	4	3	2,572,536	3,206,027
Banshee Breeze, 1995 m., by Unbridled	3	18	10	5	2	2,784,798	3,102,350
Bewitch, 1945 m., by Bull Lea	5	55	20	10	11	462,605	3,098,480
Miesque, 1984 m., by Nureyev	3	16	12	3	1	2,070,163	3,029,958
Beautiful Pleasure, 1995 m., by Maudlin	5	25	10	5	2	2,734,078	3,007,086
Estrapade, 1980 m., by *Vaguely Noble	4	30	12	5	5	1,937,142	2,978,644
Top Flight, 1929 m., by *Dis Donc	2	16	12	0	0	275,900	2,967,736
Tosmah, 1961 m., by Tim Tam	4	39	23	6	2	612,588	2,967,715
Safely Kept, 1986 m., by Horatius	4	31	24	2	3	2,194,206	2,935,450
Busher, 1942 m., by War Admiral	3	21	15	3	1	334,035	2,908,332
Ashado, 2001 f., by Saint Ballado	2	14	9	3	2	2,870,440	2,883,279
Dance in the Mood (Jpn), 2001 f., by Sunday Silence	1	9	3	3	0	2,866,978	2,866,978
Honeymoon, 1943 m., by *Beau Pere	6	78	20	14	9	387,760	2,861,743
Old Hat, 1959 m., by Boston Doge	6	80	35	18	9	556,401	2,697,980
Affectionately, 1960 m., by Swaps	4	52	28	8	6	546,659	2,686,917
Heritage of Gold, 1995 m., by Gold Legend	4	28	16	2	4	2,381,762	2,597,803
Open Mind, 1986 m., by Deputy Minister	3	19	12	2	2	1,844,372	2,578,694
Take Charge Lady, 1999 m., by Dehere	3	22	11	7	0	2,480,377	2,571,912
Next Move, 1947 m., by Bull Lea	4	46	17	11	3	398,550	2,539,705
Xtra Heat, 1998 m., by Dixieland Heat	4	35	26	5	2	2,389,635	2,510,555
Sickle's Image, 1948 m., by Sickletoy	5	73	27	13	16	413,275	2,503,200
Gamely, 1964 m., by Bold Ruler	3	41	16	9	6	574,961	2,483,681
Sightseek, 1999 m., by Distant View	3	20	12	5	0	2,445,216	2,480,252
Bed o' Roses, 1947 m., by Rosemont	4	46	18	8	6	383,925	2,463,595
Politely, 1963 m., by *Amerigo	4	49	21	9	5	552,972	2,455,131
Goodbye Halo, 1985 m., by Halo	3	24	11	5	4	1,706,702	2,435,958
Personal Ensign, 1984 m., by Private Account	3	13	13	0	0	1,679,880	2,432,202
Perfect Sting, 1996 m., by Red Ransom	4	21	14	3	0	2,202,042	2,398,360
Very Subtle, 1984 m., by Hoist the Silver	4	29	12	6	4	1,608,360	2,370,263
Family Style, 1983 m., by State Dinner	3	35	10	8	7	1,537,118	2,348,342
Sharp Cat, 1994 m., by Storm Cat	3	22	15	3	0	2,032,575	2,307,402
Convenience, 1968 m., by Fleet Nasrullah	4	35	15	9	4	648,933	2,287,443
Hatoof, 1989 m., by Irish River (Fr)	4	21	9	4	1	1,841,070	2,254,657
Miss Alleged, 1987 m., by Alleged	3	15	5	4	3	1,757,342	2,254,203
Gallant Bloom, 1966 m., by *Gallant Man	3	22	16	1	1	535,739	2,247,391
Numbered Account, 1969 m., by Buckpasser	3	22	14	3	2	607,048	2,242,782
Trillion, 1974 m., by Hail to Reason	3	32	9	14	3	957,413	2,224,612
Pebbles (GB), 1981 m., by Sharpen Up (GB)	3	15	8	4	0	1,419,632	2,218,208
Outstandingly, 1982 m., by Exclusive Native	4	28	10	4	3	1,412,206	2,216,585
The Very One, 1975 m., by One for All	5	71	22	12	9	1,104,623	2,215,861
User Friendly (GB), 1989 m., by Slip Anchor	3	16	8	1	2	1,764,938	2,199,745
Princess Rooney, 1980 m., by Verbatim	3	21	17	2	1	1,343,339	2,192,938
Jewel Princess, 1992 m., by Key to the Mint	4	29	13	4	7	1,904,060	2,192,334
Royal Native, 1956 m., by *Royal Charger	4	49	18	13	3	422,769	2,183,208
You, 1999 m., by You and I	3	23	9	8	2	2,101,353	2,181,584
Winning Colors, 1985 m., by Caro (Ire)	3	19	8	3	1	1,526,837	2,176,884
Heavenly Prize, 1991 m., by Seeking the Gold	4	18	9	6	3	1,825,940	2,173,618

Leading Earners by Foal Crop

YOB	MALE, Sex, Sire	Yrs. Raced	St. Strts	Wins	St. Wins	Earnings	FEMALE, Sex, Sire	Yrs. Raced	St. Strts	Wins	St. Wins	Earnings
2002	Wilko, c., Awesome Aain	1	12	3	1	$934,074	Sweet Catomine, f., Storm Cat	1	4	3	3	$799,800
2001	Smarty Jones, c., Elusive Quality	2	9	8	7	7,613,155	Ashado, f., Saint Ballado	2	14	9	8	2,870,440
2000	Funny Cide, g., Distorted Humor	3	21	8	6	3,174,485	Storm Flag Flying, f., Storm Cat	3	14	7	5	1,951,828
1999	Medaglia d'Oro, h., El Prado (Ire)	4	17	8	7	5,754,720	Take Charge Lady, m., Dehere	3	22	11	9	2,480,377
1998	Pleasantly Perfect, h., Pleasant Colony	4	18	9	6	7,789,880	Azeri, m., Jade Hunter	4	24	17	14	4,079,820
1997	Captain Steve, h., Fly So Free	3	25	9	8	6,828,356	Spain, m., Thunder Gulch	4	35	9	7	3,540,542
1996	Fantastic Light, h., Rahy	4	25	12	10	8,486,957	Silverbulletday, m., Silver Deputy	3	23	15	14	3,093,207
1995	Victory Gallop, h., Cryptoclearance	3	17	9	7	3,505,895	Banshee Breeze, m., Unbridled	3	18	10	8	2,784,798
1994	Silver Charm, h., Silver Buck	4	24	12	11	6,944,369	Seeking the Pearl, m., Seeking the Gold	4	21	8	7	4,021,716
1993	Skip Away, h., Skip Trial	4	38	18	16	9,616,360	Escena, m., Strawberry Road (Aus)	4	29	11	7	2,962,639
1992	Thunder Gulch, h., Gulch	2	16	9	8	2,915,086	Serena's Song, m., Rahy	3	38	18	17	3,283,388
1991	Taiki Blizzard, h., Seattle Slew	4	23	6	3	5,523,549	Heavenly Prize, m., Seeking the Gold	4	18	9	8	1,825,940
1990	Cigar, h., Palace Music	4	33	19	15	9,999,815	Ski Paradise, m., Lyphard	3	20	6	5	1,470,588
1989	Devil His Due, h., Devil's Bag	4	41	11	9	3,920,405	Hatoof, m., Irish River (Fr)	4	21	9	8	1,841,070
1988	Best Pal, g., *Habitony	7	47	18	17	5,668,245	Dance Smartly, m., Danzig	3	17	12	10	3,263,835
1987	Unbridled, h., Fappiano	3	24	8	5	4,489,475	Miss Alleged, m., Alleged	3	15	5	4	1,757,342
1986	Sunday Silence, h., Halo	3	14	9	7	4,968,554	Safely Kept, m., Horatius	4	31	24	22	2,194,206
1985	Forty Niner, h., Mr. Prospector	2	19	11	9	2,726,000	Goodbye Halo, m., Halo	3	24	11	10	1,706,702
1984	Alysheba, h., Alydar	3	26	11	10	6,679,242	Miesque, m., Nureyev	3	16	12	11	2,070,163
1983	Ferdinand, h., Nijinsky II	4	29	8	7	3,777,978	Family Style, m., State Dinner	3	35	10	9	1,537,118
1982	Spend a Buck, h., Buckaroo	2	15	10	7	4,220,689	Lady's Secret, m., Secretariat	4	45	25	22	3,021,325
1981	Precisionist, h., Crozier	5	46	20	17	3,485,398	Life's Magic, m., Cox's Ridge	3	32	8	7	2,255,218
1980	Slew o' Gold, h., Seattle Slew	3	21	12	8	3,533,534	Estrapade, m., *Vaguely Noble	4	30	12	10	1,937,142
1979	Majesty's Prince, h., His Majesty	4	43	12	9	2,077,796	Sefa's Beauty, m., Lt. Stevens	5	52	25	11	1,171,628
1978	Silveyville, h., *Petrone	8	56	19	14	1,282,880	Sintrillium, m., Sinister Purpose	5	46	14	9	743,602
1977	Temperence Hill, h., Stop the Music	3	31	11	9	1,567,650	Bold 'n Determined, m., Bold and Brave	3	20	16	11	949,599
1976	Spectacular Bid, h., Bold Bidder	3	30	26	23	2,781,608	Track Robbery, m., No Robbery	6	59	22	13	1,098,537
1975	John Henry, g., Ole Bob Bowers	8	83	39	30	6,591,860	The Very One, m., One for All	5	71	22	13	1,104,623
1974	Seattle Slew, h., Bold Reasoning	3	17	14	9	1,208,726	Trillion, m., Hail to Reason	3	32	9	8	957,413
1973	Exceller, h., *Vaguely Noble	5	33	15	13	1,674,587	Optimistic Gal, m., Sir Ivor	2	21	13	10	686,861
1972	Foolish Pleasure, h., What a Pleasure	3	26	16	12	1,216,705	Ivanjica, m., Sir Ivor	3	15	6	5	626,682
1971	Sharp Gary, g., Carry Back	7	115	16	8	535,198	Chris Evert, m., Swoon's Son	3	15	10	7	679,475
1970	Forego, g., *Forli	6	57	34	24	1,938,957	Dahlia, m., *Vaguely Noble	5	48	15	14	1,489,105
1969	Riva Ridge, h., First Landing	3	30	17	13	1,111,497	Susan's Girl, m., Quadrangle	5	63	29	24	1,251,668
1968	Run the Gantlet, h., Tom Rolfe	3	21	9	7	559,079	Convenience, m., Fleet Nasrullah	4	35	15	8	648,933
1967	Loud, g., *Herbager	7	88	12	3	527,779	Saturnina, m., *Ballydonnell	5	107	47	8	392,195
1966	Ack Ack, h., Battle Joined	4	27	19	13	636,641	Shuvee, m., Nashua	4	44	16	15	890,445
1965	Nodouble, h., *Noholme II	4	42	13	9	846,749	Gay Matelda, m., Sir Gaylord	3	37	9	5	409,945
1964	Damascus, h., Sword Dancer	3	32	21	17	1,176,781	Gamely, m., Bold Ruler	3	41	16	13	574,961
1963	Buckpasser, h., Tom Fool	3	31	25	21	1,462,014	Politely, m., *Amerigo	4	49	21	13	552,972
1962	Tom Rolfe, h., *Ribot	3	32	16	9	671,297	Straight Deal, m., Hail to Reason	6	99	21	13	733,020
1961	Roman Brother, g., Third Brother	4	42	16	10	943,473	Tosmah, m., Tim Tam	4	39	23	16	612,588
1960	Candy Spots, h., *Nigromante	3	22	12	9	824,718	Affectionately, m., Swaps	4	52	28	18	546,659
1959	Native Diver, h., Imbros	7	81	37	33	1,026,500	Cicada, m., Bryan G.	4	42	23	18	783,674
1958	Carry Back, h., Saggy	4	62	21	14	1,241,165	Bowl of Flowers, m., Sailor	2	16	10	6	398,504
1957	Kelso, h., Your Host	8	63	39	31	1,977,896	Airmans Guide, m., One Count	3	20	13	8	315,673
1956	Sword Dancer, h., Sunglow	3	39	15	10	829,610	Royal Native, m., *Royal Charger	4	49	18	11	422,769
1955	Bald Eagle, h., *Nasrullah	4	29	12	12	692,946	Idun, m., *Royal Charger	3	30	17	9	392,490
1954	Round Table, h., *Princequillo	4	66	43	31	1,749,869	Endine, m., *Rico Monte	3	45	10	4	306,547
1953	Swoon's Son, h., The Doge	4	51	30	22	970,605	Dotted Line, m., *Princequillo	5	67	11	5	324,159
1952	Nashua, h., *Nasrullah	3	30	22	19	1,288,565	High Voltage, m., *Ambiorix	3	45	13	10	362,240
1951	Determine, h., *Alibhai	3	44	18	16	573,360	Queen Hopeful, m., Roman	5	48	18	10	365,044
1950	Find, g., Discovery	8	110	22	13	803,615	Grecian Queen, m., *Heliopolis	4	53	12	9	323,575
1949	Mark-Ye-Well, h., Bull Lea	4	40	14	11	581,910	Real Delight, m., Bull Lea	2	15	12	10	261,822
1948	Crafty Admiral, h., Fighting Fox	4	39	18	12	499,200	Sickle's Image, m., Sickletoy	5	73	27	10	413,275
1947	Oil Capitol, h., *Mahmoud	5	80	19	14	580,756	Next Move, m., Bull Lea	4	46	17	12	398,550
1946	Ponder, h., Pensive	4	41	14	11	541,275	Two Lea, m., Bull Lea	4	26	15	9	309,250
1945	Citation, h., Bull Lea	4	45	32	22	1,085,760	Bewitch, m., Bull Lea	5	55	20	15	462,605
1944	On Trust, h., *Alibhai	7	88	23	11	554,145	But Why Not, m., Blue Larkspur	5	46	12	8	295,155
1943	Assault, h., Bold Venture	6	42	18	15	675,470	Honeymoon, m., *Beau Pere	6	78	20	13	387,760
1942	Pavot, h., Case Ace	4	32	14	12	373,365	Gallorette, m., *Challenger II	5	72	21	13	445,535
1941	Stymie, h., Equestrian	7	131	35	25	918,485	Twilight Tear, m., Bull Lea	3	24	18	10	202,165
1940	Count Fleet, h., Reigh Count	2	21	16	9	250,300	Happy Issue, m., Bow to Me	9	157	27	5	225,424
1939	First Fiddle, h., *Royal Minstrel	6	95	23	10	398,610	Vagrancy, m., *Sir Gallahad III	3	42	15	9	102,480
1938	Whirlaway, h., *Blenheim II	4	60	32	22	561,161	Moon Maiden, m., *Challenger II	6	109	19	1	76,780
1937	Bimelech, h., Black Toney	3	15	11	8	248,745	Fairy Chant, m., Chance Shot	3	42	10	7	81,985
1936	Challedon, h., *Challenger II	5	44	20	17	334,660	Loveday, m., Petee-Wrack	6	85	17	5	56,225
1935	Stagehand, h., *Sickle	3	25	9	6	200,110	Jacola, m., *Jacopo	3	25	11	4	70,060
1934	War Admiral, h., Man o' War	4	26	21	15	273,240	Dawn Play, m., Clock Tower	2	14	4	3	50,800
1933	Seabiscuit, h., Hard Tack	6	89	33	26	437,730	Columbiana, m., Petee-Wrack	4	28	11	1	60,925
1932	Rosemont, h., The Porter	4	23	7	5	168,750	Esposa, m., Espino	7	96	19	15	132,055
1931	Top Row, h., Peanuts	5	42	14	11	213,870	Mata Hari, m., Peter Hastings	2	16	7	5	66,699
1930	Ladysman, h., Pompey	5	22	8	5	134,310	Swivel, m., *Swift and Sure	2	24	5	2	74,955

All-Time Leading Earners by State Where Bred 1954-2004

Alabama

MALE, YOB, Sex, Sire	Yrs Raced	Strts	Wins	SWs	Earnings	FEMALE, YOB, Sex, Sire	Yrs Raced	Strts	Wins	SWs	Earnings
Winonly, 1957 h., Olympia	5	64	21	11	$326,264	My Portrait, 1958 m., Olympia	5	94	17	3	$261,275
Lombardi Time, 1987 g., Lombardi	6	68	25	5	270,933	Rocky Turn, 1995 m., Rocky Mountain	6	62	10	0	158,335
Alpena Magic, 1990 g., L'Enjoleur	13	145	16	0	205,872	Blacksher, 1995 m., Reack Boldly	7	82	18	0	155,520
Sky Gem, 1960 h., *Quibu	4	63	12	2	197,573	Comalagold, 2000 f., Royal Empire	3	20	6	2	135,540
Alagon, 1989 g., Rajab	6	80	10	3	169,353	Vicki's Ryde, 1987 m., Society Max	7	81	24	1	130,758
Chief Tudor, 1997 g., Chief Persuasion	6	53	8	3	164,180	Teacher's Art, 1964 m., *Quibu	3	15	5	2	121,494
He's a Duster, 1991 g., Stark Duster	10	112	11	0	146,364	Georges Cherub, 1985 m., If This Be So	5	76	11	0	101,905
Ezgo, 1954 g., Olympia	6	72	12	4	135,731	Darling's Bid, 1993 m., Prospector's Bid	4	37	7	0	101,141
King Oasis, 1974 h., Island Kingdom	8	102	32	0	134,508	Jem Klip, 1988 m., Luck's Reality	8	102	12	0	81,835
Knight Tres, 1994 g., Knight of Old	8	107	16	0	130,693	Sun Block, 2000 m., Shot Block	3	12	4	1	80,417

Alaska

MALE, YOB, Sex, Sire	Yrs Raced	Strts	Wins	SWs	Earnings	FEMALE, YOB, Sex, Sire	Yrs Raced	Strts	Wins	SWs	Earnings
Austin Texas, 1988 g., Tom Tulle	7	76	9	0	$27,778	Ice Blue Moon, 1979 m., *Hard Water	4	60	4	0	$15,146
Cope Stetic, 1983 h., Romeo	3	36	3	0	9,157	Murph's Pet, 1979 m., J. R.'s Pet	3	21	2	0	7,911
Whistling Johnny, 1975 h., Whistling Kettle	2	15	1	0	3,202	Princess Will Win, 1988 m., Will Win	2	6	1	0	2,970

Arizona

MALE, YOB, Sex, Sire	Yrs Raced	Strts	Wins	SWs	Earnings	FEMALE, YOB, Sex, Sire	Yrs Raced	Strts	Wins	SWs	Earnings
Coyote Lakes, 1994 g., Society Max	8	63	20	5	$728,337	Monrow, 1996 m., Fool the Experts	5	43	17	3	$287,344
First Intent, 1989 g., Prima Voce	7	63	12	2	524,357	Knoll Lake, 1998 m., Benton Creek	5	26	12	9	270,155
Last Don B., 1987 g., Don B.	9	104	40	15	471,461	Nervous John, 1976 m., Nervous Energy	4	44	14	11	257,686
Faro, 1982 h., Crafty Drone	7	59	20	6	460,103	To the Post, 1989 m., Bold Ego	4	22	11	7	241,912
G Malleah, 1991 g., Fool the Experts	10	61	17	13	439,613	Bueno, 1992 m., Society Max	6	49	14	9	233,130
Peaked, 1985 h., Drone	6	43	16	11	398,338	Left the Latch, 1991 m., Society Max	6	40	16	5	207,848
Tropic Ruler, 1979 g., Key Rulla	4	21	11	4	395,898	The Lord's Tune, 1997 m.,	3	26	12	0	176,305
Radar Ahead, 1975 h., *Repicado II	5	17	9	4	390,125	Relaunch a Tune					
Hyder, 1997 g., Calumar	6	50	13	0	348,823	Hugafool, 1994 m., Fool the Experts	5	29	9	4	175,653
Mad Key, 1977 h., Key Rulla	7	62	21	8	288,779	La Paz, 1988 m., Hold Your Peace	4	26	8	3	175,431
						Ayanna, 1999 m., In Excess (Ire)	3	12	3	2	162,498

Arkansas

MALE, YOB, Sex, Sire	Yrs Raced	Strts	Wins	SWs	Earnings	FEMALE, YOB, Sex, Sire	Yrs Raced	Strts	Wins	SWs	Earnings
Nodouble, 1965 h., *Noholme II	4	42	13	9	$846,749	Humble Clerk, 1997 m., Humble Eleven	3	17	6	4	$503,545
Dust On the Bottle, 1995 h., Temperence Hill	7	81	11	4	683,312	Ruddy Eagle, 1990 m., Beau's Leader	6	82	15	5	468,680
						Nurse Dopey, 1987 m., Dr. Blum	4	32	16	11	456,362
Beau's Town, 1998 g., Beau Genius	4	21	12	8	611,930	Stoney Jody, 1994 m., Silver Survivor	3	39	14	1	384,813
Never Forgotten, 1984 g., Bold L. B.	8	119	15	6	499,606	Biolage, 1989 m., Hurricane Ed	7	122	12	1	294,983
E J Harley, 1992 g., Beat Inflation	10	54	17	4	456,915	Jay's Sue, 1979 m., Jahan	5	51	18	5	282,560
Lanyons Star, 1988 g., Suzanne's Star	10	127	21	4	450,915	Humble Eight, 1992 m., Seattle Battle	4	34	6	4	278,450
Temperence Time, 1996 g., Temperence Hill	6	39	10	6	436,860	Tsu Tsu Won, 1993 m., Air Forbes Won	10	117	18	0	270,878
						Cato Double, 1980 m., Nodouble	4	56	10	3	265,869
Dirty Mike, 1995 g., Temperence Hill	8	84	16	2	415,478	Turn to the Queen, 1993 m.,	4	25	6	1	263,905
Be a Agent, 1984 h., Be a Prospect	7	81	16	0	355,362	Lyphard's Ridge					
Up Limit, 1978 g., Decimator	7	68	23	4	353,216						

California

MALE, YOB, Sex, Sire	Yrs Raced	Strts	Wins	SWs	Earnings	FEMALE, YOB, Sex, Sire	Yrs Raced	Strts	Wins	SWs	Earnings
Tiznow, 1997 h., Cee's Tizzy	2	15	8	7	$6,427,830	Fran's Valentine, 1982 m., Saros (GB)	4	34	13	12	$1,375,465
Best Pal, 1988 g., *Habitony	7	47	18	17	5,668,245	Brown Bess, 1982 m., *Petrone	6	36	16	11	1,300,920
Snow Chief, 1983 h., Reflected Glory	3	24	13	12	3,383,210	Gourmet Girl, 1995 m., Cee's Tizzy	5	33	9	6	1,255,373
Bertrando, 1989 h., Skywalker	5	24	9	8	3,185,610	Lazy Slusan, 1995 m., Slewvescent	5	47	12	10	1,150,410
Free House, 1994 h., Smokester	4	22	9	8	3,178,971	Feverish, 1995 m., Pirate's Bounty	4	42	12	8	908,983
General Challenge, 1996 g., General Meeting	4	21	9	4	2,877,178	Soviet Problem, 1990 m., Moscow Ballet	4	20	15	10	905,546
						Summer Wind Dancer, 2000 m., Siberian Summer	3	18	5	4	898,762
Budroyale, 1993 g., Cee's Tizzy	7	52	17	7	2,840,810						
Nostalgia's Star, 1982 h., Nostalgia	5	59	9	7	2,154,827	Southern Truce, 1988 m., Truce Maker	6	50	19	7	867,578
Native Desert, 1993 g., Desert Classic	8	74	21	15	1,828,177	Bel's Starlet, 1987 m., Bel Bolide	6	46	13	9	863,802
Flying Continental, 1986 h., Flying Paster	6	51	12	8	1,815,938	Supercilious, 1993 m., Skywalker	5	35	10	8	843,454

Colorado

MALE, YOB, Sex, Sire	Yrs Raced	Strts	Wins	SWs	Earnings	FEMALE, YOB, Sex, Sire	Yrs Raced	Strts	Wins	SWs	Earnings
To Erin, 1976 h., Epic Journey	7	104	28	1	$392,707	Prairie Maiden, 1993 m., Badger Land	4	30	10	5	$294,784
Rusty Canyon, 1975 h., Sound Off	9	94	16	5	372,935	She's Finding Time, 1999 m., Ragtime Rascal	4	31	13	5	183,959
Personal Beau, 1996 g., Personal Flag	7	45	16	9	317,806						

MALE, YOB, Sex, Sire	Yrs Raced	Strts	Wins	SWs	Earnings	FEMALE, YOB, Sex, Sire	Yrs Raced	Strts	Wins	SWs	Earnings
Lewistown, 1992 g., Strike Gold	10	64	21	0	308,547	Windic, 1975 m., Dancing Dervish	5	55	9	1	144,097
Moro Grande, 1995 g., Fuzzy	8	43	7	5	247,119	Jennaly, 1995 m., Alydarmer	5	48	9	3	135,263
High Rover, 1965 g., Star Rover	10	110	33	10	215,701	Gentle Gil, 1981 m., Gilligan	5	53	14	2	134,828
Bitterrook, 1978 h., *David II	5	60	9	2	201,212	Broncomania, 1977 m., Marv 'n Jeff	7	58	19	7	130,418
Moonlight Maverick, 1997 h., Seattle Sleet	4	18	10	6	198,525	Astral Girl, 1988 m., The Astonisher	8	88	20	2	126,527
Defrere's Vixen, 2000 g., Defrere	4	22	5	0	197,480	Miss Bob O Lark, 1975 m., My Lark	4	58	8	0	109,255
Colorado City, 1964 h., Chevation	12	150	27	2	196,248	Slewannavan, 1997 m., Slewacide	6	36	7	2	109,053
						Charmed One, 1984 m., Dewan	5	40	2	0	107,925

Connecticut

MALE, YOB, Sex, Sire	Yrs Raced	Strts	Wins	SWs	Earnings	FEMALE, YOB, Sex, Sire	Yrs Raced	Strts	Wins	SWs	Earnings
Nantucketeer, 1998 h., Departing Prints	5	44	11	0	$189,908	Skipat, 1974 m., Jungle Cove	5	45	26	14	$614,215
Fast Smile, 1970 h., Fast Gun	6	105	32	1	142,795	Leave No Prints, 1995 m., Departing Prints	5	53	8	1	232,377
Belle's Brat, 1974 h., Precision	8	173	27	0	131,872	Onyx Fox, 1974 m., Mr. Hasty	7	105	20	0	109,451
Reserve Native, 1974 h., Native Admiral	9	146	21	0	114,496	Poker's Thunder, 1992 m., Honest Turn	6	92	17	0	108,877
Lonesome Dawn, 1994 g., Fly Till Dawn	5	43	5	0	114,235	Pation, 1977 m., Patrician	7	96	17	0	91,313
President Jim, 1960 g., *Good Shot	7	84	20	1	101,722	Naskrahoney, 1974 m., Naskra	4	38	6	1	83,201
More Coins, 1960 g., Royal Visitor	9	193	23	0	92,858	Diplomatic King, 1984 m., Diplomatic Note	3	40	12	0	75,429
Chapel Creek, 1978 h., Our Native	3	28	4	0	84,456	Good Jane, 1961 m., *Good Shot	4	45	9	1	70,563
Peace Isle, 1956 g., *Good Shot	7	117	19	0	65,579	Lady Petee, 1983 m., Hairy Business	7	63	10	0	69,977
Gisele's Banker, 1969 h., My Banker	11	115	25	0	64,499	Clown's Gal, 1977 m., The Clown	5	88	10	0	66,893

Delaware

MALE, YOB, Sex, Sire	Yrs Raced	Strts	Wins	SWs	Earnings	FEMALE, YOB, Sex, Sire	Yrs Raced	Strts	Wins	SWs	Earnings
Baitman, 1961 g., Assemblyman	8	113	27	3	$298,198	Pokey Lady, 1984 m., Georgeandthedragon	5	74	20	0	$155,275
Golden Immigrant, 1981 g., Medaille d'Or	5	47	6	0	161,380	Wing Flutter, 1969 m., Sunrise Flight	6	86	13	0	90,894
Whale, 1969 g., Impressive	10	123	18	0	119,663	Shoe Off, 1972 m., Rambunctious	4	64	10	0	76,316
Proudest Doon, 1982 h., Matsadoon	3	11	4	2	104,620	Wild Beat, 1979 m., Iron Ruler	2	7	4	0	52,980
Space to Kevin, 1984 h., 5 Travelling Music	78	9	0	9	6,530	Appear, 1969 m., Loom	3	39	7	0	47,689
						Double Hold, 1981 m., Hold Your Peace	4	28	4	0	41,915
Great Depths, 1962 h., *King of the Tudors	7	125	15	1	96,521	Foamy, 1954 m., Tide Rips	7	133	21	0	36,233
Brixton Road, 1963 h., Great Captain	8	133	13	0	58,472	Tacky Lady, 1973 m., Nail	3	50	5	0	35,834
Parish Judge, 1968 g., Delta Judge	4	85	16	0	52,301	Wedge, 1969 m., Fulcrum	3	60	12	0	32,172
Devilfish, 1953 g., Greek Song	7	109	12	0	50,237	Oh She May, 1979 m., Oceans Reward	5	64	7	0	25,555
Frank's Ace, 1973 h., Rock Talk	5	78	5	0	49,600						

Florida

MALE, YOB, Sex, Sire	Yrs Raced	Strts	Wins	SWs	Earnings	FEMALE, YOB, Sex, Sire	Yrs Raced	Strts	Wins	SWs	Earnings
Skip Away, 1993 h., Skip Trial	4	38	18	16	$9,616,360	Beautiful Pleasure, 1995 m., Maudlin	5	25	10	7	$2,734,078
Silver Charm, 1994 h., Silver Buck	4	24	12	11	6,944,369	Jewel Princess, 1992 m., Key to the Mint	4	29	13	10	1,904,060
Unbridled, 1987 h., Fappiano	3	24	8	5	4,489,475	Smok'n Frolic, 1999 m., Smoke Glacken	4	33	9	8	1,534,720
Precisionist, 1981 h., Crozier	5	46	20	17	3,485,398	Halo America, 1990 m., Waquoit	5	40	15	9	1,460,992
Peace Rules, 2000 c., Jules	3	19	9	8	3,084,278	Meadow Star, 1988 m., Meadowlake	3	20	11	10	1,445,740
Sir Bear, 1993 g., Sir Leon	8	71	19	11	2,538,422	Hollywood Wildcat, 1990 m., Kris S.	4	21	12	11	1,432,160
Gate Dancer, 1981 h., Sovereign Dancer	4	28	7	4	2,501,705	Tappiano, 1984 m., Fappiano	4	34	17	14	1,305,522
Holy Bull, 1991 h., Great Above	3	16	13	11	2,481,760	One Dreamer, 1988 m., Relaunch	4	25	12	7	1,266,067
Mecke, 1992 h., Maudlin	4	40	12	9	2,470,550	Glitter Woman, 1994 m., Glitterman	4	23	10	5	1,256,805
Marlin, 1993 h., Sword Dance (Ire)	3	26	9	6	2,448,880	Susan's Girl, 1969 m., Quadrangle	5	63	29	24	1,251,668

Georgia

MALE, YOB, Sex, Sire	Yrs Raced	Strts	Wins	SWs	Earnings	FEMALE, YOB, Sex, Sire	Yrs Raced	Strts	Wins	SWs	Earnings
Bluesthestandard, 1997 g., American Standard	4	33	15	3	$939,818	Vivace, 1993 m., Shot Gun Scott	5	40	20	15	$1,037,671
Maybe Jack, 1993 g., Classic Account	9	121	35	1	534,265	Ayrial Delight, 1992 m., Quick Dip	6	63	18	6	458,992
Southern Slew, 1986 h., Slew Machine	6	41	13	0	207,610	Bobbyrea, 1994 m., Classic Account	4	39	13	0	262,106
Fortunate Lance, 1988 g., Fortunate Prospect	6	53	11	0	186,499	Tia's Orphan Annie, 1995 m., Prospector's Halo	8	93	12	0	163,910
						Rose Darling, 1996 m., Roaring Camp	6	77	11	0	158,800
More Tell, 1996 g., Reach for More	6	56	15	0	161,430	Prime to Go, 1991 m., Classic Go Go	7	72	19	0	142,223
Rise Higher, 1991 g., Reach for More	10	119	20	0	156,289	Sarcasm, 1987 m., Noon Time Spender	9	87	11	0	136,154
My Mac Flashys, 1986 g., Flashy Mac	4	28	8	1	139,195	Rabs Lil Brit Brit, 1991 m., Classic Account	5	47	7	0	123,044
Jeshurun, 1986 h., First Sea Lord	7	73	14	0	115,333						
Reach for Ameri, 1996 g., Reach for More	7	64	9	1	109,786	Paddy's Princess, 1975 m., Irish Dude	5	64	8	0	120,750
Finally Class, 1985 h., Finally Gotcha	6	41	8	1	102,808	Victory Lark, 1980 m., Upset Victory	4	66	17	0	110,315

Hawaii

MALE, YOB, Sex, Sire	Yrs Raced	Strts	Wins	SWs	Earnings	FEMALE, YOB, Sex, Sire	Yrs Raced	Strts	Wins	SWs	Earnings
Hawaii Boy, 1970 g., Kaaba	7	87	17	0	$46,817	Mapu, 1964 m., Hauli	5	99	9	0	$19,078
Kaniala, 1957 h., Bel Canto	10	142	22	0	36,912	Punahou, 1961 m., Skip Khal	7	93	2	0	4,641
Molokai, 1962 h., Skip Khal	11	143	23	0	34,343	Lace Lady, 1973 m., Braefox	2	11	0	0	3,200
Hey Sam, 1961 h., Hauli	5	53	6	0	31,622	Webb's Trouble, 1965 m., Star Hug	3	23	3	0	2,920
Alakahi, 1963 g., Bel Canto	6	98	10	0	27,845	Iwaiha, 1962 m., Hauli	4	26	3	0	2,048
Hoanani, 1958 g., Alicane	9	129	19	0	27,817	Waipio, 1962 m., Skip Khal	3	32	1	0	1,060
Manakuke, 1955 h., Alicane	8	136	15	0	22,810	Sushila, 1962 m., Hauli	2	11	0	0	905
Kawela, 1963 h., Skip Khal	7	89	11	0	20,175	Kauhiwai, 1963 m., Bel Canto	1	12	0	0	737
Pua Nalu, 1969 h., Kaaba	2	32	5	0	17,495	Go Margo, 1959 h., Bel Canto	1	13	0	0	630
Lukanela, 1955 g., Alicane	3	48	7	0	14,544	Bel Senora, 1967 m., Hauli	3	21	1	0	498

Idaho

MALE, YOB, Sex, Sire	Yrs Raced	Strts	Wins	SWs	Earnings	FEMALE, YOB, Sex, Sire	Yrs Raced	Strts	Wins	SWs	Earnings
Gratteau, 1995 g., Synastry	8	50	14	4	$366,644	Angi Go, 1990 m., Idaho's Majesty	5	36	15	8	$437,493
L'Effaceur, 1997 g., Jestic	6	30	10	1	324,064	Lookn Mighty Fine, 1997 m., Peterhof	6	54	12	2	300,851
Lookn East, 1998 g., Eastern Echo	3	28	7	2	243,156	Lethal Leta, 1991 m., Synastry	5	32	12	8	300,602
Northern Provider, 1982 g., Staff Writer	7	51	8	2	231,619	Just Lookn, 1994 m., Synastry	2	18	8	4	213,675
Mining for Fun, 1998 g., L. B. Jaklin	6	58	7	0	208,704	Princess in Charge, 1991 m., Prince Card	5	46	7	0	193,105
San Diego Pete, 1995 g., Santiago Peak	7	63	16	4	199,210	Thou Shalt Not Lie, 1990 m., El Baba	4	39	8	1	183,687
Bojima's Majesty, 1990 g., Bojima	6	84	20	1	189,143	Printasity, 1983 m., Growler	8	81	20	0	170,279
Schuyler Road, 1992 g., Synastry	9	75	14	1	173,399	Riband, 1996 m., Lord of the Apes	6	50	11	0	166,671
Hooten Harry, 1992 g., Unable	6	64	13	0	171,367	Ladys Lil Cruiser, 1992 m., Key to the Carr	5	50	11	1	161,975
Rub, 1995 g., Sharper One	7	67	10	1	166,023	Somer Wonders, 1995 m., Synastry	6	65	13	2	161,571

Illinois

MALE, YOB, Sex, Sire	Yrs Raced	Strts	Wins	SWs	Earnings	FEMALE, YOB, Sex, Sire	Yrs Raced	Strts	Wins	SWs	Earnings
Buck's Boy, 1993 g., Bucksplasher	5	30	16	9	$2,750,148	Two Item Limit, 1998 m., Twining	3	28	7	4	$1,060,585
Polar Expedition, 1991 g., Kodiack	7	49	20	14	1,491,071	Lady Shirl, 1987 m., That's a Nice	6	41	18	10	951,523
Mystery Giver, 1998 g., Dynaformer	4	33	11	8	1,165,900	Bungalow, 1987 m., Lord Avie	3	42	17	9	850,141
Western Playboy, 1986 h., Play Fellow	5	45	8	4	1,128,449	Peach of It, 1986 m., Navajo	5	53	15	9	625,721
Bucks Nephew, 1990 g., Bucksplasher	5	45	15	8	853,618	Summer Mis, 1999 m., Summer Squall	4	23	11	6	542,662
Harham's Sizzler, 1979 h., Good Behaving	7	73	24	14	843,406	Your Ladyship, 1990 m., Moment of Hope	5	47	17	6	539,328
Beboppin Baby, 1993 g., Hatchet Man	8	64	13	3	842,540	Darley Dancer, 1988 m., Play Fellow	6	48	17	5	516,098
Tic N Tin, 1995 g., Lac Ouimet	8	92	28	9	760,840	Valid Vixen, 1985 m., Valid Appeal	4	27	10	6	492,655
Magic Doe, 1995 g., Fast Gold	8	83	17	6	756,253	Faccia Bella, 1996 m., Dixie Brass	7	57	8	4	488,442
Chicago Six, 1995 h., Wild Again	5	39	16	9	733,347	My Own Lovely Lee, 1992 m., Bucksplasher	4	34	13	6	487,149

Indiana

MALE, YOB, Sex, Sire	Yrs Raced	Strts	Wins	SWs	Earnings	FEMALE, YOB, Sex, Sire	Yrs Raced	Strts	Wins	SWs	Earnings
Hillsdale, 1955 h., Take Away	3	41	23	14	$646,935	Honky Star, 1971 m., Bupers	4	39	18	10	$353,012
Fight for Ally, 1997 g., Fit to Fight	6	31	12	6	544,029	Marciann, 1997 m., Speedy Cure	5	29	11	5	278,806
Pass Rush, 1999 h., Crown Ambassador	4	25	5	2	506,225	Senorita Ziggy, 1998 m., Senor Speedy	4	26	9	4	223,960
Navajo, 1970 h., *Grey Dawn II	5	48	22	6	351,982	Ellens Lucky Star, 1999 m., Crown Ambassador	3	19	9	6	205,105
Red's Honor, 1998 h., Glitterman	5	33	11	4	315,650	Lighting Bopers, 1996 m., Cape Storm	3	8	5	4	178,455
Vic's Rebel, 1994 g., Lac Ouimet	5	34	11	4	304,682	Maggie's Dream, 1998 m., Philadream	5	31	7	3	169,472
Pelican Beach, 1998 g., Air Forbes Won	4	34	17	1	277,817	Amanda's Crown, 1999 m., Crown Ambassador	3	21	5	3	161,152
Cancion Alegre, 1997 g., Smilin Singin Sam	6	63	13	0	241,922	Miss Dakota, 2000 f., Never Wavering	3	21	6	3	148,600
Joanies No Phony, 1997 g., Buckhar	6	67	11	1	220,126	Atractiva, 1981 m., Navajo	4	22	13	1	145,145
Key West Kid, 1997 h., Prospector's Music	5	58	17	0	214,809	Lady's Legal Ma Ja, 1997 m., Legalmumblejumble	5	43	2	1	138,678

Iowa

MALE, YOB, Sex, Sire	Yrs Raced	Strts	Wins	SWs	Earnings	FEMALE, YOB, Sex, Sire	Yrs Raced	Strts	Wins	SWs	Earnings
Sure Shot Biscuit, 1996 g., Miracle Heights	6	54	23	13	$1,025,480	Sharky's Review, 1998 m., Sharkey	4	36	15	10	$685,425
Take Me Up, 1998 g., Take Me Out	4	32	12	5	480,189	Nut N Better, 1997 m., Miracle Heights	4	28	14	9	572,828
Cowboy Stuff, 1999 h., Evansville Slew	4	23	11	4	428,280	Lady Tamworth, 1995 m., No Louder	6	68	15	3	567,058
Le Numerous, 1998 g., Numerous	5	49	9	1	307,341	Vaguely Who, 1993 m., Hittias (GB)	6	48	12	5	333,745
Fleet Flyer, 1994 g., Wind Flyer	8	53	14	3	278,428	Sumthintotalkabout, 1997 m., Kyle's Our Man	4	25	9	2	313,928
Deputy Flag, 1996 h., Personal Flag	4	23	6	2	274,586	Danzig Foxxy Woman, 1995 m., Dr. Danzig	4	28	6	4	268,707
Reuben, 1997 h., Rubiano	5	37	7	1	274,043	Sound of Gold, 1998 m., Mutakddim	5	40	13	4	268,243
D. W. Wheels, 1996 g., Owens Troupe	6	53	10	0	247,903	One Fine Shweetie, 1999 m., Shuailaan	4	29	5	2	260,587
I Z Gold, 1992 g., Royal Pavilion	7	62	12	2	247,687	Switch Lanes, 1999 m., Deerhound	3	29	7	1	227,611
Roselle Native, 1994 g., Raja Native	6	46	9	2	243,134	Trisha Runs, 1997 m., Sharkey	3	18	6	1	226,914

Kansas

MALE, YOB, Sex, Sire	Yrs Raced	Strts	Wins	SWs	Earnings
I Dancer, 1995 g., I Enclose	7	68	15	1	$270,862
Gay Revoke, 1958 h., Blue Gay	9	128	27	5	251,251
Kangaroo King, 1993 g., Tarsal	6	53	14	4	211,719
Cheryl's Gazelle, 1995 g., Discover	7	70	11	0	179,306
Rio Gambler, 1990 g., Boca Rio	8	92	17	2	168,904
Jim Dunham, 1991 g., Dunham's Gift	11	109	17	2	168,455
Morning Merry, 2000 g., Scarlet 'n Gray	3	20	7	3	168,210
Liberated Pleasure, 1990 g., Pleasure Prize	7	91	18	4	161,141
Polar Barron, 1996 g., Track Barron	7	52	13	3	159,759
Just a Eclipse, 1994 g., Dream Valley	8	56	23	5	152,277

FEMALE, YOB, Sex, Sire	Yrs Raced	Strts	Wins	SWs	Earnings
Sunnie Do It, 1994 m., Do It Again Dan	8	83	16	9	$316,722
Tiney Toast, 1989 m., Blue Jester	4	28	6	3	217,614
Shero, 1993 m., Glorious Flag	6	63	9	0	164,203
Swinging Janie Gal, 1997 m., A. M. Swinger	6	36	5	0	157,815
Queena Corrina, 1999 m., Here We Come	4	23	7	0	154,170
Amberaja, 1985 m., Kibe	7	90	23	0	141,868
Lady Take the Gold, 1989 m., Gold Ruler	8	116	17	0	137,492
Discreetly Irish, 1998 m., Big Splash	5	52	11	4	128,650
Scarlet Rumor, 1995 m., Scarlet 'n Gray	5	36	9	5	126,310
Krisi My Girl, 1995 m., Victorian Line	4	44	8	2	122,867

Kentucky

MALE, YOB, Sex, Sire	Yrs Raced	Strts	Wins	SWs	Earnings
Fantastic Light, 1996 h., Rahy	4	25	12	10	$8,486,957
Pleasantly Perfect, 1998 h., Pleasant Colony	4	18	9	6	7,789,880
Captain Steve, 1997 h., Fly So Free	3	25	9	8	6,828,356
Alysheba, 1984 h., Alydar	3	26	11	10	6,679,242
John Henry, 1975 g., Ole Bob Bowers	8	83	39	30	6,591,860
Medaglia d'Oro, 1999 h., El Prado (Ire)	4	17	8	7	5,754,720
Taiki Blizzard, 1991 h., Seattle Slew	4	23	6	3	5,523,549
Sunday Silence, 1986 h., Halo	3	14	9	7	4,968,554
Easy Goer, 1986 h., Alydar	3	20	14	12	4,873,770
Behrens, 1994 h., Pleasant Colony	4	27	9	7	4,563,500

FEMALE, YOB, Sex, Sire	Yrs Raced	Strts	Wins	SWs	Earnings
Azeri, 1998 m., Jade Hunter	4	24	17	14	$4,079,820
Spain, 1997 m., Thunder Gulch	4	35	9	7	3,540,542
Serena's Song, 1992 m., Rahy	3	38	18	17	3,283,388
Silverbulletday, 1996 m., Silver Deputy	3	23	15	14	3,093,207
Escena, 1993 m., Strawberry Road (Aus)	4	29	11	7	2,962,639
Ashado, 2001 f., Saint Ballado	2	14	9	8	2,870,440
Banshee Breeze, 1995 m., Unbridled	3	18	10	8	2,784,798
Flawlessly, 1988 m., Affirmed	5	28	16	15	2,572,536
Take Charge Lady, 1999 m., Dehere	3	22	11	9	2,480,377
Sightseek, 1999 m., Distant View	3	20	12	10	2,445,216

Louisiana

MALE, YOB, Sex, Sire	Yrs Raced	Strts	Wins	SWs	Earnings
Scott's Scoundrel, 1992 h., L'Enjoleur	6	50	22	19	$1,270,052
Zarb's Magic, 1993 g., Zarbyev	8	69	23	5	893,946
King Roller, 1991 g., Silent King	9	107	21	5	883,588
Dixie Poker Ace, 1987 g., Patriotically	8	86	27	18	850,126
Free Spirit's Joy, 1988 h., Joey Bob	5	32	8	5	841,277
Oak Hall, 1996 g., Olympio	7	43	18	9	635,067
Nijinsky's Gold, 1989 g., Lot o' Gold	7	45	10	7	622,160
Caro's Royalty, 1993 g., Spruce Bouquet	9	84	20	3	587,743
Magnify, 1993 g., Contested Colors	5	40	14	6	535,681
Zarb's Luck, 199 g., Zarbyev	6	40	11	6	520,320

FEMALE, YOB, Sex, Sire	Yrs Raced	Strts	Wins	SWs	Earnings
Sarah Lane's Oates, 1994 m., Sunshine Forever	7	77	21	15	$888,296
Fit to Scout, 1987 m., Fit to Fight	3	30	8	6	767,600
Hallowed Dreams, 1997 m., Malagra	4	30	25	17	740,144
Eskimo's Angel, 1989 m., Eskimo	5	39	11	8	701,539
Zuppardo Ardo, 1994 m., Zuppardo's Prince	5	39	14	10	667,886
Leslie's Love, 1997 m., Combat Ready	6	56	22	6	642,484
Hope List, 1990 m., List	6	81	20	7	601,475
Up the Apalachee, 1984 m., Apalachee	3	28	14	8	595,935
I Ain't Bluffing, 1994 m., Pine Bluff	3	13	8	6	582,069
Nettie Cometti, 1981 m., *Giacometti	4	33	13	8	571,900

Maine

MALE, YOB, Sex, Sire	Yrs Raced	Strts	Wins	SWs	Earnings
Seboomook, 1976 h., Sunny South	7	96	22	0	$124,837
My Secret Love, 1965 g., Busy Harvest	10	172	24	0	69,853
Sokokis, 1971 h., Midland Man	2	32	5	0	54,232
Atafu, 1966 h., Atoll	9	128	14	0	38,230
Mr. Kippers, 1967 h., Hallursan	3	43	14	0	35,397
Hyperides, 1969 h., Midland Man	9	107	16	0	28,147
Blue Katahdin, 1970 g., Black Mountain	7	115	13	0	25,534
Mr. Jazzman, 1967 h., Midland Man	5	59	12	0	25,090
Hacienda Imperal, 1962 h., Activate	7	112	13	0	17,394
Beau Harvest, 1968 h., Busy Harvest	4	71	8	0	15,044

FEMALE, YOB, Sex, Sire	Yrs Raced	Strts	Wins	SWs	Earnings
North of Boston, 1972 m., Midland Man	4	25	4	0	$40,693
Louisa Midland, 1975 m., George Lewis	3	20	5	0	40,149
Amblast, 1973 m., Blasting Charge	4	36	6	0	31,632
Limington, 1969 m., Black Mountain	2	24	4	1	25,854
Favorite Act, 1959 m., Activate	6	100	14	0	25,075
Irish Dotty, 1959 m., Activate	6	108	16	0	20,665
Carrabasset, 1977 m., George Lewis	2	18	1	0	13,180
Lilac Ribbons, 1971 m., Cap Size	2	11	2	0	10,721
Hacienda Gal, 1967 m., Busy Harvest	4	74	5	0	9,198
Jet's Tru Dan, 1978 m., Danaus	3	34	2	0	8,875

Maryland

MALE, YOB, Sex, Sire	Yrs Raced	Strts	Wins	SWs	Earnings
Cigar, 1990 h., Palace Music	4	33	19	15	$9,999,815
Awad, 1990 h., Caveat	7	70	14	11	3,270,131
Concern, 1991 h., Broad Brush	3	30	7	4	3,079,350
Broad Brush, 1983 h., Ack Ack	3	27	14	12	2,656,793
Little Bold John, 1982 g., John Alden	9	105	38	25	1,956,406
Include, 1997 h., Broad Brush	4	20	10	7	1,659,560
Valley Crossing, 1988 h., Private Account	5	48	8	4	1,616,490
Our New Recruit, 1999 h., Alphabet Soup	3	19	6	2	1,470,915
Ten Keys, 1984 h., Sir Ivor Again	5	54	21	16	1,209,211
Homebuilder, 1984 h., Mr. Prospector	4	60	11	8	1,172,153

FEMALE, YOB, Sex, Sire	Yrs Raced	Strts	Wins	SWs	Earnings
Safely Kept, 1986 m., Horatius	4	31	24	22	$2,194,206
Shine Again, 1997 m., Wild Again	5	34	14	7	1,271,840
Jameela, 1976 m., Rambunctious	4	58	27	16	1,038,704
Urbane, 1992 m., Citidancer	3	18	8	7	1,018,568
Squan Song, 1981 m., Exceller	5	36	18	14	898,444
Thirty Eight Go Go, 1985 m., Thirty Eight Paces	5	46	10	8	871,229
Wide Country, 1988 m., Magesterial	3	26	12	11	819,728
Brilliant Brass, 1987 m., Marine Brass	4	27	16	9	767,051
In the Curl, 1984 m., Shelter Half	8	85	26	10	749,891
Mz. Zill Bear, 1989 m., Salutely	6	41	15	10	740,423

Massachusetts

MALE, YOB, Sex, Sire	Yrs Raced	Strts	Wins	SWs	Earnings	FEMALE, YOB, Sex, Sire	Yrs Raced	Strts	Wins	SWs	Earnings
Rise Jim, 1976 h., Jim J.	5	52	27	12	$528,789	Isadorable, 1983 m., Moleolus	4	39	19	17	$415,018
Garemma, 1986 g., Shananie	5	43	16	1	395,583	Big Miss, 1996 m., Chief Honcho	5	76	16	5	357,834
Jini's Jet, 1998 g., A. P Jet	5	43	16	9	328,820	Sunlit Ridge, 1998 m., Sundance Ridge	5	60	16	10	346,630
Stylish Sultan, 1999 h., Sundance Ridge	4	28	13	10	301,180	Land Ahoy, 1993 m., Oh Say	7	74	14	7	242,765
Galloping Gael, 1994 h., Lost Code	6	50	9	3	297,317	Lt'l Miss D. S., 1990 m., Hiromi the Great	4	54	12	7	220,064
Second Episode, 1992 h., Potentiate	7	68	17	13	274,277	Potential Fire, 1991 m., Potentiate	6	46	10	5	202,938
Papa Ho Ho, 1993 g., On to Glory	8	87	18	6	265,882	Weepecket, 1997 m., Mr. Sparkles	6	56	8	3	184,775
Tonights the Night, 1978 h., Great Mystery	8	115	13	8	258,532	Potential Dreamer, 1991 m., Potentiate	6	76	12	4	184,247
Josiah W., 1977 h., Heat of Battle	7	104	18	2	193,244	African Princess, 1999 m., Sundance Ridge	3	34	7	5	183,930
But Jim, 1987 h., Rise Jim	10	84	12	5	188,699	Dr Margaret, 1997 m., Dr. Blum	3	23	11	6	181,100

Michigan

MALE, YOB, Sex, Sire	Yrs Raced	Strts	Wins	SWs	Earnings	FEMALE, YOB, Sex, Sire	Yrs Raced	Strts	Wins	SWs	Earnings
Tenpins, 1998 h., Smart Strike	4	17	9	5	$1,133,449	Peppen, 1994 m., Pep Up	4	37	15	11	$623,417
Secret Romeo, 1998 h., Service Stripe	5	55	23	17	865,790	Karate Miss, 1995 m., Chicanery Slew	4	38	17	14	602,465
Pongo Boy, 1992 g., Matchlite	9	87	22	12	776,184	Born to Dance, 1999 m., Service Stripe	4	28	10	8	499,719
Badwagon Harry, 1979 h., Ole Bob Bowers	9	121	19	10	742,412	Sefas Rose, 1997 m., Sefapiano	5	32	13	7	488,815
Xclusive Imp, 1994 g., Majesty's Imp	8	87	12	9	584,130	Cashier's Dream, 1999 m., Service Stripe	2	7	5	3	423,042
Thumbsucker, 1979 h., Great Sun	4	31	16	10	525,553	Agiftfrom Bertie, 1993 m., Monetary Gift	4	38	10	9	408,378
Wind Chill, 1983 h., It's Freezing	7	73	15	6	502,492	Farer Belle Lee, 1979 m., Seafarer	5	62	17	9	334,700
Solo Matt, 1986 h., Bucksplasher	4	47	12	5	453,249	My Show, 1986 m., Tilt Up	6	77	19	6	331,408
That Gift, 1997 h., Monetary Gift	6	51	18	6	450,758	North Rustim, 1978 m., Northern Native	5	61	19	15	328,002
Grand Circus Park, 1988 h., Apalachee	8	43	22	13	442,713	Upon a Thron, 1997 m., Sefapiano	3	17	9	9	324,089

Minnesota

MALE, YOB, Sex, Sire	Yrs Raced	Strts	Wins	SWs	Earnings	FEMALE, YOB, Sex, Sire	Yrs Raced	Strts	Wins	SWs	Earnings
Blair's Cove, 1985 h., Bucksplasher	6	58	17	10	$533,528	Courtly Kathy, 1991 m., Lost Code	8	89	18	4	$277,950
Super Abound, 1987 h., Superbity	4	36	6	2	398,418	Fortunate Faith, 1990 m., Fortunate Prospect	3	14	5	1	251,635
Cocoboy, 1988 g., Cozzene	13	196	30	1	371,567						
Crocrock, 1997 g., North Prospect	6	39	16	9	359,977	Princess Elaine, 1985 m., Providential (Ire)	4	27	9	6	232,240
Timeless Prince, 1987 g., Prince Forli	7	69	16	6	326,977						
It's Truly Obvious, 1992 g., Mufti	8	96	20	2	325,204	Northbound Pride, 1986 m., Proud Pocket	5	38	11	4	213,983
Ashar, 1995 g., Bucksplasher	8	53	9	5	274,654						
Bleu Victoriate, 1996 g., Victoriate	6	43	11	5	262,154	Samdanya, 1995 m., Northern Prospect	4	27	9	6	192,747
Buchman, 1987 h., Bucksplasher	3	32	8	1	254,929	Plana Dance, 1993 m., Northern Flagship	5	26	11	5	171,216
Wally's Choice, 2001 g., Quick Cut	2	13	7	4	228,090	Shabana, 1991 m., Nasty and Bold	5	48	10	2	169,412
						Wishek's Kid, 1989 m., Pappa Riccio	7	67	18	3	167,359
						Sweet Sum, 1990 m., Scroll	7	51	12	3	167,025
						Nidari, 1996 m., Northern No Trump	6	32	6	5	165,553

Mississippi

MALE, YOB, Sex, Sire	Yrs Raced	Strts	Wins	SWs	Earnings	FEMALE, YOB, Sex, Sire	Yrs Raced	Strts	Wins	SWs	Earnings
American Cowboy, 1994 g., Gold Crest	5	56	9	1	$174,867	Real Irish Hope, 1987 m., Tilt Up	5	49	15	3	$433,190
Lotsa Honey, 1981 h., Turn and Count	5	20	4	0	122,125	Miss Needlework, 1970 m., Needles	5	65	11	0	71,053
Dollars and Sense, 1991 g., Dollar Away	11	139	17	0	113,800	Miss Corinne, 1976 m., Grand Premiere	5	76	7	0	64,907
Nick's Palace, 1988 g., Palace Music	7	97	9	0	112,299	Cocoa Baker, 1994 m., Jobaker	4	39	10	0	62,478
Ruben Wizznat, 1986 h., North Rock	6	111	19	0	110,753	Pass the Money, 1987 m., Pass the Tab	5	57	10	0	59,178
Pajima, 1985 h., Wajima	4	47	8	0	98,061	Proclaiming, 1973 m., Full Value	5	89	17	0	51,700
Jobaker, 1981 h., Heir to the Line	3	15	7	3	85,119	Claire's Secret, 1991 m., Happy Hooligan	5	37	3	0	40,590
Question of Gold, 1994 g., Gold Angle	9	82	7	0	83,589	Peaches Galore, 1984 m., Hold Your Tricks	6	80	10	0	32,855
Hasty Chuto, 1992 g., Pachuto	6	82	10	0	79,196	Sweet Debbie, 2000 m., Sekari (GB)	3	23	3	0	30,800
Triple Cabin, 1981 h., Triple Bend	4	55	11	0	75,711	Defuniac, 1985 m., Dynastic	5	54	4	0	29,703

Missouri

MALE, YOB, Sex, Sire	Yrs Raced	Strts	Wins	SWs	Earnings	FEMALE, YOB, Sex, Sire	Yrs Raced	Strts	Wins	SWs	Earnings
Carjack, 1981 h., Cojak	5	72	20	0	$469,181	Peaceful River, 1979 m., Peaceful Tom	5	72	14	4	$250,990
Fort Metfield, 1994 g., Metfield	9	105	23	0	440,997	Redoy's Drive, 1994 m., Mr. Redoy	6	51	11	0	224,534
Missouri Ace, 1993 g., Taxachusetts	7	48	12	3	244,152	Arctic Quest, 1995 m., Yukon	4	53	8	0	146,511
Page Two, 1994 g., Victorious	8	100	16	0	240,522	My Sister Kate, 1993 m., Haileys Tropic	6	56	17	0	146,489
Mr. Springfield, 1989 g., Taxachusetts	11	107	24	0	216,230	Simply So, 1988 m., Gold Ruler	6	48	8	1	136,634
Pilot Knob, 1965 h., Gun Shot	10	164	37	1	186,139	Shared Reflections, 1986 m., Pursuit	6	67	12	1	114,601
Hold Me Together, 1994 g., Comet Kat	9	109	19	0	168,611	Caban Monere, 1992 m., Indian Detail	6	56	12	0	112,861
Minor Flaw, 1986 h., Rolfson	6	47	6	3	154,418	Shergars Best Shot, 1989 m., Shergar's Best (Ire)	7	90	20	0	107,596
Uncle Zip, 1967 h., Bergamot	9	151	38	0	149,950	Trip the Load, 1989 m., Positiveness	7	89	19	0	106,466
Al Berto, 1994 g., Chief Bandito	8	74	8	1	145,911	Erica Thor, 1987 m., Satan's Thunder	6	74	17	0	101,375

Montana

MALE, YOB, Sex, Sire	Yrs Raced	Strts	Wins	SWs	Earnings	FEMALE, YOB, Sex, Sire	Yrs Raced	Strts	Wins	SWs	Earnings
Payday Mackee, 1990 g., Black Mackee	9	79	17	5	$214,668	Hallelujah Angel, 1991 m., Dance Centre	6	55	12	1	$197,496
River Lord, 1979 h., Eastern Lord	8	96	15	2	204,451	Mickey's Hot Stuff, 1995 m.,	6	65	10	2	174,667
Toseek, 1993 g., Cave Creek	7	96	17	2	149,793	Mickey Le Mousse					
Big Sky Rusher, 1994 g., Cave Creek	6	49	9	3	131,714	Hatti, 1985 m., One More Slew	3	38	6	2	139,545
Sonabove, 1992 g., Son of Briartic	8	79	11	0	117,204	Montani, 1988 m., Kotani	8	92	20	1	121,780
Kelsos Kin, 1968 h., Scotsmans Bond	11	152	20	2	104,952	Breath of Dawn, 1993 m., Black Mackee	7	75	13	0	121,437
Blazing Zulu, 1980 h., Zulu Tom	7	73	12	0	96,855	Jocko Miss, 1997 m., Black Mackee	4	37	10	0	102,217
No Name Trail, 1991 g., Mr. Badger	8	56	15	2	92,558	Belle of Nassau, 1993 m.,	6	53	14	0	101,728
Flying Whitesocks, 1990 g.,	9	93	18	0	91,914	Nassau Square					
No Name Trail, 1991 g., Mr. Badger	8	56	15	2	92,558	Mission Gem, 1996 m., Prince Alert	4	35	11	1	101,223
Blushing Guest						Dancing River, 1975 m., Marketable	5	74	17	0	99,812
Bug Hall, 1999 g., Knight in Savannah	1	8	3	1	90,418	Happy Ann, 1989 m., Fiesty Fouts	7	61	11	0	88,145

Nebraska

MALE, YOB, Sex, Sire	Yrs Raced	Strts	Wins	SWs	Earnings	FEMALE, YOB, Sex, Sire	Yrs Raced	Strts	Wins	SWs	Earnings
Dazzling Falls, 1992 h., Taylor's Falls	3	20	9	7	$904,622	Orphan Kist, 1984 m., Fort Prevel	8	100	28	18	$631,997
Who Doctor Who, 1983 g., Doctor Stat	8	64	33	26	813,870	Falls Amiss, 1986 m., Taylor's Falls	4	29	15	9	312,301
Amadevil, 1974 h., Jungle Savage	7	93	33	20	653,534	G. U. Dreamer, 1985 m., Tarsal	4	39	14	4	289,219
Darla's Charge, 1987 g., Ragtime Band	10	141	30	1	447,766	Fantango Lady, 1994 m., Lytrump	5	55	22	18	279,295
Roman Zipper, 1972 h., Zip Line	9	128	31	13	392,782	Clever Kat, 1986 m., Comet Kat	6	59	23	9	260,170
Skunktail, 1989 g., Music Prince	11	103	20	12	380,075	Oglala Sue, 1998 m., Verzy	4	29	8	3	235,232
Plaza Star, 1978 h., Lt. Stevens	9	108	20	7	361,742	Face the Verdict, 1979 m., Executioner	5	66	10	1	228,799
Irish Villon, 1990 g., Verzy	7	66	17	11	311,016	St. Patty Day, 1982 m., Majestic Red	8	67	24	3	202,610
Wandarous, 1984 g., Replant	10	103	23	9	302,051	Robbers Doll, 1982 m., No Robbery	7	85	13	4	199,635
Comet Kat, 1977 h., Foreign Comet	5	71	13	7	297,408	Nasty and Brave, 1994 m.,	8	80	19	0	192,516
						Nasty and Bold					

Nevada

MALE, YOB, Sex, Sire	Yrs Raced	Strts	Wins	SWs	Earnings	FEMALE, YOB, Sex, Sire	Yrs Raced	Strts	Wins	SWs	Earnings
Y Flash, 1960 h., Flash o' Night	2	28	6	3	$226,635	Wood and Wine, 1975 m., Fleet Allied	5	54	18	4	$261,119
Times Rush, 1968 h., Indian Rush	6	75	15	7	215,332	High Estimate, 1972 m., Windy Sands	5	45	16	5	164,749
Port of the Sea, 1971 h., Port Wine	7	61	13	3	113,649	Nevada Bond, 1955 m., Bymeabond	4	40	6	1	49,250
Washoe Lea, 1977 h., Double Lea	8	58	17	0	101,979	Petrones Own, 1972 m., *Petrone	4	38	8	1	45,219
Arvoicsal, 1996 g., King Alobar	5	61	8	0	90,431	Snow Spirit, 1985 m., Feather Dollar	2	18	1	0	44,110
Noti, 1960 h., Leisure Time	1	12	3	2	89,150	Bingo Bets, 1981 m., Art's Classy Jet	5	44	10	3	39,529
Import Wine, 1975 h., Port Wine	7	68	9	0	82,928	Ingrid H., 1969 m., Mr. Busher	3	54	5	0	38,027
First Estimate, 1969 h., Windy Sands	4	47	9	0	71,337	Orbit Rose, 1995 m., Pencil Point (Ire)	2	16	6	0	34,792
Crow Creek, 1968 g., *Rapido	6	63	17	0	62,170	Dharita, 1960 m., Dharan	8	143	23	0	32,631
Pee Jay Kit, 1970 g., Nevada P. J.	5	39	11	0	61,853	Fun Finder, 1978 m., Pleasure Seeker	2	11	4	0	32,555

New Hampshire

MALE, YOB, Sex, Sire	Yrs Raced	Strts	Wins	SWs	Earnings	FEMALE, YOB, Sex, Sire	Yrs Raced	Strts	Wins	SWs	Earnings
Road to Rock, 1963 g., Ross Sea	9	187	36	2	$248,113	Lite Ft., 1981 m., Last Dance	6	71	15	0	$137,000
Trim Clipper, 1963 g., *Pallestrelli	11	127	21	0	72,419	A Wish for Abby, 1993 m.,	6	40	9	0	40,644
Mystic Clown, 1972 h., The Clown	6	23	11	0	56,230	Maudlin's Pleasure					
Easter Gloves, 1958 h., Golden Gloves	9	197	24	0	55,786	Frost Heaves, 1979 m., Buck Run	6	67	6	0	36,896
Ruff Enuff, 1971 h., *Arrebato II	7	90	18	0	51,737	Toy Party, 1962 m., Pan	11	199	22	0	34,665
Sailing Chance, 1960 h., Sailed Away	7	81	14	1	48,133	Sunapee, 1990 m., Iron Brigade	5	57	8	0	32,478
Buttonwood Star, 1990 g., Rock Dance	6	72	3	0	43,455	Pilot Fish, 1985 m., Star Spruce	4	44	1	0	26,885
Alybull, 1997 g., Alyfoe	3	16	4	0	41,944	Polly Pierce, 1980 m., Bert B. Don	4	44	5	0	25,627
Tallymead Pip, 1964 h., Pan	5	76	13	0	41,351	Arpey, 1956 m., *River War	2	20	6	1	25,160
Life's Adventure, 1993 g., Lifer	4	66	8	0	41,221	Quick Glory, 1965 m., *Reprimand II	6	84	10	0	25,155
						Pandora Dee, 1962 m., Pan	6	105	13	0	17,695

New Jersey

MALE, YOB, Sex, Sire	Yrs Raced	Strts	Wins	SWs	Earnings	FEMALE, YOB, Sex, Sire	Yrs Raced	Strts	Wins	SWs	Earnings
Friendly Lover, 1988 h., Cutlass	7	66	22	12	$1,247,670	Open Mind, 1986 m., Deputy Minister	3	19	12	11	$1,844,372
Zoffany, 1980 h., Our Native	6	36	15	11	1,225,569	Missy's Mirage, 1988 m., Stop the Music	4	28	14	9	838,894
Sewickley, 1985 h., Star de Naskra	4	32	11	5	1,017,517	Classy Mirage, 1990 m., Storm Bird	3	25	13	7	716,712
Dance Floor, 1989 h., Star de Naskra	2	16	4	3	863,299	Spruce Fir, 1983 m., Big Spruce	5	40	16	12	698,703
Frugal Doc, 1987 g., Baederwood	9	113	29	4	782,595	Private Treasure, 1988 m., Explodent	2	19	5	4	603,189
Sea of Tranquility, 1996 h., Heff	7	74	23	13	781,512	Jersey Girl, 1995 m., Belong to Me	2	11	9	7	571,136
Gators N Bears, 2000 h., Stormy Atlantic	3	25	10	6	659,750	Just Smashing, 1982 m., Explodent	5	61	25	8	532,383
Loaded Gun, 1995 h., Prosper Fager	6	58	13	8	633,272	Eleven North, 1994 m., Northern Idol	6	40	16	6	459,755
Johnny Legit, 1994 g., Double Negative	5	67	19	0	616,808	Girl Powder, 1983 m., Talc	4	44	18	10	449,447
Virginia Rapids, 1990 h., Riverman	4	37	7	5	566,018	Wild Palm, 1994 m., My Prince Charming	6	74	17	0	428,061

New Mexico

MALE, YOB, Sex, Sire	Yrs Raced	Strts	Wins	SWs	Earnings
Ciento, 1998 h., Prospector Jones	5	32	19	14	$776,014
Rocky Gulch, 2001 g., Dry Gulch	2	15	10	8	541,088
Run Johnny, 1992 g., Johnny Blade	7	52	14	6	518,790
Bold Ego, 1978 h., Bold Tactics	3	35	15	5	511,648
Runmore Mema, 1997 h., Jack Wilson	6	54	14	5	438,777
Star Smasher, 1999 h., Full Choke	3	24	12	10	437,992
Copper Case, 1977 g., Hopeful Venture	9	92	33	18	365,374
Boulderdash Bay, 1990 g., Spotter Bay	7	47	16	5	331,885
Ninety Nine Jack, 1999 g., Jack Wilson	4	29	14	7	312,625
B. G.'s Drone, 1989 h., Full Choke	7	57	14	3	294,470

FEMALE, YOB, Sex, Sire	Yrs Raced	Strts	Wins	SWs	Earnings
Shemoveslikeaghost, 2000 f., Ghostly Moves	3	18	10	7	$458,191
Yulla Yulla, 1995 m., Look See	5	27	21	14	443,022
Frosty Tail, 1980 m., It's Freezing	3	28	11	3	361,078
Espeedytoo, 1999 m., Ghost Ranch	3	24	10	6	340,564
Fearless Ego, 1985 m., Bold Ego	4	43	16	6	325,377
Bold n Special, 1983 m., Bold River (Fr)	3	22	7	3	265,541
Peachy Manners, 1981 m., Well Mannered	6	51	17	8	239,085
Lord Imajones, 1999 m., Prospector Jones	4	25	5	3	233,190
Gollygot, 1996 m., Whitebrush	5	44	13	0	231,405
Ghost Chatter, 2000 m., Ghostly Moves	3	25	8	2	226,480

New York

MALE, YOB, Sex, Sire	Yrs Raced	Strts	Wins	SWs	Earnings
Funny Cide, 2000 g., Distorted Humor	3	21	8	6	$3,174,485
Say Florida Sandy, 1994 h., Personal Flag	8	98	33	19	2,085,408
Gander, 1996 g., Cormorant	7	60	15	6	1,824,011
L'Carriere, 1991 g., Carr de Naskra	3	23	8	2	1,726,175
Fourstardave, 1985 g., Compliance	9	100	21	13	1,636,737
Fourstars Allstar, 1988 h., Compliance	6	59	14	9	1,596,760
Win, 1980 g., Barachois	5	44	14	7	1,408,980
Victory Speech, 1993 h., Deputy Minister	3	27	9	5	1,289,020
Thunder Rumble, 1989 h., Thunder Puddles	3	19	8	6	1,047,552
More to Tell, 1991 h., Moro	7	85	18	7	995,804

FEMALE, YOB, Sex, Sire	Yrs Raced	Strts	Wins	SWs	Earnings
Grecian Flight, 1984 m., Cormorant	5	40	21	14	$1,320,215
Fit for a Queen, 1986 m., Fit to Fight	5	51	13	8	1,226,429
Irish Linnet, 1988 m., Seattle Song	6	62	19	13	1,220,180
Lottsa Talc, 1990 m., Talc	6	65	21	16	1,206,248
Critical Eye, 1997 m., Dynaformer	4	38	14	5	1,060,984
Capades, 1986 m., Overskate	3	27	11	8	1,051,006
Queen Alexandra, 1982 m., Determined King	5	46	19	14	1,034,144
Dat You Miz Blue, 1997 m., Cure the Blues	4	33	14	7	806,291
Biogio's Rose, 1994 m., Polish Numbers	6	52	16	6	797,959
Perfect Arc, 1992 m., Brown Arc	3	13	10	6	668,230

North Carolina

MALE, YOB, Sex, Sire	Yrs Raced	Strts	Wins	SWs	Earnings
Bold Circle, 1986 h., Circle Home	4	55	11	3	$372,488
G H's Pleasure, 1992 g., Foolish Pleasure	7	52	9	3	356,293
Triangular, 1967 g., Blue Prince	8	72	15	3	240,059
Insideangle, 1992 h., Allen's Prospect	4	60	10	0	233,738
Moment of Triumph, 1984 h., Timeless Moment	5	50	17	1	230,427
Dump Truck, 1973 h., Four Strings	10	188	31	0	211,930
R. T. Rise n Shine, 1984 g., Secretary of War	8	132	18	0	186,887
We're Just Bluff, 1987 g., Fairway Phantom	8	86	15	0	180,435
Ben Ali's Rullah, 1989 h., Clever Trick	4	58	9	0	175,365
Gold Candy Too, 1990 g., Goldlust	4	38	11	1	172,550

FEMALE, YOB, Sex, Sire	Yrs Raced	Strts	Wins	SWs	Earnings
Top Socialite, 1982 m., Topsider	5	34	10	7	$521,944
Amanti, 1979 m., Anticipating	5	53	15	4	306,981
See Your Point, 1992 m., Rock Point	3	37	12	3	283,985
Family Effort, 1991 m., Goldlust	5	69	13	0	252,855
Hadee Mae, 1991 m., Goldlust	3	37	9	2	178,294
Flashy Concorde, 1988 h., Super Concorde	4	59	19	0	176,032
Flashy Concorde, 1988 h.,	4	59	19	0	176,032
Clever Tune, 1992 m., Tricky Tab	7	96	15	0	149,597
One More Sue, 1990 m., One More Slew	6	91	16	0	148,091
Lark's Impression, 1998 m., Above Normal	3	34	9	0	141,133
Flying Hope, 1982 m., Inverness Drive	7	85	9	0	139,808

North Dakota

MALE, YOB, Sex, Sire	Yrs Raced	Strts	Wins	SWs	Earnings
Dakota Prospect, 1997 g., Slewdledo	5	52	8	1	$131,159
Northern Ace, 1998 g., Northern Prospect	5	41	13	1	111,164
Bold Alert, 1994 g., Aferd	5	29	6	5	107,388
Stilaferd, 1994 g., Aferd	9	63	9	2	96,994
Breaker Breaker, 1997 h., Power Break	3	16	4	3	91,322
Suntana, 2000 g., Sun Man	2	14	5	4	76,005
Leeaferd, 1995 g., Aferd	8	83	9	0	73,245
Hub Cap, 1981 h., Aferd	6	50	16	4	70,597
Maddies Blues, 2000 g., Aferd	3	20	7	5	59,440
Jo Pelouse, 1970 h., Pelouse	9	127	17	0	58,715

FEMALE, YOB, Sex, Sire	Yrs Raced	Strts	Wins	SWs	Earnings
Hoist Her Flag, 1982 m., Aferd	5	43	19	11	$290,849
Creel Ribot, 1979 m., Domian	7	86	19	0	93,175
Patty Kim, 1989 m., Aferd	4	23	6	4	87,944
Strike an Image, 2001 f., Patriot Strike	2	13	4	3	67,448
Can I Lead, 1986 m., Lead Astray	8	98	23	0	60,700
Penny Bolinas, 1976 m., Bolinas Intent	6	80	11	0	49,862
Music Time, 1993 m., Ragtime Reign	7	56	8	1	44,651
Milk N Cookies, 1996 m., Continental Morn	6	53	6	0	41,745
Sheza Broad, 1989 m., Au Point	5	46	15	0	40,637
Quillos Bolinas, 1978 m., Bolinas Intent	6	91	11	0	36,785

Ohio

MALE, YOB, Sex, Sire	Yrs Raced	Strts	Wins	SWs	Earnings
Harlan's Holiday, 1999 h., Harlan	3	22	9	8	$3,632,664
Phantom On Tour, 1994 g., Tour d'Or	4	20	7	6	724,605
Kingpost, 1985 g., Stalwart	2	20	3	1	598,966
One Bold Stroke, 1995 h., Broad Brush	3	16	5	4	595,662
Royal Harmony, 1964 h., Royal Note	6	105	38	22	587,164
Stormy Deep, 1987 g., Diamond Shoal (GB)	5	53	17	8	565,672
Bill Monroe, 1978 g., Brent's Prince	6	65	24	15	466,824
Devil Time, 1997 g., Devil His Due	6	45	13	8	462,451

FEMALE, YOB, Sex, Sire	Yrs Raced	Strts	Wins	SWs	Earnings
Tougaloo, 1983 m., Lot o' Gold	5	33	13	11	$583,030
Ashwood C C, 1998 m., Cryptoclearance	5	48	17	7	579,699
Lady Cherie, 1997 m., Al Sabin	5	39	17	13	552,095
Glacial Princess, 1981 m., Brent's Prince	4	52	27	17	542,792
Sadie's Dream, 1990 m., Rare Performer	5	37	10	6	488,529
Cut the Cuteness, 1992 m., Cut Throat (GB)	5	38	13	12	411,459
Extended Applause, 1996 m., Exbourne	4	23	4	1	408,520
Safe Play, 1978 m., Sham	3	27	11	7	393,085

MALE, YOB, Sex, Sire	Yrs Raced	Strts	Wins	SWs	Earnings	FEMALE, YOB, Sex, Sire	Yrs Raced	Strts	Wins	SWs	Earnings
Major Adversary, 1992 g., Mighty Adversary	9	87	21	10	458,708	Crypto's Redjet, 1992 m., Cryptoclearance	5	39	17	8	364,640
Majestic Dinner, 1997 g., Formal Dinner	5	35	16	7	450,178	Princess Hawkins, 1981 m., Brent's Prince	6	74	12	5	354,593

Oklahoma

MALE, YOB, Sex, Sire	Yrs Raced	Strts	Wins	SWs	Earnings	FEMALE, YOB, Sex, Sire	Yrs Raced	Strts	Wins	SWs	Earnings
Clever Trevor, 1986 g., Slewacide	5	30	15	9	$1,388,841	Lady's Secret, 1982 m., Secretariat	4	45	25	22	$3,021,325
Mr Ross, 1995 g., Slewacide	6	44	18	14	1,091,046	Voladora, 1995 m., Hickory Ridge	4	53	20	10	548,622
Silver Goblin, 1991 g., Silver Ghost	6	26	16	11	1,083,895	Belle of Cozzene, 1992 m., Cozzene	4	22	9	7	522,455
Brother Brown, 1990 g., Eminency	3	20	14	8	791,448	Slide Show, 1991 m., Slewacide	4	25	12	8	347,917
Darrell Darrell, 1987 g., Boca Rio	7	53	23	13	591,646	Fullasatick, 1993 m., Derby Wish	5	43	9	3	289,611
Brush With Pride, 1992 g., Broad Brush	5	35	14	9	548,615	Mean Martha, 1978 m., Menocal	4	40	8	3	276,985
Perfec Travel, 1982 g., Inverness Drive	8	52	14	10	514,747	Caznire, 1989 m., Bold Ego	5	30	14	8	271,582
Highland Ice, 1993 g., Highland Blade	7	48	16	9	474,090	Southern Etiquette, 1988 m., Slewacide	4	27	10	6	259,459
Lucky Salvation, 1980 h., Outward Bound	8	88	22	5	467,891	Muhammad's Baby, 1986 m., Ask Muhammad	6	76	15	6	257,186
That Tat, 1998 g., Faltaat	4	40	14	5	463,585	She's a Bullet, 1991 m., T. H. Bend	6	56	13	4	254,865

Oregon

MALE, YOB, Sex, Sire	Yrs Raced	Strts	Wins	SWs	Earnings	FEMALE, YOB, Sex, Sire	Yrs Raced	Strts	Wins	SWs	Earnings
Polynesian Flyer, 1982 h., Flying Lark	5	54	14	11	$346,525	Revillew Slew, 1996 m., Can't Be Slew	6	46	13	3	$383,824
Lethal Grande, 1999 g., Corslew	4	47	14	5	243,487	Moonlit Maddie, 1998 m., Abstract	5	38	12	6	207,358
Lark's Legacy, 1981 g., Flying Lark	8	104	24	8	240,199	La Famille, 1981 m., Bob Mathias	8	80	14	0	193,105
Annie's Turn, 1977 h., Joyous Turn	6	64	16	4	203,516	Valeri's Delight, 1984 m., Dr. Valeri	4	28	10	1	181,415
Weinhard, 1996 g., Falstaff	5	69	8	0	202,688	Solda Holme, 1986 m., Jeff's Companion	7	47	21	2	163,977
Family Fox, 1979 h., Bob Mathias	6	95	17	0	196,973	Cruisin' Two Su, 1983 m., Dr. Valeri	4	30	10	2	155,380
Strong Award, 1965 h., Strong Ruler	11	118	29	3	189,361	Solamente Un Vez, 1983 m., Relaunch	3	17	6	3	126,470
Supreme Lark, 1977 h., Flying Lark	8	112	24	5	186,799	Just Out Run, 1988 m., Just the Time	6	64	11	4	125,976
Praise Jay, 1964 h., Jaybil	5	54	12	6	186,578	Swoon's Bid, 1990 m., Swoon	7	81	14	0	116,999
Prince Aglo, 1990 g., Sea Aglo	5	47	8	3	184,735	Felicity Rose, 1997 m., Tip On Slew	3	21	4	0	111,065

Pennsylvania

MALE, YOB, Sex, Sire	Yrs Raced	Strts	Wins	SWs	Earnings	FEMALE, YOB, Sex, Sire	Yrs Raced	Strts	Wins	SWs	Earnings
Smarty Jones, 2001 c., Elusive Quality	2	9	8	7	$7,613,155	Go for Wand, 1987 m., Deputy Minister	2	13	10	8	$1,373,338
Alphabet Soup, 1991 h., Cozzene	4	24	10	7	2,990,270	Bessarabian, 1982 m., Vice Regent	3	37	18	14	1,032,640
With Anticipation, 1995 g., Relaunch	8	48	15	8	2,660,543	Alice Springs, 1990 m., Val de l'Orne (Fr)	5	26	9	5	768,889
Yankee Affair, 1982 h., Northern Fling	5	55	22	15	2,282,156	Mrs. Penny, 1977 m., Great Nephew	3	22	6	6	689,609
Tikkanen, 1991 h., Cozzene	3	17	4	3	1,599,335	Classy Cathy, 1983 m., Private Account	3	15	7	4	537,970
Lil E. Tee, 1989 h., At the Threshold	3	13	7	3	1,437,506	Contredance, 1982 m., Danzig	3	21	8	5	492,700
High Yield, 1997 h., Storm Cat	2	14	4	3	1,170,196	Ambassador of Luck, 1979 m., What Luck	4	23	14	9	489,583
Unaccounted For, 1991 h., Private Account	2	17	6	2	998,468	Wonders Delight, 1986 m., Icecapade	3	36	9	4	481,521
Rochester, 1996 g., Green Dancer	7	39	10	5	974,347	My Pal Lana, 2000 m., Kris S.	3	23	6	2	463,134
Selkirk, 1988 h., Sharpen Up (GB)	3	15	6	6	843,661	After the Glitter, 1989 m., Screen King	6	51	17	8	456,786

Rhode Island

MALE, YOB, Sex, Sire	Yrs Raced	Strts	Wins	SWs	Earnings	FEMALE, YOB, Sex, Sire	Yrs Raced	Strts	Wins	SWs	Earnings
Beau Britches, 1975 h., Oxford Accent	6	89	8	2	$121,145	Good Musical, 1977 m., Rock Talk	3	45	12	0	$155,580
Gulio Cesere, 1956 h., Mel Hash	4	59	16	2	106,308	Dandy Blitzen, 1955 m., Bull Dandy	4	48	14	4	131,499
Troll By, 1973 h., Military Plume	4	28	10	3	89,914	Venomous, 1953 m., Mel Hash	4	32	15	4	107,932
Tullo, 1956 h., Bull Dandy	9	202	23	1	81,680	Dandy Princess, 1958 m., Bull Dandy	4	58	15	0	80,533
New 'tricia, 1966 h., New Rullah	9	128	22	0	68,489	Musical Sadie, 1967 m., *Good Shot	6	90	16	0	51,094
Rival Hunter, 1978 h., Oxford Accent	8	123	12	0	53,358	Farrago, 1977 m., Oxford Accent	3	22	5	0	47,153
Melpet, 1954 g., Bull Dandy	4	66	13	0	53,325	Helipat, 1954 m., Bull Dandy	5	84	6	1	45,871
Bandito Billy, 1978 h., Banderilla	5	69	14	0	51,127	Distinctive Lady, 1970 m., Times Roman	4	36	8	0	44,410
David's Success, 1957 h., Bull Dandy	8	120	19	0	49,686	Sword of Mine, 1960 m., Swift Sword	7	161	25	0	33,545
Boy Brigand, 1959 h., Bull Dandy	8	145	19	0	49,686	Nile Melody, 1957 m., Mel Hash	5	49	10	0	32,331

South Carolina

MALE, YOB, Sex, Sire	Yrs Raced	Strts	Wins	SWs	Earnings	FEMALE, YOB, Sex, Sire	Yrs Raced	Strts	Wins	SWs	Earnings
Big Rut, 1993 g., Kokand	9	91	22	7	$570,488	Double Stake, 1993 m., Kokand	4	37	11	4	$343,480
Normandy Beach, 1996 g., Sewickley	6	65	16	1	406,354	Running Cousin, 1978 m., Double Hitch	5	86	22	8	291,440
American Prince, 1998 g., Miner	5	41	6	1	346,371	Has Beauty, 1991 m., Kokand	10	106	25	0	232,156
Kiss and Run, 1968 h., Double Hitch	8	144	40	7	295,681	Frills and Ribbons, 1978 m., Double Hitch	5	77	15	1	199,354
Double Quill, 1969 h., Double Hitch	8	152	30	3	283,890						
Intelligent Male, 2000 g., Ride the Storm	3	22	7	2	257,459	Sea Trip, 1981 m., Sea Songster	5	76	12	2	194,479
Roman Report, 1983 g., Greatest Roman	7	94	23	0	256,369	Frezil, 1978 m., Double Hitch	7	88	17	1	189,019
Race 'N Brace, 1984 h., Hard Crush	5	63	19	2	242,459	Raise a Prince, 1988 m., Raise a Bid	5	54	13	2	188,653
No Complaints, 1995 g., Personal Flag	6	83	16	0	219,340	Crushem, 1979 m., Hard Crush	4	62	12	1	178,283
Dressy Time, 1977 h., Canmore	8	108	20	0	219,250	Miss Hitch, 1976 m., Double Hitch	6	54	13	3	174,470
						Winter's Work, 1989 m., Cool Corn	6	90	22	0	162,781

South Dakota

MALE, YOB, Sex, Sire	Yrs Raced	Strts	Wins	SWs	Earnings
Little Bro Lantis, 1988 g., Lost Atlantis	9	120	23	8	$719,866
Win Stat, 1977 h., Doctor Stat	8	84	22	6	438,378
Disarco's Rib, 1980 h., Libra's Rib	5	40	10	1	125,558
Atlantis Blend, 1989 g., Lost Atlantis	10	68	17	6	117,680
Right Key, 1971 h., Key Issue	8	97	22	1	108,279
Streaking On, 1975 h., Hi-Hasty	11	123	26	3	93,788
Shekmatyar, 1980 h., Bon Mot (Fr)	3	50	12	0	92,340
Officer's Call, 1971 g., Jet Man	5	53	13	3	88,543
John Jet, 1966 h., Jet Man	10	131	29	5	86,627
Rosedale Boy, 1971 h., Hi-Hasty	6	90	16	2	74,790

FEMALE, YOB, Sex, Sire	Yrs Raced	Strts	Wins	SWs	Earnings
Reen Aferd, 1985 m., Aferd	6	78	13	1	$96,107
Ferns Image, 1986 m., Aferd	8	75	15	0	82,242
Pro Raja, 1970 m., Semi-pro	4	46	15	7	74,510
Rajaja, 1978 m., Jacinto	2	29	6	1	70,330
Hi-Mini, 1969 m., Hi-Hasty	3	41	7	1	60,463
Palacity Jet, 1971 m., Jet Man	4	44	15	5	60,289
Rio Nite, 1981 m., Aferd	5	41	12	1	57,685
Dakota Diamond, 1977 m., Four Way Split	5	62	12	1	51,053
Beturio, 1979 m., *Centurio	5	62	10	0	47,893
Beautitious, 1978 m., *Restitious	5	51	8	3	44,077

Tennessee

MALE, YOB, Sex, Sire	Yrs Raced	Strts	Wins	SWs	Earnings
Slew of Damascus, 1988 g., Slewacide	7	48	16	12	$1,420,350
Startahemp, 1970 g., Hempen	8	72	25	1	282,153
Shot n' Missed, 1977 h., Naskra	3	29	12	3	228,711
Act It Out, 1979 h., An Act	5	41	11	0	211,983
Bold Ruddy, 1978 g., Captain Cee Jay	8	75	10	2	206,886
Jay Bar Toughie, 1980 h., Full Pocket	10	126	26	0	205,232
Temperence Week, 1984 g., Temperence Hill	7	117	15	0	185,026
Hold the Beans, 1977 h., Northern Fling	10	186	18	0	175,528
Charlie Jr., 1966 h., Charlevoix	9	144	25	1	159,262
Big Rock Candy, 1962 h., Morning Line	6	54	17	1	151,013

FEMALE, YOB, Sex, Sire	Yrs Raced	Strts	Wins	SWs	Earnings
Fancy Naskra, 1978 m., Naskra	5	26	8	2	$291,769
Tanya's Tuition, 1987 m., D'Accord	5	25	8	3	246,225
Tipper Time, 1992 m., Forward	6	78	13	1	171,282
Tourforsure, 1969 m., Above the Law	4	76	16	0	160,379
Alda's Will, 1993 m., Gallapiat	5	71	13	1	143,172
Southern Sweet, 1998 m., Tethra	5	29	5	0	142,642
Jay Bar Pet, 1971 m., Bold and Brave	4	65	11	0	132,240
Cellar's Best, 1985 m., Band Practice	5	59	10	1	112,800
Flee the Storm, 1979 m., Forceten	3	49	8	0	106,388
Chime, 1979 m., Bold Forbes	3	33	6	1	93,189

Texas

MALE, YOB, Sex, Sire	Yrs Raced	Strts	Wins	SWs	Earnings
Groovy, 1983 h., Norcliffe	3	26	12	12	$1,346,956
Mocha Express, 1994 h., Java Gold	4	34	16	10	960,216
Feeling Gallant, 1982 h., Gallant Gambler	6	86	19	10	846,145
Top Avenger, 1978 h., Staunch Avenger	6	57	23	11	721,237
Gold Nugget, 1995 g., Gold Legend	7	46	14	6	633,821
Jim's Orbit, 1985 h., Orbit Dancer	2	19	5	3	600,720
Appealing Breeze, 1987 h., Breezing On	2	14	9	8	553,327
Beverly Greely, 1995 g., Raja's Best Boy	8	70	18	1	482,898
Lights On Broadway, 1997 g., Majestic Light	5	49	10	5	476,335
Rare Cure, 1998 g., Rare Brick	5	51	11	6	475,450

FEMALE, YOB, Sex, Sire	Yrs Raced	Strts	Wins	SWs	Earnings
Got Koko, 1999 m., Signal Tap	3	15	7	5	$960,946
Two Altazano, 1991 m., Manzotti	3	20	9	6	709,725
Traces of Gold, 1992 m., Strike Gold	5	48	12	10	664,672
Bara Lass, 1979 m., Barachois	4	60	17	7	542,362
Take My Picture, 1982 m., Tyrant	3	28	13	7	541,273
Eagle Lake, 1998 m., Desert Royalty	4	43	13	7	477,877
Grab the Green, 1988 m., Cozzene	4	26	9	6	454,023
Darby's Daughter, 1986 m., Darby Creek Road	3	15	5	4	435,104
Sweet Misty, 1994 m., Lucky So n' So	4	45	15	8	422,005
Mastery's Gamble, 1992 m., Mastery	7	55	16	7	406,943

Utah

MALE, YOB, Sex, Sire	Yrs Raced	Strts	Wins	SWs	Earnings
Pharaoh's Heart, 1990 g., Persevered	7	67	10	2	$340,470
R Friar Tuck, 1991 g., Religiously	4	24	4	1	236,641
Indian Express, 2000 c., Indian Charlie	3	6	3	0	174,089
Charley Mc, 1993 g., High Counsel	5	25	5	2	141,813
Pierces Homeremedy, 1988 g., Humbaba	11	102	27	3	128,693
Raise a Kitten, 1985 h., Humbaba	7	78	16	2	119,102
Startinover, 1995 g., Regal Intention	7	89	8	0	93,377
Nintyfiver, 1995 g., Navegante (Chi)	8	93	16	0	88,932
Force of Habit, 1996 g., Four Seasons (GB)	5	43	5	0	88,077
Chory Four, 1999 g., Four Seasons (GB)	3	32	3	0	77,784

FEMALE, YOB, Sex, Sire	Yrs Raced	Strts	Wins	SWs	Earnings
Jones Time Machine, 1979 m., Current Concept	3	26	13	7	$329,500
Let's Get Raced, 1980 m., Joduke	5	67	14	0	137,664
Ancient River, 1983 m., Upper Nile	6	47	14	3	134,964
Lady Supreme, 1996 m., Four Seasons (GB)	4	58	6	0	80,311
Lovehmadly, 1997 m., Regal Groom	6	47	11	0	79,013
Miss Table Talk, 1994 m., Never Tabled	5	64	8	0	71,950
Synaster Angel, 1993 m., Synastry	4	29	3	0	69,495
Bay Heart, 1973 m., *Epicuro	4	35	6	0	53,655
K J Lucky Seven, 1997 m., Four Seasons (GB)	3	17	4	0	50,528
Brandy Lee, 1976 m., Joduke	4	59	14	0	48,304

Vermont

MALE, YOB, Sex, Sire	Yrs Raced	Strts	Wins	SWs	Earnings
Peter Orbit, 1971 h., Big Pete	8	90	17	0	$43,953
Tong, 1974 h., The Hammer	9	25	4	0	31,910
Persian Potentate, 1967 g., Bold Commander	5	83	7	0	30,933
Tropic Fling, 1972 h., Ribot's Fling	5	76	8	0	30,216
Rambling Ribot, 1970 h., Ribot's Fling	7	89	11	0	29,646
Mr. Kish, 1962 h., Auditing	7	94	7	0	28,695
Far West, 1975 h., Bold Legend	6	58	9	0	23,452
Pocantico, 1998 g., Slew the Knight	2	9	3	0	23,430
Fez, 1958 h., *Hafiz	6	52	14	0	23,040
Obligated Time, 1997 g., Obligato	2	13	1	0	22,954

FEMALE, YOB, Sex, Sire	Yrs Raced	Strts	Wins	SWs	Earnings
Snowshoes, 1961 m., *North Carolina	9	107	16	0	$29,685
Fling of Joy, 1969 m., Ribot's Fling	5	56	16	0	28,006
English Gin, 1966 m., *Very English	6	53	9	0	17,627
Frozen North, 1960 m., *North Carolina	6	44	7	0	17,007
Night of Dreams, 1970 m., Ribot's Fling	5	94	5	0	15,880
Clever May, 1959 m., *North Carolina	2	20	5	0	13,660
Sweet Snowdrop, 1963 m., *Reprimand II	3	19	4	0	13,410
Its Pouring, 1967 m., Rainy Lake	3	21	0	0	12,670
George's Parlay, 1966 m., Canadian Flyer	6	98	5	0	11,046
Miss Sensation, 1969 m., Motivation	5	58	5	0	8,741

Virginia

MALE, YOB, Sex, Sire	Yrs Raced	Strts	Wins	SWs	Earnings	FEMALE, YOB, Sex, Sire	Yrs Raced	Strts	Wins	SWs	Earnings
Paradise Creek, 1989 h., Irish River (Fr)	4	25	14	10	$3,401,416	Seeking the Pearl, 1994 m.,	4	21	8	7	$4,021,716
Hansel, 1988 h., Woodman	2	14	7	6	2,936,586	Seeking the Gold					
Sea Hero, 1990 h., Polish Navy	3	24	6	3	2,929,869	Sabin, 1980 m., Lyphard	4	25	18	14	1,098,341
Pleasant Tap, 1987 h., Pleasant Colony	4	32	9	6	2,721,169	Mandy's Gold, 1998 m., Gilded Time	4	24	11	7	1,081,744
Majesty's Prince, 1979 h., His Majesty	4	43	12	9	2,077,796	Miss Oceana, 1981 m., Alydar	2	19	11	9	1,010,385
Java Gold, 1984 h., Key to the Mint	2	15	9	5	1,908,832	Love Sign, 1977 m., Spanish Riddle	4	39	16	10	934,827
Simply Majestic, 1984 h., Majestic Light	4	44	18	14	1,667,713	Shuvee, 1966 m., Nashua	4	44	16	15	890,445
Colonial Affair, 1990 h.,	3	20	7	4	1,635,228	Possible Mate, 1981 m., King's Bishop	3	29	14	9	675,999
Pleasant Colony						Dismasted, 1982 m., Restless Native	3	36	14	6	629,803
Secretariat, 1970 h., Bold Ruler	2	21	16	14	1,316,808	Zoonaqua, 1990 m., Silver Hawk	6	28	5	4	611,225
Chief Honcho, 1987 h., Chief's Crown	5	34	10	4	1,265,719	Topicount, 1993 m., Private Account	4	43	9	5	607,618

Washington

MALE, YOB, Sex, Sire	Yrs Raced	Strts	Wins	SWs	Earnings	FEMALE, YOB, Sex, Sire	Yrs Raced	Strts	Wins	SWs	Earnings
Saratoga Passage, 1985 g., Pirateer	4	22	6	4	$800,212	Peterhof's Patea, 1988 m., Peterhof	5	52	16	14	$623,367
Military Hawk, 1987 g., Colonel Stevens	9	86	18	12	686,128	Rings a Chime, 1997 m., Metfield	2	13	4	2	606,315
Captain Condo, 1982 g.,	8	70	30	16	511,695	Run Away Stevie, 1989 m., Table Run	6	40	12	9	468,267
Captain Courageous						Cadette Stevens, 1988 m.,	4	30	11	10	453,539
Chinook Pass, 1979 h., Native Born	3	25	16	11	480,073	Colonel Stevens					
Funboy, 1991 h., Gumboy	5	49	13	11	478,180	Belle of Rainier, 1979 m., Windy Tide	4	43	17	14	424,526
Refried Dreams, 1993 g., Lac Ouimet	5	51	15	0	453,570	Classy Cara, 1997 m., General Meeting	2	10	4	3	405,847
Sneakin Jake, 1987 g., Table Run	8	76	16	12	439,590	Jazznwithwindy, 1994 m.,	7	71	18	0	391,739
Moscow M D, 1989 g., Moscow Ballet	8	69	16	0	435,843	Jazzing Around					
Makors Mark, 1997 h., Son of Briartic	5	29	11	6	430,753	Delicate Vine, 1984 m., Knights Choice	1	5	4	3	390,370
Snipledo, 1985 g., Slewdledo	6	45	17	5	409,905	Bonne Nuite, 1989 m., Knights Choice	5	65	16	7	376,161
						Firesweeper, 1983 m., Drum Fire	4	34	13	13	363,394

West Virginia

MALE, YOB, Sex, Sire	Yrs Raced	Strts	Wins	SWs	Earnings	FEMALE, YOB, Sex, Sire	Yrs Raced	Strts	Wins	SWs	Earnings
Soul of the Matter, 1991 h.,	4	16	7	4	$2,302,818	Evil's Pic, 1992 m., Piccolino	5	31	10	7	$437,877
Private Terms						Shes a Caper Too, 1993 m.,	6	78	12	1	291,089
Afternoon Deelites, 1992 h.,	3	12	7	6	1,061,193	Feel the Power					
Private Terms						Fancy Buckles, 2000 m., My Boy Adam	3	17	9	4	278,188
Confucius Say, 1998 g., Eastover Court	3	23	12	7	527,897	Mongo Queen, 1976 m., Mongo	3	40	8	2	277,837
Rebellious Dreamer, 1996 h.,	5	53	10	6	407,918	Sweet Annuity, 1997 m., Oh Say	5	37	9	5	260,052
My Boy Adam						Longfield Star, 1996 m., Allen's Prospect	5	41	8	3	254,077
Ardent Arab, 1992 g., Weshaam	9	77	24	2	407,475	Peacomb Hen, 1995 m., Glide	8	78	17	0	242,525
A Huevo, 1996 g., Cool Joe	3	11	6	2	389,750	Shesanothergrump, 1999 m., Weshaam	4	33	7	3	218,885
Coolmars, 1995 g., Glide	8	62	12	1	339,575	Who's Ya Mama, 1998 m.,	4	30	10	1	213,576
Me No Sissy, 1988 g., Light Years	11	123	18	2	336,011	Allen's Prospect					
Coin Collector, 1989 g., Weshaam	5	43	12	6	328,115	Spanishinquisition, 1996 m.,	5	45	7	1	208,954
Gauntlett Boy, 1986 g., Run the Gantlet	4	37	6	4	285,593	Eastover Court					

Wisconsin

MALE, YOB, Sex, Sire	Yrs Raced	Strts	Wins	SWs	Earnings	FEMALE, YOB, Sex, Sire	Yrs Raced	Strts	Wins	SWs	Earnings
Chad's Boy, 1965 h., Disdainful	9	106	31	1	$73,871	Cheetah Chick, 1977 m.,	5	36	10	0	$43,882
Hope to Sea, 1986 g., Captain Seaweed	8	86	7	0	73,400	Captain Seaweed					
Sekao, 1974 h., Oakesun	7	77	10	0	65,124	Theresadon, 1974 m., Ocala Kid	9	116	18	0	38,689
Home Swiftly, 1975 h., Swift Pursuit	7	99	18	0	63,251	Autumn Eagle, 1993 m., Curfew	6	50	6	0	32,745
Island Command, 1975 h.,	3	32	6	0	61,459	Weeds for Jennifer, 1978 m.,	3	44	9	0	28,134
Command Decision						Captain Seaweed					
Hard Liquor, 1972 g., Nahr Love	9	140	25	0	53,125	Jami Pari, 1996 m., Bold James	5	66	4	0	28,022
Racers Dream, 1984 h.,	7	92	13	0	51,583	Connie's Fashion, 1980 m., Best Award	5	76	8	0	27,105
Captain Seaweed						Polynesian Lady, 1963 m., Tropic King	6	81	16	0	27,060
Model Ribot, 1973 h., Model Fool	3	52	15	0	49,360	Pamela Jean, 1977 m., Captain Seaweed	6	71	8	0	24,200
Auat, 1998 g., Armed Truce	3	43	5	0	41,249	Balmay, 1968 m., Jomay	10	101	12	0	21,316
Bring to Papa, 1981 h., Bring to Reason	4	45	9	0	38,300	Dusty May, 1963 m., Jet Colonel	8	95	17	0	21,296

Wyoming

MALE, YOB, Sex, Sire	Yrs Raced	Strts	Wins	SWs	Earnings	FEMALE, YOB, Sex, Sire	Yrs Raced	Strts	Wins	SWs	Earnings
Peter Glory, 1956 h., New World	12	197	35	0	$81,319	Zip Pouch, 1990 m., Destroyer (SAf)	4	16	7	2	$48,981
Pappa Jeff, 1987 g., Pappagallo (Fr)	5	65	10	0	59,298	Vicsrose, 1972 m., Emma's Orphan	4	31	11	1	47,475
Toe to Toe, 1973 h., *Leandro	6	75	21	0	52,394	Sterling Memory, 1989 m.,	3	24	6	0	36,517
Chalkland, 1987 g., Chalk Hill	6	54	9	0	46,911	Hoist the Silver					
Monolo, 1979 h., *Rugger	4	38	9	3	46,701	Trivia, 1994 m., Mr. Prosperous	4	31	7	0	27,953
Mail Messenger, 1967 h., Bright Liberty	7	117	23	0	42,364	Sage Princess, 1964 m., Georgian Prinz	9	145	13	0	26,133
Khal Bell, 1962 h., Bright Liberty	6	80	11	0	41,970	Skitab, 1979 m., Hattab's Best	5	75	12	0	26,033
Living Pleasure, 1979 h., Joy of Living	8	59	7	1	40,722	Western Action, 1986 m., Ryan's Island	4	52	6	0	25,646
Supper Sport, 1974 h., Coloking	7	107	14	0	39,045	Puddin Proof, 1978 m., Proper Proof	3	52	2	0	24,798
Devil's Holiday, 1963 h., Georgian Prinz	7	70	25	1	37,289	Abiquiu Red, 1970 m., Polo Bell	4	83	10	0	24,481
						Quality Time, 1992 m., Lightning Leap	4	35	2	0	23,048

Leading 2004 Earners by State Where Bred

State	MALE, YOB, Sex, Sire	Strts	Wns	SWns	Earnings	FEMALE, YOB, Sex, Sire	Strts	Wns	SWns	Earnings
Alabama	Chief Tudor, 1997 g., Chief Persuasion	7	1	1	$36,853	Comalagold, 2000 m., Royal Empire	8	3	1	$83,590
Arizona	Newark, 2000 g., Benton Creek	9	4	3	95,204	Miss Noteworthy, 2001 f., Notebook	7	5	4	95,435
Arkansas	Beau's Town, 1998 g., Beau Genius	6	2	2	112,530	Timeless Dreamer, 2001 f., Idabel	13	4	0	74,180
California	Texcess, 2002 g., In Excess (Ire)	4	3	2	725,427	Yearly Report, 2001 f., General Meeting	7	5	5	787,500
Colorado	Cajun Pepper, 2002 g., Barricade	5	5	2	112,242	She's Finding Time, 1999 m., Ragtime Rascal	10	5	3	72,636
Connecticut	Nantucketeer, 1998 h., Departing Prints	8	2	0	31,733	Emotional Belle, 2000 m., Mixed Emotions	9	0	0	1,384
Delaware	Dog House, 1999 g., Dog Watch	5	0	0	3,914					
Florida	Southern Image, 2000 h., Halo's Image	4	3	3	1,612,150	Stay Forever, 1997 m., Stack	7	4	3	581,946
Georgia	Bluesthestandard, 1997 g., American Standard	6	1	1	132,633	Dixie Roll, 2000 m., Roaring Camp	10	1	0	29,374
Idaho	Curt's First Bid, 1999 g., Digression	10	5	0	84,335	Jayhawk Janet, 2000 m., Murrtheblurr	13	3	0	64,607
Illinois	Mystery Giver, 1998 g., Dynaformer	6	2	2	470,390	Synco Peach, 2000 m., Whadjathink	8	6	1	202,940
Indiana	Gmork, 2001 c., Cobra King	8	2	0	65,480	Ellens Lucky Star, 1999 m., Crown Ambassador	8	4	3	95,766
Iowa	Rubianos Image, 2000 h., Rubiano	12	3	1	114,076	One Fine Shweetie, 1999 m., Shuailaan	14	1	0	96,531
Kansas	Nick Missed, 2001 g., Gold Ruler	9	2	1	32,571	Queena Corrina, 1999 m., Here We Come	7	2	0	78,950
Kentucky	Pleasantly Perfect, 1998 h., Pleasant Colony	5	3	3	4,840,000	Ashado, 2001 f., Saint Ballado	8	5	5	2,259,640
Louisiana	Witt Ante, 2000 g., Upping the Ante	11	4	2	240,600	Destiny Calls, 2000 m., With Approval	8	6	3	271,670
Maryland	Our New Recruit, 1999 h., Alphabet Soup	5	2	2	1,265,795	He Loves Me, 2001 f., Not For Love	10	5	5	295,000
Massachusetts	Senor Ladd, 2001 g., Senor Conquistador	10	5	3	119,750	Ask Queenie, 2001 f., Key Contender	8	2	2	75,600
Michigan	Exclusivenjoyment, 2001 g., Quiet Enjoyment	9	3	1	131,170	Foolininthemeadow, 2002 f., Meadow Prayer	5	4	3	155,987
Minnesota	Wally's Choice, 2001 g., Quick Cut	8	5	4	199,061	Swasti, 2000 m., Beau Genius	6	4	2	77,928
Mississippi	Smalltown Slew, 2001 g., Evansville Slew	8	2	1	60,560	Sweet Debbie, 2000 m., Sekari (GB)	14	2	0	24,110
Missouri	Campinout, 1999 g., Victorious	17	5	0	83,130	Celtic Smoke, 1997 m., Cooleen Jack (Ire)	11	1	0	21,370
Montana	Badshot, 2000 g., Mr. Badger	13	3	0	26,497	Ms Knight Lane, 1999 m., Knight in Savannah	4	0	0	14,105
Nebraska	Thundering Verzy, 2001 g., Verzy	14	4	4	65,302	Sheso, 2001 f., Blumin Affair	7	4	3	36,864
Nevada	King's Option, 2001 c., Jestic	1	0	0	0	Bonnies Kaper, 2001 f., Haint	1	0	0	265
New Jersey	Gators N Bears, 2000 h., Stormy Atlantic	8	3	3	357,910	Totally Precious, 1999 m., Northern Idol	11	3	1	155,620
New Mexico	Rocky Gulch, 2001 g., Dry Gulch	10	6	6	377,179	Shemoveslikeaghost, 2000 m., Ghostly Moves	7	4	4	174,774
New York	Funny Cide, 2000 g., Distorted Humor	10	3	2	1,075,100	Board Elligible, 2000 m., Goldminers Gold	15	5	2	302,921
North Carolina	Chief's Spokesman, 2001 g., Dove Hunt	4	1	0	26,000	Chelsey's Bid, 2001 f., Chelsey Cat	9	4	0	51,000
North Dakota	Dakota Dixie, 2001 g., Dixieland Heat	11	2	1	32,626	Strike an Image, 2001 f., Patriot Strike	9	3	2	41,872
Ohio	Real Echo, 2000 g., Eastern Echo	8	5	2	128,100	Anna Em, 2001 f., Our Emblem	11	5	2	176,286
Oklahoma	Cheyenne Breeze, 1999 g., Slewacide	11	6	1	134,204	Lily of the Valley, 2000 m., Valley Crossing	12	5	0	79,320
Oregon	Lethal Grande, 1999 g., Corslew	15	6	1	111,367	Corona Del Hielo, 2001 f., Tiffany Ice	10	6	1	41,722
Pennsylvania	Smarty Jones, 2001 c., Elusive Quality	7	6	6	7,563,535	My Pal Lana, 2000 m., Kris S.	9	3	2	220,075
South Carolina	Intelligent Male, 2000 g., Ride the Storm	7	5	2	176,984	Big Wolf, 2000 m., Kokand	13	2	0	57,870
South Dakota	Doddles, 2002 g., Get Me Out	3	1	1	19,530	Platinum Sky, 2000 m., Pioneering	11	1	0	19,250
Tennessee	Tennessee Twelve, 1998 g., Out of Place	7	3	0	43,499	Valieo, 2001 f., Evansville Slew	10	1	0	43,670
Texas	Leaving On My Mind, 2002 g., Valid Expectations	13	5	4	299,873	Native Annie, 2001 f., Manzotti	9	4	3	187,050
Utah	Ten Forty Easy, 2000 h., Tinners Way	4	2	0	30,880	Seasons Promise, 2000 m., Four Seasons (GB)	7	0	0	23,630
Virginia	Separato, 2001 c., Victory Gallop	13	5	1	181,360	Misty Sixes, 1998 m., Summer Squall	8	3	2	246,074
Washington	Demon Warlock, 2000 h., Demons Begone	11	6	2	192,990	Aunt Sophie, 1998 m., Altazarr	7	3	3	108,250
West Virginia	A Huevo, 1996 g., Cool Joe	4	1	1	136,250	Original Gold, 2000 m., Slavic	4	3	1	163,020
Wisconsin	Awtair, 2000 g., Armed Truce	12	3	0	22,215	Jami Pari, 1996 m., Bold James	10	1	0	5,429
Wyoming	Thurber, 2000 g., Aide Memoire	7	0	0	1,170	Tallielane, 2000 m., Buckhar	4	2	0	1,709

Performance Rates for 2004

Performance Rates are an objective measurement of racetrack performance developed by the Jockey Club Information Systems. Performance Rates were originally developed by the Jockey Club and first published in *The Thoroughbred Record* in the 1960s. Performance Rates assign a rate to horses based on beaten lengths—who beat whom and by how much—with some adjustments made to standardize beaten distances to account for horses that were not pressed or were eased in large fields. Races in which individual horses did not finish are not counted for those horses.

Time is not a factor in Performance Rates, which are based on every start by every horse in North America in 2004. Performance Rates are expressed in lengths around a theoretical mean of zero. The average performances of the best horses in a given year are generally about 30 lengths better than an average performance of the average horse.

Two-Year-Old Males

Rank	Horse	Starts	Rating	Rank	Horse	Starts	Rating	Rank	Horse	Starts	Rating
1.	Afleet Alex	6	26.28	14.	Patriot Act	4	18.80	28.	Favorite Minit	3	17.10
2.	Devils Disciple	5	23.07	15.	Spanish Chestnut	4	18.65	29.	D'court's Speed	4	17.07
3.	Galloping Grocer	4	21.93	16.	Santana Strings	5	18.44	30.	Storm Surge	7	17.06
4.	Rockport Harbor	4	21.66	17.	Defer	3	18.34	31.	Rocky River	3	17.06
5.	Proud Accolade	5	21.00	18.	Dave the Knave	3	18.32	32.	Consolidator	5	16.98
6.	B. B. Best	7	20.63	19.	Straight Line	4	18.31	33.	Greater Good	5	16.93
7.	Sun King	4	20.33	20.	Flamenco	6	18.23	34.	Voronin	4	16.74
8.	Roman Ruler	4	20.11	21.	Closing Argument	5	18.13	35.	Upscaled	5	16.33
9.	Declan's Moon	4	19.68	22.	One Special Hoss	5	18.09	36.	Naughty New Yorker	6	16.29
10.	Rush Bay	4	19.40	23.	Cin Cin	5	18.01	37.	Uncle Denny	3	16.29
11.	Bellamy Road	4	19.32	24.	Texcess	4	17.53	38.	Walker	3	16.09
12.	Humor At Last	3	19.09	25.	Three Hour Nap	4	17.37	39.	Real Dandy	7	15.99
13.	Cajun Pepper	5	19.02	26.	Chandtrue	4	17.27	40.	Royal Moment	5	15.82
				27.	Park Avenue Ball	5	17.26	41.	Magna Graduate	5	15.81

Rank	Horse	Starts	Rating
42.	Razor	4	15.79
43.	Lunarpal	5	15.77
44.	Stormy Afternoon	4	15.62
45.	Raving Rocket	4	15.57
46.	Summerland	4	15.51
47.	Carminooch	5	15.41
48.	Giacomo	4	15.39
49.	Leon's Bull	7	15.33
50.	Funk	5	15.24

Two-Year-Old Fillies

Rank	Horse	Starts	Rating
1.	Splendid Blended	4	22.86
2.	Ready's Gal	3	22.74
3.	Punch Appeal	9	22.45
4.	Sense of Style	5	22.31
5.	In the Gold	4	22.07
6.	Salute	4	21.97
7.	Sharp Lisa	4	21.77
8.	Aclassysassylassy	7	21.35
9.	Sweet Catomine	4	21.28
10.	Seeking the Ante	4	21.24
11.	Successfully Sweet	4	21.00
12.	Play With Fire	5	20.90
13.	Enduring Will	3	20.68
14.	Aspen Tree	3	20.61
15.	Social Virtue	3	20.54
16.	Dance Away Capote	5	20.09
17.	Culinary	3	20.09
18.	Balletto (UAE)	5	20.02
19.	Miss Matched	3	19.87
20.	Alfonsina	3	19.57
21.	Speedy Deedy	3	19.55
22.	Peppermint Lilly	4	19.55
23.	Sweet Talker	5	19.52
24.	Broadway Gold	4	19.21
25.	Acey Deucey	3	18.85
26.	Yes It's Gold	7	18.40
27.	The Beter Man Can	4	18.40
28.	Hear Us Roar	3	18.02
29.	A Classic Life	3	18.00
30.	Panorama Valley	3	17.87
31.	Simply Lovely	5	17.85
32.	Burnish	4	17.77
33.	Smartest Thing	3	17.77
34.	Cee's Irish	5	17.77
35.	Sis City	7	17.75
36.	Smuggler	3	17.55
37.	Summer Raven	7	17.53
38.	Angel Trumpet	8	17.48
39.	Yodeladytoo	3	17.48
40.	Speedy Gone Sally	6	17.38
41.	Runway Model	10	17.29
42.	Darn That Girl	5	17.21
43.	Winning Season	7	17.17
44.	True Tails	4	17.02
45.	Home Ice	5	17.01
46.	Leona's Knight	9	16.97
47.	K. D.'s Shady Lady	6	16.96
48.	Classic Elegance	5	16.91
49.	Morning Gallop	4	16.89
50.	Coronado Rose	5	16.88

Three-Year-Old Males

Rank	Horse	Starts	Rating
1.	Smarty Jones	7	35.30
2.	The Cliff's Edge	8	30.17
3.	Lion Heart	7	29.85
4.	Pomeroy	5	28.80
5.	Birdstone	6	27.65
6.	Second of June	3	27.33
7.	Limehouse	5	27.23
8.	Eddington	11	27.13
9.	Read the Footnotes	3	26.66
10.	Sir Shackleton	9	26.16
11.	Borrego	8	25.92
12.	Commentator	5	25.19
13.	Tapit	4	25.15
14.	Pollard's Vision	11	24.99
15.	Swingforthefences	9	24.94
16.	Forest Danger	4	24.75

Rank	Horse	Starts	Rating
17.	A Bit O'Gold	7	24.74
18.	Song of the Sword	10	24.52
19.	Pro Prado	6	24.20
20.	Purge	8	24.00
21.	Love of Money	5	23.86
22.	Cryptograph	10	23.83
23.	Deputy Storm	3	23.83
24.	Fire Slam	9	23.50
25.	Silver Wagon	3	23.47
26.	Hi Teck Man	4	23.17
27.	Two Down Automatic	9	22.95
28.	Imperialism	9	22.80
29.	Kitten's Joy	7	22.73
30.	Saratoga County	12	22.69
31.	Rock Hard Ten	8	22.47
32.	Redskin Warrior	3	22.32
33.	Pies Prospect	14	22.31
34.	Penn Pacific	3	22.27
35.	Value Plus	5	22.22
36.	J Town	5	22.02
37.	Wynn Dot Comma	3	21.93
38.	Wimbledon	4	21.89
39.	Bwana Charlie	10	21.73
40.	Zakocity	14	21.73
41.	Royal Assault	10	21.72
42.	Katzanova	3	21.70
43.	Ice Wynnd Fire	5	21.53
44.	Tiger Heart	5	21.46
45.	Medallist	10	21.44
46.	Proper Prado	6	21.24
47.	Twice as Bad	3	21.16
48.	Britt's Jules	11	21.11
49.	Gotaghostofachance	7	20.81
50.	Perfect Moon	7	20.73

Three-Year-Old Fillies

Rank	Horse	Starts	Rating
1.	Ashado	8	30.55
2.	Madcap Escapade	5	28.55
3.	Yearly Report	7	27.94
4.	Capeside Lady	7	27.69
5.	Society Selection	9	27.24
6.	Victory U. S. A.	5	26.51
7.	Vision of Beauty	4	26.44
8.	Island Sand	7	26.19
9.	Daydreaming	8	25.23
10.	Mistda	6	25.05
11.	Path of Thunder	7	24.91
12.	Reforest	4	24.90
13.	Bending Strings	13	23.66
14.	Pawyne Princess	7	23.57
15.	Magical Illusion	6	23.55
16.	Ender's Sister	4	23.54
17.	Stellar Jayne	13	23.44
18.	House of Fortune	7	23.13
19.	Stephan's Angel	4	22.64
20.	Taittinger Rose	9	22.44
21.	Forestier	5	22.41
22.	River Belle (GB)	4	22.35
23.	Garavogue	4	22.33
24.	Spotlight (GB)	4	22.25
25.	Rare Gift	8	22.03
26.	Ginger N Sugar	3	22.03
27.	Shadow Cast	12	22.02
28.	Native Annie	9	21.91
29.	Eye Dazzler	4	21.70
30.	Wicked Wish	4	21.69
31.	Susan's Angel	12	21.64
32.	Dazzle Me	6	21.53
33.	Then She Laughs	8	21.42
34.	Little Andrea	3	21.41
35.	Placid Star	7	21.40
36.	Last Song	10	21.39
37.	Smokey Glacken	5	21.32
38.	Frenchglen	7	21.31
39.	Grey Traffic	5	21.31
40.	He Loves Me	10	21.29
41.	Sugar Punch	6	21.26
42.	Hollywood Story	7	21.12
43.	Happy Ticket	7	20.97
44.	Too Much Class	5	20.92

Rank	Horse	Starts	Rating
45.	Forest Music	7	20.88
46.	Silmaril	7	20.87
47.	Uncontrollable	3	20.81
48.	Pleasant Home	4	20.80
49.	Yoursmineours	7	20.76
50.	Friendly Michelle	7	20.73

Males, Four-Year-Olds and Older

Rank	Horse	Starts	Rating
1.	Ghostzapper	4	33.90
2.	Roses in May	6	30.25
3.	Saint Liam	5	24.98
4.	Southern Image	4	23.52
5.	Perfect Drift	9	22.94
6.	Funny Cide	10	22.89
7.	Zoning (GB)	3	22.43
8.	Newfoundland	9	22.03
9.	Magistretti	4	21.87
10.	Alumni Hall	10	21.52
11.	Wildcat Heir	7	21.41
12.	Migwaki	10	21.14
13.	Dynever	7	21.02
14.	Tenacious Affair	6	20.72
15.	Intelligent Male	7	20.71
16.	Top Shoter	6	20.61
17.	Lifestyle	4	20.60
18.	Colita	7	20.53
19.	Evening Attire	11	20.52
20.	Foreverness	5	20.51
21.	Dreadnaught	7	20.41
22.	Rize	13	20.36
23.	Speightstown	6	20.34
24.	Bowman's Band	12	20.33
25.	Dynastyle	5	20.33
26.	Presidentialaffair	8	20.26
27.	Seek Gold	9	20.24
28.	Toscani	3	20.03
29.	Mixed Up	4	19.96
30.	Clock Stopper	8	19.94
31.	Midas Eyes	5	19.91
32.	Offlee Wild	4	19.82
33.	Strong Hope	4	19.82
34.	Midway Road	8	19.67
35.	Badge of Silver	4	19.57
36.	King's Drama (Ire)	5	19.56
37.	Quantum Merit	3	19.48
38.	Angelic Aura	5	19.47
39.	Peace Rules	6	19.47
40.	Sataniste	13	19.46
41.	Sonic West	10	19.43
42.	Country Judge	12	19.42
43.	Cherokee's Boy	13	19.26
44.	Will's Journey	5	19.08
45.	Unforgettable Max	10	19.04
46.	Hawksbill	3	19.01
47.	Best Minister	6	18.99
48.	Mellowes	4	18.96
49.	Clayton's Trick	4	18.90
50.	Pleasantly Perfect	4	18.63

Females, Four-Year-Olds and Older

Rank	Horse	Starts	Rating
1.	Misty Sixes	8	23.65
2.	Sightseek	7	23.41
3.	Azeri	8	22.64
4.	Storm Flag Flying	8	22.27
5.	Original Gold	4	21.47
6.	Wonder Again	5	21.33
7.	Banished Lover	12	21.20
8.	Commercante (Fr)	4	20.89
9.	Friel's for Real	6	20.81
10.	Ribbon Cane	6	20.76
11.	Twist and Pop	10	20.58
12.	Wildwood Royal	11	20.47
13.	Nevermore	8	19.87
14.	Two Mile Hill	11	19.68
15.	Alix M	9	19.64
16.	Saintliness	4	19.58
17.	Provincial	9	19.53
18.	Board Elligible	15	19.47
19.	Angela's Love	9	19.41

Rank	Horse	Starts	Rating
20.	Shoot (GB)	4	19.33
21.	Ellens Lucky Star	8	19.27
22.	Cativa	5	19.25
23.	Dream of Summer	4	19.15
24.	Smoke Chaser	7	19.13
25.	Island Fashion	6	19.08
26.	Pampered Princess	11	19.07
27.	Finery	7	19.02
28.	Elloluv	5	18.90
29.	Randaroo	3	18.84
30.	Yet Anothernatalie	8	18.84
31.	Changing World	4	18.78
32.	Winning Chance	4	18.74
33.	Darby's Charm	7	18.73
34.	Shady Woman	12	18.73
35.	One for Rose	8	18.62
36.	Indy Groove	10	18.60
37.	Points West	11	18.58
38.	Grand Model	4	18.56
39.	Pop Princess	7	18.53
40.	Raffie's Dream	8	18.46
41.	Cloakof Vagueness	10	18.46
42.	Bounding Charm	8	18.45
43.	Improvised	8	18.31
44.	Lead Story	3	18.29
45.	Secret Request	6	18.19
46.	Redoubled Miss	12	18.19
47.	Mayo On the Side	12	18.17
48.	Tina Bull	7	18.16
49.	Golddigger Beware	9	18.13
50.	Miss Fortunate	9	18.09

Sprint Males, Three and Older

Rank	Horse	Starts	Rating
1.	Pomeroy	3	27.01
2.	Commentator	4	24.34
3.	Forest Danger	3	23.65
4.	Real Trooper	3	23.18
5.	Midas Eyes	4	22.48
6.	Penn Pacific	3	22.27
7.	Love of Money	3	22.17
8.	Sir Shackleton	3	22.04
9.	Wynn Dot Comma	3	21.93
10.	Saratoga County	8	21.75
11.	Bwana Charlie	8	21.67
12.	Fire Slam	6	21.52
13.	Wildcat Heir	7	21.41
14.	Ice Wynnd Fire	4	20.92
15.	Gotaghostofachance	5	20.84
16.	Top Shoter	6	20.61
17.	Primary Suspect	6	20.45
18.	Value Plus	3	20.43
19.	Speightstown	6	20.34
20.	Lifestyle	3	20.13
21.	Weigelia	12	20.12
22.	Toscani	3	20.03
23.	Clock Stopper	8	19.94
24.	Strong Hope	3	19.84
25.	Teton Forest	5	19.75
26.	Heckle	3	19.63
27.	Harvard Avenue	3	19.56
28.	Thunder Touch	7	19.52
29.	Willy o'the Valley	7	19.38
30.	Great Commander	5	19.35
31.	Eurosilver	3	19.23
32.	Polish Pride	3	19.00
33.	Polish Rifle	3	18.93
34.	Abbondanza	11	18.84
35.	Tango Tales	4	18.81
36.	Two Down Automatic	3	18.77
37.	Mass Media	5	18.33
38.	Work With Me	4	18.25
39.	Liquor Cabinet (Ire)	4	18.24
40.	Monty Man	3	18.23
41.	Maxwell Terrace	3	18.16
42.	Champali	8	18.15
43.	Nightmare Affair	6	18.14
44.	Medallist	7	18.14
45.	Mike's Classic	5	18.12
46.	Stratostar	3	18.05
47.	Kela	6	18.02
48.	Andiamo	4	18.00
49.	Britt's Jules	4	17.91
50.	Badge of Silver	3	17.80

Sprint Females, Three and Older

Rank	Horse	Starts	Rating
1.	Madcap Escapade	3	26.56
2.	Vision of Beauty	4	26.44
3.	Bending Strings	7	24.61
4.	Reforest	3	24.44
5.	Capeside Lady	3	24.26
6.	Wicked Wish	3	23.60
7.	Grey Traffic	3	22.74
8.	Forestier	5	22.41
9.	Ginger N Sugar	4	22.03
10.	Cherry Bomb	3	21.81
11.	Dazzle Me	6	21.53
12.	Placid Star	4	21.45
13.	Josh's Madelyn	6	21.43
14.	Then She Laughs	8	21.42
15.	Little Andrea	3	21.41
16.	Smokey Glacken	5	21.32
17.	Frenchglen	7	21.31
18.	Happy Ticket	4	21.28
19.	Sugar Punch	3	21.26
20.	Clarksburg Queen	4	20.97
21.	Forest Music	7	20.88
22.	Icy Cat	5	20.78
23.	Silmaril	3	20.65
24.	Psych	4	20.61
25.	Twilight Gallop	4	20.57
26.	Feline Story	9	20.44
27.	Bohemian Lady	5	20.43
28.	Original Gold	3	20.26
29.	Tiz a Dancer	6	20.12
30.	Angelica Slew	6	20.09
31.	Western Hemisphere	4	19.98
32.	Friendly Michelle	5	19.79
33.	Resplendency	3	19.74
34.	Fall Fashion	4	19.56
35.	Miss Noteworthy	5	19.51
36.	The K O Touch	9	19.42
37.	Muir Beach	8	19.28
38.	Mariakel	6	19.27
39.	Prall Street	3	19.15
40.	Smoke Chaser	7	19.13
41.	Alix M	6	19.05
42.	My Trusty Cat	7	19.05
43.	Strawberry Line	3	18.94
44.	Smoke Glack Attack	3	18.89
45.	Ms. Bag	3	18.87
46.	Randaroo	3	18.84
47.	Ribbon Cane	4	18.71
48.	She's a Mugs	8	18.70
49.	Oneofacat	4	18.61
50.	Simply Brilliant	4	18.56

Turf Males, Three and Older

Rank	Horse	Starts	Rating
1.	Kitten's Joy	7	22.73
2.	Magistretti	4	21.87
3.	Artie Schiller	6	20.78
4.	Foreverness	5	20.51
5.	Dreadnaught	7	20.41
6.	Mixed Up	4	19.96
7.	King's Drama (Ire)	3	19.56
8.	Quantum Merit	3	19.48
9.	Mustanfar	7	19.32
10.	Silver Ticket	5	19.31
11.	Hawksbill	3	19.01
12.	Mr O'Brien (Ire)	7	19.00
13.	Mellowes	4	18.96
14.	Sailaway	7	18.82
15.	Toasted	5	18.75
16.	Deputy Strike	5	18.45
17.	Sea Preacher	3	18.44
18.	Greek Sun	4	18.32
19.	Blackdoun (Fr)	5	18.28
20.	Wire Bound	8	18.26
21.	Royal Regalia	4	18.26
22.	Good Reward	8	18.21
23.	Icy Atlantic	7	18.07
24.	No Parole	3	17.92
25.	Cool Conductor	9	17.88
26.	Host	8	17.82
27.	Rayon	5	17.74
28.	Golden Commander	8	17.68
29.	Ay Caramba (Brz)	5	17.56
30.	Nothing to Lose	9	17.51
31.	Senor Swinger	9	17.47
32.	Stroll	5	17.47
33.	B. A. Way	8	17.43
34.	Strut the Stage	4	17.37
35.	Better Talk Now	8	17.27
36.	On the Course	5	17.16
37.	Pass Play	5	17.16
38.	Prince Arch	8	17.15
39.	Shiloh Bound	3	17.11
40.	Capital Peak	6	17.05
41.	Dr. Brendler	3	17.03
42.	Governor Brown	6	17.03
43.	Bankruptcy Court	4	17.02
44.	Timo	6	16.93
45.	Celtic Memories	9	16.87
46.	Sir Walter Rahy	5	16.78
47.	America Alive	5	16.78
48.	Maysville Slew	5	16.71
49.	Provincetown	6	16.70
50.	Ball Four	4	16.68

Turf Females, Three and Older

Rank	Horse	Starts	Rating
1.	River Belle (GB)	4	22.35
2.	Spotlight (GB)	4	22.25
3.	Sister Swank	5	21.43
4.	Wonder Again	5	21.33
5.	Path of Thunder	3	21.04
6.	Jinny's Gold	8	20.93
7.	Commercante (Fr)	4	20.89
8.	Sister Star	3	20.64
9.	Miss Vegas (Ire)	3	20.63
10.	Plenty	4	20.34
11.	Delta Sensation	7	20.00
12.	Lucifer's Stone	6	19.86
13.	Shadow Cast	4	19.81
14.	Ticker Tape (GB)	10	19.50
15.	Seducer's Song	5	19.45
16.	Shoot (GB)	4	19.33
17.	Gingham and Lace	3	19.12
18.	Finery	7	19.02
19.	Western Ransom	6	18.96
20.	Fortunate Damsel	4	18.87
21.	Changing World	4	18.78
22.	Lady Cheyne	4	18.65
23.	Dowry	3	18.63
24.	Vous	9	18.38
25.	Galloping Gal	5	18.36
26.	Lenatareese	6	18.24
27.	Art Fan	6	18.13
28.	R Obsession	6	18.06
29.	Merry Me in Spring	4	18.05
30.	Beret	5	18.03
31.	Sand Springs	5	17.97
32.	Mambo Slew	8	17.75
33.	Helen's Legacy	3	17.75
34.	Arvilla Priscilla	3	17.70
35.	Midwife	3	17.62
36.	Riskaverse	6	17.54
37.	Spring Season	5	17.49
38.	High Court (Brz)	4	17.49
39.	Film Maker	5	17.48
40.	Hour of Justice	5	17.35
41.	Rowdy	4	17.32
42.	Go Robin	4	17.30
43.	Inish Glora	5	17.18
44.	Ellens Lucky Star	4	17.11
45.	Mona Rose	4	17.10
46.	Aud	9	17.10
47.	On the Bus	7	17.07
48.	Eternal Melody (NZ)	4	16.93
49.	Humaita (Ger)	9	16.90
50.	Super Brand (SAf)	3	16.78

Experimental Free Handicap

The Experimental Free Handicap, published annually by the Jockey Club, is based on a hypothetical 1⅛-mile race for two-year-olds on dirt. Walter S. Vosburgh, the legendary Jockey Club handicapper, compiled the first Experimental Free Handicap in 1933. He placed Sanford Stakes winner First Minstrel atop his list at 126 pounds, although the filly Mata Hari at 122 pounds effectively was the highweight when considering the five-pound sex allowance then in effect. The 126-pound high weight became the standard impost for a champion of average accomplishment.

Vosburgh, who had been the racing secretary at New York tracks since 1894, retired in 1934, and no Experimental Free Handicap was prepared for that year. John B. Campbell assumed the task in 1935 and continued to compile the list until his death in '54.

Campbell, also racing secretary at the New York tracks, wrote in a 1943 letter that his Experimental Free Handicap was intended primarily as a forecast of how the horses would perform as three-year-olds. The Experimental, he wrote, "is based mainly upon my opinion of what the two-year-olds will accomplish as three-year-olds and at distances of a mile and a furlong or greater."

Following Campbell's death, Frank E. "Jimmy" Kilroe assigned the weights through 1960. Thomas Trotter, who compiled the list through 1972, followed him.

Starting in 1969, at the behest of the Jockey Club, the thrust of the Experimental was changed from a prediction of future performance to a prediction of accomplishment during the two-year-old season exclusively.

Kenneth Noe Jr. prepared the Experimental Free Handicap from 1972 through '75, and Trotter resumed the task in 1976. Beginning in 1979, a committee of three racing secretaries was chosen to establish the Experimental weights. In 1985, for the first time, separate lists were compiled for males and fillies. The 2004 Experimental Free Handicap was prepared by Frank Gabriel Jr. of Arlington Park, Mike Lakow of the New York Racing Association, and Tom Robbins of Del Mar.

The highest Experimental weight ever assigned was 132 pounds to Count Fleet in 1942; the following year, he won the Triple Crown.

Past Experimental Free Handicap Highweights

Year	Male	Female	Year	Male	Female
2004	Declan's Moon (126)	Sweet Catomine (124)	1968	Top Knight (126)	Gallant Bloom (118)
	Wilko (126)				Process Shot (118)
2003	Action This Day (126)	Halfbridled (124)	1967	Vitriolic (126)	Queen of the Stage (117)
	Cuvee (126)		1966	Successor (126)	Regal Gleam (116)
	Ruler's Court (126)		1965	Buckpasser (126)	Moccasin (120)
2002	Vindication (126)	Storm Flag Flying (123)	1964	Bold Lad (130)	Queen Empress (118)
2001	Johannesburg (126)	Tempera (123)	1963	Raise a Native (126)	Castle Forbes (115)
2000	Macho Uno (126)	Caressing (123)			Tosmah (115)
1999	Anees (126)	Cash Run (123)	1962	Never Bend (126)	Affectionately (115)
		Chilukki (123)			Smart Deb (115)
		Surfside (123)	1961	Crimson Satan (126)	Cicada (118)
1998	Answer Lively (126)	Silverbulletday (123)	1960	Hail to Reason (126)	Bowl of Flowers (120)
1997	Favorite Trick (128)	Countess Diana (125)	1959	Warfare (126)	My Dear Girl (117)
1996	Boston Harbor (126)	Storm Song (124)	1958	First Landing (126)	Quill (117)
1995	Maria's Mon (126)	My Flag (123)	1957	Jewel's Reward (126)	Idun (120)
	Unbridled's Song (126)		1956	Barbizon (126)	Alanesian (117)
1994	Timber Country (126)	Flanders (124)	1955	Career Boy (126)	Doubledogdare (116)
1993	Brocco (126)	Phone Chatter (123)			Nasrina (116)
	Dehere (126)		1954	Summer Tan (128)	HIgh Voltage (117)
1992	Gilded Time (126)	Eliza (123)	1953	Porterhouse (126)	Evening Out (118)
1991	Arazi (130)	Pleasant Stage (123)		*Turn-to (126)	
1990	Fly So Free (126)	Meadow Star (123)	1952	Native Dancer (130)	Bubbley (116)
1989	Rhythm (126)	Go for Wand (123)			Sweet Patootie (116)
1988	Easy Goer (126)	Open Mind (123)	1951	Tom Fool (126)	Rose Jet (115)
1987	Forty Niner (126)	Epitome (123)	1950	Uncle Miltie (126)	Aunt Jinny (115)
		Over All (123)			How (115)
1986	Capote (126)	Brave Raj (123)	1949	Middleground (126)	Bed o' Roses (119)
1985†	Ogygian (126)	I'm Splendid (123)	1948	Blue Peter (126)	Myrtle Charm (121)
	Tasso (126)		1947	Citation (126)	Bewitch (121)
1984	Chief's Crown (126)	Outstandingly (118)	1946	Cosmic Bomb (126)	First Flight (126)
1983	Devil's Bag (128)	Miss Oceana (120)		Double Jay (126)	
1982	Copelan (126)	Landaluce (121)	1945	Lord Boswell (128)	Beaugay (121)
	Roving Boy (126)	Princess Rooney (121)	1944	Free for All (126)	Busher (119)
1981	Deputy Minister (126)	Before Dawn (120)		Pavot (126)	
	Timely Writer (126)		1943	Pukka Gin (126)	Durazna (121)
1980	Lord Avie (126)	Heavenly Cause (120)			Miss Keeneland (121)
1979	Rockhill Native (126)	Smart Angle (120)	1942	Count Fleet (132)	Askmenow (119)
1978	Spectacular Bid (126)	Candy Eclair (119)			Good Morning (119)
		It's in the Air (119)			Chiquita Mia (115)
1977	Affirmed (126)	Lakeville Miss (119)			Ficklebush (115)
1976	Seattle Slew (126)	Sensational (119)	1941	Alsab (130)	Level Best (121)
1975	Honest Pleasure (126)	Dearly Precious (119)	1940	Whirlaway (126)	Now What (119)
		Optimistic Gal (119)	1939	Bimelech (130)	Inscoelda (116)
1974	Foolish Pleasure (127)	Ruffian (122)	1938	El Chico (126)	Jacola (116)
1973	Protagonist (126)	Talking Picture (121)	1937	Menow (126)	Rifted Clouds (115)
1972	Secretariat (129)	La Prevoyante (121)	1936	Brooklyn (126)	Forever Yours (116)
1971	Riva Ridge (126)	Numbered Account (119)	1935	Red Rain (126)	Mata Hari (122)
1970	Hoist the Flag (126)	Forward Gal (118)	1933	First Minstrel (126)	
1969	Silent Screen (128)	Fast Attack (116)			

†Starting in 1985, fillies were weighted separately.
No weights assigned in 1934.

2004 Experimental Free Handicap Colts and Geldings

Wt.	Horse	Sire—Dam, Broodmare Sire	Sts	1st	2nd	3rd	Earnings
126	Declan's Moon	Malibu Moon—Vee Vee Star, by Norquestor	4	4	0	0	$507,300
	Wilko	Awesome Again—Native Roots (Ire), by Indian Ridge	12	3	2	5	934,074
124	Afleet Alex	Northern Afleet—Maggy Hawk, by Hawkster	6	4	2	0	680,800
	Roman Ruler	Fusaichi Pegasus—Silvery Swan, by Silver Deputy	5	3	1	0	330,800
123	Proud Accolade	Yes It's True—Proud Ciel, by Septieme Ciel	5	3	0	0	364,130
	Sun King	Charismatic—Clever But Costly, by Clever Trick	4	1	0	2	244,850
122	Giacomo	Holy Bull—Set Them Free, by Stop the Music	4	1	1	1	119,440
	Rockport Harbor	Unbridled's Song—Regal Miss Copelan, by Copelan	4	4	0	0	210,300
121	Devils Disciple	Devil His Due—Stormfeather, by Storm Bird	5	3	2	0	161,800
120	Consolidator	Storm Cat—Good Example (Fr), by Crystal Glitters	7	2	1	1	480,260
119	Galloping Grocer	A. P Jet—Little Evie, by Northrop	4	3	1	0	150,400
118	Southern Africa	Cape Town—Al Fahda (GB), by Be My Chief	5	2	1	0	67,190
117	Chandtrue	Yes It's True—Chandelle, by Crafty Prospector	4	4	0	0	182,970
116	Flamenco	Dance Master—Libre, by Fly So Free	6	4	1	1	303,085
	Park Avenue Ball	Citidancer—Road to the Ball, by Cahill Road	5	3	1	0	278,600
115	Dubleo	Southern Halo—Secret Red, by Secretariat	9	6	1	1	360,899
	Greater Good	Intidab—Gather The Clan (Ire), by General Assembly	5	3	0	1	226,275
114	Crown Point	Honor Grades—Runaway Ashleigh, by Runaway Groom	7	2	1	0	90,847
	Lunarpal	Successful Appeal—Quiet Eclipse, by Quiet American	5	4	0	0	284,677
	Primal Storm	Storm Boot—Primistal, by Stalwart	4	2	0	1	102,798
113	Actxecutive	Noactor—Majestic Report, by Corporate Report	4	1	2	0	74,692
	Defer	Danzig—Hidden Reserve, by Mr. Prospector	3	2	1	0	108,900
	Straight Line,	Boundary—Zanti, by Strawberry Road (Aus)	6	3	1	0	166,312
	Texcess	In Excess (Ire)—Danish Alamode, by Regal Classic	4	3	1	0	725,427
112	Boston Glory	Boston Harbor—Unbridled Glory, by Unbridled	4	1	1	1	67,850
111	Better Than Bonds	Sweetsouthernsaint—Jabesh, by Vanlandingham	5	2	1	1	114,370
	Drum Major	Dynaformer—Endless Parade, by Williamstown	4	1	1	1	46,008
	Elusive Chris	Elusive Quality—Kara's Heart, by American Legion	6	2	3	0	122,570
	Leaving On My Mind	Valid Expectations—Sudden Attraction	13	5	2	3	299,873
	Patriot Act	A.P. Indy—Classic Value, by Copelan	4	0	2	1	114,885
	Seattles Best Joe	Personable Joe—First Class Action, by Chisos	5	3	1	0	99,415
	Seize the Day	Montbrook—Dignified Woman, by World Appeal	3	1	0	1	36,650
	Storm Surge	Storm Cat—Especially, by Mr. Prospector	7	4	1	0	192,770
110	Bellamy Road	Concerto—Hurry Home Hillary, by Deputed Testamony	3	2	0	0	140,400
	Boggy Creek	Menifee—Hail the Queen, by Danzatore	5	3	0	0	120,111
	Cajun Pepper	Barricade—Cajun Cutie, by Truce Maker	5	5	0	0	112,242
	Closing Argument	Successful Appeal—Mrs. Greeley, by Mr. Greeley	5	2	2	1	421,984
	Evil Minister	Deputy Minister—Evil's Pic, by Piccolino	5	2	0	1	120,530
	Gold Joy	Joyeux Danseur—Lizzie Worthington, by Gold Seam	6	2	1	1	110,002
	Wallstreet Scandal	Mt. Livermore—Naughty, by River Special	4	1	2	0	106,909
109	B. B. Best	Yes It's True—Bold Juana, by John Alden	7	4	0	1	360,710
	Cin Cin	Precocity—Home Together, by Homebuilder	5	3	0	1	157,140
	Funk	Unbridled's Song—Verbal Volley, by Oh Say	5	2	1	1	74,960
	Magoo's Magic	Awesome Again—Slew the Queen, by Seattle Slew	4	2	1	0	70,358
	Three Hour Nap	Afternoon Deelites—Pilgrim's Treasure, by Pilgrim	4	3	0	0	158,400
108	Anthony J.	Tiger Ridge—Sly Stylist, by Sovereign Dancer	5	1	1	1	213,630
	Bushwacker	Outflanker—Musical Score, by Romantic Lead	3	1	1	0	41,000
	Littlebitofzip	Littlebitlively—Kafaf, by Zilzal	7	1	1	2	85,328
	Sunny Sky (Fr)	Septieme Ciel—Silicon Run, by Commanche Run	7	3	0	2	74,967
	Tadreeb	Theatrical (Ire)—Space Time (Fr), by Bering (GB)	4	1	0	0	32,224
107	G P's Black Knight	Tiger Ridge—Ample Time, by Wolf Power (SAf)	7	2	2	1	89,500
	Rey de Cafe	Kingmambo—Commodities, by Private Account	6	2	2	0	113,204
106	Chips Are Down	Distorted Humor—Tiy Buster, by Housebuster	6	2	2	0	74,825
	D'court's Speed	Doneraile Court—Velvet Panther, by Pentaquod	4	1	2	0	44,800
	Killenaule	Fusaichi Pegasus—Tipically Irish, by Metfield	9	4	3	2	198,540
	Maximus C	Coronado's Quest—Long Silence, by Alleged	3	1	0	1	45,250
	Wild Desert	Wild Rush—Desert Radiance, by Desert Wine	8	2	2	1	89,636
	Winsomemoneyhoney	Spinning World—Fleeting Honey, by Afleet	2	1	1	0	35,570
105	Cherokee Chase	Rizzi—Cherokyfrolicflash, by Green Dancer	9	2	0	3	79,890
	City Code	Carson City—Valid Affect, by Valid Appeal	5	2	0	2	52,040
	Doctor Voodoo	Petionville—Go Ahead and Cry, by Belong to Me	7	3	1	2	109,745
	Major League	Magic Cat—Quick Grey, by El Prado (Ire)	8	2	3	0	97,100
	Rush Bay	Cozzene—Seoul, by Deputy Minister	4	1	2	1	87,755
	Winning Expression	Western Expression—Miss Winning Sweep, by End Sweep	5	1	2	0	78,138
104	Diamond Isle	Gilded Time—Polish Legacy, by Polish Navy	4	1	1	2	122,030
	Hal's Image	Halo's Image—Mia's Hope, by Rexson's Hope	11	1	1	3	56,040
	Magna Graduate	Honor Grades—Peacock Alley, by Fast Play	5	2	1	1	76,832
	Positive Prize	Prized—Hushi, by Riverman	5	4	0	1	106,663
	Ready Ruler	More Than Ready—Reina Victoriosa (Arg), by Interprete	7	2	2	2	114,470
	Smooth Bid	Rubiano—Miss Fizz, by Spectacular Bid	5	2	2	1	77,410
	Spanish Chestnut	Horse Chestnut (SAf)—Baby Rabbit, by No Sale George	4	2	2	0	84,420
103	Rubialedo	Rubiano—Runaway Cater, by Runaway Groom	7	1	1	2	54,085
	Scipion	A.P. Indy—Strawberry Reason, by Strawberry Road (Aus)	3	1	0	1	47,000
	Smoke Warning	Smoke Glacken—Secret Affair, by Secret Hello	6	1	1	1	61,275
	Upscaled	Sir Cat—Limestone Landing, by Red Ryder	5	1	0	3	65,916
102	Malanato	Malagra—Renato Jo, by Catane	7	4	1	1	99,020
	My Parade	Parade Ground—Suddenly Maria, by Stately Don	7	2	1	1	137,050
	Silver Haze	Silver Deputy—Crystal Vous, by Crystal Water	7	2	1	1	56,105

Wt.	Horse	Sire—Dam, Broodmare Sire	Sts	1st	2nd	3rd	Earnings
101	Chattahoochee War	War Chant—Buffalo Berry (Ire), by Sri Pekan	2	1	0	0	29,400
	Dusty Minister	Open Forum—Sister of Darkness, by Geiger Counter	7	2	1	1	53,930
	Elusive Thunder	Thunder Gulch—Be Elusive, by With Approval	7	2	1	0	75,420
	Social Probation	Jules—Satinet, by Olympio	5	2	1	0	60,900
	Woody's Apache	Cryptoclearance—Take Sara, by Regal Remark	8	1	2	3	36,990
100	Favorite Minit	Favorite Trick—Minit Towinit, by Malagra	3	2	1	0	57,150
	Fusaichi Rock Star	Wild Wonder—Grannies Feather, by At Full Feather	4	1	0	1	48,366
	Reno Bob	Miesque's Son—Odner's Jewel, by Chief's Crown	8	2	1	3	52,678
	Storm Creek Rising	Storm Creek—Goulash, by Mari's Book	5	1	3	1	65,490

2004 Experimental Free Handicap Fillies

Wt.	Horse	Sire—Dam, Broodmare Sire	Sts	1st	2nd	3rd	Earnings
124	Sweet Catomine	Storm Cat—Sweet Life, by Kris S.	4	3	1	0	$799,800
117	Balletto (UAE)	Timber Country—Destiny Dance, by Nijinsky II	5	3	2	0	614,000
	Sense of Style	Thunder Gulch—Save Me the Waltz (Ire), by Kings Lake	5	3	0	0	369,000
	Splendid Blended	Unbridled's Song—Valid Blend, by Valid Appeal	4	3	1	0	327,400
115	Ready's Gal	More Than Ready—Exquisite Mistress, by Nasty and Bold	3	2	1	0	155,200
114	Inspiring	Golden Missile—Arches of Gold, by Strike Gold	2	2	0	0	115,800
	Runway Model	Petionville—Ticket to Houston, by Houston	10	4	2	2	580,598
	Souvenir Gift	Souvenir Copy—Alleged Gift, by Alleged	5	3	2	0	211,760
113	Sharp Lisa	Dixieland Band—Winter's Gone, by Dynaformer	4	1	2	0	171,600
	Sis City	Slew City Slew—Smart Sis, by Beau Genius	7	3	0	2	282,980
112	In the Gold	Golden Missile—Incinerate, by Groovy	4	1	1	1	83,062
111	Classic Elegance	Carson City—Taegu, by Halo	6	3	0	1	204,006
	Dance Away Capote	Capote—Ingot's Dance Away, by Gate Dancer	5	2	1	0	124,450
	Paddy's Daisy	King of Kings (Ire)—Mrs. Paddy, by Woodman	6	4	0	0	186,336
	Play With Fire	Boundary—Realm, by Mr. Prospector. Claiborne Farm (Ky.)	5	1	0	2	107,000
110	Melhor Ainda	Pulpit—Potrinner (Arg), by Potrillazo	2	2	0	0	76,920
	Punch Appeal	Successful Appeal—Okanagan Dawn, by Two Punch	9	6	0	1	389,840
109	Broadway Gold	Seeking the Gold—Miss Doolittle, by Storm Cat	4	2	0	0	107,420
	Culinary	El Amante—Volunteer (Arg), by Ski Champ	3	2	0	0	78,000
	Louvain (Ire)	Sinndar—Flanders, byCommon Grounds	6	2	2	2	87,143
	Northern Mischief	Yankee Victor—Rhondaling (GB), by Welsh Pageant	5	1	0	1	77,260
	Toll Taker	Bernstein—Tappanzee, by Bet Big	6	3	0	1	114,240
108	Chocolate Brown	Lion Hearted—Twin Lights, by Holy Bull	3	2	0	0	76,206
	Enduring Will	Arch—Jodie Faster, by Theatrical (Ire)	3	2	1	0	78,800
	Hello Lucky	Lucky Lionel—Mystery Number, by Secret Hello	7	3	0	2	142,140
	Short Route	Mud Route—Short Call, by Phone Trick	5	2	1	0	106,995
107	Conveyor's Angel	Conveyor—Supreme Angel, by Prince Valid	6	2	1	0	82,530
	Megascape	Cape Canaveral—Bigger Half, by Megaturn	5	3	0	1	161,740
	Summer Raven	Summer Squall—Rahy Rose, by Rahy	7	2	2	1	168,910
106	Buzz Song	Unbridled's Song—Buzzovertomyhouse, by Drone	3	2	0	1	92,100
	Culture Clash	Petionville—Antonia Bin (Ire), by Sadler's Wells	4	1	0	0	41,400
	Hear Us Roar	Lion Hearted—Grand Slalom, by Broad Brush	3	3	0	0	128,680
	Memorette	Memo (Chi)—Forever Fondre, by Shahrastani	6	2	1	1	158,325
	Take a Check	Touch Gold—Groovy Feeling, by Groovy	8	2	3	0	84,955
105	Double D Appeal	Successful Appeal—Wicked Diablo, by Diablo	3	2	0	1	73,530
	Kota	Indian Charlie—Silverbulletlover, by Gulch	7	2	2	3	139,450
	Queens Plaza	Forestry—Kew Garden, by Seattle Slew	4	2	0	0	89,327
104	Angel Trumpet	Cape Canaveral—Tricki Mae, by Phone Trick	8	3	3	1	146,456
	Bella Banissa	Good and Tough—Banissa, by Lear Fan	3	0	2	0	37,630
	Im a Dixie Girl	Dixie Union—Im Out First, by Allen's Prospect	9	3	1	1	150,200
	No Bull Baby	Indian Charlie—Slumgullion, by Conquistador Cielo	6	2	1	0	129,720
	Royal Copenhagen (Fr)	Inchinor (GB)—Amnesia, by Septieme Ciel	4	2	2	0	68,417
103	Aspen Tree	Holy Bull—Rockaroller, by Dixieland Band	3	1	2	0	47,061
	Dansetta Light	Colony Light—Dolly's Back, by At the Threshold	9	4	1	0	165,080
	Jill Robin L	Precocity—Jo Zak, by Vilzak	8	1	2	0	49,500
	K. D.'s Shady Lady	Maria's Mon—Annie's Apple, by Shawklit Won	6	1	3	1	77,320
	La Maitresse (Ire)	Desert King—Banariya, by Lear Fan	7	1	1	2	31,392
	Limited Entry	Carson City—Grand Betty, by Copelan	3	1	1	0	52,780
	My Miss Storm Cat	Sea of Secrets—Urmia, by Meadowlake	2	1	0	1	38,616
	Smuggler	Unbridled—Inside Information, by Private Account	3	2	1	0	75,800
102	Berbatim	Bernstein—Word Harvest, by Verbatim	4	2	1	0	56,120
	Leona's Knight	Suave Prospect—P. M.'s Hope, by Rexson's Hope	9	3	0	2	126,400
	Paragon Queen	Lord Carson—Storm Struck, by Storm Bird	7	1	4	0	85,540
	Running Bobcats	Running Stag—Backatem, by Notebook	8	4	2	1	108,680
	Secrets Galore	Honour and Glory—Galore, by Gulch	6	1	2	1	60,083
	She's a Jewel	Successful Appeal—Binawin, by Binalong	5	2	0	1	70,600
101	Gotta Rush	Wild Rush—Silver Stockings, by Seattle Sleet	4	2	0	2	61,556
	Lady Glade	Straight Man—Meetmenow, by Shimatoree	2	1	1	0	41,340
	Ninadivina	Cape Town—Cecelia Be Mine, by Lomond	9	3	0	1	86,174
	Salute	Unbridled—Personal Ensign, by Private Account	4	1	2	1	87,326
	Winning Season	Lemon Drop Kid—Topicount, by Private Account	7	2	1	2	99,655
100	Darn That Girl	Darn That Alarm—Diplomatic Girl, by Gallapiat	5	1	1	0	60,234
	Malika's Gold	Gold Case—Mucci Baby, by Cozzene	4	2	0	0	74,400
	Miss Matched	Formal Gold—Ivory Princess (Ire), by Cure the Blues	3	1	1	0	72,200
	Western Princess	Gone West—My Last Alibi, by Deputy Minister	3	1	0	1	34,073
	Wild Chick	Forest Wildcat—Open Window, by Trempolino	2	1	0	1	37,200

American Match Races

Match races, a prominent part of American Thoroughbred racing through the mid-1970s, slowed to a trickle after Ruffian's fatal showdown with Foolish Pleasure at Belmont Park on July 6, 1975. Of all the match races in North America during the 20th century, very few were contested after the undefeated filly shattered her right front ankle and was euthanized the next day. Only nine of those 13 were in the United States, and none of them commanded the national attention given the Ruffian–Foolish Pleasure match and such earlier match races as Seabiscuit–War Admiral and Nashua–Swaps.

Match races in America were mostly winner take all and trace back to the early 1820s, when American Eclipse engaged in and won two matches. Similarly, the great sire Lexington won twice in head-to-head competition in the 1850s. Since Domino defeated Clifford by three-quarters of a length in a one-mile match race at Sheepshead Bay Racetrack in New York on September 6, 1894, 15 match races have contained at least one starter who was recognized officially or unofficially as a champion. (*Daily Racing Form* first designated champions in 1936.) Thirteen of the 15 races offered wagering, and favorites lost nine of them. None was more noteworthy than War Admiral's loss to Seabiscuit in 1938, and none was more one-sided than Miss Musket's 50-length loss to Chris Evert on July 20, 1974, at Hollywood Park.

To appreciate America's greatest match races, it is necessary to understand the hype and expectations heading into them. For more than a year, racing fans had clamored for a match-up of Seabiscuit and War Admiral, the two dominant horses of the late 1930s. When the two finally met, they were the only entrants in the $1\frac{3}{16}$-mile Pimlico Special Stakes on November 1, 1938. A record crowd of 40,000 turned out to see Seabiscuit, a five-year-old grandson of Man o' War, take on War Admiral, a four-year-old son of Man o' War who had won the 1937 Triple Crown and 16 of 17 starts prior to the match.

Seabiscuit, breaking from the second post position, was sent off at 2.20-to-1 under George Woolf; War Admiral, thought to be the quicker from the gate, was 0.25-to-1 under Charley Kurtsinger. War Admiral was expected to lead at the start, but Seabiscuit outbroke him. Seabiscuit had been on the lead in just one of his previous 13 starts.

War Admiral made several moves at his opponent and once drew within a nose, but Seabiscuit had plenty left and won by four lengths in track-record time of 1:56.60.

Nearly 17 years later, Kentucky Derby winner Swaps went off as the 3-to-10 favorite against Preakness and Belmont Stakes winner Nashua in the $100,000 Washington Park Match Race at 1¼ miles on August 31, 1955. Swaps was undefeated as a three-year-old and owner-breeder Rex Ellsworth had returned him to California after he defeated Nashua by 1½ lengths in the 1955 Derby. Nashua's only loss in 11 starts had been in the Derby. Swaps was the favorite under Bill Shoemaker, while Nashua was 6-to-5 with Eddie Arcaro. Nashua won by 6½ lengths, leading from start to finish.

The race that effectively ended top-level match races pitted Foolish Pleasure, 1975 Kentucky Derby winner, against undefeated Ruffian, a three-year-old filly who never had been headed in ten career starts, all against other fillies. Jacinto Vasquez was the regular rider of both horses and chose to ride Frank Whiteley-trained Ruffian in the nationally televised race. Ruffian went off at 0.40-to-1; Foolish Pleasure was 0.90-to-1.

Ruffian broke from the rail and narrowly led Foolish Pleasure through a blazing first quarter-mile in :22⅕ on Belmont's deep 1¼-mile chute. Shortly after they entered the main track, however, Ruffian broke down and swerved to the outside. Foolish Pleasure finished the race under Braulio Baeza. Ruffian, who fought her handlers when coming out of anesthetic after surgery, reinjured her leg, and was euthanized early on July 7. Match races since then never have been the same.—*Bill Heller*

Significant Match Races, 1820 to 2003

Winner, Age, Sex	Loser, Age, Sex	Race	Date	Track	Distance	Time
Soviet Problem, 4, f.	Mamselle Bebette, 4, f.	Match Race	8/21/1994	Del Mar	5fT	:56.58
Soviet Problem, 4, f.	Lazor, 4, g.	Match Race	5/12/1994	Golden Gate Fields	6f	1:08.55
Who Doctor Who, 5, g.	Explosive Girl, 4, f.	Match Race	7/23/1988	Ak-Sar-Ben	1m 70y	1:42.00
Foolish Pleasure, 3, c.	Ruffian, 3, f.	Great Match Race	7/6/1975	Belmont Park	1¼m	2:02.80
Chris Evert, 3, f.	Miss Musket, 3, f.	Hollywood Special S.	7/20/1974	Hollywood Park	1¼m	2:02.00
Jovial John, 4, g.	Blunt Man, 9, h.	Match Race	11/16/1972	Cahokia Downs	5f	1:00.80
Convenience, 4, f.	Typecast, 6, m.	Hollywood Park Match Race	6/17/1972	Hollywood Park	1⅛m	1:47.60
Nasharco, 4, c.	Nancycee, 4, f.	Match Race	4/10/1966	Turf Paradise	5½f	1:10.20
Nancycee, 4, f.	Nasharco, 4, c.	Match Race	3/20/1966	Turf Paradise	5f	:56.20
Short Nail, 2, c.	Florida Cracker, 2, c.	Match Race	12/4/1962	Garden State	6f	1:13.40
Cesca, 2, f.	Aim n Fire, 2, c.	Match Race	7/7/1962	Woodbine	5½f	1:04.60
Wichita Maid, 4, f.	Gilhooley, 5, m.	Australian Welcome Inv. Match Race	8/19/1961	Centennial	5½f	1:04.40
Routeen, 2, f.	Modest Step, 2, f.	Latonia Match Race	10/1/1960	Latonia	6f	1:13.60
Roman Colonel, 4, c.	Benedicto, 5, g.	Special Match Race	6/11/1960	Detroit Race Course	6f	1:10.40
Lori Lynn, 4, f.	*Salmon Peter, 9, g.	Inv. Match Race	8/22/1959	Centennial	1¼m	2:05.00
Wildoath, 3, c.	War Marshal, 4, c.	Special Match Race	10/12/1957	Fresno	$1\frac{1}{16}$m	1:43.60
Noorahge, 4, c.	Early Bull, 7, h.	Dapper Dan Match Race	9/14/1957	Wheeling Downs	6½f	1:24.00
Queen Doris, 3, f.	Molly Darling, 4, f.	Inv. Match Race	7/28/1956	Centennial	5½f	1:05.60
Nashua, 3, c.	Swaps, 3, c.	Washington Park Match Race	8/31/1955	Washington Park	1¼m	2:04.20
Virginia Fair, 2, f.	Virden, 2, f.	Inv. Match Race	8/15/1952	Edmonton	abt 5f	1:00.40
Capot, 3, c.	Coaltown, 4, c.	Pimlico Special	10/28/1949	Pimlico	$1\frac{3}{16}$m	1:56.80
Armed, 6, g.	Assault, 4, c.	The Special	9/27/1947	Belmont Park	1¼m	2:02.80
Busher, 3, f.	Durazna, 4, f.	Match Race	8/29/1945	Washington Park	1m	1:37.80
Alsab, 3, c.	Whirlaway, 4, c.	Narragansett Championship	9/19/1942	Narragansett	$1\frac{3}{16}$m	1:56.40
Lavengro, 7, g.	*Sir Winsome, 4, c.	Pacific Coast Sprint Championship	8/16/1942	Longacres	6f	1:10.00
Wise Moss, 3, f.	Sweet Willow, 4, f.	New Hampshire Special	11/22/1941	Rockingham	6f	1:11.20
Alsab, 2, c.	Requested, 2, c.	Match Race	9/23/1941	Belmont Park	6½f	1:16.00
Unerring, 3, f.	Flying Lill, 3, f.	Match Race	8/31/1939	Washington Park	1m	1:37.80
Seabiscuit, 5, h.	War Admiral, 4, c.	Pimlico Special	11/1/1938	Pimlico	$1\frac{3}{16}$m	1:56.60
Seabiscuit, 5, h.	*Ligaroti, 6, h.	Special Stake Race	8/12/1938	Del Mar	1⅛m	1:49.00

Winner, Age, Sex	Loser, Age, Sex	Race	Date	Track	Distance	Time
Myrtlewood, 4, f.	Miss Merriment, 5, m.	Special Sweepstakes	10/24/1936	Keeneland	6f	1:11.80
Clang, 3, g.	Myrtlewood, 3, f.	Match Race	10/12/1935	Coney Island	6f	1:09.20
Myrtlewood, 3, f.	Clang, 3, g.	Match Race	9/25/1935	Hawthorne	6f	1:10.80
*Winooka, 5, c.	Onrush, 3, g.	International Match Race	9/16/1933	Longacres	6f	1:14.00
Zev, 3, c.	In Memoriam, 4, c.	Match Race	11/17/1923	Churchill Downs	1¼m	2:06.60
Sarazen, 2, g.	Happy Thoughts, 2, f.	Laurel Special	10/26/1923	Laurel Park	6f	1:14.00
Zev, 3, c.	*Papyrus, 3, c.	International Race	10/20/1923	Belmont Park	1½m	2:35.40
Man o' War, 3, c.	Sir Barton, 4, c.	Kenilworth Park Gold Cup	10/12/1920	Kenilworth	1¼m	2:03.00
*Hourless, 3, c.	*Omar Khayyam, 3, c.	American Champion S.	10/18/1917	Laurel Park	1¼m	2:02.00
Novelty, 2, c.	Textile, 2, c.	Two-Year-Old Special	8/17/1910	Saratoga	6f	1:13.20
Dick Welles, 3, c.	Grand Opera, 4, c.	Special Race	8/14/1903	Harlem	1m	1:37.40
Ethelbert, 4, c.	Jean Beraud, 4, c.	Special Sweepstakes	6/2/1900	Gravesend	1¼m	2:08.20
Admiration, 3, f.	May Hempstead, 3, f.	Match Race	7/1/1899	Coney Island	1m	1:40.20
dh-Domino, 3, c.	dh-Henry of Navarre, 3, c.	The Third Special	9/15/1894	Brooklyn	1⅛m	1:55.50
dh-Domino, 2, c.	dh-Dobbins, 2, c.	Match Race	8/31/1893	Coney Island	abt 6f	1:12.60
Kingston, 7, h.	Van Buren, 3, c.	Match Race	8/31/1891	Garfield Park, Chicago	1 1/16m	1:50.75
Longstreet, 5, h.	Tenny, 5, h.	Match Race	8/1/1891	Morris Park	1¼m	2:07.50
Salvator, 4, c.	Tenny, 4, c.	Match Race	6/25/1890	Sheepshead Bay	1¼m	2:05.00
Troubadour, 4, c.	Miss Woodford, 5, m.	Special Race	6/29/1886	Coney Island	1¼m	2:08.75
Miss Woodford, 5, m.	Freeland, 6, g.	Match Race	8/20/1885	Monmouth Park	1¼m	2:09.50
Miss Woodford, 4, f.	Drake Carter, 4, g.	Match Race	9/18/1884	Sheepshead Bay	2½m	4:28.75
Crickmore, 3, g.	Hindoo, 3, c.	Brighton Beach Purse	9/17/1881	Sheepshead Bay	1½m	2:36.25
Hiawassa, 2, f.	Memento, 2, f.	Match Race	8/20/1881	Monmouth Park	6f	1:16.50
Eole, 3, c.	Getaway, 3, c.	Match Race	8/12/1881	Saratoga	1⅝m	2:52.25
Onondaga, 2, c.	Sachem, 2, c.	Match Race	6/25/1881	Sheepshead Bay	6f	1:15.50
Geranium, 3, f.	Marathon, 3, g.	Match Race	6/23/1881	Sheepshead Bay	1m	1:45.00
Marathon, 3, g.	Geranium, 3, f.	Match Race	6/4/1881	Jerome Park	1m	1:53.00
Luke Blackburn, 3, c.	Uncas, 4, c.	Match Race	9/14/1880	Gravesend Park	1½m	2:42.50
Spartan, 3, c.	Bramble, 3, c.	Match Race	7/6/1878	Monmouth Park	1¼m	2:16.00
Ten Broeck, 6, h.	Mollie McCarthy, 5, m.	Match Race	7/4/1878	Louisville	4m	heats
Mollie McCarthy, 5, m.	Jake, 5, h.	Match Race	3/2/1878	Sacramento	2m	heats
Jake, 4, c.	Madge Duke, 3, f.	Match Race	11/29/1877	San Francisco	2m	heats
Rappahannock, 4, c.	Kilburn, 6, g.	Match Race	10/26/1877	Pimlico	2m	heats
Bazil, 3, g.	Cloverbrook, 3, c.	Match Race	6/18/1877	Jerome Park	1¼m	2:12.75
Shirley, 3, g.	Resolute, 6, h.	Match Race	10/28/1876	Pimlico	2m	3:44.50
Shylock, 5, h.	Vaultress, 3, f.	Match Race	7/18/1874	Monmouth Park	2m	3:46.50
Joe Daniels, 4, c.	Nell Flaherty, 6, m.	Match Race	12/25/1873	San Francisco	1½m	2:46.00
Girl of the Period, 4, f.	Ophelia, 4, f.	Match Race	10/4/1873	Jerome Park	4f	heats
Shylock, 4, c.	M. A. B., 4, f.	Match Race	10/4/1873	Jerome Park	1½m	heats
Survivor, 3, c.	Aerolite, 3, c.	Match Race	7/21/1873	Monmouth Park	1m	1:46.00
Thad Stevens, 8, h.	Ben Wade, 4, c.	Match Race	6/28/1873	Oakland	2m	heats
Nell Flaherty, 6, m.	Abi, 4, f.	Match Race	6/28/1873	Oakland	1m	heats
Thad Stevens, 8, h.	Nettie Brown, 5, m.	Match Race	3/1/1873	San Francisco	1m	heats
Alarm, 2, c.	Inverary, 2, f.	Match Race	8/16/1871	Saratoga	1m	1:47.50
Virgil, 6, h.	Chalmette, 6, h.	Match Race	5/20/1871	New Orleans	2m	heats
Nannie McNairy, 7, m.	Sarah McDonald, 4, f.	Match Race	12/4/1869	New Orleans	6f	1:20.00
Finesse, 2, f.	Intrigue, 2, f.	Match Race	10/6/1869	Jerome Park	1m	1:52.25
Intrigue, 2, f.	El Dorado, 2, c.	Match Race	6/6/1869	Jerome Park	6f	1:25.75
*Glenelg, 3, c.	Rapture, 3, f.	Match Race	6/3/1869	Jerome Park	1m	1:49.25
Miss Alice, 2, f.	c. by Censor, 2	Match Race	6/3/1869	Jerome Park	1m	1:54.25
Nannie McNairy, 6, m.	Lewis E. Smith, 5, h.	Match Race	4/8/1869	New Orleans	4f	:49.75
Nannie McNairy, 5, m.	Le Noir, 6, m.	Match Race	12/7/1868	New Orleans	4f	:54.50
Maid of Honor, 4, f.	Trovatore, 5, m.	Match Race	11/7/1868	Jerome Park	1m	1:51.25
Raquette, 3, c.	Redwing, 3, f.	Match Race	11/9/1867	Jerome Park	1m	1:48.50
DeCourcy, 3, c.	Maid of Honor, 3, f.	Match Race	5/25/1867	Jerome Park	1m	heats
Tornado, 6, h.	Minnie C., 6, m.	Match Race	1/22/1867	New Orleans	1m	1:52.50
Derringer, 4, c.	Susie B. Moore, 5, m.	Match Race	1/14/1867	San Francisco	1m	heats
Maid of Honor, 2, f.	Redwing, 2, f.	Match Race	10/3/1866	Jerome Park	6f	1:21.00
Mike Edwards, 5, g.	Red Oak, 11, g.	Match Race	5/15/1866	St. Louis	2m	3:20.25
Lewis E. Smith, 2, c.	Maiden, 3, f.	Match Race	4/20/1866	New Orleans	1m	heats
Ooltawa, 5, h.	Muggins, 4, c.	Match Race	1/13/1866	Nashville	1m	heats
Flora, 5, m.	Pele, 6, m.	Match Race	1/6/1866	San Francisco	4m	heats
Norfolk, 4, c.	Lodi, 5, h.	Match Race	9/23/1865	Sacramento	3m	heats
Norfolk, 4, c.	Lodi, 5, h.	Match Race	9/18/1865	Sacramento	2m	heats
Norfolk, 4, c.	Lodi, 5, h.	Match Race	5/23/1865	San Francisco	2m	heats
Kentucky, 3, c.	Aldebaran, 4, c.	Match Race	9/17/1864	Paterson, New Jersey	2m	heats
Lexington, 5, h.	Lecomte, 5, h.	Jockey Club Purse	4/14/1855	New Orleans	4m	heats
Lexington, 3, c.	Sallie Waters, 4, f.	Match Race	5/27/1853	New Orleans	3m	heats
Peytona, 6, m.	Fashion, 8, m.	Great Sectional Match Race	5/13/1845	Union Course	4m	heats
Fashion, 5, m.	Boston, 9, h.	North vs. South Match Race	5/10/1842	Union Course	4m	heats
Boston, 7, h.	Gano	Match Race	12/7/1840	Augusta, Georgia	4m	heats
Black Maria	Brilliant		10/23/1839	Union Course		
Portsmouth, h.	Boston, 6, h.	Match Race	4/16/1839	Petersburg, Virginia	2m	heats
Arietta, f.	Ariel, 8, m.	Match Race	5/8/1830	Union Course	2m	3:44.00
Flirtilla, f.	Ariel, 3, f.	Match Race	10/31/1825	Union Course	3m	heats
Ariel, 3, f.	Lafayette, 3, c.	Match Race	10/3/1825	Union Course	1m	heats
American Eclipse, 9, h.	Henry, 4, c.	Match Race	5/27/1823	Union Course	4m	heats
American Eclipse, 8, h.	Sir Charles, c.	Match Race	11/20/1822	Washington, D.C.	4m	heats

Notable Walkovers Since 1930

Walkovers are rare in Thoroughbred racing if only because competition is at the heart of the sport. The most recent walkover occurred in 1997 when Sharp Cat's two opponents, Alzora and Toda Una Dama (Arg) were scratched from the Bayakoa Handicap (G2) after December rains turned Hollywood Park's track muddy. Prior to that, champion Spectacular Bid walked over when Winter's Tale, Temperence Hill, and Dr. Patches were scratched from the 1980 Woodward Stakes (G1).

In consecutive years, Calumet Farm champions Coaltown and Citation walked over in Maryland races. Coaltown was unopposed in the 1949 Edward Burke Handicap at Havre de Grace, and Citation had no opponents entered against him in the 1948 Pimlico Special.

Although walkovers usually involve only one horse, two horses with the same owner may walk over if they are entered in a race and no horses oppose them. Here are several of the most important walkovers since 1930.

Walkovers, 1930 to 2003

Horse, Age, Sex	Race (Grade)	Date	Track	Distance	Final Time
Sharp Cat, 3, f	Bayakoa H. (G2)	12/07/1997	Hollywood Park	1¹⁄₁₆m	1:42.68
Spectacular Bid, 4, c	Woodward S. (G1)	9/20/1980	Belmont Park	1¼m	2:02.40
Coaltown, 4, c	Edward Burke H.	4/23/1949	Havre De Grace	1¹⁄₁₆m	1:52.20
Citation, 3, c	Pimlico Special	10/29/1948	Pimlico Race Course	1³⁄₁₆m	1:59.80
Stymie, 5, h	Saratoga Cup	8/31/1946	Saratoga Race Course	1¾m	3:07.40

Scale of Weights

The scale of weights provides a guideline to the weights that horses carry at different ages and over different distances. As in many standards in Thoroughbred racing, the current scale of weights evolved over time.

The earliest Thoroughbred races in the 17th century were run at catch weights—whatever the rider, usually the owner, weighed. As racing became more sophisticated, various methods were tried to make contests more fair as well as more competitive, including assigning different weights according to the height of the horse, known as "give-and-take" weights.

That concept eventually evolved into assigning different weights to horses of differing perceived abilities. The first recorded handicap race was the Subscription Handicap Plate at Newmarket in 1785.

In 1740, the English Parliament established minimum weights for horses of different ages. Those weights were not meant to be assigned to horses of different ages in the same race, however.

In the mid-19th century, Admiral Henry Rous, British racing's de facto dictator, applied and expanded the concept to horses of different ages in the same race. Rous published the world's first weight-for-age scale in his 1850 book *On the Laws and Practice of Horse Racing*. Rous's scale also recognized that Thoroughbreds mature steadily from ages two through four; he assigned different weights at different distances for every month of the year.

All subsequent scales essentially have been refinements of Rous's work. The scale of weights listed below is the official scale used by American racing secretaries.

Distance and Age	Jan.	Feb.	Mar.	Apr.	May	June	July	Aug.	Sept.	Oct.	Nov.	Dec.
Half mile												
2 years	x	x	x	x	x	x	x	105	108	111	114	114
3 years	117	117	119	119	121	123	125	126	127	128	129	129
4 years	130	130	130	130	130	130	130	130	130	130	130	130
5 years & up	130	130	130	130	130	130	130	130	130	130	130	130
6 furlongs												
2 years	x	x	x	x	x	x	x	102	105	108	111	111
3 years	114	114	117	117	119	121	123	125	126	127	128	128
4 years	129	129	130	130	130	130	130	130	130	130	130	130
5 years & up	130	130	130	130	130	130	130	130	130	130	130	130
1 mile												
2 years	x	x	x	x	x	x	x	x	96	99	102	102
3 years	107	107	111	111	113	115	117	119	121	122	123	123
4 years	127	127	128	128	127	126	126	126	126	126	126	126
5 years & up	128	128	128	128	127	126	126	126	126	126	126	126
1¼ miles												
2 years	x	x	x	x	x	x	x	x	x	x	x	x
3 years	101	101	107	107	111	113	116	118	120	121	122	122
4 years	125	125	127	127	127	126	126	126	126	126	126	126
5 years & up	127	127	127	127	127	126	126	126	126	126	126	126
1½ miles												
2 years	x	x	x	x	x	x	x	x	x	x	x	x
3 years	98	98	104	104	108	111	114	117	119	121	122	122
4 years	124	124	126	126	126	126	126	126	126	126	126	126
5 years & up	126	126	126	126	126	126	126	126	126	126	126	126
2 miles												
3 years	96	96	102	102	106	109	112	114	117	119	120	120
4 years	124	124	126	126	126	126	126	125	125	124	124	124
5 years & up	126	126	126	126	126	126	126	125	125	124	124	124

(a) In races of intermediate lengths, the weights for the shorter distance are carried.

(b) In races exclusively for three-year-olds or four-year-olds, the weight is 126 lbs., and in races exclusively for two-year-olds, it is 122 lbs.

(c) In all races except handicaps and races where the conditions expressly state to the contrary, the scale of weights is less, by the following: for two-year-old fillies, 3 lbs.; for three-year-old and up fillies and mares, 5 lbs. before September 1, and 3 lbs. thereafter.

(d) In all handicaps that close more than 72 hours prior to the race the top weight shall be not less than 126 lbs., except in handicaps for fillies and mares, the top weight shall not be less than 126 lbs. less the sex allowance at the time of the race.

Oldest Male Grade 1 Stakes Winners Since 1976

Age	Horse, YOB, Sex, Sire	Year, Race
9	John Henry, 1975 g., by Ole Bob Bowers	1984 Budweiser Million, Hollywood Invitational H., Sunset H., Turf Classic
	John's Call, 1991 g., by Lord At War (Arg)	2000 Sword Dancer Invitational H., Turf Classic Invitational S.
	Super Diamond, 1980 g., by Pass the Glass	1989 San Antonio H.
8	Affirmed Success, 1994 g., by Affirmed	2002 Carter H.
	Cetewayo, 1994 h., by His Majesty	2002 Gulfstream Park Breeders' Cup H.
	John Henry, 1975 g., by Ole Bob Bowers	1983 Hollywood Turf Cup
	Mashkour, 1983 h., by Irish River (Fr)	1991 San Juan Capistrano Invitational H.
	Redattore (Brz), 1995 h., by Roi Normand	2003 Shoemaker Breeders' Cup Mile S.
	Sir Bear, 1993 g., by Sir Leon	2001 Gulfstream Park H.
7	A Huevo, 1996 g., by Cool Joe	2003 Frank J. De Francis Memorial Dash S.
	Ancient Title, 1970 h., by Gummo	1977 San Antonio S.
	Awad, 1990 h., by Caveat	1997 Sword Dancer Invitational H.
	Bemo, 1970 g., by Maribeau	1977 United Nations H.
	Cardmania, 1986 g., by Cox's Ridge	1993 Breeders' Cup Sprint
	Designed for Luck, 1997 g., by Rahy	2004 Shoemaker Breeders' Cup Mile S.
	Down the Aisle, 1993 h., by Runaway Groom	2000 United Nations H.
	Elmhurst, 1990 g., by Wild Again	1997 Breeders' Cup Sprint
	Forego, 1970 g., by *Forli	1977 Metropolitan H., Woodward H.
	Grand Flotilla, 1987 h., by Caro (Ire)	1994 Hollywood Turf H.
	John Henry, 1975 g., by Ole Bob Bowers	1982 Oak Tree Invitational H., Santa Anita H.
	Jumping Hill, 1972 h., by Hillary	1979 Widener H.
	Key Contender, 1988 h., by Fit to Fight	1995 Suburban H.
	Kona Gold, 1994 g., by Java Gold	2001 San Carlos H.
	Ladies Din, 1995 g., by Din's Dancer	2002 Shoemaker Breeders' Cup Mile S.
	Noble Dancer (GB), 1972 h., by Prince de Galles	1979 San Luis Rey S., United Nations H.
	Passinetti, 1996 g., by Slew o' Gold	2003 San Juan Capistrano Invitational H.
	Pleasant Variety, 1984 h., by Pleasant Colony	1991 San Luis Rey S.
	Red Bishop, 1988 h., by Silver Hawk	1995 San Juan Capistrano Invitational H.
	River Keen (Ire), 1992 h., by Keen	1999 Jockey Club Gold Cup, Woodward S.
	Sabona, 1982 h., by Exclusive Native	1989 Californian S.
	Sandpit (Brz), 1989 h., by Baynoun (Ire)	1996 Caesars International H., Hollywood Turf H.
	Special Ring, 1997 g., by Nureyev	2004 Eddie Read H.
	Steinlen (GB), 1983 h., by Habitat	1990 Hollywood Turf H.
	Val's Prince, 1992 g., by Eternal Prince	1999 Man o' War S., Turf Classic Invitational S.
	Winter's Tale, 1976 g., by Arts and Letters	1983 Suburban H.
	With Anticipation, 1995 g., by Relaunch	2002 Man o' War S., Sword Dancer Invitational H., United Nations H.
	Yankee Affair, 1982 h., by Northern Fling	1989 Man o' War S., Turf Classic, United Nations H.
	Zoffany, 1980 h., by Our Native	1987 San Luis Rey S.

Oldest Female Grade 1 Stakes Winners Since 1976

Age	Horse, YOB, Sex, Sire	Year, Race
8	Brown Bess, 1982 m., by *Petrone	1990 Santa Barbara H.
7	Brown Bess, 1982 m., by *Petrone	1989 Ramona H., Yellow Ribbon Invitational S.
	Halo America, 1990 m., by Waquoit	1997 Apple Blossom H.
	Paseana (Arg), 1987 m., by Ahmad	1994 Santa Margarita Invitational H.
6	Ack's Secret, 1976 m., by Ack Ack	1982 Santa Barbara H., Santa Margarita Invitational H.
	Anka Germania (Ire), 1982 m., by Malinowski	1988 Sword Dancer H.
	Annoconnor, 1984 m., by Nureyev	1990 Santa Ana H.
	Astra, 1996 m., by Theatrical (Ire)	2002 Beverly Hills H., Gamely Breeders' Cup H.
	Azeri, 1998 m., by Jade Hunter	2004 Apple Blossom H., Go for Wand H., Overbrook Spinster S.
	Bayakoa (Arg), 1984 m., by Consultant's Bid	1990 Breeders' Cup Distaff, Milady H., Santa Margarita H., Santa Maria H., Spinster S.
	Dahlia, 1970 m., by *Vaguely Noble	1976 Hollywood Invitational H.
	Estrapade, 1980 m., by *Vaguely Noble	1986 Arlington Million, Oak Tree Invitational S.
	Exchange, 1988 m., by Explodent	1994 Matriarch S.
	Exotic Wood, 1992 m., by Rahy	1998 Santa Maria H., Santa Monica H.
	Fact Finder, 1979 m., by Staff Writer	1985 Matriarch Invitational S., Santa Barbara H.
	Far Out Beast, 1987 m., by Far Out East	1993 Flower Bowl H.
	Flawlessly, 1988 m., by Affirmed	1994 Ramona H.
	Gourmet Girl, 1995 m., by Cee's Tizzy	2001 Apple Blossom H., Vanity H.
	Happyanunoit (NZ), 1995 m., by Yachtie	2001 Gamely Breeders' Cup H.
	Heatherten, 1979 m., by Forceten	1985 Hempstead H.
	Jameela, 1976 m., by Rambunctious	1982 Delaware H.
	Kalookan Queen, 1996 m., by Lost Code	2002 Ancient Title Breeders' Cup H., Santa Monica H.
	Kostroma (Ire), 1986 m., by Caerleon	1992 Beverly D. S., Santa Barbara H.
	Lazy Slusan, 1995 m., by Slewvescent	2001 Milady Breeders' Cup H., Santa Margarita Invitational H.
	Little Brianne, 1985 m., by Coastal	1991 Santa Margarita Invitational H., Santa Maria H.

Age	Horse, YOB, Sex, Sire	Year, Race
	Miss Huntington, 1977 m., by Torsion	1983 Apple Blossom H.
	Noches De Rosa (Chi), 1998 m., by Stagecraft (GB)	2004 Gamely Breeders' Cup H.
	One Dreamer, 1988 m., by Relaunch	1994 Breeders' Cup Distaff
	Paseana (Arg), 1987 m., by Ahmad	1993 Apple Blossom H., Milady H., Spinster S.
	Queens Court Queen, 1989 m., by Lyphard	1995 Santa Margarita Invitational H., Santa Maria H.
	Quick Mischief, 1986 m., by Distinctive Pro	1992 John A. Morris H.
	Re Toss (Arg), 1987 m., by Egg Toss	1993 Vanity H.
	Sefa's Beauty, 1979 m., by Lt. Stevens	1985 Apple Blossom H.
	Southern Truce, 1988 m., by Truce Maker	1994 Santa Monica H.
	Stop Traffic, 1993 m., by Cure the Blues	1999 Santa Monica H.
	The Very One, 1975 m., by One for All	1981 Santa Barbara H.
	Track Robbery, 1976 m., by No Robbery	1982 Apple Blossom H., Spinster S.
	Twice the Vice, 1991 m., by Vice Regent	1997 Vanity H.
	Windsharp, 1991 m., by Lear Fan	1997 Beverly Hills H.

Oldest Male Graded Stakes Winners Since 1976

Age	Horse, YOB, Sex, Sire	Year, Race
9	Affirmed Success, 1994 g., by Affirmed	2003 Toboggan H. (G3)
	Bet On Sunshine, 1992 g., by Bet Big	2001 Aristides H. (G3), Phoenix Breeders' Cup S. (G3)
	Desert Waves, 1990 g., by Alysheba	1999 King Edward Breeders' Cup H. (Can-G2)
	John Henry, 1975 g., by Ole Bob Bowers	1984 Budweiser Million (G1), Hollywood Invitational H. (G1), Sunset H. (G1), Turf Classic (G1), Golden Gate H. (G3)
	John's Call, 1991 g., by Lord At War (Arg)	2000 Sword Dancer Invitational H. (G1), Turf Classic Invitational S. (G1)
	Kona Gold, 1994 g., by Java Gold	2003 El Conejo H. (G3)
	Parose, 1994 g., by Parlay Me	2003 Durham Cup H. (Can-G3)
	Sir Bear, 1993 g., by Sir Leon	2002 Skip Away H. (G3)
	Softshoe Sure Shot, 1986 g., by Bolger	1995 San Carlos H. (G2)
	Soviet Line (Ire), 1990 g., by Soviet Star	1999 Maker's Mark Mile S. (G3)
	Sunny Sunrise, 1987 g., by Sunny's Halo	1996 John B. Campbell H. (G3)
	Super Diamond, 1980 g., by Pass the Glass	1989 San Antonio H. (G1)
8	Affirmed Success, 1994 g., by Affirmed	2002 Carter H. (G1)
	Ancient Title, 1970 g., by Gummo	1978 San Pasqual H. (G2)
	Best of the Rest, 1995 h., by Skip Trial	2003 Skip Away H. (G3)
	Bet On Sunshine, 1992 g., by Bet Big	2000 Aristides H. (G3)
	Blaze O'Brien, 1987 g., by Interco	1995 Inglewood H. (G3)
	Cardmania, 1986 g., by Cox's Ridge	1994 San Carlos H. (G2)
	Cetewayo, 1994 h., by His Majesty	2002 Gulfstream Park Breeders' Cup H. (G1), Stars and Stripes Breeders' Cup Turf H. (G3)
	Chorwon, 1993 g., by Cozzene	2001 Kentucky Cup Turf H. (G3)
	Coyote Lakes, 1994 g., by Society Max	2002 Gallant Fox H. (G3)
	Dancing Guy, 1995 g., by Robyn Dancer	2003 Memorial Day H. (G3)
	Deputy Inxs, 1991 g., by Silver Deputy	1999 Durham Cup H. (Can-G3), Vigil H. (Can-G3)
	First Intent, 1989 g., by Prima Voce	1997 Potrero Grande Breeders' Cup H. (G2), Bing Crosby Breeders' Cup H. (G3)
	Flag Down, 1990 h., by Deputy Minister	1998 Gulfstream Park Breeders' Cup H. (G2)
	Forlitano (Arg), 1981 h., by Good Manners	1989 Bougainvillea H. (G2)
	Fourstardave, 1985 g., by Compliance	1993 Poker S. (G3)
	Friendly Lover, 1988 h., by Cutlass	1996 Philadelphia Park Breeders' Cup H. (G3)
	Glick, 1996 h., by Theatrical (Ire)	2004 San Simeon H. (G3)
	Inevitable Leader, 1979 h., by Mr. Leader	1987 Ark-La-Tex H. (G3)
	John Henry, 1975 g., by Ole Bob Bowers	1983 Hollywood Turf Cup (G1), American H. (G2)
	John's Call, 1991 g., by Lord At War (Arg)	1999 Laurel Turf Cup S. (G3)
	Key Lory, 1994 h., by Key to the Mint	2002 Red Bank H. (G3)
	King's Swan, 1980 g., by King's Bishop	1988 Bold Ruler S. (G2), Tom Fool S. (G2), Assault H. (G3), Grey Lag H. (G3), Stymie H. (G3)
	Kona Gold, 1994 g., by Java Gold	2002 Los Angeles H. (G3)
	Letthebighossroll, 1988 g., by Flying Paster	1996 Triple Bend Breeders' Cup H. (G3)
	Mashkour, 1983 h., by Irish River (Fr)	1991 San Juan Capistrano Invitational H. (G1)
	Men's Exclusive, 1993 g., by Exclusive Ribot	2001 Palos Verdes H. (G2), Vernon O. Underwood S. (G3)
	P Day, 1995 g., by Private Terms	2003 Baltimore Breeders' Cup H. (G3)
	Parose, 1994 g., by Parlay Me	2002 Woodbine Slots Cup H. (Can-G3)
	Punch Line, 1990 g., by Two Punch	1998 Fall Highweight H. (G2), Forest Hills H. (G2)
	Redattore (Brz), 1995 h., by Roi Normand	2003 Shoemaker Breeders' Cup Mile S. (G1), Citation H. (G2), Frank E. Kilroe Mile H. (G2), San Gabriel H. (G2)
	*Royal Derby II, 1969 h., by Bally Royal	1977 San Luis Obispo H. (G2), San Marcos H. (G3)
	Sandpit (Brz), 1989 h., by Baynoun (Ire)	1997 San Marcos H. (G2)
	Silveyville, 1978 h., by *Petrone	1986 San Marcos H. (G3)
	Sir Bear, 1993 g., by Sir Leon	2001 Gulfstream Park H. (G1)
	Son of a Pistol, 1992 g., by Big Pistol	2000 San Carlos H. (G2)

Age	Horse, YOB, Sex, Sire	Year, Race
	Soviet Line (Ire), 1990 g., by Soviet Star	1998 Robert F. Carey Memorial H. (G3)
	Stalwars, 1985 h., by Stalwart	1993 National Jockey Club H. (G3)
	Super Diamond, 1980 g., by Pass the Glass	1988 San Pasqual H. (G2)
	Truce Maker, 1978 h., by Ack Ack	1986 Tanforan H. (G3)
	Variety Road, 1983 h., by Kennedy Road	1991 William P. Kyne H. (G3)
	Yankee Affair, 1982 h., by Northern Fling	1990 Red Smith H. (G2)

Oldest Female Graded Stakes Winners Since 1976

Age	Horse, YOB, Sex, Sire	Year, Race
8	Brown Bess, 1982 m., by *Petrone	1990 Santa Barbara H. (G1)
	Paseana (Arg), 1987 m., by Ahmad	1995 Hawthorne H. (G2)
7	Avie Jane, 1984 m., by Lord Avie	1991 Thoroughbred Club of America S. (G3)
	Brown Bess, 1982 m., by *Petrone	1989 Ramona H. (G1), Yellow Ribbon Invitational S. (G1), California Jockey Club H. (G3), Countess Fager H. (G3), Yerba Buena H. (G3)
	Exchange, 1988 m., by Explodent	1995 Orchid H. (G2)
	Fieldy (Ire), 1983 m., by Northfields	1990 Beaugay H. (G3), Lady Canterbury H. (G3)
	Gaily Gaily (Ire), 1983 m., by Cure the Blues	1990 Modesty H. (G3)
	Halo America, 1990 m., by Waquoit	1997 Apple Blossom H. (G1), Louisville Breeders' Cup H. (G2)
	Irish Linnet, 1988 m., by Seattle Song	1995 New York H. (G2), Noble Damsel H. (G3)
	Marshua's River, 1987 m., by Riverman	1994 Buckram Oak H. (G3), Suwannee River H. (G3)
	Miss Unnameable, 1984 m., by Great Neck	1991 Bewitch S. (G3)
	Paseana (Arg), 1987 m., by Ahmad	1994 Santa Margarita Invitational H. (G1), Chula Vista H. (G2)
	Quidnaskra, 1995 m., by Halo	2002 Gallorette H. (G3)
	Scotzanna, 1992 m., by Silver Deputy	1999 First Lady H. (G3)
	Sefa's Beauty, 1979 m., by Lt. Stevens	1986 Sixty Sails H. (G3)
	Sintrillium, 1978 m., by Sinister Purpose	1985 Affectionately H. (G3)
	Skipat, 1974 m., by Jungle Cove	1981 Barbara Fritchie H. (G3)
	Spook Express (SAf), 1994 m., by Comic Blush	2001 WinStar Galaxy S. (G2), Honey Fox H. (G3), Suwannee River H. (G3)
	Stay Forever, 1997 m., by Stack	2004 WinStar Galaxy S. (G2), Mint Julep H. (G3)
	Survive, 1984 m., by Pass the Glass	1991 A Gleam H. (G2)
	Tocopilla (Arg), 1990 m., by El Basco	1997 The Very One H. (G3)

Oldest Male Stakes Winners Since 1976

Age	Horse, YOB, Sex, Sire	Year, Race
12	Bold Sundance, 1989 g., by Bold Ryan	2001 Gene Francis & Associates S.
	Island Day Break, 1985 g., by Time to Explode	1997 Claiming Series #2 H., Cowboy Bar Claiming H., OMO Construction H.
	Leaping Plum, 1991 g., by Lightning Leap	2003 Grasmick H.
	Mayruncouldfly, 1974 h., by Cheapers' David	1986 Rocking Chair Invitational H.
11	Antiash, 1978 h., by Anticipating	1989 Memorial Day H.
	Bad Toda Bone, 1992 g., by Taj Alriyadh	2003 Keddie's Track & Western Wear S.
	Brush Count, 1968 h., by Fleet Burn	1979 Governor's H.
	Curribot, 1977 g., by Little Current	1988 Albuquerque H., Sunland Park H.
	Dobi Pay, 1971 h., by Dobi Deenar	1982 Buck Buchanan Memorial H.
	Major Zee, 1993 g., by Dayjur	2004 Parnitha S.
	Prexy Machree, 1970 h., by Prexy	1981 Vernon Sayler Memorial S.
	Sir Echo, 1991 g., by Herat	2002 Yankee Affair S.
	Spend, 1985 g., by Draconic	1996 Pinon H.
10	Alias Jake, 1979 h., by Ingrained	1989 San Juan Downs H.
	All American Kid, 1972 g., by Count of Honor	1982 Centennial H.
	Aran Island, 1994 g., by Irish River (Fr)	2004 Old Timers S.
	Bay Rocket, 1987 g., by Forbidden Pleasure	1997 Independence Day H.
	Better Choice, 1994 g., by Variety Road	2004 Inaugural H.
	Blue Mercenary, 1972 h., by Blue Serenade	1982 Robert Hall H.
	Brush Count, 1968 h., by Fleet Burn	1978 Governor's H.
	Caro's Royalty, 1993 g., by Spruce Bouquet	2003 Brother Brown S.
	Castelets, 1979 g., by King's Bishop	1989 Viburnum S.
	Clarinet King, 1976 h., by His Majesty	1986 Royal Vale S.
	Crimson Victory, 1968 h., by Crimson Satan	1978 Gemini H.
	Curribot, 1977 g., by Little Current	1987 Clyde Tingley H., Sunland Park H.
	D. Guilford, 1986 g., by Guilford Road	1996 Basil Hall S.
	Energetic King, 1979 h., by On the Sly	1989 Doublrab H.
	Fluid Gold, 1992 g., by Strike Gold	2002 Chippewa Downs Open S.
	Groovy Add Vice, 1991 g., by Groovy	2001 Georgia Bragging Rights S.
	John's Call, 1991 g., by Lord At War (Arg)	2001 Cape Henlopen H.
	Leaping Plum, 1991 g., by Lightning Leap	2001 Grasmick H.
	Lost Again, 1994 g., by Lost Code	2004 Dempsey Gibbons Thoroughbred H.
	March Speed, 1980 h., by Curra Boy	1990 Wyoming Centennial Series S. #1
	Mr. I R S, 1992 g., by Minshaanshu Amad	2002 B Cup S.

Age	Horse, YOB, Sex, Sire	Year, Race
	Nosho, 1991 g., by Falstaff	2001 Frank Figueroa Memorial Starter S.
	Oil Man, 1994 g., by Black Tie Affair (Ire)	2004 Arizona County Fair Distance Series S.
	Olden Ring, 1988 g., by Silver Ring (Fr)	1998 FSIN/SIGA Mile H.
	On the Edge, 1987 g., by L'Enjoleur	1997 I-80 S., Prairie Meadows H.
	Papa Ho Ho, 1993 g., by On to Glory	2003 Rise Jim S.
	Passport Money, 1982 g., by Dogwood Passport	1992 Early Bird Allowance S.
	Polar Ridge, 1988 g., by Cox's Ridge	1998 Con Jackson Claiming H.
	Prolanzier, 1990 g., by Copelan	2000 Private Terms S., Waquoit S.
	Quiet I'm Thinking, 1986 g., by Zen	1996 Ten Thousand Lakes S.
	Quite a Day, 1968 g., by Prince Khaled	1978 Pomona H.
	Rebuff, 1985 g., by Cold Reception	1995 Chieftain H.
	Right Ribot, 1976 h., by Right Reason	1986 Au Revoir H., Buck Buchanan Memorial H.
	Rosy Way, 1989 g., by Lord Avie	1999 Carl "Cub" Klahr Memorial H., City of Trees H., Govenor's Cup H., Stars And Stripes H.
	Sir Echo, 1991 g., by Herat	2001 Yankee Affair S.
	Skunktail, 1989 g., by Music Prince	1999 Dowd Mile H., Nebraskaland H.
	Smile for Action, 1971 h., by Fleet Action	1981 Brown Palace H.
	Stilaferd, 1994 g., by Aferd	2004 Chippewa Downs Open Thoroughbred S.
	Thou Art Handy, 1974 h., by Captain Courageous	1984 Yakima Speed H.
	Tonights the Night, 1978 h., by Great Mystery	1988 Massachusetts Stallion S.
	Wilkes, 1985 g., by Traffic Cop	1995 Independence Day H.
	Willy Fiddle, 1976 h., by Roan Will	1986 Inaugural H., Stars and Stripes H.
	Wise Dusty, 1991 g., by Bishop Northcraft	2001 HBPA Kelly Kip S.

Oldest Female Stakes Winners Since 1976

Age	Horse, YOB, Sex, Sire	Year, Race
10	Alex Marie, 1992 m., by Trooper Seven	2002 Buttons and Bows S.
	Chrystal Gail, 1973 m., by Special Dunce	1983 Carlton Cup, Dale Buick H.
	Favorite Pleasure, 1966 m., by *Favorite Prince	1976 Vicki Merrill H.
	Judge Smiles, 1991 m., by Judge Smells	2001 Matron H.
	Physical Law, 1982 m., by Wardlaw	1992 Merrimack Valley H.
9	All That Glitters, 1994 m., by Goldlust	2003 Buckland S., Somethingroyal S.
	Astral Moon, 1973 m., by *The Knack II	1982 Anniversary S.
	Crystal Cinders, 1994 m., by Incinderator	2003 Ralph Taylor/Vance Davenport Memorial S.
	Due to Win, 1995 m., by Lac Ouimet	2004 Cornucopia H., Fleur de Lis S., Matron H.
	Ghetto Doll, 1976 m., by Dendron	1985 Red Camelia H.
	Judge Smiles, 1991 m., by Judge Smells	2000 Matron H.
	Just Like Mama, 1975 m., by *Tenerosa	1984 Ladies H.
	Okie Miss, 1989 m., by Competitiveness	1998 Interior Royal Bank Futurity
	Petrina Above, 1995 m., by Great Above	2004 Barb's Dancer S., U Can Do It H.
	Run Around Sue, 1995 m., by Coach George	2004 Falls Amiss H.
	Sea Kindly, 1973 m., by Night Invader	1982 Bed of Roses S.
	St. Patty Day, 1982 m., by Majestic Red	1991 South Sioux City H.
	Sum Day Flowers, 1981 m., by Jenny's Boy	1990 Raton Mile H.
	Wychnor (NZ), 1985 m., by Truly Vain	1994 Toolie's Country H.

Oldest Male Winners Since 1976

Age	Horse, YOB, Sex, Sire	Track	Date	Race Condition
17	Behavin Jerry, 1964 h., Ambehaving	Com	9/7/1981	$1,500 clm
	Golden Arrow, 1961 h., Fort Salonga	GBF	9/25/1978	1,500 clm
16	Double Express, 1980 g., Viking Ruler	GF	7/6/1996	1,600 clm
	Maxwell G., 1961 h., Author	TuP	1/22/1977	2,000 clm
	Playing Politics, 1982 g., In Reality	Suf	1/4/1998	4,000 clm
	Silver Fir, 1963 h., Swoon's Son	FL	10/24/1979	2,000 clm
	Stonehenge, 1960 h., Call Over	Com	8/13/1976	1,500 clm
15	Beaver Cat, 1962 g., Brown Beaver	Bil	9/10/1977	1,000 clm
	Best Beau, 1962 h., Beauguerre	Poc	5/27/1977	1,500 clm
	Double Express, 1980 g., Viking Ruler	GF	7/29/1995	1,600 clm
		MeP	8/19/1995	1,600 clm
	Dr. Hecker, 1967 g., Clem Pac	MF	8/23/1982	1,500 clm
	Flyingphere, 1961 g., Mr. Hemisphere	FL	11/21/1976	1,500 clm
	Jymfyg, 1965 h., Beau Max	FL	10/28/1980	2,000 clm
	Lexington Park, 1967 g., Quadrangle	Com	5/22/1982	2,000 clm
	Lindsey-Jan, 1965 h., *Silver King II	GBF	7/23/1980	2,000 clm
	Maxwell G., 1961 h., Author	Haw	5/6/1976	4,000 clm
	Mayruncouldfly, 1974 h., Cheapers' David	SJD	8/5/1989	2,000 clm
	Montana Winds, 1967 h., Windy Sands	Com	7/24/1982	2,000 clm
	Nellies Joy, 1977 g., Immediate Joy	MeP	8/16/1992	1,250 clm
	Northern Broadway, 1988 g., Northern Magus	Beu	4/3/2003	3,500 clm
	Playing Politics, 1982 g., In Reality	Suf	4/23/1997	4,000 clm

Age	Horse, YOB, Sex, Sire	Track	Date	Race Condition
	Royal Rouser, 1968 g., Speed Rouser	Bil	8/18/1983	1,600 clm
	Sagely, 1970 h., Sage and Sand	FL	5/12/1985	3,500 clm
	Sailawayin, 1967 g., Bal Harbour	FP	9/18/1982	2,500 clm
	Satans Story, 1968 h., Crimson Satan	MF	8/24/1983	2,000 clm
	Sharon Caper, 1983 g., Cartesian	Nmp	9/6/1998	4,000 clm
	Silver Fir, 1963 h., Swoon's Son	FL	10/28/1978	1,500 clm
	Snappy Nashville, 1964 h., Nashville	YM	2/17/1979	1,600 clm
14	Alpena Magic, 1990 g., L'Enjoleur	InD	5/27/2004	4,000 clm
	Ariel Beau, 1967 h., Ariel Streak	Beu	9/26/1981	2,500 clm
	Northern Broadway, 1988 g., Northern Magus	Beu	10/16/2002	3,500 clm
	Rhinasti, 1988 g., Rinoso	Eur	6/16/2002	2,500 clm
	Son Coming, 1986 g., Son of Briartic	StP	6/10/2000	3,000 clm
		NP	9/3/2000	3,000 clm

Oldest Female Winners Since 1976

Age	Horse, YOB, Sex, Sire	Track	Date	Race Condition
14	Gloriella, 1964 m., *Nathoo	GBF	9/14/1978	$1,500 clm
		GBF	9/18/1978	1,500 clm
13	Double the Count, 1980 m., Gala Double	BGD	10/27/1993	3,200 clm
	Fuzzy White, 1964 m., Roman Line	FD	1/21/1977	2,000 clm
		FD	1/28/1977	2,000 clm
	Gather Round, 1963 m., Blenban	GBF	9/22/1976	1,500 clm
	Gloriella, 1964 m., *Nathoo	MF	8/25/1977	1,500 clm
	Jackie H., 1965 m., Greek Star	Nar	8/3/1978	1,500 clm
	Johns Sis, 1965 m., Be Joyful	Bil	10/1/1978	1,000 clm
	Mabel My Love, 1970 m., *Puerto Madero	GBF	9/20/1983	2,000 clm
	Passive Loss, 1987 m., Highland Blade	Suf	5/21/2000	4,000 clm
	Vain Lass, 1964 m., *Newbus	LaD	1/29/1977	2,500 clm
12	Brandy Star, 1968 m., *Northern Star	CT	8/17/1980	1,600 clm
	Chotin, 1967 m., *Belliqueux	GBF	9/12/1979	1,500 clm
	College Fiddler, 1966 m., College Boy	PJ	8/19/1978	1,250 clm
	Culottes, 1965 m., *Khaled	Boi	5/25/1977	700 alw
	Doge Hill, 1967 m., Boston Doge	MF	8/25/1979	2,000 clm
		Nmp	9/2/1979	1,500 clm
	Everfast, 1966 m., Gordian Knot	GBF	10/2/1978	1,500 clm
	Favorite Pleasure, 1966 m., *Favorite Prince	AsD	6/11/1978	2,000 clm
	Flash Thru, 1967 m., Nir Thru	MD	8/1/1979	2,200 str
	Gambolak, 1964 m., Sid's Gambol	Nmp	9/2/1976	1,500 clm
	Gene's Hobby, 1974 m., Fincastle	MD	9/13/1986	1,500 clm
	Gloriella, 1964 m., *Nathoo	BD	9/24/1976	1,500 clm
	Johns Sis, 1965 m., Be Joyful	Reg	9/13/1977	1,500 clm
	Lindarella, 1966 m., *Bel Canto II	EIP	7/28/1978	2,500 clm
	Mabel My Love, 1970 m., *Puerto Madero	MF	8/20/1982	1,500 clm
	Mama Doc, 1964 m., Double Brandy	CT	3/27/1976	1,500 clm
	My Encore, 1964 m., Encore Fer	GM	7/5/1976	1,500 clm
	Old Toy, 1975 m., Obsolete	ErD	5/16/1987	2,500 clm
	Platters Honey, 1965 m., Platter	FL	6/25/1977	1,500 clm
	Polyego, 1965 m., Egotistical	FL	3/19/1977	1,500 clm
	Rainbow Gold, 1966 m., *Mont d'Or	MF	8/25/1978	1,500 clm
	Serenity Empress, 1986 m., Klassy Charger	FE	8/17/1998	5,000 clm
	Shore to Shore, 1987 m., Proctor	EIP	7/1/1999	4,000 clm
	Sis Jane, 1966 m., Hay Hook	RD	6/25/1978	2,500 clm
	Texas Toy, 1969 m., Green Hornet	RD	5/30/1981	2,500 clm
	Troublesome Sal, 1964 m., War Trouble	EIP	8/20/1976	2,000 clm
11	Aurora Sister, 1968 m., Cloud Chief	Sun	3/24/1979	2,500 clm
	Bun's Barmaid, 1971 m., Solid Circle	GF	7/31/1982	2,000 clm
	Count Tricia, 1969 m., Count Me Out	Bil	8/11/1980	1,600 clm
	Dreamolark, 1970 m., Meno Dream	Ril	2/14/1981	1,250 clm
	Easy Mission, 1968 m., Mon Easy	Com	8/31/1979	1,500 clm
		Wat	11/5/1979	1,500 clm
	Flash Thru, 1967 m., Nir Thru	MD	8/5/1978	4,000 clm
	Gene's Hobby, 1974 m., Fincastle	MD	5/27/1985	2,000 clm
	Nolowblows, 1969 m., Uppercut	Nmp	9/5/1980	1,500 clm
	Peyton Sissy, 1974 m., Desi	LaM	9/22/1985	2,500 clm
	Phil's Hope, 1969 m., Philately	Pla	6/29/1980	3,200 clm
	Renest, 1967 m., Iamarelic	FL	10/8/1978	1,500 clm
	Risha, 1969 m., *Grand Applause	FL	4/11/1980	4,000 clm
	Special Party, 1969 m., Special Notice	Nmp	9/5/1980	1,500 clm
	Supreme Fleet, 1969 m., *Pallestrelli	Poc	10/7/1980	2,000 clm
	Texas Toy, 1969 m., Green Hornet	RD	8/16/1980	2,500 clm

The Claiming Game

Claiming races are the heart of almost every racing meet in America. In 2003, nearly two-thirds of all races (66.5%) were either straight claiming or maiden claiming. The horses that populate those races are an eclectic band of warriors whose common bond is their owners' willingness to lose them for a specified price as soon as the race is over.

The claimers are typified by such horses as Creme de La Fete, a chestnut gelding who went to post with a price on his head in all but 20 of his 151 career starts in the late 1970s and early '80s. His claiming prices ranged from $7,000 to $72,500.

Creme de La Fete was so well known that he was saluted in a ceremony at Aqueduct. The National Horsemen's Benevolent and Protective Association annually selects a claimer of the year, and the Claiming Crown held each summer has given more attention to the sport's foot soldiers.

But publicity for claimers is rare, accorded usually to horses that were claimed early in their careers and developed into champions, as Stymie did in the 1940s. Or, the attention goes to horses that ran in claiming races but were not taken, such as two-time Horse of the Year John Henry or 1999 Horse of the Year Charismatic.

Most claimers toil in anonymity, week after week, start after start, battling their infirmities as much as the competition. Most males are geldings and race well past their prime.

Claiming races have been a part of Thoroughbred racing for more than three centuries, though they began in England in a much different fashion and were called selling races.

In a story in the January 1972 issue of *The Thoroughbred of California*, Barry H. Irwin uncovered the original set of horse racing rules used in England in 1698, '99, and 1700 for races "at Thettford in the Countys of Norfolke and Suffolke" for the last Friday in September of each year. Eight noblemen and 11 commoners wrote 15 conditions for the races. One was that every owner would sell every horse entered for "Thirty Guineys" and that the "Contributors present shall throw dice" and that "the Purchaser will be he who throwes most at three."

More than 300 years later, if more than one claim is entered on a particular horse, the winner is determined by lot by the stewards. Getting to that point took several revisions once racing became established in the United States.

According to the Jockey Club's 1828 *Racing Calendar*, the owner of the second-place finisher in a selling race was entitled to purchase the winner for a specified sum. That rule was modified to allow all losing owners in a race to buy the winner, with the option to purchase determined by the order of finish. If the owner of the second-

place horse did not want the winner, the option to buy passed to the third-place finisher.

In the early 1900s, Canadian racetracks introduced the concept of sealed bids for the winner being submitted within 15 minutes after the race. A similar rule was approved by the Kentucky Association on September 1, 1916, and used at the 1917 spring race meeting in Lexington.

On opening day that spring, April 28, the Kentucky Association approved a Claiming Race Rule that allowed all horses in a claiming race to be purchased, and it set down the chilling reality for the person making a claim. The purchaser would become the owner of the horse "whether he be alive or dead, sound or unsound, or injured during the race or after it." To this day, the claim takes effect as soon as the starting gate opens. If a claimed horse dies during the race, the person who claimed it must not only buy the horse but also pay to remove the horse from the track and pay its burial fees.

Claiming races were well received and soon spread to East Coast tracks in the 1920s. However, selling races remained a part of the Jockey Club's rules of racing to the 1950s. By the 1940s, the selling race had become a variation of a claiming race in which only the winner was auctioned off for at the least the offering price. All other horses in the race were eligible to be claimed for the stated claiming price.

Claiming rules today vary modestly from one racing jurisdiction to another, but two basic concepts apply in almost all of them. First, any licensed trainer or owner who has had at least one starter at a race meeting may claim any horse at that meeting, although an owner or trainer who lost the last horse of his stable on a claim at the previous meeting is eligible to make a claim. Second, for a period of 30 days, the horse must race for at least 25% more than the price for which it was claimed. For example, a horse claimed for $10,000 cannot start in a claiming race for less than $12,500 for 30 days. Under those restrictions, the horse is frequently referred to as being "in jail," ostensibly because the new owner does not have the freedom to place him at any claiming price. Some racing jurisdictions have experimented with eliminating jail time. In addition, the claimed horse cannot be sold privately to another party in the 30-day period, and the horse cannot race at another track until the end of the race meet at which it was claimed.

For every claimer, there is a claiming trainer, and, like their horses, some have risen to prominence. Hirsch Jacobs, who led the nation in victories 11 times between 1933 and '44, may have been the first great claiming trainer. Jacobs claimed Stymie from a maiden claimer for $1,500 on June 8, 1943, and Stymie rewarded him by winning more than $900,000.

On the West Coast, one of the most prominent claiming trainers was R. H. "Red" McDaniel, who led the nation in victories from 1950 through 1954. In 1955, McDaniel saddled a winner at Golden Gate Fields and a few minutes later jumped to his death from the San Francisco Bay Bridge.

Claimers have been an integral part of the success of father-son Racing Hall of Fame members Marion and Jack Van Berg. Jack Van Berg led the nation's trainers in victories nine times, including a still-record 496 wins in 1976.

Frank "Pancho" Martin won 11 New York training titles, the first in 1971 and then ten straight from 1973 through 1982. The Cuban-born Martin explained his training philosophy in a 1972 magazine article: "The most important thing to remember is to treat your cheapest horse as good as your best," Martin said. "Give a claimer the same care you give a stakes horse, and he'll win for you in his own class. If you improve a horse, move him up in company, but never ask him to do the impossible."

Three of Martin's greatest claimers were Manassa Mauler, a $12,800 claim who won the 1959 Wood Memorial Stakes and earned $359,171; Autobiography, a $29,000 claim who won the '72 Jockey Club Gold Cup over Key to the Mint and Riva Ridge; and *Big Shot II, a $25,000 claim who won a $100,000 stakes, the '71 Century Handicap.

Though Bobby Frankel shifted his base of operations to California in 1972, he had consider-

able success with claimers in his six New York seasons before heading west. In that period, Frankel developed claimers Barometer, Baitman, and Pataha Prince into stakes winners. Barometer, claimed for $15,000, won the 1970 Suburban Handicap and earned $174,584. Baitman, who was seven years old when Frankel claimed him for $15,000, earned more than $150,000 after the claim. In California, Frankel claimed Wickerr for $50,000 and then won the 1981 and '82 Eddie Read Handicaps (G1) with him. Wickerr also won the 1981 Del Mar Handicap (G2).

West Virginia-based Dale Baird led the nation's trainers in victories 15 times from 1971 through '99, almost exclusively with claimers. He was displaced as America's top trainer by victories in 2000 and '01 by Scott Lake, who races simultaneously at several tracks in the Northeast. Steve Asmussen was the 2002 leader by wins.

Fifty-two years after Stymie was claimed for $1,500, a first-time starter at Hollywood Park named Budroyale was claimed in a maiden race for $32,000 by trainer Dan Hendricks for Decoury W. Graham. Budroyale was subsequently claimed twice more for $40,000 and for $50,000 before he matured to win several graded stakes, finish second in the 1999 Breeders' Cup Classic (G1), and earn more than $2.8-million, most of it for small-scale owner Jeffrey Sengara. Such horses as Stymie and Budroyale are the exceptions, but the hope of finding a diamond in the rough keeps many owners and trainers in the claiming game.

—*Bill Heller*

North American Claiming Races in 2004

Claiming races remain a significant part of Thoroughbred racing in North America, both in terms of the number of races and the purse money distributed in them. In 2004, the number of claiming races declined slightly from the previous year, but purses paid to claimers rebounded to record levels after a sizable drop

in '03. In 2004, 39,010 claiming races were held in North America, 101 fewer than in '03, but the percentage of claiming races remained unchanged at 66.5%. Total claiming purses were $446.8-million, up from $436.2-million in 2003. The percentage of total purse money going to claimers ticked up slightly to 37.9%.

Claiming Races in North America, 1997-2004

Year	Number of Races	% of Races	Total Claiming Purses	% of Purses	Average Purse	Number of Claims	Value of All Claims	Average Claim Price
2004	39,010	66.5%	$446,836,040	37.9%	$11,454	16,307	$209,586,963	$12,853
2003	39,111	66.5%	436,172,397	37.8%	11,152	14,777	202,646,625	13,714
2002	39,351	65.9%	444,901,718	38.0%	11,306	15,912	207,807,725	13,060
2001	39,655	65.5%	428,916,774	37.4%	10,816	14,974	200,883,275	13,415
2000	39,103	64.5%	393,469,977	36.0%	10,062	14,682	202,498,225	13,792
1999	39,420	65.6%	367,718,557	36.5%	9,328	13,909	177,754,863	12,780
1998	40,194	65.7%	354,541,816	36.6%	8,821	12,466	150,608,500	12,080
1997	42,368	66.7%	327,460,399	36.8%	7,729	11,703	136,154,325	11,634

Claims by Category at United States Tracks in 2004

Claiming Price Range	No. of Starts	No. Claims	% of Claimed	% of All of Claims	Total Value of Claims	Average Claim Price
Less than $1,000	0	0	0.0%	0.0%	$0	$0
$1,000 to $2,499	2,033	44	2.2%	0.3%	80,600	1,832
$2,500 to $4,999	80,495	2,847	3.5%	18.7%	9,984,950	3,507
$5,000 to $7,499	65,704	3,277	5.0%	21.6%	17,332,000	5,289

Claiming Price Range	No. of Starts	No. Claims	% of Claimed	% of All of Claims	Total Value of Claims	Average Claim Price
$7,500 to $9,999	33,148	1,628	4.9%	10.7%	12,563,500	7,717
$10,000 to $14,999	49,837	2,880	5.8%	18.9%	31,631,500	10,983
$15,000 to $19,999	22,055	1,481	6.7%	9.7%	23,575,500	15,919
$20,000 to $29,999	27,009	1,594	5.9%	10.5%	36,723,000	23,038
$30,000 to $39,999	11,364	674	5.9%	4.4%	21,651,500	32,124
$40,000 to $49,999	6,021	392	6.5%	2.6%	15,805,000	40,319
$50,000 to $74,999	4,947	334	6.8%	2.2%	17,997,500	53,885
$75,000 and up	1,050	50	4.8%	0.3%	4,025,000	80,500
Totals	**303,663**	**15,201**	**5.0%**	**100.0%**	**$191,370,050**	**$12,589**

Claims by Category at Canadian Tracks in 2004

Claiming Price Range	No. of Starts	No. Claims	% of Claimed	% of All of Claims	Total Value of Claims	Average Claim Price
Less than $1,000	0	0	0.0%	0.0%	$0	$0
$1,000 to $2,499	1,008	14	1.4%	1.3%	29,500	$2,107
$2,500 to $4,999	3,044	78	2.6%	7.1%	268,725	3,445
$5,000 to $7,499	7,314	154	2.1%	13.9%	833,750	5,414
$7,500 to $9,999	4,684	130	2.8%	11.8%	1,022,813	7,868
$10,000 to $14,999	4,543	206	4.5%	18.6%	2,355,000	11,432
$15,000 to $19,999	3,140	149	4.7%	13.5%	2,397,625	16,091
$20,000 to $29,999	3,434	222	6.5%	20.1%	5,023,000	22,626
$30,000 to $39,999	1,336	59	4.4%	5.3%	1,911,500	32,398
$40,000 to $49,999	983	61	6.2%	5.5%	2,492,500	40,861
$50,000 to $74,999	604	28	4.6%	2.5%	1,500,000	53,571
$75,000 and up	151	5	3.3%	0.5%	382,500	76,500
Totals	**30,241**	**1,106**	**3.7%**	**100.0%**	**$18,216,913**	**$16,471**

United States Claiming Activity by State and Track in 2004

	No. of Horses Claimed	Total Value of Claims	Avg. Price of Claim
Arizona			
Apache County Fair	1	$1,000	$1,000
Cochise County Fair	1	1,250	1,250
Flagstaff	4	7,000	1,750
Gila County Fair	1	2,000	2,000
Mohave County Fair	1	1,000	1,000
Rillito Park	2	2,500	1,250
Santa Cruz County Fair	2	2,750	1,375
Turf Paradise	456	2,533,350	5,556
Yavapai Downs	55	166,300	3,024
Total Arizona	**523**	**$2,717,150**	**$5,195**
Arkansas			
Oaklawn Park	241	$3,760,000	$15,602
Total Arkansas	**241**	**$3,760,000**	**$15,602**
California			
Bay Meadows	516	$6,655,950	$12,899
Bay Meadows Fair	40	499,700	12,493
Del Mar	292	7,847,000	26,873
Fairplex Park	68	798,250	11,739
Ferndale	2	8,200	4,100
Fresno	15	59,500	3,967
Golden Gate Fields	508	6,325,750	12,452
Hollywood Park	373	10,521,000	28,206
Los Alamitos	204	650,200	3,187
Pleasanton	41	288,600	7,039
Sacramento	33	191,500	5,803
Santa Anita Park	548	15,849,500	28,922
Santa Rosa	50	483,550	9,671
Solano County Fair	40	338,150	8,454
Stockton	31	158,050	5,098
Total California	**2,761**	**$50,674,900**	**$18,354**
Colorado			
Arapahoe Park	16	$87,450	$5,466
Total Colorado	**16**	**$87,450**	**$5,466**
Delaware			
Delaware Park	498	$7,007,250	$14,071
Total Delaware	**498**	**$7,007,250**	**$14,071**
Florida			
Calder Race Course	351	$5,591,500	$15,930
Gulfstream Park	416	8,966,250	21,553

	No. of Horses Claimed	Total Value of Claims	Avg. Price of Claim
Little Everglades	1	25,000	25,000
Tampa Bay Downs	232	2,380,500	10,261
Total Florida	**1,000**	**$16,963,250**	**$16,963**
Idaho			
Les Bois Park	18	$55,800	$3,100
Total Idaho	**18**	**$55,800**	**$3,100**
Illinois			
Arlington Park	397	$6,647,500	$16,744
Fairmount Park	64	319,850	4,998
Hawthorne Race Course	425	4,888,500	11,502
Total Illinois	**886**	**$11,855,850**	**$13,381**
Indiana			
Hoosier Park	77	$401,000	$5,208
Indiana Downs	33	179,750	5,447
Total Indiana	**110**	**$580,750**	**$5,280**
Iowa			
Prairie Meadows Racetrack	92	$1,003,250	$10,905
Total Iowa	**92**	**$1,003,250**	**$10,905**
Kansas			
The Woodlands	13	$52,000	$4,000
Total Kansas	**13**	**$52,000**	**$4,000**
Kentucky			
Churchill Downs	436	$8,450,000	$19,381
Ellis Park	115	1,202,500	10,457
Keeneland	95	1,857,500	19,553
Kentucky Downs	4	55,000	13,750
Turfway Park	203	2,132,250	10,504
Total Kentucky	**853**	**$13,697,250**	**$16,058**
Louisiana			
Delta Downs	235	$1,769,000	$7,528
Evangeline Downs	193	1,065,000	5,518
Fair Grounds	302	5,322,500	17,624
Louisiana Downs	116	1,393,750	12,015
Total Louisiana	**846**	**$9,550,250**	**$11,289**
Maryland			
Laurel Park	241	$3,591,000	$14,900
Pimlico	348	5,032,000	14,460
Timonium	13	190,000	14,615
Total Maryland	**602**	**$8,813,000**	**$14,640**

	No. of Horses Claimed	Total Value of Claims	Avg. Price of Claim
Massachusetts			
Suffolk Downs	189	$1,368,750	$7,242
Total Massachusetts	**189**	**$1,368,750**	**$7,242**
Michigan			
Great Lakes Downs	32	$166,000	$5,188
Total Michigan	**32**	**$166,000**	**$5,188**
Minnesota			
Canterbury Park	78	$631,000	$8,090
Total Minnesota	**78**	**$631,000**	**$8,090**
Montana			
Great Falls	3	$6,500	$2,167
Western Montana Fair	3	7,500	2,500
Yellowstone Downs	1	2,500	2,500
Total Montana	**7**	**$16,500**	**$2,357**
Nebraska			
Columbus Races	32	$121,500	$3,797
Fonner Park	45	193,500	4,300
Horsemen's Atokad Down's	6	26,000	4,333
Horsemen's Park	2	18,000	9,000
Lincoln State Fair	33	105,500	3,197
Total Nebraska	**118**	**$464,500**	**$3,936**
New Jersey			
Atlantic City Race Course	2	$40,000	$20,000
Monmouth Park	302	4,524,500	14,982
The Meadowlands	75	1,498,250	19,977
Total New Jersey	**379**	**$6,062,750**	**$15,997**
New Mexico			
Ruidoso Downs	29	$162,050	$5,588
Sunland Park	229	2,007,750	8,767
SunRay Park	12	69,000	5,750
The Downs at Albuquerque	25	142,000	5,680
Total New Mexico	**295**	**$2,380,800**	**$8,071**
New York			
Aqueduct	300	$7,726,000	$25,753
Belmont Park	185	6,274,500	33,916
Finger Lakes	136	855,750	6,292
Saratoga Race Course	113	4,357,500	38,562
Total New York	**734**	**$19,213,750**	**$26,177**
Ohio			
Beulah Park	44	$211,500	$4,807
River Downs	78	424,500	5,442
Thistledown	166	734,500	4,425
Total Ohio	**288**	**$1,370,500**	**$4,759**
Oklahoma			
Blue Ribbon Downs	1	$5,000	$5,000
Fair Meadows at Tulsa	19	100,000	5,263
Remington Park	64	483,000	7,547
Total Oklahoma	**84**	**$588,000**	**$7,000**
Oregon			
Grants Pass	4	$10,800	$2,700
Portland Meadows	102	343,800	3,371
Total Oregon	**106**	**$354,600**	**$3,345**

	No. of Horses Claimed	Total Value of Claims	Avg. Price of Claim
Pennsylvania			
Penn National Race Course	230	$1,255,750	$5,460
Philadelphia Park	602	6,110,250	10,150
Total Pennsylvania	**832**	**$7,366,000**	**$8,853**
Texas			
Lone Star Park	376	$4,401,500	$11,706
Manor Downs	1	6,250	6,250
Retama Park	34	245,500	7,221
Sam Houston Race Park	73	600,000	8,219
Total Texas	**484**	**$5,253,250**	**$10,854**
Virginia			
Colonial Downs	24	$318,500	$13,271
Total Virginia	**24**	**$318,500**	**$13,271**
Washington			
Emerald Downs	216	$1,895,750	$8,777
Total Washington	**216**	**$1,895,750**	**$8,777**
West Virginia			
Charles Town Races	2166	$12,535,250	$5,787
Mountaineer Race Track	709	4,562,500	6,435
Total West Virginia	**2,875**	**$17,097,750**	**$5,947**
Wyoming			
Wyoming Downs	1	$3,500	$3,500
Total Wyoming	**1**	**$3,500**	**$3,500**

Canadian Claiming Activity by Province and Track in 2004

	No. of Horses Claimed	Total Value of Claims	Avg. Price of Claim
Alberta			
Lethbridge	16	$46,500	$2,906
Northlands Park	139	2,051,000	14,755
Stampede Park	115	1,643,000	14,287
Total Alberta	**270**	**3,740,500**	**13,854**
British Columbia			
Hastings Race Course	186	$2,143,000	$11,522
Kin Park	1	3,000	3,000
Total British Columbia	**187**	**$2,146,000**	**$11,476**
Manitoba			
Assiniboia Downs	87	$461,188	$5,301
Total Manitoba	**87**	**$461,188**	**$5,301**
Ontario			
Fort Erie	131	$1,052,500	$8,034
Woodbine	411	10,764,500	26,191
Total Ontario	**542**	**$11,817,000**	**$21,803**
Saskatchewan			
Marquis Downs	19	$50,225	$2,643
Total Saskatchewan	**19**	**$50,225**	**$2,643**

Horses With Highest Earnings After First Claim in 2004

Horse, YOB, Sex, Sire	Claiming Price	Wins After Claim	Earnings After Claim
Star Over the Bay, 1998 g., Cozzene	$80,000	3	$430,000
Flamethrowintexan, 2001 g., Way West (Fr)	40,000	5	332,513
Choctaw Nation, 2000 g., Louis Quatorze	40,000	4	289,200
My Snookie's Boy, 2001 c., Crafty Friend	50,000	2	283,866
Sis City, 2002 f., Slew City Slew	50,000	2	263,000
Cologny, 2000 m., Go for Gin	25,000	5	238,408
Market Garden, 2000 m., Bold Badgett	40,000	3	218,398
Classic Endeavor, 1998 h., Silver Buck	35,000	5	212,400
Silver Impulse, 2002 f., Silver Charm	62,500	2	198,218

Horse, YOB, Sex, Sire	Claiming Price	Wins After Claim	Earnings After Claim
Yougottawanna, 1999 g., Candi's Gold	$50,000	4	$183,059
Separato, 2001 c., Victory Gallop	40,000	5	172,900
Diligent Gambler, 2001 c., Diligence	25,000	7	171,800
Long Term Success, 1999 g., Sandpit (Brz)	10,000	4	168,090
Lava Man, 2001 g., Slew City Slew	50,000	1	162,000
Demon Warlock, 2000 h., Demons Begone	25,000	4	159,340
Upturn, 2000 g., Distorted Humor	65,000	4	155,480
Slim Dusty, 1999 g., Anjiz	40,000	3	153,860
Discreet Hero, 1998 g., Honour and Glory	40,000	3	150,987
Miss Grindstone, 1999 m., Grindstone	50,000	2	146,565
Thermal Ablasion, 1999 m., Unusual Heat	40,000	4	145,916
Sky Diamond, 2000 g., Sky Classic	35,000	3	145,580
Twist and Pop, 1999 m., Oliver's Twist	22,500	4	145,240
Scooter Roach, 1999 g., Mi Cielo	62,500	1	145,109
Heroic Sight, 1998 g., Sea Hero	14,000	7	144,530
Childress, 1998 m., Evansville Slew	25,000	4	142,750
Revello, 1998 g., Memo (Chi)	40,000	2	141,108
Seventeen Above, 2001 f., Partner's Hero	25,000	4	138,396
Ojibway, 2001 g., Bugatti Reef (Ire)	50,000	4	136,995
Jake Skate, 2000 h., Arch	40,000	3	134,720
Beyond Brilliant, 1998 g., High Brite	32,000	5	134,428
Latenite Special, 2001 f., Super Special	10,000	4	133,523
Sterling Gold, 1999 g., Mutakddim	40,000	4	130,175
Tiger Shrimp, 2000 g., Alphabet Soup	20,000	3	128,310
Geardown, 2000 g., High Brite	20,000	3	127,677
Willie Dunn, 2001 g., Bold n' Flashy	20,000	3	127,264
Juliet's Kiss, 2001 f., Kissin Kris	20,000	2	126,112
Devil Badgett, 2000 g., Bold Badgett	25,000	3	125,976
Big Tease, 2000 m., Gold Token	30,000	3	125,000

Leading Earners After First Claim, 1991-2004

Horse, YOB, Sex, Sire	Initial Claim Price	Date of Claim	Starts After Claim	Wins After Claim	Earnings After Claim
Budroyale, 1993 g., by Cee's Tizzy	$32,000	12/9/1995	52	17	$2,837,610
Ladies Din, 1995 g., by Din's Dancer	32,000	7/30/1997	35	11	1,896,854
Native Desert, 1993 g., by Desert Classic	32,000	10/10/1996	72	20	1,815,827
Say Florida Sandy, 1994 h., by Personal Flag	70,000	9/14/1997	85	27	1,774,748
Peeping Tom, 1997 g., by Eagle Eyed	40,000	3/24/2000	51	15	1,367,297
River Keen (Ire), 1992 h., by Keen	100,000	12/4/1998	16	3	1,338,880
Lazy Slusan, 1995 m., by Slewvescent	20,000	10/22/1997	45	11	1,142,196
Full Moon Madness, 1995 g., by Half a Year	32,000	6/25/1997	45	15	1,094,205
Shake You Down, 1998 g., by Montbrook	65,000	3/12/2003	16	10	1,093,244
Recoup the Cash, 1990 g., by Copelan	15,000	6/3/1993	67	22	1,090,713
License Fee, 1995 m., by Black Tie Affair (Ire)	75,000	9/2/1998	34	13	1,084,276
Early Pioneer, 1995 g., by Rahy	62,500	10/25/1998	22	7	1,068,815
Mr. Epperson, 1995 g., by Cabrini Green	50,000	7/10/1998	63	15	1,024,974
One for Rose, 1999 m., by Tejano Run	40,000	10/4/2002	21	11	1,022,823
Parose, 1994 g., by Parlay Me	15,000	7/22/1998	69	18	1,005,894
Elated Guy, 1989 g., by Brave Shot (GB)	40,000	8/22/1991	63	9	941,904
One Way Love, 1995 h., by Regal Classic	50,000	11/1/1997	37	14	937,095
Bluesthestandard, 1997 g., by American Standard	22,500	4/25/2001	32	14	930,218
Pie N Burger, 1998 g., by Twining	62,500	9/13/2000	42	14	920,533
Dancing Guy, 1995 g., by Robyn Dancer	18,000	11/25/1997	90	21	912,953
Shoop, 1991 m., by Double Sonic	25,000	8/26/1995	70	11	911,515
Designed for Luck, 1997 g., by Rahy	62,500	12/17/1999	24	9	901,100
Tour of the Cat, 1998 g., by Tour d'Or	25,000	11/11/2000	46	13	867,861
Royal Haven, 1992 g., by Hail Emperor	75,000	8/6/1995	37	16	847,161
Beboppin Baby, 1993 g., by Hatchet Man	32,000	7/13/1996	64	13	830,990
Judge T C, 1991 h., by Judge Smells	30,000	6/11/1993	27	11	825,960
Arromanches, 1993 h., by Relaunch	12,500	6/24/1996	75	30	800,224
Moscow Burning, 2000 m., by Moscow Ballet	25,000	8/7/2003	16	5	776,550
Adminniestrator, 1997 g., by Incinderator	32,000	3/31/2000	40	9	761,716
Coyote Lakes, 1994 g., by Society Max	12,500	10/26/1996	59	19	724,337
Classic Endeavor, 1998 h., by Silver Buck	75,000	9/2/2000	54	16	713,293
Sharp Appeal, 1993 h., by World Appeal	50,000	7/14/1995	39	12	712,346
Irisheyesareflying, 1996 h., by Flying Continental	12,500	2/20/1999	36	8	711,736
Ninebanks, 1998 g., by Smokester	50,000	8/3/2001	30	10	698,283

Horse, YOB, Sex, Sire	Initial Claim Price	Date of Claim	Starts After Claim	Wins After Claim	Earnings After Claim
Esteemed Friend, 1994 g., by Gulch	$50,000	8/21/1997	51	17	$677,417
Same Old Wish, 1990 g., by Lyphard's Wish (Fr)	35,000	8/4/1994	49	5	675,935
Chicago Six, 1995 h., by Wild Again	18,000	9/2/1999	29	15	675,147
Golden Tent, 1989 g., by Shelter Half	50,000	5/15/1994	105	17	673,903
Mr. Sinatra, 1994 h., by Mining	75,000	8/22/1997	53	10	667,205
Chris's Bad Boy, 1997 g., by Marquetry	10,000	11/13/2001	30	16	666,688
Boom Towner, 1988 g., by Obligato	50,000	9/1/1993	56	16	663,070
My Cousin Matt, 1999 g., by Matty G	85,000	9/25/2002	20	4	655,100
Wicapi, 1992 g., by Waquoit	20,000	1/11/1996	54	17	651,601
Iron Gavel, 1990 g., by Time for a Change	15,500	11/18/1993	77	24	646,408
Tic N Tin, 1995 g., by Lac Ouimet	25,000	10/2/1999	76	24	645,395
Freedom Crest, 1996 g., by To Freedom	32,000	6/10/1999	28	7	641,400
Oro de Mexico, 1994 g., by Well Decorated	80,000	3/14/1997	60	9	638,950
Praise From Dixie, 1996 g., by Dixie Brass	62,500	5/7/2000	52	9	631,557
Morluc, 1996 h., by Housebuster	50,000	1/15/1999	34	10	628,088
Echo Eddie, 1997 g., by Restless Con	20,000	11/20/1999	27	8	627,084
Sassy Hound, 1997 g., by Deerhound	14,500	1/6/2000	43	14	619,298
Lil Personalitee, 1997 g., by Personal Flag	62,500	8/4/2000	49	11	615,566
Theresa's Tizzy, 1994 m., by Cee's Tizzy	20,000	7/25/1997	31	13	612,171
Boston Common, 1999 g., by Boston Harbor	50,000	6/23/2001	32	12	605,317
Devine Wind, 1996 g., by American Chance	40,000	5/10/2000	38	11	604,683
Watchman's Warning, 1995 g., by Carnivalay	35,000	6/28/1998	75	12	600,700
Fit for a King, 1993 g., by General Meeting	16,000	11/9/1996	31	15	598,618
Greatsilverfleet, 1990 g., by On to Glory	62,500	5/12/1993	69	15	593,637
Back Ring Al, 1992 g., by Allen's Prospect	25,000	1/15/1995	104	25	590,679
Slerp, 1989 h., by Slewpy	40,000	1/17/1992	31	9	588,842
Truly a Judge, 1998 g., by Judge T C	50,000	3/7/2001	37	11	587,981
Halory Leigh, 2000 m., by Halory Hunter	75,000	6/5/2003	17	6	587,312
Nappelon, 1992 m., by Bold Revenue	35,000	2/9/1995	58	14	584,720
Ringaskiddy, 1996 g., by Slewvescent	50,000	3/13/1999	47	4	583,631
Countess Steffi, 1989 m., by Geiger Counter	25,000	8/16/1991	33	11	580,835
Poor But Honest, 1990 g., by Nasty and Bold	17,500	5/18/1994	28	11	579,230

Horses With Most Wins After First Claim in 2004

Horse, YOB, Sex, Sire	Claiming Price	Wins After Claim	Earnings After Claim
Out of Pride, 1999 m., Out of Place	$6,250	8	$100,655
Kipper's an Angel, 1999 g., Kipper Kelly	10,000	8	92,200
Aly's Leader, 1997 m., Alyten	5,000	8	85,235
Diligent Gambler, 2001 c., Diligence	25,000	7	171,800
Heroic Sight, 1998 g., Sea Hero	14,000	7	144,530
Smooth Lover, 1999 g., Suave Prospect	14,000	7	124,410
Proud Tears, 2000 m., Proud and True	4,000	7	121,624
Lone Traveler, 1998 g., Judge Smells	7,500	7	117,727
Home Deed, 1998 m., Alydeed	4,000	7	82,380
Gimme the Willys, 1998 m., Walter Willy (Ire)	10,000	7	80,900
The Niner Account, 1998 g., Unaccounted For	20,000	6	120,210
Dorst, 2001 g., Dance Brightly	25,000	6	114,560
Firststatedeposit, 1998 g., Deposit Ticket	20,000	6	112,800
Late Expectations, 2001 g., Valid Expectations	10,000	6	110,800
Concisely, 2000 g., Horatius	5,000	6	87,983
Wicklow Highlands, 1996 h., Temperence Hill	18,000	6	87,010
Mister Riley, 2000 g., Mister Jolie	6,250	6	71,520
Transcendent, 1999 g., Muhtafal	3,500	6	71,030
Pine Brook, 2000 g., Meadow Flight	5,000	6	69,693
Regal Watch, 2000 g., Cobra King	8,000	6	66,865
Savvy Girl, 2000 m., Valid Expectations	5,000	6	60,597
Sea Power, 2000 h., Grindstone	30,000	6	60,520
Senfully Easy, 1999 m., Mr. Easy Money	6,250	6	56,560
Thebigbrushoff, 2000 g., Schossberg	4,000	6	55,490
Song Dancer, 1998 h., Unbridled's Song	8,000	6	53,321
Lunar Bounty, 1999 g., Migrating Moon	15,000	6	50,455
Fortunate One, 1998 g., Fortunate Prospect	3,500	6	49,585
Private American, 2001 c., Quiet American	20,000	6	47,760
How Say You, 2001 c., Caller I. D.	16,000	6	45,795
River Monster, 1999 h., Meadow Monster	16,000	6	44,870
Rich March, 1998 g., Rizzi	3,500	6	44,323

Horse, YOB, Sex, Sire	Claiming Price	Wins After Claim	Earnings After Claim
Yankee Ruler, 1996 g., Yankee Fan	$7,000	6	$35,789
Chief Cahill, 2000 g., High Brite	3,200	6	34,775
Legal Thief, 1997 g., Pirate's Bounty	2,000	6	28,697
Knines Dream, 1995 g., Crystal Tas	3,200	6	28,121
Mr. Melcap, 1999 g., Victory Speech	2,500	6	21,013
Miner's Surprise, 2000 g., Prized	4,000	6	18,254
Baldjim, 1996 g., Katowice	2,000	6	10,870

Horses With Most Wins After First Claim, 1991-2004

Horse, YOB, Sex, Sire	Initial Claim Price	Date of Claim	Starts After Claim	Wins After Claim	Earnings After Claim
Sawmill Run, 1988 g., by It's Freezing	$4,000	6/28/1992	125	35	$224,514
Mankato, 1988 g., by Meadowlake	15,000	3/17/1992	145	34	330,856
Maybe Jack, 1993 g., by Classic Account	15,000	4/18/1997	106	33	511,945
Oh So Fabulous, 1992 g., by Singular	6,250	2/21/1997	97	33	229,402
It's the Wind, 1989 g., by Contare	5,000	3/1/1992	123	32	202,300
Meine Empress, 1989 m., by Rex Imperator	14,000	9/12/1992	75	32	145,190
The Mighty Zip, 1988 g., by Fire Dancer	5,000	10/5/1992	121	32	223,453
J V Bennett, 1993 g., by Key to the Mint	32,000	6/20/1996	90	31	375,729
Adorable Racer, 1992 g., by Two's a Plenty	3,500	2/13/1996	103	30	333,622
Arromanches, 1993 h., by Relaunch	12,500	6/24/1996	75	30	800,224
Belle's Ruckus, 1985 g., by Bold Ruckus	5,000	7/11/1992	106	30	156,856
Out for Gold, 1990 g., by Gold Crest	35,000	1/6/1993	179	30	284,711
Sgt. Ivor, 1990 g., by Ivor Street	5,000	1/28/1994	157	30	165,012
Tate Express, 1992 g., by Naevus	12,500	12/29/1995	137	30	236,159
Bell Buzzer, 1990 g., by Sauce Boat	4,000	11/17/1994	101	29	111,630
Cope With Peace, 1988 h., by Copelan	10,000	2/20/1992	109	29	182,749
Mahrally, 1991 g., by Ballydoyle	6,250	8/1/1994	142	29	146,535
Secret Service Man, 1992 g., by Shot Gun Scott	18,000	8/2/1996	98	29	290,043
Boca Ratony, 1988 g., by Boca Rio	14,000	7/31/1993	103	28	75,934
Gold Digs, 1987 g., by Regal and Royal	4,000	4/5/1992	103	28	150,206
Spacemaker, 1988 g., by Sunny Clime	5,000	10/11/1992	83	28	148,711
Victory Tower, 1990 g., by Singular	10,000	8/20/1993	152	28	151,654
Exuberant's Tip, 1990 g., by Exuberant	30,000	6/26/1992	87	27	116,315
Fit for Royalty, 1988 g., by Fighting Fit	9,000	4/9/1993	135	27	206,439
Northern Broadway, 1988 g., by Northern Magus	5,000	5/10/1992	160	27	108,542
Rosy Way, 1989 g., by Lord Avie	20,000	8/22/1993	46	27	88,779
Say Florida Sandy, 1994 h., by Personal Flag	70,000	9/14/1997	85	27	1,774,748
Scent a Grade, 1992 g., by Foolish Pleasure	5,000	7/20/1995	86	27	172,910
Win Man, 1985 g., by Con Man	8,250	2/23/1992	66	27	262,792

Horses With Most Claiming Wins in 2004

Horse, YOB, Sex, Sire	Starts	Claiming Wins	Claiming Earnings
Diligent Gambler, 2001 c., by Diligence	15	9	$196,400
Warrior's Dance, 2000 g., by Forever Dancer	16	9	77,900
Co Twining Niner, 1999 g., by Twining	16	8	33,420
Miner's Surprise, 2000 g., by Prized	14	8	24,646
Baby Book, 1999 m., by Repriced	14	7	38,674
Chief Cahill, 2000 g., by High Brite	14	7	37,850
Fatal Caper, 2000 m., by Town Caper	16	7	109,200
Herpotofgold, 2000 m., by Mutakddim	20	7	40,411
Hook Call (Brz), 1995 g., by Exile King	11	7	78,120
Knines Dream, 1995 g., by Crystal Tas	16	7	34,294
Regal Watch, 2000 g., by Cobra King	17	7	78,430
Rize, 1996 g., by Theatrical (Ire)	13	7	137,160
Senfully Easy, 1999 m., by Mr. Easy Money	10	7	62,335
Time to Be Sassy, 1999 g., by Temper Time	19	7	32,320
Transcendent, 1999 g., by Muhtafal	16	7	79,414
Vantage Star, 2001 f., by Tactical Advantage	19	7	71,915

Horses With Most Claiming Wins, 1991-2004

No. Claiming Wins	Horse, YOB, Sex, Sire	Claiming Starts	Claiming Earnings	Total Earnings
36	Boca Ratony, 1988 g., by Boca Rio	117	$107,020	$123,587
34	Best Boy's Jade, 1989 g., by Raja's Best Boy	134	170,982	223,983
32	Mankato, 1988 g., by Meadowlake	139	299,146	381,821
32	Spacemaker, 1988 g., by Sunny Clime	91	145,020	174,097
31	Sawmill Run, 1988 g., by It's Freezing	123	195,437	251,404
31	Smart Graustark, 1990 h., by Special Graustark	94	51,057	52,487
30	Dundee Maverick, 1989 g., by Implore	110	112,638	125,220

No. Claiming Wins	Horse, YOB, Sex, Sire	Claiming Starts	Claiming Earnings	Total Earnings
30	Gold Digs, 1987 g., by Regal and Royal	107	$151,805	$182,566
30	Halo Round My Head, 1988 m., by Gregorian	97	112,852	130,383
29	Thar He Blows, 1988 g., by Dewan Keys	143	75,020	80,867
29	The Mighty Zip, 1988 g., by Fire Dancer	114	183,953	265,341
28	Inspector Moomaw, 1987 g., by Entropy	128	184,689	207,948
28	It's the Wind, 1989 g., by Contare	102	163,627	207,100
28	Northern Broadway, 1988 g., by Northern Magus	163	119,212	127,096
28	Sgt. Ivor, 1990 g., by Ivor Street	151	143,856	173,316
28	Son Coming., 1986 g., by Son of Briartic	130	128,806	136,579
28	Two the Twist, 1987 g., by Two's a Plenty	141	292,975	496,488
28	Wilowy's Image, 1989 m., by Mongo's Image	70	130,208	154,698
27	Bon to Run, 1992 g., by Search for Gold	130	119,427	132,833
27	Elegant Bo, 1987 g., by Swelegant	121	153,132	199,284
27	Monsignor K., 1987 g., by Gala Harry	158	130,434	138,286
27	Oh So Fabulous, 1992, g., by Singular	88	173,081	286,339
27	Out for Gold, 1990 g., by Gold Crest	169	253,929	313,896
27	Primetime Pirate, 1991 g., by Word Pirate	114	65,705	71,368
27	Regal Peace, 1988 m., by Peace for Peace	112	113,460	115,383
27	Sheila K., 1988 m., by Family Doctor	127	117,413	117,833

Horses Claimed Most Times, 1991-2004

No. Times Claimed	Horse, YOB, Sex, Sire	Aggregate Claim Price	Average Claim Price	Starts	Wins	Earnings
22	Sound System, 1993 g., by by Waquoit	$170,000	$7,727	105	28	$306,101
20	Above the Crowd, 1993 g., by by Housebuster	541,500	27,075	88	24	461,886
20	Game Skipper, 1992 g., by Skip Trial	165,000	8,250	128	19	237,043
19	North Salem, 1994 h., by Badger Land	243,500	12,816	106	17	297,236
18	Brisa, 1995 m., by Prince of Fame	84,500	4,694	96	10	148,676
18	Erhard, 1996 g., by by Gallant Prospector	157,000	8,722	75	13	111,011
18	Nauset Flash, 1987 g., by Parfaitement	204,000	11,333	164	20	299,579
18	Out for Gold, 1990 g., by by Gold Crest	171,500	9,528	187	33	313,896
18	Sharp n Strong, 1992 m., by Stalwart	226,000	12,556	86	14	290,071
18	Tenfortynine, 1998 g., by Ide	92,000	5,111	53	11	154,932
17	Halos Wonder, 1993 m., by Hay Halo	109,750	6,456	77	18	140,509
17	Imua Keoki, 1991 g., by Qui Native	178,500	10,500	86	17	201,224
17	Palace Heroine, 1996 m., by Fort Chaffee	94,000	5,529	77	10	173,574
17	Retail Sales, 1995 m., by Tour d'Or	171,500	10,088	96	19	205,712
17	Rich Coins, 1998 h., by Rizzi	335,500	19,735	72	12	315,111
17	Shot On Stage, 1991 g., by Gold Stage	154,000	9,059	129	12	184,274
17	Takeitlikeaman, 1991 g., by Exuberant	148,000	8,706	111	14	291,699
17	Wings of Jones, 1996 g., by by Seneca Jones	146,000	8,588	84	18	354,722

Horses Claimed Most Times in 2004

No. Times Claimed	Horse, YOB, Sex, Sire	Average Claim Price	Tracks Where Claimed	2004 Race Record
11	Mr. Kuck, 1997 g., by Wallenda	$4,727	CT	15-5-2-2, $60,430
9	Milky Bar (Chi), 1996 g., by The Great Shark	5,333	CT	13-2-0-0, 32,260
9	Red Hot Secret, 2000 g., by Mr. Greeley	7,444	CT	14-2-4-2, 55,039
9	Tour of the Rose, 1997 m., by Tour d'Or	4,722	CT	15-6-3-2, 91,568
8	Caroline's Candy, 2000 m., by Weshaam	4,750	CT	14-3-2-2, 53,180
8	Dirty Harryette, 1999 m., by Unaccounted For	9,063	CT	12-2-2-1, 50,185
8	Four Girls, 1999 m., by Foxhound	4,688	CT, Pen	14-3-2-1, 54,358
8	Lucky Larue, 2000 g., by Barbeau	4,000	CT	12-2-4-1, 27,880
8	Mary Carlisle, 1999 m., by Katowice	7,188	CT	15-2-3-4, 53,446
8	Prospector Who, 1999 g., by Crafty Prospector	3,625	CT	16-5-3-2, 57,271
8	Senfully Easy, 1999 m., by Mr. Easy Money	10,531	BM, Dmr, Fpx, GG, Hol	10-7-1-2, 62,335
7	Alkarnak, 1997 g., by Cryptoclearance	7,000	Del, GP	18-2-4-3, 31,030
7	Andrea's Angel, 2001 f., by Candi's Gold	15,643	BM, Dmr, GG, Hol	15-4-3-2, 49,000
7	Chuck Yeager, 2000 g., by Well Decorated	4,571	Tdn, TP	21-2-6-3, 21,307
7	Cool Cash, 1999 h., by Pentelicus	3,571	CT	15-4-0-3, 48,983
7	Cove Hill Missle, 1999 m., by Buckhar	20,000	Aqu, Bel, Pha	13-4-3-2, 77,880
7	Court Shenanigans, 1995 g., by Petersburg	15,071	Dmr, Fpx, GG, Hol, SA	12-3-2-2, 47,710
7	Devil's Gulch, 1999 g., by Thunder Gulch	19,857	Del, GP	12-3-6-1, 67,030
7	Devil's Mark, 1998 g., by Miner's Mark	11,000	Med, Mth, Pha, Tam	20-5-5-2, 68,922
7	Donde Estaras, 2000 m., by Always Silver	7,750	Del, GP	16-3-3-4, 44,010
7	Fine Results, 2000 m., by Repriced	5,500	Mnr	10-2-4-1, 36,343
7	First Arrival, 1996 m., by Deputed Testamony	10,500	CT, Lrl	15-3-0-2, 59,790
7	Gators Get, 1998 g., by Level Sands	10,214	CT	16-6-2-2, 95,149
7	Gravel Gertie, 1999 m., by Perfecting	7,071	CT	21-3-4-1, 48,492
7	Haint You Grand, 2001 g., by Haint	17,143	Dmr, Fpx, GG, Hol, SA	16-4-1-4, 77,660

No. Times Claimed	Horse, YOB, Sex, Sire	Average Claim Price	Tracks Where Claimed	2004 Race Record
7	Liberty Quest, 2000 g., by Concerto	$4,214	CT	15-2-5-1, $42,400
7	Linkoman, 1997 g., by Turkoman	5,714	Aqu, CT, Mnr	18-0-3-3, 22,068
7	Lord Burleigh, 1999 g., by Langfuhr	7,179	Del, GP	14-2-3-2, 37,142
7	Magicleigh, 1999 m., by Magic Prospect	3,571	CT	12-2-2-3, 26,848
7	Natural Style, 1997 h., by Valiant Nature	11,357	Dmr, GG, Hol, SA	14-2-2-6, 38,882
7	Opus Won, 1997 h., by Fit to Fight	5,000	CT	8-1-1-3, 20,150
7	Outta Luck, 1999 m., by Conveyor	5,857	CT	15-4-4-2, 56,870
7	Pounding, 1997 g., by Prospector's Music	8,929	CT	11-0-3-2, 27,346
7	Proud Patrolman, 1998 g., by Proud Irish	4,093	GG, Sac, SR	19-4-5-4, 37,011
7	Radon, 1999 m., by Lord Carson	21,071	BM, Dmr, GG, Hol, SA	14-3-2-2, 54,645
7	Storm's Secret, 1998 m., by Storm Creek	4,357	CT	14-4-3-2, 43,088
7	Sweet Peaches, 2000 m., by Oraibi	5,071	CT	14-2-5-1, 44,385
7	Trophy Case, 1998 g., by Keep Dreaming	10,714	CT, Lrl	15-4-3-1, 63,795
7	Two Thirty Seven, 2000 g., by Siberian Summer	13,857	DeD, Hol, SA	15-4-1-1, 44,890

Horses Claimed Most Times Consecutively in 2004

Cons. Claims	Horse, YOB, Sex, Sire	Starts	Wins	Earnings
7	Magicleigh, 1999 m., by Magic Prospect	12	2	$26,848
7	Opus Won, 1997 h., by Fit to Fight	8	1	20,150
6	Dirty Harryette, 1999 m., by Unaccounted For	12	2	50,185
6	Milky Bar (Chi), 1996 g., by The Great Shark	13	2	32,260
6	Personal Stash, 1998 g., by Air Forbes Won	8	1	16,284
6	Rally Mode, 1999 g., by Hasty Spirit	12	2	26,967
6	Rustic, 1999 m., by Schossberg	9	3	29,797
5	Banshee Boy, 2000 g., by Regal Intention	12	2	25,355
5	Cat Crusher, 1999 h., by Patton	11	2	26,950
5	Cool Cash, 1999 h., by Pentelicus	15	4	48,983
5	Daily Report, 1999 m., by Editor's Note	15	3	28,874
5	Damn the Torpedoes, 1997 g., by Cox's Ridge	7	2	43,920
5	Deer Creek Lady, 2001 f., by Valley Crossing	21	2	31,828
5	Flightofthebuffalo, 1999 g., by Sultry Song	10	3	64,590
5	Harbor of Grace, 1996 g., by Deputed Testamony	7	4	33,829
5	Lucky Larue, 2000 g., by Barbeau	12	2	27,880
5	Mister Stip, 2000 g., by Mister Jolie	13	5	91,905
5	Senfully Easy, 1999 m., by Mr. Easy Money	10	7	62,335
5	Skip the Promise, 2001 f., by Skip Trial	9	2	32,405
5	Starry Heaven, 1998 g., by Odyle	8	3	30,570
5	Stylish Mission, 1997 m., by Missionary Ridge (GB)	11	1	19,628
5	Suspicious, 2000 m., by Defrere	6	3	48,520
5	Tizagal, 1998 m., by Cee's Tizzy	8	3	52,890
5	Triple Jim, 1995 g., by Triple Sec	13	4	18,220
5	Zacharov, 1994 g., by Cool Victor	10	0	22,615

Horses Claimed Most Consecutive Times, 1991-2004

Horse, YOB, sex, sire	Cons. Claims	Initial Claim Price	Wins During Claim Period	Earnings During
I Wood Be a Winner, 1995 g., by Knight Skiing	9	$6,250	22	$280,329
Red Hot Secret, 2000 g., by Mr. Greeley	9	7,500	2	49,380
Adjustable Note, 1993 g., by Native Prospector	8	5,000	2	22,230
Blazing Wind, 1997 g., by Zero for Conduct	7	4,000	2	43,707
Dirty Harryette, 1999 m., by Unaccounted For	7	12,500	6	128,478
Magicleigh, 1999 m., by Magic Prospect	7	5,000	3	43,294
Mapeb, 1997 h., by Wallenda	7	3,500	8	72,960
Mr. Sundancer, 1995 g., by Allen's Prospect	7	17,500	12	124,593
Opus Won, 1997 h., by Fit to Fight	7	40,000	6	70,890
Personal Stash, 1998 g., by Air Forbes Won	7	7,500	4	63,407
Rally Mode, 1999 g., by Hasty Spirit	7	10,000	2	30,394
Silver Mystery, 1994 m., by Norquestor	7	16,000	8	126,247
Well Travelled, 1999 h., by Fortunate Prospect	7	25,000	7	89,130
Castlebright, 1998 m., by Bagdad Road	6	20,000	7	123,880
Catch If You Can, 1990 g., by Big Burn	6	8,000	11	57,238
Cien Seas, 1997 g., by Cien Fuegos	6	7,500	4	44,135
Crijinsky, 1989 g., by Sir Jinsky	6	8,000	7	53,330
Foyt Sparkler, 1988 g., by Foyt	6	12,500	6	59,342
Imablazinbeauty, 2000 m., by Semoran	6	10,000	9	94,570
Just Wyatt, 1995 g., by Claim	6	17,500	15	56,555
Lambourne, 1995 g., by Exbourne	6	12,500	3	46,294
Milky Bar (CHI), 1996 g., by The Great Shark	6	20,000	8	147,480
Millennium Song, 1998 h., by Maudlin	6	16,000	7	102,875

Horse, YOB, sex, sire	Cons. Claims	Initial Claim Price	Wins During Claim Period	Earnings During
Nasty Newt, 1989 g., by Nasty and Bold	6	$10,000	9	$53,691
Parlay Cory, 1995 g., by Parlay Me	6	5,500	4	28,161
Pell Mell, 1998 g., by Press Card	6	2,500	9	81,889
Remission, 1997 m., by Superbity	6	8,000	3	32,615
Rustic, 1999 m., by Schossberg	6	20,000	4	61,193
Sound System, 1993 g., by Waquoit	6	18,500	26	261,930
Sox On Top, 1995 g., by Black Moonshine	6	35,000	10	223,854
Stroker, 1999 g., by Forest Wildcat	6	5,000	4	47,794
Tender Hearted, 1995 m., by Bello	6	20,000	2	87,268
Tenfortynine, 1998 g., by Ide	6	4,000	6	96,269
U. R. My Hope, 1997 g., by Sir Leon	6	20,000	5	89,922
Where's Sally, 1996 m., by Mi Cielo	6	12,500	8	86,994

Claiming Crown

The Claiming Crown, started in 1999 by the Thoroughbred Owners and Breeders Association and the National Horsemen's Benevolent and Protective Association, is promoted as a championship event for the sport's hard-working claimers, and it certainly offers generous purses, a total of $550,000 spread over six races. The event has been described as the "granddaddy of all starter allowances," which are races limited to horses that have started for a specific claiming price or less within a specified period of time. To be eligible for the Claiming Crown races, the horse must have made at least one start at the stated claiming price or lower within the prior year. The claiming prices range from $5,000 or less for the $50,000 Claiming Crown Iron Horse to $25,000 or less for the $150,000 Claiming Crown Jewel. All races are for horses three years old and up, with weight allowances made to three-year-olds and females. A seventh race, the $100,000 Claiming Crown Tiara, was run in 1999 and 2000.

Owners must nominate their horses to the Claiming Crown program for $100 by April 15 or $500 by May 27, with a race specified by the latter date. Supplemental entries, at 5% of the purse, are permitted until July 1. Pre-entries are made 11 days before the races, and entries are taken three days in advance of the event. A maximum of 14 horses can start in each race; if more than 14 horses are entered for a race, winners of official preview races will be given preference to start, as will the two highest-ranked Canterbury Park-based horses in each category. The remainder of the field will be selected according to a points system based on finish position and quality of races. For instance, a winner of a graded stakes race will receive 12 points, and the third finisher in a claimer or starter race with a price below that of the Claiming Crown contest will receive one point. Pre-entry, entry, and starting fees range from $1,000 for the Iron Horse to $3,000 for the Jewel.

The Claiming Crown has been held each year at Canterbury Park near Minneapolis with the exception of 2002, when the races were held at Philadelphia Park. The 2005 Claiming Crown was scheduled for July 16 at Canterbury Park.

Claiming Crown Emerald S.

Canterbury Park, three-year-olds and up, starters for a claiming price of $20,000 or less, 1 1/16 miles, turf. Held July 17, 2004, with a gross value of $125,000. First held in 2000. Stakes record 1:41.66 (2000 P. D. Lucky).

Year	Winner	Jockey	Second	Third	Strs	Time	1st Purse
2004	Stage Player, 5, 124	T. A. Baze	Bristolville, 8	He Flies, 6	14	1:42.20	$68,750
2003	Image, 5, 122	J. A. Krone	W. W. Robin de Hood, 5	Mega Gift, 6	10	1:42.12	68,750
2002	Nowrass (GB), 6, 122	J. Valdivia Jr.	Grade One, 6	Taylorman (NZ), 7	9	1:46.66	68,750
2001	Al's Dearly Bred, 4, 120	S. Martinez	Metatonia, 6	Concielo, 5	11	1:42.22	68,750
2000	P. D. Lucky, 5, 124	R. Perez	Felite Patet, 6	G. R. Rabbit, 7	8	1:41.66	55,000

Sponsored by Daily Racing Form 2001. Held at Philadelphia Park 2002.

Claiming Crown Express S.

Canterbury Park, three-year-olds and up, starters for a claiming price of $7,500 or less, 6 furlongs, dirt. Held July 17, 2004, with a gross value of $47,000. First held in 1999. Stakes record 1:09.29 (2002 Talknow).

Year	Winner	Jockey	Second	Third	Strs	Time	1st Purse
2004	Chisholm, 7, 124	J. Campbell	Setthehook, 5	Devil's Con, 5	8	1:10.10	$27,500
2003	Landler, 4, 122	R. Fogelsonger	Pelican Peach, 5	Spooky Mulder, 5	10	1:09.65	27,500
2002	Talknow, 5, 124	E. Trujillo	Danny E, 4	Wise Sweep, 6	8	1:09.29	27,500
2001	The Maccabee, 5, 122	J. Flores	Lord of Time, 4	Hot Affair, 5	10	1:09.68	27,500
2000	Spit Polish, 8, 122	J. Flores	Modesto, 5	Citizen's Arrest, 5	10	1:10.74	27,500
1999	Pioneer Spirit, 5, 120	W. Martinez	Satchmo, 5	Exclusive Example, 5	10	1:10.45	33,000

Sponsored by Winticket.com 2001. Held at Philadelphia Park 2002.

Claiming Crown Glass Slipper S.

Canterbury Park, three-year-olds and up, fillies and mares, starters for a claiming price of $12,500 or less, 6 1/2 furlongs, dirt. Held July 17, 2004, with a gross value of $70,500. First held in 1999. Stakes record 1:16.68 (2001 French Teacher).

Year	Winner	Jockey	Second	Third	Strs	Time	1st Purse
2004	Banished Lover, 6, 124	T. Clifton	Moving Fever, 4	Flaming Night, 5	8	1:17.29	$41,250
2003	Mum's Gold, 4, 124	N. Santagata	Margarita's Garden, 4	Sentimentalromance, 7	9	1:16.82	41,500
2002	Won Moro, 5, 122	G. Melancon	Dandy Dulce, 4	Playmera, 5	9	1:17.01	41,500

Year	Winner	Jockey	Second	Third	Strs	Time	1st Purse
2001	French Teacher, 5, 120	M. Johnston	Beauty's Due, 4	Lost Judgement, 5	13	1:16.68	41,250
2000	A Lot of Mary, 5, 124	J. Flores	Pretty Lilly, 5	Cinderella Island, 7	10	1:16.75	33,000
1999	You're a Lady, 5, 124	W. Martinez	Castle Blaze, 6	Dazzling Danielle, 6	8	1:44.33	41,250

Held at Philadelphia Park 2002. 1¹/₁₆ miles 1999.

Claiming Crown Iron Horse S.

Canterbury Park, three-year-olds and up, starters for a claiming price of $5,000 or less, 1¹/₁₆ miles, dirt. Held July 17, 2004, with a gross value of $48,500. First held in 1999. Stakes record 1:43.45 (2000 Gingerboy).

Year	Winner	Jockey	Second	Third	Strs	Time	1st Purse
2004	Superman Can, 4, 122	S. Stevens	Rough Draft, 7	Gram's Folly, 6	11	1:44.26	$27,500
2003	Ghoastly Prize, 5, 120	B. Walker Jr.	Entrepreneurship, 6	Shut Out Time, 7	12	1:44.99	27,500
2002	Ruskin, 9, 120	J. Flores	Regal Tour, 4	Entrepreneurship, 5	7	1:45.37	27,500
2001	Secret Squall, 6, 122	L. Quinonez	Home a Winner, 7	Gothard, 4	13	1:45.75	27,500
2000	Gingerboy, 6, 122	M. Guidry	Irish Bacon, 7	Your Draw, 5	9	1:43.45	27,500
1999	A Point Well Made, 6, 120	D. Bell	Higher Desire, 7	Unruly Zeal, 7	9	1:45.65	27,500

Sponsored by Vetrap 2001. Held at Philadelphia Park 2002.

Claiming Crown Jewel S.

Canterbury Park, three-year-olds and up, starters for a claiming price of $25,000 or less, 1¹/₈ miles, dirt. Held July 17, 2004, with a gross value of $145,500. First held in 1999. Stakes record 1:49.17 (2003 Daunting).

Year	Winner	Jockey	Second	Third	Strs	Time	1st Purse
2004	Intelligent Male, 4, 120	E. M. Martin Jr.	Musique Toujours, 4	Rize, 8	11	1:49.62	$82,500
2003	Daunting, 5, 122	J. A. Krone	Freeze Alert, 6	Patton's Victory, 5	8	1:49.17	82,500
2002	Truly a Judge, 4, 122	J. Valdivia Jr.	Quiet Mike, 5	Prince Iroquois, 5	9	1:50.39	85,500
2001	Sing Because, 8, 124	J. Valdivia Jr.	Halo Kris, 4	Banner Salute, 4	8	1:50.74	82,500
2000	B Flat Major, 5, 126	R. Madrigal Jr.	Shot of Gold, 5	Snohomish Loot, 5	7	1:49.72	68,750
1999	One Brick Shy, 4, 120	E. M. Martin Jr.	Honest Venture, 6	Captain Ripperton, 4	14	1:50.79	82,500

Held at Philadelphia Park 2002.

Claiming Crown Rapid Transit S.

Canterbury Park, three-year-olds and up, starters for a claiming price of $16,000 or less, 6¹/₂ furlongs, dirt. Held July 17, 2004, with a gross value of $94,000. First held in 1999. Stakes record 1:15.47 (2003 Pioneer Boy).

Year	Winner	Jockey	Second	Third	Strs	Time	1st Purse
2004	Heroic Sight, 6, 124	T. Glasser	Quote Me Later, 4	Satan's Code, 6	8	1:15.56	$55,000
2003	Pioneer Boy, 5, 124	R. Wilson	Debonair Joe, 4	Bensalem, 6	10	1:15.47	55,000
2002	Risen Warrior, 6, 124	S. Elliott	Yavapai, 6	Largenadincharge, 6	9	1:16.10	55,000
2001	Sassy Hound, 4, 124	M. Johnston	Crowns Runner, 8	Exert, 4	13	1:16.18	55,000
2000	Teddy Boy, 6, 124	M. Guidry	Bion, 6	Taylor's Day, 6	9	1:16.90	41,250
1999	Aplomado, 6, 120	L. A. Pincay Jr.	Emperor Tigere, 5	Oto No Icy, 5	12	1:16.27	55,000

Held at Philadelphia Park 2002.

Claiming Crown Tiara S.

Canterbury Park, three-year-olds and up, fillies and mares, starters for a claiming price of $20,000 or less twice since July 31, 1999, 1¹/₁₆ miles, dirt. Held August 7, 1999, with a gross value of $96,000. First held in 1999. Stakes record 1:42.14 (2000 Look to the Day).

Year	Winner	Jockey	Second	Third	Strs	Time	1st Purse
2000	Look to the Day, 6, 118	P. Nolan	Vengeful Val, 7	Pine Baroness, 4	10	1:42.14	$55,000
1999	Taffy, 4, 120	T. T. Doocy	Partial Prift, 4	Frosty Peace, 4	14	1:17.37	68,750

Not held 2001-'04. 6¹/₂ furlongs 1999.

Some of the Best Claimers

Following are some of the most prominent horses who either were claimed prior to outstanding careers on the racetrack or at stud or started in claiming races but went unclaimed.

ASPIDISTRA—1954 b. m., Better Self—Tilly Rose, by Bull Brier. 14-2-2-2, $5,115. Bred by King Ranch, Aspidistra was purchased by William L. McKnight's Minnesota Mining & Manufacturing Co. employees as a 70th birthday gift in 1957. Aspidistra, named for a hardy house plant, then was in the midst of a nondescript racing career that did not improve after her purchase. For McKnight, she raced for a $6,500 claiming tag. Retired after one racing season at age three, she became the foundation of McKnight's Tartan Farms in Florida, producing 1968 Horse of the Year Dr. Fager and champion sprinter Ta Wee.

BOOM TOWNER—1988 b. g., Obligato—Perfect Profile, by Stop the Music. 82-29-16-14, $962,391. Boom Towner began his eight-year career in a $5,000 maiden claimer at Rockingham Park, winning by 10¾ lengths. He won the 1992 Toboggan Handicap (G3) and was claimed the following year for $50,000 by trainer Mike Hushion for Barry Schwartz. In Hushion's care, Boom Towner won the 1993 Boojum (G3) and Sport Page (G3) Handicaps, both at Aqueduct. He won the Toboggan again in 1994.

BROWN BESS—1982 dk. b. or br. m., *Petrone—Chickadee, by Windy Sands. 36-16-8-6, $1,300,920. Brown Bess's owner-breeder, Calbourne Farm, put her at risk only once, for $50,000 in a Bay Meadows Race Course claimer on September 28, 1986. It was her first start on grass, and she finished second by a nose. Brown Bess would thrive on the grass, winning the 1989 Yellow Ribbon Invitational Stakes (G1) and the Ramona

Handicap (G1) on her way to an Eclipse Award as champion turf female.

BUDROYALE—1993 b. g., Cee's Tizzy—Cee's Song, by Seattle Song. 52-17-12-2, $2,840,810. First-time starter Budroyale was taken for $32,000 by trainer Dan Hendricks from breeder/co-owner Cecilia Straub-Rubens on December 9, 1995, at Hollywood Park. Budroyale was subsequently claimed for $40,000 by trainer Nick Canani on August 17, 1997, and for $50,000 by trainer Ted West for Jeffrey Sengara on February 15, 1998. He won the 1998 San Bernardino Handicap (G2) and in '99 scored victories in the Goodwood Breeders' Cup Handicap (G2), the Mervyn LeRoy Handicap (G2), and the Longacres Mile Handicap (G3). He was second five times, including the Breeders' Cup Classic (G1). In 2000, Budroyale won the San Antonio Handicap (G2) the same year his full brother Tiznow won the first of his two Breeders' Cup Classics.

CHARISMATIC—1996 ch. h., Summer Squall—Bail Babe, by Drone. 17-5-2-4, $2,038,064. Charismatic won only one of his first 13 starts and only raced four more times in his career. Trained by D. Wayne Lukas and owned by Robert and Beverly Lewis, Charismatic was placed first in a $62,500 claimer at Santa Anita Park on February 11, 1999. After finishing second in the El Camino Real Derby (G3) at Bay Meadows Race Course, Charismatic was a soundly beaten fourth in the Santa Anita Derby (G1). He subsequently won the Coolmore Lexington Stakes (G2), the Kentucky Derby (G1), and the Preakness Stakes (G1) before finishing third in the Belmont Stakes (G1), in which he sustained two fractures of his right foreleg. He was voted 1999 champion three-year-old male and Horse of the Year.

CREME DE LA FETE—1976 dk. c. g., Creme Dela Creme—Bridge Day, by *Tudor Minstrel. 151-40-27-16, $460,350. After winning his career debut by a nose as a two-year-old at Keeneland Race Course in 1978, Creme de La Fete finished fifth of six in the Bashford Manor Stakes at Churchill Downs. Unlike many two-year-olds that fade from the racing scene, Creme de La Fete would make 149 more starts. His two best years were in 1981, when he won 12 of 26 starts and $123,180, and in '83, when he won nine of 30 starts and earned $127,240.

DEPUTED TESTAMONY—1980 b. h., Traffic Cop—Proof Requested, by Prove It. 20-11-3-0, $674,329. Owned by Francis Sears and trained by J. William Boniface, Deputed Testamony was not competitive in his first start, finishing sixth by 12¾ lengths in a $25,000 maiden claimer at Bowie Race Course on September 21, 1982. In his next start, the colt won a $22,500 maiden claimer at Keystone Race Track, and Boniface put him at risk once more, in a $40,000 open claimer at the Meadowlands. Deputed Testamony won by three lengths and was not claimed. The following year, he won the Preakness Stakes (G1) and Monmouth Park's Haskell Invitational Handicap (G1). He won his two 1984 starts, including a track-record effort in the City of Baltimore Handicap, before retiring to stud at Boniface's Bonita Farm, the place of his birth.

GAIL'S BRUSH—1991 b. m., Broad Brush—Parade of Roses, by Blues Parade. 39-11-5-4, $250,701. Claimed by John E. Salzman Jr. on November 25, 1995, for $25,000, Gail's Brush made only two starts for the Maryland trainer before she was picked up by owner-trainer Edwin T. Broome from a $40,000 claimer on grass at Gulfstream Park in early 1996. Gail's Brush, whose performance had improved dramatically when switched to grass, made only six starts for Broome, but they included consecutive victories in the 1996 Eatontown Handicap (G3),

Columbiana Handicap, Politely Stakes, and Rumson Stakes.

GOLDEN TENT—1989 dk. b. or br. g., Shelter Half—Jump for Gold, by Search for Gold. 114-21-27-17, $732,793. By the standards of racing in the new century, Golden Tent is made of iron. He started once at three and then made 113 starts through 2001. Golden Tent was claimed seven times, four within a little more than four months in 1999 at the age of ten. Trainer Mike Hushion claimed Golden Tent three times for Barry Schwartz, for whom the gelding finished second in the 1998 Bold Ruler Handicap (G3) and third in the Fall Highweight Handicap (G2) that year.

JEWEL PRINCESS—1992 b. m., Key to the Mint—Jewell Ridge, by Melyno (Ire). 29-13-4-7, $1,904,060. An Eclipse Award winner as outstanding older female after winning the 1996 Breeders' Cup Distaff (G1), Jewel Princess began her career with a third-place finish in a $20,000 maiden claimer at Calder Race Course on October 27, 1994. She won her next start in a $30,000 maiden claimer and never looked back. In the care of Wally Dollase, Jewel Princess won the 1996 Vanity Invitational Handicap (G1) in addition to the Distaff, and in '97 she won the Santa Maria (G1) and Santa Margarita Invitational (G1) Handicaps. At the 2000 Keeneland November breeding stock sale, she was sold for $4.9-million to Coolmore Stud principal owner John Magnier.

JOHN HENRY—1975 b. g., Old Bob Bowers—Once Double, by Double Jay. 83-39-15-9, $6,591,860. John Henry raced five times in claiming races in 1978 but was not claimed. Purchased privately for $27,500 by Sam Rubin in 1978, he made his final claiming start for Sam and Dorothy Rubin's Dotsam Stable at $35,000 on June 28, 1978, at Belmont Park and won by 14 lengths. Trained by Robert Donato, Victor "Lefty" Nickerson, and Ron McAnally, he was Horse of the Year in 1981 and '84 as well as a four-time champion turf male and once champion older male. He retired as the richest North American Thoroughbred of all time.

KING COMMANDER—1949 dk. b. or br. g., Brown King—Guinea Egg, by *Cohort. 67-17-15-6, $100,295. King Commander made 27 of his first 31 starts in claimers although he was claimed only once, for $5,000 at Aqueduct in 1952. Converted to steeplechase after winning three of 32 starts on the flat, King Commander won 14 of 35 starts over fences and was voted champion steeplechase horse in 1954.

KING'S SWAN—1980 b. h., King's Bishop—Royal Cygnet, by *Sea-Bird. 107-31-19-18, $1,924,845. King's Swan already had won 11 of 44 starts and $212,350 when he was claimed in 1985 for $80,000 by trainer Richard Dutrow. The following year, King's Swan won eight of 15 starts, including the Vosburgh Stakes (G1) and Boojum Handicap (G3), and earned $451,207. At seven, he won three Grade 3 stakes in 12 starts and earned $477,218. He was even better at eight, winning five graded stakes, including the Bold Ruler (G2) and Tom Fool (G2) Stakes in 14 starts and banking $539,681.

KOBUK KING—1966 dk. b. or br. h., One-Eyed King—Winby, by Crafty Admiral. 68-12-10-11, $173,921. After showing considerable promise as a two-year-old in 1968, winning three of 13 starts and finishing second in the El Camino Stakes at Bay Meadows Race Course, Kobuk King went zero-for-three as a three-year-old and zero-for-19 at four. Claimed for $15,000 in 1971, Kobuk King found himself and scored consecutive victories in the Cabrillo Handicap at Del Mar, the

Tanforan Handicap at Bay Meadows, and Santa Anita Park's Carleton F. Burke Invitational Handicap for co-owners Allegre Stable and Ron McAnally, who trained the horse.

LADY MARYLAND—1934 gr. m., Sir Greysteel—Palestra, by *Prince Palatine. 82-18-14-14, $31,067. The 1939 champion handicap mare, Lady Maryland made 19 of her 82 starts in claimers and was taken for $2,500 in her 28th career start by B. B. Archer. Her final start in a claimer was as a four-year-old for $4,500 at Havre de Grace. She was not claimed and quickly improved in her five-year-old season, winning the Carroll and Ritchie Handicaps at Pimlico Race Course.

LAKEVILLE MISS—1975 dk. b. or br. m., Rainy Lake—Hew, by Blue Prince. 14-7-4-1, $371,582. While Affirmed and Alydar slugged it out for two-year-old male honors in 1977, the juvenile filly championship was taken by the strapping Lakeville Miss, who possessed a blue-collar pedigree and started her career as a $25,000 maiden claimer for owner-breeder Randolph Weinsier. She won a 5½-furlong claiming race at Belmont Park by four lengths on June 30 and never started again for a claiming tag. Trained by Jose Martin, Lakeville Miss won the Matron (G1) and Frizette (G1) Stakes at Belmont and the Selima Stakes (G1) at Laurel Race Course. She concluded her career with a four-length win in the 1978 Coaching Club American Oaks (G1).

LEAVE IT TO BEEZER—1993 b. g., Henbane—Blue Shocker, by Copelan. 75-22-11-13, $587,086. Although he had lost ten straight races, six-year-old Leave It to Beezer was claimed for $32,000 by trainer Scott Lake for Leo Gaspari Racing Stable on December 22, 1999. His third-place finish that day extended his losing streak to 11. Lake backed off on the gelding's training regimen, and Leave It to Beezer responded by winning nine of 15 starts, including the Salvator Mile Handicap (G3) at Monmouth Park and the Baltimore Breeders' Cup Handicap (G3) at Pimlico on the way to earning $350,830 in 2000.

McKAYMACKENNA—1989 b. m., Ends Well—Amuse, by Secretariat. 38-15-6-2, $581,322. R Kay Stable claimed McKaymackenna for $35,000 from a Belmont Park race in which she was beaten by more than 35 lengths. Sloppy tracks like the one she encountered at Belmont on May 16, 1992, were not to her liking; turf racing was her game. After trainer Gary Sciacca claimed her, she won seven grass stakes, including the 1993 Beaugay Handicap (G3) and Noble Damsel Stakes (G3).

PARKA—1958 br. g., *Arctic Prince—Manchon, by *Blenheim II. 93-27-14-18, $446,236. Bred by Marion duPont Scott and unraced at two, Parka was claimed for $10,000 in his 11th career start by Warren A. "Jimmy" Croll Jr. for client Rachel Carpenter. Parka won that Atlantic City Race Course race by a head, and Croll entered him in a $13,000 claimer 15 days later. He won that race by eight lengths and never raced in a claimer again. He was 1965 champion grass horse off victories in the Bougainvillea Handicap at Hialeah Park, the Kelly-Olympic and United Nations Handicaps at Atlantic City, and Aqueduct's Long Island Handicap in his final career start.

PEAT MOSS—1975 b. g., *Herbager—Moss, by Round Table. 55-15-7-9, $635,517. A little more than one year after winning a $10,000 claimer, Claiborne Farm-bred Peat Moss came within a head of upsetting John Henry in the 1981 Jockey Club Gold Cup (G1). Owned and trained by Murray Garren, Peat Moss loved to go a distance, winning the 1980 Display Handicap (G3) at 2¼ miles and the 1980 and '81 Kelso Handicap at two miles.

PORT CONWAY LANE—1969 gr. h., Bold Commander—*Grey Taffety, by Grey Sovereign. 242-52-39-36, $431,593. Port Conway Lane spent most of his lengthy career in claimers, although he started his career in allowance and stakes races, including a second-place finish in the 1971 Marlboro Nursery Stakes. He won Pimlico Race Course's City of Baltimore Handicap twice, in 1974 and '75, as well as Bowie Race Course's '74 Bowie Handicap and '75 Terrapin Handicap. By the end of 1976, however, he was racing principally in claimers and continued to do so through '83.

***PRINCEQUILLO**—1940 b. h., by Prince Rose—*Cosquilla, by *Papyrus. 33-12-5-7, $96,550. Exported from England in 1941, *Princequillo was offered for a $2,500 claiming price by owner Anthony Pelleteri on August 20, 1942. Taking him for Boone Hall Stable was Horatio Luro, who would develop *Princequillo into a multiple stakes winner during World War II. At Claiborne Farm, he proved to be an outstanding stallion, leading the general sire list in 1957 and '58 and topping the broodmare sire list eight times in North America and once in England.

SEABISCUIT—1933 b. h., Hard Tack—Swing On, by Whisk Broom II. 89-33-15-13, $437,730. Long before he became a top handicap horse, Seabiscuit lost the first 17 races of his career, including three defeats in $2,500 claimers and a loss in a $4,000 claimer at Havre de Grace in April 1935. Nobody took him, and later Wheatley Stable sold him to Charles Howard. Under the care of Racing Hall of Fame trainer Tom Smith, Seabiscuit went on to spectacular success, including a seven-stakes win streak in 1937, when he was champion handicap horse. The following year, he was voted Horse of the Year and handicap champion.

STYMIE—1941 ch. h., Equestrian—Stop Watch, by On Watch. 131-35-33-28, $918,485. Taken in his third lifetime start for $1,500 by Hirsch Jacobs, Stymie became the richest Thoroughbred of all time by his retirement in 1949, a record that only lasted until Citation moved past him in 1950. In his prime from ages four through seven, he won 28 of 69 starts, including the Saratoga Cup Stakes and the Gallant Fox, Metropolitan, Grey Lag, Aqueduct, and Sussex Handicaps twice each.

TIMELY WRITER—1979 b., c., Staff Writer—Timely Roman, by Sette Bello. 15-9-1-2, $605,491. A $13,000 yearling purchase owned by Peter and Francis Martin and trained by Dominic Imprescia, Timely Writer made his debut with an eighth-length victory in a $30,000 maiden claimer at Monmouth Park. He subsequently won Saratoga Race Course's Hopeful Stakes (G1) and the Champagne Stakes (G1) at Belmont Park, earning him co-highweight with Eclipse Award champion Deputy Minister on the 1981 Experimental Free Handicap. At three, he won the Flamingo Stakes (G1) and Florida Derby (G1), but surgery for an intestinal blockage knocked him out of the Triple Crown races. He returned in the fall but sustained a fatal breakdown in the Jockey Club Gold Cup (G1).

VIDEOGENIC—1982 b. m., Caucasus—Video Babe, by T.V. Commercial. 73-20-9-10, $1,154,360. Trainer Gasper Moschera convinced owner Albert Davis to claim Videogenic for $100,000 on May 24, 1985. She was not much to look at, but she could run, winning 11 stakes races after the claim, including the 1985 Ladies Handicap (G1) at Aqueduct and the 1986 Santa Ana Handicap (G1) at Santa Anita Park. She won more than $1-million for Davis on the racetrack and was sold as a broodmare prospect for $625,000 at the 1988 Keeneland November breeding stock sale.

RACETRACKS
Racetracks of North America
Arizona

Apache County Fair

Location: 825 W 4th St. N, Saint Johns, Az. 85936-0357
Phone: (928) 337-4364
Fax: (520) 337-2783
Abbreviation: SJ

Racing Dates
2004: September 11-September 19, 4 days
2005: September 17-September 25, 4 days

Fastest Times of 2004 (Dirt)
4 furlongs: Pass Them Quick, :44.60, September 19, 2004
5 1/2 furlongs: Go Get Em Harry, 1:06.40, September 19, 2004
6 furlongs: Fastfoot Freddie, 1:13.00, September 19, 2004
6 1/2 furlongs: My Jewel, 1:20.80, September 18, 2004
7 furlongs: Napa Spring, 1:25.60, September 18, 2004

Cochise County Fair

Location: 3677 N Leslie Canyon Rd., Douglas, Az. 85607-6304
Phone: (520) 364-3819
Fax: (520) 364-1175
E-Mail: cochisefair@theriver.com
Year Founded: 1924
Abbreviation: DG

Officers
President: Nick Forsythe
General Manager: Karen Strongin
Vice President: Bill Thomas Sr.
Stewards: Robert Clink, Violet Smith

Racing Dates
2004: April 10-April 18, 4 days
2005: April 9-April 17, 4 days

Attendance
Average Daily Recent Meeting: 2,625, 2004
Total Attendance Recent Meeting: 10,500, 2004

Handle
Average All Sources Recent Meeting: $28,836, 2004
Total All Sources Recent Meeting: $115,344, 2004

Fastest Times of 2004 (Dirt)
a3 furlongs: Maria Ferrante, :38.00, April 11, 2004
5 1/2 furlongs: High Riser, 1:05.00, April 18, 2004
6 furlongs: Crystal Sound, 1:11.20, April 17, 2004
7 furlongs: Luxury Leader, 1:25.20, April 18, 2004
1 mile: Oil Man, 1:40.20, April 18, 2004

Coconino County Fair

Location: HC 39 Box 3A, Flagstaff, Az. 86001
Phone: (928) 774-5139
Fax: (928) 774-2572
Website: co.coconino.az.us/parks
E-Mail: parks2@co.coconino.az
Year Founded: 1954
Abbreviation: Flg
Acreage: 400
Number of Stalls: 320
Seating Capacity: 3,500

Ownership
Coconino County Parks and Recreation

Officers
General Manager: Linda Kellogg
Racing Secretary: JIm Davis
Director of Operations: Linda Kellogg
Director of Finance: Kelly Burkhart
Director of Marketing: Jennifer Hartin
Director of Mutuels: Jerry Doolittle
Stewards: Robert Clink, Rita Fresquez, Violet Smith
Track Announcer: Craig Willis
Track Photographer: Double B Photography
Track Superintendent: Dave Stewart

Racing Dates
2004: July 2-July 5, 4 days
2005: July 1-July 4, 4 days

Track Layout
Main Circumference: 5/8 Mile
Main Width: 75 Feet

Attendance
Average Daily Recent Meeting: 2,750
Highest Single Day Record: 2,600
Highest Single Meet Record: 12,000
Total Attendance Recent Meeting: 11,000, 4 days
Lowest Single Day Record: 800
Total All Sources Recent Meeting: $1,682,199
Total On-Track Recent Meeting: $316,486

Fastest Times of 2004 (Dirt)
a3 furlongs: Brite Nite, :39.60, July 3, 2004
5 1/2 furlongs: Marina Mon, 1:09.00, July 4, 2004; Mr. Plum, 1:09.00, July 4, 2004
6 furlongs: A J Dustdevil, 1:14.80, July 2, 2004
6 1/2 furlongs: Alkatraz Island, 1:22.80, July 4, 2004
7 furlongs: Notate, 1:26.80, July 4, 2004
1 mile: Summer Prince, 1:43.60, July 4, 2004

Gila County Fair

Location: P.O. Box 2193, Globe, Az. 85502-2193
Phone: (928) 473-3521
Fax: (520) 473-4122
Abbreviation: GCF

Racing Dates
2004: September 25-October 3, 4 days
2005: October 1-October 9, 4 days

Fastest Times of 2004 (Dirt)
3 furlongs: Go Lively, :35.00, October 10, 2004
5 furlongs: Last Caper, 1:01.20, October 9, 2004
5 1/2 furlongs: Hermosilla, 1:08.00, October 2, 2004
6 furlongs: Napa Spring, 1:15.40, October 9, 2004; Occupied, 1:15.40, October 2, 2004
7 furlongs: Our Mud Pie, 1:33.60, October 10, 2004
1 1/16 miles: Dyna King, 1:55.60, October 10, 2004

Graham County Fair

Location: 527 E Armory Rd., Safford, Az. 85546-2231
Phone: (928) 428-7180
Fax: (928) 348-0023
E-Mail: cfaunce@graham.az.gov
Year Founded: 1965
Dates of Inaugural Meeting: 1965
Abbreviation: Saf
Acreage: 220

Officers

President: Phil Curtis
General Manager: Casey Faunce
Director of Racing: Casey Faunce
Racing Secretary: Tom Figueroa
Secretary: Jessie Hines
Director of Operations: Larry Jensen
Director of Mutuels: Jerome Doolittle
Vice President: Jon Haralson
Horsemen's Liaison: Robert Pledge
Stewards: Robert Clink, Roy Snedigar, Violet Smith
Track Announcer: Red Davis
Track Photographer: Double D
Track Superintendent: Jim Gutierrez

Racing Dates

2004: March 27-April 4, 4 days
2005: April 2-April 10, 4 days

Attendance

Average Daily Recent Meeting: 650, 2004
Total Attendance Recent Meeting: 2,600, 2004

Handle

Average All Sources Recent Meeting: $17,248, 2004
Total All Sources Recent Meeting: $68,991, 2004

Track Records, Main Dirt

4 furlongs: In The Military, :44 2/5
5 1/2 furlongs: Dusty Orchid, 1:05 2/5
6 furlongs: Bendabout's Trump, 1:11 1/5
7 furlongs: Hum Dewey Slew, 1:26 3/5
1 1/16 miles: Cop Out, 1:46 3/5, March 31, 2001

Fastest Times of 2004 (Dirt)

4 furlongs: Midnight Rider, :46.60, March 28, 2004
5 1/2 furlongs: Occupied, 1:08.40, March 28, 2004
6 furlongs: Pero Dinero, 1:14.80, March 27, 2004
7 furlongs: Summer Prince, 1:27.00, March 28, 2004
1 mile: Chehalis, 1:46.00, April 4, 2004

Greenelee County Fair

Location: P.O. Box 123, Duncan, Az. 85534-0123
Phone: (928) 359-2032
Fax: (928) 359-2721
Abbreviation: Dun

Officers

Racing Secretary: Tom Figueroa
Director of Mutuels: Jerry Doolittle
Director of Publicity: Douglas Barlow
Stewards: Roy Snedigar, Violet Smith
Track Announcer: Tom Figueroa

Racing Dates

2004: March 13-March 21, 4 days
2005: March 12-March 20, 4 days

Attendance

Average Daily Recent Meeting: 509, 2004
Total Attendance Recent Meeting: 2,035, 2004

Handle

Average All Sources Recent Meeting: $22,147, 2004
Total All Sources Recent Meeting: $88,589, 2004

Track Records, Main Dirt

5 furlongs: Ack Like A Dancer, 1:00, March 26, 2000
5 1/2 furlongs: Fire In The Hole, 1:05 1/5
6 furlongs: Please Explain, 1:11 1/5, March 25, 2000
7 furlongs: Saros Irish Luck, 1:24 1/5
1 1/16 miles: Sunburst, 1:47 4/5

Fastest Times of 2004 (Dirt)

5 furlongs: High Riser, 1:00.40, March 20, 2004
5 1/2 furlongs: Two Timing Paul, 1:06.00, March 21, 2004
a6 furlongs: Ice Out There, 1:10.80, March 13, 2004
7 furlongs: Chehalis, 1:27.20, March 21, 2004; Ice Out There, 1:27.20, March 21, 2004

Mohave County Fair

Location: 2600 Fairgrounds Blvd., Kingman, Az. 86401-4169
Phone: (928) 753-2636
Fax: (928) 753-8383
Abbreviation: MoF

Officers

Chairman: Mike Burton

Attendance

Average Daily Recent Meeting: 950, 2004
Total Attendance Recent Meeting: 3,801, 2004

Handle

Average All Sources Recent Meeting: $28,349, 2004
Total All Sources Recent Meeting: $113,394, 2004

Fastest Times of 2004 (Dirt)

4 furlongs: Fly With Hope, :44.40, May 15, 2004
5 1/2 furlongs: Fastfoot Freddie, 1:06.20, May 16, 2004
6 furlongs: Tooties Teddy, 1:13.60, May 9, 2004
7 furlongs: Alltime Blues, 1:28.00, May 15, 2004
1 1/16 miles: Oil Man, 1:45.20, May 16, 2004

Rillito Park

Location: 4502 N. 1st Ave., Tucson, Az. 85718
Phone: (520) 293-5011
Fax: (520) 293-1187
Year Founded: 1943
Dates of Inaugural Meeting: November 1, 1953
Abbreviation: Ril
Number of Stalls: 500
Seating Capacity: 2,500

Ownership

Pima County

Officers

General Manager: Patricia White
Director of Racing: Patricia White
Racing Secretary: Josephine Stavers
Secretary: Patricia White
Treasurer: Patricia White
Director of Finance: Patricia White
Director of Marketing: Jim Collins
Director of Mutuels: Patrick Kelly
Vice President: Timothy Kelly
Director of Publicity: Jim Collins
Horsemen's Liaison: Doreen Rawls
Stewards: James Dreyer
Track Announcer: Craig Willis
Track Photographer: Coady Photography
Track Superintendent: Bo Pafford
Horsemen's Bookkeeper: Doreen J. Rawls
Security: Lisa Pina

Racing Dates

2004: January 17-February 29, 14 days
2005: January 22-March 6, 14 days

Track Layout

Main Circumference: 5 furlongs
Main Track Chute: 4 furlongs and 6 1/2 furlongs
Main Width: 80 feet
Main Length of Stretch: 660 feet

Attendance

Average Daily Recent Meeting: 2,887, 2004
Highest Single Day Record: 4,526, January 17, 2004
Total Attendance Recent Meeting: 40,411, 2004
Lowest Single Day Record: 1,782, February 8, 2003

Handle
Average All Sources Recent Meeting: $96,495, 2004
Average On-Track Recent Meeting: $81,568, 2004
Total All Sources Recent Meeting: $1,350,928, 2004
Total On-Track Recent Meeting: $1,141,951, 2004
Highest Single Day On-Track Record Recent Meet: $118,159, February 29, 2004
Highest Single Day Record Recent Meet: $136,895, February 29, 2004

Leaders
Recent Meeting, Leading Jockey: Fernando Manuel Gamez, 12, 2004; James Daniel Schwartz, 12, 2004
Recent Meeting, Leading Trainer: Bill K. Earle, 6, 2004

Track Records, Main Dirt
4 furlongs: Blushing God, :44.40, February 3, 2001
5 1/2 furlongs: Corrino Bay, 1:04.60, February 4, 2001
6 furlongs: Turf's Bounty, 1:10 1/5, November 25, 1989
6 1/2 furlongs: Club Champ, 1:15.80, February 18, 1996
7 furlongs: Stalk the Table, 1:22.60, January 29, 1994
Other: 3 furlongs, Alice Be Gay, :36, March 2, 1974; 3 1/2 furlongs, Slow Dancing, :40 3/5, March 22, 1981; a6 furlongs, Loomis Trail, 1:20, February 15, 2000

Principal Races
Dr. Dale Shirley S., Budweiser Mile S.

Notable Events
Rillito Park Weiner Cup

Fastest Times of 2004 (Dirt)
4 furlongs: Go Mike, :44.60, January 17, 2004
5 1/2 furlongs: Gold Fevers Gift, 1:04.80, January 31, 2004
6 furlongs: Boyisdue, 1:10.80, February 21, 2004; Bridled Gold, 1:10.80, January 18, 2004
6 1/2 furlongs: Gold Fevers Gift, 1:17.00, February 22, 2004
7 furlongs: Grand Canyon, 1:24.20, February 15, 2004; Ice Out There, 1:24.20, February 1, 2004
1 1/16 miles: Realignment, 1:45.80, January 31, 2004

Santa Cruz County Fair

Location: P.O. Box 85, Sonoita, Az. 85637-0085
Phone: (520) 455-5553
Fax: (520) 455-5330
Website: www.sonoitafairgrounds.com
E-Mail: sccfra@theriver.com
Abbreviation: Son
Acreage: 36.5
Number of Stalls: 180
Seating Capacity: 2,200

Officers
Chairman: Burton S. Kruglick
President: Bob Morrison
General Manager: Maralyn Parker
Director of Racing: Scott McDaniel
Racing Secretary: Jim Davis
Secretary: Bob Bambauer
Treasurer: Foster Drummond
Director of Mutuels: Jerry Doolittle
Vice President: Dean Fish
Director of Publicity: Scott McDaniel
Stewards: Robert Clink, Floyd Campbell, Rita Fresquez
Track Announcer: Jim Davis
Track Photographer: Double B Photo
Track Superintendent: Harold Hager

Racing Dates
2004: April 24-May 2, 4 days
2005: April 30-May 8, 4 days

Track Layout
Main Circumference: 4 furlongs

Attendance
Average Daily Recent Meeting: 3,824, 2004
Total Attendance Recent Meeting: 15,295, 2004

Handle
Average All Sources Recent Meeting: $46,936, 2004
Total All Sources Recent Meeting: $187,743, 2004

Principal Races
Lewis Memorial, Sonoita Derby, Figueroa Memorial, Kelly Memorial, Desert Classic

Fastest Times of 2004 (Dirt)
5 furlongs: Gold Fevers Gift, :59.60, May 2, 2004
5 1/2 furlongs: Saxmeamemo, 1:05.00, May 2, 2004
6 furlongs: Areallyniceguy, 1:10.40, April 25, 2004
7 furlongs: Fastfoot Freddie, 1:28.40, May 1, 2004
1m 70 yds: Dyna King, 1:47.40, April 24, 2004

Turf Paradise

A Phoenix tradition for nearly a half-century, Turf Paradise has survived several ownership changes and the dramatic reshaping of Thoroughbred racing to remain a vital part of the winter racing scene. Turf Paradise was the vision of businessman Walter Cluer, who purchased 1,400 acres of desert land in 1954 and transformed it into a racetrack, which opened its doors on January 7, 1956. Cluer owned the track until 1980. The track's next two owners, Herb Owens and Robert Walker, added a turf course and off-track betting, respectively. Hollywood Park purchased the track in 1994 and weathered an influx of Native American casino gambling in Arizona before selling the track to Phoenix developer Jerry Simms in June 2000. In November 2002, Arizona voters rejected slot machines at the state's racetracks and approved more machines at Native American casinos.

Location: 1501 W Bell Rd., Phoenix, Az. 85023-3411
Phone: (602) 942-1101
Fax: (602) 942-8659
Website: www.turfparadise.com
E-Mail: contact@turfparadise.net
Year Founded: 1955
Dates of Inaugural Meeting: January 7, 1956
Abbreviation: TuP
Acreage: 1,400
Number of Stalls: 1,700
Seating Capacity: 7,284

Officers
President: Randy Fozzard
General Manager: Randy Fozzard
Director of Racing: Shawn Swartz
Racing Secretary: Shawn Swartz
Director of Operations: Brian Whitman
Director of Communications: Vincent Francia
Director of Marketing: Vincent Francia
Director of Mutuels: Jack Mullen
Vice President: Dave Johnson
Director of Publicity: Vincent Francia
Director of Simulcasting: Jack Mullen
Horsemen's Liaison: Debbie Zimmerman
Stewards: Jerry Nicodemus
Track Announcer: Luke Kruytbosch
Track Photographer: Coady Photography
Track Superintendent: Terry Brown

Racing Dates
2004: September 26, 2003-May 16, 2004, 170 days
2005: October 1, 2004-May 22, 2005, 165 days

Track Layout
Main Circumference: 1 mile
Main Track Chute: 3 furlongs
Main Track Chute: 6 1/2 furlongs
Main Width: 80 feet
Main Turf Circumference: 7 furlongs

Main Turf Chute: 1/8 mile
Main Turf Width: 73 feet
Main Turf Length of Stretch: 999 feet

Attendance
Highest Single Day Record: 16,000 est., March 18, 1984

Mutuel Records
Highest Win: $287.60, Gaye Rest, May 23, 1974
Lowest Win: $170.20, Garfield Red, December 12, 1980
Highest Exacta: $17,092.20, May 8, 1988
Highest Trifecta: $42,774, October 18, 1987
Highest Daily Double: $5,355, April 24, 1985
Highest Pick 6: $137,372, March 3, 1986

Leaders
Career, Leading Jockey by Titles: Sam Powell, 16
Career, Leading Owner by Titles: Dennis Weir, 10
Career, Leading Trainer by Titles: Richard Hazelton, 27

Records
Single Day Jockey Wins: Marty Wentz, Ray York, 7
Single Meet, Leading Jockey by Wins: Pat Steinberg, 225
Single Meet, Leading Trainer by Wins: Bart Hone, 88

Track Records, Main Dirt
4 furlongs: Beau Madison, :45.00, March 30, 1957
4 1/2 furlongs: Kathryn's Doll, :50 2/5, April 9, 1967
5 furlongs: Zip Pocket, :55 2/5, April 22, 1967
5 1/2 furlongs: Plenty Zloty, 1:01.10, April 18, 1995
6 furlongs: G Malleah, 1:06.60, April 8, 1995
6 1/2 furlongs: Lost in the Fog, 1:13.55, December 26, 2004
7 furlongs: Free Duty, 1:26 1/5, January 23, 1985
1 mile: Mr. Pappion, 1:33.20, January 30, 1993
1 1/16 miles: Down the Isle, 1:39 1/5, February 11, 1987
1 1/8 miles: Our Forbes, 1:47.60, November 29, 1996
1 3/16 miles: Erin Glen, 1:55.3, January 15, 1967
1 1/4 miles: Truly a Pleasure, 2:01.40, March 26, 1995
1 3/8 miles: Bloom n Character, 2:15 2/5, April 12, 1980
1 1/2 miles: Spinney, 2:29.2, April 30, 1961
1 5/8 miles: Masked Rider, 2:44.40, February 10, 2002; Swelter, 2:44.40, February 29, 2004
1 3/4 miles: Arsenal, 2:55 2/5, February 7, 1971
2 miles: Vermejo, 3:24, April 20, 1969
Other: 2 furlongs, Wandering Boy, :21 1/5, December 5, 1965; 3 furlongs, Never Shamed, :31.60, April 1, 1996

Track Records, Main Turf
4 1/2 furlongs: Dan's Groovy, :50.34, December 17, 2004; Dysfunctional Lady, :50.34, December 26, 2004
5 furlongs: Honor the Hero, :56.20, February 5, 1995
7 furlongs: Lord Pleasant, 1:22.80, October 12, 1992
7 1/2 furlongs: Black Bart, 1:27.54, November 6, 2004
1 mile: Prose (Ire), 1:34.83, March 27, 2001
1 1/16 miles: Caesour, 1:40.40, February 5, 1995
1 1/8 miles: Narghile, 1:48, February 1, 1987
1 3/8 miles: Turk Flyer, 2:16.11, April 14, 2001
1 1/2 miles: Senator McGuire, 2:29 3/5, May 22, 1988
Other: 1 7/8 miles, Shadows Fall, 3:09 2/5, May 17, 1987

Principal Races
Phoenix Gold Cup, Turf Paradise Derby, Turf Paradise Breeders' Cup

Fastest Times of 2004 (Dirt)
2 furlongs: Cover Now, :21.50, March 30, 2004
4 1/2 furlongs: Muley Tune, :52.06, May 2, 2004
5 furlongs: Rojo Rogue, :56.26, October 10, 2004
5 1/2 furlongs: Expert, 1:01.36, April 13, 2004
6 furlongs: Taiaslew, 1:07.42, February 21, 2004
6 1/2 furlongs: Lost in the Fog, 1:13.55, December 26, 2004
1 mile: Black Bart, 1:33.68, March 1, 2004
1 1/16 miles: Mambo Train, 1:42.07, February 7, 2004
1 1/8 miles: Nabatean, 1:50.81, December 3, 2004
1 1/4 miles: Stormie Britches, 2:03.49, February 10, 2004
1 5/8 miles: Swelter, 2:44.40, February 29, 2004

Fastest Times of 2004 (Turf)
4 1/2 furlongs: Dan's Groovy, :50.34, December 17, 2004; Dysfunctional Lady, :50.34, December 26, 2004

7 1/2 furlongs: Black Bart, 1:27.54, November 6, 2004
1 mile: Magnificent Val, 1:35.05, May 1, 2004
1 1/16 miles: Irish Warrior, 1:40.89, February 7, 2004
1 1/8 miles: Bristolville, 1:48.57, March 29, 2004
1 3/8 miles: Bristolville, 2:16.12, April 25, 2004
1 7/8 miles: Fade to Blue, 3:11.97, May 16, 2004

Yavapai Downs

The story of Yavapai Downs actually involves two tracks. Located in Arizona's Prescott Valley region, Yavapai opened its doors in 2001, replacing Prescott Downs, a half-mile oval that had been in operation since 1913. While Prescott was known for its rustic atmosphere and occasionally wild bullring racing, Yavapai quickly established a reputation as a more refined track, with modern amenities and a one-mile oval. The $23-million facility was completed in 13 months, almost one year ahead of schedule, allowing it to open in May 2001. The physical plant features a three-story clubhouse and grandstand with Arizona's Mingus Mountains as a backdrop. The backstretch offers stabling for 1,200 horses. During its first four meets, average purses exceeded $30,000 per day. Prescott, Arizona's summer racing home for the better part of nine decades, was the site of Racing Hall of Fame jockey Pat Day's first victory.

Location: P.O. Box 26557, Prescott Valley, Az. 86312-6557
Phone: (928) 775-8000
Fax: (928) 445-0408
Website: www.yavapaidownsatpv.com
E-Mail: jim@yavapaidownsatpv.com
Year Founded: 2001
Dates of Inaugural Meeting: May-September, 2001
Abbreviation: Yav
Acreage: 200
Number of Stalls: 1,500
Seating Capacity: 5,000

Ownership
Yavapai County Fair Association

Officers
President: Bob Gray
General Manager: James Grundy
Director of Racing: Don Rogers
Racing Secretary: John Everly
Secretary: James Pickering
Treasurer: Jim Pickering
Director of Operations: Gary Spiker
Director of Admissions: Janet Howard
Director of Finance: Sharon Fischer
Director of Marketing: James Grundy
Director of Mutuels: Bob Chisholm
Vice President: Jean Knight
Director of Publicity: Sharon Fischer
Director of Sales: James Grundy
Director of Simulcasting: Don Rogers
Stewards: Floyd Campbell, Rita Fresquez, Violet Smith
Track Announcer: Greg Wry
Track Photographer: Coady Photography
Track Superintendent: Bubba French

Racing Dates
2004: May 29-September 7, 60 days
2005: May 28-September 6, 60 days

Track Layout
Main Circumference: 1 mile
Main Track Chute: 1/4 mile
Main Track Chute: 6 furlongs
Main Width: 75 feet
Main Length of Stretch: 1,280 feet

Handle
Single Day All Sources Handle: $1,280,000, June 7, 2003

Leaders
Recent Meeting, Leading Horse: Royal Groove, 5, 2004
Recent Meeting, Leading Jockey: Wilson Omar Diequez, 46, 2004
Recent Meeting, Leading Trainer: Bill Brashears, 39, 2004

Track Records, Main Dirt
4 1/2 furlongs: Red Spark, :50.20, September 7, 2004
5 furlongs: Canyon's Wildcat, :56.40, August 9, 2004
5 1/2 furlongs: Hemandan, 1:02.36, August 13, 2002
6 furlongs: Miss Pixie, 1:08.12, August 24, 2002
1 mile: Heightenedinterest, 1:35.01, June 3, 2002
1 1/16 miles: Gusto Forzado, 1:42.63, June 24, 2002
1 1/8 miles: Moonray, 1:49.40, June 25, 2002
1 1/4 miles: Cajun Bound, 2:03.20, August 18, 2003

Principal Races
Yavapai Downs TB Futurity, Yavapai H., Mile Hi H., Yavapai Classic

Interesting Facts
Previous Names and Dates: Prescott Downs

Fastest Times of 2004 (Dirt)
4 1/2 furlongs: Red Spark, :50.20, September 7, 2004
a4 1/2 furlongs: Half Penny, :49.60, July 25, 2004
5 furlongs: Canyon's Wildcat, :56.40, August 9, 2004
5 1/2 furlongs: Along Came George, 1:02.80, June 8, 2004; Madigan, 1:02.80, July 11, 2004
6 furlongs: Madigan, 1:08.80, August 2, 2004; Red Spark, 1:08.80, June 27, 2004; Seveneightone East, 1:08.80, August 22, 2004
1 mile: Sideways, 1:36.80, July 24, 2004
1 1/16 miles: Royal Groove, 1:43.80, August 16, 2004
1 1/8 miles: Captain Speed, 1:53.80, June 19, 2004
1 1/4 miles: Papa's Got Gin, 2:06.40, August 9, 2004

Arkansas

Oaklawn Park

Arkansas's leading tourist attraction is Oaklawn Park in the resort community of Hot Springs. The track first opened in 1905 but closed two years later due to political problems in the state. The track reopened in 1916 under the ownership of Louis Cella, whose great-nephew, Charles Cella, is the track's current president and board chairman. Oaklawn, which offers live racing from January to mid-April, attracts runners from across the United States for its Racing Festival of the South. The festival features at least one stakes race each day on the final eight days of the meet, ending with the $500,000 Arkansas Derby (G2), which was first run in 1936. Other major races include the Apple Blossom Handicap (G1) for fillies and mares and the $500,000-guaranteed Oaklawn Handicap (G2) for older horses. In 2004, Oaklawn Park and the Cella family received the Eclipse Award of Merit for their contributions to racing.

Location: 2705 Central Ave., Hot Springs, Ar. 71901-7515
Phone: (501) 623-4411
Phone: (800) 625-5926
Fax: (501) 624-4950
Website: www.oaklawn.com
E-Mail: winning@oaklawn.com
Year Founded: 1904
Dates of Inaugural Meeting: February 24, 1905
Abbreviation: OP
Acreage: 120
Number of Stalls: 1,600
Seating Capacity: 26,200

Officers
President: Charles J. Cella
General Manager: R. Eric Jackson
Racing Secretary: Patrick J. Pope
Director of Operations: Craig Holtz
Director of Mutuels: Bobby Geiger
Director of Publicity: Terry Wallace
Director of Simulcasting: Bobby Geiger
Horsemen's Liaison: Debbie Keene
Stewards: John Ferrara Jr., Johnnie Johnson, Larry Snyder
Track Announcer: Terry Wallace
Track Photographer: Jeff Coady
Track Superintendent: Jerry Garner

Racing Dates
2004: January 23-April 10, 55 days
2005: January 21-April 16, 55 days

Track Layout
Main Circumference: 1 mile
Main Track Chute: 6 furlongs
Main Width: 70 feet
Main Length of Stretch: 1,155 feet

Attendance
Average Daily Recent Meeting: 12,455, 2004; 12,842, 2005
Highest Single Day Record: 71,203, April 19, 1986
Record Daily Average for Single Meet: 23,272, 1983
Highest Single Meet Record: 1,419,650, 1984
Total Attendance Recent Meeting: 685,074, 2004; 706,328, 2005

Handle
Average All Sources Recent Meeting: $4,973,133, 2004; $5,239,263, 2005
Average On-Track Recent Meeting: $1,032,937, 2004; $1,052,129, 2005
Record Daily Average for Single Meet: $5,288,620, 2002
Single Day All Sources Handle: $15,133,537, April 15, 2000
Total All Sources Recent Meeting: $273,522,302, 2004; $288,159,518, 2005
Total On-Track Recent Meeting: $56,811,557, 2004; $57,867,109, 2005

Mutuel Records
Highest Win: $350.80, Phaltup, March 7, 1950
Highest Exacta: $3,915.20, April 8, 1994
Highest Trifecta: $46,395, March 12, 1998
Highest Daily Double: $6,902, March 30, 1971
Highest Pick 3: $36,686.80, February 17, 1996
Highest Pick 6: $818,693.40, February 15, 1995

Leaders
Career, Leading Jockey by Titles: Pat Day, 12
Career, Leading Trainer by Titles: Henry Forrest, 11
Recent Meeting, Leading Jockey: John McKee, 71, 2004
Recent Meeting, Leading Owner: Highway 1 Racing Stable, 12, 2004
Recent Meeting, Leading Trainer: Cole Norman, 56, 2004

Records
Single Day Jockey Wins: Larry Snyder, 6, April 1, 1969; Pat Day, 6, February 17, 1986; Pat Day, 6, March 11, 1993; Pat Day, 6, February 20, 1995
Single Meet, Leading Jockey by Wins: Pat Day, 137, 1986
Single Meet, Leading Trainer by Wins: David Vance, 50, 1974

Track Records, Main Dirt
4 furlongs: Crimson Saint, :44 4/5, April 1, 1971
4 1/2 furlongs: Montague, :53, March 29, 1937
5 furlongs: Miss Brendy, :57 3/5, February 22, 1966
5 1/2 furlongs: Sis Pleasure Fager, 1:02 3/5, February 15, 1984
6 furlongs: Karen's Tom, 1:07 4/5, April 16, 1990
1 mile: Whitebrush, 1:34 2/5, March 10, 1984
1m 70 yds: Win Stat, 1:38 2/5, March 7, 1984
1 1/16 miles: Heatherten, 1:40 1/5, April 18, 1984; Hang On Slewpy, 1:40 1/5, April 20, 1991
1 1/8 miles: Snow Chief, 1:46 3/5, April 17, 1987
1 3/16 miles: Brassy, 1:57 2/5, March 29, 1952
1 1/4 miles: Out of Fire, 2:04, March 31, 1937

1 3/8 miles: Homeplace, 2:20 3/5, March 29, 1961
1 1/2 miles: Dapper, 2:31 3/5, March 30, 1957
1 3/4 miles: Flag Carrier, 2:58, April 18, 1987
Other: 3 furlongs, Gay Whip, :33 2/5, March 7, 1967 and Hempen's Song, February 16, 1971; 2 miles 70 yds, Turntable, 3:34, March 27, 1942

Principal Races
Apple Blossom H. (G1), Arkansas Derby (G2), Azeri Breeders' Cup S. (G2), Rebel S. (G3), Count Fleet Sprint H. (G3)

Fastest Times of 2004 (Dirt)
5 1/2 furlongs: Western Roar, 1:03.67, March 27, 2004
6 furlongs: Abbi's Choice, 1:08.75, March 10, 2004
1 mile: Fourth Floor, 1:36.86, April 3, 2004
1 1/16 miles: Azeri, 1:41.24, April 3, 2004
1 1/8 miles: Peace Rules, 1:48.26, April 3, 2004
1 3/16 miles: Luck Arrives, 1:58.66, March 25, 2004
1 3/4 miles: Spin Time, 3:05.96, April 10, 2004

California

Bay Meadows Fair

Location: 2600 S Delaware St., San Mateo, Ca. 94403-1902
Phone: (650) 574-7223
Fax: (650) 345-6826
Website: www.sanmateocountyfair.com
Abbreviation: BMF
Number of Stalls: 1,535

Ownership
San Mateo County Fair

Officers
President: Chris Carpenter
General Manager: Jennifer Burleson
Director of Racing: Hiro Higashi
Racing Secretary: C. Gregory Brent Jr.
Director of Mutuels: Bryan Wayte
Director of Publicity: Tom Ferrall
Director of Simulcasting: Kay Webb
Stewards: Pam Berg
Stewards: Darrel McHargue
Stewards: John Herbuveaux
Track Announcer: Tony Calo
Track Photographer: Vassar Photography
Track Superintendent: Robert Turman
Security: Jerry Gonzalez

Racing Dates
2004: August 11-August 23, 12 days
2005: August 10-August 22, 12 days

Track Layout
Main Circumference: 1 mile
Main Track Chute: 6 furlongs and 1 1/4 miles
Main Length of Stretch: 990 feet
Main Turf Circumference: 7 furlongs

Attendance
Average Daily Recent Meeting: 2,152, 2004
Total Attendance Recent Meeting: 25,818, 2004

Handle
Average All Sources Recent Meeting: $2,406,836, 2004
Average On-Track Recent Meeting: $551,386, 2004
Total All Sources Recent Meeting: $28,882,030, 2004
Total On-Track Recent Meeting: $6,616,631, 2004

Leaders
Recent Meeting, Leading Jockey: Dennis Carr, 14, 2004
Recent Meeting, Leading Trainer: John F. Martin, 7, 2004

Principal Races
Mid-Peninsula Stakes

Fastest Times of 2004 (Dirt)
5 furlongs: Gottahavemilk, :59.04, August 11, 2004
5 1/2 furlongs: Strategically, 1:03.10, August 13, 2004
6 furlongs: Jagged Ice, 1:09.01, August 21, 2004
1 mile: No Toro, 1:35.80, August 19, 2004
1 1/16 miles: Magicjakenjohn, 1:43.65, August 18, 2004

Fastest Times of 2004 (Turf)
5 furlongs: Unforgetabull, :56.43, August 11, 2004
7 1/2 furlongs: Midwife, 1:30.31, August 13, 2004
1 mile: Motel Staff, 1:35.16, August 15, 2004
1 1/16 miles: Lost Bride, 1:43.29, August 14, 2004

Bay Meadows Race Course

Located 20 miles south of San Francisco in San Mateo, Bay Meadows Race Course was founded in 1934 by the innovative William P. Kyne, who helped to bring about the legalization of pari-mutuel wagering in California a year earlier. At Bay Meadows, Kyne introduced the totalizator system, photo-finish camera, and the still-popular daily double wager. Bay Meadows also was the site of the first all-enclosed starting gate in America in 1939 and, on October 27, 1945, the destination point of the first equine air passenger when El Lobo, a Thoroughbred, was flown from Los Angeles to an airstrip adjacent to Bay Meadows. Bay Meadows was the only California racetrack allowed to operate during World War II as Kyne pledged all profits to various war relief projects. In 1951, Coaltown captured the Children's Hospital Handicap, another charity fundraiser. Bay Meadows introduced the El Camino Real Derby (G3) in 1982 as a prep for the Kentucky Derby (G1), and 17 years later Charismatic finished second by a head in the race (to Cliquot) before winning the Derby and Preakness Stakes (G1). Magna Entertainment Corp. leased the track from 2001 through '04, and Bay Meadows Land Co., which owns the property, resumed operation of the facility in 2005.

Location: 2600 South Delaware St., San Mateo, Ca. 94403-1904
Phone: (650) 574-7223
Fax: (650) 803-8168
Website: www.baymeadows.com
E-Mail: webmaster@baymeadows.com
Year Founded: 1934
Dates of Inaugural Meeting: November 3, 1934
Abbreviation: BM
Acreage: 90
Number of Stalls: 900
Seating Capacity: 12,000

Ownership
Bay Meadows Land Co.

Officers
President: F. Jack Liebau
General Manager, Administration: Bernie Thurman
General Manager, Operations: Mike Ziegler
Director of Racing: Richard J. Lewis
Racing Secretary: Tom Doutrich
Secretary: Gary Cohn
Treasurer: Daniel Newman
Director of Operations: Mike Scalzo
Director of Mutuels: Bryan Wayte
Vice President: Mike Scalzo
Vice President: Dyan Grealish
Director of Publicity: Tom Ferrall
Director of Sales: Dyan Grealish
Director of Simulcasting: Kay Webb
Stewards: Darrel McHargue, Dennis Nevin, John Herbuveaux
Track Announcer: Tony Calo

Track Photographer: William Vassar
Track Superintendent: Robert Turman
Asst. Racing Secretary: C. Gregory Brent, Jr.
Security: Jerry Gonzalez
Promotions/Events: Robin McHargue

Racing Dates

2004: April 7-June 20, 55 days; September 3-November 7, 49 days
2005: February 2-May 8, 71 days; September 3-October 16, 33 days

Track Layout

Main Circumference: 1 mile
Main Track Chute: 6 furlongs and 1 1/4 miles
Main Width: Homestretch: 85 feet; Backstretch: 75 feet
Main Length of Stretch: 990 feet
Main Turf Circumference: 7 furlongs 32 feet
Main Turf Width: 75 feet

Attendance

Average Daily Recent Meeting: 3,587, Spring 2004; 2,662, Fall 2004
Highest Single Day Record: 29,300, April 17, 1948
Total Attendance Recent Meeting: 197,280, Spring 2004; 130,443, Fall 2004

Handle

Average All Sources Recent Meeting: $3,926,996, Spring 2004; $3,437,937, Fall 2004
Average On-Track Recent Meeting: $809,246, Spring 2004; $632,042, Fall 2004
Single Day On-Track Handle: $8,660,396, November 6, 1999
Total All Sources Recent Meeting: $215,984,763, Spring 2004; $168,458,900, Fall 2004
Total On-Track Recent Meeting: $44,508,557, Spring 2004; $30,970,050, Fall 2004
Highest Single Day Recent Meet: $9,793,536, May 1, 2004, Spring; $8,426,524, October 30, 2004, Fall

Mutuel Records

Highest Win: $599.80
Highest Exacta: $2,108
Highest Daily Double: $5,231
Highest Pick 6: $1,132,466
Highest Other Exotics: $1,298.80, Quinella; $347,970.40, Pick Nine

Leaders

Career, Leading Jockey by Titles: Russell Baze, 32
Recent Meeting, Leading Jockey: Russell Baze, 90, Spring 2004; Russell Baze, 92, Fall 2004
Recent Meeting, Leading Trainer: Jerry Hollendorfer, 64, Spring 2004; Jerry Hollendorfer, 47, Fall 2004

Records

Single Day Jockey Wins: John Adams, 6, April 7, 1938; John Longden, 6, November 22, 1947; Bill Shoemaker, 6, October 13, 1950; William Harmatz, 6, September 23, 1954; Ralph Neves, 6, October 24, 1961; Russell Baze, 6, September 1, 1984; Russell Baze, 6, January 31, 1999

Track Records, Main Dirt

4 furlongs: Ima Dear, :46 2/5, April 2, 1935
4 1/2 furlongs: Metatron, :50.59, May 24, 2001
5 furlongs: Trickey Trevor, :56.01, October 27, 2004
5 1/2 furlongs: Rio Oro, 1:01.60, October 7, 2001
6 furlongs: Black Jack Road, 1:07 1/5, October 28, 1990
7 1/2 furlongs: Lookabout, 1:30 2/5, November 26, 1936
1 mile: Aristocratical, 1:33 3/5, September 10, 1983
1m 70 yds: Redress, 1:41 3/5, December 10, 1934
1 1/16 miles: Hoedown's Day, 1:38 2/5, October 23, 1983
1 1/8 miles: Super Moment, 1:46 1/5, December 8, 1980
1 3/16 miles: Force of Reason, 1:52 4/5, November 5, 1983
1 1/4 miles: Ask Father, 2:00 2/5, September 28, 1968
1 1/2 miles: Cattle Creek, 2:27 3/5, December 12, 1979
1 5/8 miles: Rag King, 2:43 1/5, December 15, 1990
1 3/4 miles: Tornillo, 2:57 3/5, November 21, 1936
Other: 2 furlongs, Royalette, :21.11, April 12, 2002; 3 1/2 furlongs, Harrogate, :40 4/5, March 16, 1935

Track Records, Main Turf

4 1/2 furlongs: Santano, :50.38, May 17, 2001
5 furlongs: Excessive Barb, :56.32, May 30, 2004
7 furlongs: First Flyer, 1:24.35, September 25, 1997
7 1/2 furlongs: Hegemony (Ire), 1:28 4/5, October 12, 1985
1 mile: Staff Rider, 1:34.68, August 28, 1993
1 1/16 miles: Dreamer, 1:40.21, August 17, 1997
1 1/8 miles: Ocean Queen, 1:47.80, October 12, 1996
1 3/8 miles: Peu a Peu, 2:16.39, May 18, 2002
1 1/2 miles: Swiss Conviction, 2:31.46, October 12, 1998
2 miles: Lighting Star, 3:28.39, March 23, 1997
Other: a1 1/8 miles, Mula Gula, 1:45.34, September 25, 1999; a1 3/8 miles, Handsome Weed, 2:17.10, October 24, 1991

Principal Races

Bay Meadows Breeders' Cup H. (G3), Bay Meadows Derby (G3), San Francisco Breeders' Cup Mile H. (G2), Yerba Buena Breeders' Cup H. (G3), Bay Meadows Breeders' Cup Sprint H. (G3)

Interesting Facts

Bay Meadows is the longest continually operating racetrack in California and is home to the longest-running stakes race in the state, the Bay Meadows H. (G3).

Notable Events

Labor Day Family Day Infield Party

Fastest Times of 2004 (Dirt)

2 furlongs: Tricky Secret, :21.69, April 22, 2004
4 1/2 furlongs: Whatsthenameman, :51.81, June 13, 2004
5 furlongs: Trickey Trevor, :56.01, October 27, 2004
5 1/2 furlongs: Lunar Lion, 1:02.88, April 16, 2004
6 furlongs: Green Team, 1:07.41, September 11, 2004
1 mile: Cree, 1:34.51, September 12, 2004
1 1/16 miles: Yougottawanna, 1:40.08, May 31, 2004
1 1/8 miles: Trieste's Honor, 1:47.95, April 17, 2004

Fastest Times of 2004 (Turf)

5 furlongs: Excessive Barb, :56.32, May 30, 2004
7 1/2 furlongs: Adreamisborn, 1:29.66, April 17, 2004
1 mile: Singletary, 1:35.16, April 24, 2004
1 1/16 miles: Hippogator, 1:41.46, April 10, 2004
1 1/8 miles: Cat Alert, 1:50.40, May 5, 2004
a1 1/8 miles: Needwood Blade (GB), 1:46.55, October 2, 2004
1 3/8 miles: B. Z. Jones, 2:20.01, October 15, 2004

Del Mar

Known as the track "where the surf meets the turf," Del Mar is renowned for its laid-back atmosphere and rich purses. The Del Mar style is a legacy of the film stars who helped build it, principally Bing Crosby and Pat O'Brien. But the track's beginnings were rocky. In the mid-1930s, the 22nd District Agricultural Association began to build a fair grounds with a one-mile racetrack and grandstand north of San Diego, and Crosby formed the Del Mar Turf Club to lease the facility for ten years. But the agricultural district soon ran out of money, and Crosby and O'Brien borrowed almost $600,000 to complete the project. The track opened on July 3, 1937, with Crosby greeting the first patron through the turnstiles. The following year, the crooner wrote "Where the Surf Meets the Turf" and sang it on opening day; it still is played every day at the track. Del Mar was closed during World War II, serving as a Marine training center and an assembly center for B-17 wing ribs. It reopened in 1945, and the lease was extended through 1959. In 1970, a group of prominent California owners and breeders formed the Del Mar Thoroughbred Club and leased the facility for 20 years. The lease was extended for another 20 years in 1990. A rebuilt Del Mar grandstand and clubhouse costing $80-million were completed in 1993, two years after the first running of the track's now-signature event, the Pacific Classic Stakes (G1).

Location: 2260 Jimmy Durante Blvd., P.O. Box 700, Del Mar, Ca. 92014
Phone: (858) 755-1141
Fax: (858) 792-1477
Website: www.delmarracing.com
E-Mail: marys@dmtc.com
Year Founded: 1937
Dates of Inaugural Meeting: July 3-July 31, 1937
Abbreviation: Dmr
Acreage: 350
Number of Stalls: 2,100
Seating Capacity: 14,304

Officers
Chairman: Robert S. Strauss
President: Joe Harper
General Manager: Joe Harper
Director of Racing: Thomas S. Robbins
Racing Secretary: Thomas S. Robbins
Director of Operations: Tim Read
Director of Finance: Michael R. Ernst
Director of Marketing: Josh Rubinstein
Director of Mutuels: Bill Navarro
Vice President: Craig R. Fravel
Director of Publicity: Daniel G. Smith
Director of Sales: Jackie King
Director of Simulcasting: Paul Porter
Horsemen's Liaison: Lisa Iaria
Stewards: David Samuel, George Slender, Ingrid Fermin
Track Announcer: Trevor Denman
Track Photographer: Benoit and Associates
Track Superintendent: Robert Sanchez

Racing Dates
2004: July 21-September 8, 43 days
2005: July 20-September 7, 43 days

Track Layout
Main Circumference: 1 mile
Main Track Chute: 7 furlongs and 1 1/4 miles
Main Width: 80 feet
Main Length of Stretch: 919 feet
Main Turf Circumference: 7 1/2 furlongs
Main Turf Chute: 1 1/8 miles diagonal
Main Turf Width: 63 feet
Main Turf Length of Stretch: 761 feet
Training Track: 1/2 mile

Attendance
Average Daily Recent Meeting: 17,052, 2004
Highest Single Day Record: 44,181, August 10, 1996
Record Daily Average for Single Meet: 19,776, 1985
Highest Single Meet Record: 733,237, 2004
Total Attendance Recent Meeting: 733,237, 2004
Highest Single Day Recent Meet: 39,346, July 21, 2004

Handle
Average All Sources Recent Meeting: $10,968,546, 2004
Average On-Track Recent Meeting: $2,377,744, 2004
Record Daily Average for Single Meet: $3,861,247, 1987
Single Day On-Track Handle: $5,657,840, August 15, 1987
Single Day All Sources Handle: $22,857,785, August 15, 1998
Total All Sources Recent Meeting: $471,647,459, 2004
Total On-Track Recent Meeting: $102,242,996, 2004
Highest Single Day On-Track Recent Meet: $4,552,878, August 22, 2004
Highest Single Day Recent Meet: $20,458,547, August 22, 2004
Record Total All Sources for Single Meet: $471,647,459, 2004
Record average all sources single meet: $10,968,546, 2004

Mutuel Records
Highest Win: $263.40, Cipria, September 1, 1955
Highest Exacta: $2,383, August 7, 1987
Highest Trifecta: $13,405.50, July 28, 1997
Highest Daily Double: $7,720, August 27, 2004
Highest Pick 3: $20,080.30, August 20, 2000
Highest Pick 6: $2,100,017, August 1, 2004
Highest Other Exotics: $133,013.40, Superfecta, September 6, 1998; $43,602.40, Place Pick All, September 8, 2002

Highest Quinella: $1,374, July 28, 1997
Highest Pick 4: $49,571.60, July 23, 2003

Leaders
Career, Leading Jockey by Titles: William Shoemaker, 7
Career, Leading Owner by Titles: Golden Eagle Farm, 6
Career, Leading Trainer by Titles: Farrell W. Jones, 11
Career, Leading Jockey by Stakes Wins: Chris McCarron, 134
Career, Leading Trainer by Stakes Wins: Charles Whittingham, 74
Career, Leading Jockey by Wins: Laffit Pincay Jr., 1,011
Career, Leading Trainer by Wins: Ron McAnally, 409
Recent Meeting, Leading Horse: Blackdoun (Fr), Top Money, 3 each, 2004
Recent Meeting, Leading Jockey: Corey S. Nakatani, 54, 2004
Recent Meeting, Leading Owner: Robert D. Bone, 8, 2004
Recent Meeting, Leading Trainer: Doug O'Neill, 28, 2004

Records
Single Day Jockey Wins: William Shoemaker, 6, September 4, 1954; Rudy Rosales, 6, September 6, 1969; Laffit Pincay Jr., 6, July 28, 1976; Laffit Pincay Jr., 6, July 29, 1978
Single Day Trainer Wins: R. H. "Red" McDaniel, 4, September 4, 1954; R. H. "Red" McDaniel, 4, September 6, 1954; Farrell W. Jones, 4, August 13, 1964; Ron McAnally, 4, August 20, 1989; Jack Van Berg, 4, August 3, 1995
Single Meet, Leading Jockey by Wins: William Shoemaker, 94, 1954
Single Meet, Leading Trainer by Wins: R. H. "Red" McDaniel, 47, 1954

Track Records, Main Dirt
5 furlongs: Soldier Girl, :56 2/5, August 13, 1964
5 1/2 furlongs: Ack Ack, 1:02 1/5, September 12, 1970; Lakeside Trail, 1:02 1/5, August 18, 1974; Little Mustard, 1:02 1/5, September 5, 1974; Brainstorming, 1:02 1/5, August 28, 1991
6 furlongs: King of Cricket, 1:07 3/5, August 22, 1973
6 1/2 furlongs: Native Paster, 1:13 3/5, September 4, 1988
7 furlongs: Solar Launch, 1:20, August 10, 1990
1 mile: Precisionist, 1:33 1/5, August 1, 1988
1 1/16 miles: Windy Sands, 1:40, August 4, 1962; Native Diver, 1:40, August 7, 1965; Matching, 1:40, August 18, 1982
1 1/8 miles: Latin Touch, 1:46, September 1, 1979
1 3/16 miles: Four By Five, 1:56 2/5, August 16, 1954
1 1/4 miles: Candy Ride (Arg), 1:59.11, August 24, 2003
1 1/2 miles: Spring Boy, 2:29 2/5, August 16, 1958
1 5/8 miles: Ormolu, 2:45, August 24, 1957
1 3/4 miles: Lurline B., 2:57 2/5, August 26, 1949
2 miles: Pilot Anne, 3:24 1/5, September 2, 1949
Other: a1 3/16 miles, Ancient Title,1:55 2/5, September 5, 1977

Track Records, Main Turf
5 furlongs: Maria's Mirage, :55.06, July 28, 2003
7 1/2 furlongs: Syncopate, 1:27 4/5, August 24, 1981
1 mile: Touch of the Blues, 1:32.22, August 2, 2003
1 1/16 miles: Allover, 1:39.84, August 27, 2003
1 1/8 miles: Special Ring, 1:45.87, July 27, 2003
1 3/8 miles: Crazy Ensign, 2:12.07, August 29, 2003
Other: a7 1/2 furlongs, Buck Price, 1:27 2/5, September 8, 1975

Principal Races
Pacific Classic (G1), Del Mar Oaks (G1), Del Mar Debutante (G1), Eddie Read H. (G1), John C. Mabee H. (G1), Bing Crosby H. (G1)

Fastest Times of 2004 (Dirt)
5 furlongs: Starleena, :58.82, July 25, 2004
5 1/2 furlongs: Cash in the Bank, 1:03.48, September 6, 2004
6 furlongs: Our New Recruit, 1:08.25, September 6, 2004
6 1/2 furlongs: Attack Alert, 1:14.98, August 21, 2004
7 furlongs: Kela, 1:21.17, August 15, 2004
1 mile: Perfect Moon, 1:35.09, September 3, 2004
1 1/16 miles: Daunting, 1:42.00, July 25, 2004
1 1/8 miles: B. Z. Jones, 1:51.09, August 5, 2004
1 1/4 miles: Pleasantly Perfect, 2:01.17, August 22, 2004

Fastest Times of 2004 (Turf)
5 furlongs: De Valmont (Aus), :55.10, August 12, 2004
1 mile: Special Rate, 1:33.25, August 28, 2004
1 1/16 miles: Cayoke (Fr), 1:39.93, August 20, 2004
1 1/8 miles: Special Ring, 1:45.90, July 25, 2004
1 3/8 miles: Star Over the Bay, 2:12.71, August 29, 2004

Fairplex Park

For more than 80 years, the Los Angeles County Fair Association has offered racing at Fairplex Park. In recent decades, the fair meeting has given the major Southern California circuit a welcome break between the Del Mar and Oak Tree at Santa Anita meets in September. The inaugural Los Angeles County Fair was conducted in 1922, a five-day meet over a half-mile track. By the mid-1930s, after pari-mutuel wagering had been legalized in California, the fair was extended to a 17-day meeting. The Barretts Ltd. sales pavilion is located adjacent to the track.

Location: 1101 W McKinley Ave., Pomona, Ca. 91768-1639
Phone: (909) 865-4545
Fax: (909) 623-8170
Website: www.fairplex.com
E-Mail: info@fairplex.com
Year Founded: 1922
Dates of Inaugural Meeting: 1922
Abbreviation: Fpx
Acreage: 487
Number of Stalls: 1,306
Seating Capacity: 10,000

Officers
Chairman: Stephen C. Morgan
President: James E. Henwood
General Manager: George Bradrica
Director of Racing: Terry Gilligan
Racing Secretary: Richard Wheeler
Director of Operations: Dwight Richards
Director of Communications: Scott Kelly
Director of Finance: Mike Seder
Director of Marketing: Scott Kelly
Vice President: Dale Coleman, Dwight Richards, Mike Seder
Director of Publicity: Wendy Talarico
Stewards: David Samuel, Tom Ward, Will Meyers
Track Announcer: Trevor Denman
Track Photographer: Benoit & Asssociates

Racing Dates
2004: September 10-September 26, 17 days
2005: September 9-September 25, 17 days

Track Layout
Main Circumference: 5/8 mile
Main Track Chute: 1/4 mile
Main Track Chute: 1 1/8 miles
Main Width: 75 feet
Main Length of Stretch: 660 feet

Attendance
Average Daily Recent Meeting: 13,711, 2004
Highest Single Day Record: 28,300, September 25, 1948
Record Daily Average for Single Meet: 18,749, 1998
Highest Single Meet Record: 337,491, 1998
Total Attendance Recent Meeting: 102,255, 2004

Handle
Average All Sources Recent Meeting: $4,467,647, 2004
Average On-Track Recent Meeting: $530,437, 2004
Record Daily Average for Single Meet: $3,861,247, 1987
Single Day On-Track Handle: $4,112,091, September 27, 1987
Single Day All Sources Handle: $10,200,000, September 27, 2003
Total All Sources Recent Meeting: $74,250,009, 2004
Total On-Track Recent Meeting: $11,435,086, 2004

Highest Single Day Record Recent Meet: $9,196,965, September 25, 2004

Mutuel Records
Highest Win: $182.20, Uncle Fox, September 21, 1976
Highest Exacta: $5,645, September 13, 1986
Highest Trifecta: $29,278.80, September 30, 1996
Highest Daily Double: $4,362.40, September 17, 1990
Highest Pick 6: $199,346.60, September 13, 1999
Highest Other Exotics: $30,497, $1 Superfecta, September 19, 2000

Leaders
Recent Meeting, Leading Jockey: Martin Pedroza, 51, 2004
Recent Meeting, Leading Trainer: Doug O'Neill, 16, 2004
Career, Leading Jockey by Stakes Wins: David Flores, 52
Career, Leading Trainer by Stakes Wins: Mel Stute, 42
Career, Leading Jockey by Wins: Martin Pedroza, 349
Career, Leading Trainer by Wins: Mel Stute, 172

Records
Single Day Jockey Wins: David Flores, 6, September 20, 1992
Single Day Jockey Wins: David Flores, 6, September 30, 1992
Single Day Trainer Wins: Jerry Fanning, 4, September 24, 1984
Single Day Trainer Wins: Gordon Campbell, 4, September 30, 1967
Single Meet, Leading Jockey by Wins: David Flores, 48, 1991
Single Meet, Leading Trainer by Wins: Mel Stute, 13, 1986

Track Records, Main Dirt
4 furlongs: Nashua's Asset, :45.55, September 15, 2002
6 furlongs: Drouilly's Boy, 1:09 1/5, September 19, 1989
6 1/2 furlongs: Bundle of Iron, 1:15 1/5, September 23, 1986
7 furlongs: Best of Time, 1:22.66, September 16, 2000
1 1/16 miles: Monte Parnes (Arg), 1:41 3/5, September 29, 1990
1 1/8 miles: Dachi's Folly, 1:48 2/5, September 29, 1990
1 3/8 miles: Mummy's Pleasure, 2:15, September 28, 1986

Principal Races
Barretts Juvenile S., Barretts Debutante S., Ralph M. Hinds Pomona Invitational H., Las Madrinas H., Pomona Derby

Interesting Facts
Achievements/Milestones: Track was expanded to 5/8 mile in 1986

Notable Events
Mel Stute inaugural inductee into Fairplex Park Hall of Fame, September 27, 2003
Julie Krone rode in and won Pomona Derby, September 27, 2003.

Fastest Times of 2004 (Dirt)
a4 furlongs: Sealed With a Kiss, :44.79, September 13, 2004
6 furlongs: Strategically, 1:10.03, September 25, 2004
6 1/2 furlongs: Madringa, 1:15.42, September 21, 2004
7 furlongs: Magical Dust, 1:22.53, September 26, 2004
1 1/16 miles: Verkade, 1:42.48, September 11, 2004
a1 1/8 miles: Semi Lost, 1:48.95, September 25, 2004
1 3/8 miles: Sigfreto, 2:17.34, September 26, 2004

Ferndale

Location: 1250 5th St., Ferndale, Ca. 95536-9712
Phone: (707) 786-9511
Fax: (707) 786-9450
Website: www.humboldtcountyfair.org
E-Mail: humcou1@northcoast.com
Year Founded: 1896
Abbreviation: Fer
Number of Stalls: 258 permanent, 200 portable
Seating Capacity: 2,200

Ownership
County of Humboldt

Officers

Chairman: Irv Parlato
President: Irv Parlato
General Manager: Stuart Titus
Director of Racing: Stuart Titus
Racing Secretary: Ella Robinson
Director of Operations: Stuart Titus
Director of Marketing: Stuart Titus
Director of Mutuels: George Vidak
Vice President: Bill Branstetter, Valerie Davis
Director of Publicity: Stuart Titus
Stewards: Will Myers, Grant Baker
Track Announcer: John McGary
Track Superintendent: Steve Woods

Racing Dates

2004: August 12-August 22, 10 days
2005: August 11-August 22, 10 days

Track Layout

Main Circumference: 1/2 mile
Main Track Chute: 5 furlongs
Main Track Chute: 7 furlongs
Main Length of Stretch: 530 feet

Attendance

Average Daily Recent Meeting: 2,176, 2004
Total Attendance Recent Meeting: 21,759, 2004

Handle

Average All Sources Recent Meeting: 205,548, 2004
Average On-Track Recent Meeting: 69,908, 2004
Total All Sources Recent Meeting: $2,055,481, 2004
Total On-Track Recent Meeting: 699,081, 2004

Leaders

Recent Meeting, Leading Horse: Designer Image, 3, 2004
Recent Meeting, Leading Jockey: Victor Miranda, 11, 2004
Recent Meeting, Leading Trainer: Warren Shelley, 8, 2004

Principal Races

Les Mademoiselle S., Humboldt County Marathon

Fastest Times of 2004 (Dirt)

3 furlongs: Distance Power, :33.73, August 19, 2004
5 furlongs: Sizzlin Hot Summer, :58.23, August 21, 2004
6 1/2 furlongs: Drivers Seat, 1:19.15, August 14, 2004
7 furlongs: Suck Um Up Bro, 1:24.96, August 16, 2004
1 1/16 miles: Scattering, 1:46.67, August 21, 2004
1 5/8 miles: Clip, 2:47.04, August 22, 2004

Fresno

Location: 1121 S Chance Ave., Fresno, Ca. 93702-3707
Phone: (559) 650-3247
Fax: (559) 650-3226
Website: www.fresnofair.com
E-Mail: info@fresnofair.com
Year Founded: 1883
Abbreviation: Fno

Ownership

State of California

Officers

Chairman: Ardie Der Manouel
President: Susan Good
Director of Racing: Dan White
Racing Secretary: Charlie Palmer
Director of Publicity: Cohen Communications
Track Superintendent: Dave Wood

Racing Dates

2004: October 6-October 17, 11 days
2005: October 5-October 16, 11 days

Attendance

Average Daily Recent Meeting: 6,310, 2004
Total Attendance Recent Meeting: 69,412, 2004

Handle

Average All Sources Recent Meeting: $528,793, 2004
Average On-Track Recent Meeting: $283,428, 2004
Total All Sources Recent Meeting: $5,816,727, 2004
Total On-Track Recent Meeting: $3,117,712, 2004
Single Day All Sources Handle: $633,000, 2003

Leaders

Recent Meeting, Leading Jockey: Modesto Linares, 15, 2004
Recent Meeting, Leading Trainer: Dennis Hopkins, 6, 2004

Principal Races

Bulldog S.

Fastest Times of 2004 (Dirt)

5 furlongs: Byreasonofinsanity, :56.79, October 9, 2004
5 1/2 furlongs: Double Seeded, 1:03.53, October 14, 2004
6 furlongs: Two Out of Three, 1:07.50, October 8, 2004
1 mile: Strategically, 1:34.79, October 16, 2004
1 1/8 miles: Potri Cacho (Arg), 1:48.09, October 9, 2004

Golden Gate Fields

On April 29, 1949, a 19-year-old apprentice jockey from Texas named Bill Shoemaker rode Shafter V. to victory in the second race at Golden Gate Fields in Albany, California. That win marked the first of a then-record 8,833 career victories for Shoemaker, a Racing Hall of Fame jockey. Several famous horses also have raced at the San Francisco-area track. Citation, the 1948 Triple Crown winner, defeated champion handicap horse *Noor in the '50 Golden Gate Mile Handicap, setting a world record for one mile in the process. Silky Sullivan captured his first stakes victory in the 1957 Golden Gate Futurity and went on to win 12 of 27 career starts and earned more than $150,000. In February 1941, entrepreneur Edward "Slip" Madigan opened the track, then known as the Albany Turf Club. The track closed after its first five days of racing due to flooding from heavy rains. During World War II, the United States Navy used Golden Gate as a landing base for amphibious craft. Racing resumed in 1947 after the water problem was solved, and in '71 the track added a turf course. In 1989, Ladbroke Group purchased Golden Gate for $41-million. As it wound down its North American racing operations, Ladbroke sold the facility to Magna Entertainment Corp. in 1999.

Location: 1100 Eastshore Hwy, Albany, Ca. 94710
Phone: (510) 559-7300
Fax: (510) 559-7467
Website: www.goldengatefields.com
E-Mail: help@goldengatefields.com
Year Founded: 1941
Dates of Inaugural Meeting: February 1, 1941, 5 days
Abbreviation: GG
Acreage: 225
Number of Stalls: 1,425
Seating Capacity: 14,750

Ownership

Magna Entertainment Corp.

Officers

Chairman: Frank Stronach
Chief Executive Officer: Jim McAlpine
General Manager: Peter Tunney
Director of Racing: Richard Lewis
Racing Secretary: Tom Doutrich
Secretary: Gary Cohn
Treasurer: Barbara Helm
Director of Mutuels: Bryan Wayte
Vice President: Bernie Thurman, Calvin Rainey, Michael A. Scalzo, Michael Ziegler

Director of Publicity: Tom Ferrall
Director of Sales: Dyan Grealish
Director of Simulcasting: Kay Webb
Horsemen's Liaison: Jenny Scullin
Stewards: Dennis Nevin, John Herbuveaux, Darrel McHargue
Track Announcer: Tony Calo
Track Photographer: William Vassar
Track Superintendent: Juan Meza
Security: Jerry Gonzalez
Promotions/Events: Robin McHargue

Racing Dates
2004: November 5, 2003-April 4, 2004 109 days
2005: November, 10, 2004-January 30, 2005, 59 days; May 11-June 19, 29 days; October 19-December 19, 46 days

Track Layout
Main Circumference: 1 mile
Main Width: 78 feet
Main Length of Stretch: 1,000 feet
Main Turf Circumference: 9/10 mile
Main Turf Chute: 3/16 mile
Main Turf Width: 65 feet

Attendance
Average Daily Recent Meeting: 2,235, 2004/2005
Highest Single Day Record: 33,039 October 18, 1947
Total Attendance Recent Meeting: 131,879, 2004/2005

Handle
Average All Sources Recent Meeting: $3,784,767, 2004/2005
Average On-Track Recent Meeting: $561,837, 2004/2005
Single Day All Sources Handle: $6,638,222, January 31, 2004
Total All Sources Recent Meeting: $223,301,272.20, 2004/2005
Total On-Track Recent Meeting: $33,148,373.10, 2004/2005

Mutuel Records
Highest Win: $322.60, Pasadena Slim, October 28, 1957
Highest Exacta: $2,270.20, January 18, 1997
Highest Trifecta: $38,689.20, January 18, 1997
Highest Daily Double: $8,711.40, November 16, 1960
Highest Pick 3: $18,851, December 13, 1998
Highest Pick 6: $1,074,405.80, May 23, 1990
Highest Other Exotics: $63,954, Superfecta, March 2, 2002

Leaders
Career, Leading Jockey by Titles: Russell Baze, 25
Career, Leading Trainer by Titles: Jerry Hollendorfer, 23
Recent Meeting, Leading Jockey: Russell Baze, 80, 2004/2005
Recent Meeting, Leading Trainer: Jerry Hollendorfer, 50, 2004/2005

Records
Single Day Jockey Wins: Russell Baze, 7, April 16, 1992
Single Day Trainer Wins: Walter Greenman, 5, November 25, 1970; Ace Gibson, 5, February 24, 1971; Jerry Hollendorfer, 5, May 1, 1996; Jerry Hollendorfer, 5, January 23, 1997
Single Meet, Leading Jockey by Wins: Russell Baze, 178, 1992
Single Meet, Leading Trainer by Wins: Jerry Hollendorfer, 89, 1990

Track Records, Main Dirt
4 furlongs: Glenbar, :47, March 12, 1952
4 furlongs: Giddy Up, :47, March 25, 1952
4 1/2 furlongs: Victory Found, :50.30, April 30, 1992
5 furlongs: Contradiction, :56.12, January 1, 2003
5 1/2 furlongs: Linear Lights, 1:01.99, February 25, 2004
6 furlongs: El Dorado Shooter, 1:07.55, January 20, 2001
1 mile: Caros Love, 1:33, February 13, 1988
1 1/16 miles: Restless Con, 1:39.50, June 24, 1991
1 1/8 miles: Simply Majestic, 1:45, April 2, 1988
1 3/16 miles: Fleet Bird, 1:52 3/5, October 24, 1953
1 1/4 miles: *Noor, 1:58 1/5, June 24, 1950
1 3/8 miles: Forin Sea, 2:18 3/5, October 3, 1959
1 1/2 miles: Bo Donna, 2:29 2/5, June 8, 1979
1 3/4 miles: Sirmark, 2:57 1/5, October 16, 1948
2 miles: Mantourist, 3:25 4/5, October 23, 1948
Other: 2 furlongs, Black Wagner, :21.75, March 26, 2004

Track Records, Main Turf
4 1/2 furlongs: Bonne Nuite, :50.58, May 22, 1994
5 furlongs: Black Tornado, :56, May 10, 1975; L'Natural, :56, May 28, 1977; Goldie's Goldian, :56, May 27, 1978
7 1/2 furlongs: Clever Song, 1:28, May 25, 1986; His Honor, 1:28, April 25, 1981; Struttin' George, 1:28, May 5, 1979
1 mile: Don Alberto, 1:33 2/5, March 22, 1980
1 1/16 miles: Announcer, 1:40 2/5, April 16, 1977
1 1/8 miles: Blues Traveller (Ire), 1:47.71, May 14, 1994
1 3/8 miles: John Henry, 2:13, May 6, 1984
1 1/2 miles: Silveyville, 2:27 2/5, June 10, 1984; Kings Island (Ire), 2:27 2/5, June 9, 1985; Val Danseur, 2:27 2/5, June 8, 1986
2 miles: Never-Rust, 3:25 3/5, June 26, 1988
Other: 2 3/8 miles, Situada (Chi), 4:10 4/5, June 25, 1990

Principal Races
El Camino Real Derby (G3), Golden Gate Breeders' Cup H. (G3), Berkeley H. (G3).

Notable Events
Crab and wine festival for charity, Beer Fest for charity.

Fastest Times of 2004 (Dirt)
2 furlongs: Black Wagner, :21.75, March 26, 2004
5 furlongs: Northern Tide, :56.34, January 10, 2004
5 1/2 furlongs: Linear Lights, 1:01.99, February 25, 2004
6 furlongs: Twentythreejaybird, 1:07.56, February 20, 2004
1 mile: Snorter, 1:33.92, March 27, 2004
1 1/16 miles: Yougottawanna, 1:40.67, February 28, 2004
1 1/8 miles: Desert Boom, 1:49.14, December 5, 2004

Fastest Times of 2004 (Turf)
4 1/2 furlongs: Santano, :50.25, April 2, 2004
1 mile: High Alert, 1:35.78, March 18, 2004
1 1/16 miles: Motel Staff, 1:41.94, March 20, 2004
1 1/8 miles: Tronare (Chi), 1:48.48, March 14, 2004

Hollywood Park

Hollywood Park sprung to life in 1938 when the Hollywood Turf Club was formed with Warner Brothers executive Jack L. Warner as its chairman. Several Hollywood power brokers, including actors (Ralph Bellamy), singers (Bing Crosby), and studio executives (Walt Disney, Darryl Zanuck) were among the original shareholders. Not everything has had a Hollywood ending at the track, however. A fire in 1949 destroyed the club's physical plant and forced racing over to Santa Anita Park for one year. The track reopened in time for a typical Hollywood finish when Citation won the 1951 Hollywood Gold Cup and became racing's first equine millionaire in the process. Hollywood again was the backdrop of history 28 years later when Affirmed won the Hollywood Gold Cup (G1) to break racing's $2-million barrier. In 1983, John Henry became the first $4-million earner when he won the Hollywood Turf Cup (G1). The first Breeders' Cup championship day was staged at Hollywood in 1984. The event returned in 1987 and again in '97. Hollywood has not been immune from controversy. An expensive rebuilding of the track—including an extension of the track to 1⅛ miles and construction of a new clubhouse structure, the Pavilion of the Stars—preceded the first Breeders' Cup, and fans resented the move of the finish line toward the new facility. A bitter fight for control of the track raged in the late 1980s and early '90s, and the struggle was resolved in February '91 when R. D. Hubbard wrested control from longtime executive Marjorie Lindheimer Everett in a proxy fight. Hubbard immediately launched a multimillion-dollar renovation program that spruced up the track and transformed the clubhouse pavilion into a card-club casino. As a part of that project, the finish line was returned to its original location. In 1999, Churchill Downs Inc. bought Hollywood Park (excluding the card club) for $140-million. On December 10, 1999, Laffit Pincay Jr. became the winningest rider in racing history with a triumph at Hollywood, surpassing the record of 8,833 wins of Bill Shoemaker.

Location: 1050 South Prairie Ave., Inglewood, Ca. 90301-4460
Phone: (310) 419-1500
Fax: (310) 672-4664
Website: www.hollywoodpark.com
Year Founded: 1938
Dates of Inaugural Meeting: June 10, 1938
Abbreviation: Hol
Acreage: 240
Number of Stalls: 1,958
Seating Capacity: 10,000

Ownership
Churchill Downs Inc.

Officers
Chairman: Thomas H. Meeker
President: Rick Baedeker
General Manager: Eual Wyatt Jr.
Director of Racing: Martin Panza
Racing Secretary: Martin Panza
Director of Operations: Don Barney
Director of Communications: Michael P. Mooney
Director of Marketing: Christy Tucker
Director of Mutuels: Robert D. Poole
Vice President: Allen Gutterman, John Long, Steve Arnold
Director of Publicity: Michael P. Mooney
Director of Simulcasting: Tim Barden
Horsemen's Liaison: Diana Hudak
Stewards: George Slender, Pete Pedersen, Thomas Ward
Track Announcer: Vic Stauffer
Track Photographer: Benoit and Associates
Track Superintendent: Dennis Moore
Asst. Racing Secretary: Richard Wheeler
Promotions/Events: Deann Fruhling
Security: Don Barney

Racing Dates
2004: April 21-July 18, 65 days; November 3-December 20, 36 days
2005: April 22-July 17, 64 days; November 9-December 19, 31 days

Track Layout
Main Circumference: 1 1/8 miles
Main Track Chute: 7 1/2 furlongs
Main Width: Homestretch: 92 feet; Backstretch: 82 feet
Main Length of Stretch: 990 feet
Main Turf Circumference: 1 mile and 145 feet
Main Turf Width: 64 feet
Main Turf Length of Stretch: 990 feet
Training Track: 1/2 mile

Attendance
Average Daily Recent Meeting: 8,348, Spring/Summer 2004; 6,216, Fall 2004
Highest Single Day Record: 80,348, May 4, 1980
Highest Single Meet Record: 2,398,528, Spring/Summer 1980
Record Daily Average for Single Meet: 34,516, Spring/Summer 1965
Total Attendance Recent Meeting: 542,597, Spring/Summer 2004; 223,766, Fall 2004

Handle
Average All Sources Recent Meeting: $9,029,461, Spring/Summer 2004; $7,577,663, Fall 2004
Average On-Track Recent Meeting: $1,750,708, Spring/Summer 2004; $1,285,280, Fall 2004
Record Daily Average for Single Meet: $5,486,172, 1985
Single Day All Sources Handle: $67,096,242, November 2, 1997

Total All Sources Recent Meeting: $586,914,975, Spring/Summer 2004; $272,795,855, Fall 2004
Total On-Track Recent Meeting: $113,796,028, Spring/Summer 2004; $46,270,068, Fall 2004
Highest Single Day Record Recent Meet: $24,198,385.60, May 1, 2004, Spring/Summer
Highest Single Day On-Track Recent Meet: $4,885,425.30, May 1, 2004, Spring/Summer

Mutuel Records
Highest Win: $361.80, Family Flair, June 29, 1989
Highest Exacta: $6,989.40, May 11, 1991
Highest Trifecta: $28,294, July 17, 1997
Highest Daily Double: $6,141.60, July 10, 1962
Highest Pick 3: $137,200.20, December 17, 1993
Highest Pick 6: $1,312,808.60, May 19, 2004
Highest Other Exotics: $190,769.80, Superfecta, November 11, 1994
Highest Pick 4: $90,470.50, June 20, 2004

Leaders
Career, Leading Jockey by Titles: Bill Shoemaker, 18
Career, Leading Owner by Titles: Juddmonte Farms, 6
Career, Leading Trainer by Titles: Robert Frankel, 12
Recent Meeting, Leading Jockey: Tyler Baze, 59, Spring/Summer 2004; Rene Douglas, 37, Fall 2004
Recent Meeting, Leading Owner: Robert D. Bone, 11, Spring/Summer 2004
Recent Meeting, Leading Trainer: Jeff Mullins, 37, Spring/Summer 2004; Doug O'Neill, 17, Fall 2004
Career, Leading Jockey by Stakes Wins: Laffit Pincay Jr., 285
Career, Leading Jockey by Wins: Laffit Pincay Jr., 3,049
Career, Leading Trainer by Wins: Charlie Whittingham, 859

Records
Single Day Jockey Wins: Bill Shoemaker, 6, June 20, 1953; Laffit Pincay Jr., 6, May 27, 1968; Bill Shoemaker, 6, June 24, 1970; Kent Desormeaux, 6, July 3, 1992
Single Day Trainer Wins: Allen Drumheller Sr., 5, July 4, 1955
Single Meet, Leading Jockey by Wins: Laffit Pincay Jr., 148, 1974
Single Meet, Leading Owner by Wins: Marion R. Frankel, 55, 1972
Single Meet, Leading Trainer by Wins: Robert Frankel, 60, 1972

Track Records, Main Dirt
4 1/2 furlongs: Bridge of Royalty, :50.59, May 4, 1995
5 furlongs: Diligent Prospect, :56.29, May 30, 2004
5 1/2 furlongs: Hombre Rapido, 1:01.67, December 20, 2002
6 furlongs: Apalachee Ridge, 1:07.52, December 12, 1997
6 1/2 furlongs: Lucky Forever, 1:13.24, May 20, 1995
7 furlongs: Mazel Trick, 1:19.97, June 27, 1999
7 1/2 furlongs: Awesome Daze, 1:26.26, November 23, 1997
1 mile: Greinton (GB), 1:32 3/5, June 9, 1985
1 1/16 miles: Power Forward, 1:40, December 19, 1987; Crafty Friend, 1:40, July 12, 1997; New Journey, 1:40, November 27, 1997
1 1/8 miles: Gentlemen (Arg), 1:45.35, December 22, 1996
1 3/16 miles: Dig for It, 1:54.85, May 30, 2001
1 1/4 miles: Greinton (GB), 1:58 2/5, June 23, 1985
1 3/8 miles: Golden Ticket, 2:13.42, December 21, 2002
1 5/8 miles: Ol' Henry, 2:42.50, June 27, 1997
1 3/4 miles: Roman Cuzzin, 2:56.77, July 21, 1997

Track Records, Main Turf
5 1/2 furlongs: Pembroke, 1:00.46, July 15, 1995
6 furlongs: Answer Do, 1:07, December 15, 1990
1 mile: Megan's Interco, 1:32.64, May 22, 1994
1 1/16 miles: Leroidesanimaux (Brz), 1:38.45, May 1, 2004
1 1/8 miles: Fastness (Ire), 1:44.78, November 25, 1995
1 3/16 miles: Kudos, 1:51.99, April 25, 2001
1 1/4 miles: Bien Bien, 1:57.75, May 31, 1993
1 1/2 miles: Talloires, 2:23.55, July 21, 1996
Other: a1 1/8 miles, Zoffany, 1:44 4/5, November 16, 1985; a1 3/4 miles, Big Warning, 2:50 2/5, December 22, 1990

Principal Races
Fall: Hollywood Derby (G1), Hollywood Starlet S. (G1), Hollywood Futurity (G1), Hollywood Turf Cup H. (G1), Matriarch S. (G1)

Spring/Summer: Hollywood Gold Cup H. (G1), American Invitational Oaks (G1), Shoemaker Breeders' Cup Mile S. (G1), Charles Whittingham Memorial H. (G1), Gamely Breeders' Cup H. (G1)

Notable Events

Gold Rush in April, Autumn Turf Festival on Thanksgiving weekend

Fastest Times of 2004 (Dirt)

4 1/2 furlongs: Chandtrue, :50.83, April 29, 2004
5 1/2 furlongs: Scarlett Memories, 1:02.19, December 12, 2004
6 furlongs: Taste of Paradise, 1:08.04, December 5, 2004
6 1/2 furlongs: Greg's Gold, 1:14.30, November 3, 2004
7 furlongs: Indian Country, 1:20.69, December 18, 2004
7 1/2 furlongs: Anziyan Royalty, 1:27.30, November 13, 2004
1 1/16 miles: Awesome Dividend, 1:40.69, December 20, 2004
1 1/8 miles: Truly a Judge, 1:47.06, December 11, 2004
1 1/4 miles: Total Impact (Chi), 2:00.72, July 10, 2004

Fastest Times of 2004 (Turf)

5 furlongs: Excusabull, :58.28, June 20, 2004
5 1/2 furlongs: King Robyn, 1:00.60, April 23, 2004
1 mile: Designed for Luck, 1:32.81, May 31, 2004
1 1/8 miles: Bayamo (Ire), 1:46.60, July 4, 2004
1 1/4 miles: Gallant (GB), 1:59.04, April 21, 2004
1 1/2 miles: Remonte, 2:26.45, May 30, 2004

Los Alamitos Race Course

Thoroughbreds have competed at Los Alamitos Race Course in Cypress, California, since 1994, when the track received permission to begin offering races for the breed. Los Alamitos primarily had been known as a Quarter Horse track since 1947, when nonpari-mutuel racing debuted at the track built by Frank Vessels on his ranch. In 1951, Los Alamitos received approval to begin holding pari-mutuel racing. After Vessels's death in 1963, his son Frank Vessels Jr. took over operation of the track, which five years later began offering night racing. After Vessels Jr.'s death in 1974, his wife, Millie, assumed the track's presidency and became one of the first women to hold a leadership position in Thoroughbred racing. In 1984, Los Alamitos was sold to Hollywood Park and entered a period of decline. Five years later, businessmen and harness-racing enthusiasts Lloyd Arnold and Chris Bardis bought the facility. Edward C. Allred, a physician and the all-time leading breeder of Quarter Horses by earnings, then purchased a majority interest in Los Alamitos and today is sole owner of the track, which also offers Paint, Appaloosa, and Arabian racing.

Location: 4961 Katella Ave., Los Alamitos, Ca. 90720-2721
Phone: (714) 820-2800
Fax: (714) 820-2689
Website: www.losalamitos.com
E-Mail: larace@losalamitos.com
Year Founded: 1946
Dates of Inaugural Meeting: 1951
Abbreviation: LA
Number of Stalls: 1,400
Seating Capacity: 13,000

Ownership

Edward C. Allred

Officers

Chairman: Edward C. Allred
Director of Racing: Ronald Church
Racing Secretary: Ronald Church
Secretary: G. Michael Lyon

Treasurer: Kathleen Chavez
Director of Operations: Howard Knuchell
Director of Finance: Robert M. Passero
Director of Marketing: Orlando Gutierrez
Director of Mutuels: Robert DiGiovanni
Vice President: John T. Seibly
Director of Publicity: Orlando Gutierrez
Director of Sales: Vandi Ekins
Director of Simulcasting: Melodie Knuchell
Horsemen's Liaison: Vandi Ekins
Stewards: Albert Christiansen, Martin Hamilton, Merlin Volzke
Track Announcer: Ed Burgart
Track Photographer: Scott Martinez
Track Superintendent: Rick Hughes
Promotions/Events: Vandi Ekins
Chief executive officer: Edward C. Allred
Asst. Racing Secretary: Edward Reese

Racing Dates

2004: December 26, 2003-December 19, 2004, 203 days
2005: December 26, 2004-December 18, 2005, 206 days

Track Layout

Main Circumference: 5 furlongs
Main Track Chute: 550 yards and 4 1/2 furlongs
Main Width: Homestretch: 100 feet; Backstretch: 90 feet
Main Length of Stretch: 558 feet

Attendance

Average Daily Recent Meeting: 4,663, 2004
Highest Single Day Record: 19,970, May 6, 1983
Highest Single Meet Record: 1,046,158, 1994
Record Daily Average for Single Meet: 9,492, 1970
Total Attendance Recent Meeting: 932,609, 2004

Handle

Average All Sources Recent Meeting: $1,281,868, 2004
Average On-Track Recent Meeting: $255,278, 2004
Record Daily Average for Single Meet: $1,281,868, 2004
Single Day All Sources Handle: $2,379,112, November 1, 2003
Total All Sources Recent Meeting: $260,219,285, 2004
Total On-Track Recent Meeting: $51,821,434, 2004
Record Total All Sources for Single Meet: $260,219,285, 2004
Highest Single Day Record Recent Meet: $1,995,758, June 19, 2004

Mutuel Records

Highest Exacta: $8,650.30, August 30, 1996
Highest Trifecta: $27,386.10, July 27, 1996
Highest Daily Double: $2,107.90, June 12, 1997
Highest Pick 3: $12,017.60, August 21, 1991
Highest Other Exotics: Superfecta, $21,198, July 12, 1997

Leaders

Career, Leading Jockey by Titles: Alex Bautista, 3
Career, Leading Trainer by Titles: Charles S. Treece, 6
Recent Meeting, Leading Jockey: Guillermo Gutierrez, 57, 2004
Recent Meeting, Leading Trainer: Jesus Nunez, 66, 2004
Career, Leading Jockey by Wins: Alex Bautista, 393
Career, Leading Trainer by Wins: Charles S. Treece, 282

Track Records, Main Dirt

4 1/2 furlongs: Valiant Pete, :49.20, August 11, 1990

Principal Races

Los Alamitos Million Futurity, Golden State Million, Ed Burke Million, Champion of Champions

Interesting Facts

Achievements/Milestones: Los Alamitos is the home of the richest horse race of any breed in California—the $1.3-million Los Alamitos Million.

Notable Events

California Breeders Champions Night, Wiener Dog Nationals

Fastest Times of 2004 (Dirt)

4 1/2 furlongs: Gravitate, :50.18, February 21, 2004

Oak Tree Racing Association at Santa Anita

In 1968, Southern California horsemen Clement Hirsch, Jack K. Robbins, and Louis R. Rowan approached Santa Anita Park President Robert P. Strub with a proposal for a brief, high-quality fall meeting at the Arcadia track. Except for the brief Fairplex Park meet, the Southern California racing calendar was empty between the close of Del Mar in September and the opening of Santa Anita's winter-spring meet each December 26. (Hollywood Park then had only a spring-summer meet.) Strub initially resisted, but Santa Anita officials finally agreed to try a fall meet under the auspices of the Oak Tree Racing Association, headed by Hirsch, in October 1969. In case the idea flopped, Oak Tree's directors had to guarantee the first day's purses. The initial 20-day fall meet was a success, and Oak Tree has become an important part of the racing scene in Southern California and nationally. Oak Tree secured rights to stage the third Breeders' Cup championship day in 1986, and the event attracted an on-track crowd of 69,155, the largest crowd to that time. Oak Tree hosted the championship day in 1993 and 2003. In addition, Oak Tree's stakes serve as leading prep races for the Breeders' Cup championship events. Hirsch died in 2000 and was succeeded as Oak Tree president by Robbins.

Location: 285 W. Huntington Dr., Arcadia, Ca. 91007-3439
Phone: (626) 574-7223
Fax: (626) 446-9565
Website: www.oaktreeracing.com
E-Mail: info@oaktreeracing.com
Year Founded: 1969
Dates of Inaugural Meeting: October 7, 1969
Abbreviation: SA

Ownership
Oak Tree Racing Association

Officers
President: Dr. Jack K. Robbins
Executive Vice President: Sherwood C. Chillingworth
General Manager: Jack McDaniel
Director of Racing: Michael J. Harlow
Racing Secretary: Michael J. Harlow
Secretary: Thomas R. Capehart
Treasurer: Barbara Helm
Director of Operations: Richard Price
Director of Mutuels: Randy Hartzell
Director of Publicity: Vince Bruun
Director of Simulcasting: Aaron Vercruysse
Stewards: Pete Pedersen, Thomas Ward, Jack Williams
Track Announcer: Trevor Denman
Track Photographer: Benoit and Associates
Track Superintendent: Steve Wood
Asst. Racing Secretary: Richard D. Wheeler
Security: Dick Honaker

Racing Dates
2004: September 29-October 31, 26 days
2005: September 28-November 6, 31 days

Attendance
Average Daily Recent Meeting: 9,270, 2004
Highest Single Day Record: 69,155, November 1, 1986
Highest Single Meet Record: 858,652, 1985
Record Daily Average for Single Meet: 28,822, 1982
Highest Single Day Recent Meet: 24,450, October 16, 2004
Total Attendance Recent Meeting: 241,016, 2004

Handle
Average All Sources Recent Meeting: $8,524,715, 2004
Average On-Track Recent Meeting: $1,959,964, 2004

Record Daily Average for Single Meet: $10,237,220, 1998
Single Day On-Track Handle: $17,171,465, October 25, 2003
Single Day All Sources Handle: $120,788,128, October 25, 2003
Record Total All Sources for Single Meet: $327,591,053, 1998
Highest Single Day On-Track Record Recent Meet: $5,393,351.90, October 30, 2004
Highest Single Day Recent Meet: $19,563,395.50, October 30, 2004
Record Total for Single Meet: $169,252,456, 1987
Total All Sources Recent Meeting: $221,642,588, 2004
Total On-Track Recent Meeting: $50,959,066, 2004

Mutuel Records
Highest Win: $269.20, Arcangues, November 6, 1993
Highest Exacta: $3,022.20, September 26, 2001
Highest Trifecta: $52,892.50, September 26, 2001
Highest Daily Double: $5,000, October 13, 1990
Highest Pick 3: $174,331.80, October 18, 1991
Highest Pick 6: $1,010,221.20, October 19, 1994
Highest Other Exotics: $73,093.90, Superfecta, October 15, 2000; $57,062.50, Place Pick All, November 11, 1995
Highest Pick 4: $58,803.30, September 26, 2001
Highest Quinella: $1,949.60, September 26, 2001

Leaders
Career, Leading Jockey by Titles: Laffit Pincay Jr., 6
Career, Leading Owner by Titles: Elmendorf, 3
Career, Leading Trainer by Titles: Robert Frankel, 6
Career, Leading Jockey by Stakes Wins: Chris McCarron, 74
Career, Leading Trainer by Stakes Wins: Charles Whittingham, 68
Career, Leading Jockey by Wins: Laffit Pincay Jr., 671
Career, Leading Trainer by Wins: Robert Frankel, 233
Recent Meeting, Leading Horse: West War, 2, 2004
Recent Meeting, Leading Jockey: Corey Nakatani, 21, 2004
Recent Meeting, Leading Owner: Jerome and Ann Moss, 6, 2004
Recent Meeting, Leading Trainer: Mike Mitchell, 13, 2004

Records
Single Day Jockey Wins: Steve Valdez, 6, October 15, 1973; Darrel McHargue, 6, October 25, 1979; Patrick Valenzuela, 6, October 21, 1988; Martin Pedroza, 6, October 31, 1992

Track Records, Main Dirt
5 furlongs: Zero Henry, :57.78, October 23, 1996
5 1/2 furlongs: Davy Be Good, 1:02.17, November 14, 1993
6 furlongs: Beira, 1:07 4/5, October 13, 1974; Grenzen, 1:07 4/5, October 7, 1978; Hawkin's Special, 1:07 4/5, October 27, 1978
6 1/2 furlongs: Enjoy the Moment, 1:14.15, October 8, 1998
7 furlongs: Ancient Title, 1:20 4/5, October 18, 1972
1 mile: Salud y Pesetas, 1:33 4/5, October 7, 1987
1 1/16 miles: Cajun Prince, 1:40 1/5, October 9, 1982
1 1/8 miles: My Sonny Boy, 1:46, November 3, 1990
1 1/4 miles: King Pellinore, 2:00, November 6, 1976
1 1/2 miles: Whisk Spree, 2:29.17, October 16, 1993

Track Records, Main Turf
1 mile: Urgent Request (Ire), 1:32.44, October 5, 1996
1 1/8 miles: Kostroma (Ire), 1:43.92, October 20, 1991
1 1/4 miles: Double Discount, 1:57 2/5, October 9, 1977
1 1/2 miles: Hawkster, 2:22 4/5, October 14, 1989
Other: a6 1/2 furlongs, El Cielo, November 3, 2001

Principal Races
Yellow Ribbon S. (G1), Clement L. Hirsch Memorial Turf Championship S. (G1), Ancient Title Breeders' Cup H. (G1), Oak Tree Breeders' Cup Mile S. (G2), Goodwood Breeders' Cup H. (G2)

Notable Events
California Cup

Fastest Times of 2004 (Dirt)
2 furlongs: Whatsthenameman, :21.09, April 15, 2004
5 1/2 furlongs: Boston Common, 1:02.35, January 1, 2004

6 furlongs: Amerindio (Arg), 1:07.81, January 2, 2004
6 1/2 furlongs: My Master (Arg), 1:14.58, September 29, 2004
7 furlongs: Unfurl the Flag, 1:20.11, February 21, 2004
1 mile: Buddy Gil, 1:34.73, April 16, 2004
1 1/16 miles: St Averil, 1:41.62, January 17, 2004
1 1/8 miles: Pleasantly Perfect, 1:47.25, January 31, 2004
1 1/4 miles: Southern Image, 2:01.64, March 6, 2004

Fastest Times of 2004 (Turf)
a6 1/2 furlongs: Lennyfromalibu, 1:11.13, January 22, 2004
1 mile: Golden Dragon (GB), 1:32.88, January 22, 2004
1 1/8 miles: Little Ghazi, 1:45.93, March 24, 2004
1 1/4 miles: Star Over the Bay, 1:58.70, October 3, 2004
1 1/2 miles: Meteor Storm (GB), 2:26.03, March 20, 2004
a1 3/4 miles: Meteor Storm (GB), 2:45.98, April 18, 2004

Pleasanton

Location: 4501 Pleasanton Ave., Pleasanton, Ca. 94566
Phone: (925) 426-7600
Fax: (925) 426-7599
Website: www.alamedacountyfair.com
E-Mail: info@alamedacountyfair.com
Year Founded: 1939
Abbreviation: Pln
Number of Stalls: 700
Seating Capacity: 6,808

Officers
Chairman: Billie Sherwood
President: Tony Macchiano
General Manager: Rick K. Pickering
Director of Racing: Rick K. Pickering
Racing Secretary: Rick K. Pickering
Treasurer: Ted Holder
Director of Marketing: April Chase
Director of Mutuels: Brian Wayte
Vice President: Anthony Varni
Director of Publicity: April Chase
Director of Simulcasting: Jeanne Wasserman
Stewards: Pam Berg, Will Meyers
Track Announcer: John McGary
Track Photographer: Photos by Frank
Track Superintendent: Toni Applebee
Chief executive officer: Rick K. Pickering
Asst. Racing Secretary: Linda Anderson

Racing Dates
2004: June 30-July 11, 11 days
2006: June 28-July 9, 11 days
2005: June 29-July 10, 11 days

Track Layout
Main Circumference: 1 mile
Main Track Chute: 2 furlongs and 6 furlongs
Main Width: 60 feet
Main Length of Stretch: 1,085 feet

Attendance
Average Daily Recent Meeting: 4,374, 2004
Total Attendance Recent Meeting: 48,112, 2004

Handle
Average All Sources Recent Meeting: $2,979,668, 2004
Average On-Track Recent Meeting: $572,578, 2004
Single Day On-Track Handle: $908,604, July 6, 2003
Single Day All Sources Handle: $4,586,825, July 3, 2004
Total All Sources Recent Meeting: $32,776,343, 2004
Total On-Track Recent Meeting: $6,298,354, 2004
Highest Single Day Record Recent Meet: $4,586,825, July 3, 2004

Leaders
Recent Meeting, Leading Jockey: Russell Baze, 11, 2004
Recent Meeting, Leading Trainer: Jerry Hollendorfer, 9, 2004

Track Records, Main Dirt
4 1/2 furlongs: French Invader,: 51.20, June 27, 1996
5 furlongs: Wind Water, :56.20, July 4, 2004
5 1/2 furlongs: Boundary Ridge, 1:02, June 29, 1993
6 furlongs: Sloat Blvd, 1:08.09, July 5, 2004
1m 70 yds: Call It, 1:38.01, July 5, 2003
1 1/16 miles: Marwood, 1:40.04, July 5, 2004

Principal Races
Juan Gonzalez Memorial S., Everett Nevin Alameda County Futurity, Sam J. Whiting Memorial H., Alameda County Fillies and Mares H., Alameda H.

Fastest Times of 2004 (Dirt)
4 1/2 furlongs: Scatterman, :52.28, July 1, 2004
5 furlongs: Wind Water, :56.20, July 4, 2004
5 1/2 furlongs: Zadar, 1:02.34, July 11, 2004
6 furlongs: Sloat Blvd, 1:08.09, July 5, 2004
1m 70 yds: Sharp Looking Dude, 1:39.20, July 11, 2004
1 1/16 miles: Marwood, 1:40.04, July 5, 2004

Sacramento

Location: 1600 Exposition Blvd., Sacramento, Ca. 95815-5104
Phone: (916) 263-3279
Fax: (916) 263-3198
Website: www.bigfun.org
E-Mail: delliott@calexpo.com
Year Founded: 1963
Abbreviation: Sac
Number of Stalls: 1,000
Seating Capacity: 7,100

Ownership
State of California

Officers
Chairman: Ed Phillips
General Manager: Norbert Bartosik
Director of Racing: David Elliott
Racing Secretary: Grant Baker
Director of Operations: Kate Snider
Director of Marketing: Sally Ash
Director of Mutuels: George Vidak
Director of Publicity: Alex Traverso
Stewards: Pam Berg, Thomas Ward, Will Meyers
Track Announcer: John McGary
Track Photographer: Vassar Photography
Track Superintendent: Steve Wood

Racing Dates
2004: August 25-September 6, 12 days
2005: August 24-September 5, 12 days

Track Layout
Main Circumference: 1 mile
Main Track Chute: 6 furlongs
Main Track Chute: 1 1/4 miles
Main Length of Stretch: 990 feet

Attendance
Average Daily Recent Meeting: 5,451, 2004
Total Attendance Recent Meeting: 65,414, 2004

Handle
Average All Sources Recent Meeting: $1,636,606, 2004
Average On-Track Recent Meeting: $270,502, 2004
Total All Sources Recent Meeting: $19,639,267, 2004
Total On-Track Recent Meeting: $3,246,023, 2004
Single Day All Sources Handle: $4,223,537, August 23, 2003

Leaders
Recent Meeting, Leading Jockey: Victor Miranda, 15, 2004
Recent Meeting, Leading Trainer: Rene Amescua, 8, 2004

Principal Races
Governor's H., Earlene McCabe Derby

Notable Events
Dachshund Derby

Fastest Times of 2004 (Dirt)
5 1/2 furlongs: U Betcha Joe, 1:02.68, August 29, 2004
6 furlongs: Jet West, 1:08.60, August 29, 2004
1 mile: Beaudazzler, 1:35.80, August 27, 2004
1 1/16 miles: Brisote, 1:42.57, September 4, 2004
1 1/8 miles: Yougottawanna, 1:48.37, August 28, 2004

Santa Anita Park

With the San Bernardino Mountains as a backdrop, an undulating downhill turf course, and an abundance of quality racing, Santa Anita Park symbolizes racing's possibilities. On a big race day, with a sizable crowd in the stands and quality Thoroughbreds on the track, the Arcadia track is one of the world's finest facilities. The story of Santa Anita is told in two parts. The first part is the original track, the dream of early 20th century California entrepreneur E. J. "Lucky" Baldwin. Opened in 1907, the track gave Los Angeles racing fans a tantalizing glimpse of racing as an opulent spectacle. But Baldwin's death two years later and the lack of legal pari-mutuel wagering in California postponed the Santa Anita dream until the 1930s. When pari-mutuel wagering was legalized in 1933, the Los Angeles Turf Club was organized under the leadership of Dr. Charles H. Strub, and it built a $1-million facility near the site of Baldwin's track. Opened in 1934, the track's inaugural 1934-'35 racing season featured two races that immediately had an impact on the national racing calendar, the Santa Anita Handicap and the Santa Anita Derby. Now Grade 1 races, they continue to have an important place on the spring schedule. With a $100,000 purse for its inaugural running, the Big 'Cap immediately became one of America's best-known races. The race and its $1-million purse today draw some of the best handicap runners from around North America. The Santa Anita Derby is one of the top Kentucky Derby (G1) prep races and has been utilized by recent Kentucky Derby winners Silver Charm, Real Quiet, Charismatic, and Giacomo. Legendary jockey Bill Shoemaker rode in his final race at Santa Anita in February 1990. The track hosts the important Oak Tree Racing Association meet each fall. Magna Entertainment Corp. purchased the track in December 1998 for $126-million.

Location: 285 W. Huntington Dr, Arcadia, Ca. 91007-3439
Phone: (626) 574-7223
Fax: (626) 574-6682
Website: www.santaanita.com
E-Mail: sainfo@santaanita.com
Year Founded: 1934
Dates of Inaugural Meeting: December 25, 1934
Abbreviation: SA
Acreage: 320
Number of Stalls: 2,000
Seating Capacity: 26,000

Ownership
Magna Entertainment Corp.

Officers
Chairman: Frank Stronach
President: Ron Charles
General Manager: George Haines
Director of Racing: Michael J. Harlow
Racing Secretary: Rick Hammerle

Secretary: Gary M. Cohn
Treasurer: Barbara Helm
Director of Operations: Richard Price
Director of Finance: Douglas R. Tatters
Director of Marketing: Stuart A. Zanville
Director of Mutuels: Randy Hartzell
Vice President: George Haines
Director of Publicity: Vince Bruun
Director of Sales: Dyan Grealish
Director of Simulcasting: Mary Forney
Stewards: Pete Pedersen, Thomas Ward, Jack Williams
Track Announcer: Trevor Denman
Track Photographer: Benoit and Associates
Track Superintendent: Steve Wood
Asst. Racing Secretary: Richard D. Wheeler
Chief executive officer: Jim McAlpine
Security: Dick Honaker

Racing Dates
2004: December 26, 2003-April 18, 2004, 84 days
2005: December 26, 2004-April 18, 2005, 84 days

Track Layout
Main Circumference: 1 mile
Main Track Chute: 7 furlongs and 1 1/4 miles
Main Width: Homestretch: 85 feet; Backstretch: 80 feet
Main Length of Stretch: 990 feet
Main Turf Circumference: 7 furlongs
Main Turf Chute: a6 1/2 furlongs or a1 3/4 miles

Attendance
Average Daily Recent Meeting: 8,900, 2003/2004; 7,874, 2004/2005
Highest Single Day Record: 85,527, March 3, 1985
Highest Single Meet Record: 2,936,086, 1983/1984
Record Daily Average for Single Meet: 35,247, 1946/1947
Total Attendance Recent Meeting: 747,640, 2003/2004; 677,193, 2004/2005

Handle
Average All Sources Recent Meeting: $9,926,759, 2003/2004; $8,317,029.22, 2004/2005
Average On-Track Recent Meeting: $2,245,199, 2003/2004; $1,327,811.38, 2004/2005
Record Daily Average for Single Meet: $6,176,295, 1986/1987
Single Day All Sources Handle: $25,282,789, April 8, 2000
Highest Single Day Record Recent Meet: $21,975,321, April 3, 2004
Highest Single Day On-Track Record Recent Meet: $5,599,755, April 3, 2004
Total All Sources Recent Meeting: $833,847,722, 2003/2004; $706,947,483.50, 2004/2005
Total On-Track Recent Meeting: $188,596,686, 2003/2004; $112,863,967, 2004/2005

Mutuel Records
Highest Win: $673.40, Playmay, February 4, 1938
Highest Exacta: $1,502.50, February 15, 2002
Lowest Exacta: $1.60, April 1, 2001
Highest Trifecta: $21,771.80, February 6, 1999
Lowest Trifecta: $4.30, April 16, 1999
Highest Daily Double: $4,330, January 31, 2001
Lowest Daily Double: $4.40, April 5, 2002
Highest Pick 3: $73,527.30, February 16, 1997
Lowest Pick 3: $2.00, March 9, 1997
Highest Pick 6: $1,567,984.60, March 3, 2004
Lowest Pick 6: $106.20, March 16, 1986
Highest Other Exotics: $187,651.20, Superfecta, February 21, 1999; $47,393.10, Place Pick All, March 7, 1998
Lowest Other Exotics: $19.20, Superfecta, March 4, 2000; $27.70, Place Pick All, February 14, 2003
Lowest Pick 4: $31.10, March 4, 2001
Highest Quinella: $1,482.80, February 3, 2000
Lowest Quinella: $2.20, March 8, 2003
Highest Stakes Win: $55.60, Debonair Joe, December 26, 2002
Highest Pick 4: $124,199.10, December 27, 2003

Leaders

Career, Leading Jockey by Titles: William Shoemaker, 17
Career, Leading Owner by Titles: Elmendorf, 4; Golden Eagle Farm, 4
Career, Leading Trainer by Titles: Farrell W. Jones, 8; Bob Baffert, 8
Career, Leading Jockey by Stakes Wins: William Shoemaker, 260
Career, Leading Trainer by Stakes Wins: Charles Whittingham, 204
Career, Leading Jockey by Wins: Laffit Pincay Jr., 2,860
Career, Leading Trainer by Wins: Charles Whittingham, 869

Records

Single Day Jockey Wins: Laffit Pincay Jr., 7, March 14, 1987
Single Day Trainer Wins: Clyde Van Dusen, 4, February 6, 1941; Farrell Jones, 4, January 5, 1962; M. E. "Buster" Millerick, 4, December 29, 1965; Charles Whittingham, 4, February 9, 1967; Bobby Frankel, 4, January 3, 1976; Bobby Frankel, 4, March 26, 1981
Single Meet, Leading Jockey by Wins: Laffit Pincay Jr., 138, 1970/1971
Single Meet, Leading Trainer by Wins: Gary Jones, 47, 1975/1976; Bob Baffert, 47, 1997/1998

Track Records, Main Dirt

4 furlongs: Valiant Pete, :44 1/5, April 20, 1991
4 1/2 furlongs: Willy Float, :51 2/5, March 23, 1972
5 furlongs: Zero Henry, :57.78, October 23, 1996
5 1/2 furlongs: Kona Gold, 1:01.74, January 3, 1999
6 furlongs: Sunny Blossom, 1:07 1/5, December 30, 1989
6 1/2 furlongs: Son of a Pistol, 1:13.71, April 4, 1998
7 furlongs: Spectacular Bid, 1:20, January 5, 1980
1 mile: Ruhlmann, 1:33 2/5, March 5, 1989
1 1/16 miles: Efervescente (Arg), 1:39.18, January 6, 1993
1 1/8 miles: Star Spangled, 1:45 4/5, March 24, 1979
1 1/4 miles: Spectacular Bid, 1:57 4/5, February 3, 1980
1 3/8 miles: Be Faithful, 2:15 1/5, February 9, 1946
1 1/2 miles: Queen's Hustler, 2:27 1/5, February 19, 1973
1 5/8 miles: Ace Admiral, 2:39 4/5, July 23, 1949
1 3/4 miles: *Noor, 2:52 4/5, March 4, 1950
2 miles: Durango, 3:26 1/5, February 2, 1935; Fuego, 3:26 1/5, June 30, 1945; Jimmy John, 3:26 1/5, March 9, 1946
Other: 2 furlongs, Beautiful Moment, :21, April 3, 1996; 3 furlongs, King Rhymer, :32, February 27, 1947; 2 1/4 miles, English Harry, 3:55 3/5, February 16, 1940; 2 1/2 miles, Big Ed, 4:22, February 23, 1940; 3 miles, English Harry, 5:20 1/5, March 1, 1940

Track Records, Main Turf

1 mile: Atticus, 1:31.89, March 1, 1997
1 1/8 miles: Kostroma (Ire), 1:43.92, October 20, 1991
1 1/4 miles: Double Discount, 1:57 2/5, October 9, 1977; Bequest, 1:57.50, March 31, 1991
1 1/2 miles: Hawkster, 2:22 4/5, October 14, 1989
Other: a6 1/2 furlongs, Lennyfromalibu, 1:11.13, January 22, 2004; a1 1/2 miles, *Practicante, 2:26 2/5, February 21, 1972; a1 3/4 miles, Bienamado, 2:42.96, April 14, 2001

Principal Races

Santa Anita H. (G1), Santa Anita Derby (G1), Santa Anita Oaks (G1), Santa Margarita H. (G1), Frank E. Kilroe Mile H. (G1)

Notable Events

Sunshine Millions

Fastest Times of 2004 (Dirt)

2 furlongs: Whatsthenameman, :21.09, April 15, 2004
5 1/2 furlongs: Boston Common, 1:02.35, January 1, 2004
6 furlongs: Amerindio (Arg), 1:07.81, January 2, 2004
6 1/2 furlongs: My Master (Arg), 1:14.58, September 29, 2004
7 furlongs: Unfurl the Flag, 1:20.11, February 21, 2004
1 mile: Buddy Gil, 1:34.73, April 16, 2004
1 1/16 miles: St Averil, 1:41.62, January 17, 2004
1 1/8 miles: Pleasantly Perfect, 1:47.25, January 31, 2004
1 1/4 miles: Southern Image, 2:01.64, March 6, 2004

Fastest Times of 2004 (Turf)

a6 1/2 furlongs: Lennyfromalibu, 1:11.13, January 22, 2004
1 mile: Golden Dragon (GB), 1:32.88, January 22, 2004
1 1/8 miles: Little Ghazi, 1:45.93, March 24, 2004
1 1/4 miles: Star Over the Bay, 1:58.70, October 3, 2004
1 1/2 miles: Meteor Storm (GB), 2:26.03, March 20, 2004
a1 3/4 miles: Meteor Storm (GB), 2:45.98, April 18, 2004

Santa Rosa

Location: 1350 Bennett Valley Rd., Santa Rosa, Ca. 95403
Phone: (707) 545-4200
Phone: (800) 454-7223
Fax: (707) 573-9342
Website: www.sonomacountyfair.com
E-Mail: publicity@sonomacountyfair.com
Year Founded: 1936
Abbreviation: SR
Number of Stalls: 1,022

Officers

President: Dave Lewers
General Manager: G. James Moore
Racing Secretary: C. Gregory Brent Jr.
Secretary: Annette O'Kelley
Treasurer: Cam Parry
Director of Mutuels: George Vidak
Vice President: John Serres
Director of Publicity: Cammie Noah
Stewards: Darrel McHargue, Grant Baker, Pam Berg
Track Announcer: Vic Stauffer
Track Superintendent: Steve Wood

Racing Dates

2004: July 28-August 9, 12 days
2005: July 27-August 8, 12 days

Track Layout

Main Circumference: 1 mile
Main Track Chute: 6 furlongs and 1 1/4 miles
Main Length of Stretch: 1,145.8 feet

Attendance

Average Daily Recent Meeting: 5,296, 2004
Total Attendance Recent Meeting: 63,556, 2004

Handle

Average All Sources Recent Meeting: $3,079,422, 2004
Average On-Track Recent Meeting: $499,904, 2004
Total All Sources Recent Meeting: $36,953,006, 2004
Total On-Track Recent Meeting: $5,998,847, 2004
Single Day All Sources Handle: $4,128,001, August 2, 2003

Leaders

Recent Meeting, Leading Jockey: Russell Baze, 15, 2004
Recent Meeting, Leading Trainer: Jerry Hollendorfer, 8, 2004

Principal Races

Joseph T. Grace H., Ernest Finley H., Luther Burbank H., James F. Lyttle S., Cavonnier Juvenile S., Elie Destruel S.

Fastest Times of 2004 (Dirt)

4 1/2 furlongs: Solicitor, :51.14, August 5, 2004
5 furlongs: Crisane, :57.68, August 4, 2004
5 1/2 furlongs: Welcome Aboard, 1:02.78, August 4, 2004
6 furlongs: Halo Cat, 1:08.10, July 31, 2004
1 mile: Starspell, 1:35.56, July 31, 2004
1 1/16 miles: Calkins Road, 1:41.29, August 7, 2004

Stockton

Location: 1658 S. Airport Way, Stockton, Ca. 95206
Phone: (209) 466-5041
Fax: (209) 466-5739
Website: www.sanjoaquinfair.com

E-Mail: fun@sanjoaquinfair.com
Year Founded: 1933
Dates of Inaugural Meeting: August 1934
Abbreviation: Stk
Number of Stalls: 756
Seating Capacity: 5,660

Officers

President: Greg O'Leary
General Manager: Forrest J. White
Director of Racing: Forrest J. White
Racing Secretary: Robert Moreno
Director of Operations: Roger Huber
Director of Marketing: Lea Isetti
Director of Mutuels: George Vidak
Vice President: Wayne Watanabe
Director of Publicity: Lea Isetti
Stewards: Grant Baker, Pam Berg, Will Meyers
Track Announcer: John McGary
Track Photographer: Photo by Frank
Track Superintendent: Steve Wood

Racing Dates

2004: June 16-June 27, 10 days
2005: June 15-June 26, 10 days
2006: June 14-June 25, 10 days

Track Layout

Main Circumference: 1 mile
Main Track Chute: 6 furlongs and 1 1/4 miles
Main Width: 80 feet
Main Length of Stretch: 1,003 feet

Attendance

Average Daily Recent Meeting: 4,514, 2004
Total Attendance Recent Meeting: 45,145, 2004

Handle

Average All Sources Recent Meeting: $1,638,640, 2004
Average On-Track Recent Meeting: $214,939, 2004
Total All Sources Recent Meeting: $16,386,402, 2004
Total On-Track Recent Meeting: $2,149,393, 2004
Highest Single Day Record Recent Meet: $3,207,475, June 27, 2004

Leaders

Recent Meeting, Leading Jockey: Ken Tohill, 14, 2004
Recent Meeting, Leading Trainer: Barry Holmes, 5, 2004

Track Records, Main Dirt

5 furlongs: Shining Prince, :55.80, June 26, 1994
5 1/2 furlongs: Whirley Side, 1:02.15, June 16, 2004
6 furlongs: Lynn's Notebook, 1:07.80, June 25, 1995
1 mile: Flying Cuantal, 1:33.40, June 15, 1997
1 1/16 miles: Athenia Green (GB), 1:40.40, June 28, 1992
1 1/8 miles: Episodic, 1:49.20, June 27, 1993
1 1/4 miles: Ali Kato, 2:01 3/5, August 17, 1986

Fastest Times of 2004 (Dirt)

4 1/2 furlongs: Ex Federali, :50.67, June 24, 2004
5 furlongs: Gray Mike, :57.70, June 16, 2004
5 1/2 furlongs: Whirley Side, 1:02.15, June 16, 2004
6 furlongs: Strategically, 1:09.31, June 20, 2004
1 mile: Givemethreedimes, 1:36.01, June 24, 2004

Vallejo

Location: 900 Fairgrounds Dr., Vallejo, Ca. 94589
Phone: (707) 644-4401
Fax: (707) 642-7947
Website: www.scfair.com
E-Mail: pskelton@scfair.org
Year Founded: 1950
Dates of Inaugural Meeting: June 16, 1951
Abbreviation: Sol
Number of Stalls: 1,004
Seating Capacity: 6,500

Ownership

County of Solano

Officers

Chairman: Raymond Simonds
President: Michael Freese
General Manager: Joe Barkett
Director of Racing: Joe Barkett
Racing Secretary: Gregory Brent
Director of Operations: Stephan Hales
Director of Mutuels: George Vidak
Vice President: William Luiz
Director of Publicity: Pam Hamilton
Stewards: Pam Berg, Darrel McHargue, Will Meyers
Track Announcer: John McGary
Track Photographer: Photos by Frank
Track Superintendent: Trackmasters Inc.
Asst. Racing Secretary: Linda Anderson

Racing Dates

2004: July 14-July 26, 11 days
2005: July 13-July 25, 11 days

Track Layout

Main Circumference: 7 furlongs
Main Track Chute: 6 furlongs
Main Length of Stretch: 1,085 feet

Attendance

Average Daily Recent Meeting: 1,475, 2004
Highest Single Day Record: 18,127, June 14, 1980
Total Attendance Recent Meeting: 16,229, 2004

Handle

Average All Sources Recent Meeting: $2,729,403, 2004
Total All Sources Recent Meeting: $30,023,430, 2004

Leaders

Recent Meeting, Leading Jockey: Russell Baze, 11, 2004
Recent Meeting, Leading Trainer: Jerry Hollendorfer, 6, 2004

Track Records, Main Dirt

4 1/2 furlongs: Genuine Sparky, :51.38, July 20, 2002
5 furlongs: One Bad Shark, :56.60, July 14, 2002
5 1/2 furlongs: Ridgewood High, 1:02 1/5, July 18, 1982
6 furlongs: Salta's Pride, 1:07.80, July 13, 1996
1 mile: Kamalii King, 1:34 4/5, July 18, 1982
1 1/16 miles: Hoedown's Day, 1:39 4/5, July 24, 1983
1 1/8 miles: Baffi's Eagle, 1:48 2/5, July 17, 1984
1 1/4 miles: Super Sonet, 2:03 2/5, June 20, 1974
1 3/8 miles: Rain Storm, 2:15 4/5, June 22, 1973
1 1/2 miles: Always King, 2:32 3/5, June 24, 1978

Principal Races

Solano County Juvenile Filly S., Vacaville H., Fairfield S.

Fastest Times of 2004 (Dirt)

4 1/2 furlongs: Polish Magic, :51.45, July 26, 2004
5 furlongs: High Zone, :58.12, July 17, 2004
5 1/2 furlongs: Don't Know Diddley, 1:04.06, July 26, 2004
6 furlongs: Jagged Ice, 1:09.20, July 24, 2004
1 mile: Snoopy Cat, 1:37.68, July 23, 2004
1 1/16 miles: Uncle Brother, 1:45.67, July 25, 2004
1 1/8 miles: Dandi Candi, 1:52.96, July 24, 2004

Colorado

Arapahoe Park

    One of racing's quiet survivors, Denver-area Arapahoe Park has survived a disastrous launch, increased gambling competition, and disputes with horsemen to remain a summer racing fixture in the Rocky Mountains region. The track opened in the mid-1980s, replacing longtime Denver track Centennial Park. But its location southeast of Denver was far from any interstate highways; interest in the track was negligible, and it was closed for several years after its opening. The track reopened in the early 1990s but has struggled to develop a fan base amid competition from a state lottery and Native American casinos, which were legalized in the state in the early '90s. A dispute between the track's former owner, Wembley USA, and horsemen over racing dates nearly forced the cancellation of the 2000 race meet. Arapahoe and other Wembley properties were sold to BLB Investors for $455-million in 2005.

Location: 26000 E. Quincy Ave., Aurora, Co. 80016-2026
Phone: (303) 690-2400
Fax: (303) 690-6730
Website: *www.wembleyco.com*
E-Mail: Arapahoe@Wembleyusa.com
Dates of Inaugural Meeting: May 24, 1984
Abbreviation: Arp
Acreage: 297
Number of Stalls: 1,500
Seating Capacity: 2,000

Ownership
BLB Investors

Officers
Chairman: Ty Howard
President: Ty Howard
General Manager: Bruce Seymore
Director of Racing: Bill Powers
Racing Secretary: Bill Powers
Director of Marketing: Jessica Costello
Director of Mutuels: Kathy Keeley
Director of Simulcasting: Bill Powers
Stewards: Rick Evans, Joe Gibson
Track Announcer: Bill Rogan
Track Superintendent: Paul Guerrieri

Racing Dates
2004: July 3-September 6, 39 days
2005: June 10-August 28, 37 days

Track Layout
Main Circumference: 1 mile
Main Track Chute: 7 furlongs and 1 1/4 miles
Main Width: 90 feet
Main Length of Stretch: 1,029 feet

Attendance
Average Daily Recent Meeting: 1,055, 2004
Total Attendance Recent Meeting: 39,062, 2004

Handle
Average All Sources Recent Meeting: $85,139, 2004
Average On-Track Recent Meeting: $37,878, 2004
Single Day All Sources Handle: $361,000, August 5, 2003
Total All Sources Recent Meeting: $5,162,969, 2004
Total On-Track Recent Meeting: $1,401,489, 2004

Leaders
Recent Meeting, Leading Jockey: Travis Wales, 40, 2004
Recent Meeting, Leading Trainer: Jon G. Arnett, 31, 2004

Track Records, Main Dirt
4 furlongs: Et Tu Brutus, :44.60, July 26, 2004
4 1/2 furlongs: V G's Catch, :50.40, June 23, 2002; Hugs Legacy, :50.40, July 19, 2004
5 furlongs: NYCity, :56, July 13, 2002
5 1/2 furlongs: Choppers Passion, 1:02.20, June 22, 2001; Ladysgottheooks, 1:02.20, September 4, 2004
6 furlongs: Absolutely True, 1:08.20, July 11, 2004
6 1/2 furlongs: Pray for Bridge, 1:18.60, August 25, 1995
7 furlongs: Daring Pegasus, 1:21.20, July 4, 2003
1 mile: Honor Bright, 1:35.20, August 7, 1993
1m 70 yds: Naskra's Advocate, 1:38.20, July 23, 1993
1 1/16 miles: Run At Night, 1:42.20, August 14, 2004
1 1/8 miles: Glaring, 1:50.20, August 13, 1995

1 1/4 miles: Builder's Boy, 2:05.40, June 26, 1992
1 1/2 miles: Calgary Classic, 2:33.20, July 24, 1993
1 3/4 miles: Read My Mind, 3:02, August 9, 1992
2 miles: Little Reeves, 3:28.40, August 27, 1994

Principal Races
Gold Rush Futurity, Colorado Derby, Inaugural S., Arapahoe Park Sprint H., Molly Brown H.

Fastest Times of 2004 (Dirt)
4 furlongs: Et Tu Brutus, :44.60, July 26, 2004
4 1/2 furlongs: Hugs Legacy, :50.40, July 19, 2004
5 furlongs: Lukfata Louis, :56.60, August 16, 2004
5 1/2 furlongs: Ladysgottheooks, 1:02.20, September 4, 2004
6 furlongs: Absolutely True, 1:08.20, July 11, 2004
7 furlongs: Personal Beau, 1:21.40, August 1, 2004
1 mile: All American Chris, 1:36.00, July 31, 2004
1m 70 yds: Vannacide, 1:42.80, August 7, 2004
1 1/16 miles: Run At Night, 1:42.20, August 14, 2004
1 1/8 miles: Personal Beau, 1:50.80, August 29, 2004
1 1/2 miles: Sneffels Street, 2:35.60, September 6, 2004

Delaware

Delaware Park

Competition from racetracks in neighboring Pennsylvania, Maryland, and New Jersey forced the closure of historic Delaware Park in Stanton in September 1982. In late 1983, Maryland developer William Rickman Sr. acquired Delaware Park in partnership with Maryland horseman William Christmas, and the track ran abbreviated meets in the spring and fall of '84. Rickman's son, William Rickman Jr., managed track operations and in 1994 helped to secure state approval for installing slot machines at the track. Delaware's slots facility opened in December 1995, and revenues from the slots have more than tripled purses. The Wilmington-area track was designed by banker and horseman William duPont Jr. and became a haven for summer racing fans throughout the Mid-Atlantic region. The track's richest race, the Delaware Handicap (G2), debuted in 1937 as the New Castle Handicap and has been won by some of the sport's leading fillies and mares.

Location: 777 Delaware Park Blvd., Wilmington, De. 19804
Phone: (302) 994-2521
Fax: (302) 994-3567
Website: *www.delpark.com*
E-Mail: programs@delawarepark.com
Year Founded: 1937
Abbreviation: Del

Ownership
William Rickman

Officers
Chairman: William M. Rickman
President: William M. Rickman Jr.
Racing Secretary: Sam Abbey
Director of Operations: Andrew Gentile
Director of Communications: Mike McGinnis
Director of Marketing: Pam Cunningham
Director of Mutuels: Scott Loomis
Director of Publicity: Jennifer Oberle
Horsemen's Liaison: Joe'Lyn Rigione
Stewards: Dennis Lima, Fritz Burkhardt, Jack Houghton Jr.
Track Announcer: John Curran
Track Photographer: Hoofprints Inc.
Track Superintendent: Bob D. Beaubien
Asst. Racing Secretary: Chris Camac
Security: Kathy Harer
Horsemen's Bookkeeper: Cindy Houghton

Racing Dates
2004: April 24-November 7, 134 days
2005: April 30-November 13, 135 days

Track Layout
Main Circumference: 1 mile
Main Track Chute: 6 furlongs and 1 1/4 miles
Main Width: 100 feet
Main Length of Stretch: 995 feet
Main Turf Circumference: 7 furlongs

Attendance
Average Daily Recent Meeting: 1,465, 2004
Total Attendance Recent Meeting: 196,312, 2004

Handle
Average All Sources Recent Meeting: $675,986, 2004
Average On-Track Recent Meeting: $136,071, 2004
Single Day All Sources Handle: $1,131,434, October 30, 2004
Total All Sources Recent Meeting: $90,582,118, 2004
Total On-Track Recent Meeting: $18,233,483, 2004

Leaders
Recent Meeting, Leading Horse: Regal Watch, 6, 2004
Recent Meeting, Leading Jockey: Ramon Dominguez, 198, 2004
Recent Meeting, Leading Owner: Michael Gill, 40, 2004
Recent Meeting, Leading Trainer: Scott Lake, 96, 2004

Track Records, Main Dirt
4 1/2 furlongs: Erlton, :51.80, May 5, 1998
5 furlongs: Milky Way Gal, :56.20, July 29, 1989
5 1/2 furlongs: Dontcloseyoureyes, 1:03, October 14, 1990
6 furlongs: Damitrius, 1:08.20, September 2, 1980
1 mile: Ashlar, 1:35.20, June 25, 1960
1m 70 yds: Distinct Vision, 1:39.20, August 25, 2003
1 1/16 miles: Lies of Omission, 1:41.20, July 4, 1998
1 1/8 miles: Victoria Park, 1:47.40, June 18, 1960
1 3/16 miles: Gold Star Deputy, 1:56.72, October 31, 1999
1 1/4 miles: Coup de Fusil, 1:59.80, July 25, 1987
1 1/2 miles: Bam, 2:31, June 26, 1948
1 5/8 miles: Flying Restina Run, 2:45.40, September 4, 2000
1 3/4 miles: Cer Vantes, 2:56.40, June 27, 1951
2 miles: Dixies Act, 3:29.40, August 10, 1975
Other: 2 furlongs, Glitter River, :21.60, September 5, 2000; 2m 70 yds, Wolfe Tone, 3:34, November 7, 1993; 2 1/4 miles, Sanguine Sword, 3:58.60, July 2, 1986

Track Records, Main Turf
5 furlongs: Mujado, :56.16, July 27, 2002
1 mile: Hanover Hollywood, 1:34.74, August 3, 2002
1 1/16 miles: Charabanc, 1:40.20, July 20, 1963
1 1/8 miles: Foufa's Warrior, 1:47.44, July 20, 2003
1 3/8 miles: Cool Prince, 2:12.40, July 3, 1965
1 1/2 miles: Revved Up, 2:26.46, July 20, 2003
2 miles: Verdance, 3:24.40, September 21, 1986
Other: 1 7/8 miles, El Moro, 3:11.80, July 22, 1963; 2 3/8 miles, Lively London, 4:09, July 25, 1986; 2 7/8 miles, Call Louis, 5:08.20, August 24, 1986

Principal Races
Delaware H. (G2), Delaware Oaks (G2), Leonard Richards S. (G3), Kent Breeders' Cup (G3), Endine H. (G3)

Notable Events
Delaware Handicap Festival of Racing, Owners Day

Fastest Times of 2004 (Dirt)
4 1/2 furlongs: Lady Glade, :52.56, May 24, 2004
5 furlongs: Curb, :57.87, September 19, 2004
5 1/2 furlongs: Procreate, 1:03.56, September 4, 2004
6 furlongs: Toscani, 1:08.99, June 15, 2004
1 mile: Max Forever, 1:36.62, May 8, 2004
1m 70 yds: Pay the Preacher, 1:41.19, July 20, 2004
1 1/16 miles: Country Be Gold, 1:43.00, August 21, 2004
1 1/8 miles: Loving (Brz), 1:48.43, September 11, 2004
1 3/16 miles: Lyracist, 1:57.73, October 2, 2004
1 1/4 miles: Loving (Brz), 2:02.74, May 18, 2004
1 1/2 miles: Chopper Won, 2:35.73, July 18, 2004

Fastest Times of 2004 (Turf)
5 furlongs: Satan's Code, :56.26, September 13, 2004
a5 furlongs: Tight Spin, :57.17, September 27, 2004
1 mile: Executive Mansion, 1:36.69, September 8, 2004
a1 miles: Garden Dance, 1:39.36, August 23, 2004
1 1/16 miles: Natalie Beach (Arg), 1:41.73, September 13, 2004
a1 1/16 miles: Skip n' Jump, 1:43.48, July 4, 2004
1 1/8 miles: Sportscaster, 1:48.90, September 12, 2004
a1 1/8 miles: Nationalistic (Ire), 1:51.88, September 25, 2004
1 3/8 miles: Alternate, 2:20.07, July 17, 2004

Florida

Calder Race Course

Calder Race Course, which offers racing from late April through early January, is located in Miami next to Pro Player Stadium, home of the National Football League's Miami Dolphins. Built by real-estate businessman Stephen A. Calder, the track was granted summer racing dates for 1970. Because the track was under construction, those dates were run at Tropical Park. Calder officially opened on May 6, 1971, debuting an all-weather synthetic track surface designed by 3M that remained in place until 1992. In 1972, Tropical Park closed and began holding its meet at Calder; the last several weeks of each year's season are known as the Tropical Park meet. From 1980-'84, Calder underwent $10.5-million in improvements. In 1988, Thoroughbred owner-breeder Bertram R. Firestone bought Calder. Three years later, Kawasaki Leasing Inc. assumed control of the track. The track underwent a $1-million renovation of its first floor, and in 1995 it added full-card simulcasting. In 1999, Churchill Downs Inc. bought Calder for approximately $86-million. Today, Calder features three racing events: the Florida Stallion Stakes, a series of races for offspring of Florida stallions; Festival of the Sun, a $1.6-million day of racing highlighted by the finals of the Florida Stallion Stakes series; and Summit of Speed, sprint stakes races with combined purses totaling $1.9-million. Calder opened a card club in May 2004.

Location: 21001 N W 27th Ave., Miami, Fl. 33056
Phone: (305) 625-1311
Fax: (305) 620-2569
Website: *www.calderracecourse.com*
E-Mail: customerservice@calderracecourse.com
Year Founded: 1971
Dates of Inaugural Meeting: May 6, 1971
Abbreviation: Crc
Acreage: 220
Number of Stalls: 1,800
Seating Capacity: 15,000

Ownership
Churchill Downs Inc.

Officers
Chairman: Thomas H. Meeker
President: C. Kenneth Dunn
General Manager: Michael Abes
Director of Racing: Robert D. Umphrey
Racing Secretary: Robert D. Umphrey
Secretary: Rebecca C. Reed
Treasurer: Michael Abes
Director of Admissions: Bill Keers
Director of Marketing: Michael Cronin
Director of Mutuels: Edward Mackie Sr.
Vice President: Michael Cronin, Michael Abes
Director of Publicity: Michele Blanco

Director of Simulcasting: Diane Stoess
Stewards: Charles Camac, Jeffrey Noe, Kevin Sheen
Track Announcer: Bobby Neuman
Track Photographer: Jim Lisa
Track Superintendent: Steve Cross
Director of Security: Tony Otero
Horsemen's Bookkeeper: Nelly Torrente

Racing Dates
2004: April 26-October 23, 123 days
2005: April 25-October 16, 122 days

Track Layout
Main Circumference: 1 mile
Main Track Chute: 7 furlongs and 1 1/4 miles
Main Width: Homestretch: 80 feet; Backstretch: 75 feet
Main Length of Stretch: 990 feet
Main Turf Circumference: 7 furlongs
Main Turf Chute: 1 1/8 miles
Main Turf Width: 67 feet
Main Turf Length of Stretch: 986 feet

Attendance
Average Daily Recent Meeting: 4,429, 2004
Highest Single Day Record: 23,103, May 4, 1985
Record Daily Average for Single Meet: 9,401, 1976
Highest Single Meet Record: 1,113,017, 1975
Total Attendance Recent Meeting: 544,745, 2004
Lowest single meet record: 544,745, 2004

Handle
Average All Sources Recent Meeting: $3,017,450, 2004
Average On-Track Recent Meeting: $385,675, 2004
Record Daily Average for Single Meet: $1,206,739, 1986
Single Day On-Track Handle: $2,954,162, May 7, 1988
Single Day All Sources Handle: $10,843,994, July 10, 2004
Total All Sources Recent Meeting: $371,146,341, 2004
Total On-Track Recent Meeting: $47,438,009, 2004
Highest Single Day Recent Meet: $10,843,994, July 10, 2004

Mutuel Records
Highest Win: $345.40, Lou Glory, September 12, 1991
Lowest Win: $2.10, Isle O'Style, June 12, 1974; $2.10, June 16, 2001
Highest Exacta: $31,133.20, November 3, 1972
Lowest Exacta: $3.40, August 16, 1989
Highest Trifecta: $58,432.40, October 25, 1986
Lowest Trifecta: $10.40, July 31, 1994
Highest Daily Double: $2,671, July 2, 1976
Lowest Daily Double: $3.20, September 16, 1992
Highest Pick 3: $39,548.80, April 26, 2004
Lowest Pick 3: $9, September 12, 2000
Highest Other Exotics: $74,622, Superfecta, October 26, 1996
Lowest Other Exotics: $33.40, Superfecta, August 7, 1995
Highest Pick 4: $10,846.70, April 26, 2004
Lowest Pick 4: $59.10, October 12, 2002

Leaders
Career, Leading Jockey by Titles: Eibar Coa, 4
Career, Leading Trainer by Titles: William P. White, 9
Recent Meeting, Leading Jockey: Eddie Castro, 154, 2004
Recent Meeting, Leading Owner: Michael Sherman, 39, 2004
Recent Meeting, Leading Trainer: William P. White, 48, 2004
Career, Leading Jockey by Stakes Wins: Gene St. Leon, 73
Career, Leading Trainer by Stakes Wins: Frank Gomez, 89
Career, Leading Jockey by Wins: Gene St. Leon, 1,310
Career, Leading Trainer by Wins: Emanuel Tortora, 977

Records
Single Day Jockey Wins: George Gomez, 6, May 12, 1977; Walter Guerra, 6, October 3, 1979; Rene Douglas, 6, July 15, 1995; Eibar Coa, 6, September 7, 1998
Single Day Trainer Wins: Arnold N. Winick, 5, September 16, 1972; Stanley Hough, 5, May 12, 1977
Single Meet, Leading Jockey by Wins: Walter Guerra, 193, 1979
Single Meet, Leading Trainer by Wins: Stanley Hough, 110, 1977

Track Records, Main Dirt
4 furlongs: Diamond Studs, :46.21, July 14, 2001
4 1/2 furlongs: Gold Phantom, :51.86, September 16, 2001
5 furlongs: Honest, :57.61, July 1, 1996
5 1/2 furlongs: Bernard's Candy, 1:04.39, August 9, 2002
6 furlongs: Forty One Carats, 1:08.95, October 7, 2000
6 1/2 furlongs: Tour of the Cat, 1:15.99, August 17, 2002
7 furlongs: Constant Escort, 1:21.82, September 28, 1996
1 mile: High Ideal, 1:36.25, September 15, 2001
1m 70 yds: Halo's Image, 1:41.78, October 31, 1995
1 1/16 miles: Castlebrook, 1:42.55, September 15, 2001
1 1/8 miles: Jumping Hill, 1:50, December 30, 1978
1 3/16 miles: Arctic Honeymoon, 1:59 3/5, January 3, 1987
1 1/4 miles: Wicapi, 2:05.08, June 24, 1996
1 1/2 miles: Lead'm Home, 2:32 3/5, December 31, 1977
1 5/8 miles: Timberlea Tune, 2:50 1/5, October 16, 1971
1 3/4 miles: *Detective II, 3:03 1/5, October 23, 1971
2 miles: *Detective II, 3:30 1/5, November 11, 1971
Other: 2 furlongs, Baby Shark, :20.81, July 13, 2002

Track Records, Main Turf
5 furlongs: Whenthedoveflies, :54.78, May 23, 2004
7 furlongs: Carterista, 1:22.36, June 19, 1993
7 1/2 furlongs: Court Lark, 1:26.54, July 16, 1994
1 mile: Dillonmyboy, 1:33.66, October 30, 2000
1 1/16 miles: He's Crafty, 1:39.27, December 28, 2004
1 1/8 miles: The Vid, 1:44.99, November 25, 1995
1 3/8 miles: King's Design, 2:13.18, July 23, 1999
1 1/2 miles: Flag Down, 2:24.11, December 16, 1995
2 miles: Skate On Thin Ice, 3:21.89, January 2, 1996

Principal Races
Princess Rooney H. (G2), Smile Sprint H. (G3), Calder Derby (G3), Miami Mile Breeders' Cup H. (G3), Florida Stallion Stakes Series

Notable Events
Summit of Speed, Festival of the Sun, Juvenile Showcase

Fastest Times of 2004 (Dirt)
2 furlongs: Pembroke Hall, :21.65, July 10, 2004
4 1/2 furlongs: Lucky Frolic, :52.27, August 21, 2004
5 furlongs: Paradise Dancer, :58.06, November 25, 2004
5 1/2 furlongs: All Hail Stormy, 1:04.50, December 27, 2004
6 furlongs: Weigelia, 1:09.64, May 9, 2004
6 1/2 furlongs: Iron Boy, 1:17.18, December 18, 2004
7 furlongs: Medallist, 1:22.62, December 18, 2004
1 mile: Kristine's King, 1:38.28, June 7, 2004
1m 70 yds: Cin Cin, 1:46.30, October 2, 2004
1 1/16 miles: Island Skipper, 1:45.46, July 9, 2004
1 1/8 miles: Pies Prospect, 1:50.74, December 18, 2004
1 1/4 miles: Thunder Squall, 2:10.37, June 28, 2004
1 1/2 miles: Dajudge, 2:40.55, June 5, 2004

Fastest Times of 2004 (Turf)
5 furlongs: Whenthedoveflies, :54.78, May 23, 2004
7 1/2 furlongs: Winter Ghost, 1:27.89, December 16, 2004
1 mile: Romolo's Fritzi, 1:34.18, July 11, 2004
1 1/16 miles: He's Crafty, 1:39.27, December 28, 2004
1 1/8 miles: Host (Chi), 1:45.74, December 4, 2004
1 3/8 miles: Iowa's Image, 2:24.53, July 19, 2004
1 1/2 miles: Dreadnaught, 2:26.60, December 18, 2004

Gulfstream Park

Since the 1940s, Gulfstream Park, located north of Miami in Hallandale, Florida, has been a favorite winter destination for horsemen and annually offers high-quality winter racing. Gulfstream opened in February 1939 but went bankrupt and closed after four days of racing. In 1944, James Donn Sr., who owned a local floral shop and was a creditor of the track, reopened Gulfstream. In 1952, the Florida Derby (now G1) debuted and became a major stop on the road to the Kentucky Derby (G1). Ten winners of the race, including Northern Dancer, Unbridled, Thunder Gulch, and Monarchos, went on to win the Kentucky Derby. Gulfstream in 1989 held the first of the track's three Breeders' Cup championship days. In 1999, Frank Stronach-led Magna Entertainment Corp. purchased Gulfstream for $95-million. In 2003, Magna opened Palm Meadows Training Center, a 304-acre training facility located near Boynton Beach, and began a rebuilding of the track itself in 2004. Voters in Broward County, where Gulfstream is located, authorized slot machines at the track in 2005.

Location: 901 S Federal Hwy, Hallandale Beach, Fl. 33009-7199
Phone: (954) 454-7000
Phone: (800) 771-TURF
Fax: (954) 457-6357
Website: www.gulfstreampark.com
Year Founded: 1944
Dates of Inaugural Meeting: February 1-4, 1939
Abbreviation: GP
Acreage: 256
Number of Stalls: 1,454
Seating Capacity: 20,300

Ownership
Magna Entertainment Corp.

Officers
Chairman: Frank Stronach
President: Scott Savin
General Manager: Scott Savin
Director of Racing: David F. Bailey
Racing Secretary: David F. Bailey
Director of Operations: Dennis Testa
Director of Admissions: David Lang
Director of Communications: Joe Tanenbaum
Director of Finance: Richard Odum
Director of Marketing: Mike Tanner
Director of Mutuels: Edward Mackie
Director of Simulcasting: Mike Tanner
Horsemen's Liaison: Raina Chingos-Gunderson
Stewards: Charles Camac, Jeffrey Noe, Walter Blum
Track Announcer: Vic Stauffer
Track Photographer: Equi-Photo/Bill Denver
Track Superintendent: John Grillon
Security: Rick Buhrmaster

Racing Dates
2004: January 3-April 25, 92 days
2005: January 3-April 24, 86 days

Track Layout
Main Circumference: 1 mile
Main Track Chute: 3 furlongs
Main Track Chute: 7 furlongs
Main Width: 80 feet
Main Length of Stretch: 952 feet, 2 inches
Main Turf Circumference: 7 furlongs
Main Turf Chute: 1 1/8 miles
Main Turf Width: 70 feet
Main Turf Length of Stretch: 921 feet
Training Track: Palm Meadows

Attendance
Average Daily Recent Meeting: 8,574, 2004
Highest Single Day Record: 45,124, November 6, 1999
Highest Single Meet Record: 1,096,404, 1991
Record Daily Average for Single Meet: 15,528, 1979
Total Attendance Recent Meeting: 780,235, 2004

Handle
Average All Sources Recent Meeting: $9,010,000, 2004; $9,161,000, 2005
Average On-Track Recent Meeting: $1,670,330, 2004
Record Daily Average for Single Meet: $2,121,121, 1998
Single Day On-Track Handle: $7,993,485, March 12, 1994
Single Day All Sources Handle: $21,102,814, March 16, 1996
Total All Sources Recent Meeting: $819,910,000, 2004; $787,846,000, 2005
Total On-Track Recent Meeting: $152,000,000, 2004

Mutuel Records
Highest Win: $404.00, Concert Grand, February 14, 1993
Lowest Win: $2.10, Honest Pleasure, April 3, 1976; $2.10, Spectacular Bid, February 7, 1979; $2.10, Spectacular Bid, March 6, 1979
Highest Exacta: $8,948.80, March 13, 1987
Lowest Exacta: $3.80, March 6, 1979; $3.80, March 10, 1991
Highest Trifecta: $96,751.80, January 31, 1993
Lowest Trifecta: $9.60, March 6, 1979
Highest Daily Double: $6,683.60, January 28, 1972
Lowest Daily Double: $6.00, January 14, 1995
Highest Pick 3: $63,737.60, January 26, 1995
Lowest Pick 3: $9.80, February 22, 1994
Highest Pick 6: $301,585.80, February 24, 1996

Leaders
Career, Leading Jockey by Titles: Jorge Chavez, 4
Career, Leading Trainer by Titles: A. N. Winick, 12
Recent Meeting, Leading Jockey: Edgar Prado, 62, 2005
Recent Meeting, Leading Trainer: Todd Pletcher, 36, 2005
Career, Leading Jockey by Stakes Wins: Jerry Bailey

Records
Single Day Jockey Wins: Jerry Bailey, 7, March 11, 1995
Single Meet, Leading Jockey by Wins: Julio Pezua, 97, 1987; Wigberto Ramos, 97, 1991; Jerry Bailey, 97, 1996
Single Meet, Leading Trainer by Wins: William I. Mott, 39, 1996

Track Records, Main Dirt
4 furlongs: Piet, :46 1/5, April 3, 1947; Growing Up, :46 1/5, March 12, 1949
4 1/2 furlongs: Iron Rail, :51 2/5, April 6, 1960
5 furlongs: Boston Brat, :56.35, January 17, 2003
5 1/2 furlongs: Rare Rock, 1:02.50, January 3, 1998
6 furlongs: Mr. Prospector, 1:07 4/5, March 31, 1973
6 1/2 furlongs: Federal Hill, 1:15, March 25, 1957; Alydeed, 1:15, March 6, 1993
7 furlongs: Elusive Quality, 1:20, February 21, 1997
1m 70 yds: Blacksburg, 1:39, February 6, 1994
1 1/16 miles: Saxony Warrior, 1:40 1/5, March 6, 1973
1 1/8 miles: Jumping Hill, 1:46 2/5, February 3, 1979
1 3/16 miles: Michael's Choice, 1:56, March 23, 1960; Sal's Boat, 1:56, April 22, 1960
1 1/4 miles: Mat Boy (Arg), 1:59, March 24, 1984
1 3/8 miles: Blacktype, 2:15 2/5, March 17, 1956; Bayluc, 2:15 2/5, April 2, 1960
1 1/2 miles: Buffalo Lark, 2:27 3/5, April 12, 1975
1 5/8 miles: Toulouse, 2:43 2/5, April 7, 1956
1 3/4 miles: Tisbury, 2:57 2/5, April 20, 1953
2 miles: Undue Influence, 3:25.73, March 16, 1997
Other: 2 1/2 furlongs, Rich Coins, :28, March 31, 2000; 2 1/2 furlongs, Sonnyhero, :28, April 5, 2000; 3 furlongs, El Macho, :32 1/5, February 26, 1974; 1 7/8 miles, Pharawell, 3:13 4/5, April 8, 1947; 2 miles 70 yds, Pharawell, 3:53 4/5, April 17, 1947

Track Records, Main Turf
5 furlongs: True Love's Secret, :56.16, April 11, 2004
1 mile: Lure, 1:32.90, October 31, 1992
1 1/16 miles: Garbu, 1:39.33, March 13, 1999
1 1/8 miles: Proud Man, 1:45.69, January 24, 2004
1 3/8 miles: Yagli, 2:10.73, February 6, 1999
1 1/2 miles: Unite's Big Red, 2:23, March 6, 1999
2 miles: Sabinus, 3:22 2/5, April 17, 1971

Principal Races
Florida Derby (G1), Donn H. (G1), Gulfstream Park Breeders' Cup H. (G1), Fountain of Youth S. (G2), Sunshine Millions

Interesting Facts
Trivia: Bill Shoemaker rode the last winner of his career (Beau Genius) in the 1990 Hallandale Handicap. Turf course opened in 1959.

Notable Events
Major concerts every Saturday and Sunday

Fastest Times of 2004 (Dirt)

3 furlongs: Shocking Dunn, :33.38, April 24, 2004
5 furlongs: Cripple Creek, :56.48, March 3, 2004
5 1/2 furlongs: Lilah, 1:03.29, February 11, 2004
6 furlongs: Alke, 1:08.30, January 8, 2004
6 1/2 furlongs: House Party, 1:15.55, March 7, 2004
7 furlongs: Randaroo, 1:21.42, February 8, 2004; Value Plus, 1:21.42, February 14, 2004
1m 70 yds: Smooth Lover, 1:41.96, April 16, 2004
1 1/16 miles: Puzzlement, 1:42.39, January 3, 2004
1 1/8 miles: Medaglia d'Oro, 1:47.68, February 7, 2004
1 1/4 miles: Jackpot, 2:02.80, April 3, 2004

Fastest Times of 2004 (Turf)

5 furlongs: True Love's Secret, :56.16, April 11, 2004
a5 furlongs: Desirable Moment, :55.61, March 28, 2004
1 mile: Silver Tree, 1:33.38, February 21, 2004
a1 miles: Marco's Word, 1:36.11, January 29, 2004
1 1/16 miles: Steadfast and True, 1:40.50, January 3, 2004
a1 1/16 miles: Alnahaam (Ire), 1:42.15, April 7, 2004
1 1/8 miles: Proud Man, 1:45.69, January 24, 2004
a1 1/8 miles: Slew Valley, 1:48.58, March 12, 2004
1 3/8 miles: Hard Buck (Brz), 2:11.56, February 22, 2004
a1 3/8 miles: Host, 2:19.14, March 19, 2004
1 1/2 miles: In Hand, 2:26.27, February 22, 2004
a1 1/2 miles: Host, 2:34.65, March 1, 2004

Hialeah Park

Location: 105 E 21st St., P.O. Box 158, Hialeah, Fl. 33010
Phone: (305) 885-8000
Phone: (708) 614-1830
Fax: (305) 887-8006
Website: *www.hialeahpark.com*
Year Founded: 1924
Dates of Inaugural Meeting: January 25, 1925
Abbreviation: Hia
Acreage: 220
Number of Stalls: 1,631
Seating Capacity: 20,000

Ocala Training Center

Location: 1701 SW 60th Ave., Ocala, Fl. 34474-1800
Phone: (352) 237-2154
Fax: (352) 237-3566
Website: *www.obssales.com*
E-Mail: obs@obssales.com
Abbreviation: OTC

Officers

Director of Racing: Bob Gulick
Racing Secretary: Rick Coyne
Director of Operations: Royal Logan
Stewards: Bobby Wingo, Charles Camac, Tommy Trotter
Track Announcer: Phil Saltzman
Track Photographer: Jim Lisa
Track Superintendent: John Barbazon

Racing Dates

2004: March 15, 1 day
2005: March 21, 1 day

Fastest Times of 2004 (Dirt)

5 furlongs: Vision in Flight, :57.80, March 15, 2004
6 furlongs: Baronage, 1:10.60, March 15, 2004
1 1/16 miles: Doc's Doll, 1:44.20, March 15, 2004; Humorously, 1:44.20, March 15, 2004

Tampa Bay Downs

Tampa Bay Downs, the only Thoroughbred track on Florida's gulf coast, opened on February 18, 1926, as Tampa Downs. The initial 39-day meet was orchestrated by Harvey Mayers, a businessman from Ohio, and Churchill Downs executive Col. Matt J. Winn. Renamed Sunshine Park in 1947, it became known as the "Santa Anita of the South" in the '50s, a nickname provided by legendary sportswriters Grantland Rice, Red Smith, and Arthur Daley, who frequented the track while covering baseball spring training. Following the sale of the track, its name was changed to Florida Downs in 1965 and to Tampa Bay Downs in 1980. On February 12, 1981, jockey Julie Krone scored the first victory of her Racing Hall of Fame career on Lord Farkle. Tampa Bay Downs has since added a picnic area, year-round simulcasting, a seven-furlong turf course, a luxurious Sports Gallery featuring an extensive video racing library, an updated grandstand with private work stations, central air conditioning, and a renovated deli, bar, and pizza area. In 2004, the track opened a card room.

Location: 11225 Race Track Rd., Oldsmar, Fl. 34677-7007
Phone: (813) 855-4401
Phone: (800) 200-4434
Fax: (813) 854-3539
Website: *www.tampabaydowns.com*
E-Mail: customerservice@tampabaydowns.com
Year Founded: 1926
Dates of Inaugural Meeting: February 18, 1926
Abbreviation: Tam
Acreage: 450
Number of Stalls: 1,462
Seating Capacity: 6,000

Ownership

Stella Thayer and Howell Ferguson

Officers

President: Stella F. Thayer
General Manager: Peter Berube
Director of Racing: Robert Clark
Racing Secretary: Robert Clark
Secretary: Howell Ferguson
Treasurer: Stella F. Thayer
Director of Admissions: Melissa Wirth
Director of Communications: Margo Flynn
Director of Finance: Greg Gelyon
Director of Marketing: Margo Flynn
Director of Mutuels: Frank White
Vice President: Lorraine King, Peter Berube, Robert Cassanese
Director of Publicity: Margo Flynn
Director of Sales: Nicole McGill
Director of Simulcasting: Cathy Dwyer
Horsemen's Liaison: Margo Flynn
Stewards: Dennis Lima, Charles Miranda, Heriberto Rivera Jr.
Track Announcer: Richard Grunder
Track Photographer: Tom Cooley
Track Superintendent: Tom McLaughlin
Security: Robert Kibbey
Asst. Racing Secretary: Edward P. Cantlon Jr.
Horsemen's Bookkeeper: Amanda Carlin

Racing Dates

2004: December 13, 2003-May 2, 2004, 93 days
2005: December 11, 2004-May 8, 2005, 94 days

Track Layout

Main Circumference: 1 mile
Main Track Chute: 3 furlongs and 7 furlongs
Main Width: 75 feet
Main Length of Stretch: 976 feet
Main Turf Circumference: 7 furlongs
Main Turf Chute: 1/4 mile
Main Turf Width: 80 feet

Attendance

Average Daily Recent Meeting: 3,495, 2004; 3,513, 2005
Highest Single Day Record: 9,765, April 8, 1990
Highest Single Meet Record: 457,414, 1988/1989
Total Attendance Recent Meeting: 325,025, 2004; 330,248, 2005

Handle
Average All Sources Recent Meeting: $3,166,051, 2004; $3,410,092, 2005
Average On-Track Recent Meeting: $293,959, 2004; $300,530, 2005
Single Day On-Track Handle: $1,336,000, May 4, 2002
Single Day All Sources Handle: $5,353,782, March 14, 2003
Total All Sources Recent Meeting: $294,442,708, 2004; $320,548,667, 2005
Total On-Track Recent Meeting: $27,338,223, 2004; $28,249,856, 2005

Mutuel Records
Highest Win: $249, March 23, 1988
Highest Trifecta: $50,617, January 26, 1999
Highest Daily Double: $3,320, January 17, 1950
Highest Pick 3: $12,913.40, January 9, 2001
Highest Other Exotics: $9,754, Perfecta, February 8, 1973; $33,237.50, Superfecta, January 12, 1999
Highest Quinella: $5,067.60, February 21, 1995

Leaders
Career, Leading Jockey by Titles: Bill Henry, 4
Career, Leading Trainer by Titles: Don Rice, 6
Career, Leading Jockey by Stakes Wins: William Henry, 21
Career, Leading Owner by Stakes Wins: Harold Queen, 6
Career, Leading Trainer by Stakes Wins: Don Rice, 8
Recent Meeting, Leading Jockey: Jesus Castanon, 101, 2004
Recent Meeting, Leading Trainer: Don Rice, 35, 2004

Records
Single Day Jockey Wins: Richard Depass, 7, March 15, 1980
Single Day Owner Wins: Christos Gatis, 3, April 10, 2001
Single Day Trainer Wins: Kathleen O'Connell, 4, February 23, 2003
Single Meet, Leading Jockey by Wins: Willie Martinez, 123, 1991/1992; William Henry, 123, 1992/1993
Single Meet, Leading Trainer by Wins: Don Rice, 44, 2001/2002

Track Records, Main Dirt
4 furlongs: Camp Izard, :46.80, May 1, 1993
4 1/2 furlongs: Geronimo J., :52 4/5, March 16, 1984
5 furlongs: Arion Fair, :57 1/5, March 20, 1982; Mr. Buffum, :57.28, March 17, 2002
5 1/2 furlongs: Schmoopy, 1:03.55, March 17, 2000
6 furlongs: Bootlegger's Pet, 1:09, January 26, 1974
7 furlongs: Oh So Striking, 1:22.60, April 5, 1997
7 1/2 furlongs: Secret Romeo, 1:22.62, January 22, 2002
1 mile: Double Prince, 1:42 3/5, February 8, 1966; Rianan, 1:42 3/5, February 11, 1966
1m 40 yds: Mistum, 1:41 1/5, March 21, 1981
1m 70 yds: Deep Thought, 1:41 4/5, January 21, 1956
1 1/16 miles: Sunny Prospector, 1:43 2/5, March 29, 1989
1 1/8 miles: Las Olas, 1:48 2/5, November 21, 1968
1 3/16 miles: Warning Flag, 1:59 3/5, January 25, 1986
1 1/4 miles: Finale Puer, 2:07 2/5, March 7, 1959
1 3/8 miles: Rugged Zeal, 2:20.68, April 23, 2002
1 1/2 miles: Royal Jacopo, 2.33, March 12, 1955
1 5/8 miles: Most Valiant, 2:48.20, March 29, 1997
1 3/4 miles: Our Day, 3:00 2/5, March 20, 1957
2 miles: Boss Man Jarett, 3:30.30, April 24, 1999
Other: 2 furlongs, Silver Dollar Boy, :21 4/5, January 18, 1990; 3 furlongs, Hot Star, :33 2/5, February 14, 1980; 3 furlongs, Wynn Dot Comma, :33.40, April 21, 2003; 1 7/8 miles, Best Hearted, 3:18 3/5, March 22, 1986; 2 miles 70 yds, Turkey Foot Road, 3:39 4/5, March 22, 1969; 2 1/16 miles, Mystic Fox, 3:37 3/5, March 27, 1988

Track Records, Main Turf
5 furlongs: Nicole's Dream, :56, March 16, 2003
1 mile: Lucky J J, 1:33.79, February 12, 2000
1 1/16 miles: Legs Galore, 1:39.65, February 20, 1999
1 1/8 miles: Lilys Cousin, 1:46.34, May 6, 2000
1 3/8 miles: Fun n' Gun, 2:24.06, March 30, 2002
1 1/2 miles: Top Senor, 2:31.60, February 26, 2002
Other: a5 furlongs, Milky Way Guy, :57.38, January 5, 2004; a1 mile, Mercedes Song, 1:36.80, January 12, 1999; a1 1/16 miles, Ben's Quitoxe, 1:41.23, December 28, 1999; a1 1/8 miles, Guardianofthegate, 1:48.33, April 6, 2003; a1 1/2 miles, Top Senor, 2:31.60, February 26, 2002

Principal Races
Tampa Bay Derby (G3), Hillborough S. (G3), Florida Oaks

Interesting Facts
Previous Names and Dates: Tampa Downs (1926-1946), Sunshine Park (1947-1964), Florida Downs (1965-1979)

Notable Events
Florida Cup Day

Fastest Times of 2004 (Dirt)
3 furlongs: Tooke Tooke, :36.00, April 25, 2004
5 furlongs: Dirtymoposse, :57.66, February 28, 2004
5 1/2 furlongs: Rebel's Mission, 1:04.03, April 20, 2004
6 furlongs: Sea Span, 1:10.42, January 3, 2004; Silver Dynasty, 1:10.42, April 24, 2004
6 1/2 furlongs: O'Malley, 1:16.99, December 31, 2004
7 furlongs: Above the Wind, 1:23.78, January 24, 2004
1 1/16 miles: Limehouse, 1:43.99, March 14, 2004
1 1/8 miles: Northernprospector, 1:52.37, April 19, 2004
1 3/8 miles: Improvised, 2:23.09, March 16, 2004

Fastest Times of 2004 (Turf)
5 furlongs: Mighty Patriot, :56.24, April 10, 2004
a5 furlongs: Whenthedoveflies, :57.23, April 20, 2004
1 mile: Awol Soldier, 1:35.66, April 10, 2004
a1 miles: Mr. Fran Man, 1:38.74, April 19, 2004
1 1/16 miles: Burning Roma, 1:41.68, February 14, 2004
a1 1/16 miles: Casino Casey, 1:44.75, April 18, 2004
1 1/8 miles: Mile, 1:49.79, April 27, 2004
a1 1/8 miles: Restage, 1:48.03, May 1, 2004
a1 3/8 miles: Galic Boy, 2:17.40, March 9, 2004

Tropical Park

Tropical Park no longer has a physical presence but remains alive as the late fall-early winter meeting at Calder Race Course in northwest Miami. The Tropical Park meet at Calder Race Course runs from late October until the first days of January, which approximates the traditional Tropical Park spot in the South Florida rotation. Starting in the late 1940s, Tropical operated from late November until mid-January. Tropical Park first was a greyhound track and opened as a Thoroughbred track on December 26, 1931, in Coral Gables, a suburb southwest of Miami. The track was sold in 1941 and went through two ownership changes in the early 1950s. Tropical was host for the first Calder meeting in 1970 and for that season used an experimental, synthetic Tartan track, developed by Minnesota Mining and Manufacturing Co., inside the main, one-mile oval. Calder's investors, including 3M Chairman William L. McKnight, bought out Tropical with the intention of moving its dates to the new track. Tropical closed on January 15, 1972, and was transformed into a municipal park. Several of Calder's graded stakes races are held during the Tropical Park meeting. Tropical Park still maintains separate meet records from Calder for leading jockey, trainer, and other categories, although track records are the same for both.

Location: 21001 N W 27th Ave., Miami, Fl. 33056
Phone: (305) 625-1311
Fax: (305) 620-2569
Website: www.calderracecourse.com
E-Mail: customerservice@calderracecourse.com
Year Founded: 1972
Abbreviation: Crc

Ownership
Churchill Downs Inc.

Officers
Chairman: Thomas H. Meeker
President: C. Kenneth Dunn

General Manager: Michael Abes
Director of Racing: Robert D. Umphrey
Racing Secretary: Robert D. Umphrey
Secretary: Rebecca C. Reed
Treasurer: Michael Abes
Director of Marketing: Michael Cronin
Director of Mutuels: Edward Mackie Sr.
Vice President: Michael Cronin, Michael Abes
Director of Publicity: Michele Blanco
Director of Simulcasting: Diane Stoess
Stewards: Charles Camac, Jeffrey Noe, Kevin Sheen
Track Announcer: Bobby Neuman
Track Photographer: Jim Lisa
Track Superintendent: Steve Cross
Director of Security: Tony Otero
Horsemen's Bookkeeper: Nelly Torrente

Racing Dates
2004: October 24, 2004-January 2, 2005, 55 days
2005: October 17, 2005-January 2, 2006, 59 days

Track Layout
Main Circumference: 1 mile
Main Track Chute: 7 furlongs and 1 1/4 miles
Main Width: Homestretch: 80 feet; Backstretch: 75 feet
Main Length of Stretch: 990 feet
Main Turf Circumference: 7 furlongs
Main Turf Chute: 1 1/8 miles
Main Turf Width: 67 feet
Main Turf Length of Stretch: 986 feet

Attendance
Average Daily Recent Meeting: 4,408, 2004/2005
Highest Single Day Record: 17,671, January 14, 1978
Highest Single Day Recent Meet: 12,141, January 1, 2005
Total Attendance Recent Meeting: 242,420, 2004/2005

Handle
Average All Sources Recent Meeting: $4,370,422, 2004/2005
Average On-Track Recent Meeting: $441,781, 2004/2005
Record Daily Average for Single Meet: $1,475,680, 1988
Single Day On-Track Handle: $2,793,767, January 7, 1989
Single Day All Sources Handle: $9,461,604, December 29, 2001
Record Total for Single Meet: $73,784,024, 1988
Total All Sources Recent Meeting: $240,373,189, 2004/2005
Total On-Track Recent Meeting: $24,297,975, 2004/2005
Highest Single Day Recent Meet: $8,169,829, December 18, 2004

Mutuel Records
Highest Win: $447.40, December 23, 1986
Lowest Win: $2.20, December 18, 1972
Highest Exacta: $10,837.20, December 18, 1988
Lowest Exacta: $4.80, December 18, 1972
Highest Trifecta: $52,398, January 6, 1979
Lowest Trifecta: $11.40, December 9, 1993
Highest Daily Double: $7,907.80, December 14, 1973
Lowest Daily Double: $6.40, April 18, 1992
Highest Pick 3: $28,275, December 21, 1993
Lowest Pick 3: $15.80, December 17, 1988
Highest Other Exotics: $68,684.20, Superfecta, November 16, 1996
Lowest Other Exotics: $37.80, Superfecta, November 16, 1995
Lowest Pick 4: $52.50, November 16, 2002
Highest Pick 4: $77,762.40, December 30, 2000

Leaders
Career, Leading Jockey by Titles: Jacinto Vasquez, 5
Career, Leading Trainer by Titles: Stanley Hough, 5; William White, 5
Recent Meeting, Leading Jockey: Eddie Castro, 83, 2004/2005
Recent Meeting, Leading Owner: Michael Sherman, 17, 2004/2005
Recent Meeting, Leading Trainer: Daniel Hurtak, 21, 2004/2005
Career, Leading Jockey by Stakes Wins: Jerry Bailey, 26
Career, Leading Trainer by Stakes Wins: Luis Olivares, 18; Martin D. Wolfson, 18
Career, Leading Jockey by Wins: Eibar Coa, 537
Career, Leading Trainer by Wins: Emanuel Tortora, 368

Records
Single Day Jockey Wins: Jacinto Vasquez, 6, December 22, 1990; Rene Douglas, 6, December 8, 1993; Javier Castellano, 6, December 31, 2000
Single Meet, Leading Jockey by Wins: Cornelio Velasquez, 84, 2002/2003
Single Meet, Leading Trainer by Wins: Stanley Hough, 35, 1978/1979; John Tammaro, 35, 1988

Track Records, Main Dirt
4 furlongs: Diamond Studs, :46.21, July 14, 2001
4 1/2 furlongs: Gold Phantom, :51.86, September 16, 2001
5 furlongs: Honest, :57.61, July 1, 1996
5 1/2 furlongs: Bernard's Candy, 1:04.39, August 9, 2002
6 furlongs: Forty One Carats, 1:08.95, October 7, 2000
6 1/2 furlongs: Tour of the Cat, 1:15.99, August 17, 2002
7 furlongs: Constant Escort, 1:21.82, September 28, 1996
1 mile: High Ideal, 1:36.25, September 15, 2001
1m 70 yds: Halo's Image, 1:41.78, October 31, 1995
1 1/16 miles: Castlebrook, 1:42.55, September 15, 2001
1 1/8 miles: Jumping Hill, 1:50, December 30, 1978
1 3/16 miles: Arctic Honeymoon, 1:59 3/5, January 3, 1987
1 1/4 miles: Wicapi, 2:05.08, June 24, 1996
1 1/2 miles: Lead'm Home, 2:32 3/5, December 31, 1977
1 5/8 miles: Timberlea Tune, 2:50 1/5, October 16, 1971
1 3/4 miles: *Detective II, 3:03 1/5, October 23, 1971
2 miles: *Detective II, 3:30 1/5, November 11, 1971
Other: 2 furlongs, Baby Shark, :20.81, July 13, 2002

Track Records, Main Turf
5 furlongs: Whenthedoveflies, :54.78, May 23, 2004
7 furlongs: Carterista, 1:22.36, June 19, 1993
7 1/2 furlongs: Court Lark, 1:26.54, July 16, 1994
1 mile: Dillonmyboy, 1:33.66, October 30, 2000
1 1/16 miles: He's Crafty, 1:39.27, December 28, 2004
1 1/8 miles: The Vid, 1:44.99, November 25, 1995
1 3/8 miles: King's Design, 2:13.18, July 23, 1999
1 1/2 miles: Flag Down, 2:24.11, December 16, 1995
2 miles: Skate On Thin Ice, 3:21.89, January 2, 1996

Principal Races
La Prevoyante H. (G2), W. L. McKnight H. (G2), Tropical Park Derby (G3), Frances A. Genter S. (G3), Fred W. Hooper H. (G3)

Notable Events
The Florida Million, Grand Slam I, II and III

Fastest Times of 2004 (Dirt)
2 furlongs: Pembroke Hall, :21.65, July 10, 2004
4 1/2 furlongs: Lucky Frolic, :52.27, August 21, 2004
5 furlongs: Paradise Dancer, :58.06, November 25, 2004
5 1/2 furlongs: All Hail Stormy, 1:04.50, December 27, 2004
6 furlongs: Weigelia, 1:09.64, May 9, 2004
6 1/2 furlongs: Iron Boy, 1:17.18, December 18, 2004
7 furlongs: Medallist, 1:22.62, December 18, 2004
1 mile: Kristine's King, 1:38.28, June 7, 2004
1m 70 yds: Cin Cin, 1:46.30, October 2, 2004
1 1/16 miles: Island Skipper, 1:45.46, July 9, 2004
1 1/8 miles: Pies Prospect, 1:50.74, December 18, 2004
1 1/4 miles: Thunder Squall, 2:10.37, June 28, 2004
1 1/2 miles: Dajudge, 2:40.55, June 5, 2004

Fastest Times of 2004 (Turf)
5 furlongs: Whenthedoveflies, :54.78, May 23, 2004
7 1/2 furlongs: Winter Ghost, 1:27.89, December 16, 2004
1 mile: Romolo's Fritzi, 1:34.18, July 11, 2004
1 1/16 miles: He's Crafty, 1:39.27, December 28, 2004
1 1/8 miles: Host (Chi), 1:45.74, December 4, 2004
1 3/8 miles: Iowa's Image, 2:24.53, July 19, 2004
1 1/2 miles: Dreadnaught, 2:26.60, December 18, 2004

Idaho

Jerome Racing
Location: 406 N Buchanan St., Jerome, Id. 83338-2319
Phone: (208) 324-7057
Fax: (208) 324-7059
Abbreviation: Jrm

Racing Dates
2004: June 12- June 19, 3 days
2005: June 18- June 25, 3 days

Les Bois Park

Located in Boise on the Western Idaho Fairgrounds, Les Bois Park is one of the largest racetracks in the Northwest and annually holds the Idaho Cup for state-bred Thoroughbreds, Quarter Horses, Paints, and Appaloosas. Les Bois, which is French for "the woods," opened in May 1970, six years after pari-mutuel wagering was legalized in Idaho. The track had difficult times in the late 1980s, when a downturn in horse racing caused the track owners, the Ada County Commission, to put the Les Bois lease up for auction. A group of horsemen led by veterinarian Chris Christian won the lease for $100 per month and successfully lobbied for full-card simulcasting, which turned the track around and allowed it to increase its purses. In April 2002, the track was leased to former professional basketball player Arnell Jones and his wife, Lanae, but their Lariat Productions failed to make required payments to Ada County in 2005. The track features Thoroughbreds, Quarter Horses, Appaloosas, and Paints racing from early May to mid-August. Les Bois was the launching pad for Racing Hall of Fame jockey Gary Stevens, who scored his first career victory at the track aboard Little Star in 1979.

Location: 5610 Glenwood Rd., Boise, ID 83714-1338
Phone: (208) 376-3991
Fax: (208) 378-4032
Year Founded: 1970
Abbreviation: Boi

Ownership
Lariat Productions, lessee

Officers
Chairman: Lanae Jones
President: Lanae Jones
General Manager: Duayne Didericksen
Director of Racing: Fred Snapp
Racing Secretary: Fred Snapp
Director of Publicity: Hugh Mellon
Track Superintendent: Roger White

Racing Dates
2004: May 1-August 8
2005: May 4-August 14, 47 days

Attendance
Average Daily Recent Meeting: 920, 2004
Total Attendance Recent Meeting: 42,298, 2004

Handle
Average On-Track Recent Meeting: $26,321, 2004
Total On-Track Recent Meeting: $1,210,753, 2004

Leaders
Recent Meeting, Leading Horse: Classical Guitar, 4, 2004; Mini Me, 4, 2004; Smoke and Ice, 4, 2004
Recent Meeting, Leading Jockey: Berkley Packer, 64, 2004
Recent Meeting, Leading Trainer: Kevin Knudsen, 22, 2004

Principal Races
Idaho Cup

Notable Events
Idaho Cup Day

Fastest Times of 2004 (Dirt)
4 1/2 furlongs: Annie Oakleaf, :53.20, July 4, 2004
5 furlongs: Crooked Key, :56.60, June 27, 2004
6 1/2 furlongs: Hair Jordan, 1:17.60, July 11, 2004
7 furlongs: The Gray Jaklin, 1:23.80, July 11, 2004
7 1/2 furlongs: Reno Bound, 1:31.80, July 4, 2004
1 mile: Crooked Key, 1:38.00, July 31, 2004; Paradise Wild, 1:38.00, July 31, 2004
1 1/4 miles: Find My Halter, 2:06.60, August 15, 2004

Oneida County Fair

Location: P.O. Box 13, Malad City, Id. 83252-0013
Phone: (208) 766-4706
Phone: (805) 565-1125
Fax: (208) 766-4707
Abbreviation: One
Acreage: 30
Number of Stalls: 93
Seating Capacity: 1,000

Officers
President: David Moss
Director of Racing: Deon Jones
Secretary: Deon Jones
Director of Marketing: Jim Moss
Vice President: Bob Hobson
Director of Publicity: Jim Moss
Director of Simulcasting: Linda Daniels

Track Layout
Main Circumference: 1/2 mile
Main Width: 60 feet
Main Length of Stretch: 300 yds

Pocatello Downs

Location: 10588 Fairgrounds Road, Pocatello, Id. 83204
Phone: (208) 238-1721
Fax: (208) 238-1763
Abbreviation: PoD

Racing Dates
2004: May 15-June 6, 9 days
2005: May 14-June 5, 9 days

Rupert Downs

Location: P.O. Box 263, Rupert, Id. 83350-0263
Phone: (208) 436-9748
Fax: (208) 436-8063
Abbreviation: Rup

Racing Dates
2004: July 3-July 11, 5 days
2005: July 2-July 10, 5 days

Illinois

Arlington Park

Arlington Park first opened on October 13, 1927, and has been home to many firsts in Thoroughbred racing. Located northwest of Chicago in Arlington Heights, the track became the first in Illinois to offer turf races in 1934. In 1966, Laffit Pincay Jr. recorded his first United States victory there on his way to a place in the

Racing Hall of Fame and a record 9,530 victories. In 1981, Arlington became the world's first track to host a $1-million race for Thoroughbreds when it inaugurated the Arlington Million Stakes (G1). The first running was won by John Henry, who returned to win the race in 1984. Today, the Million is part of Arlington's International Festival of Racing, which also includes the Beverly D. (G1) and Secretariat (G1) Stakes. On July 31, 1985, fire destroyed Arlington's clubhouse, causing the track to shift most of its remaining races to Hawthorne Race Course. The exception was the Million, which was held on August 25 at Arlington, and more than 35,000 fans watched the race from tents and temporary facilities during what would be dubbed the "Miracle Million." Those efforts led to Arlington becoming the first racetrack to earn an Eclipse Award. Arlington was rebuilt lavishly by Chicago-area industrialist Richard Duchossois, who closed the track for two seasons—1998 and '99—due to unfavorable economic and regulatory conditions. Arlington reopened in 2000 and the Arlington Million was resumed. Also in 2000, Churchill Downs Inc. purchased the track and assumed about $80-million in loans, while Duchossois received close to 4-million shares of common stock in Churchill.

Location: 2200 W Euclid Ave., Arlington Heights, Il. 60006
Phone: (847) 385-7500
Fax: (847) 385-7251
Website: www.arlingtonpark.com
E-Mail: track@arlingtonpark.com
Year Founded: 1926
Dates of Inaugural Meeting: October 13, 1927
Abbreviation: AP
Number of Stalls: 2,140
Seating Capacity: 35,000

Ownership
Churchill Downs Inc.

Officers
Chairman: Richard L. Duchossois
President: Clifford C. Goodrich
Racing Secretary: Frank G. Gabriel Jr.
Treasurer: Dan Peters
Director of Operations: Ted G. Nicholson
Director of Admissions: Bill Adams
Director of Communications: Dan Leary
Director of Finance: Michael Cody
Director of Marketing: Keith Darby
Director of Mutuels: Jack Lisowski
Vice President: William A. Thayer Jr.
Director of Sales: Tom Maloney
Stewards: Eddie Arroyo, Joseph K. Lindeman, Steve Morgan, Peter Kosiba Jr.
Track Announcer: John G. Dooley
Track Photographer: Bob Benoit and Associates
Track Superintendent: Javier Barajas
Security: Dan Centracchio

Racing Dates
2004: May 14-September 19, 96 days
2005: May 13-September 18, 94 days

Track Layout
Main Circumference: 1 1/8 miles
Main Track Chute: 6 1/2 furlongs
Main Track Chute: 7 furlongs
Main Track Chute: 7 1/2 furlongs
Main Track Chute: 1 mile
Main Width: 90 feet
Main Length of Stretch: 1,049 feet
Main Turf Circumference: 1 mile
Main Turf Chute: 1 1/4 miles

Main Turf Width: 150 feet
Main Turf Length of Stretch: 1,020 feet
Training Track: 5 furlongs

Attendance
Average Daily Recent Meeting: 7,572, 2004
Highest Single Day Record: 50,638, July 4, 1938
Total Attendance Recent Meeting: 726,923, 2004

Handle
Average All Sources Recent Meeting: $4,190,711, 2004
Average On-Track Recent Meeting: $579,713, 2004
Single Day On-Track Handle: $13,568,209, October 26, 2002
Single Day All Sources Handle: $108,513,107, October 26, 2002
Total All Sources Recent Meeting: $402,308,299, 2004
Total On-Track Recent Meeting: $55,652,458, 2004
Highest Single Day Recent Meet: $17,913,433, August 14, 2004 (Arlington Million Day)

Mutuel Records
Highest Win: $382, Ivalinda, August 12, 1963
Highest Exacta: $6267, August 7, 1991
Highest Trifecta: $58,116.20, September 14, 2001
Highest Daily Double: $3,835.20, July 5, 1939
Highest Pick 3: $21,775.40, June 11, 1990
Highest Pick 6: $269,253.60, September 25, 1984
Highest Other Exotics: $52,686, Superfecta, August 13, 1995; $2,701, Quinella, September 3, 2000; $16,349.30, Pick 5, October 26, 2002

Leaders
Career, Leading Jockey by Titles: Earlie Fires, 6
Career, Leading Owner by Titles: Calumet Farm, 9
Career, Leading Trainer by Titles: Richard Hazelton, 8; William Hal Bishop, 8
Career, Leading Jockey by Stakes Wins: Earlie Fires, 100
Career, Leading Owner by Stakes Wins: Calumet Farm, 58
Career, Leading Trainer by Stakes Wins: Harry Trotsek, 45
Career, Leading Jockey by Wins: Earlie Fires, 2,709
Career, Leading Trainer by Wins: Richard Hazelton, 1,114
Recent Meeting, Leading Horse: Cloudy's Knight, 4, 2004
Recent Meeting, Leading Jockey: Rene Douglas, 125, 2004
Recent Meeting, Leading Owner: Frank Calabrese, 26, 2004
Recent Meeting, Leading Trainer: Frank Kirby, 32, 2004

Records
Single Day Jockey Wins: Pat Day, 8, September 13, 1989
Single Meet, Leading Jockey by Wins: Shane Sellers, 219, 1991
Single Meet, Leading Owner by Wins: Frank Calabrese, 66, 2002
Single Meet, Leading Trainer by Wins: Wayne Catalano, 64, 2002

Track Records, Main Dirt
4 1/2 furlongs: Wheat Penny, :51.64, June 8, 2000; Bold America, :51.64, June 28, 2002
5 furlongs: Staunch Avenger, :57 1/5, June 29, 1970; Heisanative, :57 1/5, June 12, 1971; Shecky Greene, :57 1/5, June 15, 1972; Zarb's Magic, :57.31, September 7, 2002
5 1/2 furlongs: Hey That's Great, 1:02 3/5, June 27, 1992
6 furlongs: Taylor's Special, 1:08, August 22, 1986
6 1/2 furlongs: Pentelicus, 1:14 1/5, July 14, 1990
7 furlongs: Tumiga, 1:20 2/5, July 13, 1968
7 1/2 furlongs: I'll Raise You One, 1:28 4/5, August 3, 1987; Apt to Be, 1:28.81, September 15, 2004
1 mile: Dr. Fager, 1:32 1/5, August 24, 1968
1m 70 yds: Geo. Groom, 1:42 4/5, October 25, 1927
1 1/16 miles: Kindly Manner, 1:41 2/5, August 22, 1977; Mojave, 1:41 2/5, June 30, 1981
1 1/8 miles: Spectacular Bid, 1:46 1/5, July 19, 1980
1 3/16 miles: Tenpins, 1:55.07, September 29, 2002
1 1/4 miles: Private Thoughts, 1:59 2/5, August 20, 1977
1 3/8 miles: Playdale, 2:15 2/5, July 19, 1932
1 1/2 miles: El Misterio, 2:28 1/5, September 5, 1960
1 5/8 miles: Fool's Robbery, 2:45 3/5, July 5, 1973

1 3/4 miles: *Deux-Moulins, 2:59 2/5, July 14, 1955
2 miles: Swede of Norfolk, 3:26 2/5, August 15, 1970
Other: 1 5/16 miles, Rush Home, 2:10, August 7, 1971; 1 5/16 miles, Evanescent, 2:10, July 18, 1993; 2 1/4 miles, *Djem, 4:05 3/5, July 30, 1953

Track Records, Main Turf

5 furlongs: Distinctive Mr. B, :56.36, September 15, 2001
5 1/2 furlongs: Marley's Revenge, 1:02.44, September 19, 2004
1 mile: Gee Can He Dance, 1:34.50, September 4, 1995
1m 70yds: Pass the Brandy, 1:38 4/5, July 25, 1970
1 1/16 miles: Zeeruler, 1:41, September 7, 1992
1 1/8 miles: Mr. Leader, 1:47 2/5, July 4, 1970; Jinski's World, 1:47 2/5, July 6, 1991; World Class Splash, 1:47.40, July 11, 1992
1 3/16 miles: Reluctant Guest, 1:53 1/5, September 1, 1990
1 1/4 miles: Awad, 1:58.69, August 27, 1995
1 1/2 miles: Cetewayo, 2:27.50, July 6, 2002
1 5/8 miles: Coincident, 2:45, July 26, 1951
1 3/4 miles: *Pennsburg, 3:02 3/5, July 5, 1941
2 miles: Penaway, 3:25 2/5, July 24, 1953
Other: 2 1/16 miles, *Deux-Moulins, 3:30 4/5, July 28, 1955; 2 1/8 miles, English Harry, 3:45, July 30, 1941

Principal Races

Arlington Million (G1), Beverly D. S. (G1), Secretariat S. (G1), Washington Park H. (G2), American Derby (G2)

Interesting Facts

Trivia: June 24, 2003, jockey Rene Douglas won seven races, including first five on the card, from nine mounts.
Previous Names and Dates: Arlington International Racecourse
Achievements/milestones: July 31, 1985, destroyed by fire. June 28, 1989, rebuilt track opened.

Notable Events

International Festival of Racing (Arlington Million Day)

Fastest Times of 2004 (Dirt)

4 1/2 furlongs: Raving Rocket, :52.51, May 31, 2004
5 furlongs: French Account, :57.33, July 9, 2004
5 1/2 furlongs: He's Hammered, 1:04.29, August 8, 2004
6 furlongs: Gold Storm, 1:08.65, August 28, 2004
6 1/2 furlongs: Coach Jimi Lee, 1:15.59, June 11, 2004
7 furlongs: Formal Decree, 1:22.25, May 20, 2004
7 1/2 furlongs: Apt to Be, 1:28.81, September 15, 2004
1 mile: Ajedrez (Arg), 1:35.28, July 4, 2004
1 1/8 miles: Alumni Hall, 1:49.46, July 10, 2004
1 3/16 miles: Eye of the Tiger, 1:56.87, July 31, 2004
1 1/4 miles: Ta Ta Baby, 2:07.17, September 18, 2004
1 1/2 miles: Covering Ground, 2:33.37, June 12, 2004

Fastest Times of 2004 (Turf)

5 furlongs: Glitterbdancing, :57.17, September 5, 2004; Miners Gamble, :57.17, August 8, 2004
a5 furlongs: Be Factual, :57.10, August 13, 2004
5 1/2 furlongs: Marley's Revenge, 1:02.44, September 19, 2004
1 mile: Color by d'Or, 1:35.84, August 1, 2004
a1 miles: Hug Me Hug Me, 1:36.53, August 13, 2004
1 1/16 miles: Cloudy's Knight, 1:42.57, September 18, 2004
a1 1/16 miles: Lord Carmen, 1:42.32, June 30, 2004
1 1/8 miles: Ticker Tape (GB), 1:48.63, September 18, 2004
a1 1/8 miles: Dynareign, 1:48.84, July 30, 2004
1 3/16 miles: Simple Exchange (Ire), 1:54.93, July 24, 2004
1 1/4 miles: Kitten's Joy, 1:59.65, August 14, 2004
1 1/2 miles: Proud Partner, 2:33.52, July 25, 2004
a1 1/2 miles: Private Bound, 2:29.34, August 13, 2004

Fairmount Park

Fairmount Park, located in Collinsville, about 30 minutes east of St. Louis, opened on September 26, 1925. The track was built to resemble a small Churchill Downs

by Col. E. R. Bradley, who owned four Kentucky Derby winners, and Col. Matt Winn, who made the Kentucky Derby at Churchill a sporting institution. In 1947, Fairmount became the first one-mile oval racetrack in the world to provide lighting for night Thoroughbred racing. Fairmount's most famous horseman is jockey Dave Gall, who retired in 1999 with 7,396 wins, placing him among Thoroughbred racing's winningest jockeys. Fairmount, which has been owned since 1969 by Ogden Services Corp., has struggled to compete against riverboat gambling casinos throughout the St. Louis area in recent years.

Location: 9301 Collinsville Rd., Collinsville, Il. 62234-1729
Phone: (618) 345-4300
Fax: (618) 344-8218
Website: *www.fairmountpark.com*
E-Mail: fmtpark@fairmountpark.com
Year Founded: 1924
Dates of Inaugural Meeting: September 26, 1925
Abbreviation: FP
Acreage: 190
Number of Stalls: 1,080
Seating Capacity: 3,148

Ownership

Fairmount Park Inc.

Officers

Chairman: William Stiritz
President: Brian F. Zander
General Manager: Brian F. Zander
Director of Racing: Bobby Pace
Racing Secretary: Bobby Pace
Treasurer: Joe Ruppert
Director of Operations: Joe Ruppert
Director of Marketing: Gregg Smith
Director of Mutuels: Mike Heidemann
Vice President: Joe Ruppert
Director of Publicity: Jon Sloane
Director of Sales: Linda Schwaegel
Director of Simulcasting: Greg Graves
Stewards: Jeff Bowen, Dave Smith, Roger Duff
Track Superintendent: Frank Killian

Racing Dates

2004: March 26-September 18, 101 days
2005: March 25-September 17, 102 days

Track Layout

Main Circumference: 1 mile
Main Track Chute: 6 furlongs and 1 1/4 miles
Main Width: Homestretch: 80 feet; Backstretch: 70 feet
Main Length of Stretch: 1,050 feet

Attendance

Average Daily Recent Meeting: 3,191, 2004
Total Attendance Recent Meeting: 322,249, 2004

Handle

Average All Sources Recent Meeting: $291,697, 2004
Average On-Track Recent Meeting: $134,044, 2004
Total All Sources Recent Meeting: $29,461,395, 2004
Total On-Track Recent Meeting: $13,538,441, 2004

Leaders

Recent Meeting, Leading Jockey: Ramsey Zimmerman, 180, 2004
Recent Meeting, Leading Trainer: Ralph Martinez, 143, 2004

Track Records, Main Dirt

4 furlongs: Aledo, :45.60, June 2, 1994
4 1/2 furlongs: Vague Promise, :51 3/5, May 19, 1978
5 furlongs: Slight in the Rear, :56 4/5, July 25, 1989
5 1/2 furlongs: Sarof Jr., 1:03 2/5, June 5, 1980

6 furlongs: Ye Country, 1:08 3/5, November 26, 1977
1 mile: Dusty Appeal, 1:37.40, June 20, 1992
1m 70 yds: Dusty Appeal, 1:39 4/5, July 30, 1989
1 1/16 miles: Lt. Lao, 1:40 4/5, July 22, 1989
1 1/8 miles: Andover Man, 1:47 3/5, August 26, 1989
1 1/4 miles: Leaddrop, 2:03, July 2, 1989
1 1/2 miles: *Firth of Tay, 2:33, September 21, 1927
1 5/8 miles: Monthazar, 2:48, November 3, 1973
1 3/4 miles: Lightin Bill, 3:02 4/5, October 14, 1939
2 miles: East Royalty, 3:32.60, December 1, 1991
Other: 2 furlongs, Fantan Sam, :21 2/5, November 22, 1989;
2 miles 70 yds, King Boogie, 3:33 3/5, September 1, 1984;
2 1/16 miles, Tim Trefle, 3:38 4/5, September 10, 1983; 2
1/8 miles, Lucrest, 3:46 1/5, September 24, 1983; 2 1/4 miles,
Baye Dawn, 4:00, October 8, 1983; 2 1/2 miles, Cat Walk,
4:29, October 22, 1983

Notable Events
Party at the Park, Ultra Thursdays

Fastest Times of 2004 (Dirt)
4 furlongs: Peepsight, :47.40, March 26, 2004
4 1/2 furlongs: Diamond Leap, :53.20, March 26, 2004; Miner's
Wish, :53.20, March 27, 2004
5 furlongs: Haunted Forrest, :58.60, August 28, 2004
5 1/2 furlongs: Island N Abreeze, 1:04.40, May 4, 2004; Spanish Curse, 1:04.40, May 14, 2004
6 furlongs: Wildwood Royal, 1:09.20, May 1, 2004
1 mile: One Call Close, 1:38.00, May 4, 2004
1m 70 yds: Fax Dance, 1:41.20, May 13, 2004
1 1/4 miles: Slew the City, 2:04.40, August 20, 2004

Hawthorne Race Course

For nearly 100 years, members of the Carey family
have overseen Hawthorne Race Course in the near
Chicago suburb of Stickney. In 1909, Thomas Carey
bought the track from horseman and noted gambler
Ed Corrigan, who had opened the track in 1891. Under
Corrigan's ownership, Hawthorne closed when the
state Senate banned racing in Chicago in 1905, and
new owner Carey attempted over the next several years
to revive racing. He finally succeeded in 1922. In 1928,
the track's most notable race, the Hawthorne Gold Cup
(G2), debuted. Among the winners of the Hawthorne
Gold Cup are five-time Horse of the Year Kelso, 1968
Horse of the Year Dr. Fager, and 1991 Horse of the
Year Black Tie Affair (Ire). In 1977, a fire destroyed
Hawthorne's grandstand, and the remainder of its meet
was held at Sportsman's Park, located a block away.
Racing returned to the track in 1980 when a new grand-
stand was built. Over the years, Hawthorne also has
conducted harness racing. In late 2002, Hawthorne
merged with Sportsman's Park, with Thomas F. Carey
III becoming president of the new entity, Hawthorne
National. Sportsman's Park was sold for development
and its racing dates and major races are now run at
Hawthorne.

Location: 3501 S Laramie Ave., Cicero, Il. 60804-4503
Phone: (708) 780-3700
Fax: (708) 780-3753
Website: www.hawthorneracecourse.com
E-Mail: jim@hawthorneracecourse.com
Year Founded: 1890, by Edward Corrigan
Dates of Inaugural Meeting: May 20, 1891
Abbreviation: Haw
Acreage: 119
Number of Stalls: 2,100
Seating Capacity: 18,000

Officers
Chairman: Patricia Bidwell
President: Thomas F. Carey III
General Manager: Thomas F. Carey III
Director of Racing: Gary M. Duch
Racing Secretary: Gary M. Duch
Secretary: P. J. Mudro
Director of Operations: Thomas F. Carey III
Director of Communications: Jim Miller
Director of Marketing: Joe Scurto
Director of Mutuels: Michael P. Hart
Vice President: Mary Patton Pitocchelli
Director of Publicity: Jim Miller
Director of Sales: Pam Dorr
Director of Simulcasting: Lorene Heninger
Horsemen's Liaison: Tim Becker
Stewards: Eddie Arroyo, Joseph K. Lindeman, Steve Morgan
Track Announcer: Peter Galassi
Track Photographer: Four Footed Fotos
Track Superintendent: Gregorio Cardenas
Security: Dennis Taylor

Racing Dates
2004: February 27-May 13, 47 days; September 20, 2004-Jan-
uary 2, 2005, 67 days
2005: February 25-May 10, 54 days; September 23-Decem-
ber 31, 70 days

Track Layout
Main Circumference: 1 mile
Main Track Chute: 6 1/2 furlongs
Main Width: 75 feet
Main Length of Stretch: 1,320 feet
Main Turf Circumference: 7 furlongs, 148 feet

Attendance
Average Daily Recent Meeting: 2,484, Spring 2004; 2,068,
Fall 2004
Total Attendance Recent Meeting: 116,744, Spring 2004;
138,575, Fall 2004
Highest Single Day Record: 37,792, September 6, 1937

Handle
Average All Sources Recent Meeting: $2,380,828, Spring
2004; $2,785,202, Fall 2004
Average On-Track Recent Meeting: $224,518, Spring 2004;
$199,275, Fall 2004
Total All Sources Recent Meeting: $111,898,907, Spring
2004; $186,608,567, Fall 2004
Total On-Track Recent Meeting: $10,552,359, Spring 2004;
$13,351,407, Fall 2004
Record Daily Average for Single Meet: $3,575,861, 1996
Single Day On-Track Handle: $10,300,640, May 5, 2001

Leaders
Career, Leading Jockey by Wins: Earlie Fires, 1,117

Records
Single Day Jockey Wins: Johnny Heckman, 7, October 1, 1956
Single Day Trainer Wins: Mike Reavis, 5, November 2, 2002
Single Meet, Leading Jockey by Wins: Mark Guidry, 137, 1995
Single Meet, Leading Trainer by Wins: Richard Hazelton, 48,
1976

Track Records, Main Dirt
4 1/2 furlongs: Joanies Bella, :51.80, May 28, 2001
5 furlongs: De La Concorde, :57, November 11, 1992
5 1/2 furlongs: Marluel's Troy, 1:02 2/5, November 2, 1976
6 furlongs: Satan's Poppy, 1:08 1/5, October 21, 1978
6 1/2 furlongs: Dee Lance, 1:14 2/5, August 27, 1988
1 mile: Actuary, 1:37 1/5, July 17, 1923; Hopeless, 1:37 1/5,
August 29, 1925
1m 70 yds: Soldat Bleu, 1:39 1/5, July 27, 1988
1 1/16 miles: Sensitive Prince, 1:39 3/5, September 23, 1978
1 1/8 miles: *Zografos, 1:46 3/5, October 9, 1974
1 3/16 miles: Lindy's Lad, 1:59 2/5, November 12, 1980
1 1/4 miles: Gladwin, 1:58 4/5, October 1, 1970; Group Plan,
1:58 4/5, October 19, 1974

1 1/2 miles: David, 2:29 3/5, October 1, 1969
1 5/8 miles: Viale (Uru), 2:47, December 10, 2000
1 3/4 miles: America Fore, 3:02 1/5, October 2, 1943
Other: 2 furlongs, Minty Flavors, :20.88, May 14, 1999; 1 13/16 miles, Stiffelio (Ire), 3:14 3/5, November 15, 1997; 2 miles 70 yds, Sun N Shine, 3:30 2/5, October 19, 1974

Track Records, Main Turf

5 furlongs: Sulemark, :56, October 25, 1992
7 furlongs: Glassy Dip, 1:22 3/5, May 30, 1977
7 1/2 furlongs: Joey Jr., 1:27 1/5, November 5, 1989
1 mile: Soviet Line (Ire), 1:33.40, July 25, 1998
1 1/16 miles: Bendecida, 1:40.53, September 6, 1999
1 1/8 miles: Rainbows for Life, 1:44 3/5, October 13, 1991
1 3/16 miles: Royal Glint, 1:54 2/5, September 28, 1974; Sari's Baba, 1:54 2/5, September 24, 1985
1 1/4 miles: Pass the Line, 2:00 2/5, August 10, 1985
1 3/8 miles: Shayzari (Ire), 2:15 1/5, September 3, 1988
1 1/2 miles: Lord Comet, 2:26.87, October 27, 1999
1 3/4 miles: Neverest, 2:58 4/5, August 31, 1973

Principal Races

Hawthorne Gold Cup (G2), Illinois Derby (G2), National Jockey Club H. (G3), Sixty Sails H. (G3), Hawthorne Derby (G3).

Interesting Facts

Trivia: First major U.S. track to use an electric timer (1931). Track announcer Phil Georgeff entered the Guiness Book of World Records when he called his 85,000th race on August 13, 1988.

Fastest Times of 2004 (Dirt)

4 1/2 furlongs: Midnight Miss, :53.53, May 4, 2004
6 furlongs: Wonone, 1:08.97, December 5, 2004
6 1/2 furlongs: Big Talkin Man, 1:15.99, December 11, 2004
1m 70 yds: Noble Ruler, 1:41.77, March 26, 2004
1 1/16 miles: Dancefortyniner, 1:43.25, December 4, 2004
1 1/8 miles: Ten Most Wanted, 1:49.54, April 17, 2004
1 1/4 miles: Freefourinternet, 2:03.34, October 2, 2004

Fastest Times of 2004 (Turf)

1 mile: Scooter Roach, 1:34.51, October 9, 2004
1 1/16 miles: Great Bloom, 1:41.10, May 2, 2004
1 1/8 miles: Cool Conductor, 1:47.89, October 16, 2004

Indiana

Hoosier Park

In 1989, Indiana approved pari-mutuel wagering, and the state's first pari-mutuel racetrack, Hoosier Park, opened its inaugural season of Standardbred racing in 1994. Thoroughbred racing debuted at Hoosier in 1995. Located northeast of Indianapolis in Anderson, the $10-million track was developed by majority owner Churchill Downs Inc. as the company's first racing interest outside Kentucky. Hoosier annually holds a Thoroughbred meet. For 2004, Hoosier hosted two graded stakes, the $500,000 Indiana Derby (G2) and the $350,000 Indiana Breeders' Cup Oaks (G3). A competitor, Indiana Downs, opened on April 1, 2003, only 40 miles from its facility.

Location: 4500 Dan Patch Circle, Anderson, In. 46013-3165
Phone: (765) 642-7223
Phone: (800) 526-7223
Fax: (765) 644-0467
Website: www.hoosierpark.com
E-Mail: info@hoosierpark.com
Year Founded: 1994
Dates of Inaugural Meeting: September 1-October 28, 1995
Abbreviation: Hoo
Acreage: 105
Number of Stalls: 1080
Seating Capacity: 15,000

Ownership

Churchill Downs Inc. and Centaur

Officers

Chairman: Thomas H. Meeker
President: Richard B. Moore
General Manager: Richard B. Moore
Director of Racing: Raymond "Butch" Cook
Racing Secretary: Raymond "Butch" Cook
Secretary: Rebecca Reed
Treasurer: Steven L. Wilkening
Director of Operations: Kevin Mack
Director of Admissions: Sue Walters
Director of Communications: Thomas F. Bannon
Director of Finance: Steven L. Wilkening
Director of Marketing: Donna Smith
Director of Mutuels: Randy Westerman
Vice President: Donald R. Richardson
Director of Publicity: Thomas F. Bannon
Director of Sales: Jim Garrett
Director of Simulcasting: Randy Westerman
Horsemen's Liaison: Kathryn Bonham
Stewards: Gary I. Wilfert, James Higginbottom, Mike Manganello
Track Announcer: Steve Cross
Track Photographer: Jim Linscott
Track Superintendent: John Betts
Security: James Leist
Horsemen's Bookkeeper: Karen Baker
Asst. Racing Secretary: Michael Smith

Racing Dates

2004: September 2-November 21, 59 days
2005: September 3-November 25, 60 days

Track Layout

Main Circumference: 7 furlongs
Main Track Chute: 6 furlongs
Main Width: 90 feet
Main Length of Stretch: 1,255 feet

Attendance

Average Daily Recent Meeting: 955, 2004
Highest Single Day Record: 10,827, October 7, 2000
Highest Single Meet Record: 95,468, 1995
Record Daily Average for Single Meet: 2,273, 1995
Total Attendance Recent Meeting: 56,345, 2004

Handle

Average All Sources Recent Meeting: $1,303,110, 2004
Average On-Track Recent Meeting: $76,321, 2004
Record Daily Average for Single Meet: $1,465,497, 2003
Single Day On-Track Handle: $2,207,621, November 14, 2003
Total All Sources Recent Meeting: $76,883,506, 2004
Total On-Track Recent Meeting: $4,502,937, 2004
Highest Single Day Recent Meet: $2,083,118, November 6, 2004

Mutuel Records

Highest Win: $291.40, Mi Serenade, October 19, 2001
Highest Exacta: $3,212.60, September 10, 2000
Highest Trifecta: $34,077.20, November 22, 2002
Highest Daily Double: $5,986.40, October 17, 2002
Highest Pick 3: $8,952.00, November 22, 2002
Highest Other Exotics: $36,602.80, Superfecta, November 28, 2003

Leaders

Career, Leading Jockey by Titles: Jon Court, 3
Career, Leading Owner by Titles: Highway 1 Racing Stable, 3
Career, Leading Trainer by Titles: Ralph Martinez, Gary Patrick, Stanley Roberts, 2 each
Recent Meeting, Leading Jockey: Ramsey Zimmerman, 92, 2004
Recent Meeting, Leading Trainer: Ralph Martinez, 62, 2004
Career, Leading Jockey by Stakes Wins: Jon Court, 13
Career, Leading Owner by Stakes Wins: McKee Stables, 9
Career, Leading Trainer by Stakes Wins: Dale Romans, 17
Career, Leading Jockey by Wins: Terry Thompson, 393
Career, Leading Owner by Wins: Louis O'Brien, 131
Career, Leading Trainer by Wins: Gary Patrick, 168

Records

Single Day Jockey Wins: Terry Thompson, 7, November 18, 2001

Single Day Trainer Wins: David Pate, 3, October 11, 1995; Bernard Flint, 3, November 4, 1995; Kathleen Cooper, 3, September 20, 1996; Stephen Dunn, 3, September 14, 1997; Stanley Roberts, 3, October 2, 1998; Barbara McBride, 3, September 14, 1999; Stanley Roberts, 3, October 29, 1999; Stanley Roberts, 3, September 22, 2000; Michael Mann, 3, October 20, 2001; Gary Patrick, 3, September 22, 2002; Ralph Martinez, 3, September 5, 2003; Ralph Martinez, 3, September 17, 2003; Ralph Martinez, 3, October 24, 2003; Ralph Martinez, 3, November 28, 2003

Single Meet, Leading Jockey by Wins: Terry Thompson, 122, 2001

Single Meet, Leading Owner by Wins: Louis O'Brien, 66, 2003

Single Meet, Leading Trainer by Wins: Ralph Martinez, 66, 2003

Track Records, Main Dirt

5 furlongs: Jimmy Jones, :58.39, October 9, 2004
5 1/2 furlongs: Moro Oro, 1:02.20, September 20, 1996; Chukker Creek, 1:02.20, November 24, 1996
6 furlongs: Moro Oro, 1:07.40, November 16, 1996
1 mile: Vic's Rebel, 1:33.40, October 13, 1998
1 1/16 miles: Alydar's Rib, 1:41, November 1, 1996
1 1/8 miles: Henbane's Cat, 1:54.47, October 2, 2004
1 1/2 miles: Got Brass, 2:36.88, October 30, 2004
1 5/8 miles: Open Space, 2:41.20, November 16, 1996
Other: 1 9/16 miles, Our Forbes, 2:39.20, November 7, 1997; 1 7/8 miles, Raw New, 3:16.20, December 1, 2000

Principal Races

Indiana Derby (G2), Indiana Breeders' Cup Oaks (G3), Michael Schaefer Mile

Notable Events

Indiana Derby Gala, Ladies' Night

Fastest Times of 2004 (Dirt)

5 furlongs: Jimmy Jones, :58.39, October 9, 2004
5 1/2 furlongs: Mr Mag, 1:04.23, October 2, 2004
6 furlongs: Mr. Mink, 1:09.93, September 19, 2004
1 mile: Added Edge, 1:35.85, November 13, 2004
1 1/16 miles: Daydreaming, 1:43.65, October 1, 2004
1 1/8 miles: Henbane's Cat, 1:54.47, October 2, 2004
1 1/2 miles: Got Brass, 2:36.88, October 30, 2004

Indiana Downs

Located in Shelbyville, about 40 miles southeast of Indianapolis, Indiana Downs held its inaugural Thoroughbred meet in 2003. Construction of the $35-million track was opposed by Hoosier Park, but the red-and-white grandstand facility opened on schedule for its inaugural 2002 Standardbred meet. Owned by Oliver Racing LLC and LHT Capital LLC, the track opened its first off-track betting facility in February 2003 in Evansville, near Churchill-owned Ellis Park, and in 2004 opened an OTB facility across the Ohio River from Louisville, home of Churchill Downs. Beginning in 2003, Indiana Downs and Hoosier split the state subsidy generated by a tax on riverboat admissions.

Location: 4200 N Michigan Rd., Shelbyville, In. 46176-8515
Phone: (317) 421-0000
Phone: (866) 478-7223
Fax: (317) 421-0100
Website: www.indianadowns.com
E-Mail: info@indianadowns.com
Year Founded: 2002
Dates of Inaugural Meeting: April 11-May 26, 2003
Abbreviation: InD

Ownership

Indianapolis Downs LLC

Officers

Chairman: Ross Mangano
President: Ralph Ross
General Manager: Jon Schuster
Director of Racing: Raymond Cook
Racing Secretary: Raymond Cook
Secretary: Michael Keller
Treasurer: Richard Roggeveen
Director of Operations: Eddie Matson
Director of Marketing: Liza Markle-Bell
Director of Mutuels: Eddie Matson
Vice President: Paul Estridge Jr.
Director of Publicity: Joe Thompson
Stewards: Denny Oelschlager, Gary Wilfert, Rick Evans
Track Announcer: Dominic Polito
Track Photographer: Jeff Coady
Security: Dave Scranton

Racing Dates

2004: April 16-June 20, 48 days
2005: April 15-June 18, 48 days

Mutuel Records

Highest Pick 6: $322,561.40, August 9, 2004

Principal Races

Oliver S., Checkered Flag S., First Lady S., Indiana Sires Derby, Veterans S.

Fastest Times of 2004 (Dirt)

4 1/2 furlongs: Woodside Parkway, :51.20, June 18, 2004
5 furlongs: Roll the Gold, :57.85, May 6, 2004
5 1/2 furlongs: Savoya On Ice, 1:03.30, June 11, 2004
6 furlongs: Tee to Green, 1:10.17, April 23, 2004
1 mile: Way Fleeter, 1:37.74, May 19, 2004
1m 70 yds: Cowboy's Limelite, 1:41.92, April 16, 2004
1 1/16 miles: Roberto Royale, 1:44.00, June 16, 2004
1 1/8 miles: Dr. Robbie, 1:52.79, May 31, 2004
1 1/4 miles: Pleasant Italian, 2:06.35, June 9, 2004

Fastest Times of 2004 (Turf)

5 furlongs: Captain Larkin, :57.14, June 4, 2004
a5 furlongs: Fit to Keep, :58.64, June 11, 2004
7 1/2 furlongs: Crackerbox Palace, 1:29.89, June 4, 2004
1 mile: If I Were You, 1:36.51, May 23, 2004
a1 miles: Dashing Princess, 1:39.73, June 11, 2004
1 1/16 miles: If I Were You, 1:41.94, June 6, 2004
a1 1/16 miles: General Lee, 1:43.82, June 9, 2004
1 3/8 miles: Parisky, 2:11.37, June 20, 2004

Iowa

Prairie Meadows Racetrack

The Thoroughbred industry in Iowa received a boost when Prairie Meadows Racetrack in Altoona, not far from Des Moines, opened in 1989. But financial difficulties forced the track to file for bankruptcy in 1991 and to close for live racing in '92. The following year, Prairie Meadows became the property of Polk County, which today leases the facility to the not-for-profit Racing Association of Central Iowa. The track's future was secured in 1995 when slot machines were installed, with a portion of revenues significantly increasing race purses. Today, Prairie Meadows's live racing schedule begins with a Thoroughbred meet that is followed by a mixed meet for Thoroughbreds and Quarter Horses, and concludes with a harness racing season. One of the track's most popular events is the Iowa Classic, a ten-race event for state-bred Thoroughbreds and Quarter Horses.

Location: 1 Prairie Meadows Dr., Altoona, Ia. 50009-0901
Phone: (515) 967-1000
Phone: (800) 325-9015
Fax: (859) 288-1081
Website: *www.prairiemeadows.com*
E-Mail: marylou.coady@prairiemeadows.com
Year Founded: July 19, 1984
Dates of Inaugural Meeting: March 1-15, 1989
Abbreviation: PrM
Acreage: 233
Number of Stalls: 1,350
Seating Capacity: 7,000

Officers
Chairman: Jack Bishop
President: Robert A. Farinella
General Manager: Robert A. Farinella
Director of Racing: Derron D. Heldt
Racing Secretary: Daniel J. Doocy
Secretary: Shirley Kleywegt
Director of Finance: Pat Fox
Director of Marketing: Tom Manning
Director of Mutuels: Mark Loewe
Vice President: Gary Palmer
Director of Publicity: Mary Lou Coady
Director of Simulcasting: Mark Loewe
Horsemen's Liaison: Chuck Schott
Stewards: Gerald Hobby, Ralph D'Amico, Rick Sackett
Track Announcer: Jim McAulay
Track Photographer: Jack Coady Jr.
Track Superintendent: Bob Gorla
Asst. Racing Secretary: Tom Davis

Racing Dates
2004: April 16-July 4, 49 days; July 9-September 25, 47 days
2005: April 21-July 4, 47 days; July 8-September 24, 48 days

Track Layout
Main Circumference: 1 mile
Main Track Chute: 2 furlongs and 6 furlongs
Main Width: Homestretch: 90 feet; Backstretch: 60 feet
Main Length of Stretch: 1,033 feet
Training Track: 5/8 mile

Attendance
Average Daily Recent Meeting: 9,091, Spring 2004; 8,525, Summer 2004
Total Attendance Recent Meeting: 445,459, Spring 2004; 400,675, Fall 2004

Handle
Average On-Track Recent Meeting: $79,777, Spring 2004; $57,976, Summer 2004
Record Daily Average for Single Meet: $580,430, Fall 2002
Single Day On-Track Handle: $488,070, May 5, 1990
Total On-Track Recent Meeting: $3,909,080, Spring 2004; $2,724,855, Summer 2004

Mutuel Records
Lowest Win: $2.20
Highest Exacta: $2,424.20, May 19, 1997
Lowest Exacta: $3.60, July 28, 1994
Highest Trifecta: $35,761.40, August 31, 2002
Lowest Trifecta: $7.80, July 22, 2000
Highest Daily Double: $2,216, September 24, 1998
Lowest Daily Double: $3.00, August 28, 2004

Leaders
Career, Leading Jockey by Titles: Glenn Corbett, 5
Career, Leading Owner by Titles: River Ridge Ranch, 6
Career, Leading Trainer by Titles: Dick R. Clark, 15
Recent Meeting, Leading Jockey: Timothy T. Doocy, 78, Spring 2004; Timothy T. Doocy, 54, Summer 2004
Recent Meeting, Leading Trainer: Dick R. Clark, 52, Spring 2004; Dick R. Clark, 43, Summer 2004
Career, Leading Owner by Wins: Maggi Moss, 140
Career, Leading Trainer by Wins: Dick R. Clark, 505

Records
Single Day Jockey Wins: Terry Thompson, 6, May 20, 2002
Single Meet, Leading Jockey by Wins: Kelly Murray, 101, 1989
Single Meet, Leading Owner by Wins: Maggi Moss, 35, 2004
Single Meet, Leading Trainer by Wins: Gary Ryan, 76, 1989

Track Records, Main Dirt
4 furlongs: Straight Fever, :46.20, July 16, 1993
4 1/2 furlongs: Southern Alert, :51.24, May 7, 2002
5 furlongs: Dayjob, :56, May 1, 1999
5 1/2 furlongs: Leaping Plum, 1:02.50, August 5, 1997
6 furlongs: Coach Jimi Lee, 1:07.85, July 4, 2004
1 mile: Tartine, 1:35, August 11, 1998
1m 70 yds: Northwest Hill, 1:39.69, July 4, 2003
1 1/16 miles: Excessivepleasure, 1:40.82, July 5, 2003
1 1/8 miles: Beboppin Baby, 1:46.62, July 4, 1998
1 1/4 miles: Famous Event, 2:02.60, June 23, 1995
1 1/2 miles: Famous Event, 2:32, July 9, 1995
1 5/8 miles: Sir Star, 2:44.3, May 12, 1989
2 miles: Gritti Marco, 3:26, July 28, 1995
Other: 2 furlongs, Dashboard Drummer, :22.20, May 9, 2003

Principal Races
Prairie Meadows Cornhusker Breeders' Cup H. (G2), Iowa Oaks (G3), Iowa Derby, Iowa Sprint H., Iowa Classic

Fastest Times of 2004 (Dirt)
4 1/2 furlongs: Panorama Valley, :52.13, May 11, 2004
5 furlongs: Panorama Valley, :57.05, July 1, 2004
5 1/2 furlongs: Sterling's Lad, 1:03.33, May 24, 2004
6 furlongs: Coach Jimi Lee, 1:07.85, July 4, 2004
1 mile: Wildwood Royal, 1:35.75, May 21, 2004
1m 70 yds: Northwest Hill, 1:40.09, May 30, 2004
1 1/16 miles: Wildwood Royal, 1:41.44, June 12, 2004
1 1/8 miles: Roses in May, 1:46.63, July 3, 2004
1 1/4 miles: Reactionary, 2:03.80, May 30, 2004
2 miles: Old Man's Delite, 3:32.25, September 25, 2004

Kansas

Anthony Downs

Location: 521 East Sherman, P.O. Box 444, Anthony, Ks. 67003-0444
Phone: (620) 842-3796
Fax: (620) 842-3797
Website: *www.anthonydownsraces.com*
Year Founded: 1904
Abbreviation: AnF

Ownership
Anthony Fair Association

Officers
President: Dan Bird
Racing Secretary: Norris E. Gwin
Secretary: Terry Allen
Treasurer: Mel Kitts
Vice President: Joe Wilcox
Director of Publicity: Tom Morris
Track Announcer: John Ridenhour
Security: John Blevins
Asst. Racing Secretary: Rita Osborn

Racing Dates
2004: July 16-July 25, 6 days
2006: July 14-July 23, 6 days
2005: July 15-July 24, 6 days

Track Layout
Main Circumference: 4 furlongs

Attendance
Average Daily Recent Meeting: 1,112, 2004
Total Attendance Recent Meeting: 6,670, 2004

Handle
Average All Sources Recent Meeting: $41,552, 2004
Total All Sources Recent Meeting: $249,312, 2004
Highest Single Day Recent Meet: $73,000, July, 25, 2004

Leaders
Recent Meeting, Leading Horse: Overprint, 2, 2004
Recent Meeting, Leading Jockey: Richard M. Vasquez, 7, 2004
Recent Meeting, Leading Trainer: Joe Frederick Thomas, Sr., 4, 2004

Principal Races
Anthony Downs Derby, Anthony Thoroughbred Futurity, Harper County H., Anthony Fair H., Gene Francis and Associates S., Kansas Bred Centennial H.

Notable Events
Kansas City BBQ Society Contest

Fastest Times of 2004 (Dirt)
4 1/2 furlongs: Appealing Promise, :56.46, July 17, 2004
5 furlongs: Hawks Slugger, 1:01.39, July 25, 2004
a5 furlongs: Sunset Cruise, 1:01.72, July 18, 2004
6 1/2 furlongs: Marlin's Ruler, 1:21.54, July 25, 2004
7 furlongs: Donut Beat All, 1:31.93, July 17, 2004
1 1/16 miles: Overprint, 1:53.42, July 24, 2004
a1 1/16 miles: Overprint, 1:54.54, July 17, 2004

Eureka Downs

Eureka Downs, located 60 miles east of Wichita, runs a mixed horse meet on weekends and holidays from the first week of May through July 4. The five-furlong track, which dates to 1872, raced Standardbreds in the late 1940s and was the site of Kansas's first pari-mutuel race for Thoroughbreds on September 3, 1988. The track closed in 1991 and reopened in '93 with the Greenwood County Fair Association and the Kansas Quarter Horse Racing Association co-licensed as operators. Eureka Downs races Thoroughbreds, Quarter Horses, Appaloosas, Paints, and mules. Nonbetting mule contests began in the late 1990s and proved so popular that they were added to the pari-mutuel menu.

Location: 210 N Jefferson St., P.O. Box 228, Eureka, Ks. 67045
Phone: (620) 583-5528
Fax: (620) 583-5381
Website: www.eurekadowns.com
E-Mail: info@eurekadowns.com
Year Founded: 1993
Abbreviation: Eur

Officers
Director of Publicity: Coralee Farley

Racing Dates
2004: May 3-July 5, 20 days
2005: May 7-July 10, 20 days

Track Layout
Main Circumference: 5 furlongs

Fastest Times of 2004 (Dirt)
4 furlongs: Notus, :45.53, June 6, 2004
6 furlongs: Reign of Class, 1:13.65, June 26, 2004
7 furlongs: Clever Red, 1:29.37, June 12, 2004

The Woodlands

Opened in September 1989 for greyhound racing, The Woodlands began Thoroughbred racing on May 24, 1990. The track, located in the northwest corner of Kansas City, offers a 26-day mixed horse racing meet for Thoroughbreds and Quarter Horses in October and year-round greyhound racing on a separate track. The three types of racing have been conducted concurrently since 1990. The Woodlands set a single-day attendance record of 22,015 in its first year of Thoroughbred operation with a wallet giveaway. The track's then-parent company filed for bankruptcy protection from its creditors in 1996. The track was sold in 1998 to William M. Grace, principal owner of the St. Jo Frontier Casino in St. Joseph, Missouri.

Location: 9700 Leavenworth Rd., Kansas City, Ks. 66109-3551
Phone: (913) 299-9797
Phone: (800) 695-RACE
Fax: (913) 299-9804
Website: www.woodlandskc.com
E-Mail: info@woodlandskc.com
Year Founded: 1989
Dates of Inaugural Meeting: May 24, 1990
Abbreviation: Wds
Acreage: 700
Number of Stalls: 1,250
Seating Capacity: 4,250

Ownership
Kansas Racing LLC

Officers
General Manager: James Gartland
Director of Racing: Doug Schoepf
Racing Secretary: Doug Schoepf
Secretary: Larry Seckington
Director of Operations: Kevin King
Director of Finance: Charles Wheeler
Director of Marketing: Connie Loebsack
Director of Mutuels: Carl Schroll
Vice President: Bruce Schmitter
Director of Publicity: Connie Loesback
Director of Sales: Denise Souza
Director of Simulcasting: Jayme LaRocca
Stewards: Trudy Lyons, Sam Lato, Robert Stovall
Track Announcer: Keith Nelson
Horsemen's Bookkeeper: Judy Laster
Security: Robert Fritz

Racing Dates
2004: September 20-October 31, 30 days
2005: September 24-October 29, 26 days

Track Layout
Main Circumference: 1 mile
Main Track Chute: 6 furlongs
Main Length of Stretch: 1,030 feet

Attendance
Average Daily Recent Meeting: 1,480, 2004
Highest Single Day Record: 22,015, July 22, 1990
Total Attendance Recent Meeting: 44,405, 2004

Handle
Average All Sources Recent Meeting: $197,168, 2004
Average On-Track Recent Meeting: $61,411, 2004
Total All Sources Recent Meeting: $5,915,065, 2004
Total On-Track Recent Meeting: $1,842,343, 2004
Highest Single Day Record Recent Meet: $338,479, October 25, 2004

Leaders
Recent Meeting, Leading Horse: Tushar, 3, 2004; Wind Twister, 3, 2004
Recent Meeting, Leading Jockey: Alex Birzer, 31, 2004
Recent Meeting, Leading Trainer: Timothy Gleason, 19, 2004

Track Records, Main Dirt
4 furlongs: King of Diamonds, :45.80, October 10, 2001
4 1/2 furlongs: Lanyons Star, :51 2/5, June 29, 1990
5 furlongs: Jungle Merit, :57.40, October 29, 1993
5 1/2 furlongs: Axe Age, 1:03.20, August 15, 1993
6 furlongs: Great Immunity, 1:08.50, June 30, 1991
1 mile: French Fritter, 1:36, June 1, 1991
1m 70 yds: Holly's Wind, 1:40 2/5, June 24, 1990
1 1/16 miles: Axle Lode, 1:42.80, September 22, 1996
1 1/8 miles: Model Age, 1:49 4/5, July 18, 1990
1 3/16 miles: Old Man's Delite, 1:58, October 21, 2003
1 1/4 miles: Midway Mail, 2:03.20, September 10, 1993
1 1/2 miles: He's a Valentine, 2:33.20, October 14, 1994
1 3/4 miles: Mark of Strength, 3:02, November 5, 1993

Principal Races
Manhattan H., Sunflower H., Kansas Oaks, Woodlands Derby, Woodlands H.

Fastest Times of 2004 (Dirt)
5 furlongs: Scarlet Jeff, 1:00.00, September 26, 2004
5 1/2 furlongs: Fast Senorita, 1:04.20, October 22, 2004
6 furlongs: Ww Conquistador, 1:09.60, September 25, 2004
1 mile: Rapadash (Ire), 1:38.60, September 24, 2004
1m 70 yds: Lady Riss, 1:44.00, October 23, 2004; Luckymata, 1:44.00, October 17, 2004; Winaprize, 1:44.00, September 26, 2004
1 1/16 miles: Wildwood Royal, 1:45.00, October 10, 2004
1 1/8 miles: Gun Runner, 1:53.00, October 16, 2004
1 3/4 miles: Gun Runner, 3:03.40, October 31, 2004

Kentucky

Churchill Downs

Churchill Downs in Louisville is arguably the world's best-known racetrack, and its premier event, the Kentucky Derby (G1), is widely recognized as the sport's best-known race. First staged in 1875, the Derby is one of America's oldest continually run races and annually attracts an on-track throng exceeding 140,000, the nation's largest crowd for a Thoroughbred race, as well as worldwide television audience in the millions. The Derby has been held at Churchill since the track opened on its current site in 1875. Col. M. Lewis Clark Jr., the track's founder, built the first grandstand on land he secured from uncles John and Henry Churchill. Churchill Downs had financial problems for the first 28 years of its existence, forcing its sale by Clark and subsequent owners until Col. Matt Winn and partners bought the track in 1902. The track, whose famous Twin Spires date from 1895, today is owned by Churchill Downs Inc., which also owns Hollywood Park near Los Angeles, Arlington Park near Chicago, Calder Race Course in Miami, Ellis Park in western Kentucky, and Fair Grounds in New Orleans. It also is part-owner of Hoosier Park in Indiana. Churchill has hosted five runnings of the Breeders' Cup, beginning in 1988 and most recently in 2000. In 2005, Churchill completed a $121-million renovation project, including a $95-million rebuilding of the track's clubhouse.

Location: 700 Central Ave., Louisville, Ky. 40208-1200
Phone: (502) 636-4400
Phone: (800) 28-DERBY
Fax: (502) 636-4430
Website: www.churchilldowns.com
E-Mail: info@kyderby.com
Year Founded: 1875

Dates of Inaugural Meeting: May 17, 1875
Abbreviation: CD
Acreage: 147
Number of Stalls: 1,404
Seating Capacity: 41,851

Ownership
Churchill Downs Inc.

Officers
Chairman: Carl Pollard
President: Steve Sexton
General Manager: Jim Gates
Director of Racing: Doug Bredar
Racing Secretary: Doug Bredar
Vice President of Operations: David Sweazy
Director of Admissions: Ray Pait Jr.
Vice President of Communications: John Asher
Director of Marketing: Stacey Meier
Director of Mutuels: Rick Smith
Director of Publicity: Tony Terry
Horsemen's Liaison: J. L. "Buck" Wheat
Stewards: Richard S. Leigh, Steve Obrekaitis, Mickey Sample
Track Announcer: Luke Kruytbosch
Track Photographer: Four Footed Fotos
Track Superintendent: Raymond "Butch" Lehr Jr.
Chief executive officer: Thomas H. Meeker

Racing Dates
2004: April 24-July 4, 53 days; October 31-November 27, 21 days
2005: April 30-July 10, 52 days; October 30-November 26, 21 days

Track Layout
Main Circumference: 1 mile
Main Track Chute: 1 1/4 miles
Main Width: Homestretch: 80 feet; Backstretch: 79 feet
Main Length of Stretch: 1,234.5 feet
Main Turf Circumference: 7 furlongs
Main Turf Width: 80 feet

Attendance
Average Daily Recent Meeting: 11,955, Spring 2004; 7,467, Fall 2004
Highest Single Day Record: 163,628, May 4, 1974
Highest Single Meet Record: 811,446, Spring 1988
Record Daily Average for Single Meet: 20,066, Spring 1944
Total Attendance Recent Meeting: 633,016, Spring 2004; 156,305, Fall 2004

Handle
Average All Sources Recent Meeting: $11,204,112, Spring 2004; $7,798,867, Fall 2004
Average On-Track Recent Meeting: $1,644,246, Spring 2004; $1,100,251, Fall 2004
Record Daily Average for Single Meet: $2,054,901, Spring 1997
Total All Sources Recent Meeting: $593,817,958, Spring 2004; $163,776,216, Fall 2004
Total On-Track Recent Meeting: $87,145,043, Spring 2004; $23,105,268, Fall 2004
Highest Single Day Recent Meet: $141,088,445, May 1, 2004 - Derby day; $12,070,673, November 26, 2004

Mutuel Records
Highest Win: $495.60, Gold and Rubles, November 21, 1978
Highest Exacta: $9,814.80, May 7, 2005
Highest Trifecta: $133,134.80, May 7, 2005
Highest Daily Double: $6,818.20, October 29, 1984
Highest Pick 3: $114,156, November 4, 2000
Highest Pick 6: $1,168,136, June 25, 2003
Highest Other Exotics: $1,728,507, Superfecta, May 7, 2005

Leaders
Career, Leading Jockey by Titles: Pat Day, 34
Career, Leading Owner by Titles: Kenneth and Sarah Ramsey, 9

Career, Leading Trainer by Titles: D. Wayne Lukas, 11
Recent Meeting, Leading Jockey: Rafael Bejarano, 81, Spring 2004; John McKee, 27, Fall 2004
Recent Meeting, Leading Owner: Kenneth and Sarah Ramsey, 19, Spring 2004; Overbrook Farm, 5, Fall 2004
Recent Meeting, Leading Trainer: Steve Asmussen, 35, Spring 2004; Steve Asmussen, 14, Fall 2004
Career, Leading Owner by Stakes Wins: Calumet Farm, 32
Career, Leading Trainer by Stakes Wins: William I. Mott, 65
Career, Leading Jockey by Wins: Pat Day, 2,340
Career, Leading Trainer by Wins: William I. Mott, 525

Records
Single Day Jockey Wins: Pat Day, 7, June 20, 1984
Single Meet, Leading Jockey Wins: Pat Day, 169, 1983
Single Meet, Leading Trainer by Wins: William I. Mott, 54, 1984

Track Records, Main Dirt
4 furlongs: Fair Phantom, :46 3/5, May 7, 1921; Casey :46 3/5, May 9, 1921; Miss Joy, :46 3/5, May 10, 1921
4 1/2 furlongs: Chilukki, :51, April 28, 1999
5 furlongs: Put Me In, :56.61, June 10, 2004
5 1/2 furlongs: Cashier's Dream, 1:02.52, July 7, 2002
6 furlongs: Kona Gold, 1:07.77, November 4, 2000
6 1/2 furlongs: Love At Noon, 1:14.34, May 5, 2001
7 furlongs: Alannan, 1:20.50, May 5, 2001
7 1/2 furlongs: Miss Lodi, 1:28.08, June 1, 2002
1 mile: Chilukki, 1:33.57, November 4, 2000
1m 70 yds: The Porter, 1:41 3/5, May 30, 1919
1 1/16 miles: Yes Sir, 1:41 3/5, November 25, 1970
1 1/8 miles: Victory Gallop, 1:47.28, June 12, 1999
1 3/16 miles: Bonnie Andrew, 1:58 3/5, November 14, 1942
1 1/4 miles: Secretariat, 1:59 2/5, May 5, 1973
1 3/8 miles: Elliott, 2:20 3/5, October 15, 1906
1 1/2 miles: A Storm Is Brewing, 2:32.02, June 17, 2001
1 5/8 miles: Tupolev (Arg), 2:49 2/5, July 23, 1983
1 3/4 miles: Caslon Bold, 2:59.64, July 4, 1995
2 miles: Libertarian, 3:22.26, November 28, 1998
Other: 1m 20 yds, Frog Legs, 1:39, May 13, 1913; 1m 50 yds, Hodge, 1:41 4/5, October 4, 1916; 1m 100 yds, The Caxton, 1:49 1/5, May 16, 1902; 2 1/16 miles, Hi Neighbor, 3:40 4/5, November 11, 1949; 2 1/4 miles, Raincoat, 3:53, October 7, 1915; 3 miles, Ten Broeck, 5:26 1/5, September 3, 1876; 4 miles, Sotemia, 7:10 4/5, October 7, 1912

Track Records, Main Turf
5 furlongs: Are You Down, :55.57, May 14, 2003
1 mile: Jaggery John, 1:33.78, July 4, 1995
1 1/16 miles: Ever With You, 1:40.82, November 7, 2001
1 1/8 miles: Lure, 1:46.34, April 30, 1993
1 3/8 miles: Snake Eyes, 2:13, May 22, 1997
1 1/2 miles: Tikkanen, 2:26.50, November 5, 1994

Principal Races
Spring Meet: Kentucky Derby (G1), Kentucky Oaks (G1), Woodford Reserve Turf Classic S. (G1), Humana Distaff H. (G1), Stephen Foster H. (G1)
Fall Meet: Clark H. (G2), Kentucky Jockey Club S. (G2), Golden Rod S. (G2), Falls City H. (G2), Churchill Downs Distaff H. (G2)

Notable Events
Fall Meet: Churchill Downs Chili Cook-Off
Spring Meet: Kentucky Derby, Festival in the Field, Brew and Barbecue Fest

Fastest Times of 2004 (Dirt)
4 1/2 furlongs: Primal Storm, :51.29, April 29, 2004
5 furlongs: Put Me In, :56.61, June 10, 2004
5 1/2 furlongs: Run Sarah Run, 1:03.94, July 3, 2004
6 furlongs: Clock Stopper, 1:08.67, June 9, 2004
6 1/2 furlongs: Tina Bull, 1:15.63, July 4, 2004
7 furlongs: Speightstown, 1:21.38, May 1, 2004
7 1/2 furlongs: Friendly Michelle, 1:28.26, April 29, 2004
1 mile: Halory Leigh, 1:35.05, November 7, 2004
1 1/16 miles: Added Edge, 1:42.44, May 8, 2004
1 1/8 miles: Alumni Hall, 1:49.66, June 10, 2004
1 1/4 miles: Mr. Mabee, 2:03.71, May 8, 2004
1 1/2 miles: Rupert Herd, 2:32.84, July 4, 2004

Fastest Times of 2004 (Turf)
5 furlongs: Anna Em, :55.97, June 23, 2004
1 mile: Quantum Merit, 1:34.15, July 3, 2004
1 1/16 miles: Salcombe (GB), 1:41.51, May 23, 2004
1 1/8 miles: Shaconage, 1:46.75, June 26, 2004
1 3/8 miles: Two Dot Slew, 2:16.71, May 6, 2004

Ellis Park

Ellis Park near Henderson, holds the distinction of being the only racetrack where soybeans are grown in the infield. Built in 1922 and designed after Saratoga Race Course, the track located on an island in the Ohio River near Evansville, Indiana, was originally named Dade Park and intended for harness racing. Within one month of its opening, the track replaced harness racing with Thoroughbred racing. Dade Park was plagued with financial problems and in 1923 and '24, the only racing held was for race cards on Labor Day weekend. In 1924, James C. Ellis, who owned construction and oil enterprises, purchased the track for $35,100 and reopened it for Thoroughbred racing in 1925. In 1954, two years before Ellis's death, the track's name was changed to James C. Ellis Park. In 1998, Churchill Downs Inc. purchased Ellis, and its purses have benefited from full-card simulcasting revenues. However, Churchill Downs Inc. announced in 2003 that it had lost money on Ellis and intended to sell it. Ellis's richest race each year is the $200,000 Gardenia Handicap (G3) for fillies and mares.

Location: P.O. Box 33, Henderson, Ky. 42419-0033
Phone: (812) 425-1456
Fax: (812) 425-3725
Website: www.ellisparkracing.com
Year Founded: 1922 (as Dade Park)
Dates of Inaugural Meeting: November 8, 1922
Abbreviation: EIP
Acreage: 214
Number of Stalls: 1,142
Seating Capacity: 7,750

Officers
President: Steve Sexton
General Manager: Paul D. Kuerzi
Director of Racing: Doug Bredar
Racing Secretary: Doug Bredar
Director of Operations: Robert A. Jackson
Director of Admissions: Marianne Wagner
Director of Finance: Tom Hattenbach
Director of Marketing: Bob Cunningham
Director of Mutuels: Jeff Hall
Vice President: Paul D. Kuerzi
Director of Publicity: Luke Kruytbosch
Director of Simulcasting: Robert A. Jackson
Horsemen's Liaison: Donna Porter
Stewards: Ronald Herbstreit, Steve Obrekaitis, Warren C. Groce
Track Announcer: Luke Kruytbosch
Track Photographer: Four Footed Photos
Track Superintendent: Glenn Thompson

Racing Dates
2004: July 7-September 6, 54 days
2005: July 13-September 5, 48 days

Track Layout
Main Circumference: 1 1/8 miles
Main Track Chute: 7 furlongs and 1 mile
Main Width: Homestretch: 100 feet; Backstretch: 85 feet
Main Length of Stretch: 1,175 feet
Main Turf Circumference: 1 mile

Attendance
Average Daily Recent Meeting: 2,540, 2004
Total Attendance Recent Meeting: 137,169, 2004
Highest Single Day Record: 15,500 est., September 4, 1967

Handle
Average All Sources Recent Meeting: $2,758,509, 2004
Average On-Track Recent Meeting: $184,786, 2004
Total All Sources Recent Meeting: $148,959,508, 2004
Total On-Track Recent Meeting: $9,978,475, 2004

Leaders
Career, Leading Jockey by Titles: Leroy Tauzin, 7
Career, Leading Trainer by Titles: Bernard S. Flint, 10
Recent Meeting, Leading Horse: Boom Baby, 3, 2004; Rainbow Boy, 3, 2004; Unrullah Bull, 3, 2004
Recent Meeting, Leading Jockey: Rafael Bejarano, 85, 2004
Recent Meeting, Leading Trainer: Bobby Barnett, 13, 2004

Records
Single Day Jockey Wins: Willie Martinez, 8
Single Day Trainer Wins: Wayne Bearden, 5, August 7, 1997
Single Meet, Leading Jockey by Wins: Mike McDowell, 89, 1986
Single Meet, Leading Owner by Wins: Tom Dorris, 20, 1978
Single Meet, Leading Trainer by Wins: Angel Montano, 34, 1976

Track Records, Main Dirt
5 furlongs: White Image, :57 3/5, July 9, 1988
5 1/2 furlongs: Mount Forloon, 1:03 2/5, July 17, 1988
6 furlongs: Stubilem, 1:09, July 1, 1982
6 1/2 furlongs: American Chance, 1:15, July 16, 1994
7 furlongs: Josh's Madelyn, 1:21.37, September 5, 2004
1 mile: Still Waving, 1:34 3/5, August 13, 1988
1 1/8 miles: Lt. Lao, 1:47 3/5, August 27, 1988
1 1/4 miles: Won Du Loup, 2:03, September 4, 1988
1 3/8 miles: Ramona Jay, 2:23, August 24, 1985
1 1/2 miles: Unaccountable, 2:29 3/5, July 23, 1988
1 5/8 miles: Sir Lightning, 2:45.80, August 9, 1992
1 3/4 miles: Bondi, 3:00, August 27, 1966
2 miles: Classic Deal, 3:25 3/5, August 21, 1988
Other: 2 1/4 miles, Bondi, 3:54, September 5, 1966

Track Records, Main Turf
5 1/2 furlongs: Bettybird, 1:00.52, August 21, 2002
1 mile: Slewper Imp, 1:32.60, July 16, 1995; Suffragette, 1:32.60, July 24, 1999
1 1/16 miles: Majestic Jove, 1:39.20, August 27, 1997
1 1/8 miles: Yaqthan (Ire), 1:44.60, September 2, 1996
1 1/4 miles: Ye Slew, 1:59.60, August 6, 1994
1 1/2 miles: Our Forbes, 2:25.40, August 10, 1994
2 miles: Irish Harbour, 3:20.20, September 2, 1996

Principal Races
Gardenia S. (G3), HBPA H., Don Bernhardt S., A. M. Fisher Debutante S., J. C. Ellis Juvenile S.

Interesting Facts
Previous Names and Dates: Dade Park

Notable Events
Family Day, Year-Round Simulcasting

Fastest Times of 2004 (Dirt)
5 furlongs: Kathy Lynn, :58.19, September 6, 2004
5 1/2 furlongs: Lucky Baldwin, 1:03.79, August 26, 2004
6 furlongs: Sterling Gold, 1:09.38, August 25, 2004
6 1/2 furlongs: Padlock, 1:16.06, July 11, 2004
7 furlongs: Josh's Madelyn, 1:21.37, September 5, 2004
1 mile: Added Edge, 1:35.34, August 28, 2004
1 1/8 miles: Angela's Love, 1:49.54, August 7, 2004

Fastest Times of 2004 (Turf)
5 1/2 furlongs: Speedy Sonata, 1:00.84, July 15, 2004
1 mile: Quidditch Player, 1:33.71, September 5, 2004
1 1/16 miles: G P Fleet, 1:39.22, September 6, 2004
1 1/8 miles: Strident Fellow, 1:49.28, August 20, 2004
1 1/4 miles: Kiawah, 2:03.88, August 29, 2004
1 1/2 miles: Powdered Wig, 2:40.86, July 11, 2004

Keeneland Race Course

Some tracks offer nothing more than an endless procession of live and simulcast races. But a few American tracks offer a sense of history and a state of mind. Keeneland Race Course falls into the latter category. Since its opening meet in October 1936, the Lexington track has developed a unique identity. The stately facility offers two short, marquee meetings—including races such as the Blue Grass Stakes (G1) in the spring and the Spinster Stakes (G1) in the fall—in an attractive setting. Profits from Keeneland's lucrative sales arm help to finance purses and make them among the highest in the country. The Keeneland Association was incorporated in 1935 and purchased 147.5 acres of land, including an ornate clubhouse and training track, from J. O. "Jack" Keene, to build the facility. Lexington, bereft of racing after the Kentucky Association track closed earlier in the 1930s, quickly embraced the new facility, and more than 25,000 people attended the inaugural nine-day meeting. Crowds in excess of 25,000 on a single day are common at Keeneland, whose meets attract a wide range of spectators, including veteran racegoers, local business executives, socialites, breeders, and college students.

Location: 4201 Versailles Rd., P.O. Box 1690, Lexington, Ky. 40588-1690
Phone: (859) 254-3412
Fax: (859) 255-2484
Website: www.keeneland.com
E-Mail: webmaster@keeneland.com
Year Founded: 1935
Dates of Inaugural Meeting: October 15-24, 1936
Abbreviation: Kee
Acreage: 907
Number of Stalls: 1,845
Seating Capacity: 7,000

Ownership
Keeneland Association Inc.

Officers
President: Nick Nicholson
Director of Racing: W. B. Rogers Beasley
Racing Secretary: Ben Huffman
Secretary: William T. Bishop III
Treasurer: Jessica A. Green
Director of Operations: James A. Perry
Director of Communications: R. James Williams
Director of Finance: Jessica A. Green
Director of Marketing: Fran Taylor
Director of Mutuels: Robert A. Butcher
Vice President: Harvie B. Wilkinson
Director of Sales: Geoffrey G. Russell
Director of Simulcasting: Maggie Johnson
Horsemen's Liaison: Kathleen Torok
Stewards: Ronald L. Herbstreit, R. Spencer Leigh III, Michael K. Sample
Track Announcer: Kurt Becker
Track Photographer: Bill Straus, Patrick Lang
Track Superintendent: Sammy Garland, Jerry Huff, Jimmy Young
Asst. Racing Secretary: Allison A. DeLuca
Horsemen's Bookkeeper: Pam Barker

Racing Dates
2004: April 2-April 23, 15 days; October 8-October 30, 17 days
2005: April 8-April 29, 16 days; October 7-October 29, 17 days

Track Layout
Main Circumference: 1 1/16 miles
Main Track Chute: 4 1/2 furlongs and 7 furlongs

Main Width: 77 feet
Main Length of Stretch: 1,174 ft.
Main Turf Circumference: 7 1/2 furlongs
Main Turf Length of Stretch: 1,190 ft.
Training Track: 5 furlongs

Attendance

Average Daily Recent Meeting: 15,522, Spring 2004; 13,389, Fall 2004
Highest Single Day Record: 33,621, April 16, 2005
Record Daily Average for Single Meet: 15,522, Spring 2004
Highest Single Meet Record: 232,826, Spring 2004
Total Attendance Recent Meeting: 232,826, Spring, 2004; 227,620, Fall 2004
Lowest Single Day Record: 1,294, October 16, 1936

Handle

Average All Sources Recent Meeting: $9,078,739, Spring 2004; $6,963,411, Fall 2004
Average On-Track Recent Meeting: $1,449,426, Spring 2004; $1,176,412, Fall 2004
Record Daily Average for Single Meet: $1,558,917, Spring 1988
Single Day On-Track Handle: $2,902,234, April 16, 2005
Single Day All Sources Handle: $17,076,993, April 14, 2001
Total All Sources Recent Meeting: $136,181,075, Spring 2004; $118,377,987, Fall 2004
Total On-Track Recent Meeting: $21,741,390, Spring 2004; $19,999,000, Fall 2004
Highest Single Day Recent Meet: $3,196,259, April 10, 2004, Spring Meet; $2,610,576, October 9, 2004, Fall Meet

Mutuel Records

Highest Win: $255.40, Rip Dabbs, October 8, 1988
Lowest Win: $2.10, Spectacular Bid, April 26, 1979
Highest Exacta: $5,200.40, October 27, 1993
Lowest Exacta: $3.60, April 13, 1988
Highest Trifecta: $37,832, October 28, 1995
Lowest Trifecta: $7.80, April 3, 2004
Highest Daily Double: $5,796.40, April 19, 1961
Lowest Daily Double: $4.60, October 12, 1983
Highest Pick 3: $49,628.60, April 6, 1997
Lowest Pick 3: $8.80 April 21, 1990
Highest Pick 6: $160,628.90, October 16, 2003
Lowest Pick 6: $74.80, October 9, 1991
Highest Other Exotics: Pick Five, $7,172.30, October 18, 2001; Superfecta, $120,550, October 24, 2001
Lowest Other Exotics: Pick Four, $21.50, April 19, 2001; Pick Five, $375.80, October 12, 2001; Quinella, $2.60, October 5, 2003; Superfecta, $43.00, April 21, 2004
Highest Stakes Win: $222.60, Foxy Dean, October 13, 1984, Alcibiades S.
Highest Pick 4: $56,235.80, October 11, 2003
Highest Quinella: $1,535.40, October 8, 2004

Leaders

Career, Leading Jockey by Titles: Pat Day, 22
Career, Leading Owner by Titles: T. A. and J. E. Grissom, 14
Career, Leading Trainer by Titles: D. Wayne Lukas, 15
Recent Meeting, Leading Jockey: Pat Day, 21, Spring 2004; Rafael Bejarano, 26, Fall 2004
Recent Meeting, Leading Owner: Heiligbrodt Racing Stable, Kenneth L. and Sarah K. Ramsey, 5 each, Spring 2004; G. Watts Humphrey, Jr., 7, Fall 2004
Recent Meeting, Leading Trainer: Steven M. Asmussen, 9, Spring 2004; Steven M. Asmussen, Nicholas P. Zito, 11 each, Fall 2004
Career, Leading Jockey by Stakes Wins: Pat Day, 95
Career, Leading Owner by Stakes Wins: Claiborne Farm, 24
Career, Leading Trainer by Stakes Wins: D. Wayne Lukas, 50
Career, Leading Jockey by Wins: Pat Day, 918
Career, Leading Owner by Wins: William S. Farish, 174
Career, Leading Trainer by Wins: D. Wayne Lukas, 254

Records

Single Day Jockey Wins: Randy Romero, 6, April 7, 1990; Craig Perret, 6, April 18, 1990

Single Day Trainer Wins: William I. Mott, 4, April 9, 1995
Single Meet, Leading Jockey by Wins: Pat Day, 45, Fall 1991
Single Meet, Leading Owner by Wins: Calumet Farm, 12, Spring 1941; Mr. and Mrs. Robert F. Roberts, 12, Fall 1968
Single Meet, Leading Trainer by Wins: D. Wayne Lukas, 22, Fall 1989

Track Records, Main Dirt

4 1/2 furlongs: Quick Swoon, :51, April 20, 1966; Royality Note, :51, April 23, 1968; Bend the Times, :51, April 8, 1980
6 furlongs: Anjiz, 1:07.78, October 9, 1993
6 1/2 furlongs: Number One Sheikh, 1:14.70, October 11, 2000
7 furlongs: Binalong, 1:20.39, October 13, 1993
1 1/16 miles: Din's Dancer, 1:40 4/5, October 9, 1990
1 1/8 miles: Midway Road, 1:46.78, April 22, 2004
1 3/16 miles: Arch, 1:53.87, October 11, 1998
1 1/4 miles: Political Fact, 2:02.21, October 15, 1993
1 5/8 miles: Put-in-Bay, 2:45, October 13, 1967; Mr. Copy Chief, 2:45, October 20, 1971
Other: 7 furlongs 184 feet, Lamb Chop, 1:24 3/5, October 10, 1963

Track Records, Main Turf

5 1/2 furlongs: Chris's Thunder, 1:01.72, October 8, 2000
1 mile: Perfect Soul (Ire), 1:33.54, April 9, 2004
1 1/16 miles: Quiet Resolve, 1:40.30, April 27, 2000
1 1/8 miles: Memories of Silver, 1:45.81, October 5, 1996
1 3/16 miles: Happyanunoit (NZ), 1:53.91, October 15, 1999
1 1/2 miles: Bursting Forth, 2:27.54, April 22, 1999
1 5/8 miles: Royal Strand (Ire), 2:38.68, October 24, 1999

Principal Races

Fall: Lane's End Breeders' Futurity (G1), Shadwell Turf Mile S. (G1), Overbrook Spinster S. (G1), Queen Elizabeth II Challenge Cup (G1), Darley Alcibiades S. (G2)
Spring: Blue Grass S. (G1), Ashland S. (G1), Stonerside Beaumont S. (G1), Maker's Mark Mile S. (G2), Commonwealth Breeders' Cup (G2), Coolmore Lexington S. (G2).

Fastest Times of 2004 (Dirt)

4 1/2 furlongs: Classic Elegance, :51.39, April 16, 2004
6 furlongs: Champali, 1:08.72, October 8, 2004
6 1/2 furlongs: Tricky Devil, 1:14.96, October 8, 2004
7 furlongs: Halory Leigh, 1:22.44, October 10, 2004
a7 furlongs: Commentator, 1:25.19, October 14, 2004
1 1/16 miles: Roses in May, 1:42.61, April 17, 2004
1 1/8 miles: Midway Road, 1:46.78, April 22, 2004
1 3/16 miles: Confirmed, 1:57.94, October 10, 2004
1 1/4 miles: Regal Reproach, 2:05.37, October 22, 2004

Fastest Times of 2004 (Turf)

5 1/2 furlongs: Soaring Free, 1:01.78, April 10, 2004
1 mile: Perfect Soul (Ire), 1:33.54, April 9, 2004
1 1/16 miles: Intercontinental (GB), 1:41.41, April 18, 2004
1 1/8 miles: Stage Call (Ire), 1:47.03, April 9, 2004
1 3/16 miles: Stay Forever, 1:57.08, October 10, 2004
1 1/2 miles: Art Variety (Brz), 2:27.89, April 7, 2004
2 1/2 miles: Hirapour (Ire), 4:41.48, April 16, 2004

Kentucky Downs

Straddling the Kentucky-Tennessee state border adjacent to Interstate 65, Kentucky Downs has enjoyed a short, colorful history. Opened in 1990 as Dueling Grounds Race Course—the track site was reputed to be the scene of several 19th century duels—the turf-only racecourse was conceived as a simulcasting facility with one day of live steeplechase racing a year. But ownership controversies dogged the facility until the late 1990s, when businessman Brad Kelley, Turfway Park, and Churchill Downs purchased the facility. Kelley owns 52%, and the tracks each hold 24%. Track officials have found ways to make Kentucky Downs's turf-only status pay off. The track now offers a series of turf stakes on the flat to coincide partly with the Kentucky Cup series of dirt-only races at Turfway Park in Florence, Kentucky.

Location: 5629 Nashville Rd., Franklin, Ky. 42135
Phone: (270) 586-7778
Fax: (270) 586-8080
Website: www.kentuckydowns.com
Year Founded: 1996
Dates of Inaugural Meeting: April 22, 1990
Abbreviation: KD

Ownership
Kentucky Downs LLC

Officers
General Manager: Ryan Driscoll
Racing Secretary: Richard Leigh
Director of Operations: Jon Goodman
Director of Mutuels: Shelley Spears
Director of Simulcasting: Mary Troilo
Track Superintendent: Tommy Sullivan

Racing Dates
2004: September 18-September 28, 7 days
2005: September 17-September 27, 7 days

Track Layout
Main Turf Circumference: 1 5/16 miles

Leaders
Career, Leading Jockey by Titles: Jon Court, 2
Recent Meeting, Leading Jockey: Rafael Bejarano, 12, 2004
Recent Meeting, Leading Trainer: W. Elliott Walden, 3, 2004

Records
Single Meet, Leading Jockey by Wins: Jon Court, 8

Track Records, Main Turf
6 furlongs: Morluc, 1:09.66, September 23, 2000
7 furlongs: Slew of Deuces, 1:22.77, September 18, 2000
1 mile: Rob 'n Gin, 1:35.00, September 19, 1998
1 1/2 miles: Yaqthan (Ire), 2:27.60, September 19, 1998

Principal Races
Kentucky Cup Turf (G3)

Interesting Facts
Previous Names and Dates: Dueling Grounds 1990-1996

Fastest Times of 2004 (Turf)
6 furlongs: Black Escort, 1:10.49, September 28, 2004
7 furlongs: Pass Play, 1:23.48, September 21, 2004
1 mile: Sand Springs, 1:36.88, September 25, 2004
1 1/2 miles: Mythique, 2:32.96, September 28, 2004

Turfway Park

Turfway Park is the Northern Kentucky successor to Old Latonia, a track that opened in the Latonia section of Covington in 1883 and shut down in 1939. In the late 1950s, an investor group built a new Latonia Race Course in Florence, approximately ten miles from the former site, and it opened on August 27, 1959. On April 9, 1986, Nashville real-estate developer Jerry Carroll and partners bought Latonia for $13.5-million and renamed it Turfway Park. Carroll undertook an extensive renovation program and raised the purse of the track's spring race for three-year-old Triple Crown prospects, the Jim Beam Stakes (G2), to $500,000 in 1987. The race's purse would peak at $750,000 when it lost its initial sponsor and became the Galleryfurniture.com Stakes for 1999 only. In 2002, the race became the Lane's End

Spiral Stakes, and in 2003 it was renamed the Lane's End Stakes. During Carroll's tenure, Turfway was a leader in offering intertrack wagering in Kentucky (1988) and in promoting legislation for full-card simulcasting in '94. Also in 1994, Turfway launched its Kentucky Cup Day of Champions, a September event featuring five stakes races. Carroll and partners sold the track to a partnership led by the Keeneland Association for $37-million on January 15, 1999. For its 2005 fall meeting, Turfway renovated its track by putting in Polytrack, becoming the first track in North America to install the synthetic surface as its main track.

Location: 7500 Turfway Rd., Florence, Ky. 41042-1342
Phone: (859) 371-0200
Phone: (800) 733-0200
Fax: (859) 647-4730
Website: www.turfway.com
E-Mail: info@turfway.com
Year Founded: 1986 as Turfway Park
Dates of Inaugural Meeting: August 27, 1959 (Latonia); April 9, 1986 (Turfway Park)
Abbreviation: TP
Acreage: 197
Number of Stalls: 1,200

Ownership
Keeneland Association, Harrah's Entertainment, GTech

Officers
President: Robert N. Elliston
General Manager: Greg Schmitz
Director of Racing: Richard S. Leigh
Racing Secretary: Richard S. Leigh
Treasurer: Clifford Reed
Director of Operations: Greg Schmitz
Director of Marketing: Brian Gardner
Director of Mutuels: Kenny Kramer
Vice President: Clifford Reed
Director of Publicity: Sherry Pinson
Director of Simulcasting: Mary Troilo
Stewards: Ronald Herbstreit, Brooks A. Becraft III, Michael Sample
Track Announcer: Mike Battaglia
Track Photographer: Patrick Lang
Track Superintendent: Daniel Chapman
Chief executive officer: Robert N. Elliston
Horsemen's Bookkeeper: Terry Moore
Asst. Racing Secretary: Tyler B. Picklesimer

Racing Dates
2004: January 1-April 1, 66 days; September 8-October 7, 22 days; November 28-December 31, 24 days
2005: January 1-April 7, 69 days; September 7-October 6, 22 days; November 27-December 31, 25 days

Track Layout
Main Circumference: 1 mile
Main Track Chute: 1/4 mile and 6 1/2 furlongs
Main Width: Backstretch: 50 feet; Homestretch: 90 feet
Main Length of Stretch: 970 feet

Attendance
Average Daily Recent Meeting: 2,148, Winter/Spring 2004; 2,161, Fall 2004; 1,223, Holiday 2004
Highest Single Day Record: 22,480, March 25, 2000
Highest Single Meet Record: 354,867, Spring 1988
Record Daily Average for Single Meet: 5,377, Spring 1988
Total Attendance Recent Meeting: 118,157, Winter/Spring 2004; 47,538, Fall 2004; 26,909, Holiday 2004

Handle
Average All Sources Recent Meeting: $2,515,253, Winter/Spring 2004; $2,441,845, Fall 2004; $2,453,986, Holiday 2004
Average On-Track Recent Meeting: $412,205, Winter/Spring 2004; $302,420, Fall 2004; $284,948, Holiday 2004

Single Day On-Track Handle: $3,223,778, April 2, 1994
Total All Sources Recent Meeting: $138,338,918, Winter/Spring
2004; $53,720,595, Fall 2004; $53,987,705, Holiday 2004
Total On-Track Recent Meeting: $22,671,267, Winter/Spring
2004; $6,653,252, Fall 2004; $6,268,860, Holiday 2004
Highest Single Day Recent Meet: $7,164,448, March 20,
2004 (Winter/Spring); $5,859,538, September 18, 2004 (Fall);
$3,743,774, December 4, 2004 (Holiday)

Mutuel Records
Highest Exacta: $6,777.20, January 29, 1988
Lowest Exacta: $3.20, September 26, 1998
Highest Trifecta: $101,694.80, February 21, 1996
Lowest Trifecta: $5.20, September 26, 1998
Highest Daily Double: $4,575.80, December 12, 1986
Lowest Daily Double: $5, September 24, 1994
Highest Pick 3: $35,920, September 7, 2002
Lowest Pick 3: $13.00, December 2, 2001
Highest Pick 6: $1,474,380, March 23, 1988
Highest Other Exotics: $106,848.20, Superfecta, March 20,
2004

Leaders
Career, Leading Jockey by Titles: Willie Martinez, 9
Career, Leading Trainer by Titles: Bernard Flint, 20
Recent Meeting, Leading Jockey: Rafael Bejarano, 150, Win-
ter/Spring 2004; Rafael Bejarano, 35, Fall 2004; Dean Sarvis,
39, Holiday 2004
Recent Meeting, Leading Owner: M.Y. Stables, 6, Winter/Spring
2004; Kenneth and Sarah Ramsey, 5, Fall 2004; Louis O'Brien,
6, Holiday 2004
Recent Meeting, Leading Trainer: Gregory Foley, 24,
Winter/Spring 2004; Robert Holthus, 9, Fall 2004; Bernard
Flint, George Leonard III and Wayne Mogge, 7 each, Holi-
day 2004
Career, Leading Jockey by Stakes Wins: Pat Day, 37
Career, Leading Trainer by Stakes Wins: D. Wayne Lukas, 35

Records
Single Day Jockey Wins: Rafael Bejarano, 7, March 12, 2004
Single Day Trainer Wins: Bernard Flint, 4; George Isaacs, 4;
D. Wayne Lukas, 4; Harry Trotsek, 4; V. R. Wright, 4
Single Meet, Leading Jockey by Wins: Rafael Bejarano, 150,
Winter/Spring 2004
Single Meet, Leading Trainer by Wins: Bernard S. Flint, 44,
Winter/Spring 2003

Track Records, Main Dirt
5 furlongs: Cindy's Hobby, :56.93, January 7, 2004
5 1/2 furlongs: Da'White Judge, 1:03.54, September 29, 1979
6 furlongs: Appealing Skier, 1:08.24, September 21, 1996;
Partner's Hero, 1:08.24, March 29, 1998
6 1/2 furlongs: Boone's Mill, 1:14.32, December 30, 1995
1 mile: Secreto's Hideaway, 1:34.12, March 5, 1994
1m 70 yds: Venture, 1:40 3/5, September 2, 1963
1 1/16 miles: Anet, 1:40.73, March 29, 1997
1 1/8 miles: Hansel, 1:46.70, March 30, 1991
1 3/16 miles: Roman Justice, 1:58 3/5, December 24, 1966
1 1/4 miles: Executor, 2:03.82, December 29, 2000
1 3/8 miles: Briarwick, 2:21, December 10, 1968
1 1/2 miles: Fast Dish, 2:29.19, March 26, 2004
1 5/8 miles: Bluegrass Warrior, 2:46.61, February 23, 1991
1 3/4 miles: Bluegrass Warrior, 2:59, March 10, 1990
2 miles: Bluegrass Warrior, 3:23.90, March 30, 1991
Other: 2 furlongs, Sizzling Lisa, :21 3/5, December 2, 1979;
3 furlongs, Cut Glass, :34 3/5, March 27, 1976; 1 11/16 miles,
Sestos, 2:56 1/5, January 1, 1969

Principal Races
Lane's End S. (G2), Kentucky Cup Classic H. (G2), Kentucky
Cup Juvenile S. (G3), Kentucky Cup Sprint S. (G3), Turfway
Breeders' Cup S. (G3), Turfway Park Fall Championship S.
(G3), Kentucky Cup Juvenile Fillies S.

Interesting Facts
Previous Names and Dates: Latonia Race Course (1959-1986)

Notable Events
Kentucky Cup Day of Champions

Fastest Times of 2004 (Dirt)
5 furlongs: Cindy's Hobby, :56.93, January 7, 2004
5 1/2 furlongs: Western Honoree, 1:03.75, March 26, 2004
6 furlongs: Nattitude, 1:08.49, March 26, 2004
6 1/2 furlongs: King of Speed, 1:15.84, March 28, 2004
1 mile: Smiling Sky, 1:35.36, March 25, 2004
1 1/16 miles: Angela's Love, 1:40.85, March 27, 2004
1 1/8 miles: Discreet Hero, 1:47.52, December 18, 2004
1 1/4 miles: Sultry Mood, 2:05.26, February 19, 2004
1 1/2 miles: Fast Dish, 2:29.19, March 26, 2004

Louisiana

Delta Downs

Lee Berwick, a prominent Quarter Horse breeder
and owner and a former president of the American
Quarter Horse Association, opened the first Delta Downs
as a nonpari-mutuel match track on his farm at St.
Joseph, Louisiana, on the banks of the Mississippi River.
He moved the operation to Vinton, Louisiana, two hours
northeast of Houston, Texas, and opened Delta Downs
in 1973. Berwick served as track president until 1997,
when his daughter, Kathryn, succeeded him in the position. In 1999, the Berwicks sold Delta Downs for more
than $10-million to Shaun Scott and Jinho Cho, who
began renovating the facility in hopes of installing slot
machines. In 2001, the track was sold for $125-million
to Las Vegas-based Boyd Gaming Corp., which owns
casinos in Louisiana, Nevada, Illinois, and Mississippi.
In October 2001, Boyd received approval from the
Louisiana Gaming Control Board to operate 1,700 slot
machines. Delta Downs offers racing for Thoroughbreds as well as a separate season for Quarter Horses
and Paints. The slots have resulted in sizable increases
in Thoroughbred purses, with the average daily distribution increasing to $180,196 with an average purse of
$18,020 for its 2004-'05 season.

Location: 2717 Delta Downs Dr, P.O. Box 175, Vinton, La.
70668-6025
Phone: (337) 589-0708
Phone: (800) 589-7441
Fax: (337) 589-2399
Website: www.deltadowns.com
Year Founded: 1973
Abbreviation: DeD
Acreage: 240
Number of Stalls: 1320

Ownership
Boyd Gaming Corp.

Officers
General Manager: Jack Bernsmeier
Director of Racing: Chris Warren
Racing Secretary: Trent McIntosh
Director of Finance: Tony Demahy
Director of Marketing: Adrian King
Director of Simulcasting: Chris Warren
Stewards: Aaron Emigh, Duane Domingue, Judy Dugas
Track Announcer: Donald Stevens
Track Photographer: Coady Photography
Security: Ben Crimm

Racing Dates
2004: October 31, 2003-March 17, 2004, 86 days
2005: October 1, 2004-April 2, 2005, 101 days

Track Layout
Main Circumference: 6 furlongs
Main Track Chute: 5 furlongs

Main Track Chute: 1 1/16 miles
Main Width: 70 feet
Main Length of Stretch: 660 feet

Handle
Average All Sources Recent Meeting: $1,407,762, 2004/2005
Average On-Track Recent Meeting: $39,847, 2004/2005
Total All Sources Recent Meeting: $140,776,251, 2004/2005
Total On-Track Recent Meeting: $3,984,683, 2004/2005
Highest Single Day Record Recent Meet: $2,206,902, December 30, 2004

Leaders
Recent Meeting, Leading Horse: Starofmynight, 6, 2004/2005
Recent Meeting, Leading Jockey: Guy Smith, 121, 2004/2005
Recent Meeting, Leading Owner: Carrol Castille, 18, 2004/2005
Recent Meeting, Leading Trainer: Keith Bourgeois, 54, 2004/2005

Track Records, Main Dirt
4 furlongs: Rock Afire, :46 1/5, December 10, 1994
4 1/2 furlongs: Road to Seattle, :52, January 15, 1998
5 furlongs: Britt's Jules, :57.49, November 5, 2003
6 1/2 furlongs: Chief Okie Dokie, 1:18.76, February 8, 2002
7 furlongs: Norms Promise, 1:24 3/5, March 2, 1975
7 1/2 furlongs: Junior Gent, 1:33 1/5, March 14, 1974
1 mile: Freon Flier, 1:37.52, March 10, 2002
1m 70 yds: Thriller, 1:42 2/5, September 27, 1973
1 1/16 miles: Norms Promise, 1:43 1/5, March 23, 1975
1 1/8 miles: Lucky Silence, 1:55 2/5, February 18, 1994
1 3/16 miles: Ponderosa Lark, 2:03 3/5, October 31, 1975
1 1/4 miles: Shy Bull, 2:10 1/5, November 3, 1974
1 3/8 miles: Ponderosa Lark, 2:27 1/5, December 15, 1974
1 1/2 miles: Art Work, 2:41 1/5, December 11, 1974
2 miles: Can Em, 3:43 4/5, December 10, 1988
Other: 1 5/16 miles, Gentleman Mike, 2:17 3/5, December 1, 1974; 1 9/16 miles, Golden Foil, 2:46.86, March 27, 2004

Principal Races
Delta Jackpot S.

Interesting Facts
Trivia: Three alligators live in the infield

Fastest Times of 2004 (Dirt)
4 1/2 furlongs: Thrilling Request, :52.98, March 19, 2004
5 furlongs: Swim Easy, :57.91, January 14, 2004
6 1/2 furlongs: Prince Slew, 1:19.21, January 2, 2004
7 furlongs: Happy Ticket, 1:25.86, November 12, 2004
7 1/2 furlongs: Mahebo, 1:35.84, January 15, 2004
1 mile: Monty Man, 1:38.21, March 27, 2004
1 1/16 miles: Kodema, 1:45.00, March 27, 2004
1 1/4 miles: No Net Needed, 2:13.49, December 22, 2004
1 3/8 miles: Mac's Mark, 2:28.12, February 20, 2004
1 9/16 miles: Golden Foil, 2:46.86, March 27, 2004

Evangeline Downs

Located in Louisiana's colorful Cajun country, Evangeline Downs is known as the cradle of jockeys. Racing Hall of Fame members Eddie Delahoussaye and Kent Desormeaux as well as leading jockeys Shane Sellers and Mark Guidry all won their first races at the track. Several nationally known horses also have competed at Evangeline. In 1977, a two-year-old named John Henry won two of three starts at Evangeline and scored his first stakes win in the Lafayette Futurity. From that beginning, John Henry went on to earn more than $6.5-million and was voted Horse of the Year in 1981 and '84. In 1999 and 2000, Louisiana-bred Hallowed Dreams won 16 consecutive races, including six at Evangeline. The track, which offers some Quarter Horse racing, conducts live racing from mid-April to early September. The track's future includes a new location and slot machines, which began generating purse money in December 2003. In 2005, the track moved to Opelousas to take advantage of a state law that permits slot machines at racetracks if authorized by local parishes. The new track has a grandstand that seats nearly 6,000 fans, a one-mile dirt oval, and a turf course inside the main track.

Location: 2235 Creswell Ln. Ext, Opelousas, La. 70570
Phone: (337) 594-3000
Phone: (800) 349-0687
Fax: (337) 594-3166
Website: www.evangelinedowns.com
E-Mail: evdinfo@evangelinedowns.com
Year Founded: 1966
Dates of Inaugural Meeting: April 28, 1966
Abbreviation: EvD
Acreage: 750 acres
Number of Stalls: 1,000
Seating Capacity: 6,000

Ownership
Peninsula Gaming

Officers
President: Michael S. Luzich
General Manager: David A. Yount
Director of Racing: Warren C. Groce
Racing Secretary: Warren C. Groce
Director of Finance: Steve Darbonne
Director of Mutuels: Rachel Conway
Director of Publicity: Sean D. Beirne
Director of Simulcasting: Sean D. Beirne
Horsemen's Liaison: Dayne Dugas
Stewards: Benny Rayburn, Brook Hawkins, Norris Gwin
Track Announcer: Sean D. Beirne
Track Photographer: S.C.I. Photography
Chief executive officer: M. Brent Stevens
Security: Joseph Albarado

Racing Dates
2004: April 1-September 6, 92 days
2005: April 7-September 5, 88 days

Track Layout
Main Circumference: 1 mile
Main Turf Circumference: 7 furlongs

Attendance
Average Daily Recent Meeting: 1,201, 2004
Highest Single Day Record: 8,218, July 4, 1975
Total Attendance Recent Meeting: 110,575, 2004

Handle
Average All Sources Recent Meeting: $1,277,950, 2004
Average On-Track Recent Meeting: $102,499, 2004
Record Daily Average for Single Meet: $1,531,758, 2000
Single Day All Sources Handle: $2,052,653, July 1, 1999
Total All Sources Recent Meeting: $117,571,392, 2004
Total On-Track Recent Meeting: $9,429,942, 2004
Highest Single Day Recent Meet: $1,940,990, April 2, 2004

Mutuel Records
Highest Win: $412.20, Princely Greek, April 26, 1987
Highest Exacta: $24,213.90, August 1, 1982
Highest Trifecta: $37,995, August 23, 1997

Leaders
Career, Leading Trainer by Titles: Don Cormier Sr., 8 (consecutive 1992-1999)
Recent Meeting, Leading Jockey: Brian J. Hernandez Jr., 99, 2004
Recent Meeting, Leading Trainer: Keith Bourgeois, 60, 2004

Records

Single Day Jockey Wins: Gerard Melancon, 6, 1984; Shane Sellers, 6, 1985; James Avant, 6, 1988; Curt Bourque, 6, 1989; Curt Bourque, 6, 1991; James Avant, 6, 1995; Kirk LeBlanc, 6, 1995
Single Meet, Leading Jockey by Wins: Curt Bourque, 141; Randy Romero, 141
Single Meet, Leading Trainer by Wins: Don Cormier Sr., 91, 1996

Track Records, Main Dirt

4 furlongs: Rare Trip, :46 3/5, May 20, 1977
4 1/2 furlongs: Bag in Hand, :51.60, August 28, 2000
5 furlongs: Hallowed Dreams, :57.40, July 3, 1999; Fuse It, :57.40, April 24, 2004
5 1/2 furlongs: Money Is the Key, 1:03.40, August 26, 2004
6 furlongs: Rail, 1:09.20, July 22, 1995
7 1/2 furlongs: Top Silk, 1:31.40, June 2, 1991; Kreems View, 1:31.40, April 2, 2004
1 mile: Selma's Boy, 1:36 3/5, July 12, 1981; Winning Connection, 1:36.60, August 19, 2000
1m 40 yds: Mr. D's Prank, 1:43 3/5, July 11, 1983
1m 70 yds: State Commander, 1:42, April 22, 1991
1 1/16 miles: Nin's Pick, 1:43 2/5, June 19, 1977
1 1/8 miles: Report to Glory, 1:50.80, August 9, 1993
1 3/16 miles: Pasquale G., 2:01.2, July 31, 1977
1 1/4 miles: Nageire, 2:10 4/5, June 3, 1972
1 3/8 miles: Stubzy, 2:22 2/5, September 12, 1970
1 1/2 miles: Just for Charlie, 2:41 2/5, September 15, 1986
1 5/8 miles: Lucky Man, 2:49.60, August 4, 2000
2 miles: Gray Gardner, 3:31 3/5, August 27, 1990
Other: 1 7/16 miles, Red and Bold, 2:30 1/5, July 31, 1988; 1 7/8 miles, Concho County, 3:19.40, August 18, 2000

Principal Races

D. S. "Shine" Young Memorial Futurity, Evangeline Mile, Lafayette S.

Notable Events

All American Fourth of July Festival

Fastest Times of 2004 (Dirt)

2 1/2 furlongs: Flutter Butterfly, :27.00, July 10, 2004
4 1/2 furlongs: Mr. Excellent, :52.00, June 3, 2004
5 furlongs: Fuse It, :57.40, April 24, 2004
5 1/2 furlongs: Money Is the Key, 1:03.40, August 26, 2004
6 furlongs: Swim Easy, 1:10.00, June 25, 2004
7 1/2 furlongs: Kreems View, 1:31.40, April 2, 2004
1 mile: Pie N Burger, 1:37.80, August 14, 2004
1m 70 yds: No Its Not, 1:43.60, April 10, 2004
1 1/16 miles: Kiss a Native, 1:46.00, May 1, 2004

Fair Grounds

Thoroughbred racing has been conducted at the site of Fair Grounds in New Orleans with few interruptions since 1853, when a racetrack named Union Course held its first Thoroughbred meeting. The track, which has been called Fair Grounds since the 1860s, served as a military camp during the Civil and Spanish-American Wars. At times, changing political climates have halted racing, and devastating fires destroyed the facility in 1919 and '93. Fair Grounds survived, and some of the sport's most famous racehorses have run there. Legendary distaffer Pan Zareta died of pneumonia at Fair Grounds in 1918 and was buried at the track. Kentucky Derby winner Black Gold, winner of the Louisiana Derby at Fair Grounds in 1924, was fatally injured in the Salome Handicap in '28 and was buried in the track's infield. Other noted horses who have raced at Fair Grounds include 1941 Triple Crown winner Whirlaway, winner of the inaugural Louisiana Handicap in '42; multiple Fair Grounds stakes winner Master Derby, who

captured the '75 Preakness Stakes (G1); and Silverbulletday, who won two Fair Grounds stakes during her '99 championship season. The Krantz family bought the track in 1990 and rebuilt the track after the 1993 fire. A $34.5-million grandstand and clubhouse opened on November 27, 1997. The track filed for bankruptcy in 2003 after a ruinous, $89.9-million court judgment to horsemen involving video-poker revenue, and it was sold in 2004 for $47-million to Churchill Downs Inc.

Location: 1751 Gentilly Blvd., New Orleans, La. 70119-2133
Phone: (504) 944-5515
Fax: (504) 944-2511
Website: www.fairgroundsracecourse.com
E-Mail: webmaster@fgno.com
Year Founded: 1872
Dates of Inaugural Meeting: April 13, 1872
Abbreviation: FG
Acreage: 145
Number of Stalls: 1,950
Seating Capacity: 6,500

Ownership

Churchill Downs Inc.

Officers

Chairman: Thomas H. Meeker
President: Randall E. Soth
General Manager: Randall E. Soth
Director of Racing: Ben Huffman
Racing Secretary: Ben Huffman
Secretary: Rebecca C. Reed
Treasurer: Michael E. Miller
Director of Finance: Will Bienvenu
Director of Marketing: Lenny Vangilder
Director of Mutuels: Gordon M. Robertson
Vice President: Andrew G. Skehan
Director of Publicity: Lenny Vangilder
Director of Sales: Karen A. Robicheaux
Horsemen's Liaison: Brook Hawkins
Stewards: William Hartack, Larry Munster, Peter Kosiba
Track Announcer: John G. Dooley
Track Photographer: Louis Hodges Jr.
Track Superintendent: Paul Gregoire
Asst. Racing Secretary: David M. Heitzmann
Security: David B. Martin

Racing Dates

2004: November 27, 2003-March 28, 2004, 80 days
2005: November 25, 2004-March 27, 2005, 82 days
2006: November 24, 2005-March 26, 2006, 83 days

Track Layout

Main Circumference: 1 mile
Main Track Chute: 2 furlongs
Main Width: Homestretch: 75 feet; Backstretch: 70 feet
Main Length of Stretch: 1,346 feet
Main Turf Circumference: 7 furlongs

Attendance

Average Daily Recent Meeting: 2,104, 2004/2005
Total Attendance Recent Meeting: 172,550, 2004/2005
Highest Single Day Record: 23,662, November 27, 1969

Handle

Average All Sources Recent Meeting: $4,184,980, 2004/2005
Average On-Track Recent Meeting: $221,481, 2204/2005
Total All Sources Recent Meeting: $343,168,377, 2004/2005
Total On-Track Recent Meeting: $18,161,344, 2004/2005
Single Day On-Track Handle: $2,696,741, March 28, 1982
Single Day All Sources Handle: $11,310,990, March 12, 2005
Highest Single Day Recent Meet: $11,310,990, March 12, 2005

Mutuel Records

Highest Win: $500.60, Grey Hip, March 16, 1933
Lowest Win: $2.20, C J's Star, January 3, 2002
Highest Exacta: $3,015.60, November 23, 2000

Lowest Exacta: $2.20, January 3, 2002
Highest Daily Double: $2,917, January 5, 1971
Lowest Daily Double: $5.20, March 10, 2002
Highest Pick 3: $23,731.40, December 26, 1999
Lowest Pick 3: $12.60, December 23, 2000
Highest Pick 6: $108,848.20, March 29, 1999
Highest Other Exotics: Superfecta, $133,156.40, January 13, 2001
Lowest Other Exotics: $28.20 Superfecta, December 1, 2001

Leaders

Career, Leading Jockey by Titles: Ronald Ardoin, 6
Career, Leading Trainer by Titles: Jack Van Berg, 10
Recent Meeting, Leading Horse: Skip Irish, 5, 2004/2005
Recent Meeting, Leading Jockey: Robby Albarado, 101, 2004/2005
Recent Meeting, Leading Owner: Michael Gill, 43, 2004/2005
Recent Meeting, Leading Trainer: Steven M. Asmussen, 67, 2004/2005

Records

Single Day Jockey Wins: James P. Bowlds, 6, March 11, 1965; E. J. Perrodin, 6, November 18, 1979; Randy Romero, 6, February 8, 1984; V. L. "Billy" Smith, 6, March 15, 1990; Shane Romero, 6, February 10, 1991; Shane Romero, 6, February 24, 1991
Single Day Trainer Wins: several times; most recent was: Thomas Amoss, 4, January 19, 1995
Single Meet, Leading Jockey by Wins: Randy Romero, 181, 1983/1984
Single Meet, Leading Trainer by Wins: Jack Van Berg, 92, 1973/1974

Track Records, Main Dirt

4 furlongs: Blue Carbon, :46 1/5, March 18, 1967
4 1/2 furlongs: Debs Mini Bars, :52 1/5, March 8, 1971
5 furlongs: Posse, :57.35, February 10, 2003
5 1/2 furlongs: Toby's Success, 1:03.20, January 26, 2004
6 furlongs: Mountain General, 1:08.03, November 28, 2002
7 furlongs: For Fair, 1:24 2/5, February 8, 1915
7 1/2 furlongs: Begue, 1:33 3/4, March 30, 1896
1 mile: Kitwe, 1:35.94, March 26, 1998
1m 40 yds: Total Rage, 1:38.52, March 23, 1997
1m 70 yds: Zevson, 1:41, November 26, 1936
1 1/16 miles: Pie in Your Eye, 1:42.02, March 19, 1994
1 1/8 miles: Phantom On Tour, 1:48.13, March 8, 1998
1 3/16 miles: Half Magic, 1:56 1/5, March 21, 1977
1 1/4 miles: It's the One, 2:01 4/5, March 21, 1982; Westheimer, 2:01 4/5, March 24, 1985; Herat, 2:01 4/5, March 16, 1986
1 3/8 miles: Carroll Road, 2:18 1/5, January 30, 1965; Tahuna, 2:18 1/5, March 6, 1965
1 1/2 miles: Tahuna, 2:32 2/5, March 13, 1965
1 5/8 miles: Major Mansir, 2:49 3/5, January 4, 1904; From Afar, 2:49 3/5, February 27, 1954
1 3/4 miles: Aladdin Prince, 3:01 2/5, April 5, 1981
2 miles: Bolster, 3:28 1/5, February 7, 1920
Other: 2 furlongs, Baloma, :21 4/5, February 14, 1952; 3 furlongs, Henry's Baby, :33 4/5, February 15, 1971; 3 furlongs, It's the Law, :33 4/5, February 18, 1976; 3 1/2 furlongs, Silver Finn, :41, February 24, 1925; 1m 20 yds, Lucky R., 1:40 3/5, January 1, 1916; 1m 20 yds, Grumpy, 1:40 3/5, February 5, 1916; 1 9/16 miles, Retintin, 2:42 4/5, March 28, 1970; 1 7/8 miles, Julius Caesar, 3:19, February 27, 1900; 2 miles 70 yds, Omar, 3:39 1/5, March 3, 1940; 2 1/16 miles, Quib's Bally, 3:47 1/5, March 6, 1948; 2 1/4 miles, Marvin Neal, 3:56, February 23, 1907; 3 miles, Colonist, 5:35, February 17, 1906; 4 miles, Major Mansir, 8:04 3/5, March 21, 1903

Track Records, Main Turf

a5 1/2 furlongs: My Lord, 1:02.90, March 27, 2004
a7 1/2 furlongs: Northcote Road, 1:29.26, March 7, 2000
a1 mile: Great Bloom, 1:35.57, March 20, 2004
a1 1/16 miles: Dixie Poker Ace, 1:42, January 8, 1994
a1 1/8 miles: Mystery Giver, 1:48.29, March 21, 2004
a1 3/8 miles: Present the Colors, 2:17 1/5, April 4, 1982
a1 1/2 miles: Palace Panther (Ire), 2:32, April 6, 1986
Other: a1 9/16 miles, To the Floor, 2:40.26, March 29, 1999

Principal Races

Louisiana Derby (G2), Fair Grounds Oaks (G2), New Orleans H. (G2), Mervin H. Muniz Jr. Memorial H. (G2)

Interesting Facts

Previous Names and Dates: Union Race Course 1872-1952

Notable Events

Louisiana Champions Day

Fastest Times of 2004 (Dirt)

5 1/2 furlongs: Toby's Success, 1:03.20, January 26, 2004
6 furlongs: Cat Genius, 1:08.83, March 14, 2004
1 mile: Classic Par, 1:36.71, February 19, 2004
1m 40 yds: Yessirgeneralsir, 1:38.53, March 4, 2004
1 1/16 miles: Wimbledon, 1:42.71, March 7, 2004
1 1/8 miles: Peace Rules, 1:48.61, February 29, 2004

Fastest Times of 2004 (Turf)

a5 1/2 furlongs: My Lord, 1:02.90, March 27, 2004
a7 1/2 furlongs: Unigold, 1:30.12, March 28, 2004
a1 miles: Great Bloom, 1:35.57, March 20, 2004
a1 1/16 miles: Mr. Sulu, 1:43.58, March 26, 2004
a1 1/8 miles: Mystery Giver, 1:48.29, March 21, 2004

Louisiana Downs

Louisiana Downs, located near Shreveport in Bossier City, opened in 1974. Built by the late shopping-center developer Edward DeBartolo Sr., the track introduced the Super Derby (now G2) in 1980, and since then the fall race has attracted leading three-year-olds. The first running was won by Temperence Hill, winner of that year's Belmont Stakes (G1). Two three-year-olds—Sunday Silence in 1989 and Tiznow in 2000—used the Super Derby as a steppingstone to victory in the Breeders' Cup Classic (G1) and Horse of the Year honors in their respective years. DeBartolo's racetrack holdings were sold following his death, and Louisiana Downs was acquired by his son-in-law, John York II. In November 2001, a group of investors headed by Shreveport lawyer Jim Davis announced plans to buy Louisiana Downs. In 2002, Harrah's Entertainment Corp. acquired approximately 95% of Louisiana Downs and opened a casino with 905 slot machines in 2003. By 2005, the renamed Harrah's Louisiana Downs had more than 1,400 machines. Harrah's valued the purchase, including renovations, at $183.4-million.

Location: 8000 E Texas St., Bossier City, La. 71111-7016
Phone: (318) 742-5555
Phone: (800) 551-2361
Fax: (318) 741-2615
Website: www.ladowns.com
E-Mail: bburgess@harrahs.com
Year Founded: 1974
Dates of Inaugural Meeting: October 30, 1974-January 26, 1975
Abbreviation: LaD
Acreage: 350
Number of Stalls: 1,360
Seating Capacity: 17,240

Ownership

Harrah's Entertainment

Officers

General Manager: Patrick Dennehy
Director of Racing: Patrick J. Pope
Racing Secretary: Patrick J. Pope
Director of Operations: Cliff D. Burge
Director of Admissions: Tom Stedman
Director of Finance: Kelly Castete

Director of Marketing: Jennifer Ray
Director of Mutuels: Holly Romain
Vice President: Ray A. Tromba
Director of Sales: Tom Showalter
Director of Simulcasting: Dick Pollock
Stewards: Coleman Lloyd, Johnnie Johnson, Judy Dugas
Track Announcer: Frank Mirahmadi
Track Photographer: Reed Palmer Photography
Track Superintendent: George McDermott

Racing Dates
2004: May 14-October 31, 102 days
2005: April 29-October 9, 93 days

Track Layout
Main Circumference: 1 mile
Main Track Chute: 7 furlongs
Main Track Chute: 1 1/4 miles
Main Width: 80 feet
Main Length of Stretch: 1,010 feet
Main Turf Circumference: 7 furlongs 50 feet
Main Turf Width: 70 feet
Main Turf Length of Stretch: 940 feet

Attendance
Highest Single Day Record: 26,513, May 26, 1986

Handle
Average All Sources Recent Meeting: $2,020,091, 2004
Average On-Track Recent Meeting: $201,060, 2004
Total All Sources Recent Meeting: $206,049,256, 2004
Total On-Track Recent Meeting: $20,508,129, 2004
Single Day On-Track Handle: $4,371,781, September 27, 1987
Single Day All Sources Handle: $6,763,853, October 2, 1999

Mutuel Records
Highest Win: $249, B.J.'s Spruce, June 21, 1996
Lowest Win: $2.20, Appealing Breeze, 1989; $2.20, Richman, 1990; $2.20, Morning Meadow, 1993; $2.20, Runaway Venus, 1999; $2.20, Smart Ring, 1999
Highest Exacta: $2,780.80, May 1, 1994
Lowest Trifecta: $18.90, August 19, 1994
Highest Daily Double: $5,556.20, October 14, 1976
Highest Pick 3: $37,286.20, June 6, 1992
Lowest Pick 3: $11.80, September 12, 1994
Highest Pick 6: $555,287, May 25, 1991
Highest Other Exotics: $52,017.60, Superfecta, June 2, 1996

Leaders
Career, Leading Jockey by Titles: Ronald Ardoin, 6; Larry Snyder, 6
Career, Leading Owner by Titles: John Franks, 18
Career, Leading Trainer by Titles: Frank Brothers, 6
Career, Leading Jockey by Stakes Wins: Ronald Ardoin
Career, Leading Owner by Stakes Wins: John Franks, 144
Career, Leading Trainer by Stakes Wins: Frank Brothers
Career, Leading Jockey by Wins: Ronald Ardoin, 2,773
Career, Leading Trainer by Wins: C. W. Walker, 820

Records
Single Day Jockey Wins: Ricky Frazier, 7, October 27, 1984
Single Day Trainer Wins: Jack Van Berg, 5, December 5, 1976; Frank Brothers, 5, May 16, 1982; Frank Brothers, 5, September 3, 1984
Single Meet, Leading Jockey by Wins: Ronald Ardoin, 198, 1993
Single Meet, Leading Owner by Wins: John Franks, 65, 1983
Single Meet, Leading Trainer by Wins: Frank Brothers, 99, 1987

Track Records, Main Dirt
4 1/2 furlongs: Sondor, :51 3/5, May 16, 1984
5 furlongs: Oh Mar, :57.21, September 25, 2000
5 1/2 furlongs: Fighting K, 1:02.84, September 11, 1993
6 furlongs: Tangent, 1:08 4/5, April 28, 1984
6 1/2 furlongs: Prince of the Mt., 1:14.98, May 23, 1996
7 furlongs: Carrysport, 1:21 3/5, July 4, 1984
1m 70 yds: Country Jim, 1:39 2/5, July 4, 1982
1 1/16 miles: Nelson, 1:41.44, August 15, 1993

1 1/8 miles: Mocha Express, 1:48.14, July 24, 1999
1 3/16 miles: Jungle Pocket, 1:57 2/5, August 15, 1984
1 1/4 miles: Tiznow, 1:59.84, September 30, 2000
1 1/2 miles: Frankie's Pal, 2:31 4/5, September 3, 1990
1 3/4 miles: Frankie's Pal, 2:58 4/5, October 14, 1990
2 miles: Vain Lass, 3:35 1/5, November 16, 1975
Other: 1 13/16 miles, Stage Door Joey, 3:09.91, September 20, 1992

Track Records, Main Turf
5 furlongs: Mo Dinero, :55.40, September 26, 1999
7 1/2 furlongs: Chuck n Luck, 1:28 2/5, August 5, 1989
1 mile: Cherokee Circle, 1:34 1/5, July 24, 1983
1 1/16 miles: Clever Song, 1:40 1/5, August 11, 1985
1 1/4 miles: Tali Hai, 2:04.19, August 31, 1997
1 3/8 miles: Semillero (Chi), 2:13 1/5, October 21, 1985

Principal Races
Super Derby (G2)

Fastest Times of 2004 (Dirt)
4 1/2 furlongs: Silver Haze, :53.20, June 18, 2004
5 furlongs: Open Promise, :57.60, June 25, 2004
5 1/2 furlongs: Top Commander, 1:03.45, May 22, 2004
6 furlongs: Zarb's Dahar, 1:09.22, October 23, 2004
6 1/2 furlongs: Varoom, 1:16.26, August 29, 2004
7 furlongs: Demon's Prince, 1:22.29, May 27, 2004
1m 70 yds: Pie N Burger, 1:41.08, May 23, 2004
1 1/16 miles: Rose Hunter, 1:43.20, August 12, 2004
1 1/8 miles: Fantasticat, 1:51.40, September 25, 2004

Fastest Times of 2004 (Turf)
5 furlongs: Our Love, :56.05, October 30, 2004
a5 furlongs: Top Commander, :54.96, July 22, 2004
7 1/2 furlongs: Excessive Behavior, 1:28.75, May 28, 2004
a7 1/2 furlongs: Due to Win Again, 1:27.88, July 16, 2004
1 mile: Onlycook Half Ofit, 1:36.11, October 24, 2004
a1 mile: Renegade Rogue, 1:34.21, May 21, 2004
1 1/16 miles: Cajole, 1:41.73, July 25, 2004
a1 1/16 miles: Due to Win Again, 1:41.38, September 11, 2004
a1 1/4 miles: Bedillion, 2:09.35, August 6, 2004

Maryland

Laurel Park

Located in Laurel, midway between Baltimore and Washington, D.C., Laurel Park became a part of the Magna Entertainment Corp. family when the company headed by Frank Stronach bought a majority interest in the Maryland Jockey Club in 2002. Racing began at Laurel in 1911, and, three years later, New York City grocery entrepreneur James Butler acquired the track and hired Col. Matt Winn as the track's general manager. In 1947, the Maryland Jockey Club bought the track from Butler's estate, but the state's racing commission refused to permit Pimlico Race Course's dates to be moved to Laurel. Baltimore industrialist Morris Schapiro purchased the track in 1950 and put his youngest son, John D. Schapiro, in charge. Two years later, Laurel debuted the Washington, D.C., International, a turf stakes that was the first North American race to become a major annual target of European horses. Among the winners of the race was Racing Hall of Fame member Kelso in 1964. (The race was suspended after the 1994 running.) In 1984, Schapiro sold Laurel to a group of investors headed by Frank De Francis. In late 1986, De Francis and partners bought Pimlico, thus consolidating ownership of Maryland's major tracks. De Francis died in 1989 and was succeeded as president by his son, Joe, who remains a minority owner with his sister, Karin. Laurel's main track and turf course were rebuilt in 2004 and early 2005.

Location: P.O. Box 130, Laurel, Md. 20725-0130
Phone: (301) 725-0400
Phone: (800) 638-1859
Fax: (301) 725-4561
Website: www.marylandracing.com
E-Mail: webmaster@marylandracing.com
Year Founded: 1911
Dates of Inaugural Meeting: October 2, 1911
Abbreviation: Lrl
Acreage: 360
Number of Stalls: 880
Seating Capacity: 5,185

Ownership
Magna Entertainment Corp. and Maryland Jockey Club

Officers
Chairman: Frank Stronach
President: Joseph A. De Francis
Racing Secretary: Georganne Hale
Executive Vice President: James Gagliano
Director of Operations: Louis J. Raffetto Jr.
Director of Communications: Mike Gathagan
Director of Finance: Douglas J. Illig
Director of Marketing: Carrie L. Everly
Stewards: John Burke III, William J. Passmore, Phillip E. Grove
Track Announcer: Dave Rodman
Track Photographer: James McCue
Track Superintendent: John Olsen

Racing Dates
2004: January 1-March 28, 62 days
2005: January 26-April 17, 61 days; August 10-August 26; September 7-December 31

Track Layout
Main Circumference: 1 1/8 miles
Main Track Chute: 7 furlongs
Main Width: 75 feet
Main Length of Stretch: 1,344 feet
Main Turf Circumference: 1 mile
Main Turf Width: 70 feet
Main Turf Length of Stretch: 990 feet

Attendance
Average Daily Recent Meeting: 6,870, Winter/Spring 2005
Highest Single Day Record: 40,276, November 11, 1958
Total Attendance Recent Meeting: 419,094, Winter/Spring 2005

Handle
Average All Sources Recent Meeting: $3,958,065, 2004; $4,257,377, Winter/Spring 2005
Total All Sources Recent Meeting: $245,400,000, 2004; $259,700,000, Winter/Spring 2005

Leaders
Career, Leading Trainer by Titles: King T. Leatherbury, 25

Records
Single Day Jockey Wins: Chuck Baltazar, 7, 1969; Horatio Karamanos, 7, October 26, 2002
Single Meet, Leading Jockey by Wins: Edgar Prado, 197, Winter 1998/1999
Single Meet, Leading Trainer by Wins: King T. Leatherbury, 86, Winter 1995

Track Records, Main Dirt
4 1/2 furlongs: Weighmaster, :52 2/5, April 13, 1964
5 furlongs: Dave's Friend, :57, November 21, 1980
5 1/2 furlongs: Crossing Point, 1:02.45, November 1, 2002
6 furlongs: Richter Scale, 1:07.95, July 15, 2000
6 1/2 furlongs: Ebonizer, 1:15 2/5, November 23, 1990
7 furlongs: Tappiano, 1:21 2/5, February 12, 1989
7 1/2 furlongs: Tidal Surge, 1:29.52, March 12, 1994
1 mile: Skipper's Friend, 1:34 2/5, December 6, 1980
1 1/16 miles: Willard Scott, 1:41 4/5, November 16, 1985
1 1/8 miles: Excellent Tipper, 1:47.64, July 5, 1992
1 3/16 miles: Testing, 1:54.51, October 21, 2000
1 1/4 miles: Richie the Coach, 1:59.96, November 23, 1996
1 3/8 miles: Amber Wave, 2:17 4/5, November 28, 1968
1 3/4 miles: Asserche, 2:58.51, February 13, 1994

Track Records, Main Turf
5 furlongs: Sikkim, :57 2/5, November 21, 1967
5 1/2 furlongs: Oops I Am, 1:02.20, June 14, 1994
6 furlongs: Texas Glitter, 1:08, October 28, 2000
1 mile: Portsmouth, 1:34, October 30, 1965
1 1/16 miles: Water Moccasin, 1:39 2/5, June 15, 1987
1 1/8 miles: Finder's Choice, 1:46.13, October 24, 1992
1 3/16 miles: Guilded Youth, 1:53.70, June 27, 1998
1 1/4 miles: Dynamic Trick 1:58.42, October 22, 2000
1 1/2 miles: Kelso, 2:23 4/5, November 11, 1964
2 miles: Summer Ensign, 3:23.64, June 15, 1993

Principal Races
Frank J. De Francis Dash (G1), General George H. (G2), Barbara Fritchie H. (G2), Laurel Futurity (G3), Selima S. (G3)

Notable Events
Maryland Million Day, SprintFest Weekend, Laurel Community Day

Fastest Times of 2004 (Dirt)
5 1/2 furlongs: Alarm the C. E. O., 1:03.33, February 7, 2004
6 furlongs: Pull Over Please, 1:09.28, February 4, 2004
7 furlongs: Well Fancied, 1:22.49, February 16, 2004
1 1/16 miles: Paparazzi, 1:43.27, January 28, 2004
1 1/8 miles: Ole Faunty, 1:49.05, February 14, 2004

Pimlico Race Course

The first horse to win a stakes race at Baltimore's Pimlico Race Course during the track's inaugural season in 1870 is the namesake of one of the world's most famous horse races. Preakness, a colt by legendary 19th-century sire Lexington, won the Dinner Party Stakes that year, and in 1873 the Preakness Stakes (now G1) made its debut. The race was not run in 1891, '92, or '93, and then it was held in New York for 15 years before it was returned to Pimlico in 1909. The Preakness now is the middle jewel of the Triple Crown and is run on the third Saturday in May. The day before the Preakness, Pimlico runs the race's three-year-old filly counterpart, the Black-Eyed Susan Stakes (G2). Another of the track's most famous races is the Pimlico Special Handicap (G1), which in 1938 captured the attention of the nation when Seabiscuit defeated War Admiral in a two-horse race. Magna Entertainment Corp. purchased majority ownership of Pimlico and Laurel near Washington, D.C., for $50.6 million in 2002. The two tracks share host duties for the Maryland Million, a day of racing for state-breds. Pimlico long has been called "Old Hilltop," a nickname that dates from the era when a small rise in the infield was a favorite gathering place for trainers and racing fans. The hill was removed in 1938, but the nickname remained.

Location: 5201 Park Heights Ave., Baltimore, Md. 21215-5117
Phone: (410) 542-9400
Fax: (410) 466-2521
Website: www.marylandracing.com
E-Mail: webmaster@marylandracing.com
Year Founded: 1743 (Maryland Jockey Club)
Dates of Inaugural Meeting: October 25, 1870
Abbreviation: Pim
Acreage: 140
Number of Stalls: 500
Seating Capacity: 14,852

Ownership
Magna Entertainment Corp. and Maryland Jockey Club

Officers
Chairman: Frank Stronach
President: Joseph A. De Francis
Racing Secretary: Georganne Hale
Director of Operations: Louis J. Raffetto Jr.

Director of Communications: Mike Gathagan
Director of Finance: Douglas J. Illig
Director of Marketing: Carrie L. Everly
Director of Mutuels: Dave Scheing
Executive Vice President: James L. Gagliano, Karin M. De Francis
Director of Sales: Keith Leacock
Director of Simulcasting: Dennis Smoter
Horsemen's Liaison: Phoebe Hayes
Stewards: John Burke III, Phillip E. Grove, William J. Passmore
Track Announcer: Dave Rodman
Track Superintendent: Jamie Richardson
Security: Willie Coleman
Asst. Racing Secretary: Clayton Beck, Jillian Sofarelli

Racing Dates

2004: March 31-June 6, 48 days; July 31-August 27, 16 days; September 9-January 17, 81 days
2005: April 20-June 12, 39 days

Track Layout

Main Circumference: 1 mile
Main Track Chute: 6 furlongs and 1 1/4 miles
Main Width: 70 feet
Main Length of Stretch: 1,152 feet
Main Turf Circumference: 7 furlongs

Attendance

Highest Single Day Record: 112,668, May 15, 2004

Handle

Average All Sources Recent Meeting: $4,892,000, Spring 2004; $2,321,800, Summer 2004
Average On-Track Recent Meeting: $1,772,700, Spring 2004; $1,266,000, Summer 2004
Single Day All Sources Handle: $87,858,878, May 15, 2004
Single Day On-Track Handle: $11,084,415, May 21, 2005
Single Day All Sources Handle: $91,028,704, May 21, 2005
Total All Sources Recent Meeting: $265,000,000, Spring 2004; $52,300,000, Summer 2004
Total On-Track Recent Meeting: $115,228,116, Spring 2004; $35,400,000, Summer 2004
Highest Single Day Record Meet: $87,858,878, May 15, 2004

Mutuel Records

Highest Win: $574, Cadeaux, May 7, 1913
Lowest Win: $2.10, War Admiral, November 3, 1937
Highest Exacta: $5,223.60, May 27, 1989
Lowest Exacta: $2.60, March 28, 1981
Highest Trifecta: $73,278, March 15, 1982
Highest Daily Double: $5,932.20, December 1, 1955
Highest Pick 6: $294,169, March 8, 1986
Highest Other Exotics: $414,243.90, Twin Trifecta, April 4, 1991
Highest Pick 4: $36,227.50, May 16, 2001

Leaders

Career, Leading Jockey by Titles: Edgar Prado, 14
Career, Leading Trainer by Titles: King T. Leatherbury, 25
Recent Meeting, Leading Jockey: Steve Hamilton, 49, Spring 2004; Erick Rodriquez and Chip Van Hassel, 16, Summer 2004; Ryan Fogelsonger, 83, Fall 2004
Recent Meeting, Leading Trainer: Dale Capuano, 25, Spring 2004; Dale Capuano, 6, Summer 2004; Dale Capuano, 30, Fall 2004

Records

Single Day Jockey Wins: Paul Nicol Jr., 7, June 8, 1983
Single Meet, Leading Jockey by Wins: Kent Desormeaux, 184, Spring 1989
Single Meet, Leading Trainer by Wins: King T. Leatherbury, 100, 1976

Track Records, Main Dirt

4 furlongs: Gavotte, :47 2/5, May 4, 1925
4 1/2 furlongs: Countess Diana, :51.50, June 6, 1997
5 furlongs: Kingmaker, :56.46, September 27, 2003
5 1/2 furlongs: Higher Strata, 1:02.46, July 29, 1995
6 furlongs: Northern Wolf, 1:09, August 18, 1990; Xtra Heat, 1:09, August 18, 2001
7 furlongs: Zeus, 1:26, May 3, 1921
1 mile: June Grass, 1:37 3/5, May 2, 1923
1m 70 yds: Sabotage, 1:41 2/5, December 17, 1958
1 1/16 miles: Deputed Testamony, 1:40 4/5, May 19, 1984; Poor But Honest, 1:40.80, September 9, 1995
1 1/8 miles: Private Terms, 1:47 1/5, May 27, 1989
1 3/16 miles: Farma Way, 1:52.55, May 11, 1991
1 1/4 miles: Manzotti, 2:01 4/5, March 19, 1988
1 3/8 miles: Narwhal, 2:16 2/5, December 15, 1962
1 1/2 miles: War Trophy, 2:29 2/5, November 8, 1948
1 5/8 miles: Market Wise, 2:43 1/5, November 13, 1941
1 3/4 miles: Blue Hills, 2:55 2/5, October 25, 1949
2 miles: Everett, 3:25 3/5, October 31, 1920
Other: 1 11/16 miles, Post Morton, 2:57 4/5, December 7, 1957; 2 miles 70 yds, Filisteo, 3:30 4/5, October 31, 1941; 2 1/16 miles, Beau Diable, 3:35 3/5, December 10, 1960; 2 1/4 miles, Edith Cavell, 3:52 1/5, November 13, 1926; 2 1/2 miles, Miss Grillo, 4:14 3/5, November 12, 1948

Track Records, Main Turf

5 furlongs: Yankee Wildcat, :55.99, June 4, 2004
7 furlongs: Lofty Peak, 1:23 1/5, May 14, 1956
1 mile: North East Bound, 1:33.42, May 7, 2000
1 1/16 miles: Air Attack, 1:40.33, May 27, 1991
1 1/8 miles: Mr O'Brien (Ire), 1:46.34, May 15, 2004
1 3/16 miles: Bayard Park, 2:01, May 7, 1966
1 3/8 miles: Dunsinyne, 2:13.74, June 22, 1997
1 1/2 miles: Fort Marcy, 2:27 2/5, May 9, 1970
Other: 1 7/8 miles, Brightly, 3:17, December 1, 1955

Principal Races

Preakness S. (G1), Pimlico Special (G1), Black-Eyed Susan S. (G2), Dixie H. (G2), Maryland Breeders' Cup H. (G3)

Notable Events

Preakness S. (G1) - middle Jewel of Triple Crown

Fastest Times of 2004 (Dirt)

4 1/2 furlongs: Downthehill, :53.15, June 3, 2004
5 furlongs: Avalino, :57.20, October 7, 2004
5 1/2 furlongs: Devil On the Moon, 1:03.50, October 1, 2004
6 furlongs: Wildcat Heir, 1:09.45, November 20, 2004
1 1/16 miles: Spicy Stuff, 1:42.20, September 10, 2004
1 1/8 miles: The Lady's Groom, 1:48.23, April 17, 2004
1 3/16 miles: Presidentialaffair, 1:55.58, October 9, 2004

Fastest Times of 2004 (Turf)

5 furlongs: Yankee Wildcat, :55.99, June 4, 2004
1 mile: Jaki's Magic, 1:35.64, June 3, 2004
1 1/16 miles: Ocean Drive, 1:40.85, May 15, 2004
1 1/8 miles: Mr O'Brien (Ire), 1:46.34, May 15, 2004

Timonium

Although Timonium's annual live meeting, run in conjunction with the Maryland State Fair, lasts only a few days through Labor Day, it attracts more than a half-million fans each year to the community located near Baltimore's northern border. In 2001, Timonium lost two dates of its usual ten dates because of insufficient purses but still had a successful meet. In 2002 and 2003, the track again ran eight dates. In the early 1980s, it raced as many as 42 days, but its season was sharply reduced in 1985 when Maryland's mile tracks began running year-round. Timonium, which struggled in the early 1990s until the addition of simulcasting both into and out of the track, is operated by the not-for-profit Maryland State Fair and Agricultural Society Inc., which directs all profits to the fair, 4-H Club awards, and improvements. Racing at Timonium began in September 1887. Its five-eighths-mile track has a four-furlong chute and a 6½-furlong chute.

Location: 2200 Block York Rd., Timonium, Md. 21094
Phone: (410) 252-0200
Fax: (910) 561-5610
Website: *www.marylandstatefair.com*
E-Mail: msfair@msn.com
Year Founded: 1878
Abbreviation: Tim
Acreage: 100
Number of Stalls: 600
Seating Capacity: 4,850

Ownership
Maryland State Fair and Agricultural Society Inc.

Officers
Chairman: F. Grove Miller
President: Howard M. Mosner Jr.
General Manager: Howard M. Mosner Jr.
Racing Secretary: Georganne Hale
Director of Mutuels: Richard Insley
Stewards: Phillip Grove, John Burke III, William Passmore
Track Announcer: Dave Rodman
Track Superintendent: Don Denmyer

Racing Dates
2004: August 28-September 6, 10 days
2005: August 27-September 5, 8 days
2006: August 26-September 4, 8 days

Track Layout
Main Circumference: 5/8 mile
Main Track Chute: 4 furlongs and 6 1/2 furlongs
Main Width: 70 feet
Main Length of Stretch: 700 feet

Attendance
Average Daily Recent Meeting: 3,965, 2004
Highest Single Day Record: 17,306, September 4, 1967
Total Attendance Recent Meeting: 31,719, 2004

Handle
Average All Sources Recent Meeting: $2,026,592, 2004
Average On-Track Recent Meeting: $354,516, 2004
Single Day On-Track Handle: $2,452,514, August 29, 1998
Total All Sources Recent Meeting: $16,212,581, 2004
Total On-Track Recent Meeting: $2,836,143, 2004
Highest Single Day Recent Meet: $2,506,120, August, 28, 2004

Leaders
Recent Meeting, Leading Jockey: Eric Camacho, 12, 2004;
Erick D. Rodriguez, 12, 2004
Recent Meeting, Leading Trainer: Gary Capuano, 4, 2004;
Kenneth M. Cox, 4, 2004

Principal Races
Alma North S., Taking Risks S.

Interesting Facts
Achievements/Milestones: Trainer King T. Leatherbury won
his 6,000th race on August 23, 2003 at Timonium.

Fastest Times of 2004 (Dirt)
4 furlongs: Woodford Cat, :45.76, September 3, 2004
a6 1/2 furlongs: Ribbon Cane, 1:16.41, September 4, 2004
1 mile: All Things French, 1:40.16, September 6, 2004
1 1/16 miles: Captain Chessie, 1:46.65, September 6, 2004

Massachusetts

Brockton Fair

Location: P.O. Box 6, Brockton, Ma. 02303-0006
Phone: (508) 586-8000
Fax: (508) 821-3239
Website: *www.brocktonfair.com*
E-Mail: sue@brocktonfair.com
Abbreviation: BF

Racing Dates
2004: July 2-July 11
2005: June 30-July 10

Northampton Fair

Location: P.O. Box 305, Fair St., Northampton, Ma. 01061-
0305
Phone: (413) 584-2237
Fax: (413) 586-1297
Website: *www.3countyfair.com*
E-Mail: hampfair@valinet.com
Year Founded: 1818 (fair)
Dates of Inaugural Meeting: 1942
Abbreviation: Nhp
Acreage: 50+
Number of Stalls: 450
Seating Capacity: 2,400

Ownership
Hampshire, Franklin and Hampden Agricultural Society

Officers
President: Dayne Tracy
General Manager: Bruce Shallcross
Director of Racing: Sandy Stanisewski
Racing Secretary: Thomas Creel
Treasurer: Norman Roy
Director of Operations: John Renaud
Director of Communications: Dayne Tracy
Director of Marketing: Sandy Stanisewski
Director of Mutuels: Jack Kovalski
Vice President: Frank Basile
Director of Publicity: Sandy Stanisewski
Director of Simulcasting: Sandy Stanisewski
Horsemen's Liaison: Art Lyman
Stewards: Richard Tobin, William Keene
Track Announcer: Peter Kules
Track Photographer: CB Photo
Track Superintendent: Joseph Jasinki

Racing Dates
2004: September 3-September 19, 10 days
2005: September 2-September 18, 10 days

Track Layout
Main Circumference: 1/2 mile

Leaders
Recent Meeting, Leading Horse: Come to Pass, 3, 2004
Recent Meeting, Leading Jockey: Willie Belmonte, 16, 2004
Recent Meeting, Leading Trainer: Samuel Keyrouze, 8, 2004

Principal Races
Northampton S., Mortgage Specialists Fair Challenge I, Mortgage Specialists Fair Challenge II

Interesting Facts
Achievements/Milestones: Oldest agricultural fair in country.

Suffolk Downs

    Built in just 62 days for $2-million by the Eastern
Racing Association, Suffolk Downs opened before an
estimated crowd of 35,000 in East Boston on July 10,
1935, as the nation's only racetrack with a concrete
grandstand. Just one month later, 52,726 fans set a
Suffolk attendance record that still stands. Suffolk's
signature race, the Massachusetts Handicap (G2), was
inaugurated in 1935, and it has been won by such
champions as Seabiscuit in 1937 and two-time Mass-
Cap winners Cigar and Skip Away in the 1990s. To
conserve purse money for a longer meet, the Mass-

Cap was canceled in 2003 and 2005. Legendary promoter Bill Veeck carded chariot races, livestock giveaways, and mock Indian battles in the infield during his tenure there in 1969 and '70. He also successfully sued the state to allow children to attend the races. Following a two-year shutdown in 1990 and '91, James B. Moseley's and John Hall's Sterling Suffolk Racecourse Ltd. leased the track and Thoroughbred racing returned to Boston. In 1997, Suffolk Racecourse LLC bought Suffolk for $40-million. Suffolk received a major boost at the end of 2001 when the state legislature authorized $3-million in tax revenue and uncashed winning tickets to be used for purses. Rockingham Park's abandonment of Thoroughbred racing in 2003 resulted in a restructuring of Suffolk's racing season.

Location: 111 Waldemar Ave., East Boston, Ma. 02128-1035
Phone: (617) 567-3900
Fax: (617) 561-5100
Website: www.suffolkdowns.com
E-Mail: publicity@suffolkdowns.com
Year Founded: 1935
Dates of Inaugural Meeting: July 10-August 10, 1935, 28 days
Abbreviation: Suf
Acreage: 190
Number of Stalls: 1,380
Seating Capacity: 9,505

Ownership
Sterling Suffolk Racecourse LLC

Officers
Chairman: Patricia Moseley
President: John L. Hall II
General Manager: Joe Fatalo
Director of Racing: L. J. Pambianchi Jr.
Racing Secretary: L. J. Pambianchi Jr.
Secretary: Charles A. Baker III
Director of Operations: Robert M. O'Malley
Director of Finance: Mary Walukiewicz
Director of Marketing: JoEllen Coen
Director of Mutuels: James R. Alcott
Director of Publicity: Christian Teja
Director of Sales: Dominic Terlizzi
Stewards: Edward Canhon Jr., William Keen, Susan Walsh
Track Announcer: T. D. Thornton
Track Photographer: Chip Bott
Track Superintendent: Steve Pini

Racing Dates
2004: May 1-November 27, 119 days
2005: April 30-November 19, 117 days

Track Layout
Main Circumference: 1 mile
Main Track Chute: 6 furlongs and 1 1/14 miles
Main Width: Homestretch: 90 feet; Backstretch: 70 feet
Main Length of Stretch: 1,030 feet
Main Turf Circumference: a7 furlongs
Main Turf Width: 65 to 70 feet
Main Turf Length of Stretch: 1,030 feet

Attendance
Average Daily Recent Meeting: 3,421, 2004
Highest Single Day Record: 52,726, August 10, 1935
Record Daily Average for Single Meet: 18,388, 1945
Total Attendance Recent Meeting: 407,113, 2004

Handle
Average All Sources Recent Meeting: $1,108,258, 2004
Average On-Track Recent Meeting: $145,778, 2004
Record Daily Average for Single Meet: $1,164,240, 1946
Single Day On-Track Handle: $2,175,836, May 30, 1960

Single Day All Sources Handle: $5,867,414, May 31, 1997
Total All Sources Recent Meeting: $131,882,718, 2004
Total On-Track Recent Meeting: $17,347,549, 2004
Highest Single Day Recent Meet: $3,641,441, June 19, 2004

Mutuel Records
Highest Win: $445, Sue Harper, June 14, 1940
Highest Exacta: $9,923.80, January 13, 1985
Highest Trifecta: $51,778, January 13, 1985
Lowest Trifecta: $7.40, May 30, 1998
Highest Daily Double: $16,515, May 25, 1979
Lowest Daily Double: $3.60, May 30, 1998
Highest Pick 3: $10,515.40, December 26, 1992
Lowest Pick 3: $11, April 21, 1993; $11, December 3, 2001
Highest Pick 6: $25,399, November 28, 1982
Highest Other Exotics: $9,923.80, Perfecta, January 13, 1985; $23,079.40, Superfecta, March 27, 1996
Lowest Other Exotics: $3.60, Perfecta, November 10, 1985

Leaders
Recent Meeting, Leading Horse: Kipper's an Angel, 8, 2004
Recent Meeting, Leading Jockey: Winston Thompson, 154, 2004
Recent Meeting, Leading Trainer: John Rigattieri, 93, 2004

Records
Single Day Jockey Wins: Leroy Moyers, 7, July 4, 1967
Single Meet, Leading Jockey by Wins: S. Elliott, 381, 1989
Single Meet, Leading Trainer by Wins: W. W. Perry, 140, 1989

Track Records, Main Dirt
4 furlongs: Crimson Streak, :45 2/5, April 6, 1970
4 1/2 furlongs: Lovely Gypsy, :51 4/5, May 7, 1965; Happy Voter, :51 4/5, May 16, 1966
5 furlongs: Rene Depot, :57 2/5, June 25, 1972
5 1/2 furlongs: Four Cards Too, 1:04.11, May 1, 2004
6 furlongs: Canal, 1:08 1/5, May 16, 1966
1 mile: Back Bay Brave, 1:35 1/5, July 12, 1986
1m 70 yds: Half Breed, 1:40, May 23, 1964; Half an Hour, 1:40.10, January 22, 1997
1 1/16 miles: Talent Show, 1:41 4/5, May 12, 1962; Bear the Palm, 1:41 4/5, July 3, 1977
1 1/8 miles: Skip Away, 1:47.27, May 30, 1998
1 3/16 miles: Shut Out, 1:55 2/5, July 4, 1942
1 1/4 miles: Helioscope, 2:01, May 19, 1955
1 1/2 miles: Connie Rab, 2:30 3/5, May 15, 1954
1 5/8 miles: Count Fire, 2:45 2/5, June 23, 1962
1 3/4 miles: Toulouse, 2:58 2/5, June 16, 1956
2 miles: Hutch, 3:35 2/5, August 1, 1950
Other: 2 furlongs, Adriano's Girl, :21.94, June 4, 1997; 2 miles 70 yds, On the Square, 3:39 4/5, April 16, 1973; 2 1/16 miles, Bold Fencer, 3:35 4/5, April 18, 1983; 2 1/4 miles, Fundy Bay, 3:54 1/5, December 9, 1973

Track Records, Main Turf
a5 furlongs: Bishop Ridley, :57 1/5, July 19, 1987; Concorde Cal, :57 1/5, October 30, 1994
a7 1/2 furlongs: Times Ahead, 1:32 2/5, September 3, 1988
a1 mile: Diablo Reigns, 1:39.35, September 15, 2003
a1m 70yds: Alphabetical, 1:42.07, June 30, 2004
a1 1/16 miles: Landing Court, 1:44.91, October 26, 1994
a1 3/8 miles: Chompion, 2:20 4/5, July 18, 1970; Gaybrook Swan, 2:20 4/5, July 18, 1970 (Dead Heat)
a1 1/2 miles: *Akbar Khan, 2:30 3/5, June 17, 1957
a2 miles: Jean-Pierre, 3:19 1/5, June 28, 1969
Other: a1 15/16 miles, Jamf, 3:11 1/5, July 4, 1975

Principal Races
Massachusetts H. (G2), James B. Moseley Breeders' Cup H.

Notable Events
Hot Dog Safari (a fund-raiser for JoeyFund/Cystic Fibrosis Foundation)

Fastest Times of 2004 (Dirt)
5 furlongs: Sweet Promises, :57.75, July 6, 2004
5 1/2 furlongs: Four Cards Too, 1:04.11, May 1, 2004

6 furlongs: Gators N Bears, 1:09.24, June 19, 2004
1 mile: Future Fantasy, 1:37.77, November 23, 2004
1m 70 yds: Milky Way Guy, 1:41.76, June 2, 2004
1 1/16 miles: Jini's Jet, 1:44.96, July 5, 2004
1 1/8 miles: Offlee Wild, 1:49.14, June 19, 2004
1 1/4 miles: Colonial Loot, 2:10.59, September 15, 2004

Fastest Times of 2004 (Turf)
a5 furlongs: Last Slew, :57.80, June 26, 2004
a7 1/2 furlongs: Laredo Lil, 1:32.91, June 19, 2004
a1 miles: Helen's Legacy, 1:39.80, July 12, 2004
a1m 70 yds: Alphabetical, 1:42.07, June 30, 2004
a1 1/16 miles: Final Prophecy, 1:46.66, September 4, 2004

Michigan

Great Lakes Downs

Great Lakes Downs was born in 1999 out of the necessity to preserve live racing in Michigan following the shuttering of Ladbroke-owned Detroit Race Course. Located at the site of a former Standardbred track in Muskegon, Great Lakes Downs came together quickly as a group of horse owners and racing enthusiasts raised the capital to renovate the facility and prepare for racing. After an understated first meeting in 1999, the track gained national attention in the winter of 2000 when Frank Stronach-led Magna Entertainment Corp., in the midst of a track-buying spree, added Great Lakes Downs to its holdings. In early 2003, Magna reported that Great Lakes was losing money and wrote down the book value of the track. Magna has received preliminary local approval to build a new track near Detroit.

Location: 4800 S Harvey St., Muskegon, Mi. 49444-9762
Phone: (231) 799-2400
Fax: (231) 798-3120
Website: *www.greatlakesdowns.com*
E-Mail: glweb@greatlakesdowns.com
Year Founded: 1999
Abbreviation: GLD

Ownership
Magna Entertainment Corp.

Officers
Chairman: Frank Stronach
General Manager: Amy MacNeil
Racing Secretary: Allan Plever
Director of Marketing: Mary Jane Shrauger
Vice President: Blake Tohana, Donald Amos, Gary Cohn, Douglas Tatters, Frank DeMarco Jr.
Director of Publicity: Mary Jane Shrauger
Stewards: Charlie Miranda, Heriberto Rivera Jr., and Daryl Parker
Track Announcer: Matt Hook
Track Superintendent: John Pollert

Racing Dates
2004: April 25-October 30, 118 days
2005: May 16-October 31, 102 days

Track Layout
Main Circumference: 5 furlongs
Main Track Chute: 4 furlongs and 7 furlongs
Main Width: 80 feet
Main Length of Stretch: 580 feet

Leaders
Recent Meeting, Leading Horse: Co Twining Niner, 8, 2004
Recent Meeting, Leading Jockey: T. D. Houghton, 196, 2004
Recent Meeting, Leading Trainer: Gerald S. Bennett, 94, 2004

Track Records, Main Dirt
4 furlongs: Dinner Band, :45.87, May 15, 2001
5 1/2 furlongs: Deputy Stripe, 1:06, July 22, 2002
6 furlongs: Above the Wind, 1:12.65, June 12, 2004
6 1/2 furlongs: Cool Rain Falling, 1:20, July 26, 2002
7 furlongs: Secret Romeo, 1:24.77, September 2, 2001
1 mile: Secret Romeo, 1:40, October 29, 2001
1m 70 yds: Secret Romeo, 1:49.50, November 4, 2000
1 1/16 miles: That Monetary, 1:47.28, August 27, 2001
1 1/8 miles: The Bold Bruiser, 1:54.11, October 28, 2000
Other: 2 furlongs, Skirt in the Wind, :23.52, June 22, 1999

Interesting Facts
Achievements/milestones: Jockey Terry Houghton rode his 3,000th winner on June 3, 2002 at Great Lakes Downs.

Fastest Times of 2004 (Dirt)
4 furlongs: Sailing Factor, :46.90, June 25, 2004
5 1/2 furlongs: Secret Romeo, 1:07.57, April 25, 2004
6 furlongs: Above the Wind, 1:12.65, June 12, 2004
6 1/2 furlongs: Sultry Danse, 1:21.32, October 2, 2004
7 furlongs: Methodist (Ire), 1:27.63, August 29, 2004
1 mile: Woodlyon, 1:42.82, June 1, 2004
1 1/16 miles: Cats Copy, 1:49.95, September 17, 2004
1 1/8 miles: Dancin for Gold, 1:57.63, October 9, 2004
1 5/16 miles: You'redusty, 2:22.81, September 8, 2004

Mt. Pleasant Meadows

Location: 500 N Mission Rd., P.O. Box 220, Mount Pleasant, Mi. 48858-4600
Phone: (989) 773-0012
Fax: (989) 773-7616
Abbreviation: MPM

Officers
Director of Publicity: Geoff Huntly

Racing Dates
2004: May 1-September 26, 36 days
2005: May 7-September 25, 36 days

Track Layout
Main Circumference: 4 furlongs
Main Width: 60 feet

Fastest Times of 2004 (Dirt)
2 furlongs: Unbridled Speed, :22.31, July 11, 2004
4 furlongs: Bugsy N Tuff, :50.22, September 26, 2004
4 1/2 furlongs: Cargi, :54.79, June 13, 2004
5 furlongs: Eckmo, 1:02.28, September 5, 2004
5 1/2 furlongs: Eckmo, 1:08.82, August 28, 2004
1m 70 yds: Francis Albert, 1:53.82, September 12, 2004

Minnesota

Canterbury Park

Canterbury Park is located in Shakopee, southwest of Minneapolis and St. Paul. When the track first opened in 1985, three years after Minnesota legalized parimutuel wagering, it was known as Canterbury Downs, and its ownership group included the Santa Anita Operating Co. In 1990, the track was purchased by Ladbroke Racing Corp., but, due to declining business, closed in '92. One year later, Irwin Jacobs, a Twin Cities financier, purchased the track and sold it to businessman and breeder Curtis Sampson, Sampson's son Randy, and partner Dale Schenian. Four months later, the owners held an initial public offering of the newly created Canterbury Park Holding Corp. The track, which reopened in 1995 as Canterbury Park, offers Thoroughbred racing and some Quarter Horse racing during its live racing season, which runs from mid-May through early September. In 1999, Canterbury held the first running of the Claiming Crown, which quickly became recognized as a major sporting event in Minnesota, and has been held at the Shakopee track every year but one. The Canterbury Card Club opened in 2000 at the track, and its revenues supplement race purses.

Location: 1100 Canterbury Rd., Shakopee, Mn. 55379-1867
Phone: (952) 445-7223
Phone: (800) 340-6361
Fax: (952) 496-6480
Website: www.canterburypark.com
E-Mail: cbypark@canterburypark.com
Year Founded: 1985
Dates of Inaugural Meeting: June 26, 1985
Abbreviation: Cby
Acreage: 355
Number of Stalls: 1,620
Seating Capacity: 22,830

Officers
Chairman: Curtis Sampson
President: Randall Sampson
General Manager: Randall Sampson
Director of Racing: Nat Wess
Racing Secretary: Douglas Schoepf
Treasurer: Richard Primuth
Director of Operations: Casey Shannon
Director of Finance: David Hansen
Director of Marketing: Jennifer Lauermann
Director of Mutuels: Mike Newlin
Vice President: Mike Garin, Mark Erickson, John Harty
Director of Simulcasting: Eric Halstrom
Horsemen's Liaison: Mary Green
Stewards: Jim Higgenbottom, Noble Hay, David Moore
Track Announcer: Paul Allen
Track Photographer: Brian Malarkey Photography
Track Superintendent: Moe Nye
Security: Patrick Shannon

Racing Dates
2004: May 14-September 6, 68 days
2005: May 7-September 5, 69 days

Track Layout
Main Circumference: 1 mile
Main Track Chute: 3 1/2 furlongs, 6 1/2 furlongs, 1 1/4 miles
Main Turf Circumference: 7 furlongs
Main Turf Chute: 1 1/16 miles

Attendance
Average Daily Recent Meeting: 4,977, 2004
Highest Single Day Record: 27,439, April 24, 1987
Total Attendance Recent Meeting: 333,457, 2004

Handle
Average All Sources Recent Meeting: $791,923, 2004
Average On-Track Recent Meeting: $528,394, 2004
Single Day On-Track Handle: $2,265,404, June 28, 1987
Total All Sources Recent Meeting: $53,058,841, 2004
Total On-Track Recent Meeting: $35,402,364, 2004
Highest Single Day Recent Meet: $3,632,968, July 17, 2004

Leaders
Career, Leading Jockey by Titles: Luis Quinonez, 5
Career, Leading Owner by Titles: Stephen Herold, 2, Curtis Sampson, 2, Valene Farm, 2, Steve Richardson, 2
Career, Leading Trainer by Titles: Pat Cuccurullo, 3, Doug Oliver, 3, David Van Winkle, 3
Recent Meeting, Leading Horse: Chisholm, 6, 2004
Recent Meeting, Leading Jockey: Derek Bell, 92, 2004
Recent Meeting, Leading Owner: Steve Richardson, 14, 2004
Recent Meeting, Leading Trainer: Hugh Robertson, 53, 2004

Track Records, Main Dirt
4 1/2 furlongs: Gallapiat's Song, :51.27, June 23, 1991
5 furlongs: Tonight Rainbow, :57, May 31, 2004
5 1/2 furlongs: Nickel Slot, 1:02 4/5, May 17, 1989
6 furlongs: So Long Seoul, 1:08 3/5, May 6, 1990; Iwazza Bad Boy, 1:08.60, August 18, 1996
6 1/2 furlongs: Don's Irish Melody, 1:14, June 12, 1988
1 mile: Minneapple, 1:35 1/5, September 27, 1987
1m 70 yds: Come Summer, 1:40 1/5, August 18, 1985; J. P. Jet, 1:40.20, August 3, 2002; Silver Zipper, 1:40.20, August 10, 2002
1 1/16 miles: Wally's Choice, 1:41.74, August 22, 2004
1 1/8 miles: Olympio, 1:46.47, July 7, 1991
1 1/4 miles: John Bullit, 2:04 3/5, July 25, 1986
1 1/2 miles: Loustros (GB), 2:32 3/5, August 28, 1987
1 3/4 miles: Luciole (Arg), 2:59 4/5, October 12, 1985
2 miles: My Tulles Free, 3:25 3/5, September 1, 1986
Other: a3 furlongs, Bye for Now, :40, June 30, 1985; 3 1/2 furlongs, In Moderation, :39.11, May 26, 1997

Track Records, Main Turf
5 furlongs: Win the Crowd, :56.31, August 21, 2004
7 1/2 furlongs: Honor the Hero, 1:28, June 18, 1995
1 mile: Go Go Jack, 1:33.40, June 3, 1995
1m 70yds: Numchuek, 1:39 1/5, July 6, 1988
1 1/16 miles: Little Bro Lantis, 1:40.20 June 16, 1995
1 1/8 miles: Fluffkins, 1:44, July 22, 1995
1 3/8 miles: Treizieme, 2:12 3/5, August 3, 1986
Other: a7 1/2 furlongs, Kiltartan Cross, 1:27.80, August 11, 1991; a1 mile, Kiltartan Cross, 1:33.40, July 10, 1991; a1m 70yds, Tainer's Toy, 1:39.20, August 10, 1991; a1 1/16 miles, Diplomat's Reward, 1:41.20, July 17, 1999; a1 3/8 miles, Le Fabulous Song, 2:14.80, October 20, 1991; 1 7/8 miles, John Bullit, 3:11 2/5, September 26, 1987; a1 7/8 miles, Mark of Stregth, 3:11.40, September 12, 1992

Principal Races
Lady Canterbury Breeders' Cup S., Claiming Crown - Jewel S., Emerald S., Rapid Transit S., Tiara S., Glass Slipper S., Iron Horse S., Express S.

Interesting Facts
Previous Names and Dates: Canterbury Downs 1984-1994

Fastest Times of 2004 (Dirt)
3 1/2 furlongs: George L Brown, :39.63, May 29, 2004
5 furlongs: Tonight Rainbow, :57.11, May 31, 2004
5 1/2 furlongs: Aces Full, 1:03.15, August 20, 2004
6 furlongs: Bistro Mathematics, 1:08.85, August 15, 2004
6 1/2 furlongs: Heroic Sight, 1:15.56, July 17, 2004
1 mile: Our Best Man, 1:35.30, August 14, 2004
1m 70 yds: Try for Par, 1:40.59, August 13, 2004
1 1/16 miles: Wally's Choice, 1:41.74, August 22, 2004
1 1/8 miles: Intelligent Male, 1:49.62, July 17, 2004

Fastest Times of 2004 (Turf)
5 furlongs: Win the Crowd, :56.31, August 21, 2004
7 1/2 furlongs: Sajjan, 1:29.91, September 2, 2004
a7 1/2 furlongs: Turk Flyer, 1:29.62, July 29, 2004
1 mile: Be My Friend, 1:35.55, June 20, 2004; Now Playing, 1:35.55, August 22, 2004
a1 miles: Southern Spring, 1:35.36, July 23, 2004
1 1/16 miles: Ghostly Gate, 1:41.89, June 19, 2004
a1 1/16 miles: Verzene, 1:42.00, August 13, 2004
1 3/8 miles: Dontbotherknocking, 2:20.64, September 6, 2004

Montana

Great Falls

Location: 400 3rd Ave. N W, Great Falls, Mt. 59404
Phone: (406) 727-8900

Fax: (406) 452-8955
Website: www.mtexpopark.com
E-Mail: info@mtexpopark.com
Year Founded: 1931
Abbreviation: GF

Ownership
Cascade County MT

Officers
General Manager: Bill Ogg
Director of Racing: Bill Ogg
Racing Secretary: Shorty Martin
Director of Operations: John Scott
Director of Marketing: Lori Cox
Director of Publicity: Lori Cox
Stewards: Raleigh Swensaud, John Regan, Tim Doughty
Track Superintendent: Joe McCracken

Racing Dates
2004: July 3-August 1, 9 days
2005: July 4-July 3, 10 days

Leaders
Recent Meeting, Leading Jockey: B. Buck Harris, 10, 2004
Recent Meeting, Leading Trainer: Janis Schoepf, 6, 2004

Principal Races
Treasure State Futurity, Lewis and Clark Derby, Big Sky H.

Fastest Times of 2004 (Dirt)
5 furlongs: Rogan Slew, :59.60, July 30, 2004
a5 furlongs: Redinal, 1:04.80, July 18, 2004
a5 1/4 furlongs: Alleged Feu, 1:04.40, August 1, 2004; Chevron Fleet, 1:04.40, August 1, 2004
7 furlongs: Fruit Rapport, 1:26.40, August 1, 2004; Streak a Roani, 1:26.40, August 1, 2004
1m 70 yds: Cabreo, 1:46.20, August 1, 2004

Helena Downs

Location: P.O. Box 9706, Helena, Mt. 59604-9706
Phone: (406) 457-9492
Abbreviation: Hln

Marias Fair

Location: P.O. Box 924, Shelby, Mt. 59474-0924
Phone: (406) 337-3600
Abbreviation: MaF

Racing Dates
2004: July 16-July 18, 3 days
2005: July 23-July 24, 2 days

Fastest Times of 2004 (Dirt)
5 furlongs: Plenty of Talk, 1:00.00, July 25, 2004
a6 furlongs: Clever At Midnight, 1:11.00, July 25, 2004
7 furlongs: Lost Again, 1:25.80, July 24, 2004
1m 70 yds: Neighborhood Bully, 1:48.60, July 25, 2004

Miles City Bucking Horse Sale

Location: P.O. Box 127, Miles City, Mt. 59301-0127
Phone: (406) 232-1210
Abbreviation: MC

Racing Dates
2004: May 9-May 16, 3 days
2005: May 15-May 22, 3 days

Fastest Times of 2004 (Dirt)
5 furlongs: Blade Ae, 1:05.00, May 15, 2004
5 1/2 furlongs: Fruit Rapport, 1:08.60, May 15, 2004

Northwest Montana Fair

Location: 256 N Meridian Rd., Kalispell, Mt. 59901-3850
Phone: (406) 758-5810
Fax: (406) 758-5808
Abbreviation: Ksp

Racing Dates
2004: August 20-August 29, 5 days
2005: August 19-August 28, 5 days

Fastest Times of 2004 (Dirt)
5 furlongs: Plenty of Sass, 1:01.80, August 20, 2004
6 furlongs: Tickle Me Malmo, 1:13.60, August 21, 2004
7 furlongs: Lucky Bounty, 1:27.60, August 20, 2004

Western Montana Fair and Races

Location: 1101 South Ave. W, Missoula, Mt. 59801-7907
Phone: (406) 721-3247
Fax: (406) 728-7479
Website: www.westernmontanafair.com
E-Mail: thinton@westernmontanafair.com
Year Founded: 1876
Abbreviation: WMF
Acreage: 40 Acres
Number of Stalls: 356
Seating Capacity: 3,000

Officers
General Manager: Scot Meader
Racing Secretary: Francis "Shorty" Martin
Director of Operations: Toni Hinton
Director of Marketing: Toni Hinton
Director of Mutuels: Teri Lerch
Director of Publicity: Toni Hinton
Stewards: Walt Horning, Ron Read, Raleigh Swensrud
Track Announcer: Phil Benson, Bruce Micklus
Track Superintendent: Wilber Phillips
Horsemen's Bookkeeper: Mary Wallace

Racing Dates
2004: August 10-August 15, 6 days
2005: August 9-August 14, 6 days

Leaders
Recent Meeting, Leading Horse: Stitch n' Weave, 3, 2004
Recent Meeting, Leading Jockey: Russell David Kingrey, 11, 2004
Recent Meeting, Leading Trainer: John Stabenfeldt, 4, 2004

Track Records, Main Dirt
5 furlongs: Seattle Cue, :59.60, August 13, 2004
1 1/16 miles: Early Shove, 1:44.40, August 11, 1996
1 1/8 miles: Rulvic, 1:53 2/5, August 23, 1986

Principal Races
Darrell Ost Memorial S., Rose Blossom H., Cluff Sprint S., Western Montana Fair Thoroughbred Derby, Western Montana Fair Thoroughbred Futurity

Fastest Times of 2004 (Dirt)
5 furlongs: Seattle Cue, :59.60, August 13, 2004
a5 furlongs: Secret Victory, 1:07.00, August 13, 2004
a5 1/4 furlongs: Popescu (Brz), 1:05.00, August 12, 2004
6 1/2 furlongs: Shouldbevictory, 1:22.20, August 15, 2004
1 1/16 miles: Sarah Oteka, 1:52.20, August 14, 2004
1 1/8 miles: Staged Reality, 1:55.40, August 15, 2004
1 5/8 miles: Neighborhood Bully, 2:57.20, August 14, 2004

Yellowstone Downs

Location: P.O. Box 1138, Billings, Mt. 59103-1138
Phone: (406) 869-5251
Fax: (406) 869-5253
Website: *www.yellowstonedowns.com*
E-Mail: racing@yellowstonedowns.com
Abbreviation: YD

Officers
Director of Publicity: Ben Carlson

Racing Dates
2004: August 21-September 19
2005: August 19-September 25, 14 days

Fastest Times of 2004 (Dirt)
5 1/4 furlongs: Deadly Talons, 1:02.40, September 26, 2004
7 furlongs: Harbour Axe, 1:27.60, September 19, 2004
1m 70 yds: Excellenceinmotion, 1:47.00, September 26, 2004

Nebraska

Columbus Races

Opened in the 1950, Columbus Races in Columbus, 90 miles northwest of Lincoln, is operated on the Platte County Agricultural Society Fairgrounds. It was at Columbus that Racing Hall of Fame trainer Marion H. Van Berg and his son, Jack, also a Racing Hall of Fame member, began their careers. The elder Van Berg operated a sales barn, offering hogs, cattle, and horses, in addition to running his stable. Columbus usually conducts a 24-day summer meet from late July through mid-September, racing on Fridays, Saturdays, and Sundays. Extensive simulcasting is also offered. The five-eighths-mile oval has a 6½-furlong chute. A record crowd of 8,856 attended on September 3, 1973. The record handle of $719,725 was set exactly 11 years later.

Location: 822 15th St., Columbus, Ne. 68601-5370
Phone: (402) 564-0133
Fax: (402) 564-0990
Website: *www.agpark.com*
E-Mail: agpark@megavision.com
Year Founded: June 2, 1941
Dates of Inaugural Meeting: July 1942
Abbreviation: Cls
Acreage: 160 Acres
Number of Stalls: 1,000
Seating Capacity: 4,000

Officers
Chairman: Lynn Anderson
General Manager: Gary Bock
Director of Racing: Dennis Kochevar
Racing Secretary: Dennis Kochevar
Secretary: Gary Kruse
Treasurer: Gary Kruse
Director of Operations: Gary Bock
Director of Finance: Gary Kruse
Director of Mutuels: Leon Ebel
Vice President: Eldon Engel
Director of Publicity: Gary Bock
Director of Simulcasting: Gary Bock
Stewards: Jim Haberlan, Rol Schaal, Quient Schaffer
Track Announcer: Keith Nelson
Track Photographer: Coady Photography
Track Superintendent: Bill Lusche

Racing Dates
2004: July 23-September 12, 22 days
2005: July 28-September 11, 24 days

Track Layout
Main Circumference: 5 furlongs
Main Track Chute: 4 furlongs and 6 1/2 furlongs
Main Width: 80 feet
Main Length of Stretch: 650 feet

Attendance
Highest Single Day Record: 8,856, September 3, 1973

Handle
Single Day On-Track Handle: $719,725, September 3, 1984

Leaders
Recent Meeting, Leading Horse: Chex, 3, 2004; Whats Gonna, 3, 2004; Majestic Glitter, 3, 2004
Recent Meeting, Leading Jockey: Filmer Munaylla, 32, 2004
Recent Meeting, Leading Trainer: David C. Anderson, 24, 2004

Track Records, Main Dirt
4 furlongs: Kips Flyer, :39 4/5, August 11, 2000
6 furlongs: Eve's Choice, 1:10 2/5, August 27, 1994
6 1/2 furlongs: Jae Ranch, 1:17, August 12, 1984
1m 70 yds: Ilafan, 1:41.40, September 9, 1984
1 1/16 miles: Foreign Intent, 1:44.40, September 21, 1974

Principal Races
Amadevil S., Columbus Breeders Special, Columbus Futurity, Columbus Debutante, Stevens S.

Notable Events
Super Saver Sunday, Let the Bets Roll Saturdays

Fastest Times of 2004 (Dirt)
3 1/2 furlongs: Festive Fellow, :41.00, July 23, 2004
6 furlongs: Coz He's Mean, 1:13.40, August 14, 2004; Nakayama Jazz, 1:13.40, September 11, 2004; Wabaroani, 1:13.40, August 14, 2004
6 1/2 furlongs: Midlothian, 1:19.40, September 4, 2004
1m 70 yds: High Tech Racing, 1:44.60, September 3, 2004
1 1/16 miles: Lord Ale, 1:49.40, August 13, 2004

Fonner Park

The closing of Omaha's Ak-Sar-Ben racecourse in 1995 dealt a serious blow to Nebraska racing. But Fonner Park in Grand Island has been one of the tracks to keep the flame flickering in the Cornhusker State with its down-home brand of racing. The 280-acre facility staged its first race meet in 1954. Fonner Park is operated by a not-for-profit organization, with the track's profits going to charitable and community activities in the Grand Island region. With the advent of telephone-account wagering in Nebraska in October 2001, Fonner officials sought to reach more of the state's bettors. The five-furlong facility has never been known as a racing mecca, but some interesting horses have competed at Fonner. One of them is sprinter Leaping Plum, who in 2001 won his seventh consecutive renewal of the opening-week Grasmick Handicap. The gelding also won the Coca-Cola Sprint Handicap four consecutive times (1995-'98).

Location: 700 E Stolley Park Rd., Grand Island, Ne. 68802
Phone: (308) 382-4515
Fax: (308) 384-2753
Website: *www.fonnerpark.com*
E-Mail: fonnerpark@aol.com
Year Founded: 1951
Dates of Inaugural Meeting: April 29, 1954

Abbreviation: Fon
Acreage: 240
Number of Stalls: 1,100
Seating Capacity: 5,766

Officers
President: Gary Rosacker
General Manager: Hugh Miner Jr.
Director of Racing: Douglas Schoepf
Racing Secretary: Douglas Schoepf
Secretary: Larry Toner
Treasurer: Roger Luebbe
Director of Operations: Bruce A. Swihart
Director of Marketing: Linda Wilhelmy
Director of Mutuels: William McConnell
Vice President: Doyle Hulme, Barry Sandstrom, Jim Cannon
Director of Simulcasting: Todd W. Otto
Stewards: James Haberlan, R. W. Shaal, Dennis Kochevar
Track Announcer: Matt Hook
Track Photographer: Coady Photography
Track Superintendent: Rick L. Danburg

Racing Dates
2004: February 14-May 8, 38 days
2005: February 11-May 7, 38 days

Track Layout
Main Circumference: 5/8 mile
Main Track Chute: 4 furlongs and 6 1/2 furlongs
Main Width: 70 feet
Main Length of Stretch: 700 feet
Training Track: 1/2 mile

Attendance
Highest Single Day Record: 10,387, April 2, 1977

Handle
Single Day On-Track Handle: $1,204,660, April 16, 1983

Mutuel Records
Highest Win: $520.40, Black Ticket, March 10, 1977
Lowest Win: $2.20, Ben's Whiz, March 30, 1974; $2.20, Real Style, March 30, 1974; $2.20, I'ma Game Master, April 29, 1995
Highest Exacta: $5,421, March 28, 1994
Lowest Exacta: $4, May 6, 2000
Highest Trifecta: $26,474.40, March 30, 1990
Lowest Trifecta: $14.60, March 15, 1998
Highest Daily Double: $5,451.20, March 18, 1977
Lowest Daily Double: $5, March 10, 1994; $5, April 21, 1995
Highest Pick 3: $13,800.80, February 27, 1988
Lowest Pick 3: $3.20, March 18, 2000
Highest Other Exotics: $17,526.60, Superfecta, March 23, 2001
Lowest Other Exotics: $271.40, Superfecta, March 4, 2001

Leaders
Career, Leading Jockey by Titles: R. D. Williams, 9
Career, Leading Trainer by Titles: Tim Gleason, 8

Records
Single Day Jockey Wins: Ken Shino, 8, April 2, 2000
Single Day Trainer Wins: Tim Gleason, 5, February 18, 1989; Marvin Johnson, 5, February 26, 2000; Marvin Johnson, 5, April 2, 2000
Single Meet, Leading Jockey by Wins: Perry Compton, 85, 2000
Single Meet, Leading Trainer by Wins: M. A. Johnson, 50, 2000

Track Records, Main Dirt
4 furlongs: Leaping Plum, :44.20, February 17, 1996
5 1/2 furlongs: Little L.M., 1:04 2/5, April 12, 1975
6 furlongs: Orphan Kist, 1:10, April 8, 1989
6 1/2 furlongs: Majority of One, 1:17, March 18, 1989
1 mile: Brian's Star, 1:36 3/5, April 9, 1986; High On Laraka, 1:36 3/5, April 19, 1986
1m 70 yds: Shamtastic, 1:40, April 26, 1986; Advice, 1:40, April 25, 1987

1 1/16 miles: Sahara King, 1:43, April 27, 1996
1 1/8 miles: Potro, 1:51.40, April 25, 1993
1 3/8 miles: Meat Loaf, 2:22 2/5, April 29, 1970
Other: 1 7/16 miles, Wenga, 2:30 2/5, May 1, 1968

Principal Races
Gus Fonner H.

Fastest Times of 2004 (Dirt)
4 furlongs: Missy Can Do, :45.20, February 14, 2004; Tonight Rainbow, :45.20, February 21, 2004
6 furlongs: Death Trappe, 1:11.60, March 13, 2004; Tonight Rainbow, 1:11.60, April 9, 2004
6 1/2 furlongs: Southern Alert, 1:18.20, May 1, 2004
1 mile: Okie Style, 1:38.80, May 8, 2004
1m 70 yds: Lovely Slew, 1:44.00, May 7, 2004; Soul Obsession, 1:44.00, May 8, 2004
1 1/16 miles: Sonic West, 1:46.80, April 24, 2004
1 1/8 miles: J. R. Honor, 1:52.40, May 8, 2004

Horsemen's Atokad Downs

Live Thoroughbred racing in Nebraska did not die when Omaha's Ak-Sar-Ben closed in 1995 after 74 years. Ak-Sar-Ben, which was torn down in 1997, is Nebraska spelled backward. Atokad is Dakota spelled backward, and the track is located in Dakota County, in the state's northwest corner near the South Dakota border. The five-eighths-mile track in South Sioux City opened on September 20, 1956. Atokad conducted a late-summer meeting in most years, though it did not race from 1998 through 2000. A single-day meet was resurrected in 2001 by Robert E. Lee, president of the Nebraska Horsemen's and Benevolent Protective Association, and three days of racing were scheduled for mid-September 2005. A record crowd of 6,200 attended on October 18, 1958. The record handle of $483,486 was set on November 9, 1980.

Location: 1524 Atokad Dr., P.O. Box 796, South Sioux City, Ne. 68776
Phone: (402) 494-5722
Fax: (402) 241-0410
E-Mail: atokad@cableone.net
Year Founded: 1951
Dates of Inaugural Meeting: September 20, 1956
Abbreviation: Ato
Acreage: 50
Seating Capacity: 3,112

Ownership
Nebraska Horsemen's Benevolent and Protective Association

Officers
President: Donald Everett
General Manager: Gregory Hosch
Director of Racing: Gregory Hosch
Racing Secretary: Gregory Hosch
Treasurer: Patricia Shefland
Director of Operations: Linda Wunderlin
Director of Marketing: Linda Wunderlin
Vice President: William Vannoy
Director of Publicity: Linda Wunderlin
Stewards: Dennis Kochevar, Quient Schaffer
Track Announcer: Buddy Haar
Track Photographer: Coady Services
Track Superintendent: Moe Nye
Security: Titan Security Inc.
Horsemen's Bookkeeper: Patricia Shefland

Racing Dates
2004: September 17-September 19, 3 days
2005: September 16-September 18, 3 days

Track Layout
Main Circumference: 5 furlongs
Main Track Chute: 6 1/2 furlongs and 1 1/8 miles
Main Width: 68 feet
Main Length of Stretch: 660 feet

Attendance
Average Daily Recent Meeting: 1,833, 2004
Highest Single Day Record: 6,200, October 18, 1958
Total Attendance Recent Meeting: 5,500, 2004

Handle
Average All Sources Recent Meeting: $85,604, 2004
Average On-Track Recent Meeting: $50,929, 2004
Single Day On-Track Handle: $483,486, November 9, 1980
Total All Sources Recent Meeting: $256,813, 2004
Total On-Track Recent Meeting: $152,787, 2004

Leaders
Recent Meeting, Leading Jockey: Dennis Collins, 2, 2004;
Perry Compton, 2, 2004
Recent Meeting, Leading Trainer: David Anderson, 3, 2004

Track Records, Main Dirt
4 furlongs: Shining Sea, :44.40, June 28, 1992
5 1/2 furlongs: Slipped in Space, 1:05 1/5, October 24, 1976
6 furlongs: Don Rivers, 1:11 2/5, October 28, 1966
6 1/2 furlongs: Spanish Key, 1:16 2/5, October 24, 1970
1 mile: Quilla Sue, 1:38, October 30, 1973
1m 70 yds: No Mystery, 1:42 1/5, November 5, 1976
1 1/16 miles: Great Commander, 1:43 3/5, November 3, 1973
1 1/8 miles: Reason to Explode, 1:50.20, July 13, 1991
1 3/8 miles: Barker's Tip, 2:20, October 17, 1964
2 miles: Navy Grey, 3:30 1/5, October 30, 1962; Middle Road,
3:30 1/5, November 21, 1976
Other: a4 furlongs, Classy Fleet, :43 4/5, November 19, 1977;
a6 furlongs, Urgent Valentine, 1:16.40, July 20, 2003; 1 7/16
miles, Echo Bar, 2:28, October 30, 1968; a1 7/16 miles, Duke
of Badgerland, 2:29.60, November 6, 1996

Fastest Times of 2004 (Dirt)
6 furlongs: Bingo's Orphan, 1:11.80, September 17, 2004
a6 1/2 furlongs: What About David, 1:15.80, September 19,
2004
1 mile: Rockport Road, 1:42.00, September 17, 2004
1m 70 yds: J. R. Honor, 1:45.20, September 18, 2004; Verzy
Tune, 1:45.20, September 17, 2004
1 1/16 miles: Therlo, 1:47.60, September 18, 2004

Horsemen's Park

Boasting a simulcasting facility that offers wagering on 18 to 21 racetracks daily, Horsemen's Park opened on January 3, 1998, for simulcasting in Omaha, four miles south of the former Ak-Sar-Ben site. Two live races were held each day on two consecutive days in July 1998 by the Nebraska Horsemen's Benevolent and Protective Association, which owns and operates the track. The meet was expanded to four days in 2003, with $500,000 now offered in purses each year. The track is a five-eighths-mile oval. The simulcasting facility offers seating for 3,000 and contains 675 closed-circuit monitors.

Location: 6303 Q St., Omaha, Ne. 68117-1696
Phone: (402) 731-2900
Fax: (402) 731-5122
Website: www.horsemenspark.com
E-Mail: horsemenspark@horsemenspark.com
Year Founded: 1998
Dates of Inaugural Meeting: January 3, 1998
Abbreviation: HPO
Seating Capacity: 3,000

Ownership
Nebraska Horsemen's Benevolent and Protective Association

Officers
President: William Vannoy
General Manager: Dick Moore
Racing Secretary: Gregory C. Hosch
Treasurer: Patricia Shefland
Director of Marketing: Dick Moore
Director of Mutuels: Mary Palais, Mary Snelling
Vice President: Donald Everett
Director of Publicity: Dick Moore
Director of Simulcasting: Patricia Shefland
Stewards: Jim Haberlan, Rol Shaal, Quient Schaffer
Track Superintendent: Tim Hurd

Racing Dates
2004: July 15-July 18, 4 days
2005: July 21-July 24, 4 days

Track Layout
Main Circumference: 5 furlongs
Main Width: 65 feet
Main Length of Stretch: 680 feet

Leaders
Recent Meeting, Leading Jockey: Robert Dean Williams, 4,
2004
Recent Meeting, Leading Trainer: Herb Riecken, 2, 2004

Principal Races
Omaha H., Queen's H.

Fastest Times of 2004 (Dirt)
6 furlongs: Chiming, 1:12.40, July 15, 2004
1 mile: Stormy Impact, 1:38.60, July 18, 2004
1 3/8 miles: My Dad's Bad, 2:23.00, July 16, 2004

State Fair Park

Location: P.O. Box 81223, Lincoln, Ne. 68501
Phone: (402) 474-5371
Fax: (402) 473-4114
Website: www.statefair.org
Abbreviation: Lnn

Officers
General Manager: Patrick Lloyd
Director of Marketing: Christine Rasmussen
Director of Mutuels: Mark Jensen
Director of Publicity: Heather Manion
Track Announcer: Keith Nelson
Track Superintendent: Scott Yound

Racing Dates
2004: May 14-July 11, 34 days
2005: May 13-July 17, 37 days

Track Layout
Main Circumference: 5 furlongs

Leaders
Recent Meeting, Leading Horse: Paid Vacation, 3, 2004;
Carmella, 3, 2004
Recent Meeting, Leading Jockey: Robert Dean Williams, 70,
2004
Recent Meeting, Leading Trainer: David C. Anderson, 29, 2004

Records
Single Day Jockey Wins: Robert D. Williams, 8, September
29, 1984

Interesting Facts
Trivia: Triple dead heat for win on October 23, 1981; at the
time one of only 17 such instances since 1940 and the only
one ever in Nebraska. On July 18, 1999, a national record
for a place payoff was set at $493.

Fastest Times of 2004 (Dirt)
4 furlongs: Slotsfan, :48.00, June 6, 2004
4 1/2 furlongs: Jack Black and Ice, :50.60, May 22, 2004
6 furlongs: Hawaiian Symphony, 1:11.00, May 14, 2004
1 mile: Red Hot Fox, 1:38.20, May 16, 2004
1m 70 yds: J. R. Honor, 1:41.60, May 16, 2004
1 1/16 miles: Who Devil Who, 1:47.80, June 27, 2004
1 3/8 miles: Gun Runner, 2:26.40, June 20, 2004
2 miles: My Dad's Bad, 3:35.80, July 4, 2004

New Hampshire

Rockingham Park

Location: P.O. Box 47, Salem, N.H. 03079-0047
Phone: (603) 898-2311
Fax: (603) 898-7284
Website: www.rockinghampark.com
E-Mail: track@rockinghampark.com
Year Founded: 1906
Dates of Inaugural Meeting: June 28, 1906
Abbreviation: Rkm
Acreage: 325
Number of Stalls: 1,400
Seating Capacity: 15,000

Ownership
Rockingham Venture Inc.

Officers
Chairman: Max Hugel
President: Dr. Thomas Carney
General Manager: Edward M. Callahan
Secretary: Kathleen Brothers
Treasurer: Robert G. Tolman
Director of Admissions: Laurence M. Murphy
Director of Marketing: Lynne Snierson
Director of Mutuels: Kathleen Brothers
Vice President: Edward J. Keelan, Edward M. Callahan
Director of Publicity: Lynne Snierson
Director of Simulcasting: Laurence M. Murphy
Stewards: Thomas Smith, Carl Gambardella, Edward Cantlon
Track Announcer: John Vitale
Track Photographer: Lawson Brouse
Track Superintendent: Raymond S. Messina
Security: John Burns

Racing Dates
2004: September 5, 1 day
2005: September 4, 1 day

Track Layout
Main Circumference: 1 mile
Main Track Chute: 6 furlongs, 1 1/4 miles
Main Width: 83 feet
Main Turf Circumference: 7 furlongs
Main Turf Chute: 1 1/8 miles

Attendance
Average Daily Recent Meeting: 2,195, 2004
Highest Single Day Record: 41,509, September 6, 1965
Total Attendance Recent Meeting: 2,195, 2004

Handle
Average All Sources Recent Meeting: $109,559, 2004
Average On-Track Recent Meeting: $62,784, 2004
Single Day On-Track Handle: $2,669,721, September 2, 1968
Total All Sources Recent Meeting: $109,559, 2004
Total On-Track Recent Meeting: $62,784, 2004
Highest Single Day Record Recent Meet: $109,559, September 5, 2004

Leaders
Career, Leading Jockey by Titles: Rudy Baez, 10
Recent Meeting, Leading Jockey: Orlando Bocachica, 2, 2004
Recent Meeting, Leading Trainer: George R. Handy, 2, 2004

Records
Single Day Jockey Wins: Willie Turnbull, 7, July 31, 1942; Rudy Baez, 7, September 27, 1991
Single Meet, Leading Jockey by Wins: Harry Vega, 302, 1989

Track Records, Main Dirt
4 furlongs: Maria's Brown Eyes, :46 1/5, May 28, 1987
4 1/2 furlongs: Kipper Katz, :52.44, June 25, 1997
5 furlongs: Sneaky Pal, :56 4/5, July 8, 1974
5 1/2 furlongs: Bama Redd, 1:03 4/5, May 21, 1987
6 furlongs: Dandy Blitzen, 1:08 4/5, August 29, 1959
1m 40 yds: Zafarrancho (Arg), 1:38 1/5, June 19, 1987
1 1/16 miles: Herbalist, 1:42, August 19, 1972
1 1/8 miles: Dr. Fager, 1:48 1/5, July 15, 1967
1 1/4 miles: Dr. Fager, 1:59 4/5, September 2, 1967
1 1/2 miles: Girder, 2:29 3/5, October 10, 1953
Other: 2 miles 40 yds, Zagora, 3:34 2/5, September 2, 1985; 2 1/4 miles, Usable, 3:58 2/5, September 4, 1978; 2 1/2 miles, Bert Leo B., 4:23 3/5, July 5, 1978

Track Records, Main Turf
1 mile: Rode to Ankara, 1:37.19, June 24, 1993
1 1/16 miles: Simply Majestic, 1:42 3/5, June 18, 1989; Paris Opera, 1:42 3/5, July 4, 1990
1 1/8 miles: Statesmanship, 1:48.49, June 20, 1998
1 3/8 miles: Autonomo, 2:20.80, June 15, 1991
Other: 1 7/8 miles, Hypnotizer, 3:15 3/5, August 19, 1989

Interesting Facts
Trivia: Mentioned in the movie "The Sting"

Fastest Times of 2004 (Turf)
1 1/16 miles: Ringing Rock, 1:46.28, September 5, 2004
a1 1/8 miles: Edgefield, 1:50.29, September 5, 2004

New Jersey

Atlantic City Race Course

When Atlantic City Race Course opened on July 22, 1946, its roster of stockholders read more like the A-list from a Hollywood party than investors in a racetrack in McKee City, 13 miles from the Jersey Shore resort. Bob Hope, Frank Sinatra, Harry James, Xavier Cugat, and Sammy Kaye were among the initial shareholders. John B. Kelly Sr., an Olympic gold-medal rower, brick magnate, and father of the late Princess Grace of Monaco, was Atlantic City's first president. Kelly was succeeded in 1960 by radio and television pioneer Leon Levy, whose son Robert succeeded him. An innovator who arranged the nation's first full-card simulcast from Meadowlands racetrack in September 1983, the younger Levy also raced 1987 Belmont Stakes (G1) winner Bet Twice and champion sprinter Housebuster. Crowds of more than 30,000 turned out to see such races as the United Nations Handicap (G1), first run in 1953, and such outstanding horses as Dr. Fager, Round Table, and Mongo. The disruption of the New Jersey circuit with the 1977 Garden State Park fire and the opening of Atlantic City's first casinos the following year hurt the track's business and led to a gradual reduction in its schedule. Atlantic City conducted a six-day, all-turf meet in 1999 and 2000, and it raced ten days in 2001 to qualify for year-round, full-card simulcasting. Atlantic City was sold to Greenwood Racing for $13-million in August 2001. Atlantic City runs a brief, all-turf meet at its McKee City plant each year.

Location: 4501 Black Horse Pike, Mays Landing, N.J. 08330-3142
Phone: (609) 641-2190

Fax: (609) 645-8309
Website: *www.acracecourse.com*
E-Mail: mgallagherbugdon@aol.com
Year Founded: 1944
Dates of Inaugural Meeting: July 22, 1946
Abbreviation: Atl
Acreage: 255
Seating Capacity: 10,000

Ownership
Greenwood Racing Inc.

Officers
Chairman: Harold Handel
President: Harold Handel
Director of Racing: Sal Sinatra
Racing Secretary: Sal Sinatra
Secretary: Frank McDonnell
Treasurer: Anthony D. Ricci
Director of Publicity: Maureen Gallagher Bugdon
Director of Simulcasting: Geri Mercer
Track Photographer: World Wide Racing Photos
Track Superintendent: William Gatto

Racing Dates
2004: May 5-May 19, 4 days
2005: April 29-May 13, 4 days

Track Layout
Main Circumference: 1 1/8 miles
Main Track Chute: 7 furlongs
Main Width: 100 feet
Main Length of Stretch: 947.29 feet
Main Turf Circumference: 1 mile
Main Turf Width: 100 feet

Leaders
Recent Meeting, Leading Jockey: Danielle Hodsdon, 3, 2004; Stewart Elliott, 3, 2004
Recent Meeting, Leading Trainer: Jonathan E. Sheppard, 3, 2004; Thomas H. Voss, 3, 2004

Fastest Times of 2004 (Turf)
5 furlongs: Hostility, :55.86, May 13, 2004
5 1/2 furlongs: Scattering Breezes, 1:02.39, May 13, 2004
1 mile: Adinatha, 1:36.73, May 13, 2004
1 1/16 miles: Cateress, 1:43.87, May 13, 2004
1 1/2 miles: Serazzo, 2:28.10, May 5, 2004
2 1/8 miles: Military Man, 4:01.01, May 19, 2004
a2 1/8 miles: Tallow, 4:03.12, May 19, 2004

Monmouth Park

The first Monmouth Park opened in July 1870 and was located three miles from Long Branch, New Jersey. The track's early years included performances by some of the era's most famous horses, including Longfellow and Miss Woodford, the latter the first racehorse to earn $100,000. However, Monmouth fell victim to changing times, and it closed in 1893 after New Jersey outlawed wagering. Fifty years later, pari-mutuel wagering was legalized, and a group of investors led by Amory L. Haskell built a new Monmouth in 1946 at its current location in Oceanport. Since then, the track known for its easy-going, seaside ambiance has been a popular destination for some of the sport's leading Thoroughbreds. The track's richest race is the Haskell Invitational Handicap (G1), a $1-million race for three-year-olds and the first major East Coast event after the Triple Crown races. Monmouth also features the United Nations Handicap (G1), which formerly was run at Atlantic City Race Course. The Philip H. Iselin Breeders' Cup Handicap (G3), named in honor of a former Monmouth president, formerly was known as the Monmouth Handicap, which was inaugurated in 1884. In 2007, Monmouth is scheduled to host the Breeders' Cup World Thoroughbred Championships.

Location: Oceanport Ave., P.O. Box MP, Oceanport, N.J. 07757
Phone: (732) 222-5100
Fax: (732) 571-8658
Website: *www.monmouthpark.com*
E-Mail: mpinfo@njsea.com
Year Founded: Original: 1870; Current Track: 1946
Dates of Inaugural Meeting: July 30, 1870
Abbreviation: Mth
Acreage: 500
Number of Stalls: 1,600
Seating Capacity: 18,000

Ownership
New Jersey Sports and Exposition Authority

Officers
President: George R. Zoffinger
General Manager: Robert J. Kulina
Racing Secretary: Michael P. Dempsey
Director of Operations: Horace Smith
Director of Admissions: Joseph J. Cieri
Director of Finance: James Jemas
Director of Marketing: Peter Verdee
Director of Publicity: William Knauf
Director of Simulcasting: John S. Grasty
Horsemen's Liaison: Mary Beth Yates
Stewards: Samuel Boulmetis Sr., Harvey I. Wardell Jr., Stephen Pagano
Track Announcer: Larry Collmus
Track Photographer: Bill Denver/Equi Photo
Track Superintendent: Dave Harrington
Security: William Kudlacik

Racing Dates
2004: May 29-September 26, 87 days
2005: May 14-September 25, 90 days

Track Layout
Main Circumference: 1 mile
Main Track Chute: 6 furlongs
Main Track Chute: 1 1/4 miles
Main Width: 100 feet
Main Length of Stretch: 985 feet
Main Turf Circumference: 7 furlongs
Main Turf Chute: 1 1/16 miles
Main Turf Chute: 1 1/8 miles
Main Turf Width: 90 feet

Attendance
Average Daily Recent Meeting: 7,085, 2004
Total Attendance Recent Meeting: 790,433, 2004
Highest Single Day Record: 53,638, August 3, 2003
Record Daily Average for Single Meet: 20,907, 1957
Highest Single Meet Record: 1,150,658, 1981

Handle
Average All Sources Recent Meeting: $4,197,758, 2004
Average On-Track Recent Meeting: $1,347,641, 2004
Total All Sources Recent Meeting: $364,595,940, 2004
Total On-Track Recent Meeting: $117,244,821, 2004
Record Daily Average for Single Meet: $1,997,807, 1970
Single Day All Sources Handle: $11,407,470, 1999

Mutuel Records
Highest Win: $229.20, July 15, 1951
Lowest Win: $2.10, Skip Away, August 30, 1998; $2.10, Silverbulletday, July 10, 1999
Highest Trifecta: $62,172, June 15, 1978
Lowest Trifecta: $17.60, July 29, 1985
Highest Daily Double: $3,962.50, July 19, 1952
Lowest Daily Double: $2.80, June 3, 1995

Leaders

Career, Leading Jockey by Titles: Joe Bravo, 10
Career, Leading Trainer by Titles: Budd Lepman, 5; John H. Forbes, 5; Juan Serey, 5
Recent Meeting, Leading Horse: Rat Like Cunning, 4, 2004; Quiet Desperation, 4, 2004
Recent Meeting, Leading Jockey: Joe Bravo, 96, 2004
Recent Meeting, Leading Trainer: Timothy Hills, 36, 2004

Records

Single Day Jockey Wins: Walter Blum, 6, June 9, 1961; Chris Antley, 6, July 30, 1984; Julie Krone, 6, August 19, 1987; Joe Bravo, 6, August 31, 1994
Single Day Trainer Wins: J. Willard Thompson, 4, November 8, 1975; Robert Klesaris, 4, July 10, 1987; John H. Forbes, 4, August 28, 1989
Single Meet, Leading Jockey by Wins: Chris Antley, 171, 1984
Single Meet, Leading Trainer by Wins: John Tammaro III, 55, 1974; J. Willard Thompson, 55, 1975

Track Records, Main Dirt

5 furlongs: Camden Harbor, :56.22, June 18, 1991
5 1/2 furlongs: American Royale, 1:02.96, July 21, 1991
6 furlongs: Gilded Time, 1:07.84, August 8, 1992
1 mile: Forty Niner, 1:33 4/5, July 16, 1988
1m 70 yds: Presidentialaffair, 1:38.85, July 5, 2004
1 1/16 miles: Formal Gold, 1:40.20, August 23, 1997
1 1/8 miles: Spend a Buck, 1:46 4/5, August 17, 1985; Jolie's Halo, 1:46.80, August 8, 1992
1 3/16 miles: Okamsel, 1:59 3/5, June 20, 1951
1 1/4 miles: Carry Back, 2:00 2/5, July 14, 1962; Majestic Light, 2:00 2/5, August 30, 1977
1 1/2 miles: Chappys Joy, 2:34 1/5, August 5, 1989
1 3/4 miles: *Halconero, 3:04 1/5, August 5, 1950

Track Records, Main Turf

5 furlongs: Klassy Briefcase, :54.97, June 8, 1991
1 mile: Double Booked, 1:33.34, June 2, 1991
1 1/16 miles: Mi Narrow, 1:39.40, July 11, 1999
1 1/8 miles: Batique, 1:46.19, June 16, 2001
1 3/16 miles: *Dorienne, 2:01, June 30, 1953
1 1/4 miles: Muzzle, 2:08 2/5, July 10, 1953
1 3/8 miles: Balto Star, 2:12.78, July 5, 2003
1 1/2 miles: Agacode, 2:29 2/5, June 14, 1985

Principal Races

Haskell Invitational H. (G1), United Nations S. (G1), Molly Pitcher Breeders' Cup H. (G2), Monmouth Breeders' Cup Oaks (G2), Philip H. Iselin Breeders' Cup H. (G3)

Notable Events

August 3, 2003, Haskell Day, 53,638 in attendance; largest crowd ever for a horse race in New Jersey.

Fastest Times of 2004 (Dirt)

5 furlongs: Sing Me Back Home, :56.34, August 14, 2004
5 1/2 furlongs: A One Rocket, 1:03.36, June 5, 2004
6 furlongs: War's Prospect, 1:08.67, August 14, 2004
1 mile: Presidentialaffair, 1:35.27, July 25, 2004
1m 70 yds: Presidentialaffair, 1:38.85, July 5, 2004
1 1/16 miles: Capeside Lady, 1:42.18, August 15, 2004
1 1/8 miles: Ghostzapper, 1:47.66, August 21, 2004

Fastest Times of 2004 (Turf)

5 furlongs: Blakelock, :55.24, June 26, 2004
1 mile: Frisky Spider, 1:33.95, June 19, 2004
1 1/16 miles: Kathir, 1:39.88, June 27, 2004
1 1/8 miles: Lord Louis, 1:47.39, June 26, 2004
1 3/8 miles: Request for Parole, 2:13.37, July 3, 2004
a2 1/2 miles: Sur La Tete, 4:38.61, September 26, 2004

The Meadowlands

Meadowlands racetrack, located on former marshland in East Rutherford, has been the economic engine of the Meadowlands Sports Complex. Built by the New Jersey Sports and Exposition Authority for $340-million, the complex includes the Continental Airlines Arena, home of basketball's New Jersey Nets and hockey's New Jersey Devils, and Giants Stadium, where the New York Giants and Jets play football. Meadowlands, which held its first Thoroughbred meet in September 1977, has been host to several memorable events in racing history. In 1978, Dr. Patches upset Seattle Slew in the Paterson Handicap. John Henry, once the sport's all-time leading earner, closed his career with a stunning, come-from-behind victory in the Ballantine's Scotch Classic Handicap in 1984. Four years later, Alysheba set a 1¼-mile track record when he captured the Meadowlands Cup Handicap (G1) during his Horse of the Year campaign. Meadowlands, whose world-renowned Standardbred meet runs from December through August, conducts Thoroughbred racing in the fall.

Location: 50 State Hwy 120, East Rutherford, N.J. 07073-2131
Phone: (201) 935-8500
Fax: (201) 460-4042
Website: www.thebigm.com
E-Mail: MRotella@njsea.com
Year Founded: 1976
Dates of Inaugural Meeting: September 6, 1977
Abbreviation: Med
Acreage: 220
Number of Stalls: 1,760
Seating Capacity: 4,650

Ownership

New Jersey Sports and Exposition Authority

Officers

Chairman: Carl J. Goldberg
President: George Zoffinger
General Manager: Christopher McErlean
Racing Secretary: Michael Dempsey
Secretary: Marvin Schmelzer
Treasurer: Joseph M. Forgione
Director of Operations: Marcello Esposito
Director of Admissions: Marianne Rotella
Director of Communications: Carol Hodes
Director of Finance: Jim Jemas
Director of Marketing: Glenn Cademartori
Director of Mutuels: Robert Halpin
Director of Publicity: Carol Hodes
Director of Simulcasting: Alex Dadoyan
Horsemen's Liaison: Mary Beth Yates
Stewards: James Edwards, Stephan Pagano, Harvey I. Wardell Jr.
Track Announcer: Dave Johnson, Sam McKee, Ken Warkentin
Track Photographer: Equi-Photo
Track Superintendent: Robert Ashelman
Asst. Racing Secretary: John Perlow

Racing Dates

2004: October 1-November 13, 32 days
2005: September 30-November 12, 30 days

Track Layout

Main Circumference: 1 mile
Main Track Chute: 1 1/4 miles
Main Track Chute: 6 furlongs
Main Width: 90 feet
Main Length of Stretch: 990 feet
Main Turf Circumference: 7 furlongs

Attendance

Average Daily Recent Meeting: 4,113, 2004
Highest Single Day Record: 41,155
Highest Single Meet Record: 1,772,209, 1977
Record Daily Average for Single Meet: 17,901, 1977
Total Attendance Recent Meeting: 135,730, 2004
Lowest Single Meet Record: 135,730, 2004

Handle

Average All Sources Recent Meeting: $2,204,704, 2004
Average On-Track Recent Meeting: $418,276, 2004
Record Daily Average for Single Meet: $2,619,909, 1994
Single Day All Sources Handle: $5,025,645, 1994
Total All Sources Recent Meeting: $70,550,528, 2004
Total On-Track Recent Meeting: $13,384,832, 2004
Highest Single Day Recent Meet: $933,628, October 8, 2004

Mutuel Records

Highest Win: $354.80, Great Normand, 1990
Lowest Win: $2.20, Spectacular Bid, 1979

Leaders

Career, Leading Jockey by Titles: Joe Bravo, 8
Career, Leading Trainer by Titles: John Forbes, 7
Career, Leading Jockey by Stakes Wins: Angel Cordero, 27; Jorge Velasquez, 27
Career, Leading Trainer by Stakes Wins: Philip G. Johnson, 17
Career, Leading Jockey by Wins: Nick Santagata, 961
Career, Leading Trainer by Wins: John H. Forbes, 590
Recent Meeting, Leading Horse: Melody's Slasher, 3, 2004
Recent Meeting, Leading Jockey: Stewart Elliot, 37, 2004
Recent Meeting, Leading Trainer: Patricia Farro, 11, 2004

Records

Single Day Jockey Wins: Julie Krone, 6, September 19, 1989
Single Day Trainer Wins: John Forbes, 4, November 8, 1978
Single Meet, Leading Jockey by Wins: Joe Bravo, 142, 1994
Single Meet, Leading Owner by Wins: William C. Martucci, 34
Single Meet, Leading Trainer by Wins: John Forbes, 47, 1982; Joseph Pierce Jr., 47, 1982; John Forbes, 47, 1990

Track Records, Main Dirt

5 furlongs: Stu's Choice, :55.95, September 6, 1996
5 1/2 furlongs: King Bold Reality, 1:04 1/5, September 15, 1983
6 furlongs: Hay Cody, 1:07.81, September 6, 1996
1 mile: On the Tour, 1:34.43, November 10, 1999
1m 70 yds: Schedule (GB), 1:37.90, October 15, 2004
1 1/16 miles: Black Forest, 1:40.39, September 26, 1998
1 1/8 miles: Forty One Carats, 1:45.50, October 29, 1999
1 3/16 miles: Key Lory, 1:53.88, November 20, 1999
1 1/4 miles: Alysheba, 1:58 4/5, October 14, 1988

Track Records, Main Turf

5 furlongs: Special Occasion, :55.17, September 4, 2000
1 mile: True Diplomacy, 1:34, September 8, 1989
1m 70yds: Cape Playhouse, 1:38, October 25, 1978
1 1/16 miles: Wanderkin, 1:39 2/5, September 30, 1988
1 3/8 miles: Rice, 2:12.02, September 25, 1998

Principal Races

Meadowlands Breeders' Cup S. (G2), Pegasus S. (G3), Cliff Hanger H. (G3), Violet H. (G3)

Fastest Times of 2004 (Dirt)

5 furlongs: Cumby Texas, :56.37, November 5, 2004
5 1/2 furlongs: Lieutenant Danz, 1:04.75, October 9, 2004
6 furlongs: Special Judge, 1:08.62, October 6, 2004
1 mile: Simply Awesome, 1:35.17, October 15, 2004
1m 70 yds: Schedule (GB), 1:37.90, October 15, 2004
1 1/16 miles: Roaring Fever, 1:41.83, October 29, 2004
1 1/8 miles: Pies Prospect, 1:48.57, October 1, 2004

Fastest Times of 2004 (Turf)

5 furlongs: Worldwind Romance, :56.11, October 8, 2004
1 mile: Theartfuldutchman, 1:34.98, October 12, 2004
1m 70 yds: Hourly Storm, 1:40.01, October 23, 2004
1 1/16 miles: Wizard of Gold, 1:41.46, October 13, 2004
1 3/8 miles: Macaw (Ire), 2:14.20, October 29, 2004

New Mexico

Ruidoso Downs

Located 7,000 feet above sea level in the pine-covered mountains of southeastern New Mexico, Ruidoso

Downs long has been a popular destination for Southwestern horsemen and racing fans seeking to escape the summer heat. Since 1959, the track has held Quarter Horse racing's richest and most famous event, the All American Futurity, which in 1978 became the world's first $1-million horse race. Leading trainers such as D. Wayne Lukas and Bob Baffert raced Quarter Horses at Ruidoso before switching to Thoroughbred racing. Thoroughbred racing also is a fixture at Ruidoso, where purses have increased significantly due to revenues from the Billy the Kid Casino, which opened at the track in 1999. Ruidoso has a unique track configuration for the two breeds that compete at the track. A separate straightaway for Quarter Horses is located on the outside of the seven-furlong Thoroughbred oval.

Location: P.O. Box 449, Ruidoso Downs, N.M. 88346-0449
Phone: (505) 378-4431
Fax: (505) 378-4631
Website: *ruidosodownsracing.com*
E-Mail: info@ruidownsracing.com
Dates of Inaugural Meeting: July 1, 1947
Abbreviation: Rui
Number of Stalls: 2,000
Seating Capacity: 7,000

Officers

Chairman: R. D. Hubbard
President: Bruce Rimbo
General Manager: Rick Baugh
Racing Secretary: Robert Junk
Secretary: Edward Burger
Treasurer: Edward Burger
Director of Operations: Richard Swenor
Director of Marketing: Neal Mullarky
Director of Mutuels: Deano McTeigue
Vice President: Edward Burger
Director of Simulcasting: Kristian Lovelace
Stewards: Bobby Allison, Bruce Brinkley, Jerry Nicodemus
Track Announcer: Jim McAulay
Track Photographer: Instant Images
Track Superintendent: Mike Dorame
Security: Richard Swenor

Racing Dates

2004: May 28-September 6, 60 days
2005: May 27-September 5, 60 days

Track Layout

Main Circumference: 7 furlongs
Main Track Chute: 6 furlongs
Main Track Chute: 1 1/8 miles
Main Length of Stretch: 656 feet

Attendance

Highest Single Day Record: 17,009, September 2, 2002

Handle

Single Day On-Track Handle: $1,469,740, September 1, 2003

Leaders

Recent Meeting, Leading Jockey: Alfredo J. Juarez Jr., 34, 2004; Carlos D. Madeira, 34, 2004
Recent Meeting, Leading Trainer: Joel Marr, 18, 2004

Track Records, Main Dirt

4 1/2 furlongs: Becca's Shoulder, :52, June 25, 2004
5 furlongs: King of Stars, :57.20, July 30, 1999
5 1/2 furlongs: Jack Wilson, 1:02.80, August 8, 1992; Rocky Gulch, 1:02.80, August 1, 2004
6 furlongs: Jack Wilson, 1:08.80, August 16, 1992; Ninety Nine Jack, 1:08.80, July 8, 2004
6 1/2 furlongs: Mr. Tattoo, 1:17 3/5, July 4, 1973
7 furlongs: Fill Mackis Cup, 1:24 2/5, July 15, 1984
7 1/2 furlongs: Last Don B., 1:31, May 29, 1993
1 mile: Set Records, 1:37, July 28, 1995; Strong Arm Robbery, 1:37, September 1, 2001

1m 70 yds: Brogander, 1:45 1/5, January 1, 1954
1 1/16 miles: Lucky Bluff, 1:43.40, September 2, 2001
1 1/8 miles: Run John, 1:53.40, July 5, 1996
1 1/4 miles: Best Finish (GB), 2:08.20, September 7, 1998
1 3/8 miles: Start Jumpin, 2:24 1/5, August 18, 1990
1 1/2 miles: Decidedly Henry C., 2:37, August 19, 1989
1 5/8 miles: More Than Glory, 2:25.80, August 15, 1992

Principal Races

First Lady H., Free Spirits S., Fern Sawyer H., Ruidoso Oaks, Governor's H.

Fastest Times of 2004 (Dirt)

2 1/2 furlongs: Doctor Dragon, :27.80, August 29, 2004
4 1/2 furlongs: Beccas' Shoulder, :52.00, June 25, 2004
5 furlongs: Twilight Diamond, :56.60, July 17, 2004
5 1/2 furlongs: Rocky Gulch, 1:02.80, August 1, 2004
6 furlongs: Ninety Nine Jack, 1:08.80, July 18, 2004
7 1/2 furlongs: Ninety Nine Jack, 1:31.40, August 1, 2004; Southern Twilight, 1:31.40, July 1, 2004
1 mile: Don't Strike Out, 1:37.20, June 20, 2004
1 1/16 miles: Southern Twilight, 1:44.40, September 5, 2004
1 1/8 miles: Fin Entertainment, 1:55.60, August 22, 2004
1 1/4 miles: Fin Entertainment, 2:09.40, September 6, 2004

Sunland Park

Opened in 1959, Sunland Park was built just across the state line from El Paso, Texas, in New Mexico, which unlike its neighbor allowed pari-mutuel wagering. Sunland launched the career of several notable horsemen and horses. Jerry Bailey, one of Thoroughbred racing's all-time leading riders, began his career at the track in 1974. Bold Ego, who won Sunland's Riley Allison Futurity in 1980, captured the '81 Arkansas Derby (G1) and ran second in the Preakness Stakes (G1). In the mid-1990s, the track nearly closed because of competition from Native American casinos and pari-mutuel racing in Texas and Oklahoma. New Mexico horsemen and racetracks successfully lobbied for legalizing slot machines at tracks, and Sunland's casino opened in February 1999. With a portion of casino revenues earmarked to purses, the quality of racing improved significantly.

Location: 1200 Futurity Dr, Sunland Park, N.M. 88063-9057
Phone: (505) 589-1131
Fax: (505) 589-1518
Website: www.sunland-park.com
E-Mail: sunland-info@sunland-park.com
Year Founded: 1959
Dates of Inaugural Meeting: October 9, 1959
Abbreviation: Sun
Number of Stalls: 1,600
Seating Capacity: 5,710

Ownership

Stan E. Fulton

Officers

President: Harold Payne
General Manager: Harold Payne
Director of Racing: Dustin Dix
Racing Secretary: Norm Amundson
Director of Operations: Dustin Dix
Director of Finance: Charlie Casiao
Director of Marketing: Adeline Rogers
Director of Mutuels: Dustin Dix
Director of Publicity: Eric Alwan
Director of Sales: Connie Blevins
Director of Simulcasting: Charles Chrisman
Horsemen's Liaison: Donna Martin
Stewards: Bruce Brinkly, Bob Allison, Richard Lidberg

Track Announcer: Robert Geller
Track Photographer: Bill Pitt Jr.
Track Superintendent: Bob Patty
Security: Oscar Renteria

Racing Dates

2004: November 19, 2003-April 11, 2004, 80 days
2005: November 5, 2004-April 3, 2005, 87 days
2006: December 2, 2005-April 16, 2006, 79 days

Track Layout

Main Circumference: 1 mile
Main Track Chute: 6 1/2 furlongs
Main Track Chute: 1 1/4 miles
Main Width: 80 feet
Main Length of Stretch: 990 feet

Attendance

Average Daily Recent Meeting: 3,612, 2004/2005
Total Attendance Recent Meeting: 314,200, 2004/2005
Highest Single Day Record: 8,494

Handle

Average All Sources Recent Meeting: $733,478, 2004/2005
Average On-Track Recent Meeting: $125,311, 2004/2005
Total All Sources Recent Meeting: $63,812,618, 2004/2005
Total On-Track Recent Meeting: $10,902,019, 2004/2005
Single Day All Sources Handle: $2,194,229, February 3, 2004

Leaders

Career, Leading Jockey by Titles: Bobby Harmon, 8
Career, Leading Trainer by Titles: Bob E. Arnett, 12
Recent Meeting, Leading Horse: Cassie's Casper, 6, 2004/2005; Daring Pegasus, 6, 2004/2005
Recent Meeting, Leading Jockey: Ken Tohill, 109, 2004/2005
Recent Meeting, Leading Trainer: Steve Asmussen, 47, 2004/2005

Records

Single Meet, Leading Trainer by Wins: Ramon Gonzalez, 37

Track Records, Main Dirt

4 furlongs: Tamran's Jet, :44 4/5, March 22, 1968
4 1/2 furlongs: Bold Liz, :50 2/5, March 25, 1972
5 furlongs: Jimmy Jones, :55.90, February 7, 2004
5 1/2 furlongs: Treasure Hunt, 1:02.1, January 28, 2003
6 furlongs: Yet Anothernatalie, 1:08.24, December 11, 2004
6 1/2 furlongs: Funny Meeting, 1:14.84
1 mile: Mr. Trieste, 1:35.38, December 7, 2004
1 1/16 miles: Butte City, 1:41.92, December 12, 2004
1 1/8 miles: Winsham Lad, 1:48 1/5, January 8, 1961; Prenupcial, 1:48 1/5, April 28, 1962
1 3/16 miles: Mickey J., 1:58 1/5, November 14, 1970
1 1/4 miles: Curribot, 2:01 2/5, May 6, 1984
1 3/8 miles: Hot Deck, 2:19 2/5, January 10, 1970
1 5/8 miles: Rush Line, 2:47 3/5, April 6, 1969

Principal Races

WinStar Derby, WinStar/Sunland Park Oaks, Borderland Derby

Interesting Facts

Achievements/milestones: Casino opened February 2, 1999

Fastest Times of 2004 (Dirt)

2 furlongs: Oso Tricky, :21.86, March 5, 2004
4 1/2 furlongs: Ring of the Run, :51.92, March 23, 2004
5 furlongs: Jimmy Jones, :55.90, February 7, 2004
5 1/2 furlongs: Values of the Hunt, 1:02.70, March 28, 2004
6 furlongs: Yet Anothernatalie, 1:08.24, December 11, 2004
6 1/2 furlongs: Bang, 1:14.29, March 6, 2004
1 mile: Mr. Trieste, 1:35.38, December 7, 2004
1 1/16 miles: Butte City, 1:41.92, December 12, 2004
1 1/8 miles: My Buba Boy, 1:50.15, January 20, 2004
1 1/4 miles: Money Set, 2:10.02, April 11, 2004

SunRay Park

SunRay Park in Farmington, New Mexico, is located in an area called the Four Corners region, where northwestern New Mexico, northeastern Arizona, southeastern Utah, and southwestern Colorado meet. The racetrack, which offers Thoroughbred and Quarter Horse racing, originally was known as San Juan Downs; it was built by San Juan County at the county fairgrounds and opened in 1984. Declining business forced the track to close after its 1993 season. SunRay Gaming of New Mexico LLC secured a ten-year option to operate the track, which was renamed SunRay Park and reopened in October 1999. SunRay Gaming's interest in reviving horse racing at the facility largely was based on its ability to operate a casino with slot machines. A portion of revenues from the slots enhances race purses.

Location: 39 Road 5568, Farmington, N.M. 87401-1466
Phone: (505) 566-1200
Fax: (505) 326-4292
Website: www.sunraygaming.com
E-Mail: racing@sunraygaming.com
Year Founded: 1984
Abbreviation: SrP
Number of Stalls: 1,298
Seating Capacity: 3,000

Ownership
SunRay Gaming of New Mexico LLC

Officers
General Manager: Byron Campbell
Director of Racing: Lonnie Barber Jr.
Racing Secretary: Hank Demoney
Director of Operations: Toni Authurs
Director of Finance: Brad Bohem
Director of Marketing: Tony Montano
Director of Mutuels: Natalie Swisher
Director of Publicity: Tony Montano
Director of Simulcasting: Toni Authurs
Stewards: Bob Allison, Bruce Brinkley, Vicki Eikleberry
Track Announcer: Jeff Munson
Track Photographer: Coady Photography
Track Superintendent: Gary Kretchmer
Security: Leonard Demoney
Asst. Racing Secretary: Gordon Graham
Horsemen's Bookkeeper: Toby Demoney

Racing Dates
2004: August 2-November 2, 44 days
2005: July 2-September 5, 38 days

Attendance
Average Daily Recent Meeting: 1,140, 2004
Total Attendance Recent Meeting: 50,160, 2004

Handle
Average All Sources Recent Meeting: $142,942, 2004
Average On-Track Recent Meeting: $22,852, 2004
Total All Sources Recent Meeting: $6,289,457, 2004
Total On-Track Recent Meeting: $1,005,493, 2004
Highest Single Day Recent Meet: $234,122, October 4, 2004

Leaders
Recent Meeting, Leading Jockey: Ken Tohill, 55, 2004
Recent Meeting, Leading Trainer: Dan Dennison, 20, 2004

Track Records, Main Dirt
4 furlongs: Absolutely True, :44.60, November 16, 2003
4 1/2 furlongs: Sky Diver, :49.80, October 10, 2003
6 furlongs: Unbridled Set, 1:11.40, October 11, 1999
6 1/2 furlongs: Herecomesthemannow, 1:15.60, September 22, 2003

7 furlongs: Oh Gracie, 1:22.60, September 25, 2000
7 1/2 furlongs: Dalt's Kingpin, 1:28.60, November 17, 2003
1 mile: Ben Told, 1:35.60, October 15, 2000
1 1/8 miles: Line Gauge, 1:48.80, November 21, 1999

Principal Races
New Mexico Breeders' Derby, New Mexico Breeders' Distaff H., New Mexico Breeders' Association H., Aztec Oaks, Totah Futurity

Fastest Times of 2004 (Dirt)
4 1/2 furlongs: Swift for Sure, :50.40, September 27, 2004
6 1/2 furlongs: Swift for Sure, 1:16.80, August 2, 2004
7 furlongs: Miss Noteworthy, 1:22.80, August 28, 2004
7 1/2 furlongs: Elbow Creek, 1:32.20, October 25, 2004
1 mile: Swift for Sure, 1:36.40, October 19, 2004
1 1/8 miles: Pleasant Bend, 1:50.40, November 2, 2004

The Downs at Albuquerque

The Downs at Albuquerque, located on the New Mexico State Fairgrounds in Albuquerque, features Thoroughbred and Quarter Horse racing each spring and during the 17-day New Mexico State Fair in September. The fair dates from 1881, while its race meet, which opened in October 1938, is the oldest in New Mexico. The New Mexico State Fair Futurity for Quarter Horses debuted in 1946 and is the oldest continuously run stakes race for the breed. One notable Thoroughbred horseman who competed at Albuquerque early in his career was jockey Mike Smith, a New Mexico native who became a Racing Hall of Fame member in 2003. In 1990, the track debuted The Lineage, a day of racing exclusively for state-bred Thoroughbreds and Quarter Horses. With assistance from its slots casino, which opened in 1999, the track has been able to solidify its business and increase purses.

Location: 201 California St. NE, Albuquerque, N.M. 87108-1802
Phone: (505) 266-5555
Fax: (505) 268-1970
Website: www.abqdowns.com
E-Mail: donc@abqdowns.com
Year Founded: 1938
Abbreviation: Alb

Officers
President: Paul Blanchard
General Manager: Craig Smith
Director of Racing: Don Cook
Racing Secretary: Roddy Taylor
Director of Operations: Beth McKinney
Director of Finance: Charles DeNolf
Director of Marketing: Michael Lazarus
Director of Mutuels: Barbra Hewson
Director of Simulcasting: Beth McKinney
Track Superintendent: Tony Martinez

Racing Dates
2004: April 9-July 5, 53 days; September 10-September 26, 17 days
2005: April 2-June 12, 42 days; September 9-September 25, 17 days

Track Layout
Main Circumference: 1 mile
Main Length of Stretch: 1,114 feet

Track Records, Main Dirt
4 furlongs: Chipper J., :45.76, May 6, 2001
4 1/2 furlongs: Silver Matt, :51.22, June 17, 2000
5 furlongs: Scout Revolt, :56.35, December 12, 1998

5 1/2 furlongs: Yulla Yulla, 1:01.68, September 23, 2000
6 furlongs: Huggin the Rail, 1:08.44, September 29, 1996; Ninety Nine Jack, 1:08.44, May 2, 2004
6 1/2 furlongs: Shellerton, 1:14.92, May 18, 2001
1 mile: Dashing Forbes, 1:35.74, September 16, 1994
1 1/16 miles: Ciento, 1:40.60, September 22, 2001
1 1/8 miles: Brew, 1:48.47, June 3, 2001
1 3/16 miles: Savage Wind, 2:05 4/5, September 23, 1981
1 1/4 miles: Luedke, 2:03.69, April 14, 1996
1 1/2 miles: Luedke, 2:33.73, September 25, 1994
1 5/8 miles: Vikings Shield, 2:43 2/5, April 17, 1988
Other: 1 13/16 miles, Vermejo, 3:05 2/5, September 27, 1970

Principal Races
The Downs at Albuquerque H.

Fastest Times of 2004 (Dirt)
5 furlongs: Lukfata Louis, :56.79, April 24, 2004
5 1/2 furlongs: Dayjurette, 1:02.56, April 9, 2004
6 furlongs: Ninety Nine Jack, 1:08.44, May 2, 2004
6 1/2 furlongs: Blossom Belle, 1:15.41, May 1, 2004
7 furlongs: Angelica Slew, 1:22.11, September 24, 2004
1 mile: Wolfwithintegrity, 1:35.84, May 23, 2004
1 1/16 miles: Ciento, 1:44.24, June 12, 2004
1 1/8 miles: Latenite Trick, 1:49.30, September 26, 2004
1 1/2 miles: Hammerin, 2:34.34, July 5, 2004
1 13/16 miles: Megan's Man, 3:10.04, September 26, 2004

New York

Aqueduct

Occupying roughly half of the New York Racing Association's year-round schedule, the track known as the Big A offers racing in winter, spring, and fall. Aqueduct opened as a six-furlong track in New York's Queens Borough on September 27, 1894. Site of the only triple dead heat in a stakes race—Brownie, Bossuet, and Wait a Bit hit the wire together in the Carter Handicap on June 10, 1944—Aqueduct was torn down in 1956 and completely rebuilt over three years. For four years, from 1964 through 1967, Aqueduct played host to the Belmont Stakes while Belmont Park was rebuilt. An all-time record crowd of 73,435 watched Gun Bow win the Metropolitan Handicap on Memorial Day, May 31, 1965. In 1975, the one-mile inner dirt track was completed, allowing racing throughout the winter. Six years later, Aqueduct opened Equestris, a 300-foot-long, $7-million facility for 1,600 diners. A $3-million renovation in 1985 prior to its only Breeders' Cup championship day expanded Aqueduct's paddock and grandstand. The spring meet's principal race is the Wood Memorial Stakes (G1), a Kentucky Derby (G1) prep, and the Cigar Mile Handicap (G1) is one of its fall features. The New York Legislature in 2001 authorized video-lottery terminals to be installed at the track, and a slot-machine contractor, MGM Mirage, was chosen in 2003.

Location: 1100 Rockaway Blvd., P. O. Box 90, Jamaica, N.Y. 11417
Phone: (718) 641-4700
Fax: (718) 322-3814
Website: www.nyra.com/aqueduct
E-Mail: gmathes@nyrainc.com
Year Founded: 1894
Dates of Inaugural Meeting: September 27, 1894
Abbreviation: Aqu
Capsule description: The Big A
Acreage: 192
Number of Stalls: 547
Seating Capacity: 17,000

Ownership
New York Racing Association Inc.

Officers
Chairman and Chief Executive: Charles E. Hayward
Racing Secretary: Michael S. Lakow
Treasurer: John Giombarrese
Director of Admissions: Jerry A. Davis Jr.
Senior Vice President: William A. Nader
Director of Mutuels: Patrick Mahony
Director of Simulcasting: Elizabeth Bracken
Horsemen's Liaison: Carmen Barrera
Stewards: Dr. W. Theodore Hill, David Hicks, Carmine Donofrio
Track Announcer: Tom Durkin
Track Photographer: Adam Coglianese, Bob Coglianese
Track Superintendent: Jerry Porcelli
Security: John Tierney

Racing Dates
2004: January 1-May 2, 88 days; October 27-December 31, 42 days
2005: January 1-May 1, 85 days; November 2-December 31, 39 days

Track Layout
Main Circumference: 1 1/8 miles
Main Width: 100 feet
Main Length of Stretch: 1,155.6 feet
Main Turf Circumference: 7 furlongs
Inner Circumference: 1 mile

Attendance
Average Daily Recent Meeting: 3,874, Winter/Spring 2004; 3,235, Fall 2004; 3,178, Winter/Spring 2005
Highest Single Day Record: 73,435, May 31, 1965
Total Attendance Recent Meeting: 344,786, Winter/Spring 2004; 135,883, Fall 2004; 263,774, Winter/Spring 2005

Handle
Average All Sources Recent Meeting: $8,663,317, Winter/Spring 2004; $8,467,211, Fall 2004; $7,765,246, Winter/Spring 2005
Average On-Track Recent Meeting: $1,288,331, Winter/Spring 2004; $699,725, Fall 2004; $1,094,629, Winter/Spring 2005
Single Day On-Track Handle: $8,171,520, November 2, 1985
Total All Sources Recent Meeting: $771,035,213, Winter/Spring 2004; $355,622,845, Fall 2004; $644,515,418, Winter/Spring 2005
Total On-Track Recent Meeting: $114,661,459, Winter/Spring 2004; $29,388,457, Fall 2004; $90,854,207, Winter/Spring 2005

Mutuel Records
Highest Win: $434, Markobob, September 3, 1943
Highest Pick 6: $1,210,287, January 17, 2004

Records
Single Day Jockey Wins: Michael Venezia, 6, December 7, 1964; Rudy L. Turcotte, 6, December 2, 1969; Angel Cordero Jr., 6, March 12, 1975; Ron Turcotte, 6, March 5, 1976; Steve Cauthen, 6, January 22, 1977; Steve Cauthen, 6, April 7, 1977; Steve Cauthen, 6, November 29, 1977; Mike Smith, 6, January 13, 1992; Mike Smith, 6, January 30, 1992; Jorge Chavez, 6, February 18, 1996; Shaun Bridgmohan, 6, February 15, 1998

Track Records, Main Dirt
4 1/2 furlongs: About to Burst, :51 3/5, August 26, 1984
6 furlongs: Kelly Kip, 1:07.54, April 10, 1999
6 1/2 furlongs: Coronado's Quest, 1:14.35, October 26, 1997
7 furlongs: Artax, 1:20.04, May 2, 1999
1 mile: Easy Goer, 1:32 2/5, April 8, 1989
1 1/8 miles: Riva Ridge, 1:47, October 15, 1973
1 3/16 miles: Riva Ridge, 1:52 2/5, July 4, 1973
1 1/4 miles: Damascus, 1:59 1/5, July 20, 1968
1 3/8 miles: Demi's Bret, 2:12.31, October 26, 1997
1 1/2 miles: Going Abroad, 2:26 1/5, Octboer 12, 1964
1 5/8 miles: Sharp Gary, 2:40 2/5, December 13, 1975
1 3/4 miles: Malmo, 2:53.73, March 30, 1996
2 miles: Kelso, 3:19 1/5, October 31, 1964
Other: 1 5/16 miles, Gold Star Deputy, 2:07.32, April 10, 1999; 1 7/8 miles, Erin Bright, 3:12 4/5, April 18, 1985; 2 1/4 miles, Paraje, 3:47 4/5, December 15, 1973

Track Records, Inner Dirt

4 1/2 furlongs: Call Me Up, :52.29, February 16, 1998
6 furlongs: Captain Red, 1:07.93, February 26, 2003
1 mile: Tejano Couture, 1:35.79, March 9, 2000
1m 70yds: Carry My Colors, 1:38.92, February 5, 2000
1 1/16 miles: Autoroute, 1:41, December 19, 1992
1 1/8 miles: Conveyor, 1:47.33, March 6, 1993
1 3/16 miles: Victoriously, 1:54.42, January 25, 1998
1 1/4 miles: Transient Trend, 2:01.53, December 21, 1995
1 1/2 miles: Piling, 2:29 3/5, March 13, 1983
1 5/8 miles: Relaxing, 2:42 2/5, December 13, 1980
1 3/4 miles: Sophie's Friend, 2:56.73, February 10, 1996
2 miles: Charlie Coast, 3:24 4/5, February 21, 1979
Other: 2 1/16 miles, Rollix, 3:38 4/5, February 3, 1983; 2 1/8 miles, Peat Moss, 3:40 3/5, January 31, 1981; 2 1/4 miles, Field Cat, 3:51 4/5, December 31, 1981

Track Records, Main Turf

1 mile: Possible Mate, 1:34 3/5, November 1, 1985; Tax Dodge, 1:34 3/5, November 1, 1985
1 1/16 miles: Spindrift (Ire), 1:40.88, May 6, 2000
1 1/8 miles: Slew the Dragon, 1:47, November 3, 1985
1 3/8 miles: Fluorescent Light, 2:14 1/5, November 7, 1978
1 1/2 miles: Pebbles (GB), 2:27, November 2, 1985
2 miles: Putting Green, 3:30 2/5, November 23, 1984

Principal Races

Wood Memorial (G1), Carter H. (G1), Cigar Mile H. (G1), Demoiselle S. (G2), Remsen S. (G2)

Notable Events

First East Coast track to host Breeders' Cup in 1985.

Fastest Times of 2004 (Dirt)

4 1/2 furlongs: Chocolate Brown, :53.01, April 8, 2004
6 furlongs: Primary Suspect, 1:08.81, October 30, 2004
6 1/2 furlongs: Black Silk (GB), 1:15.96, November 27, 2004
7 furlongs: Pico Central (Brz), 1:20.22, April 10, 2004
7 1/2 furlongs: Imafavoritetrick, 1:28.54, November 27, 2004
1 mile: Lion Tamer, 1:33.46, November 27, 2004
1m 70 yds: Pay Per Win, 1:41.28, February 12, 2004; Song of the Sword, 1:41.28, March 5, 2004
1 1/16 miles: Seattle Fitz (Arg), 1:42.13, January 17, 2004
1 1/8 miles: Kissin Saint, 1:48.33, April 7, 2004
1 3/16 miles: Scott, 1:56.57, March 26, 2004
1 1/4 miles: Limero (Arg), 2:04.76, December 10, 2004
1 5/16 miles: Angelic Aura, 2:09.63, April 10, 2004
1 5/8 miles: Tamburello (Chi), 2:43.95, December 29, 2004

Fastest Times of 2004 (Turf)

1 mile: I Met Somebody, 1:35.27, May 1, 2004
1 1/16 miles: Chilly Rooster, 1:42.47, April 24, 2004
1 1/8 miles: Host (Chi), 1:49.95, October 30, 2004
1 3/8 miles: Latino (Per), 2:16.68, October 27, 2004
1 1/2 miles: Eleusis, 2:31.51, November 6, 2004

Belmont Park

With a 1½-mile oval, Belmont Park on Long Island is the largest racetrack in North America, and its huge grandstand has a 90,000-person capacity. Originally built for $2.5-million and opened on May 4, 1905, Belmont is host to the third leg of the Triple Crown, the Belmont Stakes (G1), which was named for German-born financier August Belmont I. The first Belmont Stakes was run in 1867 at Jerome Park and was moved to Morris Park in 1890. Within a few years of Belmont's opening, antigambling legislation shut the track in 1911 and '12. The track reopened in 1913. The grandstand was rebuilt in 1920, raising seating capacity to 17,500. In 1963, deterioration of the grandstand forced a five-year closure while the current facility was constructed for $30.7-million. In those years, the Belmont and most of the track's races and dates were run at Aqueduct. Belmont has played host to four runnings of the Breeders' Cup

World Thoroughbred Championships, in 1990, '95, 2001, and '05. The 2001 running of the championship event marked the first international sporting event to be held in the New York City area following the September 11, 2001, terrorist attack on the World Trade Center.

Location: 2150 Hempstead Pike, Elmont, N.Y. 11003-1551
Phone: (516) 488-6000
Fax: (516) 352-0919
Website: www.nyra.com/belmont
E-Mail: nyra@nyra.com
Year Founded: 1905
Dates of Inaugural Meeting: May 4, 1905
Abbreviation: Bel
Acreage: 430
Number of Stalls: 2,200
Seating Capacity: 32,941

Ownership

New York Racing Association Inc.

Officers

Chairman and Chief Executive: Charles E. Hayward
Racing Secretary: Michael S. Lakow
Treasurer: John Giombarrese
Director of Admissions: Jerry A. Davis Jr.
Director of Mutuels: Patrick Mahony
Senior Vice President: William A. Nader
Director of Simulcasting: Elizabeth Bracken
Horsemen's Liaison: Carmen Barrera
Stewards: Dr. W. Theodore Hill, David Hicks, Carmine Donofrio
Track Announcer: Tom Durkin
Track Photographer: Adam Coglianese, Bob Coglianese
Track Superintendent: Jerry Porcelli
Security: John Tierney

Racing Dates

2004: May 5-July 25, 60 days; September 10-October 24, 33 days
2005: May 4-July 24, 60 days; September 9-October 30, 38 days

Track Layout

Main Circumference: 1 1/2 miles
Main Length of Stretch: 1,097 feet
Main Turf Circumference: 1 5/16 miles
Inner Turf Circumference: 1 3/16 miles
Training Track: 7 furlongs

Attendance

Average Daily Recent Meeting: 8,319, Spring/Summer 2004; 5,189, Fall 2004
Highest Single Day Record: 120,139, June 5, 2004
Total Attendance Recent Meeting: 499,166, Spring/Summer 2004; 171,251, Fall 2004

Handle

Average All Sources Recent Meeting: $12,086,814, Spring/Summer 2004; $9,083,735, Fall 2004
Average On-Track Meeting Record: $1,327,224, Spring/Summer 2004; $1,055,489, Fall 2004
Single Day On-Track Handle: $14,461,402, June 5, 2004
Single Day All Sources Handle: $114,887,594, June 5, 2004
Total All Sources Recent Meeting: $725,208,823, Spring/Summer 2004; $299,763,265, Fall 2004
Total On-Track Recent Meeting: $79,633,440, Spring/Summer 2004; $34,831,133, Fall 2004
Highest Single Day Record Recent Meet: $114,887,594, June 5, 2004
Highest Single Day On-Track Recent Meet: $14,461,402, June 5, 2004

Mutuel Records

Highest Exacta: $5,454, June 1, 1985

Records

Single Day Jockey Wins: Jorge Velasquez, 6, July 9, 1981
Single Meet, Leading Trainer by Wins: Todd Pletcher, 40, Spring/Summer 2003

Track Records, Main Dirt
5 furlongs: Kelly Kip, :55.75, June 21, 1996
5 1/2 furlongs: Mike's Classic, 1:02.26, June 20, 2004
6 furlongs: Artax, 1:07.66, October 16, 1999
6 1/2 furlongs: Bear Fan, 1:14.46, June 5, 2004
7 furlongs: Left Bank, 1:20.17, July 4, 2002
1 mile: Najran, 1:32.24, May 7, 2003
1 1/16 miles: Rock and Roll, 1:39.51, June 13, 1998
1 1/8 miles: Secretariat, 1:45 2/5, September 15, 1973
1 3/16 miles: Lueders, 1:56, June 24, 1982
1 1/4 miles: In Excess (Ire), 1:58 1/5, July 4, 1991
1 3/8 miles: Victoriously, 2:14.72, October 16, 1997
1 1/2 miles: Secretariat, 2:24, June 9, 1973

Track Records, Main Turf
6 furlongs: Masterclass, 1:07.31, May 24, 1992
7 furlongs: Officialpermission, 1:19.88, July 23, 2000
1 mile: Elusive Quality, 1:31.63, July 4, 1998
1 1/16 miles: Fortitude, 1:38.53, September 6, 1997
1 3/8 miles: Influent, 2:11.06, July 13, 1997
1 1/2 miles: Fantastic Light, 2:24.36, October 27, 2001
2 miles: King's General (GB), 3:20 2/5, July 4, 1983

Track Records, Inner Turf
1 1/16 miles: Roman Envoy, 1:39.38, May 23, 1992
1 1/8 miles: Artie Schiller, 1:45.50, September 26, 2004
1 1/4 miles: Paradise Creek, 1:57.79, June 11, 1994
1 3/8 miles: With Approval, 2:10 1/5, June 17, 1990

Principal Races
Belmont S. (G1), Metropolitan H. (G1), Mother Goose S. (G1), Suburban H. (G1), Manhattan H. (G1)

Fastest Times of 2004 (Dirt)
5 furlongs: June the Tiger, :57.12, June 6, 2004
5 1/2 furlongs: Mike's Classic, 1:02.26, June 20, 2004
6 furlongs: Speightstown, 1:08.04, June 5, 2004
6 1/2 furlongs: Bear Fan, 1:14.46, June 5, 2004
7 furlongs: Ghostzapper, 1:20.42, July 4, 2004
7 1/2 furlongs: Commentator, 1:27.44, September 24, 2004
1 mile: Ahpo Here, 1:34.80, October 1, 2004
1 1/16 miles: Medallist, 1:40.02, July 11, 2004
1 1/8 miles: Seattle Fitz (Arg), 1:46.30, June 12, 2004
1 1/4 miles: Peace Rules, 1:59.52, July 3, 2004
1 1/2 miles: Birdstone, 2:27.50, June 5, 2004

Fastest Times of 2004 (Turf)
6 furlongs: Copyco, 1:10.02, July 11, 2004
7 furlongs: Old Forester, 1:20.84, October 11, 2004
1 mile: Christine's Outlaw, 1:32.46, July 10, 2004; Literary Row, 1:32.46, June 17, 2004
1 1/16 miles: Delta Princess, 1:38.64, July 3, 2004
1 1/8 miles: Artie Schiller, 1:45.50, September 26, 2004
1 1/4 miles: Meteor Storm (GB), 1:59.34, June 5, 2004
1 3/8 miles: Kicken Kris, 2:12.19, July 17, 2004
1 1/2 miles: Gunning For, 2:29.91, October 16, 2004
2 1/2 miles: Sur La Tete, 4:36.53, June 3, 2004

Finger Lakes

In Native American lore, the Finger Lakes region of upstate New York was created when the Great Spirit placed his hand down on the land to create the series of long, thin lakes. Finger Lakes Race Track, which is located 20 miles from Rochester in Farmington, opened May 23, 1962, and offers racing from mid-April to early December. Owned by Finger Lakes Racing Association Inc., the track has featured Eclipse Award-winning sprinters Not Surprising, Groovy, and Safely Kept. Fio Rito shipped out of the western New York track to win the 1981 Whitney Handicap (G1) at Saratoga Race Course. In 2001, Shesastonecoldfox became the first horse based at Finger Lakes to compete in the Breeders' Cup World Thoroughbred Championships. The

$150,000 New York Derby, which has been held at Finger Lakes since 1969, annually is the track's richest race. Video lottery terminals began operation at the track in February 2004.

Location: 5857 Route 96, P.O. Box 25250, Farmington, N.Y. 14425-0250
Phone: (585) 924-3232
Fax: (585) 924-3967
Website: *www.fingerlakesracetrack.com*
E-Mail: marketing@dncinc.com
Year Founded: 1962
Dates of Inaugural Meeting: May 23, 1962
Abbreviation: FL
Acreage: 450
Number of Stalls: 1,214
Seating Capacity: 6,000

Ownership
Delaware North Companies

Officers
President: Christian Riegle
General Manager: Christian Riegle
Director of Racing: Brad Lewis
Racing Secretary: Joe Colasacco
Director of Finance: Jay Underkofler
Director of Marketing: Steven Martin
Director of Mutuels: David Bridger
Director of Publicity: Steven Martin
Director of Sales: Sue Pines
Director of Simulcasting: Patrick Placito
Horsemen's Liaison: Kim DeLong
Stewards: Rick Coyne, Richard Hanson, Stuart Rainey
Track Announcer: Ross Morton
Track Photographer: Tom Cooley
Track Superintendent: Rick Brongo
Asst. Racing Secretary: Carl Anderson
Security: Dan Martin

Racing Dates
2004: April 16-November 27, 160 days
2005: April 15-November 29, 160 days

Track Layout
Main Circumference: 1 mile
Main Track Chute: 6 furlongs and 1 1/4 miles
Main Width: 85 feet
Main Length of Stretch: 960 feet

Attendance
Average Daily Recent Meeting: 1,477, 2004
Highest Single Day Record: 15,344, September 3, 1962
Highest Single Meet Record: 698,113, 1974
Record Daily Average for Single Meet: 5,032, 1962
Total Attendance Recent Meeting: 236,322, 2004
Lowest Single Meet Record: 190,353, 2003

Handle
Average All Sources Recent Meeting: $875,718, 2004
Average On-Track Recent Meeting: $88,218, 2004
Record Daily Average for Single Meet: $348,608, 1982
Single Day On-Track Handle: $765,580, September 24, 1978
Single Day All Sources Handle: $2,549,108, October 3, 1989
Total All Sources Recent Meeting: $140,522,469, 2004
Total On-Track Recent Meeting: $14,114,914, 2004
Highest Single Day Recent Meet: $1,495,186, April 26, 2004

Mutuel Records
Highest Pick 6: $161,490, June 21, 2001

Leaders
Career, Leading Jockey by Titles: Kevin Whitley, 9
Career, Leading Trainer by Titles: Michael S. Ferraro, 18
Recent Meeting, Leading Horse: Karakorum Dixie, 7, 2004
Recent Meeting, Leading Jockey: John Davila, Jr., 136, 2004
Recent Meeting, Leading Trainer: Chris Englehart, 136, 2004

Records
Single Day Jockey Wins: Robert Messina, 6, November 23, 2001
Single Meet, Leading Jockey by Wins: John Grabowski, 233, 2000
Single Meet, Leading Trainer by Wins: Chris Englehart, 136, 2004

Track Records, Main Dirt
4 1/2 furlongs: Top End, :50.60, April 8, 1998
5 furlongs: Wonderous Wise, :57 1/5, April 11, 1989; Bobby's Code, :57.20, April 8, 1998
5 1/2 furlongs: Hilary Star, 1:02 4/5, April 16, 1989; With It, 1:02.80, June 12, 1994; What a Rollick, 1:02.80, December 12, 1994
6 furlongs: Kelly Kip, 1:08.20, June 20, 1998
1 mile: Transact, 1:36.20, August 29, 1994; Fling n Roll, 1:36.20, November 29, 1995
1m 70 yds: C B Account, 1:40, July 6, 1997
1 1/16 miles: Fit for Royalty, 1:43, May 19, 1997
1 1/8 miles: Copper Mount, 1:48.80, August 27, 1994
1 3/16 miles: North Warning, 1:58.40, July 10, 1994
1 1/4 miles: Caramba, 2:05 1/5, July 11, 1987
1 1/2 miles: Brave Beast, 2:33.70, September 22, 1991
1 5/8 miles: North Warning, 2:46.60, September 4, 1994
Other: 2 furlongs, Broadway Blondie, :21.80, April 3, 1998

Principal Races
New York Derby, New York Breeders' Futurity, New York Oaks

Notable Events
$10.5-million gaming floor with 1,010 video lottery terminals opened in 2004.

Fastest Times of 2004 (Dirt)
4 1/2 furlongs: Carrie's Turn, :51.68, April 16, 2004
5 furlongs: Wild Bill Hiccup, :57.84, April 30, 2004
5 1/2 furlongs: Trumpster, 1:03.52, August 22, 2004
6 furlongs: Top Shoter, 1:09.02, August 21, 2004
1 mile: A R Spun, 1:40.21, April 24, 2004
1m 70 yds: Halo Malone, 1:41.15, August 27, 2004
1 1/16 miles: Halo Malone, 1:44.53, September 6, 2004
1 1/8 miles: Dulce de Leche, 1:53.63, July 4, 2004
1 1/4 miles: Strider's Rocket, 2:09.32, September 10, 2004

Saratoga Race Course

An American landmark and one of the world's leading sports venues, Saratoga Race Course operates six weeks each year and draws huge crowds to the foothills of the Adirondack Mountains in historic Saratoga Springs, approximately 25 miles north of Albany. Saratoga set records for total attendance, average attendance, and single-day attendance in 2003. Opened August 2, 1864, Saratoga Race Course is the oldest existing track in America. Major renovations of the facility occurred in 1902, '28, '40, '65, '85, and 2000, when $8-million was spent to remodel the track's three main entrances, construct state-of-the-art jockeys' quarters, and restore an elegant 19th-century fountain in front of the clubhouse gate. Known as the "graveyard of champions," Saratoga has been host to many of Thoroughbred racing's greatest upsets, none more notable than Man o' War's only career loss to Upset in the 1919 Sanford Stakes. Other noteworthy upsets were Gallant Fox's loss in the 1930 Travers Stakes to 100-to-1 longshot Jim Dandy; Onion's shocking victory over Secretariat in the 1973 Whitney Stakes (G2); and Runaway Groom's 1982 Travers Stakes (G1) upset of Conquistador Cielo. Racing at Saratoga is enhanced annually by the inductions at the National Museum of Racing Hall of Fame, Fasig-Tipton's yearling sale, and the Jockey Club Round Table Conference.

Location: P.O. Box 564, Saratoga Springs, N.Y. 12866-0564
Phone: (518) 584-6200
Fax: (518) 587-4646
Website: www.nyra.com/saratoga
E-Mail: nyra@nyra.com
Year Founded: 1863
Dates of Inaugural Meeting: August 3-6, 1863
Abbreviation: Sar
Acreage: 350
Number of Stalls: 1,830
Seating Capacity: 18,000

Ownership
New York Racing Association, Inc.

Officers
Chairman and Chief Executive: Charles E. Hayward
Racing Secretary: Michael S. Lakow
Treasurer: John Giombarrese
Director of Admissions: Jerry A. Davis Jr.
Director of Finance: John Giombarrese
Senior Vice President: William A. Nader
Director of Mutuels: Patrick Mahony
Director of Simulcasting: Elizabeth Bracken
Horsemen's Liaison: Carmen Barrera
Stewards: Dr. W. Theodore Hill, David Hicks, Carmine Donofrio
Track Announcer: Tom Durkin
Track Photographer: Adam Coglianese, Bob Coglianese
Track Superintendent: Jerry Porcelli
Security: John Tierney

Racing Dates
2004: July 28-September 6, 36 days
2005: July 27-September 5, 36 days

Track Layout
Main Circumference: 1 1/8 miles
Main Track Chute: 7 furlongs
Main Length of Stretch: 1,144 feet
Main Turf Circumference: 1 mile
Main Turf Length of Stretch: 1,144 feet
Inner Turf Circumference: 7 furlongs
Inner Turf Length of Stretch: 1,164 feet
Training Track: 7 furlongs turf
Training Track: 1 mile

Attendance
Average Daily Recent Meeting: 26,762, 2004
Highest Single Day Record: 69,523, August 4, 2002
Highest Single Meet Record: 1,049,309, 2003
Record Daily Average for Single Meet: 29,147, 2003
Total Attendance Recent Meeting: 963,432, 2004

Handle
Average All Sources Recent Meeting: $15,810,827, 2004
Average On-Track Recent Meeting: $3,242,486, 2004
Record Daily Average for Single Meet: $3,742,773, 1993
Single Day On-Track Handle: $7,887,462, August 19, 1995
Total All Sources Recent Meeting: $545,171,412, 2004
Total On-Track Recent Meeting: $116,729,508, 2004

Mutuel Records
Highest Trifecta: $63,624, August 22, 1974
Highest Daily Double: $4,313.90, August 27, 1945

Leaders
Career, Leading Jockey by Titles: Angel Cordero Jr., 13
Career, Leading Trainer by Titles: Bill Mott, 7
Recent Meeting, Leading Horse: Mighty David, 3, 2004
Recent Meeting, Leading Jockey: John R. Velazquez, 65, 2004
Recent Meeting, Leading Trainer: Todd A. Pletcher, 35, 2004

Records
Single Day Jockey Wins: John Velazquez, 6, September 3, 2001
Single Meet, Leading Jockey by Wins: John Velazquez, 65, 2004
Single Meet, Leading Trainer by Wins: Todd Pletcher, 35, 2003; Todd Pletcher, 35, 2004

Track Records, Main Dirt
5 furlongs: Fabulous Force, :56.71, August 18, 1993
5 1/2 furlongs: Mayakovsky, 1:03.32, July 25, 2001
6 furlongs: Spanish Riddle, 1:08, August 18, 1972
6 1/2 furlongs: Topsider, 1:14 2/5, August 1, 1979
7 furlongs: Darby Creek Road, 1:20 3/5, August 8, 1978
1 mile: Key Contender, 1:34.72, August 9, 1992
1 1/8 miles: Tri Jet, 1:47, August 3, 1974; Left Bank, 1:47.04, August 3, 2002
1 3/16 miles: Winter's Tale, 1:54 3/5, August 21, 1982
1 1/4 miles: General Assembly, 2:00, August 18, 1979
1 5/8 miles: Green Highlander, 2:43.57, August 15, 1991
2 miles: James Boswell, 3:26, August 11, 1983

Track Records, Main Turf
1 1/16 miles: Fourstardave, 1:38.91, July 29, 1991
1 1/8 miles: Tentam, 1:45 2/5, August 10, 1973; Waya (Fr), 1:45 2/5, August 21, 1978
1 3/16 miles: Phi Beta Doc, 1:51.61, September 1, 1999
1 5/8 miles: Tom Swift, 2:37, August 23, 1978

Track Records, Inner Turf
1 mile: L'Oiseau d'Argent, 1:33.42, August 5, 2004
1 1/16 miles: Roman Envoy, 1:39.99, August 3, 1992
1 1/8 miles: Amarettitorun, 1:46.22, July 26, 1997
1 3/8 miles: Babinda (GB), 2:12, July 26, 1997
1 1/2 miles: Awad, 2:23.20, August 9, 1997

Principal Races
Travers S. (G1), Whitney S. (G1), Hopeful S. (G1), Alabama S. (G1), Sword Dancer Invitational H. (G1)

Fastest Times of 2004 (Dirt)
5 furlongs: Galloping Grocer, :56.88, August 22, 2004
5 1/2 furlongs: Lady Carmen, 1:04.14, August 26, 2004
6 furlongs: Speightstown, 1:08.04, August 14, 2004
6 1/2 furlongs: Midas Eyes, 1:14.82, August 25, 2004
7 furlongs: Pomeroy, 1:20.99, August 28, 2004
1 1/8 miles: Purge, 1:47.56, August 8, 2004
1 3/16 miles: Decoder, 1:58.37, August 11, 2004
1 1/4 miles: Evening Attire, 2:00.83, August 22, 2004

Fastest Times of 2004 (Turf)
1 mile: L'Oiseau d'Argent, 1:33.42, August 5, 2004
1 1/16 miles: Nothing to Lose, 1:39.50, August 28, 2004
1 1/8 miles: Artie Schiller, 1:47.71, August 9, 2004
1 3/16 miles: Governor Brown, 1:53.11, August 28, 2004
1 3/8 miles: Arvada (GB), 2:14.12, September 5, 2004
1 1/2 miles: Host, 2:28.09, September 6, 2004
1 5/8 miles: Spanish Spur (GB), 2:46.29, August 16, 2004
2 1/16 miles: Praise the Prince (NZ), 3:41.13, August 12, 2004
2 3/8 miles: Tres Touche, 4:19.46, September 2, 2004

North Dakota

North Dakota Horse Park

Location: 901 28th St. SW, Fargo, ND 58103-2314
Phone: (701) 235-1288
Fax: (701) 293-6779
Website: www.northdakotahorsepark.org
Abbreviation: Far
Acreage: 113
Number of Stalls: 400

Officers
President: Ken Pawluk
Director of Racing: Leslie A. Schmidt
Racing Secretary: Carol Sivak
Secretary: Jim Tilton
Treasurer: Susan Bala
Director of Finance: Susan Bala
Director of Marketing: Dale Chilson
Vice President: Rick Buchholz
Stewards: Randy Blaseg
Track Announcer: Bubby Haar
Track Superintendent: Glen Thompson

Racing Dates
2004: August 6-September 6, 15 days
2005: August 5-September 5, 15 days

Track Layout
Main Circumference: 6 1/2 furlongs
Main Track Chute: 2 furlongs and 6 furlongs
Main Width: 80 feet

Leaders
Recent Meeting, Leading Jockey: Scot A. Schindler, 13, 2004
Recent Meeting, Leading Trainer: John Ness, 12, 2004

Principal Races
North Dakota Bred Derby, North Dakota Bred Futurity, North Dakota First Lady's Cup, E.K. Rolfson Sr. Memorial S.

Fastest Times of 2004 (Dirt)
4 furlongs: Cash Converter, :48.60, August 29, 2004
5 furlongs: Halo's Echo, 1:00.00, September 5, 2004; Programmed Appeal, 1:00.00, September 4, 2004
5 1/2 furlongs: Maddies Blues, 1:06.60, August 21, 2004
6 furlongs: Senor Prado, 1:13.00, August 14, 2004
7 furlongs: My Statue, 1:28.60, September 6, 2004; Seven No Tremp, 1:28.60, August 28, 2004
1 mile: Maddies Blues, 1:41.40, September 6, 2004
1 1/2 miles: Old Man's Delite, 2:40.60, September 6, 2004

Ohio

Beulah Park

Ohio's oldest racetrack, Beulah Park is located in Grove City, south of Columbus. Operating since 1923, the track offered a spring meet that once was a popular stopping point for horses in transit from Florida to New York. Beulah was started by successful paving contractor Robert J. Dienst. After Dienst's death, ownership of the track passed to his son, Robert Y. Dienst. In 1983, the younger Dienst sold Beulah, which passed through a succession of owners and was known as Darby Downs from 1983 to '86. Current owner Charles Ruma restored the track's original name in 1986. Under Ruma's leadership, Beulah was the first Ohio track to offer simulcasting, phone wagering, and Internet wagering through its www.winticket.com website, the online portal of AmericaTab, which is principally owned by Beulah and River Downs. Along with Thistledown and River Downs, Beulah shares host duties for the annual Best of Ohio day, which offers five stakes races for Ohio-breds.

Location: P.O. Box 850, Grove City, Oh. 43123-0850
Phone: (614) 871-9600
Fax: (614) 871-0433
Website: www.beulahpark.com
E-Mail: mweiss@beulahpark.com
Year Founded: 1923
Dates of Inaugural Meeting: April 21, 1923
Abbreviation: Beu
Number of Stalls: 1,200
Seating Capacity: 7,200

Ownership
Charles Ruma

Officers
President: Charles J. Ruma
General Manager: Michael Weiss
Racing Secretary: Ed Vomacka
Director of Admissions: Holly Freking
Director of Finance: Jim McKinney
Director of Operations: Holly Freking

Director of Marketing: Hugh Mellon
Director of Mutuels: Holly Freking
Director of Publicity: Hugh Mellon
Director of Simulcasting: Brian DeJong
Stewards: Herb Clark, Jim Beck, Joe DeLuca
Track Announcer: Bill Downes
Track Photographer: Harry Kaplan
Track Superintendent: Ernest Ratcliff

Racing Dates
2004: January 10-May 1, 75 days; September 18-December 21, 67 days
2005: January 8-May 7, 74 days; September 24-December 20

Track Layout
Main Circumference: 1 mile
Main Width: 78 feet
Main Length of Stretch: 1,100 feet
Main Turf Circumference: 6 furlongs, less 223 feet

Track Records, Main Dirt
5 furlongs: Love Pappa Mucci, :56.75, February 11, 1994
5 1/2 furlongs: North and South, 1:02.52, February 1, 2004
6 furlongs: Devil Time, 1:08.32, April 10, 2004
1 mile: Appygolucky, 1:35.47, January 17, 2003
1m 70 yds: King's Wailea, 1:40.15, November 19, 1993
1 1/16 miles: Din's Dancer, 1:40 4/5, November 3, 1990
1 1/8 miles: Lord Try On, 1:48.96, September 26, 1992
1 3/16 miles: World of Magic, 1:55, September 21, 1991
1 1/4 miles: On the Scent, 2:00.22, October 19, 1991
1 1/2 miles: Doctor's Romance, 2:29.50, March 26, 1994
1 5/8 miles: Big Beans, 2:46, October 5, 1957
1 3/4 miles: Dot Your Eye, 2:57 3/5, October 20, 1971
Other: 2 furlongs, Go Chop, :21 3/5, May 7, 1989; 2 miles 70 yds, Benomen, 3:29.81, November 20, 1993; 2 1/16 miles, She Looks Great, 3:41 2/5, November 28, 1983; 2 1/8 miles, Second City, 3:48 4/5, November 25, 1984; 2 1/4 miles, Hallay's Pride, 3:48.90, May 4, 1991

Track Records, Main Turf
1 mile: Gaelic Cross, 1:35 2/5, September 23, 1987
1m 70yds: Twin To Win, 1:41, October 24, 1986
1 3/8 miles: Syncospin, 2:12 3/5, September 25, 1987
1 5/8 miles: Nigilik, 2:48 1/5, October 24, 1986

Fastest Times of 2004 (Dirt)
4 1/2 furlongs: Mercer's Launch, :51.29, April 6, 2004
5 furlongs: Shamrocks Fibber, :57.30, December 16, 2004
5 1/2 furlongs: North and South, 1:02.52, February 1, 2004
6 furlongs: Devil Time, 1:08.32, April 10, 2004
1 mile: Don't Hang Up, 1:37.20, December 16, 2004
1m 70 yds: Calliehadaprenup, 1:42.53, January 24, 2004
1 1/16 miles: Floater, 1:46.08, May 1, 2004
1 1/8 miles: Bocciolo, 1:52.63, January 17, 2004
1 3/16 miles: Explosive Test, 2:01.56, February 15, 2004
1 1/4 miles: Count On My Word, 2:06.18, November 21, 2004
1 1/2 miles: Round Rock, 2:37.18, November 9, 2004
1 3/4 miles: Chief Cahill, 3:05.88, November 30, 2004
2 miles: Scout Me, 3:31.97, December 21, 2004
2 1/4 miles: Calliehadaprenup, 4:02.17, May 1, 2004

River Downs

With the Ohio River serving as an attractive and sometimes destructive backdrop, River Downs has been part of the southern Ohio racing scene for more than 75 years. The track at Cincinnati's eastern edge opened in July 1925 as Coney Island racetrack. A crowd of 10,000 packed the facility for opening day, according to River Downs historians, and the track was off to a fast start. But the floods of 1937 put a temporary stop to that. The track rebuilt following the flood and reopened as River Downs. Sixty years later, the track again endured major Ohio River flooding, but once more the track was cleaned up and reopened. The track's grandstand had undergone an extensive renovation in the 1980s. River Downs offers a pair of quality two-year-old stakes every year in the Cradle and the Bassinet (for fillies). The 1984 Cradle was won by Spend a Buck, who won the following year's Kentucky Derby (G1). River Downs was one of the first tracks at which Racing Hall of Fame jockey Steve Cauthen competed.

Location: 6301 Kellogg Ave., P.O. Box 30286, Cincinnati, Oh. 45230
Phone: (513) 232-8000
Fax: (513) 232-1412
Website: www.riverdowns.com
E-Mail: info@riverdowns.com
Year Founded: 1925
Dates of Inaugural Meeting: July 6, 1925
Abbreviation: RD
Number of Stalls: 1,350
Seating Capacity: 9,350

Ownership
Dr. J. David Rutherford Partnership

Officers
Chairman: Dr. J. David Rutherford
President: Jack Hanessian
Vice President: Martin J. Stringer
General Manager: Jack Hanessian
Director of Racing: Ed Vomacka
Racing Secretary: Ed Vomacka
Director of Operations: Kathy Ewing
Director of Communications: John Engelhardt
Director of Marketing: John Engelhardt
Director of Mutuels: Larry Alexander
Director of Publicity: John Engelhardt
Director of Simulcasting: Vince Cyster
Stewards: Mike Manganello, Ron Tomlinson
Track Announcer: Brian de Jong
Track Photographer: Patrick Lang Photography
Track Superintendent: Jim Cornett
Asst. Racing Secretary: Tim Richardson

Racing Dates
2004: April 9-September 6, 121 days
2005: April 15-September 5, 120 days

Track Layout
Main Circumference: 1 mile
Main Track Chute: 3/4 mile
Main Track Chute: 1 1/4 mile
Main Width: 80 feet
Main Length of Stretch: 1,117 feet
Main Turf Circumference: 7 furlongs

Leaders
Career, Leading Jockey by Stakes Wins: Eugene Sipus Jr., 25; Sebastian Madrid, 25
Career, Leading Owner by Stakes Wins: Woodburn Farm, 16
Career, Leading Trainer by Stakes Wins: James E. Morgan, 52
Recent Meeting, Leading Jockey: Dean Sarvis, 167, 2004
Recent Meeting, Leading Owner: Billy Hays, 12, 2004
Recent Meeting, Leading Trainer: Joe Woodard, 14, 2004

Track Records, Main Dirt
4 1/2 furlongs: One Bad Dude, :52.20, July 9, 2004
5 furlongs: Banker's Forbes, :57.60, June 7, 1994
5 1/2 furlongs: Tazua, 1:03, August 1, 1964
6 furlongs: Francine M., 1:08 3/5, July 4, 1969
1 mile: Dondougold, 1:36 1/5, July 25, 1970; Alladin Rib, 1:36 1/5, August 8, 1988
1m 70 yds: South Dakota, 1:40, August 4, 1945
1 1/16 miles: Ingenero White, 1:41 4/5, July 5, 1969; Irish Dude, 1:41 4/5, July 5, 1969

1 1/8 miles: Brown Sugar, 1:49, September 2, 1925
1 1/4 miles: Crusader, 2:02, July 24, 1926
1 1/2 miles: South Dakota, 2:30 3/5, July 1, 1950
1 5/8 miles: Sada, 2:45 3/5, Ocotber 13, 1934
1 3/4 miles: Brigler, 2:59 3/5, October 19, 1940
2 miles: South Dakota, 3:21 2/5, July 8, 1950
Other: 1 11/16 miles, Distribute, 2:51 3/5, September 7, 1940; 1 7/8 miles, Shot Bills, 3:26 3/5, August 19, 1979; 2 miles 70 yds, Omar, 3:33 3/5, September 2, 1940; 2 1/4 miles, Almac, 3:54, October 31, 1936; 2 1/2 miles, Here Come Midge, 4:30 4/5, June 17, 1972; 3 miles 70 yds, Gloria Dream, 5:32 2/5, August 9, 1972

Track Records, Main Turf

4 1/2 furlongs: Adena, :50 4/5, June 19, 1971
5 furlongs: Boston Storm, :56.20, June 5, 2005
7 1/2 furlongs: Stormy Deep, 1:28 2/5, August 15, 1990
1 mile: Bad News Blues, 1:34.20, July 23, 1994
1 1/16 miles: Franchise Player, 1:40.60, June 12, 1994
1 3/8 miles: Hi Rise, 2:15.60, August 15, 2000
1 1/2 miles: Rebel Thunder, 2:28, June 28, 1996
Other: 1 7/16 miles, Dina's Pl'ymate, 2:25, August 30, 1969

Principal Races
Cradle S., Bassinet S.

Interesting Facts
Previous Names and Dates: Coney Island 1925-1937

Notable Events
Crade Stakes Week-end

Fastest Times of 2004 (Dirt)

4 1/2 furlongs: One Bad Dude, :52.20, July 9, 2004
5 furlongs: Ben's Reflection, :57.80, August 21, 2004
5 1/2 furlongs: Hank's Rib, 1:04.60, April 27, 2004
6 furlongs: Smoke Stack Jack, 1:10.20, August 27, 2004
1 mile: S Table Dancer, 1:39.40, August 27, 2004; Woodsnwaters, 1:39.40, August 2, 2004
1m 70 yds: Better Road, 1:44.00, May 13, 2004
1 1/16 miles: Bellamy Road, 1:45.00, September 6, 2004
1 1/8 miles: Malalco, 1:53.80, June 13, 2004
1 1/4 miles: Hopso (Ire), 2:08.00, July 11, 2004
1 1/2 miles: Northern Rain, 2:40.00, August 30, 2004
1 5/8 miles: Convexity, 2:52.00, August 10, 2004

Fastest Times of 2004 (Turf)

5 furlongs: Rollin Me Out, :56.60, June 22, 2004
7 1/2 furlongs: Ben's Reflection, 1:28.60, July 10, 2004
1 mile: Bannerstone, 1:35.80, June 8, 2004; Hopso (Ire), 1:35.80, June 29, 2004
1 1/16 miles: Brent's Challanger, 1:42.40, June 20, 2004; Tracemark, 1:42.40, June 8, 2004
1 3/8 miles: Western Stranger, 2:16.00, June 27, 2004
1 1/2 miles: Thelightsareon, 2:30.00, July 25, 2004
1 7/8 miles: Round Rock, 3:10.80, September 6, 2004

Thistledown

Thistledown in suburban Cleveland is the home of Ohio's most important race, the Ohio Derby (G2). Opened on July 20, 1925, Thistledown was owned and operated by the DeBartolo Corp. from 1959 through '99, when the track was purchased by Magna Entertainment Corp. Thistledown has inside its grandstand an interactive Starting Gate educational museum, which features exhibits, weekly handicapping seminars, and information on racing in Ohio. In 2000, the track reconfigured the outdoor paddock area, adding more than 9,000 square feet and such amenities as picnic tables, television monitors, and mutuel windows. The North Randall track typically races from April through the end of December.

Location: 21501 Emery Rd., Cleveland, Oh. 44128-4513
Phone: (216) 662-8600
Fax: (216) 662-5339
Website: www.thistledown.com
E-Mail: info@thistledown.com
Year Founded: 1925
Dates of Inaugural Meeting: July 20, 1925
Abbreviation: Tdn
Acreage: 128
Number of Stalls: 1560
Seating Capacity: 3,800

Ownership
Magna Entertainment Corp.

Officers
Chairman: Frank Stronach
General Manager: William D. Murphy
Director of Racing: L. William Couch
Racing Secretary: L. William Couch
Treasurer: Rita Seuffert
Director of Operations: David Ellsworth
Director of Communications: Heather McColloch
Director of Finance: Blake Tohana
Director of Marketing: Brent Reitz
Director of Mutuels: Bob Hickey
Director of Publicity: Heather McColloch
Director of Simulcasting: Greg Davis
Stewards: Joel McCullar, J. David Rollinson, Kim Sawyer
Track Announcer: Matt Hook
Track Photographer: Jeff Zamaiko
Track Superintendent: John Banno
Horsemen's Bookkeeper: Rita Rojas

Racing Dates
2004: April 8-December 31, 184 days
2005: April 8-December 23, 187 days

Track Layout
Main Circumference: 1 mile
Main Track Chute: 6 furlongs and 1 1/4 miles
Main Width: 95 feet
Main Length of Stretch: 978 feet

Attendance
Highest Single Day Record: 19,411, June 18, 1978
Record Daily Average for Single Meet: 7,049, 1954
Highest Single Meet Record: 986,095, 1979

Handle
Average All Sources Recent Meeting: $1,224,390, 2004
Average On-Track Recent Meeting: $136,743, 2004
Single Day On-Track Handle: $3,851,575, July 24, 1999
Total All Sources Recent Meeting: $225,287,772, 2004
Total On-Track Recent Meeting: $25,160,673, 2004

Mutuel Records
Highest Win: $500.20, Nobody's Secret, November 22, 1995
Highest Daily Double: $4,553.40, June 8, 1967
Highest Pick 6: $89,306.20, November 29, 1985

Leaders
Career, Leading Jockey by Titles: Michael Rowland, 28
Career, Leading Trainer by Titles: Gary Johnson, 24
Recent Meeting, Leading Jockey: Huber Villa-Gomez, 152, 2004
Recent Meeting, Leading Owner: Rodney Faulkner, 50, 2004
Recent Meeting, Leading Trainer: Rodney Faulkner, 82, 2004
Career, Leading Jockey by Stakes Wins: Julio Felix, 12

Records
Single Day Jockey Wins: Buddy Haas, 6, August 28, 1933; John Adams, 6, September 2, 1942; Danny Weiler, 6, August 12, 1961; Anthony Rini, 6, June 12, 1970; Antonio Graell, 6, February 21, 1976; Benny Feliciano, 6, June 18, 1978; Antonio Graell, 6, November 14, 1980; Tony Graell, 6, December 13, 1982; Michael Rowland, 6, March 29, 1991; Brian Mills, 6, August 28, 1993; Michael Rowland, 6, October 19, 1999

Single Day Trainer Wins: Gary Johnson, 6, November 27, 1999
Single Meet, Leading Jockey by Wins: Antonio Graell, 93, Summit Meet 1976
Single Meet, Leading Trainer by Wins: Gary Johnson, 42, Cranwood Meet 2001

Track Records, Main Dirt
4 furlongs: Ifufeelfroggyleap, :45.30, October 8, 2004
4 1/2 furlongs: Onion Roll, :51.57, November 20, 1992
5 furlongs: Great Allegiance, :57.56, May 18, 1997
5 1/2 furlongs: Down Thepike Mike, 1:03.20, August 10, 1998
6 furlongs: Fancy Threat, 1:08 2/5, November 21, 1987
1 mile: Setting Limits, 1:35 3/5, November 17, 1989
1m 40 yds: Ifthisbe Britches, 1:38 3/5, December 8, 1989; North Island, 1:38 3/5, December 9, 1989
1m 70 yds: Wisdom Seeker, 1:40.92, July 22, 1995
1 1/16 miles: Entitled To Star, 1:41.32, November 25, 1995
1 1/8 miles: Smarten, 1:45 2/5, June 17, 1979
1 3/16 miles: Smoke Screen, 1:55 3/5, July 17, 1954
1 1/4 miles: Pert Near, 2:03, December 1, 1979
1 1/2 miles: Martha's Wave, 2:31 4/5, June 18, 1955
1 5/8 miles: Alsang, 2:46, August 8, 1936
1 3/4 miles: Mala Kee, 2:57 3/5, July 19, 1957
2 miles: Likely Advice, 3:27, December 15, 1980
Other: 2 furlongs, Onion Roll, :20.95, September 27, 1993; 1 9/16 miles, Military Girl, 2:44 1/5, June 13, 1942; 2 miles 40 yds, Winning Mark, 3:29 2/5, July 20, 1940; 2 1/16 miles, Bunker, 3:32 4/5, July 13, 1955; 2 1/8 miles, Lonely Cloud, 3:52.65, July 3, 1992; 2 3/16 miles, Current Data, 3:54 3/5, December 5, 1981; 2 1/4 miles, Son Richard, 3:54 3/5, August 27, 1938; 2 11/16 miles, Bea Beauty, 4:47 4/5, September 8, 1973; 3 miles 40 yds, Bea Beauty, 5:31 4/5, September 22, 1973; 3 5/8 miles, Eastern Promise, 6:49 3/5, October 6, 1973

Principal Races
Ohio Derby (G2), Cleveland Gold Cup S., Rose DeBartolo Memorial S., Governor's Buckeye Cup S.

Fastest Times of 2004 (Dirt)
4 furlongs: Ifufeelfroggyleap, :45.30, October 8, 2004
4 1/2 furlongs: Clever Jimmy C, :52.44, August 22, 2004; Herpotofgold, :52.44, August 20, 2004
5 furlongs: Pockets, :58.48, September 30, 2004
5 1/2 furlongs: Gatebuster, 1:04.58, June 4, 2004
6 furlongs: Jay's Impact, 1:09.28, December 16, 2004
1 mile: American Guy, 1:38.96, July 17, 2004; Clever Jimmy C, 1:38.96, October 1, 2004
1m 40 yds: Wire Leader, 1:42.69, April 8, 2004
1m 70 yds: Regency's Honor, 1:41.51, December 16, 2004
1 1/16 miles: Ashwood C C, 1:44.60, May 29, 2004
1 1/8 miles: Brass Hat, 1:49.50, June 12, 2004
1 1/4 miles: Real Echo, 2:05.36, September 6, 2004

Oklahoma

Blue Ribbon Downs

Blue Ribbon Downs, located near Sallisaw, Oklahoma, was developed by Blue Ribbon Ranch owner Bill Hedge on ranch property. It first offered racing in 1960 as a nonpari-mutuel racetrack, with all business operations based in Hedge's house. In 1973, Hedge sold the track to a group of investors. A decade later, Blue Ribbon was the first track to offer pari-mutuel racing in Oklahoma, but fire destroyed its grandstand two weeks before the 1983 meet was to open. Within one week, a new grandstand was erected. The track's richest Thoroughbred race is the Oklahoma-bred Thoroughbred Futurity for two-year-olds. The track conducts Thoroughbred, Quarter Horse, Appaloosa, and Paint racing from mid-February to early December. In 2004, the Ok-

lahoma Legislature approved electronic gaming and nonhouse card games for Blue Ribbon and two other state tracks.

Location: 3700 W Cherokee, P.O. Box 489, Sallisaw, Ok. 74955
Phone: (918) 775-7771
Fax: (918) 775-5805
Website: *www.blueribbondowns.net*
E-Mail: brd@blueribbondowns.net
Year Founded: 1960
Abbreviation: BRD
Acreage: 165
Number of Stalls: 1064 Stalls

Ownership
Backstretch LLC

Officers
General Manager: Frank Deal
Racing Secretary: Shirley Ellis
Treasurer: Julie Tillman
Director of Operations: Sandy Farmer
Director of Marketing: Robin Akers
Director of Mutuels: Janine Schaub
Director of Publicity: Robin Akers
Horsemen's Liaison: Jinx Blades
Stewards: Bill Brown, Bill McNutt, Tom Clark
Track Announcer: Fred Davis
Track Photographer: Gene Wilson and Associates
Track Superintendent: Darrin Toney
Security: Randel Dillard

Racing Dates
2004: February 21-May 1; August 6-October 30
2005: February 19-May 7, 27 days; August 6-October 30, 33 days

Track Layout
Main Circumference: 7/8 mile oval
Main Length of Stretch: 845 feet

Attendance
Total Attendance Recent Meeting: 58,816, Spring 2004

Leaders
Recent Meeting, Leading Jockey: Debbie Freeman, 26, Spring 2004
Recent Meeting, Leading Trainer: Rex Brooks, 19, Spring 2004

Track Records, Main Dirt
4 furlongs: Iwontbeback, :44.35, July 3, 1995
4 1/2 furlongs: Rebel's Jon, :50.35, June 29, 1996
5 furlongs: Pow Wow Al, :56.45, May 27, 1996
5 1/2 furlongs: Rebel's Jon, 1:02, October 1, 1995
6 furlongs: Rebel's Jon, 1:08.45, July 9, 1995
7 furlongs: Prententious Chief, 1:23, September 10, 1995
7 1/2 furlongs: Karate Kick, 1:29.35, September 17, 1994
1 mile: Staged Attraction, 1:36.15, June 10, 1989
1 1/16 miles: Just Ask Rudy, 1:43.15, April 6, 1996
1 1/8 miles: Long On Rowdy, 1:49.35, July 17, 1994
1 1/4 miles: Dare More, 2:03.35, August 28, 1994
1 3/8 miles: Say It All, 2:17.15, October 1, 1995
1 1/2 miles: Mr Sanhedrin, 2:32.35, November 14, 1993
1 5/8 miles: Sharp's Caliber, 2:47.15, December 11, 1994

Principal Races
Blue Ribbon Derby, Blue Ribbon Futurity, Black Gold Program

Fastest Times of 2004 (Dirt)
4 furlongs: As de Oro, :46.13, March 14, 2004
4 1/2 furlongs: C. C.'s Crane Man, :52.30, August 15, 2004
5 furlongs: C. C.'s Crane Man, :58.87, February 22, 2004
5 1/2 furlongs: Copper Classic, 1:03.88, October 17, 2004
6 furlongs: Tallest Timber, 1:11.00, April 18, 2004
7 1/2 furlongs: Jimmy Mack, 1:33.60, October 17, 2004
1 mile: Rein Man, 1:39.78, November 7, 2004

Fair Meadows at Tulsa

Offering nighttime Thoroughbred, Quarter Horse, Paint, and Appaloosa racing on its five-furlong oval, Fair Meadows at Tulsa is one of the entertainment facilities located at Expo Square, which hosts the Tulsa State Fair and some 400 other events each year. Fair Meadows, which has been conducting live racing since 1989, is located on a former auto-racing oval and is next to the stadium of the Tulsa Drillers, the Class AA minor-league baseball team affiliated with the Colorado Rockies. During racing season, a giant net between the stadium and Fair Meadows keeps foul balls from landing on the track's final turn. Expo Square includes an amusement park, water park, and hotel, and Fair Meadows offers a state-of-the-art simulcast facility that operates year-round.

Location: 4145 E 21st St., Tulsa, Ok. 74114-2108
Phone: (918) 743-7223
Fax: (918) 743-8053
Website: *www.fairmeadows.com*
Dates of Inaugural Meeting: 1988 (Summer)
Abbreviation: FMT
Number of Stalls: About 700
Seating Capacity: 10,000

Officers
General Manager: Ron Shotts
Director of Racing: Ron Shotts
Director of Marketing: Richard Linihan
Director of Mutuels: Fred Davis
Director of Publicity: Richard Linihan
Director of Simulcasting: Kevin Jones
Horsemen's Liaison: Nina Parrish
Track Photographer: Gene Wilson and Associates
Track Superintendent: Jim Parrish

Racing Dates
2004: May 27-July 25, 32 days
2005: May 26-July 23, 32 days

Track Layout
Main Circumference: 5/8 mile
Main Track Chute: 350 yards
Main Length of Stretch: 300 yards

Leaders
Recent Meeting, Leading Jockey: Curtis Kimes, 20, 2004
Recent Meeting, Leading Trainer: Mike Teel, 8, 2004

Track Records, Main Dirt
4 furlongs: Only Cash, :44.40, May 30, 1997
5 1/2 furlongs: Double Jack 1:03.40, August 1, 2001
6 furlongs: Carsoni, 1:10.80, August 3, 1995
6 1/2 furlongs: Assension Crozier, 1:16.80, August 20, 1994
1 mile: Judge North, 1:37, August 5, 1995
1 1/16 miles: Citation Rock, 1:46, September 11, 1991
1 1/8 miles: Demascus Slew, 1:51.78, May 30, 1998
1 3/8 miles: Second Avie, 2:20, August 5, 1995
1 5/8 miles: Phantom Cottage, 2:51.80, August 1, 1992

Fastest Times of 2004 (Dirt)
4 furlongs: Abbi's Choice, :44.60, June 19, 2004
5 1/2 furlongs: Magdelena May, 1:05.20, June 25, 2004
6 furlongs: Goldleafed Mirror, 1:11.40, July 10, 2004
6 1/2 furlongs: Kiddo, 1:18.60, June 25, 2004; Senor Realidad, 1:18.60, July 9, 2004
1 mile: Shiloh Billy, 1:38.40, June 12, 2004

Remington Park

Built by the late Edward J. DeBartolo, Remington Park opened its gates on September 1, 1988, and was purchased by Magna Entertainment Corp. in October 1999 after average daily attendance had plummeted from a high of 11,263 in 1989 to 2,517 in 1998. The track began a new era in 2001 with the addition of lights, thus allowing night racing. Thoroughbreds race during a summer-fall meet from mid-August to late November, and Quarter Horses are featured in a spring meet. The track's feature Thoroughbred race is the Oklahoma Derby (G3), which was to be run for the 17th time in 2005. Customers have multiple choices for settings, including the Players Sports Bar, the Silks Restaurant, the Eclipse Restaurant, and luxurious private suites. Approval of electronic gaming devices and nonhouse card games at Remington and two other state tracks was expected to boost purses beginning as early as 2005.

Location: 1 Remington Pl, Oklahoma City, Ok. 73111-7101
Phone: (405) 424-1000
Fax: (405) 425-3297
Website: *www.remingtonpark.com*
E-Mail: Scott.Wells@Remingtonpark.com
Dates of Inaugural Meeting: September 1, 1988
Abbreviation: RP
Number of Stalls: 1,312

Ownership
Magna Entertainment Corp.

Officers
Chairman: Frank Stronach
Chief Executive Officer: Jim McAlpine
President: Corey S. Johnsen
General Manager: Scott Wells
Director of Racing: Larry Craft
Racing Secretary: Mike Shamburg
Director of Operations: Matt Vance
Director of Admissions: Diane Bynum
Director of Marketing: Dale Day
Director of Mutuels: Carrie Kluck
Vice President: Jeff Greco
Director of Publicity: Marilyn Toney
Director of Sales: Sharon Lair
Director of Simulcasting: Fred Hutton
Stewards: Mike Corey, Charlie Cox, Norma Calhoun, David Southard
Track Announcer: Don Stevens
Track Photographer: Reed Palmer
Track Superintendent: James Porter
Security: Mike Chapple

Racing Dates
2004: August 6-December 5, 65 days
2005: August 5-November 28, 66 days

Track Layout
Main Circumference: 1 mile
Main Track Chute: 7 furlongs
Main Track Chute: 1 3/8 miles
Main Width: 100 feet
Main Length of Stretch: 990 feet
Main Turf Circumference: 7 furlongs
Main Turf Chute: 1 1/8 miles
Main Turf Width: 80 feet
Main Turf Length of Stretch: 990 feet

Attendance
Average Daily Recent Meeting: 1,589, 2004
Highest Single Day Record: 26,411, February 29, 1992
Record Daily Average for Single Meet: 11,128, 1988
Total Attendance Recent Meeting: 103,272, 2004

Handle
Average All Sources Recent Meeting: $558,656, 2004
Average On-Track Recent Meeting: $77,875, 2004
Record Daily Average for Single Meet: $1,310,542, 1990

Single Day On-Track Handle: $2,808,243, February 24, 1990
Total All Sources Recent Meeting: $36,312,665, 2004
Total On-Track Recent Meeting: $5,061,888, 2004
Highest Single Day Recent Meet: $1,026,502, December 5, 2004

Mutuel Records
Highest Win: $254.20, Cherokee County, October 28, 2001
Highest Exacta: $5,495.80, December 3, 1988
Highest Trifecta: $58,662.40, February 24, 1995
Highest Daily Double: $2,969.60, September 2, 2000
Highest Pick 3: $18,057.60, November 13, 1994
Highest Other Exotics: $38,968.80, Superfecta, December 1, 1996

Leaders
Career, Leading Jockey by Titles: Pat Steinberg, 9
Career, Leading Trainer by Titles: Donnie Von Hemel, 11
Career, Leading Jockey by Stakes Wins: Don Pettinger, 108
Career, Leading Owner by Stakes Wins: Barbara and John Smicklas, 20
Career, Leading Trainer by Stakes Wins: Donnie Von Hemel, 115
Career, Leading Jockey by Wins: Don Pettinger, 1,266
Recent Meeting, Leading Horse: George Taylor, 5, 2004
Recent Meeting, Leading Jockey: Quincy Hamilton, 94, 2004
Recent Meeting, Leading Owner: Gary Owens, 26, 2004
Recent Meeting, Leading Trainer: Roger Engel, 36, 2004

Records
Single Day Jockey Wins: Tim Doocy, 6, December 5, 1993; Cliff Berry, 6, September 30, 2001
Single Day Trainer Wins: Wade White, 5, November 17, 1993
Single Meet, Leading Jockey by Wins: Tim Doocy, 127, 1997
Single Meet, Leading Owner by Wins: John Franks, 22, Fall 1988
Single Meet, Leading Trainer by Wins: Joe Petalino, 69, 1998

Track Records, Main Dirt
4 1/2 furlongs: Payday Two, :52.20, February 26, 2000
5 furlongs: Highland Ice, :57.20, December 3, 1999
5 1/2 furlongs: Run Johnny, 1:02, September 26, 1997
6 furlongs: Smoke of Ages, 1:08, September 29, 1991
6 1/2 furlongs: Kangaroo King, 1:14.40, July 26, 1997
7 furlongs: Golden Gear, 1:20 2/5, March 18, 1995
1 mile: White Wheels, 1:35.40, August 17, 1997
1m 70 yds: Marked Tree, 1:39.60, March 13, 1993
1 1/16 miles: Valid Bonnet, 1:41.20, July 26, 1997
1 1/8 miles: Classic Cat, 1:48, August 30, 1998
1 3/16 miles: Wild Rush, 1:53.60, August 10, 1997
1 1/4 miles: Double Platinum, 2:03.40, October 10, 1999
1 3/8 miles: Wild and Comfy, 2:17.96, October 18, 2002
1 1/2 miles: Bid the Zeal, 2:31.40, October 24, 1998
Other: 3 furlongs, Raisable Adversary, :31.20, August 29, 1999

Track Records, Main Turf
5 furlongs: Precious Luck, :55.73, September 26, 2004
7 1/2 furlongs: Foreign Justice, 1:27.46, August 27, 2004
1 mile: No More Hard Times, 1:33.80, September 20, 1992
1 1/16 miles: Burbank, 1:39.20, August 30, 1997
1 1/8 miles: Major Rhythm, 1:46.22, September 6, 2004
1 3/8 miles: Vergennes, 2:13.00, September 3, 2000
2 miles: Big Notice, 3:29, November 20, 1993

Principal Races
Oklahoma Classics, E. J. DeBartolo Memorial Breeders' Cup, Oklahoma Derby, Remington-MEC Mile

Fastest Times of 2004 (Dirt)
3 furlongs: Desert Wolf Girl, :32.86, August 7, 2004
5 furlongs: Tough Pilgrim, :57.34, August 27, 2004
5 1/2 furlongs: Calling Randy, 1:03.82, August 14, 2004
6 furlongs: Day Trader, 1:08.93, August 27, 2004
6 1/2 furlongs: Expensive Risk, 1:15.79, November 6, 2004
7 furlongs: Casual Attitude, 1:22.45, December 5, 2004
1 mile: Spurred On, 1:37.22, October 30, 2004
1m 70 yds: Clever Red, 1:41.03, August 29, 2004

1 1/16 miles: George Taylor, 1:43.11, September 25, 2004
1 1/8 miles: Wally's Choice, 1:50.26, November 21, 2004
1 3/8 miles: George Taylor, 2:19.22, November 26, 2004

Fastest Times of 2004 (Turf)
5 furlongs: Precious Luck, :55.73, September 26, 2004
7 1/2 furlongs: Foreign Justice, 1:27.46, August 27, 2004
1 mile: Cherylville Slew, 1:34.93, September 5, 2004
1 1/16 miles: Maysville Slew, 1:42.33, August 14, 2004
1 1/8 miles: Major Rhythm, 1:46.22, September 6, 2004
1 3/8 miles: George Taylor, 2:20.00, October 18, 2004
1 1/2 miles: Cumulus, 2:38.38, November 8, 2004

Will Rogers Downs

Will Rogers Downs is located on 210 acres just east of Claremore and approximately 25 miles from downtown Tulsa. No racing was conducted from 2001 through 2005, but live racing was scheduled to resume after Oklahoma approved gaming at Will Rogers and two other state tracks in 2004 and the facility was purchased by the Cherokee Nation, which announced a $2-million renovation. The track is home to rodeos as well as Will Rogers County Jamborees every other Saturday night, presenting a family-oriented country show and concert.

Location: 20900 S 4200 Rd., Claremore, Ok. 74017-4295
Phone: (918) 343-5900
Fax: (918) 343-6399
Website: www.willrogersdowns.com

Racing Dates
2005: November 5-December 11, 12 days

Oregon

Grants Pass

Location: 1451 Fairgrounds Rd., P.O. Box 282, Grants Pass, Or. 97526
Phone: (541) 476-3215
Fax: (541) 476-1027
Website: www.jocofair.com
E-Mail: jackie@jocofair.com
Abbreviation: GrP

Officers
General Manager: Al Westoff
Director of Racing: Al Westoff
Racing Secretary: Michael P. Fliger
Director of Operations: Allan Westhoff
Director of Marketing: Gary Davison
Director of Publicity: Gary Davison
Stewards: Blair Smith
Track Superintendent: Carl Stallings

Racing Dates
2004: May 15-July 5, 16 days
2005: May 14-July 4, 16 days

Leaders
Recent Meeting, Leading Horse: Nevets, 4, 2004
Recent Meeting, Leading Jockey: Twyla Beckner, 28, 2004
Recent Meeting, Leading Trainer: Judi Yearout, 8, 2004

Fastest Times of 2004 (Dirt)
4 1/2 furlongs: Sizzlin Cisco, :51.40, June 27, 2004
5 furlongs: Primecat, :58.20, July 3, 2004
5 1/2 furlongs: Ancient Traveler, 1:04.40, May 15, 2004
6 1/2 furlongs: Teri Time, 1:17.20, May 16, 2004

Portland Meadows

Founded by Bay Meadows Race Course builder William Kyne, Portland Meadows has a rich history dating to September 14, 1946, when a crowd of 10,000 watched the nation's first evening Thoroughbred racing card. General Electric Co., which devised the lighting system, boasted at the time: "This system, the first of its kind, has enough power to light a four-lane super highway from Portland to Salem (a distance of more than 40 miles)." But Portland Meadows officials were powerless to fight the Vanport flood, which in 1948 forced cancellation of the track's season after just 13 cards and caused $250,000 in damage. The track was hit again in the early-morning hours of April 25, 1970, when a fire razed the grandstand. Portland Meadows was rebuilt, opening its 1971 season before a record crowd of 12,635. Portland Meadows served as an early proving ground for Racing Hall of Fame jockey Gary Stevens, who won two riding titles there in the early 1980s. New Portland Meadows Inc. operated the track from 1991 until it leased the track to Magna Entertainment Corp. in mid-2001. In 2002, Magna purchased the long-term operating rights to Portland Meadows.

Location: 1001 N Schmeer Rd., Portland, Or. 97217-7505
Phone: (503) 285-9144
Fax: (503) 286-9763
Website: www.portlandmeadows.com
E-Mail: info@portlandmeadows.com
Year Founded: 1945
Dates of Inaugural Meeting: September 14, 1946
Abbreviation: PM
Acreage: 100+
Number of Stalls: 850
Seating Capacity: 4,450

Ownership
Magna Entertainment Corp.

Officers
General Manager: Chris Dragone
Director of Racing: Jerry Kohls
Treasurer: Stacey M. Whearty
Director of Operations: Patrick Kerrison
Director of Mutuels: Keith Jones
Director of Publicity: Patrick Kerrison
Director of Simulcasting: Patrick Kerrison
Stewards: Robert Blair, James Smith, Ray Youngren
Track Photographer: Jeff Fisher Photography

Racing Dates
2004: October 18, 2003-April 26, 2004, 80 days
2005: October 16, 2004-April 24, 2005, 78 days

Track Layout
Main Circumference: 1 mile
Main Track Chute: 6 furlongs and 1 1/4 mile
Main Length of Stretch: 990 feet

Attendance
Average Daily Recent Meeting: 203, 2003/2004
Total Attendance Recent Meeting: 16,245, 2003/2004
Highest Single Day Record: 12,635, February 6, 1971

Handle
Average All Sources Recent Meeting: $283,690, 2003/2004; $273,379, 2004/2005
Average On-Track Recent Meeting: $32,768, 2003/2004; $33,035, 2004/2005
Total All Sources Recent Meeting: $22,695,233, 2003/2004; $21,323,537, 2004/2005
Total On-Track Recent Meeting: $2,621,449, 2003/2004; $2,576,714, 2004/2005

Leaders
Recent Meeting, Leading Horse: Big Al T, 8, 2004/2005
Recent Meeting, Leading Jockey: Javier A. Ortega, 72, 2004/2005
Recent Meeting, Leading Trainer: Jonathan Nance, 48, 2004/2005

Track Records, Main Dirt
4 furlongs: Wayne S., :47, May 22, 1947
4 1/2 furlongs: Star Expresso, :51.80, April 3, 1999
5 furlongs: Pajone's Hostess, :58, January 6, 1977
5 1/2 furlongs: My Runaway, 1:02 4/5, January 6, 1977
6 furlongs: Lethal Grande, 1:09.01, March 30, 2003
1 mile: Star of Kuwait, 1:36 1/5, May 11, 1975
1m 70 yds: Beau Julian, 1:41 1/5, May 14, 1979
1 1/16 miles: Me Brave, 1:43 1/5, May 5, 1969
1 1/8 miles: Hannibal Khal, 1:48 4/5, December 30, 1978
1 3/16 miles: Kitsap Kid, 1:58 2/5, April 27, 1968
1 1/4 miles: True Enough, 2:03.20, April 9, 1994
1 1/2 miles: Martins Lemon, 2:32, May 13, 1973
1 3/4 miles: Moribana, 2:58 3/5, May 27, 1972
2 miles: Martins Lemon, 3:27 3/5, May 20, 1973

Principal Races
Portland Meadows Mile, Oregon Derby, Oregon Oaks, Janet Wineberg S., OS West Oregon Futurity

Fastest Times of 2004 (Dirt)
4 1/2 furlongs: More Heart, :52.41, March 5, 2004
5 furlongs: Holiday Coins, :58.38, October 18, 2004
5 1/2 furlongs: Gold for Ghost, 1:04.22, October 18, 2004
6 furlongs: Slewicide Cruise, 1:09.76, October 16, 2004
1 mile: Seedoubleyoubee, 1:38.39, October 18, 2004
1 1/16 miles: Green Flair, 1:46.50, October 30, 2004; Sensationalsonny, 1:46.50, December 4, 2004
1 1/8 miles: Yesss, 1:53.36, January 24, 2004
1 1/4 miles: Theyjustdontgetit, 2:09.92, April 5, 2004
1 1/2 miles: Theyjustdontgetit, 2:37.55, April 24, 2004

Tillamook County Fair

Location: 4603 3rd St., Tillamook, Or. 97141-2943
Phone: (503) 842-2272
Fax: (503) 842-3314
Abbreviation: Til

Officers
General Manager: Jerry Underwood
Director of Racing: Mel Tupper
Racing Secretary: Lonnie Craig
Track Photographer: Roger Nielson

Racing Dates
2004: August 12-August 14, 3 days
2005: August 11-August 13, 3 days

Track Layout
Main Circumference: 5 furlongs

Fastest Times of 2004 (Dirt)
a5 furlongs: Cee'z the Dream, 1:03.80, August 14, 2004
a1 1/16 miles: Hayden Storm, 2:04.40, August 14, 2004

Pennsylvania

Penn National Race Course

Built by a group of Central Pennsylvania investors, Penn National Race Course is located 13 miles from the state capital, Harrisburg. It staged its first race meeting on August 30, 1972. The following year, Penn National bought the racing license of defunct Pitt Park and began an essentially year-round racing schedule. In 1978, Penn

National built the state's first turf course. Led by principal owner Peter D. Carlino, Penn National has been an innovator in Pennsylvania's racing industry. Philadelphia-area businessman Carlino bought one of the track's operating licenses in 1974 and the other in '83. With legalization of telephone betting in 1982, Penn National began the commonwealth's first account-wagering system, and the following year it began the first cable-television broadcast of its races. Following legislative approval of off-track wagering in 1989, Penn National built and operated six facilities in Central Pennsylvania. In 1994, the track's parent company, Penn National Gaming Inc., held an initial public stock offering. With those proceeds and subsequent stock issues, Penn National has financed the acquisitions of Charles Town Races, a Thoroughbred track in West Virginia, and Pocono Downs, a Standardbred track near Wilkes-Barre, Pennsylvania, as well as casino properties. Pocono Downs was sold in 2005 after Penn National Gaming received legislative approval for slot machines at its namesake track.

Location: P.O. Box 32, Grantville, Pa. 17028-0032
Phone: (717) 469-2211
Fax: (717) 469-2910
Website: *www.pennnational.com*
E-Mail: pnrc@pngaming.com
Year Founded: 1972
Dates of Inaugural Meeting: August 30, 1972-December 31, 1972
Abbreviation: Pen
Acreage: 600
Number of Stalls: 1,200
Seating Capacity: 9,570

Ownership
Penn National Gaming Inc.

Officers
President: Peter M. Carlino
General Manager: Richard T. Schnaars
Racing Secretary: Paul Jenkins
Treasurer: David Meno
Director of Admissions: Carole Kneasel
Director of Marketing: Frederick D. Lipkin
Director of Mutuels: Carole Kneasel
Director of Publicity: Frederick D. Lipkin
Director of Sales: Grace Vazquez
Director of Simulcasting: Chris Camplese
Stewards: Robert Campbell, Rodney Peters, Thomas Crouse
Track Announcer: John Bogar
Track Photographer: Gill's Positive Images
Track Superintendent: Robert Longenecker
Security: Glenn Firestone

Racing Dates
2004: January 3-December 31, 201 days
2005: January 5-December 30, 203 days

Track Layout
Main Circumference: 1 mile
Main Track Chute: 6 furlongs and 1 1/4 miles
Main Length of Stretch: 990 feet
Main Turf Circumference: 7 furlongs

Attendance
Highest Single Day Record: 15,442, August 2, 1980

Handle
Single Day On-Track Handle: $2,173,921, December 26, 1998

Mutuel Records
Highest Win: $343.40, Busy Lady, Decemeber 20,1977
Highest Exacta: $8,430, April 13, 1988
Highest Trifecta: $42,886.50, May 27, 1980
Lowest Daily Double: $27,985.80, July 11, 1975
Highest Other Exotics: Twin Trifecta, $543,014, June 14, 1988

Leaders
Recent Meeting, Leading Horse: Migwaki, 9, 2004
Recent Meeting, Leading Jockey: Thomas Clifton, 166, 2004; William Otero, 166, 2004
Recent Meeting, Leading Owner: Danny Chen, 57, 2004
Recent Meeting, Leading Trainer: Bruce Kravets, 145, 2004

Track Records, Main Dirt
4 furlongs: Gross, :46 1/5, April 13, 1973
4 1/2 furlongs: Rita's Best, :50.3, April 27, 2001
5 furlongs: On The Phone, :56.60, July 13, 1996
5 1/2 furlongs: Cortan, 1:03 1/5, May 29, 1978
6 furlongs: Jiva Coolit, 1:08 4/5, May 22, 1977
1 mile: Vambourine, 1:36 1/5, June 12, 1977
1m 70 yds: A Letter to Harry, 1:41 1/5, September 10, 1978
1 1/16 miles: A Letter to Harry, 1:41 1/5, September 10, 1978
1 1/8 miles: Collection Agent, 1:49 4/5, August 22, 1987
1 3/16 miles: Bar Tab, 1:55 2/5, October 14, 1972
1 1/4 miles: Adda Nickell, 2:03 3/5, October 30, 1976
1 1/2 miles: Holly Holme, 2:31 2/5, September 29, 1973
1 5/8 miles: New Episode, 2:45, May 18, 2001
1 3/4 miles: Chasqui, 3:00, June 21, 1980
2 miles: Finny Flyer, 3:28, May 25, 1974

Track Records, Main Turf
5 furlongs: Bop, :54.61, August 3, 2002
1 mile: The Very One, 1:33 1/5, July 15, 1979
1m 70yds: Aborigine, 1:37 1/5, August 20, 1978
1 1/16 miles: Told, 1:38, September 14, 1980
1 1/2 miles: Coalitioncandidate, 2:27, May 27, 1991

Principal Races
Pennsylvania Governor's Cup H., Jenny Wade H.

Fastest Times of 2004 (Dirt)
2 furlongs: Pensglitter, :20.71, October 9, 2004
4 1/2 furlongs: Joe Pag, :51.07, November 18, 2004
5 furlongs: Snap Hook, :57.52, March 18, 2004
5 1/2 furlongs: Window B, 1:03.23, November 20, 2004
6 furlongs: Fly by Moonlight, 1:09.51, November 10, 2004
1 mile: S W Pocket Money, 1:38.02, May 22, 2004
1m 70 yds: Tiffany Gold, 1:42.27, November 17, 2004
1 1/16 miles: Devilish Dove, 1:44.98, July 7, 2004
1 1/8 miles: Migwaki, 1:53.98, March 25, 2004
1 3/16 miles: Tiffany Gold, 2:00.17, December 16, 2004
1 1/4 miles: Migwaki, 2:05.10, July 2, 2004
1 1/2 miles: Mendham, 2:33.98, May 20, 2004
1 3/4 miles: Mendham, 3:02.43, April 22, 2004
2 miles: Salaverry, 3:35.16, September 4, 2004

Fastest Times of 2004 (Turf)
5 furlongs: Sport d'Hiver, :56.06, July 7, 2004
1 mile: Wekiva Luck, 1:35.36, July 10, 2004
1m 70 yds: Proven Promise, 1:39.63, July 9, 2004
1 1/16 miles: Shoot for the Loot, 1:41.52, May 27, 2004

Philadelphia Park

Built reluctantly and inexpensively in the early 1970s, the track now known as Philadelphia Park has had a difficult history. But, it has emerged as a leader in providing fan amenities and phone wagering in its region. When racing first arrived in Pennsylvania in the late 1960s, both Thoroughbred and Standardbred racing were conducted at Liberty Bell Park in Philadelphia's Northeast section. But with regional lawmakers insisting on a separate Thoroughbred facility, Keystone Race Track was built for $20-million approximately one mile north of Liberty Bell in Bensalem Township, across the city border in Bucks County. It opened in November 1974 with two ownership groups, which often feuded. Keystone inaugurated the track's signature race, the Pennsylvania Derby (G3), in 1979, and phone betting was authorized in 1982. In 1984, Robert Brennan-controlled International Thoroughbred Breeders Inc. bought Keystone for $37.5-million to avoid competition for its Garden State Park, which opened in April 1985 (and closed in 2001). Brennan's company renamed the track Philadelphia Park and spent several million dollars renovating the grandstand and the racing surface, including the addition of a turf course. Financially failing International Thoroughbred Breeders sold the track to Greenwood Racing, headed by British bookmaking executives Robert Green and William Hogwood, for $67-million in 1990, the year in which the track opened the first of its five off-track betting facilities. In May 1999, Philadelphia Park completed an acclaimed $4-million renovation of its first floor.

Location: P.O. Box 1000, Bensalem, Pa. 19020-8512
Phone: (215) 639-9000
Fax: (215) 639-0337
Website: www.philadelphiapark.com
E-Mail: mgallagherbugobn@aol.com
Year Founded: 1969
Dates of Inaugural Meeting: 1969
Abbreviation: Pha
Acreage: 417
Number of Stalls: 1,700
Seating Capacity: 8,700

Officers
President: Robert W. Green
Chiif Executive Officer: Harold G. Handel
Director of Racing: Salvatore Sinatra
Racing Secretary: Salvatore Sinatra
Director of Finance: Anthony Ricci
Director of Marketing: James Milligan
Director of Mutuels: William Barnes
Senior Vice President: Andrew Green, Len Carey Sr.
Director of Publicity: Keith Jones
Director of Simulcasting: Geri Mercer
Stewards: John P. Hicks, Johnathan S. Gerweck, Samuel A. Boulmetis Jr.
Track Announcer: Keith Jones
Track Superintendent: Stan James

Racing Dates
2004: January 1-December 31, 214 days
2005: January 1-December 31, 220 days

Track Layout
Main Circumference: 1 mile
Main Track Chute: 1 1/4 miles
Main Track Chute: 7 furlongs
Main Width: 80 feet
Main Length of Stretch: 974 feet
Main Turf Circumference: 7 furlongs
Main Turf Chute: 1 1/8 miles
Main Turf Width: 80 feet
Main Turf Length of Stretch: 1,060 feet

Mutuel Records
Highest Win: $588.80, Oak Tree, February 17, 1982
Highest Exacta: $6,792.60, November 18, 1976
Highest Trifecta: $55,608.90, November 1, 1976
Highest Daily Double: $2,943.40, December 13, 1976

Attendance
Average Daily Recent Meeting: 3,627, 2004
Total Attendance Recent Meeting: 776,196, 2004

Handle
Average All Sources Recent Meeting: $276,143, 2004
Average On-Track Recent Meeting: $139,873, 2004
Total All Sources Recent Meeting: $59,094,517, 2004
Total On-Track Recent Meeting: $29,932,788, 2004
Highest Single Day Record Recent Meet: $1,264,332, September 6, 2004

Leaders
Career, Leading Jockey by Titles: Rick Wilson, 9
Career, Leading Trainer by Titles: Efrain T. Garcia, 5
Career, Leading Jockey by Stakes Wins: Rick Wilson, 75
Career, Leading Trainer by Stakes Wins: Dennis Heimer, 56
Recent Meeting, Leading Jockey: Jose Flores, 168, 2004
Recent Meeting, Leading Owner: Jack Armstrong, 43, 2004
Recent Meeting, Leading Trainer: Scott Lake, 136, 2004

Records
Single Meet, Leading Jockey by Wins: Stewart Elliott, 237, 2003
Single Meet, Leading Trainer by Wins: David Vance, 172, 1976

Track Records, Main Dirt
4 furlongs: Heres a Tip, :45, June 11, 1982
4 1/2 furlongs: Distinctive Hat, :51.48, May 2, 1994
5 furlongs: My Favorite Grub, :56, September 7, 1998
5 1/2 furlongs: Saint Verre, 1:02.65, July 17, 2000
6 furlongs: Iron Punch, 1:07.89, July 29, 2000
6 1/2 furlongs: Tricky Mister, 1:14.40, June 21, 1998
7 furlongs: Flaming Bridle, 1:20.61, September 28, 1999
1 mile: Regal Count, 1:34 4/5, December 5, 1985
1m 70 yds: Tragedy, 1:38.70, December 12, 1995
1 1/16 miles: Cool Spring Park, 1:40 4/5, November 4, 1974
1 1/8 miles: Selari Spirit, 1:47, November 30, 1974
1 3/16 miles: Southern Shade, 1:56 2/5, October 20, 1984
1 1/4 miles: It's Always Archie, 2:02, November 23, 1974
1 1/2 miles: Laugh a Minute, 2:31, January 4, 1992
1 5/8 miles: River Wolf, 2:46 2/5, October 13, 1990
1 3/4 miles: Johnny's Silencer, 2:57 4/5, December 17, 1988
2 miles: Perfect to a Tee, 3:25.87, September 2, 1996
Other: 2 furlongs, Queen Millie, :21.32, January 30, 1994; 1 9/16 miles, Laugh a Minute, 2:40.85, January 18, 1992; 1 11/16 miles, Laugh a Minute, 2:53.20, December 21, 1991; 1 13/16 miles, Fire North, 3:04.80, March 14, 1992; 1 7/8 miles, Haberdasher, 3:13 3/5, October 17, 1987; 2 1/8 miles, Heavy Medal Man, 3:39.59, April 25, 1992; 2 1/4 miles, Transfer Ticket, 3:56, December 31, 1988; 2 1/2 miles, Half Chance, 4:24.15, May 25, 1992

Track Records, Main Turf
5 furlongs: Lou's Bucks, :56, September 20, 1998
7 1/2 furlongs: Here Comes Scott, 1:30.85, September 10, 1994
1 mile: Lake Cecebe, 1:35 3/5, June 28, 1986
1m 70yds: Rolfe's Ruby, 1:39 2/5, June 21, 1986; Marlish, 1:39 2/5, August 13, 1986
1 1/16 miles: Whatever For, 1:40 2/5, June 22, 1986
1 1/8 miles: Whatever For, 1:46 1/5, September 1, 1986
1 3/8 miles: Juanca (Arg), 2:16 2/5, September 1, 1986
1 1/2 miles: Lord Zada, 2:28.38, June 10, 2000
2 miles: Chippenham Park, 3:28 4/5, September 1, 1990

Principal Races
Pennsylvania Derby (G2), Cotillion H. (G2)

Interesting Facts
Previous Names and Dates: Keystone Race Track 1974-1984

Fastest Times of 2004 (Dirt)
4 1/2 furlongs: Chazmandu, :53.87, June 29, 2004
5 furlongs: Cumby Texas, :56.60, August 17, 2004
5 1/2 furlongs: Nautical But Nice, 1:02.79, January 9, 2004
6 furlongs: Abbondanza, 1:08.11, October 2, 2004
6 1/2 furlongs: Hey Stretch, 1:15.34, January 12, 2004
7 furlongs: Mister Stip, 1:21.21, January 11, 2004
1 mile: Senor Charismatic, 1:35.71, January 21, 2004
1m 70 yds: Baryshnikov's Song, 1:40.38, December 18, 2004
1 1/16 miles: Ashado, 1:41.68, October 2, 2004
1 1/8 miles: Love of Money, 1:48.42, September 6, 2004
1 1/4 miles: Let's Behave, 2:06.09, July 27, 2004

Fastest Times of 2004 (Turf)
5 furlongs: Aberdian (Ire), :57.53, May 31, 2004
a5 furlongs: Concisely, :57.76, September 25, 2004
7 1/2 furlongs: Hook Call (Brz), 1:32.43, June 22, 2004
a7 1/2 furlongs: Campfire Burning, 1:36.70, July 10, 2004
1 mile: Fleetway, 1:38.39, September 26, 2004

a1 miles: Hereafter, 1:43.38, August 14, 2004
1m 70 yds: Shoot for the Loot, 1:42.23, September 25, 2004
a1m 70 yds: Storm Watch, 1:46.22, July 17, 2004
1 1/16 miles: Lady of the Future, 1:43.80, July 3, 2004
a1 1/16 miles: R. Encounter, 1:49.11, August 14, 2004
1 1/8 miles: Mittens, 1:52.68, September 7, 2004
1 3/8 miles: Gimme the Willys, 2:19.18, June 28, 2004
1 1/2 miles: In Hand, 2:33.32, June 5, 2004
a2 1/16 miles: Thegooddieyoung, 3:44.44, October 10, 2004

South Dakota

Brown County Fair

Location: 25 Market St., P.O. Box 1104, Aberdeen, S.D. 57401-4224
Phone: (605) 226-3464
Fax: (605) 226-2521
Abbreviation: BCF

Racing Dates
2004: May 15-May 31, 7 days
2005: May 14-May 30, 7 days

Fort Pierre Horse Races

Location: P.O. Box 426, Fort Pierre, S.D. 57532-0426
Phone: (605) 223-2178
Abbreviation: FtP

Racing Dates
2004: April 17-May 2, 7 days
2005: April 16-May 8, 8 days

Texas

Gillespie County Fairgrounds

Location: P.O. Box 526, Fredericksburg, Tx. 78624-0526
Phone: (830) 997-2359
Fax: (830) 997-4923
Website: *www.gillespiefair.com*
E-Mail: gcffa@ctesc.net
Year Founded: 1886
Dates of Inaugural Meeting: 1886
Abbreviation: Gil
Number of Stalls: 200
Seating Capacity: 3,000

Officers
President: James R. Wahrmund
General Manager: Ron Ersch
Director of Racing: Mike Burleson
Racing Secretary: Scott Sherwood
Secretary: Paula C. Flowerday
Treasurer: Greg Knopp
Director of Mutuels: Lee Delong
Vice President: Jerry Durst
Director of Simulcasting: Scott Sherwood
Stewards: Donnie Walker, Jerry Burgess, John Ferrera, Norman Morrison
Track Photographer: White Oak Studio
Track Superintendent: Dorman Schmidt

Racing Dates
2004: July 3-August 29, 8 days
2005: July 2-August 28, 8 days

Track Layout
Main Circumference: 5 furlongs
Main Width: 28 yards

Attendance
Average Daily Recent Meeting: 1,723, 2004
Total Attendance Recent Meeting: 13,784, 2004

Handle
Average All Sources Recent Meeting: $143,691, 2004
Average On-Track Recent Meeting: $143,691, 2004
Total All Sources Recent Meeting: $1,149,534, 2004
Total On-Track Recent Meeting: $1,149,534, 2004

Leaders
Recent Meeting, Leading Horse: Truth Endures, 2, 2004
Recent Meeting, Leading Jockey: Salvador Perez, 6, 2004
Recent Meeting, Leading Trainer: Marvin Hayes, 2, 2004; Gabe Newman, 2, 2004

Track Records, Main Dirt
5 1/2 furlongs: Jamie Boy, 1:07.60, June 18, 1994
7 furlongs: Power Ego, 1:27.20, August 23, 1998

Fastest Times of 2004 (Dirt)
5 1/2 furlongs: Truth Endures, 1:09.19, August 28, 2004
6 furlongs: Unruly Sun, 1:16.30, July 18, 2004
7 furlongs: Victory Day, 1:29.61, August 29, 2004

Lone Star Park

One decade after Texas legalized pari-mutuel racing, Lone Star Park at Grand Prairie opened in 1997 and joined Sam Houston Race Park in Houston and Retama Park near San Antonio as the three major tracks in the state. Located in the Dallas-Fort Worth metropolitan area, Lone Star was built for $96-million by the Lone Star Jockey Club, a group headed by real estate moguls Trammell Crow and his son, Harlan, of Trammell Crow Co. The track's sale to Magna Entertainment Corp. for $99-million, including assumption of debt, was completed in 2002. The All-Star Jockey Championship, started by Lone Star and now sponsored by the National Thoroughbred Racing Association, brings the nation's leading riders to the track for a ten-race competition. Texas-bred Thoroughbreds take center stage for the Stars of Texas Day. Lone Star was host to the Breeders' Cup World Thoroughbred Championships in 2004.

Location: 1000 Lone Star Pkwy, Grand Prairie, Tx. 75050-7941
Phone: (972) 263-7223
Phone: (800) 795-7223
Fax: (972) 237-1155
Website: *www.lonestarpark.com*
E-Mail: darrenr@lonestarpark.com
Dates of Inaugural Meeting: April 17, 1997
Abbreviation: LS
Acreage: 315
Number of Stalls: 1,594
Seating Capacity: 12,000

Ownership
Magna Entertainment Corp.

Officers
Chairman: Frank Stronach
President: Corey S. Johnsen
General Manager: Jeffrey Greco
Director of Racing: Larry A. Craft
Racing Secretary: Larry A. Craft
Treasurer: Paula Dowell
Director of Communications: Darren Rogers
Director of Finance: Paula Dowell
Director of Marketing: Kristen Schweitzer
Director of Mutuels: Don Fontenot
Vice President: Jeffrey Greco

Director of Publicity: Darren Rogers
Director of Simulcasting: Mindy Freeland
Horsemen's Liaison: Rainey Brookfield
Stewards: Jerry Burgess, Norman Morrison, Dennis Sidener
Track Announcer: John Lies
Track Photographer: Reed Palmer
Track Superintendent: Ron Moore

Racing Dates

2004: April 15-July 11, 63 days; October 1-31, 19 days
2005: April 14-July 17, 67 days

Track Layout

Main Circumference: 1 mile
Main Track Chute: 7 furlongs; 1 1/4 miles
Main Width: 90 feet
Main Length of Stretch: 930 feet
Main Turf Circumference: 7 furlongs
Main Turf Chute: 1 1/8 miles
Main Turf Width: 80 feet
Main Turf Length of Stretch: 900 feet

Attendance

Average Daily Recent Meeting: 8,700, Spring 2004; 9,800, Fall 2004
Highest Single Day Record: 53,717, October 30, 2004
Highest Single Meet Record: 715,900, 1998
Record Daily Average for Single Meet: 9,800, 1998; 9,800 Fall 2004
Total Attendance Recent Meeting: 548,100, Spring 2004; 186,200, Fall 2004
Highest Single Day Recent Meet: 53,717, October 30, 2004

Handle

Average All Sources Recent Meeting: $1,770,000, Spring 2004
Average On-Track Recent Meeting: $540,000, Spring 2004
Single Day On-Track Handle: $13,326,726, October 30, 2004
Single Day All Sources Handle: $120,863,117, October 30, 2004
Total All Sources Recent Meeting: $111,510,000, Spring 2004
Total On-Track Recent Meeting: $34,020,000, Spring 2004
Highest Single Day On-Track Recent Meet: $13,326,726, October 30, 2004
Highest Single Day Recent Meet: $120,863,117, October 30, 2004

Mutuel Records

Highest Win: $231.40, Purse Stealer, May 26, 2001
Highest Exacta: $6,900.00, May 26, 2001
Highest Trifecta: $117,108, May 26, 2001
Highest Daily Double: $3,016.80, July 18, 1998
Highest Pick 3: $33,651.00, May 28, 2001
Highest Pick 6: $39,891.80, April 26, 1998
Highest Other Exotics: $96,993, Superfecta, May 28, 2001
Highest Stakes Win: $114.00, Thatsusintheolbean, 1997 Alysheba Breeders' Cup
Highest Quinella: $1,103.80, June 8, 2002
Highest Pick 4: $18,069.00, July 2, 2003

Leaders

Career, Leading Jockey by Titles: Corey Lanerie, 4
Career, Leading Owner by Titles: Ken Murphy, 3
Career, Leading Trainer by Titles: Steve Asmussen, 5
Recent Meeting, Leading Jockey: Eddie Martin Jr., 87, Spring 2004
Recent Meeting, Leading Owner: Kagele Brothers Inc., 27, Spring 2004
Recent Meeting, Leading Trainer: Steve Asmussen, 82, Spring 2004
Career, Leading Jockey by Stakes Wins: Corey Lanerie, 22
Career, Leading Owner by Stakes Wins: Heiligbrodt Racing Stable, 8
Career, Leading Trainer by Stakes Wins: Steve Asmussen, 31
Career, Leading Jockey by Wins: Corey Lanerie, 470
Career, leading owner by wins: Ken Murphy, 72
Career, Leading Trainer by Wins: Steve Asmussen, 509

Records

Single Day Jockey Wins: Ronald Ardoin, 6, July 17, 1997, Anthony Lovato, 6, July 3, 2001
Single Day Trainer Wins: Steve Asmussen, 7, July 14, 2002
Single Meet, Leading Jockey by Wins: Corey Lanerie, 102, 1999
Single Meet, Leading Owner by Wins: Ken Murphy, 26, 2003
Single Meet, Leading Trainer by Wins: Cole Norman, 98, 2003

Track Records, Main Dirt

4 1/2 furlongs: Ruby Be Mine, :51.30, April 30, 2004
5 furlongs: Joyful Tune, :56.25, May 5, 2002
5 1/2 furlongs: That Tat, 1:01.88, April 11, 2003
6 furlongs: Savorthetime, 1:07.82, May 31, 2004
6 1/2 furlongs: Spiritbound, 1:14.16, May 3, 1997
7 furlongs: Yearly Report, 1:20.67, October 29, 2004
1 mile: Isitingood, 1:34.44, April 20, 1997
1 1/16 miles: Dixie Dot Com, 1:40.53, May 28, 2001
1 1/8 miles: Ashado, 1:48.26, October 30, 2004
1 3/16 miles: Moosekabear, 1:56.21, May 10, 1997
1 1/4 miles: Ghostzapper, 1:59.02, October 30, 2004
1 1/2 miles: Tali Hai, 2:32.57, July 5, 1997
1 3/4 miles: Sir Moon Dancer, 3:00.46, July 19, 1998
Other: 2 1/2 furlongs, Yes He Will, :26.53, October 7, 1997

Track Records, Main Turf

5 furlongs: Caro's Royalty, :55.60, June 28, 1997, Icy Morn, :55.60, June 28, 1997
7 1/2 furlongs: Special Moments, 1:28.20, May 24, 1998
1 mile: Kiraday, 1:33.56, July 4, 1997
1 1/16 miles: Sharpest Image (Ire), 1:40.05, June 12, 1998
1 1/8 miles: Yaqthan (Ire), 1:45.54, May 25, 1998
1 3/8 miles: Rugged Bugger, 2:13.53, May 10, 1998
1 1/2 miles: Final Val, 2:28.20, July 4, 1998

Principal Races

Lone Star Park H. (G3), WinStar Distaff H. (G3), Texas Mile S. (G3), Lone Star Derby (G3), Dallas Turf Cup H.

Interesting Facts

Achievements/milestones: Lone Star Park handled a daily average of $2.39 million during its inaugural 1997 meeting, which ranked No. 1 among all U.S. racetracks built since 1970. As an encore, Lone Star Park became the first racetrack in modern history to increase attendance in its second year of operation - from 712,673 customers during the 1997 Thoroughbred season to 715,995 in 1998.

Notable Events

National Thoroughbred Racing Association All-Star Jockey Championship, Lone Star Million Day

Fastest Times of 2004 (Dirt)

4 1/2 furlongs: Ruby Be Mine, :51.30, April 30, 2004
5 furlongs: Aloha Bold, :56.26, May 1, 2004
5 1/2 furlongs: Smile Away, 1:03.08, May 20, 2004
6 furlongs: Savorthetime, 1:07.82, May 31, 2004
6 1/2 furlongs: Canadian River, 1:14.94, May 31, 2004
7 furlongs: Yearly Report, 1:20.67, October 29, 2004
1 mile: Wishingitwas, 1:35.41, October 30, 2004
1 1/16 miles: Yessirgeneralsir, 1:41.29, May 31, 2004
1 1/8 miles: Ashado, 1:48.26, October 30, 2004
1 1/4 miles: Ghostzapper, 1:59.02, October 30, 2004
1 5/16 miles: Gabriel's Pat, 2:12.34, October 22, 2004

Fastest Times of 2004 (Turf)

5 furlongs: Nicole's Dream, :56.09, October 16, 2004
7 1/2 furlongs: Janeian (NZ), 1:28.24, April 17, 2004
1 mile: Breach of Promise, 1:35.08, April 15, 2004
1 1/16 miles: Promise of War, 1:41.61, October 1, 2004
1 1/8 miles: Aud, 1:48.41, October 3, 2004
1 3/8 miles: Ouija Board (GB), 2:18.25, October 30, 2004
1 1/2 miles: Better Talk Now, 2:29.70, October 30, 2004

Manor Downs

Thoroughbred racing debuted in 2002 at Manor Downs, a small racetrack near Austin, Texas, that long had offered only straightaway Quarter Horse and Paint racing. Ordered by the Texas Racing Commission to improve its racetrack to accommodate Thoroughbred racing, Manor (pronounced May-ner) spent more than $4-million to expand its oval to 7½ furlongs and to renovate the barn area and other sections. Manor, which is owned by Frances Tapp, was among the tracks in Texas's far-flung nonpari-mutuel circuit that flourished before legislation allowing pari-mutuel wagering was passed in 1987.

Location: 9211 Hill Ln., Manor, Tx. 78653
Phone: (512) 272-5581
Fax: (512) 278-1892
Website: www.manordowns.com
E-Mail: manordowns@aol.com
Abbreviation: Man

Ownership
Frances Tapp

Officers
Chairman: Howard Phillips
President: Howard Phillips
General Manager: Howard Phillips
Director of Racing: Howard Phillips
Racing Secretary: Melanie Posey
Treasurer: Howard Phillips
Director of Operations: Howard Phillips
Director of Marketing: Howard Phillips
Vice President: Howard Phillips
Stewards: Joe McWilliams, Chuck Nuber, Donnie Walker
Track Superintendent: Robert Allan Key

Racing Dates
2004: February 28-April 25, 18 days
2005: March 5-April 24, 16 days

Attendance
Average Daily Recent Meeting: 3,155, 2004
Total Attendance Recent Meeting: 56,791, 2004

Handle
Average All Sources Recent Meeting: $69,437, 2004
Average On-Track Recent Meeting: $69,437, 2004
Total All Sources Recent Meeting: $1,249,872, 2004
Total On-Track Recent Meeting: $1,249,872, 2004

Principal Races
Manor Downs Thoroughbred Futurity Trials, Manor Downs Distaff, Tony Sanchez Memorial Mile S., Manor Downs Thoroughbred Futurity

Fastest Times of 2004 (Dirt)
4 furlongs: Rockin Early, :45.95, February 29, 2004
4 1/2 furlongs: Lovely Secret, :51.21, April 4, 2004
5 1/2 furlongs: Luckyustoo, 1:04.86, March 20, 2004
6 furlongs: Dirtdobler, 1:10.80, April 24, 2004
7 1/2 furlongs: C Ya, 1:32.12, March 27, 2004
1 mile: Triple Time, 1:38.92, March 28, 2004

Retama Park

One of the country's newest racing facilities, Retama Park opened in April 1995 in Selma, 15 minutes northeast of San Antonio. The racetrack is both uniquely named—for the green-limbed deciduous tree or shrub native to south and west Texas—and uniquely designed, with its mission-style, five-tiered grandstand featuring arched entranceways, food courts, the Terrace Dining Room, the Race Book and Sports Bar, and the Player's Club for Turf and Field Club members. The track's original investors hired well-known racing executive Robert

J. Quigley to oversee construction of the $79-million plant and the track's opening, but the facility failed to meet its modest wagering projections. In 1996, Retama was purchased by Call Now Inc., which still operates the track.

Location: 1 Retama Pkwy, Selma, Tx. 78154-3808
Phone: (210) 651-7000
Fax: (210) 651-7099
Website: www.retamapark.com
E-Mail: run@retamapark.com
Year Founded: 1989
Dates of Inaugural Meeting: April 7, 1995
Abbreviation: Ret
Acreage: 226
Number of Stalls: 1,288
Seating Capacity: 6,800

Officers
Chairman: Joe R. Straus Jr.
Chief Executive Officer: Bryan P. Brown
President: Joe R. Straus Jr.
General Manager: Robert W. Pollock
Director of Racing: Larry A. Craft
Racing Secretary: Larry A. Craft
Director of Marketing: Doug Vair
Director of Mutuels: Jackie F. Hart
Vice President: Bryan P. Brown
Director of Publicity: Doug Vair
Director of Simulcasting: Steven M. Ross
Security: Richard L. Cole
Stewards: John Ferrara, Chuck Nuber, Donnie Walker
Track Announcer: Don Alexander
Track Photographer: Coady Photography
Track Superintendent: Jesse L. Cardenas

Racing Dates
2004: July 23-September 25, 39 days
2005: August 5-October 15, 43 days

Track Layout
Main Circumference: 1 mile
Main Track Chute: 7 furlongs
Main Width: 110 feet
Main Length of Stretch: 990 feet
Main Turf Circumference: 7 furlongs
Main Turf Chute: 1 1/8 miles
Main Turf Width: 90 feet

Attendance
Average Daily Recent Meeting: 4,169, 2004
Total Attendance Recent Meeting: 162,591, 2004
Highest Single Day Record: 16,827, April 7, 1995
Highest Single Meet Record: 452,421, 1995
Record Daily Average for Single Meet: 4,713, 1995

Handle
Average All Sources Recent Meeting: $794,571, 2004
Average On-Track Recent Meeting: $116,544, 2004
Total All Sources Recent Meeting: $30,988,269, 2004
Total On-Track Recent Meeting: $4,545,216, 2004
Record Daily Average for Single Meet: $429,562
Single Day On-Track Handle: $705,712, April 7, 1995
Single Day All Sources Handle: $2,502,823, October 27, 2001

Leaders
Recent Meeting, Leading Jockey: Roman Chapa, 59, 2004
Recent Meeting, Leading Trainer: Danny Pish, 41, 2004

Mutuel Records
Highest Win: $136.40, Icy's Baba, August 15, 1999

Records
Single Meet, Leading Jockey by Wins: Corey Lanerie, 99, 1995, Ted Gondron, 99, 1996
Single Meet, Leading Owner by Wins: Carolyn A. Crowly, 17, 1996
Single Meet, Leading Trainer by Wins: Steve Asmussen, 48, 1995

Notable Events
Fifty-Cent Friday Nights

Track Records, Main Dirt
4 1/2 furlongs: Raise a Tab, :51.06, August 1, 1998
5 furlongs: Teed Off, :56.20, August 20, 2000
5 1/2 furlongs: Bailando, 1:02.90, May 13, 1995
6 furlongs: Bucharest, 1:08.82, May 10, 1995
6 1/2 furlongs: Heavily Armed, 1:15.30, August 30, 1997
7 furlongs: Bucharest, 1:22.05, May 24, 1995
1 mile: Mr. Pappion, 1:36.90, May 11, 1995
1 1/16 miles: Heavily Armed, 1:43.20, September 20, 1997
1 1/8 miles: Fletcher's Pride, 1:51.43, August 14, 1998
1 1/4 miles: Call Me Wild, 2:04.01, September 3, 1995
1 3/8 miles: Slews Minister, 2:19.95, October 28, 2000
Other: 2 1/2 furlongs, Texas Hope, :28.20, June 28, 1998; 1 5/16 miles, Opening Remark, 2:13.99, September 5, 1996

Track Records, Main Turf
5 furlongs: Fearless Peer, :56.00, October 10, 2001
7 1/2 furlongs: Call Me Wild, 1:28.43, September 17, 1995
1 mile: Eagle Lake, 1:34.54, October 4, 2003
1 1/16 miles: Fly Slama Jama, 1:40.79, October 4, 2003
1 1/8 miles: Untraceable, 1:48.13, August 10, 1996
1 3/8 miles: Point Click, 2:18.09, October 18, 2003
Other: 1 13/16 miles, Misting Rain, 3:13.22, September 28, 1996

Principal Races
El Joven S., La Senorita S.

Fastest Times of 2004 (Dirt)
4 1/2 furlongs: One Special Judge, :51.69, July 24, 2004
5 furlongs: Jimmy Jones, :58.38, September 16, 2004
5 1/2 furlongs: Jabibti (Per), 1:03.82, July 30, 2004; True Solution, 1:03.82, August 21, 2004
6 furlongs: Gold Storm, 1:10.20, July 23, 2004
6 1/2 furlongs: High Strike Zone, 1:16.52, September 25, 2004
7 furlongs: True Solution, 1:23.95, September 4, 2004
1 mile: Monty Man, 1:37.64, September 10, 2004
1 1/16 miles: Gabriel's Pat, 1:47.45, July 23, 2004

Fastest Times of 2004 (Turf)
5 furlongs: Seneca Song, :56.04, September 18, 2004
7 1/2 furlongs: Honorable Pic, 1:28.77, August 21, 2004
1 mile: Sanibel Sunset, 1:35.59, September 25, 2004
1 1/16 miles: Fly Slama Jama, 1:41.97, July 31, 2004

Sam Houston Race Park

In April 1994, Sam Houston Race Park opened as the first Class I racetrack in Texas, which had outlawed pari-mutuel wagering for more than 50 years. Built for $85-million and named for one of the state's founding fathers, the racetrack in northwest Houston is a part of the Class I Texas racing circuit that includes Lone Star Park in the Dallas-Fort Worth metroplex and Retama Park near San Antonio. Sam Houston, which conducts nighttime racing, holds a fall-winter-spring Thoroughbred meet and hosts Quarter Horse racing in the summer. The track's signature event is Texas Champions Day, which offers nine lucrative stakes races for state-breds. Sam Houston's majority owner is MAXXAM Inc., a Houston-based Fortune 500 company involved in aluminum, forest products, and real estate that is chaired by Texas native Charles Hurwitz. The track is the home of the Houston Equine Research Organization, a not-for-profit group that works to promote the welfare of racehorses through research and also offers a successful racehorse adoption program.

Location: 7575 N Sam Houston Parkway W, Houston, Tx. 77064-3417
Phone: (281) 807-8700
Fax: (281) 807-8777
Website: *www.shrp.com*
Year Founded: 1994
Dates of Inaugural Meeting: April 29, 1994
Abbreviation: Hou
Acreage: 230
Number of Stalls: 1,250
Seating Capacity: 18,000

Ownership
Maxxam Inc.

Officers
Chairman: Charles E. Hurwitz
President: Robert L. Bork
General Manager: Robert L. Bork
Racing Secretary: Eric M. Johnston
Vice President of Operations: Ann McGovern
Director of Admissions: Todd Duckett
Director of Communications: Martha Claussen
Vice President of Finance: Mike Vitek
Director of Marketing: Kerry Graves
Director of Mutuels: Kim Pomposelli
Director of Publicity: Martha Claussen
Director of Sales: Kerry Graves
Director of Simulcasting: Steve Hofmann
Horsemen's Liaison: Sherry Wolter
Stewards: John Ferrara, Joe McWilliams, Ricky Walker
Track Announcer: Michael Chamberlain
Track Photographer: Jack Coady
Track Superintendent: Greg Johnson
Security: Donald Ahrens

Racing Dates
2004: October 23, 2003-April 10, 2004, 89 days
2005: November 17, 2004-April 10, 2005, 69 days; October 26-December 23, 34 days

Track Layout
Main Circumference: 1 mile
Main Track Chute: 7 furlongs; 1 1/4 miles
Main Width: 90 feet
Main Length of Stretch: 966 feet
Main Turf Circumference: 7 furlongs
Main Turf Chute: 1 1/8 miles
Main Turf Width: 80 feet

Attendance
Highest Single Day Record: 24,316, July 4, 2003

Handle
Single Day On-Track Handle: $3,557,018, December 7, 2002
Single Day All Sources Handle: $5,740,955, December 7, 2002

Records
Single Day Jockey Wins: Austin Lovelace, 7, December 10, 1994
Single Day Trainer Wins: Gilbert Ciavaglia, 5, February 23, 1997
Single Meet, Leading Jockey by Wins: Steve Bourque, 120, 2000/2001
Single Meet, Leading Owner by Wins: John Franks, 24, 1994/1995
Single Meet, Leading Trainer by Wins: Steve Asmussen, 57, 2002/2003

Track Records, Main Dirt
4 1/2 furlongs: Prime Time Man, :51.70, February 12, 2004
5 furlongs: Endofthestorm, :57.21, October 25, 2003
5 1/2 furlongs: Bucharest, 1:02.92, April 13, 1996
6 furlongs: Bucharest, 1:08.88, May 11, 1994
6 1/2 furlongs: Brass Jacks, 1:15.74, May 21, 1994
7 furlongs: Bucharest, 1:21.27, May 4, 1996
1 mile: Catalissa, 1:36.33, March 8, 2003

1m 70 yds: Capt. Tiff's Beau, 1:40.52, October 24, 1998
1 1/16 miles: Desert Air, 1:42.74, February 13, 1999
1 1/8 miles: Lost Soldier, 1:48.75, May 3, 1997
1 1/4 miles: Sauvage Isn't Home, 2:04.75, December 29, 1995
1 1/2 miles: Final Val, 2:32.99, February 20, 1998
1 3/4 miles: Final Val, 3:01.50, March 13, 1998
2 miles: Final Val, 3:31.29, April 3, 1998

Track Records, Main Turf
5 furlongs: Go Scotty, :56.93, March 6, 1999
1 mile: Solo Attack, 1:36.16, March 17, 2001
1 1/16 miles: Luna Delight, 1:43.24, December 4, 1998
1 1/8 miles: Chorwon, 1:47.65, March 6, 1999
1 1/2 miles: Commander Calhoun, 2:32.56, October 3, 1996

Principal Races
John B. Connally Breeders' Cup Turf H., Sam Houston Texan Juvenile S., Maxxam Gold Cup H.

Interesting Facts
Trivia: First Class 1 racetrack in Texas

Fastest Times of 2004 (Dirt)
4 1/2 furlongs: Prime Time Man, :51.70, February 12, 2004
5 furlongs: Spider Dann, :57.48, March 4, 2004
5 1/2 furlongs: The Student (Arg), 1:03.42, December 9, 2004
6 furlongs: Cheyenne Breeze, 1:09.61, February 21, 2004
6 1/2 furlongs: Nuttyboom, 1:16.59, December 17, 2004
7 furlongs: Catalissa, 1:22.56, March 20, 2004
1 mile: Native Annie, 1:37.78, November 20, 2004
1m 70 yds: Idealism, 1:42.81, December 4, 2004
1 1/16 miles: Goosey Moose, 1:43.74, November 20, 2004
1 1/8 miles: Sir Cherokee, 1:51.76, January 17, 2004

Fastest Times of 2004 (Turf)
5 furlongs: Sound of Gold, :57.96, February 28, 2004
1 mile: Viva Pentelicus, 1:38.22, January 10, 2004
1 1/16 miles: Lavender Baby, 1:45.44, January 9, 2004
1 1/8 miles: Warleigh, 1:53.01, April 10, 2004
1 1/2 miles: Nordan's Image, 2:39.87, April 9, 2004

Virginia

Colonial Downs

Colonial Downs has featured a high standard of racing since its opening in 1997, and the facility has slowly built a local brand name and a national following for its simulcast signal. Constructed in New Kent County approximately 24 miles from Richmond, the track is the only facility to open in Virginia since pari-mutuel wagering was legalized in 1993. The track features seating for 6,000 in an attractive setting. Colonial's ten-furlong dirt track is one of North America's largest, and its turf course has drawn praise. Its operations are run by the Maryland Jockey Club. Colonial originally raced in late summer and early fall but switched to a 25-day, early summer meeting in 2001. In mid-2001, principal investor Jeffrey Jacobs bought out the track's shareholders and transformed Colonial into a private company.

Location: 10515 Colonial Downs Pkwy, New Kent, Va. 23124
Phone: (804) 966-7223
Fax: (804) 966-1565
Website: www.colonialdowns.com
E-Mail: info@colonialdowns.com
Year Founded: 1997
Dates of Inaugural Meeting: September 1-October 12, 1997
Abbreviation: Cnl
Acreage: 345
Number of Stalls: 1,050
Seating Capacity: 6,000

Ownership
Jeffrey Jacobs

Officers
Chairman: Jeffrey Jacobs
President: Ian M. Stewart
General Manager: John E. Mooney
Director of Racing: R. Clayton Beck
Senior Vice President: Jerry Monahan
Racing Secretary: Clayton R. Beck
Treasurer: Iain Woolnough
Vice President of Finance: Tom Hamilton
Director of Marketing: Darrell Wood
Director of Mutuels: Lori Heath
Director of Publicity: Darrell Wood
Director of Sales: Teresa Harver
Director of Simulcasting: Jeanna Bonzek
Horsemen's Liaison: Linda Gil
Stewards: Jean Chalk, Stan Bowker, William Passmore
Track Announcer: Dave Rodman
Track Photographer: Full Stride Productions
Track Superintendent: Wes Sheldon
Security: Dale Moser

Racing Dates
2004: June 11-July 26, 34 days
2005: June 17-August 9, 40 days

Track Layout
Main Circumference: 1 1/4 miles
Main Track Chute: 1 1/8 miles
Main Width: 80 feet
Main Length of Stretch: 1,290.50 feet
Main Turf Circumference: 7 1/2 furlongs to 1 1/8 miles, depending on rail position
Main Turf Width: 180 feet
Main Turf Length of Stretch: 1,123.62 feet

Attendance
Average Daily Recent Meeting: 2,155, 2004
Highest Single Day Record: 13,468, September 1, 1997
Highest Single Meet Record: 108,900, 1997
Record Daily Average for Single Meet: 3,630, 1997
Total Attendance Recent Meeting: 73,270, 2004

Handle
Average All Sources Recent Meeting: $1,058,747, 2004
Average On-Track Recent Meeting: $197,577, 2004
Record Daily Average for Single Meet: $197,577, 2004
Single Day All Sources Handle: $3,084,466, July 10, 2004
Total All Sources Recent Meeting: $34,149,432, 2004
Total On-Track Recent Meeting: $6,515,498, 2004
Highest Single Day Recent Meet: $3,084,466, July 10, 2004

Leaders
Career, Leading Jockey by Titles: Mario Pino, 3
Career, Leading Trainer by Titles: A. Ferris Allen III, 5
Recent Meeting, Leading Jockey: Ryan Fogelsonger, 53, 2004
Recent Meeting, Leading Trainer: Phil Schoenthal, 22, 2004
Career, Leading Jockey by Wins: Mario Pino, 184
Career, Leading Trainer by Wins: A. Ferris Allen III, 76

Records
Single Day Jockey Wins: Mario Pino, 7, July 7, 2002
Single Meet, Leading Jockey by Wins: Edgar Prado, 59, 1997
Single Meet, Leading Trainer by Wins: A. Ferris Allen III, 25, 1997

Track Records, Main Dirt
5 furlongs: Timothy Mac, :55.74, July 1, 2003
5 1/2 furlongs: Bid Wild, 1:02.68, July 1, 2003
6 furlongs: Satan's Code, 1:08.48, June 27, 2004
6 1/2 furlongs: Cool Ken Jane, 1:16.60, September 7, 1997
7 furlongs: Sky Watch, 1:20.87, September 1, 1997
1 mile: Mt. Carson, 1:35.07, June 26, 2004
1 1/16 miles: Gold Token, 1:41.09, September 13, 1998
1 1/8 miles: Our Toby, 1:48.95, October 4, 1997
1 1/4 miles: Macgyver, 2:03.54, September 1, 1997
1 1/2 miles: Lord Mendelson, 2:30.13, September 4, 2000

Track Records, Main Turf
5 furlongs: Bop, :55.85, June 22, 2002
5 1/2 furlongs: Devereux, 1:01.93, September 24, 1999
6 furlongs: Tyaskin, 1:08.11, September 20, 1998
1 1/16 miles: Lonesome Sound, 1:41.28, September 18, 1998
1 1/8 miles: Kerfoot Corner, 1:47.40, September 26, 1998
1 3/16 miles: Jacsonzac, 1:54.41, October 10, 1998
1 1/4 miles: Phi Beta Doc, 1:59.97, October 2, 1999
1 1/2 miles: Attention Mark, 2:31.76, September 11, 1998
1 5/8 miles: Beluga, 2:45.80, September 26, 1998

Track Records, Inner Turf
5 furlongs: Smart Sunny, :56.02, September 8, 2000
5 1/2 furlongs: Smart Sunny, 1:02.94, September 13, 1998
1 mile: La Reine's Terms, 1:34.24, September 17, 1998
1 1/16 miles: Grass Roots, 1:41.01, October 8, 1999
1 1/8 miles: Steak Scam, 1:48.71, September 25, 1999
1 1/4 miles: Franc, 2:03.02, September 9, 2000
1 1/2 miles: Winsox, 2:27.04, September 28, 1998
1 5/8 miles: Our Game, 2:44.82, September 24, 1999

Principal Races
Virginia Derby (G3), All Along Breeders' Cup S. (G3), Colonial Turf Cup S., Virginia Oaks

Fastest Times of 2004 (Dirt)
5 furlongs: General Tommy, :56.66, June 28, 2004
5 1/2 furlongs: Smart Grace, 1:03.85, July 24, 2004
6 furlongs: Satan's Code, 1:08.48, June 27, 2004
7 furlongs: Biloxi Pride, 1:22.90, July 13, 2004
1 mile: Mt. Carson, 1:35.07, June 26, 2004
1 1/16 miles: Dream Deliverer, 1:42.90, July 26, 2004
1 1/8 miles: Commander's Affair, 1:49.68, June 25, 2004

Fastest Times of 2004 (Turf)
5 furlongs: Tight Spin, :56.95, July 2, 2004
5 1/2 furlongs: Dream Counter, 1:03.67, July 5, 2004
1 mile: Halo's Alarm, 1:37.32, July 6, 2004
1 1/16 miles: Spring Season, 1:43.14, July 2, 2004
1 1/8 miles: Film Maker, 1:50.08, July 10, 2004
1 3/16 miles: Outcome, 1:58.37, July 23, 2004
1 1/4 miles: Kitten's Joy, 2:01.22, July 10, 2004
1 7/8 miles: Moneytrain (Ger), 3:22.83, June 13, 2004
2 1/4 miles: Racey Dreamer, 4:10.34, July 11, 2004

Washington

Dayton Days
Location: RR 1 Box 163, Dayton, Wa. 99328
Phone: (509) 382-2954
Abbreviation: Day

Officers
President: Phil Eades

Racing Dates
2004: May 29-May 31, 3 days
2005: May 28-May 30, 3 days

Fastest Times of 2004 (Dirt)
5 furlongs: Rogan Slew, 1:03.20, May 31, 2004
6 1/2 furlongs: Chrissy de Rio, 1:26.40, May 30, 2004
1 1/16 miles: Tender Offer (IRE), 1:51.00, May 31, 2004

Emerald Downs
Emerald Downs returned Thoroughbred racing to the Seattle area when it opened in 1996. Since the 1930s, the hub of Northwest racing had been Longacres, which was sold in '90 to aircraft manufacturer Boeing Co. After Longacres held its last season of racing in 1992, Yakima Meadows in Yakima became its short-term successor.

A group of investors headed by Ron Crockett, who formerly was involved in an airline-related company, built Emerald for $83-million. The track, which offers racing from mid-April to mid-September, became the new host of the Northwest's most famous race when the Longacres Mile Handicap (G3) was first held at the track during its inaugural season.

Location: 2300 Emerald Downs Dr, Auburn, Wa. 98001-1633
Phone: (253) 288-7000
Phone: (888) 931-8400
Fax: (253) 288-7010
Website: www.emeralddowns.com
Dates of Inaugural Meeting: June 20, 1996
Abbreviation: EmD
Acreage: 167
Number of Stalls: 1,276

Officers
President: Ron Crockett
Director of Racing: Paul Ryneveld
Director of Operations: Bob Fraser
Vice President: Jack E. Hodge Jr.
Horsemen's Liaison: Jan McDowell
Track Announcer: Robert Geller
Track Photographer: Reed Palmer

Racing Dates
2004: April 16-September 20, 90 days
2005: April 15-October 16, 101 days

Track Layout
Main Circumference: 1 mile
Main Track Chute: 6 1/2 furlongs and 1 1/4 miles
Main Width: 90 feet
Main Length of Stretch: 1,033 feet

Handle
Average All Sources Recent Meeting: $1,227,000, 2004
Single Day On-Track Handle: $3,037,581, August 24, 2003
Total All Sources Recent Meeting: $110,430,000, 2004

Mutuel Records
Highest Win: $142.80, My Lady Boots, July 27, 1997
Lowest Win: $2.40, Youcan'ttakeme, June 1, 2003
Highest Exacta: $2,317.80, August 28, 1998
Lowest Exacta: $2.10, June 1, 2003
Highest Trifecta: $27,356.90, July 3, 2002
Lowest Trifecta: $11.80, August 24, 1997; $11.80, August 28, 1999
Highest Daily Double: 1,464.80, July 5, 1999
Lowest Daily Double: $4.40, August 24, 1997
Highest Pick 3: $19,219.40, July 27, 1996
Lowest Pick 3: $4.70, May 8, 1997
Highest Pick 6: $217,140, June 8, 1997
Lowest Pick 6: $146.20, August 31, 1997
Highest Other Exotics: $15,487.20, Superfecta, June 2, 2002; $9,248.20, Pick 4, September 21, 2003
Lowest Other Exotics: $75.20, Superfecta, May 22, 1999
Highest Stakes Win: $85.20, Edneator, August 20, 2000, Longacres Mile

Leaders
Career, Leading Jockey by Stakes Wins: Gallyn Mitchell, 39
Career, Leading Trainer by Stakes Wins: Bud Klokstad, 37
Career, Leading Jockey by Wins: Gallyn Mitchell, 697
Career, Leading Owner by Wins: Ron Crockett, 101
Career, Leading Trainer by Wins: Tim McCanna, 387
Recent Meeting, Leading Horse: Duke of Kent, 5, 2004
Recent Meeting, Leading Jockey: Ricky Frazier, 109, 2004
Recent Meeting, Leading Trainer: Frank Lucarelli, 52, 2004

Records
Single Day Jockey Wins: Kevin Radke, 6, September 2, 2002
Single Day Trainer Wins: Jim Penney, 5, September 6, 1998

Track Records, Main Dirt
4 1/2 furlongs: I. M. Adevil, :50.60, May 30, 1999; Pacificat, :50.60, May 21, 2000

5 furlongs: Jazzy Mac, :55.40, August 20, 2000; Victor Slew, :55.40, August 24, 2003
5 1/2 furlongs: Willie the Cat, 1:01.20, April 16, 2004
6 furlongs: Blue Tejano, 1:07.60, June 7, 2002; Salt Grinder, 1:07.60, May 21, 2005
6 1/2 furlongs: Sabertooth, 1:13, May 22, 2005
1 mile: Sky Jack, 1:33, August 24, 2003
1 1/16 miles: Kid Katabatic, 1:39.60, July 26, 1998
1 1/8 miles: Flying Notes, 1:45.40, September 2, 2002
1 1/4 miles: Rapid Stream, 2:01.80, August 15, 1998
1 1/2 miles: Keen Line, 2:30.60, September 6, 1997
2 miles: Kavil, 3:26.80, November 1, 1996
Other: 2 furlongs, Midnight Cruiser, :21.40, May 4, 2000; Adventure Man, :21.40, May 10, 2000

Principal Races
Mt. Rainier Breeders' Cup, Seattle Slew Breeders' Cup, Washington Breeders' Cup Oaks, Emarld Downs Breeders' Cup Distaff, Emerald Downs Breeders' Cup Derby

Fastest Times of 2004 (Dirt)
2 furlongs: Fairest Warning, :22.40, April 25, 2004
4 1/2 furlongs: Rosieontop, :51.40, June 3, 2004; T's So Shy, :51.40, June 18, 2004
5 furlongs: Pool Boy, :56.00, April 24, 2004; Prize Weaver, :56.00, August 22, 2004
5 1/2 furlongs: Willie the Cat, 1:01.20, April 16, 2004
6 furlongs: Willie the Cat, 1:07.80, April 25, 2004
6 1/2 furlongs: Best On Tap, 1:13.60, May 31, 2004
1 mile: Poker Brad, 1:33.80, May 30, 2004
1 1/16 miles: Demon Warlock, 1:40.60, September 19, 2004
1 1/8 miles: Poker Brad, 1:46.60, July 25, 2004
1 1/4 miles: Big Bad Bue, 2:03.00, July 30, 2004
1 1/2 miles: Duke of Kent, 2:31.40, August 15, 2004
2 miles: Horatio, 3:22.60, September 20, 2004

Playfair Race Course

Location: 202 N Altamont St., Spokane, Wa. 99202
Phone: (509) 534-0505
Fax: (509) 534-0101
Year Founded: 1901
Abbreviation: Pla
Number of Stalls: 1,000+

Officers
President: Bruce Wagar
General Manager: Daniel McCanna
Director of Racing: Ted Martin
Racing Secretary: Mike Pfliger
Director of Marketing: Tom Blaine
Vice President: Amy Haven

Track Layout
Main Circumference: 5 furlongs
Main Length of Stretch: 704 feet

Sun Downs

Location: P.O. Box 6662, Kennewick, Wa. 99336-0639
Phone: (509) 582-5434
Fax: (509) 586-9780
Year Founded: 1969
Abbreviation: SuD
Number of Stalls: 400
Seating Capacity: 6,000

Ownership
Tri-City Horse Racing Association

Officers
President: Cliff Schellinger
General Manager: Nancy Sorick
Director of Racing: Nellie Schellinger
Racing Secretary: Shorty Martin

Treasurer: Nancy Sorick
Director of Marketing: Des Ritari
Director of Mutuels: Helen Lizotte
Vice President: William Henderson
Director of Publicity: Des Ritari
Stewards: Bob Lightfoot, Frank O'Leary, Charles Landells
Track Announcer: Zane Torester
Track Superintendent: Jimmie McDonnell
Security: Benton-Franklin, Mounted Posse

Racing Dates
2004: April 3-May 2, 10 days
2005: April 9-May 8, 10 days

Handle
Single Day On-Track Handle: $61,785, 2003

Fastest Times of 2004 (Dirt)
4 furlongs: Whistle Tester, :47.00, May 2, 2004
6 furlongs: R C's Star Power, 1:15.20, May 1, 2004
6 1/2 furlongs: Zee Chalupa, 1:22.80, May 2, 2004
7 furlongs: Tender Offer (IRE), 1:27.40, May 2, 2004

Waitsburg Race Track

Location: P.O. Box 391, Waitsburg, Wa. 99361-0391
Phone: (509) 337-6623
Fax: (509) 337-6026
Year Founded: 1911
Abbreviation: Wts

Ownership
Community-Non Profit

Officers
President: Dan McKinley
Director of Racing: Terry Hofer
Racing Secretary: Shorty Martin
Treasurer: Terry Jaloy
Vice President: Karen Mohney

Racing Dates
2004: May 15-May 16, 2 days
2005: May 21-May 22, 2 days

Handle
Single Day On-Track Handle: $35,000, May 17, 2003

Leaders
Recent Meeting, Leading Jockey: David Deforest Brown, 3, 2004; Mark Allen Boag, 3, 2004
Recent Meeting, Leading Trainer: Randy Abrahamson, 3, 2004

Principal Races
Queens Futurity, Glover Memorial

Fastest Times of 2004 (Dirt)
a5 furlongs: Incredible You, 1:05.80, May 15, 2004
6 1/2 furlongs: Umatilla Ridge, 1:24.40, May 15, 2004
1 1/16 miles: Tender Offer (Ire), 1:48.80, May 16, 2004

Walla Walla

Location: PO Drawer G, Walla Walla, Wa. 99362-0036
Phone: (509) 527-3247
Fax: (509) 527-3259
Abbreviation: WW
Number of Stalls: 180
Seating Capacity: 3,000

Officers
Chairman: Dick Monahan
President: Dallas Thompson
General Manager: Cory Hewitt

Director of Racing: Dick Monahan
Racing Secretary: Debbie Delaney
Secretary: Terry Atchison
Director of Marketing: Cory Hewitt
Director of Mutuels: Ted Tucker
Vice President: Ted Tucker
Director of Publicity: Cory Hewitt
Stewards: Frank O'Leary, Dave Dayton, Robert Lightfoot
Track Announcer: Pete O'Laughlin
Track Photographer: Roger Neilsen
Track Superintendent: Craig Strange
Security: Dick Moeller

Racing Dates
2004: May 8-May 9, 2 days; September 3-September 5, 3 days
2005: May 14-May 15, 2 days; September 2-September 4, 3 days

Track Layout
Main Circumference: 4 furlongs
Main Track Chute: 6 furlongs
Main Length of Stretch: 150 yards

Leaders
Recent Meeting, Leading Jockey: Mark Allen Boag, 4, Spring 2004; Bobbie Jean Brown, 1, Fall 2004; Nikeela Black, 1, Fall 2004
Recent Meeting, Leading Trainer: James R. Craig, 3, Spring 2004; Abel Borg, 2, Fall 2004

Fastest Times of 2004 (Dirt)
a5 furlongs: Corey's Special, 1:04.00, May 9, 2004
7 furlongs: Courting Chance, 1:29.40, May 8, 2004

West Virginia

Charles Town Races

Founded in 1933 by Albert Boyle, Charles Town Races in Charles Town has been wholly owned by Penn National Gaming Inc. since 2000. The company also owns Penn National Race Course in Pennsylvania as well as other gaming and resort facilities. Penn National Gaming bought a majority interest in Charles Town after local voters approved slot machines at the track in 1996. Charles Town Races has seen its fortunes improve dramatically since the slot machines were installed. Purses for horse racing receive a portion of revenues on slot-machine play at Charles Town, which has more than 3,800 machines at the track. The track's marquee event is the West Virginia Breeders' Classic, a series of races that showcase runners bred, sired, or raised in the state, and is highlighted by the $250,000 West Virginia Breeders' Classic. Charles Town completed a multimillion-dollar remodeling project, including a new racing surface, in August 2004.

Location: P.O. Box 551, Charles Town, W.V. 25414-0551
Phone: (304) 725-7001
Phone: (800) 795-7001
Fax: (304) 724-4326
Website: www.charlestownraces.com
Year Founded: 1933
Dates of Inaugural Meeting: December 2, 1933
Abbreviation: CT
Number of Stalls: 1,500
Seating Capacity: 3,550

Ownership
Penn National Gaming

Officers
President: James Buchanan
General Manager: Richard Moore

Director of Racing: James E. Hammond
Racing Secretary: James E. Hammond
Director of Operations: Ameet Patel
Director of Marketing: Mike McCarthy
Director of Mutuels: Joy Lushbaugh
Vice President: John Finamore
Director of Publicity: Jeff Gilleas
Stewards: Danny Wright, Ismael L. Trejo, L. Robert Lotts
Track Announcer: Jeff Cernik
Track Photographer: Mike Montgomery
Track Superintendent: Doug Bowling

Racing Dates
2004: January 1-December 31, 258 days
2005: January 1-December 31

Track Layout
Main Circumference: 6 furlongs
Main Track Chute: 4 1/2 furlongs and 1 5/16 miles
Main Length of Stretch: 660 feet

Attendance
Highest Single Day Record: 21,480, September 17, 1981

Handle
Single Day On-Track Handle: $2,047,873, May 3, 2003

Records
Single Day Jockey Wins: Travis Dunkelberger, 7, March 30, 2000

Track Records, Main Dirt
4 1/2 furlongs: It's Only Money, :50.36, July 4, 1999
6 1/2 furlongs: Jet Appeal, 1:17, January 6, 1976
7 furlongs: Ohmylove, 1:24, January 7, 1976
1 1/16 miles: My Sister Pearl, 1:43.83, January 4, 2001
1 1/8 miles: A Huevo, 1:50.10, October 10, 1999
1 1/4 miles: Belle d'Amour, 2:05 3/5, June 28, 1941
1 1/2 miles: Guasave Breeze, 2:34, June 9, 1972

Principal Races
Charles Town Dash, Breeders' Classics

Notable Events
Owners Day, Jockeys Across America

Fastest Times of 2004 (Dirt)
4 furlongs: Choctaw Ridge, :44.86, October 8, 2004
4 1/2 furlongs: Tender Toes, :50.85, August 1, 2004
6 1/2 furlongs: Bryceslittlesecret, 1:18.38, October 27, 2004
7 furlongs: Jazzy Jay, 1:25.05, December 26, 2004
1 1/16 miles: Prince Benjamin, 1:46.12, May 1, 2004
1 1/8 miles: Cherokee's Boy, 1:52.95, July 18, 2004

Mountaineer Race Track and Gaming Resort

Mountaineer Race Track in Chester, West Virginia, was recognized in 2001 as one of the top small businesses in the United States when Forbes magazine ranked MTR Gaming Group Inc., which owns the track, seventh among the top 200 such enterprises. Much of Mountaineer's success resulted from the legalization of slot machines in 1993, which increased revenues and enabled the track to offer higher purses. In 2003, the track received approval for 500 additional slot machines, enabling it to operate a maximum of 3,500 slot machines. MTR Gaming, headed by Edson "Ted" Arneault, also owns a golf course, hotel, spa, theater, and other entertainment facilities at the track's location. The track was known as Waterford Park when it was opened in 1951 by the Charles Town Jockey Club; the facility was renamed Mountaineer Park in

'87 and Mountaineer Race Track in 2001. Mountaineer offers year-round racing four nights a week. The West Virginia Derby (G3), worth $750,000 in 2005, is the richest race to be run in West Virginia history. In 2003, MTR Gaming Group bought Scioto Downs, an Ohio harness track, and in late 2002 it received approval from the Pennsylvania Horse Racing Commission to build a $56-million Thoroughbred track, Presque Isle Downs, near Erie, but court appeals delayed the project.

Location: P.O. Box 358, RR 2, Chester, W.V. 26034-0358
Phone: (304) 387-8300
Phone: (800) 804-0468
Fax: (304) 387-8303
Website: www.mtrgaming.com
E-Mail: info@mtrgaming.com
Year Founded: 1951
Dates of Inaugural Meeting: May 16, 1951
Abbreviation: Mnr
Capsule Description: Live racing year-round, casino, hotel, spa, fitness center, and golf course
Number of Stalls: 1164
Seating Capacity: 7,400

Ownership
MTR Gaming Group Inc.

Officers
Chairman: Edson R. Arneault
Chief Executive Officer: Ted Arneault
President: Edson R. Arneault
Director of Racing: Rose Mary Williams
Racing Secretary: Joseph Narcavish
Vice President: Patrick Arneauult
Director of Publicity: Tamara Pettit
Stewards: Jim O'Brien, Larry Dupuy, Steve Kourpas
Track Announcer: Jim Dolan
Track Photographer: Ethel Riser

Racing Dates
2004: January 19-December 28, 219 Days
2005: January 15-December 27, 238 days

Track Layout
Main Circumference: 1 mile
Main Track Chute: 6 furlongs and 1 1/4 miles
Main Width: 80 feet
Main Length of Stretch: 905.31 feet
Main Turf Circumference: 7 furlongs

Attendance
Average Daily Recent Meeting: 6,168, 2004
Total Attendance Recent Meeting: 1,357,085, 2004
Highest Single Day Record: 17,934, August 10, 2002

Handle
Average All Sources Recent Meeting: $155,214, 2004
Average On-Track Recent Meeting: $61,440, 2004
Total All Sources Recent Meeting: $33,991,816, 2004
Total On-Track Recent Meeting: $13,455,284, 2004
Single Day On-Track Handle: $966,508, May 8, 1973
Single Day All Sources Handle: $2,513,911, 2003

Track Records, Main Dirt
4 1/2 furlongs: Ameri Brilliance, :50.16, August 7, 2004
5 furlongs: Last At the Table, :56.16, April 1, 2000
5 1/2 furlongs: The Dancer, 1:02.24, December 29, 2000
6 furlongs: Hustler, 1:07.81, August 11, 2001
1 mile: Find the Mine, 1:33,86, July 4, 2000
1m 40 yds: Ski Sez, 1:39.83, March 9, 1996
1m 70 yds: Mort, 1:38.81, April 1, 2000
1 1/16 miles: It's Reality, 1:41.75, December 23, 2000
1 1/8 miles: Western Pride, 1:47.20, August 11, 2001
1 3/16 miles: No Spend No Glow, 1:56.95, May 19, 2001
1 1/4 miles: Georgie Porgie, 2:03.69, August 6, 1995
1 1/2 miles: Pete's Skianno, 2:31.43, June 10, 2000

1 5/8 miles: Prince Swivel, 2:45, September 8, 1973
1 3/4 miles: Chased Again, 2:58.58, July 18, 1959
2 miles: Sovereign M.D., 3:27.66, December 10, 2000
Other: 2 furlongs, Promised Cruise, :21, June 23, 1990; 2 1/16 miles, Sovereign M.D., 3:28.40, December 30, 2000

Track Records, Main Turf
4 1/2 furlongs: Cake n' Steak, :50, August 9, 1993
5 furlongs: Fina Dur, :55.52, September 6, 1999
7 furlongs: On To Richmond, 1:21.40, June 16, 2002
7 1/2 furlongs: Magical Madness, 1:27.48, May 22, 2002
1 mile: La Reine's Term, 1:33.49, September 2, 2002
1m 70yds: Fast and Friendly, 1:34, September 7, 1964; Poteau, 1:34, July 25, 1982
1 3/8 miles: Sunset Party, 2:13.23, September 26, 1999
1 1/2 miles: Guild Hall, 2:33.20, June 20, 1969
1 3/4 miles: Pleasant Company, 2:55.11, August 15, 2004
Other: 1 7/8 miles, Code's Best, 3:08.23, September 4, 2000

Principal Races
West Virginia Derby (G3), Harvey Arneault Breeders' Cup Memorial S., West Virginia Governor's S., West Virginia Senate President's Breeders' Cup S.

Interesting Facts
Previous Names and Dates: Waterford Park

Fastest Times of 2004 (Dirt)
4 1/2 furlongs: Ameri Brilliance, :50.16, August 7, 2004
5 furlongs: Buckeye Bert, :57.01, February 2, 2004
5 1/2 furlongs: Regal Road, 1:03.53, February 2, 2004
6 furlongs: Kasparov, 1:09.25, August 16, 2004
1 mile: Banished Lover, 1:36.74, February 16, 2004
1m 70 yds: Ask the Lord, 1:42.25, June 5, 2004
1 1/16 miles: Wiggins, 1:43.37, August 7, 2004
1 1/8 miles: Sir Shackleton, 1:49.16, August 7, 2004
1 3/16 miles: Sataniste, 2:01.53, May 15, 2004
1 1/4 miles: Mt. Ouray, 2:06.20, July 31, 2004
1 1/2 miles: Actuary's Son, 2:34.72, October 16, 2004
1 5/8 miles: Pleasant Company, 2:49.21, October 31, 2004
1 3/4 miles: Pleasant Company, 3:06.58, November 16, 2004
2 miles: Sir Dorset, 3:34.00, December 7, 2004

Fastest Times of 2004 (Turf)
4 1/2 furlongs: Long Star, :50.23, June 21, 2004
5 furlongs: Nicole's Dream, :55.78, September 5, 2004
7 furlongs: Soldier Song, 1:21.88, June 8, 2004
7 1/2 furlongs: Burning Marque, 1:28.39, July 11, 2004
1 mile: Chance Dance, 1:34.09, September 6, 2004
1 3/8 miles: Crystallo, 2:15.86, June 27, 2004
1 3/4 miles: Pleasant Company, 2:55.11, August 15, 2004
1 7/8 miles: Pleasant Company, 3:10.35, September 6, 2004

Wyoming

Wyoming Downs

Though it is one of North America's least-known Thoroughbred facilities, Wyoming Downs has been providing racing to southwestern Wyoming for nearly 20 years. Located just north of Evanston, Wyoming Downs offers Thoroughbred and Quarter Horse racing, with most emphasis on the latter. The track's top races are Quarter Horse events, the Silver Dollar and Diamond Classic Futurities, each with estimated purses of $100,000. For Thoroughbreds, the top event is the $4,000-added Bettie Bullock Memorial Derby for three-year-olds. Wyoming Downs, which races during the summer, also operates four off-track betting facilities that offer simulcast wagering year-round. In 2003, the track's OTB facilities added Instant Racing, an electronic pari-mutuel game developed at Oaklawn Park in Arkansas.

Location: 10180 Highway 89 N, Evanston, Wy. 82930-9020
Phone: (307) 789-0511
Fax: (702) 212-6662
Website: *www.wyomingdowns.com*
E-Mail: info@wydowns.com
Year Founded: 1985
Dates of Inaugural Meeting: 1985
Abbreviation: Wyo
Acreage: 200
Seating Capacity: approx. 5,000

Ownership
Wyoming Horseracing Inc.

Officers
President: Eric L. Nelson
General Manager: Dale Parker
Director of Racing: Dale Parker
Racing Secretary: Dale Parker
Director of Operations: Joan Ramos
Director of Admissions: Ethellynn Sims, Linda Willoughby
Director of Finance: Lorie Anderson-Miller
Director of Marketing: Kortney Kettleson
Director of Mutuels: Jerry Doolittle
Director of Publicity: Nina Earll
Director of Simulcasting: Jodi Lopez
Stewards: Susan Barret, WPC
Track Announcer: John Nielson
Track Photographer: Gene Wilson & Associates
Track Superintendent: Angel Lopez

Racing Dates
2004: June 26-August 22, 18 days
2005: June 25-August 21, 18 days

Track Layout
Main Circumference: 7 furlongs
Main Track Chute: 550 yards

Principal Races
Blane Schvaneveldt Futurity, Cowboy Classic Futurity, Diamond Classic, Governor's Cup, Silver Dollar Futurity

Fastest Times of 2004 (Dirt)
4 1/2 furlongs: Popescu (Brz), :52.49, July 10, 2004
a4 1/2 furlongs: Mackay Man, :52.01, August 8, 2004
5 furlongs: Cheese Puff, :56.77, August 21, 2004
5 1/2 furlongs: Fire Ball John, 1:03.46, August 22, 2004
6 furlongs: Fire Ball John, 1:08.86, August 15, 2004
7 1/2 furlongs: Air Forbes Too, 1:31.26, August 7, 2004
1 mile: Quiet Syns, 1:38.53, August 22, 2004

Canada

Alberta

Evergreen Park (Grand Prairie)

Location: Grand Prairie Fairgrounds, Box 370, Grand Prairie, Ab. T8V 3A5
Phone: (780) 532-3279
Phone: (940) 594-6804
Fax: (780) 539-0373
Abbreviation: GPr

Racing Dates
2004: July 9-August 22
2005: July 8-August 21, 22 days

Leaders
Recent Meeting, Leading Horse: Lafleur, 3, 2004; Welder's Flash, 3, 2004
Recent Meeting, Leading Jockey: Scott Sterr, 14, 2004
Recent Meeting, Leading Trainer: Stan Marks, 8, 2004

Fastest Times of 2004 (Dirt)
4 furlongs: Ding Dong Dandy, :47.20, August 1, 2004
5 1/2 furlongs: Irish Intrigue, 1:07.60, August 1, 2004; Lafleur, 1:07.60, July 16, 2004; Miss Combo, 1:07.60, August 15, 2004; Miss Combo, 1:07.60, August 22, 2004
6 furlongs: First Hoedown, 1:13.40, August 7, 2004; Welder's Flash, 1:13.40, August 20, 2004
6 1/2 furlongs: Hy Nick, 1:20.00, August 13, 2004
7 furlongs: Lafleur, 1:25.40, August 15, 2004
1 mile: Ezee Target, 1:40.60, August 14, 2004
1 1/16 miles: Chief Joseph, 1:50.40, July 25, 2004
1 1/8 miles: Moe Boots, 1:55.00, August 22, 2004

Lethbridge

Location: 3401 Parkside Dr S, Lethbridge, Ab. T1J 1G6
Phone: (403) 380-1905
Fax: (403) 380-1903
Website: *www.rockymountainturfclub.com*
E-Mail: racedot@telusplanet.net
Year Founded: 1911
Abbreviation: Lbg
Number of Stalls: 300
Seating Capacity: 3,000

Ownership
Rocky Mountain Turf Club

Officers
President: Max Gibb
Director of Racing: Dorothy 'Dot' Stein
Racing Secretary: Jim Ralph
Director of Marketing: Rose Rossi
Director of Publicity: Rose Rossi
Stewards: D. G. Rees, Scott Dahl
Track Announcer: Murray Slough
Track Photographer: Coady Photo

Racing Dates
2004: May 1-June 13; August 28-October 24
2005: May 7-July 3, 23 days; September 3-October 30, 27 days

Track Layout
Main Circumference: 4 furlongs

Leaders
Recent Meeting, Leading Jockey: Scott Sterr, 15, 2004
Recent Meeting, Leading Trainer: Mel Berkram, 5, 2004

Principal Races
Alberta Bred S., Autotote Derby, Open S.

Notable Events
Chuckwagon Racing, Street Machine Weekend, Hot Rod 50's Weekend

Fastest Times of 2004 (Dirt)
3 furlongs: Reality Belle, :35.20, September 11, 2004
5 furlongs: Docs Tyrant, :59.40, September 18, 2004; Express Post, :59.40, June 20, 2004
5 1/2 furlongs: Lovers Son, 1:07.00, June 5, 2004
6 furlongs: High Powered Mack, 1:12.20, September 4, 2004
a6 furlongs: First Hoedown, 1:09.20, June 20, 2004
7 furlongs: Fruit Rapport, 1:24.40, June 19, 2004
1 1/16 miles: Barton's Breeze, 1:48.40, October 31, 2004; Streak a Roani, 1:48.40, October 31, 2004
1 1/8 miles: Candid Remark, 1:52.20, October 31, 2004
1 3/16 miles: Cabreo, 2:04.20, October 3, 2004

Millarville Race Society

Location: General Delivery Box 68, Millarville, Ab. T0L 1L0
Phone: (403) 931-3411
Fax: (403) 931-3411
Abbreviation: Mil

Racing Dates
2004: July 1, 1 day
2005: July 1, 1 day

Leaders
Recent Meeting, Leading Jockey: Peter McAleney, 1, 2004; Laurina Bugeaud, 1, 2004
Recent Meeting, Leading Trainer: Marlon Draper, 1, 2004; Nellie Opal Pigeau, 1, 2004

Fastest Times of 2004 (Dirt)
5 furlongs: By Yourself Lady, 1:02.60, July 1, 2004
7 furlongs: Fancy Batchler, 1:30.40, July 2, 2004; Piston Broke, 1:30.40, July 2, 2004
1 1/8 miles: Diamond Passer, 1:54.80, July 1, 2004

Northlands Park

Like many Canadian racetracks, Northlands Park in Edmonton races both Thoroughbreds and Standardbreds. Both breeds enjoy richer purses due to the arrival of slot machines. In late December 2001, Northlands received 250 additional machines to double its original total as part of a $42-million racing rehabilitation project under Alberta Premier Ralph Klein, an amateur harness driver, former TV reporter, and former Calgary mayor. Opened in July 1925 as Edmonton Racetrack, the track was renamed Northlands Park in January 1964. Northlands conducts harness racing from early March through mid-June and Thoroughbred racing from late June through late October.

Location: Northlands Spectrum, P.O. Box 1480, Edmonton, Ab. T5J 2N5
Phone: (780) 471-7379
Fax: (403) 471-7134
Website: www.northlands.com
E-Mail: racing@northlands.com
Year Founded: 1879
Abbreviation: NP
Number of Stalls: 1,100
Seating Capacity: 9,000

Officers
President: Dale Leschiutta
General Manager: Ken Knowles
Director of Racing: Les Butler
Racing Secretary: Fred Hilts
Director of Operations: Kevin Behm
Director of Communications: Jonathan Huntington
Director of Finance: Ken Baker
Director of Marketing: Stephanie Hughes
Director of Mutuels: Glen Weir
Vice President: Jerry Bouma, Jim Campbell
Director of Publicity: Jonathan Huntington
Director of Simulcasting: Glen Weir
Stewards: Conrad Dick, Robert Noda, Wayne Armstrong
Track Announcer: Mike Dimoff
Track Photographer: Ryan Haynes
Track Superintendent: Ron Grift

Racing Dates
2004: June 25-October 30, 72 days
2005: June 24-October 29, 72 days

Track Layout
Main Circumference: 5/8 mile
Main Track Chute: 6 1/2 furlongs
Main Width: 70 feet
Main Length of Stretch: 625 feet

Attendance
Highest Single Day Record: 15,922, August 25, 1973

Handle
Single Day On-Track Handle: $1,652,940, August 16, 1990

Leaders
Recent Meeting, Leading Jockey: Quincy Welch, 108, 2004
Recent Meeting, Leading Trainer: Ron K. Smith, 39, 2004

Track Records, Main Dirt
5 1/2 furlongs: So Long Fellas, 1:04 2/5, August 16, 1975
6 furlongs: Sageata, 1:09.80, July 22, 1984; Lynn's Dream, 1:09.80, July 8, 2000
6 1/2 furlongs: Timely Ruckus, 1:15.40, June 26, 1999
1 mile: Bagfull, 1:35 4/5, May 16, 1981
1 1/16 miles: Chilcoton Blaze, 1:42 4/5, August 4, 1984
1 3/8 miles: Slyly Gifted, 2:15 4/5, August 30, 1986
1 5/8 miles: Racey Richard, 2:46, September 1, 1986
Other: 3 1/2 furlongs Steel Penny Black, :38 1/5, June 14, 1984; 1 5/16 miles, Arctic Laur, 2:09, August 20, 1995

Principal Races
Canadian Derby (Can-G3), Alberta Centennial S., Speed to Spare S., City of Edmonton Distaff H., Alberta Breeders' H.

Fastest Times of 2004 (Dirt)
3 1/2 furlongs: Love's Conquest, :39.40, July 24, 2004
5 1/2 furlongs: Forever Rascal, 1:05.80, August 13, 2004; Northtown Will, 1:05.80, September 12, 2004
6 furlongs: Jade Peony, 1:11.80, October 8, 2004; Northern Neechitoo, 1:11.80, August 29, 2004; Regal Legacy, 1:11.80, July 24, 2004; Regal Legacy, 1:11.80, August 13, 2004
6 1/2 furlongs: Deputy Country, 1:17.20, August 2, 2004; James Logan, 1:17.20, August 7, 2004; Think Fast, 1:17.20, August 15, 2004
1 mile: Sixthirtyjoe, 1:37.40, August 15, 2004
1 1/16 miles: Sweet Monarch, 1:44.80, August 13, 2004
1 5/16 miles: Kat Kool, 2:12.60, August 7, 2004
1 3/8 miles: Beau Brass, 2:20.20, September 11, 2004
1 5/8 miles: Badshot, 2:51.00, October 2, 2004

Stampede Park

Though it is famous for its annual Calgary Stampede rodeo, Stampede Park is also a longtime part of the Thoroughbred racing scene in Alberta. Thoroughbred racing debuted at Stampede in 1974, with the facility offering racing on a five-furlong oval and stabling for 1,400 horses. Though the track's seating of 25,000 is snug during the Calgary Stampede in July, it has been more than adequate for racing; the track's record attendance is 6,167, set on August 15, 1981. Stampede conducts a spring Thoroughbred meet from early April through mid-June and a Standardbred meet in the summer and early fall. Its major Thoroughbred race is the $100,000 Alberta Derby (Can-G3) in mid-June. In 2004, a competing organization, United Horsemen of Alberta, was awarded the license to operate racing in the Calgary area from 2007 to 2017, and the group will build a $70-million track to open in April 2007.

Location: 2300 Stampede Trail SE, Calgary, Ab. T2P 2K8
Phone: (403) 261-0214
Fax: (403) 261-0526
Website: www.stampede-park.com
E-Mail: stpracing@calgarystampede.com
Abbreviation: StP
Number of Stalls: 1,400
Seating Capacity: 25,000

Officers
Chairman: Steve Allan
President: Steve Allan
Vice President: Gordon Fache, Doug Armitage
General Manager: Steve Edwards
Director of Racing: Dave Chalack
Racing Secretary: Barry McGrath

Director of Mutuels: Sheri Holmes
Vice President: George Brookman, Steve Allen
Director of Publicity: Patti Hunt
Director of Simulcasting: Sheri Holmes
Stewards: A. C. Dick, A. Lennox, W. Armstrong
Track Announcer: Joe Carbury
Track Photographer: Neil Webster
Track Superintendent: Kevin Hannon

Racing Dates
2004: April 2-June 20, 47 days
2005: April 1-June 19, 47 days

Attendance
Average Daily Recent Meeting: 2,081, 2004
Highest Single Day Record: 6,167, August 15, 1981
Total Attendance Recent Meeting: 95,722, 2004

Handle
Average All Sources Recent Meeting: $264,473, 2004
Average On-Track Recent Meeting: $112,241, 2004
Total All Sources Recent Meeting: $12,165,775, 2004
Total On-Track Recent Meeting: $5,163,099, 2004

Leaders
Recent Meeting, Leading Jockey: Quincy Welch, 65, 2004
Recent Meeting, Leading Trainer: Ron K. Smith, 29, 2004

Principal Races
Alberta Derby

Fastest Times of 2004 (Dirt)
3 1/2 furlongs: Speedy Gone Sally, :41.00, June 19, 2004
4 furlongs: Dance Me Free, :44.00, April 3, 2004
6 furlongs: Jade Peony, 1:09.80, April 21, 2004; Sixthirtyjoe, 1:09.80, June 4, 2004
1 mile: Fuhr Ore, 1:37.60, June 2, 2004; Fussy's Kid, 1:37.60, May 19, 2004
1 1/16 miles: Affordable Fun, 1:44.00, June 4, 2004

British Columbia

Hastings Racecourse

For more than 80 years, the racing scene in the Canadian province of British Columbia has focused on the tract of land where Hastings Park currently stands. From 1994 to 2002, the not-for-profit Pacific Racing Association managed racing at Hastings, which conducts Thoroughbred racing at the five-furlong facility usually from April through November. Woodbine Entertainment Group bought the facility in 2002, and in 2004 sold it to Great Canadian Gaming Corp. for $15.7-million. First opened in 1920, Hastings reached its peak as a racing facility in the early 1980s, when the track sometimes drew crowds of 20,000 or more. The track also has appealed to Vancouver's expanding Asian population by offering simulcast wagering from Hong Kong.

Location: Hastings Racecourse, Vancouver, B.C. V5K 3N8
Phone: (604) 254-1631
Phone: (800) 677-7702
Fax: (604) 251-0411
Website: *www.hastingsracecourse.com*
E-Mail: comments@hastingsracecourse.com
Year Founded: 1889 (Exhibition Park); 1994 (Hastings Racecourse)
Dates of Inaugural Meeting: 1920
Abbreviation: Hst
Acreage: 45
Number of Stalls: 1,000
Seating Capacity: 5,600

Ownership
Great Canadian Gaming Corp.

Officers
Chairman: Ross J. McLeod
President: Anthony Martin
General Manager: Michael Brown
Racing Secretary: Lorne Mitchell
Treasurer: Vickie Heese
Director of Marketing: Cindy Bugden
Vice President: Michael Brown
Director of Publicity: Howard Blank
Stewards: Douglas F. Scott, Keith G. Smith, Wayne J. Russell
Track Announcer: Dan Jukich
Track Photographer: Winner's Photography
Track Superintendent: Drew Levere
Horsemen's Bookkeeper: Merrilee Elliott

Racing Dates
2004: April 17-November 28, 71 days
2005: April 16-November 27, 83 days

Track Layout
Main Circumference: 5 furlongs, 208 feet
Main Track Chute: 6 1/2 furlongs and 1 1/8 miles
Main Width: 65 feet
Main Length of Stretch: 513 feet

Attendance
Highest Single Day Record: 21,156, July 9, 1982

Handle
Average All Sources Recent Meeting: $764,723, 2004
Average On-Track Recent Meeting: $349,234, 2004
Single Day On-Track Handle: $2,612,316, July 9, 1982
Total All Sources Recent Meeting: $53,217,443, 2004
Total On-Track Recent Meeting: $24,795,649, 2004
Highest Single Day Recent Meet: $1,171,719, June 5, 2004

Mutuel Records
Highest Win: $508.10, 1953
Highest Exacta: $4,092, 1962
Highest Trifecta: $21,806.20, 1982
Highest Daily Double: $4,863.10, 1995
Highest Pick 3: $11,474, 1993
Highest Other Exotics: $920,411.70, Sweep 6, 1982; $63,326.70, Win 4, 1988; $42,946, Superfecta, June 13, 2004

Leaders
Career, Leading Jockey by Titles: Chris Loseth, 8
Career, Leading Trainer by Titles: Harold Barroby, 10
Career, Leading Jockey by Stakes Wins: Chris Loseth, 204
Career, Leading Trainer by Stakes Wins: Harold Barroby, 143
Career, Leading Jockey by Wins: Chris Loseth, 3,551
Career, Leading Trainer by Wins: Harold Barroby, 1,196
Recent Meeting, Leading Horse: Pioneer Pete, 5, 2004; Rampoldi, 5, 2004; Regal Red, 5, 2004
Recent Meeting, Leading Jockey: Pedro Alvarado, 130, 2004
Recent Meeting, Leading Owner: Diglett Stable, 19, 2004
Recent Meeting, Leading Trainer: Dino Condilenios, 37, 2004

Records
Single Day Jockey Wins: Chris Loseth, 8, April 9, 1984
Single Day Trainer Wins: George Cummings, 5, November 8, 1992
Single Meet, Leading Jockey by Wins: Mark Patzer, 173, 1991
Single Meet, Leading Trainer by Wins: Lance Giesbrecht, 76, 1997

Track Records, Main Dirt
6 furlongs: Great Discretion, 1:10 2/5, May 10, 1969; Humphrey Lad, 1:10 2/5, April 13, 1988; Sir Khaled, 1:10 2/5, April 15, 1988
6 1/2 furlongs: Torque Converter, 1:15, July 1, 1996
1m 70 yds: Westbury Road, 1:40 2/5, July 29, 1967
1 1/16 miles: Coral Isle, 1:42 1/5, July 28, 1973; No Time Flat, 1:42 1/5, August 12, 1987; Timely Stitch, 1:42.20, July 6, 1996
1 1/8 miles: Artic Son, 1:46.80, August 3, 1998
1 3/8 miles: Irish Bear, 2:14 2/5, October 17, 1987
1 1/2 miles: Lucky Son, 2:29, August 25, 1995

1 3/4 miles: Glen Gower, 2:59, September 23, 1987
Other: a3 1/2 furlongs,Turn to Knight, :41.1/5, May 27, 1990; 3 1/2 furlongs, Flying Memo, :39.40, October 26, 2003; a6 furlongs, Count the Green, 1:10 4/5, April 17, 1971; 1 7/16 miles, Who's in Command, 2:23, August 10, 1987; a1 1/2 miles, Golden Gentry, 2:29 2/5, September 20, 1987; 1 11/16 miles, Glen Gower, 2:51 1/5, September 9, 1987; 2 1/16 miles, Laddie's Prince, 3:30, October 7, 1987; a2 1/16 miles, High Hawk, 3:48 2/5, October 16, 1983; 2 1/8 miles, Mr. Chancellor, 3:38 4/5, October 18, 1987

Principal Races
Ballerina Breeders' Cup S. (Can-G3), British Columbia Breeders' Cup Oaks (Can-G3), British Columbia Derby (Can-G3), Premier's H. (Can-G3), Ascot Graduation S.

Notable Events
British Columbia Cup Day

Fastest Times of 2004 (Dirt)
3 1/2 furlongs: Avenging Kat, :39.70, September 11, 2004
6 furlongs: April Foolish, 1:12.18, April 24, 2004; Bates, 1:12.18, April 25, 2004
6 1/2 furlongs: Dancewithavictor, 1:15.74, May 22, 2004
1 1/16 miles: Metatron, 1:42.41, August 2, 2004
1 1/8 miles: Royal Place, 1:49.08, July 1, 2004
1 3/8 miles: Woody's Dancer, 2:19.05, August 2, 2004
1 1/2 miles: Woody's Dancer, 2:30.91, September 11, 2004
1 3/4 miles: Sea Navigator, 2:59.47, October 2, 2004

Kamloops

Location: 479 Chilcotin St., Kamloops, B.C. V2H 1G4
Phone: (250) 314-9645
Fax: (250) 828-0836
Website: www.kamloopsonlineoffline.com
E-Mail: kxa@mail.ocis.net
Year Founded: 1895
Abbreviation: Kam
Number of Stalls: 310
Seating Capacity: 2000

Ownership
Kamloops Exhibition Association

Officers
Chairman: Luigi Sale
President: Luigi Sale
Director of Racing: Luigi Sale
Racing Secretary: Jim Rogers
Vice President: Dave Carswell
Director of Publicity: Lugi Sale
Stewards: Jim Rogers
Track Announcer: Keith Reid
Track Superintendent: Jim Larson

Racing Dates
2004: May 23-June 27, 5 days; August 8-September 5, 5 days
2005: May 22-June 26, 5 days; August 6-September 4, 5 days

Leaders
Recent Meeting, Leading Jockey: Ronald Bilodeau, 3, 2004
Recent Meeting, Leading Trainer: Jake Born, 2, 2004

Fastest Times of 2004 (Dirt)
a4 1/2 furlongs: Jewels Again, :50.05, May 30, 2004; J. R. Jazz, :50.05, June 13, 2004
a6 1/2 furlongs: Jewels Again, 1:19.37, June 6, 2004
a1 miles: Tender Offer (IRE), 1:38.45, August 15, 2004

Kin Park

Location: P.O. Box 682, Vernon, B.C. V1T 6M6
Phone: (250) 542-5759
Fax: (250) 542-9317
Abbreviation: Kin

Racing Dates
2004: July 11-August 1, 4 days
2005: July 9-July 30, 4 days

Leaders
Recent Meeting, Leading Horse: Tammy Star, 2, 2004
Recent Meeting, Leading Jockey: Caroline Stinn, 3, 2004
Recent Meeting, Leading Trainer: Garry Saitz, 3, 2004

Fastest Times of 2004 (Dirt)
a4 furlongs: Tammy Star, :44.33, July 11, 2004
a6 furlongs: Chief Swan, 1:11.89, August 1, 2004
6 1/2 furlongs: Getta Klew, 1:22.20, July 11, 2004
a6 1/2 furlongs: Tender Offer (Ire), 1:20.00, July 18, 2004
a1 1/16 miles: Eager Lee, 1:45.62, August 1, 2004

Sunflower Downs

Location: P.O. Box 584, Princeton, B.C. V0H 1W0
Phone: (250) 295-6380
Fax: (250) 295-7322
Abbreviation: SnD

Officers
President: Brad Hope
General Manager: Jack Powell
Director of Racing: Joe Horton
Treasurer: Evelyn Beale
Director of Mutuels: Roberta Baron
Vice President: Brad Carter
Director of Publicity: June Hope
Stewards: Elaine Covert, Merv Nelson, Sten Matell
Track Announcer: Keith Reid

Racing Dates
2005: June 30-July 2, 3 days

Manitoba

Assiniboia Downs

Assiniboia Downs continues a rich tradition of horse racing in Winnipeg, dating from the last quarter of the 19th century. Racing enthusiast and businessman Jack Hardy built Assiniboia, which opened in 1958 to replace Polo Park, a 30-year-old track located on property that became a shopping center. In 1974, Jim Wright bought the track and racing prospered under his leadership. By the early 1990s, however, competition from other gambling forms made the track unprofitable. In 1993, Assiniboia was sold to its current owners, the Manitoba Jockey Club, a not-for-profit organization that solidified its future by pouring profits from video lottery terminals and full-card simulcasting back into the facility. Assiniboia, which offers live racing from early May through September, was the first track in Canada to offer pick-six and telephone-account wagering. The track's richest race, the Manitoba Derby (Can-G3), has been run at Assiniboia since 1960. In 1970, Queen Elizabeth II and Prince Philip attended the race as part of Manitoba's centennial year. The winner was Fanfreluche, a Northern Dancer filly who was that year's Canadian Horse of the Year as well as an Eclipse Award winner as North America's champion three-year-old filly. Her son L'Enjoleur won the Manitoba Derby in 1975, the year in which he earned his second Canadian Horse of the Year title.

Location: 3975 Portage Ave., Winnipeg, Mb. R3K 2E9
Phone: (204) 885-3330
Fax: (204) 831-5348
Website: www.assiniboiadowns.com
E-Mail: info@assiniboiadowns.com
Dates of Inaugural Meeting: 1958
Abbreviation: AsD
Number of Stalls: 936
Seating Capacity: 6,000

Ownership
Manitoba Jockey Club

Officers
President: Harvey Warner
General Manager: Sharon Gulyas
Director of Racing: Derren Dunn
Racing Secretary: Ray Miller
Secretary: Barry Anderson
Treasurer: Kris Nancoo
Director of Operations: Derren Dunn
Director of Finance: Kris Nancoo
Director of Marketing: Pat Tymkin
Director of Mutuels: Glenn Passey
Vice President: Dr. Norm Elder
Director of Publicity: Ernest Nairn
Director of Sales: Jamie Sullivan
Director of Simulcasting: Glenn Passey
Stewards: Craig MacDonald, Hazel Bochinski, Jack Wash, Larry Huber
Track Announcer: Derren Dunn
Track Photographer: Gerry Hart
Track Superintendent: Bob Timlick
Horsemen's Bookkeeper: Louise Russell
Asst. Racing Secretary: Dustin Davis
Security: Tim McDonald

Racing Dates
2004: May 2-October 3, 69 days
2005: May 1-October 2, 75 days

Track Layout
Main Circumference: 1 3/16 miles
Main Width: 80 feet
Main Length of Stretch: 990 feet
Training Track: 1/2 mile

Attendance
Highest Single Day Record: 13,276, August 6, 1979

Handle
Average All Sources Recent Meeting: $127,270, 2004
Average On-Track Recent Meeting: $86,821, 2004
Single Day On-Track Handle: $713,756, September 5, 1988
Total All Sources Recent Meeting: $8,857,499.41, 2004
Total On-Track Recent Meeting: $6,045,488.60, 2004
Highest Single Day Recent Meet: $339,622.76, August 2, 2004

Mutuel Records
Highest Win: $474.20, May 31, 1986
Highest Exacta: $3,514.80, May 16, 1998
Highest Trifecta: $40,026.60, May 18, 1981
Highest Daily Double: $4,235.50, July 23, 1971
Highest Pick 3: $3,269.40, June 28, 1998
Highest Pick 4: $14,584.95, September 1, 1986

Leaders
Career, Leading Jockey by Titles: Bobby Stewart, 5
Career, Leading Trainer by Titles: Clayton Gray, 7
Recent Meeting, Leading Jockey: Travis Hightower, 98, 2004
Recent Meeting, Leading Trainer: Ardell Sayler, 40, 2004
Career, Leading Jockey by Wins: Ken Hendricks, 1,619
Career, Leading Trainer by Wins: Gary Danelson, 1010

Records
Single Day Jockey Wins: Jim Sorenson, 7, June 23, 1976

Track Records, Main Dirt
4 furlongs: Northern Spike, :44.40, April 23, 1982
4 1/2 furlongs: Astral Moon, :50.80, May 1, 1982
5 furlongs: Northern Spike, :56.40, May 9, 1982
5 1/2 furlongs: Sunny Famous, 1:02.80, September 19, 1992
6 furlongs: Mr. Quill, 1:09, October 10, 1981; Nephrite, 1:09, October 8, 1989
7 furlongs: Victor's Pride, 1:23.20, August 16, 1978
1 mile: *Gladiatore II, 1:35.80, July 7, 1972; Tower of Shan, 1:35.80, June 24, 1990
1 1/16 miles: Goa, 1:41.60, July 23, 1988
1 1/8 miles: Overskate, 1:47.60, September 9, 1978
1 1/4 miles: Nifty (Fr), 2:05, September 20, 1986; Northern Debut, 2:05, October 3, 1993

Principal Races
Gold Breeders' Cup, Manitoba Derby, Matron Breeders' Cup, Winnipeg Futurity

Fastest Times of 2004 (Dirt)
4 1/2 furlongs: Rich Rubies, :53.40, July 1, 2004
5 furlongs: Bally Cat, :59.20, August 6, 2004; Proud Princely, :59.20, July 23, 2004
5 1/2 furlongs: Runnin' the River, 1:05.80, June 4, 2004
6 furlongs: Dearest Jack, 1:11.00, September 18, 2004; Gus Again, 1:11.00, September 24, 2004
7 1/2 furlongs: Iwoodificould, 1:32.20, July 18, 2004
1 mile: Northern Affair, 1:38.20, August 2, 2004
1 1/16 miles: Shanghied, 1:44.60, July 11, 2004
1 1/8 miles: Shanghied, 1:51.80, August 29, 2004

Ontario

Fort Erie

Founded in 1897, Fort Erie is one of Canada's oldest racetracks. Located in southern Ontario across the border from Buffalo, New York, the track began its premier event, the Prince of Wales Stakes, in 1959 with the help of prominent Ontario horseman E. P. Taylor. The race for three-year-old Canadian-breds now has become the second leg of Canada's Triple Crown. Taylor-bred Northern Dancer made his career debut at Fort Erie in August 1963. The following year, the Nearctic colt became the first Canadian-bred to win the Kentucky Derby. The track now is owned by Nordic Gaming Corp., which consists of three business interests from southern Ontario and two foreign investors. It underwent $30-million in renovations in 1999 to prepare for 1,200 slot machines that help to support the racing operation.

Location: 230 Catherine Street, P.O. Box 1130, Fort Erie, On. L2A 5N9
Phone: (905) 871-3200
Fax: (905) 994-36229
Website: www.forterieracing.com
E-Mail: femedia@forterieracetrack.com
Dates of Inaugural Meeting: June 16, 1897
Abbreviation: FE
Number of Stalls: 1,300
Seating Capacity: 4,000

Ownership
Nordic Gaming

Officers
General Manager: Eddie Lynn
Director of Racing: Herb McGirr
Racing Secretary: Tom Gostlin
Treasurer: Bonnie Loubert
Director of Operations: Alan Gouck
Director of Communications: Brian Blessing, Daryl Wells

Director of Finance: Bonnie Loubert
Director of Marketing: Herb McGirr
Director of Mutuels: Chad Gates
Director of Publicity: Brian Blessing, Daryl Wells
Director of Simulcasting: Chad Gates
Track Announcer: Daryl Wells
Track Photographer: Patricia Burns
Track Superintendent: Ken McSwain

Racing Dates
2004: May 1-September 6, 81 days
2005: May 1-October 31, 108 days

Track Layout
Main Circumference: 1 mile
Main Width: 75 feet
Main Length of Stretch: 1,060 feet
Main Turf Circumference: 7 furlongs

Handle
Average All Sources Recent Meeting: $824,085, 2004
Average On-Track Recent Meeting: $130,808, 2004
Total All Sources Recent Meeting: $10,595,432, 2004
Total On-Track Recent Meeting: $66,750,886, 2004
Highest Single Day Recent Meet: $1,336,927, July 27, 2004

Leaders
Recent Meeting, Leading Horse: Thunder Bull, 5, 2004
Recent Meeting, Leading Jockey: Neil Poznanzky, 71, 2004
Recent Meeting, Leading Owner: Bruno Schickendanz, 18, 2004; Michael Barkowski, 18, 2004
Recent Meeting, Leading Trainer: Tom Agosti, 27, 2004

Track Records, Main Dirt
4 furlongs: Kirk's Dandy, :47 2/5, May 2, 1957
4 1/2 furlongs: Dawn Deluxe, :52, April 17, 1971; Dozen Dancer, :52, April 24, 1971; Trade Wagon, :52, May 8, 1968
5 furlongs: Cool Shot, :56.60, July 15, 1995
5 1/2 furlongs: Emotionally, 1:03.60, June 28, 1997; Just a Lord, 1:03.60, June 15, 1991
6 furlongs: Deputy Carson, 1:08.85, September 9, 2001
6 1/2 furlongs: Muzledick, 1:15, August 10, 1968
1m 70 yds: Myrtle Irene, 1:39.80, August 26, 1994
1 1/8 miles: Laurie's Dancer, 1:48, August 23, 1972
1 3/16 miles: Bruce's Mill, 1:53.20, July 31, 1994

Track Records, Main Turf
5 furlongs: Oh Mar, :56.99, September 9, 2002
7 furlongs: Native Vigil, 1:22.10, July 2, 1991
1 mile: Fifth and a Jigger, 1:34.30, June 10, 1991
1 1/16 miles: Road of War, 1:40.80, June 19, 1994

Principal Races
Prince of Wales S., Labatt Bison City S.

Fastest Times of 2004 (Dirt)
2 furlongs: Bermuda Triangle, :21.61, August 3, 2004
5 furlongs: Krz Ruckus, :57.31, June 12, 2004
6 furlongs: Krz Ruckus, 1:10.26, July 1, 2004
6 1/2 furlongs: A Nice Splash, 1:16.12, August 21, 2004
1m 70 yds: Secret Secret Star, 1:42.42, August 2, 2004
1 1/16 miles: Ginger Gold, 1:43.49, June 15, 2004
1 1/8 miles: Prince of Rhodes, 1:53.12, August 16, 2004
1 3/16 miles: A Bit O'Gold, 1:57.69, July 18, 2004
1 1/4 miles: Gist of Art, 2:09.57, July 24, 2004
1 3/4 miles: Gist of Art, 3:08.50, August 10, 2004
2m 70 yds: Attonotauto, 3:40.05, September 5, 2004

Fastest Times of 2004 (Turf)
5 furlongs: Major Zee, :58.12, July 25, 2004
a5 furlongs: Famous Fury, :59.07, August 27, 2004
a7 furlongs: Long Term Success, 1:22.76, June 29, 2004
1 mile: Lindsey's Dove, 1:37.82, September 4, 2004
a1 miles: Whiskey Wizard, 1:39.82, July 1, 2004
1 1/16 miles: Hanlan, 1:43.39, June 28, 2004
a1 1/16 miles: Silent Thunder, 1:45.91, July 13, 2004
a1 3/8 miles: Chimes Rebel, 2:21.53, July 1, 2004

Woodbine

The addition of 1,700 slot machines in March 2000 substantially increased purses and made Canada's best-known racetrack into a financial success after years of operating under a burdensome debt load. After installing the slot machines, the organization that owns the track changed its name from the Ontario Jockey Club to the Woodbine Entertainment Group. Woodbine, located in the Toronto suburb of Rexdale, is home of the Queen's Plate Stakes, first run in 1860 and North America's oldest continually run stakes race. With a unique track arrangement on its 650 acres, Woodbine is the only track in North America to conduct Standardbred and Thoroughbred racing on the same day. Its 1½-mile grass course, the E. P. Taylor Turf Course, features the longest stretch run in North America, 1,440 feet. Inside the turf course is the one-mile dirt track, which was completely rebuilt in 1994. Inside the main dirt track is a seven-eighths-mile, 85-foot-wide harness track. Woodbine's rich history dates to 1874, when the track opened on what was then the eastern outskirts of Toronto, which is now Toronto's downtown. That track's name was changed to Old Woodbine in 1956 and then renamed Greenwood Raceway in 1963. The present Woodbine opened on June 12, 1956. In 1996, Woodbine became the first track outside the United States to host the Breeders' Cup, and it drew a record Woodbine crowd of 42,243. Besides the Queen's Plate, Woodbine hosts the $1.5-million Canadian International (Can-G1) and the $1-million Atto Mile Stakes (Can-G1), which has evolved into an important stakes for grass horses aiming for the Breeders' Cup Mile (G1).

Location: 555 Rexdale Blvd., Rexdale, On. M9W 5L2
Phone: (416) 675-7223
Phone: (888) 675-RACE
Fax: (416) 213-2126
Website: www.woodbineentertainment.com
E-Mail: csd@woodbineentertainment.com
Year Founded: 1874
Dates of Inaugural Meeting: June 12-July 14 1956; October 1-November 17, 1956
Abbreviation: WO
Acreage: 650
Number of Stalls: 1,860
Seating Capacity: 12,000

Ownership
Woodbine Entertainment Group

Officers
Chairman: David S. Willmot
President: David S. Willmot
Director of Racing: Chris Evans
Racing Secretary: Steve Lym
Secretary: Robert Careless
Executive Vice President: J. W. Ormiston
Director of Operations: Al Dymon
Director of Admissions: Steve Mitchell
Director of Communications: Glenn Crouter
Director of Finance: Tom Valiquette
Director of Marketing: Nick Eaves
Director of Mutuels: Sean Pinsonneault
Vice President: Hugh M. Mitchell
Director of Publicity: John Siscos
Director of Sales: Joseph Araujo
Director of Simulcasting: Debbie Chomiak
Stewards: R. Grubb, G. Lindberg, L. Phelan
Track Announcer: Dan Loiselle
Track Photographer: Michael Burns
Track Superintendent: Brian Jabelman
Asst. Racing Secretary: Sheryl McSwain
Horsemen's Bookkeeper: F. Courtney

Racing Dates

2004: April 17-December 12, 167 days
2005: April 16-December 11, 167 days

Track Layout

Main Circumference: 1 mile
Main Track Chute: 2 furlongs and 7 furlongs
Main Width: 85 feet
Main Length of Stretch: 975 feet
Main Turf Circumference: 1 1/2 miles
Main Turf Chute: 1 1/8 miles
Main Turf Width: Homestretch: 100 feet; Backstretch: 120 feet
Main Turf Length of Stretch: 1,440 feet
Inner Circumference: 7 furlong harness track

Attendance

Highest Single Day Record: 42,243, October 26, 1996

Handle

Average All Sources Recent Meeting: $2,026,042, 2004
Single Day On-Track Handle: $6,884,357, October 26, 1996
Single Day All Sources Handle: $67,738,890, October 26, 1996
Total All Sources Recent Meeting: $338,349,020, 2004

Mutuel Records

Highest Win: $794.20, Waverley Steps, June 24, 1968
Highest Exacta: $6,405, June 11, 1995
Lowest Exacta: $2.70, June 16, 1991
Highest Trifecta: $123,279, November 28, 1999
Lowest Trifecta: $11.60, August 11, 1998
Highest Daily Double: $5,497.50, June 16, 1978
Lowest Daily Double: $3.80, May 20, 1998
Highest Pick 3: $10,881.80, June 29, 1991
Lowest Pick 3: $1.80, July 28, 1991
Highest Other Exotics: $123,372.30, Win 4, June 15, 1988; $466,671.65, Super 7, July 1, 1989; $34,900.35, Superfecta, November 4, 2001
Lowest Other Exotics: $21.75, Win 4, April 29, 1995; $221.50, Super 7, May 10, 1997; $86.30, Superfecta, July 5, 2000

Leaders

Career, Leading Jockey by Titles: Sandy Hawley, 19
Career, Leading Trainer by Titles: Frank Merrill, 30
Recent Meeting, Leading Jockey: Todd Kabel, 156, 2004
Recent Meeting, Leading Owner: Stronach Stables, 44, 2004
Recent Meeting, Leading Trainer: Sid Attard, 73, 2004

Records

Single Day Jockey Wins: Richard Grubb, 7, May 16, 1967; Sandy Hawley, 7, May 22, 1972; Sandy Hawley, 7, October 10, 1974

Track Records, Main Dirt

4 1/2 furlongs: Hallmarked, :50.40, March 24, 1996; Written Approval, :50.40, March 25, 1996
5 furlongs: Jack and Emma, :55.95, April 5, 2003
5 1/2 furlongs: Uncle Woger, 1:02.70, April 4, 1999
6 furlongs: Chris's Bad Boy, 1:08.05, November 29, 2003
6 1/2 furlongs: Fair Juror, 1:14 3/5, October 17, 1961; Saoirse, 1:14.78, October 16, 1999
7 furlongs: Oronero, 1:20.60, December 6, 1995
1m 70 yds: Regal Courser, 1:39.60, August 8, 1998
1 1/16 miles: Kiridashi, 1:40.80, August 17, 1996
1 1/8 miles: Glorious Song, 1:48, July 1, 1981
3/16 miles: Runnin Roman, 1:55 4/5, September 15, 1974
1 1/4 miles: Alphabet Soup, 2:01, October 26, 1996
1 3/8 miles: Lovely Sunrise, 2:17, October 26, 1974
1 1/2 miles: Norcliffe, 2:29 1/5, October 29, 1977
1 5/8 miles: *Eugenia II, 2:43 2/5, October 27, 1956
1 3/4 miles: Major Pots, 2:52.60, December 8, 1994
Other: 3 furlongs, Noble Herod, :33 3/5, May 5, 1978; 1 7/8 miles, Flying Commander, 3:13.29, December 2, 2001

Track Records, Main Turf

6 furlongs: Wild Zone, 1:07.60, July 7, 1996
6 1/2 furlongs: Chris's Bad Boy, 1:14.27, August 7, 2004
7 furlongs: Soaring Free, 1:19.38, July 24, 2004
1 mile: Royal Regalia, 1:31.84, July 1, 2004
1 1/16 miles: Jet Freighter, 1:39.20, June 4, 1995; Honolulu

Gold, 1:39.20, July 11, 1996; Western Express, 1:39.20, July 12, 1998
1 1/8 miles: Bold Ruritana, 1:45.20, June 18, 1995
1 1/4 miles: Arbalest, 2:01, June 15, 1995; Set Ablaze, 2:01, July 5, 1996
1 3/8 miles: Shoal Water, 2:12.37, July 25, 2004
1 1/2 miles: Raintrap (GB), 2:25.60, October 16, 1994
Other: a1 1/8 miles, Surging River, 1:42.87, August 8, 2004; a1 1/4 miles, Desert Waves, 2:02.40, July 24, 1995; a1 1/4 miles, Murad, 2:02.40, June 4, 1998; a1 3/8 miles, Chief Bearhart, 2:16, July 25, 1996; a1 1/2 miles, Mr. Lucky Junction, 2:29.60, July 26, 1996

Track Records, Inner Turf

5 furlongs: Deputy Regent, :58, July 4, 1982
1 mile: Charlie Barley, 1:34 4/5, May 28, 1989; Myrtle Irene, 1:34 4/5, September 19, 1993
1 1/16 miles: Overskate, 1:40 4/5, June 3, 1979; Seattle Sangue, 1:40 4/5, June 17, 1990
1 1/4 miles: Mill Native, 2:00, June 26, 1983
1 3/8 miles: Wayover, 2:19 1/5, June 26, 1985
1 1/2 miles: Great Stake, 2:34, July 5, 1985

Principal Races

Atto Mile (Can-G1), Canadian International (Can-G1), Queen's Plate, Breeders' S., Woodbine Oaks

Interesting Facts

Previous Names and Dates: Ontario Jockey Club 1881-2001
Achievements/milestones: Hosted Arlington Million in 1988; Hosted Breeders' Cup in 1996

Notable Events

In January 2004, the company launched hpibet.com, an internet wagering site.

Fastest Times of 2004 (Dirt)

4 1/2 furlongs: Fortunate Trip, :51.67, May 9, 2004
5 furlongs: Priceless Legend, :57.32, April 30, 2004
5 1/2 furlongs: Cheyenne Spring, 1:03.81, April 30, 2004
6 furlongs: Chris's Bad Boy, 1:08.75, April 17, 2004
6 1/2 furlongs: Winter Garden, 1:15.57, August 22, 2004
7 furlongs: Mobil, 1:21.81, May 1, 2004
1m 70 yds: Tic Tac Man (Aus), 1:41.08, August 11, 2004
1 1/16 miles: Sky Diamond, 1:42.74, September 4, 2004
1 1/8 miles: Slim Dusty, 1:50.98, October 17, 2004
1 3/16 miles: Questing Knight, 1:59.23, August 7, 2004
1 1/4 miles: Mobil, 2:03.34, July 1, 2004
1 1/2 miles: Daddy Cool, 2:35.49, November 20, 2004
1 3/4 miles: Daddy Cool, 3:03.52, December 12, 2004
1 7/8 miles: Mr. Perpetuity, 3:19.50, December 12, 2004

Fastest Times of 2004 (Turf)

6 furlongs: Hour of Justice, 1:07.83, August 2, 2004
6 1/2 furlongs: Chris's Bad Boy, 1:14.27, August 7, 2004
7 furlongs: Soaring Free, 1:19.38, July 24, 2004
1 mile: Royal Regalia, 1:31.84, July 1, 2004
1 1/16 miles: Hour of Justice, 1:40.13, August 28, 2004
1 1/8 miles: P. J.'s Paulie Boy, 1:46.68, June 12, 2004
a1 1/8 miles: Surging River, 1:42.87, August 8, 2004
1 1/4 miles: King of Siam, 2:01.68, July 2, 2004
a1 1/4 miles: Charming Proposal, 2:04.18, September 12, 2004
1 3/8 miles: Shoal Water, 2:12.37, July 25, 2004
1 1/2 miles: Strut the Stage, 2:25.87, September 6, 2004
a1 1/2 miles: Burst of Fire, 2:31.66, September 15, 2004

Saskatchewan

Marquis Downs

Marquis Downs in Saskatoon has offered live racing since 1969. With a five-furlong track and a grandstand capacity of 4,500, Marquis is part of the Saskatoon Prairieland Exhibition, a multipurpose facility that includes meeting and exhibition halls and a casino. Rac-

ing annually takes place from May through September.
Location: P.O. Box 6010, Saskatoon, Sk. S7K 4E4
Phone: (306) 242-6100
Phone: (888) 931-9333
Fax: (306) 242-6907
Website: *www.saskatoonex.com*
E-Mail: contactus@saskatoonex.com
Dates of Inaugural Meeting: August 18, 1969
Abbreviation: MD
Number of Stalls: 750
Seating Capacity: 3,027

Officers
President: Les Cannam
Racing Secretary: Rick Fior
Treasurer: Dan Kemppainen
Director of Communications: Marlene Rochelle
Director of Marketing: Maurice Neault
Vice President: Rick Holm
Director of Simulcasting: Doug King
Stewards: Doug Schneider, Terry Harkness, Margo Tutt
Track Announcer: Steve Tatarniuk
Track Superintendent: Dennis Paules
Chief Executive Officer: Mark Regier

Racing Dates
2004: May 28-September 11, 30 days
2005: May 27-September 10, 30 days

Track Layout
Main Circumference: 5 furlongs
Main Track Chute: 7 furlongs and 1 1/8 miles
Main Width: 90 feet
Main Length of Stretch: 660 feet

Attendance
Average Daily Recent Meeting: 791, 2004
Total Attendance Recent Meeting: 22,943, 2004

Handle
Average On-Track Recent Meeting: $22,367, 2004
Total On-Track Recent Meeting: $648,654, 2004
Highest Single Day Record Recent Meet: $31,841, August 7, 2004

Leaders
Recent Meeting, Leading Jockey: Serge Rocheleau, 56, 2004
Recent Meeting, Leading Trainer: Don Bjarnarson, 19, 2004; Hubert Pilon, 19, 2004

Track Records, Main Dirt
4 furlongs: Zizzilin, :45, May 8, 1981
5 1/2 furlongs: Mickey's Mark, 1:04 2/5, July 28, 1980
6 furlongs: Shotgun Annie, 1:10 2/5, August 7, 1981
6 1/2 furlongs: Christmas Country, 1:18.60, August 1, 1994
7 furlongs: T.V. Fling, 1:24 1/5, August 28, 1988
1 mile: Three for You, 1:37 1/5, June 12, 1981
1 1/16 miles: Little Bo, 1:42, September 1, 1984
1 1/8 miles: Zance, 1:49 3/5, October 10, 1988
1 3/8 miles: Secret Cipher, 2:18, October 15, 1983
1 5/8 miles: Bright Bern, 2:48, July 31, 1976
1 3/4 miles: Lloyd's Admiral, 3:01 2/5, October 19, 1986
Other: 3 1/2 furlongs, Kid Dynamo, :40 2/5, June 20, 1977; a4 furlongs, Royal Alibi, :45 1/5, May 20, 1978; a6 1/2 furlongs, Shona Rae, 1:17.80, June 11, 1992; a7 furlongs, Graceful Klinchit, 1:23.60, August 31, 1991; a1 1/8 miles, Easy Riser, 1:49 2/5, August 25, 1980; 1 5/16 miles, Extrapolate, 2:13, August 29, 1993; a1 1/2 miles, Spring Sunsation, 2:35, September 26, 1993

Principal Races
Saskatchewan Derby, Prairie Lily Sales S., Heritage Day (4 Saskatchewan-bred races)

Interesting Facts
Trivia: Jockey Tim Moccasin rode 14 consecutive winners August 24 through September 1, 2001, believed to be a North American record

Fastest Times of 2004
4 furlongs: Double Time, :46.53, May 28, 2004
6 furlongs: Double Time, 1:12.06, June 26, 2004
6 1/2 furlongs: Fargo Forbes, 1:22.45, August 21, 2004
7 furlongs: Party in the Park, 1:25.35, August 6, 2004
1 mile: Beau Ring, 1:39.53, July 23, 2004
1 1/16 miles: Noble Dane, 1:45.45, September 11, 2004

Puerto Rico

El Comandante

Located in Canovanas, El Comandante has been the island's racing outlet for decades. To many racing fans, El Comandante is probably best known for producing Bold Forbes and Mister Frisky. A dual-classic winner and 1976 champion three-year-old male in the United States, Bold Forbes began his career at El Comandante. So did Mister Frisky, who started his unbeaten string here in 1989 before coming to the United States and going off as the favorite in the 1990 Kentucky Derby (G1), in which he finished eighth. In recent years, El Comandante has added a sophisticated network of off-track wagering outlets and a daily television racing report. The subsidiary of Virginia-based Equus Gaming Co. that operates El Comandante filed for bankruptcy in 2004. Also in 2004, Puerto Rico authorized 6,500 slot machines for the track's off-track betting system.

Location: P.O. Box 1675, Canovanas, P.R. 00729-1675
Phone: (787) 641-6060
Fax: (787) 876-5170
Website: *www.comandantepr.com*
E-Mail: nidnal@comandantepr.com
Year Founded: 1976
Abbreviation: ElC
Acreage: 257
Number of Stalls: 1,500+

Ownership
El Comandante Management Co.

Officers
President: Charles A. Caprill
General Manager: Alejandro Fuentes Fernandez
Director of Racing: Marcos Rivera Puga
Racing Secretary: Angel Ayala
Treasurer: Stanley Pinkerton
Director of Mutuels: Wilma Curet
Director of Publicity: Nidnal J. Adrover
Stewards: Ronan Lozada, Jose Landrau, Ruben Diaz
Track Photographer: Ivan Baella

Racing Dates
2004: January 1-December 31
2005: January 1-December 31

Track Layout
Main Circumference: 1 mile
Main Track Chute: 7 furlongs

Leaders
Career, Leading Owner by Titles: Villa Real
Career, Leading Trainer by Titles: Maximo Gomez
Career, Leading Jockey by Stakes Wins: Wilfredo Rohena
Career, Leading Jockey by Wins: Juan Carlos Diaz

Principal Races
Derby Puertorriqueno, Copa Gobernador, Copa San Juan, Clasico Antonio Fernandez Castrillon, Clasico Internacional del Caribe

North American Racetracks

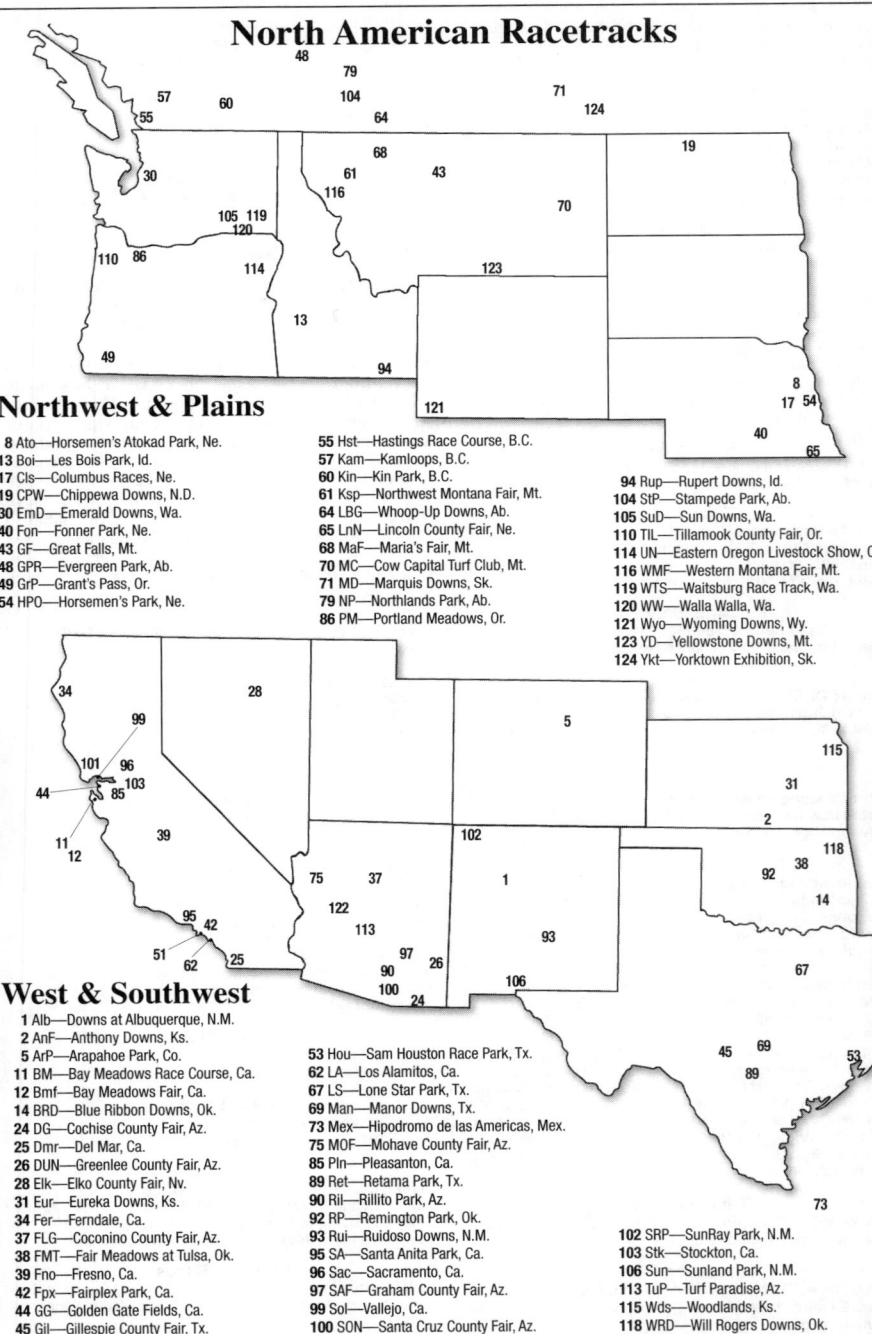

Northwest & Plains

8 Ato—Horsemen's Atokad Park, Ne.
13 Boi—Les Bois Park, Id.
17 Cls—Columbus Races, Ne.
19 CPW—Chippewa Downs, N.D.
30 EmD—Emerald Downs, Wa.
40 Fon—Fonner Park, Ne.
43 GF—Great Falls, Mt.
48 GPR—Evergreen Park, Ab.
49 GrP—Grant's Pass, Or.
54 HPO—Horsemen's Park, Ne.

55 Hst—Hastings Race Course, B.C.
57 Kam—Kamloops, B.C.
60 Kin—Kin Park, B.C.
61 Ksp—Northwest Montana Fair, Mt.
64 LBG—Whoop-Up Downs, Ab.
65 LnN—Lincoln County Fair, Ne.
68 MaF—Maria's Fair, Mt.
70 MC—Cow Capital Turf Club, Mt.
71 MD—Marquis Downs, Sk.
79 NP—Northlands Park, Ab.
86 PM—Portland Meadows, Or.

94 Rup—Rupert Downs, Id.
104 StP—Stampede Park, Ab.
105 SuD—Sun Downs, Wa.
110 TIL—Tillamook County Fair, Or.
114 UN—Eastern Oregon Livestock Show, Or.
116 WMF—Western Montana Fair, Mt.
119 WTS—Waitsburg Race Track, Wa.
120 WW—Walla Walla, Wa.
121 Wyo—Wyoming Downs, Wy.
123 YD—Yellowstone Downs, Mt.
124 Ykt—Yorktown Exhibition, Sk.

West & Southwest

1 Alb—Downs at Albuquerque, N.M.
2 AnF—Anthony Downs, Ks.
5 ArP—Arapahoe Park, Co.
11 BM—Bay Meadows Race Course, Ca.
12 Bmf—Bay Meadows Fair, Ca.
14 BRD—Blue Ribbon Downs, Ok.
24 DG—Cochise County Fair, Az.
25 Dmr—Del Mar, Ca.
26 DUN—Greenlee County Fair, Az.
28 Elk—Elko County Fair, Nv.
31 Eur—Eureka Downs, Ks.
34 Fer—Ferndale, Ca.
37 FLG—Coconino County Fair, Az.
38 FMT—Fair Meadows at Tulsa, Ok.
39 Fno—Fresno, Ca.
42 Fpx—Fairplex Park, Ca.
44 GG—Golden Gate Fields, Ca.
45 Gil—Gillespie County Fair, Tx.
51 Hol—Hollywood Park, Ca.

53 Hou—Sam Houston Race Park, Tx.
62 LA—Los Alamitos, Ca.
67 LS—Lone Star Park, Tx.
69 Man—Manor Downs, Tx.
73 Mex—Hipodromo de las Americas, Mex.
75 MOF—Mohave County Fair, Az.
85 Pln—Pleasanton, Ca.
89 Ret—Retama Park, Tx.
90 Ril—Rillito Park, Az.
92 RP—Remington Park, Ok.
93 Rui—Ruidoso Downs, N.M.
95 SA—Santa Anita Park, Ca.
96 Sac—Sacramento, Ca.
97 SAF—Graham County Fair, Az.
99 Sol—Vallejo, Ca.
100 SON—Santa Cruz County Fair, Az.
101 SR—Santa Rosa, Ca.

102 SRP—SunRay Park, N.M.
103 Stk—Stockton, Ca.
106 Sun—Sunland Park, N.M.
113 TuP—Turf Paradise, Az.
115 Wds—Woodlands, Ks.
118 WRD—Will Rogers Downs, Ok.
122 Yav—Yavapai Downs, Az.

Abbreviations and Locations

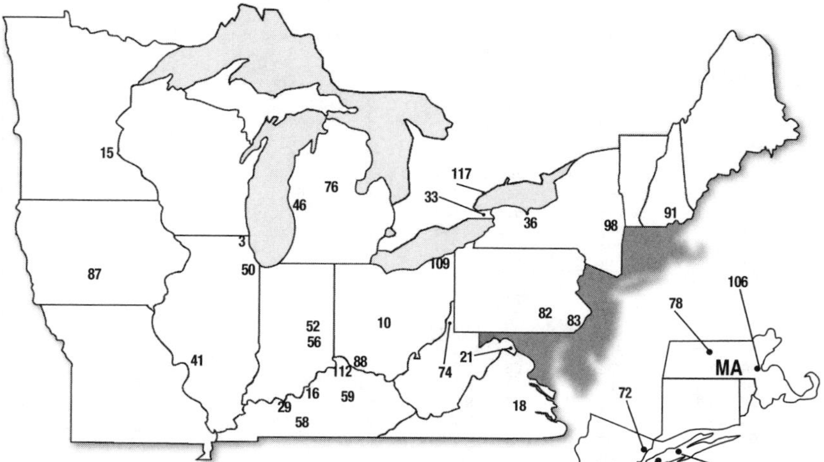

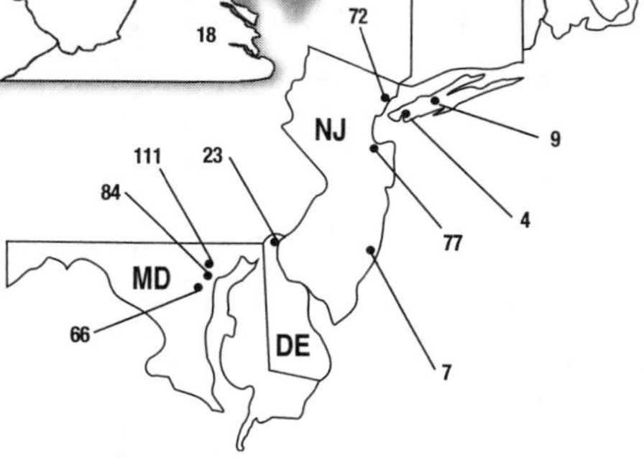

15

117

46 76 33

3 36 98 91

50 109

87 106

78

82 83

52 10

56

41 88 21 72 MA

16 12 74 18

29 59

58 NJ 9

Northeast & Midwest

111 23 4

84 77

3 AP—Arlington Park, Ill.
4 Aqu—Aqueduct, N.Y.
6 AsD—Assiniboia Downs, Mb.
7 Atl—Atlantic City Race Course, N.J.
9 Bel—Belmont Park, N.Y.
10 Beu—Beulah Park, Oh.
15 Cby—Canterbury Park, Mn.
16 CD—Churchill Downs, Ky.
18 Cnl—Colonial Downs, Va.
21 CT—Charlestown Races, W.V.
23 Del—Delaware Park, De.
29 EIP—Ellis Park, Ky.
33 FE—Fort Erie, On.
36 FL—Finger Lakes, N.Y.
41 FP—Fairmount Park, Il.
46 GLD—Great Lakes Downs, Mi.
50 Haw—Hawthorne Park, Il.
52 Hoo—Hoosier Park, In.
56 Ind—Indiana Downs, In.
58 KD—Kentucky Downs, Ky.

MD 66

DE 7

59 Kee—Keeneland Race Course, Ky.
66 Lrl—Laurel Park, Md.
72 Med—Meadowlands, N.J.
74 Mnr—Mountaineer Race Track, W.V.
76 MPM—Mount Pleasant Meadows, Mi.
77 Mth—Monmouth Park, N.J.
78 Nmp—Northampton Fair, Ma.
82 Pen—Penn National Race Course, Pa.
83 Pha—Philadelphia Park, Pa.
84 Pim—Pimlico Race Course, Md.

87 PrM—Prairie Meadows Racetrack, Ia.
88 RD—River Downs, Oh.
91 Rkm—Rockingham Park, N.H.
98 Sar—Saratoga Race Course, N.Y.
106 Suf—Suffolk Downs, Ma.
109 Tdn—Thistledown, Oh.
111 Tim—Timonium, Md.
112 TP—Turfway Park, Ky.
117 WO—Woodbine, On.

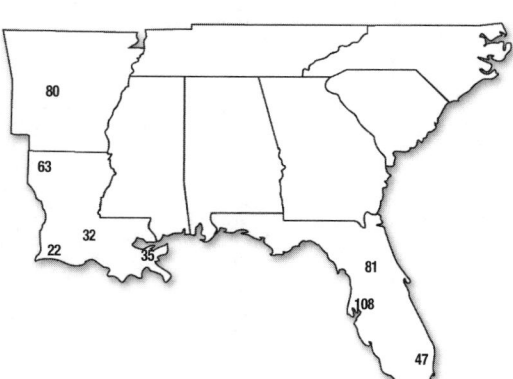

80

63

32

22 35 81

108

47

Southeast

20 Crc—Calder Race Course, Fl.
22 DeD—Delta Downs, La.
27 EIC—El Comandante, P.R.
32 Evd—Evangeline Downs, La.
35 FG—Fair Grounds, La.
47 GP—Gulfstream Park, Fl.
63 LaD—Louisiana Downs, La.
80 OP—Oaklawn Park, Ar.
81 OTC—Ocala Training Center, Fl.
108 Tam—Tampa Bay Downs, Fl.

North American Purse Distribution by Year

Year	No. of runners	No. of races	Total purses	Average purse	Per Runner Average	Median
2004	73,915	58,686	$1,177,769,795	$20,069	$15,934	$5,877
2003	73,614	58,813	1,154,238,845	19,626	15,680	5,714
2002	72,504	59,712	1,170,169,267	19,597	16,139	6,003
2001	70,942	60,538	1,146,337,367	18,936	16,159	6,010
2000	69,230	60,579	1,093,661,241	18,053	15,798	5,796
1999	68,435	60,118	1,008,162,608	16,770	14,732	5,310
1998	68,419	61,141	968,366,929	15,838	14,153	4,939
1997	69,067	63,491	888,667,752	13,997	12,867	4,425
1996	70,371	64,263	845,916,706	13,163	12,021	3,937
1995	72,316	68,197	815,987,125	11,965	11,283	3,702
1994	74,939	70,617	770,426,193	10,910	10,280	3,314
1993	78,763	72,224	748,415,925	10,362	9,502	2,850
1992	83,468	77,711	771,136,296	9,989	9,238	2,731
1991	86,483	78,671	761,446,198	9,679	8,805	2,433
1990	89,722	79,971	775,006,519	9,691	8,637	2,376
1989	91,436	82,726	771,421,230	9,325	8,437	2,218
1988	90,482	79,589	736,698,230	9,256	8,142	2,127
1987	89,504	80,376	704,372,435	8,763	7,870	2,101
1986	86,022	77,732	661,826,092	8,514	7,694	2,070
1985	82,548	75,687	641,658,553	8,478	7,773	2,158
1984	78,253	74,396	599,348,425	8,056	7,659	2,345
1983	74,540	71,034	544,260,167	7,662	7,302	2,435
1982	69,505	71,515	526,587,096	7,363	7,576	2,703
1981	65,797	70,881	507,007,953	7,153	7,706	2,865
1980	64,499	68,236	449,631,322	6,589	6,971	2,524
1979	63,728	69,406	414,629,063	5,974	6,506	2,440
1978	62,937	69,498	367,163,242	5,283	5,834	n/a
1977	61,960	68,826	335,720,312	4,878	5,418	2,189
1976	61,084	69,480	318,680,094	4,587	5,217	2,100
1975	58,818	68,203	291,194,571	4,270	4,951	2,058
1974	56,524	65,288	262,942,547	4,027	4,652	1,904
1973	54,812	62,264	233,662,724	3,753	4,263	1,764
1972	52,561	59,417	210,435,265	3,542	4,004	1,647

Data reflect all Thoroughbred purses distributed to racehorses in North America, excluding Mexico and Puerto Rico, from Jockey Club Information Systems data. Steeplechase races are excluded.

Top 25 Race Meetings
by Average Attendance in 2004

Rank	Meet	Racing Dates	Total Attendance	Average Attendance
1	Saratoga Race Course	36	$963,432	26,762
2	Del Mar	43	733,237	17,052
3	Keeneland Race Course (Spring)	17	232,826	15,522
4	Fairplex Park	17	102,255	13,711
5	Keeneland Race Course (Fall)	17	227,620	13,389
6	Oaklawn Park	55	706,328	12,842
7	Churchill Downs (Spring)	53	633,616	11,955
8	Oak Tree at Santa Anita	26	241,016	9,270
9	Lone Star Park	63	*548,100	*8,700
10	Hollywood Park (Spring)	65	542,597	8,348
11	Belmont Park (Spring)	60	499,166	8,319
12	Santa Anita Park	86	677,193	7,874
13	Bay Meadows (Spring)	71	427,290	7,769
14	Arlington Park	96	726,923	7,572
15	Churchill Downs (Fall)	21	156,305	7,467
16	Monmouth Park	87	790,433	7,085
17	Laurel Park	62	419,094	6,870
18	Hollywood Park (Fall)	36	223,766	6,216
19	Bay Meadows (Fall)	33	290,447	5,927
20	Belmont Park (Fall)	33	171,251	5,189
21	Canterbury Park	68	333,457	4,977
22	Los Alamitos	203	932,609	4,663
23	Calder Race Course	123	544,745	4,429
24	Tropical Park at Calder	55	242,420	4,408
25	Retama Park	39	162,591	4,169

*Including Breeders' Cup World Championships day

Top 25 Race Meetings by Average All-Sources Wagering in 2004

Rank	Meet	Racing Dates	Total All-Sources Wagering	Average All-Sources Wagering
1	Saratoga Race Course	36	$545,171,412	$15,810,827
2	Del Mar	43	580,375,067	13,497,095
3	Belmont Park (Spring)	60	725,208,823	12,086,814
4	Churchill Downs (Spring)	53	593,817,958	11,204,112
5	Gulfstream Park	86	787,846,000	9,161,000
6	Belmont Park (Fall)	33	299,763,265	9,083,735
7	Keeneland Race Course (Spring)	17	136,181,075	9,078,739
8	Hollywood Park (Spring)	65	586,914,975	9,029,461
9	Aqueduct (Spring)	88	771,035,213	8,663,317
10	Oak Tree at Santa Anita	26	221,642,588	8,524,715
11	Aqueduct (Fall)	42	355,622,845	8,467,211
12	Santa Anita Park	86	706,947,483	8,317,029
13	Churchill Downs (Fall)	21	163,776,216	7,798,867
14	Hollywood Park (Fall)	36	272,795,855	7,577,663
15	Keeneland Race Course (Fall)	17	118,377,987	6,963,411
16	Oaklawn Park	55	288,159,518	5,239,263
17	Pimlico Race Course (Spring)	48	265,000,000	4,862,000
18	Fairplex Park	17	74,250,009	4,467,647
19	Tropical Park at Calder	55	240,373,189	4,370,422
20	Monmouth Park	87	364,595,940	4,197,758
21	Arlington Park	96	402,308,299	4,190,711
22	Fair Grounds	82	343,168,377	4,184,980
23	Laurel Park	62	245,400,000	3,958,065
24	Bay Meadows (Spring)	71	215,984,763	3,926,996
25	Bay Meadows (Fall)	33	168,458,900	3,437,937

Top 25 Race Meetings by Average On-Track Wagering in 2004

Rank	Meet	Racing Dates	Total On-Track Wagering	Average On-Track Wagering
1	Saratoga Race Course	36	$116,729,508	$3,242,486
2	Del Mar	43	102,242,996	2,377,744
3	Oak Tree at Santa Anita	26	50,959,066	1,959,964
4	Pimlico Race Course (Spring)	48	115,228,116	1,772,700
5	Hollywood Park (Spring)	65	113,796,028	1,750,708
6	Churchill Downs (Spring)	53	87,145,043	1,644,246
7	Keeneland Race Course (Spring)	17	21,741,390	1,449,426
8	Monmouth Park	87	117,244,821	1,347,641
9	Santa Anita Park	86	112,863,967	1,327,811
10	Aqueduct (Spring)	88	114,661,459	1,288,331
11	Hollywood Park (Fall)	36	46,270,068	1,285,280
12	Pimlico Race Course (Fall)	16	35,400,000	1,266,000
13	Keeneland Race Course (Fall)	17	19,999,000	1,176,412
14	Churchill Downs (Fall)	21	23,105,268	1,100,251
15	Belmont Park (Fall)	33	34,831,133	1,055,489
16	Oaklawn Park	55	57,867,109	1,052,129
17	Bay Meadows (Spring)	71	44,508,557	809,246
18	Aqueduct (Fall)	42	29,388,457	699,725
19	Bay Meadows (Fall)	33	30,970,050	632,042
20	Tampa Bay Downs	94	57,642,806	619,815
21	Arlington Park	96	55,652,458	579,713
22	Lone Star Park	63	*34,020,000	*540,000
23	Fairplex Park	17	11,435,086	530,437
24	Canterbury Park	68	35,402,364	528,394
25	Tropical Park at Calder	55	24,297,975	441,781

*Including Breeders' Cup World Championships day

Revenues to States From Horse Racing

For a few decades, horse racing was the golden goose for state governments, as shown in the table of current-dollar revenues prepared by the Association of Racing Commissioners International. The revenues cover all forms of horse racing, but a substantial portion of the total is derived from Thoroughbred racing.

When the effects of inflation are removed from the figures using the United States Commerce Department's gross domestic product implicit price deflator, the peak period for state taxation of horse racing was from 1962 through '80, when inflation-adjusted state revenues exceeded $1.3-billion annually. State revenues topped out in 1975 at $2.1-billion in deflated dollars.

In both current and inflation-adjusted dollars, state revenues began a sharp decline in the 1980s as states reduced their pari-mutuel tax rates. By 1983, inflation-adjusted revenues had fallen below $1-billion, and by 1995 those revenues had slipped below $500-million. With two exceptions, 1990 and '95, current-dollar revenues to the state have declined from the preceding 12 months in every year since 1988.

Year	Current Dollars	Deflated Dollars
1965	$369,892,036	$1,641,411,298
1964	350,095,928	1,581,925,480
1963	316,570,791	1,452,292,830
1962	287,930,030	1,334,925,263
1961	264,853,077	1,244,727,310
1960	258,039,385	1,226,364,645
1959	243,388,655	1,172,900,848
1958	222,049,651	1,083,274,715
1957	216,747,621	1,081,682,907
1956	207,456,272	1,069,748,218
1955	186,989,588	997,650,259
1954	178,015,828	966,584,286
1953	167,426,465	917,757,304
1952	142,489,696	790,643,081
1951	117,250,564	661,759,589
1950	98,366,167	595,040,633
1949	95,327,053	582,968,768
1948	95,803,364	584,808,717
1947	97,926,984	631,542,525
1946	94,035,859	672,357,064
1945	65,265,405	522,541,273
1944	55,971,233	460,062,740
1943	38,194,727	321,342,142
1942	22,005,278	195,099,548
1941	21,128,173	201,893,674
1940	16,145,182	164,612,378
1939	10,369,807	106,960,361
1938	9,576,335	97,817,518
1937	8,434,792	83,653,595
1936	8,611,538	89,100,238
1935	8,386,255	87,740,688
1934	6,024,193	64,292,348

Revenue to States from Horse Racing

Year	Current Dollars	Deflated Dollars
2002	$346,799,090	$333,637,106
2001	351,511,182	343,363,174
2000	367,786,590	367,786,590
1999	392,201,085	400,744,968
1998	431,722,361	447,510,533
1997	441,768,972	463,002,255
1996	443,882,538	472,960,127
1995	455,764,292	494,825,844
1994	451,546,549	500,278,697
1993	471,735,474	533,752,135
1992	491,259,606	568,686,237
1991	523,249,392	619,640,699
1990	623,839,806	764,603,268
1989	584,888,183	744,549,344
1988	596,202,319	787,648,055
1987	608,351,461	831,126,648
1986	587,357,677	824,361,652
1985	625,159,697	896,762,006
1984	650,262,852	961,145,299
1983	641,387,176	983,617,060
1982	652,888,463	1,040,857,799
1981	680,199,584	1,150,560,030
1980	712,727,523	1,318,815,615
1979	680,919,798	1,374,262,933
1978	673,063,831	1,470,952,709
1977	700,239,986	1,637,911,644
1976	714,629,120	1,777,861,280
1975	780,081,431	2,052,737,832
1974	645,980,984	1,860,276,412
1973	585,201,524	1,837,425,112
1972	531,404,550	1,761,600,975
1971	512,838,417	1,773,852,226
1970	486,403,097	1,766,554,431
1969	461,498,886	1,764,881,586
1968	426,856,448	1,713,388,384
1967	394,381,913	1,650,616,971
1966	388,452,125	1,676,096,501

Minimum Age to Attend and Wager at U.S. Racetracks

State	Minimum Age	Legal Wagering Age
Arizona	None	18
Arkansas	Under 16 with adult	18
California	None	18
Colorado	None	18
Delaware	Under 18 with adult	18
Florida	Under 18 with adult	18
Idaho	None	18
Illinois	Under 17 with adult	17
Indiana	Under 17 with adult	18
Iowa	Under 18 with adult	21
Kansas	Under 18 with adult	18
Kentucky	None	18
Louisiana	6	21
Maryland	None	18
Massachusetts	None	18
Michigan	None	18
Minnesota	Under 18 with adult	18
Montana	None	18
Nebraska	Under 18 with adult	19
New Hampshire	Under 18 with adult	18
New Jersey	Under 18 with adult	18
New Mexico	Under 18 with adult	18
New York	Under 18 with adult	18
Ohio	Under 18 with adult	18
Oklahoma	6	18
Oregon	12 after 6 p.m.	18
Pennsylvania	None	18
Puerto Rico	None	18
Texas	Under 16 with adult	21
Virginia	None	18
Washington	None	18
West Virginia	None	18
Wyoming	None	19

PEOPLE
Leading Owners of 2004

Along with bettors, Thoroughbred owners are the primary source of the billions of dollars of investments that make the Thoroughbred industry the living, breathing, wonderful thing that it is. Owners spend well over $1-billion annually purchasing Thoroughbreds of various descriptions at public auctions and by private contract, thus taking on the privilege and responsibility of paying further untold sums for their training, veterinary care, board, and other expenses. In return, owners in North America get a shot at roughly $1-billion annually in purses.

Total purses are divided among thousands of owners but, in the natural order of things, some do better than others. The following lists rate the accomplishments of owners in 2004 according to various criteria. The annual THOROUGHBRED TIMES leading owners list ranks owners according to three equally weighted criteria: 1) total earnings, 2) average earnings per starter, and 3) total number of winners. That weighted list purposely favors quality over quantity.

Leading Owners by Purses Won
North American Earnings Only

Year	Name	Wins	Earnings
2004	Michael J. Gill	486	$10,811,211
2003	Michael J. Gill	425	9,236,530
2002	Stronach Stables	122	8,347,017
2001	Richard A. Englander	405	9,784,822
2000	Stronach Stables	162	11,133,785
1999	Stronach Stables	124	6,221,147
1998	Stronach Stables	91	7,221,416
1997	Allen E. Paulson	66	5,259,107
1996	Allen E. Paulson	88	6,686,629
1995	Allen E. Paulson	62	5,626,396
1994	Golden Eagle Farm	95	3,674,692
1993	Golden Eagle Farm	102	3,613,828
1992	Golden Eagle Farm	112	4,487,959
1991	Sam-Son Farm	29	3,613,473
1990	Kinghaven Farms	66	5,041,280
1989	Ogden Phipps	25	5,438,034
1988	Ogden Phipps	35	5,858,168
1987	Eugene V. Klein	81	4,904,247
1986	John Franks	250	4,463,115
1985	Hunter Farm	10	3,662,989
1984	John Franks	172	3,073,036
1983	John Franks	183	2,645,884
1982	Viola Sommer	136	2,183,706
1981	Elmendorf	57	1,928,102
1980	Harbor View Farm	103	2,208,901

THOROUGHBRED TIMES Leading Owners of 2004

Rankings based on formula that gives equal weighting to three statistical categories for performance in 2004: 1) total earnings; 2) average earnings per starter; and 3) total number of winners. A minimum of ten starters is required to be considered for inclusion. Names of owners are of individual property lines as reported by the Jockey Club. No attempt was made to consolidate names where an owner had more than one partnership or property line. Statistics are for North America only and for racing in 2004.

Rank	Owner	No. Strs	No. Wnrs	No. SWs	SWs/ Strs	No. GSWs	GSWs/ Strs	Total Earnings	Average Earnings/ Starter	Leading Earner	Earnings of Leading Earner
1	Sam-Son Farm	58	28	8	13.8%	7	12.1%	$4,830,939	$83,292	Soaring Free	$1,113,862
2	Eugene and Laura Melnyk	113	62	8	7.1%	3	2.7%	4,446,767	39,352	Speightstown	1,045,556
3	Stronach Stables	143	67	9	6.3%	4	2.8%	7,189,592	50,277	Ghostzapper	2,590,000
4	Heiligbrodt Racing Stable	75	44	7	9.3%	4	5.3%	2,997,977	39,973	Lady Tak	439,412
5	Robert and Beverly Lewis	67	31	7	10.5%	5	7.5%	3,043,330	45,423	Consolidator	480,260
6	Juddmonte Farms	33	20	6	18.2%	6	18.2%	3,454,794	104,691	Sightseek	1,011,350
7	Pin Oak Stable	42	26	5	11.9%	2	4.8%	2,013,577	47,942	I Thee Wed	314,337
8	Ken and Sarah Ramsey	114	55	5	4.4%	2	2.6%	5,784,964	50,745	Roses in May	1,723,277
9	Dogwood Stable	60	37	6	10.0%	2	3.3%	1,786,556	29,776	Limehouse	367,000
10	Jay Em Ess Stable	41	21	5	12.2%	3	7.3%	2,284,103	55,710	Declan's Moon	507,300
11	Live Oak Plantation	50	33	4	8.0%		0.0%	1,939,052	38,781	Broadway View	180,213
12	Robert D. Bone	119	64	4	3.4%	2	1.7%	3,014,791	25,334	Stage Player	383,645
13	Padua Stables	46	23	6	13.0%	4	8.7%	1,847,253	40,158	Proud Accolade	364,130
14	Richard A. Englander	106	52	4	3.8%		0.0%	2,438,549	23,005	My Cousin Matt	208,200
15	Michael J. Gill	604	290	13	2.2%	1	0.2%	10,811,211	17,899	Umpateedle	216,160
16	Maggi Moss	108	62	5	4.6%		0.0%	1,986,173	18,390	Fine Stormy	126,456
17	Edmund A. Gann	20	13	8	40.0%	7	35.0%	2,639,725	131,986	Peace Rules	1,024,288
18	Gary A. Tanaka	36	14	5	13.9%	4	11.1%	3,112,187	86,450	Pico Central (Brz)	1,013,000
19	Rosendo G. Parra	93	47	4	4.3%	1	1.1%	2,096,019	22,538	Even the Score	343,272
20	Darley Stable	65	25	4	6.2%	3	4.6%	2,234,797	34,381	Balletto (UAE)	614,000
21	Overbrook Farm	82	39	3	3.7%		0.0%	2,256,719	27,521	Clock Stopper	292,725
22	Flying Zee Stable	93	49	3	3.2%		0.0%	2,218,064	23,850	Golden Commander	133,149
23	Edward P. Evans	54	23	5	9.3%	1	1.9%	1,981,871	36,700	Gygistar	295,320
24	Everest Stables Inc.	63	24	4	6.4%	1	1.6%	2,036,755	32,329	Island Fashion	615,000
25	Tracy Farmer	21	16	3	14.3%	1	4.8%	1,823,046	86,812	Sir Shackleton	566,105
26	Stoneside Stable	40	17	7	17.5%	2	5.0%	1,560,244	39,006	Danieltown	279,361
27	Gumpster Stable	105	57	2	1.9%		0.0%	2,142,198	20,402	Clever Electrician	220,870
28	Buckram Oak Farm	67	40	2	3.0%	1	1.5%	1,919,336	28,647	Last Song	205,520
29	Golden Eagle Farm	69	29	2	2.9%	1	1.5%	2,105,726	30,518	Yearly Report	787,500
30	Paranack Stable	73	34	2	2.7%		0.0%	2,004,251	27,455	Song of the Sword	258,600
31	Mrs. E. Paul Robsham	31	19	4	12.9%	2	6.5%	1,420,947	45,837	Canadian Frontier	194,562

Rank	Owner	No. Strs	No. Wnrs	No. SWs	SWs/ Strs	No. GSWs	GSWs/ Strs	Total Earnings	Average Earnings/ Starter	Leading Earner	Earnings of Leading Earner
32	Dale Baird	221	97		0.0%		0.0%	$2,002,813	$9,063	Free Expresso	$77,449
33	Frank D. Di Giulio Jr.	21	12	4	19.1%	2	9.5%	1,748,615	83,267	Brass in Pocket	371,038
34	Augustin Stable	66	26	3	4.6%	1	1.5%	1,517,857	22,998	My Pal Lana	220,075
35	K. K. Sangara	36	21	3	8.3%	1	2.8%	1,371,131	38,087	Sweet Problem	249,205
36	Stan E. Fulton	54	20	3	5.6%	2	3.7%	1,726,957	31,981	Fire Slam	427,381
37	Mr. and Mrs. Martin J. Wygod	43	16	3	7.0%	3	7.0%	1,753,972	40,790	Sweet Catomine	799,800
38	John D. Murphy	54	32	3	5.6%		0.0%	1,140,793	21,126	The Lady's Groom	262,520
39	Steven M. Asmussen	138	80	1	0.7%		0.0%	1,490,707	10,802	Promise of War	52,820
40	Dominion Bloodstock, Derek Ball, and Hugh Galbraith	35	21	2	5.7%		0.0%	1,370,014	39,143	Moonshine Justice	283,914
41	James McIngvale	19	11	4	21.1%	2	10.5%	1,396,671	73,509	Wimbledon	412,400
42	Louis D. O'Brien	133	101	1	0.8%		0.0%	1,407,559	10,583	Moe B Dick	68,258
43	Mary and Chester Broman	38	19	2	5.3%	1	2.6%	1,487,891	39,155	Friends Lake	611,800
44	Bruno Schickedanz	110	54		0.0%		0.0%	1,452,233	13,202	The King N Rob	130,200
45	Frank Carl Calabrese	130	56	1	0.8%		0.0%	1,295,698	9,967	Nebraska Moon	103,760
46	Danny J. Chen	111	67		0.0%		0.0%	1,216,464	10,959	Rose of Etbauer	52,000
47	B. Wayne Hughes	50	22	2	4.0%	1	2.0%	1,269,571	25,391	Teton Forest	222,000
48	Puglisi Stables	31	16	3	9.7%		0.0%	1,101,587	35,535	Misty Sixes	246,074
49	J. Paul Reddam	31	16	3	9.7%	2	6.5%	1,140,168	36,780	Tangle (Ire)	218,669
50	Robert V. LaPenta	13	9	2	15.4%	2	15.4%	2,001,302	153,946	The Cliff's Edge	1,010,000
51	Marylou Whitney Stables	19	11	2	10.5%	2	10.5%	1,628,890	85,731	Birdstone	1,236,600
52	Peter Vegso	34	20	2	5.9%	2	5.9%	1,164,891	34,262	Silver Tree	328,060
53	Franks Farms	85	26	2	2.4%	1	1.2%	1,260,812	14,833	Adreamisborn	251,740
54	Ogden Mills Phipps	16	9	3	18.8%	3	18.8%	1,780,647	111,290	Daydreaming	483,180
55	Valene Farms	28	19	4	14.3%		0.0%	858,357	30,656	Outright Buck	152,300
56	G. Watts Humphrey Jr.	59	23	3	5.1%		0.0%	1,073,816	18,200	Rey de Cafe	113,204
57	William S. Farish	28	15	3	10.7%	1	3.6%	1,044,381	37,299	Midway Road	372,015
58	Klaravich Stables Inc.	23	14	2	8.7%	1	4.4%	1,178,597	51,243	Swingforthefences	385,745
59	Michael B. Tabor	14	8	4	28.6%	2	14.3%	1,877,867	134,133	Magistretti	764,000
60	Harris Farms Inc.	40	20	2	5.0%	1	2.5%	1,103,810	27,595	Alphabet Kisses	326,910
61	Willmott Stables Inc.	18	10	4	22.2%	2	11.1%	1,352,569	75,143	Eddington	605,360
62	Jayeff B Stables	46	21	2	4.4%		0.0%	1,075,404	23,378	Schedule (GB)	102,240
63	M. Y. Stables Inc.	55	29	4	7.3%		0.0%	764,459	13,899	Ben's Reflection	109,880
64	Edward E. Turner	84	38		0.0%		0.0%	1,136,940	13,535	Trumpets Delight	82,963
65	Mr. and Mrs. Jerome S. Moss	57	25	1	1.8%	1	1.8%	1,185,965	20,806	Belleski	136,567
66	New Farm	23	17	2	8.7%	1	4.4%	929,275	40,403	Wildcat Heir	305,860
67	Turf Express Inc.	107	48	1	0.9%		0.0%	990,830	9,260	Intelligent Male	130,684
68	John D. Gunther	18	9	3	16.7%	3	16.7%	1,350,580	75,032	Bending Strings	495,150
69	Alpine Stable Ltd.	47	23	1	2.1%		0.0%	1,166,006	24,809	Chris's Bad Boy	261,480
70	Tucci Stables	21	14	1	4.8%	1	4.8%	1,198,671	57,080	One for Rose	489,832
71	Gary Owens	102	51	2	2.0%		0.0%	918,582	9,006	The Niner Account	120,210
72	Amerman Racing Stables	32	13	1	3.1%	1	3.1%	1,454,199	45,444	Adoration	607,304
73	Gilbert G. Campbell	36	22	2	5.6%	1	2.8%	873,245	24,257	Friel's for Real	204,450
74	Kagele Brothers Inc.	42	31	2	4.8%		0.0%	760,393	18,105	Pie N Burger	112,000
75	Monarch Stables Inc.	58	36		0.0%		0.0%	976,129	16,830	Joann Jr	98,890
76	Michael H. Sherman	84	41		0.0%		0.0%	953,833	11,355	Gloried Dancer	72,640
77	James W. and Marcia S. Equils	65	27		0.0%		0.0%	995,369	15,313	Direct Male	61,200
78	Runnin Horse Farm Inc.	43	23	1	2.3%		0.0%	972,398	22,614	Hotstufanthensome	124,050
79	Robert L. Cole Jr.	51	31	1	2.0%	1	2.0%	911,082	17,864	Shake You Down	278,604
80	J D Farms	22	12	3	13.6%		0.0%	920,455	41,839	Secret Request	355,250
81	Joseph V. Shields Jr.	13	11	3	23.1%	2	15.4%	835,148	64,242	Passing Shot	185,460
82	Jerry Hollendorfer and George Todaro	80	42		0.0%		0.0%	879,905	10,999	Raise the Heat	91,213
83	Kelynack Racing Stable Inc.	34	14	1	2.9%		0.0%	1,175,422	34,571	Heyahohowdy	186,067
84	Aaron U. and Marie D. Jones	16	10	3	18.8%	1	6.3%	960,621	60,039	Value Plus	220,900
85	Ogden Mills Phipps, et al.	10	8	2	20.0%	1	10.0%	1,020,649	102,065	Storm Flag Flying	563,248
86	Richard, Bertram, and Elaine Klein	40	13	2	5.0%	1	2.5%	991,126	24,778	G P Fleet	247,786
87	Gustav Schickedanz	18	10	3	16.7%	1	5.6%	954,606	53,034	Mobil	440,213
88	Kinsman Stable	28	15	3	10.7%	2	7.1%	744,677	26,596	Ebony Breeze	255,360
89	Peachtree Stable	25	16	1	4.0%		0.0%	913,993	36,560	Flamenco	303,085
90	Team Block	23	11	2	8.7%	1	4.4%	972,618	42,288	Mystery Giver	470,390
91	Jack J. Armstrong	76	39		0.0%		0.0%	798,903	10,512	Carried Away	44,477
92	Pyrite Stables	50	25	2	4.0%		0.0%	716,156	14,323	Tour the Hive	88,558
93	Glen Hill Farm	30	15	3	10.0%		0.0%	734,532	24,484	Indy Groove	160,545
94	Allen E. Paulson Living Trust	13	8	1	7.7%	1	7.7%	1,396,642	107,434	Azeri	1,035,000
95	Erdenheim Farm	26	13	2	7.7%	1	3.9%	807,398	31,054	Play Bingo	172,230
96	Nelson Bunker Hunt	34	17	2	5.9%		0.0%	767,765	22,581	Souris	166,150
97	Mercedes Stables LLC	19	11	2	10.5%	2	10.5%	923,998	48,631	Laura's Lucky Boy	246,730
98	Courtlandt Farms	24	12	2	8.3%	1	4.2%	808,845	33,702	Film Maker	422,000
99	Jacks or Better Farm Inc.	33	16	3	9.1%		0.0%	709,102	21,488	Hear No Evil	182,500
100	Martin S. Schwartz	10	8	2	20.0%		0.0%	943,070	94,307	Bowman's Band	439,334

Leading Owners by Earnings in 2004

Owner	No. Strs	No. Wnrs	Total Earnings
Michael J. Gill	604	290	$10,811,211
Someday Farm	4	2	7,584,305
Stronach Stables	143	67	7,189,592
Ken and Sarah Ramsey	114	55	5,784,964
Sam-Son Farm	58	28	4,830,939
Eugene and Laura Melnyk	113	62	4,446,767
Juddmonte Farms	33	20	3,454,794
Gary A. Tanaka	36	14	3,112,187
Robert and Beverly Lewis	67	31	3,043,330
Robert D. Bone	119	64	3,014,791
Heiligbrodt Racing Stable	75	44	2,997,977
Starlight Stables, Paul Saylor, and Johns Martin	3	2	2,672,374
Edmund A. Gann	20	13	2,639,725
Richard A. Englander	106	52	2,438,549
Jay Em Ess Stable	41	21	2,284,103
Overbrook Farm	82	39	2,256,719
Darley Stable	65	25	2,234,797
Flying Zee Stable	93	49	2,218,064
Gumpster Stable LLC	105	57	2,142,198
Golden Eagle Farm	69	29	2,105,726
Rosendo G. Parra	93	47	2,096,019
Everest Stables	63	24	2,036,755
Pin Oak Stable	42	26	2,013,577
Paraneck Stable	73	34	2,004,251
Dale Baird	221	97	2,002,813
Robert V. LaPenta	13	9	2,001,302
Maggi Moss	108	62	1,986,173
Edward P. Evans	54	23	1,981,817
Live Oak Plantation	50	33	1,939,052
Buckram Oak Farm	67	40	1,919,336
Michael B. Tabor	14	8	1,877,867
Padua Stables	46	23	1,847,253
Michael Tabor and Derrick Smith	6	4	1,832,620
Tracy Farmer	21	16	1,823,046
Dogwood Stable	60	37	1,786,556
Ogden Mills Phipps	16	9	1,780,647
Mr. & Mrs. Martin J. Wygod	43	16	1,753,972
Frank D. Di Giulio Jr.	21	12	1,748,615
Stan E. Fulton	54	20	1,726,957

Leading Owners by Average Earnings per Starter in 2004

(Minimum of 10 Starters)

Owner	No. Strs	No. Wnrs	Average Earnings per Starter
Robert V. LaPenta	13	9	$153,946
Diamond A Racing Corp.	12	5	136,740
Michael B. Tabor	14	8	134,133
Edmund A. Gann	20	13	131,986
Marge and Irving Cowan	10	7	125,632
Ogden Mills Phipps	16	9	111,290
Allen Paulson Living Trust	13	8	107,434
Juddmonte Farms	33	20	104,691
Ogden Mills Phipps, et al.	10	8	102,065
Fox Ridge Farm Inc.	11	7	97,873
Chiefswood Stable	14	7	95,412
Martin S. Schwartz	10	8	94,307
Tracy Farmer	21	16	86,812
Gary A. Tanaka	36	14	86,450

Owner	No. Strs	No. Wnrs	Average Earnings per Starter
Marylou Whitney Stables	19	11	85,731
Brushwood Stable	11	6	85,425
Sam-Son Farm	58	28	83,292
Frank D. Di Giulio Jr.	21	12	83,267
Stonecrest Farm	12	4	77,212
Sheikh Maktoum bin Rashid al Maktoum	10	5	77,055
Willmott Stables Inc.	18	10	75,143
John D. Gunther	18	9	75,032
James McIngvale	19	11	73,509
Anstu Stables	13	8	69,134
Joseph Allen	12	7	68,049
Joseph V. Shields Jr.	13	11	64,242
Aaron U. and Marie D. Jones	16	10	60,039
Equirace.com LLC	10	3	57,972
Tucci Stables	21	14	57,080
Jay Em Ess Stable	41	21	55,710
T N T Stud	18	6	54,313
Gustav Schickedanz	18	10	53,034
Green Lantern Stables	10	5	51,453
Klaravich Stables	23	14	51,243
Ken and Sarah Ramsey	114	55	50,745
Stronach Stables	143	67	50,277
Michael House	10	7	49,120
Bruce Lunsford	13	4	48,741
Mercedes Stables	19	11	48,631

Leading Owners by Number of Stakes Winners in 2004

Owner	No. Strs	No. Wnrs	No. SWs
Michael J. Gill	604	290	13
Stronach Stables	143	67	9
Eugene and Laura Melnyk	113	62	8
Edmund A. Gann	20	13	8
Sam-Son Farm	58	28	8
Robert and Beverly Lewis	67	31	7
Stonerside Stable	40	17	7
Heiligbrodt Racing Stable	75	44	7
Padua Stables	46	23	6
Dogwood Stable	60	37	6
Juddmonte Farms	33	20	6
Ken and Sarah Ramsey	114	55	5
Edward P. Evans	54	23	5
Gary A. Tanaka	36	14	5
Pin Oak Stable	42	26	5
Maggi Moss	108	62	5
Dennis E. Weir	44	21	5
Jay Em Ess Stable	41	21	5
Frank D. Di Giulio Jr.	21	12	4
James McIngvale	19	11	4
Darley Stable	65	25	4
Willmott Stables Inc.	18	10	4
Kristine and John Richter	20	9	4
Richard A. Englander	106	52	4
M. Y. Stables Inc.	55	29	4
Michael B. Tabor	14	8	4
Everest Stables Inc.	63	24	4
Live Oak Plantation	50	33	4
Valene Farms	28	19	4
Rosendo G. Parra	93	47	4
Robert D. Bone	119	64	4
Mrs. E. Paul Robsham	31	19	4

Leading Owners by Stakes Wins in 2004

Owner	No. Stakes Starts	No. Stakes Wins
Michael J. Gill	157	20
Heiligbrodt Racing Stable	70	16
Eugene and Laura Melnyk	67	14
Sam-Son Farm	60	14
Juddmonte Farms	35	13
Ken and Sarah Ramsey	54	13
Stronach Stables	56	13
Edmund A. Gann	37	12
Robert and Beverly Lewis	58	11
Stonerside Stable	41	10
Dennis E. Weir	40	9
Frank D. DiGiulio Jr.	23	8
Everest Stables	71	8
Pin Oak Stable	46	8
Michael B. Tabor	21	8
Gary A. Tanaka	57	8
G. Chris Coleman	21	7
Dogwood Stable	42	7
Jay Em Ess Stable	21	7
J D Farms	33	7
Rosendo G. Parra	72	7
Caridad Inc.	28	6
Martin L. Cherry	24	6
Richard A. Englander	24	6
Edward P. Evans	49	6
Jim Ford, Deron Pearson, and Jack Sweesy	23	6
Franks Farms	38	6
Stan E. Fulton	30	6
Golden Eagle Farm	23	6
John D. Gunther	28	6
Arnold Heppner	13	6
Linwood Stables	14	6
M. Y. Stables	19	6
Padua Stables	30	6
Mrs. E. Paul Robsham	23	6
Howard and Penny Scarberry	26	6
Someday Farm	7	6
Starlight Stables, Paul Saylor, and Johns Martin	14	6
Michael Tabor and Derrick Smith	19	6
Larry R. Teague	9	6
Mr. and Mrs. Martin J. Wygod	13	6

Owner	No. Strs	No. Wnrs	No. SWs	SWs/ Strs
Sheikh Maktoum bin Rashid al Maktoum	10	5	2	20.0%
Kristine and John Richter	20	9	4	20.0%
Vincent Papandrea	10	7	2	20.0%
Ogden Mills Phipps, et al.	10	8	2	20.0%
Nico Nierenberg	10	6	2	20.0%
Swift Thoroughbreds	10	6	2	20.0%
Martin S. Schwartz	10	8	2	20.0%
Ronald C. Waranch	10	6	2	20.0%
Michael House	10	7	2	20.0%
Green Lantern Stables	10	5	2	20.0%
Peter Redekop B.C.	10	6	2	20.0%
Frank D. Di Giulio Jr.	21	12	4	19.1%
Aaron U. and Marie D. Jones	16	10	3	18.8%
Ogden Mills Phipps	16	9	3	18.8%
Fox Ridge Farm Inc.	11	7	2	18.2%
Richard P. Hogue Jr.	11	6	2	18.2%
Juddmonte Farms	33	20	6	18.2%
Lawrence Goichman	11	6	2	18.2%
Stoneway Farm LLC	11	6	2	18.2%
Canyon Farms	11	4	2	18.2%
William L. Hedrick	11	2	2	18.2%

Leading Owners by Number of Graded Stakes Winners in 2004

Owner	No. Strs	No. Wnrs	No. GSWs	GSWs/ Strs
Edmund A. Gann	20	13	7	35.0%
Sam-Son Farm	58	28	7	12.1%
Juddmonte Farms	33	20	6	18.2%
Robert and Beverly Lewis	67	31	5	7.5%
Gary A. Tanaka	36	14	4	11.1%
Heiligbrodt Racing Stable	75	44	4	5.3%
Padua Stables	46	23	4	8.7%
Stronach Stables	143	67	4	2.8%
Darley Stable	65	25	3	4.6%
Jay Em Ess Stable	41	21	3	7.3%
Eugene and Laura Melnyk	113	62	3	2.7%
Ken and Sarah Ramsey	114	55	3	2.6%
Ogden Mills Phipps	16	9	3	18.8%
Mr. & Mrs. Martin J. Wygod	43	16	3	7.0%
Joseph Allen	12	7	3	25.0%
John D. Gunther	18	9	3	16.7%
Michael Tabor and Derrick Smith	6	4	3	50.0%
Marsha Naify and Woodside Farms	7	4	2	28.6%
Noctis LLC, Neil Papiano, and Steve Taub	7	4	2	28.6%
Starlight Stables, Paul Saylor, and Johns Martin	3	2	2	66.7%
Mrs. E. Paul Robsham	31	19	2	6.5%
Stonerside Stable	40	17	2	5.0%
Robert D. Bone	119	64	2	1.7%
Moyglare Stud Farm	3	3	2	66.7%
Kinross Farm	20	8	2	10.0%
T N T Stud	18	6	2	11.1%
Michael B. Tabor	14	8	2	14.3%
Joseph V. Shields Jr.	13	11	2	15.4%
Prestonwood Farm	6	6	2	33.3%
Pin Oak Stable	42	26	2	4.8%
Godolphin Racing	6	2	2	33.3%
Kinsman Stable	28	15	2	7.1%
Dogwood Stable	60	37	2	3.3%
J. Paul Reddam	31	16	2	6.5%

Leading Owners by Percent of Stakes Winners from Starters in 2004
(Minimum of 10 Starters)

Owner	No. Strs	No. Wnrs	No. SWs	SWs/ Strs
Edmund A. Gann	20	13	8	40.0%
G. Chris Coleman	10	5	3	30.0%
Michael B. Tabor	14	8	4	28.6%
Sandra Hall Trust	11	9	3	27.3%
Joseph Allen	12	7	3	25.0%
Anstu Stables	13	8	3	23.1%
Margaret Root	13	5	3	23.1%
Joseph V. Shields Jr.	13	11	3	23.1%
Charles Cono	13	6	3	23.1%
Willmott Stables Inc.	18	10	4	22.2%
James McIngvale	19	11	4	21.1%
Rowell Enterprises Inc.	10	6	2	20.0%

Leading Owners by Graded Stakes Wins in 2004

Owner	No. Graded Stakes Starts	No. Graded Stakes Wins
Juddmonte Farms	33	13
Ken and Sarah Ramsey	37	11
Sam-Son Farm	39	11
Edmund A. Gann	31	9
Robert and Beverly Lewis	37	8
Stronach Stables	25	8
Heiligbrodt Racing Stable	19	7
Eugene and Laura Melnyk	28	7
Gary A. Tanaka	48	7
Starlight Stables, Paul Saylor, and Johns Martin	13	6
Michael Tabor and Derrick Smith	19	6
John D. Gunther	25	5
Jay Em Ess Stable	15	5
Mr. and Mrs. Martin J. Wygod	7	5
Joseph Allen	20	4
Bonnie and Sy Baskin	9	4
Edgewood Farm	12	4
Kinross Farm	7	4
Padua Stables	16	4
Ogden Mills Phipps	10	4
T N T Stud	10	4
Michael B. Tabor	12	4

Leading Owners by Most Grade 1 Stakes Wins in 2004

Owner	No. G1 Starts	No. G1 Wins
Gary A. Tanaka	27	6
Juddmonte Farms	17	5
Kenneth L. and Sarah K. Ramsey	13	4
Allen E. Paulson Living Trust	8	3
Edmund A. Gann	10	3
Starlight Stables, Paul Saylor, and Johns Martin	9	3
Michael Tabor and Derrick Smith	9	3
Mr. and Mrs. Martin J. Wygod	5	3
Blahut Stables, Kagele Brothers, Allen Tepper,, et al.	3	2
Marge and Irving M. Cowan	7	2
Diamond A Racing Corp.	7	2
Eldon Farm	6	2
Estate of Barracuda Stables	4	2
Godolphin Racing	4	2
Jim Ford, Deron Pearson, and Jack Sweesy	4	2
Kinross Farm	5	2
Robert B. and Beverly J. Lewis	8	2
Marylou Whitney Stables	4	2
Sam-Son Farm	13	2
Someday Farm	3	2
Spendthrift Farm, Chuck Kidder, Nancy Cole, and Nick Strong	8	2
Stronach Stables	4	2
Michael B. Tabor	5	2
The Two Bit Racing Stable	3	2

Leading Owners by Most Grade 1 Stakes Winners in 2004

Owner	No. G1 Starters	No. G1 Winners
Edmund A. Gann	6	3
Juddmonte Farms	10	3
Kenneth L. and Sarah K. Ramsey	7	3
Michael Tabor and Derrick Smith	4	3
Gary A. Tanaka	13	3
Diamond A Racing Corp.	3	2
Godolphin Racing	4	2
Robert B. and Beverly J. Lewis	3	2
Sam-Son Farm	9	2
Michael B. Tabor	2	2
Mr. and Mrs. Martin J. Wygod	3	2

Leading Owners by Number of Wins in 2004

Owner	No. Strs	No. Wnrs	No. Wins
Michael J. Gill	604	290	484
Louis D. O'Brien	133	101	230
Dale Baird	221	97	128
Steven M. Asmussen	138	80	122
Gumpster Stable LLC	105	57	114
Robert D. Bone	119	64	113
Danny J. Chen	111	67	110
Stronach Stables	143	67	108
Richard A. Englander	106	52	103
Bruno Schickedanz	110	54	101
Maggi Moss	108	62	98
Eugene and Laura Melnyk	113	62	93
Ken and Sarah Ramsey	114	55	83
Frank Carl Calabrese	130	56	83
Flying Zee Stable	93	49	79
Gary Owens	102	51	78
Monarch Stables Inc.	58	36	77
Heiligbrodt Racing Stable	75	44	75
M. Y. Stables Inc.	55	29	73
Rosendo G. Parra	93	47	70
Jack J. Armstrong	76	39	69
Joseph Clark Faulkner	48	30	68
Buddy Lee Racing Stable	71	46	66
Turf Express Inc.	107	48	66
Michael H. Sherman	84	41	64
Edward E. Turner	84	38	60
Jerry Hollendorfer and George Todaro	80	42	57
Rodney C. Faulkner	49	27	56
Billy Hays	78	38	55
Hwy 1 Racing Stable LLC	68	31	55
Jerry Hollendorfer	63	34	54
Overbrook Farm	82	39	54
R. Gary Patrick	60	32	53
Kagele Brothers Inc.	42	31	51
Robert L. Cole Jr.	51	31	50
Robert and Beverly Lewis	67	31	49

Most Wins for an Owner on One Day in 2004

Wins	Owner	Date	Track(s)
6	Michael J. Gill	1/2/2004	Aqu, CT, Lrl, SA
	Michael J. Gill	7/24/2004	Cnl, CT, Del, Mth, Suf
	Louis D. O'Brien	5/28/2004	AP, FP, Ind
5	Michael J. Gill	7/23/2004	Cnl, CT, Mth
	Michael J. Gill	7/17/2004	Cnl, CT, Del, Mth, Suf
	Michael J. Gill	9/10/2004	CT, Mth, Pim
	Michael J. Gill	6/12/2004	Cnl, CT, Mth, Suf
	Michael J. Gill	10/16/2004	Bel, CT, Del, LS, Med, Pha, Pim, Suf
	Michael J. Gill	12/17/2004	CT, FG, Pen, Pha, Pim

Most Wins for an Owner
on One Program in 2004

Wins	Owner	Date	Track
4	Michael J. Gill	1/15/2004	Lrl
	Michael J. Gill	5/14/2004	Pim
	Elaine M. Gross	3/20/2004	Beu
	Louis D. O'Brien	3/26/2004	FP
	Louis D. O'Brien	4/3/2004	FP

Wins	Owner	Date	Track
4	Louis D. O'Brien	4/6/2004	FP
	Louis D. O'Brien	4/17/2004	FP
	Louis D. O'Brien	5/11/2004	FP
	Louis D. O'Brien	7/20/2004	FP
	Louis D. O'Brien	6/25/2004	FP
	Louis D. O'Brien	8/20/2004	FP
	Louis D. O'Brien	10/21/2004	Hoo
	William Stiritz	5/8/2004	FP

Leading Owners by Most Purses in a Year (1980-2004)

Owner	Year	Earnings	Leading Earner (Earnings)
Stronach Stables	2000	$11,133,785	Perfect Sting ($1,367,000)
Michael J. Gill	2004	10,811,211	Umpateedle ($216,160)
Richard A. Englander	2001	9,784,822	Elektraline ($222,383)
Michael J. Gill	2003	9,236,530	Highway Prospector ($290,397)
Stronach Stables	2002	8,347,017	Milwaukee Brew ($1,590,000)
The Thoroughbred Corp.	2001	8,000,763	Point Given ($3,350,000)
The Thoroughbred Corp.	2002	7,887,915	War Emblem ($3,125,000)
Someday Farm	2004	7,584,305	Smarty Jones ($7,563,535)
Richard A. Englander	2002	7,530,362	Boston Common ($303,177)
Stronach Stables	2003	7,289,114	Milwaukee Brew ($743,000)
Stronach Stables	1998	7,221,416	Awesome Again ($3,845,990)
Stronach Stables	2004	7,193,867	Ghostzapper ($2,590,000)
Juddmonte Farms	2001	6,806,015	Aptitude ($1,410,000)
Allen E. Paulson	1996	6,686,629	Cigar ($2,510,000)
Stronach Stables	2001	6,539,481	Macho Uno ($563,400)
Juddmonte Farms	2003	6,265,030	Empire Maker ($1,936,200)
Stronach Stables	1999	6,221,147	Golden Missile ($838,240)
Overbrook Farm	1996	5,996,242	Boston Harbor ($1,906,325)
The Thoroughbred Corp.	2000	5,880,705	Spain ($1,979,500)
Ogden Phipps	1988	5,858,168	Seeking the Gold ($2,145,620)
Kenneth and Sarah Ramsey	2004	5,855,964	Roses in May ($1,723,277)
Edmund A. Gann	2003	5,848,681	Medaglia d'Oro ($1,990,000)
John Franks	1999	5,735,827	Littlebitlively ($868,303)
Michael J. Gill	2002	5,639,292	Rusty Spur ($180,610)
Golden Eagle Farm	1999	5,630,399	General Challenge ($1,658,100)
Allen E. Paulson	1995	5,626,396	Cigar ($3,670,000)
Golden Eagle Farm	1998	5,590,971	Excellent Meeting ($773,824)
Juddmonte Farms	2000	5,496,951	Chester House ($1,408,500)
Allen E. Paulson	1998	5,483,756	Escena ($2,032,425)
Ogden Phipps	1989	5,438,034	Easy Goer ($3,837,150)
Godolphin Racing	2001	5,359,804	Fantastic Light ($2,896,615)
Richard A. Englander	2003	5,347,231	My Cousin Matt ($237,500)
Allen E. Paulson	1997	5,259,107	Ajina ($979,175)
Juddmonte Farms	2002	5,172,287	Beat Hollow (GB) ($1,437,150)
John Franks	1998	5,145,343	Precocity ($868,630)
Michael E. Pegram	1999	5,128,905	Silverbulletday ($1,707,640)
Eugene V. Klein	1988	5,093,091	Winning Colors ($1,347,746)
Overbrook Farm	1999	5,052,194	Cat Thief ($3,020,500)
Kinghaven Farms	1990	5,041,280	Izvestia ($2,486,667)
Richard A. Englander	2000	4,927,214	Watchman's Warning ($210,862)
Eugene V. Klein	1987	4,904,247	Success Express ($737,207)
Sam-Son Farm	2004	4,830,939	Soaring Free ($1,113,862)
Sam-Son Farm	2000	4,698,712	Quiet Resolve ($967,871)
The Thoroughbred Corp.	1999	4,598,903	Anees ($609,200)
Gaillard-Hancock-Whittingham	1989	4,580,404	Sunday Silence ($4,578,454)
Golden Eagle Farm	1992	4,487,959	Best Pal ($955,000)
Edward P. Evans	2002	4,472,047	Summer Colony ($992,500)
John Franks	1986	4,463,115	Herat ($541,000)
Eugene and Laura Melnyk	2004	4,447,689	Speightstown ($1,045,556)
Golden Eagle Farm	1997	4,420,911	Career Collection ($482,005)
John Franks	1990	4,386,593	Beyond Perfection ($345,614)
Carolyn H. Hine	1997	4,347,895	Skip Away ($4,089,000)
Frank H. Stronach	1996	4,271,752	Cash Deposit ($269,072)
Frank H. Stronach	1997	4,246,073	Wild Rush ($614,780)
Kinghaven Farms	1989	4,136,174	With Approval ($1,772,150)
Eugene and Laura Melnyk	2003	4,123,765	Strong Hope ($582,360)
John Franks	1997	4,084,085	Halo America ($528,012)
John Franks	2003	4,083,255	Chatter Chatter ($383,470)
Gary A. Tanaka	2002	4,078,701	Golden Apples (Ire) ($1,111,680)
Golden Eagle Farm	2000	4,060,324	General Challenge ($1,198,118)

Leading Breeders of 2004

Thoroughbred breeding is played out on an international stage, and very often the top-ranked breeders in North America have overseas addresses. For instance, the three leading breeders in the 2003 THOROUGHBRED TIMES rankings were Juddmonte Farms, Flaxman Holdings Ltd., and the brothers Wertheimer. The 2004 season provided a different type of list of leading breeders, however, as purely American operations hold down the top three positions.

Atop the 2004 list were Aaron and Marie Jones, veterans of the racing and breeding game who bred two '04 champions, three-year-old filly Ashado and champion sprinter Speightstown. Second in the rankings was Margaux Stud, a Kentucky-based operation that bred Roses in May, second to Ghostzapper in the Breeders' Cup Classic (G1).

Four of the ten top-ranked breeders for 2004 were based outside the United States, and one was Canada's perennial leading breeder Sam-Son Farm, which bred and raced Soaring Free, Horse of the Year in his native Canada. Two others, Haras Don Alberto and Haras Firmamento, are South American breeders with a prominent U.S. runner, Total Impact (Chi) in the case of Haras Don Alberto and Star Parade (Arg) for Firmamento.

Also among the top ten in the THOROUGHBRED TIMES rankings were two organizations with deep roots in the American Turf: Phipps Stable and Marylou Whitney Stables. The operation of Ogden Mills Phipps and his family had two graded stakes winners from 16 starters in 2004, and the widow of C. V. Whitney raced Birdstone, winner of the Belmont (G1) and Travers (G1) Stakes.

The four criteria for rankings in the THOROUGHBRED TIMES standings are: 1) total earnings; 2) average earnings per starter; 3) percentage of stakes winners from starters; and 4) percentage of graded stakes winners from starters. These criteria clearly favor quality over quantity, and they certainly lean toward smaller-scale breeders who had a very good year. And so it was in 2004.

For the second consecutive year, Frank Stronach's Adena Springs led all North American breeders by earnings, with more than $14-million.

Leading Breeders by Purses Won

Year	Name	Wins	Purses Won
2004	Adena Springs	383	$14,122,256
2003	Adena Springs	296	11,542,871
2002	Mockingbird Farm	516	11,175,975
2001	Mockingbird Farm	390	9,550,610
2000	Harry T. Mangurian Jr.	495	10,757,845
1999	Harry T. Mangurian Jr.	490	10,851,459
1998	Mr. and Mrs. John Mabee	270	8,221,982
1997	Allen E. Paulson	248	7,723,615

THOROUGHBRED TIMES Leading Breeders of 2004

Rankings based on formula that gives equal weighting to four statistical categories for performance in 2004: 1) total earnings; 2) average earnings per starter; 3) percent stakes winners from starters; and 4) percent graded stakes winners from starters. A minimum of ten starters is required to be considered for inclusion. Names of breeders are of individual property lines as reported by the Jockey Club. No attempt was made to consolidate names where a breeder had more than one partnership or property line. Statistics are for North America only and for racing in 2004.

Rank	Breeder	No. strs	No. wnrs	No. SWs	SWs/ strs	No. GSWs	GSWs/ strs	Total earnings	Average earnings/ starter	Leading earner	Earnings of leading earner
1	Aaron U. and Marie D. Jones	25	13	4	16.0%	2	8.0%	$4,033,129	$161,325	Ashado	$2,259,640
2	Margaux Farm	12	10	2	16.7%	1	8.3%	1,954,443	162,870	Roses in May	1,723,277
3	Phipps Stable	16	11	2	12.5%	2	12.5%	1,849,454	115,591	Storm Flag Flying	963,248
4	Haras Don Alberto	14	8	4	28.6%	3	21.4%	1,514,686	108,192	Total Impact (Chi)	793,430
5	Chiefswood Stables	10	6	1	10.0%	1	10.0%	1,203,501	120,350	Niigon	864,610
6	Clovelly Farms	12	6	1	8.3%	1	8.3%	1,434,561	119,547	Pleasantly Perfect	1,240,000
7	Sam-Son Farm	53	28	7	13.2%	6	11.3%	4,782,501	90,236	Soaring Free	1,113,862
8	Tri-County Farms	10	6	1	10.0%	1	10.0%	983,266	98,327	Magistretti	764,000
9	Marylou Whitney Stables	16	10	1	6.3%	1	6.3%	1,480,547	92,534	Birdstone	1,236,600
10	Haras Firmamento	18	10	3	16.7%	3	16.7%	1,509,506	83,861	Star Parade (Arg)	483,670
11	Juddmonte Farms	63	34	7	11.1%	7	11.1%	4,975,947	78,983	Sightseek	1,011,350
	Tracy Farmer	11	6	2	18.2%	1	9.1%	961,910	87,446	Sir Shackleton	566,105
13	Wind Hill Farm	13	6	1	7.7%	1	7.7%	1,101,341	84,719	Stellar Jayne	992,169
14	Beclawat Stable	19	10	1	5.3%	1	5.3%	1,569,669	82,614	A Bit O'Gold	1,060,790
15	Dr. William A. Reed and Stonecrest Farm	11	4		0.0%		0.0%	1,080,872	98,261	Perfect Drift	947,595
16	Newchance Farm	13	2	1	7.7%	1	7.7%	1,050,026	80,771	Peace Rules	1,024,288
17	John D. Gunther	18	12	2	11.1%	2	11.1%	1,252,717	69,595	Bending Strings	495,150
18	Cypress Farms 1991	15	11	2	13.3%	1	6.7%	1,015,269	67,685	Kela	710,212
19	Fox Ridge Farm	15	9	1	6.7%	1	6.7%	1,024,087	68,272	Riskaverse	717,472
20	Moloney and Thompson	13	8	2	15.4%	1	7.7%	867,690	66,745	Flamethrowintexan	368,813
21	Ogden Mills Phipps	21	14	2	9.5%	2	9.5%	1,268,176	60,389	Daydreaming	483,180
22	Chris Nolan	11	7	1	9.1%	1	9.1%	718,328	65,303	Colonial Colony	607,625
23	Wimborne Farm	47	24	4	8.5%	1	2.1%	2,793,360	59,433	Better Talk Now	1,407,000
24	Lucy G. Bassett	14	7	1	7.1%	1	7.1%	808,811	57,772	Adoration	607,304
25	Cherry Valley Farm,	17	12	2	11.8%	1	5.9%	926,980	54,528	Pomeroy	296,250
26	Brushwood Stable	12	9	1	8.3%	1	8.3%	660,755	55,063	Cat Fighter	206,060
27	Darley	13	1	1	7.7%	1	7.7%	705,618	54,278	Balletto (UAE)	614,000
28	William S. Farish Jr.	13	8	3	23.1%	2	15.4%	691,497	53,192	Shadow Cast	267,480

Rank	Breeder	No. Strs	No. Wnrs	No. SWs	SWs/ Strs	No. GSWs	GSWs/ Strs	Total Earnings	Average Earnings/ Starter	Leading Earner	Earnings of Leading Earner
29	G. Watts Humphrey	15	4	2	13.3%	1	6.7%	$760,601	$50,707	Newfoundland	$523,750
30	Larry R. Teague	13	6	2	15.4%		0.0%	676,860	52,066	Rocky Gulch	377,179
31	Sabine Stable	31	13	2	6.5%	1	3.2%	1,520,195	49,039	Lion Heart	1,080,000
32	Kenneth L. and Sarah K. Ramsey	100	63	7	7.0%	2	2.0%	4,784,649	47,846	Kitten's Joy	1,625,796
33	John Zamora	10	8	1	10.0%		0.0%	508,232	50,823	Cozy Guy	324,504
34	Kilroy Thoroughbred Partnership	10	9		0.0%		0.0%	527,275	52,728	Bankruptcy Court	139,450
35	Allen E. Paulson	70	36	4	5.7%	3	4.3%	3,141,512	44,879	Azeri	1,035,000
36	Vinery	11	6	3	27.3%	1	9.1%	519,777	47,252	Hollywood Story	287,105
37	Hopewell Investments	19	12	2	10.5%		0.0%	857,069	45,109	My Snookie's Boy	312,766
38	McKee Stables	23	11	1	4.4%	1	4.4%	1,016,962	44,216	Champali	634,398
39	Reade Baker	13	7	1	7.7%		0.0%	606,993	46,692	Ontheqt	128,575
40	Wertheimer et Frere	28	10	3	10.7%	3	10.7%	1,167,813	41,708	Olmodavor	367,000
41	Chester and Mary R. Broman	33	18	2	6.1%	1	3.0%	1,386,411	42,012	Friends Lake	611,800
42	John Franks and Jonabell Farm	11	6	1	9.1%	1	9.1%	497,951	45,268	Adreamisborn	257,740
43	Buckingham Farm	11	5	1	9.1%	1	9.1%	496,593	45,145	He Loves Me	295,000
44	Mr. & Mrs. Charles McGinnes	34	23	5	14.7%		0.0%	1,409,433	41,454	Aggadan	263,371
45	WinStar Farm,	75	45	4	5.3%	2	2.7%	3,053,300	40,711	Funny Cide	1,075,100
46	Sentinel Thoroughbred Farms	11	7	1	9.1%		0.0%	491,213	44,656	A to the Z	312,612
47	Arthur I. Appleton	124	71	4	3.2%	2	1.6%	5,005,602	40,368	Southern Image	1,612,150
48	Flaxman Holdings	27	16	1	3.7%		0.0%	1,116,382	41,347	King of Happiness	161,802
49	Rainbow Stables	14	11	1	7.1%		0.0%	599,419	42,816	Heroic Sight	145,370
50	John W. Rooker	16	7	1	6.3%		0.0%	676,805	42,300	Bowman's Band	439,334
51	L. William Heiligbrodt	10	4	1	10.0%	1	10.0%	433,472	43,347	Lunarpal	284,677
52	Willmott Stable	16	8	1	6.3%	1	6.3%	653,364	40,835	Aud	257,578
53	Stonerside Stable	69	27	8	11.6%	3	4.4%	2,643,157	38,307	The Cliff's Edge	1,010,000
54	William Sorokolit	20	10	1	5.0%	1	5.0%	802,025	40,101	Classic Stamp	425,043
55	Patricia Blass	10	8	1	10.0%		0.0%	433,858	43,386	Wildcat Shoes	116,725
56	Pin Oak Stud	55	37	5	9.1%	2	3.6%	2,098,583	38,156	I Thee Wed	314,337
57	Joseph Allen	15	10	1	6.7%	1	6.7%	593,267	39,551	Rare Gift	161,220
58	Mt. Brilliant Farm	31	17	4	12.9%	2	6.5%	1,161,519	37,468	Josh's Madelyn	245,172
59	Adena Springs	378	219	15	4.0%	6	1.6%	14,225,036	37,632	Ghostzapper	2,590,000
60	Gustav Schickedanz	38	22	3	7.9%	1	2.6%	1,415,871	37,260	Mobil	440,213
61	Enrique R. Ubarri	10	9	2	20.0%	2	20.0%	403,620	40,362	Hispanica	157,720
62	Casino Royale Farms	11	9	1	9.1%		0.0%	445,463	40,497	Caught in the Rain	138,820
63	Eugene Melnyk	39	25	2	5.1%		0.0%	1,455,796	37,328	Arch Hall	187,342
64	Green Lantern Stables	14	7	2	14.3%		0.0%	541,836	38,703	Ender's Sister	317,580
	Nancy W. Mitchell	12	8		0.0%		0.0%	487,987	40,666	Slim Dusty	233,553
66	Mr. & Mrs. Gerald Nielsen	15	9	1	6.7%	1	6.7%	573,264	38,218	Quantum Merit	280,585
67	Windways Farm	17	13		0.0%		0.0%	662,083	38,946	Wild Desert	89,636
68	Kinghaven Farms	40	22	2	5.0%		0.0%	1,475,008	36,875	Just in Case Jimmy	272,825
69	Shadwell Farm	40	20	2	5.0%	1	2.5%	1,454,289	36,357	Mustanfar	394,716
70	Knob Hill Stable	25	14	3	12.0%		0.0%	924,452	36,978	Clubay	115,440
71	James C. Spence	11	9	1	9.1%	1	9.1%	428,571	38,961	Golden Sonata	166,000
72	Everest Stables	112	59	7	6.3%	3	2.7%	3,931,983	35,107	Island Fashion	615,000
73	Kennelot Stables	10	4	2	20.0%	1	10.0%	387,908	38,791	Raylene	210,134
74	Ron E. Gomez	30	11	1	3.3%		0.0%	1,099,711	36,657	Texcess	725,427
75	O'Sullivan Farms	11	7	1	9.1%		0.0%	428,923	38,993	Earth Power	121,830
76	Robert H. and Bea Roberts	47	27	2	4.3%	2	4.3%	1,651,951	35,148	Request for Parole	757,100
77	J. V. Shields Jr.	34	23	3	8.8%	2	5.9%	1,183,739	34,816	Passing Shot	185,460
78	New Farm	22	13	2	9.1%	1	4.6%	784,760	35,671	Wildcat Heir	305,860
79	Edward P. Evans	140	73	10	7.1%	5	3.6%	4,775,260	34,109	Saint Liam	618,760
80	Thomas L. Nichols	12	11		0.0%		0.0%	461,077	38,423	Keys to the Heart	100,800
81	Colts	16	10	2	12.5%		0.0%	577,277	36,080	Strength and Honor	183,145
82	Thomas/Lakin	47	27	4	8.5%	1	2.1%	1,600,801	34,060	Capeside Lady	266,220
83	James D. Haley	12	5	1	8.3%	1	8.3%	443,666	36,972	Toasted	315,680
84	Four Horsemen's Ranch	28	12	1	3.6%	1	3.6%	970,925	34,676	Star Over the Bay	493,960
85	Cheryl A. Curtin	18	11	1	5.6%	1	5.6%	626,368	34,798	Limehouse	367,000
86	Hickory Tree Farm	12	7	2	16.7%		0.0%	436,815	36,401	With Patience	178,750
87	W. S. Farish	58	30	6	10.3%	1	1.7%	1,928,086	33,243	Midway Road	372,015
88	Moyglare Stud Farm	11	4	2	18.2%	2	18.2%	395,355	35,941	Where We Left Off (GB)	194,480
89	Berkshire Stud	13	7	2	15.4%		0.0%	461,490	35,499	High Peaks	114,501
90	Ed and Sharon Hudon	10	8	1	10.0%		0.0%	369,872	36,987	Black Bart	254,720
91	Edition Farm	13	9	2	15.4%		0.0%	458,770	35,290	Then She Laughs	117,140
92	Gainsborough Farm	25	8	2	8.0%	1	4.0%	829,896	33,196	Musical Chimes	438,300
93	John H. Peace	13	8		0.0%		0.0%	468,590	36,045	Points West	125,630
94	Vegso Racing Stable	26	17	1	3.9%	1	3.9%	865,702	33,296	Silver Tree	328,060
95	TAC Holdings	35	24	2	5.7%	1	2.9%	1,145,832	32,738	Film Maker	470,430
96	W. S. Farish & Kilroy Tbred Partnership	10	7	1	10.0%		0.0%	364,544	36,454	Eavesdropper	118,214
97	Glory Days Breeding	35	17	1	2.9%	1	2.9%	1,113,407	31,812	Purge	562,734
98	Rutledge Farm	10	8	1	10.0%	1	10.0%	343,307	34,331	Sur La Tete	209,310
99	Paul R. and Mary Anne Denes	10	9	1	10.0%		0.0%	347,555	34,756	Cervelo	82,570
100	Marion G. Montanari	23	14	1	4.4%	1	4.4%	730,778	31,773	Proud Accolade	364,130

Leading Breeders by Earnings in 2004

Breeder	No. Strs	No. Wnrs	Total Earnings
Adena Springs	378	219	$14,225,036
John Franks	548	301	10,300,563
Farnsworth Farms	429	235	8,696,897
Someday Farm	2	1	7,563,853
Mr. and Mrs. John C. Mabee	204	123	5,063,818
Arthur I. Appleton	125	71	5,042,948
Juddmonte Farms	63	34	4,975,947
Kenneth L. and Sarah K. Ramsey	102	64	4,813,119
Sam-Son Farm	53	28	4,782,501
Edward P. Evans	140	73	4,775,260
Sez Who Thoroughbreds	198	115	4,604,294
Brereton C. Jones	240	128	4,339,870
Aaron U. and Marie D. Jones	25	13	4,033,129
Everest Stables	112	59	3,931,983
Allen E. Paulson	70	36	3,141,512
Overbrook Farm	135	66	3,129,500
Mr. and Mrs. Martin J. Wygod	116	56	3,109,849
WinStar Farm	75	45	3,053,300
Mockingbird Farm	170	90	3,039,895
Haras Santa Isabel	167	113	2,916,814
Gilbert G. Campbell	156	86	2,899,795
Wimborne Farm	48	25	2,812,351
Stonerside Stable	70	27	2,643,617
Charles Nuckols Jr. and Sons	108	64	2,563,680
Harris Farms	101	58	2,554,661
Ro Parra	98	51	2,378,427
J & D Farms	113	61	2,332,831
Live Oak Stud	81	46	2,264,685
Pin Oak Stud	55	37	2,098,583
Margaux Farm	12	10	1,954,443
W. S. Farish	57	29	1,926,514
Phipps Stable	16	11	1,849,454
Dr. D. W. Frazier	114	67	1,820,209
Hill 'n' Dale Farm	51	29	1,732,227
Robert H. and Bea Roberts	50	29	1,669,347
Thomas and Lakin	47	27	1,600,801
Tommy Town Thoroughbreds	83	53	1,591,302
Flying Zee Stables	70	37	1,575,491
Foxwood Plantations	63	33	1,573,737
Beclawat Stables	20	10	1,569,669
The Thoroughbred Corp.	54	28	1,525,910
Haras Don Alberto	14	8	1,514,686
Ronald E Gomez	46	22	1,512,428
Firmamento	18	10	1,509,506
Donald R. Dizney	93	58	1,509,480
Marylou Whitney Stables	16	10	1,480,547

Breeder	No. Strs	No. Wnrs	Average Earnings per Starter
Marylou Whitney Stables	16	10	$92,534
Sam-Son Farm	53	28	90,236
Tracy Farmer	11	6	87,446
Wind Hill Farm	13	6	84,719
Haras Firmamento	18	10	83,861
Newchance Farm	13	2	80,771
Juddmonte Farms	63	34	78,983
Beclawat Stables	20	10	78,483
Fox Ridge Farm	15	9	68,272
Cypress Farms 1991	15	11	67,685
Sabine Stables	13	6	67,565
Moloney and Thompson	13	8	66,745
John D. Gunther	19	12	65,932
Chris Nolan	11	7	65,303
Ogden Mills Phipps	21	14	60,389
Robert W. Camac	10	5	59,177
Wimborne Farm	48	25	58,591
Lucy G. Bassett	14	7	57,772
Sabine Stable	25	12	57,399
Brushwood Stable	12	9	55,063
Cherry Valley Farm	17	12	54,528
Darley	13	1	54,278
Jan, Mace, and Samantha Siegel	13	8	53,966
William S. Farish Jr.	13	8	53,192
Kilroy Thoroughbred Partnership	10	9	52,728
Larry R. Teague	13	6	52,066
Vinery	11	6	47,232
Kenneth L. and Sarah K. Ramsey	102	64	47,187
Reade Baker	13	7	46,692
William Sorokolit	15	7	45,537

Leading Breeders by Average Earnings per Starter in 2004
(Minimum of 10 Starters)

Breeder	No. Strs	No. Wnrs	Average Earnings per Starter
Margaux Farm	12	10	$162,870
Aaron U. and Marie D. Jones	25	13	161,325
Madeline A. Paulson	10	6	120,587
Chiefswood Stables	10	6	120,350
Clovelly Farms	12	6	119,547
Phipps Stable	16	11	115,591
Haras Don Alberto	14	8	108,192
Tri-County Farms	10	6	98,327
Dr. William A. Reed and Stonecrest Farm	11	4	98,261

Leading Breeders by Stakes Wins in 2004

Breeder	Stakes Starts	Stakes Wins
John Franks	170	26
Adena Springs	170	19
Kenneth L. & Sarah K. Ramsey	77	17
Juddmonte Farms	46	16
Farnsworth Farms	123	13
Aaron U. & Marie D. Jones	33	13
Sam-Son Farm	59	13
Edward P. Evans	80	12
Everest Stables	96	12
W. S. Farish	53	12
Mr. & Mrs. John C. Mabee	48	11
Larry R. Teague	18	11
Overbrook Farm	61	10
Stonerside Stable Ltd.	57	10
Arthur I. Appleton	67	9
Foxwood Plantation	40	9
Harris Farms	45	9
Sez Who Thoroughbreds	80	9
Mr. & Mrs. Martin J. Wygod	32	9
Haras Santa Isabel	70	8
J D Farms	47	8
Mr. & Mrs. Charles McGinnes	37	8
Pin Oak Stud	44	8
Billingsley Creek Ranch	19	7
Hill 'n' Dale Farms	28	7
Kinghaven Farms Ltd.	25	7
Live Oak Stud	46	7
Richter Family Trust	30	7
Dennis E. Weir	34	7

Leading Breeders by Stakes Winners in 2004

Breeder	Stakes Starters	Stakes Winners
John Franks	59	17
Adena Springs	75	15
Edward P. Evans	25	10
Farnsworth Farms	44	9
Sez Who Thoroughbreds	37	8
Stonerside Stable Ltd.	18	8
Everest Stables	30	7
Juddmonte Farms	19	7
Mr. & Mrs. John C. Mabee	29	7
Kenneth L. Ramsey & Sarah K. Ramsey	21	7
Richter Family Trust	12	7
Sam-Son Farm	21	7
W. S. Farish	18	6
Foxwood Plantation	17	6
Haras Santa Isabel	26	6
Harris Farms	17	6
Overbrook Farm	22	6
Cobra Farm	7	5
Foxfield	15	5
Mr. & Mrs. Charles McGinnes	12	5
Charles Nuckols Jr. & Sons	17	5
Pin Oak Stud	15	5
Tommy Town Thoroughbreds	16	5
Mr. & Mrs. Martin J. Wygod	17	5
Arthur I. Appleton	24	4
Gilbert G. Campbell	22	4
Haras Don Alberto	6	4
Jacks Or Better Farm	13	4
J D Farms	17	4
Aaron U. & Marie D. Jones	8	4
Brereton C. Jones	28	4
Live Oak Stud	19	4
Mt. Brilliant Farm	6	4
Orion Stables	12	4
Allen E. Paulson	20	4
Dr. & Mrs. Jack B. Root Jr.	7	4
Carolyn Sleeter	7	4
The Thoroughbred Corp.	11	4
Thomas-Lakin	9	4
Triple AAA Ranch	22	4
Dennis E. Weir	15	4
Wimborne Farm	6	4
WinStar Farm	10	4

Leading Breeders by Graded Wins in 2004

Breeder	Graded Starts	Graded Wins
Juddmonte Farms	42	16
Adena Springs	58	10
Sam-Son Farm	36	10
Aaron U. & Marie D. Jones	15	9
Kenneth L. & Sarah K. Ramsey	30	8
Firmamento	22	6
Everest Stables	47	5
Allen E. Paulson	22	5
Mr. & Mrs. Martin J. Wygod	10	5
James D. Conway & Thomas C. Mueller	9	4
Edward P. Evans	35	4
John Franks	35	4
John D. Gunther	21	4

Breeder	Graded Starts	Graded Wins
Haras Fronteira	6	4
Mr. & Mrs. John C. Mabee	12	4
Arthur I. Appleton	24	3
Lucy G. Bassett	6	3
Marjorie Cowan & Irving Cowan	9	3
Car Colston Hall Stud	7	3
Cypress Farms 1991	9	3
Four Horsemen's Ranch	5	3
Haras Bage Do Sul	4	3
Haras Don Alberto	22	3
Haras du Mezeray	5	3
Margaux Farm	4	3
McKee Stables	6	3
Newchance Farm	5	3
Madeleine A. Paulson	12	3
Ogden Mills Phipps	8	3
Phipps Stable	13	3
Pin Oak Stud	15	3
Brice Ridgely	3	3
Robert H. & Bea Roberts	13	3
Rutledge Farm	6	3
Stiftung Gestut Fahrhof	8	3
Charles A. Smith	9	3
Paul Smith	7	3
Someday Farm	4	3
Stonerside Stable Ltd.	22	3
Wesley Ward	4	3
Wertheimer et Frere	17	3
Wind Hill Farm	12	3
WinStar Farm	20	3

Leading Breeders by Graded Stakes Winners in 2004

Breeder	Graded Starters	Graded Winners
Juddmonte Farms	16	7
Adena Springs	28	6
Sam-Son Farm	16	6
Edward P. Evans	13	4
Everest Stables	18	3
Firmamento	4	3
John Franks	14	3
Haras Don Alberto	5	3
Allen E. Paulson	9	3
Stonerside Stable Ltd.	8	3
Wertheimer et Frere	8	3
Mr. & Mrs. Martin J. Wygod	6	3
Arthur I. Appleton	10	2
William S. Farish Jr.	3	2
John D. Gunther	4	2
Aaron U. & Marie D. Jones	3	2
Mr. & Mrs. John C. Mabee	5	2
Moyglare Stud Farm Ltd.	2	2
Mt. Brilliant Farm	4	2
Madeleine A. Paulson	2	2
Ogden Mills Phipps	3	2
Phipps Stable	3	2
Pin Oak Stud	5	2
Kenneth L. & Sarah K. Ramsey	10	2
Robert H. & Bea Roberts	3	2
Sabine Stables	2	2
Sez Who Thoroughbreds	8	2
J. V. Shields Jr.	7	2
Stiftung Gestut Fahrhof	2	2
Win Star Farm	6	2

Leading Breeders by Most Grade 1 Stakes Wins in 2004

Breeder	No. G1 Starts	No. G1 Wins
Juddmonte Farms	37	6
Aaron U. and Marie D. Jones	16	4
Haras Fronteira	4	3
Allen E. Paulson	12	3
Kenneth L. and Sarah K. Ramsey	8	3
Mr. and Mrs. Martin J. Wygod	5	3
Adena Springs	7	2
Aga Khan's Studs	4	2
Arthur I. Appleton	5	2
Beclawat Stable	4	2
Car Colston Hall Stud	4	2
Marjorie and Irving Cowan	6	2
Haras Don Alberto	6	2
Haras Firmamento	8	2
John A. Manfuso	4	2
Phipps Stable	6	2
Rutledge Farm	5	2
Sam-Son Farm	12	2
Someday Farm	3	2
Marylou Whitney Stables	4	2
Wimborne Farm Inc.	6	2
Wind Hill Farm	8	2

Leading Breeders by Most Grade 1 Winners in 2004

Breeder	No. G1 Starters	No. G1 Winners
Juddmonte Farms	23	4
Haras Don Alberto	3	2
Aaron U. and Marie D. Jones	4	2
Phipps Stable	2	2
Kenneth L. and Sarah K. Ramsey	3	2
Sam-Son Farm	8	2
Mr. and Mrs. Martin J. Wygod	3	2

Leading Breeders by Number of Winners in 2004

Breeder	No. Strs	No. Wnrs
John Franks	548	301
E. Farnsworth Farms	429	235
Adena Springs	378	219
Brereton C. Jones	240	128
Mr. and Mrs. John C. Mabee	204	123
Sez Who Thoroughbreds	198	115
Haras Santa Isabel	167	113
Mockingbird Farm	170	90
Gilbert G. Campbell	156	86
Edward P. Evans	140	73
Arthur I. Appleton	125	71
Dr. D. W. Frazier	114	67
Potrero Los Llanos	100	67
Overbrook Farm	135	66
Charles Nuckols, Jr. and Sons	108	64
Kenneth L. Ramsey and Sarah K. Ramsey	102	64
J & D Farms	113	61
Everest Stables	112	59
Donald R. Dizney	93	58
Harris Farms	101	58
Mr. and Mrs. Martin J. Wygod	116	56
Tommy Town Thoroughbreds	83	53
Joseph Adcock	96	51

Breeder	No. Strs	No. Wnrs
Ro Parra	98	51
Live Oak Stud	81	46
WinStar Farm	75	45
Liberation Farm and Oratis Thoroughbreds	68	44
Highland Farms	79	40
E & D Enterprises	76	39
Arthur B. Hancock, III	71	37
Flying Zee Stables	70	37
Hermitage Farm L L C	67	37
Pin Oak Stud	55	37
Allen E. Paulson	70	36
Foxfield	59	36
Juddmonte Farms	63	34
Ocala Stud Farms	57	34
Brylynn Farm	58	33
Double D Farm Corp.	84	33
Foxwood Plantations	63	33
Hargus S. Sexton and Sandra Sexton	74	33
Meadowbrook Farms	57	33

Leading Breeders by Number of Wins in 2004

Breeder	No. Strs	No. Wnrs	No. Wins
John Franks	548	301	542
Farnsworth Farms	429	235	473
Adena Springs	378	219	400
Haras Santa Isabel	167	113	285
Brereton C. Jones	240	128	220
Sez Who Thoroughbreds	198	115	205
Mr. and Mrs. John C. Mabee	204	123	201
Gilbert G. Campbell	156	86	184
Mockingbird Farm	170	90	170
Arthur I. Appleton	125	71	160
Potrero Los Llanos	100	67	142
Edward P. Evans	140	73	138
Dr. D. W. Frazier	114	67	124
Charles Nuckols Jr. and Sons	108	64	115
J & D Farms	113	61	113
Kenneth L. and Sarah K. Ramsey	102	64	109
Harris Farms	101	58	106
Mr. and Mrs. Martin J. Wygod	116	56	105
Overbrook Farm	135	66	104
Everest Stables	112	59	101
Donald R. Dizney	93	58	93
Ro Parra	98	51	90
Live Oak Stud	81	46	84
Allen E. Paulson	70	36	77
Joseph Adcock	96	51	77
Tommy Town Thoroughbreds	83	53	77
South River Ranch	47	28	74
WinStar Farm	75	45	73
Liberation Farm and Oratis Thoroughbreds	68	44	67
Ocala Stud Farms	57	34	67
W. S. Farish	57	29	66
Foxwood Plantations	63	33	65
Jose Carro	49	23	64
Pin Oak Stud	55	37	64
Flying Zee Stables	70	37	63
Triple AAA Ranch	49	31	63
Hargus S. and Sandra Sexton	74	33	62
E & D Enterprises	76	39	61
Foxfield	59	36	61
Hermitage Farm	67	37	61

Leading Trainers of 2004

Training Thoroughbred racehorses is a tough way to make a living. The days are long and most trainers are on the job before the sun climbs over the stable area and are there when the last race is run. Increasingly, the job entails considerable travel and mastering the complexities of running a million-dollar business. Not only must the trainer understand the personalities of his owners—some of whom invariably will be more difficult to handle than others—but he or she also must devise and execute a plan of action that leads from the auction ring to the winner's circle.

Indeed, the hopes and aspirations of all trainers are focused on the winner's circle. To win is to please everyone—the owner, the breeder, the stallion manager, the jockey, and the stable staff. For the trainer, day money to train the horse yields a subsistence living at best, and getting to the winner's circle yields the greatest monetary reward. While the money is important, most trainers thrive on getting to the winner's circle.

The THOROUGHBRED TIMES Leading Trainers of 2004 table recognizes those who have succeeded at a tough job. The rankings are based on four criteria: 1) total purses; 2) average earnings per starter; 3) percentage of stakes winners from starters; and 4) number of winners. These criteria favor quality over quantity but nonetheless recognize the importance of getting to the winner's circle.

Leading Trainers by Purses Won

North American Earnings Only

Year	Trainer	Wins	Purses
2004	Todd A. Pletcher	240	$17,511,923
2003	Robert J. Frankel	114	19,143,289
2002	Robert J. Frankel	117	17,750,340
2001	Robert J. Frankel	101	14,607,446
2000	Bob Baffert	145	11,793,355
1999	Bob Baffert	169	16,842,332
1998	Bob Baffert	138	12,604,110
1997	D. Wayne Lukas	175	10,351,397
1996	D. Wayne Lukas	192	15,967,609
1995	D. Wayne Lukas	194	12,852,843
1994	D. Wayne Lukas	147	9,249,577
1993	Robert J. Frankel	78	8,928,602
1992	D. Wayne Lukas	246	10,061,240
1991	D. Wayne Lukas	289	15,953,757
1990	D. Wayne Lukas	267	14,508,871
1989	D. Wayne Lukas	305	16,103,998
1988	D. Wayne Lukas	318	17,842,358
1987	D. Wayne Lukas	343	17,502,110
1986	D. Wayne Lukas	259	12,344,520
1985	D. Wayne Lukas	218	11,155,188
1984	D. Wayne Lukas	131	5,838,221
1983	D. Wayne Lukas	78	4,267,261
1982	Charles E. Whittingham	62	4,586,077
1981	Charles E. Whittingham	74	3,991,877
1980	Lazaro S. Barrera	99	2,971,626

THOROUGHBRED TIMES Leading Trainers of 2004

Rankings based on formula that gives equal weighting to four statistical categories for performance in 2004: 1) total purses; 2) average earnings per starter; 3) percent stakes winners from starters; and 4) number of winners. A minimum of ten starters is required to be considered for inclusion. Statistics are for North America only and for racing in 2004.

Rank	Trainer	No. Strs	No. Wnrs	No. SWs	SWs/ Strs	No. GSWs	GSWs/ Strs	Total Purses	Average Earnings/ Starter	Leading Earner	Earnings of Leading Earner
1	Todd A. Pletcher	234	134	36	15.4%	24	10.3%	$17,511,923	$74,837	Ashado	$2,259,640
2	Robert J. Frankel	147	79	30	20.4%	26	17.7%	15,605,911	106,163	Ghostzapper	2,590,000
3	Richard E. Dutrow Jr.	161	91	17	10.6%	6	3.7%	7,436,771	46,191	Saint Liam	618,760
4	Bob Baffert	155	67	20	12.9%	12	7.7%	7,535,753	48,618	Yearly Report	787,500
5	William I. Mott	170	80	18	10.6%	5	2.9%	5,690,580	33,474	Stroll	348,524
6	H. Allen Jerkens	64	40	11	17.2%	5	7.8%	4,447,477	69,492	Society Selection	929,700
7	Jeff Mullins	180	87	16	8.9%	5	2.8%	6,832,640	37,959	Summer Wind Dancer	598,905
8	Nicholas P. Zito	100	54	11	11.0%	5	5.0%	6,967,742	69,677	Birdstone	1,236,600
9	Mark R. Frostad	59	29	8	13.6%	7	11.9%	4,912,015	83,254	Soaring Free	1,113,862
10	Robert P. Tiller	61	37	8	13.1%	2	3.3%	3,939,642	64,584	Brass in Pocket	371,038
11	Steven M. Asmussen	585	346	33	5.6%	11	1.9%	14,003,445	23,937	Lady Tak	439,412
12	Kiaran P. McLaughlin	122	50	12	9.8%	9	7.4%	5,525,744	45,293	Bending Strings	471,150
13	Claude R. McGaughey III	59	28	7	11.9%	5	8.5%	4,208,832	71,336	Storm Flag Flying	963,248
14	Patrick L. Biancone	36	20	6	16.7%	5	13.9%	3,397,917	94,387	Lion Heart	1,080,000
15	Doug O'Neill	270	113	14	5.2%	4	1.5%	7,001,387	25,931	Pohave	450,740
16	Kenneth G. McPeek	92	49	9	9.8%	3	3.3%	3,418,025	37,152	Prince Arch	405,746
17	Julio C. Canani	59	28	7	11.9%	6	10.2%	3,350,745	56,792	Sweet Catomine	799,800
18	Bernard S. Flint	132	66	10	7.6%	2	1.5%	3,513,043	26,614	Runway Model	580,598
19	Robert E. Holthus	82	45	9	11.0%	2	2.4%	2,635,551	32,141	Greater Good	226,275
20	Christophe Clement	107	45	9	8.4%	6	5.6%	3,541,781	33,101	Proud Man	313,334
21	James A. Jerkens	47	22	7	14.9%	2	4.3%	2,471,946	52,595	Artie Schiller	467,578
22	Stanley M. Hough	56	30	6	10.7%	3	5.4%	2,910,662	51,976	Request for Parole	757,100
23	Jerry Hollendorfer	328	185	13	4.0%	4	1.2%	5,922,484	18,056	Adreamisborn	257,740
24	Bruce N. Levine	109	62	7	6.4%	0	0.0%	3,535,539	32,436	Clever Electrician	220,870
25	Dale L. Romans	174	74	8	4.6%	4	2.3%	7,010,345	40,289	Roses in May	1,723,277
26	H. Graham Motion	112	52	7	6.3%	3	2.7%	4,358,674	38,917	Better Talk Now	1,407,000
27	Cole Norman	233	141	10	4.3%	0	0.0%	3,721,732	15,973	Pie N Burger	241,200
28	Timothy F. Ritchey	83	47	6	7.2%	1	1.2%	2,991,693	36,044	Afleet Alex	680,800
29	Sid C. Attard	59	39	4	6.8%	2	3.4%	3,844,401	65,159	One for Rose	489,832
30	D. Wayne Lukas	123	46	7	5.7%	5	4.1%	5,567,299	45,263	Azeri	1,035,000

Rank	Trainer	No. Strs	No. Wnrs	No. SWs	SWs/ Strs	No. GSWs	GSWs/ Strs	Total Purses	Average Earnings/ Starter	Leading Earner	Earnings of Leading Earner
31	Hugh H. Robertson	109	60	9	8.3%	1	0.9%	2,133,342	19,572	Three Hour Nap	158,400
32	James M. Cassidy	36	11	4	11.1%	3	8.3%	2,580,222	71,673	Ticker Tape (GB)	1,159,075
33	Richard E. Mandella	57	17	5	8.8%	5	8.8%	3,075,262	53,952	Pleasantly Perfect	1,240,000
34	Guadalupe Preciado	106	59	7	6.6%		0.0%	2,464,075	23,246	Caught in the Rain	138,820
35	Michael Stidham	102	48	8	7.8%	1	1.0%	2,228,860	21,852	Herculated	233,200
36	Mark A. Hennig	115	47	6	5.2%	2	1.7%	3,954,798	34,390	Eddington	605,360
37	John C. Servis	66	39	3	4.6%	2	3.0%	8,922,686	135,192	Smarty Jones	7,563,535
38	Timothy A. Hills	126	60	6	4.8%	1	0.8%	3,075,524	24,409	Mooji Moo	203,500
38	Wallace A. Dollase	34	15	5	14.7%	3	8.8%	1,864,907	54,850	Meteor Storm (GB)	529,800
40	Donnie K. Von Hemel	118	63	7	5.9%	1	0.9%	2,285,398	19,368	Cryptograph	257,398
41	Reade Baker	77	33	5	6.5%	1	1.3%	2,844,159	36,937	Touchnow	327,283
42	Steve Klesaris	113	61	5	4.4%		0.0%	3,189,251	28,223	Misty Sixes	246,074
43	Neil D. Drysdale	52	24	4	7.7%	2	3.9%	2,630,399	50,585	Musical Chimes	438,300
44	Vladimir Cerin	84	41	5	6.0%	4	4.8%	2,796,647	33,293	Even the Score	343,272
45	Thomas M. Amoss	161	90	5	3.1%		0.0%	3,617,785	22,471	Cat Genius	203,030
46	Roger L. Attfield	57	23	4	7.0%	1	1.8%	2,777,942	48,736	Perfect Soul (Ire)	391,549
47	John W. Sadler	117	49	6	5.1%	2	1.7%	2,970,367	25,388	Victory Encounter	274,287
48	Neil J. Howard	40	21	4	10.0%	3	7.5%	1,938,175	48,454	Midway Road	372,015
49	Mark E. Casse	110	38	6	5.5%	1	0.9%	2,946,340	26,785	Higher World	213,210
50	Patrick J. Kelly	43	14	4	9.3%	2	4.7%	2,093,089	48,676	Riskaverse	717,472
51	Mike R. Mitchell	132	65	4	3.0%	2	1.5%	3,834,120	29,046	Kela	710,212
52	Benjamin M. Feliciano Jr.	71	37	7	9.9%		0.0%	1,665,721	23,461	Crossing Point	124,615
53	Ronald L. McAnally	73	20	5	6.9%	3	4.1%	2,475,331	33,909	Sweet Return (GB)	446,180
54	Patrick Gallagher	55	28	5	9.1%	3	5.5%	1,883,313	34,242	Domestic Dispute	293,428
55	Kristin Mulhall	51	17	5	9.8%	3	5.9%	1,875,297	36,771	Imperialism	539,000
56	Mark Shuman	328	107	6	1.8%	1	0.3%	4,130,231	12,592	Umpateedle	209,160
57	Martin D. Wolfson	61	23	6	9.8%	2	3.3%	1,710,079	28,034	Stay Forever	581,946
58	Allen Iwinski	123	60	4	3.3%	1	0.8%	3,001,695	24,404	My Snookie's Boy	283,866
59	Carl A. Nafzger	81	35	4	4.9%	3	3.7%	2,732,948	33,740	Mayo On the Side	405,241
60	Scott A. Lake	423	219	5	1.2%	2	0.5%	7,405,329	17,507	Shake You Down	278,604
61	Michael W. Dickinson	62	28	4	6.5%	3	4.8%	2,036,362	32,845	Tapit	477,500
62	Dallas Stewart	70	33	4	5.7%	2	2.9%	2,170,555	31,008	Clock Stopper	292,725
63	Craig Dollase	60	28	4	6.7%	1	1.7%	1,951,256	32,521	Tangle (Ire)	218,669
64	Barclay Tagg	51	22	3	5.9%	2	3.9%	2,335,781	45,800	Funny Cide	1,075,100
65	Donald Chatlos Jr.	17	8	2	11.8%	1	5.9%	1,528,196	89,894	Singletary	1,192,910
66	Anthony L. Reinstedler	44	19	5	11.4%	1	2.3%	1,435,674	32,629	Aud	257,578
67	W. Bret Calhoun	194	98	4	2.1%	1	0.5%	2,733,984	14,093	Janeian (NZ)	177,820
68	Richard A. Violette Jr.	76	28	4	5.3%	1	1.3%	2,213,729	29,128	Swingforthefences	385,745
69	Gregory D. Foley	78	42	4	5.1%	1	1.3%	2,014,950	25,833	Champali	634,398
70	David R. Bell	51	26	3	5.9%	1	2.0%	2,019,903	39,606	I Thee Wed	314,337
71	Daniel J. Vella	57	25	3	5.3%	1	1.8%	2,198,573	38,571	Mark One	378,988
72	John Charles Zimmerman	164	104	3	1.8%		0.0%	2,554,021	15,573	Banished Lover	164,753
73	Chris M. Block	54	31	4	7.4%		0.0%	1,586,382	29,377	Fort Prado	98,612
74	Laura de Seroux	35	7	3	8.6%	3	8.6%	1,664,329	47,552	Total Impact (Chi)	793,430
75	Edward Plesa Jr.	100	41	5	5.0%		0.0%	1,821,259	18,213	B. B. Best	360,710
76	Edward T. Allard	73	47	4	5.5%	1	1.4%	1,587,655	21,749	Friel's for Real	204,450
77	Michael R. Matz	58	24	3	5.2%	1	1.7%	1,928,354	33,247	Kicken Kris	727,000
78	George Weaver	88	35	4	4.6%	2	2.3%	1,918,713	21,804	Saratoga County	237,390
79	Paulo H. Lobo	35	12	2	5.7%	2	5.7%	1,923,033	54,944	Pico Central (Brz)	1,139,000
80	Marcelo Polanco	50	17	3	6.0%	1	2.0%	1,806,333	36,127	Island Fashion	615,000
81	Michael Machowsky	54	17	2	3.7%	1	1.9%	2,486,767	46,051	Southern Image	1,612,150
82	Josie Carroll	72	29	3	4.2%		0.0%	1,990,780	27,650	Mr. Sulu	140,456
83	William P. White	118	52	5	4.2%		0.0%	1,667,132	14,128	Cin Cin	157,140
84	Troy Young	46	26	5	10.9%		0.0%	1,201,649	26,123	Leslie's Love	189,800
85	David M. Carroll	47	24	4	8.5%	1	2.1%	1,324,580	28,183	Fire Slam	427,381
86	Michael Keogh	29	7	4	13.8%	2	6.9%	1,198,873	41,340	Mobil	440,213
87	Dale Capuano	150	88	2	1.3%		0.0%	2,444,277	16,295	Point Lily	108,430
88	Henry Dominguez	119	55	5	4.2%		0.0%	1,568,023	13,177	Speedy Falcon	208,512
89	George R. Arnold II	51	19	5	9.8%		0.0%	1,270,678	24,915	Ender's Sister	317,580
90	Jonathan E. Sheppard	108	39	4	3.7%	1	0.9%	1,821,893	16,869	Cherokeeinthehills	155,438
91	Gary C. Contessa	137	58	2	1.5%		0.0%	2,718,922	19,846	Angel in Harlem	105,376
92	James J. Toner	31	11	3	9.7%	2	6.5%	1,276,406	41,174	Wonder Again	611,767
93	Paul G. Aguirre	54	20	3	5.6%	1	1.9%	1,532,835	28,386	Texcess	725,427
94	Doris Hebert	142	68	4	2.8%		0.0%	1,613,345	11,362	Mr. Excellent	81,700
95	David Cotey	44	25	2	4.6%		0.0%	1,680,885	38,202	Moonshine Justice	283,914
96	Gerald S. Bennett	83	61	3	3.6%		0.0%	1,475,786	17,781	Demagoguery	108,423
97	David R. Brownlee	26	14	4	15.4%		0.0%	1,044,385	40,169	Secret Request	355,250
98	Danny Pish	152	78	4	2.6%		0.0%	1,594,907	10,493	Leaving On My Mind	299,873
99	Jennifer Pedersen	73	33	2	2.7%		0.0%	2,015,485	27,609	Song of the Sword	258,600
100	Eric Coatrieux	13	7	1	7.7%	1	7.7%	1,335,774	102,752	Niigon	864,610

Leading Trainers by Earnings in 2004

Trainer	No. Strs	No. Wnrs	Total Purses
Todd Pletcher	234	134	$17,511,923
Robert J. Frankel	147	79	15,605,911
Steven Asmussen	585	346	13,993,602
John Servis	66	39	8,922,686
Bob Baffert	155	67	7,535,753
Richard E. Dutrow Jr.	161	91	7,436,771
Scott Lake	423	219	7,405,329
Dale Romans	174	74	7,010,345
Doug O'Neill	270	113	7,001,387
Nick Zito	100	54	6,967,742
Jeff Mullins	180	87	6,832,640
Jerry Hollendorfer	328	185	5,922,484
William I. Mott	170	80	5,690,580
D. Wayne Lukas	123	46	5,567,299
Kiaran McLaughlin	122	50	5,525,744
Mark R. Frostad	59	29	4,912,015
H. Allen Jerkens	64	40	4,447,477
H. Graham Motion	112	52	4,358,674
Shug McGaughey III	59	28	4,208,832
Mark Shuman	328	107	4,130,231
Mark Hennig	115	47	3,954,798
Robert P. Tiller	61	37	3,939,642
Sid C. Attard	59	39	3,844,401
Mike R. Mitchell	132	65	3,834,120
Cole Norman	233	141	3,721,732
Tom Amoss	161	90	3,617,785
Christophe Clement	107	45	3,541,781
Bruce N. Levine	109	62	3,535,539
Bernard S. Flint	132	66	3,513,043
Ken McPeek	92	49	3,418,025
Patrick Biancone	36	20	3,397,917
Julio C. Canani	59	28	3,350,745
Steve Klesaris	113	61	3,189,251
Timothy A. Hills	126	60	3,075,524
Richard Mandella	57	17	3,075,262
Allen Iwinski	123	60	3,001,695
Timothy F. Ritchey	83	47	2,991,693
John W. Sadler	117	49	2,970,367
Mark Casse	110	38	2,946,340
Stanley M. Hough	56	30	2,910,662
Reade Baker	77	33	2,844,159
Vladimir Cerin	84	41	2,796,647
Roger Attfield	57	23	2,777,942
W. Bret Calhoun	194	98	2,733,984
Carl Nafzger	81	35	2,732,948

Leading Trainers by Average Earnings per Starter in 2004
(Minimum of 10 Starters)

Trainer	No. Strs	No. Wnrs	Average Earnings per Starter
John Servis	66	39	$135,192
Robert J. Frankel	147	79	106,163
Aidan O'Brien	10	0	103,730
Eric Coatrieux	13	7	102,752
Patrick Biancone	36	20	94,387
Donald Chatlos Jr.	17	8	89,894
Mark Frostad	59	29	83,254
Jason R. Orman	13	4	78,283
Todd A. Pletcher	234	134	74,837
Catherine Day Phillips	23	10	71,943

Trainer	No. Strs	No. Wnrs	Average Earnings per Starter
James M. Cassidy	36	11	$71,673
Shug McGaughey III	59	28	71,336
Nick Zito	100	54	69,677
H. Allen Jerkens	64	40	69,492
Kenneth B. Parsley	10	7	68,535
Sid C. Attard	59	39	65,159
Robert P. Tiller	61	37	64,584
Julio C. Canani	59	28	56,792
Paulo Lobo	35	12	54,944
Wally Dollase	34	15	54,850
Richard Mandella	57	17	53,952
Lorne Richards	18	10	52,775
James A. Jerkens	47	22	52,595
Sandra L. Slivka	12	5	52,274
Stanley M. Hough	56	30	51,976
Murray W. Johnson	20	4	51,692
Neil Drysdale	52	24	50,585
Leo S. Nechamkin II	10	7	50,334
Thomas Albertrani	21	9	49,827
Macdonald Benson	22	8	48,765
Roger Attfield	57	23	48,736
Patrick J. Kelly	43	14	48,676
Bob Baffert	155	67	48,618
Neil J. Howard	40	21	48,454
Laura de Seroux	35	7	47,552
Richard E. Dutrow Jr.	161	91	46,191
Michael Machowsky	54	17	46,051
Barclay Tagg	51	22	45,800
Kiaran McLaughlin	122	50	45,293
D. Wayne Lukas	123	46	45,263
Ronald C. Cartwright	15	12	43,560
George G. Yetsook	10	7	42,422
Laurie Lafavers	11	5	41,418

Leading Trainers by Stakes Wins in 2004

Trainer	No. Stakes Starts	No. Stakes Wins
Todd A. Pletcher	293	67
Steven M. Asmussen	299	54
Robert J. Frankel	192	51
Bob Baffert	140	29
Richard E. Dutrow Jr.	79	27
Jerry Hollendorfer	117	24
Jeff Mullins	96	21
William I. Mott	137	19
H. Allen Jerkens	85	18
Kiaran P. McLaughlin	97	18
Doug O'Neill	150	18
Dale L. Romans	83	18
Nicholas P. Zito	92	16
Bernard S. Flint	72	15
Robert P. Tiller	42	15
Christophe Clement	66	14
Mark R. Frostad	61	14
D. Wayne Lukas	92	14
Cole Norman	70	13
Martin D. Wolfson	55	13
Julio C. Canani	38	12
Robert E. Holthus	54	12
Hugh H. Robertson	46	12
Stanley M. Hough	44	11
James A. Jerkens	44	11
Kenneth G. McPeek	74	11

Trainer	No. Stakes Starts	No. Stakes Wins
Michael Stidham	61	11
Donnie K. Von Hemel	91	11
Patrick L. Biancone	59	10
Gregory D. Foley	36	10
Claude R. McGaughey III	69	10
H. Graham Motion	75	10
Guadalupe Preciado	42	10
Mark Shuman	75	10
Ron K. Smith	44	10
James M. Cassidy	59	9
Sam B. David Jr.	27	9
Kevin Eikleberry	39	9
Andrew Leggio Jr.	24	9
John C. Servis	44	9
Thomas M. Amoss	60	8
Sid C. Attard	34	8
David R. Brownlee	36	8
David M. Carroll	29	8
Wallace A. Dollase	27	8
Benjamin M. Feliciano Jr.	41	8
Timothy E. Hamm	36	8
Timothy A. Hills	57	8
Scott A. Lake	47	8
Bruce N. Levine	44	8
Ronald L. McAnally	66	8
Dan L. McFarlane	35	8
Mike R. Mitchell	40	8
Danny Pish	31	8
Edward Plesa Jr.	57	8
Merrill R. Scherer	27	8
Troy Young	50	8

Trainer	No. Strs	No. Wnrs	No. SWs
Guadalupe Preciado	106	59	7
Donnie K. Von Hemel	118	63	7
Patrick Biancone	36	20	6
Mark E. Casse	110	38	6
Kevin Eikleberry	36	19	6
Mark Hennig	115	47	6
Timothy A. Hills	126	60	6
Stanley M. Hough	56	30	6
Timothy F. Ritchey	83	47	6
Ben Root	68	30	6
John Sadler	117	49	6
Mark Shuman	328	107	6
Kelly R. Von Hemel	78	42	6
Martin D. Wolfson	61	23	6
George R. Arnold II	51	19	5
Gary W. Cross	49	27	5
David Forster	32	11	5
Ron K. Smith	64	39	5

Leading Trainers by Percent of Stakes Winners from Starters in 2004
(Minimum of 10 Starters)

Trainer	No. Strs	No. Wnrs	No. SWs	SWs/ Strs
Kenneth E. McReynolds	15	9	4	26.7%
Judy Hunter	13	8	3	23.1%
Robert J. Frankel	147	79	30	20.4%
Lyman H. Rollins	15	12	3	20.0%
Janis D. Schoepf	10	8	2	20.0%
Fern Zdunick	10	6	2	20.0%
Hubert Pilon	21	13	4	19.1%
Vannessa Hunt	22	13	4	18.2%
H. Allen Jerkens	64	40	11	17.2%
Robert J. Anderson	18	7	3	16.7%
Patrick L. Biancone	36	20	6	16.7%
Pete Dubois	12	8	2	16.7%
Kevin Eikleberry	36	19	6	16.7%
David Forster	32	11	5	15.6%
David R. Brownlee	26	14	4	15.4%
Francis M. Dullea	13	5	2	15.4%
Karen Haverty	13	8	2	15.4%
Jason R. Orman	13	4	2	15.4%
Bruce F. Phelan	13	8	2	15.4%
Todd A. Pletcher	234	134	36	15.4%
James A. Jerkens	47	22	7	14.9%
Joe Frederick Thomas	27	15	4	14.8%
Wallace A. Dollase	34	15	5	14.7%
Michael Keogh	29	7	4	13.8%
Francis P. Campitelli	22	12	3	13.6%
Mark R. Frostad	59	29	8	13.6%
William Earl Brownlee	15	6	2	13.3%
Ronald C. Cartwright	15	12	2	13.3%
Jeff Trosclair	15	9	2	13.3%
Aubrey Villyard	15	9	2	13.3%
H. Ray Ashford Jr.	38	18	5	13.2%
Robert P. Tiller	61	37	8	13.1%
Neil R. Morris	23	10	3	13.0%
Bob Baffert	155	67	20	12.9%
Anthony Mitchell	31	14	4	12.9%
Martin E. Ciresa	24	11	3	12.5%
Herb Riecken	24	14	3	12.5%
Riley Rycroft	16	6	2	12.5%
Julio C. Canani	59	28	7	11.9%
Claude R. McGaughey III	59	28	7	11.9%
Donald Chatlos Jr.	17	8	2	11.8%

Leading Trainers by Number of Stakes Winners in 2004

Trainer	No. Strs	No. Wnrs	No. SWs
Todd Pletcher	234	134	36
Steven Asmussen	585	346	33
Robert J. Frankel	147	79	30
Bob Baffert	155	67	20
William I. Mott	170	80	18
Richard E. Dutrow Jr.	161	91	17
Jeff Mullins	180	87	16
Doug O'Neill	270	113	14
Jerry Hollendorfer	328	185	13
Kiaran McLaughlin	122	50	12
H. Allen Jerkens	64	40	11
Nick Zito	100	54	11
Bernard S. Flint	132	66	10
Cole Norman	233	141	10
Christophe Clement	107	45	9
Robert E. Holthus	82	45	9
Ken McPeek	92	49	9
Hugh H. Robertson	109	60	9
Mark Frostad	59	29	8
Dale Romans	174	74	8
Michael Stidham	102	48	8
Robert P. Tiller	61	37	8
Julio C. Canani	59	28	7
Benjamin M. Feliciano Jr.	71	37	7
James A. Jerkens	47	22	7
Bruce N. Levine	109	62	7
D. Wayne Lukas	123	46	7
Shug McGaughey III	59	28	7
H. Graham Motion	112	52	7

Leading Trainers by Graded Stakes Wins in 2004

Trainer	No. Graded Stakes Starts	No. Graded Stakes Wins
Robert J. Frankel	165	44
Todd A. Pletcher	171	43
Bob Baffert	90	17
Kiaran P. McLaughlin	74	15
Steven M. Asmussen	60	14
Dale L. Romans	46	12
Mark R. Frostad	40	11
D. Wayne Lukas	63	10
Julio C. Canani	27	9
Patrick L. Biancone	42	8
Christophe Clement	41	8
Richard E. Dutrow Jr.	29	8
H. Allen Jerkens	58	8
Nicholas P. Zito	68	8
Claude R. McGaughey III	52	7
Jeff Mullins	39	7
Wallace A. Dollase	22	6
Manuel Fernandez	31	6
Richard E. Mandella	31	6
Mike R. Mitchell	25	6
James M. Cassidy	37	5
Vladimir Cerin	20	5
Maximo Gomez	31	5
Paulo H. Lobo	19	5
Ronald L. McAnally	44	5
Ramon Morales	38	5
William I. Mott	68	5
Doug O'Neill	54	5
John C. Servis	12	5
P. Douglas Fout	21	4
Jerry Hollendorfer	30	4
Stanley M. Hough	21	4
Neil J. Howard	23	4
James A. Jerkens	22	4
Kenneth G. McPeek	35	4
Neil R. Morris	7	4
H. Graham Motion	40	4
Kristin Mulhall	28	4
Juan M. Rodriguez	16	4
Martin D. Wolfson	14	4
Laura de Seroux	28	3
Julio Diaz Jr.	28	3
Michael W. Dickinson	21	3
Neil D. Drysdale	39	3
Ronald W. Ellis	6	3
Bernard S. Flint	15	3
Gregory D. Foley	9	3
Patrick Gallagher	16	3
David E. Hofmans	8	3
Robert E. Holthus	17	3
Michael Keogh	13	3
Humberto Lopez	9	3
Jorge J. Maymo	25	3
Carl A. Nafzger	31	3
John W. Sadler	25	3
Arderson Santiago	14	3
Barclay Tagg	22	3
James J. Toner	14	3
David R. Vance	17	3
Darrell Vienna	14	3
Wesley A. Ward	8	3

Leading Trainers by Number of Graded Stakes Winners in 2004

Trainer	No. Strs	No. Wnrs	No. GSWs	GSWs/ Strs
Robert J. Frankel	147	79	26	17.7%
Todd Pletcher	234	134	24	10.3%
Bob Baffert	155	67	12	7.7%
Steven Asmussen	585	346	11	1.9%
Kiaran McLaughlin	122	50	9	7.4%
Mark R. Frostad	59	29	7	11.9%
Julio C. Canani	59	28	6	10.2%
Christophe Clement	107	45	6	5.6%
Richard E. Dutrow Jr.	161	91	6	3.7%
Patrick Biancone	36	20	5	13.9%
H. Allen Jerkens	64	40	5	7.8%
D. Wayne Lukas	123	46	5	4.1%
Richard Mandella	57	17	5	8.8%
Shug McGaughey III	59	28	5	8.5%
William Mott	170	80	5	2.9%
Jeff Mullins	180	87	5	2.8%
Nick Zito	100	54	5	5.0%
Vladimir Cerin	84	41	4	4.8%
Jerry Hollendorfer	328	185	4	1.2%
Doug O'Neill	270	113	4	1.5%
Dale Romans	174	74	4	2.3%
James M. Cassidy	36	11	3	8.3%
Laura de Seroux	35	7	3	8.6%
Michael Dickinson	62	28	3	4.8%
Wally Dollase	34	15	3	8.8%
Patrick Gallagher	55	28	3	5.5%
Stanley M. Hough	56	30	3	5.4%
Neil J. Howard	40	21	3	7.5%
Ronald McAnally	73	20	3	4.1%
Ken McPeek	92	49	3	3.3%
H. Graham Motion	112	52	3	2.7%
Kristin Mulhall	51	17	3	5.9%
Carl Nafzger	81	35	3	3.7%
Sanna N. Hendriks	28	16	2	7.1%
James A. Jerkens	47	22	2	4.3%
Patrick J. Kelly	43	14	2	4.7%
Paulo Lobo	35	12	2	5.7%
Mike R. Mitchell	132	65	2	1.5%
John W. Sadler	117	49	2	1.7%
Dallas Stewart	70	33	2	2.9%
George Weaver	88	35	2	2.3%

Leading Trainers by Most Grade 1 Wins in 2004

Trainer	No. G1 Starts	No. G1 Wins
Robert J. Frankel	62	13
D. Wayne Lukas	22	6
Todd A. Pletcher	44	6
Julio C. Canani	19	5
Patrick L. Biancone	20	4
Paulo H. Lobo	12	3
Richard E. Mandella	14	3
Dale L. Romans	9	3
Nicholas P. Zito	23	3
Bob Baffert	27	2
Saeed bin Suroor	4	2
James M. Cassidy	12	2
Wallace A. Dollase	8	2
Neil D. Drysdale	17	2
Mark R. Frostad	13	2

Trainer	No. G1 Starts	No. G1 Wins
H. Allen Jerkens	19	2
Michael Machowsky	4	2
Claude R. McGaughey III	11	2
Mike R. Mitchell	8	2
Neil R. Morris	5	2
H. Graham Motion	8	2
John C. Servis	3	2
Darrell Vienna	7	2

Leading Trainers by Most Grade 1 Winners in 2004

Trainer	No. G1 Starters	No. G1 Winners
Robert J. Frankel	36	10
Patrick L. Biancone	10	4
Julio C. Canani	8	4
Todd A. Pletcher	21	4
D. Wayne Lukas	5	3
Richard E. Mandella	8	3
Bob Baffert	16	2
Saeed bin Suroor	4	2
Wallace A. Dollase	4	2
Neil D. Drysdale	10	2
Mark R. Frostad	9	2
Claude R. McGaughey III	5	2
Mike R. Mitchell	4	2
Dale L. Romans	6	2
Nicholas P. Zito	11	2

Leading Trainers by Number of Wins in 2004

Trainer	No. Strs	No. Wnrs	No. Wins
Steven Asmussen	585	346	555
Scott Lake	423	219	373
Jerry Hollendorfer	328	185	306
Cole Norman	233	141	249
Todd A. Pletcher	234	134	240
Ralph Martinez	133	101	230
John Charles Zimmerman	164	104	193
Doug O'Neill	270	113	170
Bruce M. Kravets	184	93	164
Richard E. Dutrow Jr.	161	91	163
Mark Shuman	328	107	157
Art Sherman	176	101	152
Chris J. Englehart	129	81	149
W. Bret Calhoun	194	98	148
Tom Amoss	161	90	140
Jeff Mullins	180	87	139
Dale Capuano	150	88	135
Robert J. Frankel	147	79	135
Keith L. Bourgeois	165	83	132
Dale Baird	230	100	131
Ronney W. Brown	253	90	131
John F. Martin	173	83	125
Harry F. Thompson Jr.	168	82	125
Bernard S. Flint	132	66	124
John Rigattieri	80	57	122
Danny Pish	152	78	121
Guadalupe Preciado	106	59	118
Gerald S. Bennett	83	61	117
Kevin J. Joy	187	82	117
William Mott	170	80	115
Michael V. Pino	163	72	108

Trainer	No. Strs	No. Wnrs	No. Wins
Dale Romans	174	74	108
Bruce N. Levine	109	62	107
Timothy A. Hills	126	60	103
Jeff C. Runco	189	75	103
Bob Baffert	155	67	102
Doris Hebert	142	68	102
Flint W. Stites	123	55	101
Hugh H. Robertson	109	60	100
Allen Iwinski	123	60	98
Jeffrey A. Radosevich	104	59	98
Dick R. Clark	88	56	97
Kim Hammond	98	55	97
Steve Klesaris	113	61	97
Mike R. Mitchell	132	65	97
Rodney C. Faulkner	98	46	96
David C. Anderson	102	56	94

Most Wins for a Trainers on One Day in 2004

Wins	Trainer	Date	Track(s)
10	Steven M. Asmussen	2/7/2004	DeD, FG, Hou, OP, Sun
7	Steven M. Asmussen	3/27/2004	DeD, FG, GP, Hou, OP, Sun
	Steven M. Asmussen	10/10/2004	Bel, Haw, Kee, LaD, LS
6	Steven M. Asmussen	10/8/2004	Bel, Haw, Kee, LaD, LS, Med
	Steven M. Asmussen	5/31/2004	CD, LaD, LS
	Steven M. Asmussen	7/3/2004	CD, LaD, LS
	Ralph Martinez	5/28/2004	AP, FP, InD
5	Steven M. Asmussen	7/4/2004	AP, CD, LS, PrM
	Steven M. Asmussen	7/10/2004	AP, CRC, LaD, LS
	Steven M. Asmussen	6/16/2004	AP, Bel, CD, LS
	Steven M. Asmussen	6/19/2004	CD, LaD, LS
	Steven M. Asmussen	6/4/2004	AP, Bel, CD, LaD, LS
	Steven M. Asmussen	5/30/2004	AP, CD, LaD, LS
	Steven M. Asmussen	7/29/2004	AP, ELP, LaD, Ret, Sar
	Steven M. Asmussen	10/1/2004	Haw, LaD, LS, TP
	Steven M. Asmussen	10/23/2004	Bel, Haw, LaD, LS
	Steven M. Asmussen	10/24/2004	Haw, Kee, LaD, LS
	Steven M. Asmussen	11/6/2004	CD, Haw, Med, Sun
	Steven M. Asmussen	11/7/2004	Aqu, CD, Sun
	Steven M. Asmussen	11/20/2004	Aqu, CD, DeD, Haw, Hou, Sun
	Steven M. Asmussen	11/26/2004	Aqu, CD, FG, Haw, Hou, Sun
	Steven M. Asmussen	12/18/2004	Aqu, FG, Hou, Sun
	Steven M. Asmussen	4/3/2004	Hou, Kee, OP, Sun
	Steven M. Asmussen	4/4/2004	Hou, Kee, OP, Sun
	Steven M. Asmussen	1/29/2004	DeD, FG, GP, Hou
	Jerry Hollendorfer	5/26/2004	BM
	Scott A. Lake	5/30/2004	Del, Pha
	Scott A. Lake	11/13/2004	Med, Pha, Pim
	William I. Mott	6/26/2004	Bel, CD, Pha
	Todd A. Pletcher	3/13/2004	Aqu, GP
	Todd A. Pletcher	8/30/2004	Sar
	Todd A. Pletcher	10/30/2004	Aqu, Del, LS, Med

Most Wins for a Trainers on One Program in 2004

Wins	Trainer	Date	Track
5	Steven M. Asmussen	5/31/2004	LS
	Jerry Hollendorfer	5/26/2004	BM
	Todd A. Pletcher	8/30/2004	Sar

Wins	Trainer	Date	Track
4	David C. Anderson	2/16/2004	Fon
	Steven M. Asmussen	7/4/2004	CD
	Steven M. Asmussen	11/7/2004	Sun
	Steven M. Asmussen	10/24/2004	LS
	Steven M. Asmussen	12/18/2004	Hou
	Steven M. Asmussen	3/27/2004	OP
	Gerald S. Bennett	7/12/2004	GLD
	Gerald S. Bennett	8/30/2004	GLD
	Keith L. Bourgeois	10/2/2004	DeD
	Ronney W. Brown	11/20/2004	CT
	Dick R. Clark	5/31/2004	PrM
	Dick R. Clark	7/10/2004	PrM
	Reid Gross	3/20/2004	Beu
	Doris Hebert	3/26/2004	DeD
	Jerry Hollendorfer	5/23/2004	BM
	Jerry Hollendorfer	7/31/2004	SR
	Kevin J. Joy	11/13/2004	CT
	Bruce M. Kravets	2/19/2004	Pen
	Bruce M. Kravets	4/10/2004	Pen
	Bruce M. Kravets	9/18/2004	Pen

Wins	Trainer	Date	Track
4	Bruce M. Kravets	9/25/2004	Pen
	Ralph Martinez	3/26/2004	FP
	Ralph Martinez	4/3/2004	FP
	Ralph Martinez	4/6/2004	FP
	Ralph Martinez	4/17/2004	FP
	Ralph Martinez	5/11/2004	FP
	Ralph Martinez	6/25/2004	FP
	Ralph Martinez	7/20/2004	FP
	Ralph Martinez	8/20/2004	FP
	Ralph Martinez	10/21/2004	Hoo
	Cole Norman	6/12/2004	LaD
	Cole Norman	9/2/2004	LaD
	Cole Norman	10/10/2004	LaD
	Danny Pish	10/23/2004	LS
	Todd A. Pletcher	3/13/2004	GP
	Todd A. Pletcher	6/6/2004	Bel
	Jeffrey A. Radosevich	12/13/2004	Tdn
	John M. Rodriguez	6/26/2004	Suf
	Ardell Sayler	7/18/2004	AsD
	John Charles Zimmerman	9/23/2004	Pen
	Jimmy Zook	5/8/2004	FP

Leading Trainers by Most Purses in a Year (1980-2004)

Trainer	Year	Purses	Leading Earner
Robert J. Frankel	2003	$19,143,289	Medaglia d'Oro ($1,990,000)
D. Wayne Lukas	1988	17,842,358	Gulch ($1,360,840)
Robert J. Frankel	2002	17,750,340	Medaglia d'Oro ($2,245,000)
Todd A. Pletcher	2004	17,511,923	Ashado ($2,259,640)
D. Wayne Lukas	1987	17,502,110	Tejano ($1,177,189)
Bob Hebert	1999	16,842,332	Silverbulletday ($1,707,640)
D. Wayne Lukas	1989	16,103,998	Steinlen (GB) ($1,521,378)
D. Wayne Lukas	1996	15,967,609	Boston Harbor ($1,928,605)
D. Wayne Lukas	1991	15,953,757	Farma Way ($2,598,350)
Robert J. Frankel	2004	15,605,911	Ghostzapper ($2,590,000)
Robert J. Frankel	2001	14,607,446	Skimming ($1,330,000)
D. Wayne Lukas	1990	14,508,871	Criminal Type ($2,270,290)
Steven M. Asmussen	2004	14,003,445	Lady Tak ($439,412)
D. Wayne Lukas	1995	12,852,843	Thunder Gulch ($2,644,080)
Bob Baffert	2001	12,761,034	Point Given ($3,350,000)
Bob Baffert	1998	12,608,670	Silver Charm ($2,296,506)
Todd A. Pletcher	2003	12,356,924	Balto Star ($907,500)
D. Wayne Lukas	1986	12,344,520	Lady's Secret ($1,871,053)
D. Wayne Lukas	1999	12,070,460	Cat Thief ($3,020,500)
Bob Baffert	2002	12,029,115	War Emblem ($3,125,000)
Bob Baffert	2000	11,793,355	Captain Steve ($1,882,276)
William I. Mott	1995	11,789,625	Cigar ($4,819,800)
Steven M. Asmussen	2003	11,727,910	Lady Tak ($675,350)
William I. Mott	1996	11,703,723	Cigar ($2,510,000)
Charles E. Whittingham	1989	11,402,231	Sunday Silence ($4,578,454)
D. Wayne Lukas	1985	11,155,188	Lady's Secret ($994,349)
D. Wayne Lukas	2000	10,492,317	Spain ($1,925,500)
D. Wayne Lukas	1997	10,351,397	Marlin ($1,521,600)
Steven M. Asmussen	2002	10,248,260	Easyfromthegitgo ($606,905)
Robert J. Frankel	2000	10,239,071	Chester House ($1,408,500)
D. Wayne Lukas	1992	10,061,240	Mountain Cat ($1,460,627)
William I. Mott	1998	10,012,899	Escena ($2,032,425)
Richard E. Mandella	2003	9,869,548	Pleasantly Perfect ($2,470,000)
William I. Mott	1997	9,474,680	Ajina ($979,175)
Bob Baffert	2003	9,442,281	Congaree ($1,608,000)
William I. Mott	2001	9,418,657	Hap ($919,070)
Charles E. Whittingham	1987	9,415,097	Ferdinand ($2,185,150)
D. Wayne Lukas	1994	9,249,577	Tabasco Cat ($2,164,334)
Scott A. Lake	2003	9,163,599	Shake You Down ($814,640)
Robert J. Frankel	1993	8,928,602	Bertrando ($2,217,800)
John C. Servis	2004	8,922,686	Smarty Jones ($7,563,535)
Bob Baffert	1997	8,867,128	Silver Charm ($1,638,750)
Charles E. Whittingham	1986	8,801,284	Estrapade ($1,184,800)
Todd A. Pletcher	2002	8,702,228	Left Bank ($626,146)
William I. Mott	2000	8,591,389	Snow Polina ($772,943)
Richard E. Mandella	1997	8,432,774	Gentlemen (Arg) ($2,125,300)
Ronald L. McAnally	1991	8,388,214	Festin (Arg) ($2,003,250)
Scott A. Lake	2002	8,307,347	Thunderello ($355,600)

Leading Jockeys of 2004

Jockeys have been described as pound for pound the strongest human athletes. Their task is formidable: balance by their toes on a half-ton of fury and navigate through a 35 mph stampede to the winner's circle. Often, they perform this feat seven or eight times a day. From the time they first show ability astride a horse, they are destined to pursue only this one calling—as long as they keep their weight under 112 pounds or so.

Hundreds of men and women possess the agility and ability to ride professionally and make a living as a jockey. Some transcend their peers and become leaders of their circuits or the sport. A very, very few achieve greatness. Eddie Arcaro ruled the 1940s, and Bill Shoemaker was the little man with the gifted hands through the 1960s. He passed the crown to Laffit Pincay Jr., who set a new standard of accomplishment, with more than 9,500 victories while riding on the most competitive circuits in North America.

For a decade beginning in the mid-1990s, Jerry Bailey and Pat Day were leaders in a very talented colony of North American jockeys. As they and their contemporaries began to contemplate life after racing, a new generation emerged to assume the top spots on the leader board. For the second consecutive year in 2004, John Ve-

Leading Jockeys by Purses Won

North American Earnings Only

Year	Jockey	Wins	Purses
2004	John R. Velazquez	335	$22,250,261
2003	Jerry D. Bailey	206	23,354,960
2002	Jerry D. Bailey	213	19,271,814
2001	Jerry D. Bailey	227	19,015,720
2000	Pat Day	267	17,481,863
1999	Pat Day	254	18,094,045
1998	Pat Day	276	17,380,569
1997	Jerry D. Bailey	272	15,920,743
1996	Jerry D. Bailey	297	17,815,376
1995	Jerry D. Bailey	287	16,315,288
1994	Mike E. Smith	316	15,974,592
1993	Mike E. Smith	342	14,017,365
1992	Kent J. Desormeaux	364	14,196,390
1991	Chris J. McCarron	265	14,437,083
1990	Gary L. Stevens	283	13,881,198
1989	Jose A. Santos	285	13,838,389
1988	Jose A. Santos	369	14,856,214
1987	Jose A. Santos	305	12,405,075
1986	Jose A. Santos	328	11,330,067
1985	Laffit A. Pincay Jr.	289	13,315,049
1984	Chris J. McCarron	355	11,997,588
1983	Angel Cordero Jr.	362	10,116,697
1982	Angel Cordero Jr.	397	9,675,040
1981	Chris J. McCarron	326	8,399,712
1980	Chris J. McCarron	405	7,666,100

lazquez led the THOROUGHBRED TIMES rankings of leading jockeys.

THOROUGHBRED TIMES Leading Jockeys of 2004

Rankings based on formula that gives equal weighting to three statistical categories for performance in 2004: 1) percent winners from mounts; 2) total number of wins; and 3) average earnings per mount. A minimum of 100 starters is required to be considered for inclusion. Statistics are for North America only and for racing in 2004.

Rank	Jockey	No. Mounts	No. Wins	Wins/ Mounts	No. SW	Stakes Wins/ Mounts	No. GSWs	Total Purses	Average Earnings/ Mount	Leading Earner	Earnings of Leading Earner
1	John R. Velazquez	1,325	335	25.3%	56	4.2%	40	$22,250,261	$16,793	Ashado	$1,829,640
2	Ramon A. Dominguez	1,348	382	28.3%	27	2.0%	8	11,478,569	8,515	Better Talk Now	1,365,000
3	Rafael Bejarano	1,922	455	23.7%	31	1.6%	11	12,210,108	6,353	Colonial Colony	548,665
4	Russell Baze	1,182	321	27.2%	16	1.4%	4	5,771,940	4,883	Adreamisborn	214,520
5	Edgar Prado	1,445	281	19.5%	50	3.5%	34	18,342,230	12,694	Birdstone	1,200,000
6	Corey Nakatani	1,076	220	20.5%	33	3.1%	15	12,448,657	11,569	Sweet Catomine	640,000
7	Todd Kabel	686	156	22.7%	36	5.3%	14	10,637,082	15,506	Soaring Free	1,042,500
8	Pat Day	798	172	21.6%	26	3.3%	12	10,882,222	13,637	Azeri	678,750
9	Jerry Bailey	639	147	23.0%	43	6.7%	35	14,427,544	22,578	Pleasantly Perfect	1,040,000
10	Stewart Elliott	1,357	260	19.2%	29	2.1%	8	14,516,071	10,697	Smarty Jones	7,563,535
11	Eibar Coa	1,011	209	20.7%	42	4.2%	8	7,739,268	7,655	Pollard's Vision	490,000
12	Shane Sellers	698	146	20.9%	24	3.4%	11	6,533,154	9,360	The Cliff's Edge	910,000
13	Victor Espinoza	1,331	239	18.0%	39	2.9%	27	15,902,377	11,948	Southern Image	1,612,150
14	Alex Solis	548	117	21.4%	27	4.9%	19	7,862,599	14,348	Pico Central (Brz)	660,000
15	Rene Douglas	1,296	242	18.7%	14	1.1%	6	8,495,284	6,555	Madcap Escapade	389,200
16	Joe Bravo	1,152	214	18.6%	19	1.7%	8	8,163,405	7,086	Lion Heart	670,000
17	Chad Phillip Schvaneveldt	586	144	24.6%	5	0.9%		2,653,250	4,528	Onebigbag	92,272
18	Ryan Fogelsonger	1,065	217	20.4%	15	1.4%	2	4,525,877	4,250	Art Fan	125,695
19	Patrick Husbands	748	141	18.9%	10	1.3%	2	7,432,199	9,936	Classic Stamp	419,837
20	Lonnie Meche	925	199	21.5%	16	1.7%		3,417,018	3,694	Happy Ticket	247,260
21	Tyler Baze	1,394	239	17.1%	18	1.3%	8	10,177,312	7,301	Star Over the Bay	418,800
22	Pedro V. Alvarado	533	130	24.4%	9	1.7%	1	2,216,447	4,158	See Me Through	127,911
23	Ken S. Tohill	829	194	23.4%	18	2.2%		2,825,384	3,408	Shemoveslikeaghost	174,774
24	Javier Castellano	1,277	212	16.6%	27	2.1%	14	13,023,589	10,199	Ghostzapper	2,590,000
25	Roman Chapa	956	214	22.4%	11	1.2%		3,205,914	3,353	Leaving On My Mind	281,730
26	Jeremy Rose	881	164	18.6%	6	0.7%	2	4,541,292	5,155	Afleet Alex	680,800
27	Robby Albarado	1,309	213	16.3%	29	2.2%	10	10,371,173	7,923	Stellar Jayne	944,761
28	Richard Migliore	869	149	17.2%	18	2.1%	13	8,039,995	9,252	Friends Lake	611,800
29	Patrick Valenzuela	201	45	22.4%	3	1.5%	3	1,864,873	9,278	Designed for Luck	304,180
30	Eddie M. Martin Jr.	1,300	225	17.3%	18	1.4%	4	5,658,957	4,353	Halory Leigh	201,624
31	Anthony S. Black	668	148	22.2%	7	1.1%		2,321,682	3,476	Prince Joseph	104,720

Rank	Jockey	No. Mounts	No. Wins	Wins/ Mounts	No. SW	Stakes Wins/ Mounts	No. GSWs	Total Purses	Average Earnings/ Mount	Leading Earner	Earnings of Leading Earner
32	Eddie Castro	1,547	268	17.3%	18	1.2%	2	6,074,613	3,927	Stay Forever	554,346
33	Roberto Alvarado Jr.	909	167	18.4%	5	0.6%		3,863,571	4,250	Hopelessly Devoted	135,000
34	Harry Vega	872	177	20.3%	5	0.6%		2,764,234	3,170	Lady of the Future	145,905
35	Cornelio H. Velasquez	1,584	240	15.2%	20	1.3%	8	11,086,720	6,999	Society Selection	600,000
36	Abel Castellano Jr.	1,202	200	16.6%	14	1.2%	2	5,050,996	4,202	Silmaril	178,390
37	Quincy Welch	794	173	21.8%	8	1.0%		2,274,600	2,865	Kat Kool	70,054
38	Mario Pino	920	156	17.0%	13	1.4%		4,285,750	4,658	Misty Sixes	230,520
39	Ronald J. Warren Jr.	921	167	18.1%	13	1.4%		3,298,517	3,581	Marwood	195,400
40	Steve J. Bourque	885	177	20.0%	9	1.0%		2,717,990	3,071	Kodema	90,000
41	Travis Dunkelberger	892	160	17.9%	7	0.8%		3,306,687	3,707	Crafty Carni	73,973
42	Dana G. Whitney	1,428	267	18.7%	4	0.3%		4,184,757	2,931	Sataniste	75,490
43	Gary Stevens	264	48	18.2%	9	3.4%	5	3,477,524	13,172	Rock Hard Ten	407,600
44	Mike Smith	688	110	16.0%	17	2.5%	13	7,823,902	11,372	Total Impact (Chi)	721,000
45	Chad K. Murphy	861	157	18.2%	6	0.7%		2,985,318	3,467	Danieltown	161,606
46	Dennis Carr	936	170	18.2%	1	0.1%	1	3,209,457	3,429	Attack Force	90,590
47	James McAleney	682	110	16.1%	8	1.2%	4	5,981,418	8,770	I Thee Wed	314,337
48	Rick Wilson	108	24	22.2%	3	2.8%		553,885	5,129	Friel's for Real	52,050
49	Timothy T. Doocy	1,029	187	18.2%	15	1.5%	1	3,259,729	3,168	Wild Wild West	103,530
50	Kent Desormeaux	690	108	15.7%	17	2.5%	10	8,661,263	12,553	Ticker Tape (GB)	1,077,295
51	Gerard Melancon	1,267	205	16.2%	22	1.7%	1	4,711,881	3,719	Fantasticat	312,000
52	Eusebio Razo Jr.	979	159	16.2%	6	0.6%	2	4,254,204	4,345	Eye of the Tiger	210,000
53	Martin Pedroza	823	138	16.8%	10	1.2%	1	3,711,847	4,510	Truly a Judge	87,600
54	Manoel R. Cruz	1,192	201	16.9%	13	1.1%		4,126,181	3,462	Kaufy Mate	150,000
55	Monte Clifton Berry	1,191	234	19.7%	6	0.5%		3,180,955	2,671	Maysville Slew	198,600
56	Roberto M. Gonzalez	965	163	16.9%	11	1.1%	4	3,467,832	3,594	Ema Bovary (Chi)	521,780
57	Charles C. Lopez	654	107	16.4%	6	0.9%	3	3,984,081	6,092	Gators N Bears	282,440
58	Julio A. Garcia	416	76	18.3%	8	1.9%		1,773,518	4,263	Hear No Evil	108,500
59	Jozbin Z. Santana	750	131	17.5%	9	1.2%	1	2,667,243	3,556	He Loves Me	289,000
60	Dyn Panell	717	159	22.2%	4	0.6%		1,815,546	2,532	Senor Ladd	119,750
61	Brian Joseph Hernandez Jr.	1,463	243	16.6%	4	0.3%		4,399,917	3,007	Gigawatt	78,715
62	John McKee	1,444	210	14.5%	12	0.8%	3	6,062,316	4,198	Greater Good	226,275
63	Kevin Radke	338	65	19.2%	1	0.3%		1,169,456	3,460	Heavenly Humor	38,640
64	David Flores	873	123	14.1%	20	2.3%	13	8,364,997	9,582	Board Elligible	903,600
65	Pablo Fragoso	1,174	164	14.0%	10	0.9%	3	7,159,551	6,098	Board Elligible	219,445
66	Angel R. Quinones	1,208	199	16.5%	2	0.2%		3,736,142	3,093	Fort Smith	58,600
67	Larry J. Sterling Jr.	786	125	15.9%	6	0.8%		3,115,016	3,963	Synco Peach	194,940
68	Terry J. Thompson	638	109	17.1%	7	1.1%	1	2,244,212	3,518	Island Sand	334,400
69	Carlos H. Marquez Jr.	765	119	15.6%	12	1.6%	2	3,508,554	4,586	Golden Sonata	130,000
70	Jose Santos	982	137	14.0%	20	2.0%	12	7,599,843	7,739	Funny Cide	1,025,100
71	Mark Guidry	785	120	15.3%	7	0.9%	2	3,900,613	4,969	Angela's Love	184,260
72	Ramsey Zimmerman	1,294	326	25.2%	7	0.5%		2,597,885	2,008	Moe B Dick	65,128
73	Julian Pimentel	740	112	15.1%	10	1.4%	1	4,121,065	5,569	Hey Chub	115,667
74	Bobby J. Walker Jr.	509	93	18.3%	2	0.4%		1,635,756	3,214	Cobra Lady	81,189
75	Jose Luis Flores	925	178	19.2%		0.0%		2,303,693	2,490	Oliver Street	60,725
76	Mick Ruis	1,052	171	16.3%	8	0.8%		3,291,219	3,129	Very Vegas	174,998
77	Michael J. Luzzi	780	114	14.6%	9	1.2%	1	4,689,488	6,012	Shake You Down	166,500
78	Rickey Walcott	702	138	19.7%	5	0.7%		1,835,637	2,615	Sixthirtyjoe	98,714
79	Francine Villeneuve	391	67	17.1%	4	1.0%		1,457,356	3,727	Wholelottabourbon	207,255
80	Christopher A. Emigh	1,188	175	14.7%	4	0.3%	1	4,268,280	3,593	Allspice	178,594
81	Glenn W. Corbett	833	156	18.7%	6	0.7%		2,143,377	2,573	Switch Lanes	96,180
82	Jose C. Caraballo	711	106	14.9%	5	0.7%		2,961,983	4,166	Play Bingo	121,830
83	Corey J. Lanerie	1,095	165	15.1%	8	0.7%	1	3,602,925	3,290	Ole Rebel	145,600
84	Elvis Joseph Perrodin	550	86	15.6%	12	2.2%		2,140,481	3,892	Old Lee	140,550
85	Joe M. Castro	442	76	17.2%	3	0.7%	1	1,442,296	3,263	A B Noodle	112,175
86	Casey T. Lambert	925	151	16.3%	6	0.7%		2,640,954	2,855	Berdelia	170,498
87	Dino Luciani	461	67	14.5%	3	0.7%	1	3,164,150	6,864	Kissed by a Prince	167,986
88	Jono C. Jones	670	91	13.6%	8	1.2%	2	5,978,103	8,923	A Bit O'Gold	1,060,790
89	Abdiel Toribio	497	80	16.1%	7	1.4%		1,761,540	3,544	Cin Cin	157,140
90	John Jacinto	1,139	202	17.7%	12	1.1%		2,747,169	2,412	Katlin's Rocket	96,180
91	Seth B. Martinez	674	114	16.9%	8	1.2%		1,911,756	2,836	Vazandar	101,742
92	Javier Santiago	642	88	13.7%	5	0.8%	3	4,237,653	6,601	Wimbledon	402,600
93	Willie Martinez	1,057	152	14.4%	6	0.6%	3	3,636,500	3,440	Brass Hat	516,780
94	Carl James Woodley	880	156	17.7%		0.0%		2,175,423	2,472	Honey Hit	88,787
95	Craig Perret	226	33	14.6%	4	1.8%	2	1,809,832	8,008	Halory Leigh	190,746
96	Christopher P. DeCarlo	447	65	14.5%	18	4.0%	2	2,379,824	5,324	Capeside Lady	248,795
97	Alfredo J. Juarez Jr.	652	119	18.3%	11	1.7%		1,652,933	2,535	Hush's Gold	82,905
98	Tony Noguez	337	62	18.4%	6	1.8%		954,415	2,832	Icy Lane	105,870
99	Pedro A. Rodriguez	722	143	19.8%	2	0.3%		1,577,404	2,185	Wild Bill Hiccup	54,840
100	Donald R. Pettinger	474	72	15.2%	8	1.7%	2	1,716,614	3,622	Cryptograph	257,398

Leading Jockeys by Earnings in 2004

Jockey	No. Mounts	No. Wins	Total Purses
John R. Velazquez	1,325	335	$22,250,261
Edgar Prado	1,445	281	18,342,230
Victor Espinoza	1,331	239	15,902,377
Stewart Elliott	1,357	260	14,516,071
Jerry Bailey	639	147	14,427,544
Javier Castellano	1,277	212	13,023,589
Corey Nakatani	1,076	220	12,448,657
Rafael Bejarano	1,922	455	12,210,108
Ramon A. Dominguez	1,348	382	11,478,569
Cornelio Velasquez	1,584	240	11,086,720
Pat Day	798	172	10,882,222
Todd Kabel	686	156	10,637,082
Robby Albarado	1,309	213	10,371,173
Tyler Baze	1,394	239	10,177,312
Kent Desormeaux	690	108	8,661,263
Rene Douglas	1,296	242	8,495,284
David Flores	873	123	8,364,997
Joe Bravo	1,152	214	8,163,405
Richard Migliore	869	149	8,039,995
Alex Solis	548	117	7,862,599
Mike Smith	688	110	7,823,902
Eibar Coa	1,011	209	7,739,268
Jose Santos	982	137	7,599,843
Patrick Husbands	748	141	7,432,199
Pablo Fragoso	1,174	164	7,159,551
Shaun Bridgmohan	1,256	153	7,071,254
Shane Sellers	698	146	6,533,154
Eddie Castro	1,547	268	6,074,613
John McKee	1,444	210	6,062,316
Emile Ramsammy	935	94	6,009,954
James McAleney	682	110	5,981,418
Jono C. Jones	670	91	5,978,103
Russell Baze	1,182	321	5,771,940
Eddie M. Martin Jr.	1,300	225	5,658,957
Jose Valdivia Jr.	757	76	5,643,270
Jorge Chavez	927	119	5,280,942
Abel Castellano Jr.	1,202	200	5,050,996
Gerard Melancon	1,267	205	4,711,881
Aaron Gryder	966	113	4,711,511
Michael Luzzi	780	114	4,689,488
Jon Kenton Court	771	82	4,606,598

Leading Jockeys by Average Earnings per Starter in 2004
(Minimum of 20 Mounts)

Jockey	No. Mounts	No. Wins	Average Earnings per Starter
Jerry Bailey	639	147	22,578
John R. Velazquez	1,325	335	16,793
Todd Kabel	686	156	15,506
Alex Solis	548	117	14,348
Pat Day	798	172	13,637
Gary Stevens	264	48	13,172
Edgar Prado	1,445	281	12,694
Kent Desormeaux	690	108	12,553
Victor Espinoza	1,331	239	11,948
Corey Nakatani	1,076	220	11,569
Mike Smith	688	110	11,372
Stewart Elliott	1,357	260	10,697

Jockey	No. Mounts	No. Wins	Average Earnings per Starter
Javier Castellano	1,277	212	$10,199
Patrick Husbands	748	141	9,936
David Flores	873	123	9,582
Shane Sellers	698	146	9,360
Patrick Valenzuela	201	45	9,278
Richard Migliore	869	149	9,252
Jono C. Jones	670	91	8,923
James McAleney	682	110	8,770
Ramon A. Dominguez	1,348	382	8,515
Craig Perret	226	33	8,008
Robby Albarado	1,309	213	7,923
Robert C. Landry	529	58	7,835
Tony Farina	47	6	7,763
Jose Santos	982	137	7,739
Eibar Coa	1,011	209	7,655
Eric Saint-Martin	68	11	7,583
Jose Valdivia Jr.	757	76	7,455
Tyler Baze	1,394	239	7,301
Brice Blanc	551	65	7,230
Joe Bravo	1,152	214	7,086
Cornelio Velasquez	1,584	240	6,999
Dino Luciani	461	67	6,864
Slade Callaghan	555	73	6,796
Javier Santiago	642	88	6,601
Steven R. Bahen	544	69	6,578
David Clark	429	55	6,570
Rene Douglas	1,296	242	6,555
Emile Ramsammy	935	94	6,428
James McKnight	210	25	6,378
Rafael Bejarano	1,922	455	6,353
Pablo Fragoso	1,174	164	6,098
Charles C. Lopez	654	107	6,092
Michael J. Luzzi	780	114	6,012
Jon Kenton Court	771	82	5,975
Richard Dos Ramos	364	35	5,790
Jorge Chavez	927	119	5,697
Shaun Bridgmohan	1,256	153	5,630
Gerry Olguin	415	44	5,605
Julian Pimentel	740	112	5,569
Constant Montpellier	592	62	5,404
Christopher DeCarlo	447	65	5,324
Jose A. Velez Jr.	516	60	5,323
Jeremy Rose	881	164	5,155
Norberto Arroyo Jr.	825	108	5,150
Danny Sorenson	287	38	5,146
Rick Wilson	108	24	5,129

Leading Jockeys by Number of Stakes Wins in 2004

Jockey	No. Mounts	No. Wins	No. Stakes Wins
John R. Velazquez	1,325	335	56
Edgar Prado	1,445	281	50
Jerry Bailey	639	147	43
Eibar Coa	1,011	209	42
Victor Espinoza	1,331	239	39
Todd Kabel	686	156	36
Corey Nakatani	1,076	220	33
Rafael Bejarano	1,922	455	31
Robby Albarado	1,309	213	29
Stewart Elliott	1,357	260	29

Jockey	No. Mounts	No. Wins	No. Stakes Wins
Javier Castellano	1,277	212	27
Ramon A. Dominguez	1,348	382	27
Alex Solis	548	117	27
Pat Day	798	172	26
Shane Sellers	698	146	24
Gerard Melancon	1,267	205	22
David Flores	873	123	20
Jose Santos	982	137	20
Cornelio Velasquez	1,584	240	20
Joe Bravo	1,152	214	19
Tyler Baze	1,394	239	18
Eddie Castro	1,547	268	18
Christopher DeCarlo	447	65	18
Eddie M. Martin Jr.	1,300	225	18
Richard Migliore	869	149	18
Ken S. Tohill	829	194	18
Kent Desormeaux	690	108	17
Mike Smith	688	110	17
Russell A. Baze	1,182	321	16
Jorge Martin Bourdieu	676	95	16
Lonnie Meche	925	199	16
Brice Blanc	551	65	15
Jose Valdivia Jr.	757	76	15

Jockey	Stakes Mounts	Stakes Wnrs
Kent J. Desormeaux	88	12
Lonnie Meche	58	12
Ken S. Tohill	39	12
Jose Valdivia Jr.	67	11
Norberto Arroyo Jr.	55	10
Aaron T. Gryder	61	10
Patrick Husbands	53	10
John Jacinto	45	10
Carlos H. Marquez Jr.	52	10
John McKee	64	10
Martin A. Pedroza	47	10
Julian Pimentel	59	10
Emile Ramsammy	66	10
Pablo Fragoso	66	9
Michael J. Luzzi	53	9
Berkley R. Packer	20	9
Luis E. Perez	26	9
Elvis Joseph Perrodin	50	9
Mario G. Pino	43	9
Javier Santiago	76	9
Gary L. Stevens	65	9
Ronald J. Warren Jr.	25	9

Leading Jockeys by Number of Stakes Winners in 2004

Jockey	Stakes Mounts	Stakes Wnrs
John R. Velazquez	139	44
Edgar S. Prado	165	43
Eibar Coa	129	38
Jerry D. Bailey	129	31
Victor Espinoza	138	31
Corey S. Nakatani	110	26
Ramon A. Dominguez	91	24
Rafael Bejarano	106	23
Robby Albarado	124	22
Javier Castellano	113	22
Todd Kabel	52	22
Alex O. Solis	66	22
Pat Day	120	20
Stewart Elliott	99	20
Cornelio H. Velasquez	148	20
Shane J. Sellers	62	19
David Romero Flores	104	18
Joe Bravo	108	17
Gerard Melancon	69	17
Christopher P. DeCarlo	51	16
Eddie M. Martin Jr.	79	16
Jose A. Santos	108	16
Tyler Baze	108	15
Richard Migliore	89	14
Mike E. Smith	88	14
Russell A. Baze	45	13
Brice Blanc	66	13
Eddie Castro	79	13
Timothy T. Doocy	39	13
Rene R. Douglas	98	13
Ryan Fogelsonger	53	13
Scott A. Stevens	60	13
Abel Castellano Jr.	62	12
Manoel R. Cruz	67	12

Leading Jockeys by Percent of Stakes Wins from Mounts in 2004
(Minimum of 10 Mounts)

Jockey	No. Mounts	No. Wins	No. Stakes Wins	Stakes Wins/ Mounts
Lanfranco Dettori	13	3	3	23.1%
Kieren Fallon	11	4	2	18.2%
Jerry Bailey	639	147	43	6.7%
Larry D. Payne	30	5	2	6.7%
Chris Bowen	19	4	1	5.3%
Todd Kabel	686	156	36	5.3%
Melissa Marshall	20	5	1	5.0%
Alex Solis	548	117	27	4.9%
Paul Green	22	1	1	4.6%
Cody House	23	1	1	4.4%
Eric Saint-Martin	68	11	3	4.4%
Serge Rocheleau	188	56	8	4.3%
Eibar Coa	1,011	209	42	4.2%
Ralph Garcia Jr.	24	7	1	4.2%
Russell Kingrey	96	28	4	4.2%
John Velazquez	1,325	335	56	4.2%
Jay Conklin	253	60	10	4.0%
Christopher DeCarlo	447	65	18	4.0%
James Bo White	52	10	2	3.9%
Berkley R. Packer	348	73	13	3.7%
Roger Butterfly	83	13	3	3.6%
Travis Hamilton	56	7	2	3.6%
Shannon Wippert	165	31	6	3.6%
Edgar Prado	1,445	281	50	3.5%
Shane Sellers	698	146	24	3.4%
Gary Stevens	264	48	9	3.4%
Pat Day	798	172	26	3.3%
Peter McAleney	218	44	7	3.2%
Corey Nakatani	1,076	220	33	3.1%
Scott Sterr	291	61	9	3.1%
Scot A. Schindler	99	19	3	3.0%
Victor Espinoza	1,331	239	39	2.9%
Hugh Cade Huston	68	9	2	2.9%

Leading Jockeys by Number of Graded Stakes Wins in 2004

Jockey	No. Mounts	No. Wins	No. Graded Stakes Wins	Graded Wins/ Mounts
John R. Velazquez	1,325	335	40	3.0%
Jerry Bailey	639	147	35	5.5%
Edgar Prado	1,445	281	34	2.4%
Victor Espinoza	1,331	239	27	2.0%
Alex Solis	548	117	19	3.5%
Corey Nakatani	1,076	220	15	1.4%
Javier Castellano	1,277	212	14	1.1%
Todd Kabel	686	156	14	2.0%
David Flores	873	123	13	1.5%
Richard Migliore	869	149	13	1.5%
Mike Smith	688	110	13	1.9%
Pat Day	798	172	12	1.5%
Jose A. Santos	982	137	12	1.2%
Rafael Bejarano	1,922	455	11	0.6%
Shane Sellers	698	146	11	1.6%
Robby Albarado	1,309	213	10	0.8%
Kent Desormeaux	690	108	10	1.5%
Tyler Baze	1,394	239	8	0.6%
Brice Blanc	551	65	8	1.5%
Joe Bravo	1,152	214	8	0.7%
Eibar Coa	1,011	209	8	0.8%
Ramon A. Dominguez	1,348	382	8	0.6%
Stewart Elliott	1,357	260	8	0.6%
Jose Valdivia Jr.	757	76	8	1.1%
Cornelio Velasquez	1,584	240	8	0.5%
Rene Douglas	1,296	242	6	0.5%
Jon Court	771	82	5	0.7%
Gary Stevens	264	48	5	1.9%
Russell Baze	1,182	321	4	0.3%
Jorge Chavez	927	119	4	0.4%
Roberto M. Gonzalez	965	163	4	0.4%
Eddie M. Martin Jr.	1,300	225	4	0.3%

Leading Jockeys by Number of Graded Stakes Winners in 2004

Jockey	GS Mounts	GS Wnrs
John R. Velazquez	85	30
Edgar S. Prado	108	29
Jerry D. Bailey	95	26
Victor Espinoza	73	20
Alex O. Solis	48	15
David Romero Flores	64	12
Mike E. Smith	59	12
Javier Castellano	54	11
Corey S. Nakatani	69	11
Pat Day	80	10
Todd Kabel	18	10
Richard Migliore	47	10
Rafael Bejarano	46	9
Jose A. Santos	58	9
Shane J. Sellers	34	9
Robby Albarado	67	8
Eibar Coa	52	8
Cornelio H. Velasquez	81	8
Brice Blanc	42	7
Joe Bravo	41	7
Kent J. Desormeaux	51	7
Ramon A. Dominguez	42	7
Rene R. Douglas	45	6

Jockey	GS Mounts	GS Wnrs
Jose Valdivia Jr.	44	6
Tyler Baze	62	5
Stewart Elliott	31	5
Matthew Otis McCarron	10	5
Gary L. Stevens	39	5
Russell A. Baze	13	4
Eddie M. Martin Jr.	16	4
Calvin H. Borel	23	3
Shaun Bridgmohan	29	3
Jorge F. Chavez	59	3
Jon Kenton Court	34	3
Lanfranco Dettori	10	3
Pablo Fragoso	26	3
Roberto M. Gonzalez	7	3
Charles C. Lopez	12	3
James McAleney	17	3
Javier Santiago	38	3
Patrick A. Valenzuela	15	3

Leading Jockeys by Most Grade 1 Wins in 2004

Jockey	No. G1 Starts	No. G1 Wins
Edgar S. Prado	53	11
Jerry D. Bailey	45	9
Victor Espinoza	37	9
John R. Velazquez	57	9
Kent J. Desormeaux	30	6
Mike E. Smith	36	5
Alex O. Solis	18	4
Robby Albarado	25	3
Tyler Baze	25	3
Javier Castellano	21	3
Pat Day	38	3
Lanfranco Dettori	9	3
Ramon A. Dominguez	22	3
Stewart Elliott	7	3
David R. Flores	27	3
Corey S. Nakatani	37	3
Jose A. Santos	20	3

Leading Jockeys by Most Grade 1 Stakes Winners in 2004

Jockey	No. G1 Starters	No. G1 Winners
Edgar S. Prado	40	10
Jerry D. Bailey	35	9
Victor Espinoza	27	7
John R. Velazquez	33	7
Kent J. Desormeaux	18	5
Mike E. Smith	28	5
Tyler Baze	24	3
Lanfranco Dettori	9	3
David Romero Flores	21	3
Corey S. Nakatani	31	3
Jose A. Santos	14	3
Alex O. Solis	13	3
Robby Albarado	17	2
Rafael Bejarano	11	2
Javier Castellano	16	2
Pat Day	25	2
Ramon A. Dominguez	13	2
Rene R. Douglas	14	2

Jockey	No. G1 Starters	No. G1 Winners
Stewart Elliott	5	2
Todd Kabel	5	2
Gary L. Stevens	16	2
Jose Valdivia Jr.	14	2
Cornelio H. Velasquez	19	2

Leading Jockeys by Number of Wins in 2004

Jockey	No. Mounts	No. Wnrs	No. Wins
Rafael Bejarano	1,922	386	455
Ramon A. Dominguez	1,348	316	382
John R. Velazquez	1,325	250	335
Ramsey Zimmerman	1,294	218	326
Russell Baze	1,182	247	321
T. D. Houghton	1,517	223	284
Edgar Prado	1,445	232	281
Eddie Castro	1,547	211	268
Dana G. Whitney	1,428	205	267
Stewart Elliott	1,357	203	260
Dean Sarvis	1,278	204	255
Rodney A. Prescott	1,784	210	251
Brian Hernandez Jr.	1,463	200	243
Rene Douglas	1,296	208	242
Cornelio H. Velasquez	1,584	222	240
Tyler Baze	1,394	194	239
Victor Espinoza	1,331	191	239
Deshawn L. Parker	1,606	187	238
Monte Clifton Berry	1,191	180	234
Eddie M. Martin Jr.	1,300	191	225
Corey Nakatani	1,076	170	220
Ryan Fogelsonger	1,065	177	217
Joe Bravo	1,152	179	214
Roman Chapa	956	169	214
Robby Albarado	1,309	174	213
Javier Castellano	1,277	175	212
Perry Wayne Ouzts	1,447	168	212
John McKee	1,444	175	210
Eibar Coa	1,011	183	209
Gerard Melancon	1,267	159	205
John Jacinto	1,139	157	202
Manoel R. Cruz	1,192	159	201
Abel Castellano Jr.	1,202	169	200
Marco A. Ccamaque	1,298	160	200
Lonnie Meche	925	149	199
Angel R. Quinones	1,208	162	199

Leading Jockeys by Number of Winners in 2004

Jockey	No. Mounts	No. Wnrs
Rafael Bejarano	1,922	386
Ramon A. Dominguez	1,348	316
John R. Velazquez	1,325	250
Russell Baze	1,182	247
Edgar Prado	1,445	232
T. D. Houghton	1,517	223
Cornelio Velasquez	1,584	222
Ramsey Zimmerman	1,294	218
Eddie Castro	1,547	211
Rodney A. Prescott	1,784	210
Rene Douglas	1,296	208
Dana G. Whitney	1,428	205
Dean Sarvis	1,278	204
Stewart Elliott	1,357	203
Brian Joseph Hernandez Jr.	1,463	200
Tyler Baze	1,394	194
Victor Espinoza	1,331	191
Eddie M. Martin Jr.	1,300	191
Deshawn L. Parker	1,606	187
Eibar Coa	1,011	183
Monte Clifton Berry	1,191	180
Joe Bravo	1,152	179
Ryan Fogelsonger	1,065	177
John McKee	1,444	175
Javier Castellano	1,277	175
Robby Albarado	1,309	174
Corey Nakatani	1,076	170
Abel Castellano Jr.	1,202	169
Roman Chapa	956	169
Perry Wayne Ouzts	1,447	168
Angel R. Quinones	1,208	162
Marco A. Camaque	1,298	160
Manoel R. Cruz	1,192	159
Gerard Melancon	1,267	159
John Jacinto	1,139	157
Timothy T. Doocy	1,029	154

Leading Jockeys by Career Purses
North American Earnings
Through December 31, 2004

Jockey	Career Purses
1. Pat Day	$296,581,177 +
2. Jerry Bailey	277,480,425 +
3. Chris J. McCarron	257,717,924
4. Gary L. Stevens	211,941,256 +
5. Laffit A. Pincay Jr.	208,379,702
6. Eddie J. Delahoussaye	192,469,869
7. Alex O. Solis	178,833,290 +
8. Kent J. Desormeaux	174,754,972 +
9. Jose A. Santos	174,665,633 +
10. Mike E. Smith	168,693,562 +
11. Corey S. Nakatani	150,224,654 +
12. Edgar S. Prado	148,871,832 +
13. Jorge F. Chavez	142,586,640 +
14. John R. Velazquez	142,017,395 +
15. Angel Cordero Jr.	137,063,998
16. Richard Migliore	134,306,238 +
17. Russell A. Baze	131,317,547 +
18. Patrick A. Valenzuela	127,663,331 +
19. Shane J. Sellers	122,431,794
20. Robbie G. Davis	115,737,627
21. Craig Perret	104,292,244
22. David Flores	102,294,389 +
23. Jorge Velasquez	98,538,544
24. Chris W. Antley	92,277,031
25. Robby Albarado	91,283,463 +
26. Eddie Maple	91,097,360
27. Julie A. Krone	90,122,764
28. Mario G. Pino	87,222,324 +
29. Jean-Luc Samyn	85,652,345 +
30. Jacinto Vasquez	83,235,740
31. Aaron T. Gryder	82,683,986 +
32. Todd Kabel	82,663,742 +
33. Joe Bravo	81,862,049 +
34. Mark Guidry	81,160,699 +
35. Victor Espinoza	78,108,034 +

+ Active through May 26, 2005

Leading Jockeys by Career Wins

Jockey	Career Wins
1. Laffit Pincay Jr.	9,530
2. Russell Baze	8,959 +
3. Bill Shoemaker	8,833
4. Pat Day	8,778 +
5. David Gall	7,396
6. Chris McCarron	7,139
7. Angel Cordero Jr.	7,057
8. Jorge Velasquez	6,795
9. Sandy Hawley	6,449
10. Larry Snyder	6,388
11. Eddie Delahoussaye	6,384
12. Carl Gambardella	6,349
13. Earlie Fires	6,322 +
14. John Longden	6,032
15. Jerry Bailey	5,780 +
16. Mario Pino	5,506 +
17. Edgar Prado	5,323 +
18. Jacinto Vasquez	5,231
19. Ronnie Ardoin	5,225
20. Robert Colton	4,976
21. Rick Wilson	4,934 +
22. Rudy Baez	4,875
23. Gary Stevens	4,838 +
24. Anthony Black	4,833 +
25. Eddie Arcaro	4,779
26. Perry Ouzts	4,769 +
27. Mark Guidry	4,680 +
28. Don Brumfield	4,573
29. Timothy Doocy	4,532 +
30. Kent Desormeaux	4,511 +
31. Mike Smith	4,474 +
32. Steve Brooks	4,451
33. Craig Perret	4,406 +
34. Eddie Maple	4,398
35. Walter Blum	4,382
36. Randy Romero	4,294
37. Jeff Lloyd	4,276
38. Bill Hartack	4,272
39. Ray Sibille	4,264
40. Alex Solis	4,195 +
41. Avelino Gomez	4,081
42. Shane Sellers	4,070
43. Richard Migliore	4,064 +
44. Jorge Chavez	4,050 +
45. Hugo Dittfach	4,000
46. Mike Rowland	3,996
47. Phil Grove	3,991
48. Jose Santos	3,916 +
49. Randall Meier	3,868
50. R. D. Williams	3,839

+Active jockeys; statistics through May 11, 2005

Female Jockeys
With More Than 1,000 Wins

	Wins	Active Years
Julie Krone	3,704	1981-2004
Patti Cooksey	2,136	1979-2004
Jill Jellison	1,771	1982-2005
Vicky Aragon Baze	1,769	1985-2001
Dodie Cartier Duys	1,760	1983-2004
Rosemary Homeister Jr.	1,727	1977-2004
Cindy Noll	1,631	1990-2005
Vicki Warhol	1,607	1979-2004

	Wins	Active Years
Lillian Kuykendall	1,419	1980-2001
Jerri Elizabeth Nichols	1,393	1988-2005
Lori Wydick	1,308	1984-2005
Mary Randall Doser	1,273	1985-2005
Donna Barton Brothers	1,130	1987-1998
Cynthia Herman Medina	1,116	1986-2004
Diane Nelson	1,090	1986-2005
Patti Barton	1,085	1969-1984
Sandi Lee Gann	1,067	1987-2005

Through May 11, 2005

Most Wins by a Jockey
on One Day in 2004

Wins	Jockey	Date	Track(s)
7	Rafael Bejarano	3/12/2004	TP
	Quincy Welch	8/14/2004	NP
6	Robby Albarado	3/11/2004	FG
	Rafael Bejarano	2/28/2004	TP
	Rafael Bejarano	6/19/2004	CD, Ind
	Rafael Bejarano	1/2/2004	TP
	Rafael Bejarano	9/21/2004	KD
	Perry Compton	4/10/2004	Fon
	Joel Cruz Ramos	5/31/2004	ElC
	Ryan Fogelsonger	9/18/2004	Pim
	Curtis Kimes	4/30/2004	Fon
	Lester Cash Knight	11/19/2004	Hoo
	Eddie M. Martin Jr.	1/18/2004	FG
	Orlando Mojica	5/7/2004	Ind, RD
	Rodney A. Prescott	5/8/2004	Ind, RD
	Brandon Whitacre	5/14/2004	CT, Pim
	Robert Dean Williams	7/2/2004	LnN

Most Wins by a Jockey
on One Program in 2004

Wins	Jockey	Date	Track
7	Rafael Bejarano	3/12/2004	TP
	Quincy Welch	8/14/2004	NP
6	Robby Albarado	3/11/2004	FG
	Rafael Bejarano	2/28/2004	TP
	Rafael Bejarano	9/21/2004	KD
	Rafael Bejarano	1/2/2004	TP
	Perry Compton	4/10/2004	Fon
	Joel Cruz Ramos	5/31/2004	ElC
	Ryan Fogelsonger	9/18/2004	Pim
	Curtis Kimes	4/30/2004	Fon
	Lester Cash Knight	11/19/2004	Hoo
	Eddie M. Martin Jr.	1/18/2004	FG
	Robert Dean Williams	7/2/2004	LnN

Most Consecutive Wins
by Jockey in 2004

Wins	Jockey	Date(s)	Track(s)
8	Carlos Nieto	10/20-22/2004	Pen
	Robert Dean Williams	5/21-22/2004	LnN
7	Taylor M. Hole	4/2-3/2004	Pen
6	Frank T. Alvarado	12/1-2/2004	GG
	Thomas Clifton	11/1-4/2004	Pha, Pen
	Julio E. Felix	11/1-4/2004	Tdn
	Ted D. Gondron	11/6-7/2004	Sun
	John A. Grabowski	2/10-16/2004	TuP, GG
	Pedro A. Rodriguez	5/23-24/2004	FL
	Ken S. Tohill	8/3-7/2004	SRP
	John R. Velazquez	5/26-27/2004	Bel

Notable Names in Racing's Past

(Names of Racing Hall of Fame members are in boldface italics.)

As much as great horses are central to the sport, Thoroughbred racing and breeding would not exist without the important individuals of the past who worked to perfect the breed or sport and who performed with distinction within the industry. Here are outstanding individuals from racing's history, with members of the Racing Hall of Fame noted in boldface italics.

Adams, Frank D. "Dooley," 1927-2004. Jockey, trainer. Leading steeplechase jockey 1946, '49-'55; inducted into Racing Hall of Fame in '70. Rode 337 winners, including Neji, Elkridge, Oedipus, Refugio, and Floating Isle. Trained Subversive Chick.

Adams, John H., 1914-'95. Jockey, trainer. Leading jockey 1937, '42, '43; inducted into Racing Hall of Fame in '65; George Woolf Memorial Jockey Award in '56. Rode 3,270 winners, including *Kayak II, Hasty Road. Trained J. O. Tobin. Won 1954 Preakness Stakes aboard Hasty Road.

Aga Khan III, Sultan Sir Mahomed Shah, 1877-1957. Ismaili Muslim leader. Owner of Gilltown, Sheshoon, Ballymany, Sallymount, and Ongar Studs in Ireland; Haras de la Coquenne, Haras de Marly-la-Ville, Haras de Saint-Crespin in France. Leading owner in England 13 times; leading breeder in England eight times. Bred *Bahram, *Nasrullah, *Tulyar, *Mahmoud, *Alibhai, *Khaled, *Masaka; owned Mumtaz Mahal, *Blenheim II. Grandfather of current Aga Khan.

Alexander, Alexander J., 1824-1902. Iron works, farming. Owner of Woodburn Stud, Kentucky. Stood leading sire Lexington. Leading breeder. Bred Duke of Magenta, Spendthrift, Tom Bowling, Tom Ochiltree, Harry Bassett, Joe Daniels, Fellowcraft, Fonso, etc. Brother of Robert A. Alexander.

Alexander, Robert A., 1819-'67. Iron works, farming. Founder of Woodburn Stud, Kentucky. Stood leading sire Lexington. Leading breeder. Bred Norfolk, Asteroid, Maiden, Virgil, Preakness, etc. Brother of Alexander J. Alexander.

Annenberg, Moses L., 1878-1942. Publisher. Published *Daily Racing Form* 1922-'42, *Morning Telegraph.* Founded Triangle Publications.

Annenberg, Walter, 1908-2002. Former publisher, *Daily Racing Form.* Took control of his family's Triangle Publications Inc. in 1940 and built largest private publishing empire in the country; ambassador to Great Britain 1968-'74. Sold publishing enterprises by late 1980s. Son of publisher Moses Annenberg.

Arcaro, Eddie, 1916-'97. Jockey. Inducted into Racing Hall of Fame in 1958; George Woolf Memorial Jockey Award in '53. Rode 4,779 winners, including Whirlaway, Citation, Bold Ruler, Nashua. Won two Triple Crowns, five Kentucky Derbys, six Preakness Stakes, and six Belmont Stakes.

Archer, Fred, 1857-'86. Jockey. Winner of 12 consecutive riding titles in England (1874-'85) and rode 2,748 career winners, a record that stood for 57 years. Won 21 classic races, including five Epsom Derbys with Silvio, Bend Or, Iroquois, Melton, *Ormonde.

Atkinson, Ted F., 1916-2005. Jockey, racing official. Leading jockey by money won 1944, '46; leading jockey by races won 1944, '46; inducted into Racing Hall of Fame in '57; George Woolf Memorial Jockey Award in '57. Rode 3,795 winners, including Tom Fool, Gallorette, Devil Diver. Rode 1953 Horse of the Year Tom Fool to

handicap triple crown; first jockey whose mounts earned more than $1-million in one year (1946).

Bacon, Mary, 1948-'91. Pioneer female jockey; rode 286 winners.

Baldwin, Elias J. "Lucky," 1828-1909. Mining, investments. Owned Rancho el Santa Anita, California. Bred and owned Emperor of Norfolk, Volante, Rey El Santa Anita, Americus. Built original Santa Anita Park racetrack.

Barbee, George, ca. 1855-1941. Jockey. Inducted into Racing Hall of Fame in 1996. Rode Saxon, Survivor, Shirley, Jacobus. Won the first Preakness Stakes aboard Survivor in 1873; won two other Preakness Stakes and one Belmont Stakes.

Barrera, Lazaro, 1924-'91. Trainer. Eclipse Award trainer 1976-'79; leading trainer by money won 1977-'80; inducted into Racing Hall of Fame in '79. Trained more than 140 stakes winners and six champions, including Affirmed, Bold Forbes.

Bassett, Carroll K., 1905-'72. Jockey. Inducted into Racing Hall of Fame in 1972. Rode more than 100 steeplechase winners, including Battleship, Peacock, Night Retired, Passive, Sable Muff. Rode Battleship to victory in the American Grand National and two National Steeplechase Hunt Cups.

Beard, Louis A., 1888-1954. Farm manager, racing executive. Managed Greentree Stud 1927-'48. Co-founder and president, Keeneland Race Course; co-founder, American Thoroughbred Breeders' Association; co-founder, Grayson Foundation.

Bedwell, H. Guy, 1876-1951. Trainer. Leading trainer by races won in 1909, '12-'17; leading trainer by money won 1918-'19; inducted into Racing Hall of Fame in 1971. Trained 2,160 winners, including Sir Barton, Billy Kelly. First trainer to saddle a Triple Crown winner (Sir Barton in 1919); won 16 races in 14 days in 1910.

Belmont, August I, 1816-'90. Banker. President of American Jockey Club (Jerome Park) 1866-'86. Owner of Nursery Stud in New York and later in Kentucky. Leading owner. Bred and owned Woodbine, Potomac, Fides, Prince Royal; also owned Glenelg, Fenian, *The Ill-Used.

Belmont, August II, 1853-1924. Banker. First president of Belmont Park; chairman, Jockey Club 1895-1924; chairman, Belmont Park. Owned Nursery Stud, Kentucky. Leading breeder. Bred Man o' War, Fair Play, Tracery, Beldame; also owned *Hourless, Henry of Navarre.

Bieber, Isidor, 1887-1974. Restaurateur, gambler. Co-owner of Bieber-Jacobs Stable, Stymie Manor, Maryland. Leading breeder 1964-'67; co-breeder of Hail to Reason, Allez France, Affectionately, Straight Deal; also co-owned Stymie, Searching.

Bobinski, Kazimierz, 1905-'69. Russian-born pedigree authority. In collaboration with Stefan Zamoyski, authored the landmark *Family Tables of Racehorses, Volumes I & II,* which expanded on the work of Bruce Lowe and Hermann Goos.

Bostwick, George, 1909-'82. Jockey, trainer. Leading amateur steeplechase jockey 1928-'32, '41; leading steeplechase trainer 1940, '51, '55; inducted into Racing Hall of Fame in 1968. Rode 87 winners, including Chenango, Escapade, Sussex, Darkness. Trained Neji and Oedipus. Played on six United States championship polo teams.

Boussac, Marcel, 1889-1980. Textile tycoon. Leading French breeder 19 times, winner of the Prix du Jockey-Club (French Derby) 12 times. Bred notable racehorses or sires Tourbillon, Pharis, Djebel, *Goya II, and *Ambiorix. In 1950 became first foreign owner to lead English owners list, the year he won the Epsom Derby with Galcador. Also bred and owned two-time Prix de l'Arc de Triomphe winner Corrida.

Bowie, Oden, 1826-'94. Railways, politician. Maryland governor 1869-'72; first president of Pimlico Race Course in 1870. Owner of Fairview Plantation, Maryland. Bred Catesby, Crickmore.

Bradley, Edward R., 1859-1946. Gambler. Owner of Idle Hour Stock Farm, Kentucky. Bred and owned Blue Larkspur, Bimelech, Black Helen, Busher, Bubbling Over. Bred and owned four Kentucky Derby winners and imported foundation mare *La Troienne.

Brady, James Cox Jr., 1908-'71. Investments. Chairman of Jockey Club 1961-'69; chairman of New York Racing Association 1961-'69. Owner of Dixiana Farm, Kentucky, and Hamilton Stable. Bred Long Look, War Plumage, Jungle Cove. Co-founder of Monmouth Park, American Horse Council; oversaw rebuilding of Belmont Park. Father of Nicholas J. Brady, United States treasury secretary 1988-'93, and chairman of the Jockey Club 1976-'82.

Brooks, Steve, 1922-'79. Jockey. Leading jockey in 1949; inducted into Racing Hall of Fame in 1963; George Woolf Memorial Jockey Award in 1962. Rode 4,451 winners, including Two Lea, Citation, Round Table. Rode Ponder in 1949 Kentucky Derby.

Brown, Edward D. "Brown Dick," 1850-1906. Trainer, jockey. Inducted into Racing Hall of Fame in 1984. Trained Ben Brush, Plaudit, Spendthrift, Hindoo. Rode Asteroid to an undefeated 9-for-9 record in 1864-'65.

Brown, Harry D. "Curly," 1863-1930. Restaurateur, racetrack executive. Founder and first president of Arlington Park; built Laurel Park, Oriental Park. Owned Brown Shasta Farm, California.

Bruce, Benjamin G., 1827-'91. Publisher. Founder and editor of the *Livestock Record* 1875-'91 (predecessor of *The Thoroughbred Record*). Brother of Sanders D. Bruce.

Bruce, Sanders D., 1825-1902. Hotelier, publisher. Co-editor of *Turf, Field and Farm* 1865-1902. Compiler of first four volumes of *American Stud Book*. Brother of Benjamin G. Bruce.

Bull, Phil, 1910-'89. Handicapper, gambler, owner, breeder, publisher. In 1948 launched *Timeform*, a British Thoroughbred industry information service that annually assesses the individual merits of thousands of runners. Founded Hollins Stud; bred champion Romulus.

Burch, Preston, 1884-1978. Trainer, breeder, owner. Leading trainer in 1950; inducted into Racing Hall of Fame in 1963. Trained more than 70 stakes winners, including George Smith, Sailor, Flower Bowl, Bold. Bred Gallorette. Trained stakes winners in New York, Canada, Cuba, France, and Italy. Wrote influential book on training, *Training Thoroughbred Horses*. Son of William P. Burch; father of Racing Hall of Fame trainer J. Elliott Burch.

Burch, William P., 1846-1926. Trainer. Inducted into Racing Hall of Fame in 1955. Trained Grey Friar, My Own, Decanter. First of three generations of Hall of Fame trainers. Father of Preston Burch.

Burke, Carleton F., 1882-1962. Banker, farmer. First chairman of California Horse Racing Board 1933-'39.

Burlew, Fred, 1871-1927. Trainer. Inducted into Racing Hall of Fame in 1973. Trained 32 stakes winners and two champions, including Beldame, Morvich, Inchcape.

Burns, Tommy H., 1879-1913. Jockey. Leading jockey by races won in 1898-'99; inducted into Racing Hall of Fame in 1983. Rode 1,333 winners, including Broomstick, Imp, Caughnawaga. Set an American record in the 1¼-mile Brighton Beach Handicap aboard Broomstick.

Butler, James Sr., 1855-1934. Grocery-chain owner. Owner of Empire City racetrack. Owner of East View Farm, New York. Bred Questionnaire, Sting, Pebbles, Spur; owned Comely.

Butler, James II, 1891-1940. Grocery-chain owner. President of Empire City Racing Association. Owner of East View Farm, New York.

Butwell, James, 1896-1956. Jockey, racing official. Leading jockey in 1912; leading jockey by races won in '20; inducted into Racing Hall of Fame in '84. Rode 1,402 winners, including Roamer, Sweep, Hilarious, Maskette. Leading American jockey by number of wins at the time of his retirement.

Byers, J. Dallett "Dolly," 1898-1966. Jockey, trainer. Leading steeplechase jockey 1918, '21, '28; leading jockey by money won in '28; inducted into Racing Hall of Fame in '67. Rode 149 winners, including Jolly Roger, Fairmount. Trained Tea-Maker, Lovely Night, Invader. Won the Temple Gwathmey Steeplechase Handicap five years in a row.

Byrnes, Matthew, 1854-1933. Jockey, trainer. Rode Glenelg, Kingfisher; trained Racing Hall of Fame members Parole, Salvator, Firenze.

Caldwell, Thomas, 1928-2001. Auctioneer. Auctioneer and director of auctions for the Keeneland Association 1975-2001. Owned Gavel Ranch, Oregon.

Campbell, John B., 1876-1954. Racing executive. Racing secretary and handicapper at New York tracks 1935-'54. Handicapped three-way dead heat in 1944 Carter Handicap.

Capossela, Fred, 1903-'91. Famed race caller at New York racetracks 1943-'71.

Cassidy, Mars, 1862-1929. Racing executive. Legendary starter at New York racetracks 1902-'29. Father of Marshall Cassidy.

Cassidy, Marshall, 1892-1968. Racing executive. Executive secretary of Jockey Club. Developed first modern starting gate; developed modern photo-finish camera; instituted first film patrol and saliva tests; founded Jockey Club Round Table meetings. Son of Mars Cassidy.

Cella, Charles, 1875-1940. Hotelier, theater owner. Founder of Oaklawn Park; co-owner of Fort Erie racetrack.

Chenery, Christopher T., 1886-1973. Utilities. First president of Thoroughbred Owners and Breeders Association. Owner of Meadow Stud, Virginia. Bred Secretariat, Riva Ridge, Hill Prince, Cicada, First Landing, Sir Gaylord. Co-founder of New York Racing Association.

Childs, Frank E., 1886-1973. Trainer. Inducted into Racing Hall of Fame in 1968. Trained 23 stakes winners, including *Tomy Lee, Canina, Dinner Gong. Known for his ability to turn claiming horses into stakes winners.

Chinn, Philip T., 1874-1962. Horse trader. Owner of Himyar Stud, Kentucky. Bred 58 stakes winners, including Miss Merriment, Black Maria, In Memoriam, High Resolve. Leading consignor at Saratoga in 1920s; sold then-record $70,000 yearling in '27.

Clark, Henry S., 1904-'99. Trainer. Inducted into Racing Hall of Fame in 1982. Trained 37 stakes winners and one champion, including Tempted, Cyane, Endine, Obeah. Twice won back-to-back Delaware Handicaps.

Clark, John C., 1891-1974. Advertising executive. President of Hialeah Park 1940-'54; first president of Thoroughbred Racing Associations 1942-'43. Owned Sun Briar Court, New York. Bred Charlie McAdam, Accomplish.

Clark, John H. "Trader," 1919-'96. Horse trader, author. President, Thoroughbred Breeders of Kentucky. Author of *Trader Clark.*

Clark, Meriwether Lewis, 1846-'99. Racing executive. Founder and president of Louisville Jockey Club. Founder of Kentucky Derby in 1875. Established first uniform scale of weights in America.

Clay, Albert, (1917-2002). Farmer, burley warehousing. Breeder or co-breeder of at least 20 stakes winners, including Albert the Great, Seaside Attraction, Gorgeous, Pompeii, George Navonod; helped to found the American Horse Council and was instrumental in establishing the University of Kentucky's Maxwell H. Gluck Equine Research Center. Father of Three Chimneys Farm owner Robert Clay.

Clay, Ezekiel F., 1841-1920. Farmer, breeder. President, Kentucky Racing Association. Co-owner of Runnymede Farm, Kentucky. Chairman of Kentucky Racing Commission. Bred Hanover, Sir Dixon, Miss Woodford, Raceland.

Clay, Henry, 1777-1852. Lawyer, politician. Owner of Ashland Stud, Kentucky. Bred Heraldry. Father of John M. Clay.

Clay, John M., 1820-'87. Farmer, breeder. Owner of Ashland Stud, Kentucky. Bred Kentucky, Maggie B. B., Daniel Boone, Simon Kenton, Gilroy, Star Davis, Lodi, Day Star. Son of Henry Clay.

Cocks, W. Burling, 1915-'98. Trainer. Leading steeplechase trainer 1949, '65, '73, '80; inducted into Racing Hall of Fame in '85; F. Ambrose Clark Award in '73. Trained 49 stakes winners, including six American Grand National winners. Trained Zaccio, Down First.

Coe, William R., 1869-1955. Insurance, financier. Owner of Shoshone Farm, Kentucky. Bred and owned Pompey, Pompoon; owned Ladysman, Cleopatra, Black Maria, Pilate.

Cole, Ashley T., 1876-1965. New York industry leader. Chairman of the New York State Racing Commission 1945-'65; president of the National Association of State Racing Commissioners. Involved in organizing the not-for-profit New York Racing Association, in building the new Aqueduct Race Course, and in developing the New York breeders awards program.

Coltiletti, Frank, 1904-'87. Jockey, trainer, racing official. Inducted into Racing Hall of Fame in 1970. Rode 667 winners, including Mars, Crusader, Sun Beau. Won Preakness Stakes at age 17 aboard Broomspun in 1921.

Combs, Leslie II, 1901-'90. Breeder. Owner of Spendthrift Farm, Kentucky. Leading breeder in 1972. Chairman of Kentucky Racing Commission. Bred 247 stakes winners, including Majestic Prince, Myrtle Charm, Idun, Mr. Prospector. Originated modern stallion syndicates in 1950s.

Conway, James P., 1910-'84. Trainer. Inducted into Racing Hall of Fame in 1996. Trained 43 stakes winners and five champions, including Chateaugay, Primonetta, Grecian Queen. Won 1963 Kentucky Derby and Belmont Stakes with three-year-old champion colt Chateaugay.

Corrigan, Edward, 1854-1924. Railway investor. Founded Hawthorne Race Course. Raced *McGee.

Corum, M. W. "Bill," 1895-1958. President of Churchill Downs (1949-'58). Sports writer for the New York *Journal-American*. In 1925 coined the phrase "run for the roses" to describe the Kentucky Derby.

Cowdin, John E., 1859-1941. Silk merchant. President of Queens County Jockey Club (Aqueduct).

Crawford, Robert H. "Specs," 1897-1975. Jockey, trainer. Leading steeplechase jockey 1919-'20, '22, '26; inducted into Racing Hall of Fame in '73. Rode 139 winners, including Jolly Roger, Fairmount, Lytle, Erne II. Won four American Grand Nationals.

Croker, Richard "Boss," 1841-1922. Real estate, politician. Head of New York's Tammany Hall political machine. Owner of Glencairn Stud, Ireland. Bred Orby, Rhodora, Grand Parade.

Cromwell, Thomas B., 1871-1957. Publisher, bloodstock agent. Founded *The Blood-Horse*, Cromwell Bloodstock agency. Credited with refining past performance charts.

Crosby, H. L. "Bing," 1903-'77. Entertainer. First president of Del Mar Turf Club 1936-'46. Co-owner of Binglin Stock Farm, California. Owned *Meadow Court, *Ligaroti, *Don Bingo, *Blackie II.

Daingerfield, Algernon, 1867-1941. Racing executive. Executive secretary of Jockey Club. Son of Foxhall Daingerfield.

Daingerfield, Elizabeth, 1870-1951. Farm manager. Owner of Haylands Farm. Managed Wickliffe Stud, Faraway Farm. Managed leading sires Man o' War, High Time. Daughter of Foxhall Daingerfield.

Daingerfield, Foxhall A., ca. 1840-1913. Farm manager. Managed stud careers of Domino, Commando, Ben Brush, Kingston at Castleton Stud, Kentucky. Father of Algernon and Elizabeth Daingerfield.

Daingerfield, J. Keene, 1910-'93. Racing executive, author. Kentucky state steward 1973-'85. Eclipse Award of Merit in 1989. Author of *Training for Fun and Profit (Maybe)*. Grandson of Foxhall Daingerfield.

Daly, Marcus, 1842-1900. Mining. Owner of Bitter Root Stock Farm, Montana. Bred *Ogden, Tammany; owned Hamburg.

Daly, William C. "Father Bill," 1837-1931. Trainer. Famous mentor of Racing Hall of Fame jockeys James McLaughlin, Snapper Garrison, Winnie O'Connor, Danny Maher.

DeBartolo, Edward J., 1909-'94. Real estate developer. Owned Louisiana Downs, Thistledown, Remington Park. Special Eclipse Award in 1988.

De Francis, Frank, 1927-'89. Lawyer, racing executive. Owner of King of Mardi Gras, Hail Emperor. Led groups to buy Laurel Park in 1984 and Pimlico Race Course in '86, thus consolidating ownership of Maryland racetracks.

de Kwiatkowski, Henryk, 1924-2003. Aviation. Owner of Calumet Farm, Kentucky; Kennelot Stable. Joe Palmer Award in 1993. Owned Conquistador Cielo, De La Rose, Danzig, Stephan's Odyssey, Sabin. Bought bankrupt Calumet Farm for $17-million at public auction in 1992.

DeLancey, James, 1732-1801. Real estate. Owner of Bouwerie Farm, New York. Bred Maria Slamerkin, Bashaw. Imported *DeLancey's Cub mare (great American foundation mare), *Lath, *Wildair.

Donn, James Sr., 1887-1972. Landscaping contractor, nursery owner. Chairman of Gulfstream Park 1944-'72. Grandfather of former Gulfstream Park executive Douglas Donn.

Donoghue, Steve, 1884-1945. Jockey. Winner of ten consecutive riding titles in England (1914-'23). Rode six Epsom Derby winners: Humorist, Captain Cuttle, *Papyrus, Manna, Pommern, Gay Crusader. Rode 1,840 winners in a 33-year career.

Doswell, Thomas W., 1792-1890. Tobacco plantations. Owner of Bullfield Plantation. Bred Planet, Eolus, Algerine, Morello, Fanny Washington; owner of Knight of Ellerslie, Nina, Abd-el-Kader. Mentor and partner of Capt. Richard Hancock, who established Ellerslie Stud.

Drayton, Spencer, 1911-'94. FBI special agent who, upon recommendation of J. Edgar Hoover, in 1946 became the first head of the Thoroughbred Racing Protective Bureau. Served as TRPB president until his retirement in 1978. Inaugurated lip tattoos as a means of horse identification.

Duke, William, 1858-1926. Trainer. Inducted into Racing Hall of Fame in 1956. Trained Flying Ebony, Coventry. Won the 1924 French Derby with *Pot Au Feu; won '25 Kentucky Derby with Flying Ebony; won '25 Preakness Stakes with Coventry.

Dunn, Neville, 1904-'57. Publisher, editor. Editor of *The Thoroughbred Record* 1941-'57. Co-founder of Thoroughbred Club of America.

duPont, William Jr., 1897-1966. Banker. Owner of Walnut Hall Farm, Virginia. Bred and owned Parlo, Berlo, Rosemont, Fairy Chant, Ficklebush; owned Fair Star, Dauber. Founder of Delaware Park.

Duryea, Herman B., 1862-1916. Investments. Owner of Haras du Gazon, France. Leading owner in 1904, when leasing W. C. Whitney's horses. Co-Bred and owned *Durbar II, Banshee, *Sweeper; also co-owned Irish Lad.

Dwyer, Michael F., 1847-1906. Meat processor. Leading owner. Owned or co-owned Hindoo, Hanover, Miss Woodford, Kingston, Luke Blackburn, Bramble, Ben Brush, Tremont, etc. Brother of Philip J. Dwyer.

Dwyer, Philip J., 1843-1917. Meat processor. President of Brooklyn Jockey Club (Gravesend), Queens County Jockey Club (Aqueduct). Leading owner. Co-owned Hindoo, Hanover, Miss Woodford, Kingston, Luke Blackburn, Bramble, Tremont, etc. Brother of Michael F. Dwyer.

Easton, William, ca. 1850-1909. Auctioneer. American representative of Tattersalls; auctioneer for Fasig-Tipton Co. First great American auctioneer.

Ellis, James C., 1872-1956. Oilman, banker, Thoroughbred breeder, racetrack owner. In 1925 he acquired Dade Park racetrack in Henderson, Kentucky, at court auction. Thirty years later the track's name was changed to James C. Ellis Park.

Ellsworth, Rex, 1907-'97. Rancher. Owner of Ellsworth Farm, California. Leading owner and breeder 1962-'63. Bred and owned Swaps, Candy Spots, Olden Times, Prove It; owned *Prince Royal II; imported *Khaled.

Engelhard, Charles W., 1917-'71. Precious metals. Owner of Cragwood Stable. Leading owner in England in 1970. Owned Nijinsky II, *Hawaii, Assagai, Ribocco, Ribero, Halo, Mr. Leader, Indiana.

Ensor, Lavelle "Buddy," 1900-'47. Jockey. Inducted into Racing Hall of Fame in 1962. Rode 411 winners, including Exterminator, Grey Lag, Hannibal. Rode 33 winners in 11 days, including five of six races on one of those days, in 1919.

Estes, Joseph A., 1902-'70. Journalist. Editor of *The Blood-Horse* 1930-'63. Devised Average Earnings Index; established Jockey Club Statistical Bureau.

Evans, Thomas Mellon, 1910-'97. Mergers and acquisitions. Owner of Buckland Farm. Bred and owned Pleasant Colony, Pleasant Tap, Pleasant Stage.

Fairbairn, Robert A., 1867-1951. Financier. Owner of Fairholme Farm, Kentucky. Bred Gallahadion, Hoop, Jr. Co-owner of *Sir Gallahad III, *Blenheim II.

Fasig, William B., 1846-1902. Auctioneer. Co-founder of Fasig-Tipton Co. in 1898. Conducted first equine auctions in Madison Square Garden.

Fator, Laverne, 1900-'36. Jockey. Leading jockey 1925-'26; inducted into Racing Hall of Fame in '55. Rode 1,075 winners, including Grey Lag, Black Maria, Pompey, Scapa Flow. Won consecutive runnings of Belmont Futurity and Carter and Gazelle Handicaps.

Feustel, Louis, 1884-1970. Trainer. Leading trainer in 1920; inducted into Racing Hall of Fame in '64. Trained two champions and Man o' War, Rock View, Ordinance, Ladkin. Won 20 of 21 races with Man o' War.

Field, Marshall W. III, 1893-1956. Publisher, retailer. Bred High Quest, High Strung, Escutcheon, Clang, Eclair; owned Nimba, Stimulus.

Fink, Jule, 1913-'90. Thoroughbred owner-breeder and noted handicapper. Known as one of the "Speed Boys," his gambling success resulted in Jockey Club refusing to renew his owner's license in 1949. His subsequent suit against Jockey Club led to a significant reduction in the club's power over racing, but the New York State Racing and Wagering Board continued the ban until 1967. He was a partner in 1966 Santa Anita Derby winner Boldnesian.

Finney, Humphrey S., 1903-'84. Auctioneer. Chairman of Fasig-Tipton Co. 1952-'84. Founded *Maryland Horse*; author of *A Stud Farm Diary, Fair Exchange*. Father of John M. S. Finney.

Finney, John M. S., 1934-'94. Auctioneer. President Fasig-Tipton Co. 1968-'89. Son of Humphrey Finney.

Fisher, Charles T., 1880-1964. Automobile manufacturer. Owner of Dixiana Farm, Kentucky. Bred Spy Song, Mata Hari, Sweep All, Star Reward.

Fitzsimmons, James E. "Sunny Jim," 1874-1966. Trainer. Leading trainer 1930, '32, '36, '39, '55; inducted into Racing Hall of Fame in '58. Trained 2,275 winners, 155 stakes winners, including Triple Crown winners Gallant Fox and Omaha, and eight champions, including Bold Ruler, Nashua, Granville.

Franks, John, 1925-2004. Oil production. Owner of Franks Farms, Louisiana; Louisiana Stallions, Louisiana; Southland Farm, Florida. Co-owner of Heatherten Farm, Maryland. Leading owner by money won 1983-'84, '86, '93; leading owner by races won in 1983-'84, '86-'89; leading breeder by races won 1988-'93; leading owner by races won in '89; leading owner by money won in '93; Eclipse Award owner in 1983-'84, '93-'94. Bred and owned Answer Lively, Derby Wish, Kissin Kris. Bred Sharp Cat, Royal Anthem. Owned Heatherten, Dave's Friend, Top Avenger. Earned $3.1-million in 1984, then a single-season record for owners.

Gaines, John R., 1928-2005. Breeder. Former chairman, Breeders' Cup Ltd. Founder of Gainesway Farm, Kentucky. Eclipse Award of Merit in 1984; John W. Galbreath Award in '93. Bred Halo, Silent King, Time Limit. Owned Bold Bidder, Oil Royalty. Founder of Breeders' Cup, Kentucky Horse Park; assisted in developing the Maxwell H. Gluck Center for Equine Research at the University of Kentucky.

Galbreath, John W., 1897-1988. Real estate developer. Owned Darby Dan Farm, Kentucky and Ohio. Eclipse Award, Man of the Year in 1972. Bred and owned Roberto, Chateaugay, Primonetta, Little Current, Graustark, His Majesty, Proud Truth, Proud Clarion. Instrumental in rebuilding of Belmont Park and Aqueduct.

Garner, J. Mack, 1900-'36. Jockey. Leading jockey by races won in 1915; leading jockey by money won in '29; inducted into Racing Hall of Fame in '69. Rode 1,346 winners, including Cavalcade, Blue Larkspur. Won 1934 Kentucky Derby on Cavalcade.

Garrison, Edward R. "Snapper," 1868-1930. Jockey, stable agent, trainer, racing official. Inducted into Racing Hall of Fame in 1955. By his estimate, rode more than 700 winners, including Firenze, Tammany. His come-from-behind style immortalized as "Garrison finish."

Gaver, John M., 1900-'82. Trainer. Leading trainer 1942, '51; inducted into Racing Hall of Fame in '66. Trained 73 stakes winners and four champions, including Tom Fool, Capot, Stage Door Johnny, Devil Diver. Won the handicap triple crown with Tom Fool in 1953.

Genter, Frances S., 1898-1992. Household appliances manufacturer. Owned Frances S. Genter Stable. Eclipse Award owner in 1990. Bred and owned In Reality, Smile; owned Unbridled, My Dear Girl, Rough'n Tumble.

Gentry, Olin B., 1900-'90. Farm manager. Managed Idle Hour Stock Farm, Darby Dan Farm. Planned matings for 188 stakes winners, 20 champions, five Kentucky Derby winners. Father of Kentucky breeder Tom Gentry.

Gluck, Maxwell F., 1899-1984. Apparel stores. Owner of Elmendorf Farm. Eclipse Award outstanding owner in 1977; leading owner '77, '81; leading breeder '73, '81. Bred and owned Protagonist, Talking Picture, Big Spruce, Hold Your Peace; owned Prince John. Donation endowed Maxwell F. Gluck Equine Research Center at University of Kentucky.

Gomez, Avelino, 1929-'80. Jockey. Leading Canadian jockey seven times; North American leading jockey in 1966; inducted into Racing Hall of Fame in '82. Rode 4,081 winners, including Ridan, Buckpasser, Affectionately.

Graham, Florence N. "Elizabeth Arden," 1885-1966. Cosmetics manufacturer. Owner of Maine Chance Farm, Kentucky. Leading owner in 1945. Bred Gun Bow, Jewel's Reward, Jet Action; owned Jet Pilot, Beaugay, Myrtle Charm, Star Pilot, Mr. Busher, Lord Boswell.

Grayson, Cary T., 1878-1938. Physician. Owner of Blue Ridge Farm, Virginia. Bred Insco, My Own, Happy Argo; also owned High Time. Co-founder of Grayson Foundation.

Griffin, Henry "Harry," 1876-1955. Jockey. Inducted into Racing Hall of Fame in 1956. Rode 569 winners, including The Butterflies, Henry of Navarre. One of the original investors in Hollywood Park.

Guerin, O. Eric, 1924-'93. Jockey. Leading apprentice jockey in 1942; inducted into Racing Hall of Fame in '72. Rode 2,712 winners, including Native Dancer, Bed o' Roses, Jet Pilot. Rode Native Dancer in 20 of his 21 victories (in 22 starts).

Guest, Raymond R., 1907-'91. Investments. Owner of Powhatan Plantation, Virginia; Ballygoran Stud, Ireland. Bred and owned Tom Rolfe, Chieftain; bred Cascapedia; owned Sir Ivor, Larkspur.

Guggenheim, Harry F., 1890-1971. Publisher, mining. Owner of Cain Hoy Stable. Leading breeder in England in 1963. Bred and owned Never Bend, Bald Eagle, Ack Ack, Cherokee Rose, Red God; bred Ragusa, Crafty Admiral; owned Dark Star, *Turn-to. Co-founder of New York Racing Association.

Haggin, James Ben Ali, 1821-1914. Lawyer, mining. Owner of Elmendorf Farm, Kentucky; Rancho del Paso, California. Bred Firenze, Africander, Tyrant, Waterboy, Tournament; owned Salvator, Ben Ali.

Haggin, Louis L. II, 1913-'80. Real estate. Chairman of Keeneland Association 1970-'80; president of Thoroughbred Racing Associations 1967-'68; co-founder of Thoroughbred Breeders of Kentucky. Bred and owned Himalayan, Harbor Springs, Tingle. Great-grandson of James Ben Ali Haggin.

Hagyard, Charles W., 1901-'95. Veterinarian. Owner of Hagyard Farm, Kentucky. Breeder of Rough'n Tumble, Rising Market. Stood Hail to Reason, Promised Land. Co-founder of Hagyard-Davidson-McGee equine clinic.

Hancock, Arthur B. Jr. "Bull," 1910-'72. Breeder. President of American Thoroughbred Breeders' Association. Owner of Claiborne Farm, Kentucky, and Ellerslie Stud, Virginia. Leading breeder 1958-'59, '68-'69. Breeder of Round Table, Gamely, Apalachee, Moccasin, Doubledogdare, Bayou, Lamb Chop. Imported and syndicated *Nasrullah, *Ambiorix, *Herbager; stood Bold Ruler, Nijinsky II, *Princequillo, Round Table. Son of A. B. Hancock Sr.; father of Kentucky breeders Arthur B. Hancock III (Stone Farm) and Seth Hancock (Claiborne Farm).

Hancock, Arthur B. Sr., 1875-1957. Breeder. President of Breeders' Sales Co. Founder and owner of Claiborne Farm, Kentucky; owner of Ellerslie Stud, Virginia. Leading breeder 1935-'37, '39, '43. Breeder of Johnstown, Beaugay, Cleopatra, St. James, Jacola, Nimba, Jet Pilot. Imported and syndicated *Sir Gallahad III, *Blenheim II. Son of Richard J. Hancock, father of Arthur B. "Bull" Hancock Jr.

Hancock, Richard J., 1838-1912. Breeder. Founder of Ellerslie Stud, Virginia. Bred Knight of Ellerslie, Elkwood, Eon, Eole, Eolist. Father of A. B. Hancock Sr.

Hanes, John W., 1892-1988. Textiles, investments. Co-founder and first chairman of New York Racing Association; president of National Museum of Racing Hall of Fame. Bred Idun; owned Bold Bidder.

Harbut, Will, 1885-1947. Groom. Stud groom of Man o' War. Coined well-known phrase, "He was the mostest hoss."

Harding, William G., 1808-'86. Farming, railways. Owner of Belle Meade Stud, Tennessee. Bred Vandalite. Stood leading sires *Priam, Vandal, *Bonnie Scotland.

Harper, John, 1803-'74. Farmer. Owner of Nantura Stock Farm, Kentucky. Bred Longfellow, Ten Broeck, Rhynodyne, Fanny Holton.

Harriman, W. Averill, 1891-1986. Railways, politician. Owner of Arden Farm Stable. Owned Chance Play, Ladkin, Mary Jane. As governor of New York (1955-'59) aided formation of New York Racing Association.

Haskell, Amory L., 1894-1966. Automobiles, safety glass. President of Monmouth Park 1946-'66; president of Thoroughbred Racing Associations 1954-'55. Owner of Blue Sparkler. Aided campaign to legalize pari-mutuel wagering in New Jersey.

Hatton, Charles W., 1906-'75. Journalist. President, New York Turf Writers Association. Eclipse Special Award in 1974. Popularized concept of American Triple Crown.

Hawkins, Abe, Birthdate unknown-1867. Jockey. A slave when he rode Lecompte to victory over Lexington in an 1854 match race, was perhaps the first African-American professional athlete to gain national and international prominence.

Headley, Duval A., 1910-'87. Horseman. President, Keeneland Race Course; president, Thoroughbred Club of America. Owner of Manchester Farm, Kentucky. Breeder of Tom Fool, Dark Mirage, Aunt Ginny. Trained 23 stakes winners, including champions Menow, Apogee. Nephew of Hal Price Headley.

Headley, Hal Petit, 1856-1921. Timber interests. Founder of Beaumont Farm, Kentucky. Bred and owned Ornament. Father of Hal Price Headley.

Headley, Hal Price, 1888-1962. Timber, burley. First president of Keeneland Race Course. Owner of Beaumont Farm, Kentucky. Bred and owned Menow, Alcibiades, Askmenow, Handy Mandy, Chacolet. Co-founder of Keeneland Association; co-founder of American Thoroughbred Breeders' Association. Father of Kentucky breeder Alice Headley Chandler (Mill Ridge Farm).

Healey, Thomas J., 1866-1944. Trainer, racing official. Inducted into Racing Hall of Fame in 1955. Trained three champions, Equipoise, Top Flight, Campfire. Won five Preakness Stakes.

Helis, William G., 1887-1950. Oil exploration. Co-owner of Fair Grounds. Owner of Helis Stock Farm, New Jersey. Owned Cosmic Bomb, Rippey, Salmagundi.

Hern, Maj. William Richard "Dick," (1921-2002). Trainer. Four-time leading British trainer; won 17 classics, including Epsom Derby three times; trained unbeaten Brigadier Gerard; trained for Queen Elizabeth II.

Hernandez, Joe, 1909-'72. Race caller at Santa Anita Park 1935-'72 and Hollywood Park.

Hertz, John D., 1879-1961 and **Frances**, 1881-1963. Taxis and rental cars. Co-owner of Arlington Park. Owner of Stoner Creek Stud, Kentucky; Leona Farm, Illinois. Bred and owned Count Fleet, Anita Peabody, Prince John, Fleet Nasrullah, Blue Banner, Count of Honor; owned Reigh Count.

Hervey, John L., 1870-1947. Journalist. Racing historian and author under pen name of "Salvator." Author of *Racing in America*, Vols. 1, 2, 4.

Hildreth, Samuel, 1866-1929. Trainer, owner. Leading trainer by money won nine times; leading trainer by races won 1921, '27; leading owner by money won 1909-'10, '11; inducted into Racing Hall of Fame in '55. Trained Grey Lag, Zev. Trained ten champions, seven Belmont Stakes winners.

Hine, Hubert "Sonny," 1931-2000. Trainer. Elected to Racing Hall of Fame in 2003. Trained Skip Away, Guilty Conscience, Skip Trial, Technology.

Hirsch, Clement L., 1914-2000. Canned foods. Co-founder and president of Oak Tree Racing Association. Eclipse Award for distinguished service in 1999. Owner of *Figonero, June Darling, *Snow Sporting, Magical Mile, Magical Maiden.

Hirsch, Mary (Mrs. Charles McLennan), 1914-'63. Trainer. First licensed woman trainer in 1933. Owner (with Charles McLennan) of Cowpens Farm, Maryland. Trained stakes winner No Sir. Daughter of Max Hirsch.

Hirsch, Max, 1880-1969. Trainer, jockey, owner, breeder. Inducted into Racing Hall of Fame in 1959. Trained more than 100 stakes winners and six champions, including Assault, Sarazen, Middleground, Bold Venture, Gallant Bloom. Won 1946 Triple Crown with Assault. Father of William J. "Buddy" Hirsch, Mary Hirsch.

Hirsch, William J. "Buddy," 1909-'97. Trainer. Inducted into Racing Hall of Fame in 1982. Trained 56 stakes winners and one champion, Gallant Bloom. Owned stakes winner Columbiana. Son of Max Hirsch.

Hitchcock, Thomas, 1861-1941. Trainer. Inducted into Racing Hall of Fame in 1973. Trained three champions: Good and Plenty, Salvidere, Annibal. Captained America's first international polo team.

Hollingsworth, Kent, 1930-'99. Journalist. Editor of *The Blood-Horse* 1963-'87; president of Thoroughbred Club of America 1974-'75; president of National Museum of Racing Hall of Fame 1982-'86.

Hoomes, John, 1755-1805. Stagecoaches. Founder of Virginia Jockey Club. Imported *Diomed, *Spread Eagle, *Buzzard.

Hooper, Fred W., 1898-2000. Highway construction. Owner of Hooper Farm, Florida. Eclipse Award outstanding breeder 1975, '82; Eclipse Award of Merit in '92. Bred and owned Susan's Girl, Precisionist, Crozier, Tri Jet, Copelan; owned Hoop, Jr., Olympia, Education. Brought Racing Hall of Fame jockeys Braulio Baeza, Laffit Pincay Jr., and Jorge Velasquez to United States.

Howard, Charles S., 1881-1950. Automobile dealer, real estate. Leading owner 1937, '40. Owner of Seabiscuit, *Noor, *Kayak II.

Hughes, Hollie, 1888-1981. Trainer. Inducted into Racing Hall of Fame in 1973. Trained more than 20 stakes winners, including, *Tourist II. Trained 1916 Kentucky Derby winner George Smith.

Hunter, John, 1833-1914. Real estate. First chairman of the Jockey Club 1894-'95; co-founder of Saratoga Race Course. Owner of Annieswood Stud, New York. Owner of Kentucky, Sultana; bred and owned Alarm, Olitipa, Rhadamanthus.

Hyland, John J., Birthdate unknown-1913. Trainer. Inducted into Racing Hall of Fame in 1956. Trained six champions, including Beldame, Henry of Navarre, His Highness, The Butterflies.

Isaacs, Harry Z., 1904-'90. Clothing manufacturer. Owner of Brookfield Farm, Maryland. Bred and owned Intentionally, Intent, Itsabet.

Iselin, Philip H., 1902-'76. Clothing manufacturer. President of Monmouth Park 1966-'77. Instrumental in consolidation of year-end polls into Eclipse Awards.

Jackson, James, 1782-1840. Merchant. Owner of Forks of Cypress Farm, Alabama. Bred Peytona, Reel. Imported *Glencoe, *Galopade, *Leviathan.

Jacobs, Hirsch, 1904-'70. Owner-breeder, trainer. Leading breeder by money won 1964-'67; leading trainer by money won 1946, '60, '65; leading trainer by races won 1933-'39, '41-'44; inducted into Racing Hall of Fame in '58. Trained 3,596 winners and four champions. Bred Affectionately, Hail to Reason, Straight Deal, Personality. Co-owned and trained Hail to Reason, Stymie, Affectionately, Straight Deal.

Janney, Stuart S. Jr., 1907-'88. Lawyer, financier. Chairman, Maryland Racing Commission in 1947; president of Maryland Horse Breeders Association. Owner of Locust Hill Farm, Maryland. Bred and owned Ruffian, Icecapade, Buckfinder, Private Terms. Father of Maryland breeder Stuart S. Janney III.

Jeffords, Walter M. Sr., 1883-1960. Investments. President of Grayson Foundation; president of National Museum of Racing Hall of Fame 1954-'60. Owner of Faraway Farm, Kentucky. Bred and owned One Count, Pavot, Bateau, Kiss Me Kate, Scapa Flow, Snow Goose.

Jerome, Leonard W., 1817-'91. Financier. Built Jerome Park in 1866; president of Coney Island Jockey Club (Sheepshead Bay racetrack). Owned Kentucky, Fleetwing, Decoursey.

Johnson, Albert, 1900-'66. Jockey, trainer. Leading jockey by money won in 1922; inducted into Racing Hall of Fame in '71. Rode 503 winners, including Exterminator, American Flag, Crusader. Rode two Kentucky Derby winners.

Johnson, Phil G., 1925-2004. Trainer. Inducted into Racing Hall of Fame in 1997. Trained Quiet Little Table, *Amen II, Maplejinsky, Match the Hatch, Naskra, Nasty and Bold, Volponi.

Johnson, William Ransom, 1782-1849. Trainer. Inducted into Racing Hall of Fame in 1986. Trained more than 20 champions, including Boston, Sir Archy. First great American trainer, called the "Napoleon of the Turf;" won 61 of 63 races during a two-year period.

Johnston, Elwood B., 1909-'81. California industry leader. Established Old English Rancho in the 1930s. Founder of the HBPA's California division. North America's leading breeder of stakes winners in 1972, with 13; co-leader in '71 (nine). Breeder of more than 100 stakes winners, including Real Good Deal, Special Warmth, MacArthur Park, Impressive Style, June Darling, Fleet Treat, Admirably, Generous Portion. Bought and raced Fleet Nasrullah.

Jones, Ben A., 1882-1961. Trainer. Leading trainer by money won 1941, '43-'44, '52; inducted into Racing Hall of Fame in '58. Trained 11 champions, including Whirlaway, Lawrin, Bewitch, Twilight Tear, Armed. Won record six Kentucky Derbys. Father of Horace A. "Jimmy" Jones.

Jones, Horace A. "Jimmy," 1906-2001. Trainer. Leading trainer by money won 1947-'49, '57, '61; inducted into Racing Hall of Fame in '59. Trained 54 stakes winners and seven champions, including Citation, Armed, Coaltown, Tim Tam. First trainer to win more than $1-million in purses. Son of Ben Jones.

Jones, Warner L., 1916-'94. Distiller, breeder. Chairman of Churchill Downs 1984-'92; president of Thoroughbred Breeders of Kentucky. Owner of Hermitage Farm, Kentucky. Eclipse Award of Merit in 1990. Breeder of Dark Star, Lomond, Is It True, Seattle Dancer, Northern Trick, Woodman, King's Bishop. Sold world-record $13.1-million yearling in 1984; co-founder of the American Horse Council.

Joyner, Andrew Jackson, 1861-1943. Trainer. Leading trainer by races won in 1908; inducted into Racing Hall of Fame in '55. Trained five champions, including Ethelbert, St. James, Whisk Broom II.

Keck, Howard B., 1913-'96. Oil production. Bred Ferdinand; bred and owned Turkish Trousers, Bagdad, Fiddle Isle, Tell, etc.

Keene, Foxhall P., 1867-1941. Sportsman. Owner of Domino, Cap and Bells. Purchased Domino for $3,000 as a yearling. Son of James R. Keene.

Keene, James R., 1838-1913. Financier. Owner of Castleton Stud, Kentucky. Leading owner 1905-'08; leading breeder. Bred and owned Colin, Commando, Peter Pan, Sweep, Kingston, Sysonby, Cap and Bells; owned Domino, Spendthrift. Prime mover in formation of the Jockey Club in late 1893. Father of Foxhall P. Keene.

Kenner, Duncan F., 1813-'87. Sugar planter. President, Louisiana Jockey Club. Owner of Blue Bonnet. Owned slave jockey Abe Hawkins.

Kilmer, Willis Sharpe, 1868-1940. Patent-medicine distributor. Owner of Court Manor Stud, Virginia; Sun Briar Court, New York. Bred and owned Sun Beau, Sally's Alley, Chance Sun; owned Exterminator, *Sun Briar; bred Reigh Count.

Kilroe, Frank E. "Jimmy," 1912-'96. Racing executive. Racing secretary and handicapper at Santa Anita Park 1953-'90 and at New York tracks 1954-'59. Eclipse Award of Merit in 1979.

Kirkpatrick, Haden, 1911-'88. Publisher, journalist. Publisher, editor of *The Thoroughbred Record* 1941-'80.

Kleberg, Robert J., 1896-1974. Rancher, oilman. Owner of King Ranch, Kentucky and Texas. Leading owner in 1954. Bred and owned Assault, Middleground, Gallant Bloom, Dawn Play, Stymie, Miss Cavandish; owned High Gun, But Why Not, Bridal Flower.

Klein, Eugene V., 1921-'90. Automobile dealer. Leading owner 1985, '87; Eclipse Award owner 1985-'87. Owned Lady's Secret, Winning Colors, Capote, Life's Magic, Tank's Prospect, Open Mind, Family Style.

Knapp, Willie, 1888-1972. Jockey, trainer, racing official. Inducted into Racing Hall of Fame in 1969. Rode 649 winners, including Exterminator, Upset. Won 1919 Sanford Stakes aboard Upset, handing Man o' War his only loss.

Knight, Henry H., 1889-1959. Automobile dealer. Owner of Almahurst Farm and Coldstream Stud, Kentucky. Bred Nail, Cosmah. Stood leading sires *Bull Dog, *Heliopolis.

Kummer, Clarence, 1899-1930. Jockey. Leading jockey by money won in 1920; inducted into Racing Hall of Fame in '72. Rode 464 winners, including Man o' War, Sir Barton, Exterminator, Sarazen. Defeated French champion *Epinard by a head aboard Ladkin in 1924 International Special.

Kurtsinger, Charles F., 1906-'46. Jockey. Leading jockey by money won 1931, '37; inducted into Racing Hall of Fame in '67. Rode 721 winners. Won 1931 Kentucky Derby with Twenty Grand; rode War Admiral to victory in 1937 Triple Crown.

Kyne, William P., 1887-1957. Racing executive. General manager of California Jockey Club (Bay Meadows Race Course) 1934-'57; owner of Portland Meadows racetrack 1946-'57. Promoted passage of California pari-mutuel law in 1933.

Lakeland, William, 1853-1914. Trainer. Trained Domino, Hamburg, *Ogden, Electioneer, Exile. Co-breeder and co-owner of Commando.

Laurin, Lucien, 1912-2000. Trainer, jockey. Eclipse Award trainer in 1972; inducted into Racing Hall of Fame in '77. Trained 36 stakes winners and three champions: Secretariat, Quill, Riva Ridge. Trained 1972-'73 Horse of the Year Secretariat to Triple Crown.

LeRoy, Mervyn, 1900-'87. Movie producer. President of Hollywood Park 1951-'85. Co-bred and owned Honeymoon, Stepfather, Honey's Alibi.

Lewis, J. Howard, 1862-1947. Trainer. Inducted into Racing Hall of Fame in 1969. Trained 14 steeplechase champions, including Bushranger, Fairmount.

Lindheimer, Benjamin F., 1891-1960. Real-estate developer. Chairman of Arlington Park 1938-'60, Washington Park 1934-'60. Father of Marjorie Everett, former chief executive of Hollywood Park.

Loftus, Johnny, 1895-1976. Jockey, trainer. Leading jockey by money won in 1919; inducted into Racing Hall of Fame in '59. Rode 580 winners, including Man o' War, Sir Barton, Pan Zareta. First jockey to win the Triple Crown, aboard Sir Barton in 1919.

Longden, John, 1907-2003. Jockey, trainer. Leading jockey by races won in 1938, '47-'48; leading jockey by money won in 1943, '45; inducted into Racing Hall of Fame in '58; Special Eclipse Award in '94; George Woolf Memorial Jockey Award in '52; Avelino Gomez Memorial Award in '85. Rode then-record 6,032 winners, including Count Fleet, Busher, *Noor. Trained Majestic Prince, Jungle Savage, Baffle. Founded Jockeys' Guild with Eddie Arcaro and Sam Renick in 1940. Only man to both ride (Count Fleet) and train (Majestic Prince) a Kentucky Derby winner.

Lord Derby (Edward Stanley, 12th Earl of Derby), 1752-1834. A pillar of 18th-century British racing, he was responsible for founding the Epsom Oaks (1779) and Epsom Derby (1780), the latter bearing his family name after he won a coin toss with Sir Charles Bunbury. Won 1787 Derby with Sir Peter Teazle.

Lord Derby (Edward Stanley, 17th Earl of Derby), 1865-1948. Bred then-record 19 English classic winners, including Hyperion, Sansovino, Fairway, Swynford, Colorado, and *Watling Street. Also bred influential sires Phalaris, Pharos, *Sickle, and *Pharamond II. Generally acknowledged as one of the most successful owners-breeders in British Turf history.

Lorillard, George, 1843-'86. Tobacco sales. President of Monmouth Park. Owner of Westbrook Stable. Leading owner 1877-'80. Owned Tom Ochiltree, Spinaway, Duke of Magenta, Harold, Saunterer, Grenada.

Lorillard, Pierre, 1832-1901. Tobacco sales. Owner of Rancocas Stud, New Jersey. Bred and owned Wanda, Exile, Sibola, Dewdrop, Hiawasse; owned Iroquois, Parole, Saxon, Democrat. First American to win Epsom Derby, with Iroquois in 1881; inspired formation of the Board of Control (predecessor to the Jockey Club) in 1891.

Luro, Horatio, 1901-'91. Trainer. Inducted into Racing Hall of Fame in 1980. Trained 43 stakes winners, including Northern Dancer, *Kayak II, Decidedly, *Princequillo, *Miss Grillo.

Mabee, John C., 1921-2002. Grocery chain owner. Chairman, Del Mar Thoroughbred Club. Co-owner with wife Betty of Golden Eagle Farm, California. Eclipse Award breeder 1991, '97, '98. Bred and owned Best Pal, Event of the Year, General Challenge, Jeanne Jones, Worldly Manner. Founding member of the board of directors of Breeders' Cup Ltd.; Del Mar's largest growth occurred under his leadership.

MacBeth, Don, 1949-'87. Jockey. George Woolf Memorial Jockey Award in 1987. Rode Chief's Crown, Temperence Hill, Silver Buck, Half Iced. Inspired formation of injured jockey's fund that bears his name.

Macomber, A. Kingsley, 1876-1955. Banker, oilman. Important owner-breeder in California and France. Worked in 1920s to bring big-time horse racing to California; founder of the New Pacific Coast Jockey Club; also owned Haras du Quesnay in France, Mira Monte Stock Farm in California. Owned Parth, Rose Prince; imported *North Star III.

Madden, John E., 1856-1929. Trainer, owner, breeder. Owner of Hamburg Place. Leading breeder 1917-'27; leading trainer 1901-'03; inducted into Racing Hall of Fame in '83. Trained at least 38 stakes winners and eight champions. Bred Grey Lag, Sir Barton, Old Rosebud; owned Hamburg; trained Hamburg, Plaudit, Sir Martin. Bred five Kentucky Derby winners.

Maher, Danny, 1881-1916. Jockey. Leading jockey in U.S. in 1898; leading jockey in England 1908, '13; inducted into Racing Hall of Fame in '55. Rode 1,771 winners, including *Rock Sand, Spearmint, Cicero.

Maloney, James W., 1909-'84. Trainer. Inducted into Racing Hall of Fame in 1989. Trained 42 stakes winners and two champions, including Gamely, Lamb Chop, Princessnesian.

Markey, Lucille P. (Wright), 1897-1982. Investments. Owner of Calumet Farm, Kentucky. Leading breeder 1950-'57, '61; leading owner 1952, '56-'58, '61. Bred and owned Alydar, Fabius, Tim Tam, Our Mims, Forward Pass, Davona Dale, Iron Liege, Barbizon, Before Dawn.

Mars, Ethel V., 1884-1945. Confectioner. Owner of Milky Way Farm, Tennessee. Leading owner in 1936. Owned Gallahadion, Forever Yours, Sky Larking, Case Ace, Reaping Reward.

Mayer, Louis B., 1885-1957. Movie producer. Owner of Louis B. Mayer Stock Farm, California. Bred Honeymoon, Your Host, On Trust, Clem, Lurline B.; imported *Alibhai, *Beau Pere.

McAtee, J. Linus "Pony," 1897-1963. Jockey. Leading jockey in 1928; inducted into Racing Hall of Fame in '56. Rode 930 winners, including Exterminator, Twenty Grand, Jack High. Won 1927, '28 Kentucky Derby.

McCarthy, Clem, 1883-1962. Sportscaster. First radio broadcast of Kentucky Derby in 1928; broadcast Derby from 1928-'50.

McCreary, Conn, 1921-'79. Jockey, trainer. Inducted into Racing Hall of Fame in 1975. Rode 1,263 winners, including Racing Hall of Fame members Stymie, Twilight Tear, Armed, Searching. Trained three stakes winners.

McDaniel, Henry, 1867-1948. Trainer. Co-leading trainer by races won in 1922; inducted into Racing Hall of Fame in '56. Trained 1,041 recorded winners and four champions, including Exterminator, Reigh Count, Sun Beau.

McDaniel, Robert H. "Red," 1911-'55. Trainer. Leading trainer by races won 1950-'54. Trained *Poona II, Blue Reading.

McGrath, H. Price, 1814-'81. Tailor, bookmaker. Owner of McGrathiana Stud, Kentucky. Bred first Kentucky Derby winner Aristides, Thora, Tom Bowling.

McKinney, Rigan, 1908-'85. Jockey, trainer, breeder. Leading amateur steeplechase jockey 1933-'34, '36, '38; inducted into Racing Hall of Fame in '68. Rode 138 winners, including Green Cheese, Beacon Hill, Annibal. Trained Navigate, Drift, The Heir. Won American Grand National aboard Green Cheese in 1931.

McKnight, William L., 1888-1978. Industrialist. Chairman, Minnesota Mining and Manufacturing Co. 1949-'66. Co-founder of Calder Race Course. Owner of Tartan Farms, Florida. Eclipse Award, Man of the Year, in 1974. Leading breeder in 1990. Bred and owned Dr. Fager, Ta Wee, Dr. Patches; bred Unbridled.

McLaughlin, James, 1861-1927. Jockey. Leading jockey 1884-'87; inducted into Racing Hall of Fame in 1955. Rode Hindoo, Tecumseh, Tremont, Firenze. Won 1881 Kentucky Derby on Hindoo; won '85 Preakness Stakes aboard Tecumseh; won six Belmont Stakes.

McLennan, Joseph, 1868-1933. Racing executive. Racing secretary at Hialeah Park, Arlington Park.

Meadors, Joel C. "Skeets," 1896-1967. Photographer.

Mellon, Paul, 1908-'99. Investments, banking. Owner of Rokeby Stud, Virginia. Eclipse Award owner-breeder in 1971; breeder in '86; Award of Merit in '93. Bred and owned Mill Reef, Arts and Letters, Key to the Mint, Fort Marcy, Sea Hero, Quadrangle, Run the Gantlet, Java Gold; owned Fit to Fight, Summer Guest, Blue Banner.

Miller, Walter, 1890-1959. Jockey. Leading jockey 1906-'07; inducted into Racing Hall of Fame in '55. Rode 1,904 winners, including Colin, Ballot, Peter Pan, Whimsical. Won 388 races in 1906 (at age 16), a record that stood until Racing Hall of Fame jockey William Shoemaker tied the mark 44 years later in 1950 and broke it in '52.

Mills, James P., 1909-'87, and **Alice**, 1912-2000. Aviation. Owner of Hickory Tree Farm, Virginia. Bred and owned Committed, Believe It, Terpsichorist, Hagley; owned Devil's Bag, Gone West.

Mills, Ogden, 1884-1937. Investments. Co-owner of Wheatley Stable. Bred Seabiscuit, Edelweiss; owned Dice, Diavolo, Dark Secret. Brother of Mrs. H. C. Phipps.

Molter, William, 1910-'60. Trainer. Leading trainer by races won 1946-'49; leading trainer by money won 1954, '56, '58, '59; inducted into Racing Hall of Fame in '60. Trained 2,158 winners and 48 stakes winners, including Round Table, Determine, T. V. Lark.

Mori, Eugene, 1898-1975. Banker, real-estate developer. Builder and president of Garden State Park 1942-'72; owned Hialeah Park 1954-'72. Owner of East Acres Farm, New Jersey. Bred Tosmah; owned Alma North, Cosmah. Promoted pari-mutuel wagering in New Jersey.

Morris, Francis, 1810-'86. Shipping. Owner of Morris Stud, New York. Bred and owned Ruthless, Relentless, Narragansett. Aided Leonard W. Jerome in founding of American Jockey Club and Jerome Park in 1866.

Morris, Green B., 1837-1920. Owner, trainer. Leading owner in 1902. Trained Apollo, Sir Dixon, Strathmeath, *Star Ruby.

Morris, John A., 1892-1985. Financier. President of Thoroughbred Racing Associations, Jamaica Racetrack. Eclipse Award, Man of the Year, in 1975. Bred and owned Missile Belle, Proudest Roman, L'Heureux; owned Missile. Great-grandson of Francis Morris.

Morrissey, John, 1831-'78. Prizefighter, gambler, politician. Co-founder of Saratoga Race Course in 1863.

Mulholland, W. F. "Bert," 1884-1968. Trainer. Inducted into Racing Hall of Fame in 1967. Trained 832 winners, 57 stakes winners, and five champions, including Jaipur, Eight Thirty, Lucky Draw, Battlefield. Trained for George D. Widener for more than 40 years.

Munnings, Sir Alfred, 1878-1959. Painter. Greatest English painter of horses of 20th century.

Murphy, Isaac, 1860-'96. Jockey, trainer, owner. Inducted into Racing Hall of Fame in 1955. Rode 530 recorded winners, including Falsetto, Firenze, Salvator, Emperor of Norfolk. First jockey to win three Kentucky Derbys; first jockey elected to Racing Hall of Fame. Won with 44% of his mounts.

Neloy, Eddie, 1921-'71. Trainer. Leading trainer by money won 1966-'68; inducted into Racing Hall of Fame in '83. Trained 60 stakes winners and five champions, including Buckpasser, Bold Lad, Gun Bow.

Neves, Ralph, 1921-'95. Jockey. Inducted into Racing Hall of Fame in 1960; George Woolf Memorial Jockey Award in '54. Rode 3,771 winners, sixth all-time by wins at retirement; rode 173 stakes winners, including Round Table, Native Diver. Rode five winners at Bay Meadows after track announcer declared him "deceased" following an accident the previous day.

Newman, Neil, 1886-1951. Journalist. Wrote under the pen name of "Roamer." Author of *Famous Horses of the American Turf* series 1930-'32.

Niarchos, Stavros, 1909-'96. Shipping. Owner of Haras de Fresnay-le-Buffard, France; Oak Tree Farm, Kentucky. Bred and owned Miesque, Spinning World,

Kingmambo, Hernando (Fr), Hector Protector, Machiavellian; owned Nureyev.

Niccolls, Richard, 1624-'72. Soldier, politician. Founded first American racecourse, Newmarket, at Salisbury Plain (near modern Hempstead), Long Island, New York.

Notter, Joe, 1890-1973. Jockey. Leading jockey by money won in 1908; inducted into Racing Hall of Fame in '63. Rode Regret, Whisk Broom II, Colin. First jockey to ride a filly, Regret, to victory in the Kentucky Derby (1915); first jockey to win handicap triple crown, on Whisk Broom II.

O'Connor, Winnie, 1884-1947. Jockey, trainer. Leading jockey in 1901; inducted into Racing Hall of Fame in '56. Rode 1,229 winners in United States and France, including Yankee, Reina. One of "Father Bill" Daly's "Five Aces."

Odom, George M., 1883-1964. Jockey, trainer. Inducted into Racing Hall of Fame in 1955. Rode 527 winners, including Broomstick, Delhi, Banastar. Trained Busher, Pasteurized. Won the Belmont Stakes as a jockey and later as a trainer.

O'Farrell, Joe, 1912-'82. Breeder. President, Florida Breeders' Sales Co. Owner of Ocala Stud, Florida. Bred Roman Brother, Office Queen, My Dear Girl. Stood Rough'n Tumble. Primary founder of Florida breeding industry.

Olin, John M., 1892-1982. Small-arms munitions. Bred and owned Cannonade; owned Bold Bidder, Northfields.

O'Neill, Frank, 1886-1960. Jockey. Inducted into Racing Hall of Fame in 1956. Rode Beldame, Roseben, *Prince Palatine, Spion Kop. Also successful jockey in France and England.

Palmer, Joe H., 1904-'52. Journalist. Author of *This Was Racing, American Racehorses* series 1944-'51.

Parke, Burley, 1905-'77. Trainer. Inducted into Racing Hall of Fame in 1986. Trained 37 stakes winners and three champions: Roman Brother, *Noor, Raise a Native. *Noor beat Citation in four consecutive stakes races. Brother of Ivan Parke.

Parke, Ivan, 1908-'95. Jockey, trainer. Leading jockey by races won in 1923, '24 (his first two years of racing); leading jockey by money won in '24; inducted into Racing Hall of Fame in '78. Rode 419 winners, including Backbone. Trained 27 stakes winners, including Exclusive Native, Hoop, Jr. Brother of Burley Parke.

Patrick, Gilbert "Gilpatrick," 1812-ca. 1880. Jockey. Inducted into Racing Hall of Fame in 1970. Rode Ruthless, Boston, Kentucky, Lexington. Rode first Belmont Stakes winner, Ruthless, in 1867.

Paulson, Allen E., 1922-2000. Aviation. Owner of Brookside Farm, Kentucky. Eclipse Award breeder in 1993; owner '95 and '96. Owned and bred Cigar, Ajina, Escena, Fraise; owned Theatrical (Ire), Strawberry Road (Aus), Blushing John, Arazi, Paradise Creek; bred Azeri.

Payson, Mrs. Charles S. (Joan Whitney), 1903-'75. Publisher, investments. Co-owner of Greentree Stud. Leading owner in 1951. Owned and bred Stage Door Johnny, Capot, Bowl Game, Late Bloomer, The Axe II, Cohoes, Stop the Music; owned Tom Fool. Daughter of Mr. and Mrs. Payne Whitney; sister of John Hay Whitney.

Pelleteri, Anthony, 1893-1952. Trainer, racing executive. Won the 1941 Santa Anita Handicap with 90-to-1 Bay View, and developed stakes winners Bull Reigh and Andy K. In 1941 Pelleteri organized a partnership that saved the historic Fair Grounds racetrack in New Orleans from being auctioned and subdivided; served as the track's executive vice president until his death.

Penna, Angel, 1923-'92. Trainer. Leading trainer in Argentina in 1952; leading trainer in Venezuela in '54; leading trainer in France in '74; inducted into Racing Hall of Fame in '88. Trained more than 250 stakes winners, including Allez France, Relaxing, San San, Private Account.

Perry, William Haggin, 1911-'93. Investments. Owner of Waterford Farm, Virginia. Co-owned and co-bred Gamely, Lure, Revidere, Coastal, Lamb Chop, Boldnesian.

Phipps, Mrs. Henry C. (Gladys Mills), 1883-1970. Investments. Owner of Wheatley Stable. Leading owner in 1966. Bred and owned Bold Ruler, Bold Lad, Seabiscuit, High Voltage, Misty Morn, Queen Empress, Successor, Bold Bidder, Castle Forbes. Mother of leading owner-breeder Ogden Phipps; sister of Ogden Mills.

Phipps, Ogden, 1908-2002. Investments. Chairman, Jockey Club 1964-'74; former chairman New York Racing Association. Leading owner by money won 1988, '89; Eclipse Award breeder in '88; Eclipse Award owner 1988, '89; Eclipse Award of Merit 2002; Mr. Fitz Award in '89. Bred and owned Buckpasser, Easy Goer, Private Account. Bred and raced Personal Ensign, who was unbeaten in 13 starts.

Piatt, Thomas, 1877-1965. Farmer, tobacco. First president of Thoroughbred Club of America; president, Breeders' Sales Co. Owner of Brookdale Farm, Kentucky. Bred Alsab, Donau. Father of Thomas Carr Piatt.

Piatt, Thomas Carr, 1900-'53. Farmer, tobacco. President, Breeders' Sales Co. 1949-'53. Owner of Crestwood Farm, Kentucky. Co-breeder of Occupation, Occupy, Errard. Son of Thomas Piatt.

Pincus, Jacob, 1838-1918. Trainer, jockey. Leading trainer in 1869; inducted into Racing Hall of Fame in '88. Trained Glenelg, Eagle, Richmond. Trained Iroquois, first American winner of the Epsom Derby.

Pollard, John "Red," 1909-1981. Canadian-born jockey. Rode his first Thoroughbred winner in 1926. In mid-1930s began association with C. S. Howard, owner of Seabiscuit, whom he rode to many important victories—although not in the famed 1938 match against War Admiral. Retired after injury-plagued 30-year career. Later inducted into the Canadian Racing Hall of Fame.

Porter, William T., 1809-'58. Publisher. Founded *Spirit of the Times* magazine in 1831.

Price, Jack, 1908-'95. Trainer. Trained 1961 Kentucky Derby and Preakness Stakes winner Carry Back, whom he bred out of the $265 mare Joppy.

Purdy, Samuel, 1785-1836. Jockey. Inducted into Racing Hall of Fame in 1970. Semi-retired when pulled from the crowd to replace American Eclipse's jockey at the Union Course in 1823, winning the next two heats to win the match over Henry.

Rasmussen, Leon, 1915-2003. Journalist. "Bloodlines" columnist, *Daily Racing Form*. Walter Haight Award in 1987; Engelhard Award in '87. Bred and owned Apollo, Nanetta. Popularized Dr. Steven A. Roman's dosage system in his column.

Reiff, John, 1885-1974. Jockey. Leading jockey in France in 1902; inducted into Racing Hall of Fame in '56. Rode 1,016 winners, including Orby, Tagalie, Retz, Moia. Among the top ten jockeys for ten seasons in France; won two Epsom Derbys and one French Derby.

Rice, Daniel, 1896-1975, and **Ada L.**, 1899-1977. Stock and grain broker. Co-owners of Arlington Park 1940-'68. Owners of Danada Farm, Kentucky. Bred and owned Lucky Debonair, Pucker Up, Proud Delta, Delta Judge, Advocator.

Rice, Grantland, 1880-1954. Journalist. Covered most major sports for the New York *Herald Tribune*, but horse racing was a favorite. Among the great racing events he covered was the 1938 Seabiscuit-War Admiral match.

Richards, A. Keene, 1827-'81. Sugar and cotton planter. Owner of Blue Grass Park Stud, Kentucky. Owned *Australian, Starke, War Dance. Bred Fenian, Target, Eliza Davis, Ulrica.

Richards, Sir Gordon, 1904-'86. Jockey. Champion British flat jockey 26 times in 34 seasons of racing. First to ride more than 4,000 winners, he retired in 1954 with a then-world record 4,870 career victories. In 1953 he became the first professional jockey to be knighted.

Richards, Leonard P., Birthdate and date of death unknown. Chemical manufacturer. Second chairman of the Delaware Racing Commission.

Riddle, Samuel D., 1862-1951. Textiles. Owner of Faraway Farm, Kentucky; Glen Riddle Stable. Leading owner in 1925. Owned Man o' War; bred and owned War Admiral, Crusader, American Flag, War Relic.

Riggs, William P., 1874-1936. Racetrack executive. Secretary of the Maryland Jockey Club; a driving force behind the revival of Pimlico Race Course and return of Preakness Stakes to Maryland in 1909.

Robertson, Alfred, 1911-'75. Jockey. Inducted into Racing Hall of Fame in '71; New York Turf Writers Association's best jockey in 1942. Rode 1,856 winners, including Top Flight, Whirlaway, Riverland, Sky Larking. Twice rode six winners in a single day.

Robertson, William H. P., 1920-'82. Journalist. Editor of *The Thoroughbred Record* 1962-'78. Author of *History of Thoroughbred Racing in America, Hoofprints of the Century.*

Roebling, Joseph M., 1909-'80. Building contractor. Owner of Harbourton Stud, New Jersey. Bred and owned Blue Peter, Fall Aspen, Rainy Lake.

Rogers, John W., ca. 1850-1908. Trainer. Inducted into Racing Hall of Fame in 1955. Trained 11 champions, including Artful, Modesty. Trained Artful to win the 1904 Belmont Futurity, giving Sysonby the only defeat of his career.

Rolapp, R. Richards, 1941-'93. Lawyer. President of American Horse Council 1978-'93.

Ross, John K. L., 1876-1951. Railways. Leading owner 1918-'19. Owned Sir Barton, Billy Kelly, Cudgel.

Rous, Adm. Henry J., 1795-1877. English Jockey Club steward, Turf reformer, handicapper. Published *Handbook on the Laws of Racing*, which included the first standard scale of weights. Established and enforced strict standards and banned unsavory characters. Often referred to as the "Father of the Turf."

Rowan, Louis R., 1911-'88. Investments. Original shareholder in Santa Anita Racetrack; six-term president of the California Thoroughbred Breeders Association; conceived California Cup; founding director of Oak Tree Racing Association and Del Mar Thoroughbred Club. Founding chairman of the Winners Foundation.

Rowe, James Sr., 1857-1929. Trainer, jockey. Leading jockey 1871-'73; leading trainer 1908, '13, '15; inducted into Racing Hall of Fame in '55. Trained 34 horses regarded as champions, more than any other Hall of Fame trainer. Trained Colin, Miss Woodford, Regret, Luke Blackburn, Hindoo.

Runyon, Damon, 1884-1946. Journalist, sports columnist, author, humorist. Many of his short stories had to do with gambling and horse racing. Most famous for writing *Guys and Dolls*, although probably best known in racing for the poem "Gimme a Handy Guy Like Sande," about jockey Earl Sande.

Salman, Ahmed bin, 1958-2002. Publisher, Saudi royal family. Owner of The Thoroughbred Corp. Bred and owned Point Given, Spain. Owned Sharp Cat, Jewel Princess, Oath, Anees, Royal Anthem, War Emblem.

Salmon, Walter J., ca. 1880-1953. Real estate. Owner of Mereworth Farm. Leading breeder in 1946. Bred Discovery, Display, Dr. Freeland, Battleship (first American-bred and -owned winner of England's Grand National Steeplechase), Free For All; owned Vigil.

Samuel, Ernest, 1930-2000. Steel distribution. Owner of Sam-Son Farm, Ontario and Florida. Eclipse Award owner in 1991; leading owner and breeder in '91. Bred and raced more than 100 stakes winners, including Dance Smartly, Sky Classic, Chief Bearhart.

Sande, Earl, 1899-1968. Jockey, trainer. Leading jockey 1921, '23, '27; leading trainer in '38; inducted into Racing Hall of Fame in '55. Rode 968 winners, including Gallant Fox, Zev, Man o' War. Trained Stagehand, Sceneshifter. Won three Kentucky Derbys, five Belmont Stakes, and five Jockey Club Gold Cups.

Sanford, John, 1851-1939. Carpet mills, politician. Owner of Hurricane Stud, New York. Bred and raced *Affection, *Snob II, Sir John Johnson, *Donnacona; owned George Smith. Son of Stephen Sanford.

Sanford, Milton H., 1812-'83. Cotton mills. Owner of Preakness Stud, New Jersey; North Elkhorn Farm, Kentucky. Bred Vagrant, Vigil; also owned Preakness, Virgil, Monarchist. Stood leading sire Glenelg.

Sanford, Stephen, 1826-1913. Carpet mills. Owner of Hurricane Stud, New York. Raced only homebreds, which he gave Indian names, including Caughnawaga, Chuctununda, and Mohawk II. Stood Clifford, *Voter. Father of John Sanford.

Sangster, Robert, 1936-2004. Betting pools, investments. Co-owner of Coolmore Stud; owner of Swettenham Stud. Renowned owner-breeder who helped to fuel the 1980s boom at Thoroughbred yearling sales, with partners purchased a yearling for world-record $13.1-million in '85, campaigned more than 800 stakes winners, including champions The Minstrel, Alleged, Caerleon, and homebred Sadler's Wells; five-time leading owner in England.

Schapiro, John, 1914-2002. Racetrack executive. President of Laurel Park. Eclipse Award of Merit in 1980; *Sports Illustrated*'s Racing Man of the Year in 1960; Inaugurated the Washington, D.C., International at Laurel in 1952.

Scott, Marion duPont, 1891-1983. Investments. Owner of Montpelier Farm, Virginia. Bred more than 50 stakes winners, including Mongo, Parka, Neji, Soothsayer; owned Proud Delta, Battleship. Founded Carolina Cup Steeplechase in Camden, South Carolina. Member of syndicate that imported *Blenheim II.

Seagram, Joseph E., 1841-1919. Distiller. Member of Canadian Parliament. President of Ontario Jockey Club. Bred and raced Inferno, Belle Mahone. Won 15 King's (Queen's) Plates.

Shaffer, Charles B., 1859-1943. Oil production. Owner of Coldstream Stud, Kentucky. Bred Bull Lea, Occupation, Occupy, Star Pilot, Reaping Reward, Plucky Play. Stood leading sires *Bull Dog, *Heliopolis. Father of E. E. Dale Shaffer.

Shaffer, E. E. Dale, 1917-'74. Oil production. Founder of Detroit Race Course; chairman of Kentucky Racing Commission 1950-'51; president of Michigan Racing Association; president of Thoroughbred Racing Associations 1960-'61. Owner of Coldstream Stud, Kentucky. Leading breeder in 1945. Bred Sweet Patootie, Star

Pilot, Johns Joy. Stood leading sires *Bull Dog, *Heliopolis. Son of Charles Shaffer.

Shilling, Carroll, 1882-1950. Jockey. Leading jockey in 1910; inducted into Racing Hall of Fame in '70. Rode 969 winners, including Colin, Sir Martin, Fitz Herbert, King James. Won 1912 Kentucky Derby aboard Worth.

Shoemaker, William, 1931-2003. Jockey, trainer. President, Jockeys' Guild in 1975-'90. Leading jockey by money won in 1958-'64; inducted into Racing Hall of Fame in '58; Special Eclipse Award in '76; Eclipse Award jockey in '81; Eclipse Award of Merit in '81; George Woolf Memorial Jockey Award in '51; Mike Venezia Award in '90. Rode then-record 8,833 winners and 1,009 stakes winners, including Swaps, Spectacular Bid, Round Table, Ack Ack, Forego, John Henry, Prove It, Olden Times, Sword Dancer. Trained Fire the Groom, Alcando (Ire). First jockey to reach $100-million in earnings; mounts earned more than $123-million in purses. Paralyzed in single-car accident April 8, 1991.

Simms, Edward F., 1870-1938. Oil production. Owner of Xalapa Farm, Kentucky. Bred Coventry; owned Eternal, My Play.

Simms, Willie, 1870-1927. Jockey. Leading jockey in 1894; inducted into Racing Hall of Fame in 1977. Rode 1,125 winners, including Henry of Navarre, Ben Brush, Plaudit, Commanche. Won back-to-back Belmont Stakes (1893-'94) aboard Commanche and Henry of Navarre.

Sinclair, Harry F., 1876-1956. Oil production. Owner of Rancocas Stud, New Jersey. Leading owner 1921-'23. Bred and owned Mad Play, Ariel; owned Zev, Grey Lag, Mad Hatter.

Skinner, John S., 1788-1851. Publisher. Founded *American Turf Register* in 1830.

Sloan, James F. "Tod," 1874-1933. Jockey. Inducted into Racing Hall of Fame in 1955. Rode Hamburg, Clifford. Credited with popularizing the use of shortened stirrups in United States and England.

Sloane, Isabel Dodge, 1898-1962. Automobile heiress. Owner of Brookmeade Stud, Virginia. First female leading owner 1934, '50. Bred and owned Sword Dancer, Bowl of Flowers, Bold, Sailor, Greek Ship; owned Cavalcade, High Quest.

Smith, George "Pittsburgh Phil," 1862-1905. Gambler. Most successful gambler of Victorian era, died a millionaire.

Smith, Robert A., 1869-1942. Trainer, owner. Leading trainer 1933-'34; inducted into Racing Hall of Fame in '76. Trained more than 27 stakes winners and three champions, including 1934 Horse of the Year Cavalcade, High Quest. Owned Articulate. Won 1934 Kentucky Derby with Cavalcade.

Smith, Tom "Silent Tom," 1879-1957. Trainer. Leading trainer 1940, '45; inducted into Racing Hall of Fame in 2001. Trained 29 stakes winners and six champions, including Seabiscuit, Jet Pilot, *Kayak II. Trained 1947 Kentucky Derby winner Jet Pilot.

Smithwick, Alfred "Paddy," 1927-'73. Jockey. Leading steeplechase jockey by races won 1956-'58, '62; inducted into Racing Hall of Fame in '73. Rode 398 winners, including Neji, Bon Nouvel, Elkridge. Won two American Grand Nationals aboard Neji. Trained two stakes winners.

Sommer, Sigmund, 1917-'79. Real estate. Leading owner 1971-'72. Owned 29 stakes winners, including Autobiography, Sham, Never Bow.

Spreckels, Adolph, 1857-1924. Sugar merchant. President of Pacific Coast Jockey Club. Owner of Napa Stock Farm, California. Bred Morvich; bred and owned Runstar.

Stanford, Leland, 1824-'93. Politician. Governor of California 1861-1863; United States senator 1885-1893; founder of Stanford University. Developed Palo Alto Stock Farm. In 1872 hired photographer to prove that all of a horse's feet are off the ground at one point in the gallop.

Stephens, Woodford C. "Woody," 1913-'98. Trainer. Eclipse Award trainer in 1983; inducted into Racing Hall of Fame in '76. Trained 131 stakes winners and 11 champions, including Swale, Conquistador Cielo, Never Bend. Won five consecutive Belmont Stakes (1982-'86).

Stout, James, 1914-'76. Jockey, racing official. Inducted into Racing Hall of Fame in 1968. Rode Johnstown, Granville, Assault, Omaha, Stymie. Finished in the first triple win dead heat in a major stakes aboard Bousset in the 1944 Carter Handicap.

Strub, Charles H., 1884-1958. Baseball team owner, real estate, investments. Founder of Santa Anita Park. Father of Robert P. Strub.

Strub, Robert P., 1919-'93. Real estate. President of Los Angeles Turf Club (Santa Anita Park); chairman, Santa Anita Operating Co.; president of Thoroughbred Racing Associations 1963-'64. Eclipse Award of Merit in 1992. Son of Charles H. Strub.

Stull, Henry, 1851-1913. Noted American equine painter. First to accurately portray racehorses at a gallop. Owned Swarthmore.

Sutcliffe, Leonard S., 1880-1937. Photographer. Published photographic volumes *Thoroughbred Sires* and *Famous Mares in America.*

Swigert, Daniel, 1833-1912. Breeder. Founded Elmendorf Farm, Kentucky. Leading breeder. Bred Spendthrift, Hindoo, Salvator, Tremont, Baden-Baden. Managed Woodburn Stud. Father-in-law of Leslie Combs Sr.

Swinebroad, George W., 1901-'75. Auctioneer. Legendary auctioneer at Keeneland and Saratoga. Hammered down first $100,000 yearling in 1961.

Swope, Herbert Bayard, 1882-1958. Journalist, investments. Chairman of New York Racing Commission.

Taral, Fred, 1867-1925. Jockey, trainer. Inducted into Racing Hall of Fame in 1955. Rode 1,437 winners, including Domino, Henry of Navarre, Dr. Rice, Ramapo. Rode Domino to nine consecutive victories in 1893.

Tasker, Col. Benjamin Jr., 1720-'60. Planter. Prominent owner-breeder during Colonial era. Owner of Belair Stud, Maryland. Imported great racemare *Selima from England in 1750, notable sire *Othello; bred Pacolet, Selim.

Tayloe, John II, 1721-'79. Planter. Owner of Mount Airy Stud, Virginia. Bred Yorick, Ariel, Bellair; owned *Selima, Moreton's Traveller. Father of John Tayloe III.

Tayloe, John III, 1771-1828. Planter. Owner of Mount Airy Stud, Virginia. Bred American foundation sire Sir Archy, Lady Lightfoot, Grey Diomed, Calypso. Imported *Castianira, dam of Sir Archy. Son of John Tayloe II.

Taylor, Charles P. B., 1935-'97. Journalist, investments. Owner of Windfields Farm, Canada and Maryland; chairman, Canadian Jockey Club; vice president, Breeders' Cup Inc. Son of Edward P. Taylor.

Taylor, Edward P., 1901-'89. Brewing. President, Ontario Jockey Club and Canadian Thoroughbred Horse Society. Owner of Windfields Farm, Canada and Maryland. Leading breeder 1974-'80; Eclipse Award breeder 1977, '83. Bred and owned Northern Dancer, Nearctic, Victoria Park; bred Nijinsky II, El Gran Senor, Devil's Bag, The Minstrel, Secreto, Shareef Dancer, Storm Bird, Viceregal. Father of Charles P. B. Taylor.

Taylor, Joe, 1924-2003. Noted Kentucky horseman and author, whose sons founded Taylor Made Farm and Taylor Made Sales Agency, manager of Gainesway Farm from 1950 to '90.

Ten Broeck, Richard, 1809-'92. Gambler, sportsman. Owner of Metairie Race Course, Louisiana. Bred Umpire; owned Lexington, Lecompte, Prioress, *Eclipse, Starke. Conducted first successful invasion of England with American-breds in 1860s.

Tenney, Meshach, 1907-'93. Trainer. Leading trainer 1962-'63; inducted into Racing Hall of Fame in '91. Trained 36 stakes winners and one champion, including Swaps, Candy Spots, Olden Times, Prove It. Won 1955 Kentucky Derby with Swaps.

Tesio, Federico, 1869-1954. Breeder. Acclaimed Italian breeder of *Ribot, Nearco, Donatello II, Niccolo Dell'Arca. Bred and owned 20 Italian Derby winners. Author of *Breeding the Racehorse.*

Thomas, Barak G., 1826-1906. Planter, publisher. Noted owner-breeder in post-Civil War America. Founded Dixiana Farm, Kentucky. Bred and owned Himyar; bred Domino, Correction.

Thompson, Henry J. "Derby Dick," 1881-1937. Trainer. Inducted into Racing Hall of Fame in 1969. Trained 373 recorded winners and five champions, including Blue Larkspur, Burgoo King, Bubbling Over. First trainer to saddle four Kentucky Derby winners.

Tipton, Edward A., 1855-1930. Auctioneer. Co-founder of Fasig-Tipton Co. in 1898. Sold company to E. J. Tranter. Manager of Bitter Root Stud, Montana, 1896-1900.

Tranter, Enoch J., 1875-1938. Auctioneer. Owner of Fasig-Tipton Co. 1904-'38. Revolutionized Thoroughbred auction business in America. Launched annual yearling sale at Saratoga.

Travers, William R., 1819-'87. Stockbroker, raconteur. First president of Saratoga Association. Owned Kentucky, Alarm, Sultana.

Trotsek, Harry, 1912-'97. Trainer. Inducted into Racing Hall of Fame in 1984. Trained 96 stakes winners and two champions; trained Moccasin, Hasty Road, *Stan. Expert handler of imported horses; coached young jockeys at his jockey school in the 1940s.

Troye, Edward, 1808-'74. Painter. Prolific equine portraitist; his subjects included Lexington, Boston, and many of America's great mid-19th-century Thoroughbreds.

Tuckerman, Bayard J., 1889-1974. Jockey, breeder, owner. First president of Suffolk Downs. Inducted into Racing Hall of Fame in 1973. Rode Homestead. Bred Lavender Hill. Leading amateur jockey.

Turner, Nash, 1881-1937. Jockey, trainer, owner. Inducted into Racing Hall of Fame in 1955. Rode Imp, Flying Star, Goldsmith, Irish Lad. Rider of Imp, the first filly to win the Suburban Handicap in 1899; won 1906 Prix du Jockey-Club (French Derby).

Van Berg, Marion H., 1896-1971. Trainer, owner. Leading owner by money won 1965, '68-'70; leading owner by races won 1952, '54, '56, '60-'70; inducted into Racing Hall of Fame in '70. Trained more than 1,470 winners and six stakes winners, including *Estacion, Rose Bed. Father of Racing Hall of Fame trainer Jack Van Berg.

Vanderbilt, Alfred G., 1912-'99. Investments. Chairman, New York Racing Association; president, Belmont Park and Pimlico Race Course. Owner of Sagamore

Farm, Maryland. Eclipse Award of Merit in 1994. Bred and owned Native Dancer, Next Move, Bed o' Roses, Now What, Petrify; owned Discovery; bred Conniver, Miss Disco.

Van Ranst, Cornelius W., Birthdate and date of death unknown. Owned American Eclipse, *Messenger.

Veitch, Sylvester, 1910-'96. Trainer. Inducted into Racing Hall of Fame in 1977. Trained 44 stakes winners and five champions, including Counterpoint, Career Boy. Trained Horse of the Year Counterpoint, who won the 1951 Belmont Stakes. Father of trainer John Veitch.

Vosburgh, Walter, 1855-1938. Handicapper, author. Racing secretary, Westchester Racing Association (Belmont Park) 1894-1934. Author of *Racing in America 1866-1921;* Turf editor of *Spirit of the Times.* Originated Experimental Free Handicap in 1933.

Waggoner, William T., 1852-1934. Oil production, rancher. Early 20th-century force in Texas racing. Owner of 3D's Stock Farm, Texas. Built Arlington Downs racetrack, Texas, in 1929.

Walden, R. Wyndham, Birthdate unknown-1905. Trainer. Inducted into Racing Hall of Fame in 1970. Trained 101 stakes winners, including Duke of Magenta, Grenada, Saunterer. Trained seven Preakness Stakes winners, five consecutively.

Walsh, Michael G., 1906-'93. Trainer. Leading steeplechase trainer by races won 1953-'55; leading steeplechase trainer by money won 1953-'54, '60; inducted into Racing Hall of Fame in '75; F. Ambrose Clark Award in '75. Trained 31 stakes winners.

Ward, Sherrill, 1911-'84. Trainer. Eclipse Award trainer in 1974; inducted into Racing Hall of Fame in '78. Trained 20 stakes winners and two champions, including Forego, Summer Tan, and Idun. Trained Forego to Horse of the Year honors in 1975 and '76.

Warfield, Elisha, 1781-1859. Physician. Co-founder of the Kentucky Association racetrack, Lexington. Owner of The Meadows Stud, Kentucky. Breeder of Lexington, Berthune, Alice Carneal. Known as the "Father of the Kentucky Turf."

Welch, Aristides J., 1811-'90. Owner of Erdenheim Stud, Pennsylvania. Bred Iroquois, Parole, Sensation, Harold, Spinaway. Stood leading sire *Leamington.

Wells, Thomas J., 1803-'62. Sugar planter. President of Metairie Race Course. Bred Lecomte, Prioress; owned Reel.

Werblin, David A. "Sonny," 1910-'91. Entertainment and sports executive. First president of New Jersey Sports and Exposition Authority (originally the Meadowlands and now including Monmouth Park). Owner of Silent Screen, Process Shot.

Westrope, Jack, 1918-'58. Jockey. Leading jockey in 1933 at age 15, when he rode 301 winners. Inducted into Racing Hall of Fame in 2002.

Whitney, Cornelius V., 1899-1992. Investments. First president of National Museum of Racing Hall of Fame. Owner of C. V. Whitney Farm, Kentucky. Leading breeder 1933, '34, '38, '60; leading owner 1930-'33, '60. Bred more than 175 stakes winners. Bred and owned Counterpoint, Silver Spoon, Career Boy, First Flight; owned Equipoise, Top Flight. Son of Harry Payne Whitney.

Whitney, Harry Payne, 1872-1930. Investments. Owner of Brookdale Stud, New Jersey; Whitney Farm, Kentucky. Leading breeder 1926-'32; leading owner 1913, '20, '24, '26, '27, '29. Bred and owned Regret, Equipoise, Top Flight, Whisk Broom II, Whichone, Whiskery, Pennant, Upset, John P. Grier, Prudery. Father of C. V. Whitney.

Whitney, Mrs. Payne (Helen Hay), 1876-1944. Investments. "First Lady of the American Turf." Owner of Greentree Stud, Kentucky. Leading owner and breeder in 1942. Bred and owned Twenty Grand, Shut Out, Devil Diver, First Minstrel. Mother of John Hay Whitney and Joan Whitney (Mrs. Charles S.) Payson.

Whitney, John Hay "Jock," 1904-'82. Investments, publisher. Co-founder of American Thoroughbred Breeders' Association. Co-owner of Greentree Stud, Kentucky; owner of Mare's Nest Farm, Kentucky. Leading owner in 1951. Bred and raced Stage Door Johnny, Capot, Late Bloomer, Bowl Game, The Axe II, Cohoes, Stop the Music; owned Tom Fool. Stood The Porter.

Whitney, W. Payne, 1875-1927. Investments. Owner of Greentree Stud, Kentucky. Son of William C. Whitney; brother of H. P. Whitney; father of John Hay Whitney and Joan Whitney (Mrs. Charles S.) Payson.

Whitney, William C., 1841-1904. Transportation, oil production. President of Saratoga Race Course. Owner of La Belle Stud, Kentucky. Leading owner 1901, '03. Owned Volodyovski, Plaudit, Artful, Endurance By Right, Nasturtium; bred Artful, Tanya. Father of Harry Payne and W. Payne Whitney.

Whittingham, Charles E., 1913-'99. Trainer. Leading trainer 1970-'73, '75, '81, '82; Eclipse Award trainer 1971, '82, '89; inducted into Racing Hall of Fame in '74. Trained 252 stakes winners and 11 champions, including Ack Ack, Sunday Silence, Ferdinand, Turkish Trousers. All-time leading trainer at Hollywood Park and Santa Anita Park; trained two Kentucky Derby winners.

Wickham, John, 1763-1839. Lawyer. Bred champion and leading sire Boston, Tuckahoe.

Widener, George D., 1889-1971. Investments. Chairman of the Jockey Club 1950-'64; president, National Museum of Racing; president, Belmont Park. Owner of Old Kenney Farm, Kentucky; Erdenheim Stud, Pennsylvania. Bred and owned more than 100 stakes winners, including Jaipur, Eight Thirty, What a Treat, Jamestown, High Fleet, Platter, Stefanita, Jester, Seven Thirty, Rare Treat. Nephew of Joseph E. Widener.

Widener, Joseph E., 1871-1943. Investments. President of Hialeah Park, Belmont Park. Owner of Elmendorf Farm, Kentucky. Leading breeder in 1940. Bred Polynesian, Peace Chance, Osmand; owned Chance Shot. Imported leading sire *Sickle. Father of P. A. B. Widener II; uncle of George D. Widener.

Widener, Peter A. B. II, 1896-1952. Investments. Owner of Elmendorf Farm, Kentucky. Son of Joseph E. Widener.

Williamson, Ansel, ca. 1806-'81. Trainer. Inducted into Racing Hall of Fame in 1998. Trained Aristides, Tom Bowling, Brown Dick, Virgil. Trained first Kentucky Derby winner, Aristides.

Willmot, Donald G., 1917-'94. Brewer, investments. Owner of Kinghaven Farm, Ontario. Leading owner in 1990. Bred and owned With Approval, Izvestia, Steady Growth, Candle Bright, Bayford, Play the King, Carotene; co-owner of Deputy Minister.

Winfrey, G. Carey, 1885-1962. Trainer, owner. Inducted into Racing Hall of Fame in 1975. Trained 16 stakes winners and one champion, including Dedicate, Squared Away, Bulwark, Martyr. Stepfather of William C. Winfrey.

Winfrey, William C., 1916-'94. Trainer. Leading trainer in 1964; inducted into Racing Hall of Fame in '71. Trained 38 stakes winners and seven champions, including Native Dancer, Bed o' Roses, Next Move, Bold Lad. Trained Native Dancer, who retired in 1954 with 21 wins in 22 starts. Stepson of G. Carey Winfrey.

Winkfield, Jimmy, 1882-1974. Jockey. Inducted into the Racing Hall of Fame in 2004. Won the 1901 and '02 Kentucky Derbys aboard His Eminence and Alan-a-Dale, respectively, becoming the last African-American rider to capture the Louisville classic. In 1904 became a leading rider in Russia; later competed in Poland, Romania, Germany, and France.

Winn, Col. Matt. G., 1861-1949. Racing executive. President of Louisville Jockey Club. Legendary racetrack promoter, developed Kentucky Derby into world-class event.

Winters, Theodore, 1823-'94. Mining. Owner of Rancho del Rio, California; Rancho del Sierra, Nevada. Bred Emperor of Norfolk, Yo Tambien, El Rio Rey, Rey del Rey, Thad Stevens; owned Norfolk.

Withers, David D., 1821-1972. Banker. President, Monmouth Park. Owner of Brookdale Farm, New Jersey. Bred Requital, Laggard, Kinglike.

Wood, Eugene D., Birthdate unknown-1924. Racing executive. Treasurer of the Metropolitan Jockey Club (Jamaica). Namesake of Wood Memorial Stakes.

Woodford, Catesby, 1849-1923. President of Kentucky Racing Association. Owner of Raceland Farm, Kentucky. Co-owner of Runnymede Stud, Kentucky. Stood Hindoo, *Star Shoot. Co-breeder of Miss Woodford, Hanover, Sir Dixon.

Woodward, William Jr., 1920-'55. Banker, sportsman. Owner of Belair Stud. Owned Nashua.

Woodward, William Sr., 1876-1953. Banker. Chairman of the Jockey Club 1930-'50. Owner of Belair Stud, Maryland. Leading owner in 1939. Part of syndicate that imported *Sir Gallahad III. Bred and owned Gallant Fox, Omaha, Nashua, Granville, Vagrancy.

Woolf, George "The Iceman," 1910-'46. Jockey. Leading jockey by money won 1942, '44; inducted into Racing Hall of Fame in '55. Rode 721 winners, including Seabiscuit, Whirlaway, Challedon. Won the Belmont Futurity three straight years, the first running of the Santa Anita Derby, and the Preakness Stakes.

Workman, Raymond "Sonny," 1909-'66. Jockey. Leading jockey by races won 1930, '33, '35; leading jockey by money won 1930, '32; inducted into Racing Hall of Fame in '56. Rode 1,169 winners, including Equipoise, Top Flight, Discovery.

Wright, Warren, 1875-1950. Baking powder, investments. Owner of Calumet Farm, Kentucky. Leading breeder 1941, '44, '47-'50; leading owner 1941, '43-'44, '46-'49. Bred and owned Citation, Whirlaway, Pensive, Ponder, Coaltown, Bewitch, Hill Gail, Twilight Tear, Real Delight, Armed; owned Nellie Flag, Bull Lea. Stood leading sire Bull Lea, Sun Again, Chance Play.

Yoshida, Zenya, 1921-'93. Breeder. Owner of Shadai Farm, Japan; Fontainebleau Farm, Kentucky. Leading Japanese breeder 20 times. Bred Amber Shadai, Gallop Dyna, Dyna Gulliver, Vega; co-owned Wajima; stood Northern Taste, Sunday Silence.

Young, Col. Milton S., 1851-1918. Retail hardware, real estate. Chairman of Kentucky Racing Commission. Owner of McGrathiana Stud, Kentucky. Leading breeder in 1890. Bred Broomstick, Yankee; stood Hanover.

Young, William T., 1918-2004. Foods, storage. Owner of Overbrook Farm, Kentucky. Eclipse Award breeder in 1994. Bred and owned Storm Cat, Tabasco Cat, Cat Thief, Boston Harbor, Flanders, Surfside, Golden Attraction, Grindstone. Owned Editor's Note.

Contemporary Individuals in Racing and Breeding

(Names of Racing Hall of Fame members are in boldface italics.)

Abdullah, Khalid, 1942-. Investments. Owner of Juddmonte Farms, Kentucky and England. Eclipse Award breeder in 1995, 2001-'03; Eclipse Award owner in '92, 2003; P.A.B. Widener Trophy in '93; honorary member of Great Britain's Jockey Club in '83. Bred Ryafan, Wandesta (GB), Commander in Chief, Warning (GB), Banks Hill (GB), Empire Maker. Owned Known Fact, Dancing Brave, Rainbow Quest. Member of the ruling family of Saudi Arabia; first Arab owner to win a British classic (Two Thousand Guineas [English-G1] with Known Fact in 1980).

Abercrombie, Josephine, 1926-. Oil production, boxing promoter. Owner of Pin Oak Farm, Kentucky. Member of Jockey Club. Bred and owned Laugh and Be Merry, Peaks and Valleys. Co-owned Maria's Mon. Bred Elocutionist, Touching Wood.

Aga Khan IV, Karim, 1936-. Investments, Ismaili Muslim leader. Owner of Gilltown Stud, Sheshoon Stud in Ireland; Haras de Bonneval in France. Bred and owned Shergar, Sinndar, Kahyasi, Daylami (Ire), Kalanisi (Ire), Dalakhani. Built Aiglemont training facility near Chantilly, France, in 1977; continued breeding operations begun by his grandfather, Aga Khan III, and his father, Aly Khan.

Aitcheson, Joe Jr., 1929-. Jockey. Leading steeplechase jockey 1961, '63-'64, '67-'70; inducted into Racing Hall of Fame in '78; first jockey to receive the F. Ambrose Clark Memorial Award in '75. Rode 478 winners, including Amber Diver, Bon Nouvel, Tuscalee, Top Bid, Soothsayer, Inkslinger. Won eight Virginia Gold Cups, seven Carolina Cups, and two Colonial Cups.

Alexander, Helen, 1951-. Investments. Member of Jockey Club. President, Thoroughbred Club of America, 1989-'91. Owner of Middlebrook Farm, Kentucky. Bred Twining. Bred and owned Althea, Aishah, Aquilegia. Granddaughter of Robert J. Kleberg.

Allbritton, Joseph, 1924-. Publishing, banking, broadcasting, real estate. Owner of Lazy Lane Farms, Kentucky and Virginia. Member of Jockey Club. Owned Hansel, Secret Hello, Life At the Top, Kittiwake.

Anthony, John Ed, 1939-. Timber. Owner of Shortleaf Farm, Arkansas; president of Loblolly Stable. Member of Jockey Club. Bred and owned Temperence Hill, Vanlandingham, Prairie Bayou. Owned Cox's Ridge. Established the Exercise Induced Pulmonary Hemorrhage Fund after his Demons Begone bled during the 1987 Kentucky Derby (G1).

Appleton, Arthur, 1915-. Electrical manufacturing. Owner of Bridlewood Farm, Florida. Bred and owned Jolie's Halo, Wild Event. Owned Skip Trial. One of stockholders of *The Florida Horse.*

Asmussen, Cash, 1962-. Jockey. Leading jockey by money won in 1979; leading jockey in France 1985-'86, '88-'90; Eclipse Award as apprentice jockey in '79. Rode Suave Dancer, Hector Protector, Mill Native, Northern Trick. Won inaugural Japan Cup aboard Mairzy Doates in 1981; three times won five races on a single card in New York. Brother of trainer Steve Asmussen.

Asmussen, Steven, 1965-. Trainer. Leading trainer by wins in 2002 and '04. Saddled record 555 winners in '04. Brother of Cash Asmussen.

Avioli, Greg, 1964-. Lawyer, lobbyist. Executive vice president of legislative and corporate planning, National Thoroughbred Racing Association; former NTRA president and deputy commissioner; chaired NTRA Wagering Systems Task Force. Formerly senior vice president, International Sports and Entertainment Strategies.

Bacharach, Burt, 1929-. Composer. Co-owner of Country Roads Farm, West Virginia. Thoroughbred Owners and Breeders Association Award for outstanding owner-breeder 1995-'96. Bred and owned Heartlight No. One, Afternoon Deelites, Soul of the Matter.

Baeza, Braulio, 1940-. Jockey, trainer. Leading jockey by money won 1965-'68, '75; Eclipse Award jockey 1972, '75; inducted into Racing Hall of Fame in '76; George Woolf Memorial Jockey Award in '68. Rode 3,140 winners, including Buckpasser, Dr. Fager, Ack Ack, Gallant Bloom, Affectionately, Chateaugay. Trained Double Zeus. Rode Buckpasser to one-mile record in 1966 and then lowered it aboard Dr. Fager in '68.

Baffert, Bob, 1953-. Trainer. Leading trainer by money won, 1998-2001; Eclipse Award trainer 1997-'99; United Thoroughbred Trainers of America's Trainer of the Year in '98; Mr. Fitz Award in '97. Trained Chilukki, Real Quiet, Silverbulletday, Silver Charm, Point Given, War Emblem. Won a record 13 stakes at Del Mar in 2000; only trainer to win Kentucky Derby (G1) and Preakness Stakes (G1) in consecutive years (1997-'98).

Bailey, Jerry, 1957-. Jockey. President, Jockeys' Guild, 1990-'97. Leading jockey by money won 1995-'98, 2001-'03; inducted into Racing Hall of Fame in '95; Eclipse Award jockey 1995-'97, 2000-'03; George Woolf Memorial Jockey Award in '92; Mike Venezia Award in '93. Rode Cigar, Fit to Fight, Black Tie Affair (Ire), Sea Hero. In 1996, rode Cigar to his 16th consecutive win; rode seven winners on Florida Derby (G1) day program in '95; successfully lobbied for protective vests to be worn by all jockeys; won handicap triple crown with Fit to Fight in '84.

Baird, Dale, 1935-. Trainer. Leading American trainer by annual winners 15 times. On November 5, 2004, became the first trainer to saddle more than 9,000 career winners. Inducted into National HBPA Hall of Fame in 2001. Based at Mountaineer Racetrack in West Virginia. Special Eclipse Award in 2004.

Bandoroff, Craig, 1955-. Farm owner, consignor. Owner of Denali Stud, Kentucky. One of country's leading consignors of yearlings, broodmares, and weanlings.

Barr, John, 1929-. Real estate. Owner, Los Amigos Thoroughbred Farm in Temecula, California; Member and steward, Jockey Club; director, Oak Tree Racing Association; secretary-treasurer, Richard Nixon Presidential Library. Races horses as Oakcrest Stable.

Barton, Patti, 1945-. Jockey. Helped break gender barrier when she became one of the first female jockeys in 1969. Retired in 1984 as world's winningest female rider, with 1,202 victories. Mother of former jockey and television personality Donna Barton Brothers and trainer Jerry Barton.

Bassett, James E. "Ted" III, 1921-. Racing executive. Former chairman, Keeneland Association; former president, Breeders' Cup Ltd.; also served as chairman, Equibase Co.; president, Thoroughbred Racing Associations; chairman, Kentucky Horse Park; president, Thoroughbred Club of America. Co-owner of Lanark Farm, Kentucky. Eclipse Award of Merit in 1995;

John W. Galbreath Award in '91; Turf and Field Club Award in '84; Joe Palmer Award in '86; John A. Morris Award in '97; Lord Derby Award in '98.

Baugh, Rollin, 1937-. Bloodstock agent. California-based agent maintains international trade, especially to Japan. Brokered sales of Forty Niner, Charismatic, Captain Steve, and Chief Bearhart to Japan. Member, Jockey Club. Director of Del Mar, Tranquility Farm Thoroughbred retirement facility.

Baze, Russell, 1958-. Jockey. Leading jockey by races won 1992-'96, 2002; inducted into Racing Hall of Fame in '99; Special Eclipse Award in '95; Isaac Murphy Award 1995-2003; George Woolf Memorial Jockey Award in 2002. Rode Hawkster, Both Ends Burning, Itsallgreektome, Lost in the Fog. Won 24 stakes races in 1998; won 400 races a year 11 times in 12 years; won 9,000th race in 2005.

Beasley, Rogers W. B., 1949-. Racing executive. Director of racing for Keeneland Association since 2001; previously director of sales for Keeneland for 19 years; led the initiative to introduce preferred sessions to the September sale and to inaugurate the April two-year-olds in training sales.

Beck, Graham, 1929-. Mining, investments, vintner. Owner of Gainesway, Kentucky; Silvercrest Farm, Kentucky; Midway Farm, Kentucky; Highlands Farm, South Africa; Maine Chance Farm, South Africa; Noreen Stud, South Africa. Bred Pompeii, Real Cozzy, Irish Prize. Co-owned Timber Country.

Bell, Headley, 1954-. Bloodstock agent. Son of Mill Ridge Farm owner Alice Chandler; maternal grandson of Hal Price Headley, co-founder of Keeneland. Past board member, Thoroughbred Club of America, Sales Integrity Sales Force.

Bell, John A. III, 1918-. Owner, breeder, bloodstock agent. Member of Jockey Club. Director, Thoroughbred Owners and Breeders Association; president, Thoroughbred Club of America in 1954; former president, Farm Manager's Club. Owned Jonabell Farm, Kentucky. Bred Battlefield, Aglimmer, One for All, Never Say Die. Owned Epitome. Former president of *The Blood-Horse* magazine; acquired half-interest in Cromwell Bloodstock Agency in 1950.

Bell, Reynolds Jr., 1952-. Bloodstock agent. Son of Mill Ridge Farm owner Alice Chandler; maternal grandson of Hal Price Headley, co-founder of Keeneland. Member, Jockey Club. Vice president, Thoroughbred Owners and Breeders Association. Former manager of Mill Ridge Farm. Past president, Thoroughbred Club of America.

Bellocq, Pierre "Peb," 1926-. Caricaturist. Special Eclipse Award in 1980; John Hervey Award 1965-'66, '68; Knights of Arts and Letters Award in '90; Golden Horseshoe Award in '91. Achieved international acclaim as *Daily Racing Form*'s caricaturist; has murals at Aqueduct, Churchill Downs, Oaklawn Park, and Arlington Park; founded the Amateur Riders Club of the Americas with son Remi Bellocq.

Bellocq, Remi, 1961-. Marketing, organization executive. Former marketing director at Turf Paradise and Santa Anita Park. Became executive director of the National Horsemen's Benevolent and Protective Association in 2001. Son of Pierre Bellocq.

Berube, Paul, 1941-. Retired president of the Thoroughbred Racing Protective Bureau. Background in military intelligence; TRPB agent and vice president 1965-'88.

Biancone, Patrick, 1952-. Trainer. Trained All Along (Fr) to North America Horse of the Year title in 1983 with sweep of three turf races carrying a $1-million bonus; All Along also won the Prix de l'Arc de Triomphe (Fr-G1) that year. Also won Arc in 1984 with Sagace (Fr). Trained champion Bikala, Strawberry Road (Aus), Triptych, Palace Music. Came to the United States in 2000 after suspension for a medication positive in Hong Kong.

Biszantz, Gary, 1934-. Golf-club manufacturer. Chairman of Thoroughbred Owners and Breeders Association. Jockey Club member; Breeders' Cup director. Owns 350-acre Cobra Farm in Lexington. Owned Old Trieste, Running Flame (Fr), Admise (Fr), Lord Grillo (Arg), homebred Cobra King. Co-founder of Cobra Golf, sold in 1996 to American Brands.

Blum, Walter, 1934-. Jockey, racing official. Former president, Jockeys' Guild. Leading jockey by races won 1963-'64; inducted into Racing Hall of Fame in '87; George Woolf Memorial Jockey Award in '64. Rode 4,382 winners, including Affectionately, Gun Bow, Forego, Mr. Prospector, Pass Catcher, Summer Scandal, Boldnesian, Priceless Gem, Lady Pitt.

Bonnie, Edward S. "Ned," 1929-. Lawyer, steeplechase horseman. Of counsel, Frost Brown Todd LLC, Louisville. Member, Jockey Club. Former director, National Steeplechase Association, Thoroughbred Owners and Breeders Association, Kentucky Thoroughbred Association. With wife Nina, received 2002 First USA Bank/USA Equestrian Lifetime Achievement Award. Responsible for National Steeplechase and Kentucky protective helmet regulations for jockeys.

Boulmetis, Sam Sr., 1927-. Jockey, racing official. Inducted into Racing Hall of Fame in 1973. Rode 2,783 winners. Rode Tosmah, Helioscope, Dedicate. Longtime steward at New Jersey tracks.

Bowen, Edward L., 1942-. Industry executive, author. President, Grayson-Jockey Club Research Foundation. Editor-in-chief, *The Blood-Horse*, 1987-'92. Author of 15 books, including *The Jockey Club Illustrated History of Racing*, *Matriarchs*, and *Man o' War*.

Brady, Nicholas J., 1930-. Financier. Chairman, Jockey Club, 1974-'82; United States treasury secretary 1988-'93; Co-owner of Mill House Stable. Bred and owned Sensational, Furiously, Meritus. Son of James Cox Brady Jr.

Bramlage, Larry, 1952-. Veterinarian. President, American Association of Equine Practitioners in 2003-'04. Member of Jockey Club. Jockey Club Gold Medal in 1994; British Equine Veterinary Association's Special Award of Merit in '98. Developed and improved ways to repair serious bone fractures.

Brennan, Niall, 1961-. Bloodstock agent, pinhooker. Owner of Niall Brennan Stables, Florida. Leading two-year-old consignor in 2000-'04. Sold Ecton Park, Jersey Girl, Kurofune, Read the Footnotes, Whitmore's Conn, Yonaguska.

Broman, Chester, 1935-. Building contractor. President of Clifford Broman & Sons Inc. in Babylon, New York. Trustee, New York Racing Association; New York Thoroughbred Breeders board of directors. Owner of Chestertown Farm, New York. With his wife, Mary, owned and bred Friends Lake.

Brumfield, Don, 1938-. Jockey, racing official. Inducted into Racing Hall of Fame in 1996; George Woolf Memorial Jockey Award in '88. Rode 4,573 winners, including Forward Pass, Alysheba, Gold Beauty, Our Mims, Old Hat. Retired in 1989 with the most wins in Churchill Downs's (925) and Keeneland Race Course's (716) history.

Brunetti, John, 1931-. President and owner of Hialeah Park, which he purchased in 1978; track has not conducted racing since 2001. Owner of Red Oak Farm, Florida; owned Strolling Belle.

Burch, J. Elliott, 1922-. Trainer. Leading trainer by money won in 1969; inducted into Racing Hall of Fame in '80. Trained more than 30 stakes winners and six champions, including Sword Dancer, Fort Marcy, Arts and Letters, Bowl of Flowers, Run the Gantlet, Key to the Mint. Son of Hall of Fame trainer Preston Burch; grandson of Hall of Fame trainer William Burch.

Burge, Doug, 1971-. Industry executive. Executive vice president and general manager, California Thoroughbred Breeders Association, 1997-.

Campbell Jr., Alex, 1928-. Thoroughbred owner-breeder, philanthropist. Member, Jockey Club. Director, Breeders' Cup Ltd. Retired from tobacco business in 1989. Helped to develop Thoroughbred Park in Lexington. Co-owner, Grade 1 winner Goodbye Halo. Owner and breeder of Mr Purple.

Campbell, W. Cothran "Cot," 1927-. Advertising, racing syndicates. President of Dogwood Stable, South Carolina. John W. Galbreath Award in 1992. Owned Summer Squall, Storm Song, Dominion (GB). Popularized racing syndicates; wrote *Lightning in a Jar: Catching Racing Fever*.

Carey, Thomas, 1932-. Racing executive. President and general manager, Hawthorne Race Course. Inducted into Chicago Sports Hall of Fame in 1998. Instrumental in rebuilding Hawthorne after fire in 1978.

Casner, William, 1948-. Heavy equipment. Partner in WinStar Farm, Kentucky. Board of advisers, The Race for Education scholarship foundation. Vice chairman and co-founder, Kentucky Equine Education Project (KEEP). Member, board of directors of the University of Kentucky's Maxwell H. Gluck Equine Research Center, National Thoroughbred Racing Association's Political Action Committee. In WinStar name, bred Funny Cide, One Cool Cat. Owned Awesome Humor, Bet Me Best, Byzantium (Brz), and Pompeii. Co-owner of Ipi Tombe (Zim), Crimson Palace. Stands Tiznow, Distorted Humor, Victory Gallop. Stood Kris S.

Casse, Mark, 1961-. Trainer, consignor, bloodstock agent. Former private trainer and director of operations for Mockingbird Farm, Florida. Leading trainer at Woodbine in 2002. Trained Exciting Story, Dark Ending, Added Edge.

Cauthen, Steve, 1960-. Jockey. Leading jockey by races won in 1977; inducted into Racing Hall of Fame in '94; Eclipse Award apprentice jockey in '77; Eclipse Award jockey in '77; Eclipse Award of Merit in '77; George Woolf Memorial Jockey Award in '84. Rode 2,794 winners, including Affirmed, Oh So Sharp (Ire), Old Vic, Johnny D., Diminuendo, Indian Skimmer. Rode Affirmed to Triple Crown in 1978; only jockey to win the Kentucky, Epsom, Irish, French, and Italian Derbys; at 18, youngest jockey to win Kentucky Derby.

Cella, Charles, 1936-. Real estate, racing executive. President, Oaklawn Park; president, Thoroughbred Racing Associations 1975-'76. TRA's youngest president in 1975. Eclipse Award of Merit 2004. Owned Northern Spur (Ire), Out of Hock, Crafty Shaw.

Chace, Baden P. "Buzz," 1941-. Bloodstock agent. Since 1983, buyer of racing prospects for various clients. Selected Breeders' Cup winners Unbridled's Song and champion Artax, Belmont Stakes (G1) winner Sarava, and numerous Grade 1 winners.

Chandler, Alice Headley, 1927-. Farm owner. Chairwoman, Maxwell F. Gluck Equine Research Center; former chairwoman, Kentucky Racing Commission; president, Kentucky Thoroughbred Owners and Breeders Association; former president, Kentucky Thoroughbred Associaton; director, Keeneland Association. Member of Jockey Club. Owner of Mill Ridge Farm, Kentucky. Bred and owned Keeper Hill. Bred Sir Ivor, Secret Hello, Ciao, Flemensfirth.

Chavez, Jorge, 1961-. Jockey. Leading jockey in New York 1994-'99; Eclipse Award jockey in '99. Rode Monarchos, Artax, Beautiful Pleasure, A P Valentine, Affirmed Success. Rode six winners on single card at Gulfstream Park in 1999.

Chenery, Helen "Penny," 1931-. Investments. President, Thoroughbred Owners and Breeders Association, 1976-'84. Former owner of Meadow Stud and Meadow Stable, Virginia. Bred Alada. Owned Secretariat, Riva Ridge. First woman to head a major national racing organization; one of the first three women inducted into Jockey Club, in 1983.

Chillingworth, Sherwood, 1926-. Executive vice president of Oak Tree Racing Association. Jockey Club member; board of NTRA Investments; ex-officio member of NTRA Thoroughbred Industry Council; vice chairman of Santa Anita Realty 1994-'96.

Clay, Robert N., 1946-. Farm owner. President, Thoroughbred Owners and Breeders Association, 1990-'93; past president, National Thoroughbred Association and Thoroughbred Club of America. Member of Jockey Club. Co-owner of Three Chimneys Farm, Kentucky. John W. Galbreath Award in 1995. Bred and owned Hidden Lake, Gorgeous. Bred Seaside Attraction, Subordination.

Combs II, Brownell, 1933-. Former president and chairman of Spendthrift Farm; former Kentucky Racing Commission chairman. Son of Leslie Combs II, renowned commercial horse salesman, stallion syndicator, and founder of Spendthrift Farm in 1930s. Pleaded guilty in 2001 to federal income tax fraud charges.

Cooksey, Patricia, 1958-. Jockey. Second all-time leading female jockey with more than 2,100 winners and purse earnings of $20-million. Captured four riding titles at Turfway Park. All-time leading female rider at Churchill Downs. In 1985 became first female to ride in the Preakness Stakes (G1) (sixth on Tajawa). Member of the Kentucky Athletic Hall of Fame. Mr. Fitz Award 2004. Mike Venezia Memorial Award 2004. Retired 2004.

Cordero, Angel Jr., 1942-. Jockey, jockey's agent. Leading jockey by money won 1976, '82-'83; leading jockey by races won in '68; inducted into Racing Hall of Fame in '88; Eclipse Award jockey 1982-'83; George Woolf Memorial Jockey Award in '72; Mike Venezia Award in '92. Rode 7,076 winners, including Seattle Slew, Slew o' Gold, All Along (Fr), Bold Forbes, Broad Brush. Won jockey's title at Saratoga 13 times, 11 consecutively.

Couto, Drew, 1959-. Lawyer. President, Thoroughbred Owners of California. Former president, Thoroughbred Owners and Breeders Association.

Craig, Sidney, 1932- and **Craig, Jenny,** 1932-. Diet foods. Owners of Rancho del Rayo training center in California. Owned 1992-'93 champion older female Paseana (Arg), Exchange, Dr Devious (Ire), Alpride (Ire).

Croll, Warren A. "Jimmy" Jr., 1920-. Trainer. Inducted into Racing Hall of Fame in 1994; United Thoroughbred Trainers of America Outstanding Trainer Award in '94; Big Sport of Turfdom Award in '95; Mr. Fitz Award in '95. Owned and trained Holy Bull. Trained Mr. Prospector, Bet Twice, Parka, Forward Gal, Housebuster.

Day, Pat, 1953-. Jockey. President, Jockeys' Guild, 2000-'01. Leading jockey by races won 1982-'84, '86, '90-'91; inducted into Racing Hall of Fame in '91; Eclipse Award jockey in 1984, '86-'87, '91; George Woolf Memorial Jockey Award in '85; Mike Venezia Award in '95; Mr. Fitz Award in 2000. Rode Wild Again, Flanders, Lady's Secret, Easy Goer, Summer Squall, Tank's Prospect, Louis Quatorze, Lil E. Tee, Dance Smartly. All-time leader by earnings among jockeys and third-highest number of winners; set a record for most stakes won (60) in a single season in 1991; rode seven winners in one day at Churchill Downs in '84; won on eight of nine mounts at Arlington Park in '89.

De Francis, Joseph, 1955-. Racing executive, lawyer. President, Maryland Jockey Club; president, Pimlico Race Course and Laurel Park. Son of Frank De Francis.

Delahoussaye, Eddie, 1951-. Jockey. Leading jockey in 1978; inducted into Racing Hall of Fame in '93; George Woolf Memorial Jockey Award in '81. Rode A.P. Indy, Princess Rooney, Prized, Gato Del Sol, Sunny's Halo, Pleasant Stage, Thirty Slews, Gate Dancer. One of four jockeys to win consecutive Kentucky Derbys, in 1982-'83. Retired in early 2003.

Delp, Grover G. "Bud," 1932-. Trainer. Eclipse Award trainer in 1980. Inducted into Racing Hall of Fame in 2002. Trained Spectacular Bid, Include, Timeless Native, Aspro, Silent King.

Desormeaux, Kent, 1970-. Jockey. Leading jockey by races won 1987-'89; leading jockey by money won in '92; inducted into Racing Hall of Fame in 2004; Eclipse Award apprentice jockey in '87; Eclipse Award jockey 1989, '92; George Woolf Memorial Jockey Award in '93. Rode Fusaichi Pegasus, Real Quiet, Kotashaan (Fr); Risen Star. Won record 598 races in 1989; won six races on a single card at Hollywood Park in 1992.

Dickinson, Michael, 1950-. Trainer. Owner of Tapeta Farm, Maryland. Trained Da Hoss, Fleet Renee, Cetewayo, Tapit. Trained first five finishers in England's Cheltenham Gold Cup in 1983.

DiMauro, Steve Sr., 1932-. Trainer. Owner of DiMauro Farm, New York. Eclipse Award trainer in 1975. Bred Flip's Pleasure, Father Don Juan. Trained Wajima, Dearly Precious, Nagurski, Father Don Juan.

Dixon, F. Eugene, 1923-. Investments. Owner of Erdenheim Farm in Pennsylvania, formerly owned by his uncle George D. Widener. Member of Jockey Club; chairman of the Pennsylvania Horse Racing Commission. Former owner of Philadelphia 76ers basketball team.

Dizney, Donald R., 1942-. Health care, banking. Founder and chairman, United Medical Corp. Owner of Double Diamond Farm in Ocala. President, Florida Thoroughbred Breeders' and Owners' Association. Member and steward of the Jockey Club. Bred and co-owned Grade 1 winner Wekiva Springs.

Donn, Douglas, 1947-. Racing executive. President of Gulfstream Park racetrack 1978-2000; chairman of the board 2000-'04, after the track was purchased by Magna Entertainment Corp. Grandson of late Gulfstream owner James Donn Sr.

Dreyfus, Jack J. Jr., 1913-. Financier. Chairman, New York Racing Association, in 1969 and '75. Owner Hobeau Farm, Florida. Member of Jockey Club. Leading owner by money won in 1967; Eclipse Award of Merit in '76. Bred and owned Beau Purple, Duck Dance, Never Bow, Step Nicely. Exacta introduced in New York betting under his direction; his Beau Purple upset Kelso three times.

Drysdale, Neil, 1947-. Trainer. Inducted into Racing Hall of Fame in 2000. Trained A.P. Indy, Fusaichi Pegasus, Princess Rooney, Tasso, Hollywood Wildcat, Fiji (GB), Bold 'n Determined.

Duchossois, Richard L., 1921-. Industrialist. Chairman, Arlington Park. Owner of Hill 'N Dale Farm, Illinois. Special Eclipse Award in 1989; Eclipse Award of Merit in 2004. Special Sovereign Award in '88; Lord Derby Award in '88; Jockey Club Medal in '86; Jockey Agents' Benevolent Association's Man of the Year in '90. Member of Jockey Club. Bred Explosive Darling. Rebuilt Arlington Park after the track was destroyed by fire in 1985; under his leadership, Arlington received a Special Eclipse Award in '85, the first awarded to a racetrack.

Duncker, C. Stephen, 1958-. Industry executive. Co-chairman, New York Racing Association, 2005-. Former co-chief operating officer, NYRA, 2003-'04. Member, Jockey Club. Chairman, American Graded Stakes Committee. Trustee, Thoroughbred Owners and Breeders Association. Former managing director, Goldman Sachs. Bred and owned multiple Grade 2 winner Middlesex Drive.

duPont, Allaire (Mrs. Richard C.), 1913-. Investments. Owner of Woodstock Farm, Maryland; Bohemia Stable, Maryland. Member of Jockey Club. Thoroughbred Owners and Breeders Association award for Maryland in 1984. Bred and owned Politely, Believe the Queen. Bred and raced Kelso, only five-time Horse of the Year (1960-'64); one of the first three women inducted into Jockey Club, in 1983.

Englander, Richard, 1959-. Investments. Eclipse Award owner in 2001, when he led the nation with stable earnings of $9,784,822, and in '02.

Evans, Edward P. "Ned," 1942-. Publishing. Owner of Spring Hill Farm, Virginia. Member of Jockey Club. Bred and owned Minstrella, Prenup, Raging Fever, Fairy Garden, Colonial Minstrel. Owned Withallprobability. Brother of Robert S. Evans; son of Thomas Mellon Evans.

Evans, Robert S. "Shel," 1944-. Manufacturing. Owner of Winter Haven Farm, Florida; Courtland Farm, Maryland. Member of Jockey Club. Bred and owned Sewickley, Shared Interest. Bred Forestry, Cash Run. Brother of Edward P. Evans; son of Thomas Mellon Evans.

Everett, Marjorie L., 1921-. Racing executive. Former chairman and chief executive officer, Hollywood Park; former owner, Arlington Park; former owner, Washington Park. Undertook major improvements at Hollywood Park, including expanding the circumference of the track, building the Cary Grant Pavilion, and improving the backstretch; successfully lobbied for inaugural Breeders' Cup to be held at Hollywood Park in 1984.

Fabre, Andre, 1945-. Trainer. Champion French trainer 1987-2004. Won five Prix de l'Arc de Triomphes (Fr-G1), three Breeders' Cup events—the 1993 Classic (G1) with 134-to-1 Arcangues; 1990 Turf (G1) with In the Wings (GB); and 2001 Filly and Mare Turf (G1) with Banks Hill (GB). Also trained Trempolino, Swain (Ire), Subotica (Fr), Sagamix (Fr), Zafonic.

Farish, William S., 1939-. Investments. Chairman, Churchill Downs, 1992-2001. Vice chairman of Jockey Club. President and owner of Lane's End, Kentucky. Eclipse Award breeder in 1992, '99; P.A.B. Widener Trophy in '92. Bred or co-bred A.P. Indy, Mineshaft, Law

Society, Lemon Drop Kid, Charismatic, Summer Squall, Prospectors Delite. Owned Bee Bee Bee, Miss Brio (Chi), Sweet Revenge. Former chairman of the Breeders' Cup executive committee; United States ambassador to Great Britain and Northern Ireland, 2001-2004. Nephew of Martha Gerry.

Farish, William "Bill" Jr., 1964-. Business manager and sales director of Lane's End, Kentucky. Son of William S. Farish. Member of the Jockey Club. Board member, Kentucky Thoroughbred Association, Breeders' Cup Ltd, Thoroughbred Owners and Breeders Association, Maxwell H. Gluck Equine Research Center. Former president, Thoroughbred Club of America. Owned and bred Grade 2 winner Shadow Cast and bred Grade 1 winner Burning Roma.

Farmer, Tracy, 1939-. Auto dealer. Owns Farmer Automotive Group Inc. in Louisville and has dealerships in Atlanta and Florida. University of Kentucky Board of Trustees, 1979-'91. Chairman, Kentucky Democratic Party, 1981. Owner of Shadowlawn Farm, Kentucky. Co-owned Hidden Lake, Joyeux Danseur; raced Albert the Great.

Fenwick Jr., Charles, 1948-. Auto dealer; steeplechase jockey, trainer. Trained and rode *Dosdi to two National Steeplechase Association Timber Horse of the Year titles. In 1980 rode *Ben Nevis II to victory in England's Grand National Steeplechase. Trained 1987 Eclipse Award-winning steeplechaser Inlander (GB) and timber champions Buck Jakes, Free Throw, Sugar Bee.

Ferguson, John, 1960-. Bloodstock agent, racing manager. Purchased Pentire, E Dubai, Dubai Destination, Essence of Dubai, Moon Ballad. Chief buying agent and racing manager for Sheikh Mohammed bin Rashid al Maktoum.

Fick, Dan, 1948-. Industry executive. Executive vice president and executive director of the Jockey Club. Chairman of the Racing Medication and Testing Consortium. Former senior vice president of racing for the American Quarter Horse Association. Credited with revitalizing the Race Track Chaplaincy of America.

Fires, Earlie, 1947-Jockey. Leading apprentice jockey in 1965; inducted into Racing Hall of Fame in 2001; George Woolf Memorial Jockey Award in 1991. Rode In Reality, War Censor, Dike, Abe's Hope, Pattee Canyon, Woozem, Gallant Romeo. Won seven races from eight mounts in a single day at Arlington Park in 1983; won all six mounts in one day at Hawthorne Race Course in '89.

Firestone, Bertram S., 1931-and **Firestone, Diana**, 1932-. Real estate, investments. Owner, Calder Race Course and Gulfstream Park 1988-'91. Owner of Catoctin Stud, Virginia. Eclipse Award owner in 1980. Owned Genuine Risk. Bred and owned Theatrical (Ire), Paradise Creek, April Run (Ire), Honest Pleasure, What a Summer.

Fishback, Jerry, 1947-. Jockey, bloodstock agent. Leading steeplechase jockey by races won 1971, '73-'75, '77; leading steeplechase jockey by money won in '85; inducted into Racing Hall of Fame in '92. Rode 301 winners, including Cafe Prince, Flatterer. Won the Temple Gwathmey Steeplechase Handicap six times; won four Carolina Cups and four International Gold Cups.

Ford, Gerald, 1944-. Banker and insurer. Chairman of Dallas-based First Acceptance Corp., formerly Liberte Investments Inc., of which he owns approximately 45%. In 2000, bought 815 acres of former Brookside Farm in Kentucky for approximately $11-million and renamed it Diamond A Farms. Also owns 120,000-acre Diamond A Ranch in New Mexico. Raced Pleasantly Perfect, winner of the 2003 Breeders' Cup Classic (G1) and 2004 Dubai World Cup (UAE-G1). Also raced home-bred Minister Eric.

Foreman, Alan, 1950-. Lawyer. Chairman and chief executive officer, Thoroughbred Horsemen's Association. Creator of Mid-Atlantic Thoroughbred Championship (MATCH) series; general counsel for the Maryland Thoroughbred Horsemen's Association.

Forsythe, John, 1918-. Actor. Director, Hollywood Park. Owner of Big Train Farm. Eclipse Award of Merit in 1988. Owned Targa. Longtime Eclipse Awards dinner host.

Francis, Dick, 1920-. Jockey, author. International best-selling author of 39 mystery novels about horse racing. England's champion steeplechase jockey of 1953-'54 when he rode for the Queen Mother. Published first novel—*Dead Cert*—in 1962 and last—*Shattered*—in 2000. Winner of three Edgar Allen Poe Awards for best mystery novel.

Frankel, Robert, 1941-. Trainer. Leading trainer by money won in 1993, 2002-'03; inducted into Racing Hall of Fame in '95; Eclipse Award trainer in 1993, 2000-'03. Trained Bertrando, Possibly Perfect, Wandesta (GB), Marquetry, Squirtle Squirt, Empire Maker, Medaglia d'Oro, Ghostzapper. Once called the king of claimers for his ability to turn claiming horses into winners; won a record 60 races at Hollywood Park during his first year in California (1972). Established earnings record and mark for most Grade 1 victories in a year in 2003.

Fravel, Craig, 1958-. Lawyer, racetrack executive. Executive vice president, Del Mar Thoroughbred Club, 1990-. Director, NTRA; member, Equibase Management Committee.

Fuller, Peter S., 1923-. Automobile dealer. John A. Morris Award in 1985. Bred and owned Dancer's Image, Mom's Command, Shananie, Donna's Time.

Fulton, Stanley, 1931-. Owner of Sunland Park Racetrack and Casino, New Mexico; consultant, Anchor Gaming; Thoroughbred owner, philanthropist. Leading buyer at 2003 Fasig-Tipton Kentucky select yearling sale.

Gann, Edmund A., 1923-. Commercial fisheries, banking. Entered racing in 1960s when a fishing buddy offered him half-interest in a filly to settle a debt. Owned more than 35 stakes winners, including Pay the Butler, Al Mamoon, Medaglia d'Oro, Peace Rules, Midas Eyes, You.

Garland, Bruce, 1950-. Racing executive. Senior executive vice president of racing for New Jersey Sports and Exposition Authority; vice chairman of Harness Tracks of America; serves on board of the Thoroughbred Racing Associations and U.S. Trotting Association. In 2003 elected to the NTRA board representing independent Mid-Atlantic region racetracks; formerly executive director of New Jersey Racing Commission.

Gaylord, E. K. II, 1957-. Chairman and executive producer, Gaylord Films. Board of directors, Gaylord Entertainment Co. Member, Breeders' Cup board of directors. Director, National Cowboy & Western Heritage Center. Breeder, owner, owns Lazy E Ranch in Edmond, Oklahoma. Son of E. L. Gaylord, part-owner of 1980 Kentucky Derby (G1) runner-up Rumbo and graded stakes winner Cactus Road.

Gentry, Tom, 1937-. Bloodstock agent, breeder. Former owner of Tom Gentry Farm, Kentucky. Bred Royal Academy, Brazen, Marfa, Terlingua, Pancho Villa, Artichoke. Leading Keeneland consignor in 1970s, '80s. Son of Olin Gentry.

Gerry, Martha Farish, 1918-. Investments. Owner of Lazy F Ranch, Texas. Member of Jockey Club. Bred and owned Forego, Maid of France, Clef d'Argent, French Colonial. Bred and raced three-time Horse of the Year Forego, who earned nearly $2-million from 1973-'78. Aunt of William S. Farish.

Gertmenian, L. Wayne, 1939-. President, Jockeys' Guild; president and chief executive officer, Matrix Capital Associates; professor of economics and management, Graziadio School of Business and Management, Pepperdine University.

Gill, Michael, 1956-. Mortgage banking. Led all owners in the United States by wins and earnings in 2003-'04; finished second among U.S. owners by wins in 2002 and '00. Broke records at Gulfstream and Monmouth Parks for wins in 2003.

Hamilton, Lucy Young, 1952-. Co-owner of Overbrook Farm in Lexington. Member, Jockey Club. Daughter of the late William T. Young and widow of trainer Francois Boutin.

Hancock, Arthur B. III, 1943-. Breeder. Owner of Stone Farm, Kentucky. Member of Jockey Club. Mr. Fitz Award in 1990. Bred and owned Sunday Silence, Gato Del Sol, Goodbye Halo. Co-bred Fusaichi Pegasus. Stood leading sire Halo. Brother of Seth Hancock; son of Arthur B. "Bull" Hancock Jr.

Hancock, Dell, 1952-. Co-owner of Claiborne Farm and spokesperson for the Paris, Kentucky, breeding operation. Member and steward, Jockey Club; chairman, Grayson-Jockey Club Research Foundation. Daughter of the late A. B. "Bull" Hancock Jr.

Hancock, Richard E., 1940-. Industry executive. Executive vice president and chief executive officer for the Florida Thoroughbred Breeders' and Owners' Association since 1988. Board member, National Thoroughbred Retirement Foundation and the Florida Division of the Thoroughbred Retirement Foundation.

Hancock, Seth, 1949-. Breeder. Director, Churchill Downs; director, Keeneland Association. Member of Jockey Club. President of Claiborne Farm, Kentucky. Eclipse Award breeder 1979, '84. Bred and owned Swale, Forty Niner, Lure. Bred Wajima, Nureyev, Caerleon. Organized a syndicate to acquire Secretariat for more than $6-million. Stood Mr. Prospector, Unbridled, Danzig. Stands Seeking the Gold. Brother of Arthur B. Hancock III; son of Arthur B. "Bull" Hancock Jr.

Harper, Joseph, 1943-. Racing executive. President and chief executive officer of Del Mar Thoroughbred Club since 1990; president of Thoroughbred Racing Associations, 2003-'04. Member of Jockey Club; former executive vice president and general manager of Oak Tree Racing Association; grandson of Cecil B. DeMille.

Harris, John C., 1943-. Breeder, agricultural products. Past president, California Thoroughbred Breeders Association; director, Thoroughbred Owners of California. Member of Jockey Club. Owner of Harris Farms, California. Bred and owned Soviet Problem.

Handel, Harold G. "Hal," 1947-. Racing executive. Chief executive officer of Greenwood Racing Inc. operator of Philadelphia Park, since 1998. President of the Thoroughbred Racing Associations,1997-'98. Former executive vice president of the New Jersey Sports and Exposition Authority, owner of the Meadowlands and Monmouth Park racetracks; former executive director and legal counsel for New Jersey Racing Commission.

Hartack, William J., 1932-. Jockey, racing official. Leading jockey by races won in 1955-'57, '60; leading jockey by money won in 1956-'57; inducted into Racing Hall of Fame in '59. Rode 4,272 winners, including Northern Dancer, Tim Tam, Majestic Prince. First jockey to earn $3-million in one year (1957); won five Kentucky Derbys (aboard Iron Liege in 1957, Venetian Way in '60, Decidedly in '62, Northern Dancer in '64, and Majestic Prince in '69).

Hawley, Sandy, 1949-. Jockey. Leading jockey by races won in 1970, '72-'73, '76; leading rider in Canada nine times; inducted into Racing Hall of Fame in '92; inducted into Canada's Hall of Fame in '86; Eclipse Award jockey in '76; George Woolf Memorial Jockey Award in '76; Sovereign Award in 1978, '88; Avelino Gomez Memorial Award in '86; Joe Palmer Award in '98. Rode 6,449 winners, including Youth, Desert Waves, Kiridashi, Smart Strike, Highland Vixen. First jockey to win more than 500 races in one season (1973).

Hayward, Charles, 1950-. Racetrack executive. President and chief executive officer, New York Racing Association, 2004-. Former president and chief executive officer *Daily Racing Form*. Member, NYRA board of trustees, 1995-'99.

Heiligbrodt, William, 1941-. Retired from banking, financial services, and funeral services. Campaigned more than 55 stakes winners. Board member, Texas Thoroughbred Association and Texas Horse Racing Hall of Fame. With wife, Corinne, raced 2003 Grade 1 winner Lady Tak and top sprinter Posse.

Hettinger, John, 1933-. Investments, real estate. Director, Breeders' Cup Ltd. Owner of Akindale Farm, New York. Member of Jockey Club. Special Eclipse Award in 2000. Bred and owned Warfie, Yestday's Kisses, Chase the Dream, Genuine Regret. Instrumental in founding the Racehorse Adoption Referral Program; chairman emeritus of the Grayson-Jockey Club Research Foundation; major shareholder, Fasig-Tipton Co.

Hickey, Jay, 1944-. Lawyer, lobbyist. President, American Horse Council. Represented equine organizations, horse owners, and horse breeders during his time as a practicing lawyer.

Hirsch, Joe, 1929-. Journalist. Co-founder and first president of the National Turf Writers Association 1959-'60. Lord Derby Award in 1985; Jockey Club Medal in '89; Mr. Fitz Award in '98; Walter Haight Award in '84; Joe Palmer Award in '94; Eclipse Award of Merit in '92; Eclipse Award for outstanding newspaper writing in '79. Longtime executive columnist of *Daily Racing Form;* retired in late 2003.

Hollendorfer, Jerry, 1949-. Trainer. All-time leading trainer in Northern California. Trained more than 4,300 winners through mid-2005. Won Bay Meadows Race Course and Golden Gate Fields training titles more than 20 times consecutively; won Golden Gate title 22 consecutive times. Trained Lite Light, King Glorious, Pike Place Dancer, Event of the Year.

Hubbard, R. D., 1935-. Glass manufacturing. Former chairman and chief executive officer, Hollywood Park; owner, Ruidoso Downs. Owner of Crystal Springs

Farm, Kentucky; Frontera Farm, New Mexico. Owned Gentlemen (Arg), Talloires, Leger Cat (Arg), Fit to Lead, Invited Guest, Mistico (Chi). Co-founded the Shoemaker Foundation in 1990 to help horsemen who have had catastrophic accidents or illnesses.

Hughes, B. Wayne, 1933-. Warehousing, philanthropist. Founder and president of Public Storage, of which he and his family own 39%. Director, Thoroughbred Owners and Breeders Association. Founder, Parker Hughes Cancer Center in Minnesota. Bought Spendthrift Farm in 2004. Owner of Action This Day, Joyeux Danseur, Shake the Yoke (GB), Trishyde.

Humphrey, G. Watts Jr., 1944-. Investments, manufacturing. Vice president, Breeders' Cup; director, Keeneland Association; steward of Jockey Club. Owner of Shawnee Farm, Kentucky. Bred Creme Fraiche, Sacahuista. Owned Likely Exchange, Amherst Wayside, Noble Damsel, Sorbet.

Hunt, Nelson Bunker, 1926-. Oil production. Owned Bluegrass Farm, Kentucky. Eclipse Award breeder in 1976, '85, '87; P.A.B. Widener Trophy in '85-'87. Bred and owned Dahlia, Youth, Empery, Trillion, Estrapade. Owned *Vaguely Noble, Exceller, Glorious Song. Bred Dahlia, the first mare to earn more than $1-million.

Icahn, Carl, 1936-. Financier. Owner of Foxfield Thoroughbreds, Kentucky. John A. Morris Award in 1990. Bred Blushing K. D., Great Navigator, Vaudeville, Helmsman, Brave Tender. Owned Meadow Star, Rose's Cantina, Colonial Waters.

Janney, Stuart III, 1948-. Financier. Former chairman, Thoroughbred Owners and Breeders Association. Steward of Jockey Club. Bred and owned Coronado's Quest, Warning Glance, Deputation, Mesabi Maiden. Aided in the formation of the National Thoroughbred Racing Association.

Jerkens, H. Allen, 1929-. Trainer. Leading trainer in New York in 1957, '62, '66, '69; inducted into Racing Hall of Fame in '75; Eclipse Award trainer in '73; Mr. Fitz Award in 2001. Trained more than 150 stakes winners, including Sky Beauty, Onion, Beau Purple, Duck Dance, Prove Out. Known as the "Giant Killer" for training horses who upset champions Secretariat, Kelso, Forego, and Buckpasser. Father of trainer Jimmy Jerkens.

Johnsen, Corey, 1955-. Racing executive. Magna Entertainment Corp. vice president and president of Lone Star Park; former general manager, Remington Park; created the All-Star Jockey Championship in 1997; played a key role in the development, construction, and opening of Lone Star and Remington; produced Eclipse Award-winning television program while at Louisiana Downs. Elected president of TRA in 2005.

Jolley, LeRoy, 1938-. Trainer. Inducted into Racing Hall of Fame in 1987. Trained Foolish Pleasure, Honest Pleasure, Genuine Risk, What a Summer, Manila, Meadow Star. Won the Kentucky Derby in 1980 with filly Genuine Risk. Son of trainer Moody Jolley.

Jones, Aaron U., 1921-. and **Jones, Marie**. Timber. Bred and owned Lemhi Gold, Western, Tiffany Lass. Owned Riboletta (Brz), Forestry, Plenty of Light. Bred Speightstown, Ashado.

Jones, Brereton C., 1939-. Breeder, politician. Director, Breeders' Cup Ltd.; past president and director, Thoroughbred Club of America. Owner of Airdrie Stud, Kentucky. Bred Desert Wine, Southjet, Formidable Lady, Dansil. Owned By Land by Sea, Imp Society, Silver Medallion. Helped persuade Breeders' Cup to supplement purses at tracks around the country in addition to the Breeders' Cup day events; inaugurated Kentucky Thoroughbred Development Fund while governor of Kentucky, 1991-'95, co-founder of Kentucky Equine Education Project.

Jones, John T. L. Jr., 1935-. Breeder. Owner and general manager, Walmac International, Kentucky. One of the founding members of the Breeders' Cup Ltd.; stood Alleged, Nureyev, Phone Trick.

Jones, Richard I. G., 1938-. Lawyer, bloodstock agent. Co-founded Walnut Green Bloodstock with brother Russell B. Jones Jr. Member, Jockey Club. Breeding and racing manager for Christiana Stables.

Jones, Russell B. Jr., 1935-. Bloodstock agent. President and chief operating officer, Walnut Green Bloodstock, which he co-founded with brother Richard I. G. Jones. Member, Jockey Club. General manager of Morven Stud, 1991-2000.

Karches, Peter, 1951-. Industry executive. Co-chairman, New York Racing Association, 2005-. Former co-chief operating officer, NYRA, 2003-'04. Former vice chairman, NYRA board of trustees. Member, Jockey Club. Trustee, Thoroughbred Owners and Breeders Association. Former president and chief operating officer, Morgan Stanley Dean Witter Securities Group. Campaigned graded stakes winners Dynever, Statesmanship, Fast Decision.

Kelly, Tommy J., 1919-. Trainer. Inducted into Racing Hall of Fame in 1993. Trained Plugged Nickle, Colonel Moran, Droll Role, Pet Bully, Globemaster. Co-owner of Evening Attire. Father of trainer Pat Kelly.

Kimmel, John, 1954-. Veterinarian, trainer. Conditioned 1997 champion Hidden Lake. In veterinary practice, 1980-'87. Has saddled nearly 1,000 winners and the earners of more than $40-million. Father, Caesar Kimmel, has owned racehorses for 30 years.

Krantz, Bryan, 1960-. Racing executive. past president and general manager, Fair Grounds Race Course; owner, Jefferson Downs. Built new grandstand after a fire destroyed Fair Grounds's physical plant in 1993.

Krone, Julie, 1963-. Jockey. Inducted into Racing Hall of Fame in 2000. All-time leading female jockey with more than 3,700 victories. First woman to win a Triple Crown race (Colonial Affair, 1993 Belmont Stakes [G1]) and Breeders' Cup race (Halfbridled, 2003 Breeders' Cup Juvenile Fillies [G1]).

Lake, Scott, 1965-. Trainer. Manages a stable of approximately 150 horses, mostly claimers. Leading North American trainer by wins in 2001 with 406, and in 2003 with 455. Trained former claimers Shake You Down and My Cousin Matt to Grade 2 victories.

Lavin, A. Gary, V.M.D., 1937-. Veterinarian. President of American Association of Equine Practitioners, 1994; AAEP's Lavin Cup, an annual award for commitment to horse welfare, in his honor. Founded Longfield Farm in Goshen, Kentucky, in 1979. Elected to Jockey Club in 1994, the first veterinarian chosen in 100 years. Past president, Kentucky Thoroughbred Association.

Lewis, Robert, 1924- and **Lewis, Beverly**, 1927-. Beer distributor. Eclipse Award of Merit in 1997; Big Sport of Turfdom Award in '95. Robert is member of Jockey Club. Owned Silver Charm, Charismatic, Serena's Song, Timber Country, Hennessy. Won two-thirds of the Triple Crown in 1997 and '99 (with Silver Charm and Charismatic, respectively).

Levy, Robert P., 1931-. Chemical storage. Former owner, Atlantic City Race Course; former president, Thoroughbred Racing Associations. Owner of Muirfield East, Maryland. Owned Housebuster, Smoke Glacken, Bet Twice. Inaugurated full-card simulcasting in 1983.

Liebau, F. Jack, 1938-. Lawyer, racetrack executive. President, Bay Meadows Racing Assocation; former president, Santa Anita Park. Member of Jockey Club. Owner of Valley Creek Farm, California. Owned Yashgan (GB), Boo La Boo, Forzando (GB), Kadial (Ire).

Little, Donald, 1934-. Financial management. Owner of Centennial Farms, Virginia. Owned Colonial Affair, Rubiano, King Cugat. Past president of the United States Polo Association; organizes racing syndicates.

Lukas, D. Wayne, 1935-. Trainer. Leading trainer by money won in 1983-'92, '94-'97; leading trainer by races won in 1987-'90; leading trainer by stakes races won in 1985-'92; inducted into Racing Hall of Fame in '99; Eclipse Award trainer in 1985-'87, '94; John W. Galbreath Award in '98. Leading trainer of Eclipse Award winners. Trained Lady's Secret, Thunder Gulch, Timber Country, Gulch, Flanders, Tabasco Cat, Codex, Charismatic. First trainer to reach both $100-million and $200-million in earnings; first trainer to win two Breeders' Cup races in one day (in 1985) and three races in one day (in '88); transformed modern training with entrepreneurial methods.

Lyster, Wayne G. III, 1948-. Owner, Ashview Farm, Kentucky. Former chairman, Kentucky Racing Commission. Co-bred champion Johannesburg; bred stakes winners At the Half, Lu Ravi.

Mabee, Betty, 1921-. Owner of Golden Eagle Farm near Ramona, California. Along with late husband, John, who died in 2002, won Eclipse Award as outstanding breeder in 1991, '97, and '98. Campaigned $5-million winner Best Pal, $2-million earners General Challenge and Dramatic Gold, and millionaire Excellent Meeting.

Madden, Preston, 1934-and **Madden, Anita**, 1933-. Real estate development. Owner of Hamburg Place, Kentucky. Bred Alysheba, Pink Pigeon, Miss Carmie, Romeo, Kentuckian. Owned T. V. Lark. Stood leading sire T. V. Lark; Anita Madden was the first female member of the Kentucky State Racing Commission.

Magnier, John, 1948-. Farm owner, breeder. Owner of Coolmore Stud, Ireland; Coolmore Stud, Australia; Ashford Stud, Kentucky; Creek View Farm, Kentucky. Bred Galileo (Ire), Sadler's Wells, Dr Devious (Ire). Originated shuttle-stallion concept; expanded mare books; stood Be My Guest, El Gran Senor, Danehill. Stands Sadler's Wells, Woodman.

Maktoum, Sheikh Hamdan bin Rashid al, 1945-. Deputy ruler of Dubai; minister of finance and industry for United Arab Emirates; UAE representative to OPEC. Owns Shadwell Farm in Kentucky, Shadwell Estate, Nunnery Stud, England; Derrinstown Stud, Ireland. Leading owner in England, 1995. Bred and owned Nashwan, Erhaab, Salsabil (Ire); partner with brothers Mohammed and Maktoum in Godolphin Racing.

Maktoum, Sheikh Maktoum bin Rashid al, 1943-. Ruler of Dubai; vice president and prime minister of United Arab Emirates. Owner of Gainsborough Farm, Kentucky; Woodpark Stud, Ballysheehan Stud, Ireland; Gainsborough Stud, England. Owned Shareef Dancer, Touching Wood, Shadeed, Ma Biche. Partner in Godolphin Racing with brothers Mohammed and Hamdan.

Maktoum, Sheikh Mohammed bin Rashid al, 1949-. Crown prince of Dubai. Owner of Raceland Farm, Kentucky; Darley at Jonabell, Kentucky; Dalham Hall Stud, England; Kildangan Stud, Ireland; Darley Australia, Australia. Bred and owned Dubai Millennium, Intrepidity (GB), In the Wings (GB), Swain (Ire). Owned Oh So Sharp (GB), Daylami (Ire), Pebbles (GB). Created Godolphin Racing, Dubai World Cup (UAE-G1).

Mandella, Richard, 1950-. Trainer. Inducted into Racing Hall of Fame in 2001. Trained Kotashaan (Fr), Phone Chatter, Dixie Union, Gentlemen (Arg), Halfbridled, Johar, Pleasantly Perfect, Wild Rush, and Dare and Go, who won the Pacific Classic (G1) in 1996, ending Cigar's 16-race winning streak. Won record four Breeders' Cup races in 2003.

Mangurian, Harry T. Jr., 1926-. Real estate development, construction. Former owner, Mockingbird Farm. Member, Jockey Club. Eclipse Award of Merit, 2002. Leading breeder in North America by earnings and races won, 1999-2002. First chairman of Ocala Breeders' Sales Co. Past director, Breeders' Cup Ltd., Florida Thoroughbred Breeders' and Owners' Association. Bred or owned more than 150 stakes winners, including Appealing Skier, Desert Vixen, Gilded Time, Successful Appeal, Valid Appeal. Former owner, Boston Celtics.

Maple, Edward, 1948-. Jockey. Began riding in Ohio and West Virginia, moved to New Jersey in 1970 and New York in '71. Rode champions Conquistador Cielo, Devil's Bag; won the Belmont Stakes (G1) with Temperence Hill and Creme Fraiche. Won 4,398 races and earned more than $105-million; rode Secretariat in champion's last career start, 1973 Canadian International. George Woolf Memorial Jockey Award in 1995; retired from racing in 1998 immediately after receiving the Mike Venezia Award.

Martin, Frank "Pancho," 1925-. Trainer. Leading trainer by money won in 1974; leading trainer in New York in 1973-'82; inducted into Racing Hall of Fame in '81. Trained 51 stakes winners and two champions, including Autobiography, Outstandingly, Sham, Manassa Mauler, Rube the Great.

Marzelli, Alan, 1954-. Racing executive. President and chief operating officer of Jockey Club since January 1, 2003; chairman of Equibase Co. LLC since 1996. Joined Jockey Club in 1983 as chief financial officer and later became executive vice president.

McAlpine, James R., 1946-. Former president and chief executive officer, Magna Entertainment Corp; vice chairman of corporate development for Magna.

McAnally, Ron, 1932-. Trainer. Inducted into Racing Hall of Fame in 1990; Eclipse Award trainer in 1981, '91-'92; Mr. Fitz Award in '92. Trained John Henry, Bayakoa (Arg), Tight Spot, Paseana (Arg), Northern Spur (Ire).

McCarron, Chris, 1955-. Jockey, racetrack executive. Leading jockey by races won in 1974-'75, '80; leading jockey by money won in 1980-'81, '84, '91; inducted into Racing Hall of Fame in '89; Eclipse Award apprentice jockey in '74; Eclipse Award jockey in '80; George Woolf Memorial Jockey Award in '80; Mike Venezia Award in '91. Rode Alysheba, John Henry, Lady's Secret, Sunday Silence, Tiznow. Retired in 2002 as leading earner among jockeys with $264-million; along with his wife, Judy, and comedian Tim Conway, created the Don MacBeth Memorial Fund for disabled jockeys. General manager of Santa Anita Park in 2003-'04.

McDonald, Reiley, 1957-. Bloodstock agent. Partner, Eaton Sales Inc. Kentucky. Owner, Indian Hills Farm and Athens-Woods Farm, Kentucky. Former vice president, Fasig-Tipton Co., former president, Stallion Access. Driving force behind development of Thoroughbred Retirement Foundation's Secretariat Center, located at Kentucky Horse Park, for rehabilitation and adoption of Thoroughbreds. Board member, Keeneland Association, University of Kentucky's Maxwell H. Gluck Equine Research Center, Kentucky Horse Park. Sold Banshee Breeze, Grand Slam, Hawk Wing, High Yield, Russian Rhythm, Victory Gallop, Yes It's True. Owned Nasty Storm.

McGaughey, Claude R. "Shug" III, 1951-. Trainer. Eclipse Award trainer in 1988; inducted into Racing Hall of Fame in 2004. Trained Easy Goer, Rhythm, Inside Information, Heavenly Prize, My Flag, Storm Flag Flying and Personal Ensign, unbeaten in 13 races; won five graded stakes at Belmont Park on Breeders' Cup preview day in 1993.

McKathan, J. B., 1966- and **McKathan, Kevin**, 1968-. Bloodstock agents. Owners of McKathan Brothers Training Facility in Ocala; purchased for clients Silver Charm, Real Quiet, Silverbulletday, Captain Steve.

McKay, Jim (Jim McManus), 1921-. Broadcaster. Eclipse Award of Merit in 2000; Big Sport of Turfdom Award in 1987; Joe Palmer Award in 2000. Member of Jockey Club. Co-founder of Maryland Million; broadcast host of Triple Crown 1975-2000 on ABC.

McMahon, Gerald F. "Jerry," 1950-. Sales company executive. President and general manager, Barretts Equine Sales Ltd. Previously vice president, Fasig-Tipton California.

McNair, Robert, 1937- and **McNair, Janice**, 1936-. Investments, NFL team owner. Owner of Stonerside Stable, Kentucky; training facilities in Aiken, South Carolina and Saratoga Springs, New York. Co-bred Fusaichi Pegasus; bred and owned Congaree. Owned Chilukki, Tuzla (Ire). Co-owned Coronado's Quest, Touch Gold. Robert is member of Jockey Club.

Meeker, Thomas, 1943-. Racing executive. President, Churchill Downs Inc.; president, Thoroughbred Racing Associations, 1991-'92. John W. Galbreath Award in 1999. Beginning in 1984, implemented a $25-million, five-year improvement plan for Churchill, including a $3.6-million turf course and a $2.8-million paddock. Undertook $121-million renovation of Churchill in 2002; oversaw expansion of Churchill Downs Inc. to encompass tracks from coast to coast.

Melnyk, Eugene, 1959-. Pharmaceuticals. Owns Ottawa Senators of the National Hockey League. Owner, Winding Oaks Farm, Florida. Member, New York Racing Association board of trustees. Co-recipient of National Turf Writers Association 2002 Joe Palmer Award for contributions to racing. Campaigns horses with wife, Laura. Co-owned Archers Bay; owned Graeme Hall, Harmony Lodge, Marley Vale, Pico Teneriffe, Strong Hope, Tweedside, Speightstown.

Metzger, Dan, 1963-. Racing executive. President of Thoroughbred Owners and Breeders Association since 1999. Former director of marketing services and licensing for Breeders' Cup Ltd.

Meyerhoff, Robert, 1924-. Real estate development. Owner of Fitzhugh Farm, Maryland. Bred and owned Broad Brush, Concern, Include, Valley Crossing.

Meyocks, Terry, 1951-. Racing executive. Former president and chief operating officer of New York Racing Association. Former vice president of racing for NYRA; former racing secretary at Calder Race Course, director of racing at Gulfstream Park.

Miller, Leverett, 1931-. Owner-breeder. With wife, Linda, owns and operates T-Square Stud in Fairfield, Florida. Campaigns in Eton blue silks of late uncle C.V. Whitney. Bred Silver Wagon. Member, Jockey Club. Board member, Breeders' Cup, Florida Thoroughbred Breeders' and Owners' Association. Former board member, Ocala Breeders' Sales Co.

Miller, MacKenzie "Mack," 1921-. Trainer, breeder. Inducted into Racing Hall of Fame in 1987; Mr. Fitz Award in '96. Member of Jockey Club. Trained 72 stakes winners, including champions Leallah, Assagai, Hawaii, and *Snow Knight. Trained Fit to Fight to New York handicap triple crown in 1984; trained Sea Hero to Kentucky Derby victory in 1993. Bred De La Rose, Lite Light, Chilukki.

Moran, Elizabeth "Betty," 1932-. Investments. Owner of Brushwood Stable, Pennsylvania. Bred Russian Rhythm, High Yield. Owned Creme Fraiche. Won English Grand National Steeplechase Handicap with Papillon in 2000.

Mott, William, 1953-. Trainer. Inducted into Racing Hall of Fame in 1998; Eclipse Award in 1995-'96. Trained Cigar, Paradise Creek, Ajina, Theatrical (Ire), Geri, Escena, Wekiva Springs. Trained Cigar for 16 consecutive victories from 1994-'96.

Nafzger, Carl, 1941-. Trainer. Eclipse Award trainer in 1990; Big Sport of Turfdom Award in '90. Trained Unbridled, Banshee Breeze, Unshaded, Vicar, Solvig. Wrote *Traits of a Winner: The Formula for Developing Thoroughbred Racehorses* in 1994.

Nerud, John A., 1913-. Trainer, breeder. President of Tartan Farms, Florida, 1959-'89. Inducted into Racing Hall of Fame in 1972. Trained 27 stakes winners and five champions, including Dr. Fager, Ta Wee, Delegate, Intentionally, Dr. Patches, *Gallant Man. Bred and owned Cozzene, Fappiano. Dr. Fager is the only horse to win four championships in one year.

Niarchos-Gouazé, Maria, Investments. Director, Breeders' Cup Ltd. Owner of Haras de Fresnay-le-Buffard, France. In partnership with her brothers, breeds under the name Flaxman Holdings Ltd. Bred and owned champion Aldebaran, Dream Well (Fr), Sulamani (Ire), Bago, Six Perfections (Fr), Divine Proportions. Daughter of shipping magnate Stavros Niarchos.

Nicholson, George "Nick," 1947-. Racing executive. President and chief executive officer, Keeneland Association; executive director, Jockey Club 1989-2000; former chief operating officer, National Thoroughbred Racing Association; president, Thoroughbred Club of America in '91. Jockey Club Gold Medal in 1998. Involved in the planning and development of the Kentucky Horse Park; played key role in formation of Equibase; helped to pull industry together to support the National Thoroughbred Racing Association.

Noe, Kenneth Jr. "Kenny," 1928-. Former racing executive. New York Racing Association chairman and chief executive officer 1995-2000. NYRA president, general manager 1994-'95. president, general manager of Calder Race Course 1979-'90. Member of Jockey Club.

Nuckols, Charles Jr., 1922-. Breeder. Former president, Thoroughbred Club of America; director, Keeneland Association. Member of Jockey Club. Owner of Nuckols Farm, Kentucky. Bred Hidden Lake, Habi-

tat, Decathlon, Typecast. Co-bred War Emblem. Co-authored the Kentucky Thoroughbred Development Fund legislation.

O'Brien, Aidan, 1969-. Trainer. Won then-record 23 Grade/Group 1 races in 2001. Trains for Coolmore Stud and partners at Ballydoyle, Ireland. Won 2001-'02 Epsom Derby (Eng-G1) with Galileo (Ire) and High Chaparral (Ire), respectively. Trained Giant's Causeway, King of Kings (Ire), Milan (GB), Imagine (Ire), Stravinsky, Hawk Wing, Rock of Gibraltar (Ire), Ballingarry (Ire), Johannesburg, Footstepsinthesand.

O'Brien, Vincent, 1917-. Legendary Irish trainer. Founded Ballydoyle training center in Ireland; with John Magnier and Robert Sangster established Coolmore Stud in 1975. Trained winners of 27 Irish classics, 16 English classics, and in 1977 saddled then-record 22 Group 1 winners. Trained Nijinsky II, Roberto, Golden Fleece, Sir Ivor, The Minstrel, Alleged. In a 2003 *Racing Post* poll, he was voted the all-time most important figure in English racing.

O'Byrne, Dermot "Demi," 1944-. Bloodstock agent, veterinarian. Purchased Thunder Gulch, Honour and Glory, High Yield, Fasliyev, Stravinsky, King of Kings (Ire), Johannesburg. Chief talent spotter for Coolmore Stud-Michael Tabor partnerships.

O'Farrell, J. Michael Jr., 1948-. Breeder. First vice president, Florida Thoroughbred Breeders' and Owners' Association. Member of Jockey Club. Owner of Ocala Stud Farm, Florida. Bred Bolshoi Boy, Proudest Duke, Queen Alexandra. Son of Joe O'Farrell.

Oxley, John C., 1937- and **Oxley, Debbie,** 1951-. Oil production. John is steward of Jockey Club. Owner of Fawn Leap Farm, Kentucky. Bred and owned Pyramid Peak. Owned Monarchos, Beautiful Pleasure, Sky Mesa.

Pape, William L., 1930-. Auto dealership. Former president, National Steeplechase Association. Co-bred champions Flatterer and Martie's Anger; owned champion Athenian Idol.

Paragallo, Ernie, 1958-. Investment banking, computer software. In name of Paraneck Stable, raced 1999 champion sprinter Artax; also campaigned 1995 Breeders' Cup Juvenile (G1) winner Unbridled's Song, 1999 Wood Memorial Stakes (G2) winner Adonis.

Payson, Virginia Kraft, 1930-. Investments. Owner of Payson Stud, Kentucky. Bred and owned St. Jovite, L'Carriere. Owned Carr de Naskra. Bred 2002 champions Vindication and Farda Amiga. Owner and operator of Payson Park training center in Florida.

Pegram, Mike, 1952-. Fast food franchises. Owned Real Quiet, Silverbulletday, Isitingood, Thirty Slews, Captain Steve.

Perret, Craig, 1951-. Jockey. Eclipse Award jockey in 1990; George Woolf Memorial Jockey Award in '98. Rode Unbridled, Housebuster, Safely Kept, Eillo, Rhythm, Alydeed, Bet Twice. Won a record-tying 57 stakes in 1990.

Phillips, John W., 1952-. Investments, lawyer. Member of Jockey Club. Managing partner of Darby Dan Farm, Kentucky. Bred and owned Memories of Silver, Sunshine Forever, Brian's Time, Soaring Softly. Grandson of John W. Galbreath.

Phipps, Ogden Mills "Dinny," 1940-. Investments. Chairman, Jockey Club; former chairman, New York Racing Association; director, Grayson-Jockey Club Research Foundation. Eclipse Award of Merit in 1978. Bred and owned Inside Information, Rhythm, Educated Risk, Storm Flag Flying. Co-bred and owned Successor. Son of Ogden Phipps.

Piggott, Lester, 1936-. Retired jockey, trainer. Champion English jockey 11 times. Won more than 5,300 races, including record 30 English classics. Winner of the Epsom Derby record nine times; Ascot Gold Cup 11 times; Irish Derby five times; and the 1990 Breeders' Cup Mile (G1) at age 54. Rode Nijinsky II, Sir Ivor, Roberto, The Minstrel, Alleged. Imprisoned a year for tax evasion 1987-'88 before resuming his riding career.

Pincay, Laffit Jr., 1946-. Jockey. Leading jockey by money won in 1970-'74, '79, '85; leading jockey by races won in '71; inducted into Racing Hall of Fame in '75 ; Eclipse Award jockey in 1971, '73-'74, '79, '85; Special Eclipse Award in '99; George Woolf Memorial Jockey Award in '70. Big Sport of Turfdom Award in '85. Rode Affirmed, John Henry, Gamely, Susan's Girl, Desert Vixen, Genuine Risk. Broke Bill Shoemaker's lifetime win record on December 10, 1999, with his 8,834th victory; first jockey to win seven races on a single card at Santa Anita Park, in '87; first jockey to win more than 9,000 races. Retired on April 24, 2003, with a record 9,530 victories and purse earnings of $237-million.

Pletcher, Todd, 1967-. Trainer. Annually among the top ten North American trainers by earnings and was leader by in 2004 with $17.5-million. Eclipse Award as outstanding trainer, 2004. Son of horseman Jake Pletcher and a longtime assistant to Racing Hall of Fame trainer D. Wayne Lukas. Trained champions Ashado, Left Bank, Speightstown; Grade 1 winners include Archers Bay, Ashado, Balto Star, Harlan's Holiday, Jersey Girl.

Polk, Hiram Jr., M.D., 1936-. Surgeon, breeder. Retired chair, University of Louisville School of Medicine surgery department. Member, Jockey Club. Breeder and co-owner of multiple stakes winner Mrs. Revere.

Pollard, Carl, 1938-. Health care executive. Chairman, Churchill Downs Inc.; president, Kentucky Derby Museum. Owner of Hermitage Farm, Kentucky. Owned Caressing, Sheepscot, Duck Trap, Take Me Out.

Powell, Lonny, 1959-. Racing executive. Vice president of public affairs, Youbet.com Inc.; former president of Association of Racing Commissioners International. Former president of Santa Anita Park.

Prado, Edgar, 1967-. Jockey. Peru native among national leaders by earnings; second in 2004 with $18.3-million. Registered 5,000th career victory in 2004; won Belmont Stakes (G1) with Birdstone (2004) and Sarava ('02). Led all North American riders by victories with 536 in 1997, 474 in '98, and 402 in '99.

Ramsey, Kenneth L., 1935-. Cellular telephones. In 1990s, acquired cellular telephone franchises along Interstate 75 in northeastern Georgia and southeastern Kentucky. Acquired Almahurst Farm in 1994 and renamed it Ramsey Farm. With wife, Sarah, won Eclipse Award as outstanding owner in 2004. Owner of 2004 champion turf male Kitten's Joy, Grade 1 winner Roses in May.

Reddam, J. Paul, 1955-. Finance. Founder, Ditech.com, an Internet-based mortgage company that he sold in 1999 to General Motors. President, Cash Call, a consumer loan company. Former Standardbred syndicator claimed his first Thoroughbred in 1988. Owner, Metropolitan Handicap (G1) winner Swept Overboard, millionaire Elloluv, and 2004 Breeders' Cup Juvenile (G1) winner Wilko.

Richardson, J. David, M.D., 1945-. Vascular surgeon. Member, Jockey Club; past president, Kentucky Thoroughbred Association; co-bred and raced Mrs. Revere.

Rickman, William Sr., 1924-. Racing executive, owner-breeder. Chairman of Delaware Park. Bought Delaware Park in 1983, reopened it after a one-year shutdown, and turned it into profitable enterprise. Introduced slots in 1995. Son William Rickman Jr. is president and chief executive. Also owns Ocean Downs harness track and holds license to build a new track in Allegany County, Maryland.

Roark, John, 1940-. Lawyer. In private practice in Temple, Texas. President of the National Horsemen's Benevolent and Protective Association. Former president, Texas Thoroughbred Partnership. Director, National Thoroughbred Racing Association.

Robertson, Walter, 1949-. Auctioneer. President, Fasig-Tipton Co.; former president, Thoroughbred Club of America. Auctioneer at the Calumet Farm sale in 1992.

Robbins, Jack K., V.M.D., 1921-. Veterinarian, racing executive. President, founding director of Oak Tree Racing Association; Jockey Club member; director of Grayson-Jockey Club Research Foundation; distinguished life member of American Association of Equine Practitioners. Father of trainer Jay Robbins, Del Mar Director of Racing Tom Robbins, and former Hollywood Park President Don Robbins.

Robinson, J. Mack, 1923-. Financier, philanthropist. Member, Jockey Club. Family owns Rosehill Plantation in Thomasville, Georgia. Daughter Jill raced 1994 champion sprinter Cherokee Run. Honored as owner of the year by the Georgia Thoroughbred Owners and Breeders Association. Chief benefactor of J. Mack Robinson College of Business at Georgia State University.

Romero, Randy, 1957-. Jockey. Father, Lloyd, was Quarter Horse trainer; film *Casey's Shadow* was based on his Louisiana family; won Breeders' Cup races with champions Sacahuista (1987 Distaff [G1]), Personal Ensign (1988 Distaff), and Go for Wand (1989 Juvenile Fillies [G1]). Sustained life-threatening burns in a 1983 accident in Oaklawn Park jockeys' room. Won 4,294 races, earned more than $75-million.

Rotz, John L., 1934-. Jockey, racing official. Leading jockey by stakes winners in 1968-'69; inducted into Racing Hall of Fame in '83; George Woolf Memorial Jockey Award in '73. Rode 2,908 winners. Rode Gallant Bloom, Ta Wee, Carry Back, Dr. Fager, Silent Screen.

Russell, Geoffrey, 1961-. Keeneland director of sales since 2001. Previously assistant director of sales, 1996-2001; also worked at Goffs Bloodstock Sales and Fasig-Tipton.

Sahadi, Jenine, 1963-. Trainer. First female to win a Breeders' Cup race on the flat, champion Lit de Justice in the 1996 Breeders' Cup Sprint (G1) and Elmhurst in the same race in 1997. First female to saddle a Santa Anita Derby (G1) winner, The Deputy (Ire) in 2000. Also trained stakes winners Grand Flotilla, and Creston. Daughter of Fred Sahadi, founder of Cardiff Stud.

Sampson, Curtis, 1933-. Telecommunications. Chairman of Canterbury Park Holding Corp.; bought closed track in 1994 with partners and reopened it in 1995. Entered racing in 1987 as an owner; among Minnesota's leading breeders.

Sams, Timothy H., 1944-. Breeder. Indiana Horse Racing Commission member, 1998-2002. Indiana Horse Racing Commission vice chairman, 2002. Member, Jockey Club. Former director, Breeders' Cup Ltd., Indiana Thoroughbred Breed Development Advisory Committee.

Samuel-Balaz, Tammy, Investments. Co-owner of Sam-Son Farm, Canada and Florida. Bred and owned Dancethruthedawn, Scatter the Gold, Catch the Ring, Mountain Angel, Quiet Resolve. Daughter of Ernest Samuel.

Santos, Jose, 1961-. Jockey. Leading jockey by money won in 1986-'89; Eclipse Award jockey in '88; George Woolf Memorial Jockey Award in '99. Rode Lemon Drop Kid, Skip Away, Colonial Affair, Chief Bearhart, Volponi, Funny Cide. Led all jockeys by money won with a then-record $14.86-million in 1988; rode 13 winners in three days at Aqueduct in '88. Won 2003 Kentucky Derby (G1) and Preakness Stakes (G1) on Funny Cide.

Santulli, Richard, 1944-. Aviation. Co-owner of Jay-eff B Stable. Member of Jockey Club. Bred and owned Ciro. Owned Safely Kept, Banshee Breeze, Korveya.

Savin, Scott, 1960-. Owner, executive. President, Gulfstream Park; former president, Florida Horsemen's Benevolent and Protective Association. Owned Bet Big, Cheshire Kitten. Grandson of A. I. "Butch" Savin, owner of Mr. Prospector.

Scherf, Christopher, 1951-. Racing executive. Executive vice president of Thoroughbred Racing Associations since 1988; president of TRA Enterprises. Serves on the American Horse Council's Racing and Government Affairs committees. Former sportswriter for the Louisville *Courier-Journal* and United Press International; director of press relations for the New York Racing Association, 1978-'81.

Schickendanz, Gustav, 1929-. President and CEO of family construction and development company. Owner of Schonberg Farm in Nobleton, Ontario. Bred and owned 2003 Canadian Triple Crown winner and Canadian Horse of the Year Wando and 2004 Canadian champion Mobil. Also campaigned Sovereign Award winners Glanmire (1997 sprinter) and Langfuhr (1996 sprinter).

Schiff, Peter G., 1952-. Financier. Trustee, New York Racing Association. Member, Jockey Club. Owner of Fox Ridge Farm. Owned Christiecat, Riskaverse, Token Dance, Wortheroatsingold. Son of John Schiff.

Schulhofer, Flint S. "Scotty," 1926-. Trainer. Inducted into Racing Hall of Fame in 1992. Trained 80 stakes winners, including champions Ta Wee, Mac Diarmida, Smile, Fly So Free, Lemon Drop Kid, Rubiano; also trained Cryptoclearance. Father of trainer Randy Schulhofer.

Schwartz, Barry, 1942-. Clothing executive. Former chairman and chief executive officer, New York Racing Association. Member of Jockey Club. Owner of Stonewall Farm, New York. Bred and owned Beru, Patricia J. K. Owned Three Ring.

Seitz, Fred, 1946-. Consignor, breeder. Former president, Thoroughbred Club of America and Kentucky Thoroughbred Association; director, Keeneland Association. Owner, Brookdale Farm, Kentucky, which stood Deputy Minister and stands Forest Wildcat, Crafty Prospector, Silver Deputy, With Approval. Bred Bluebird in partnership.

Sexton, Steve, 1959-. Racetrack executive. President of Churchill Downs. Former executive vice president of Arlington Park; former executive vice president and general manager of Lone Star Park; former general manager of Thistledown racetrack.

Sheppard, Jonathan, 1940-. Trainer, breeder. Owner of Ashwell Stables, Pennsylvania. President, National Steeplechase Association. Leading steeplechase trainer by money won in 1973-'90, '92-'95; inducted into Racing Hall of Fame in '90. Trained more than 120 stakes winners, including champions Cafe Prince, Flatterer, Athenian Idol, Martie's Anger, Jimmy Lorenzo (GB),

Highland Bud. Also trained Storm Cat, With Anticipation. Co-bred Martie's Anger, Flatterer.

Sherman, Michael, 1940-. Breeder. Owner and president of Farnsworth Farms, Florida. Leading breeder by stakes winners in 1994-'95; Eclipse Award breeder in '96. Bred Beautiful Pleasure, Jewel Princess, Mecke, Frisk Me Now, Once Wild.

Shields, Joseph V. Jr., 1938-. Investment manager, owner-breeder. Chairman and CEO of Shields & Co., brokerage and investment management firm. Vice chairman, New York Racing Association, member of the Jockey Club, trustee of National Museum of Racing Hall of Fame, Thoroughbred Owners and Breeders Association; director of Grayson-Jockey Club Research Foundation. Owner-breeder of Wagon Limit, Passing Shot, House Party, Puzzlement, Limit Out.

Sikura, John G., 1958-. Thoroughbred owner and breeder. Owner of Hill 'n' Dale Farm and Hill 'n' Dale Sales Agency in Kentucky. Breeder or co-breeder of Grade 1-Group 1 winners Hawk Wing and Touch Gold. Son of Hill 'n' Dale founder John Sikura Jr.

Smith, Mike, 1965-. Jockey. Elected to Racing Hall of Fame in 2003. Leading jockey by races won in 1994; Eclipse Award jockey in 1993-'94; Mike Venezia Award in '94; George Woolf Memorial Jockey Award in 2000. Rode Holy Bull, Lure, Skip Away, Azeri, Unbridled's Song, Coronado's Quest, Vindication, Giacomo. Won record 66 stakes in 1994. Through mid-2005, won more than 4,500 races and earned more than $170-million.

Smith, Tim, 1948-. Racing executive. Former commissioner of National Thoroughbred Racing Association, 1998-2004. Helped increase national television exposure for horse racing. President, Friends of New York Racing, founded February 2005.

Smithwick, D. M. "Mike," 1929-. Trainer. Inducted into Racing Hall of Fame in 1971. Trained 52 stakes winners and six champions. Trained Neji, Bon Nouvel, Ancestor, Mako, Top Bid, Straight and True. Trained Neji to three championships in 1955, '57, and '58; trained the first two winners (Top Bid and Inkslinger) of the Colonial Cup. Brother of Racing Hall of Fame jockey Paddy Smithwick.

Solis, Alex, 1964-. Jockey. Among top ten leading riders by career earnings. Panama native first rode in U.S. in 1982; recipient of the first Bill Shoemaker Award in 2003 for outstanding achievement on the Breeders' Cup program; rode two winners, Johar in Breeders' Cup Turf (G1) dead heat and Pleasantly Perfect in the Breeders' Cup Classic (G1). Also rode Pleasantly Perfect to win in 2004 Dubai World Cup (UAE-G1).

Sommer, Viola (Mrs. Sigmund), 1921-. Real estate. Leading owner in 1982; Eclipse Award owner in '82. Member of Jockey Club. Bred and owned Bottled Water. Owned Sham, Ten Below, Tom Swift.

Steinbrenner, George, 1930-. Shipping. Director, Florida Thoroughbred Breeders' and Owners' Association. Owner of Kinsman Farm, Florida. Bred and owned Concerto, Diligence, Eternal Prince; owned Bellamy Road. Former co-owner Florida Downs (later Tampa Bay Downs). Managing partner, New York Yankees.

Stevens, Gary, 1963-. Jockey. President, Jockeys' Guild, 1995-2000. Leading jockey by money won in 1990; inducted into Racing Hall of Fame in '97; Eclipse Award jockey in '98; George Woolf Memorial Jockey Award in '96. Rode more than 4,800 winners, including Point Given, Silver Charm, Winning Colors, Thunder Gulch, Hennessy, Broad Brush. Youngest rider to earn more than $100-million in purses, in 1993.

Stoute, Sir Michael, 1945-. Trainer. Five-time champion trainer in England. Trained Epsom Derby (Eng-G1) winners Shergar (1981), Shahrastani ('86), Kris Kin (2003), North Light ('04), and Unite (Ire), stakes winners Sonic Lady, Shareef Dancer, Melodist, Ivor's Image, Ajdal, Saddlers' Hall, Marwell (Ire), Zilzal, Opera House (GB), Ezzoud (Ire), Russian Rhythm, Islington (Ire).

Strauss, Robert S., 1918-. Lawyer, diplomat. Chairman of Del Mar Thoroughbred Club since 2002. Jockey Club member. Former FBI special agent; ambassador to the Soviet Union 1991-'92; President Carter's representative to the Middle East peace negotiations; winner of the Presidential Medal of Freedom '81; chairman of the Democratic National Committee 1973-'76. Bred Last Tycoon (Ire).

Strawbridge, George Jr., 1937-. Investments. Former president, National Steeplechase Association. Member of Jockey Club. Owner of Augustin Stables, Pennsylvania. F. Ambrose Clark Award in 1979. Bred and owned Tikkanen, Selkirk, Silver Fling, With Anticipation. Bred Treizieme, Turgeon. Owned Cafe Prince, Mo Bay.

Stronach, Frank, 1932-. Auto-parts manufacturer. Chairman, Magna International Corp., Magna Entertainment Corp. Owner of Adena Springs Farm, Kentucky; Adena Springs North, Ontario; Adena Springs South, Florida. Owner of Stronach Stable. Eclipse Award owner in 1998-2000; Eclipse Award breeder in '00 and '04; eight Sovereign Awards as owner of year and four Sovereign Awards as breeder of year. Bred and owned Macho Uno, Perfect Sting, Ghostzapper. Co-owned Touch Gold, Glorious Song. Also bred and owned Awesome Again, richest Canadian-bred runner of all-time with $4,374,590. Through Magna Entertainment, purchased Thoroughbred racetracks Santa Anita Park, Gulfstream Park, Thistledown, Golden Gate Fields, Remington Park, Great Lakes Downs, Portland Meadows, Lone Star Park; majority of Pimlico Race Course and Laurel Park.

Stute, Melvin F., 1927-. Trainer. Trained two Eclipse Award winners in 1986, Preakness Stakes (G1) winner Snow Chief and Breeders' Cup Juvenile Fillies (G1) winner Brave Raj. Also trained Very Subtle, winner of the 1987 Breeders' Cup Sprint (G1). Brother of trainer Warren Stute.

Suroor, Saeed bin, 1967-. Trainer. Leading trainer in England by money won in 1995. Trained Dubai Millennium, Fantastic Light, Swain (Ire), E Dubai, Lammtarra, Mark of Esteem (Ire). Head trainer for Godolphin Racing; won the Emirates World Series in 1999 with Daylami (Ire), Fantastic Light (2000-'01), and Grandera in 2002.

Switzer, David, 1945-. Executive director of Kentucky Thoroughbred Association. Board member of University of Kentucky-Gluck Research Foundation.

Tabor, Michael, 1941-. Former betting shop owner, investments. Owned or co-owned Thunder Gulch, Montjeu (Ire), Desert King, Honour and Glory, Johannesburg, Galileo (Ire), High Chaparral (Ire).

Tanaka, Gary, 1943-. Stockbroker, co-owner of Amerindo Investment Advisors Inc. Frequently bought proven horses in Europe and raced them in California. Owned User Friendly (GB), Dernier Empereur, Donna Viola (GB), Dreams Gallore, Golden Apples (Ire). Charged with improper use of client funds in 2005.

Taylor, Duncan, 1956-. Farm owner. Co-owner (with brothers Frank, Ben, and Mark) of Taylor Made Farm and Sales Agency, Kentucky. Sold more than $1-billion total value of horses at public auctions since 1978. Stands Unbridled's Song, Forestry. Son of Joe Taylor.

Taylor, Mickey, 1940- and **Taylor, Karen**, 1940-. Timber. Owned and bred Slew o' Gold, Slewpy. Co-owned Seattle Slew, who won 14 of 17 starts, including the Triple Crown in 1977, and earned $1.2-million.

Thomas, Becky, 1957- . Bloodstock agent. Co-founder of Lakland and Lakland North with partners Lewis and Brenda Lakin. Owns and operates Sequel Bloodstock, which consigns at two-year-old sales.

Troutt, Kenny, 1948-. Telecommunications. Partner in WinStar Farm, Kentucky. Trustee, Thoroughbred Owners and Breeders Association; director, Breeders Cup Ltd. In WinStar name, bred Funny Cide, One Cool Cat. Owned Awesome Humor, Bet Me Best, Byzantine (Brz), and Pompeii. Co-owner of Ipi Tombe (Zim), Crimson Palace. Stands Tiznow, Distorted Humor, Victory Gallop. Stood Kris S.

Turcotte, Ron, 1941-. Jockey. Leading jockey by stakes won in 1972-'73; inducted into Racing Hall of Fame in '79; George Woolf Memorial Jockey Award in '79. Rode 3,032 winners, including Secretariat, Damascus, Northern Dancer, Riva Ridge, Shuvee, Dark Mirage, Fort Marcy. Won Triple Crown in 1973 aboard Secretariat. Paralyzed in 1978 spill.

Turner, William H. "Billy," 1941-. Trainer. Trained Seattle Slew through his three-year-old season to become the first undefeated American Triple Crown winner. Also trained Czaravich. Rode in steeplechase races from 1958-'62; assistant to Racing Hall of Fame trainer W. Burling Cocks before going on his own in 1966.

Ussery, Robert N., 1935-. Jockey. Inducted into Racing Hall of Fame in 1980. Rode 3,611 winners, including Hail to Reason, Bally Ache, Bramalea, Never Bow. Fifth by money won among jockeys at retirement; finished first in two consecutive Kentucky Derbys, aboard Proud Clarion (1967) and Dancer's Image ('68, disqualified, placed last).

Valpredo, Don, 1939-. Agriculture. Director, Thoroughbred Owners of California, Breeders' Cup Ltd.; Member, Jockey Club. President, Ridge Ginning Co.; Director, Kern Ridge Growers, Arvin Edison Water Storage District. Son of John Valpredo.

Van Berg, Jack, 1936-. Trainer. Leading trainer by races won in 1968-'70, '72, '74, '76, '83-'84, '86; leading trainer by money won in '76; inducted into Racing Hall of Fame in '85; Eclipse Award trainer in '84; Big Sport of Turfdom Award in '87; Jockey Club Gold Medal in '87; Mr. Fitz Award in '88. Trained Alysheba, Gate Dancer. Holds record for most races won in a single year (496 in 1976); trained champion Alysheba, who retired with a then-record total earnings of $6,679,242; 6,000th career win in February 1995. Son of Racing Hall of Fame trainer Marion Van Berg.

Van Clief, Daniel G. Jr., 1948-. Racing executive. Commissioner, National Thoroughbred Racing Association; president, Breeders' Cup Ltd.; chairman, Fasig-Tipton Co.; member of Jockey Club. Co-owner of Nydrie Stud, Virginia. Eclipse Award of Merit in 1998; Jockey Club Medal in '84. Worked to put together Breeders' Cup day of championship races; key figure in development of NTRA.

Van de Kamp, John, 1936-. Lawyer, association executive. Past president, Thoroughbred Owners of California; director, National Thoroughbred Racing Association. Gathered support in the TOC to pass account wagering bill; lobbied for horse industry tax relief measures in California.

VanMeter II, Tom, D.V.M., 1957-. Veterinarian, sales agent, owner-breeder. Co-owner with Reiley McDonald of Eaton Sales, Kentucky. Owner of Victory U. S. A., Be Gentle; raced Brahms; co-bred Mr. Mellon.

Varola, Francesco, 1922-. Author, bloodstock adviser. Author of *Typology of the Racehorse*; added to the dosage theory by creating aptitudinal classes in which he categorized each *chef-de-race* stallion.

Vasquez, Jacinto, 1944-. Jockey, trainer. Inducted into Racing Hall of Fame in 1998. Rode winners of 5,231 races, including Ruffian, Genuine Risk, Princess Rooney, Forego. Nation's 15th all-time winning jockey at his retirement in 1996; rode Ruffian to victory in the New York filly triple crown in '75.

Veitch, John, 1945-. Executive, former trainer. Deputy director, Kentucky Horse Racing Authority. Trained Davona Dale, Our Mims, Before Dawn, Proud Truth. Trained Alydar, who finished second behind Affirmed in all three Triple Crown races in 1978. Son of Racing Hall of Fame trainer Sylvester Veitch.

Velasquez, Jorge, 1946-. Jockey. Leading jockey by races won in 1967; leading jockey by money won in '69; leading jockey by stakes races won in '85; inducted into Racing Hall of Fame in '90; George Woolf Memorial Jockey Award in '86. Rode 6,795 winners, including Alydar, Chris Evert, Davona Dale, Lady's Secret, Shuvee, Fort Marcy. Won the New York filly triple crown with Chris Evert in 1974 and Davona Dale in '79; first jockey to win six of six races in New York, in '81.

Velazquez, John R., 1971-. Jockey. Eclipse Award jockey, 2004; North American leading rider by earnings in 2004 with $22.2-million. Rode winners of six Breeders' Cup races: Ashado, Speightstown, Da Hoss, Caressing, Starine, and Storm Flag Flying.

Valenzuela, Patrick, 1962-. Jockey. Rode Sunday Silence to win 1989 Kentucky Derby (G1) and Preakness Stakes (G1). Winner of seven Breeders' Cup races. Youngest rider ever to win Santa Anita Derby (G1), with Codex in 1980. First jockey to sweep five major California meet titles, 2003. Career interrupted repeatedly by alcohol and drug abuse.

Walsh, Thomas 1940-. Jockey. Leading American steeplechase rider in 1960 and '66; fifth-ranked all-time American steeplechase jockey with 253 victories. Regular rider of champions Barnabys Bluff, Bon Nouvel, and Mako. Won American Grand National six times, five years in succession, 1959-'63. Inducted into Racing Hall of Fame in 2005.

Ward, John T. Jr., 1945-. Trainer. Owner of Sugar Grove Farm, Kentucky; John T. Ward Stables, Kentucky. Trained Monarchos, Beautiful Pleasure, Darling My Darling, Jambalaya Jazz, Pyramid Peak. Nephew of Racing Hall of Fame trainer Sherrill Ward.

Waterman, Scot, D.V.M., 1966-. Veterinarian, industry executive. Executive director, Racing Medication and Testing Consortium. Recipient of North American Pari-Mutuel Regulators Association's Winner's Circle Award, 2004. Thoroughbred owner and breeder.

Watters Jr., Sidney 1917-. Trainer. Champion steeplechase trainer in 1951, '56, '61, and '63, co-leader by wins in '48 and '71. Leading steeplechase trainer by earnings in 1956, '63, and '71. Trained champions Amber Diver and Shadow Brook. On flat, trained 1970 champion two-year-old male Hoist the Flag and '83 three-year-old male Slew o' Gold. Inducted into Racing Hall of Fame as a steeplechase trainer in 2005.

Weber, Charlotte, 1942-. Investments. Member of Jockey Club. Owner of Live Oak Stud, Florida. Bred and owned Peaceful Union, Gnome Home, Medieval Man, Laser Light, Sultry Song, High Fly, Sultry Sun.

Weisbord, Barry, 1950-. Publisher. Joe Palmer Award in 1992. Co-owned Safely Kept. Created the American Championship Racing Series in 1991; created the Matchmaker Breeders' Exchange, the first centralized market for stallion seasons and shares.

West, R. Smiser. Dentist, breeder. Owner of Waterford Farm, Kentucky. Co-breeder of Lite Light, De La Rose, Chilukki.

Whiteley, Frank Jr., 1915-. Trainer. Inducted into Racing Hall of Fame in 1978. Trained 35 stakes winners and four champions, including Damascus, Forego, Ruffian, Tom Rolfe.

Whitney, Marylou, 1926-. Investments. Owner of Whitney Farm, Kentucky; Blue Goose Stable, Kentucky. Bred and owned Silver Buck, Bird Town, Birdstone. Long known for her Derby Eve parties and for her parties in Saratoga Springs, New York. Widow of C. V. Whitney; married to John Hendrickson.

Willmot, David, 1950-. Breeder, investments. President, Woodbine Entertainment Group, formerly Ontario Jockey Club. Owner of Kinghaven Farms, Canada. John W. Galbreath Award in 2001; Sovereign Award in 1998. Bred and owned Talkin Man, Poetically, Alywow, Play the King, Summer Mood, With Approval. Successfully lobbied for legislation to add slot machines at Woodbine racetrack; Kinghaven became the first Canadian stable to earn more than $2-million, in 1986. Son of Donald Willmot.

Wolfson, Louis, 1912-. and **Wolfson, Patrice.** Investments. Owner of Harbor View Farm, Florida. Leading breeder in 1970-'71. Bred and owned Affirmed, Flawlessly, Exclusive Native, It's In the Air, Outstandingly. Owned Raise a Native. Bred and raced two-time Horse of the Year Affirmed, winner of the Triple Crown in 1978. Bred and owned Racing Hall of Fame Flawlessly. Patrice Wolfson is daughter of Racing Hall of Fame trainer Hirsch Jacobs.

Wygod, Martin, 1940-. Executive, owner-breeder. Chairman and chief executive of WebMD. Sold his Medco Containment Services Inc. to Merck & Co. for $6.5-billion in 1994. Owns River Edge Farm and 102-acre property in Rancho Santa Fe, both in California. Member of the Jockey Club. With wife, Pam, bred and owned champion Sweet Catomine.

Ycaza, Manuel, 1938-. Jockey. Inducted into Racing Hall of Fame in 1977. Rode 2,367 winners, including Ack Ack, Dr. Fager, Damascus, Sword Dancer, Gamely, Dark Mirage, Never Bend. Won first New York filly triple crown with Dark Mirage in 1968.

Yoshida, Teruya, 1947-. Breeder. Owner, president of Shadai Farm, founded by his late father, Zenya Yoshida. With brothers Haruya and Katsumi, owns Shadai Stallion Station, home to Japan's leading sire in 20 of the last 21 years, including ten-time leader Northern Taste and eight-time leader Sunday Silence. Vice chairman of the Japanese Racing Horse Association.

Zilber, Maurice, 1926-. Trainer. Ten times leading trainer during the 1950s in his native Egypt; leading trainer in France. Trained Racing Hall of Fame members Dahlia and Exceller, and Trillion, Youth, Argument (Fr), Hippodamia.

Zito, Nick, 1948-. Trainer. Elected to Racing Hall of Fame in 2005. Trained Kentucky Derby (G1) winners Go for Gin (1994) and Strike the Gold ('91), Preakness Stakes (G1) winner Louis Quatorze, Belmont Stakes (G1) winner Birdstone, plus A P Valentine, Thirty Six Red, Bird Town.

Industry Awards

Eric Beitia Memorial Award

Awarded annually by the New York Racing Association to the leading apprentice jockey at the NYRA tracks. Named for the leading apprentice of 1980 who died November 28, 1983, at age 21 of a gunshot wound a week earlier.

2004	Pablo Fragoso
2003	Pablo Fragoso
2002	Lorenzo Lezcano
2001	Lorenzo Lezcano
2000	Norberto Arroyo Jr.
1999	Ariel Smith
1998	Shaun Bridgmohan
1997	Phil Teator
1996	Jose Trejo
1995	Ramon Perez
1994	Dale Beckner
1993	Caesar Bisono
1992	Gerry Brocklebank
1991	Rafael Mojica Jr.
1990	Paul Toscano
1989	Jose Martinez
1988	Brian Peck
1987	David Nuesch
1986	David Nuesch, Edward Thomas Baird
1985	Wesley Ward
1984	Wesley Ward
1983	Declan Murphy

Big Sport of Turfdom Award

Sponsored by the Turf Publicists of America and awarded to the individual or individuals whose cooperation with the media enhances coverage and brings favorable attention to Thoroughbred racing.

2004	John Servis
2003	Sackatoga Stable
2002	Ken and Sue McPeek
2001	Laura Hillenbrand
2000	Laffit Pincay Jr.
1999	D. Wayne Lukas
1998	Mike Pegram
1997	Bob Baffert
1996	Cigar, Allen Paulson, Bill Mott, Jerry Bailey
1995	Robert and Beverly Lewis
1994	Warren "Jimmy" Croll Jr.
1993	Chris McCarron
1992	Angel Cordero Jr.
1991	Hammer and Oaktown Stable
1990	Carl Nafzger
1989	Tim Conway
1988	Julie Krone
1987	Jack Van Berg
1986	Jim McKay
1985	Laffit Pincay Jr.
1984	John Henry
1983	Joe Hirsch
1982	Woody Stephens
1981	John Forsythe
1980	Jack Klugman
1979	Laz Barrera
1978	Ron Turcotte
1977	Steve Cauthen

1976	Telly Savalas
1975	Francis P. Dunne
1974	Eddie Arcaro
1973	Penny Chenery
1972	John Galbreath
1971	Burt Bacharach
1970	Saul Rosen
1969	Bill Shoemaker
1968	John Nerud
1967	Allaire duPont
1966	E. P. Taylor

F. Ambrose Clark Award

Presented periodically by the National Steeplechase Association to those who promote, improve, or encourage steeplechase racing. Named for a renowned steeplechase owner.

2004	Stephen P. Groat
2002	George A. Sloan
2001	John A. Wayt Jr.
1995	John T. von Stade
1991	Beverly Steinman
1988	William L. Pape
1982	Mrs. Miles Valentine
1980	Charles Fenwick Jr.
1979	George Strawbridge Jr.
1978	Morris H. Dixon
1977	Alfred M. Hunt
1976	Joseph Aitcheson Jr.
1975	Michael Walsh
1974	John Cooper
1973	W. Burling Cocks
1972	Russell M. Arundel
1971	Raymond G. Woolfe
1970	Raymond R. Guest
1969	Mrs. Odgen Phipps
1968	John W. Hanes
1967	S. Bryce Wing
1966	Crompton Smith Jr.
1965	Marion duPont Scott

Coman Humanitarian Award

Presented by Kentucky Thoroughbred Owners and Breeders for contributions to better human relations in the Thoroughbred industry. Named for KTOB Executive Director William C. Coman. No longer awarded.

2002	Alice Chandler
2001	Sheikh Mohammed bin Rashid al Maktoum
2000	Benjamin Roach, M.D.
1999	J. David Richardson, M.D.
1998	Gary Biszantz
1997	Dr. John T. Bryans
1996	Larry Weber
1994	Paul Mellon
1993	John A. Bell III
1992	Charles Nuckols Jr.
1991	William T. Young
1990	Carl Icahn
1989	Tim Conway
1988	Jim and Linda Ryan
1987	Jay Spurrier
1986	James E. "Ted" Bassett III
1985	Drs. Charles Hagyard, Arthur Davidson,

and William McGee
1984 Keene Daingerfield
1983 Brownell Combs
Maxwell Gluck

Dogwood Dominion Award

Sponsored by Dogwood Stable and presented to the "unsung heroes" of racing, especially in the backstretch areas. Named for Dominion (GB), Dogwood's first graded stakes winner who raced from 1974 to '78.

2004 Pam Berg
2003 Neftali "Junior" Gutierrez
2002 Jim Greene and Shirley Edwards
2001 Julian "Buck" Wheat
2000 Katherine Todd Smith
1999 Danny Perlsweig
1998 Donald "Peanut Butter" Brown
1997 Nick Caras
1996 Grace Belcuore
1995 Peggy Sprinkles
1994 Howard "Gelo" Hall
1993 H. W. "Salty" Roberts

Charles W. Engelhard Award

Presented by Kentucky Thoroughbred Owners and Breeders for outstanding media coverage of the Thoroughbred industry.

2004 *Seabiscuit*
2003 Ercel Ellis Jr.
2002 Television Games Network
2001 John Henderson ("Thoroughbred Week")
2000 Ray Paulick (*The Blood-Horse*)
1999 Maryjean Wall (Lexington *Herald-Leader*)
1998 David Heckerman (*The Blood-Horse*)
1997 Jim Bolus
1996 Kenny Rice (WTVQ-TV)
1994 Jay Hovdey (*The Blood-Horse*)
John Asher (WHAS Radio)
1993 Jennie Rees (Louisville *Courier-Journal*)
1992 Josh Pons (*Country Life Diary*)
1991 Cawood Ledford
1990 Jim McKay (ABC)
1989 Lewis Owens (Lexington *Herald-Leader*)
1988 Anheuser-Busch
1987 Jim Wilburn and Chris Lincoln
(Winner Communications)
1986 Leon Rasmussen (*Daily Racing Form*)
1985 Dick Enberg (NBC)
1984 NBC Sports
1983 Cawood Ledford
1982 Tom Hammond
1981 *The Thoroughbred Record*
1980 Billy Reed (Louisville *Courier-Journal*)
1979 Logan Bailey (*Daily Racing Form*)
1978 Kent Hollingsworth (*The Blood-Horse*)
1977 Jim McKay (ABC)
1976 Heywood Hale Broun (CBS)
1975 Robert Wussler (CBS)
1974 Joe Hirsch (*Daily Racing Form*)
1973 Jack Whitaker (CBS)
1972 Hugh "Mickey" McGuire
(*Daily Racing Form*)
1971 Red Smith (New York *Times*)
1970 Win Elliott (CBS Radio)

John W. Galbreath Award

Sponsored by the University of Louisville's Equine Industry Program, the award named for the Darby Dan Farm owner honors equine-industry entrepreneurs.

2004 Judith Forbis
2003 Frank "Scoop" Vessels
2002 William S. Morris III
2001 David Willmot
2000 Denny Gentry
1999 Tom Meeker
1998 D. Wayne Lukas
1997 John M. Lyons
1996 B. Thomas Joy
1995 Robert Clay
1994 Ami Shinitzky
1993 John Gaines
1992 W. Cothran "Cot" Campbell
1991 James E. "Ted" Bassett III
1990 John A. Bell III

Avelino Gomez Memorial Award

Sponsored by Woodbine, the award named for jockey Avelino "El Perfecto" Gomez is presented to the Canadian-born, -raised, or -based jockey who has made a significant contribution to Thoroughbred racing. North America's leading rider in 1966, Gomez died of injuries incurred in a three-horse spill in the Canadian Oaks on June 21, 1980.

2005 Sam Krasner
2004 Francine Villeneuve
2003 Robert Landry
2002 Richard Dos Ramos
2001 Chris Loseth
2000 Jim McKnight
1999 David Clark
1998 Irwin Driedger
1997 Richard Grubb
1996 David Gall
1995 Don Seymour
1994 Not awarded
1993 Larry Attard
1992 Robin Platts
1991 Hugo Dittfach
1990 Lloyd Duffy
1989 Jeff Fell
1988 Chris Rogers
1987 Don MacBeth
1986 Sandy Hawley
1985 John Longden
1984 Ron Turcotte

John K. Goodman Alumni Award

University of Arizona Race Track Industry Program award for a program graduate who has achieved distinction in the racing industry. Named for one of the program's founders.

2004 Phil O'Hara
2003 Patricia McQueen
2002 Todd Pletcher
2001 Luke Kruytbosch
2000 Ann McGovern
1999 Lonny Powell
1998 Dan Fick
1997 Bob Baffert

Walter Haight Award

Presented by the National Turf Writers Association for excellence in Turf writing. Named for Washington Post racing columnist and handicapper known for his humorous style.

2004	Steve Haskin
2003	Russ Harris
2002	Billy Reed
2001	Gary West (Dallas *Morning News*)
2000	Bill Christine (Los Angeles *Times*)
1999	Jennie Rees (Louisville *Courier-Journal*)
1998	Andrew Beyer (Washington *Post*)
1997	Jim Bolus
1996	Ed Schuyler Jr. (Associated Press)
1995	Jay Hovdey
1994	Ed Bowen
1993	Jack Mann (New York *Herald-Tribune*)
1992	Mike Barry (*Kentucky Irish American* and The Louisville *Times*) Bill Nack (*Sports Illustrated*)
1991	Bob Harding (Newark *Star-Ledger*)
1990	Kent Hollingsworth (*The Blood-Horse*)
1989	William Leggett (Thoroughbred Times)
1988	Leon Rasmussen (*Daily Racing Form*)
1987	Si Burick (Dayton *Daily News*)
1986	Ed Comerford (*Newsday*)
1985	Sam McCracken (Boston *Globe*)
1984	Joe Hirsch (*Daily Racing Form*)
1983	Fred Russell (Nashville *Banner*)
1982	Joe Agrella (Chicago *Sun-Times*)
1981	Bill Robertson (*The Thoroughbred Record*)
1980	Joe Nichols (New York *Times*)
1979	Barney Nagler (*Daily Racing Form*)
1978	Nelson Fisher (San Diego *Union*)
1977	Red Smith (New York *Times*)
1976	Saul Rosen (*Daily Racing Form*)
1975	Don Fair (*Daily Racing Form*)
1974	Raleigh Burroughs (*Turf and Sport Digest*)
1973	George Ryall (*The New Yorker*)
1972	Jimmy Doyle (Cleveland *Plain Dealer*)

Hardboot Award

Sponsored by Kentucky Thoroughbred Owners and Breeders.

2004	Diane Perkins
2003	Henry White
2002	Charles Nuckols Jr. Virginia Kraft Payson
2001	Robert Courtney Sr.
2000	Carlos Perez
1999	Dr. and Mrs. R. Smiser West Mr. and Mrs. MacKenzie Miller

Joe Hirsch Breeders' Cup Newspaper Writing Award

Sponsored by Breeders' Cup Ltd. and the National Thoroughbred Racing Association, the award named for the longtime Daily Racing Form columnist honors excellence in newspaper coverage of the previous year's Breeders' Cup World Thoroughbred Championships.

2004	Jay Privman
2003	Pat Forde
2002	Jay Privman

2001	Pat Forde
2000	Robert Edmondson
1999	Dick Jerardi
1998	Jennie Rees
1997	Pat Forde
1996	Dick Jerardi
1995	Jay Posner

Jockey Club Medal of Honor

Awarded periodically by the Jockey Club for meritorious service to the Thoroughbred industry.

1998	Nick Nicholson and Alan Marzelli
1994	Larry Bramlage, D.V.M.
1993	Kenny Noe Jr.
1992	R. Richards Rolapp
1991	Dr. Manuel Gilman
1990	Dr. Charles Randall
1989	Joe Hirsch
1988	Dennis Swanson
1987	Jack Van Berg
1986	Richard Duchossois
1985	Jean Romanet
1984	D. G. Van Clief Jr.

Lavin Cup

Sponsored by the American Association of Equine Practitioners and awarded to a nonveterinary individual or organization that has demonstrated exceptional compassion for horses or has developed and enforced guidelines for horses' welfare. Named for Kentucky veterinarian A. Gary Lavin, AAEP president in 1994.

2004	Herb and Ellen Moelis
2003	Professional Rodeo Cowboys Association
2002	Dayton O. Hyde
1999	Tom Dorrance
1998	Thoroughbred Retirement Foundation
1997	American Quarter Horse Association
1996	California Horse Racing Board

Bill Leggett Breeders' Cup Magazine Writing Award

Sponsored by Breeders' Cup Ltd. and the National Thoroughbred Racing Association, award named for the late Sports Illustrated and Thoroughbred Times writer honors excellence in magazine coverage of the previous year's Breeders' Cup World Thoroughbred Championships.

2004	Michele MacDonald
2003	Billy Reed
2002	Billy Reed
2001	Tom Law
2000	Bill Heller
1999	Tom LaMarra
1998	Robbie Henwood
1997	Glenye Cain
1996	Jay Hovdey
1994	Jay Hovdey

William H. May Award

Awarded by Association of Racing Commissioners International for distinguished service to racing. Named for a former president of National Association of State Racing Commissioners.

2005	Lonny Powell
2004	Race Track Chaplaincy of America
2003	American Association of Equine Practitioners
2002	American Quarter Horse Association
2001	John R. Gaines
2000	R. D. Hubbard
1999	Bob and Beverly Lewis
1998	Fred Noe
1997	James E. "Ted" Bassett III
1996	Allen Paulson
1995	Paul Mellon
1994	Joe Hirsch
1993	Tony Chamblin
1992	Bill Shoemaker
1991	Jockey Club
1990	James P. Ryan
1989	Stanley Bergstein
1988	*Daily Racing Form*
1987	Breeders' Cup Ltd.
1986	Robert H. Strub

Mr. Fitz Award

Sponsored by National Turf Writers Association, award named for Racing Hall of Fame trainer James E. "Sunny Jim" Fitzsimmons honors individuals who typify the spirit of horse racing.

2004	Patti Cooksey
2003	Sackatoga Stable
2002	Chris McCarron
2001	H. Allen Jerkens
2000	Pat Day
1999	Bob and Beverly Lewis
1998	Joe Hirsch
1997	Bob Baffert
1996	MacKenzie Miller
1995	Warren "Jimmy" Croll
1994	Jeff Lukas
1993	Angel Cordero Jr.
1992	Ron McAnally
1991	Frances Genter
1990	Arthur B. Hancock III
1989	Ogden Phipps
1988	Jack Van Berg
1987	Laffit Pincay Jr.
1986	Arlington Park management
1985	John Henry
1984	Penny Chenery
1983	Fred Hooper
1982	Bill Shoemaker, Woody Stephens
1981	Jack Klugman

Isaac Murphy Award

Named for 19th-century black jockey who won with 44% of his career mounts, National Turf Writers Association award honors jockey with highest winning percentage for the year.

2004	Ramon Dominguez
1995-2003	Russell Baze

Jerry Frutkoff Preakness Photography Award

Sponsored by Pimlico Race Course and Nikon, for best Preakness Stakes (G1) photo from previous year.

Renamed for longtime Maryland Jockey Club photographer who died in 2003.

2005	Gary Hershorn (Reuters)
2004	Jeff Snyder (*The Blood-Horse*)
2003	Skip Dickstein (*The Blood-Horse*)
2002	Molly Riley (Reuters)

Old Hilltop Award

Presented by Pimlico Race Course for distinction in Thoroughbred racing reporting. Name derives from Pimlico's nickname.

2005	Jay Privman (*Daily Racing Form*)
	Scott Garceau (WMAR-TV)
2004	Gary West (Dallas *Morning News*)
	Bruce Cunningham (*WBFF-TV*)
2003	John Patti (WBAL-AM)
	Steve Haskin (*The Blood-Horse*)
2002	Stan Charles (Baltimore radio)
	Michele MacDonald (THOROUGHBRED TIMES)
2001	Keith Mills (WMAR-TV)
	Jennie Rees (Louisville *Courier-Journal*)
2000	Marty Bass (WJZ-TV)
	Joe Kelly (Turf historian)
1999	Harry Kakel (WMAR-TV)
	Pohla Smith (Pittsburgh *Post-Gazette*)
1998	Ed Kiernan (WBAL Radio)
	Vinnie Perrone (*Maryland Turf Writers*)
1997	Reid Cherner (*USA Today*)
	Chris Lincoln (ESPN)
1996	Dan Farley (*Racing Post*)
	George Michael (WRC-TV)
1995	Charlsie Cantey (ABC Sports)
	Neil Milbert (Chicago *Tribune*)
1994	Ed Schuyler Jr. (*Associated Press*)
	Jim West (WBAL Radio)
1993	Jim Bolus (free-lance journalist)
	John Buren (WJZ TV)
1992	Dave Johnson (ABC Sports)
	Maryjean Wall (Lexington *Herald-Leader*)
1991	Sam Lacy (Baltimore *Afro-American*)
	Demmie Stathopolos (*Sports Illustrated*)
1990	Bill Tanton (Baltimore *Evening Sun*)
	Shelby Whitfield (ABC Radio)
1989	Bill Christine (Los Angeles *Times*)
	John Steadman (Baltimore *Evening Sun*)
1988	Ed Bowen (*The Blood-Horse*)
	Bill Nack (*Sports Illustrated*)
1987	Jack Dawson (WMAR-TV)
	Dave Feldman (Chicago *Sun-Times*)
1986	Vince Bagli (WBAL-TV)
	Shirley Povich (Washington *Post*)
1985	Howard Cosell (ABC Sports)
	Sam McCracken (Boston *Globe*)
1984	Jim McKay (ABC Sports)
	Billy Reed (Louisville *Courier-Journal*)
1983	Jack Whitaker (ABC Sports)
	Dale Austin (Baltimore *Sun*)
1982	Russ Harris (New York *Daily News*)
	Kent Hollingsworth (*The Blood-Horse*)
1981	William Leggett (*Sports Illustrated*)
	Jack Mann (Baltimore *Evening Sun*)
1980	Edwin Pope (Miami *Herald*)
	Snowden Carter (*Maryland Horse*)
1979	Whitney Tower (*Sports Illustrated*)
	Joe Kelly (Washington *Star*)

1979	William C. Phillips (*Daily Racing Form*)
1978	Win Elliott (CBS)
	Joe Hirsch (*Daily Racing Form*)
	Bob Maisel (Baltimore *Sun*)
1977	William Boniface (Baltimore *Sun*)
	Barney Nagler (*Daily Racing Form*)
	Charles Lamb (*News American*)
1976	Red Smith (New York *Times*)
	Raoul Carlisle (Arkansas *Times Herald*)

Joe Palmer Award

National Turf Writers Association Award for meritorious service to racing. Named for New York Herald-Tribune Turf writer known for his overall appreciation of the sport.

2004	Noble Threewitt
2003	Laffit Pincay Jr.
2002	Richard Duchossois, Eugene Melnyk
2001	Shirley Day Smith
2000	Jim McKay
1999	Kent Hollingsworth
1998	Sandy Hawley
1997	Jim Bolus
1996	Allen Paulson
1995	Mark Kaufman
1994	Joe Hirsch
1993	Henryk de Kwiatkowski
1992	Barry Weisbord
1991	Joe Burnham
1990	James P. Ryan
1989	Claude "Shug" McGaughey III
1988	Charlie Whittingham
1987	Alfred Vanderbilt
1986	James E. "Ted" Bassett III
1985	John Gaines
1984	E. P. Taylor
1983	David "Sonny" Werblin
1982	Frank "Jimmy" Kilroe
1981	Keene Daingerfield, Marion duPont Scott
1980	Chick Lang Sr., Leo O'Donnell
1979	Laz Barrera
1978	Steve Cauthen
1977	Nelson Bunker Hunt
1976	Fred Hooper
1975	I. J. Collins
1974	Secretariat
1973	John Galbreath
1972	Paul Mellon
1971	Bill Shoemaker
1970	Warner Jones Jr.
1969	Raymond Guest
1968	Marion Van Berg
1967	John Longden
1966	Marshall Cassidy
1965	John Schapiro
1964	Wathen Knebelkamp

Joan F. Pew Award

Sponsored by the Association of Racing Commissioners International and awarded to racing commissioner who demonstrates vision and vitality. Named for first woman member of Pennsylvania Horse Racing Commission and first woman president of National Association of State Racing Commissioners.

2005	Lynda Tanaka
2004	Cecil Alexander
2003	Norman I. Barron
2002	Stan Sadinsky
2001	Basil Plasteras
2000	Timothy "Ted" Connors
1999	Robin Traywick Williams
1998	Jon McKinnie
1997	Arthur Khoury
1996	Not awarded
1995	Not awarded
1994	Gil Moutray
1993	Joe Neglia
1992	Joanne McAdam
1991	Dr. Glenn Blodgett
1990	Frank Drea
1989	Richard Corbisiero Jr.
1988	Dr. James Smith
1987	Eric Braun

Red Smith Award

Churchill Downs award for outstanding print coverage of the Kentucky Derby (G1) in four categories. Named for late New York Times columnist.

Feature Story

2004	C. Ray Hall (Louisville *Courier-Journal*)
2003	Mike Kane ([Schenectady] *Daily Gazette*)
2002	Jennie Rees (Louisville *Courier-Journal*)
2001	Bill Christine (Los Angeles *Times*)
2000	Jerry Izenberg (Newark *Star-Ledger*)
1999	Jay Privman (*Daily Racing Form*)
1998	Matt Graves (Albany *Times Union*)
1997	Jennie Rees (Louisville *Courier-Journal*)
1996	Dave Koerner
	(Louisville *Courier-Journal*)
1995	Bob Fortus (New Orleans *Times-Picayune*)
1994	Rick Bozich (Louisville *Courier-Journal*)
1993	Rick Bozich (Louisville *Courier-Journal*)
1992	Tom Archdeacon (Dayton *Daily News*)
1991	Dave Koerner (Louisville *Courier-Journal*)
1990	Jim Wells (St. Paul *Pioneer-Press*)
1989	Steve Crist (New York *Times*)
1988	Bill Christine (Los Angeles *Times*)
1987	Hubert Mizell (St. Petersburg *Times*)
1986	Bill Christine (Los Angeles *Times*)
1985	Dick Fenlon (Columbus *Dispatch*)
1984	Stan Hochman (Philadelphia *Daily News*)
1983	Jim Bolus (Louisville *Times*)

Advance Story

2004	Richard Rosenblatt (Associated Press)
2003	Rick Bozich (Louisville *Courier-Journal*)
2002	Rick Bozich (Louisville *Courier-Journal*)
2001	Mike Kane ([Schenectady] *Daily Gazette*)
2000	Rick Bozich (Louisville *Courier-Journal*)
1999	Rick Bozich (Louisville *Courier-Journal*)
1998	Vic Ziegel (New York *Daily News*)
1997	Matt Graves (Albany *Times Union*)
1996	Steve Haskin (*Daily Racing Form*)
1995	Blackie Sherrod (Dallas *Morning News*)
1994	Billy Reed (Lexington *Herald-Leader*)
1993	Rick Bozich (Louisville *Courier-Journal*)
1992	Vic Ziegel (New York *Daily News*)
1991	Steve Woodward (*USA Today*)
1990	Jerry Izenberg (New York *Post*)

1989	Rick Bozich (Louisville *Courier-Journal*)
1988	Billy Reed (Lexington *Herald-Leader*)
1987	Billy Reed (Lexington *Herald-Leader*)
1986	Bob Harding (Newark *Star-Ledger*)
1985	Jack Patterson (Akron *Beacon-Journal*)
1984	Bill Christine (Los Angeles *Times*)
1983	Peter Finney
	(New Orleans *Times-Picayune*)

Sunday Wrap-Up

2004	Pat Forde (Louisville *Courier-Journal*)
2003	Richard Rosenblatt (*Associated Press*)
2002	Mike Kane ([Schenectady] *Daily Gazette*)
2001	Jennie Rees (Louisville *Courier-Journal*)
2000	Mike Kane ([Schenectady] *Daily Gazette*)
1999	Mike Kane ([Schenectady] *Daily Gazette*)
1998	Jay Privman (New York *Times*)
1997	Jay Privman (New York *Times*)
1996	Billy Reed (Lexington *Herald-Leader*)
1995	Chuck Culpepper
	(Lexington *Herald-Leader*)
1994	Tom Archdeacon (Dayton *Daily News*)
1993	Jennie Rees (Louisville *Courier-Journal*)
1992	Bill Christine (Los Angeles *Times*)
1991	Tom Archdeacon (Dayton *Daily News*)
1990	Billy Reed (Lexington *Herald-Leader*)
1989	Jay Privman (Los Angeles *Daily News*)
1988	Jay Privman (Los Angeles *Daily News*)
1987	Bill Christine (Los Angeles *Times*)
1986	Paul Moran ([Long Island] *Newsday*)
1985	Tom McEwen (Tampa *Tribune*)
1984	Billy Reed (Louisville *Courier-Journal*)
1983	Billy Reed (Louisville *Courier-Journal*)

Monday Wrap-Up

2004	Steve Haskin (*The Blood-Horse*)
2003	Tom Law (Thoroughbred Times)
2002	Lew Freedman (Chicago *Tribune*)
2001	John Harrell (Thoroughbred Times)
2000	Steve Haskin (*The Blood-Horse*)
1999	Steve Haskin (*The Blood-Horse*)
1998	Bill Nack (*Sports Illustrated*)
1997	Dick Jerardi (Philadelphia *Daily News*)
1996	Greg Boeck (*USA Today*)
1995	Bill Nack (*Sports Illustrated*)
1994	Chuck Culpepper
	(Lexington *Herald-Leader*)
1993	Jack Murray (Cincinnati *Enquirer*)
1992	Harry King (*Associated Press*)
1991	Dick Jerardi (Philadelphia *Daily News*)
1990	Rick Bozich (Louisville *Courier-Journal*)
1989	Tom Cushman (San Diego *Tribune*)
1988	Stan Hochman (Philadelphia *Daily News*)
1987	Dick Jerardi (Philadelphia *Daily News*)
1986	Stan Hochman (Philadelphia *Daily News*)
	Edwin Pope (Miami *Herald*)
1985	Stan Hochman (Philadelphia *Daily News*)
1984	Dave Anderson (New York *Times*)
1983	Tom Jackson (Washington *Times*)

UTTA Outstanding Trainer of the Year Award

No longer awarded.

2001	John T. Ward Jr.
2000	Bobby Frankel
1999	D. Wayne Lukas
1998	Bob Baffert
1997	Pat Byrne
1996	Hubert "Sonny" Hine
1995	Bill Mott
1994	Warren "Jimmy" Croll Jr.
1993	Claude R. "Shug" McGaughey III
1992	H. Allen Jerkens
1991	Frank Brothers

Clay Puett Award

Sponsored by the University of Arizona Race Track Industry Program, for long-term, multifaceted, or far-reaching contributions to the racing industry. Named for creator of modern starting gate.

2004	Trudy McCaffery
2003	W. Cothran "Cot" Campbell
2002	John and Betty Mabee and family
2001	Joe Hirsch
2000	John Gaines
1999	Vessels family
1998	Brady family
1997	Hancock family
1996	Phipps family
1995	Allen Paulson
1994	Clement Hirsch

University of Arizona Race Track Industry Program Distinguished Service Award

2004	Not awarded
2003	Fred Stone
2001	Bob Benoit
2000	Stan Bergstein
1999	*Daily Racing Form*
1998	Sherwood Chillingworth
1997	Bennett Liebman
	Ronald Sultemeier
1996	Joe Harper
1995	Lonny Powell
1994	Rukin Jelks
1993	John Goodman
	Dr. Darrel Metcalfe
	Vessels family
1992	Dan Fick

University of Arizona Race Track Industry Program Distinguished Senior Award

2004	Jon Hansen
2003	Heather Meacham
2002	Stacia Mumm
2001	Laura Plato
2000	Scot Waterman
1999	Sable Downs
1998	Mike Hummel
1997	Valora Kilby

Alfred Gwynne Vanderbilt Award

New York Turf Writers Association award for individual or group that did the most for racing. Named for owner-breeder of Native Dancer; formerly known as the John A. Morris Award.

2003	Joe Hirsch
2002	Hans Stahl
2001	Barry K. Schwartz
2000	Kenny Noe Jr.
1999	Alfred Gwynne Vanderbilt
1998	Carolyn and Hubert "Sonny" Hine
1997	Skip Away
1996	James "Ted" Bassett
1995	Cigar
1994	Holy Bull
1993	Paul Mellon
1992	Allen Gutterman
1991	Barry Weisbord,
	American Championship Racing Series
1989	John Gaines
	Whitney Tower
1988	Linda and Jim Ryan
1987	David "Sonny" Werblin
1986	ESPN/Thoroughbred Sports Television
1985	Peter Fuller
	John Galbreath
	Fred Hooper
1984	John Nerud
1983	Allaire duPont
1982	Helen "Penny" Chenery
	Frank "Jimmy" Kilroe
1981	Sam Rubin
1980	Jack Klugman
1979	Louis and Patrice Wolfson
1978	Affirmed
	Alydar
1977	Ogden Mills Phipps
1976	Marion duPont Scott
1975	Eddie Arcaro
	Johnny Longden
	Warren Mehrtens
	William "Smokey" Saunders
	Ron Turcotte
	Jack Dreyfus Jr.
1974	Martha F. Gerry
1973	Secretariat
1972	John H. "Jack" Krumpe
	Arthur B. "Bull" Hancock Jr.
1971	Jacques D. Wimpfheimer
1970	Charles W. Engelhard
	Sen. Thomas Morton
1969	Raymond Guest
1968	John W. Hanes
1967	Robert J. Kleberg Jr.
1966	Jack Dreyfus
1965	James Cox Brady
1964	Allaire duPont
1963	Alfred Gwynne Vanderbilt
1962	Capt. Harry F. Guggenheim
1961	Francis Dunne
1960	Capt. Harry F. Guggenheim
1959	John W. Hanes
1958	Marshall Cassidy
1957	C. V. Whitney
1956	George Widener

1953	Walter Jeffords
1952	C. V. Whitney
1951	John Hay Whitney
1950	Saratoga Association
1949	Marshall Cassidy
	George Widener
1948	Lou Smith
1947	Dr. Charles H. Strub
1946	John Blanks Campbell
1944	Harry Parr III
1943	Lincoln Plaut
1942	Herbert Bayard Swope
1941	Alfred Gwynne Vanderbilt
1940	Herbert Bayard Swope
1939	George H. Bull
1938	Alfred Gwynne Vanderbilt
1937	Mrs. Payne Whitney
1936	Alfred Gwynne Vanderbilt

P.A.B. Widener II Trophy

Sponsored by Kentucky Thoroughbred Owners and Breeders and presented to breeder whose Kentucky-bred horses have performed the best based on a point system. Named for owner-breeder who raced under Elmendorf Farm.

2004	Aaron and Marie Jones
2003	Juddmonte Farms
2002	Allen Paulson
2001	Juddmonte Farms
2000	Adena Springs
1999	Overbrook Farm
1998	Mr. and Mrs. John C. Mabee
1997	Juddmonte Farms
1996	Juddmonte Farms
1995	Juddmonte Farms
1994	Overbrook Farm
1993	Juddmonte Farms
1992	William S. Farish and partners
1991	Verne Winchell
1990	Calumet Farm
1989	Ogden Phipps
1988	Ogden Phipps
1987	Nelson Bunker Hunt
1986	Nelson Bunker Hunt
1985	Nelson Bunker Hunt
1984	Hancock family
1983	Hancock family
1982	Fred Hooper
1981	Verna Lehmann
1980	Verna Lehmann
1979	Hancock family
1978	Randolph Weinsier
1977	Ben Castleman
1976	Ogden Mills Phipps
1975	Hancock family
1974	John Galbreath
1973	Maxwell H. Gluck
1972	Leslie Combs

David F. Woods Memorial Award

Presented by Pimlico Race Course for best Preakness Stakes (G1) story from previous year. Named for longtime racetrack publicist and Baltimore *Evening Sun* columnist.

2005	Dick Jerardi (Philadelphia *Daily News*)
2004	Sean Clancy (*Mid-Atlantic Thoroughbred*)
2003	Bill Finley (New York *Times*)
2002	Jay Privman (*Daily Racing Form*)
2001	Tom LaMarra (*The Blood-Horse*)
2000	Rick Snider (Washington *Times*)
1999	Bill Mooney (*The Backstretch*)
1998	Jay Hovdey (*Daily Racing Form*)
1997	Jay Hovdey (*Daily Racing Form*)
1996	Steve Haskin (*Daily Racing Form*)
1995	Bill Finley (New York *Daily News*)
1994	Jay Posner (San Diego *Union-Tribune*)
1993	Bill Mooney (*The Blood-Horse*)
1992	Jay Hovdey (*The Blood-Horse*)
1991	Bill Christine (Los Angeles *Times*)
1990	Bill Christine (Los Angeles *Times*)
1989	Larry Bortstein
	(Orange County *Register*)
1988	Don Clippinger
	(*The Thoroughbred Record*)
	Bob Roberts (Cleveland *Plain Dealer*)
1987	Billy Reed (Lexington *Herald-Leader*)
1986	Dave Kindred
	(Atlanta *Constitution-Journal*)
1985	George Vecsey (New York *Times*)
1984	Jack Murphy (Cincinnati *Enquirer*)
1983	John Schulian (Chicago *Sun-Times*)
1982	Billy Reed (Louisville *Courier-Journal*)

George Woolf Memorial
Jockey Award

Sponsored by Santa Anita Park and awarded to jockey whose career and character earn esteem for themselves and Thoroughbred racing, based on a vote of their fellow jockeys. Named for Racing Hall of Fame jockey George "Iceman" Woolf, who died January 4, 1946, a day after incurring severe head injuries in a spill at Santa Anita.

2005	Ray Sibille
2004	Robby Albarado
2003	Edgar Prado
2002	Russell Baze
2001	Dean Kutz
2000	Mike Smith
1999	Jose Santos
1998	Craig Perret
1997	Alex Solis
1996	Gary Stevens
1995	Eddie Maple
1994	Phil Grove
1993	Kent Desormeaux
1992	Jerry Bailey
1991	Earlie Fires
1990	John Lively
1989	Larry Snyder
1988	Don Brumfield
1987	Don MacBeth
1986	Jorge Velasquez
1985	Pat Day
1984	Steve Cauthen
1983	Marco Castaneda
1982	Patrick Valenzuela

1981	Eddie Delahoussaye
1980	Chris McCarron
1979	Ron Turcotte
1978	Darrel McHargue
1977	Frank Olivares
1976	Sandy Hawley
1975	Fernando Toro
1974	Alvaro Pineda
1973	John Rotz
1972	Angel Cordero Jr.
1971	Jerry Lambert
1970	Laffit Pincay Jr.
1969	John Sellers
1968	Braulio Baeza
1967	Donald Pierce
1966	Alex Maese
1965	Walter Blum
1964	Manuel Ycaza
1963	Ismael Valenzuela
1962	Steve Brooks
1961	Peter Moreno
1960	Bill Harmatz
1959	Bill Boland
1958	Merlin Volzke
1957	Ted Atkinson
1956	John Adams
1955	Ray York
1954	Ralph Neves
1953	Eddie Arcaro
1952	John Longden
1951	Bill Shoemaker
1950	Gordon Glisson

Mike Venezia Memorial Award

Named for the popular New York jockey who was killed in an on-track accident on October 13, 1988, the Mike Venezia Memorial Award honors jockeys who exemplify extraordinary sportsmanship and citizenship.

2004	Patti Cooksey
2003	Richard Migliore
2002	Dean Kutz
2001	Mike Luzzi
2000	Jorge Chavez
1999	Gary Stevens
1998	Eddie Maple
1997	Robbie Davis
1996	Laffit Pincay Jr.
1995	Pat Day
1994	Mike Smith
1993	Jerry Bailey
1992	Angel Cordero Jr.
1991	Chris McCarron
1990	Bill Shoemaker
1989	Mike Venezia

White Horse Award

Sponsored by the Race Track Chaplaincy of America to honor an industry member for a specific act of heroism.

| 2004 | John Woodley |
| 2003 | Leigh Grey |

BREEDING
Development of Breeding Industry

Because the English aristocracy developed the Thoroughbred, the first harbingers of anything remotely resembling a Thoroughbred breeding industry necessarily appeared in England. Kings James I, Charles I, and especially Charles II were crucially important in importing Arabian stallions and broodmares in the 17th century.

When Charles I was deposed and beheaded by the Puritans in 1649, his stud at Tutbury was inventoried and dispersed, thus providing some of the earliest written records on the foundations of many modern pedigrees. Principal beneficiaries of that dispersal were members of Yorkshire's Darcy family, whose head, James Darcy Sr., was appointed Master of the Horse to Charles II. The Darcys, whose principal stud farm was at Sedbury in northern Yorkshire, were closely connected by marriage to other prominent early Yorkshire breeders: the Wyvil, Gascoigne, Hutton, and Villiers (the Dukes of Buckingham) families.

The Yorkshire land holdings of those families centered the early English breeding industry in that county, but Charles II chose the more southerly Suffolk village of Newmarket in East Anglia as his racing headquarters and established Newmarket racecourse in the 1660s. Newmarket's Rowley Mile, the course over which the Two Thousand Guineas (Eng-G1) and One Thousand Guineas (Eng-G1) are run,

is named after Charles II, whose nickname in his more mature days was "Old Rowley."

The English lords who followed the royal family's lead in breeding racehorses owned estates all over the country, and each established their principal stud farms according to the location of their lands. For example, the various Earls of Derby's principal stud farms were at Knowsley, near Liverpool, while the Dukes of Newcastle's (and later Dukes of Portland's) stud was at Welbeck Abbey, near Newcastle. Newmarket's place as the headquarters of English racing eventually led to a cluster of breeding farms in the surrounding area, but English stud farms are still scattered throughout the country.

Printed Record

The early Yorkshire breeders often kept meticulous, handwritten records of their breeding activities in private stud books, some of which have survived. The earliest printed record that included pedigrees was John Cheney's *Racing Calendar*, an annual volume of race results that first appeared in 1727. After Cheney's death in 1751, competing calendars produced by John Pond, Reginald Heber, and William Pick appeared, and the competition continued until James Weatherby established his version of the *Racing Calendar* as the sole authority, beginning in 1773.

Although Cheney included pedigree infor-

Jersey Act

America's Thoroughbred industry was nearly destroyed between 1908 and '10 when antiwagering legislation swept the country—closing many racetracks, slashing purses to minuscule levels for those that remained open, and rendering American bloodstock all but worthless at home. Desperate breeders thus began to look abroad for racing opportunities and markets for their horses.

English breeders were disturbed by this sudden influx of foreign bloodstock onto European shores. They had long perceived themselves as the world's supplier of Thoroughbreds and feared that American horses for sale in great numbers would threaten the international demand for their own products. In 1913, England's Jockey Club, chaired by the seventh Earl of Jersey, sought to protect its breeders' interests by enacting a rule that effectively barred American bloodstock from the Thoroughbred canon, but not from racing.

Known as the Jersey Act, the rule designated as "half-bred" any horse that did not trace in every pedigree line "without flaw" to foundation stock recorded in the earliest volumes of England's *General Stud Book*, which much of the world accepted as an industry bible. The Jersey Act thus labeled as half-breds many American Thoroughbreds whose distant ancestors had been lost in the chaos of revolution and civil war. Although the rule was not retroactive, after 1913 horses carrying the blood of Lexington, Hanover, Domino, Spendthrift, Ben Brush, and other influential American progenitors no longer were admitted into the *General Stud Book*.

This discriminatory rule ultimately worked to America's advantage. For more than three decades and through two world wars, Americans imported top English bloodstock to enrich their breeding programs, while England could not look to America to do the same. While America acquired such horses as *Mahmoud, *Sir Gallahad III, and *Bull Dog, England had no access to Man o' War, Bull Lea, or Black Toney—halfbreds one and all under the Jersey Act.

In June 1949, the Jersey Act was quietly repealed. Lady Wentworth, a respected British pedigree authority and historian, applauded the action as long overdue and described the Jersey Act as "a mistake that made us look rather foolish." Under the revised rule, admission to the *General Stud Book* required only eight or nine proven crosses of pure blood and "such performances of its immediate family on the Turf as to warrant the belief in the purity of its blood."

mation on prominent runners in his annual volumes, it was Heber who first requested pedigree information from breeders in a standardized format. But no one attempted to collect this information into a separate book until Weatherby published Volume 1 of the *General Stud Book* in 1791. Based largely on private stud books and the various *Racing Calendars*, especially Pick's reconstruction of pre-Cheney races and pedigrees, Volume 1 of the *General Stud Book* was revised five times, with the final edition published in 1891.

The *Racing Calendar* and the *General Stud Book* gave the nascent Thoroughbred industry the kind of documentation required for expansion to other countries. Although records of racing in America extend back almost to the earliest English colonization, the first Thoroughbred recorded as imported to the New World in the *American Stud Book* is *Bulle (or Bully) Rock, by Darley Arabian, listed as imported to Virginia, "before the Revolution," specifically in 1730.

Virginia and Maryland became the first centers for breeding racehorses in America, led by the Tayloe family of Virginia and the Tasker family in Maryland. Given the primitive conditions of Colonial America, it is little wonder that many early records of imported Thoroughbreds and their produce in America were lost, and other records were reconstructed or fabricated at later dates.

As in England, early racing in America was the province of aristocratic families, and further progress by American breeders did not occur until the disruption caused by the American Revolution had thoroughly passed. The importation of *Diomed in 1799 proved pivotal because he established the first enduring American sire line through his son Sir Archy, great-grandsire of Lexington.

Commercial Beginnings

It was Lexington who cemented the transfer of the breeding industry west across the Appalachian Mountains to Kentucky. If any one man is the founder of the American commercial breeding industry, that person is Robert A.S.C. Alexander, who purchased Lexington for his Woodburn Stud near the city of Lexington in 1855. Lexington's success as 16-time leading sire and the many top racehorses that Alexander and his brother Alexander J. Alexander sold at Woodburn's annual yearling auctions enticed many other breeders to locate their stud farms in the Bluegrass.

The Alexanders also were among the sponsors of what became the definitive *American Stud Book*, after several false starts. George W. Jeffreys published the *Virginia Stud Book* in 1828, but the first comprehensive attempt at an American Stud Book was Patrick Nisbett Edgar's *American Race-Turf Register, Sportsman's Herald, and General Stud Book*, published in 1833.

Unfortunately, Edgar's work included a stunning number of obvious inaccuracies, some of which remain in the official record. As in England, several competitors, including John S. Skinner and William T. Porter, published versions of Racing Calendars or Stud Books before Sanders D. Bruce's *American Stud Book, Volume 1,* appeared in 1868.

Although Bruce's book retained some of Edgar's errors and created some of its own, it was a considerable advance on previous offerings. It rapidly became the official record and was purchased by the American Jockey Club in May 1897 for $35,000. That purchase was the first step toward the Jockey Club's current position as the breed registry and the keeper of the sport's records.

Early American race results were recorded primarily by periodicals such as Porter's *Spirit of the Times* and Bruce's *Turf, Field, and Farm*. *Daily Racing Form* and the *Morning Telegraph* took over these functions in the late 19th century, and the *Racing Form* became the de facto newspaper of record by the 1920s. In 1991, the Jockey Club and the Thoroughbred Racing Associations formed Equibase Co. to develop the official database of the Thoroughbred industry, and in '98 Equibase became the data provider to the *Racing Form* as well.

Designating Imported Horses

In its earliest years, the *American Stud Book* designated horses imported to North America for racing or breeding with "Imported" or "Imp." before the horse's name.

This practice changed in 1906 with publication of the *American Stud Book's* Volume 9. Its preface noted: "While the general features of this volume remain the same as Volume 8, it has been found necessary, in order to avoid a two-volume work, to condense the subject matter in every way possible, the most radical change being the substitution of an * in place of the word Imported wherever possible.

"The prefix Imported has been omitted from the fol-lowing horses, they having been foaled in the United States, viz.: Bel Demonio, Donald A., Dundee, Flax Spinner, Glenelg, Keene, Loiterer, Pontiac, Paladin, Uncommon and Victory."

The asterisk, which preceded such notable names in American breeding history as *Nasrullah and *Ribot, was eliminated in 1975. An introductory note to the *American Stud Book, Foals of 1981*, states: "The practice of designating imported horses with an asterisk (*) was discontinued in 1975, and from that time forward, the country of origin is reflected in the suffix attached to the name. The asterisk or suffix is omitted in the cases of horses which were imported in utero."

Key Figures

Key figures in the development of an American commercial breeding industry on the foundation laid by the Alexanders were John E. Madden, Arthur B. Hancock Sr. and his son Arthur B. "Bull" Hancock Jr., Leslie Combs II, and John R. Gaines. A hands-on horseman who bred and trained his own horses with a keen eye for profit, Madden bred five Kentucky Derby winners at Hamburg Place, named for his first great coup with the great racehorse and sire Hamburg.

Hancock Sr. founded Claiborne Farm near Paris, Kentucky, in 1908 and stood Celt, who became the first of 11 leading American sires who won 29 sire championships at Claiborne during the 20th century.

Combs modernized both the stallion-syndication process and yearling salesmanship at his Spendthrift Farm near Lexington. He stood leading sires Exclusive Native and Seattle Slew, but it was his recruitment of wealthy clients to the sales ring and the breeding industry that helped set the stage for the bloodstock boom of the 1970s and '80s.

Combs's success made clear that big money could be made by breeding and selling potential racehorses, but it was Gaines who developed the syndication of stallions into a highly lucrative enterprise. An innovative thinker, Gaines also created the concept of the Breeders' Cup, which came to fruition in 1984, and he was one of the founders of the National Thoroughbred Association, which was quickly subsumed by the industry-backed National Thoroughbred Racing Association in 1998.

From its beginnings as a passionate pursuit of a few aristocratic Englishmen, Thoroughbred racing and breeding have developed into a worldwide, multibillion-dollar industry. Though still primarily a business for the wealthy, Thoroughbreds are now produced in every condition from the brick palaces of the Bluegrass and Newmarket to, quite literally, suburban back yards.—*John P. Sparkman*

Registration Rules for Breeding
Copyright © 2005 The Jockey Club

History of Registration

The Jockey Club, an organization dedicated to improving Thoroughbred breeding and racing, registers more than 30,000 Thoroughbred foals each year, introducing them to the *American Stud Book* following a disciplined process of initiation that began more than 300 years ago.

Early in the 17th century, three stallions brought to England—the Darley Arabian, the Godolphin Arabian, and the Byerly Turk—became the foundation sires of the Thoroughbred industry. In 1791, James Weatherby published the first stud book, the *General Stud Book*. It listed the pedigrees of 387 mares that could each be traced to one of three descendants of the foundation sires: Eclipse, a direct descendant of the Darley Arabian; Matchem, a grandson of the Godolphin Arabian; and Herod, a great-great-grandson of the Byerly Turk.

In America, Patrick Edgar attempted to publish a national stud registry in 1833 but was unsuccessful. One year later, John Skinner reprinted the entire *General Stud Book* and added the existing pedigrees of American horses at the end. Following Skinner's effort, the pedigree section of *Mason's Farrier* was the only available resource until 1867, when John H. Wallace published *Wallace's American Stud Book*. Wallace soon abandoned the enterprise, which was a financial failure, and turned his attention to compiling the American Trotting Registry.

One year later, Col. Sanders D. Bruce published the *American Stud Book*. On May 17, 1897, the Jockey Club acquired the rights to Bruce's work for $35,000. Now, more than 100 years later, the Jockey Club continues to maintain the *American Stud Book* to ensure the integrity of the breed.

Today, registering a Thoroughbred is as simple as logging onto the Internet. Through Jockey Club Interactive Registration™ (*www.registry.jockeyclub.com*), owners and breeders can complete registration forms, submit digital photos, review a database of active names, and check the status of a registration. A goal of the Jockey Club is to provide a virtual foal certificate that will eliminate paper, which can be lost, destroyed, or illegally altered, while at the same time providing real-time access to all registry-related information.

How to Register

All requirements of the Principal Rules and Requirements of the *American Stud Book* must be met within one year of a foal's originally reported foaling date.

Step 1

For foals of 2001 and after, the foal's sire and dam must be genetically typed. For foals of 2000 and earlier, the foal's sire and dam must be blood-typed.

Step 2

Report of Mares Bred (Deadline: August 1 each year)

Stallion owners must file a report of all Thoroughbred mares bred to a stallion in a breeding season (February-July).

Step 3

Live Foal/No Foal Report (Deadline: Within 30 days after foaling)

1. The owner of record of each broodmare in the Jockey Club files will receive a preprinted Live Foal/No Foal Report. Note: All changes of mare ownership should be reported to the Jockey Club immediately.

2. The Live Foal/No Foal Report must be filed no later than 30 days following the birth of a foal, or in Jan-

uary if the mare was not bred. Note: The registration services department at the Jockey Club should be contacted immediately if a preprinted Live Foal/No Foal Report is not received by the time the foal is born.

Step 4

Genetic-Typing (Deadline: Within 45 days of receipt of genetic typing kit)

1. Within 180 days of the foaling date, a Registration and Genetic Typing Kit will be mailed to the address shown on the Live Foal/No Foal Report. Note: If genetic typing kit is not used within 45 days, the genetic typing process may have to be restarted at an additional fee.

2. Mane hairs pulled/blood drawn from the foal must be mailed to the laboratory shown on the preprinted mailer.

Notes:

Helpful hints for taking a DNA sample:

• Clean the mane comb thoroughly before pulling the mane.

• Grasp the mane close to the neck to help ensure you get roots.

• Do not try to pull a sample if the mane is wet.

Helpful hints for drawing blood:

• If, for some reason, a syringe must be used to draw blood, insert needle through stopper and depress plunger on syringe slowly.

• Do not remove stoppers or chemicals from tubes.

• Do not shake tubes; turn them end over end.

• Refrigerate blood if not mailing the same day. (Do not put tubes in Styrofoam container during refrigeration, and do not freeze the sample).

• Do not mail samples on the weekend or immediately before a holiday. (If samples are untestable on receipt by laboratory, another kit will be mailed and the process must be repeated.)

Step 5

Registration/Genetic Typing/Blood-Typing Form (Deadline: Send to the Jockey Club when DNA/blood sample is mailed to lab. Before sending to the Jockey Club, be certain that):

1. Both sides of form are completed, including:

i) Written description of markings, indicating:

• All white markings.

• All flesh-colored markings.

• All dark and chestnut markings on coronet.

• All head and neck cowlicks (except cowlick at the very top of forehead).

• Any other distinguishing characteristics.

ii) Signature by foal's owner or authorized agent.

iii) One to six name choices. (This could avoid additional naming fees.)

2. A set of four color photos is enclosed, clearly showing color and all markings from the front, back, and both sides. Note: Do not take photographs until the foal has shed its "baby hair."

3. The Stallion Service Certificate (acquired from the stallion owner) is attached.

4. Fee payment is enclosed.

How to Name a Horse

A. A name may be claimed on the Registration Application, on a Name Claiming Form, or through Interactive Registration™ at *www.registry.jockeyclub.com*. Name selections should be listed in order of prefer-ence. Names will be assigned based upon availability and compliance with the naming rules as stated herein. Names may not be claimed or reserved by telephone. When a foreign language name is submitted, an English translation must be furnished to the Jockey Club. An explanation must accompany "coined" or "made-up" names that have no apparent meaning. Horses born in the United States, Puerto Rico, or Canada and currently reside in another country must be named by the Jockey Club through the Stud Book Authority of their country of residence.

B. If a valid attempt to name a foal is submitted to the Jockey Club by February 1 of the foal's two-year-old year and such a name is determined not eligible for use, no fee is required for a subsequent claim of name for that foal. If a valid attempt to name a foal is not submitted to the Jockey Club by February 1 of the foal's two-year-old year, a fee is required to claim a name for such a foal.

C. A reserved name must be used within one year (365 days) from the day it was reserved. Reserved names cannot be used until written notification requesting the assignment of the name to a specific horse is received by the Registry Office. If the reserved name is not used within one year (365 days) from its reservation, it will become available for any horse. A fee is required to reserve a name.

D. A foal's name may be changed at any time prior to starting in its first race. Ordinarily, no name change will be permitted after a horse has started in its first race or has been used for breeding purposes. However, in the event a name must be changed after a horse has started in its first race, both the old and new names should be used until the horse has raced three times following the name change. The prescribed fee and the Certificate of Foal Registration must accompany any request to the Registry Office for a change of name.

E. Names of horses over ten years old may be eligible if they are not excluded and have not been used during the preceding five years either in breeding or racing.

Names of geldings and horses that were never used for breeding or racing may be available five years from the date of their death as reported.

F. The following classes of names are not eligible for use:

1. Names consisting of more than 18 letters (spaces and punctuation marks count as letters).

2. Initials such as C.O.D., F.O.B., etc.

3. Names ending in "filly," "colt," "stud," "mare," "stallion," or any similar horse-related term.

4. Names consisting entirely of numbers, except numbers above 30 may be used if they are spelled out.

5. Names ending with a numerical designation such as "2nd" or "3rd," whether or not such a designation is spelled out.

6. Names of persons unless written permission to use their name is on file with the Jockey Club.

7. Names of "famous" people no longer living unless approval is granted by the Board of Stewards of the Jockey Club.

8. Names of "notorious" people.

9. Names of racetracks or graded stakes races.

10. Recorded names such as assumed names or stable names.

11. Names clearly having commercial significance, such as trade names.

12. Copyrighted material, titles of books, plays, motion pictures, popular songs, etc., unless the applicant furnishes the Jockey Club with proof that the copyright has been abandoned or that such material has not been used within the past five years.

13. Names that are suggestive or have a vulgar or obscene meaning; names considered in poor taste; or names that may be offensive to religious, political, or ethnic groups.

14. Names that are currently active either in racing or breeding, and names similar in spelling or pronunciation to such names.

15. Permanent names and names similar in spelling or pronunciation to permanent names. The list of criteria to establish a permanent name is as follows:

a. Horses in the Racing Hall of Fame;

b. Horses that have been voted Horse of the Year;

c. Horses that have won an Eclipse Award;

d. Horses that have won a Sovereign Award (Canadian champions);

e. Annual leading sire and broodmare sire by progeny earnings;

f. Cumulative money winners of $2-million or more;

g. Horses that have won the Kentucky Derby (G1), Preakness Stakes (G1), Belmont Stakes (G1), Jockey Club Gold Cup (G1), Breeders' Cup Classic (G1), or Breeders' Cup Turf (G1); and

h. Horses included in the International List of Protected Names.

G. In addition to the provisions of this rule, the Registrar of the Jockey Club reserves the right of approval on all name requests.

Age Definitions

Foal: A young horse of either sex in its first year of life.

Suckling: A foal of any sex in its first year of life while it is still nursing.

Weanling: A foal of any sex in its first year of life after being separated from its dam.

Yearling: A colt, filly, or gelding in its second calendar year of life (beginning January 1 of the year following its birth).

Two-Year-Old: A colt, filly, or gelding in its third calendar year of life (beginning January 1 of the year following its yearling year).

Color Definitions

The following colors are recognized by the Jockey Club:

Bay: The entire coat of the horse may vary from a yellow-tan to a bright auburn. The mane, tail, and lower portion of the legs are always black, unless white markings are present.

Black: The entire coat of the horse is black, including the muzzle, flanks, mane, tail, and legs, unless white markings are present.

Chestnut: The entire coat of the horse may vary from a red-yellow to a golden-yellow. The mane, tail, and legs are usually variations of coat color, unless white markings are present.

Dark Bay or Brown: The entire coat of the horse will vary from a brown, with areas of tan on the shoulders, head, and flanks, to a dark brown, with tan areas seen only in the flanks and/or muzzle. The mane, tail, and lower portion of the legs are always black, unless white markings are present.

Gray or Roan: In order to reduce the number of corrections involving the colors gray and roan, the Jockey Club has combined these colors into one color category. This does not change the individual definitions of the colors for gray and roan and in no way impacts on the two-coat color inheritance principle as stated in a previous rule.

Gray: The majority of the coat of the horse is a mixture of black and white hairs. The mane, tail, and legs may be either black or gray, unless white markings are present.

Roan: The majority of the coat of the horse is a mixture of red and white hairs or brown and white hairs. The mane, tail, and legs may be black, chestnut, or roan, unless white markings are present.

Palomino: The entire coat of the horse is golden-yellow, unless white markings are present. The mane and tail are usually flaxen.

White: A rare color not to be confused with the colors gray or roan. The entire coat, including the mane, tail, and legs, is white and no other color should be present.

Breeding Terminology

Bred (Mated): Any filly or mare that has undergone the physical act of breeding (mating).

Bred (Area Foaled): The term "bred" is sometimes used to describe the location where a foal was born; i.e., Kentucky-bred, New York-bred, etc.

Breeder: The breeder of a foal is the owner of the dam at the time of foaling, unless the dam was under a lease or foal-sharing agreement at the time of foaling. In that case, the person(s) specified by the terms of the agreement is (are) the breeder of the foal.

Stallion: A male horse that is used to produce foals.

Sire: A male horse that has produced, or is producing, foals.

Broodmare: A filly or mare that has been bred (mated) and is used to produce foals.

Dam: A female horse that has produced, or is producing, foals.

Maiden: A filly or mare that has never been bred (mated).

In Foal (Pregnant) Broodmare: A filly or mare that was bred (mated), conceived, and is currently in foal (pregnant).

Aborted: A term used to describe a broodmare that has been pronounced in foal (pregnant) based on an examination of 42 days or more post breeding (mating) and lost her foal prematurely; or a broodmare from whom an aborted fetus has been observed.

Barren (Not Pregnant): A term used to describe a filly or mare, other than a maiden mare, that was bred (mated) and did not conceive during the last breeding season.

Breeding (Mating): The physical act of a stallion mounting a broodmare with intromission and ejaculation of semen into the reproductive tract.

Gender Terminology

Colt: An entire male horse four years old or younger.

Horse: When reference is made to gender, a "horse" is an entire male five years old or older.

Ridgling ("rig"): A lay term used to describe either a monorchid or cryptorchid.

Cryptorchid: A male horse of any age that has no testes in his scrotum but was never gelded (the testes are undescended).

Monorchid: A male horse of any age that has only one testicle in his scrotum (the other testicle was either removed or is undescended).

Gelding: A male horse of any age that is unsexed (had both testicles removed).

Filly: A female horse four years old or younger.

Mare: A female horse five years old or older.

Deadlines

Report of Mares Bred (Stallion Reports): This report must be filed no later than August 1 of the breeding year.

Live Foal/No Foal Report (Mare Reports):
• Reporting live foal information. This report must be filed within 30 days after the foaling date.
• Reporting no foal information. This report must be filed no later than 30 days after the intended foaling date or in January if the mare was not bred.

Foal Registration: All requirements must be completed by one year from the foaling date, including genetic typing, to avoid paying an additional fee.

Naming: Must be named by February 1 of two-year-old year to avoid paying a fee.

Death: Must be reported within 30 days after the death.

Export: Requirements must be met within 60 days after the horse's departure to avoid paying an additional fee.

Foreign Registration: All requirements must be met within 60 days after the horse's arrival to avoid paying an additional fee.

Geldings: Should be reported immediately.

Sold Without Pedigree: Should be reported within 60 days after the date of sale.

Fees

Foal Registration Fees: If all requirements are met within one calendar year from foaling date (includes genetic typing of the foal and parentage verification, as well as ownership transfers and corrections): $200

By December 31 of yearling year: $525
By December 31 of two-year-old year: $775
After December 31 of two-year-old year: $2,000
Reserved Names: $75
Foal-Naming Fee: After February 1 of the foal's two-year-old year. (Before this date, no fee is required): $50

Name-Change Fee: $100
Genetic Typing Fees:
Genetic typing, entry into the Ownership Registry: $80
Additional Genetic Typing: $80 (or retyping as required by the Jockey Club)
Duplicate Certificate Fee: $150
Corrected Certificate Fee (six months after original certificates issued): $50

Certificate of Exportation Fees:
If all requirements are completed within 60 days of the horse's departure from the United States, Canada, or Puerto Rico: $150
If all requirements are completed after 60 days of the horse's departure from the United States, Canada, or Puerto Rico: $400
Certificate of Foreign Registration Fees:
If all requirements are completed within 60 days of the horse's arrival in the United States, Canada, or Puerto Rico: $150
If all requirements are completed after 60 days and up until one year of the horse's arrival in the United States, Canada, or Puerto Rico: $400
If all requirements are not completed within one year of the horse's arrival in the United States, Canada, or Puerto Rico, and the horse is eligible for late registration: $750
Horses registered in the *American Stud Book* returning from a foreign country: $150
Thirty-day foreign racing permit fee:
If application is received within 30 days of the horse's arrival in the United States, Canada, or Puerto Rico: $150
Express handling fee: $100

How to Contact the Jockey Club:

Address: The Jockey Club, 821 Corporate Dr., Lexington, Ky. 40503-2794
Telephone: (859) 224-2700
Registration Services: (800) 444-8521
Fax: (859) 224-2710
Website: *www.jockeyclub.com*
Jockey Club Interactive Registration™
Website: *www.registry.jockeyclub.com*

Brief History of Foal Identification

When registering Thoroughbreds in North America, foal identification traditionally has been documented by markings, both narrative descriptions of the distinctive characteristics and diagrams of those markings.

For instance, the breeder would be required to describe any white markings and their locations, as well as any flesh-colored areas and markings on the coronet, when applicable. If the horse had a blaze, the breeder would include a diagram of the horse's head and the shape of the blaze.

Over time, photographs of the horse and any markings became a requirement of foal registration. This process occurred gradually, beginning when breeders would attach photographs of the markings with the registration application. The Jockey Club Registry began accepting digital photos in 2001.

Beginning with the foal crop of 1987, blood-typing for parentage verification was made a requirement for registration.

Advances in technology allowed the Jockey Club to begin DNA verification of parentage with the foal crop of 2001. Within 180 days of the foaling date, breeders receive a registration and genetic typing kit. The genetic typing kit, which contains instructions for pulling mane hairs and drawing blood, must be returned within 45 days.

Current registration practices still require breeders to include a narrative of all markings as well as four-color photographs of the foal from the front, back, and both sides to document the markings.

Foal Registration

Foal registration for all Thoroughbreds in North America—the United States, Canada, and Puerto Rico—is performed by the Jockey Club, which was founded in 1894 and is a not-for-profit organization dedicated to improving the Thoroughbred breed. To be registered in the *American Stud Book*, which is maintained by the Jockey Club, the parentage of all foals must be verified, a process that today includes DNA typing of all

stallions, broodmares, and foals.

Registration of American Thoroughbreds was started by Col. Sanders D. Bruce, a Kentuckian who spent a lifetime researching pedigrees of American Thoroughbreds. He published the first volume of the *American Stud Book* in 1868, and he produced six volumes of the registry. In 1897, the Jockey Club purchased all rights to the *American Stud Book*.

Foal Registration by State in North America in 2003

Alabama 63	Iowa...........................415	New Hampshire.............2	Texas 1,733
Alaska...........................3	Kansas 107	New Jersey.................328	Utah..............................49
Arizona 337	Kentucky.................8,641	New Mexico................707	Vermont..........................2
Arkansas 285	Louisiana...............1,516	New York 1,927	Virginia 483
California 3,745	Maine............................2	North Carolina.............35	Virgin Islands.................1
Colorado....................251	Maryland....................980	North Dakota................52	Washington 699
Connecticut 1	Massachusetts 80	Ohio...........................576	West Virginia..............438
Delaware 0	Michigan....................329	Oklahoma..................900	Wisconsin.......................8
Florida 4,394	Minnesota..................259	Oregon 236	Wyoming.......................17
Georgia........................66	Mississippi 25	Pennsylvania 986	**Total U.S. 32,700**
Hawaii............................0	Missouri 35	Rhode Island 0	**Total Canada 2,479**
Idaho..........................162	Montana.....................101	South Carolina.............57	**Total Puerto Rico......498**
Illinois 897	Nebraska...................163	South Dakota...............56	**Total Crop............35,677**
Indiana........................505	Nevada........................12	Tennessee...................34	

Trend of Foal Registration in North America

Year	United States	Change	Canada	Change	Puerto Rico	Change	Total	Change
2005	34,070*	0.0%	2,580*	0.2%	550*	-0.9%	**37,200***	0.0%
2004	34,070*	0.1%	2,575*	6.2%	555*	0.9%	**37,200***	0.5%
2003	32,700*	0.2%	2,479*	1.1%	498*	-4.2%	**35,677***	0.2%
2002	32,650	-5.8%	2,452	-5.1%	519	-11.9%	**35,621**	-5.9%
2001	34,663	-0.1%	2,584	4.9%	589	4.8%	**37,836**	0.3%
2000	34,707	2.6%	2,464	1.2%	562	-13.5%	**37,733**	2.2%
1999	33,831	2.7%	2,435	4.1%	650	-11.4%	**36,916**	2.5%
1998	32,944	2.6%	2,340	2.5%	734	-0.8%	**36,018**	2.5%
1997	32,116	-0.4%	2,284	-4.7%	740	1.9%	**35,140**	-0.6%
1996	32,241	1.1%	2,397	-2.0%	726	11.2%	**35,364**	1.1%
1995	31,882	-0.7%	2,445	-5.6%	653	3.3%	**34,980**	-1.0%
1994	32,117	-5.0%	2,591	-4.5%	632	4.5%	**35,340**	-4.8%
1993	33,820	-3.5%	2,713	-2.3%	605	-0.8%	**37,138**	-3.4%
1992	35,050	-8.1%	2,777	-8.2%	610	-2.9%	**38,437**	-8.0%
1991	38,149	-5.4%	3,025	-5.3%	628	1.8%	**41,802**	-5.3%
1990	40,333	-8.9%	3,193	-4.9%	617	-1.4%	**44,143**	-8.5%

*Estimated or incomplete

Annual Foal Registration in North America

2005 ....37,200*	1982 42,894	1959 12,240	1936 5,042	1913 1,722
2004 ....37,200*	1981 38,669	1958 11,377	1935 5,038	1912 1,900
2003 ....37,000*	1980 35,679	1957 10,832	1934 4,924	1911 2,040
2002 35,621	1979 32,904	1956 10,112	1933 5,158	1910 1,950
2001 37,836	1978 31,510	1955 9,610	1932 5,256	1909 2,340
2000 37,733	1977 30,036	1954 9,064	1931 5,266	1908 3,080
1999 36,916	1976 28,809	1953 9,040	1930 5,137	1907 3,780
1998 36,018	1975 28,271	1952 8,811	1929 4,903	1906 3,840
1997 35,140	1974 27,586	1951 8,944	1928 4,503	1905 3,800
1996 35,364	1973 26,811	1950 9,095	1927 4,182	1904 3,990
1995 34,980	1972 25,726	1949 8,770	1926 3,632	1903 3,440
1994 35,340	1971 24,301	1948 8,434	1925 3,272	1902 3,600
1993 37,138	1970 24,361	1947 7,705	1924 2,921	1901 3,784
1992 38,437	1969 23,848	1946 6,579	1923 2,763	1900 3,476
1991 41,802	1968 22,910	1945 5,819	1922 2,352	1899 3,080
1990 44,143	1967 21,876	1944 5,650	1921 2,035	1898 2,940
1989 48,235	1966 20,228	1943 5,923	1920 1,833	1897 2,992
1988 49,220	1965 18,846	1942 6,427	1919 1,665	1893-'96.....5,940*
1987 50,917	1964 17,343	1941 6,805	1918 1,950	1803-'92.....3,950*
1986 51,296	1963 15,917	1940 6,003	1917 1,680	*Estimated
1985 50,433	1962 14,870	1939 6,316	1916 2,128	
1984 49,247	1961 13,794	1938 5,696	1915 2,120	
1983 47,237	1960 12,901	1937 5,535	1914 1,702	

Evolution of the Breed

In genetic terms, the Thoroughbred is a hybrid, created by crossing two or possibly more breeds of horses to produce an animal with specific characteristics. One of those breeds was the Arabian horse, but the exact identities of other contributors are considerably less clear.

Early records do not identify most of the mares mated to the many Arabian, Barb, and Turk (all are varieties of Arabians) stallions imported to England after the Markham Arabian's acquisition by King James I. Although the Markham Arabian was the first Arabian whose importation was noted by history, no doubt others, both males and females, were transported from the Middle East over several centuries, beginning with the Crusades of the 12th and 13th centuries. However, many horses called Arabians or Barbs in the *General Stud Book* were certainly not purebreds.

These imports were crossed with native English stock over many generations. By the time the modern Thoroughbred was created, there were two varieties of pony-sized English and Irish racehorses known as Hobbies and Galloways, and Oriental imports of the time were not much larger. Both English breeds certainly carried Oriental blood, but no one knows how much. Before the Puritan revolution in 1649, the royal stud of King James I and his ill-fated son King Charles I probably included mares of both mixed English and Oriental blood and pure-bred Arabians. These mares came to be called "royal mares" and now stand as the earliest known female ancestors of several modern female families.

The surge of importations that began with the restoration of King Charles II in 1660 included both males and females. With King Charles leading the way, the English nobility engaged in fierce competition to produce better, faster racehorses, and they quickly learned that the more Arabian

Estimated Relationships of Some Important Horses to Modern Thoroughbreds

Horse (Year of Birth)	Percentage Relationship
Herod (1758)	17.2%
Eclipse (1764)	15.2%
Highflyer (1774)	12.8%
Godolphin Arabian (1724)	12.7%
Partner (1718)	11.4%
Regulus (1739)	9.4%
St. Simon (1881)	8.7%
Stockwell (1849)	8.7%
Curwen Bay Barb mare (1710)	8.4%
Birdcatcher (1833)	7.4%
Pocahontas (1837)	7.0%
Matchem (1748)	6.3%
Flying Childers (1715)	5.7%
Darley Arabian (ca. 1700)	5.3%
*Teddy (1913)	4.9%
Byerley Turk (ca. 1680)	4.6%
Curwen Bay Barb (ca. 1695)	4.4%
Hyperion (1930)	4.2%
*Nasrullah (1940)	4.2%
Bald Galloway (ca. 1700)	4.0%

Figures based on an unpublished statistical study. Percentages of horses born since about 1850 may change slightly.

blood their stock could claim, the better chance they had.

Foundation Sires

The arrivals of the Byerley Turk, Place's White Turk, the Curwen Bay Barb, the Darley Arabian, and finally the Godolphin Arabian (around 1730) sharply accelerated the development of the breed. The Darley Arabian sired Flying Childers, generally recognized as the first great Thoroughbred, in 1714. Through Flying Childers's full brother Bartlett's Childers, the Darley Arabian

The Darley Arabian

Of the Thoroughbred's three male-line foundation sires, only the Darley Arabian was almost certainly a pure-bred Arabian. The Godolphin Arabian was probably a Turcoman-Arabian cross, while the Byerley Turk may have been born in England, sired by another Turcoman-Arabian cross horse whose identity is uncertain.

Probably born in what is now Syria in 1700, the Darley Arabian was purchased in Aleppo, then part of the Ottoman Empire, by English merchant Thomas Darley in '04 and shipped to his brother Richard Darley at Aldby Park near York, England. The Darley Arabian was said to be of the "keheilan" or "manicca" breed, the subset of Arabians then most prized by Bedouins. Ottoman law forbade the sale of any pure-bred Arabian to a foreigner, but Darley's merchant connections in Aleppo allowed him to spirit the horse out of the country.

The Darley Arabian mostly covered his owner's broodmares, but one of the few outside mares bred to him was Leonard Childers's Betty Leedes, by Careless, who produced Flying Childers in 1714 and his full brother Bartlett's Childers in '15. Flying Childers was unbeaten and considered by far the fastest horse until that time. Darley Arabian also sired the good racehorses Almanzor, Cupid, and Brisk.

Although Flying Childers was a successful sire, his brother Bartlett's Childers—unraced because he was a bleeder—carried on the line. He sired the good racehorse Squirt, who in turn sired Marske, sire of Eclipse (1764). Eclipse in turn founded the male lines that lead to the modern lines of Phalaris (Northern Dancer, *Nasrullah, Native Dancer), St. Simon (*Ribot and *Princequillo), Hyperion, Domino, *Teddy, and Blandford.

established today's dominant male line, leading to Phalaris and his descendants.

The Godolphin Arabian was the most prepotent immediate influence among the three founding male-line sires, establishing the male line that leads to dual Breeders' Cup Classic (G1) winner Tiznow. Although the Godolphin Arabian male line is now far less prominent than that of the Darley Arabian, almost 13% of the genes of the modern Thoroughbred come from the Godolphin Arabian, according to modern statistical studies.

The male line tracing to the Byerley Turk achieved dominance in the late 18th century through his great-great-grandson Herod. By 1825, inbreeding to Herod had reached its limit, and his overall influence began to decline. Today, his male line appears to be headed for extinction, with tendrils hanging on in Europe through Ahonoora and in Australia through Century. Nevertheless, more than 17% of the genes of the modern Thoroughbred come from Herod.

Beneficiary of the intense early inbreeding to Godolphin Arabian and Herod was the Darley Arabian line. The line from Flying Childers was prominent for approximately 50 years, but descendants of his unraced full brother, the bleeder Bartlett's Childers, gained ascendance through his great-grandson Eclipse, foaled in

1764. Eclipse was the greatest of the four-milers, and during his stud career a shift began from the four-mile heat racing that had been popular since King Charles's era to "dash" racing over shorter distances, exemplified by the Epsom Derby, founded in 1780 and contested at one mile that year.

Eclipse and Herod surpassed all other stallions of their time in producing the speedier, more brilliant horse necessary for dash racing. Added together, Herod, Godolphin Arabian, and Eclipse account for 45% of the genes of the modern Thoroughbred.

In the same time period that surviving male lines were being whittled down to three, female lines descending from approximately 100 foundation mares listed in Volume 1 of the *General Stud Book* were cut in half. That, of course, does not mean that those additional foundation mares and stallions had no influence on the development of the breed. Indeed, their names persist, sometimes with great influence, in the nether reaches of pedigrees.

Exportation of the Thoroughbred to other countries, particularly to North America, Australia, and Argentina, inevitably resulted in the introduction of female lines not found in the *General Stud Book*. The chaotic circumstances of Colonial and Revolutionary America meant that

---

Averages for the Breed

Averages for the breed statistics are designed to provide a baseline to evaluate the performances of contemporary racehorses, sires, and dams. Statistics shown in the column on the left below reflect the worldwide performances of all named foals born in North America between 1987-'96. Statistics in the column on the right reflect the same data for foals by the top 1% of all sires by total earnings for the same decade. All statistics are based on data in the Jockey Club Information System's worldwide database. The Jockey Club database includes complete records for racing in United States, Canada, Puerto Rico, England, Ireland, France, Germany, Italy, Japan, Australia, Hong Kong, Saudi Arabia, Argentina, Brazil, and United Arab Emirates for some, but not all of the years covered by these statistics.

Statistics below are designed to give a snapshot of what an average "good" horse should accomplish.

	Foals 1987-'96	Foals by Top 1% of Sires
Starters/foals	69.4%	85%
Winners/foals (starters)	46.1% (66.4%)	65.5% (77%)
Repeat winners/foals (starters)	35.1% (50.5%)	53.4% (62.8%)
Stakes winners/foals (starters)	3.4% (4.9%)	9% (10.6%)
Graded SW/foals (starters)	0.8% (1.1%)	3.6% (4.2%)
Grade 1 SW/foals (starters)	0.2% (0.3%)	1.1% (1.3%)
Stakes-placed/foals (starters)	5.3% (7.6%)	11.8% (13.9%)
2-year-old starters/foals	34%	46.8%
2yo winners/foals (% 2yo starters)	11.3% (33.3%)	18.6% (39.8%)
2yo SW/foals (% 2yo starters)	1% (3%)	2.4% (5.1%)
3-year-old starters/foals	59.9%	76.9%
4-year-old starters/foals	44.6%	56.8%
5-year-old and up starters/foals	27.6%	35.9%
Average career starts/foal	14.8	18.6
Average career starts/starter	21.3	21.9
Average win distance in furlongs	6.82	7.24
Average win distance on turf in furlongs	8.29	8.47
Average earnings/starter	$34,002	$79,011
Average earnings/starter male (female)	$40,187 ($27,569)	$98,643 ($58,294)
Average earnings/start	$1,594	$3,615
Average earnings/start male (female)	$1,647 ($1,521)	$3,619 ($3,609)
Average Racing Index (RI)	1.16	2.36

records were lost on many legitimate members of the breed and invented for many who doubtless were not.

Such chaos inevitably led to controversy. When American racing collapsed early in the 20th century due to antigambling hysteria, England's Turf authority, the Jockey Club, essentially banned American-bred stock from the hallowed pages of the *General Stud Book* when American exports threatened to flood the market. Fortunately for the future of the breed, the Jersey Act of 1913 excluding American-breds included a provision that grandfathered in American-bred stock already included in earlier volumes.

Within 40 years, descendants of those acceptable American-breds—including such horses as Nearco and his son *Nasrullah—and descendants of French-bred Tourbillon (branded as a half-bred by the Jersey Act because of his American antecedents) dominated English racing, which forced the repeal of these exclusionary rules.

Changing Conditions

The descendants of Eclipse's great-grandson Whalebone through his great-great-grandson Stockwell proved especially adaptable to the pattern of English racing established by the five classic races (Two Thousand Guineas, One Thousand Guineas, Epsom Derby, Epsom Oaks, and St. Leger Stakes). Stockwell led the English sire list eight times and his great-grandson, unbeaten Triple Crown winner *Ormonde, is widely considered the best racehorse of the 19th century. The male line of *Ormonde lives on tenuously through the descendants of Damascus.

The inauguration of several valuable races outside the classic pattern in the 1890s changed the requirements of English racing at about the same time that an invasion of American jockeys changed race-riding. After American riders such as Tod Sloan and Danny Maher proved the virtues of setting a faster pace, male-line descendants of one stallion, Phalaris, gradually proved the most capable of adapting to the new conditions.

A top-class sprinter during World War I, Phalaris sired two sets of full brothers who established powerful male lines: Pharos and Fairway, and *Sickle and *Pharamond II. Pharos and his descendants generally sired heavier, more muscular horses with speed, while the Fairways tended toward taller, lighter individuals. Today the Fairway line hangs by the thread of Lord At War (Arg), while Pharos reigns supreme through descendants of his grandsons *Nasrullah, sire of Bold Ruler, and Nearctic, sire of Northern Dancer.

*Sickle led the U.S. sire list twice, and his brother *Pharamond II finished second to him in 1938. *Sickle's great-grandson Native Dancer, another heavy, powerful horse, established the second most dominant male line in modern pedigrees, that descending from his grandson Mr. Prospector.

In 300 years, the Thoroughbred breed has evolved from a small, relatively lightly made animal designed to gallop 3½ miles at a sedate pace and then sprint for a half-mile. It has become a much larger, heavier, proportionally shorter-legged animal designed primarily for high speeds from the start over distances up to 1¼ miles. Without much doubt, Flying Childers would hardly recognize his modern descendants.

—John P. Sparkman

Breeding Theories

Flying Childers was the first great racehorse who clearly could be defined as a Thoroughbred. Undoubtedly, his breeder, Leonard Childers, had a theory to explain why his greatest creation was so fast. In the three centuries since Flying Childers first saw daylight in 1714, it is certain that most breeders were equally sure they knew why their latest champion could run a hole in the wind.

Over time, however, breeders' ideas about why one horse runs faster than another have coalesced into a remarkably small set of concepts. Breeding theories range from vaguely general precepts such as "breed the best to the best and hope for the best" to highly specific constructs such as the many varieties of dosage theory.

Breed the Best to the Best

The logic behind the broadest of these ideas—breed the best to the best—is obvious. If speed in the racehorse is determined to a degree by inheritance, then it is logical to assume that the fastest horses—both male and female—have the best chances to pass on their abilities to their offspring.

The history of the breed has shown irrefutably that this assumption is true. In general, the horses that turn out to be the best sires are almost always high-class racehorses themselves. The correlation between racecourse ability and sire success is, of course, far from guaranteed but undeniably positive.

The case for the female of the species is less clear but still undeniable. On average, the best racemares become more successful broodmares than those females that showed less ability on the racecourse. Thus, if a high-class racehorse is mated to a high-class racemare, the breeder theoretically increases the probability that another high-class racehorse will result.

Because probability is capricious, the odds are still against the breeder. The most successful stallions in history have sired only about 25% stakes winners. Individual broodmares may achieve higher percentages, but percentages based on the relatively small numbers of foals from those mares are meaningless in the larger picture.

So, breeding the best to the best certainly works, on average. However, it is far too general a precept to satisfy many Thoroughbred breeders—and of no use whatsoever to those who cannot afford to buy the best, most expensive racing prospects, both male and female.

Inbreeding

For the first 100 years or so of the Thoroughbred's existence as a distinct, definable breed, the number of horses bred each year was so small that inbreeding was inevitable.

Inbreeding, as most commonly used by Thoroughbred breeders, means the repetition of one or more names at least once on both the sire's and dam's side of a pedigree within the first four or five generations. In genetic terms, inbreeding reduces the number of different and distinct gene alleles available to appear in the genome of the new individual. Thus, it increases the chances that the offspring of that mating will display uniform and specific characteristics.

Inbreeding is therefore used in animal husbandry to fix type—that is, to create a more uniform subspecies, which is exactly what Thoroughbred breeders were doing in the 18th century.

The process of creating the Thoroughbred was largely one of inbreeding to certain prepotent stallions and mares—often very closely. For example, the third dam of Flying Childers is listed in the *General Stud Book*'s Volume 1—detailing the genesis of the Thoroughbred breed—as being by the excellent 17th-century racehorse and sire Spanker and out of Spanker's own dam, the Old Morocco mare. That's about as close as inbreeding can get.

The best racehorses of the 18th century and early 19th century were almost invariably closely inbred to a succession of great stallions, beginning with the Godolphin Arabian and continuing through Eclipse, Herod, and the latter's son Highflyer. By about 1825, the genes of those four stallions were so highly concentrated in the Thoroughbred that breeders were forced to seek outcrosses. Since that time, inbreeding has gone in and out of fashion, and a few great breeders, notably French breeder Marcel Boussac, have used its principles to create great racehorses, sires, and broodmares.

Inbreeding is described in contemporary industry texts by a shorthand method that denotes the name and location in the five-cross pedigree of the individual or individuals to which the subject horse is inbred. Thus "inbred 3x4 to Northern Dancer" means that the name of Northern Dancer appears in the third generation on the sire's side of the pedigree and in the fourth generation of the dam's side.

Some Famous Inbred Horses

Horse (Year of Birth)	Inbreeding	Accomplishment
Spanker mare (ca 1690)	2x1 Old Morocco mare	Third dam of Flying Childers
Rachel (1763)	2x3 Godolphin Arabian	Dam of Highflyer, undefeated, 13-time leading sire
Eclipse (1764)	3x4 Snake mare	Unbeaten champion, sire line founder
Prunella (1788)	3x3 Blank	Dam of three classic winners, grandam of seven others
Sir Archy (1802)	3x4 Herod	American foundation sire
Boston (1833)	3x3 *Diomed	Greatest American four-miler
Lexington (1850)	3x4 Sir Archy	16-time leading American sire
Galopin (1872)	3x3 Voltaire	Epsom Derby winner, sire of St. Simon
Americus (1892)	3x3 Lexington	Key horse in pedigree of *Nasrullah
Flying Fox (1896)	3x2 Galopin	English Triple Crown, grandsire of *Teddy
Bromus (1905)	2x3 Springfield	Dam of Phalaris
Bayardo (1906)	4x2 Galopin	English champion, sire of two Triple Crown winners
Havresac II (1915)	2x3 St. Simon	Leading Italian sire, broodmare sire of Nearco
*Ksar (1918)	3x2 Omnium II	Prix de l'Arc de Triomphe winner, sire of Tourbillon
Pharos (1920)	4x3 St. Simon	Champion Stakes winner, sire of Nearco, Pharis
Hyperion (1930)	4x3 St. Simon	Epsom Derby winner, six-time leading sire
Coronation (1946)	2x2 Tourbillon	Prix de l'Arc de Triomphe winner
*Turn-to (1951)	3x3 Pharos	Sire of sires Hail to Reason, Sir Gaylord, Cyane, Best Turn
Broad Brush (1983)	3x3 *Turn-to	Leading sire of 1995

A more accurate method would be to calculate the inbreeding coefficient, or percentage of inbreeding, to that individual. By that method, the inbreeding coefficient of a horse inbred 3x4 to Northern Dancer would be 1.56%.

Nicks

Thoroughbred breeding is of necessity both a retrospective and a predictive art. Early Thoroughbred breeders could not help but notice the efficacy of inbreeding to certain stallions and mares, and the repeated success of combining certain sires and broodmares also became apparent. For reasons that are now obscure, this pattern of combining a specific sire and broodmares sired by another stallion became known as a nick.

Perhaps the best early example of a nick was the combination of the immortal racehorse and great sire Eclipse and mares by the even-greater sire Herod. This direct cross produced 1784 Epsom Derby winner Serjeant. The reverse cross of Herod on an Eclipse mare produced 1783 St. Leger Stakes winner Phenomenom, but the real gold mine for breeders was in the innumerable crosses of sons of Eclipse on mares by Herod or his sons, and sons of Herod on mares by Eclipse or his sons. That more generalized nick was preserved in the breed most notably through 1793 Derby winner Waxy (by Eclipse's son Pot8O's out of a Herod mare), tail-male ancestor of the Phalaris male line.

Phalaris, a foal of 1913, contributed to the most famous 20th-century nick. The four current male lines tracing to Phalaris all descend from sons out of Chaucer mares. *Sickle (Raise a Native line) and *Pharamond II (Buckpasser line) were both foaled by Selene, by Chaucer, while Pharos (*Nasrullah and Northern Dancer lines) and Fairway (Lord At War [Arg] line) were both sons of Scapa Flow, by Chaucer.

Contemporary advocates of the nicking theory have compiled and marketed nicking information that evaluates various crosses according to percentage of stakes winners or graded winners produced by all exemplars of that cross. To accumulate sufficient numbers of exemplars of the cross to be statistically meaningful, these formulations frequently extend the concept to include grandsons or great-grandsons of a particular sire crossed on granddaughters or great-granddaughters of another sire.

At that point, such data are focusing on the hypothetical power of one individual in the third generation of a pedigree and another in the fourth while ignoring the rest of the pedigree. Even at the sire–broodmare sire level, statistical studies

of some of the most famous nicks such as the *Nasrullah–*Princequillo cross have not been encouraging.

Still, the fact that certain crosses such as Phalaris–Chaucer have had extraordinary impact on the breed lends some credence to the concept.

Bruce Lowe Numbers

For the first 150 years of the Thoroughbred as a distinct breed, breeding theories focused almost entirely on the influence of stallions. Toward the end of the 19th century, however, an Australian, Bruce Lowe, and a German, Herman Goos, independently began to trace every mare in the General Stud Book back to the earliest female ancestor recorded in Volume 1. Both found that every mare traced to one of about 50 of approximately 100 original foundation mares recorded in Volume 1.

Goos published his results in Family Tables of English Thoroughbred Stock, a monumental work that was the foundation for the even more monumental Family Tables of Racehorses by Kazimierz Bobinski and Stefan Zamoyski in 1953. Goos noted that some female lines had been much more successful than others, but Lowe went several steps further. The Australian numbered each family according to the cumulative number of winners of the Epsom Derby, Epsom Oaks, and St. Leger Stakes each had produced up to his era. Thus, the female line tracing to Tregonwell's Natural Barb mare was named the Number 1 family, and that tracing to the Burton Barb mare was Number 2. In all, 49 families were numbered.

Based on their success rates, Lowe designated families 1 through 5 as his "running" families. He also designated families 3, 8, 11, 12, and 14 his "sire" families, based on his judgment that the highest number of successful sires occurred in those families. He called those family numbers "figures." He then developed several theories of breeding racehorses based on combinations of those families. His theories were published posthumously in 1895 in Breeding Race Horses by the Figure System.

Lowe's system ignored the fact that the primary reason families 1 through 5 produced the most classic winners was that they had produced the most foals in pretty much the same proportions. Numerical superiority, not innate hereditary superiority, accounted for the differences. His theories on breeding also ignored the fact that the original foundation mares were so many generations removed from contemporary horses that their genetic influences were statistically negligible.

Bruce Lowe's theories were promoted assiduously by his editor, English journalist and bloodstock agent William Allison. Lowe's theories were widely influential around the turn of the 20th century, especially in America, where Allison's purchases of broodmares formed the basis for James R. Keene's stud. Genetic science in the 20th century proved Lowe's theories were useless, but his numbering system of female lines has remained a valuable contribution.

Vuillier Dosage

The late 19th century was a remarkably fertile period for pedigree research. At about the same time Lowe and Goos were tracing their female lines, French cavalry officer Col. Jean-Joseph Vuillier overheard two men arguing over whether Eclipse or Herod was the more influential sire and set out to answer the question statistically. To do so, Vuillier compiled complete pedigrees of more than 650 high-class racehorses, mostly winners of the English classics that Lowe used.

Although he apparently had no knowledge of either theory, Vuillier correctly applied a modern Mendelian interpretation of Galton's Law of genetic inheritance, which states that each parent contributes 50% of the genetic material to their offspring on average. Extending his pedigrees to a minimum of 12 generations, he assigned a value of 1 to a name that appeared in the 12th generation, a value of 2 in the 11th, 4 in the tenth, 8 in the ninth, and on down to a value of 2,048 for first-generation parents.

To determine the percentage contribution of Eclipse and Herod, Vuillier added up the numbers for each occurrence in each generation. Vuillier found that when he averaged the results for his 650 pedigrees, Herod's average number was 750 while Eclipse's average was only 568. He also discovered that Herod's son Highflyer was almost as influential as Eclipse with an average of 543.

In pursuing his research over 15 years, Vuillier noticed that other, more recent ancestors also accumulated high numbers, and he compiled figures that he called "dosages" for 11 more stallions and one mare, Pocahontas. Vuillier's dosages are, in fact, remarkably accurate representations of the percentage of genetic influence on the classic Thoroughbred of the 15 horses in his classification.

Since classic winners were frequently the most successful sires of future generations, Vuillier reasoned that the breed as a whole would and should move in the same direction as the classic pedigree. Thus, he concluded the object of a breed-

Vuillier dosages
First Series
Horse	Dosage
Herod (1758)	750
Eclipse (1764)	568
Highflyer (1774)	543

Second Series
Birdcatcher (1833)	288
Touchstone (1831)	351
Pocahontas (1837)	313
Voltaire (1826)	186
Pantaloon (1824)	140
Melbourne (1834)	184
Bay Middleton (1833)	127
Gladiator (1833)	95

Third Series
Stockwell (1849)	340
Newminster (1848)	295

Fourth Series
St. Simon (1881)	420
Galopin (1872)	405
Isonomy (1875)	280
Hampton (1872)	260
Hermit (1864)	235
Bend Or (1877)	210

ing program should be to produce pedigrees with the same dosages as his classic pedigrees.

To facilitate this process, Vuillier devised the *ecart* system. *Ecart* is a French word that translates loosely to mean mathematical difference. For any potential mating using Vuillier's system, the breeder could calculate the dosages of the prospective foal. The difference between the prospective dosages and the ideal is the *ecart*. The object of Vuillier's system was to reduce the ecart as much as possible.

Vuillier published his findings privately in volumes 1 and 2 of *Les Croisements Rationnels* (Rational Breeding) in 1903 and '27. The Aga Khan hired him to manage his stud in 1925, but Vuillier died shortly thereafter. His widow took over and arranged the Aga Khan's matings for more than 30 years. During that period, the Aga Khan was the most successful and influential breeder in the world, with his stud producing such great racehorses and sires as *Bahram, *Mahmoud, and *Nasrullah. The Vuillier system, privately modernized and updated, is still in use by the current Aga Khan.

Varola Dosage
Vuillier's method was not widely available and

was difficult to execute because it required constructing 12-generation pedigrees and keeping track of mathematical data in an era long before computers. Italian journalist Francesco Varola built on Vuillier's work in his *Typology of the Racehorse*, published in 1974. Since Vuillier's published series of influential stallions extended only through the late 19th century, Varola updated and vastly expanded this list of influential stallions. His initial work identified 120 more horses, all born in the 20th century.

Unlike Vuillier, Varola did not utilize Galton's Law in his formulation, applying equal value to an appearance by a given stallion regardless of the generation of the pedigree in which he appeared. Recognizing that the modern Thoroughbred racehorse is much more specialized than in Vuillier's day, Varola divided his 120 stallions initially into five groups defined by his judgment of the type of influence they exerted on the breed.

His five categories—Brilliant, Intermediate, Classic, Stout, and Professional—were based partly on sociological concepts, partly on physical type and racecourse expression, and partly on inspiration. Varola eventually split the Brilliant group into Brilliant and Transbrilliant and Stout into Solid and Rough, but the original five categories quickly became associated in the public mind with varying degrees of stamina. Varola has consistently disavowed this interpretation.

Varola arranged the names of all his "*chefs-de-race*" in a "dosage diagram," dividing the names of each *chef-de-race* (chief of the breed) that occurs in a given pedigree into the five (or seven) categories and totaling the number of occurrences, regardless of generation. The resulting series of numbers offered breeders a thumbnail picture of the balance in a pedigree among all of Varola's different aptitudes.

Varola's chief contribution may be his insight into the increasing specialization of the Thoroughbred into sprinters, stayers, and middle-distance horses, among others, and his recognition that human sociology plays a role in determining the type of racehorse produced in different countries in different eras.

Roman Dosage

In the 1980s, Steve Roman, an American chemistry professor, developed a system combining some of the aspects of the Vuillier and Varola dosage systems. Considering only the first four generations of a pedigree, Roman assigned a numerical value of 16 to any *chef-de-race* that appeared in the first generation of a pedigree, eight to a second-generation *chef*, four for the third generation, and two for the fourth.

Roman interpreted Varola's five original categories strictly in terms of stamina, with Brilliant horses defined as those contributing extreme speed but little stamina, while Professional *chefs* contributed stamina but little speed. Applying the appropriate value according to generation for each occurrence of a *chef*'s name and adding those values up for each of Varola's five aptitudinal categories, Roman devised a "dosage profile" meant to give breeders insight into the relative stamina inherent in a given pedigree.

Roman invented the "dosage index," a single number that is calculated by dividing the total points in the Brilliant and Intermediate categories plus half the Classic points by the total of the points in the Stout and Professional categories plus the other half of the Classic points. The resultant figure is intended to predict a horse's ability to stay classic distances.

Applying his ideas to the history of the Kentucky Derby (G1), Roman found that almost all Derby winners since the 1930s had dosage indexes of 4.00 or less. Leon Rasmussen of *Daily Racing Form* popularized Roman's ideas in the 1980s and early '90s, and, though several Kentucky Derby winners have subsequently defied their Roman dosage, his theories remain popular.

Modern Genetics

The science of genetics, like the other physical sciences, made enormous strides during the 20th century. Though published earlier, Mendel's laws were virtually unknown at the turn of the 20th century, but early in the 21st century the complete human genome was mapped. Science had progressed from crossbreeding garden peas to cloning sheep and other large mammals.

None of this progress has significantly affected Thoroughbred breeding. An equine genome mapping project is under way, but even that should have no immediate effect on the breed because knowing the location of genes does not reveal the traits or characteristics they control. Even coat-color genetics, once thought to be a relatively simple dominance series consisting of gray, bay (or brown), and chestnut alleles, proved to be not so simple because white Thoroughbreds began to appear about 30 years ago.

The problem is that the traits that produce a successful racehorse are not governed by single genes. Factors such as speed, stamina, temperament, and soundness are each dependent on thousands of different genes working together with the environment to create outstanding racehorses.—*John P. Sparkman*

SIRES

Leading Sires by Progeny Earnings in 2004

Worldwide earnings for stallions who stand in North America or stood in North America if pensioned or dead.

◆ Denotes freshman sire.

Sire	Strs	Wnrs	SWs	Leading Earner (Earnings)	Total Earnings
Elusive Quality, Ky.	139	80	5	Smarty Jones ($7,563,535)	$10,865,792
Kingmambo, Ky.	183	74	14	King Kamehameha ($3,743,956)	10,701,986
El Prado (Ire), Ky.	200	102	16	Kitten's Joy ($1,625,796)	10,089,174
Storm Cat, Ky.	141	78	19	Seeking the Dia ($1,407,809)	9,843,341
A.P. Indy, Ky.	188	99	21	Friends Lake ($611,800)	9,129,720
Saint Ballado, Dead	179	90	4	Ashado ($2,259,640)	8,403,410
Tale of the Cat, Ky.	226	123	12	Lion Heart ($1,080,000)	7,707,398
Hennessy, Ky.	313	139	10	Grand Armee ($694,556)	7,649,836
Grand Slam, Ky.	178	96	13	Cafe Olympus ($875,328)	7,592,130
Royal Academy, Ky.	337	149	12	Bullish Luck ($1,459,267)	7,491,965
Unbridled's Song, Ky.	227	103	13	Domestic Dispute ($413,428)	7,458,540
Awesome Again, Ky.	117	61	5	Ghostzapper ($2,590,000)	7,120,028
Smart Strike, Ky.	136	84	12	Soaring Free ($1,113,862)	6,895,919
Carson City, Dead	186	101	10	Pollard's Vision ($1,022,020)	6,872,455
Silver Deputy, Ky.	176	92	6	Divine Silver ($1,121,192)	6,840,598
Langfuhr, Ky.	281	133	10	Imperialism ($542,000)	6,755,258
Dynaformer, Ky.	159	72	9	Perfect Drift ($947,595)	6,690,523
Alphabet Soup, Ky.	178	105	11	Our New Recruit ($1,265,795)	6,645,156
Pleasant Colony, Dead	54	24	4	Pleasantly Perfect ($4,840,000)	6,503,225
Thunder Gulch, Ky.	270	96	8	Sense of Style ($369,000)	6,197,381
Distorted Humor, Ky.	188	98	13	Funny Cide ($1,075,100)	5,878,454
Gone West, Ky.	158	67	6	Speightstown ($1,045,556)	5,723,453
Belong to Me, Ky.	193	101	8	Ocean Drive ($505,900)	5,591,936
Not For Love, Md.	180	102	10	Love of Money ($491,500)	5,441,941
Devil His Due, Ky.	199	103	9	Roses in May ($1,723,277)	5,333,966
Smoke Glacken, Ky.	150	100	9	Smok'n Frolic ($258,220)	5,144,394
Pleasant Tap, Ky.	137	70	5	Tap Dance City ($2,548,869)	5,137,415
Mt. Livermore, Ky.	166	80	3	Meiner Morgen ($902,935)	4,928,153
Kris S., Dead	109	51	10	Rock Hard Ten ($790,380)	4,919,496
Roar, Ca.	235	137	11	Little Jim (Arg) ($393,510)	4,735,903
Pulpit, Ky.	110	54	7	Purge ($562,734)	4,657,206
Gulch, Ky.	153	75	7	The Cliff's Edge ($1,010,000)	4,636,769
Honour and Glory, Ky.	308	136	6	Meisho Eishi ($200,309)	4,572,499
Cozzene, Ky.	127	64	5	Star Over the Bay ($493,960)	4,465,272
Cherokee Run, Ky.	172	102	6	During ($307,614)	4,458,711
Crafty Prospector, Ky.	150	92	5	Pies Prospect ($473,865)	4,392,606
Gold Fever, N.Y.	162	91	1	A Bit O'Gold ($1,060,790)	4,305,789
Regal Classic, N.Y.	207	96	4	Regal Roller ($604,314)	4,267,459
Quiet American, Ky.	163	89	6	Josh's Madelyn ($245,172)	4,267,329
Skip Away, Ky.	129	81	8	Crystal Violet ($440,312)	4,149,053
Rahy, Ky.	156	74	4	Designed for Luck ($311,180)	4,090,201
Indian Charlie, Ky.	101	68	8	Bwana Charlie ($349,690)	4,039,306
Unbridled, Dead	110	48	3	Niigon ($864,610)	4,033,237
In Excess (Ire), Ca.	109	60	7	Texcess ($725,427)	4,013,762
Sky Classic, Ky.	155	73	4	Nothing to Lose ($643,200)	4,012,881
Grindstone, Ky.	101	51	6	Birdstone ($1,236,600)	4,011,484
Forest Wildcat, Ky.	178	94	9	Wildcat Heir ($305,860)	3,953,310
Distant View, Ky.	132	57	5	Sightseek ($1,011,350)	3,948,371
Gilded Time, Ky.	203	94	5	Barely a Moment ($297,269)	3,943,857
Mr. Greeley, Ky.	176	92	3	Eishin Marukamu ($223,596)	3,836,834
Touch Gold, Ky.	136	61	4	Eishin Weiden ($455,417)	3,835,091
Valid Expectations, Tx.	134	82	9	Leaving On My Mind ($299,873)	3,817,376
Dixieland Band, Ky.	162	58	5	Bowman's Band ($439,334)	3,811,282
Storm Boot, Ky.	178	97	7	Very Vegas ($195,498)	3,805,301
Defrere, N.J.	125	74	5	Le Mars Girl ($1,224,177)	3,804,509
Petionville, Ky.	122	66	6	Island Fashion ($615,000)	3,777,418
Theatrical (Ire), Ky.	142	53	10	Laura's Lucky Boy ($246,730)	3,620,282
Runaway Groom, Ky.	175	101	8	The Lady's Groom ($262,520)	3,565,797
Rubiano, Ky.	139	71	7	Taiki Helios ($272,973)	3,563,588
Deputy Commander, Ky.	143	65	5	Grab Your Heart ($674,075)	3,556,078
Holy Bull, Ky.	146	73	2	Pohave ($450,740)	3,549,269
American Chance, Dead	123	58	7	Bending Strings ($495,150)	3,540,624
Seeking the Gold, Ky.	132	47	9	Seeking My Love ($392,411)	3,537,611
Wild Again, Pens	123	60	6	Offlee Wild ($335,640)	3,524,640
Halo's Image, Fl.	111	59	2	Southern Image ($1,612,150)	3,478,969

Sire	Strs	Wnrs	SWs	Leading Earner (Earnings)	Total Earnings
Honor Grades, Dead	157	67	2	Adoration ($607,304)	$3,401,423
Allen's Prospect, Dead	193	102	4	Crossing Point ($124,615)	3,351,884
Maria's Mon, Ky.	169	90	3	Grass Volante ($336,497)	3,330,421
Glitterman, Ky.	144	78	6	Champali ($634,398)	3,329,448
With Approval, Ky.	156	83	3	Destiny Calls ($271,670)	3,325,911
Housebuster, W.V.	84	34	4	Meisho Jako ($382,489)	3,325,909
Woodman, Ky.	304	97	4	Pretty Trio ($186,903)	3,317,073
Boundary, Ky.	119	62	4	Pomeroy ($296,250)	3,276,912
Polish Numbers, Dead	135	74	7	Chrusciki ($174,770)	3,251,105
Jade Hunter, Ky.	133	69	4	Azeri ($1,035,000)	3,223,660
Broad Brush, Pens	98	46	5	Nobo True ($925,316)	3,202,412
Peaks and Valleys, Ky.	175	97	6	Higher World ($213,210)	3,200,200
Cryptoclearance, Ky.	223	111	3	Cryptograph ($257,398)	3,196,824
Victory Gallop, Ky.	93	53	8	Victory U. S. A. ($263,267)	3,177,973
Marquetry, Ky.	169	83	3	Chris's Bad Boy ($261,480)	3,169,037
Deputy Minister, Dead	142	60	4	Miss Fortunate ($190,165)	3,131,205
Lit de Justice, Ca.	120	66	4	Hour of Justice ($243,953)	3,119,319
Arch, Ky.	89	56	6	Prince Arch ($405,946)	3,102,878
Miswaki, Dead	99	47	6	Sir Shackleton ($566,105)	3,093,767
Louis Quatorze, Md.	206	96	6	Choctaw Nation ($301,800)	3,069,073
General Meeting, Ca.	92	51	6	Yearly Report ($787,500)	3,061,344
Danzig, Pens	76	32	4	Antonius Pius ($460,158)	3,058,659
Souvenir Copy, Ca.	128	71	2	Souvenir Gift ($211,760)	3,043,851
Black Tie Affair (Ire), W.V.	113	32	2	Evening Attire ($420,040)	3,035,936
Stormy Atlantic, Ky.	130	72	5	Gators N Bears ($357,910)	3,029,930
Mutakddim, Ky.	174	92	5	Lady Tak ($439,412)	3,010,332
Dixie Brass, Dead	112	67	0	South Wing ($168,862)	2,958,921
Salt Lake, Ky.	191	95	7	Big Shark ($215,280)	2,947,013
Pioneering, Ky.	112	67	6	Danieltown ($279,361)	2,935,944
Two Punch, Md.	135	78	5	Bronze Abe ($241,900)	2,930,173
Out of Place, Ky.	153	77	2	Royal Place ($137,696)	2,885,560
A. P Jet, N.Y.	147	76	4	Travelator ($187,915)	2,857,664
Northern Afleet, Ky.	65	46	6	Afleet Alex ($680,800)	2,832,405
Diesis (GB), Ky.	111	39	3	Magistretti ($782,981)	2,814,342
Formal Gold, Ca.	112	70	5	Caballero Negro ($168,440)	2,807,120
Bold Executive, On.	88	45	4	Blonde Executive ($414,263)	2,800,055
Sword Dance (Ire), Pens	144	72	3	Eagle Sword ($447,692)	2,792,114
Gold Case, Ky.	132	80	5	Randaroo ($181,365)	2,779,607
Judge T C, N.Y.	120	64	3	Request for Parole ($757,100)	2,779,583
Sultry Song, Ky.	103	47	4	Singletary ($1,192,910)	2,769,904
Whiskey Wisdom, On.	77	42	4	Moonshine Justice ($283,914)	2,745,065
Bertrando, Ca.	139	75	3	Black Rock Road ($173,040)	2,723,491
Afternoon Deelites, La.	127	59	4	Water Goran ($271,779)	2,714,590
Montbrook, Fl.	129	74	8	Shake You Down ($278,604)	2,699,931
Stravinsky, Ky.	153	64	7	Cool Conductor ($298,295)	2,690,506
Kissin Kris, Ky.	145	79	3	Juliet's Kiss ($165,572)	2,653,613
Smokester, Ca.	136	83	3	Areyoutalkintome ($268,352)	2,651,586
Formal Dinner, Fl.	149	89	3	Formal Miss ($152,550)	2,610,191
Tactical Advantage, Dead	156	80	2	Omar Alejandro ($234,440)	2,591,706
Cape Town, Ky.	93	56	6	Susan's Angel ($338,540)	2,581,439
Storm Creek, Ca.	168	80	3	Hopelessly Devoted ($499,260)	2,578,300
Slew City Slew, Ky.	142	77	8	Sis City ($282,980)	2,563,286
Silver Ghost, Ky.	138	70	5	Caribbean Cruiser ($228,140)	2,562,744
Notebook, Dead	121	73	7	R Obsession ($148,800)	2,554,963
Dance Brightly, Ky.	121	75	2	Mr. Whitestone ($135,460)	2,490,493
High Brite, Ca.	129	80	5	Super High ($170,760)	2,484,565
Forestry, Ky.	68	34	11	Teton Forest ($222,000)	2,469,000
Sir Cat, Ky.	130	80	2	Joyful Spirit H K ($176,412)	2,444,329
Tomorrows Cat, N.Y.	120	56	4	West Virginia ($302,345)	2,439,783
Lear Fan, Pens	116	50	6	Freedom Hawk ($288,064)	2,425,915
Pentelicus, Dead	161	90	2	Fines Creek ($80,274)	2,359,411
Subordination, Ky.	65	42	3	Gene Crisis ($903,596)	2,317,218
Fortunate Prospect, Fl.	112	70	1	Credit Gal ($93,475)	2,276,768
Lite the Fuse, Pa.	109	62	3	Ablo ($191,040)	2,238,964
Pine Bluff, Ky.	99	54	4	Bear Fan ($496,180)	2,232,827

Sire	Strs	Wnrs	SWs	Leading Earner (Earnings)	Total Earnings
Wekiva Springs, Fl.	136	82	3	Merry Me in Spring ($124,700)	$2,212,824
Double Honor, Fl.	122	70	5	Honorable Buck ($119,975)	2,205,631
Silver Hawk, Pens	89	27	5	Wonder Again ($611,767)	2,184,114
Siberian Summer, Ca.	85	50	3	Summer Wind Dancer ($598,905)	2,176,034
Summer Squall, Pens	75	39	8	Misty Sixes ($246,074)	2,168,567
Patton, Pa.	118	71	3	Yessirgeneralsir ($278,250)	2,158,848
Conquistador Cielo, Dead	119	70	3	Taste of Paradise ($134,095)	2,151,806
Suave Prospect, Fl.	103	57	3	Umpateedle ($216,160)	2,150,261
Robyn Dancer, N.M.	131	65	0	Aspen Flower ($95,270)	2,133,820
Take Me Out, N.Y.	102	62	4	Put Me In ($261,222)	2,102,959
Is It True, Fl.	114	61	3	Sweet Problem ($249,205)	2,090,452
Phone Trick, N.Y.	127	69	1	Cloud Walker ($106,844)	2,067,784
Capote, Pens	107	48	4	Daddy Cool ($243,358)	2,030,788
Prized, Ky.	88	40	4	Brass Hat ($624,430)	2,014,410
Cee's Tizzy, Ca.	108	59	1	Kid Royal ($96,260)	2,003,525
Helmsman, Ca.	84	49	2	Emerald Earrings ($285,406)	2,001,575
Wheaton, Pa.	106	68	2	Wheaton's Aly ($101,200)	1,977,903
Line In The Sand, Fl.	160	77	1	City Line Ave ($87,746)	1,961,765
Archers Bay, Dead	56	29	2	Archers Bow ($198,145)	1,954,905
Citidancer, Md.	80	45	4	Park Avenue Ball ($278,600)	1,950,292
Dove Hunt, Tx.	103	59	5	Whenthedoveflies ($139,160)	1,936,351
Unusual Heat, Ca.	49	25	4	Lennyfromalibu ($172,639)	1,932,697
Lost Soldier, Ky.	132	63	2	Semi Lost ($163,070)	1,925,518
Mazel Trick, Pa.	80	41	1	Tricky Taboo ($138,026)	1,922,919
Kiridashi, On.	72	35	3	Financingavailable ($294,151)	1,906,365
Partner's Hero, Md.	93	49	2	Seventeen Above ($139,236)	1,903,686
Malibu Moon, Ky.	70	35	4	Declan's Moon ($507,300)	1,900,933
Personal Flag, Pens	137	63	2	Priscilla's Flag ($122,180)	1,900,450
Meadowlake, Ky.	107	54	2	Flemish Cap ($79,320)	1,894,552
Fit to Fight, Ky.	112	66	2	Certifiably Crazy ($144,729)	1,886,785
Tour d'Or, Fl.	128	67	2	Tour of the Rose ($91,568)	1,879,527
Swiss Yodeler, Ca.	98	56	2	Mr. Fondue ($99,028)	1,873,892
Lord Carson, Ca.	125	64	1	Paragon Queen ($85,540)	1,872,790
Siphon (Brz), Ky.	144	54	1	I'm the Tiger ($187,580)	1,859,322
Friendly Lover, Ia.	125	59	1	Win Me Over ($114,434)	1,856,359
Old Trieste, Dead	70	30	3	Maltese Heat ($375,607)	1,845,458
Favorite Trick, Fl.	131	61	4	Tight Spin ($109,430)	1,818,819
Mecke, Fl.	83	39	1	Supah Blitz ($446,280)	1,813,243
Menifee, Ky.	59	34	4	Can Ihavethisdance ($152,568)	1,807,034
Wild Zone, Ky.	144	69	2	Berdelia ($173,248)	1,805,285
Will's Way, Pa.	69	36	1	Lion Tamer ($592,380)	1,794,551
Pembroke, Ky.	113	64	2	Niclie ($140,670)	1,790,804
Concerto, Fl.	67	43	5	Bellamy Road ($140,400)	1,784,637
Rizzi, N.Y.	122	70	1	Ritta ($120,696)	1,776,151
Tactical Cat, Ky.	62	34	3	Dazzle Me ($265,276)	1,764,122
Mi Cielo, Ia.	75	28	1	Eishin Champ ($224,553)	1,757,996
Open Forum, Tx.	112	51	1	Open Concert ($136,457)	1,750,730
Benchmark, Ca.	77	39	3	Silent Sighs ($317,500)	1,745,504
Memo (Chi), Ca.	86	50	7	McCann's Mojave ($177,140)	1,734,700
Artax, N.Y.	75	37	1	Friendly Michelle ($335,754)	1,732,921
Banker's Gold, Pa.	91	50	0	Lukelynn ($83,522)	1,732,515
◆Successful Appeal, Ky.	22	15	6	Closing Argument ($421,984)	1,727,557
Ide, La.	88	53	0	Ide Be Gone ($134,700)	1,703,591
Mister Jolie, Dead	87	56	1	Coordinadora ($144,534)	1,701,103
Bold Badgett, Dead	72	30	3	Market Garden ($246,658)	1,698,327
Ghazi, Mn.	93	52	2	On the Bus ($171,220)	1,681,718
Lucky Lionel, Ok.	91	52	3	Hello Lucky ($142,140)	1,680,436
Doneraile Court, Ky.	77	49	3	Ruckus in Court ($138,775)	1,677,313
Unreal Zeal, Il.	120	70	4	Really Royal ($92,900)	1,675,579
Sandpit (Brz), Dead	143	70	2	Long Term Success ($177,750)	1,674,759
Demidoff, Il.	81	55	5	Setemup Joe ($105,920)	1,673,839
Valid Wager, Ca.	90	51	2	Irish Wager ($92,671)	1,672,648
Beau Genius, Ca.	110	58	4	My Creed ($140,790)	1,668,539
Editor's Note, Ky.	111	51	2	Lead Story ($235,740)	1,653,889
Swain (Ire), Ky.	74	23	3	Shell Game ($558,153)	1,644,477
Lac Ouimet, Ky.	100	59	4	Dreadnaught ($264,043)	1,632,445
Stormin Fever, Ky.	91	42	2	After the Tone ($112,507)	1,614,022
Cobra King, Ca.	81	46	2	Something Ventured ($114,920)	1,610,191
Vying Victor, B.C.	107	50	4	Alabama Rain ($136,784)	1,609,040
Devil's Bag, Dead	91	38	2	Symboli Devil ($269,514)	1,608,768

Leading Sires by Average Earnings per Runner in 2004
Minimum of 25 Starters

Sire	Strs	Wnrs	Average
Pleasant Colony, Dead	54	24	$120,430
Elusive Quality, Ky.	139	80	78,171
Storm Cat, Ky.	141	78	69,811
Awesome Again, Ky.	117	61	60,855
Kingmambo, Ky.	183	74	58,481
Smart Strike, Ky.	136	84	50,705
El Prado (Ire), Ky.	200	102	50,446
A.P. Indy, Ky.	188	99	48,562
Saint Ballado, Dead	179	90	46,946
Kris S., Dead	109	51	45,133
Northern Afleet, Ky.	65	46	43,575
Grand Slam, Ky.	178	96	42,652
Pulpit, Ky.	110	54	42,338
Dynaformer, Ky.	159	72	42,079
Danzig, Pens	76	32	40,246
◆Dixie Union, Ky.	25	14	40,029
Indian Charlie, Ky.	101	68	39,993
Grindstone, Ky.	101	51	39,718
Housebuster, W.V.	84	34	39,594
Unusual Heat, Ca.	49	25	39,443
Silver Deputy, Ky.	176	92	38,867
Pleasant Tap, Ky.	137	70	37,499
Alphabet Soup, Ky.	178	105	37,332
Carson City, Dead	186	101	36,949
In Excess (Ire), Ca.	109	60	36,824
Unbridled, Dead	110	48	36,666
Forestry, Ky.	68	34	36,309
Gone West, Ky.	158	67	36,224
Whiskey Wisdom, On.	77	42	35,650
Subordination, Ky.	65	42	35,650
Matty G, Ky.	39	25	35,432
Cozzene, Ky.	127	64	35,160
Archers Bay, Dead	56	29	34,909
Arch, Ky.	89	56	34,864
Smoke Glacken, Ky.	150	100	34,296
Victory Gallop, Ky.	93	53	34,172
◆Yes It's True, Ky.	42	16	34,115
Tale of the Cat, Ky.	226	123	34,104
General Meeting, Ca.	92	51	33,275
Unbridled's Song, Ky.	227	103	32,857
Broad Brush, Pens	98	46	32,678
Skip Away, Ky.	129	81	32,163
Bold Executive, On.	88	45	31,819
Halo's Image, Fl.	111	59	31,342
Distorted Humor, Ky.	188	98	31,268
Miswaki, Dead	99	47	31,250
Petionville, Ky.	122	66	30,962
Menifee, Ky.	59	34	30,628
Defrere, N.J.	125	74	30,436
Gulch, Ky.	153	75	30,306
Not For Love, Md.	180	102	30,233
Foxtrail, On.	41	17	30,094
◆Fusaichi Pegasus, Ky.	43	19	30,001

Leading Sires by Median Earnings per Runner in 2004
Minimum of 25 Starters

Sire	Strs	Wnrs	Median
Indian Charlie, Ky.	101	68	$23,175
Smoke Glacken, Ky.	150	100	22,523
Whiskey Wisdom, On.	77	42	21,232
Smart Strike, Ky.	136	84	20,657
Dixie Brass, Dead	112	67	20,420
Storm Cat, Ky.	141	78	19,501
A.P. Indy, Ky.	188	99	19,106
Sahm, Ky.	30	23	18,464
Archers Bay, Dead	56	29	18,168
Victory Gallop, Ky.	93	53	17,900
Barbeau, Dead	29	17	17,879
Ormsby, N.Y.	29	21	17,673
Arch, Ky.	89	56	17,365
Grand Slam, Ky.	178	96	16,444

Sire	Strs	Wnrs	Median
Good and Tough, N.Y.	47	31	$16,125
Formal Gold, Ca.	112	70	16,101
Carson City, Dead	186	101	16,063
Military, Ky.	36	21	15,963
Cape Town, Ky.	93	56	15,600
Royal Merlot, P.R.	29	25	15,470
Valid Expectations, Tx.	134	82	15,468
Pulpit, Ky.	110	54	15,306
Quaker Ridge, Fl.	28	21	15,301
Unusual Heat, Ca.	49	25	15,270
Not For Love, Md.	180	102	15,192
Elusive Quality, Ky.	139	80	15,153
Menifee, Ky.	59	34	15,115
Doneraile Court, Ky.	77	49	15,001
Skip Away, Ky.	129	81	14,940
Pioneering, Ky.	112	67	14,838
Tactical Cat, Ky.	62	34	14,828
Quiet American, Ky.	163	89	14,460
Saint Ballado, Dead	179	90	14,450
Matty G, Ky.	39	25	14,435
Yarrow Brae, Md.	55	29	14,409
Valiant Nature, W.V.	45	23	14,344
West Acre, Fl.	45	30	14,280
Awesome Again, Ky.	117	61	14,050
Silver Deputy, Ky.	176	92	13,879
Ops Smile, Pa.	45	27	13,864
Forestry, Ky.	68	34	13,745
Cozzene, Ky.	127	64	13,740
◆Dixie Union, Ky.	25	14	13,709
Malibu Moon, Ky.	70	35	13,585
Tale of the Cat, Ky.	226	123	13,500

Leading Sires by Number of Winners in 2004

Sire	Strs	Wnrs	Wnrs/Strs
Royal Academy, Ky.	337	148	43.9%
Hennessy, Ky.	310	138	44.5%
Roar, Ca.	235	137	58.3%
Honour and Glory, Ky.	308	135	43.8%
Langfuhr, Ky.	281	133	47.3%
Tale of the Cat, Ky.	226	123	54.4%
Cryptoclearance, Ky.	223	111	49.8%
Alphabet Soup, Ky.	178	105	59.0%
Devil His Due, Ky.	199	103	51.8%
Unbridled's Song, Ky.	227	103	45.4%
Allen's Prospect, Dead	193	102	52.8%
Cherokee Run, Ky.	172	102	59.3%
El Prado (Ire), Ky.	200	102	51.0%
Not For Love, Md.	180	102	56.7%
Belong to Me, Ky.	193	101	52.3%
Carson City, Dead	186	101	54.3%
Runaway Groom, Ky.	175	101	57.7%
Smoke Glacken, Ky.	150	100	66.7%
A.P. Indy, Ky.	188	99	52.7%
Distorted Humor, Ky.	188	98	52.1%
Peaks and Valleys, Ky.	175	97	55.4%
Storm Boot, Ky.	178	97	54.5%
Grand Slam, Ky.	178	96	53.9%
Louis Quatorze, Md.	206	96	46.6%
Thunder Gulch, Ky.	270	96	35.6%
Woodman, Ky.	303	96	31.7%
Salt Lake, Ky.	191	95	49.7%
Forest Wildcat, Ky.	178	94	52.8%
Gilded Time, Ky.	203	94	46.3%
Regal Classic, N.Y.	202	94	46.5%
Crafty Prospector, Ky.	150	92	61.3%
Mr. Greeley, Ky.	176	92	52.3%
Mutakddim, Ky.	174	92	52.9%
Silver Deputy, Ky.	176	92	52.3%
Gold Fever, N.Y.	162	91	56.2%
Maria's Mon, Ky.	169	90	53.3%
Pentelicus, Dead	161	90	55.9%
Saint Ballado, Dead	179	90	50.3%
Formal Dinner, Fl.	149	89	59.7%
Quiet American, Ky.	163	89	54.6%
Smart Strike, Ky.	136	84	61.8%

Sire	Strs	Wnrs	Wnrs/Strs
Marquetry, Ky.	169	83	49.1%
Smokester, Ca.	136	83	61.0%
With Approval, Ky.	156	83	53.2%
Slewdledo, Wa.	141	82	58.2%
Valid Expectations, Tx.	134	82	61.2%
Wekiva Springs, Fl.	136	82	60.3%
Skip Away, Ky.	129	81	62.8%

Leading Sires by Number of Wins in 2004

Sire	Strs	Wnrs	Wins
Roar, Ca.	235	137	237
Langfuhr, Ky.	281	133	235
Hennessy, Ky.	310	138	225
Royal Academy, Ky.	337	148	222
Honour and Glory, Ky.	308	135	200
Tale of the Cat, Ky.	226	123	200
Not For Love, Md.	180	102	195
Alphabet Soup, Ky.	178	105	194
Devil His Due, Ky.	199	103	190
Smoke Glacken, Ky.	150	100	185
El Prado (Ire), Ky.	200	102	184
Storm Boot, Ky.	178	97	184
Formal Dinner, Fl.	149	89	179
Unbridled's Song, Ky.	227	103	176
Belong to Me, Ky.	193	101	175
Carson City, Dead	186	101	175
Quiet American, Ky.	163	89	175
Mutakddim, Ky.	174	92	174
Pentelicus, Dead	161	90	173
Runaway Groom, Ky.	175	101	173
Distorted Humor, Ky.	188	98	172
Cherokee Run, Ky.	172	102	167
Silver Deputy, Ky.	176	92	166
Cryptoclearance, Ky.	223	111	165
Salt Lake, Ky.	191	95	165
Allen's Prospect, Dead	193	102	163
A.P. Indy, Ky.	188	99	163
Valid Expectations, Tx.	134	82	161
Crafty Prospector, Ky.	150	92	160
Regal Classic, N.Y.	202	94	159
Gold Fever, N.Y.	162	91	158
High Brite, Ca.	129	80	158
Peaks and Valleys, Ky.	175	97	156
Smart Strike, Ky.	136	84	156
Fortunate Prospect, Fl.	112	70	155
Grand Slam, Ky.	178	96	155
Gilded Time, Ky.	203	94	154
Louis Quatorze, Md.	206	96	154
Kissin Kris, Ky.	145	79	151
With Approval, Ky.	156	83	151
Smokester, Ca.	136	83	150
Defrere, N.J.	125	74	149
Skip Away, Ky.	129	81	149
Glitterman, Ky.	144	78	146
Tactical Advantage, Dead	156	80	146
Pioneering, Ky.	112	67	145
Thunder Gulch, Ky.	270	96	145
Wheaton, Pa.	106	68	145
Indian Charlie, Ky.	101	68	144
Maria's Mon, Ky.	169	90	142
Sword Dance (Ire), Pens	144	72	142
Saint Ballado, Dead	179	90	141
Marquetry, Ky.	169	83	140
Gold Case, Ky.	132	80	139
Pembroke, Ky.	113	64	139
Woodman, Ky.	303	96	139
Forest Wildcat, Ky.	178	94	138
Rizzi, N.Y.	122	70	137

Leading Sires by Number of Stakes Winners in 2004

Sire	Strs	Wnrs	SWs	SWins
A.P. Indy, Ky.	188	99	21	28
Storm Cat, Ky.	141	78	19	28
El Prado (Ire), Ky.	200	102	16	28

Sire	Strs	Wnrs	SWs	SWins
Kingmambo, Ky.	183	74	14	22
Distorted Humor, Ky.	188	98	13	18
Grand Slam, Ky.	178	96	13	19
Unbridled's Song, Ky.	227	103	13	19
Royal Academy, Ky.	337	148	12	18
Smart Strike, Ky.	136	84	12	21
Tale of the Cat, Ky.	226	123	12	15
Alphabet Soup, Ky.	178	105	11	18
Forestry, Ky.	68	34	11	13
Roar, Ca.	235	137	11	15
Carson City, Dead	186	101	10	18
Hennessy, Ky.	310	138	10	14
Kris S., Dead	109	51	10	14
Langfuhr, Ky.	281	133	10	14
Not For Love, Md.	180	102	10	18
Theatrical (Ire), Ky.	142	53	10	10
Devil His Due, Ky.	199	103	9	13
Dynaformer, Ky.	159	72	9	10
Forest Wildcat, Ky.	178	94	9	11
Seeking the Gold, Ky.	132	47	9	11
Smoke Glacken, Ky.	150	100	9	12
Valid Expectations, Tx.	134	82	9	15
Belong to Me, Ky.	193	101	8	15
Indian Charlie, Ky.	101	68	8	11
Montbrook, Fl.	129	74	8	10
Runaway Groom, Ky.	175	101	8	9
Skip Away, Ky.	129	81	8	11
Summer Squall, Pens	75	39	8	10
Thunder Gulch, Ky.	270	96	8	9
Victory Gallop, Ky.	93	53	8	8

Leading Sires by Number of Graded Stakes Winners in 2004

Sire	Strs	Wnrs	GSWs	GSWins
Storm Cat, Ky.	141	78	11	15
A.P. Indy, Ky.	188	99	9	11
Unbridled's Song, Ky.	227	103	8	11
Hennessy, Ky.	310	138	7	12
Royal Academy, Ky.	337	148	7	11
El Prado (Ire), Ky.	200	102	6	16
Kingmambo, Ky.	183	74	5	10
Pulpit, Ky.	110	54	5	5
Roar, Ca.	235	137	5	23
Tale of the Cat, Ky.	226	123	5	9
Theatrical (Ire), Ky.	142	53	5	5
Alphabet Soup, Ky.	178	105	4	5
Awesome Again, Ky.	117	61	4	7
Carson City, Dead	186	101	4	7
Dynaformer, Ky.	159	72	4	4
Grand Slam, Ky.	178	96	4	7
Gulch, Ky.	153	75	4	4
Kris S., Dead	109	51	4	6
Not For Love, Md.	180	102	4	4
Pleasant Colony, Dead	54	24	4	6
Smart Strike, Ky.	136	84	4	7
Arch, Ky.	89	56	3	6
Belong to Me, Ky.	193	101	3	8
Danzig, Pens	76	32	3	4
Diesis (GB), Ky.	111	39	3	3
Forestry, Ky.	68	34	3	3
◆Giant's Causeway, Ky.	70	19	3	5
Gone West, Ky.	158	67	3	6
Grindstone, Ky.	101	51	3	4
Langfuhr, Ky.	281	133	3	5
Louis Quatorze, Md.	206	96	3	5
Miswaki, Dead	99	47	3	5
Mutakddim, Ky.	174	92	3	8
Regal Classic, N.Y.	202	94	3	7
Saint Ballado, Dead	179	90	3	7
Silver Hawk, Pens	89	27	3	5
Sky Classic, Ky.	155	73	3	4
Smoke Glacken, Ky.	150	100	3	3
Stormy Atlantic, Ky.	130	72	3	4
Touch Gold, Ky.	136	61	3	4
Wild Again, Pens	123	60	3	3

Leading Juvenile Sires
by Progeny Earnings in 2004

Worldwide earnings for stallions who stood in North America in year of conception of two-year-olds of 2004.

♦ Denotes freshman sire.

Sire	Strs	Wnrs	SWs	Leading Earner (Earnings)	Total Earnings
Storm Cat, Ky.	32	16	4	Sweet Catomine ($799,800)	$1,927,589
♦Successful Appeal, Ky.	22	15	6	Closing Argument ($421,984)	1,727,557
♦Yes It's True, Ky.	42	16	4	Proud Accolade ($364,130)	1,432,823
♦Fusaichi Pegasus, Ky.	43	19	4	Roman Ruler ($330,800)	1,290,041
♦Giant's Causeway, Ky.	70	19	4	Shamardal ($359,680)	1,277,448
Awesome Again, Ky.	26	10	2	Wilko ($934,074)	1,268,720
Valid Expectations, Tx.	35	18	3	Leaving On My Mind ($299,873)	1,084,955
In Excess (Ire), Ca.	12	6	2	Texcess ($725,427)	1,019,531
♦Dixie Union, Ky.	25	14	2	Siberian Hobby ($189,161)	1,000,713
Thunder Gulch, Ky.	60	16	4	Sense of Style ($369,000)	974,268
♦Cape Canaveral, Ky.	34	13	4	Megascape ($161,740)	970,633
Petionville, Ky.	29	9	2	Runway Model ($580,598)	970,054
Unbridled's Song, Ky.	23	11	3	Splendid Blended ($327,400)	952,594
♦Precise End, Jpn	31	13	2	Seiun Vivace ($223,231)	939,157
♦More Than Ready, Ky.	45	20	3	Ready's Gal ($155,200)	938,813
Malibu Moon, Ky.	27	9	3	Declan's Moon ($507,300)	872,112
A.P. Indy, Ky.	27	10	2	Exhaust Note ($243,218)	864,646
Victory Gallop, Ky.	30	11	3	Victorious Ami ($188,600)	855,175
Touch Gold, Ky.	33	10	0	Eishin Weiden ($455,417)	828,060
Carson City, Dead	35	16	2	Classic Elegance ($204,006)	823,737
Northern Afleet, Ky.	13	8	1	Afleet Alex ($680,800)	814,430
A. P Jet, N.Y.	46	16	2	Galloping Grocer ($150,400)	772,446
Kingmambo, Ky.	31	8	2	Divine Proportions ($481,006)	771,303
Whiskey Wisdom, On.	14	9	3	Moonshine Justice ($283,914)	759,611
Foxtrail, On.	24	8	2	Wholelottabourbon ($286,230)	739,773
Wild Event, Fl.	18	10	1	Aclassysassylassy ($498,800)	722,940
Gilded Time, Ky.	36	19	2	Emit Time ($138,685)	705,449
Tale of the Cat, Ky.	35	15	0	Canadian Gem ($125,580)	702,090
Indian Charlie, Ky.	16	10	3	World Avenue ($167,486)	678,991
Honour and Glory, Ky.	60	18	1	Green Belt ($85,439)	664,619
Wheaton, Pa.	41	23	2	Departing Now ($71,106)	646,346
Smart Strike, Ky.	26	11	3	Pelham Bay ($126,777)	632,789
Peaks and Valleys, Ky.	32	14	3	Higher World ($213,210)	620,332
Stormy Atlantic, Ky.	48	20	1	Frosty Royalty ($74,060)	618,677
Afternoon Deelites, La.	32	13	2	Three Hour Nap ($158,400)	618,194
Boundary, Ky.	18	8	1	Eishin Aswan ($182,116)	615,333
Swiss Yodeler, Ca.	37	15	0	Mr. Fondue ($99,028)	611,810
Maria's Mon, Ky.	38	15	1	K. D.'s Shady Lady ($77,320)	603,549
Danzig, Pens	19	10	2	Ad Valorem ($258,357)	601,180
Forest Wildcat, Ky.	34	19	0	Get Wild ($62,365)	597,253
Double Honor, Fl.	39	21	2	Cut the Mustard ($70,400)	591,645
Southern Halo, Arg	29	7	2	Dubleo ($360,899)	591,544
Stormin Fever, Ky.	37	14	2	Sweet Talker ($99,760)	581,927
Charismatic, Jpn	42	13	1	Sun King ($244,850)	579,193
Stravinsky, Ky.	34	10	2	Golden Stravinsky ($173,249)	577,898
♦Yankee Victor, Ky.	31	15	0	Maltese Victor ($84,314)	576,742
Silver Charm, Jpn	33	11	1	Silver Impulse ($202,662)	576,568
Cherokee Run, Ky.	30	14	1	Cherokee Path ($98,365)	559,275
Spinning World, Ire	25	12	1	Cheerful World ($179,206)	556,637
Wild Rush, Jpn	24	8	1	Wild Remarks ($100,442)	552,834
Menifee, Ky.	25	10	1	Boggy Creek ($120,111)	540,178
♦Bernstein, Ky.	23	12	2	Sweet Solairo ($133,683)	534,631
Pulpit, Ky.	26	8	1	Bhagavadgita ($102,736)	529,449
♦Running Stag, Fl.	34	11	1	Running Bobcats ($108,680)	529,072
Smoke Glacken, Ky.	24	15	2	Clemson You ($63,310)	528,325
♦Tiger Ridge, Fl.	26	11	1	Anthony J. ($213,630)	518,486
Cape Town, Ky.	22	13	2	Ninadivina ($86,174)	516,547
♦Sweetsouthernsaint, Fl.	27	13	1	Better Than Bonds ($114,370)	516,211
♦Straight Man, Fl.	34	13	0	South Battle Man ($97,637)	510,843
Grand Slam, Ky.	29	11	0	Countach ($81,106)	500,886
Wild Zone, Ky.	42	15	1	Berdelia ($173,248)	499,683
♦Old Topper, Ca.	19	10	2	Shout to the North ($132,292)	498,815
Lord Carson, Ca.	34	16	0	Paragon Queen ($85,540)	498,791
King of Kings (Ire), Swi	38	12	1	Paddy's Daisy ($186,336)	489,777
Devil His Due, Ky.	42	16	1	Devils Disciple ($161,800)	483,537

Leading Juvenile Sires by Average Earnings per Runner in 2004
Minimum of 10 Starters

Sire	Strs	Wnrs	Average
In Excess (Ire), Ca.	12	6	$84,961
◆Successful Appeal, Ky.	22	15	78,525
Northern Afleet, Ky.	13	8	62,648
Storm Cat, Ky.	32	16	60,237
Whiskey Wisdom, On.	14	9	54,258
Awesome Again, Ky.	26	10	48,797
Indian Charlie, Ky.	16	10	42,437
Unbridled's Song, Ky.	23	11	41,417
Wild Event, Fl.	18	10	40,163
◆Dixie Union, Ky.	25	14	40,029
Boundary, Ky.	18	8	34,185
◆Yes It's True, Ky.	42	16	34,115
Petionville, Ky.	29	9	33,450
Malibu Moon, Ky.	27	9	32,300
A.P. Indy, Ky.	27	10	32,024
Danzig, Pens	19	10	31,641
Valid Expectations, Tx.	35	18	30,999
Seattle Slew, Dead	12	5	30,896
Foxtrail, On.	24	8	30,824
◆Precise End, Jpn	31	13	30,295
◆Fusaichi Pegasus, Ky.	43	19	30,001

Leading Juvenile Sires by Median Earnings per Runner in 2004
Minimum of 10 Starters

Sire	Strs	Wnrs	SWs Median
Whiskey Wisdom, On.	14	9	$33,319
◆Successful Appeal, Ky.	22	15	28,703
Indian Charlie, Ky.	16	10	23,430
Good and Tough, N.Y.	15	7	20,540
Military, Ky.	10	6	18,705
Compadre, On.	10	5	18,605
Cape Town, Ky.	22	13	18,143
Smoke Glacken, Ky.	24	15	17,490
◆Lion Hearted, Md.	14	10	16,926
Mister Jolie, Dead	10	7	16,829
Victory Gallop, Ky.	30	11	14,676
Star of Valor, Dead	10	5	14,384
Wild Event, Fl.	18	10	13,785
◆Untuttable, Fl.	15	7	13,742
◆Dixie Union, Ky.	25	14	13,709
◆Bernstein, Ky.	23	12	13,620

Leading Juvenile Sires by Number of Winners in 2004

Sire	Strs	Wnrs	Wnrs/Strs
Wheaton, Pa.	41	23	56.1%
Double Honor, Fl.	39	21	53.8%
Slew Gin Fizz, Fl.	38	21	55.3%
◆More Than Ready, Ky.	45	20	44.4%
Stormy Atlantic, Ky.	48	20	41.7%
◆Catienus, N.Y.	33	19	57.6%
Forest Wildcat, Ky.	34	19	55.9%
◆Fusaichi Pegasus, Ky.	43	19	44.2%
◆Giant's Causeway, Ky.	70	19	27.1%
Gilded Time, Ky.	36	19	52.8%
Honour and Glory, Ky.	60	18	30.0%
Valid Expectations, Tx.	35	18	51.4%
Family Calling, Fl.	34	17	50.0%
A. P Jet, N.Y.	46	16	34.8%
Carson City, Dead	35	16	45.7%
Devil His Due, Ky.	42	16	38.1%
Lord Carson, Ca.	34	16	47.1%
Storm Cat, Ky.	32	16	50.0%
Thunder Gulch, Ky.	60	16	26.7%
◆Yes It's True, Ky.	42	16	38.1%
Fortunate Prospect, Pens	25	15	60.0%
Maria's Mon, Ky.	38	15	39.5%
Smoke Glacken, Ky.	24	15	62.5%
◆Successful Appeal, Ky.	22	15	68.2%
Swiss Yodeler, Ca.	37	15	40.5%
Tale of the Cat, Ky.	35	15	42.9%
Wild Zone, Ky.	42	15	35.7%
◆Yankee Victor, Ky.	31	15	48.4%

Leading Juvenile Sires by Number of Wins in 2004

Sire	Strs	Wnrs	Wins
Wheaton, Pa.	41	23	36
Valid Expectations, Tx.	35	18	34
Double Honor, Fl.	39	21	32
◆Successful Appeal, Ky.	22	15	31
Slew Gin Fizz, Fl.	38	21	28
Stormy Atlantic, Ky.	48	20	28
◆Fusaichi Pegasus, Ky.	43	19	27
◆Giant's Causeway, Ky.	70	19	27
◆More Than Ready, Ky.	45	20	27
◆Yes It's True, Ky.	42	16	26
Storm Cat, Ky.	32	16	25
◆Cape Canaveral, Ky.	34	13	23
◆Catienus, N.Y.	33	19	23
Gilded Time, Ky.	36	19	23
Carson City, Dead	35	16	22
Devil His Due, Ky.	42	16	22
Family Calling, Fl.	34	17	22
Forest Wildcat, Ky.	34	19	22
Fortunate Prospect, Pens	25	15	22
Robyn Dancer, N.M.	43	13	22
◆Sweetsouthernsaint, Fl.	27	13	22
Tale of the Cat, Ky.	35	15	22
Thunder Gulch, Ky.	60	16	22
Bartok (Ire), Ca.	32	13	21
Honour and Glory, Ky.	60	18	21
Wild Zone, Ky.	42	15	21
A. P Jet, N.Y.	46	16	20
Peaks and Valleys, Ky.	32	14	20
Smoke Glacken, Ky.	24	15	20
Stravinsky, Ky.	34	10	20
Swiss Yodeler, Ca.	37	15	20
Unbridled's Song, Ky.	23	11	20

Leading Juvenile Sires by Number of Stakes Winners in 2004

Sire	Strs	Wnrs	SWs	SWins
◆Successful Appeal, Ky.	22	15	6	12
◆Cape Canaveral, Ky.	34	13	4	6
◆Fusaichi Pegasus, Ky.	43	19	4	7
◆Giant's Causeway, Ky.	70	19	4	6
Storm Cat, Ky.	32	16	4	7
Thunder Gulch, Ky.	60	16	4	5
◆Yes It's True, Ky.	42	16	4	8
Danjur, Dead	12	7	3	4
Indian Charlie, Ky.	16	10	3	4
Malibu Moon, Ky.	27	9	3	6
◆More Than Ready, Ky.	45	20	3	3
Peaks and Valleys, Ky.	32	14	3	5
Rubiano, Dead	31	11	3	3
Smart Strike, Ky.	26	11	3	4
Unbridled's Song, Ky.	23	11	3	4
Valid Expectations, Tx.	35	18	3	8
Victory Gallop, Ky.	30	11	3	3
Whiskey Wisdom, On.	14	9	3	5

Leading Juvenile Sires by Number of Graded Stakes Winners in 2004

Sire	Strs	Wnrs	GSWs	GSWins
◆Giant's Causeway, Ky.	70	19	3	5
Storm Cat, Ky.	32	16	3	5
Danzig, Pens	19	10	2	2
Unbridled's Song, Ky.	23	11	2	3
◆Yes It's True, Ky.	42	16	2	2

Leading Freshman Sires
by Progeny Earnings in 2004

Worldwide earnings for stallions who stood in North America in 2001
and whose oldest foals were two-year-olds in '04. ◆ Denotes freshman sire.

Sire	Strs	Wnrs	SWs	Leading Earner (Earnings)	Total Earnings
◆Successful Appeal, Ky.	22	15	6	Closing Argument ($421,984)	$1,727,557
◆Yes It's True, Ky.	42	16	4	Proud Accolade ($364,130)	1,432,823
◆Fusaichi Pegasus, Ky.	43	19	4	Roman Ruler ($330,800)	1,290,041
◆Giant's Causeway, Ky.	70	19	4	Shamardal ($359,680)	1,277,448
◆Dixie Union, Ky.	25	14	2	Siberian Hobby ($189,161)	1,000,713
◆Cape Canaveral, Ky.	34	13	4	Megascape ($161,740)	970,633
◆Precise End, Jpn	31	13	2	Seiun Vivace ($223,231)	939,157
◆More Than Ready, Ky.	45	20	3	Ready's Gal ($155,200)	938,813
◆Monashee Mountain, Ky.	54	16	3	Le Giare ($170,535)	765,499
◆Rossini, Ky.	60	16	2	Tournedos ($140,546)	639,706
◆Yankee Victor, Ky.	31	15	0	Maltese Victor ($84,314)	576,742
◆Bernstein, Ky.	23	12	2	Sweet Solairo ($133,683)	534,631
◆Running Stag, Fl.	34	11	1	Running Bobcats ($108,680)	529,072
◆Tiger Ridge, Fl.	26	11	1	Anthony J. ($213,630)	518,486
◆Sweetsouthernsaint, Fl.	27	13	1	Better Than Bonds ($114,370)	516,211
◆Straight Man, Fl.	34	13	0	South Battle Man ($97,637)	510,843
◆Old Topper, Ca.	19	10	2	Shout to the North ($132,292)	498,815
◆High Yield, Ky.	36	13	0	Stormy Jim ($72,290)	481,309
◆War Chant, Ky.	19	12	2	Up Like Thunder ($99,265)	467,887
◆Catienus, N.Y.	33	19	1	Kathern's Cat ($79,603)	451,551
◆Lion Hearted, Md.	14	10	2	Hear Us Roar ($128,680)	398,927
◆Dance Master, Fl.	9	5	1	Flamenco ($303,085)	397,740
◆Cat Thief, Ky.	22	10	0	Eishin Boston ($83,041)	388,530
◆Stephen Got Even, Ky.	25	8	0	Didycheatamandhowe ($76,330)	386,429
◆Western Expression, N.Y.	20	7	0	Summerland ($83,973)	384,961
◆Lemon Drop Kid, Ky.	23	8	1	Winning Season ($99,655)	375,459
◆Chester House, Dead	29	9	1	Exceptional Ride ($106,303)	337,105
◆Golden Missile, Ky.	24	6	1	Inspiring ($115,800)	332,496
◆Chief Seattle, Ky.	24	9	0	Bold Outlook ($68,400)	304,361
◆Anees, Dead	19	5	1	Swither ($128,826)	280,239
◆Magic Cat, Tx.	29	11	1	Major League ($97,100)	279,934
◆Vicar, Ky.	29	9	0	Crafty Vixen ($47,620)	278,996
◆Untuttable, Fl.	15	7	1	Favalora ($52,390)	277,473
◆Intidab, Ky.	6	3	1	Greater Good ($226,275)	255,219
◆Littlebitlively, La.	22	7	0	Littlebitofzip ($85,328)	223,864
◆Greenwood Lake, Ky.	16	7	0	Extra Bases ($71,097)	211,194
◆Richter Scale, Ky.	14	5	1	Quite a Ruckus ($110,653)	204,013
◆Wised Up, Fl.	15	7	0	Wise Briana ($45,460)	191,359
◆Meadow Prayer, Mi.	6	2	1	Foolininthemeadow ($155,987)	168,542
◆Storm and a Half, Ar.	12	5	2	Z Storm ($39,220)	166,425
◆Devonwood, Dead	15	5	1	Speedy Gone Sally ($71,444)	153,358
◆Muqtarib, Ca.	8	3	2	Whatsthenameman ($75,855)	149,932
◆Unbridled Jet, Md.	26	2	0	Media Alert ($28,580)	133,071
◆Deputy Diamond, La.	25	7	0	One Tough Deputy ($20,117)	127,081
◆Elnadim, Ire	7	3	0	Wild as Elle ($78,315)	124,009
◆Kelly Kip, N.Y.	12	4	0	My Kip ($32,350)	122,343
◆Royal Anthem, Ky.	26	5	0	Prince T. ($25,480)	116,711
◆Commendable, Kor	15	6	0	Sue Me ($35,418)	113,743
◆Karen's Cat, Tx.	6	3	0	Cat Tourn ($71,028)	109,430
◆Aljabr, Ky.	14	6	0	Where's Bailey ($35,200)	104,777
◆Badge, N.Y.	9	3	0	Pretty Partisan ($59,200)	101,194
◆Untold Gold, Dead	3	2	1	Hush's Gold ($82,905)	100,917
◆Sasha's Prospect, Fl.	9	4	0	Denium Cowgirl ($44,260)	92,608
◆The Deputy (Ire), Ky.	16	5	0	Deputy French ($19,500)	89,025
◆Best of Luck, Ky.	30	2	0	Best One ($30,145)	85,644
◆Robb, W.V.	5	3	0	Miss Angel ($32,141)	85,482
◆Malek (Chi), Ca.	12	1	0	Musica Si ($43,089)	81,757
◆King of Scat, Ok.	12	6	1	S C King ($18,984)	79,732
◆Lightning Al, P.R.	2	2	1	Lightning Al Boy ($39,480)	78,610
◆Silic (Fr), Ky.	7	2	0	Katie Can Dance ($54,217)	74,701
◆Behrens, Ky.	9	3	0	Sueno Del Mar ($30,930)	73,570
◆Sea Twister, Dead	3	2	2	Wind Twister ($52,360)	72,960
◆Makula King, Dead	3	3	0	Always Picked On ($43,090)	70,330
◆Close Up, N.J.	5	2	0	Joey P. ($57,240)	69,500
◆Adcat, Fl.	11	4	0	Swift Mercedes ($21,620)	69,354

Leading Freshman Sires by Average Earnings per Runner in 2004
Minimum of 10 Starters

Sire	Strs	Wnrs	Average
◆Successful Appeal, Ky.	22	15	$78,525
◆Dixie Union, Ky.	25	14	40,029
◆Yes It's True, Ky.	42	16	34,115
◆Precise End, Jpn	31	13	30,295
◆Fusaichi Pegasus, Ky.	43	19	30,001
◆Cape Canaveral, Ky.	34	13	28,548
◆Lion Hearted, Md.	14	10	28,495
◆Old Topper, Ca.	19	10	26,253
◆War Chant, Ky.	19	12	24,626
◆Bernstein, Ky.	23	12	23,245
◆More Than Ready, Ky.	45	20	20,863
◆Tiger Ridge, Fl.	26	11	19,942
◆Western Expression, N.Y.	20	7	19,248
◆Sweetsouthernsaint, Fl.	27	13	19,119
◆Yankee Victor, Ky.	31	15	18,605
◆Untuttable, Fl.	15	7	18,498
◆Giant's Causeway, Ky.	70	19	18,249
◆Cat Thief, Ky.	22	10	17,660
◆Lemon Drop Kid, Ky.	23	8	16,324
◆Running Stag, Fl.	34	11	15,561
◆Stephen Got Even, Ky.	25	8	15,457
◆Straight Man, Fl.	34	13	15,025
◆Anees, Dead	19	5	14,749
◆Richter Scale, Ky.	14	5	14,572
◆Monashee Mountain, Ky.	54	16	14,176

Leading Freshman Sires by Median Earnings per Runner in 2004
Minimum of 10 Starters

Sire	Strs	Wnrs	Median
◆Successful Appeal, Ky.	22	15	$28,703
◆Lion Hearted, Md.	14	10	16,926
◆Untuttable, Fl.	15	7	13,742
◆Dixie Union, Ky.	25	14	13,709
◆Bernstein, Ky.	23	12	13,620
◆Old Topper, Ca.	19	10	12,880
◆War Chant, Ky.	19	12	11,836
◆Yankee Victor, Ky.	31	15	11,760
◆Western Expression, N.Y.	20	7	10,587
◆Precise End, Jpn	31	13	9,778
◆More Than Ready, Ky.	45	20	9,525
◆Lemon Drop Kid, Ky.	23	8	9,000
◆Greenwood Lake, Ky.	16	7	8,721
◆Fusaichi Pegasus, Ky.	43	19	7,395
◆Cape Canaveral, Ky.	34	13	7,198

Leading Freshman Sires by Number of Winners in 2004

Sire	Strs	Wnrs	Wnrs/Strs
◆More Than Ready, Ky.	45	20	44.4%
◆Catienus, N.Y.	33	19	57.6%
◆Fusaichi Pegasus, Ky.	43	19	44.2%
◆Giant's Causeway, Ky.	70	19	27.1%
◆Monashee Mountain, Ky.	54	16	29.6%
◆Rossini, Ky.	60	16	26.7%
◆Yes It's True, Ky.	42	16	38.1%
◆Successful Appeal, Ky.	22	15	68.2%
◆Yankee Victor, Ky.	31	15	48.4%
◆Dixie Union, Ky.	25	14	56.0%
◆Cape Canaveral, Ky.	34	13	38.2%
◆High Yield, Ky.	36	13	36.1%
◆Precise End, Jpn	31	13	41.9%
◆Straight Man, Fl.	34	13	38.2%
◆Sweetsouthernsaint, Fl.	27	13	48.1%
◆Bernstein, Ky.	23	12	52.2%
◆War Chant, Ky.	19	12	63.2%
◆Magic Cat, Tx.	29	11	37.9%
◆Running Stag, Fl.	34	11	32.4%
◆Tiger Ridge, Fl.	26	11	42.3%
◆Cat Thief, Ky.	22	10	45.5%
◆Lion Hearted, Md.	14	10	71.4%
◆Old Topper, Ca.	19	10	52.6%
◆Chester House, Dead	29	9	31.0%
◆Chief Seattle, Ky.	24	9	37.5%
◆Vicar, Ky.	29	9	31.0%
◆Lemon Drop Kid, Ky.	23	8	34.8%
◆Stephen Got Even, Ky.	25	8	32.0%

Leading Freshman Sires by Number of Wins in 2004

Sire	Strs	Wnrs	Wins
◆Successful Appeal, Ky.	22	15	31
◆Monashee Mountain, Ky.	54	16	28
◆Fusaichi Pegasus, Ky.	43	19	27
◆Giant's Causeway, Ky.	70	19	27
◆More Than Ready, Ky.	45	20	27
◆Rossini, Ky.	60	16	27
◆Yes It's True, Ky.	42	16	26
◆Cape Canaveral, Ky.	34	13	23
◆Catienus, N.Y.	33	19	23
◆Sweetsouthernsaint, Fl.	27	13	22
◆Dixie Union, Ky.	25	14	19
◆Bernstein, Ky.	23	12	18
◆Yankee Victor, Ky.	31	15	17
◆High Yield, Ky.	36	13	16
◆Precise End, Jpn	31	13	16
◆Running Stag, Fl.	34	11	16
◆Straight Man, Fl.	34	13	16
◆Old Topper, Ca.	19	10	15
◆Lion Hearted, Md.	14	10	13
◆Magic Cat, Tx.	29	11	13
◆Tiger Ridge, Fl.	26	11	13
◆War Chant, Ky.	19	12	13
◆Untuttable, Fl.	15	7	12
◆Chester House, Dead	29	9	11
◆Cat Thief, Ky.	22	10	10
◆Chief Seattle, Ky.	24	9	10
◆Dance Master, Fl.	9	5	9
◆Lemon Drop Kid, Ky.	23	8	9
◆Stephen Got Even, Ky.	25	8	9
◆Vicar, Ky.	29	9	9

Leading Freshman Sires by Number of Stakes Winners in 2004

Sire	Strs	Wnrs	SWs	SWins
◆Successful Appeal, Ky.	22	15	6	12
◆Cape Canaveral, Ky.	34	13	4	6
◆Fusaichi Pegasus, Ky.	43	19	4	7
◆Giant's Causeway, Ky.	70	19	4	6
◆Yes It's True, Ky.	42	16	4	8
◆Monashee Mountain, Ky.	54	16	3	4
◆More Than Ready, Ky.	45	20	3	3
◆Bernstein, Ky.	23	12	2	3
◆Dixie Union, Ky.	25	14	2	3
◆Lion Hearted, Md.	14	10	2	3
◆Muqtarib, Ca.	8	3	2	2
◆Old Topper, Ca.	19	10	2	2
◆Precise End, Jpn	31	13	2	2
◆Rossini, Ky.	60	16	2	2
◆Sea Twister, Dead	3	2	2	3
◆Storm and a Half, Ar.	12	5	2	2
◆War Chant, Ky.	19	12	2	2

Leading Freshman Sires by Number of Graded Stakes Winners in 2004

Sire	Strs	Wnrs	GSWs	GSWins
◆Giant's Causeway, Ky.	70	19	3	5
◆Rossini, Ky.	60	16	2	2
◆Yes It's True, Ky.	42	16	2	2
◆Bernstein, Ky.	23	12	1	1
◆Cape Canaveral, Ky.	34	13	1	1
◆Fusaichi Pegasus, Ky.	43	19	1	2
◆Golden Missile, Ky.	24	6	1	1
◆Intidab, N.Y.	6	3	1	2
◆Monashee Mountain, Ky.	54	16	1	1
◆Successful Appeal, Ky.	22	15	1	2

Leading Broodmare Sires by Progeny Earnings in 2004

Worldwide earnings for broodmare sires who stand or last stood
in North America or had 25 North American starters in 2004.

Sire	Strs	Wnrs	SWs	Leading Earner (Earnings)	Total Earnings
Mr. Prospector, Dead	495	223	26	Hookipa Wave ($1,058,933)	$20,311,039
Sadler's Wells, Ire	487	182	26	Heavenly Romance ($1,109,499)	16,088,687
Caerleon, Dead	468	181	15	Silk Famous ($2,449,025)	15,718,983
Nureyev, Dead	365	158	16	Bago ($1,729,227)	15,051,204
Danzig, Pens	403	181	22	Soaring Free ($1,113,862)	14,869,560
Dixieland Band, Ky.	382	201	17	Delta Blues ($2,525,023)	14,780,849
Woodman, Ky.	492	229	23	Belmont Patty ($576,369)	12,609,726
Deputy Minister, Dead	386	194	15	Magistretti ($782,981)	12,062,534
Affirmed, Dead	321	155	10	Pleasantly Perfect ($4,840,000)	11,613,950
Rainbow Quest, Eng	264	108	15	North Light ($1,961,555)	11,129,341
Seattle Slew, Dead	362	152	20	Erimo Maxim ($896,428)	10,841,650
Nijinsky II, Dead	283	104	5	Dance in the Mood (Jpn) ($2,866,978)	10,711,838
Alydar, Dead	297	125	9	Hishi Atlas ($1,188,500)	10,454,410
Seeking the Gold, Ky.	202	96	11	Seeking the Dia ($1,407,809)	10,277,353
Storm Cat, Ky.	325	141	6	Speightstown ($1,045,556)	10,233,773
Storm Bird, Dead	391	188	16	Birdstone ($1,236,600)	9,951,443
Miswaki, Dead	395	175	15	Memory Keanu ($528,882)	9,913,083
Mining, Jpn	162	83	6	Zenno Rob Roy ($6,681,748)	9,503,430
Smile, Dead	84	41	3	Smarty Jones ($7,563,535)	8,841,684
Alleged, Dead	335	143	17	Sulamani (Ire) ($1,611,523)	8,754,741
Lyphard, Dead	319	128	8	Peer Gynt ($685,962)	8,472,188
Clever Trick, Dead	347	170	9	Elegant Fashion ($1,118,838)	8,388,286
Kris S., Dead	261	133	11	Sweet Catomine ($799,800)	8,154,967
Gulch, Ky.	218	99	7	Refuse To Bend (Ire) ($766,803)	7,843,272
Halo, Dead	342	162	8	Bwana Charlie ($349,690)	7,615,552
Riverman, Dead	314	107	7	Makybe Diva ($2,410,921)	7,506,552
Green Dancer, Dead	364	150	14	Happy Tomorrow ($458,178)	7,227,291
Valid Appeal, Dead	324	174	8	Eagle Sword ($447,692)	7,206,999
Lear Fan, Pens	222	102	8	Kitten's Joy ($1,625,796)	7,152,205
Private Account, Dead	324	149	10	Menhoubah ($400,035)	7,139,793
Wild Again, Pens	318	156	8	Osumi Stayer ($309,401)	7,124,581
Bold Ruckus, Dead	244	134	10	My Vintage Port ($383,302)	7,031,181
Vice Regent, Dead	290	138	4	Eye of the Sphynx ($688,340)	6,857,641
Crafty Prospector, Ky.	321	170	9	Spicule ($674,567)	6,720,167
Afleet, Jpn	220	98	6	Sidewinder ($548,283)	6,629,778
Pleasant Colony, Dead	274	138	8	Bowman's Band ($439,334)	6,599,836
Cure the Blues, Dead	305	151	7	Cajun Beat ($326,800)	6,507,405
Forty Niner, Jpn	210	106	10	Sepia Memory ($538,840)	6,354,730
Sovereign Dancer, Dead	258	140	8	Kela ($710,212)	6,331,124
Gone West, Ky.	225	103	12	Toyo Atlanta ($343,076)	6,236,912
Royal Academy, Ky.	236	78	11	Rule of Law ($1,233,320)	6,203,544
Alysheba, KSA	175	84	6	Bullish Luck ($1,459,267)	6,074,560
Silver Hawk, Pens	214	93	7	Ticker Tape (GB) ($1,159,075)	6,058,768
Topsider, Dead	210	110	5	Kite Hill Wind ($1,025,937)	6,052,194
Majestic Light, Dead	305	145	4	Artie Schiller ($467,578)	6,032,423
Irish River (Fr), Dead	346	134	13	Felicia ($495,011)	5,992,258
Slew o' Gold, Pens	238	98	5	Monopole ($701,330)	5,966,311
Chief's Crown, Dead	239	103	7	Eddington ($605,360)	5,907,639
Devil's Bag, Dead	276	129	6	Balto Star ($410,834)	5,827,648
Saratoga Six, N.M.	221	111	10	Madcap Escapade ($536,400)	5,604,202
Conquistador Cielo, Dead	313	148	7	My Cousin Matt ($208,200)	5,486,019
Fappiano, Dead	214	101	6	Meiner Polonaise ($303,039)	5,362,357
Ogygian, Jpn	176	77	9	Divine Silver ($1,121,192)	5,316,664
Cox's Ridge, Dead	270	134	7	Swingforthefences ($385,745)	5,310,154
Be My Guest, Dead	331	121	9	Naniwa Victory ($611,799)	5,282,732
Blushing Groom (Fr), Dead	190	79	6	Haafhd ($772,558)	5,265,791
Naskra, Dead	119	50	7	Perfect Drift ($947,595)	5,255,719
Capote, Pens	222	103	5	Roar Emotion ($328,652)	5,223,293
Strawberry Road (Aus), Dead	170	105	9	Eishin Hampton ($741,422)	5,200,586
The Minstrel, Dead	238	93	8	Grey Swallow ($1,041,518)	5,114,916
Star de Naskra, Dead	208	102	6	Singletary ($1,192,910)	5,104,862
Spectacular Bid, Dead	237	119	14	Bare Necessities ($328,970)	5,083,726
Phone Trick, N.Y.	279	138	10	Eye of the Tiger ($296,450)	4,967,533
Regal Classic, N.Y.	170	87	3	Texcess ($725,427)	4,737,668
Rahy, Ky.	223	99	6	Even the Score ($343,272)	4,617,731

Leading Broodmare Sires
by Average Earnings per Runner in 2004
Minimum of 25 Starters

Sire	Strs	Wnrs	Average
Smile, Dead	84	41	$105,258
Rhythm, Ca.	34	10	63,157
Olympio, Ca.	41	20	59,506
Mining, Jpn	162	83	58,663
Seeking the Gold, Ky.	202	96	50,878
Northern Dancer, Dead	95	32	46,568
Naskra, Dead	119	50	44,166
Easy Goer, Dead	70	32	43,550
Mari's Book, Dead	93	50	43,324
Rainbow Quest, Eng	264	108	42,157
Bailjumper, Dead	58	27	41,396
Nureyev, Dead	365	158	41,236
Mr. Prospector, Dead	495	223	41,032
Kingmambo, Ky.	65	29	40,275
Quiet American, Ky.	68	31	39,254
Dixieland Band, Ky.	382	201	38,693
Highland Park, Dead	62	34	37,953
Nijinsky II, Dead	283	104	37,851
Citidancer, Md.	46	29	37,849
Danzig, Pens	403	181	36,897
Diablo, Jpn	53	32	36,645
Risen Star, Dead	96	47	36,181
Affirmed, Dead	321	155	36,181
Gulch, Ky.	218	99	35,978
Alydar, Dead	297	125	35,200
Alysheba, KSA	175	84	34,712

Leading Broodmare Sires
by Median Earnings per Runner in 2004
Minimum of 25 Starters

Sire	Strs	Wnrs	Median
Akureyri, Dead	27	17	$16,945
Jolie's Halo, Jpn	48	28	15,598
Cherokee Fellow, Dead	48	32	15,360
Citidancer, Md.	46	29	15,070
Diablo, Jpn	53	32	14,000
Skip Trial, Fl.	91	55	13,975
Carson City, Dead	151	88	13,880
Unreal Zeal, Il.	82	47	13,495
Bold Ruckus, Dead	244	134	13,432
Silver Deputy, Ky.	126	72	13,046
Secret Hello, Dead	36	22	13,024
Jaklin Klugman, Dead	25	12	12,755
Proud Appeal, Dead	38	22	12,692
Red Ransom, Eng	168	95	12,442
Strawberry Road (Aus), Dead	170	105	12,264
Falstaff, Pens	39	22	12,124
Medaille d'Or, Dead	27	16	12,120
Pleasant Colony, Dead	274	138	11,755
Storm Cat, Ky.	325	141	11,497
Deputed Testamony, Pens	51	32	11,362

Leading Broodmare Sires
by Number of Winners in 2004

Sire	Strs	Wnrs	Wnrs/Strs
Woodman, Ky.	492	229	46.5%
Mr. Prospector, Dead	495	223	45.1%
Dixieland Band, Ky.	382	201	52.6%
Deputy Minister, Dead	386	194	50.3%
Storm Bird, Dead	391	188	48.1%
Sadler's Wells, Ire	487	182	37.4%
Caerleon, Dead	468	181	38.7%
Danzig, Pens	403	181	44.9%
Miswaki, Dead	395	175	44.3%
Valid Appeal, Dead	324	174	53.7%
Clever Trick, Dead	347	170	49.0%
Crafty Prospector, Ky.	321	170	53.0%
Halo, Dead	342	162	47.4%
Nureyev, Dead	365	158	43.3%
Wild Again, Pens	318	156	49.1%
Affirmed, Dead	321	155	48.3%
Seattle Slew, Dead	362	152	42.0%
Cure the Blues, Dead	305	151	49.5%
Green Dancer, Dead	364	150	41.2%

Leading Broodmare Sires
by Number of Wins in 2004

Sire	Strs	Wnrs	Wins
Woodman, Ky.	492	229	380
Mr. Prospector, Dead	495	223	370
Dixieland Band, Ky.	382	201	356
Deputy Minister, Dead	386	194	331
Crafty Prospector, Ky.	321	170	319
Valid Appeal, Dead	324	174	300
Storm Bird, Dead	391	188	296
Miswaki, Dead	395	175	288
Danzig, Pens	403	181	286
Clever Trick, Dead	347	170	280
Sadler's Wells, Ire	487	182	278
Seattle Slew, Dead	362	152	274
Caerleon, Dead	468	181	265
Green Dancer, Dead	364	150	265
Affirmed, Dead	321	155	264
Conquistador Cielo, Dead	313	148	263
Halo, Dead	342	162	262
Bold Ruckus, Dead	244	134	260
Vice Regent, Dead	290	138	250
Nureyev, Dead	365	158	249
Wild Again, Pens	318	156	248
Cure the Blues, Dead	305	151	244
Majestic Light, Dead	305	145	239

Leading Broodmare Sires by Number
of Stakes Winners in 2004

Sire	Strs	Wnrs	SWs	GSWins
Mr. Prospector, Dead	495	223	26	30
Sadler's Wells, Ire	487	182	26	37
Woodman, Ky.	492	229	23	31
Danzig, Pens	403	181	22	35
Seattle Slew, Dead	362	152	20	27
Alleged, Dead	335	143	17	24
Dixieland Band, Ky.	382	201	17	28
Nureyev, Dead	365	158	16	24
Storm Bird, Dead	391	188	16	23
Caerleon, Dead	468	181	15	16
Deputy Minister, Dead	386	194	15	19
Miswaki, Dead	395	175	15	19
Rainbow Quest, Eng	264	108	15	24
Green Dancer, Dead	364	150	14	23
Spectacular Bid, Dead	237	119	14	19
Irish River (Fr), Dead	346	134	13	13
Gone West, Ky.	225	103	12	19
Roberto, Dead	155	64	12	16
Kris S., Dead	261	133	11	18
Royal Academy, Ky.	236	78	11	19
Seeking the Gold, Ky.	202	96	11	17

Leading Broodmare Sires by Number
of Graded Stakes Winners in 2004

Sire	Strs	Wnrs	GSWs	GSWins
Sadler's Wells, Ire	487	182	13	19
Mr. Prospector, Dead	495	223	11	14
Seattle Slew, Dead	362	152	9	12
Dixieland Band, Ky.	382	201	8	17
Rainbow Quest, Eng	264	108	8	14
Alleged, Dead	335	143	7	10
Danzig, Pens	403	181	7	10
Green Dancer, Dead	364	150	7	7
Trempolino, Fr	175	66	7	8
Irish River (Fr), Dead	346	134	6	6
Royal Academy, Ky.	236	78	6	11
Southern Halo, Arg	189	86	6	17
Caerleon, Dead	468	181	5	5
Deputy Minister, Dead	386	194	5	7
Halo, Dead	342	162	5	9
Lear Fan, Pens	222	102	5	12
Night Shift, Ire	285	107	5	7
Nureyev, Dead	365	158	5	12
Roberto, Dead	155	64	5	7
Silver Hawk, Pens	214	93	5	8

Leading Sires by Progeny Earnings in North America in 2004

Earnings in North America only for stallions represented by at least one starter in North America in 2004, regardless of where the stallion stands or stood.

Sire	Strs	Wnrs	SWs	Leading Earner (Earnings)	Total Earnings
Elusive Quality, Ky.	133	78	5	Smarty Jones ($7,563,535)	$10,720,197
A.P. Indy, Ky.	161	86	20	Friends Lake ($611,800)	8,247,185
El Prado (Ire), Ky.	174	95	16	Kitten's Joy ($1,625,796)	8,074,726
Storm Cat, Ky.	103	56	14	Storm Flag Flying ($963,248)	6,709,124
Saint Ballado, Dead	156	82	4	Ashado ($2,259,640)	6,614,013
Smart Strike, Ky.	129	80	11	Soaring Free ($1,113,862)	6,466,414
Awesome Again, Ky.	104	58	5	Ghostzapper ($2,590,000)	6,312,464
Tale of the Cat, Ky.	170	98	10	Lion Heart ($1,080,000)	6,031,213
Unbridled's Song, Ky.	152	76	12	Even the Score ($343,272)	5,853,286
Carson City, Dead	174	96	10	Pollard's Vision ($1,022,020)	5,573,739
Langfuhr, Ky.	180	99	10	Imperialism ($542,000)	5,477,557
Not For Love, Md.	179	102	10	Love of Money ($491,500)	5,439,082
Devil His Due, Ky.	194	102	9	Roses in May ($1,723,277)	5,306,747
Dynaformer, Ky.	137	58	7	Perfect Drift ($947,595)	5,237,939
Alphabet Soup, Ky.	175	102	11	Mark One ($378,988)	5,132,114
Wild Rush, Jpn	124	74	8	Stellar Jayne ($992,169)	5,083,484
Grand Slam, Ky.	154	86	12	Fire Slam ($427,381)	5,018,973
Distorted Humor, Ky.	121	72	12	Funny Cide ($1,075,100)	4,975,215
Smoke Glacken, Ky.	145	96	9	Smok'n Frolic ($258,220)	4,788,030
Silver Deputy, Ky.	157	84	5	Bare Necessities ($328,970)	4,173,168
Kris S., Dead	84	40	9	Rock Hard Ten ($790,380)	4,089,972
Roar, Ca.	147	93	7	Roar Emotion ($328,652)	4,017,308
Belong to Me, Ky.	135	76	7	Ocean Drive ($505,900)	4,003,212
Gold Fever, N.Y.	137	82	1	A Bit O'Gold ($1,060,790)	3,991,329
Gulch, Ky.	99	61	7	The Cliff's Edge ($1,010,000)	3,942,828
Quiet American, Ky.	145	81	5	Josh's Madelyn ($245,172)	3,921,154
In Excess (Ire), Ca.	109	60	7	Texcess ($725,427)	3,913,762
Cherokee Run, Ky.	166	98	6	During ($287,614)	3,913,080
Unbridled, Dead	103	46	3	Niigon ($864,610)	3,873,111
Pulpit, Ky.	98	50	6	Purge ($562,734)	3,846,835
Petionville, Ky.	120	65	5	Island Fashion ($615,000)	3,762,674
Hennessy, Ky.	141	75	6	Madcap Escapade ($536,400)	3,756,724
Jules, Dead	112	60	5	Peace Rules ($1,024,288)	3,744,481
Sky Classic, Ky.	144	69	3	Nothing to Lose ($643,200)	3,730,335
Valid Expectations, Tx.	132	82	9	Leaving On My Mind ($299,873)	3,704,481
Storm Boot, Ky.	174	96	7	Very Vegas ($195,498)	3,636,827
Forest Wildcat, Ky.	169	92	7	Wildcat Heir ($305,860)	3,578,080
American Chance, Dead	120	59	7	Bending Strings ($495,150)	3,562,824
Runaway Groom, Ky.	169	100	8	The Lady's Groom ($262,520)	3,543,534
Grindstone, Ky.	96	48	5	Birdstone ($1,236,600)	3,518,346
Halo's Image, Fl.	110	59	2	Southern Image ($1,612,150)	3,478,969
Crafty Prospector, Ky.	133	82	5	Pies Prospect ($473,865)	3,416,322
Indian Charlie, Ky.	96	66	8	Bwana Charlie ($349,690)	3,416,093
Skip Away, Ky.	124	78	8	Muir Beach ($228,710)	3,388,311
Tabasco Cat, Dead	102	57	5	Freefourinternet ($527,693)	3,362,777
Allen's Prospect, Dead	192	102	4	Crossing Point ($124,615)	3,349,787
Glitterman, Ky.	142	78	6	Champali ($634,398)	3,329,448
Polish Numbers, Dead	131	73	7	Chrusciki ($174,770)	3,202,386
Touch Gold, Ky.	129	58	4	Medallist ($291,375)	3,194,085
Boston Harbor, Jpn	130	78	6	Swingforthefences ($385,745)	3,174,292
Gone West, Ky.	86	45	4	Speightstown ($1,045,556)	3,156,314
Regal Classic, N.Y.	143	73	3	Inish Glora ($433,730)	3,120,289
With Approval, Ky.	146	79	3	Destiny Calls ($271,670)	3,093,320
Cryptoclearance, Ky.	217	107	3	Cryptograph ($257,398)	3,086,516
Royal Academy, Ky.	114	59	3	Academic Angel ($210,520)	3,085,878
Wild Again, Pens	110	56	6	Offlee Wild ($335,640)	3,082,344
Gilded Time, Ky.	145	77	4	Clock Stopper ($292,725)	3,070,001
General Meeting, Ca.	92	51	6	Yearly Report ($787,500)	3,061,344
Honour and Glory, Ky.	169	89	6	Battle Won ($192,829)	3,054,428
Honor Grades, Dead	137	65	2	Adoration ($607,304)	3,030,510
Peaks and Valleys, Ky.	171	96	6	Higher World ($213,210)	3,028,164
Stormy Atlantic, Ky.	129	71	5	Gators N Bears ($357,910)	3,015,854
Souvenir Copy, Ca.	124	69	2	Souvenir Gift ($171,760)	3,006,286
West by West, Tur	149	82	2	Sonic West ($367,813)	3,004,410
Jade Hunter, Ky.	110	58	4	Azeri ($1,035,000)	2,999,080

Leading Sires by Average Earnings per Runner in North America in 2004
Minimum of 25 Starters

Sire	Strs	Wnrs	Average
Elusive Quality, Ky.	133	78	$80,603
Talkin Man, Ire	26	10	68,440
Danehill, Dead	27	9	65,570
Storm Cat, Ky.	103	56	65,137
Pleasant Colony, Dead	44	23	62,452
Awesome Again, Ky.	104	58	60,697
Diesis (GB), Ky.	28	11	58,964
A.P. Indy, Ky.	161	86	51,225
Smart Strike, Ky.	129	80	50,127
Kris S., Dead	84	40	48,690
El Prado (Ire), Ky.	174	95	46,406
Northern Afleet, Ky.	64	45	44,206
Danzig, Pens	38	18	42,825
Saint Ballado, Dead	156	82	42,398
Distorted Humor, Ky.	121	72	41,117
Wild Rush, Jpn	124	74	40,996
Gulch, Ky.	99	61	39,827
Silver Hawk, Pens	27	10	39,737
Unusual Heat, Ca.	49	25	39,443
Pulpit, Ky.	98	50	39,253
Unbridled's Song, Ky.	152	76	38,508
Distant View, Ky.	58	32	38,453
Dynaformer, Ky.	137	58	38,233
Forestry, Ky.	65	33	37,626
Unbridled, Dead	103	46	37,603

Leading Sires by Median Earnings per Runner in North America in 2004
Minimum of 25 Starters

Sire	Strs	Wnrs	Median
A.P. Indy, Ky.	161	86	$22,744
Smoke Glacken, Ky.	145	96	22,345
Indian Charlie, Ky.	96	66	22,323
Whiskey Wisdom, On.	77	42	21,232
Smart Strike, Ky.	129	80	20,713
Dixie Brass, Dead	112	67	20,420
Storm Cat, Ky.	103	56	19,800
Sahm, Ky.	25	20	19,000
Archers Bay, Dead	56	29	18,168
Barbeau, Dead	29	17	17,879
Ormsby, N.Y.	29	21	17,673
Gulch, Ky.	99	61	17,262
Tactical Cat, Ky.	58	32	17,012
Formal Gold, Ca.	108	70	17,000
Military, Ky.	35	21	16,990
Distorted Humor, Ky.	121	72	16,825
Victory Gallop, Ky.	85	49	16,810
Tale of the Cat, Ky.	170	98	16,775
Wild Rush, Jpn	124	74	16,581
Awesome Again, Ky.	104	58	16,142
Good and Tough, N.Y.	45	31	16,125

Leading Sires by Number of Winners in North America in 2004

Sire	Strs	Wnrs	Wnrs/ Strs
Cryptoclearance, Ky.	217	107	49.3%
Not For Love, Md.	179	102	57.0%
Alphabet Soup, Ky.	175	102	58.3%
Devil His Due, Ky.	194	102	52.6%
Allen's Prospect, Dead	192	102	53.1%
Runaway Groom, Ky.	169	100	59.2%
Langfuhr, Ky.	180	99	55.0%
Tale of the Cat, Ky.	170	98	57.6%
Cherokee Run, Ky.	166	98	59.0%
Storm Boot, Ky.	174	96	55.2%
Carson City, Dead	174	96	55.2%
Smoke Glacken, Ky.	145	96	66.2%
Peaks and Valleys, Ky.	171	96	56.1%
El Prado (Ire), Ky.	174	95	54.6%
Roar, Ca.	147	93	63.3%
Forest Wildcat, Ky.	169	92	54.4%
Honour and Glory, Ky.	169	89	52.7%
Pentelicus, Dead	155	89	57.4%
Maria's Mon, Ky.	167	87	52.1%
Formal Dinner, Fl.	145	87	60.0%
A.P. Indy, Ky.	161	86	53.4%
Grand Slam, Ky.	154	86	55.8%
Silver Deputy, Ky.	157	84	53.5%

Leading Sires by Number of Wins in North America in 2004

Sire	Strs	Wnrs	Wins
Not For Love, Md.	179	102	195
Devil His Due, Ky.	194	102	188
Alphabet Soup, Ky.	175	102	186
Storm Boot, Ky.	174	96	182
Smoke Glacken, Ky.	145	96	180
Roar, Ca.	147	93	177
Formal Dinner, Fl.	145	87	177
Langfuhr, Ky.	180	99	176
El Prado (Ire), Ky.	174	95	173
Runaway Groom, Ky.	169	100	172
Pentelicus, Dead	155	89	169
Allen's Prospect, Dead	192	102	163
Carson City, Dead	174	96	163
Tale of the Cat, Ky.	170	98	162
Valid Expectations, Tx.	132	82	161
Cherokee Run, Ky.	166	98	161
Quiet American, Ky.	145	81	160
Cryptoclearance, Ky.	217	107	160
High Brite, Ca.	128	80	158

Leading Sires by Number of Stakes Winners in North America in 2004

Sire	Strs	Wnrs	SWs	SWins
A.P. Indy, Ky.	161	86	20	27
El Prado (Ire), Ky.	174	95	16	28
Storm Cat, Ky.	103	56	14	21
Grand Slam, Ky.	154	86	12	18
Unbridled's Song, Ky.	152	76	12	18
Distorted Humor, Ky.	121	72	12	17
Smart Strike, Ky.	129	80	11	20
Forestry, Ky.	65	33	11	13
Alphabet Soup, Ky.	175	102	11	17
Not For Love, Md.	179	102	10	18
Langfuhr, Ky.	180	99	10	14
Tale of the Cat, Ky.	170	98	10	13
Carson City, Dead	174	96	10	18
Devil His Due, Ky.	194	102	9	13
Smoke Glacken, Ky.	145	96	9	12
Valid Expectations, Tx.	132	82	9	15
Kris S., Dead	84	40	9	13

Leading Sires by Number of Graded Stakes Winners in North America in 2004

Sire	Strs	Wnrs	GSWs	GSWins
A.P. Indy, Ky.	161	86	9	11
Unbridled's Song, Ky.	152	76	8	11
Storm Cat, Ky.	103	56	8	12
El Prado (Ire), Ky.	174	95	6	17
Wild Rush, Jpn	124	74	5	7
Hennessy, Ky.	141	75	4	5
Smart Strike, Ky.	129	80	4	7
Tale of the Cat, Ky.	170	98	4	6
Awesome Again, Ky.	104	58	4	7
Pulpit, Ky.	98	50	4	5
Grand Slam, Ky.	154	86	4	7
Not For Love, Md.	179	102	4	4
Kris S., Dead	84	40	4	6
Theatrical (Ire), Ky.	75	33	4	4
Gulch, Ky.	99	61	4	4
Dynaformer, Ky.	137	58	4	4
Danehill, Dead	27	9	4	7
Carson City, Dead	174	96	4	7

Leading Juvenile Sires by Progeny Earnings in North America in 2004

Earnings in North America only for stallions represented by at least one starter in North America in 2004, regardless of where the stallion stands or stood. ♦ Denotes freshman sire.

Sire	Strs	Wnrs	SWs	Leading Earner (Earnings)	Total Earnings
♦Successful Appeal, Ky.	22	15	6	Closing Argument ($421,984)	$1,727,557
Storm Cat, Ky.	18	7	3	Sweet Catomine ($799,800)	1,616,329
♦Yes It's True, Ky.	40	15	4	Proud Accolade ($364,130)	1,424,382
Awesome Again, Ky.	23	9	2	Wilko ($833,580)	1,100,214
Valid Expectations, Tx.	34	18	3	Leaving On My Mind ($299,873)	1,084,955
In Excess (Ire), Ca.	12	6	2	Texcess ($725,427)	1,019,531
♦Cape Canaveral, Ky.	31	12	4	Megascape ($161,740)	961,092
Petionville, Ky.	27	8	2	Runway Model ($580,598)	955,310
♦Fusaichi Pegasus, Ky.	22	7	3	Roman Ruler ($330,800)	923,385
Thunder Gulch, Ky.	50	15	3	Sense of Style ($369,000)	916,731
Malibu Moon, Ky.	27	9	3	Declan's Moon ($507,300)	872,112
Unbridled's Song, Ky.	19	9	3	Splendid Blended ($327,400)	870,306
♦More Than Ready, Ky.	35	17	3	Ready's Gal ($155,200)	848,557
Carson City, Dead	35	16	2	Classic Elegance ($204,006)	823,737
Northern Afleet, Ky.	13	8	1	Afleet Alex ($680,800)	814,430
A. P Jet, N.Y.	46	16	2	Galloping Grocer ($150,400)	772,446
Whiskey Wisdom, On.	14	9	3	Moonshine Justice ($283,914)	759,611
Foxtrail, On.	24	8	2	Wholelottabourbon ($286,230)	739,773
Wild Event, Fl.	18	10	1	Aclassysassylassy ($498,800)	722,940
♦Precise End, Jpn	29	12	2	Accurate ($115,688)	709,293
♦Dixie Union, Ky.	21	11	2	Im a Dixie Girl ($150,200)	695,666
Victory Gallop, Ky.	25	8	3	Victorious Ami ($188,600)	653,377
Wheaton, Pa.	41	23	2	Departing Now ($71,106)	646,346
Smart Strike, Ky.	26	11	3	Pelham Bay ($126,777)	632,789
Tale of the Cat, Ky.	30	14	0	Canadian Gem ($125,580)	629,414
Timber Country, Jpn	4	1	1	Balletto (UAE) ($614,000)	623,056
Peaks and Valleys, Ky.	32	14	3	Higher World ($213,210)	620,332
Afternoon Deelites, La.	32	13	2	Three Hour Nap ($158,400)	618,194
Swiss Yodeler, Ca.	37	15	0	Mr. Fondue ($99,028)	611,810
Stormy Atlantic, Ky.	47	19	1	Frosty Royalty ($74,060)	604,601
Double Honor, Fl.	39	21	2	Cut the Mustard ($70,400)	591,645
Forest Wildcat, Ky.	31	18	0	Get Wild ($62,365)	580,525
Silver Charm, Jpn	32	11	1	Silver Impulse ($202,662)	572,633
A.P. Indy, Ky.	19	7	1	Dance With Ravens ($223,820)	547,981
Maria's Mon, Ky.	38	14	0	K. D.'s Shady Lady ($77,320)	546,303
Menifee, Ky.	25	10	1	Boggy Creek ($120,111)	540,178
Cherokee Run, Ky.	29	13	1	Cherokee Path ($98,365)	530,736
♦Running Stag, Fl.	34	11	1	Running Bobcats ($108,680)	529,072
♦Bernstein, Ky.	18	11	2	Sweet Solairo ($133,683)	525,467
Smoke Glacken, Ky.	23	14	2	Clemson You ($63,310)	520,337
♦Tiger Ridge, Fl.	26	11	1	Anthony J. ($213,630)	518,486
♦Sweetsouthernsaint, Fl.	27	13	1	Better Than Bonds ($114,370)	516,211
Wild Rush, Jpn	22	8	1	Wild Remarks ($100,442)	514,205
Indian Charlie, Ky.	15	9	3	Kota ($139,450)	511,505
Charismatic, Jpn	38	11	1	Sun King ($244,850)	501,387
Wild Zone, Ky.	42	15	1	Berdelia ($173,248)	499,683
♦Old Topper, Ca.	19	10	2	Shout to the North ($132,292)	498,815
Lord Carson, Ca.	34	16	0	Paragon Queen ($85,540)	498,791
Southern Halo, Arg	12	5	2	Dubleo ($360,899)	490,571
Honour and Glory, Ky.	46	15	1	Secrets Galore ($60,083)	488,491
Robyn Dancer, N.M.	42	13	0	Gloried Dancer ($72,640)	480,700
Gilded Time, Ky.	24	14	1	Diamond Isle ($122,030)	478,366
Devil His Due, Ky.	39	15	1	Devils Disciple ($161,800)	467,071
Rubiano, Dead	31	11	3	Smooth Bid ($77,410)	464,271
Stormin Fever, Ky.	32	12	2	Sweet Talker ($99,760)	460,800
Cape Town, Ky.	20	12	2	Ninadivina ($86,174)	456,305
♦Catienus, N.Y.	31	19	1	Kathern's Cat ($79,603)	451,551
Distorted Humor, Ky.	28	11	1	Humor At Last ($92,805)	451,206
Slew City Slew, Ky.	20	9	1	Sis City ($282,980)	432,131
Leestown, La.	32	10	2	Equestrian Girls ($115,820)	430,376
Doneraile Court, Ky.	21	11	0	Get Down ($70,080)	423,669
Meadow Monster, Md.	26	13	1	Monster Chaser ($138,280)	423,620
Bartok (Ire), Ca.	32	13	0	Sip One for Mom ($52,600)	422,829
♦Yankee Victor, Ky.	29	13	0	Northern Mischief ($77,260)	416,929
Allen's Prospect, Dead	40	11	1	What's Up Lonely ($85,020)	414,045

Leading Juvenile Sires by Average Earnings per Runner in North America in 2004
Minimum of 10 Starters

Sire	Strs	Wnrs	Average
Storm Cat, Ky.	18	7	$89,796
In Excess (Ire), Ca.	12	6	84,961
◆Successful Appeal, Ky.	22	15	78,525
Northern Afleet, Ky.	13	8	62,648
Whiskey Wisdom, On.	14	9	54,258
Awesome Again, Ky.	23	9	47,835
Unbridled's Song, Ky.	19	9	45,806
◆Fusaichi Pegasus, Ky.	22	7	41,972
Southern Halo, Arg	12	5	40,881
Wild Event, Fl.	18	10	40,163
◆Yes It's True, Ky.	40	15	35,610
Petionville, Ky.	27	8	35,382
Indian Charlie, Ky.	15	9	34,100
◆Dixie Union, Ky.	21	11	33,127
Malibu Moon, Ky.	27	9	32,300
Valid Expectations, Tx.	34	18	31,910
◆Cape Canaveral, Ky.	31	12	31,003
Foxtrail, On.	24	8	30,824

Leading Juvenile Sires by Median Earnings per Runner in North America in 2004
Minimum of 10 Starters

Sire	Strs	Wnrs	Median
Whiskey Wisdom, On.	14	9	$33,319
◆Successful Appeal, Ky.	22	15	28,703
Indian Charlie, Ky.	15	9	23,400
Good and Tough, N.Y.	15	7	20,540
Military, Ky.	10	6	18,705
Compadre, On.	10	5	18,605
◆Bernstein, Ky.	18	11	18,335
Cape Town, Ky.	20	12	18,143
Smoke Glacken, Ky.	23	14	17,820
◆Lion Hearted, Md.	14	10	16,926
Mister Jolie, Dead	10	7	16,829
Royal Academy, Ky.	11	6	15,600
Doneraile Court, Ky.	21	11	15,200

Leading Juvenile Sires by Number of Winners in North America in 2004

Sire	Strs	Wnrs	Wnrs/Strs
Wheaton, Pa.	41	23	56.1%
Slew Gin Fizz, Fl.	38	21	55.3%
Double Honor, Fl.	39	21	53.8%
◆Catienus, N.Y.	31	19	61.3%
Stormy Atlantic, Ky.	47	19	40.4%
Valid Expectations, Tx.	34	18	52.9%
Forest Wildcat, Ky.	31	18	58.1%
Family Calling, Fl.	33	17	51.5%
◆More Than Ready, Ky.	35	17	48.6%
Lord Carson, Ca.	34	16	47.1%
A. P Jet, N.Y.	46	16	34.8%
Carson City, Dead	35	16	45.7%
Fortunate Prospect, Fl.	25	15	60.0%
Devil His Due, Ky.	39	15	38.5%
Wild Zone, Ky.	42	15	35.7%
Thunder Gulch, Ky.	50	15	30.0%
Honour and Glory, Ky.	46	15	32.6%
◆Successful Appeal, Ky.	22	15	68.2%
◆Yes It's True, Ky.	40	15	37.5%
Swiss Yodeler, Ca.	37	15	40.5%

Leading Juvenile Sires by Number of Wins in North America in 2004

Sire	Strs	Wnrs	Wins
Wheaton, Pa.	41	23	36
Valid Expectations, Tx.	34	18	34
Double Honor, Fl.	39	21	32
◆Successful Appeal, Ky.	22	15	31
Slew Gin Fizz, Fl.	38	21	28

Sire	Strs	Wnrs	Wins
Stormy Atlantic, Ky.	47	19	27
◆Yes It's True, Ky.	40	15	25
◆More Than Ready, Ky.	35	17	24
◆Catienus, N.Y.	31	19	23
Family Calling, Fl.	33	17	22
◆Cape Canaveral, Ky.	31	12	22
◆Sweetsouthernsaint, Fl.	27	13	22
Fortunate Prospect, Fl.	25	15	22
Carson City, Dead	35	16	22
Robyn Dancer, N.M.	42	13	22
Forest Wildcat, Ky.	31	18	21
Wild Zone, Ky.	42	15	21
Tale of the Cat, Ky.	30	14	21
Bartok (Ire), Ca.	32	13	21

Leading Juvenile Sires by Number of Stakes Winners in 2004

Sire	Strs	Wnrs	SWs	SWins
◆Successful Appeal, Ky.	22	15	6	12
◆Yes It's True, Ky.	40	15	4	8
◆Cape Canaveral, Ky.	31	12	4	6
Malibu Moon, Ky.	27	9	3	6
◆Fusaichi Pegasus, Ky.	22	7	3	6
Victory Gallop, Ky.	25	8	3	3
◆More Than Ready, Ky.	35	17	3	3
Whiskey Wisdom, On.	14	9	3	5
Indian Charlie, Ky.	15	9	3	3
Storm Cat, Ky.	18	7	3	6
Rubiano, Dead	31	11	3	3
Smart Strike, Ky.	26	11	3	4
Danjur, Dead	12	7	3	4
Peaks and Valleys, Ky.	32	14	3	4
Thunder Gulch, Ky.	50	15	3	4
Unbridled's Song, Ky.	19	9	3	4
Valid Expectations, Tx.	34	18	3	8

Leading Juvenile Sires by Number of Graded Stakes Winners in North America in 2004

Sire	Strs	Wnrs	GSWs	GSWins
Storm Cat, Ky.	18	7	2	4
◆Yes It's True, Ky.	40	15	2	2
Unbridled's Song, Ky.	19	9	2	3
Northern Afleet, Ky.	13	8	1	1
Storm Boot, Ky.	25	7	1	1
El Amante, Tx.	5	2	1	1
A.P. Indy, Ky.	19	7	1	1
Boundary, Ky.	12	4	1	1
Concerto, Fl.	15	10	1	1
Southern Halo, Arg	12	5	1	2
Petionville, Ky.	27	8	1	2
Afternoon Deelites, La.	32	13	1	1
Peaks and Valleys, Ky.	32	14	1	1
Carson City, Dead	35	16	1	2
Timber Country, Jpn	4	1	1	1
Summer Squall, Pens	9	3	1	1
◆Successful Appeal, Ky.	22	15	1	2
Danzig, Pens	7	4	1	1
Souvenir Copy, Ca.	16	4	1	1
Citidancer, Md.	6	3	1	1
Deputy Minister, Dead	17	6	1	1
Slew City Slew, Ky.	20	9	1	1
◆Cape Canaveral, Ky.	31	12	1	3
Malibu Moon, Ky.	27	9	1	3
◆Bernstein, Ky.	18	11	1	1
◆Sinndar, Ire	1	1	1	1
◆Fusaichi Pegasus, Ky.	22	7	1	2
◆Brave Act (GB), Ind	1	1	1	1
King of Kings (Ire), Swi	12	1	1	1
Thunder Gulch, Ky.	50	15	1	2
◆Intidab, N.Y.	4	1	1	2
Awesome Again, Ky.	23	9	1	1
◆Golden Missile, Ky.	24	6	1	1

Leading Freshman Sires by Progeny Earnings in North America in 2004

Earnings in North America only for stallions represented by at least one starter in North America in 2004, regardless of where the stallion stands or stood. ◆ Denotes freshman sire.

Sire	Strs	Wnrs	SWs	Leading Earner (Earnings)	Total Earnings
◆Successful Appeal, Ky.	22	15	6	Closing Argument ($421,984)	$1,727,557
◆Yes It's True, Ky.	40	15	4	Proud Accolade ($364,130)	1,424,383
◆Cape Canaveral, Ky.	31	12	4	Megascape ($161,740)	961,092
◆Fusaichi Pegasus, Ky.	22	7	3	Roman Ruler ($330,800)	923,385
◆More Than Ready, Ky.	35	17	3	Ready's Gal ($155,200)	848,557
◆Precise End, Jpn	29	12	2	Accurate ($115,688)	709,293
◆Dixie Union, Ky.	21	11	2	Im a Dixie Girl ($150,200)	695,666
◆Running Stag, Fl.	34	11	1	Running Bobcats ($108,680)	529,072
◆Bernstein, Ky.	18	11	2	Sweet Solairo ($133,683)	525,467
◆Tiger Ridge, Fl.	26	11	1	Anthony J. ($213,630)	518,486
◆Sweetsouthernsaint, Fl.	27	13	1	Better Than Bonds ($114,370)	516,211
◆Old Topper, Ca.	19	10	2	Shout to the North ($132,292)	498,815
◆Catienus, N.Y.	31	19	1	Kathern's Cat ($79,603)	451,551
◆Yankee Victor, Ky.	29	13	0	Northern Mischief ($77,260)	416,929
◆Straight Man, Fl.	33	12	0	Straightlittlelady ($60,184)	413,206
◆Lion Hearted, Md.	14	10	2	Hear Us Roar ($128,680)	398,927
◆Dance Master, Fl.	8	5	1	Flamenco ($303,085)	397,740
◆Western Expression, N.Y.	20	7	0	Summerland ($83,973)	384,961
◆Lemon Drop Kid, Ky.	17	7	1	Winning Season ($99,655)	353,961
◆Golden Missile, Ky.	24	6	1	Inspiring ($115,800)	332,496
◆Chester House, Dead	25	9	1	Exceptional Ride ($106,303)	326,963
◆Stephen Got Even, Ky.	22	7	0	Didycheatamandhowe ($76,330)	314,967
◆War Chant, Ky.	14	7	1	Up Like Thunder ($99,265)	306,168
◆Chief Seattle, Ky.	24	9	0	Bold Outlook ($68,400)	304,361
◆High Yield, Ky.	27	8	0	Stormy Jim ($72,290)	299,331
◆Anees, Dead	19	5	1	Swither ($128,826)	280,239
◆Magic Cat, Tx.	29	11	1	Major League ($97,100)	279,934
◆Vicar, Ky.	29	9	0	Crafty Vixen ($47,620)	278,996
◆Untuttable, Fl.	14	7	1	Favalora ($52,390)	263,005
◆Cat Thief, Ky.	19	8	0	Steal the Show ($35,250)	238,135
◆Intidab, N.Y.	4	1	1	Greater Good ($226,275)	232,834
◆Littlebitlively, La.	22	7	0	Littlebitofzip ($85,328)	223,864
◆Richter Scale, Ky.	14	5	1	Quite a Ruckus ($110,653)	204,013
◆Wised Up, Fl.	15	7	0	Wise Briana ($45,460)	191,359
◆Greenwood Lake, Ky.	14	7	0	Extra Bases ($71,097)	175,395
◆Meadow Prayer, Mi.	6	2	1	Foolininthemeadow ($155,987)	168,542
◆Storm and a Half, Ar.	12	5	2	Z Storm ($39,220)	166,425
◆Devonwood, Dead	15	5	1	Speedy Gone Sally ($71,444)	153,358
◆Muqtarib, Ca.	8	3	2	Whatsthenameman ($75,855)	149,932
◆Unbridled Jet, Md.	26	2	0	Media Alert ($28,580)	133,071
◆Deputy Diamond, La.	25	7	0	One Tough Deputy ($20,117)	127,081
◆Kelly Kip, N.Y.	12	4	0	My Kip ($32,350)	122,343
◆Giant's Causeway, Ky.	17	2	0	My Typhoon (Ire) ($31,710)	113,805
◆Commendable, Kor	14	6	0	Sue Me ($35,418)	113,743
◆Karen's Cat, Tx.	6	3	0	Cat Tourn ($71,028)	109,430
◆Badge, N.Y.	9	3	0	Pretty Partisan ($59,200)	101,194
◆Untold Gold, Dead	3	2	1	Hush's Gold ($82,905)	100,917
◆Sasha's Prospect, Fl.	9	4	0	Denium Cowgirl ($44,260)	92,608
◆The Deputy (Ire), Ky.	16	5	0	Deputy French ($19,500)	89,025
◆Best of Luck, Ky.	30	2	0	Best One ($30,145)	85,644
◆Robb, W.V.	5	3	0	Miss Angel ($32,141)	85,482
◆Malek (Chi), Ca.	12	1	0	Arch Stanton ($26,315)	81,757
◆King of Scat, Ok.	12	6	1	S C King ($18,984)	79,732
◆Lightning Al, P.R.	2	2	1	Lightning Al Boy ($59,480)	78,610
◆Royal Anthem, Ky.	17	2	0	Prince T. ($25,480)	74,392
◆Behrens, Ky.	7	3	0	Sueno Del Mar ($30,930)	73,008
◆Sea Twister, Dead	3	2	2	Wind Twister ($52,360)	72,960
◆Makula King, Dead	3	3	0	Always Picked On ($43,090)	70,330
◆Close Up, N.J.	5	2	0	Joey P. ($57,240)	69,500
◆B. J.'s Mark, La.	4	1	1	Maid in China ($64,500)	69,345
◆Crowd Pleaser, Md.	19	3	0	Assemblyman ($15,530)	68,567
◆Brushed On, Dead	7	1	0	Brushme On ($38,128)	68,190
◆Aljabr, Ky.	5	3	0	Where's Bailey ($35,200)	65,945
◆Adcat, Fl.	10	3	0	Swift Mercedes ($21,620)	64,752
◆Millions, N.Y.	5	2	0	Millibrook ($34,491)	63,767

Leading Freshman Sires by Average Earnings per Runner in North America in 2004
Minimum of 10 Starters

Sire	Strs	Wnrs	Average
◆Successful Appeal, Ky.	22	15	$78,525
◆Fusaichi Pegasus, Ky.	22	7	41,972
◆Yes It's True, Ky.	40	15	35,610
◆Dixie Union, Ky.	21	11	33,127
◆Cape Canaveral, Ky.	31	12	31,003
◆Bernstein, Ky.	18	11	29,193
◆Lion Hearted, Md.	14	10	28,495
◆Old Topper, Ca.	19	10	26,253
◆Precise End, Jpn	29	12	24,458
◆More Than Ready, Ky.	35	17	24,244
◆War Chant, Ky.	14	7	21,869
◆Lemon Drop Kid, Ky.	17	7	20,821
◆Tiger Ridge, Fl.	26	11	19,942
◆Western Expression, N.Y.	20	7	19,248
◆Sweetsouthernsaint, Fl.	27	13	19,119
◆Untuttable, Fl.	14	7	18,786
◆Running Stag, Fl.	34	11	15,561
◆Anees, Dead	19	5	14,749
◆Richter Scale, Ky.	14	5	14,572
◆Catienus, N.Y.	31	19	14,566
◆Yankee Victor, Ky.	29	13	14,377
◆Stephen Got Even, Ky.	22	7	14,317
◆Storm and a Half, Ar.	12	5	13,869
◆Golden Missile, Ky.	24	6	13,854
◆Chester House, Dead	25	9	13,079
◆Wised Up, Fl.	15	7	12,757
◆Chief Seattle, Ky.	24	9	12,682
◆Cat Thief, Ky.	19	8	12,533
◆Greenwood Lake, Ky.	14	7	12,528
◆Straight Man, Fl.	33	12	12,521
◆High Yield, Ky.	27	8	11,086
◆Devonward, Dead	15	5	10,224
◆Kelly Kip, N.Y.	12	4	10,195
◆Littlebitlively, La.	22	7	10,176

Leading Freshman Sires by Median Earnings in North America in 2004
Minimum of 10 Starters

Sire	Strs	Wnrs	Median
◆Successful Appeal, Ky.	22	15	$28,703
◆Bernstein, Ky.	18	11	18,335
◆Lion Hearted, Md.	14	10	16,926
◆Dixie Union, Ky.	21	11	13,709
◆Old Topper, Ca.	19	10	12,880
◆More Than Ready, Ky.	35	17	12,600
◆Untuttable, Fl.	14	7	12,419
◆Yankee Victor, Ky.	29	13	11,640
◆War Chant, Ky.	14	7	11,204
◆Lemon Drop Kid, Ky.	17	7	10,978
◆Western Expression, N.Y.	20	7	10,587
◆Precise End, Jpn	29	12	9,778
◆Catienus, N.Y.	31	19	9,585
◆Cape Canaveral, Ky.	31	12	9,480
◆Greenwood Lake, Ky.	14	7	8,721
◆Chester House, Dead	25	9	7,400
◆Chief Seattle, Ky.	24	9	6,862
◆Tiger Ridge, Fl.	26	11	6,790
◆Stephen Got Even, Ky.	22	7	6,482
◆King of Scat, Ok.	12	6	6,470
◆Storm and a Half, Ar.	12	5	6,403
◆Wind Whipper, Fl.	11	5	6,140
◆Wised Up, Fl.	15	7	5,755
◆Kelly Kip, N.Y.	12	4	5,745

Leading Freshman Sires by Number of Winners in North America in 2004

Sire	Strs	Wnrs	Wnrs/Strs
◆Catienus, N.Y.	31	19	61.3%
◆More Than Ready, Ky.	35	17	48.6%
◆Successful Appeal, Ky.	22	15	68.2%
◆Yes It's True, Ky.	40	15	37.5%
◆Sweetsouthernsaint, Fl.	27	13	48.1%
◆Yankee Victor, Ky.	29	13	44.8%
◆Cape Canaveral, Ky.	31	12	38.7%
◆Precise End, Jpn	29	12	41.4%
◆Straight Man, Fl.	33	12	36.4%
◆Bernstein, Ky.	18	11	61.1%
◆Dixie Union, Ky.	21	11	52.4%
◆Magic Cat, Tx.	29	11	37.9%
◆Running Stag, Fl.	34	11	32.4%
◆Tiger Ridge, Fl.	26	11	42.3%
◆Lion Hearted, Md.	14	10	71.4%
◆Old Topper, Ca.	19	10	52.6%
◆Chester House, Dead	25	9	36.0%
◆Chief Seattle, Ky.	24	9	37.5%
◆Vicar, Ky.	29	9	31.0%
◆Cat Thief, Ky.	19	8	42.1%
◆High Yield, Ky.	27	8	29.6%
◆Deputy Diamond, La.	25	7	28.0%
◆Fusaichi Pegasus, Ky.	22	7	31.8%
◆Greenwood Lake, Ky.	14	7	50.0%
◆Lemon Drop Kid, Ky.	17	7	41.2%
◆Littlebitlively, La.	22	7	31.8%
◆Stephen Got Even, Ky.	22	7	31.8%
◆Untuttable, Fl.	14	7	50.0%
◆War Chant, Ky.	14	7	50.0%
◆Western Expression, N.Y.	20	7	35.0%
◆Wised Up, Fl.	15	7	46.7%

Leading Freshman Sires by Number of Wins in North America in 2004

Sire	Strs	Wnrs	Wins
◆Successful Appeal, Ky.	22	15	31
◆Yes It's True, Ky.	40	15	25
◆More Than Ready, Ky.	35	17	24
◆Catienus, N.Y.	31	19	23
◆Cape Canaveral, Ky.	31	12	22
◆Sweetsouthernsaint, Fl.	27	13	22
◆Bernstein, Ky.	18	11	17
◆Running Stag, Fl.	34	11	16
◆Dixie Union, Ky.	21	11	15
◆Old Topper, Ca.	19	10	15
◆Precise End, Jpn	29	12	15
◆Straight Man, Fl.	33	12	15
◆Yankee Victor, Ky.	29	13	15
◆Fusaichi Pegasus, Ky.	22	7	14
◆Lion Hearted, Md.	14	10	13
◆Magic Cat, Tx.	29	11	13
◆Tiger Ridge, Fl.	26	11	13

Leading Freshman Sires by Number of Stakes Winners in North America in 2004

Sire	Strs	Wnrs	SWs	SWins
◆Successful Appeal, Ky.	22	15	6	12
◆Cape Canaveral, Ky.	31	12	4	6
◆Yes It's True, Ky.	40	15	4	8
◆Fusaichi Pegasus, Ky.	22	7	3	6
◆More Than Ready, Ky.	35	17	3	3
◆Bernstein, Ky.	18	11	2	2
◆Dixie Union, Ky.	21	11	2	3
◆Lion Hearted, Md.	14	10	2	3
◆Muqtarib, Ca.	8	3	2	2
◆Old Topper, Ca.	19	10	2	2
◆Precise End, Jpn	29	12	2	2
◆Sea Twister, Dead	3	2	2	3
◆Storm and a Half, Ar.	12	5	2	2

Leading Freshman Sires by Number of Graded Stakes Winners in North America in 2004

Sire	Strs	Wnrs	GSWs	GSWins
◆Yes It's True, Ky.	40	15	2	2
◆Bernstein, Ky.	18	11	1	1
◆Cape Canaveral, Ky.	31	12	1	1
◆Fusaichi Pegasus, Ky.	22	7	1	2
◆Golden Missile, Ky.	24	6	1	1
◆Intidab, N.Y.	4	1	1	2
◆Successful Appeal, Ky.	22	15	1	2

Leading Broodmare Sires by Progeny Earnings in North America in 2004

Earnings in North America only for broodmare sires represented by at least one starter in North America in 2004, regardless of where the stallion stands or stood.

Sire	Strs	Wnrs	SWs	Leading Earner (Earnings)	Total Earnings
Dixieland Band, Ky.	330	187	15	Southern Image ($1,612,150)	$11,642,430
Relaunch, Dead	330	191	11	Ghostzapper ($2,590,000)	9,651,766
Deputy Minister, Dead	316	171	12	Magistretti ($764,000)	9,045,078
Smile, Dead	77	41	3	Smarty Jones ($7,563,535)	8,828,709
Mr. Prospector, Dead	252	131	15	Rock Hard Ten ($790,380)	8,455,083
Bold Ruckus, Dead	233	133	10	My Vintage Port ($383,302)	6,936,952
Storm Bird, Dead	245	134	12	Birdstone ($1,236,600)	6,828,690
Danzig, Pens	174	95	15	Soaring Free ($1,113,862)	6,739,945
Kris S., Dead	228	120	10	Sweet Catomine ($799,800)	6,498,894
Valid Appeal, Dead	307	168	8	Splendid Blended ($327,400)	6,003,726
Clever Trick, Dead	309	158	7	Nothing to Lose ($643,200)	5,962,071
Affirmed, Dead	226	126	7	Pleasantly Perfect ($1,240,000)	5,632,493
Seattle Slew, Dead	225	101	14	Seattle Fitz (Arg) ($404,810)	5,604,896
Storm Cat, Ky.	226	109	6	Speightstown ($1,045,556)	5,431,964
Pleasant Colony, Dead	226	122	6	Bowman's Band ($439,334)	5,307,643
Vice Regent, Dead	239	119	4	Eye of the Sphynx ($688,340)	5,221,369
Crafty Prospector, Ky.	287	160	8	Chandtrue ($182,970)	5,196,942
Woodman, Ky.	207	123	12	Wildwood Royal ($203,100)	5,127,172
Sovereign Dancer, Dead	220	120	8	Kela ($710,212)	5,060,150
Wild Again, Pens	252	131	7	Cheiron ($293,822)	5,048,826
Conquistador Cielo, Dead	271	139	7	My Cousin Matt ($208,200)	5,045,487
Miswaki, Dead	248	131	10	Destiny Calls ($271,670)	4,962,741
Alleged, Dead	173	90	8	Sulamani (Ire) ($900,000)	4,865,796
Star de Naskra, Dead	180	94	6	Singletary ($1,192,910)	4,783,678
Cox's Ridge, Dead	229	120	6	Swingforthefences ($385,745)	4,730,575
Regal Classic, N.Y.	160	87	3	Texcess ($725,427)	4,719,710
Private Account, Dead	232	119	8	My Trusty Cat ($311,290)	4,717,532
Cure the Blues, Dead	236	123	7	Cajun Beat ($226,800)	4,646,586
Nureyev, Dead	110	59	6	Sightseek ($1,011,350)	4,617,463
Green Dancer, Dead	199	91	11	I Thee Wed ($314,337)	4,614,536
Halo, Dead	259	135	7	Bwana Charlie ($349,690)	4,446,896
Seeking the Gold, Ky.	127	70	9	Riskaverse ($717,472)	4,326,198
Phone Trick, N.Y.	233	122	9	Eye of the Tiger ($296,450)	4,310,331
Spectacular Bid, Dead	184	104	11	Bare Necessities ($328,970)	4,306,432
Smarten, Dead	174	86	9	Love of Money ($491,500)	4,300,213
Saratoga Six, N.M.	181	93	10	Madcap Escapade ($536,400)	4,191,892
Forty Niner, Jpn	165	92	9	Island Sand ($391,937)	4,156,777
Mr. Leader, Dead	188	86	6	Lion Heart ($1,080,000)	4,124,141
Naskra, Dead	112	45	6	Perfect Drift ($947,595)	3,882,591
Majestic Light, Dead	233	112	4	Artie Schiller ($467,578)	3,850,670
Mari's Book, Dead	82	45	4	Ashado ($2,259,640)	3,846,576
Copelan, Dead	176	94	7	Purge ($562,734)	3,801,365
Alydar, Dead	181	83	4	Pohave ($450,740)	3,799,514
Broad Brush, Pens	178	101	5	Aud ($257,578)	3,779,808
Baldski, Dead	136	65	7	Better Talk Now ($1,407,000)	3,759,395
Carson City, Dead	141	81	10	See Me Through ($157,041)	3,741,117
Lear Fan, Pens	133	69	3	Kitten's Joy ($1,625,796)	3,729,793
Mt. Livermore, Ky.	208	98	8	Cryptograph ($257,398)	3,717,151
Rahy, Ky.	169	78	6	Even the Score ($343,272)	3,713,792
Dynaformer, Ky.	139	67	10	Hollywood Story ($287,105)	3,705,950
Devil's Bag, Dead	211	101	4	Balto Star ($410,834)	3,664,742
Strawberry Road (Aus), Dead	145	91	6	Bedanken ($222,555)	3,653,252
Lost Code, Dead	192	107	4	Coconut Girl ($154,686)	3,623,002
Two Punch, Md.	145	78	5	Punch Appeal ($389,840)	3,568,234
Stalwart, Dead	174	93	7	Simply Lovely ($288,240)	3,549,729
Silver Deputy, Ky.	113	64	9	Roman Ruler ($330,800)	3,495,506
Caveat, Dead	163	84	3	Organ Grinder ($414,813)	3,494,668
Fit to Fight, Ky.	192	96	6	Royal Assault ($301,501)	3,491,674
Nijinsky II, Dead	130	61	2	Balletto (UAE) ($614,000)	3,475,525
Meadowlake, Ky.	207	106	6	Open Concert ($136,457)	3,456,953
Afleet, Jpn	156	81	6	Catboat ($184,598)	3,439,386
Gone West, Ky.	127	61	8	Misty Sixes ($246,074)	3,420,998
Topsider, Dead	148	87	4	Chris's Bad Boy ($261,480)	3,405,282
Capote, Pens	174	87	4	Roar Emotion ($328,652)	3,392,640
Secretariat, Dead	200	90	4	Perfect Soul (Ire) ($391,549)	3,378,391

Leading Broodmare Sires by Average Earnings per Runner in North America in 2004
Minimum of 25 Starters

Sire	Strs	Wnrs	Average
Smile, Dead	77	41	$114,659
Rainbow Quest, Eng	30	11	53,618
Mari's Book, Dead	82	45	46,909
Easy Goer, Dead	45	26	46,415
Nureyev, Dead	110	59	41,977
Olympio, Ca.	37	19	41,878
Danzig, Pens	174	95	38,735
Citidancer, Md.	44	28	37,203
Sadler's Wells, Ire	47	23	36,583
Dixie Brass, Dead	28	12	35,308
Dixieland Band, Ky.	330	187	35,280
Naskra, Dead	112	45	34,666
Seeking the Gold, Ky.	127	70	34,065
Kingmambo, Ky.	25	16	33,822
Mr. Prospector, Dead	252	131	33,552
Quiet American, Ky.	61	29	33,315
Alydeed, Ab.	43	25	32,186
Dayjur, Ky.	57	32	31,576
Shimatoree, Dead	26	12	31,027
Silver Deputy, Ky.	113	64	30,934
Hawkster, Jpn	50	24	30,562

Leading Broodmare Sires by Median Earnings per Runner in North America in 2004
Minimum of 25 Starters

Sire	Strs	Wnrs	Median
Akureyri, Dead	26	16	$15,793
Kingmambo, Ky.	25	16	15,770
Cherokee Fellow, Dead	48	32	15,360
Citidancer, Md.	44	28	15,070
Secret Hello, Dead	33	21	14,575
Skip Trial, Fl.	87	53	14,500
Bold Ruckus, Dead	233	133	14,480
Easy Goer, Dead	45	26	14,465
Rainbow Quest, Eng	30	11	14,230
Jolie's Halo, Jpn	47	28	14,180
Carson City, Dead	141	81	14,038
Strawberry Road (Aus), Dead	145	91	13,800
Stately Don, Jpn	35	16	13,716
Sir Harry Lewis, Eng	26	17	13,569
Silver Deputy, Ky.	113	64	13,535
Dayjur, Ky.	57	32	13,431

Leading Broodmare Sires by Number of Winners in North America in 2004

Sire	Strs	Wnrs	Wnrs
Relaunch, Dead	330	191	57.9%
Dixieland Band, Ky.	330	187	56.7%
Deputy Minister, Dead	316	171	54.1%
Valid Appeal, Dead	307	168	54.7%
Crafty Prospector, Ky.	287	160	55.7%
Clever Trick, Dead	309	158	51.1%
Conquistador Cielo, Dead	271	139	51.3%
Halo, Dead	259	135	52.1%
Storm Bird, Dead	245	134	54.7%
Bold Ruckus, Dead	233	133	57.1%
Mr. Prospector, Dead	252	131	52.0%
Miswaki, Dead	248	131	52.8%
Wild Again, Pens	252	131	52.0%
Affirmed, Dead	226	126	55.8%
Cure the Blues, Dead	236	123	52.1%
Woodman, Ky.	207	123	59.4%
Phone Trick, N.Y.	233	122	52.4%
Pleasant Colony, Dead	226	122	54.0%
Cox's Ridge, Dead	229	120	52.4%
Kris S., Dead	228	120	52.6%
Sovereign Dancer, Dead	220	120	54.5%
Private Account, Dead	232	119	51.3%
Vice Regent, Dead	239	119	49.8%
Majestic Light, Dead	233	112	48.1%
Storm Cat, Ky.	226	109	48.2%

Leading Broodmare Sires by Number of Wins in North America in 2004

Sire	Strs	Wnrs	Wins
Dixieland Band, Ky.	330	187	334
Relaunch, Dead	330	191	312
Crafty Prospector, Ky.	287	160	298
Deputy Minister, Dead	316	171	293
Valid Appeal, Dead	307	168	292
Clever Trick, Dead	309	158	263
Bold Ruckus, Dead	233	133	258
Conquistador Cielo, Dead	271	139	254
Mr. Prospector, Dead	252	131	236
Miswaki, Dead	248	131	228
Vice Regent, Dead	239	119	226
Affirmed, Dead	226	126	220
Halo, Dead	259	135	220
Storm Bird, Dead	245	134	219
Pleasant Colony, Dead	226	122	217

Leading Broodmare Sires by Number of Stakes Winners in North America in 2004

Sire	Strs	Wnrs	SWs	SWins
Danzig, Pens	174	95	15	23
Dixieland Band, Ky.	330	187	15	26
Mr. Prospector, Dead	252	131	15	18
Seattle Slew, Dead	225	101	14	21
Deputy Minister, Dead	316	171	12	16
Storm Bird, Dead	245	134	12	18
Woodman, Ky.	207	123	12	16
Green Dancer, Dead	199	91	11	18
Relaunch, Dead	330	191	11	19
Spectacular Bid, Dead	184	104	11	13
Bold Ruckus, Dead	233	133	10	20
Carson City, Dead	141	81	10	13
Dynaformer, Ky.	139	67	10	13
Kris S., Dead	228	120	10	17
Miswaki, Dead	248	131	10	13
Saratoga Six, N.M.	181	93	10	13
Forty Niner, Jpn	165	92	9	11
Phone Trick, N.Y.	233	122	9	12
Seeking the Gold, Ky.	127	70	9	12
Silver Deputy, Ky.	113	64	9	15
Smarten, Dead	174	86	9	12

Leading Broodmare Sires by Number of Graded Stakes Winners in North America in 2004

Sire	Strs	Wnrs	GSWs	GSWins
Mr. Prospector, Dead	252	131	8	10
Dixieland Band, Ky.	330	187	7	15
Danzig, Pens	174	95	6	10
Green Dancer, Dead	199	91	6	6
Seattle Slew, Dead	225	101	6	8
Deputy Minister, Dead	316	171	4	6
Halo, Dead	259	135	4	7
Kris S., Dead	228	120	4	7
Alleged, Dead	173	90	3	3
Clever Trick, Dead	309	158	3	8
Copelan, Dead	176	94	3	5
Dynaformer, Ky.	139	67	3	3
Gone West, Ky.	127	61	3	3
Mr. Leader, Dead	188	86	3	4
Naskra, Dead	112	45	3	4
Quiet American, Ky.	61	29	3	4
Rahy, Ky.	169	78	3	5
Relaunch, Dead	330	191	3	8
Seeking the Gold, Ky.	127	70	3	4
Spectacular Bid, Dead	184	104	3	3
Star de Naskra, Dead	180	94	3	6
Storm Bird, Dead	245	134	3	4
Trempolino, Fr	49	23	3	4
Valid Appeal, Dead	307	168	3	4

Leading Worldwide Sires by 2004 Earnings

Worldwide earnings for stallions represented by one starter in any of the following countries: United States, Canada, Puerto Rico, England, Ireland, France, Italy, Germany, United Arab Emirates, Saudi Arabia, Australia, Brazil, Argentina, Japan, and Hong Kong.

Sire, YOB, Sire	Loc	2004 Stud Fee	Strs	Wnrs	SWs/Stk Wins	Leading Earner (Earnings)	Progeny Earnings
SUNDAY SILENCE, 86, by Halo	Dead		520	231	37/45	Zenno Rob Roy (Jpn) ($6,681,748)	$83,748,391
DANEHILL, 86, by Danzig	Dead		489	220	45/73	North Light (Ire) ($1,961,555)	25,628,375
DANCE IN THE DARK, 93, by Sunday Silence	Jpn.	N/A	266	81	4/5	Delta Blues (Jpn) ($2,525,023)	22,852,146
BRIAN'S TIME, 85, by Roberto	Jpn.	N/A	230	74	7/12	Time Paradox (Jpn) ($3,408,062)	20,715,297
FUJI KISEKI, 92, by Sunday Silence	Jpn.	N/A	293	84	6/8	Osumi Cosmo (Jpn) ($997,553)	16,462,585
END SWEEP, 91, by Forty Niner	Dead		335	153	6/7	Sweep Tosho (Jpn) ($2,118,418)	14,923,219
FORTY NINER, 85, by Mr. Prospector	Jpn.	N/A	142	55	5/9	Meiner Select (Jpn) ($1,601,061)	14,500,136
SADLER'S WELLS, 81, by Northern Dancer	Ire.	N/A	280	116	30/38	Diaghilev (Ire) ($1,426,762)	12,762,392
TONY BIN, 83, by Kampala	Dead		88	31	5/5	Narita Century (Jpn) ($1,419,924)	12,722,671
AFLEET, 84, by Mr. Prospector	Jpn.	N/A	188	56	2/3	Hikari Zirconia (Jpn) ($1,077,989)	12,660,735
SAKURA BAKUSHIN O, 89, by Sakura Yutaka O	Jpn.	N/A	171	59	2/2	She is Tosho (Jpn) ($731,284)	11,926,438
ELUSIVE QUALITY, 93, by Gone West	Ky.	$50,000	139	80	5/15	Smarty Jones ($7,563,535)	10,865,792
KINGMAMBO, 90, by Mr. Prospector	Ky.	$225,000	183	74	14/22	King Kamehameha (Jpn) ($3,743,956)	10,703,786
BUBBLE GUM FELLOW, 93, by Sunday Silence	Jpn.	N/A	229	61	1/1	Taiki Alpha (Jpn) ($377,929)	10,519,356
WARNING (GB), 85, by Known Fact	Dead		120	41	6/9	Sunningdale (Jpn) ($1,680,778)	10,288,189
EL PRADO (Ire), 89, by Sadler's Wells	Ky.	$75,000	200	102	16/28	Kitten's Joy ($1,625,796)	10,102,201
TIMBER COUNTRY, 92, by Woodman	Jpn.	N/A	166	46	5/7	Admire Don (Jpn) ($3,251,772)	10,038,791
STORM CAT, 83, by Storm Bird	Ky.	$500,000	141	78	19/28	Seeking the Dia ($1,407,809)	9,843,341
A.P. INDY, 89, by Seattle Slew	Ky.	$300,000	188	99	21/28	Friends Lake ($611,800)	9,129,720
TAIKI SHUTTLE, 94, by Devil's Bag	Jpn.	N/A	142	40	2/4	Golden Cast (Jpn) ($939,760)	8,942,241
SAINT BALLADO, 89, by Halo	Dead		179	90	4/9	Ashado ($2,259,640)	8,403,410
HENNESSY, 93, by Storm Cat	Ky.	$35,000	321	146	10/17	Grand Armee (Aus) ($1,352,194)	8,140,276
TAMAMO CROSS, 84, by C B Cross	Jpn.	N/A	112	24	2/3	My Sole Sound (Jpn) ($1,123,516)	7,986,548
JADE ROBBERY, 87, by Mr. Prospector	Dead		196	47	0/0	Senoe Dyna (Jpn) ($468,139)	7,899,656
TALE OF THE CAT, 94, by Storm Cat	Ky.	$75,000	229	125	13/16	Lion Heart ($1,080,000)	7,896,568
MEJIRO RYAN, 87, by Amber Shadai	Jpn.	N/A	144	42	2/3	Dream Come Come (Jpn) ($876,016)	7,884,645
TWINING, 91, by Forty Niner	Jpn.	N/A	187	88	3/4	Meiner Zest (Jpn) ($350,348)	7,642,542
ROYAL ACADEMY, 87, by Nijinsky II	Ky.	$20,000	348	160	14/20	Bullish Luck ($1,459,267)	7,610,907
GRAND SLAM, 95, by Gone West	Ky.	$75,000	178	96	13/19	Cafe Olympus ($875,328)	7,592,355
MARVELOUS SUNDAY, 92, by Sunday Silence	Jpn.	N/A	92	25	2/3	Silk Famous (Jpn) ($2,449,025)	7,536,776
UNBRIDLED'S SONG, 93, by Unbridled	Ky.	$125,000	227	103	13/19	Domestic Dispute ($413,428)	7,458,540
AWESOME AGAIN, 94, by Deputy Minister	Ky.	$75,000	117	61	5/9	Ghostzapper ($2,590,000)	7,120,028
WILD RUSH, 94, by Wild Again	Jpn.	N/A	133	78	9/13	Personal Rush ($1,165,761)	7,030,902
SMART STRIKE, 92, by Mr. Prospector	Ky.	$25,000	136	84	12/21	Soaring Free ($1,113,862)	6,895,919
LANGFUHR, 92, by Danzig	Ky.	$25,000	292	141	10/14	Imperialism ($542,000)	6,882,723
CARSON CITY, 87, by Mr. Prospector	Dead		186	101	10/18	Pollard's Vision ($1,022,020)	6,872,455
SILVER DEPUTY, 85, by Deputy Minister	Ky.	$40,000	176	92	6/15	Divine Silver ($1,121,192)	6,840,598
FRENCH DEPUTY, 92, by Deputy Minister	Jpn.	N/A	164	81	6/8	Ambroise (Jpn) ($598,484)	6,757,166
DEHERE, 91, by Deputy Minister	Jpn.	N/A	197	84	4/5	Keiai Guard (Jpn) ($801,741)	6,718,776
SPINNING WORLD, 93, by Nureyev	Ire.	$21,952	208	81	8/9	World Scale ($444,298)	6,704,563
DYNAFORMER, 85, by Roberto	Ky.	$75,000	159	72	9/10	Perfect Drift ($947,595)	6,703,864
EL CONDOR PASA, 95, by Kingmambo	Dead		126	41	1/1	Vermilion (Jpn) ($500,222)	6,678,978
FUSAICHI CONCORDE, 93, by Caerleon	Jpn.	N/A	101	21	2/3	Osumi Haruka (Jpn) ($1,252,860)	6,669,890
ALPHABET SOUP, 91, by Cozzene	Ky.	$10,000	178	105	11/18	Our New Recruit ($1,265,795)	6,645,156
COMMANDER IN CHIEF, 90, by Dancing Brave	Jpn.	N/A	183	31	2/3	Meisho Kio (Jpn) ($743,817)	6,558,871
PLEASANT COLONY, 78, by His Majesty	Dead		54	25	4/7	Pleasantly Perfect ($4,840,000)	6,511,198
THUNDER GULCH, 92, by Gulch	Ky.	$50,000	284	102	8/9	Sense of Style ($369,000)	6,386,209
WHITE MUZZLE (GB), 90, by Dancing Brave	Jpn.	N/A	62	24	2/2	Ingrandire (Jpn) ($1,485,928)	6,343,119
DISTORTED HUMOR, 93, by Forty Niner	Ky.	$50,000	190	101	13/18	Funny Cide ($1,075,100)	6,084,127
SAKURA LAUREL, 91, by Rainbow Quest	Jpn.	N/A	98	23	2/2	Lingus Laurel (Jpn) ($513,274)	5,988,754
HELISSIO, 93, by Fairy King	Eng.	$10,702	174	37	0/0	Meisho Kachidoki (Jpn) ($592,327)	5,870,687
PENTIRE., 92, by Be My Guest	Jpn.	N/A	94	33	3/4	Meiner Amundsen (Jpn) ($948,911)	5,764,669
GONE WEST, 84, by Mr. Prospector	Ky.	$125,000	158	67	6/12	Speightstown ($1,045,556)	5,723,984
ADJUDICATING, 89, by Danzig	Jpn.	N/A	84	19	3/3	Adjudi Mitsuo (Jpn) ($1,922,509)	5,684,381
MAYANO TOP GUN, 92, by Brian's Time	Jpn.	N/A	117	29	2/2	Precise Machine (Jpn) ($998,599)	5,605,141
BELONG TO ME, 89, by Danzig	Ky.	$25,000	193	101	8/15	Ocean Drive ($505,900)	5,591,936
DESERT KING, 94, by Danehill	Aus.	N/A	250	91	6/6	Makybe Diva (GB) ($3,956,143)	5,528,426
LAMMTARRA, 92, by Nijinsky II	Jpn.	N/A	135	31	1/1	Maruka Senryo (Jpn) ($406,946)	5,468,414
TOKAI TEIO, 88, by Symboli Rudolf (Jpn)	Jpn.	N/A	86	18	2/2	Meiner Solomon (Jpn) ($954,192)	5,460,138
NOT FOR LOVE, 90, by Mr. Prospector	Md.	$25,000	180	102	10/18	Love of Money ($491,500)	5,441,941
DEVIL HIS DUE, 89, by Devil's Bag	Ky.	$7,500	199	104	9/13	Roses in May ($1,723,277)	5,355,018
SPECIAL WEEK, 95, by Sunday Silence	Jpn.	N/A	125	41	1/1	Smooth Baritone (Jpn) ($503,905)	5,264,880
MACHIAVELLIAN, 87, by Mr. Prospector	Dead		187	85	7/10	Right Approach (GB) ($948,690)	5,261,552
BOSTON HARBOR, 94, by Capote	Jpn.	N/A	143	84	6/7	Sepia Memory (Jpn) ($538,840)	5,248,056
SMOKE GLACKEN, 94, by Two Punch	Ky.	$25,000	150	100	9/12	Smok'n Frolic ($258,220)	5,139,994

Leading General Sire by Year

Year	General Sire	Earnings	Year	General Sire	Earnings	Year	General Sire	Earnings
2004	Elusive Quality	$10,865,792	1955	*Nasrullah	$1,433,660	1906	*Meddler	$151,243
2003	Kris S.	11,497,747	1954	*Heliopolis	1,406,638	1905	Hamburg	153,160
2002	Dehere	9,337,302	1953	Bull Lea	1,155,846	1904	*Meddler	222,555
2001	Danehill	13,542,612	1952	Bull Lea	1,630,847	1903	*Ben Strome	106,965
2000	Storm Cat	9,269,521	1951	Count Fleet	1,160,847	1902	Hastings	113,865
1999	Storm Cat	10,383,259	1950	*Heliopolis	852,292	1901	Sir Dixon	165,682
1998	Deputy Minister	8,526,094	1949	Bull Lea	991,842	1900	Kingston	116,368
1997	Deputy Minister	8,581,511	1948	Bull Lea	1,334,027	1899	*Albert	95,975
1996	Palace Music	5,231,734	1947	Bull Lea	1,259,718	1898	Hanover	118,590
1995	Sadler's Wells	5,862,410	1946	*Mahmoud	638,025	1897	Hanover	122,374
1994	Broad Brush	5,397,181	1945	War Admiral	591,352	1896	Hanover	86,853
1993	Danzig	5,082,552	1944	Chance Play	431,100	1895	Hanover	106,908
1992	Danzig	6,932,569	1943	*Bull Dog	372,706	1894	*Sir Modred	134,318
1991	Danzig	6,997,402	1942	Equipoise	437,141	1893	Himyar	249,502
1990	Alydar	6,661,455	1941	*Blenheim II	378,981	1892	Iroquois	183,026
1989	Halo	7,525,638	1940	*Sir Gallahad III	305,610	1891	Longfellow	189,334
1988	Mr. Prospector	9,575,605	1939	*Challenger II	316,281	1890	*St. Blaise	189,005
1987	Mr. Prospector	5,877,385	1938	*Sickle	327,822	1889	*Rayon d'Or	175,877
1986	Lyphard	4,045,447	1937	The Porter	292,262	1888	Glenelg	130,746
1985	Buckaroo	4,145,272	1936	*Sickle	209,800	1887	Glenelg	120,031
1984	Seattle Slew	5,361,259	1935	Chance Play	191,465	1886	Glenelg	114,088
1983	Halo	2,773,637	1934	*Sir Gallahad III	180,165	1885	Virgil	73,235
1982	His Majesty	2,675,823	1933	*Sir Gallahad III	136,428	1884	Glenelg	98,862
1981	Nodouble	2,499,946	1932	Chatterton	210,040	1883	*Billet	89,998
1980	Raja Baba	2,483,352	1931	*St. Germans	315,585	1882	*Bonnie Scotland	103,475
1979	Exclusive Native	2,872,605	1930	*Sir Gallahad III	422,200	1881	*Leamington	139,219
1978	Exclusive Native	1,969,867	1929	*Chicle	289,123	1880	*Bonnie Scotland	135,700
1977	Dr. Fager	1,593,079	1928	High Time	307,631	1879	*Leamington	70,837
1976	What a Pleasure	1,622,159	1927	Fair Play	361,518	1878	Lexington	50,198
1975	What a Pleasure	2,011,878	1926	Man o' War	408,137	1877	*Leamington	41,700
1974	T. V. Lark	1,242,000	1925	Sweep	237,564	1876	Lexington	90,570
1973	Bold Ruler	1,488,622	1924	Fair Play	296,102	1875	*Leamington	64,518
1972	Round Table	1,199,932	1923	The Finn	285,759	1874	Lexington	51,889
1971	Northern Dancer	1,288,580	1922	*McGee	222,491	1873	Lexington	71,565
1970	Hail to Reason	1,400,839	1921	Celt	206,167	1872	Lexington	71,515
1969	Bold Ruler	1,357,144	1920	Fair Play	269,102	1871	Lexington	109,095
1968	Bold Ruler	1,988,427	1919	*Star Shoot	197,233	1870	Lexington	120,360
1967	Bold Ruler	2,249,272	1918	Sweep	139,057	1869	Lexington	56,375
1966	Bold Ruler	2,306,523	1917	*Star Shoot	131,674	1868	Lexington	68,340
1965	Bold Ruler	1,091,924	1916	*Star Shoot	138,163	1867	Lexington	54,030
1964	Bold Ruler	1,457,156	1915	Broomstick	94,387	1866	Lexington	92,725
1963	Bold Ruler	917,531	1914	Broomstick	99,043	1865	Lexington	58,750
1962	*Nasrullah	1,474,831	1913	Broomstick	76,009	1864	Lexington	28,440
1961	*Ambiorix	936,976	1912	*Star Shoot	79,973	1863	Lexington	14,235
1960	*Nasrullah	1,419,683	1911	*Star Shoot	53,895	1862	Lexington	9,700
1959	*Nasrullah	1,434,543	1910	Kingston	85,220	1861	Lexington	22,425
1958	*Princequillo	1,394,540	1909	Ben Brush	75,143	1860	Revenue	49,450
1957	*Princequillo	1,698,427	1908	Hastings	154,061			
1956	*Nasrullah	1,462,413	1907	Commando	270,345			

Leading Juvenile Sire by Year

Year	Juvenile Sire	Earnings	Year	Juvenile Sire	Earnings	Year	Juvenile Sire	Earnings
2004	Storm Cat	$1,927,589	1983	Alydar	$1,136,063	1962	*Nasrullah	$574,231
2003	Tale of the Cat	2,077,206	1982	Olden Times	948,900	1961	Bryan G.	428,810
2002	Storm Cat	2,540,238	1981	Hoist the Flag	680,753	1960	*My Babu	437,240
2001	Hennessy	1,766,695	1980	Raja Baba	807,335	1959	Determine	413,765
2000	Honour and Glory	1,436,584	1979	Mr. Prospector	529,665	1958	*Turn-to	463,280
1999	Storm Cat	1,570,026	1978	Secretariat	600,617	1957	Jet Jewel	360,402
1998	Storm Cat	1,686,995	1977	In Reality	432,596	1956	*Nasrullah	422,573
1997	Phone Trick	1,737,764	1976	Raja Baba	419,872	1955	*Nirgal	293,800
1996	Capote	2,756,558	1975	What a Pleasure	611,071	1954	*Nasrullah	625,692
1995	Storm Cat	1,281,030	1974	What a Pleasure	387,748	1953	Roman	550,966
1994	Woodman	1,303,362	1973	Raise a Native	311,002	1952	Polynesian	341,730
1993	Storm Cat	1,567,979	1972	Bold Ruler	541,990	1951	Menow	274,700
1992	Storm Cat	1,729,366	1971	First Landing	551,120	1950	War Relic	272,182
1991	Blushing Groom (Fr)	1,295,629	1970	Hail to Reason	473,244	1949	Roman	227,604
1990	Woodman	1,310,633	1969	Prince John	418,183	1948	War Admiral	346,260
1989	Mr. Prospector	1,514,223	1968	Bold Ruler	609,243	1947	Bull Lea	420,940
1988	Seattle Slew	946,433	1967	Bold Ruler	1,126,844	1946	*Mahmoud	283,983
1987	Mr. Prospector	1,566,919	1966	Bold Ruler	941,493	1945	*Sickle	183,510
1986	Rajab	950,335	1965	Tom Fool	592,871	1944	Case Ace	230,525
1985	Fappiano	1,232,408	1964	Bold Ruler	967,814	1943	*Bull Dog	178,344
1984	Danzig	2,146,530	1963	Bold Ruler	343,585	1942	*Bull Dog	221,332

Leading Freshman Sire by Year

Year	Freshman Sire	Earnings	Year	Freshman Sire	Earnings	Year	Freshman Sire	Earnings
2004	Successful Appeal	$1,727,557	1994	Red Ransom	$817,550	1984	Danzig	$2,146,530
2003	Stravinsky	1,271,620	1993	Seeking the Gold	939,642	1983	Alydar	1,136,063
2002	Grand Slam	1,403,880	1992	Forty Niner	578,567	1982	Seattle Slew	666,755
2001	Valid Expectations	1,397,911	1991	Capote	1,185,886	1981	Turn and Count	283,279
2000	Honour and Glory	1,436,584	1990	Woodman	1,310,633	1980	Foolish Pleasure	536,783
1999	Cherokee Run	1,369,126	1989	Secreto	584,023	1979	L'Enjoleur	201,116
1998	End Sweep	947,013	1988	Chief's Crown	760,842	1978	Mr. Prospector	309,168
1997	Gilded Time	730,106	1987	Crafty Prospector	349,405	1977	Roberto	359,285
1996	Salt Lake	850,954	1986	Sportin' Life	781,754	1976	Raja Baba	419,872
1995	Farma Way	818,043	1985	Fappiano	1,232,408	1975	Al Hattab	217,630

Leading Broodmare Sire by Year

Year	Broodmare Sire	Earnings	Year	Broodmare Sire	Earnings	Year	Broodmare Sire	Earnings
2004	Mr. Prospector	$20,311,039	1983	Buckpasser	$3,479,749	1962	War Admiral	$1,654,396
2003	Mr. Prospector	21,425,839	1982	Prince John	3,072,150	1961	Bull Lea	1,632,559
2002	Mr. Prospector	9,725,924	1981	Double Jay	3,453,131	1960	Bull Lea	1,915,881
2001	Mr. Prospector	11,430,437	1980	Prince John	3,423,135	1959	Bull Lea	1,481,291
2000	Mr. Prospector	10,390,642	1979	Prince John	2,856,004	1958	Bull Lea	1,646,812
1999	Mr. Prospector	11,124,523	1978	Crafty Admiral	2,298,048	1957	*Mahmoud	1,593,782
1998	Mr. Prospector	9,364,191	1977	Double Jay	2,696,490	1956	*Bull Dog	1,683,908
1997	Mr. Prospector	9,829,817	1976	*Princequillo	2,763,189	1955	*Sir Gallahad III	1,499,162
1996	Seattle Slew	9,105,905	1975	Double Jay	2,233,642	1954	*Bull Dog	1,780,267
1995	Seattle Slew	8,291,630	1974	Olympia	2,292,178	1953	*Bull Dog	1,941,345
1994	Nijinsky II	7,606,160	1973	*Princequillo	3,079,810	1952	*Sir Gallahad III	1,656,221
1993	Nijinsky II	7,179,266	1972	*Princequillo	2,717,859	1951	*Sir Gallahad III	1,707,823
1992	Secretariat	7,345,089	1971	Double Jay	2,053,235	1950	*Sir Gallahad III	1,376,629
1991	Northern Dancer	6,030,243	1970	*Princequillo	2,451,785	1949	*Sir Gallahad III	1,393,104
1990	*Grey Dawn II	6,211,259	1969	*Princequillo	2,189,583	1948	*Sir Gallahad III	1,468,648
1989	Buckpasser	10,111,605	1968	*Princequillo	2,104,439	1947	*Sir Gallahad III	1,458,309
1988	Buckpasser	7,593,450	1967	*Princequillo	2,302,065	1946	*Sir Gallahad III	1,529,393
1987	Hoist the Flag	5,516,181	1966	*Princequillo	2,007,184	1945	*Sir Gallahad III	1,020,235
1986	Prince John	4,468,468	1965	Roman	2,394,944	1944	*Sir Gallahad III	1,024,290
1985	Speak John	5,187,865	1964	War Admiral	2,028,459	1943	*Sir Gallahad III	703,301
1984	Buckpasser	5,111,391	1963	Count Fleet	1,866,809	1942	*Chicle	533,572

Most Times as Leading General Sire (1830-2004)

16	Lexington (1861-'74, '76, '78)
8	Bold Ruler (1963-'69, '73)
	*Glencoe (1847, '49-'50, '54-'58)
5	Bull Lea (1947-'49, '52-'53)
	*Leviathan (1837-'39, '43, '48)
	*Nasrullah (1955-'56, '59-'60, '62)
	Sir Charles (1830-'33, '36)
	*Star Shoot (1911-'12, '16-'17, '19)
4	Glenelg (1884, '86-'88)
	Hanover (1895-'98)
	*Leamington (1875, '77, '79, '81)
	*Priam (1842, '44-'46)
	*Sir Gallahad III (1930, '33-'34, '40)
3	Boston (1851-'53)
	Broomstick (1913-'15)
	Danzig (1991-'93)
	Fair Play (1920, '24, '27)

Before 1860, leading sire was determined by number of wins.

Most Times as Leading Juvenile Sire (1942-2004)

7	Storm Cat (1992-'93, '95, '98-'99, 2002, '04)
6	Bold Ruler (1963-'64, '66-'68, '72)
3	Mr. Prospector (1979, '87, '89)
	*Nasrullah (1954, '56, '62)
	Woodman (1990, '94, '98)
2	*Bull Dog (1942-'43)
	Raja Baba (1976, '80)
	What a Pleasure (1974-'75)

Most Times as Leading Broodmare Sire (1942-2004)

12	*Sir Gallahad III (1939, 1943-'52, '55)
8	Mr. Prospector (1997-2004)
	*Princequillo (1966-'70, '72-'73, '76)
4	Buckpasser (1983-'84, '88-'89)
	Bull Lea (1958-'61)
	Double Jay (1971, '75, '77, '81)
	Prince John (1979-'80, '82, '86)

Most Times as Leading General Sire in Consecutive Years (1830-2004)

14	Lexington (1861-'74)
7	Bold Ruler (1963-'69)
5	*Glencoe (1854-'58)
4	Hanover (1895-'98)
	Sir Charles (1830-'33)
3	Boston (1851-'53)
	Broomstick (1913-'15)
	Bull Lea (1947-'49)
	Danzig (1991-'93)
	Glenelg (1886-'88)
	*Leviathan (1837-'39)
	*Priam (1844-'46)
2	Bull Lea (1952-'53)
	Deputy Minister (1997-'98)
	Exclusive Native (1978-'79)
	*Glencoe (1849-'50)
	Mr. Prospector (1987-'88)

2	*Nasrullah (1955-'56)
	*Nasrullah (1959-'60)
	*Princequillo (1957-'58)
	*Sir Gallahad III (1933-'34)
	*Star Shoot (1911-'12)
	*Star Shoot (1916-'17)

Before 1860, leading sire was determined by number of wins.

Most Times as Leading Juvenile Sire in Consecutive Years (1942-2004)

3	Bold Ruler (1966-'68)
2	Bold Ruler (1963-'64)
	*Bull Dog (1942-'43)
	Storm Cat (1992-'93)
	Storm Cat (1998-'99)
	What a Pleasure (1974-'75)

Most Times as Leading Broodmare Sire in Consecutive Years (1942-2004)

9	Sir Gallahad III (1943-'52)
8	Mr. Prospector (1997-2004)
5	*Princequillo (1966-'70)
4	Bull Lea (1958-'61)
2	Buckpasser (1983-'84)
	Buckpasser (1988-'89)
	*Bull Dog (1953-'54)
	Nijinsky II (1993-'94)
	Prince John (1979-'80)
	*Princequillo (1972-'73)
	Seattle Slew (1995-'96)

Profiles of Leading Sires

2004—ELUSIVE QUALITY, 1993 b. h., Gone West—Touch of Greatness, by Hero's Honor. Bred in Kentucky by Silver Springs Stud Farm Inc. and H. Costelloe. Raced in name of Sheikh Mohammed bin Rashid al Maktoum and his Darley operation. 20-9-3-2, $413,284. Half brother to stakes winner Rossini. Trained by Bill Mott, won 1998 Poker H. (G3), world record for mile on turf, 1:31.63; Jaipur H. (G3), set seven-furlong track record at Gulfstream Park, 1:20.17, on dirt. Stands at Gainsborough Farm in Versailles, Kentucky, and shuttled to Australia in 2003 and 2004. Through 2004, sire of 16 stakes winners (8% from foals), including five group or graded stakes winners, with progeny earnings of $15,202,580. Sire of Smarty Jones, 2004 champion three-year-old male, $7,613,155, and Elusive City, 2003 highweighted two-year-old on French Free Handicap. Substantial part of 2004 progeny earnings, $10,876,981, from Smarty Jones, who received a $5-million bonus from Oaklawn Park for winning the Rebel S., Arkansas Derby (G2), and Kentucky Derby (G1).

2003—KRIS S., 1977 dk. b. or br. h., Roberto—Sharp Queen, by *Princequillo. Bred in Florida by John Brunetti Jr.'s Red Oak Farm. Raced by estate of Lloyd Schuneman and partners. 5-3-1-0, $53,350. Won 1980 Bradbury S. Entered stud in 1982 at Joseph and Barbara LaCroix's Meadowbrook Farm in Florida; moved to Prestonwood Farm in Kentucky in 1994; acquired by WinStar Farm when it purchased Prestonwood's assets. To 2005, sire of 87 stakes winners (10% of foals), including 41 graded stakes winners, with total progeny earnings of $74,390,143. His four champions are: Symboli Kris S, 2002-'03 Horse of the Year in Japan, $8,401,282; Hollywood Wildcat, 1993 champion three-year-old filly, $1,432,160; Soaring Softly, 1999 champion turf female, $1,270,433; and Action This Day, 2003 champion two-year-old male, $817,200. Also sire of Kris Kin, winner of the 2003 Epsom Derby (Eng-G1). Sire of sires. Died in 2002.

2002—DEHERE, 1991 b. h., Deputy Minister—Sister Dot, by Secretariat. Bred in Kentucky by Robert E. Brennan's Due Process Stable. 9-6-2-0, $723,712. Champion two-year-old male in 1993. Trained by Reynaldo Nobles, swept Saratoga Race Course's three major juvenile races culminating with the Hopeful Stakes (G1); also won the Champagne Stakes (G1) at two, won the Fountain of Youth Stakes (G2) but broke down before the Triple Crown races. Retired initially to Ashford Stud and sold to Japan in 1999. To 2005, sire of 55 stakes winners (7%), including multiple Grade 1 winner Take Charge Lady, 2000 Puerto Rican champion imported two-year-old colt Mi Amigo Guelo, and Belle Du Jour, highweighted two-year-old filly on the 1999 Australian Free Handicap.

2001—DANEHILL, 1986 b. h., Danzig—Razyana, by His Majesty. Bred in Kentucky by Juddmonte Farms. 9-4-1-2, $321,064. Highweighted sprinter at three on European Free Handicap. Retired to Coolmore Stud, Ireland, in 1990. From 1991 through 2001, shuttled annually to Coolmore Australia; in 2002, covered mares on Southern Hemisphere schedule in Ireland. Stood in Japan in 1996. Leading sire in Australia six times; leading sire in France 2001, '02. To 2005, sire of 287 stakes winners (12%) and 17 champions. Best runners: European highweights Rock of Gibraltar (Ire), Banks Hill (GB), Desert King, Mozart (Ire), Tiger Hill; Hong Kong Horse of the Year Fairy King Prawn; and Australian champions Dane Ripper, Danewin, Catbird, and Merlene. In 2001, set a single-season record with 48 stakes winners. Died May 13, 2003, at Coolmore.

2000, 1999—STORM CAT, 1983 dk. b. or br. h., Storm Bird—Terlingua, by Secretariat. Bred in Pennsylvania by W. T. Young Storage Inc., raced for W. T. Young. 8-4-3-0, $570,610. Won Young America Stakes (G1) and finished second by a nose to champion Tasso in 1985 Breeders' Cup Juvenile (G1). Entered stud in 1988 at Overbrook Farm in Kentucky for initial fee of $25,000; by 2002, stood for American high of $500,000. To 2005, sire of 132 stakes winners (13%), including North American champion Storm Flag Flying, European highweight Giant's Causeway, and major American winners Tabasco Cat, Cat Thief, and Sharp Cat. Led juvenile sire list a record seven times, 1992-'93, '95, '98-'99, 2002, '04.

1998, 1997—DEPUTY MINISTER, 1979 dk. b. or br. h., Vice Regent—Mint Copy, by Bunty's Flight. Bred in Canada by Mr. and Mrs. Morton Levy's Centurion Farms. 22-12-2-2, $696,964. Canadian Horse of the Year in 1981; Eclipse- and Sovereign Award-winning two-year-old male. Half-interest purchased by Kinghaven Farm midway through two-year-old season; purchased by Robert Brennan's Due Process Stable prior to 1982 season. Entered stud in 1984 at Windfields Farm Maryland; relocated in 1988 to Brookdale Farm in Kentucky. Sire of 82 stakes winners (8%) to 2005, including 12 millionaires. Best include Racing Hall of Fame member Go for Wand; two-time champion and filly triple crown winner Open Mind; 1993 champion juvenile male and 2002 leading sire Dehere; 1998 Breeders' Cup Classic (G1) winner Awesome Again. Broodmare sire of more than 105 stakes winners. Died September 10, 2004.

1996—PALACE MUSIC, 1981 ch. h., The Minstrel—Come My Prince, by Prince John. Bred in Kentucky by Mereworth Farm. Sold for $130,000 to Nelson Bunker Hunt at 1982 Keeneland July and raced for partnership of Hunt and Allen Paulson. 21-7-5-3, $918,700. Group 1 and Grade 1 turf stakes winner in England and North America. Stood one season at Hunt's Bluegrass Farm in Kentucky, then moved in 1988 to Paulson's Brookside Farm. Shuttled between Kentucky and New Zealand for several years before relocating permanently in 1991 to Australia, where he was pensioned in 2005. Was 1996 leading U.S. sire due to one horse—Cigar, a two-time Horse of the Year and leading American money winner ($9,999,815). Also sire of several important Australasian runners, including 1992 champion stayer Naturalism; also sire of South Africa two-year-old champion Palace Line. To 2005, sire of 33 stakes winners.

1995—SADLER'S WELLS, 1981 b. h., Northern Dancer—Fairy Bridge, by Bold Reason. Bred in Kentucky by Swettenham Stud and Partners. 11-6-3-0, $713,690. Winner of 1984 Irish Two Thousand Guineas (Ire-G1) and Eclipse Stakes (Eng-G1). Stands at Coolmore Stud in Ireland. Leading sire in England and Ireland in 1990, 1992-2004, a modern-record 13 consecutive years; leading sire in France in '93, '99. To 2005, sire of 17 champions and 257 stakes winners (14%), including 144 group or graded winners. Best include champions High Chaparral (Ire), Montjeu (Ire), Galileo (Ire), Northern Spur (Ire), Old Vic, Barathea (Ire), Islington (Ire).

1994—BROAD BRUSH, 1983 b. h., Ack Ack—Hay Patcher, by Hoist the Flag. Bred in Maryland by Robert E. Meyerhoff and raced three seasons for Meyerhoff. 27-14-5-5, $2,656,793. Winner of Santa Anita Handicap (G1), Suburban Handicap (G1), etc. Syndicated and entered stud in 1988 at Gainesway Farm in Kentucky. To 2005, sire of 86 stakes winners (13%), including 2002 champion three-year-old filly Farda Amiga, 1994 Breeders' Cup Classic

(G1) winner Concern, $4-million-earner Broad Appeal (in Japan), and 2001 North American Grade 1 winners Include and Pompeii. Pensioned December 1, 2004.

1993, 1991-'92—DANZIG, 1977 b. h., Northern Dancer—Pas de Nom, by Admiral's Voyage. Bred in Pennsylvania by Derry Meeting Farm and William S. Farish. Sold for $310,000 to Henryk de Kwiatkowski at the 1978 Saratoga yearling sale. 3-3-0-0, $32,400. Undefeated New York allowance winner before injury ended his career. Entered stud in 1981 at Claiborne Farm. To 2005, sire of more than 180 stakes winners (18%), including champions in U.S., Canada, Japan, England, France, Ireland, Spain, and United Arab Emirates. Best runners: 1984 two-year-old male champion Chief's Crown, two-time Breeders' Cup Mile (G1) winner Lure, and 1991 Canadian Triple Crown winner Dance Smartly. To 2005, broodmare sire of 127 stakes winners, including 2000 Kentucky Derby (G1) winner Fusaichi Pegasus. Pensioned July 13, 2004.

1990—ALYDAR, 1975 ch. h, Raise a Native—Sweet Tooth, by On-and-On. Bred in Kentucky by Calumet Farm. 26-14-9-1, $957,195. Won 1978 Blue Grass Stakes (G1), Florida Derby (G1), etc.; second to Affirmed in all three 1978 Triple Crown races. Entered stud in 1980 at Calumet Farm and became leading American freshman sire of 1983. Sired 77 stakes winners (11%) in 11 crops, with career progeny earnings of $60,604,510. Best runners include Horses of the Year Alysheba (1988) and Criminal Type ('90), North American champions Easy Goer, Turkoman, and Althea, and 1991 Kentucky Derby (G1) winner Strike the Gold. Broodmare sire of 136 stakes winners and earners of $144-million to 2005. Died at age 15 at Calumet on November 15, 1990, following a leg injury of suspicious cause.

1989, 1983—HALO, 1969 dk. b. or br. h., Hail to Reason—Cosmah, by Cosmic Bomb. Bred in Kentucky by John R. Gaines. Purchased for $100,000 by Charles Engelhard at 1970 Keeneland July yearling sale. 31-9-8-5, $259,553. Won 1974 United Nations Handicap (G1). Sold for $600,000 to stand in England, but sale fell through upon discovery he was a cribber. Syndicated for $30,000 per share and retired in 1974 to Windfields Farm Maryland. In 1984, was sold based on $36-million valuation and moved to Stone Farm in Kentucky. Sire of 63 stakes winners (8%), including champion and Racing Hall of Fame member Sunday Silence, all-time leading sire in Japan; 1983 Kentucky Derby winner Sunny's Halo; and champions Glorious Song and Devil's Bag. Broodmare sire of more than 135 stakes winners. Pensioned in 1997 and died at Stone Farm on November 28, 2000, at age 31.

1988, 1987—MR. PROSPECTOR, 1970 b. h., Raise a Native—Gold Digger, by Nashua. Bred in Kentucky by Leslie Combs II. Sold for a sale-topping $220,000 at 1971 Keeneland July sale to Abraham I. "Butch" Savin, for whom he won the Gravesend and Whirlaway Handicaps and set a Gulfstream Park track record, six furlongs in 1:07⅗, in 1973. 14-7-4-2, $112,171. Retired in 1975 to Savin's Aisco Farm in Florida and was top freshman sire of '78. Moved to Claiborne Farm in Kentucky in 1981. Sired 180 stakes winners (15%) and 16 champions to 2005, including Gulch, Forty Niner, Conquistador Cielo, and Woodman. Broodmare sire of more than 285 stakes winners. Leading broodmare sire eight times. Died of peritonitis at Claiborne Farm on June 1, 1999, at age 29.

1986—LYPHARD, 1969 b. h., Northern Dancer—Goofed, by *Court Martial. Bred in Pennsylvania by Mrs. J. O. Burgwin. Sold for $35,000 as a weanling at 1969 Keeneland November sale; resold as a yearling in Ireland for $38,000. 12-6-1-0, $195,427. Became one of Europe's top milers,

winning 1972 Prix de la Foret and Prix Jacques le Marois while racing for Mrs. Pierre Wertheimer. Retired in 1973 and stood five seasons in France, where he was twice leading sire and subsequently was twice leading broodmare sire. For 1978 season, moved to Gainesway Farm in Kentucky and syndicated. Sired 115 stakes winners (14%) and eight champions, including Manila, Dancing Brave, and Three Troikas (Fr). Broodmare sire of 206 stakes winners to 2005. Pensioned in 1996. Died June 10, 2005.

1985—BUCKAROO, 1975 b. h., Buckpasser—Stepping High, by No Robbery. Bred in Kentucky by Greentree Stud. 18-5-5-1, $138,604. Won 1978 Saranac (G2) and Peter Pan (G3) Stakes. Retired to Greentree in 1980. Sold privately in 1985 to Gary and Stephen Wolfson and moved to Happy Valley Farm in Florida. Relocated in 1991 to Florida Stallion Station and again in '92 to Bridlewood Farm near Ocala. Leading sire of 1985 due largely to Horse of the Year and Kentucky Derby (G1) winner Spend a Buck, who received a $2-million bonus for winning the Jersey Derby (G3). Also sired millionaires Roo Art and Lite the Fuse among 29 stakes winners from 17 crops. Died of kidney failure on July 30, 1996, at the University of Florida School of Veterinary Medicine at age 21.

1984—SEATTLE SLEW, 1974 dk. b. or br. h., Bold Reasoning—My Charmer, by Poker. Bred in Kentucky by Ben Castleman. Sold at 1975 Fasig-Tipton Kentucky July sale for $17,500 to partnership of Mickey and Karen Taylor and Jim and Sally Hill. 17-14-2-0, $1,208,726. Champion at two, three, and four, Horse of the Year at three; in 1977, became first to win American Triple Crown while undefeated. Retired in 1979 to Spendthrift Farm in Kentucky but later relocated to Three Chimneys Farm; moved to Hill 'n' Dale Farm shortly before his death. Sired 112 stakes winners (10%) through 2005, including Horse of the Year and top sire A.P. Indy, champions Slew o' Gold, Vindication, Surfside, Swale, Capote, and Landaluce. First to sire winners of $5-million in a single season (1984). Noted sire of sires. Broodmare sire of Cigar; twice leading broodmare sire; broodmare sire of 139 stakes winners, including nine champions, to 2005. Died on May 7, 2002, at Hill 'n' Dale in Kentucky, at age 28.

1982—HIS MAJESTY, 1968 b. h., *Ribot—Flower Bowl, by *Alibhai. Bred in Kentucky by Mr. and Mrs. John W. Galbreath. Full brother to Graustark. 22-5-6-3, $99,430. Only stakes victory was 1971 Everglades Stakes. Syndicated for $2-million valuation and retired in 1974 to his birthplace, Darby Dan Farm, where he remained throughout a 23-season stud career. Sired 59 stakes winners (9%) and champions in U.S., Italy, Canada, Panama, and Mexico. Best include 1981 champion and dual-classic winner Pleasant Colony, '91 grass champion Tight Spot, and $2-million earner Majesty's Prince. Maternal grandsire of leading international sire Danehill and 95 other stakes winners. Died at Darby Dan on September 21, 1995, at age 27.

1981—NODOUBLE, 1965 ch. h., *Noholme II—Abla-Jay, by Double Jay. Bred in Arkansas by Gene Goff. 42-13-11-5, $846,749. Two-time champion handicap horse, 1969-'70; known as "Arkansas Traveler" because he won stakes in seven states. Winner of 1969 Santa Anita Handicap, '70 Metropolitan Handicap, etc. Retired in 1971 and stood at four different farms from California to Florida before moving in '86 to Three Chimneys Farm in Kentucky. Sired 91 stakes winners (14%), including two-time Canadian Horse of the Year Overskate, Japan Cup (Jpn-G1) winner Mairzy Doates, and world record-setter Double Discount. Broodmare sire of 89 stakes winners to 2005. Pensioned in 1988. Died of colic at Three Chimneys on April 26, 1990, at age 25.

1980—RAJA BABA, 1968 b. h., Bold Ruler—Missy Baba, by *My Babu. Bred in Kentucky by Michael G. Phipps. 41-7-12-9, $123,287. Modest stakes winner retired in 1974 to Hermitage Farm in Kentucky and sired 62 stakes winners (10%), including 1987 champion and Breeders' Cup Distaff (G1) winner Sacahuista, two-time Mexican Horse of the Year Gran Zar (Mex), and Canadian champion sprinter Summer Mood. Broodmare sire of more than 75 stakes winners of $67.6-million to 2004. Pensioned at Hermitage in 1987 and died on October 9, 2002.

1979, 1978—EXCLUSIVE NATIVE, 1965 ch. h., Raise a Native—Exclusive, by Shut Out. Bred in Florida by Harbor View Farm. 13-4-4-3, $169,013. Won 1968 Arlington Classic Stakes but far better sire than racehorse. Entered stud in 1969 at Spendthrift Farm in Kentucky for a fee of $1,500. Eventually sired 66 stakes winners (13%), including Racing Hall of Fame members Affirmed and Genuine Risk—the former an American Triple Crown winner, the latter only the second filly to win the Kentucky Derby (G1). Syndicated in 1972 for $1.8-million. Broodmare sire of 97 stakes winners. Died of cancer at Spendthrift Farm on April 21, 1983, at age 18.

1977—DR. FAGER, 1964 b. h., Rough'n Tumble—Aspidistra, by Better Self. Bred in Florida by William L. McKnight's Tartan Farms. 22-18-2-1, $1,002,642. Horse of the Year in 1968. Set world record mile of 1:32⅕ at Arlington Park carrying 134 pounds. Syndicated for $3.2-million in 1968 and entered stud the next year at Tartan Farms in Florida, where he sired nine crops. His 35 stakes winners (13%) include 1978 champion sprinter Dr. Patches, '75 champion juvenile filly Dearly Precious, and '77 Canadian Horse of the Year L'Alezane. Broodmare sire of 98 stakes winners, including notable sires Fappiano and Quiet American. Inducted into the Racing Hall of Fame in 1971. Died at Tartan Farms on August 5, 1976, at age 12, from torsion of the large colon.

1976, 1975—WHAT A PLEASURE, 1965 ch. h., Bold Ruler—Grey Flight, by *Mahmoud. Bred in Kentucky by Wheatley Stable. 18-6-5-2, $164,935. Won Hopeful Stakes and was fourth in 1967 Experimental Free Handicap. Sold in 1968 to Howard Sams. Entered stud the following year at Sams's Waldemar Farm in Florida. Sired 50 stakes winners (10%), including Foolish Pleasure and Honest Pleasure, juvenile champions in 1974 and '75, respectively. Syndicated in 1976 for $8-million. Twice top juvenile sire by money won. Broodmare sire of 83 stakes winners, including champion juveniles Gilded Time and Tasso. Died of a heart attack at Waldemar Farm on March 13, 1983, at age 18.

1974—T. V. LARK, 1957 b. h., *Indian Hemp—Miss Larksfly, by Heelfly. Bred in California by Dr. Walter D. Lucas and raised in a half-acre paddock. Sold for $10,000 to Chase McCoy at 1958 Del Mar yearling sale. 72-19-13-6, $902,194. Champion grass horse of 1961 with victory over Kelso in Washington, D.C., International. Sold for $600,000 to syndicate headed by Preston Madden and retired in 1963 to Hamburg Place in Kentucky. First crop included world record-setter Pink Pigeon. Sired 53 stakes winners and 35% stakes horses from winners—Did not establish an enduring male line but became broodmare sire of Racing Hall of Fame filly Chris Evert. Died at Hamburg on March 6, 1975, at age 18.

1973, 1963-'69—BOLD RULER, 1954 dk. b. h., 1954, *Nasrullah—Miss Disco, by Discovery. Bred in Kentucky by Wheatley Stable. 33-23-4-2, $764,204. Racing Hall of Fame member, 1957 Horse of the Year. Retired to Claiborne Farm in 1959 and began his reign as perennial leading sire four years later. Became the dominant force in American breeding throughout the 1960s and '70s, leading by progeny earnings seven times in succession, eight times overall—more than any other 20th-century stallion. Also six times leading juvenile sire. Sired 43% stakes horses from starters, 82 stakes winners (22%), and 11 champions, among them Secretariat, Gamely, Wajima, and Bold Bidder. Broodmare sire of 119 stakes winners, although he never led in that category. Died of cancer at Claiborne on July 12, 1971, at age 17.

1972—ROUND TABLE, 1954 b. h., *Princequillo—*Knight's Daughter, by Sir Cosmo. Bred in Kentucky by Claiborne Farm. Sold privately in 1957 to Travis Kerr. 66-43-8-5, $1,749,869. Set or equaled 16 track, American, and world records. Horse of the Year in 1958, three-time champion grass horse, and world's leading money-earner at retirement. Entered stud in 1960 at Claiborne Farm. Made international impact, siring 83 stakes winners (21%) from 19 crops, including champions in England, Ireland, France, and Canada. Did not establish significant male line, although several sons proved useful stallions. Broodmare sire of 125 stakes winners, including champions Outstandingly, De La Rose, and Bowl Game. Inducted into Racing Hall of Fame in 1972. Pensioned in 1978 and died at Claiborne on June 13, 1987, at age 33.

1971—NORTHERN DANCER, 1961 b. h., Nearctic—Natalma, by Native Dancer. Bred in Canada by E. P. Taylor. 18-14-2-2, $580,647. Champion in Canada and U.S., won 1964 Kentucky Derby, Preakness Stakes. Entered stud in 1965 at Windfields Farm in Canada but later relocated to Windfields's Maryland division. Syndicated in 1970 for $2.4-million. Became one of the most sought-after commercial stallions of all time, with numerous offspring selling at auction for $1-million and more. Leading sire in England four times. Leading U.S. broodmare sire in 1991. Former international leader by stakes winners, with 146—including 23 champions and noted sires Sadler's Wells, Nijinsky II, Danzig, Lyphard, Nureyev, and Storm Bird. Daughters produced 242 stakes winners (19 champions) to 2005. Inducted into the Racing Hall of Fame in 1976. Died of colic at Windfields in Maryland on November 16, 1990, at age 29. Buried at Windfields, Canada.

1970—HAIL TO REASON, 1958 br. h., *Turn-to—Nothirdchance, by Blue Swords. Bred in Kentucky by Bieber-Jacobs Stable. 18-9-2-2, $328,434. Champion at two. Sesamoid injury forced retirement in 1961 to Hagyard Farm in Kentucky. Syndicated for $1,085,000. Leading sire and juvenile sire of 1970, and also among leading sires in England and France. Sired 43 stakes winners (13%), including 1970 co-Horse of the Year Personality and fillies Trillion, Straight Deal, and Regal Gleam. Several sons became top sires, including two-time American leader Halo and 1972 Epsom Derby winner Roberto, both of whom kept his male line alive. Daughters produced millionaires Allez France, Triptych, Royal Glint, Colonial Waters, and 110 additional stakes winners. Died at Hagyard on February 24, 1976, at age 18.

1962, 1959-'60, 1955-'56—*NASRULLAH, 1940 b. h., Nearco—Mumtaz Begum, by *Blenheim II. Bred in Ireland by the Aga Khan. 10-5-1-2, $15,259. Champion at two in England and classic-placed at three but generally a disappointment due to tendency to sulk before and during races. Entered stud in 1944 at Great Barton Stud in England; sold and relocated the next year to Brownstown Stud in Ireland. Purchased in 1950 for approximately $400,000 by A. B. Hancock on behalf of an American syndicate and sent to Claiborne Farm in Kentucky for '51 breeding season. Sired 93 international stakes winners (22%) and established an enduring male line through

Racing Hall of Fame son Bold Ruler and English-raced sons Red God and Grey Sovereign. Reigned five times as leading sire in America and once in England. Broodmare sire of 159 stakes winners. Suffered fatal heart attack at Claiborne on May 26, 1959, at age 19.

1961—*AMBIORIX, 1946 dk. b. h., Tourbillon—Lavendula, by Pharos. Bred in France by Marcel Boussac. 7-4-2-0, $25,165. Champion at two in France, winning Grand Criterium, and added the Prix Lupin at three before being narrowly beaten in the Prix du Jockey-Club (French Derby). Three-quarter brother to champion *My Babu. After failing to acquire *My Babu, A. B. Hancock purchased *Ambiorix in 1949 for syndication in America. Entered stud at Claiborne Farm in Kentucky the following year and ultimately sired 51 stakes winners (12%), including champion two- and three-year-old filly High Voltage. Leading sire of 1961 when runners included major winners Ambiopoise, Hitting Away, Make Sail, and Sarcastic. Also a successful broodmare sire, leading the list in England in 1963. Pensioned in 1972 and died at Claiborne in January '75 at age 29.

1958, 1957—*PRINCEQUILLO, 1940 b. h., Prince Rose—*Cosquilla, by *Papyrus. Bred in England by American Laudy Lawrence. 33-12-5-7, $96,550. Imported to U.S. as a yearling, leased to Anthony Pelleteri at two, and claimed for $2,500 by future Racing Hall of Fame trainer Horatio Luro for Dimitri Djordjaze. Became a top stayer, with victories including the 1943 Jockey Club Gold Cup. Retired in 1945 to A. B. Hancock's Ellerslie Farm in Virginia for $250 fee. Moved two years later to Claiborne Farm in Kentucky. Racing Hall of Fame members Round Table and Hill Prince were among his 65 stakes winners (13%), and *Princequillo arguably was one of America's two greatest broodmare sires (along with *Sir Gallahad III) of the 20th century. Was eight times atop broodmare sire list; his daughters produced 170 stakes winners, including champions Secretariat, Mill Reef, Fort Marcy, Key to the Mint, and Bold Lad. Died at Claiborne on July 18, 1964, at age 24.

1954, 1950—*HELIOPOLIS, 1936 b. h., Hyperion—Drift, by Swynford. Bred in England by Lord Derby. 15-5-2-1, $71,216, stakes winner at two and three in England, third in 1939 Epsom Derby. Imported to America the following year by Charles B. Shaffer and finished last after sulking in his only U.S. start, an allowance race at Hialeah Park. Retired in 1941 to Shaffer's Coldstream Stud in Kentucky. Sold in 1951 to Henry Knight and relocated to Almahurst Farm. Among his 53 stakes winners (15%) were 1954 Belmont Stakes victor and champion High Gun, and champion fillies Grecian Queen, Parlo, Berlo, and Aunt Jinny. Died at Almahurst on April 2, 1959, at age 23.

1953, 1952, 1947-'49—BULL LEA, 1935 b. h., *Bull Dog—Rose Leaves, by Ballot. Bred in Kentucky by Coldstream Stud. 27-10-7-3, $94,825. Sold as a yearling for $14,000 to Calumet Farm. A moderately accomplished racehorse, he won the Widener Handicap and Blue Grass Stakes. Retired to Calumet in 1940 for a $750 fee and became one of the greatest American sires of all time. Sired 57 stakes winners (15%), including a record seven Racing Hall of Fame members—Citation, Armed, Coaltown, Bewitch, Two Lea, Real Delight, and Twilight Tear. In 1947, became first stallion with single-season progeny earnings of $1-million. Four-time leading broodmare sire of 105 stakes winners. Died and buried at Calumet on June 16, 1964, at age 29.

1951—COUNT FLEET, 1940 br. h., Reigh Count—Quickly, by Haste. Bred in Kentucky by Mrs. John D. Hertz. 21-16-4-1, $250,300. In the Hertz colors, won 1943 Triple Crown, taking Belmont Stakes by 25 lengths. Retired in 1945 to Stoner Creek Farm near Paris, Kentucky, where he remained for the next 30 years. Outstanding sire and even better broodmare sire, leading in the latter category in 1963 and in the top five ten times. Among his 39 stakes winners (9%) were back-to-back Horses of the Year and Belmont Stakes winners Counterpoint (1951) and One Count ('52). Daughters produced 118 stakes winners and seven champions, including Racing Hall of Fame member Kelso. Pensioned in 1966. Count Fleet was inducted into the Racing Hall of Fame in 1961. He died at Stoner Creek on December 3, 1973, at age 33.

1946—*MAHMOUD, 1933 gr. h., *Blenheim II—Mah Mahal, by Gainsborough. Bred in France by the Aga Khan. 11-4-2-3, $86,439. Champion at three in England in 1936 when he won the Epsom Derby in record time. Entered stud at Newmarket in 1937. Purchased in 1940 by C. V. Whitney for about $85,000 and imported to stand at his Kentucky farm. Prior to his arrival, gray Thoroughbreds were spurned by many prominent American breeders, but *Mahmoud made the color acceptable. Sired 66 stakes winners, including U.S. champions Oil Capitol, The Axe II, and First Flight, and European champions *Majideh and Donatella. Leading broodmare sire of 1957 and among leaders throughout the '60s. Daughters produced 139 stakes winners, including Racing Hall of Fame members *Gallant Man and Silver Spoon. Died at C. V. Whitney Farm on September 18, 1962, at age 29.

1945—WAR ADMIRAL, 1934 br. h., Man o' War—Brushup, by Sweep. Bred in Kentucky by Samuel D. Riddle and raced for Glen Riddle Stable. 26-21-3-1, $273,240. Racing Hall of Fame runner is generally acknowledged as Man o' War's best son, both on the track and in the stud. Won 1937 Triple Crown and stood alongside Man o' War at Faraway Farm in Kentucky. Sire of 40 stakes winners (11%), including 1945 Horse of the Year Busher, champion Blue Peter, and the great racemares-broodmares Searching and Busanda. Twice leading broodmare sire of 113 stakes winners, including champions Buckpasser, Hoist the Flag, and Affectionately. Died on October 30, 1959, at age 25 and buried next to Man o' War at Faraway. Remains were exhumed, along with his sire's, in the 1970s, and reinterred at Kentucky Horse Park.

1944, 1935—CHANCE PLAY, 1923 ch. h., Fair Play—*Quelle Chance, by Ethelbert. Bred in Kentucky by August Belmont II. 39-16-9-2, $137,946. A handsome horse who resembled his sire, he raced for W. Averill Harriman's Log Cabin Stable and was considered the best horse of the year in 1927. Retired in 1929, stood at farms from Kentucky to New York until purchased by Warren Wright, who made him one of first stallions to stand at Calumet Farm in Lexington. Sired 23 stakes winners (7%), including 1939 champion juvenile filly Now What and '45 Jockey Club Gold Cup winner Pot o' Luck. Pensioned in 1947 following heart attack. Euthanized at Calumet on July 6, 1950, at age 27 and buried in the farm's cemetery.

1943—*BULL DOG, 1927 b. or br. h., *Teddy—Plucky Liege, by Spearmint. Bred in France by Jefferson Davis Cohn. 8-2-1-0, $7,802. Stakes winner at three in France. Full brother to leading sire *Sir Gallahad III and half brother to top European sires Bois Roussel and Admiral Drake. Imported by Charles B. Shaffer in 1930 to stand at his Coldstream Stud in Kentucky. Top runners include champion two-year-olds Occupy and Our Boots and five-time leading American sire Bull Lea. Sired 52 stakes winners (15%) in 18 crops, and 27% of his starters were of stakes class. In 1953, he supplanted *Sir Gallahad III atop broodmare sire list and subsequently led that list three times. His daughters produced 89 stakes winners and four champions. Pensioned in 1948. Died at Coldstream on October 10, 1954, at age 27.

1942—EQUIPOISE, 1928 ch. h., Pennant—Swinging, by Broomstick. Bred in Kentucky by Harry Payne Whitney. 51-29-10-4, $338,610. First great racehorse to carry colors of Whitney's son, Cornelius Vanderbilt Whitney. Nicknamed the "Chocolate Soldier" because of his dark chestnut color and combative spirit, he was an American champion at ages two, four, and five. Entered stud at C. V. Whitney Farm in 1935. Sired just four crops and 74 foals, nine of whom won stakes (12%), including 1940 champion juvenile filly Level Best and 1942 Kentucky Derby and Belmont Stakes winner Shut Out. Broodmare sire of 1946 Triple Crown winner Assault. First foals were two-year-olds when he died of enteritis at age ten on August 4, 1938. Inducted into Racing Hall of Fame in 1957.

1941—*BLENHEIM II, 1927 br. h., Blandford—Malva, by Charles O'Malley. Bred in England by Lord Carnarvon. Sold as yearling to the Aga Khan for about $20,000. 10-5-3-0, $73,060. Injury forced retirement following victory in 1930 Epsom Derby. Stood in Europe for six seasons, siring 1936 Epsom Derby winner *Mahmoud, Italian champion Donatello II. Sold in 1936 for reported $250,000 to an American syndicate and sent to Claiborne Farm in Kentucky. Sire of more than 45 stakes winners, including 1941 American Triple Crown winner Whirlaway and '43 champion handicap mare Mar-Kell. Broodmare sire of more than 120 stakes winners, including *Nasrullah and Kentucky Derby winners Ponder, Hill Gail, and Kauai King. Died at Claiborne on May 26, 1958, at age 31.

1940, 1933-'34, 1930—*SIR GALLAHAD III, 1920 b. h., *Teddy—Plucky Liege, by Spearmint. Bred in France by Jefferson Davis Cohn. 24-11-3-3, $17,009, Poule d'Essai des Poulains (French Two Thousand Guineas), match with *Epinard, etc. Full brother to leading sire *Bull Dog, half brother to top European sires Bois Roussel and Admiral Drake. Stood 1925 season in France, then sold for $125,000 to U.S. syndicate headed by A. B. Hancock. First important American stallion syndication. Stood at Claiborne Farm in Kentucky for remainder of career. First U.S. crop included 1930 Triple Crown winner Gallant Fox, and with two crops racing he led general sire list for the first of four times. Sired 56 stakes winners (10%), including three Kentucky Derby victors and several champions. Not a notable sire of sires but an all-time great broodmare sire, leading in that category 12 times. Died and buried at Claiborne on July 8, 1949, at age 29.

1939—*CHALLENGER II, 1927 b. h., Swynford—Sword Play, by Great Sport. Bred in England by the National Stud. 2-2-0-0 $10,930, Richmond S., Clearwell S., ranked third on English Free Handicap, one pound above future leading American sire *Blenheim II. Classic engagements canceled upon death of owner Lord Dewar under the rules then in force. Sold for reported $100,000 to William L. Brann and Robert Castle and imported to U.S. but injured in paddock accident before he could race again. Stood 17 seasons at Brann's Glade Valley Farm in Maryland, the first leading sire to spend his entire career outside Kentucky since *Sir Modred in 1894. Sired 34 stakes winners (11%), including future Racing Hall of Fame members Challedon and Gallorette. Died at Glade Valley on December 23, 1948, at age 21.

1938, 1936—*SICKLE, 1924 br. h., Phalaris—Selene, by Chaucer. Bred in England by Lord Derby. 10-3-4-2, $23,629, stakes winner at two, third in the 1927 Two Thousand Guineas. Half brother to the great racehorse and sire Hyperion, full brother to *Pharamond II. Stood one sea-

son in England before being imported under a lease agreement in 1930 by Joseph E. Widener, who eventually purchased him for a reported $100,000. Sent to Widener's Elmendorf Farm in Kentucky, where he replaced deceased Fair Play as the stud's leading stallion. Sired 22% stakes horses from foals, with 41 stakes winners (14%), including champions Stagehand, Star Pilot, and *Gossip II. Broodmare sire of 57 stakes winners, including 1951 Horse of the Year Counterpoint. Died on December 26, 1943, at Elmendorf at age 19.

1937—THE PORTER, 1915 b. h., Sweep—Ballet Girl, by St. Leonards. Bred in Kentucky by David Stevenson. Raced for Samuel Ross and later Edward McLean. 52-26-10-8, $89,249, Annapolis Handicap, etc. Stood barely 15 hands. From 1922-'31 stood at McLean Stud in Virginia. At age 16, purchased for $27,000 at McLean's 1931 dispersal by Mrs. John Hay Whitney and sent to Kentucky. Sired 11% stakes winners from foals, with the best of his 34 stakes winners being 1937 Santa Anita Handicap winner Rosemont, '37 Suburban Handicap winner Aneroid, and the top juvenile Porter's Mite. Died at Mare's Nest Farm in Kentucky on October 23, 1944, at age 29.

1932—CHATTERTON, 1919 ch. h., Fair Play—Chit Chat, by *Rock Sand. Bred in Kentucky by August Belmont II. 32-15-5-4, $26,565. Bred like Man o' War, by Fair Play out of *Rock Sand mare. Sold privately and raced for Frank J. Kelley. Multiple stakes winner in Midwest, though not a top runner. Stood 1924 in California but after Kelley's death sent to Claiborne Farm in Kentucky. Remained there except for 1932 season when leased to Arrowbrook Farm in Illinois. His position atop list was due almost entirely to 1932 champion and Belmont Stakes winner Faireno. Also sired 1928 champion juvenile filly Current and nine other stakes winners. Died at Claiborne of kidney ailment on July 14, 1933, at age 14.

1931—*ST. GERMANS, 1921 b. h., Swynford—Hamoaze, by Torpoint. Bred in England by Lord Astor. 20-9-4-4, $44,793, Coronation Cup, Doncaster Cup, etc., second in Epsom Derby. Imported by Payne Whitney to stand at his Greentree Stud. Advertised "for private use only" in early years. He suffered from low fertility and averaged fewer than ten foals per crop, but those were highly successful. Best of 23 stakes winners (13%) was Twenty Grand, winner of the Kentucky Derby and Belmont Stakes; two-time handicap champion Devil Diver; and 1936 Kentucky Derby-Preakness Stakes winner Bold Venture. Twenty Grand was sterile, and several prominent male-line descendants experienced fertility problems. Died at Greentree Stud on May 18, 1929, at age 18 following attack of enteritis.

1929—*CHICLE, 1913 b. h., Spearmint—Lady Hamburg II, by Hamburg. Bred in France by Harry Payne Whitney but raced in U.S. 10-3-0-2, $4,765. Had soundness problems but nonetheless won Champagne Stakes and Brooklyn Derby (now Dwyer Stakes). Entered stud in Kentucky at H. P. Whitney Farm for fee of $500. Fee later raised as high as $1,500. Bad tempered, kept muzzled as a stallion for safety of farm workers. Sired six stakes winners from first 13-foal crop and about 40 overall—including champion juveniles Whichone and Mother Goose. Leading broodmare sire of 1942. Died May 20, 1939, at age 26, at C. V. Whitney Farm near Lexington.

1928—HIGH TIME, 1916 ch. h., Ultimus—Noonday, by Domino. Bred in Kentucky by Wickliffe Stud of Corrigan and McKinney. 7-1-0-1, $3,950, Hudson S., 3rd Great American S. Highly inbred to Domino, with three crosses in first three generations. Beautiful physical specimen, sold at auction as two-year-old for $8,500. Career limited by throat problems. Won Aqueduct's Hudson Stakes in track-record time for five furlongs. Retired at three to Haylands Stud in 1919 but was not well received by Kentucky breeders. In later years, changed ownership several times before settling at Dixiana Farm in Kentucky. Sired about 40 stakes winners, including Racing Hall of Fame champion gelding Sarazen and 1928 champion juvenile colt High Strung. Leading broodmare sire of 1940. Died at Dixiana on November 20, 1937, at age 21.

1927, 1924, 1920—FAIR PLAY, 1905 ch. h., Hastings— *Fairy Gold, by Bend Or. Bred in Kentucky by August Belmont II. 32-10-11-3, $86,950. Racing Hall of Fame runner had misfortune to come along in same crop as unbeatable Colin. Won 1908 Lawrence Realization. When betting was outlawed in New York, shipped to England, where heavy weight assignments and a deteriorating attitude led to a 6-0-0-0 record. Retired to Nursery Stud in 1910. When Belmont died in 1924, sold at age 20 on $100,000 bid to Joseph Widener. Renowned for producing stamina, the three-time leading sire got champions Chance Play and Mad Hatter but was immortalized as sire of Man o' War, through whom his male line survives today. Leading broodmare sire in 1931, '34, and '38. Died at age 24 in paddock at Elmendorf Farm in Kentucky on December 16, 1929.

1926—MAN O' WAR, 1917 ch. h., Fair Play—Mahubah, by *Rock Sand. Bred in Kentucky by August Belmont II. 21-20-1-0, $249,465. Sold at auction as yearling for $5,000 to Samuel Riddle. Became one of the greatest racehorses of all time, winning Preakness and Belmont Stakes. Retired in 1921 to Hinata Stock Farm but soon moved to Faraway Farm, both in Kentucky. Instant success, led general sire list with only three crops racing. Top runners include future Racing Hall of Fame members War Admiral and Crusader as well as six other American champions. Also a great broodmare sire. As Riddle's private stallion, did not receive the best mares but nonetheless sired 64 stakes winners, 17% of foals. Died at age 30 at Faraway on November 1, 1947. Thousands attended funeral, which was nationally broadcast on radio and filmed for newsreels. Grave and larger-than-life bronze statue relocated in late 1970s to Kentucky Horse Park.

1925, 1918—SWEEP, 1907 br. h., Ben Brush—Pink Domino, by Domino. Bred in Kentucky by James R. Keene. 13-9-2-2, $59,998, champion at two in 1909 when he won the Futurity Stakes and added the Belmont Stakes at three. Sold at 1913 Keene estate dispersal at Madison Square Garden for $17,500 to partnership of John Barbee, J. C. Carrick, and Andrew Stone. Led broodmare sire list twice and twice was leader by number of two-year-old winners. Sired more than 40 stakes winners. Top runners include 1918 champion juvenile Eternal and handicap star The Porter, leading sire of 1937. Died at age 24 from "indigestion" on August 15, 1931, at Glen-Helen Stud in Kentucky.

1923—THE FINN, 1912 bl. h., *Ogden—Livonia, by *Star Shoot. Bred in Kentucky by John E. Madden. 50-19-10-6, $38,965. Raced initially for Madden before being sold to H. C. Hallenbeck. Victories included Belmont and Withers Stakes as well as Metropolitan, Manhattan, and Havre de Grace Handicaps. Generally regarded as champion three-year-old colt of 1915. Madden later bought him back and in 1923 he was sold again, for $100,000, to W. R. Coe. Stood thereafter at Hinata Stock Farm in Kentucky. Sired Kentucky Derby winners Flying Ebony and Zev, the latter America's first racehorse to top $300,000 in earnings (1924). Died at Hinata on September 4, 1925, from "inflammation of the bowels," at age 13.

1922—*MCGEE, 1900 b. h., White Knight—Remorse, by Hermit. Bred in England by Lord Bradford. 53-24-14-5,

$18,391, Fleetfoot H., etc. Only foal by an unraced stallion. Sold cheaply as yearling to Ed Corrigan and imported to U.S. Raced in Midwest, a minor stakes winner of 24 races. Primarily a sprinter—set American 5½-furlong record in 1903. Retired to Corrigan's Freeland Stud near Lexington, then sold in 1908 for $1,300 to Charles Moore. Relocated to nearby Mere Hill Stud where his 1909 fee was $50. Sired at least 20 stakes winners, most notably the great gelding Exterminator and Donerail, winner of 1913 Kentucky Derby at 91.45-to-1. His last foal was conceived in 1930 when *McGee was 30 years old. Prior to his death at Mere Hill on September 18, 1931, he was believed to be the oldest stallion in Kentucky.

1921—CELT, 1905 ch. h., Commando—*Maid Of Erin, by Amphion. Bred in Kentucky by James R. Keene. 6-4-1-1, $29,975. Lightly raced winner of 1908 Brooklyn Handicap, overshadowed by unbeaten stablemate Colin, another son of Commando. Stood initially at Castleton Stud, then leased for 1912 to stand at Hancock family's Ellerslie Stud in Virginia. Though lease expired in 1913, A. B. Hancock acquired him that fall for $20,000 at Keene's estate dispersal. Returned to Ellerslie to sire a total of at least 29 stakes winners. In 1930, was top broodmare sire when Gallant Fox swept the Triple Crown. Died at age 14 in 1919.

1919, 1916-'17, 1911-'12—*STAR SHOOT, 1898 ch. h., Isinglass—Astrology, by Hermit. Bred in England by Maj. Eustace Loder. 10-3-1-3, $34,747, National Breeders' Produce S., etc. A good two-year-old, developed wind problems at three and was unplaced in two starts that season. Because he was from a family not noted for producing good sires, he was sold to America and entered stud in 1902 at Runnymede Farm in Kentucky, where he was an immediate success. Purchased privately by John Madden in 1912 and relocated to Hamburg Place. One of the most influential American-based stallions of his time; his sons included future Racing Hall of Fame members Grey Lag and Sir Barton. In 1916, had record 29 juvenile winners. Died of pneumonia at Hamburg on November 19, 1919, at age 21.

1915, 1913-'14—BROOMSTICK, 1901 b. h., Ben Brush— *Elf, by Galliard. Bred in Kentucky by Col. Milton Young. 39-14-11-5, $74,730, Travers S., etc. Young acquired *Elf for $250 in foal with Broomstick. Colt was owned privately to race for coal millionaire Samuel Brown. Racing Hall of Fame runner raced through age four. Retired in 1906 to Brown's Senorita Stud in Kentucky. Sold for $7,250 two years later at estate sale of his owner to H. P. Whitney. Eventually sired about 25% stakes winners from foals—nearly 60 in all—including the first New York handicap triple crown winner, Whisk Broom II; the first filly Kentucky Derby winner, Regret; 1911 Derby winner Meridian; and '12 Two Thousand Guineas winner *Sweeper. Died at C. V. Whitney Farm in Kentucky, on March 24, 1931, at age 30.

1910, 1900—KINGSTON, 1884 br. h., Spendthrift—*Kapanga, by Victorious. Bred in Kentucky by James R. Keene. 138-89-33-12, $140,195, First Special S., etc. Raced through age ten, primarily for Phil and Mike Dwyer. His 89 career victories remains an all-time record, and for about one year (1892-'93) he reigned as America's leading money earner. Entered stud in 1895 at Eugene Leigh's La Belle Farm in Kentucky for a $150 fee. Moved in a few years to Keene's Castleton Farm near Lexington, where he stood privately with leading sires Ben Brush and Commando. Represented by Futurity Stakes winners Ballyhoo Bey (1900) and Novelty ('10), as well as 1900 Belmont Stakes winner Ildrim. Died at Castleton on December 4, 1912, at age 28.

1909—BEN BRUSH, 1893 b. h., Bramble—Roseville, by Reform. Bred in Kentucky by Catesby Woodford and Ezekiel Clay. 40-25-5-5, $65,208. Small, plain, and tough, a superb racehorse, and Racing Hall of Fame member. Sold as yearling for $1,200 to Eugene Leigh and Ed Brown, and again at three for reported $25,000 to Mike Dwyer. Won 1896 Kentucky Derby and '97 Suburban Handicap. Sold to James R. Keene for stud duty at Castleton Farm in Kentucky. Following Keene's death in 1913, acquired for $10,000 by Kentucky Senator Johnson Camden and lived out his days at Camden's Hartland Stud near Versailles. Established noted male line that endured for decades. Best offspring include three-time leading American sire Broomstick and two-time leader Sweep. Died at age 25 on June 8, 1918.

1908, 1902—HASTINGS, 1893 br. h., Spendthrift—*Cinderella, by Tomahawk or Blue Ruin. Bred in Kentucky by Dr. J. D. Neet. 21-10-8-0, $16,340. Raced at two for Gideon and Daly. Upon dispersal of that stable at Sheepshead Bay in 1895, acquired for $37,000 by August Belmont II. Won 1896 Belmont Stakes, although generally not regarded as a top racehorse. Entered stud in 1898 at Belmont's Nursery Stud in Kentucky and was known for his savage disposition. Sire of champion filly Gunfire (1899), but by far his best was the 1905 colt Fair Play, the future sire of Man o' War. Died at Nursery Stud in 1917 at age 24 following an attack of paralysis.

1907—COMMANDO, 1898 b. h., Domino—Emma C., by *Darebin. Bred in Kentucky by James R. Keene. 9-7-2-0, $58,196. Coarse and heavily muscled, he did not resemble his handsome sire but was at least his equal on the racecourse. In James R. Keene's colors, won 1901 Belmont Stakes. The Racing Hall of Fame member retired to Keene's Castleton Stud in 1902 to take the place of Domino, who died at age six in 1897. Immediate success at stud but, like his sire, he died young. From three crops and 27 foals, sired ten stakes winners, among them Racing Hall of Fame members Peter Pan and Colin and influential sires Celt and Ultimus. Died of tetanus at Castleton in early March 1905 at age seven.

1906, 1904—*MEDDLER, 1890 b. h., *St Gatien—Busybody, by Petrarch. Bred in England by George Abington Baird. 3-3-0-0, $16,689, Dewhurst S., etc. By an Epsom Derby winner and out of an Epsom Oaks winner. Unraced after two-year-old season following the death of his owner, which, under rules in force at the time, voided his nominations to the three-year-old classics. Sold in 1893 for $76,000 to American William Forbes, who stood him initially at Neponset Stud in Massachusetts. Upon Forbes's death in 1897, sold to W. C. Whitney for $49,000 and moved to La Belle Stud in Kentucky. Sold at 1904 Whitney estate dispersal for $51,000. Represented by champion fillies Trigger, Tangle, and Tanya (winner of 1905 Belmont Stakes). When American racing was decimated by 1909 antiwagering legislation, relocated to France, where he died on April 17, 1916, at Haras de Fresnay-le-Buffard in Normandy at age 26.

1905—HAMBURG, 1895 b. h., Hanover—Lady Reel, by Fellowcraft. Bred in Kentucky by C. J. Enright. Sold for $1,250 as yearling to John E. Madden, who later named his famous breeding farm, Hamburg Place, for the Racing Hall of Fame member. 21-16-3-2, $60,380, Lawrence Realization, etc. Sold privately for $40,001 to Marcus Daly in 1898. Stood two seasons at Daly's Bitter Root Stud in Montana. After Daly's death in 1900, sold for $60,000 to W. C. Whitney, who sent him to La Belle Stud in Kentucky. At 1904 Whitney dispersal, sold for $70,000 to Whitney's son Harry Payne Whitney, who took him to Brookdale Stud in New Jersey. Sired Racing Hall of Fame filly Art-

ful, champions Borrow, Hamburg Belle, Burgomaster, and Rosie O'Grady, and foundation mare Frizette. Died at Brookdale on September 15, 1915, at age 20.

1903—*BEN STROME, 1886 b. h., Bend Or—Strathfleet, by The Scottish Chief. Bred in England by the Duke of Westminster. 35-3-6-6, $2,975. Big (16.2 hands tall), good-looking, and beautifully bred, but a poor racehorse in England. Entered stud in 1894 at Thomas J. Carson's Dixiana Farm in Kentucky. When his first foals were yearlings, Dixiana advertised that a limited number of approved mares would be accepted by special contract, which meant at no cost. By 1904, his fee had jumped to $300, one of the highest in the country. Most noted as sire of Racing Hall of Fame member Roseben, but offspring also included juvenile champions Eugenia Burch and Highball. Died at Dixiana in 1909 at age 23.

1901—SIR DIXON, 1885 br. h., *Billet—Jaconet, by *Leamington. Bred in Kentucky by Col. Ezekiel Clay. 29-10-7-7, $54,915. Sold for $1,125 as yearling to Green B. Morris, who resold him at three for $20,000 to Mike and Phil Dwyer. A high-strung, delicate type, he was unable to endure the tough campaigns favored by the Dwyers but nevertheless scored victories in the 1888 Belmont, Withers, and Travers Stakes. Stood his entire career at Clay's Runnymede Stud in Kentucky. Sired champions Butterflies, Blue Girl, Kilmarnock, and Running Water, and 1905 Kentucky Derby winner Agile. Died on March 23, 1909, at age 14 after breaking his right hip in a paddock accident.

1899—*ALBERT, 1882 b. h., Albert Victor—Hawthorn Bloom, by Kettledrum. Bred in England by Sir Richard Jardine. 6-1-1-0, $2,547. A racehorse of modest talents, won a minor stakes at Newcastle as a two-year-old. Imported as a stallion by Alfred Withers. Later spent most of his breeding career at the Adelbert Stud of Williams and Radford near Hopkinsville, Kentucky. Advertised for a $100 fee in 1896, with a reference to him as "the most uniform sire of winners in America—they mature early and make great campaigners." Not an outstanding sire, his best was probably 1899 juvenile champion Mesmerist and the good filly Hatasoo, an ancestress of many top racehorses. Believed to have died in 1907, because his last five foals arrived the following spring.

1898, 1895-'97—HANOVER, 1884 ch. h., Hindoo—Bourbon Belle, by *Bonnie Scotland. Bred in Kentucky at Col. Ezekiel Clay's Runnymede Farm. 50-32-14-2, $118,887, champion three-year-old, 1887 Belmont Stakes, etc. Sold as a yearling for $1,350 to Phil and Mike Dwyer. Won 17 consecutive races at two and three and ultimately retired with American earnings record. One of America's better all-time stallions, his best by far was Racing Hall of Fame member Hamburg. Hanover was valued at $100,000 when he died on March 23, 1899, at McGrathiana Stud in Kentucky at age 15. Cause of death was said to be blood poisoning caused by a leg injury. He was originally buried at McGrathiana, but his skeleton was later exhumed for research and display.

1894—*SIR MODRED, 1877 b. h., Traducer—Idalia, by Cambuscan. Bred in New Zealand by Middle Park Stud. Among the foremost racehorses of his day in New Zealand, with victories in the Canterbury Derby, Canterbury Cup, and Metropolitan Stakes. Imported to California in 1885 by James Ben Ali Haggin. In 1894, became the first California-based stallion to lead the American sire list with his offspring won 137 races and $134,318. Notable offspring include champion Tournament, 1893 Belmont Stakes winner Comanche, 1890 Travers Stakes winner Sir John, and the outstanding fillies Gloaming and Lucania. Stood at Haggin's 44,000-acre Rancho del Paso near Sacramento, where he was pensioned for several seasons prior to his death due to infirmities of old age in June 1904 at age 27.

1893—HIMYAR, 1875 b. h., Alarm—Hira, by Lexington. Bred in Kentucky by Maj. Barak Thomas. 27-14-6-4, $11,650, Phoenix Hotel Stakes, etc. Finished second in 1878 as one of the heaviest favorites ever for the Kentucky Derby. High-strung, nervous, and hard to train, considered primarily a speed horse. Entered stud in 1882 at Thomas's Dixiana Farm near Lexington and got, among others, immortal racehorse and sire Domino and '98 Kentucky Derby winner Plaudit. In 1893, due largely to Domino, he established a single-season progeny earnings record of $259,252, which stood for 24 years. Died at age 30 on December 30, 1905, and was buried at Dixiana under a tombstone that reads: "Speed springs eternal from his ashes."

1892—IROQUOIS, 1878 br. h., *Leamington—Maggie B.B., by *Australian. Bred by Aristides Welch at Erdenheim Stud in Pennsylvania. 26-12-4-3, $99,707. Sold as a yearling to tobacco magnate Pierre Lorillard, who sent him to race in England. First American-bred winner of Epsom Derby and St. Leger Stakes; finished second in the Two Thousand Guineas. Wall Street briefly halted trading to celebrate news of his Derby triumph. Returned to U.S., he raced three times without success, probably because of pulmonary bleeding. Retired to stud at W. H. Johnson's Belle Meade Farm, where he died in 1899 at age 21. His offspring included champion Tammany.

1891—LONGFELLOW, 1867 br. h., *Leamington—Nantura, by Brawner's Eclipse. Bred, owned, and trained by John Harper. 16-13-2-0, $11,200. Standing a towering 17 hands, he was named for his long legs and not for the noted poet. One of the great racehorses of the 1870s, an injury forced his retirement to Harper's Nantura Stud near Midway, Kentucky. Sired more than 40 stakes winners, including Kentucky Derby winners Leonatus and Riley, 1886 Preakness winner The Bard, and champions Thora and Freeland. A dominant bay, it was said that all his foals but one were bay or brown. Died at Nantura on November 5, 1893, and was buried with a marker that reads: "King of Racers and King of Stallions."

1890—*ST. BLAISE, 1880 ch. h., Hermit—Fusee, by Marsyas. Bred in England by Lord Alington. 16-7-2-1, $41,066. Won 1883 Epsom Derby. Imported for $30,000 in 1885 by August Belmont I to stand at his Nursery Stud in Kentucky. Following Belmont's death, sold at auction in 1891 by Tattersalls of New York for a then-world record $100,000. Purchased on a solitary bid by Charles Reed of Tennessee. Not successful for Reed, sold at auction again in 1902 for $8,300 to James Ben Ali Haggin of Elmendorf Farm, Kentucky, but subsequently purchased privately by August Belmont II. At age 22, he returned to Nursery Stud to live out his days. Best runners include 1890 Futurity Stakes winner Potomac and '96 Preakness Stakes winner Margrave. Died in October 1909 at age 29.

1889—*RAYON D'OR, 1876 ch. h., Flageolet—Araucaria, by Ambrose. Bred in France by Haras de Dangu. 28-15-7-4, $110,207. Won from five to 18 furlongs, including 1879 St. Leger, and carried up to 132 pounds to victory. Imported in 1883 by W. L. Scott, who paid nearly $40,000 for him and stood him initially at his Algeria Stud in Pennsylvania. When Algeria dispersed in 1892, purchased by August Belmont II and moved to Nursery Stud in Kentucky. Sired many top runners, including Brooklyn Handicap winner Tenny, Futurity Stakes winner Chaos, and Banquet, winner of 62 races and $118,872. Died from "fever" on July 15, 1896, at Nursery Stud at age 20.

1888, 1886–'87, 1884—GLENELG, 1866 b. h., Citadel—*Babta, by Kingston. Imported in utero by R. W. Cameron,

who earlier had imported four-time leading sire *Leamington. Foaled at Cameron's Clifton Farm in New York. 18-10-5-2, $23,340. Purchased as a yearling by August Belmont I for $2,000. Big, bad-tempered, and prone to colic, he nonetheless won the 1869 Travers Stakes and other important races. After his racing days, he was sold to Milton H. Sanford for $10,000. His many outstanding runners include Racing Hall of Fame mare Firenze. Died on October 23, 1897, at age 31 at the farm of Tyree Bate in Castalian Springs, Tennessee.

1885—VIRGIL, 1864 dk. b. h., Vandal—Hymenia, by *Yorkshire. Bred in Woodford County, Kentucky, by Hyman C. Gratz. 10-7-2-1, $2,950, Sequel S. three times, etc. A beautiful, nearly black horse, owned during his racing days by Milton Sanford, primarily a sprinter in an era that prized stamina (although he won once at two miles). Initially had few opportunities as a stallion and was even broken to harness and used to pull a carriage. Sold cheaply in 1874. When his son Vagrant won the 1876 Kentucky Derby, Virgil was repurchased by Sanford. He subsequently sired Racing Hall of Fame member Hindoo (also a great sire) and unbeaten Tremont. Died at Quindaro Stud in Kentucky in 1893 at age 29.

1883—*BILLET, 1865 br. h., Voltigeur—Calcutta, by Flatcatcher. Bred in England by James Smith. 18-5-3-1, $3,983. Insignificant racehorse in England, racing most often in selling races. Imported to America in 1869 and stood several seasons in Illinois. After son Elias Lawrence established a Saratoga three-year-old record in 1878, was moved to Runnymede Stud in Paris, Kentucky, where he remained until his death on January 17, 1889, at age 24. Top runners include Racing Hall of Fame member Miss Woodford, the first American Thoroughbred to top $100,000 in earnings, and 1901 leading sire Sir Dixon.

1882, 1880—*BONNIE SCOTLAND, 1853 b. h., Iago—Queen Mary, by Gladiator. Bred in England by William I'Anson. 4-2-1-0, $6,308. Lightly raced and never truly sound because of an injury as a foal, won Liverpool St. Leger and Doncaster Stakes. Imported to America in 1857, believed to have stood originally in Ohio before relocating to Gen. W. G. Harding's famous Belle Meade Stud near Nashville, Tennessee. Offspring include Racing Hall of Fame member Luke Blackburn, 1883 Belmont Stakes winner George Kinney, and champion Bramble. Died in his paddock at Belle Meade on February 2, 1880, at age 27.

1881, 1879, 1877, 1875—*LEAMINGTON, 1853 br. h., Faugh-a-Ballagh—mare by Pantaloon. Bred in England by Mr. Halford. 24-8-3-3, $33,446, Goodwood S., Tradesmen's Plate twice, etc. Imported in 1865 by R. W. Cameron of New York after standing six seasons in England. In U.S., stood first at Bosque Bonita Stud in Kentucky, later at Cameron's Clifton Stud on Staten Island, and finally at Aristides Welch's Erdenheim Stud near Philadelphia. Sire of Racing Hall of Fame members Longfellow and Parole, inaugural Kentucky Derby winner Aristides, and Iroquois, first American-bred winner of the Epsom Derby. Many of his best offspring were out of Lexington mares and were raced by the Lorillard brothers, George and Pierre, who dominated American racing during the 1870s and '80s. Died at Erdenheim on May 6, 1878, at age 25.

1878, 1876, 1861–'74—LEXINGTON, 1850 b. h., Boston—Alice Carneal, by *Sarpedon. Bred in Kentucky by Dr. Elisha Warfield. 7-6-1-0, $56,600, Great Post S., etc. Sold to Richard Ten Broeck as a three-year-old and in 1855 set an American four-mile record of 7:19¾. By then, he was going blind and was sold for $15,000 to R. A. Alexander of Woodburn Stud, Kentucky. He stood at that Midway farm his entire career except for an interlude in Illinois for his own safety during the Civil War. As with *Glencoe, a number of his offspring were utilized as Civil War mounts. His many outstanding runners include champions Kentucky, Asteroid, Norfolk, Duke of Magenta, Harry Bassett, Sultana, and Tom Bowling. Lexington's post-Civil War fee of $500 was unprecedented. His male-line survived into the 20th century, and numerous crosses of his name are still present in far branches of modern pedigrees. The 16-time leading sire died on July 1, 1875, at age 25. His skeleton is in the possession of the Smithsonian Institution in Washington, D.C.

1860—REVENUE, 1843 b. h., *Trustee—Rosalie Somers, by Sir Charles. Bred in Virginia by statesman John M. Botts. 21-16-5-0. Son of a leading sire and champion racemare. Stood at Botts's farm in Virginia, where he sired the great Planet, widely viewed as the best American racehorse in the era preceding the Civil War, compiling a 31-27-4-0 record and surpassing Peytona as America's top earner with $69,700, a mark that stood for 20 years. In 1860, Revenue became the first stallion to lead an American sire list based on earnings ($49,450) rather than races won (the previously recognized standard), although he led by wins as well. He died in Virginia in September 1868 at age 25.

1859—*ALBION, 1837 bl. h., Cain or Actaeon—Panthea, by Comus or Blacklock. Bred in England; reportedly was a successful racehorse in America during the early 1840s. A reliable sire of winners during pre-Civil War years and later an outstanding broodmare sire. Died in 1859 at age 22 in Sumner County, Tennessee.

1858, 1854-'57, 1849-'50, 1847—*GLENCOE, 1831 ch. h., Sultan—Trampoline, by Tramp. Bred in England by Lord Jersey. 10-8-1-1, $33,459. Winner of 1834 Two Thousand Guineas, third in Epsom Derby. Stood one season in England, getting legendary broodmare Pocahontas. Imported in 1836 by James Jackson, who reportedly paid $10,000 for him. Swaybacked but otherwise handsome, he was much admired by breeders of the day. Stood from 1837-'44 in Alabama; 1845-'48 in Tennessee; and 1849-'57 in Kentucky as property of A. Keene Richards, an ardent secessionist who allegedly turned over many of his offspring for use as Confederate mounts during the Civil War. Sired the great mares Reel and Peytona, the latter America's leading money winner from 1845-'61 ($62,400), as well as top sons Star Davis and Vandal. Died of "lung fever" on August 25, 1857, at Blue Grass Park in Georgetown, Kentucky.

1853, 1851-'52—BOSTON, 1833 b. h., Timoleon—Sister to Tuckahoe, by Ball's Florizel. Bred in Virginia by John Wickham. 45-40-2-1, $51,700. Sold at two for $800 to Nathaniel Rives to satisfy a gaming debt. Racing Hall of Fame member won 30 four-mile heat races. Nicknamed "Old White Nose" for his distinctively blazed face, his vicious temper struck fear into the hearts of his handlers. Sire of Racing Hall of Fame member Lexington and his great rival, Lecomte (also known as Lecompte), as well as the great racemare Nina, dam of Planet. Died in 1850 at age 17 at Col. E. M. Blackburn's farm in Woodford County, Kentucky.

1848 (co-leader), 1843, 1837-'39—*LEVIATHAN, 1823 ch. h., Muley—Coxcomb's dam, by Windle. Bred in England by Mr. Painter. 19-15-3-0, $11,096, Dee S., etc. At 16 hands, large for his time. Imported in 1830 by James Jackson of Alabama. Not well received at first because of his enormous size. In 1838, became America's first $100,000 sire when his progeny won 92 races. At one time, his $75 fee was the highest in America. Stood in Tennessee, man-

aged by Col. George Elliott. Died in Gallatin, Tennessee, in 1846, at age 23 from "inflammation of the bowels."

1848 (co-leader)—*TRUSTEE, 1829 ch. h., Catton—Emma, by Whisker. 11-4-3-3, $7,446, Claret S., etc. Third in 1832 Epsom Derby in first career start. Brother to 1835 Epsom Derby winner Mundig, half brother to '43 Derby winner Cotherstone. Imported in 1835 by Commodore Robert Stockton, later senator from New Jersey. Not well received by American breeders and moved often during his stud career. Stood in New York between 1836-'41; Virginia in 1842; Kentucky in 1843-'44; Virginia in 1845-'46; and back to New York in 1847, where he remained until his death at age 27. Sire of Racing Hall of Fame filly Fashion, the great mare Levity, and leading 1860 American sire Revenue. Died in 1856 at West Farms, Westchester County, New York.

1846, 1844-'45, 1842—*PRIAM, 1827 b. h., Emilius—Cressida, by Whisker. Bred in England by Sir John Shelley. 16-14-1-1, $65,100. Winner of the 1830 Epsom Derby, Goodwood Cup. Considered the greatest English racehorse of his era. Imported in 1837 by Merritt and Co. for $15,000, then believed to be a record. Leading American sire four times. Sire of Epsom Oaks winners Crucifix, Miss Letty, and Industry before his importation. Sire in America of Margaret Wood, Little Trick, Lucy Long. Died in Tennessee in 1847 at age 20.

1841, 1840—MEDOC, 1829 ch. h., American Eclipse—Young Maid of the Oaks, by *Expedition. Bred in New York by James Bathgate. 5-4-1-0, $5,300. Greatest son of American Eclipse. Entered stud in Kentucky in 1835. His offspring won 61 races in 1840 and 51 races the following year. Sire of top four-miler Grey Medoc, Bob Letcher, Mary Morris, Picayune. Broke his near foreleg when he stepped in a hole during exercise in 1839 and died at age ten from the injury at Col. William Buford's farm in Woodford County, Kentucky.

1836, 1830-'33—SIR CHARLES, 1816 ch. h., Sir Archy—*Citizen mare, by *Citizen. Won 20 of 25 starts. Believed to have been bred in Virginia by W. R. Johnson. Ancestry of his dam questioned; some referred to her as a "cart mare" whose pedigree had been fabricated. Dominant in long heat races throughout the South. Beaten while lame in final start, 1822 match with American Eclipse for the national championship in Washington, D.C. Died on June 7, 1833, at age 17 at George Johnson's Earnscliffe Plantation, Virginia. Sired the great racemares Trifle, Bonnets o' Blue, and Rosalie Somers, and notable racehorse and sire Wagner.

1835—BERTRAND, 1821 b. h., Sir Archy—Eliza, by *Bedford. Bred in South Carolina by Col. John R. Spann. Won 13 of 16 starts. In 1826, he was sold to Hutchcraft and Co. and sent to Kentucky, where he stood his entire 12-season career, and was said to have covered between 175 and 200 mares per season. He is credited with vastly improving the Thoroughbred of the Bluegrass region. His best include John Bascombe, Richard Singleton, and Queen Mary. Died in Hopkinsville, Kentucky, in 1838 at age 17.

1834—MONSIEUR TONSON, 1822 b. h., Pacolet—Madam Tonson, by Top Gallant. Bred in Tennessee by Thomas Foxhall. Won 11 of 12 starts; only defeat was his first start as a two-year-old. William R. Johnson, the "Napoleon of the Turf" in America, bought him for $10,000. Stood initially in Virginia, later in North Carolina, and finally was sent to Kentucky, where he died. Sire of South Carolina champion Argyle and many other winners.

Note: Prior to 1860, leading sires were based on races won rather than progeny earnings.

All-Time Leading Sires

The sire lists on the following pages do not include steeplechase statistics.

All-Time Leading North American Sires by Total Worldwide Earnings

Through 2004

Name, YOB, Sire	Where Stood	Earnings
Danzig, 1977, by Northern Dancer	U.S.	$99,556,642
Mr. Prospector, 1970, by Raise a Native	U.S.	97,447,749
Storm Cat, 1983, by Storm Bird	U.S.	88,477,589
Woodman, 1983, by Mr. Prospector	U.S., Aus.	84,352,903
Seattle Slew, 1974, by Bold Reasoning	U.S.	81,583,061
Crafty Prospector, 1979, by Mr. Prospector	U.S.	80,266,499
Nureyev, 1977, by Northern Dancer	Fr., U.S.	77,012,560
Wild Again, 1980, by Icecapade	U.S.	75,017,266
Kris S., 1977, by Roberto	U.S.	71,649,425
Deputy Minister, 1979, by Vice Regent	U.S.	69,848,682
Miswaki, 1978, by Mr. Prospector	U.S.	66,932,003
Cozzene, 1980, by Caro (Ire)	U.S.	65,281,346
Pleasant Colony, 1978, by His Majesty	U.S.	63,959,403
Dixieland Band, 1980, by Northern Dancer	U.S.	63,728,367
Seeking the Gold, 1985, by Mr. Prospector	U.S.	62,685,431
Royal Academy, 1987, by Nijinsky II	Ire., Jpn., U.S., Aus.	62,444,489
Gulch, 1984, by Mr. Prospector	U.S.	62,058,597
Theatrical (Ire), 1982, by Nureyev	U.S.	61,880,608
A.P. Indy, 1989, by Seattle Slew	U.S.	61,335,520
Rahy, 1985, by Blushing Groom (Fr)	U.S.	61,019,534
Alydar, 1975, by Raise a Native	U.S.	60,556,180
Broad Brush, 1983, by Ack Ack	U.S.	59,340,176
Gone West, 1984, by Mr. Prospector	U.S.	58,795,401
Conquistador Cielo, 1979, by Mr. Prospector	U.S.	58,594,427
Mt. Livermore, 1981, by Blushing Groom (Fr)	U.S.	57,783,133
Cure the Blues, 1978, by Stop the Music	U.S.	55,700,274
Kingmambo, 1990, by Mr. Prospector	U.S.	55,434,617
Nijinsky II, 1967, by Northern Dancer	U.S.	55,220,808
Silver Deputy, 1985, by Deputy Minister	U.S.	52,427,525
Green Dancer, 1972, by Nijinsky II	Fr., U.S.	52,382,493
Affirmed, 1975, by Exclusive Native	U.S.	50,645,810
Carson City, 1987, by Mr. Prospector	U.S.	50,613,762
Dynaformer, 1985, by Roberto	U.S.	50,311,864
Lyphard, 1969, by Northern Dancer	Fr., U.S.	49,924,053
Valid Appeal, 1972, by In Reality	U.S.	47,954,560
Runaway Groom, 1979, by Blushing Groom (Fr)	U.S.	47,588,024
Silver Hawk, 1979, by Roberto	U.S.	46,969,579
Phone Trick, 1982, by Clever Trick	U.S.	46,930,502
Vice Regent, 1967, by Northern Dancer	Can.	46,818,245
Devil's Bag, 1981, by Halo	U.S.	46,767,816
Bold Ruckus, 1976, by Boldnesian	Can.	45,951,188
Black Tie Affair (Ire), 1986, by Miswaki	U.S., Jpn.	45,592,473
Halo, 1969, by Hail to Reason	U.S.	44,392,274
Irish River (Fr), 1976, by Riverman	Fr., U.S.	44,235,384
Clever Trick, 1976, by Icecapade	U.S.	43,907,862
Private Account, 1976, by Damascus	U.S.	43,840,114
Riverman, 1969, by Never Bend	Fr., U.S.	43,690,887
Allen's Prospect, 1982, by Mr. Prospector	U.S.	43,536,488
El Prado (Ire), 1989, by Sadler's Wells	U.S.	43,225,237
Mr. Leader, 1966, by Hail to Reason	U.S.	43,052,638
Diesis (GB), 1980, by Sharpen Up (GB)	U.S.	42,881,802
Cox's Ridge, 1974, by Best Turn	U.S.	42,301,880
Capote, 1984, by Seattle Slew	U.S.	42,215,119
Unbridled, 1987, by Fappiano	U.S.	41,425,962

All-Time Leading Sires by Number of Winners Worldwide

Through 2004

Name, YOB, Sire	Where Stood	Wnrs
Danehill, 1986, by Danzig	Ire., Jpn., Aus.	1,234
Woodman, 1983, by Mr. Prospector	U.S., Aus.	849
Sadler's Wells, 1981, by Northern Dancer	Ire.	818
Sunday Silence, 1986, by Halo	Jpn.	787
Mr. Prospector, 1970, by Raise a Native	U.S.	750
Royal Academy, 1987, by Nijinsky II	Ire., Jpn., U.S., Aus.	746
Night Shift, 1980, by Northern Dancer	Eng., U.S., Ire.	706
Last Tycoon (Ire), 1983, by Try My Best	Ire., Aus, Jpn., N.Z.	686
Southern Halo, 1983, by Halo	Arg., U.S., Jpn.	678
Mr. Leader, 1966, by Hail to Reason	U.S.	667
Bluebird, 1984, by Storm Bird	Ire., Aus.	653
Miswaki, 1978, by Mr. Prospector	U.S.	651
Alzao, 1980, by Lyphard	Ire., Aus.	646
Clever Trick, 1976, by Icecapade	U.S.	638
Crafty Prospector, 1979, by Mr. Prospector	U.S.	630
Allen's Prospect, 1982, by Mr. Prospector	U.S.	627
Dixieland Band, 1980, by Northern Dancer	U.S.	622
Danzig, 1977, by Northern Dancer	U.S.	621
Runaway Groom, 1979, by Blushing Groom (Fr)	U.S.	610
Green Dancer, 1972, by Nijinsky II	Fr., U.S.	598
Phone Trick, 1982, by Clever Trick	U.S.	591
Wild Again, 1980, by Icecapade	U.S.	589
Caerleon, 1980, by Nijinsky II	Ire., Aus.	586
Geiger Counter, 1982, by Mr. Prospector	Can., U.S., Aus.	585
Be My Guest, 1974, by Northern Dancer	Ire.	582
Valid Appeal, 1972, by In Reality	U.S.	561
Conquistador Cielo, 1979, by Mr. Prospector	U.S.	552
Cure the Blues, 1978, by Stop the Music	U.S.	551
Kris S., 1977, by Roberto	U.S.	545
Mt. Livermore, 1981, by Blushing Groom (Fr)	U.S.	538
Riverman, 1969, by Never Bend	Fr., U.S.	536
Pirate's Bounty, 1975, by Hoist the Flag	U.S.	528
Storm Cat, 1983, by Storm Bird	U.S.	526
Irish River (Fr), 1976, by Riverman	Fr., U.S.	523
Seattle Slew, 1974, by Bold Reasoning	U.S.	517
Cryptoclearance, 1984, by Fappiano	U.S.	516
Fortunate Prospect, 1981, by Northern Prospect	U.S.	516
Fit to Fight, 1979, by Chieftain	U.S.	513
Afleet, 1984, by Mr. Prospector	U.S., Jpn.	511
Deputy Minister, 1979, by Vice Regent	U.S.	510

All-Time Leading Sires of Stakes Winners Worldwide

Through 2004

Name, YOB, Sire	Where Stood	SWs
Danehill, 1986, by Danzig	Ire., Jpn., Aus.	273
Sadler's Wells, 1981, by Northern Dancer	Ire.	233
Danzig, 1977, by Northern Dancer	U.S.	184
Mr. Prospector, 1970, by Raise a Native	U.S.	180
Nijinsky II, 1967, by Northern Dancer	U.S.	153
Northern Dancer, 1961, by Nearctic	Can., U.S.	146
Nureyev, 1977, by Northern Dancer	Fr., U.S.	137
Southern Halo, 1983, by Halo	Arg., U.S., Jpn.	133
Sunday Silence, 1986, by Halo	Jpn.	130
Storm Cat, 1983, by Storm Bird	U.S.	129
Riverman, 1969, by Never Bend	Fr., U.S.	127
Caerleon, 1980, by Nijinsky II	Ire., Aus.	125
*Sir Tristram, 1971, by Sir Ivor	N.Z.	124
Lyphard, 1969, by Northern Dancer	Fr., U.S.	114
Seattle Slew, 1974, by Bold Reasoning	U.S.	111
Roy, 1983, by Fappiano	Chi., U.S., Brz., Arg.	108
Vice Regent, 1967, by Northern Dancer	Can.	104
Royal Academy, 1987, by Nijinsky II	Ire., Jpn., U.S., Aus.	102
Dixieland Band, 1980, by Northern Dancer	U.S.	100

Name, YOB, Sire	Where Stood	SWs
Miswaki, 1978, by Mr. Prospector	U.S.	97
Woodman, 1983, by Mr. Prospector	U.S., Aus.	96
Alleged, 1974, by Hoist the Flag	U.S.	94
Rainbow Quest, 1981, by Blushing Groom (Fr)	Eng.	94
Alzao, 1980, by Lyphard	Ire., Aus.	93
*Nasrullah, 1940, by Nearco	Ire., U.S.	93
Sir Ivor, 1965, by Sir Gaylord	Ire., U.S.	92
Blushing Groom (Fr), 1974, by Red God	U.S.	91
Habitat, 1966, by Sir Gaylord	Ire.	89
Nodouble, 1965, by *Noholme II	U.S.	89
Relaunch, 1976, by In Reality	U.S.	88
Valid Appeal, 1972, by In Reality	U.S.	88
Nearco, 1935, by Pharos	Eng.	87
Crafty Prospector, 1979, by Mr. Prospector	U.S.	86
Green Dancer, 1972, by Nijinsky II	Fr., U.S.	86
Hyperion, 1930, by Gainsborough	Eng.	86
Night Shift, 1980, by Northern Dancer	Eng., U.S., Ire.	86
Broad Brush, 1983, by Ack Ack	U.S.	85
Affirmed, 1975, by Exclusive Native	U.S.	84
Irish River (Fr), 1976, by Riverman	Fr., U.S.	84
Kris S., 1977, by Roberto	U.S.	84
Zabeel, 1986, by *Sir Tristram	N.Z.	84
Mr. Leader, 1966, by Hail to Reason	U.S.	83
Round Table, 1954, by *Princequillo	U.S.	83
Bold Ruler, 1954, by *Nasrullah	U.S.	82
Roberto, 1969, by Hail to Reason	U.S.	82
Wild Again, 1980, by Icecapade	U.S.	82

All-Time Leading Sires by Percentage of Stakes Winners Worldwide
Through 2004

Name, YOB, Sire	Where Stood	Percent SWs
Northern Dancer, 1961, by Nearctic	Can., U.S.	22.6%
Bold Ruler, 1954, by *Nasrullah	U.S.	22.4%
*Nasrullah, 1940, by Nearco	Ire., U.S.	21.9%
Round Table, 1954, by *Princequillo	U.S.	20.5%
Hoist the Flag, 1968, by Tom Rolfe	U.S.	19.9%
*Sea-Bird, 1962, by Dan Cupid	U.S.	18.9%
Nearco, 1935, by Pharos	Eng.	17.9%
Nijinsky II, 1967, by Northern Dancer	U.S.	17.7%
Blushing Groom (Fr), 1974, by Red God	U.S.	17.4%
Kalamoun, 1970, by Zeddaan	Ire., Fr.	17.1%
Danzig, 1977, by Northern Dancer	U.S.	17.0%
Nureyev, 1977, by Northern Dancer	Fr., U.S.	17.0%
*Mahmoud, 1933, by *Blenheim II	Eng., U.S.	16.6%
Never Bend, 1960, by *Nasrullah	U.S.	16.5%
Tentam, 1969, by Intentionally	U.S.	16.1%
Philately, 1962, by *Princequillo	U.S.	16.0%
Roberto, 1969, by Hail to Reason	U.S.	16.0%
*Amerigo, 1955, by Nearco	U.S.	15.7%
Mill Reef, 1968, by Never Bend	Eng.	15.7%
Sea Aglo, 1971, by *Sea-Bird	U.S.	15.6%
*Heliopolis, 1936, by Hyperion	U.S.	15.3%
*Ribot, 1952, by Tenerani	Ity., Eng., U.S.	15.2%
Nedayr, 1935, by Neddie	U.S.	15.1%
Vice Regent, 1967, by Northern Dancer	Can.	15.1%
Mr. Prospector, 1970, by Raise a Native	U.S.	15.0%
Bull Lea, 1935, by *Bull Dog	U.S.	14.9%
Eight Thirty, 1936, by Pilate	U.S.	14.7%
*Herbager, 1956, by Vandale	U.S.	14.5%
Chop Chop, 1940, by Flares	Can.	14.4%
In Reality, 1964, by Intentionally	U.S.	14.4%
Native Dancer, 1950, by Polynesian	U.S.	14.4%
Pelouse, 1951, by Pavot	U.S.	14.3%
Nearctic, 1954, by Nearco	Can., U.S.	14.2%
*Royal Charger, 1942, by Nearco	Ire., U.S.	14.2%

All-Time Leading Sires of Group or Graded Stakes Winners Worldwide
Through 2004

Name, YOB, Sire	Where Stood	GSWs
Danehill, 1986, by Danzig	Ire., Jpn., Aus.	154
Sadler's Wells, 1981, by Northern Dancer	Ire.	135
Mr. Prospector, 1970, by Raise a Native	U.S.	111
Danzig, 1977, by Northern Dancer	U.S.	103
Nijinsky II, 1967, by Northern Dancer	U.S.	97
Southern Halo, 1983, by Halo	Arg., U.S., Jpn.	95
Roy, 1983, by Fappiano	Chi., U.S., Brz., Arg.	83
*Sir Tristram, 1971, by Sir Ivor	N.Z.	82
Storm Cat, 1983, by Storm Bird	U.S.	81
Northern Dancer, 1961, by Nearctic	Can., U.S.	77
Nureyev, 1977, by Northern Dancer	Fr., U.S.	77
Caerleon, 1980, by Nijinsky II	Ire., Aus.	67
Riverman, 1969, by Never Bend	Fr., U.S.	67
Lyphard, 1969, by Northern Dancer	Fr., U.S.	64
Ghadeer, 1978, by Lyphard	Brz.	62
Zabeel, 1986, by *Sir Tristram	N.Z.	60
Seattle Slew, 1974, by Bold Reasoning	U.S.	59
Blushing Groom (Fr), 1974, by Red God	U.S.	58
Alleged, 1974, by Hoist the Flag	U.S.	57
Habitat, 1966, by Sir Gaylord	Ire.	56
Rainbow Quest, 1981, by Blushing Groom (Fr)	Eng.	55
Fitzcarraldo, 1981, by Cipayo	Arg.	51
Royal Academy, 1987, by Nijinsky II	Ire., U.S., Jpn., Aus.	51
Cipayo, 1974, by Lacydon	Arg.	48
Alydar, 1975, by Raise a Native	U.S.	46
Sir Ivor, 1965, by Sir Gaylord	Ire., U.S.	44
*Vaguely Noble, 1965, by Vienna	U.S.	44
Green Dancer, 1972, by Nijinsky II	Fr., U.S.	43
Diesis (GB), 1980, by Sharpen Up (GB)	U.S.	42
Elliodor, 1977, by Lyphard	S.Af.	42
Roberto, 1969, by Hail to Reason	U.S.	42
Affirmed, 1975, by Exclusive Native	U.S.	41
Bluebird, 1984, by Storm Bird	Ire., Aus.	41
Damascus, 1964, by Sword Dancer	U.S.	41
Egg Toss, 1977, by Buckpasser	Arg.	41
Gone West, 1984, by Mr. Prospector	U.S.	41
Irish River (Fr), 1976, by Riverman	Fr., U.S.	41
Alzao, 1980, by Lyphard	Ire., Aus.	40
Clackson, 1976, by I Say	Brz.	40
Dixieland Band, 1980, by Northern Dancer	U.S.	40
Theatrical (Ire), 1982, by Nureyev	U.S.	40
A.P. Indy, 1989, by Seattle Slew	U.S.	39
Caro (Ire), 1967, by Fortino II	Fr., U.S.	39
Foveros, 1976, by Averof	S.Af.	39
Marscay, 1979, by Biscay	Aus.	39
Mill Reef, 1968, by Never Bend	Eng.	39
Fairy King, 1982, by Northern Dancer	Ire., Aus.	38
Kris S., 1977, by Roberto	U.S.	38
Last Tycoon (Ire), 1983, by Try My Best	Ire., Aus., Jpn., N.Z.	38
Majestic Light, 1973, by Majestic Prince	U.S.	38
Wild Again, 1980, by Icecapade	U.S.	38

All-Time Leading Sires by Grade 1 or Group 1 Stakes Winners Worldwide
Through 2004

Name, YOB, Sire	Where Stood	G1Ws
Sadler's Wells, 1981, by Northern Dancer	Ire.	65
Danehill, 1986, by Danzig	Ire., Jpn., Aus.	62
Mr. Prospector, 1970, by Raise a Native	U.S.	48
Roy, 1983, by Fappiano	Chi., U.S., Brz., Arg.	47
Southern Halo, 1983, by Halo	Arg., U.S., Jpn.	46
*Sir Tristram, 1971, by Sir Ivor	N.Z.	45
Danzig, 1977, by Northern Dancer	U.S.	43

Name, YOB, Sire	Where Stood	G1Ws
Nijinsky II, 1967, by Northern Dancer	U.S.	34
Storm Cat, 1983, by Storm Bird	U.S.	30
Nureyev, 1977, by Northern Dancer	Fr., U.S.	29
Zabeel, 1986, by *Sir Tristram	N.Z.	29
Seattle Slew, 1974, by Bold Reasoning	U.S.	27
Northern Dancer, 1961, by Nearctic	Can., U.S.	26
Blushing Groom (Fr), 1974, by Red God	U.S.	25
Ghadeer, 1978, by Lyphard	Brz.	25
Lyphard, 1969, by Northern Dancer	Fr., U.S.	25
Riverman, 1969, by Never Bend	Fr., U.S.	24
*Vaguely Noble, 1965, by Vienna	U.S.	23
Alleged, 1974, by Hoist the Flag	U.S.	22
Caerleon, 1980, by Nijinsky II	Ire., Aus.	22
Cipayo, 1974, by Lacydon	Arg.	21
Alydar, 1975, by Raise a Native	U.S.	20
Fitzcarraldo, 1981, by Cipayo	Arg.	20
Caro (Ire), 1967, by Fortino II	Fr., U.S.	19
Habitat, 1966, by Sir Gaylord	Ire.	19
Mill Reef, 1968, by Never Bend	Eng.	19
Rainbow Quest, 1981, by Blushing Groom (Fr)	Eng.	18
Star Way, 1977, by *Star Appeal	N.Z.	18
Sunday Silence, 1986, by Halo	Jpn.	18

All-Time Leading Sires by Progeny Earnings Worldwide
Through 2004

Name, YOB, Sire	Where Stood	Earnings
Sunday Silence, 1986, by Halo	Jpn.	$492,826,443
Tony Bin, 1983, by Kampala	Jpn.	191,538,308
Danehill, 1986, by Danzig	Ire., Jpn., Aus.	188,585,737
Brian's Time, 1985, by Roberto	Jpn.	185,570,821
Northern Taste, 1971, by Northern Dancer	Jpn.	132,606,792
Afleet, 1984, by Mr. Prospector	U.S., Jpn.	116,024,911
Sadler's Wells, 1981, by Northern Dancer	Ire.	112,978,598
Real Shadai, 1979, by Roberto	Jpn.	106,622,303
Danzig, 1977, by Northern Dancer	U.S.	99,556,642
Mr. Prospector, 1970, by Raise a Native	U.S.	97,447,749
Caerleon, 1980, by Nijinsky II	Ire., Aus.	94,298,936
Storm Cat, 1983, by Storm Bird	U.S.	88,477,589
Jade Robbery, 1987, by Mr. Prospector	Jpn.	88,010,339
Forty Niner, 1985, by Mr. Prospector	U.S., Jpn.	87,466,347
Woodman, 1983, by Mr. Prospector	U.S., Aus.	84,381,931
Sakura Yutaka O, 1982, by Tesco Boy	Jpn.	83,365,879
Amber Shadai, 1977, by Northern Taste	Jpn.	81,891,714
Seattle Slew, 1974, by Bold Reasoning	U.S.	81,585,747
Last Tycoon (Ire), 1983, by Try My Best	Ire., Aus., Jpn., N.Z.	80,288,677
Crafty Prospector, 1979, by Mr. Prospector	U.S.	80,266,520
Nureyev, 1977, by Northern Dancer	Fr., U.S.	77,016,576
Wild Again, 1980, by Icecapade	U.S.	75,017,266
Nihon Pillow Winner, 1980, by Steel Heart	Jpn.	71,700,582
Kris S., 1977, by Roberto	U.S.	71,649,425
Tamamo Cross, 1984, by C B Cross	Jpn.	71,232,860
Deputy Minister, 1979, by Vice Regent	U.S.	69,848,682
Miswaki, 1978, by Mr. Prospector	U.S.	66,932,554
Dancing Brave, 1983, by Lyphard	Eng., Jpn.	66,087,655
Cozzene, 1980, by Caro (Ire)	U.S.	65,281,346
Pleasant Colony, 1978, by His Majesty	U.S.	63,967,376
Dixieland Band, 1980, by Northern Dancer	U.S.	63,728,367
Seeking the Gold, 1985, by Mr. Prospector	U.S.	62,731,873
Royal Academy, 1987, by Nijinsky II	Ire., Jpn., U.S., Aus.	62,534,537
Commander in Chief, 1990, by Dancing Brave	Jpn.	62,429,730
Gulch, 1984, by Mr. Prospector	U.S.	62,058,597
Theatrical (Ire), 1982, by Nureyev	U.S.	61,881,415
A.P. Indy, 1989, by Seattle Slew	U.S.	61,335,520
Rahy, 1985, by Blushing Groom (Fr)	U.S.	61,024,748
Soccer Boy, 1985, by Dictus	Jpn.	60,854,694
Alydar, 1975, by Raise a Native	U.S.	60,556,180

All-Time Leading North American Broodmare Sires by Progeny Earnings Worldwide
Through 2004

Name, YOB, Sire	Where Stood	Earnings
Mr. Prospector, 1970, by Raise a Native	U.S.	$216,241,370
Nijinsky II, 1967, by Northern Dancer	U.S.	189,069,609
Northern Dancer, 1961, by Nearctic	Can., U.S.	160,877,939
Danzig, 1977, by Northern Dancer	U.S.	157,857,703
Lyphard, 1969, by Northern Dancer	Fr., U.S.	156,386,818
Alydar, 1975, by Raise a Native	U.S.	135,547,872
Blushing Groom (Fr), 1974, by Red God	U.S.	133,536,619
Seattle Slew, 1974, by Bold Reasoning	U.S.	131,884,010
Nureyev, 1977, by Northern Dancer	Fr., U.S.	131,199,741
Secretariat, 1970, by Bold Ruler	U.S.	129,554,667
Vice Regent, 1967, by Northern Dancer	Can.	113,437,850
Halo, 1969, by Hail to Reason	U.S.	112,563,414
Riverman, 1969, by Never Bend	Fr., U.S.	108,443,113
Damascus, 1964, by Sword Dancer	U.S.	100,368,545
Affirmed, 1975, by Exclusive Native	U.S.	99,650,815
Roberto, 1969, by Hail to Reason	U.S.	95,613,174
Raise a Native, 1961, by Native Dancer	U.S.	94,545,027
Miswaki, 1978, by Mr. Prospector	U.S.	94,412,632
Green Dancer, 1972, by Nijinsky II	Fr., U.S.	90,397,737
Alleged, 1974, by Hoist the Flag	U.S.	89,819,773
In Reality, 1964, by Intentionally	U.S.	88,082,805
*Grey Dawn II, 1962, by *Herbager	U.S.	87,832,616
Key to the Mint, 1969, by Graustark	U.S.	85,277,038
Graustark, 1963, by *Ribot	U.S.	85,105,715
Caro (Ire), 1967, by Fortino II	Fr., U.S.	84,942,245
Sir Ivor, 1965, by Sir Gaylord	Ire., U.S.	82,268,887
*Vaguely Noble, 1965, by Vienna	U.S.	81,160,409
Storm Bird, 1978, by Northern Dancer	U.S.	77,852,063
Valid Appeal, 1972, by In Reality	U.S.	76,869,955
Fappiano, 1977, by Mr. Prospector	U.S.	76,866,914
Tom Rolfe, 1962, by *Ribot	U.S.	73,704,517
Mr. Leader, 1966, by Hail to Reason	U.S.	72,803,056
Deputy Minister, 1979, by Vice Regent	U.S.	69,342,731
Drone, 1966, by Sir Gaylord	U.S.	68,412,011
The Minstrel, 1974, by Northern Dancer	U.S.	68,139,968

All-Time Leading Broodmare Sires by Progeny Earnings Worldwide
Through 2004

Name, YOB, Sire	Where Stood	Earnings
Northern Taste, 1971, by Northern Dancer	Jpn.	$434,024,451
Mr. Prospector, 1970, by Raise a Native	U.S.	216,241,370
Nijinsky II, 1967, by Northern Dancer	U.S.	189,069,609
Tosho Boy, 1973, by Tesco Boy	Jpn.	173,669,692
Northern Dancer, 1961, by Nearctic	Can., U.S.	160,877,939
Danzig, 1977, by Northern Dancer	U.S.	157,857,703
Lyphard, 1969, by Northern Dancer	Fr., U.S.	156,386,818
Alydar, 1975, by Raise a Native	U.S.	135,547,872
Blushing Groom (Fr), 1974, by Red God	U.S.	133,536,619
Seattle Slew, 1974, by Bold Reasoning	U.S.	131,884,010
Nureyev, 1977, by Northern Dancer	Fr., U.S.	131,199,741
Secretariat, 1970, by Bold Ruler	U.S.	129,554,667
Bravest Roman, 1972, by Never Bend	U.S., Jpn.	113,854,323
Vice Regent, 1967, by Northern Dancer	Can.	113,437,850
Halo, 1969, by Hail to Reason	U.S.	112,563,414
Riverman, 1969, by Never Bend	Fr., U.S.	108,443,113
Tesco Boy, 1963, by Princely Gift	Jpn.	100,844,222
Damascus, 1964, by Sword Dancer	U.S.	100,368,545
Affirmed, 1975, by Exclusive Native	U.S.	99,650,815
Roberto, 1969, by Hail to Reason	U.S.	95,613,174
Raise a Native, 1961, by Native Dancer	U.S.	94,545,027

Name, YOB, Sire	Where Stood	Earnings
Miswaki, 1978, by Mr. Prospector	U.S.	94,412,632
Caerleon, 1980, by Nijinsky II	Ire., Aus.	92,914,198
Mill George, 1975, by Mill Reef	Jpn.	92,417,640
Green Dancer, 1972, by Nijinsky II	Fr., U.S.	90,397,737
Alleged, 1974, by Hoist the Flag	U.S.	89,819,773
Partholon, 1960, by Milesian	Jpn.	89,200,006
In Reality, 1964, by Intentionally	U.S.	88,082,805
*Grey Dawn II, 1962, by *Herbager	U.S.	87,832,616
Key to the Mint, 1969, by Graustark	U.S.	85,277,038
Graustark, 1963, by *Ribot	U.S.	85,105,715
Caro (Ire), 1967, by Fortino II	Fr., U.S.	84,942,245
Sadler's Wells, 1981, by Northern Dancer	Ire.	83,113,823
Sir Ivor, 1965, by Sir Gaylord	Ire., U.S.	82,268,887
*Vaguely Noble, 1965, by Vienna	U.S.	81,160,409
Storm Bird, 1978, by Northern Dancer	U.S.	77,852,063
Valid Appeal, 1972, by In Reality	U.S.	76,869,955
Fappiano, 1977, by Mr. Prospector	U.S.	76,866,914
Dancer's Image, 1965, by Native Dancer	U.S., Fr., Jpn.	75,473,717

All-Time Leading Broodmare Sires by Stakes Winners Worldwide
Through 2004

Name, YOB, Sire	Where Stood	SWs
Mr. Prospector, 1970, by Raise a Native	U.S.	279
Northern Dancer, 1961, by Nearctic	Can., U.S.	235
Nijinsky II, 1967, by Northern Dancer	U.S.	233
Habitat, 1966, by Sir Gaylord	Ire.	217
Lyphard, 1969, by Northern Dancer	Fr., U.S.	198
Raise a Native, 1961, by Native Dancer	U.S.	181
Hyperion, 1930, by Gainsborough	Eng.	174
*Princequillo, 1940, by Prince Rose	U.S.	170
Prince John, 1953, by *Princequillo	U.S.	169
Riverman, 1969, by Never Bend	Fr., U.S.	165
*Vaguely Noble, 1965, by Vienna	U.S.	162
*Nasrullah, 1940, by Nearco	Ire., U.S.	159
Secretariat, 1970, by Bold Ruler	U.S.	158
Damascus, 1964, by Sword Dancer	U.S.	156
Nearco, 1935, by Pharos	Eng.	154
Northfields, 1968, by Northern Dancer	Ire., Aus., S.Af.	154
Sir Ivor, 1965, by Sir Gaylord	Ire., U.S.	149
*Sir Gallahad III, 1920, by *Teddy	U.S.	147
In Reality, 1964, by Intentionally	U.S.	146
*Sir Tristram, 1971, by Sir Ivor	N.Z.	146
Fleet Nasrullah, 1955, by *Nasrullah	U.S.	145
Graustark, 1963, by *Ribot	U.S.	142
Green Dancer, 1972, by Nijinsky II	Fr., U.S.	142
Blushing Groom (Fr), 1974, by Red God	U.S.	138
Roberto, 1969, by Hail to Reason	U.S.	138
Buckpasser, 1963, by Tom Fool	U.S.	137
*Mahmoud, 1933, by *Blenheim II	Eng., U.S.	137
Seattle Slew, 1974, by Bold Reasoning	U.S.	134
Nureyev, 1977, by Northern Dancer	Fr., U.S.	133
Halo, 1969, by Hail to Reason	U.S.	132
Alleged, 1974, by Hoist the Flag	U.S.	131
Shirley Heights, 1975, by Mill Reef	Eng.	131
Alydar, 1975, by Raise a Native	U.S.	128
*Grey Dawn II, 1962, by *Herbager	U.S.	127
Danzig, 1977, by Northern Dancer	U.S.	126
Mill Reef, 1968, by Never Bend	Eng.	124
Round Table, 1954, by *Princequillo	U.S.	124
Big Game, 1939, by *Bahram	Eng.	122
*Court Martial, 1942, by Fair Trial	Eng., U.S.	121
Nashua, 1952, by *Nasrullah	U.S.	121
*Blenheim II, 1927, by Blandford	Fr., U.S.	118
Bold Ruler, 1954, by *Nasrullah	U.S.	118
Count Fleet, 1940, by Reigh Count	U.S.	118
Caro (Ire), 1967, by Fortino II	Fr., U.S.	117

All-Time Leading Broodmare Sires by Group or Graded Stakes Winners Worldwide
Through 2004

Name, YOB, Sire	Where Stood	GSWs
Mr. Prospector, 1970, by Raise a Native	U.S.	124
Nijinsky II, 1967, by Northern Dancer	U.S.	110
Northern Dancer, 1961, by Nearctic	Can., U.S.	104
Habitat, 1966, by Sir Gaylord	Ire.	102
Northfields, 1968, by Northern Dancer	Ire., Aus., S.Af.	97
Lyphard, 1969, by Northern Dancer	Fr., U.S.	81
Riverman, 1969, by Never Bend	Fr., U.S.	81
*Sir Tristram, 1971, by Sir Ivor	N.Z.	81
*Vaguely Noble, 1965, by Vienna	U.S.	75
Nureyev, 1977, by Northern Dancer	Fr., U.S.	67
Prince John, 1953, by *Princequillo	U.S.	67
Roberto, 1969, by Hail to Reason	U.S.	67
Seattle Slew, 1974, by Bold Reasoning	U.S.	67
Sir Ivor, 1965, by Sir Gaylord	Ire., U.S.	66
Buckpasser, 1963, by Tom Fool	U.S.	64
Shirley Heights, 1975, by Mill Reef	Eng.	64
Graustark, 1963, by *Ribot	U.S.	63
Green Dancer, 1972, by Nijinsky II	Fr., U.S.	63
Blushing Groom (Fr), 1974, by Red God	U.S.	60
Alydar, 1975, by Raise a Native	U.S.	59
Mill Reef, 1968, by Never Bend	Eng.	59
Secretariat, 1970, by Bold Ruler	U.S.	59
Sovereign Edition, 1962, by Sovereign Path	N.Z.	59
Alleged, 1974, by Hoist the Flag	U.S.	58
Raise a Native, 1961, by Native Dancer	U.S.	57
Round Table, 1954, by *Princequillo	U.S.	57
Damascus, 1964, by Sword Dancer	U.S.	56
Ghadeer, 1978, by Lyphard	Brz.	55
Key to the Mint, 1969, by Graustark	U.S.	52
Vain, 1966, by Wilkes	Aus.	52
Busted, 1963, by Crepello	Eng.	51
Bold Ruler, 1954, by *Nasrullah	U.S.	49
Sadler's Wells, 1981, by Northern Dancer	Ire.	49
The Minstrel, 1974, by Northern Dancer	U.S.	49
Halo, 1969, by Hail to Reason	U.S.	46
Caro (Ire), 1967, by Fortino II	Fr., U.S.	45
Logical, 1972, by Buckpasser	Arg.	45
*Ribot, 1952, by Tenerani	Ity., Eng., U.S.	44
Bletchingly, 1970, by Biscay	Aus.	43
In Reality, 1964, by Intentionally	U.S.	43
Sir Gaylord, 1959, by *Turn-to	U.S.	43
Danzig, 1977, by Northern Dancer	U.S.	42
*Le Fabuleux, 1961, by Wild Risk	Fr., U.S.	42
Stage Door Johnny, 1965, by Prince John	U.S.	42

All-Time Leading Broodmare Sires by Group 1 or Grade 1 Winners Worldwide
Through 2004

Name, YOB, Sire	Where Stood	G1Ws
Northfields, 1968, by Northern Dancer	Ire., Aus., S.Af.	43
Nijinsky II, 1967, by Northern Dancer	U.S.	42
Northern Dancer, 1961, by Nearctic	Can., U.S.	40
Mr. Prospector, 1970, by Raise a Native	U.S.	34
Riverman, 1969, by Never Bend	Fr., U.S.	30
Buckpasser, 1963, by Tom Fool	U.S.	29
Lyphard, 1969, by Northern Dancer	Fr., U.S.	29
*Vaguely Noble, 1965, by Vienna	U.S.	29
*Sir Tristram, 1971, by Sir Ivor	N.Z.	28
Ghadeer, 1978, by Lyphard	Brz.	27
Habitat, 1966, by Sir Gaylord	Ire.	27
Key to the Mint, 1969, by Graustark	U.S.	26
Sovereign Edition, 1962, by Sovereign Path	N.Z.	26
Nureyev, 1977, by Northern Dancer	Fr., U.S.	24

Name, YOB, Sire	Where Stood	G1Ws
Graustark, 1963, by *Ribot	U.S.	23
Logical, 1972, by Buckpasser	Arg.	23
Green Dancer, 1972, by Nijinsky II	Fr., U.S.	22
Prince John, 1953, by *Princequillo	U.S.	22
Secretariat, 1970, by Bold Ruler	U.S.	22
Sir Ivor, 1965, by Sir Gaylord	Ire., U.S.	22
Waldmeister, 1961, by Wild Risk	Brz.	22
High Top, 1969, by Derring-Do	Eng.	20
Roberto, 1969, by Hail to Reason	U.S.	20
Round Table, 1954, by *Princequillo	U.S.	20
Seattle Slew, 1974, by Bold Reasoning	U.S.	20
Shirley Heights, 1975, by Mill Reef	Eng.	20
Stage Door Johnny, 1965, by Prince John	U.S.	20
Zamazaan, 1965, by Exbury	Aus.	20
Alydar, 1975, by Raise a Native	U.S.	19
Blushing Groom (Fr), 1974, by Red God	U.S.	19
Caro (Ire), 1967, by Fortino II	Fr., U.S.	19
Darshaan, 1981, by Shirley Heights	Ire.	19
*Le Fabuleux, 1961, by Wild Risk	Fr., U.S.	18
Raise a Native, 1961, by Native Dancer	U.S.	18
Sadler's Wells, 1981, by Northern Dancer	Ire.	18
Busted, 1963, by Crepello	Eng.	17
Le Filou, 1946, by Vatellor	Fr.	17

All-Time Leading Sires by Number of Millionaires

(Names of Millionaires)

134   **Sunday Silence** (Admire Boss, Admire Groove, Admire Max, Admire Vega, Agnes Arashi, Agnes Flight, Agnes Gold, Agnes Partner, Agnes Special, Agnes Tachyon, Air Gang Star, Air Shakur, Albireo, Azuma Sanders, Believe [Jpn], Big Gold, Black Tuxedo, Born King, Bright Sunday, Bubble Gum Fellow, Chapel Concert, Cheers Brightly, Cheers Grace, Cheers Message, Cheers Silence, Chokai Ryoga, Chunyi, Coin Toss, Croupier Star, Daitaku Surgeon, Daiwa el Cielo, Daiwa Major, Daiwa Rouge, Dance in the Dark, Dance in the Mood [Jpn], Dance Partner [Jpn], Diamond Biko, Divine Light, Durandal, Egao o Misete, Eishin Rudens [Jpn], Emerald Isle, Er Nova, Fuji Kiseki, Fusaichi Airedale, Fusaichi Run Heart, Fusaichi You Can, Genuine, Glorious Sunday, Gold Allure, Hallelujah Sunday, Happy Path, Hat Trick, Heart's Cry, Heavenly Romance, Higher Game, Hustler, Iron Reality, Isao Heat, Ishino Sunday, Jo Big Bang, King of Daiya, King of Sunday, Kiss Me Tender, Limitless Bid, Lincoln, Machikane Akatsuki, Magic Kiss, Manhattan Cafe, Maruka Candy, Maruka Komachi, Marvelous Sunday, Meisho Domenica, Meisho Odo, Millennium Bio, Miscast, Monopole, Neo Universe, Noblesse Oblige, Not Seldom, Orange Peel, Otomeno Inori, Painted Black, Peace of World, Peer Gynt, Ponderosa, Prime Stage, Quiet Day, Reportage, Rosado, Rosebud, Rosen Kavalier, Royal Cancer, Royal Touch, Saikyo Sunday, Sakura President, Shinin' Ruby, Shinko Singular, Silence Suzuka, Silent Cruise, Silent Deal, Silent Happiness, Silent Hunter, Silent Savior, Special Week, Starry Heaven, Stay Gold, Still in Love, Stinger [Jpn], Stormy Sunday, Sunday Branch, Sunday Kaiser, Sunday Sarah, Sun Place, Sunrise Pegasus, Suzuka Mambo, Tagano Silence, Tayasu Meadow, Tayasu Tsuyoshi, Tiger Cafe, Time to Change, T.M.Sunday, T M Tenrai, Tokai Oza, To the Victory, Vita Rosa, Waltz Dancer, What a Reason, Win Duel, Win Marvelous, Win Radius, Yamanin Respect, Yukino Sun Royal, Zenno Rob Roy)

46   **Tony Bin** (Air Dublin, Air Groove, Air Thule, Bu O, Christmas Tree, Daddy's Dream, Derby Regno, Eighty Grow, Eishin One Schon, Emocion, Felicitar, Freeway Heart, Gemmy Dress, Happy Look, Inter Licence, Irish Dance, Island Oja, Jungle Pocket, Ken Tony O, Lady Pastel, Leningrad, Long Kaiun, Lord Cronos, Lord Platinum, Maquereau, Misuzu Chardon, Narita Century, Nobori Yukio, North Flight, Offside Trap, Royce and Royce, Sakura Chitose O, Sakura Victoria, Sidewinder, Spring Coat, Tai Kalamoun, Tayasu Intime, Telegnosis, Tenzan Seiza, Towa Treasure, Vega, Wedding Honey, Winning Ticket, Yuki Slugger, Yuki Vivace, Yu One Protect)

38   **Danehill** (Air Eminem, Air Smap, Aquarelliste, Arena, Banks Hill [GB], Breaktime, Catbird, Dane Ripper, Danewin, Desert King, Dr More, The Duke, Elvstroem, Fairy King Prawn, Fastnet Rock, Fine Motion, Flying Spur, Gaily Flash, Gamble Rose, Generalist, Ha Ha, Jeune King Prawn, Johan Cruyff, Lord Flag, Lucky Owners, Machikane Jindaiko, Mayano Absolute, Merlene, Midtown [Ire], North Light, Nothin' Leica Dane, Planet Ruler, Rock of Gibraltar [Ire], Scintillation, Tamamo Ruby King, Tiger Hill, Tsukuba Symphony, Uncle Super)

32   **Brian's Time** (Admire Gale, Automatic, Big Gold, Brilliant Road, Chokai Carol, Dantsu Flame, En Dehors, Erimo Brian, Erimo Dandy, Erimo Maxim, Mayano Top Gun, Meine Nouvelle, Meiner Brian, Meiner Max, M.I.Blanc, Narita Brian, Narita Luna Park, No Reason, Osumi Stayer, Phalaenopsis, Port Brian's, Silk Justice, Silk Prima Donna, Silky Lagoon, Spring Verbena, Sunny Brian, Tanino Gimlet, Teruno Shingeki, Time Paradox, Toho Emperor, Toho Kelly, Toho Shiden, Treasure)

29   **Northern Taste** (Adorable, Agnes Handsome, Air Deja Vu, Best Darjeeling, Big Fight, Big Shori, Daiwa Geant, Elizabeth Rose, Fashion Show, Inter Flag, King Admire, Kris the Brave, Kyoei Forte, Lady Gossip, Main Caster, Manjuden Kabuto, Matikanetannhauser, Nifty Dancer, Northern Rainbow, Northern Way, Osumi Best, Plantain Ciecle, Queen Sonnet, Razor Moon, Samani Beppin, Scarlet Bouquet, Shinin' Racer, Sing Like Talk, Slew O'Dyna)

25   **Sadler's Wells** (Ballingarry [Ire], Barathea [Ire], Beat Hollow [GB], Brian Boru [GB], Carnegie [Ire], Daliapour [Ire], Diaghilev, Doyen, Dream Well [Fr], Dushyantor, Galileo [Ire], High Chaparral [Ire], In the Wings [GB], Islington [Ire], Kayf Tara, King's Theatre [Ire], Montjeu [Ire], Northern Spur [Ire], Old Vic, Opera House [GB], Perfect Soul [Ire], Powerscourt [GB], Refuse To Bend [Ire], Sage Wells, Salsabil [Ire])

23   **Amber Shadai** (Bebop, Best Tie Up, Camphor Best, Golden Hour, Headship, Hikaru Palo Santo, Hokusei Amber, Jealous Guy, Kachidoki Ryu, Kamino Cremona, Kamino Cresse, Kanahara Dragon, Kanetoshi Governor, Long Shikotei, Meiner Blau, Meisho Genie, Meisho Taikan, Meisho Yoshiie, Mejiro Ryan, Mercury Mannish, Osumi Leopard, Towa Nagon, Tsurumaru Zamurai)

22   **Caerleon** (Apotheose, Biwa Heidi, Corwyn Bay [Ire], Daiwa Caerleon, Fusaichi Concorde, Generous, Green Blitz, Ibuki Perceive [Jpn], Kostroma [Ire], Kurokami, Lord Successor, L-Way Win, Marienbard, Matikaneharesugata, Missionary Ridge [GB], Paradise Hills, Passacaglia [Jpn], Princess Carla, Shinko Lovely, Volga [Ire], Warrsan, Zenno El Cid)

18   **Real Shadai** (Air Real, Beauty Make, Big Symbol, Daiichi Joyful, Daiwa Oshu, Grass Position, Hagino Real King, Ibuki Maikagura, King Pharaoh, Monsieur Siecle, Osumi Shadai, Rice Shower, Run for the Dream, Stage Champ, Sunrise Flag, Sunrise Jaeger, Turf Genius, Wedding Cake)

18   **Tamamo Cross** (First Sonia, Fuji One Man Cross, Hiro de Cross, Inter Unique, Kanetsu Cross, Kanoya Battlecross, Latir, Love is Dream, Makoto Raiden, Mayano Poseidon, My Sole Sound, Narita Daido, Tamamo Highway, Tamamo Inazuma, T.M.Tokkyu, White Happiness, Win Generale, Yamanin Recall)

16   **Danzig** (Agnes World, Biko Pegasus, Chief's Crown, Dance Smartly, Danzig Connection, Dispute, Dumaani, Hikari Cermet, Lure, Magnaten, Pine Bluff, Polish Navy, Stephan's Odyssey, Versailles Treaty, War Chant, Yamanin Paradise)

16   **Sakura Yutaka O** (Air Jihad, Alegrar, Dynamite Daddy, Higashi Majorca, Mayano Dempsey, Nishino Daio, Osumi Max, Sakura Bakushin O, Sakura Candle, Sakura Senai O, Sistina, Tenzan Yutaka, Tunante, Umeno Fiber, World Now, Yukino Bijin)

15   **Afleet** (A Fleets Dancer, Big Fleet, Big Wolf, Check the Luck, Gaily Condor, Gaily Magnum, Golden Jack, Hikari Zirconia, Icarus' Dream, Ishiyaku Mach, Preeminence [Jpn], Primo Ordine [Jpn], Rikiai Taikan, Saqalat, Sterling Rose)

15   **Dancing Brave** (Chokai Raijin, Commander in Chief, Dancing Surpass, Erimo Chic, Erimo Pixy, Green Planet, Joten Brave, King Halo, Kyoei March, Leo Ryuho, Snark Suzuran, Tagajo Noble, T.M.Ocean, T.M.Top Dan, White Muzzle [GB])

14   **Mr. Prospector** (Aldebaran, Chester House, Dancethruthedawn, Educated Risk, Forty Niner, Fusaichi Pegasus, Gulch, Homebuilder, Jet Around, Rhythm, Seeking the Gold, Shake Hand, Syourinomegami, Tank's Prospect)

14   **Nihon Pillow Winner** (Bell Winner, Cheers Hope, Dandy Commando, Flower Park, Foundry Short, Kyoei Bonanza, Mega Stardom, Memory Catch, Nihonpillow Prince, Nihon Pillow Study, Towa Darling, Towa Ia Novia, Towa Winner, Yamanin Zephyr)

14   **Nureyev** (Alwuhush, Annoconnor, Atticus, Black Hawk [GB], Good Journey, Heart Lake, Legacy Hunter, Lord Kirov, Miesque, Peintre Celebre, Skimming, Soviet Star, Spinning World, Theatrical [Ire])

Leading 2004 Sires by State and Province Where Bred

Earnings of horses as reported bred in states and provinces, regardless of where sire stands or stood.
Limited to sires with 2004 progeny earnings of $5,000 or more by horses bred in that state or province.

Alabama

Sire, YOB, Sire	Strs	Wnrs	Wins	SWs	Leading Runner (Earnings)	Total Earnings
Royal Empire, 1994, by Forty Niner	16	6	10	1	Comalagold ($83,590)	$182,812
Shot Block, 1987, by Relaunch	6	3	3	0	Sun Block ($31,697)	61,139
Valid Victorious, 1994, by Valid Appeal	6	1	2	0	Valid's Beauty ($24,331)	39,091
Abity, 1990, by Superbity	2	1	1	1	Scotties Abity ($30,060)	38,025
Chief Persuasion, 1983, by Liege Lord	1	1	1	1	Chief Tudor ($36,853)	36,853

Arizona

Sire, YOB, Sire	Strs	Wnrs	Wins	SWs	Leading Runner (Earnings)	Total Earnings
Benton Creek, 1993, by Septieme Ciel	60	33	67	4	Newark ($95,204)	$636,936
Society Max, 1982, by Mr. Prospector	28	18	28	1	Carte Madera ($43,170)	296,930
Chopin, 1994, by Mr. Prospector	17	11	20	3	Imdabossau ($49,490)	185,344
Chanate, 1995, by Storm Cat	27	9	15	1	Sauceonside ($60,600)	174,778
Barricade, 1993, by Riverman	27	15	31	0	Barricaded ($30,500)	174,045

Arkansas

Sire, YOB, Sire	Strs	Wnrs	Wins	SWs	Leading Runner (Earnings)	Total Earnings
Bold Anthony, 1990, by Bold Ruckus	38	18	34	1	Quote Me Later ($103,617)	$506,359
Idabel, 1986, by Mr. Prospector	33	16	29	0	Timeless Dreamer ($74,180)	436,527
Stutz Blackhawk, 1977, by Mr. Prospector	29	13	30	0	Tindell ($61,880)	269,164
Big Pistol, 1981, by Romeo	28	12	22	1	B J's Pistol ($53,070)	267,830
Forever Dancer, 1988, by Dixieland Band	15	7	20	0	Warrior's Dance ($78,800)	242,304

California

Sire, YOB, Sire	Strs	Wnrs	Wins	SWs	Leading Runner (Earnings)	Total Earnings
In Excess (Ire), 1987, by Siberian Express	93	53	94	5	Texcess ($725,427)	$3,296,538
General Meeting, 1988, by Seattle Slew	81	44	69	6	Yearly Report ($787,500)	2,747,464
Smokester, 1988, by Never Tabled	129	77	142	3	Areyoutalkintome ($268,352)	2,498,820
High Brite, 1984, by Best Turn	117	73	143	4	Super High ($170,760)	2,196,143
Siberian Summer, 1989, by Siberian Express	77	46	85	3	Summer Wind Dancer ($598,905)	2,146,878

Colorado

Sire, YOB, Sire	Strs	Wnrs	Wins	SWs	Leading Runner (Earnings)	Total Earnings
Barricade, 1993, by Riverman	1	1	5	1	Cajun Pepper ($112,242)	$112,242
Coverallbases, 1989, by Capote	12	5	9	2	Cut of Music ($42,959)	105,943
Air Forbes Won, 1979, by Bold Forbes	2	1	3	1	Socko ($100,734)	101,508
Music Master, 1981, by Marshua's Dancer	6	2	7	1	Long Range ($47,108)	96,668
Defrere, 1992, by Deputy Minister	2	2	5	0	Defrere's Vixen ($81,930)	90,905

Connecticut

Sire, YOB, Sire	Strs	Wnrs	Wins	SWs	Leading Runner (Earnings)	Total Earnings
Departing Prints, 1982, by Dactylographer	1	1	2	0	Nantucketeer ($31,733)	$31,733

Florida

Sire, YOB, Sire	Strs	Wnrs	Wins	SWs	Leading Runner (Earnings)	Total Earnings
Jules, 1994, by Forty Niner	94	52	95	5	Peace Rules ($1,024,288)	$3,398,393
End Sweep, 1991, by Forty Niner	119	60	118	1	Agnes Wing ($1,136,535)	3,383,745
Halo's Image, 1991, by Halo	100	51	98	2	Southern Image ($1,612,150)	3,166,222
Sword Dance (Ire), 1984, by Nijinsky II	141	71	139	3	Eagle Sword ($447,692)	2,682,874
Stormy Atlantic, 1994, by Storm Cat	119	68	123	3	Icy Atlantic ($216,720)	2,551,964

Georgia

Sire, YOB, Sire	Strs	Wnrs	Wins	SWs	Leading Runner (Earnings)	Total Earnings
American Standard, 1980, by In Reality	1	1	1	1	Bluesthestandard ($132,633)	$132,633
Roaring Camp, 1991, by Forty Niner	18	3	4	0	Dixie Roll ($29,374)	118,522
Grub, 1983, by Mr. Prospector	3	3	5	0	Georgia Glory ($36,610)	73,269
Birdonthewire, 1989, by Proud Birdie	1	1	1	0	Nors' Proud Birdie ($34,480)	34,480
Classic Account, 1985, by Private Account	1	1	2	0	Maybe Jack ($25,070)	25,070

Idaho

Sire, YOB, Sire	Strs	Wnrs	Wins	SWs	Leading Runner (Earnings)	Total Earnings
L. B. Jaklin, 1984, by Jaklin Klugman	9	6	12	1	Mining for Fun ($54,390)	$104,461
Digression, 1987, by Seattle Slew	2	2	6	0	Curt's First Bid ($84,335)	89,529
Shergar's Best (Ire), 1983, by Shergar	16	9	15	1	Sheer Sweetness ($16,383)	83,037
Fabulous Champ, 1989, by Somethingfabulous	18	9	14	1	Hey Fabulous ($15,445)	79,880
Murrtheblurr, 1977, by Torsion	5	2	4	0	Jayhawk Janet ($64,607)	73,445

Illinois

Sire, YOB, Sire	Strs	Wnrs	Wins	SWs	Leading Runner (Earnings)	Total Earnings
Cartwright, 1990, by Forty Niner	92	49	91	2	Wiggins ($181,920)	$1,512,444
Unreal Zeal, 1980, by Mr. Prospector	53	25	42	1	Lady Riss ($68,036)	583,208
Dynaformer, 1985, by Roberto	2	1	2	1	Mystery Giver ($470,390)	473,105
Classified Facts, 1993, by Seattle Slew	17	12	19	0	Call Me Dorie ($76,460)	445,165
French Deputy, 1992, by Deputy Minister	3	2	4	1	Phantom Mask ($309,950)	431,757

Indiana

Sire, YOB, Sire	Strs	Wnrs	Wins	SWs	Leading Runner (Earnings)	Total Earnings
Presidential Order, 1993, by Danzig	42	16	35	2	Sir Traver ($56,501)	$457,771
Crown Ambassador, 1994, by Storm Cat	31	19	32	2	Ellens Lucky Star ($95,766)	374,344
Moro Oro, 1993, by Moro	23	18	25	1	Free Bonus ($80,100)	361,757
Jacquelyn's Groom, 1988, by Runaway Groom	29	14	19	0	Fe's Groom ($32,370)	256,084
Lil E. Tee, 1989, by At the Threshold	17	12	20	1	Tee's Pearl ($76,200)	246,108

Iowa

Sire, YOB, Sire	Strs	Wnrs	Wins	SWs	Leading Runner (Earnings)	Total Earnings
Blumin Affair, 1991, by Dynaformer	39	22	32	0	Yoyo Jabo ($58,978)	$536,435
Sharkey, 1987, by Sharpen Up (GB)	30	14	19	1	Sharky's Review ($87,412)	289,836
Mercedes Won, 1986, by Air Forbes Won	21	11	17	0	Mingo Mohawk ($73,788)	288,273
Wild Invader, 1991, by Seattle Slew	21	12	22	0	Wild Fiesta ($51,293)	253,215
Devil His Due, 1989, by Devil's Bag	12	7	11	0	Mr. Mingo ($49,545)	198,045

Kansas

Sire, YOB, Sire	Strs	Wnrs	Wins	SWs	Leading Runner (Earnings)	Total Earnings
Gold Ruler, 1980, by Mr. Prospector	32	13	27	4	Nick Missed ($32,571)	$196,517
Big Splash, 1988, by Ziggy's Boy	11	5	7	1	Discreetly Irish ($31,640)	81,760
Here We Come, 1988, by Mr. Prospector	1	1	2	0	Queena Corrina ($78,950)	78,950
Sea Twister, 1996, by Ghazi	2	2	6	2	Wind Twister ($52,360)	66,980
Scarlet 'n Gray, 1986, by Secreto	5	2	4	0	C T King Oftheroad ($25,970)	61,369

Kentucky

Sire, YOB, Sire	Strs	Wnrs	Wins	SWs	Leading Runner (Earnings)	Total Earnings
Storm Cat, 1983, by Storm Bird	130	69	106	13	Seeking the Dia ($1,407,809)	$9,314,938
El Prado (Ire), 1989, by Sadler's Wells	142	71	130	11	Kitten's Joy ($1,625,796)	8,514,189
A.P. Indy, 1989, by Seattle Slew	175	95	154	19	Daydreaming ($483,180)	7,966,154
Saint Ballado, 1989, by Halo	142	70	108	4	Ashado ($2,259,640)	7,457,814
Grand Slam, 1995, by Gone West	145	79	121	10	Cafe Olympus ($875,328)	6,576,397

Louisiana

Sire, YOB, Sire	Strs	Wnrs	Wins	SWs	Leading Runner (Earnings)	Total Earnings
Zarbyev, 1984, by Nureyev	68	35	54	3	Zarb's Dahar ($157,835)	$1,186,292
Excavate, 1988, by Mr. Prospector	91	44	61	2	Bebe Garcon ($84,733)	1,148,128
Bag, 1989, by Devil's Bag	96	40	64	2	Cheerful Bag ($64,629)	1,054,406
Forty Won, 1991, by Forty Niner	57	30	48	0	Forty Dolls ($73,142)	891,096
Leestown, 1994, by Seattle Slew	65	24	37	3	Old Lee ($151,705)	888,148

Maryland

Sire, YOB, Sire	Strs	Wnrs	Wins	SWs	Leading Runner (Earnings)	Total Earnings
Not For Love, 1990, by Mr. Prospector	96	50	99	5	Love of Money ($491,500)	$2,947,166
Allen's Prospect, 1982, by Mr. Prospector	118	65	103	4	Crossing Point ($124,615)	2,107,339
Polish Numbers, 1987, by Danzig	69	37	70	5	Chrusciki ($174,770)	1,718,765
Two Punch, 1983, by Mr. Prospector	69	41	78	3	Bronze Abe ($241,900)	1,685,150
Malibu Moon, 1997, by A.P. Indy	34	21	35	3	Declan's Moon ($507,300)	1,345,025

Massachusetts

Sire, YOB, Sire	Strs	Wnrs	Wins	SWs	Leading Runner (Earnings)	Total Earnings
Sundance Ridge, 1986, by Cox's Ridge	10	4	7	3	Stylish Sultan ($64,090)	$219,010
Senor Conquistador, 1991, by Conquistador Cielo	10	5	9	1	Senor Ladd ($119,750)	176,892
A. P Jet, 1989, by Fappiano	3	2	6	1	Jini's Jet ($95,150)	123,660
Red Scamper, 1985, by Icecapade	7	5	8	0	Deer Danny Boy ($27,961)	84,308
Genuine Reward, 1993, by Rahy	2	2	6	0	Genuine Regard ($47,750)	78,872

Michigan

Sire, YOB, Sire	Strs	Wnrs	Wins	SWs	Leading Runner (Earnings)	Total Earnings
Matchlite, 1983, by Clever Trick	42	21	31	1	Dancin for Gold ($133,179)	$530,735
Native Factor, 1987, by Foolish Pleasure	24	17	37	2	Timely Factor ($98,025)	447,413
Quiet Enjoyment, 1989, by Ogygian	22	15	24	1	Exclusivenjoyment ($131,170)	354,178
Monetary Gift, 1978, by Gold and Myrrh	21	14	29	0	Deb's Favoite Gift ($60,828)	250,730
Pauliano, 1991, by Fappiano	26	8	20	0	Everglide ($46,505)	241,178

Minnesota

Sire, YOB, Sire	Strs	Wnrs	Wins	SWs	Leading Runner (Earnings)	Total Earnings
Demidoff, 1990, by Mr. Prospector	10	7	13	3	Vazandar ($105,306)	$345,536
Quick Cut, 1994, by Storm Cat	26	13	20	1	Wally's Choice ($199,061)	341,997
North Prospect, 1980, by Mr. Prospector	17	7	11	1	Crocrock ($75,680)	179,514
Wolf Power (SAf), 1978, by Flirting Around	2	2	6	1	Lt. Sampson ($76,050)	132,896
Quaker Hill, 1991, by Alydar	9	4	4	0	Quakers Surprise ($31,856)	105,332

Mississippi

Sire, YOB, Sire	Strs	Wnrs	Wins	SWs	Leading Runner (Earnings)	Total Earnings
Evansville Slew, 1992, by Slew City Slew	1	1	2	1	Smalltown Slew ($60,560)	$60,560
Blushing Star, 1993, by Blushing John	5	2	3	0	Go Star Buster ($32,580)	47,755
To a Wild Kris, 1992, by Kris S.	1	1	1	0	Charlie Riddell ($27,490)	27,490
Homo Sapiens, 1993, by Big Bronk	2	1	2	1	Heart to Heart ($21,820)	24,530
Sekari (GB), 1994, by Polish Precedent	1	1	2	0	Sweet Debbie ($24,110)	24,110

Missouri

Sire, YOB, Sire	Strs	Wnrs	Wins	SWs	Leading Runner (Earnings)	Total Earnings
Victorious, 1980, by Explodent	6	5	13	0	Campinout ($83,130)	$140,873
Wood Reply, 1992, by Woodman	5	4	6	0	Reply N Aces ($16,760)	41,632
Metfield, 1988, by Seattle Slew	1	1	4	0	Fort Metfield ($28,163)	28,163
Mandamus, 1992, by Mining	4	2	3	0	Silly Girl ($20,290)	23,260
Lucky South, 1990, by Lucky North	2	2	3	0	Pass the Luck ($14,860)	22,968

Montana

Sire, YOB, Sire	Strs	Wnrs	Wins	SWs	Leading Runner (Earnings)	Total Earnings
Black Mackee, 1976, by Captain Courageous	17	8	15	0	Ponoka ($24,874)	$92,021
Mr. Badger, 1979, by Mr. Leader	6	3	6	0	Badshot ($26,497)	50,088
Streaker Gotchey, 1982, by Osage Streaker	2	1	3	1	Streak a Roani ($20,232)	20,232
Weekend Guest, 1987, by Mr. Prospector	1	1	4	1	Bizzyweekend ($19,711)	19,711
Grey West, 1994, by Gone West	7	2	5	0	Little Gusher ($10,646)	19,693

Nebraska

Sire, YOB, Sire	Strs	Wnrs	Wins	SWs	Leading Runner (Earnings)	Total Earnings
Verzy, 1982, by Vice Regent	39	23	39	1	Thundering Verzy ($65,302)	$368,989
Lytrump, 1985, by Lypheor (GB)	24	11	22	1	Jitterbug Joy ($36,733)	214,710
Blumin Affair, 1991, by Dynaformer	15	7	15	1	Sheso ($36,864)	132,246
Night Above, 1982, by Great Above	14	7	10	2	Death Trappe ($41,245)	131,267
Yankee Fan, 1984, by Our Native	17	8	18	1	Yankee Ruler ($40,969)	119,359

New Jersey

Sire, YOB, Sire	Strs	Wnrs	Wins	SWs	Leading Runner (Earnings)	Total Earnings
Private Interview, 1992, by Nureyev	53	23	36	0	John's Interview ($94,299)	$1,098,766
Northern Idol, 1986, by Northrop	35	20	32	5	Totally Precious ($155,620)	938,586
Evening Kris, 1985, by Kris S.	26	12	20	0	Cowboy Chili ($100,800)	597,876
Not For Love, 1990, by Mr. Prospector	16	11	16	0	Cuba ($78,220)	394,656
Stormy Atlantic, 1994, by Storm Cat	1	1	3	1	Gators N Bears ($357,910)	357,910

New Mexico

Sire, YOB, Sire	Strs	Wnrs	Wins	SWs	Leading Runner (Earnings)	Total Earnings
Prospector Jones, 1992, by Mr. Prospector	58	27	51	3	Hat Creek ($157,804)	$1,040,993
Devon Lane, 1993, by Storm Cat	44	23	36	2	Scarzane ($119,104)	816,158
In Excessive Bull, 1994, by In Excess (Ire)	60	33	46	2	Leon's Bull ($101,714)	717,403
Ghostly Moves, 1992, by Silver Ghost	29	8	18	1	Shemoveslikeaghost ($174,774)	638,023
Jack Wilson, 1988, by Encino	24	14	22	1	Ninety Nine Jack ($173,821)	477,974

New York

Sire, YOB, Sire	Strs	Wnrs	Wins	SWs	Leading Runner (Earnings)	Total Earnings
Dixie Brass, 1989, by Dixieland Band	85	50	86	0	South Wing ($168,862)	$2,426,674
A. P Jet, 1989, by Fappiano	119	60	97	3	Travelator ($187,915)	2,339,737
Tomorrows Cat, 1995, by Storm Cat	95	43	67	2	West Virginia ($302,345)	2,053,655
Distorted Humor, 1993, by Forty Niner	13	7	17	4	Funny Cide ($1,075,100)	1,643,943
Distinctive Pro, 1979, by Mr. Prospector	83	40	71	0	Distinctive Kitten ($145,197)	1,494,072

North Carolina

Sire, YOB, Sire	Strs	Wnrs	Wins	SWs	Leading Runner (Earnings)	Total Earnings
Chelsey Cat, 1998, by Storm Cat	16	8	20	0	Chelsey's Bid ($51,000)	$203,011
Above Normal, 1985, by Great Above	15	5	7	0	Silks N Roses ($29,677)	91,906
Minister's Mark, 1997, by Deputy Minister	1	1	1	0	Rich Lady Anne ($35,074)	35,074
Dove Hunt, 1991, by Danzig	1	1	1	0	Chief's Spokesman ($26,000)	26,000
Quaker Ridge, 1996, by Forty Niner	1	1	2	0	Quakerism ($23,820)	23,820

North Dakota

Sire, YOB, Sire	Strs	Wnrs	Wins	SWs	Leading Runner (Earnings)	Total Earnings
Patriot Strike, 1989, by General Assembly	4	2	4	1	Strike an Image ($41,872)	$56,280
Aferd, 1976, by Hoist the Flag	6	5	8	2	Maddies Blues ($14,530)	38,037
Dixieland Heat, 1990, by Dixieland Band	1	1	2	1	Dakota Dixie ($32,626)	32,626
Capitalimprovement, 1989, by Dixieland Band	1	1	2	1	Northrnimprovement ($28,520)	28,520
Northern Prospect, 1976, by Mr. Prospector	1	1	2	0	Northern Ace ($19,562)	19,562

Ohio

Sire, YOB, Sire	Strs	Wnrs	Wins	SWs	Leading Runner (Earnings)	Total Earnings
Mercer Mill, 1994, by Forty Niner	43	23	31	1	Mercer's Launch ($77,680)	$373,594
Stalwars, 1985, by Stalwart	34	17	32	0	Joann's Joy ($37,283)	314,817
Noble Cat, 1995, by Storm Cat	22	4	12	1	Fierce Cat ($80,000)	251,298
Flight Forty Nine, 1991, by Forty Niner	29	13	24	0	Wirebender ($38,758)	248,119
Our Emblem, 1991, by Mr. Prospector	2	2	7	2	Anna Em ($176,286)	247,536

Oklahoma

Sire, YOB, Sire	Strs	Wnrs	Wins	SWs	Leading Runner (Earnings)	Total Earnings
Here We Come, 1988, by Mr. Prospector	67	31	58	2	George Taylor ($93,883)	$663,274
Slewacide, 1980, by Seattle Slew	43	22	43	2	Cheyenne Breeze ($134,204)	583,826
Muldoon, 1995, by Kingmambo	33	17	25	0	La Brieanna ($47,465)	222,238
Notable Cat, 1995, by Storm Cat	37	18	26	1	Sooner Pride ($45,305)	217,948
Harriman, 1984, by Lord Gaylord	25	10	16	1	Dusty Spike ($58,490)	204,264

Oregon

Sire, YOB, Sire	Strs	Wnrs	Wins	SWs	Leading Runner (Earnings)	Total Earnings
Baquero, 1995, by Forty Niner	43	22	28	5	Chiltepin ($24,660)	$202,916
Abstract, 1993, by Danzig	22	15	34	3	Moonlit Maddie ($36,266)	182,899
Corslew, 1990, by Seattle Slew	5	4	11	2	Lethal Grande ($111,367)	157,906
Cisco Road, 1990, by Northern Baby	29	18	29	1	Ransome Road ($16,248)	113,304
Gold Meridian, 1982, by Seattle Slew	36	14	27	0	B J's Black Gold ($13,912)	88,313

Pennsylvania

Sire, YOB, Sire	Strs	Wnrs	Wins	SWs	Leading Runner (Earnings)	Total Earnings
Elusive Quality, 1993, by Gone West	5	2	7	1	Smarty Jones ($7,563,535)	$7,592,015
Not For Love, 1990, by Mr. Prospector	35	20	49	3	Presidentialaffair ($285,040)	1,240,206
Roanoke, 1987, by Pleasant Colony	67	35	64	0	Sunshine Johanne ($83,217)	927,322
Allen's Prospect, 1982, by Mr. Prospector	31	20	35	0	Gold Dancer ($92,980)	582,116
French Deputy, 1992, by Deputy Minister	4	3	6	0	Nobo Jack ($219,914)	458,275

South Carolina

Sire, YOB, Sire	Strs	Wnrs	Wins	SWs	Leading Runner (Earnings)	Total Earnings
Kokand, 1985, by Mr. Prospector	40	18	33	0	Fooler ($83,580)	$449,655
Ride the Storm, 1994, by Storm Cat	4	2	8	1	Intelligent Male ($176,984)	207,312
Miner, 1993, by Forty Niner	14	8	13	0	American Prince ($28,630)	152,171
Valiant Lark, 1980, by Buffalo Lark	3	1	4	0	Fully Packed ($77,299)	87,934
Signal, 1993, by Forty Niner	6	3	3	0	Niner's Echo ($37,559)	83,036

South Dakota

Sire, YOB, Sire	Strs	Wnrs	Wins	SWs	Leading Runner (Earnings)	Total Earnings
Get Me Out, 1996, by Capote	6	3	3	1	Doddles ($19,530)	$38,000
Storm of the Night, 1993, by Storm Cat	3	2	3	0	My Pink Panther ($9,392)	20,901
Pioneering, 1993, by Mr. Prospector	1	1	1	0	Platinum Sky ($19,250)	19,250
Mr. O. P., 1986, by Naskra	12	3	3	0	Senor Mas ($4,460)	17,137
Crowning Season (GB), 1990, by Danzig	1	1	1	0	Hitchinpost Louie ($11,286)	11,286

Tennessee

Sire, YOB, Sire	Strs	Wnrs	Wins	SWs	Leading Runner (Earnings)	Total Earnings
Evansville Slew, 1992, by Slew City Slew	1	1	1	0	Valieo ($43,670)	$43,670
Out of Place, 1987, by Cox's Ridge	1	1	3	0	Tennessee Tuxedo ($43,499)	43,499
Smilin Singin Sam, 1991, by Smile	5	2	2	0	Sister Strut ($24,157)	42,817
Mr. Beasley, 1993, by Farma Way	3	2	2	0	Stormin ($22,443)	29,727
Rockamundo, 1990, by Key to the Mint	1	1	2	0	Bin Rockin' ($24,555)	24,555

Texas

Sire, YOB, Sire	Strs	Wnrs	Wins	SWs	Leading Runner (Earnings)	Total Earnings
Valid Expectations, 1993, by Valid Appeal	66	41	83	6	Leaving On My Mind ($299,873)	$1,766,891
Hadif, 1986, by Clever Trick	86	56	95	1	Fleeta Dif ($100,000)	1,016,557
Marked Tree, 1990, by Forty Niner	74	36	65	0	Timber ($48,135)	703,809
Sunny's Halo, 1980, by Halo	70	26	47	1	Charming Socialite ($152,210)	624,504
Seneca Jones, 1990, by Alydar	34	21	39	1	Seneca Summer ($64,240)	510,049

Utah

Sire, YOB, Sire	Strs	Wnrs	Wins	SWs	Leading Runner (Earnings)	Total Earnings
Four Seasons (GB), 1990, by Sadler's Wells	16	5	10	0	Seasons Promise ($23,630)	$126,526
Tinners Way, 1990, by Secretariat	1	1	2	0	Ten Forty Easy ($30,880)	30,880
Regal Groom, 1987, by Runaway Groom	1	1	3	0	Lovehermadly ($17,640)	17,640
Isnad, 1986, by Topsider	3	2	4	0	Is a Gay Time ($8,750)	16,115
Bustopher Jones, 1996, by Storm Cat	5	2	4	1	Bus Express ($10,322)	15,856

Virginia

Sire, YOB, Sire	Strs	Wnrs	Wins	SWs	Leading Runner (Earnings)	Total Earnings
Secret Hello, 1987, by Private Account	23	12	27	2	Standard Bearer ($88,813)	$444,031
Ball's Bluff, 1991, by Cox's Ridge	8	7	14	1	Bluffie Slew ($107,810)	373,328
Summer Squall, 1987, by Storm Bird	2	2	4	1	Misty Sixes ($246,074)	281,586
Stormin Fever, 1994, by Storm Cat	11	5	10	0	After the Tone ($112,507)	265,590
Thunder Rumble, 1989, by Thunder Puddles	16	6	9	0	Arctic Rumble ($46,680)	252,692

Washington

Sire, YOB, Sire	Strs	Wnrs	Wins	SWs	Leading Runner (Earnings)	Total Earnings
Slewdledo, 1981, by Seattle Slew	130	75	119	4	Carla Rose ($85,800)	$1,450,393
Demons Begone, 1984, by Elocutionist	57	32	60	1	Demon Warlock ($192,990)	688,323
Game Plan, 1993, by Danzig	57	34	61	1	Melanyhasthepapers ($56,820)	651,877
Basket Weave, 1981, by Best Turn	82	47	80	3	Arco Iris ($45,421)	645,275
Petersburg, 1986, by Danzig	42	23	38	2	Court's in Session ($134,485)	514,239

West Virginia

Sire, YOB, Sire	Strs	Wnrs	Wins	SWs	Leading Runner (Earnings)	Total Earnings
Weshaam, 1983, by Fappiano	35	16	29	3	Miss Roberson ($102,658)	$874,158
My Boy Adam, 1987, by Encino	54	18	26	1	Fancy Buckles ($108,820)	809,860
Feel the Power, 1982, by Raise a Native	24	10	17	1	Earth Power ($121,830)	466,103
Native Slew, 1985, by Raise a Native	18	5	10	1	Do No Wrong ($42,820)	220,079
Oh Say, 1978, by Hoist the Flag	6	4	5	0	Tienneman Square ($118,501)	197,183

Wisconsin

Sire, YOB, Sire	Strs	Wnrs	Wins	SWs	Leading Runner (Earnings)	Total Earnings
Armed Truce, 1981, by Bold Forbes	4	2	4	0	Awtair ($22,215)	$32,001
Bold James, 1984, by Bold Reason	1	1	1	0	Jami Pari ($5,429)	5,429

Puerto Rico

Sire, YOB, Sire	Strs	Wnrs	Wins	SWs	Leading Runner (Earnings)	Total Earnings
Royal Merlot, 1993, by Forty Niner	29	25	59	3	Hispanica ($157,720)	$732,847
Fappiano's Star, 1988, by Fappiano	42	29	61	0	Little Franky Boy ($82,522)	631,032
Eqtesaad, 1991, by Danzig	38	31	56	0	Estrellero ($48,788)	488,683
Sejm, 1987, by Danzig	32	20	44	0	El Incondicional ($44,930)	423,787
Cagey Bidder, 1991, by Seeking the Gold	23	15	43	1	Bancada ($62,434)	370,640

Alberta

Sire, YOB, Sire	Strs	Wnrs	Wins	SWs	Leading Runner (Earnings)	Total Earnings
Regal Remark, 1982, by Vice Regent	59	37	67	2	The Cashew Queen ($57,162)	$772,198
Weekend Guest, 1987, by Mr. Prospector	57	32	59	6	Kellys Guest ($71,890)	760,042
Brass Minister, 1988, by Deputy Minister	40	15	31	1	A Shaky Start ($154,356)	507,552
Pole Position, 1976, by Draft Card	27	16	24	1	Curious Gamble ($42,474)	379,325
Chapel Creek, 1978, by Our Native	37	16	27	0	Sweet Creek ($76,378)	353,545

British Columbia

Sire, YOB, Sire	Strs	Wnrs	Wins	SWs	Leading Runner (Earnings)	Total Earnings
Vying Victor, 1989, by Flying Paster	92	45	74	4	Alabama Rain ($136,784)	$1,457,001
Katahaula County, 1988, by Bold Ruckus	59	31	47	3	Socorro County ($146,249)	976,672
Regal Intention, 1985, by Vice Regent	61	34	55	0	My Miss Emily ($105,087)	851,378
On Target, 1992, by Forty Niner	57	29	55	3	Regal Red ($140,313)	821,514
Alfaari, 1989, by Danzig	50	22	37	0	Sonofawac ($52,450)	611,265

Manitoba

Sire, YOB, Sire	Strs	Wnrs	Wins	SWs	Leading Runner (Earnings)	Total Earnings
His Excellence, 1993, by El Gran Senor	22	12	20	1	Your Excellence ($65,654)	$183,754
Buie, 1990, by Fappiano	14	8	11	1	Stonewall Harris ($44,091)	147,404
Circulating, 1990, by Bold Ruckus	22	12	12	1	Danger Pay ($34,992)	123,046
Langfuhr, 1992, by Danzig	2	2	2	0	Albarino ($72,108)	90,708
Act Smart, 1992, by Smarten	10	4	6	1	Coal Smudge ($53,291)	81,900

Ontario

Sire, YOB, Sire	Strs	Wnrs	Wins	SWs	Leading Runner (Earnings)	Total Earnings
Smart Strike, 1992, by Mr. Prospector	23	16	33	3	Soaring Free ($1,113,862)	$3,221,216
Bold Executive, 1984, by Bold Ruckus	85	44	81	4	Blonde Executive ($414,263)	2,748,142
Whiskey Wisdom, 1993, by Wild Again	67	35	56	4	Moonshine Justice ($283,914)	2,547,144
Archers Bay, 1995, by Silver Deputy	51	27	40	2	Archers Bow ($198,145)	1,863,829
Kiridashi, 1992, by Bold Ruckus	66	34	54	3	Financingavailable ($294,151)	1,814,841

Quebec

Sire, YOB, Sire	Strs	Wnrs	Wins	SWs	Leading Runner (Earnings)	Total Earnings
Kiridashi, 1992, by Bold Ruckus	2	1	5	0	Brigadoon ($44,209)	$76,779
Accelerator, 1994, by A.P. Indy	1	1	1	0	Castle Prospect ($64,213)	64,213
Western Gentleman, 1990, by Gone West	1	1	2	0	Sterling Prospect ($39,110)	39,110
Favorite Trick, 1995, by Phone Trick	2	2	4	0	Sungold Beauty ($31,980)	38,910
Oakmont, 1991, by Alydar	3	2	2	0	Diablesse ($28,695)	36,467

Saskatchewan

Sire, YOB, Sire	Strs	Wnrs	Wins	SWs	Leading Runner (Earnings)	Total Earnings
Royal Quiz, 1984, by Real Emperor	16	6	10	4	Bleu Royale ($15,140)	$73,635
Pole Position, 1976, by Draft Card	8	2	5	0	Spirit to Spare ($50,938)	72,893
Shaheen, 1994, by Danzig	18	9	13	3	Danzig Ballerina ($11,388)	62,119
Stop the Stage, 1985, by Gold Stage	10	6	9	0	Megan's Way ($12,260)	54,734
Clash of Steel, 1985, by Deputy Minister	8	6	14	1	Steel Copy ($12,046)	40,202

Stallion Syndications

In part because the definition of stallion syndication has changed over the decades, pinpointing the first syndication contract is difficult, if not impossible. However, the earliest syndication agreement comparable in form and intent to modern syndicates was that of Tracery in 1923. That agreement between the syndicators, the International Horse Agency and Exchange and a group of 30 subscribers, placed a value of $219,840 on the 1912 St. Leger winner, who was the sire of '23 Epsom Derby victor *Papyrus.

The principle behind that syndicate and all subsequent ones was to spread the risk of purchasing a very expensive breeding horse (and, in Tracery's case, returning him from Argentina). From the beginning of the Thoroughbred breeding industry in the late 17th century right up to the 20th century, Thoroughbred breeding was essentially a private affair, with rich aristocrats wholly owning stallions and breeding mostly their own mares to those sires.

As Thoroughbred breeding slowly became more commercial in the late 19th and early 20th centuries, a new method of financing was required, both to spread the risk of failure and to ensure that a stallion received an appropriate number and quality of mares. Syndication was the answer. In Tracery's case, spreading the risk was a wise strategy because the stallion died after only one season at stud in England.

In a modern syndicate agreement, individuals agree to purchase a specific percentage of ownership in a stallion—the percentage ownership is determined by the number of shares—with payment for that percentage interest usually spread in installments over several years. In return, the buyer of a syndicate share gains the right to breed one or more mares to that stallion each year without additional payments (except for agreed maintenance fees). The syndicate manager normally receives a specified number of free nominations each year as compensation.

The similarity to buying stock market shares is evident. The syndicate manager receives capital to pay for a major capital asset, and shareholders gain the possibility of dividends from the share through sale of the nomination or value of the produce. Shares also may be sold later to other investors at a profit (or loss), just as in the stock market, although syndication agreements may place restrictions on the transfer of the shares.

Although the first clearly identifiable syndicate was English, Americans soon became active syndicators. Arthur B. Hancock of Claiborne Farm formed a four-man partnership in 1926 to purchase the high-class French miler *Sir Gallahad III for $125,000. When *Sir Gallahad III sired Triple Crown winner Gallant Fox in his

Chronology of Record Stallion Syndications

Stallion	Year	Price	Farm	Seller	Share Price	No. Shares
Fusaichi Pegasus	2000	†$60,000,000	Ashford Stud (Ky.)	Fusao Sekiguchi	$1,500,000	40
Lammtarra	1996	42,000,000	Arrow Stud (Jpn)	Dalham Hall Stud	1,050,000	40
Shareef Dancer	1983	40,000,000	Dalham Hall Stud (Eng)	Aston Upthorpe Stud	1,000,000	40
Conquistador Cielo	1982	36,400,000	Claiborne Farm (Ky.)	Henryk de Kwiatkowski (retained 10 shares)	910,000	40
Storm Bird	1981	30,000,000	Ashford Stud (Ky.)	Robert Sangster, et al.	750,000	40
Spectacular Bid	1980	22,000,000	Claiborne Farm (Ky.)	Hawksworth Farm (retained 20 shares)	550,000	40
Troy	1979	16,500,000	Highclere Stud (Eng)	Sir Michael Sobell and Arnold Weinstock	412,500	40
Alleged	1978	16,000,000	Walmac-Warnerton Int.'l. (Ky.)	Robert Sangster, et al.	400,000	40
Seattle Slew	1978	12,000,000	Spendthrift Farm (Ky.)	Wooden Horse Investments (retained 20 shares)	300,000	40
The Minstrel	1977	9,000,000	Windfields Farm (Md.)	Robert Sangster, et al.	250,000	36
What a Pleasure	1976	8,000,000	Waldemar Farm (Ky.)	Waldemar (retained 16 shares)	250,000	32
Wajima	1975	7,200,000	Spendthrift Farm (Ky.)	East-West Stable (retained 20 shares)	200,000	36
Secretariat	1973	6,080,000	Claiborne Farm (Ky.)	Meadow Stable	190,000	32
Nijinsky II	1970	5,440,000	Claiborne Farm (Ky.)	Charles W. Englehard (retained 10 shares)	170,000	32
*Vaguely Noble	1969	5,000,000	Gainesway (Ky.)	Nelson Bunker Hunt and Dr. Robert Franklyn	125,000	40
Buckpasser	1967	4,800,000	Claiborne Farm (Ky.)	Ogden Phipps (retained 16 shares)	150,000	32
Raise a Native	1967	2,625,000	Spendthrift Farm (Ky.)	Louis Wolfson and Leslie Combs	75,000	35
Graustark	1966	2,400,000	Darby Dan Farm (Ky.)	John W. Galbreath	60,000	40
Tom Fool	1960	1,750,000	Greentree Stud (Ky.)	Greentree Stud	50,000	35
Nashua	1955	1,251,200	Spendthrift Farm (Ky.)	Estate of William Woodward Jr.	39,200	32
*Tulyar	1952	697,500	Irish National Stud (Ire)	H. H. Aga Khan	17,438	40
The Phoenix	1948	619,920	Ballykisteen Stud (Ire)	Fred Myerscough	15,498	40
*Alibhai	1948	500,000	Spendthrift Farm (Ky.)	Louis B. Mayer	16,667	30
Stardust	1945	451,360	Gilltown Stud (Ire)	H. H. Aga Khan	11,284	40
Tehran	1945	403,000	Barton Stud (Eng)	Prince Aly Khan	10,075	40
*Blenheim II	1936	240,000	Claiborne Farm (Ky.)	H. H. Aga Khan	30,000	8
Tracery	1923	219,400	Cobham Stud (Eng)	Senor Unzue	5,485	40

†Estimated value

first crop, making him leading sire for the first of four times, the syndication process gained impetus in America. In 1936, Hancock syndicated another leading sire, *Blenheim II, for a record price, $240,000. In his first crop, *Blenheim II sired Triple Crown winner Whirlaway.

The record returned to England in 1945 when the good young sires Stardust and Tehran were syndicated in rapid succession, but the record price returned to America in '48 when Leslie Combs II purchased *Alibhai from Louis B. Mayer as a replacement for Combs's first syndicated horse, *Beau Pere, who died before covering a mare.

Combs also syndicated Nashua, the first $1-

million stallion, as a four-year-old in 1956. The record price remained in America until 1983 (except for a brief period in '79) when Sheikh Mohammed bin Rashid al Maktoum syndicated his Irish Derby (Ire-G1) winner, Shareef Dancer, for a reported $40-million.

That reported price signifies one of the problems with modern syndications. With values soaring to astronomical figures, stallion managers now often decline to publish the exact price per share or contract terms. Thus, the $60-million to $70-million figure for current record holder Fusaichi Pegasus is based on approximate figures released by the syndicate manager and private communications from syndicate members.

Most Expensive North American Stallion Syndications

Stallion	Year	Price	Farm	Seller	Share Price	No. Shares
Fusaichi Pegasus	2000	$60,000,000	Ashford Stud (Ky.)	Fusao Sekiguchi	†$1,500,000	40
Point Given	2001	50,000,000	Three Chimneys Farm (Ky.)	The Thoroughbred Corp.	1,000,000	50
Smarty Jones	2004	39,000,000	Three Chimneys Farm (Ky.)	Someday Farm	650,000	60
Conquistador Cielo	1982	36,400,000	Claiborne Farm (Ky.)	Henryk de Kwiatkowski	910,000	40
Devil's Bag	1983	36,000,000	Claiborne Farm (Ky.)	Hickory Tree Farm	900,000	40
Halo	1984	36,000,000	Stone Farm (Ky.)	Windfields Farm	900,000	40
Storm Bird	1981	30,000,000	Ashford Stud (Ky.)	Robert Sangster, et al.	750,000	40
Lemon Drop Kid	2000	30,000,000	Lane's End (Ky.)	Jeanne Vance	750,000	40
Assert (Ire)	1982	25,000,000	Windfields Farm (Md.)	Robert Sangster	625,000	40
Cigar	1996	25,000,000	Ashford Stud (Ky.)	Allen Paulson	500,000	50
Spectacular Bid	1980	22,000,000	Claiborne Farm (Ky.)	Hawksworth Farm	550,000	40
Mr. Prospector	1980	20,000,000	Claiborne Farm (Ky.)	Aisco Farm	500,000	40
Chief's Crown	1984	20,000,000	Three Chimneys Farm (Ky.)	Star Crown Stable	500,000	40
Secreto	1984	20,000,000	Calumet Farm (Ky.)	Luigi Miglietti	500,000	40
Unbridled	1996	19,000,000	Claiborne Farm (Ky.)	Frances A. Genter	475,000	40
Aloma's Ruler	1982	18,880,000	Mare Haven Farm (Ky.)	Nathan Scherr	472,000	40
Riverman	1979	18,000,000	Gainesway (Ky.)	Haras du Quesnay	450,000	40
Skip Away	1998	18,000,000	Hopewell Farm (Ky.)	Carolyn Hine	400,000	45
Alleged	1978	16,000,000	Walmac-Warnerton Int'l. (Ky.)	Robert Sangster, et al.	400,000	40
Saratoga Six	1984	16,000,000	North Ridge Farm (Ky.)	Eugene Klein, et al.	400,000	40
A P Valentine	2000	16,000,000	Ashford Stud (Ky.)	Celtic Pride Stable	N/A	N/A
Exceller	1979	15,000,000	Gainesway (Ky.)	Nelson Bunker Hunt	375,000	40
Northjet	1981	15,000,000	Airdrie Stud (Ky.)	Serge Fradkoff	375,000	40
Coronado's Quest	1998	15,000,000	Claiborne Farm (Ky.)	Stuart Janney and Stonerside Stable	300,000	50
Affirmed	1979	14,400,000	Spendthrift Farm (Ky.)	Harbor View Farm	400,000	36
Shahrastani	1986	14,400,000	Three Chimneys Farm (Ky.)	H. H. Aga Khan	400,000	36
Nureyev	1981	14,200,000	Walmac-Warnerton Int.'l. (Ky.)	Stavros Niarchos	355,000	40
Risen Star	1988	14,000,000	Walmac Int.'l. (Ky.)	Louis Roussell III and Ronnie Lamarque	350,000	40
Desert Wine	1984	13,000,000	Cardiff Stud Farms (Ca.)	Cardiff Stud Farms and T90 Ranch	325,000	40
L'Emigrant	1983	13,000,000	Gainesway (Ky.)	Stavros Niarchos	325,000	40
Seattle Slew	1978	12,000,000	Spendthrift Farm (Ky.)	Wooden Horse Investments	300,000	40
Fappiano	1981	12,000,000	Tartan Farms (Fl.)	John Nerud	300,000	40
Flying Paster	1981	12,000,000	Cardiff Stud Farms (Ca.)	B. J. Ridder	300,000	40
Pleasant Colony	1981	12,000,000	Buckland Farm (Ky.)	Thomas M. Evans	300,000	40
Bering (GB)	1986	12,000,000	Walmac Int.'l. (Ky.)	Alec Head	300,000	40
Aldebaran	2002	12,000,000	Darby Dan Farm (Ky.)	Niarchos Family	300,000	40
Tale of the Cat	1998	11,600,000	Ashford Stud (Ky.)	Phantom House Stable	290,000	40
Noble Nashua	1981	11,000,000	Schoenborn Brothers Farm (N.Y.)	Flying Zee Stable	275,000	40
Cure the Blues	1986	11,000,000	Pillar Stud (Ky.)	Gilltown Stud	275,000	40
General Assembly	1986	11,000,000	Pillar Stud (Ky.)	Gilltown Stud	275,000	40
Cresta Rider	1981	10,000,000	Gainesway (Ky.)	Stavros Niarchos	250,000	40
Lord Avie	1981	10,000,000	Lane's End (Ky.)	SKS Stable	250,000	40
Master Willie	1981	10,000,000	Windfields Farm (Md.)	William Barnett	250,000	40
A.P. Indy	1992	10,000,000	Lane's End (Ky.)	Tomonoru Tsurumaki	250,000	40
Kingmambo	1993	10,000,000	Lane's End (Ky.)	Niarchos Family	250,000	40
Lure	1994	10,000,000	Claiborne Farm (Ky.)	Claiborne Farm and Nicole Perry Gorman	250,000	40
Grand Slam	1998	10,000,000	Ashford Stud (Ky.)	Baker, Cornstein, and Mack	250,000	40
War Chant	2000	10,000,000	Three Chimneys Farm (Ky.)	Irving Cowan	200,000	50
Slew o' Gold	1983	9,600,000	Three Chimneys Farm (Ky.)	Equusequity Stable	240,000	40
The Minstrel	1977	9,000,000	Windfields Farm (Md.)	Robert Sangster, et al.	250,000	36

†Estimated value

Leading Stud Farms of 2004

Minimum of 20 starters in 2004, worldwide earnings. Includes all active stallions at each farm in 2004 and deceased or pensioned stallions that last stood at those farms. Order is based on stallion progeny earnings, average earnings per starter, percentage of stakes winners from starters, and percentage of graded stakes winners from starters. Each category is assigned equal weight.

Rank	Farm (State)	Stallion Earnings	Avg. Earnings	SWs/Strs	GSWs/Strs
1	Overbrook Farm (Ky.)	$31,082,948	$35,810	6.45%	2.65%
2	Adena Springs Kentucky (Ky.)	30,839,956	38,792	5.28%	2.39%
3	Lane's End (Ky.)	73,285,326	32,086	5.47%	1.75%
4	Taylor Made Farm (Ky.)	24,349,222	32,684	5.10%	2.28%
5	WinStar Farm (Ky.)	15,017,196	35,169	7.96%	1.87%
6	Claiborne Farm (Ky.)	33,069,871	26,060	3.70%	1.65%
	Three Chimneys Farm (Ky.)	21,685,403	25,971	4.43%	1.56%
8	Ashford Stud (Ky.)	58,665,979	23,106	3.82%	1.50%
9	Gainsborough Farm (Ky.)	15,257,984	47,385	3.42%	0.93%
10	Mill Ridge Farm (Ky.)	9,108,845	29,671	3.58%	1.95%
11	Northview Stallion Station (Md.)	16,698,014	22,968	4.40%	0.83%
12	Brookdale Farm (Ky.)	21,868,968	26,540	3.28%	0.85%
13	Hill 'n' Dale Farms (Ky.)	20,667,154	20,771	3.42%	1.51%
14	Walmac Farm (Ky.)	13,034,662	20,303	4.21%	1.40%
15	Rancho San Miguel (Ca.)	12,007,896	18,675	4.51%	1.71%
	Gainesway (Ky.)	30,080,415	22,398	3.35%	0.89%
17	Vessels Stallion Farm (Ca.)	5,722,040	28,468	4.48%	1.00%
18	Airdrie Stud (Ky.)	16,638,028	21,721	3.13%	0.78%
19	Pin Oak Stud (Ky.)	10,891,107	21,439	2.76%	0.98%
20	O'Sullivan Farms (W.V.)	9,493,559	24,659	2.86%	0.78%
21	Crestwood Farm (Ky.)	9,557,715	22,489	3.29%	0.71%
	Ocala Stud Farm (Fl.)	14,246,571	17,831	4.26%	0.63%
23	Gardiner Farms Ltd. (On.)	4,942,183	23,991	3.88%	0.97%
24	Darley (Ky.)	8,662,277	22,736	2.62%	1.31%
25	Lane's End Texas (Tx.)	8,964,884	19,574	3.93%	0.66%
26	McMahon of Saratoga (N.Y.)	12,523,820	18,975	2.27%	1.06%
27	Vinery Kentucky (Ky.)	10,723,192	17,102	3.67%	0.48%
28	Bridlewood Farm (Fl.)	7,240,292	22,912	2.53%	0.63%
29	Hopewell Farm (Ky.)	7,956,015	20,505	3.09%	0.52%
30	Juddmonte Farms (Ky.)	5,419,430	23,563	3.04%	0.43%
31	Creston Farms (Ky.)	3,924,741	19,239	3.43%	0.98%
32	Golden Eagle Farm (Ca.)	7,939,630	21,229	2.41%	0.53%
	Windfields Farm (On.)	8,534,253	24,108	2.54%	0.28%
34	Margaux Farm (Ky.)	8,877,243	19,425	2.63%	0.44%
35	Metropolitan Stud (N.Y.)	12,723,077	21,347	1.68%	0.34%
36	Magali Farms (Ca.)	4,862,009	20,689	2.55%	0.43%
	River Edge Farm (Ca.)	4,735,107	19,730	2.92%	0.42%
38	Darby Dan Farm (Ky.)	8,264,481	18,406	2.23%	0.45%
39	Stone Farm (Ky.)	4,428,884	18,301	3.31%	0.41%
	Wafare Farm (Ky.)	9,194,468	13,744	2.39%	0.60%
41	Walnford Stud (N.J.)	5,522,756	24,990	2.26%	0.00%
42	Spendthrift Farm (Ky.)	10,314,109	16,663	2.10%	0.32%
43	Murmur Farm (Md.)	7,214,979	15,063	2.30%	0.63%
	Country Life Farm (Md.)	6,837,656	17,947	2.62%	0.26%
45	Clear Creek Stud (La.)	9,645,080	16,572	2.06%	0.34%
46	Rockin' River Ranch (Ia.)	7,278,240	15,891	1.75%	0.87%
47	Harris Farms (Ca.)	8,549,782	17,272	2.22%	0.20%
	Millennium Farms (Ky.)	4,577,923	18,385	2.41%	0.40%
49	Farnsworth Farms (Fl.)	10,541,618	16,975	2.09%	0.00%
	Stonehedge Farm South (Fl.)	4,091,345	19,765	1.93%	0.48%
	Pin Oak Lane Farm (Pa.)	10,265,289	17,638	1.89%	0.17%
52	Buck Pond Farm (Ky.)	6,182,567	16,710	2.70%	0.00%
53	Sugar Maple Farm (N.Y.)	7,097,373	19,498	2.20%	0.00%
54	Reigle Heir Farms (Pa.)	10,865,008	15,724	1.59%	0.29%
55	Elite Thoroughbreds (La.)	4,864,014	16,322	2.35%	0.34%
56	Red River Farms (La.)	8,938,526	12,380	2.08%	0.14%
57	Valor Farm (Tx.)	4,818,723	13,311	2.49%	0.28%
58	Hidden Point Farm (Fl.)	6,168,358	16,493	1.87%	0.00%
59	El Dorado Farms (Wa.)	3,316,418	9,959	2.70%	0.30%
60	Oklahoma Equine (Ok.)	3,325,960	15,257	1.83%	0.46%
	Milfer Farm (N.Y.)	5,689,250	16,587	2.04%	0.00%
62	Blooming Hills Farm (Ca.)	4,342,954	12,516	1.44%	0.58%
63	Payson Stud (Ky.)	3,013,318	13,951	1.85%	0.46%
64	Fleming Thoroughbred Farm (Az.)	2,408,719	11,525	3.83%	0.00%
65	Rising Hill Farm (Fl.)	5,893,999	14,168	1.92%	0.00%
	Hideaway Farms (Ca.)	4,772,759	10,220	1.93%	0.21%

Leading Stud Farms of 2004

OVERBROOK FARM—Location: Lexington. Founded: 1972. Principals: Bill Young and Lucy Young Hamilton. Acreage: 2,400. Stallions for 2005: Cape Canaveral, Cape Town, Cat Thief, Grindstone, Jump Start, Pioneering, Storm Cat, Tactical Cat. Graded or group stakes winners in 2004 by Overbrook stallions: Birdstone, Consolidator, Good Reward, Storm Flag Flying, Sweet Catomine.

ADENA SPRINGS KENTUCKY—Location: Versailles, Kentucky. Founded: 1989. Principal: Frank Stronach. Acreage: 1,800. Stallions for 2005: Alphabet Soup, Awesome Again, Congaree, El Prado (Ire), Gold Case, Golden Missile, Milwaukee Brew, Olmodavor, Sligo Bay (Ire), Touch Gold. Graded or group stakes winners of 2004 by Adena Springs Kentucky stallions: Alphabet Kisses, Ghostzapper, Kitten's Joy, Medaglia d'Oro, Midas Eyes, Our New Recruit, Wilko.

LANE'S END—Location: Versailles, Kentucky. Founded: 1979. Principals: Mr. and Mrs. William S. Farish. Acreage: 3,000. Stallions for 2005: A.P. Indy, Belong to Me, Came Home, City Zip, Dixieland Band, Dixie Union, Fit to Fight, Gulch, King Kugat, Kingmambo, Langfuhr, Lemon Drop Kid, Mineshaft, Pine Bluff, Pleasantly Perfect, Pleasant Tap, Silver Ghost, Smart Strike, Stephen Got Even. Graded or group stakes winners of 2004 by Lane's End stallions: A. P. Adventure, Divine Proportions, Eye of the Sphynx, Friends Lake, King Mamehameha, Menhoubah, Pt's Grey Eagle, Rule of Law, Russian Rhythm, Soaring Free, The Cliff's Edge.

TAYLOR MADE FARM—Location: Nicholasville, Kentucky. Founded: 1976. Principals: Duncan, Ben, Frank, and Mark Taylor: Acreage: 1,600. Stallions for 2005: Forestry, Northern Afleet, Our Emblem, Real Quiet, Unbridled's Song. Graded or group stakes winner of 2004 by Taylor Made stallions: Friendly Michele, Splendid Blended.

WINSTAR FARM—Location: Versailles, Kentucky. Founded: 2000. Principals: Bill Casner and Kenny Troutt. Acreage: 1,450. Stallions for 2005: Distorted Humor, Speightstown, Tiznow, Victory Gallop. Graded or group stakes winners of 2004 by WinStar stallions: Funny Cide, Rinky Dink.

CLAIBORNE FARM—Location: Paris, Kentucky. Founded: 1910. President: Seth Hancock. Acreage: 2,764. Stallions for 2005: Arch, Boundary, During, Flatter, Horse Chestnut (SAf), Monarchos, Out of Place, Private Terms, Pulpit, Seeking the Gold, Stroll, Strong Hope. Graded or graded stakes winners of 2004 by Claiborne stallions: Ad Valorem, Lucifer's Stone, Pomeroy, Stroll, Tapit.

THREE CHIMNEYS FARM—Location: Midway, Kentucky. Founded: 1972. Principals: Mr. and Mrs. Robert N. Clay. Acreage: 1,700. Stallions for 2005: Albert the Great, Dynaformer, Point Given, Rahy, Sky Mesa, Smarty Jones, War Chant, Yes It's True. Graded or group stakes winners of 2004 by Three Chimneys stallions: Designed for Luck, Riskaverse.

ASHFORD STUD—Location: Versailles, Kentucky. Founded: 1984. Principals: John Magnier. Acreage: 2,000. Stallions for 2005: Black Minnaloushe, Chapel Royal, Fusaichi Pegasus, Giant's Causeway, Grand Slam, Hennessy, High Yield, Hold That Tiger, Honour and Glory, Johannesburg, Lion Heart, Monashee Mountain, Royal Academy, Stravinsky, Tale of the Cat, Thunder Gulch, Van Nistelrooy, Woodman. Graded stakes winners of 2004 by Ashford stallions: Durban Thunder, Lion Heart, Madcap Escapade, Marenostrum, Sense of Style, Shamardal.

GAINSBOROUGH FARM—Location: Versailles, Kentucky. Founded: 1984 Principal: Sheikh Maktoum bin Rashid al Maktoum. Acreage: 1,987. Stallions for 2005: Elusive Quality, Quiet American, Shadeed. Graded stakes winners of 2004 by Gainsborough stallions: Elusive Diva, Smarty Jones.

MILL RIDGE FARM—Location: Lexington. Founded: 1962. Principals: Alice Headley Chandler and Dr. John Chandler. Acreage: 1,050. Stallions for 2005: Diesis (GB), Gone West, Johar. Graded stakes winners of 2004 by Mill Ridge stallions: Magistretti, Speightstown.

WALMAC FARM—Location: Lexington. Founded: 1936. Principals: John T. L. Jones III and Robert Trussell. Acreage: 1,300. Stallions for 2005: Cactus Ridge, Eavesdropper, Gentlemen (Arg), Leelanau, Minardi, Salt Lake, Scatmandu, Sea of Secrets, Successful Appeal, Tenpins, Tumblebrutus, Zavata. Graded or group stakes winners in 2004 by Walmac stallions: Bachelor Duke, Salt Champ (Arg).

NORTHVIEW STALLION STATION—Location: Chesapeake City, Maryland. Founded: 1989. Principals: Richard Golden, Allaire duPont, and Tom Bowman. Acreage: 400. Stallions for 2005: Crowd Pleaser, Diamond, Domestic Dispute, Great Notion, Lion Hearted, Not For Love, Partner's Hero, Polish Miner, Two Punch, Waquoit.

BROOKDALE FARM—Location: Versailles, Kentucky. Founded: 1983. Principal: Fred Seitz. Acreage: 500. Stallions for 2005: Crafty Prospector, Forest Wildcat, Newfoundland, Silver Deputy, With Approval. Graded or group stakes winners in 2004 by Brookdale stallions: Var, Wildcat Heir, Lion Tamer.

HILL 'N' DALE FARMS—Location: Lexington. Founded: 1987. Principal: John G. Sikura. Acreage: 524. Stallions for 2005: Buddha, Candy Ride (Arg), Doneraile Court, El Corredor, Jade Hunter, Marquetry, Medaglia d'Oro, Mutakddim, Saarland, Stormy Atlantic, Theatrical (Ire), Vindication, Vision and Verse. Graded or group stakes winners in 2004 by Hill 'n' Dale stallions: Artemisa, Azeri, Lady Tak.

RANCHO SAN MIGUEL—Location: San Miguel, California. Founded: 1999. Principal: Tom Clark. Acreage: 250. Stallions for 2005: Corslew, Formal Gold, Marino Marini, Roar, Storm Creek. Graded or group stakes winners of 2004 by Rancho San Miguel stallions: Forty Doriana, Forty Fabuloso, Forty Greeta, Forty Marchanta, Forty Mirage.

GAINESWAY FARM—Location: Lexington. Founded: 1962. Principal: Graham Beck. Acreage: 1,500. Stallions for 2005: Birdstone, Cozzene, K One King, Luhuk, Mt. Livermore, Officer, Orientate, Sir Cat, Smoke Glacken, Subordination, Sunday Break (Jpn), Tapit, Ten Most Wanted. Graded stakes winners of 2004 by Gainesway stallions: Star Over the Bay, Rosa Miss, Zanzibar.

VESSELS STALLION FARM—Location: Bonsall, California. Founded: 1983. Principals: Frank "Scoop" Vessels III and Bonnie Vessels. Acreage: 450. Stallions for 2005: Apollo, In Excess (Ire), Jackpot, Momentum. Graded or group stakes winners in 2004 by Vessels Stallion Farm stallions: Musical Chimes.

Live Foal Report for 2004

Reflecting both increased optimism within the Thoroughbred industry and Kentucky's recovery from mare reproductive loss syndrome (MRLS), live foals of 2004 in North America rose to 39,835 as of the end of the year, the Jockey Club reported. That figure represented approximately 95% of live foal reports expected by the Jockey Club. At the same time a year earlier, 38,797 live foals had been reported for the 2003 crop, 2.7% below the 2004 live-foal crop.

Kentucky, recovering from the MRLS disaster that cut into the 2001 crop and reduced the '02 crop substantially, posted a 2004 live-foal crop of 14,476, up 10.7% from 13,076 live foals reported at the end of '03. The 2003 Kentucky crop in turn had been up 6.5% from the MRLS-depleted crop of 12,276 live foals in '02. With Kentucky's foal losses down considerably, the state's live-foal rate rose from 60% in 2002 to 72% in '04. Across North America, the live foal rate was 63%. Among states with large breeding industries, Kentucky returned to the top by live-foal rate; California, the 2003 leader, had a '04 rate of 69%, and Florida matched the overall average.

Kentucky's 2004 crop represented more than one-third of all live foals in North America, 36.3%. Florida had the second-largest foal crop, 4,229 foals, followed by California at 4,045, Texas at 1,835, New York at 1,703, Louisiana at 1,598, and Maryland at 1,081.

With a large number of mares bred to him and a high rate of live foals, Tale of the Cat led North America by 2004 live foals with 157. The Ashford Stud stallion had been bred to 192 mares in 2003 and had a live-foal rate of 82%. Two other Ashford stallions with large books ranked second and third. Grand Slam, bred to 197 mares, had 151 live foals (77%), and Johannesburg had 150 live foals from 192 breedings (78%). California-based Bertrando was bred to considerably fewer mares in 2003, 86 compared with 179 in 2002, but he maintained one of the highest live-foal figures, 92%. His live-foal rate in 2003 had been 88%. California-based Swiss Yodeler, with 115 live foals, was the leading sire of foals standing outside of Kentucky.

Leading Stallions by 2004 Foals

Stallion	Mares Bred	Live Foals	Live Foal Rate	State	Stallion	Mares Bred	Live Foals	Live Foal Rate	State
Tale of the Cat	192	157	82%	Ky.	High Yield	125	93	74%	Ky.
Grand Slam	197	151	77%	Ky.	Yes It's True	122	93	76%	Fl.
Johannesburg	192	150	78%	Ky.	Fusaichi Pegasus	114	92	81%	Ky.
Stormy Atlantic	189	146	77%	Ky.	Mizzen Mast	123	92	75%	Ky.
Buddha	164	141	86%	Ky.	Storm Cat	116	92	79%	Ky.
Distorted Humor	156	136	87%	Ky.	Tactical Cat	123	92	75%	Ky.
Mr. Greeley	164	125	76%	Ky.	Victory Gallop	142	92	65%	Ky.
Giant's Causeway	143	121	85%	Ky.	In Excess (Ire)	111	91	82%	Ca.
Orientate	141	120	85%	Ky.	Montbrook	117	90	77%	Fl.
El Corredor	160	116	73%	Ky.	Brahms	117	89	76%	Ky.
Swiss Yodeler	143	115	80%	Ca.	Chief Seattle	122	89	73%	Ky.
Langfuhr	144	114	79%	Ky.	Golden Missile	107	89	83%	Ky.
Mutakddim	163	113	69%	Ky.	Cherokee Run	131	88	67%	Ky.
Include	153	111	73%	Ky.	Exploit	119	88	74%	Ky.
Elusive Quality	143	110	77%	Ky.	Forest Wildcat	110	88	80%	Ky.
Honour and Glory	139	108	78%	Ky.	Officer	115	87	76%	Ky.
Royal Academy	141	106	75%	Ky.	Point Given	104	87	84%	Ky.
Stormin Fever	150	106	71%	Ky.	Stravinsky	131	87	66%	Ky.
Yonaguska	149	106	71%	Ky.	Belong to Me	109	86	79%	Ky.
Holy Bull	131	104	79%	Ky.	Dynaformer	104	86	83%	Ky.
Smart Strike	119	103	87%	Ky.	Stephen Got Even	107	85	79%	Ky.
Tiznow	132	103	78%	Ky.	Awesome Again	101	83	82%	Ky.
Chester House	126	102	81%	Ky.	Came Home	106	82	77%	Ky.
Sea of Secrets	142	102	72%	Ky.	Mazel Trick	103	82	80%	Ky.
Lemon Drop Kid	120	101	84%	Ky.	Gone West	100	81	81%	Ky.
Maria's Mon	121	101	83%	Ky.	More Than Ready	109	81	74%	Ky.
Aptitude	132	99	75%	Ky.	Valid Wager	104	81	78%	Ca.
Broken Vow	127	99	78%	Ky.	Jump Start	101	80	79%	Ky.
Thunder Gulch	130	99	76%	Ky.	Artax	122	79	65%	Ky.
Unbridled's Song	110	97	88%	Ky.	Bertrando	86	79	92%	Ca.
Catienus	117	96	82%	Ky.	Carson City	101	79	78%	Ky.
Touch Gold	117	96	82%	Ky.	Comic Strip	108	79	73%	Ca.
Dixie Union	122	94	77%	Ky.	Forestry	111	79	71%	Ky.
Forest Camp	128	94	73%	Ky.	Indian Charlie	121	79	65%	Ky.
Storm Boot	119	94	79%	Ky.	Pure Prize	104	79	76%	Ky.
Street Cry (Ire)	131	94	72%	Ky.	Gentlemen (Arg)	105	78	74%	Ky.
Deputy Commander	114	93	82%	Ky.	Gulch	97	78	80%	Ky.
Devil His Due	133	93	70%	Ky.	Kingmambo	97	78	80%	Ky.
					Monarchos	92	78	85%	Ky.

Live Foals by Stallions by State and Province in 2004

State	Stallions	Mares Bred	Live Foals	Live Foal Rate	State	Stallions	Mares Bred	Live Foals	Live Foal Rate
Alabama	23	121	58	48%	Ohio	108	667	343	51%
Alaska	1	2	1	50%	Oklahoma	211	1,607	814	51%
Arizona	65	656	338	52%	Oregon	53	435	274	63%
Arkansas	65	580	306	53%	Pennsylvania	115	1,042	574	55%
California	397	5,852	4,045	69%	Rhode Island	2	2	1	50%
Colorado	85	501	264	53%	South Carolina	24	150	51	34%
Delaware	1	1	1	100%	South Dakota	16	129	40	31%
Florida	257	6,709	4,229	63%	Tennessee	23	91	44	48%
Georgia	20	119	55	46%	Texas	395	3,252	1,835	56%
Idaho	53	295	151	51%	Utah	34	122	58	48%
Illinois	112	1,152	600	52%	Vermont	2	3	1	33%
Indiana	103	878	421	48%	Virginia	71	457	285	62%
Iowa	49	630	342	54%	Washington	99	1,080	603	56%
Kansas	32	196	84	43%	West Virginia	82	1,002	548	55%
Kentucky	380	20,185	14,476	72%	Wisconsin	15	58	22	38%
Louisiana	222	2,791	1,598	57%	Wyoming	14	33	13	39%
Maine	2	5	0	0%	Puerto Rico	70	756	530	70%
Maryland	92	1,695	1,081	64%	Virgin Islands	1	2	2	100%
Massachusetts	24	93	50	54%	Unknown	21	59	19	32%
Michigan	73	531	318	60%					
Minnesota	37	346	194	56%	**Canada Province**				
Mississippi	16	69	33	48%	Alberta	92	899	449	50%
Missouri	32	108	51	47%	British Columbia	65	772	452	59%
Montana	41	196	103	53%	Manitoba	22	213	82	38%
Nebraska	44	356	169	47%	New Brunswick	1	2	1	50%
Nevada	8	18	11	61%	Nova Scotia	1	1	1	100%
New Hampshire	1	1	1	100%	Ontario	129	1,612	958	59%
New Jersey	36	327	209	64%	Quebec	2	9	0	0%
New Mexico	161	1,540	808	52%	Saskatchewan	20	124	60	48%
New York	157	2,772	1,703	61%					
North Carolina	18	71	33	46%	**Totals**	**4,312**	**63,450**	**39,835**	**63%**
North Dakota	17	75	42	56%					

Stallions With Live Foals in 2004
(As of December 31, 2004; Minimum of Ten Mares Bred)

Stallion	Mares Bred	Fls	Live Foal Rate	Stallion	Mares Bred	Fls	Live Foal Rate	Stallion	Mares Bred	Fls	Live Foal Rate
Alabama				Glorious Bid	12	4	33%	Cee's Tizzy	57	46	81%
Casey On Deck	12	8	67%	Idabel	12	6	50%	Cherokee Colony	14	12	86%
Power of Mind	13	3	23%	Ile St. Louis (Chi)	16	8	50%	Chimineas	11	9	82%
Royal Empire	22	12	55%	Kipling	23	14	61%	Chullo (Arg)	19	16	84%
Turn Out	10	5	50%	Mongol Warrior	20	11	55%	Clure	17	14	82%
Arizona				Olympic Prospector	20	3	15%	Cobra King	17	9	53%
Al Ghazi	27	21	78%	Proper Reality	10	7	70%	Comet Shine	22	16	73%
Barricade	10	6	60%	Smolderin Heart	35	22	63%	Comic Strip	108	79	73%
Benton Creek	35	27	77%	Southern Forest	10	5	50%	Commitment	37	10	27%
Big Sky Chester	13	10	77%	Storm and a Half	64	40	63%	Compelling Sound	11	8	73%
Buck Strider	41	21	51%	Tough Hombre	17	8	47%	Corslew	16	15	94%
Chanate	21	14	67%	Unbridled's Risk	17	12	71%	Crowning Storm	59	38	64%
Chancery Court	11	9	82%	Valley Crossing	51	23	45%	Dance Floor	29	17	59%
E. W. Cat	11	5	45%	**California**				Desert Classic	10	6	60%
Local Artist	12	6	50%	All Thee Power	12	6	50%	Desert Secret (Ire)	17	3	18%
Midnight Royalty	39	28	72%	Alymagic	21	19	90%	Devon Lane	37	24	65%
Racey Remarque	17	11	65%	Anziyan	18	12	67%	Discover	16	8	50%
Relaunch a Tune	10	5	50%	Apollo	17	15	88%	Dixie Dot Com	40	34	85%
Reversal	17	9	53%	Avenue of Flags	31	18	58%	Dominique's Cat	16	11	69%
Sideburn	24	13	54%	Bartok (Ire)	34	18	53%	Downtown Seattle	13	6	46%
Snowbound	142	61	43%	Beau Genius	60	48	80%	Dumaani	15	11	73%
Society Max	16	10	63%	Benchmark	91	72	79%	Elegant Fellow	20	10	50%
South Boy (Jpn)	10	7	70%	Bertrando	86	79	92%	Endow	13	6	46%
Star of Halo	23	6	26%	Bienamado	26	16	62%	Event of the Year	39	30	77%
T. G. Dewey	13	7	54%	Boomerang	11	7	64%	Fabulous Champ	10	7	70%
Truce Maker	19	1	5%	Born Wild	12	10	83%	Falstaff	12	7	58%
Arkansas				Bouccaneer (Fr)	33	15	45%	Fine n' Majestic	25	15	60%
A. P. Million	10	3	30%	Brave Romane	20	15	75%	Flom's Prospector	14	5	36%
Bold Anthony	48	27	56%	Bring the Heat	28	15	54%	Flying Continental	45	34	76%
Cinnamon Creek	25	14	56%	Built for Pleasure	23	19	83%	Flying Victor	15	10	67%
Cornish Snow	13	9	69%	Bustopher Jones	25	16	64%	For Really	34	18	53%
Etbauer	15	7	47%	Cactus Creole	20	9	45%	Free House	51	36	71%
				Candi's Gold	21	12	57%	Fruition	15	12	80%
				Category Five	12	9	75%	Fun Devil	22	16	73%
								Fusaichi Accele	23	11	48%
								Future Storm	56	44	79%

Stallion	Mares Bred	Fls	Live Foal Rate
Game Plan	48	37	77%
General Meeting	70	43	61%
Globalize	16	13	81%
Guarani	12	9	75%
Haint	17	9	53%
Half a Year	10	8	80%
Half Term	10	7	70%
Helmsman	35	23	66%
High Brite	79	60	76%
High Demand	24	21	88%
Holding Court	20	10	50%
Hoolie	13	7	54%
Houston	27	14	52%
Hunter's Glory	12	6	50%
Illinois Storm	51	37	73%
In Excess (Ire)	111	91	82%
Iron Cat	17	11	65%
Ito the Hammer	13	9	69%
Iz a Saros	13	5	38%
Joyeux Danseur	16	8	50%
Kessem Power (NZ)	26	19	73%
Kid Capote	12	10	83%
King Excess	13	9	69%
Lacey Evitan	13	10	77%
Lake George	17	11	65%
Laramie's Deputy	21	11	52%
Larry the Legend	41	28	68%
Last Lion	14	10	71%
Latin American	35	25	71%
Lit de Justice	50	38	76%
Lord Carson	91	69	76%
Lucayan Prince	10	8	80%
Mach One	15	10	67%
Madraar	69	55	80%
Majesterian	27	20	74%
Makaleha	12	9	75%
Malek (Chi)	22	16	73%
Memo (Chi)	38	33	87%
Miesque's Son	13	10	77%
Moms From Dixie	13	4	31%
Moscow Ballet	34	24	71%
Mr. Broad Blade	23	8	35%
Mud Route	66	50	76%
Muqtarib	43	34	79%
Newton's Law (Ire)	15	13	87%
Nineeleven	33	29	88%
Northern Devil	15	13	87%
Old Topper	78	57	73%
Ole'	22	8	36%
Olympio	35	27	77%
One Man Army	19	16	84%
Perfect Mandate	62	49	79%
Persian Turban (Ire)	19	11	58%
Peyrano (Arg)	11	5	45%
Phonetics	13	11	85%
Poteen	25	21	84%
Proud Irish	35	24	69%
Puerto Madero (Chi)	15	10	67%
Pulzarr	10	7	70%
Rahy's Quackerjack	26	20	77%
Rainbow Blues (Ire)	14	10	71%
Raise Suzuran	36	25	69%
Red	26	12	46%
Replicate	17	9	53%
Rhythm	31	18	58%
Richly Blended	61	40	66%
Rio Verde	37	28	76%
River Flyer	17	15	88%
Roar	82	49	60%
Robannier	15	9	60%
Rocket Cat	22	17	77%
Royal Cat	26	22	85%
Royal Regatta (Ire)	11	8	73%
Score Quick	15	11	73%
Seattle Bound	30	23	77%
Sharan (GB)	18	13	72%
Sharp Victor	10	3	30%
Siberian Summer	52	40	77%
Silver Ray	10	4	40%
Six Below	26	14	54%
Skimming	101	68	67%
Slew of Angels	28	13	46%

Stallion	Mares Bred	Fls	Live Foal Rate
Slew the Bride	12	11	92%
Slewvescent	33	20	61%
Smokester	39	25	64%
Smooth Runner	14	9	64%
Soft Gold (Brz)	21	19	90%
Sought After	24	11	46%
Strike Gold	11	7	64%
Suggest	26	18	69%
Surachai	47	29	62%
Swiss Yodeler	143	115	80%
Taskmaster	11	5	45%
The Elfee Child	11	5	45%
Tinners Way	13	12	92%
Tom Cruiser	11	8	73%
Town Caper	23	15	65%
Trail City	25	19	76%
Tribal Rule	73	60	82%
Tricky Creek	18	16	89%
Truckee	16	12	75%
Truly Met	17	7	41%
Turkoman	61	34	56%
T. U. Slew	15	5	33%
Twin Spires	19	15	79%
Tychonic (GB)	17	9	53%
Unbridled's Love	12	8	67%
Until Sundown	19	19	100%
Unusual Heat	97	74	76%
Valid Wager	104	81	78%
Vermont	23	9	39%
Via Lombardia (Ire)	12	10	83%
Walter Willy (Ire)	15	8	53%
Western Fame	67	58	87%
Wild Deputy	24	22	92%
Worldly Manner	14	10	71%

Colorado

Stallion	Mares Bred	Fls	Live Foal Rate
A Man of Class	14	8	57%
Annual Tradition	25	13	52%
Capote's Promise	13	7	54%
Cash Deposit	39	19	49%
Conquistador Deoro	31	16	52%
Crafty Harold	15	9	60%
Dash Ahead	13	6	46%
Eishin Masamune (Jpn)	27	19	70%
Kennedy Factor	13	6	46%
Oliver's Twist	48	35	73%
Prospectors Gamble	10	6	60%
Sinceilostmybaby	12	2	17%

Florida

Stallion	Mares Bred	Fls	Live Foal Rate
Absent Russian	14	10	71%
Adcat	100	50	50%
Big Jewel	12	7	58%
B L's Appeal	31	24	77%
Bucksplasher	10	6	60%
Byars	19	15	79%
Capture the Gold	26	13	50%
Cimarron Secret	18	13	72%
Classic Cat	18	11	61%
Cloud Cover	58	27	47%
Cloud Hopping	56	36	64%
Cohiba	18	11	61%
Colony Light	56	43	77%
Concerto	118	74	63%
Concorde's Tune	46	26	57%
Crafty Dude	12	8	67%
Cyberspace	73	40	55%
Dance Master	31	21	68%
Darn That Alarm	13	10	77%
Dawn Quixote	10	7	70%
Delaware Township	42	33	79%
Diligence	20	10	50%
Double Honor	92	62	67%
Dr. Caton	20	9	45%
Dr. Gigolo	10	6	60%
Eltish	65	42	65%
Emmanuel	10	1	10%
Exchange Rate	53	40	75%
Fabulous Frolic	12	8	67%
Family Calling	44	26	59%
Fappie's Notebook	36	21	58%

Stallion	Mares Bred	Fls	Live Foal Rate
Fast 'n Royal	15	10	67%
Flame Thrower	40	22	55%
Forbidden Apple	50	31	62%
Formal Dinner	60	31	52%
Fortunate Move	12	6	50%
Fortunate Prospect	33	21	64%
French Envoy	83	54	65%
Gibson County	20	13	65%
Gold Alert	30	18	60%
Golden Gear	53	31	58%
Graeme Hall	77	69	90%
Greenwood Lake	40	24	60%
Groomstick	12	7	58%
Halos and Horns	42	22	52%
Halo's Image	71	48	68%
Hazaam	20	4	20%
Holiday Thunder	10	4	40%
Holy Mountain	18	10	56%
Honor Glide	70	45	64%
Hunting Hard	21	9	43%
Impeachment	35	21	60%
Invisible Ink	39	25	64%
Is It True	53	34	64%
Island Whirl	19	10	53%
Kissin Kris	58	41	71%
Lake Austin	60	37	62%
Lexicon	45	29	64%
Limit Out	18	10	56%
Line In The Sand	74	46	62%
Littlebitlively	53	36	68%
Lost Soldier	83	55	66%
Lucky North	30	20	67%
Magabird	12	8	67%
Marco Bay	11	2	18%
Master Bill	39	23	59%
Max's Pal	72	53	74%
Mecke	72	41	57%
Metfield	18	13	72%
Middlesex Drive	27	14	52%
Migrating Moon	25	17	68%
Monsieur Cat	28	20	71%
Montbrook	117	90	77%
Mount McKinley	20	12	60%
Native Regent	23	19	83%
Noactor	15	9	60%
Northern Afleet	109	74	68%
Northern Trend	40	27	68%
Notebook	62	40	65%
Outflanker	105	71	68%
Outofthebox	104	75	72%
Palance	11	9	82%
Personal First	45	23	51%
Pistols and Roses	32	20	63%
Precocity	29	18	62%
Premiership	18	11	61%
Prime Timber	58	32	55%
Proud and True	30	17	57%
Proudest Romeo	34	29	85%
Put It Back	85	48	56%
Quaker Ridge	78	43	55%
R. Cooper	17	11	65%
Reality Road	21	16	76%
Reprized	42	28	67%
Robyn Dancer	59	44	75%
Safely's Mark	21	11	52%
Salty Sea	23	15	65%
Seacliff	24	11	46%
Semoran	21	10	48%
Skip Trial	58	27	47%
Slew Gin Fizz	67	52	78%
Snow Ridge	96	67	70%
Snuck In	110	66	60%
Songandaprayer	83	49	59%
Stack	27	20	74%
Star of Valor	11	9	82%
Statesmanship	13	2	15%
Stone Bridge	14	10	71%
Straight Man	100	55	55%
Suave Prospect	114	75	66%
Successful Appeal	68	44	65%
Sweetsouthernsaint	121	74	61%
Texas Glitter	103	61	59%

Stallion	Mares Bred	Fls	Live Foal Rate
Thats Our Buck	30	12	40%
The Silver Move	36	18	50%
Three Wonders	114	77	68%
Tiger Ridge	121	72	60%
Tour d'Or	54	38	70%
Trippi	116	72	62%
Unbridled Time	100	59	59%
Untuttable	61	40	66%
Way West (Fr)	52	33	63%
Weekend Cruise	61	37	61%
Wekiva Springs	45	30	67%
West Acre	90	67	74%
Wild Escapade	20	16	80%
Wild Event	100	58	58%
Wind Whipper	67	39	58%
Win M All	13	3	23%
Winter Glitter	10	5	50%
Wised Up	36	23	64%
Yes It's True	122	93	76%

Georgia

Stallion	Mares Bred	Fls	Live Foal Rate
Prospector Street	19	9	47%
Roaring Camp	19	10	53%
Roundup	12	5	42%

Idaho

Stallion	Mares Bred	Fls	Live Foal Rate
Carmen's Baby	10	4	40%
Chisos	23	6	26%
Coastal Voyage	13	10	77%
Kings Blood (Ire)	25	16	64%
Pirate's Gulch	10	6	60%
Renteria	15	11	73%
Sebrof	11	3	27%
Silent Generation	15	6	40%
Starmaniac	30	16	53%
Thunderah	20	16	80%

Illinois

Stallion	Mares Bred	Fls	Live Foal Rate
Alaskan Frost	45	22	49%
A Lee Rover	15	0	0%
Allen Charge	21	12	57%
Awesome Cat	31	20	65%
Bold Revenue	18	6	33%
Canyon Run	13	8	62%
Cartwright	89	50	56%
Cat Creek Slew	15	4	27%
Catastrophic	13	4	31%
Chicago Six	19	13	68%
City by Night	29	18	62%
Classified Facts	48	23	48%
Conte Di Savoya	29	13	45%
Demidoff	15	14	93%
Denouncer	24	14	58%
Diazo	14	6	43%
Electric Blue	24	0	0%
Fact Book	14	8	57%
Garcon Rouge	13	8	62%
Hannibal Cat	10	6	60%
He's a Tough Cat	26	18	69%
Inexcess Express	15	10	67%
Mahie Gold	14	6	43%
Marte	18	11	61%
Nooo Problema	12	9	75%
Powerful Goer	22	10	45%
Rigging	15	11	73%
Sabona	18	13	72%
Seattle Morn	32	24	75%
Shadow Launcher	14	7	50%
Shakeel	11	6	55%
Sir Spellbinder	27	20	74%
Unbridled Success	16	3	19%
Unite	22	4	18%
Unreal Zeal	36	27	75%
Western Playboy	10	6	60%
Zagor	17	9	53%

Indiana

Stallion	Mares Bred	Fls	Live Foal Rate
Avalli	15	3	20%
Black Moonshine	15	6	40%
Board Member	14	9	64%

Stallion	Mares Bred	Fls	Live Foal Rate
Cat Power	22	7	32%
Classy Prospector	28	13	46%
Colonel Bradley	10	5	50%
Colossus	14	1	7%
Commemorate	21	15	71%
Conscience Clear	27	16	59%
Crown Ambassador	64	38	59%
D. C. Tenacious	13	6	46%
Fast Ferdie	13	10	77%
Fiscal	12	4	33%
Indy Mood	11	6	55%
Jackson's Gap	19	10	53%
Keynote	12	1	8%
Launch a Leader	12	8	67%
Le Casque Gris	21	9	43%
Monroan	12	5	42%
Moro Oro	19	14	74%
Once Wild	11	2	18%
Philadream	18	13	72%
Plenty Chilly	14	2	14%
Presidential Order	14	3	21%
Radio Daze	14	5	36%
Stylish Senor	11	7	64%
Tracker	17	17	100%
Tricon	19	8	42%
Unbridled Man	32	10	31%
Unloosened	19	10	53%
Waki Warrior	31	14	45%
Winning Bid	24	13	54%

Iowa

Stallion	Mares Bred	Fls	Live Foal Rate
Battle Cry	13	10	77%
Brassy Wells	10	9	90%
Cape Storm	30	13	43%
Cat's Debut	19	9	47%
Deputy Slew	12	4	33%
Dignitas	28	17	61%
Doug Fir	39	19	49%
Exclusivengagement	15	5	33%
Friendly Lover	72	40	56%
H. J. Baker	11	2	18%
Honest Ensign	19	10	53%
Humming	13	9	69%
Kyle's Our Man	12	10	83%
Mocha Express	33	17	52%
Night Runner	18	9	50%
Purdue King	17	8	47%
Sharkey	51	30	59%
Supremo	40	22	55%
Tiger Talk	21	14	67%
West Buoyant	10	1	10%
Wild Invader	28	21	75%

Kansas

Stallion	Mares Bred	Fls	Live Foal Rate
Admiral Indy	18	9	50%
Another Good Deed	13	3	23%
Dansil	20	2	10%
Prospector's Treat	12	5	42%
So Ever Clever	17	11	65%
Speedy Nijinsky	17	6	35%

Kentucky

Stallion	Mares Bred	Fls	Live Foal Rate
Acceptable	28	23	82%
Afternoon Deelites	67	47	70%
Albert the Great	83	63	76%
Aljabr	58	50	86%
Alphabet Soup	73	62	85%
Anees	29	17	59%
Anet	19	14	74%
Announce	36	22	61%
A.P. Indy	97	74	76%
Aptitude	132	99	75%
A P Valentine	15	7	47%
Arch	62	47	76%
Artax	122	79	65%
Atticus	35	25	71%
Austinpower (Jpn)	18	13	72%
Awesome Again	101	83	82%
Bahri	39	32	82%
Banker's Gold	86	61	71%
Barkerville	41	16	39%

Stallion	Mares Bred	Fls	Live Foal Rate
Basic	18	5	28%
Bates Motel	18	8	44%
Beautiful Indy	23	16	70%
Behrens	67	53	79%
Belong to Me	109	86	79%
Bernstein	74	47	64%
Best of Luck	46	34	74%
Bianconi	98	61	62%
Birdonthewire	23	7	30%
Black Minnaloushe	93	62	67%
Boundary	59	36	61%
Brahms	117	89	76%
Bright Launch	28	20	71%
Broad Brush	47	37	79%
Broken Vow	127	99	78%
Buddha	164	141	86%
Came Home	106	82	77%
Canaveral	16	11	69%
Cape Canaveral	63	55	87%
Cape Town	66	42	64%
Capote	80	52	65%
Carolina Kid	56	19	34%
Carson City	101	79	78%
Catienus	117	96	82%
Cat Thief	90	74	82%
Charles Bridge	13	6	46%
Cherokee Run	131	88	67%
Chester House	126	102	81%
Chief Seattle	122	89	73%
Clever Trick	38	18	47%
Commendable	94	71	76%
Composer	18	7	39%
Confide	17	11	65%
Coronado's Quest	82	64	78%
Count the Time	21	14	67%
Cozzene	63	53	84%
Crafty Friend	81	56	69%
Crafty Prospector	59	38	64%
Cryptoclearance	105	76	72%
Dance Brightly	34	19	56%
Danzig	48	31	65%
Dayjur	66	43	65%
Deerhound	20	15	75%
Deputy Commander	114	93	82%
Deputy Minister	71	55	77%
Devil His Due	133	93	70%
Devil's Bag	54	38	70%
Diesis (GB)	58	48	83%
Distant View	54	43	80%
Distorted Humor	156	136	87%
Dixieland Band	59	51	86%
Dixieland Heat	39	23	59%
Dixie Union	122	94	77%
Doneraile Court	127	76	60%
Down the Aisle	38	17	45%
Dynaformer	104	86	83%
Ecton Park	112	68	61%
Editor's Note	25	19	76%
E Dubai	108	50	46%
El Corredor	160	116	73%
El Prado (Ire)	90	71	79%
Elusive Quality	143	110	77%
Evansville Slew	91	50	55%
Explicit	62	40	65%
Exploit	119	88	74%
Fast Play	29	17	59%
Favorite Trick	72	49	68%
Fit to Fight	30	19	63%
Five Star Day	98	66	67%
Flying Chevron	26	19	73%
Forest Camp	128	94	73%
Forestry	111	79	71%
Forest Wildcat	110	88	80%
Formal Gold	59	40	68%
Frisk Me Now	31	17	55%
Fusaichi Pegasus	114	92	81%
General Royal	52	34	65%
Gentlemen (Arg)	105	78	74%
Geri	31	19	61%
Giant's Causeway	143	121	85%
Gilded Time	106	68	64%
Glitterman	91	66	73%

Stallion	Mares Bred	Fls	Live Foal Rate
Go for Gin	31	23	74%
Gold Case	76	56	74%
Golden Missile	107	89	83%
Gone West	100	81	81%
Grand Slam	197	151	77%
Grindstone	36	22	61%
Gulch	97	78	80%
Hap	51	27	53%
Hennessy	111	69	62%
High Yield	125	93	74%
Hold for Gold	25	18	72%
Holy Bull	131	104	79%
Home At Last	10	7	70%
Honour and Glory	139	108	78%
Horse Chestnut (SAf)	74	47	64%
Include	153	111	73%
Indian Charlie	121	79	65%
Irgun	16	10	63%
Jade Hunter	74	52	70%
Jambalaya Jazz	38	27	71%
Johannesburg	192	150	78%
Jump Start	101	80	79%
Kanjinsky	10	4	40%
King Cugat	69	55	80%
Kingmambo	97	78	80%
K One King	21	12	57%
K. O. Punch	34	20	59%
Labeeb (GB)	32	20	63%
Lac Ouimet	32	20	63%
Langfuhr	144	114	79%
Lasting Approval	12	8	67%
Lear Fan	70	54	77%
Leelanau	34	21	62%
Lemon Drop Kid	120	101	84%
Lil E. Tee	29	17	59%
Lil's Lad	61	37	61%
Lion Cavern	27	21	78%
Lite the Fuse	66	50	76%
Littleexpectations	65	42	65%
Louis Quatorze	34	21	62%
Lucky Lionel	28	16	57%
Luhuk	63	45	71%
Lure	16	4	25%
Malabar Gold	99	66	67%
Mancini	21	15	71%
Manndar (Ire)	14	11	79%
Maria's Mon	121	101	83%
Marquetry	84	56	67%
Matty G	82	65	79%
Mazel Trick	103	82	80%
Meadowlake	81	57	70%
Menifee	88	74	84%
Military	21	13	62%
Millennium Wind	102	73	72%
Minardi	46	32	70%
Miswaki	44	14	32%
Mizzen Mast	123	92	75%
Monarchos	92	78	85%
Mongoose	40	31	78%
More Than Ready	109	81	74%
Mr. Greeley	164	125	76%
Mt. Livermore	73	53	73%
Mula Gula	19	12	63%
Mutakddim	163	113	69%
Northern Spur (Ire)	10	6	60%
Officer	115	87	76%
Old Kentucky Home	30	22	73%
Ordway	77	42	55%
Orientate	141	120	85%
Our Emblem	92	71	77%
Out of Place	69	52	75%
Parade Ground	24	15	63%
Peaks and Valleys	61	46	75%
Pembroke	39	19	49%
Petionville	61	50	82%
Pikepass	132	76	58%
Pine Bluff	56	40	71%
Pioneering	49	30	61%
Pleasant Tap	60	45	75%
Point Given	104	87	84%
Polish Navy	33	20	61%
Private Terms	41	25	61%

Stallion	Mares Bred	Fls	Live Foal Rate
Prized	33	18	55%
Pulpit	85	68	80%
Pure Prize	104	79	76%
Pyramid Peak	35	24	69%
Quiet American	71	50	70%
Rahy	92	71	77%
Real Quiet	106	76	72%
Red Bullet	88	56	64%
Red Ransom	91	70	77%
Repriced	33	19	58%
Richter Scale	73	52	71%
Rod and Staff	13	8	62%
Romanov (Ire)	11	6	55%
Royal Academy	141	106	75%
Royal Anthem	58	41	71%
Runaway Groom	53	42	79%
Running Stag	98	74	76%
Sahm	49	37	76%
Salt Lake	97	67	69%
Sandpit (Brz)	12	8	67%
Saratoga Six	29	19	66%
Scatmandu	90	57	63%
Scorpion	78	27	35%
Sea of Secrets	142	102	72%
Seeking the Gold	79	56	71%
Sefapiano	29	20	69%
Service Stripe	92	64	70%
Shadeed	20	14	70%
Silic (Fr)	55	33	60%
Silver Charm	101	75	74%
Silver Deputy	104	76	73%
Silver Ghost	45	32	71%
Silver Hawk	47	26	55%
Siphon (Brz)	55	40	73%
Sir Cat	60	40	67%
Skip Away	96	57	59%
Sky Classic	63	50	79%
Slew City Slew	73	50	68%
Smart Strike	119	103	87%
Smoke Glacken	101	76	75%
Souvenir Copy	53	38	72%
Stalwart	14	7	50%
Stephen Got Even	107	85	79%
Storm Boot	119	94	79%
Storm Cat	116	92	79%
Storm Creek	56	37	66%
Stormin Fever	150	106	71%
Stormy Atlantic	189	146	77%
Stormy Look	12	11	92%
Stravinsky	131	87	66%
Street Cry (Ire)	131	94	72%
Subordination	16	10	63%
Sultry Song	94	57	61%
Summer Squall	10	4	40%
Swain (Ire)	39	29	74%
Syncline	49	21	43%
Tactical Cat	123	92	75%
Tale of the Cat	192	157	82%
Talk Is Money	57	42	74%
Tejano Run	47	27	57%
Theatrical (Ire)	74	49	66%
The Deputy (Ire)	107	66	62%
The Name's Jimmy	13	5	38%
Thousand Ores	11	6	55%
Thunder Gulch	130	99	76%
Thunderello	90	57	63%
Tiznow	132	103	78%
Touch Gold	117	96	82%
Twining	68	53	78%
Unbridled's Song	110	97	88%
Vicar	67	45	67%
Victory Gallop	142	92	65%
Vision and Verse	74	52	70%
Wagon Limit	32	19	59%
War Chant	90	77	86%
Wavering Monarch	33	21	64%
Wild Again	40	18	45%
Wild Rush	38	36	95%
Wild Wonder	33	18	55%
Will's Way	48	33	69%
With Approval	73	58	79%
Woodman	74	50	68%

Stallion	Mares Bred	Fls	Live Foal Rate
Yankee Victor	88	64	73%
Yonaguska	149	106	71%
You and I	40	25	63%

Louisiana

Stallion	Mares Bred	Fls	Live Foal Rate
Abajo	86	45	52%
A Corking Limerick	28	15	54%
Aloha Prospector	22	11	50%
Autocracy	23	18	78%
Bag Ir	13	9	69%
Battle Launch	13	2	15%
Bayou Hebert	12	9	75%
Belek	36	20	56%
Busterwaggley	30	18	60%
Capote's Gone	11	6	55%
Carnovali	21	11	52%
Change Takes Time	12	7	58%
Choosing Choice	20	13	65%
Contested Colors	12	7	58%
Corwyn	18	13	72%
Deputy Diamond	46	32	70%
Direct Hit	40	17	43%
Distant Mirage (Ire)	15	5	33%
Erlton	32	25	78%
Esplanade Ridge	16	5	31%
Fair Decor	11	3	27%
Finest Hour	65	38	58%
Forty Won	20	13	65%
Gift of Gib	14	7	50%
Gold Tribute	56	40	71%
Goodbye Doeny	16	12	75%
Grim Reaper	12	5	42%
High Energy	12	2	17%
Hold Hands	10	3	30%
Holy Sting	27	15	56%
Homebuilder	31	18	58%
Huff	13	3	23%
Ide	79	54	68%
I'ma Hell Raiser	15	6	40%
In a Walk	21	13	62%
Jaunatxo	28	18	64%
Jolie's Frolic	14	7	50%
Kimberlite Pipe	41	25	61%
Kipper Kelly	29	17	59%
Laabity	29	18	62%
Lake Holme	17	7	41%
Leestown	82	58	71%
Like a Soldier	12	5	42%
Malagra	20	14	70%
Many a Wish	10	4	40%
Mighty	21	9	43%
Moonlight Dancer	12	1	8%
Mr. Shawklit	18	15	83%
Mr. Sparkles	16	9	56%
Mutah	12	4	33%
My Friend Max	18	12	67%
Nelson	18	11	61%
Northern Niner	16	11	69%
On Target	51	39	76%
Our Shining Hour	28	18	64%
Out of the Crisis	31	13	42%
Planet Earth	18	8	44%
Prince of the Mt.	40	30	75%
Pulling Punches	30	22	73%
Royal Strand (Ire)	10	5	50%
Ruby Hill	12	7	58%
Safe Prospect	24	15	63%
Saint's Honor	10	7	70%
Scott's Scoundrel	12	4	33%
Sharp Frosty	39	20	51%
Shrubs	18	11	61%
Silky Sweep	31	17	55%
Stately Slew	18	3	17%
Storm Day	91	66	73%
Strategic Intent	18	9	50%
Thunder Breeze	10	7	70%
Time Bandit	53	32	60%
Tirade	19	9	53%
Toolighttoquit	17	9	53%
Top Venture	34	26	76%
Tricky	17	4	24%
Trophy Hunter	12	6	50%

Stallion	Mares Bred	Fls	Live Foal Rate
Twilight Agenda	21	16	76%
Upping the Ante	36	23	64%
Valid Belfast	76	44	58%
Viva Deputy	19	15	79%
Western Gentleman	23	10	43%
Winter Halo	16	9	56%
Wire Me Collect	37	22	59%
Worldly Ways (GB)	31	13	42%
Zarbyev	38	18	47%

Maryland

Stallion	Mares Bred	Fls	Live Foal Rate
Allen's Prospect	109	74	68%
Ameri Valay	10	7	70%
Appealing Skier	28	17	61%
Awad	20	12	60%
Carnivalay	23	3	13%
Citidancer	48	21	44%
Concern	35	16	46%
Crowd Pleaser	37	27	73%
Crypto Star	40	20	50%
Deputed Testamony	10	4	40%
Diamond	75	51	68%
Disco Rico	66	37	56%
Dumyat	21	17	81%
Eastern Echo	91	65	71%
In Case	17	11	65%
Jazz Club	78	44	56%
Larrupin'	11	5	45%
Lion Hearted	73	50	68%
Malibu Moon	75	47	63%
Meadow Monster	65	49	75%
Mojave Moon	50	43	86%
Not For Love	102	74	73%
Ops Smile	17	15	88%
Partner's Hero	97	73	75%
Polish Miner	51	40	78%
Purple Passion	11	6	55%
Rubiyat	11	4	36%
Storm Broker	23	14	61%
Swear by Dixie	15	11	73%
Two Punch	92	66	72%
Unbridled Jet	56	30	54%
Waquoit	30	20	67%
Wayne County (Ire)	13	7	54%
Yarrow Brae	28	17	61%

Massachusetts

Stallion	Mares Bred	Fls	Live Foal Rate
Senor Conquistador	13	4	31%
Sundance Ridge	16	11	69%

Michigan

Stallion	Mares Bred	Fls	Live Foal Rate
Binalong	33	18	55%
Collateral Attack	11	8	73%
Creative	15	9	60%
Daylight Savings	10	9	90%
Demaloot Demashoot	30	21	70%
Grand Circus Park	12	8	67%
Great Alliegance	11	6	55%
Island Storm	10	7	70%
Matchlite	20	15	75%
Native Factor	28	21	75%
Ocala Slew	21	14	67%
Pappa Joe	11	6	55%
Pauliano	18	11	61%
Quick and Dirty	17	0	0%
Quiet Enjoyment	16	13	81%
Research	22	14	64%
Treasury	20	14	70%
Why Change	15	11	73%
Will Be Dancing	12	3	25%

Minnesota

Stallion	Mares Bred	Fls	Live Foal Rate
Boundless	18	9	50%
Dixie Power	13	8	62%
Ghazi	60	38	63%
Lakeshore Road	35	22	63%
Late Edition	10	6	60%
North Prospect	20	10	50%
Olaf	11	6	55%
Quaker Hill	10	3	30%

Stallion	Mares Bred	Fls	Live Foal Rate
Quick Cut	20	12	60%
Shot of Gold	27	17	63%
Tahkodha Hills	17	11	65%
Victor's Gent	15	7	47%

Mississippi

Stallion	Mares Bred	Fls	Live Foal Rate
House Burner	13	9	69%
Minister Slew	13	7	54%
Valid Victorious	10	4	40%

Missouri

Stallion	Mares Bred	Fls	Live Foal Rate
Dark Hyacinth	10	8	80%

Montana

Stallion	Mares Bred	Fls	Live Foal Rate
Bujones	10	5	50%
Khalsa	14	6	43%
Perry Road	11	3	27%
Rubio First (Arg)	16	10	63%
Son's Corona	11	0	0%
Unbridled Desire	11	11	100%
White Tie Tryst	13	6	46%

Nebraska

Stallion	Mares Bred	Fls	Live Foal Rate
American Pace	11	5	45%
Blumin Affair	25	20	80%
Box Buster	31	15	48%
Coach George	10	2	20%
Dazzling Falls	19	9	47%
Fighting Fantasy	15	6	40%
Glenview	15	3	20%
Gray Raider	12	3	25%
Itaka	23	13	57%
Military Tune	16	10	63%
Miracle Heights	11	8	73%
More to Tell	12	5	42%
Not So Fast	15	7	47%
Shawklit Player	14	7	50%
Silver Launch	31	16	52%

New Jersey

Stallion	Mares Bred	Fls	Live Foal Rate
Bugatti Reef (Ire)	14	7	50%
Close Up	23	10	43%
Defrere	73	49	67%
G. P.'s Krugerrand	11	8	73%
Honor Defend	12	4	33%
Mr. Nugget	25	13	52%
Mr. Sinatra	20	15	75%
My Prince Charming	10	7	70%
Perfect	11	9	82%
Private Interview	34	26	76%
Unlimited Sky	12	5	42%

New Mexico

Stallion	Mares Bred	Fls	Live Foal Rate
Adams Trail	19	7	37%
Aledo	18	7	39%
Alnaab	27	10	37%
B. G.'s Drone	14	9	64%
Blind Man's Bluff	10	6	60%
Caracal	17	7	41%
Carmen's Glory	15	8	53%
Chimes Band	63	31	49%
Con Artist	11	2	18%
Copelan's Pache	23	13	57%
Dee Lance	12	9	75%
Deep Gold	24	22	92%
Desert God	14	9	64%
Devil Begone	17	7	41%
Digging In	48	30	63%
Dome	53	32	60%
Eishin Storm	23	14	61%
Elegant Cat	19	10	53%
Forever Whirl	12	7	58%
General Gem	10	8	80%
Ghost Ranch	13	5	38%
Ghostly Moves	41	27	66%
Gold Decorum	12	4	33%
Golden Ransom	16	11	69%
Gone Hollywood	11	9	82%
He's a Looker	13	3	23%
Highland Park	12	5	42%

Stallion	Mares Bred	Fls	Live Foal Rate
Hit a Jackpot	26	15	58%
In Excessive Bull	29	21	72%
King's Wailea	14	10	71%
L'Africain Bleu (Fr)	14	8	57%
Launch a Dream	10	5	50%
Lazy Lode (Arg)	26	15	58%
Le Grande Danseur	28	16	57%
Lesters Boy	12	6	50%
Mizaj	20	8	40%
Mountain Metal	21	9	43%
Mr. Groush	16	8	50%
Not Tricky	31	6	19%
Old Chapel	13	5	38%
Pallets	10	8	80%
Paramour	15	9	60%
Parentheses	31	16	52%
Patsyprospect	25	9	36%
Polish Love	10	6	60%
Prince of Fame	21	15	71%
Prospector Jones	18	15	83%
Red Prairie	11	10	91%
R. Payday	20	10	50%
Sadler Slew	27	15	56%
Sandia Slew	17	5	29%
Shooter	10	3	30%
Silver Season	11	8	73%
Spreadthealarm	14	3	21%
Starship Commander	13	4	31%
Storm Ashore	13	3	23%
Tap N Snap	22	13	59%
Thatsusintheolbean	21	11	52%
The Trader's Echo	20	15	75%
Thunder Falcon	13	1	8%

New York

Stallion	Mares Bred	Fls	Live Foal Rate
Abaginone	22	18	82%
Abuzaid	14	7	50%
Adios My Friend	14	11	79%
Adonis	32	17	53%
All Gone	12	8	67%
American Chance	55	39	71%
American Standard	10	5	50%
A. P Jet	30	17	57%
Aristotle	13	6	46%
Badge	16	10	63%
Brushed On	29	15	52%
Captain Bodgit	25	15	60%
Carry My Colors	15	11	73%
City Zip	101	62	61%
Cozy Drive	15	8	53%
Crimson Guard	10	6	60%
Crusader Sword	13	6	46%
Danzatame	16	8	50%
David	18	12	67%
Deputy Cat	24	15	63%
Distinctive Pro	44	33	75%
Freud	77	56	73%
Full Quiver	14	3	21%
Gold Fever	49	31	63%
Gold Token	48	26	54%
Gone for Real	13	7	54%
Good and Tough	114	77	68%
Go West	10	4	40%
Halissee	20	13	65%
Halory Hunter	11	7	64%
Intidab	19	10	53%
Judge T C	88	57	65%
Kelly Kip	59	25	42%
Kettle Won	10	6	60%
Key Contender	30	19	63%
Kingsboro	12	7	58%
King's Grant	13	6	46%
Legion Field	18	12	67%
Lycius	40	23	58%
Malibu Wesley	15	5	33%
Manlove	18	14	78%
Mesopotamia	15	9	60%
Mighty Magee	16	5	31%
Millions	24	10	42%
Ormsby	48	31	65%
Performing Magic	12	10	83%
Personal Flag	21	5	24%
Phone Trick	78	54	69%

Stallion	Mares Bred	Fls	Live Foal Rate
Polish Pro	22	11	50%
Precise End	57	45	79%
Radio Star	63	42	67%
Raffie's Majesty	21	16	76%
Rage	24	17	71%
Regal Classic	82	58	71%
Reign Road	13	9	69%
River Keen (Ire)	30	14	47%
Rizzi	55	37	67%
Rock and Roll	39	22	56%
Rodeo	11	11	100%
Satellite Sun	34	23	68%
Sea Salute	22	11	50%
Senor Speedy	21	13	62%
Signal Tap	38	22	58%
Slice of Reality	11	7	64%
Smokin Mel	20	16	80%
Spectacular Bid	10	5	50%
Take Me Out	47	35	74%
Tank's Number	19	11	58%
The Wicked North	12	10	83%
Tomorrows Cat	50	30	60%
Top Account	24	10	42%
Treasure Cove	24	14	58%
Tri Line	10	7	70%
Watch the Bird	13	10	77%
Well Noted	34	19	56%
Western Borders	17	8	47%
Western Expression	83	48	58%
Wheelaway	83	60	72%
Williamstown	42	17	40%

North Carolina

Stallion	Mares Bred	Fls	Live Foal Rate
Chelsey Cat	19	11	58%

North Dakota

Stallion	Mares Bred	Fls	Live Foal Rate
Codys Key	14	11	79%
Speed Calling	12	7	58%

Ohio

Stallion	Mares Bred	Fls	Live Foal Rate
Academy Award	42	19	45%
Ago	11	4	36%
Coax Me Chad	11	2	18%
Colony Key	10	4	40%
Cool Quaker	18	1	6%
Devious	11	6	55%
Flight Forty Nine	11	9	82%
French Legionaire	11	8	73%
Gold Market	27	20	74%
Iroquois Park	27	6	22%
Keep It Down	10	6	60%
Left Banker	10	8	80%
Mahogany Hall	27	12	44%
Mambo Game	10	5	50%
Mercer Mill	32	25	78%
Noon Prospect	13	6	46%
Parents' Reward	17	12	71%
Political Folly	19	12	63%
Pride of Burkaan	10	6	60%
Sun Master	11	3	27%
Winthrop	29	21	72%
Yeti	10	1	10%

Oklahoma

Stallion	Mares Bred	Fls	Live Foal Rate
Alamocitos	20	7	35%
Aurium	11	4	36%
Baltimore Gray	17	7	41%
Beat the Feet	12	7	58%
Bonus Time Cat	35	19	54%
Burbank	23	11	48%
Chazerahy	13	4	31%
Cherokee Dan	15	0	0%
Cherokee Five	11	2	18%
Chief's Reward	15	6	40%
Comstock Lode	10	9	90%
Concorde Cal	12	6	50%
Coordinator	23	9	39%
Deodar	16	10	63%
Double Niner	20	11	55%
Ecstatic Ride	13	1	8%

Stallion	Mares Bred	Fls	Live Foal Rate
Expense Account	13	7	54%
Fistfite	40	20	50%
French Seventyfive	11	9	82%
Garbu	18	11	61%
Ghost Tension	18	12	67%
Harriman	10	7	70%
Have Fun	33	14	42%
Haymarket (GB)	13	5	38%
Here We Come	16	11	69%
Inca Chief	23	6	26%
Indy Talent	14	7	50%
Ivory Dreams	11	5	45%
King of Scat	57	23	40%
Leave a Legacy	13	7	54%
Lost Opportunity	10	5	50%
Maghnatis	10	4	40%
Magna	20	11	55%
Major Henry	16	10	63%
Mi Selecto	68	44	65%
Moro	13	7	54%
Muldoon	12	6	50%
New Way	12	10	83%
Notable Cat	63	47	75%
Officer of Court	15	2	13%
Prospector's Music	77	50	65%
Raise a Rascal	11	4	36%
Reel On Reel	12	10	83%
Rojo Dinero	10	7	70%
Star of the Crop	21	15	71%
Stromboli	12	7	58%
Tarakam	11	5	45%
Track Barron	14	5	36%
Undeniable	14	4	29%
Unome	12	5	42%
Western Challenge (GB)	13	4	31%
Wild Colony	12	3	25%

Oregon

Stallion	Mares Bred	Fls	Live Foal Rate
Abstract	19	11	58%
Airdrie Apache	21	20	95%
Bagshot	17	12	71%
Baquero	29	17	59%
Cascadian	15	10	67%
Ex Marks the Cop	42	27	64%
Gold Meridian	10	6	60%
Klinsman (Ire)	22	19	86%
Mr. Easy Money	15	8	53%
Ochoco	36	25	69%
Prospected	19	13	68%
Rob 'n Gin	10	6	60%
Superior Success	14	7	50%
Tiffany Ice	18	13	72%
True Confidence	30	20	67%

Pennsylvania

Stallion	Mares Bred	Fls	Live Foal Rate
Activist	17	13	76%
Aquarian Prince	12	4	33%
Attorney	16	8	50%
Bankbook	10	3	30%
Bombardier	16	8	50%
Brian Is Golden	10	8	80%
Caller I. D.	64	44	69%
Cat's Career	33	23	70%
Clash by Night	48	26	54%
Coastal Storm	40	29	73%
Contemplate	14	8	57%
Corporate Report	12	8	67%
Deposit Ticket	23	14	61%
Fastness (Ire)	35	23	66%
Fini Cassette	10	4	40%
Flying Pidgeon	20	8	40%
Foligno	12	9	75%
Harry the Hat	28	13	46%
Miner's Mark	41	17	41%
Patton	66	39	59%
Pin Stripe	12	5	42%
Pok Ta Pok	18	6	33%
Ponche	30	11	37%
Power by Far	24	14	58%
Quarry	18	10	56%
Rip Cat	14	4	29%
Roanoke	12	5	42%

Stallion	Mares Bred	Fls	Live Foal Rate
Turn West	15	8	53%
Turnofthecentury	10	7	70%
U So Bad	13	5	38%
Western Echo	20	8	40%

South Carolina

Stallion	Mares Bred	Fls	Live Foal Rate
Just a Miner	17	3	18%
Lad	10	3	30%
Prime Legacy	13	7	54%
Ride the Storm	14	2	14%
Stormville	10	2	20%

South Dakota

Stallion	Mares Bred	Fls	Live Foal Rate
Neff Lake	22	0	0%
Storm of the Night	47	13	28%

Tennessee

Stallion	Mares Bred	Fls	Live Foal Rate
Defense Witness	10	1	10%
Doppler	10	4	40%
Head West	20	12	60%
Prince Nureyev	10	4	40%

Texas

Stallion	Mares Bred	Fls	Live Foal Rate
Aggie Southpaw	34	21	62%
American Champ	13	7	54%
Asabashi	12	3	25%
Assault Cat	14	7	50%
Ben's Ridge (GB)	12	6	50%
Big Lukey	10	3	30%
Blowing Rock	11	0	0%
Boone's Mill	36	19	53%
Bugatti	29	4	14%
Capote's Prospect	18	9	50%
Captain Countdown	51	27	53%
Carlisle Bay	20	16	80%
Cat Strike	18	11	61%
Cien Fuegos	12	10	83%
City Street	19	11	58%
Clever Return	10	6	60%
Commanchero	84	55	65%
Crafty	15	11	73%
Dove Hunt	36	25	69%
El Amante	17	12	71%
Exciting Story	39	28	72%
Exclusive Zone	12	8	67%
Fashion Find	25	12	48%
Festival of Light	89	61	69%
Fiend	10	5	50%
Flying Kris	10	5	50%
Gen Stormin'norman	24	14	58%
Gold Legend	23	19	83%
Goldmine (Fr)	10	3	30%
Gold Regent	31	17	55%
Gone East	12	3	25%
Groovy Jett	12	9	75%
Hadif	49	28	57%
Heather's Prospect	15	10	67%
Hollycombe	23	11	48%
Holzmeister	18	10	56%
Hunter's Phone	10	1	10%
Hurlingham	15	11	73%
Imperial Cat	12	4	33%
Indian Prospector (Fr)	12	8	67%
Irish Open	46	15	33%
Itron	10	3	30%
Karen's Cat	75	42	56%
Magic Cat	29	19	66%
Marked Tree	28	20	71%
Meacham	14	9	64%
Myrmidon	14	8	57%
Mystery Storm	15	14	93%
Naevus	31	21	68%
Night Beat	29	19	66%
Omega Man	11	3	27%
Once a Sailor	19	13	68%
Open Forum	73	45	62%
Pancho Villa	52	30	58%
Pepper M.	11	6	55%
Pollock's Luck	17	7	41%
Porto Varas	12	6	50%
Proud Halo	11	6	55%

Stallion	Mares Bred	Fls	Live Foal Rate
Rare Brick	31	19	61%
Report On Rain	11	1	9%
River Squall	22	16	73%
Roo Art	11	10	91%
Saxton	12	4	33%
Seattle Sleet	10	6	60%
Secret Claim	10	9	90%
Seeking a Home	24	15	63%
Seneca Jones	41	25	61%
Shadow Caster	10	6	60%
Southern Romance	11	0	0%
Star Programmer	70	49	70%
Stay Sound	11	6	55%
Stephene Mon Amour	12	7	58%
Storm Walk	12	7	58%
Sunny's Halo	10	4	40%
Texas City	11	8	73%
Touch Tone	28	19	68%
Touring Dancer	10	6	60%
Trancus	17	8	47%
Trapp Mountain	21	13	62%
Tricky Prospect	10	2	20%
Truluck	67	39	58%
Uncle Abbie	37	24	65%
Under David's Wing	12	5	42%
Valid Expectations	54	40	74%
Wajir	15	8	53%
Warfield	11	3	27%
Western City	11	7	64%
Western Trader	15	6	40%
Wild Phantom	10	5	50%
Wild Zone	44	34	77%
Won Song	12	5	42%
Z Smart Prospect	12	9	75%

Utah

Stallion	Mares Bred	Fls	Live Foal Rate
Classic Chrys	13	11	85%
Crystal Gazer	19	7	37%

Virginia

Stallion	Mares Bred	Fls	Live Foal Rate
Ball's Bluff	15	9	60%
Expelled	43	25	58%
Forest Service	16	7	44%
Fred Astaire	14	7	50%
Hay Halo	29	17	59%
Housebuster	83	55	66%
Mighty Forum (GB)	10	8	80%
One More Power	20	13	65%
Prenup	22	13	59%
Prospect Bay	19	15	79%
Rock Point	15	14	93%
Two Smart	15	9	60%

Washington

Stallion	Mares Bred	Fls	Live Foal Rate
Adventure Road	10	6	60%
Basket Weave	21	10	48%
Beefchopper	11	6	55%
Cahill Road	47	31	66%
Cisco Road	29	17	59%
Commandperformance	11	5	45%
Defensive Play	17	14	82%
Delineator	14	8	57%
Desert Wine	13	8	62%
Detox	16	10	63%
Flying With Eagles	21	13	62%
Free At Last	47	28	60%
He's Tops	46	28	61%
Ihtimam	33	18	55%
Katowice	23	14	61%
Kentucky Lucky	16	12	75%
La Saboteur	13	5	38%
Liberty Gold	42	30	71%
Liquid Gold	18	14	78%
Matricule	61	25	41%
Midway Magistrate	19	12	63%
M. P. Fancy Man	10	6	60%
Ore Grade	13	9	69%
Our Boy Harvey	20	5	25%
Petersburg	53	27	51%
Raisor's Edge	23	8	35%
Sampson	14	5	36%

Stallion	Mares Bred	Fls	Live Foal Rate
Slewdledo	75	55	73%
Stolen Gold	18	8	44%
Swing and Miss	20	8	40%
Tahoe City	10	7	70%
Tamourad	10	3	30%
Tribunal	46	30	65%
Tristaino	15	6	40%
Tropic Lightning	12	9	75%

West Virginia

Stallion	Mares Bred	Fls	Live Foal Rate
Arromanches	18	5	28%
Castine	35	18	51%
Citislipper	11	7	64%
Civilisation	54	36	67%
Dancinwiththedevil	11	7	64%
Eastover Court	14	7	50%
Emancipator	36	16	44%
Explosive Red	13	7	54%
Greenspring Willy	13	1	8%
Kokand	60	39	65%
Lt. Gulch	10	1	10%
Luftikus	69	44	64%
Makin	82	50	61%
Medford	19	9	47%
My Boy Adam	21	16	76%
Native Slew	14	6	43%
Our Valley View	18	8	44%
Proper Texan	13	6	46%
Robb	18	7	39%
Roxbury Park	12	10	83%
Run Softly	23	16	70%
Satchmo's Band	11	6	55%
Select Session	12	5	42%
Slew O'Quoit	20	10	50%
Sprizzo	10	8	80%
Strike Adduce	23	15	65%
Stritzel	18	6	33%
Tank	10	6	60%
Truculent Schular	21	11	52%
Valiant Nature	35	25	71%
Weshaam	22	8	36%
Western Cat	53	28	53%

Alberta

Stallion	Mares Bred	Fls	Live Foal Rate
Banjo	18	7	39%
Brass Minister	16	6	38%
Brunswick	14	10	71%
Castle Arms	13	7	54%
Ciano Cat	41	25	61%
Desperately	19	6	32%
Devonwood	28	17	61%
Dr. Adagio	35	24	69%
Easy Climb	17	2	12%
Fast Account	13	5	38%
Go Gary Go	32	15	47%
Ground Stroke	12	4	33%
Hail the Ruckus	24	10	42%
Haus of Dehere	29	18	62%
Hurricane Center	38	14	37%
Important Notice	12	4	33%
Just a Cat	49	19	39%
Magic Prospect	18	10	56%
Nicholas Ds	10	8	80%
Othello	31	12	39%
Rebmec	15	8	53%
Regal Remark	21	10	48%
Rosetti	47	25	53%
Royal Rumpus	10	8	80%
Seattle Syn	15	5	33%
Smithfield	20	8	40%
The Key Rainbow (Ire)	18	7	39%
Weekend Guest	24	12	50%

British Columbia

Stallion	Mares Bred	Fls	Live Foal Rate
Alfaari	29	18	62%
Alybro	11	9	82%
Baron de Vaux	24	7	29%
Captain Collins (Ire)	19	12	63%
Devil On Ice	13	5	38%
Digital Dan	16	11	69%
Dixieland Brass	15	11	73%

Stallion	Mares Bred	Fls	Live Foal Rate
Dixieland Diamond	20	8	40%
Dramatic Show	11	10	91%
Feu d'Enfer	21	15	71%
Funboy	10	5	50%
Katahaula County	79	55	70%
Light of Mine	16	8	50%
Mass Market	45	34	76%
Millennium Allstar	33	20	61%
Net Asset	11	6	55%
Persian Star	12	8	67%
Regal Intention	30	20	67%
Repletion	10	3	30%
Silver Fox	27	10	37%
Stephanotis	44	34	77%
Vying Victor	58	45	78%
Wandering	14	3	21%
Western Trick	12	6	50%
Yoonevano	59	32	54%

Manitoba

Stallion	Mares Bred	Fls	Live Foal Rate
Act Smart	14	7	50%
Akado	12	1	8%
Boanerges	12	7	58%
Chinese Gold	18	6	33%
Circulating	26	12	46%
Gentle Kent	15	6	40%
Gold Hat	10	7	70%
Saratoga Express	11	2	18%
Shrike	17	6	35%
Silver of Silver	20	7	35%

Ontario

Stallion	Mares Bred	Fls	Live Foal Rate
A Fleets Dancer	63	43	68%
Alydeed	28	15	54%
Alystar Slew	15	12	80%
Ascot Knight	47	34	72%
Ashbury	20	7	35%
Bluesbreaker	13	0	0%
Bold Executive	80	54	68%
Bold n' Flashy	61	36	59%
Brite Adam	25	12	48%
Canyon Creek (Ire)	14	7	50%
Cat's At Home	80	53	66%
Compadre	58	26	45%
Crown Attorney	58	32	55%
Domasca Dan	28	10	36%
Eh	10	5	50%
Elajjud	17	7	41%
Foxtrail	51	31	61%
Highland Ruckus	15	9	60%
I Can't Believe	20	14	70%
It's too Late	11	9	82%
Kinshasa	66	25	38%
Kiridashi	33	20	61%
Like the Prospects	13	5	38%
Minstrel Dancer	11	7	64%
Not Impossible (Ire)	18	11	61%
One Way Love	63	51	81%
Parisianprospector	39	25	64%
Perigee Moon	45	31	69%
Porto Foricos	17	9	53%
Randy Regent	37	25	68%
Regal Discovery	17	6	35%
Sea Wall	13	7	54%
Shelly's Charmer	11	8	73%
Swampster	10	6	60%
Tejabo	15	11	73%
Tethra	44	28	64%
Tough Call	13	12	92%
Trajectory	82	52	63%
Valid Trefaire	22	13	59%
War Deputy	27	17	63%
Whiskey Wisdom	18	10	56%
Wonneberg	12	8	67%

Saskatchewan

Stallion	Mares Bred	Fls	Live Foal Rate
Blowin de Turn	12	5	42%
Linkage	14	11	79%
No Malice	11	6	55%
Stop the Stage	14	7	50%
You've Got Action	14	7	50%

Report of Mares Bred for 2004

In 2004, the long, slow decline in the number of active stallions in North America continued. However, the number of mares bred stayed relatively the same, at least through the early returns, continuing a trend in which the number of mares bred has stayed in a narrow range for more than a decade.

As of December 31, 2004, the Jockey Club reported that 3,766 stallions in North America had been bred to mares in 2004. That figure was down 13.2% from the 4,339 active stallions reported in 2003. But more breedings were likely to be reported for 2004, which would bring the figure closer to that of '03.

The stallion population in the two largest North American breeding nations has been declining for more than a decade. In 1992, the Jockey Club reported that 6,753 stallions were bred to mares. From 1992 to 2003, then, there was a 35.7% decline in the number of stallions bred to at least one mare.

In 1988, the first year the Jockey Club began reporting on the number of stallions and number of mares bred by year, there were 8,638 active stallions and a total of 88,682 mares were bred.

The 62,574 mares reported as bred in 2004 were close to the number of mares reported bred in '03, and with more breedings to be reported, the 2004 number of mares bred should exceed the '03 number when the final tally is made.

Kentucky led North America by most mares bred in 2004, when the state's 352 stallions were bred to 20,346 mares. California had the largest number of stallions, 378, followed by Kentucky and Texas (319).

The equation of more mares and fewer stallions has yielded larger stallion books. In 1992, the average stallion book was 9.4 mares. In 2004, the average book stood at 16.6 mares, a 76.6% increase. In Kentucky, the average stallion book also has increased dramatically. At 31.1 mares per stallion in 1992, the Kentucky average rose to 57.8 mares in 2004.

The Kentucky figures, in particular, emphasized the influence of huge stallion books on the breeding industry. For the second consecutive year, no stallion was bred to more 200 mares. Hold That Tiger, however, was bred to 199 mares, and two other sires, Fusaichi Pegasus and Grand Slam, were each bred to more than 190 mares. The record total for most mares bred was Thunder Gulch's 216 in 2001. More than 110 stallions were bred to 100 or more mares in 2004; while most of those stallions were based in Kentucky, other jurisdictions with stallions bred to 100 or more mares were Florida, Maryland, California, and Ontario.

Leading Stallions by Mares Bred

(As of December 31, 2004)

Stallion, Location	Mares Bred	Stallion, Location	Mares Bred	Stallion, Location	Mares Bred	Stallion, Location	Mares Bred
Hold That Tiger, Ky.	199	High Yield, Ky.	138	Flatter, Ky.	116	Kingmambo, Ky.	105
Fusaichi Pegasus, Ky.	193	Broken Vow, Ky.	137	Gold Case, Ky.	116	Najran, Ky.	105
Grand Slam, Ky.	191	Cat Thief, Ky.	137	Golden Missile, Ky.	116	Vicar, Ky.	105
Van Nistelrooy, Ky.	186	Halo's Image, Fl.	134	Smoke Glacken, Ky.	116	Cactus Ridge, Ky.	104
Tale of the Cat, Ky.	185	Smart Strike, Ky.	134	Storm Cat, Ky.	116	Indian Charlie, Ky.	104
Doneraile Court, Ky.	184	Yonaguska, Ky.	134	Victory Gallop, Ky.	116	Malabar Gold, Ky.	104
Stormy Atlantic, Ky.	183	Sunday Break (Jpn), Ky.	132	In Excess (Ire), Ca.	115	Mineshaft, Ky.	104
Buddha, Ky.	182	Carson City, Ky.	131	Orientate, Ky.	115	Wiseman's Ferry, N.Y.	104
Johannesburg, Ky.	175	Cherokee Run, Ky.	130	Posse, Ky.	115	Zavata, Ky.	104
Chief Seattle, Ky.	166	Giant's Causeway, Ky.	130	Storm Creek, Ca.	114	Belong to Me, Ky.	103
Mutakddim, Ky.	162	Mizzen Mast, Ky.	130	Holy Bull, Ky.	112	Bold Executive, On.	103
Proud Citizen, Ky.	157	Aptitude, Ky.	129	Lemon Drop Kid, Ky.	112	Silver Charm, Ky.	103
El Corredor, Ky.	156	Officer, Ky.	129	Tactical Cat, Ky.	112	Sligo Bay (Ire), Ky.	103
Gulf Storm, Fl.	155	Street Cry (Ire), Ky.	129	Empire Maker, Ky.	111	Texas Glitter, Fl.	103
Honour and Glory, Ky.	152	Northern Afleet, Fl.	128	Richter Scale, Ky.	111	Thunder Gulch, Ky.	103
Full Mandate, Fl.	151	Lion Hearted, Md.	127	Three Wonders, Fl.	111	Wheelaway, N.Y.	103
More Than Ready, Ky.	151	Mr. Greeley, Ky.	127	Forest Wildcat, Ky.	110	Not For Love, Md.	102
Malibu Moon, Ky.	149	Jump Start, Ky.	125	Sky Mesa, Ky.	110	Yankee Gentleman, Ky.	102
Tiger Ridge, Fl.	149	Petionville, Ky.	125	Macho Uno, Fl.	109	Aldebaran, Ky.	101
Trippi, Fl.	147	Matty G, Ky.	124	Outofthebox, Fl.	109	Dixie Union, Ky.	101
Distorted Humor, Ky.	146	Millennium Wind, Ky.	123	Pulpit, Ky.	109	Double Honor, Fl.	101
E Dubai, Ky.	143	Tiznow, Ky.	123	Successful Appeal, Fl.	109	Ecton Park, Ky.	101
Stravinsky, Ky.	143	Hennessy, Ky.	122	Dynaformer, Ky.	108	Silver Deputy, Ky.	101
Kafwain, Ky.	142	Yes It's True, Fl., Ky.	122	Came Home, Ky.	106	Trust N Luck, Ky.	101
Forestry, Ky.	141	Benchmark, Ca.	121	El Prado (Ire), Ky.	106	Albert the Great, Ky.	100
Langfuhr, Ky.	141	Deputy Commander, Ky.	120	Milwaukee Brew, Ky.	106	Concorde's Tune, Fl.	100
Elusive Quality, Ky.	140	Montbrook, Fl.	119	Snuck In, Fl.	106	Horse Chestnut (SAf), Ky.	100
Stephen Got Even, Ky.	140	Repent, Fl.	119	Touch Gold, Ky.	106	Leestown, La.	100
Vindication, Ky.	140	Alphabet Soup, Ky.	118	Devil His Due, Ky.	105	Gone West, Ky.	99
Harlan's Holiday, Ky.	138	Unbridled's Song, Ky.	118	Forest Camp, Ky.	105	Storm Day, La.	99
						Unusual Heat, Ca.	99

Stallions and Mares Bred in the United States, Canada, and North America, 1992-2004

Year	U.S. Stallions	U.S. Mares Bred	Avg. Book	Canada Stallions	Canada Mares Bred	Avg. Book	Total NA Stallions	Total NA Mares Bred	Avg. Book
2004	3,485	58,883	16.9	281	3,691	13.1	3,766	62,574	16.6
2003	4,006	59,170	14.8	333	3,585	10.8	4,339	62,755	14.5
2002	4,154	60,163	14.5	347	3,562	10.3	4,501	63,725	14.2
2001	4,326	60,239	13.9	338	3,539	10.5	4,664	63,778	13.7
2000	4,419	60,827	13.8	352	3,462	9.8	4,771	64,289	13.5
1999	4,396	57,301	13.0	350	3,431	9.8	4,746	60,732	12.8
1998	4,513	55,914	12.4	386	3,544	9.2	4,899	59,458	12.1
1997	4,675	54,944	11.8	414	3,652	8.8	5,089	58,596	11.5
1996	4,882	54,571	11.2	427	3,700	8.7	5,309	58,271	11.0
1995	5,182	55,435	10.7	425	3,656	8.6	5,607	59,091	10.5
1994	5,365	55,275	10.3	430	3,730	8.7	5,795	59,005	10.2
1993	5,801	56,269	9.7	453	3,973	8.8	6,254	60,242	9.6
1992	6,263	59,607	9.5	490	4,159	8.5	6,753	63,766	9.4

Stallions and Mares Bred by State and Province
(As of December 31, 2004)

State	Stallions	Mares Bred	State	Stallions	Mares Bred	State	Stallions	Mares Bred
Alabama	25	136	Mississippi	14	72	Vermont	3	4
Alaska	1	3	Missouri	17	73	Virginia	53	387
Arizona	53	485	Montana	42	181	Washington	94	1,160
Arkansas	68	593	Nebraska	36	360	West Virginia	77	1,048
California	378	5,757	Nevada	6	15	Wisconsin	7	22
Colorado	62	431	New Jersey	25	257	Wyoming	6	19
Connecticut	1	1	New Mexico	148	1,528	Puerto Rico	54	776
Florida	228	6,935	New York	144	2,654	Virgin Islands	2	4
Georgia	20	116	North Carolina	17	61	Unknown	16	69
Idaho	45	308	North Dakota	19	110			
Illinois	111	1,067	Ohio	83	515	**Canada Province**		
Indiana	87	702	Oklahoma	171	1,488	Alberta	73	922
Iowa	45	505	Oregon	46	449	British Columbia	58	786
Kansas	25	189	Pennsylvania	109	1,003	Manitoba	21	184
Kentucky	352	20,346	Rhode Island	1	1	New Brunswick	2	3
Louisiana	229	3,092	South Carolina	24	140	Nova Scotia	1	1
Maryland	67	1,603	South Dakota	9	111	Ontario	102	1,619
Massachusetts	17	68	Tennessee	13	56	Quebec	4	13
Michigan	57	544	Texas	319	2,882	Saskatchewan	20	163
Minnesota	32	341	Utah	27	216	**Totals**	**3,766**	**62,574**

Stallions Bred to Five or More Mares in 2004
(As of December 31, 2004)

Stallion	Mares Bred	Stallion	Mares Bred	Stallion	Mares Bred	Stallion	Mares Bred
ALABAMA		E. W. Cat	11	Cornish Snow	18	**CALIFORNIA**	
Casey On Deck	11	Fool the Experts	7	Croydon	7	Acclaimed Honor	5
Dantesque (Ire)	6	Hidden City	21	Cubes Ozzy	6	All Thee Power	5
Guaranteed	5	Jeep Shot	6	Distant Mirage (Ire)	13	Alymagic	11
Power of Mind	14	Local Artist	6	Etbauer	18	American Day	12
Royal Empire	22	Midnight Royalty	38	Explosive Ridge	7	America's Storm	19
Schembechler	5	Ronton	18	Father Steve	15	Anziyan	14
Special Coach	6	Santoni	5	Glorious Bid	21	Apollo	6
Turn Out	12	Sideburn	31	Harlan Traveler	8	Arctic White	5
Whambam	10	Slew Mood	13	I'am Cured	5	Arthur L.	8
Youngs Neck Arod	15	Speed Dial	6	Idabel	17	Avanzado (Arg)	36
		Star of Halo	14	Ile St. Louis (Chi)	27	Bartok (Ire)	95
ARIZONA		Teddy Boy	5	Joy's Report	8	Beau Genius	66
Al Ghazi	24	T. G. Dewey	12	Macabe	43	Benchmark	121
Benton Creek	52	Zigtrick (Fr)	7	Monarch's Maze	21	Bertrando	65
Big Sky Chester	28			No Catch	6	Bienamado	17
Bonus Bucks	5	**ARKANSAS**		Proper Reality	13	Bien Rullah	9
Buck Strider	45	American General	10	Proper Ridge	5	Birdonthewire	28
Chanate	27	A. P. Million	17	Siberian Pine	5	Bonus Money (GB)	7
Chancery Court	13	Bob's Prospect	7	Smolderin Heart	35	Boomerang	12
Directed Energy	5	Bold Anthony	45	Southern Forest	13	Bouccaneer (Fr)	31
Ellusive Quest	11	Cathode	8	Storm and a Half	70	Brave Romane	13
Equinox	7	Cinnamon Creek	20	Tough Hombre	8	Bring the Heat	17
				Trust No Lawyer	11		

Stallion	Mares Bred	Stallion	Mares Bred	Stallion	Mares Bred	Stallion	Mares Bred
Broadway Moon	5	Kris Kross	9	Siberian Summer	48	Sagebrush Sam	9
Bucky Raj	7	Lacey Evitan	15	Silver Ray	6	Scott's Dream	10
Built for Pleasure	29	Lake George	6	Simply Majestic	5	Silver Saint	13
Bustopher Jones	11	Lake William	57	Sir Dennis	8	Spellbounder	13
Cactus Creole	10	Laramie's Deputy	26	Sir Fir	8	The Rufus	7
Candi's Gold	13	Larry the Legend	41	Six Below	14	Top Villa	10
Capsized	58	Last Lion	9	Skimming	94		
Caros Love	7	Latin American	18	Slew of Angels	6	**FLORIDA**	
Category Five	21	Lit de Justice	51	Slewvescent	24	Adcat	80
Cee's Tizzy	81	Lord Carson	82	Smokester	55	Adonis	15
Chatelain (Arg)	5	Lord Charmer	8	Smooth Runner	19	A. P. Five Hundred	21
Cherokee Colony	13	Lost in Paradise	5	Snow Blink	7	Arrested	29
Chimineas	10	Mach One	8	Soft Gold (Brz)	30	Arts and Toys	6
Chullo (Arg)	32	Madraar	57	Sought After	14	Awesome of Course	10
Citibanker	7	Majesterian	11	Soul of the Matter	17	Awesome Sword	8
Cobra King	35	Makaleha	10	Speed Jaro (Fr)	9	Band Is Passing	14
Comet Shine	26	Malek (Chi)	33	Stage Colony	6	Best of the Rest	13
Comic Strip	42	Mechon Tom (Arg)	19	Storm Creek	114	Big Jewel	14
Corslew	16	Memo (Chi)	30	Stormy Jack	43	B L's Appeal	41
Crowning Storm	43	Michael's Flyer	13	Strike Gold	9	Brief Ruckus	10
Cutlass Reality	7	Moms From Dixie	15	Suggest	14	Broadway Beau	6
Dance Floor	7	Mongol Warrior	9	Surachai	18	Brushing Up	8
Decarchy	73	Moscow Ballet	30	Swiss Yodeler	63	Bucksplasher	6
Definite Edge	19	Mr. Broad Blade	12	Synastry	11	Capture the Gold	10
Desert Classic	13	Mr. Procrastinator	7	Tactical Heir	10	Carlisle Bay	7
Devon Lane	34	Mr. Publisher	16	Takin It Deep	19	China Grind	8
Dismissed	14	Mt. Bellewood	14	Tannersmyman	13	Cimarron Secret	15
Dixie Dot Com	39	Mud Route	47	Taskmaster	7	Classic Cat	55
Dominique's Cat	17	Muqtarib	62	Thinkin Problem	10	Cloud Cover	23
Done Dancing	10	Music d'Enfer	5	Tom Cruiser	5	Cloud Hopping	42
Downtown Seattle	12	My King (Ger)	7	Toughness	5	Cohiba	5
D's Bertrando	16	Naevus Star	6	Town Caper	6	Colony Light	39
Dumaani	14	National Saint	16	Trail City	16	Concerto	32
Elegant Fellow	13	Native Storm	6	Tribal Rule	78	Concorde's Tune	100
Emerald Jig	9	Newton's Law (Ire)	14	Tricky Creek	19	Conquista Fager	10
Epic Honor	22	Nineeleven	28	Truckee	18	Conscience Clear	5
Event of the Year	13	Now Voyager	5	Truly Met	26	Crown Delite	7
Expressionist	5	Old Topper	59	Turkoman	42	Cyberspace	38
Faculty	7	Ole'	18	T. U. Slew	12	Dance Master	33
Fargo	6	Oly Ogy	7	Twin Spires	8	Dance the Ballado	9
Fine n' Majestic	22	Olympio	12	Unbridled's Love	24	Dawn Quixote	8
Flom's Prospector	15	One Man Army	22	Unusual Heat	99	De Hero	5
Flying Continental	27	Outing	8	Valid Fast	7	Delaware Township	84
Flying Victor	15	Perfect Mandate	97	Valid Wager	79	Deputy Wild Cat	36
For Really	24	Persian Turban (Ire)	16	Vermont	6	Diligence	22
Free House	45	Peyrano (Arg)	12	Vernon Castle	6	D. J. Cat	5
Freespool	54	Pharisien (Fr)	5	Via Lombardia (Ire)	28	Double Honor	101
Fruition	12	Phonetics	44	Walter Willy (Ire)	11	Dr. Caton	11
Fun Devil	13	Pine for Java	6	Western Fame	21	Dr. Gigolo	11
Fusaichi Zenon (Jpn)	10	Poteen	16	Wings Bash (Ire)	7	Drewman	94
Future Storm	41	Pride of Slew	7	Worldly Manner	12	Eltish	72
Game Plan	43	Proud Irish	37	You and I	55	Essence of Dubai	87
General Meeting	17	Puerto Madero (Chi)	23	Zanferrier	13	Exchange Rate	81
Globalize	30	Rahy's Quackerjack	5			Express Tour	35
Golden Gear	46	Rainbow Blues (Ire)	16	**COLORADO**		Family Calling	57
Gotham City	45	Raise Suzuran	14	Alydarmer	5	Fappie's Notebook	35
Guarani	24	Raz Lea	6	A Man of Class	13	Fast 'n Royal	16
Haint	20	Really Honest	12	Annual Tradition	17	Fiery Best	7
Half Term	16	Red	18	Basic Rate	7	First Tour	14
Helmsman	18	Regent Act	10	Bumbury Did It	5	Flame Thrower	62
Here Comes Big C	12	Replicate	20	Capote's Promise	11	Forbidden Apple	62
High Brite	55	Rhythm	28	Cash Deposit	18	Formal Dinner	39
High Demand	35	Richly Blended	50	Cats and Dogs	15	Fortunate Prospect	6
Highland Gold	22	Ride the Rails	26	Conquistador Deoro	16	French Envoy	40
Holding Court	12	Rio Verde	71	Coverallbases	7	Full Mandate	151
Houston	16	River Flyer	5	Crafty Harold	8	Georgia Two	11
Huddle Up	6	Roar	73	Dash Ahead	12	Gibson County	31
Hunter's Glory	8	Robannier	18	Eishin Masamune (Jpn)	31	Graeme Hall	58
Iam the Iceman	12	Rocket Cat	35	Ernie Tee	11	Greatness	82
Illinois Storm	54	Roman Dancer	22	Exploding Rainbow	5	Gulf Storm	155
I'madrifter	5	Roots and Ropes	5	Free and Equal	7	Hadrian's Wall	20
In Excess (Ire)	115	Royal Cat	32	Gripfast	5	Halos and Horns	36
Indy Film	6	Royal Regatta (Ire)	6	Habitony's Ace	7	Halo's Image	134
Irish Ways (Ire)	5	Royal Walk	7	Kennedy Factor	7	Henriques	7
Iron Cat	33	Russian Courage	6	Majorbigtimesheet	17	Hesabull	6
Iz a Saros	6	Safarado (Ire)	5	Montego Bay	7	Honor Glide	75
Kahuna Jack	11	Score Early	7	Mr. Gehrig	11	Impeachment	54
Kessem Power (NZ)	15	Score Quick	12	My Memoirs (GB)	5	Indy King	40
Kid Capote	10	Seattle Bound	12	Oliver's Twist	49	Invisible Ink	34
King Excess	11	Seattle Proud	7	Pragmatic	7	Is It True	35
King George's Way	5	Seeking Greatness	5	Really A Rainbow	5	Kissin Kris	31
King of the Hunt	10	Sharan (GB)	15				

Stallion	Mares Bred
Lake Austin	9
Lexicon	59
Lido Palace (Chi)	80
Lightnin N Thunder	74
Line In The Sand	23
Lite the Fuse	36
Littlebitlively	21
Lordhyexecutioner	6
Lost Soldier	44
Lucky North	9
Macho Uno	109
Master Bill	28
Max's Pal	68
Mecke	33
Mesne Process	8
Metfield	18
Middlesex Drive	16
Migrating Moon	31
Mongoose	39
Monsieur Cat	23
Montbrook	119
Mount McKinley	37
Niganithat	5
No Dreamer	6
Northern Afleet	128
Northern Trend	53
Outofthebox	109
Palance	15
Personal First	28
Pistols and Roses	11
Point in Time	12
Precocity	24
Presailist	7
Private Talk	8
Proud and True	29
Proudest Romeo	52
Pure Precision	67
Put It Back	86
Quaker Ridge	21
R. Cooper	20
Recommended List	15
Red Bullet	87
Repent	119
Reprized	10
Robyn Dancer	62
Rocket Ryan	5
Running Stag	86
Safely's Mark	17
Salty Sea	30
Sasha's Prospect	6
Scorpion	55
Scottish Halo	13
Shanawi (Ire)	35
Skip to the Stone	70
Skip Trial	30
Sky Glory	8
Slew Gin Fizz	41
Smooth Jazz	87
Snow Ridge	78
Snuck In	106
Songandaprayer	80
Stack	9
Stark Ridge	8
Stone Bridge	14
Straight Man	73
Suave Prospect	70
Successful Appeal	109
Sweetsouthernsaint	42
Texas Glitter	103
Thats Our Buck	10
The Kaiser	6
The Silver Move	16
Three Wonders	111
Tiger Ridge	149
Tour d'Or	32
Trippi	147
True Enough	22
Unbridled Time	94
Untuttable	70
War Secretary	5
Weekend Cruise	66
Wekiva Springs	34
West Acre	72
Wild Escapade	11
Wild Event	53
Wind Whipper	38
Wised Up	24
Yes It's True	120

GEORGIA

Stallion	Mares Bred
Hurry to Dinner	7
KingfishKing	5
Level Sands	11
Play Both Ends	10
Roaring Camp	17
Roundup	16
Slew the Slewor	9
St. Alydar	10
Yourplaceormine	5

IDAHO

Stallion	Mares Bred
Carmen's Baby	6
Chisos	14
Coastal Voyage	47
Fabulous Champ	8
Judith's Wild One	6
Kings Blood (Ire)	28
Pirate's Gulch	13
Pulzarr	12
Reversal	17
Ring of Mordor	6
Secret Prince	6
Silent Generation	5
Smart Chip	7
Starmaniac	28
Tavasco	14
Thunderah	23
Turtle Member	6

ILLINOIS

Stallion	Mares Bred
Alaskan Frost	27
A Lee Rover	6
Allen Charge	15
Awesome Cat	14
Bold Revenue	15
Canyon Run	14
Cartwright	83
Catastrophic	7
Cherokee Saga	5
Chicago Six	20
City by Night	14
Classic Account	16
Classified Facts	32
Conte Di Savoya	29
Crimson Classic	10
Demidoff	25
Denouncer	13
Diazo	6
Fact Book	11
Fairway Topper	5
Fascio (Arg)	6
Gogarty (Ire)	6
Hasten To Add	8
He's a Tough Cat	27
Honour Attendant	21
Inexcess Express	9
Irgun	54
Lens	7
Mahie Gold	10
Marte	21
My Magical Star	5
Nassau Hall	6
Nooo Problema	12
One Little Hustler	8
Pirate Stronghold	7
Pleasant Minstrel	5
Posh	33
Powerful Goer	26
Regal Code	7
Rigging	13
Roman Truce	8
Royal Roberto	11

Stallion	Mares Bred
Sabona	25
Seattle Morn	24
Shadow Launcher	8
Shakeel	7
Shore Breeze	35
Sir Spellbinder	15
S'No Business	7
Supeona	12
The Name's Jimmy	6
Theran	7
Tiger Tiger	8
Tough Call	8
Unbridled Success	14
Unloosened	12
Unreal Zeal	50
Valid Vengeance	6
Viareggio (Ire)	8
Zagor	15
Z Z Cat	7

INDIANA

Stallion	Mares Bred
Announce	22
Arromanches	26
Assembly Dancer	5
Avalli	11
Bartlettsunbridled	7
Black Moonshine	17
Blase	11
Cat Power	9
Colonel Bradley	14
Commemorate	23
Could Be Me	8
Crown Ambassador	29
D. C. Tenacious	5
Dewdle's Dancer	12
Dixie Road	10
Easy Scoop	7
Fast Ferdie	9
Fiscal	10
Gallant Step	7
Garcon Rouge	12
Green Stamp	7
Hit the Roof	5
Indian Territory	23
Indy Mood	21
Jacquelyn's Groom	14
Keynote	16
King Tiara	7
Le Casque Gris	12
Miswaki Bandit	12
Monroan	9
Montreal Red	10
Moro Oro	15
New York Prospect	10
Once Wild	11
Plenty Chilly	15
Presidential Order	27
Prince Guistino	6
Ripsaw	5
Sixto G	11
Speedy Cure	11
Stylish Senor	6
Summer Ransom	6
Swiss Trick	12
Timeraker	12
Tracker	8
Tricon	14
Unbridled Man	25
Waki Warrior	9
War Poet	8

IOWA

Stallion	Mares Bred
Arz	6
Brassy Wells	12
Bravo Bull	22
Buzz Saw	16
Canaveral	11
Cape Storm	10
Cat's Debut	8
De Guerin	8
Deputy Slew	11

Stallion	Mares Bred
Dignitas	16
Doug Fir	24
Friendly Lover	43
Fugitive	6
H. J. Baker	8
Humming	12
Kyle's Our Man	13
Maze Craze	7
Mocha Express	20
Night Runner	6
One Hundred Slews	19
Sharkey	24
So Private	5
Supremo	21
Tiger Talk	12
Too Much Ice	7
Trump an Ace	9
Valley Crossing	28
West Buoyant	15
Wild Gold	30
Wild Invader	12
Winter Glitter	32

KANSAS

Stallion	Mares Bred
Admiral Indy	27
Another Good Deed	10
Fortifier	11
Ianomami (Ire)	10
Life Interest	7
Polly's Comet	12
Prospector's Treat	20
Reality's Conquest	9
So Ever Clever	13
Speedy Nijinsky	7
Testafly	6
Torey Ridge	13
Tricky Six	13

KENTUCKY

Stallion	Mares Bred
Acceptable	16
Albert the Great	100
Aldebaran	101
Aljabr	29
Alphabet Soup	118
A.P. Indy	97
Aptitude	129
Aramus	5
Arch	88
Artax	74
Atticus	27
Austinpower (Jpn)	12
Austin Powers (Ire)	15
Awesome Again	91
Ballado Chieftan	12
Barkerville	26
Basic	18
Behaviour (GB)	8
Behrens	64
Belong to Me	103
Bernstein	84
Best of Luck	38
Black Minnaloushe	96
Booklet	13
Boundary	37
Brahms	92
Bright Launch	29
Broad Brush	26
Broken Vow	137
Buddha	182
Cactus Ridge	104
Came Home	106
Cape Canaveral	66
Cape Town	82
Carolina Kid	11
Carson City	131
Castle Gandolfo	71
Cat Doctor	16
Cat Thief	137
Century City (Ire)	72
Changeintheweather	84
Cherokee Run	130

Stallion	Mares Bred	Stallion	Mares Bred	Stallion	Mares Bred	Stallion	Mares Bred
Chief Seattle	166	Kafwain	142	Rojo Dinero	17	**LOUISIANA**	
Commendable	63	Kanjinsky	10	Royal Academy	90	Abajo	32
Composer	10	King Cugat	45	Royal Anthem	54	A Corking Limerick	8
Cozzene	49	Kingmambo	105	Ruckus Hosner	5	Afternoon Deelites	80
Crafty Friend	41	K One King	16	Runaway Groom	56	Almostashar	30
Crafty Prospector	50	K. O. Punch	31	Sahm	52	Aloha Prospector	26
Cryptoclearance	58	Kutsa	15	Salt Lake	95	American Tribute	8
Dance Brightly	32	Labeeb (GB)	29	Saratoga Six	22	A. P. Delta	44
Danzig	45	Lac Ouimet	30	Scatmandu	43	Autocracy	12
David Copperfield	31	Langfuhr	141	Sea of Secrets	85	Bag Ir	9
Dayjur	40	Lear Fan	49	Seeking the Gold	78	Beanie Babe	9
Deerhound	12	Leelanau	45	Service Stripe	80	Belek	14
Deputy Commander	120	Lee's Badger	8	Shadeed	12	Bermuda Cedar	6
Deputy Minister	64	Lemon Drop Kid	112	Silic (Fr)	53	Big Dawgs Brick	6
Devil His Due	105	Lil E. Tee	20	Silver Charm	103	B. J.'s Mark	11
Devil Power	5	Line Rider	16	Silver Deputy	101	Blare of Trumpets	10
Devil's Bag	53	Lion Cavern	15	Silver Ghost	25	Blue Grass Magic	5
Diesis (GB)	60	Littleexpectations	55	Siphon (Brz)	64	Bold Pac Man	7
Distant View	67	Luhuk	53	Sir Cat	54	Busterwaggley	9
Distorted Humor	146	Malabar Gold	104	Skip Away	61	Canboulay	6
Dixieland Band	52	Malibu Moon	149	Sky Classic	34	Catastrophe	24
Dixieland Heat	23	Mancini	21	Sky Mesa	110	Change Takes Time	7
Dixie Union	101	Maria's Mon	66	Slew City Slew	62	Cherokee Beau	9
Doneraile Court	184	Marquetry	59	Slide to the Left	6	Cherokee Tin	5
Down the Aisle	40	Matty G	124	Sligo Bay (Ire)	103	Choosing Choice	24
Dynaformer	108	Mazel Trick	64	Smart Strike	134	Classic Alliance	10
Ecton Park	101	Meadowlake	76	Smoke Glacken	116	Combat Ready	7
Editor's Note	33	Menifee	70	Souvenir Copy	41	Contested Colors	9
E Dubai	143	Military	49	State Craft	6	Corwyn	7
El Corredor	156	Millennium Wind	123	Stephen Got Even	140	Count the Time	16
El Prado (Ire)	106	Milwaukee Brew	106	St. Jovite	6	Crowning Decision	9
Elusive Quality	140	Minardi	86	Storm Boot	77	Dagwood	5
Empire Maker	111	Mineshaft	104	Storm Cat	116	Dakota Pride	6
En Tete	5	Misbah	15	Stormin Fever	95	Daring Bid	9
Evansville Slew	85	Miswaki	6	Stormy Atlantic	183	Deputy Diamond	40
Exclusive Enough	7	Mizzen Mast	130	Stravinsky	143	Direct Hit	36
Explicit	63	Monarchos	76	Street Cry (Ire)	129	Disciple	7
Exploit	88	More Than Ready	151	Subordination	15	Doeny Rain	9
Fadaaei	5	Morluc	38	Sultry Song	64	Dr. Lewis	10
Fast Play	33	Mr. Greeley	127	Sunday Break (Jpn)	132	Dream Tripper	10
Favorite Trick	27	Mr Henrysee	10	Swain (Ire)	66	Easyfromthegitgo	54
Fit to Fight	25	Mt. Livermore	55	Swing Lord	10	Erlton	33
Five Star Day	87	Mula Gula	6	Syncline	50	Escrito	27
Flatter	116	Mutakddim	162	Tactical Cat	112	Esplanade Ridge	10
Flying Chevron	8	Najran	105	Tale of the Cat	185	Eulogize	11
Forest Camp	105	No Dice	5	Talk Is Money	93	Exclusive Scout	7
Forestry	141	Northern Charm	6	Tejano Run	32	Far Out Wadleigh	8
Forest Wildcat	110	Northern Spur (Ire)	11	Theatrical (Ire)	53	Fenter	9
Formal Gold	53	Officer	129	The Deputy (Ire)	42	Finder's Gold	25
Frisk Me Now	15	Old Kentucky Home	24	Thousand Ores	6	Finest Hour	90
Fusaichi Pegasus	193	Orientate	115	Thunder Gulch	103	Fly Cry	20
General Royal	37	Our Emblem	63	Thunderello	92	Forty Won	26
Gentlemen (Arg)	9	Out of Place	59	Tiznow	123	Gift of Gib	11
Giant's Causeway	130	Peaks and Valleys	26	Touch Gold	106	Global Mission	20
Gilded Time	90	Pembroke	28	Trust N Luck	101	Golden Slew	19
Glitterman	76	Perfect Vision	35	Two Chiefs	5	Gold Tribute	66
Go for Gin	20	Peruvian	9	Two Point Two Mill	9	Goodbye Doeny	10
Gold Case	116	Petionville	125	Unbridled's Song	118	Grim Reaper	15
Golden Missile	116	Phone the King	5	Valid Lightning	7	Handkerchief (Arg)	8
Gold Spring (Arg)	8	Pikepass	72	Van Nistelrooy	186	Hat Trick X Three	7
Gone West	99	Pine Bluff	69	Vicar	105	Hervy	6
Grand Slam	191	Pioneering	33	Victory Gallop	116	Hold Hands	8
Greenwood Lake	91	Pleasant Tap	72	Vindication	140	Holy Sting	26
Grindstone	91	Point Given	95	Vision and Verse	71	Homebuilder	13
Gulch	83	Polish Navy	25	Volponi	80	Huff	8
Hap	43	Posse	115	Wagon Limit	38	Hyperborean	5
Harlan's Holiday	138	Private Terms	54	War Chant	57	Ide	74
Hennessy	122	Prized	39	Wavering Monarch	18	In a Walk	44
High Yield	138	Proud Citizen	157	Waving Past	5	Jaunatxo	15
Hold for Gold	34	Pulpit	109	Wheaton	12	Jitterbug Chief	7
Hold That Tiger	199	Pure Prize	81	Whywhywhy	95	Joe Who (Brz)	8
Holy Bull	112	Pyramid Peak	14	Wild Again	20	Kadhaaf	11
Home At Last	7	Quiet American	87	Wild Wonder	54	Keats	24
Honour and Glory	152	Raheeb	7	Will's Way	12	Kimberlite Pipe	25
Horse Chestnut (SAf)	100	Rahy	79	Winning Bid	9	King of Tap	6
Hussonet	83	Rather Bold	5	With Approval	68	Kipper Kelly	30
Include	93	R C Indy Go	7	Woodman	71	Kukulcan	10
Indian Charlie	104	Real Quiet	64	Yankee Gentleman	102	Laabity	30
Jade Hunter	43	Repriced	29	Yankee Victor	94	Lake Holme	7
Jambalaya Jazz	47	Richter Scale	111	Yonaguska	134	Leestown	100
Johannesburg	175	Ringer's Wildcat	10	Zavata	104	Like a Soldier	12
Jump Start	125	Rod and Staff	14				

Stallion	Mares Bred
Lunar Shadow	6
Malagra	20
Malibu Wesley	18
Middle Man	5
Mighty	16
Mike's Little Man	9
Mister Herbert	6
Montana Dreamin'	6
Moonlight Dancer	8
Mr. John	10
Mr. Shawklit	9
Mr. Sparkles	15
Mulberry Five	5
Munch n' Nosh	8
Mutah	5
My Friend Max	16
Native Regent	16
No Limit Soldier	7
Northern Niner	22
On Target	35
On the Sauce	5
Oro Bandito	6
Our Diablo	10
Our Shining Hour	17
Out of the Crisis	36
Parting Guest	10
Piccolino	19
Placid Fund	24
Planet Earth	12
Political Whit	8
Power and Peace	7
Prince of the Mt.	21
Prospector's Gift	34
Pulling Punches	26
Rail	10
Regreta	5
Road Rush	7
Royal Strand (Ire)	6
Ruby Hill	15
Rum Isle	6
Run Production	21
Rush	11
Safe Prospect	15
Saint's Honor	6
Sanctuary	6
Schumaker	6
Sea Soul	6
Secluded Hunt	6
Secret Odds	20
Sefapiano	56
Shrubs	6
Silky Sweep	43
Sky Raider	6
Slew the Surgeon	11
Spiritbound	5
Sport Hunter	6
Storm Day	99
Storm Passage	39
Storm Walk	10
Supremo Secret	7
Thank the Bank	11
Thunder Breeze	11
Time Bandit	71
Toolighttoquit	13
Top Venture	28
Tourist	17
Tricky	27
Trophy Hunter	5
Twilight Agenda	15
Two Punch Sonny	5
Upping the Ante	33
Valid Belfast	36
Valid Bidder	32
Virginia Carnival	13
Viva Deputy	18
Walnut Hall	5
Warp Speed Scottie	9
Western Echo	17
Western Gentleman	15
Westport Landing	6
Winter Halo	10
Wire Me Collect	26

Stallion	Mares Bred
Worldly Ways (GB)	41
Zarbyev	35
Zephruss	5

MARYLAND

Stallion	Mares Bred
Ameri Valay	8
Appealing Skier	33
Boy Done Good	7
Cat Country	10
Citidancer	32
Crowd Pleaser	33
Cruisin' Dixie	8
Crypto Star	36
Deputed Testamony	9
Diamond	42
Disco Rico	48
Eastern Echo	35
Fleet Foot	19
Innkeeper	6
Jazz Club	38
Larrupin'	23
Lion Hearted	127
Louis Quatorze	77
Marciano	5
Meadow Monster	46
Mojave Moon	65
Mokhieba	12
No Armistice	74
Not For Love	102
Ops Smile	11
Outflanker	73
Parker's Storm Cat	70
Partner's Hero	58
Polish Miner	54
Purple Passion	12
Rock Slide	69
Root Boy	5
Seeking Daylight	52
Smart Guy	7
Two Punch	85
Unbridled Jet	52
Waquoit	38
Wayne County (Ire)	11
Who's Your Daddy	11
Yarrow Brae	35
Yoh May Kenta	10

MASSACHUSETTS

Stallion	Mares Bred
Papa Juliet	6
Senor Conquistador	11
Silk Broker	5
Storm of Angels	15
Sundance Ridge	5

MICHIGAN

Stallion	Mares Bred
Allie's Punch	10
Awesome Arnold	10
Binalong	21
Career Best	12
Circus Surprise	10
Clock Radio	10
Collateral Attack	13
Creative	12
Crimson Guard	23
Daylight Savings	26
Demaloot Demashoot	37
Elusive Hour	28
Equality	41
Fast Five Six	6
Favorite Express	9
Great Allegiance	11
Gulch It	5
Hunting Hard	15
Intermediary	5
Island Storm	7
Matchlite	15
Meadow Prayer	9
Mr. Katowice	10
Native Factor	18
Ocala Slew	12

Stallion	Mares Bred
Override Battle	9
Pauliano	24
Predecessor	6
Quiet Enjoyment	16
Research	17
Sea Legs	6
Silent Era	5
Sky Approval	9
Treasury	11
Ulises	10
West Palm	9
Wind Chill	8

MINNESOTA

Stallion	Mares Bred
Boundless	18
Creditworthy	6
Dixie Power	23
Dynomania	10
Emailit	10
Foolish Lover	7
Gazebo	17
Ghazi	49
Jack's Storm	5
Lakeshore Road	13
La Pete	8
Late Edition	19
Olaf	9
Polished Brass	10
Quaker Hill	10
Quick Cut	17
Shot of Gold	31
Shotiche	7
Silk Song	9
Tahkodha Hills	27
Victor's Gent	16

MISSISSIPPI

Stallion	Mares Bred
Glitzi's Classic	5
House Burner	11
Mara o' Chino	6
Minister Slew	18
Valid Victorious	10

MISSOURI

Stallion	Mares Bred
Bananas	8
Hubba Hubba	11
Isaypete	7
Seattle Sun	9

MONTANA

Stallion	Mares Bred
C Spot Go	7
Double Dewars	10
Grey West	7
Khalsa	17
Let's Talk	9
Lifes Reward	10
Peacenfreedom	9
Polish	9
Rubio First (Arg)	5
Signoretto (Fr)	5
Silesia Flash	7
Twig n' Berries	7
Unbridled Desire	13
White Tie Tryst	12

NEBRASKA

Stallion	Mares Bred
Alyfoe	5
Blumin Affair	28
Box Buster	22
Dazzling Falls	19
Fortuoso	16
Glenview	20
Godolphin Cat	15
Golden Dice	6
Gourami	5
Gray Raider	20
Lytrump	6
Military Tune	19
Miracle Heights	9

Stallion	Mares Bred
More to Tell	7
Niner Bush	7
Not So Fast	19
Raja's Charter	9
Shawklit Player	20
Silent Bluff	35
Silver Launch	15
Yankee Fan	17

NEVADA

Stallion	Mares Bred
A Firm Seven	5
King Alobar	5

NEW JERSEY

Stallion	Mares Bred
Bugatti Reef (Ire)	6
Close Up	21
Contemplate	11
Defrere	69
Deputy Warlock	9
Evening Kris	24
Funny Frolic	6
Gerosa	15
Honor Defend	13
Imaginary Sword	5
Mr. Nugget	22
My Prince Charming	9
Private Interview	20
Tree	9

NEW MEXICO

Stallion	Mares Bred
Ack's Gold	5
Adios Mundo	8
Aledo	18
Alnaab	13
Bay Head King	29
Bayou the Moon	5
B. G.'s Drone	11
Call Me Cat	5
Caracal	8
Carmen's Glory	8
Chain of Command	9
Chimes Band	93
Chopin	9
Claudius	26
Comic Genius	36
Con Artist	15
Confide	9
Copelan's Pache	30
Daytime Dancer	7
Dee Lance	8
Deep Gold	20
Desert God	19
Devil Begone	15
Digging In	7
Doctor Roy A.	5
Dome	58
Don Lux	11
Dry Gulch	7
Eishin Seattle	6
Eishin Storm	21
Elegant Cat	22
Elk's Uz	5
El Sancho	16
Ferrara	16
Forever Whirl	6
General Gem	9
Ghost Ranch	8
Ghostly Moves	45
Golden Ransom	14
Gone Hollywood	9
Groomstick	20
Gun Bay	5
H. E. Miller	5
He's a Looker	5
Hezafastgold	7
Hit a Jackpot	27
Indian Runner	6
In Excessive Bull	52
Insinger	6
Istintaj	29
Lazy Lode (Arg)	33

Stallion	Mares Bred	Stallion	Mares Bred	Stallion	Mares Bred	Stallion	Mares Bred
Le Grande Danseur	12	Hook and Ladder	76	Alladin Rib	8	In Case	18
Lesters Boy	16	Intidab	7	Brolly	9	Indy Talent	13
Liberty Run	11	Its Acedemic	5	Camp Izard	7	Island City	6
Maid's Minister	7	Jager	5	Devil's Luck	6	It'sallinthechase	26
Mesquite Flat	12	Judge T C	62	Donthelumbertrader	5	Jazzman's Prospect	12
Mizaj	12	Kelly Kip	15	Farms	8	Jet K.	7
Mountain Metal	29	Kettle Won	10	Flight Forty Nine	6	Kelly S	6
Mr. Groush	16	Key Contender	11	Forest Gazelle	16	Kidd Cat	7
Mt. Hot	5	King's Grant	5	Gold Market	18	King Crypto	7
Not Tricky	26	Lacotte (Ire)	6	Holditholditholdit	6	King of Scat	47
Old Chapel	5	Legion Field	19	Iroquois Park	10	Kipling	27
Pallets	8	Let Goodtimes Roll	6	Keep It Down	11	Kukenhof	11
Paramour	13	Limit Out	10	King Tutta	29	Leave a Legacy	13
Parentheses	11	Lycius	39	Lake Superior	5	Lendell Ray	6
Passer Magnum	5	Manlove	9	Left Banker	5	Lesley's Express	6
Patsyprospect	21	Mayakovsky	52	Lived It Up	6	Letthedreambegin	5
Premeditation	7	Mighty Magee	8	Mahogany Hall	9	Lucky Lionel	31
Prince of Fame	10	Millions	13	Mambo Game	18	Maghnatis	20
Reality Play	5	Not a Corgi	11	Mercer Mill	25	Magics in the Wind	18
Red Prairie	9	Nunzio	10	Musical Dreamer	5	Magna	10
Retsina Run	7	Obligato	19	Pacific Waves	5	Major Henry	21
R. Payday	5	Ommadon	10	Parents' Reward	16	Mambo King	11
Sadler Slew	15	Ormsby	14	Part the Waters	5	Mister Deville	6
Schizoid	8	Our Frankie	10	Polish Spray	15	Moment of Crisis	5
Seacliff	30	Performing Magic	20	Political Folly	19	Muldoon	10
Shooter	9	Phone Trick	46	Pride of Burkaan	6	My Home Phone	8
Sleepless Morn	7	Polish Pro	18	Private School	7	My Liege	13
Stake a Claim	6	Precise End	52	Quietamericanforce	7	My Rare Verdict	7
Storm Ashore	25	Prime Timber	31	Round Four	6	Naroctive	7
Sunday Minister	7	Raffie's Majesty	19	Runto the Mountain	6	Notable Beaux	10
Tap N Snap	9	Rage	12	San Mont Andreas	6	Notable Cat	70
Thatsusintheolbean	35	Regal Classic	47	Winthrop	31	Officer of Court	7
The Trader's Echo	26	Reign Road	6	Yeti	8	Overview	20
Ticketless	6	River Keen (Ire)	27			Pistol's Cowboy	6
Tilt the Odds	7	Rizzi	11	**OKLAHOMA**		Plentyofit	7
To Teras	7	Rock and Roll	27			Polar Ice Caps	5
Touchdown Ky	13	Rodeo	12	Actor	8	Probable	5
Untold Gold	30	Satellite Sun	33	Alamocitos	37	Prospector's Music	47
Valet Man	12	Say Florida Sandy	71	All Storm	13	Raise a Rascal	15
Wild Deputy	14	Say Uncle	5	Alybel	5	Reardon Steel	8
You Know How It Is	8	Sea Salute	6	Amazing Connection	7	Reavealing Gold	5
		Senor Speedy	13	Avies Copy	5	Reel On Reel	8
NEW YORK		Signal Tap	10	Backoff Dude	5	River Eagle	6
		Silver Music	10	Back Packer	6	Riverside	11
Adios My Friend	9	Slice of Reality	15	Baltimore Gray	16	Search for Green	5
Allawinir	5	Smokin Mel	13	Bluffy	6	Sebastian	5
All Gone	8	Strategic Mission	18	Board Member	19	Speak	11
American Chance	48	Take Me Out	33	Bonus Time Cat	14	Star of the Crop	21
American Standard	9	Tank's Number	6	Burbank	25	Stromboli	24
A. P Jet	32	The Wicked North	5	Carr Tech	12	Taconic Road	5
Aristotle	11	Thriller	5	Charleys Gamble	5	Thingamajig	5
Badge	20	Tomorrows Cat	64	Cherokee Dan	15	Ti Valley	6
Be Accountable	7	Top Account	22	Christmas Storm	5	Unome	23
Captain Bodgit	27	Treasure Cove	19	Comstock Lode	15	Way Wild	8
Carry My Colors	13	Tri Line	12	Concern	28	Well Honed	5
Catienus	84	Watch the Bird	10	Confederate Hero	15	Wertaloona	9
City Hall Slew	8	Well Noted	25	Cool Cat	14	Western Challenge (GB)	13
City Zip	83	Western Borders	41	Coordinator	14	Who's John Galt	7
Comeonmom	13	Western Expression	86	Cuzzin Jeb	8	Wolf Touch	5
Country Squire	6	Wheelaway	103	Deal an Ace	5	Wolfire	12
Crafty C. T.	44	Williamstown	33	Defensive Bid	7		
Crusader Sword	25	Wiseman's Ferry	104	Deodar	26	**OREGON**	
David	11			Double Niner	7		
Daygata	18	**NORTH CAROLINA**		Dr. Dalton	6	Abstract	13
Deputy Cat	6			Easy Friend	7	Airdrie Apache	19
Desert Warrior	73	Chelsey Cat	22	Fistfite	27	Bagshot	19
Distinctive Pro	29	Programable	10	Flameout	7	Baquero	47
Dream Run	50			French Seventyfive	6	Cascadian	36
Dynamite Song	14	**NORTH DAKOTA**		Garbu	8	Crypt de Chine	6
Entepreneur	9			Ghost Tension	14	Dr. Litin	34
Freud	49	Castle Howard	8	Golden Dodger	8	Ex Marks the Cop	35
Full Quiver	6	Cross Morant	6	Harriman	13	Gold Meridian	7
Gold Fever	55	Far North Road	6	Have Fun	14	Klinsman (Ire)	13
Goldminers Gold	13	Gold Spats	14	Haymarket (GB)	9	Magic Level	5
Gold Token	74	Paranoide (Arg)	17	Heir Nijinsky	6	Nucay	8
Gone for Real	6	Patriot Strike	8	Here We Come	27	Ochoco	25
Good and Tough	74	Skipper Kipper	5	High Wide N Handsome	5	Prince Stanley	6
Griffinite	49	Speed Calling	14	Holy Notes	5	Prospected	24
Halissee	10	Win Lose Or Draw	8	House of Sport	19	Rob 'n Gin	12
Halory Hunter	14			Inagroove	6	Sound of Rhythm	10
Harbor Boy	9	**OHIO**		Inca Chief	32	Steel Ruhlr	5
Harry K.	7	Academy Award	29				
		Ago	20				

Stallion	Mares Bred
Superior Success	8
Tiffany Ice	12
True Confidence	37

PENNSYLVANIA

Stallion	Mares Bred
Activist	16
Aisle	7
Alyzig	19
Animation	8
Aquarian Prince	6
Attorney	10
Banker's Gold	77
Brian Is Golden	11
Caller I. D.	28
Cat's Career	29
Coastal Storm	43
Company Approval	7
Corporate Report	6
Count On Steve	10
Dark Mystery	5
Deposit Ticket	10
Digamist	8
Duckhorn	60
Dusty Screen	8
Erland	8
Fair Skies	6
Fastness (Ire)	20
Federal Trial	7
Fini Cassette	8
Flying Pidgeon	22
Give Us an Encore	5
G. P.'s Kruggerand	5
Harry the Hat	30
Jd's Determination	6
Knockadoon	14
Lil's Lad	26
Lord At Law	7
Lucky Clone	10
Mr. Sinatra	11
Munaadel	10
My Favorite Grub	12
National News	12
Native Comedy	5
Ocean Splash	9
Patton	52
Pin Stripe	13
Pok Ta Pok	19
Ponche	23
Power by Far	15
Reigning King	7
Rip Cat	7
Roanoke	8
Running Copelan	6
Sheryar	12
Special Times	13
Spectaculardynasty	6
Tekken (Ire)	5
Traffic Zack	12
Tricky Mister	6
Turn West	13
Turnofthecentury	15
Two Davids	8
U So Bad	6
Valid Request	10
Westminster	8
Wild West	23

SOUTH CAROLINA

Stallion	Mares Bred
Buckhar	5
Cat in Town	6
Charleston Man	6
Cockpit	7
East of Easy	5
Go West	9
Just a Miner	17
Lad	21
Nines Wild	6
Ride the Storm	7
Ring	12
Roll Again	10
Whisky Creek	6

SOUTH DAKOTA

Stallion	Mares Bred
Crafty Ridan	11
Crowning Season (GB)	17
Finn McCool	12
Khatef	6
Modern Day Moses	6
Storm of the Night	51

TENNESSEE

Stallion	Mares Bred
Code Talker	6
Doppler	11
Head West	13
Sir Wayma	5

TEXAS

Stallion	Mares Bred
Aggie Southpaw	31
Aggressive Chief	8
American Champ	21
American Spirit	12
Anniversary M.	6
A.p Jetter	11
A P Valentine	20
Asabashi	7
Assault Cat	15
Ataka Crypto	9
Authenticate	86
Ben's Ridge (GB)	10
Big Lukey	9
Blowing Rock	7
Blue Eyed Streaker	6
Boone's Mill	37
Boston Rebel	7
Brandan's Bid	5
Capitalimprovement	6
Capote's Prospect	11
Captain Countdown	51
Cat Strike	16
Cherokee Runaway	7
Cici Cici	6
Cien Fuegos	8
City Street	53
Clever Return	6
Cold Bid	6
Cold Hearted Man	6
Commanchero	34
Courtney's Native	5
Crafty	10
Dancer's Ghost	11
Diogenes	6
Discos My Name	5
Dot's Silver B.	5
Dove Hunt	36
Dynameaux	10
Early Flyer	42
Eastern Memories (Ire)	5
El Amante	16
El Sacrificio	5
Emerald Affair	7
Endless Queue	5
Excellent Secret	12
Exciting Story	26
Exclusive Zone	7
Falkenham (GB)	6
Fashion Find	5
Fat Francis	5
Festive	7
Fiend	10
Fifty Stars	13
Fincher Branch	6
Flaming Quest (GB)	12
Flying Kris	14
Gen Stormin'norman	29
Gilded Crusader	5
Gold Alert	15
Gold Legend	28
Goldmine (Fr)	10
Gold Regent	35
Gone East	13
Grand Jewel	12
Groovy Jett	7

Stallion	Mares Bred
Hadif	10
Half Fast George	6
Heather's Prospect	11
Hello Houston	8
Hollycombe	11
Holzmeister	20
Hometown Favorite	12
Houston Slue	8
Hurlingham	7
Ile de Jinsky	5
Imperial Cat	7
Indian Prospector (Fr)	10
Irish Open	33
Island Born	8
Itaka	10
Itron	11
Jadacus	12
Jolie's Wild Again	5
Karen's Cat	55
Kentucky Jazz	7
Kingkiowa	13
King of the Heap	7
Leafy	9
Lil Honcho	8
Lockstockandhouse	6
Lucky So n' So	8
Magic Cat	58
Malthus	8
Marked Tree	34
Meacham	18
Memento	11
Miswaki Gold	8
Mr. Cellular	10
Myrmidon	18
Mystery Storm	21
Naevus	19
Never Bend Better	7
New Trieste	32
Night Beat	6
Noble Savage (Ire)	9
Olmos	14
Omega Man	6
Once a Sailor	18
Open Forum	36
Ore Deal	18
Pancho Villa	26
Pepper M.	11
Pollock's Luck	10
Porto Varas	12
Power Storm	8
Proud Halo	11
Raja's Best Boy	12
Rare Brick	16
Regent Minister	7
Report On Rain	5
River Squall	19
Ruhlmann	9
Saints n' Sinners	5
Saucey Avenger	9
Saxton	8
Seattle Pattern	10
Seattle Sleet	38
Secret Claim	7
Secreteex	6
Seeking a Home	19
Semoran	5
Seneca Jones	65
Shadow Caster	8
Side	6
Siebe	5
Simon Lord Lovat	5
Sir Bedivere	28
Star Programmer	65
Storm Broker	14
Struggler (GB)	8
Sudden Storm	6
Swamp	14
Texas City	11
The Great Prize	7
The Prime Minister	7

Stallion	Mares Bred
Tinners Way	25
Top Gear	7
Tory Hole	7
Touch Tone	31
Traffic Circle	5
Trancus	17
Trapp Mountain	11
Treetopper	6
Tricky Prospect	5
Truluck	50
Twin Rocket Power	5
Uncle Abbie	30
Uncommon Valor	7
Under David's Wing	8
Valid Expectations	80
Waco Connection	9
Wajir	15
Wake Up Alarm	7
Western City	10
Western Trader	13
Wild Zone	44
Z Smart Prospect	19

UTAH

Stallion	Mares Bred
Albright Avenue	6
Bagdad Road	6
Classic Chrys	14
Crystal Gazer	13
Mi Selecto	91
Regal Groom	10
Serve the Flag	8
Taillevent	10
Thunder Falcon	20

VIRGINIA

Stallion	Mares Bred
Aaron's Gold	12
Ball's Bluff	12
Black Tie Affair (Ire)	92
Bop	32
Forest Service	8
Fred Astaire	15
Hay Halo	11
Housebuster	48
Hurricane State	6
Husband	6
Mighty Forum (GB)	8
Near the Limit	5
Pleasant Dancer	5
Prenup	5
Prospect Bay	10
Rock Point	8
Selective Pro	8
Slew the Deputy	5
Star Trace	5
Tagish	8
Tom Cobbley	5
Zillionair	5

WASHINGTON

Stallion	Mares Bred
Basket Weave	11
Beefchopper	5
Cahill Road	49
Chinquapin Charlie	5
Chumaree	12
Cisco Road	23
Commandperformance	10
Consigliere (GB)	9
Defensive Play	17
Delineator	16
Detox	21
Dixieland Glo	15
Eastern Money	10
Flying With Eagles	6
Free At Last	39
Gold Saga	10
Hampton Bay	21
He's Tops	60
Ihtimam	40
Ito the Hammer	8
Jazzing Around	5

Stallion	Mares Bred
Just Ruler	9
Kansas City	7
Katowice	25
Kentucky Lucky	30
Liberty Gold	49
Liquid Gold	5
Makors Mark	33
Matricule	62
Midway Magistrate	9
My Grand Indy	5
Name for Norm	6
Pacific Missioner	7
Petersburg	34
Polish Gift	28
Raisor's Edge	15
Red Storm Rising	16
Rojo Warrior	7
Salty's Tuko	7
Slewdledo	76
Snowbound	84
Stolen Gold	19
Tahoe City	13
Tamourad	12
Tribunal	65
Tristaino	14
Tropic Lightning	8
Vitesse	8
Zayzoom	15

WEST VIRGINIA

Stallion	Mares Bred
Castine	37
Citislipper	17
Civilisation	49
Constant Escort	5
Copelan Too	11
Cowboy Carson	7
Creative Act	8
Dancinwiththedevil	18
Danish Gold	9
Devon Deputy	24
Emancipator	45
Endeavouring	27
Ghostly Minister	15
Green Fee	24
Kokand	54
Luftikus	50
Make Your Mark	9
Makin	61
Master's Honey	6
Meadow Mango	7
Medford	28
My Boy Adam	23
Native Slew	12
One More Power	22
Our Valley View	22
Peak Dancer	7
Proper Texan	13
Raft	6
Reparations	17
Rich Deeds	13
Robb	9
Roxbury Park	6
R. S. V. P. Please	9
Rugby	8
Runaway Macho	9
Run Softly	27
Sandlot Star	6
Satchmo's Band	8
Select Session	10
Sequoia Slew	26
Siouxperheart	5
Slew O'Quoit	18
Standing On Edge	13
Strike Adduce	10
Stritzel	6
Twin Bridges	8
Valiant Nature	22
Way West (Fr)	56
Weshaam	16
Western Cat	29
Windsor Castle	31
Zizou	7

WISCONSIN

Stallion	Mares Bred
Prospect Feature	7
Radevore (GB)	5

WYOMING

Stallion	Mares Bred
Aide Memoire	5
King's Gent	6

PUERTO RICO

Stallion	Mares Bred
Balcony	17
Bargello	13
Be Frank	30
Billions	37
Blustery	16
Cape Cod	20
Casanova Star	13
Crowd	16
D' Coach	33
Don Serafin	7
El Jibaro	10
El Justo	17
Eqtesaad	42
Fappiano's Star	55
Figure of Speech	5
Fort La Roca	24
Glitman	11
Goldwater	8
Hard Charger	13
Just Typical	31
King's Crown	15
Laurentide	8
Lightning Al	18
Millonario	27
Monoestrellado	6
Mr. Proud	7
Myfavorite Place	37
Nather	7
Ordway	16
Plano Pleasure	5
Royal Merlot	45
Stag Dinner	8
Stake Procpect	9
Sudden Thunder	51
Sutters Pond	9
Tamhid	11
Virtua Cop	28
Wonder Bird	17

ALBERTA

Stallion	Mares Bred
Banjo	6
Brass Minister	23
Brunswick	24
Cache In	7
Candid Cameron	10
Commitisize	38
Deal Breaker	7
Desperately	19
Devonwood	37
Dr. Adagio	43
Dubious Connection	5
Easy Climb	12
Esteem	24
Fast Account	8
Go Gary Go	36
Ground Stroke	11
Half a Year	38
Haus of Dehere	40
Hurricane Center	26
Important Notice	11
Just a Cat	37
King's Nest	7
Lenado Road	18
Linkage	17
Magic Prospect	10
Mint	19
Misnomer	13
Nicholas Ds	15
Othello	30
Parlay Me	7

Stallion	Mares Bred
Proud Exchange	8
Ranger (Fr)	6
Real West	7
Rebmec	10
Regal Remark	17
Rocanville	13
Rosetti	51
Royal Rumpus	9
Seattle Syn	13
Smile Again	43
Smithfield	6
Stevie Ruckus	6
The Fed	6
The Key Rainbow (Ire)	12
Tiger Trap	18
Tossofthecoin	22
Weekend Guest	8
Young Devil	8
Zuppardo's Future	8

BRITISH COLUMBIA

Stallion	Mares Bred
Alfaari	28
Alybro	12
Amaruk	10
Baron de Vaux	8
Bright Valour	33
Captain Collins (Ire)	13
Devil On Ice	12
Digital Dan	25
Dixieland Brass	8
Dixieland Diamond	17
Feu d'Enfer	15
Finality	37
Flaming West	17
Funboy	5
Incitatus (Bar)	5
J. L. Sullivan	5
Katahaula County	57
King of Cats	10
Light of Mine	30
Mass Market	33
Millennium Allstar	30
Mombo Gambo	7
Net Asset	12
Nightofthegaelics	12
Noble Lyphard	13
Orchid's Devil	8
Persian Star	8
Regal Intention	34
Silver Fox	13
Stephanotis	67
Synastry Express	7
Vying Victor	66
Walkinwithapproval	12
Wandering	12
Welbred Fred	8
Yoonevano	48

MANITOBA

Stallion	Mares Bred
Act Smart	16
Akado	5
Battle Cat	28
Boanerges	7
Chinese Gold	21
Circulating	14
Crystal Gulch	12
Gentle Kent	15
Get Me Out	8
Honorable Hero	6
Sunset Ridge	9
Tabib	7
Ten Keys	7
Transferred	11

ONTARIO

Stallion	Mares Bred
A Fleets Dancer	49
Alydeed	20
Alystar Slew	14
Ascot Knight	24

Stallion	Mares Bred
Ashbury	17
Bold Executive	103
Bold n' Flashy	39
Breezy Meadow	5
Brite Adam	23
Catahoula Parish	6
Catinental	8
Cat's At Home	54
Ciano Cat	63
Compadre	43
Cool Groom	9
Cracker's Folly	7
Crown Attorney	9
Domasca Dan	35
D'wildcat	56
Elajjud	18
Endeavor	17
Explosive Victory	5
Fort Chaffee	25
Foxtrail	8
Guaranteed Gold	6
Gun Power	11
Hierarch	7
Highland Ruckus	6
I Can't Believe	6
Inspired Prospect	5
Iskandar Elakbar	6
King Riviera	7
Kinshasa	59
Kiridashi	15
Like the Prospects	17
Magic Walk	5
Matter of Honor	5
Minstrel Dancer	6
My Way Only	6
Not Impossible (Ire)	34
One Way Love	74
Parisianprospector	19
Paynes Bay	83
Perigee Moon	46
Pete's Sake	8
Porto Foricos	26
Raj Waki	19
Randy Regent	40
Regal Discovery	6
Salty Note	18
Sambuca On Ice	9
Sato	14
Sea Wall	17
Shelly's Charmer	12
Tejabo	9
Tempolake	9
Tethra	48
Trajectory	88
Valid N Bold	17
Valid Trefaire	12
Wake At Noon	10
War Deputy	17
Whiskey Wisdom	37
Wonneberg	14
Yellow Creek	14

QUEBEC

Stallion	Mares Bred
Oronero	9

SASKATCHEWAN

Stallion	Mares Bred
Blowin de Turn	10
Bluegrass Spirit	19
Good Evening Sir	8
High Firm	19
McCallister's Risk	5
Nation Wide News	8
Northern Sleeper	5
Royal Quiz	6
Satellite Signal	5
Shaheen	16
Slew Express	9
Whiskey Bill	7
You've Got Action	24

BROODMARES
Broodmares of the Year
As awarded by the Kentucky Thoroughbred Owners and Breeders Association

2004—DEAR BIRDIE
1987 ch. m., Storm Bird—Hush Dear, by Silent Screen
Breeder, Echo Valley Horse Farm Inc. (Ky.). **Owner**, Marylou Whitney.
Dam of 11 foals, 10 starters, all winners, including **BIRD TOWN**, 4 wins, $871,251, 2003 champion three-year-old filly, 2003 Kentucky Oaks (G1), etc.; **BIRDSTONE**, 5 wins, $1,575,600, 2004 Belmont S. (G1), etc.

2003—PROSPECTORS DELITE
1989 ch. m., Mr. Prospector—Up the Flagpole,
by Hoist the Flag
Breeder, W. S. Farish (Ky.). **Owners**, William S. Farish, James Elkins Jr., and W. Temple Webber Jr.
Dam of 5 foals, all winners, including **MINESHAFT**, 10 wins, $2,283,402, 2003 Horse of the Year, 2003 champion older male, 2003 Jockey Club Gold Cup S. (G1), etc.; **TOMISUE'S DELIGHT**, 7 wins, $1,207,537, 1998 Personal Ensign H. (G1), **ROCK SLIDE, MONASHEE MOUNTAIN, DELTA MUSIC**.

2002—TOUSSAUD
1989 dk. b. or br. m., El Gran Senor—Image of Reality,
by In Reality
Breeder, Juddmonte Farms Inc. (Ky.). **Owner**, Juddmonte Farms Inc.
Dam of 9 foals, 6 starters, 5 winners, including **CHESTER HOUSE**, 6 wins, $1,944,545, 2000 Arlington Million S. (G1), etc.; **EMPIRE MAKER**, 4 wins, $1,985,800, 2003 Belmont S. (G1), etc.; **HONEST LADY**, 6 wins, $894,168, 2000 Santa Monica H. (G1), etc.; **CHISELLING**, 3 wins, $410,000, 2002 Secretariat S. (G1), etc.; **DECARCHY**, 6 wins, $703,862, 2002 Frank E. Kilroe Mile H. (G2), etc.

2001—TURKO'S TURN
1992 ch. m., Turkoman—Turbo Launch, by Relaunch
Breeder, John F. Dolan (Ky.). **Owner**, The Thoroughbred Corp.
Dam of 8 foals, 4 winners, including **POINT GIVEN**, 9 wins, $3,968,500, 2001 Horse of the Year, 2001 champion three-year-old male, 2001 Preakness S. (G1), etc.

2000—PRIMAL FORCE
1987 b. m., Blushing Groom (Fr)—Prime Prospect,
by Mr. Prospector
Breeders, Mr. and Mrs. Bertram R. Firestone (Ky.). **Owner**, Frank Stronach.
Dam of 9 foals, 4 starters, all winners, including **MACHO UNO**, 6 wins, $1,851,803, 2000 champion two-year-old male, 2000 Breeders' Cup Juvenile (G1), etc.; **AWESOME AGAIN**, 9 wins, $4,374,590, 1998 Breeders' Cup Classic (G1), etc.

1999—ANNE CAMPBELL
1973 b. m., Never Bend—Repercussion, by *Tatan
Breeder, Mill House (Ky.). **Owner**, Arthur B. Hancock III.
Dam of 14 foals, 10 starters, 7 winners, including **MENIFEE**, 5 wins, $1,732,000, 1999 Haskell Invitational H. (G1), etc.; **DESERT WINE**, 8 wins, $1,618,043, 1984 Hollywood Gold Cup (G1), etc.

1998—IN NEON
1982 b. m., Ack Ack—Shamara, by Dewan
Breeder, Clairmont Farm (Ky.). **Owner**, John Franks.
Dam of 7 foals, all starters, 6 winners, including **SHARP CAT**, 15 wins, $2,032,575, 1998 Beldame S. (G1), etc.; **ROYAL ANTHEM**, 6 wins, $1,876,876, 1998 Canadian International S. (Can-G1), etc.; **STAR RECRUIT**, 5 wins, $807,200, 1991 Alysheba S. (G3), etc.

1997—SLIGHTLY DANGEROUS
1979 b. m., Roberto—Where You Lead, by Raise a Native
Breeder, Alan Clore (Ky.). **Owner**, Juddmonte Farms.
Dam of 13 foals, 11 starters, 10 winners, including **COMMANDER IN CHIEF**, 5 wins, $1,311,514, 1993 champion three-year-old male in Eur, 1993 Epsom Derby (Eng-G1), etc.; **WARNING (GB)**, 8 wins, $937,280, 1987 champion two-year-old male in Eng, 1988 champion three-year-old male in Eng, 1988 Queen Elizabeth II S. (Eng-G1), etc.; **YASHMAK**, 4 wins, $529,382, 1997 Flower Bowl Invitational H. (G1), etc.; **DUSHYANTOR**, 5 wins, $1,197,570, 1996 Great Voltigeur S. (Eng-G2), **JIBE**.

1996—PERSONAL ENSIGN
1984 b. m., Private Account—Grecian Banner,
by Hoist the Flag
Breeder, Ogden Phipps (Ky.). **Owner**, Ogden Phipps, Phipps Stable.
Dam of 9 foals, 8 starters, all winners, including **MY FLAG**, 6 wins, $1,557,057, 1995 Breeders' Cup Juvenile Fillies (G1), etc.; **MINER'S MARK**, 6 wins, $967,170, 1993 Jockey Club Gold Cup (G1), etc.; **TRADITIONALLY**, 5 wins, $495,660, 2001 Oaklawn H. (G1).

1995—NORTHERN SUNSET (Ire)
1977 ch. m., Northfields—Moss Greine, by *Ballymoss
Breeder, Basil Brindly (Ire). **Owner**, Virginia Kraft Payson.
Dam of 13 foals, 12 starters, 11 winners, including **ST. JOVITE**, 6 wins, $1,604,439, 1992 Horse of the Year in Eur, 1991 champion two-year-old male in Ire, 1992 Irish Derby (Ire-G1), etc.; **SALEM DRIVE**, 13 wins, $1,046,065, 1987 Bougainvillea H. (G2), etc.; **LAC OUIMET**, 13 wins, $817,863, 1986 Jim Dandy S. (G2), etc.; **L'CARRIERE**, 8 wins, $1,726,175, 1996 Saratoga Cup H. (G3), etc.

Broodmares of the Year

Year	Broodmare	Year	Broodmare	Year	Broodmare	Year	Broodmare
2004	Dear Birdie	1989	Relaxing	1974	Cosmah	1959	*Knight's Daughter
2003	Prospectors Delite	1988	Grecian Banner	1973	Somethingroyal	1958	Miss Disco
2002	Toussaud	1987	Banja Luka	1972	*Moment of Truth II	1957	Belle Jeep
2001	Turko's Turn	1986	Too Bald	1971	Iberia	1956	Swoon
2000	Primal Force	1985	Dunce Cap II	1970	Levee	1955	Iron Reward
1999	Anne Campbell	1984	Hasty Queen II	1969	All Beautiful	1954	Traffic Court
1998	In Neon	1983	Courtly Dee	1968	Delta	1953	Gaga
1997	Slightly Dangerous	1982	Best in Show	1967	Kerala	1952	Ace Card
1996	Personal Ensign	1981	Natashka	1966	Juliets Nurse	1951	*Alpenstock III
1995	Northern Sunset (Ire)	1980	Key Bridge	1965	Pocahontas	1950	Hildene
1994	Fall Aspen	1979	Smartaire	1964	Maid of Flight	1949	Easy Lass
1993	Glowing Tribute	1978	Primonetta	1963	Misty Morn	1948	Our Page
1992	Weekend Surprise	1977	Sweet Tooth	1962	Track Medal	1947	Potheen
1991	Toll Booth	1976	*Gazala II	1961	Striking	1946	Bloodroot
1990	Kamar	1975	Shenanigans	1960	Siama		

1994—FALL ASPEN

1976 ch. m., Pretense—Change Water, by Swaps
Breeder, Joseph M. Roebling (Ky.). **Owner**, John Magnier.
Dam of 14 foals, 13 starters, 12 winners, including **TIMBER COUNTRY**, 5 wins, $1,560,400, 1994 champion two-year-old male, 1995 Preakness S. (G1), etc.; **BIANCONI**, 3 wins, $134,520, 1998 Diadem S. (Eng-G2); **FORTWOOD**, 3 wins, $359,995, 1993 Grand Prix de Paris (Fr-G1), etc.; **NORTHERN ASPEN**, 5 wins, $253,678, 1987 Gamely H. (G1), etc.; **HAMAS (Ire)**, 5 wins, $237,814, 1993 Juddy Cup S. (Eng-G2), etc.; **COLORADO DANCER (Ire)**, 3 wins, $203,389, 1989 Prix de Pomone (Fr-G2), etc.; **ELLE SEULE**, 3 wins, $101,478, 1986 Prix d'Astarte (Fr-G2); **MAZZACANO (GB)**, 3 wins, $153,421, 1989 Goodwood Cup (Eng-G3); **PRINCE OF THIEVES**, 2 wins, $368,474.

1993—GLOWING TRIBUTE

1973 b. m., Graustark—Admiring, by Hail to Reason
Breeder, Paul Mellon (Va.). **Owner**, John R. Gaines.
Dam of 12 foals, 10 starters, 9 winners, including **SEA HERO**, 6 wins, $2,929,869, 1993 Kentucky Derby (G1), etc.; **HERO'S HONOR**, 8 wins, $499,025, 1984 Bowling Green H. (G1), etc.; **GLOWING HONOR**, 6 wins, $296,450, 1988, '89 Diana H. (G2), etc.; **WILD APPLAUSE**, 5 wins, $240,136, 1984 Diana H. (G2), etc.; **CORONATION CUP**, 3 wins, $172,181, 1994 Nijana S. (G3); **MACKIE**, 3 wins, $164,579, 1996 Busher S. (G3); **SEATTLE GLOW**, 4 wins, $69,023.

1992—WEEKEND SURPRISE

1980 b. m., Secretariat—Lassie Dear, by Buckpasser
Breeders, W. S. Farish III and W. S. Kilroy (Ky.). **Owners**, W. S. Farish III and W. S. Kilroy.
Dam of 14 foals, 12 starters, 9 winners, including **A.P. INDY**, 8 wins, $2,979,815, 1992 Horse of the Year, 1992 champion three-year-old male, 1992 Belmont S. (G1), etc.; **SUMMER SQUALL**, 3 wins, $1,844,282, 1990 Preakness S. (G1), etc.; **WELCOME SURPRISE**, 2 wins, $143,574, 2000 Dogwood S. (G3); **EAVESDROPPER**, 3 wins, $167,794.

1991—TOLL BOOTH

1971 b. m., Buckpasser—Missy Baba, by *My Babu
Breeder, John M. Schiff (Ky.). **Owner**, Lazy Lane Farms.
Dam of 12 foals, all starters, 11 winners, including **PLUGGED NICKLE**, 11 wins, $647,206, 1980 champion sprinter, 1980 Florida Derby (G1), etc.; **CHRISTIECAT**, 11 wins, $799,745, 1992 Flower Bowl H. (G1), etc.; **KEY TO THE BRIDGE**, 7 wins, $289,747, 1988 Beaugay H. (G3); **TOLL FEE**, 7 wins, $333,917; **TOLL KEY**, 9 wins, $290,218; **IDLE GOSSIP**, 5 wins, $101,721; **TOKENS ONLY**, 4 wins, $50,455.

1990—KAMAR

1976 b. m., Key to the Mint—Square Angel, by Quadrangle
Breeder, E. P. Taylor (Can). **Owner**, Heronwood Farm.
Dam of 9 foals, 8 starters, 7 winners, including **KEY TO THE MOON**, 13 wins, $714,536, 1984 champion three-year-old male in Can, 1984 Discovery H. (G3), etc.; **GORGEOUS**, 8 wins, $1,171,370, 1989 Ashland S. (G1), etc.; **SEASIDE ATTRACTION**, 4 wins, $272,541, 1990 Kentucky Oaks (G1); **HIAAM**, 3 wins, $48,081, 1986 Princess Margaret S. (Eng-G3), etc.

1989—RELAXING

1976 b. m., Buckpasser—Marking Time, by To Market
Breeder, Ogden Phipps (Ky.). **Owner**, Ogden Phipps.
Dam of 12 foals, all starters, all winners, including **EASY GOER**, 14 wins, $4,873,770, 1988 champion two-year-old male, 1989 Belmont S. (G1), etc.; **EASY NOW**, 4 wins, $359,466, 1992 Go for Wand S. (G1), etc.; **CADILLACING**, 7 wins, $268,137, 1988 Ballerina S. (G1), etc.

1988—GRECIAN BANNER

1974 dk. b. or br. m., Hoist the Flag—*Dorine, by Aristophanes
Breeder, Ogden Phipps (Ky.). **Owner**, Ogden Phipps.
Dam of 7 foals, 5 starters, all winners, including **PERSONAL ENSIGN**, 13 wins, $1,679,880, 1988 champion older female, 1996 Broodmare of the Year, 1988 Breeders' Cup Distaff (G1), etc.; **PERSONAL FLAG**, 8 wins, $1,258,924, 1988 Suburban H. (G1), etc.

1987—BANJA LUKA

1968 b. m., Double Jay—Legato, by Dark Star
Breeder, Howard B. Keck (Ky.). **Owner**, Howard B. Keck.
Dam of 9 foals, all starters, 7 winners, including **FERDINAND**, 8 wins, $3,777,978, 1987 Horse of the Year, 1987 champion older male, 1986 Kentucky Derby (G1), etc.; **DONNA INEZ**, 4 wins, $101,275; **JAYSTON**, 7 wins, $92,143; **DANCING**, 4 wins, $77,925; **ANCIENT ART**, 4 wins, $74,250; **PLINTH**, 3 wins, $65,980.

1986—TOO BALD

1964 dk. b. or br. m., Bald Eagle—Hidden Talent, by Dark Star
Breeder, H. F. Guggenheim (Ky.). **Owner**, North Ridge Farm.
Dam of 12 foals, 11 starters, all winners, including **CAPOTE**, 3 wins, $714,470, 1986 champion two-year-old male, 1986 Breeders' Cup Juvenile S. (G1), etc.; **EXCELLER**, 15 wins, $1,674,587, 1978 Jockey Club Gold Cup (G1), etc.; **VAGUELY HIDDEN**, 8 wins, $239,313, 1990 New Jersey Turf Classic S. (G3); **AMERICAN STANDARD**, 5 wins, $180,120; **BALDSKI**, 7 wins, $103,214.

1985—DUNCE CAP II

1960 dk. b. or br. m., Tom Fool—Bright Coronet, by Bull Lea
Breeder, Greentree Stud Inc. (Ky.). **Owner**, Greentree Stud Inc.
Dam of 10 foals, 8 starters, all winners, including **LATE BLOOMER**, 11 wins, $512,040, 1978 champion older female, 1978 Beldame S. (G1), etc.; **JOHNNY APPLESEED**, 4 wins, $91,910, 1976 Louisiana Derby (G2); **LATE ACT**, 9 wins, $661,089, 1985 Cliff Hanger H. (G3), etc.

1984—HASTY QUEEN II

1963 dk. b. or br. m., One Count—Queen Hopeful, by Roman
Breeder, A. E. Reuben (Ky.). **Owners**, Robert E. Courtney and Robert B. Congleton.
Dam of 16 foals, 14 starters, 12 winners, including **FIT TO FIGHT**, 14 wins, $1,042,075, 1984 Brooklyn H. (G1), etc.; **HASTY FLYER**, 10 wins, $293,663, 1974 Round Table H. (G3), etc.; **HASTY TAM**, 16 wins, $211,738; **PLAYFUL QUEEN**, 5 wins, $101,837; **MICHAEL NAVONOD**, 6 wins, $86,380; **HASTY CUTIE**, 8 wins, $63,639.

1983—COURTLY DEE

1968 dk. b. or br. m., Never Bend—Tulle, by War Admiral
Breeder, Donald Unger (Ky.). **Owners**, Helen Alexander, David Aykroyd, and Helen Groves.
Dam of 18 foals, 17 starters, 15 winners, including **ALTHEA**, 8 wins, $1,275,255, 1983 champion two-year-old filly, 1984 Arkansas Derby (G1), etc.; **ALI OOP**, 7 wins, $174,020, 1976 Sapling S. (G1); **KETOH**, 3 wins, $173,550, 1985 Cowdin S. (G1); **AQUILEGIA**, 8 wins, $446,081, 1993 New York H. (G2), etc.; **TWINING**, 5 wins, $238,140, 1994 Peter Pan S. (G2), etc.; **AISHAH**, 6 wins, $169,340, 1990 Rare Perfume S. (G2); **NATIVE COURIER**, 14 wins, $522,635, 1981 Bernard Baruch H. (G3), etc.; **PRINCESS OOLA**, 5 wins, $108,291.

1982—BEST IN SHOW

1965 ch. m., Traffic Judge—Stolen Hour, by Mr. Busher
Breeder, Philip Connors (Ky.). **Owners**, Mr. and Mrs. Darrell Brown.
Dam of 17 foals, 12 starters, 9 winners, including **MALINOWSKI**, 2 wins, 1975 champion two-year-old in Ire, 1976 Ladbroke Craven S. (Eng-G3); **BLUSH WITH PRIDE**, 6 wins, $536,807, 1982 Kentucky Oaks (G1), etc.; **GIELGUD**, 1 win, $56,635, 1980 Champagne S. (Eng-G2); **MONROE**, 3 wins, $34,422, 1980 Ballyogan S. (Ire-G3), etc.

1981—NATASHKA

1963 dk. b. or br. m., Dedicate—Natasha, by *Nasrullah
Breeder, Greentree Stud Inc. (Ky.). **Owner**, W. S. Farish III.
Dam of 9 foals, 7 starters, all winners, including **GREGORIAN**, 4 wins, $194,912, 1980 Joe McGrath Memorial S. (Ire-G1), etc.; **TRULY BOUND**, 9 wins, $382,449, 1980 Arlington-Washington Lassie S. (G2), etc.; **IVORY WAND**, 5 wins, $97,452, 1976 Test S. (G3); **BLOOD ROYAL**, 4 wins, $28,870, 1975 Jockey Club Cup (Eng-G3), etc.; **ARKADINA**, 2 wins, $79,830, Athasi S. (Ire-G3), etc.

1980—KEY BRIDGE

1959 b. m., *Princequillo—Blue Banner, by War Admiral
Breeder, Paul Mellon (Va.). **Owner**, Paul Mellon.
Dam of 11 foals, 8 starters, 7 winners, including **FORT MARCY**, 21 wins, $1,109,791, 1970 Horse of the Year, 1967, '68, '70 champion turf male, 1970 champion older male, 1967, '70 Washington D.C. International S., etc.; **KEY TO THE MINT**, 14 wins, $576,015, 1972 champion three-year-old male, 1973 Suburban H. (G1), etc.; **KEY TO CONTENT**, 7 wins, $354,772, 1981 United Nations H. (G1), etc.; **KEY TO THE KINGDOM**, 7 wins, $109,590, 1974 Stymie H. (G3).

1979—SMARTAIRE

1962 dk. b. or br. m., *Quibu—Art Teacher, by Olympia
Breeder, F. W. Hooper (Al.). **Owners**, Mr. and Mrs. James P. Ryan.
Dam of 12 foals, all starters, 10 winners, including **SMART ANGLE**, 7 wins, $414,217, 1979 champion two-year-old filly, 1979 Frizette S. (G1), etc.; **SMARTEN**, 11 wins, $716,426, 1979 American Derby (G2), etc.; **QUADRATIC**, 6 wins, $233,941, 1977 Cowdin S. (G2); **SMART HEIRESS**, 6 wins, $154,999.

1978—PRIMONETTA

1958 ch. m., Swaps—Banquet Bell, by Polynesian
Breeder, John W. Galbreath (Ky.). **Owner**, John W. Galbreath.
Dam of 7 foals, 6 starters, all winners, including **CUM LAUDE LAURIE**, 8 wins, $405,207, 1977 Beldame S. (G1), etc.; **PRINCE THOU ART**, 3 wins, $167,902, 1975 Florida Derby (G1); **MAUD MULLER**, 3 wins, $138,383, 1974 Gazelle H. (G2), etc.; **GRENFALL**, 4 wins, $19,467, 1971 Gallinule S. (Ire-G2), etc.

1977—SWEET TOOTH

1965 b. m., On-and-On—Plum Cake, by Ponder
Breeder, Calumet Farm (Ky.). **Owner**, Calumet Farm.
Dam of 13 foals, 10 starters, 8 winners, including **OUR MIMS**, 6 wins, $368,034, 1977 champion three-year-old filly, 1977 Coaching Club American Oaks (G1), etc.; **ALYDAR**, 14 wins, $957,195, 1978 Blue Grass S. (G1), etc.; **SUGAR AND SPICE**, 5 wins, $257,046, 1980 Mother Goose S. (G1), etc.

1976—*GAZALA II

1964 dk. b. or br. m, Dark Star—*Belle Angevine, by L'Amiral
Breeder, Nelson Bunker Hunt (Fr). **Owner**, Nelson Bunker Hunt.
Dam of 10 foals, 8 starters, 6 winners, including **YOUTH**, 8 wins, $716,146, 1976 champion three-year-old in Fr, 1976 champion turf male, 1976 Prix du Jockey Club (Fr-G1), etc.; **MISSISSIPIAN**, 3 wins, $248,520, 1973 champion two-year-old in Fr, 1973 Grand Criterium (Fr-G1), etc.; **GONZALES**, 4 wins, $103,968, 1980 Irish St. Leger (Ire-G1), etc.; **SILKY BABY**, 2 wins, $51,351, 1981 Prix de Guiche (Fr-G3); **BEST OF BOTH**, 6 wins, $242,150.

1975—SHENANIGANS

1963 gr. m., Native Dancer—Bold Irish, by Fighting Fox
Breeder, Stuart S. Janney Jr. (Md.). **Owner**, Locust Hill Farm.
Dam of 6 foals, all winners, including **RUFFIAN**, 10 wins, $313,428, 1974 champion two-year-old filly, 1975 champion three-year-old filly, 1975 Filly Triple Crown, 1975 Coaching Club American Oaks (G1), etc.; **ICECAPADE**, 13 wins, $256,468, 1973 William duPont Jr. H. (G2), etc.; **BUCKFINDER**, 9 wins, $230,513, 1978 William duPont Jr. H. (G2), etc.

1974—COSMAH

1953 b. m., Cosmic Bomb—Almahmoud, by *Mahmoud
Breeder, Henry H. Knight (Ky.). **Owner**, John R. Gaines.
Dam of 15 foals, 10 starters, 9 winners, including **TOSMAH**, 23 wins, $612,588, 1963 champion two-year-old filly, 1964 champion three-year-old filly, 1964 champion handicap female, 1964 Beldame S., etc.; **HALO**, 9 wins, $259,553, 1974 United Nations H. (G1), etc.; **FATHERS IMAGE**, 7 wins, $173,318; **MARIBEAU**, 4 wins, $20,925.

1973—SOMETHINGROYAL

1952 b. m., *Princequillo—Imperatrice, by Caruso
Breeder, Mr. C. T. Chenery (Va.). **Owner**, Meadow Stable.
Dam of 18 foals, 15 starters, 11 winners, including **SECRE-**
TARIAT, 16 wins, $1,316,808, 1972, 1973 Horse of the Year, 1972 champion two-year-old male, 1973 champion three-year-old male, 1973 champion turf male, 1973 Triple Crown, 1973 Kentucky Derby (G1), etc.; **SIR GAYLORD**, 10 wins, $237,404, 1961 Sapling S., etc.; **FIRST FAMILY**, 7 wins, $188,040, 1966 Gulfstream Park H., etc.; **SYRIAN SEA**, 6 wins, $178,245, 1967 Selima S., etc.

1972—*MOMENT OF TRUTH II

1959 ch. m., Matador—Kingsworthy, by Kingstone
Breeder, Mrs. M. Clarke (GB). **Owner**, Cragwood Estates.
Dam of 9 foals, all winners, including **CONVENIENCE**, 15 wins, $648,933, 1973 Vanity H. (G1), etc.; **NIGHT ALERT**, 3 wins, $121,268, 1980 Prix Jean Prat (Fr-G2), etc.; **INDULTO**, 27 wins, $466,789, 1966 Withers S., etc.; **PROLIFERATION**, 7 wins, $66,680; **PUNTILLA**, 3 wins, $64,255.

1971—IBERIA

1954 ch. m., *Heliopolis—War East, by *Easton
Breeder, L. S. MacPhail (Md.). **Owner**, Meadow Stable.
Dam of 10 foals, all starters, 8 winners, including **RIVA RIDGE**, 17 wins, $1,111,497, 1971 champion two-year-old male, 1973 champion older male, 1972 Kentucky Derby, etc.; **HYDROLOGIST**, 10 wins, $277,958, 1970 Excelsior H., etc.; **POTOMAC**, 3 wins, $37,361.

1970—LEVEE

1953 ch. m., Hill Prince—Bourtai, by Stimulus
Breeder, Claiborne Farm (Ky.). **Owner**, Whitney Stone.
Dam of 11 foals, 9 starters, 7 winners, including **SHUVEE**, 16 wins, $890,445, 1970, 1971 champion handicap mare, 1969 Filly Triple Crown, 1969 Coaching Club American Oaks, etc.; **ROYAL GUNNER**, 6 wins, $334,650; **NALEE**, 8 wins, $141,631, 1963 Black-Eyed Susan S., etc.; **A. T'S OLIE**, 6 wins, $82,211.

1969—ALL BEAUTIFUL

1959 ch. m., Battlefield—Parlo, by *Heliopolis
Breeder, William duPont Jr. (Va.). **Owner**, Paul Mellon.
Dam of 12 foals, 11 starters, 9 winners, including **ARTS AND LETTERS**, 11 wins, $632,404, 1969 Horse of the Year, 1969 champion three-year-old male, 1969 champion handicap horse, 1969 Belmont S., etc.

1968—DELTA

1952 b. m., *Nasrullah—Bourtai, by Stimulus
Breeder, Claiborne Farm (Ky.). **Owner**, Claiborne Farm.
Dam of 10 foals, all starters, 9 winners, including **OKAVANGO**, 6 wins, $153,802, 1975 San Pasqual H. (G2), etc.; **DIKE**, 7 wins, $351,274, 1969 Wood Memorial S., etc.; **CANAL**, 33 wins, $280,358; **CABILDO**, 22 wins, $267,265; **SHORE**, 6 wins, $62,357.

1967—KERALA

1958 b. m., *My Babu—Blade of Time, by *Sickle
Breeder, Greentree Stud Inc. (Ky.). **Owner**, Mrs. Thomas M. Bancroft.
Dam of 13 foals, 9 starters, 8 winners, including **DAMASCUS**, 21 wins, $1,176,781, 1967 Horse of the Year, 1967 champion three-year-old male, 1967 champion handicap male, 1967 Preakness S., etc.

1966—JULIETS NURSE

1948 dk. b. or br. m., Count Fleet—Nursemaid, by Luke McLuke
Breeder, Mrs. Roy Carruthers (Ky.). **Owner**, J. Graham Brown.
Dam of 13 foals, all starters, 11 winners, including **RUN FOR NURSE**, 22 wins, $253,145; **GALLANT ROMEO**, 15 wins, $202,401, 1966 Vosburgh H., etc.; **WOOZEM**, 7 wins, $163,083, 1966 Demoiselle S., etc.; **DUTIFUL**, 5 wins, $80,780.

1965—POCAHONTAS

1955 dk. b. or br. m., Roman—How, by *Princequillo
Breeder, H. B. Delman (Ky.). **Owner**, Raymond Guest.
Dam of 9 foals, 5 starters, all winners, including **TOM ROLFE**, 16 wins, $671,297, 1965 champion three-year-old male, 1965 Preakness S., etc.; **LADY REBECCA**, 2 wins, $26,434, 1974 Prix Vanteaux (Fr-G3); **CHIEFTAIN**, 13 wins, $405,256, 1964 Governor's Gold Cup, etc.; *WENONA, 3 wins, Blandford S. (Ire), etc.

1964—MAID OF FLIGHT
1951 dk. b. or br. m., Count Fleet—Maidoduntreath,
        by Man o' War
Breeder, Mrs. Silas B. Mason (Ky.). **Owner**, Mrs. Richard C.
duPont.
Dam of 11 foals, 10 starters, 9 winners, including **KELSO**, 39
wins, $1,977,896, 1960, '61, '62, '63, '64 Horse of the Year,
1960 champion three-year-old male, 1961, '62, '63, '64
champion handicap horse, 1960, '61, '62, '63, '64 Jockey
Club Gold Cup, etc.

1963—MISTY MORN
1952 b. m., *Princequillo—Grey Flight, by *Mahmoud
Breeder, Wheatley Stable (Ky.). **Owner**, Mrs. H. C. Phipps.
Dam of 10 foals, 8 starters, 7 winners, including **SUCCES-
SOR**, 7 wins, $532,254, 1966 champion two-year-old, 1966
Champagne S., etc.; **BOLD LAD**, 14 wins, $516,465, 1964
champion two-year-old, 1964 Champagne S., etc.; **SUN-
RISE FLIGHT**, 11 wins, $380,995, 1963 Gallant Fox H., etc.;
BEAUTIFUL DAY, 7 wins, $160,007; **BOLD CONSORT**, 6
wins, $38,147.

1962—TRACK MEDAL
1950 dk. b. or br. m., *Khaled—Iron Reward, by *Beau Pere
Breeder, Rex C. Ellsworth (Ca.). **Owner**, Greentree Stud.
Dam of 10 foals, 8 starters, 6 winners, including **OUTING
CLASS**, 6 wins, $229,759, 1962 Hopeful S., etc.; *O'HARA**,
8 wins, $202,180, 1966 Sunset H.; **TUTANKHAMEN**, 12
wins, $157,530, 1962 Manhattan H.; **FOOL'S GOLD II**, 1
win, 1962 Musidora S. (Eng), etc.

1961—STRIKING
1947 b. m., War Admiral—Baby League, by Bubbling Over
Breeder, Ogden Phipps (Ky.). **Owner**, Ogden Phipps.
Dam of 15 foals, 12 starters, 11 winners, including **HITTING
AWAY**, 13 wins, $309,079, 1961 Dwyer H., etc.; **BATTER
UP**, 7 wins, $166,504, 1962 Black-Eyed Susan S., etc.; **MY
BOSS LADY**, 4 wins, $64,174; **GLAMOUR**, 6 wins, $60,775;
BASES FULL, 3 wins, $17,627.

1960—SIAMA
1947 b. m., Tiger—China Face, by Display
Breeder, E. K. Thomas (Ky.). **Owner**, Harry F. Guggenheim.
Dam of 9 foals, 5 starters, all winners, including **BALD EAGLE**,
12 wins, $692,946, 1960 champion handicap male, 1959,
1960 Washington D.C. International, etc.; **ONE-EYED KING**,
15 wins, $266,281, 1960 Arlington H., etc.; **DEAD AHEAD**,
8 wins, $73,645.

1959—*KNIGHT'S DAUGHTER
1941 b. m., Sir Cosmo—Feola, by Friar Marcus
Breeder, King George VI (GB). **Owner**, Claiborne Farm.
Dam of 7 foals, all starters, 6 winners, including **ROUNDTABLE**,
43 wins, $1,749,869, 1958 Horse of the Year, 1957, 1958,
'59 champion turf male, 1958, '59 champion older male, 1957
Hollywood Gold Cup, etc.; **MONARCHY**, 7 wins, $85,737;
*LOVE GAME**.

1958—MISS DISCO
1944 b. m., Discovery—Outdone, by Pompey
Breeder, Alfred G. Vanderbilt (Md.). **Owner**, Mrs. H. C. Phipps.
Dam of 11 foals, 7 starters, all winners, including **BOLD RULER**,
23 wins, $764,204, 1957 Horse of the Year, 1957 champion
three-year-old male, 1958 champion sprinter, 1957 Preakness S., etc.; **INDEPENDENCE**, 12 wins, $132,088; **NASCO**,
7 wins, $71,930.

1957—BELLE JEEP
1949 b. m., War Jeep—Model Beauty,
        by *Blenheim II
Breeder, Maine Chance Farm (Ky.). **Owner**, Maine Chance
Farm.
Dam of 14 foals, 12 starters, all winners, including **JEWEL'S
REWARD**, 7 wins, $448,592, 1957 champion two-year-old
male, 1957 Champagne S., etc.; **TRIPLE CROWN**, 4 wins,
$128,874, 1974 San Jacinto S. (G2), etc.; **LORD JEEP**, 11
wins, $64,504; **EVASIVE ACTION**, 3 wins, $47,004.

1956—SWOON
1942 ch. m, Sweep Like—Sadie Greenock, by Greenock
Breeder, E. Gay Drake (Ky.). **Owner**, E. Gay Drake.
Dam of 10 foals, all starters, 8 winners, including **SWOON'S
SON**, 30 wins, $970,605, 1956 American Derby, etc.; **DO-
GOON**, 28 wins, $220,360, 1954 Hawthorne Juvenile H., etc.

1955—IRON REWARD
1946 b. m., *Beau Pere—Iron Maiden, by War Admiral
Breeder, W. W. Naylor (Ca.). **Owner**, Rex Ellsworth.
Dam of 11 foals, 9 starters, 5 winners, including **SWAPS**, 19
wins, $848,900, 1956 Horse of the Year, 1956 champion
handicap horse, 1955 Kentucky Derby, etc.; **THE SHOE**, 10
wins, $105,000, 1958 Cinema H., etc.; **LIKE MAGIC**, 10
wins, $87,872.

1954—TRAFFIC COURT
1938 dk. b. or br. m., Discovery—Traffic, by Broomstick
Breeder, C. V. Whitney (Ky.). **Owner**, Clifford Mooers.
Dam of 3 foals, all winners, including **HASTY ROAD**, 14 wins,
$541,402, 1953 champion two-year-old male, 1954 Preak-
ness S., etc.; **TRAFFIC JUDGE**, 13 wins, $432,450, 1957
Suburban H., etc.

1953—GAGA
1942 b. m., *Bull Dog—Alpoise, by Equipoise
Breeder, A. C. Ernst (Ky.). **Owner**, Duval Headley.
Dam of 5 foals, all winners, including **TOM FOOL**, 21 wins,
$570,165, 1953 Horse of the Year, 1951 champion two-year-
old male, 1953 champion sprinter, 1953 champion older
male, 1953 Surburban H., etc.; **AUNT JINNY**, 5 wins, $106,020,
1950 champion two-year-old filly, 1950 Demoiselle S., etc.

1952—ACE CARD
1942 b. m., Case Ace—Furlough, by Man o' War
Breeder, Walter M. Jeffords (Pa.). **Owner**, Mrs. Walter M.
Jeffords.
Dam of 12 foals, all starters, 11 winners, including **ONE COUNT**,
9 wins, $245,625, 1952 Horse of the Year, 1952 champion
three-year-old male, 1952 Belmont S., etc.; **POST CARD**, 14
wins, $170,525; **MY CARD**, 7 wins, $98,404, 1963 Selima S.;
YILDIZ, 7 wins, $90,475, 1951 Flamingo S., etc.

1951—*ALPENSTOCK III
1936 dk. b. or br. m., Apelle—Plymstock,
        by Polymelus
Breeder, Cliveden Stud (GB). **Owner**, Mereworth Farm.
Dam of 13 foals, 10 starters, 8 winners, including **RUHE**, 11
wins, $294,490, 1951 Blue Grass S., etc.; **STURDY ONE**,
13 wins, $202,970, 1951 Tanforan H., etc.; **ALLADIER**, 9
wins, $61,712, 1951 Breeders' Futurity, etc.

1950—HILDENE
1938 b. m., Bubbling Over—Fancy Racket, by *Wrack
Breeder, Xalapa Farm (Ky.). **Owner**, Meadow Stable.
Dam of 13 foals, 12 starters, 9 winners, including **HILL PRINCE**,
17 wins, $422,140, 1950 Horse of the Year, 1949 champion
two-year-old male, 1950 champion three-year-old male, 1951
champion older male, 1950 Preakness S., etc.;
FIRST LANDING, 19 wins, $779,577, 1958 champion two-
year-old male, 1958 Champagne S., etc.; **THIRD BROTHER**,
9 wins, $310,787; **MANGOHICK**, 23 wins, $115,115; **PRINCE
HILL**, 8 wins, $98,300.

1949—EASY LASS
1940 bl. m., *Blenheim II—Slow and Easy, by Colin
Breeder, Calumet Farm (Ky.). **Owner**, Calumet Farm.
Dam of 7 foals, all starters, 6 winners, including **COALTOWN**,
23 wins, $415,675, 1949 Horse of the Year, 1948 cham-
pion sprinter, 1949 champion older male, 1949 Washington Park H., etc.; **WISTFUL**, 13 wins, $213,060, 1949
champion three-year-old filly, 1949 Coaching Club of America Oaks, etc.; **ROSEWOOD**, 9 wins, $92,950; **FANFARE**,
9 wins, $46,140.

1948—OUR PAGE
1940 b. m., Blue Larkspur—Occult, by *Dis Donc
Breeder, Woodvale Farm (Oh.). **Owner**, Royce C. Martin.

Dam of 5 foals, all winners, **BULL PAGE**, 9 wins, $25,730, 1951 Horse of the Year in Canada, 1951 champion older horse in Canada, 1951 Canadian Championship S.; **NAVY PAGE**, 21 wins, $127,322, 1953 Jerome H., etc.; **SPORT PAGE**, 4 wins, $79,175; **BROTHER TEX**, 8 wins, $77,633; **PAGE BOOTS**, 3 wins, $51,635.

1947—POTHEEN
1928 dk. b. or br. m., Wildair—Rosie O'Grady, by Hamburg
Breeder, H. P. Whitney (Ky.). Owner, Calumet Farm.
Dam of 12 foals, 11 starters, 9 winners, including **BEWITCH**, 20 wins, $462,605, 1947 champion two-year-old filly, 1949 champion older female, 1947 Washington Park Futurity,

etc.; **POT O' LUCK**, 14 wins, $239,150, 1945 Jockey Club Gold Cup, etc.; **LOT O LUCK**, 9 wins, $46,950.

1946—BLOODROOT
1932 b. m., Blue Larkspur—*Knockany Bridge, by Bridge of Earn
Breeder, Idle Hour Stock Farm (Ky.). Owner, Ogden Phipps.
Dam of 13 foals, 11 starters, 8 winners, including **ANCESTOR**, 26 wins, $237,956, 1959 champion steeplechaser, 1952 Discovery H., etc.; **BE FAITHFUL**, 14 wins, $189,040, 1947 Hawthorne Gold Cup H., etc.; **BRIC A BAC**, 13 wins, $103,225, 1945 San Juan Capistrano H., etc.; **BIMLETTE**, 4 wins, $28,065, 1946 Frizette S.

Leading Broodmares by Progeny Earnings
Worldwide Leaders, 1930-2004

Broodmare, YOB, Sire—Dam	Fls.	Strs.	Wnrs.	SWs	Progeny Earnings	Leading Earner	Earnings
Once Wed, 1984, Blushing Groom (Fr)—Noura	11	10	7	1	$18,431,882	T.M.Opera O	$16,200,337
Pacificus, 1981, Northern Dancer—Pacific Princess	11	10	7	3	18,135,348	Narita Brian	9,296,552
Dancing Key, 1983, Nijinsky II—Key Partner	12	12	9	4	17,658,796	Dance Partner (Jpn)	5,973,652
Katies (Ire), 1981, Nonoalco—Mortefontaine	15	11	10	5	11,222,779	Hishi Amazon	6,981,102
Vega, 1990, Tony Bin —Antique Value	3	3	3	3	11,133,819	Admire Don	7,655,421
Happy Trails, 1984, Posse—Roycon (GB)	11	10	8	3	10,468,390	Shinko Lovely	4,596,546
Ingot Way, 1981, Diplomat Way—Ingot	14	10	9	1	10,383,641	Skip Away	9,616,360
Solar Slew, 1982, Seattle Slew—Gold Sun (Arg)	11	7	7	2	10,363,980	Cigar	9,999,815
Golden Sash, 1988, Dictus—Dyna Sash	10	9	6	2	10,262,342	Stay Gold	8,682,142
All Dance, 1978, Northern Dancer—All Rainbows	12	11	7	2	9,715,535	Tap Dance City	8,986,709
Tokai Natural, 1982, Nice Dancer—Tokai Midori	13	12	10	2	9,713,663	Tokai Teio	4,698,139
Cee's Song, 1986, Seattle Song—Lonely Dancer	12	9	6	4	9,680,428	Tiznow	6,427,830
Floral Magic, 1985, Affirmed—Rare Lady	9	7	7	1	9,582,529	Narita Top Road	8,389,594
Campaign Girl, 1987, Maruzensky—Lady Shiraoki	3	2	2	1	9,519,113	Special Week	9,346,435
Roamin Rachel, 1990, Mining—One Smart Lady	6	5	3	2	9,420,770	Zenno Rob Roy	8,994,210
Dyna Carle, 1980, Northern Taste—Shadai Feather	9	9	8	1	9,368,616	Air Groove	6,832,242
Mejiro Aurola, 1978, Remand—Mejiro Iris	11	6	5	2	9,270,538	Mejiro McQueen	7,618,803
Princess Reema, 1984, Affirmed—First Fling	14	12	10	3	9,193,481	Meisho Doto	8,088,202
Takeno Falcon, 1982, Philip of Spain—Cool Fair	9	8	5	1	9,125,759	Hokuto Vega	8,300,301
Tree of Knowledge (Ire), 1977, Sassafras (Fr)—Sensibility	10	7	5	1	9,019,381	Taiki Blizzard	5,523,549
Reru du Temps, 1982, Maruzensky—Kei Tsunami	9	6	5	2	8,891,809	Mejiro Bright	6,848,423
Chancey Squaw, 1991, Chief's Crown—Alliance	7	4	3	2	8,864,677	Agnes Digital	8,095,160
Jood, 1989, Nijinsky II—Kamar	9	7	5	2	8,782,122	Fantastic Light	8,486,957
Sakura Clare, 1982, Northern Taste—Clare Bridge	13	9	5	2	8,742,526	Sakura Chitose O	5,178,760
Croupier Lady, 1983, What Luck—Question d'Argent	10	9	6	1	8,584,517	Genuine	5,455,575
Cocotte, 1983, Troy—Gay Milly	13	10	7	5	8,509,877	Fine Motion	4,427,083
Tee Kay, 1991, Gold Meridian—Tri Argo	5	4	4	1	8,495,310	Symboli Kris S	8,401,282
Mejiro Beauty, 1982, Partholon—Mejiro Nagasaki	8	8	8	1	8,403,145	Mejiro Dober	6,240,681
Powerful Lady, 1981, Maruzensky—Roch Tesco	17	12	9	2	8,371,802	Winning Ticket	3,359,368
Legacy of Strength, 1982, Affirmed—Katonka	13	12	9	2	8,332,266	Stinger (Jpn)	3,467,289
Sakura Hagoromo, 1984, Northern Taste—Clear Amber	10	8	8	1	8,276,014	Sakura Bakushin O	4,800,631
Sawayaka Princess, 1986, Northern Taste—Scotch Princess	9	8	8	2	8,227,837	Durandal	4,278,144
White Narubi, 1974, *Silver Shark—Never Narubi	15	5	3	2	8,155,897	Oguri Cap	6,940,077
Tenzan Otome, 1983, Maruzensky—Mombetsu Kachidoki	10	8	6	2	8,123,127	Osumi Jet	4,915,054
Regal State, 1983, Affirmed—La Trinite (Fr)	11	9	4	2	7,921,508	Pleasantly Perfect	7,789,880
Pointed Path (GB), 1984, Kris—Silken Way	10	9	6	2	7,859,158	Neo Universe	5,263,786
Comaz, 1983, Danzig—Middlemarch	9	6	4	2	7,851,751	Sterling Rose	4,692,919
Warranty Applied, 1986, Monteverdi (Ire)—Implied Warranty	10	9	8	1	7,814,621	Eishin Preston	7,408,086
Urakawa Miyuki, 1981, *Habitony—Kemmaru Midori	11	9	6	1	7,671,685	Nice Nature	5,232,135
Crafty Wife, 1985, Crafty Prospector—Wife Mistress	11	10	9	2	7,642,281	Big Shori	2,984,808
Never Ichiban, 1971, Never Beat—Miss Nanba Ichiban	14	9	6	1	7,636,765	Daitaku Helios	4,629,341
I'll Get Along, 1992, Smile—Dont Worry Bout Me	5	2	2	1	7,628,590	Smarty Jones	7,613,155
Bel Sheba, 1970, Lt. Stevens—Belthazar	13	13	11	5	7,594,619	Alysheba	6,679,242
Rosita, 1986, Mill George—Mellow Madang	10	9	6	2	7,585,690	Kanetsu Fleuve	3,635,744
Alp Me Please, 1981, Blushing Groom (Fr)—Swiss	7	6	2	1	7,567,701	Mayano Top Gun	7,463,557
Fairy Doll, 1991, Nureyev—Dream Deal	5	5	3	3	7,528,262	To the Victory	5,303,281
Mountain Queen, 1982, Nizon—Yamaka Queen	14	10	7	1	7,484,436	Kyoto City	5,622,437
Dream Vision, 1986, Northern Taste—Honey Dreamer	10	10	8	2	7,417,161	Utopia	2,975,654
Daltawa, 1989, Miswaki—Damana (Fr)	7	5	4	3	7,416,156	Daylami (Ire)	4,614,762
Spring Never, 1992, Sakura Yutaka O—Never Ichiban	5	5	2	2	7,343,798	Daitaku Bertram	3,682,964
Ameriflora, 1989, Danzig—Graceful Touch	7	5	5	2	7,290,188	Grass Wonder	5,987,405
The Last Word, 1987, Northern Taste—Gloria Wave	10	9	6	2	7,223,769	Fast Friend	5,896,693
Bonnie's Poker, 1982, Poker—What a Surprise	12	10	6	1	7,097,159	Silver Charm	6,944,369

Leading Broodmares by 2004 Progeny Earnings in North America

Broodmare, YOB, Sire—Dam	Earnings	Leading Earner	Earnings
I'll Get Along, 1992, Smile—Dont Worry Bout Me	$7,563,535	Smarty Jones	$7,563,535
Baby Zip, 1991, Relaunch—Thirty Zip	2,592,250	Ghostzapper	2,590,000
Goulash, 1993, Mari's Book—Wise Bride	2,370,170	Ashado	2,259,640
Tell a Secret, 1977, Speak John—Secret Retreat	1,723,277	Roses in May	1,723,277
Bendita, 1985, Baldski—Bonne Note (Fr)	1,680,561	Better Talk Now	1,407,000
Kitten's First, 1991, Lear Fan—That's My Hon	1,627,076	Kitten's Joy	1,625,796
Pleasant Dixie, 1995, Dixieland Band—Pleasant Jolie	1,612,150	Southern Image	1,612,150
Dear Birdie, 1987, Storm Bird—Hush Dear	1,265,314	Birdstone	1,236,600
Regal State, 1983, Affirmed—La Trinite (Fr)	1,244,680	Pleasantly Perfect	1,240,000
Joiski's Star, 1991, Star de Naskra—Joi'ski	1,193,221	Singletary	1,192,910
Dancing With Wings, 1988, Danzig—Loudrangle	1,181,502	Soaring Free	1,113,862
Argent Du Bois, 1996, Silver Hawk—Wiener Wald	1,159,075	Ticker Tape (GB)	1,159,075
Sheila Purple (Brz), 1990, Purple Mountain—Ecoute	1,139,000	Pico Central (Brz)	1,139,000
Annasan, 1994, Corporate Report—Amber Ryder	1,118,361	A Bit O'Gold	1,060,790
Belle's Good Cide, 1993, Slewacide—Belle of Killarney	1,110,900	Funny Cide	1,075,100
Satin Sunrise, 1990, Mr. Leader—Logic	1,080,000	Lion Heart	1,080,000
Viviana, 1990, Nureyev—Nijinsky Star	1,077,910	Sightseek	1,011,350
Silken Cat, 1993, Storm Cat—Silken Doll	1,050,556	Speightstown	1,045,556
Zodiac Miss (Aus), 1989, Ahonoora—Capricornia	1,035,000	Azeri	1,035,000
Hold to Fashion, 1989, Hold Your Peace—Toga Toga	1,024,288	Peace Rules	1,024,288
Etats Unis, 1995, Dixieland Band—Hometown Queen	1,022,020	Pollard's Vision	1,022,020
Zigember, 1993, Danzig—Red Ember	1,010,000	The Cliff's Edge	1,010,000
My Flag, 1993, Easy Goer—Personal Ensign	1,001,540	Storm Flag Flying	963,248
To the Hunt, 1985, Relaunch—Royal Advocator	992,169	Stellar Jayne	992,169
Nice Gal, 1985, Naskra—Vigal	947,595	Perfect Drift	947,595
Love That Jazz, 1994, Dixieland Band—Love From Mom	929,700	Society Selection	929,700
Soul Dream, 1990, Alleged—Normia (GB)	900,000	Sulamani (Ire)	900,000
Maggy Hawk, 1994, Hawkster—Qualique	875,689	Afleet Alex	680,800

Most Graded/Group Stakes Winners for a Broodmare
(1930-2004)

8 Fall Aspen (1976, Pretense—Change Water, by Swaps). 14 foals, 13 starters, 12 winners, 9 stakes winners, 8 graded/group stakes winners (Fort Wood [Fr-G1], Hamas [Ire] [Eng-G1], Timber Country [G1], Northern Aspen [G1], Colorado Dancer [Ire] [Fr-G2], Bianconi [Eng-G2], Elle Seule [Fr-G2], Mazzacano [GB] [Eng-G3])

7 Courtly Dee (1968, Never Bend—Tulle, by War Admiral). 18 foals, 17 starters, 15 winners, 8 stakes winners, 7 graded/group stakes winners (Ali Oop [G1], Althea [G1], Ketoh [G1], Aishah [G2], Aquilegia [G2], Twining [G2], Native Courier [G3])

6 Dahlia (1970, *Vaguely Noble—Charming Alibi, by Honeys Alibi). 13 foals, 11 starters, 8 winners, 6 stakes winners, 6 graded/group stakes winners (Dahar [G1], Dahlia's Dreamer [G1], Delegant [G1], Rivlia [G1], Wajd [Fr-G2], Llandaff [G2])

Glowing Tribute (1973, Graustark—Admiring, by Hail to Reason). 12 foals, 10 starters, 9 winners, 7 stakes winners, 6 graded/group stakes winners (Hero's Honor [G1], Sea Hero [G1], Glowing Honor [G2], Wild Applause [G2], Coronation Cup [G3], Mackie [G3])

5 Blessings (Fr) (1971, Floribunda—*Marabelle, by Miralgo). 17 foals, 11 starters, 8 winners, 6 stakes winners, 5 graded/group stakes winners (Bleding [Arg] [Arg-G1], Sings [Arg-G1], Blue Boss [Aus-G3], Blue Bles [Arg-G3], Flibless [Arg-G3])

Chaldee (1978, Banner Sport—Gevar, by Right of Way). 13 foals, 7 starters, 6 winners, 5 stakes winners, 5 graded/group stakes winners (Potrichal [Arg] [Arg-G1], Potrinner [Arg] [Arg-G1], Potrizaris [Arg] [Arg-G1], Potridee [Arg] [Arg-G1], Sun Banner [Arg-G3])

Coup de Folie (1982, Halo—Raise the Standard, by Hoist the Flag). 12 foals, 10 starters, 7 winners, 5 stakes winners, 5 graded/group stakes winners (Coup de Genie [Fr-G1], Exit to Nowhere [Fr-G1], Machiavellian [Fr-G1], Hydro Calido [Fr-G2], Ocean of Wisdom [Fr-G3])

5 Eight Carat (1975, *Pieces of Eight II—Klairessa [GB], by *Klairon). 10 foals, 12 starters, 5 winners, 5 stakes winners, 5 graded/group stakes winners (Marquise [NZ-G1], Our Diamond Lover [NZ-G1], Kaapstad [Aus-G1], Mouawad [Aus-G1], Octagonal [Aus-G1])

Halory (1984, Halo—Cold Reply, by Northern Dancer). 14 foals, 12 starters, 9 winners, 5 stakes winners, 5 graded/group stakes winners (Van Nistelrooy [Ire-G2], Halory Hunter [G2], Brushed Halory [G3], Key Lory [G3], Prory [G3])

Hasili (1991, Kahyasi—Kerali, by High Line). 6 foals, 5 starters, 5 winners, 5 stakes winners, 5 graded/group stakes winners (Banks Hill [GB] [G1], Heat Haze [GB] [G1], Intercontinental [GB] [G1], Cacique [Fr-G2], Dansili [GB] [Fr-G2])

***Lupe II** (1967, Primera—Alcoa, by Alycidon). 10 foals, 9 starters, 8 winners, 5 stakes winners, 5 graded/group stakes winners (Lascaux [Fr-G2], Louveterie [Fr-G3], Legend of France [Eng-G3], Leonardo Da Vinci [Fr] [Eng-G3], L'Ile Du Reve [Eng-G3])

Princess Tracy (Ire) (1981, Ahonoora—Princess Ru, by Princely Gift). 10 foals, 9 starters, 7 winners, 5 stakes winners, 5 graded/group stakes winners (Tracy's Element [Aus] [SAf-G1], Danasinga [Aus-G1], Topasannah [SAf-G2], Cullen [Aus-G3], Towkay [Aus-G3])

Summoned (1978, Crowned Prince—Sweet Life, by *Pardao). 16 foals, 15 starters, 12 winners, 5 stakes winners, 5 graded/group stakes winners (Zeditave [Aus-G1], Alannon [Aus-G3], Pampas Fire [Aus-G3], Square Deal [Aus-G3], Zedagal [Aus-G3])

Toussaud (1989, El Gran Senor—Image of Reality, by In Reality). 9 foals, 6 starters, 5 winners, 5 stakes winners, 5 graded/group stakes winners (Chester House [G1], Chiselling [G1], Empire Maker [G1], Honest Lady [G1], Decarchy [G2])

Most Stakes Winners for a Broodmare
(1930-2004)

9 **Fall Aspen** (1976, Pretense—Change Water, by Swaps). 14 foals, 13 starters, 12 winners, 9 stakes winners (Bianconi, Colorado Dancer [Ire], Elle Seule, Fort Wood, Hamas [Ire], Mazzacano [GB], Northern Aspen, Prince of Thieves, Timber Country)

Fallow (1957, *Worden—Galloway Queene, by Colombo). 16 foals, 11 starters, 12 winners, 9 stakes winners (Fact [Arg], Factory, Fairly [Arg], Fallowed, Far, *Farm, Farmer, Fazenda [Arg], *Fizz)

Grey Flight (1945, *Mahmoud—Planetoid, by Ariel). 15 foals, 15 starters, 14 winners, 9 stakes winners (Bold Princess, Bold Queen, Full Flight, Gray Phantom, Misty Day, Misty Flight, Misty Morn, Signore, What a Pleasure)

8 **Astronomie** (1932, Asterus—Likka, by Sardanapale). 10 foals, 9 starters, 8 winners, 8 stakes winners (Arbar, Arbele, *Asmena, Caracalla, Estremadur, Floriados, Marsyas II, Pharas)

Courtly Dee (1968, Never Bend—Tulle, by War Admiral). 18 foals, 17 starters, 15 winners, 8 stakes winners (Aishah, Ali Oop, Althea, Aquilegia, Ketoh, Native Courier, Princess Oola, Twining)

Retorica (1955, Snob—Rochelle, by Selim Hassan). 12 foals, 9 starters, 8 winners, 8 stakes winners (*Legent II, Leon II, Lioness, *Lirio, Llegador [Arg], Locomotor, *Lostalo, Ruizero [Arg])

7 **Bold Pat** (1975, Bold Destroyer—Bolerita, by Bolero). 14 foals, 14 starters, 13 winners, 7 stakes winners (A Bold Embrace, Arctic Pat, Bay Is O. K., Bold Fawn, Elegant Black, Milden's Girl, Pat's Bold Brat)

Dan's Dream (1961, Your Host—Rosella, by War Relic). 15 foals, 15 starters, 12 winners, 7 stakes winners (Costly Dream, Dream 'n Be Lucky, El Corazon, Go On Dreaming, Jesta Dream Away, Once Upon a Star, Royal Knightmare)

Donatella (1939, *Mahmoud—Delleana, by Clarissimus). 13 foals, 12 starters, 10 winners, 7 stakes winners (*Daumier, De Dreux, Delaroche, *Dominate II, *Donatellina II, Donna Lydia, Duccio)

Flying B. G. (1978, Barachois—Up Alone, by Solo Landing). 16 foals, 12 starters, 11 winners, 7 stakes winners (B. G.'s Drone, Burgone Gimmetwo, Draconic's B. G., Flying Drone, Soiree, Talent Connection, Texas Holdem)

Glowing Tribute (1973, Graustark—Admiring, by Hail to Reason). 12 foals, 10 starters, 9 winners, 7 stakes winners (Coronation Cup, Glowing Honor, Hero's Honor, Mackie, Sea Hero, Seattle Glow, Wild Applause)

Here's Lookn Adder (1983, Superbity—Sarah Blue Eyes, by Explodent). 13 foals, 10 starters, 9 winners, 7 stakes winners (Drumm Valley, Jessen, Just Lookn, Lookn At a Blurr, Lookn At Another, Peak Out, Takin It Deep)

Moccasin (1963, Nantallah—*Rough Shod II, by Gold Bridge). 9 foals, 8 starters, 7 winners, 7 stakes winners (Apalachee, Belted Earl, Brahms, Flippers, Indian, Nantequos, Scuff)

My Dear Girl (1957, Rough'n Tumble—Iltis, by War Relic). 15 foals, 14 starters, 13 winners, 7 stakes winners (Gentle Touch, In Reality, My Dear Lady, Really and Truly, Return to Reality, Superbity, Watchfulness)

Qui Royalty (1977, Native Royalty—Qui Blink, by Francis S.). 14 foals, 12 starters, 10 winners, 7 stakes winners (Appointed One, Bakharoff, Demonry, Emperor Jones, Majlood, Sum, Thyer)

Roar n' Honey (1965, Hezahoney—Rip 'n Roar, by Rippey). 14 foals, 12 starters, 11 winners, 7 stakes winners (Bar Tender, Dandy Man, My Favorite Gal, One That Got Away, Singh Honey, Sonny Says, St. Aubin)

Soumida (1953, Tehran—*Sou'wester, by Blue Peter). 10 foals, 9 starters, 9 winners, 7 stakes winners (Sarcelle, Senechal, Siska, Solidor, Solon, Sorana, *Soudard)

7 **Toll Booth** (1971, Buckpasser—Missy Baba, by *My Babu). 13 foals, 12 starters, 11 winners, 7 stakes winners (Christiecat, Idle Gossip, Key to the Bridge, Plugged Nickle, Tokens Only, Toll Fee, Toll Key)

Up the Flagpole (1978, Hoist the Flag—The Garden Club, by *Herbager). 11 foals, 10 starters, 10 winners, 7 stakes winners (Allied Flag, Flagbird, Fold the Flag, Long View, Prospectors Delite, Runup the Colors, Top Account)

6 **Accra** (1941, Annapolis—Ladala, by Ladkin). 11 foals, 11 starters, 10 winners, 6 stakes winners (Mandingo, Mongo, Nahodah, Nala, Neji, Songai)

Adriana (1944, Arjaman—Adriatica, by Janitor). 15 foals, 14 starters, 11 winners, 6 stakes winners (Ametta, Anatol, Andrea II, Appell, Aspiration, *Ataturk II)

Alta Mira (1948, *Don Bingo—Music Hall, by Snark). 9 foals, 9 starters, 6 stakes winners (Collin Baykey, Craig D., Donn Baykey, Ky. Miracle, Ky. Music, Son of Donn)

Annie Edge (Ire) (1980, Nebbiolo—Friendly Court, by Be Friendly). 12 foals, 11 starters, 8 winners, 6 stakes winners (Rimrod, Rory Creek, Seebe, Selkirk, Skillington, Syncline)

Apostille (1944, Astrophel—Polititia, by Comedy King). 8 foals, 6 starters, 6 winners, 6 stakes winners (Apostol, Bingo, Poisson Volant, Postboy, Postman, Virgule)

Banja Luka (1968, Double Jay—Legato, by Dark Star). 9 foals, 9 starters, 7 winners, 6 stakes winners (Ancient Art, Dancing, Donna Inez, Ferdinand, Jayston, Plinth)

Bargain (1943, Millero—Bonne Fille, by Bermejo). 7 foals, 7 starters, 6 winners, 6 stakes winners (Corbar, Dadiva, Moon Shine, Postwar, *Propina, Shilling)

Battle Creek Girl (1977, His Majesty—Far Beyond, by Nijinsky II). 20 foals, 17 starters, 15 winners, 6 stakes winners (Everhope, Parade Ground, Parade Leader, Speed Dialer, Tricky Creek, Wavering Girl)

Blessings (Fr) (1971, Floribunda—*Marabelle, by Miralgo). 17 foals, 11 starters, 8 winners, 6 stakes winners (Bleding [Arg], Blue Bles, Blue Boss, Flibless, Fritz, Sings)

Blue Denim (1940, Blue Larkspur—Judy O'Grady, by Man o' War). 15 foals, 14 starters, 11 winners, 6 stakes winners (Blue Prince, Green Baize, Piano Jim, Policeman Day, Suleiman, Tahiti)

Confirm (1977, Proudest Roman—Spanked, by Cornish Prince). 17 foals, 16 starters, 11 winners, 6 stakes winners (Autumn Glitter, Confirmed Dancer, Hollycombe, Ron Bon, Saratoga Sizzle, Yolanda)

Dahlia (1970, *Vaguely Noble—Charming Alibi, by Honeys Alibi). 13 foals, 11 starters, 8 winners, 6 stakes winners (Dahar, Dahlia's Dreamer, Delegant, Llandaff, Rivlia, Wajd)

Doff the Derby (1981, Master Derby—Margarethen, by *Tulyar). 12 foals, 10 starters, 9 winners, 6 stakes winners (Generous, Imagine, Osumi Tycoon, Strawberry Roan [Ire], Wedding Bouquet [Ire], Windy Triple K.)

Dumka (1971, Kashmir II—Faizebad [Fr], by *Prince Taj). 8 foals, 8 starters, 7 winners, 6 stakes winners (Dafayna, Dalsaan, Dayzaan, Dolka [Ire], Dolpour, Doyoun)

Eterna (1954, Atabor—Eme, by Lord Wembley). 9 foals, 7 starters, 7 winners, 6 stakes winners (El Califa, *El Fakir, El Faraon, Envidiada [Arg], Esporazo, Eternelle)

Floral Victory (1962, Victoria Park—La Belle Rose, by Le Lavandou). 17 foals, 15 starters, 13 winners, 6 stakes winners (Floral Dancer, Happy Victory, Nonparrell, Northern Ballerina, Snow Blossom, Victego)

Fun House (1958, The Doge—Recess, by Count Fleet). 9 foals, 9 starters, 9 winners, 6 stakes winners (Court Ruling, Funny Cat, Fun Palace, Good Manners, King's Palace, Yes Sir)

Gran Corrida (1961, Prince d'Or—Gay Ega, by Gay Boy). 14 foals, 7 starters, 6 winners, 6 stakes winners (A Esperar, Galopon, Grandeza Real, Grandor Real, Gran Real, Real Corrida)

6   *Green Valley II (1967, *Val de Loir—Sly Pola, by Spy Song). 15 foals, 14 starters, 13 winners, 6 stakes winners (Ercolano, Green Dancer, Pink Valley, Sir Raleigh, Soviet Lad, Val Danseur)

Hasty Queen II (1963, One Count—Queen Hopeful, by Roman). 16 foals, 14 starters, 12 winners, 6 stakes winners (Fit to Fight, Hasty Cutie, Hasty Flyer, Hasty Tam, Michael Navonod, Playful Queen)

Height of Fashion (Fr) (1979, Bustino—Highclere [GB], by Queen's Hussar). 12 foals, 10 starters, 8 winners, 6 stakes winners (Alwasmi, Mukddaam, Nashwan, Nayef, Sarayir, Unfuwain)

Il Mondo (1968, Promised Land—Nunzi Nunzi, by *Endeavour II). 13 foals, 13 starters, 8 winners, 6 stakes winners (Balimondo, Craftsmypapa, Mondanza, Mondo Lea, Mondolu, Turnin Doe)

Imperatrice (1938, Caruso—Cinquepace, by Brown Bud). 16 foals, 13 starters, 10 winners, 6 stakes winners (Imperial Hill, Imperium, Scattered, Speedwell, Squared Away, Yemen)

Kazanlik (1960, Ommeyad—Rose Supreme, by Supreme Court). 13 foals, 10 starters, 8 winners, 6 stakes winners (Boabdil, Darling Bud, Frances Jordan, Gay George, *Lark Rise II, Orient Rose)

Lapel (1935, Apelle—Lampeto, by Tetratema). 9 foals, 9 starters, 9 winners, 6 stakes winners (Carlist, Cassock, Durante, Golden Spur, Red Carnation, Val d'Assa)

Loudrangle (1974, Quadrangle—Lady Known as Lou, by Nearctic). 9 foals, 7 starters, 7 winners, 6 stakes winners (Dancing With Wings, No Louder, Ruling Angel, Slew of Angels, Tiffany Tam, Tilt My Halo)

Missy Baba (1958, *My Babu—*Uvira II, by Umidwar). 14 foals, 12 starters, 12 winners, 6 stakes winners (Chokri, Dromba, Gay Missile, Master Bold, Raja Baba, Sauce Boat)

Modena (1983, Roberto—Mofida [GB], by Right Tack). 9 foals, 9 starters, 9 winners, 6 stakes winners (Elmaamul, High Walden, Modern Day, Modernise, Modesta, Reams of Verse)

Nas-Mahal (1959, *Nasrullah—*Love Game, by Big Game). 12 foals, 11 starters, 9 winners, 6 stakes winners (Beja, Celine, Craelius, Epidaurus, Tell, Turkish Trousers)

No Class (1974, Nodouble—Classy Quillo, by Outing Class). 8 foals, 7 starters, 7 winners, 6 stakes winners (Always a Classic, Classic Reign, Classy 'n Smart, Grey Classic, Regal Classic, Sky Classic)

Patsy Dru (1959, Alorter—Patsy, by Escadru). 17 foals, 17 starters, 15 winners, 6 stakes winners (Astaconda, Great Commander, Levant, Patsy's Reign, Prom Crasher, Shotgun Pat)

Phase (1939, Windsor Lad—Lost Soul, by Solario). 14 foals, 12 starters, 9 winners, 6 stakes winners (Narrator, Neasham Belle, Netherton Maid, None Nicer, No Pretender, Setting Star)

6   Picture Light (1954, *Court Martial—Queen of Light, by Borealis). 13 foals, 11 starters, 9 winners, 6 stakes winners (Dazzling Light, Father Christmas, Illuminous, Miss Pinkie, Photo Flash, Welsh Pageant)

Polite Society (1952, War Admiral—Doggin' It, by *Bull Dog). 12 foals, 12 starters, 12 winners, 6 stakes winners (Big Brigade, Blue Society, La Gentillesse, Long Position, Montjuich, Rising Market)

*Queen's Statute (1954, Le Lavandou—Statute, by Son-in-Law). 14 foals, 13 starters, 13 winners, 6 stakes winners (Court Royal, Dance Act, Down North, Epic Queen, Menedict, North of the Law)

Radiant Light (1953, Sayajirao—Wakening Light, by Eight Thirty). 13 foals, 8 starters, 7 winners, 6 stakes winners (Grand Slam, Mairona [Chi], Mediatore, Metapio, Morgan, *Morgana II)

Ripeck (1959, *Ribot—Kyak, by Big Game). 10 foals, 10 starters, 9 winners, 6 stakes winners (Anchor, Balinger, Bireme, Buoy, Fluke, *Kedge)

Stafaralla (1935, Solario—Mirawala, by Phalaris). 14 foals, 8 starters, 7 winners, 6 stakes winners (Anwar, Inshalla, Iran, Kerman, *Norooz, Tehran)

Sun Princess (1937, Solario—Mumtaz Begum, by *Blenheim II). 13 foals, 11 starters, 9 winners, 6 stakes winners (Alassio, *Flaneur II, Lucky Bag, *Royal Charger, Royal Justice, Tessa Gillian)

Tata (1938, Tresiete—Tacana, by Leteo). 6 foals, 6 starters, 6 winners, 6 stakes winners (Taia, Taimado, Taitao, Talon, Tatai, Tolpan)

Theresina (1927, Diophon—Teresina, by Tracery). 13 foals, 10 starters, 8 winners, 6 stakes winners (*Benane, Byculla, Eboo, *Nemrod, Tambara, Turkhan)

Tokamura (1940, Navarro—Tofanella, by Apelle). 16 foals, 13 starters, 12 winners, 6 stakes winners (Tanaka, Theodorica, Titano, Tommaso Da Modena, *Tommaso Guidi, *Toulouse Lautrec)

Vera Me (1979, Polar Night—Vera Jae, by Gaylord's Feather). 13 foals, 13 starters, 11 winners, 6 stakes winners (Amazonpassage, Heatherforyou, Jessica Jae, Mebazaar, Polar Barron, Steaksonme)

Verdura (1948, *Court Martial—Bura, by *Bahram). 12 foals, 11 starters, 11 winners, 6 stakes winners (Avon's Pride, Gratitude, Heathen, Highest Hopes, Patroness, Pharsalia)

Yakima Swinger (1974, Canadian Gil—Eternal Heeler, by Heeler). 12 foals, 11 starters, 11 winners, 6 stakes winners (Bucks for Bob, Hat Rock, Lyon Swinger, Rock On Merit, Sarajevo Merit, Slightly Sinister)

Zanzara (1951, Fairey Fulmar—Sunright, by Solario). 17 foals, 14 starters, 13 winners, 6 stakes winners (Duke Ellington, Enrico, Enticement, Farfalla, Matatina, Showdown)

Most Foals for a Broodmare
(1930-2004)

Broodmare, YOB, Pedigree	Fls.	Strs.	Wnrs.	Wins	Earnings
*Betsy Ross II (1939, *Mahmoud—*Celerina, by *Teddy)	23	19	13	44	$152,943
Day Line (1963, *Day Court—Fast Line, by Mr. Busher)	21	17	14	42	421,940
Alanette (1962, Alarullah—Jaconet, by *Jacopo)	20	18	9	33	128,897
Battle Creek Girl (1977, Hoist the Flag—Far Beyond, by Nijinsky II)	20	17	15	80	4,255,073
Bold Bikini (1969, Boldnesian—Ran-Tan, by Summer Tan)	20	14	12	37	974,619
Bright Festive (1966, Festive—Bright Cirrus, by Solferino)	20	1	0	0	0
Capulet (1977, Gallant Romeo—Indaba, by Sir Gaylord)	20	16	10	55	594,709
Cequillo (1956, *Princequillo—Boldness, by *Mahmoud)	20	18	14	81	1,031,646
Feather Bed (1961, Johns Joy—Silly Sara, by *Rustom Sirdar)	20	17	13	60	305,357
Jettapari (1979, Tri Jet—Annulment, by Manifesto)	20	15	12	71	986,420
Such 'n Such (1974, Ack Ack—Long Stemmed Rose, by Jacinto)	20	16	11	46	735,875
Tie a Bow (1979, Dance Spell—Bold Bikini, by Boldnesian)	20	14	8	34	457,515
Wayward Miss (1966, Brumeux—Miss Contrary, by Cannobie)	20	16	4	26	12,805
Wind in Her Sails (1972, Mr. Leader—Bunch of Daisies, by Sir Gaylord)	20	13	12	44	375,991
Wisp O'Will (1964, New Policy—Miss Willow, by Oil Capitol)	20	16	14	70	894,640

Steeplechase performances are not included in statistics

Most Consecutive Foals for a Broodmare
(1930-2004)

Broodmare, YOB, Pedigree	Foals	Consecutive Foals
Bold Bikini (1969, Boldnesian—Ran-Tan, by Summer Tan)	20	**19**
Photo Flash (1965, *Match II—Picture Light, by *Court Martial)	19	**19**
Sarasail (1966, Hitting Away—*Sail Riona, by *Royal Charger)	19	**19**
Such 'n Such (1974, Ack Ack—Long Stemmed Rose, by Jacinto)	20	**19**
Gallant Lady (1930, *Sir Gallahad III—*Peroration, by Clarissimus)	18	**18**
Maxencia (Fr) (1977, Tennyson—Matuschka, by *Orsini II)	18	**18**
So What (1978, Iron Ruler—Merry Mama, by Prince John)	17	**18**
Trinity (1978, Logical—Trinidad, by Make Tracks)	18	**18**
Whitewood (1960, *Worden—Solarist, by Supreme Court)	18	**18**

Most Wins by Broodmare's Offspring
(1930-2004)

Broodmare, YOB, Sire—Dam	Foals	Starters	Winners	Starts	Wins	Earnings
Slow and Easy (1922, Colin—*Shyness)	15	14	11	962	182	$287,417
*Adorable II (1925, Sardanapale—Incredule)	15	13	12	1,175	181	164,936
Cotton Candy (1945, Stimulus—Sugar Bird)	13	12	12	1,109	178	359,502
Transit (1926, *Chicle—*Traverse)	10	10	10	1,169	178	308,632
*Clonaslee (1922, Orpiment—Bullet Proof)	18	17	16	1,170	176	258,219
Sag Rock (1930, Rock Man—Atomin)	13	12	11	981	170	237,689
Dame Mariechen (1931, High Time—Carrie Hogan)	14	14	14	1,149	167	254,771
Pevensea (1935, Enoch—Truly Movin)	13	13	13	1,177	166	167,298
Lady Excellent (1932, Nocturnal—Falco)	14	13	12	1,180	165	185,899
Ginogret (1941, *Gino—Sunlygret)	12	12	12	982	164	223,038
Alondra (1947, War Admiral—Lady Lark)	17	17	15	1,173	163	496,993
Doggerel (1935, *Bull Dog—Shenanigan)	10	9	9	1,113	163	200,484
Jemima Lee (1929, General Lee—Miss Jemima)	15	15	14	860	163	219,609
Sassaby (1931, Broomstick—Saucy Sue)	9	9	9	1,112	163	321,217
Agnes Ayres (1923, King James—Sweet Mary)	15	14	12	1,201	161	364,151
Lady Floyd (1924, Sir Martin—Fruit Cake)	13	11	10	1,015	159	151,435
Much Ado (1921, Ed Crump)	14	13	13	1,026	159	93,168
Vanrose (1920, Vandergrift)	13	10	9	993	159	123,744
Blame (1921, *Wrack—Censure)	11	10	9	1,153	157	132,321
Balking (1935, Balko—Bodega)	11	11	10	853	156	426,263
*Miss Turley (1924, Bachelor's Jap—Raftonia)	12	12	11	967	154	74,273
New Melody (1952, Bimelech—Melodious)	13	13	13	961	154	688,387
Mary Kelly (1926, Ormondale—Starina)	14	14	13	1,097	153	136,548
Kind Annie (1938, Brilliant—*Chaucer Girl)	12	11	10	992	152	273,962
Daunt (1925, Lucullite—Dauntless)	13	13	13	817	151	230,505
Knightess (1929, *Bright Knight—Markiluna)	13	13	10	1,005	151	175,222
Lucy T. (1933, Whichone—*Refugee III)	13	11	9	1,092	151	254,071
Cariboo Lass (1928, *Marcus—Mary Fuller)	13	12	11	1,115	150	126,034
Softie (1943, Flares—Sicklefeather)	16	15	13	1,073	150	338,172
*Flamante (1926, Flamboyant—*Flaminia)	11	10	10	960	149	210,627
Maradadi (1930, Stimulus—Virginia L.)	18	18	13	1,065	148	428,469
Vinnie (1948, Vincentive—Glorious Time)	15	14	11	851	148	422,519
Accra (1941, Annapolis—Ladala)	11	11	10	646	146	1,632,463
Happy Factor (1941, Benefactor—Miss Jemima)	13	10	10	940	146	337,080
Lady Gallivant (1922, *Hourless—*Lady's Gauntlet)	11	10	10	1,049	146	148,508
Hastily Yours (1936, John P. Grier—*Hastily)	14	12	11	1,080	145	692,799
Mintairy (1927, Mint Briar—*Airy Fairy)	10	10	10	776	145	195,913
Panoramic (1932, Chance Shot—Dustwhirl)	11	11	11	975	144	686,387
Pennant Girl (1929, *Rire Aux Larmes—Flying Pennant)	14	14	10	848	144	254,551
Royalite (1922, Lucullite—Royal Ensign)	9	8	8	853	144	122,635
*Valdina Spirea (1940, Canon Law—*Spiraea II)	14	14	13	1,157	143	413,361
Cushion (1917, Nonpareil—Hassock)	12	9	9	617	142	140,109
Predicament (1929, *Waygood—Precipitate)	15	13	13	1,024	142	184,201
Brown Maiden (1933, Brown Bud—Tailor Maid)	10	10	10	1,165	140	202,886
Miss Velocity (1957, Spy Song—Fairy Dancer)	18	17	17	1,174	140	560,219
Scuttle (1928, Whiskaway—Sea Tale)	11	11	11	927	140	199,437
Glacial (1926, *Hourless—*Snowcapt)	15	15	13	1,093	139	199,418
Sis Tartan (1947, Port au Prince—Tartan Betsy)	10	10	9	824	139	343,586
Sly Marie (1962, Neptune—*Marie Lou)	12	12	11	911	139	523,325
Greedy Girl (1926, *Vulcain—Grasp)	12	10	10	817	137	196,899
*Legend of the Lake (1929, Dark Legend—Narrow Water)	10	10	7	766	137	105,120
Nancy Clay (1923, *Wrack—Nancy Lee)	14	12	11	854	137	163,667
Baffling Miss (1927, Baffling—Miss Merle)	4	4	4	764	136	86,250
Dog Show (1940, *Bull Dog—Pomp and Glory)	16	15	15	892	136	361,952
Annabell Lee (1926, *Volta—Compose)	12	11	11	774	135	288,719
May Morning (1935, Pompey—Howdy)	9	9	9	1,087	135	227,415
Nortell (1955, El Mono—Control Board)	12	12	12	864	135	477,660

Most Winners for a Broodmare
(1930-2004)

Broodmare, YOB, Sire—Dam	Foals	Starters	Winners	SWs	Earnings
*Mindrum Maid (1939, *Mahmoud—Imp)	17	17	17	0	$149,615
Miss Velocity (1957, Spy Song—Fairy Dancer)	18	17	17	0	560,219
Arizona Jubilee (1964, Spotted Moon—The Frog Hook)	19	17	16	1	271,893
*Clonaslee (1922, Orpiment—Bullet Proof)	18	17	16	1	258,219
Dear Guinevere (1977, Fearless Knight—Brave and Free)	19	17	16	1	1,449,872
Lady Ambassador (1959, Hill Prince—Your Hostess)	17	17	16	1	880,817
Northern Beauty (1955, Borealis—Fleeting Beauty)	18	15	16	2	260,119
Pia Mia (1968, Pia Star—Surprise Lady)	18	18	16	3	933,832
Sable Lady (1927, *Waygood—Kolinsky)	17	17	16	0	180,004
Admittance (1946, Maeda—Stitches)	15	15	15	0	208,098
Alondra (1947, War Admiral—Lady Lark)	17	17	15	2	496,993
Amazer (1967, Mincio—*Alzara)	17	17	15	2	1,916,353
Battle Creek Girl (1977, His Majesty—Far Beyond)	20	17	15	6	4,255,073
Blinking Owl (1938, *Pharamond II—Baba Kenny)	19	16	15	0	195,196
Bold Essence (1977, Native Charger—Cologne)	16	16	15	1	1,048,236
Bold Pythian (1975, Bold Reason—Pythian)	18	18	15	0	589,322
Bonnie Blade (1976, Blade—Promised Princess)	16	16	15	1	1,053,597
Cherry Lady (1973, Bold Lad—Cherry Fool)	16	15	15	1	773,746
Courtly Dee (1968, Never Bend—Tulle)	18	17	15	8	3,446,275
Dancing Liz (1972, Northern Dancer—Crimson Queen)	16	16	15	1	1,215,005
Day and a Half (1972, Time Tested—Jolly)	18	16	15	2	942,371
Dog Show (1940, *Bull Dog—Pomp and Glory)	16	15	15	1	361,952
Don't Honey Me (1977, Triple Bend—Honey Deb)	16	15	15	1	1,363,547
Godzilla (1972, Gyr—Gently)	15	15	15	2	4,353,027
Grecian Coin (1960, Royal Coinage—Greek Pillar)	17	15	15	0	787,886
Maxencia (Fr) (1977, Tennyson—Matuschka)	18	17	15	2	396,667
Mideau (1942, *Bull Dog—Wild Waters)	18	18	15	1	509,729
Miss Cotton (1962, Swoon's Son—Always Movin)	16	15	15	4	959,195
Newsun (1973, Penowa Rullah—Sunshine Bright)	16	16	15	2	1,273,538
Our Patty (1933, Brown Bud—Perjury)	17	15	15	0	141,309
Patsy Dru (1959, Alorter—Patsy)	17	17	15	6	459,604
Peace Please (1978, Hold Your Peace—Please Say Yes)	16	16	15	1	839,910
Pines Lady (1966, Pinebloom—Lady Peabody)	15	15	15	0	497,559
Poker's Errand (1974, Poker—Gallant Lesina)	18	17	15	1	621,568
Proof Enough (1969, Prove It—Theonia)	16	16	15	3	910,495
Ribbon Duster (1973, Dust Commander—First Ribbon)	17	16	15	1	596,754
Stepping High (1969, No Robbery—*Bebop II)	17	17	15	2	1,377,143
Sweet Tulle (1978, Tom Tulle—Little Divy)	17	17	15	0	281,628
Tattooed Miss (1960, Mark-Ye-Well—Mossy Number)	18	18	15	2	375,182
Tweentzel Pie (1966, Four-and-Twenty—Peachywillow)	16	16	15	2	633,905
Wolf Hands (1963, All Hands—Wolf Bait)	16	16	15	3	462,595

Most Starts by Broodmare's Offspring
(1930-2004)

Broodmare, YOB, Sire—Dam	Foals	Starters	Winners	Starts	Earnings
Our Patty (1933, Brown Bud—Perjury)	17	15	15	1,275	$141,309
Mrs. Burke (1923, *Berrilldon—Pinkie)	12	11	11	1,248	104,588
Admittance (1946, Maeda—Stitches)	15	15	15	1,217	208,098
Mica (1924, Fair Play—Malachite)	9	8	8	1,215	106,918
Tabset (1938, Upset Lad—McTab)	12	12	12	1,212	194,434
Agnes Ayres (1923, King James—Sweet Mary)	15	14	12	1,201	364,151
Lina Clark (1919, Delhi—Prism)	13	13	11	1,187	115,562
Lady Excellent (1932, Nocturnal—Falco)	14	13	12	1,180	185,899
Dark Victory (1929, *Traumer—Sun Vive)	11	11	10	1,179	213,242
Pevensea (1935, Enoch—Truly Movin)	13	13	13	1,177	167,298
*Adorable II (1925, Sardanapale—Incredule)	15	13	12	1,175	164,936
Miss Velocity (1957, Spy Song—Fairy Dancer)	18	17	17	1,174	560,219
Alondra (1947, War Admiral—Lady Lark)	17	17	15	1,173	496,993
*Clonaslee (1922, Orpiment—Bullet Proof)	18	17	16	1,170	258,219
Transit (1926, *Chicle—*Traverse)	10	10	10	1,169	308,632
Brown Maiden (1933, Brown Bud—Tailor Maid)	10	10	10	1,165	202,886
*Valdina Spirea (1940, Canon Law—*Spiraea II)	14	14	13	1,157	413,361
Blame (1921, *Wrack—Censure)	11	10	9	1,153	132,321
Respite (1922, Hilarious—Lucinda)	13	12	9	1,151	134,844
Dame Mariechen (1931, High Time—Carrie Hogan)	14	14	14	1,149	254,771
Galful (1940, Hadagal—Armful)	16	16	13	1,136	183,184
Hurry Home (1921, *Omar Khayyam)	14	13	10	1,128	105,900

Broodmare, YOB, Sire—Dam	Foals	Starters	Winners	Starts	Earnings
Happy Seas (1939, *Happy Argo—Golden Billows)	12	10	9	1,120	$188,979
Cariboo Lass (1928, *Marcus—Mary Fuller)	13	12	11	1,115	126,034
Doggerel (1935, *Bull Dog—Shenanigan)	10	9	9	1,113	200,484
Asianna (1935, Wise Counsellor—Asia)	13	11	10	1,112	185,443
Miss Dora (1918, Jack Atkin)	14	10	9	1,112	83,443
Sassaby (1931, Broomstick—Saucy Sue)	9	9	9	1,112	321,217

Oldest Broodmares to Produce a Winner
(1930-2004)

Broodmare, YOB, Pedigree	Foals	1st Winner	Age Foaled Last Winner
Miss Jubilee (1951, Cassis—Bacchante, by Questionnaire)	5	16	31
Sumpinextra (1952, Super Duper—Ariels Elite, by Ariel)	10	19	30
Faila Suit (1957, Faila—Follow Suit, by Revoked)	9	12	28

Oldest Broodmares to Produce a Stakes Winner
(1930-2004)

Broodmare, YOB, Pedigree	Fls.	1st SW	Age Foaled Last SW	Stakes Winner
Fantasy Miss (1975, Dumpty's Cutter—Caminar, by Last Round)	13	12	26	Fanteria
Mary's Fantasy (1973, Olympian King—Fantasy Dream, by Everett Jr.)	12	12	26	Perfect Fantasy
Beaconaire (1974, *Vaguely Noble—Ole Liz, by Double Jay)	14	6	25	Binya (Ger)
Brown Berry (1960, Mount Marcy—Brown Baby, by Phalanx)	19	8	25	Hours After
Conejo Bonita (1949, Trace Call—Downy Pillow, by Morvich)	10	25	25	Coneja's Con Man
Fairy Sprite (1953, Papa Redbird—Fairy Fleet, by Broadside)	11	15	25	Orphan Annye
Fire's Gem (1961, *Royal Gem II—Fire Fire Fire, by Attention)	13	22	25	Lassafras
Floral Victory (1962, Victoria Park—La Belle Rose, by Le Lavandou)	16	6	25	Floral Dancer
Green Finger (1958, Better Self—Flower Bed, by *Beau Pere)	17	12	25	Blandford Park
Heat of Holme (1970, *Noholme II—Heat Lamp, by Better Self)	18	4	25	Speed On Holme
Hill of Sheba (1964, Federal Hill—Sheba S., by Errard King)	13	17	25	Apart
Knightly Spritely (1975, Knightly Dawn—Craim Check, by Terrang)	17	11	25	Spritely Walker
Little Blush (1968, *Day Court—Beaukiss, by *Mahmoud)	14	7	25	Cartofel
Melanie's Girl (1958, Nashua—*Nebroda, by Nearco)	14	8	25	Hagley's Relic
Phanatam (1941, Mokatam—Phantom Fairy, by *Negofol)	12	25	25	Jacks Again
Sooni (1970, Buckpasser—Missy Baba, by *My Babu)	16	20	25	Black Cash
*Uvira II (1938, Umidwar—Lady Lawless, by Son-in-Law)	13	6	25	Francis U.

Most Millionaires Produced by a Broodmare

No. Millionaires	Broodmare, YOB, Sex, Pedigree	Millionaires
5	Dancing Key, 1983 m., Nijinsky II—Key Partner, by Key to the Mint	Air Dublin ($3,401,386), Air Gang Star ($1,260,218), Dance in the Dark ($3,459,758), Dance in the Mood (Jpn) ($2,931,889), Dance Partner (Jpn) ($5,973,652)
	Miyabi Sakurako, 1989 m., Northern Taste—Dyna Freeway, by Dictus	Freeway Heart ($1,114,742), King of Sunday ($1,177,838), Royal Cancer ($1,502,256), Win Duel ($1,272,018), Win Marvelous ($1,151,464)
4	Millracer, 1983 m., *Le Fabuleux—Marston's Mill, by In Reality	Agnes Special ($1,083,054), Fuji Kiseki ($1,319,239), Shinin' Racer ($1,915,140), Super License ($1,214,916)
3	Antique Value, 1979 m., Northern Dancer—Moonscape, by Tom Fool	Maquereau ($1,245,865), NewsValue ($1,246,690), Vega ($2,105,918)
	Croupier Lady, 1983 m., What Luck—Question d'Argent, by Tentam	Croupier Star ($1,257,929), Genuine ($5,455,575), What a Reason ($1,074,212)
	Eileen's Moment, 1982 m., For The Moment—Sailaway, by *Hawaii	Agnes Arashi ($1,108,588), Agnes Partner ($1,011,810), Lil E. Tee ($1,437,506)
	First Act, 1986 m., Sadler's Wells—Arkadina, by *Ribot	Heavenly Romance ($1,607,574), Mr Big Ben ($1,027,220), Reportage ($1,258,839)
	Happy Trails, 1984 m., Posse—Roycon (GB), by High Top	Happy Path ($2,117,320), Shinko Lovely (4,596,546), Taiki Marshal ($1,910,894)
	Legacy of Strength, 1982 m., Affirmed—Katonka, by Minnesota Mac	Legacy of Zelda ($1,256,666), Silent Happiness ($1,870,725), Stinger (Jpn) ($3,467,289)
	National Flag, 1986 m., Dictus—Dyna World, by Huntercombe	Daiwa Geant ($1,117,364), Inter Flag ($2,498,883), Maruka Komachi ($1,672,369)
	Northern Sunset (Ire), 1977 m., Northfields—Moss Greine, by *Ballymoss	L'Carriere ($1,726,175), Salem Drive ($1,046,065), St. Jovite ($1,604,439)
	Powerful Lady, 1981 m., Maruzensky—Roch Tesco, by Tesco Boy	Marubutsu Powerful ($1,100,278), Royal Touch ($2,795,933), Winning Ticket ($3,359,368)
	Rosa Nay, 1988 m., Lyphard—Riviere Doree, by Secretariat	Rosado ($3,686,146), Rose Colour ($1,044,385), Vita Rosa ($1,541,127)
	Scarlet Bouquet, 1988 m., Northern Taste—Scarlet Ink, by Crimson Satan	Daiwa Major ($1,447,648), Daiwa Rouge ($1,097,647), Glorious Sunday ($1,069,293)
	Vega, 1990 m., Tony Bin—Antique Value, by Northern Dancer	Admire Boss ($1,101,340), Admire Don ($7,566,441), Admire Vega ($2,466,038)

AUCTIONS
History of Thoroughbred Auctions

By far the oldest brand name in Thoroughbred racing is Tattersalls, the English auction company founded by the eponymous Richard Tattersall at London's Hyde Park Corner in 1766. Tattersalls (the appropriate apostrophe was lost at some point in its history) remains the preeminent European auction house and has served as the model for Thoroughbred sales companies throughout the world.

Richard Tattersall expanded his position as the leading seller of Thoroughbreds by providing a dining room for Jockey Club members, and his descendants (who remained in charge of the company for more than 200 years) transferred its headquarters to Newmarket in 1870.

The first American to attempt to emulate Tattersalls's success was English-educated William Easton, who served as Tattersalls's American representative for the last quarter of the 19th century and in 1879 established his own company, the American Horse Exchange, which he later merged with Tattersalls of New York. Easton was the auctioneer at the famous dispersal of August Belmont I's breeding stock in 1891, when Charles Reed made the first $100,000 bid at auction to acquire leading sire *St. Blaise.

Several competitors for Easton's company emerged in the 1890s, principally Powers-Hunter and the Fasig Co. William B. Fasig began auctioneering in his native Cleveland in the early 1890s, and Easton soon invited him to join Tattersalls. The English company chose to sell its American division after the financial panic of 1893, and Fasig took control. In 1898, he took on a partner, Edward A. Tipton, giving the company its now-familiar name, Fasig-Tipton.

Fasig's assistant Enoch J. Tranter took control of the company when Fasig abandoned ship after another panic in 1907, and Tranter established the Saratoga yearling sale in '17. Saratoga has remained the backbone of Fasig-Tipton ever since, through the stewardship of Humphrey S. Finney, his son John M. S. Finney, and the current management led by D. G. Van Clief Jr.

The commercial breeding industry began in both England and the U.S. around the middle of the 19th century. William Blenkiron's Middle Park Stud was the first famously successful commercial breeding operation in England, sending a long succession of high-priced horses to the annual Tattersalls October yearling sale.

Robert A.S.C. Alexander was the key figure in establishing Thoroughbred breeding as a viable commercial endeavor in the U.S. through the foundation of his Woodburn Stud near Lexington in the 1850s. Though hampered by the Civil War, Woodburn held annual yearling sales at the Kentucky farm until 1890. Those sales drew buyers from all over the U.S., and its success—plus the presence of 16-time leading sire Lexington at Woodburn—effectively concentrated the breeding industry in the Bluegrass.

Several small sales companies sprung up in Kentucky over the decades but died just as quickly, primarily because most buyers were in the East. Once Woodburn's star faded, they rarely could be enticed to Kentucky to buy horses. Petroleum rationing during World War II prevented Kentucky breeders from shipping their horses to Saratoga in 1943, however, and Fasig-Tipton agreed to hold a sale in a tent on the grounds of Keeneland Race Course in Lexington. That sale included eventual 1945 Kentucky Derby winner Hoop, Jr.

Kentucky breeders liked the idea so much that by the next year they had formed their own cooperative company, Breeders' Sales Co., and purchased Fasig-Tipton's Lexington sales pavilion, which was dismantled and reconstructed at Keeneland. Breeders' Sales Co. merged with Keeneland in 1962 to become the sales division of the Keeneland Association.

Benefiting from the worldwide success of American-breds over the last 50 years, Keeneland has become the world's largest and most successful sales company. Keeneland sold the first $100,000 yearling, $130,000 Swapson in 1961; the first $1-million yearling, Canadian Bound at $1.5-million in '76; and the world-record-priced yearling, Seattle Dancer, at $13.1-million in '85.

Fasig-Tipton re-established itself in Kentucky in the 1970s, selling three Kentucky Derby (G1) winners in five years, including Triple Crown winner Seattle Slew, but its strategy differs from Keeneland's. While Keeneland's sales are based almost exclusively at its facility in Lexington, Fasig-Tipton spreads a wider net with sales at six locations in five states, often serving regional markets as well as national ones.

As the breeding industry has grown, regional markets have also begun to support their own sales organizations, most notably Ocala Breeders' Sales Co. in Florida. OBSC, founded in 1974, grew out of the two-year-old sales industry that began in the late 1950s when one of the first Florida breeders, Carl Rose, started selling his two-year-olds to trainers at Hialeah Park.

In the late 1980s, Barretts Equine Ltd. was formed to build a sales pavilion and to conduct sales on the Los Angeles County Fair Grounds in Pomona. Barretts's two-year-old sales were particularly successful when Japanese buyers were active in the market in the early 1990s.

—John P. Sparkman

Auction Review of 2004

In 1999, North America's Thoroughbred marketplace capped a spectacular eight-year boom in prices and production by soaring over the $1-billion mark for the first time in history. The terrorist attacks against the United States during the 2001 Keeneland September yearling sale and the subsequent U.S. invasions of Afghanistan and Iraq slowed spending for the next couple of years, but the market began to rebound in 2003.

The market essentially completed its return to 2000 levels—and sometimes exceeded them—in '04, when total expenditures in all market categories combined soared past the $1-billion mark once again, topping out at $1,054,388,413, second-highest total in history and a 23.3% increase on the '03 total. Average auction price for a Thoroughbred, $52,203, surpassed the record set in 2000 because more than 1,000 fewer horses were sold in '04.

All North American Thoroughbred Sales

Year	No. Sold (Chg)	Total Sales (Chg)	Average (Chg)
2004	20,198 (6.8%)	$1,054,388,413 (23.3%)	**$52,203** (15.5%)
2003	18,916 (2.8%)	855,123,171 (11.5%)	45,206 (8.4%)
2002	18,397 (−4.1%)	767,048,402 (−9.4%)	41,694 (−5.5%)
2001	19,191 (−9.6%)	846,478,571 (−22.5%)	44,108 (−14.3%)
2000	**21,225** (5.5%)	**1,091,872,249** (9.0%)	51,443 (3.3%)
1999	20,117 (2.4%)	1,001,718,775 (20.9%)	49,795 (18.1%)
1998	19,653 (5.1%)	828,664,233 (18.3%)	42,165 (12.6%)
1997	18,698 (−0.9%)	700,362,250 (12.8%)	37,457 (13.9%)
1996	18,871 (1.9%)	620,712,382 (17.9%)	32,892 (15.7%)
1995	18,518 (3.0%)	526,647,938 (17.4%)	28,440 (13.9%)
1994	17,972 (8.2%)	448,685,293 (23.1%)	24,966 (13.7%)
1993	16,605 (−5.0%)	364,519,425 (4.5%)	21,952 (9.9%)
1992	17,471 (−7.9%)	348,939,344 (−13.0%)	19,972 (−5.5%)
1991	18,977 (−10.3%)	401,102,091 (−19.8%)	21,136 (−10.6%)
1990	21,153 (−1.7%)	500,167,261 (−12.8%)	23,645 (−11.3%)
Highest figures in boldface.			

Huge investments by just a few buyers such as Sheikh Mohammed bin Rashid al Maktoum in the yearling market ($34-million at Keeneland September) and Jess Jackson in the broodmare market ($21-million at Keeneland November) fueled the upward trend, but the number of deep-pocketed buyers investing at all levels of the market clearly increased.

Yearlings

Because yearlings make up more than half of the total North American Thoroughbred market and are generally the glamour boys and girls of the trade, it is hardly surprising that the overall market almost always goes in the same direction as the yearling market. That has seldom been more evident than in the last half of 2003 and all of '04.

Since Sheikh Mohammed reinvigorated the yearling market by spending $20.9-million at the 2003 Keeneland September yearling sale, prices in the segment have steadily moved upward. The 2003 Keeneland November sale, which accounts for more than 90% of the market for breeding stock, rose sharply, and the market for two-year-olds in training reached historic heights early in '04. The Fasig-Tipton Kentucky July sale of selected yearlings kicked off the yearling sales year in acceptable fashion, and, after a slight hiccup at Fasig-Tipton's Saratoga sale of selected yearlings, Keeneland September exceeded all expectations, fueled once again by Sheikh Mohammed, who returned to spend more than $34-million.

North American Yearling Sales

Year	No. Sold (Chg)	Total Sales (Chg)	Average (Chg)
2004	9,421 (6.9%)	$496,937,672 (17.0%)	$52,748 (9.4%)
2003	8,812 (−1.3%)	424,854,888 (8.5%)	48,213 (10%)
2002	8,928 (−1.7%)	391,472,126 (−17.3%)	43,848 (−15.9%)
2001	9,081 (−4.7%)	473,487,556 (−8.9%)	52,140 (−4.4%)
2000	**9,527** (9.4%)	**519,775,432** (18.2%)	**54,558** (8.0%)
1999	8,705 (5.4%)	439,800,627 (24.2%)	50,523 (17.8%)
1998	8,260 (2.5%)	354,191,040 (15.1%)	42,880 (12.3%)
1997	8,057 (0.4%)	307,689,262 (11.0%)	38,189 (10.6%)
1996	8,026 (1.8%)	277,221,538 (13.9%)	34,540 (11.9%)
1995	7,882 (1.8%)	243,392,908 (15.6%)	30,880 (13.6%)
1994	7,744 (3.8%)	210,460,233 (12.4%)	27,177 (8.3%)
1993	7,460 (−6.0%)	187,232,894 (5.9%)	25,098 (12.6%)
1992	7,993 (−3.0%)	176,825,683 (−17.3%)	22,290 (−14.8%)
1991	8,179 (−8.5%)	213,940,466 (−20.3%)	26,157 (−12.9%)
1990	8,937 (−3.8%)	268,378,588 (−10.8%)	30,030 (−7.4%)
Highest figures in boldface.			

This powerful upward trend resulted in a brightly glittering statistics for 2004:

- 9,421 yearlings sold, up 6.9% and the second-highest number on record;
- Total proceeds rose 17% to $496,937,672, also the second-highest number in history;
- Average price climbed 9.4% to $52,748, again second-best of all time;
- Median went up 8.3% to $13,000;
- Top price more than doubled from $3.8-million to $8-million; and
- Buy-back rate remained stable at 24.8%.

The most remarkable fact to be gleaned from the list of leading buyers of yearlings in 2004 was not the $49.3-million spent worldwide on yearlings by Sheikh Mohammed through his principal agent, John Ferguson, but that 122 different buyers spent $1-millon or more on Thoroughbred yearlings. In 2003, 101 different buyers matched the same total expenditure.

Only 16 of those 122 buyers paid $1-million or more for an individual yearling worldwide, compared with 19 in 2003. The clear conclusion was that more buyers were acquiring more horses rather than investing a small fortune in a few very high-priced yearlings.

Through Ferguson, Sheikh Mohammed spent more than anyone else, as he has in five of six years through 2004 and for nine years dating back to 1991. Demi O'Byrne, who represents Michael Tabor and John Magnier, Sheikh Mohammed's principal rivals on the international stage, was second in 2004, spending $37.2-million. O'Byrne and Ferguson have been first or second on the leading buyers list for six consecutive years.

Japanese trainer Hideyuki Mori, on behalf of owner Fusao Sekiguchi, bid $8-million for a handsome chestnut colt by the year's leading commercial yearling sire, Storm Cat, out of Welcome Surprise (a stakes-winning half sister to the year's second-leading sire of yearlings, A.P. Indy) at the Keeneland September sale. That was easily the year's top price, the fourth-highest-priced yearling of all time, and the highest since Seattle Dancer sold for a world-record $13.1-million at the 1985 Keeneland July sale.

Storm Cat, the world's most expensive stallion at $500,000 per nomination, was the only American sire whose progeny averaged more than $1-million in 2004. His gaudy average of $1,406,715 was almost double that of A.P. Indy. Galileo (Ire) easily won the international race for leading first-year sire of yearlings. Taylor Made Sales Agency, which passed the $1-billion mark in total sales since its inception in 1997 at the 2004 Keeneland November sale, headed the list of leading consignors by total proceeds for the fourth consecutive year.

Two-Year-Olds

Buyers at sales of two-year-olds in training broke practically every significant historical record for juveniles sold at public auction. During a 90-minute period at the Fasig-Tipton Calder sale of selected two-year-olds in training, the world-record price for a juvenile was broken not once, but twice.

Overall figures for the year were:
- 2,908 horses sold, down 3.7% from 2003;
- Total proceeds of $171,333,601, up 23% and a record;
- Average price up 27.7% to a record $58,918;
- Median up 17.6% to a record $20,000;
- Buy-back rate down to 26.9% from 32.4% in 2003;
- Fusaichi Samurai shattered the world-record price on a $4.5-million bid from Fusao Sekiguchi;
- Dubai Escapade set a record of $2-million for a filly in training at auction;
- A record eight juveniles sold for $1-million or more; and
- Pinhookers posted a record $22.1-million profit.

Buyers' largesse spread over the breadth of the market. The record number of horses sold for seven-figure prices raised the top 10% of the market by 34%, but that was not the highest percentage rise. Buyers willing to pay for horses substantially below the top of the price scale resulted in two positive developments for the market: Average price soared 20.3% or more for the bottom 40% of the market, and overall buy-back rate dipped below 30% for the first time since 1997.

North American Juvenile Sales		
Year No. Sold (Chg)	Total Sales (Chg)	Average (Chg)
2004 2,908 (–3.7%)	**$171,333,601 (23.0%)**	**$58,918 (27.7%)**
2003 3,019 (11.6%)	139,296,135 (8.1%)	46,140 (–3.1%)
2002 2,706 (0.0%)	128,870,834 (1.4%)	47,624 (1.4%)
2001 2,705 (–11.1%)	127,056,203 (–17.9%)	46,971 (–7.7%)
2000 3,043 (5.0%)	154,807,648 (0.1%)	50,873 (–4.7%)
1999 2,897 (–2.9%)	154,648,585 (13.4%)	53,382 (16.9%)
1998 2,985 (12.3%)	136,318,616 (12.9%)	45,668 (0.5%)
1997 2,657 (–0.8%)	120,694,031 (2.9%)	45,425 (14.1%)
1996 2,946 (–0.5%)	117,263,901 (23.9%)	39,804 (24.5%)
1995 2,961 (–0.2%)	94,666,095 (23.1%)	31,971 (23.3%)
1994 2,966 (–0.3%)	76,905,149 (26.7%)	25,929 (27.1%)
1993 2,976 (0.1%)	60,716,936 (7.8%)	20,402 (7.7%)
1992 2,974 (–16.1%)	56,349,005 (–12.0%)	18,947 (4.9%)
1991 3,546 (–5.4%)	64,026,814 (–16.3%)	18,056 (–11.5%)
1990 **3,750** (14.2%)	76,510,757 (49.1%)	20,403 (30.6%)
Highest figures in boldface.		

Also, profit margins rose despite a rising yearling market in 2003. Rate of return rose sharply from 44.5% in 2003 to 81.2% in '04, which also was a record. Niall Brennan Stables sold two of the three highest-priced juveniles ever sold at auction and 156 horses for $16,836,900.

Sekiguchi was second on the leading buyers list behind John Ferguson, who spent $15.5-million for 20 horses on behalf of Sheikh Mohammed. Ferguson signed for four of the eight seven-figure juveniles. Sekiguchi's big splash in the marketplace pushed overall Japanese investment to $16.6-million, highest since 1996.

Weanlings

Weanlings constituted the only segment of the Thoroughbred marketplace that suffered a general decline in 2004, but that drop might be seen as the last, indirect vestiges of mare reproductive loss syndrome (MRLS), which struck the Kentucky foal crops of 2001 and '02. Higher weanling prices, up 28.6% in 2003, left pinhookers with little room to make money on weanlings bought for resale as yearlings in 2004, which resulted in lower profits. Thus, weanling-to-yearling pinhookers were in no mood to pay high prices for foals in 2004. Unlike 2003, no weanlings by top sire Storm Cat were on offer in 2004, and the market had no high-profile dispersal such as The Thoroughbred Corp. dispersal in '03. The results can be seen in the following overall numbers for North American weanling sales:
- Number sold rose 14.5% to 1,939;
- Total proceeds climbed 5.7% to $71,716,550;
- Average price fell 7.7% to $36,986;
- Buy-back rate rose to 25.9% from 23.3%; and
- Median rose 15.4% to $15,000.

As has become the norm in recent years, the year's highest-priced foals sold at the Japan Race

Horse Association's July sale. In fact, the four highest-priced weanlings—three of them by Sunday Silence's highly regarded young son Dance in the Dark—sold at the JRHA sale. Top price among North American weanlings did not come at the Keeneland November breeding stock sale's exclusive selected sessions, but on that sale's third day, when John Sikura paid $1.15-million for an Unbridled's Song filly who is a half sister to English champion two-year-old Shamardal.

Despite the decline, the market level remained high enough for breeders to make a profit, on average. Average price of $38,208 for the 1,864 weanlings for whom a 2003 stud fee was reported was exactly 2.5 times the average stud fee; the profitability standard is generally regarded to be 2-to-1 for weanlings.

North American Weanling Sales

Year	No. Sold (Chg)	Total Sales (Chg)	Average (Chg)
2004	1,939 (14.5%)	$71,716,550 (5.7%)	$36,986 (–7.7%)
2003	1,693 (8.7%)	67,866,478 (39.8%)	40,087 (28.6%)
2002	1,557 (–19.2%)	48,549,515 (–7.2%)	31,181 (14.9%)
2001	1,926 (–17.9%)	52,288,439 (–37.6%)	27,149 (–24.0%)
2000	**2,345** (2.4%)	83,755,053 (–14.6%)	35,716 (–16.7%)
1999	2,289 (0.5%)	**98,087,172** (9.8%)	**42,852** (9.3%)
1998	2,278 (9.0%)	89,303,995 (32.8%)	39,203 (21.8%)
1997	2,090 (–3.4%)	67,251,828 (10.1%)	32,178 (14.0%)
1996	2,164 (8.3%)	61,094,609 (17.0%)	28,232 (8.1%)
1995	1,999 (5.4%)	52,221,842 (26.2%)	26,124 (19.7%)
1994	1,896 (23.4%)	41,374,263 (14.2%)	21,822 (–7.5%)
1993	1,536 (2.3%)	36,233,360 (51.1%)	23,589 (47.8%)
1992	1,502 (4.8%)	23,974,936 (–17.9%)	15,962 (–21.7%)
1991	1,433 (–8.2%)	29,199,004 (2.8%)	20,376 (12.0%)
1990	1,561 (5.1%)	28,403,069 (–19.1%)	18,195 (–23.0%)

Highest figures in boldface.

Gone West led the list of American-based sires of weanlings, but his total included a $2.59-million foal sold at the JRHA sale. Leading 2004 sire Elusive Quality was second with eight weanlings averaging $306,875, without benefit of a Japanese sale.

Taylor Made Sales Agency led American consignors, selling 96 weanlings for $7,759,800, and Ferguson, acting for Sheikh Mohammed, led all buyers with 18 purchases in North America, Japan, and England for $3,846,742. Fusao Sekiguchi set a world record of $4.54-million for a Dance in the Dark foal at the JRHA sale in July, about four months after he paid about the same world-record price for a two-year-old at the Fasig-Tipton Calder sale of selected two-year-olds in training.

Broodmares

In response to an 18-month surge in the yearling and juvenile markets, average price for broodmares in North America soared to record levels in 2004 and total proceeds climbed to the third-highest total on record. Positive vibes in the broodmare market pushed year-end North American figures into record or near-record territory on several fronts:

- 5,355 broodmares or broodmare prospects were sold, up 7.5%;
- Average price up 27.5% to a record $55,694;
- Total proceeds up 37% to $298,241,142, third-highest on record;
- Median up 34% to $9,000, joint-second highest in history;
- 36 broodmares sold for $1-million or more, second-highest in history; and
- Buy-back rate declined from 26% to 21.7%.

The Keeneland November breeding stock sale annually constitutes about 60% of the total market for broodmares and broodmare prospects, and the 2004 auction included 34 of the 36 seven-figure broodmare transactions in North America (five more were recorded at Tattersalls's Newmarket December sale in England). The year's most expensive broodmare was I'll Get Along, dam of dual classic winner Smarty Jones. Gaines-Gentry Thoroughbreds paid $5-million for I'll Get Along, in foal to Smarty Jones's sire, Elusive Quality, at the Fasig-Tipton Kentucky November sale on the day before Keeneland November began.

Smarty Jones's popularity helped to make 12-year-old I'll Get Along something of an anomaly among the most expensive broodmares. Of the 36 seven-figure mares, only six, including I'll Get Along, were ten years old or older. Breeders focused instead on young broodmares and were willing to pay a substantial premium either for graded-stakes racing class or a highly fashionable pedigree. Best example of a mare combining youth, beauty, race record, and pedigree proved to be Santa Catarina, the Keeneland November sale topper purchased in foal to A.P. Indy for $4.8-million by Eaton Sales, agent.

North American Broodmare Sales

Year	No. Sold (Chg)	Total Sales (Chg)	Average (Chg)
2004	5,355 (7.5%)	$298,241,142 (37.0%)	**$55,694** (27.5%)
2003	4,983 (5.1%)	217,672,620 (13.3%)	43,683 (7.8%)
2002	4,741 (–6.3%)	192,082,219 (2.1%)	40,515 (9.0%)
2001	5,059 (–12.7%)	188,107,111 (–40.7%)	37,183 (–32.1%)
2000	**5,797** (3.9%)	**317,398,250** (6.4%)	54,752 (2.4%)
1999	5,582 (1.7%)	298,397,805 (24.4%)	53,457 (22.3%)
1998	5,489 (8.5%)	239,875,672 (25.1%)	43,701 (15.3%)
1997	5,058 (0.9%)	191,764,648 (22.7%)	37,913 (21.5%)
1996	5,011 (2.6%)	156,304,244 (24.2%)	31,192 (21.0%)
1995	4,883 (6.6%)	125,836,989 (12.8%)	25,770 (5.8%)
1994	4,579 (10.2%)	111,520,366 (46.9%)	24,355 (33.3%)
1993	4,154 (–2.8%)	75,910,215 (–1.4%)	18,274 (1.5%)
1992	4,274 (–9.4%)	76,970,720 (–7.3%)	18,009 (2.3%)
1991	4,718 (–11.9%)	83,053,742 (–19.6%)	17,604 (–8.7%)
1990	5,356 (–10.6%)	103,263,519 (–36.0%)	19,280 (–28.5%)

Highest figures in boldface.

The most significant new buyer was Kendall Jackson Winery founder Jess Jackson, buyer of more than 90 of leading buyer Narvick International's 94 purchases for $21,924,000. Taylor Made Sales Agency led all consignors, selling 289 mares for $38,705,200.—*John P. Sparkman*

Highest-Priced Yearlings of 2004

Horse	Consignor	Buyer	Sale	Price
C., by Storm Cat—Welcome Surprise	Lane's End, agent	Hideyuki Mori	Kee Sept.	$8,000,000
C., by Storm Cat—Bless	Taylor Made Sales Agency, agent for ClassicStar	Hideyuki Mori	Kee Sept.	3,400,000
C., by Kingmambo—Zuri	Dromoland Farm, agent	John Ferguson Bloodstock	Kee Sept.	3,100,000
C., by A.P. Indy—Sahara Gold	Lane's End, agent for Stonerside Stables	John Ferguson Bloodstock	Kee Sept.	3,100,000
C., by Kingmambo—Crown of Crimson	Lakland LLC, agent	Shadwell Estate Co. Ltd.	Kee Sept.	2,850,000
C., by Unbridled's Song—Cruising Haven	Paramount Sales, agent	Demi O'Byrne	Kee Sept.	2,800,000
C., by Danehill—Bordighera	Trickledown Stud	Demi O'Byrne	Tatt Oct.	2,154,421
C., by Danzig—Scads	Claiborne Farm, agent	Demi O'Byrne	Kee Sept.	2,000,000
C., by Galileo (Ire)—Regina Maria	Runnymede Farm, agent	Demi O'Byrne	Kee Sept.	1,900,000
C., by Forestry—Clever Bertie	Taylor Made Sales Agency, agent	Buzz Chace, agent	Kee Sept.	1,900,000
C., by Giant's Causeway—Alaska Queen	Gainesway, agent	Team Valor	F-T Saratoga	1,850,000
C., by Seeking the Gold—Angel Fever	Stone Farm, agent for Stone Farm and Stonerside Stable	Hideyuki Mori	Kee Sept.	1,800,000
F., by Storm Cat—Warm Mood	Lane's End, agent	John Ferguson Bloodstock	Kee Sept.	1,700,000
C., by Danehill—Fiji (GB)	Eaton Sales, agent	Demi O'Byrne	Kee Sept.	1,500,000
F., by Fusaichi Pegasus—Golden Oriole	Michael C. Byrne, agent	Skara Glen Stables	Kee Sept.	1,500,000
F., by A.P. Indy—Seebe	Derry Meeting Farm, agent	W. S. Farish	F-T Saratoga	1,500,000
C., by Danehill—Rockerlong	Hascombe Stud	Demi O'Byrne	Tatt Oct.	1,405,057
F., by Storm Cat—Jewel Princess	Eaton Sales, agent	Roger King	F-T Saratoga	1,400,000
C., by Danzig—Shouldnt Say Never	Lane's End, agent	John Ferguson Bloodstock	Kee Sept.	1,400,000
C., by Sadler's Wells—Bex	Camas Park Stud, Ireland	Nobutaka Tada	Tatt Oct.	1,311,387
C., by Galileo (Ire)—Balisada	Hascombe Stud	Charles P. Gordon-Watson	Tatt Oct.	1,310,431
C., by Grand Slam—Sheza Honey	Michael C. Byrne, agent	Demi O'Byrne	Kee Sept.	1,300,000
C., by A.P. Indy—Warrior Queen	Eaton Sales, agent	Fleetwood/NW Management	Kee Sept.	1,300,000
F., by Storm Cat—Strategic Maneuver	Eaton Sales, agent	Reynolds Bell, agent	Kee Sept.	1,300,000
F., by Unbridled's Song—Towering Success	Paramount Sales, agent	Brushwood Stable	Kee Sept.	1,250,000
C., by Storm Cat—Program Pick	Eaton Sales, agent	Shadwell Estate Co. Ltd.	Kee Sept.	1,250,000
C., by Giant's Causeway—Statuette	Dromoland Farm, agent	Demi O'Byrne	Kee Sept.	1,150,000
C., by Unbridled's Song—Mesmerized	Paramount Sales, agent	William B. Haines	F-T Saratoga	1,150,000
F., by Storm Cat—Gone to the Moon	Hill 'n' Dale Sales Agency, agent	Roger King	F-T Saratoga	1,100,000
C., by Forestry—Christmas in Aiken	Taylor Made Sales Agency, agent	John Ferguson Bloodstock	Kee Sept.	1,100,000
C., by Danehill—Heavenly Whisper	Highclere Stud	Demi O'Byrne	Tatt Oct.	1,086,577
C., by Sadler's Wells—Sumoto	Watership Down Stud	Demi O'Byrne	Tatt Oct.	1,085,786
F., by Giant's Causeway—Touch of Greatness	Three Chimneys Sales, agent	Reynolds Bell, agent	Kee Sept.	1,050,000
C., by Rahy—Crystal Crossing (Ire)	Four Star Sales, agent	John Ferguson Bloodstock	Kee Sept.	1,050,000
C., by Giant's Causeway—Smokey Mirage	Brookdale Sales, agent for Audley Farm	John Ferguson Bloodstock	Kee Sept.	1,000,000
C., by A.P. Indy—Million Gift (Jpn)	Taylor Made Sales Agency, agent	Michael J. Ryan, agent	Kee Sept.	1,000,000
C., by Storm Cat—Gone to Venus	Three Chimneys Sales, agent	Robert and Beverly Lewis	F-T Saratoga	1,000,000
F., by Danehill—Hotelgenie Dot Com	Catridge Farm Stud	Demi O'Byrne	Tatt Oct.	974,173
C., by Elusive Quality—Cercida	Dromoland Farm, agent	John Ferguson Bloodstock	F-T Ky. July	950,000
C., by Forestry—Concentric	Taylor Made Sales Agency, agent	John Ferguson Bloodstock	Kee Sept.	950,000
C., by Kingmambo—Possibly Perfect	Ashleigh Stud	John Ferguson Bloodstock	Kee Sept.	950,000
F., by Seattle Slew—Pleasant Temper	Eaton Sales, agent	Lael Stables	Kee Sept.	950,000
C., by Kingmambo—String Quartet (Ire)	Eaton Sales, agent	Shadwell Estate Co. Ltd.	Kee Sept.	950,000
F., by Danehill—Brigitta (Ire)	Watership Down Stud	BBA (Ireland)	Tatt Oct.	936,705
F., by Seeking the Gold—Corona Lake	Mill Ridge Sales, agent	Buzz Chace, agent	Kee Sept.	925,000
C., by War Chant—Safely Kept	Lakland LLC, agent	Narvick International	Kee Sept.	900,000
F., by Gone West—England's Rose	Vinery	John Ferguson Bloodstock	Kee Sept.	900,000
C., by Pulpit—Mountain Girl	Lane's End, agent	John Ferguson Bloodstock	Kee Sept.	900,000
F., by Kingmambo—Sweet and Ready	Gainesway, agent	Narvick International	F-T Saratoga	900,000
C., by Grand Slam—Bisbee	Three Chimneys Sales, agent	Fleetwood/NW Management	F-T Saratoga	900,000
C., by Giant's Causeway—Serape	Middlebrook Farm, agent	John Ferguson Bloodstock	Kee Sept.	875,000
C., by Grand Lodge—Native Twine (GB)	Haras de Bois Carrouges	Richard O'Gorman Bloodstock	Deauville Aug.	851,690
C., by Elusive Quality—First Glimmer	Taylor Made Sales Agency, agent	Buzz Chace, agent	Kee Sept.	850,000
C., by Giant's Causeway—Devine Beauty	Hopewell Farm, agent	Demi O'Byrne	Kee Sept.	850,000
F., by Storm Cat—Nannerl	Taylor Made Sales Agency, agent for ClassicStar	John Ferguson Bloodstock	Kee Sept.	850,000
F., by Storm Cat—Pennant Fever	Lane's End, agent	Edward Evans	Kee Sept.	850,000
F., by Green Desert—Simaat	Camas Park Stud	John Magnier	Goffs Orby	830,397
C., by Cozzene—Avie's Fancy	Seven Fold Farm, agent for Gunsmith Stables	Lane's End Bloodstock, agent	F-T Ky. July	825,000
C., by Giant's Causeway—Fountain Lake	Taylor Made Sales Agency, agent	Robert Baker and Bill Mack	Kee Sept.	825,000
C., by Rahy—Balistroika	Eaton Sales, agent	Shadwell Estate Co. Ltd.	Kee Sept.	825,000
C., by Point Given—Classic Threat	Anderson Farms, agent	Robert and Beverly Lewis	Kee Sept.	800,000
F., by Seattle Slew—Ski Dancer	Lane's End, agent	B. Wayne Hughes	Kee Sept.	800,000
C., by A.P. Indy—Ring of Fire	Lane's End, agent	John Ferguson Bloodstock	Kee Sept.	800,000
C., by Giant's Causeway—Sweeping Story	Taylor Made Sales Agency, agent	John Ferguson Bloodstock	Kee Sept.	800,000
F., by A.P. Indy—Kelli Cat	Taylor Made Sales Agency, agent	Buzz Chace, agent	Kee Sept.	800,000
F., by Touch Gold—Arches of Gold	Threave Main Stud, agent	B. Wayne Hughes	Kee Sept.	800,000

Highest-Priced Weanlings of 2004

Horse	Consignor	Buyer	Sale	Price
C., by Dance in the Dark—Air Groove	Northern Farm	Fusao Sekiguchi	Japan July	$4,537,037
C., by Gone West—Seattle Sunset	Northern Farm	Fusao Sekiguchi	Japan July	2,592,593
C., by Dance in the Dark—Subtle Change	Shadai Farm	Big Red Farm	Japan July	1,851,852
C., by Dance in the Dark—Star Ballerina	Shadai Farm	Takaya Shimakawa	Japan July	1,583,333
F., by Unbridled's Song—Helsinki (GB)	Taylor Made Sales Agency, agent	John Sikura	Kee Nov.	1,150,000
C., by Danehill—Zarawa	Tullamaine Castle Stud, Ireland	BBA (Ireland)	Tatt Dec.	995,708
C., by Agnes Tachyon—Fair Deal	Northern Farm	Miduki Noda	Japan July	953,704
F., by Danehill—Knight's Baroness	Watership Down Stud	Peter J. Doyle Bloodstock	Tatt Dec.	927,375
C., by Kurofune—Really Happy	Northern Farm	Riichi Kondo	Japan July	925,926
C., by Jungle Pocket—Admire Sunday	Northern Farm	Fusao Sekiguchi	Japan July	925,926
C., by Agnes Tachyon—Sawayaka Princess	Shadai Farm	Takaya Shimakawa	Japan July	925,926
C., by Taiki Shuttle—Seazun	Northern Farm	RRA Co. Ltd.	Japan July	916,667
C., by Barathea (Ire)—Interruption	Shadai Farm	Takaya Shimakawa	Japan July	787,037
C., by Brian's Time—Palatial Affaire	Chiyoda Farm	Makoto Kaneko	Japan July	768,519
C., by Dance in the Dark—Bubble Dream (Fr)	Paca Paca Farm	Soda Noen Co., Ltd.	Japan July	750,000
C., by Gone West—Donna Viola (GB)	Shadai Farm	Danox Co Ltd.	Japan July	740,741
F., by Gone West—Dance Swiftly	Taylor Made Sales Agency, agent	Maurice W. Miller, agent	Kee Nov.	700,000
C., by Black Hawk (GB)—Dancing Sunday	Shadai Farm	Fusao Sekiguchi	Japan July	666,667
C., by White Muzzle (GB)—Croupier Star	Shadai Farm	Genichiro Tahara	Japan July	657,407
F., by French Deputy—Silver Lane	Paca Paca Farm	Makoto Kaneko	Japan July	657,407
C., by Grand Slam—Heavenly Cat	Viking Stud, agent for Twin Hopes Farm	Glen Hill Farm	Kee Nov.	650,000
C., by Jungle Pocket—Sunday Picnic	Shadai Farm	Takaya Shimakawa	Japan July	638,889
F., by War Chant—Dissemble	Indian Creek (Dave C. Parrish Jr.), agent	Stewart L. Armstrong	Kee Nov.	625,000
C., by Manhattan Cafe—Eternal Beat	Oiwake Farm	Masatsugu Takezono	Japan July	620,370
C., by Manhattan Cafe—Royal Successor	Northern Farm	Fusao Sekiguchi	Japan July	620,370
C., by Rock of Gibraltar (Ire)—Onereuse	Paget Bloodstock, Ireland	Shadwell Estate Co. Ltd.	Tatt Dec.	585,711
F., by Pulpit—Mila	Claiborne Farm, agent	Lael Stables/Nicoma Bloodstock, agent	Kee Nov.	575,000
F., by Giant's Causeway—Halo America	Hill 'n' Dale Sales Agency, agent for Estate of John Franks	Robert Ogden	Kee Nov.	575,000
C., by Fusaichi Pegasus—Primaly	Oiwake Farm	Makoto Kaneko	Japan July	574,074
C., by Agnes Tachyon—Race Cam	Excelmanagement	Danox Co Ltd.	Japan July	564,815
C., by Jungle Pocket—Shinko Beauty	Northern Farm	Miduki Noda	Japan July	555,556
C., by Elusive Quality—Barbara Sue	Taylor Made Sales Agency, agent	John Ferguson Bloodstock	Kee Nov.	550,000
C., by Dance in the Dark—Dalinda	Northern Farm	Masaru Shimada	Japan July	537,037
C., by Fusaichi Pegasus—Gracie Lady (Ire)	Ashford Stud, agent	Foxtale Farm	Kee Nov.	535,000
C., by French Deputy—Katies First	Northern Farm	RRA Co. Ltd.	Japan July	518,519
C., by Brian's Time—Sweet Orchid	Symboli Stud	Shoji Ogiwara	Japan July	509,259
C., by Elusive Quality—Silver Tornado	Runnymede Farm, agent	John Ferguson Bloodstock	Kee Nov.	500,000
C., by Agnes Tachyon—Air Sharon	Shadai Farm	Takao Watanabe	Japan July	472,222
C., by Brian's Time—Matikanehatusimada	Shadai Farm	Danox Co Ltd.	Japan July	462,963
C., by Jungle Pocket—Crafty Wife	Northern Farm	Yasushi Tsumura	Japan July	462,963
C., by Elusive Quality—Valid Warning	Claiborne Farm, agent	John Ferguson Bloodstock	Kee Nov.	450,000
C., by Giant's Causeway—Esther Rose	Claiborne Farm, agent	Dromoland Farm	Kee Nov.	450,000
C., by Mr. Greeley—Hard Knocker	Knockgriffin Farm, agent	Eldon Farm Equine	Kee Nov.	440,000
C., by Dance in the Dark—Northern Princess	Northern Farm	RRA Co. Ltd.	Japan July	439,815
C., by Agnes Tachyon—Toccoa	Northern Farm	Daiwa Shoji Co.	Japan July	430,556
F., by Rock of Gibraltar (Ire)—Qhazeenah (GB)	Norelands Stud, Ireland	BBA (Ireland)	Tatt Dec.	429,521
F., by Kurofune—Sun Spring (Arg)	Northern Farm	Makoto Kaneko	Japan July	425,926
C., by French Deputy—Silent Prayer	Shadai Farm	Takaya Shimakawa	Japan July	425,926
C., by Agnes Tachyon—Aiesha Powell	Shadai Farm	Daiwa Shoji Co.	Japan July	421,296
C., by Crafty Prospector—Lilac Lane	Shiraoi Farm	Makoto Kaneko	Japan July	416,667
F., by Dixie Union—Be a Prospector	Brookdale Sales, agent for Joseph and William Stavola	Robert E. Courtney, agent	Kee Nov.	400,000
C., by War Chant—Peu a Peu (Ger)	Oiwake Farm	Takashi Suzuki	Japan July	398,148
F., by French Deputy—Real Number (Arg)	Northern Farm	Makoto Kaneko	Japan July	393,519
C., by Kurofune—Rubia	Northern Farm	Daiwa Shoji Co.	Japan July	393,519
C., by Johannesburg—La Martina (GB)	Nuthurst Farm Stud	Bolton Grange	Tatt Dec.	390,474
C., by Tanino Gimlet—Cheerful	Northern Farm	Danox Co Ltd.	Japan July	388,889
C., by Seeking the Gold—Glamorous	Toyosato Bokujo	Gold Horse Club Co. Ltd.	Japan July	388,889
F., by Giant's Causeway—Million Stories	Highclere Sales, agent	Gus Bell, agent	F-T Ky. Nov.	385,000
C., by Fuji Kiseki—Spring Sonnett	Shadai Farm	Lucky Field Co.	Japan July	379,630
C., by Fuji Kiseki—Air Peace	Shadai Farm	Broodmare Co., Ltd.	Japan July	379,630
F., by Jungle Pocket—Sermon Time	Northern Farm	Hanzawa Co. Ltd.	Japan July	379,630
C., by Special Week—Fusaichi Yoko	Shadai Farm	Fusao Sekiguchi	Japan July	379,630
C., by Admire Vega—Dancing Auntie	Northern Farm	Fusao Sekiguchi	Japan July	375,000
F., by Fusaichi Pegasus—Silent Eskimo	Hill 'n' Dale Sales Agency, agent for Estate of John Franks	Frederic Sauque, agent	Kee Nov.	375,000
C., by Agnes Tachyon—Northern Maia	Northern Farm	Yoshio Komurasaki	Japan July	370,370
C., by Agnes Tachyon—Admise (Fr)	Shadai Farm	Daiwa Shoji Co.	Japan July	370,370

Highest-Priced Two-Year-Olds of 2004

Horse	Consignor	Buyer	Sale	Price
Fusaichi Samurai, c., by Fusaichi Pegasus—Hidden Storm	Kirkwood Stables, agent	Fusao Sekiguchi	F-T Calder	$4,500,000
Chekhov, c., by Pulpit—In My Cap	Niall Brennan Stables, agent	Demi O'Byrne	Kee April	3,300,000
Dubai Dreamer, c., by Stephen Got Even—Blacktie Bid	Niall Brennan Stables, agent	John Ferguson Bloodstock	F-T Calder	3,100,000
Dubai Escapade, f., by Awesome Again—Sassy Pants	Jerry Bailey Sales Agency, agent	John Ferguson Bloodstock	Barretts March	2,000,000
Mutanabi, c., by Wild Rush—Freudenau	W. D. North, agent	John Ferguson Bloodstock	Ocala Calder	1,600,000
Timsaah, c., by Rubiano—Magari	H. T. Inc., agent for Cam Allard	John Ferguson Bloodstock	F-T Calder	1,500,000
Radetzky, c., by Dixie Union—Sneaky Quiet	Solitary Oak Farm, agent	Demi O'Byrne	Kee April	1,400,000
Storm Cat Johnny, c., by Storm Cat—Add	Hoby and Layna Kight, agent	Robert V. LaPenta	F-T Calder	1,050,000
Fusaichi Seishiro, c., by Fusaichi Pegasus—Lyric Fantasy (Ire)	Bansha House Stables	Fusao Sekiguchi	Tatt April	980,595
Woodford Gale, c., by Distorted Humor—Zuppardo Ardo	Niall Brennan Stables, agent for Estate of John Franks	John Ferguson Bloodstock	Ocala April	975,000
Daddy Joe, c., by Unbridled's Song—Vennila Cream	Hoby and Layna Kight, agent	Baden Chace	F-T Calder	900,000
Fusaichi Rock Star, c., by Wild Wonder—Grannies Feather	Jessie and Stacy Longoria	Fusao Sekiguchi	F-T Calder	825,000
She's a Devil Slew, f., by Seattle Slew—She's a Devil Due	Robert N. Scanlon, agent	Fleetwood/NW Management	Kee April	800,000
Deputy Grant, c., by Deputy Minister—Win Crafty Lady	Eddie Woods, agent	B. Wayne Hughes	F-T Calder	800,000
Coach Kent, c., by Fusaichi Pegasus—Rokeby Rosie	Eaton Sales, agent for Jeanne G. Vance	Aaron and Marie Jones	Kee April	750,000
Bremmer, c., by Distorted Humor—Dare to Be Me	Tony Bowling and Bobby Dodd, agent	John Ferguson Bloodstock	F-T Calder	750,000
One Smart Deputy, c., by Silver Deputy—Awful Smart	Maurice W. Miller, agent	Roger L. Attfield	F-T Calder	700,000
War Plan, c., by Fusaichi Pegasus—Li Law	Robert N. Scanlon, agent	Brian Morgan, agent	F-T Calder	700,000
Collegiate Honor, c., by Double Honor—Camptown Miss	Farnsworth Farms, agent	William J. Condren	Ocala April	675,000
Rachel's Song, f., by Tale of the Cat—Too too Divine	Hartley/De Renzo Thoroughbreds, agent	Michael J. Ryan, agent	F-T Calder	650,000
Notable Tiger, c., by Tiger Ridge—Notable Girl	Hartley/De Renzo Thoroughbreds, agent	John Ferguson Bloodstock	Ocala March	650,000
Fashion Cat, f., by Forest Wildcat—Hold to Fashion	Leprechaun Racing, agent	Bar S Ranch	F-T Calder	630,000
Edwardo's Cavalier, c., by Pulpit—Silent Greeting	M & H Training and Sales, agent	Michael J. Ryan, agent	F-T Calder	625,000
Going Wild, c., by Golden Missile—Pola	Maurice W. Miller, agent	Robert and Beverly Lewis	F-T Calder	600,000
Nasema's Slam, f., by Grand Slam—Nasema	Equine Legacy Farm, agent	Fleetwood/NW Management	F-T Calder	600,000
Should Be Royalty, f., by Pine Bluff—Malley	Jerry Bailey Sales Agency, agent	Demi O'Byrne	Barretts March	600,000
Swissle Stick, c., by Swiss Yodeler—Miss Soft Sell	Wavertree Stables, agent	Robert and Beverly Lewis	Barretts March	600,000
Yankee Million, f., by Yankee Victor—Betamillion Bock	Niall Brennan Stables, agent	Narvick International	Ocala March	575,000
True Integrity, c., by Honour and Glory—Defer West	Jerry Bailey Sales Agency, agent	Narvick International	Barretts March	575,000
For All We Know, f., by Stephen Got Even—Over All	Niall Brennan Stables, agent	John C. Oxley	F-T Calder	550,000
Walk In The Park, c., by Montjeu (Ire)—Classic Park	Mocklershill Stables	BBA (Ireland)	Tatt April	529,521
Happy As Larry, c., by Yes It's True—Don't Be Blue	Niall Brennan Stables, agent	John Ferguson Bloodstock	F-T Calder	525,000
Play Ballado, f., by Saint Ballado—Piccolo Player	Cary Frommer, agent	John C. Oxley	F-T Calder	525,000
Quiet Money, c., by Seattle Slew—Discreet Account	Nick de Meric, agent	R. A. Violette	F-T Calder	500,000
Materialism, c., by Not For Love—Gala Goldie's Best	M & H Training and Sales, agent	John Ferguson Bloodstock	F-T Calder	500,000
Devil At Sea, c., by Devil His Due—Atlantique du Nord	Indian Prairie Ranch, agent	John H. Peace	F-T Calder	500,000
Smokum Sam, c., by Smoke Glacken—Flo White	Costanzo Sales	John Ferguson Bloodstock	Ocala April	500,000
Western Acres, c., by West Acre—Y'All Sing	Eisaman Equine Services, agent	Kaaren J. Biggs	Ocala April	500,000
Ridges In Time, c., by Tiger Ridge—Winning Journey	Sequel Bloodstock, agent	Bruno DeBerdt, agent	Barretts March	500,000
Jim's Smokin Pinot, c., by Victory Gallop—Buck's Lady	Terry Oliver, agent	Never Tell Farm LLC	Barretts March	500,000
Gold Siphon, f., by Siphon (Brz)—Misty Music	Nick de Meric, agent	Aaron and Marie Jones	Kee April	500,000
Fusaichi Forza, c., by Polish Numbers—Student Wife	Kirkwood Stables, agent	Fusao Sekiguchi	Kee April	500,000
Brazilian, f., by Stravinsky—Golden Pond (Ire)	Robert N. Scanlon, agent	John P. Fort	Kee April	500,000
Storm Silk, c., by Stormin Fever—Carpenter's Lace	Wavertree Stables, agent	John Ferguson Bloodstock	F-T Calder	500,000
Spanish Chestnut, c., by Horse Chestnut (SAf)—Baby Rabbit	Ocala Oaks and Don R. Graham	Demi O'Byrne	Ocala Calder	500,000
Siphon City, c., by Siphon (Brz)—Carsona	Cleveland Wheeler, agent for Straightaway Farm	Demi O'Byrne	Ocala Calder	500,000
Notta Saint, c., by Saint Ballado—Sapphire Beads	Tony Bowling and Bobby Dodd, agent	Aaron and Marie Jones	Kee April	475,000
Unnamed, f., by Danehill—Supamova	Bansha House Stables	Keishiro Kanamori	Tatt April	470,686
Theschemeofthings, f., by Grand Slam—Schematic	Niall Brennan Stables, agent	Never Tell Farm LLC	Kee April	460,000
Paragon Queen, f., by Lord Carson—Storm Struck	B.C.3 Thoroughbreds, agent for Timberline	Robert and Beverly Lewis	Barretts March	450,000
Desert Breeze, c., by Deputy Minister—Date Stone	Niall Brennan Stables, agent	David Moore	Kee April	450,000
Buddy Got Even, c., by Stephen Got Even—Gem Treck	Murray Smith, agent	Fleetwood/NW Management	F-T Calder	450,000
Krisheba, c., by Kissin Kris—In Reverence	Kirkwood Stables, agent for Estate of John Franks	La Cresta Farm	Barretts March	450,000
Compulsive, c., by Chief Seattle—Helen's Pick	Paul Sharp, agent	James McIngvale	Ocala March	450,000
Proud Accolade, c., by Yes It's True—Proud Ciel	Eisaman Equine Services, agent	Padua Stables	Ocala March	450,000
Writer's Walk, c., by Yankee Victor—Mesmerized	Stephens Thoroughbreds, agent for Paragon Farms	Joseph Brocklebank, agent	Ocala March	450,000
Lady H, f., by Silver Deputy—Livia B	Niall Brennan Stables, agent	Charles and Marianne	FTMMAY	450,000

Highest-Priced Broodmares and Broodmare Prospects of 2004

Horse (Covering Sire), Age	Consignor	Buyer	Sale	Price
I'll Get Along (Elusive Quality), 12	Brent Fernung, agent for CloverLeaf Farms II	Gaines-Gentry Thoroughbreds	F-T Ky Nov.	$5,000,000
Santa Catarina (A.P. Indy), 4	Denali Stud, agent for Robert and Beverly Lewis	Eaton Sales, agent	Kee Nov.	4,800,000
Unbridled Elaine (Forestry), 6	Taylor Made Sales Agency, agent	John Ferguson Bloodstock	Kee Nov.	4,400,000
Take Charge Lady (Seeking The Gold), 5	Three Chimneys Sales, agent	Eaton Sales, agent	Kee Nov.	4,200,000
Helsinki (GB) (Cherokee Run), 11	Taylor Made Sales Agency, agent	Christy Grassick	Kee Nov.	3,900,000
Stellar Jayne, 3	Spendthrift Farm, agent	John Ferguson Bloodstock	Kee Nov.	3,600,000
Dessert (Kingmambo), 4	Lane's End, agent	Shadwell Farm	Kee Nov.	3,600,000
Cat Fighter, 4	Hill 'n' Dale Sales Agency, agent	Live Oak Stud	Kee Nov.	2,300,000
Storm Beauty (A.P. Indy), 9	Denali Stud, agent for Robert and Beverly Lewis	Brushwood Stable	Kee Nov.	2,200,000
Be Gentle (A.P. Indy), 3	Eaton Sales, agent	Diamond A Farms	Kee Nov.	2,100,000
Blithe (A.P. Indy), 3	Stone Farm, agent for Stonerside Stable and Stone Farm	Reynolds Bell, agent	Kee Nov.	2,000,000
Dimitrova, 4	Indian Creek (Dave C. Parrish Jr.), agent	Abbott Bloodstock	Kee Nov.	2,000,000
Miss Lodi (A.P. Indy), 5	Denali Stud, agent	Skara Glen Stables	Kee Nov.	2,000,000
Better Than Honour (Mineshaft), 8	Lane's End, agent	BBA (Ireland)	Kee Nov.	2,000,000
Words Of War (Storm Cat), 15	Stone Farm, agent for Stonerside Stable and Stone Farm	Malibu Farm	Kee Nov.	1,950,000
Gaviola (Gone West), 7	Eaton Sales, agent for Twilite Farms	ClassicStar LLC	Kee Nov.	1,900,000
Golden Sonata (A.P. Indy), 5	Hartwell Farm, agent	Skara Glen Stables	Kee Nov.	1,900,000
Elloluv, 4	Three Chimneys Sales, agent	Frank Stronach	Kee Nov.	1,750,000
Happily Unbridled (Storm Cat), 6	Taylor Made Sales Agency, agent	Frederic Sauque, agent	Kee Nov.	1,700,000
Ipi Tombe (Zim) (Sadler's Wells), 6	Denali Stud, agent	James S. Delahooke	Tatt Dec.	1,659,514
Profit Column (Storm Cat), 11	Claiborne Farm, agent	ClassicStar LLC	Kee Nov.	1,600,000
Renaissance Lady (Elusive Quality), 3	Denali Stud, agent for Robert and Beverly Lewis	Summer Wind Farm	Kee Nov.	1,600,000
Kenmist (Rock Of Gibraltar [Ire]), 10	European Sales Management	Penfold Bloodstock	Tatt Dec.	1,513,086
Got Koko, 5	Brereton C. Jones, agent	Narvick International	Kee Nov.	1,500,000
Stylish (A.P. Indy), 6	Lane's End, agent	Malibu Farm	Kee Nov.	1,500,000
Halo America (Vindication), 14	Hill 'n' Dale Sales Agency, agent for Estate of John Franks	John G. Sikura	Kee Nov.	1,450,000
Unbridled Beauty (Tale of the Cat), 3	Denali Stud, agent for Robert and Beverly Lewis	Forging Oaks Farm LLC	Kee Nov.	1,400,000
Cat Fighter, 4	Kristin A. Mulhall, agent	John G. Sikura	BESMAR	1,350,000
Fashion Star (Vindication), 12	Bluegrass T'bred. Svs., agent for Carl Rosen Assoc.	Summer Wind Farm	Kee Nov.	1,300,000
Time Ahead (Dalakhani), 4	Jamie Railton, agent	BBA (Ireland)	Tatt Dec.	1,269,040
Silver Tornado (Lemon Drop Kid), 6	Runnymede Farm, agent	BBA (Ireland)	Kee Nov.	1,250,000
Smok'n Frolic, 5	Three Chimneys Sales, agent for Dogwood Stable	Adena Springs	Kee Nov.	1,250,000
Renashaan (Pivotal), 15	The Castlebridge Consignment	Tim Hyde	Tatt Dec.	1,249,516
Dublino, 5	Narvick International, agent	Cheveley Park Stud	Kee Nov.	1,200,000
Fairest Cape, 2	Michael C. Byrne, agent	Skara Glen Stables	Kee Nov.	1,200,000
Nonsuch Bay, 5	Mill Ridge Sales, agent	Never Tell Farm LLC	Kee Nov.	1,150,000
She's A Beauty (Fusaichi Pegasus), 4	Paramount Sales, agent	Manganaro LLC	Kee Nov.	1,100,000
Airwave, 4	Kingstone Warren Stables	BBA (Ireland)	Tatt Dec.	1,073,803
Mer De Corail (Ire) (Giant's Causeway), 5	Eaton Sales, agent	France Pur Sang and 6 C Racing Ltd.	Kee Nov.	1,050,000
Rubywood (Giant's Causeway), 4	Ashview Farm LLC	Reynolds Bell, agent	Kee Nov.	1,000,000
Mila (Dixie Union), 6	Claiborne Farm, agent	Claiborne Farm	Kee Nov.	1,000,000
Australie, 3	New England Stud	Ballygallon Stud Ltd.	Tatt Dec.	976,185
Ebaraya (Ire) (Machiavellian), 5	Pegasus Farms Ltd., Ireland	Skara Glen Stables	Tatt Dec.	976,185
Frizzante, 5	Pegasus Stables	London Thoroughbred Services	Tatt Dec.	976,185
Star Begonia (GB) (Fasliyev), 9	Michael C. Byrne, agent	Shadai Farm	Kee Nov.	975,000
Tropical Blossom (Silver Deputy), 6	Mill Ridge Sales, agent	Katsumi Yoshida	Kee Nov.	950,000
Nevermore, 4	Brookdale Sales, agent	Vin Cox Bloodstock Pty. Ltd.	Kee Nov.	950,000
Danelissima, 3	Glebe House Stables, Ireland	Netherfield House Stud	Tatt Dec.	917,613
Megans Bluff (Mineshaft), 7	Three Chimneys Sales, agent	Eldon Farm Equine	Kee Nov.	900,000
Carib Lady (Ire) (Gone West), 5	Taylor Made Sales Agency, agent	Shadai Farm	Kee Nov.	900,000
Fordyce (Victory Gallop), 10	Taylor Made Sales Agency, agent	Diamond A Farms	Kee Nov.	875,000
Zonk (Gone West), 6	Taylor Made Sales Agency, agent	J. Fred Miller	F-T Ky Nov.	875,000
Avie's Fancy (Elusive Quality), 13	Seven Fold Farm, agent for Gunsmith Stables	ClassicStar LLC	F-T Ky Nov.	850,000
Silent Eskimo (Vindication), 9	Hill 'n' Dale Sales Agency, agent for Estate of John Franks	ClassicStar LLC	Kee Nov.	850,000
Ms. Strike Zone (Empire Maker), 10	Gainesway, agent	Shadai Farm	Kee Nov.	850,000
Reina Blanca (GB) (Lemon Drop Kid), 4	Lane's End, agent	BBA (Ireland)	Kee Nov.	850,000
Beckys Shirt (Woodman), 13	Hill 'n' Dale Sales Agency, agent	BBA (Ireland)	Kee Jan.	850,000
Lindy Wells (Fusaichi Pegasus), 4	Lane's End, agent	Narvick International	Kee Nov.	825,000

Chronological Review of Major 2004 Sales

Sale	No. Sold	Total	Change	Average	Change	Highest Price
January						
Keeneland January horses of all ages	1,260	$49,362,600	58.3%	$39,177	48.9%	$850,000
Ocala Breeders' Sales Co. winter mixed	690	7,864,000	57.5%	11,397	32.4%	300,000
Heritage Place winter mixed	121	409,900	103.8%	3,388	24.6%	29,000
Barretts Equine Ltd. winter mixed	517	4,057,300	−8.4%	7,848	−7.2%	425,000
February						
Fasig-Tipton Midlantic winter mixed	132	1,303,000	174.7%	9,871	122.6%	59,000
Ocala Breeders' Sales Co. selected two-year-olds in training	112	15,266,000	19.9%	136,304	25.2%	1,600,000
Tattersalls Ltd. February	118	1,674,041	29.7%	14,187	31.9%	131,095
Stallion Access February seasons and shares	24	337,800	−22.0%	14,075	−22.0%	45,000
Fasig-Tipton Kentucky winter mixed	394	4,713,100	49.1%	11,962	7.9%	235,000
Fasig-Tipton Florida selected two-year-olds in training	142	41,586,000	43.0%	292,859	40.0%	4,500,000
March						
Barretts Equine Ltd. March selected two-year-olds in training	131	20,181,200	65.0%	154,055	8.3%	2,000,000
Fair Grounds Sales Co. selected two-year-olds in training	44	479,400	14.6%	10,895	−19.3%	27,000
Evangeline Downs two-year-olds in training	127	1,398,800	1,136.8%	11,014	55.8%	70,000
Ocala Breeders' Sales Co. selected two-year-olds in training	245	22,563,000	24.0%	92,094	38.2%	650,000
Adena Springs two-year-olds in training	57	2,228,000	14.4%	39,088	24.4%	310,000
Fasig-Tipton Texas two-year-olds in training	192	3,507,800	41.6%	18,270	12.1%	160,000
April						
Iowa Thoroughbred Breeders and Owners two-year-olds in training	7	72,500		10,357		32,000
Keeneland April two-year-olds in training	108	24,037,000	12.1%	222,565	32.9%	3,300,000
Louisiana Thoroughbred Breeders Sales Co. spring mixed	155	871,900	321.3%	5,625	74.0%	45,000
Tattersalls Ltd. breeze-up two-year-olds in training	130	11,907,338	74.9%	91,595	73.6%	980,595
Ocala Breeders' Sales Co. spring two-year-olds in training	774	23,183,000	55.5%	29,952	41.2%	975,000
May						
Barretts Equine Ltd. May two-year-olds in training	189	7,053,000	−1.9%	37,317	22.5%	350,000
Illinois Thoroughbred Breeders and Owners Foundation two-year-olds in training and horses of racing age	21	173,800	−68.9%	8,276	−46.7%	29,000
Fasig-Tipton Midlantic two-year-olds in training	354	13,227,800	34.9%	37,367	22.7%	450,000
June						
Michigan Thoroughbred Owners and Breeders Association two-year-olds in training and horses of racing age	10	48,400	19.2%	4,840	−16.6%	8,000
Ocala Breeders' Sales Co. June two-year-olds in training and horses of racing age	331	7,538,600	61.2%	22,775	24.2%	200,000
Heritage Place spring mixed	24	41,650	146.4%	1,735	−7.6%	7,000
Barretts Equine Ltd. summer two-year-olds in training and horses of racing age	93	1,254,800		13,492		110,000
July						
Tattersalls Ltd. July mixed sale	368	10,114,503	82.6%	27,485	42.4%	251,119
Japan Racing Horse Association selected foal	234	71,129,628	18.9%	303,973	7.2%	4,537,037
Stemman's Summer mixed	84	117,750		1,402		10,000
Fasig-Tipton Kentucky selected yearling	338	38,620,000	36.9%	114,260	22.8%	950,000
Charles Town Thoroughbred Horse Sales Co. July mixed	44	65,750		1,494		10,000
August						
Minnesota Thoroughbred Association state-bred yearling	36	312,500	62.3%	8,681	−0.8%	37,000
Louisiana Thoroughbred Breeders Sales Co. summer mixed	140	551,000	30.0%	3,936	6.7%	80,000
Fasig-Tipton Saratoga selected yearling	150	45,705,000	−5.3%	304,700	−2.8%	1,850,000
Fasig-Tipton New York Saratoga preferred yearling	112	5,596,500	6.0%	49,969	20.2%	180,000
California Thoroughbred Breeders Association Del Mar August yearling	57	2,749,000	−11.5%	48,228	39.8%	250,000
Ruidoso Thoroughbred yearling	189	1,598,550	3.0%	8,458	17.7%	127,000
Indiana Thoroughbred Owners and Breeders Association horses of all ages	34	47,000	−23.6%	1,382	−28.1%	3,600
Michigan Thoroughbred Owners and Breeders Association yearling	42	211,800	20.0%	5,043	20.0%	31,000
L'Agence Francaise Deauville August yearling sale	373	34,567,556	15.3%	92,674	8.5%	851,690
C.T.H.S. Alberta division summer yearling	147	927,448	8.0%	6,309	6.5%	31,542
Ocala Breeders' Sales Co. selected and open yearling	891	18,361,400	43.4%	20,608	32.5%	235,000
Fasig-Tipton Texas summer yearling	270	3,360,800	24.8%	12,447	1.2%	130,000
September						
Washington Thoroughbred Breeders Association summer yearling	152	2,541,800	−1.8%	16,722	3.3%	92,000
C.T.H.S. Manitoba division yearling	23	69,985	−34.8%	3,043	16.2%	8,261
C.T.H.S. Ontario division selected Canadian-bred yearling	171	4,772,373		27,909		199,015

Sale	No. Sold	Total	Change	Average	Change	Highest Price
C.T.H.S. Ontario division open Canadian-bred yearling	128	703,807		5,498		27,787
Keeneland September yearling	3,370	324,904,300	18.6%	96,411	4.5%	8,000,000
C.T.H.S. British Columbia division summer mixed	123	1,155,247	32.8%	9,392	23.0%	54,072
Iowa Thoroughbred Breeders and Owners Assoc. fall mixed	72	370,150	56.8%	5,141	45.9%	36,000
Oregon Thoroughbred Breeders' Association annual mixed	97	209,550	38.4%	2,160	14.1%	10,000
Goffs Bloodstock Sales Ltd. Orby Sale	738	54,097,807	43.3%	73,303	−35.7%	1,044,408
California Thoroughbred Breeders Association Northern California yearling	130	893,600		6,874		47,000
California Thoroughbred Breeders Association Golden State Stables Dispersal	14	36,500		2,607		6,000
New York Thoroughbred Breeders' Sales Co. mixed	191	1,224,200		6,409		57,000
October						
Ohio Thoroughbred Breeders and Owners Midwest Regional mixed	55	144,900	25.7%	2,635	48.5%	14,000
C.T.H.S. Ontario division fall mixed	56	105,490	−76.1%	1,884	−37.0%	14,928
Breeders Sales Co. of Louisiana fall mixed	181	1,199,950	−1.7%	6,630	22.7%	50,000
Fasig-Tipton Midlantic Eastern fall yearling	493	10,791,500	29.6%	21,889	19.9%	500,000
Barretts Equine Ltd. October preferred yearling	242	3,233,750	0.6%	13,363	−1.9%	170,000
Tattersalls Ltd. October yearling part 1	512	98,550,914	20.6%	192,482	153.0%	2,154,421
C.T.H.S. Alberta division fall mixed	89	134,303	−5.5%	1,509	−27.8%	10,782
Louisiana Thoroughbred Breeders Sales Co. winter mixed	85	220,400	−10.0%	2,593	−16.4%	22,500
Ocala Breeders' Sales Co. fall mixed	708	10,521,800	50.6%	14,861	55.7%	120,000
Tattersalls Ltd. October yearling part 2	818	24,298,808		29,705		244,812
Arizona Thoroughbred Breeders Association fall mixed	167	915,950	2.8%	5,485	−12.6%	47,000
Heritage Place fall mixed	40	100,050	−0.7%	2,501	36.5%	14,500
Barretts Equine Ltd. fall mixed	419	2,274,300	−20.5%	5,428	−2.7%	165,000
Fasig-Tipton Kentucky October yearling	511	8,317,200	−9.8%	16,276	−6.8%	230,000
Charles Town Thoroughbred Horse Sales Co. October mixed	41	69,500		1,695		13,000
November						
Stallion Access fall selected seasons and shares	25	448,100	−56.2%	17,924	−26.4%	95,000
Fasig-Tipton Kentucky fall selected mixed	267	22,938,300	251.6%	85,911	58.0%	5,000,000
Keeneland November breeding stock	2,873	279,680,200	18.5%	97,348	7.8%	4,800,000
Tattersalls Ltd. December mixed	1,574	103,188,959	−7.1%	65,558	0.2%	1,659,514
December						
Washington Thoroughbred Breeders Association winter mixed	213	878,050	20.3%	4,122	−14.2%	40,000
Fasig-Tipton Midlantic December mixed	363	3,862,300	42.9%	10,640	41.7%	160,000
Fasig-Tipton Texas mixed	180	825,300	51.8%	4,585	24.8%	34,000

Histories of Major Sales

Following are the histories of several prominent Thoroughbred auctions in North America. The sales are listed by type of sale, with the order within each category determined by total sales.

Keeneland September Yearlings

Year	Offered	Sold	Gross	Chg	Average	Chg	High Price
2004	4,359	3,370	$324,904,300	18.6%	$96,411	4.5%	$8,000,000
2003	3,819	2,968	273,925,300	29.9%	92,293	28.5%	3,800,000
2002	3,840	2,934	210,809,000	−17.1%	71,850	−18.2%	2,500,000
2001	4,003	2,895	254,190,600	−12.9%	87,803	−0.3%	6,400,000
2000	4,302	3,313	291,827,100	25.2%	88,085	13.8%	6,800,000
1999	3,788	3,011	233,020,800	37.2%	77,390	30.3%	3,900,000
1998	3,528	2,860	169,811,800	9.8%	59,375	9.2%	2,100,000
1997	3,396	2,844	154,666,800	12.7%	54,384	16.3%	2,300,000
1996	3,649	2,936	137,233,800	5.5%	46,742	6.2%	1,400,000
1995	3,495	2,955	130,085,300	24.4%	44,022	18.4%	1,200,000
1994	3,264	2,812	104,552,900	19.8%	37,181	6.1%	625,000
1993	2,862	2,492	87,308,100	11.3%	35,035	23.0%	775,000
1992	3,188	2,754	78,427,400	1.2%	28,478	−4.0%	400,000
1991	3,065	2,612	77,511,000	−10.7%	29,675	−0.5%	900,000
1990	3,310	2,909	86,756,500	12.8%	29,823	−12.6%	535,000
1989	2,578	2,253	76,887,600	19.2%	34,127	20.7%	700,000
1988	2,752	2,281	64,500,600	−10.8%	28,277	−14.6%	625,000
1987	2,452	2,182	72,289,100	28.9%	33,130	11.3%	1,100,000
1986	2,175	1,884	56,097,000	−9.1%	29,775	−10.8%	525,000
1985	2,172	1,849	61,741,900	10.6%	33,392	5.1%	440,000
1984	2,173	1,757	55,803,400	−10.4%	31,761	−4.5%	675,000
1983	2,245	1,848	61,766,100	30.9%	33,423	1.0%	735,000
1982	1,644	1,426	47,202,800	−20.6%	33,102	18.6%	400,000
1981	2,442	2,131	59,486,500	19.2%	27,915	3.7%	600,000
1980	1,967	1,855	49,922,800	50.9%	26,913	40.9%	310,000
1979†	N/A	1,733	33,082,200	47.2%	19,098	35.6%	300,000
1978	N/A	1,596	22,474,000	21.2%	14,081	8.2%	142,000
1977	N/A	1,425	18,538,500	14.3%	13,009	21.1%	200,000

Year	Offered	Sold	Gross	Chg	Average	Chg	High Price
1976	N/A	1,510	16,216,400	38.7%	10,739	12.8%	$200,000
1975	N/A	1,228	11,688,000	-5.1%	9,518	23.7%	110,000
1974	N/A	1,601	12,315,700	17.7%	7,693	-5.8%	100,000

First held in current format in 1960. From 1944 to '48, fall yearlings were part of a mixed sale format. In 1949, approximately half the yearlings were sold in a separate October sale and the remainder in a November breeding stock sale. In 1950, yearlings were in a separate session of breeding stock sale. In 1951, fall yearling sales were separated from breeding stock by a week. Selected sessions were inaugurated in 1989.
† Before 1980, gross sales include RNAs. N/A Not available.

Keeneland July Selected Yearlings

Year	Offered	Sold	Gross	Chg	Average	Chg	High Price
2002	146	87	$ 42,385,000	-32.9%	$487,184	-31.4%	$3,100,000
2001	132	89	63,212,000	-21.7%	710,247	14.4%	4,000,000
2000	180	130	80,732,000	5.1%	621,015	6.7%	3,600,000
1999	181	132	76,815,000	6.8%	581,932	20.5%	3,000,000
1998	201	149	71,932,000	15.0%	482,765	35.0%	4,000,000
1997	236	175	62,565,000	7.1%	357,514	2.2%	1,500,000
1996	204	167	58,430,000	25.8%	349,880	41.6%	1,700,000
1995	225	188	46,450,000	2.6%	247,074	5.9%	1,250,000
1994	257	194	45,265,000	-8.3%	233,325	-1.2%	1,050,000
1993	251	209	49,350,000	4.7%	236,124	-9.3%	1,050,000
1992	266	181	47,120,000	-35.8%	260,331	-18.8%	1,700,000
1991	300	229	73,443,000	-21.0%	320,712	10.8%	2,600,000
1990	416	321	92,920,000	-19.9%	289,470	-4.7%	2,900,000
1989	448	382	115,978,000	18.5%	303,607	-17.5%	2,800,000
1988	323	266	97,845,000	-10.1%	367,838	-1.3%	3,500,000
1987	344	292	108,839,000	4.5%	372,736	-9.5%	3,700,000
1986	291	253	104,174,000	-24.2%	411,755	-23.3%	3,600,000
1985	292	256	137,505,000	-17.2%	537,129	-10.5%	13,100,000
1984	320	277	166,155,000	12.8%	599,838	14.0%	8,250,000
1983	301	280	147,330,000	53.4%	526,179	52.9%	10,200,000
1982	297	279	96,027,000	7.5%	344,183	32.5%	4,250,000
1981	369	344	89,342,000	55.3%	259,715	29.6%	3,500,000
1980	301	287	57,522,000	21.2%	200,425	28.8%	1,700,000
1979†	N/A	305	47,448,000	11.4%	155,567	27.9%	1,600,000
1978	N/A	350	42,579,000	54.0%	121,654	42.5%	1,300,000
1977	N/A	324	27,651,000	20.0%	85,343	28.2%	725,000
1976	N/A	346	23,035,000	25.6%	66,575	24.1%	1,500,000
1975	N/A	342	18,344,000	7.2%	53,637	0.3%	715,000
1974	N/A	320	17,116,500	-13.9%	53,489	-5.9%	625,000

First held in 1943. Not held 2003 to '05.
† Before 1980, gross sales include RNAs. N/A Not available.

Fasig-Tipton Saratoga Selected Yearlings

Year	Offered	Sold	Gross	Chg	Average	Chg	High Price
2004	191	150	$45,705,000	-5.3%	$304,700	-2.8%	$3,300,000
2003	196	154	48,257,000	36.9%	313,357	24.5%	2,700,000
2002	196	140	35,242,000	-43.5%	251,729	-34.7%	1,300,000
2001	201	162	62,412,000	49.0%	385,259	26.0%	3,300,000
2000	173	137	41,901,000	7.6%	305,847	17.0%	4,200,000
1999	201	149	38,957,000	13.8%	261,456	23.7%	3,000,000
1998	220	162	34,246,000	23.7%	211,395	15.3%	1,700,000
1997	205	151	27,691,000	1.4%	183,384	13.5%	1,400,000
1996	220	169	27,311,000	21.1%	161,604	26.2%	630,000
1995	207	176	22,545,000	21.4%	128,097	32.5%	440,000
1994	241	192	18,566,000	53.4%	96,698	3.9%	520,000
1993	162	130	12,101,000	0.5%	93,085	-4.2%	350,000
1992	152	124	12,046,000	-20.0%	97,145	-19.4%	525,000
1991	168	125	15,062,000	-54.3%	120,496	-42.5%	800,000
1990	219	157	32,923,000	3.7%	209,701	-12.8%	1,500,000
1989	170	132	31,745,000	-12.0%	240,492	19.4%	1,750,000
1988	259	179	36,054,000	-23.1%	201,419	-16.6%	1,500,000
1987	237	194	46,871,000	22.0%	241,603	29.0%	2,400,000
1986	253	205	38,407,000	-24.3%	187,351	-27.7%	1,625,000
1985	233	196	50,760,000	6.1%	258,980	4.0%	2,700,000
1984	235	192	47,825,000	10.9%	249,089	17.8%	4,600,000
1983	248	204	43,127,000	19.6%	211,407	19.6%	3,000,000
1982	243	204	36,053,000	-5.7%	176,730	10.0%	2,100,000
1981	265	238	38,222,000	47.6%	160,597	44.5%	1,200,000
1980	253	233	25,900,000	26.3%	111,159	13.3%	1,600,000
1979†	N/A	209	20,502,000	22.2%	98,096	22.2%	650,000
1978	N/A	209	16,771,500	39.4%	80,246	40.0%	800,000
1977	N/A	210	12,035,000	14.5%	57,310	29.2%	375,000
1976	N/A	237	10,510,700	23.3%	44,349	19.6%	550,000
1975	N/A	230	8,525,700	2.3%	37,068	-0.4%	260,000
1974	N/A	224	8,337,100	-13.6%	37,219	-12.9%	350,000

First held in 1917. Not held 1943-'45, because of World War II travel restrictions.
† Before 1980, gross sales include RNAs. N/A Not available.

Fasig-Tipton Kentucky July Selected Yearlings

Year	Offered	Sold	Gross	Chg	Average	Chg	High Price
2004	452	338	$38,620,000	36.9%	$114,260	22.8%	$950,000
2003	425	303	28,202,000	−11.3%	93,076	−4.8%	800,000
2002	536	325	31,790,000	37.3%	97,815	0.1%	700,000
2001	381	237	23,148,000	−11.6%	97,671	25.7%	625,000
2000	517	337	26,186,500	17.9%	77,705	3.6%	525,000
1999	361	296	22,211,000	58.2%	75,037	35.3%	525,000
1998	340	253	14,036,500	43.9%	55,480	5.3%	220,000
1997	238	185	9,751,000	−2.6%	52,708	36.3%	290,000
1996	393	259	10,013,500	52.2%	38,662	4.0%	300,000
1995	227	177	6,580,500	16.6%	37,178	18.5%	200,000
1994	245	180	5,645,000	24.1%	31,361	−0.8%	170,000
1993	173	144	4,550,500	95.2%	31,601	−6.5%	147,000
1992	97	69	2,331,000	−35.0%	33,783	−0.1%	115,000
1991	154	106	3,585,000	−28.8%	33,821	−16.8%	140,000
1990	143	124	5,038,500	−44.5%	40,633	−12.3%	140,000
1989	240	196	9,080,500	−34.2%	46,329	−27.8%	255,000
1988	296	215	13,795,500	0.0%	64,165	13.0%	475,000
1987	309	243	13,797,000	−35.7%	56,778	−29.1%	450,000
1986	365	268	21,465,500	−26.7%	80,095	−10.1%	400,000
1985	421	329	29,297,500	−17.8%	89,050	−13.6%	730,000
1984	428	346	35,648,000	−13.7%	103,029	−2.7%	900,000
1983	439	390	41,302,000	37.1%	105,903	35.0%	1,750,000
1982	459	384	30,118,000	−0.2%	78,432	11.7%	1,000,000
1981	502	430	30,186,000	43.7%	70,200	32.0%	1,300,000
1980	441	395	21,010,500	56.2%	53,191	31.7%	325,000
1979†	N/A	333	13,450,000	19.5%	40,390	23.7%	310,000
1978	N/A	353	11,258,500	57.4%	32,659	36.5%	205,000
1977	N/A	299	7,154,900	151.0%	23,929	50.3%	255,000
1976	N/A	179	2,850,100	84.0%	15,922	49.0%	75,000
1975	N/A	145	1,549,000	287.8%	10,683	12.3%	110,000
1974	N/A	42	399,400	−48.3%	9510	13.2%	30,000

First held in 1972. Held at Newtown Paddocks since 1975.
† Before 1980, gross sales include RNAs. N/A Not available.

Fasig-Tipton Calder Selected Two-Year-Olds in Training

Year	Offered	Sold	Gross	Chg	Average	Chg	High Price
2005	267	147	$50,132,000	20.6%	$341,034	16.4%	$5,200,000
2004	223	142	41,586,000	43%	292,859	40%	4,500,000
2003	246	139	29,077,000	−1.4%	209,187	−1.4%	1,400,000
2002	254	139	29,479,000	4.6%	212,079	2.3%	1,000,000
2001	237	136	28,186,000	−16.3%	207,250	−4.0%	1,000,000
2000	264	156	33,690,000	0.9%	215,962	17.1%	1,950,000
1999	296	181	33,386,000	26.9%	184,453	33.9%	1,100,000
1998	302	191	26,303,000	13.6%	137,712	14.2%	1,000,000
1997	297	192	23,162,000	1.7%	120,635	16.1%	780,000
1996	309	219	22,765,000	22.2%	103,950	11.1%	875,000
1995	306	199	18,624,000	39.0%	93,588	31.3%	550,000
1994	276	188	13,403,000	17.7%	71,293	25.2%	390,000
1993	318	200	11,386,000	−8.0%	56,930	−3.9%	450,000
1992	292	209	12,376,000	14.1%	59,215	−5.5%	350,000
1991	299	173	10,846,000	−24.6%	62,694	−17.2%	375,000
1990	269	190	14,383,000	36.0%	75,700	18.8%	625,000
1989	233	166	10,579,000	−13.1%	63,729	−1.1%	360,000
1988	296	189	12,175,500	4.4%	64,421	−2.3%	275,000
1987	243	177	11,666,000	21.0%	65,910	24.4%	315,000
1986	232	182	9,640,000	56.8%	52,967	25.8%	525,000
1985	208	146	6,146,000	8.2%	42,096	−11.0%	325,000
1984	179	120	5,678,000	−20.5%	47,317	−2.6%	360,000
1983	206	147	7,144,000	—	48,599	—	195,000

First held in 1983.

Keeneland April Two-Year-Olds in Training

Year	Offered	Sold	Gross	Chg	Average	Chg	High Price
2005	176	105	$17,040,500	−22.6%	$162,290	−25.5%	$800,000
2004	183	101	22,012,000	2.7%	217,941	30.1%	3,300,000
2003	198	128	21,440,000	20.8%	167,500	−3.7%	950,000
2002	178	102	17,749,500	19.1%	174,015	6.3%	850,000
2001	146	91	14,898,000	−19.2%	163,714	8.3%	775,000
2000	195	122	18,435,000	−0.7%	151,107	0.1%	825,000
1999	179	123	18,560,000	33.3%	150,894	0.8%	2,000,000
1998	125	93	13,925,000	−3.5%	149,731	52.6%	725,000
1997	210	147	14,427,000	0.9%	98,143	−14.9%	900,000
1996	195	124	14,305,000	20.6%	115,363	11.8%	400,000
1995	169	115	11,865,000	3.3%	103,174	41.0%	700,000
1994	219	157	11,491,500	69.0%	73,194	15.2%	400,000
1993	136	107	6,800,500	—	63,556	—	300,000

First held in 1993.

Ocala Breeders' Sales Co. Calder Two-Year-Olds in Training

Year	Offered	Sold	Gross	Chg	Average	Chg	High Price
2005	158	109	$14,921,000	-2.3%	**$136,890**	0.4%	$600,000
2004	169	112	15,266,000	19.9%	136,403	25.2%	**1,600,000**
2003	166	117	12,733,000	-2.4%	108,829	-4.9%	1,200,000
2002	175	114	13,041,000	-7.7%	114,395	10.2%	500,000
2001	188	136	14,124,000	-9.5%	103,853	-5.5%	900,000
2000	226	142	15,599,000	-5.2%	109,852	6.8%	550,000
1999	204	160	**16,454,000**	31.0%	102,838	25.2%	525,000
1998	193	153	12,564,000	20.5%	82,118	20.5%	430,000
1997	184	153	10,428,000	12.0%	68,157	16.4%	300,000
1996	218	159	9,314,000	19.5%	58,579	6.7%	275,000
1995	181	142	7,794,500	24.7%	54,891	24.7%	270,000
1994	202	142	6,248,500	9.4%	44,004	14.0%	350,000
1993	200	148	5,712,000	8.6%	38,595	2.7%	325,000
1992	182	140	5,261,000	-1.5%	37,579	2.7%	260,000
1991	218	146	5,341,000	-17.6%	36,582	-14.2%	135,000
1990	205	152	6,478,000	18.3%	42,618	23.0%	360,000
1989	209	158	5,474,500	-5.8%	34,649	-2.8%	302,000
1988	231	163	5,811,500	-20.4%	35,653	-13.5%	140,000
1987	**232**	**177**	7,298,500	0.1%	41,234	-3.3%	175,000
1986	207	171	7,290,500	71.6%	42,635	28.5%	250,000
1985	173	128	4,247,500	—	33,184	—	135,000

First held in 1985 at Hialeah Park. Held at Calder Race Course since 1986.

Barretts Equine Ltd. Selected Two-Year-Olds in Training

Year	Offered	Sold	Gross	Chg	Average	Chg	High Price
2005	145	88	$14,360,500	4.6%	$163,188	-6.1%	$1,900,000
2004	128	79	13,728,000	12.3%	173,722	22%	2,000,000
2003	166	86	12,228,000	11.7%	142,186	-5.2%	**2,700,000**
2002	121	73	10,950,000	8.6%	150,000	5.6%	1,900,000
2001	130	71	10,085,000	-41.7%	142,042	-21.1%	750,000
2000	170	96	17,287,000	-21.4%	180,073	-20.6%	2,000,000
1999	172	97	21,995,000	-3.2%	**226,753**	30.8%	2,000,000
1998	200	131	22,711,000	-28.9%	173,366	-21.8%	1,000,000
1997	255	144	31,926,000	-3.3%	221,708	7.4%	1,100,000
1996	233	160	**33,016,000**	56.1%	206,350	56.1%	900,000
1995	274	160	21,148,000	57.4%	132,175	61.3%	900,000
1994	240	164	13,440,000	51.6%	81,951	39.6%	700,000
1993	237	151	8,863,400	-7.5%	58,698	-5.1%	430,000
1992	280	155	9,584,000	-33.0%	61,832	-20.1%	370,000
1991	**317**	185	14,313,000	-12.8%	77,368	-7.6%	600,000
1990	270	**196**	16,405,000	—	83,699	—	700,000

First held in 1990.

Keeneland November Breeding Stock

Year	Offered	Sold	Gross	Chg	Average	Chg	High Price
2004	3,736	2,873	$279,680,200	18.5%	$97,348	7.8%	$4,800,000
2003	3,337	2,614	236,070,900	26.1%	90,310	14.6%	**7,100,000**
2002	2,982	2,377	187,230,000	4.3%	78,767	9.9%	4,000,000
2001	3,383	2,506	179,568,600	-41.0%	71,655	-22.9%	4,000,000
2000	**4,367**	3,277	304,549,800	-4.1%	92,936	1.3%	4,900,000
1999	4,227	**3,461**	**317,666,000**	20.0%	91,784	17.2%	4,700,000
1998	4,312	3,379	264,657,700	23.7%	78,324	10.3%	7,000,000
1997	3,673	3,013	213,979,800	25.4%	71,019	17.6%	1,400,000
1996	3,451	2,826	170,691,800	21.2%	60,400	22.5%	2,600,000
1995	3,505	2,855	140,822,300	16.3%	49,325	1.6%	2,500,000
1994	2,932	2,494	121,056,900	32.5%	48,539	10.3%	2,700,000
1993	2,300	2,075	91,342,900	24.6%	44,021	16.6%	1,150,000
1992	2,324	1,942	73,337,200	-11.6%	37,764	-9.7%	1,100,000
1991	2,281	1,984	82,938,400	-18.0%	41,804	5.8%	1,400,000
1990	3,061	2,558	101,107,700	-34.8%	39,526	-43.1%	2,300,000
1989	2,518	2,235	155,161,300	36.7%	69,423	22.3%	4,600,000
1988	2,401	2,000	113,517,600	-4.1%	56,759	-15.8%	1,900,000
1987	1,999	1,756	118,358,900	-5.3%	67,403	-3.4%	2,600,000
1986	2,159	1,791	125,022,700	-22.0%	69,806	-27.3%	5,400,000
1985	2,076	1,668	160,207,100	5.1%	96,047	-7.7%	5,500,000
1984	1,915	1,465	152,373,200	-9.6%	104,009	-1.4%	4,600,000
1983	1,977	1,598	168,518,600	44.6%	**105,456**	42.8%	5,250,000
1982	1,989	1,578	116,538,700	-1.7%	73,852	28.4%	3,800,000
1981	2,491	2,060	118,494,900	26.4%	57,522	13.2%	2,150,000
1980	2,024	1,845	93,746,700	40.0%	50,811	44.4%	2,000,000
1979†	N/A	1,903	66,968,300	50.6%	35,191	23.6%	1,600,000
1978	N/A	1,562	44,472,200	21.2%	28,471	11.6%	800,000

Year	Offered	Sold	Gross	Chg	Average	Chg	High Price
1977	N/A	1,439	36,699,400	33.2%	25,503	28.1%	$575,000
1976	N/A	1,384	27,548,800	70.4%	19,905	35.8%	1,000,000
1975	N/A	1,103	16,163,700	−3.5%	14,654	30.8%	295,000
1974	N/A	1,495	16,751,200	−33.6%	11,205	−29.9%	385,000

First held in 1944.
† Before 1980, gross sales include RNAs. N/A Not available.

Keeneland January Horses of All Ages

Year	Offered	Sold	Gross	Chg	Average	Chg	High Price
2005	**1,765**	1,361	$53,418,000	8.2%	$39,249	0.2%	$1,350,000
2004	1,602	1,260	49,362,600	58.3%	39,177	48.9%	850,00
2003	1,600	1,185	31,186,000	−10.1%	26,317	−28.9%	475,000
2002	1,135	937	34,689,200	−12.5%	37,022	12.7%	**3,600,000**
2001	1,667	1,207	39,657,700	−34.9%	32,856	−33.1%	1,700,000
2000	1,605	1,241	60,951,200	43.7%	**49,115**	39.3%	5,000,000
1999	1,452	1,203	42,410,900	−20.2%	35,254	−23.1%	3,250,000
1998	1,378	1,160	53,164,800	121.1%	45,832	91.2%	3,400,000
1997	1,156	1,003	24,042,300	−20.6%	23,970	−21.0%	710,000
1996	1,220	997	30,263,400	56.2%	30,354	61.2%	1,800,000
1995	1,195	1,029	19,377,700	29.5%	18,832	7.0%	375,000
1994	948	850	14,960,600	25.5%	17,601	24.0%	210,000
1993	1,018	840	11,918,600	−37.5%	14,189	−36.4%	210,000
1992	952	855	19,066,000	−14.2%	22,299	38.9%	650,000
1991	1,670	**1,385**	22,229,900	9.9%	16,050	−33.1%	685,000
1990	983	844	20,234,200	−1.8%	23,974	5.9%	2,100,000
1989	1,083	901	20,469,300	−66.7%	22,718	−53.1%	745,000
1988	1,382	1,268	**61,450,100**	291.4%	48,462	102.5%	2,500,000
1987	796	656	15,701,800	−23.1%	23,936	−22.5%	1,750,000
1986	836	661	20,411,100	0.5%	30,879	−10.8%	3,000,000
1985	754	587	20,317,400	−5.1%	34,612	−13.3%	1,250,000
1984	693	536	21,399,100	11.8%	39,924	−1.8%	2,500,000
1983	602	471	19,139,700	−15.4%	40,636	29.3%	825,000
1982	860	720	22,626,600	−4.3%	31,426	24.7%	1,000,000
1981	1,073	938	23,640,900	25.3%	25,204	3.9%	1,000,000
1980	856	778	18,874,000	115.6%	24,260	105.1%	850,000
1979†	N/A	740	8,753,000	18.7%	11,828	15.9%	145,000
1978	N/A	723	7,375,200	41.6%	10,201	15.0%	215,000
1977	N/A	587	5,208,500	5.0%	8,873	23.4%	310,000
1976	N/A	690	4,961,700	−1.8%	7,191	13.5%	295,000
1975	N/A	798	5,053,900	19.3%	6,333	1.3%	100,000
1974	N/A	678	4,238,000	10.1%	6,251	8.1%	122,000

First held in 1956. Not held 1958-'60.
† Before 1980, gross sales include RNAs. N/A Not available.

Highest-Priced Horses of All Time
North American Top-Priced Yearlings
(With Subsequent Race Record)

$13,100,000	SEATTLE DANCER, 1984 c., Nijinsky II—My Charmer, by Poker. Consignor: Warner L. Jones Jr.; Buyer: BBA (England), agent for Robert Sangster and partners. 1985 Keeneland July. 5 starts, 2 wins, $152,413, in France and Ireland, SW, Ire-G2.
10,200,000	SNAAFI DANCER, 1982 c., Northern Dancer—My Bupers, by Bupers. Consignor: Crescent Farm; Buyer: Aston Upthorpe Stud, agent for Sheikh Mohammed bin Rashid al Maktoum. 1983 Keeneland July. Unraced.
8,250,000	IMPERIAL FALCON, 1983 c., Northern Dancer—Ballade, by *Herbager. Consignor: Windfields Farm; Buyer: BBA (England), agent for Robert Sangster and partners. 1984 Keeneland July. 3 starts, 2 wins, $13,395, in Ireland.
8,000,000	UNNAMED, 2003 c., Storm Cat—Welcome Surprise, by Seeking the Gold. Consignor: Lane's End, agent; Buyer: Hideyuki Mori. 2004 Keeneland September. Unraced.
7,100,000	JAREER, 1983 c., Northern Dancer—Fabuleux Jane, by *Le Fabuleux. Consignor: Bruce Hundley, agent for Ralph C. Wilson Jr.; Buyer: Darley Stud Management. 1984 Keeneland July. 9 starts, 1 win, $5,591, in England and North America.
7,000,000	LAA ETAAB, 1984 c., Nijinsky II—Crimson Saint, by Crimson Satan. Consignor: Tom Gentry; Buyer: Gainsborough Farm. 1985 Keeneland July. Unraced.
6,800,000	TASMANIAN TIGER, 1999 c., Storm Cat—Hum Along, by Fappiano. Consignor: Lane's End, agent; Buyer: Demi O'Byrne. 2000 Keeneland September. 25 starts, 3 wins, $154,543, in Ireland and Hong Kong.
6,500,000	AMJAAD, 1983 c., Seattle Slew—Desiree, by Raise a Native. Consignor: Spendthrift Farm, agent for Mr. and Mrs. Louis E. Wolfson and Mrs. Ethel D. Jacobs; Buyer: Darley Stud Management. 1984 Keeneland July. 4 starts, unplaced, in England, Ireland, and North America.
6,400,000	VAN NISTELROOY, 2000 c., Storm Cat—Halory, by Halo. Consignor: Lane's End, agent for Stonerside Stable; Buyer: Demi O'Byrne. 2001 Keeneland September. 6 starts, 3 wins, $229,980, in England, Ireland, and North America, SW, Ire-G2.
5,500,000	ALAJWAD, 2000, c., Storm Cat—La Affirmed, by Affirmed. Consignor: Eaton Sales, agent; Buyer: John Ferguson Bloodstock. 2001 Keeneland September. 6 starts, 2 wins, $77,445, in North America and United Arab Emirates.
5,400,000	OBLIGATO, 1983 c., Northern Dancer—Truly Bound, by In Reality. Consignor: Windfields Farm; Buyer: BBA (Ireland), agent for Robert Sangster and partners. 1984 Keeneland July. 2 starts, unplaced, in Ireland.
5,300,000	KING'S CONSUL, 1999 c., Kingmambo—Battle Creek Girl, by His Majesty. Consignor: Lane's End, agent; Buyer: John Ferguson Bloodstock. 2000 Keeneland September. 8 starts, 1 win, $40,759, in England and North America.
5,100,000	WASSL TOUCH, 1983 c., Northern Dancer—Queen Sucree, by *Ribot. Consignor: North Ridge Farm; Buyer: Darley Stud Management. 1984 Keeneland July. 6 starts, 3 wins, $30,168, in Ireland, SW.

4,600,000	PARLANDO, 1983 c., Northern Dancer—Bubbling, by Stage Door Johnny. Consignor: Wild Oak Plantation; Buyer: BBA (Ireland), agent for Robert Sangster and partners. 1984 Fasig-Tipton Saratoga. Unraced.
	PROFESSOR BLUE, 1983 c., Northern Dancer—Mississippi Mud, by Delta Judge. Consignor: Lane's End; Buyer: BBA (England), agent for Stavros Niarchos. 1984 Keeneland July. 7 starts, placed, $5,171, in France and North America.
4,400,000	MOON'S WHISPER, 1999 f., Storm Cat—East of the Moon, by Private Account. Consignor: Lane's End; Buyer: Shadwell Estate Co. Ltd. 2000 Keeneland September. Unraced.
	Shah Jehan, 1999 c., Mr. Prospector—Voodoo Lily, by Baldski. Consignor: Lane's End, agent; Buyer: Demi O'Byrne. 2000 Keeneland September. 30 starts, 4 wins, $238,238, in North America, Ireland, England, and France, spl, G3.
4,250,000	EMPIRE GLORY, 1981 c., Nijinsky II—Spearfish, by Fleet Nasrullah. Consignor: Glencoe Farm; Buyer: BBA (Ireland). 1982 Keeneland July. 6 starts, 2 wins, $35,420, in Ireland, SW, Ire-G3.
	FOXBORO, 1982 c., Northern Dancer—Desert Vixen, by In Reality. Consignor: North Ridge Farm; Buyer: BBA (England), agent for Robert Sangster and partners. 1983 Keeneland July. 1 start, unplaced, in Ireland.
4,200,000	DISTINCTION, 1999 c., Seattle Slew—Omi, by Wild Again. Consignor: Double Diamond Farm; Buyer: David J. Shimmon. 2000 Fasig-Tipton Saratoga. 3 starts, $78,058.
4,100,000	**GALLANT ARCHER**, 1982 c., Nijinsky II—Belle of Dodge Me, by Creme dela Creme. Consignor: E. A. Seltzer and Parlina; Buyer: Aston Upthorpe Stud, agent for Sheikh Mohammed bin Rashid al Maktoum. 1983 Keeneland July. 16 starts, 5 wins, $294,477, in England and North America, SW, G3.
4,000,000	**ELNAWAAGI**, 1983 c., Roberto—Gurkhas Band, by Lurullah. Consignor: Keswick Stables; Buyer: Darley Stud Management. 1984 Fasig-Tipton Saratoga. 11 starts, 4 wins, $23,607, in England and Germany, SW.
	FUSAICHI PEGASUS, 1997 c., Mr. Prospector—Angel Fever, by Danzig. Consignor: Stone Farm, agent; Buyer: Fusao Sekiguchi. 1998 Keeneland July. 9 starts, 6 wins, $1,994,400, SW, G1.
	SHOWLADY, 1999 f., Theatrical (Ire)—Claxton's Slew, by Seattle Slew. Consignor: Brookside Farms; Buyer: John Ferguson Bloodstock. 2000 Keeneland September. 6 starts, 2 wins, $158,640, SW.
	WARHOL, 2000 c., Saint Ballado—Charm a Gendarme, by Batonnier. Consignor: Taylor Made Sales Agency, agent; Buyer: Demi O'Byrne. 2001 Keeneland July. 4 starts, 1 win, $18,809, in England and Ireland.
3,900,000	DUBAI TO DUBAI, 1998 c., Kris S.—Mr. P's Princess, by Mr. Prospector. Consignor: Harold Harrison; Buyer: John Ferguson Bloodstock. 1999 Keeneland September. 11 starts, 3 wins, $152,319, in North America and United Arab Emirates.
3,800,000	HASHIMIYA, 2002 f., Gone West—Touch of Greatness, by Hero's Honor. Consignor: Three Chimneys Sales, agent; Buyer: John Ferguson Bloodstock. 2003 Keeneland September. 2 starts, unplaced, $1,250, in England and United Arab Emirates.
	HOYER, 2000 c., Mr. Prospector—Destination Mir, by Cherokee Colony. Consignor: Lazy E Ranch; Buyer: John Ferguson Bloodstock. 2001 Keeneland September. Unraced.
3,750,000	ALCHAASIBIYEH, 1983 f., Seattle Slew—Fine Prospect, by Mr. Prospector. Consignor: Spendthrift Farm; Buyer: Darley Stud Management. 1984 Keeneland July. 6 starts, placed, $2,098, in England.
3,700,000	VIRTUOSA, 2000 f., Seeking the Gold—Escena, by Strawberry Road (Aus). Consignor: Denali Stud, agent for Falls Creek Farm; Buyer: Reynolds Bell, agent. 2001 Keeneland July. 10 starts, 1 win, $39,470.
	WARRSHAN, 1986 c., Northern Dancer—Secret Asset, by Graustark. Consignor: Hermitage Farm; Buyer: Darley Stud Management. 1987 Keeneland July. 11 starts, 4 wins, $125,928, in England and North America, SW, Eng-G3.
3,600,000	ACT OF DUTY, 2000 c., Mr. Prospector—Nuryette, by Nureyev. Consignor: Three Chimneys Sales, agent for Warner L. Jones Farm; Buyer: John Ferguson Bloodstock. 2001 Keeneland July. 3 starts, placed, $2,954, in England and United Arab Emirates.
	America's Storm, 1999 c., Storm Cat—Lilly Capote, by Capote. Consignor: Hartwell Farm, agent; Buyer: Padua Stables and Gaines-Gentry. 2000 Keeneland September. 17 starts, 3 wins, $106,230, spl.
	BORN PERFECT, 1999 f., Mr. Prospector—Molly Girl, by Seattle Slew. Consignor: Mr. and Mrs. John C. Mabee; Buyer: Padua Stables. 2000 Keeneland July. Unraced.
	NORTHERN STATE, 1985 c., Northern Dancer—South Ocean, by New Providence. Consignor: Windfields Farm; Buyer: Darley Stud Management. 1986 Keeneland July. 4 starts, 1 win, $2,137, in England.
	OLYMPIC, 2002 c., Danzig—Queena, by Mr. Prospector. Consignor: Middlebrook Farm, agent; Buyer: Demi O'Byrne. 2003 Keeneland September. 1 start, placed, $3,615, in Ireland.
3,500,000	BALLYDOYLE, 1980 c., Northern Dancer—South Ocean, by New Providence. Consignor: Windfields Farm; Buyer: BBA (Ireland). 1981 Keeneland July. 4 starts, 1 win, $2,542, in Ireland.
	ROYAL ACADEMY, 1987 c., Nijinsky II—Crimson Saint, by Crimson Satan. Consignor: Barry L. Weisbord, trustee for Tom Gentry; Buyer: Vincent O'Brien. 1988 Keeneland July. 7 starts, 4 wins, $758,994, in England, Ireland, and North America, SW, G1. Highweighted at 3 on European and Irish Free Handicaps 7-9½ furlongs.
3,400,000	BLESSED STORM, 2003 c., Storm Cat—Bless, by Mr. Prospector. Consignor: Taylor Made Sales Agency, agent for Classic-Star; Buyer: Hideyuki Mori. 2004 Keeneland September. Unraced.
	INKLING, 1997 f., Seeking the Gold—Number, by Nijinsky II. Consignor: Claiborne Farm and Nicole Perry Gorman; Buyer: Demi O'Byrne. 1998 Keeneland January. 1 start, 1 win, $6,847, in Ireland.
	SOPHISTICAT, 1999 f., Storm Cat—Serena's Song, by Rahy. Consignor: Robert and Beverly Lewis; Buyer: Demi O'Byrne. 2000 Keeneland July. 12 starts, 3 wins, $443,394, in England, Ireland, France, and North America, SW, Eng-G1.
3,300,000	AUTHENTICATE, 1999 c., Gone West—Lakeway, by Seattle Slew. Consignor: Eaton Sales, agent; Buyer: Padua Stables. 2000 Keeneland July. Unraced.
	HABAYEB, 2000 f., Storm Cat—Gone to Venus, by Gone West. Consignor: Taylor Made Sales Agency, agent; Buyer: John Ferguson Bloodstock. 2001 Fasig-Tipton Saratoga select. 6 starts, 2 wins, $30,871, in England and North America.
	NEWFOUNDLAND, 2000 c., Storm Cat—Clear Mandate, by Deputy Minister. Consignor: Lane's End, agent; Buyer: Demi O'Byrne. 2001 Keeneland September. 22 starts, 7 wins, $677,534, in England, Ireland, and North America, SW, G3.
	SHAREEF DANCER, 1980 c., Northern Dancer—Sweet Alliance, by Sir Ivor. Consignor: Windfields Farm; Buyer: Aston Upthorpe Stud. 1981 Keeneland July. 5 starts, 2 wins, $236,978, in England and Ireland, SW, Ire-G1, Champion three-year-old male in England and Ireland.

North American Top-Priced Two-Year-Olds

$5,200,000	UNNAMED, 2003 c., Tale of the Cat—Carry All, by Devil's Bag. Consignor: Robert N. Scanlon, agent; Buyer: Darley. 2005 Fasig-Tipton Florida February.
4,500,000	FUSAICHI SAMURAI, 2002 c., by Fusaichi Pegasus—Hidden Storm, by Storm Cat. Consignor: Kirkwood Stables, agent. Buyer: Fusao Sekiguchi. 2004 Fasig-Tipton Florida February. 1 start, 1 win, $21,000.
3,300,000	CHEKHOV, 2002 c., by Pulpit—In My Cap, by Vice Regent. Consignor: Niall Brennan Stables, agent; Buyer: Demi O'Byrne. 2004 Keeneland April. 3 starts, placed, $17,566.
3,100,000	DUBAI DREAMER, 2002 c., by Stephen Got Even—Blacktie Bid, by Black Tie Affair (Ire). Consignor: Niall Brennan Stables, agent. Buyer: John Ferguson Bloodstock. 2004 Fasig-Tipton Florida February. 3 starts, placed, $2,890, in England and United Arab Emirates.

3,000,000	UNNAMED, 2003 c., Forestry—Rare Bird, by Rahy. Consignor: Tony Bowling and Bobby Dodd, agent; Buyer: Demi O'Byrne. 2005 Fasig-Tipton Florida February.
2,900,000	UNNAMED, 2003 c., Grand Slam—Dama, by Storm Cat. Consignor: Maurice W. Miller, agent; Buyer: Darley. 2005 Fasig-Tipton Florida February.
2,700,000	DIAMOND FURY, 2001 g., Sea of Secrets—Swift Spirit, by Tasso. Consignor: Sequel Bloodstock, agent. Buyer: Charles Fipke. 2003 Barretts March. 12 starts, 2 wins, $81,580.
2,000,000	DUBAI ESCAPADE, 2002 f., by Awesome Again—Sassy Pants, by Saratoga Six. Consignor: Jerry Bailey Sales Agency, agent. Buyer: John Ferguson Bloodstock. 2004 Barretts March. 2 starts, 1 win, $16,250, in England and United Arab Emirates.
	GOTHAM CITY, 1998 c., Saint Ballado—What a Reality, by In Reality. Consignor: Jerry Bailey Sales Agency. Buyer: David J. Shimmon. 2000 Barretts March. 2 starts, unplaced, $2,880.
	LA SALLE STREET, 1997 c., Not for Love—Three Grand, by Assert (Ire). Consignor: H. T. Stables, agent, for Cam Allard. Buyer: Demi O'Byrne. 1999 Keeneland April. 3 starts, placed, $3,420.
	MOROCCO, 1997 c., Brocco—Roll Over Baby, by Rollin On Over. Consignor: Sequel Bloodstock, agent. Buyer: The Thoroughbred Corp. 1999 Barretts March. 16 starts, 4 wins, $133,640.
1,950,000	YONAGUSKA, 1998 c., Cherokee Run—Marital Spook, by Silver Ghost. Consignor: Niall Brennan Stables, agent. Buyer: Demi O'Byrne. 2000 Fasig-Tipton Florida February. 18 starts, 6 wins, $536,355, SW, G1.
1,900,000	ATLANTIC OCEAN, 2000 f., Stormy Atlantic—Super Chef, by Seattle Slew. Consignor: Chapman Farms. Buyer: The Thoroughbred Corp. 2002 Barretts March. 19 starts, 5 wins, $678,210, SW, G3.
	WHAT A SONG, 2003 c., Songandaprayer—What a Knight, by Tough Knight. Consignor: Murray Smith, agent; Buyer: Robert B. Lewis and Beverly J. Lewis. 2005 Barretts March. Unraced.
1,650,000	HARMONY LODGE, 1998 f., Hennessy—Win Crafty Lady, by Crafty Prospector. Consignor: Eddie Woods, agent. Buyer: Eugene Melnyk. 2000 Fasig-Tipton Florida February. 24 starts, 10 wins, $851,120, SW, G1.
1,600,000	MUTANABI, 2002 c., by Wild Rush—Freudenau, by Meadowlake. Consignor: W. D. North, agent. Buyer: John Ferguson Bloodstock. 2004 Ocala Breeders' Sales Co. February. 2 starts, placed, $3,171, in England.
1,500,000	TIMSAAH, 2002 c., by Rubiano—Magari, by Quack. Consignor: H. T. Inc., agent for Cam Allard. Buyer: John Ferguson Bloodstock. 2004 Fasig-Tipton Florida February. Unraced.
	UNNAMED, 2003 c., Golden Missile—Ms. Copelan, by Copelan. Consignor: Wavertree Stables, agent; Buyer: Demi O'Byrne. 2005 Fasig-Tipton Florida February.
	UNNAMED, 2003 f., Storm Cat—Turbo Launch, by Relaunch. Consignor: Hartley/De Renzo Thoroughbreds, LLC, agent; Buyer: Demi O'Byrne. 2005 Fasig-Tipton Florida February.
1,400,000	LION HEART, 2001 c., Tale of the Cat—Satin Sunrise, by Mr. Leader. Consignor: Robert N. Scanlon, agent. Buyer: Demi O'Byrne. 2003 Fasig-Tipton Florida February. 10 starts, 5 wins, $1,390,800, SW, G1.
	RADETZKY, 2002 c., Dixie Union—Sneaky Quiet, by Seeking the Gold. Consignor: Solitary Oak Farm, agent; Buyer: Demi O'Byrne. 2004 Keeneland April. Unraced.
1,300,000	MINSTRESS, 1983 f., The Minstrel—Fleet Victress, by *King of the Tudors. Consignor: Newstead Farm Trust. Buyer: W. S. Farish. 1985 Newstead Farm Trust Dispersal. 19 starts, 5 wins, $147,399, SW.
1,250,000	LE CHAT, 1998 c., Storm Cat—Adorable Micol, by Riverman. Consignor: Hartley/De Renzo Thoroughbreds, agent. Buyer: John Moynihan, agent. 2000 Fasig-Tipton Florida February. 3 starts, 1 win, $28,470.
	LOCHLIN SLEW, 1997 f., Seattle Slew—Lochlin, by Screen King. Consignor: M. W. Miller III, agent. Buyer: B. Wayne Hughes. 1999 Keeneland April. Unraced.
1,200,000	CHAPEL ROYAL, 2001 c., Montbrook—Cut Class Leanne, by Cutlass. Consignor: Ocala Stud Farms. Buyer: Demi O'Byrne. 2003 Ocala Breeders' Sales Co. February. 8 starts, 3 wins, $495,571, SW, G2.
	DANCE MASTER, 1997 c., Gone West—Nijinsky's Lover, by Nijinsky II. Consignor: Jerry Bailey Sales Agency. Buyer: Padua Stables. 1999 Barretts March. 19 starts, 4 wins, $196,455, SW, G2.
	TASK, 1996 f., Mr. Prospector—Department, by Secretariat. Consignor: Claiborne Farm and Nicole Perry Gorman. Buyer: Course Investment. 1998 Keeneland January. 3 starts, unplaced, $405, in France.
1,100,000	I'M PERSUADED, 1997 c., Deputy Minister—The Way We Were, by Avatar. Consignor: The Kindergarten Farm, agent. Buyer: Narvick International. 1999 Keeneland April. 7 starts, 1 win, $38,900.
	PRATHER, 1997 c., Brocco—Dazzling Dixie, by Dixieland Band. Consignor: Welcome Gate Farm, agent. Buyer: Aaron and Marie Jones. 1999 Fasig-Tipton Florida February. Unraced.
	SCATMANDU, 1995 c., Storm Cat—Princess Alydar, by Alydar. Consignor: Jerry Bailey Sales Agency, agent, for Bailey-Ellenberg Select. Buyer: John C. Kimmel, agent. 1997 Barretts March. 16 starts, 6 wins, $330,789, SW, G3.

North American Top-Priced Weanlings

$2,500,000	MAGIC OF LIFE, 1985 f., Seattle Slew—Larida, by Northern Dancer. Consignor: Newstead Farm Trust. Buyer: British Bloodstock Agency (England). 1985 Newstead Farm Trust Dispersal. 9 starts, 4 wins, $254,841, in England, SW, Eng-G1.
2,400,000	CARPOCRATES, 2003 c., Storm Cat—Spain, by Thunder Gulch. Consignor: Three Chimneys Sales, agent. Buyer: Dromoland Farm. 2003 Keeneland November. Unraced.
2,300,000	GHASHTAH, 1987 f., Nijinsky II—My Charmer, by Poker. Consignor: Hermitage Farm. Buyer: Shadwell Estate Co. Ltd. 1987 Warner L. Jones Jr. Dispersal. Unraced.
1,500,000	KING CHARLEMAGNE, 1998 c., Nureyev—Race the Wild Wind, by Sunny's Halo. Consignor: Ashford Stud, agent. Buyer: Demi O'Byrne. 1998 Keeneland November. 6 starts, 5 wins, $200,211, in England, Ireland, and France, SW, Fr-G1.
1,450,000	Juniper, 1998 c., Danzig—Meadow Flyer, by Alydar. Consignor: Taylor Made Sales Agency, agent. Buyer: Demi O'Byrne. 1998 Keeneland November. 6 starts, 1 win, $37,214, in England and Ireland, spl, Eng-G2.
1,400,000	RESTORATION, 1999 c., Sadler's Wells—Madame Est Sortie (Fr), by Longleat. Consignor: Eaton Sales, agent for Padua Stables. Buyer: M. W. Miller III, agent. 1999 Keeneland November. Unraced.
	SERENA'S CAT, 2003 f., Storm Cat—Serena's Tune, by Mr. Prospector. Consignor: Hill 'n' Dale Sales Agency, agent. Buyer: Dell Ridge Farm. 2003 Keeneland November. Unraced.
	SECRET THYME, 2003 f., Storm Cat—Garden Secrets, by Time for a Change. Consignor: Eaton Sales. Buyer: Brushwood Stable. 2003 Keeneland November. Unraced.
	WINTHROP, 1996 c., Storm Cat—Tinnitus, by Restless Wind. Consignor: John R. Gaines Thoroughbreds, agent. Buyer: Demi O'Byrne. 1996 Keeneland November. Unraced.
1,300,000	NEW TRIESTE, 1999 c., A.P. Indy—Lovlier Linda, by Vigors. Consignor: John R. Gaines Thoroughbreds, agent. Buyer: Paul Shanahan. 1999 Keeneland November. 1 start, unplaced, $1,500.
1,200,000	Net Dancer, 1989 f., Nureyev—Doubles Partner, by Damascus. Consignor: Bruce Hundley, agent for Ralph C. Wilson Jr. and Oxford Stable. Buyer: E. Hudson. 1989 Keeneland November. 13 starts, 2 wins, $46,225, spl.

SHE'S A BEAUTY, 2000 f., Storm Cat—Now That's Funny, by Saratoga Six. Consignor: Gaines-Gentry Thoroughbreds. Buyer: Timothy Hyde. 2000 Keeneland November. 3 starts, placed, $1,772, in Ireland.

TIDE CAT, 1998 f., Storm Cat—Maytide, by Naskra. Consignor: John R. Gaines Thoroughbreds, agent. Buyer: Brad Martin, agent for 505 Farms. 1998 Keeneland November. Unraced.

1,175,000   RAZEEN, 1987 c., Northern Dancer—Secret Asset, by Graustark. Consignor: Hermitage Farm. Buyer: Darley Stud Management. 1987 Warner L. Jones Jr. Dispersal. 9 starts, 3 wins, $106,665, in England and North America, SW.

1,150,000   A. P. PETAL, 2000 f., A.P. Indy—Golden Petal, by Mr. Prospector Consignor: Taylor Made Sales Agency, agent. Buyer: B. Wayne Hughes. 2000 Keeneland November. Unraced.

UNNAMED, 2004 f., Unbridled's Song—Helsinki (GB), by Machiavellian. Consignor: Taylor Made Sales Agency, agent; Buyer: John Sikura. 2004 Keeneland November.

1,100,000   HOLD THAT TIGER, 2000 c., Storm Cat—Beware of the Cat, by Caveat. Consignor: Lane's End, agent for Ten Broeck Farm. Buyer: Demi O'Byrne. 2000 Keeneland November. 10 starts, 3 wins, $644,235 in England, France, Ireland, and North America, SW, Fr-G1, Champion two-year-old male in Europe.

WOROOD, 1985 f., *Vaguely Noble—Farouche, by Northern Dancer. Consignor: Newstead Farm Trust. Buyer: British Bloodstock Agency (England). 1985 Newstead Farm Trust Dispersal. 16 starts, 3 wins, $82,067, in France, SW.

1,050,000   SEASIDE ATTRACTION, 1987 f., Seattle Slew—Kamar, by Key to the Mint. Consignor: Hermitage Farm. Buyer: Monty Hinton. 1987 Warner L. Jones Jr. Dispersal. 12 starts, 4 wins, $272,541, SW, G1.

WILDCAT QUEEN, 2000 f., Storm Cat—Jetapat, by Tri Jet. Consignor: Brereton C. Jones, agent. Buyer: Bradley and Bowden, agent. 2000 Keeneland November. 5 starts, 1 win, $33,595.

North American Top-Priced Broodmares

$7,100,000   CASH RUN, 1997, Seeking the Gold—Shared Interest, by Pleasant Colony. (Storm Cat). Consignor: Taylor Made Sales Agency, agent. Buyer: John Magnier. 2003 Keeneland November.

7,000,000   KORVEYA, 1982, Riverman—Konafa, by Damascus. (Woodman). Consignor: Claiborne Farm, agent. Buyer: Reynolds Bell Jr., agent. 1998 Keeneland November.

MISS OCEANA, 1981, Alydar—Kittiwake, by *Sea-Bird. (Northern Dancer). Consignor: Newstead Farm Trust. Buyer: Foxfield. 1985 Newstead Farm Trust mixed sale.

6,100,000   WINDSHARP, 1991, Lear Fan—Yes She's Sharp, by Sharpen Up (GB). (Gone West). Consignor: Mill Ridge Sales, agent. Buyer: John Ferguson Bloodstock. 2003 Keeneland November.

6,000,000   PRICELESS FAME, 1975, Irish Castle—Comely Nell, by Commodore M. (Seattle Slew). Consignor: Highclere, agent for Joseph O. Morrissey. Buyer: Darley Stud Management. 1984 Fasig-Tipton Kentucky November.

5,500,000   PRINCESS ROONEY, 1980, Verbatim—Parrish Princess, by Drone. (Danzig). Consignor: Stone Farm agent. Buyer: Wichita Equine. 1985 Keeneland November.

5,400,000   LADY'S SECRET, 1982, Secretariat—Great Lady M., by Icecapade. Consignor: D. Wayne Lukas, agent for Eugene V. Klein. Buyer: Fasig-Tipton Bloodstock, agent. 1987 Night of the Stars, Fasig-Tipton Kentucky November.

LIFE'S MAGIC, 1981, Cox's Ridge—Fire Water, by Tom Rolfe. (Mr. Prospector). Consignor: Mel Hatley Racing Stables, agent. Buyer: Eugene V. Klein. 1986 Keeneland November.

5,300,000   SPAIN, 1997, Thunder Gulch—Drina, by Regal and Royal. (Storm Cat). Consignor: Three Chimneys Sales. Buyer: Dromoland Farm. 2003 Keeneland November.

5,250,000   PRODUCER, 1976, Nashua—*Marion, by Tantieme. (Northern Dancer). Consignor: Walnut Green, agent for Carelaine Stable. Buyer: BBA (England). 1983 Keeneland November.

5,000,000   I'LL GET ALONG, 1992, Smile—Dont Worry Bout Me, by Foolish Pleasure. (Elusive Quality).Consignor: Brent Fernung, agent for CloverLeaf Farms Ii; Buyer: Gaines-Gentry Thoroughbreds. 2004 Fasig-Tipton Kentucky November.

MACKIE, 1993, Summer Squall—Glowing Tribute, by Graustark. (Mr. Prospector). Consignor: Eaton Sales, agent. Buyer: Britton House Stud. 2000 Keeneland January.

4,900,000   JEWEL PRINCESS, 1992, Key to the Mint—Jewell Ridge, by Melyno (Ire). (Storm Cat). Consignor: Lane's End, agent. Buyer: John Magnier. 2000 Keeneland November.

4,800,000   SANTA CATARINA, 2000, Unbridled—Purrfectly, by Storm Cat. (A.P. Indy). Consignor: Denali Stud, agent for Robert and Beverly Lewis; Buyer: Eaton Sales, agent. 2004 Keeneland November.

4,700,000   CATCHASCATCHCAN (GB), 1995, Pursuit of Love—Catawba, by Mill Reef. (Danzig). Consignor: Claiborne Farm, agent. Buyer: Lyons Demesne. 2000 Keeneland November.

DANCE DESIGN (Ire) , 1993, Sadler's Wells—Elegance in Design (Ire), by Habitat. (A.P. Indy). Consignor: Eaton Sales, agent for Padua Stables. Buyer: Hugo Lascelles, agent. 1999 Keeneland November.

4,600,000   IT'S IN THE AIR, 1976, Mr. Prospector—A Wind Is Rising, by Francis S. (Seattle Slew). Consignor: Hill 'n' Dale Sales Agency. Buyer: Darley Stud Management. 1984 Keeneland November.

MYHRR, 1997, Mr. Prospector—Miesque, by Nureyev. Consignor: Lane's End, agent. Buyer: Reynolds Bell Jr., agent. 2000 Keeneland November.

WINGLET, 1988, Alydar—Highest Trump, by Bold Bidder. (Storm Cat). Consignor: Lane's End, agent for Brookside Farms. Buyer: John Magnier. 1999 Keeneland November.

4,500,000   ESTRAPADE, 1980, *Vaguely Noble—Klepto, by No Robbery. Consignor: Blue Grass Farm, agent. Buyer: Allen E. Paulson. 1985 Keeneland November.

LIFE'S MAGIC, 1981, Cox's Ridge—Fire Water, by Tom Rolfe. (Alydar). Consignor: D. Wayne Lukas, agent for Eugene V. Klein. Buyer: Shadwell Estate Co. Ltd. 1987 Night of the Stars, Fasig-Tipton Kentucky November.

TWO RINGS, 1970, Round Table—Allofthem, by Bagdad. (Nijinsky II). Consignor: Mint Lane Farm, agent for Kinghaven Farms. Buyer: Due Process Stable. 1983 Keeneland November.

4,400,000   UNBRIDLED ELAINE, 1998, Unbridled's Song—Carols Folly, by Taylor's Falls. (Forestry). Consignor: Taylor Made Sales Agency, agent; Buyer: John Ferguson Bloodstock. 2004 Keeneland November.

4,200,000   MAGICAL ALLURE, 1995, General Meeting—Rare Lady, by Never Bend. (Storm Cat). Consignor: Eaton Sales, agent for Mr. and Mrs. John C. Mabee. Buyer: Shadwell Estate Co. Ltd. 2000 Keeneland November.

TAKE CHARGE LADY, 1999, Dehere—Felicita, by Rubiano. (Seeking The Gold). Consignor: Three Chimneys Sales. agent. Buyer: Eaton Sales, agent. 2004 Keeneland November.

4,100,000   LOVE SIGN, 1977, Spanish Riddle—Native Nurse, by Graustark (Seattle Slew). Consignor: Three Chimneys Farm. Buyer: Arthur I. Appleton. 1984 Keeneland November.

SANGUE (Ire), 1978, Lyphard—Prodice (Fr), by Prominer. (Seattle Slew). Consignor: Henry Moreno, agent for R. Charlene Parks. Buyer: Nelson Bunker Hunt. 1984 Keeneland November.

Highest Yearling Prices Through the Years

Public interest in record prices paid for Thoroughbreds at public auction soared in the 1970s and '80s, when the record price for a yearling racing prospect exceeded $1-million. Yet there has always been a record-priced yearling ever since the first yearling was sold. Just when that may have been, no one can say with certainty, but the first really famous record-priced yearling was Sceptre, a lovely brown filly foaled in 1899 at the Duke of Westminster's Eaton Stud in England. Breeder and owner of *Ormonde, the greatest racehorse of the 19th century, and his grandson Flying Fox, winner of the Triple Crown in the year of Sceptre's birth, the Duke died late in 1899, forcing the dispersal of his bloodstock.

Sceptre, by the great Persimmon out of *Ormonde's full sister Ornament, by Bend Or, and with the looks to match her purple pedigree, came up for sale in 1900 at the Tattersalls Newmarket July sale, then one of the two most important auctions in England. Victorian England was scandalized when the gambler Robert Sievier outbid the late Duke's son and heir to acquire Sceptre for 10,000 guineas ($51,133 at the contemporary exchange rate).

Sceptre proved more than worth the price, though her racing career was somewhat scarred by the roller-coaster fortunes of Sievier, who won and lost fortunes betting on horses and cards for the two years he owned her. Sometimes training the great filly himself, Sievier could not resist attempting betting coups with Sceptre, running her in inappropriate races, such as the Lincolnshire Handicap against older males in her first start at three. Sceptre overcame such abuse, winning four of the five English classics of 1902 (she finished fourth in the Epsom Derby), and is still acclaimed as one of the greatest racemares of all time.

Sceptre's successors as world-record-priced yearlings have never achieved quite the same level of fame or accomplishment, but overall the race records of the 21 successive record-priced yearlings have been quite good. Of the 21 listed in the accompanying chart, five (including Sceptre) have become champions or classic winners, and four more won recognized stakes races. Thus, nine of the 21 record-priced yearlings listed, or 42.9%, were stakes winners, which is far superior to the breed average of about 3%.

On the other hand, only two, Sceptre and Majestic Prince, recaptured their purchase price in purse money on the racecourse, and there were certainly some very expensive failures. Hustle On, who wrested the record away from the English (though he himself was American-bred only by virtue of his dam being imported while carrying him), never raced. His immediate successor, New Broom, could not win in nine starts, the same dismal record as the $1.6-million Hoist the King.

Perhaps the saddest tale of any record-priced yearling, though, is that of Colonel Payne, the Fairway colt out of Golden Hair, by Golden Sun, purchased for 15,000 guineas ($78,278) by Dorothy Paget at Tattersalls Doncaster yearling sale in 1936. An eccentric English-born granddaughter of William C. Whitney, founder of the Whitney family's bloodstock empire, Paget generally refused to grant her horses a name until they had won a race, a practice then permissible under English rules. Colts that failed to meet her standards, she habitually had shot.

The Golden Hair colt ran with promise in his only outing at two, finishing third in the National Breeders' Produce Stakes, then the richest two-year-old race in England. Unfortunately, he proved to be the victim of his owner's eccentricities and never reappeared on the racecourse or anywhere else.—*John P. Sparkman*

Progression of Top-Priced Yearlings

Price	Year	Horse, Sex, Breeding	Sale	Consignor	Buyer	Race record
$13,100,000	1985	SEATTLE DANCER c., Nijinsky II—My Charmer	Keeneland July	Warner L. Jones Jr.	BBA England (agent for Robert Sangster)	5-2-1-1, $152,413 Gallinule S. (Ire-G2) etc.
10,200,000	1983	SNAAFI DANCER c., Northern Dancer—My Bupers	Keeneland July	Crescent Farm	Aston Upthorpe Stud (Sheikh Mohammed bin Rashid al Maktoum)	unraced
4,250,000	1982	EMPIRE GLORY c., Nijinsky II—Spearfish	Keeneland July	Glencoe Farm	BBA Ireland (agent for Robert Sangster)	6-2-2-2, $35,420, Royal Whip S. (Ire-G3) etc.
3,500,000	1981	BALLYDOYLE c., Northern Dancer—South Ocean	Keeneland July	Windfields Farm	BBA Ireland (agent for Robert Sangster)	4-1-1-0, $2,542
1,700,000	1980	LICHINE c., Lyphard—Stylish Genie	Keeneland July	Carelaine Farm, Getty, Riordan, Heerman, agent	BBA England (agent for Stavros Niarchos)	16-3-1-4, $71,527, Prix de Guiche etc.
1,600,000	1979	HOIST THE KING c., Hoist the Flag—Royal Dowry	Keeneland July	Tom Gentry	Kazuo Nakamura	9-0-1-1, $6,977
1,500,000	1976	CANADIAN BOUND c., Secretariat—Charming Alibi	Keeneland July	Bluegrass Farm	Blue Meadows Farm, agent (Ted Burnett, John Sikura, and partners)	4-0-1-0, $4,769
625,000	1974	KENTUCKY GOLD c., Raise a Native—Gold Digger	Keeneland July	Spendthrift Farm	Wallace A. Gilroy	7-1-0-3, $5,950
600,000	1973	WAJIMA c., Bold Ruler—*Iskra	Keeneland July	Claiborne Farm	James A. Scully (agent for Zenya Yoshida and partners)	16-9-5-0, $537,837, Champion 3-year-old male, Travers S. (G1) etc.
510,000	1970	CROWNED PRINCE c., Raise a Native—Gay Hostess	Keeneland July	Spendthrift Farm	Frank McMahon	4-2-0-0, $37,883, champion 2-year-old in England, Dewhurst S., etc.

Price	Year	Horse, Sex, Breeding	Sale	Consignor	Buyer	Race record
$250,000	1967	MAJESTIC PRINCE c., Raise a Native—Gay Hostess	Keeneland July	Spendthrift Farm	Frank McMahon	10-9-1-0, $414,200, Kentucky Derby, Preakness S., etc.
200,000	1966	BOLD DISCOVERY c., Bold Ruler—La Dauphine	Keeneland July	Spendthrift Farm	Frank McMahon	3-0-0-0, $0
170,000	1964	ONE BOLD BID c., Bold Ruler—Forgetmenow	Keeneland July	Warner L. Jones Jr.	Mrs. Velma Morrison	unraced
130,000	1961	SWAPSON c., Swaps—Obedient	Keeneland July	Spendthrift Farm	John M. Olin	31-8-3-5, $26,766
118,492 (28,000g)	1945	SAYAJIRAO c., Nearco—Rosy Legend	Tattersalls Doncaster	Sir Eric Ohlson	Gaekwar of Baroda	16-6-6-3, $96,647, champion 3-year-old in England, St. Leger S. etc.
78,278 (15,000g)	1936	Colonel Payne c., Fairway—Golden Hair	Tattersalls Doncaster	Viscount Furness	Dorothy Paget	1-0-0-1, $494, 3rd National Breeders' Produce S.
75,000	1928	NEW BROOM c., Whisk Broom II—Payment	Fasig-Tipton Saratoga	Mrs. T. J. Regan	C.V.B. Cushman	9-0-2-1, $275
70,000	1927	HUSTLE ON c., Hurry On—*Fatima II	Fasig-Tipton Saratoga	Himyar Stud	W. R. Coe	unraced
55,724 (14,500g)	1920	BLUE ENSIGN c., The Tetrarch—Blue Tit	Tattersalls Doncaster	Sledmere Stud	Lord Glanely	1-0-0-0, $0
53,492 (11,500g)	1919	WESTWARD HO c., Swynford—Blue Tit	Tattersalls Doncaster	Sledmere Stud	Lord Glanely	6-2-0-0, $3,989, Great Yorkshire S., 3rd St. Leger S.
51,133 (10,000g)	1900	SCEPTRE f., Persimmon—Ornament	Tattersalls Newmarket July	Estate of Duke of Westminster	Robert Sevier	25-13-4-4, $192,544 champion 3-year-old, champion older horse, Epsom Oaks etc.

Top-Priced Yearlings by Year

High-priced yearlings have a poor reputation in the Thoroughbred industry. Although statistics show that, on average, the higher the price paid for a yearling the better the racehorse, high-priced failures such as the $10.2-million Snaafi Dancer, who never raced, are remembered more readily than success stories such as the $2.9-million Horse of the Year A.P. Indy. Even the world's record-priced yearling, the $13.1-million Seattle Dancer, is regarded as a failure though he won a Group 2 race in Europe.

In the years since Fasig-Tipton first began selling yearlings at Saratoga, 24 of the 92 top-priced yearlings each year (there were six ties) have become stakes winners. That 26% strike rate is obviously far higher than the 3% average of stakes winners to foals for the breed.

Yearling buyers appear to have greatly improved their selection techniques over the last few decades. The record of top-priced yearlings for the first half of the 20th century was little better than that of the average horse. But in the 36 years since 1969 Kentucky Derby winner Majestic Prince sold for $250,000 at Keeneland July in 1967, 15 year-toppers have become stakes winners. —*John P. Sparkman*

Most Expensive North American Yearlings by Year

Year Sold	Horse	Sex, Sire—Dam	Price	Sale	Buyer	Race Record
2004	UNNAMED	c., Storm Cat—Welcome Surprise	$8,000,000	Kee Sept	Hideyuki Mori	unraced
2003	HASHIMIYA	f., Gone West—Touch of Greatness	3,800,000	Kee Sept	John Ferguson Bldstk.	1-0-0-0, $0
2002	ONE COOL CAT	c., Storm Cat—Tacha	3,100,000	Kee July	Demi O'Byrne	10-5-0-1, $568,086, Champion 2yo male in Europe, Phoenix S. (Ire-G1), etc.
2001	VAN NISTELROOY	c., Storm Cat—Halory	6,400,000	Kee Sept	Demi O'Byrne	6-3-1-1, $229,980, EBF Futurity S. (Ire-G2), etc.
2000	TASMANIAN TIGER	c., Storm Cat—Hum Along	6,800,000	Kee Sept	Demi O'Byrne	25-3-1-1, $154,543
1999	DUBAI TO DUBAI	c., Kris S.—Mr. P's Princess	3,900,000	Kee Sept	John Ferguson Bldstk.	11-3-1-2, $152,319
1998	FUSAICHI PEGASUS	c., Mr. Prospector—Angel Fever	4,000,000	Kee July	Fusao Sekiguchi	9-6-2-0, $1,994,400, Kentucky Derby (G1), etc.
1997	SASHA'S PROSPECT	c., Mr. Prospector—Missy's Mirage	2,300,000	Kee Sept	Padua Stables	10-1-0-0, $37,200
1996	PARGATA KING	c., Storm Cat—Alpargata	1,700,000	Kee July	Fusao Sekiguchi	1-0-0-0, $0
1995	CONSTANT WISH	f., Mr. Prospector—Daring Bidder	1,250,000	Kee July	Demi O'Byrne	unraced
1994	Golden Colors	f., Mr. Prospector—Winning Colors	1,050,000	Kee July	Pegasus Bloodstock	10-3-1-0, $509,963, 2nd Daily Hai Queen Cup
1993	GOLDEN LEGEND	c., Mr. Prospector—Reminiscing	1,050,000	Kee July	John R. Gaines, agt.	6-0-0-0, $5,700
1992	NUMEROUS	c., Mr. Prospector—Number	1,700,000	Kee July	Finney Bloodstock, agt.	18-4-2-2, $255,348, Derby Trial S. (G3) etc.
1991	JEUNE HOMME	c., Nureyev—Alydariel	2,600,000	Kee July	Morio Sakurai	20-4-5-3, $431,724, Citation S. (G2), etc.
1990	A.P. INDY	c., Seattle Slew—Weekend Surprise	2,900,000	Kee July	BBA (Ire)	11-8-0-1, $2,979,815, Horse of the Year, champion 3yo male, Breeders' Cup Classic (G1), etc.
1989	NORTHERN PARK	c., Northern Dancer—Mrs. Penny	2,800,000	Kee July	Zenya Yoshida	30-4-7-4, $171,493, Grand Prix de Villeurbanne
1988	ROYAL ACADEMY	c., Nijinsky II—Crimson Saint	3,500,000	Kee July	Vincent O'Brien	7-4-2-0, $758,994, European Hwt. at 3, 7-9½ f., Breeders' Cup Mile (G1) etc.

Year Sold	Horse	Sex, Sire—Dam	Price	Sale	Buyer	Race Record
1987	WARRSHAN	c., Northern Dancer—Secret Asset	$3,700,000	Kee July	Darley Stud Mgt.	11-4-0-3, $125,928, Gordon S. (Eng-G3) etc.
1986	NORTHERN STATE	c., Northern Dancer—South Ocean	3,600,000	Kee July	Darley Stud Mgt.	4-1-0-0, $2,137
1985	SEATTLE DANCER	c., Nijinsky II—My Charmer	13,100,000	Kee July	BBA (Eng), agt. for Robert Sangster	5-2-1-1, $152,413, Gallinule S. (Ire-G2) etc.
1984	IMPERIAL FALCON	c., Northern Dancer—Ballade	8,250,000	Kee July	BBA (Eng)	3-2-0-0, $13,395
1983	SNAAFI DANCER	c., Northern Dancer—My Bupers	10,200,000	Kee July	Aston Upthorpe Stud	unraced
1982	EMPIRE GLORY	c., Nijinsky II—Spearfish	4,250,000	Kee July	BBA (Ire), agt. for Robert Sangster	6-2-2-2, $35,420, Royal Whip S. (Ire-G3) etc.
1981	BALLYDOYLE	c., Northern Dancer—South Ocean	3,500,000	Kee July	BBA (Ire), agt. for Robert Sangster	4-1-1-0, $2,542
1980	LICHINE	c., Lyphard—Stylish Genie	1,700,000	Kee July	BBA (Ire), agt. for Stavros Niarchos	16-3-1-4, $71,527, Prix de Suresnes etc.
1979	HOIST THE KING	c., Hoist the Flag—Royal Dowry	1,600,000	Kee July	Kazuo Nakamura	9-0-1-1, $6,977
1978	NUREYEV	c., Northern Dancer—Special	1,300,000	Kee July	BBA (Eng)	3-2-0-0, $42,522, champion miler in France, Prix Thomas Bryon (Fr-G3) etc.
1977	FOREIGN SECRETARY	c., Secretariat—Lady Victoria	725,000	Kee July	BBA (Ire)	11-3-1-1, $47,375
1976	CANADIAN BOUND	c., Secretariat—Charming Alibi	1,500,000	Kee July	Blue Meadows Farm, agt.	4-0-1-0, $4,769
1975	ELEGANT PRINCE	c., Raise a Native—Gay Hostess	715,000	Kee July	Franklin Groves	unraced
1974	KENTUCKY GOLD	c., Raise a Native—Gold Digger	625,000	Kee July	Wallace A. Gilroy	7-1-0-3, $5,950
1973	WAJIMA	c., Bold Ruler—*Iskra	600,000	Kee July	James A. Scully, agt. for Zenya Yoshida & partners	16-9-5-0, $537,837, champion 3-year-old male, Travers S. (G1) etc.
1972	Riboquill	c., *Ribot—Quill	230,000	Kee July	Cromwell Bloodstock	11-3-1-1, $46,875, 3rd Grand Prix de Deauville (Fr-G2)
1971	PASS	c., Buckpasser—*Casaque Grise	235,000	FT Sara	Marion duPont Scott	unraced
1970	CROWNED PRINCE	c., Raise a Native—Gay Hostess	510,000	Kee July	Frank McMahon	4-2-0-0, $37,883, champion two-year-old in Eng., Dewhurst S. etc.
1969	KNIGHTS HONOR	c., Round Table—Vestment	210,000	Kee July	Bert W. Martin	4-0-1-1, $1,670
1968	REINE ENCHANTEUR	f., *Sea-Bird—*Libra	405,000	Kee July	W. P. Rosso	7-1-1-5, $9,305
1967	MAJESTIC PRINCE	c., Raise a Native—Gay Hostess	250,000	Kee July	Frank McMahon	10-9-1-0, $414,200, Kentucky Derby, Preakness S., etc.
1966	BOLD DISCOVERY	c., Bold Ruler—La Dauphine	200,000	Kee July	Frank McMahon	3-0-0-0, $0
1965	ROYAL MATCH	f., *Turn-to—Cosmah	140,000	Kee July	Arnold Winick, agt.	unraced
1964	ONE BOLD BID	c., Bold Ruler—Forgetmenow	170,000	Kee July	Mrs. Velma Morrison	unraced
1963	LENSO	c., Swaps—*Blue Star II	85,000	Kee July	Leonard Sasso	5-0-0-1, $420
1962	GOLDEN GORSE	f., Swaps—*Auld Alliance	83,000	FT Sara	J. T. Skinner, agt.	2-0-0-2, $735
1961	SWAPSON	c., Swaps—Obedient	130,000	Kee July	John M. Olin	31-8-3-5, $26,766
1960	NASHOLIN	c., Nashua—*Pashmina	75,000	Kee July	N. McLeod	25-2-0-3, $7,955
1959	ROYAL DRAGOON	c., *Royal Charger—Grecian Queen	80,000	Kee July	C. G. Raible	9-1-2-1, $5,050
	GLOBEMASTER	c., *Heliopolis—No Strings	80,000	FT Sara	Penowa Farms	27-10-9-2, $355,423, Wood Memorial S. etc.
1958	PRINCE BLESSED	c., *Princequillo—Dog Blessed	77,000	Kee July	Kerr Stables	35-8-6-4, $255,805, Hollywood Gold Cup S. etc.
1957	LAW AND ORDER	c., *Nasrullah—In Bloom	65,000	Kee July	J. H. Rouse Farm, agt. for King Ranch	unraced
1956	*RISE 'N SHINE	c., Hyperion—Deodara	$87,000	FT Sara	Mrs. M. E. Lunn	43-4-2-1, $17,515
1955	TULSAN	c., *Nasrullah—In Bloom	80,000	Kee July	Forrest Lindsay Farm	25-2-2-3, $8,050
1954	NALUR	c., *Nasrullah—Lurline B	86,000	Kee July	F. J. Adams Syndicate	20-2-1-0, $6,575
1953	ROMAN BOAT	f., Roman—Boat	59,000	Kee July	Duntreath Farm	4-1-0-0, $1,950
1952	LADYBREATH	f., Roman—Miss Brief	46,000	Kee July	Chester Gates, agt.	7-1-0-0, $2,100
1951	PERFECTION	f., Bull Lea—Lady Lark	60,000	Kee July	C. S. Jones	31-3-4-4, $30,600, Playa del Rey S., etc.
1950	FARAHAAN	f., *Mahmoud—Aphaona	35,000	FT Sara	William Post	3-0-0-1, $725
1949	Unification	c., War Admiral—Summer Time	37,000	Kee July	William Helis	80-6-11-14, $24,015, 3rd Dominion Day H.
	OLD ROWLEY	c., Menow—Risk	37,000	Kee July	Moody Jolley, agt.	9-2-1-1, $5,275
1948	DESTINO	c., *Beau Pere—Sun Lady	52,000	FT Sara	King Ranch	7-0-4-1, $3,400
1947	Spotted Bull	c., *Bull Dog—Spotted Beauty	45,000	Kee July	Jaclyn Stable	19-4-1-2, $12,850, 3rd Will Rogers H.
1946	LA CHICUELA	f., *Blenheim II—La Chica	54,000	Kee July	J. P. Smith	14-1-2-2, $4,100
	SILVER QUEEN	f., War Admiral—Danise M	54,000	Kee July	Maine Chance Farm	16-1-1-1, $3,650
1945	SIR GALLASCENE	c., *Sir Gallahad III—*Scenery II	46,000	Kee July	C. C. Tanner	54-15-3, $8,175
	BLUE FANTASY	f., Blue Larkspur—Risk	46,000	Kee July	Leslie Combs II, agt. for Elizabeth Nightingale Graham	unraced
1944	COLONY BOY	c., Eight Thirty—Heritage	46,000	Kee July	Leslie Combs II, agt. for Elizabeth Arden (Graham)	17-5-0-3, $39,750, Walden S., etc.
1943	PERICLES	c., *Blenheim II—Risk	66,000	FT Kee	William Helis	5-2-0-1, $5,200
1942	BOY KNIGHT	c., *Sir Gallahad III—Heloise	9,000	FT Sara	Crispin Oglebay	36-5-2-10, $44,145, Wilmington H., etc.
1941	BULRUSHES	c., *Bull Dog—Spur Flower	10,000	FT Sara	Ogden Phipps	196-25-40-33, $24,232
1940	REAPER'S BLADE	c., *Sickle—Friendly Gal	18,000	FT Sara	Brookmeade Stable	15-3-2-2, $3,425
1939	TOM-TOM	c., *Sir Gallahad III—Percussion	20,000	FT Sara	Manhasset Stable	unraced
	Lord Kitchener	c., *Blenheim II—Argosie	20,000	FT Sara	Samuel D. Riddle	38-4-5-7, $9,726, 3rd Travers S. etc.

Year Sold	Horse	Sex, Sire—Dam	Price	Sale	Buyer	Race Record
1938	Romanov	c., *Ksar—Duration	$22,000	FT Sara	Brookmeade Stable	28-2-3-3, $4,756, 3rd Lawrence Realization H.
1937	TEMULAC	c., *Sir Gallahad III—Marching Along	26,000	FT Sara	Calumet Farm	69-7-5-11, $6,732
1936	FARRELL	c., *Sir Gallahad III—Sari	18,000	FT Sara	Milky Way Farms	100-12-19-13, $9,999
1935	WINGED VICTORY	c., Victorian—Grief	13,000	FT Sara	Milky Way Farms	97-7-16-11, $7,130
1934	TEDDY BOY	c., *Teddy—Superstitious	11,500	FT Sara	Calumet Farm	32-1-3-5, $1,425
1933	CALUMET DICK	c., Gallant Fox—*Martha Snow	13,000	FT Sara	Calumet Farm	51-17-6-8, $72,515, Dixie H.
1932	THE TRIUMVIR	c., Pompey—Cowslip	14,500	FT Sara	Greentree Stable	176-12-15-15, $10,935
1931	CARRY THE NEWS	c., The Porter—Cypher Code	16,000	FT Sara	J. H. Whitney	20-1-3-6, $1,665
1930	TEXAS KNIGHT	c., *Sir Gallahad III—Fasnet	30,000	FT Sara	Three D's Stock Farm	82-8-5-11, $6,390
	GALA FLIGHT	f., *Sir Gallahad III—*Starflight	30,000	FT Sara	Griffin Watkins	25-3-0-4, $3,425
1929	War	c., Man o' War—Milky Way	45,000	FT Sara	Sagamore Stable	61-8-13-4, $8,280, 2nd Brookdale H.
1928	NEW BROOM	c., Whisk Broom II—Payment	75,000	FT Sara	C.V.B. Cushman	9-0-2-1, $275
1927	HUSTLE ON	c., Hurry On—*Fatima II	70,000	FT Sara	W. R. Coe	unraced
1926	TUSKEGEE	c., Black Toney—Humanity	35,000	FT Sara	E. M. Byers	43-10-7-8, $11,925 Belgrade Claiming S.
1925	WAR FEATHERS	c., Man o' War—*Tuscan Red	50,500	FT Sara	Hamilton Farms	7-1-10, $1,350
1924	BLASISTA	c., Eternal—*Aquamarine	16,000	FT Sara	William Zeigler Jr.	5-0-0-0, $0
1923	FLYING EBONY	c., The Finn—Princess Mary	21,000	FT Sara	G. A. Cochran	13-6-1-2, $62,420, Kentucky Derby, etc.
1922	THE TRAMP	c., The Finn—Kate Adams	12,500	FT Sara	Montfort Jones	1-0-0-0, $0
1921	COEUR DE LION	c., Fair Play—*Couronne de Laurier	8,600	FT Sara	Rancocas Stable	288-48-50-43, $33,165
1920	PIRATE GOLD	c., Rock View—Gold	14,000	FT Sara	Greentree Stable	157-20-34-20, $23,258
1919	SUN TURRET	c., Sunstar—Marian Hood	25,000	FT Sara	J.K.L. Ross	103-6-5-11, $3,855
1918	Royal Jester	c., Black Jester—*Primula II	14,500	FT Sara	J.K.L. Ross	33-1-9-7, $4,381, 2nd Earl Grey H., etc.
1917	*HURON	c., *Sweeper—Zuna	4,000	FT Sara	Joseph E. Widener	105-28-20-14, $17,131, Windon H., etc.
	THE SAINT	c., Sain—Nannette	4,000	FT Sara	Samuel D. Riddle	unraced

†† Through May 1, 2004

Leading Sires of Top-Priced Yearlings

Northern Dancer	7
*Sir Gallahad III	7
Mr. Prospector	6
Storm Cat	5
Raise a Native	4
*Blenheim II	3
*Nasrullah	3
Bold Ruler	3
Nijinsky II	3
Roman	3
Swaps	3

Leading Consignors of Top-Priced Yearlings

Arthur B. Hancock Sr.	12
Spendthrift Farm/ Leslie Combs II	9
Lane's End	5
Hermitage Farm/ Warner L. Jones	4
Windfields Farm	4
Claiborne Farm	3
Robert A. Fairbarn	3
Himyar Stud/Phil T. Chinn	3

Leading Buyers of Top-Priced Yearlings

†Sheikh Mohammed bin Rashid al Maktoum	5
British Bloodstock Agency (Eng)	4
British Bloodstock Agency (Ire)	4
Demi O'Byrne	4
Greentree Stud	4
Calumet Farm	3
Maine Chance Farm/ Elizabeth Arden	3
Frank McMahon	3
‡Fusao Sekiguchi	3

† Includes those bought in the name of Aston Upthorpe Stud, Darley Stud Management, and John Ferguson Bloodstock
‡ Includes horses bought for Fusao Sekiguchi by Hideyuki Mori

---

Sales Average of All Horses by Year

Year	Average	Change	Deflated Average
2004	$52,205	15.5%	$48,240
2003	45,206	8.4%	42,648
2002	41,694	−5.5%	40,055
2001	44,108	−14.3%	43,086
2000	51,443	3.3%	51,443
1999	49,795	18.1%	50,880
1998	42,165	12.6%	43,707
1997	37,457	13.9%	39,257
1996	32,892	15.7%	35,047
1995	28,440	13.9%	30,877
1994	24,966	13.7%	27,660
1993	21,952	9.9%	24,838
1992	19,972	−5.5%	23,120
1991	21,136	−10.6%	25,030
1990	23,645	−11.3%	28,980
1989	26,648	−1.1%	33,922
1988	26,957	−6.0%	35,613
2002	$47,624	1.4%	$45,752
2001	46,971	−7.7%	45,882
2000	50,873	−4.7%	50,873
1999	53,382	16.9%	54,545
1998	45,668	0.5%	47,338
1997	45,425	14.1%	47,608
1996	39,804	24.5%	42,411
1995	31,971	23.3%	34,711
1994	25,929	27.1%	28,727
1993	20,402	7.7%	23,084
1992	18,947	4.9%	21,933
1991	18,056	−11.5%	21,382
1990	20,403	30.0%	25,007
1989	15,690	−5.2%	19,973
1988	16,542	5.4%	21,854

Two-Year-Olds in Training Sales Average by Year

Year	Average	Change	Deflated Average
2004	$58,918	27.7%	$54,443
2003	46,140	−3.1%	43,529

Yearling Sales Average by Year

Year	Average	Change	Deflated Average
2004	$52,748	9.4%	$48,741
2003	48,213	10.0%	45,485
2002	43,848	−15.9%	42,124
2001	52,140	−4.4%	50,931
2000	54,558	8.0%	54,558
1999	50,523	17.8%	51,624
1998	42,880	12.3%	44,448

Year	Average	Change	Deflated Average
1997	$38,189	10.6%	$40,025
1996	34,540	11.9%	36,803
1995	30,880	13.6%	33,527
1994	27,177	8.3%	30,110
1993	25,098	12.6%	28,398
1992	22,290	-14.8%	25,803
1991	26,157	-12.9%	30,976
1990	30,030	-6.4%	36,806
1989	32,097	-2.0%	40,859
1988	32,748	-7.3%	43,264

Year	Average	Change	Deflated Average
1992	$15,962	-21.7%	$18,478
1991	20,376	12.0%	24,130
1990	18,195	-23.0%	22,301
1989	23,635	50.1%	30,087
1988	15,743	-55.5%	20,798

Weanling Sales Average by Year

Year	Average	Change	Deflated Average
2004	$36,986	-7.7%	$34,177
2003	40,087	28.6%	37,819
2002	31,181	14.9%	29,955
2001	27,149	-24.0%	26,520
2000	35,716	-16.7%	35,716
1999	42,852	9.3%	43,786
1998	39,203	21.8%	40,637
1997	32,178	14.0%	33,725
1996	28,232	8.1%	30,081
1995	26,124	19.7%	28,363
1994	21,822	-7.5%	24,177
1993	23,589	47.8%	26,690

Broodmare Sales Average by Year

Year	Average	Change	Deflated Average
2004	$55,694	27.5%	$51,464
2003	43,683	7.8%	41,211
2002	40,515	9.0%	38,922
2001	37,183	-32.1%	36,321
2000	54,752	2.4%	54,752
1999	53,457	22.3%	54,622
1998	43,701	15.3%	45,299
1997	37,913	21.5%	39,735
1996	31,192	21.0%	33,235
1995	25,770	5.8%	27,979
1994	24,355	33.3%	26,983
1993	18,274	1.5%	20,676
1992	18,009	2.3%	20,847
1991	17,604	-8.7%	20,847
1990	19,280	-29.4%	23,620
1989	27,291	-0.1%	34,741
1988	27,328	7.3%	36,103

Pinhooking in American Auctions

No one knows exactly how the terms pinhooking or pinhooker entered the English language—or at least Thoroughbred racing's esoteric subset of Shakespeare's tongue—but the practice and profession have become far more common, lucrative, and important to the industry since the early 1990s, when the market for two-year-olds exploded.

Pinhooking is a variation on the capitalist concept of wholesale versus retail. The pinhooker buys a horse—for example, a yearling at auction—with the express purpose of reselling that horse at a later auction, almost always a sale of two-year-olds in training. Thus, the pinhooker tries to purchase at a relatively low price (wholesale) and resell later at a higher price (retail). In between, the pinhooker makes further investments of time and money trying to improve the quality of the wholesale purchase in hopes of cashing in on a retail sale.

Pinhooking is a business with high risks and the potential for high rewards, as illustrated by the following tables, which detail the most and least successful pinhooks on record.

Most Successful Pinhooks by Total Gain (through 3/30/2005)

Yearling to Juvenile

$4,230,000 FUSAICHI SAMURAI, 2002 dk b/br. c., Fusaichi Pegasus—Hidden Storm, by Storm Cat. **Yearling Purchase:** $270,000, 2003 Fasig-Tipton New York Saratoga select yearling, by White Horse Stables. **Juvenile Sale:** $4,500,000, 2004 Fasig-Tipton Florida Calder February, consigned by Kirkwood Stables, agent, purchased by Fusao Sekiguchi. 1,566.7% gain. 1-1-0-0, $21,000.

$3,130,000 CHEKHOV, 2002 b. c., Pulpit—In My Cap, by Vice Regent. **Yearling Sale:** $170,000, 2003 Keeneland September, by Michael J. Ryan, agent. **Juvenile Sale:** $3,300,000, 2004 Keeneland April, consigned by Niall Brennan Stables, agent, purchased by Demi O'Byrne. 1,841.2% gain. 3-0-1-1, $17,566.

$2,943,000 DUBAI DREAMER, 2002 gr/ro. c., Stephen Got Even—Blacktie Bid, by Black Tie Affair (Ire). **Yearling Purchase:** $157,000, 2003 Fasig-Tipton Kentucky select yearling, by Michael J. Ryan, agent. **Juvenile Sale:** $3,100,000, 2004 Fasig-Tipton Florida Calder February, consigned by Niall Brennan Stables, agent, purchased by John Ferguson. 1,874.5% gain. 3-0-1-0, $2,890.

$2,800,000 Unnamed, 2003 b. c., Forestry—Rare Bird, by Rahy. **Yearling Purchase:** $200,000, 2004 Fasig-Tipton Kentucky select yearling, by Tony Bowling and Bobby Dodd. **Juvenile Sale:** $3,000,000, 2005 Fasig-Tipton Florida Calder February, consigned by Tony Bowling and Bobby Dodd, agent, purchased by Demi O'Byrne. 1,400% gain. Unraced.

$2,670,000 DIAMOND FURY, 2001 ch. g., Sea of Secrets—Swift Spirit, by Tasso. **Yearling Purchase:** $30,000, 2002 Fasig-Tipton Kentucky select yearling, by Becky Thomas.

Juvenile Sale: $2,700,000, 2003 Barretts March, consigned by Sequel Bloodstock, agent, purchased by Charles Fipke. 8,900% gain. 12-2-2-2, $81,580.

$2,450,000 Unnamed, 2003 dk b/br. c., Grand Slam—Dama, by Storm Cat. **Yearling Purchase:** $450,000, 2004 Fasig-Tipton Kentucky select yearling, by Maurice W. Miller, agent. **Juvenile Sale:** $2,900,000, 2005 Fasig-Tipton Florida Calder February, consigned by Maurice W. Miller, agent, purchased by Darley. 544.4% gain. Unraced.

$1,925,000 DUBAI ESCAPADE, 2002 b. f., Awesome Again—Sassy Pants, by Saratoga Six. **Yearling Purchase:** $75,000, 2003 Keeneland September, by Gulf Coast Farms. **Juvenile Sale:** $2,000,000, 2004 Barretts March, consigned by Jerry Bailey Sales Agency, agent, purchased by John Ferguson Bloodstock. 2,566.7% gain. 2-1-0-0, $16,250.

$1,869,000 ATLANTIC OCEAN, 2000 dk b/br. c., Stormy Atlantic—Super Chef, by Seattle Slew. **Yearling Purchase:** $31,000, 2001 Keeneland September, by James K. Chapman. **Juvenile Sale:** $1,900,000, 2002 Barretts March, consigned by Chapman Farms, purchased by The Thoroughbred Corp. 6,029.0% gain. 19-5-3-2, G3, $678,210.

$1,825,000 MOROCCO, 1997 ch. h., Brocco—Roll Over Baby, by Rollin On Over. **Yearling Purchase:** $175,000, 1998 Fasig-Tipton New York Saratoga select yearling, by Alfred T. Eldredge. **Juvenile Sale:** $2,000,000, 1999 Barretts March, consigned by Sequel Bloodstock, agent, purchased by The Thoroughbred Corp. 1,042.9% gain. 16-4-0-1, $133,640.

$1,805,000 **YONAGUSKA**, 1998 dk b/br. h., Cherokee Run—Marital Spook, by Silver Ghost. **Yearling Purchase:** $145,000, 1999 Keeneland September, by Michael J. Ryan, agent. **Juvenile Sale:** $1,950,000, 2000 Fasig-Tipton Florida Calder February, consigned by Niall Brennan, agent, purchased by Demi O'Byrne. 1,244.8% gain. 18-6-1-5, G1, $536,355.

$1,805,000 WHAT A SONG, 2003 dk b/br. c., Songandaprayer—What a Knight, by Tough Knight. **Yearling Purchase:** $95,000, 2004 Fasig-Tipton Kentucky select yearling, by M.S.T.S. **Juvenile Sale:** $1,900,000, 2005 Barretts March, consigned by Murray Smith, agent, purchased by Robert B. and Beverly J. Lewis. 1,900% gain. Unraced.

$1,780,000 LA SALLE STREET, 1997 dk b/br. h., Not For Love—Three Grand, by Assert (Ire). **Yearling Purchase:**

$220,000, 1998 Fasig-Tipton Midlantic Eastern fall yearling, by Cam Allard. **Juvenile Sale:** $2,000,000, 1999 Keeneland April, consigned by Cam Allard, purchased by Demi O'Byrne. 809.1% gain. 3-0-1-0, $3,420.

$1,555,000 MUTANABI, 2002 b. c., Wild Rush—Freudenau, by Meadowlake. **Yearling Purchase:** $45,000, 2003 OBSC August, by Ricky Leppala. **Juvenile Sale:** $1,600,000, 2004 OBSC February, consigned by W.D. North, agent, purchased by John Ferguson. 3,455.6% gain. 2-0-1-1, $3,171.

$1,360,000 TIMSAAH, 2002 gr/ro. c., Rubiano—Magari, by Quack. **Yearling Purchase:** $140,000, 2003 Fasig-Tipton Kentucky select yearling, by Cam Allard. **Juvenile Sale:** $1,500,000, 2004 Fasig-Tipton Florida Calder February, consigned by Cam Allard, purchased by John Ferguson. 971.4% gain. Unraced.

Most Successful Pinhooks by Percentage Gain (through 3/30/2005)

Yearling to Juvenile

8,900.0%   DIAMOND FURY, 2001 ch. g., Sea of Secrets—Swift Spirit, by Tasso. **Yearling Purchase:** $30,000, 2002 Fasig-Tipton Kentucky select yearling, by Becky Thomas. **Juvenile Sale:** $2,700,000, 2003 Barretts March, consigned by Sequel Bloodstock, agent, purchased by Charles Fipke. $2,670,000 gain. 12-2-2-2, $81,580.

6,029.0%   **ATLANTIC OCEAN**, 2000 dk b/br..f., Stormy Atlantic—Super Chef, by Seattle Slew. **Yearling Purchase:** $31,000, 2001 Keeneland September, by James K. Chapman. **Juvenile Sale:** $1,900,000, 2002 Barretts March, consigned by Chapman Farms, purchased by The Thoroughbred Corp. $1,869,000 gain. 19-5-3-2, G3, $678,210.

4,900.0%   AFTERNOON QUE, 2002 dk b/br. c., Afternoon Deelites—How 'bout Chris, by Unbridled. **Yearling Purchase:** $5,000, 2003 Fasig-Tipton Midlantic Eastern fall yearling, by M & H Training and Sales. **Juvenile Sale:** $250,000, 2004 OBSC March, consigned by M & H Training and Sales, agent, purchased by West Point Thoroughbreds. $245,000 gain. Unraced.

4,687.2%   **Major Adonis**, 1997 b. g., Major Impact—Adonara, by Strawberry Road (Aus). **Yearling Purchase:** $4,700, 1998 Fasig-Tipton Kentucky October, by Bea and Robert H. Roberts. **Juvenile Sale:** $225,000, 1999 Keeneland November, consigned by Bea and Robert H. Roberts, purchased by Eugene N. Melnyk. $220,300 gain. 16-2-3-2, spl, $100,926.

3,650.0%   HYPER NAKAYAMA, 1995 dk b/br. h., Well Decorated—Tea and Roses, by Fleet Nasrullah. **Yearling Purchase:** $8,000, 1996 Keeneland January, by Donna M. Wormser. **Juvenile Sale:** $300,000, 1997 OBSC February, consigned by Donna M. Wormser, agent, purchased by Heatherway, agent. $292,000 gain. 24-4-7-4, $1,002,590.

3,650.0%   IRREVOCABLE, 2001 b. f., Our Emblem—Northern Glance, by Nijinsky II. **Yearling Purchase:** $3,200, 2002 Keeneland January, by Burden Creek Farm. **Juvenile**

Sale: $120,000, 2003 Keeneland April, consigned by American Equistock and Parrish Farms, purchased by John C. Kimmel. $116,800 gain. 4-0-1-0, $3,465.

3,455.6%   MUTANABI, 2002 b. c., Wild Rush—Freudenau, by Meadowlake. **Yearling Purchase:** $45,000, 2003 OBSC August, by Ricky Leppala. **Juvenile Sale:** $1,600,000, 2004 OBSC February, consigned by W.D. North, agent, purchased by John Ferguson. $1,555,000 gain. 2-0-1-1, $3,171.

3,125.8%   SMOKUM SAM, 2002 ch. c., Smoke Glacken—Flo White, by Whitesburg. **Yearling Purchase:** $15,500, 2003 Keeneland September, by Samerin Oaks. **Juvenile Sale:** $500,000, 2004 OBSC April, consigned by Costanzo Sales, purchased by John Ferguson Bloodstock, agent. $484,500 gain. 1-1-0-0, $7,988.

2,995.2%   NOTABLE TIGER, 2002 dk b/br. c., Tiger Ridge—Notable Girl, by What a Pleasure. **Yearling Purchase:** $21,000, 2003 OBSC August, by Hartley/De Renzo Thoroughbreds LLC. **Juvenile Sale:** $650,000, 2004 OBSC March, consigned by Hartley/De Renzo Thoroughbreds LLC, agent, purchased by John Ferguson Bloodstock. $629,000 gain. Unraced.

2,677.8%   JIM'S SMOKIN PINOT, 2002 dk b/br. c., Victory Gallop—Buck's Lady, by Alleged. **Yearling Purchase:** $18,000, 2003 Keeneland September, by Tony Bowling and Bobby Dodd. **Juvenile Sale:** $500,000, 2004 Barretts March, consigned by Terry Oliver, agent, purchased by NeverTell Farm LLC. $482,000 gain. 4-0-2-0, $19,970.

2,650.0%   **FUSAICHI ROCK STAR**, 2002 gr/ro. c., Wild Wonder—Grannies Feather, by At Full Feather. **Yearling Purchase:** $30,000, 2003 OBSC August, by Jessie Longoria. **Juvenile Sale:** $825,000, 2004 Fasig-Tipton Florida Calder February, consigned by Jessie and Stacy Longoria, purchased by Fusao Sekiguchi. $795,000 gain. 5-2-0-1, G2, $138,366.

Least Successful Pinhooks by Total Loss (through 3/30/2005)

Yearling to Juvenile

–$590,000 HANNAH'S WISH, 1998 dk b/br. h., Kris S.—Admise (Fr), by Highest Honor (Fr). **Yearling Purchase:** $900,000, 1999 Keeneland September, by Narvick International. **Juvenile Sale:** $310,000, 2000 Barretts July, consigned by 505 Farms, purchased by Hollywood Bloodstock. –65.6% loss. Unraced.

–$300,000 EVIL MINISTER, 2002 ch. c., Deputy Minister—Evil's Pic, by Piccolino. **Yearling Purchase:** $500,000, 2003 Fasig-Tipton New York Saratoga select yearling, by Ventures Partnership. **Juvenile Sale:** $200,000, 2004 Fasig-Tipton Florida Calder February, consigned by Kings Equine, agent, purchased by Namcook Stable. –60% loss. 6-2-0-1, G3, $120,530.

–$285,000 DAMASCUS LAD, 1984 b. h., Damascus—Great Lady M., by Icecapade. **Yearling Purchase:** $425,000, 1985 Keeneland July select, by Cardiff Stud Farms. **Juvenile Sale:** $140,000, 1986 C.T.S. March, consigned by

Cardiff Stud Farms, purchased by Central Farms. –67.1% loss. 3-0-1-1, $9,375.

–$280,000 Unnamed, 2003 dk b/br. f., Arch—Questress, by Seeking the Gold. **Yearling Purchase:** $360,000, 2004 Keeneland September, by Whitehorse Stables. **Juvenile Sale:** $80,000, 2005 Fasig-Tipton Florida Calder February, consigned by Solitary Oak Farm, agent, purchased by Germania Farms. –77.8% loss. Unraced.

–$260,891 RAILBIRD (Ire), 1995 ch. h., Caerleon—My Lady's Key, by Key to the Mint. **Yearling Purchase:** $302,891, 1996 Goffs Orby, by Kenneth E. Ellenberg. **Juvenile Sale:** $42,000, 1997 Barretts March, consigned by Bailey-Ellenberg Select, purchased by Waldon Randall Welty. –86.1% loss. 16-1-3-3, $11,165.

–$250,000 RUSH TO DEFEND, 2000 b. c., Wild Rush—Mary Sloan, by Woodman. **Yearling Purchase:** $500,000, 2001 Fasig-Tipton Kentucky select yearling, by Paul Collins, agent. **Juvenile Sale:** $250,000, 2002 Fasig-Tipton Florida Calder February, consigned by Eddie Woods, agent, purchased by Chester Broman. –50% loss. 11-1-1-0, $18,485.

–$220,000 **OVERVIEW**, 1998 b. h., Kingmambo—Long View, by Damascus. **Yearling Purchase:** $300,000, 1999 Fasig-Tipton New York Saratoga select yearling, by Two Bucks Stable, agent. **Juvenile Sale:** $80,000, 2000 Keeneland April, consigned by Jerry Bailey Sales Agency, agent, purchased by John C. Oxley. –73.3% loss. 14-2-1-4, SW, $105,831.

–$220,000 **COLONY STAR**, 1995 dk b/br. m., Pleasant Colony—Star Glimmer, by General Assembly. **Yearling Purchase:** $250,000, 1996 Keeneland July select, by Cam Allard. **Juvenile Sale:** $30,000, 1997 Keeneland April, consigned by H. T. Stables, agent, purchased by Henri Mastey. –88% loss. 1-0-0-0, $150.

–$210,000 **PLUNKIT**, 2002 b. c., Lemon Drop Kid—April Starlight, by Storm Bird. **Yearling Purchase:** $500,000, 2003 Fasig-Tipton Kentucky select yearling, by Jeanne G. Vance. **Juvenile Sale:** $290,000, 2004 Keeneland April, consigned by Jeanne G. Vance, purchased by Robert B. and Beverly J. Lewis. –42% loss. 5-0-2-1, $25,480.

–$203,000 **JETTIN HIGH**, 2002 ch. c., High Yield—Rhodesia, by Polish Navy. **Yearling Purchase:** $220,000, 2003 Keeneland September, by White Horse Stables. **Juvenile Sale:** $17,000, 2004 Keeneland April, consigned by Kirkwood Stables, agent, purchased by Gary Owens. –92.3% loss. 5-1-0-0, $10,335.

–$200,000 **HONOR ME**, 1998 ch. g., Honor Grades—Bo K., by Raise a Native. **Yearling Purchase:** $350,000, 1999 Fasig-Tipton Kentucky select yearling, by Cam Allard. **Juvenile Sale:** $150,000, 2000 Fasig-Tipton Midlantic two-year-olds in training, consigned by H. T. Stables, agent, purchased by Dan Butler. –57.1% loss. 38-13-10-4, SW, $329,088.

–$200,000 **GREENSKEEPER**, 2003 b. f., Unbridled's Song—Defining Style, by Out of Place. **Yearling Purchase:** $300,000, 2004 Fasig-Tipton Kentucky select yearling, by Hoby Kight. **Juvenile Sale:** $100,000, 2005 Fasig-Tipton Florida Calder February, consigned by Hoby and Layna Kight, agent, purchased by Shadai Farm. –66.7% loss. Unraced.

–$185,000 **BOB'S CLOG BUSTER**, 1996 b. h., Beau Genius—Told It All, by Told. **Yearling Purchase:** $200,000, 1997 Keeneland September, by Louie J. Roussel. **Juvenile Sale:** $15,000, 1998 Fasig-Tipton Florida Calder February, consigned by Jockey Club Farm, agent, purchased by Ralph C. Sessa. –92.5% loss. Unraced.

–$185,000 **CIELO'S DANCE**, 1995 b. m., Danzig—Orlanova, by Conquistador Cielo. **Yearling Purchase:** $335,000, 1996 Fasig-Tipton New York Saratoga select yearling, by Hartley/De Renzo Thoroughbreds LLC. **Juvenile Sale:** $150,000, 1997 Barretts March, consigned by Hartley/De Renzo Thoroughbreds LLC, purchased by Thomas F. VanMeter. –55.2% loss. Unraced.

Least Successful Pinhooks by Percentage Loss (through 3/30/2005)
Yearling to Juvenile

–96.7%   PLEASANT DAYS, 1996 b. h., Pleasant Tap—Elusive Bird, by Storm Bird. **Yearling Purchase:** $180,000, 1997 Keeneland September, by Silky Green. **Juvenile Sale:** $6,000, 1998 Barretts Spring two-year-olds in training and horses of racing age, consigned by Nick de Meric, agent, purchased by Gloria Haley. –$174,000 loss. 2-0-1-0, $1,400.

–96.3%   CEO SIS, 1994 b. m., Unbridled—Cruisie, by Assert (Ire). **Yearling Purchase:** $190,000, 1995 Fasig-Tipton New York Saratoga select yearling, by John Galbreath, agent. **Juvenile Sale:** $7,000, 1996 Keeneland November, consigned by Darby Dan Farm, agent, purchased by Carlos S. E. Moore, agent. –$183,000 loss. 5-2-0-1, $66,041.

–92.5%   BOB'S CLOG BUSTER, 1996 b. h., Beau Genius—Told It All, by Told. **Yearling Purchase:** $200,000, 1997 Keeneland September, by Louie J. Roussel. **Juvenile Sale:** $15,000, 1998 Fasig-Tipton Florida Calder February, consigned by Jockey Club Farm, agent, purchased by Ralph C. Sessa. –$185,000 loss. Unraced.

–92.5%   BEN'S QUEST, 2002 ch. c., Coronado's Quest—Donna Karan (Chi), by Roy. **Yearling Purchase:** $160,000, 2003 Keeneland September, by Becky Thomas. **Juvenile Sale:** $12,000, 2004 Keeneland April, consigned by Sequel Bloodstock, agent, purchased by Moneylane Farms. –$148,000 loss. 2-1-0-0, $6,075.

–92.3%   JETTIN HIGH, 2002 ch. c., High Yield—Rhodesia, by Polish Navy. **Yearling Purchase:** $220,000, 2003 Keeneland September, by White Horse Stables. **Juvenile Sale:** $17,000, 2004 Keeneland April, consigned by Kirkwood Stables, agent, purchased by Gary Owens. –$203,000 loss. 5-1-0-0, $10,335.

–92.1%   GOTTA TEMPER, 1999 b. m., Pleasant Colony—Omnia, by Green Dancer. **Yearling Purchase:** $140,000, 2000 Keeneland September, by Murray Smith, agent. **Juvenile Sale:** $11,000, 2001 Keeneland April, consigned by Murray Smith, agent, purchased by Wheeler Racing. –$129,000 loss. 20-3-6-3, $63,806.

–91.9%   CAL'S BABY, 1998 dk b/br. m., Smart Strike—Silver Dollar Kate, by Green Dancer. **Yearling Purchase:** $185,000, 1999 Keeneland September, by James Cassels. **Juvenile Sale:** $15,000, 2000 Keeneland April,

consigned by Hartley/De Renzo Thoroughbreds LLC, agent, purchased by Shah Stables. –$170,000 loss. 24-4-2-8, $110,150.

–91.7%   HONOUR TOPPER, 2002 b. g., Honour and Glory—Chart Topper, by Groovy. **Yearling Purchase:** $120,000, 2003 Fasig-Tipton Kentucky select yearling, by Michael J. Ryan, agent. **Juvenile Sale:** $10,000, 2004 Fasig-Tipton Midlantic two-year-olds in training, consigned by Niall Brennan Stables, agent, purchased by John E. Salzman. –$110,000 loss. 5-1-1-0, $9,175.

–91.6%   MIRANDOLA, 1990 b. m., Ogygian—Miramani, by Slew o' Gold. **Yearling Purchase:** $125,000, 1991 Keeneland September, by Michael J. Ryan, agent. **Juvenile Sale:** $10,500, 1992 Keeneland November, consigned by King Ranch Farm, purchased by Ocean Blue Stables, agent. –$114,500 loss. 2-0-0-0, $0.

–91.3%   PHILTHEDEPUTY, 1997 b. h., Silver Deputy—Philharmonia (Ire), by Caerleon. **Yearling Purchase:** $100,000, 1998 Fasig-Tipton Kentucky select yearling, by Sarem Stable. **Juvenile Sale:** $8,700, 1999 OBSC April, consigned by Niall Brennan, agent, purchased by Eureka Farm. –$91,300 loss. 7-0-1-0, $1,823.

–91.3%   VIC'S TIME, 1997 ch. h., Gilded Time—Regal Grant, by Mr. Prospector. **Yearling Purchase:** $160,000, 1998 Fasig-Tipton New York Saratoga select yearling, by Kenneth E. Ellenberg. **Juvenile Sale:** $14,000, 1999 Fasig-Tipton New York Saratoga two-year-olds and horses of racing age, consigned by Jerry Bailey Sales Agency, agent, purchased by John Shaw. –$146,000 loss. 10-0-1-0, $5,816.

–90.9%   SWEET PERSUASION, 1993 b. m., Devil's Bag—Ivory Idol, by Alydar. **Yearling Purchase:** $110,000, 1994 Keeneland September, by D. Wayne Lukas. **Juvenile Sale:** $10,000, 1995 Keeneland November, consigned by Denali Stud, agent, purchased by Dermot Carty. –$100,000 loss. 1-0-1-0, $6,800.

–89.7%   Athena's Glory, 1981 ch. h., In Reality—Eleven Pleasures, by What a Pleasure. **Yearling Purchase:** $175,000, 1982 Keeneland July select, by W. S. Farish III. **Juvenile Sale:** $18,000, 1983 OBSC March, consigned by Waldemar Farms, agent, purchased by C & K Stable. –$157,000 loss. 60-6-5-12, spl, $67,515.

Most Successful Pinhooks by Total Gain (through 3/30/2005)

Weanling to Yearling

$1,180,000 DUBAI TOUCH, 1999 dk b/br. h., Saint Ballado—Jettin Diplomacy, by Roman Diplomat. **Weanling Purchase:** $220,000, 1999 Keeneland November, by B.M.K. Equine. **Yearling Sale:** $1,400,000, 2000 Keeneland July select, consigned by Hartwell Farm, agent, purchased by John Ferguson Bloodstock. 536.4% gain. 9-0-0-0, $3,868.

$1,100,000 SEEKING AN ALIBI, 2002 ch. c., Storm Cat—Seeking Regina, by Seeking the Gold. **Weanling Purchase:** $500,000, 2002 Keeneland November, by Bradley Thoroughbred Brokerage. **Yearling Sale:** $1,600,000, 2003 Keeneland September, consigned by Eaton Sales, agent, purchased by John Ferguson Bloodstock. 220% gain. 2-0-0-0, $0.

$1,015,000 TALK IS MONEY, 1998 ch. h., Deputy Minister—Isle Go West, by Gone West. **Weanling Purchase:** $785,000, 1998 Keeneland November, by Smithfield Investments. **Yearling Sale:** $1,800,000, 1999 Keeneland September, consigned by Dromoland Farm, agent, purchased by Baden P. "Buzz" Chace, agent. 129.3% gain. 7-2-1-1, SW, $104,110.

$1,000,000 LIFESTYLE, 2000 b. c., Indian Charlie—Inlaw, by Gold Seam. **Weanling Purchase:** $100,000, 2000 Keeneland November, by Holiday Stables. **Yearling Sale:** $1,100,000, 2001 Keeneland September, consigned by Paternostro & Herbener, agent, purchased by The Thoroughbred Corp. 1,000% gain. 4-2-0-0, $49,500.

$938,000 WEATHERMAN, 1998 ch. h., Summer Squall—Plucky Maid, by Housebuster. **Weanling Purchase:** $62,000, 1998 Keeneland November, by Plaza Stud. **Yearling Sale:** $1,000,000, 1999 Keeneland September, consigned by Jim J. FitzGerald, agent, purchased by Stonerside Stable. 1,512.9% gain. 4-1-1-1, $38,280.

$900,000 DUBAI TIGER, 1999 b. h., Storm Cat—Toga Toga Toga, by Saratoga Six. **Weanling Purchase:** $900,000, 1999 Keeneland November, by Tim Hyde. **Yearling Sale:** $1,800,000, 2000 Keeneland September, consigned by Eaton Sales, agent, purchased by John Ferguson Bloodstock. 100% gain. 8-2-1-1, $106,510.

$900,000 Unnamed, 2003 b. c., Grand Slam—Sheza Honey, by Honey Jay. **Weanling Purchase:** $400,000, 2003 Keeneland November, by Michael Byrne. **Yearling Sale:** $1,300,000, 2004 Keeneland September, consigned by Michael C. Byrne, agent, purchased by Demi O'Byrne. 225% gain. Unraced.

$888,000 EALING PARK, 1999 dk b/br. h., Saint Ballado—Jeannie the Meanie, by Rare Performer. **Weanling Purchase:** $62,000, 1999 Keeneland November, by Phillip Frances McCarthy. **Yearling Sale:** $950,000, 2000 Keeneland September, consigned by Taylor Made Sales Agency, agent, purchased by Eugene N. Melnyk. 1,432.3% gain. 6-0-0-0, $3,500.

$850,000 STORMIN' HEAVEN, 1998 ch. h., Hennessy—Afleet Francais, by Afleet. **Weanling Purchase:** $350,000, 1998 Keeneland November, by Greenwood Farm. **Yearling Sale:** $1,200,000, 1999 Keeneland July select, consigned by Eaton Sales, agent, purchased by Robert B. Hess, agent. 242.9% gain. 12-4-0-1, $124,224.

$800,000 FUTURE MINISTER, 1999 b. h., Deputy Minister—Brink, by Forty Niner. **Weanling Purchase:** $500,000, 1999 Keeneland November, by Ballard Stable. **Yearling Sale:** $1,300,000, 2000 Keeneland July select, consigned by Taylor Made Sales Agency, agent, purchased by John Ferguson Bloodstock. 160% gain. 11-1-3-1, $62,678.

$800,000 HANNAH'S WISH, 1998 dk b/br. h., Kris S. —Admise (Fr), by Highest Honor (Fr). **Weanling Purchase:** $100,000, 1998 Fasig-Tipton Kentucky fall mixed, by The Lads. **Yearling Sale:** $900,000, 1999 Keeneland September, consigned by The Lads, purchased by Narvick International. 800% gain. Unraced.

$800,000 SECRET POND, 1999 dk b/br. h., Mr. Prospector—Golden Pond (Ire), by Don't Forget Me. **Weanling Purchase:** $600,000, 1999 Keeneland November, by Horse France. **Yearling Sale:** $1,400,000, 2000 Keeneland July select, consigned by Lakland LLC, agent, purchased by Katsumi Yoshida. 133.3% gain. Unraced.

Most Successful Pinhooks by Percentage Gain (through 3/30/2005)

Weanling to Yearling

11,233.3% TORTONI, 2000 dk b/br. c., Candy Stripes—Our Dani, by Homebuilder. **Weanling Purchase:** $1,500, 2000 Keeneland November, by Pasco Bloodstock. **Yearling Sale:** $170,000, 2001 OBSC August, consigned by Summerfield, agent, purchased by Journeyman Bloodstock, agent. $168,500 gain. 8-1-1-1, $25,880.

8,048.1% DUKE OF DESTINY, 2003 dk b/br. c., Pikepass—Dutch's Duchess, by Roy. **Weanling Purchase:** $2,700, 2003 Keeneland November, by Benedict A. Mohit. **Yearling Sale:** $220,000, 2004 OBSC August, consigned by Kaizen Sales, agent, purchased by Martin L. Cherry. $217,300 gain. Unraced.

6,566.7% GOLDEN TONES, 2001 b. c., Seeking the Gold—Bethany, by Dayjur. **Weanling Purchase:** $6,000, 2001 Keeneland November, by Jay Rodgers. **Yearling Sale:** $400,000, 2002 Keeneland September, consigned by Taylor Made Sales Agency, agent, purchased by Robert B. and Beverly J. Lewis. $394,000 gain. 3-1-1-0, $35,720.

6,566.7% KING BRIDLE, 1998 b. h., Unbridled—Life's Magic, by Cox's Ridge. **Weanling Purchase:** $3,000, 1998 Keeneland November, by Lori Tanel. **Yearling Sale:** $200,000, 1999 Keeneland September, consigned by Susan Y. Foreman, agent, purchased by David and Jill Heerensperger. $197,000 gain. 23-1-1-1, $11,948.

4,900.0% UNTOLD STORY, 1995 b. h., Theatrical (Ire) —Committed Miss, by Key to Content. **Weanling Purchase:** $4,000, 1995 Keeneland November, by Bruce Hundley. **Yearling Sale:** $200,000, 1996 Keeneland September, consigned by James B. Keogh, agent, purchased by Newmarket International. $196,000 gain. 23-0-0-1, $1,654.

3,788.9% Unnamed, 1994 b. h., Lord At War (Arg) —Corking, by Sensitive Prince. **Weanling Purchase:** $4,500, 1994 Keeneland November, by Chad R. Schumer, agent. **Yearling Sale:** $175,000, 1995 Fasig-Tipton Kentucky select yearling, consigned by Clarkland Farm, agent, purchased by Baden P. "Buzz" Chace, agent. $170,500 gain. Unraced.

3,300.0% AIR TOUCH, 1996 ch. h., Phone Trick—Serna, by Cox's Ridge. **Weanling Purchase:** $5,000, 1996 Keeneland November, by Green Meadow Farm. **Yearling Sale:** $170,000, 1997 Keeneland September, consigned by Taylor Made Sales Agency, agent, purchased by Supervent Inc. $165,000 gain. 1-0-0-0, $0.

3,181.3% LORD ADMIRAL, 1982 b. g., Topsider—Tumbling Dancer, by Dancer's Image. **Weanling Purchase:** $16,000, 1982 Keeneland November, by Charles St. George. **Yearling Sale:** $525,000, 1983 Keeneland September, consigned by Ashleigh Stud Farm, purchased by BBA (England). $509,000 gain. 1-0-0-0, $100.

3,150.0% WINDSOR COURT, 1998 dk b/br. g., Southern Halo—Her Grace, by Northern Flagship. **Weanling Purchase:** $8,000, 1998 Keeneland November, by Rachel Holden. **Yearling Sale:** $260,000, 1999 Keeneland September, consigned by Tri-County Farm, agent, purchased by James T. Scatuorchio. $252,000 gain. 43-3-10-3, $90,640.

2,300.0% Faah Emiss, 1998 b. h., Is It True—Change the Set, by Gold Stage. **Weanling Purchase:** $5,000, 1998 Keeneland November, by Barbara Crabtree. **Yearling Sale:** $120,000, 1999 OBSC August, consigned by Beth Bayer, agent, purchased by Cam Allard. $115,000 gain. 31-4-8-2, spl, $149,777.

Least Successful Pinhooks by Total Loss (through 3/30/2005)

Weanling to Yearling

−$800,000 NEW TRIESTE, 1999 ch. h., A.P. Indy—Lovlier Linda, by Vigors. **Weanling Purchase:** $1,300,000, 1999 Keeneland November, by Paul Shanahan. **Yearling Sale:** $500,000, 2000 Keeneland September, consigned by Eaton Sales, agent, purchased by Daniel M. Borislow. −61.5% loss. 1-0-0-0, $1,500.

−$475,000 **WISEMAN'S FERRY**, 1999 ch. h., Hennessy—Emmaus, by Silver Deputy. **Weanling Purchase:** $775,000, 1999 Keeneland November, by Indian Hill Farm. **Yearling Sale:** $300,000, 2000 Keeneland September, consigned by Eaton Sales, agent, purchased by Hugo Merry Bloodstock. −61.3% loss. 16-4-3-2, G3, $825,266.

−$375,000 SPORTS HERO, 1999 dk b/br. h., Mr. Prospector—Alysoft, by Alydar. **Weanling Purchase:** $775,000, 1999 Keeneland November, by High Mills Farm. **Yearling Sale:** $400,000, 2000 Fasig-Tipton New York Saratoga select yearling, consigned by Lakland LLC, agent, purchased by Select Equine. −48.4% loss. 2-2-0-0, $26,890.

−$350,000 Manhattan Skyline, 1999 dk b/br. m., Spinning World—Crystal Cream, by Secretariat. **Weanling Purchase:** $550,000, 1999 Keeneland November, by Farfellow Farms. **Yearling Sale:** $200,000, 2000 Keeneland July select, consigned by Taylor Made Sales Agency, agent, purchased by Jockey Club Farm. −63.6% loss. 11-4-5-0, spl, $141,255.

−$325,000 CARELESS ALY, 1991 ch. m., Alydar—Careless Notion, by Jester. **Weanling Purchase:** $350,000, 1991 Keeneland November, by Mandysland Farm. **Yearling Sale:** $25,000, 1992 Keeneland September, consigned by Joe Riggs, agent, purchased by Helen C. Alexander, agent. −92.9% loss. Unraced.

−$270,000 SIR BEDIVERE, 1999 ch. h., Unbridled—Bold Windy, by Bold Tropic (SAf). **Weanling Purchase:** $400,000, 1999 Keeneland November, by Narvick International. **Yearling Sale:** $130,000, 2000 Keeneland November, consigned by 505 Farm, purchased by Leprechaun Racing, agent. −67.5% loss. 7-1-0-1, $12,630.

−$250,000 **Truckle Feature**, 2000 dk b/br. c., Saint Ballado—Magic Gleam, by Danzig. **Weanling Purchase:** $275,000, 2000 Keeneland November, by Indian Hill Farm. **Yearling Sale:** $25,000, 2001 Keeneland September, consigned by Eaton Sales, agent, purchased by Straightaway Farm, agent. −90.9% loss. 10-2-1-2, spl, $151,460.

−$240,000 SPINNING MISS, 1999 ch. m., Spinning World—Bemissed, by Nijinsky II. **Weanling Purchase:** $575,000, 1999 Keeneland November, by Narvick International. **Yearling Sale:** $335,000, 2000 Keeneland September, consigned by 505 Farm, purchased by Brushwood Stable. −41.7% loss. 6-0-0-0, $300.

−$198,000 VICTORYTONITEHEY, 2001 b. c., Victory Gallop—Fancy Ruler, by Half a Year. **Weanling Purchase:** $225,000, 2001 Keeneland November, by Springvalley Farm. **Yearling Sale:** $27,000, 2002 Fasig-Tipton Kentucky October, consigned by Denali Stud, agent, purchased by Rocket City Stables. −88% loss. 11-1-0-1, $13,360.

−$183,000 Unnamed, 2003 dk b/br. f., Red Ransom—British Columbia (GB), by Selkirk. **Weanling Purchase:** $190,000, 2003 Keeneland November, by Arosa Farms. **Yearling Sale:** $7,000, 2004 Keeneland September, consigned by Arosa Farms, purchased by John Collins. −96.3% loss. Unraced.

−$175,000 **GOVERNOR BROWN**, 2000 ch. c., Kingmambo—Miss Mistletoes (Ire), by The Minstrel. **Weanling Purchase:** $485,000, 2000 Keeneland November, by Chestnut Hill Farm. **Yearling Sale:** $310,000, 2001 Keeneland September, consigned by Eaton Sales, agent, purchased by Dan Kenny, agent. −36.1% loss. 12-3-2-4, G3, $157,299.

−$163,000 SUMMIT STORM, 1999 b. h., Storm Cat—Refinancing, by *Forli. **Weanling Purchase:** $350,000, 1999 Keeneland November, by Richard Nip. **Yearling Sale:** $187,000, 2000 Keeneland September yearling internet RNA auction, consigned by Paternostro & Herbener, agent, purchased by Three Chimneys Farm. −46.6% loss. Unraced.

Least Successful Pinhooks by Percentage Loss (through 3/30/2005)

Weanling to Yearling

−96.3% Unnamed, 2003 dk b/br. f., Red Ransom—British Columbia (GB), by Selkirk. **Weanling Purchase:** $190,000, 2003 Keeneland November, by Arosa Farms. **Yearling Sale:** $7,000, 2004 Keeneland September, consigned by Arosa Farms, purchased by John Collins. −$183,000 loss. Unraced.

−93.8% RING DANG DO, 2000 b. c., Red Ransom—Laurentine, by Private Account. **Weanling Purchase:** $130,000, 2000 Keeneland November, by Bridlestown Stud. **Yearling Sale:** $8,000, 2001 Keeneland September, consigned by Dromoland Farm, agent, purchased by Kern/Lillingston Associates. −$122,000 loss. 19-1-2-4, $2,240.

−92.9% CARELESS ALY, 1991 ch. m., Alydar—Careless Notion, by Jester. **Weanling Purchase:** $350,000, 1991 Keeneland November, by Mandysland Farm. **Yearling Sale:** $25,000, 1992 Keeneland September, consigned by Joe Riggs, agent, purchased by Helen C. Alexander, agent. −$325,000 loss. Unraced.

−92.9% CUM LAUDE, 1999 dk b/br. g., Honor Grades—Jody G., by Roberto. **Weanling Purchase:** $175,000, 1999 Keeneland November, by Grade I Bloodstock. **Yearling Sale:** $12,500, 2000 Fasig-Tipton Kentucky October, consigned by Darby Dan Farm, agent, purchased by Kenneth Ayres. −$162,500 loss. 23-4-2-4, $33,897.

−92.0% CATRINA ERINA, 1998 ch. m., Candy Stripes—Erina, by Slewpy. **Weanling Purchase:** $100,000, 1998 Keeneland November, by Green Hall Stud. **Yearling Sale:** $8,000, 1999 Fasig-Tipton Kentucky October, consigned by Taylor Made Sales Agency, agent, purchased by Ted Latour. −$92,000 loss. 18-4-2-4, $31,905.

−91.3% Unnamed, 2003 dk b/br. f., Stormin Fever—Down the Street, by Ghazi. **Weanling Purchase:** $150,000, 2003 Keeneland November, by Tyra Holdings. **Yearling Sale:** $13,000, 2004 Fasig-Tipton Midlantic Eastern fall yearling, consigned by Bluewater Sales LLC, agent, purchased by Lincoln Avenue Partners. −$137,000 loss. Unraced.

−90.9% **Truckle Feature**, 2000 dk b/br. c., Saint Ballado—Magic Gleam, by Danzig. **Weanling Purchase:** $275,000, 2000 Keeneland November, by Indian Hill Farm. **Yearling Sale:** $25,000, 2001 Keeneland September, consigned by Eaton Sales, agent, purchased by Straightaway Farm, agent. −$250,000 loss. 10-2-1-2, spl, $151,460.

−90.0% PRINCESA ALEXA, 2003 ch. f., Broken Vow—Gail's Falcon, by Imperial Falcon. **Weanling Purchase:** $100,000, 2003 Keeneland November, by Barron Bloodstock. **Yearling Sale:** $10,000, 2004 Keeneland September, consigned by Highclere Sales, agent, purchased by Eric B. Peng. −$90,000 loss. Unraced.

−90.0% RING WARRIOR, 1999 gr/ro. h., K. O. Punch—Quiet Sound, by Quiet American. **Weanling Purchase:** $110,000, 1999 Keeneland November, by Horse France. **Yearling Sale:** $11,000, 2000 Keeneland September, consigned by Hopewell Farm, agent, purchased by Jim Snavely. −$99,000 loss. 5-1-0-2, $5,372.

−89.5% COOL AMERICAN, 2001 b. f., Real Quiet—With Your Approval, by With Approval. **Weanling Purchase:** $105,000, 2001 Keeneland November, by Jon Freston, agent. **Yearling Sale:** $11,000, 2002 Keeneland September, consigned by Eaton Sales, agent, purchased by John R. Parker. −$94,000 loss. 2-0-0-0, $0.

Most Successful Pinhooks by Total Gain (through 3/30/2005)

Weanling to Juvenile

$860,000 **Brave Quest**, 1997 b. h., Miswaki—Cousin Margaret, by Topsider. **Weanling Purchase:** $90,000, 1997 Fasig-Tipton Kentucky fall mixed, by Richard Spoor. **Juvenile Sale:** $950,000, 1999 Fasig-Tipton Florida Calder February, consigned by Robert N. Scanlon, agent, purchased by John C. Oxley. 955.6% gain. 7-4-1-1, spl, $164,502.

$815,000 SOMETHING ELSE, 1995 ch. m., Seeking the Gold—Rythmical, by Fappiano. **Weanling Purchase:** $185,000, 1995 Keeneland November, by BBA (England). **Juvenile Sale:** $1,000,000, 1997 Barretts March, consigned by Kirkwood Stables, agent, purchased by The Thoroughbred Corp. 440.5% gain. 3-0-2-0, $18,144.

$750,000 Unnamed, 2003 b. c., Indian Charlie—Tupelo Belle, by Turkoman. **Weanling Purchase:** $150,000, 2003 Keeneland November, by Gage Hill Stable. **Juvenile Sale:** $900,000, 2005 Barretts March, consigned by H. T. Stables, agent, purchased by John W. Sadler, agent. 500% gain. Unraced.

$725,000 UNCOMMON VALOR, 1997 b. h., Kris S. —Patchiano, by Fappiano. **Weanling Purchase:** $75,000, 1997 Keeneland November, by Tom Reeves. **Juvenile Sale:** $800,000, 1999 Fasig-Tipton Florida Calder February, consigned by Robert J. Harris, agent, purchased by Team Valor. 966.7% gain. 5-3-1-0, $86,200.

$600,000 DEBIT ACCOUNT, 1996 b. m., Mr. Prospector—Awesome Account, by Lyphard. **Weanling Purchase:** $350,000, 1996 Keeneland November, by Cypress Farms. **Juvenile Sale:** $950,000, 1998 Barretts March, consigned by Bailey-Ellenberg Select, purchased by Demi O'Byrne. 171.4% gain. 9-3-0-0, $70,260.

$565,000 GOLDEN PENNY, 2000 b. f., Touch Gold—Penny's Growl, by Strike Gold. **Weanling Purchase:** $85,000, 2000 Keeneland November, by The Narrows. **Juvenile Sale:** $650,000, 2002 Keeneland April, consigned by Tony Bowling and Bobby Dodd, agent, purchased by Robert B. and Beverly J. Lewis. 664.7% gain. 18-2-3-3, $65,634.

$558,000 NASEMA'S SLAM, 2002 dk b/br. f., Grand Slam—Nasema, by Encino. **Weanling Purchase:** $42,000, 2002 Keeneland November, by Luann Baker. **Juvenile**

Sale: $600,000, 2004 Fasig-Tipton Florida Calder February, consigned by Equine Legacy Farm, agent, purchased by Fleetwood and NW Management. 1,328.6% gain. 1-0-1-0, $9,000.

$530,000 SWISSLE STICK, 2002 ch. c., Swiss Yodeler—Miss Soft Sell, by Siyah Kalem. **Weanling Purchase:** $70,000, 2002 Keeneland November, by Terry Oliver, agent. **Juvenile Sale:** $600,000, 2004 Barretts March, consigned by Wavertree Stables, agent, purchased by Robert B. and Beverly J. Lewis. 757.1% gain. 10-1-2-0, $42,030.

$490,000 GOLDEN BAND, 1999 ch. m., Dixieland Band—Honey Bee Gold, by Drone. **Weanling Purchase:** $285,000, 1999 Keeneland November, by Cam Allard. **Juvenile Sale:** $775,000, 2001 Keeneland April, consigned by H. T. Stables, agent, purchased by Bob Baffert, agent. 171.9% gain. 6-1-2-2, $61,240.

$480,000 SARANOIA, 2000 dk b/br. c., Seattle Slew—Sharp Call, by Sharpen Up (GB). **Weanling Purchase:** $320,000, 2000 Keeneland November, by Chad Johnson, agent. **Juvenile Sale:** $800,000, 2002 Fasig-Tipton Florida Calder February, consigned by Terry Oliver, agent, purchased by Michael Gill. 150% gain. 6-0-1-1, $12,970.

$450,000 MARIANNE'S CAT, 2003 ch. f., Tale of the Cat—Marianne's Song, by Unbridled's Song. **Weanling Purchase:** $50,000, 2003 Keeneland November, by J. L. Simmons Bloodstock. **Juvenile Sale:** $500,000, 2005 Fasig-Tipton Florida Calder February, consigned by Ocala Oaks and Don R. Graham, agent, purchased by Demi O'Byrne. 900% gain. Unraced.

$425,000 RENUMBERED, 1999 b. h., Polish Numbers—Launchette, by Relaunch. **Weanling Purchase:** $40,000, 1999 Fasig-Tipton Midlantic December mixed, by Josham Farms. **Juvenile Sale:** $465,000, 2001 Fasig-Tipton Florida Calder February, consigned by Tony Bowling and Bobby Dodd, agent, purchased by F. Eugene Dixon. 1,062.5% gain. 8-1-0-1, $11,424.

$420,000 CONCERT STAR, 1996 b. h., Dehere—Minett, by Fappiano. **Weanling Purchase:** $230,000, 1996 Keeneland November, by Cypress Farms. **Juvenile Sale:** $650,000, 1998 Barretts March, consigned by Bailey-Ellenberg Select, purchased by Cabin Creek Farm. 182.6% gain. 14-2-0-1, $105,290.

Most Successful Pinhooks by Percentage Gain (through 3/30/2005)

Weanling to Juvenile

6,900.0% MR. ELUSIVE, 2000 dk b/br. c., Elusive Quality—Capote's Joy, by Capote. **Weanling Purchase:** $1,500, 2000 Keeneland November, by Silverwood, agent. **Juvenile Sale:** $105,000, 2002 Barretts Equine Ltd. spring two-year-olds in training, consigned by Timber Creek, agent, purchased by Larry O. and Veralene Hillis. $103,500 gain. 24-5-2-0, $87,728.

5,900.0% EISHIN GONZALES, 1997 b. h., Take Me Out—Aunt Mockey, by Our Native. **Weanling Purchase:** $4,500, 1997 Fasig-Tipton Kentucky fall mixed, by William D. Snyder. **Juvenile Sale:** $270,000, 1999 Fasig-Tipton Florida Calder February, consigned by Sequel Bloodstock, agent, purchased by Silky Green. $265,500 gain. 19-3-1-0, $308,887.

5,455.6% BIG BIG CASINO, 1998 dk b/br. h., Pioneering—Kelly's Super Pet, by Muscovite. **Weanling Purchase:** $1,800, 1998 Keeneland November, by Shari Kepsel. **Juvenile Sale:** $100,000, 2000 Barretts Equine Ltd. spring two-year-olds in training, Fairplex Park, consigned by Jerry Bailey Sales Agency, agent, purchased by Bruno de Berdt, agent. $98,200 gain. 4-1-1-1, $25,520.

4,185.7% OUR EMM, 2001 dk b/br. c., Our Emblem—Thoughts, by Seattle Slew. **Weanling Purchase:** $3,500, 2001 Keeneland November, by Clouston Farm. **Juvenile Sale:** $150,000, 2003 Keeneland April, consigned by American Equistock and Parrish Farms, purchased by International Equine Acquisitions. $146,500 gain. Unraced.

3,488.2% Mancari's Rose, 1996 b. m., Glitterman—Puddin Hill, by Afleet. **Weanling Purchase:** $8,500, 1996 Keeneland

November, by Jockey Club Farm. **Juvenile Sale:** $305,000, 1998 OBSC March, consigned by Jockey Club Farm, agent, purchased by William Bronstad. $296,500 gain. 6-1-0-1, spl, $33,275.

2,578.6% PRIME TIMBER, 1996 b. h., Sultry Song—Wine Taster, by Nodouble. **Weanling Purchase:** $14,000, 1996 Keeneland November, by Donna M. Wormser. **Juvenile Sale:** $375,000, 1998 OBSC February, consigned by Donna M. Wormser, agent, purchased by Aaron U. Jones. $361,000 gain. 17-4-4-0, G2, $621,238.

2,000.0% MAYAKOVSKY, 1999 dk b/br. h., Matty G—Joy to Raise, by Raise a Man. **Weanling Purchase:** $10,000, 1999 O.B.S. fall, by Gold Circle Racing. **Juvenile Sale:** $210,000, 2001 OBSC April, consigned by Eisaman Equine Services, agent, purchased by Robert N. Scanlon, agent. $200,000 gain. 9-3-1-0, G3, $275,200.

1,900.0% BEE MOUNTAIN, 1999 gr/ro. h., Cahill Road—Blockbuster Lady, by Northern Jove. **Weanling Purchase:** $15,000, 1999 Keeneland November, by J. S. Northern. **Juvenile Sale:** $300,000, 2001 OBSC March, consigned by Eisaman Equine Services, agent, purchased by Choctaw Racing Stable. $285,000 gain. 9-4-1-1, $81,775.

1,900.0% STORM HEARTED, 2002 b. f., Lion Hearted—Shallah, by Proud Truth. **Weanling Purchase:** $12,000, 2002 Fasig-Tipton Midlantic December mixed, by Short Term Stable. **Juvenile Sale:** $240,000, 2004 Barretts March, consigned by Paula Capestro Bloodstock, agent, purchased by C R K Stable. $228,000 gain. Unraced.

Least Successful Pinhooks by Total Loss (through 3/30/2005)
Weanling to Juvenile

–$325,000 NIJINSKY'S CROWN, 1999 ch. h., Gone West—Nijinsky's Lover, by Nijinsky II. **Weanling Purchase:** $725,000, 1999 Keeneland November, by R. A. Adkinson. **Juvenile Sale:** $400,000, 2001 Fasig-Tipton Florida Calder February, consigned by Robert N. Scanlon, agent, purchased by B.T.A. Stable. –44.8% loss. 3-0-0-0, $0.

–$245,000 Alive With Hope, 1991 ch. m., Alydar—Awesome Account, by Lyphard. **Weanling Purchase:** $400,000, 1991 Keeneland November, by Oaktown Stable. **Juvenile Sale:** $155,000, 1993 Keeneland November, consigned by Jonabell Farm, agent, purchased by Millhouse. –61.3% loss. 18-6-2-3, spl, $184,631.

–$210,000 HATSURATSU, 2000 ch. c., Pulpit—Afare, by Meadowlake. **Weanling Purchase:** $360,000, 2000 Keeneland November, by Bohanon-Walden LLC. **Juvenile Sale:** $150,000, 2002 Fasig-Tipton Florida Calder February, consigned by Maurice W. Miller, agent, purchased by Everglades Stable. –58.3% loss. 11-3-2-0, $419,354.

–$193,000 SEGUIN, 1997 ch. h., Miswaki—Anytimeatall, by It's Freezing. **Weanling Purchase:** $195,000, 1997 Keeneland November, by Horse France. **Juvenile Sale:** $2,000, 1999 Keeneland April, consigned by Hartley/De Renzo Thoroughbreds LLC, agent, purchased by Spring Farm. –99% loss. 13-1-1-3, $24,774.

–$179,000 GRAY EMBLEM, 2002 gr/ro. f., Our Emblem—Lingquoit, by Waquoit. **Weanling Purchase:** $200,000, 2002 Keeneland November, by Venture One Partnership. **Juvenile Sale:** $21,000, 2004 OBSC April, consigned by SAB Training, agent, purchased by Gary Owens. –89.5% loss. 1-0-0-0, $0.

–$175,000 PRICELY GEM, 2003 b. c., Honour and Glory—Thirty Six Carat, by Meadowlake. **Weanling Purchase:** $210,000, 2003 Keeneland November, by Jack Smith. **Juvenile Sale:** $35,000, 2005 Barretts March, consigned by Excel Bloodstock, agent, purchased by NJ Cal Breeders. –83.3% loss. Unraced.

–$163,000 PAPPA'S MONEY, 1996 ch. g., St. Jovite—Queen of Bronze, by Roberto. **Weanling Purchase:** $180,000, 1996 Keeneland November, by Cypress Farms. **Juvenile Sale:** $17,000, 1998 Barretts March, consigned by Bailey-Ellenberg Select, purchased by Dale V. Ray. –90.6% loss. 10-1-0-0, $4,552.

–$158,000 CHET, 2002 dk b/br. c., Chester House—King's Pact, by Slewacide. **Weanling Purchase:** $170,000, 2002 Keeneland November, by Dromoland Farm and Hartwell Farm. **Juvenile Sale:** $12,000, 2004 Keeneland April, consigned by Robert N. Scanlon, agent, purchased by Rosebud Stable. –92.9% loss. 9-1-0-1, $8,890.

–$140,000 NO BID, 1995 b. m., Rahy—Learycal, by Lear Fan. **Weanling Purchase:** $165,000, 1995 Keeneland November, by Ward C. Pitfield. **Juvenile Sale:** $25,000, 1997 Keeneland April, consigned by Kirkwood Stables, agent, purchased by Philip M. Hauswald, agent. –84.8% loss. Unraced.

–$140,000 UNDEFINED, 2001 gr/ro. c., Unbridled's Song—Star On the Move, by Blade. **Weanling Purchase:** $250,000, 2001 Keeneland November, by Wood Ridge Thoroughbreds. **Juvenile Sale:** $110,000, 2003 Fasig-Tipton Florida Calder February, consigned by Terry Oliver, agent, purchased by Estable. –56% loss. 6-0-2-1, $53,691.

–$131,000 Unnamed, 1998 ch. h., Forest Wildcat—Musical Precedent, by Seattle Song. **Weanling Purchase:** $140,000, 1998 Keeneland November, by A. Cafferrata. **Juvenile Sale:** $9,000, 2000 Fasig-Tipton Midlantic two-year-olds in training, consigned by Eddie Woods, agent, purchased by Sean C. Magee, agent. –93.6% loss. Unraced.

–$130,000 TRY AGAIN LEN, 2000 ch. c., Silver Deputy—Nickle Lady, by Plugged Nickle. **Weanling Purchase:** $150,000, 2000 Keeneland November, by Talus Bloodstock. **Juvenile Sale:** $20,000, 2002 OBSC March, consigned by Niall Brennan, agent, purchased by Jeff Pitzer. –86.7% loss. 3-1-0-0, $13,237.

Least Successful Pinhooks by Percentage Loss (through 3/30/2005)
Weanling to Juvenile

–99.0% SEGUIN, 1997 ch. h., Miswaki—Anytimeatall, by It's Freezing. **Weanling Purchase:** $195,000, 1997 Keeneland November, by Horse France. **Juvenile Sale:** $2,000, 1999 Keeneland April, consigned by Hartley/De Renzo Thoroughbreds LLC, agent, purchased by Spring Farm. –$193,000 loss. 13-1-1-3, $24,774.

–93.6% Unnamed, 1998 ch. h., Forest Wildcat—Musical Precedent, by Seattle Song. **Weanling Purchase:** $140,000, 1998 Keeneland November, by A. Cafferrata. **Juvenile Sale:** $9,000, 2000 Fasig-Tipton Midlantic two-year-olds in training, consigned by Eddie Woods, agent, purchased by Sean C. Magee, agent. –$131,000 loss. Unraced.

–92.9% CHET, 2002 dk b/br. c., Chester House—King's Pact, by Slewacide. **Weanling Purchase:** $170,000, 2002 Keeneland November, by Dromoland Farm and Hartwell Farm. **Juvenile Sale:** $12,000, 2004 Keeneland April, consigned by Robert N. Scanlon, agent, purchased by Rosebud Stable. –$158,000 loss. 9-1-0-1, $8,890.

–90.6% PAPPA'S MONEY, 1996 ch. g., St. Jovite—Queen of Bronze, by Roberto. **Weanling Purchase:** $180,000, 1996 Keeneland November, by Cypress Farms. **Juvenile Sale:** $17,000, 1998 Barretts March, consigned by Bailey-Ellenberg Select, purchased by Dale V. Ray. –$163,000 loss. 10-1-0-0, $4,552.

–90.0% ROYAL TROMP'E, 2001 b. f., Cozzene—Attractive Crown, by Chief's Crown. **Weanling Purchase:** $100,000, 2001 Keeneland November, by Michael R. Duffy. **Juvenile Sale:** $10,000, 2003 Fasig-Tipton Midlantic two-year-olds in training, consigned by Eddie Woods, agent, purchased by Kathleen P. Mongeon, agent. –$90,000 loss. 8-0-2-0, $20,170.

–89.5% GRAY EMBLEM, 2002 gr/ro.f., Our Emblem—Lingquoit, by Waquoit. **Weanling Purchase:** $200,000, 2002 Keeneland November, by Venture One Partnership. **Juvenile Sale:** $21,000, 2004 OBSC April, consigned by SAB Training, agent, purchased by Gary Owens. –$179,000 loss. 1-0-0-0, $0.

–88.7% MEADOWLAKE JOHN, 2000 b.c., Meadowlake—Flowers for M'lady, by Stage Door Johnny. **Weanling Purchase:** $115,000, 2000 Keeneland November, by Granite Hill. **Juvenile Sale:** $13,000, 2002 Fasig-Tipton Midlantic two-year-olds in training, consigned by Eddie Woods, agent, purchased by Jeffrey Gasperini. –$102,000 loss. 15-2-1-1, $39,783.

–88.6% JUDITH'S DEPUTY, 1999 ch. m., Silver Deputy—Solar Display, by Diesis (GB). **Weanling Purchase:** $140,000, 1999 Keeneland November, by Green Bridge Stud. **Juvenile Sale:** $16,000, 2001 OBSC April, consigned by Robert N. Scanlon, agent, purchased by Harvey Tenenbaum. –$124,000 loss. Unraced.

–86.7% TRY AGAIN LEN, 2000 ch. c., Silver Deputy—Nickle Lady, by Plugged Nickle. **Weanling Purchase:** $150,000, 2000 Keeneland November, by Talus Bloodstock. **Juvenile Sale:** $20,000, 2002 OBSC March, consigned by Niall Brennan, agent, purchased by Jeff Pitzer. –$130,000 loss. 3-1-0-0, $13,237.

–85.3% SWEETIEPIEOFMYEYE, 2000 dk b/br. f., Red Ransom—Brittan Lee, by Forty Niner. **Weanling Purchase:** $150,000, 2000 Keeneland November, by Geraldine Scullion. **Juvenile Sale:** $22,000, 2002 Keeneland April, consigned by Robert N. Scanlon, agent, purchased by Dick Lossen, agent. –$128,000 loss. 5-1-1-1, $7,468.

–85.0% SKY TO WIN, 1996 ch. h., Fly So Free—Yoda, by Proudest Roman. **Weanling Purchase:** $100,000, 1996 Keeneland November, by Rollin W. Baugh, agent. **Juvenile Sale:** $15,000, 1998 Barretts Spring two-year-olds in training and horses of racing age, consigned by Rollin W. Baugh, agent, purchased by J. J. Eaton Racing Stable. –$85,000 loss. Unraced.

Notable Dispersals

Because of their selective and exclusive nature, dispersals have long been noted for high prices and long-term influence on the breeding industry. Most frequently, dispersals occur when a major breeder dies or decides to retire. Historically, that has meant that high-class bloodlines previously unavailable are on the market, attracting the most ambitious and wealthy breeders of a younger generation.

The first notable American dispersal was in 1891 when the stud of the late August Belmont I totaled $515,150. A large chunk of the total receipts came from Charles Reed's astonishing

record bid of $100,000 for that year's leading sire, *St. Blaise.

Marcus Daly was a buyer at Belmont's dispersal, and when Daly died nine years later, financiers W. C. Whitney and James R. Keene were buyers at the dispersal of Daly's Bitter Root Stud. Whitney's and Keene's dispersals a few years later provided the foundations for the studs of Whitney's descendants and other great American breeders, including E. R. Bradley's Idle Hour Stock Farm.

The current record is $46,912,800 set by the dispersal of Nelson Bunker Hunt's Bluegrass Farm in 1988.

Notable North American Bloodstock Dispersals

Year	Dispersal	No. Sold	Total	Avg.	Notable Horses	Sale Company
1998	Fares Farm (Issam Fares)	232	$26,805,400	$115,541	Lady's Secret, Miss Alleged, November Snow	Keeneland
1998	Claiborne Farm/Nicole Perry Gorman	34	21,205,000	623,676	Limit	Keeneland
1997	Buckland Farm (Thomas Mellon Evans)	124	12,563,000	101,315	Meteor Stage	Keeneland
1996	Windfields Farm (Charles Taylor)	68	7,238,000	106,441	Baltic Sea, La Lorgnette	Keeneland
1992	Rokeby Stable (Paul Mellon)	32	6,294,600	196,706	Glowing Tribute, Wild Applause	
1991	Calumet Farm	185	15,068,500	81,451	Stick to Beauty, Tis Juliet	Keeneland
1989	Oxford Stable (Ralph C. Wilson Jr.)	46	18,572,700	379,034	Arazi, Fabuleux Jane	Keeneland
1989	Eugene Klein	114	29,623,000	259,851	Open Mind, Winning Colors, Lady's Secret	Keeneland, Fasig-Tipton Co.
1988	Nelson Bunker Hunt	580	46,912,800	80,884	Dahlia, Sangue (Ire), Highest Trump	Keeneland
1987	Hermitage Farm (Warner L. Jones Jr.)	130	32,676,500	251,358	My Charmer, Kamar, Seaside Attraction	Keeneland
1987	Tartan Farms/John Nerud	194	25,634,000	132,134	Unbridled, Gana Facil, Funistrada	Fasig-Tipton Co.
1986	Spendthrift Farm	163	19,171,700	117,618	Lillian Russell, Anne Campbell	Keeneland
1985	Newstead Farm (Hardin family)	42	37,186,000	885,381	Miss Oceana, Magic of Life, White Star Line	Fasig-Tipton Co.
1972	George D. Widener	69	6,643,700	96,286	What a Treat, Patelin, Seven Thirty	Fasig-Tipton Co.
1972	A. B. Hancock Jr./W. H. Perry	35	2,580,000	73,714	Sham, Apalachee	Fasig-Tipton Co.
1969	Cain Hoy Stable (Harry F. Guggenheim)	137	4,751,200	34,688	Riverman, Bold Reason, Too Bald, San San	Keeneland, Fasig-Tipton Co.
1967	Charlton Clay	18	796,100	44,228	Rose Bower, Leallah	Keeneland
1967	Maine Chance Farm (Elizabeth N. Graham)	83	1,270,700	15,310	Ribbons and Bows	Keeneland
1966-'70	Bieber-Jacobs Stable	175	3,851,000	22,005	Admiring, Priceless Gem	Keeneland, Timonium, Saratoga, Ocala, Pomona
1965	William duPont Jr.	51	2,401,300	47,084	Berlo, Parlo, All Beautiful	Maryland Breeders Sales Co.
1958	Louis B. Mayer	59	821,000	13,915	Popularity	Fasig-Tipton
1955-'56	Belair Stud (William Woodward Jr.)	59	2,475,600	41,959	Segula, Vagrancy	Keeneland
1955	Almahurst Farm (Henry Knight)	68	1,035,800	15,232	Almahmoud	Fasig-Tipton Co.
1951	Coldstream Stud (C.B. Shaffer)	48	990,500	20,635	Be Faithful, Spotted Beauty	Keeneland
1947-'50	Louis B. Mayer	248	4,479,650	18,063	Busher, Your Host, Honeymoon	Fasig-Tipton Co.
1935	Shoshone Stud (W. R. Coe)	86	201,090	2,338	Pompey, Pilate	Fasig-Tipton Co.
1925	Nursery Stud (August Belmont II)	68	782,000	11,500	Fair Play, *Quelle Chance	Joseph E. Widener
1913	Castleton Stud (James R. Keene)	45	229,000	5,088	Peter Pan, Colin, Sweep, Ultimus	Kentucky Sales Co.
1905	Rancho del Paso (James B. A. Haggin)	401	405,325	1,010	*Watercress, Colonial	Fasig-Tipton Co.
1904	LaBelle Stud (W. C. Whitney)	91	463,650	5,095	Hamburg, *Meddler, Endurance by Right	Fasig-Tipton Co.
1901	Bitter Root Stud (Marcus Daly)	186	406,525	2,185	Hamburg, *Pastorella	Fasig-Tipton Co.
1891	Nursery Stud (August Belmont I)	102	515,150	5,050	*St. Blaise	Tattersalls of New York

ORGANIZATIONS
Jockey Club

The Jockey Club, one of the Thoroughbred industry's most powerful and influential organizations, derives much of its strength from its position as the registration agency for all North American Thoroughbreds and from a membership comprising most of the sport's leading breeders and owners. In its distant past, the Jockey Club also was a regulator of racing; today, it has utilized advancing computer technology to expand its role and influence.

The Jockey Club grew out of meetings in late 1893 in which leading owners addressed the question of how to reform an unruly and corrupt racing industry. Two years earlier, prominent owner Pierre Lorillard had founded the Board of Control, but it largely represented the interests of racetrack owners, many of whom also were leading owners of racehorses. Alarmed that the racetrack owners might reduce purses, James R. Keene and seven fellow owners and breeders met on December 23 and 27, 1893, in a New York hotel to form an organization that represented the interests of both racetracks and racehorse owners. The goals of the organization were "not only to encourage the development of the Thoroughbred horse, but to establish racing on such a footing that it may command the interests as well as the confidence and favorable position of the public."

The organization was formally incorporated on February 9, 1894, as the Jockey Club, taking its name from the foundation institution in England. John Hunter was the first chairman of the American organization.

Although the Jockey Club today maintains the *American Stud Book*, it did not set out in 1894 to fulfill that function. Since 1868, Col. Sanders D. Bruce had been publishing a stud book of American pedigrees, and the Jockey Club wrote to him that it "does not propose to publish a stud book, but to keep a record of foals in the interest and for the protection of racing." The parallel projects proved to be incompatible, however, and on May 17, 1897, the Jockey Club purchased the six volumes of the *American Stud Book* previously published by Bruce, plus all related works and copyrights, for $35,000.

One of the Jockey Club's original goals was to bring order to racing in New York and New Jersey, and it played a significant role in developing the rules of racing for the East Coast and eventually the entire United States. Its influence in that area waned as the system of state racing commissions developed in the 1930s and it lost a court case involving Jule Fink in the '50s, but it remains the official registrar of racing silks in New York.

Maintaining the sport's integrity has been the thread that runs through the Jockey Club's history, and the organization has been at the forefront of precise identification of horses. The Jockey Club adopted the photographing of night eyes—the structure on the inside of the leg that in the horse is the equivalent of a fingerprint—as a method of identifying Thoroughbreds. In the 1970s, the Jockey Club adopted blood-typing as an identification tool, and, with the foal crop of 2001, began DNA testing as a definitive verification of parentage.

In July 1953, Jockey Club Chairman George D. Widener convened in New York a meeting of 18 owners, racing officials, and journalists to discuss a wide range of issues facing the industry. The following year, the meeting was moved to Saratoga Springs, New York, and now is known as the Jockey Club Round Table Conference on Matters Pertaining to Racing.

The Jockey Club has developed the world's most extensive database of race records and pedigrees of Thoroughbreds. It has complete information for all North American racing from 1930 to the present. In recent years it has been able to work with other countries' registrars to obtain complete racing information and pedigrees from the world's major racing countries. The Jockey Club also has utilized its technology to develop a family of subsidiaries and affiliated companies.

Lexington Office
821 Corporate Dr.
Lexington, Ky. 40503
Phone: (859) 224-2700
Fax: (859) 224-2710
Website: *www.jockeyclub.com*

New York Office
40 East 52nd St.
New York, N.Y. 10022
Phone: (212) 371-5970
Fax: (212) 371-6123

Officers
Chairman: Ogden Mills Phipps
Vice Chairman: William S. Farish
Secretary-Treasurer: James C. Brady
President: Alan Marzelli
Executive Vice President, Executive Director: Dan Fick
Executive Vice President, Chief Financial Officer: Laura Barillaro
Executive Vice President, Chief Administrative Officer: James L. Gagliano

Stewards

John Barr	James C. Brady
Donald Dizney	William S. Farish
Dell Hancock	G. Watts Humphrey Jr.
Stuart S. Janney III	John C. Oxley
Ogden Mills Phipps	

Members

Josephine E. Abercrombie	Helen C. Alexander
Joseph L. Allbritton	John Ed Anthony
William Backer	Charles Baker
John Barr	James E. Bassett III
Rollin Baugh	John A. Bell III
Reynolds Bell Jr.	Gary Biszantz
Edward S. Bonnie	Frank A. Bonsal Jr.
James C. Brady	Nicholas F. Brady
Larry Bramlage, D.V.M.	Michael C. Byrne
Alexander G. Campbell Jr.	Thomas R. Capehart
Charles J. Cella	Alice H. Chandler
Helen B. Chenery	Sherwood C. Chillingworth
Duke of Devonshire CBE	Robert N. Clay
F. Eugene Dixon Jr.	Donald R. Dizney
Allan R. Dragone	Jack J. Dreyfus Jr.
Richard L. Duchossois	C. Steven Duncker
William duPont III	Allaire duPont
Edward P. Evans	Robert S. Evans

William S. Farish
Hugh A. Fitzsimons Jr.
John K. Goodman
Lucy Young Hamilton
Dell Hancock
Joseph W. Harper
John Hettinger
G. Watts Humphrey Jr.
Richard I. G. Jones
Peter F. Karches
Robert B. Lewis
William C. MacMillen Jr.
Frank L. Mansell
James K. McManus
Robert E. Meyerhoff
MacKenzie Miller
Kenneth Noe Jr.
Michael O'Farrell Jr.
John H. Peace
Hiram C. Polk Jr., M.D.
Ogden Mills Phipps
Reuben F. Richards
Jack K. Robbins, V.M.D.
Timothy H. Sams
Joseph V. Shields Jr.
Barry Schwartz
Viola Sommer
George Strawbridge Jr.
Stella Thayer
Donald J. Valpredo
Frank "Scoop" Vessells III
Charlotte C. Weber
David Willmot
William T. Young Jr.

William S. Farish Jr.
Martha F. Gerry
Louis L. Haggin III
Arthur B. Hancock III
Seth W. Hancock
John C. Harris
E. Edward Houghton
Stuart S. Janney III
Russell B. Jones Jr.
Gary Lavin
F. Jack Liebau
Harry T. Mangurian Jr.
J. W. Y. Martin Jr.
Robert McNair
Leverett Miller
Nick Nicholson
Charles Nuckols Jr. J .
John C. Oxley
John W. Phillips
Carl Pollard
David P. Reynolds
J. David Richardson, M.D.
J. Mack Robinson
Richard Santulli
Peter G. Schiff
Mace Siegal
Robert S. Strauss
Shirley H. Taylor
Oakleigh B. Thorne
Daniel G. Van Clief Jr.
Joseph Walker Jr.
Wheelock Whitney
Martin Wygod

Jockey Club Chairmen

Chairman	Term
Ogden Mills Phipps	February 10, 1983—present
August Belmont IV	May 3, 1982—February 10, 1983
Nicholas F. Brady	January 12, 1974—April 19, 1982
Odgen Phipps	January 7, 1964—January 12, 1974
George D. Widener	January 12, 1950—January 7, 1964
William Woodward	November 3, 1930—January 12, 1950
Frank K. Sturgis	December 30, 1924—November 3, 1930
August Belmont II	January 24, 1895—December 10, 1924
John Hunter	March 1, 1894—January 24, 1895

Jockey Club subsidiaries
Jockey Club Information Systems Inc.

The Jockey Club Information Systems Inc., incorporated in 1989, is a wholly owned subsidiary of Jockey Club Holdings Inc. All profits from its activities are reinvested in the Thoroughbred industry and helps to finance industry projects. The organization has three divisions: Information Services, Cataloguing, and Software Sales and Consulting. In 2000, it launched equineline.com, (*www.equineline.com*), an Internet-based information and communication network. Through equineline, the Jockey Club sells information—pedigrees of horses, race records, sire progeny records, produce records of dams, etc.—online to customers. Under the equineline banner, the Lexington-based organization has launched management programs for horse owners and breeders, trainers, and farms.

Phone: (859) 224-2800 or (800) 333-1778
Fax: (859) 224-2810
Website: *www.tjcis.com*
Chairman and Chief Executive Officer: Carl E. Hamilton

Secretary-Treasurer: Laura Barillaro
Board Members: Reynolds Bell Jr., C. Steven Duncker, Robert S. Evans, Carl E. Hamilton, Alan Marzelli, John Phillips, and Ogden Mills Phipps

InCompass

InCompass, a wholly owned subsidiary of Jockey Club Holdings Inc., was created in November 2001. Formerly known as McKinnie Systems, InCompass provided recordkeeping and operational assistance to racing offices and horsemen's bookkeepers at more than 70 client racetracks in 2004. Functions include attendance and wagering tracking, race entries, and horsemen's bookkeeper applications.

Phone: (859) 296-3000 or (800) 625-4664
Fax: (859) 296-3010
Website: *www.incompass-solutions.com*
Chairman: Alan Marzelli
President: David Haydon
Secretary-Treasurer: Laura Barillaro

Grayson-Jockey Club Research Foundation

Established in 1940 to raise funds for equine veterinary research, the Grayson Foundation was combined in 1989 with the similarly chartered Jockey Club Research Foundation. The Lexington-based foundation, which solicits contributions from the Thoroughbred community, allocated nearly $850,000 in research grants in 2004, raising its total contributions to nearly $10-million since the merger. In 2001 and '02, it contributed more than $250,000 for research into mare reproductive loss syndrome (MRLS).

Phone: (859) 224-2850
Fax: (859) 224-2853
Website: *www.grayson-jockeyclub.org*
E-mail: contactus@grayson-jockeyclub.org

Chairman: Dell Hancock
Chairman Emeritus: John Hettinger
Secretary-Treasurer: Laura Barillaro
President: Edward L. Bowen
Vice President of Development: Nancy C. Kelly
Board Members: Josephine Abercrombie, William Backer, Larry Bramlage, D.V.M., William Condren, Adele Dilschneider, Allaire duPont, William Farish Jr., John Goodman, Lucy Young Hamilton, Dell Hancock, Joseph W. Harper, Eugene Melnyk, Leverett Miller, Kenneth Noe Jr., John M. B. O'Connor, John C. Oxley, Ogden Mills Phipps, Hiram Polk Jr., M.D., Jack Robbins, V.M.D., and Joseph V. Shields Jr.

The Jockey Club Foundation

Established in 1943, the Jockey Club Foundation provides confidential financial assistance to needy members of the Thoroughbred industry and their families. The New York-based foundation distributed more than $600,000 in 2004.

Phone: (212) 521-5305
Fax: (212) 371-6123
Website: *www.tjcfoundation.org*
Trustees: John Hettinger, C. Steven Duncker, D. G. Van Clief Jr.
Secretary-Treasurer: Laura Barillaro
Executive Director: Nancy C. Kelly

National Thoroughbred Racing Association

With its founding in 1998, the National Thoroughbred Racing Association immediately became one of the industry's leading organizations. The NTRA originated in part from a "Guest Commentary" by Lexington advertising executive Fred Pope in the August 27, 1993, issue of THOROUGHBRED TIMES. Pope, an associate of Breeders' Cup founder John Gaines, suggested that horse owners pool their media rights—the images of their horses in races—and establish a major league of racing. With the funds generated from simulcasting the sport's leading races, the proposed owners' association—the National Thoroughbred Association—would market the sport to the American public.

The industry was not ready for Pope's idea in 1993, but three years later full-card simulcasting had exploded across the nation and provided a new stream of revenue for racing. Former Carter White House aides Hamilton Jordan and Tim Smith were hired by Pope and Gaines to sell the NTA concept to the Thoroughbred industry. Although not accepted by the racetracks, Pope's idea—that the sport needed a national presence and national marketing—gained momentum, and in March 1997 four industry organizations—Breeders' Cup Ltd., the Jockey Club, Keeneland Association, and Oak Tree Racing Association—put up $1-million each as seed money for a new organization to market the sport. In a short time, the new entity was named the National Thoroughbred Racing Association, and the efforts of the NTA were effectively folded into it. (The NTA formally merged into the NTRA in August 1998, and Pope was compensated for his intellectual property.)

Even with the backing of industry leaders, the NTRA was not a sure bet to be supported by racetracks and national organizations. Breeders' Cup President D. G. Van Clief Jr., serving as the NTRA's interim chief executive, and Jockey Club Executive Director Nick Nicholson traveled throughout the country to sell the concept of a national office to market racing to industry participants. They gained sufficient backing and a business plan was released in December 1997. The NTRA formally began operation on April 1, 1998. Its first commissioner and chief executive officer was Smith, who, after leaving the White House, had served as deputy commissioner of the Professional Golfers' Association Tour and had helped to reorganize the Association of Tennis Professionals Tour.

The NTRA's first priority was marketing, and it produced an edgy, attention-grabbing national television advertisement featuring actress Lori Petty. Industry members, however, panned the ad, and the NTRA could not replicate its success through subsequent marketing campaigns, including spots that featured actor Rip Torn. In its first years, the NTRA ventured beyond marketing, opening subsidiary operations such as NTRA Services, NTRA Investments, NTRA Productions (for television production), and NTRA Charities. The NTRA became the producer of the Eclipse Awards, assuming a role formerly held by Thoroughbred Racing Associations.

By the end of 1999, several racetrack executives, including Magna Entertainment Corp.'s Frank Stronach and a group of Mid-Atlantic track owners, complained that the NTRA had veered away from its original marketing mandate and had entered business enterprises where it was in competition with tracks, notably by operating a telephone-wagering hub in Oregon for Television Games Network. Some of the Mid-Atlantic tracks pulled out of the NTRA but returned later, while Stronach was appeased when more racetrack representation was added to the NTRA board of directors, including a seat for a Stronach representative. Also that year, NTRA transferred operation of the Oregon hub to TVG.

NTRA's continuing budget deficits contributed to a decision in 2000 to merge many of its operations with Breeders' Cup Ltd., and the merger took place on January 1, 2001. Smith remained commissioner and Van Clief became the NTRA's vice chairman. By the end of 2001, many NTRA functions had been melded into the Breeders' Cup operation. Smith resigned in 2004, and Van Clief was named commissioner on an interim basis. His appointment became permanent in April 2005.

In recent years, the NTRA has worked to build the sport's fan base through increased television exposure, consumer research, and promotion of the Breeders' Cup World Thoroughbred Championships. The NTRA has increased its lobbying and group-purchasing efforts, and it has proved effective in crisis management, particularly in the 2002 Breeders' Cup Ultra Pick Six scandal.

2525 Harrodsburg Rd.
Lexington, Ky. 40504
Phone: (859) 223-5444
Fax: (859) 223-3945
Website: *www.ntra.com*
E-mail: ntra@ntra.com

Commissioner and Chief Executive Officer: D. G. Van Clief Jr.
Executive Vice President: Robert Clay

Directors: John Amerman, Robert Elliston, Alan Foreman, Craig Fravel, Bruce Garland, Charles Hayward, G. Watts Humphrey Jr., Jim McAlpine, Tom Meeker, Nick Nicholson, Ogden Mills Phipps, John Roark, D. G. Van Clief Jr.

Thoroughbred Racing Associations

In January 1942, racing's representatives to the National Association of State Racing Commissioners convention perceived themselves to be in a war-related emergency and convened a meeting that March in Chicago. The object of the meeting initially was to pull together all elements of the industry into a single ruling organization.

The two-day meeting that began on March 19, 1942, would not yield an overall ruling body for the fractious and fragmented industry. However, at that meeting, 33 executives of 22 racetracks formed the Thoroughbred Racing Associations of the United States, with Hialeah Park President John C. Clark as its first president. The organization was formally incorporated on May 22, 1942. (The name subsequently was changed to the Thoroughbred Racing Associations of North America when Canada's tracks joined the organization.)

Representatives to the March 1942 meeting realized that they could not conduct racing throughout the war strictly as an entertainment vehicle, and the Turf Committee of America was formed to raise funds to support the war effort.

New challenges awaited in the postwar years; chief among them was the integrity of the sport. In 1946, at the behest of Federal Bureau of Investigation Director J. Edgar Hoover (an avid racing fan), the TRA formed the Thoroughbred Racing Protective Bureau. A former FBI agent, Spencer J. Drayton, became the first director of the TRPB and instituted practices such as fingerprinting of all licensees, from hotwalkers to owners.

Drayton became the TRA's executive vice president in 1960, and his appointment resulted in the resignation of five racetracks. He retired in 1974, and, since '76, the TRA has had only two executive vice presidents, J. B. Faulconer and Christopher N. Scherf (since 1988).

In 1950, the TRA had begun to select its own end-of-year champions, which sometimes differed from those chosen by the *Daily Racing Form*, which established its poll in 1936. Faulconer was given the task of unifying the championships in 1971. Then president of Turf Publicists of America, Faulconer brought together the TRA, *Daily Racing Form*, and the National Turf Writers Association to launch the Eclipse Awards that year. In the late 1990s, the National Thoroughbred Racing Association supplanted the TRA as the industry's representative to the Eclipse Awards.

420 Fair Hill Dr., Suite 1
Elkton, Md. 21921-2573
Phone: (410) 392-9200

Fax: (410) 398-1366
Website: *www.tra-online.com*
e-mail: info@tra-online.com

President: Corey S. Johnsen
Vice Presidents: C. Kenneth Dunn, David S. Willmot
Secretary: Robert L. Bork
Treasurer: William I. Fasy
Executive Vice President: Christopher N. Scherf

Directors: Don Amos, Charles W. Bidwill III, Robert L. Bork, Michael Brown, Thomas F. Carey III, Charles J. Cella, Sherwood C. Chillingworth, Joseph A. De Francis, Dennis O. Dowd, Steve Duncker, C. Kenneth Dunn, Robert N. Elliston, Robert A. Farinella, James L. Gagliano, William Gallo Jr., Clifford C. Goodrich, Robert W. Green, Harold G. Handel, Joseph W. Harper, Charles E. Hayward, Corey S. Johnsen, Peter Karches, Robert P. Levy, F. Jack Liebau, Jim McAlpine, Christopher McErlean, Hugh M. Miner Jr., Jerry M. Monahan, Richard E. Moore, Howard M. Mosner Jr., Nick Nicholson, William M. Rickman Jr., Charles J. Ruma, Randall D. Sampson, Christopher N. Scherf, Richard T. Schnaars, Sal Sinatra, Randall E. Soth, Ronald A. Sultemeier, Stella F. Thayer, Ray A. Tromba, Scott Wells, David S. Willmot

TRA Presidents

Term	President	Representing
1942-'43	John C. Clark	Hialeah
1944-'46	Henry A. Parr II	Pimlico
1947-'48	James E. Dooley	Narragansett
1949-'50	Donald P. Ross Sr.	Delaware
1951-'52	Alfred G. Vanderbilt	Belmont
1953-'54	John A. Morris	Jamaica
1955-'56	Amory L. Haskell	Monmouth
1957-'58	James D. Stewart	Hollywood
1959-'60	John G. Cella	Oaklawn
1961-'62	E. E. Dale Shaffer	Detroit Race Course
1963-'64	Robert P. Strub	Santa Anita
1965-'66	Edward P. Taylor	Ontario Jockey Club
1967-'68	Louis Lee Haggin II	Keeneland
1969-'70	John D. Schapiro	Laurel
1971-'73	James E. Brock	Ak-Sar-Ben
1973-'75	Frank M. Basil	New York Racing Association
1975-'76	Charles J. Cella	Oaklawn
1977-'78	Baird C. Brittingham	Delaware
1979-'80	Robert S. Gunderson	Bay Meadows
1981-'82	Lynn Stone	Churchill Downs
1983-'84	Morris J. Alhadeff	Longacres
1985-'86	James E. Bassett III	Keeneland
1987-'88	Gerard J. McKeon	New York Racing Association
1989-'90	Robert P. Levy	Atlantic City
1991-'92	Thomas H. Meeker	Churchill Downs
1993-'94	David M. Vance	Remington
1995-'96	Clifford C. Goodrich	Santa Anita
1997-'98	Harold G. Handel	New Jersey Sports and Exposition Authority
1999-2000	Stella F. Thayer	Tampa Bay Downs
2001-'02	Bryan G. Krantz	Fair Grounds
2003-'04	Joseph W. Harper	Del Mar
2005-'06	Corey S. Johnsen	Lone Star Park

Thoroughbred Racing Protective Bureau

Modeled after the Federal Bureau of Investigation and initially staffed by former FBI agents, the Thoroughbred Racing Protective Bureau is the investigative and security arm of the Thoroughbred Racing Associations of North America. The TRPB was founded in January 1946 to protect the integrity of the sport.

420 Fair Hill Dr., Suite 2
Elkton, Md. 21921-2573
Phone: (410) 398-2261
Fax: (410) 398-1499

Web site: *www.trpb.com*
E-mail: trpbinfo@trpb.com
President and Treasurer: Franklin J. Fabian
Vice President and Secretary: James P. Gowen
Chairman: John E. Mooney
Vice Chairman: Bryan Krantz
Directors: Robert L. Bork, Charles J. Cella, Sherwood Chillingworth, C. Kenneth Dunn, Franklin J. Fabian, James L. Gagliano, Bryan Krantz, Chris McErlean, Terence J. Meyocks, John E. Mooney, Nick Nicholson, Richard Schnaars, Stella F. Thayer

Equibase

Equibase Co. LLC, a general partnership of the Thoroughbred Racing Associations of North America (TRA) and the Jockey Club, is the official source of all racehorse past performances and racing data in North America. It was founded in 1991 because the racetracks and racing authorities at that time did not possess their own database of racing performance, nor did they have free access to the information. Rather, an independent daily newspaper, *Daily Racing Form,* compiled and owned all racing records of horses starting in North America.

For decades previous, racetracks published an official program containing official betting numbers and such basic information as a horse's pedigree, owner, trainer, jockey, post position, morning-line betting odds, and colors of each owner's racing silks. Past performances were the exclusive province of the *Daily Racing Form.*

Equibase began operation in 1991 with its own chart callers for the purpose of creating past-performance lines that could be used in programs sold by racetracks. (The charts, a statistical description of a race and each horse's running position, are the raw materials of past-performance lines.) To help subsidize the start-up, each participating track pledged 25 cents from each program sold to be paid to Equibase. While some tracks began to publish magazine-sized official programs with Equibase past performances, a significant competitor to *Daily Racing Form* emerged when *Racing Times,* backed by England-based publishing magnate Robert Maxwell, began operation. *Racing Times* purchased its past-performance lines from Equibase. *Racing Times* was making inroads into the *Racing Form*'s monopoly when Maxwell drowned off the Canary Islands in late 1991, and his empire collapsed.

The magazine-sized programs, which usually sold for about one-third of the price of *Daily Racing Form,* gradually became popular with race-goers, which sharply reduced *Daily Racing Form*'s circulation. In 1998, after years of negotiations between the two parties, Equibase became the sole data-collection agency, with *Daily Racing Form* dropping its collection efforts and thereafter purchasing its racing information from Equibase. Today, Equibase provides information to more than 100 tracks and 1,100 simulcast outlets, as well as to *Daily Racing Form, Sports-Eye,* several online resellers, and the industry's major interactive wagering services.

Since repaying all start-up costs in 1997, Equibase profits have been shared among the TRA and its limited-partner racetracks (66%) and the Jockey Club (33%) in the form of dividends. In 2004, Equibase distributed dividends of $2.4-million to its partners. Equibase employs 45 full-time employees, 90 chart callers, and several part-time employees.

The company also serves the sport's fan base through its website, *www.equibase.com,* which offers a wide array of handicapping information and services geared toward every level of handicapper. Among the products available are race programs with handicapping information in easy-to-understand formats for new and existing fans. These pages were developed in conjunction with the National Thoroughbred Racing Association. The Equibase Virtual Stable, the exclusive notification service of the NTRA, delivers entry, workout, and result notices for horses that fans wish to follow. Virtual Stable also features a race series notification service that allows fans to monitor the progress of leading contenders for the Triple Crown and Breeders' Cup races in the months leading up to those events.

In July 2002, it purchased AXCIS Information Network Inc., a provider of electronic handicapping information, through its Track Master product. In April 2004, Equibase hired Philip O'Hara as its president and chief executive officer.

821 Corporate Dr.
Lexington, Ky. 40503-2794
Phone: (859) 224-2860 or (800) 333-2211
Fax: (859) 224-2811
Website: *www.equibase.com*

Chairman: Alan Marzelli
President and Chief Executive Officer: Philip O'Hara
Executive Vice President and Chief Operating Officer: Hank Zeitlin
Secretary: Christopher N. Scherf
Treasurer: Laura Barillaro
Management Committee: Sherwood Chillingworth, C. Steven Duncker, Dan Fick, Craig Fravel, Alan Marzelli, Jim McAlpine, William A. Nader, Nick Nicholson, Ogden Mills Phipps, Steve Sexton, Ray Tromba, Michael Weiss

National Industry Organizations

**American Academy
of Equine Art
c/o Kentucky Horse Park**
4089 Iron Works Pkwy.
Lexington, Ky. 40511
Ph: (859) 281-6031
Fax: (859) 281-6043
E-mail: julieb@aaea.net
Website: www.aaea.net
President: Werner Rentsch

**American Association
of Equine Practitioners**
4075 Iron Works Pkwy.
Lexington, Ky. 40511
Ph: (859) 233-0147
Fax: (859) 233-1968
E-mail: aepoffice@aaep.org
Website: www.aaep.org
President: Scott Palmer, V.M.D.

American Farriers Assn.
4059 Iron Works Pkwy., Ste. 1
Lexington, Ky. 40511
Ph: (859) 233-7411
Fax: (859) 231-7862
E-mail: farriers@americanfarriers.org
Website: www.american
farriers.org
President: Craig Trnka

American Horse Council
1616 H Street NW, 7th floor
Washington, D.C. 20006
Ph: (202) 296-4031
Fax: (202) 296-1970
E-mail: ahc@horsecouncil.org
Website: www.horsecouncil.org
President: James J. Hickey Jr.

**American Horse
Protection Assn.**
1000 29th St. NW., Ste. T-100
Washington, D.C. 20007
Ph: (202) 965-0500
Fax: (202) 965-9621
Website: www.ahpa.us

Animal Transportation Assn.
111 East Loop North
Houston, Tx. 77029
Ph: (713) 532-2177
Fax: (713) 532-2166
E-mail: info@aata-animaltransport.org
Website: www.aata-animal
transport.org

**Association of Racing
Commissioners Int.'l**
2343 Alexandria Dr., Ste. 200
Lexington, Ky. 40504-3276
Ph: (859) 224-7070
Fax: (859) 224-7071
E-mail: support@arci.com
Website: www.arci.com
Chairman: Frank Zanzuccki
President: Ed Martin

Breeders' Cup Ltd.
P.O. Box 4230
Lexington, Ky. 40544-4230
Ph: (859) 223-5444
Fax: (859) 223-3945
E-mail: breederscup@breederscup.com
Website: www.breederscup.com
President: D. G. Van Clief Jr.

**Canadian Veterinary
Medical Assn.**
339 Booth St.
Ottawa, ON K1R 7K1 Canada
Ph: (613) 236-1162
Fax: (613) 236-9681
E-mail: admin@cvma-acmv.org
Website: www.canadian
veterinarians.net

**Grayson-Jockey Club
Research Foundation**
821 Corporate Dr.
Lexington, Ky. 40503
Ph: (859) 224-2850
Fax: (859) 224-2853
E-mail: grayson@jockeyclub.com
Website: www.jockeyclub.com
President: Edward L. Bowen

**Horsemen's Benevolent
and Protective Assn.
(National)**
4063 Iron Works Pkwy.,
Bldg. B, Ste. 2
Lexington, Ky. 40511-8905
Ph: (859) 259-0451
Fax: (859) 259-0452
E-mail: racing@hbpa.org
Website: www.hbpa.org
Executive Director: Remi Bellocq
President: John Roark

Jockey Club of Canada
P.O. Box 66; Station B
Etobicoke, Ontario M9W 5K9 Canada
Ph: (416) 675-7756
Fax: (416) 675-6378
E-mail: jockeyclub@bellnet.ca
Website: www.jockeyclub
canada.com
Chairman: Michael C. Byrne

Jockeys' Guild
P.O. Box 150
Monrovia, Ca. 91017
Ph: (626) 305-5605
Fax: (626) 305-5615
E-mail: info@jockeysguild.com
Website: www.jockeysguild.com
President: Wayne Gertmenian
Chairman: Tomey Jean Swan

National Horse Carriers Assn.
2053 Buck Ln.
Lexington, Ky. 40511
Ph: (859) 255-9406
Website: www.nationalhorse
carriers.com
Chairman: Robert D. Maxwell

**National Museum of
Racing and Hall of Fame**
191 Union Ave.
Saratoga Springs, New York 12866-3566
Ph: (518) 584-0400
Fax: (518) 584-4574
E-mail: nmrinfo@racingmuseum.net
Website: www.racingmuseum.org
Director: Peter Hammell

National Steeplechase Assn.
400 Fair Hill Dr.
Elkton, Md. 21921-2573
Ph: (410) 392-0700
Fax: (410) 392-0706
E-mail: steeplechs@aol.com
Website: www.national
steeplechase.com
President: Jonathan Sheppard

**National Thoroughbred
Racing Assn.**
2525 Harrodsburg Rd., 5th Fl.
Lexington, Ky. 40504-3359
Ph: (859) 223-5444
Fax: (859) 245-6868
E-mail: ntra@ntra.com
Website: www.ntra.com
Commissioner: D. G. Van Clief Jr.

National Turf Writers Assn.
1244 Meadow Ln.
Frankfort, Ky. 40601
Ph: (502) 875-4864
E-mail: dliebman@bloodhorse.com
President: Mike Kane

**North American Pari-Mutuel
Regulators Assn.**
120 North Third Street; Ste 100
Bismarck, N.D. 58501
Ph: (701) 221-2142
Fax: (701) 255-7979
E-mail: pbowlinger@napraonline.com
Website: www.napraonline.com
Executive Director: Paul Bowlinger

The Jockey Club
40 E. 52nd St.
New York, N.Y. 10022
Ph: (212) 371-5970
Fax: (212) 371-6123
E-mail: comments@jockeyclub.com
Website: www.jockeyclub.com
Chairman: Ogden Mills Phipps

Thoroughbred Club of America
P.O. Box 8098
Lexington, Ky. 40533-8098
Ph: (859) 254-4282
Fax: (859) 231-6131
President: Benny Bell Williams

**Thoroughbred Owners and
Breeders Assn.**
P.O. Box 4367
Lexington, Ky. 40544-4367
Ph: (859) 276-2291
Fax: (859) 276-2462
E-mail: TOBA@toba.org
Website: www.toba.org
President: Dan Metzger

Thoroughbred Racing Assns.
of North America
420 Fair Hill Dr., Ste. 1
Elkton, Md. 21921-2573
Ph: (410) 392-9200
Fax: (410) 398-1366

E-mail: info@tra-online.com
Website: www.tra-online.com
President: Corey Johnsen
Executive Vice President: Chris Scherf

Thoroughbred Racing
Protective Bureau
420 Fair Hill Dr., Ste. 2
Elkton, Md. 21921
Ph: (410) 398-2261

Fax: (410) 398-1499
E-mail: trpbinfo@trpb.com
Website: www.trpb.com
President: Paul W. Berube

Triple Crown Productions
700 Central Ave.
Louisville, Ky. 40208-1200
Ph: (502) 636-4405
Fax: (502) 636-4554
E-mail: triplecrown@
   kentuckyderby.com
Website: www.visatriple
   crown.com
President: Thomas H. Meeker
Executive Vice President:
   Edward Seigenfeld

Turf Publicists of America
P.O. Box 90
Jamaica, N.Y. 11417
Ph: (718) 641-4700
Fax: (718) 843-7673
E-mail: jlee@nyrainc.com
Website: www.turfpublicists.com
President: John Lee

United Thoroughbred
Trainers of America
P.O. Box 7065
Louisville, Ky. 40257-0065
Ph: (502) 499-9201
Fax: (502) 893-0026

State and Provincial Racing Organizations

Alabama
Alabama Horsemen's
Benevolent and
Protective Assn.
1523 Indian Hills
Hartselle, Al. 35640
Ph: (256) 773-3592
Fax: (256) 773-5370
E-mail: alahbpa@aol.com
President: Skip Drinkard

Birmingham Racing
Commission
2101 6th Ave. N., Ste. 725;
   Colonial Plaza
Birmingham, Al. 35203
Ph: (205) 328-7223
E-mail: ledadimperio@bellsouth.net
Executive Secretary: W. Kip Keefer

Arizona
Arizona Horsemen's
Benevolent and
Protective Assn.
P.O. Box 43636
Phoenix, Az. 85080
Ph: (602) 942-3336
Fax: (602) 866-3790
E-mail: azhbpa@qwest.net
President: Kevin Eikleberry

Arizona Racing Commission
1110 W. Washington, Suite 260
Phoenix, Az. 85007
Ph: (602) 364-1700
Fax: (602) 364-1703
E-mail: ador@azracing.gov
Website: www.racing.state.az.us
Executive Director: Geoffrey Gonsher
Chairman: Bob Ford

Arizona Thoroughbred
Breeders Assn.
P.O. Box 41774
Phoenix, Az. 85080
Ph: (602) 942-1310
Fax: (602) 942-8225
E-mail: atba@worldnet.att.net
Website: www.atba.net
President: Bradley Rollins

University of Arizona
Race Track Industry Program
845 N. Park Ave., Ste. 370
Tucson, Az. 85721
Ph: (520) 621-5660
Fax: (520) 621-8239
Website: www.ua-rtip.org
Director: Douglas Reed

Arkansas
Arkansas Horse Council
P.O. Box 737
Jasper, Ar. 72641
Ph: (870) 446-6226
Fax: (870) 446-6226
E-mail: footloose1126@
   jasper.yournet.com
Website: www.twb.net/ahc

Arkansas Horsemen's
Benevolent and
Protective Assn.
P.O. Box 1670
Hot Springs, Ar. 71902
Ph: (501) 623-7641
Fax: (501) 623-1350
E-mail: arhbpa@aol.com
President: Dr. Earl Bellamy

Arkansas Racing Commission
1515 W. 7th St.
P.O. Box 3076
Little Rock, Ar. 72203
Ph: (501) 682-1467
Fax: (501) 682-5273
E-mail: bob.cohee@dfa.state.ar.us
Website: www.accessarkansas
   .org/dfa/racing/
Chairman: Cecil Alexander

Arkansas Thoroughbred
Breeders and
Horsemen's Assn.
P.O. Box 21641
Hot Springs, Ar. 71903-1641
Ph: (501) 624-6328
Fax: (501) 623-5722
E-mail: atbha@direclynx.net
Website: www.atbha.com
President: David Bunn

California
California Assn. of
Thoroughbred Racetracks
980 9th St., Ste. 1550
Sacramento, Ca. 95814-2735
Ph: (916) 449-6820
Fax: (916) 449-6830

California Horse Racing Board
1010 Hurley Wy., Ste. 300
Sacramento, Ca. 95825
Ph: (916) 263-6000
Fax: (916) 263-6042
E-mail: roym@chrb.ca.gov
Website: www.chrb.ca.gov
Executive Director: Ingrid Fermin
Chairman: John C. Harris

California Thoroughbred
Breeders Assn.
P.O. Box 60018
Arcadia, Ca. 91066-6018
Ph: (626) 445-7800
Fax: (626) 574-0852
E-mail: ctbanfo@ctba.com
Website: www.ctba.com
President: Keith Card

California Thoroughbred Farm
Managers Assn.
5580 46th St.
Riverside, Ca. 92509
Ph: (760) 942-4789
Fax: (760) 942-2985
E-mail: c2carville@sbcglobal.net
Website: www.thoroughbredinfo.
   com/showcase/ctfma.htm
President: Kimberley Carville

California Thoroughbred Horse-
men's Foundation
P.O.Box 660129
Arcadia, Ca. 91066-6251
Ph: (626) 446-0169
Fax: (626) 447-6251

California Thoroughbred
Trainers
285 West Huntington
Arcadia, Ca. 91066
Ph: (626) 447-2145
Fax: (626) 446-0270
E-mail: caltrnrs@pacbell.net

Website: www.thoroughbredinfo.
  com/showcase/CTT.htm
President: Jenine Sahadi

**Thoroughbred Owners
of California**
285 W. Huntington Dr.
Arcadia, Ca. 91007
Ph: (626) 574-6620
Fax: (626) 821-1515
E-mail: santaanita@toconline.com
Website: www.toconline.com
President: Drew Couto

Colorado
Colorado Racing Commission
1881 Pierce St., Ste. 108
Lakewood, Co. 80214
Ph: (303) 205-2990
Fax: (303) 205-2950
E-mail: racing@spike. dor.state.co.us
Executive Director: Daniel J. Hartman
Chairman: Dr. Gene Naugle

**Colorado Thoroughbred
Breeders Assn.**
4701 Marion St., Ste. 203
Denver, Co. 80216
Ph: (303) 294-0260
Fax: (303) 294-0260
E-mail: ctba@worldnet.att.net
Website: www.toba.
  org/state/coindex.html
President: F. A. Heckendorf

Delaware
**Delaware Thoroughbred
Racing Commission**
2320 S. DuPont Hwy.
Dover, De. 19901
Ph: (302) 698-4599
Fax: (302) 697-4748
E-mail: john.wayne@state.de.us
Executive Director: John F. Wayne
Chairman: Bernard J. Daney

**Delaware Thoroughbred
Horsemen's Association**
777 Delaware Park Blvd.
Wilmington, De. 19804
Ph: (302) 994-2521
Fax: (302) 994-3392
E-mail: dpha@aol.com
Website: www.dtha.com
Executive Director: Bessie Gruwell

Florida
**Florida Horsemen's
Benevolent and
Protective Assn.**
P.O. Box 1808
Opa Locka, Fl. 33055
Ph: (305) 625-4591
Fax: (305) 625-5259
E-mail: fhbpa@bellsouth.net
Website: www.fhbba.org
President: Linda Mills
Executive Director: Kent Stirling

**Florida Division of
Pari-Mutuel Wagering**
1940 N. Monroe St.
Tallahassee, Fl. 32399-1035
Ph: (850) 488-9130
Fax: (850) 488-0550
Website: www.myflorida.com

**Florida Thoroughbred Breeders'
and Owners' Assn.**
801 SW. 60th Ave.
Ocala, Fl. 34474-1827
Ph: (352) 629-2160
Fax: (352) 629-3603
E-mail: ftboa@aol.com
Website: www.ftboa.com
President: Donald Dizney
Executive Vice President:
  Richard E. Hancock

**Florida Thoroughbred
Farm Managers**
6998 NW. Highway 27, Ste. 106B
Ocala, Fl. 34482
Ph: (352) 401-3535
Fax: (352) 401-3533
E-mail: ftfm@atlantic.net
Website: www.flfarmmanagers
  .com
President: Bobby Jones

Horse Protection Assn. of Florida
20690 NW. 130th Ave.
Micanopy, Fl. 32667
Ph: (352) 466-4366
E-mail: hpaf@bellsouth.net
Website: www.hpaf.org
Executive Director: Morgan Silver

Sunshine State Horse Council
P.O. Box 4158
North Fort Myers, Fl. 33918-4158
Ph: (727) 731-2999
E-mail: vicshadyl@aol.com
Website: www.sshc.org
President: Vicki Lawry

Georgia
**Georgia Thoroughbred Owners
and Breeders Assn.**
3340 Peachtree Rd. N.E., Ste. 2540
Tower Place
Atlanta, Ga. 30326
Ph: (866) 664-8622
Fax: (866) 924-8622
E-mail: gtoba@bellsouth.net
Website: www.gtoba.com
Senior Adviser: Jack Damico

Idaho
**Idaho Horsemen's
Benevolent and
Protective Assn.**
P.O. Box 140143
Boise, Id. 83714
Ph: (208) 939-0650
President: Sam Stephenson

Idaho Racing Commission
P.O. Box 700
Meridian, Id. 83680
Ph: (208) 884-7080
Fax: (208) 884-7098
E-mail: ardie.noyes@isp.idaho.gov
Executive Director: Jack O. Baker
Chairman: Dr. Michael Lineberry

Idaho Thoroughbred Assn.
3085 N. Cole Rd. Ste. 113
Boise, Id. 83704
Ph: (208) 375-5930
Fax: (208) 375-5959
E-mail: ita3@mindspring.com
Website: www.idaho
  thoroughbred.org
President: Frank Edmunds

**Idaho Thoroughbred
Breeders Assn.**
3085 N. Cole Rd., Ste. 113
Boise, Id. 83704
Ph: (208) 375-5930
Fax: (208) 375-5959
E-mail: ita@micron.net
Website: www.idaho
  thoroughbred.org

Illinois
**Chicago Horsemen's Benevolent
and Protective Assn.**
138 West Station St.
Barrington, Il. 60010
Ph: (847) 382-3484
Fax: (847) 382-9579
President: Noel Hickey

**Illinois Horsemen's Benevolent
and Protective Assn.**
P.O. Box 429
Caseyville, Il. 62232-0429
Ph: (618) 345-7724
Fax: (618) 344-9049
President: John Wainwright

Illinois Racing Board
100 W. Randolph St., Ste. 7-701
Chicago, Il. 60601
Ph: (312) 814-2600
Fax: (312) 814-5062
E-mail: racing board@irb.state.il.us
Website: www.state.il.us/agency/irb
Chairwoman: Lorna Propes

**Illinois Thoroughbred Breeders
and Owners Foundation**
P.O. Box 336
Caseyville, Il. 62232
Ph: (618) 344-3427
Fax: (618) 346-1051
E-mail: itbofh@apci.net
Website: www.illinoisracingnews
  .com/itbof.htm
President: John D. Bauman

Indiana
Indiana Horse Council
225 S. East St. Ste. 738
Indianapolis, In. 46202
Ph: (317) 692-7115

Fax: (317) 692-7350
E-mail: operations@indianahorse council.org
Website: www.indianahorse council.org
President: Dave Howell

Indiana Horsemen's Benevolent and Protective Assn.
4500 Dan Patch Cir.
Anderson, In. 46013
Ph: (317) 894-1520
Fax: (317) 894-1530
E-mail: hbpaofin@aol.com
President: Dan Horrell

Indiana Racing Commission
150 W. Market St., ISTA Center, Ste. 530
Indianapolis, In. 46204
Ph: (317) 233-0148
Fax: (317) 233-4470
Executive Director: Joe Gorajec
Chairman: Alan Armstrong

Indiana Thoroughbred Owners and Breeders Assn.
P.O. Box 3753
Carmel, In. 46082-3753
Ph: (800) 450-9895
E-mail: info@itoba.com
Website: www.itoba.com
President: Jerry C. Walker

Iowa
Iowa Horsemen's Benevolent and Protective Assn.
P.O. Box 163
Altoona, Ia. 50009
Ph: (515) 967-4804
Fax: (515) 967-4963
E-mail: iahbpa@aol.com
President: Leroy Gessman

Iowa Racing Commission
717 E. Court Ave., Ste. B
Des Moines, Ia. 50309 4934
Ph: (515) 281-7352
Fax: (515) 242-6560
E-mail: irgc@irgc.state.ia.us
Website: www.state.ia.us/irgc
Chairman: Michael Mahaffey

Iowa Thoroughbred Breeders and Owners Assn.
1 Prairie Meadows Dr.
Altoona, Ia. 50009
Ph: (515) 957-3002
Fax: (515) 967-1368
E-mail: itboa@prairiemeadows.com
Website: www.iowa thoroughbred.com
President: Ray Shattuck

Kansas
Kansas Horse Council
8831 Quail Lane; Ste. 201
Manhattan, Ks. 66502
Ph: (785) 776-0662
Fax: (785) 770-8558
E-mail: office@kansashorsecouncil.com

Website: www.kansashorse council.com
President: Dr. Ken Haggard

Kansas Horsemen's Benevolent and Protective Assn.
16585 SW. 90th Ave.
Zenda, Ks. 67159
Ph: (316) 243-6641
President: Ralph Lilja

Kansas Racing & Gaming Commission
3400 SW. Van Buren St.
Topeka, Ks. 66611-2228
Ph: (785) 296-5800
Fax: (785) 296-0900
E-mail: kracing@cjnetworks.com
Website: www.access kansas.org/krc
Executive Director: Tracy T. Diel
Chairman: Gene Olander

Kansas Thoroughbred Assn.
215 Monroe Dr.
Fredonia, Ks. 66736
Ph: (316) 378-4772
Fax: (316) 378-4772
President: Dwight Daniels

Kentucky
Kentucky Equine Education Project
4047 Ironworks Pkway
Lexington, Ky. 40511
Ph: (859) 259-0007
Fax: (859) 259-0511
E-mail: info@horseswork.com
Website: www.equinealliance.com
President: Brereton Jones

Kentucky Horse Council
4063 Iron Works Pkway
Building B; Ste. 2
Lexington, Ky. 40511
Ph: (800) 459-4677
Fax: (859) 299-9849
E-mail: tjburc01@gwise.louisville.edu
Website: www.kentuckyhorse.org
President: Terri Burch

Kentucky Horsemen's Benevolent and Protective Assn.
Churchill Downs
Louisville, Ky. 40209
Ph: (502) 363-1077
Fax: (502) 367-6800
E-mail: info@kyhbpa.org
Website: www.hbpa.org
President: Susan Bunning

Kentucky Horse Racing Authority
4063 Iron Works Pkwy., Bldg B
Lexington, Ky. 40511-8434
Ph: (859) 246-2040
Fax: (859) 246-2039
E-mail: krc.info@mail.state.ky.us
Chairman: Bill Street

Kentucky Thoroughbred Assn.
4079 Iron Works Pkwy.
Lexington, Ky. 40511-8483
Ph: (859) 381-1414
Fax: (859) 233-9737
E-mail: contact@kta-ktob.com
Website: www.kta-ktob.com
President: John Ward Jr.

Kentucky Thoroughbred Farm Managers Club
P.O. Box 4688
Lexington, Ky. 40544-4688
Ph: (859) 296-4279
E-mail: kyfarmclub@aol.com
Website: www.ktfmc.org
President: Charles Koch

Kentucky Thoroughbred Owners and Breeders
4079 Iron Works Pkwy.
Lexington, Ky. 40511-8483
Ph: (859) 259-1643
Fax: (859) 233-9737
E-mail: contact@kta-ktob.com
Website: www.kta-ktob.com
President: John Ward Jr.

Louisiana
Louisiana Horsemen's Benevolent and Protective Assn.
1535 Gentilly Blvd.
New Orleans, La. 70119
Ph: (504) 945-1555
Fax: (504) 945-1579
E-mail: lahbpa@aol.com
Website: www.hbpa.org
President: Oran Trahan

Louisiana Racing Commission
320 N Carrollton Ave., Ste. 2-B
New Orleans, La. 70119
Ph: (504) 483-4000
Fax: (504) 483-4898
E-mail: cgardiner@lrc.state.la
Website: www.horseracing.la.gov
Executive Director: Charles Gardiner
Chairman: Bob Wright

Louisiana Thoroughbred Breeders Assn.
P.O. Box 24650
New Orleans, La. 70184
Ph: (504) 947-4676
Fax: (504) 943-2149
E-mail: ltba@iamerica.net
Website: www.louisianabred.com
President: Warren Harang III

Maryland
Maryland Horse Breeders Assn.
P.O. Box 427
Timonium, Md. 21094
Ph: (410) 252-2100
Fax: (410) 560-0503
E-mail: info@marylandthoroughbred.com
Website: www.mdhorsebreeders .com
President: William Boniface

Maryland Horse Council
P.O. Box 233
Lisbon, Md. 21765
Ph: (410) 489-7826
Fax: (410) 489-7828
E-mail: admin@mail.mdhorsecouncil
.org
Website: www.mdhorsecouncil
.org
President: LuAnne Levens

Maryland Million Ltd.
P.O. Box 365
Timonium, Md. 21094
Ph: (410) 252-2100
Fax: (410) 252-0503
E-mail: info@marylandthoroughbred
.com
Website: www.mdhorsebreeders
.com/Million
President: Michael Pons

Maryland Racing Commission
500 N. Calvert St., Rm. 201
Baltimore, Md. 21202-3651
Ph: (410) 230-6330
Fax: (410) 333-8308
E-mail: racing@dllr.state.md.us
Chairman: Thomas F. McDonough

**Maryland Thoroughbred
Horsemen's Assn.**
6314 Windsor Mill Rd.
Baltimore, Md. 21207
Ph: (410) 265-6842
Fax: (410) 265-6841
E-mail: mdhorsemen@erols.com
Website: www.mdhorsebreeders
.com/mtha
President: Richard Hoffberger

Massachusetts
**Massachusetts Racing
Commission**
1 Ashburton Pl., Rm. 1313
Boston, Ma. 02108
Ph: (617) 727-2581
Fax: (617) 227-6062
E-mail: elizabeth.barry@state.ma.us
Website: www.state.ma.us/src
Chairman: Joseph Betro

**Massachusetts Thoughtbred
Breeders Association**
20 Norumbega Street
Cambridge, Ma. 02138
Ph: (617) 492-7217
E-mail: mtba@comcast.net
Website: www.massbreds.com
Chairman: George Brown

**New England Horsemen's
Benevolent and Protective
Association**
P.O. Box 388
Revere, Ma. 02151
Ph: (617) 567-3900
Fax: (617) 569-3797
Website: www.hbpa.org
President: Mario DeStefano

Michigan
**Michigan Horsemen's
Benevolent and
Protective Assn.**
4800 S. Harvey
Muskegon, Mi. 49444
Ph: (231) 798-2250
Fax: (517) 552-0004
E-mail: mihbpa@aol.com
Website: www.mihbpa.com
President: Robert Miller

Michigan Racing Commission
Office of Racing Commissioner
37650 Professional Center Dr., Ste. 105-A
Livonia, Mi. 48154-1100
Ph: (734) 462-2400
Fax: (734) 462-2429
E-mail: perroned9@michigan.gov
Website: www.mi.gov/horseracing
Commissioner: Christine C. White

**Michigan Thoroughbred Owners
and Breeders Association**
4800 Harvey St.
Muskegon, Mi. 49444
Ph: (231) 798-7721
Fax: (231) 798-7612
E-mail: mtoba@iserv.net
Website: www.mtoba.com
President: Patti M. Dickinson

Minnesota
**Minnesota Horsemen's
Benevolent and
Protective Assn.**
1100 Canterbury Rd.
Shakopee, Mn. 55379
Ph: (952) 496-6442
Fax: (952) 496-6443
E-mail: mnhbpa@pclink.com
Website: www.hbpa.org
President: Tom Metzen Sr.

Minnesota Racing Commission
P.O. Box 630
Shakopee, Mn. 55379
Ph: (952) 496-7950
Fax: (952) 496-7954
E-mail: richard.krueger@state.mn.us
Website: www.mnrace.
commission.state.msn.us
Executive Director: Richard Krueger

Minnesota Thoroughbred Assn.
1100 Canterbury Rd.
Shakopee, Mn. 55379
Ph: (952) 496-3770
Fax: (952) 496-3672
E-mail: mtassoc@voyager.net
Website: www.mtassoc.com
President: Craig Biorn

Mississippi
**Mississippi Thoroughbred
Owners and Breeders Assn.**
107 Sundown Rd.
Madison, Ms. 39110
Ph: (601) 856-8293
President: Bruns Myers Jr.

Missouri
Missouri Equine Council
P.O. Box 608
Fulton, Mo. 65251
Ph: (800) 313-3327
E-mail: info@mo-equine.org
Website: www.mo-equine.org
President: Hattie Fancis

Missouri Racing Commission
P.O. Box 1847
Jefferson City, Mo. 65102
Ph: (573) 526-4080
Fax: (573) 526-1999
E-mail: angie.franks@mgc.dps.mo.gov

Montana
**Montana Horsemen's
Benevolent and
Protective Assn.**
139 New Dracut Hill Rd.
Vaughn, Mt. 59487
Ph: (406) 452-2135
Fax: (406) 727-2663
President: R. C. Foster

Montana Racing Commission
P.O. Box 200512
Helena, Mt. 59620-0512
Ph: (406) 444-4287
Fax: (406) 444-4305
E-mail: mstark@state.mt.us
Website: www.
discoveringmontana.com/liv
Executive Director: Sam Murfitt

Nebraska
**Nebraska Horsemen's
Benevolent and
Protective Assn.**
6406 South 150th Street
Omaha, Ne. 68137
Ph: (402) 438-4684
Fax: (402) 438-4793
E-mail: nebrhbpa@radiks.net
President: Donald Everett

Nebraska Racing Commission
P.O. Box 95014
Lincoln, Ne. 68509-5014
Ph: (402) 471-4155
Fax: (402) 471-2339
E-mail: denny@leelawoffice.com
Website: www.horseracing. state.ne.us
Chairman: Dennis Lee

**Nebraska Thoroughbred
Breeders Assn.**
P.O. Box 2215
Grand Island, Ne. 68802
Ph: (308) 384-4683
Fax: (308) 384-9172
E-mail: ntbai@kdsi.net
President: Jim Cranwell

New Hampshire
New Hampshire Horse Council
273 Poor Farm Rd.
New Ipswich, N.H. 03071
Ph: (603) 456-3230
E-mail: eqnfun@earthlink.net

Website: *www.nhhorse council.com*
President: Jill Lorenz

New Hampshire Pari-Mutuel Commission
78 Regional Drive
Concord, N.H. 03301-8530
Ph: (603) 271-2158
Fax: (603) 271-3381
E-mail: paul.kelley@racing.nh.gov
Executive Director: Paul M. Kelley
Chairman: Timothy J. Connors

New Jersey
New Jersey Racing Commission
P.O. Box 088
Trenton, N.J. 08625
Ph: (609) 292-0613
Fax: (609) 599-1785
Website: *www.njpublicsafety .org/racing*
Executive Director: Frank Zanzuccki
Chairman: John Tucker

Thoroughbred Breeders' Assn. of New Jersey
444 N. Ocean Blvd.
Long Branch, N.J. 07740
Ph: (732) 870-9718
Fax: (732) 870-9719
E-mail: info@njbreds.com
Website: *www.njbreds.com*
President: Michael Harrison

New Mexico
New Mexico Horse Breeders' Assn.
P.O. Box 36869
Albuquerque, N.M. 87176-6869
Ph: (505) 262-0224
Fax: (505) 265-8009
E-mail: nmhba@worldnet.att.net
Website: *www. nmhorse breeders.com*
President: Kay M. Thurman

New Mexico Horse Council
P.O. Box 10206
Albuquerque, N.M. 87184-0206
Ph: (505) 345-8959
Fax: (505) 565-3223
E-mail: burtonranch@yahoo.com
Website: *www.nmhorse council.org*
President: Laura Burton

New Mexico Racing Commission
300 San Mateo Blvd. NE., Ste. 110
Albuquerque, N.M. 87108
Ph: (505) 841-6400
Fax: (505) 841-6413
E-mail: nmrc@state.nm.us
Website: *www.nmrc.state.nm.us*
Chairman: Eddie Fowler

New York
Finger Lakes Horsemen's Benevolent and Protective Association
P.O. Box 25250
Farmington, N.Y. 14425

Ph: (585) 924-3004
Fax: (585) 924-1433
E-mail: flhbpa@frontiernet.net
President: Paul Steckel

Genesee Valley Breeders Association
P.O. Box 301
Shortsville, N.Y. 14548-0301
Ph: (585) 289-8524
Fax: (585) 289-8524
Website: *www.nybreds.com/ GVBA/index.html*

New York State Horse Council
44 Eggleston Ln.
Westport, N.Y. 12993
Ph: (518) 962-2316
E-mail: kinggeo@westelcom.com
Website: *www.nyshc.org*
President: George King

New York State Racing and Wagering Board
1 Watervliet Ave. Ext., Ste. 2
Albany, N.Y. 12206-1668
Ph: (518) 453-8460
Fax: (518) 453-8490
E-mail: info@racing.state.ny.us
Website: *www.racing.state.ny.us*
Chairman: Michael Hoblock Jr.

New York Thoroughbred Breeders
57 Phila St., 2nd Fl.
Saratoga Springs, N.Y. 12866
Ph: (518) 587-0777
Fax: (518) 587-1551
E-mail: nytb@nybreds.com
Website: *www.nybreds.com*
Executive Director: Dennis Brida

New York State Thoroughbred Breeding and Development
1 Penn Plaza, Ste. 725
New York, N.Y. 10119
Ph: (212) 465-0660
Fax: (212) 465-8205
E-mail: nybreds@nybreds.com
Website: *www.nybreds.com*
Chairman: William Levin

New York Thoroughbred Horsemen's Assn.
P.O. Box 170070
Jamaica, N.Y. 11417
Ph: (718) 848-5045
Fax: (718) 848-9269
Website: *www.nytha.com*
President: Richard Bomze

North Carolina
North Carolina Horse Council
4904 Waters Edge Dr., Ste. 290
Raleigh, N.C. 27606
Ph: (919) 854-1990
Fax: (919) 854-1989
E-mail: cindy@nchorsecouncil.com
Website: *www.nchorsecouncil.com*
President: Glenn Petty

North Carolina Thoroughbred Breeders Assn.
2103 Orange Factory Rd.
Bahama, N.C. 27503
Ph: (919) 471-0131
Fax: (919) 286-9421
President: Robert Sanford

North Dakota
North Dakota Racing Commission
500 North 9th St.
Bismarck, N.D. 58501
Ph: (701) 328-4290
Fax: (701) 328-4300
E-mail: htessman@state.nd.us
Website: *www.ndracing commission.com*
Chairman: James Boehm

Ohio
Ohio Horsemen's Benevolent and Protective Assn.
3684 Park St.
Grove City, Oh. 43123
Ph: (614) 875-1269
Fax: (614) 875-0786
E-mail: ohio-hbpa@rrohio.com
Website: *www.ohio-hbpa.com*
President: Gus George

Ohio Racing Commission
77 S. High St., 18th Fl.
Columbus, Oh. 43215-6108
Ph: (614) 466-2757
Fax: (614) 466-1900
E-mail: can@osrc.state.oh.us
Website: *www.racing.ohio.gov*
Chairman: Norman I. Baron

Ohio Thoroughbred Breeders and Owners Assn.
6024 Harrison Ave., Ste. 13
Cincinnati, Oh. 45248-1621
Ph: (513) 574-5888
Fax: (513) 574-2313
E-mail: gb.otbo@fuse.net
Website: *www.otbo.com*
President: Dennis Heebink

Oklahoma
Oklahoma Horsemen's Benevolent and Protective Assn.
1 Remington Pl.
Oklahoma City, Ok. 73111
Ph: (405) 427-8753
Fax: (405) 427-7099
E-mail: okhbpa@earthlink.net
Website: *www.okhbpa.com*
President: Joe Lucas

Oklahoma Racing Commission
2401 NW 23rd St.; Ste 78
Oklahoma City, Ok. 73107
Ph: (405) 943-6472
Fax: (405) 943-6474
E-mail: ohrc@socket.net
Website: *www.ohrc.org*
Chairman: Ray Bayliff

Oklahoma Thoroughbred Assn.
2000 SE. 15th St., Bldg. 450, Ste. A
Edmond, Ok. 73013
Ph: (405) 330-1006
Fax: (405) 330-6206
E-mail: info@otawins.com
Website: *www.otawins.com*
President: Chuck Clugston

Oregon
**Oregon Horsemen's Benevolent
and Protective Assn.**
11919 N. Jantzen Ave.; PMB #585
Portland, Or. 97217
Ph: (503) 285-4941
Fax: (503) 285-4942
E-mail: ohbpa@aol.com
Website: *www.oregonhbpa.com*
President: Dave Benson

Oregon Racing Commission
800 NE Oregon St. #11; Ste. 310
Portland, Or. 97232
Ph: (503) 731-4052
Fax: (503) 731-4053
E-mail: carol.n.morgan@state.or.us
Website: *www.orednet.org*
Executive Director: Jodi N. Hanson
Chairman: Stephen S. Walters

**Oregon Thoroughbred
Breeders Assn.**
P.O. Box 17248
Portland, Or. 97217
Ph: (503) 285-0658
Fax: (503) 285-0659
E-mail: otba@quest.net
Website: *www.thoroughbred
info.com/showcase/otba.htm*
President: Gary Martin

Pennsylvania
Pennsylvania Equine Council
P.O. Box 21
Dallas, Pa. 18612
Ph: (888) 304-0281
E-mail: expo2002@hky.com
Website: *www.pennsylvania
equinecouncil.com*
President: Walter Jeffers

**Pennsylvania Horse
Breeders Assn.**
701 E. Baltimore Pk., Ste. C-1
Kennett Square, Pa. 19348
Ph: (610) 444-1050
Fax: (610) 444-1051
E-mail: exsec@pabred.com
Website: *www.pabred.com*
President: Ray Hamm
Executive Secretary:
Dr. Richard Reveley

**Pennsylvania Horsemen's
Benevolent and
Protective Assn.**
P.O. Box 88
Grantville, Pa.17028
Ph: (717) 469-2970
Fax: (717) 469-7714
E-mail: pahbpa@paonline.com
President: John Wames

**Pennsylvania Horse
Racing Commission**
2301 N. Cameron St., Rm. 304
Harrisburg, Pa. 17110
Ph: (717) 787-1942
Executive Director: Benjamin H. Nolt Jr.
Chairman: F. Eugene Dixon Jr.

**Pennsylvania Thoroughbred
Horsemen's Assn.**
P.O. Box 300
Bensalem, Pa. 19020-0300
Ph: (215) 638-2012
Fax: (215) 638-2919
President: Lawrence Riviello

South Carolina
**South Carolina Thoroughbred
Owners and Breeders**
Rte. 1, Box 19-A
Wando, S.C. 29492
Ph: (803) 432-3388
Fax: (803) 432-5777
E-mail: info@sctoba.org
Website: *www.sctoba.org*
President: Lee Christian

South Dakota
**South Dakota Commission
on Gaming**
118 W. Capitol Ave.
Pierre, S.D. 57501
Ph: (605) 773-6050
Fax: (605) 773-6053
E-mail: gaminginfo@state.sd.us
Website: *www.state.sd.us/ drr2
/reg/gaming*
Executive Director: Larry Eliason
Chairman: Ralph "Chip" Kemnitz

Texas
**Texas Horsemen's Benevolent
and Protective Assn.**
P.O. Box 142533
Austin, Tx. 78714
Ph: (512) 467-9799
Fax: (512) 467-9790
E-mail: wobanan@texashorsemen.com
Website: *www.texashorsemen.com*
Executive Director: Tommy Azopardi

Texas Racing Commission
P.O. Box 12080
Austin, Tx. 78711-2080
Ph: (512) 833-6699
Fax: (512) 833-6907
E-mail: paula.flowerday@txrc.state.tx.us
Website: *www.txrc.state.tx.us*
Executive Secretary:
Paula C. Flowerday
Chairman: R. Dyke Rogers

Texas Thoroughbred Assn.
P.O. Box 14967
Austin, Tx. 78761
Ph: (512) 458-6133
Fax: (512) 453-5919
E-mail: info@texasthoroughbred.com
Website: *www.texas
thoroughbred.com*
President: Larry T. Smith

Vermont
Vermont Horse Council
146 Bent Hill Rd.
Braintree, Vt. 05060
Ph: (802) 728-6303
E-mail: rose@kdpyield.com
Website: *www.vthorsecouncil.org*
President: Terry Rose

Virginia
**Virginia Horsemen's Benevolent
and Protective Assn.**
38 Garrett St.
Warrenton, Va. 20186
Ph: (540) 347-0033
Fax: (540) 675-1103
E-mail: race@vhpa.org
Website: *www.vhbpa.org*
President: Robin Richards

Virginia Racing Commission
10700 Horsemen's Rd.
New Kent, Va. 23124
Ph: (804) 966-7400
Fax: (804) 966-7418
E-mail: stanley.bowker@
vrc.Virginia.gov
Website: *www.vrc.state.va.us*
Chairwoman: Annie D. W. Poulson

Virginia Thoroughbred Assn.
38-C Garrett St.
Warrenton, Va. 20186-3107
Ph: (540) 347-4313
Fax: (540) 347-7314
E-mail: vta@vabred.org
Website: *www.vabred.org*
President: Deborah A. Easter

Washington
**Northwest Horsemen's
Benevolent and
Protective Assn.**
P.O. Box 40141
Spokane, Wa. 99202
Ph: (509) 536-5123
Fax: (509) 536-5145
President: Jay Healy

**Washington Horsemen's
Benevolent and
Protective Assn.**
3702 W. Valley Hwy., Ste. 210
Auburn, Wa. 98001
Ph: (206) 804-6822
Fax: (206) 804-6899
E-mail: seabiscuit@msn.com
President: Larry Hills

**Washington Horse
Racing Commission**
6326 Martin Way, Ste. 209
Olympia, Wa. 98516
Ph: (360) 459-6462
Fax: (360) 459-6461
E-mail: psorby@whrc.state.wa.us
Website: *www.whrc.wa.gov*
Chairman: Gary Christenson

**Washington Thoroughbred
Breeders Assn.**
P.O. Box 1499
Auburn, Wa. 98071-1499

Ph: (253) 288-7878
Fax: (253) 288-7890
E-mail: maindesk@washington
thoroughbred.com
Website: *www.washington
thoroughbred.com*
President: David Thorner

**Washington Thoroughbred
Farm Managers Assn.**
P.O. Box 857
Enumclaw, Wa. 98022
Ph: (253) 288-7897
Fax: (253) 288-7890
E-mail: maindesk@washington
thoroughbred.com
Website: *www.washington
thoroughbred.com/IndAddrs/
WTFMA.htm*

West Virginia
**Charles Town Horsemen's
Benevolent and Protective
Assn.**
P.O. Box 581
Charles Town, W.V. 25414
Ph: (304) 725-1535
Fax: (304) 728-2113
E-mail: cthbpa@earthlink.net
President: Ann C. Hilton

**Mountaineer Park Horsemen's
Benevolent and Protective
Assn.**
P. O. Box 358
Chester, W.V. 26034
Ph: (304) 387-9772
Fax: (304) 387-1925
E-mail: hbpa@raex.com
President: Charles Bailey

**West Virginia
Breeders Classics Ltd.**
P.O. Box 1251
Charles Town, W.V. 25414
Ph: (304) 725-0709
Fax: (540) 687-6927
E-mail: wvbcmbn@erols.com
Website: *www.wvbc.com*
President: Sam Huff

**West Virginia
Racing Commission**
106 Dee Dr.
Charleston, W.V. 25311
Ph: (304) 558-2150
Fax: (304) 558-6319
Email: oliver8@saintjoes.net
Website: *www.wvf.state.wv.us/
racing*
Chairman: Andrew A. Payne III

**West Virginia Thoroughbred
Breeders Assn.**
P.O. Box 626
Charles Town, W.V. 25414
Ph: (304) 725-7001
President: Cynthia O'Bannon

Wyoming
**Wyoming Pari-Mutuel
Commission**
2515 Warren Ave., Ste. 301
Cheyenne, Wy. 82002
Ph: (307) 777-5887
Fax: (307) 777-6005
E-mail: flamb@state.wy.us
Website: *parimutuel.state.wy.us*
Executive Director: Frank R. Lamb

Canada
**Alberta Division
Canadian Thoroughbred
Horse Society**
225 17th Ave. SW. #401
Calgary, AB T2S 2T8 Canada
Ph: (403) 229-3609
Fax: (403) 244-6909
E-mail: cthsalta@telusplanet.net
Website: *www.cthsalta.com*
President: Gordon Wilson

Alberta Horse Racing
9707 110th St., #720
Edmonton, AB T5K 2L9 Canada
Ph: (780) 415-5432
Fax: (780) 488-5105
Website: *www.thehorses.com*
Chairman: Dr. David Reid

**British Columbia Division
Canadian Thoroughbred
Horse Society**
17687 56A Ave.
Surrey, BC V3S 1G4 Canada
Ph: (604) 574-0145
Fax: (604) 574-5868
E-mail: cthsbc@axionet.com
Website: *www.cthsbc.org*

**Canada Horsemen's Benevolent
and Protective Assn.**
609 W. Hastings St. No. 888
Vancouver, BC V6B 4W4 Canada
Ph: (604) 647-2211
Fax: (604) 647-0095
E-mail: bpm@jcbailey-ca.com
President: Mel Snow

**Division of Racing
of British Columbia**
4603 Kingsway, Ste. 408
Burnaby, BC V5H 4M4 Canada
Ph: (604) 660-7400
Fax: (604) 660-7414
E-mail: gaming.branch@gems1
.gov.bc.ca
Website: *www.pssg.gov.bc.ca/gaming*
Director: Sam Hawkins

**Eastern Canadian
Thoroughbred Assn.**
Longview Farm, RR 4, 159 Lowe Rd.
Ashton, ON K0A 1B0 Canada
Ph: (613) 257-5837
Fax: (613) 257-5837
E-mail: kenne58@attglobal.net
Website: *www.ecta-equine.ca*
President: Patricia Enright

**Horse Council of
British Columbia**
27336 Fraser Highway
Aldergrove, BC V4W 3N5 Canada
Ph: (604) 856-4304
Fax: (604) 856-4302
E-mail: administration@hcbc.ca
Website: *www.horsecouncil bc.com*
President: Sue Thompson

**Manitoba Division Canadian
Thoroughbred Horse Society**
Westdale Box 46152
Winnipeg, MB R3R 3S3 Canada
Ph: (204) 832-1702
Fax: (204) 831-6735
E-mail: info@cthsmb.ca
Website: *www.cthsmb.ca*
President: Brent Hrymak

Manitoba Horse Council
200 Main St., Ste. 207
Winnipeg, MB R3C 4M2 Canada
Ph: (204) 925-5718
Fax: (204) 925-5737
E-mail: admin1mhc@sport.mb.ca
Website: *www.manitobahorse
council.ca*

Manitoba Racing Commission
P.O. Box 46086 RPO Westdale
Winnipeg, MB R3R 3S3 Canada
Ph: (204) 885-7770
Fax: (204) 831-0942
E-mail: dwilliams@manitoba
horsecomm.org
President: Bob Parker
Chairman: Norman Kalinski

**Ontario Division Canadian
Thoroughbred Horse Society**
P.O. Box 172
Rexdale, ON M9W 5L1 Canada
Ph: (416) 675-3602
Fax: (416) 675-9405
E-mail: cthsont@idirect.com
Website: *www.cthsont.com*

Ontario Equestrian Federation
9120 Leslie St.; Ste. 203
Richmond Hill, ON L4B 3J9 Canada
Ph: (905) 709-6545
Fax: (905) 709-1867
E-mail: horse@horse.on.ca
Website: *www.horse.on.ca*

Ontario Horse Breeders Assn.
P.O. Box 520
Caledon, ON L0N ICO Canada
Ph: (519) 942-3527

**Ontario Horsemen's
Benevolent and
Protective Assn.**
135 Queens Plate Dr., Ste. 370
Toronto, ON M9W 6V1 Canada
Ph: (416) 747-5252
Fax: (416) 747-9606
Website: *www.hbpa.on.ca*
E-mail: general@hbpa.com
President: Conrad Cohen

Ontario Racing Commission
20 Dundas St. W.; 9th Fl.
Toronto, ON M5G2C2 Canada
Ph: (416) 327-0520
Fax: (416) 325-3478
E-mail: wendy.hoogeveen@cbs
.gov.on.ca
Chairman: Lynda Tanaka

**Quebec Division Canadian
Thoroughbred Horse Society**
3 Chemindes Chavaux Lac Quindon
Quebec, J0R 1B0 Canada
Ph: (450) 224-4020

**Saskatchewan Division
Canadian Thoroughbred
Horse Society**
1229 Spadina Crescent W.

Saskatoon, SK S7M 1P4 Canada
Ph: (306) 242-9128
Fax: (306) 665-5829
E-mail: dturner@sk.sympatico.ca

Saskatchewan Horse Federation
2205 Victoria Ave.
Regina, SK S4P 0S4 Canada
Ph: (306) 780-9244
Fax: (306) 525-4009
E-mail: sk.horse@sasktel.net
Website: www.saskhorsefed.com
President: Murray Acton

Puerto Rico

**Puerto Rico Thoroughbred
Breeders Assn.**
Centro de Seguros Bldg.; Ste. 312

Ponce de Leon Ave. 701
San Juan, P.R. 00907
Ph: (787) 725-8715
Fax: (787) 725-8606
E-mail: criadores@icepr.com

Mexico

Mexico Racing Commission
Fuente de Templanza No. 6, P. H.
Col. Tecamachalco,
Naucalpan, Edo. De Mexico
Mexico City 53950
Ph: 011(52) 5 293-0264
Fax: 011 (52) 5 294-7928
E-mail: cnccg@aol.com

Charitable Organizations
National

American Horse Defense Fund
Trina Bellak
Ph: (866) 983-3456
E-mail: AHDForg@aol.com
Website: www.ahdf.org

Blue Horse Charities
Leslie McCammish
Ph: (859) 255-1555
E-mail: lmccammish@fasigtipton.com
Website: www.bluehorsecharities.org

CANTER
Jo Anne Normile
Ph: (734) 455-0639
Website: www.canterusa.org

**Disabled Jockeys'
Endowment Inc.**
1540 S. Lewis St.
Anaheim, Ca. 92805-6423
Ph: (714) 491-3436
Fax: (714) 502-8480
E-mail: info@jockeysguild.com
Chairman: David A. Woodcock

**Don MacBeth Memorial
Jockey Fund**
P.O. Box 18470
Encino, Ca. 91416
Ph: (310) 550-4542
Fax: (818) 981-6914
E-mail: info@macbethfund.org
Website: www.macbethfund.org

Equine Advocates
Susan Wagner
Ph: (845) 278-3095
Website: www.equineadvocates.com

Equine Protection Network
Christine Barry
Website: www.equineprotection
network.com

**Grayson-Jockey Club
Research Foundation**
821 Corporate Dr.

Lexington, Ky. 40503
Ph: (859) 224-2850
Fax: (859) 224-2853
E-mail: grayson@jockeyclub.com
Website: www.jockeyclub.com/
grayson.html
President: Edward L. Bowen

HoofPAC.com
Cathleen Doyle
Website: www.hoofpac.com

Humane Society of U.S.
Ph: (818) 501-2275
Website: www.hsus.org

The Jockey Club Foundation
40 East 52nd St.
New York, N.Y. 10022
Phone: (212) 521-5305
Fax: (212) 371-6123
E-mail: nkelly@jockeyclub.com
Website: www.tjcfoundation.org
Executive Director: Nancy C. Kelly

**Kentucky Horse
Park Foundation**
4089 Iron Works Pk.
Lexington, Ky. 40511
Ph: (859) 255-5727
Fax: (859) 254-7121
E-mail: khpf@mis.net
Website: www.kyhorsepark.com/khp
/foundation

**Maryland Horsemen's
Assistance Fund**
6314 Windsor Mill Rd.
Baltimore, Md. 21207
Ph: (410) 265-6843
Fax: (410) 265-6841
E-mail: mdassistance@erols.com
Website: www.mdhorsemen.com

**National Horse
Protection Coalition**
Ph: (202) 333-4936
Website: www.horse-protection.org

**Racehorse Adoption
Referral Program**
Ph: (877) 576-NTRA
Website: www.ntra.com

**Race Track Chaplaincy
of America**
P.O. Box 91640
Los Angeles, Ca. 90009
Ph: (310) 419-1640
Fax: (310) 419-1642
E-mail: etorres@
racetrackchaplaincy.org
Website: www.racetrack
chaplaincy.org
President: Edward Smith
Executive Director: Dr. Enrique Torres
Director of Development:
Edward Donnally

Recycle Racehorses
E-mail: delahorse@aol.com
Website: members2.boardhost
.com/hollihorse

ReRun
P.O. Box 113
Helmetta, N.J. 08828
Ph: (732) 521-1370
E-mail: rerunnj@comcast.net
Website: www.rerun.org

ReRun
Laurie Lane
Ph: (859) 289-7786
Website: www.rerun.org

Second Career Racehorses
25 S. Division
Grand Rapids, Mi. 49503
Ph: (616) 913-2790
Fax: (616) 913-2801
E-mail: scr@cybernet-usa.com
Website: www.secondcareerrace
horses.org

Shoemaker Foundation
P.O. Box 17026
Ingelwood, Ca. 90308-7026

Ph: (310) 419-1503
Fax: (310) 672-3899

Thoroughbred Charities of America
P.O. Box 3856
Midway, Ky. 40347
Ph: (859) 312-5531
E-mail: liz@speedbeam.com
Website: www.thoroughbred charities.org
President: Herb Moelis
Executive Director: Liz Harris

Thoroughbred Retirement Foundation
450 Shrewsbury Plaza, Ste. 351
Shrewsbury, N.J. 07702
Ph: (800) 728-1660

Fax: (802) 496-3276
E-mail: trf@trfinc.org
Website: www.trfinc.org
Executive Director: Diana Pikulski
Operations Director: Fred Winters
Adoptions and Retirement Coordinator: Missy Klick

United Pegasus Foundation
102 S. First Ave.
Arcadia, Ca. 91006
Ph: (626) 279-1306
E-mail: unitedpegasus@yahoo.com
Website: www.unitedpegasus.com

Winners Foundation
285 W. Huntington Dr.
Arcadia, Ca. 91007

Ph: (626) 574-6498
Fax: (626) 821-9091
E-mail: robert.fletcher@santaanita.com
Executive Director: Bob Fletcher

Winners Federation
P.O. Box 46098
Chicago, Il. 60646-0098
Ph: (847) 477-3551
Fax: (847) 982-6559
E-mail: winfed2002@yahoo.com
Website: www.winners federation.org
President: Peggy Goetsch
Vice President: Dr. Barbara Wilmes
Executive Director: Don Clippinger

Thoroughbred Retirement and Rescue

Alabama
Alabama Equine Rescue
Ph: (205) 680-1862
E-mail: AERescue2000@yahoo.com
Website: www.aerescue.netfirms.com

Foal Train
Liz Creamer
Ph: (251) 545-7980
E-mail: tugonurhrt@aol.com
Website: www.foaltrain.com

Alaska
Alaska Equine Rescue
Sally Clampitt
Ph: (888) 588-4677 or (888) LUV-HORSE
E-mail: aer@alaskaequinerescue.com
Website: www.alaskaequinerescue.com

Arizona
Hacienda de los Milagros
Wynne Zaugg
Ph: (520) 636-5348
Website: www.haciendadelosmilagros. org

Hooved Animal Humane Society
E-mail: hahsofazcv@yahoo.com
Website: www.hahsofaz.com

Maricopa County Horse Rescue
Ph: (623) 434-5602
Website: www.werescuehorses.com

TheHorseRescue@aol.com
Mesa Equine Sanctuary
Website: www.dhhrescue.com

Rescue A Horse.com
Holly Marino
Ph: (602) 689-8825
E-mail: holly@rescueahorse.com
Website: www.rescueahorse.com

X-S Ranch Livestock Rescue & Sanctuary
Website: www.xs-ranch.20m.com

Arkansas
Ozland Horse Rescue
Website: myozland.tripod.com/ ozlandhorserescue/

ReRun
Jennifer Keller
Ph: (501) 997-8581
E-mail: jkeller@rerun.org
Website: www.rerun.org

California
California Equine Retirement Foundation
34033 Kooden Rd.
Winchester, Ca. 92596
Grace Belcuore
Ph: (909) 926-4190
Fax: (909) 926-4181
E-mail: cerf@pe.net
Website: www.cerfhorses.org

Equus Sanctuary
Ph: (530) 931-0108
Website: www.equus.org

Exceller Fund to Rescue Horses
17172 Armstead St.
Grandada Hills, Ca. 91344
E-mail: Bonnie.Mizrahi@excellerfund.org
Website: www.excellerfund.org

Glen Ellen Vocational Academy (GEVA)
Pam Berg
Ph: (707) 527-8092
E-mail: gef@vom.com
Website: www.glenellenfarms.com/geva

Jack Auchterlonie Memorial Equine Sanctuary (JAMES)
Fran Becker
Ph: (760) 362-1357
E-mail: james29palms@aol.com
Website: www.jamesrescue.com

Phoenix Equine Foundation
Teri Rohm
Ph: (707) 833-4774
E-mail: Jeanie@ap.net

Redwings Horse Sanctuary
Ph: (831) 386-0135
E-mail: info@redwings.org
Website: www.redwings.org

Return to Freedom
Neda De Mayo
Ph: (805) 737-9246

E-mail: info@returntofreedom.org
Website: www.returntofreedom.org

Southern California Equine Foundation
Leigh Gray
Ph: (909) 590-0988
Website: www.scef-inc.com

Tranquility Farm
Priscilla Clark
Ph: (661) 823-0307
Website: www.tranquilityfarmtbs.org

True Innocents Equine Rescue
Ph: (909) 360-1464
E-mail: info@tierrescue.org
Website: www.tierrescue.org

United Pegasus Foundation
Helen Meredith
Ph: (626) 279-1306
E-mail: unitedpegasus@yahoo.com
Website: www.unitedpegasus.com

Colorado
Colorado Horse Rescue
Nan Millett
Ph: (720) 494-1414
Website: www.chr.org

Friends of Horses Rescue & Adpt.
Bill Stiffler
Ph: (877) 229-7483
Website: www.getahorse.org

Lasso Horse Rescue
Larry Simms
Ph: (970) 264-0095
Website: www.lassohorserescue.org

Rocky Mountain Foal Rescue
Pam Pietsch
Ph: (719) 683-5880
E-mail: rmfr@qwest.net
Website: www.rockymountainfoal rescue.org

7 Star Mustang Sanctuary
K. S. Brown
Ph: (719) 942-3753
E-mail: info@7starsanctuary.org

Connecticut

Citizens for Animal Protection
P.O. Box 1496
Litchfield, Ct. 06759
Ph: (203) 699-8447
Fax: (203) 699-8447
E-mail: capinc@usa.net
Website: www.geocities.com/
Petsburgh/Zoo/7966

Greener Pastures Rescue
E-mail: 4asteed@steedread.com
Website: www.greenerpastures
rescue.org

HORSE of Connecticut
Patty Wahlers
Ph: (860) 868-1960
E-mail: horseofct@yahoo.com

**New Haven Animal Rescue
Association**
E-mail: care4animals@mail.com

Delaware

Horse Lovers United
Lorraine Truitt
Ph: (410) 749-3599
Website: www.horseloversunited.com

Summer Wind Stables
Elena DiSilvestro
Ph: (877) SMRWIND
Website: www.summerwindstables.com

**Tri State Equine Rescue and
Adoption**
Ph: (302) 492-0492
Website: www.tristateequine.org

Florida

Adopt-A-Horse
Judy Detore
Ph: (863) 382-4483
Website: www.adoptahorse.com

**Back in the Saddle
Horse Adoption (BITS)**
Pam Rayl
Ph: (904) 284-5852
E-mail: info@bitshorseadopt.org
Website: www.bitshorseadopt.org

**Equine Rescue & Adoption
Foundation**
Ph: (561) 627-1198
E-mail: info@equinerescuefl.org
Website: www.equinerescuefl.org

Friends of the EIA Horse
Debbie Barwick
Ph: (954) 492-0168
Website: www.eiahorses.org

**Heavenly Meadows Horse
Rescue**
Vicky Hammond
Ph: (850) 773-9991
E-mail: info@heavenlymeadows.org
Website: www.heavenlymeadows.org

HOPE
Tara McDonald
Ph: (813) 417-6386
E-mail: hope4tbreds@aol.com

Hope For Horses
Ph: (772) 785-5309
E-mail: info@hopeforhorses.net
E-mail: hope4horses@hotmail.com
Website: www.hopeforhorses.net

Horse Protection Association
Morgan Silver
Ph: (352) 466-4366
Website: www.hpaf.org

Retirement Home for Horses
Peter Gregory
Ph: (386) 462-1001
E-mail: rhh@millcreekfarm.com
Website: www.millcreekfarm.org

Whispering Winds Ranch
Ph: (352) 472-3925
E-mail: taini2727@aol.com
Website: www.whisperingwindsranch
.homestead.com

Georgia

**Begin Again Farms
Equine Shelter**
Rhonda Jackson
E-mail: Beginagainfarms@aol.com
Website: www.beginagainfarms.com

Exceller Fund to Rescue Horses
Karla Phaneuf
Ph: (770) 998-7368
Website: www.excellerfund.org

Georgia Equine Rescue League
Marty Paulk
Ph: (770) 464-0138
E-mail: info@gerlltd.org
Website: www.gerlltd.org

**Horse Rescue, Relief
& Retirement**
Cheryl Flanagan
Ph: (770) 886-5419
Website: www.savethehorses.org

Idaho

Orphan Acres
Ph: (208) 882-9293
E-mail: orphan_acres@hotmail.com

Illinois

CANTER
Denise Fillo
Ph: (630) 850-5548
Website: www.canterusa.org

Crosswinds Equine Rescue
Ph: (217) 832-2010
Website: www.crosswindseqresq.org

Hooved Animal Humane Society
Lydia Miller
Ph: (815) 337-5563
Email: info@hahs.org
Website: www.hahs.org

ReRun
Gingy Cody
Ph: (847) 428-9371
Website: www.rerun.org

Indiana

Indiana Horse Rescue
Ph: (765) 659-5209
Website: www.esfrescue.com

Moon Winds Rescue
Ph: (765) 676-5798
Website: www.moonwindsrescue.com

Iowa

Lazy R Equine Rescue
Karen Ralston
Ph: (563) 652-4593
E-mail: granny2000@earthlink.net
Website: www.angelfire.com/ia2/
lazyriowa/main.html

Kentucky

**Casey Creek Horse
Rescue & Adoption Inc.**
Kenneth Holland
Ph: (270) 789-4198
E-mail: desperado_55@yahoo.com
Website: www.homestead.com/cchra/
cchra.html

Old Friends
Michael Blowen
Ph: (859) 846-9995
Website: www.oldfriendsequine.org

ReRun
Shon Wylie
Ph: (859) 289-7786
E-mail: rerunhorse@kih.net
Website: www.rerun.org

Louisiana

Hopeful Haven Equine Rescue
Debra Barlow
Ph: (318) 925-4272
Website: www.hopefulhaven.com

Maine

**Standardbred Pleasure Horse
Organization**
Website: www.sphomaine.net

Maryland

Days End Farm Horse Rescue
15856 Frederick Rd.
Lisbon, Md. 21765
Kathy Schwartz
Ph: (301) 854-5037
E-mail: defhr@erols.com
Website: www.defhr.org

Equine Rescue & Rehabilitation
Deborah Fran
Ph: (410) 343-2142
Website: www.horserescue.com

Fox Shadow Foundation
Jeannie Meade
Ph: (410) 673-2634
E-mail: foxshadow@dmv.com

Greener Pastures Equine Sanctuary
Wendy Moon
Ph: (410) 885-2198
Website: www.thoroughbredcharities.org

Horse Lovers United
Lorraine Truitt
Ph: (410) 749-3599
Website: www.horseloversunited.com

HorseNet Horse Rescue
Ph: (410) 795-8989
Website: www.horsenethorse
rescue.org

Lost & Found Horse Rescue
Kelly Young
Ph: (717) 428-9701
Website: www.lfhr.org

Mid Atlantic Horse Rescue
Beverly Strauss
Ph: (302) 376-7297
Website: www.midatlantichorse
rescue.org

New Life Equine Rescue
Ph: (301) 305-0702
Website: www.nler.org

Royal Equine Rescue & Sanctuary Inc.
Alyssa Taylor
Ph: (443) 417-0069
E-mail: alyssa@rersi.org
Website: www.rersi.org

The Keep at Andelain Farm Inc.
Wendy Moulton
Ph: (301) 271-4191
E-mail: thekeep@andelainfarm.com
Website: www.horsessavingkids.org

Massachusetts
Eye of the Storm Equine Rescue
Nina Arbella
Ph: (978) 897-8866
Website: www.equine-rescue.com

Suffolk Downs
Lori Lindermann
Ph: (617) 567-3900
Website: www.suffolkdowns.com

Michigan
Broken Pine Ranch Horse Rescue
E-mail: brokenpineranch@myway.com

CANTER
Jo Anne Normile
Ph: (734) 455-0639
Website: www.canterusa.org

Great Lakes Hooved Animal Rescue
Ph: (616) 837-1144
Website: www.hoovedrescue.org

Horses' Haven
P.O. Box 166
Howell, Mi. 48884

Ph: (517) 548-4880
E-mail: horseshaven@earthlink.net
Website: www.ismi.net/horseshaven

Hugs2Horses Inc.
Ph: (517) 223-3263
Website: www.hugs2horses.com

Second Chance Thoroughbred Adoption
Dale Berryhill
Website: www.horsenetwork.com/
second chance/

Minnesota
A & L Equine Sanctuary
Laurie Parsons
Ph: (218) 397-2397
Website: www.aandlequinesanctuary
.com

Midwest Horse Adoption Program
E-mail: mwhorseadoption@yahoo.com

Minnesota Hooved Animal Rescue and Rehabilitation Station
Ph: (763) 856-3119
Website: www.mnhoovedanimal
rescue.org

The Original Funny Farm
Website: www.geocities.com/original
funnyfarm

Save Our Souls Equine Rescue (SOSER)
Ph: (218) 637-2168
E-mail: rescue@soser.us
Website: www.soser.us

Missouri
D-D Farm, Animal Sanctuary
Deb Tolentino
E-mail: vhatfie@fableview.org

Fableview Equine Rescue
Valerie O'Brien
Ph: (660) 747-0531
Website: www.fableview.org

Pientka Horse Rescue
Cheryl Pientka
Ph: (816) 690-7442

Rainbow Ridge Ranch Horse Sanctuary
E-mail: info@rainbowridgeranch.org
Website: www.rainbowridgeranch.org

Montana
Angels Among Us Equine Rescue
Michelle Sudan
Ph: (406) 249-5016
E-mail: pinball@centurytel.net

Montana Large Animal Sanctuary
Ph: (406) 741-3823
Website: www.mtanimalsanctuary.com

Nevada
Miracle Horse Rescue
Ph: (775) 751-1101
Website: www.miraclehorse.com

New Hampshire
Live and Let Live Farm
Teresa Paradise
Ph: (603) 798-5615
Website: www.liveandletlivefarm.org

New Hampshire Equine Humane Assn.
27 Main St.
Goffstown, N.H. 03045
Ph: (603) 497-5900
E-mail: nhehainfo@aol.com
Website: nheha.org

Turtle Rock Rescue
Ken Terry
Ph: (603) 585-9995
Website: www.equineextra.com

New Jersey
Lost & Found Horse Rescue
Kelly Young
Ph: (717) 428-9701
Website: www.lfhr.org

Mylestone Equine Rescue
Susan Thompson
Ph: (908) 995-9300
Website: www.mylestone.org

ReRun
Laurie Lane
Ph: (732) 521-4752
Website: www.rerun.org

New Mexico
Horse Stories
Carolyn M. Bertin
Ph: (505) 281-9675
Website: www.horsestories.org

Perfect Harmony Animal Rescue
Ph: (505) 824-2130
Website: www.perfectharmony.bizland
.com

The Horse Shelter
Jan Bandler
Ph: (505) 984-3235
Website: www.thehorseshelter.org

New York
Balanced Innovative Teaching Strategies
Lynn Cross
Ph: (518) 794-8104
E-mail: lynn@h-o-r-s-e.org
Website: www.h-o-r-s-e.org

Crane Mountain Valley Horse Rescue
Nancy Van Wie or Eddie Mrozik
Ph: (518) 623-3470
Website: www.cmvhr.org

Equine Advocates
Susan Wagner
Ph: (518) 245-1599
Website: www.equineadvocates.com

**Equine Rescue of
Orange County**
Lynda Broas
Ph: (845) 733-6085
Website: www.equinerescue.org

Equine Rescue Resource
Colleen Segarra
Ph: (845) 744-1728
Website: www.equineresecueresource
.com

HiHopes For Horses
Donna O'Leary
Website: www.hihopes.com

**H.O.R.S.E. Rescue
and Sanctuary**
Chris Dodge
Ph: (585) 584-8210
Website: www.hrsny.org

New York Horse Rescue
Mona Kanciper
Ph: (631) 874-9420
E-mail: mona@nyhr.org

ReRun
Sue Swart
Ph: (315) 598-2898
Website: www.rerun.org

Tender Mercy Equine Rescue
Ph: (716) 471-4796
Website: www.tendermercyrescue.com

**Western New York
Equine Sanctuary**
CarolAnn Piazza
Ph: (716) 438-0182
E-mail: cpiazza912@aol.com

North Carolina
Carolina Equine Society
Stephen Hill
Ph: (336) 768-1514
Website: www.carolinaequine
society.org

Horse Protection Society of NC
Joan Benson
Ph: (704) 855-2978
Website: www.horseprotection.org

**United States Equine Rescue
League**
Jacalyn Ackerman
Ph: (336) 720-9757
Website: www.userl.org

North Dakota
Sleipnir Horse Sanctuary
Scott and Ame Smith
Ph: (701) 782-4217
Website: sleipnirsanctuary.tripod.com

Ohio
CANTER
Nancy Scott
Ph: (330) 697-4460
Website: www.canterusa.org/ohio

Happy Trails
Annette Fisher
Ph: (330) 296-5914
Website: www.happytrailsfarm.org

Last Chance Corral
Victoria Goss
Ph: (740) 594-4336
Website: www.lastchancecorral.org

**Lost Acres Horse Rescue
& Rehabilitation**
Sissy Burggraf
Ph: (740) 779-6761
Website: www.geocities.com/sblahrr

**New Vocations Racehorse
Adoption Program**
3293 Wright Rd.
Laura, Oh. 45337-9706
Dot Morgan
Ph: (937) 947-4020
Fax: (937) 947-3201
E-mail: dot@horseadoption.com
Website: www.horseadoption.com

Second Chance Horse Rescue
Daniel's Thoroughbred Farm
Alice Crow
Ph: (513) 200-0808
E-mail: info@secondchancehorse
rescue.com
Website: www.secondchancehorse
rescue.com

Oregon
**Emerald Valley Equine
Assistance**
Sandy
Ph: (541) 935-3906
Website: www.eveahr.com

Equine Angels
Ph: (541) 874-3517
E-mail: equineangels@aol.com

Pennsylvania
**Angel Acres Horse
Haven Rescue**
Jo Deibel
Ph: (717) 225-3212
Website: www.angelacreshorsehaven
rescue.com

Another Chance for Horses
Kathy George
Ph: (434) 384-9465
Website: www.anotherchance
forhorses.com

Bran Manor Equine Rescue
Tru Marabella
Ph: (610) 587-1098
Website: www.angelfire.com/ri2/
branmanorrescue

Bright Futures Farm
44793 Harrison Rd.
Spartansburg, Pa. 16434
Ph: (814) 827-8270
Fax: (814) 827-8278
E-mail: info@brightfuturesfarm.org
Website:
www.brightfuturesfarm.org

High Hope
Joa Haas
Ph: (610) 273-7521
E-mail: lizajoa@aol.com

Hooved Animal Welfare Council
Ph: (814) 899-0960
E-mail: majek25@hotmail.com

Last Chance Ranch
Lori Benetz
Ph: (215) 538-2077
Website: www.lastchanceranch.org

Lost & Found Horse Rescue
Kelly Young
Ph: (717) 428-9701
Website: www.lfhr.org

**Paradise Equine Adoption &
Youth Ministry**
Ph: (724) 775-4470
Website: www.paradiseequine
adoption.org

Ryerss Farm for Aged Equines
Joseph Donahue
Ph: (610) 469-0533
Website: www.ryerss.com

Whispering Acres
Dan Beachel
Ph: (570) 966-9374
Website: www.geocities.com/
whisperingacres

**Wind Ridge Farm Equine
Sanctuary**
Gary Barnes
Ph: (717) 432-2959

South Carolina
PEER
Bernie Peeples
Ph: (843) 871-1909
Website: www.peer-horserescue.org

**South Carolina Awareness,
Rescue**
Karen Metze
Ph: (888) 866-8744

South Dakota
Black Hills Wildhorse Sanctuary
Dayton Hyde
Website: www.wildmustangs.com

Tennessee
Angel Rescue and Transport
Lena M. Frensley
Ph: (615) 740-0964
E-mail: LenaFrensley@angelrescue.com
Website: www.angelrescue.com

Horse Haven of Tennessee
Nina Margetson
Ph: (865) 609-4030
Website: www.horsehavenoftn.com

Texas
Animals First
Holly Christian
Ph: (936) 228-0434
E-mail: animals1strescue@hotmail.com
Website: www.animals1st.com

Brighter Days Horse Refuge
Jeanie Weatherholz
Ph: (830) 510-6607
Website: www.brighterdays
horserefuge.org

Equiserve Equine Rescue
Janice McCoy
Ph: (817) 220-0775
E-mail: jlmccoy@equiserveequine
rescue.org
Website: www.equiserveequinerescue
.org

Exceller Fund to Rescue Horses
Barbara Kraus
Ph: (972) 874-7486
Website: www.excellerfund.org

Habitat For Horses
Ph: (409) 935-0277
Website: www.habitatforhorses.org

Hope for Horses
Ph: (972) 734-6218
Website: www.hopeforhorses.org

Humane Help Animal Rescue
Ph: (432) 229-4295
Website: www.freewebs.com/hhar

Last Refuge
Carol Chapman
Ph: (972) 962-7706
Website: www.geocities.com/
~lastrefuge

Lone Star Equine Rescue
P.O. Box 627
Haslet, Tx. 76052
Jennny Williams
Ph: (979) 776-9396
Ph: (817) 439-0412
Fax: (817) 439-0412
E-mail: info@lser.org
Website: www.lser.org

**Sam Houston Race Park
Adopt-a-Horse**
Ph: (281) 807-8700
Website: www.shrp.com

Shady Oaks Ranch
LeAnn Souser
Ph: (817) 648-0122
E-mail: leann@shadyoaksranch.com
Website: www.shadyoaksranch.com

**Southwestern Equine Rescue
Foundation**
Christy Clements
Ph: (469) 384-0230
E-mail: cclements@earthlink.net

**United States Equine Sanctuary
& Rescue**
Daniele Pruitt
Ph: (877) 720-1685
E-mail: dpruitt@usesr
Website: www.usesr.org

Vermont
**Humane Organization
for Un-Raceables**
Terry Holden
Ph: (802) 644-2759
E-mail: HORSEVT@sover.net

Spring Hill Horse Rescue
Gina Brown
Ph: (802) 247-2857
E-mail: Springhillrescue@aol.com

Virginia
**Dream Catcher Farm Horse
Sanctuary**
Website: www.horsesanctuary.com

Equine Rescue League
P.O. Box 4366
Leesburg, Va. 20177
Pat Rogers
Ph: (703) 771-1240
E-mail: bubbasays2@aol.com
Website: www.equinerescueleague.org

Horse Lovers United
Lorraine Truitt
Ph: (410) 749-3599
Website: www.horseloversunited.com

Lost & Found Horse Rescue
Kelly Young
Ph: (717) 428-9701
Website: www.lfhr.org

ReRun
Paul Linn
Ph: (434) 369-5433
Website: www.rerun.org

Roanoke Valley Horse Rescue
Pat Gillar
Ph: (540) 797-1999
Website: www.rvhr.com

The Laughing Horse Sanctuary
Tom and Julia Durfee
Ph: (434) 927-5298
Website: www.laughinghorse.org

Washington
**Broken Oaks Equine
Retirement Center**
Jean and Gary Pratt
Ph: (509) 767-1461
E-mail: gpratt@gorge.net
Website: www.brokenoaks.org

**Hooved Animal Rescue
of Thurston County**
Joyce Bell
Website: www.har-otc.com

People Helping Horses
Ph: (360) 920-6444
Website: www.peoplehelpinghorses.com

ReRun
Jody Peetz
Ph: (425) 313-5982
Website: www.rerun.org

Sleepy Hollow Horse Rescue
Sarah Schak
Ph: (509) 488-7669
Website: www.sleepy-hollow.org

**Whidbey Island Rescue
of Equines**
Becky Montoya
Ph: (360) 675-9252
Website: www.petfinder.org/shelters/
WA151.html

West Virginia
CANTER
Allison Conrad
Ph: (301) 728-6062
Website: www.canterusa.org

C & M Equine Rescue
Michelle Eddy
Website: www.cmranch.org

Second Wind Adoption Program
Ph: (304) 873-3121
E-mail: secondwindadopt@aol.com
Website: www.crossedsabers.com

Wisconsin
Central States Horse Rescue
Website: www.cshr.50megs.com

**Midwest Horse
Welfare Foundation**
Scott Bayerl
Ph: (715) 387-0555
E-mail: yukon@tznet.com
Website: www.equineadoption.com

Prairie-Woods Horse Rescue
Ph: (715) 246-5323
E-mail: info@prairie-woods.org

Canada
Foalquest
Wendy Ellis
Website: www.pmufoalquest.com

Heaven Can Wait
Claire Malcolm
Ph: (705) 359-3766
Website: www.heavencanwaitequine
rescue.org

**LongRun Thoroughbred
Retirement**
Vicki Pappas
Ph: (416) 675-3993
Website: www.longrunretirement.com

NetPets
Karen Briggs
Ph: (905) 352-2662
Website: www.netpets.com

**New Stride Thoroughbred
Retirement**
Cathy Sheppard
Ph: (604) 255-7652

Sales Companies

**Agence Francaise
de Vente du Pur-Sang**
32 Ave. Hocquart de Turtot No.51
Deauville, 14800 France
Ph: 33 2 31 81 81 00
Fax: 33 2 31 81 81 01
E-mail: af@deauville-sales.com
Website: *www.deauville-sales.com*
President: Philippe Augier

**Arizona Thoroughbred
Breeders Assn.**
P.O. Box 41774
Phoenix, Az. 85080
Ph: (602) 942-1310
Fax: (602) 942-8225
E-mail: atba@worldnet.att.net
Website: *www.atba.net*
President: Bradley Rollins

Barretts Equine Ltd.
P.O. Box 2010
Pomona, Ca. 91769
Ph: (909) 629-3099
Fax: (909) 629-2155
E-mail: barrettseq@aol.com
Website: *www.barretts.com*
President: Gerald F. McMahon

Breeders Sales Co. of Louisiana
P.O. Box 24650
New Orleans, La. 70184
Ph: (504) 947-4676
Fax: (504) 943-2149
E-mail: *ltba@iamerica.net*
President: Bryan Krantz

**California Thoroughbred
Breeders Sales**
P.O. Box 60018
Arcadia, Ca. 91066-6018
Ph: (626) 445-7800
Fax: (626) 574-0852
E-mail: cookie@ctba.com
Website: *www.ctba.com*
Sales Coordinator:
Cookie Hackworth

Canadian Breeders Sales
P.O. Box 10 Station B
Etobicoke, ON M9W 5K9 Canada
Ph: (416) 674-1460
Fax: (416) 675-6430

**Doncaster Bloodstock
Sales Ltd.**
Auction Mart Offices, Hawick
Roxburghshire, TD9 9NN England
Ph: 44 (1450) 372222
Fax: 44 (1450) 378017
E-mail: winners@dbsauctions.com
Website: *www.dbsauctions.com*
Managing Director: Henry G. Beeby

Fair Grounds Sales Co.
1751 Gentilly Blvd. N.
New Orleans, La. 70152
Ph: (504) 944-5515
Fax: (504) 944-2511
Website: *www.fgno.com/sales*

Fasig-Tipton Co.
2400 Newtown Pk.
Lexington, Ky. 40583
Ph: (859) 255-1555
Fax: (859) 254-0794
E-mail: info@fasigtipton.com
Website: *www.fasigtipton.com*
President: Walt Robertson
**Executive Vice President and Chief
Operating Officer:** Boyd T. Browning Jr.

Fasig-Tipton Florida
3641 SE 22nd Ave.
Ocala, Fl. 34471
Ph: (352) 368-6623
Fax: (352) 368-6733
E-mail: ppenny@fasigtipton.com
Website: *www.fasigtipton.com*
Director of Two-Year-Old Sales:
Peter Penny

Fasig-Tipton Midlantic
356 Fair Hill Dr., Ste. C
Elkton, Md. 21921
Ph: (410) 392-5555
Fax: (410) 392-5556
Website: *www.fasigtipton.com*
Sales Coordinator: Paget Bennett

Goffs Bloodstock Sales Ltd.
Kildare Paddocks Kill
County Kildare, Ireland
Ph: 353 (45) 886600
Fax: 353 (45) 877119
E-mail: sales@goffs.ie
Website: *www.goffs.com*
Chairman: Michael Osborne
Managing Director: Matt Mitchell

Heritage Place Sales Co.
2829 S. MacArthur Blvd.
Oklahoma City, Ok. 73128
Ph: (405) 682-4551
Fax: (405) 686-1267
E-mail: info@heritageplace.com
Website: *www.heritageplace.com*
General Manager: Clayton Keys

**Illinois Thoroughbred Breeders
and Owners Foundation**
P.O. Box 336
Caseyville, Il. 62232
Ph: (618) 344-3427
Fax: (618) 346-1051
E-mail: itboffp@apci.net
Website: *www.illinoisracingnews
.com/itbof.htm*
President: John Bauman

**Iowa Thoroughbred Breeders
and Owners Assn.**
1 Prairie Meadows Dr.
Altoona, Ia. 50009
Ph: (515) 957-3002
Fax: (515) 957-1368
E-mail: itboa@prairiemeadows.com
Website: *www.iowa
thoroughbred.com*
President: Ray Shattuck

Japan Racing Horse Assn.
Northern Horse Park
114-7, Misawa
Tomakomai
Hokkaido, Japan
Ph: 81-144-58-2812
E-mail: info@jrha.or.jp
Website: *www.jrha.or.jp/eng*

Keeneland Association
4201 Versailles Rd.
Lexington, Ky. 40592-1690
Ph: (859) 254-3412
Fax: (859) 288-4348
E-mail: sales@keeneland.com
Website: *www.keeneland.com*
President: Nick Nicholson
Director of Sales: Geoffrey G. Russell

**Louisiana Thoroughbred
Breeders Sales Co.**
P.O. Box 789
Carencro, La. 70520
Ph: (337) 896-6152
Fax: (337) 896-6153
E-mail: ltbscl1@aol.com
President: Charles Ashy Sr.

Magic Millions Sales
28 Ascot Ct.
Bundall, QLD 9726 Australia
Ph: 61 (7) 5538 8933
Fax: 61 (7) 5531 7082
E-mail: info@magicmillions.com.au
Website: *www.magicmillions.com.au*
Chairman: Gerry Harvey

**Michigan Thoroughbred
Owners and Breeders
Association**
4800 Harvey St.
Muskegon, Mi. 49444
Ph: (231) 798-7721
Fax: (231) 798-7612
E-mail: mtoba@iserv.net
Website: *www.mtboa.com*

Ocala Breeders' Sales Co.
P.O. Box 99
Ocala, Fl. 34478
Ph: (352) 237-2154
Fax: (352) 237-3566
E-mail: obs@obssales.com
Website: *www.obssales.com*
Director of Sales: Tom Ventura

**Ohio Thoroughbred Breeders
and Owners Assn.**
6024 Harrison Ave. Ste. 13
Cincinnati, Oh. 45248-1621
Ph: (513) 574-0440
Fax: (513) 574-2313
E-mail: gb.otbo@fuse.net
Website: *www.otbo.com*
President: Dennis Heebink

**Ontario Division
Canadian Thoroughbred
Horse Society**
P.O. Box 172
Rexdale, ON M9W 5L1 Canada
Ph: (416) 675-3602

Fax: (416) 675-9405
E-mail: cthsont@idirect.com
Website: www.cthsont.com

Oregon Thoroughbred Breeders Assn.
P.O. Box 17248
Portland, Or. 97217
Ph: (503) 285-0658
Fax: (503) 285-0659
E-mail: otba@gwest.net
Website: www.thoroughbredinfo
.com/showcase/otba.htm
Executive Director: Ursula V. Gibbons

Puerto Rico Breeders Sales Co.
Edificio Mercantil Plaza; Ste. 1515
Ave. Ponce de Leon
Hecto Rey, P.R. 00918
Ph: (787) 725-8715

Ruidoso Horse Sales Co.
P.O. Box 909
Ruidoso Downs, N.M. 88346
Ph: (505) 378-4474
Fax: (505) 378-4788
E-mail: ruihorse@zianet.com

Website: www.ruidosodowns
racing.com
President: Lowell Neumayer

San Antonio Horse Sale Co.
6514 N. New Braunfels Ave.
San Antonio, Tx. 78209-3828
Ph: (210) 824-7552
Fax: (210) 824-7562
Email: sahsc@aol.com
Sales Manager: Bart Sherwood

Tattersalls Ltd.
Terrace House
Newmarket, Suffolk, CB8 9BT Great Britain
Ph: 44 (1638) 665931
Fax: 44 (1638) 660850
E-mail: sales@tattersalls.com
Website: www.tattersalls.com
Chairman: Edmond Mahony

Tattersalls (Ireland) Ltd.
Fairyhouse, Ratoath
County Meath, Ireland
Ph: 353 (1) 8864300
Fax: 353 (1) 8864303

E-mail: info@tattersalls.ie
Website: www.tattersalls.ie
Chairman: Edmond Mahony

Tennessee Breeders Sales Co.
2474 Old Natchez Trace Rd.
Franklin, Tn. 37069-6302
Ph: (615) 373-8197

Thomas Sales Co.
10410 N. Yale Ave.
Sperry, Ok. 74073
Ph: (918) 288-7308
Fax: (918) 288-7330
E-mail: thomas.sales@worldnet.att.net
President: Robert Thomas

Washington Thoroughbred Breeders Assn.
P.O. Box 1499
Auburn, Wa. 98071-1499
Ph: (253) 288-7878
Fax: (253) 288-7890
E-mail: maindesk@washington
thoroughbred.com
Website: www.washington
thoroughbred.com
Sales and Research: Pamela Voss

Publicly Owned Companies With Thoroughbred-Industry Holdings

Boyd Gaming Corp.

A newcomer to the horse racing industry, Boyd Gaming hit a home run when it purchased Delta Downs in Vinton, Louisiana, in 2001. Purses and wagering have increased substantially since the Las Vegas-based company opened its Delta Downs slots pavilion in early 2002. With the Boyd family controlling nearly half of the common stock, the company has 17 gaming properties in Nevada, Mississippi, Illinois, and Indiana, in addition to Louisiana. It is developing the Borgata casino hotel in Atlantic City, New Jersey, with MGM Mirage. Boyd Gaming owns the Stardust Hotel and Casino in Las Vegas and has two adjacent properties in Tunica, Mississippi—Sam's Town and Isle of Capri. In 2004, it bought Harrah's Shreveport, Louisiana, casino for $190-million and Las Vegas-based Coast Casinos for $820-million.

Headquarters: 2950 Industrial Rd., Las Vegas, Nv. 89109-1150
Phone: (702) 792-7200
Website: www.boydgaming.com
Chairman and CEO: William S. Boyd
President: Keith E. Smith
Symbol, exchange: BYD, New York Stock Exchange
Employees: 19,293
2004 Revenues: $1.73-billion
2004 Net Profit: $111.5-million

Canterbury Park Holding Corp.

Canterbury Downs opened in 1985 outside Minneapolis, and, like several other tracks debuting in that era, such as the Birmingham Turf Club and the rebuilt Garden State Park, it struggled for survival as it failed to meet expectations for pari-

mutuel handle and attendance. Ladbroke Racing bought the track in 1990 but closed it two years later. In late 1993, investor Irwin Jacobs bought the property and sold it a few months later to a group headed by Curtis A. Sampson, owner of a successful Minnesota telecommunications company. Randall Sampson, his son and an investor in the track, became president of Canterbury. The elder Sampson spearheaded an initial public offering in 1994, and the track, with its name changed to Canterbury Park, reopened for live racing in 1995. Boosted by full-card simulcasting, Canterbury posted its first profit in 1997 and showed further gains when its card club opened in 2000.

Headquarters: 1100 Canterbury Road, Shakopee, Mn. 55379
Phone: (952) 445-7223
Website: www.canterburypark.com
Chairman: Curtis A. Sampson
President and CEO: Randall D. Sampson
Symbol, exchange: ECP, American Stock Exchange
Employees: 1,086
2004 Revenues: $54.9-million
2004 Net Profit: $3.9-million

Churchill Downs Inc.

For more than a half-century, Churchill Downs has been America's best-known racetrack, but financial difficulties in the early 1980s almost led to a takeover. Warner Jones, a prominent breeder, stepped in and reorganized the company, bringing in lawyer Thomas Meeker as president and chief executive officer in 1984. Over the next two decades, Churchill Downs Inc. became a heavyweight within the racetrack industry, occupying top spots with Magna Entertainment Corp. and the New York Racing Association. Churchill's expansion began rather modestly, building Hoosier Park as a controlling partner and buying Ellis Park in western Kentucky. But the pace accelerated after Magna's Frank Stronach began his acquisitions in 1998, and Churchill bought Calder Race Course, Hollywood Park, and Arlington Park. In 2003, Churchill officials put Ellis up for sale and in 2005 explored a possible sale of Hollywood Park. In 2004, Churchill acquired Fair Grounds in New Orleans for $47-million, and in 2005 it was authorized to install slot machines there.

Headquarters: 700 Central Avenue, Louisville, Ky. 40208
Phone: (502) 636-4400
Website: www.churchilldownsincorporated.com
Chairman: Carl F. Pollard
President and CEO: Thomas H. Meeker
Employees: 2,500
Symbol, exchange: CHDN, NASDAQ
2004 Revenues: $463.1-million
2004 Net Profit: $9.1-million

Gemstar-TV Guide International Inc.

Television Games Network, the racing industry's first national provider of televised races by cable and satellite signal, became a part of Gemstar-TV Guide International when Gemstar bought out TV Guide in 2002. In turn, Gemstar-TV Guide is 41% owned by Rupert Murdoch's News Corp. After restating 2002 earnings and reporting a $6.4-billion loss, the company had further losses in 2003 and 2004. TVG continued to show improved performance, however, with 2004 wagering of $303.5-million, up 42% from 2003.

Headquarters: 6922 Hollywood Blvd., 12th Fl. Los Angeles, Ca. 90028
Phone: (323) 817-4600
Website: www.gemstartvguide.com
Chairman: Anthea Disney
Chief Executive: Rick Battista
Employees: 2,011
Symbol, exchange: GMST, NASDAQ
2004 Revenues: $732.3-million
2004 Net Loss: $94.4-million

GTECH Holdings Corp.

The world's largest operator of lottery systems, GTECH Holdings Corp. has an interest in the racing industry from its one-third ownership of Turfway Park. A wholly owned GTECH subsidiary, Dreamport Inc., formally holds the ownership interest in the Northern Kentucky track. Dreamport also is a part-owner of Suffolk Downs in East Boston, Massachusetts, and provides technological services to several pari-mutuel operations, including Harrington Raceway in Delaware. If Turfway's performance has proved to be disappointing, it is a small piece of GTECH, which supplies or operates lotteries for more than 80 customers in 44 countries.

Headquarters: 55 Technology Wy., West Greenwich, R.I. 02817
Phone: (401) 392-1000
Website: www.gtech.com
Chairman: Robert M. Dewey Jr.
President: William B. Turner
Employees: 4,900
Symbol, exchange: GTK, New York Stock Exchange
2004 Revenues: $1.26-billion
2004 Net Profit: $196.4-million

Harrah's Entertainment Inc.

The world's largest casino company, Harrah's Entertainment Inc. has been increasing its involvement in the pari-mutuel industry. By virtue of a loan to Turfway Park, Harrah's became a one-third owner of the Northern Kentucky track when Keeneland led a buyout of Jerry Carroll and his partners in January 1999. In August 2002, Harrah's announced it was buying 95% of Louisiana Downs. The attraction was the arrival of slot machines at the Bossier City track in 2003, and a new slots casino opened there in '04. The company's total investment in Louisiana Downs, including the purchase price, was estimated at $183-million.

Headquarters: One Harrah's Ct., Las Vegas, Nv. 89119
Phone: (702) 407-6000
Website: www.harrahs.com
Chairman President, and CEO: Gary W. Loveman
Employees: 46,600
Symbol, exchange: HET, New York Stock Exchange
2004 Revenues: $4.55-billion
2004 Net Profit: $367.7-million

International Game Technology

International Game Technology became a player in the pari-mutuel industry with its 2001 purchase of Anchor Gaming, owner of United Tote Co. IGT acquired Anchor for more than $1.3-billion in stock, and the attraction was Anchor's slot-machine and lottery-related businesses. A private group of investors, including United Tote managers, bought the totalizator company in 2003.

Headquarters: 9295 Prototype Dr., Reno, Nv. 89521
Phone: (775) 448-7777
Website: www.igtonline.com
Chairman and CEO: Thomas J. Matthews
Employees: 4,900
Symbol, exchange: IGT, New York Stock Exchange
2004 Revenues: $2.48-billion
2004 Net Profit: $488.7-million

Magna Entertainment Corp.

Spun off from Frank Stronach-controlled Magna International in 1999, Magna Entertainment Corp. has quickly become the biggest player in the racetrack industry. Stronach's buying spree began with Santa Anita Park in 1998 and has grown to no fewer than 13 tracks, including ones that it leases. In addition to Santa Anita, Magna has acquired another top-level track, Gulfstream Park in South Florida, and in 2002 completed its purchase of Lone Star Park in the Dallas-Fort Worth metroplex for $80-million and assumption of $20-million in debt. Also in 2002, Magna added a Triple Crown track to its portfolio when it acquired controlling interest in Pimlico Race Course and Laurel Park. Magna rolled out its XpressBet system for phone wagering, and in early 2003 unveiled HorseRacing TV, a cable-television network featuring races from the 13 Magna-owned or -affiliated tracks and 60 other racetracks.

Headquarters: 337 Magna Dr., Aurora, ON L4G 7K1, Canada
Phone: (905) 726-2462
Website: www.magnaent.com
Chairman: Frank Stronach
President and CEO: W. Thomas Hodgson
Employees: 5,300
Symbol, exchange: MECA, NASDAQ
2004 Revenues: $731.6-million
2004 Net Loss: $95.6-million

MAXXAM Inc.
A highly diversified company that has stirred controversy with its past acquisitions, MAXXAM Inc. offers a range of products from aluminum to lumber to live horse racing. Its principal source of revenues is Kaiser Aluminum, of which it owns approximately 62%. MAXXAM also owns Pacific Lumber, which owns more than 2,000 acres of commercial timberlands in Humboldt County, California. In addition, MAXXAM owns commercial and residential properties in several states and Puerto Rico. Its Sam Houston Race Park investment has been hurt in recent years by slot machines at Delta Downs in Louisana, a short distance from the Texas border.

Headquarters: 5847 San Felipe, Ste. 2600, Houston, Tx. 77057
Phone: (713) 975-7600
Website: None
Chairman and CEO: Charles E. Hurwitz
President: Paul N. Schwartz
Employees: 1,775
Symbol, exchange: MXM, American Stock Exchange
2004 Revenues: $336.6-million
2004 Net Loss: $46.6-million

MGM Mirage
Headed by horse owner J. Terrence Lanni, MGM Mirage made an inroad into the Thoroughbred industry in 2004 when it became a partner with the New York Racing Association in a slots pavilion at Aqueduct. In 2005, it was promised that its slots operation would continue past the expiration of the NYRA racing franchise in 2007. The world's second-largest gaming company, MGM Mirage owns such high-profile properties as the Bellagio, Mirage, and MGM Grand Hotel in Las Vegas. Kirk Kerkorian, the company's founder, owns 57% of MGM Mirage.

Headquarters: 3600 Las Vegas Blvd. S., Las Vegas, Nv. 89109
Phone: (702) 693-7120
Website: www.mgmmirage.com
Chairman and CEO: J. Terrence Lanni
President: James J. Murren
Employees: 40,000
Symbol, exchange: MGG, New York Stock Exchange
2004 Revenues: $4.24-billion
2004 Net Profit: $412.4-million

MTR Gaming Group Inc.
Edson R. "Ted" Arneault thought he was simply helping a friend sell woebegone Mountaineer Park in 1992, but he ended up in the middle of a campaign to legalize video lottery terminals at West Virginia's racetracks. The effort succeeded, and Mountaineer became its hot property. MTR, of which Arneault owns approximately 13%, changed the name of the Chester facility to Mountaineer Racetrack and Gaming Resort to emphasize that it has both racing and more than 3,000 slot machines. In 2002, MTR opened a hotel on the site and hosted its first graded race, the West Virginia Derby (G3). It has been granted a license to build a new racetrack, Presque Isle Downs, near Erie, Pennsylvania, and it owns Scioto Downs, a standardbred track near Columbus, Ohio. In 2004 it bought Binion's Horseshoe Casino, in downtown Las Vegas. In 2005, the facility was renamed Binion's Gambling Hall and Hotel.

Headquarters: Rte. 2 S., Chester, W.V. 26034
Phone: (304) 387-5712
Website: www.mtrgaming.com
Chairman, President, and CEO: Edson R. "Ted" Arneault
Employees: 2,750
Symbol, exchange: MNTG, NASDAQ
2004 Revenues: $315.2-million
2004 Net Profit: $14.5-million

Penn National Gaming Inc.
From relatively modest beginnings as the owner of a regional racetrack near Harrisburg, Pennsylvania, Penn National Gaming has grown into the nation's seventh-largest publicly owned gaming company. Under Chairman and Chief Executive Officer Peter M. Carlino, son of the racetrack's principal owner, the company made profitable investments in off-track betting facilities in Central Pennsylvania, bought Pocono Downs and its off-track facilities, and then moved into gaming with its purchase of Charles Town Races in 1996. With extensive remodeling and slot machines, Charles Town has prospered and so has Penn National Gaming. It owns several casino properties and in 2004 obtained authorization to install slot ma-

chines at Penn National Race Course. Because it cannot own two Pennsylvania gaming facilities, Penn National sold Pocono Downs and its five OTB sites to the Mohegan Tribal Gaming Authority for $280-million in 2005.

Headquarters: 825 Berkshire Blvd., Ste. 200, Wyomissing, Pa. 19610
Phone: (610) 373-2400
Website: *www.pennnational.com*
Chairman and CEO: Peter M. Carlino
President: Kevin DeSanctis
Employees: 12,126
Symbol, exchange: PENN, NASDAQ
2004 Revenues: $1.14-billion
2004 Net Profit: $71.4-million

Scientific Games Corp.

Autotote Corp., a leading provider of pari-mutuel equipment and services, acquired Scientific Games Holdings Corp. in September 2000, and the combined company took the name Scientific Games Corp. A. Lorne Weill, who had been chairman and chief executive officer of Autotote since 1992, took over those positions in the new company. Scientific Games is a leading provider of instant lottery tickets, and Autotote controlled approximately 65% of the racetrack pari-mutuel market through 2002. In late 2002, the company gained wide attention when an employee and two of his friends conspired to fix a winning ticket, worth $3-million, for the Breeders' Cup Ultra Pick Six at Arlington Park. The three quickly were indicted and sentenced for wire fraud, and Autotote took steps to improve security in its pari-mutuel operations.

Headquarters: 750 Lexington Ave., 25th Fl., New York, N.Y. 10022
Phone: (212) 754-2233
Website: *www.scientificgames.com*
Chairman and CEO: A. Lorne Weill
Employees: 3,550
Symbol, exchange: SGMS, NASDAQ
2004 Revenues: $725.5-million
2004 Net Profit: $65.7-million

Youbet.com Inc.

After a rocky start, interactive wagering company Youbet.com is making some headway in racetrack wagering over the Internet. A membership service with an Oregon wagering hub, Youbet.com offers wagering on races in most states as well as Canada, Australia, South Africa, and Hong Kong. Charles F. "Chuck" Champion became Youbet.com's president in 2002 and put in place operational and management changes that resulted in the company's first profit in 2004, $4.6-million on revenues of $65.2-million.

Headquarters: 5901 De Soto Ave., Woodland Hills, Ca. 91367
Phone: (818) 668-2100
Website: *www.youbet.com*
Chairman, President and CEO: Charles F. Champion
Employees: 81
Symbol, exchange: UBET, NASDAQ
2004 Revenues: $65.2-million
2004 Net Profit: $4.6-million

Revenues and Profit or Loss in Millions of Dollars

Company (Symbol)	Revenues	Profit (Loss)	Year-End Stock Price
Boyd Gaming Corp. (BYD)	$1,734.1	$111.5	$41.65
Canterbury Park Holding Corp. (ECP)	54.9	3.9	20.20
Churchill Downs Inc. (CHDN)	463.1	9.1	44.70
Gemstar-TV Guide International Inc. (GMST)	732.3	−94.4	5.92
GTECH Holdings Corp. (GTK)	1,257.2	196.4	25.95
Harrah's Entertainment Inc. (HET)	4,548.3	367.7	66.89
International Game Technology (IGT)	2,484.8	488.7	34.38
Magna Entertainment Corp. (MECA)	731.6	−95.6	6.02
MAXXAM Inc. (MXM)	347.5	−46.6	32.80
MGM Mirage (MGG)	4,238.1	412.4	72.74
MTR Gaming Group Inc. (MNTG)	315.2	14.5	10.56
Penn National Gaming Inc. (PENN)	1,140.	71.4	60.55
Scientific Games Corp. (SGMS)	725.5	65.7	23.84
Youbet.com Inc. (UBET)	65.2	4.6	5.06

Racetrack Stock Closing Prices by Year

Company (Symbol)	2004	2003	2002	2001	2000	1999
Boyd Gaming Corp. (BYD)	$41.65	$16.14	$14.05	$6.50	$3.4375	$5.1825
Canterbury Park Holding Corp. (ECP)	20.20	16.95	13.27	7.20	7.50	5.6875
Churchill Downs Inc. (CHDN)	44.70	36.37	38.18	36.97	29.8125	22.5625
Gemstar-TV Guide International Inc. (GMST)	5.92	5.07	3.25	27.70	46.125	71.25
GTECH Holdings Corp. (GTK)	25.95	49.49	27.86	45.29	20.5625	22.00
Harrah's Entertainment Inc. (HET)	66.89	49.77	39.60	37.01	26.375	26.4375
International Game Technology (IGT)	34.38	35.70	75.92	68.30	48.00	20.3125
Magna Entertainment Corp. (MECA)	6.02	5.05	6.20	7.00	4.75	
MAXXAM Inc. (MXM)	32.80	18.95	9.30	17.50	15.1875	42.875
MGM Mirage (MGG)	72.74	37.61	32.97	28.87	28.1875	50.1325
MTR Gaming Group Inc. (MTRG)	10.56	10.30	7.96	16.00	4.75	3.0675
Penn National Gaming Inc. (PENN)	60.55	23.12	15.86	30.34	10.1875	9.00
Scientific Games Corp. (SGMS)	23.84	16.97	7.26	8.75	2.95	3.25
Youbet.com Inc. (UBET)	5.06	2.51	0.77	0.51	0.9687	4.3125

INTERNATIONAL
Review of the 2004 Racing Season

No name in the history of Thoroughbred racing is better known than that of Derby. The 10th Lord Derby was an avid racing fan in the early 1700s, and in 1779 the 12th Earl established the sport's first filly classic, the Oaks, which was named for the family's residence in Woodmansterne, Surrey. The 12th Lord Derby won that first Oaks with Bridget, and, at a lavish dinner celebrating the race, a contest for three-year-old colts to complement the Oaks was proposed. According to Derby family legend, the dinner guests insisted that the race should be named for either Derby or his friend Sir Charles Bunbury, also an influential racing figure of that era. The issue was decided by a coin toss, Lord Derby won, and the first Derby, held a year later in 1780, was won by Bunbury's Diomed. In 1787, Lord Derby scored his first victory in the race with Sir Peter Teazle, who would sire four Derby winners and two Oaks winners. Lord Derby's famous "black jacket and white cap" silks made their first appearance at Newmarket in 1788 (the colors previously were green and white stripes).

After a long period of inactivity and neglect, the 16th Lord Derby, Frederick Arthur, and his son, Lord Stanley, returned the family to prominence in the sport. The family stud near Liverpool was restored, and in 1893 the center of the family's racing activities moved to Newmarket with the legendary George Lambton as private trainer. Lord Stanley, who became the 17th Earl in 1908, took the family's operations to new heights. Among his 20 classic winners was Hyperion, the 1933 Derby winner who proved to be an influential sire on both sides of the Atlantic Ocean.

After the death of the 17th Earl in 1948, the Stanley operation had few major successes. The lone major winner for the 18th Lord Derby was Teleprompter (GB), a gelding who won the 1985 Arlington Million Stakes (G1). The stud also produced his half sister, Selection Board, a nonwinner who in 2001 foaled Ouija Board (GB), a dual classic winner and a Breeders' Cup winner in North America who was among the top horses racing in Europe in '04. Voted the Cartier Horse of the Year over Prix de l'Arc de Triomphe (Fr-G1) winner Bago and another top three-year-old filly, Attraction, Ouija Board was the only horse raced in 2004 by the 19th Lord Derby, Edward Richard William Stanley. In a year that was, with the exception of Bago, a relatively weak one for European males, fillies excelled. Soviet Song, a four-year-old Marju filly, was voted the end-of-season Cartier Award as outstanding older horse.

Ouija Board, the first classic winner for Lord Derby's Stanley House Stud since Sun Stream swept the 1945 One Thousand Guineas and Oaks, started her 2004 season with an easy, six-length score in Newmarket's Pretty Polly Stakes on May 2. Trainer Edward Dunlop then sent her out for a devastating seven-length victory in the Epsom Oaks (Eng-G1) on June 4. On six weeks' rest, the Cape Cross (Ire) filly came back to win the Darley Irish Oaks (Ire-G1) by a length. Scratched from the Aston Upthorpe Yorkshire Oaks (Eng-G1) because of soft ground, Ouija Board trained up to the Arc on October 3 and finished third when her late charge was 1½ lengths short of overhauling Bago.

One of the few European horses dispatched to Texas for the 21st Breeders' Cup, Ouija Board at first was ticketed to the Breeders' Cup Turf (G1) at her preferred distance of 1½ miles, but the Stanley House brain trust and Dunlop decided to keep her against members of her own sex in the Breeders' Cup Filly and Mare Turf (G1), in which she went off as the 9-to-10 favorite and won by 1½ lengths.

While Ouija Board had had a respectable but hardly noteworthy juvenile season, Attraction sparkled as a two-year-old and was weighted at 119 pounds, only two pounds behind Bago, the male champion, on the International Classifications of 2003. She hardly lost any of her glimmer at three for trainer Mark Johnston. After nearly ten months away from the racecourse, she won the One Thousand Guineas (Eng-G1) by a half-length over Sundrop and added the Irish One Thousand Guineas (Ire-G1) by a length over Alexander Goldrun. In mid-June, she scored a brilliant 2½-length victory in the Coronation Stakes (Eng-G1). The Efisio filly sustained her first career defeat when Soviet Song beat her in Newmarket's Falmouth Stakes (Eng-G1) on July 6. Dispatched to Deauville to oppose males in the Prix du Haras de Fresnay-le-Buffard Jacques le Marois (Fr-G1), she became bogged down on soft turf and finished tenth behind winner Whipper. Second again to Soviet Song in the Matron Stakes (Ire-G1) at Leopardstown, she finished her season with a victory in the Sun Chariot Stakes (Eng-G1) at Newmarket on October 2. In many years, Attraction's stellar season would have been sufficient to gain the three-year-old filly title, but Ouija Board's campaign trumped her.

At the end of the 2003 season, Bago had been regarded as the leading classics contender, but when minor physical problems delayed his return to the races, six three-year-olds divvied up the major spring events. Haafhd, from the stud of Sheikh Hamdan bin Rashid al Maktoum, won the Two Thousand Guineas (Eng-G1) at 5.50-to-

1 odds. Odds-on American Post was a lucky winner of the Gainsborough Poule d'Essai des Poulains (Fr-G1), the French Two Thousand Guineas equivalent, and Bachelor Duke upset the Irish Two Thousand Guineas (Ire-G1). The three European Derbys had three different winners: North Light captured the Epsom Derby (Eng-G1); Blue Canari won the Prix du Jockey-Club (Fr-G1) (French Derby); and Grey Swallow took the Irish Derby (Ire-G1).

Bago, bred and owned by the Niarchos family, returned to fine form in late spring for trainer Jonathan Pease. On the Prix du Jockey-Club undercard, he ran his unbeaten streak to five with a three-length victory in the Prix Jean Prat (Fr-G1); later in June, he fought hard for a half-length win at 1-to-10 odds in the Juddmonte Grand Prix de Paris (Fr-G1). His unbeaten streak ended in the Juddmonte International Stakes (Eng-G1), in which he met older rivals for the first time and finished third, 1½ lengths behind winner Sulamani (Ire). To prepare the Nashwan colt for the Arc, Pease sent him into the Prix Niel (Fr-G2), but the result was more troubling than the Juddmonte. On soft ground at Longchamp, Bago failed to overtake front-running Valixir and Prospect Park and finished a length back in third at 4-to-5 odds. Bettors abandoned Bago in the Arc and sent him off at 10-to-1, but he surged in the final yards to a half-length victory over Cherry Mix. Bago's owners decided not to send him to the United States for the Breeders' Cup.

As some commentators noted at the time, older foreign horses did not go to Texas for the Breeders' Cup, not so much because of the weather, which was pleasant, or the ground, which was yielding, but because the division had little depth. Sulamani made the trip across the Atlantic Ocean, but his target was the Canadian International Stakes (Can-G1) on October 24, six days before the Breeders' Cup races. Against decidedly mundane competition, he went off at 0.85-to-1 odds at Woodbine and won by 1½ lengths over Simonas. Among the top older males, Godolphin Racing's son of Her-

nando (Fr) probably was the year's best and closed out the season with his only two 2004 victories. Other members of the division had their moments in the spotlight and then faded from view. At Royal Ascot in June, Rakti won the Prince of Wales's Stakes (Eng-G1) at 3-to-1—Sulamani finished fourth as the 2.75-to-1 favorite—and he returned to Ascot in September to win the Queen Elizabeth II Stakes (Eng-G1). But those were his only 2004 victories. Refuse To Bend (Ire), the 2003 Two Thousand Guineas winner, also had two major victories, the Queen Anne Stakes (Eng-G1) at Ascot and the Eclipse Stakes (Eng-G1) at Sandown, but his other 2004 starts were decidedly mediocre. Godolphin's Doyen won the King George VI and Queen Elizabeth Stakes (Eng-G1) as the 1.10-to-1 favorite but went badly off form thereafter.

The year's most consistent older runner proved to be Soviet Song, a homebred of the vast Elite Racing Club who had four victories in 2004, all at a mile. After defeats in two minor early-season stakes, the four-year-old filly won the Ridgewood Pearl Stakes (Ire-G2) at the Curragh in May and then was a courageous second to Refuse To Bend in the Queen Anne. Over the summer, she put together three marvelous races, defeating Attraction by 2½ lengths in the Falmouth, besting males in the Sussex Stakes (Eng-G1) at Goodwood, and again taking the measure of Attraction in the Matron. She ended her 2004 season with a dull effort behind Rakti in the Queen Elizabeth II.

The juvenile division sported two undefeated champions. Shamardal won his three 2004 starts, all by open lengths. After an easy maiden win for Johnston, the Giant's Causeway colt won the Vintage Stakes (Eng-G2) and set all the pace in the Darley Dewhurst Stakes (Eng-G1). The leading filly, Divine Proportions, was divinely perfect in five starts for the Niarchos family and trainer Pascal Bary. She defeated males handily in the Prix Morny (Fr-G1) at Deauville in August and successfully stepped up to a mile in winning the Prix Marcel Boussac (Fr-G1) at Longchamp on the Arc program.—*Don Clippinger*

Richest International Races of 2004

Race (Grade)	Purse	Track	Distance	Date	Winner	1st Purse
Dubai World Cup (UAE-G1)	$6,000,000	Nad al Sheba, United Arab Emirates	9.94f	3/27	Pleasantly Perfect	$3,600,000
Japan Cup (Jpn-G1)	4,686,838	Tokyo, Japan	11.93f	11/28	Zenno Rob Roy	2,469,753
Arima Kinen	3,341,817	Nakayama, Japan	12.43f	12/26	Zenno Rob Roy	1,767,292
Tokyo Yushun	3,115,965	Tokyo, Japan	11.93f	5/30	King Kamehameha	1,726,012
Melbourne Cup (Aus-G1)	3,101,710	Flemington, Australia	15.91f	11/2	Makybe Diva	2,092,720
Kikuka Sho	2,549,948	Kyoto, Japan	14.91f	10/24	Delta Blues	1,437,290
Derby S. (Eng-G1)	2,500,696	Epsom, England	a12f	6/5	North Light	1,450,404
Japan Cup Dirt	2,467,218	Tokyo, Japan	10.44f	11/28	Time Paradox	1,302,040
Tenno Sho (Fall)	2,422,657	Tokyo, Japan	9.94f	10/31	Zenno Rob Roy	1,281,659
Takarazuka Kinen (Jpn-G1)	2,377,984	Hanshin, Japan	10.94f	6/27	Tap Dance City	1,257,359
Tenno Sho (Spring)	2,323,059	Kyoto, Japan	15.91f	5/2	Ingrandire	1,229,433
Hong Kong Cup (HK-G1)	2,314,800	Sha Tin, Hong Kong	9.94f	12/12	Alexander Goldrun	1,311,720
Golden Slipper S. (Aus-G1)	2,274,000	Rosehill, Australia	5.97f	4/3	Dance Hero	1,384,608
W. S. Cox Plate (Aus-G1)	2,233,290	Moonee Valley, Australia	9.94f	10/23	Savabeel	1,493,790

Race (Grade)	Purse	Track	Distance	Date	Winner	1st Purse
Satsuki Sho	$2,187,795	Nakayama, Japan	9.94f	4/18	Daiwa Major	$1,231,902
Yushun Himba	2,042,679	Tokyo, Japan	11.93f	5/23	Daiwa el Cielo	1,142,301
Dubai Duty Free (UAE-G1)	2,000,000	Nad al Sheba, United Arab Emirates	8.83f	3/27	(DH) Paolini (Ger), Right Approach	800,000
Dubai Golden Shaheen (UAE-G1)	2,000,000	Nad al Sheba, United Arab Emirates	5.97f	3/27	Our New Recruit	1,200,000
Dubai Sheema Classic (UAE-G1)	2,000,000	Nad al Sheba, United Arab Emirates	11.93f	3/27	Polish Summer (GB)	1,200,000
UAE Derby (UAE-G2)	2,000,000	Nad al Sheba, United Arab Emirates	8.83f	3/27	Lundy's Liability (Brz)	1,200,000
Prix de l'Arc de Triomphe (Fr-G1)	1,985,920	Longchamp, France	11.93f	10/3	Bago	1,134,755
Oka Sho	1,961,395	Hanshin, Japan	7.95f	4/11	Dance in the Mood (Jpn)	1,098,360
Queen Elizabeth II Commemorative Cup	1,852,748	Kyoto, Japan	10.94f	11/14	Admire Groove	984,215
Doncaster H. (Aus-G1)	1,848,746	Randwick, Australia	7.95f	4/12	Private Steer	1,204,466
Hong Kong Mile (HK-G1)	1,800,400	Sha Tin, Hong Kong	7.95f	12/12	Firebreak	1,028,800
Hong Kong Vase (HK-G1)	1,800,400	Sha Tin, Hong Kong	11.93f	12/12	Phoenix Reach (Ire)	1,028,800
Hong Kong Derby	1,796,200	Sha Tin, Hong Kong	9.94f	3/21	Lucky Owners	1,041,796
Queen Elizabeth II Cup (HK-G1)	1,794,800	Sha Tin, Hong Kong	9.94f	4/25	Diaghilev	1,025,600
Mile Championship	1,790,601	Kyoto, Japan	7.95f	11/21	Durandal	947,032
Takamatsunomiya Kinen	1,745,841	Chukyo, Japan	5.97f	3/28	Sunningdale	924,037
February S.	1,690,761	Tokyo, Japan	7.95f	2/22	Admire Don	894,039
Sprinters S.	1,667,931	Nakayama, Japan	5.97f	10/3	Calstone Light O	881,595
Yasuda Kinen	1,666,470	Tokyo, Japan	7.95f	6/6	Tsurumaru Boy	882,120
International Cup (Sin-G1)	1,644,017	Singapore, Malaysia	9.94f	5/16	Epalo (Ger)	922,041
NHK Mile Cup	1,610,576	Tokyo, Japan	7.95f	5/9	King Kamehameha	854,340
JBC Classic	1,600,040	Ohi, Japan	9.94f	11/3	Admire Don	941,200
Shuka Sho	1,596,989	Kyoto, Japan	9.94f	10/17	Sweep Tosho	850,263
Caulfield Cup (Aus-G1)	1,582,615	Caulfield, Australia	11.93f	10/16	Elvstroem	997,815
Tancred S. (Aus-G1)	1,532,623	Rosehill, Australia	11.93f	4/3	Grand Zulu	1,002,023
Canadian International S. (Can-G1)	1,500,000	Woodbine, Canada	a12f	10/24	Sulamani (Ire)	900,000
Irish Derby (Ire-G1)	1,477,925	The Curragh, Ireland	12f	6/27	Grey Swallow	895,632
Australian Derby (Aus-G1)	1,461,425	Randwick, Australia	11.93f	4/10	Starcraft	953,365
King George VI and Queen Elizabeth S. (Eng-G1)	1,374,301	Ascot, England	a12f	7/24	Doyen	797,094
Prix du Jockey Club (Fr-G1)	1,351,899	Chantilly, France	11.93f	6/6	Blue Canari	772,476
Tokyo Daishoten	1,309,136	Ohi, Japan	9.94f	12/29	Adjudi Mitsuo	770,080
Hong Kong Sprint (HK-G1)	1,286,000	Sha Tin, Hong Kong	4.97f	12/12	Silent Witness	733,020
Stayers S.	1,209,022	Nakayama, Japan	17.9f	12/4	Daitaku Bertram	636,681
CBC Sho	1,186,474	Chukyo, Japan	5.97f	12/29	Precious Cafe	625,306
Sankei Osaka Hai	1,177,902	Hanshin, Japan	9.94f	4/4	Neo Universe	619,862
Nikkei Sho	1,165,782	Nakayama, Japan	12.43f	3/27	Win Generare	614,074
Nikkei Shinshun Hai	1,156,820	Kyoto, Japan	11.93f	1/18	Silk Famous	609,256
American Jockey Club Cup	1,155,909	Nakayama, Japan	9.5f	1/25	Dantsu Judge	608,190
Hanshin Daishoten (Jpn-G2)	1,151,520	Hanshin, Japan	14.91f	3/21	Lincoln	605,653
Hanshin Juvenile Fillies	1,134,964	Hanshin, Japan	7.95f	12/5	Shonan Peintre	600,514
Nakayama Kinen	1,134,828	Nakayama, Japan	8.83f	2/29	Sakura President	597,992
Kyoto Kinen	1,132,308	Kyoto, Japan	10.94f	2/21	Silk Famous	596,442
Victoria Derby (Aus-G1)	1,130,840	Flemington, Australia	12.43f	10/30	Plastered	737,667
Sapporo Kinen	1,127,160	Sapporo, Japan	9.94f	8/22	Fine Motion	593,159
Mainichi Okan (Jpn-G2)	1,124,761	Tokyo, Japan	8.83f	10/10	Telegnosis	591,865
Kyoto Daishoten (Jpn-G2)	1,124,029	Kyoto, Japan	11.93f	10/10	Narita Century	591,353
Irish Champion S. (Ire-G1)	1,121,110	Leopardstown, Ireland	10f	9/11	Azamour	710,201
Kinko Sho	1,117,417	Chukyo, Japan	9.94f	5/29	Tap Dance City	588,158
Sankei Sho All Comers	1,111,008	Nakayama, Japan	10.94f	9/26	Tosen Dandy	584,314
Hanshin Himba S.	1,108,988	Hanshin, Japan	7.95f	12/19	Heavenly Romance	586,409
Asahi Hai Futurity S.	1,100,572	Nakayama, Japan	7.95f	12/12	Meiner Recolte	582,122
Swan S.	1,094,834	Kyoto, Japan	6.96f	10/30	Tamamo Hot Play	579,314
Copa Republica Argentina	1,060,563	Tokyo, Japan	12.43f	11/7	Leningrad	559,130
Keio Hai Spring Cup (Jpn-G2)	1,014,472	Tokyo, Japan	6.96f	5/16	Win Radius	536,821
Meguro Kinen	1,000,679	Tokyo, Japan	12.43f	5/22	Chakra	528,144
Atto Mile (Can-G1)	1,000,000	Woodbine, Canada	1m	9/19	Soaring Free	600,000
Godolphin Mile (UAE-G2)	1,000,000	Nad al Sheba, United Arab Emirates	7.95f	3/27	Firebreak	600,000
Queen's Plate S.	1,000,000	Woodbine, Canada	10f	6/27	Niigon	600,000

Progression of Richest International Race, 1980-2004

Purse	Race	Track	Country	Year	Winner	1st Purse
$6,000,000	Dubai World Cup (UAE-G1)	Nad al Sheba	U.A.E.	2000	Dubai Millennium	$3,600,000
5,000,000	Dubai World Cup (UAE-G1)	Nad al Sheba	U.A.E.	1999	Almutawakel (GB)	3,000,000
4,689,920	Breeders' Cup Classic (G1)	Churchill Downs	U.S.	1998	Awesome Again	2,662,400
4,030,400	Breeders' Cup Classic (G1)	Hollywood Park	U.S.	1997	Skip Away	2,288,000
4,000,000	Dubai World Cup	Nad al Sheba	U.A.E.	1996	Cigar	2,400,000
3,389,470	Japan Cup (Jpn-G1)	Tokyo	Japan	1994	Marvelous Crown	1,784,713
2,748,000	Breeders' Cup Classic (G1)	Churchill Downs	U.S.	1991	Black Tie Affair (Ire)	1,560,000
2,739,000	Breeders' Cup Classic (G1)	Hollywood Park	U.S.	1984	Wild Again	1,350,000
1,049,725	Hollywood Futurity (G1)	Hollywood Park	U.S.	1983	Fali Time	549,849
1,000,000	Arlington Million Invitational	Arlington Park	U.S.	1981	John Henry	600,000
641,093	Derby S. (Eng-G1)	Epsom	England	1980	Henbit	387,439

Major International Races
Canada
Atto Mile Stakes

Grade 1, Woodbine, Ontario, three-year-olds and up, 1 mile, turf. Held September 19, 2004, with a gross value of $1,000,000. First held in 1997.

Year	Winner	Jockey	Second	Third	Strs	Time	1st Purse
2004	Soaring Free, 5	T. Kabel	Perfect Soul (Ire), 6	Royal Regalia, 6	11	1:32.72	$600,000
2003	Touch of the Blues (Fr), 6	K. J. Desormeaux	Soaring Free, 4	Perfect Soul (Ire), 5	11	1:33.39	600,000
2002	Good Journey, 6	P. Day	†Chopinina, 4	Nuclear Debate, 7	13	1:33.27	600,000
2001	Numerous Times, 4	P. Husbands	Affirmed Success, 7	Quiet Resolve, 6	14	1:32.79	600,000
2000	Riviera (Fr), 6	J. R. Velazquez	Arkadian Hero, 5	Affirmed Success, 6	13	1:33.18	600,000
1999	‡Quiet Resolve, 4	R. C. Landry	Rob 'n Gin, 5	Jim and Tonic (Fr), 5	15	1:33.19	630,000
1998	Labeeb (GB), 6	K. J. Desormeaux	Jim and Tonic (Fr), 4	Poteen, 4	11	1:33.00	450,000
1997	Geri, 5	C. W. Antley	Helmsman, 5	Crown Attorney, 4	12	1:36.20	300,000

‡Woodbine Mile S. 1997-'98. Hawksley Hill (Ire) finished first, DQ to fourth, 1999. †Denotes female.

Breeders' Stakes

Not graded, Woodbine, Ontario, three-year-olds, Canadian-foaled, 1½ miles, turf. Held August 8, 2004, with a gross value of $500,000. First held in 1889.

Year	Winner	Jockey	Second	Third	Strs	Time	1st Purse
2004	A Bit O'Gold	J. Jones	Burst of Fire	Silver Ticket	11	2:27.15	$300,000
2003	Wando	P. Husbands	Shoal Water	Colorful Judgement	8	2:28.69	300,000
2002	Portcullis	S. Callaghan	El Soprano	Mountain Beacon	10	2:29.80	300,000
2001	†Sweetest Thing	J. S. McAleney	Flaming Sky	†Asia	6	2:29.90	300,000
2000	Lodge Hill	M. E. Smith	Master Stuart	Scatter the Gold	7	2:28.97	300,000
1999	†Free Vacation	L. L. Gulas	John the Drummer	American Falcon	13	2:28.45	195,000
1998	†Pinafore Park	R. C. Landry	Patriot Love	Comet Kris	9	2:30.20	180,000
1997	John the Magician	S. R. Bahen	†One Emotion	†Heaven to Earth	12	2:35.60	175,860
1996	Chief Bearhart	M. Walls	Firm Dancer	Sealaunch	9	2:28.60	171,120
1995	Charlie's Dewan	C. Perret	Mt. Sassafras	Dagda	13	2:26.40	182,700
1994	Basqueian	J. M. Lauzon	Pagagar	Testalino	5	2:47.80	149,739
1993	Peteski	C. Perret	Flashy Regent	English Toff	4	2:30.40	237,549
1992	Blitzer	D. J. Seymour	†Classic Reign	Rodin	11	2:35.60	180,000

Held at Fort Erie 1994. †Denotes female.

Canadian International Stakes

Grade 1, Woodbine, Ontario, three-year-olds and up, 1½ miles, turf. Held October 24, 2004, with a gross value of $1,500,000. First held in 1938.

Year	Winner	Jockey	Second	Third	Strs	Time	1st Purse
2004	Sulamani (Ire), 5	L. Dettori	Simonas (Ire), 5	Brian Boru (GB), 4	10	2:28.64	$900,000
2003	Phoenix Reach (Ire), 3	M. Dwyer	Macaw (Ire), 4	Brian Boru (GB), 3	10	2:33.62	900,000
2002	Ballingarry (Ire), 3	M. J. Kinane	Falcon Flight (Fr), 6	Yavana's Pace (Ire), 10	8	2:31.68	900,000
2001	Mutamam (GB), 6	R. Hills	Paolini (Ger), 4	Lodge Hill, 4	12	2:28.46	900,000
2000	Mutafaweq, 4	L. Dettori	Williams News, 5	Daliapour (Ire), 4	12	2:27.62	900,000
1999	Thornfield, 5	R. A. Dos Ramos	Fruits of Love, 4	Courteous (GB), 4	9	2:32.39	936,000
1998	Royal Anthem, 3	G. L. Stevens	Chief Bearhart, 5	Parade Ground, 3	8	2:29.60	630,000
1997	Chief Bearhart, 4	J. A. Santos	Down the Aisle, 4	Romanov (Ire), 3	8	2:29.00	600,000
1996	Singspiel (Ire), 4	G. L. Stevens	Chief Bearhart, 3	Mecke, 4	7	2:33.20	600,000
1995	Lassigny, 4	P. Day	Mecke, 3	Hasten To Add, 5	15	2:29.80	653,250
1994	Raintrap (GB), 4	R. G. Davis	†Alywow, 3	Volochine (Ire), 3	9	2:25.60	606,900
1993	Husband, 3	C. B. Asmussen	Cozzene's Prince, 6	Regency (GB), 3	11	2:36.40	623,100
1992	‡Snurge, 5	R. T. R. Quinn	Ghazi, 3	Wiorno (GB), 4	14	2:39.00	636,000

Rothmans Ltd. International S. 1992-'95. ‡Wiorno (GB) finished first, DQ to third, 1992. †Denotes female.

E. P. Taylor Stakes

Grade 1, Woodbine, Ontario, three-year-olds and up, fillies and mares, 1¼ miles, turf. Held October 24, 2004, with a gross value of $750,000. First held in 1956.

Year	Winner	Jockey	Second	Third	Strs	Time	1st Purse
2004	Commercante (Fr), 4	J. Velazquez	Punctilious (GB), 3	Classic Stamp, 4	8	2:04.02	$450,000
2003	Volga (Ire), 5	R. Migliore	Tigertail, 4	Hi Dubai (GB), 3	10	2:05.68	450,000
2002	Fraulein (GB), 3	K. Darley	Alasha (Ire), 3	Volga (Ire), 4	6	2:10.03	450,000
2001	Choc Ice (Ire), 3	J. P. Murtagh	Volga (Ire), 3	Spring Oak (GB), 3	13	2:03.01	300,000
2000	Fly for Avie, 5	T. Kabel	Lady Upstage (Ire), 3	Innuendo (Ire), 5	6	2:02.78	300,000
1999	Insight (Fr), 4	M. E. Smith	Cerulean Sky (Ire), 3	Midnight Line, 4	8	2:05.34	300,000
1998	Zomaradah (GB), 3	G. L. Stevens	Tresoriere, 4	Griselda, 3	8	2:02.40	273,600
1997	Kool Kat Katie (Ire), 3	O. Peslier	Mousse Glacee (Fr), 3	L'Annee Folle (Fr), 4	9	2:02.00	206,460
1996	Wandering Star, 3	W. H. McCauley	Flame Valley, 3	Carling (Fr), 4	8	2:04.60	204,120
1995	Timarida (Ire), 3	L. Dettori	Matiara, 3	Bold Ruritana, 5	7	2:03.60	213,120
1994	Truly a Dream (Ire), 4	C. J. McCarron	Bold Ruritana, 4	Hero's Love, 6	9	2:01.60	207,180
1993	Hero's Love, 5	E. Fires	Dance for Donna, 4	Lady Shirl, 6	11	2:14.40	204,300
1992	Hatoof, 3	W. R. Swinburn	Urban Sea, 3	Hero's Love, 4	12	2:07.80	210,960

Prince of Wales Stakes

Not graded, Fort Erie, Ontario, three-year-olds, Canadian-foaled, 1³/₁₆ miles, dirt. Held July 18, 2004, with a gross value of $500,000. First held in 1929.

Year	Winner	Jockey	Second	Third	Strs	Time	1st Purse
2004	A Bit O'Gold	J. Jones	Niigon	His Smoothness	7	1:57.69	$300,000
2003	Wando	P. Husbands	Arco's Gold	Shoal Water	7	1:55.84	300,000
2002	Le Cinquieme Essai	B. T. Bochinski	Bravely	Anglian Prince	12	1:56.53	300,000
2001	Win City	C. Montpellier	†Dancethruthedawn	Brushing Bully	6	1:56.14	210,000
2000	Scatter the Gold	T. Kabel	For Our Sake	Cool N Collective	7	1:56.01	170,280
1999	†Gandria	C. Montpellier	Woodcarver	Euchre	8	1:56.23	155,700
1998	Archers Bay	R. C. Landry	Nite Dreamer	One Way Love	6	1:55.20	118,500
1997	Cryptocloser	W. Martinez	C. C. On Ice	Rabbit in a Hat	7	1:56.00	117,660
1996	Stephanotis	M. Walls	Firm Dancer	Kristy Krunch	7	1:55.20	121,620
1995	Kiridashi	L. Attard	Regal Discovery	Mt. Sassafras	6	1:55.00	121,800
1994	Bruce's Mill	C. Perret	Basqueian	Parental Pressure	4	1:53.20	87,296
1993	Peteski	D. Penna	Flashy Regent	Cheery Knight	8	1:54.40	72,203
1992	Benburb	L. Attard	Alydeed	Judge Carson	6	1:57.40	107,700

†Denotes female.

Queen's Plate Stakes

Not graded, Woodbine, Ontario, three-year-olds, Canadian-foaled, 1¼ miles, dirt. Held June 27, 2004, with a gross value of $1,000,000. First held in 1860.

Year	Winner	Jockey	Second	Third	Strs	Time	1st Purse
2004	Niigon	R. Landry	A Bit O'Gold	Will He Crow	13	2:04.72	$600,000
2003	Wando	P. Husbands	Mobil	Rock Again	12	2:02.48	600,000
2002	T J's Lucky Moon	S. R. Bahen	Anglian Prince	Forever Grand	13	2:06.88	600,000
2001	†Dancethruthedawn	G. Boulanger	Win City	Brushing Bully	10	2:03.78	600,000
2000	Scatter the Gold	T. Kabel	I and I	For Our Sake	16	2:05.53	600,000
1999	Woodcarver	M. Walls	†Gandria	Euchre	17	2:03.13	300,000
1998	Archers Bay	K. J. Desormeaux	Brite Adam	Kinkennie	13	2:02.20	300,000
1997	Awesome Again	M. E. Smith	Cryptocloser	Sovereign Storm	14	2:04.20	255,420
1996	Victor Cooley	E. Ramsammy	Stephanotis	Kristy Krunch	13	2:03.80	255,480
1995	Regal Discovery	T. Kabel	Freedom Fleet	Mt. Sassafras	14	2:03.80	261,660
1994	Basqueian	J. M. Lauzon	Bruce's Mill	Parental Pressure	11	2:03.40	276,420
1993	Peteski	C. Perret	Cheery Knight	Janraffole	11	2:04.20	218,600
1992	Alydeed	C. Perret	Grand Hooley	Benburb	12	2:04.60	228,900

†Denotes female.

England

Derby S.

Group 1, Epsom, three-year-olds, 1½ miles and 10 yards, turf. Held June 4, 2005, with a gross value of $2,266,250. First held in 1780.

Year	Winner	Jockey	Second	Third	Strs	Time	1st Purse
2005	Motivator	J. P. Murtagh	Walk In The Park	Dubawi	13	2:35.60	$1,314,425
2004	North Light	K. Fallon	Rule of Law	Let The Lion Roar (GB)	14	2:33.72	1,491,719
2003	Kris Kin	K. Fallon	The Great Gatsby	Alamshar	20	2:33.35	1,373,453
2002	High Chaparral (Ire)	J. P. Murtagh	Hawk Wing	Moon Ballad (Ire)	12	2:39.45	1,249,424
2001	Galileo (Ire)	M. J. Kinane	Golan (Ire)	Tobougg (Ire)	12	2:33.20	800,342
2000	Sinndar	J. P. Murtagh	Sakhee	Beat Hollow (GB)	15	2:36.75	918,981
1999	Oath	K. Fallon	Daliapour (Ire)	Beat All	16	2:37.43	990,671
1998	High-Rise (Ire)	O. Peslier	City Honours	Border Arrow	15	2:33.88	978,679
1997	Benny the Dip	W. Ryan	Silver Patriarch	Romanov (Ire)	13	2:34.77	971,448
1996	Shaamit	M. Hills	Dushyantor	Shantou	20	2:35.05	804,894
1995	Lammtarra	W. R. Swinburn	Tamure (Ire)	Presenting	15	2:32.31	805,687
1994	Erhaab	W. Carson	King's Theatre (Ire)	Colonel Collins	25	2:34.16	717,662
1993	Commander in Chief	M. J. Kinane	Blue Judge	Blues Traveller (Ire)	16	2:34.51	693,078
1992	Dr Devious (Ire)	J. A. Reid	St. Jovite	Silver Wisp	18	2:36.19	649,473

Gold Cup

Group 1, Royal Ascot Racecourse, four-year-olds and up, about 2½ miles, turf. Held June 17, 2004, with a gross value of $442,940. First held in 1807.

Year	Winner	Jockey	Second	Third	Strs	Time	1st Purse
2004	Papineau, 4	L. Dettori	Westerner, 5	Darasim, 6	13	4:20.90	$256,905
2003	Mr Dinos, 4	K. Fallon	Persian Punch, 10	Pole Star, 5	12	4:20.15	233,581
2002	Royal Rebel, 6	J. P. Murtagh	Vinnie Roe, 4	Wareed, 4	15	4:25.64	199,184
2001	Royal Rebel, 5	J. P. Murtagh	Persian Punch, 8	Jardines Lookout, 4	12	4:18.90	172,432
2000	Kayf Tara, 6	M. J. Kinane	Far Cry, 5	Compton Ace, 4	11	4:24.53	184,308
1999	Enzeli, 4	J. P. Murtagh	Invermark, 5	Kayf Tara, 5	17	4:18.85	191,662
1998	Kayf Tara, 4	L. Dettori	Double Trigger, 7	Three Cheers, 4	16	4:32.36	198,132
1997	Celeric, 5	P. Eddery	Classic Cliche, 5	Election Day, 5	13	4:26.19	187,197
1996	Classic Cliche, 4	M. J. Kinane	Double Trigger, 5	Nononito, 5	14	4:23.20	182,980
1995	Double Trigger, 4	J. Weaver	Moonax, 4	Admiral's Well, 5	7	4:20.25	178,465
1994	Arcadian Heights, 6	M. Hills	Vintage Crop, 7	Sonus, 5	9	4:27.67	169,666
1993	Drum Taps, 7	L. Dettori	Assessor, 4	Turgeon, 7	10	4:32.57	166,410
1992	Drum Taps, 6	L. Dettori	Arcadian Heights, 4	Turgeon, 6	6	4:18.20	198,590

King George VI and Queen Elizabeth Stakes

Group 1, Ascot Racecourse, three-year-olds and up, about 1½ miles, turf. Held July 24, 2004, with a gross value of $1,374,300. First held in 1951.

Year	Winner	Jockey	Second	Third	Strs	Time	1st Purse
2004	Doyen, 4	L. Dettori	Hard Buck (Brz), 5	Sulamani (Ire), 5	11	2:33.18	$797,094
2003	Alamshar, 3	J. P. Murtagh	Sulamani (Ire), 4	Kris Kin, 3	12	2:33.26	700,742
2002	Golan (Ire), 4	K. Fallon	Nayef, 4	Zindabad (Fr), 6	9	2:29.70	636,448
2001	Galileo (Ire), 3	M. J. Kinane	Fantastic Light, 5	Hightori, 4	12	2:27.71	619,745
2000	Montjeu (Ire), 4	M. J. Kinane	Fantastic Light, 4	Daliapour (Ire), 4	7	2:29.98	654,023
1999	Daylami (Ire), 5	L. Dettori	Nedawi, 4	Fruits of Love, 4	8	2:29.35	539,676
1998	Swain (Ire), 6	L. Dettori	High-Rise (Ire), 3	Royal Anthem, 3	8	2:29.60	587,463
1997	Swain (Ire), 5	J. A. Reid	Pilsudski (Ire), 5	Helissio, 4	8	2:36.45	490,509
1996	Pentire, 4	M. Hills	Classic Cliche, 4	Shaamit, 3	8	2:28.11	457,867
1995	Lammtarra, 3	L. Dettori	Pentire, 3	Strategic Choice, 4	7	2:31.01	445,877
1994	King's Theatre (Ire), 3	M. J. Kinane	White Muzzle (GB), 4	Wagon Master, 4	12	2:28.92	408,813
1993	Opera House (GB), 5	M. Roberts	White Muzzle (GB), 3	Commander in Chief, 3	10	2:33.94	409,307
1992	St. Jovite, 3	S. Craine	Saddlers' Hall (Ire), 4	Opera House (GB), 4	8	2:30.85	497,878

Oaks S.

Group 1, Epsom, three-year-old fillies, 1½ miles and 10 yards, turf. Held June 3, 2005, with a gross value of $696,503. First held in 1779.

Year	Winner	Jockey	Second	Third	Strs	Time	1st Purse
2005	Eswarah	R. Hills	Something Exciting	Pictavia	12	2:39.00	$403,971
2004	Ouija Board (GB)	K. Fallon	All Too Beautiful	Punctilious	7	2:35.41	376,585
2003	Casual Look	M. Dwyer	Yesterday (Ire)	Summitville	15	2:38.07	387,744
2002	Kazzia (Ger)	L. Dettori	Quarter Moon (Ire)	Shadow Dancing	14	2:44.52	297,009
2001	Imagine	M. J. Kinane	Flight of Fancy	Relish The Thought (Ire)	14	2:36.70	292,125
2000	Love Divine	T. R. Quinn	Kalypso Katie (Ire)	Melikah (Ire)	16	2:43.11	288,823
1999	Ramruma	K. Fallon	Noushkey	Zahrat Dubai (GB)	10	2:38.72	286,775
1998	Shahtoush (Ire)	M. J. Kinane	Bahr (GB)	Midnight Line	8	2:38.23	289,342
1997	Reams of Verse	K. Fallon	Gazelle Royale	Crown of Light	12	2:35.59	297,432
1996	Lady Carla (GB)	P. Eddery	Pricket	Mezzogiorno	11	2:35.55	309,279
1995	Moonshell (Ire)	L. Dettori	Dance a Dream (GB)	Pure Grain (GB)	10	2:35.44	236,037
1994	Balanchine	L. Dettori	Wind in Her Hair (Ire)	Hawajiss	10	2:40.37	223,758
1993	Intrepidity (GB)	M. Roberts	Royal Ballerina (Ire)	Oakmead (Ire)	14	2:34.19	228,404
1992	User Friendly (GB)	G. Duffield	All At Sea	Pearl Angel (GB)	7	2:39.77	269,851

One Thousand Guineas

Group 1, Newmarket, three-year-old fillies, 1 mile, turf. Held May 1, 2005, with a gross value of $653,216. First held in 1814.

Year	Winner	Jockey	Second	Third	Strs	Time	1st Purse
2005	Virginia Waters	K. Fallon	Maids Causeway	Vista Bella	20	1:36.50	$378,865
2004	Attraction	K. Darley	Sundrop (Jpn)	Hathrah (Ire)	16	1:36.78	347,265
2003	Russian Rhythm	K. Fallon	Six Perfections (Fr)	Intercontinental (GB)	19	1:38.43	292,747
2002	Kazzia (Ger)	L. Dettori	Snowfire (GB)	Alasha	17	1:37.85	250,612
2001	Ameerat (GB)	P. Robinson	Muwakleh (GB)	Toroca	15	1:38.30	250,473
2000	Lahan (GB)	R. Hills	Princess Ellen (GB)	Petrushka (Ire)	18	1:36.38	221,517
1999	Wince	K. Fallon	Wannabe Grand (Ire)	Valentine Waltz (Ire)	22	1:37.91	206,757
1998	Cape Verdi (Ire)	L. Dettori	Shahtoush (Ire)	Exclusive	16	1:37.86	214,081
1997	Sleepytime (Ire)	K. Fallon	Oh Nellie	Dazzle	15	1:37.66	169,872
1996	Bosra Sham	P. Eddery	Matiya (Ire)	Bint Shadayid	13	1:37.75	151,461
1995	Harayir	R. Hills	Aqaarid	Moonshell (Ire)	14	1:36.72	178,983
1994	Las Meninas (Ire)	J. A. Reid	Balanchine	Coup de Genie	15	1:36.71	166,127
1993	Sayyedati (GB)	W. R. Swinburn	Niche	Ajfan	12	1:37.34	163,969
1992	Hatoof	W. R. Swinburn	Marling (Ire)	Kenbu (Fr)	14	1:39.45	192,254

St. Leger S.

Group 1, Doncaster, three-year-olds, 1¾ miles and 132 yards, turf. Held September 11, 2004, with a gross value of $718,560. First held in 1776.

Year	Winner	Jockey	Second	Third	Strs	Time	1st Purse
2004	Rule of Law	K. McEvoy	†Quiff (GB)	Tycoon (GB)	9	3:06.29	$431,136
2003	Brian Boru (GB)	J. P. Spencer	High Accolade	Phoenix Reach (Ire)	12	3:04.64	386,040
2002	Bollin Eric	K. Darley	Highest	Bandari	8	3:02.92	374,640
2001	Milan (GB)	M. J. Kinane	Demophilos	Mr Combustible	10	3:05.10	326,629
2000	Millenary	T. R. Quinn	Air Marshall	Chimes At Midnight	11	3:02.58	315,018
1999	Mutafaweq	R. Hills	†Ramruma	Adair	9	3:02.75	353,664
1998	Nedawi	J. A. Reid	†High and Low	Sunshine Street	9	3:05.61	335,898
1997	Silver Patriarch	P. Eddery	Vertical Speed	The Fly (GB)	10	3:06.92	295,420
1996	Shantou	L. Dettori	Dushyantor	Samraan	11	3:05.10	271,692
1995	Classic Cliche	L. Dettori	Minds Music	Istiidaad	10	3:09.74	259,794
1994	Moonax	P. Eddery	Broadway Flyer	Double Trigger	8	3:04.19	236,950
1993	Bob's Return	P. Robinson	Armiger	Edbaysaan	9	3:07.85	292,567
1992	†User Friendly (GB)	G. Duffield	Sonus	Bonny Scot	9	3:05.48	323,139

†Denotes female.

Two Thousand Guineas

Group 1, Newmarket, three-year-olds, 1 mile, turf. Held April 30, 2005, with a gross value of $610,304. First held in 1809.

Year	Winner	Jockey	Second	Third	Strs	Time	1st Purse
2005	**Footstepsinthesand**	K. Fallon	Rebel Rebel	Kandidate	19	1:36.10	$353,976
2004	**Haafhd**	R. Hills	Snow Ridge	Azamour	14	1:36.74	322,787
2003	**Refuse To Bend (Ire)**	P. J. Smullen	Zafeen	Norse Dancer	20	1:37.98	292,747
2002	**Rock of Gibraltar (Ire)**	J. P. Murtagh	Hawk Wing	Redback	22	1:36.50	250,612
2001	**Golan (Ire)**	K. Fallon	Tamburlaine (Ire)	Frenchmans Bay	18	1:37.40	250,473
2000	**King's Best**	K. Fallon	Giant's Causeway	Barathea Guest	27	1:37.77	265,820
1999	**Island Sands**	L. Dettori	Enrique	Mujahid	16	1:37.14	276,426
1998	**King of Kings (Ire)**	M. J. Kinane	Lend a Hand (GB)	Border Arrow	18	1:39.25	286,219
1997	**Entrepreneur**	M. J. Kinane	Revoque	Poteen	16	1:35.64	213,832
1996	**Mark of Esteem (Ire)**	L. Dettori	Even Top (Ire)	Bijou d'Inde	13	1:37.59	184,212
1995	**Pennekamp**	T. Jarnet	Celtic Swing	Bahri	11	1:35.16	190,487
1994	**Mister Baileys (GB)**	J. Weaver	Grand Lodge	Colonel Collins	23	1:35.08	194,491
1993	**Zafonic**	P. Eddery	Barathea (Ire)	Bin Ajwaad	14	1:35.32	173,569
1992	**Rodrigo de Triano**	L. Piggott	Lucky Lindy	Pursuit of Love	16	1:38.37	203,189

France

Gainsborough Poule d'Essai des Poulains (French Two Thousand Guineas)

Group 1, Longchamp, three-year-olds, colts, 1,600 meters (7.9536 furlongs), turf. Held May 15, 2005, with a gross value of $504,920. First run in 1883.

Year	Winner	Jockey	Second	Third	Strs	Time	1st Purse
2005	**Shamardal**	L. Dettori	Indesatchel	Gharir	15	1:39.20	$288,511
2004	**American Post**	R. Hughes	Diamond Green (Fr)	Byron	7	1:36.50	247,048
2003	**Clodovil**	C. Soumillon	Catcher In The Rye	Krataios	10	1:36.40	217,809
2002	**‡Landseer (GB)**	M. J. Kinane	Medecis (GB)	Bowman	13	1:36.80	176,111
2001	**Vahorimix**	C. Soumillon	Clearing	Denon	12	1:35.40	133,600
2000	**Bachir**	L. Dettori	Berine's Son	Valentino	7	1:39.40	140,100
1999	**Sendawar**	G. Mosse	Dansili (GB)	Kingsalsa	15	1:36.20	162,600
1998	**Victory Note**	J. A. Reid	Muhtathir (GB)	Desert Prince (Ire)	12	1:34.50	168,500
1997	**Daylami (Ire)**	G. Mosse	Loup Sauvage	Visionary (Fr)	6	1:42.60	175,700
1996	**Ashkalani**	G. Mosse	Spinning World	Tagula	10	1:37.60	193,200
1995	**Vettori**	L. Dettori	Atticus	Petit Poucet (GB)	8	1:40.40	210,920
1994	**Green Tune**	O. Doleuze	Turtle Island	Psychobabble (Ire)	7	1:37.40	177,230
1993	**Kingmambo**	C. B. Asmussen	Bin Ajwaad	Hudo	10	1:39.10	187,740
1992	**Shanghai**	F. Head	Rainbow Corner (GB)	Lion Cavern	9	1:38.20	180,800

‡Noverre finished first, DQ to 12th, 2002.

Gainsborough Poule d'Essai des Pouliches (French One Thousand Guineas)

Group 1, Longchamp, three-year-old fillies, 1,600 meters (7.9536 furlongs), turf. Held May 15, 2005, with a gross value of $504,920. First held in 1883.

Year	Winner	Jockey	Second	Third	Strs	Time	1st Purse
2005	**Divine Proportions**	C. Lemaire	Toupie	Ysoldina	8	1:38.50	$288,511
2004	**Torrestrella (Ire)**	O. Peslier	Grey Lilas	Miss Mambo	13	1:35.70	247,048
2003	**Musical Chimes**	C. Soumillon	Maiden Tower (GB)	Etoile Montante	12	1:36.00	217,809
2002	**Zenda (GB)**	R. Hughes	Firth of Lorne (Ire)	Sophisticat	17	1:37.30	176,111
2001	**Rose Gypsy (GB)**	M. J. Kinane	Banks Hill (GB)	Lethals Lady (GB)	15	1:36.70	133,600
2000	**Bluemamba**	T. Jarnet	Peony	Alshakr	11	1:40.20	140,100
1999	**Valentine Waltz (Ire)**	R. Cochrane	Karmifira (Fr)	Calando	14	1:36.00	162,600
1998	**Zalaiyka**	G. Mosse	Cortona	La Nuit Rose	14	1:35.70	168,500
1997	**Always Loyal**	F. Head	Seebe	Red Camellia	7	1:40.20	175,700
1996	**Ta Rib**	W. Carson	Shake the Yoke (GB)	Sagar Pride (Ire)	9	1:38.70	193,200
1995	**Matiara**	F. Head	Carling (Fr)	Shaanxi	16	1:42.40	210,920
1994	**East of the Moon**	C. B. Asmussen	Agathe	Belle Argentine	8	1:37.10	177,230
1993	**Madeleine's Dream**	C. B. Asmussen	Ski Paradise	Gold Splash	8	1:36.40	187,740
1992	**Culture Vulture**	T. R. Quinn	Hydro Calido	Guislaine (Fr)	9	1:37.00	180,800

Prix de Diane (French Oaks)

Group 1, Chantilly, three-year-olds, fillies, 2,100 meters (10.439 furlongs), turf. Held June 12, 2005, with a gross value of $969,760. First held in 1843.

Year	Winner	Jockey	Second	Third	Strs	Time	1st Purse
2005	**Divine Proportions**	C. Lemaire	Argentina	Paita	10	2:06.30	$554,121
2004	**Latice (Ire)**	C. Soumillon	Millionaia	Grey Lilas	17	2:07.00	352,925
2003	**Nebraska Tornado**	R. Hughes	Time Ahead	Musical Chimes	10	2:08.10	320,955
2002	**Bright Sky (Ire)**	D. Boeuf	Dance Routine	Ana Marie	15	2:07.60	260,302
2001	**Aquarelliste**	D. Boeuf	Nadia (GB)	Time Away	12	2:09.50	220,490
2000	**Egyptband**	O. Doleuze	Volvoreta (GB)	Goldamix (Ire)	14	2:08.50	203,420
1999	**Daryaba**	G. Mosse	Star of Akkar	Visionnaire (Fr)	14	2:16.10	224,700
1998	**Zainta**	G. Mosse	Abbatiale	Insight (Fr)	11	2:11.20	235,340
1997	**Vereva**	G. Mosse	Mousse Glacee (Fr)	Brilliance (Fr)	12	2:08.20	240,520

Year	Winner	Jockey	Second	Third	Strs	Time	1st Purse
1996	Sil Sila	C. B. Asmussen	Miss Tahiti	Matiya (Ire)	12	2:07.30	$269,080
1995	Carling (Fr)	T. Thulliez	Matiara	Tryphosa	12	2:07.70	282,240
1994	East of the Moon	C. B. Asmussen	Her Ladyship	Agathe	9	2:07.90	248,850
1993	Shemaka	G. Mosse	Baya	Dancienne (Fr)	14	2:16.00	260,582
1992	Jolypha	P. Eddery	Sheba Dancer (Fr)	Verveine	12	2:09.50	259,770

Prix de l'Arc de Triomphe

Group 1, Longchamp, three-year-olds and up, 2,400 meters (11.9303 furlongs), turf. Held October 3, 2004, with a gross value of $1,985,920. First held in 1920.

Year	Winner	Jockey	Second	Third	Strs	Time	1st Purse
2004	Bago (Fr), 3	T. Gillet	Cherry Mix (Fr), 3	†Ouija Board (GB), 3	19	2:25.00	$1,134,755
2003	Dalakhani, 3	C. Soumillon	Mubtaker, 6	High Chaparral (Ire), 4	13	2:32.30	1,002,738
2002	Marienbard, 5	L. Dettori	Sulamani (Ire), 3	High Chaparral (Ire), 3	16	2:26.70	899,704
2001	Sakhee, 4	L. Dettori	†Aquarelliste, 3	Sagacity, 3	17	2:36.10	840,000
2000	Sinndar, 3	J. P. Murtagh	†Egyptband, 3	†Volvoreta (GB), 3	10	2:25.80	806,400
1999	Montjeu (Ire), 3	M. J. Kinane	El Condor Pasa, 4	Croco Rouge, 4	14	2:38.50	654,000
1998	Sagamix, 3	O. Peslier	†Leggera (Ire), 3	Tiger Hill, 3	14	2:34.50	724,000
1997	Peintre Celebre, 3	O. Peslier	Pilsudski (Ire), 5	†Borgia (Ger), 3	18	2:24.60	677,600
1996	Helissio, 3	O. Peslier	Pilsudski (Ire), 4	Oscar Schindler, 4	16	2:29.90	771,600
1995	Lammtarra, 3	L. Dettori	Freedom Cry (GB), 4	Swain (Ire), 3	16	2:31.80	811,600
1994	Carnegie (Ire), 3	T. Jarnet	Hernando (Fr), 4	Apple Tree (Fr), 5	20	2:31.10	754,440
1993	†Urban Sea, 4	E. Saint-Martin	White Muzzle (GB), 3	Opera House (GB), 5	23	2:37.90	879,050
1992	Subotica (Fr), 4	T. Jarnet	User Friendly (GB), 3	Vert Amande, 4	18	2:39.00	1,039,500

†Denotes female.

Prix du Jockey-Club (French Derby)

Group 1, Chantilly, three-year-olds, 2,100 meters (10.44 furlongs), turf. Held June 5, 2005, with a gross value of $1,833,750. First held in 1836.

Year	Winner	Jockey	Second	Third	Strs	Time	1st Purse
2005	Shamardal	L. Dettori	Hurricane Run	Rocamadour	17	2:09.00	$1,047,805
2004	Blue Canari	T. Thulliez	Prospect Park	Valixir	15	2:25.20	776,435
2003	Dalakhani	C. Soumillon	Super Celebre	Coroner	7	2:26.70	706,102
2002	Sulamani (Ire)	T. Thulliez	Act One	Simeon (GB)	15	2:25.00	569,080
2001	Anabaa Blue	C. Soumillon	Chichicastenango	Grandera	14	2:27.90	517,200
2000	Holding Court	P. Robinson	Lord Flasheart	Circus Dance	14	2:31.80	359,750
1999	Montjeu (Ire)	C. B. Asmussen	Nowhere to Exit	Rhagaas	8	2:33.50	395,500
1998	Dream Well (Fr)	C. B. Asmussen	Croco Rouge	Sestino (Ire)	13	2:29.30	417,250
1997	Peintre Celebre	O. Peslier	Oscar	Astarabad	14	2:29.60	433,500
1996	Ragmar	G. Mosse	Polaris Flight	Le Destin	15	2:27.20	484,250
1995	Celtic Swing	K. Darley	Poliglote (GB)	Winged Love	11	2:32.80	504,000
1994	Celtic Arms (Fr)	G. Mosse	Solid Illusion	Alriffa	15	2:31.30	444,375
1993	Hernando (Fr)	C. B. Asmussen	Dernier Empereur	Hunting Hawk	11	2:27.20	465,325
1992	Polytain	L. Dettori	Marignan	Contested Bid	17	2:30.30	463,875

Prix Royal-Oak (French St. Leger)

Group 1, Longchamp, three-year-olds and up, 3,100 meters (15.41 furlongs), turf. Held October 24, 2004, with a gross value of $253,480.

Year	Winner	Jockey	Second	Third	Strs	Time	1st Purse
2004	Westerner, 5	S. Pasquier	†Behkara, 4	Alcazar, 9	8	3:28.90	$144,838
2003	Westerner, 4	D. Boeuf	Alcazar, 8	†Behkara, 3	14	3:31.20	94,007
2002	Mr Dinos, 3	D. Boeuf	†Sulk (Ire), 3	Clety, 6	7	3:38.50	84,347
2001	Vinnie Roe, 3	P. J. Smullen	Generic, 6	Germinis, 7	13	3:37.80	54,440
2000	Amilynx, 4	O. Peslier	San Sebastian, 6	Tajoun, 6	11	3:33.40	51,280
1999	Amilynx, 3	O. Peslier	Tajoun, 5	Northerntown, 3	7	3:40.60	65,200
1998	Tiraaz, 4	G. Mosse	†Erudite, 3	Asolo, 4	7	3:58.40	72,840
1997	†Ebadiyla, 3	G. Mosse	†Snow Princess, 5	Oscar Schindler, 5	11	3:26.50	67,160
1996	†Red Roses Story (Fr), 4	V. Vion	Moonax, 5	†Helen of Spain, 4	5	3:38.40	77,840
1995	Sunshack (GB), 4	T. Jarnet	Shrewd Idea (GB), 5	†Sunrise Song, 4	7	3:16.20	81,160
1994	Moonax, 3	P. Eddery	Always Earnest, 6	†Dalara, 3	7	3:28.90	75,444
1993	Raintrap (GB), 3	P. Eddery	Mashaallah, 5	Sonus, 4	8	3:45.80	70,324
1992	Assessor, 3	T. R. Quinn	†Always Friendly, 4	†Sought Out, 4	12	3:35.80	83,160

†Denotes female.

Ireland

Irish Derby

Group 1, The Curragh, three-year-olds, 1½ miles, turf. Held June 27, 2004, with a gross value of $1,429,777. First held in 1866.

Year	Winner	Jockey	Second	Third	Strs	Time	1st Purse
2004	Grey Swallow	P. Smullen	North Light	Tycoon (GB)	10	2:28.70	$837,101
2003	Alamshar	J. P. Murtagh	Dalakhani	Roosevelt	9	2:28.20	837,101
2002	High Chaparral (Ire)	M. J. Kinane	Sholokhov	Ballingarry (Ire)	9	2:32.20	678,466
2001	Galileo (Ire)	M. J. Kinane	Morshdi	Golan (Ire)	12	2:27.10	551,571

Year	Winner	Jockey	Second	Third	Strs	Time	1st Purse
2000	Sinndar	J. P. Murtagh	Glyndebourne (Ire)	Ciro	11	2:33.90	$584,814
1999	Montjeu (Ire)	C. B. Asmussen	Daliapour (Ire)	Tchaikovsky	10	2:30.10	583,427
1998	Dream Well (Fr)	C. B. Asmussen	City Honours	Desert Fox	10	2:44.30	592,554
1997	Desert King	C. Roche	Dr Johnson	Loup Sauvage	10	2:32.50	601,322
1996	Zagreb	P. Shanahan	Polaris Flight	His Excellence	13	2:30.60	546,276
1995	Winged Love	O. Peslier	Definite Article (GB)	Annus Mirabilis (Fr)	13	2:30.10	556,247
1994	†Balanchine	L. Dettori	King's Theatre (Ire)	Colonel Collins	9	2:32.70	515,040
1993	Commander in Chief	P. Eddery	Hernando (Fr)	Foresee	11	2:31.20	524,676
1992	St. Jovite	C. Roche	Dr Devious (Ire)	Contested Bid	10	2:25.10	591,093

†Denotes female.

Darley Irish Oaks

Group 1, The Curragh, three-year-old fillies, 1½ miles, turf. Held July 18, 2004, with a gross value of $497,960. First run in 1895.

Year	Winner	Jockey	Second	Third	Strs	Time	1st Purse
2004	Ouija Board (GB)	K. Fallon	Punctilious	Hazarista	7	2:28.20	$295,290
2003	Vintage Tipple	L. Dettori	L'Ancresse (Ire)	Casual Look	11	2:28.30	252,990
2002	Margarula	K. Manning	Quarter Moon (Ire)	Lady's Secret	12	2:37.40	204,023
2001	Lailani (GB)	L. Dettori	Mot Juste (GB)	Karsavina (Ire)	12	2:30.50	137,466
2000	Petrushka (Ire)	J. P. Murtagh	Melikah (Ire)	Inforapenny	10	2:31.20	133,775
1999	Ramruma	K. Fallon	Sunspangled	Sister Bella	7	2:33.00	153,443
1998	Winona (Ire)	J. P. Murtagh	Kitza (Ire)	Bahr (GB)	9	2:39.80	157,965
1997	Ebadiyla	J. P. Murtagh	Yashmak	Brilliance (Fr)	11	2:33.70	170,988
1996	Dance Design (Ire)	M. J. Kinane	Shamadara	Key Change	6	2:29.70	192,348
1995	Pure Grain (GB)	J. A. Reid	Russian Snows	Valley of Gold	10	2:33.60	185,279
1994	Bolas (GB)	P. Eddery	Hawajiss	Gothic Dream	10	2:37.60	171,295
1993	Wemyss Bight (GB)	P. Eddery	Royal Ballerina (Ire)	Oakmead (Ire)	11	2:35.00	162,573
1992	User Friendly (GB)	G. Duffield	Market Booster	Arrikala	9	2:33.10	212,040

Irish One Thousand Guineas

Group 1, The Curragh, three-year-old fillies, 1 mile, turf. Held May 22, 2005, with a gross value of $502,440. First held in 1922.

Year	Winner	Jockey	Second	Third	Strs	Time	1st Purse
2005	Saoire	M. J. Kinane	Penkenna Princess	Luas Line	18	1:41.50	$282,874
2004	Attraction	K. Darley	Alexander Goldrun	Illustrious Miss	15	1:37.60	278,190
2003	Yesterday (Ire)	M. J. Kinane	Six Perfections (Fr)	Dimitrova	8	1:40.80	252,889
2002	Gossamer (GB)	J. P. Spencer	Quarter Moon (Ire)	Starbourne	15	1:45.50	198,135
2001	Imagine	J. A. Heffernan	Crystal Music	Toroca	16	1:41.10	138,443
2000	Crimplene (Ire)	P. Robinson	Amethyst (Ire)	Storm Dream (Ire)	13	1:39.80	133,195
1999	Hula Angel	M. Hills	Golden Silca (GB)	Dazzling Park	17	1:38.80	151,446
1998	Tarascon	J. P. Spencer	Kitza (Ire)	La Nuit Rose	13	1:38.40	120,461
1997	Classic Park	S. Craine	Strawberry Roan (Ire)	Caiseal Ros (Ire)	10	1:42.20	128,119
1996	Matiya (Ire)	W. Carson	Dance Design (Ire)	My Branch	12	1:39.80	131,497
1995	Ridgewood Pearl (GB)	C. Roche	Warning Shadows	Khaytada	10	1:43.90	137,791
1994	Mehthaaf	W. Carson	Las Meninas (Ire)	Relatively Special (GB)	10	1:49.00	127,067
1993	Nicer (Ire)	M. Hills	Goodnight Kiss	Danse Royale (Ire)	14	1:44.20	174,235
1992	Marling (Ire)	W. Swinburn	Market Booster	Tarwiya	9	1:41.10	196,988

Irish St. Leger S.

Group 1, The Curragh, three-year-olds and up, 1¾ miles, turf. Held September 18, 2004, with a gross value of $456,467. First held in 1915.

Year	Winner	Jockey	Second	Third	Strs	Time	1st Purse
2004	Vinnie Roe, 6	P. J. Smullen	Brian Boru (GB), 4	First Charter, 5	13	3:03.90	$205,389
2003	Vinnie Roe, 5	P. J. Smullen	Gamut, 4	Powerscourt (GB), 3	6	2:25.90	203,410
2002	Vinnie Roe, 4	P. J. Smullen	Pugin, 4	Ballingarry (Ire), 3	8	2:59.00	171,824
2001	Vinnie Roe, 3	P. J. Smullen	Millenary, 4	Marienbard, 4	8	2:58.40	153,159
2000	Arctic Owl, 6	D. Harrison	Yavana's Pace, 8	Mutafaweq, 4	8	3:02.20	110,412
1999	Kayf Tara, 5	L. Dettori	Yavana's Pace, 7	Silver Patriarch, 5	5	3:12.50	143,953
1998	Kayf Tara, 4	J. A. Reid	Silver Patriarch, 4	†Delilah (Ire), 4	7	3:05.70	131,690
1997	Oscar Schindler, 5	S. Craine	Persian Punch, 4	†Whitewater Affair, 4	7	3:06.40	132,223
1996	Oscar Schindler, 4	S. Craine	†Key Change, 3	Sacrament, 5	9	2:59.10	137,349
1995	Strategic Choice, 4	T. R. Quinn	Moonax, 4	Oscar Schindler, 3	7	3:00.90	141,290
1994	Vintage Crop, 7	M. J. Kinane	†Rayseka, 4	†Kithanga, 4	8	3:07.30	133,045
1993	Vintage Crop, 6	M. J. Kinane	Assessor, 4	Foresee, 3	8	3:06.70	123,262
1992	Mashaallah, 4	S. Cauthen	Snurge, 5	Drum Taps, 6	9	3:02.01	163,314

†Denotes female.

Irish Two Thousand Guineas

Group 1, The Curragh, three-year-olds, 1 mile, turf. Held May 21, 2005, with a gross value of $456,467. First held in 1921.

Year	Winner	Jockey	Second	Third	Strs	Time	1st Purse
2005	Dubawi	L. Dettori	Oratorio	Democratic Deficit	8	1:41.60	$287,898
2004	Bachelor Duke	S. Sanders	Azamour	Grey Swallow	8	1:40.00	288,072
2003	Indian Haven	J. F. Egan	France (GB)	Tout Seul	16	1:41.50	245,265
2002	Rock of Gibraltar (Ire)	M. J. Kinane	Century City (Ire)	Della Francesca	7	1:47.30	209,239

Year	Winner	Jockey	Second	Third	Strs	Time	1st Purse
2001	Black Minnaloushe	J. P. Murtagh	Mozart (Ire)	Minardi	12	1:41.40	$138,443
2000	Bachir	L. Dettori	Giant's Causeway	Cape Town	8	1:39.80	137,926
1999	Saffron Walden	O. Peslier	Enrique	Orpen	10	1:38.10	151,379
1998	Desert Prince (Ire)	O. Peslier	Fa-Eq	Second Empire (Ire)	7	1:35.80	169,717
1997	Desert King	C. Roche	Verglas (Ire)	Romanov (Ire)	12	1:38.30	171,383
1996	Spinning World	C. B. Asmussen	Rainbow Blues (Ire)	Beauchamp King	10	1:38.80	175,902
1995	Spectrum	J. A. Reid	Adjareli	Bahri	9	1:40.30	187,592
1994	Turtle Island	J. A. Reid	Guided Tour	Ridgewood Ben	9	1:50.10	169,989
1993	Barathea (Ire)	M. Roberts	Fatherland (Ire)	Massyar (Ire)	11	1:43.00	175,777
1992	Rodrigo de Triano	L. Piggott	Ezzoud (Ire)	Brief Truce	6	1:41.00	198,616

United Arab Emirates
Dubai World Cup

Group 1, Nad al Sheba, three-year-olds and up, 2,000 meters (9.9419 furlongs), dirt. Held March 26, 2005, with a gross value of $6,000,000. First held in 1996.

Year	Winner	Jockey	Second	Third	Strs	Time	1st Purse
2005	Roses in May, 5, 126	J. Velazquez	Dynever	Choctaw Nation	12	2:02.17	$3,600,000
2004	Pleasantly Perfect, 6, 126	A. Solis	Medaglia d'Oro, 5	Victory Moon, 5	12	2:00.24	3,600,000
2003	Moon Ballad (Ire), 4, 126	L. Dettori	Harlan's Holiday, 4	Nayef, 5	11	2:00.48	3,600,000
2002	Street Cry (Ire), 4, 126	J. D. Bailey	Sei Mi, 6	Sakhee, 5	11	2:01.18	3,600,000
2001	Captain Steve, 4, 126	J. D. Bailey	†To the Victory, 5	Hightori, 5	12	2:00.47	3,600,000
2000	Dubai Millennium, 4, 126	L. Dettori	Behrens, 6	Public Purse, 6	13	2:00.65	3,600,000
1999	Almutawakel (GB), 5, 126	R. Hills	Malek (Chi), 6	Victory Gallop, 4	8	2:00.65	3,000,000
1998	Silver Charm, 4, 126	G. L. Stevens	Swain (Ire), 6	Loup Sauvage, 4	9	2:04.29	2,400,000
1997	Singspiel (Ire), 5, 126	J. D. Bailey	Siphon (Brz), 6	Sandpit (Brz), 8	12	2:01.91	2,400,000
1996	Cigar, 6, 126	J. D. Bailey	Soul of the Matter, 5	L'Carriere, 5	11	2:03.84	2,400,000

1996-'97 listed race.

English Triple Crown

Throughout its long history, the English Triple Crown has proved to be as elusive as its younger American cousin, and perhaps even more so. Approaching its third century, the English Triple Crown has been won only 15 times. Since Gainsborough became the 13th winner in 1918, only two more have followed: unbeaten *Bahram in 1935 and the brilliant Nijinsky II in '70.

The English Triple Crown for three-year-olds, dating from 1809, consists of the one-mile Two Thousand Guineas (Eng-G1) at Newmarket in May, the 1½-mile Epsom Derby (Eng-G1) at Epsom Downs in June, and the St. Leger Stakes (Eng-G1) at 1¾ miles and 127 yards at Doncaster Race Course in September. Over the years, there has been some variance in the distances of the three races, and alternative races were used during war years.

The St. Leger Stakes was named for the popular local sportsman Lt. Col. Anthony St. Leger. Alabaculia was the first winner of the St. Leger Stakes in 1776. Four years later, *Diomed, later imported to the United States, won the initial running of the Epsom Derby. The first Two Thousand Guineas was taken by Wizard in 1809, nine years after Champion became the first three-year-old to win both the Epsom Derby and the St. Leger Stakes. In 1813, Sir Charles Bunbury's Smolensko became the first to win the Two Thousand Guineas and the Epsom Derby.

Forty years later in 1853, West Australian became the first to win all three stakes. He was followed by Gladiateur (1865), Lord Lyon (1866), *Ormonde (1886), Common (1891), Isinglass (1893), Galtee More (1897), Flying Fox (1899), Diamond Jubilee (1900), *Rock Sand (1903), Pommern (1915), Gay Crusader (1917), Gainsborough (1918), *Bahram (1935), and Nijinsky II (1970).

In today's racing world, the English Triple Crown is a prize not pursued. The most recent horse with a chance to seize the crown, 1989 Two Thousand Guineas (Eng-G1) and Epsom Derby (Eng-G1) victor Nashwan, was withheld from the St. Leger Stakes (Eng-G1) by owner Sheikh Hamdan bin Rashid al Maktoum to point for the Prix de l'Arc de Triomphe (Fr-G1), in which he did not start because of injury.

Following are the 15 English Triple Crown winners:

WEST AUSTRALIAN—1850 b. h., Melbourne–Mowerina, by Touchstone. 10-9-1-0, $68,615. Known popularly as "the West," West Australian gave owner-breeder John Bowes his fourth and final Epsom Derby victory. Trained by John Scott, West Australian ran second in the Criterion Stakes to Speed the Plough and then beat his rival in the Glasgow Stakes as a two-year-old. At three, West Australian won the Two Thousand Guineas by a half-length over the Duke of Bedford's Sittingbourne and the Epsom Derby by a desperate neck over the same opponent. West Australian won the St. Leger easily, and at four won the Triennial Stakes and the Ascot Gold Cup. Though not widely regarded as a success at stud, he sired The Wizard, the 1860 Two Thousand Guineas winner, and his son *Australian sired Spendthrift, tail-male ancestor of the Man o' War male line that leads to Tiznow.

GLADIATEUR—1862 b. h., Monarque–Miss Gladiator, by Gladiator. 19-16-0-1, $236,537. French-bred and -owned Gladiateur shattered the notion that England's Thoroughbreds were superior when he won the 1865 Two Thousand Guineas, earning the gleeful nickname "Avenger of Waterloo" among the French. Trained at Newmarket by Tom Jennings, he added the Epsom Derby "in a canter" and the St. Leger. In between, he traveled to his native France and captured that country's greatest race at the time, the Grand Prix de Paris. At four, Gladiateur won the Gold Cup at Ascot by 40 lengths after reputedly trailing by 300 yards at one point. He was not a success at stud.

LORD LYON—1863 b. h., Stockwell–Paradigm, by Paragone. 19-15-3-1, $180,497. Leased to Richard Sutton, the second son of Sir Richard Sutton, and trained by James Dover, Lord Lyon dead-heated with Redan in the Champagne Stakes for two-year-olds at Doncaster and then won the Criterion and Troy Stakes at Newmarket. After winning the Two Thousand Guineas by one length over Monarch of the Glen, Lord Lyon completed the Triple Crown by beating Savernake by a head in the Epsom Derby and the same rival by inches in the St. Leger. The following year, Lord Lyon won the Ascot Biennial and the Stockbridge Cup. His most famous offspring were *Ormonde's rival Minting, winner of the 1886 Grand Prix de Paris, and '77 Oaks winner Placida.

*ORMONDE—1883 b. h., Bend Or–Lily Agnes, by Macaroni. 16-16-0-0, $138,340. Considered by many as the finest Thoroughbred of the 19th century, the Duke of Westminster's *Ormonde was unbeaten in his 16-race career despite developing a wind infirmity. At four in the Hardwicke Stakes, he bested Grand Prix de Paris winner Minting. *Ormonde sired just seven foals in his first season at stud in England, but that crop included Orme, a multiple major stakes winner and sire of 1899 Triple Crown winner Flying Fox. After a stint in Argentina, *Ormonde was purchased by William O'Brien Macdonough, an American, for $150,000 in 1893 and stood in California. From 1894 through 1905, *Ormonde sired just 17 foals, but 12 started and five, including Ormondale, won stakes races.

COMMON—1888 br. h., Isonomy–Thistle, by Scottish Chief. 5-4-0-1, $77,567. Owned by his breeder, Lord Allington, and Sir Frederick Johnstone, Common was a colt with dubious joints and thus was not raced at two by trainer John Porter. Common made his debut in the 1891 Two Thousand Guineas, and his profuse sweating prompted Prince Soltykoff to remark, "He's very well named." Uncommon on the Newmarket course, Common won easily. He won the Epsom Derby by two lengths in a downpour and subsequently won the St. James's Palace Stakes before finishing third in the Eclipse Stakes. In the final start of his only racing season, Common completed the Triple Crown by winning the St. Leger by one length. Common's progeny included 1898 One Thousand Guineas winner Nun Nicer and Mushroom, who became a successful stallion in Belgium.

ISINGLASS—1890 b. h., Isonomy–Deadlock, by Wenlock. 12-11-1-0, $279,231. Despite soundness problems that he passed on to his progeny, Isinglass lost only once for his owner, Col. Harry McCalmont, in a four-year career. Isinglass suffered the only loss in his three-year-old campaign when he was defeated by Raeburn in the Lancashire Plate at Manchester, giving the winner ten pounds over an inadequate distance. At four, Isinglass captured the Princess of Wales's Stakes, Eclipse Stakes, and Jockey Club Stakes. As a five-year-old, he won the 1895 Ascot Gold Cup and retired as the sport's all-time money winner. Isinglass stood at his owner's Cheveley Park Stud near Newmarket and sired three British classic winners as well as *Star Shoot, who was North America's leading sire five times and leading broodmare sire five times.

GALTEE MORE—1894 b. h., Kendal–Morganette, by Springfield. 13-11-1-0, $131,312. Galtee More, named after a peak in the Galtee Mountains, was owned by John Gubbins, who used his considerable inheritance from an uncle to open two stud farms, one of which housed Galtee More's sire, Kendal. Trained by Sam Darling, Galtee More won the Molecomb Stakes, the Rous Plate, and the Middle Park Plate as a two-year-old. At three in 1897, Galtee More completed the Triple Crown by taking the St. Leger by three-quarters of a length over the filly Chelandry. At the end of his racing career, Galtee More was sold by Gubbins to the Russian government, and the stallion subsequently was purchased by German interests. His most noteworthy progeny was Orchidee II, dam of Oleander, leading German sire in the 1930s and '40s. Galtee More's half brother Ard Patrick won the Epsom Derby in 1902.

FLYING FOX—1896 b. h., Orme–Vampire, by Galopin. 11-9-2-0, $194,867. A large colt with beautiful shoulders, Flying Fox became the Duke of Westminster's second Triple Crown winner despite a difficult temperament that most likely came from his aptly named dam. At two in 1898, Flying Fox won the New, Stockbridge Foal, and Criterion Stakes, and he finished second in both the Imperial Produce Stakes and the Middle Park Plate. Flying Fox was unbeaten at three and ended his career with a four-length victory in the Jockey Club Stakes. Flying Fox sired French classic winner Val d'Or, and his grandson *Teddy (by French Derby winner Ajax) became an important influence on North American bloodlines through full brothers *Sir Gallahad III and *Bull Dog.

DIAMOND JUBILEE—1897 b. h., St. Simon–Perdita, by Hampton. 16-6-5-1, $142,131. Owned by the Prince of Wales, Diamond Jubilee was described as "ferocious, with a nature more befitting the bullring than the racecourse." He was found to be a cryptorchid (and thus spared from gelding) after finishing unplaced in his first two starts at two. Diamond Jubilee's trainer, Richard Marsh, gave Diamond Jubilee's groom, 18-year-old Herbert Jones, a chance to ride the ridgling, and Diamond Jubilee won the Two Thousand Guineas by four lengths. He won the Epsom Derby by a half-length and the St. Leger by one length. After standing at stud in England, he was sold in 1906 to Las Ortegas Stud in Argentina, where he was the leading sire from 1914 through '16. Diamond Jubilee was a full brother to the outstanding racehorse Persimmon, winner of the Epsom Derby and the St. Leger in 1896.

*ROCK SAND—1900 br. h., Sainfoin–Roquebrune, by St. Simon. 20-16-1-3, $221,703. Although he hobbled along at a trot and canter, *Rock Sand would fully extend himself at a gallop once warmed up and never finished unplaced in his career. He won six stakes races as a two-year-old in 1902, and at three he won the St. James's Palace Stakes and Bennington Stakes in addition to the Triple Crown contests. He won the Hardwicke, Princess of Wales's, Lingfield Park Plate, First Foal, and the Jockey Club Stakes at four. Best known for his success as a broodmare sire, *Rock Sand sired Mahubah, dam of Man o' War. *Rock Sand's other leading daughters included Hour Glass, dam of Blue Glass and *Hourless, and Tea Biscuit, dam of Hard Tack.

*Rock Sand's most accomplished sons were Tracery, winner of the St. James's Palace and the Eclipse Stakes and one of the leading sires in England for many years in the 1920s; Friar Rock, who won the 1916 Belmont Stakes and Suburban Handicap in the United States; and 1916 Preakness Stakes winner Damrosch.

POMMERN—1912 b. h., Polymelus–Merry Agnes, by St. Hilaire. 10-7-1-0, $75,165. A homebred of Solomon B. Joel, Pommern won the Richmond Stakes at Goodwood and the Imperial Produce Stakes at Kemptonat age two. Steve Donoghue was engaged to ride Pommern in his unusual three-year-old season. Pommern won the 1915 Two Thousand Guineas comfortably at Newmarket. With World War I raging across the English Channel in France, Epsom Downs was requisitioned by the military, and Pommern scored a two-length victory in the substitute for the Epsom Derby, the New Derby at 1½ miles on Newmarket's July Course. He then won the substitute for the St. Leger, the 1¾-mile September Stakes at Newmarket. In his only start at four, Pommern won the June Stakes at Newmarket. His best offspring were Adam's Apple, who won the 1927 Two Thousand Guineas; Pondoland, second in the '22 Two Thousand Guineas; and Glommen, who won the '26 Goodwood Cup.

GAY CRUSADER—1914 b. c., Bayardo–Gay Laura, by Beppo. 10-8-2-0, $53,530. Bred and owned by A. W. "Fairie" Cox, Gay Crusader was the first foal of his dam and from his sire's first crop. Trained by Alec Taylor, Gay Crusader was a small colt who developed sore shins in June of his two-year-old season. He made a late start that year, losing his debut before winning the Criterion Stakes. After finishing second in his three-year-old debut in the Column Produce Stakes, Gay Crusader won the 1917 Two Thousand Guineas by a head over Magpie, who also was trained by Taylor. With Magpie exported to Australia, Gay Crusader won the Epsom Derby, which was delayed until July 31 because of World War I, by four lengths. He then won the September Stakes, the St. Leger substitute.

Gay Crusader also won the Newmarket Gold Cup, Champion Stakes, and Lowther Stakes. A tendon injury ended his career before his first start as a four-year-old. At stud, his best were Hot Night, second in the 1927 Epsom Derby, and Hurstwood, third in the '24 Derby.

GAINSBOROUGH—1915 b. h., Bayardo–Rosedrop, by St. Frusquin. 9-5-2-1, $67,021. Lady Jane Douglas bred Gainsborough and became the first woman to own an Epsom Derby winner when the colt took the 1918 classic. Gainsborough gave his sire, Bayardo, a second straight Triple Crown winner. Gainsborough, who was twice champion sire, sired Hyperion, the 1933 Epsom Derby winner who went on to be England's leading sire six times. Gainsborough also sired 1932 Two Thousand Guineas winner Orwell and Solario, who was England's leading sire in 1937 and its leading broodmare sire in 1949 and '50. Gainsborough died in 1945 at the age of 30 and was buried at Gainsborough Stud, which was originally named Harwood Stud.

*BAHRAM**—1932 br. h., Blandford–Friar's Daughter, by Friar Marcus. 9-9-0-0, $212,816. A large colt who grew to 16.2 hands, *Bahram was bred and raced in England by the Aga Khan. Unbeaten in nine career starts through his three-year-old season, *Bahram won the National Produce, Rous Memorial, Gimcrack, and Middle Park Stakes at two. In addition to sweeping the Triple Crown at three, he won the St. James's Palace Stakes. England's second-leading sire in 1940, he was sold for $160,000 to an American syndicate that included Alfred G. Vanderbilt, Walter P. Chrysler, James Cox Brady, and S. W. Labrot. *Bahram stood in Maryland and Virginia before being sold in 1945 to stand in Argentina. *Bahram's 25 stakes winners included 1940 St. Leger and Irish Derby winner Turkhan, '40 Irish Oaks winner Queen of Shiraz, and '42 Two Thousand Guineas winner Big Game, who became the leading sire in England in '48, and the excellent sire Persian Gulf, winner of the '44 Coronation Cup.

The Influence of England's Triple Crown Worldwide

Although England's Triple Crown is the original and perhaps most difficult Triple Crown in the world to win, historically it has served as a model for racing programs around the globe. Virtually every major racing country has its set of Guineas, Derbys, and St. Legers, or their equivalents. As in most aspects of Thoroughbred racing, England, the birthplace of the Thoroughbred, established the pattern that the rest of the world adapted for its own local purposes, and the idea of a series of classic tests for three-year-olds is universal.

The Triple Crown in the United States evolved into the familiar Kentucky Derby (G1), Preakness Stakes (G1), and Belmont Stakes (G1) early in the 20th century, but several American racing jurisdictions in the 19th century attempted to establish Triple Crown series more closely modeled on the English pattern. For example, the Withers, Belmont, and Lawrence Realization Stakes were originally intended to be New York's version of the English series.

Other former English colonies such as Australia and New Zealand likewise established Guineas-Derby-St. Leger series, and those races still exist in Antipodean lands, though it has been many years since they have been a serious objective as a series for owners and trainers. As racing throughout the world has become more specialized, winning a Triple Crown over a variety of distances as wide as that in England has increasingly difficult.

Argentina, historically the most important South American racing country, established its own series, the Polla de Potrillos (Arg-G1), Gran Premio Jockey Club (Arg-G1), and Gran Premio Nacional (Arg-G1) over 1,600 meters, 2,000

meters, and 2,500 meters, respectively, but went one better than the English. The Argentines also required their best three-year-olds to beat older horses in the 2,400-meter Gran Premio Carlos Pellegrini (Arg-G1) to win their Quadruple Crown. Twenty three-year-olds have captured the Argentine Triple Crown since 1902, with Refinado Tom (Arg) in '96 the most recent winner. Only ten horses, the last being the great *Forli in 1966, have completed the Quadruple Crown.

English fillies have an opportunity to win their version of the Triple Crown, though no filly has ever completed the Two Thousand Guineas (Eng-G1), Epsom Derby (Eng-G1), St. Leger (Eng-G1) triple. Two fillies, however, have won four of the five English classics, failing only to capture the Derby. Formosa in 1868 dead-heated in the Two Thousand and won the One Thousand Guineas, Epsom Oaks, and St. Leger. Sceptre won the One Thousand, Two Thousand, Oaks, and St. Leger in 1902 but was beaten into fourth place in the Derby by Ard Patrick.

Nine fillies have won a "fillies Triple Crown" consisting of the One Thousand Guineas, Oaks, and St. Leger:

1985	Oh So Sharp (GB), ch. f., Kris—Oh So Fair, by Graustark
1955	Meld, b. f., Alycidon—Daily Double, by Fair Trial
1942	Sun Chariot, b. f., Hyperion—Clarence, by Diligence
1904	Pretty Polly, ch. f., Gallinule—Admiration, by Saraband
1902	Sceptre, b. f., Persimmon—Ornament, by Bend Or
1892	La Fleche, br. f., St. Simon—Quiver, by Toxophilite
1874	Apology, ch. f., Adventurer—Mandragora, by Rataplan
1871	Hannah, b. f., King Tom—Mentmore Lass, by Melbourne
1868	Formosa, ch. f., Buccaneer—Eller, by Chanticleer

NIJINSKY II—1967 b. h., Northern Dancer–Flaming Page, by Bull Page. 13-11-2-0, $667,220. Bred in Canada by E. P. Taylor and owned by Charles W. Engelhard, Nijinsky II was Northern Dancer's first international champion. He was a powerful, sickle-hocked colt who more closely resembled his dam than his diminutive sire. Trained by Vincent O'Brien, Nijinsky II was a champion in England and Ireland at two in 1969. He won the Two Thousand Guineas at odds of 4-to-7, the Epsom Derby at 11-to-8 odds, and the St. Leger at 2-to-7 odds, all under Lester Piggott. That year, Nijinsky II also won the Irish Sweeps Derby and the King George VI and Queen Elizabeth Stakes. His only defeats were in his final two starts, the Prix de l'Arc de Triomphe and Champion Stakes. At stud at Claiborne Farm in Kentucky, he was England's leading sire in 1986 and North America's leading broodmare sire in '93 and '94. Nijinsky II at one time was the all-time leading sire of stakes winners with 155, surpassing the record of his sire. Nijinsky II sired 11 champions, including 1987 North American Horse of the Year Ferdinand, '83 French champion Caerleon, two-time English champion Ile de Bourbon, and two undefeated winners of the Epsom Derby, Golden Fleece and Lammtarra.—*Bill Heller*

2004 World Thoroughbred Racehorse Rankings

European-Based Two-Year-Olds

Rating	Horse	YOB, Sex	Sire—Dam, Broodmare Sire	Trained	2004 Record, Earnings
123	Shamardal	2002 c.	Giant's Causeway—Helsinki (GB), by Machiavellian	GB	3-3-0-0, $359,680
122	Ad Valorem	2002 c.	Danzig—Classy Women, by Relaunch	Ire	3-3-0-0, 258,357
	Dubawi	2002 c.	Dubai Millennium—Zomaradah (GB), by Deploy	GB	3-3-0-0, 194,816
120	Rebuttal	2002 c.	Mr. Greeley—Reboot, by Rubiano	GB	4-1-2-1, 101,332
119	Wilko	2002 c.	Awesome Again—Native Roots (Ire), by Indian Ridge	GB, USA	12-3-2-5, 934,074
117	Divine Proportions	2002 f.	Kingmambo—Myth to Reality (Fr), by Sadler's Wells	Fr	5-5-0-0, 481,006
	Motivator	2002 c.	Montjeu (Ire)—Out West, by Gone West	GB	2-2-0-0, 228,080
	Oratorio	2002 c.	Danehill—Mahrah, by *Vaguely Noble	Ire	7-4-2-0, 599,157
116	Berenson	2002 c.	Entrepreneur—On Air, by Chief Singer	Ire	2-1-1-0, 85,957
	Early March	2002 c.	Dansili (GB)—Emplane, by Irish River (Fr)	Fr	4-2-1-0, 154,716
	Iceman	2002 c.	Polar Falcon—Virtuous, by Exit to Nowhere	GB	6-2-2-1, 188,766
	Layman	2002 c.	Sunday Silence—Laiyl (Ire), by Nureyev	Fr	4-2-1-1, 175,082
	Montgomery's Arch	2002 c.	Arch—Inny River, by Seattle Slew	GB	4-2-0-1, 156,729
114	Damson	2002 f.	Entrepreneur—Tadkiyra (Ire), by Darshaan	Ire	5-4-0-1, 413,988
	Etlaala	2002 c.	Selkirk—Portelet, by Night Shift	GB	3-2-0-0, 119,618
	Librettist	2002 c.	Danzig—Mysterial, by Alleged	GB	3-2-0-0, 32,788
	Satchem	2002 c.	Inchinor (GB)—Mohican Princess, by Shirley Heights	GB	5-3-1-0, 86,493
113	Fraloga	2002 f.	Grand Lodge—Fragrant Hill, by Shirley Heights	Fr	3-1-0-1, 55,894
	Galeota	2002 c.	Mujadil—Refined, by Statoblest	GB	6-3-0-0, 97,169
	Helios Quercus	2002 c.	Diableneyev—Criss Cross, by Crystal Palace	Fr	8-6-0-0, 315,949
	Perfectperformance	2002 c.	Rahy—Balistroika, by Nijinsky II	GB	5-3-1-0, 156,517
	Playful Act	2002 f.	Sadler's Wells—Magnificient Style, by Silver Hawk	GB	4-3-1-0, 297,320
	Russian Blue	2002 c.	Danehill—Soviet Artic, by Bering (GB)	Ire	8-3-1-3, 225,675
	Soar	2002 f.	Danzero—Splice, by Sharpo	GB	5-3-1-0, 180,929
	Titian Time	2002 f.	Red Ransom—Timely (GB), by Kings Lake	GB	4-1-2-1, 86,978
112	Albert Hall	2002 c.	Danehill—Al Theraab, by Roberto	Ire	3-1-2-0, 193,530
	Intrigued	2002 f.	Darshaan—Last Second (Ire), by Alzao	GB	3-1-0-1, 28,975
	Magical Romance	2002 f.	Barathea (Ire)—Shouk, by Shirley Heights	GB	5-3-0-0, 220,381
	Manduro	2002 c.	Monsun—Mandellicht, by Be My Guest	Ger	2-2-0-0, 109,166
	Portrayal	2002 f.	Saint Ballado—True Glory (Ire), by In the Wings (GB)	Fr	6-1-1-2, 66,631
	Yehudi	2002 c.	Sadler's Wells—Bella Vitessa, by Thatching	Ire	3-2-1-0, 115,440
111	Andronikos	2002 c.	Dr Fong—Arctic Air, by Polar Falcon	GB	5-3-1-0, 122,308
	Laverock	2002 c.	Octagonal—Sky Song, by Sadler's Wells	Fr	3-1-0-2, 47,061
	Maids Causeway	2002 f.	Giant's Causeway—Vallee des Reves, by Kingmambo	GB	7-3-3-1, 234,174
	Paita	2002 f.	Intikhab—Prada, by Lagunas	Ger	2-2-0-0, 160,520
	Queen of Poland	2002 f.	Halling—Polska, by Danzig	GB	4-2-1-0, 69,536
	Suez	2002 f.	Green Desert—Repeat Warning, by Warning (GB)	GB	3-2-1-0, 128,762
	Tony James	2002 c.	Xaar—Sunset Ridge, by Green Tune	GB	6-2-0-0, 163,322
	Tremar	2002 c.	Royal Applause (GB)—Sabina, by Prince Sabo	GB	7-2-1-1, 66,756
110	Caesar Beware	2002 g.	Daggers Drawn—Red Shareef, by Marju	GB	4-3-1-0, 416,954
	Captain Hurricane	2002 c.	Desert Style—Ravine, by Indian Ridge	GB	5-1-2-0, 103,472
	Centifolia	2002 f.	Kendor—Djayapura, by Fabulous Dancer	Fr	5-4-0-0, 196,969
	Chateau Istana	2002 c.	Grand Lodge—Miss Queen, by Miswaki	GB	6-3-0-0, 127,652
	Cougar Cat	2002 c.	Storm Cat—Excellent Meeting, by General Meeting	Ire	3-1-1-0, 37,363
	Council Member	2002 c.	Seatle Slew—Zoe Montana, by Seeking the Gold	GB	5-1-3-0, 79,031
	Dash To The Top	2002 f.	Montjeu (Ire)—Millennium Dash, by Nashwan	GB	3-1-1-1, 52,618
	Footstepsinthesand	2002 c.	Giant's Causeway—Glatisant, by Rainbow Quest	Ire	2-2-0-0, 73,850
	Gorella	2002 f.	Grape Tree Road (GB)—Exciting Times, by Jeune Homme	Fr	4-1-1-1, 27,765
	Henrik	2002 c.	Primo Dominie—Clincher Club, by Polish Patriot	GB	3-1-1-1, 66,800
	Mona Lisa (GB)	2002 f.	Giant's Causeway—Colorsnap, by Shirley Heights	Ire	4-0-1-0, 23,539
	Mystical Land	2002 c.	Xaar—Samsung Spirit, by Statoblest	GB	7-1-4-1, 111,211
	Scandinavia	2002 c.	Fusaichi Pegasus—Party Cited, by Alleged	Ire	5-1-3-0, 65,263
	Walk In The Park	2002 c.	Montjeu (Ire)—Classic Park, by Robellino	Fr	5-1-1-3, 69,446
	Windsor Knot	2002 c.	Pivotal—Triple Tie, by The Minstrel	GB	3-2-0-0, 57,106

Extended, Three and Up, Turf

Rating	Horse	YOB, Sex	Sire—Dam, Broodmare Sire	Trained	2004 Record, Earnings
120	Rule of Law	2001 h.	Kingmambo—Crystal Crossing (Ire), by Royal Academy	GB	5-2-2-0, $1,233,320
119	Papineau	2000 h.	Singspiel (Ire)—Early Rising, by *Grey Dawn II	GB	3-3-0-0, 390,292
	Vinnie Roe	1998 h.	Definite Article (GB)—Kayu, by Tap On Wood	Ire	4-1-3-0, 774,367
118	Westerner	1999 h.	Danehill—Walensee, by Troy	Fr	7-4-2-0, 500,063
117	Millenary	1997 h.	Rainbow Quest—Ballerina, by Dancing Brave	GB	5-3-0-2, 309,835
117	Mr Dinos	1999 h.	Desert King—Spear Dance, by Gay Fandango	GB	3-0-1-0, 62,897
115	Ingrandire	1999 h.	White Muzzle (GB)—Marilyn Momoko, by Real Shadai	Jpn	4-1-2-0, 1,485,928
115	Maraahel	2001 c.	Alzao—Nasanice, by Nashwan	GB	4-1-2-0, 120,252
115	Mikado	2001 c.	Sadler's Wells—Free At Last (GB), by Shirley Heights	Ire	5-1-0-1, 88,387
116	Quiff	2001 f.	Sadler's Wells—Wince, by Selkirk	GB	4-2-1-1, 465,753

Long, Three and Up, Turf

Rating	Horse	YOB, Sex	Sire—Dam, Broodmare Sire	Trained	2004 Record, Earnings
127	Doyen	2000 h.	Sadler's Wells—Moon Cactus, by Kris	GB	5-2-1-0, $1,047,627
126	Bago	2001 c.	Nashwan—Moonlight's Box, by Nureyev	Fr	5-3-0-2, 1,729,227
125	Cherry Mix	2001 c.	Linamix—Cherry Moon, by Quiet American	Fr	7-2-3-2, 626,464
123	Grey Swallow	2001 c.	Daylami (Ire)—Style of Life, by The Minstrel	Ire	6-2-0-1, 1,041,518
122	Kitten's Joy	2001 c.	El Prado (Ire)—Kitten's First, by Lear Fan	USA	8-6-2-0, 1,625,796
	North Light	2001 c.	Danehill—Sought Out, by Rainbow Quest	GB	4-2-1-0, 1,961,555
	Zenno Rob Roy	2000 h.	Sunday Silence—Roamin Rachel, by Mining	Jpn	7-3-3-0, 6,681,748
121	Better Talk Now	1999 g.	Talkin Man—Bendita, by Baldski	USA	8-2-2-0, 1,407,000
120	Acropolis	2001 c.	Sadler's Wells—Dedicated Lady, by Pennine Walk (Ire)		2-1-0-0, 161,307
	Hard Buck (Brz)	1999 h.	Spend a Buck—Social Secret, by Secreto	USA	6-1-3-0, 840,526
	Ouija Board (GB)	2001 f.	Cape Cross (Ire)—Selection Board, by Welsh Pageant	GB	5-4-0-1, 1,659,958
	Tap Dance City	1997 h.	Pleasant Tap—All Dance, by Northern Dancer	Jpn	4-2-1-0, 2,548,869
	Tycoon (GB)	2001 c.	Sadler's Wells—Fleeting Glimpse, by Rainbow Quest	Ire	5-0-0-3, 325,494
119	Shirocco	2001 c.	Monsun—So Sedulous, by The Minstrel	Ger	6-3-1-2, 699,292
118	Bandari	1999 h.	Alhaarth—Miss Audimar, by Mr. Leader	GB	10-4-0-2, 238,846
	Electrocutionist	2001 c.	Red Ransom—Elbaaha (GB), by Arazi	Ity	4-3-1-0, 219,259
	Gamut	1999 h.	Spectrum—Greektown, by Ela-Mana-Mou	GB	5-2-1-0, 450,073
	Let The Lion Roar (GB)	2001 c.	Sadler's Wells—Ballerina (Ire), by Dancing Brave	GB	6-1-1-2, 409,828
117	Cosmo Bulk	2001 c.	Zagreb—Iseno Tosho, by Tosho Boy	Jpn	8-3-2-0, 2,626,305
	Egerton	2001 c.	Groom Dancer—Enrica, by Niniski	Ger	7-0-3-0, 209,349
	King Kamehameha	2001 c.	Kingmambo—Manfath (Ire), by Last Tycoon (Ire)	Jpn	6-5-0-1, 3,743,956
	Magistretti	2000 h.	Diesis (GB)—Ms. Strike Zone, by Deputy Minister	USA	7-1-2-0, 782,981
	Mubtaker	1997 h.	Silver Hawk—Gazayil, by Irish River (Fr)	GB	3-1-0-0, 215,103
	Quiff	2001 f.	Sadler's Wells—Wince, by Selkirk	GB	4-2-1-1, 465,753
	Simonas	1999 g.	Sternkoenig—Sistadari, by Shardari	Ger	8-3-1-0, 479,639
116	Blue Canari	2001 c.	Acatenango—Delicieuse Lady, by Trempolino	Fr	6-1-0-2, 802,195
	Delta Blues	2001 c.	Dance in the Dark—Dixie Splash, by Dixieland Band	Jpn	11-4-1-1, 2,525,023
	Mr O'Brien (Ire)	1999 g.	Mukaddamah—Laurel Delight, by Presidium (GB)	USA	9-3-1-1, 514,050
	Policy Maker	2000 h.	Sadler's Wells—Palmeraie, by Lear Fan	Fr	6-2-1-0, 622,311
	Silk Famous	1999 h.	Marvelous Sunday—Saint Sailor, by Caerleon	Jpn	6-2-1-2, 2,449,025
	Valixir	2001 c.	Trempolino—Vadlamixa, by Linamix	Fr	6-3-0-2, 359,411
115	Film Maker	2000 m.	Dynaformer—Miss Du Bois, by Mr. Prospector	USA	6-1-2-1, 470,430
	Groom Tesse	2001 c.	Groom Dancer—Vicomtesse Mag, by Highest Honor (Fr)	Ity	4-2-1-0, 589,109
	Lincoln	2000 h.	Sunday Silence—Grace Admire, by Tony Bin	Jpn	4-1-0-1, 916,649
	Narita Century	1999 h.	Tony Bin—Princess Liebe, by Northern Taste	Jpn	8-3-1-0, 1,419,924
	Percussionist	2001 c.	Sadler's Wells—Magnificient Style, by Silver Hawk	GB	8-2-1-1, 238,931
	Phoenix Reach	2000 h.	Alhaarth—Carroll's Canyon, by Hatim	GB	5-1-0-0, 1,038,393
	Polish Summer (GB)	1997 h.	Polish Precedent—Hunt the Sun, by Rainbow Quest	Fr	7-2-0-0, 1,316,120
	Prospect Park	2001 c.	Sadler's Wells—Brooklyn's Dance (Fr), by Shirley Heights	Fr	7-3-3-0, 451,901
	Request For Parole	1999 h.	Judge T C—Madison's Quest, by Deputy Minister	USA	10-3-2-0, 757,100
	Senex	2000 h.	Pelder—Septima, by Touching Wood	Ger	6-2-0-2, 402,886
	Vallee Enchantee	2000 m.	Peintre Celebre—Verveine, by Lear Fan	Fr	5-0-0-2, 291,543
	Wonder Again	1999 m.	Silver Hawk—Ameriflora, by Danzig	USA	5-2-0-1, 611,767

Intermediate, Three and Up, Turf

Rating	Horse	YOB, Sex	Sire—Dam, Broodmare Sire	Trained	2004 Record, Earnings
124	Haafhd	2001 c.	Alhaarth—Al Bahathri, by Blushing Groom (Fr)	GB	5-3-0-0, $772,558
123	Azamour	2001 c.	Night Shift—Asmara, by Lear Fan	Ire	5-2-1-2, 1,191,232
123	Sulamani (Ire)	1999 h.	Hernando (Fr)—Soul Dream, by Alleged	GB	5-2-1-1, 1,611,523
121	Norse Dancer	2000 h.	Halling—River Patrol (GB), by Rousillon	GB	10-1-2-1, 626,062
	Refuse To Bend (Ire)	2000 h.	Sadler's Wells—Market Slide, by Gulch	GB	7-2-0-1, 766,803
120	Powerscourt (GB)	2000 h.	Sadler's Wells—Rainbow Lake, by Rainbow Quest	Ire	9-1-2-2, 903,837
	Warrsan	1998 h.	Caerleon—Lucayan Princess, by High Line	GB	9-2-1-1, 1,114,442
117	Chorist	1999 m.	Pivotal—Choir Mistress, by Chief Singer	GB	5-2-1-2, 427,797
	Epalo (Ger)	1999 h.	Lando (Ger)—Evening Kiss, by Kris	Ger	5-2-2-1, 1,141,228

Rating	Horse	YOB, Sex	Sire—Dam, Broodmare Sire	Trained	2004 Record, Earnings
117	Kicken Kris	2000 h.	Kris S.—Kicken Grass, by Jade Hunter	USA	6-2-0-1, $727,000
	Latice (Ire)	2001 f.	Inchinor (GB)—Laramie, by Gulch	Fr	5-2-0-0, 387,142
	Touch of Land (Fr)	2000 h.	Lando (Ger)—Touch of Class, by Be My Guest	Fr	7-2-1-2, 446,700
	Voix du Nord	2001 c.	Valanour (Ire)—Dame Edith, by Top Ville	Fr	2-2-0-0, 208,171
116	Alexander Goldrun	2001 f.	Gold Away (Ire)—Renashaan, by Darshaan	Ire	7-4-2-0, 1,801,721
	Altieri	1998 h.	Selkirk—Minya, by Blushing Groom (Fr)	Ity	5-3-0-0, 386,428
	Ikhtyar	2000 h.	Unfuwain—Sabria, by Miswaki	GB	6-0-1-3, 133,515
	Intendant	2001 c.	Lando (Ger)—Incenza, by Local Suitor	Ger	5-2-0-1, 121,830
	Meteor Storm (GB)	1999 h.	Bigstone (Ire)—Hunt the Sun, by Rainbow Quest	USA	6-3-0-1, 529,800
	Millemix	2001 c.	Linamix—Milesime, by Riverman	Fr	3-1-2-0, 136,085
	Mister Monet	2001 c.	Peintre Celebre—Breyani, by Commanche Run	GB	6-4-1-0, 200,631
	Soldier Hollow	2000 h.	In the Wings (GB)—Island Race, by Common Grounds	Ger	9-4-2-0, 350,376
115	Artie Schiller	2001 c.	El Prado (Ire)—Hidden Light, by Majestic Light	USA	8-5-1-0, 467,578
	Cacique	2001 c.	Danehill—Hasili, by Kahyasi	Fr	7-4-2-0, 388,323
	Execute	1997 h.	Suave Dancer—She's My Lovely, by Sharpo	Fr	4-1-1-0, 164,949
	Kalaman now Oriental Magic	2000 h.	Desert Prince (Ire)—Kalamba, by Green Dancer	GB/HK	6-2-1-1, 255,573
	Lune d'Or	2001 f.	Green Tune—Luth D'Or (Fr), by Noir et Or	Fr	7-4-0-1, 359,744
	Millionaia	2001 f.	Peintre Celebre—Moonlight Dance, by Alysheba	Fr	4-1-3-0, 167,619
	Sabiango (Ger)	1998 h.	Acatenango—Spirit of Eagles, by Beau's Eagle	USA	4-2-0-0, 334,000
	Star Over the Bay	1998 g.	Cozzene—Lituya Bay, by Empery	USA	9-5-1-0, 439,960

Mile, Three and Up, Turf

Rating	Horse	YOB, Sex	Sire—Dam, Broodmare Sire	Trained	2004 Record, Earnings
123	Rakti	1999 h.	Polish Precedent—Ragera, by Rainbow Quest	GB	6-2-0-0, $655,822
122	Haafhd	2001 c.	Alhaarth—Al Bahathri, by Blushing Groom (Fr)	GB	5-3-0-0, 772,558
	Lucky Story	2001 c.	Kris S.—Spring Flight, by Miswaki	GB	4-0-2-0, 123,288
121	Refuse To Bend (Ire)	2000 h.	Sadler's Wells—Market Slide, by Gulch	GB	7-2-0-1, 766,803
120	Durandal	1999 h.	Sunday Silence—Sawayaka Princess, by Northern Taste	Jpn	4-1-2-0, 1,726,862
119	Soviet Song	2000 m.	Marju—Kalinka, by Soviet Star	GB	8-4-2-1, 973,999
118	Attraction	2001 f.	Efisio—Flirtation, by Pursuit of Love	GB	7-4-2-0, 1,210,348
	Bachelor Duke	2001 c.	Miswaki—Gossamer, by Seattle Slew	GB	3-1-0-0, 279,700
	Nayyir	1998 g.	Indian Ridge—Pearl Kite, by Silver Hawk	GB	6-0-2-1, 382,238
	Singletary	2000 h.	Sultry Song—Joiski's Star, by Star de Naskra	USA	6-3-2-1, 1,192,910
	Snow Ridge	2001 c.	Indian Ridge—Snow Princess, by Ela-Mana-Mou	GB	2-0-1-0, 117,348
	Somnus	2000 g.	Pivotal—Midnight's Reward, by Night Shift	GB	6-2-2-0, 401,733
	Whipper	2001 c.	Miesque's Son—Myth to Reality (Fr), by Sadler's Wells	Fr	6-2-1-0, 389,850
117	Ancient World	2000 h.	Spinning World—Headline (GB), by Machiavellian	GB	7-3-2-0, 440,010
	Antonius Pius	2001 c.	Danzig—Catchascatchcan (GB), by Pursuit of Love	Ire	9-0-1-2, 460,158
	Chic	2000 m.	Machiavellian—Exclusive, by Polar Falcon	GB	6-2-1-1, 247,186
	Diamond Green (Fr)	2001 c.	Green Desert—Diamonaka, by Akarad	Fr	7-0-4-1, 306,046
	King Kamehameha	2001 c.	Kingmambo—Manfath (Ire), by Last Tycoon (Ire)	Jpn	6-5-0-1, 3,743,956
	Russian Rhythm	2000 m.	Kingmambo—Balistroika, by Nijinsky II	GB	1-1-0-0, 204,160
	Special Ring	1997 g.	Nureyev—Ring Beaune, by Bering (GB)	USA	3-1-0-0, 240,000
116	Bayamo (Ire)	1999 g.	Valanour (Ire)—Clare Bridge, by Little Current	USA	5-2-2-0, 272,400
	Grey Lilas	2001 f.	Danehill—Kenmist, by Kenmare	Fr	7-4-2-1, 547,572
	Mr O'Brien (Ire)	1999 g.	Mukaddamah—Laurel Delight, by Presidium (GB)	USA	9-3-1-1, 514,050
	Prince Kirk	2000 h.	Selkirk—Princess Manila, by Manila	Ity	3-2-0-1, 189,575
	Stroll	2000 h.	Pulpit—Maid for Walking (GB), by Prince Sabo	USA	5-1-1-0, 348,524
	Tsurumaru Boy	1998 h.	Dance in the Dark—Tsurumaru Girl, by Soccer Boy	Jpn	5-1-0-0, 1,071,080
115	American Post	2001 c.	Bering (GB)—Wells Fargo, by Sadler's Wells	Fr	5-3-0-0, 346,005
	Artie Schiller	2001 c.	El Prado (Ire)—Hidden Light, by Majestic Light	USA	8-5-1-0, 467,578
	Designed for Luck	1997 g.	Rahy—Fantastic Look, by Green Dancer	USA	4-1-1-0, 311,180
	Firebreak	1998 h.	Charnwood Forest (Ire)—Breakaway, by Song	GB	5-3-1-0, 1,792,050
	Intercontinental (GB)	2000 m.	Danehill—Hasili, by Kahyasi	USA	6-4-1-0, 592,386
	Nothing to Lose	2000 h.	Sky Classic—Cherlindrea, by Clever Trick	USA	9-2-3-1, 643,200
	Paolini	1997 h.	Lando (Ger)—Prairie Darling, by Stanford	Ger	5-1-0-0, 800,000
	Passing Glance	1999 h.	Polar Falcon—Spurned, by Robellino	GB	4-1-0-0, 89,988
	Salselon	1999 h.	Salse—Heady, by Rousillon	GB	10-0-3-3, 224,709
	Sweet Return (GB)	2000 h.	Elmaamul—Sweet Revival, by Claude Monet	USA	7-2-1-1, 446,180
	Telegnosis	1999 h.	Tony Bin—Make a Wish, by Northern Taste	Jpn	6-1-2-1, 1,395,504
	Wonder Again	1999 m.	Silver Hawk—Ameriflora, by Danzig	USA	5-2-0-1, 611,767

Sprint, Three and Up, Turf

Rating	Horse	YOB, Sex	Sire—Dam, Broodmare Sire	Trained	2004 Record, Earnings
117	Var	1999 h.	Forest Wildcat—Loma Preata, by Zilzal	GB	5-3-1-0, $209,038
115	Ashdown Express	1999 g.	Ashkalani—Indian Express, by Indian Ridge	GB	9-0-2-1, 133,483
	Bahamian Pirate	1995 g.	Housebuster—Shining Through, by Deputy Minister	GB	15-4-1-0, 272,020
	Cape of Good Hope	1998 g.	Inchinor (GB)—Cape Merino, by Clantime	HK	11-0-4-4, 1,013,000
	Calstone Light O	1998 h.	Warning (GB)—Oshima Lucia, by Crystal Glitters	Jpn	5-2-1-1, 1,470,483

Rating	Horse	YOB, Sex	Sire—Dam, Broodmare Sire	Trained	2004 Record, Earnings
	Patavellian	1998 g.	Machiavellian—Alessia, by Caerleon	GB	5-0-0-3, $70,958
	Pivotal Point	2000 g.	Pivotal—True Precision, by Presidium (GB)	GB	9-4-1-0, 304,544
	Tante Rose	2000 m.	Barathea (Ire)—My Branch, by Distant Relative (Ire)	GB	3-3-0-0, 317,589
	The Tatling	1997 g.	Perugino—Aunty Eileen, by Ahonoora	GB	12-2-4-3, 417,987

Long, Three and Up, Dirt

Rating	Horse	YOB, Sex	Sire—Dam, Broodmare Sire	Trained	2004 Record, Earnings
120	Birdstone	2001 c.	Grindstone—Dear Birdie, by Storm Bird	USA	6-3-0-0, $1,236,600

Intermediate, Three and Up, Dirt

Rating	Horse	YOB, Sex	Sire—Dam, Broodmare Sire	Trained	2004 Record, Earnings
130	Ghostzapper	2000 h.	Awesome Again—Baby Zip, by Relaunch	USA	4-4-0-0, $2,590,000
128	Smarty Jones	2001 c.	Elusive Quality—I'll Get Along, by Smile	USA	7-6-1-0, 7,563,535
126	Pleasantly Perfect	1998 h.	Pleasant Colony—Regal State, by Affirmed	USA	5-3-1-1, 4,840,000
124	Medaglia d'Oro	1999 h.	El Prado (Ire)—Cappucino Bay, by Bailjumper	USA	2-1-1-0, 1,500,000
123	Roses In May	2000 h.	Devil His Due—Tell a Secret, by Speak John	USA	6-5-1-0, 1,723,277
122	Southern Image	2000 h.	Halo's Image—Pleasant Dixie, by Dixieland Band	USA	4-3-1-0, 1,612,150
120	Birdstone	2001 c.	Grindstone—Dear Birdie, by Storm Bird	USA	6-3-0-0, 1,236,600
119	Peace Rules	2000 h.	Jules—Hold to Fashion, by Hold Your Peace	USA	6-3-0-0, 1,024,288
	Perfect Drift	1999 g.	Dynaformer—Nice Gal, by Naskra	USA	9-0-5-2, 947,595
117	Azeri	1998 m.	Jade Hunter—Zodiac Miss (Aus), by Ahonoora	USA	8-3-2-0, 1,035,000
	Ashado	2001 f.	Saint Ballado—Goulash, by Mari's Book	USA	8-5-2-1, 2,259,640
	Lion Heart	2001 c.	Tale of the Cat—Satin Sunrise, by Mr. Leader	USA	7-2-3-0, 1,080,000
	Total Impact (Chi)	1998 h.	Stuka—Pebbles, by Manos de Piedra	USA	11-1-5-2, 988,390
116	Funny Cide	2000 g.	Distorted Humor—Belle's Good Cide, by Slewacide	USA	10-3-2-3, 1,075,100
115	Admire Don	1999 h.	Timber Country—Vega, by Tony Bin	Jpn	7-3-2-0, 3,251,772
	Evening Attire	1998 g.	Black Tie Affair (Ire)—Concolour, by Our Native	USA	11-1-6-0, 420,040
	Island Fashion	2000 m.	Petionville—Danzigs Fashion, by A Native Danzig	USA	7-2-1-0, 615,000
	Midway Road	2000 h.	Jade Hunter—Fleet Road, by Magesterial	USA	8-4-1-0, 372,015
	Society Selection	2001 f.	Coronado's Quest—Love That Jazz, by Dixieland Band	USA	9-3-3-1, 929,700
	The Cliff's Edge	2001 c.	Gulch—Zigember, by Danzig	USA	8-1-4-2, 1,010,000
	Time Paradox	1998 h.	Brian's Time—Jolie Zaza, by Alzao	Jpn	12-5-1-2, 3,408,062

Mile, Three and Up, Dirt

Rating	Horse	YOB, Sex	Sire—Dam, Broodmare Sire	Trained	2004 Record, Earnings
123	Ghostzapper	2000 h.	Awesome Again—Baby Zip, by Relaunch	USA	4-4-0-0, $2,590,000
122	Southern Image	2000 h.	Halo's Image—Pleasant Dixie, by Dixieland Band	USA	4-3-1-0, 1,612,150
119	Peace Rules	2000 h.	Jules—Hold to Fashion, by Hold Your Peace	USA	6-3-0-0, 1,024,288
	Perfect Drift	1999 g.	Dynaformer—Nice Gal, by Naskra	USA	9-0-5-2, 947,595
	Saint Liam	2000 h.	Saint Ballado—Quiet Dance, by Quiet American	USA	5-2-2-1, 618,760
118	Smarty Jones	2001 c.	Elusive Quality—I'll Get Along, by Smile	USA	7-6-1-0, 7,563,535
	Azeri	1998 m.	Jade Hunter—Zodiac Miss (Aus), by Ahonoora	USA	8-3-2-0, 1,035,000
	Sightseek	1999 m.	Distant View—Viviana, by Nureyev	USA	7-4-1-0, 1,011,350
117	Ashado	2001 f.	Saint Ballado—Goulash, by Mari's Book	USA	8-5-2-1, 2,259,640
116	Adoration	1999 m.	Honor Grades—Sewing Lady, by Key to the Mint	USA	5-3-1-0, 607,304
115	Admire Don	1999 h.	Timber Country—Vega, by Tony Bin	Jpn	7-3-2-0, 3,251,772
	Dynever	2000 h.	Dynaformer—Flamboyance, by Zilzal	USA	7-1-3-0, 254,694
	Even the Score	1998 h.	Unbridled's Song—Ashtabula, by Rahy	USA	4-2-0-2, 343,272
	Firebreak	1999 h.	Charnwood Forest (Ire)—Breakaway, by Song	GB	5-3-1-0, 1,792,050
	Lundy's Liability (Brz)	2000 h.	Candy Stripes—Emerald Counter, by Geiger Counter	USA	5-2-1-0, 1,542,500
	Purge	2001 c.	Pulpit—Copelan's Bid Gal, by Copelan	USA	8-3-1-0, 562,734
	Read the Footnotes	2001 c.	Smoke Glacken—Baydon Belle, by Al Nasr (Fr)	USA	3-1-0-0, 210,000
	Ten Most Wanted	2000 h.	Deputy Commander—Wanted Again, by Criminal Type	USA	2-1-0-0, 165,000
	The Cliff's Edge	2001 c.	Gulch—Zigember, by Danzig	USA	8-1-4-2, 1,010,000

Sprint, Three and Up, Dirt

Rating	Horse	YOB, Sex	Sire—Dam, Broodmare Sire	Trained	2004 Record, Earnings
123	Pico Central (Brz)	1999 h.	Spend a Buck—Sheila Purple (Brz), by Purple Mountain	USA	7-5-0-2, $1,139,000
122	Speightstown	1998 h.	Gone West—Silken Cat, by Storm Cat	USA	6-5-0-1, 1,045,556
118	Kela	1998 h.	Numerous—Bolshoi Comedy, by Sovereign Dancer	USA	9-3-1-0, 710,212
	Midas Eyes	2000 h.	Touch Gold—Bayou Plans, by Bayou Hebert	USA	5-2-1-0, 258,600
116	Strong Hope	2000 h.	Grand Slam—Shining Through, by Deputy Minister	USA	4-1-1-1, 185,100
115	Azeri	1998 m.	Jade Hunter—Zodiac Miss (Aus), by Ahonoora	USA	8-3-2-0, 1,035,000
	Bluesthestandard	1997 g.	American Standard—Bob's Blue, by Bob's Dusty	USA	6-1-2-1, 132,633
	Ema Bovary (Chi)	1999 m.	Edgy Diplomat—Coqueta, by Domineau	USA	5-4-1-0, 521,780
	Island Fashion	2000 m.	Petionville—Danzigs Fashion, by A Native Danzig	USA	7-2-1-0, 615,000
	My Cousin Matt	1999 g.	Matty G—Conquistamiss, by Conquistador Cielo	USA	8-1-0-2, 208,200
	Our New Recruit	1999 h.	Alphabet Soup—Delta Danielle, by Lord Avie	USA	5-2-0-1, 1,265,795
	Pohave	1998 g.	Holy Bull—Trail Robbery, by Alydar	USA	8-3-3-2, 450,740

Cartier Awards

Established in 1991, the Cartier Awards are European racing's closest equivalent to the Eclipse Awards. Winners are determined by points earned in pattern races and votes of racing experts and Daily Telegraph *readers.*

Award of Merit
2004	David and Patricia Thompson
2003	Lord John Oaksey
2002	Khalid Abdullah
2001	John Magnier
2000	Aga Khan
1999	Peter Walwyn
1998	Head family
1997	Sir Peter O'Sullevan
1996	Frankie Dettori
1995	John Dunlop
1994	Lord Hartington
1993	Francois Boutin
1992	Lester Piggott
1991	Henri Chalhoub

Horse of the Year
2004	Ouija Board (GB)
2003	Dalakhani
2002	Rock of Gibraltar (Ire)
2001	Fantastic Light
2000	Giant's Causeway
1999	Daylami (Ire)
1998	Dream Well (Fr)
1997	Peintre Celebre
1996	Helissio
1995	Ridgewood Pearl (GB)
1994	Barathea (Ire)
1993	Lochsong (GB)
1992	User Friendly (GB)
1991	Arazi

Millennium Award of Merit
2000	Queen Elizabeth II

Two-Year-Old Filly
2004	Divine Proportions
2003	Attraction
2002	Six Perfections (Fr)
2001	Queen's Logic
2000	Superstar Leo
1999	Torgau (Ire)
1998	Bint Allayl
1997	Embassy (GB)
1996	Pas de Reponse
1995	Blue Duster
1994	Gay Gallanta
1993	Lemon Souffle (GB)
1992	Lyric Fantasy (Ire)
1991	Culture Vulture

Two-Year-Old Colt
2004	Shamardal
2003	One Cool Cat
2002	Hold That Tiger
2001	Johannesburg
2000	Tobougg (Ire)
1999	Fasliyev
1998	Aljabr
1997	Xaar
1996	Bahamian Bounty
1995	Alhaarth
1994	Celtic Swing
1993	First Trump
1992	Zafonic
1991	Arazi

Three-Year-Old Filly
2004	Ouija Board (GB)
2003	Russian Rhythm
2002	Kazzia (Ger)
2001	Banks Hill (GB)
2000	Petrushka (Ire)
1999	Ramruma
1998	Cape Verdi (Ire)
1997	Ryafan
1996	Bosra Sham
1995	Ridgewood Pearl (GB)
1994	Balanchine
1993	Intrepidity (GB)
1992	User Friendly (GB)
1991	Kooyonga (Ire)

Three-Year-Old Colt
2004	Bago
2003	Dalakhani
2002	Rock of Gibraltar (Ire)
2001	Galileo (Ire)
2000	Sinndar
1999	Montjeu (Ire)
1998	Dream Well (Fr)
1997	Peintre Celebre
1996	Helissio
1995	Lammtarra
1994	King's Theatre (Ire)
1993	Commander in Chief
1992	Rodrigo de Triano
1991	Suave Dancer

Stayer
2004	Westerner
2003	Persian Punch
2002	Vinnie Roe
2001	Persian Punch
2000	Kayf Tara
1999	Kayf Tara
1998	Kayf Tara
1997	Celeric
1996	Nononito
1995	Double Trigger
1994	Moonax
1993	Vintage Crop
1992	Drum Taps
1991	Turgeon

Sprinter
2004	Somnus
2003	Oasis Dream (GB)
2002	Continent
2001	Mozart (Ire)
2000	Nuclear Debate
1999	Stravinsky
1998	Tamarisk
1997	Royal Applause (GB)
1996	Anabaa (Ire)
1995	Hever Golf Rose (GB)
1994	Lochsong (GB)
1993	Lochsong (GB)
1992	Mr Brooks (GB)
1991	Sheikh Albadou (GB)

Older Horse
2004	Soviet Song
2003	Falbrav (Ire)
2002	Grandera
2001	Fantastic Light
2000	Kalanisi (Ire)
1999	Daylami (Ire)
1998	Swain (Ire)
1997	Pilsudski (Ire)
1996	Halling
1995	Further Flight
1994	Barathea (Ire)
1993	Opera House (GB)
1992	Mr Brooks (GB)
1991	Terimon

Special Award
2002	Tony McCoy
1994	Vincent O'Brien

Lord Derby Awards

Presented by the British Horserace Writers and Photographers Association for overall excellence.

Service to International Racing
2003	Khalid Abdullah
2002	Nick Clarke
2001	Pam Blatz-Murff
2000	Aga Khan
1999	Michael Osborne
1998	James E. "Ted" Bassett III
1997	Geoffrey Gibbs
1996	Flying Grooms
1995	Maj. Gen. Guy Watkins
1994	Robert Sangster
1993	Francois Boutin
	Niarchos family
1992	Maktoum family
1991	John Dunlop

1990	Louis Romanet
1989	Michael Byrne
1988	Richard Duchossois
1987	Yves Saint-Martin
1986	John Gaines
1985	Lord Derby
1984	Ivan Straker
1983	Paul Mellon
1982	Jean Romanet
1981	Joe Hirsch

Outstanding Achievement Award (George Ennor Trophy)
2004	Peter Willett
2003	Pat Eddery

2002	Ian Balding
2001	Graham Rock
2000	Johnny Murtagh
1999	Peter Walwyn
1998	Capt. Tim Forster
1997	Sir Peter O'Sullevan
1996	Peter Easterby
1995	Lester Piggott
1994	Vincent O'Brien
1993	Dermot Weld

Outstanding Achievement Award (President's Trophy)
2004	George Ennor
2003	Lord John Oaksey

2002	Not awarded
2001	John Reid
2000	Ray Cochrane
1999	Jack Berry
1998	Not awarded
1997	Maj. Dick Hern
1996	Not awarded
1995	Jim Old Stable staff

International
Trainer of the Year

2004	Ed Dunlop
2003	Pascal Bary
2002	Demot Weld
2001	Aidan O'Brien
2000	Saeed bin Suroor
1999	Saeed bin Suroor
1998	Saeed bin Suroor
1997	Sir Michael Stoute
1996	Sir Michael Stoute
1995	Peter Chapple-Hyam
1994	John Dunlop
1993	John Dunlop
1992	Paul Cole
1991	Paul Cole
1990	Paul Cole
1989	Henry Cecil
1988	Luca Cumani
1987	Paul Cole
1986	Michael Stoute
1985	Clive Brittain
1984	Ian Balding
1983	Luca Cumani
1982	John Dunlop
1981	Ian Balding

Owner of the Year

2004	Lord Derby
2003	Jim Lewis
2002	Sir Alex Ferguson
2001	Susan Magnier
	Michael Tabor
2000	Aga Khan
1999	Michael Tabor
1998	The Summit Partnership
1997	Peter Winfield
1996	Godolphin Racing
1995	Godolphin Racing
1994	Jeff Smith
1993	Robert Sangster
1992	Bill Gredley
1991	Prince Fahd Salman
1990	Sheikh Hamdan bin
	Rashid al Maktoum
1989	Sheikh Hamdan bin
	Rashid al Maktoum
1988	Jim Joel
1987	Louis Freedman
1986	Khalid Abdullah
1985	Lord Howard de Walden
1984	Eric Moller
1983	Robert Barnett
1982	Paul Mellon
1981	Aga Khan
1980	Pat Muldoon
1979	Snailwell Stud
1978	David McCall
1977	Queen Elizabeth II
1976	Daniel Wildenstein
1975	Carlo Vittadini
1974	Peter O'Sullevan
1973	Louis Freedman
1972	Lady Beaverbrook

1971	John and Jean Hislop
1970	Charles Engelhard and
	David McCall
1969	Earl of Rosebery
1968	Lord Allendale
1967	Jim Joel

Trainer of the Year

2004	Saeed bin Suroor
2003	Sir Michael Stoute
2002	Mark Johnston
2001	Aidan O'Brien
2000	John Oxx
1999	Henry Cecil
1998	Saeed bin Suroor
1997	Sir Michael Stoute
1996	Henry Cecil
1995	John Dunlop
1994	Mark Johnston
1993	Richard Hannon
1992	Richard Hannon
1991	Paul Cole
1990	Jack Berry
1989	Maj. Dick Hern
1988	David Chapman
1987	Henry Cecil
1986	Sir Michael Stoute
1985	Henry Cecil
1984	Roy Sheather
1983	John Dunlop
1982	David Chapman
1981	Guy Harwood
1980	Maj. Dick Hern
1979	Henry Cecil
1978	Michael Stoute
1977	Vincent O'Brien
1976	Henry Cecil
1975	Maj. Dick Hern
1974	Peter Walwyn
1973	Arthur Budgett
1972	Bruce Hobbs
1971	Ian Balding
1970	Vincent O'Brien
1969	Harvey Leader
1968	Sir Cecil Boyd-Rochfort
1967	Sir Noel Murless

Jockey of the Year

2004	Frankie Dettori
2003	Kieren Fallon
2002	Richard Hughes
2001	Michael Kinane
2000	Kevin Darley
1999	Richard Quinn
1998	Kieren Fallon
1997	Kieren Fallon
1996	Frankie Dettori
1995	Frankie Dettori
1994	Frankie Dettori
1993	Kevin Darley
1992	Michael Roberts
1991	Alan Munro
1990	Frankie Dettori
1989	Willie Carson
1988	Michael Roberts
1987	Steve Cauthen
1986	Pat Eddery
1985	Steve Cauthen
1984	Steve Cauthen
1983	Willie Carson
1982	Lester Piggott
1981	Lester Piggott
1980	Lester Piggott

1979	Joe Mercer
1978	Greville Starkey
1977	Willie Carson
1976	Brian Taylor
1975	Joe Mercer
1974	Pat Eddery
1973	Tony Murray
1972	Edward Hide
1971	Willie Carson
1970	Lester Piggott
1969	Geoff Lewis
1968	Sandy Barclay
1967	Doug Smith

National Hunt Owner of the Year
(Awarded 1969-'73)

1973	Noel le Mare
1972	Mrs. John Rogerson
1971	Col. Bill Whitbread
1970	Bryan Jenks
1969	Edward Courage

National Hunt
Trainer of the Year

2004	Henrietta Knight
2003	Philip Hobbs
2002	Henrietta Knight
2001	Martin Pipe
2000	Noel Chance
1999	Paul Nichols
1998	Martin Pipe
1997	Martin Pipe
1996	Jim Old
1995	Kim Bailey
1994	David Nicholson
1993	Nigel Twiston-Davies
1992	Mary Reveley
1991	Martin Pipe
1990	Martin Pipe
1989	Martin Pipe
1988	David Elsworth
1987	Nicky Henderson
1986	Nicky Henderson
1985	Capt. Tim Forster
1984	Jenny Pitman
1983	Michael Dickinson
1982	Michael Dickinson
1981	Peter Easterby
1980	Peter Easterby
1979	Peter Easterby
1978	Fred Winter
1977	Peter Easterby
1976	Tony Dickinson
1975	Gordon Richards
1974	Donald "Ginger" McCain
1973	Fulke Walwyn
1972	David Barons
1971	Fred Winter
1970	Arthur Stephenson
1969	Colin Davies
1968	Fred Rimell

National Hunt
Jockey of the Year

2004	Tony McCoy
2003	Tony McCoy
2002	Tony McCoy
2001	Tony McCoy
2000	Tony McCoy
1999	Tony McCoy
1998	Tony McCoy
1997	Tony McCoy
1996	Tony McCoy

1995	Norman Williamson	1996	Ian Willows	1991	*Express and Star*)	
1994	Aidrian Maguire	1995	Sidney Outen	1990	Tony Morris (*Racing Post*)	
1993	Richard Dunwoody		John Sayers	1989	Michael Seely (*The Times*)	
1992	Peter Niven	1994	Vicki Harris	1988	Geoff Lester (*Sporting Life*)	
1991	Peter Scudamore		Ron Thomas	1987	Peter Goodall (Press	
1990	Peter Scudamore	1993	John Cullen		Association)	
1989	Peter Scudamore		Geoff Thompson	1986	Peter O'Sullevan (BBC)	
1988	Chris Grant	1992	Johnny East	1985	Jim Stanford (*Daily Mail*)	
1987	Peter Scudamore		Bill Palmer	1984	John Sharratt (Raceform)	
1986	Peter Scudamore	1991	Harvey Ewart	1983	Bill Garland (Press	
1985	John Francome		Steven Rose		Association)	
1984	John Francome	1990	Steve Fox	1982	George Ennor (*Sporting Life*)	
1983	John Francome		Colin Nutter	1981	Jonathan Powell (*Sunday	
1982	Peter Scudamore	1989	Brian Delaney		People*)	
1981	Bob Champion		Meg MacDonald	1980	Michael Seely (*The Times*)	
1980	Jonjo O'Neil	1988	Peter Heaney	1979	Christopher Poole (*Evening	
1979	Tommy Carmody		Kevin Murrell		Standard*)	
1978	Jonjo O'Neill	1987	Alison Dean	1978	Tim Richards (*Daily Mirror*)	
1977	Tommy Stack	1986	Glyn Foster	1977	Brough Scott (*Sunday Times*)	
1976	Jeff King	1985	Jimmy Swales	1976	Peter Willett (*Sporting	
1975	Tommy Stack	1984	Syd McGahey		Chronicle*)	
1974	Richard Pitman	1983	Raymond Campbell	1975	Peter Scott (*Daily Telegraph*)	
1973	Ron Barry	1982	Linda McCauley	1974	Tom Cosgrove (London	
1972	Bob Davies	1981	Olga Nicholson		*Evening News*)	
1971	Graham Thorner	1980	Alan Welborne	1973	Richard Baerlein (*The	
1970	Terry Biddlecombe	1979	Jack Kidd		Guardian/Observer*)	
1969	Stan Mellor	1978	Nigel Atkinson	1972	Roger Mortimer (*Sunday Times*)	
1968	Brian Fletcher	1977	John Hallum	1971	Clive Graham (*Daily Express*)	
1967	Josh Gifford	1976	Mervyn Heath		Peter O'Sullevan (*Daily Express*)	
		1975	John Vickers	1970	George Stevens (Birmingham	

Stable Staff of the Year

2004	Jock Brown, Brian Clothworthy, Ian Wilder		**Journalist of the Year** **(Clive Graham Trophy)**		*Post & Mail*)	
2003	Albert "Corky" Browne	2004	Alan Lee (*The Times*)	1969	Geoffrey Hamlyn (*Sporting Life*)	
	Johnny Worrall	2003	Clare Balding	1968	John Lawrence (*Daily	
	Dennis Wright		(BBC and *Evening Standard*)		Telegraph*)	
2002	Tom Townsend		Doug Moscrop	1967	Quintin Gilbey (*Sporting	
	Dave Goodwin		(Newcastle *Journal*)		Chronicle*)	
2001	Rodney Boult	2002	Tom O'Ryan (*Racing Post*)			
	Peter Maughan	2001	Alan Lee (*The Times*)		**Photographer of the Year**	
	Jimmy Scott	2000	Alan Amies (Raceform)	2004	Dan Abraham	
2000	George Charlton	1999	Alastair Down (*Racing Post*)	2003	Ed Whitaker (*Racing Post*)	
	John Smillie	1998	Claude Duval (*The Sun*)	2002	Ed Whitaker (*Racing Post*)	
1999	Rachel Hume	1997	Rodney Masters (*Racing Post*)	2001	Anne Grossick (free-lance)	
	Robynne Watton	1996	David Ashforth (*Sporting Life*)	2000	John Grossick (free-lance)	
1998	Michael Leaman	1995	Richard Evans (*The Times*)	1999	Ed Whitaker (*Racing Post*)	
	Geoff Snook	1994	Alastair Down (*Sporting Life*)	1998	Alec Russell (free-lance)	
1997	Jack Nelson	1993	Paul Haigh (*Racing Post*)	1997	Mark Cranham (free-lance)	
	Eddie Watt	1992	Jim McGrath (*Daily Telegraph*)		**Broadcaster of the Year**	
1996	Harry Buckle	1991	John Sexton (Wolverhampton		**(Sir Peter O'Sullevan Trohy)**	
				2004	Clare Balding (*BBC*)	

Major International Racetracks

Argentina
Argentino de Palermo

Located in the Palermo district close to downtown Buenos Aires and familiarly known as Palermo, Hipodromo Argentino opened on May 7, 1876. Originally a Standardbred facility offering just one Thoroughbred race daily, the track changed to full-time Thoroughbred racing on August 18, 1883, and was the first racetrack in Argentina to feature a totalizator. A sales pavilion, veterinary hospital and laboratory, equine institute, and museum complement the racetrack, which is home of the Gran Premio Nacional (Arg-G1), Argentina's equivalent of the Kentucky Derby (G1) and third race of the Argentine Triple Crown. Two of its most famous winners were *Yatasto in 1951 and *Forli in '66. Another major stakes race is the Polla de Potrillos (Arg-G1) (Argentine Two Thousand Guineas), the first race of the Triple Crown, in September. Racing is held over a 2,410-meter,* left-

handed track with three chutes. (*See conversion table from metric to English distances in Reference section.)

Location: Ave. Del Libertador 4101, Capital Federal, Buenos Aires
Phone: 541 (47) 782-800
Fax: 541 (47) 746-807
Website: *www.palermo.com.ar*
E-Mail: Palermo@satlink.com
Abbreviation: HAr
Principal Races: Comparacion (Arg-G1), Criadores (Arg-G1), De Honor (Arg-G1), De las Americas-Internacional (Arg-G1), Jorge de Atucha (Arg-G1), Nacional (Arg-G1), Polla de Potrancas (Arg-G1), Polla de Potrillos (Arg-G1), Santiago Luro (Arg-G1), Seleccion (Arg-G1)

La Plata

The first racetrack in Argentina to hold evening race cards, Hipodromo de La Plata opened on September

14, 1884. Situated approximately 35 miles south of Buenos Aires, the track is in the city of La Plata in the province of Buenos Aires. The track's proximity to a railway station makes it easily accessible by public transportation. The left-handed, elliptical dirt track is 2,000 meters (9.94 furlongs, or approximately 1¼ miles) with two chutes. As many as 145 racing dates are held annually.

Location: La Plata, Pica de Buenos Aires
Phone: 541 (21) 211-071
Fax: 541 (21) 42-390
Abbreviation: LP
Principal Races: Dardo Rocha Internacional (Arg-G1), Joachin V. Gonzalez Internacional (Arg-G1), Ciudad de La Plata Internacional (Arg-G1), Seleccion de Potrancas (Arg-G1)

San Isidro

Located 14 miles north of Buenos Aires on the edge of the Pampas, San Isidro Racecourse was founded on December 8, 1935, by the Jockey Club Argentino. San Isidro hosts the Gran Premio Carlos Pellegrini-Internacional (Arg-G1), the country's most important race, which is the final leg of the San Isidro Triple Crown. *Yatasto won the Carlos Pellegrini in 1952 before a record crowd of 104,810. *Forli accomplished the feat in 1966 and was then imported to the United States. A daily card consists of as many as 14 races, which begin in midafternoon and conclude at night under lights. Two overlapping, left-handed turf courses—the main one is 2,738 meters—have three chutes.

Location: 504 Avenue Marquez, San Isidro 1642
Phone: 54 (11) 4743-4010
Website: *www.hipodromosanisidro.com.ar*
E-Mail: jchsi@overnet.com.ar
Abbreviation: SI
Principal Races: 25 de Mayo (Arg-G1), Carlos Pellegrini-Internacional (Arg-G1), Copa de Oro (Arg-G1), De Potrancas (Arg-G1), Estrellas Sprint (Arg-G1), Estrellas Distaff (Arg-G1), Estrellas Junior Sprint (Arg-G1), Estrellas Juvenile Fillies (Arg-G1), Estrellas Sprint (Arg-G1), Felix de Alzaga Unzue-Internacional (Arg-G1), Gran Criterium (Arg-G1), Jockey Club (Arg-G1)

Australia
Ascot

Located along the Swan River in the heart of Perth, capital city of Western Australia, Ascot features the Perth Cup (Aus-G2), first contested in 1879. In 1982, the track underwent a major renovation. It has a left-handed course of 2,000 meters with a 300-meter straight. Three different chutes are used to start Ascot's three major races: the Perth Cup, the Western Australian Turf Club Derby (Aus-G1) at 2,400 meters, and the Railway Stakes (Aus-G1) at 1,600 meters.

Location: 70 Grandstand Road, Ascot, WA 6104
Phone: 61 (08) 9277-0713
Fax: 61 (08) 9277-0710
Website: *www.waturf.org.au*
E-Mail: perthracing@perthracing.org.au
Abbreviation: AsR
Chairman: E. Van Heemst
Chief Executive: P. D. Neck
Principal Races: Railway S. (Aus-G1), West Australian Turf Club Derby (Aus-G1), Perth Cup (Aus-G2)

Canterbury

Canterbury Racecourse, located approximately seven miles southwest of Sydney's central business district, is easily accessible by public transportation and offers ample free parking. Its intimate, 1,600-meter track affords spectators a close view of the 34 race cards conducted annually by the Sydney Turf Club. Racing is usually held on Thursday evenings, with occasional Saturday-evening programs, including the beginning of the rich Autumn Golden Slipper Festival. Programs of eight to ten races are held on the right-handed turf course. In July 2002, Sydney Turf Club officials announced that the Canterbury facility would not be sold for development. The 1,800-meter Canterbury Guineas (Aus-G1) for three-year-olds is the track's top race.

Location: King Street, Canterbury, NSW 2193
Phone: 61 (02) 9930-4000
Fax: 61 (02) 9930-4098
Website: *www.stc.com.au*
E-Mail: sydturf@stc.com.au
Abbreviation: Cby
Chairman: Bruce McHugh
Chief Executive: Michael T. Kenny
Principal Races: Canterbury Guineas (Aus-G1)

Caulfield

Situated about five miles southeast of Melbourne, Caulfield Racecourse has a rich history that traces to August 5, 1876. In 1996, the Melbourne Racing Club (formerly the Victoria Amateur Turf Club) widened the track to 30 meters around the entire circumference and lengthened the straight by 43 meters. Affectionately known as "the Heath," Caulfield is home to the Caulfield Carnival each spring, which features three major stakes: the 2,400-meter Caulfield Cup (Aus-G1), the 1,600-meter Caulfield Guineas (Aus-G1) for three-year-olds, and the 1,600-meter Vinery Australia Thousand Guineas (Aus-G1) for three-year-old fillies. The Autumn Carnival offers Victoria's richest race for two-year-olds, the AAMI Blue Diamond Stakes (Aus-G1) at 1,200 meters. Caulfield stages 20 dates of racing during the year.

Location: P.O. Box 231, 22 Station Street, Caulfield, VIC 3145
Phone: 61 (3) 9257-7200
Fax: 61 (3) 9257-7210
Website: *www.melbourneracingclub.net.au*
E-Mail: contact@melbourneracingclub.net.au
Abbreviation: Cau
Chairman: Kevin A. Hayes
Chief Executive: Peter J. Sweeney
General Manager: John Green
Director of Racing: John Faulkner
Director of Marketing: Chris West
Principal Races: Blue Diamond Stakes (Aus-G1), Caulfield Cup (Aus-G1), Caulfield Guineas (Aus-G1), Underwood Stakes (Aus-G1), Vinery Australia Thousand Guineas (Aus-G1)

Doomben

Doomben Track, formerly the Doomben Park Recreation Grounds Ltd., was opened in 1933 by the Brisbane Amateur Turf Club, which subsequently changed its name to the Brisbane Turf Club. Called the "Garden Racecourse," Doomben was used as a base by United States troops during World War II. The track underwent an extensive renovation in 1982 and now hosts 40 race dates, 25 of them on Saturdays, each year. Its major races include the Doomben 10,000 Stakes (Aus-G1), formerly the T. M. Ahern Memorial Stakes, and the Doomben Cup (Aus-G1) at 2,200 meters. Another highlight is the six-day Winter Racing Carnival. Doomben is adjacent to Eagle Farm Racecourse, the principal track in Brisbane, Queensland's capital. The track is approximately four miles from Brisbane's central business district and a short distance from Brisbane Airport.

Location: P.O. Box 168, Hamilton Central, Queensland 4007
Phone: 61 (07) 3268-6800
Fax: 61 (07) 3868-1281
Website: www.doomben.com
E-Mail: btc@doomben.com
Abbreviation: Doo
Chairman: Ian Baxter
Chief Executive Officer: Sean Kelk
Principal Races: Doomben 10,000 Stakes (Aus-G1), Doomben Cup (Aus-G1)

Eagle Farm

Located on the northern side of Brisbane in Ascot, Eagle Farm boasts a long history and excellent equine facilities. Its racing started on August 14, 1865, under the Queensland Turf Club, which was founded in 1863 by a group of 53 sportsmen. The training facilities include two turf tracks, a wood-fiber track, a sand track, two exercise rings, and an equine swimming pool. The main turf track is approximately 2,026 meters with a single chute. Horses race clockwise and must navigate a slight uphill climb heading for the finish line. During World War II, Eagle Farm was used as a military base by both Australian and United States troops. For those five years, the Queensland Turf Club held race meetings at Albion Park.

Location: P.O. Box 21, Hamilton Central, Queensland 4007
Phone: 61 (07) 3268-2171
Fax: 61 (07) 3868-2410
Website: www.qtc.org
E-Mail: info@qtc.org
Abbreviation: EF
Principal Races: Brisbane Cup (Aus-G1), Queensland Derby (Aus-G1), Queensland Oaks (Aus-G1), Sires' Produce S. (Aus-G1), Stradbroke H. (Aus-G1), The T. J. Smith S. (Aus-G1)

Flemington

A breathtaking course with Melbourne's skyline as a backdrop, Flemington has staged racing since 1840, and the Melbourne Cup (Aus-G1), its famed stakes race at about two miles on the first Tuesday of November, is regarded as a national holiday. On the morning of the Melbourne Cup, a service held at St. Francis's Church is followed by a carnival on Burke Street, Melbourne's central thoroughfare. Up to 100,000 spectators fill Flemington on Melbourne Cup day to celebrate the stakes first run in 1861. The winner of the first Melbourne Cup, Archer, was reported to have walked more than 500 miles from his stable in New South Wales to enter the race. In 1930, *Phar Lap won the race after surviving an attempt on his life while training at Flemington. He was hidden in the ensuing days, arrived at the track just minutes before post time, and won the race in a canter. The legendary runner is honored by a bronze statue outside an entrance to the track. Flemington also holds the Victoria Derby (Aus-G1), first run in 1855 and the oldest established race in Australia. The left-handed, 2,300-meter turf course has a 1,200-meter straight chute.

Location: 400 Epsom Road, Flemington, Victoria 3031
Phone: 61 (130) 072-7575
Website: www.vrc.net.au
E-Mail: customerservice@vrc.net.au
Abbreviation: Fle
Chairman: R. M. Fitzroy
Vice Chairman: Peter Barnett
Principal Races: Australian Cup (Aus-G1), Australian Guineas (Aus-G1), MacKinnon S. (Aus-G1), Lightning S. (Aus-G1), Melbourne Cup (Aus-G1), Sires' Produce S. (Aus-G1), Victoria Derby (Aus-G1)

Moonee Valley

Located less than four miles from central Melbourne, Moonee Valley was founded by William Samuel Cox in 1883. The Cox Plate (Aus-G1), Australia's most important weight-for-age race, is run at Moonee Valley one week before the Melbourne Cup at Flemington. First run in 1922, the Cox Plate was won by *Phar Lap in '30 and '31. In a historic running of the Cox Plate in 1986, Bonecrusher edged fellow New Zealand champion Our Waverley Star by a neck. Moonee Valley offers a wide range of amenities, including a 1,000-seat dining room, glass-enclosed dining boxes, 20 bars, and electronic gaming machines, which were added in 1992. The 1,800-meter, left-handed course is more rectangular than oval, with very sharp turns and short straights, putting a high premium on agility and speed. It is intersected by a diagonal straight course. Inside the main course are hurdle and steeplechase courses.

Location: McPherson Street, Moonee Ponds, Victoria 03039
Phone: 61 (130) 079-7959
Fax: 61 (03) 9326-0090
Website: www.mvrc.net.au
E-Mail: customerservice@mvrc.net.au
Abbreviation: Moo
Principal Races: Manikato S. (Aus-G1), W. S. Cox Plate (Aus-G1)

Morphettville

Located along the Anzac Highway in Adelaide, South Australia, Morphettville is operated by the South Australian Jockey Club. Founded in 1860, Morphettville holds its principal meet in May, when it stages the South Australian Derby (Aus-G1), the South Australian Oaks (Aus-G1), and the Adelaide Cup (Aus-G1). The 2,300-meter course has a short straight of nearly 400 meters. The track's grandstand was razed in 1976 and replaced by a modern facility, and a multimillion-dollar renovation of the course itself was completed in 2002.

Location: P. O. Box 1695, Anzac Highway and Morphett Road, Morphettville, Adelaide, SA 5001
Phone: 61 (88) 295-0111
Fax: 61 (88) 376-2099
Website: www.sajc.com.au
Abbreviation: Mor
Ownership: South Australian Jockey Club
President: Peter Lewis
Vice President: John Naffine
Chief Executive: Steve Ploubidis
Principal Races: Adelaide Cup (Aus-G1), Goodwood Handicap (Aus-G1), Robert Sangster Stakes (Aus-G1), South Australian Derby (Aus-G1)

Rosehill Gardens

Located about 14 miles west of Sydney, Rosehill frequently is called Sydney's garden course and is home to Australia's premier race for two-year-olds, the 1,200-

meter Golden Slipper Stakes (Aus-G1), first contested in 1957. The beautifully landscaped track was constructed on Australia's most historic agricultural property, Elizabeth Farm, and major festivals are held in both the spring and autumn. The about 2,000-meter course features a 400-meter straight. Races of 1,200 meters (5.97 furlongs) start in the center of the course and traverse a long bend into the straight. Training facilities include Equitrack, grass, sand, and cinder training tracks with stabling available adjacent to the track.

Location: James Ruse Drive, P.O. Box 21, Rosehill, NSW 2142
Phone: 61 (29) 930-4000
Fax: 61 (29) 930-4099
Website: www.stc.com.au
E-Mail: sydturf@stc.com.au
Abbreviation: Roh
President: Bruce William McHugh
Vice President: Alan Francis Brown
Chief Executive Officer: Michael T. Kenny
Principal Races: George Ryder S. (Aus-G1), Golden Slipper S. (Aus-G1), H. E. Tancred S. (Aus-G1), Rosehill Guineas (Aus-G1), Storm Queen/Arrowfield Stud S. (Aus-G1)

Royal Randwick

Home of the Australian Jockey Club, Randwick has conducted racing since 1860, when the club relocated from Homebush. The inaugural running of the Australian Jockey Club St. Leger (Aus-G2) was held in 1841 at Homebush but was moved to Randwick when the track opened. The first A.J.C. Derby (Aus-G1) was run in 1861. The Sydney Cup (Aus-G1) was first contested in April 1865. Randwick, which is close to Sydney, holds racing festivals in both the spring at the start of October and in the fall in April. The major stakes in the spring is the Metropolitan (Aus-G1) at 2,600 meters. The A.J.C. Derby, Doncaster Handicap (Aus-G1), and Queen Elizabeth Stakes (Aus-G1) are contested in the fall. Randwick's 2,218-meter course with four chutes circles an infield lake and is considered one of the most demanding in Australia.

Location: Alison Road, Randwick, NSW 2031
Phone: 61 (29) 663-8400
Fax: 61 (29) 662-6292
Website: www.ajc.org.au
Abbreviation: Ran
Chairman: Bill Rutledge
Vice Chairman: Treve Williams
Principal Races: A.J.C. Australian Derby (Aus-G1), A.J.C. Australian Oaks (Aus-G1), Champagne S. (Aus-G1), Doncaster H. (Aus-G1), Sires' Produce S. (Aus-G1), Spring Champion S. (Aus-G1), Sydney Cup (Aus-G1)

Victoria Park

Founded in 1788, Victoria Park is the South Australian capital city of Adelaide's second-oldest racetrack and the largest track in the country. Located less than a mile from the city center in the Adelaide City Parklands, Victoria Park has two turf courses, one 2,361 meters in circumference with a 601-meter straight, and an inner course of 1,961 meters with a 479-meter straight. Known as "the Course of Natural Beauty," the track also has a 1,000-meter straight. Victoria Park stages the Adelaide Guineas (Aus-G3), among other stakes races. Each December, it is host to Christmas Twilight, a race program that benefits the South Australia Variety Club.

Location: Wakefield Street and Fullarton Road, Rose Park, Adelaide, SA 5001
Phone: 61 (88) 223-5466
Fax: 61 (88) 223-4669
Website: www.sajc.com.au
Year Founded: 1888
Abbreviation: VP
Ownership: South Australian Jockey Club
President: Peter Lewis
Vice President: John Naffine
Chief Executive: Steve Ploubidis
Principal Races: Adelaide Guineas (Aus-G3)

Warwick Farm

Warwick Farm Racecourse, operated by the Australian Jockey Club, is located about 18 miles from Sydney and is renowned for its picnic atmosphere. Racing is conducted on an oblong, 1,937-meter oval with a straight of just 326 meters. The track has a chute for races between 1,000 and 1,400 meters, and it also has two short chutes for 1,600-meter and 2,400-meter races. Front-runners tend to do well because of Warwick Farm's sharp turns, which can force late closers very wide. The track opened in 1925 and resumed racing in '52 after being closed through World War II. Its J.M.B. Carr Grandstand was built in 1982.

Location: Hume Highway, Warwick Farm, Sydney NSW 2031
Phone: 61 (29) 602-6199
Fax: 61 (29) 821-2150
Website: www.ajc.org.au
Abbreviation: WF
Chairman: Treve Williams
General Manager: Jeff Haynes
Chief Executive: Tony King
Principal Races: Chipping Norton Stakes (Aus-G1), George Main Stakes (Aus-G1)

Brazil
Cidade Jardim

Just minutes from downtown Sao Paulo, Cidade Jardim offers year-round turf and dirt racing on left-handed courses. Cidade Jardim opened on January 25, 1941, after Brazilian racing officials decided that Mooca, the track in the center of Sao Paulo, was too small and too crowded. Today, Cidade Jardim is a sprawling facility that houses many important Brazilian racing authorities, including the Stud-Book Brazileiro. Cidade Jardim's main turf course is an about 2,000-meter oval with a dirt course of about 1,800 meters. Cidade Jardim also encompasses a training center with two dirt training tracks, a stud farm, and an exhibition center for cultural and scientific activities.

Location: Sao Paulo
Phone: 55 (11) 2161-8300
Website: www.hcj.com.br
E-Mail: hcj@hcj.com.br
Abbreviation: CJ
Principal Races: Consagracao (Brz-G1), Derby Paulista (Brz-G1), Diana (Brz-G1), Jockey Club de Sao Paulo (Brz-G1), Organizacao Sulamericana de Fomento ao Puro Sangue de Corrida (Brz-G1), Oswaldo Aranha (Brz-G1), Presidente da Republica (Brz-G1), Sao Paulo (Brz-G1)

La Gavea

With the Statue of Christ the Redeemer atop Corcovado Mountain in Rio de Janeiro serving as a dramatic backdrop, La Gavea is located adjacent to Lake Rodrigo de Freitas. An outer, 2,120-meter turf course rings a 2,036-meter dirt track with two separate turns out of the home straight. Though racing was conducted in Brazil as early as 1825, betting was not allowed until '72. In that year, the Jockey Club Brazileiro was formed, which led to the opening of La Gavea. La Gavea's spring season in October and November features the Gran Premio Linneo de Paula Machado (Brz-G1), among other stakes. Racing is held year-round on Saturdays and Sundays.

Location: Rio de Janeiro
Website: *www.jcb.com.br*
Abbreviation: Gav
Principal Races: Proprietarios do Cavalo de Corrida (Brz-G1), Brasil (Brz-G1), Cruzeiro do Sul (Brz-G1), Diana (Brz-G1), Jockey Club Brasileiro (Brz-G1), Linneo de Paula Machado (Brz-G1), Presidente da Republica (Brz-G1)

Taruma

Located ten minutes from downtown Curitiba, a city of 2.3-million people that is the capital of the state of Parana, Taruma races year-round under the ownership of Jockey Club do Parana. Opened on December 2, 1873, Taruma has an 1,800-meter course. Its biggest race, the 2,400-meter Gran Premio International Parana (Brz-G1), is run in December.

Location: Avenue Victor Ferreira Do Amaral, Curitiba Parana
Phone: 55 (41) 366-2121
Abbreviation: Tma
Chairman: Cesar de Paula ou Alessandro Reichel
Principal Races: Gran Premio International Parana (Brz-G1)

Chile
Club Hipico de Santiago

Lush, beautiful, and close to the center of Santiago, Club Hipico de Santiago encompasses more than 200 acres and is full of gardens, lakes, tennis courts, and fountains. Members of the Chilean bourgeoisie created Club Hipico in 1869, and its first race was run on September 20, 1870. Club Hipico is home to the oldest stakes race in South America, the El Ensayo (Chi-G1), first run in 1873 for three-year-old colts and fillies. The track stages as many as 16 races a day, usually on Mondays and Thursdays in January, February, and March, and on Sundays during other months.

Location: Avenida Blanco Encalada, Santiago
Phone: 56 (2) 693-9600
Fax: 56 (2) 683-7074
Website: *www.clubhipico.cl*
Abbreviation: CDS
Principal Races: Club Hipico de Santiago (Chi-G1), El Ensayo (Chi-G1), Las Oaks (Chi-G1), Polla de Potrancas (Chi-G1), Polla de Potrillos (Chi-G1)

Hipodromo Chile

Founded in 1904 by a group of 19 breeders, owners, and trainers, Hipodromo Chile is located ten minutes north of Santiago and near the Comodo Merino Benitez Airport. Racing is conducted on every other Wednesday and every Saturday year-round on a 1,645-meter, left-handed dirt track. A nearby sales complex, conducting two-year-olds in training sales in the spring and fall, complement the racing.

Location: 1715 Avenue Hipodromo Chile, Independencia, Santiago 02753
Phone: 56 (2) 270-9237
Fax: 56 (2) 777-2089
Website: *www.hipodromo.cl*
E-Mail: rrpp@hipodromochile.cl or sugerencias@hipodromochile.cl
Abbreviation: HC
President: Juan Cuneo Solari
General Manager: Luis I. Salas
Vice President: Orlando Mercado Labbe
Executive Director: Luis Solar Feuereisen
Principal Races: Dos Mil Guineas (Chi-G1), Gran Criterium (Chi-G1), Gran Premio Hipodromo Chile (Chi-G1), Mil Guineas (Chi-G1), St. Leger (Chi-G1)

Vina del Mar

Hipodromo de Vina del Mar is operated by the Valparaiso Sporting Club. Thirteen to 17 dates are held annually on Wednesdays and Fridays, and races range from 800 meters to 2,400 meters. The two main turf courses and dirt training track can accommodate 600 horses. El Derby (Chi-G1), the third race of the Chilean Triple Crown, is contested at 2,400 meters (11.93 furlongs) on turf.

Location: Los Castanos 404, Vina Del Mar
Phone: 56 (3) 268-9393
Fax: 56 (3) 297-6700
Website: *www.sporting.cl*
E-Mail: sporting@sporting.cl
Abbreviation: Val
Principal Races: Copa de Plata Italo Traverso (Chi-G1), El Derby (Chi-G1)

England
Aintree

Located a short distance from Liverpool, Aintree is home to the world's best-known steeplechase race, the Grand National, a 4½-mile marathon in early April over 30 tall, testing fences. The Grand National was first run at Aintree in 1839, when the striking bay Lottery won the third running of a race known then as the Grand Liverpool Steeplechase, which was held at another site in its first two years.

In the 1990s, animal-rights protests forced the taming of the 2¼-mile Grand National course's more terrifying fences. Most notable was the filling of Becher's Brook, named for Captain Martin Becher, who fell at its tall fence and tumbled into the creek after his mount allegedly was impeded by Lottery. The Chair, one of two obstacles on the 16-fence course that are jumped only once, stands 5'2" tall, and its landing side is higher than the takeoff side. As many as 40 horses can start in the Grand National, but often only a handful of horses complete the race.

Location: Ormskirk Road, Aintree, Liverpool L9 5AS
Phone: 44 (151) 523-2600
Fax: 44 (151) 522-2920
Website: *www.aintree.co.uk*
E-Mail: aintree@rht.net
Abbreviation: Ain
General Manager: Charles Barnett
Director of Operations: Alastair Warwick
Principal Races: Grand National Steeplechase

Ascot

Host of the traditional Royal Meeting in June as well as racing throughout the year in both National Hunt and flat divisions, Ascot is owned by Queen Elizabeth II. Queen Anne marked the course out in Windsor Park, and racing began there in August 1711. The National Hunt course was added in 1965. The Royal Meeting begins with the queen and her royal party driving down the straight mile in horse-drawn carriages to the applause of the crowd, with the men sporting top hats and morning suits and the women wearing elegant hats. Traditionally, the first race is the Queen Anne Stakes (Eng-G1), and the races that follow offer a wide variety of competition from sprinters to stayers. No Ascot race is more demanding than the 2½-mile Ascot Gold Cup (Eng-G1), first run in 1807. The St. James's Palace Stakes (Eng-G1), the King George VI and Queen Elizabeth Stakes (Eng-G1), the King Edward VII Stakes (Eng-G2), the Queen Elizabeth II Stakes (Eng-G1), the Coronation Stakes (Eng-G1) for fillies, and the Meon Valley Stud Fillies' Mile (Eng-G1) are among Ascot's most definitive events. The flat course at Ascot is a right-handed triangular oval of 1¾ miles with two mile chutes. Ascot, which was previously held in a private trust, underwent a $347-million renovation beginning in 2002 and, after closing in September 2004, was scheduled to reopen in 2006.

Location: Ascot Racecourse, Berkshire SL5 7JX
Phone: 44 (134) 487-6876
Fax: 44 (134) 462-8299
Website: www.ascot.co.uk
E-Mail: enquiries@ascot.co.uk
Abbreviation: Asc
Chairman: Duke of Devonshire CBE
Chief Executive: Douglas Erskin-Crum
Director of Operations: Ronnie Wilkie
Commercial and Finance Director: Janet Walker
Other Officials: Directors: Mark Davies, Johnny Weatherby, John Varley, Simon Murray
Principal Races: Coronation S. (Eng-G1), Gold Cup S. (Eng-G1), King George VI and Queen Elizabeth S. (Eng-G1), Prince of Wales's S. (Eng-G1), Queen Elizabeth II S. (Eng-G1), St. James's Palace S. (Eng-G1)
Ascot Redevelopment: Ascot closed for 20 months at the end of September 2004 to embark on its $347-million redevelopment and was scheduled to reopen for the 2006 Royal Meeting.

Cheltenham

Located in the Cotswolds in west-central England, Cheltenham is a stunning racecourse that is host each March to the National Hunt Festival, which features the Cheltenham Gold Cup and Champion Hurdle Stakes, championship races for their respective divisions. The 2001 Cheltenham festival was canceled because of the foot-and-mouth disease outbreak that winter, and in most years the festival is standing-room only. The first Gold Cup was held in 1819 as a three-mile flat race on Cleeve Hill, which overlooks the current course. When crowds grew to 50,000, a grandstand was constructed, but it was torn down when an antigambling sentiment swept the area in the 1820s. Racing was re-established at the current site in Prestbury Park in 1831, but no racing was conducted there from the 1840s through the '90s. Barry Bingham purchased the course, refurbished it, built a new grandstand and running rails, and launched the festival in 1902 as a two-day event. A third day was added in 1923, and a fourth day was inaugurated in 2005. The Gold Cup was reinstituted in 1924, and three years later the Champion Hurdle was added. Cheltenham has separate left-handed steeplechase and hurdle courses, with a testing, uphill run to the finish post. Among the heroes of Cheltenham are Dorothy Paget's Golden Miller, who won five consecutive runnings of the Gold Cup (1932-'36), and trainer Michael Dickinson, who saddled the first five finishers in the 1983 Gold Cup.

Location: Prestbury Park, Cheltenham, Gloucestershire GL50 4SH
Phone: 44 (124) 251-3014
Fax: 44 (124) 222-227
Website: www.cheltenham.co.uk
E-Mail: cheltenham@rht.net
Abbreviation: Chm
Ownership: Racecourse Holdings Trust
Chairman: Lord Vestey
General Manager: Edward W. Gillespie
Principal Races: Champion Hurdle S., Cheltenham Gold Cup

Doncaster

Home of the final race of the English Triple Crown, the St. Leger Stakes (Eng-G1) in September, Doncaster has hosted racing since 1776. Doncaster runs flat and jump races on separate courses. The pear-shaped, left-handed main course is nearly two miles in circumference. The St. Leger meeting begins with the filly version of the St. Leger Stakes, the Park Hill Stakes (Eng-G3). The Doncaster Cup (Eng-G3), first run in 1766 and the oldest race still run by the Jockey Club, the Champagne Stakes (Eng-G2), May Hill Stakes (Eng-G3), and the Flying Childers Stakes (Eng-G2) for two-year-olds precede the St. Leger, the oldest of the English classics and named for popular local sportsman Lt. Col. Anthony St. Leger. Winners of the St. Leger Stakes include Hambletonian in 1795, Champion (the first horse to win the Epsom Derby and St. Leger Stakes) in 1800, and West Australian, who became the first Triple Crown winner 53 years later. Nijinsky II became the most recent English Triple Crown winner in 1970. The Racing Post Trophy Stakes (Eng-G1) is Doncaster's most significant juvenile race.

Location: The Grandstand, Leger Way, South Yorkshire, Doncaster DN2 6BB
Phone: 44 (130) 230-4200
Fax: 44 (130) 232-3271
Website: www.doncaster-racecourse.com
E-Mail: info@doncasterracing.co.uk
Year Founded: 1776
Abbreviation: Don
Ownership: Doncaster Metropolitan Borough Council
Chairman: Councillor Bill Mordue
General Manager: Steven Clarke
Principal Races: Racing Post Trophy S. (Eng-G1), St. Leger S. (Eng-G1), Champagne S. (Eng-G2)

Epsom Downs

Thoroughbreds have been racing at Epsom, 15 miles south of London in Surrey, for more than 350 years. In 1648, a party of Royalists held races there, and the first recorded race meet was in 1661 on Banstead Downs, which is part of Epsom Downs. The jewel of the racing year is the Epsom Derby (Eng-G1), which traditionally had been run on the first Wednesday in June but now has been moved successfully to the Saturday five weeks after the Two Thousand Guineas (Eng-G1) at Newmarket on the first Saturday of May or, less commonly, the last Saturday in April. First run in 1780, one year after the initial running of the Epsom Oaks (Eng-G1), the 1½-mile

Derby is the middle leg of the English Triple Crown. Epsom has other important stakes during its season, with meets beginning in April and concluding in September of each year. The major races include the Coronation Cup (Eng-G1) and the Diomed Stakes (Eng-G3). The course features a downhill run to the final turn, the world-famous Tattenham Corner, and an uphill pull to the finish.

Location: The Racecourse, Epsom Downs, Surrey KT18 5LQ
Phone: 44 (137) 272-6311
Fax: 44 (137) 274-8253
Website: *www.epsomderby.co.uk*
E-Mail: epsom@rht.net
Abbreviation: Eps
General manager: S. H. Wallis
Principal Races: Coronation Cup (Eng-G1), Epsom Derby (Eng-G1), Epsom Oaks (Eng-G1)

Goodwood

Located amid rolling countryside on Sussex Downs 60 miles southwest of London, Goodwood traces its history to the Duke of Richmond, who first hosted racing on his estate in 1802. The fifth Duke of Richmond improved the quality of racing at Goodwood by making it part of the English social circuit, a task made easier by the development of a railroad network to transport horses and racegoers to the estate. The about one-mile Sussex Stakes (Eng-G1), the about two-mile Goodwood Cup (Eng-G2), the six-furlong Richmond Stakes (Eng-G2), and the 1¼-mile Nassau Stakes (Eng-G1) for fillies and mares are the major races of the annual July meeting, though racing is also held in May, June, August, and October. Goodwood also is host to the Celebration Mile Stakes (Eng-G2) at the end of August. Goodwood has a skewered figure-eight, right-handed course with a six-furlong straight that allows horses to finish in front of Goodwood's restaurant atop the grandstand.

Location: Goodwood, Chichester, West Sussex PO18 0PS
Phone: 44 (124) 375-5022
Fax: 44 (124) 375-5025
Website: *www.goodwood.co.uk*
E-Mail: racing@goodwood.co.uk
Year Founded: 1802
Abbreviation: Goo
Ownership: Goodwood Estate Co. Ltd.
President: Duke of Richmond
General Manager: Rod Fabricius
Director of Marketing: Dan Downie
Principal Races: Nassau S. (Eng-G1), Sussex S. (Eng-G1)

Haydock Park

Located north of Liverpool, Haydock Park Racecourse was created as a successor to the nearby Old Golborne Heath course, home of the Newton Races, which flourished in the 1750s. Haydock conducted its first race in 1899. Haydock's 1⅞-mile track has a tight top bend, and the Sprint Cup Stakes (Eng-G1) is staged each September. A new grandstand was completed in 1982.

Location: Newton-Le-Willows, Merseyside WA12 0HQ
Phone: 44 (194) 272-5963
Fax: 44 (194) 227-0879
Website: *www.haydock-park.co.uk*
E-Mail: haydockpark@rht.net
Abbreviation: Hay
Chairman: W. T. Whittle
Chief Executive: Adam Waterworth
Principal Races: Haydock Sprint Cup S. (Eng-G1)

Kempton Park

Located a 35-minute train ride from Waterloo Station, Kempton Park advertises itself as "London's Racecourse," and it is nine miles south of Heathrow Airport. Built by S. H. Hyde, Kempton Park conducted its first race meet in July 1878. During World War II, the track housed German prisoners of war, and racing resumed in 1947. The track's major race is the King George VI Chase on Boxing Day, December 26, each year, and it also stages flat race meets during the year. In 2005, Kempton announced plans to transform itself into a night-time all-weather track for flat racing while retaining its steeplechase fixtures on turf.

Location: Staines Road East, Sunbury, Middlesex TW16 5AQ
Phone: 44 (193) 278-2292
Fax: 44 (193) 278-2044
Website: *www.kempton.co.uk*
E-Mail: kempton@rht.net
Abbreviation: Kem
Managing Director: Julian Thick
Clerk of the Course: Brian Clifford

Lingfield Park

Set on 300 acres in the Surrey countryside south of London, Lingfield Park is one of Great Britain's most modern racetracks, featuring year-round flat racing on its all-weather artificial-surface track.

Owned by Arena Leisure, Lingfield was the first of England's all-weather tracks, but its Equitrack surface increasingly drew complaints. In late 2001, the racecourse replaced Equitrack with Polytrack, a synthetic surface composed of polypropylene, polyester, Lycra, silica sand, and rubber, covered by a wax coating. The surface, which cost $4.2-million, has been praised by jockeys and trainers. The all-weather track is 1¼-miles around, with a quarter-mile stretch and a quarter-mile chute for 1½-mile races. Lingfield also has a 1¼-mile, left-handed turf course with a 3½-furlong run-in and a 1⅞-mile steeplechase course.

Location: Lingfield Park Racecourse, Lingfield, Surrey RH7 6PQ
Phone: 44 (134) 283-1705
Fax: 44 (134) 283-5874
Website: *www.lingfield-racecourse.co.uk*
E-Mail: info@lingfieldpark.co.uk
Year Founded: 1890
Abbreviation: Lin
Ownership: Arena Leisure
Chairman and President: Ian Renton
General Manager: Clive Stephens
Principal Races: Derby Trial S. (Eng-G3), Oaks Trial, Winter Derby, Spring Cup

Newbury

Located west of London, Newbury has its own railway station just yards from the attractive left-handed racecourse. The course measures more than 1¾ miles with a slightly undulating straight mile ideal for galloping.

Fifteen days of flat racing extend from April through October, and steeplechase meets are conducted during the colder months. Its major flat races include the one-mile Juddmonte Lockinge Stakes (Eng-G1), and its premier race over fences is the Hennessy Cognac Gold Cup.

Newbury, which opened in 1905, resulted from a chance meeting between well-known trainer John Porter and King Edward VII. It quickly became known as one of the country's best courses, but the course has been pressed into other duties during wartime. Newbury was requisitioned during World War I and was used for troops, supplies, tank testing and repair, and as a prisoner of war camp. In World War II, the track became a major American base and prisoner of war camp.

Racing resumed on April 1, 1949, and now features elegant surroundings, including a sky-lighted "Long Bar" overlooking the track on the first floor and 41 private boxes. The New Grandstand, which opened in 2000, features several exhibition spaces as well as conference rooms for up to 1,000 delegates. The course also features an 18-hole, par 71 golf course and a 20-bay driving range. A leisure center with a swimming pool and gymnasium also are on the property.

Location: The Racecourse, Newbury, Berskhire RG14 7NZ
Phone: 44 (16) 354-0015
Fax: 44 (16) 355-28354
Website: www.newbury-racecourse.co.uk
E-Mail: info@newbury-racecourse.co.uk
Abbreviation: Nby
Chairman: Sir David Sieff
General Manager: Mark Kershaw
Principal Races: Juddmonte Lockinge S. (Eng-G1)

Newmarket

Newmarket is the headquarters of British racing, and its racecourse is a fitting complement to the training gallops to the east of the course. An observer once said: "Newmarket is one of the only places where a man can go racing; elsewhere he merely goes to the races, which isn't the same thing at all." Racing has been held at Newmarket, a Suffolk town 60 miles northeast of London, for more than 350 years. Newmarket's racing spans the entire British flat season, with the spring season featuring the year's first classics, the Two Thousand Guineas (Eng-G1) and One Thousand Guineas (Eng-G1), down its one-mile Rowley Mile Course on the first weekend in May. In the fall, the Champion Stakes (Eng-G1), Cheveley Park Stakes (Eng-G1), Middle Park Stakes (Eng-G1), and Dewhurst Stakes (Eng-G1) are contested across the flat, a 1¼-mile straight that includes the Rowley course. Longer races, such as the rich Cesarewitch Handicap over 2¼ miles, require the use of a ten-furlong extension of the Rowley Mile in a backward, L-shape configuration that extends through the ancient "Devil's Dike." Between those spring and fall events, racing is conducted on the July Course, a straight that connects to the Rowley course. The July Cup (Eng-G1) is the major July stakes. Though Charles I decided Newmarket would be an ideal place to race his horses, his son, Charles II, created the course and the straight mile derives its name from his nickname, "Old Rowley." In 1665, he founded the Newmarket Town Plate, a race that is still contested in a different form. With its uphill finish and no turns, Newmarket provides a severe test of stamina.

Location: Westfield House, The Links, Newmarket, Suffolk CB8 0TG
Phone: 44 (163) 866-3482
Fax: 44 (163) 866-3044
Website: www.newmarketracecourses.co.uk
E-Mail: newmarket@rht.net
Year founded: 1664
Abbreviation: New
Ownership: Racecourse Holdings Trust
Chairman: Richard Hambro
General Manager: Lisa Hancock

Clerk of the Course: Michael Prosser
Principal Races: Champion S. (Eng-G1), Cheveley Park S. (Eng-G1), Dewhurst S. (Eng-G1), July Cup S. (Eng-G1), One Thousand Guineas S. (Eng-G1), Two Thousand Guineas S. (Eng-G1)

Sandown Park

Only 14 miles south of central London, Sandown Park opened in 1875 and was the first totally enclosed racecourse in the country. The course was the brainchild of Lt. Col. Owen Williams, and his brother, Hwfa (pronounced "Hoofer"), was instrumental in Sandown Park's development, serving as chairman and clerk of the course for 50 years. The grandstand, rebuilt in 1973 for approximately $5-million, sits on a hill overlooking the racecourse. The right-handed, 1⅛-mile course includes a downhill run to the back straight and a substantial uphill pull to the homestretch. A five-furlong, uphill straight course runs through the main course. Sandown Park's major stakes race is the 1¼-mile Eclipse Stakes (Eng-G1) in July. It was first run in 1886 and, at the time, was the country's richest stakes race. In the spring, Sandown features the Whitbread Gold Cup, the National Hunt season's final major race over steeplechase fences. Flat racing is held in short meets from late April through the beginning of October. A $33.4-million renovation of the grandstand was completed in early 2002.

Location: Portsmouth Road, Esher, Surrey KT10 9AJ
Phone: 44 (137) 246-3072
Fax: 44 (137) 246-5205
Website: www.sandown.co.uk
E-Mail: sandown@rht.net
Abbreviation: San
Ownership: Racecourse Holdings Trust
Chief Executive: Andrew Coppell
General Manager: Steve Brice
Principal Races: Eclipse S. (Eng-G1)

York

Referred to by many as England's Ascot of the North, York is home to the popular Ebor Festival in mid-August at the Knavesmire, common land 20 minutes from the city of York that has featured racing since 1731. The wide horseshoe-shaped, two-mile, unenclosed course has a 4½-furlong straight after a left-handed turn. Two separate chutes are used for sprints of six and seven furlongs. York came to prominence in 1767 when the Gimcrack Club was founded to honor the champion Gimcrack, who won 26 races between 1764 and '71. The club members organized the York meeting to attract the best horses to the North, and by the 1840s the August meeting featured the Ebor Handicap, Yorkshire Oaks (Eng-G1), and the Gimcrack Stakes (Eng-G2). The Nunthorpe Stakes (Eng-G1) was added in 1903. In 1851, one of the most famous match races in Turf history pitted Epsom Derby winners The Flying Dutchman and Voltigeur, who had inflicted the former's only loss the previous year in the Doncaster Cup. More than 100,000 fans turned out to see the rematch, won by The Flying Dutchman. More than a century later, the Benson & Hedges Gold Cup (Eng-G1), now known as the Juddmonte International Stakes, was created to match two champions of the 1970s, Mill Reef and Brigadier Gerard. Mill Reef broke down before the race, but John Galbreath's Epsom Derby (Eng-G1) victor Roberto handed Brigadier Gerard his only career defeat and set a course record.

Location: The Racecourse, York, North Yorkshire YO23 1EX
Phone: 44 (190) 462-0911
Fax: 44 (190) 461-1071
Website: *www.yorkracecourse.co.uk*
E-Mail: enquiries@yorkracecourse.co.uk
Year Founded: 1731
Abbreviation: Yor
Chairman: N.H.T. Wrigley
Chief Executive and Clerk of the Course: William Derby
Principal Races: Aston Upthorpe Yorkshire Oaks (Eng-G1), Juddmonte International S. (Eng-G1), Nunthorpe S. (Eng-G1), Gimcrack S. (Eng-G2)

France

Chantilly

Racing at Chantilly, a village approximately 20 miles north of Paris, is held every June in front of the palatial Les Grandes Ecuries (literally, "the big stables") and the Chateau de Chantilly. The palatial stables were built by the Prince de Conde, who believed he would be reincarnated as a horse. The estate includes a lavish stable that can house 250 horses. Chantilly, surrounded by woods, lakes, and 250 acres of greenery, also serves as France's principal training center, with as many as 10 trainers and 3,000 horses using its sand, all-weather, and turf training tracks. Chantilly's premier races are the 2,100-meter Prix du Jockey-Club (Fr-G1), first run in 1836 and popularly known as the French Derby, for three-year-olds, and the 2,100-meter (10.44-furlong) Prix de Diane (Fr-G1) (French Oaks) for three-year-old fillies, begun in '41.

Location: 16 Avenue du General Leclerc, BP 90209, Chantilly 60631
Phone: 33 (34) 462-4100
Fax: 33 (34) 457-3489
Abbreviation: Chy
Chief Executive: Mathieu Vincent
Principal Races: Prix de Diane (Fr-G1), Prix du Jockey-Club (Fr-G1), Prix Jean Prat (Fr-G1)

Deauville

Deauville, sometimes referred to as the Saratoga of France, held its first meet in 1864, the same year as Saratoga Race Course's first meet. It runs a short meeting in August, as Saratoga did for decades, and also features a major sale of yearlings, as does Saratoga. Deauville was founded by the Duke of Morny to cater to Parisian society vacationing on the Normandy coast. The setting allows horses to gallop on the beach or in the surf. There is also polo in the afternoons and the casino in the evenings for entertainment, as well as innumerable first-rate restaurants. Deauville offers a top-class, 1,600-meter stakes, the Prix du Haras de Fresnay-le-Buffard Jacques Le Marois (Fr-G1), and the 1,200-meter Prix Morny (Fr-G1) for two-year-olds. Deauville is a right-handed course of 2,200 meters with a 1,600-meter chute on one end and a short chute on the other. Another major stakes, the Grand Prix de Deauville (Fr-G2), is held on the last Sunday of the meeting.

Location: 45 Avenue Hocquart de Turtot, BP 43300, Deauville 14800
Phone: 33 (23) 114-2000
Fax: 33 (23) 114-2001
Abbreviation: Dea
Chief Executive: Yves Deshayes

Principal Races: Prix du Haras de Fresnay-le-Buffard Jacques le Marois (Fr-G1), Prix Maurice de Gheest (Fr-G1), Prix Morny (Fr-G1)

Longchamp

Emperor Napoleon III traveled by boat on the Seine River to attend Longchamp's first day of racing on April 27, 1857, and he was joined at the Paris track by nearly 10,000 countrymen. Finishing second in the first of five races that afternoon was Miss Gladiator, the dam of Gladiateur, who became a legend as the first French-bred horse to win the Epsom Derby. For Gladiateur's first start after the English classic, 150,000 racegoers turned out to watch him win the Grand Prix de Paris (now a Group 1 race) at Longchamp.

But the race for which Longchamp is best known is the Prix de l'Arc de Triomphe (Fr-G1), first contested in 1920. Horses from both England and Italy took on France's best, and the first winner was Comrade, owned and bred by Frenchman Evremond de Saint-Alary, trained in England by Peter Gilpin, and ridden by Australian jockey Frank Bullock. The 2,400-meter race on the first Sunday in October was an instant international success and has become Europe's championship race.

Other Longchamp stakes have longer histories. The Grand Prix de Paris was inaugurated in 1863 and for a century was France's most important race for three-year-olds. Following the modern trend, its distance was reduced from 3,000 meters to 2,000 meters in 1987. It was lengthened again to 2,400 meters in 2005. The first classics of each year, the 1,600-meter Poule d'Essai des Poulains (Fr-G1) (French Two Thousand Guineas) and Poule d'Essai des Pouliches (Fr-G1) (French One Thousand Guineas) for three-year-olds and three-year-old fillies, respectively, are run in May. The Poule d'Essai des Poulains was first run in 1840, while the Poule d'Essai des Pouliches debuted in '83. Longchamp's right-handed course has a long and testing homestretch with a slightly uphill finish.

Location: Route des Tribunes, Bois de Boulogne, Paris 75116
Phone: 33 (14) 430-7500
Fax: 33 (14) 430-7599
Abbreviation: Lch
Chief Executive: Gerard Grandchamp
Principal Races: Grand Prix de Paris (Fr-G1), Poule d'Essai des Poulains (Fr-G1), Poule d'Essai des Pouliches (Fr-G1), Prix de l'Arc de Triomphe (Fr-G1), Prix du Moulin de Longchamp (Fr-G1), Prix Ganay (Fr-G1), Prix Marcel Boussac (Fr-G1)

Maisons-Laffitte

Secluded near the Saint-Germain forest just west of Paris and home to some 1,800 Thoroughbreds conditioned by more than 80 trainers, Maisons-Laffitte offers one of Europe's most pleasant settings for Thoroughbred racing. Its 2,000-meter straight course, rivaled only by the Rowley Mile at Newmarket in England, is complemented by both right- and left-handed courses to accommodate 35 racing dates from the end of March until the end of July and from early September through early December.

The Prix Robert Papin (Fr-G2) is the first major stakes for two-year-olds each year, while other juvenile stakes, such as the Criterium de Maisons-Laffitte (Fr-G2), are run later in the meet. Among the course's top races for two-year-old fillies is the Prix Miesque (Fr-G3), named for the outstanding filly who won two North American championships with her triumphs in the 1987 and '88 Breeders' Cup Mile (G1).

Miesque won the Prix Imprudence at Maisons-Laffitte immediately before her victory in the 1987 One Thousand Guineas (Eng-G1). Among other champions who have raced at Maisons-Laffitte are *Sea-Bird, Nureyev, Arctic Tern, *Match II, Exbury, and Relko.

Set on more than 120 acres, Maisons-Laffitte is home to the Museum of the Racecourse, which was opened in 1990 and allows fans to review the history of racing by walking through magnificent rooms of an ancient castle.

Location: 1 Avenue de la Pelouse, Maisons-Laffitte 78600
Phone: 33 (13) 962-9095
Fax: 33 (13) 962-7608
Abbreviation: ML
Chief Executive: Martial de Rouffignac
Principal Races: Prix Robert Papin (Fr-G2), Prix Miesque (Fr-G3)

Saint-Cloud

The most frequently used Parisian track, Saint-Cloud hosts racing from February through July and from September through December. Its history extends to 1901 when the Societe du Demi-Sang was thrown out of Vincennes by the army and retreated to a strip of land owned by Edmond Blanc to continue racing. After World War I, the course was given to the Societe Sportive d'Encouragement, which supervised Thoroughbred racing at Maisons-Laffitte. The major stakes race at Saint-Cloud is the Grand Prix de Saint-Cloud (Fr-G1), which began in 1904 under the name Prix du President de la Republique. *Sea-Bird, fellow Arc winners Rheingold and Sagace (Fr), and Epsom Derby winners Relko and Teenoso all won races at Saint-Cloud, which also was the site of *Vaguely Noble's lone three-year-old defeat.

The 1,600 meter Criterium International (Fr-G1) was inaugurated in 2001 after the distance of the Grand Criterium (Fr-G1) at Longchamp was changed from 1,600 meters to 1,400 meters. Saint-Cloud's left-handed, 2,200-meter course is dissected by a 600-meter straight.

Location: 1 Rue du Camp Canadien, Saint-Cloud 92210
Phone: 33 (14) 771-6926
Fax: 33 (14) 771-3774
Abbreviation: StC
Chief Executive: Christian Leger
Principal Races: Criterium de Saint-Cloud (Fr-G1), Criterium International (Fr-G1), Grand Prix de Saint-Cloud (Fr-G1)

Germany
Baden-Baden

Set among the foothills of the Black Forest nine miles northwest of Baden-Baden, Baden-Baden Racecourse was the idea of Edouard Benazet, who offered visitors to the world-famous spa not only Thoroughbred racing but also a casino. When the casino closed in 1872, racing was taken over by the Internationale Club, which today supervises racing in short meets from May through June and from August through September. The nearby attractions include a casino, the vineyards of Rebland, Old Town, theaters, concerts, and elegant boutiques. Baden-Baden hosts the Grosser Preis von Baden (Ger-G1) and the Grosser Mercedes-Benz Preis (Ger-G2). The three overlapping, left-handed courses at Baden-Baden are named Old Course, New Course, and Straight Course.

Location: Lichtentaler Alley 8, Baden-Baden 76530
Phone: 49 (72) 292-1120
Fax: 49 (72) 2121-1222
Website: www.baden-galopp.de
E-Mail: club@baden-galopp.de
Abbreviation: Bad
Chairman: Hartmann Freiherr von Richthofen
Chief Executive: Frank Joyeux
Principal Races: Grosser Preis von Baden (Ger-G1)

Dusseldorf

Located in a hilly, wooded park on the edge of the Grafenberg Forest in Dusseldorf's Broich district, Dusseldorf Racecourse is the site of one of Germany's richest races, the Deutschland-Preis (Ger-G1), which is contested in late July. Other important stakes include the Henkel-Rennen (Ger-G2) (German One Thousand Guineas) in early May and the Grosser Preis von Dusseldorf (Ger-G3) in mid-October. The hilly, undulating, right-hand track features a sharp bend.

Location: Rennbahnstr 20, Dusseldorf 40629
Phone: 49 (21) 162-2885
Fax: 49 (21) 1610-7730
Website: www.duesseldorf-galopp.de
Abbreviation: Dus
Chairman: Peter Endres
Chief Executive: Detlef Meimann
Principal Races: Deutschland-Preis (Ger-G1), Henkel-Rennen (Ger-G2), Grosser Preis von Dusseldorf (Ger-G3)

Hamburg

Hamburg is the home of the Deutsches Derby (Ger-G1), a 2,400-meter race for three-year-olds first contested in 1869 under the management of the Hamburger Renn-Club. Hamburg's other major stakes races are the Hansa-Preis (Ger-G2) at 2,100 meters, the Deutscher Herold-Preis (Ger-G3) at the same distance, and the 1,200-meter Holsten-Trophy (Ger-G3). The racetrack is about six miles from Hamburg and is accessible by the motorway from Berlin, subway, and bus. Racing is conducted from the end of June through early July on a right-handed turf course of approximately 2,000 meters.

Location: Rennbahnstr 96, Hamburg 22111
Phone: 49 (40) 651-8229
Fax: 49 (40) 655-6615
Website: www.galopp-derby.de
E-Mail: deutsches-derby@t-online.de
Abbreviation: Hbg
Chairman: Franz-Guenther von Gaertner
Chief Executive: Guenther Gudert
Principal Races: Deutsches Derby (Ger-G1)

Koln

Situated in the Cologne neighborhood of Weidenpesch, Koln Racecourse is a flat, right-handed track with a 2½-furlong straight. Top stakes at Koln include the Europa-Preis (Ger-G1), the Gerling-Preis (Ger-G2), the Mehl-Mulhens-Rennen (Ger-G2) (German Two Thousand Guineas), and the Union-Rennen (Ger-G2).

Location: Rennbahnstr 152, Weidenpesch, Koln 50737
Phone: 49 (221) 974-5050
Fax: 49 (221) 974-5055
Abbreviation: Kol
Chairman: Baron Georg von Ullman
Chief Executive: Benedikt Fassbender
Principal Races: Europa-Preis (Ger-G1), Gerling-Preis (Ger-G2), Mehl-Mulhens-Rennen (Ger-G2) (German Two Thousand Guineas), and Union-Rennen (Ger-G2)

Mulheim

Located in western Germany, Mulheim is host to the country's longest flat race, the 3,400-meter Silbernes Band der Ruhr. Mulheim is a right-handed track with a 2½-furlong straight. The Preis der Diana-Deutsches Stuten-Derby (Ger-G1) (German Oaks) is contested in mid-June.

Location: Akazienallee 80-82, Mulheim Ruhr 45478
Phone: 49 (20) 857-001
Fax: 49 (20) 857-005
Abbreviation: Mul
Chairman: Bodo Scheibel
Chief Executive: Michael Kunst
Principal Races: Preis der Diana-Deutsches Stuten-Derby (Ger-G1)

Hong Kong
Happy Valley

Surrounded today by Hong Kong's skyscrapers, Happy Valley was built on reclaimed marshland and has held racing since 1846. Training horses is not easy on the 31-square-mile island, now under the control of the People's Republic of China, but the rich purses attract horsemen whose runners are housed in high-rise stables. Overshadowed by Sha Tin, Happy Valley conducts a 60-day racing season that lasts from September through June.

Location: 2 Sports Road, Happy Valley
Phone: 852 (2) 895-1523
Fax: 852 (2) 966-8111
Website: www.happyvalleyracecourse.com
Abbreviation: HV

Sha Tin

In 1959, Sir John Saunders, then chairman of the Royal Hong Kong Jockey Club, proposed creating a racetrack in Sha Tin Bay to alleviate overcrowding at Happy Valley. After three years of planning, the project of reclaiming 250 acres from the bay was begun. The soil needed for the project was taken from the top of one of the nearby mountains, which allowed development of that property and paid the track's construction costs.

Working around the clock on a tight, three-year schedule, Sha Tin opened as planned on October 7, 1978, with an expansive grandstand that encompasses 16½ acres. A 1,900-meter turf course encircles an all-weather dirt track. Sha Tin's major races are the Hong Kong Derby for four-year-olds, run every February at the start of the Chinese New Year since 1990, the Hong Kong Cup (HK-G1), the Hong Kong Vase (HK-G1), the Hong Kong Mile (HK-G1), and the Hong Kong Sprint (HK-G1).

Location: New Territories
Phone: 852 (2) 695-6223
Website: www.shatinracetrack.com
E-Mail: shatinracing@hongkong.com
Abbreviation: ST
Chief Executive: Lawrence T. Wong
Principal Races: Hong Kong Cup (HK-G1), Hong Kong Mile (HK-G1), Hong Kong Sprint (HK-G1), Hong Kong Vase (HK-G1), Queen Elizabeth II Cup (HK-G1)

Ireland
Leopardstown

Roughly six miles from Dublin, Leopardstown overcame a troubled past. Nine years after its opening in 1888, the five-furlong course was found to be only 4½ furlongs long. Capt. George Quin, who headed a syndicate that had purchased the course, constructed a new five-furlong course that was not well received. Finally, Richard "Boss" Croker, owner of 1907 Irish Derby and Epsom Derby winner Orby, purchased additional land and a larger course was constructed. Leopardstown was owned by Fred Clarke until he sold the track to the Irish Racing Board in 1967. Two years later, Leopardstown received an extensive facelift, reopening in 1971 with a new grandstand, an enclosed betting hall, new dining and bar facilities, and a new stable area. Another renovation in 1988 extended the grandstand and added 16 private boxes. Race meets are held at Leopardstown from mid-March through mid-November over a left-handed turf course of about 2,800 meters. Leopardstown's premier race is the Irish Champion Stakes (Ire-G1).

Location: Leopardstown Racecourse, Foxrock, Dublin 00018
Phone: 353 (1) 289-0500
Fax: 353 (1) 289-2634
Website: www.leopardstown.com
E-Mail: info@leopardstown.com
Abbreviation: Leo
Chairman: Joseph Donnelly
Principal Races: Irish Champion S. (Ire-G1)

The Curragh

According to legend, St. Bridget was offered as much of the Curragh plain as she could cover with her cloak. Unfurling the cloak from her shoulder, she threw it to cover the whole plain of Kildare. When she gathered up her cloak, the land was covered in the richest and deepest grass imaginable—ideal for training and racing Thoroughbreds. Match races have been held there for centuries. The first recorded one was in 1634 when the Earl of Ormond beat Lord Digby in a four-mile race. The first race recorded at the Curragh was in 1741, and the first Irish Derby (Ire-G1) was held in 1866. By 1921, all five Irish classic stakes were contested at the Curragh. Joining the Derby were the Irish Oaks (Ire-G1), the Irish St. Leger (Ire-G1), the Irish Two Thousand Guineas (Ire-G1), and the Irish One Thousand Guineas (Ire-G1). Located 30 miles west of Dublin, the Curragh offers race meets from mid-March to the beginning of November. The horseshoe-shaped, right-handed course is two miles in length with an uphill, straight run-in of three furlongs to the finish line.

Location: Tara Court, Dublin Road Naas, Co. Kildare
Phone: 353 (4) 544-1205
Fax: 353 (4) 544-1442
Website: www.curragh.ie
E-Mail: info@curragh.ie
Abbreviation: Cur
General Manager: Paul Hensey
Principal Races: Irish Derby (Ire-G1), Irish Oaks (Ire-G1), Irish One Thousand Guineas (Ire-G1), Irish St. Leger (Ire-G1), Irish Two Thousand Guineas (Ire-G1), Moyglare Stud S. (Ire-G1), National S. (Ire-G1), Phoenix S. (Ire-G1), Tattersalls Gold Cup (Ire-G1)

Italy
Capannelle

Less than eight miles from the Colosseum in Rome, Capannelle opened in 1926. The grandstand, turf course, and interior dirt course are close to an ancient Roman aqueduct and are not far from St. Peter's Basilica in the Vatican City. Race meets are held from March to mid-June and from September through November on right-handed turf and sand courses that are slightly uphill near the start and slightly downhill near the finish. National Hunt races also are conducted. Top stakes races include the Premio Presidente della Repubblica (Ity-G1) for four-year-olds and up, the Derby Italiano (Ity-G1) for three-year-olds, and the Premio Roma (Ity-G1) for three-year-olds and older. Capannelle's training facilities include 2,600-meter turf and dirt tracks, another turf course inside them, and a 1,200-meter sand track around the stabling area.

Location: Viaduct Appia Nuova 1255, Rome 00178
Phone: 39 (6) 716-771
Fax: 39 (6) 7167-7213
Website: *www.capannelle-galoppo.it*
E-Mail: capannel@tin.it
Abbreviation: Rom
Chief Executive: Ing. Elio Pautasso
Principal Races: Derby Italiano (Ity-G1), Premio Presidente della Repubblica (Ity-G1), Premio Roma (Ity-G1)

San Siro

Racing began at San Siro in 1888 on a racecourse designed by architect Giulio Valerio. In 1909, a training center was added to the facility located just north of downtown Milan. Today, approximately 200 acres of training grounds include two turf tracks, two sand tracks, and a nearby all-weather track. San Siro's racecourse consists of three right-handed, overlapping turf courses of 2,800, 2,000, and 1,800 meters. Race meets are held from mid-March through July and from September to mid-November. Its premier races are the Oaks d'Italia (Ity-G1) for three-year-old fillies, the Gran Criterium (Ity-G1) for two-year-olds, and the Gran Premio di Milano (Ity-G1) and the Premio del Jockey Club (Ity-G1) for three-year-olds and up.

Location: Viaduct Ippodromo 100, Milan 20155
Phone: 39 (24) 821-6215
Fax: 39 (24) 820-1721
Abbreviation: Mil
Chief Executive: Alessandro Berardelli
Principal Races: Gran Criterium (Ity-G1), Gran Premio di Milano (Ity-G1), Oaks d'Italia (Ity-G1), Premio di Capua V. (Ity-G1), Premio Jockey Club (Ity-G1)

Japan
Hanshin

The newest of the Japan Racing Association's four major tracks, Hanshin opened in 1949 and is about 12 miles from Osaka. Hanshin completed an extensive modernization in 1991 and races from March through June and in September and December. A lush, wide, right-handed turf course—slightly downhill in the backstretch and slightly uphill in the homestretch—encircles a dirt track.

On the second Sunday in April, Hanshin stages the 1,600-meter Oka Sho (Japan's equivalent of the one-mile One Thousand Guineas [Eng-G1]), named for the cherry blossoms in bloom at that time each year. Other major stakes include the all-age Grand Prix Takarazuka Kinen (Jpn-G1) in mid-June and the Hanshin Sansai Himba Stakes in early December for two-year-old fillies.

Location: 1-1 Komano-cho, Takarazuka-shi, Hyogo 665-0053
Phone: 81(79) 851-7151
Website: *www.jair.jrao.ne.jp/courses/jra/jra004.html*
Abbreviation: Hsn
Principal Races: Takarazuka Kinen (Jpn-G1), Oka Sho

Kyoto

Another of the major Japan Racing Association tracks, Kyoto Racecourse is located six miles south of Kyoto and stages racing in January, February, April, May, October, and November over a 1,900-meter, right-handed turf course that is uphill in the backstretch. Enclosed within the main course is a dirt course, an inner turf course, and a huge lake. A mammoth walking ring allows thousands of fans to see horses prepare for their race. The Spring Tenno Sho (Emperor's Cup) is a 3,200-meter endurance stakes for four-year-olds and older held on the last Sunday in April. In November, three major stakes are held on successive Sundays: the 3,000-meter Kikuka Sho (Japanese St. Leger) for three-year-olds, the final leg of the Japanese Triple Crown; the 2,400-meter Queen Elizabeth Cup, which is the concluding race of the Japanese filly triple crown; and the 1,600-meter Mile Championship.

Location: 32 Yoshijima, Watashibashima-machi, Fushimi-ku, Kyoto 612-8265
Phone: 81 (75) 631-3131
Website: *www.jair.jrao.ne.jp/courses/jra/jra003.html*
Abbreviation: Kyo
Principal Races: Kikuka Sho, Mile Championship, Queen Elizabeth Cup, Spring Tenno Sho

Nakayama

Located 12 miles east of Tokyo, Nakayama Racecourse features two broad turf courses and a dirt course inside them. The outer course is 1,840 meters, and the inner grass course 1,667 meters. The dirt course is 1,493 meters. All three courses have a modest uphill run over the last 200 meters to the finish line. The track also has a steeplechase course in its infield. Among the racecourse's major races are the Arima Kinen, the Sprinters Stakes, and Satsuki Sho, which is Japan's equivalent of the Two Thousand Guineas for three-year-olds.

Location: 1-1-1 Kosaku, Funabashi-shi, Chiba 273-0037
Website: *www.jair.jrao.ne.jp/courses/jra/jra002.html*
Abbreviation: Nak
Principal Races: Arima Kinen, Satsuki Sho, Sprinters Stakes

Tokyo

Home of Japan's premier race, the Japan Cup (Jpn-G1), Tokyo Racecourse at Fuchu, 15 miles west of Tokyo, was built in 1933. The 1,878-meter interior dirt course is based on the design of American courses but is uniquely fine-tuned to handle Japan's heavier precipitation. The track is packed firmly with a layer of mountain sand and covered with loose river sand, giving horses a strong bottom underneath and a surface on top to absorb impact and ease stress on their legs. The undulating turf course is 2,116 meters. The Japan Cup, which is run left-handed on turf at 2,400 meters, begins on a 400-meter straight run that minimizes the impact of poor post position. On the same weekend, the $2-million Japan Cup Dirt is run. The course underwent extensive renovations in 2002.

Location: 1-1 Hiyoshi-cho, Fuchu-shi, Tokyo 183-0024
Phone: 81 (42) 363-3141
Website: *www.jair.jrao.ne.jp/courses/jra/jra001.html*
Abbreviation: Tok
Principal Races: Japan Cup (Jpn-G1), Japan Cup Dirt

New Zealand

Avondale

Operated by the Avondale Jockey Club, which was formed in 1889, Avondale is located near Auckland and hosts 14 racing dates each year. The original left-handed course was just under a mile in circumference. It was enlarged to 1⅛ miles and converted to a right-handed course a few years later.

Location: Ash Street, 103 Avondale, Auckland
Phone: 64 (09) 828-3309
Fax: 64 (09) 828-3099
Website: www.ajc.co.nz
E-Mail: admin@ajc.co.nz
Abbreviation: Avo
President: Graham Reddaway
Secretary: Jim Patterson
Principal Races: Avondale Gold Cup H. (NZ-G1), Avondale Guineas (NZ-G1)

Ellerslie

Several of New Zealand's Group 1 races are held at Ellerslie, including the New Zealand Derby (NZ-G1) and the Easter Handicap (NZ-G1). The track, approximately five miles from New Zealand's largest city, Auckland, boasts an elegant grandstand and beautifully maintained grounds. Racing was first conducted about one mile from Ellerslie on January 5, 1842, but the present site was not used until May 25, 1874, a national holiday to observe Queen Victoria's birthday. Ellerslie's major stakes races are held from December 26 through January 2 and during the first week in June. The main track is a 1,870-meter, right-handed turf course with a finishing straight of 380 meters that is slightly downhill.

Location: Greenlane, Auckland
Phone: 64 (9) 524-4069
Fax: 64 (9) 524-8680
Website: www.ellerslie.co.nz
E-Mail: davel@ellerslie.co.nz
Abbreviation: Ell
Chairman: G. J. Clatworthy
Chief executive: Chris Weaver
Director of racing: Andrew Castles
Principal Races: Auckland Cup (NZ-G1), Easter H. (NZ-G1), Ellerslie Sires' Produce S. (NZ-G1), New Zealand Derby (NZ-G1)

Hawke's Bay

Racing dates back to 1845 at Hawke's Bay, located near the cities of Napier and Hastings on the eastern shore of New Zealand's northern island. The four racing clubs using the racetrack, however, did not unite until 1989. Now, 14 dates are conducted annually. The highlight of the year is the Spring Carnival, which is held over five weeks in August and September and features the Kelt Capital Stakes (NZ-G1), the richest weight-for-age race in New Zealand. The Hawke's Bay Cup Handicap (NZ-G2), the country's second-oldest race, was first contested in 1860.

Location: Prospect Road, Box 1046, Hastings
Phone: 64 (6) 873-4545
Fax: 64 (6) 6876-6488
Website: www.hb-racing.co.nz
E-Mail: comeracing@hb-racing.co.nz
Abbreviation: HB
Chief Executive: John McGifford
Principal Races: Kelt Capital S. (NZ-G1), Hawke's Bay Gold Cup (NZ-G2), Mudway PartsWorld Stakes (NZ-G2), Hawke's Bay Guineas (NZ-G3)

Otaki

Otaki Racecourse, located at the north end of Otaki on Kapiti island, has an 1,800-meter, left-handed track and is home of the Otaki-Maori Racing Club. Organized racing has been held at Otaki since the 1850s, and the Otaki-Maori Racing Club dates from 1866. In September 2000, the Levin Racing Club, Wellington Race Club, and Masterson Racing Club joined with the Otaki Maori Racing Club to form Capital Racing. The four clubs, each of which had been facing financial difficulties before the 2000 agreement, combine to run 27 days a year at Otaki, which is easily accessible by railroad from Wellington, at the southern tip of New Zealand's northern island. The WFA Stakes (NZ-G1) is staged there.

Location: P.O. Box 13, Otaki
Phone: 64 (6) 364-8078
Fax: 64 (6) 364-8079
E-Mail: otaki_maorirc@xtra.co.nz
Abbreviation: Oki
Chief Executive: A. J. Castles
Principal Races: WFA Stakes (NZ-G1)

Riccarton Park

The Canterbury Jockey Club was formed in 1854, and the following year began racing at Riccarton Park Racecourse, which is located ten minutes from the center of Christchurch, New Zealand's second-largest city, on the southern island. Among the races held at Riccarton are the New Zealand Two Thousand Guineas (NZ-G1), New Zealand One Thousand Guineas (NZ-G1), and the New Zealand Cup Handicap (NZ-G2).

Location: Racecourse Road, Riccarton, Christchurch
Phone: 64 (3) 342-8928
Fax: 64 (3) 342-6114
Website: www.riccartonpark.co.nz/cjc
E-Mail: enquiries@riccartonpark.co.nz
Abbreviation: Ric
Chief Executive: Tim Mills
Principal Races: New Zealand One Thousand Guineas (NZ-G1), New Zealand Two Thousand Guineas (NZ-G1), New Zealand Cup Handicap (NZ-G2)

Te Rapa

Located north of Hamilton on New Zealand's northern island, Te Rapa Racecourse is operated by the Waikato Racing Cup and conducts 18 days of racing annually. Flat racing is conducted on a left-handed, 1,800-meter track with two chutes. Te Rapa has an expansive galloping track, tree-lined paddocks, and a large grandstand. Among its major races are the Waikato Draught Sprint Stakes (NZ-G1), Whakanui Stud International Stakes (NZ-G1), and the Cambridge Stud Sir Tristram Fillies Classic Stakes (NZ-G2).

Location: P.O. Box 10050, Te Rapa, Hamilton
Phone: 64 (7) 849-2839
Fax: 64 (7) 849-1211
Website: www.waikatoracing.co.nz
E-Mail: info@waikatoracing.co.nz
Abbreviation: TeR
Chairman: David Smith
Vice Chairman: Peter McCowan
General Manager: A. C. Enting
Principal Races: Waikato Draught Sprint Stakes (NZ-G1), Whakanui Stud International (NZ-G1), Cambridge Stud Sir Tristram Fillies Classic Stakes (NZ-G2)

Trentham

Located about 20 miles north of New Zealand's capital city, Wellington, Trentham was founded in 1870, not long after the city itself was built. Trentham's figure-eight steeplechase course is ringed by a wide, 2,000-meter turf course with a 450-meter home straight. Its major races include the Wellington Cup Handicap (NZ-G1), the Telegraph Handicap (NZ-G1), and the New Zealand Oaks (NZ-G1). Trentham was home of the country's top yearling sale for more than six decades. In its second year in 1928, the sale included a chestnut colt bought for 160 guineas. Named *Phar Lap, he was sent to Australia and made racing history. In 1988, the sale was shifted north, closer to the major breeding operations in the country.

Location: Racecourse Road, Trentham, Upper Hutt, Wellington
Phone: 64 (4) 528-9611
Fax: 64 (4) 528-4166
Website: www.trentham.co.nz
E-Mail: wrc@trentham.co.nz
Abbreviation: Tre
President: R. Dixon
Chief Executive: E. C. Jansen
Principal Races: New Zealand Oaks (NZ-G1), Telegraph H. (NZ-G1), Thorndon Mile H. (NZ-G1), Wellington Cup H. (NZ-G1)

Peru
Monterrico

Racing in Peru was held in the 19th century at a small racetrack called Cancha Meiggs, and successively was conducted at Hipodromo de Santa Beatriz and San Felipe before the opening of the Monterrico Race Track in Lima on December 18, 1960. Racing is conducted year-round on Tuesday and Thursday evenings, Saturdays, and Sundays. The left-handed track has both a dirt track and a grass course. On December 8, 1997, Panama native Laffit Pincay Jr. and Peruvian-born Edgar Prado, Jorge Chavez, and Julio Pezua represented the United States in an international riders competition at Monterrico. Juan Jose Paule of Argentina and Peruvian Edwin Talaverano tied for first place in the three-race event. Monterrico's premier races form the Quadruple Crown. All of Peru's more than 40 graded races are run at Monterrico.

Location: Avenue El Derby, Santiago De Surco, Lima
Phone: 51 (1) 610-3000
Website: www.monterricoenlared.com
Abbreviation: Mon
President: Herbert Moebius Castaneda
Principal Races: Derby Nacional (Per-G1), Jockey Club del Peru (Per-G1)

Singapore
Singapore Racecourse

Singapore Racecourse at Kranji in the northern part of Singapore is the host of the Singapore Airlines International Cup (Sin-G1). The stakes race is contested at 1¼ miles in May over the 2,000-meter, left-handed track. The race was canceled in 2003 because of the severe acute respiratory syndrome (SARS) outbreak. Another major stakes is the Singapore KrisFlyer Sprint (Sin-G3). With three training tracks, the track accommodates approximately 1,000 horses. Horses are sta-

bled in either air-conditioned or naturally ventilated stalls in barns separated by large courtyards. The four-story grandstand can accommodate 30,000 people.

Location: 1 Turf Club Avenue, Kranji 73807
Phone: 65 (6) 879-1000
Fax: 65 (6) 871-010
Website: www.turfclub.com.sg
Abbreviation: Sin
President: Yu Pang Fey
Principal Races: International Cup (Sin-G1)

South Africa
Clairwood

Clairwood, operated by the Gold Circle Racing and Gaming Group in Merebank, is host of the 2,000-meter Champions Cup (SAf-G1) in late July. A flat, left-handed track of approximately 2,500 meters in circumference, Clairwood features a 1,200-meter straight that is used for all sprints. The start for 1,400-meter races begins very close to the turn, often resulting in a scramble for good position early, especially in large fields.

Location: 89 Barrier Lane, Clairwood 4052
Phone: 27 (31) 469-1020
Fax: 27 (31) 469-0607
Website: www.goldcircle.co.za
E-Mail: info@goldcircle.co.za
Abbreviation: Cla
Chief Executive: Ken McArthur
Principal Races: Champions Cup (SAf-G1), Gold Challenge S. (SAf-G1), Mercury Sprint Stakes (SAf-G1)

Greyville

Located in a complex that includes a championship golf course, Greyville has conducted racing just outside the city of Durban since 1844. In 1897, the Durban Turf Club took over the track's administration. The 2,000-meter Durban July Handicap (SAf-G1), the country's most prestigious race, is held on the first Saturday of the month and attracts crowds of up to 60,000. Other major stakes are the South African Guineas (SAf-G1) in May, the South African Fillies Guineas (SAf-G1), and the Daily News Two Thousand (SAf-G1). The right-handed, pear-shaped turf course of about 2,800 meters features tight turns and a straight of nearly 500 meters.

Location: 150 Avondale Road, Greyville Box 40, Durban 04000
Phone: 27 (31) 309-4545
Fax: 27 (31) 309-2553
Abbreviation: Grv
Principal Races: Daily News Two Thousand (SAf-G1), Durban July H. (SAf-G1), Garden Province S. (SAf-G1), Gold Cup (SAf-G1), Premier's Champion S. (SAf-G1), South African Fillies Guineas (SAf-G1), South African Guineas (SAf-G1)

Kenilworth

Serving the Cape Town region, Kenilworth boasts three tracks. Its largest course is 2,800 meters with a 600-meter run-in. Known as the "new course," this left-handed oval is used primarily in summer and is regarded as one of the fairest in South Africa. A smaller, 2,700-meter, left-handed course has a 450-meter run-in and is utilized mostly in the winter months. In addition, a 1,200-meter straight course bisects the infield on a diagonal, and the three courses come together only in the galloping-out area. The straight course is one of the stiffest tests in South African racing, with a climb for the first 200 meters and another rise in the final 200 meters.

Location: Rosmead Avenue, Box 53073, Kenilworth 7700, Cape Town 07745
Phone: 27 (21) 700-1600
Fax: 27 (21) 762-1919
Website: www.goldcircle.co.za
E-Mail: info@goldcircle.co.za
Abbreviation: Ken
Ownership: Western Province Racing
Principal Races: Graham Beck Wines Cape Derby (SAf-G1), J & B Met S. (SAf-G1)

Scottsville

Located near Pietermaritzburg, Scottsville conducted its first race meet on April 3, 1886. Racing is held on 14 Saturdays, two holidays, and 17 weekdays throughout the year on a right-handed, oval turf course approximately 2,270 meters in circumference. Nearby training centers in Ashburton, Clairwood Park, and Summerveld accommodate 2,000 horses for approximately 50 trainers. Scottsville hosts the South African Fillies Sprint (SAf-G1) and the Golden Spur Stakes (SAf-G1). Like Clairwood, it is owned by the Gold Circle Racing and Gaming Group.

Location: 45 New England Road, P. O. Box 101064, Durban, Scottsville 03201
Phone: 27 (33) 345-3405
Fax: 27 (33) 394-1141
Website: www.goldcircle.co.za
E-Mail: info@goldcircle.co.za
Abbreviation: Sco
Principal Races: Allan Robertson Fillies Championship (SAf-G1), Gold Medallion (SAf-G1), Golden Spur S. (SAf-G1), South African Fillies Sprint (SAf-G1)

Turffontein

Only two miles south of Johannesburg, Turffontein has been home to racing since 1887, just one year after the first Thoroughbred race was held in the city. While maintaining its traditions, including a Royal Box, Turffontein has been thoroughly modernized. The grandstand, rebuilt in the 1970s, allows a panoramic view of the course, and the Ascot Bar and Lounge, Caradoc Room, and Lawn Enclosure give fans many alternatives for enjoying their day at the races. The course has its own water source, which allows for beautiful lawns, numerous flower gardens, meticulously maintained trees and shrubs, and a bird sanctuary. Racing is conducted mostly on Saturdays on a testing, uphill, right-handed turf course of 2,658 meters. Its single chute allows for a 1,200-meter straight. Turffontein also has a 2,000-meter grass training track and four sand training tracks. The South Africa Derby (SAf-G1), Champion Stakes (SAf-G1), and Horse Chestnut 1,600 Stakes (SAf-G1), formerly the President's Cup, are three of Turffontein's biggest races.

Location: Turf Club Street, P. O. Box 183, Turffontein, Gauteng 2190, Johannesburg 02000
Phone: 27 (11) 681-5000
Fax: 27 (11) 683-3407
Website: www.aro.co.za/source/profiles/tracks/ turf.htm
Abbreviation: Tff

Principal Races: Champion S. (SAf-G1), Empress Club S. (SAf-G1), Gold Bowl (SAf-G1), Horse Chestnut 1,600 S. (SAf-G1), South Africa Derby (SAf-G1), South Africa Nursery (SAf-G1), Summer Cup (SAf-G1), Triple Crown 1,600 (SAf-G1), Triple Tiara 1,600 (SAf-G1)

United Arab Emirates
Nad al Sheba

Offering the world's richest race—the $6-million Dubai World Cup (UAE-G1)—and no betting on any of its races, Nad al Sheba Racecourse is located within the tiny sheikhdom of Dubai in the United Arab Emirates. First laid out in 1986 and resurfaced in 1997 before the third running of the World Cup, the 2,200-meter (1⅜-mile), left-handed dirt course has three chutes. A left-handed turf course inside the dirt course is composed of Bermuda hybrid grass, which thrives in hot and humid climates. Two-time North American Horse of the Year Cigar won the inaugural Dubai World Cup in 1996 to give the stakes instant credibility. Also on the Dubai World Cup program are the Dubai Duty Free Stakes (UAE-G1), the Dubai Golden Shaheen (UAE-G1), the Dubai Sheema Classic (UAE-G1), the United Arab Emirates Derby (UAE-G2), and the Godolphin Mile (UAE-G2). The Dubai World Cup Committee pays a wide array of costs for visiting horses competing in Dubai, including roundtrip airfare.

Location: City Tower 1, 2nd Floor, Office 206, P. O. Box 9305, Dubai
Phone: 971 (4) 332-2277
Fax: 971 (4) 332-2288
Website: www.dubairacingclub.com
E-Mail: info@dubairacingclub.com
Abbreviation: Nad
Chairman: Saeed H. Al Tayer
General Manager: Jerry Kilby
Principal Races: Dubai Duty Free S. (UAE-G1), Dubai Golden Shaheen (UAE-G1), Dubai Sheema Classic (UAE-G1), Dubai World Cup (UAE-G1), Godolphin Mile (UAE-G2), United Arab Emirates Derby (UAE-G2)

Uruguay
Maronas National Racetrack

Shuttered for 5½ years, historic Maronas National Racetrack reopened in June 2003 after a multimillion-dollar renovation by its lessees, Hipica Rioplatense and Lone Star Park, a Magna Entertainment Corp. property. The Montevideo track, which dates from the mid-1870s, is owned by the Republic of Uruguay, and the partnership holds a 30-year lease on the track and concessions. By its first anniversary, the track was offering an average of almost ten races a day and was attracting increasingly larger crowds and wagering. The track's reopening also was credited with stimulating the Uruguayan breeding industry. The track, which also has four off-track facilities with slot machines and 20 OTBs for race wagering, simulcasts its races around the world and began sending Group 1 races into the United States in early 2005.

Location: 3540 Jose Maria Guerra, Montevideo
Phone: 598 (2) 511-7777
Fax: 598 (2) 511-9961
Website: www.maronas.com.uy
E-Mail: info@maronas.com.uy
Abbreviation: Man
Principal Races: Gran Premio Jose Pedro Ramirez

International Sire Lists
Leading Sires by Earnings by Country for 2004
(By Racing Season for Southern Hemisphere Countries)

Argentina

Sire	Strs	Wnrs	SWs	Leading Earner (Earnings)	Total Earnings
Roy	84	43	6	Don Incauto ($140,964)	$626,813
Luhuk	104	69	10	Macadamia ($27,632)	558,940
Southern Halo	95	47	10	Sebastiano ($39,288)	498,129
Roar	90	57	6	Forty Marchanta (Arg) ($71,467)	488,514
Mutakddim	87	57	4	Major Leader ($22,984)	439,059
Lode	94	44	5	Best Bob ($30,255)	400,553
Equalize	104	55	4	Postergada ($26,323)	385,024
Interprete	106	49	6	Inminente ($39,710)	363,647
Engrillado	77	33	2	Basko Pinton ($141,441)	332,872
Louis Quatorze	87	45	3	Louis Fifteen ($37,813)	328,159

Australia

Sire	Strs	Wnrs	SWs	Leading Earner (Earnings)	Total Earnings
Danehill	212	102	19	Elvstroem ($1,890,239)	$8,159,244
Zabeel	211	99	16	Savabeel ($1,983,410)	7,283,366
Redoute's Choice	115	59	15	Stratum ($1,545,150)	5,845,235
Desert King	121	50	3	Makybe Diva ($3,956,143)	5,382,450
Encosta de Lago	236	98	6	Alinghi (Aus) ($1,523,321)	5,188,695
Flying Spur	258	116	11	Wager ($228,050)	3,884,693
Hennessy	136	69	4	Grand Armee ($1,729,627)	3,137,168
Rubiton	134	57	3	Patezza ($1,154,146)	2,685,041
Snippets	186	81	6	Sky Cuddle ($323,598)	2,407,314
Danzero	173	60	5	Danni Martine ($536,265)	2,293,566

Brazil

Sire	Strs	Wnrs	SWs	Leading Earner (Earnings)	Total Earnings
Roi Normand	166	81	9	Glaire ($32,424)	$487,221
Royal Academy	79	50	10	Macbeth ($86,854)	423,291
Choctaw Ridge	134	71	9	Loving New ($36,932)	418,334
Fast Gold	165	74	5	Total Gold ($17,983)	367,481
Dodge	109	56	4	Omaggio ($52,040)	326,538
Minstrel Glory	167	88	5	Malvacea ($11,419)	310,637
Midnight Tiger	140	72	1	Appointment ($11,473)	276,623
Mensageiro Alado	94	44	4	Sinistro ($33,309)	256,665
Jules	96	46	2	Notificado (BRZ) ($26,602)	246,074
Irish Fighter	110	52	1	Princesa Desejada ($30,056)	238,022

Canada

Sire	Strs	Wnrs	SWs	Leading Earner (Earnings)	Total Earnings
Smart Strike	35	23	4	Soaring Free ($946,740)	$3,286,698
Bold Executive	77	39	4	Blonde Executive ($414,263)	2,603,323
Whiskey Wisdom	70	35	4	Moonshine Justice ($283,914)	2,556,883
Archers Bay	48	27	2	Archers Bow ($198,145)	1,869,921
Kiridashi	65	28	3	Financingavailable ($294,151)	1,736,463
Langfuhr	32	19	4	Mobil ($436,463)	1,569,807
Regal Classic	35	18	2	Inish Glora ($433,730)	1,556,923
Lit de Justice	31	18	1	Hour of Justice ($228,953)	1,414,774
Vying Victor	87	44	4	Alabama Rain ($136,784)	1,402,319
Gold Fever	11	7	1	A Bit O'Gold ($1,060,790)	1,383,416

England

Sire	Strs	Wnrs	SWs	Leading Earner (Earnings)	Total Earnings
Sadler's Wells	121	44	11	Doyen ($1,047,627)	$5,082,034
Danehill	106	47	8	North Light ($1,599,446)	3,624,421
Pivotal	89	51	9	Salamanca ($273,260)	2,384,072
Efisio	78	39	3	Attraction ($879,649)	2,074,505
Kingmambo	52	21	5	Rule of Law ($1,180,915)	2,014,186
Barathea (Ire)	90	34	3	Tante Rose ($317,589)	1,885,494
Selkirk	87	39	7	Favourable Terms ($365,145)	1,873,521

Sire	Strs	Wnrs	SWs	Leading Earner (Earnings)	Total Earnings
Machiavellian	87	34	2	Mephisto ($336,729)	$1,753,246
Polar Falcon	80	35	6	Iceman ($188,766)	1,562,560
Cape Cross (Ire)	66	33	8	Ouija Board (GB) ($404,477)	1,518,057

England/Ireland

Sire	Strs	Wnrs	SWs	Leading Earner (Earnings)	Total Earnings
Sadler's Wells	199	83	23	Doyen ($1,047,627)	$7,248,096
Danehill	132	67	17	North Light ($1,904,758)	5,444,637
Pivotal	93	53	9	Chorist ($414,222)	2,729,354
Efisio	81	39	3	Attraction ($1,210,348)	2,414,119
Kingmambo	62	27	6	Rule of Law ($1,233,320)	2,354,141
Barathea (Ire)	113	39	5	Tante Rose ($317,589)	2,195,566
Night Shift	111	40	2	Azamour ($1,191,232)	2,177,342
Selkirk	101	46	7	Favourable Terms ($365,145)	2,067,930
Cape Cross (Ire)	77	37	8	Ouija Board (GB) ($699,767)	2,057,539
Marju	78	30	8	Soviet Song ($973,999)	2,010,115

France

Sire	Strs	Wnrs	SWs	Leading Earner (Earnings)	Total Earnings
Linamix	107	56	10	Cherry Mix ($626,464)	$3,163,044
Danehill	38	18	7	Grey Lilas ($547,572)	2,398,965
Sadler's Wells	62	21	4	Prospect Park ($451,901)	1,893,864
Nashwan	21	7	1	Bago ($1,636,755)	1,887,864
Green Tune	97	38	3	Delfos ($197,365)	1,710,010
Highest Honor (Fr)	101	44	2	Frosted Aclaim ($96,341)	1,450,061
Bering (GB)	84	30	3	American Post ($308,495)	1,439,532
Take Risks	89	32	2	My Risk ($149,105)	1,288,716
Anabaa	76	36	5	Marshall ($135,187)	1,282,284
Kendor	76	26	4	Centifolia ($196,969)	1,260,380

Germany

Sire	Strs	Wnrs	SWs	Leading Earner (Earnings)	Total Earnings
Monsun	103	50	9	Shirocco ($512,167)	$1,882,789
Big Shuffle	147	67	10	Pepperstorm ($128,703)	1,490,143
Lomitas (GB)	80	37	4	Malinas ($248,846)	784,080
Dashing Blade	96	37	3	Kahlua ($75,278)	669,368
Caerleon	3	1	1	Warrsan ($603,100)	605,138
Tiger Hill	37	19	5	Saldentigerin ($170,820)	513,293
Platini	95	42	2	Deva ($50,817)	476,114
Law Society	59	27	2	Rotteck ($154,400)	464,652
Lando (Ger)	43	21	3	Intendant ($121,830)	454,174
Goofalik	78	42	1	Spatzolita ($32,677)	444,203

Hong Kong

Sire	Strs	Wnrs	SWs	Leading Earner (Earnings)	Total Earnings
Danehill	79	35	4	Lucky Owners ($1,300,358)	$7,998,326
El Moxie	5	3	2	Silent Witness ($1,940,879)	2,318,695
Royal Academy	14	7	1	Bullish Luck ($1,459,267)	2,030,328
Snippets	26	11	0	Town Of Fionn ($620,282)	1,894,928
Sadler's Wells	6	2	1	Diaghilev ($1,426,762)	1,646,354
Gaius	1	1	1	Cheerine Kid ($1,469,277)	1,469,277
Danewin	6	4	1	Elegant Fashion ($1,103,860)	1,451,765
Marju	18	10	0	Classa For Ever ($303,092)	1,316,452
Gold Away (Ire)	1	1	1	Alexander Goldrun ($1,311,720)	1,311,720
Flying Spur	17	7	0	Firebolt ($213,901)	1,281,507

Ireland

Sire	Strs	Wnrs	SWs	Leading Earner (Earnings)	Total Earnings
Sadler's Wells	100	39	12	Powerscourt (GB) ($302,510)	$2,166,062
Danehill	44	21	9	North Light ($305,312)	1,820,216
Daylami (Ire)	9	3	1	Grey Swallow ($1,014,848)	1,054,107
Night Shift	19	5	1	Azamour ($802,795)	902,808
Marju	27	4	4	Soviet Song ($303,967)	624,898
Cape Cross (Ire)	17	5	1	Ouija Board (GB) ($295,290)	539,482
Entrepreneur	38	10	1	Damson ($301,792)	537,025
Sri Pekan	27	6	1	Tropical Lady ($272,758)	497,517
Spectrum	46	7	1	Addario (Ire) ($137,776)	449,770
Storm Cat	15	9	3	Grand Reward ($76,692)	440,259

Italy

Sire	Strs	Wnrs	SWs	Leading Earner (Earnings)	Total Earnings
Sri Pekan	96	54	2	Rumba Loca ($202,043)	$1,872,720
Desert Prince (Ire)	29	17	3	Ceprin ($272,733)	1,177,820
Love the Groom	81	34	0	Maktub (Ity) ($106,832)	924,802
Groom Dancer	15	10	1	Groom Tesse ($589,106)	874,556
Marju	40	19	1	Marbye ($113,428)	743,411
Shantou	74	29	0	Quality Son ($56,574)	680,329
Selkirk	10	7	3	Altieri ($386,428)	642,337
Zafonic	22	13	0	Principe Di Galles ($123,470)	640,758
In the Wings (GB)	32	13	2	Soldier Hollow ($194,490)	632,554
Orpen	27	15	1	Kaypen ($78,077)	628,024

Japan

Sire	Strs	Wnrs	SWs	Leading Earner (Earnings)	Total Earnings
Sunday Silence	495	216	35	Zenno Rob Roy ($6,681,748)	$82,853,357
Dance in the Dark	266	81	4	Delta Blues ($2,525,023)	22,852,146
Brian's Time	228	72	6	Time Paradox ($3,408,062)	20,579,857
Fuji Kiseki	222	61	4	Osumi Cosmo ($997,553)	15,928,669
Forty Niner	126	47	5	Meiner Select ($1,541,061)	14,218,232
Tony Bin	88	31	5	Narita Century ($1,419,924)	12,722,671
Afleet	181	53	2	Hikari Zirconia ($1,077,989)	12,572,976
Sakura Bakushin O	171	59	2	She is Tosho ($731,284)	11,926,438
End Sweep	95	45	5	Sweep Tosho ($2,118,418)	11,609,886
Bubble Gum Fellow	191	49	0	Taiki Alpha ($377,929)	10,215,095

Saudi Arabia

Sire	Strs	Wnrs	SWs	Leading Earner (Earnings)	Total Earnings
Another Review	57	18	8	Nabae Aljood ($53,215)	$373,373
Mirror Black	33	6	2	Tayhoor ($43,012)	127,233
Barathea (Ire)	4	2	2	La Zia ($56,119)	126,663
Voleris	21	6	1	Raq Qaass ($36,581)	113,647
Torrey Canyon	18	7	2	Ramz Alkhail ($40,005)	112,181
Blue Judge	10	3	1	Ghazhyah ($73,315)	108,941
Razor	3	2	1	Mahboobat Salman ($92,753)	101,031
Point House	5	1	1	Hub Alriyadh ($82,044)	90,417
Indian Ridge	5	3	1	Adhwa ($43,722)	89,744
Arazi	2	2	1	Shibl ($82,301)	88,710

Puerto Rico

Sire	Strs	Wnrs	SWs	Leading Earner (Earnings)	Total Earnings
Royal Merlot	29	25	3	Hispanica ($157,720)	$732,847
Fappiano's Star	42	29	0	Little Franky Boy ($82,522)	631,032
Eqtesaad	38	31	0	Estrellero ($48,788)	488,683
Sejm	32	20	0	El Incondicional ($44,930)	423,787
Cagey Bidder	23	15	1	Bancada ($62,434)	370,640
Balcony	27	16	1	Mueca ($127,900)	366,261
Goldgalliano (Ire)	26	16	0	Chiquitina ($48,369)	345,700
Concerto	9	6	2	Special Concerto ($135,700)	330,122
Sunshine Jimmy	27	11	1	Malcadi ($75,740)	313,688
Run Turn	23	13	0	Queen Native ($42,144)	293,730

United Arab Emirates

Sire	Strs	Wnrs	SWs	Leading Earner (Earnings)	Total Earnings
Pleasant Colony	2	2	2	Pleasantly Perfect ($3,600,000)	$3,717,378
Machiavellian	22	12	1	Right Approach ($891,000)	1,477,650
Candy Stripes	5	2	1	Lundy's Liability (Brz) ($1,242,500)	1,276,233
El Prado (Ire)	4	2	0	Medaglia d'Oro ($1,200,000)	1,248,275
Polish Precedent	3	1	1	Polish Summer (GB) ($1,200,000)	1,208,306
Alphabet Soup	1	1	1	Our New Recruit ($1,200,000)	1,200,000
Al Mufti	2	1	1	Victory Moon ($940,000)`	940,000
Grand Slam	5	1	0	Alke ($400,000)	819,155
Lando (Ger)	1	1	1	Paolini (Ger) ($800,000)	800,000
Charnwood Forest (Ire)	5	2	1	Firebreak ($600,000)	606,602

Leading Sires by Year

Argentina*

Year	Sire, YOB, Sire	Earnings
2004	Roy, 1983, by Fappiano	$626,813
2003	Roar, 1993, by Forty Niner	642,453
2002	Southern Halo, 1983, by Halo	553,695
2001	Roy, 1983, by Fappiano	818,389
2000	Southern Halo, 1983, by Halo	1,632,869
1999	Southern Halo, 1983, by Halo	1,490,119
1998	Southern Halo, 1983, by Halo	1,883,179
1997	Southern Halo, 1983, by Halo	2,010,382

Australia*

Year	Sire, YOB, Sire	Earnings
2004	Danehill, 1986, by Danzig	$8,159,244
2003	Danehill, 1986, by Danzig	5,723,877
2002	Danehill, 1986, by Danzig	4,031,267
2001	Danehill, 1986, by Danzig	4,033,288
2000	Danehill, 1986, by Danzig	4,080,825
1999	Danehill, 1986, by Danzig	4,952,018
1998	Zabeel , 1986, by *Sir Tristram	6,793,635
1997	Danehill, 1986, by Danzig	5,034,265

Brazil*

Year	Sire, YOB, Sire	Earnings
2004	Roi Normand, 1983, by Exclusive Native	$487,221
2003	Choctaw Ridge, 1989, by Mr. Prospector	415,765
2002	Fast Gold, 1979, by Mr. Prospector	427,914
2001	Choctaw Ridge, 1989, by Mr. Prospector	563,482
2000	Minstrel Glory, 1980, by The Minstrel	530,018
1999	Roi Normand, 1983, by Exclusive Native	278,000
1998	Bright Again, 1987, by Wild Again	397,767
1997	Punk, 1984, by Ringaro	406,900

Canada

Year	Sire, YOB, Sire	Earnings
2004	Smart Strike, 1992, by Mr. Prospector	$3,286,698
2003	Langfuhr, 1992, by Danzig	3,783,111
2002	Regal Classic, 1985, by Vice Regent	2,777,503
2001	Regal Classic, 1985, by Vice Regent	2,663,430
2000	Regal Classic, 1985, by Vice Regent	2,778,491
1999	Regal Classic, 1985, by Vice Regent	2,000,300
1998	Silver Deputy, 1985, by Deputy Minister	2,097,515
1997	Bold Ruckus, 1976, by Boldnesian	1,859,252

England

Year	Sire, YOB, Sire	Earnings
2004	Sadler's Wells, 1981, by Northern Dancer	$5,082,034
2003	Sadler's Wells, 1981, by Northern Dancer	3,023,989
2002	Sadler's Wells, 1981, by Northern Dancer	3,006,898
2001	Sadler's Wells, 1981, by Northern Dancer	3,977,732
2000	Sadler's Wells, 1981, by Northern Dancer	2,606,967
1999	Fairy King, 1982, by Northern Dancer	1,962,154
1998	Nashwan, 1986, by Blushing Groom (Fr)	1,524,720
1997	Silver Hawk, 1979, by Roberto	1,488,473

England and Ireland

Year	Sire, YOB, Sire	Earnings
2004	Sadler's Wells, 1981, by Northern Dancer	$7,248,096
2003	Sadler's Wells, 1981, by Northern Dancer	5,823,175
2002	Sadler's Wells, 1981, by Northern Dancer	5,562,690
2001	Sadler's Wells, 1981, by Northern Dancer	5,738,357
2000	Sadler's Wells, 1981, by Northern Dancer	3,676,718
1999	Sadler's Wells, 1981, by Northern Dancer	2,952,410
1998	Sadler's Wells, 1981, by Northern Dancer	2,626,355
1997	Sadler's Wells, 1981, by Northern Dancer	2,241,578

France

Year	Sire, YOB, Sire	Earnings
2004	Linamix, 1987, by Mendez	$3,163,044
2003	Darshaan, 1981, by Shirley Heights	2,433,602
2002	Danehill, 1986, by Danzig	1,952,836
2001	Danehill, 1986, by Danzig	1,630,129
2000	Highest Honor (Fr), 1983, by Kenmare	$1,424,916
1999	Sadler's Wells, 1981, by Northern Dancer	2,155,310
1998	Linamix, 1987, by Mendez	1,929,004
1997	Nureyev, 1977, by Northern Dancer	2,139,852

Germany

Year	Sire, YOB, Sire	Earnings
2004	Monsun, 1990, by Konigsstuhl	$1,882,789
2003	Big Shuffle, 1984, by Super Concorde	1,341,355
2002	Monsun, 1990, by Konigsstuhl	1,278,658
2001	Big Shuffle, 1984, by Super Concorde	917,938
2000	Monsun, 1990, by Konigsstuhl	1,361,406
1999	Dashing Blade, 1987, by Elegant Air	1,223,849
1998	Big Shuffle, 1984, by Super Concorde	1,040,915
1997	Acatenango, 1982, by Surumu	1,484,293

Hong Kong

Year	Sire, YOB, Sire	Earnings
2004	Danehill, 1986, by Danzig	$7,998,326
2003	Danehill, 1986, by Danzig	8,562,038
2002	Danehill, 1986, by Danzig	6,308,554
2001	Danehill, 1986, by Danzig	5,549,309
2000	Rahy, 1985, by Blushing Groom (Fr)	3,106,199
1999	Danehill, 1986, by Danzig	3,089,946
1998	Danehill, 1986, by Danzig	2,779,929
1997	Green Desert, 1983, by Danzig	850,035

Ireland

Year	Sire, YOB, Sire	Earnings
2004	Sadler's Wells, 1981, by Northern Dancer	$2,166,062
2003	Sadler's Wells, 1981, by Northern Dancer	2,799,276
2002	Sadler's Wells, 1981, by Northern Dancer	2,555,792
2001	Sadler's Wells, 1981, by Northern Dancer	1,760,625
2000	Sadler's Wells, 1981, by Northern Dancer	1,069,751
1999	Sadler's Wells, 1981, by Northern Dancer	1,710,136
1998	Sadler's Wells, 1981, by Northern Dancer	1,150,913
1997	Danehill, 1986, by Danzig	1,198,712

Italy

Year	Sire, YOB, Sire	Earnings
2004	Sri Pekan, 1992, by Red Ransom	$1,872,720
2003	Sri Pekan, 1992, by Red Ransom	1,585,694
2002	Love the Groom, 1984, by Blushing Groom (Fr)	979,041
2001	Roi Danzig, 1986, by Danzig	908,189
2000	Roi Danzig, 1986, by Danzig	847,389
1999	Sikeston, 1986, by Lear Fan	800,283
1998	Love the Groom, 1984, by Blushing Groom (Fr)	1,250,469
1997	Love the Groom, 1984, by Blushing Groom (Fr)	1,490,432

Japan

Year	Sire, YOB, Sire	Earnings
2004	Sunday Silence, 1986, by Halo	$82,853,357
2003	Sunday Silence, 1986, by Halo	69,943,962
2002	Sunday Silence, 1986, by Halo	52,709,704
2001	Sunday Silence, 1986, by Halo	53,790,988
2000	Sunday Silence, 1986, by Halo	53,883,429
1999	Sunday Silence, 1986, by Halo	45,579,976
1998	Sunday Silence, 1986, by Halo	33,925,214
1997	Sunday Silence, 1986, by Halo	29,390,122

United Arab Emirates

Year	Sire, YOB, Sire	Earnings
2004	Pleasant Colony, 1978, by His Majesty	$3,717,378
2003	Singspiel (Ire), 1992, by In the Wings (GB)	4,155,117
2002	Machiavellian, 1987, by Mr. Prospector	4,082,712
2001	Fly So Free, 1988, by Time for a Change	3,600,000
2000	Seeking the Gold, 1985, by Mr. Prospector	3,675,318
1999	Machiavellian, 1987, by Mr. Prospector	3,165,733
1998	Silver Buck, 1978, by Buckpasser	2,400,000
1997	In the Wings (GB), 1986, by Sadler's Wells	2,420,558

*Southern Hemisphere seasons

Sovereign Awards

Inaugurated in 1975, the Sovereign Awards honor outstanding horses and individuals in Canadian racing. Administered by the Jockey Club of Canada, Sovereign Awards are presented in ten horse categories, including Canadian Horse of the Year. In addition, a Broodmare of the Year award is presented.

Sovereign Awards are awarded to individuals in five categories: owner, breeder, trainer, jockey, and apprentice jockey. In addition, the E. P. Taylor Award of Merit is presented periodically.

Some of Canada's best runners have been honored with Eclipse Awards. Most recently, 1997 Canadian Horse of the Year Chief Bearhart was voted an Eclipse Award as champion turf male. In 1991, Canadian Triple Crown winner and Canadian Horse of the Year Dance Smartly was honored with an Eclipse Award as champion three-year-old filly, and 1981 Canadian Horse of the Year Deputy Minister won the champion juvenile male Eclipse Award for that season.

Sovereign recipients are selected by a panel of sportswriters, broadcasters, and racing officials across Canada. Horses need not be bred in Canada, but they must make at least three starts in Canada to be eligible for each year's awards.

2004 Sovereign Awards
Soaring Free, Horse of the Year. Continuing a trend that established itself in the late 1990s,

the 2004 Sovereign Awards went to horses who excelled in Ontario and had few outings, if any, in the United States. Sam-Son Farm's homebred Soaring Free, who was 2004 Horse of the Year and champion turf male, made three excursions into the lower 48 and came back with one victory in a Grade 3 race and a creditable fourth in the Breeders' Cup Mile (G1).

By the Sam-Son homebred Smart Strike and out of homebred Dancing With Wings, Soaring Free hardly soared in his first racing season, as a three-year-old in 2002. He had two victories, a maiden score and an allowance win, both at Woodbine. Trainer Mark Frostad said Soaring Free's performance improved after he was gelded at the end of his three-year-old season.

Principally a turf sprinter who could carry his speed a mile, Soaring Free was Canada's champion sprinter in 2003, a year in which he won the Nearctic (Can-G2) and Play the King (Can-G3) Handicaps and finished a close second in the Atto Mile Stakes (Can-G1). Sent to Santa Anita Park, he finished fifth in the Breeders' Cup Mile.

Frostad started Soaring Free's 2004 season at Keeneland Race Course in the 5½-furlong Shakertown Stakes (G3) on turf, which the five-year-old won by 1½ lengths. He next started on the dirt in Pimlico Race Course's Maryland Breeders' Cup Handicap (G3), and finished a dismal eighth. Until

History of the Sovereign Awards

Year	E. P. Taylor Award of Merit†	Owner	Breeder	Trainer	Jockey	Apprentice Jockey
2004	Not awarded	Sam-Son Farm	Sam-Son Farm	Robert Tiller	Todd Kabel	Corey Fraser
2003	Not awarded	Stronach Stable	Sam-Son Farm	Robert Tiller	Todd Kabel	Julia Brimo
2002	Not awarded	Stronach Stable	Sam-Son Farm	Roger Attfield	Patrick Husbands	Chantal Sutherland
2001	Not awarded	Sam-Son Farm	Sam-Son Farm	Robert Tiller	Patrick Husbands	Chantal Sutherland
2000	Mike Harris	Sam-Son Farm	Sam-Son Farm	Mark Frostad	Patrick Husbands	Cory Clark
1999	George Hendrie	Stronach Stable	Frank Stronach	Mark Frostad	Patrick Husbands	Ben Russell
1998	David Willmot	Stronach Stable	Frank Stronach	Michael Wright Jr.	David Clark	Helen Vanek
1997	Not awarded	Frank Stronach	Frank Stronach	Mark Frostad	Emile Ramsammy	Rui Pimentel
1996	Not awarded	Minshall Farms	Minshall Farms	Barbara Minshall	Emile Ramsammy	Neil Poznansky
1995	Charles Taylor	Frank Stronach	Kinghaven Farms	Danny Vella	Todd Kabel	Dave Wilson
1994	Jack Kenney	Frank Stronach	Kinghaven Farms	Danny Vella	Robert Landry	Dave Wilson
1993	Not awarded	Frank Stronach	Kinghaven Farms	Roger Attfield	Robert Landry	Constant Montpellier
1992	Col. Charles Baker	Knob Hill Stable	Knob Hill Stable	Philip England	Todd Kabel	Stanley Bethley
1991	Ernest Samuel	Sam-Son Farm	Sam-Son Farm	Jim Day	Mickey Walls	Mickey Walls
1990	James Wright	Kinghaven Farms	Kinghaven Farms	Roger Attfield	Don Seymour	Mickey Walls
1989	George C. Frostad	Kinghaven Farms	Kinghaven Farms	Roger Attfield	Don Seymour	Maree Richards
1988	Sandy Hawley	Sam-Son Farm	Sam-Son Farm	Jim Day	Sandy Hawley	Jim McAleney
1987	Larry Regan	Kinghaven Farms	Kinghaven Farms	Roger Attfield	Don Seymour	Jim McAleney
1986	D. G. Willmot	D. G. Willmot	D. G. Willmot	Roger Attfield	Larry Attard	Todd Kabel
1985	George Gardiner	Ernest Samuel	E. P. Taylor	Jim Day	Don Seymour	Nancy Jumpsen
1984	Jim Coleman	Ernest Samuel	Frank Stronach	Mike Doyle	Chris Loseth	Robert King
1983	Joe Thomas	B. K. Yousif	Mr. and Mrs. Russell Bennett	Bill Marko	Larry Attard	Robert King
1982	Jean-Louis Levesque	D. G. Willmot	D. G. Willmot	Bill Marko	Lloyd Duffy	Richard Dos Ramos
1981	Jim Bentley	Dave Kapchinsky	Tom Webb	Ron Brock	Erwin Driedger	Richard Dos Ramos
1980	Jack Stafford	Ernest Samuel	Mr. and Mrs. Marvin Hamilton	Gerry Belanger	Gary Stahlbaum	Valerie Thompson
1979	George C. Hendrie	James Shields	D. G. Willmot	Jim Day	Robin Platts	Ray Creighton
1978	Ron Turcotte	Conn Smythe	Jean-Louis Levesque	F. H. Merrill	Sandy Hawley	Ron Hansen
1977	E. P. Taylor	Bory Margolus	Conn Smythe	Red Smith	Avelino Gomez	Brad Smythe
1976	Jack Diamond	George Gardiner	E. P. Taylor	Lou Cavalaris	Chris Rogers	Chris Loseth
1975	E. P. Taylor	Jack Stafford	Bory Margolus	Gil Rowntree	Hugo Dittfach	Jeff Fell

†Formerly known as Man of the Year

his start at Lone Star Park in the Breeders' Cup Mile, Soaring Free was restricted to Woodbine's turf course and was reunited with champion jockey Todd Kabel, who rode him to five consecutive victories—all as the race favorite.

After an allowance win in early June, Soaring Free led at every call to win the six-furlong Highlander Handicap (Can-G3) on June 27. He then was stretched out to his preferred distance, seven furlongs, with impressive results. On July 24, he scored a second consecutive victory in the Ontario Jockey Club Stakes, setting all the pace and coming home in 1:19.38, a course record. Again at seven furlongs, Soaring Free collected his second straight Play the King victory.

His Play the King effort set him up for a second shot at the $1-million Atto Mile. Although he drew the outside starting stall in a field of 11, Soaring Free blasted away from the gate and set a withering pace—:46.01 to the half-mile marker and six furlongs in 1:09.19—before turning back the challenge of 2003 Canadian male turf champion Perfect Soul (Ire) inside the furlong pole. Soaring Free won by three-quarters of a length in 1:32.72 on a firm turf course. In the Breeders' Cup Mile, Soaring Free again attempted to wire his field but faded to finish fourth, beaten 2½ lengths by winner Singletary.

Individuals receiving 2004 Sovereign Awards: **Sam-Son Farm, outstanding breeder and owner.** The operation founded by the late Ernest Samuel collected its seventh title as outstanding breeder, including the last five in succession, and it displaced Frank Stronach as outstanding owner. It was the eighth leading owner title for Sam-Son and its first since 2000. Sam-Son raced two homebred 2004 champions, Horse of the Year and champion turf male Soaring Free and Eye of the Sphynx, champion three-year-old filly. As a breeder, Sam-Son had seven stakes winners and earnings of more than $4.7-million. The racing operation won 47 races with earnings of $4,830,939. Ernie Samuel's daughter, Tammy Samuel-Balaz, oversees the Sam-Son operation, which is based in Milton, Ontario, near Toronto.

Robert Tiller, outstanding trainer. Canada's champion trainer with 15 stakes victories in 2004, Bob Tiller collected his third Sovereign Award in four years. At his Woodbine base, he won 68 races (second to Sid Attard's 73) and earned $3,877,986, behind only Mark Frostad's $4.9-million. One of Tiller's stakes winners was Simply Lovely, champion two-year-old filly.

Todd Kabel, outstanding jockey. The Manitoba native collected his second consecutive Sovereign Award and his fourth title overall. His 2004 season mirrored the success of his 2003 campaign, when his mounts won more than $11-million, a record for a Canadian jockey. In 2004, Kabel recorded 156 victories, all of them at Woodbine, and his mounts earned $10,467,572. The regular rider of Canadian Horse of the Year Soaring Free, Kabel won with 23% of his mounts.

Corey Fraser, outstanding apprentice jockey. At 27, he was one of the sport's older apprentice jockeys, but he compiled a solid record at Woodbine, winning 66 races from 469 mounts and his mounts earned $2,352,043. He finished eighth in the track's 2004 standings.

History of the Sovereign Awards

Year	Horse of the Year	Two-Year-Old Filly	Two-Year-Old Male	Three-Year-Old Filly	Three-Year-Old Male
2004	Soaring Free	Simply Lovely	Wholelottabourbon	Eye of the Sphynx	A Bit O'Gold
2003	Wando	My Vintage Port	Judiths Wild Rush	Too Late Now	Wando
2002	Wake At Noon	Brusque	Added Edge	Lady Shari	Le Cinquieme Essai
2001	Win City	Ginger Gold	Rare Friends	Dancethruthedawn	Win City
2000	Quiet Resolve	Poetically	Highland Legacy	Catch the Ring	Kiss a Native
1999	Thornfield	Hello Seattle	Exciting Story	Gandria	Woodcarver
1998	Chief Bearhart	Fantasy Lake	Riddell's Creek	Kirby's Song	Archers Bay
1997	Chief Bearhart	Primaly	Dawson's Legacy	Cotton Carnival	Cryptocloser
1996	Mt. Sassafras	Larkwhistle	Cash Deposit	Silent Fleet	Victor Cooley
1995	Peaks and Valleys	Silken Cat	Gomtuu	Scotzanna	Peaks and Valleys
1994	Alywow	Honky Tonk Tune	Talkin Man	Alywow	Bruce's Mill
1993	Peteski	Term Limits	Comet Shine	Deputy Jane West	Peteski
1992	Benburb	Deputy Jane West	Truth of It All	Hope for a Breeze	Benburb
1991	Dance Smartly	Buckys Solution	Free At Last	Dance Smartly	Bolulight
1990	Izvestia	Dance Smartly	Rainbows for Life	Lubicon	Izvestia
1989	With Approval	Wavering Girl	Sky Classic	Blushing Katy	With Approval
1988	Play the King	Legarto	Mercedes Won	Tilt My Halo	Regal Intention
1987	Afleet	Phoenix Factor	Regal Classic	One From Heaven	Afleet
1986	Ruling Angel	Ruling Angel	Blue Finn	Carotene	Golden Choice
1985	Imperial Choice	Stage Flite	Grey Classic	La Lorgnette	Imperial Choice
1984	Dauphin Fabuleux	Deceit Dancer	Dauphin Fabuleux	Classy 'n Smart	Key to the Moon
1983	Travelling Victor	Ada Prospect	Prince Avatar	Northern Blossom	Bompago
1982	Frost King	Candle Bright	Sunny's Halo	Avowal	Runaway Groom
1981	Deputy Minister	Choral Group	Deputy Minister	Rainbow Connection	Frost King
1980	Glorious Song	Rainbow Connection	Bayford	Par Excellance	Ben Fab
1979	Overskate	Par Excellance	Allan Blue	Kamar	Steady Growth
1978	Overskate	Liz's Pride	Medaille d'Or	La Voyageuse	Overskate
1977	L'Alezane	L'Alezane	Overskate	Northernette	Dance in Time
1976	Norcliffe	Northernette	Sound Reason	Bye Bye Paris	Norcliffe
1975	L'Enjoleur	Seraphic	Proud Tobin	Momigi	L'Enjoleur

Horse of the Year
Turf Male
SOARING FREE, 1999 dk. b. or br. g., Smart Strike—Dancing With Wings, by Danzig. 2004 Record: 8-6-0,0, $1,113,862. Career: 22-13-3-0, $1,917,544. Owner-breeder: Sam-Son Farm (On.). Trainer: Mark R. Frostad. In 2004, won Atto Mile S. (Can-G1), Shakertown S. (G3), Highlander H. (Can-G3), Play the King H. (Can-G3), Ontario Jockey Club S. (course record).

Two-Year-Old Male
WHOLELOTTABOURBON, 2002 ch. g., Foxtrail—Regretfully, by Lit de Justice. 2004 record: 5-4-1-0, $286,230. Breeder: Bobby Ray Rankin (Ky.). Owner: M.A.D. Racing Stables and Martha Gonzalez. Trainer: Nicholas Gonzalez. In 2004, won Colin S., Silver Deputy S., Bull Page S.; 2nd Victoria S.

Two-Year-Old Filly
SIMPLY LOVELY, 2002 dk. b. or br. f., Bold Executive—Belle Affair, by Stalwart. 2004 record: 5-3-1-0, $288,240. Breeder: Garland E. Williamson (On.). Owner: Rocco A. Marcello. Trainer: Robert P. Tiller. In 2004, won Fanfreluche S., Muskoka S., Victorian Queen S.

Three-Year-Old Male
A BIT O'GOLD, 2001 ch. g., Gold Fever—Annasan, by Corporate Report: 2004 record: 7-4-3-0, $1,060,790. Career: 11-7-3-0, $1,290,819. Breeder: Beclawat Stable (On.). Owner: The Two Bit Racing Stable. Trainer: Catherine Day Phillips. In 2004, won Prince of Wales S., Breeders' S., Ontario Derby, Plate Trial S.; 2nd Queen's Plate S., Woodbine Slots Cup H. (Can-G3), Queenston S.

Three-Year-Old Filly
EYE OF THE SPHYNX, 2001 b. f., Smart Strike—Queen of Egypt, by Vice Regent. 2004 and career record: 7-4-2-0, $688,340. Owner-breeder: Sam-Son Farm (On.). Trainer: Mark R. Frostad. In 2004, won Selene S. (Can-G2), Woodbine Oaks, Fury S.; 2nd Bison City S., Wonder Where S.

Older Male
MOBIL, 2000 b. c., Langfuhr—Kinetigal, by Naskra. 2004 record: 8-3-2-0, $440,213. Career: 23-11-5-1, $1,507,924. Owner-breeder: Gustav Schickedanz (On.). Trainer: Michael Koegh. In 2004, won Dominion Day H. (Can-G3), Vigil H. (Can-G3), Halton S.; 2nd Chinese Cultural Centre S. (Can-G2), Durham Cup H. (Can-G3).

Older Female
ONE FOR ROSE, 1999 dk. b. or br. m., Tejano Run—Saucyladygaylord, by Lord Gaylord. 2004 record: 8-4-2-0, $489,832. Career: 22-12-4-2, $1,047,243. Breeder: Hill'N'Dale Farms (On.). Owner: Tucci Stables. Trainer: Sid C. Attard. In 2004, won Maple Leaf S. (Can-G3), Ontario Matron H., Seagram Cup S., Algoma S.; 2nd Belle Mahone S.

History of the Sovereign Awards

Year	Older Female	Older Male	Turf Female†	Turf Male	Sprinter	Broodmare of the Year
2004	One for Rose	Mobil	Soaring Free	Inish Glora	Blonde Executive	Annasan
2003	One for Rose	Phantom Light	Inish Glora	Perfect Soul (Ire)	Soaring Free	Radiant Ring
2002	Small Promises	Wake At Noon	Chopinina	Portcullis	Wake At Noon	First Class Gal
2001	Mountain Angel	A Fleets Dancer	Sweetest Thing	Numerous Times	Mr. Epperson	Dance Smartly
2000	Saoirse	One Way Love	Heliotrope	Quiet Resolve	One Way Love	Primarily
1999	Magic Code	Deputy Inxs	Free Vacation	Thornfield	Deputy Inxs	Sharpening Up
1998	Santa Amelia	Terremoto	Colorful Vices	Chief Bearhart	Deputy Inxs	Fleet Courage
1997	Woolloomooloo	Chief Bearhart	Woolloomooloo	Chief Bearhart	Glanmire	Charming Sassafras
1996	Windsharp	Mt. Sassafras	Windsharp	Chief Bearhart	Langfuhr	Amelia Bearhart
1995	Bold Ruritana	Basquelan	Bold Ruritana	Hasten To Add	Scotzanna	Sea Regent
1994	Pennyhill Park	King Ruckus		Alywow	King Ruckus	Rainbow Connection
1993	Dance for Donna	Cozzene's Prince		Hero's Love	Apelia	Bold Debra
1992	Wilderness Song	Rainbows for Life		Rainbows for Life	King Corrie	Ballade
1991	Avant's Gold	Sky Classic		Sky Classic	King Corrie	Classy 'n Smart
1990	Diva's Debut	Twist the Snow		Izvestia	Twist the Snow	Shy Spirit
1989	Proper Evidence	Steady Power		Charlie Barley	Mr. Hot Shot	Passing Mood
1988	Carotene	Play the King		Carotene	Play the King	Polite Lady
1987	Carotene	Play the King		Carotene	Play the King	Arctic Vixen
1986	Bessarabian	Let's Go Blue		Carotene	New Connection	Loudrangle
1985	Lake Country	Ten Gold Pots		Imperial Choice	Summer Mood	No Class
1984	Sintrillium	Canadian Factor		Bounding Away	Diapason	Friendly Ways
1983	Eternal Search	Travelling Victor		Kingsbridge	Fraud Squad	Two Rings
1982	Eternal Search	Frost King		Frost King	Avowal	Yonnie Girl
1981	Glorious Song	Driving Home		Ben Fab	Eternal Search	Native Flower
1980	Glorious Song	Overskate		Overskate	La Voyageuse	Hangin Round
1979	La Voyageuse	Overskate		Overskate		Fitz's Fancy
1978	Christy's Mount	Giboulee		Overskate		Fanfreluche
1977	Reasonable Win	Norcliffe		Momigi		Doris White
1976	Momigi	Victorian Prince		Victorian Prince		Northern Minx
1975	Victorian Queen	Rash Move		Victorian Queen		Reasonable Wife

†1995 marks the first year the award for turf horse to be divided into male and female categories.

Sprinter

BLONDE EXECUTIVE, 2001 ch. f., Bold Executive—Dream Smartly, by Smarten. 2004 record: 6-5-0-0, $414,263. Career: 13-8-1-1, $610,591, Owner-breeder: Bruno Brothers Farm (On.). Trainer: A. R. Loney. In 2004, won Duchess S. (Can-G3), Lady Angela S., La Prevoyante S., Passing Mood S.

Turf Female

INISH GLORA, 1998 b. m., Regal Classic—Star Guest, by Assert (Ire). 2004 record: 5-3-2-0, $433,730. Career: 32-9-9-4, $977,618. Breeder: C. G. Scott, D.V.M. (On.). Owner: Robert J. Costigan. Trainer: Macdonald Benson. In 2004,

won Nassau S. (Can-G3), Victoriana S.; 2nd Canadian H. (Can-G2), Dance Smartly H. (Can-G3).

Broodmare of the Year

ANNASAN, 1994 ch. m., Corporate Report—Amber Ryder, by Red Ryder. Race record: 11-1-1-2, $23,892. Owner-breeder: Beclawat Stable (On.). Through 2004, dam of four foals, three starters, three winners, two stakes winners, and one champion. Dam of A Bit O'Gold (by Gold Fever), 2004 champion three-year-old male, won Breeders' S., Prince of Wales S., Ontario Derby, etc.; Arco's Gold (by Gold Fever), won 2002 Coronation Futurity.

Canadian Triple Crown Winners

Year	Winner	Owner	Trainer	Jockey(s)
2003	Wando	G. Schickedanz	M. Keogh	P. Husbands
1993	Peteski	E. I. Mack	R. Attfield	C. Perret, D. Penna
1991	Dance Smartly	Sam-Son Farm	J. E. Day	P. Day
1990	Izvestia	Kinghaven Farms	R. Attfield	D. J. Seymour
1989	With Approval	Kinghaven Farms	R. Attfield	D. J. Seymour
1963	Canebora	Windfields Farm	G. McCann	M. Ycaza, H. Dittfach
1959	New Providence	Windfields Farm	G. McCann	R. Ussery, A. Gomez

Canadian Horse Racing Hall of Fame

Founded in 1976, the Canadian Horse Racing Hall of Fame recognizes the people and horses who have established the roots of Canadian racing. The Hall of Fame was originally a list of inductees until a permanent site was established in 1997 at the west entrance of Woodbine.

Horses (Year Inducted)
Ace Marine 1952 (2003)
Afleet 1984 (1992)
*Anita's Son 1956 (2005)
Arise 1946 (1983)
Awesome Again 1994 (2001)
Belle Geste 1968 (1990)
Bull Page 1947 (1977)
Bunty Lawless 1935 (1976)
Canadiana 1950 (1978)
Casa Camara 1944 (2000)
Carotene 1983 (2003)
Chief Bearhart 1993 (2002)
Chop Chop 1940 (1977)
Ciboulette 1961 (1983)
Classy 'n Smart 1981 (2004)
Cool Reception 1964 (2005)
Dance Smartly 1988 (1995)
Deputy Minister 1979 (1988)
Duchess of York 1923 (1976)
E. Day 1960 (1989)
Fanfreluche 1967 (1981)
Flaming Page 1959 (1980)
Frost King 1978 (1986)
Gallant Kitty 1916 (1977)
George Royal 1961 (1976)
Glorious Song 1976 (1995)
He's a Smoothie 1963 (2003)
Horometer 1931 (1976)
Inferno 1930 (1976)
Izvestia 1987 (1999)
Joey 1930 (1976)
Kennedy Road 1968 (2000)
Kingarvie 1943 (1976)
Langcrest 1961 (1984)
Langfuhr 1992 (2004)
La Prevoyante 1970 (1976)
Major Presto 1963 (1982)
Martimas 1896 (2001)
Mona Bell 1935 (2000)
Nearctic 1954 (1977)
New Providence 1956 (1982)

Nijinsky II 1967 (1976)
No Class 1974 (1997)
Norcliffe 1973 (2005)
Northern Dancer 1961 (1976)
Northernette 1974 (1987)
Overskate 1975 (1993)
Queensway 1929 (2003)
Runaway Groom 1979 (2001)
Shepperton 1939 (1976)
Sir Barton 1916 (1976)
Sky Classic 1987 (1998)
South Shore 1918 (2000)
Sunny's Halo 1980 (1986)
Terror 1866 (1996)
The Minstrel 1974 (1979)
Vice Regent 1967 (1989)
Victoria Park 1957 (1976)
Windfields 1943 (2002)
With Approval 1986 (1993)
Wonder Where 1956 (2004)
Yellow Rose 1837 (1996)
Youville 1939 (1977)

Jockeys (Year Inducted)
Ted Atkinson (2002)
Larry Attard (2001)
Hugo Dittfach (1983)
Jeff Fell (1993)
Jim Fitzsimmons (1984)
Norman "Dude" Foden (2000)
David Gall (1993)
Avelino Gomez (1977)
Sandy Hawley (1986)
Charles "Chick" Lang (1990)
Herb Lindberg (1991)
Charles Littlefield (2000)
John Longden (1976)
Don MacBeth (1988)
Frank Mann (2000)
Richard "Dick" O'Leary (2000)
Robin Platts (1997)
John "Red" Pollard (1982)

Pat Remillard (1979)
Chris Rogers (1977)
William "Smokey" Saunders (1976)
Don Seymour (1999)
Ron Turcotte (1980)
R. B. "Bobby" Watson (1998)
Headley Woodhouse (1980)
George Woolf (1976)

Trainers (Year Inducted)
A. E. "Burt" Alexandra (2002)
Roger Attfield (1999)
Macdonald "Mac" Benson (2002)
James "Jim" Bentley (1981)
Charles Boyle (2001)
W. H. "Bill" Bringloe (2000)
Donald "Duke" Campbell (1984)
Lou Cavalaris Jr. (1995)
John Dyment Jr. (2001)
Morris Fishman (2001)
Harry Giddings (1985)
R. K. "Doc" Hodgson (2001)
Gord Huntley (1998)
Roy Johnson (2003)
Lucien Laurin (1978)
Barry Littlefield (2000)
Edward "Ted" Mann (1982)
Gordon "Pete" McCann (1980)
Frank Merrill Jr. (1981)
J. C. "Jerry" Meyer (1999)
John Nixon (2002)
John Passero (2000)
Gil Rowntree (1997)
F. H. "Fred" Schelke (2002)
Ronald K. "Red" Smith (2004)
Joseph "Yonnie" Starr (1979)
Austin Irwin "Butch" Taylor (1987)
J. J. "Johnny" Thorpe (2002)
John R. Walker (2000)
Arthur Warner (1984)
James White (1996)
Ed Whyte (2001)

REFERENCE
Rules of Racing

The following model rules were developed by the Association of Racing Commissioners International and the North American Pari-Mutuel Regulators Association. Although individual states implement their own regulations for how racing is conducted in their jurisdictions, the model rules combine both time-tested concepts and new developments in the Thoroughbred sport. The following rules encompass the running of the race. Other model rules include such matters as racing officials, medications, and pari-mutuel wagering.

I. Entries and Nominations
A. Entering
No horse shall be qualified to start unless it has been and continues to be entered.

B. Procedure
1. Entries and nominations shall be made with the racing secretary and shall not be considered until received by the racing secretary, who shall maintain a record of time of receipt of them for a period of one year.

2. An entry shall be in the name of the horse's licensed owner and made by the owner, trainer, or a licensed designee of the owner or trainer.

3. Races printed in the condition book shall have preference over substitute and extra races.

4. An entry must be sent in writing, by telephone, or facsimile machine to the racing secretary. The entry must be confirmed in writing should the stewards or the racing secretary so request.

5. The person making an entry shall clearly designate the horse so entered.

6. No alteration may be made in any entry after the closing of entries, but an error may be corrected with permission of the stewards.

7. No horse may be entered in more than one race (with the exception of stakes races) to be run on the same day on which pari-mutuel wagering is conducted.

8. Any permitted medication or approved change of equipment must be declared at time of entry.

C. Limitation as to Spouses
No entry in any race shall be accepted for a horse owned wholly or in part by, or trained by, a person whose husband or wife is under license suspension at time of such entry; except that, if the license of a jockey has been suspended for a routine riding offense, the stewards may waive this rule.

D. Coupled Entries
1. Two or more horses entered in a race shall be joined as a mutuel entry and single betting interest if they are owned or leased in whole or in part by the same owner or are trained by a trainer who owns or leases any interest in any of the other horses in the race, except that entries may be uncoupled in stakes races.

2. No more than two horses having common ties through ownership or training may be entered in an overnight race. Under no circumstances may both horses of a coupled entry start to the exclusion of a single entry. When making a coupled entry, a preference for one of the horses must be made.

E. Nominations
1. Any nominator to a stakes race may transfer or declare such nomination prior to closing.

2. Joint nominations and entries may be made by any one of joint owners of a horse, and each such owner shall be jointly and severally liable for all payments due.

3. Death of a horse, or a mistake in its entry when such horse is eligible, does not release the nominator or transferee from liability for all stakes fees due. No fees paid in connection with a nomination to a stakes race that is run shall be refunded, except as otherwise stated in the conditions of a stakes race.

4. Death of a nominator to a stakes race shall not render void any subscription, entry, or right of entry. All rights, privileges, and obligations shall be attached to the legal heirs of the decedent or the successor owner of the horse.

5. When a horse is sold privately or at public auction or claimed, stakes engagements shall be transferred automatically to its new owner, except when the horse is transferred to a person whose license is suspended or who is otherwise unqualified to race or enter the horse; then such nomination shall be void as of the date of such transfer.

6. All stakes fees paid toward a stakes race shall be allocated to the winner unless otherwise provided by the conditions for the race. If a stakes race is not run for any reason, all such nomination fees paid shall be refunded.

F. Closings
1. Entries for purse races and nominations to stakes races shall close at the time designated by the association in previously published conditions for such races. No entry, nomination, or declaration shall be accepted after such closing time; except in the event of an emergency or if an overnight race fails to fill, the racing secretary may, with the approval of a steward, extend such closing time.

2. Except as otherwise provided in the conditions for a stakes race, the deadline for accepting nominations and declarations is midnight of the day of closing, provided they are received in time for compliance with every other condition of the race.

G. Number of Starters in a Race
The maximum number of starters in any race shall be limited to the number of starting positions afforded by the association starting gate and its extensions. The number of starters may be further limited by the number of horses that, in the opinion of the stewards, can be afforded a safe, fair, and equal start.

H. Split or Divided Races
1. In the event a race is canceled or declared off, the association may split any overnight race for which post positions have not been drawn.

2. Where an overnight race is split, forming two or more separate races, the racing secretary shall give notice of not less than 15 minutes before such races are closed to grant time for making additional entries to such split races.

I. Post Positions
Post positions for all races shall be determined by lot and shall be publicly drawn in the presence of a steward or steward designee.

J. Also-Eligible List

1. If the number of entries for a race exceeds the number of horses permitted to start, the racing secretary may create and post an also-eligible list.

2. If any horse is scratched from a race for which an also-eligible list was created, a replacement horse shall be drawn from the also-eligible list into the race in order of preference. If none is preferred, a horse shall be drawn into the race from the also-eligible list by public lot.

3. Any owner or trainer of a horse on the also-eligible list who does not wish to start the horse in such race shall so notify the racing secretary prior to scratch time for the race, thereby forfeiting any preference to which the horse may have been entitled.

4. A horse that draws into a straightaway race from the also-eligible list shall start from the post position vacated by the scratched horse. In the event more than one horse is scratched, post positions of horses drawing in from the also-eligible list shall be determined by public lot.

5. A horse that draws into a nonstraightaway race from the also-eligible list shall start from the outermost post position. In the event more than one horse is scratched, post positions of horses drawing in from the also-eligible list shall be determined by public lot.

K. Preferred List

The racing secretary shall maintain a list of entered horses eliminated from starting by a surplus of entries, and these horses shall constitute a preferred list and have preference. The manner in which the preferred list shall be maintained and all rules governing such list shall be the responsibility of the racing secretary. Such rules must be submitted to the racing commission 30 days prior to the commencement of the race meeting and are subject to the approval of the commission.

II. Declarations and Scratches

Declarations and scratches are irrevocable.

A. Declarations

1. A "declaration" is the act of withdrawing an entered horse from a race prior to the closing of entries.

2. The declaration of a horse before closing shall be made by the owner, trainer, or their licensed designee in the form and manner prescribed in these rules.

B. Scratches

1. A "scratch" is the act of withdrawing an entered horse from a contest after the closing of entries.

2. The scratch of a horse after closing shall be made by the owner, trainer, or their licensed designee, with permission from the stewards.

3. A horse may be scratched from a stakes race for any reason at any time up until 45 minutes prior to post time for that race.

4. No horse may be scratched from an overnight race without approval of the stewards.

5. In overnight races, horses that are physically disabled or sick shall be permitted to be scratched first. Should horses representing more than ten betting interests in the daily double or exotic wagering races, or horses representing more than eight betting interests in any other overnight race, remain in after horses with physical excuses have been scratched, then owners or trainers may be permitted at scratch time to scratch horses without physical excuses down to such respective minimum numbers for such races. This privilege shall be determined by lot if an excessive number of owners or trainers wish to scratch their horses.

6. Entry of any horse that has been scratched or excused from starting by the stewards because of a physical disability or sickness shall not be accepted until the expiration of three racing days after such horse was scratched or excused and the horse has been removed from the Veterinarian's List by the official veterinarian.

III. Weights

A. Allowances

1. Weight allowance must be claimed at time of entry and shall not be waived after the posting of entries, except by consent of the stewards.

2. A horse shall start with only the allowance of weight to which it is entitled at time of starting, regardless of its allowance at time of entry.

3. Horses not entitled to the first weight allowance in a race shall not be entitled to any subsequent allowance specified in the conditions.

4. Claim of weight allowance to which a horse is not entitled shall not disqualify it unless protest is made in writing and lodged with the stewards at least one hour before post time for that race.

5. A horse shall not be given a weight allowance for failure to finish second or lower in any race.

6. No horse shall receive allowance of weight nor be relieved extra weight for having been beaten in one or more races, but this rule shall not prohibit maiden allowances or allowances to horses that have not won a race within a specified period or a race of a specified value.

7. Except in handicap races that expressly provide otherwise, two-year-old fillies shall be allowed three pounds, and fillies and mares three years old and upward shall be allowed five pounds before September 1 and three pounds thereafter in races where competing against male horses.

B. Penalties

1. Weight penalties are obligatory.

2. Horses incurring weight penalties for a race shall not be entitled to any weight allowance for that race.

3. No horse shall incur a weight penalty or be barred from any race for having been placed second or lower in any race.

4. Penalties incurred and allowances due in steeplechase or hurdle races shall not apply to races on the flat, and vice versa.

5. The reports, records, and statistics as published by *Daily Racing Form*, Equibase, or other recognized publications shall be considered official in determining eligibility, allowances, and penalties, but may be corrected.

C. Weight Conversions

For the purpose of determining weight assignments and/or allowances for imported horses, the following weight conversions shall be used:

1. 1 kilogram equals 2¼ pounds
2. 1 Stone equals 14 pounds

IV. Workouts

A. Requirements

A horse shall not start unless it has participated in an official race or has an approved timed workout satisfactory to the stewards. The workout must have occurred at a pari-mutuel or commission-recognized facility within the previous 30 days. A horse that has not started for a period of 60 days or more shall be ineligible to race until it has completed a timed workout approved by the stewards prior to the day of the race in which the horse is entered. The association may impose more stringent workout requirements.

B. Identification

1. Unless otherwise prescribed by the stewards or the commission, the official lip tattoo must have been affixed to a horse's upper lip or other identification method approved by the appropriate breed registry and the commission applied prior to its participation in workouts from the gate, schooling races, or workouts required for removal from the Stewards' List, Starter's List, Veterinarian's List, or Bleeder List.

2. The trainer or exercise rider shall take each horse scheduled for an official workout to be identified by the clocker or clocker's assistant immediately prior to the workout.

3. A horse shall be properly identified by its lip tattoo or other identification method approved by the appropriate breed registry and the commission immediately prior to participating in an official timed workout.

4. The trainer or trainer's designee shall be required to identify the distance the horse is to be worked and the point on the track where the workout will start.

C. Information Dissemination

Information regarding a horse's approved timed workout or workouts shall be furnished to the public prior to the start of the race for which the horse has been entered.

D. Restrictions

A horse shall not be taken onto the track for training or a workout except during hours designated by the association.

V. Ineligible Horses

A horse is ineligible to start in a race when:

1. It is not stabled on the grounds of the association or present by the time established by the commission;

2. Its breed registration certificate is not on file with the racing secretary or horse identifier, unless the racing secretary has submitted the certificate to the appropriate breed registry for correction;

3. It is not fully identified and tattooed on the inside of the upper lip or identified by any other method approved by the appropriate breed registry and the commission;

4. It has been fraudulently entered or raced in any jurisdiction under a different name, with an altered registration certificate or altered lip tattoo or other identification method approved by the appropriate breed registry and the commission;

5. It is wholly or partially owned by a disqualified person or a horse is under the direct or indirect training or management of a disqualified person;

6. It is wholly or partially owned by the spouse of a disqualified person or a horse is under the direct or indirect management of the spouse of a disqualified person, in such cases, it being presumed that the disqualified person and spouse constitute a single financial entity with respect to the horse, which presumption may be rebutted;

7. The stakes or entrance money for the horse has not been paid in accordance with the conditions of the race;

8. The losing jockey mount fee is not on deposit with the horsemen's bookkeeper;

9. Its name appears on the Starter's List, Stewards' List, or Veterinarian's List;

10. It is a first-time starter and has not been approved to start by the starter;

11. It is owned in whole or in part by an undisclosed person or interest;

12. It lacks sufficient official published workouts or race past performance(s);

13. It has been entered in a stakes race and has subsequently been transferred with its engagements, unless the racing secretary has been notified of such prior to the start;

14. It is subject to a lien that has not been approved by the stewards and filed with the horsemen's bookkeeper;

15. It is subject to a lease not filed with the stewards;

16. It is not in sound racing condition;

17. It has had a surgical neurectomy performed on a heel nerve that has not been approved by the official veterinarian;

18. It has been trachea tubed to artificially assist breathing;

19. It has been blocked with alcohol or otherwise drugged or surgically denerved to desensitize the nerves above the ankle;

20. It has impaired eyesight in both eyes;

21. It is barred or suspended in any recognized jurisdiction;

22. It does not meet the eligibility conditions of the race;

23. Its owner or lessor is in arrears for any stakes fees, except with approval of the racing secretary;

24. Its owner(s), lessor(s), and/or trainer have not completed the licensing procedures required by the commission;

25. It is by an unknown sire or out of an unknown mare; or

26. There is no current negative test certificate for Equine Infectious Anemia attached to its breed registration certificate, as required by statute.

VI. Running of the Race
A. Equipment

1. No whip shall be used unless it has affixed to the end of it a looped leather "popper" not less than 1¼ inches in width and not over 3 inches in length, and is "feathered" above the "popper" with not less than three rows of leather "feathers," each "feather" not less than 1 inch in length. No whip shall exceed 31 inches in length. All whips are subject to inspection and approval by the stewards.

2. No bridle shall exceed two pounds.

3. A horse's tongue may be tied down with clean bandages, gauze, or tongue strap.

4. No licensee may add blinkers to a horse's equipment or discontinue their use without the prior approval of the starter, the paddock judge, and the stewards.

5. No licensee may change any equipment used on a horse in its last race in this jurisdiction without approval of the paddock judge.

B. Racing Numbers

1. Each horse shall carry a conspicuous saddlecloth number corresponding to the official number given that horse on the official program.

2. In the case of a coupled entry that includes more than one horse, each horse in the entry shall carry the same number, with a different distinguishing letter following the number. As an example, two horses in the same entry shall appear in the official program as 1 and 1A.

3. Each horse in the mutuel field shall carry a separate number or may carry the same number with a distinguishing letter following the number.

C. Jockey Requirements

1. Jockeys shall report to the jockeys' quarters at the time designated by the association. Jockeys shall report their engagements and any overweight to the clerk of scales. Jockeys shall not leave the jockeys' quarters except to ride in scheduled races until all of their riding engagements of the day have been fulfilled, except as approved by the stewards.

2. A jockey who has not fulfilled all riding engagements who desires to leave the jockeys' quarters must first receive the permission of the stewards and must be accompanied by an association security guard.

3. While in the jockeys' quarters, jockeys shall have no contact or communication with any person outside the jockeys' quarters other than commission personnel and officials, an owner or trainer for whom the jockey is riding, or a representative of the regular news media, except with the permission of the stewards. Any communication permitted by the stewards may be conducted only in the presence of the clerk of scales or other person designated by the stewards.

4. Jockeys shall be weighed out for their respective mounts by the clerk of scales not more than 30 minutes before post time for each race.

5. Only valets employed by the association shall assist jockeys in weighing out.

6. A jockey must wear a safety vest when riding in any official race. The safety vest shall weigh no more than two pounds and be designed to provide shock-absorbing protection to the upper body of at least a rating of five as defined by the British Equestrian Trade Association (BETA).

7. A jockey's weight shall include his or her clothing, boots, saddle and its attachments, and any other equipment except the whip, bridle, bit or reins, safety helmet, safety vest, blinkers, goggles, and number cloth.

8. Seven pounds is the limit of overweight any horse is permitted to carry.

9. Once jockeys have fulfilled their riding engagements for the day and have left the jockeys' quarters, they shall not be readmitted to the jockeys' quarters until after the entire racing program for that day has been completed, except with permission of the stewards.

D. Paddock to Post

1. Each horse shall carry the full weight assigned for that race from the paddock to the starting post, and shall parade past the stewards' stand, unless excused by the stewards. The post parade shall not exceed 12 minutes, unless otherwise ordered by the stewards. It shall be the duty of the stewards to ensure that the horses arrive at the starting gate as near to post time as possible.

2. After the horses enter the track, no jockey may dismount nor entrust his or her horse to the care of an attendant unless, because of accident occurring to the jockey, the horse, or the equipment, and with the prior consent of the starter. During any delay during which a jockey is permitted to dismount, all other jockeys may dismount and their horses may be attended by others. After the horses enter the track, only the jockey, an assistant starter, the official veterinarian, the racing veterinarian, or an outrider or pony rider may touch the horse before the start of the race.

3. If a jockey is injured on the way to the post, the horse shall be returned to the paddock or any other area designated by the stewards, resaddled with the appropriate weight, and remounted with a replacement jockey.

4. After passing the stewards' stand in parade, the horses may break formation and proceed to the post

in any manner unless otherwise directed by the stewards. Once at the post, the horses shall be started without unnecessary delay.

5. Horses shall arrive at the starting post in post-position order.

6. In case of accident to a jockey or his or her mount or equipment, the stewards or the starter may permit the jockey to dismount and the horse to be cared for during the delay, and may permit all jockeys to dismount and all horses to be attended to during the delay.

7. If a horse throws its jockey on the way from the paddock to the post, the horse must be returned to the point where the jockey was thrown, where it shall be remounted and then proceed over the route of the parade to the post. The horse must carry its assigned weight from paddock to post and from post to finish.

8. If a horse leaves the course while moving from paddock to post, the horse shall be returned to the course at the nearest practical point to that at which it left the course, and shall complete its parade to the post from the point at which it left the course, unless ordered scratched by the stewards.

9. No person shall willfully delay the arrival of a horse at the post.

10. The starter shall load horses into the starting gate in any order deemed necessary to ensure a safe and fair start. Only the jockey, the racing veterinarian, the starter, or an assistant starter shall handle a horse at the post.

E. Post to Finish

1. The Start

a. The starter is responsible for assuring that each participant receives a fair start.

b. If, when the starter dispatches the field, any door at the front of the starting-gate stalls should not open properly due to a mechanical failure or malfunction or should any action by any starting personnel directly cause a horse to receive an unfair start, the stewards may declare such a horse a nonstarter.

c. Should a horse, not scratched prior to the start, not be in the starting-gate stall, thereby causing it to be left when the field is dispatched by the starter, the horse shall be declared a nonstarter by the stewards.

d. Should an accident or malfunction of the starting gate or other unforeseeable event compromise the fairness of the race or the safety of race participants, the stewards may declare individual horses to be nonstarters, exclude individual horses from one or more pari-mutuel pools, or declare a "no contest" and refund all wagers except as otherwise provided in the rules involving multi-race wagers.

2. Interference, Jostling, or Striking

a. A jockey shall not ride carelessly or willfully so as to permit his or her mount to interfere with, impede, or intimidate any other horse in the race.

b. No jockey shall carelessly or willfully jostle, strike, or touch another jockey or another jockey's horse or equipment.

c. No jockey shall unnecessarily cause his or her horse to shorten its stride so as to give the appearance of having suffered a foul.

3. Maintaining a Straight Course

a. When the way is clear in a race, a horse may be ridden to any part of the course, but if any horse swerves or is ridden to either side so as to interfere with, impede, or intimidate any other horse, it is a foul.

b. The offending horse may be disqualified if, in the opinion of the stewards, the foul altered the finish of the race, regardless of whether the foul was accidental, willful, or the result of careless riding.

c. If the stewards determine the foul was intentional or due to careless riding, the jockey may be held responsible.

d. In a straightaway race, every horse must maintain position as nearly as possible in the lane in which it starts. If a horse is ridden, drifts, or swerves out of its lane in such a manner that it interferes with, impedes, or intimidates another horse, it is a foul and may result in the disqualification of the offending horse.

4. Disqualification

a. When the stewards determine that a horse shall be disqualified for interference, they may place the offending horse behind such horses as in their judgment it interfered with, or they may place it last.

b. If a horse is disqualified for a foul, any horse or horses in the same race owned or trained by the same interests, whether coupled or uncoupled, may also be disqualified.

c. When a horse is disqualified for interference in a time-trial race, for the purposes of qualifying only, it shall receive the time of the horse it is placed behind plus one-hundredth of a second penalty or more exact measurement if photo-finish equipment permits, and shall be eligible to qualify for the finals or consolations of the race on the basis of the assigned time.

d. Possession of any electrical or mechanical stimulating or shocking device by a jockey, horse owner, trainer, or other person authorized to handle or attend to a horse shall be prima-facie evidence of a violation of these rules and is sufficient grounds for the stewards to scratch or disqualify the horse.

e. The stewards may determine that a horse shall be unplaced for the purpose of purse distribution and time-trial qualification.

5. Horses Shall Be Ridden Out

All horses shall be ridden out in every race. A jockey shall not ease up or coast to the finish without reasonable cause, even if the horse has no apparent chance to win prize money. A jockey shall give a best effort during a race, and each horse shall be ridden to win.

6. Use of Whips

a. Although the use of a whip is not required, any jockey who uses a whip during a race shall do so only in a manner consistent with exerting his or her best efforts to win.

b. In all races where a jockey will ride without a whip, an announcement of such fact shall be made over the public address system.

c. No electrical or mechanical device or other expedient designed to increase or retard the speed of a horse, other than the whip approved by the stewards, shall be possessed by anyone or applied by anyone to the horse at any time on the grounds of the association during the meeting, whether in a race or otherwise.

d. Whips shall not be used on two-year-old horses before April 1 of each year.

e. Prohibited use of the whip includes whipping a horse:

i. On the head, flanks, or on any other part of its body other than the shoulders or hindquarters except when necessary to control a horse;

ii. During the post parade or after the finish of the race except when necessary to control the horse;

iii. Excessively or brutally, causing welts or breaks in the skin;

iv. When the horse is clearly out of the race or has obtained its maximum placing;

v. Persistently even though the horse is showing no response under the whip; or

vi. Striking another rider or horse.

7. Horse Leaving the Racecourse

If a horse leaves the racecourse during a race, it must turn back and resume the race from the point at which it originally left the course.

8. Order of Finish

a. The official order of finish shall be decided by the stewards with the aid of the photo-finish camera, and in the absence of the photo-finish film strip, the video replay. The photo finish and video replay are only aids in the stewards' decision. The decision of the stewards shall be final in all cases.

b. The nose of the horse shall determine the placement of the horse in relationship to other horses in the race.

9. Returning After the Finish

a. After a race has been run, the jockey shall ride promptly to the place designated by the stewards, dismount, and report to the clerk of scales to be weighed in. Jockeys shall weigh in with all pieces of equipment with which they weighed out.

b. If a jockey is prevented from riding to the designated unsaddling area because of an accident or illness to the jockey or the horse, the jockey may walk or be transported to the scales or may be excused from weighing in by the stewards.

10. Unsaddling

a. Only persons authorized by the stewards may assist the jockey with unsaddling the horse after the race.

b. No one shall place a covering over a horse before it is unsaddled.

11. Weighing In

a. A jockey shall weigh in at least at the same weight at which he or she weighed out, and if under that weight by more than two pounds, his or her mount shall be disqualified from any portion of the purse money.

b. In the event of such disqualification, all money wagered on the horse shall be refunded unless the race has been declared official.

c. No jockey shall weigh in at more than two pounds over the proper or declared weight, excluding the weight attributed to inclement weather conditions and/or of health and safety equipment approved by the stewards.

12. Dead Heats

a. When two horses run a dead heat for first place, all purses or prizes to which first and second horses would have been entitled shall be divided equally between them; and this principle applies in dividing all purses or prizes whatever the number of horses running a dead heat and whatever places for which the dead heat is run.

b. In a dead heat for first place, each horse involved shall be deemed a winner and liable to penalty for the amount it shall receive.

c. When a dead heat is run for second place and an objection is made to the winner of the race and sustained, the horses that ran a dead heat shall be deemed to have run a dead heat for first place.

d. If the dividing owners cannot agree as to which of them is to have a cup or other prize that cannot be divided, the question shall be determined by lot by the stewards.

VII. Protests, Objections, and Inquiries
A. Stewards to Inquire

1. The stewards shall take cognizance of foul riding and, upon their own motion or that of any racing offi-

cial or person empowered by this chapter to object or complain, shall make diligent inquiry or investigation into such objection or complaint when properly received.

2. In determining the extent of disqualification, the stewards in their discretion may:

a. Declare null and void a track record set or equaled by a disqualified horse or any horses coupled with it as an entry;

b. Affirm the placing judges' order of finish and hold the jockey responsible if, in the stewards' opinion, the foul riding did not affect the order of finish; or

c. Disqualify the offending horse and hold the jockey blameless if in the stewards' opinion the interference to another horse in a race was not the result of an intentional foul or careless riding on the part of a jockey.

B. Race Objections

1. An objection to an incident alleged to have occurred during the running of a race shall be received only when lodged with the clerk of scales, the stewards, or their designees, by the owner, the authorized agent of the owner, the trainer, or the jockey of a horse engaged in the same race.

2. An objection following the running of any race must be filed before the race is declared official, whether all or some riders are required to weigh in or the use of a "fast official" procedure is permitted.

3. The stewards shall make all findings of fact as to all matters occurring during and incident to the running of a race, shall determine all objections and inquiries, and shall determine the extent of disqualification, if any, of horses in the race. Such findings of fact and determinations shall be final.

C. Prior Objections

1. Objections to the participation of a horse entered in any race shall be made to the stewards in writing, signed by the objector, and filed not later than one hour prior to post time for the first race on the day that the questioned horse is entered. Any such objection shall set forth the specific reason or grounds for the objection in such detail so as to establish probable cause for the objection. The stewards upon their own motion may consider an objection until such time as the horse becomes a starter.

2. An objection to a horse entered in a race may be made on, but not limited to, the following grounds or reasons:

a. A misstatement, error, or omission in the entry under which a horse is to run;

b. The horse entered to run is not the horse it is represented to be at the time of entry, or the age was erroneously given;

c. The horse is not qualified to enter under the conditions specified for the race, or the allowances are improperly claimed or not entitled the horse, or the weight to be carried is incorrect under the conditions of the race;

d. The horse is owned in whole or in part, or leased or trained by a person ineligible to participate in racing or otherwise ineligible to own a racehorse as provided in these rules; or

e. The horse was entered without regard to a lien filed previously with the racing secretary.

3. The stewards may scratch from the race any horse that is the subject of an objection if they have reasonable cause to believe that the objection is valid.

D. Protests

1. A protest against any horse that has started in a race shall be made to the stewards in writing, signed by the protestor, within 72 hours of the race exclusive of nonracing days. If the incident upon which the protest is based occurs within the last two days of the meeting, such protest may be filed with the commission within 72 hours exclusive of Saturdays, Sundays, or official holidays. Any such protest shall set forth the specific reason or reasons for the protest in such detail as to establish probable cause for the protest.

2. A protest may be made on any of the following grounds:

a. Any grounds for objection as set forth in this chapter;

b. The order of finish as officially determined by the stewards was incorrect due to oversight or errors in the numbers of the horses that started the race;

c. A jockey, trainer, owner, or lessor was ineligible to participate in racing as provided in this chapter;

d. The weight carried by a horse was improper by reason of fraud or willful misconduct; or

e. An unfair advantage was gained in violation of the rules.

3. Notwithstanding any other provision in this article, time limitation on the filing of protests shall not apply in any case in which fraud or willful misconduct is alleged, provided the stewards are satisfied that the allegations are bona fide and verifiable.

4. No person shall file any objection or protest knowing the same to be inaccurate, false, untruthful, or frivolous.

5. The stewards may order any purse, award, or prize for any race withheld from distribution pending the determination of any protest. In the event any purse, award, or prize has been distributed to an owner or for a horse that by reason of a protest or other reason is disqualified or determined to be not entitled to such purse, award, or prize, the stewards or the commission may order such purse, award, or prize returned and redistributed to the rightful owner or horse. Any person who fails to comply with an order to return any purse, award, or prize erroneously distributed shall be subject to fines and suspension.

Preference Date System

Racing secretaries long have struggled with two problems: Not enough horses for a race in the track's condition book, which details prospective races for the meet, and too many horses for a specific race.

When a race has too few entries, the racing-office staff must make calls to trainers and solicit them to enter horses in the race. This process is widely known as "hustling," and a starter that is entered for such a race is often referred to as a "hustled horse."

A race with too many entrants presents a different set of problems. Often, the race can be split. When other overnight races on the card are slow to fill, a racing secretary may choose to split a popular race, a maiden special weight race for instance, into two or three or more separate races.

If splitting a race is not feasible, the racing secretary needs a system that determines the eligible horses that will get starting positions. Racing offices long used the "star system," under which a horse denied a starting place in an oversubscribed race was given a star. A horse excluded twice from a race would get two stars. Under the star system, horses with the most stars received preference for the next race with the same conditions.

Many tracks now have changed to a "preference date system," which is similar to the star system but simpler to maintain. In the preference date system, the horses with the earliest preference date get into the race first.

As an example of how the preference date rules system is used, following are the preference date rules of Golden Gate Fields and Bay Meadows Race Course in Northern California:

Preference Date System

All horses whose foal certificates are registered with the racing secretary on the first day of entries will receive an entry date for that day. Thereafter, horses will receive entry dates for the day their foal certificates are registered with the racing secretary. Such entry dates will be good for any category.

1. In all races, winners are preferred.

2. Maidens will not be eligible to receive an entry date in any race until their papers are on file with the racing office at the time of the draw. Entry dates for maidens are good for any maiden race.

3. Horses drawn into races and horses on the also-eligible list that draw into races will receive a running date corresponding to the date on which they are to run, and lose all dates previously held.

4. Horses on the Veterinarian's, Stewards' or Starter's List cannot establish a date. They will not be permitted to enter until they have been approved to start. Horses placed on these lists will keep their dates if they ran in the particular race in which they made the list. Horses that are scratched and placed on a list will be given a scratch date for the day of that race.

5. In all cases, an entry date takes preference over a running date of the same day and a running date takes preference over a scratch date of the same day.

6. Horses drawn on the overnight (either in the race or on the also-eligible) and scratched will lose their date and acquire a scratch date corresponding to the day of the race, unless otherwise specified by the stewards. Any horse on the also-eligible list that is declared will retain its preference date if the scratch is not activated. Other scratched horses will be treated in the following manner:

a. Runaway in the paddock—Entry date for day of race.

b. Runaway in the post parade—Entry date for day of race.

c. Flip in the gate prior to the start—Scratch date for day of race.

d. Scratched for insufficient works—Scratch date for day of race.

e. Scratched because of incorrect markings—Scratch date for day of race.

f. Ineligible to race in which drawn into—Scratch date for day of race.

g. Scratched because of breakdown in transportation to the track—Retains original date.

h. Scratched at the gate and not put on any list—Scratch date for day of race.

i. Entered in the wrong race by delegated agent or trainer—Scratch date for day of race.

j. Horse hurt in gate due to accident involving another horse—Retains original date.

k. Horse left behind the gate—Retains original date.

7. Horses that have established a date at the current meeting will lose that preference date should they race elsewhere.

8. Stakes races are not considered in the preference date system.

9. In no way does the claiming, ownership transfer, or trainer transfer of a horse affect the preference date.

10. Maidens, when entered in a winners' race, will retain original date.

11. Horses entered will initially receive an entry date corresponding to the date on which they are entered.

12. A same-owner entry cannot exclude a single entry except when race preferences indicate otherwise. Trainers must declare at time of entry if he or she has a same-owner or different-owner entry in the race. All same-owner entries must have a declared first and second choice at entry time.

How Jockeys Are Paid

Leading jockeys often will be paid upfront fees when they travel to ride a horse in a stakes race, but most jockeys are compensated according to a table of fees based on race purse and finish position of the horse they ride. Joint model rules of the Association of Racing Commissioners International and the North American Pari-Mutuel Regulators Association contain a suggested fee table, although fees vary from one track or state to another. Following is the model fee schedule as published in 2005.

In the absence of a written agreement, the following jockey mount fees apply:

Purse	Winning Mount	2nd-Place Mount	3rd-Place Mount	Losing Mount
$599 and Under	$33	$33	$33	$33
$600-699	$36	$33	$33	$33
$700-999	10% Win Purse	$33	$33	$33
$1,000-1,499	10% Win Purse	$33	$33	$33
$1,500-1,999	10% Win Purse	$33	$33	$33
$2,000-3,499	10% Win Purse	$35	$33	$33
$3,500-4,999	10% Win Purse	$45	$40	$38
$5,000-9,999	10% Win Purse	$55	$45	$40
$10,000-14,999	10% Win Purse	$65	$50	$45
$15,000-24,999	10% Win Purse	5% Place Purse	5% Show Purse	$50
$25,000-49,999	10% Win Purse	5% Place Purse	5% Show Purse	$55
$50,000-99,999	10% Win Purse	5% Place Purse	5% Show Purse	$65
$100,000 & Up	10% Win Purse	5% Place Purse	5% Show Purse	$80
				$105

How to Handicap a Race

Handicapping a horse race is fun and intellectually challenging, and it also can be profitable. That does not mean you are destined to retire to a life of luxury if you learn how to handicap, but you can have winning afternoons and even winning years at the racetrack.

There is no feeling in the world quite like the one when you have correctly handicapped a race, a feeling that is tangibly rewarded if you bet your selection. Picking a winner evokes a feeling of pride, as well as bragging rights with your friends. Handicapping is an intellectual exercise, a skill that should improve as you become more experienced—as long as you are realistic.

Wagering at racetracks is pari-mutuel, which means bettors are competing against other bettors every single race. (See following section on pari-mutuel wagering and odds.) There is no single right way to handicap. But a good start is setting up a realistic framework.

Framework of Reality

You are not going to win every race. Nobody does. The reality of horse racing is that, year after year, at every track in North America, favorites in Thoroughbred racing win 25% to 35% of the time. In other words, the betting public is wrong two out of three times. If you can correctly handicap vulnerable favorites, you will be able to identify overlays, which are horses whose odds are higher than they should be. Correctly finding one or two overlays can allow you to have a successful afternoon. An underlay is a horse whose odds are shorter than justified by past performances or physical condition.

A fundamental point here is that there is a difference between handicapping and wagering. Money management, deciding which races to bet and how to bet them, with countless options available, is an entirely different ballgame. But, money management also is a skill you can hone. For now, remember that there are no rules saying you have to bet every race or even any race.

Reading Past Performance Lines

The raw materials for handicapping any race are the past-performance lines, the statistical picture of each horse's previous starts. These past-performance lines can be found in *Daily Racing Form* or a program published by the track. The *Racing Form*, which is a newspaper, provides more information in its past-performance lines than the track program, which is printed in a magazine format.

To understand the past-performance lines, you must first learn the abbreviations and terms in the accompanying boxes. You cannot handicap without reading and comprehending past-performance lines; doing so is easier than it appears.

Track Condition Abbreviations

Thoroughbred racing is contested on dirt and turf, the latter also called grass. The abbreviations for track conditions:

Dirt	Turf
ft: fast	**hd:** hard
gd: good	**fm:** firm
sy: sloppy	**gd:** good
my: muddy	**yl:** yielding
wf: wet fast	**sf:** soft
s: sealed track	

The conditions for each race appear at the top of all the horses' past-performance lines, defining which horses are eligible. The race may be limited to fillies, two-year-olds, horses that have only won a certain number of races or a certain amount of money, or horses bred in a particular state. If it is a claiming race, the claiming, or purchase, price is indicated.

The horses' names are listed in post-position order in the *Racing Form*. A track program lists the horses by the numbers they will be wearing on their saddlecloths in the race. That is the number you will use when placing a bet.

In case of an entry—when one betting number covers more than one horse because two horses have the same trainer or the same owner—horses will be designated as 1 and 1A. The horse closest to the rail will be 1, the other 1A. If there is a second entry in the same race, those two horses will be designated 2 and 2B. A single bet covers all horses in an entry.

Located just above the program numbers are the preliminary odds set by a racetrack employee to reflect how she or he believes the betting in that race will proceed. These are known as morning-line or program-line odds.

Now, let's examine a single past-performance line, that of 2004 Kentucky Derby (G1) winner Smarty Jones for the 2004 Preakness Stakes (G1) at Pimlico Race Course on May 15. (These past performances are courtesy of Equibase LLC, which provides past-performance information to *Daily Racing Form* and track programs.)

At the far left is the number on Smarty Jones's saddlecloth, seven, which was the post position he drew for the Preakness. (He actually broke from the sixth starting stall out from the rail because The Cliff's Edge, who had been entered to run in the Preakness, was scratched because of a foot ailment.) Above the saddlecloth number appeared his program-line odds. For the Preakness, Smarty Jones initially was the 8-to-5 favorite in the track oddsmaker's betting line. (The Cliff's Edge was scratched after the program page went to the printer, and Smarty Jones's odds were lowered to 6-to-5 after the scratch.)

8-5
7 SMARTY JONES (L)

ch. c. 3 Elusive Quality—I'll Get Along
by Smile
126
Bred in Pa. by Someday Farm
BLUE, blue "C" on white ball, blue dots on white sleeves, blue cap

Owner: SOMEDAY FARM
Trainer: JOHN C. SERVIS
Jockey: STEWART ELLIOTT

2004:	5	5	0	0	$6,713,535
2003:	2	2	0	0	$49,620
Life:	7	7	0	0	$6,763,155
Turf:	0	0	0	0	$0
Off Dirt:	2	2	0	0	$6,484,800

01May04	CD10	sly	1¼	$0{:}46^{73}$	$1{:}37^{35}$	$2{:}04^{06}$	3	Ky Derby(G1)-1000k	**87**	13	$4^{2\,1/2}$	$2^{1\,1/2}$	2^{hd}	1^{hd}	$1^{2\,3/4}$	Elliott S	126	*4.10	Smarty Jones$^{2\,3/4}$ Lion Heart$^{3\,1/4}$ Imperialism^{2}	Stalked, bid, clear	18
10Apr04	OP9	my	1⅛	$0{:}46^{95}$	$1{:}11^{71}$	$1{:}49^{41}$	3	ArkDerby(G2)-1000k	**97**	11	$2^{1/2}$	$2^{1/2}$	1^{hd}	1^{3}	$1^{1\,1/2}$	Elliott S	122	*1.00	*Smarty Jones*$^{1\,1/2}$ Borrego$^{1\,1/2}$ Pro Prado$^{3\,1/2}$	Cleared at will, driving	11
20Mar04	OP10	fst	1¹⁄₁₆	$0{:}47^{65}$	$1{:}12^{10}$	$1{:}42^{07}$	3	Rebel-200k	**91**	7	2^{1}	2^{1}	$2^{1/2}$	1^{1}	$1^{3\,1/4}$	Elliott S	122	3.50	*Smarty Jones*$^{3\,1/4}$ Purge$^{3\,3/4}$ Pro Prado$^{3\,3/4}$	Kicked strongly clear	9
28Feb04	OP9	fst	1	$0{:}45^{87}$	$1{:}11^{25}$	$1{:}37^{57}$	3	Southwest-100k	**87**	6	$2^{1\,1/2}$	$2^{2\,1/2}$	2^{hd}	1^{2}	$1^{3/4}$	Elliott S	122	*.50	*Smarty Jones*$^{3/4}$ *TwoDownAtomtc*$^{1/2}$ Pro Prado$^{7\,1/4}$	Chased, took over, driving	9
03Jan04	Aqu8	fst	1^{70}	$0{:}47^{03}$	$1{:}11^{78}$	$1{:}41^{42}$	3	CountFleet-81k	**89**	7	3^{1}	3^{1}	2^{hd}	$1^{1/2}$	1^{5}	Elliott S	116	*.40	*Smarty Jones*^{5} Risky Trick^{6} Mr. Spock$^{1/2}$	Stumbled start, 3 wide	7
22Nov03	Pha9	fst	7f	$0{:}21^{88}$	$0{:}44^{28}$	$1{:}21^{88}$	2	[S] PennaNurse-56k	**93**	1	10	1^{2}	$1^{2\,1/2}$	1^{8}	1^{15}	Elliott S	117	*.70	*Smarty Jones*^{15} Salty Punch$^{2\,1/4}$ Isle of Mirth$^{1\,1/2}$	Off slow, dominated	11
09Nov03	Pha6	fst	6f	$0{:}45^{32}$	$0{:}57^{86}$	$1{:}11^{19}$	2	Md Sp Wt-23k	**84**	8	4	2^{hd}	1^{5}	1^{6}	$1^{7\,3/4}$	Elliott S	118	*1.10	*Smarty Jones*$^{7\,3/4}$ *Deputy Rummy*$^{2\,3/4}$ Speedwell Beau^{6}	Handy score	10

Workouts: •24Apr04 CD 5f gd :58 B *1/34* •03Apr04 OP 5f fst :58.3 H *1/21* •13Mar04 OP 5f fst :58.3 H *1/35* •18Feb04 OP 6f fst 1:13 H *1/8* •11Feb04 OP 7f fst 1:29.3 H *1/1*

(L) - Treated with furosemide; (L*) - First time using furosemide; (O) Off of furosemide

Beneath the name is specific information about that horse: color (ch. for chestnut), sex (c. for colt), age (3), sire (Elusive Quality), dam (I'll Get Along), sire of the dam (Smile), where he was bred (Pennsylvania), and who bred him (Someday Farm). The capital letter L in parentheses after Smarty Jones's name indicates that he was treated with the diuretic furosemide, an antibleeding medication that for decades was known by the trade name Lasix. The veterinary formulation now is sold under the trade name Salix. Some horses improve dramatically the first time they are treated with the medication.

Underneath or to the right of that information is a description of the owner's silks (blue with blue C in white ball, blue dots on white sleeves, and white cap), the weight he will carry (126 pounds), and the names of the owner (Someday Farm), trainer (John C. Servis), and jockey (Stewart Elliott).

The horse's race record is in the upper right. It contains the racing record for the current season and the previous year—number of starts, followed by wins, seconds, thirds, and earnings—a lifetime record, and the horse's record on turf and off dirt (wet) tracks. Before the Preakness, Smarty Jones had raced twice on a wet (off dirt) track, winning both times.

The horse's past performances are beneath all that information. Each past-performance line is a summary of that horse's performance in a race, starting with the most recent race on top.

The past-performance line can be split into thirds. Let's start with the left one-third of Smarty Jones's previous start, the Kentucky Derby:

01May04 CD10 sy 1¼ :46.73 1:37.35 2:04.06 3 Ky Derby(G1) 1000k

In order, this identifies Smarty Jones's most recent race, which occurred on May 1, 2004, and was the tenth race at Churchill Downs (CD10). The track condition was sloppy (sy) after a torrential downpour in midafternoon, and the distance was 1¼ miles (1¼). Next are the fractions of the leader in that race. Equibase past-performance lines at this distance list only the time of the race leader after a half-mile (46.73 seconds), after one mile (one minute and 37.35 seconds), and the final time of the winner, two minutes and 4.06 seconds (2:04.06). *Daily Racing Form* gives additional fractions of the race, which often are useful in handicapping. The next number, 3, signifies that the race was limited to three-year-olds. The name of the race with its grade follows, Ky Derby (G1), and then is the purse in thousands of dollars. (With Smarty Jones collecting a $5-million bonus from Oaklawn Park for winning two of the Arkansas track's stakes races and the Derby, the actual purse for the 2004 Kentucky Derby was $6,184,800.)

The next set of numbers reveals how the race was run and gives additional information on Smarty Jones's performance in that race.

87 13 $4^{2\,1/2}$ $2^{1\,1/2}$ 2^{hd} 1^{hd} $1^{2\,3/4}$ ElliottS 126

The first number, 87, was Smarty Jones's speed rating in the Derby. The higher the number, the better the race. In general, any speed rating above 90 is considered very good, and a number above 100 is exceptional. The speed figure is an effort to give Smarty Jones's performance in that race an absolute rating so it can be compared to other races at other tracks and at other distances. Equibase employees are responsible for the speed ratings in track programs, while Racing Form speed ratings are compiled by Andrew Beyer. The Beyer rating for Smarty Jones in the Derby was an exceptional 107.

The next number, 13, indicated Smarty Jones's post position, meaning he was the 13th horse out from the rail in the starting gate. The numbers with superscript figures tell how Smarty Jones ran his race. The first number indicates Smarty Jones was fourth, 2½ lengths behind the leader ($4^{2\,1/2}$) after a half-mile, and then second by 1½ lengths at the next point of call, after three-quarters of a mile. He was second by a head (2^{hd}) at the succeeding point of call after one mile, which is the top of Churchill Down's stretch. He was first by a head (1^{hd}) at the midstretch call, which is always one-eighth of a mile (one furlong) from the finish line. The final set of numbers indicates that Smarty Jones won the Kentucky Derby by two and three-quarter lengths ($1^{2\,3/4}$). In summary, Smarty Jones was fourth, then second, got a head in front in midstretch, and won by 2¾ lengths.

Next in the past-performance line are the jockey's name, Stewart Elliott (ElliottS), and the weight Smarty Jones carried, 126 pounds. All horses in the Kentucky Derby carry the same weight, although fillies get a five-pound weight allowance and carry 121 pounds.

Now, let's look at the final third of the past-performance line.

*4.10 Smarty Jones ²³⁄₄ Lion Heart ³¹⁄₄ Imperialism ² Stalked, bid, clear 18

The first number (*4.10) was Smarty Jones's final odds in the Derby, 4.10-to-1, and the asterisk indicates that he was the race's betting favorite. Favorites rarely go off at such long odds, but Derby favorites have had relatively high odds after Churchill Downs instituted wagering on all horses in the race and the fields are so large. The odds are followed by the names of the top three finishers, each with the distance they finished ahead of the horse immediately behind them. Smarty Jones finished 2¾ lengths in front of Lion Heart, who finished second, 3¼ lengths in front of Imperialism. In turn, Imperialism finished two lengths ahead of the fourth-place finisher (Limehouse). The summary of the finish is followed by a description of Smarty Jones's performance and the type of trip he had in the race. He closely followed the pace of Lion Heart, the early front-runner (stalked), launched his winning bid on Churchill's final turn (bid), and pulled away from his opponents through the final furlong (clear) for a relatively easy victory. If a horse encountered trouble in the race, the comments might be, depending on the circumstances, "slow start," "lacked room," or "bothered." The final number, 18, is the total number of starters in the 2004 Derby.

Beneath the horse's past-performance lines are recent workouts. Workouts can be very important, especially for horses returning to the races after layoffs and for first-time starters. Also, they can indicate a horse reaching the peak of fitness at just the right time. These workout lines contain the date of the workout, the racetrack

or training center where it occurred, the distance, the track condition, the time, whether the horse was breezing (not at full speed) or working handily (under urging from its rider), and how that workout compared with all the horses that worked the same distance that morning on that particular track.

Smarty Jones's most recent workout line was:
• **Apr24 CD 5f gd :58 B 1/34**

In order, on April 24 at Churchill, Smarty Jones worked five furlongs on a track rated as good in 58 seconds while not at full speed (breezing), and his workout was the fastest of 34 at that distance that day. The typographical bullet at the beginning of the line also denotes that Smarty Jones's workout was the fastest of the day; thus, those efforts are known as bullet workouts.

The workout was notable for two reasons. First, Smarty Jones had indicated that he was ready for a powerful effort in the Derby. He was not working at top speed and still was the fastest five-furlong time that day. Also, :58 is a very fast time for a five-furlong workout of any kind, and producing that effort over a wet track (gd, for good) only emphasized how ready he was for the Derby. Second, Servis had the colt right where he wanted him after the Derby and did not feel a workout was necessary before the Preakness. Servis certainly was correct. Smarty Jones went off as the 7-to-10 favorite and won the Preakness by a record 11½ lengths.

Both track program and *Daily Racing Form* past-performance lines provide a bare outline of a race. Full details are found in the charts, which are compiled by Equibase at North American tracks. The charts provide more detailed information on how the race was run and footnotes that describe each horse's trip in that race. Serious handicappers will frequently save all the charts from one track to provide details unavailable in the past-performance lines because of space limitations. (For more on how to read a chart, see "How to Read a Chart.")

Types of Bets

Win Your horse must finish first to collect.

Place Your horse must finish first or second.

Show Your horse must finish first, second, or third.

Quinella You bet two horses and they must finish first and second in either order.

Exacta You bet two horses and they must finish first and second in exact order.

Exacta box A multiple bet in which you select two or more horses and bet all combinations of them finishing first and second.

Exacta wheel You bet one horse to win and every other horse in the field to finish second.

Trifecta or triple You bet three horses and they must finish first, second, and third in exact order.

Trifecta box or triple box A multiple bet in which you select three or more horses and they must finish first, second, and third in any order.

Superfecta You bet four horses and they must finish first, second, third, and fourth in exact order.

Superfecta box You bet four or more horses and they must finish first, second, third, and fourth in any order.

Daily (or instant, late, or middle) double You must pick the winners of two consecutive races.

Pick three or pick four You must pick the winners of three or four consecutive races.

Pick six You must pick the winners of six consecutive races. A consolation payoff for those who pick five winners usually is offered.

Three Schools of Handicapping

There are three main schools of handicapping, each posing different questions. Class asks: How much ability has this horse shown, and what has been the quality of its competition? Form asks: How has this horse performed most recently, and how is it likely to race today? Speed simply asks: How fast is this horse?

Handicappers have been arguing for decades over the relative importance of the three schools. An understanding of each will aid your handicapping.

Class

Class can be measured by the level of competition the horse has faced in its prior races. For this reason, past-performance lines should be read from the bottom line (least recent) to the top (most recent) to see how a horse is coming into today's race and whether it has previously faced other horses in this race. (See box, "Five Ways to Improve Your Handicapping.") Let's say you are handicapping a race for $10,000 claimers. Horse A's last race was in an $8,000 claimer, which he won. He is now moving up to $10,000. But previously in his past-performance lines, he may have already run in $10,000 claiming races or for an even higher claiming price. How he previously performed at that level could be vital information in evaluating his chances when moving up to the $10,000 level today.

A second gauge of class is a horse's average earnings per start. Horse B has made $50,000 in his career from ten starts. Horse C has made $55,000 in his career from 25 starts. Horse B's average earnings per start, $5,000, are considerably higher than Horse C, whose average per start is $2,200. Be aware, though, that money does not mean everything. Earnings in races restricted to horses bred in one state—for example, those bred in New York or New Jersey—can inflate a horse's earnings and present a distorted picture of its ability to compete in the race you are handicapping.

A third way to measure class is by the number of wins a horse has or does not have. Chronic losers should be avoided. If a maiden has had ten or more starts without a win, stay away. If an allowance horse has had 15 starts or more with only one win, stay away. This strategy may not work every time, but in the long run you will save yourself a lot of money by avoiding horses that find a way to lose and frequently are overbet because they often come close to winning.

When a horse with back class—as evidenced by career earnings—has been racing poorly and then shows a dramatic, sudden improvement, it is giving a sign of life. John Little was a perfect example. The six-year-old gelding had won more than $350,000 in his career, but very little of it was earned in the two years prior to an $18,000 claiming race at Belmont Park on September 29, 2004. For 2003 and 2004, he had no wins and just one second in 17 starts.

However, in his previous race, a $20,000 claimer on August 27, 2004, at Saratoga Race Course, he showed dramatic improvement, rallying from 11th, 13¼ lengths behind the leader after a half-mile, to finish fifth by 2¼ lengths as part of an entry at 30.50-to-1. To do so, he had raced his final three furlongs in the seven-furlong race in under 37 seconds, a very good time, in his first start for a new

Racing Terms and Comments

Here are some terms commonly used in racing news stories and chart footnotes. Additional terms can by found in the following section, Glossary of Common Racing and Breeding Terms.

Apprentice A rider at the beginning of his career. Horses with apprentice jockeys carry five, seven, or ten pounds less than their rivals.

Bolted The horse made a sharp, sudden move to the extreme outside.

Bore in or bore out Instead of racing in a straight line, the horse veered inside or outside.

Boxed in The horse was trapped with nowhere to move.

Brushed The horse made light contact with another horse.

Dogs Pylons or traffic cones put around a course to protect the area on the inside near the rail. Horses that work around dogs cover more distance on turns. The symbol (d) is used to denote dogs were up in a workout.

Driving The horse was all out to win.

Entry Two or more horses are coupled in the wagering because of common ownership or, in some jurisdictions, the same trainer. You bet on one and collect if either member of the entry wins.

Field Two or more horses coupled as one betting entity. Just as in an entry, you get more than one horse and collect if any horse in the betting field wins.

Furlong One-eighth of a mile.

Furosemide A diuretic commonly used in American Thoroughbred racing to prevent or limit pulmonary bleeding. Trade name is Salix (formerly Lasix).

Gamely The horse showed courage while racing.

Greenly The horse showed inexperience by racing erratically.

Handily The horse won comfortably.

Hung The horse made an apparent winning move but then failed to sustain it.

Ridden out The jockey continued to ride the winning horse to the wire without undo urging.

Route A race of one mile or longer.

Saved ground The horse raced on the inside, thereby taking a shorter route around the track.

Sprint A race shorter than one mile.

Steadied The jockey had to physically stop his riding motion because of traffic problems.

Taken up The jockey had to restrain his or her mount severely, usually because of traffic problems or interference.

Unruly The horse acted up before the start.

Used up The horse expended all its energy by contesting the pace early in the race.

Willingly The horse continued to run its best without urging.

trainer, Robert Barbara. For whatever reason, John Little had come to life and figured to move forward again. Sent off at odds of 7.80-to-1 as part of an entry, John Little won by 3½ lengths and returned $17.60 on September 29.

Form

Horses are athletes, not machines. Even the best horses cannot maintain their highest level of performance for an extended period of time, which is why Cigar's 16-race winning streak in the mid-1990s was so remarkable.

Experienced horses tend to run in form cycles. They are either moving forward or backward. Many times, horses tip off which direction they are headed in a previous race, a workout, or both. If a horse had been performing very poorly for several races and then showed a sign of life by rallying from ninth to fourth, it may very well improve again in its next start and win.

If a horse that had been racing well throws in a poor performance, the handicapper must ask whether there was a legitimate excuse. Did the horse get overextended in a speed duel, get forced wide, or run into traffic? Did that problem cause the poor effort or simply disguise diminished form? Again, going through all the horse's past-performance lines will frequently provide clues. If a horse races wide in four of five starts, there is a likelihood it will do so again if it draws an outside post position.

You should expect young horses to improve, especially if they have shown a hint of ability in their first race or two. The first race at Belmont Park on October 8, 2004, provides a good example. The race was a six-furlong maiden claimer for two-year-old fillies whose claiming prices were $35,000 to $45,000. Seven of the eight fillies entered had raced previously. The lone first-time starter was Trance, who was trained by Christophe Clement, a top-shelf horseman whose specialties are grass and distance races. Of Trance's ten workouts, nine were extremely slow, and the other, four furlongs in :49.43 on September 20, was modest, only the 46th fastest of 89 horses going a half-mile at Belmont that morning. She would go off at 30.50-to-1 and finish sixth.

Three of the seven other fillies were dropping from maiden-special-weight races to maiden claimers for the first time. The horse in the rail starting position, Jet Set Joan, had finished seventh by 15¼ lengths at 28.25-to-1 in her lone start, on May 27, but was adding blinkers and the antibleeding medication furosemide (indicated by "L" in her past-performance lines). The filly in the third post position, Clearly Kathy, had raced once on dirt, finishing ninth by 13 lengths, and twice on grass, finishing third and then 12th. The horse in the seventh starting stall, Honoring Carolyn, had shown early speed in all three of her starts, finishing third and eighth in sprints before stretching out to a mile and finishing fifth.

Of the other fillies, two had made their debuts in the same race, a $75,000 maiden claimer on September 1 at Saratoga. Brillant Success finished seventh by 7¼ lengths at 6.60-to-1, and She Can Punch finished eighth by 10¼ lengths at 28.75-to-1. Marlindsey had raced in a $50,000 maiden claimer, rallying to be a distant fourth at 22.50-to-1 in her debut at Saratoga.

Five Ways to Improve Your Handicapping

1. **Always handicap past-performance lines from the bottom (least recent) to the top.** This strategy immediately gives you an advantage over other bettors who only look at each horse's top two or three lines. By going from the bottom up, you will consistently turn up important information that others may be missing. For example, two or three horses in the race you are handicapping already may have competed against each other. Or the claimer you are considering has previously won at today's level or at a higher level several races back. At the very least, handicapping from the bottom up assures that you will have a better picture of how each horse is coming into today's race.

2. **Use all the available tools.** *Daily Racing Form* and many track programs have added a wealth of information in recent years. Trainer statistics are priceless with first-time starters, horses trying turf for the first time, horses adding or removing blinkers, or horses racing following a claim or layoff. The horse-by-horse analysis in the *Form* also has useful information, especially on two-year-olds with little or no form available. Subscribe to Thoroughbred Times and peruse the sire statistics, especially for grass horses and two-year-olds.

3. **Watch as many races as you can.** Familiarity improves handicapping. Watch replays of races. If your track has a replay center, use it to check out the horses you are considering. Look for horses that had trouble or legitimate excuses for poor finishes. Take notes, and watch recap shows nightly. The more you see, the better you will do.

4. **Practice.** Take a few minutes and jot down what you think will be the final odds for each horse in the next race. Then note the closing odds and see how close you were. If you do this exercise repeatedly, you will quickly develop a sense of value. Do the same thing with horses racing on grass for the first time. Cover up a horse's statistics and predict on the basis of its pedigree how you believe the horse will perform on turf. This exercise takes only seconds, and it can increase your knowledge of grass pedigrees. Do the same with horses on wet tracks.

5. **Identify key races.** If you have correctly evaluated one horse's previous start, use that information to evaluate other horses coming out of the same race. One right opinion can lead to others. Also, be aware that not all races are relevant to your handicapping and scratch out meaningless races, such as grass starts when handicapping a dirt race.

That left St. John Dress, who had made two starts. In a six-furlong, maiden special weight race at Saratoga, she showed brief speed, running third behind the leader by a half-length through an initial quarter-mile in :22.54 before tiring badly and finishing tenth, beaten 23½ lengths. After a seven-week freshening, she dropped to a $50,000 maiden claimer at Belmont and carried her speed much farther in a 7½-furlong race, second by a length after a first quarter-mile in :22.89 and second by a length after a half-mile in :46.84. She tired again to finish fourth by 13 lengths in a field of eight. She had shown marked improvement in her second start and had every right to continue improving in the six-furlong race, for which trainer Bill Mott added Salix and blinkers. She made perfect sense in a race where the only other front-runner, Honoring Carolyn, was coming out of a route race, which might dull her speed in a sprint. It did. Sent off at 3.10-to-1, St. John Dress led throughout to win by 3¾ lengths over Brillant Success, the .75-to-1 favorite who chased in second the entire way, and finished 9½ lengths clear of She Can Punch in third.

Speed

If every race went to the horse with the highest speed figure, racing would become quite boring and not much fun to bet on. Speed is part of the equation, not the answer. Speed must always be considered in context. If a horse is a front-runner with good early speed, is he the lone speed in the race? Or will he be pressured? And, if so, how hard will he be pressed?

There is a world of difference between a horse running loose on the lead—running freely without pressure from other horses—and being pressed hard on the lead by one or more others. If there are three speed horses in a race, has any one of them ever rated from just off the pace? If so, has that horse won when doing so? Maybe the horse has a past-performance line four races back with that same scenario.

This is another reason to go over a horse's past-performance lines from the bottom up. For example, a race might contain three speed horses—they usually break sharply from the gate and dictate the early pace of the race. Examine the three speed horses' opening quarter-mile and half-mile times in each of their races. If one of them routinely runs a quarter in :22 and a half in :45, while the other two show :23 and :46 splits, it is reasonable to assume the other two horses will not make the lead and therefore should be discarded.

If a horse has shown speed and tired under early pressure, make sure it will be pressured again in today's race. If not, it may be able to go gate to wire, which means leading from start to finish. Also, some speed horses must be on the lead to win, and watch out for those that will not extend themselves when they do not make the lead.

Always be sure to differentiate speed in sprints from speed in races at one mile or longer, which are known as route races. A front-runner in a longer race may be able to determine the early pace while running the first half-mile in 48 seconds. If entered in a sprint, the same horse might be required to run a :46 half-mile to be on the lead.

What is Good Speed?

Almost any Thoroughbred can go a furlong (one-eighth mile) in 12 seconds (:12) and two furlongs in :24. Maintaining or exceeding that rate an additional furlong or furlongs constitutes a sharp workout, be it three furlongs in :36, four furlongs in :48, five furlongs in a minute, or six furlongs in 1:12. Factor in that training tracks are slower than main tracks, so a good workout on a training track should be given greater consideration.

Changes

Change is good, sometimes. Change is worth noting all the time, be it equipment, the use of Salix, track surface, or a change in jockey, trainer, or both. The most common equipment change is the addition or removal of blinkers. Blinkers tend to keep a horse more focused because its field of sight has been narrowed. Subsequently, most horses adding blinkers show more early speed. Conversely, horses that have blinkers removed may show less speed. Again, it is important to check a horse's past-performance lines to see whether it had ever raced with (or without) blinkers and how it performed.

Horses using Salix for the first time frequently improve greatly. Other horses improve the second time they use Salix, presumably because they become accustomed to its diuretic effects. Past performances in *Daily Racing Form* and some past-performance programs reveal how much of a difference Salix can make. For example, Live Doppler finished fourth by 18½ lengths in a one-mile, $25,000 maiden claimer at Aqueduct without Salix in on March 21, 2001. Treated with Salix a few hours before his next race under the same conditions and at the same distance, he finished second by 2½ lengths. It was the same track, same distance, and same level of competition, but a vastly different result.

A change from dirt to grass or vice versa can be a defining moment for many horses. Many times, there is absolutely no connection between a horse's form on dirt and grass. When a horse has raced on dirt and is making its first grass start, check *Daily Racing Form* statistics for the trainer's record with first-time turf horses and read the *Form*'s analysis of the race, which frequently discusses that horse's grass pedigree.

Types of Races

allowance race A race for which eligibility and weight to be carried are determined by the specific conditions of the race, such as number of career wins, earnings, or time since previous win. The lowest-level allowance race is for horses that have not won one race other than maiden or claiming. At the highest level, allowance conditions are written for horses that have not won a specific amount of purse money in their careers or within a specified period of time, such as $100,000 in the previous 12 months, or, for example, nonwinners of two races worth $40,000 (usually referring to the purse to the winner) since March 15. Allowance races are generally the second-best type of race on a card, behind stakes races.

claiming race A race for horses that can be purchased (claimed) immediately from that race for the price specified at the time of entry. The claimed horse becomes the new owner's property as soon as the starting gate opens, regardless if the horse finishes, but the previous owner collects any purse money earned by the claimed horse from that race. Claims must be entered before the race, usually ten to 15 minutes before post time depending on the state rules, and they can be made only by a person who is eligible to make claims under state rules. If more than one owner puts in a claim for the same horse, the disposition of the horse is determined by lot by the stewards. Claiming races are generally of lower class than allowance races. The lower the claiming price, the lower the class, and also the lower the purse.

futurity A stakes race, usually for two-year-olds, that is restricted to horses whose owners have made nomination payments shortly after the horse's birth and subsequently have made sustaining payments to maintain the horse's eligibility. As field sizes and quality of futurities dwindled in the 1980s, this type of race became relatively rare, and nominating conditions changed as a result. In 1972, for instance, the first payment for the Futurity Stakes (G1) at Belmont Park had to have been made by August 15, 1970, the year the horses were foaled. By 1990, the subscription deadline was May 1, 1990, for a race to be run in September 1990. Two years later, the Futurity became a stakes race, with nominations closing 17 days before the race.

handicap race A race, usually of stakes caliber, in which the racing secretary determines the amount of weight each horse will carry based on career record and current form. In theory, the handicapper seeks to assign weights so that all starters finish at the same time in a dead heat to win. Handicap races formerly placed high weight assignments on such champions as Kelso (won the 1964 Straight Face Handicap with 136 pounds) and Forego (won the 1977 Nassau County Handicap with 136 pounds), but few top-weight assignments now exceed 126 pounds.

maiden claiming race A race for nonwinning horses that can be purchased immediately from that race for a specified price (see claiming race).

maiden race A race for horses that have never won a race. Maiden races are either maiden special weight, with all horses assigned a specified weight, or maiden claiming. Additional conditions may apply, such as the race being restricted to state-breds.

optional claiming A race that is both a claiming race, for those horses entered to be claimed for a specific price, and an allowance race, for those whose owners do not enter them to be claimed.

overnight handicap A race where owners do not pay to enter their horses but are assigned weights by the racing secretary. These races generally offer some of the higher purses, on a par with the best allowance races but below stakes race purses.

restricted race A race whose starters are limited to those eligible under specified conditions, such as horses that were bred in the state where the race is held, were offered or sold at a specific sale, or by their previous winnings.

stakes race A race that is generally the highest quality race offered by a track. For stakes, owners pay a fee to nominate and enter their horses in the starting gate, with the track putting up added money to make up the difference in the total purse. Stakes races are generally the richest races run at each track and attract the best horses on the grounds, plus horses coming in from other tracks or states when the purse money is high enough to attract shippers.

starter allowance An allowance race for horses that have started for a specified minimum claiming price within a specified time. For example, some starter allowances are restricted to horses that have started for a claiming price of $10,000 or less in the previous year. Conditions of the race, meaning the weight carried, are determined by allowances.

starter handicap A race similar to a starter allowance, except the horses are assigned weights by the track racing secretary, based on current ability and form rather than allowance conditions.

Jockey changes can be important if there is a significant difference in the two riders' abilities. When a horse switches riders from a Gary Stevens to a Jerry Bailey, the impact is minimal because they are both Racing Hall of Fame jockeys. A switch from a jockey with a poor record to Bailey or vice versa is significant. When there is a rider switch, check the two riders' records.

Jockeys, just like horses, can perform at different levels on dirt and grass. Bailey is one of the top jockeys on dirt, but on grass he is in a class by himself. Other jockeys win less frequently in turf races. Usually, apprentices do better on dirt than on grass.

Layoffs

Once a horse has resumed racing after a layoff, there should not be long gaps between its races or in its workouts. These absences often are a sign of unsoundness. If a horse races well, shows no workouts for a month, and then races again, be wary. If there is a gap of more than a month between workouts, something most likely happened to stop this horse's training.

Use the statistics in the *Daily Racing Form* to see a trainer's percentage of winners with horses off significant layoffs. And go through the horse's past-performance lines from the bottom up to see if it has ever raced off similar layoffs. If it has raced off layoffs, how did it do?

Post Positions

Post positions are extremely important in turf racing because most turf courses are inside the main dirt track, thus making the turns much tighter. You can check how many winners are coming from each post position on the dirt track and grass course in the *Daily Racing Form* or program. Invariably, you will find that horses from the extreme outside posts have not done well on grass. For example, at the Pimlico 2001 spring meet from March 28 through May 6, post position eight was zero-for-14, post nine one-for-13, and post positions 10 through 12 produced no winners. You should factor that information into your handicapping. If a horse breaks from the 12 post, races wide, and rallies for fourth, it may do much better in its next start with a better post position.

On some dirt courses, races at seven furlongs and one mile may be more difficult for horses breaking from the first post position, immediately next to the rail. If a horse lacks early speed, it most likely will get caught behind faster pacesetters and will be trapped behind horses when ready to make a run at the leaders.

Trainer Patterns

Trainers have patterns and proclivities, and you should be aware of them. Some are more adept with older horses, while others excel with two-year-olds. Some do equally well on grass and dirt, while others definitely do not. Some train their horses hard, and others train lightly and allow their horses to reach peak fitness by racing them. Some trainers can have their horses fit to race off long layoffs, but others never do.

Thanks to the innovations by *Daily Racing Form* over the last few years, much of that information is readily available to all handicappers in the trainer statistics at the bottom of each horse's past-performance lines. They will show each trainer's percentage of winners with horses coming off layoffs, first time on grass, first-time starters, first start after claiming a horse, stretching out from sprint to route, and other significant statistics. Trainers also can have winning and losing streaks. If a trainer has been struggling but does well with a couple of horses, other horses in the barn may be ready to perform better, too.

Handicapping Two-Year-Olds

Handicapping horses with established form is difficult enough. Handicapping a two-year-old maiden race loaded with first-time starters is even more daunting. Here are some clues. First-time starters with several good workouts—for example, four furlongs in :48 or :49 and five furlongs in 1:00 or 1:01—do as well as those with one blazing bullet workout at three furlongs, in :35⅗ or :36. Some trainers' horses usually improve dramatically in their second or third starts. New York-based trainer Nick Zito is a prime example. Some stallions are extremely proficient at siring precocious two-year-olds. Other sires' progeny do well in distance races or on turf. Again, going through available statistics will help your handicapping.

Weight

In general, the longer the race, the more important is the weight assignment. If trainers regarded weight as unimportant, they would not rush to use every hot apprentice that shows up with a five-pound weight allowance.

Weight can be overrated, but the significant factor is how a horse's weight in today's race relates to the assignments of the other horses. If two horses had been close to each other in their previous start at equal weights and now one of them carries three pounds more and the other five pounds less, that eight-pound swing could mean a difference in the outcome.

Final Thought

In many ways, handicapping is comparable to a chess match. Many factors must be considered to forecast how a race will unfold and how those factors will affect the race's outcome. The process can be mind-twisting at first, but in time your handicapping will become more skillful and more fun. Good luck and good racing.—*Bill Heller*

Handicapping a Sample Race

The 57th running of the $400,000 Personal Ensign Handicap (G1) at Saratoga Race Course on August 27, 2004, attracted a field of just five fillies and mares, but one of them was 2002 Horse of the Year and 2002 and 2003 champion older female Azeri and another was 2002 champion two-year-old filly Storm Flag Flying. Azeri had won 16 of 21 career starts with three seconds. Storm Flag Flying had six wins, two seconds, and two thirds in 11 lifetime starts. Combined, they had earned more than $4.8-million. A third horse in the Personal Ensign, Roar Emotion, had won more than $500,000. Longshots Board Elligible and Nevermore completed the field for the 1¼-mile race. None of the five Personal Ensign starters had won at ten furlongs, and only one, Roar Emotion, had ever started at the demanding distance of 1¼ miles on dirt.

Here are the starters in the Personal Ensign in post-position order. Each horse's actual past performances follow.

1. Storm Flag Flying. After winning all four of her starts as a two-year-old, including her half-length victory in the 2002 Breeders' Cup Juvenile Fillies (G1), the daughter of My Flag and granddaughter of unbeaten champion Personal Ensign suggested greatness. But she raced just twice as a three-year-old because of injuries, finishing second in the Comely Stakes (G3) and a distant sixth in the Acorn Stakes (G1). Trainer Shug McGaughey never gave up on Ogden Mills Phipps's talented Storm Cat filly, and she returned at four to post two wins, a second, and two thirds in five 2004 starts before the Personal Ensign. Following her half-length victory in the Shuvee Handicap (G2), Storm Flag Flying was second to Sightseek in the Ogden Phipps Handicap (G1), in which she finished far ahead of Azeri, and then finished third by 3¾ lengths behind Azeri and Sightseek in the Go for Wand Handicap (G1). She carried three pounds more than Azeri in the Go for Wand, and would carry six pounds fewer in the Personal Ensign.

2. Azeri. This magnificent six-year-old mare had flirted with perfection, winning 14 of her first 15 starts, with one second. Though she lost her final start in 2003, finishing third and placed second via disqualification in the Lady's Secret Breeders' Cup Handicap (G2) at Santa Anita Park, she was voted champion older female for the second straight season. Then Azeri's owner switched trainers, from Laura de Seroux to D. Wayne Lukas. Though she had been off for more than six months, Azeri made a spectacular return, winning Oaklawn Park's Apple Blossom Handicap (G1) for a third consecutive year. Then Azeri lost three straight, finishing second by a head in the seven-furlong Humana Distaff Handicap (G1) to Mayo On the Side; an uncharacteristically poor eighth against males in the one-mile Metropolitan Handicap (G1), and fourth by 11¾ lengths to Sightseek in the 1¹⁄₁₆-mile Ogden Phipps. Her fans feared she might have lost her desire to race, but she smashed that theory to bits by defeating Sightseek by 1¾ lengths in her next start, the 1⅛-mile Go for Wand. With Sightseek skipping the Personal Ensign, Azeri figured to be a deserving heavy favorite, though people wondered whether her final workout, a sizzling six furlongs in 1:11.60 over the deep Oklahoma training track at Saratoga, would hinder her in her first start at ten furlongs. She had raced on or close to the lead in most of her races. She disputed a fast first half-mile of :45.73 on the way to three-quarters in 1:10.18 in the Ogden Phipps and tired badly behind Sightseek. In the Go for Wand, she ran on the lead through a softer half-mile of :47.75 on the way to three-quarters of a mile in 1:10.90.

3. Nevermore. Talk about taking a difficult step up. Nevermore, making her first career stakes start, was taking on two multiple Grade 1 stakes winners off a second by 4¼ lengths in a nonwinners of four allowance race in her return from a ten-week layoff. Her biggest assets were her connections, trainer H. James Bond and jockey Edgar Prado.

4. Roar Emotion. This speedy four-year-old filly was no slouch, having won five of 13 races with three seconds, two thirds, and earnings of more than $580,000. She had only been beaten a half-length by Storm Flag Flying when third in the Shuvee three starts earlier. Roar Emotion encountered a sloppy track in her two starts before the Personal Ensign, finishing a distant sixth in the Fleur de Lis Handicap (G2) at Churchill Downs and then a game second by 1¼ lengths to Summer Wind Dancer in the 1¼-mile Delaware Handicap (G2) at Delaware Park. She would be carrying 115 pounds, seven fewer than Azeri. Would it matter?

5. Board Elligible. This underrated, late-running four-year-old filly had four wins and two photo-finish seconds in her six previous dirt starts. Like Nevermore, she was taking a major step up, but the distance certainly would not be a problem. In her four prior dirt starts at 1⅛ miles, she had three wins and a close second.

Analysis: Azeri's rider, Pat Day, would be forced to make a crucial early decision. Roar Emotion's jockey, Jerry Bailey, was almost certain to send her to the lead, forcing Day to decide whether he would dispute a potentially fast pace. Azeri had been cooked in a speed duel in the Ogden Phipps, but she had gotten loose on

SARATOGA APPROX. POST: 5:18PM — **Exacta, Trifecta, Daily Double Wagers**

9

1 1/4 MILE (▲START ▲FINISH)

EX | TR | WIN | PLACE | SHOW

The 57th Running of THE PERSONAL ENSIGN (Grade I)
$400,000
(Up to $48,000 NYSBFOA)

STAKES. A HANDICAP FOR FILLIES AND MARES THREE YEARS OLD AND UPWARD. By subscription of $400 each, which should accompany the nomination; $2,000 to pass the entry box and $2,000 to start. The purse to be divided 60% to the winner, 20% to second, 10% to third, 5% to fourth, 3% to fifth and 2% divided equally among remaining finishers. Trophies will be presented to the winning owner, trainer and jockey. Closed Saturday, August 14, 2004 with 12 Nominations. **One Mile And One Quarter**

Track Record: General Assembly (3), 126 lbs; 2:00 (8-18-79)

Pgm # | Owner | Wgt | Jockey | Trainer

1 Red — **5-2**
Ogden Mills Phipps, et al — Black, Cherry Cap — Trainer: **Claude R. McGaughey III** (36-5-7-7)
Storm Flag Flying (L) — **116** — **John R. Velazquez** (227-65-28-30)
Dk B/ Br.f.4 Storm Cat -My Flag by Easy Goer
Br.Phipps Stable, Kentucky (Apr 11, 2000)

Life:	11	6	2	2	$1,236,828	Turf:	0	0	0	0 $0
2004:	5	2	1	2	$248,248	Off Track:	2	2	0	0 $640,000
2003:	2	0	1	0	$21,580	Distance:	0	0	0	0 $0
						Course:	2	1	0	1 $52,000

01Aug04	Sar9 ft	1⅛	:4775	1:1090	1:4786	3↑F	GoFWandHG1 -250k	60-89	1	31½	31	42	33½	33¾	Velazquez J R	117 L	3.05	**Azeri**1201¾ Sightseek1222 StormFlagFlying1177	steadied rail 1st turn	5
19Jun04	Bel9 ft	11⁄16	:4573	1:1018	1:4146	3↑F	OPhippsHG1 -300k	72-86	4	31	3½	3½	26	23¼	Velazquez J R	117 L	3.00	Sightseek1203¼ StormFlagFlying1176½ PassingShot1162	3 wide bid,no match	4
15May04	Bel8 ft	1m	:4676	1:1128	1:3610	3↑F	ShuveeHG2 -200k	52-79	2	42½	31	41	31½	1½	Velazquez J R	116 L	*1.00	StormFlagFlying116½ PassingShot117ns **RoarEmotion**1178¼	along late outside	6
27Mar04	Aqu8 ft	7f	:2281	:4635	1:2264	3↑F	DistfBCHG2 -150k	82-82	2	3	2½	32	36½	35¾	Prado E S	118 L	2.10	Randaroo1213½ Chirimoya1102¼ *StormFlagFlying* 11811¼	inside,no response	4
26Feb04	GP8 ft	170	:4655	1:1192	1:4278	4↑F	Aoc 46000nw2$/r/6mx	80-88	7	31	21½	2½	11	13¾	Velazquez J R	115 L	*.80	StormFlagFlying1153¾ RedoubledMiss1191¼ KeiaiSakura1153¼	drew away,driving	7
06Jun03	Bel10 ft	1m	:4635	1:1040	1:3529	3 F	AcornG1 -250k	70-78	1	4¾	72	77½	713	611	Velazquez J R	121 L	*1.70	BirdTown121hd *LadyTak* 1211 FinalRound1213¼	between rivals,empty	7
18Apr03	Aqu8 ft	1m	:4535	1:1012	1:3597	3 F	ComelyG3 -100k	84-82	1	31	21½	32½	27	25½	Velazquez J R	122 L	*.25	CyberSecret1225½ StormFlagFlying1223 Bonay1162¼	chased,stayed on	5
26Oct02	AP4 gd	1⅛	:4628	1:1031	1:4960	2 F	BCJuvFilG1 -1000k	89-94	3	22	32	21	2hd	1½	Velazquez J R	119 L	*.80	StormFlagFlying119½ Composure1199¾ *SantaCatarina* 1192	headed,very game	10
05Oct02	Bel6 ft	1⅛	:4758	1:1226	1:4420	2 F	FrizetteG1 -500k	74-86	3	31	2½	2½	1½	12	Velazquez J R	120 L	*.60	*StormFlagFlying* 1202 SantaCatarina12011¼ ApplebyGardens1203	when asked,shown whip	7
15Sep02	Bel6 gd	1m	:4605	1:1259	1:3852	2 F	MatronG1 -200k	82-81	2	31½	32	2hd	13	112¾	Velazquez J R	119 L	*1.40	*StormFlagFlying* 11912¾ *WildSnitch* 1191 Fircroft1195¼	greenly,kept busy	7

Workout(s): 24 Oct 04 Bel 4F ft :48.22b 7/41 — 3 Oct 04 Bel 4F ft :47.71h 5/57 — 27 Sep 04 Bel 5F ft 1:00.12b 3/45 — 20 Sep 04 Bel 4F ft :48.27b 22/89

2 White — **3-5**
Allen E. Paulson Living Trust (M. Paulson, trustee) — White, Red Yoke, Blue and Red 'AP,' Blue Sleeves, White Stars, Blue Cap — Trainer: **D. Wayne Lukas** (76-4-15-10)
Azeri (L) — **122** — **Pat Day** (97-13-16-10)
Ch.m.6 Jade Hunter -Zodiac Miss (AUS) by Ahonoora (GB)
Br.Allen E. Paulson, Kentucky (May 06, 1998)

Life:	21	16	3	0	$3,569,820	Turf:	0	0	0	0 $0
2004:	5	2	1	0	$525,000	Off Track:	1	1	0	0 $1,040,000
2003:	5	4	1	0	$817,080	Distance:	0	0	0	0 $0
						Course:	1	1	0	0 $150,000

01Aug04	Sar9 ft	1⅛	:4775	1:1090	1:4786	3↑F	GoFWandHG1 -250k	62-92	5	11½	1½	1½	1hd	11¾	Day P	120 L	2.95	Azeri1201¾ Sightseek1222 **StormFlagFlying**1177	pace,resolute,clear	5
19Jun04	Bel9 ft	11⁄16	:4573	1:1018	1:4146	3↑F	OPhippsHG1 -300k	73-79	1	1½	1hd	2½	410	411¾	Day P	123 L	*.80	Sightseek1203¼ **StormFlagFlying**1176½ PassingShot1162	set pace,tired	4
31May04	Bel9 ft	1m	:46	1:1004	1:3547	3↑	MtropltHG1 -750k	66-82	3	32½	3½	51¼	62¾	86¾	Day P	117 L	5.80	PicoCentral119¾ Bowman'sBand1142¼ StrongHope1191½	close up inside,empty	9
01May04	CD8 ft	7f	:2249	:4504	1:2278	4↑F	HmnaDstHG1 -250k	88-89	2	4	21	21½	2hd	2hd	Smith M E	125 L	*.70	MayoOntheSide114hd Azeri1257¼ Randaroo121nk	bid btwn,game rail	4
03Apr04	OP9 ft	11⁄16	:4671	1:1099	1:4124	4↑F	AplBlsmHG1 -500k	68-92	1	11	1½	11½	12½	11½	Smith M E	123 L	2.00	Azeri1231½ WildSpirit1191¾ StarParade1147¼	pace off rail,driving	6
28Sep03	SA6 ft	11⁄16	:4723	1:1129	1:4292	3↑F	LdyScBCHG2 -300k	72-88	5	54½	53½	53½	32	32¼*	Smith M E	128 BL	*.20	GotKoko118½ Elloluv1161¾ *Azeri* 1281	3wd into lane,no bid,PL2nd	6
10Aug03	Dmr8 ft	11⁄16	:4709	1:1104	1:4212	3↑F	CLHrschHG2 -300k	72-89	1	11	1½	11½	12½	13¼	Smith M E	127 BL	*.30	Azeri1273¼ *GotKoko* 118hd TropicalBlossom1084½	bit off rail,handily	5
21Jun03	Hol8 ft	1⅛	:4731	1:1066	1:4848	3↑F	VanityHG1 -250k	87-91	6	2½	1hd	2hd	11	12	Smith M E	127 BL	*.30	*Azeri* 1272 SisterGirlBlues111½ *BareNecessities* 1184½	dueled,inched clear	7
24May03	Hol8 ft	11⁄16	:4623	1:1013	1:4187	3↑F	MladyBCHG1 -200k	87-92	4	2hd	11	12½	12½	13	Smith M E	125 BL	*.20	*Azeri* 1253 Enjoy1143 TropicalBlossom1111	speed,met bids,clear	6
05Apr03	OP8 ft	1⅛	:4870	1:1238	1:43	4↑F	AplBlsmHG1 -500k	63-92	6	32	42	2½	21½	1hd	Smith M E	123 L	*.40	*Azeri* 123hd TakeChargeLady1183¼ *Mandy'sGold* 1162	restrained,4-w,game	7

Workout(s): 9 Nov 04 CD 4F ft :47.60b 3/32 — •20 Oct 04 CD 6F ft 1:13.40b 1/4 — •3 Oct 04 CD 5F ft :59.20b 1/25 — •27 Sep 04 CD 6F ft 1:12.20b 1/6

3

William L. Clifton, Jr.
Maroon, White Diamond Frame, White Diamonds on Sleeves, Maroon Cap

Nevermore (L) 110 — **Edgar S. Prado** (242-39-50-32)

Blue **15-1**
B.f.4 Unbridled -Teewinot by Vice Regent
Br.Farfellow Farms Ltd., Kentucky (Mar 26, 2000) KEESEP01 $425,000

H. James Bond (23-5-2-2)

Life:	8	3	2	0	$96,730	Turf:	1	0	0	0	$0
2004:	4	3	1	0	$84,800	Off Track:	0	0	0	0	$0
2003:	3	0	1	0	$10,580	Distance:	1	0	0	0	$0
						Course:	2	0	2	0	$19,600

01Aug04	Sar7 ft	⊗1⅛	:4951	1:1343	1:5025	4↑F	Alw 52000nw3/x	41-78	3	42½	31½	31½	32½	24¼	Velazquez J R	120	L	*1.20	*BoundingCharm* 1184¼ Nevermore1202 ViewFromtheTop1201¼	rallied for place	5
23May04	Bel7 ft	1¹⁄₁₆	:4577	1:1070	1:4331	3↑F	Alw 48000nw2/x	62-80	1	68½	67	51¾	2hd	13	Velazquez J R	124	L	4.90	Nevermore1243 LaMinuta1211 *Hanselina* 1184½	4 wide move,clear	6
18Apr04	Aqu8 ft	1⅛	:5208	1:1684	1:5381	3↑F	Alw 44000nw1/x	22-66	5	52	52½	52	21½	1nk	Luzzi M J	122	L	2.10	*Nevermore* 122nk MamboBell1175 Esther'sStar1192¼	ducked out start	5
23Feb04	GP7 ft	1¹⁄₁₆	:4801	1:1343	1:4699	4 F	Msw	47-72	5	1110	1112	55½	11	15	Velazquez J R	121	L	3.40	*Nevermore* 1215 WyeRiver1212 OldMotherGoose1212¼	4 wide, drew off	11
16Oct03	Bel3 ft	1¹⁄₁₆	:4850	1:1377	1:4603	3↑F	Msw	43-54	2	53½	35½	36	514	523½	Prado E S	119	L	*1.45	Dynarhythm1192¾ PleasantGhost1149¼ VeiledThreat119ns	chased pace, tired	6
04Oct03	Bel4 fm	T1¼	:5049	1:4123	2:0564	3↑F	Msw	80-63	8	31	41	62¼	1118	1121	Velazquez J R	119	L	3.60	KeyDefinition112nk Reverence119ns *SilverClipper* 1174	chased 3 wide, tired	11
27Aug03	Sar6 ft	1⅛	:4778	1:1216	1:5251	3↑F	Msw	67-73	6	54½	46	36½	23½	23½	Prado E S	118	L	3.00	HardasNails1183½ Nevermore1186¼ *Yarico'sPond* 1186	3 wide move, gamely	7
08Nov02	Aqu6 ft	7f	:2330	:4649	1:2398	2 F	Msw	45-72	4	8	78½	711	68¾	58½	Prado E S	120	L	7.50	HouseParty1201 CherokeeLite1201½ *Yell* 1203	some interest late	8

Workout(s): 30 Oct 04 Bel tr 4F gd :48.90b 5/16 — 23 Oct 04 Bel 4F ft :47.98b 11/52 — •7 Oct 04 Sar tr 3F ft :36.28b 1/6 — 2 Oct 04 Sar tr 6F ft 1:15.94b 1/1

4

Joseph Allen
Green and White Blocks, Green Sleeves, White Stripes, Green Cap

Roar Emotion (L) 115 — **Jerry D. Bailey** (131-29-24-23)

Yellow **4-1**
Dk B/ Br.f.4 Roar -Emotional Outburst by Capote
Br.Brenda Jones, Kentucky (Mar 30, 2000) OBSAPR02 $37,000

Kiaran P. McLaughlin (47-6-8-8)

Life:	13	5	3	2	$583,490	Turf:	0	0	0	0	$0
2004:	7	2	1	2	$276,230	Off Track:	4	1	2	0	$279,600
2003:	3	1	1	0	$150,660	Distance:	1	0	1	0	$150,000
						Course:	0	0	0	0	$0

18Jul04	Del10 sy	1¼	:4712	1:3693	2:0363	3↑F	DelHG2 -750k	63-84	5	12½	11½	12	14	21¼	Bailey J D	117	LA	3.60	SummerWindDancer1161¼ RoarEmotion1175¾ MistySixes116¾	gamely to the end	8
12Jun04	CD8 sy	1⅛	:4778	1:1285	1:5215	3↑F	FlrDLisHG2 -400k	84-74	3	11	11	1½	54½	615¾	Bailey J D	115	cL	4.00	Adoration1221¼ BareNecessities1203¾ *LaReason* 1102	bobble start, tired	6
15May04	Bel8 ft	1m	:4676	1:1128	1:3610	3↑F	ShuveeHG2 -200k	53-79	6	2½	2½	2hd	2hd	3½	Luzzi M J	117	cL	3.10	**StormFlagFlying**116½ PassingShot117ns RoarEmotion1178¼	vied outside, gamely	6
16Apr04	Kee9 ft	1¹⁄₁₆	:4763	1:1255	1:4392	4↑F	Dbldogdare -100k	62-83	6	31	31½	3nk	2hd	34	Velazquez J R	116	L	*1.80	*MayoOntheSide* 1161¾ CatFighter1162¼ RoarEmotion116½	4w, loomed, empty	8
14Mar04	GP6 ft	1⅛	:4846	1:1181	1:5107	3↑F	RampartHG2 -200k	67-69	1	11½	11	1hd	26	418½	Velazquez J R	118	L	1.50	Sightseek1217½ RedoubledMiss1132 *LeadStory* 1179	inside, nothing left	4
15Feb04	GP11 ft	1¹⁄₁₆	:4766	1:1198	1:4332	3↑F	SabinHG3 -100k	65-83	6	21	2hd	2hd	14	15½	Velazquez J R	116	L	2.20	RoarEmotion1165½ *NonsuchBay* 115¾ LeadStory1191¾	vied, drew off	9
15Jan04	GP8 ft	1¹⁄₁₆	:4775	1:1259	1:4509	4↑F	Aoc 38000nw3/x	80-83	6	11½	11	11½	11	11	Velazquez J R	117	L	*.70	*RoarEmotion* 1171 *KissMeTwice* 11712¾ PaisleyPark1171	inside, driving	8
28Jun03	Bel9 ft	1⅛	:4654	1:1163	1:5041	3 F	MthrGoosG1 -300k	92-77	6	1hd	1hd	1hd	511	519½	Santos J A	121	L	3.20	*SpokenFur* 1215¼ Yell1213¾ FinalRound1218¼	ducked out start	6
16May03	Pim10 sy	1⅛	:4771	1:1223	1:5233	3 F	BlkEySsnG2 -200k	91-90	1	11½	11½	1hd	15	1½	Velazquez J R	122	L	3.40	RoarEmotion122½ Fircroft1198½ *SantaCatarina* 1175¾	well rated 2wd, driving	8

Workout(s): 1 Nov 04 Bel 4F ft :48.76b 13/34 — 12 Oct 04 Bel 4F ft :48.12b 8/35 — 5 Oct 04 Bel 4F ft :50.55b 17/22 — •21 Sep 04 Sar tr 4F ft :48.75b 1/36

5

Rudina Stable
Gold, Black Ball, Gold 'RD,' Gold and Black Halved Sleeves, Gold Cap

Board Elligible Ⓝ (L) 112 — **Pablo Fragoso** (169-15-19-21)

Green **10-1**
Blk.f.4 Goldminers Gold -Double Boarded by Cormorant
Br.Dr. Bernard Abramovici, New York (Mar 30, 2000)

James W. Ferraro (14-1-0-0)

Life:	27	7	7	0	$298,156	Turf:	4	0	1	0	$21,166
2004:	10	4	3	0	$166,076	Off Track:	6	1	3	0	$65,340
2003:	17	3	4	0	$132,080	Distance:	1	0	0	0	$608
						Course:	2	1	0	0	$38,760

12Aug04	Sar8 sy	1⅛	:4673	1:1182	1:5078	4↑F	Aoc 60000cnd	68-84	5	66	65½	41¾	11½	14¼	Fragoso P	120	bL	3.05	BoardElligible1204¼ Childress1163¾ JaramarRain11810½	inside move, clear	6
20Jun04	Bel6 yl	T1⅛	:4736	1:1189	1:4867	3↑F S	MtVernonH -75k	71-76	1	811	69½	66¾	78¾	78½	Bridgmohan S	114	bfL	7.40	BigTease1151¾ BeebeLake114½ Raffie'sDream1143	wide, no response	8
05Jun04	Bel5 ft	1¹⁄₁₆	:4564	1:1009	1:4208	4↑F R	WhtCrntion -70k	63-83	2	98¼	75¾	53¼	1½	11¼	Castellano J	116	bcfL	14.00	BoardElligible1161¼ PrincessDixie1202 SaintlyAction1182½	stumbled start, 4 wide	9
12May04	Bel8 gd	T1¼	:5128	1:4040	2:0456	4↑F R	Sabin -60k	60-79	4	64	62¾	64¾	77½	79½	Castellano J	116	bfL	13.60	Humaita116½ Noisette123½ Primetimevalentine1161½	no response	7
16Apr04	Aqu8 ft	1⅛	:4829	1:1282	1:5019	3↑F	Alw 46000nw2/x	58-87	1	67½	66½	64¾	1hd	12½	Castellano J	121	bcfL	4.90	BoardElligible1212½ ChaseGap1223¼ RareGift1174	4 wide move, clear	6
31Mar04	Aqu8 my	1⅛	:4791	1:1306	1:5255	4↑F R	NumbAcct -60k	59-79	4	710	79½	42½	2½	2ns	Castellano J	115	bcfL	8.90	*OurTune* 115ns *BoardElligible* 1152 HotGoldenJet115ns	3 wide move, missed	7
04Mar04	Aqu6 ft	⊙1¹⁄₁₆	:4993	1:1454	1:4442	4↑F	Alw 46000nw2/x	28-73	5	64	64½	63½	1hd	2hd	Fragoso P	115⁵	bcfL	5.10	LadyLibby120hd BoardElligible1151 SuaveQueen118nk	game finish outside	6

Workout(s): 3 Oct 04 Aqu 5F ft 1:02.25b 3/6 — •20 Sep 04 Aqu ⊙ 5F ft 1:01.07b 1/5 — 22 Aug 04 Sar tr 4F my :51.48b 7/9 — 7 Aug 04 Sar 4F ft :51.12b 47/57

*(NYSBFOA) New York Breeding Fund Owner Awards. (Non Purse Monies) (L) Treated with Lasix; (L1) First Time using Lasix; (0) Coming off Lasix; Ⓝ - New York Bred

the lead in the Go for Wand. Roar Emotion's presence meant Azeri most likely would not be running free on the lead in the Personal Ensign. Azeri had not won a race by stalking from off the pace since April 2003, when she won her second Apple Blossom. Was that a reason to resist betting Azeri at 3-to-5? The lone filly with a legitimate chance to beat her, Storm Flag Flying, went off at 2.15-to-1 under John Velazquez. Roar Emotion went off at 7.10-to-1, Board Elligible was 17.10-to-1, and Nevermore 18.30-to-1.

Result: Day decided to let Roar Emotion set the pace, keeping Azeri 1½ lengths back in second through an initial quarter-mile in :23.15 and a half-mile in :46.26. Azeri went after Roar Emotion on the far turn and took command after three-quarters in 1:09.78 and a mile in 1:35.94. Azeri had a 1½-length lead at the top of Saratoga's stretch, but Storm Flag Flying, a patient third the entire way, surged to challenge. Azeri held her off until the eighth pole, but then Storm Flag Flying took over, winning by 1¼ lengths in 2:03.63. Azeri gamely saved second by a half-length over Nevermore.—*Bill Heller*

How To Read a Race Chart

A race chart is a comprehensive explanation of exactly how a race unfolded and how it was won or lost. Experienced handicappers often save charts of all races at the tracks they play most often because the charts are the most definitive written description of a race. To read a chart, you need to understand the terminology and abbreviations used to summarize the details of a race. Let's look at the accompanying example on this page.

Personal Ensign H.- Grade 1
Purse: $400,000 Guaranteed

NINTH RACE
Saratoga
August 27, 2004

Stakes. Purse $400,000. 3 years old and up, fillies and mares. 1¼ miles dirt. Track: Fast

Value of race: $392,000. Value to winner: $240,000; second: $80,000; third: $40,000; fourth: $20,000; fifth, $12,000.

P# Horse	Wgt	M/Eqt	PP	¼	½	¾	Mile	Str.	Fin.	Jockey	Odds
1 Storm Flag Flying	116	L	1	3²¹²	3³¹²	3²¹²	3¹¹²	1ʰᵈ	1¹¹⁴	J R Velazquez	2.15
2 Azeri	122	L	2	2³¹²	2⁶	2⁷	1¹¹²	2²¹²	2¹²	P Day	.60
3 Nevermore	114	L	3	4⁶	4⁴¹²	4¹¹²	4³	3³	3⁴¹²	E S Prado	18.30
5 Board Elligible	112	L b	5	5	5	5	5	4⁷	4¹⁶	P Fragoso	17.10
4 Roar Emotion	115	L c	4	1¹¹²	1¹¹²	1ʰᵈ	2ʰᵈ	5	5	J D Bailey	7.10

OFF AT 5:18. Start: Good for all. Won: Driving. Temp: 78°. Weather: Cloudy
Time of race: :23.15, :46.26, 1:09.78, 1:35.94, 2:03.63.

Total W/P/S Pool: $680,050
Mutuel Payoffs

1—Storm Flag Flying $6.30	$2.50	$2.10	
2—Azeri	2.30	2.10	
3—Nevermore		2.10	

EXACTA 1-2 PAID $11.00   Total Pool: $467,919
TRIFECTA 1-2-3 PAID $50.50   Total Pool: $272,368

Winner: Storm Flag Flying, dk.b. or br. f., by Storm Cat—My Flag, by Easy Goer
Bred in Kentucky by Phipps Stable

STORM FLAG FLYING was unhurried while racing away from the rail early on, was patiently handled on the backstretch, advanced three wide approaching the stretch, responded when roused, collared AZERI coming to the eighth pole, dug in resolutely and was clear under the wire. AZERI raced in hand along the inside early, was eased to the outside after allowing ROAR EMOTION to set the pace, advanced outside on the backstretch, took over from that rival entering the second turn, drew clear, responded when joined by the winner in upper stretch, could not stay with that one in the final sixteenth and dug in determinedly on the rail to earn the place award. NEVERMORE was unhurried while outrun early, advanced inside on the second turn, came wide into the stretch, responded to steady pressure and finished gamely outside. BOARD ELLIGIBLE was outrun early along the inside, angled out entering the stretch and lacked a rally. ROAR EMOTION showed good speed while in hand, soon had a clear lead, set the pace along the inside, could not keep up with AZERI after entering the second turn and tired in the stretch.

Owners: (1) Phipps, Ogden Mills, et al.; (2) Allen E. Paulson Living Trust; (3) William L. Clifton Jr.; (5) Rudina Stable; (4) Joseph Allen

Trainers: (1) C R McGaughey III; (2) D W Lukas; (3) H J Bond; (5) J W Ferraro; (4) K P McLaughlin

The chart's heading lists the bare facts of the race: The Personal Ensign Handicap (G1) was the ninth race at Saratoga Race Course on August 27, 2004; it was a Grade 1 race; it was run at 1¼ miles on the main dirt track for fillies and mares three years old and older, and it had a $400,000 purse, with $240,000 to the winner and lesser amounts to the other finish positions.

The chart lists the runners according to their order of finish and provides considerable information about each horse. Following the horse's name is the actual weight she carried, an indication of race-day medication received, and the equipment used. All Personal Ensign starters were treated with the diuretic furosemide (L), which reduces pulmonary bleeding, and only Board Elligible wore blinkers (b), which help a horse to concentrate during a race.

The next figures indicate how the race was run in a numerical format. The first figure is the horse's post position, from the rail out. The next figures are the points of call in the race. The points of call—where the Equibase chart caller describes the distances separating the runners—vary depending on the distance of the race. In a six-furlong race, for instance, the points of call are after one-quarter mile, one-half mile, and the stretch call, which is always one-eighth add the finish. Races of a mile or longer add a point of call at three-quarters of a mile. Races at 1¼ miles use one-quarter mile, one-half mile, three-quarters mile, one mile, midstretch, and then the finish. The superscript number with the running position indicates how far that horse was ahead of the next horse, and the finish number indicates the margin for the winner and the distances separating the other finishers. The horse's jockey is identified next, and the last column contains the final odds on each horse. At 2.15-to-1, Storm Flag Flying was the second betting choice behind 0.60-to-1 (3-to-5) favorite Azeri.

Below the running positions is information about scratches, if any; the time the race went off; the start ("Good for all" means that every horse had a fair start); the temperature and weather; the fractional times; and the final time of the race.

Continuing down the page, the next figures report the mutuel payouts—for instance, Storm Flag Flying paid $6.30 on a $2 bet to win, $2.50 to place, and $2.10 to show—and the pool size, which is the total amount of money bet to win, place, and show.

Underneath that information is the pedigree of the winner. Storm Flag Flying is a dark bay or brown filly (dk. b. or br. f.) who is four years old. Her sire is Storm Cat, and her dam is My Flag. The sire of her dam is Easy Goer. Storm Flag Flying was bred in Kentucky by the Phipps Stable. She was in fact the last major stakes winner bred by the late Ogden Phipps, who also bred Personal Ensign and her daughter My Flag, dam of Storm Flag Flying.

Below that information is a narrative of how the race was run, written by the Equibase chart caller, followed by the owners and trainers of the starters, listed according to their horses' finish order.

About the Personal Ensign

The Personal Ensign shows how pace can affect the outcome of a race. As expected, Jerry Bailey sent Roar Emotion to the early lead, and Pat Day decided to keep Azeri in a stalking position approximately 1½ lengths behind Roar Emotion. Storm Flag Flying, the second favorite, followed Azeri in third position.

The key to the race is contained in the fractional times. The first quarter-mile went in :23.15, which—allowing for the 1½-length margin behind Roar Emotion—was roughly equal to Azeri's losing pace in the Ogden Phipps (:23.32), a race that was three-sixteenths of a mile shorter than the Personal Ensign. The pace actually picked up in the second quarter-mile of the Personal Ensign, which Roar Emotion completed in :23.11, thus making the half-mile time :46.26, with Azeri still 1½ lengths off the leader. The most telling fraction, however, was the three-quarter split. As Azeri and Day attempted to reel in Roar Emotion, the pace barely slackened, and the early leader did not surrender easily. With Roar Emotion leading by a head, the third quarter-mile went in :23.52, making the three-quarter time, 1:09.78, faster than both the Ogden Phipps (1:10.18) and the Go for Wand (1:10.90). Even a mare of Azeri's vast talent cannot maintain such a pace in a 1¼-mile race.

By contrast, Storm Flag Flying and jockey John Velazquez declined to chase such a fast pace. Trailing Azeri by 3½ lengths after a quarter-mile, Storm Flag Flying was six lengths behind her after a half-mile, and seven lengths back after six furlongs. In a distance race, those seven lengths translate into more than a second and a half. (The longtime rule of thumb is that a length equals one-fifth of a second, but the actual time required for a horse to complete one length varies in sprints and distance races.)

Azeri took the lead after a mile 1:35.94, but the early pace doomed her. Storm Flag Flying overtook her before the furlong pole—the stretch call in the chart—and coasted to a 1¼-length victory. Azeri held on for second by a half-length; still, Nevermore had gained two lengths on her in the final furlong. Board Elligible, never a factor in the race, finished fourth because Roar Emotion had exhausted herself while setting a ruinous pace through six furlongs.

—Don Clippinger

How Pari-Mutuel Wagering Began

Virtually all betting on horse races in North America, as in most countries, is conducted using the pari-mutuel wagering system. Unlike a casino, where bettors play against the house, racehorse bettors bet against each other, with the track holding the bets and, after taking out money for the track, purses, state taxes, and other mandated deductions, returning the money bet to the winning patrons after each race is run.

Unlike most traditions in North American horse racing, pari-mutuel wagering came from France rather than England. The system was devised in the mid-1860s by Pierre Oller, a Paris perfume merchant who had become disenchanted with the city's bookmakers.

Oller developed a variation of the auction pool, in which betting interests in individual horses were sold. Because fairly large sums of money were required to buy the winning interest in a favorite in the auction pools, they were not widely used by small-scale bettors. Oller's system allowed small wagers on all horses and quickly came into wide use in France. He called his wagering system perier mutuel, which means to wager among ourselves. Adopted in England, it became known as Paris mutuals, and finally pari-mutuel.

New York tracks used the pari-mutuel system (known then as Paris pools) in the early 1870s. Col. M. Lewis Clark, the founder of Churchill Downs, observed the pari-mutuels in operation during a sojourn in Europe in the early 1870s and introduced the devices at his track in 1878. (Auction pools were used in 1875, 1876, and 1877, the first three years of Churchill's existence.)

Bookmakers soon made their appearance in both New York and Louisville, and the popularity of betting with bookmakers supplanted the pari-mutuel machines. Clark abandoned pari-mutuels in 1889 at the demand of bookmakers.

In 1908, however, anti-Churchill forces took over City Hall and banned bookmaking. Col. Matt Winn, then the track's general manager, rounded up six of the old pari-mutuel machines, refurbished them, and used them for betting on the 1908 Kentucky Derby. Pari-mutuel wagering on the Derby day program that year was $67,570 ($18,300 of that total on the Derby, won by Stone Street at 23.72-to-1 odds), with another $12,669 in auction pools.

The first machines sold only one denomination of ticket, $5 for the 1908 Derby program, but by 1911 Winn had commissioned new machines that offered $2, $5, and $10 tickets. By 1914, most American tracks had switched to the pari-mutuel system as anti-gambling sentiment led to bans against bookmaking.

Betting Odds and Payouts

Pari-mutuel betting odds are based on the percentage of the net wagering pool placed on each horse. For instance, a horse sent off at even money, or 1-to-1 odds, has attracted 50% of the net wagering pool.

The net wagering pool on which the odds are based is total wagering minus deductions broadly known as takeout—money taken out for state tax, horsemen's purses, the track's share, and other deductions. Total wagering is known as handle, which the track holds until after each race is run and then returns the net balance to winning bettors.

When devising a program betting line, a line maker generally will assign odds based on 125% of handle to account for takeout.

All tracks in North America show payouts after each race on their tote boards based on a $2 wager. To figure the exact odds, for instance, at which a horse went off in the win pool, subtract the $2 bet and divide by two. If a horse paid $4.70 to win, its winning odds were 1.35-to-1 ([$4.70-$2]/2=1.35).

Exact betting odds usually are rounded down to the nearest 10 cents, although some jurisdictions round to the next lowest 5 cents.

Pari-Mutuel Odds	Percentage of Net Pool	Payout
1-to-20	95.23%	$2.10
1-to-10	90.91%	2.20
1-to-5	83.33%	2.40
2-to-5	71.42%	2.80
1-to-2	66.66%	3.00
4-to-5	55.55%	3.60
Even (1-to-1)	50.00%	4.00
7-to-5	41.67%	4.80
9-to-5	35.71%	5.60
2-to-1	33.33%	6.00
5-to-2	28.57%	7.00
3-to-1	25.00%	8.00
7-to-2	22.23%	9.00
4-to-1	20.00%	10.00
9-to-2	18.19%	11.00
5-to-1	16.67%	12.00
10-to-1	9.09%	22.00
15-to-1	6.25%	32.00
20-to-1	4.76%	42.00
30-to-1	3.23%	62.00
50-to-1	1.96%	102.00
100-to-1	0.99%	202.00

Distance Equivalents

Race distances are directly or indirectly derived from distances conventionally run in England, the cradle of Thoroughbred racing. Distances of English races are measured in the traditional English system of furlongs and miles. A furlong is 660 feet, or one-eighth of a mile, and a mile comprises eight furlongs.

France has used the metric system instituted by Napoleon since the inception of racing in that country. As racing countries around the world have adopted the metric system of measurement, racing distances often have been changed to metric equivalents.

The following table includes equivalent distances for both systems.

Furlongs to Meters

Furlongs	Miles	Approx. Meters	Exact Meters
1.00	$\frac{1}{8}$	200	201.168
2.00	$\frac{1}{4}$	400	402.336
3.00	$\frac{3}{8}$	600	603.504
4.00	$\frac{1}{2}$	800	804.672
4.50	$\frac{9}{16}$	900	905.256
5.00	$\frac{5}{8}$	1,000	1,005.840
5.50	$\frac{11}{16}$	1,100	1,106.424
6.00	$\frac{3}{4}$	1,200	1,207.008
6.50	$\frac{13}{16}$	1,300	1,307.592
7.00	$\frac{7}{8}$	1,400	1,408.176
7.50	$\frac{15}{16}$	1,500	1,508.760
8.00	1	1,600	1,609.344
8.32	1&70 yds.	1,670	1,673.717
8.50	$1\frac{1}{16}$	1,700	1,709.928
9.00	$1\frac{1}{8}$	1,800	1,810.512
9.50	$1\frac{3}{16}$	1,900	1,911.096
10.00	$1\frac{1}{4}$	2,000	2,011.680
10.50	$1\frac{5}{16}$	2,100	2,112.264
11.00	$1\frac{3}{8}$	2,200	2,212.848
11.50	$1\frac{7}{16}$	2,300	2,313.432
12.00	$1\frac{1}{2}$	2,400	2,414.016
12.50	$1\frac{9}{16}$	2,500	2,514.600
13.00	$1\frac{5}{8}$	2,600	2,615.184
13.50	$1\frac{11}{16}$	2,700	2,715.768
14.00	$1\frac{3}{4}$	2,800	2,816.352
14.50	$1\frac{13}{16}$	2,900	2,916.936
15.00	$1\frac{7}{8}$	3,000	3,017.520
15.50	$1\frac{15}{16}$	3,100	3,118.104
16.00	2	3,200	3,218.688
16.50	$2\frac{1}{16}$	3,300	3,319.272
17.00	$2\frac{1}{8}$	3,400	3,419.856
18.00	$2\frac{1}{4}$	3,600	3,621.024
19.00	$2\frac{3}{8}$	3,800	3,822.192
20.00	$2\frac{1}{2}$	4,000	4,023.360
21.00	$2\frac{5}{8}$	4,200	4,224.528
22.00	$2\frac{3}{4}$	4,400	4,425.696
23.00	$2\frac{7}{8}$	4,600	4,626.864
24.00	3	4,800	4,828.032

Meters to Furlongs

Meters	Approx. Furlongs	Approx. Miles	Exact Furlongs	Exact Miles
200	1.00	$\frac{1}{8}$	0.9942	0.1243
400	2.00	$\frac{1}{4}$	1.9884	0.2485
600	3.00	$\frac{3}{8}$	2.9826	0.3728
800	4.00	$\frac{1}{2}$	3.9768	0.4971
900	4.50	$\frac{9}{16}$	4.4739	0.5592
1,000	5.00	$\frac{5}{8}$	4.9710	0.6214
1,100	5.50	$\frac{11}{16}$	5.4681	0.6835
1,200	6.00	$\frac{3}{4}$	5.9652	0.7456
1,300	6.50	$\frac{13}{16}$	6.4623	0.8078
1,400	7.00	$\frac{7}{8}$	6.9594	0.8699
1,500	7.50	$\frac{15}{16}$	7.4565	0.9321
1,600	8.00	1	7.9536	0.9942
1,670	8.32	1&70 yds.	7.9784	0.9973
1,700	8.50	$1\frac{1}{16}$	8.4506	1.0563
1,800	9.00	$1\frac{1}{8}$	8.9477	1.1185
1,900	9.50	$1\frac{3}{16}$	9.4448	1.1806
2,000	10.00	$1\frac{1}{4}$	9.9419	1.2427
2,100	10.50	$1\frac{5}{16}$	10.4390	1.3049
2,200	11.00	$1\frac{3}{8}$	10.9361	1.3670
2,300	11.50	$1\frac{7}{16}$	11.4332	1.4292
2,400	12.00	$1\frac{1}{2}$	11.9303	1.4913
2,500	12.50	$1\frac{9}{16}$	12.4274	1.5534
2,600	13.00	$1\frac{5}{8}$	12.9245	1.6156
2,700	13.50	$1\frac{11}{16}$	13.4216	1.6777
2,800	14.00	$1\frac{3}{4}$	13.9187	1.7398
2,900	14.50	$1\frac{13}{16}$	14.4158	1.8020
3,000	15.00	$1\frac{7}{8}$	14.9129	1.8641
3,100	15.50	$1\frac{15}{16}$	15.4100	1.9263
3,200	16.00	2	15.9071	1.9884
3,300	16.50	$2\frac{1}{16}$	16.4042	2.0505
3,400	17.00	$2\frac{1}{8}$	16.9013	2.1127
3,500	17.50	$2\frac{3}{16}$	17.3984	2.1748
3,600	18.00	$2\frac{1}{4}$	17.8955	2.2369
3,700	18.50	$2\frac{5}{16}$	18.3926	2.2991
3,800	19.00	$2\frac{3}{8}$	18.8897	2.3612
3,900	19.50	$2\frac{7}{16}$	19.3868	2.4233
4,000	20.00	$2\frac{1}{2}$	19.8839	2.4855
4,100	20.50	$2\frac{9}{16}$	20.3810	2.5476
4,200	21.00	$2\frac{5}{8}$	20.8781	2.6098
4,300	21.50	$2\frac{11}{16}$	21.3752	2.6719
4,400	22.00	$2\frac{3}{4}$	21.8723	2.7340
4,500	22.50	$2\frac{13}{16}$	22.3694	2.7962
4,600	23.00	$2\frac{7}{8}$	22.8665	2.8583
4,700	23.50	$2\frac{15}{16}$	23.3636	2.9204
4,800	24.00	3	23.8607	2.9826

Countries and Measurements Used

Argentina	furlongs and meters
Australia	meters
Brazil	meters
Canada	furlongs
Chile	meters
England	furlongs
France	meters
Germany	meters
Hong Kong	meters
Ireland	furlongs
Italy	meters
Japan	meters
New Zealand	meters
United Arab Emirates	meters
United States	furlongs

Glossary of Common Racing and Breeding Terms

account wagering Betting by phone, in which a bettor must open an account with a track or an off-track agency. A synonym: phone betting.

acey-deucy Uneven stirrups, popularized by Racing Hall of Fame jockey Eddie Arcaro, who rode with his left (inside) iron lower than his right to achieve better balance on turns.

across the board A bet on a horse to win, place, and show. If the horse wins, the player collects three ways; if second, two ways (place and show); and if third, one way (show).

action 1) A horse's manner of moving. 2) A vernacular term for wagering.

added money Money added to the purse of a race by the racing association, a breeding fund, or other source. The association's money is added to the amount paid by owners in nomination, eligibility, entry, and starting fees. Added-money stakes became less common in the 1990s as more tracks went to guaranteed purses.

agent A person empowered to transact business for a stable owner or a jockey, or one empowered to sell or buy horses for an owner or a breeder.

aired Won particularly easily by open lengths.

all-age race A race for two-year-olds and up.

all out When a horse extends itself to the utmost.

allowance race A race for which the racing secretary drafts certain conditions to determine weights to be carried based on the horse's age, sex, past performance, or a combination of all three.

allowances Reductions in weights to be carried, with the adjustments based on the conditions of the race or because an apprentice jockey is on a horse. Also, a weight reduction that female horses are entitled to when racing against males or that three-year-olds receive against older horses.

also-eligible A horse officially entered for a race but not permitted to start unless the field is reduced by scratches below a specified number.

also-ran A horse that does not finish first, second, or third.

American Horse Council A national association of individuals, organizations, and companies formed as a lobbying group to represent all breeds of the horse industry. Based in Washington, D.C., the AHC works on tax regulations, import and export rules, disease prevention and control, trails and recreation enhancement, and humane concerns. Founded in 1969 as an advocate for the entire American horse industry, the AHC was founded principally by Thoroughbred interests concerned about legislation then being discussed in Congress that would have negatively affected racing and breeding.

American Stud Book Official book of foal registrations in North America maintained by the Jockey Club.

apprentice allowance Weight concession given to an apprentice rider; usually ten pounds until the fifth winner, seven pounds until the 35th winner, and five pounds for one calendar year from the 35th winner. More rarely, a three-pound allowance for a rider under contract to a specific stable or owner for two years from his or her first win. This rule varies from state to state. Apprentices do not receive a weight allowance when riding in a stakes race.

apprentice jockey Rider at the beginning of his career who has not ridden a certain number of winners within a specified period of time. Also known as a bug rider or bug boy, from the asterisk used in racing programs and past performances to denote the weight allowance such riders receive.

apron The (usually) paved area between the grandstand and the racing surface.

Association of Racing Commissioners International (RCI) Formerly the National Association of State Racing Commissioners (NASRC). Its office is based in Lexington.

asterisk Used with names of horses to denote they were imported into the United States. Practice preceded the use of country codes starting January 1, 1977.

auxiliary starting gate A second starting gate used when the number of horses in a race exceeds the capacity of the main starting gate.

average earnings index (AEI) A breeding statistic that compares racing earnings of a stallion's or mare's foals to those of all other foals racing at that time. An AEI of 1.00 is considered average, 2.00 is twice the average, 0.50 half the average, etc.

baby race A race for two-year-olds.

backstretch 1) Straight portion of the far side of the racing surface between the turns. 2) Generally, a racetrack's stable area, which often contains dormitories, a track kitchen, chapel, and recreation area for stable employees. It gained its name because most stable areas are located along the racetrack's backstretch.

bad doer A horse with a poor appetite, a condition that may be due to nervousness or other causes.

bandage Wrappings used on a horse's legs are three to six inches wide and are made of a variety of materials. In a race, they are used for support or protection against injury. Rundown bandages are used during a race to affix a pad under the fetlock to avoid injury due to abrasion when the fetlocks sink toward the ground during the weight-bearing portion of the gallop. A horse also may wear standing bandages, thick cotton wraps used during shipping and while in the stall to prevent swelling, injury, or both, or to apply medication.

bar shoe A horseshoe closed at the back to help support the frog and heel of the hoof. It is often worn by horses with quarter cracks or bruised feet.

base The portion of the track that lies under the thick top layer, or cushion. The base provides support and drainage.

battery A term for an illegal electrical device used by a jockey to stimulate a horse by electrical shock during a race. Also known as a machine or a joint.

bay A horse color that varies from a yellow tan to a bright auburn. The mane, tail, and lower portion of the legs are always black, except where white markings are present.

bearing in (or out) Deviating from a straight course. May be due to weariness, infirmity, inexperience, or the rider overusing the whip or reins to make a horse alter its course.

bell Signal sounded when the starter opens the gates or, at some tracks, to mark the close of betting.

Beyer number A handicapping tool, popularized by

author Andrew Beyer, assigning a numerical value (speed figure) to each race run by a horse based on final time and track condition. This enables different horses running at different racetracks to be objectively compared.

bid in The act of buying back a horse that does not meet a minimum price at public auction. Synonym for buy-back, reserve not attained (RNA).

Big Red Refers to either of two famous chestnut-colored horses: Man o' War or Secretariat.

Bill Daly (on the) Taking a horse to the front at the start of a race and remaining there to the finish. Term stems from "Father Bill" Daly, a famous old-time horseman who developed many great jockeys.

birthdays All Thoroughbreds born in the Northern Hemisphere celebrate their birthday on January 1. In the Southern Hemisphere, all Thoroughbred birthdays are as follows: South America, July 1; South Africa, Australia, and New Zealand, August 1.

bit A stainless steel, rubber, or aluminum bar attached to the bridle; it is placed in the bar, the space between front and back teeth in the horse's mouth, and is one of the means by which a jockey exerts guidance and control. The most common racing bit is the D-bit, named because the rings extending from the bar are shaped like the letter D. Most racing bits are snaffled (snaffle bit), which means the metal bar is made up of two pieces, connected in the middle, which leaves it free to swivel. Other bits may be used to correct specific problems, such as bearing in or out.

black A horse color that includes the hair and the skin of the muzzle, flanks, mane, tail, and legs, unless white markings are present.

black type Boldface type, used in sales catalogs and stakes results, to distinguish horses that have won or placed in a stakes race. Sales companies today have eliminated the use of black type for stakes below a certain monetary level—$15,000 in 1985; $20,000 from 1986-'89; $25,000 beginning in 1990; $30,000 beginning in 2002; $35,000 beginning in 2003; and $40,000 beginning in 2004. If a horse's name appears in boldface capital letters in a catalog or stakes results, the horse has won at least one black-type event. If the name appears in boldface type with capital and lower-case letters, the horse was second or third in at least one black-type event but has not won a black-type race.

blaze A generic term describing a large, white vertical marking on a horse's face.

blind switch A circumstance in which a rider's actions cause his or her mount to be impeded during a race when moving into a space in which the horse and rider find themselves blocked.

blinkers A cup-shaped device to limit a horse's vision and thus prevent it from swerving from objects or other horses on either side while racing. Blinker cups come in a variety of sizes and shapes to allow as little or as much vision as the trainer feels is necessary and may be attached to a hood or bridle.

blister Counterirritant causing acute inflammation; used to increase blood supply and blood flow and to promote healing in the leg.

bloodstock Horses of Thoroughbred breeding, especially such horses used for or considered in relation to racing.

bloodstock agent A person who advises or represents a buyer or a seller of Thoroughbreds at a public auction or a private sale. A bloodstock agent usually works on commission, often 5% of the purchase or sale price, and may also prepare a horse for sale.

blood typing A method of verifying a horse's parentage. Blood typing was usually completed within the first year of a horse's life and was necessary before registration papers were issued by the Jockey Club. Beginning in 2001, the Jockey Club adopted DNA technology to verify horse's parentage.

blowout A short, timed workout, usually a day or two before a race, designed to sharpen a horse's speed. Usually three-eighths or one-half mile in distance.

blue hen Used to describe an outstanding broodmare, the producer of a number of stakes winners and whose daughters, granddaughters, and great-granddaughters in turn produced important winners.

board Short for tote board, on which odds, betting pools, and other information are displayed.

boat race Slang for a fixed race.

bobble A bad step away from the starting gate, usually caused by the track surface breaking away from under a horse's hooves, causing it to duck its head or nearly go to his knees.

bolt Sudden veering from a straight course, usually to the outside rail.

bomb(er) A winning horse sent off at extremely high odds.

book 1) The group of mares being bred to a stallion in a given year. If a stallion attracts the maximum number of mares allowed by the farm manager, he has a full book. 2) A term used to describe a jockey's riding commitments with his agent.

bookie Short for bookmaker.

bookmaker A person who books bets.

bottom 1) Stamina in a horse developed over a long period of time. 2) Subsurface of a racing strip.

bottom line A Thoroughbred's breeding on the female side most specifically applied to the tail-female line listed on the bottom line of a standard pedigree diagram.

bounce A poor race run immediately after a career-best or near-best performance.

box 1) A wagering term denoting a combination bet whereby all possible numeric combinations are covered for certain horses. 2) A disadvantageous position in a race, behind and between horses. 3) A horse's stall.

boxed (in) To be trapped between, behind, or inside other horses.

brace (or bracer) Rubdown liniment used on a horse after a race or workout.

break 1) To train a young horse to wear a bridle and saddle, carry a rider, and respond to a rider's commands. Most often done when the horse is a yearling. 2) To leave from the starting gate.

breakage In pari-mutuel payoffs, which are rounded down to a nickel or dime, the pennies that are left over. Breakage may be used for any of a number of purposes. Depending upon a state's rules of racing, the money goes to the state, the track, purses, or benevolence programs.

breather Easing off on a horse for a short distance in a race to permit it to conserve or renew its strength.

bred A horse is considered to have been bred in the state or country where it was foaled.

breed-back rule Restriction imposed in some jurisdictions that, for a mare's offspring to be eligible for state-bred bonuses, the mare, after foaling, must be bred to a stallion standing in that state.

breeder Owner of the dam at time of foaling unless the dam was under a lease or foal-sharing arrangement at the time of foaling. In that case, the person specified by the terms of the agreement is the breeder of the foal.

Breeders' Cup Thoroughbred racing's year-end championship. Known as Breeders' Cup day, Breeders' Cup championship day, or beginning in 2001 as World Thoroughbred Championships, it consists of eight races conducted on one day at one of several major North American racetracks each year. (See Breeders' Cup chapter.)

Breeders' Cup Ltd. Corporate entity that oversees the Breeders' Cup program. It is a not-for-profit organization based in Lexington.

breeding fund A state fund set up to provide bonuses for state-breds.

breeding right The right to breed one mare per year to a specific stallion. Breeding rights, as opposed to stallion shares, do not usually come with bonuses (money derived from extra seasons sold), nor are they assessed expenses.

breeze (breezing) Working a horse at a moderate speed; less effort than handily.

bridge jumper A person who wagers large amounts of money, usually on short-priced horses to show, hoping to realize a small but almost certain profit.

bridle A piece of equipment, usually made of leather or nylon, that fits on a horse's head; other equipment, such as a bit and the reins, are attached to it.

broken wind Abnormality of the upper or lower respiratory tract causing loss of normal air exchange, generally resulting in reduced performance.

broodmare A mare that has been bred and is used to produce foals.

broodmare sire The maternal sire; the sire of the dam.

Broodmare Sire Index The Broodmare Sire Index is an average of the Racing Index (RI) of all foals (that started at least three times) out of the sire's daughters. For BSI to be calculated, a broodmare sire must be represented by a minimum of 75 starters lifetime.

brush 1) During a race when two horses lightly touch each other. 2) Injury that occurs when one hoof strikes the inside of the opposite limb. 3) A type of obstacle used in steeplechase racing.

bullet work The best workout time for a particular distance on a given day at a track. Derived from the printer's bullet that precedes the time of the workout in listings. Also known as a black-letter work in some parts of the country.

bullring A small racetrack, usually less than one mile in circumference.

buy-back A horse put through a public auction that fails to reach a minimum (reserve) price set by the consignor and so is retained. The consignor must pay a fee to the auction company based on a percentage of the reserve to cover the auction company's marketing, advertising, and other costs. A synonym for reserve not attained (RNA).

calk A projection on the heels of a horseshoe, similar to a cleat, on the rear shoes of a horse to prevent slipping, especially on a wet track. Also known as a sticker.

(race) call Running position of horses in a race at various points.

cast A horse positioned on its side or back and wedged against a wall, fence, or other object in such a way that it cannot get up.

chalk Wagering favorite in a race. Term dates from the days when on-track bookmakers would write current odds on a chalkboard, and the horse that was bet the most used the most chalk.

chalk player Bettor who wagers on favorites.

champion Horse or individual determined to be the outstanding performer in his or her division in a specific year. In the United States, champions are determined by the Eclipse Awards balloting.

chart A statistical picture of a race (from which past performances are compiled) showing the position and margin of each horse at designated points of call (depending on the distance of the race), as well as the horse's age, weight carried, owner, trainer, jockey, and the race's purse, conditions, payoff prices, odds, time, and other data. Before 1991, all charts were compiled by *Daily Racing Form*. From 1991 to '98, charts were compiled by both *Daily Racing Form* and Equibase; since mid-1998, charts have been compiled exclusively by Equibase.

check(ed) When a jockey slows a horse due to other horses impeding its progress.

chestnut 1) A horse color that may vary from a red-yellow to golden-yellow. The mane, tail, and legs are usually variations of coat color, except where white markings are present. 2) Horny, irregular growths found on the inside of the legs. On the forelegs, they are just above the knees. On the hind legs, they are just below the hocks. No two horses have been found to have the same chestnuts, and so chestnuts may be used for identification. Also called night eyes.

chute Extension of backstretch or homestretch to permit a straight start in a race, as opposed to starting on or near a turn.

claiming Process by which a licensed person may purchase a horse entered in a designated race for a predetermined price. When a horse has been claimed, its new owner assumes title after the starting gate opens although the former owner is entitled to all purse money earned in that race. Sometimes called halter or haltered, for the act of putting a new halter on a claimed horse so that it can be led back to its new barn.

claiming box, claims box Box in which claims are deposited before the race.

claiming race A race in which each horse entered is eligible to be purchased at a set price. Claims must be made before the race and only by licensed owners or their agents who have a horse registered to race at that meeting or who have received a claim certificate from the stewards. A claiming race in which there is an option to have horses entered to be claimed for a stated price or not eligible to be claimed is an optional claiming race.

classic 1) A race of traditional importance, usually modeled on one of the five original English classic races, and often considered part of a triple crown. 2) Used to describe a distance. The American classic distance is 1¼ miles on dirt. The European classic distance is 1½ miles on turf.

clerk of scales An official whose chief duty is to weigh the riders before and after a race to ensure proper weight is or was carried.

climbing When a horse lifts its front legs abnormally high as it gallops, causing it to run inefficiently.

clocker Individual who times workouts and races.

closer A horse that runs best in the latter part of the race, coming from off the pace.

clubhouse turn Generally, the turn on a racing oval that is closest to the clubhouse facility; usually the first turn after the finish line.

colors (horse) Colors accepted by the Jockey Club are bay, black, chestnut, dark bay or brown, gray or roan, and white. In 1996, the Jockey Club started combining gray and roan, which had been separate colors previously.

colt An ungelded (entire) male horse four years old or younger.

commingle Combining mutuel pools from off-track sites with the host track.

company Class of horses in a race or the class of horses a runner usually keeps.

comparable index (CI) Indicates the average earnings of progeny produced from mares bred to one sire when these same mares are bred to other sires. A CI of 1.00 is considered average, 2.00 is twice the average, and 0.50 half the average.

condition book(s) A series of booklets issued by a track's racing secretary setting forth conditions of races to be run at that track.

conditioner 1) A trainer. 2) A workout or race to enable a horse to attain fitness.

conditions The requirements for being able to enter a horse in a particular race as written by the track's racing secretary. Conditions may include age, sex, money or races won, weight carried, and the distance of the race.

conformation The physical makeup and bodily proportions of a horse.

connections Persons identified with a horse, such as owner, trainer, rider, and stable employees.

consolation double A payoff to holders of daily double tickets combining the winning horse in the first race of the double with a scratched horse in the second.

cooling out Restoring a horse to its normal body temperature, usually by walking, after it has become overheated during exercise or racing.

coupled (entry) Two or more horses running as an entry in a single betting unit.

cover A single breeding of a stallion to a mare.

crop 1) The number of foals by a sire in a given year. 2) All horses collectively born in the same year. 3) A jockey's whip.

cup horse A term once used to describe horses competing at the highest level of the sport in races at a distance of two miles or more.

cuppy (track) A drying and loose racing surface that breaks away under a horse's hooves.

cushion Top portion of a racetrack.

cut down Horse suffering injuries from being struck by the shoes of another horse. Or, due to a faulty stride, a horse may cut itself down.

daily double Type of wager calling for the selection of winners of two consecutive races, usually the first and second.

Daily Racing Form A daily newspaper containing news, past performance data, and handicapping infor-

mation. Founded in 1895, it is the successor of the *Morning Telegraph*. The *Morning Telegraph* was founded in 1833 and was closed during a strike by printers in 1972.

dam The female parent of a foal.

dam's sire (broodmare sire) The sire of a broodmare. Used in reference to the maternal grandsire of a foal.

dark day A day when there is no racing at the track.

dark bay or brown A horse color that ranges from brown with areas of tan on the shoulders, head, and flanks, to a dark brown, with tan areas seen only in the flanks, muzzle, or both. The mane, tail, and lower portions of the legs are always black unless white markings are present.

dark horse Probably a good horse whose full potential is unknown before a race.

dead heat Two or more horses finishing a race in a tie.

dead track Racing surface lacking resiliency.

declared In the United States, a horse withdrawn from a stakes race in advance of scratch time. In Europe, a horse confirmed to start in a race.

deep stretch A position very close to the finish line in a race.

Derby A stakes event for three-year-olds, deriving its name from Lord Derby, and usually the most important race for three-year-olds at a given track.

disqualification Change in order of finish by officials for an infraction of the rules.

distaffer A female horse.

distaff race A race for female horses.

distanced Horse so far behind the rest of the field of runners that it is out of contact and unable to regain a position of contention. A horse beaten more than 40 lengths.

dogs Rubber traffic cones (or a barrier) placed at certain distances out from the inner rail when the track is wet, muddy, soft, yielding, or heavy to prevent horses during the workout period from churning the footing along the rail.

dope 1) Any illegal drug. 2) Slang term for past performances: Readers of past performances are said to dope out a race.

dosage Although other dosage theories exist, the term is most commonly associated with the one interpreted by Dr. Steven Roman. A variation of Dr. Franco Varola's work on pedigree analysis, the system identifies patterns of ability in horses based on a list of prepotent sires, each of whom is designated a *chef-de-race*. The dosage system puts these sires into one of five categories: brilliant, intermediate, classic, solid, or professional, which are subjective judgments of speed and stamina. Sires can be listed in up to two *chef-de-race* categories. Each generation of sires is worth 16 points, divided by the number of sires; i.e., the immediate sire is worth 16 points while the four sires four generations back are worth four points apiece.

dosage index (DI) A mathematical reduction of the dosage profile to a number reflecting a horse's potential for speed or stamina. The higher the number, the more likely the horse is suited to be a sprinter. The average dosage index of all horses is about 4.00. The dosage index (DI) is derived from the dosage profile to reflect the ratio of speed to stamina in a pedigree. This is calculated by adding points from the two speed categories (brilliant and intermediate), plus half of those from the classic (middle) category, and dividing that total by the points from the two stamina categories (solid and professional), plus the other half of the classic points. The higher the DI, the more speed is imputed to be present in the pedigree. A 4.00 DI is generally the cutoff where a horse is considered not likely to be competitive at the American classic distance of 1¼ miles.

driving A horse that is all out to win and under strong urging from its jockey.

drop down A horse meeting a lower class of rival than it had been running against previously.

dwelt Extremely late in breaking from the gate.

earmuffs Equipment that covers a horse's ears to prevent it from hearing distracting sounds.

eased A horse that is gently pulled up during a race.

easily Running or winning without being pressed by rider or opposition.

Eclipse Award Thoroughbred racing's year-end awards, honoring the top horses and people in several categories. Named for the great 18th-century racehorse and sire Eclipse, who was undefeated in 18 career starts and sired the winners of 344 races. The Eclipse Awards are sponsored by the National Thoroughbred Racing Association, *Daily Racing Form*, and National Turf Writers Association. They were first awarded in 1971; previously, separate year-end champions were named by *Daily Racing Form* (beginning in 1936) and the Thoroughbred Racing Associations (beginning in 1950).

eligible Qualified to start in a race, according to conditions.

engagement 1) Stakes nomination. 2) Riding commitment.

entire An ungelded horse. In Europe, where geldings are not permitted to enter certain races, the race conditions might read: Entire colts and fillies.

entry Two or more horses with common ownership (in some cases, trained by the same trainer) that are paired as a single betting unit in one race or are placed together by the racing secretary as part of a mutuel field. Rules on entries vary from state to state. Also known as a coupled entry.

entry fee Money paid by an owner to enter a horse in a stakes race—and is what usually defines a race as a stakes. Entry fees are not required for overnight races and some invitational stakes races.

Equibase Co. A partnership between the Jockey Club and the Thoroughbred Racing Associations to establish and maintain an industry-owned, central database of racing records. Equibase past-performance information is used in track programs across North America. Formed in 1990, Equibase first collected data in '91. In 1998, it began supplying past performance information to *Daily Racing Form* and became the sole collector of racing data.

estrus (heat) Associated with ovulation; a mare usually is receptive to breeding during estrus. Referred to as horsing.

euthanize To end a horse's life by lethal injection because of a catastrophic injury or critical illness and thus prevent further pain and suffering.

evenly Neither gaining nor losing position during a race.

exacta (or perfecta) A wager in which the first two finishers in a race, in exact order of finish, must be picked. Called an exactor in Canada.

exacta box A wager in which all possible combinations using a given number of horses are bet on.

exercise rider Individual who is licensed to exercise a horse during morning training hours.

exotic (wager) Any wager other than win, place, or show that requires multiple combinations. Examples of exotic wagers: trifecta, pick six, pick three.

Experimental Free Handicap A year-end assessment of the best North American two-year-olds of the season. It is put together by a panel of racing secretaries under the auspices of the Jockey Club and is based on performances in unrestricted races. Two lists are drawn up, one for males and one for females. Only the handicap for two-year-olds is called the Experimental Free Handicap; lists for older horses are free handicaps. First started by Walter Vosburgh in 1933. Race based on Experimental was run at Aqueduct from 1940 to '56 at six furlongs (Experimental Free Handicap No. 1) and another from 1946 to '52 at 1¹⁄₁₆ miles (Experimental Free Handicap No. 2).

extended Running at top speed.

farrier Horseshoer.

fast (track) Footing that is dry, even, and resilient.

fault Weak points of a horse's conformation or its character as a racehorse.

feather Light weight. Usually refers to the weight a horse is assigned to carry in a race.

fee 1) Amount paid to a jockey for riding in a race. 2) The cost of nominating, entering, or starting a horse in a stakes race.

fetal sexing Use of ultrasonography to identify genitalia of a fetus. Optimum time to perform fetal sexing is between 60 and 75 days of gestation.

field The horses in a race.

field horse (or mutuel field) Two or more starters running as a single betting unit (entry), when there are more starters in a race than positions on the totalizator board.

filly Female horse four years old or younger.

firm A condition of a turf course corresponding to fast on a dirt track.

flag Signal manually held a short distance in front of the gate at the exact starting point of a race. In some jurisdictions, official timing starts when flag is dropped by the flagman to denote proper start.

flak jacket Similar to a jacket worn by football quarterbacks, the jockey's flak jacket protects the chest, ribs, kidneys, and back from injury.

flat race Contested over a course without obstacles to jump. Often used in the term, on the flat.

flatten out A very tired horse that slows considerably, dropping its head on a straight line with its body.

float 1) An equine dental procedure in which sharp points on the teeth are filed down. 2) The instrument with which the above procedure is performed. 3) To drag a flat plate over a wet track surface to aid in draining water.

floating Flat plate or wooden implement (float) dragged over the surface of a wet track to aid in draining water.

foal(ed) 1) A horse of either sex in its first year of life. 2) Can also denote the offspring of either a male or female parent. 3) To give birth.

Fontana safety rail An aluminum rail, in use since 1981, designed to help reduce injuries to horse and rider. It has more of an offset (slant) to provide greater clearance between the rail and the vertical posts as well as a protective cover to keep horse and rider from striking the posts.

foundation mare A mare whose descendants show high quality and have impact on the breed after many generations.

founding sires The Darley Arabian, Byerly Turk, and Godolphin Arabian. Every Thoroughbred traces its male-line parentage to one of the three founding sires.

fractional time Intermediate times recorded in a race, as at the quarter-mile, half-mile, three-quarters, etc.

free handicap A race in which no nomination fees are required. More recently, and more commonly, a ranking of horses three years old and up by weight for a theoretical race or as an intellectual challenge.

front-runner A horse whose running style is to attempt to get on or near the lead at the start of the race and to continue there as long as possible.

frozen (track) The condition of a racetrack where any moisture present is frozen.

full brother, full sister Horses that share both the same sire and dam.

furlong One-eighth of a mile, which is equal to 220 yards or 660 feet.

furosemide A medication used in the treatment of bleeders, commonly known by the trade name Salix, a diuretic. Although research has not determined definitively how furosemide reduces bleeding, it is widely believed that the diuretic effect reduces pressure within capillaries in the lungs.

futurity A race for two-year-olds in which the owners make a scheduled series of payments over a period of time to keep their horses eligible. Purses for these races vary but can be considerable.

gait The characteristic footfall pattern of a horse in motion. Thoroughbreds have four natural gaits: walk, trot, canter, and gallop. Thoroughbreds compete at a gallop.

gap An opening in the rail where horses enter and leave the course.

Garrison finish A close victory, usually from off the pace. Derived from Ed "Snapper" Garrison, a 19th-century rider known for his close finishes.

gate card A card, issued by the starter, stating that a horse is properly schooled in starting-gate procedures.

gelding A male horse of any age that has been neutered by having both testicles removed (gelded).

gentleman jockey Amateur rider, generally in steeplechases.

get Progeny of sire.

girth An elastic and leather band, sometimes covered with sheepskin, that passes under a horse's belly and is connected to both sides of the saddle.

good (track) A dirt track that is almost fast or a turf course slightly softer than firm.

grab a quarter Injury to the back of the hoof or foot caused by a horse stepping on itself (usually affects the front foot). Being stepped on from behind in the same manner usually affects the back foot. Very common in racing, the injury is usually minor.

graded race Established in 1973 to classify select stakes races in North America, at the request of European racing authorities, who had set up group races two years earlier. Grading of races is performed by a committee under the direction of the Thoroughbred Owners and Breeders Association. See graded stakes section in Racing chapter.

grandam A horse's grandmother. Also known as second dam when referring to the female line.

grandsire The grandfather of a horse; father (sire) of the horse's dam or sire.

grass slip Used in some areas, permission to exercise a horse on the turf course. Also known as a turf slip.

gray A horse color in which the majority of the coat is a mixture of black and white hairs. The mane, tail, and legs may be either black or gray unless white markings are present. Starting with foals of 1993, the color classifications gray and roan were combined as gray or roan.

Grayson-Jockey Club Research Foundation A privately financed charitable organization established in 1989, which combined the Grayson Foundation Inc. (begun in 1940) and the Jockey Club Research Foundation.

group race Designation of best races in countries outside North America. European authorities began designating races as Group 1, Group 2, and Group 3 in 1971. North American officials, under the direction of the Thoroughbred Owners and Breeders Association, began grading races in 1973.

guineas By definition, a guinea is 21 shillings, or in current usage a pound and a shilling. Thus, the guinea is equal to 1.05 pounds. Used by sales companies in England and Ireland to report sales since it includes the sales company's 5% commission.

half brother, half sister Horses out of the same dam but by different sires. Horses with the same sire and different dams are not considered half siblings in Thoroughbred racing.

halter Like a bridle, but lacking a bit and reins. Used to handle horses around the stable and when they are not being ridden.

hand Four inches. A horse's height is measured in hands and inches from the top of the shoulder (withers) to the ground; that is, 15.2 hands is 15 hands, 2 inches, or a total of 62 inches. Thoroughbreds typically range from 15 to 17 hands.

handicap 1) Race for which the track handicapper assigns the weights to be carried. 2) To make selections on the basis of past performances.

handicap horse A horse that competes in handicap races.

handicapper 1) A person, usually the racing secretary, who assigns weights to horses. 2) A bettor who is making selections based on information of horses' performances from previous starts.

handily 1) Working in the morning with a strong effort. 2) A horse racing well within itself, with little exertion, during a race.

handle Amount of money wagered in the pari-mutuels on a race, a program, during a meeting, or for a year.

hand ride Urging a horse with the hands and not using the whip.

hard A condition of a turf course where there is no resiliency to the surface.

hardboot A Kentucky horseman.

hard-knocker A tough horse that makes a lot of starts.

harrow Implement or unit with pulling teeth, or tines, used to rake and loosen the upper surface of a track.

head A margin between horses. One horse leading another by the length of its head.

head of the stretch Beginning of the straight run to the finish line.

head to head Running on even terms.

heat 1) A race decided by two or more individual races over the same distance and between the same horses on the same day. Not used in flat racing today, though it was common in the 19th century. Still used occasionally in harness racing. 2) A breeding term for estrus in a mare.

heavy Wettest possible condition of a turf course; not usually found in North America.

helmet A lightweight fiberglass cap worn by riders to prevent head injuries. It is required equipment and is not considered part of a jockey's riding weight.

high weight Refers to highest weight assigned or carried in a race.

highweight Horse assigned the highest weight on the Experimental Free Handicap, a division of the International Classifications, or one of several free handicaps in individual countries, and often viewed as the equivalent of a champion in the absence of official championships.

homebred A horse bred by its owner.

homestretch Long section of racetrack closest to the stands.

hood A covering, usually nylon, that goes over a horse's head; blinkers or earmuffs may be attached to it.

hopped A horse that has been illegally stimulated with a drug.

horse When reference is made to sex, an ungelded male five years old or older.

Horsemen's Benevolent and Protective Association A national organization of horsemen, largely composed of owners, that has divisions at many racetracks in North America to help owners and trainers negotiate purses and other issues with track management.

hotwalker A person or automatic machine that walks horses to cool them out after workouts or races.

hung A horse that does not advance its position in a race when called upon by its jockey.

icing 1) A physical therapy procedure, properly known as cryotherapy. 2) When a horse's leg or legs are placed in a tub of ice or ice packs are applied to the legs to reduce inflammation or swelling.

impost Weight carried by a horse or assigned to a horse.

inbreeding The mating of closely related individuals, resulting in a pedigree with at least one common ancestor duplicated on both sire's and dam's side of the pedigree. In Thoroughbreds, horses with one or more duplicated ancestors within the first four or five generations are generally considered inbred, while duplications of ancestors in more distant generations are often referred to as "linebreeding."

infield Area enclosed by the inner rail of the racetrack.

in hand Running under moderate control, at less than top speed.

inquiry A review of the running of the race to check into a possible infraction of the rules, called by the stewards. Also, a sign flashed by officials on the tote board on such occasions. If lodged by a jockey, it is called an objection.

in the money A horse that finishes first, second, or third in a race.

Irish rail Movable rail.

isolation barn A facility used to separate horses to ensure that disease is not carried into the area.

jail Requirement that when a claimed horse runs within 30 days of being claimed, it must run for a claiming price at least 25% higher than the price at which it was claimed.

Jockey Club Organization dedicated to the improvement of Thoroughbred breeding and racing. Incorporated February 9, 1894, in New York City, the Jockey Club serves as North America's Thoroughbred registry, responsible for the maintenance of the *American Stud Book*, a register of all Thoroughbreds foaled in the United States, Puerto Rico, and Canada; and of all Thoroughbreds imported into those countries from jurisdictions that have a registry recognized by the Jockey Club and the International Stud Book Committee.

jockey fee Sum paid to rider for competing in a race.

Jockeys' Guild National organization of professional riders.

jockey's race A race whose outcome will hinge mostly on strategic thinking by the riders; one in which riders must pay close attention to pace to keep their horses fresh for a strong finish.

jog Slow, easy gait commonly called a trot.

joint 1) Point of juncture of two bones and usually composed of fibrous connective tissue and cartilage. 2) Slang for an illegal electrical stimulation device.

jumper Steeplechase or hurdle horse.

juvenile Two-year-old horse.

key horse A single horse used in multiple combinations in an exotic wager.

kilometer One thousand meters and equal to .6214 of a mile.

lame A deviation from a normal gait due to pain in a limb or its supporting structures.

Lasix See Salix.

late double A second daily double offered during the latter part of a race program.

lead Refers to the leading leg when a horse is racing in full stride. The lead leg is the one that reaches out the farthest and bears the full weight of the horse's impact. Horses usually race on the left, or inside, lead on the turn, and on the right, or outside, lead on straightaways. Changing leads refers to the horse's ability to switch from one leading leg to the other at the proper time.

leaky-roof circuit Minor tracks.

leg up 1) To help a jockey mount a horse. 2) To improve a horse's fitness through long, slow gallops.

length A measurement approximating the length of a horse and used to describe the distances between horses in a race. A length is approximately eight feet.

listed race A stakes race just below a group race or graded race in quality.

lock Slang for a sure winner.

longe 1) A long rope or line fastened to a horse's head and held by a trainer, who causes the horse to move around in a circle. 2) A method of exercising a horse on a tether (longe line).

lug (bearing in or lugging out) Deviating from a straight course. May be due to weariness, infirmity, inexperience, or the rider overusing the whip or reins to make a horse alter its course.

maiden 1) A horse or rider who has not won a race. 2) A female horse that has never been bred.

maiden race A race for nonwinners.

mare Female horse five years old or older. Also, any female that has been bred regardless of age.

mare's month September. In theory, mares that have not run well during the summer often perform better in September.

mash Soft, moist mixture, hot or cold, of grain and other feed that is easily digested by horses.

massage Rubbing of various parts of the anatomy to stimulate healing.

match race A race between two horses.

medication list A list kept by the track veterinarian and published by the track showing which horses have been treated with legally prescribed medications.

meter The basic unit of length in the metric system. It is equal to approximately 39.37 inches. It takes 100 centimeters to make a meter and 1,000 meters to make a kilometer. To convert to inches, multiply by 39.37 (5 meters x 39.37 inches = 196.85 inches). To convert to yards, multiply by 1.1 (5 meters x 1.1 = 5.5 yards). Most European races are expressed in meters. A mile is approximately 1,600 meters, the distance at which the classic Poule d'Essai des Pouliches (Fr-G1) and the Poule d'Essai des Poulains (Fr-G1) are run. The Prix de l'Arc de Triomphe (Fr-G1) is 2,400 meters, or approximately 1½ miles; the Prix Eugene Adam (Fr-G2) is 2,000 meters, or approximately 1¼ miles. See Distance Equivalents table in preceding section.

middle distance Broadly, from one mile to 1¼ miles.

minus pool A negative mutuel pool created when a horse is so heavily played that, after deductions of state tax and commission, not enough money remains to pay the legally prescribed minimum on each winning bet. The racing association usually makes up the difference.

money rider A rider who excels in rich races.

monkey on a stick Type of riding with short stirrups popularized by riding great James F. "Tod" Sloan shortly before 1900.

morning glory Horse that performs well in morning workouts but fails to reproduce that form in races.

morning line Probable odds on each horse in a race, as determined by a mathematical formula used by the track oddsmaker, who tries to gauge both the ability of the horse and the most likely final odds as determined by the bettors. Those odds now are known as the program-line odds because they appear in the track's official program.

mud calks Special cleats that help a horse gain traction on a muddy track.

muddy (track) Condition of a racetrack that is wet but has no standing water.

mudder Horse that races well on muddy tracks. Also known as a mudlark.

mutuel pool Short for pari-mutuel pool. Sum of the wagers on a race or event, such as the win pool, daily double pool, exacta pool, etc.

muzzle 1) Nose and lips of a horse. 2) A guard placed over a horse's mouth to prevent it from biting or eating.

name (of a Thoroughbred) Names of North American Thoroughbreds are registered by the Jockey Club. They can be no longer than 18 characters, including punctuation and spaces.

National Thoroughbred Association Started as concept of advertising agency executive Fred Pope in early 1990s, with backing from owner-breeder John R. Gaines. The NTA was based on the concept that owners possess rights to their horses' images for simulcasting purposes, with the owners banding together to form a major league of racing through the pooling of simulcasting rights. Hamilton Jordan and Tim Smith were brought in to help sell the concept in 1997, and the NTA initiative eventually led to a broader industry coalition, the formation of the National Thoroughbred Racing Association. NTA officially was folded into the NTRA in August 1998.

National Thoroughbred Racing Association A not-for-profit association created by a consensus of industry factions to market the sport. Founding members were Breeders' Cup Ltd., the Jockey Club, Keeneland Association, and Oak Tree Racing Association, with each putting up $1-million in seed money. Before officially launching the office, the National Thoroughbred Association became a founding member when it ceased its existence and was rolled into the NTRA. In 2000, the Thoroughbred Owners and Breeders Association retroactively became a founding member. The NTRA first proposed a business plan to the industry in August 1997. The NTRA officially opened for business on April 1, 1998. Its first commissioner was Tim Smith. The NTRA formally merged many of its administrative functions with Breeders' Cup Ltd. on January 1, 2001. Smith resigned in 2004 and D. G. Van Clief Jr. was named commissioner.

National Museum of Racing and Hall of Fame Building in Saratoga Springs, New York, that houses a museum and a Racing Hall of Fame. The National Museum of Racing was founded in 1950. It had its first home in the old Canfield Casino, Congress Park, Saratoga Springs. It moved to its present site in 1955, when the Racing Hall of Fame was created.

near side Left side of a horse. Side on which a horse is mounted.

neck Unit of measurement. About the length of a horse's neck; a little less than one-quarter length.

nod Lowering of head. To win by a nod, a horse extends its head with its nose crossing the finish line ahead of a close competitor.

nominator One who owns a horse at the time it is named to compete in a stakes race or makes it eligible to a stakes program such as the Breeders' Cup.

North American Pari-Mutuel Regulators Association Organization founded in 1997 as a splinter group from the Association of Racing Commissioners International due to philosophical differences in practices and policies. NAPRA's original members were Alabama, Arizona, Florida, Idaho, Kansas, Minnesota, Oklahoma, Oregon, Saskatchewan, South Dakota, Wisconsin, and Wyoming. Joining the organization by June 2005 were the Alberta Racing Corp., British Columbia, Colorado, Iowa, Manitoba, Montana, Nevada, North Dakota, Pennsylvania, and Virginia.

nose Smallest advantage a horse can win by. Called a short head in Britain.

nose band A strap that goes over the bridge of a horse's nose to help secure the bridle. A figure-eight nose band goes over the bridge of the nose and under the rings of the bit to help keep the horse's mouth closed. The figure-eight nose band keeps the tongue from sliding up over the bit and is used on horses that do not like having a tongue tie used.

Oaks A stakes event for three-year-old fillies loosely patterned after England's Epsom Oaks and usually the most important race for that sex and age group at a given track.

objection Claim of foul lodged by rider, patrol judge, or other official after the running of a race.

odds-on Odds of less than even money.

oddsmaker The individual who prepares the program line for a track.

official 1) Notice displayed when a race result is confirmed. 2) Used to denote a racing official.

off side Right side of horse.

off-track betting Wagering at legalized betting outlets usually run by the tracks, management companies specializing in pari-mutuel wagering, or, in New York, by independent corporations chartered by the state. Wagers at OTB sites are usually commingled with on-track betting pools.

on the bit When a horse is eager to run. Also known as in the bridle.

on the board Finishing among the first three.

on the muscle Denotes a fit horse.

on the nose Betting a horse to win only.

optional claiming A claiming race in which there is an option to have horses entered to be claimed for a stated price or not eligible to be claimed.

outcross When a horse has no inbreeding, especially within the first five generations.

out of the money A horse that finishes worse than third.

overcheck A strap that holds the bit in place.

overgirth An elastic band that goes completely around a horse's midsection and over the saddle, to keep the saddle from slipping.

overland, overland route Racing wide throughout, outside other horses.

overlay A horse going off at higher odds than it appears to warrant based on its past performances.

overnight A sheet published by the racing secretary's office listing the entries for an upcoming racing card.

overnight race A race in which entries close in a specific number of hours before running (such as 48 hours) and does not require an entry fee, as opposed to a stakes race for which nominations close weeks and sometimes months in advance and usually requires a monetary payment for a horse to be eligible.

over-reaching Toe of hind shoe striking the forefoot or foreleg.

overweight Excess weight carried by a horse when the rider exceeds the designated weight assignment.

pacesetter The horse that is running in front (on the lead).

paddock 1) Area where horses are saddled and paraded before being taken onto the track. 2) Field on a breeding farm where horses are turned out to graze.

paddock judge Official in charge of paddock and saddling routine.

panel A slang term for a furlong.

pari-mutuel A form of wagering originated in mid-1860s by Frenchman Pierre Oller in which all money bet is distributed to those who have winning tickets after taxes, takeout, and other deductions are made. Oller called his system perier mutuel, meaning mutual stake or betting among ourselves. As this wagering method was adopted in England, it became known as Paris mutuals, and later as pari-mutuels.

parlay A multirace bet in which all winnings are subsequently wagered on a succeeding race.

part wheel Using a key horse or horses in different, but not all, possible exotic wagering combinations.

pasteboard track A lightning-fast racing surface.

past performances A horse's racing record, earnings, bloodlines, and other data, presented in composite form.

patrol judges Officials who observe the progress of a race from various vantage points around the track.

pattern race Synonym for a group race in Europe.

photo finish A result so close it is necessary to use the finish-line camera to determine the order of finish.

pick (six—or other number) A type of multirace wager in which the winners of all the included races must be selected. Pick three (sometimes called the daily triple), pick six, and pick nine are commonly used by tracks in the United States.

pill Small numbered ball used in a blind draw to decide post positions.

pinched back A horse forced back when racing in close quarters, particularly on turns.

pin firing Thermocautery intended to increase blood flow to the leg and thus to promote healing.

pinhooker A person who buys a racehorse prospect with the intention of reselling it at a profit. Examples are weanling-to-yearling pinhookers and yearling-to-juvenile pinhookers.

pipe-opener Exercise at a brisk speed.

place Second position at finish.

place bet Wager on a horse to finish first or second.

placing judge Official who posts the order of finish in a race.

plate(s) 1) A prize for a winner. Usually less valuable than a cup. 2) Generic term for lightweight horseshoes, usually made of aluminum, that are used during a race.

plater Vernacular for a claiming horse.

pocket A position in a race with horses in front and alongside.

pole(s) Markers at measured distances around the track designating the distance from the finish. The quarter pole, for instance, is one-quarter mile from the finish line, not from the start.

pony Any horse or pony that leads the parade of the field from paddock to starting gate. A horse or pony that accompanies a horse to the starting gate. Also known as a lead pony.

post 1) Starting point for a race. 2) An abbreviated version of post position.

post parade Horses going from paddock to starting gate past the stands.

post position Position of stall in starting gate from which a horse starts.

preferred list Horses with prior rights to starting, usually because they have previously been entered in races that have not filled with the minimum number of starters or they have been excluded from races that drew an excess of entries.

prep (race) A workout (or race) used to prepare a horse for a future engagement.

program line Probable odds on each horse in a race, as determined by a mathematical formula used by the track oddsmaker, who tries to gauge both the ability of the horse and the likely final odds as determined by the bettors. These odds are published in the track's official program and formerly were known as the morning line.

prop When a horse suddenly stops moving by digging its front feet into the ground.

public trainer One whose services are not exclusively engaged by a single stable and who accepts horses from a number of owners.

pull up To stop or slow a horse during or after a race or workout.

purse The total monetary amount distributed after a race to the owners of the entrants finishing in the top positions, usually five. Some racing jurisdictions may pay purse money through other places.

quarantine barn 1) A United States Department of Agriculture structure used to isolate foreign horses for a short period of time to ensure they are not carrying a disease. The structure may be at a racetrack, an airport, or a specially designated facility. Horses must be cleared by a federal veterinarian before being released from quarantine. 2) Any facility used to keep infected horses away from the general equine population.

quarter crack A vertical crack of the hoof between the toe and heel, usually extending into the coronary band.

quinella Wager in which the first two finishers must be picked in either order.

rabbit A speed horse running as an entry with another, usually a come-from-behind horse.

Racing Index Racing Index (RI) is based on the average earnings per start for all runners in the United States, Canada, England, Ireland, France, Italy, Germany, Puerto Rico, and the United Arab Emirates. RI is determined by calculating the average earnings per start, divided into males and females, of all starters in each individual country, and the average for each individual year is by definition 1.00. Median RI is much lower.

racing secretary Official who drafts conditions of races and assigns weights for handicap events.

racino A racetrack with other forms of gambling, especially slot machines.

rail The barrier on either side of the racing strip. Sometimes referred to as the fence.

rail runner Horse that prefers to run next to the inside rail.

rank A horse that refuses to settle under a jockey's handling in a race, running in a headstrong manner without respect to pace.

receiving barn Racetrack structure used to house horses shipping in for a race on a specific day. Horses trained on farms or at training centers often will be placed in the receiving barn until their races.

redboard 1) Old-time method of declaring a race official by posting a red flag or board on the tote board. 2) A mildly derogatory phrase used to describe someone who claims to have selected the winner, but always after the race.

refuse 1) When a horse will not break from the gate. 2) In jumping races, balking at a jump.

reins Long straps, usually made of leather, that are connected to the bit and used by the jockey to control the horse.

reserve A minimum price, set by the consignor, for a horse in a public auction.

reserved 1) Held for a particular engagement or race. 2) Held off the pace.

reserve not attained A minimum price, or reserve, set by the consignor for a horse at a public auction that is not met by those who are bidding. RNA.

resorption Death of an embryo or fetus before fourth month of gestation, usually followed by dehydration of the conceptus and self-dissolution of the remaining solid tissue.

ridden out A horse that finishes a race under mild urging; not as severe as driving.

ride short Using short stirrup leathers.

ridgling (rig) A term describing either a cryptorchid (neither testicle descended) or a monorchid (one

testicle descended into the scrotum).

roan A horse color in which the majority of the coat is a mixture of red and white hairs or brown and white hairs. The mane, tail, and legs may be black, chestnut, or roan unless white markings are present. Starting with foals of 1993, the color classifications of gray and roan were combined as gray or roan.

rogue Ill-tempered horse.

route A race of long distance; broadly, a race at a distance of 1⅛ miles or more in North America.

router Horse that performs well at longer distances.

run-out bit A specialty bit to prevent a horse from bearing out (or in).

saddle A Thoroughbred racing saddle is the lightest saddle used, weighing less than two pounds.

saddlecloth A cotton cloth that goes under the saddle to absorb sweat. It usually has the horse's program number on it and, often in major races, the horse's name.

saddlepad A piece of felt, sheepskin, or more usually, foam rubber, used as a base for the saddle.

Salix An antibleeder medication that had been named Lasix until the medication's manufacturer, Intervet, changed the name in 2001. Its generic name is furosemide, and it was first used in veterinary practice in 1967.

savage When a horse bites another horse or a person.

scale of weights Fixed weights to be carried by horses according to their age, sex, race distance, and time of year. See scale of weights table in the Racing chapter.

schooling Process of familiarizing a horse with the starting gate and teaching it racing practices. A horse also may be schooled in the paddock. In steeplechasing, to teach a horse to jump.

schooling list List of horses eligible to school at the starting gate before being permitted to race.

scratch To be taken out of a race before a horse starts. Trainers or owners usually scratch horses due to adverse track conditions or a horse's health. A track veterinarian can scratch a horse at any time.

second call A secondary mount of a jockey in a race in case his primary mount is scratched.

second dam Grandmother of a horse in direct female line. Also known as a grandam.

set A group of horses being exercised together.

set down 1) To be suspended, usually referring to a jockey. 2) When a jockey assumes a lower crouch in the saddle while urging the horse to pick up speed.

sex allowance Female horses (fillies and mares), according to their age and the time of year, are allowed to carry three to five pounds less when racing against males.

shadow roll A bulky piece of material, usually sheepskin or synthetic fabric, that is secured over the bridge of a horse's nose to keep it from seeing shadows on the track. Often used with horses that shy away from shadows on the track or jump them.

shank Rope or strap attached to a halter or bridle by which a horse is led.

shedrow Stable area; walking path within a barn.

sheets A handicapping tool assigning a numerical value to each race run by a horse to enable different horses running at different racetracks to be objectively compared. Two principal companies in this field are operated by Len Ragozin, the originator, and Jerry Brown.

short A horse in need of more workouts or racing to reach winning form.

show Third position at the finish.

show bet Wager on a horse to finish in the money; third or better.

shut off Unable to improve position due to being surrounded by other horses.

silks Jacket and cap worn by riders to designate the owner of the horse, or at some smaller tracks, to designate post positions (e.g., yellow for post position one, blue for two, etc.).

Silky Sullivan A term sometimes used for a horse that makes a big run from far back. Named for the horse Silky Sullivan, who once made up 41 lengths to win a six-furlong race.

simulcast A simultaneous live television transmission of a race to other tracks, off-track betting facilities, or other outlets for the purpose of wagering.

sire 1) The male parent. 2) To beget foals. According to cataloging standards and standard usage, a stallion must sire a winner to be called a sire; he is a stallion until that time.

Sire Index (SI) Sire Index is an average of the Racing Index (RI) of all foals by a sire that have started at least three times. For SI to be calculated, a sire must be represented by a minimum of three crops and 25 starters lifetime.

slipped A breeding term meaning spontaneous abortion.

sloppy A racing strip that is saturated with water and has standing water visible.

slow A racing strip that is wet on both the surface and base.

snip Small patch of white hairs on the nose or lips of a horse.

socks Solid white markings extending from the top of the hoof to the knee or hock. Also called stockings.

soft Condition of a turf course with a large amount of moisture. Horses' hooves sink deeply into the surface.

sophomores Three-year-old horses.

speed figure A handicapping tool in which a numerical value is assigned to a horse's performance.

speedy cut Injury to the inside of the knee or hock caused by a strike from another foot.

spit box A generic term describing a barn or area to which horses are taken for post-race testing. Tests may include saliva, urine, and/or blood.

spit the bit Or spit out the bit. A term referring to a tired horse that begins to run less aggressively.

split(s) Fractional times in a race in increments of one-eighth of a mile.

sprint Short race, less than one mile.

stakes A race for which the owner usually must pay a fee to run a horse. The fees can be for nominating, maintaining eligibility, entering, and starting; the track adds additional money to make up the total purse. Some stakes races are by invitation and require no payment or fee.

stakes horse A horse whose level of competition includes mostly stakes races.

stakes-placed Finished second or third in a stakes race.

stallion A male horse used for breeding.

stallion season The right to breed one mare to a specific stallion during one breeding season.

stallion share A lifetime right to breed one mare to a specific stallion each breeding season. Although generally limited to one mare per season per share, larger stallion books have in some cases allowed share owners to breed more than one mare each year. Stallion share owners are usually assessed a proportionate share of expenses and also will share in any bonuses.

stall walker Horse that moves about its stall constantly and frets rather than resting.

star 1) Any of several white markings on the forehead. (The forehead is defined as being above an imaginary line connecting the tops of the eyes.) 2) A type of credit a horse receives from the racing secretary if it is excluded from an overfilled race, giving it priority in entering future races.

starter 1) An official responsible for ensuring a fair start to the race. The starter supervises the loading of horses into the starting gate by assistant starters who collectively are known as a gate crew. The starter also has control of opening the gate. 2) A horse that is in the starting gate when the race begins, whether it runs or not.

starter race An allowance or handicap race restricted to horses that have started for a specific claiming price or less.

starting gate Partitioned mechanical device having stalls in which the horses are confined until the starter releases the stalls' front doors to begin the race.

stayer A horse that can race long distances successfully.

steadied A horse being taken in hand by its rider, usually when in close quarters.

steeplechase A race in which horses are required to jump a series of obstacles on the course. Steeplechase races in the United States are run over National Fences (artificial brush fences), natural brush fences, and timber fences. In England and Ireland, jump races are over hurdles and steeplechase fences.

step up A horse moving up in class to meet better competition.

steward Official of the race meeting responsible for enforcing the rules of racing.

stick A jockey's whip.

stirrups Metal D-shaped rings into which a jockey places his or her feet. They can be raised or lowered by shortening or lengthening the leather straps that connect the stirrups to the saddle. Also known as irons.

stockings Solid white markings extending from the top of the hoof to the knee or hock. Also called socks.

stone English system of weights is based on stones. A stone is equal to 14 pounds; thus, 126 pounds is nine stone.

(home) stretch Final straight; portion of the racetrack from the end of the final turn to the finish line.

stretch call Position of horses at the eighth pole, or one-eighth mile from the finish.

stretch runner Horse that runs fastest, relative to the pacesetters, nearing the finish of a race.

stretch turn Bend of track into the final straightaway.

stride Manner of going. Also, distance covered between successive imprints of the same hoof.

stripe A white marking running down a horse's face, starting under an imaginary line connecting the tops of the eyes.

stud 1) Male horse used for breeding. 2) A breeding farm.

stud book Registry and genealogical record of Thoroughbreds, maintained by the Jockey Club or Turf authority of another country.

subscription Fee paid by owner to nominate a horse for a stakes race or to maintain eligibility for a stakes.

substitute race Alternate race used on overnight sheets to replace a regularly scheduled race that does not fill or is canceled.

suckling A foal in its first year of life, while it is still nursing.

sulk When a horse refuses to extend itself.

swayback Horse with a prominent concave shape of the backbone, usually just behind the withers (saddle area). Lordosis.

tack Rider's racing equipment. Also applied to stable gear.

tail-male (-female) A horse's ancestry from sire to grandsire to great-grandsire, etc., tracing back to one of the three sires (or along the female line from dam to grandam to great-grandam, etc., back to the original foundation mares).

tail off Used to describe a fit horse losing its competitive edge, or, in an individual race, when a horse slows down and loses contact with the field.

taken up A horse pulled up sharply by its rider due to being in close quarters.

takeout Commission deducted from mutuel pools that is shared by the track, horsemen (in the form of purses), breeding and benevolence funds, and local and state governing bodies in the form of tax. Also called take.

tattoo A permanent, indelible mark on the inside of the upper lip used to identify the horse.

teaser A male horse used at breeding farms to determine whether a mare is ready to receive a stallion.

teletimer Electronic means to time races, including fractional times at various points of call. The lead horse trips an electronic beam of light and the clockings are transmitted instantly to the tote board.

Thoroughbred A horse that traces in all lines of its pedigree to horses registered in previous volumes of the world's Thoroughbred stud books for at least eight consecutive crosses. All modern Thoroughbreds trace in male line to one of the three founding sires—the Darley Arabian, Byerly Turk, and Godolphin Arabian. The horse also must have satisfied the rules and requirements of the Jockey Club for inclusion in the *American Stud Book*, or it is registered in a foreign stud book recognized by the Jockey Club and the International Stud Book Committee.

Thoroughbred Horsemen's Association A representative group organized on local levels primarily in Mid-Atlantic states to represent the interests of owners in negotiations with tracks on purses and other issues. Started as an alternative to the Horsemen's Benevolent and Protective Association.

Thoroughbred Racing Associations An industry group founded in 1942 and comprising about 50 racetracks in North America.

tight Vernacular for fit and ready to race.

tightener 1) A race used to give a horse a level of fitness that cannot be obtained through morning exercise alone. 2) A leg brace.

timber topper Steeplechase horse racing over post-and-rail fences.

tongue tie Strip of cloth or cloth-like material used to stabilize a horse's tongue to prevent it from choking down in a race or workout or to keep the tongue from sliding up over the bit, rendering the horse uncontrollable. Also known as a tongue strap.

top line 1) A Thoroughbred's breeding on its sire's side. 2) The visual line presented by the horse's back.

totalizator An automated pari-mutuel system that dispenses and records betting tickets, calculates and displays odds and payoffs, and provides the mechanism for cashing winning tickets. Often shortened to tote.

tote board Structure in the racetrack infield where up-to-the-minute odds and other information are listed. It may also show the amounts wagered in each mutuel pool as well as information such as jockey and equipment changes. Also known as the board.

tout Person who professes to have, and sells, advance information on a race.

track bias A racing surface that favors a particular running style or position.

track condition Physical state of the racetrack surface.

trial In Thoroughbred racing, a preparatory race created in tandem with a subsequent, more important stakes race to be run a few days or weeks later. In Europe, a trial can refer to a vigorous morning workout with other horses under race-like conditions.

trifecta A wager in which the first three finishers must be selected in exact order. Called a triactor in Canada and a triple in some parts of the United States.

trifecta box A trifecta wager in which all possible combinations using a given number of horses are bet upon.

trip An individual horse's race, with specific reference to the difficulty (or lack of difficulty) the horse had during competition, such as whether the horse was repeatedly blocked or had an unobstructed run.

Triple Crown Used generically to denote a series of three important races. In the United States, the Kentucky Derby, Preakness Stakes, and Belmont Stakes make up the Triple Crown. In England, the Two Thousand Guineas, Epsom Derby, and St. Leger Stakes. In Canada, the Queen's Plate, Prince of Wales Stakes, and Breeders' Stakes.

turn down(s) Rear shoe that is turned down—from a half-inch to one inch at the ends—to provide better traction on an off-track. Illegal in most jurisdictions.

twitch A restraining device usually consisting of a stick with a loop of rope or chain at one end, which is placed around a horse's upper lip and twisted, releasing endorphins that relax a horse and curb its fractiousness while it is being handled.

underlay A horse at shorter odds than seem warranted by its past performances.

under wraps Horse under stout restraint in a race or workout to keep it from pulling away from the competition by too large a margin.

untried 1) Not raced or tested for speed. 2) A stallion that has not been bred.

unwind Gradually withdrawing a horse from intensive training.

valet A person employed by a racing association to clean and care for a jockey's tack and other riding equipment.

walkover A race in which only one horse competes.

washed out A horse that becomes so nervous that it sweats profusely. Also known as washy or lathered (up).

weanling A foal less than one-year-old that has been separated (weaned) from its dam.

weigh in (out) The certification by the clerk of scales of a rider's weight before (after) a race. A jockey weighs in fully dressed with all equipment except for his or her helmet, whip, and flak jacket.

weight for age An allowance condition in which each entrant is assigned a weight according to its age. Females usually receive a sex allowance as well.

wheel Betting all possible combinations in an exotic wager using at least one horse as the key.

white A horse color, extremely rare, in which all the hairs are white. The horse's eyes are brown.

wire The finish line of a race.

workout A fast gallop at a predetermined distance.

yearling A horse in its second calendar year of life, beginning January 1 of the year following its birth for horses born in the Northern Hemisphere.

yielding Condition of a turf course with considerable moisture. Horses feet sink into it noticeably.

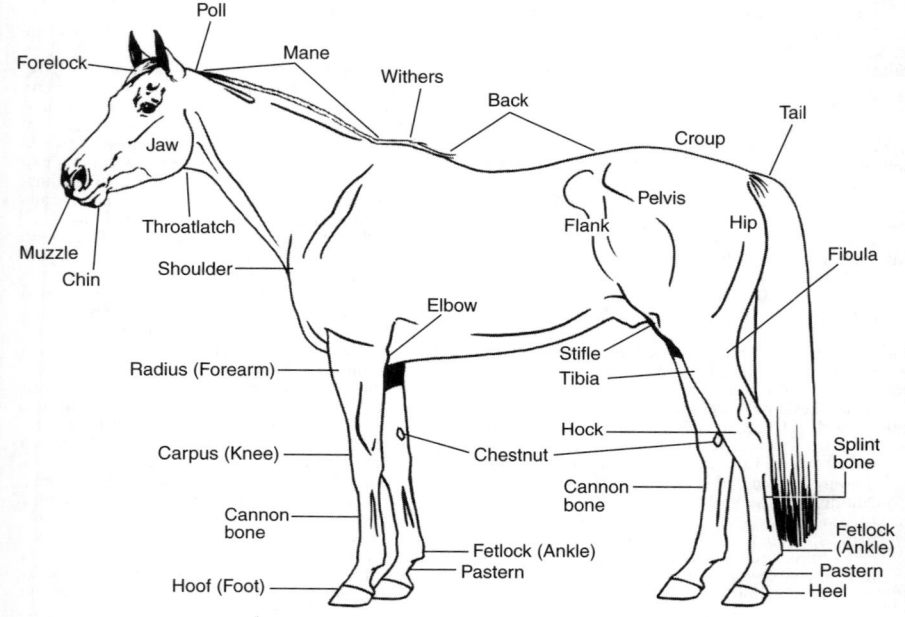

Conformation and Anatomy Terms

The following are words and expressions commonly used to describe Thoroughbred anatomy and conformation. This glossary contains many terms and definitions found in *The Media Guide to Equine Sport*, published by the American Association of Equine Practitioners.

angular limb deformity A limb that does not have correct conformation because of developmental problems in the angles of the joints.

anterior Toward the front.

back at the knee Conformation fault of foreleg. Upper leg is set back farther than lower leg, placing strain on tendons and ligaments. Synonym for calf knees.

cannon bone The third metacarpal (front leg) or metatarsal (rear leg), also referred to as the shin bone. The largest bone between the knee and ankle joints.

carpus A joint in the horse's front leg, more commonly referred to as the knee.

caudal Toward the tail.

cervical vertebrae Seven vertebrae that form the neck.

chestnut Horny growth on inside of each leg; located above the knee in the foreleg and below the hock in the hind leg. No two chestnuts are believed to be identical, and therefore were used for identification of horses in the registration process for many years. Also known as night eyes.

coccygeal vertebrae Eighteen vertebrae that form the tail in the Thoroughbred.

coffin bone The third phalanx (P3). The major bone within the confines of the hoof. Also called the pedal bone.

conformation The physical makeup and bodily proportions of a horse; how the horse is put together.

coronary band Where the hair meets the hoof. Also called the coronet.

cow hocks Abnormal conformation in which the points of the hocks turn in.

cranial Toward the head.

curb A thickening of the plantar ligament of the hock.

deep flexor tendon Present in all four legs, but injuries most commonly affect the front legs. Located on the back (posterior) of the front leg between the knee and the foot and between the hock and the foot on the rear leg. The function is to flex the digit (pastern) and knee (carpus) and to extend the elbow on the front leg and extend the hock on the rear leg. Functions in tandem with the superficial flexor tendon.

digital The part of the limb below the ankle (fetlock) joint. Includes the long and short pastern bones and the coffin bone.

digital cushion The area beneath the coffin bone in the back of the foot that separates it from the frog. The digital cushion serves as a shock absorber.

distal Away from a reference point. Usually refers to the limbs.

distal sesamoidean ligaments Attach to the bottom of the sesamoid bones, passing down and attaching to the long and short pastern bones.

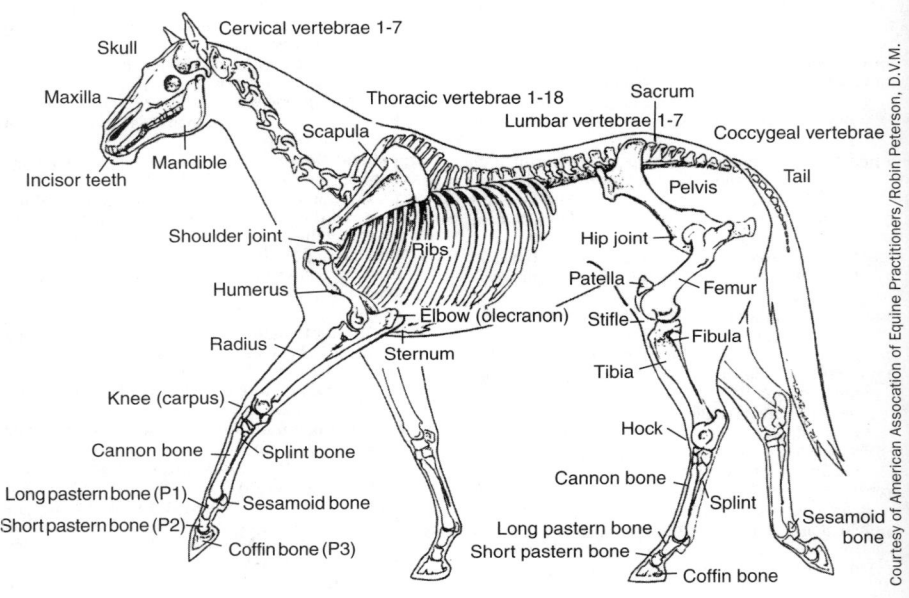

Courtesy of American Association of Equine Practitioners/Robin Peterson, D.V.M.

dorsal Up; toward the back or spine. Also used to describe the front of the lower limb below the knee (front) or hock (rear).

elbow (olecranon) Joint in forelimb that connects the humerus to the radius and ulna.

extensor tendon Extends the knee (carpus) joint, ankle joint, pastern, and foot and flexes the elbow. The muscles begin above the knee and attach to the coffin and pastern bones.

fault Weak points of a horse's conformation or its character as a racehorse.

femur Large bone of the hind limb that connects with the pelvis at the hip joint and the hind leg at the stifle joint.

fetlock Joint located between the cannon bone and the long pastern bone, also referred to as the ankle.

fibula Smaller bone in hind leg that extends half the length of the tibia and sits parallel to it. Taken together, the area from the stifle to the hock joint that includes the tibia and fibula is referred to as the gaskin.

frog The V-shaped, pliable support structure on the bottom of the foot.

hip joint Ball-and-socket joint in the hindquarters that accommodates the head of the femur.

hock A large joint just above the shin bone in the rear legs. Corresponds to the level of the knee of the front leg.

hoof The foot of the horse. Consists of several parts that play an integral role in supporting the weight of the horse.

humerus Long bone of the upper forearm that forms the point of the shoulder. The humerus connects the shoulder blade (scapula) to the radius and ulna, the two bones that compose the lower forearm.

inferior check ligament A direct continuation of the posterior (back) ligaments of the knee (carpus), located below the knee. Function is in support of the deep flexor tendon.

insensitive laminae The layer just under the wall of the hoof; similar to the human fingernail. It is an integral structure that helps attach the hoof wall to the underlying coffin bone.

joint Point of juncture of two bones and usually composed of fibrous connective tissue and cartilage.

joint capsule The sac-like structure that encloses the ends of bones in certain joints; contains synovial fluid.

ligament A band of fibrous tissue that connects bones, supports and strengthens joints, and limits the range of motion. Some ligaments support certain organs.

lumbar vertebrae Six vertebrae over the loin, immediately behind the rib cage.

mandible Lower jaw that contains teeth.

maxilla Upper jaw that contains teeth.

medial Pertaining to the middle in anatomy, nearer the median plane (the vertical plane that bisects the body into right and left halves).

metacarpal The cannon bone, located between the knee and the fetlock joint in the front leg. The cannon bone of the front leg is the third metacarpal.

metatarsal Cannon bone in the hind leg.

musculoskeletal system Consisting of the bones, muscles, ligaments, tendons, and joints of the head, vertebral column, and limbs, together with the associated muscles, tendons, ligaments, and joints.

muzzle Nose and lips of a horse.

navicular bone A small, flat bone within the confines of the hoof that helps, along with the short pastern bone and the coffin bone, to make up the coffin joint.

open knee A condition of young horses in which the physis of the knee has not closed; an immature knee. Often used to describe the status of the physis immediately above the knee and is an indicator of long-bone growth in two-year-olds.

over at the knee A leg that looks as though it has a forward arc with its center at the knee when viewed from the side.

palmer Pertaining to the back of the front limb from the knee down.

parrot mouth A horse with an extreme overbite.

pastern Bones in the area between the fetlock joint and the hoof. The joint between the long and short pastern bones is called the pastern joint. Can also be used to describe the area of the limb or to describe a specific bone: long pastern bone. Technically known as the P1 (long) and the P2 (short).

patella Bone in the stifle joint, similar to human knee cap. Ligaments attach it to the femur and the tibia.

pelvis Bone structure of the hindquarters that joins the spine around the sacrum, the fused bones of the spine. The largest structure of the pelvis is the os coxae, or hip bone.

physis The growth plate at the end of the long bones (such as the cannon bone) that lets the bone grow in length.

plantar Pertaining to the sole of the foot or back of the hind limb from the hock down.

plantar ligament The large ligament that is below and behind the hock joint.

poll The top of the head between the ears.

posterior Situated behind or toward the rear.

proximal Toward the body; the proximal cannon region is the upper portion of the cannon bone.

radius Long bone of the foreleg that extends from the elbow to the knee; principal bone of the lower forearm.

respiratory system Organ system responsible for gas exchange from nostrils to lungs.

sacral vertebrae Five fused vertebrae that make up the hip girdle.

scapula Shoulder blade in the foreleg.

sensitive laminae The area of the hoof that contains nerves and vessels.

sesamoid Two small bones (medial and lateral sesamoids) located above and at the back of the fetlock joint. Four common fractures of the sesamoids are apical (along the top of the bone), abaxial (the side of the sesamoid away from the ankle joint), midbody (sesamoid broken in half), and basilar (through the bottom) fractures. Fractures can be small chips or involve the entire bone. Surgical repair is often done by arthroscopy.

shoulder joint Ball-and-socket joint between the shoulder blade and humerus in the foreleg. Sometimes referred to as the scapulo-humeral joint.

sickle hocks Forward deviation of the lower hind leg, from the hocks to the hoof, producing the appearance of a sickle when viewed from the side. Also known as curby hocks.

splint Either of the two small bones that lie along the sides of the cannon bone.

stifle Hinge joint between the femur and tibia of the hind leg, similar to the human knee. It is the largest joint in the horse's body.

superficial flexor tendon Present in all four legs, but injuries most commonly affect the front legs. Located on the back (posterior) of the front leg between the knee and the foot and between the hock and the foot in the rear leg. Functions are to flex the digit (pastern) and knee (carpus), to extend the elbow on the front leg, and to extend the hock on the rear leg. Functions in tandem with the deep flexor tendon.

superior check ligament Fibrous band of tissue that originates above the knee and attaches to the superficial flexor tendon. Primary function is support of this tendon. Accessory ligament of the superficial flexor tendon.

suspensory ligament Originates at the back of the knee (front leg) and the back of the top part of the cannon bone (hind leg), attaching to the sesamoid bones. The lower portion of the ligament attaches the lower part of the sesamoid bones to the pastern bones. Its function is to support the fetlock. The lower ligaments that attach the sesamoid bone to the pastern bones are the distal sesamoidean ligaments.

synovial joint A movable joint that consists of articulating bone ends covered by articular cartilage held together with a joint capsule and ligaments and containing synovial fluid in the joint cavity.

synovial sheath The inner lining of a tendon sheath that produces synovial fluid. Allows ease of motion for the tendons as they cross joints.

tendon Cords of strong, white (collagen) elastic fibers that connect a muscle to a bone or other structure and transmit the forces generated by muscular contraction to the bones.

thoracic vertebrae Eighteen vertebrae in the horse's midsection that connect to the ribs.

throatlatch Point on underside of horse's head where it meets the neck.

tibia Larger of the two bones of the hind leg that extend from the stifle to the hock.

toe-in A conformation flaw in which the front of the foot angles inward and looks pigeon-toed, often causing the leg to swing outward during locomotion (paddling).

toe-out A conformation flaw in which the front of the foot faces out, often causing the leg to swing inward during locomotion (winging).

ventral Down; toward the belly.

vocal folds The membranes attached to the arytenoid cartilages in the larynx. Vibration produces vocalization.

white line When looking at the sole of the foot, the thin area between the insensitive outer hoof wall (insensitive laminae) and the inner sensitive laminae.

withers Area above the shoulder, where the neck meets the back.

Common Veterinary Terms

The following are commonly used veterinary terms. This glossary contains many terms and definitions found in the *Media Guide to Equine Sport*, published by the American Association of Equine Practitioners.

acupressure Utilizing stimulation on acupuncture points to treat an animal.

acupuncture A centuries-old therapy for treating an animal or human through the use of needles, electrical current, or moxibustion (heat and herbs) to stimulate or realign the body's electrical fields.

anhydrosis Inability to sweat in response to work output or increases in body temperature. Most commonly occurs when both temperature and humidity are high.

anterior enteritis Acute inflammation of the small intestine producing signs of abdominal distress, such as colic and diarrhea.

arthritis Inflammation of a joint. An increase in the amount of synovial fluid in the joint is a result of this inflammation.

arthroscope A thin tube containing a lens that is used for viewing areas inside a joint. Usually attached to a small video camera.

arthroscopic surgery Utilizing an arthroscope to perform surgery, eliminating the need to open the joint with a large incision to view the damaged area.

articular cartilage Cartilage that covers the ends of bones where they meet in a joint.

arytenoid cartilages Triangular cartilages in the upper part of the entrance to the larynx. Movements of the arytenoid cartilages control the diameter of the laryngeal opening.

ataxia Loss or failure of muscular coordination.

atrophy To waste away; usually used in describing muscles.

bleeder A horse that bleeds within its lungs when small capillaries that surround the lungs' air sacs (alveoli) rupture. The veterinary term is exercise-induced pulmonary hemorrhage. Blood may be seen coming out of the horse's nostrils, known as epistaxis, although it is typically discovered by an examination using a fiber-optic endoscope after exercise or racing. Hot, humid weather and cold conditions are known to exacerbate the problem. The most common preventive treatment currently available is the use of the diuretic furosemide (Salix). Less than one bleeder in 20 shows signs of epistaxis.

blister Counterirritant causing acute inflammation; used to increase blood supply and blood flow to promote healing in the leg.

bog spavin A filling with excess synovial fluid of the largest joint of the hock, called the tibial tarsal joint.

bone graft Utilizing bone taken from one part of the body to promote formation of bone in another region.

bone spavin Arthritis of the hock joint. A bone spavin that has progressed to the point that the arthritis can be seen externally is called a jack spavin.

bowed tendon A type of tendinitis. The most common injury to the tendon is a strain or bowed tendon, so named because of the appearance of a bow shape due to swelling. The most common site of injury is in the superficial flexor tendon between the knee and the ankle. Despite aggressive treatment with anti-inflammatory drugs, physical therapy, and rest, horses commonly reinjure the tendon when they return to strenuous training. Two surgeries are felt to aid horses to come back to racing: tendon splitting at the lesion site to release accumulated fluid and blood, and superior check ligament desmotomy. The latter surgery is designed to reduce forces on the tendon when the horse returns to training and racing.

breakdown When a horse suffers a potentially career-ending injury, usually to the leg.

broken wind Abnormality of the upper or lower respiratory tract causing loss of normal air exchange, generally resulting in reduced performance.

bronchodilator A drug that widens the airways in the lungs to improve breathing and to relieve muscle contraction or accumulation of mucus.

bucked shins Inflammation of the covering of the bone (periosteum) of the front surface of the cannon bone to which young horses are particularly susceptible. Usually a condition of the front legs.

bursa A sac containing synovial fluid (a natural lubricant). Its purpose is to pad or cushion and thus facilitate motion between soft tissue and bone, most commonly where tendons pass over bones.

bursitis Inflammation in a bursa that results in swelling due to accumulation of synovial fluid.

Bute Short for phenylbutazone, a nonsteroidal anti-inflammatory medication that is legal in many racing jurisdictions. Often known by the trade names Butazolidin and Butazone.

capillary refill time The amount of time it takes for blood to return to capillaries after it has been forced out, normally two seconds; usually assessed by pressing the thumb against the horse's gums. When the pressure is removed, the gum looks white but the normal pink color returns as blood flows into the capillaries.

capped elbow Inflammation of the bursa over the point of the elbow. Also known as a shoe boil.

capped hock Inflammation of the bursa over the point of the hock.

chiropractic The use of bone alignment to treat specific or general health problems.

chronic obstructive pulmonary disease Commonly known as COPD, a hyperallergenic response of the respiratory system that involves damage to the lung tissue, similar in many ways to human asthma. Affected horses may cough, develop a nasal discharge, and have a reduced tolerance for exercise. Respiratory rate is increased and lung elasticity is diminished.

chronic osselet Permanent buildup of synovial fluid in a joint, characterized by inflammation and thickening of the joint capsule over the damaged area. Usually accompanied by changes in the bone and cartilage.

clenbuterol A bronchodilator used for respiratory ailments. It is not permissible for use on race day.

closed knees A condition when the cartilaginous growth plate above the knee (distal radial physis) has turned to bone. Indicates completion of long bone growth and is one sign of maturity.

Coggins test Used to identify antigens or antibodies against equine infectious anemia.

colic Often used broadly to describe abdominal pain, it is the leading cause of death in horses. Its causes include obstruction in the large colon; a twist in the intestine that shuts off the food passageway and blocks the blood supply; or gastric ulcers.

comminuted A fracture with more than two fragments.

compound A fracture in which the damaged bone breaks through the skin. Also known as an open fracture.

condylar A fracture in the knuckle (condyle) of the lower (distal) end of a long bone such as the cannon bone or humerus (upper front limb).

congenital Present at birth.

contagious equine metritis A venereal disease. Mares may have a profuse vaginal discharge. No symptoms of CEM may be obvious in stallions.

corticosteroids Hormones (class of steroid) that are either naturally produced by the adrenal gland or man-made. They function as anti-inflammatory hormones or as hormones that regulate the chemical stability (homeostasis) of the body.

cough To expel air from the lungs in a spasmodic manner. Can be a result of inflammation or irritation to the upper airways (pharynx, larynx, or trachea) or may involve the lower airways of the lungs (deep cough).

cracked hoof A vertical split of the hoof wall. Cracks may extend upward from the bearing surface of the wall or downward from the coronary band, as the result of a defect in the band. Varying in degrees of severity, cracks can result from injuries or concussion. Hooves that are dry or thin (shelly) or improperly shod are susceptible to cracking upon concussion. Corrective trimming and shoeing may remedy mild cracks, but in severe cases, when the crack extends inward to the sensitive laminae, more extensive treatment is required, such as using screws and wires to stabilize the sides of the crack.

cribber A horse that clings to objects with its teeth and sucks air into its stomach. Also known as a wind sucker.

cryptorchid A unilateral cryptorchid is a male horse of any age that has one testicle undescended. A bilateral cryptorchid is a male horse of any age that has both testicles undescended. The Jockey Club defines cryptorchid as a male horse of any age that has both testicles undescended.

cup Refers to the irregular occlusal surface of the tooth (the surfaces that meet when a horse closes its mouth) and is used as a visual method of determining age in a horse.

curb A thickening of the plantar ligament of the hock.

degenerative joint disease Any joint problem that has progressive degeneration of joint cartilage and the underlying (subchondral) bone. Occurs most frequently in the joints below the radius in the foreleg and femur in the hind leg. Some of the more common causes include repeated trauma, conformation faults, blood disease, traumatic joint injury, subchondral bone defects, osteochondritis dissecans (OCD) lesions, and excessive intra-articular corticosteroid injections. Also known as osteoarthritis or as developmental orthopedic disease (DOD).

desmitis Inflammation of a ligament. Often a result of tearing of any number of ligament fibrils.

deworming The use of drugs (anthelmintics) to kill internal parasites, often performed by administration of oral paste or liquid or by passing a nasogastric tube into the horse's stomach.

digestible energy The amount of energy a horse is able to digest from its feed.

DMSO Dimethyl sulfoxide, a topical anti-inflammatory. Its chief characteristic is its ability to penetrate the skin and therefore act as a vehicle for medications.

dorsal displacement of the soft palate A condition in which the soft palate, located on the floor of the airway near the larynx, moves up into the airway. A minor displacement causes a gurgling sound during exercise, while in more serious cases the palate can block the airway. This is sometimes known as choking down, but the tongue does not actually block the airway. The base of the tongue is connected to the larynx, of which the epiglottis is a part. When the epiglottis is retracted, the soft palate can move up into the airway (dorsal displacement). This condition can sometimes be managed with equipment such as a figure-eight noseband or a tongue tie. In more extreme cases, surgery might be required, most commonly a myectomy.

drench Liquid administered through mouth.

Eastern equine encephalomyelitis One of several different types of encephalomyelitis that are extremely contagious, causing sickness and death in horses by affecting the central nervous system. EEE is spread by mosquitoes and can affect humans. Can be prevented by annual vaccination.

endoscope An instrument used for direct visual inspection of a hollow organ or body cavity such as the upper airway or stomach. A fiber-optic endoscope comprises a long, flexible tube that has a series of lenses and a light at the end to allow the veterinarian to view and photograph the respiratory system through the airway. Other internal organs may be viewed through a tiny surgical opening. A video endoscope has a small camera at its tip.

entrapped epiglottis A condition in which the thin membrane lying below the epiglottis moves up and covers the epiglottis. The abnormality may obstruct breathing. It is usually corrected by surgery to cut the membrane if it impairs respiratory function.

enzyme-linked immunosorbant assay A test, commonly referred to as the ELISA test, that is used after a race to detect the presence of drugs in racehorses. The post-race ELISA test was developed in the early 1990s by the University of Kentucky.

epiphysitis An inflammation in the growth plate (physis) at the ends of the long bones (such as the cannon bone). Symptoms include swelling, tenderness, and heat. Although the exact cause is unknown, contributing factors seem to be high caloric intake (either from grain or a heavily lactating mare) and a fast growth rate.

epistaxis Blood coming out of the horse's nostrils. See bleeder.

Epogen Genetically engineered form of the natural hormone erythropoietin (EPO) used to stimulate red blood cell production and thereby increase stamina. Abuse may cause fatal anemia. Banned by the Association of Racing Commissioners International as a Class 2 performance-enhancing drug.

equine protozoal myeloencephalitis Commonly called EPM. A neurological condition in a horse caused by a parasite that infects the horse's central nervous system. The cause of EPM is *Sarcocystis neurona*, a small protozoan organism that is slightly larger than a bacterium. The host necessary to complete the organism's life cycle is the opossum.

equine viral arteritis A highly contagious disease that is characterized by swelling in the legs of all horses and swelling in the scrotum of stallions. EVA can cause abortion in mares and can be shed in the semen of stallions for years after infection.

exercise-induced pulmonary hemorrhage (EIPH) See bleeder.

fissure Longitudinal crack through only one surface of a bone.

float An equine dental procedure in which sharp points on the teeth are filed down.

founder See laminitis.

fracture A break in a bone.

furosemide A medication used in the treatment of bleeders, commonly known by the trade name Salix, a diuretic.

gastric ulcers Ulceration of a horse's stomach. Often causes symptoms of abdominal distress (colic) and general unthriftiness.

gravel Infection of the hoof resulting from a crack in the white line (the border between the insensitive and sensitive laminae). An abscess usually forms in the sensitive structures and eventually breaks through at the coronet as a result of the infection.

green osselet In young horses, a swelling in the fetlock joint, particularly on the front of the joint where the cannon and long pastern bones meet. This swelling is a result of inflammation and reactive changes of the front edges of these two bones and adjacent cartilage. If the green osselet does not heal, a chronic osselet might develop with a permanent buildup of synovial fluid in the joint and inflammation and thickening of the joint capsule over the damaged area with secondary bone changes following the initial inflammation.

heaves Emphysema.

heel crack A crack on the heel of the hoof. Also called a sand crack.

hematoma A blood-filled area resulting from injury.

hyaluronic acid A normal component of joint fluid. Also can be a man-made intra-articular medication used to relieve joint inflammation.

impaction A type of colic caused by a blockage of the intestines by ingested materials (constipation).

intra-articular Within a joint.

intramuscular An injection given in a muscle.

intravenous An injection given in a vein.

ischemia Deficiency of blood supply, either temporary or permanent. Caused by the shutting down of blood vessels.

lactic acid Organic acid normally present in muscle tissue, produced by anaerobic muscle metabolism as a byproduct of exercise. An increase in lactic acid causes muscle fatigue, inflammation, and pain.

lame A deviation from a normal gait due to pain in a limb or its supporting structures.

laminitis An inflammation of the sensitive laminae of the foot. Many factors are involved, including changes in the blood flow through the capillaries of the foot. Many events can cause laminitis, including ingesting toxic levels of grain, eating lush grass, systemic disease problems, high temperature, toxemia, retained placenta, excessive weight-bearing as occurs when the opposite limb is injured, and the administration of some drugs. Laminitis usually manifests itself in the front feet, develops rapidly, and is life-threatening. In mild cases, however, a horse can resume a certain amount of athletic activity. Also known as founder.

magnetic therapy Physical therapy technique using magnetic fields. The low-energy electrical field created by the magnetic field causes dilation of the blood vessels (vasodilation) and tissue stimulation. Magnetic therapy may be used on soft tissue to treat such injuries as tendinitis or bony (skeletal) injuries such as bucked shins.

mare reproductive loss syndrome In the spring of 2001, a severe outbreak believed to have been caused by Eastern tent caterpillars caused the loss in Central Kentucky of more than 500 late-term fetuses and newborn foals and almost 5,000 early-term fetuses. The economic loss to Central Kentucky's Thoroughbred industry from MLRS was estimated at more than $300-million.

metacarpal (fracture) Usually refers to a fracture of the cannon bone, located between the knee and the fetlock joint in the front leg. Also may refer to a fracture of the splint bone. The cannon bone of the front leg is the third metacarpal.

monorchid A male horse of any age that has only one testicle in his scrotum; the other testicle was either removed or is undescended.

myectomy Surgery to treat horses that displace their soft palate or have an entrapped epiglottis while racing. Two strap muscles in the neck are cut to change the position of the larynx in the airway. Believed to release backward pressure on the larynx that may pull the epiglottis off the soft palate.

nasogastric tube A long, flexible tube that reaches from the nose to the stomach.

navicular disease A degenerative disease that affects the navicular bone (small bone in the back of the foot), navicular bursa, and deep flexor tendon. Generally considered a disease of the front feet.

neurectomy A surgical procedure in which the nerve supply to the navicular area is removed. The toe and remainder of the foot retain feeling. Sometimes referred to as posterior digital neurectomy or heel nerve. Also known as nerving.

nuclear scintigraphy Radioactive isotope tracer is injected into the horse, and its body is scanned with a specialized camera to produce an image that is interpreted by a computer. Concentration of the tracer is an indication of bone remodeling or inflammation and registers as a "hot spot"—a red area on the film; areas of diminished blood flow show up as "cold spots."

oblique Fracture at an angle.

oiling Administration of mineral oil by nasogastric tube to relieve gas or to break a blockage. Preventive procedure commonly used before long van rides to prevent impaction and subsequent colic.

open knee A condition of young horses in which the physis of the knee has not closed; an immature knee. Often used to describe the status of the physis immediately above the knee and is an indicator of long bone growth in two-year-olds.

osteoarthritis A permanent form of arthritis with progressive loss of the articular cartilage in a joint.

osteochondritis dissecans A cartilaginous or bony lesion that is the result of a fragment of cartilage and its underlying bone becoming detached from an articular surface. The OCD lesions occur commonly in the knee joint and are associated with a failure in bone development.

pastern Bones located between the fetlock joint and the hoof. The joint between the long and short pastern bones is called the pastern joint.

periostitis Inflammation of the tissue (periosteum) that overlies bone. Periostitis of the cannon bone is referred to as bucked shins, while periostitis of the splint bone is called a splint, which may be expressed as a popped splint.

phenylbutazone A nonsteroidal anti-inflammatory medication that is legal in many racing jurisdictions. Trade names are Butazolidin and Butazone.

physis The growth plate at the end of the long bones (such as the cannon bone) that lets the bone grow in length.

pin firing Thermocautery intended to increase blood flow to the leg and thus to promote healing.

pulled suspensory Suspensory ligament injury (suspensory desmitis) in which some fibers of the ligament have been disrupted and some loss of support of the distal limb may have occurred.

quarter crack A crack between the toe and heel, usually extending into the coronary band.

radiograph The picture or image on film or digital medium generated by X rays.

ring bone Osteoarthritis of joints between the pastern bones (high ring bone) or just above the coronet (low ring bone).

roaring (laryngeal hemiplegia) A whistling sound made by a horse during inhalation while exercising. The condition is caused by a partial or total paralysis of the nerves controlling the muscles that elevate the arytenoid cartilages and thereby open the larynx. In severe cases, a surgical procedure known as tie-back surgery (laryngoplasty) is performed, in which a suture is inserted through the cartilage to hold it out of the airway permanently. Paralysis almost exclusively occurs on the left side and most frequently in horses over 16 hands tall.

run down Abrasion of the heel during stride.

saucer Stress fracture of the front of the cannon bone; the fracture can be straight or curved.

screw fixation A procedure in which steel-alloy screws are surgically inserted to hold together a fractured bone.

sesamoid One of two small bones located above at the back of the fetlock joint. Fractures can be small chips or involve the entire bone. Surgical repair is often done by arthroscopy.

sesamoiditis Inflammation of the sesamoid bones.

shock-wave therapy Focus of high-energy sound waves on an affected body part to trigger natural repair mechanisms. Has been shown to stimulate bone formation and produce analgesia through numbness, which has potential for abuse.

simple A fracture along a single line that does not penetrate the skin.

slab A bone fracture in a joint that extends from one articular surface to another. Most often seen in the third carpal bone of the knee.

slipped Spontaneous abortion.

splint A condition in which calcification occurs on the splint bone and causes a bump. This condition can occur in response to a fracture or other irritation to the splint bone. A common injury is a popped splint.

stress A fracture created by the repetitive impact on a bone, most often in athletic training. Usually seen in the front of the cannon bone as a severe form of bucked shins. Also seen in the tibia and causes a hard-to-diagnose hind-limb lameness.

synchronous diaphragmatic flutter A contraction of the diaphragm in synchrony with the heartbeat after strenuous exercise, giving the appearance of hiccups. Affected horses have a noticeable twitch or spasm in the flank area that may cause an audible sound, often referred to as "thumps." Most commonly seen in electrolyte-depleted or exhausted horses. The condition resolves spontaneously with rest.

synovitis Inflammation of a synovial structure, typically a synovial sheath.

tendinitis Inflammation of a tendon.

thermography Diagnostic technique utilizing instrumentation that measures temperature differences. Records the surface temperature of a horse. Unusually hot or cold areas may be indicative of some underlying pathology (deviation from the normal).

thoroughpin Swelling of the synovial sheath of the deep flexor tendon above the hock.

tie-back surgery A procedure (laryngoplasty) used to suture the arytenoid cartilage out of the airway.

toe crack A crack near the front of the hoof.

torsion A twist in the intestine.

toxemia Poisoning sometimes caused by the absorption of bacterial products (endotoxins) that form at a local source of infection.

tubing Inserting a nasogastric tube through a horse's nostril into its stomach for the purpose of providing oral medication.

twitch A restraining device, usually consisting of a stick with a loop of rope or chain at one end, that is placed around a horse's upper lip and twisted, releasing endorphins that relax a horse and curb its fractiousness while it is being handled.

tying up Known as acute rhabdomyolysis, a form of muscle cramp that ranges in severity from mild stiffness to a life-threatening disorder. A generalized condition of muscle-fiber breakdown usually associated with exercise. The cause of the muscle-fiber breakdown is uncertain. Signs include sweating, reluctance to move, stiffness, and general distress.

ultrasound 1) Diagnostic ultrasound: A technique that uses ultrasonic waves to produce images of internal structures. 2) Therapeutic ultrasound: A therapy to create heat and stimulate healing.

Venezuelan equine encephalomyelitis A highly contagious disease affecting the central nervous system that can cause illness or death in horses and humans. Abbreviated as VEE.

Western equine encephalomyelitis A highly contagious disease spread by mosquitoes that affects the central nervous system. Can be prevented by annual vaccination.

West Nile virus Encephalitis first reported in North America in 1999. Virus is harbored in birds and spread by mosquitoes to other birds, horses, and humans. Not all horses bitten by infected mosquitoes develop clinical signs, but mortality rate is 38% in those that do. Can be prevented by semiannual vaccination.

wind puff Accumulation of synovial fluid in the fetlock-joint capsule. Also known as a wind gall.

wobbler syndrome Neurological disease clinically associated with general incoordination and muscle weakness. Can be caused by an injury to the spinal cord in the area of the cervical (neck) vertebrae or is associated with malformation or degeneration of the cervical vertebrae.